15 The Military
軍事　軍事

16 Social Stratification and Mobility
社會階層及社會流動
社会階層及びその流動性

16.1 Elite Strata
社會領導階層　エリート階層

16.2 The Bourgeoisie
商人及市民階級
商人及び市民階級

16.3 The Peasantry
農民階級　農民階級

16.4 The Working Class
勞工階級　労働者階級

17 National and Higher Education
全國教育及高等教育
国民教育及び高等教育

18 National Welfare and Living Standards
全國性福利及生活水準
国民の福祉及び生活水準

19 Modernization and Directed Social Change
近代化運動及社會改革
近代化及び社会改革

25 Feuds, Banditry, and Local Paramilitary Units
械鬥、盜賊及地方武力
械鬥、匪賊行為及び地方の保安組織

26 Local Social Stratification and Mobility
地方社會之階層與流動
地方の社会階層及びその流動性

26.1 The Local Elite
地方領導階層
地方エリート階層

26.2 Businessmen
商人及市民　商人及び市民

26.3 Peasants
農民　農民

26.4 Workers
勞工　労働者

27 Elementary and Vocational Education
初等教育及職業補習教育
初等教育及び補習教育

28 Local Welfare and Living Standards
地方福利及生活水準
地方の福祉及び生活水準

29 Regional and Subethnic Variation
習俗方言等等地域性差異
習俗方言等の地域的差異

35 Veterans Associations and the Military in Society
退
在

36.1 Elite and Professional Associations
社會領導階層與專門職業之會社
エリート及び専門職業者の団体

36.2 Employers Associations
商業雇主之社團　雇用者団体

36.3 Peasant Associations and Movements
農民協會及農民運動
農民団体及び農民運動

36.4 Labor Unions and the Labor Movement
工會及勞工運動
労働組合及び労働運動

37 Educational Associations and Movements
教育團體及教育運動
教育団体及び教育運動

38 Organized Philanthropy and Mutual-Aid Societies
慈善團體及互助組織
慈善団体及び共済組合

39 Associations Based on Common Place of Origin
鄉誼組織　同郷組織

---

40 Kinship Systems in General
親屬制度通論　親族制度一般

41 Marriage and the Family
婚姻與家庭　婚姻と家庭

42 Lineages and Clanship
氏族及譜系　氏族及び系譜

43 Ancestor Worship
祖先崇祀　祖先崇拝

44 Kin Terms and Relationships
親屬關係及稱呼
親属関係及び称呼

45 Property and Inheritance
財產及繼承　財産及び相続

46 Sex
性　性

47 Female Roles and Male-Female Differences
婦女地位及男女分別
女性の地位及び男女の区別

48 Non-Kin Interpersonal Relationships
非親屬關係　非親族関係

50 Life Cycle and Age Grading
生命周期及年齡
生命周期及び年齢

51 Reproduction
生殖　生殖

52 Infancy and Childhood
嬰兒及童年　嬰児及び幼年

53 Socialization
教養化育　社会化

54 Adolescence and Youth
青春期及青年　青春期及び青年

55 Living Routines
生活起居　日常生活

56 Illness and Medicine
疾病及醫療　疾病及び医療

57 Death Practices
死亡及喪葬　死亡及び葬祭

58 Fertility and Mortality
繁殖率及死亡率
出生率及び死亡率

59 Life Histories and Biographies
生活史及傳記　生活史及び伝記

60 Idea Systems and Values in General
觀念及價值體系通論
観念及び価値体系一般

61 Personality and Behavioral Processes
人格及行爲
パーソナリティ及び行為

62 Cognition
認知　認知

63 Ethics
倫理　倫理

64 Ideology and the Great Tradition
正統思想及意識型態
正統思想及びイデオロギー

65 Folklore and Little Traditions
民俗　民間伝承

66 Self-Conception in Relation to Outsiders
「華夷」「中外」之分辨及對異族之觀念
「華夷」「中外」等異民族に対する観念

70 Chinese Scholars of Chinese Society
華人研究中國社會
中国人学者による中国社会研究

71 Non-Chinese Scholars of Chinese Society
外人研究中國社會
外国人学者による中国社会研究

72 Bibliography
書目　書誌

MODERN CHINESE SOCIETY
An Analytical Bibliography

近代中國社會研究

論著類目索引

第一冊 西文篇

施堅雅 編

洪玳珀
韋文德 參訂

MODERN CHINESE SOCIETY
An Analytical Bibliography

1. Publications in Western Languages 1644-1972

G. William Skinner, Editor

Assisted by Deborah B. Honig and Edwin A. Winckler

近代中国社会研究
文献解題索引

欧米文篇

G・ウィリアム・スキナー 編

デボラー・B・ホーニング、エドウィン・A・ウィンクラー 助修

STANFORD UNIVERSITY PRESS Stanford, California 1973

Stanford University Press
Stanford, California

Printed in the United States of America
ISBN 0-8047-0751-0
LC 70-130831

Contents

Page Guide

This is a detailed table of contents for the Bibliography and the analytical indexes, giving the page numbers of main headings. The first portion covers the Bibliography and the Historical and Geographic Indexes, all of which use the same subject headings. The second portion (p. viii) covers the Local-Systems Index, which uses geographic headings.

Local-Systems Index

Preface

The project that produced this *Bibliography* was launched in 1963 under the auspices of the Social Science Research Council by its Subcommittee on Research on Chinese Society. The Subcommittee initiated bibliographic work because available aids in Chinese studies were inadequate to meet the needs of social scientists and analytically-minded historians. Ten years later the situation is little improved. Bibliographies for anthropologists cover Africa and Latin America as a matter of course but not China, and only rarely do bibliographies for sociologists, economists, or social psychologists treat any part of the non-Western world. Social-science bibliographies almost never cover Chinese-language works, and the few that include Japanese publications typically give only English language versions of their titles. Bibliographies for China specialists concentrate either on philology and traditional history or on current events and policy questions. Only the annual *Bibliography of Asian Studies* offers scholars a reasonably adequate list of social-science publications on China; even there the coverage is limited to Western languages and the analytical apparatus is rudimentary.

The need for analytical control of the relevant bibliography became apparent only in the 1950s, when the impossibility of doing field work on the mainland turned many faces toward the libraries. At the same time, Western social scientists were coming to recognize the importance of Chinese civilization for a universal social science, and the leading scholars of Chinese institutional history were developing a social-science-like concern for rigor and quantification. Finally, as standards of performance rose, scholars became increasingly reluctant to undertake new research projects, whether in living communities or archives, without having mastered the relevant literature. Hence the Subcommittee's decision to sponsor this *Bibliography*.

Intellectually, the picture has changed only slightly since 1963; if anything, the trends described above have been accelerated. The international situation is another matter. In 1963 China was inaccessible and isolated from the family of nations, its leaders caught up in a soberly introspective and xenophobic mood. Ten years later China is relatively close at hand, a respected member of the United Nations, accessible to a broad spectrum of visitors, its leaders confident and seemingly open-minded. Few today would question the importance of Chinese society to the future of mankind.

The new situation has its dangers as well as its opportunities. For one thing, the recent reopening of China has stimulated an outpouring of superficial publications, many of them by people who see China as a nation with no significant history before 1949. The design of this project works against this misconception by placing within a single analytical frame publications on the Ch'ing, Republican, and Communist periods; on the Communist movement prior to 1949; and on Taiwan under the Republic of China as well as on the People's Republic. Another danger is stereotyping: the kind of writing about China that says more about the writer's political bias and cognitive set than about the facts of Chinese society. Here, too, this *Bibliography* serves as a corrective. Writers of all nationalities and political persuasions are considered here, their works scrutinized and selected according to uniform criteria and juxtaposed in the same analytical categories. Meanwhile, China's new visibility and stature are stimulating a wave of new scholarship in the areas of this *Bibliography*'s concern. With its publication students of Chinese society should be able to build more securely than before on what has already been accomplished.

The editors of this *Bibliography* hope it will be influential in two ways. First, we see it as striking a blow against the tendency of social scientists and historians studying Chinese society to remain isolated in discrete communities bounded by language, political alignment, and discipline. So far as possible, the formal design of this *Bibliography* simply ignores these artificial boundaries. Works in all languages and disciplines are admitted, by scholars of all political persuasions. International communication is fostered by providing English renderings of all non-English titles and by providing section and subject headings throughout in Chinese and Japanese as well as English. Interdisciplinary communication is fostered by the strictly topical as opposed to disciplinary definitions given the Subject codes. Thus, a user checking any given subsection of the Bibliography or the Historical Index across all three volumes is likely to encounter works in half a dozen languages by scholars in two or more disciplines. We planned it that way, and we think it will work.

Our second hope is that this *Bibliography* will help to bring Chinese society fully within the range of comparative and general studies, where it clearly belongs. To this end we have incorporated in our annotation scheme many of the analytical categories found useful in cross-societal comparisons; we have done our best to avoid sinological jargon and to provide glosses of names and terms for those who may need them. If this *Bibliography* serves to bring the Chinese case closer to the mainstream of social science, we will have done, however imperfectly, what we set out to do.

Acknowledgments

There is much to acknowledge in a project of this size and duration, and there are many to thank.

We may begin with sponsors. As project director, the senior editor reported until 1970 directly to the Subcommittee on Research on Chinese Society. The editors are grateful for the guidance of the Subcommittee's members during those years: Maurice Freedman, Morton H. Fried, John C. Pelzel, Irene B. Taeuber, and Ezra F. Vogel. The Subcommittee, which was originally established through independent initiative and separately funded, enjoyed a large measure of autonomy even after 1964–65, when it was brought under the fiscal jurisdiction of the Joint Committee on Contemporary China, a committee jointly sponsored by the American Council of Learned Societies and the Social Science Research Council and administered by the latter. We are grateful to the Joint Committee for encouragement and support, and in particular to John M. H. Lindbeck, its chairman from 1964 until his untimely death in 1971, whose contribution to this project was crucial to its success. We are grateful also to Pendleton Herring, former President of the Social Science Research Council, for his unfaltering moral and logistic support, and to the Council's able staff officers for the project, Bryce Wood (until 1970) and Donald S. Shoup (1970–72). To Bryce Wood, whose admirable efforts as practitioner, advocate, and public defender of social-science scholarship have benefited so many, goes our deepest gratitude for his labors in the service of our vision, in which he maintained a steady faith. Finally, for gracious and generous support during the project's final year, when it operated under the de facto aegis of Stanford University, the editors express their profound appreciation to that university's administrative officers, notably Dean Albert H. Hastorf.

Five universities have provided the project with office space and related services over the years, in each case at no cost to the project and without compensating income from overhead. In this regard, the editors give special thanks to the China Program of Cornell University, the East Asian Institute at Columbia University, the Harvard-Yenching Institute at Harvard University, the Tokyo University Libraries (specifically Sōgō Toshokan), and the Department of Anthropology at Stanford University.

Funding for the project came chiefly from public and private American foundations, the project's own sponsoring bodies, and university centers and institutes. Major grants from the National Science Foundation underwrote a large portion of operations during 1965-72, and additional federal support came from the National Endowment for the Humanities. Of the private foundations, the Carnegie Corporation of New York was the first to provide a major grant; its generous support in the early years was particularly significant. The Rockefeller Brothers Fund and the Andrew W. Mellon Foundation made important grants at two critical junctures in the project's development, and additional support was received from the Edward W. Hazen Foundation, the Starr Foundation, and the Council on Library Resources. Other substantial contributions came from the funds of the Joint Committee on Contemporary China, which was itself supported by the Ford Foundation, from the Social Science Research Council itself, and from the project's final patron, Stanford University. Particular aspects of the enterprise were supported by each of the American universities with which the project has been associated, specifically by the London-Cornell Project for Social Research, the East Asian Institute of Columbia University, the Harvard-Yenching Institute, and at Stanford University the Hoover Institution for War, Revolution and Peace, the Center for Research in International Studies, and the Center for East Asian Studies. Finally, a grant was received from the IBM Corporation. In thanking these many donors, we want particularly to express our appreciation of their officers' remarkably successful efforts to minimize procedural formalities and their willingness to continue support for a project whose completion was never a certainty.

We are grateful to Leon E. Seltzer, Director of Stanford University Press, for his responsible interest in the substance and welfare of the project as a whole, and for moral support in periods of crisis. We were supremely fortunate in having as our press editor J. G. Bell, Editor of Stanford University Press, who put his formidable talents at the service of this *Bibliography* for over five years. We have benefited from his unerring judgment, the precision of his thinking, and his capacity for keeping the forest always in focus while fussing daily with the bark and limbs and foliage of the individual trees. Whatever there is of style and grace in this publication is largely his achievement.

Contributions to the design and development of the Stanford Automated Bibliography System (see the Introduction, p. xviii) were made by David G. Hays, Martin Kay, and William F. Lake, Jr., in addition to the senior editor. Most of the programs were written and documented by Mr. Lake, with significant additions by J. William Campbell and Charles S. Tribolet, Jr.; the senior editor expresses warm appreciation to all for the high levels of intelligence, skill, and dedication brought to their tasks. We are grateful for the cooperation of successive directors and staff officers of the Campus Facility of the Stanford Computation Center. Appreciation is also extended to our automatic typesetters, Automatech Graphics Corporation in New York City, for their willingness to accommodate the very special requirements of this project and otherwise to cope with a demanding client. Special thanks are due Theodore Birnbaum, President, for countenancing risks that his business sense continually called into question, and Larry Seeger, Senior Systems Analyst, for his competent and cheerful management of operations.

The type-punching onto paper tape of citations and subsequent corrections was largely accomplished by Elsie P. Warren and Charlene Androes, who performed this demanding and seemingly endless task with intelligence, accuracy, and good humor. The front and back matter for all volumes passed through only one typewriter, that of Mrs. Androes, whose phenomenal capacity for making of that machine an instrument for perfection is acknowledged with deep admiration and gratitude.

The editors are grateful to Jill Leland for drafting the maps and to Sophie Sa Winckler for rendering the Chinese calligraphy on the title page.

Turning now to those who contributed to this volume in particular, we must pay tribute to our editorial assistants, Deborah B. Honig and Edwin A. Winckler. Ms. Honig helped with the compilation and accomplished much of the bibliographic research for this volume, spent countless hours ferreting out errors and inconsistencies from computer printouts, made a major contribution to standardizing and improving English renderings of titles, carried the heaviest burden of proofreading, and generally served as operations manager for the Western volume from 1970 to 1973. To these and myriad other tasks she brought good judgment, meticulous attention to detail, and a flair for precision. Professor Winckler served as managing editor of the Western-language volume from 1966 to 1968; he established and directed the project's Cambridge office, organized Western-language compilation and oversaw annotation in Boston-area libraries, initiated annotation operations in continental European libraries, and supervised the first efforts to prepare data for computer inputting. One of the first to grasp the significance of the project's overall design, he facilitated computerization by an initial analysis of the components and logic of the project's citation formats and made helpful contributions to the design of the annotation scheme and indexes. We regret that Professor Winckler's other commitments precluded a major role in the project after 1968, and we are correspondingly grateful for the few occasions since that time when we have had the benefit once again of his incisive thinking and organizational skill.

Several other persons performed important staff functions over the years. Richard Sorich of Columbia University served as managing editor of the Western-language volume from 1964 to 1966; he established the project's New York office and supervised Western-language compilation and annotation in New York–area libraries. His important contributions and bibliographic skills are acknowledged with sincere gratitude. Judith B. Woodward served as operations manager for the Western volume during 1967–68, and Marion Bieber during 1968–69, both with admirable efficiency. Alfred R. Haemmerli organized and coordinated the annotation effort in European libraries during 1967; his efforts were ably assisted by Frank L. Gniffke and Lenora T. Margadant. Isabelle Nagin deserves special thanks for her accomplishments in gaining initial control of the Russian-language files and associated annotation, and Carol B. Vesecky for successfully completing these operations. John R. Ziemer was largely responsible for preparing the General Index. Both Mr. Ziemer and Professor Winston Hsieh, coeditor of Volume 2, provided important back-up editorial assistance on this volume.

Exceptional service was provided gratis by four scholars to whom the editors herewith extend deep appreciation: Dr. Inga Markovits (Stanford Law School) for providing expert assistance with the English rendering of legal terms in a number of European languages; Dr. Sophia Davidovna Maliband (Institut Vostokovedeniia, Akademiia Nauk SSSR, Moscow) for ascertaining full names and years of birth for a sizable number of Russian China specialists; Dr. Robert L. Irick (Chinese Materials and Research Aids Service Center, Taipei) for cheerfully supplying endless bibliographic details on reissues published in Taiwan; and Dr. William C. Brugger (Flinders University of South Australia) for ferreting out missing data on British dissertations.

The annotators for this volume are named on p. xiv. It is they who carried the major burden of evaluation and annotation, and much of the utility of this volume rests on the soundness of their judgment and the care and rigor with which they assigned codes. The editors warmly thank each of these talented young scholars and commend the intelligence and meticulousness they brought to their exacting tasks. The Cambridge annotators mourn the tragic death in Vietnam of one of their ablest and most amiable colleagues, Thomas R. Morris.

The evaluation and annotation of Western-language publications were carried out in a large number of libraries and institutes. The editors acknowledge with particular gratitude the facilities extended, the special arrangements made, and the exceptional services rendered by the following librarians and institute directors: Dr. Richard C. Howard, Librarian, Wason Collection, Cornell University Libraries; Dr. Warren M. Tsuneishi, Chief, Orientalia Division, and Dr. Sergius Yakobson, Chief, Slavic and Central European Division, Library of Congress; Dr. Eugene W. Wu and Mr. George E. Potter of the Harvard-Yenching Library; Miss Miwa Kai and Dr. T. K. Tong of the East Asian Library, Columbia University; Mme. Jacqueline Pluet, Bibliothécaire, Maison des Sciences de l'Homme, Paris; at the Stanford University Libraries: Dr. David C. Weber, Director, Mr. Elmer M. Grieder, Associate Director, Mr. Allen B. Veaner, Assistant Director for Bibliographic Operations, Mr. Jack Plotkin, Chief Librarian, Mr. A. H. Epstein, Chief, Automation Department, and Mrs. Florence A. Chu, in charge of interlibrary loans; at the Hoover Institution, Dr. W. Glenn Campbell, Director, Mr. Richard F. Starr and Mr. Alan H. Belmont, Associate Directors, Mr. John T. Ma, Curator-Librarian of the East Asia Collection, Mrs. Arlene B. Paul, Head of Reader Services, and indeed the entire staffs of the East Asia, Eastern Europe, and Western Europe Collections.

Extraordinary cooperation was extended by a number of European scholars who provided advice and assistance to the project's evaluation and annotation efforts in their countries. Warm appreciation is expressed in particular to Professor Göran Aijmer (Ethnografiska Institutionen, Stockholms Universitet), Professor Gabriele Crespi-Reghizzi (Istituto di Diritto Comparato, Università Commerciale Luigi Bocconi, Milan), Dr. Horst Huber (Ostasiatische Seminar Universität München), Professor A. F. P. Hulsewé (Sinologisch Instituut, Leiden), the late Professor Roger Pélissier (Centre de Documentation sur l'Extrême-Orient, Ecole Pratique des Hautes Etudes, Paris), and Professor Luciano Petech (Scuola Orientale, Città Universitaria, Rome).

Other scholars and bibliographers who gave the project the benefit of their professional advice and service include Michel Cartier, Donald R. DeGlopper, Søren Egerod, Stephan Feuchtwang, Herbert Franke, Ronald Freedman, Hesung Koh, Harry J. Lamley, Lawrence J. Lau, Carl Leban, James W. Morely, David P. Mozingo, Edwin B. Parker, Stuart R. Schram, Jonathan Spence, Thein Swe, Ross Terrill, Tang Tsou, Wang Gungwu, and Boris N. Zanegin. The editors are extremely grateful for the assistance given gladly and freely by these busy people.

In its search for the full names and birth years of authors, the project has been assisted by scores of helpful persons in the archives, registries, and alumni-records offices of universities in both Europe and North America. These public servants must remain anonymous here, along with most of the reference librarians who have provided similar assistance in our search for bibliographic data. The following librarians, however, deserve mention for their extremely helpful bibliographic research on our behalf: Thomas Bolling (University of Washington Libraries), Shirley Dunwiddie (University of Minnesota Libraries), Marjorie Griffis (Union Theological Seminary Library), Sheila K. Hart (Harvard College Library), Thomas H. Kang (Library of Congress), Virginia MacDonald (National Library of Medicine), Philip A. Muntzel (Yale Divinity School Library), H. G. H. Nelson (British Museum), Jack R. Ponischil (New York Academy of Medicine Library), William E. Schevill (Museum of Comparative Zoology, Harvard University), Joyce B. Schneider (Yale University Library), and Hung I. Wang (East Asian Library, Columbia University).

Finally we specially thank those employees of the project whose administrative skills and dedication made our work run more smoothly and efficiently, notably Blyth Coghlan Carpenter, Sue Fawn Chung, Elizabeth Hardy, Ann Retzlaff Harley, Nancy J. Hodes, Emily Homonoff, Sophie Laden La, and Gregory Yahna.

This project has in effect consumed more time than the editor had to give. By way of consolation, he acknowledges with profound regret the neglect of his sons, Geoffrey, Jim, Mark, and Jeremy; the burden of silence carried by distant friends, Maurice, Katharine, Lauri, Knight, Alice, Charles, Jim, and Barbara; and the deprivations borne by those close by, Carol, Eunice, and Kathy—and dedicates this *Bibliography* to them all.

Annotators

Alexander, Ronelle J.
Ann Choong-sik
Antolini, Anthony F.
Barron, James
Bateman, Nancy
Battini, Marisa
Baumann, Mary E.
Berney, Barbara L.
Berzin, Alexander
Bland, Margaret L.
Bodman, Richard Wainwright
Bolocan, Alice Kwong
Brambilla, Elena
Brown, Carolyn T.
Byrnes, Shaun M.
Carpenter, Blyth Coghlan
Cass, Victoria B.
Chan, Ming K.
Chen, Paul
Chung, Sue Fawn
Cole, James H.
Cone, James E.
Coombs, Mary
Corwin, David M.
Crissman, Lawrence W.
DeGlopper, Donald R.
Delaforge, Gerard
Dickstein, Phyllis
Douglass, Wallace P.
Drake, Fred W.
Dreyer, Edward L.
Edmond, Russell Bradford, Jr.
Engle, Richard H.
Feuchtwang, Stephan
Glasser, Liv
Gniffke, Frank Leon
Goell, Martha
Gold, Peter F.
Graham, Albert E., Jr.
Hallgren, Claes
Hamilton, James A. G.
Harley, Ann Retzlaff
Henning, Clara
Hirsch, Thomas F.
Hodes, Nancy J.
Hom, Lawrence Bruce
Honig, Deborah B.
Hosman, Patricia D.
Hsieh, Frances
Huber, Horst
I, Ted Chih-Fan
Jacquier, Janine V.
Johnson, Graham E.
Kaufman, Barbara Gail
Kehl, Frank S.
Laden La, Sophie
Levine, Stephen
Lipman, Jonathan N.
Littrup, Leif
Lorch, Crystal C.
Mani, Ramaswamy
Margadant, Lenora Timm
Melnick, Leonard
Meyer, Raymond C.
Miller, Kenneth H.
Mohr, Mark E.
Morris, Thomas R.
Nanda, Krishna
Netolitzky, Almut
Nitefor, George
Nötten, Renate
Olsen, Larry John
Pluet, Jacqueline
Prozer, William W.
Ribner, Susan Caroline
Rondeau, Anne Dhu
Ryavec, Karl W.
Scharf, Carl Bradley
Scheinin, Ania
Schweitzer-Tong, Gary
Silin, Robert H.
Snyder, Ellen Andrea
Sorich, Richard
Spitz, Douglas C.
Strauch, Judith V.
Su, Tina Han
Szekely, Yoram B.
Tietze, Klaus
Toresella, Sergio
Trepp, Urs
Van Halsema, Franklin T.
Vesecky, Carol B.
Volins, Lilian
Wang Sung-hsing
White, Christine K.
Winckler, Edwin A.
Wong, Billy Fook-Beau
Woodard, Judith
Wycoff, William A.
Young, Ludwig
Zachman, William F.

Introduction

Special Design Features

All user-oriented bibliographies involve some system of classification according to substantive content; most bibliographies found particularly useful by scholars are also annotated. A special feature of this *Bibliography* is that classification and annotation are integrated into a single scheme. (The scheme is described in Annotation Categories, p. xxiii; its application is illustrated in Entry Formats, p. xx, and Design of Indexes, p. xl.) In the usual published bibliography, the substantive classification is used solely to achieve a single categorization for purposes of arranging citations. In this *Bibliography*, by contrast, the substantive classification is also used to generate indexes that provide multiple classifications of every work. Let us see what this innovation means in practice.

Basic dilemmas are inherent in any attempt to achieve a single categorization of bibliographic citations. A categorization that adheres rigorously to a single dimension—topical, geographic, temporal—throws away too much helpful information. A classification that subcategorizes by successive sorts on several substantive dimensions unduly fragments the citation listings: thus a topical classification into 100 categories, each having 10 historical-period subcategories, each of which in turn has 15 geographic sub-subcategories, would fragment a bibliography into 15,000 separate alphabetical listings. In practice, the search for a middle course between the Scylla of single-dimensional rigor and the Charybdis of unwieldy fragmentation has yielded three kinds of compromise: (1) the simplification of each dimension used, (2) the combination of various dimensions to create a single multidimensional categorization, and (3) the listing of citations under more than one heading.

None of these compromises can be said to work well. The annual *Bibliography of Asian studies*, which illustrates the first and most usual kind, sorts citations on two dimensions, first geographic and second topical, each greatly simplified. The geographic breakdown into four categories (China, Taiwan, Hong Kong & Macao, and two or more of these) is extremely broad, and even the more elaborated topical classification involves such all-inclusive categories as "Sociology, Anthropology, and Psychology." An example of the second kind of compromise is Yuan Tung-li's otherwise useful *China in Western literature* (New Haven, 1958), in which temporal categories (e.g. "History: Republic"), disciplinary categories (e.g. "Economic History"), topical categories (e.g. "Commercial Law"), and geographic categories (e.g. "Northeastern Provinces") are all integrated into a single categorization. A work treating the history of commercial law in Manchuria during the Republican period logically falls under each of the four illustrative headings, but it is listed under only one; which one cannot be guessed by the user, and whichever one it is, the information that would be conveyed by classification under the other three is not conveyed. The third kind of compromise, multiple listing, is best exemplified by the dictionary catalogs of research libraries, in which a book is given three or four classifications according to an omnibus listing of "subject headings" (some geographic and temporal as well as strictly topical) and the full citation is entered under each of the subject headings. Although this procedure is followed within limits by some published bibliographies, its systematic application would be too wasteful of space for bibliographies of any amplitude.

The present *Bibliography* resolves this dilemma by the use of analytical indexes. Citations are listed only once—arranged in subcategories defined by a simplification of two dimensions, one topical and one temporal—but the full differentiation of those two substantive dimensions as well as three others is made available to the user by three indexes derived from the annotation component of each entry. One index, for instance, cross-tabulates Subject codes with Historical-period codes and Sources codes; another cross-tabulates Geographic codes with Type-of-place codes and Sources codes, providing at the same time a simplification of the Historical-period coding. (For details, see Design of Indexes, p. xl.) This system not only makes more information available to the user than any other, but actually combines classifications in ways that may enable him to refine the objectives of his search.

A second and equally basic bibliographic dilemma stems from the simple fact that publications may make significant contributions to more than one subject. In virtually all published bibliographies, publications are assigned to one and only one subject category: a two-volume classical overview of Chinese society is treated no differently in this respect from a two-page article on burial practices. But this system simply does not work for publications of any complexity. A book that is devoted primarily to an analysis of lineages may also include an authoritative treatment of geomancy; yet in the usual procedure it must be assigned to either one subject or the other. An agricultural history of China may contain the sharpest thinking on Chinese urbanization found anywhere in the literature, yet standard bibliographic practice has no way of bringing it to the attention of a user seeking bibliographic help on urbanization.

The present *Bibliography* resolves this dilemma by multiple subject coding. A work may be assigned as many as sixteen Subject codes, some of them "primary," the others "secondary" (see Annotation Categories, p. xxxi). Thus the entry for the book on lineages includes in its annotation the primary codes for both geomancy and kin groups; and the entry for the history of Chinese agriculture, although listed under the main heading 14.1 Agrarian Economy, includes in its annotation primary code 11.1 for Nationwide Urbanization. Both the Historical Index and the Geographic Index list a given entry number as many times as required; that is, if an entry has, say, thirteen Subject codes, its number is listed thirteen times in each of these indexes. Thus the work on lineages that contributes to geomancy is indexed in the primary block under 62 Cognition (the subject category that covers "natural" sciences) on a par with other works devoted primarily or exclusively to geomancy; and the work on agriculture that contributes to urbanization is indexed in the primary block under 11.1 Nationwide Urbanization along with articles addressed specifically to urbanization. This arrangement makes it possible to discriminate finely in the classification of works according to the breadth of their coverage and the degree of focus. For example, the two-volume classical overview of Chinese society might be assigned the maximum complement of sixteen Subject codes, whereas the two-page article on burial might be assigned a single code only; the first would then be indexed sixteen times in the Historical Index, the second only once.

A third bibliographic dilemma follows from the axiom that you can't tell a book by its cover. Neither can you tell an article by its title, at least not with any assurance. As we have seen, many works make major contributions to several topics, only one of which is indicated by the title. Indeed, a great many such works —some thousands in this compilation—make their *major* contributions to a subject not specifically indicated by the title: thus a work whose chief contribution concerns marriage customs may show "folklore" as the only substantive word in the title. Other works have titles that are cryptic, and still others carry titles that are wholly misleading. The only completely satisfactory solution to this problem is to read or at least scan every work listed, and that is what we have done.

One result of our procedures is that apparent discrepancies between titles and annotations are not infrequent. Thus a work ostensibly concerned with labor unions may be listed in the Bibliography under 34.3 Guilds, and Local-Systems Index entries under 1.5 South China Broadly Conceived may refer the user to titles specifying "northern provinces" or "North China." The casual user may suspect an annotation error; the experienced user will reserve judgment until he has examined the work in question.

The design of this project also touches on a fourth and final concern: the nature of the bibliographic unit. In this regard librarians and scholars tend to differ. Librarians must keep tabs on physical publications as such—this book, this pamphlet, this journal—and their tendency therefore is to take the physical publication as the bibliographic unit. Scholars, by contrast, tend to take each discrete product of scholarship as their unit— not this journal but this article, not Smith's book but Lee's paper in Smith's book. We have opted for the scholar's view: there are no entries here for journals or including works, only for journal articles and inclusions. Moreover, given our scheme for encoding annotations, we inject considerations of substance into the very process of identifying the bibliographic unit (see Entry Formats, p. xxi, and Explanatory Notes, §9). All our departures from standard practice in this regard are designed to isolate the unit that can most usefully be annotated from the user's point of view.

This, we feel, is a bibliography with a difference. The user who would take advantage of its special features is invited to read the four sections that follow—Entry Formats, Annotation Categories, Design of Indexes, and Explanatory Notes—paying special heed to "Use of the Analytical Indexes," p. xlii.

Scope and Selectivity

To qualify for inclusion in this *Bibliography,* a work must meet certain standards of substance, bibliographic status, and scholarship.

Its substance must be of probable interest to social scientists and institutional historians concerned with modern Chinese society, where modern China is defined as the territory of the present People's Republic of China plus Taiwan, Hong Kong, and Macau, from 1644 to the present. The topical coverage of included works extends to most aspects of the domestic social structure, economy, polity, culture, and personality of the Han Chinese. Non-Han peoples, whether natives of China or aliens, are excluded, as are international relations and areas of scholarly interest not intimately linked to society as such, notably the biological and physical sciences, elite arts and letters, and technical linguistics. (See Annotation Categories, p. xxiii, for a detailed statement of topical coverage.)

In general, this *Bibliography* is restricted to published secondary works and excludes unpublished materials, reference works, and primary sources. An exception is made for unpublished dissertations and theses, and for two kinds of reference works: biographical dictionaries containing article-length entries based on modern scholarship, and modern bibliographical essays and annotated bibliographies. Articles in Chinese newspapers are normally considered primary sources, whereas scholarly articles in periodicals, whether or not published in Chinese or in China, are considered secondary works unless they amount in effect to a normative pronouncement or policy statement. Biographies of Chinese are included only if based on modern scholarship, the usual run of traditional biographies being considered primary sources; and memoirs and autobiographies of Chinese are included only if they contain solid empirical material or interpretations that make them equivalent to the average secondary work. (Biographies, memoirs, and autobiographies of non-Chinese persons are included only if they have something of interest to say about Chinese society.) Raw compilations of statistics published by the compilers count as primary sources; statistical compendia and statistical presentations with any appreciable element of analysis are considered secondary works. This *Bibliography* also excludes certain categories of reissues (see Explanatory Notes, §8) and translations from more accessible to less accessible languages (see Explanatory Notes, §11.1).

Most secondary works tend to be either descriptive or interpretative, to offer either new data or new interpretations of existing data. Both kinds of secondary work are needed, and in this *Bibliography* neither has priority over the other. Indeed, good data are valued not only when unaccompanied by analysis or interpretation, but even when presented in the service of a faulty analysis or a misguided interpretation; and the converse holds for original ideas and insights that are undocumented or appear to flout the rules of evidence. If we had admitted only works that presented significant new data *and* high-quality analysis, this *Bibliography* would be reduced to a pamphlet of negligible utility as a research aid.

Insofar as possible, works have been evaluated against the entire corpus of relevant scholarship, and redundant works, however acceptable in absolute terms, have been excluded. This judgment is modulated to some extent by considerations of language, since it would clearly be a disservice to exclude a major work in a language that many scholars can read on the grounds that it is obviated by a more comprehensive or authoritative publication in a language they cannot read. This principle is seldom invoked where the languages in question are restricted to English, French, and German, but it has usually been a consideration where one or both of the languages in question are Chinese, Japanese, or Russian.

AUTOMATION

Automation, in the form of computerization and automatic typesetting, is here harnessed in the service of objectives that would otherwise be out of reach. The computer has made three major contributions to our labors: it has significantly reduced human error, it has significantly increased speed of production, and it has made possible the efficient storage and effortless retrieval of the complex information here presented.

In the matter of human error, the characteristics of computers are too well known to require elaboration. In the matter of speed, the final production tape of the Bibliography section of Volume 1 was run in June 1973; it covers publications through 1972 and includes entries for some of the more important English monographs published during the first months of 1973. The three volumes were published only six months later, in December 1973. The time would have been shorter still had it been possible to automate production of the Oriental-language material of Volumes 2 and 3.

But perhaps the most significant benefit of automation is the third, the possibility it affords for cumulation, correction, and sophisticated selection. The entire file of disks and tapes on which this publication is based can be emended, updated, or otherwise augmented in any way at low cost and with minimal risk of introducing new errors. Thus a revision of this *Bibliography* would be relatively uncomplex to prepare, since such otherwise cumbersome tasks as reordering entries in the wake of deletions and additions and reassigning entry numbers would be accomplished by computer; indeed, the numbering system, which reserves 30,000 numbers for each volume, was chosen with the possibility of a subsequent expanded edition in mind. No less important than the system's flexibility is its capacity for automated data retrieval in the form of tailor-made computer printouts, e.g. specialized bibliographies consisting of any specified subset of entries in the full files, indexes based on key words in titles or any other bibliographic element, and analytical indexes based on cross-tabulation of any two or more annotation codes. Finally, there is the possibility of so-called on-line retrieval by nonspecialist users of a library's integrated retrieval system, who can thereby tap the project's files without concerning themselves with the intricacies of its design.

The project's computer programs constitute an integrated and comprehensive system. Most of the programs are written for the IBM 360/67, and PL/1 is the principal programming language. Chinese Society Bibliography Project Language (CSBPL), a specialized language for information retrieval and classification, was developed to meet the particular needs of this project, and 360 Assembler Language was employed in several heavily used subroutines to reduce processing time. The name adopted for the total package is Stanford Automated Bibliography System (SABS), "Chinese Society" being eliminated to avoid any inference that the system is limited to Chinese subjects.

SABS, together with its manual of documentation, is now in the public domain. Similarly, the project's computerized files of bibliographic data, together with the computer software for their selective retrieval, are available for legitimate use by scholars and research organizations. Inquiries concerning access should be directed to the editor at the Department of Anthropology, Stanford, Calif. 94305.

OPERATIONS

The Chinese Society Bibliography Project was initiated in 1963. By the end of 1964 the basic elements of the overall design were in place and the annotation scheme had been pretested on both Oriental and Western-language publications. Apart from some experimental work at the Cornell Computer Center in 1964–65, the development of the project's computer system got seriously under way only in 1966–67. Annotation in European and Far Eastern libraries was begun in 1967. Basic operations of the project are described in the following paragraphs.

Compilation. Citations were gleaned under the editors' direction from a variety of sources, including published bibliographies, library catalogs, cumulative indexes to journals, guides to periodical literature, and references in scholarly publications. The libraries most intensively used in compilation included four in the United States, namely the Hoover Institution at Stanford University, the Harvard-Yenching Library at Harvard University, the East Asian Library at Columbia University, and the Wason Collection in the Cornell University Libraries; three in Japan, the National Diet Library (Kokkai Toshokan), the Oriental Library (Tōyō Bunko), and the Tokyo University Libraries (Tōkyō Daigaku Toshokan); and two in the Republic of China (Taiwan), the National Central Library (Kuo-li Chung-yang T'u-shu-kuan) and the National Taiwan University Libraries (Kuo-li T'ai-wan Ta-hsüeh T'u-shu-kuan). Altogether approximately 90,000 titles were compiled.

Evaluation and coding. Each compiled publication that could be located in a library was evaluated by one of the project's 120 trained annotators, most of whom were graduate-student China specialists in history or one of the social sciences. The names of the annotators whose work contributed to this volume are given on p. xiv. Their tasks were (1) to determine whether the work fell within the project's purview and met its criteria of scholarly value, and to note any problems in these areas for the guidance of the editors, (2) to prepare and emend the bibliographic citation in accordance with the project's established formats, and (3) to provide an encoded annotation of the work's contents (see Annotation Categories, p. xxiii). This work was carried on in libraries in the Far East and Europe as well as North America (see Library Symbols, p. lxvi), but annotation was centered over the years in only a few cities: Ithaca, N.Y. (1963–65), New York City (1964–66), Cambridge, Mass. (1965–69), Stanford and Berkeley (1966–73), Taipei (1967–70), and Tokyo (1967–71). In the end, approximately 43,000 publications were annotated.

Preparation of computer input. Annotations and related control data were made machine-readable by keypunching standard 80-column data cards. Citations were made machine-readable by type-punching citation elements on paper tape. Prior to type-punching, each citation was assigned to one of four categories of formats (see Entry Formats, p. xx) and analyzed into its basic components, each of which was type-punched with an identifying alphabetical tag.

Inputting procedures. The paper-tape and data-card records, keyed to each other by identifying number, were next entered into the computer system, where each file was checked for invalid data and internal inconsistencies. After the rectification of these defects came the crucial step in processing the citation file, namely, the generation of each citation in publication format from its constituent tagged elements according to a comprehensive set of computerized rules. Computer programs then effected an initial merger of the formatted citation with its associated annotation, and flagged discrepancies between the two. With these discrepancies remedied, the basic magnetic-tape file of merged records was ready for editorial processing.

Editorial work. The file of merged records was perfected through an elaborate interaction process between computer and editors. The project's computer system includes over thirty printouts designed to pinpoint errors within merged entries, to identify unusual data combinations requiring scrutiny, to help weed out works that are duplicated or obviated by others, and to juxtapose citations of bibliographically related publications (reissues, translations, etc.). Other printouts were designed to facilitate and control the necessary bibliographic research and reinputting process. These printouts were run in sequence, with intermittent feedback of corrections into the computer system as the editors completed various steps in the process of editorial rectification. Changes in the citations were made via paper tape, annotation changes by repunching data cards, and deletions simply by removing data cards from the file prior to reinputting. The editorial process eliminated from the computerized files approximately 10,000 entries.

Production of output. Output in the form of alphabetized listings requires the generation for each citation of a "sort key," i.e. a string of characters that ensures proper alphabetization (see Explanatory Notes, §14). One of the project's generic programs produces such alphabetical listings within categories defined by any combination of annotation codes. The tape from which the Bibliography section of this volume was produced exemplifies such a listing. In this case, entries were first sorted into categories by principal subject (see Annotation Categories, p. xxxi); within each category they were then sorted into five historical-era subcategories, defined by the merger of Historical-period codes (see pp. xxxi, xli); and finally within each subcategory they were ordered alphabetically. Another generic program produces analytical indexes by cross-tabulating selected annotation codes. Three such indexes were selected for publication in this volume (see Design of Indexes, p. xl). Other types of output include listings that categorize entries according to both annotation codes and citation elements, indexes that cross-tabulate citation elements (e.g. date of publication or key words in titles) with annotation codes, and author indexes of the type used in this *Bibliography*.

Automatic typesetting. Six sections in each volume of this *Bibliography* were typeset automatically from output tapes produced by the project—the Bibliography itself, the three analytical indexes, and the two author indexes. The typesetting was done by the Videocomp 800, which produced the formatted three-column pages in this volume at a rate of two per minute. Thereafter, production followed the usual procedures of book publication.

SHORTCOMINGS

Inevitably in an endeavor of this type, reach exceeds grasp. First, we think now that the annotation scheme itself, which was necessarily frozen at an early stage because of the expense of recoding publications already processed, could be greatly improved in three of its five components, the Subject, Type-of-place, and Sources codes. Second, we regret that financial considerations prevented us from including in our coverage China's international relations and Chinese communities outside of geographic China. Third, a final modification of the central program that formats citations was precluded by lack of funds, with the result that some fairly rare entry types of a complex nature had to be presented in makeshift formats that could be achieved within the limits of the existing program.

Fourth and most important are shortcomings in our coverage within our chosen domain. We are reasonably content with our coverage of English and Japanese publications and of Chinese works published before 1949. We are not happy with our coverage of Chinese works published in the People's Republic or of the Russian, French, and German literatures in general; and for European languages with less significant literatures on China our coverage is regrettably little better than perfunctory. A special category not adequately covered is English translations of Chinese-language publications since 1949. Although most such materials fall outside our purview, the rest constitute a sizable corpus of great significance to scholarship. We have included as many such publications as time and money permitted. But an adequate culling of the entire outpouring of Chinese-to-English translations over the past 24 years was simply beyond our resources.

Fifth and finally comes the question of selectivity, which inevitably reflects to some extent the idiosyncrasies of the particular editors involved and their personal vision of what constitutes good scholarship. In reducing some 90,000 potential entries to some 31,400 actual entries, a long and tedious process involving over a hundred people, the application of our criteria has necessarily been imperfect, not only in matters of detail but in including what ought to have been excluded and excluding what ought to have been included. We can only say we did our best.

We welcome corrections and additions (for publications through 1972 only), which may be sent to Chinese Society Bibliography Project, c/o Stanford University Press, Stanford, Calif. 94305.

G.W.S.

September 1973

Entry Formats

Structure

An entry in the Bibliography normally has five elements: a number line, an author field, a title field, a publication-data field, and a subject block. The author field is eliminated for works that have no known author, editor, or compiler, and for translations appended to the citation of the original (see the example on p. xxii). The other fields are present in all entries.

A representative entry reads as follows:

> **15321** NNC O P2 G9.2 1842–1895
> Fielde, Adele Marion, 1839–1916.
> *A corner of Cathay: Studies from life among the Chinese.*
> New York: Macmillan, 1894. 11, 286 p.
> Subj 20 24 41 55 60 ▪ 17 22.2 23 28 43 45 47 50

In the number line, 15321 is the entry number. NNC is the library symbol (see p. lxvi and Explanatory Notes, §15), indicating that a copy of Fielde's book is held at the Columbia University Libraries. O is the Sources code (see p. xxxvii), indicating that the book is based heavily on personal observation. P2 is the Type-of-place code (see p. xxxvii), indicating that the book deals with urban and rural society alike. G9.2 is the Geographic code (see p. xxxii), indicating that Fielde's book treats Kwangtung province or some portion thereof. 1842–1895 is the Historical-period module (see p. xxxi) that encompasses the period of the book's concern.

The three fields that constitute the citation proper need no explanation here. Information on various specific aspects and permutations of these fields will be found in Explanatory Notes, p. xlv: for the author field, especially §1 and §2; for the title field, especially §3; for the publication-data field, especially §4 and §5. General formatting information appears in the following section.

In the subject block, the numbers are Subject codes (see p. xxiii). The five numbers in the subject block preceding the black square represent the subjects on which Fielde's book is judged to be of primary utility, namely (in the formal wording of the code designations), local communities as total systems, local economic systems, marriage and the family, living routines, and idea systems and values in general. The eight numbers following the square represent subjects on which the book is judged to be of secondary utility. This structural classification of the coding into subjects of primary and secondary utility is also followed in the Historical and Geographic Indexes.

Formatting

For purposes of formatting, all works cited in this *Bibliography* have been classified as either monographs, inclusions, journal articles, or unpublished dissertations.

Monographs

The monograph format, illustrated in the Fielde example given above, is used for published books and pamphlets cited in their entirety.

Inclusions

The inclusion format is used for chapters in books and other discrete sections of larger works:

> **10434** CSU S P2 G1.5 1949–1972
> Wiens, Herold Jacob, 1912–1971.
> 'China: The South.' In *The pattern of Asia*, edited by Norton Sydney Ginsburg. [Selective entry]
> Englewood Cliffs, N. J.: Prentice-Hall, 1958, 213–238.
> Subj 11.3 14 ▪ 21.1

The title field of an inclusion entry always contains two titles, the title of the inclusion and the title of the including work, preceded by "In."

"Selective entry" in this example is one of three standardized comments that invariably appear in inclusion entries, the others being "Sole entry" and "Analytic entry." "Sole entry" is used when no other chapter or section of the including work is cited in this *Bibliography*; "Selective entry" when at least one other chapter but not all other chapters of the including work are cited; and "Analytic entry" when all of the basic text of the including work is covered by two or more entries in this *Bibliography*. When inclusions are cited from multivolume publications, the work as a whole is considered to be the including work when the volumes are continuously paginated (see Explanatory Notes, §4.3); when they are separately paginated, the particular volume counts as the including work. Thus one volume of a multivolume work may appear as an inclusion.

Whether a given publication is considered a monograph or an including work is an editorial decision. When all or most of a work's component parts have different authors, it is normally "analyzed" as an including work: that is, such of its components as qualify for listing in this *Bibliography* are presented as separate entries. When all but one component of the work have the same author—the exception being typically an introduction or a chapter by an outside expert—we may supply two entries, one in monograph format for the book as a whole, the other in inclusion format for the outside component. Similar treatment is given a substantive appendix that deserves citation in its own right, even when its author is the author of the including work. In general, however, works written entirely by a single author are cited as monographs. If only one or a few parts of a work fall within the purview of this *Bibliography*, those parts are treated as inclusions; thus if an author's book has only one chapter on China, that chapter is cited as a sole inclusion entry. But if only a small portion of such a work falls outside our purview, a monograph entry is usual.

Other considerations affecting this decision have to do with a work's subject, geographic, and historical-period coverage. If its various components each treat a different principal subject, the work is normally analyzed into its components; if all or almost all components treat the same principal subject, it is normally treated as a monograph. Similarly, if the various components are concerned with different provinces in more than one region of China, the work is normally analyzed; if their treatment is confined to a single region, it is normally cited as a monograph. Finally, if the components all fall within the same historical-period module (e.g. 1911–1928), monograph treatment is usual; if each falls within a different module, analysis is more likely.

A work entirely written by a single author all of whose components fall within the scope of this *Bibliography* is treated as an including work (i.e. presented in the form of separate entries) only when each component, in contrast to the work as a whole, is sharply focused in time, space, or subject matter, and even then only if the work has exceptional scholarly merit.

Separate entries are not given for including works other than monographs with single other-author components. To locate other components of an including work cited in a selective or analytic inclusion entry, consult the Author Index or the Institutional Author Index under the name of the work's editor or compiler.

Journal Articles

The journal-article format is used for articles in newspapers, magazines, journals, and other periodical publications:

> **20033** NNC P P3 G9.2 1644–1895
> Eitel, Ernest John, 1838–1908.
> 'The law of testamentary succession as popularly understood and applied in China.'
> *China review* 15, 3 (Nov.–Dec. 1886), 150–155.
> SUBJ 12.2 45 ▪ 22.2 44

When it is unclear whether a publication should be considered a journal or a monograph in a series, we have tended to classify it as a journal if successive numbers are issued more or less regularly or frequently, if they carry volume and/or issue numbers in addition to dates, and if each volume or number includes more than one article.

Unpublished Dissertations

The unpublished-dissertation format is used for doctoral dissertations, masters theses, and senior theses submitted in typescript and not subsequently reproduced for public distribution:

> **17758** ICU P P2 G1.2 1895–1928
> Loh, L. S. (Lu Lin-su), 1896–1924.
> *The status of primary education in China.*
> Unpublished doctoral dissertation in Education, U. of Chicago, 1922. 224 p.
> SUBJ 27 ▪ 14.5 18 22.1

Dissertations reproduced on film for public distribution, as by University Microfilms, Inc., are cited in monograph format (see Explanatory Notes, §10.2), as are dissertations published in revised or unrevised form as books or as separately bound supplements to journals. For dissertations published as journal articles or inclusions, the article or inclusion format is used.

Special Formats

Several special formats involve nothing more than the addition of parenthetical or bracketed material to one of the citation fields. The major instances (references are to Explanatory Notes) involve series information for books (§4.5), data on the reviewed work in entries for titled reviews (§7), reissue information (§8), and dissertation data in monograph, inclusion, or journal-article entries (§10.2–3). Four other special formats, however—those for untitled reviews, serial publications, Type 1 translations, and chapters in unpublished dissertations—involve more fundamental modifications of basic formulas.

The following example illustrates the format for an untitled review:

11217 CSU P P1 G1.2 –1895
Hsu Dau-lin (Hsü Tao-lin), 1906–.
Review of *Law in Imperial China*, by Derk Bodde and Clarence Morris.
THJ new (2nd) series 8, 1/2 (Aug. 1970), 476–487.
Subj 12.2

In entries for serial publications (see Explanatory Notes, §9) the periodicity and span of publication are always indicated, along with the average size of the individual publications. The following example illustrates a monographic series:

14890 NIC P P2 G9.5 1949–1972
Hong Kong. Education Dept.
Annual summary, 1955/56–1970/71.
Hong Kong: Government Printer. Issued annually, 1956–1971. Average ca. 60 p.
Subj 17 ▪ 28 37

The Type 1 translation format is used for translations from one Western language to another (see Explanatory Notes, §11.2). An extra title field and an extra publication-data field are added for each translation cited:

15752 MCH O P2 G1.4 1644–1842
Timkovskii, Egor Fedorovich, 1790–1875.
Puteshestvie v Kitai cherez Mongoliiu v 1820 i 1821 godakh (A journey to China through Mongolia in 1820 and 1821).
St. Petersburg: Tip. Med. departamenta M-va vnutr. del, 1824. 3 vols. 388; 409; 433, 38 p.

Voyage à Pékin, à travers la Mongolie, en 1820 et 1821, edited by Julius Heinrich Klaproth.
Paris: Dondey-Dupré, 1827. 2 vols. 480; 459 p.

Travels of the Russian mission through Mongolia to China, and residence in Peking, in the years 1820–1821. Tr. by H- E- Lloyd, edited by J. H. Klaproth.
London: Longman, Rees, Orme, Brown and Green, 1827. 2 vols. 468; 496 p.
Subj 12.2 14 15 21.3 33 66 ▪ 12 14.3 16.1 22.2 24.6 55 56 57 62 63

Note that the author field is not repeated and that extra space separates the major blocks of data.

Finally, a format that is a hybrid of the standard inclusion and unpublished-dissertation formats is used to cite particular chapters in unpublished dissertations:

10892 WSU P P2 G1.1 1895–1972
Williams, Jack Francis, 1939–.
'Mapping activities of China.' In *China in maps, 1890–1960: A selective and annotated cartobibliography*, by J. F. Williams. [Sole entry]
Unpublished masters thesis in Geography, U. of Washington, 1966, 35–48.
Subj 12 36.1 70 ▪ 15

Annotation Categories

Each work cited in the Bibliography has been annotated by coding its contents five ways: by subjects on which it has something of interest to say (Subject codes); by the historical period it is concerned with (Historical-period codes); by the geographic area it covers (Geographic codes); by the type of place it focuses on, e.g. cities or rural areas (Type-of-place codes); and by the nature of its sources, e.g. personal observation or library research (Sources codes). This section discusses the five kinds of codes in the above order.

Subject Codes

Coverage

The scope of the Subject codes conforms to the restricted domain of knowledge covered by this *Bibliography*. That domain requires delimitation with respect to ethnic coverage, domestic relevance, and topical-disciplinary concern.

First, this *Bibliography* treats the Chinese people, not the peoples of China; its coverage specifically excludes non-Han aborigines and non-Chinese aliens. Nonetheless, the following groups, whether properly considered Han or non-Han, are covered here: (1) Hakkas; (2) demeaned or *déclassé* groups, such as the boat people of Kwangtung; (3) Chinese-speaking Muslims; (4) highly sinicized populations of non-Han origin, such as the Min-chia of Yunnan and the Jews of Kaifeng; and (5) persons or groups of non-Han origin involved in governing a predominantly Chinese polity within Geographic China. Most Manchus in the Ch'ing period meet one or both of the last two criteria. Also admitted by the last criterion are the governments of Manchoukuo and of Taiwan during the Japanese period, the various Japanese-sponsored governments of 1935–1945, the governments of Hong Kong and Macau, and the administrations of such foreign enclaves as Kwantung and Kiaochow and of foreign concessions in the treaty ports. (For partial exceptions to this statement of ethnic coverage, see the definitions of Subject codes 66 and 71 on p. xxxi.)

Second, this *Bibliography* treats the *domestic* social structure, economy, polity, culture, and personality of the Han Chinese. Works concerned solely with foreign policy and international relations or with foreign or international trade are specifically excluded. What counts as foreign is strictly circumscribed. Foreign trade is excluded, but not the business organization of import-export firms; foreign policy is excluded, but not the social organization in China of governmental agencies responsible for foreign affairs.

Finally, this *Bibliography* treats man in society. It excludes the biological sciences (including physical anthropology), physical geography, and the physical sciences, but includes the sociology, economics, politics, and epistemology of science. It excludes literature, fine arts, music, and most philosophy, but includes writers, artists, musicians, and philosophers as members of society. It also includes studies of folk arts and folklore and, within philosophy, empirical studies of cognition, ethics, and ideology. It excludes linguistic analysis per se, but includes the social significance of linguistic variation (code 29, p. xxviii), linguistic behavior, and semantic analyses that relate to Chinese cognition. Works treating Chinese social scientists and historians and their disciplines as specified in Subject code 70 are also included, even if what the scholars in question are studying (e.g. Shang archaeology or the grammar of the Wu dialects) falls outside our purview.

Design

There are 98 Subject codes numbered in seven "decades." The first decade (codes 10–19) covers major aspects of Chinese society in nationwide, macroanalytic, or general terms; the second decade (codes 20–29) treats the same aspects in local, microanalytic, or particular terms, and the third (codes 30–39) covers the same range of subjects in organizational terms, with emphasis on associations and movements. The fourth decade (codes 40–48) is concerned with family and kinship, and such related topics as male-female differences and property and inheritance. The fifth decade (codes 50–59) is concerned with the life cycle and existential subjects, the sixth (codes 60–66) with ideation. The three codes of the seventh decade (70–72) cover subjects of a different order: research, scholars, and bibliography. Four numbers at the end of decades, 49 and 67–69, are not used. The numbers 34 and 36, which might be expected to precede 34.1–34.3 and 36.1–36.4 respectively, are also not used as code numbers.

In general, codes in the second decade closely parallel those in the first: thus 22.1 Local Political and Social Controls obviously parallels 12.1 State Controls of the Populace, and 27 Elementary and Vocational Education is obviously related to 17 National and Higher Education. Yet the distinctions between first- and second-decade codes are by no means mechanically drawn. Two features of the scheme are worth pointing up in this regard. First, the level in the hierarchy of territorial systems at which the decade distinction is drawn varies from one pair of codes to another, in accordance with empirical and practical considerations. For instance, codes 12 and 14.5 include the county level and codes 22 and 24.5 cover only subcounty levels, since the biggest break in the hierarchy of administrative and fiscal arrangements occurs between the county level and the level just below. By contrast, for population and manpower codes (11/21, 11.1/21.1, 11.2/21.2, 11.4/21.4) the second-decade code extends all the way up to the multiprovince region, in this case because most scholarly works are limited to nationwide treatments; to draw the line lower would have exacerbated the disparate distribution of entries between the first- and second-decade codes. Other code pairs draw the distinction above or below the province. Second, definitions of many code pairs make distinctions of substance as well as level. Thus "radio and television" are coded 14.2 regardless of level, never 24.2; and conversely "supply-and-marketing cooperatives" are coded 24.3 regardless of level, never 14.3.

Most but not all of the third-decade codes echo their first- and second-decade counterparts. For example, codes 14.1, 24.1, and 34.1 all concern agriculture, and codes 15, 25, and 35 treat different aspects of the military. The continuities across decades are emphasized by the display on the front endpapers.

Decimals are used in the first three decades as a means of subordinating subcategories to categories, and in order to assign a single second digit to a large number of related subjects. Thus, the second digit 4 indicates an economic subject, and through recourse to decimals it has been used for several codes in each of the first three decades.

In designing the subject annotation scheme, we strove to approximate the optimal level of analytical differentiation. Significantly more than 98 codes would have rendered the subject indexes unduly complex and fragmented; significantly fewer would have made the index blocks unusably large. We also sought a reasonable fit between code categories and the corpus of publications being annotated. For example, economic categories are more finely differentiated than political not only because the literature on China in all languages emphasizes economic concerns, but also because our conventional subdivision of the economic domain (see codes 14.1–14.6) works much better for the literature on China than any comparable subdivision of the political domain.

Inevitably, some subject codes have much higher incidence than others. At one extreme are seven codes each used over 3,400 times in annotating the 31,443 works cited in all three volumes; at the other extreme are four codes used fewer than 340 times. Yet on the one hand, four of the seven most frequently used codes fall in the economic domain, to which 17 of the 95 substantive codes are devoted as it is; further differentiation of this domain would have thrown the logic of the entire scheme out of balance. And on the other hand, the four least frequently used codes are analytically essential: 11.1 Nationwide Urbanization and 46 Sex are generic subjects of obvious importance, while 39 Associations Based on Common Place of Origin and 44 Kin Terms and Relationships are key features of what is specifically Chinese about Chinese society. The paucity of codings in these cases is not a sufficient argument for submerging the work that has been done in these fields under more inclusive subject categories.

Each of the 98 Subject codes has a standardized short designation, which is used along with the number in the main headings of the Bibliography, the Historical Index, and the Geographic Index, and in the front endpapers. The formal wording of these standardized short designations is italicized in the definitions that follow.

Code Descriptions

10 *Chinese Society in General.* Han Chinese society as a total social system. Macroanalysis or wide-ranging description that treats most of Subjects 11–18 below.

11 *National Population.* The population of China as a whole or in greater part, provided the data are not exclusively urban (Subject 11.1). Census activity and household registration in general and throughout all or most of China. The distribution of the national population among regions or provinces.

11.1 *Nationwide Urbanization.* The urban population of all or most of China. The population of cities nationwide and the urban proportion of the total population.

11.2 *Extranational Migration and Nationwide Geo-*

graphic Mobility. Emigration from China, including migration to Hong Kong. Interregional migration except when the focus is on a single province or multiprovince region (Subject 21.2). Population movements and geographic mobility in general or nationwide; exile and banishment as forms of geographic mobility. Rural-urban migration in general or nationwide.

11.3 *Macroecology and Settlement Patterns*. Human geography in general; spatial analysis of the economy, the ecology, and human occupance at the national, regional, and provincial levels. Generic treatments of settlement types. Central-place systems: the hierarchy of market towns and cities as centers of administration, trade, and services. The distribution and redistribution of resources, including manpower, among different settlement types and territorial systems within a province or multiprovince region, and among such units; regional planning at the provincial level and higher.

11.4 *National Labor Force and Occupational Differentiation*. Manpower and the labor force at the national level, when not exclusively agricultural (Subject 16.3), blue-collar (Subject 16.4), or white-collar (Subject 16.2). Scientific and technical manpower. Occupational differentiation and division of labor in general and nationwide. Vocational choice and guidance, employment/unemployment, and incentives, wages, income, and systems of compensation at the national level when given comprehensive or cross-sectoral treatment. Corvée, multipurpose water conservancy, mass-construction projects, and public works in general.

12 *National Political System and Bureaucracy*. The state and the national polity. The civil bureaucracy; recruitment of the bureaucracy; the Ch'ing examination system as a device for political socialization and recruitment. Control of the bureaucracy by the center; rectification campaigns within the bureaucracy. The political and administrative systems at all levels of government down to and including the county, including province-level but not subprovincial municipalities.

12.1 *State Controls of the Populace*. Social, political, and ideological controls of the populace by the state or party. Propaganda; thought reform and ideological control. Public security and police systems in general or when tied to the national political system. In the People's Republic, rectification campaigns in general. (For rectification campaigns in the government bureaucracy, see Subject 12; in the controlling party, see Subject 32; in particular organizations, see Subject 32.1; among basic-level cadres, see Subject 22; and among the common people in local systems, see Subject 22.1.)

12.2 *National Legal System*. Legal codes, legal norms, and formal law, both criminal and civil. Constitutions and constitutional law at the national and provincial levels. Crime, justice, and the penal system, except for works focusing on the local level (Subject 22.2).

13 *Elite and Official Religion*. Official religion and the state cult; religion as "diffused" in the state and bureaucracy. State control of religious ideology and organization. Officially sponsored organizations for controlling and containing organized religious systems (Buddhism, Taoism, Christianity, Islam). Maoism as a national cult.

14 *National Economy and Economic Planning*. National, regional, and provincial economies in general. Macroanalytical and overall or general treatments of the economy that cover most of Subjects 14.1–14.6 below. Economic planning and the allocation of investment at the national, regional, and provincial levels; government control of the economy. Economic fluctuations, including booms and depressions. Economic development in general. Consumption and saving, capital formation, and national income.

14.1 *Agrarian Economy*. The agrarian sector of the national economy or regional economies. Agriculture, forestry, fishing, animal husbandry, and pastoralism in general or at the national and regional levels. Farm management and agricultural production in general; agricultural technology. Agricultural land use and cropping; land tenure, tenancy, and land reform in general or at the national and regional levels. Large-scale irrigation and production-related water conservancy.

14.2 *Transport and Communications*. National and regional systems of transport and communications. Roads, bridges, vehicles, and other modes of overland transport, in general and nation- or region-wide. Water transport: navigation; harbors, navigable waterways, and locks; ships, boats, and barges; transport-related water conservancy in general and nation- or region-wide. Aviation. Radio and television. The postal system at national and regional levels. Publishing and journalism of national or regional significance; books, journals, newspapers, and other publications. State control of transport and communications.

14.3 *Commerce and Services*. The commercial and service sectors of the national economy and of regional and provincial economies. Cities and their commercial hinterlands as trading systems. Interprovincial and interregional trade. Extraction from the rural economy for urban consumption; food supply. Commodity storage and warehousing, prices and pricing, and weights and measures, in general and at the provincial level and higher. Commercial law except for strictly corporation or business law (Subject 34.2). State control of commerce and services; food rationing; price control. Smuggling. The economic effects of boycotts.

14.4 *Industrial Economy*. The industrial sector of the national economy and of regional and provincial economies, including extractive (metals, minerals, and fuels), processing (of products from the agrarian sector as well as mining), power (hydroelectric, nuclear, etc.), and manufacturing industries. Industrial and technological development. Utilities and "infrastructure" other than for transport purposes (Subject 14.2). State-operated industry and state control of industry.

14.5 *State Revenue and Expenditure*. The fiscal sector of the economy at all levels of administration down to and including the county, including province-level but not subprovincial municipalities. Taxation, customs, levies, tribute, and other state revenue. Tax law. Government budgets, expenditures, and debt management, except at subcounty levels. Anti-tax and tax-protest movements.

14.6 *Financial, Monetary, and Credit Systems*. The financial sector of the national economy and of regional and provincial economies, including banking, credit, pawnbroking, and insurance. Money, currency, and inflation; stock exchanges and money markets. State control of finance, money, and credit. Credit, monetary, and banking law.

15 *The Military*. The armed forces, including army, navy, and air force. The military bureaucracy. Soldiers and other military personnel as status groups. Warfare; military norms and theory. Military control of the populace. (For police control, see Subjects 12.1/22.1.)

16 *Social Stratification and Mobility*. The stratification system as a whole. Classes and class struggle in general. Social mobility upward or downward when viewed society-wide. Prestige, power, wealth, education, occupational status, responsibility, etc., as determinants or indicators of social or class status. General or overall treatments of socioeconomic strata that cover at least three of Subjects 16.1–16.4 below. Servitude; demeaned peoples and low-status occupational groups not covered by Subjects 16.1–16.4.

16.1 *Elite Strata*. In Ch'ing China, the imperial clan, aristocracy, and nobility; the bureaucratic elite or gentry viewed as a social stratum; the lower gentry or elite strata in general or empire-wide. In the People's Republic, party and state cadres above the basic level viewed as a social stratum. Literati and intelligentsia; teachers and other professionals not oriented to business. Differentiation within the elite, and mobility within, into, and out of the elite strata.

16.2 *The Bourgeoisie*. Townspeople in general. Merchants, shopkeepers, artisans, craftsmen, industrialists, financiers, moneylenders, brokers, property owners, compradors, etc., seen as status groups or social strata. In the People's Republic, national capitalists and the petty bourgeoisie. Semiprofessionals and professionals in or associated with commerce, industry, and finance; white-collar employees in general, including salaries and employment/unemployment.

16.3 *The Peasantry*. Peasants, farmers, and fishermen seen as status groups or social strata. Labor force, employment/unemployment, incentives, and systems of compensation when limited to agriculture, forestry, and fishing (otherwise see Subject 11.4). General treatment of the masses or common people in Ch'ing China.

16.4 *The Working Class*. Labor viewed as a status group or social stratum. The industrial proletariat, including miners. The blue-collar labor force in general, including employment/unemployment, working conditions, incentives, wages, and income. Labor productivity. Labor law unless treating welfare exclusively (Subject 18).

17 *National and Higher Education*. Education in general, except when limited to the elementary level (Subject 27). In Ch'ing China, the examination system as an educational and academic institution; official schools and educational supervision; *shu-yüan* and other academies. In modern times, secondary education unless strictly vocational (Subject 27); higher education of all kinds; teachers' education and other professional education; educational supervision and administration at all levels down to the county and municipality. The sociology of the Chinese writing system. Libraries and librarianship in general.

18 *National Welfare and Living Standards*. Standards of living and poverty; cost of living and purchasing power. Welfare, public assistance, social work, public services, charity, and philanthropy in general and nationwide or when part of a supraprovincial system. Large-scale famines, disasters, and relief measures.

19 *Modernization and Directed Social Change*. Directed change, modernizing processes, movements to effect change and reform, and "campaigns"; all of these *only when* (1) they are nationwide efforts or have general national or society-wide significance *and* (2) their significance extends beyond any particular sector or aspect of society specifically coded elsewhere. (But see Subject 12.1 for rectification campaigns.) Periodization and the temporal structure of events and policies.

20 *Local Communities as Total Systems*. The community or local territorial unit as a total social system. Microanalysis or wide-ranging description that treats most of Subjects 21–28 below. General treatment of particular local systems, e.g. villages, marketing communities, communes, market towns, cities, urban wards or quarters, and counties.

21 *Regional and Local Population*. The population of local territorial systems, provinces, and multiprovince regions, except for exclusively urban units (Subject 21.1). Census activity and household registration within regions and smaller territorial units. The

distribution of regional or provincial populations among administrative units other than municipalities.

21.1 *Regional Urbanization and City Population.* The urban population of local and regional territorial systems. The urbanization of provinces and regions. The population of particular cities.

21.2 *Regional and Local Geographic Mobility.* Migration at regional, provincial, and local levels, including immigration into a particular region or province or local system. Rural-urban migration within a multiprovince region or with respect to particular cities. *Hsia-fang* (downward transfer) as urban-to-rural migration. Return-to-the-village movements.

21.3 *Microecology and Particular Settlements.* Particular settlements (villages, towns, cities) or segments thereof as ecological or spatial systems. City and town planning. Town plus hinterland as a spatial or ecological system. The distribution and redistribution of resources, including manpower, among different settlements and territorial systems, within subprovincial regions, and among such regions; subprovincial regional planning. Land utilization when not exclusively agricultural. Units of subcounty territorial administration.

21.4 *Regional Labor Force and Local Division of Labor.* Manpower and the labor force at regional, provincial, and local levels, when not exclusively agricultural (Subjects 16.3/26.3), blue-collar (Subjects 16.4/26.4), or white-collar (Subjects 16.2/26.2). Occupational differentiation, division of labor, and corvée within local systems, provinces, and regions. Vocational choice and guidance, employment/unemployment, and incentives, wages, income, and systems of compensation at regional, provincial, and local levels, when given comprehensive or cross-sectoral treatment; in particular, systems of distribution and remuneration within communes. Particular mass-construction projects and public works.

22 *Local Political Systems.* Politics and administration in particular settlements (villages, towns, cities) or segments thereof, in all subcounty territorial systems, including communes, and in subprovincial municipalities. Community leadership and power structure; in the People's Republic, basic-level cadres as leaders and administrators, and rectification of basic-level cadres. Municipal and local services other than utilities (Subject 24.4) and police (Subject 22.1).

22.1 *Local Political and Social Controls.* Social, political, and ideological controls, including public-security and police systems, in particular settlements or segments thereof and in all subcounty territorial systems. *Pao-chia* as a system of local control. In the People's Republic, rectification campaigns in local systems.

22.2 *Customary Law and Dispute Resolution.* Customary legal norms. Disputes, social unrest, disaffection, and deviant behavior in particular settlements and in all subcounty territorial systems. Mediation and other modes of dispute resolution. Crime, justice, and the penal system in local systems.

23 *Folk Religion.* The popular or folk religion in general, including deities, temples, and religious specialists (but see Subject 33 for the social *organization* of temples and sects). Shamanism, sorcery, witchcraft, and magic, except when concerned solely with health and therapy (Subject 56). Religion within particular settlements and all subcounty territorial systems, except that Christianity and Islam are included only when folk-ized. Religion as a defining and integrative factor in local systems. Religious festivals and the annual round of festivities in connection with popular religious observances.

24 *Local Economic Systems.* The local economies of particular settlements and of subprovincial territorial systems. Microanalytical and overall or general treatments of the local economy that cover most of Subjects 24.1–24.6 below. Economic planning and the allocation of investment at subprovincial levels. Consumption and saving and capital formation within local systems.

24.1 *Local Agrarian Economies.* The agrarian sector of local and provincial economies. Agriculture, forestry, fishing, animal husbandry, and pastoralism in particular settlements, local systems, and administrative units up to the provincial level. Farm management and agricultural production at the local level, unless the focus is on producers' cooperatives or other associations (Subject 34.1). Agricultural land use, land tenure, tenancy, and land reform within local systems. Local irrigation and production-related water conservancy.

24.2 *Local Transport and Communications.* Local and provincial systems of transport and communications. Roads, bridges, vehicles, and other modes of overland transport within local systems and provinces. Water transport: navigation; harbors, navigable waterways, and locks; ships, boats, and barges; transport-related water conservancy at local or provincial levels. The postal system at provincial and local levels. Local and provincial newspapers, journals, and other publishing.

24.3 *Local Commerce and Services.* The commercial and service sectors of local economies. Market towns and their hinterlands as marketing systems. Commerce and services, commodity storage and warehousing, prices and pricing, and weights and measures—all in particular cities and other localities and within subprovincial territorial systems. Consumers' cooperatives and supply-and-marketing cooperatives.

24.4 *Local Industry.* Extractive, processing, power, and manufacturing industry and utilities in particular cities and municipalities and within subprovincial territorial systems. Handicraft and cottage industry in general and in local systems. Industrial cooperatives.

24.5 *Local Revenue and Expenditure.* Taxation, customs, levies, and other revenue at the subcounty level, including cities. Public budgets, expenditures, and debt management in subcounty systems, including communes, and in subprovincial municipalities. Anti-tax and tax-protest uprisings.

24.6 *Local Finance, Money, and Credit.* Banking, credit, pawnbroking, and insurance in particular cities and other localities, and in subprovincial territorial systems. Credit cooperatives and rotating-credit societies.

25 *Feuds, Banditry, and Local Paramilitary Units.* Militia and the militarization of local systems. Local feuds and warfare. Banditry and piracy. Local uprisings, whether or not part of an explicitly anti-state movement. Particular localized military campaigns. Conscription and other recruitment for the armed forces.

26 *Local Social Stratification and Mobility.* Social stratification, differentiation, and mobility at the subcounty level, including cities. Classes and class struggle within local systems. Determinants and indicators of social or class status at the local level. Treatments of local social strata that cover at least three of Subjects 26.1–26.4 below. Demeaned peoples and low-status occupational groups in particular cities or local systems when not covered by Subjects 26.1–26.4 below.

26.1 *The Local Elite.* In Ch'ing China, gentry and landlords in the context of their native places and more inclusive local systems. Literati, intellectuals, and professionals in particular cities and other localities. In the People's Republic, cadres at the county, municipality, and lower levels; basic-level cadres viewed as a social stratum.

26.2 *Businessmen.* Townspeople in particular localities. Merchants, shopkeepers, artisans, craftsmen, industrialists, financiers, moneylenders, brokers, property owners, compradors, semiprofessionals, white-collar workers, etc., in particular cities, market towns, and counties.

26.3 *Peasants.* Peasants, farmers, and fishermen in the context of the local community. Labor force, employment/unemployment, incentives, and systems of compensation in rural local systems, including cooperatives and communes, when limited to agriculture, forestry, and fishing (otherwise see Subject 21.4).

26.4 *Workers.* Blue-collar workers, including apprentices, in particular cities, market towns, and counties. The nonagricultural labor force, including employment/unemployment, working conditions, incentives, wages, and income at the county level and below.

27 *Elementary and Vocational Education.* Primary schools and elementary education, including kindergartens. In Ch'ing and Republican China, *ssu shu* (traditional private schools), *i hsüeh* (charitable elementary schools), and other schools supported by lineages and local systems. In modern times, primary schools apart from supervision and administration at the county and municipal levels and higher; agricultural and vocational education apart from higher-level technical schools; and part-work part-study schools.

28 *Local Welfare and Living Standards.* Standards of living and poverty in particular communities; family budgets. Welfare, public assistance, social work, public services, charity, and philanthropy when community-based, autonomous, or tied only to provincial or lower-level systems. Localized famines, disasters, and relief measures.

29 *Regional and Subethnic Variation.* Cultural variation in space; variations in culture, social structure, and language from one community, territorial unit, or region to another. Regional subcultures, linguistic provinces, and speech communities. "Speech groups" (Hakka, Cantonese, Hokkien, etc.) as culturally distinctive subethnic groups. Interethnic and intergroup relations, except between Han and non-Han peoples (Subject 66). Local norms as a basis for localism, provincialism, or regionalism.

30 *Voluntary Associations and Formal Organization in General.* Principles of organization and types of organizations in Chinese society. Social bases for organizational recruitment and internal structuring. General treatments of mass movements. General or overall treatments of Chinese organizational activity or voluntary associations that cover most of Subjects 31–39 below.

31 *Social Organization of Recreation.* Associations with a primary goal of recreation, entertainment, or aesthetic expression. The social organization and business aspects of recreation, entertainment, and expressive arts, including sports, the dance, opera, theater, and cinema. Social and recreational clubs of all kinds, including gambling but excluding organized prostitution (Subject 46).

32 *Political Parties.* Parties, factions, and other political-action groups that are not avowedly anti-state. Political, ideological, and reform movements. The Kuomintang. The Chinese Communist Party after the establishment of the People's Republic. Rectification campaigns within the controlling party.

32.1 *State or Party Control of Organized Groups.* Social, political, and ideological controls of organizations by the state apparatus or controlling party. Rectification campaigns within formal organizations apart from the government bureaucracy (see Subject 12) and the controlling party (see Subject 32). *Hsia-fang* (downward transfer) as a general practice covering government, party, and nonparty formal organizations.

32.2 *Anti-State Associations.* Secret societies; sects, parties, and other organizations that are explicitly or avowedly anti-state, rebellious, or revolutionary. Organized rebellions or revolutionary movements, including the Taiping and Nien movements, the revolutionary movement prior to the Revolution of 1911, and the Communist movement prior to the establishment of the People's Republic.

33 *Religious Sects and Associations.* Specifically or primarily religious societies and organizations not under state auspices; religious sects, whether heterodox or orthodox, and the religious aspects of secret societies. The social organization of monasteries, nunneries, "vegetarian houses," temples, churches, and sects. The Christian church, Buddhism, and Islam, unless the emphasis is on folk-ization (Subject 23) or ideological control (Subject 13); the religious life of Muslims, Christians, and Jews. Religious movements; antireligious, including anti-Christian, and atheist movements.

34.1 *Agricultural Associations and Cooperatives.* Extrafamilial organization of all kinds concerned with agrarian production (agriculture, forestry, fishing), including labor exchange, pooling of implements and draft animals, crop-watching societies, and irrigation societies. Agricultural producers' cooperatives and the associated movement. In the People's Republic, collectivization in general, and specifically mutual-aid teams, cooperatives, collectives, state farms, and, within communes, brigades, teams, and work groups as units of production.

34.2 *Business Organization.* The social organization of business enterprises, shops, firms, and factories. Business administration and industrial management. Public relations, advertising, and trademarks. Business and corporation law. The comprador system. Personnel and labor management, including recruitment, apprenticeship, and management's negotiations with labor representatives; the contract-labor system. The cooperative movement in general, i.e. when more inclusive than agricultural producers' cooperatives (Subject 34.1); federations of cooperatives. Business culture and practices; values related to occupational roles in business.

34.3 *Guilds.* Associations deriving from nonagricultural occupations that are not limited to employers, capitalists and/or managers (Subject 36.2) or to employees and/or laborers (Subject 36.4). Commercial, craft, and service guilds.

35 *Veterans Associations and the Military in Society.* Organized veterans and demobilized soldiers. Interaction between the military and the civilian population. The role of the military in society.

36.1 *Elite and Professional Associations.* Professional and academic societies, including research institutes. Elitist organizations of all kinds, except those devoted specifically and solely to political action (Subjects 32 and 32.2), education (Subject 37), or charity (Subject 38).

36.2 *Employers Associations.* Associations that are explicitly limited to employers or to firms in the sense of employers, capitalists, and/or managers. Associations of employers or firms in the same line. Chambers of commerce. Business promotion.

36.3 *Peasant Associations and Movements.* Organizations of peasants other than those devoted primarily to agricultural production (Subject 34.1). The peasant or agrarian movement; peasant uprisings and "peasant" wars.

36.4 *Labor Unions and the Labor Movement.* Associations that are explicitly limited to employees or laborers. The labor movement; strikes and workers' uprisings.

37 *Educational Associations and Movements.* Associations and movements that promote education and literacy. Associations and movements that promote language and writing reforms. Fundamental-education and community-education programs and movements; the mass-education movement; the rural-reconstruction movement in its community-education aspect; educational extension programs, adult education. Uplift programs; movements to improve the quality or decorum of daily life. Educational foundations. Alumni associations.

38 *Organized Philanthropy and Mutual-Aid Societies.* Benevolent and charitable societies of all kinds. Welfare societies and agencies. Civic organizations and service clubs. Organizations for famine and disaster relief. Mutual-aid societies that are not in the first instance religious sects (Subject 33), guilds (Subject 34.3), peasant associations (Subject 36.3), labor unions (Subject 36.4), or native-place associations (Subject 39).

39 *Associations Based on Common Place of Origin.* Associations based on common membership in, or derivation from, the same settlement (same native village, town, or city) or territorial system (same township, county, prefecture, province, region, or grouping of provinces). Associations known variously in the literature as "speech-group" or dialect associations; "fellow countrymen" or native-place associations, *t'ung-hsiang hui*; regional or provincial clubs, *hui-kuan*.

40 *Kinship Systems in General.* The kinship system as a whole or in broad outline. Overall or general treatments of family and kinship that cover most of Subjects 41–47 below. "Familism" when broadly conceived; familial and extrafamilial relationships as models for behavior with non-kin.

41 *Marriage and the Family.* Betrothal and marriage, including secondary and plural marriages; marital residence. Divorce and termination of marriage. Adoption, including "little daughter-in-law" adoption. Size and composition of the family or house-

hold. The domestic economy and the division of labor within the family. Interpersonal relationships within the family and its subsystems (conjugal units, parent-child dyads, sibling sets, etc.). The social arrangements of family division; heirship and succession to the family headship. Family law.

42 *Lineages and Clanship.* Extrafamilial kin groups of all kinds. Localized and higher-order lineages. Clans and clanship. Clan and surname associations. Interlineage and interclan relationships.

43 *Ancestor Worship.* The cult of the ancestors in the household, in the ancestral hall, and at grave sites; ancestral rites and ancestor-oriented festivals such as Ch'ing-ming. Beliefs about ancestors. Ancestral halls or lineage temples.

44 *Kin Terms and Relationships.* Kinship terminology. Relationships with extrafamilial kinsmen, whether affines, agnates, or other consanguines; normative behavior toward kinsmen. Extension to nonkinsmen of kinship terminology and behavior.

45 *Property and Inheritance.* Concepts of property, ownership, and proprietorship in relation to individual persons, kin groups, and other corporate bodies; collective or corporate ownership. Inheritance of property; property arrangements in family division; property and inheritance law. Landed property except when devoted primarily to agriculture, forestry, fishing, and/or animal husbandry (Subjects 14.1/24.1), including urban real estate and land values.

46 *Sex.* Sexuality; sexual behavior and relations, homosexual as well as heterosexual. Concepts of sexuality and chastity; sexual norms; regulation of sex. Eroticism and pornography. Prostitution and other commercialized sex.

47 *Female Roles and Male-Female Differences.* Female as distinguished from male roles; the sexual division of labor. The status of women; women as a status group; women's associations; liberation of women.

48 *Non-Kin Interpersonal Relationships.* Face-to-face social relations outside the context of kin groups or formal organizations; etiquette and manners; nonkin dyadic relationships in general. Ascriptive and experiential bases for forming or activating interpersonal ties; the taxonomy of interpersonal relations. The role of "face," trust, *kan-ch'ing*, and other attributes in interpersonal relations. Friendship, comradeship, and sworn brotherhood and sisterhood. Fictive kinship, including godparenthood and ritual adoption.

50 *Life Cycle and Age Grading.* The life cycle in general; rites of passage. Concepts of the stages of life. Role differentiation based on relative or absolute age. Absolute age groups in general and specifically from the prime of life (*chuang-nien*) through old age. Status and treatment of the aged; senescence and retirement. Wide-ranging treatments of Chinese lifeways that cover most of Subjects 51–58 below.

51 *Reproduction.* Menstruation, conception, pregnancy, childbirth, and postnatal care. Barrenness and sterility. The practice of birth control, abortion, and infanticide. Birth-control campaigns.

52 *Infancy and Childhood.* Social placement and naming; rites of passage from birth to (but not including) puberty. Infant and child care, development, and maturation. Childhood activities; status of children. Abuse and protection of children; child labor. Orphanages, nurseries, and day-care centers. Children's organizations.

53 *Socialization.* Techniques of socialization and enculturation. Child training in general and with respect to weaning, food, cleanliness, sex, aggression, independence, etc. Intergenerational transmission of social norms, skills, beliefs, etc.

54 *Adolescence and Youth.* Adolescents (*shao-nien*) and youth (*ch'ing-nien*) as status groups, and as distinguished from children and adults. Middle-school and college students. Puberty and initiation. Adolescent activities. Youth organizations; youth and student movements. Juvenile delinquency.

55 *Living Routines.* Daily, weekly, monthly, etc. cycles of routine behavior. Food preparation and consumption; cuisine; nutrition. Housing and shelter; architecture. Clothing and adornment. Drinking, smoking, and drug consumption. Personal hygiene.

56 *Illness and Medicine.* Concepts of health and sickness and of specific diseases; morbidity and morbidity rates; epidemics. Therapy and medical care, including psychiatry; doctors, medical practitioners, and paramedical personnel; hospitals and clinics; druggists and pharmaceutics. Public health, sanitation, preventive medicine, and related campaigns. Health insurance.

57 *Death Practices.* Concepts of death and dying. Dying and suicide. Funerals, burials, mortuary practices. Mourning; social relationships to death.

58 *Fertility and Mortality.* Fertility rates and the results of birth control. Mortality rates, including infant mortality. Rates of natural increase. Life tables and life expectancy. Vital processes in relation to their conditioning social factors and contexts.

59 *Life Histories and Biographies.* Life histories and biographical writings that illuminate important aspects of Chinese society and culture. Concepts, purposes, and uses of biography in Chinese culture.

60 *Idea Systems and Values in General.* Culture in the sense of ideation: systems of ideas and beliefs, of expressive symbols, and of value orientations. Overall treatments of values, idea systems, ethos, and motivation that cover most of Subjects 61–65 below.

61 *Personality and Behavioral Processes.* Motivation, aggression, dependence, and other social-psychological processes. Personality development. Intelligence and IQ. Values that are qualities of the personality.

"Modal" or "basic" personality. Mental health and illness. Thought reform as process.

62 *Cognition*. Ideas about nature and man, space and time; cosmology and world view. Historiography, theology, and mythology. Fate and divination. Science and exact knowledge; ethnoscience; systems of natural "science" such as geomancy (*feng-shui*). Semantics. Games and cognitive models. Values having primary reference to cognitive systems.

63 *Ethics*. Evaluation of interpersonal relations and behavior; ethical concepts and ethical systems. Values having primary reference to interpersonal relationships or social groups; religious values as a basis of social action.

64 *Ideology and the Great Tradition*. Elitist ideology; the great tradition of Imperial China; Confucianism as ideology. Modern ideologies from the Taipings to Maoism. Political theory and theories of political economy.

65 *Folklore and Little Traditions*. Folk ideology and folklore, including folk art, folk songs, folktales, and proverbs. Idea systems and values peculiar to the common people or to the peasantry; the coverage of Subjects 61–63 above when limited to the masses.

66 *Self-Conception in Relation to Outsiders*. Definitions of in-group and out-group. The concept of "barbarians"; ethnocentrism. Xenophobia, antiforeign movements. Nationalism as a reaction formation to foreign threat. Han Chinese interrelations with non-Han peoples.

70 *Chinese Scholars of Chinese Society*. Sociology, social/cultural anthropology, ethnology, social psychology, economics, political science, modern institutional history, and other social sciences as disciplines in China. News of research in these fields by Chinese scholars; biographical data about Chinese social scientists.

71 *Non-Chinese Scholars of Chinese Society*. The study of China within the above-mentioned disciplines in countries other than China. News of research on Chinese society, culture, and personality by non-Chinese scholars; biographical data on such social scientists.

72 *Bibliography*. Bibliographies treating Chinese society. Bibliographic essays and annotated bibliographies are given a primary 72 code; secondary 72 is used for items containing unannotated bibliographies that are extraordinarily well selected or comprehensive.

Primary vs. Secondary Codings and Principal Subject

All Subject codes assigned to a given work are designated as "primary" or "secondary." This represents a relative dichotomization of *utility* and should not be confused with the conventional scholarly distinction between primary and secondary sources. As part of the formal scheme, at least one of the codes assigned must be designated primary; not more than six codes may be designated primary, and not more than ten may be designated secondary. Though on this count and others the distinction between primary and secondary is necessarily somewhat arbitrary at the borderline, we think it will save many hours of wasted effort for the average user of the Historical and Geographic Indexes (see pp. xl–xli).

One of the primary codes assigned a given work is designated its principal subject. Although this code is defined as the one that would be assigned the work if only one code were allowed, its assignment is essentially arbitrary. Its sole use is to categorize the entry for purposes of placing it in the Bibliography proper. In the two subject indexes (Historical and Geographic), principal subject codes figure no differently from other primary subject codes.

In the subject block at the end of each entry of the Bibliography, primary codes precede the black square, secondary codes follow it; both are listed in numerical order. If no secondary codes have been assigned, no black square appears in the subject block. The distinction between primary and secondary in the subject block is the basis for the classification into primary and secondary in the Historical and Geographic Indexes.

Coding Conventions

The two most general and comprehensive codes in the scheme—10 Chinese Society in General and 20 Local Communities as Total Systems—would have little utility as secondary listings and are accordingly used only in primary designations. If a primary designation is not warranted, code 10 or 20 is simply not assigned.

A first-decade code is generally taken to subsume its second-decade counterpart when the latter would in any case be designated secondary and when the distinction is one of level rather than substance. Where the application of this rule might be ambiguous, the code definitions themselves are explicit. The definition of 17 National and Higher Education, for example, begins "Education in general, except when limited to the elementary level (Subject 27)." This convention has important consequences for the efficient use of the analytical indexes (see p. xliii).

Ten of the Subject codes have a summary function: codes 10, 20, 30, 40, 50, and 60, and codes 14/24 and 16/26. This function is spelled out in the code definitions. It, too, has consequences for the efficient use of the analytical indexes (see p. xliii).

HISTORICAL-PERIOD CODES

This volume covers publications that treat the period 1644 to 1972. For annotation purposes, this span is divided into six "modules":

1644–1842	1895–1911	1928–1949
1842–1895	1911–1928	1949–1972

Except for 1972, the years that define modules are specified to the day as follows:

30 Oct. 1644	Establishment of the Ch'ing dynasty (Fu-lin declared Emperor of China)
29 Aug. 1842	Treaty of Nanking ending the Opium War
17 Apr. 1895	Treaty of Shimonoseki ending the Sino-Japanese War
10 Oct. 1911	Wuchang Uprising initiating the Revolution of 1911
10 Oct. 1928	Establishment of the National Government of China
1 Oct. 1949	Establishment of the People's Republic of China

For works whose coverage extends beyond a single module, modules are combined as necessary into a single code, e.g. 1644–1911. The 21 possible combinations are:

1644–1842					
1644–1895	1842–1895				
1644–1911	1842–1911	1895–1911			
1644–1928	1842–1928	1895–1928	1911–1928		
1644–1949	1842–1949	1895–1949	1911–1949	1928–1949	
1644–1972	1842–1972	1895–1972	1911–1972	1928–1972	1949–1972

To accommodate works that treat pre- as well as post-1644 China—e.g. a book covering late Ming and early Ch'ing—we substitute a blank space for the year 1644: thus –1842, –1895, etc. Finally, we have used the code –1644 for a few major works that are relevant to the Ch'ing period but not explicitly concerned with it or based specifically on Ch'ing data. Thus the total number of codes used is 28. Only one of the 28 possible codes is assigned a given work—the one representing the shortest period that encompasses the time span of its concern.

Note that all codes represent a span of time; works whose coverage is limited to a lesser period within that span are necessarily coded for the whole span. When the temporal coverage is exactly one calendar year (as with a yearbook or an annual review), transitional years are given single-module codes as follows:

1644: 1644–1842	1895: 1895–1911	1928: 1911–1928
1842: 1644–1842	1911: 1895–1911	1949: 1928–1949

The precise date specified for a transitional year may be ignored in coding works whose coverage extends beyond that date but not beyond that calendar year. Thus a work covering April 1900 to December 1911 is coded 1895–1911, not 1895–1928, and one covering February 1949 to July 1966 is coded 1949–1972, not 1928–1972.

Geographic Codes

Scope and Design

It will have been noted that whereas a work may be, and normally is, assigned multiple Subject codes, it is always assigned one and only one Historical-period code. All of the remaining coding dimensions, Geographic included, resemble the Historical-period code in this regard. They are singular codes, and the logic of their design closely parallels that of the Historical-period codes. A discrete set of modules is established and cumulative codes are defined as combinations of the primary modules.

The geographic modules are essentially provinces. They correspond to the list of Nationalist provinces as of 1930, except that Sikang has been combined with Szechwan (code 8.1). Taiwan is a basic module (code 9.4); Hong Kong and Macau together form another (code 9.5). Other foreign and colonial enclaves are included in the module for the province from which they were detached, as are province-level municipalities. In sum, this *Bibliography* covers the present territory of the People's Republic of China plus Taiwan, Hong Kong, and Macau. It does not cover Outer Mongolia or the Mongolian People's Republic, even for periods when Chinese suzerainty over this territory was generally recognized.

In defining the basic geographic modules, we recognize only the more enduring of the many administrative changes that have occurred over the years. For 1644–1928, we recognize boundaries reflected in the Kuang-hsü edition of *Ta Ch'ing hui tien*. For 1928–1952 we recognize the official boundaries established in 1928 by the Nationalist government, which included radically altered provincial arrangements along China's Inner Asian frontiers. The equally sweeping changes made by the government of the People's Republic in 1952–1958 required more complex decisions. We used the 1928 boundaries for Manchuria until 1954, ignoring Manchoukuo provinces, the postwar nine-province restructuring by the Nationalists, and the several boundary revisions by the Communists prior to 1954; from 1954, when the number of Manchurian provinces was once again reduced to three, bearing the same names as the 1928 Nationalist provinces but with markedly different boundaries, our coding reflects the new boundaries. The basic codes for the four Nationalist provinces in Inner Mongolia are used until the year when each was officially abolished: 1952 for Chahar, 1954 for Suiyuan and Ningsia, and 1955 for Jehol, though the code for Ningsia (code 3.4) is revived in 1958 with the establishment of Ningsia Hui A.R. The code for Sikang is used until 1955, when that province's territory was divided between Szechwan and Tibet. We recognize neither the fleeting existence of P'ing-yüan province nor the impermanent *hsien* transfers carried out in 1958–59 and undone within a year or two, but we recognize all other official rectifications of provincial boundaries from 1952 to 1968. The 1969 changes made in the provincial boundaries of the Inner Mongolian A.R. and its neighbors are not recognized. In general, for provincial boundaries after 1955 we have relied on *Chung-hua jen min kung ho kuo hsing cheng ch'ü hua chien ts'e* (Peking, 1965).

The territorial extent of our basic provincial modules is mapped at three points in time on p. xxxiv and on the back endpapers. With few exceptions, the map labeled "Ca. 1894" holds for 1644–1928, the map labeled "Ca. 1934" holds for 1928–1955, and the map labeled "Ca. 1964" holds for 1955–1972.

Our system, then, permits different referents for the same Geographic code at different times. It follows that a locality may be assigned different Geographic codes in different periods. Thus Nan-le *hsien*, which was transferred from Hopei to Honan in 1952, is coded 5.1 before the transfer and 5.4 after it; the city of Fou-hsin is coded 5.1 for Chihli prior to 1928, 3.1 for Jehol during 1928–1954, and thereafter 2.3 for Liaoning. Some thirteen reasonably important cities have changed provinces, and hence Geographic codes, since the early 1920s. These cases are symbolized by open circles on the maps and flagged as necessary in General Index entries.

The basic modules are cumulated into three levels of larger units, each with a distinctive code: eight fixed multiprovince regions (codes 2.0, 3.0, etc.), two higher-order regions (codes 1.4 and 1.5), and three territorially distinguished versions of "China" (codes 1.1, 1.2, and 1.3). Details of the cumulation scheme are set out in the chart on p. xxxv and presented graphically in the lower right-hand map on p. xxxiv, which is reproduced on the back endpapers.

In the chart a + sign means that the basic module is covered by the cumulative code; a blank means that it is not. An S marks the two anomalous cases in which a basic module is split between two cumulative codes. The logic of the numbering scheme is readily apparent. Geographic codes beginning with the digit 1 are reserved for the various "Chinas" and higher-order regions; those whose second digit is 0 are used for multiprovince regions. The first digit of each basic module is the same as the multiprovince region to which it has been assigned.

The chart shows how the basic modules build up to form ever more inclusive cumulative codes. Take row 9.5 as an example. An item that treats Hong Kong only is coded 9.5. If it treats Hong Kong and one or more of the provincial units whose codes begin with 9, say Kwangtung, it is coded 9.0. If it treats Hong Kong and some place or places in South China beyond the 9.0 region (e.g. Hong Kong and South China generally, or the Ningpo–Hong Kong trade), it is coded 1.5. If its coverage extends beyond South China—as in, say, a comparison of the two British territories of Hong Kong and Weihaiwei, in North China—the work is given the most inclusive code, 1.1. All this is conveyed by the three + signs in row 9.5.

Three anomalies require mention. (1) Code 3.0 appears as a basic code *and* as a cumulative code. It is basic when used for Inner Mongolia prior to 1928 and when used for the Inner Mongolian A.R.; it is cumulative when used for two or more of the Nationalist provinces coded 3.1–3.4 for 1928–1955 or when used for the Inner Mongolian A.R. *and* the Ningsia Hui A.R. after 1958. (2) Code 3.1 (Jehol) is shown on the chart as included in both 2.0 and 3.0. The reason is that Jehol was a part of Manchoukuo from 1933 to 1945, and 2.0 is defined during that period as consisting of two or more of four provincial modules: 2.1, 2.2, 2.3, and 3.1. A work treating Jehol alone between 1928 and 1955 is coded 3.1; a work treating Jehol plus Chahar between 1928 and 1952 is coded 3.0; but a work treating Jehol and Liaoning in 1933–1945 is coded 2.0. (3) Codes 6.1 Kiangsu and 6.2 Anhwei are shown as being partly included in 1.4 North China Broadly Conceived and partly in 1.5 South China Broadly Conceived. This is because the Huai river, usually taken as the boundary between North and South China, bisects these two provinces. In consequence, whereas two adjacent provinces in different multiprovince regions (say 7.3 Kiangsi and 9.3 Fukien) are accommodated by one of the two higher-order region codes (in this case 1.5 South China Broadly Conceived), a similar pairing involving Kiangsu or Anhwei must be coded 1.3 The Eighteen Provinces.

Code 1.0 has not been mentioned, since it is neither basic nor cumulative in the sense used here; see its definition below.

Code Definitions

1.0 *Chinese Society, Locale Unspecified.* This is the sole "general" geographic code, being defined neither as a specific territory nor as the cumulation of various territories. It refers to Han Chinese society without reference to place or in the sense of Chinese wherever found, including overseas.

1.1 *Geographic China Broadly Conceived.* The territories now included within the People's Republic of China *plus* Taiwan, Hong Kong, and Macau. Items are coded 1.1 as against 1.2 only when they explicitly mention or cover Taiwan and/or Hong Kong and Macau or when they are based in part on evidence from or observation in Taiwan and/or Hong Kong and Macau.

1.2 *Mainland China.* The territories now included within the boundaries of the People's Republic of China. As against 1.1, this code excludes Taiwan and Hong Kong; as against 1.3, it includes Manchuria (2.0), Inner Mongolia (3.0), and the western frontier territories (4.3, 4.4, and 4.5).

1.3 *The Eighteen Provinces.* The territory of the eighteen provinces of Ch'ing China after the subdivision of Kiangnan in 1662 and before the establishment of Sinkiang in 1884; see the + signs in row 1.3 of the

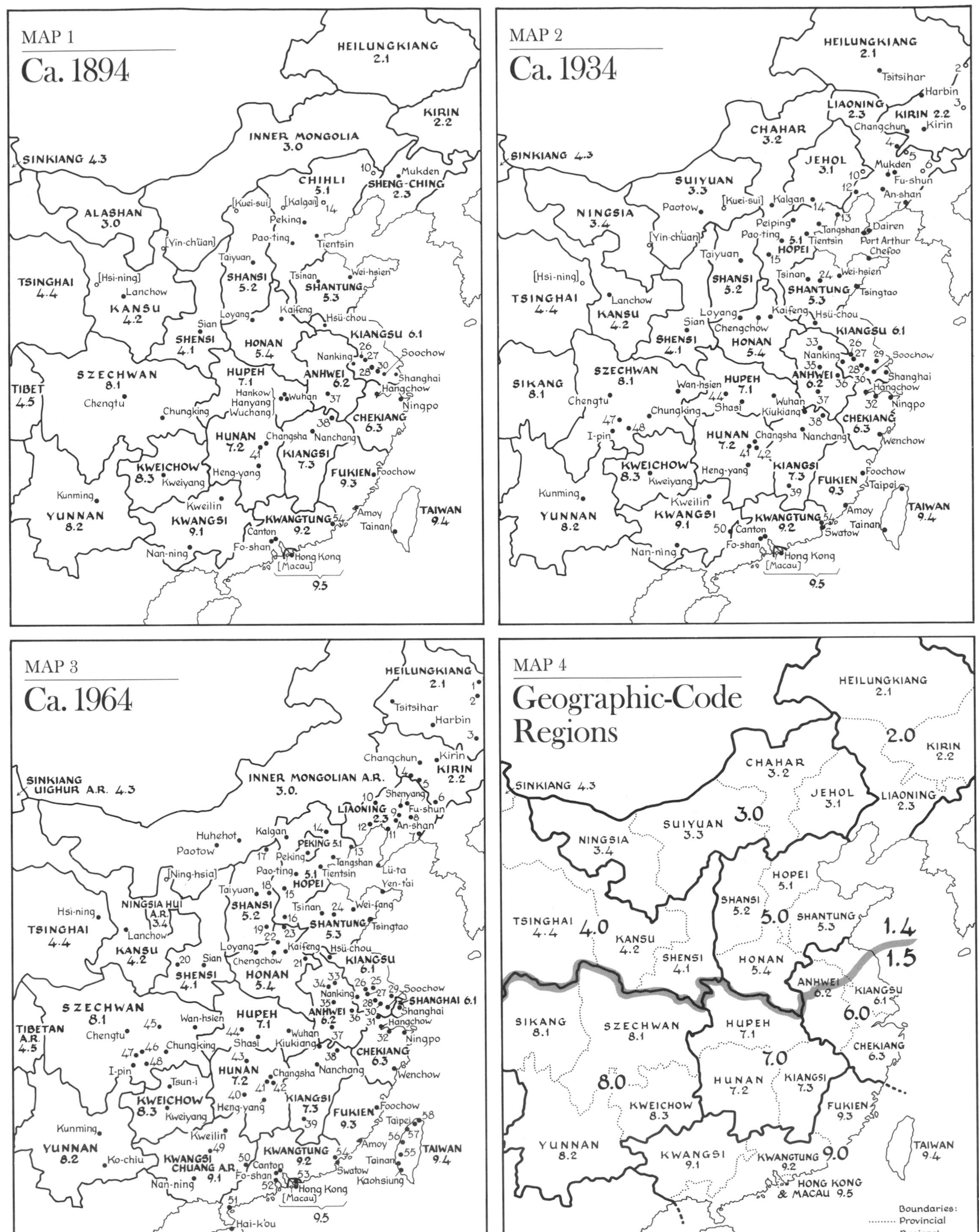

For explanation of maps and names of numbered cities, see bottom of facing panel.

BASIC CODES		Geographic China Broadly Conceived	Mainland China	18 Provinces	North China Broadly Conceived	South China Broadly Conceived	Manchuria	Inner Mongolia	NW and Far West	Northern China	East Central	Central Yangtze	SW China	SE China
		1.1	1.2	1.3	1.4	1.5	2.0	3.0	4.0	5.0	6.0	7.0	8.0	9.0
Heilungkiang	2.1	+	+		+		+							
Kirin	2.2	+	+		+		+							
Liaoning	2.3	+	+		+		+							
Inner Mongolia	3.0	+	+		+			+						
Jehol	3.1	+	+		+		(+)	+						
Chahar	3.2	+	+		+			+						
Suiyuan	3.3	+	+		+			+						
Ningsia	3.4	+	+		+			+						
Shensi	4.1	+	+	+	+				+					
Kansu	4.2	+	+	+	+				+					
Sinkiang	4.3	+	+		+				+					
Tsinghai	4.4	+	+		+				+					
Tibet	4.5	+	+			+			+					
Hopei	5.1	+	+	+	+					+				
Shansi	5.2	+	+	+	+					+				
Shantung	5.3	+	+	+	+					+				
Honan	5.4	+	+	+	+					+				
Kiangsu	6.1	+	+	+	S	S					+			
Anhwei	6.2	+	+	+	S	S					+			
Chekiang	6.3	+	+	+		+					+			
Hupeh	7.1	+	+	+		+						+		
Hunan	7.2	+	+	+		+						+		
Kiangsi	7.3	+	+	+		+						+		
Szechwan	8.1	+	+	+		+							+	
Yunnan	8.2	+	+	+		+							+	
Kweichow	8.3	+	+	+		+							+	
Kwangsi	9.1	+	+	+		+								+
Kwangtung	9.2	+	+	+		+								+
Fukien	9.3	+	+	+		+								+
Taiwan	9.4	+				+								+
Hong Kong/Macau	9.5	+				+								+

◀ **MAPS** Maps 1–3 show cities considered large (P3) in the year of the map plus selected other cities (open dots) whose G codes are affected by changes in provincial boundaries between 1894 and 1964. Map 4 shows G-code regions in relation to provinces, with provincial boundaries as of 1934.

1 Hao-kang
2 Chia-mu-ssu
3 Mu-tan-chiang
4 Ssu-p'ing
5 Liao-yüan
6 T'ung-hua
7 Tan-tung (earlier An-tung)
8 Pen-ch'i
9 Liao-yang
10 Fou-hsin
11 Ying-k'ou
12 Chin-chou
13 Ch'in-huang-tao
14 Ch'eng-te
15 Shih-chia-chuang
16 Han-tan
17 Ta-t'ung
18 Yang-ch'üan
19 Ch'ang-chih
20 Pao-chi
21 Shang-ch'iu
22 Hsin-hsiang
23 An-yang
24 Tzu-po (earlier Po-shan)
25 T'ai-chou
26 Yangchow
27 Chinkiang
28 Ch'ang-chou (also Wu-chin)
29 Nan-t'ung
30 Wusih
31 Wu-hsing (earlier Hu-chou)
32 Shao-hsing
33 Pang-fou
34 Huai-nan
35 Ho-fei
36 Wuhu
37 An-ch'ing
38 Ching-te-chen
39 Kan-chou
40 Shao-yang
41 Hsiang-t'an
42 Chu-chou
43 Ch'ang-te
44 I-ch'ang
45 Nan-ch'ung
46 Nei-chiang
47 Tzu-kung (earlier Tzu-liu-ching)
48 Lu-chou
49 Liu-chou
50 Wu-chou
51 Chan-chiang (earlier Kuang-chou-wan)
52 Chiang-men
53 Kowloon
54 Ch'ao-an (earlier Ch'ao-chou)
55 Chia-i
56 Taichung
57 Hsin-chu
58 Keelung

above chart. The precise territory of the eighteen provinces varies from one period to another, expanding or contracting with the northern boundaries of Chihli/Hopei, Shansi, Shensi, and Kansu, and with the western boundaries of Kansu, Szechwan, and Yunnan. As against 1.2, this code excludes Manchuria (2.0), Inner Mongolia (3.0), and the western frontier territories (4.3, 4.4, and 4.5); as against 1.1, it excludes these peripheral areas plus Taiwan and Hong Kong.

1.4 *North China Broadly Conceived.* The terms North China and South China are conventionally applied only to agrarian China (as opposed to the nonagrarian peripheries) and conventionally defined in terms of natural geography: the Ch'in-ling mountains in the west and the Huai river in the east. By contrast, the North China and South China of this *Bibliography* represent a dichotomization of Geographic China (i.e. 1.4 + 1.5 = 1.1), and the boundary from the Far West to Anhwei is taken as corresponding to provincial boundaries rather than to the ridges of mountain ranges. Thus 1.4 is defined as those territories of Geographic China that lie north of the southern boundaries of Sinkiang, Tsinghai, Kansu, Shensi, and Honan, and, within Anhwei and Kiangsu, north of the Huai river.

1.5 *South China Broadly Conceived.* Those territories of Geographic China that lie south of the northern boundaries of Tibet, Sikang (when applicable), Szechwan, and Hupeh, and, within Anhwei and Kiangsu, south of the Huai river, plus Taiwan and Hong Kong.

2.0 *Manchuria.* Before 1928 the provinces of Heilungkiang, Kirin, and Fengtien (formerly Sheng-ching). For 1928–1933 and 1945–1954, the provinces of Heilungkiang, Kirin, and Liaoning as defined in 1928. For 1933–1945, the territorial extent of Manchoukuo, including what the Nationalists had defined as Heilungkiang, Kirin, Liaoning, and Jehol. From 1954, the provinces of Heilungkiang, Kirin, and Liaoning as demarcated in 1954. Code 2.0 is used for any two or more of Manchuria's component provinces, including Jehol for 1933–1945.

2.1 *Heilungkiang.* Before 1928, the territory of the province as formally established in 1907. For 1928–1954, the territory of the province as demarcated in 1928. From 1954, the territory of the province as demarcated in that year.

2.2 *Kirin.* Before 1928, the territory of the province as formally established in 1907. For 1928–1954, the territory of the province as demarcated in 1928. From 1954 the territory of the province as demarcated in that year.

2.3 *Liaoning.* Before 1928, the territory of the province formally established as Fengtien in 1907 (previously known as Sheng-ching). For 1928–1954, the territory of the province of Liaoning as demarcated in 1928. From 1954, the territory of the province as demarcated in that year.

3.0 *Inner Mongolia.* Before 1928, that part of Inner Mongolia not included in established provinces. For 1928–ca. 1954, the territory comprising the Nationalist provinces of Jehol, Chahar, Suiyuan, and Ningsia; 3.0 is used for two or more of them. Also used for Japanese-sponsored Meng-chiang, 1937–1939, and its successor, the Mongolian Unified A.R., 1939–1945. From 1954, the territory of the Inner Mongolian A.R. as demarcated in that year; also used for the Inner Mongolian A.R. *and* the Ningsia Hui A.R. since 1958.

3.1 *Jehol.* Used only for 1928–1955.

3.2 *Chahar.* Used only for 1928–1952.

3.3 *Suiyuan.* Used only for 1928–1954.

3.4 *Ningsia.* Used for the Nationalist province, 1928–1954, and from 1958 for the Ningsia Hui A.R.

4.0 *Northwest and Far West.* The region comprising the following five province-level units; 4.0 is used for two or more of them.

4.1 *Shensi*

4.2 *Kansu*

4.3 *Sinkiang* (Sinkiang Uighur A.R. from 1955)

4.4 *Tsinghai*

4.5 *Tibet* (Tibetan A.R. from 1965)

5.0 *Northern China.* The region comprising the following four provinces; 5.0 is used for two or more of them.

5.1 *Hopei* (Chihli to 1928). Includes Peking and Tientsin municipalities.

5.2 *Shansi*

5.3 *Shantung*

5.4 *Honan*

6.0 *East Central China.* The region comprising the following three provinces; 6.0 is used for two or more of them.

6.1 *Kiangsu.* Includes Shanghai municipality.

6.2 *Anhwei*

6.3 *Chekiang*

7.0 *Central Yangtze Provinces.* The region comprising the following three provinces; 7.0 is used for two or more of them.

7.1 *Hupeh*

7.2 *Hunan*

7.3 *Kiangsi*

8.0 *Southwestern China.* The region comprising the following provinces; 8.0 is used for two or more of them.

8.1 *Szechwan.* For 1928–1955, includes Sikang.

8.2 *Yunnan*

8.3 *Kweichow*

9.0 *Southeastern China.* The region comprising the following provinces and territories; 9.0 is used for any two or more of these units.

9.1 *Kwangsi* (Kwangsi Chuang A.R. from 1958)
9.2 *Kwangtung*
9.3 *Fukien*
9.4 *Taiwan*
9.5 *Hong Kong and Macau.* Hong Kong includes the New Territories.

TYPE-OF-PLACE CODES

Design

Type-of-place codes are singular codes constructed of four primary modules: large cities (L), small cities (S), market towns (M), and villages (V).

Any settlement that is the nucleus of a municipality or that serves as the capital of a county or higher-level administrative unit counts as a city. So does any non-administrative settlement that ranks higher than a central market town in the hierarchy of economic central places. Residential suburbs of cities are considered part of the city even if they extend beyond the walls or municipal boundaries.

Which cities count as large in which historical periods is specified on p. xxxviii, which lists the cities alphabetically by province and provinces in numerical code order. A city is listed under more than one province if it changed provinces after achieving large-city status. Apart from dates indicating changes in provincial affiliation, the dates reflect our historical-period modules (see p. xxxi); thus 1842– means that the city is deemed to have achieved large-city status at some time during the modular period 1842–1895. Even if the change in fact came late in the modular time period, the city is coded as large throughout the period. The criterion of large size is a sliding one, ranging from a population of about 50,000 for 1644–1842 to one of about 150,000 for 1949–1972. Cities not listed on p. xxxviii are considered small for all time periods.

A market town, as distinguished from a village, is defined as any settlement in which a periodic or daily market is held, or in modern times any settlement that serves as a shopping or marketing center for a multi-village rural hinterland. As distinguished from a city, a market town does not serve as an administrative center of a county or higher-level administrative unit, does not form the nucleus of a municipality, and ranks relatively low in the functional hierarchy of economic centers.

A village is defined as a rural settlement in which no market is regularly held. The primary module V also covers the rural countryside in general, exclusive of market towns.

The various combinations of these four primary modules are grouped into seven coding categories as specified in the following definitions. The first Type-of-place code (P1), in the manner of Geographic code 1.0, is nonspecific and unrelated to the primary modules.

Code Definitions

P1 *Place Irrelevant or Type of Place Unspecified.* Used when the work is generally concerned with the total society without special reference to urban or rural sectors and without drawing rural-urban distinctions. Also used when the work treats only subjects to which place and type of place are irrelevant.

P2 *Urban* AND *Rural.* Any of the following combinations:

L + V	L + S + V	S + M + V
S + V	L + M + V	L + S + M + V

Used when the work distinguishes rural from urban or treats matters both urban, whether broadly or narrowly defined, and rural, whether broadly or narrowly defined.

P3 *Narrowly Urban: Large Cities Only.* L only. Used when the work treats one or more cities considered "large" for their time, or the class or category of such cities.

P4 *Urban, Including Smaller Cities and Hsien Capitals.* S only or L + S. Used when the work treats small cities only, or both large and small cities, or cities of unspecified size, provided market towns are not also treated.

P5 *Broadly Urban: Cities* AND *Market Towns.* Any of the following combinations:

L + M S + M L + S + M

Used when the work treats the urban sector in the most inclusive sense.

P6 *Market Towns Only.* M only.

P7 *Broadly Rural: Villages* AND *Market Towns.* M + V. Used for marketing systems and for rural communes, which almost always include at least one market town as well as villages. Also used for "peri-urban" (as opposed to suburban) areas, i.e. food-producing areas in the immediate environs of cities.

P8 *Narrowly Rural: Villages Only.* V only.

Note that in the Geographic Index, Type-of-place codes appear as italic suffixes without the initial P.

SOURCES CODES

The Sources codes are singular codes constructed of four modules as follows:

F *Field Research.* Written in significant part on the basis of data collected through social surveys, ethnographic and other systematic interviews (including interviews of informants about events displaced in time and/or space), observation by trained social scientists, and other forms of scientific research in living communities or with living informants; or on the basis of scientific investigation of artifacts and other items of material culture.

2.1 *Heilungkiang* 黑龍江
佳木斯 Chia-mu-ssu 1954– (see 2.2)
鶴崗 Hao-kang 1949–
哈爾濱 Harbin (Ha-erh-pin) 1954– (see 2.2)
牡丹江 Mu-tan-chiang 1954– (see 2.2)
齊齊哈爾 Tsitsihar (Ch'i-ch'i-ha-erh) 1928–

2.2 *Kirin* 吉林
長春 Changchun 1895–
佳木斯 Chia-mu-ssu 1949–1954 (see 2.1)
哈爾濱 Harbin (Ha-erh-pin) 1911–1954 (see 2.1)
吉林 Kirin 1911–
遼源 Liao-yüan 1954– (see 2.3)
牡丹江 Mu-tan-chiang 1949–1954 (see 2.1)
四平 Ssu-p'ing 1954– (see 2.3)
通化 T'ung-hua 1954– (see 2.3)

2.3 *Liaoning* 遼寧 (Sheng-ching 盛京 to 1907; Fengtien 奉天 1907–1928)
鞍山 An-shan 1928–
錦州 Chin-chou 1928–
大連 Dairen (Ta-lien) 1911–
阜新 Fou-hsin 1954– (see 3.1)
撫順 Fu-shun 1928–
遼陽 Liao-yang 1949–
遼源 Liao-yüan 1949–1954 (see 2.2)
旅大 Lü-ta (Port Arthur–Dairen) 1911–
本溪 Pen-ch'i 1949–
旅順 Port Arthur (Lü-shun) 1911–
瀋陽 Shenyang (earlier Mukden 奉天) 1842–
四平 Ssu-p'ing 1928–1954 (see 2.2)
丹東 Tan-tung (earlier An-tung 安東) 1911–
通化 T'ung-hua 1949–1954 (see 2.2)
營口 Ying-k'ou 1949–

3.0 *Inner Mongolia* 內蒙古 (Inner Mongolian A.R., 1954–
呼和浩特 Huhehot (Hu-ho-hao-t'e; earlier Kuei-sui 歸綏 1954– (see 3.3)
包頭 Paotow 1954– (see 3.3)

3.1 *Jehol* 熱河 (1928–1955 only)
承德 Ch'eng-te 1928–1955 (see 5.1)
阜新 Fou-hsin 1949–1955 (see 2.3)

3.2 *Chahar* 察哈爾 (1928–1952 only)
張家口 Kalgan (Chang-chia-k'ou) 1928–1952 (see 5.1)

3.3 *Suiyuan* 綏遠 (1928–1954 only)
呼和浩特 Huhehot (Hu-ho-hao-t'e; earlier Kuei-sui 歸綏) 1949–1954 (see 3.0)
包頭 Paotow 1928–1954 (see 3.0)

3.4 *Ningsia* 寧夏 (1928–1954 only; Ningsia Hui A.R., 1958–)
No large cities

4.1 *Shensi* 陝西
寶鷄 Pao-chi 1949–
西安 Sian 1644–

4.2 *Kansu* 甘肅
蘭州 Lanchow 1644–

4.3 *Sinkiang* 新疆 (Sinkiang Uighur A.R., 1955–)
哈密 Ha-mi 1949–
喀什 K'o-shih (Kashgar) 1949–
烏魯木齊 Urumchi (Wu-lu-mu-ch'i; earlier Ti-hua 廸化) 1949–

4.4 *Tsinghai* 青海
西寧 Hsi-ning 1949–

4.5 *Tibet* 西藏 (Tibetan A.R., 1965)
No large cities

5.1 *Hopei* 河北 (Chihli 直隸 to 1928) (including the province-level municipalities of Peking and Tientsin)
承德 Ch'eng-te 1955– (see 3.1)
秦皇島 Ch'in-huang-tao 1928–
邯鄲 Han-tan 1949–
張家口 Kalgan (Chang-chia-k'ou) 1911–1928, 1952– (see 3.2)
保定 Pao-ting 1842–
北京 Peking (Peiping 北平) 1644–
石家莊 Shih-chia-chuang 1928–
唐山 Tangshan 1911–
天津 Tientsin 1644–

5.2 *Shansi* 山西
長治 Ch'ang-chih 1949–
大同 Ta-t'ung 1949–
太原 Taiyuan 1644–
陽泉 Yang-ch'üan 1949–

5.3 *Shantung* 山東
芝罘 Chefoo (Yen-t'ai 烟臺) 1895–
濟南 Tsinan 1644–
青島 Tsingtao 1911–
淄博 Tzu-po (earlier Po-shan 博山) 1928–
濰坊 Wei-fang (earlier Wei-hsien 濰縣) 1842–

5.4 *Honan* 河南
安陽 An-yang 1949–
鄭州 Chengchow 1928–
新鄉 Hsin-hsiang 1949–
開封 Kaifeng 1644–
洛陽 Loyang 1644–
商丘 Shang-ch'iu 1949–

6.1 *Kiangsu* 江蘇 (including the province-level municipality of Shanghai)
常州 Ch'ang-chou (Wu-chin 武進) 1644–
鎮江 Chinkiang 1644–
徐州 Hsü-chou 1644–
南京 Nanking 1644–
南通 Nan-t'ung 1911–
上海 Shanghai 1644–
蘇州 Soochow 1644–
泰州 T'ai-chou 1949–
無錫 Wusih 1842–
揚州 Yangchow 1644–

6.2 *Anhwei* 安徽
安慶 An-ch'ing 1644–
合肥 Ho-fei 1928–
淮南 Huai-nan 1949–
蚌埠 Pang-fou 1928–
蕪湖 Wuhu 1895–

6.3 *Chekiang* 浙江
杭州 Hangchow 1644–
寧波 Ningpo 1644–
紹興 Shao-hsing 1928–
溫州 Wenchow 1895–
吳興 Wu-hsing (Hu-chou 湖州) 1949–

7.1 *Hupeh* 湖北
漢口 Hankow 1644–
宜昌 I-ch'ang 1911–
沙市 Shasi 1911–
武漢 Wuhan (Hankow 漢口, Hanyang 漢陽, and Wuchang 武昌) 1644–

7.2 *Hunan* 湖南
長沙 Changsha 1644–
常德 Ch'ang-te 1949–
株洲 Chu-chou 1928–
衡陽 Heng-yang 1842–
湘潭 Hsiang-t'an 1842–
邵陽 Shao-yang 1949–

7.3 *Kiangsi* 江西
景德鎮 Ching-te-chen 1644–
贛州 Kan-chou 1911–
九江 Kiukiang 1895–
南昌 Nanchang 1644–

8.1 *Szechwan* 四川 (including Sikang 西康, 1928–1955)
成都 Chengtu 1644–
重慶 Chungking 1644–
宜賓 I-pin 1911–
瀘州 Lu-chou 1928–
南充 Nan-ch'ung 1949–
內江 Nei-chiang 1949–
自貢 Tzu-kung (earlier Tzu-liu-ching 自流井) 1928–
萬縣 Wan-hsien 1895–

8.2 *Yunnan* 雲南
箇舊 Ko-chiu 1949–
昆明 Kunming (earlier Yün-nan-fu 雲南府) 1644–

8.3 *Kweichow* 貴州
貴陽 Kweiyang 1644–
遵義 Tsun-i 1949–

9.1 *Kwangsi* 廣西 (Kwangsi Chuang A.R., 1958–)
貴林 Kweilin 1644–
柳州 Liu-chou 1949–
南寧 Nan-ning 1644–
梧州 Wu-chou 1895–

9.2 *Kwangtung* 廣東
廣州 Canton (Kuang-chou) 1644–
湛江 Chan-chiang (earlier Kuang-chou-wan 廣州灣) 1949–
潮安 Ch'ao-an (earlier Ch'ao-chou 潮州) 1842–
江門 Chiang-men 1949–
佛山 Fo-shan 1644–
海口 Hai-k'ou 1949–
汕頭 Swatow (Shan-t'ou) 1895–

9.3 *Fukien* 福建
廈門 Amoy (Hsia-men) 1644–
福州 Foochow 1644–

9.4 *Taiwan* 臺灣
嘉義 Chia-i 1949–
新竹 Hsin-chu 1949–
高雄 Kaohsiung 1949–
基隆 Keelung 1949–
臺中 Taichung 1949–
臺南 Tainan 1644–
臺北 Taipei 1895–

9.5 *Hong Kong and Macau* 香港及澳門
香港 Hong Kong (Victoria) 1842–
九龍 Kowloon 1949–

O *Personal Observation.* Written in significant part on the basis of personal experience in and observation of Chinese society, including the usual run of journalism, reports of travels and visits, accounts and reminiscences by Chinese and foreign participants and observers, including businessmen, missionaries, diplomats, and soldiers.

P *Primary Sources.* Written in significant part on the basis of the author's own research in primary sources. All written products of Chinese society that are not descriptive-analytical or scholarly secondary works count as primary sources, including newspapers, local gazetteers, genealogies, encyclopedias, government documents and reports, and archival materials. Reference works, encyclopedias, newspapers, and the like that are not products of Chinese society do not count as primary sources.

S *Secondary Sources, Well Documented.* Written in significant part on the basis of secondary sources, i.e. scholarly or other descriptive-analytical writings about Chinese society. Reference works, encyclopedias, newspapers, and other such publications that are not products of Chinese society count as secondary sources.

Various combinations of these modules form six of the seven Sources codes. The final code, Unsupported or Poorly Documented, is independently defined.

Symbols	Headings	Definitions	
F	Field Research	F F + O	F + S F + O + S
P	Primary Sources	P	P + S
FP	Field Research *and* Primary Sources	F + P F + P + O	F + P + S F + P + O + S
O	Personal Observation	O	O + S
PO	Primary Sources *and* Personal Observation	P + O	P + O + S
S	Secondary Sources, Well Documented	S	
U	Unsupported or Poorly Documented	Used where author's sources cannot be ascertained, or are limited to secondary sources and poorly documented, if at all.	

The letter symbols in the left-hand column are used in the number line of each entry in the Bibliography, and (except U) as suffixes to entry numbers in the Historical Index. The headings in the second column are used in the Local-Systems Index.

Design of Indexes

Each volume of this *Bibliography* has six indexes, which are identical in structure across volumes:

Historical Index	Author Index
Geographic Index	Institutional Author Index
Local-Systems Index	General Index

The first three are analytical indexes, generated by computer from the annotation component of each Bibliography entry and automatically typeset. The two author indexes were generated by computer from the citation component of each Bibliography entry and also automatically typeset. The General Index was prepared manually, though not without reliance on computer output, and typeset by conventional means.

Analytical Indexes

The analytical indexes are this *Bibliography*'s most distinctive feature. They are made possible by the rigor of the annotation scheme and rendered feasible by the comprehensive automation of both data processing and typesetting. The analytical indexes have been generated by cross-tabulating three or more of the five codings that make up the annotation component of each entry. Entry numbers are grouped into subcategories by sorting on two or more dimensions; codings on one or two additional dimensions are shown by suffixes.

Historical Index

The Historical Index cross-tabulates Subject codes, Historical-period codes, and Sources codes. The first-order sort is by Subject codes without respect to their designation as primary or secondary. First-order headings are the numbers and short headings of the 98 Subject codes defined on pp. xxiv–xxxi. An entry number appears once in the index for each Subject code assigned the work, i.e. from one to sixteen times (see p. xxxi).

The second-order sort is by Historical-period codes. Since the full array set out on p. xxxii proved too fine for indexing purposes, the 21 codes were grouped into 9 categories as shown:

① 1644–1842					
② 1644–1895 1644–1911	1842–1895 1842–1911	1895–1911 ③			
④ 1644–1928	1842–1928	1895–1928	1911–1928 ⑤		
⑥ 1644–1949	1842–1949	1895–1949	1911–1949	1928–1949 ⑦	
⑧ 1644–1972	1842–1972	1895–1972	1911–1972	1928–1972	1949–1972 ⑨

Historical-period codes showing a blank (meaning pre-1644) instead of an initial date (see p. xxxii) are classified as if the first date were 1644, and the exceptional code –1644 is classified in the first category. The subheadings used in the index for these nine categories are as follows:

1 1644–1842
2 1644–1911
3 1842–1911
4 1842–1928
(including 1644–1928)
5 1911–1928
6 1911–1949
(including 1644–1949, 1842–1949)
7 1928–1949
8 1928–1972
(including 1644–1972, 1842–1972, 1911–1972)
9 1949–1972

These subheadings appear in order under each of the 98 subject main headings.

The third-order sort separates entry numbers into primary and secondary blocks following the division in the Bibliography entries. If a primary or secondary block contains more than 74 entry numbers, a fourth-order sort by citation type is made, dividing each such block into three sub-blocks: monographs (including unpublished dissertations), inclusions, and journal articles. The purpose of this fourth-order sort is simply to spare the reader the necessity of dealing with huge undifferentiated blocks of numbers.

Finally, each entry number listed in the index is followed by a Sources code symbol or a blank space representing the U symbol (see p. xxxix).

Empty categories are designated by open squares. For Subjects 10 and 20, where the secondary designation is not permitted (see p. xxxi), "*Not used*" follows the Secondary subheading.

Geographic Index

The Geographic Index cross-tabulates Subject codes, Geographic codes, Historical-period codes, and Type-of-place codes. The first-order sort is by Subject codes without respect to their designation as primary or secondary. First-order headings are the same as for the Historical Index, except that the last two headings—71 Non-Chinese Scholars of Chinese Society and 72 Bibliography—are not used.

The second-order sort is by Geographic codes, excluding 1.0 Chinese Society Locale Unspecified. Since the full geographic coding scheme (pp. xxxiii–xxxvii) is too fine for indexing purposes, the 43 codes other than 1.0 are grouped into 14 categories as follows:

Index categories	Component codes
Geographic China Broadly Conceived	1.1
Mainland China	1.2
The Eighteen Provinces	1.3
North China Broadly Conceived	1.4
Manchuria	2.0–2.3
Northern China	5.0–5.4
Northwestern China and Frontier Regions	3.0–3.4, 4.0–4.5
South China Broadly Conceived	1.5
East Central China	6.0–6.3
Central Yangtze Provinces	7.0–7.3
Southwestern China	8.0–8.3
Southeastern China	9.0–9.3
Taiwan Only	9.4
Hong Kong and Macau Only	9.5

Inner Mongolia (3.0–3.4) is combined with the Northwest and Far West (4.0–4.5) because the entry numbers for these contiguous regions are few. Taiwan (9.4) and Hong Kong and Macau (9.5) are kept separate from Southeastern China because of the especially large number of entry numbers for Taiwan and the special status of Hong Kong and Macau.

Index subheadings as given above appear in the order shown under each of the 96 subject main headings. Note that the merged coding categories appear in a logical geographic sequence that differs from the numerical order of the unmerged codes in the range 1.5 through 5.0–5.4.

Since three Subject codes—11 National Population, 11.1 Nationwide Population, and 11.4 National Labor Force and Occupational Differentiation—cannot by definition be assigned to works coded with a regional or provincial Geographic code, only the five applicable geographic subheadings are retained for these three main headings. Similarly, 10 Chinese Society in General and 14.1 Agrarian Economy cannot be assigned to works treating Taiwan only (G9.4) or Hong Kong and Macau only (G9.5); and two other Subject codes, 12 National Political System and Bureaucracy and 14 National Economy and Economic Planning, also cannot be assigned to works treating Hong Kong and Macau only. In these six cases, "*Not applicable*" follows the geographic subheading; the user should refer to the subject heading for the corresponding second-decade code.

The third-order sort separates entry numbers into primary and secondary blocks following the division in the Bibliography entries. If a primary or secondary block contains more than 75 entry numbers, a fourth-order sort by citation type is made, dividing each such block into sub-blocks of monographs, inclusions, and journal articles.

Each entry number listed in the index is followed by one or more of the letters T, R, and C. These provide a summary indication of historical era: T (Traditional) for before 1911, R (Republican) for 1911–1949, C (Contemporary) for after 1949. These suffixes are derived from the Historical-period codes in the following manner:

T	1644–1842					
	1644–1895	1842–1895				
	1644–1911	1842–1911	1895–1911			
TR	1644–1928	1842–1928	1895–1928	1911–1928	R	
	1644–1949	1842–1949	1895–1949	1911–1949	1928–1949	
TRC	1644–1972	1842–1972	1895–1972	1911–1972	1928–1972	1949–1972
					RC	C

The different letters are arranged in separate minicolumns for the user's convenience. Thus a straightedge placed just to the right of a long R minicolumn quickly sorts out those entry numbers showing an R suffix.

Finally, each entry number also shows the Type-of-place code (see p. xxxvii) as an italic number to the right of the TRC suffixes.

The use of open squares and "*Not used*" follows that in the Historical Index (see p. xl).

Local-Systems Index

The Local-Systems Index cross-tabulates Geographic codes, Type-of-place codes, Sources codes, and Historical-period codes. Since the subject dimension does not enter the design of this index, and since that dimension is the only one on which a work may be assigned multiple codes, a given entry never appears more than once in the Local-Systems Index.

The first-order sort is by Geographic codes. The fully differentiated geographic coding scheme set out on pp. xxxiii–xxxvii is used with three exceptions: 1.0 Chinese Society Locale Unspecified is omitted; the four provincial codes for Inner Mongolia, 3.1–3.4, are grouped together with cumulative code 3.0; and the codes for Sinkiang, Tsinghai, and Tibet (4.3–4.5) are grouped together with cumulative code 4.0. (These cumulations were made because of the paucity of entries for the individual provinces involved.) The 36 first-order headings of the Local-Systems Index are, with the omissions noted, those set out on the back endpapers.

The second-order sort is by Type-of-place codes (see p. xxxvii). A listing under the first subheading (1 Place Irrelevant or Type of Place Unspecified), though useless as a type-of-place subcategory, must be retained nonetheless if the listing under its geographic main heading is to be complete, i.e. if everything on (say) 5.1

is obviated, however, for the seven geographic headings that correspond to single unmerged codes in the Geographic Index as well as in the Local-Systems Index, namely 1.1–1.5 and 9.4–9.5. Accordingly, under these seven headings no entry numbers are listed under Type-of-place code 1, and the reader is referred instead to either the Historical Index or the Geographic Index, where his research objective can be more efficiently pursued by asking a more specific question keyed to the kinds of answers those indexes give.

A third-order sort of Sources codes (see p. xxxvii) applies only when a type-of-place subcategory contains more than 28 entry numbers; the seven block headings used are shown in the middle column of the table on p. xxxix. When the final sources heading (Unsupported or Poorly Documented) occurs under any of headings 1.1–1.5 and 9.4–9.5, entry numbers are suppressed and the user is referred to the Geographic Index.

When any one of the sources blocks contains more than 74 entry numbers, a fourth-order sort by citation type is made, dividing each such block into sub-blocks of monographs, inclusions, and journal articles.

Finally, each entry number listed in this index is followed by one or more of the letters T, R, and C as described above for the Geographic Index (see p. xli).

Use of the Analytical Indexes

For most research purposes, the most efficient way to use this *Bibliography* is to consult one of the analytical indexes. Which one depends, of course, on the user's objectives.

The Local-Systems Index is the natural choice for subjects defined spatially or highly specific to a province or locality (e.g. the urban geography of Kunming or the role of market towns in the Szechwan Basin), or for studies of broad scope limited to a single province (e.g. economic development in Kwangsi, the political modernization of Hunan, or the human geography of Fukien). For province-level studies, there are likely to be fewer entries under the province-level main heading in the Local-Systems Index than in the relevant regional (multiprovince) subcategories of the several subject categories that would have to be consulted in the Geographic Index. The Local-Systems Index can also play a useful supplementary role in research, e.g. by helping an historian to obtain an overview of the locality that played a crucial role in a particular movement or event, or by assisting in the choice of localities for a comparative study on a particular topic.

As for the two subject indexes, it goes without saying that when the subject is delimited in time but not in space, the Historical Index is appropriate; and that when it is delimited in space but not in time, the Geographic Index is appropriate. When the subject is delimited in neither space nor time, the Historical Index is the more efficient because each subject is subcategorized under fewer subheadings; it is easier to make use of 9 separate lists than of 14. By contrast, when the subject is to some extent delimited in both time and space, the Geographic Index is the more efficient by reason of its TRC suffixes, which provide an historical-era control that has no geographic counterpart in the Historical Index.

First-time users of this *Bibliography* may wonder why it is desirable to use the Historical Index at all for subjects that are unlimited in space and broadly delimited in time. Why not turn straight to the relevant subject heading in the Bibliography, and thence to the appropriate historical-period subheading? The answer is that many, if not most, of the entries sought will not be there. To illustrate, the Historical Index under 57 Death Practices (p. 606) lists 106 entries in primary blocks, of which only 45 are listed in the Bibliography under subject heading 57 (pp. 462–464); this is because only one of the primary Subject codes is designated the principal subject (see p. xxxi). Similarly, the subheading 1842–1911 under 57 Death Practices lists 18 entries in the primary block of which only two have code 57 as principal subject; the other sixteen, then, are listed in the Bibliography under other main headings, including not only such likely ones as 23 Folk Religion, 43 Ancestor Worship, and 65 Folklore, but such improbable ones as 17 National and Higher Education and 32 Political Parties. Also, needless to say, none of the 327 entries in the secondary blocks under heading 57 of the Historical Index appears under heading 57 of the Bibliography.

Let us now illustrate the way the analytical indexes should be used in pursuit of writings on one particular subject: rural local politics in the North China plain since 1949. Since this subject is broadly delimited in both time and space, the Geographic Index is the proper place to begin. As the Subject-code definitions show (see p. xxvii) and the General Index entry "Politics" makes clear, the most directly germane of the several relevant Subject codes is 22 Local Political Systems. The relevant subheading under this heading is "Northern China," since virtually all of the North China plain is included in the four-province region cumulated in this category (codes 5.0 and 5.1–5.4). The primary-block listing (p. 654) shows 39 entry numbers, of which 11 show the suffix C for the Contemporary (i.e. after 1949) *and* one of the rural Type-of-place codes (P7 or P8). These are the entries that should be looked up first in the Bibliography.

If these prime candidates prove insufficient for the user's research objectives, he should next make a similar selection from the secondary block under heading 22 (6 relevant entries), and then from the primary block for Northern China under 22.1 Local Political and Social Controls (4 relevant entries). If he is still unsatisfied, he may try the secondary block for Northern China under heading 22.1 (8 relevant entries), and the blocks for Northern China under 22.2 Customary Law and Dispute Resolution (p. 656), where he will find no primary entries and only two secondary entries relevant to his subject. In this manner, the analytical indexes make it possible to begin with those entries likely to yield the highest payoff for a particular subject and proceed progressively to others in order of probable utility.

The Local-Systems Index may be used to specify further a selection of entry numbers derived from the Geographic Index. Thus if our user's topic were rural local politics since 1949 in Hopei only, he would save time by checking his lists of Geographic Index entry numbers for Northern China against the Local-Systems Index listings for 5.1 Hopei and the appropriate rural subheadings (pp. 719–720) to ascertain which pertain exclusively to Hopei. Of the 11 numbers with primary Subject code 22 and geographic locus Northern China, the Local-Systems Index shows six to be concerned exclusively with Hopei: an analysis of a commune in Pu-t'ien *hsien* by an American political scientist, an article on class struggle in a commune in Fang-shan *hsien* based on personal observation by a visitor from Bangladesh, a description of the political structure of a commune in Ch'ang-li *hsien* by a French visitor, an investigation of political problems in an agricultural producers' cooperative in T'ung *hsien* translated from a Chinese journal, and two field studies of a locality in She *hsien* by a Canadian anthropologist and her English husband. Only one of these six entries, all of them a priori prime sources for the subject at hand, has 22 Local Political Systems as its principal subject; the other five appear under diverse headings in the Bibliography and can be identified as of primary utility for this user's purpose only by recourse to the analytical indexes.

Two of the coding conventions mentioned on p. xxxi have operational consequences for using the Historical and Geographic Indexes. (1) A first-decade code has generally been taken to subsume its second-decade counterpart when the latter would in any case be designated secondary and when the distinction is one of level rather than substance. It follows that if a user finds the listing for a second-decade subject (say 24.1) insufficient for his purposes, he should turn for further entries to the primary block under the corresponding first-decade code (14.1 in this example). (2) Ten of the subject codes may be used to "summarize" related subordinate codes, as specified in the definitions on pp. xxiv–xxxi. This convention has little practical significance for the codes summarized by 10, 20, and 30, but for the others—those summarized by 14/24, 16/26, 40, 50, and 60—it suggests a probable source of further useful entries. Thus if the listing for a "summarizable" code (say 26.2) proves insufficient for the user's purposes, he should turn to the primary block under the pertinent summary code (26 in this example).

AUTHOR INDEXES

Two author indexes follow the analytical indexes, the first limited to persons, the second to corporate bodies. The numbers listed in both indexes are entry numbers. For alphabetization principles, see Explanatory Notes, §14.

The Author Index provides an alphabetical listing of all personal authors, editors, compilers, and reviewers that appear in the Bibliography entries, including all variants of personal names except those consisting of initials only. Translators are not included, and pseudonyms are not identified as such. Authors whose names are identical (or identical in romanized form) are distinguished by birth and death dates or publication dates. In the case of Oriental names, no comma after the surname indicates surname-first order. To eliminate cross-references, all pertinent entry numbers for an author are listed after each variant form of his name. The entry number of a work with multiple authors appears in the index entry of each author.

The Institutional Author Index provides an alphabetical listing of corporate authors, editors, and compilers. Institutional authors that appear in two languages in the same entry (see Explanatory Notes, §2.2) are indexed under both versions. Joint editors are separately indexed. Lower-level units in nested organizations (see Explanatory Notes, §2) are referenced to the highest-level body. Thus:

> Chinese Academy of Sciences. Institute of Geography. Commune Planning Team 16465
>
> Commune Planning Team: *see* Chinese Academy of Sciences
>
> Institute of Geography: *see* Chinese Academy of Sciences

A jointly sponsored agency yields three index entries as follows (the example is hypothetical but illuminates the principle more clearly than any of the actual instances, which tend to be convoluted):

> Hong Kong Council of Social Service. Committee on Industrial Welfare 22530
> Hong Kong Trade Development Council. Committee on Industrial Welfare 22530
> Committee on Industrial Welfare: *see* Hong Kong Council of Social Service *or* Hong Kong Trade Development Council

Lower-level agencies with identical names—e.g. "Min cheng t'ing," meaning civil-affairs bureau—are referenced to as many highest-level bodies as necessary:

> Min cheng t'ing: *see* Chekiang, Hopei, *or* Kwangtung

GENERAL INDEX

The General Index does three things. It indexes the annotation scheme itself, with special attention to the

Subject and Geographic codes. It provides references, where useful, to the analytical indexes, in particular the Local-Systems Index. And it indexes key words and names that occur in English titles and English renderings of non-English titles, relying here on the computer output of a KWIC (Key word in context) program. Indexing in this manner words that appear in titles is admittedly an arbitrary and superficial procedure, but no other was feasible. When title mentions exceed 30, entry numbers are omitted in favor of page references to the relevant subcategories in the Bibliography.

General Index entries consistently prefix code numbers for three of the five annotation dimensions with an identifying capital letter: S for Subject codes, G for Geographic codes, and P for Type-of-place codes.

General Index entries are generally for five kinds of terms: place names, organizational names and terms, names of persons, historical events, and topics (e.g. banking, opium, textiles). Place names are listed in only one form, either Post Office or Wade-Giles (see Explanatory Notes, §13.1); only provinces and the more important cities and natural features are listed. Organizations are indexed by type (e.g. Rotating-credit societies, Surname associations) as well as individually (e.g. All-China Federation of Labor, Young China Party).

Explanatory Notes

The structure of Bibliography entries is discussed in Entry Formats, p. xx. Details on the annotation portion of entries—the number line at the beginning and the subject block at the end—are given in Entry Formats and elaborated in Annotation Categories, p. xxiii. The six indexes are explained in the preceding section. The notes in the present section provide further details on the citation portion of entries, including library symbols and characters.

1 Personal Authors

No author's name appears in an entry when the author's identity is not specified in the publication and could not be determined from other sources, or when the only designation of authorship is descriptive—e.g. "Our Correspondent." Authors identified by initials only are so listed.

The term "personal author," as distinguished from institutional author" (see §2), designates a person who served as author, editor, or compiler of a monograph (or monographic series), dissertation, inclusion, including work, or journal article (or journal-article series); as editor of a book or article written by another author; or as compiler or editor of an including work composed of items written by several different authors.

Whenever available, the year of birth (and where applicable, the year of death) of a personal author follows his name. When a date is putative, it is followed by a question mark; when a date is not known, a question mark appears instead.

1.1 *Preferred Forms: Western Authors*

To achieve consistency and avoid alphabetical separation of references to the same person, a single form of each personal author's name is used in every entry for that author. This *preferred form* of the author's name replaces, or precedes, any variant form or forms that may appear in the author's publications.

The preferred form of a Western author's name is the fullest version available. Initials and shortened forms of given names have been fleshed out, and given names usually omitted from the title pages of an author's work have been supplied. Thus Luther Carrington Goodrich, not L. Carrington Goodrich; Anton Pippon, not Toni Pippon; William Rhoads Murphey, III, not Rhoads Murphey. If initials only are available for given names, they are followed by dashes the first time the author's name appears in an entry:

Simon, G- Eugène Doronin, B- G-

In other respects, the preferred form of a Western author's name conforms to the author's preference, when it is known, or to conventions usually observed in the author's native language. In general, particles are retained as the initial element of surnames of authors who normally write in English; they are not treated as part of the surnames of authors who normally write in a continental European language.

The preferred form of a native Russian author's name is the transliteration of the fullest version available in cyrillic letters. (For the rules governing transliteration of Russian, see §12.4.) This principle generally holds even for Russian-speaking authors of works originally published in Western languages other than Russian (see §1.6).

For a married woman who consistently uses her husband's surname in publications or who has published under both her maiden name and her husband's surname, the preferred form consists of her given name(s), maiden name, and husband's surname.

1.2 *Preferred Forms: Oriental Authors*

For the names of native Chinese, Japanese, or Korean authors, or (in most cases) authors of Chinese, Japanese, or Korean descent, the preferred form is not normally the fullest version available. The chief reason for this differential treatment is that the preferred form of an Oriental author's name (e.g. Wellington K. K. Chan, Ilpyong John Kim) is followed by the standard transcription of the characters in the Oriental version of his name (e.g. Ch'en Chin-chiang, Kim Il-pyong) whenever they are available. Chinese, Japanese, and Korean names are transcribed according to the modified Wade-Giles, modified Hepburn, and McCune-Reischauer systems, respectively, set forth in §12. When the characters for an Oriental author's name were not available, the preferred form stands by itself.

In determining preferred forms, we have followed the author's preference (or the most widely used published form) with respect to the Oriental elements in the name. The author's spelling, hyphenation, and capitalization are respected in full, and initials that stand for Oriental names are not fleshed out, even when they represent a romanization that differs from this *Bibliography*'s standard. Initials that stand for Western given names, however, are fleshed out whenever possible. The following examples all consist solely of preferred forms followed by standard transcriptions in parentheses:

Chan, Fook-lam Gilbert (Ch'en Fu-lin)
Chao, Y. R. (Chao Yüan-jen)
Cheng, James Chester (Cheng Che-hsi)
Kitagawa, Joseph M. (Kitagawa Mitsuo)

For Oriental authors who have published only in Russian (apart from translations), the transliteration of the cyrillic title-page version is generally the preferred form:

Den Chzhun-sia (Teng Chung-hsia)
Kasai, Taichiroo (Kasai Taichirō)

Oriental authors who consistently use the surname-first order in their Western-language publications, or whose names usually appear in that order in Western-language publications (including translations), are listed with no comma after the surname:

Chou En-lai
Hsu Dau-lin (Hsü Tao-lin)
Ishikawa Shigeru
Wang Gungwu (Wang Keng-wu)

When the preferred form of an Oriental author's name is identical to the standard transcription (ignoring capitalization, hyphenation, and the order of surname and given names), it stands alone:

Banno, Masataka
Chang, Kuei-sheng
Chin Chien Yin
Hsüeh, Chün-tu

On the other hand, if there is any substantive difference, however slight, the transcription is given:

Chan, Hok-lam (Ch'en Hsüeh-lin)
Chen Po-ta (Ch'en Po-ta)
Iriye, Akira (Irie Akira)
Tschou, Tso-Tschun (Chou Tse-ch'un)

For Oriental married women, the principles governing the preferred form are the same as for Western married women. In Chinese cases, the order of transcribed names is husband's surname, maiden name, given name:

Chen, Fu-mei Chang (Ch'en Chang Fu-mei)
Chin, Ai-li Sung (Ch'en Shen Ai-li)

Manchu and Mongol authors figure in this volume only as authors of Chinese works subsequently translated into Western languages. The portions of these names that are transcriptions of Chinese characters are hyphenated following the standard established in Arthur W. Hummel, ed., *Eminent Chinese of the Ch'ing period* (Washington, D.C., 1943, 1944).

1.3 *Putative Authorship and Incomplete Names*

Unsigned or initialed works that can be ascribed with some confidence are listed under the name of the putative author, whose name, in brackets, is followed either by a dash (if the work was unsigned) or by the initials as given on the title page or elsewhere:

[La Dany, Ladislao] ———
[Li Hsiu-ch'eng] ———
[Nassunov, Nikolai?] N. N.
[Zhernakov, Vladimir Nikolaevich] V. Zh.

Dashes are used to indicate missing letters in the title-page version of a name:

IA——n, Genrikh
Volpert, Ant——

For authors identifiable by surname only (or by surname and a title like Mr. or Dr.), the missing given name is indicated by a dash:

Clavelin, *Père* ———
Musin, ———
Wittenberg, *Dr.* ———

1.4 *Variant Forms: Pseudonyms*

When a pseudonymous author's real name is known, the real name appears in brackets and the pseudonym follows:

[Gilmore, J-] Hoinos, pseud.
[Snow, Helen Foster] Nym Wales, pseud.

When the pseudonym alone is known, it is treated as the preferred form of the author's name:

Asiaticus, pseud.
Buck, Samuel, pseud.
Liu Shui Sheng, pseud.
Wong, Su-ling (Wang Shu-ling), pseud.

Some assumed names, e.g. Leon Trotsky, are treated as preferred forms in accordance with scholarly custom.

1.5 *Variant Forms Resulting from Translation*

When a Western author's works have been translated into one or more other Western languages, the title-page version of his name in the translation(s) may differ from the preferred form. In this case, the preferred form is followed by the variant forms. Initials that occur in variant forms are never fleshed out. Thus for authors whose works were translated from Russian to English and French to English, respectively:

> Berger, IAkov Mikhailovich (Ya. M. Berger)
> Wieger, Léon (Leo Wieger)

In multiple translations, the variant forms are in the order in which the translations appear in the entry. Thus for a Swedish author whose work has been published in German and French editions, cited in that order:

> Ekeberg, Karl Gustaf (Carl Gustav Ekeberg; Charles Gustave Eckeberg)

The only form of an Oriental author's name that can appear in parentheses is its standard transcription. Where translations bear variant forms of an Oriental author's name, the title-page version in the first Western-language version cited is treated as the preferred form. In the following example, from a French original translated into English, the author normally writes in French and prefers surname-first order. The surname is Sheng in Wade-Giles transcription, Cheng in the French romanization; the given name is Ch'eng in Wade-Giles, Cheng in the English title-page version, and Tcheng in the French title-page version:

> [Cheng Tcheng] Sheng-Cheng (Sheng Ch'eng)

When a character in an Oriental author's name was misidentified or misread by the translator, the correct transcription is used as the preferred form:

> Jen Pai-ko. [Tr. erroneously gives author's name as Jen Pai-i.]

Variant forms of pseudonyms that appear in translated works are treated like variant forms of true names. More than one variant of a Western pseudonym is permitted. In the following example, the author's true name appears as transcribed from the cyrillic, followed by the title-page pseudonyms as they appear in the Russian original and the German and French translations, respectively:

> [Vilenskii, Vladimir Dmitrievich] Vl. Vilenskii-Sibiriakov (W. Wilenski-Sibirjakoff; V. Vilensky-Sibiriakov), pseud.

The only permissible "variant" of an Oriental pseudonym is its standard transcription:

> Van-Min (Wang Ming), pseud.

1.6 *Other Variant Forms*

Five other classes of variant forms deserve mention. In all cases, the variant form follows the preferred form, which is enclosed in brackets.

(1) Names adopted by persons who have entered religious orders:

> [Kafarov, Petr Ivanovich] *Otets* Paladii

(2) Maiden names of women who have subsequently published under their married names:

> [Meskill, Johanna Menzel] Johanna Margarete Menzel

(3) Names of women authors identified only by their husbands' given names and surnames:

> [Richard, Mary Martin] *Mrs.* Timothy Richard

(4) Transliterations from cyrillic of names of non-Russian authors who publish original works in Russian, when the transliteration differs from the native-language version:

> [Heller, Leo N-] L. Geller

(5) Variant transliterations of names of native Russian authors whose works are published in (not translated into) another Western language:

> [Torgashev, Boris Pavlovich] Boris P. Torgasheff

1.7 *Multiple Authors*

For publications coauthored by two or three persons, full information is provided for each author:

> Buck, John Lossing, 1890–, and Yin Lien-ken (Ying Lien-keng), 1904?–.
>
> Fairbank, John King, 1907–, Alexander Eckstein, 1915–, and Lien-sheng Yang, 1914–.

For publications by more than three authors, the name of the first author is followed by "et al.," except when it is known that two or three of a larger group of authors played a particularly important role:

> Chow, L. P. (Chou Lien-pin), 1924–, et al.
>
> Freedman, Ronald, 1917–, Yuzuru John Takeshita, 1926–, et al.

1.8 *Editors, Compilers, and Translators*

Editors and compilers appear as follows at the beginning of citations:

> Boorman, Howard Lyon, 1920–, and Richard Campbell Howard, 1925–, eds.
>
> Okamatsu, Santaro (Okamatsu Santarō), 1871–1921, comp.

Where editors' or compilers' names appear in the title field, variant forms are given as necessary but dates are not given:

> Pott, Francis Lister Hawks, 1864–1947.
> 'Modern education.' In *China*, edited by Harley Farnsworth MacNair.
>
> Shih, Kuo-heng.
> *China enters the machine age: A study of labor in Chinese war industry*, edited by Fei Hsiao-tung (Fei Hsiao-t'ung).

Variant forms and standard transcriptions of personal names that appear in the author field and recur in the title field are not repeated, except for pseudonyms. To save space, when a name recurs in the same entry, any Western given names in it are spelled out only in the first occurrence:

> Wu, John C. H. (Wu Ching-hsiung), 1899–.
> 'Two forms of tortious liability in modern Chinese law.' In *The art of law and other essays, juridical and literary*, by J. C. H. Wu.

Translators' names appear as shown on the title page of the translation, whether or not this version corresponds to the preferred form.

2 Institutional Authors

The term "institutional author" refers to a corporate body that served as author, editor, or compiler of a monograph (or monograph series), dissertation, inclusion, or journal article (or journal-article series); as editor of a book or article written by another author; or as editor or compiler of an including work composed of items written by several different authors. Governmental agencies, business enterprises, political parties, and academic and research institutions all count as institutional authors. A corporate body that fits into an organizational hierarchy as a subordinate unit is referred to as "nested." When they appear in the author field, nested institutional authors are always given in large-to-small order, and middle- and upper-level agencies omitted from the publication's title page are supplied:

> Institute of Pacific Relations. American Council.
>
> T'ien-chin ta hsüeh. Chien chu hsi. Hsiao-chan kuei hua tsu.
>
> China [Ch'ing]. [Shui wu ch'u]. Hai kuan. ([Board of Customs Control]. Maritime Customs).

Acronyms and other shortened versions of institutional names are fleshed out at the beginning of citations:

> United Nations. Economic Commission for Asia and the Far East. Secretariat.

An exception is made for agencies of the U.S. government, which are cited in the truncated forms standardized by the Library of Congress.

When nested institutional authors appear as editors or compilers in the title fields of monograph, inclusion, and journal-article entries, the agencies are given in small-to-large order:

> Teng, Ssu-yü, 1906–.
> 'Some new light on the Nien movement and its effect on the fall of the Manchu dynasty.' In *Symposium on Chinese studies: Commemorating the Golden Jubilee of the University of Hong Kong, 1911–1961*, compiled by Dept. of Chinese, U. of Hong Kong.

The names of institutional as opposed to personal translators are omitted from the entry altogether.

Repetition of an institutional author already given in the author field is avoided in the title field by substituting the phrase "the agency [agencies] cited" or "the organization[s] cited." "Agency" refers to governmental authors, "organization" to all others. Thus:

> Great Britain. Admiralty. Naval Intelligence Division. Geographical Section.
> 'The ports of South China.' In *China proper, Vol. 3, Economic geography, ports and communications*, compiled by the agency cited.

2.1 *Governmental Agencies as Authors*

When an institutional author is an agency of a national government, the entry normally begins with the nation's name in the anglicized form standardized in Leon E. Seltzer, ed., *Columbia-Lippincott gazetteer of the world* (New York, 1952), except that U.S. and U.S.S.R. are always abbreviated. The major governments of modern China are distinguished as follows:

> China [Ch'ing]
> China [Republic]
> China [People's Republic]

Where institutional authors are agencies of a colonial government, the entry begins with the name of the colony, not that of the metropolitan country.

For agencies of subnational administrative units of China, "China" is omitted and the entry begins with the name of a province or municipality in Post Office spelling (see §13.1). The names of lower-level units that follow the name of the country, province, or municipality appear in the language of the country, except for colonial agencies, where the language is that of the metropolitan power.

The following examples cover the main cases:

> China [People's Republic]. Kuo wu yüan. Kuo chia t'ung chi chü.
> [Agency of a national government]
>
> Taiwan [Sōtokufu]. Bunkyōkyoku.
> [Agency of a colonial government]
>
> Hong Kong. Dept. of Commerce and Industry.
> [Agency of a colonial government]
>
> Taiwan. Min cheng t'ing.
> [Agency of a Chinese provincial government]
>
> Shanghai. She hui chü.
> [Agency of a Chinese municipal government]
>
> Honan. Teng-fang hsien cheng fu. Wen chiao chü.
> [Agency of a county government in Honan province]

2.2 *English Versions of Institutional Authors' Names*

English versions of non-English institutional authors' names are supplied when and only when the language of publication is English or an English translation is cited in the entry. For example:

> China [Republic]. Hsing cheng yüan. Nung ts'un fu hsing wei yüan hui. (Executive Yüan. Rural Reconstruction Commission).
>
> Kitaiskaia Vostochnaia zheleznaia doroga. Ekonomicheskoe biuro. (Chinese Eastern Railway. Economic Bureau), comp.

English-language versions of institutional authors have been standardized in accordance with scholarly idiom, even when a different English rendering appears on the title page.

2.3 *Joint Authorship and Jointly Sponsored Authors*

When two or more corporate bodies have collaborated in editing, compiling, or writing a publication, their names, nested or unnested, are joined by "*with*":

> Université libre de Bruxelles. Institut de sociologie Solvay. Centre d'étude des pays de l'Est *with* Centre national pour l'étude des pays à régime communiste, eds.

When an institutional author is responsible to two superior agencies or organizations, the names of the sponsoring agencies are joined by "*and.*" An institutional author jointly sponsored by two unnested agencies appears in this form:

> Hong Kong Council of Social Service *and* Hong Kong Trade Development Council. Committee on Industrial Welfare, comp.

When one or both of the sponsors is a nested agency, the phrase "*joint sponsors*" is added after the second:

> Chung-kuo nung yeh k'o hsüeh yüan (China Agricultural Sciences Institute). Nung yeh ching chi yen chiu so (Agricultural Economics Research Office) *and* Chung-kuo nung yeh k'o hsüeh yüan (China Agricultural Sciences Institute). Shan-hsi fen yüan (Shensi Sub-institute). Nung ching shih (Office of Agricultural Economics), *joint sponsors.* Tiao ch'a tsu (Investigation Team), ed.

More than two joint authors or joint sponsors necessitates a bracketed comment:

> Pei-ching i hsüeh yüan (Peking Medical College). Wei sheng hsi (Dept. of Hygiene). Hsüeh hsiao wei sheng chiao yen tsu (School Hygiene Teaching Unit) *with* Peking. Wei sheng fang i chan (Hygiene and Disease Prevention Station). Hsüeh hsiao wei sheng tsu (School Hygiene Unit). [This article has still a third joint author: Peking, Hsi-ch'eng ch'ü wei sheng fang i chan, Hsüeh hsiao wei sheng tsu (Peking, Hsi-ch'eng *ch'ü* Hygiene and Disease-Prevention Station, School Hygiene Unit).]

The first two of the examples shown above in their author-field format would appear as follows in the title field:

> . . . , jointly edited by Centre d'étude des pays de l'Est, Institut de sociologie Solvay, Université libre de Bruxelles *with* Centre national pour l'étude des pays à régime communiste.
>
> . . . , compiled by Committee on Industrial Welfare, jointly sponsored by Hong Kong Council of Social Service *and* Hong Kong Trade Development Council.

3 TITLES

Titles of books and unpublished dissertations are italicized; titles of journal articles and inclusions (i.e. chapters or papers in books) are enclosed in single quotation marks.

With respect to wording, spelling, diacritics, and hyphenation, titles are generally faithful to the title-page version. Three exceptions deserve notice: some very long titles have been shortened by the use of ellipsis dots, the German double *s* is rendered as *ss*, and the archaic Swedish *ô* is rendered as *ö* in accordance with modern usage. When a title at the head of an article or chapter is given differently in the table of contents, the latter form is ignored.

When titles of serial publications or of installments of multipart journal articles vary slightly in wording, they are followed by the comment "Title varies slightly" and only one title is supplied. When titles of installments of multipart journal articles vary considerably, they are followed by the comment "Title varies" and all variant titles are supplied.

3.1 *Capitalization and Punctuation*

The first word of a title is always capitalized. In English titles, capitalization is otherwise limited to names of persons, places, and organizations and to certain historical events for which capitalization is idiomatic. In transcribed Chinese and Japanese titles, capitalization is limited to names of persons and places. In titles in other languages, capitalization follows the conventions of the language.

Punctuation within titles has been standardized for all languages. Double quotation marks are used within titles of journal articles and inclusions—and single quotation marks within titles of books and unpublished dissertations—around words enclosed in the title-page version by quotation marks (whether single or double), guillemets, or the brackets, corner brackets, and parentheses often used as quotation marks by Chinese and Japanese typesetters. The centered dot used in Oriental copy to separate blocks of characters is rendered in transcribed titles as a word space. A subtitle is separated from the title by a comma when in strict apposition, and otherwise by a colon or, when there are two subtitles, by a combination of colon and period. Parentheses are used to enclose parenthetical material given in either brackets or parentheses on the title page. Brackets in titles are used exclusively for material supplied by the editor of this *Bibliography*.

3.2 *Title Specification*

In the case of non-English titles, bracketed material supplied by the editor of this *Bibliography*, except for dates and volume numbers, is added to the English rendering of the title. In English titles, however, all such material necessarily appears within the title itself; roman-face type is used even when the title is italicized.

Only the most recent editions (not reprintings) of books are cited, except where an earlier edition is known to be more authoritative or accurate. Data on the edition cited are appended to the title. "Mimeo." follows the titles of monographs or including works reproduced by any process other than printing.

The title field of inclusion entries normally specifies "Sole entry," "Selective entry," or "Analytic entry." The significance of this classification is explained at pp. xx–xxi.

3.3 *English Renderings*

A non-English title is immediately followed by an English rendering in parentheses except when the entry lists an English translation whose title is an acceptable version of the original or when an English rendering is provided earlier in a multiple-translation entry. Occasionally an otherwise unnecessary English rendering is supplied to incorporate essential editorial additions.

Webster's third new international dictionary is the authority for English words and phrases. Consistency across entries was sought in rendering non-English terms, departures being made only as required by context in the original or by English usage. Technical terms, organization names, names of historical events, and place names are given standardized treatment throughout. (For conventions relating to Chinese place names, see §13.)

The glosses adopted for the names of organizations and events reflect current scholarly idiom: thus "T'ung-meng Hui" is preferred to "Alliance Party," "Kuomintang" to "Nationalist Party," "Cultural Revolution" to "Great Proletarian Cultural Revolution." Where two forms are more or less equally idiomatic, both are given, e.g. "Hsing-Chung Hui [Revive China Society]." To maximize recognition, the titles of many books, journals, and newspapers are translated, e.g. "*Jen-min jih-pao* [People's daily]."

Names of historical personages are rendered in translation in the form conventional in English. For most Chinese persons this means the standardized Wade-Giles transcription of their regular name, i.e., their true surname and formal given name (*ming*). The chief exceptions are political figures from non-Mandarin-speaking areas such as Chiang Kai-shek and Sun Yat-sen, writers best known by their pseudonyms such as Lu Hsün, and scholars best known by a Western-style name such as Franklin C. H. Lee. If a person's courtesy or style name is used in the non-English title, it is rendered in English by the best known form only.

In general our desiderata in rendering titles were accuracy, correct scholarly idiom, idiomatic English, and parsimony, in that order of priority. Accuracy should be distinguished from literalness, on which little value was placed. Title-subtitle format in the original may or may not be respected, and various non-essential words are left untranslated. Nothing is bracketed that would be taken as implied by a native speaker of the language of the title: thus a Chinese title that literally means "Educational change since May 4th" is rendered "Educational change since the May Fourth Movement."

So far as possible, English renderings are designed to suggest the contents of the article. Where this cannot be done by an accurate rendering, a bracketed clarifying comment is added, e.g. "Buddha's grace and benevolence exist even in dreams [A Buddhist monk's memoirs]."

4 PUBLICATION DATA: BOOKS

Publication data are generally presented according to the conventions established by the U.S. Library of Congress. Exceptions to Library of Congress practice and conventions especially adopted for this *Bibliography* are indicated below.

4.1 *Place of Publication*

Chinese cities appear in Post Office spelling or in Wade-Giles transcription according to rules set out below (§13.1). Non-Chinese cities outside China appear in the form given in the *Columbia-Lippincott gazetteer of the world*. When a city's name has changed over time, the official name at the time of publication is used, e.g. Peiping for 1928–1949, Petrograd for 1914–1922. Places of publication that are not well known or could be confused with others of the same name are identified by state, province, or country, e.g. "Tsou-p'ing, Shantung."

When publishing houses maintain offices and distribution centers in several cities, the location of the head (editorial) office is usually cited as the sole place of publication. In a few cases, two cities are cited, e.g. "Berkeley, Los Angeles: U. of California Press."

4.2 *Publisher*

Publishers' names have been shortened to the essentials necessary for identification. Such terms as "Publishing Co.," "and Sons," and "Ltd." are omitted, along with given names and initials, unless necessary to prevent confusion with another publisher. "Press" and its equivalents in other Western languages are often omitted, but "Press" is retained for university presses to distinguish them from other university agencies:

Cambridge: Harvard U. Press

Cambridge: Harvard U., East Asian Research Center

The names of all publishers appear in the form used at the time of publication: thus "Appleton" before 1933, "Appleton-Century" from 1933 through 1947, "Appleton-Century-Crofts" beginning 1948. For privately published items, "The author[s]" appears in place of a publisher. Unascertained publishers are rendered by a dash: "Harbin: ———, 1926. 34 p."

The names of governmental agencies as publishers invariably appear in the language of the country or, in the case of colonies, of the metropolitan power, regardless of the language of publication. Other institutional authors generally appear in the language of publication. English versions are never supplied for the names of non-English publishers. When a nested institutional publisher has already been given in full in the author or title field, the lowest-level agency only is cited in publisher position. Thus, for an author field that reads "China [Republic]. Shih yeh pu. Kuo chi mao i chü. (Ministry of Industry. Bureau of Foreign Trade)," the publication-data field reads "Shanghai: Kuo chi mao i chü, 1935, 393–467."

Books are sometimes published simultaneously by different publishers. When one such publisher is in the United States and the other not, only the American edition is cited. Otherwise both are cited:

Tientsin: Hautes études; Shanghai: Université l'Aurore, 1937. 98 p.

In the case of joint publication, e.g. publication by two cooperating institutions, the names of the publishers are joined by "*with*":

Taipei: National Taiwan U., College of Law, Dept. of Sociology *with* New York: Columbia U., East Asian Institute, 1968. 35, 971 p.

When the joint publishers are located in the same city, the city name is given only once.

4.3 *Pagination*

Pagination of monograph and inclusion entries is always given in arabic numerals; roman numerals that appear as page numbers have been converted to arabic.

Front and/or back matter that is paginated continuously with the text is included in the overall page count. A page count for front or back matter that is separately paginated from the text, e.g. in roman numerals or unnumbered, is given only when such matter amounts to ten or more pages:

New York: Pantheon, 1966. 18, 341, 32 p.

Occasionally there are two separately paginated sections of front matter or back matter, each of ten pages or more, in addition to the text. In such cases, an ampersand is used:

Hong Kong: Noronha, 1898. 243, 18 & 21 p.

The abbreviation "s.p." (separately paginated) indicates that a monograph is composed of several sections, each numbered from page 1:

Paris: Rozier, 1864. s.p.

Shanghai: China Press, 1912. 186 p. [s.p.].

The abbreviation "n.p." (unpaginated) indicates the absence of page numbers:

Paris: Anisson, 1696. 2 vols. n.p.

Peking: Nachbaur, 1923. n.p. [44 p. in all]

When pagination is supplied in addition to "s.p." or "n.p.," as in the second example of each pair above, it represents a hand count.

For inclusions, pagination consists of the first and last pages of the item cited, joined by a dash. The abbreviation "s.p." is used when the entry cites one of several sections, each paginated from page 1, or an introduction separately paginated from the text:

Peking: Society for the Study of International Education, 1923. 1–20 [s.p.].

4.4 *Multivolume Works*

Pagination of multivolume works is given as follows:

London: Smith, Elder, 1870. 2 vols. 17, 444; 442 p.

London: London Printing and Publishing, 1858, 1859. 2 vols. 11, 184; 140 p.

The abbreviation "c.p." (continuously paginated) is used when each volume continues numbering from the last page of the previous volume:

Cambridge: Harvard U. Press, 1971. 2 vols. 1190 p. [c.p.].

For monographs comprising five or more volumes, only the span of years and the total number of pages are given:

Shanghai: Impr. de la Mission catholique, 1911–1938. 18 vols. 8467 p. [s.p.].

The number of the volume from which an inclusion is taken follows the year of publication of that volume:

Hong Kong: Union Research Institute, 1962, vol. 2, 231–251.

4.5 *Series*

Series information is given for both monograph and inclusion entries. It normally consists of the sponsoring organization, the series title, and the item's number in the series:

> Seattle: U. of Washington Press, 1971, 3–33. (Social Science Research Council, Studies in Chinese government and politics, 2)

When publications are part of two series, full information for each appears. Entries for all items issued by the U.S. Joint Publications Research Service show first the JPRS number and then the number in the *Monthly catalogue of United States Government publications* (abbreviated MC):

> Washington, D.C.: U.S. Joint Publications Research Service, 13 May 1965. 94 p. (JPRS 30,079; MC 11,108/1965)

The letter suffixes D and N that appear in early JPRS numbers stand for Washington, D.C. and New York City, respectively.

If the sponsoring organization has previously appeared in full as author, editor, compiler, or publisher, its name is abbreviated to capital letters:

> Washington, D.C.: American Assn. for the Advancement of Science, 1961, 59–98. (AAAS publications, 68)

If the organization or agency is a nested one that has previously appeared in full, the all-capital abbreviation of its lowest-level agency only is cited:

> Berkeley: U. of California, Center for Chinese Studies, 1968. 128 p. (CCS China research monographs, 2)

The sponsoring organization is omitted when it is clearly implied by the series title:

> New York: Columbia U. Press, 1968, 213–239. (Columbia studies in economics, 1)

5 PUBLICATION DATA: JOURNAL ARTICLES

Publication data for journal articles typically consist of journal title (in italics); volume and issue numbers; month, year, and sometimes day of issue; and running pages of the article cited. Publication data for the journals themselves are not given in the entries, but are provided in Journals Cited (p. lxviii) for all journals from which five or more articles are listed.

5.1 *Journal Titles*

Titles of journals are given in the language that appears on the journal masthead, with one exception: Oriental-language journals that also carry a Western-language title and consistently publish articles in one or more Western languages are cited by their Western-language titles. (Their Oriental-language titles are transcribed in the Journals Cited section.) Nonroman journal titles have been transcribed according to the standards set forth in §12.

Capitalization of words in journal titles follows the conventions observed in the language of the title. Initial articles in journal titles are generally dropped from titles of three or more syllables: thus *Asie et l'Afrique*, but *La Chine*. Subtitles of journals are separated from main titles by semicolons: thus *Transcultural research in mental health problems; review and newsletter.*

The following abbreviations are consistently used in journal titles:

Assn.	*Association*	*q.*	*quarterly* (noun only)
b./B.	*bulletin/Bulletin*	*r.*	*revue*
Dept.	*Department*	*U.*	*University*
j.	*journal*	*Z.*	*Zeitschrift*

These abbreviations are used for words with identical spellings in different languages, but never for their equivalents that are spelled differently. Thus, *b./B.* does duty in English, French, and German titles, but it would never be used for *biulleten'* or *bollettino*. Journal titles of two or more words may be abbreviated to initials only, depending on the length of the title and how many items from that journal are listed in this volume. A complete list of such abbreviations begins on p. lxxvii.

The series of a journal is indicated immediately following the title, "new series" being specified as required. This information is supplied in English for Oriental-language journals, otherwise in the language of the journal itself:

> *Chiao yü t'ung hsün* new (2nd) series 1, 1 (3 Jan. 1946), 1–16.
>
> *TP* 2e série 38, 1 (1947), 16–42.
>
> *Z. für Politik* neue (2.) Folge 7, 2 (1960), 241–256.

Journals bearing the same title as other journals and a few obscure journals are identified as necessary in parentheses:

> *International affairs* (London)
> *Civitas* (Mannheim)
> *Asia* (New York: American Asiatic Assn.)
> *Asia* (New York: Asia Society)

5.2 *Issue Numbers, Dates, and Pagination*

Volume and issue numbers are cited in arabic numerals, even when roman numerals or Oriental characters are used by the journal itself. Journals that give only the year of issue and the issue number show the year in volume-number position:

> *Kommunist* 1968, 7 (mai)

Unnumbered journals are so designated:

> *Shanghai market prices report* unnumbered (Jan.–Mar. 1929)

Publication months are rendered in English for Oriental-language journals, and in the language of the journal for all others. The names of months are abbreviated only in English, French, and German. The day of publication is given for journals issued more frequently than once a month.

Pagination of journal articles more than one page long invariably consists of first and last page numbers joined by a dash. The abbreviation "s.p." is used when different parts of the journal are paginated from page 1.

5.3 *Multipart Journal Articles*

Citations of articles continued in successive issues of a journal give full data for each installment:

> *A travers le monde* 6, 28 (7 juil. 1900), 222–223; 6, 29 (21 juil. 1900), 230.

For citations of multipart journal articles running to seven or more installments, the entry gives only the volume and issue numbers and dates of the first and last installments and the total number of pages:

> *Orient* (Hong Kong) 2, 1 – 2, 12 (Aug. 1951 – July 1952), 47 p. in all.

Minor changes in title are indicated by the bracketed comment "Title varies" or "Title varies slightly."

6 Bracketed Comments

In the computerized system used to format citations for this *Bibliography*, bibliographic data are rigorously analyzed into functional elements before being entered into the computer—a procedure that is essential if the data are to be automatically retrievable (see p. xv). Useful information not readily accommodated by the computer programs that format citations is added in the form of bracketed comments, which normally appear at the end of one of the citation fields. In general, bracketed comments correct, clarify, or supplement information already given in that field of the citation.

The most common categories of author-field comments concern incorrect transcriptions of Oriental author names (see §1.5), joint authorship or sponsorship by more than two corporate bodies (see §2.3), sequential authors of a serial publication (see §9), and the geographic location of an institutional author (see §13.7).

The most common categories of title-field comments concern title variation in multipart journal articles (see §5.3) and in serial publications (see §9), and specifications of translations (see §11.3 and §11.4).

The most common categories of comments in the publication-data field concern the original title of reissued works (see §8), cross-references between related entries for a single series (see §9), holding information involving more than one library (see §9), cross-references to an unpublished dissertation from derivative publications (see §10), additional translations (see §11.1), and certain cases of more or less simultaneous publication in different languages (see §11.5).

7 Reviews

This volume includes such reviews of books and journal articles as were judged to constitute a significant contribution to scholarship on the reviewer's part.

For untitled reviews, the title field begins with "Review of"; for titled reviews, the "Review of" information follows the title in brackets:

> Dernberger, Robert Franklin, 1929–.
> Review of *Foreign investment and economic development in China, 1840–1937*, by Chi-ming Hou.
>
> Meyners d'Estrey, Guillaume Henri Jean, 1829–?
> Review of 'Het huwelijken de wetgeving dienaangaande in China' (Marriage legislation in China), by J- W- Young.
>
> Briessen, Fritz van.
> 'Chinas "Gentry" und die Revolution: Zur Soziologie des Maoismus' (China's 'gentry' and the revolution: The sociology of Maoism). [Review of *China's gentry: Essays in rural-urban relations*, by Fei Hsiao-tung (Fei Hsiao-t'ung).]

Reviews whose titles consist solely of author and title data on the reviewed work are treated as untitled reviews.

Review formats do not provide publication data for the reviewed work. To locate the full citation consult the appropriate author index in the appropriate volume of this *Bibliography*. One or more of the works reviewed in a multiple review article may of course fall outside the scope of this *Bibliography*.

8 Reissues

Items originally published as monographs, inclusions, or journal articles and later reissued in whatever format with the contents unchanged are classified as reissues, and the later version is introduced by the word "reprinted." Published versions of dissertations previously "published" only on film, e.g. by University Microfilms (see §10.2), are not considered reissues. Items reissued by the original publisher are counted as reissues only if the item was out of print at the time of reissue and at least five years had elapsed since first publication.

Reissue information appears in the publication-data field in one of the forms illustrated below. The following examples illustrate reissues under the original title.

(1) "Reprinted—" for a monograph reissued as a monograph, or for a monograph, inclusion, or journal article reissued as a journal article:

> Shanghai: Impr. de la Mission catholique, 1894. 278 p. (Variétés sinologiques, 5) [Reprinted—Taipei: Ch'eng-wen, 1971. 278 p.]

(2) "Reprinted in" for a monograph, inclusion, or journal article reissued as an inclusion, or for an inclusion reissued as a journal article:

JAS 24, 1 (Nov. 1964), 3–43. [Reprinted in *Man, space and environment: Concepts in contemporary human geography*, edited by Paul Ward English and Robert Charles Mayfield. (Sole entry.) New York: Oxford U. Press, 1972, 561–601.]

(3) "Separately reprinted—" for an inclusion or a journal article reissued as a monograph:

NSEQ 9, 1 (Apr. 1936), 27–94. [Separately reprinted—Tientsin: Chihli Press, 1936. 68 p. (Nankai Institute of Economics, Industry series, 9)] [Separately reprinted—Washington, D.C.: Center for Chinese Research Materials, 1972. 68 p.]

When the title of the reissue differs from the original title, the bracketed material begins "Reprinted as" for the types of reissues shown in (1) and (2) above, and "Separately reprinted as" for the type shown in (3).

When the same item appears more or less simultaneously as two separate publications, the reissue formulas are replaced by "Also published—," "Also published as," or "Also published in":

Hong Kong: Christian Study Centre on Chinese Religion and Culture, 1969. 11, 167 p. [Also published in *Cheng feng; quarterly notes on Christianity and Chinese religion and culture* 12, 3/4 (1969), 1–167.]

When a work has been reissued under a new title, the original title and publication data are provided in a bracketed comment:

Shanghai: China United Press, 1937. 332 p. [Rev. and enl. ed. of *The Chinese railways: An historical survey*. Shanghai: China United Press, 1935. 214 p.]

Whenever possible, both the original publication and the reissue were examined. When we could not locate the original, the library symbol for the entry pertains to the reissue; this is indicated by attaching to the symbol a numerical superscript, normally [2], meaning the second publication mentioned (i.e. the reissue or the first of two or more reissues). When the original could not be located and our information on it is incomplete or unreliable, the reissue is treated as the original publication. Only in such cases does the bracketed comment begin "Reprint of" or "Reprinted from":

New York: Paragon, 1966, 150–164. [Reprinted from *American Hebrew and Jewish tribune* Jan.–Mar. 1933.]

In such cases, the library symbol indicates a holding of the reissue and no superscript is used.

9 SERIAL PUBLICATIONS

Serial publications running to three or more installments may be combined into a single entry. Such an entry may cover a series of monographs (e.g. annual reports), inclusions (e.g. recurring chapters in yearbooks), or journal articles (e.g. recurring feature articles). For such treatment, it is required that each installment be coded with the same principal subject, and that all installments fall within the same historical-period module (e.g. 1911–1928, 1928–1949). If two principal subjects or two time periods are involved, the series is presented as two separate entries; and if either portion of the divided series includes fewer than three items, the series format is abandoned for that portion.

Serial entries are also subject to a number of bibliographic constraints. If a change occurs in mid-series in place of publication, publisher, including work, or journal, what would otherwise be a single serial entry is converted to two or more. A major change in title has the same consequences, but minor changes are accommodated in a single entry, which uses the form that recurs with greatest regularity plus the bracketed comment "Title varies" or "Title varies slightly." A change of author, other things constant, is never grounds for breaking up a serial entry. Thus:

Ling Piao and Ling Feng. [Authors sequential rather than joint: Ling Piao for 1962 and 1964; Ling Feng for 1963.]
'Legal affairs' [title varies]. In *Communist China, 1962–1964*, edited by Union Research Institute.
Hong Kong: Union Research Institute. Issued annually, 1963–1965, average ca. 15 p.

Whenever what would generally be recognized as a single series is presented as two or more entries, whether because of changing substantive coverage or inconstant bibliographic features, the entries are cross-referenced to one another:

Hong Kong. Public Works Dept.
Annual departmental report by the Director of Public Works, 1950/51–1971/72. [Issues for 1946/47–1948/49 are entered as 17261.]
Hong Kong: Government Printer. Issued annually, 1951–1972. Average ca. 100 p.

When the full run of a serial publication being cited in a given entry is not known to be held at any one library, the library symbol shown (that of the library known to hold the greater part) is followed by an asterisk. An asterisked comment of the following type then appears after the publication data:

[*An exception is the issue for 1954, which is held at CSH.]

[*Exceptions are No. 1, which is held at MCH, and Nos. 4–5, which are held at JTT.]

10 DISSERTATIONS

"Dissertation" is here used as a general term for all works submitted in partial fulfillment of the requirements for an academic degree. A distinction is made in this *Bibliography*, however, between senior theses, masters theses, and doctoral dissertations, which in American universities are written for the bachelor's degree, the master's degree, and the doctorate, respectively. Despite variations from one country to another, all dissertations included in this volume have been placed in one of these three categories. Where necessary, a comment has been added for clarification.

An unpublished dissertation is included even when a summary or greatly condensed version has been published or a portion has been published in revised form, provided important substantive data remain unpublished. In such cases, the entry for the publication is cross-referenced to the dissertation entry, e.g. "[For fuller treatment, see entry -----.]."

10.1 *Unpublished Dissertations*

An unpublished dissertation is one submitted as a typescript and not subsequently reproduced for public distribution. The publication-data field is replaced by dissertation data:

> Unpublished doctoral dissertation, Faculté de droit, Université de Paris, 1968. 306, 21 p.
>
> Unpublished masters thesis in History, U. of London [School of Oriental and African Studies], 1965. 265 p.

The library symbol for an unpublished dissertation is normally that of the library of the degree-granting university.

10.2 *Published Dissertations*

A published dissertation is one that has been reproduced for distribution in essentially unrevised form, usually at or shortly after the granting of the degree. Published dissertations include those printed for limited distribution by firms that specialize in dissertation printing; those published commercially as books or parts of books, or as journal articles; and those reproduced on film for public distribution by University Microfilms, Inc., Ann Arbor, Michigan.

When a dissertation has been published, data on the dissertation follow the publication data in parentheses:

> Wiesbaden: Harrassowitz, 1959. 406 p. (Doctoral dissertation, Philosophische Fakultät, Universität München)

Citations of privately published dissertations give the dissertation printer as publisher; if no printer is listed, "The author" appears in place of a publisher:

> Cologne: The author, 1967. 197 p. (Doctoral dissertation, Wirtschafts- und sozialwissenschaftliche Fakultät, Universität Köln)

Many American universities, and some Canadian and European universities, require that copies of doctoral dissertations submitted to the university be transmitted to University Microfilms for microfilming and distribution. Abstracts of these dissertations appear, together with a publication number, in *Dissertation abstracts international,* issued monthly by University Microfilms. Entries for such dissertations give University Microfilms as the publisher and their listing date as the year of publication. The publication number from *Dissertation abstracts international* appears in parentheses. Thus:

> Ann Arbor: University Microfilms (Publ. 72-8823), 1972. 306 p. (Doctoral dissertation in Education, Columbia U. [Teachers College], 1970)

The library symbol given for all such dissertations is that of the University Microfilms Library (MAM).

10.3 *Dissertations Published in Revised Form*

A dissertation that has been revised substantially for publication is cited in standard monograph, inclusion, or journal-article format. Information on the dissertation appears in parentheses at the end, preceded by "revision of":

> 'The Hakka or "guest people": Dialect as a socio-cultural variable in southeastern China.'
> *Ethnohistory* 15, 3 (Summer 1968), 237–292. (Revision of masters thesis in Anthropology, Columbia U., 1963)
>
> *Government and politics in Kuomintang China, 1927–1937.*
> Stanford: Stanford U. Press, 1972. 14, 226 p. (Revision of *Political development in China, 1927–1937,* doctoral dissertation in Political Science, U. of Wisconsin, 1969)

The library symbol given in a revised dissertation entry is that of a library holding the published version.

11 Translations

This section discusses the criteria for including translations in this volume and certain problems of presentation. As used in this section, "Western languages" includes Turkish as well as the various European languages.

11.1 *Criteria for Inclusion*

In general, translations from more widely known to less widely known languages have been excluded. In the case of single translations, the following categories are admitted:

Language of the original	Translations admitted
English (E)	none
French (F)	into E only
German (G)	into E only
Spanish (S)	into E only
Dutch (D)	into E and F only
Russian (R)	into E, F, and G only
Italian	into E, F, and G only
Scandinavian languages	into E, F, and G only
Chinese	into E, F, and G only
Other Western languages (W)	into E, F, G, S, D, and R
Japanese	into all but W and O
Other non-Western languages (O)	into all but O

However, published translations of unpublished manuscripts are admitted regardless of the languages involved.

For multiple independent translations—translations from the original into various languages, each of which has been made directly from the original—further exclusions are made. For this purpose, the pecking order of Western languages shown above is collapsed into four groups: (1) English and French; (2) German, Spanish, Dutch, and Russian; (3) Italian and the Scandinavian languages; (4) all others. If there are translations into one or both languages in group (1), only these translations are cited; if there are no translations into group (1) languages but one or more into group (2) languages, only the group (2) translations are cited; etc.

For multiple chain translations—translations from the original into one language and then from the translated version into another language, etc.—exclusion rules are relaxed to include translations in the chain that leads from the original to an admitted translation. For example this volume contains translations from Chinese to Russian to English, even though a translation from Chinese to Russian would normally not be cited.

Entries of multiple translations that involve only Western languages follow the model of the Guillermaz example in §11.2. Title and publication data for successive translations follow the data for the first translation.

When the same material has been published in different translations, the version not chosen for the main entry is customarily cited in full in brackets:

> *CE* 2, 3 (Fall 1969), 3–14. [A different tr.—'The revolution in education in colleges of science and engineering as reflected in the struggle between the two lines at the Shanghai Institute of Mechanical Engineering.' *SCMM* 627 (16 Sept. 1968), 1–18.]

11.2 *Translation Formats*

Two basic types of translation formats are used in this volume. The *Type 1 format* is used when both the language of the original and the language(s) of the translation(s) are covered in this volume, i.e. in the case of translations involving Western languages only. The original is entered as a full citation, with any variant form of the author's name appearing in the translation included in the initial author line; a complete citation of the translation, minus the author line, follows after a space. The name of the translator, if known, follows the title of the translation. Thus:

> Guillermaz, Jacques, 1911–.
> *Histoire du Parti communiste chinois (1921–1949).*
> Paris: Payot, 1968. 450 p.
>
> *A history of the Chinese Communist Party, 1921–1949.* Tr. by Anne Destenay.
> New York: Random House, 1972. 477 p.

The *Type 2 format* is used when the language of the translation is covered by this volume but the language of the original is covered by one of the other volumes, i.e. for translations of Chinese or Japanese works into Western languages. In contrast to Type 1 formats, which are basically citations of the original, Type 2 formats are citations of the translation; title and publication data for the original follow the title of the translation. The author's name as it appears in the original (the standard transcription for Oriental authors) follows the version that appears in the translation. Thus:

> Ma, Chao-chun (Ma Ch'ao-chün), 1885–.
> *History of the labor movement in China.* Tr. by Peter Min Chi Liang of *Chung-kuo lao kung wen t'i* (Chinese labor problems); Shanghai: Min chih shu chü, 1927; 114 p.
> Taipei: China Cultural Service, 1955. 169 p.

The Type 2 format is also used for translations from one Western language to another when publication data on the original are incomplete or suspect.

Finally, as noted above, Russian translations of publications in Chinese that were subsequently translated into English, French, or German have been admitted on the assumption that many Western scholars who know English, French, or German lack a reading knowledge of either Chinese or Russian. These translations are presented in a mixture of Type 2 and Type 1 formats, the Chinese-to-Russian in Type 2 and the Russian-to-other in Type 1:

> [Miao Chu-khuan] Mjau Tschu-hwang (Miao Ch'u-huang).
> *Kratkaia istoriia Kommunisticheskoi partii Kitaia* (Brief history of the Chinese Communist Party). Tr. by A- Sergeev, R- Kudashev, and O- Rakhmanin of *Chung-kuo kung ch'an tang chien yao li shih*; Peking: Hsüeh hsi tsa chih she, 1956; 182 p.
> Moscow: Gospolitizdat, 1958. 225 p.
>
> *Kurze Geschichte der Kommunistischen Partei Chinas.* Tr. by Erich Salewski.
> Berlin: Dietz, 1960. 279 p.

11.3 *Incomplete Data*

For a translation to be cited, the following basic data on the *translation* must have been verified: the title of a monograph and its place of publication or publisher or year of publication; the title of an inclusion, the title of the including work, and its place of publication or publisher or year of publication; the title of an article, the journal title, and the journal's volume or issue number or year of issue. If these basic facts are unavailable or highly suspect, no translation is cited.

For translations involving Western languages only, one of the above sets of data on the *original* must be verified for the Type 1 format to be used. When essential data are missing, variations of the Type 2 format are used as shown below.

When the original appeared in an including work or a journal and the title of the inclusion or the journal article is not known, the citation of the original begins "Tr. from" or "Tr. by —— from " and provides as much information on the original as is known:

'The idol factory of Peking.' Tr. from *Hantverk och kultur* 1943.

'Farm settlements north of the Yellow River in western Suiyuan.' Tr. from *Shen pao chou k'an* 2, 16 (25 Apr. 1937).

When the title of the original book or journal could not be ascertained, the only information given about the original is its language:

The Chinese girl. Tr. from the Russian by E- de Laberbis.

This variation of the Type 2 format is also used for published translations of previously unpublished materials:

'An account of Macao by the Chinese Jesuit Lu Hsi-yen about 1680–90.' Tr. from the Chinese by Earl Hampton Pritchard and Kwan-wai So. [Tr. of an unpublished manuscript, *K'ai t'ien pao yao* (Precious keys to heaven), dated 1705 and held at FPN.]

11.4 *Altered Translations*

Partial, abridged, and condensed translations are cited with bracketed comments indicating the nature of the omissions. A *partial* translation is one in which large blocks of the original have been omitted but the remainder has been translated in full. An *abridged* translation is one in which many short passages have been omitted instead of or in addition to large blocks. A *condensed* translation is one in which the original or portions of it have been paraphrased in fewer words. Additional information is normally supplied in the case of partial translations:

Selivankin, S- A-.
Zametki o torgovle v Kitae.
Moscow: Gostorgizdat, 1959. 70 p.

Notes on trade in Communist China, mimeo. [Partial tr.: p. 1–52, 58–70 only]
Washington, D.C.: U.S. Joint Publications Research Service, 8 July 1960. 48 p. (JPRS 3524; MC 14,242/1960)

When the contents of an item have been substantially revised, enlarged, or otherwise altered in the process of translation, the nature and extent of the changes have been determined by comparing the original and the translation whenever possible. When the translation is in fact a revised edition of the original, it is still cited as a translation, but with a more explicit comment, e.g. "Rev. in tr.," "Greatly enlarged in tr.," or "Rev. and condensed in tr."

In cases of very partial or greatly abridged translation, recourse is had to a bracketed comment rather than to a translation format:

[Bichurin, Nikita Iakovlevich] *Otets* Iakinf, 1777–1853.
Kitai v grazhdanskom i nravstvennom sostoianii (The civil and moral state of China).
St. Petersburg: Tip. Shtaba voenno-ucheb. zavedenii, 1848. 4 vols. 33, 137; 128, 10; 152; 177 p. [For a partial tr. by Emmanuel Golitzin (vol. 4, p. 54–67 only), see 'Du chamanisme en Chine' (Shamanism in China); *Nouvelles annales des voyages* 130 (1851), 287–306.]

A summary or an abstract in a language other than the language of publication is never cited as a translation. The existence of a summary or an abstract is indicated by a bracketed comment, e.g. "With English summary" or "With French abstract." Only summaries and abstracts in languages deemed more accessible than the language of publication are mentioned.

11.5 *Multilingual Publications*

When there is no evidence to suggest that one version of a work published simultaneously in more than one language is the original and another the translation, a translation format is generally used for Western/Western and a bracketed comment for Oriental/Western publications.

For items published simultaneously in more than one language—e.g. articles from a journal with editions in different languages—place of publication, the author's native language, and the availability of editions in various languages were factors in deciding which version(s) to cite. In the case of journals regularly issued in French and English, French-language contributions by authors who normally write in French are treated as originals and the English versions as translations; English-language contributions by authors who normally write in English are cited as originals and the French versions excluded. For authors who normally write in a language other than French or English, both the French version and the English are usually cited.

Where very few libraries are known to have complete holdings of any one version of a multilingual journal, versions in several languages are cited in the hope that the user may have access to at least partial holdings in one language.

In the case of institutions (such as the League of Nations) that issue official publications simultaneously in French and English and sometimes other languages, English versions are cited, with a comment listing other-language editions. Simultaneous publication in a Western and an Oriental language is also indicated by a bracketed comment. When the Oriental version appears in the same volume or journal issue as the Western, the comment is "In Chinese as well as English"; otherwise "See vol. 2 [3] of this *Bibliography* for Chinese [Japanese] version."

12 TRANSCRIPTION STANDARDS

12.1 *Chinese*

Transcription of Chinese follows the system used in Courtnay H. Fenn, comp., *The five thousand dictionary: A Chinese-English pocket dictionary*, rev. ed. (Cambridge, Mass., 1942), which simplifies the Wade-Giles transcription by eliminating *ê* and *ŭ*, while retaining *ü*.

Because of computerization, alternative transcriptions of the same phoneme are not permitted. Where Fenn lists *-o* and *-e* as variants, this *Bibliography* opts for *o*: thus *ho, ko, k'o,* and *o,* not *he, ke, k'e,* and *e.* Where syllables ending in *-o* are phonemically distinct from those ending in *-e,* as in *cho/che,* this *Bibliography* recognizes both forms, including both versions of the one pair—*jo* vs. *je*—that Fenn treats as phonemically identical. Fenn lists three other pairs of alternative syllable transcriptions: *i/yi, lun/lün,* and *ssu/szu.* In this *Bibliography* we use *i, lun,* and *ssu.* A complete list of the Wade-Giles syllables used in this *Bibliography* is given in Volume 2, Explanatory Notes, §12.1.

Chung-kuo ta tz'u tien pien tsuan chü, ed., *Han yü tz'u tien* (Peking, 1959), issued first in 1937 under the title *Kuo yü tz'u tien,* is our authority for the pronunciation, and hence transcription, of particular characters. When a morphemic distinction exists between two pronunciations of the same character, the transcription used varies according to the meaning. In the case of variant pronunciations not correlated with morphemic differences, preference is given to a pronunciation now current in the spoken language over any "reading" pronunciation and, among spoken forms, to the pronunciation listed as primary in *Han yü tz'u tien.* In keeping with library and most scholarly practice, the characters 的 and 了 are transcribed *ti* and *liao* rather than *te* and *le.*

In the transcription of Chinese, hyphenation is limited to personal names (two-syllable given names and double surnames) and multisyllabic place names. (See §13.3 for a discussion of the complexities of hyphenation in Chinese place names.) Apart from initial syllables in titles and other bibliographic elements, capitalization is limited to personal names and place names, and within these to the first syllable of hyphenated compounds. (Note, however, that hyphenation and capitalization of Wade-Giles elements in English renderings conform to scholarly idiom. Thus the transcriptions "hsing Chung hui" and "ko lao hui" become "Hsing-Chung Hui" and "Ko-lao Hui" in an English rendering.)

12.2 *Japanese*

Transcription of Japanese follows the modified Hepburn system used in Andrew Nathaniel Nelson, comp., *The modern reader's Japanese-English character dictionary* (Rutland, Vt., 1962). This differs from the romanization system used by most other current dictionaries in only one regard: *n* preceding *m, p,* or *b* becomes *m* (e.g. "shimbun," not "shinbun"). The syllabic *n* preceding a vowel or *y* is followed by an apostrophe.

Our authorities for the pronunciation and transcription of all Japanese-language material are Katsumatsu Senkichirō, ed., *Kenkyūsha's new Japanese-English dictionary,* rev. ed. (Tokyo, 1954), and Shimmura Izuru, ed., *Kōjien,* rev. ed. (Tokyo, 1969).

Apart from the initial word in bibliographic elements, capitalization is limited to personal names and place names, as in transcribed Chinese; but personal or place names that would be hyphenated in transcribed Chinese form a single unhyphenated word in transcribed Japanese.

Word division is based on the principles enunciated in *Cataloging rules of the American Library Association and the Library of Congress: Additions and changes, 1949–1958* (Washington, D.C.: U.S. Library of Congress, 1959), pp. 48–56. Briefly, compounds consisting of two Chinese characters are written as single words; inflectional endings are affixed to the stem; postposition particles with the force of a preposition are joined without hyphens to the preceding word; other grammatical particles are considered separate words; generic terms of geographic features and territorial units of administration are separated from proper names preceding them; and compounds involving country names are written as one word where sandhi occurs and otherwise hyphenated (thus *Nitchū,* but *Chū-Nichi*).

12.3 *Korean*

Transcription of Korean follows the McCune-Reischauer system; the authority is Samuel E. Martin et al., comps., *A Korean-English dictionary* (New Haven, Conn., 1967). Practice in other respects is based on Library of Congress rules, which are largely analogous to those for Japanese.

12.4 *Russian*

Transcription standards for Russian and other languages transcribed from cyrillic follow the system adhered to in *Half a century of Soviet serials* (Washington, D.C.: U.S. Library of Congress, 1968). This system differs from current Library of Congress catalog practice in that it omits the breve accent used to mark the short *i* and the joining diacritic used to indicate that two or four roman letters are transcribed from a single cyrillic letter. Thus *nekotoryi,* not *nekotoryĭ*; *stolitsa,* not *stolit͡sa.*

In the matter of prerevolutionary orthography, we transcribe ѣ as *e,* not *ie*; and we extend the modern orthography to the titles of prerevolutionary journals that continued to be published under the same name (orthography apart) after 1918. In the titles of journals not continued into the Soviet period, the original orthography is preserved.

13 Chinese Place Names

Special pains have been taken in identifying and rendering place names. The Geographic and Type-of-place codes, integral parts of the annotation scheme, have their bibliographic counterparts in conventions designed to codify and shape scholarly idiom and to clarify and supplement the geographic information conveyed by titles.

13.1 *Post Office and Wade-Giles Forms*

The names of all cities and other settlements and of provinces and other administrative units are rendered either in Post Office spelling, which never involves hyphenation, or in Wade-Giles transcription, which never combines syllables into an unhyphenated word. The three lists below specify which Chinese localities and administrative units are rendered, in appropriate contexts, in Post Office spelling. All province and city names not on these lists are rendered exclusively by Wade-Giles transcription.

Post Office form used in this *Bibliography*	Wade-Giles transcription
PROVINCES	
Anhwei	An-hui
Chahar	Ch'a-ha-erh
Chekiang	Che-chiang
Chihli	Chih-li
Fengtien	Feng-t'ien
Fukien	Fu-chien
Heilungkiang	Hei-lung-chiang
Honan	Ho-nan
Hopei	Ho-pei
Hunan	Hu-nan
Hupeh	Hu-pei
Inner Mongolian A.R.	Nei Meng-ku *tzu chih ch'ü*
Jehol	Je-ho
Kansu	Kan-su
Kiangnan	Chiang-nan
Kiangsi	Chiang-hsi
Kiangsu	Chiang-su
Kirin	Chi-lin
Kwangsi	Kuang-hsi
Kwangsi Chuang A.R.	Kuang-hsi Chuang *tzu chih ch'ü*
Kwangtung	Kuang-tung
Kweichow	Kuei-chou
Liaoning	Liao-ning
Ningsia	Ning-hsia
Ningsia Hui A.R.	Ning-hsia Hui *tzu chih ch'ü*
Shansi	Shan-hsi
Shantung	Shan-tung
Shensi	Shan-hsi
Sikang	Hsi-k'ang
Sinkiang	Hsin-chiang
Sinkiang Uighur A.R.	Hsin-chiang Wei-wu-erh *tzu chih ch'ü*
Suiyuan	Sui-yüan
Szechwan	Ssu-ch'uan
Taiwan	T'ai-wan
Tibet	Hsi-tsang

Post Office form used in this *Bibliography*	Wade-Giles transcription
Tibetan A.R.	Hsi-tsang *tzu chih ch'ü*
Tsinghai	Ch'ing-hai
Yunnan	Yün-nan
COLONIAL ENCLAVES	
Hong Kong	Hsiang-kang
Kiaochow	Chiao-chou
Kwantung	Kuan-tung
Macau	Ao-men
Weihaiwei	Wei-hai-wei
CITIES	
Amoy	Hsia-men
Canton	Kuang-chou
Changchun	Ch'ang-ch'un
Changsha	Ch'ang-sha
Chefoo	Yen-t'ai
Chengchow	Cheng-chou
Chengtu	Ch'eng-tu
Chinkiang	Chen-chiang
Chungking	Ch'ung-ch'ing
Dairen	Ta-lien
Foochow	Fu-chou
Hangchow	Hang-chou
Hankow	Han-k'ou
Hanyang	Han-yang
Harbin	Ha-erh-pin
Huhehot	Hu-ho-hao-t'e (Kuei-sui)
Kaifeng	K'ai-feng
Kalgan	Chang-chia-k'ou
Kaohsiung	Kao-hsiung
Keelung	Chi-lung
Kirin	Chi-lin
Kiukiang	Chiu-chiang
Kowloon	Chiu-lung
Kunming	K'un-ming
Kweilin	Kuei-lin
Kweiyang	Kuei-yang
Lanchow	Lan-chou
Lhasa	La-sa
Loyang	Lo-yang
Mukden	Feng-t'ien, Shen-yang
Nanchang	Nan-ch'ang
Nanking	Nan-ching
Ningpo	Ning-po
Paotow	Pao-t'ou
Peking	Pei-ching
Peiping	Pei-p'ing
Port Arthur	Lü-shun
Shanghai	Shang-hai
Shasi	Sha-shih
Shenyang	Shen-yang
Sian	Hsi-an
Soochow	Su-chou
Swatow	Shan-t'ou
Taichung	T'ai-chung
Tainan	T'ai-nan
Taipei	T'ai-pei
Taiyuan	T'ai-yüan
Tangshan	T'ang-shan
Tientsin	T'ien-chin
Tsinan	Chi-nan
Tsitsihar	Ch'i-ch'i-ha-erh
Tsingtao	Ch'ing-tao
Urumchi	Wu-lu-mu-ch'i (Ti-hua)
Wenchow	Wen-chou
Wuchang	Wu-ch'ang
Wuhan	Wu-han
Wuhu	Wu-hu
Wusih	Wu-hsi
Yangchow	Yang-chou
Yenan	Yen-an

The province list includes all Nationalist provinces as of 1930, four earlier provinces whose Post Office forms are judged to have scholarly currency (Chihli, Fengtien, Kiangnan, and Taiwan), and the five so-called autonomous regions of the People's Republic. Among the province names excluded (i.e. judged not to have a Post Office form that has won scholarly acceptance) are those of such pre-republican provinces as Hu-kuang, Nan-ching, and Ching-shih; those of provinces created by the Manchoukuo regime and not otherwise included in the list (e.g. Lung-chiang); those of the short-lived Manchurian provinces created by the Nationalist government in the wake of World War II and not otherwise included in the list (e.g. Liao-pei); Huai-hai province, a creation of the Japanese-sponsored Nanking regime; and P'ing-yüan province, an ephemeral creation of the People's Republic. Formosa is never used as a Post Office form.

The city list is somewhat less comprehensive. It does not include all provincial capitals, not even all capitals or one-time capitals of the eighteen provinces (e.g. Pao-ting, Nan-ning, Ho-fei, and An-ch'ing are excluded). It does not include all former treaty ports (thus Ch'ing-huang-tao, not Chinwangtao; Niu-chuang, not Newchwang). And by no means does it include all large cities. The question asked is whether the Post Office form has been securely established as scholarly idiom. We think it has been for some rather small cities (e.g. Yenan) and has not been for some rather large ones (e.g. Fu-shun).

The names of many Chinese cities have changed in modern times, as has scholarly idiom. When unfamiliar forms occur in positions where the Post Office form is called for, the Wade-Giles transcription is commonly followed by the Post Office form in brackets:

> Yün-nan-fu [i.e., Kunming]
> Hsin-ching [Changchun]

Post Office forms with imperialistic connotations, notably Chefoo, Mukden, Port Arthur, and Dairen, are not idiomatic for the post-1949 period. For this period the preferred forms are "Yen-t'ai [Chefoo]," "Shenyang [Mukden]," and "Lü-ta [Port Arthur and Dairen]." The names of Lü-ta and other municipalities made up of two or three formerly separate cities (e.g. Tzu-po, Hsiang-fan, Tzu-kung) are rendered in Wade-Giles except for Wuhan.

Post Office forms are usually not followed by the generic designation. "Province" is used only in the case of Manchoukuo territorial units, and "municipality" only when the extent of the territorial unit is particularly pertinent. However, Kirin, which is the Post Office form for the city as well as the province, is always specified when appropriate as "[the city of] Kirin" or "Kirin [municipality]."

Post Office forms are consistently used as the first element of institutional authors when these are agencies of provinces, municipalities, or other subprovincial governments (see §2.1); in the English rendering of a non-English title; in specifying place of publication; and in editorially supplied comments. They are never used in transcriptions of Chinese, Japanese, or Korean material, including titles of books, articles, journals, and series, and names of publishers and series sponsors. Bastard forms such as *Kwangsi jih pao* are disallowed.

13.2 *Territorial Administrative Units*

Apart from the territorial administrative units of Manchoukuo and Japanese-controlled Taiwan, the following are the chief units represented in this volume:

Transcription	Term used in descriptive translation	Term used with place names
	PROVINCIAL LEVEL OR HIGHER	
tsung tu	governor-generalship	governor-generalship
sheng	province	NOTHING IF ON POST OFFICE LIST; OTHERWISE province
tzu chih ch'ü	autonomous region	A.R.
shih	(province-level) municipality	municipality
	INTERMEDIATE LEVEL	
tao	circuit	circuit
fu	prefecture	*fu*
chih li chou	independent department	(independent) *chou*
chih li t'ing	independent subprefecture	(independent) *t'ing*
chuan ch'ü	special district	special district
shih	(subprovincial) municipality	municipality
	HSIEN LEVEL	
hsien	county	*hsien*
chou	department	*chou*
t'ing	subprefecture	*t'ing*
tzu chih hsien	autonomous county	autonomous *hsien*
shih	(*hsien*-level) municipality	municipality
	SUB-HSIEN LEVEL	
ch'ü	district (of a *hsien*); ward (of a municipality)	IF UNNUMBERED, *ch'ü*; IF NUMBERED, ward OR district
chen	(urban) township	*chen*
hsiang	(rural) township	*hsiang*
(jen min) kung she	commune	commune
li	administrative village	*li*
pao	*pao*	*pao*
ta tui	brigade	brigade

The descriptive translation of *chen* and *hsiang* omits "urban" and "rural" when no distinction is being drawn, and the compound *chen hsiang* is translated simply "townships." For people's communes, the generic designation in a place name is always simply "commune." Since one-syllable (single-character) place names are abhorred in natural spoken Chinese, forms such as Shen *chou* and Wei *hsien* are rendered in full whenever there is editorial discretion.

Place names often contain survivals of superseded administrative arrangements. For example, "chou" occurs in the names of many Ch'ing administrative units that were not *chou* (departments) but *fu* (prefectures). Thus Fu-chou (Foochow) and Chang-chou, to mention only two examples in Fukien, were prefectures in Ch'ing times, and are thus properly rendered not Fu *chou* and Chang *chou* but Fu-chou *fu* and Chang-chou *fu*, even when the *fu* is omitted in a non-English title. After the *chou* was abolished as a distinctive unit following the Revolution of 1911, "chou" was sometimes added to place names to avoid confusion: thus, with a Hua *hsien* already in existence, Hua *chou* was renamed Hua-chou *hsien*. Another source of anachronistic error is the assignment (after 1911) of the old prefectural name to the former metropolitan *hsien* or *chou* of the prefecture; thus, using a modern gazetteer, one can readily mistake a *fu* of Ch'ing times for a *hsien*.

Taiwan place names are never given Japanese readings. Apart from the province name itself and the five cities on the Post Office list, all names, including their generic designations, are rendered in Wade-Giles transcription. For most of the Japanese period, the island was divided into *chou* (departments) and *t'ing* (subprefectures), each of which in turn was divided into *chün* and *shih*. *Chün* (districts) were subdivided into *chieh* (urban townships) and *chuang* (rural townships); *shih* (municipalities) were subdivided into *ting* (wards). In all cases, the transcribed form in italics is used in English renderings of the generic part of place names.

Manchoukuo place names are treated in English renderings like place names in China proper, except that the phrase ". . . province [Manchoukuo]" is appended to the names of all provinces: thus "Fengtien province [Manchoukuo]" is used for the small 1934–1945 province, "Fengtien" unmodified for the large province of 1907–1928.

13.3 *Central Places and Other Settlements*

Settlements are distinguished carefully in our editorial practice from administrative units. Cities and market towns, including capitals at all levels of the administrative hierarchy, are central places; all of these plus military outposts or garrison towns (*wei*), villages, and hamlets are settlements.

Imprecise terminology in Chinese and traditional Chinese cognition confound the distinction between central places and the administrative units of which they are the capitals or headquarters. In Ch'ing writings, the unspecified characters for a province are as likely to refer to the provincial capital as to the province itself. In such cases, the English rendering would show "[the capital of] Hunan [Changsha]." The name of a *hsien* in a Chinese title may in fact refer to the *hsien ch'eng*, the county capital, rather than to the county as a whole. The common or only name for some cities that serve as administrative seats is the name of the administrative unit. *Chen* following a place name may indicate a market town or the township of which that market town is the administrative seat. Many early titles use the name of a prefecture complete with *fu* to designate its capital, while others use the prefectural name without *fu* to designate the prefecture.

The necessary distinctions are made in this *Bibliography* by reserving italicized generic designations for administrative units and using hyphenated forms for central places. Thus Wei-hsien is the city, Wei *hsien* the county; Te-chou the city, Te *chou* the department; Ching-te-chen the town, Ching-te *chen* the township; Fo-shan the city, Fo-shan *chen* the township. Post Office forms are never used for subprovincial territorial units: thus Shanghai is the city and Shang-hai *hsien* the county; Chengtu is the city, Ch'eng-tu *fu* the prefecture, Ch'eng-tu *hsien* the county. Two particularly confusing cases are disentangled as follows: Yün-nan-fu is the city, Yün-nan *fu* the prefecture, Yunnan the province; Feng-t'ien-fu is the city, Feng-t'ien *fu* the prefecture, Fengtien the province. The distinction between the city as a central place and the municipality as an administrative unit is made by specifying municipality as necessary, e.g. "Chungking" unspecified vs. "Chungking municipality." In other cases distinctions are made in English. Thus "Shuang-liu hsien ch'eng" in a non-English title is rendered "the capital of Shuang-liu *hsien*."

13.4 *Nonadministrative Territories*

Some Chinese place names correspond to no particular administrative unit (e.g. North China, Central China) or refer to groupings of administrative units that have no current official standing. "Manchuria" is used wherever possible in preference to "Northeast China" or "the Northeast." Former governor-generalships are translated simply as a series of province names: thus "Liang Kuang" is rendered "Kwangtung and Kwangsi." A similar practice is followed for conventional groupings of former prefectures: thus "Su-Sung-T'ai" (a former circuit in Kiangsu) becomes "the Su-chou–Sung-chiang–T'ai-ts'ang region." For conventional groupings of *hsien*, "area" is used: thus "Ch'ao-chou" (a former prefecture in Kwangtung) becomes "the Ch'ao-chou area," and "san i" is rendered "the three-county area of Pan-yü, Nan-hai, and Shun-te."

The Post Office form Kiangnan is used for the Ch'ing province established in 1645 and subdivided in 1662 into Kiangsu and Anhwei. However, in the great majority of publication titles the term refers not to the two provinces of Kiangsu and Anhwei or their specific territory, but to nonadministrative territories of varying extent ranging from southern Kiangsu to the Lower Yangtze region. In these cases the English rendering varies in order to indicate the extent of geographic coverage.

13.5 *Natural Features*

For the following natural features, forms other than Wade-Giles are consistently used in English renderings and other positions permitting editorial discretion:

Form used in this *Bibliography*	Wade-Giles transcription
RIVERS	
Amur river	Hei-lung chiang
East River	Tung chiang
North River	Pei chiang
Pearl river	Chu chiang
Sungari river	Sung-hua chiang
Ussuri river	Wu-su-li chiang
West River	Hsi chiang
Yangtze river	Ch'ang chiang
Yellow River	Huang ho
BODIES OF WATER	
Kiaochow bay	Chiao-chou wan
Korea bay	Hsi Ch'ao-hsien wan
Gulf of Liaotung	Liao-tung wan
Gulf of Chihli	Po hai
Yellow Sea	Huang hai
Hangchow bay	Hang-chou wan
East China Sea	Tung hai
Taiwan Strait	T'ai-wan hai hsia
South China Sea	Nan hai
Hainan Strait	Ch'iung-chou hai hsia
Gulf of Tonkin	Tung-ching wan
NATURAL LAND FORMS	
Liaotung peninsula	Liao-tung pan tao
North China plain	Hua-pei p'ing yüan
Shantung peninsula	Shan-tung pan tao
Yangtze valley	Ch'ang chiang liu yü
Yangtze delta	Ch'ang chiang san chiao chou
Pearl river delta	Chu chiang san chiao chou
West River valley	Hsi chiang liu yü
Taipei basin	T'ai-pei p'en ti
Szechwan basin	Ssu-ch'uan p'en ti
Chengtu plain	Ch'eng-tu p'ing yüan
ISLANDS	
Hainan	Hai-nan (tao)
the Pescadores	P'eng-hu (tao)
Taiwan	T'ai-wan (tao)

To these lists may be added the many natural features on the Inner Asian periphery of China for which non-Chinese names are idiomatic: e.g. the Gobi desert, the Tsaidam basin, the Altai mountains.

13.6 *Railroads, Roads, and Canals*

Man-made transport routes are normally named in China by designating the two termini, the Grand Canal being a notable exception. Although the Chinese typically use a single character for each terminus, these city names are given in full in English renderings: thus "Peking-Hankow railroad," not "Ching-Han railroad." Termini not on the Post Office list are rendered in Wade-Giles and normally identified by province: "Lanchow–Hai-tung [Kiangsu] railroad." The English rendering is not always a direct fleshing out of the Chinese name: thus, for example, "Kuang-Chiu t'ieh lu," literally "Canton-Kowloon railroad," is rendered "Canton–Hong Kong railroad" in deference to established idiom.

13.7 *Editorially Supplied Geographic Data*

As a general principle, any place name mentioned in a title is identified up to the level of a province or Post-Office-form municipality. (Because of possible confusion, place names in Manchoukuo are identified all the way up to the national level.) These principles mean that all *hsien*-level units are identified by province, that all submunicipality localities are identified either by municipality alone (if on the Post Office list) or by municipality and province, and that all sub-*hsien*-level localities are identified by *hsien*-level unit and province. When not supplied by the publication itself, the necessary information was obtained from maps, gazetteers, and other reference works.

A bracketed identification beginning "i.e." is used to clarify anachronistic designations of place names, proper but unfamiliar designations, puzzling or confusing spellings in English titles, and various kinds of allusion:

> Chihli [i.e. Hopei]
> Fengtien [i.e. Liaoning]
> Ts'ang *chou* [i.e. Ts'ang *hsien*, Hopei]
> Chiang-ning-fu [i.e. Nanking]
> Sichuen [i.e. Szechwan]
> "my hometown" [i.e. Ho-fei, Anhwei]
> "the ancient capital" [i.e. Sian]
> "a Hopei village" [i.e. Hsü-chia-ch'iao, Ting *hsien*]
> "a rural town" [i.e. Chung-ho-chen, Hua-yang *hsien*, Szechwan]

Locations of universities, schools, hospitals, temples, factories, mines, and other institutions and structures situated in a specific place are supplied unless the place name forms part of the institutional name.

If no identification is supplied for a sub-*hsien*-level place name or for a site-specific institution, either the author has deliberately disguised the locality or he has failed to supply sufficient information to permit the editors to identify it. In a few cases, an annotator failed to identify a place name in a work that for some reason could not be consulted a second time.

When a work treats an extended period during which a place mentioned in the title changed its administrative status or province, the information supplied by the editor is for the end of the period.

The location of an institutional author unspecified elsewhere in the entry is given in a bracketed comment at the end of the author field:

> Chung-kuo kung ch'an tang. Chin-chou t'ieh lu chü wei yüan hui (Chinese Communist Party. Chin-chou Railroad Bureau Committee), ed. [Chin-chou is in Chin *hsien*, Liaoning.]

14 ALPHABETIZATION AND THE ORDERING OF ENTRIES

Within each subcategory of the Bibliography, entries are ordered alphabetically by author and title. No-author entries precede authored entries. Incomplete and more or less fleshed out names are alphabetized in order of completeness. Note that it is only in the alphabetization of incomplete names that personal and professional titles come into play:

J.
J. R. J.
J——n, James
Johnson, ———
Johnson, *Dr.* ———
Johnson, *Mrs.* ———
Johnson, J- R-
Johnson, J- Richard
Johnson, James Richard

Coauthored works follow works written by the first author alone, and "et al." coauthored works follow fully specified coauthored works. Entries showing the same author and title (as well as no-author entries showing the same title) are ordered by date of publication. Numbers are "alphabetized" after *z* and otherwise ordered numerically.

The alphabetization of the Author Index, the Institutional Author Index, and the General Index follows similar principles. Authors cited as initials only are excluded from both author indexes; coauthors are individually indexed.

Apart from the General Index and the various reference lists included in the front matter, all material in this *Bibliography* has been ordered by computer, which requires a precise and explicit statement of alphabetization rules. Counting translations from Oriental languages, the entries included in this volume incorporate material in twenty languages. Alphabetization rules are generally well established for languages written in roman script, but the same cannot be said of the various nonroman languages. Of these, Chinese presents the most difficult set of problems.

14.1 *Transcribed Chinese*

The system adopted in this *Bibliography* for the transcription of Chinese characters is described in §12.1. Its adoption establishes a finite list of allowable Wade-Giles syllables, and the first set of decisions to be spelled out concerns the proper ordering of this corpus of individual syllables. First, initial digraphs such as *hs, ss,* and *tz,* which may be alphabetized as if they were separate letters, are here given no special status: *hsi,* for example, is alphabetized between *ho* and *hu.* Second, the aspirate mark is treated as a diacritic: our sequence is *cha-ch'a-chai-ch'ai* rather than *cha-chai-ch'a-ch'ai* (in which the aspirate mark is considered to convert what precedes it into a distinctive letter of the alphabet) or the free variation that results from ignoring the aspirate altogether (e.g. "Ch'a-ha-erh" preceding Cha-tan). Third, *ü* is treated as a separate letter that follows *u*: our sequence is *lu-luan-lun-lung-lü-lüan-lüeh,* rather than *lu-lü-luan-lüan,* etc. (in which the double dot is treated as a diacritic) or the free variation between *lu* and *lü* or *luan* and *lüan* that results from ignoring the double dot altogether. These three decisions yield the syllable order used in the glossaries of most scholarly monographs and in such standard reference works as Fenn's *Five thousand dictionary,* Hummel's *Eminent Chinese of the Ch'ing period,* and *Revue bibliographique de sinologie* (Paris, 1955–).

Turning to the ordering of syllable sequences, the major options concern the treatment of the hyphens and word spaces that invariably separate syllables in Wade-Giles transcription. Of the many logical alternatives that could be defended, the only two that have any scholarly currency are shown in columns 1 and 2 below:

System ignoring hyphens and spaces (e.g. Klein & Clark)	Established system (e.g. Hummel)	System used in this *Bibliography*
Hsüan Hua	Hsü An-hua	Hsü An-hua
Hsü An-hua	Hsü-an-hua-i	Hsü An-huai
Hsü An-huai	Hsü-an-huai	Hsü-an-hua-i
Hsüan Huai	Hsü An-huai	Hsü-an-huai
Hsü-an-huai	Hsüan Hua	Hsüan Hua
Hsü-an-hua-i	Hsüan Hua-i	Hsüan Hua-i
Hsüan-hua-i	Hsüan-hua-i	Hsüan-hua-i
Hsüan Hua-i	Hsüan Huai	Hsüan Huai
Li Chia		Li Chia
Lin Chia		Li Pan
Ling Chia		Lin Chia
Ling Pan	same as right-hand column →	Lin Pan
Lin Pan		Ling Chia
Li Pan		Ling Pan
Lu Li-chia		Lu Li-chia
Lu Lin-chia		Lu Li-pan
Lu Ling-chia		Lu Lin-chia
Lu Ling-pan		Lu Lin-pan
Lu Lin-pan		Lu Ling-chia
Lu Li-pan		Lu Ling-pan
Ou-yang Ch'iu	same as left-hand column ←	Ou Yang-ch'iu
Ou Yang-ch'iu		Ou Yang-chung
Ou Yang-chung		Ou-yang Ch'iu
Ou-yang Chung		Ou-yang Chung

The system of column 1, used by the U.S. Board of Geographic Names and in Donald W. Klein and Anne B. Clark, *Biographic dictionary of Chinese Communism, 1921–1965* (Cambridge, Mass., 1971), ignores spaces and hyphens altogether in alphabetizing. As a result, authors with identical transcribed surnames are frequently separated, and personal and place names that happen to involve the same sequence of letters are not definitively ordered but appear in free variation (symbolized in the list by braces). The system of column 2, which is the most widely accepted, eliminates the main difficulties of the column 1 system but leaves others unresolved. This system orders sequences by discrete syllables only; that is, after letter ordering, it makes a single additional sort on spaces *or* hyphens, making no distinction between them. Our system (column 3) removes the remaining difficulties by making one further sort: within otherwise identical syllable sequences it gives precedence to word spaces over hyphens. This eliminates all free variation and thereby guarantees, among other things, that two-syllable surnames will fall together in alphabetization.

14.2 *Transcribed Japanese*

The system adopted in this *Bibliography* for the transcription of Japanese is described in §12.2. The treatment of four of its elements is moot for alphabetization purposes, namely, the macron (long-vowel symbol), the apostrophe that follows syllabic *n*, the hyphen, and the word space. One common system, used in many library catalogues, some dictionaries, and most geographical dictionaries, ignores all four elements altogether. This strict letter-by-letter alphabetization yields free variation for such diagnostic pairs as the following:

Ōkawa Kōichi	kin'en
Okawa Koichi	kinen
Chū-Nichi	rekishi jōken
chūnichi	rekishijō ken

While many standard reference works recognize the macron and the word space in their alphabetization conventions, few are consistent or explicit in their treatment of the syllabic *n* and hyphen.

The rules adopted here are as follows:

(1) The macron is treated as a diacritic. Our sequence is *kogo-kōgo-kōgō-kogu-kōgu-kōgū* rather than *kogo-kogō-kogu-kōgo-kōgu-kōgū* (in which the macron is considered to convert its vowel into a distinctive letter of the alphabet) or the free variation that results from ignoring the macron.

(2) The apostrophe that signals syllable division after *n* is considered to convert the following *y* or vowel into a distinctive letter, with *'o* immediately following *o* in the alphabet and *'y* immediately following *y*: thus *kinyū-kin'yu-kin'yū*. The advantage of letter treatment over diacritic treatment in this case is that single-syllable transcriptions of the same character are not separated and the problem of priority between diacritics is finessed.

(3) Word spaces are given precedence over letters and hyphens: thus "rekishi jōken" precedes "rekishijō ken."

(4) Hyphens are given precedence over letters. As a result single-syllable transcriptions of the same character are not separated; thus, for example, "Chū-Nichi" precedes "chūnichi."

14.3 *Other Alphabetization Conventions*

All special symbols used in the adopted transcriptions of Korean and Russian (see §12.3–4) are treated here as diacritics, and in Russian the sequences of two or four roman letters that stand for a single cyrillic letter are given no special status. These rules fix word order in the transcriptions of these two languages in accordance with our respective standards: Martin's *Korean-English dictionary* and *Half a century of Soviet serials*.

In both languages, hyphens and word spaces are treated the same as in transcribed Japanese and Chinese.

For languages written in the roman alphabet, the alphabetization conventions of each have been respected. For example, *ä*, *ö*, and *ü* in the various Germanic languages are alphabetized as *ae*, *oe*, and *ue*, respectively, whereas the diaeresis in French is ignored. (Thus *ü* is alphabetized in three different ways in German, French, and transcribed Chinese.) In names of Gaelic origin, *Mc* is alphabetized as if it were *Mac*. Spaces within a surname or a given name are ignored: e.g., Le Comte and Lecomte, De Francis and DeFrancis, are randomly interfiled. Initial articles are ignored for alphabetization purposes in the titles of all languages in which they occur.

Several pitfalls accompany the interfiling of material transcribed from Chinese, Japanese, and Korean with other forms of Chinese, Japanese, and Korean names. For example, the different Chinese surnames transcribed Cheng and Ch'eng are confounded when someone named Ch'eng prefers to drop the aspirate mark in his name, with the result that in the Bibliography, where the preferred form of the name comes first, true Chengs and Chengs by preference may be interspersed. Note, however, that the Author Index lists such authors, e.g. "Cheng Chi-pao (Ch'eng Ch'i-pao)," under both the preferred form and the transcribed form of the name. A comparable difficulty arises with institutional authors, some of which (notably governmental agencies) begin with the Post Office form, while others may begin with Wade-Giles transcriptions; in an alphabetical list "Chiang-su" and "Kiangsu" are widely separated, and even "Shan-tung" and "Shantung" do not necessarily fall together.

15 LIBRARY SYMBOLS AND HOLDING INFORMATION

Each entry in the *Bibliography* shows immediately after the entry number a library symbol in the form of three capital letters. The first letter stands for the state in the case of U.S. libraries, the province in the case of Chinese libraries, and otherwise the country; the second stands for the city, and the third for the library itself. When the key word in the name of a university library is the name of the city or state in which it is located, the third letter is U: thus the University of California Library at Berkeley is symbolized CBU, not CBC. A list of library symbols used in this volume is given below (p. lxvi).

For each entry only one library symbol is provided, normally the one for the library in which the work in question was examined. Where we know that an item is held at two or more libraries, we give precedence to libraries in the United States as opposed to other countries, and within any one country to larger and more important libraries. Unpublished dissertations are normally given the symbol of the degree-granting university's library, and dissertations published by University Microfilms are given the symbol for that organization's library, MAM.

When an entry presents data on one or more reissues and translations, thereby covering more than one discrete publication, a library symbol with no superscript number indicates a holding of the first publication cited in the entry; [2] indicates a holding of the second publication cited, [3] the third, etc. For further details, see §8 for reissues and §11.2 for translations. In the case of serial publications, if no one library holds the full span being cited, an asterisk appears after the library code and supplementary holding information is supplied in an asterisked comment (see §9). The same treatment is accorded a multivolume monograph or multipart journal article that is not known to be held in full by any one library.

16 ABBREVIATIONS

Certain journal titles are consistently abbreviated; for the rest, abbreviations are used sparingly. States and countries are abbreviated when used to identify or specify cities, and conventional abbreviations are used in the names of European cities and publishers. Organization names are sometimes abbreviated to initials, but only when the full name has already appeared in the entry. The following other abbreviations are used consistently:

Assn. Association (in names of corporate bodies only, but not abbreviated in English renderings of titles)
b./B. *bulletin/Bulletin* (in English, French, and German journal titles only)
c.p. continuously paginated (see §4.3)
comp./comps. compiler(s)
Dept. Department (in names of corporate bodies only, but not abbreviated in English renderings of titles)
ed./eds. edition; *or* editor(s)
enl. enlarged
j. *journal* (in English and French journal titles only)
MC Monthly catalogue number; i.e. number in *Monthly catalogue of United States government publications* (in further identifying works issued by the U.S. Joint Publications Research Service)
mimeo. mimeographed, i.e. reproduced by any process other than printing
n.d. no date of publication known
n.p. no place of publication known; *or* unpaginated
pseud. pseudonym
q. *quarterly* (as a noun in English journal titles only)
r. *revue* (in French journal titles only)
rev. revised
s.p. separately paginated (see §4.3 and §5.2)
tr. translation
U. University (in names of universities and university presses only)
U.S. United States
U.S.S.R. Union of Soviet Socialist Republics
Z. *Zeitschrift* (in German journal titles only)

Library Symbols

ACU Australian National U. Library, Canberra, Australia
ASU U. of Sydney Library, Sydney, Australia
CBC U. of Colorado Libraries, Boulder, Colo.
CBU U. of California Library, Berkeley, Calif.
CCU William L. Honnold Memorial Library, Claremont Graduate School and University Center, Claremont, Calif.
CHS Case Memorial Library, Hartford Seminary Foundation, Hartford, Conn.
CLS Edward L. Doheny Memorial Library, U. of Southern California, Los Angeles, Calif.
CLU University Library, U. of California, Los Angeles, Calif.
CNY Yale U. Library, New Haven, Conn.
CSB Santa Barbara Library, U. of California, Santa Barbara, Calif.
CSH Hoover Institution on War, Revolution, and Peace, Stanford U., Stanford, Calif.
CSM U. of California Medical Center Library, San Francisco, Calif.
CSU Stanford U. Libraries, Stanford, Calif.
CTU U. of Toronto Libraries, Toronto, Ont., Canada
CVB U. of British Columbia Library, Vancouver, B.C., Canada
DCK Kongelige Bibliotek, Copenhagen, Denmark
DLC U.S. Library of Congress, Washington, D.C.
DNA National Agricultural Library, U.S. Dept. of Agriculture, Washington, D.C.
ECU U. of Cambridge Libraries, Cambridge, England
ELB British Museum Library and Reading Rooms, London, England
ELE British Library of Political and Economic Science, London School of Economics and Political Science, London, England
ELL U. of Leeds Library, Leeds, England
ELO School of Oriental and African Studies Library, London, England
ELR Royal Anthropological Institute of Great Britain and Ireland, London, England
ELS U. of London Library (Senate House), London, England
ELU U. of Liverpool Library, Liverpool, England
EOB Bodleian Library, Oxford U., Oxford, England
FGU U. of Florida Libraries, Gainesville, Fla.
FPL Ecole nationale des langues orientales vivantes, Collège de France, Paris, France
FPN Bibliothèque nationale, Paris, France
GBF Universitätsbibliothek der Freien Universität, Berlin, Federal Republic of Germany
GBS Staatsbibliothek Preussischer Kulturbesitz, Berlin, Federal Republic of Germany
GBT Universitätsbibliothek der Technischen Universität, Berlin, Federal Republic of Germany
GFS Stadt- und Universitätsbibliothek/Senckenbergische Bibliothek, Frankfurt a.M., Federal Republic of Germany
GFU Universitätsbibliothek, Freiburg i.Br., Federal Republic of Germany
GGN Niedersächsische Staats- und Universitätsbibliothek, Göttingen, Federal Republic of Germany
GHT Technische Hochschule, Hanover, Federal Republic of Germany
GHU Universitätsbibliothek, Heidelberg, Federal Republic of Germany
GLU Universitätsbibliothek, Leipzig, German Democratic Republic
GMS Städtische Bibliotheken, Munich, Federal Republic of Germany
GMU Universitätsbibliothek, Munich, Federal Republic of Germany
GSU Staats- und Universitätsbibliothek, Hamburg, Federal Republic of Germany
HHU U. of Hawaii Library, Honolulu, Hawaii
HKU U. of Hong Kong Library, Hong Kong
IBU Indiana U. Libraries, Bloomington, Ind.
ICU U. of Chicago Library, Chicago, Ill.
IIU U. of Iowa Libraries, Iowa City, Iowa
ILP Purdue U. Libraries, Lafayette, Ind.
IMA Biblioteca ambrosiana, Milan, Italy
IMC Biblioteca Comunale, Milan, Italy
IMN Biblioteca Nazionale Braidense, Milan, Italy
IUU U. of Illinois Library, Urbana, Ill.
JTT Oriental Library (Tōyō Bunko), Tokyo, Japan
JTU Tokyo U. Libraries (Tōkyō Daigaku Toshokan), Tokyo, Japan
LBU Louisiana State U. Library, Baton Rouge, La.

MAM University Microfilms Library, Xerox Education Division, Ann Arbor, Mich.
MAU U. of Michigan Libraries, Ann Arbor, Mich.
MBA Cambridge Research Laboratories, Research Library, U.S. Air Force Office of Aerospace Research, Bedford, Mass.
MBJ Johns Hopkins U. Libraries, Baltimore, Md.
MBM National Library of Medicine, Bethesda, Md.
MBU Boston U. Libraries, Boston, Mass.
MCH Harvard U. Library, Cambridge, Mass.
MCM Massachusetts Institute of Technology Libraries, Cambridge, Mass.
MCY Harvard-Yenching Institute Library, Cambridge, Mass.
MMT Tufts U. Libraries, Medford, Mass.
MMU U. of Minnesota Library, Minneapolis, Minn.
MSE James Duncan Phillips Library, Essex Institute, Salem, Mass.
MSW Washington U. Library, St. Louis, Mo.
MWC Robert Hutchings Goddard Library, Clark U., Worcester, Mass.
NBO Bergen Offentlige Bibliotek, Bergen, Norway
NBU Universitetsbiblioteket, Bergen, Norway
NDD William R. Perkins Library, Duke U., Durham, N.C.
NIC Cornell U. Libraries, Ithaca, N.Y.
NNC Columbia U. Libraries, New York, N.Y.
NNF Duane Library, Fordham U., New York, N.Y.
NNJ Jewish Labor Committee Library, New York, N.Y.
NNM Missionary Research Library, Inc., New York, N.Y.
NNP New York Public Library, New York, N.Y.
NNR Rutgers U. Libraries, New Brunswick, N.J.
NNU New York U. Libraries, New York, N.Y.
NOU Universitetsbiblioteket, Oslo, Norway
NPU Princeton U. Library, Princeton, N.J.
NSU Syracuse U. Library, Syracuse, N.Y.
OCC U. of Cincinnati Library, Cincinnati, Ohio
OOC Oberlin College Library, Oberlin, Ohio
PPP Hillman Library, U. of Pittsburgh, Pittsburgh, Penna.
PPU U. of Pennsylvania Libraries, Philadelphia, Penna.
SEU U. of Edinburgh Library, Edinburgh, Scotland
SSK Kungliga Bibliotek, Stockholm, Sweden
TPH Taiwan Historical Research Commission (T'ai-wan-sheng Wen-hsien Wei-yüan-hui), Taipei, Taiwan, Republic of China
TPU National Taiwan U. Libraries (Kuo-li T'ai-wan Ta-hsüeh T'u-shu-kuan), Taipei, Taiwan, Republic of China
TPY National Central Library (Kuo-li Chung-yang T'u-shu-kuan), Taipei, Taiwan, Republic of China
WMU U. of Wisconsin Libraries, Madison, Wisc.
WSU U. of Washington Libraries, Seattle, Wash.

Journals Cited

This section gives publication data for all Western-language journals from which four or more articles are listed in this volume. More than one set of data on a journal's publication span indicates a change in its numbering system or periodicity. For journals regularly issued in more than one Western language, each title is listed; publication data appear in only one entry, to which the other entries are cross-referenced. Journals that publish articles in Chinese or Japanese as well as a Western language are listed only under the Western-language title. A transcription of the Oriental title is supplied at the end of the entry. Certain journal titles are always abbreviated; see the list on p. lxxvii. Certain words are always abbreviated in otherwise unabbreviated journal titles; see the list on p. lii.

For Western-language works translated from the Chinese or Japanese, publication data for the Oriental-language version are given in the Bibliography entry, but the Chinese- and Japanese-language journals named in such entries are not listed here. They will be found in the corresponding Journals Cited sections of Volumes 2 and 3 of this *Bibliography*.

Acta Asiatica; b. of the Institute of Eastern Culture. Tokyo: Tōhō gakkai. No. 1–, 1960–.

Acta psychologica Taiwanica (*APT*). Taipei: Kuo li T'ai-wan ta hsüeh, Li hsüeh yüan, Hsin li hsüeh hsi (National Taiwan U., College of Science, Dept. of Psychology). No. 1–, Nov. 1958 –. Bilingual: articles in English or Chinese. Chinese title: *Kuo li T'ai-wan ta hsüeh, Li hsüeh yüan, Hsin li hsüeh hsi yen chiu pao kao.*

Amerasia; a review of America and the Far East. New York. V. 1, no. 1 – v. 11, no. 7, Mar. 1937 – July 1947. Successor to *China today.*

American anthropologist (*AA*). Washington, D.C. Anthropological Society of Washington. After 1903, Lancaster, Pa.; Menasha, Wisc.; Washington, D.C.: American Anthropological Assn. and affiliated societies. V. 1, no. 1 – v. 11, no. 1, Jan. 1888 – Dec. 1898; new (2nd) series, v. 1, no. 1 –, Jan. 1899 –.

American j. of comparative law (*AJCL*). Baltimore: American Assn. for the Comparative Study of Law. V. 1, no. 1 –, Winter-Spring 1952 –.

American j. of public health. Boston; etc.: American Public Health Assn. V. 1, no. 1 –, Jan. 1911 –.

American j. of sociology (*AJS*). Chicago: American Sociological Society; U. of Chicago. V. 1, no. 1 –, July 1895 –.

American political science review (*APSR*). Baltimore: American Political Science Assn. V. 1, no. 1 –, Nov. 1906 –.

American sociological review (*ASR*). Menasha, Wisc.; Albany, N.Y.: American Sociological Society (name changed 1959 to American Sociological Assn. [Washington, D.C.]). V. 1, no. 1 –, Feb. 1936 –. Successor to *Papers and proceedings of the American Sociological Society.*

American Universities Field Staff reports, East Asian series (*AUFS-EAS*). New York: American Universities Field Staff (Hanover, N.H.). V. 1, no. 1 –, 15 Aug. 1952 –.

Annales d'hygiène et de médecine coloniales (*AHMC*). Paris: France, Ministère des colonies. V. 1, no. 1 – v. 17, no. 4?, jan.-mars 1898 – oct.-déc. 1914? Succeeded by *Annales de médecine et de pharmacie coloniales.*

Annales de géographie. Paris: Assn. de géographes français. V. 1, no. 1 –, 15 Oct. 1891 –.

Annales de la propagation de la foi (*APF*). Lyons: Assn. de la propagation de la foi. Vol. 1–103, 1822–1931; nouvelle (2e) série, no. 1–, 1932–. Successor to *Nouvelles lettres édifiantes des missions de la Chine et des Indes orientales.*

Annales des sciences politiques. Paris: Ecole libre des sciences politiques. V. 1, no. 1 – v. 25, no. 2, jan. 1886 – 1910. Title varies: v. 1, no. 1 – v. 13, no. 2, jan. 1886 – juil. 1898 issued as *Annales de l'Ecole libre des sciences politiques.* Succeeded by *R. des sciences politiques.*

Annals of the American Academy of Political and Social Science (*AAAPSS*). Philadelphia. V. 1–, July 1890 –. Successor to *Proceedings of the American Academy of Political and Social Science.*

Annals of the Assn. of American Geographers (*AAAG*). Washington, D.C. V. 1–, 1911–.

Anthropos; internationale Z. für Völker- und Sprachenkunde. Vienna; Fribourg, Switzerland; Salzburg: Leo- und Görres-Gesellschaft. V. 1, no. 1 –, Jan.-Feb. 1906 –.

Archiv für Eisenbahnwesen (*AE*). Berlin: Prussia, Ministerium der öffentlichen Arbeiten; Germany, Reichsverkehrsministerium; Deutsche Reichsbahn Gesellschaft; Deutsche Bundesbahn. V. 1–66, 1878–1943; v. 67–, 1957–.

Archiv für Schiffs- und Tropen-Hygiene (*ASTH*). Leipzig: Deutsche tropenmedizinische Gesellschaft. V. 1, no. 1 – v. 44, no. 12, 1897 – Dez. 1940. Succeeded by *Deutsche tropenmedizinische Z.*

Archiv orientálni (*AO*). Prague: Československý orientálni ústav v Praze. V. 1–, 1929–.

Artibus Asiae. Hellerau-Dresden; Ascona, Switzerland. V. 1, no. 1 –, 1925–.

Asia. New York: Asia Society. No. 1–, Spring 1964 –.

Asia; j. of the American Asiatic Assn. New York: American Asiatic Assn.; East and West Assn. V. 17, no. 1 – v. 46, no. 12, Mar. 1917 – Dec. 1946. Title varies: v. 42, no. 11, to end issued as *Asia and the Americas.* Successor to *J. of the American Asiatic Assn.* Succeeded by *United Nations world.*

Asia and the Americas: see *Asia; j. of the American Asiatic Assn.*

Asia Major. Leipzig; London. V. 1–10, 1924–1935; neue (2.) Folge, v. 1, no. 1, 1944; new (3rd) series, v. 1–, 1949–.

Asia q. Brussels: Centre d'étude du Sud-Est asiatique et de l'Extrême-Orient. V. 1971, no. 1 –. Successor to *R. du Sud-Est asiatique et de l'Extrême Orient.*

Asian folklore studies: see *Folklore studies*.
Asian forum; a quarterly j. of Asian affairs. Washington, D.C.: Pan-Asia Foundation. V. 1, no. 1 –, Jan.-Feb. 1969 –.
Asian survey (AS). Berkeley: U. of California, Institute of International Studies. V 1, no. 1 –, Mar. 1961 –. Successor to *Far Eastern survey*.
Asiatic review. Woking, Eng.: Oriental U. Institute (name changed 1903 to Oriental Institute); London; etc. V. 1, no. 1 – v. 10, no. 2, Jan. 1886 – Oct. 1890; 2nd series, v. 1, no. 1 – v. 10, no. 20, Jan. 1891 – Oct. 1895; 3rd series, v. 1, no. 1 – vol. 34, no. 68, Jan. 1896 – Oct. 1912; new (4th) series, v. 1, no. 1 – v. 50, no. 184, Jan. 1913 – Oct. 1954. Title varies: v. 1–10, 1886–1890, and 4th series, v. 1–2, 1913, issued as *Asiatic quarterly review*; 2nd and 3rd series, 1891–1912, issued as *Imperial and Asiatic quarterly review*. Succeeded by *Asian review*.
Asie française (AF). Paris: Comité de l'Asie française. V. 1, no. 1 –, avr. 1901 –. Title varies: v. 1–9, 1901–1910, issued as *B. mensuel du Comité de l'Asie française*.
Aussenpolitik; Z. für internationale Fragen. Stuttgart. V. 1, no. 1 –, Mai 1950 –.
Baessler-Archiv; Beiträge zur Völkerkunde. Leipzig; Berlin: Baessler Institut; Staatliches Museum für Völkerkunde. V. 1 – v. 25, no. 2, 1910–1943; neue (2.) Folge, v. 1–, 1952–.
Berichte der Rheinischen Missionsgesellschaft. Barmen, Germany. V. 1828/30, no. 1 –.
Bibliograficheskii sbornik Biblioteki Kitaiskoi Vostochnoi zheleznoi dorogi (BSB). Harbin: V. 1–?, 1932–? Sucessor to *Bibliograficheskii biulleten' Kitaiskoi Vostochnoi zheleznoi dorogi*.
Bijdragen tot de taal-, land- en volkenkunde van Nederlandsch-Indië (BTLV). The Hague: Koninklijk Instituut voor de Taal-, land- en volkenkunde van Nederlandsch-Indië. V. 1–, 1853–.
Biulleten' nauchnoi informatsii; trud i zarabotnaia plata (BNI). Moscow: U.S.S.R., Gosudarstvennyi komitet Soveta Ministrov, Nauchno-issledovatel'skii institut truda. V. 1–5, 1958–1962.
Blätter für vergleichende Rechtswissenschaft und Volkswirtschaftslehre (BVRV). Berlin: Internationale Vereinigung für vergleichende Rechtswissenschaft und Volkswirtschaftslehre. V. 1, no. 1 – v. 19, no. 9, 1905–1926.
Bollettino della Società geografica italiana. Florence; Rome. V. 1–12, agosto 1868 – 1875; 2a serie, v. 1–12, 1876–1887; 3a serie, v. 1–12, 1888–1899; 4a serie, v. 1–12, 1900–1911; 5a serie, v. 1–12, 1912–1923; 6a serie, v. 1–12, 1924–1935; 7a serie, v. 1–12, 1936–1947; 8a serie, v. 1–12, 1948–1959; 9a serie, v. 1–, 1960–. Title varies: 5a serie – 7a serie, v. 6, no. 11, 1912 – novembre 1941, issued as *Bollettino della Reale Società geografica italiana*; 7a serie, v. 6, no. 12 – v. 8, no. 12, dicembre 1941 – dicembre 1943, issued as *Paesi del mondo*.
B. d'information de la Commission internationale contre le régime concentrationnaire: see *Saturne*
B. de l'Association amicale franco-chinoise (BAAFC). Paris. V. 1–9/16, 1907–1917/22. Succeeded by *R. franco-chinoise*.
B. de l'Ecole française d'Extrême-Orient (BEFEO). Hanoi; Paris. V. 1–, 1901–.
B. de l'Institut international de statistique (BIIS). Rome. V. 1, no. 1 –, 1886–. Suspended publ. 1916–1923.
B. de l'Université l'Aurore (BUA). Shanghai. No. 1–19, 1909–1919; 2e série, no. 1–40, 1919–1939/40; 3e série, v. 1, no. 1 – v. 10, no. 40?, 1940 – oct. 1949?
B. de la Société de géographie. Paris. V. 1–20, 1822–1833; 2e série, v. 1–20, 1834–1843; 3e série, v. 1–14, 1844–1850; 4e série, v. 1–20, 1851–1860; 5e série, v. 1–20, 1861–1870; 6e série, v. 1–20, 1871–1880; 7e série, v. 1–20, 1881–1899. Succeeded by *Géographie*.
B. de la Société de géographie commerciale de Paris. Paris. V. 1–42, oct. 1878 – 1920; v. 43–51, 1921–1929. Succeeded by *R. économique française*.
B. de la Société de géographie de Lyon. Lyons. V. 1–23, 1875–1908; 2e série, v. 1 – v. 5, no. 1, 1908–1912; v. 1913–1936/37. Succeeded by *Etudes rhodaniennes*.
B. de la Société des études indo-chinoises de Saïgon. Saigon; Paris. V. 1–71, 1883–1923; nouvelle (2e) série, v. 1–, 1926–. Successor to *B. du Comité agricole et industriel de la Cochinchine*.
B. de la Société royale belge d'anthropologie et de préhistoire de Bruxelles (BSRB). Brussels. V. 1–, 1882–.
B. du Centre d'étude des pays de l'Est et du Centre national pour l'étude des états de l'Est. Brussels: Université libre de Bruxelles, Institut de sociologie, Centre d'étude des pays de l'Est *and* Centre national pour l'étude des pays à régime communiste (name changed July 1963 to Centre national pour l'étude des états de l'Est). V. 1, no. 1 – v. 7, no. 3, 1960–1966. Title varies: v. 1, no. 1 – v. 4, no. 2, 1960 – juin 1966, issued as *Pays communistes*.
B. économique de l'Indochine (BEI). Hanoi: Indochina, Direction de l'agriculture et du commerce (issuing agency varies); Saigon: France, Haut-commissariat en Indochine, Direction des services économiques. V. 1 – v. 55, no. 6, 1898 – juin 1952. Suspended publ. 1945, no. 2 – 1947.
B. of Concerned Asian Scholars (BCAS). Cambridge; San Francisco: Committee of Concerned Asian Scholars. No. 1–4, May 1968 – May 1969; v. 2, no. 1 –, Oct. 1969 –.
B. of the Institute of Ethnology, Academia Sinica (BIE). Taipei: Chung yang yen chiu yüan, Min tsu hsüeh yen chiu so. No. 1–, Mar. 1956 –. Bilingual: articles in English or Chinese. Chinese title: *Chung yang yen chiu yüan, Min tsu hsüeh yen chiu so chi k'an*.
B. of the International Social Security Assn. (BISSA). Montreal. V. 1, no. 1 –, Apr. 1948 –. Title varies: v. 20, no. 1 –, 1967–, issued as *International social security review*.
B. of the School of Oriental and African Studies (BSOAS). London: U. of London, School of Oriental Studies (name changed 1938 to School of Oriental and African Studies). V. 1–, 1917/20–. Title varies: v. 1–6, 1917/20–1930/32, issued as *B. of the School of Oriental Studies, London Institution*; v. 7–9, 1933/35–1937/39, issued as *B. of the School of Oriental Studies, U. of London*.
Bulletins et mémoires de la Société d'anthropologie de Paris. Paris. V. 1–6, 1860–1865; 2e série, v. 1–12, 1866–1877; 3e série, v. 1–12, 1878–1889; 4e série, v. 1–10, 1890–1899; 5e série, v. 1–10, 1900–1909; 6e série, v. 1–10, 1910–1919; 7e série, v. 1–10, 1920–1929; 8e série, v. 1–, 1930–. Title varies: 1e–5e série, 1860–1909, issued as *Bulletins de la Société d'anthropologie de Paris*.
Bulletins on Chinese education (BCE). Peking: Chinese National Assn. for the Advancement of Education. V. 1–4?, 1922–1926?
Cahiers franco-chinois (CFC). Paris. No. 1–15/16, 1959–1961.

Central Asiatic j. The Hague; Wiesbaden. V. 1, no. 1 –, 1955–.

China; een driemaandelijksch tijdschrift. Amsterdam: Nederlandsch-Chineesche Vereeniging. V. 1–14, September 1925 – Maart-Juni 1940.

China-Archiv. Berlin: Deutsch-chinesischer Verband. V. 1, no. 1 – v. 4, no. 12, Jan. 1916 – Dez. 1919. Title varies: v. 4, no. 1, to end issued as *Archiv für den Fernen Osten.* Succeeded by *Ostasiatische Rundschau.*

China critic. Shanghai. V. 1, no. 1 – v. 31, no. 6, 31 May 1928 – 7 Nov. 1940.

China j. (*CJ*). Shanghai: China Society of Science and Arts; Shanghai Chemical Society. V. 1, no. 1 – v. 35, no. 5, Jan. 1923 – Nov. 1941. Title varies: v. 1–5, 1923–1927, issued as *China j. of science and arts.*

China law review (CLR). Shanghai: Tung Wu ta hsüeh, Fa lü hsüeh yüan (Soochow U., Dept. of Law). V. 1, no. 1 – v. 11, no. 3?, Apr. 1922 – Jan. 1941? Suspended publ. July 1937 – May 1940. Bilingual: articles in English or Chinese. Chinese titles: *Fa hsüeh chi k'an; Fa hsüeh tsa chih.*

China medical j.: see *Chinese medical j.*

China medical missionary j. (*CMMJ*). Shanghai: China Medical Missionary Assn. V. 1 – v. 21, no. 2, 1887 – Oct. 1909. Succeeded by *China medical j.*

China news analysis (*CNA*). Hong Kong. No. 1–, 25 Aug. 1953 –.

China q. (*CQ*). London: Congress for Cultural Freedom (Paris); U. of London, School of Oriental and African Studies, Contemporary China Institute. No. 1–, Jan.-Mar. 1960 –.

China q. (*CQ-S*). Shanghai: China Institute of International Relations; Pan-Pacific Assn. of China; Institute of Social and Economic Research. V. 1, no. 1 – v. 6, no. 3, Sept. 1935 – Autumn 1941.

China reconstructs. Peking: China Welfare Institute. V. 1, no. 1 –, Jan.-Feb. 1952 –.

China report. New Delhi: China Study Centre. V. 1, no. 1 –, Aug. 1964 –.

China review. Hong Kong. V. 1, no. 1 – v. 25, no. 6, July 1872 – July 1901.

China's medicine (*CM*). Peking: Chung-kuo i hsüeh hui (Chinese Medical Assn.). V. 1966, no. 1 (Oct.) – v. 1968, no. 12 (Dec.)? Successor to *Chinese medical j.*

La Chine; r. bi-mensuelle illustrée. Peking. No. 1–73, 15 août 1921 – 1er jan. 1925.

Chinese Communist affairs; a bi-monthly review (*CCA*). Taipei: Chung-hua min kuo cheng chih yen chiu so (Institute of Political Research). V. 1, no. 1 – v. 6, no. 2, Mar. 1964 – Apr. 1969.

Chinese culture (*CC*). Taipei: Chung-kuo wen hua yen chiu so (Chinese Cultural Research Institute [also called Institute of Chinese Culture and Institute for Advanced Chinese Studies]). V. 1, no. 1 –, July 1957 –.

Chinese economic j. and b. (*CEJ*). Peiping: Chinese Government Bureau of Economic Information; China [Republic], Shih yeh pu, Kuo chi mao i chü (Ministry of Industry, Bureau of Foreign Trade). V. 1, no. 1 – v. 20, no. 6, Jan. 1927 – June 1937. Successor to *Chinese economic monthly.*

Chinese economic monthly (*CEM*). Peking: Chinese Government Bureau of Economic Information. V. 1, no. 1 – v. 3, no. 12, Oct. 1923 – Dec. 1926. Succeeded by *Chinese economic j. and b.*

Chinese economic studies (*CES*). White Plains, N.Y.: International Arts and Sciences Press. V. 1–, Fall 1967 –.

Chinese education (*CE*). White Plains, N.Y.: International Arts and Sciences Press. V. 1–, Spring 1968 –.

Chinese j. of administration (*CJA*). Taipei: Kuo li cheng chih ta hsüeh, Kung kung hsing cheng chi ch'i yeh kuan li chung hsin (National Chengchi U., Center for Public and Business Administration Education). No. 1–, July 1963 –. Bilingual: articles in English and/or Chinese. Chinese title: *Chung-kuo hsing cheng.*

Chinese law and government. White Plains, N.Y.: International Arts and Sciences Press. V. 1–, Spring 1968 –.

Chinese medical j. (*CMJ*). Peking; Shanghai; Washington, D.C.: China Medical Missionary Assn. (from 1925, Chung-kuo i hsüeh hui [Chinese Medical Assn.]). V. 21, no. 3 – v. 85, no. 9, Nov. 1909 – Sept. 1966. Supplementary Chengtu ed., v. 61A – v. 63A, no. 5, Oct. 1942 – Oct. 1945. Title varies: v. 21, no. 3 – v. 45, no. 12, Nov. 1909 – Dec. 1931, issued as *China medical j.* Succeeded by *China's medicine.*

Chinese medical j. (CMJ-T). Taipei: Chung-hua i hsüeh hui (Chinese Medical Assn.). V. 1, no. 1 –, Mar. 1954 –. Bilingual: articles in English or Chinese. Chinese title: *Chung-hua i hsüeh tsa chih.*

Chinese recorder (CR). Foochow; Shanghai: China Christian Educational Assn. V. 1, no. 1 – v. 72, no. 12?, June 1868 – Dec. 1941? Title varies: v. 1, no. 1 – v. 45, no. 12, June 1868 – Dec. 1914, issued as *Chinese recorder and missionary j.*; v. 70, no. 1, to end issued as *Chinese recorder and educational review.* Successor to *Missionary recorder.*

Chinese repository. Canton. V. 1, no. 1 – v. 20, no. 12, May 1832 – Dec. 1851.

Chinese social and political science review (*CSPSR*). Peiping: Chinese Social and Political Science Assn. V. 1, no. 1 – v. 24, no. 4?, Apr. 1916 – Mar. 1941?

Chinese students' monthly (*CSM*). Baltimore: Chinese Students' Alliance of Eastern States, U.S.A. V. 1 – v. 26, no. 1, 1905 – Dec. 1930.

Ch'ing-shih wen-t'i (CSWT). New Haven, St. Louis: Society for Ch'ing Studies. V. 1, no. 1 –, May 1965 –.

Chung Chi j. (CCJ). Hong Kong: Ch'ung chi shu yüan (Chung Chi College). V. 1, no. 1 –, June 1961 –. Bilingual: articles in English or Chinese. Chinese title: *Ch'ung chi hsüeh pao.*

Cina. Rome: Istituto italiano per il Medio ed Estremo Oriente. V. 1–8?, 1956–1964?

Civilisations. Brussels: Institut international des sciences politiques et sociales appliquées aux pays des civilisations différentes (name changed 1952 to Institut international des civilisations différentes). V. 1, no. 1 –, jan. 1951 –.

Civiltà cattolica. Rome. V. 1–, aprile 1850 –.

Comparative studies in society and history (CSSH). The Hague; Cambridge, Eng.: Society for the Comparative Study of Society and History. V. 1, no. 1 –, Oct. 1958 –.

Current background (*CB*). Hong Kong: U.S. Consulate General. No. 1–, 13 June 1950 –.

Current history (*CH*). New York. V. 1, no. 1 –, Sept. 1941 –. Successor to *Current history and forum* and *Events.*

Current scene; developments in Mainland China (CS). Hong Kong. V. 1, no. 1 –, 15 May 1961 –.

Daedalus. Cambridge; etc.: American Academy of Arts and Sciences (Boston). V. 1, no. 1 –, May 1846 –.

Demography. Chicago: Population Assn. of America. V. 1, no. 1 –, 1964–.
Deutsch-chinesische Rechtszeitung (*DCR*). Tsingtao. No. 1–10, Nov. 1911 – Feb. 1914.
Developing economies (*DE*). Tokyo: Ajia keizai kenkyūjo (Institute of Asian Economic Affairs). No. 1–2, Mar.-Aug. – Sept.-Dec. 1962; v. 1, no. 1 –, Jan.-June 1963 –.
Dokumentacioni bilten Instituta za medjunarodnu politiku i privredu (*DB*). Belgrade. V. 1–, 1952–.
Doneseniia Imperatorskikh rossiiskikh konsul'skikh predstavitelei za granitsei po torgovo-promyshlennym voprosam (*DIRKP*). St. Petersburg: Russia [Imperial], Ministerstvo torgovli i promyshlennosti, Otdel torgovli. No. 1–61, 1912–1916. Succeeded by *Doneseniia Rossiiskikh konsul'skikh predstavitelei za granitsei po torgovo-promyshlennym voprosam*.
East of Asia magazine (*EAM*). Shanghai. V. 1–5, 1902–1906.
Eastern horizon (*EH*). Hong Kong. V. 1, no. 1 –, July 1960 –.
Economic b. for Asia and the Far East (*EBAFE*). Bangkok: United Nations, Economic Commission for Asia and the Far East. V. 1, no. 1 –, 1950–.
Economic development and cultural change (*EDCC*). Chicago: U. of Chicago, Research Center in Economic Development and Cultural Change. V. 1, no. 1 –, Mar. 1952 –.
Economic facts (*EF*). Nanking; Chengtu: Chin-ling ta hsüeh, Nung hsüeh yüan, Nung yeh ching chi hsi (U. of Nanking, College of Agriculture, Dept. of Agricultural Economics). No. 1–55, Sept. 1936 – Apr. 1946. Bilingual (no. 1–7, 9–12 only): articles in English and Chinese. Chinese title: *Ching chi t'ung chi*.
Economic geography (*EG*). Concord, N.H.; Worcester, Mass.: Clark U. V. 1, no. 1 –, Mar. 1925 –.
Economie et politique; r. marxiste d'économie. Paris. No. 1–, avr. 1954 –.
Ekonomicheskii biulleten' (*EB*). Harbin: Kitaiskaia Vostochnaia zheleznaia doroga, Ekonomicheskoe biuro. V. 1925–1934. Supplement to *Vestnik Man'chzhurii*.
Ekonomicheskii vestnik Man'chzhurii (*EVM*). Harbin: Kitaiskaia Vostochnaia zheleznaia doroga, Ekonomicheskoe biuro. V. 1923–1924. Succeeded by *Vestnik Man'chzhurii*.
Encounter; literature, arts, politics. London: Congress for Cultural Freedom (Paris). V. 1, no. 1 –, Oct. 1953 –.
Esprit. Paris. V. 1, no. 1 – v. 36, no. 372, oct. 1932 – juin-juil. 1968; nouvelle (2e) série, v. 36, no. 373 –, août-sept. 1968 –.
Ethnos. Stockholm: Statens Etnografiska Museum. V. 1, no. 1 –, Jan. 1936 –.
Etudes. Paris: Pères de la Compagnie de Jésus. V. 1–3, 1856–1858; 2e série, v. 1–3, 1859–1861; 3e série, v. 1–13, 1862–1867; 4e série, v. 1–6, 1868–1870; 5e série, v. 1–12, 1872–1877; 6e série, v. 1–5, 1878–1880; 7e série, v. 43–, 1888–. Suspended publ. 5 June 1940 – 5 Jan. 1945. Title varies: 1e–2e série, 1856–1861, issued as *Etudes de théologie, de philosophie et d'histoire*; 4e série – 7e série, v. 50, 1862–1896, issued as *Etudes religieuses, philosophiques et historiques*.
Etudes religieuses: see *Etudes*
Extracts from China Mainland magazines (*ECMM*). Hong Kong: U.S. Consulate General. No. 1–212, 1 Aug. 1955 – 23 May 1960. Succeeded by *Selections from China Mainland magazines*.
Far Eastern economic review (*FEER*). Hong Kong. V. 1, no. 1 –, 16 Oct. 1946 –.
Far Eastern q. (*FEQ*). Ann Arbor: Far Eastern Assn. V. 1, no. 1 – v. 15, no. 4, Nov. 1941 – Aug. 1956. Succeeded by *J. of Asian studies*.
Far Eastern survey (*FES*). New York: Institute of Pacific Relations, American Council. V. 1, no. 1 – v. 30, no. 2, 3 Mar. 1932 – Feb. 1961. Succeeded by *Asian Survey*.
Folklore studies (*FS*). Peiping: Catholic U. of Peking, Museum of Oriental Ethnology; Tokyo: Society of the Divine Word Research Institute, Society for Asian Folklore. V. 1–, 1942–. Title varies: v. 23–, 1963–, issued as *Asian folklore studies*.
Foreign affairs; an American quarterly review (*FA*). New York: Council on Foreign Relations. V. 1, no. 1 –, 15 Sept. 1922 –. Successor to *J. of international relations*.
Foreign agriculture. Washington, D.C.: U.S. Dept. of Agriculture. V. 1, no. 1 –, Jan. 1937 –.
France-Asie. Saigon; Paris. V. 1, no. 1 –, 1946–. Title varies: v. 17–, 1962–, issued as *France-Asie/Asia*.
Geographical j. (*GJ*). London: Royal Geographical Society of London. V. 1, no. 1 –, Jan. 1893 –. Successor to *Proceedings of the Royal Geographical Society of London*.
Geographical magazine (*GM*). London. V. 1, no. 1 –, May 1935 –.
Geographical review (*GR*). New York: American Geographical Society of New York. V. 1, no. 1 –, Jan. 1916 –. Successor to *B. of the American Geographical Society of New York*.
Geographical teacher: see *Geography*
Geography. London: Geographical Assn. V. 1, no. 1 –, Oct. 1901 –. Title varies: v. 1–13, 1901–1926, issued as *Geographical teacher*.
Globus. Hildburghausen; Brunswick. V. 1 – v. 98, no. 24, 1861–1910. Successor to *Das Ausland*. Merged into *Petermanns geographische Mitteilungen*.
Harvard j. of Asiatic studies (*HJAS*). Cambridge: Harvard-Yenching Institute. V. 1, no. 1 –, Apr. 1936 –.
History today. London. V. 1, no. 1 –, Jan. 1951 –.
Hong Kong law. j. Hong Kong. V. 1, no. 1 –, Jan. 1971 –.
Hong Kong manager. Hong Kong: Hong Kong Management Assn. V. 1, no. 1 –, Jan.-Feb. 1965 –.
Imperial and Asiatic quarterly review: see *Asiatic review*
India q. New Delhi: Indian Council of World Affairs. V. 1, no. 1 –, Jan. 1945 –.
Industry of Free China (*IFC*). Taipei: China [Republic], Hsing cheng yüan, Ching chi an ting wei yüan hui, Kung yeh wei yüan hui (Executive Yüan, Economic Stabilization Board, Industrial Development Commission); Kuo chi ching chi ho tso fa chan wei yüan hui (Council for International Economic Cooperation and Development). V. 1, no. 1 –, Jan. 1954 –. Bilingual: articles in English or Chinese. Chinese title: *Tzu yu Chung-kuo chih kung yeh*.
Information b. (*IB*). Nanking: Council of International Affairs. V. 1 – v. 5, no. 1/2, 11 May 1936 – 27 Oct. 1937.
International j. Toronto: Canadian Institute of International Affairs. V. 1, no. 1 –, Winter 1945/46 –.
International labour review (*ILR*). Geneva: International Labour Office. V. 1, no. 1 –, 1921–.
International review of missions. Edinburgh: World Council of Churches. V. 1, no. 1 –, 1912–.
International social security review: see *B. of the International Social Security Assn.*
Internationale syndicale rouge (*ISR*): see *Krasnyi internatsional profsoiuzov*.

Internationales Archiv für Ethnographie. Leiden. V. 1–, 1888–.

Issues and studies (IS). Taipei: Chung-hua min kuo kuo chi kuan hsi yen chiu so (Institute of International Relations, Republic of China). V. 1, no. 1 –, Oct. 1964 –.

Istoricheskii vestnik; istoriko-literaturnyi zhurnal. St. Petersburg (Petrograd). V. 1–150, 1880–1917.

Izvestiia IUridicheskogo fakul'teta v g. Kharbine. Harbin: Vysshaia shkola v Kharbine, IUridicheskii fakul'tet. V. 1–12, 1925–1938.

Izvestiia Vostochnogo instituta (IVI). Vladivostok: Gosudarstvennyi dal'nevostochnyi universitet, Vostochnyi institut. V. 1–, 1899–. Title varies: 1922– issued as *Izvestiia Vostochnogo fakul'teta*.

Jahrbuch der Bodenreform. Jena. V. 1, no. 1 – v. 38, no. 1, 1905 – Apr. 1942.

Japan q. (JQ). Tokyo. V. 1, no. 1 –, Oct.-Dec. 1954 –.

J. asiatique; recueil de mémoires et de notices relatifs aux études orientales (JA). Paris: Société asiatique. V. 1–11, 1822–1827; 2e série, v. 1–16, 1828–1835; 3e série, v. 1–14, 1836–1842; 4e série, v. 1–20, 1843–1852; 5e série, v. 1–20, 1853–1862; 6e série, v. 1–20, 1863–1872; 7e série, v. 1–20, 1873–1882; 8e série, v. 1–20, 1883–1892; 9e série, v. 1–20, 1893–1902; 10e série, v. 1–20, 1903–1912; 11e série, v. 1–20, 1913–1922; v. 202–, 1923–.

J. d'hygiène. Paris: Société française d'hygiène. V. 1–20, oct. 1875 – 1914.

J. of applied sociology. Los Angeles: Southern California Sociological Society *and* U. of Southern California. V. 6, no. 1 – v. 11, no. 6, Oct. 1921 – July-Aug. 1927. Successor to *Studies in sociology*. Succeeded by *Sociology and social research*.

J. of Asian and African studies (JAAS). Leiden. V. 1, no. 1 –, Jan. 1966 –.

J. of Asian studies (JAS). Ann Arbor: Far Eastern Assn. (name changed Mar. 1957 to Assn. for Asian Studies). V. 16, no. 1 –, Nov. 1956 –. Successor to *Far Eastern q.*

J. of economic history. New York: Economic History Assn. V. 1, no. 1 –, May 1941 –.

J. of geography. Lancaster, Pa.; Chicago; etc.: National Council of Geography Teachers (1929–). V. 1, no. 1 –, Jan. 1902 –. Suspended publ. Feb.–Aug. 1907. Successor to *J. of school geography* and *B. of the American Bureau of Geography*.

J. of international affairs. New York: Columbia U., School of International Affairs. V. 1, no. 1 –, Spring 1947 –. Title varies: v. 1–5, 1947–1952, issued as *Columbia j. of international affairs*.

J. of marriage and the family. Menasha, Wisc.: National Conference on Family Relations (Chicago) (name changed 1948 to National Council on Family Relations [Chicago; Minneapolis]). V. 1, no. 1 –, Jan. 1939 –. Title varies: v. 1, no. 1 – v. 2, no. 4, Jan. 1939 – Nov. 1940, issued as *Living*; v. 3, no. 1 – v. 25, no. 4, Winter 1941 – Nov. 1963, issued as *Marriage and family living*.

J. of Oriental studies (JOS). Hong Kong: U. of Hong Kong. V. 1, no. 1 –, Jan. 1954 –. Multilingual: articles in Western languages or Chinese. Chinese title: *Tung fang wen hua*.

J. of politics. Gainesville: Southern Political Science Assn. *and* U. of Florida. V. 1, no. 1. –, Feb. 1939 –. Successor to *Proceedings of the Southern Political Science Assn.*

J. of social psychology. Worcester, Mass. V. 1, no. 1 –, Feb. 1930 –.

J. of sociology. Taipei: Kuo li T'ai-wan ta hsüeh, Fa hsüeh yüan, She hui hsüeh hsi (National Taiwan U., College of Law, Dept. of Sociology). No. 1–, Dec. 1963 –. Bilingual: articles in English or Chinese. Chinese title: *She hui hsüeh k'an*.

J. of the American Asiatic Assn. (JAAA). New York. V. 1, no. 1 – v. 15, no. 12?, July 1898 – Jan. 1917? Succeeded by *Asia; j. of the American Asiatic Assn.*

J. of the American Oriental Society (JAOS). Boston; New Haven; etc. V. 1–, 1843–.

J. of the China Branch of the Royal Asiatic Society (JRAS-CB). Shanghai. New (2nd) series, v. 19–36, 1884–1906. Successor to and succeeded by *J. of the North-China Branch of the Royal Asiatic Society*.

J. of the China Society (JCS). Taipei: Chung-kuo hsüeh hui. V. 1–, 1961–.

J. of the history of ideas. New York; Lancaster, Pa.: College of the City of New York. V. 1, no. 1 –, Jan. 1940 –.

J. of the Hong Kong Branch of the Royal Asiatic Society (JRAS-HKB). Hong Kong. V. 1–, 1960/61–.

J. of the North-China Branch of the Royal Asiatic Society (JRAS-NCB). Shanghai. V. 1–2, 1858–1860; new (2nd) series, v. 1–18, 37–73?, 1864–1883, 1907–1948? Succeeded by and successor to *J. of the China Branch of the Royal Asiatic Society*.

J. of the Royal Asiatic Society (JRAS). London. V. 1–20, 1834–1863; new (2nd) series, v. 1–21, 1864–1889; 3rd series, v. 1–, 1889–.

J. of the Royal Society of Arts. London. V. 1–, 26 Nov. 1852 –. Title varies: v. 1 – v. 56, no. 2879, 26 Nov. 1852 – 26 Jan. 1908, issued as *J. of the Society of Arts*.

J. of the West China Border Research Society (JWCBRS). Chengtu. V. 1–16, 1922/23–1945.

Journalism q. Grand Forks, N.D.; Urbana, Ill.: American Assn. of Teachers of Journalism; American Assn. of Schools and Departments of Journalism. V. 1, no. 1 –, Mar. 1924 –.

Kobe U. economic review. Kobe: Kōbe daigaku, Keizai gakubu (Kobe U., Faculty of Economics). V. 1–, 1955–.

Kommunist. Moscow: Kommunisticheskaia partiia Sovetskogo Soiuza, TSentral'nyi komitet. V. 1–28, 1924–1951; v. 1952–.

Krasnyi internatsional profsoiuzov (KIP). Moscow: Krasnyi internatsional professional'nykh soiuzov, Ispolnitel'noe biuro. V. 1–16, 30 avgusta 1921 – 1936. German, French, and English editions also published.

Die Rote Gewerkschafts-Internationale (RGI). Moscow. V. 1–13, 1921 – Feb. 1933?

Internationale syndicale rouge (ISR). Paris. No. 1–129, 31 août 1921 – août 1931; v. 1932 – v. 1933, no. 9.

R.I.L.U. magazine. London. V. 1, no. 1 – v. 2, no. 7/8, Oct. 1928 – Nov.-Dec. 1930; new (2nd) series, v. 1 – v. 3, no. 4, Feb. 1931 – May 1933. Title varies: v. 1, no. 1 – v. 2, no. 7/8, Oct. 1928 – Nov.-Dec. 1930, issued as *Red International of Labour Unions*.

Kratkie soobshcheniia Instituta narodov Azii (KSINA). Moscow: Akademiia nauk SSSR, Institut narodov Azii. No. 30, 1961; no. 39, 1963; no. 40, 1961; no. 43–, 1960–. See also *Kratkie soobshcheniia Instituta vostokovedeniia*.

Kratkie soobshcheniia Instituta vostokovedeniia (KSIV).

Moscow: Akademiia nauk SSSR, Institut vostokovedeniia. No. 1–29, 1951–1959; no. 31–38, 1958?–1960; no. 41–42, 1959–1960. See also *Kratkie soobshcheniia Instituta narodov Azii.*

Kyoto U. economic review (KUER). Kyoto: Kyōto daigaku, Keizai gakubu (Kyoto U., Faculty of Economics). V. 1, no. 1 –, July 1926 –. Suspended publ. 1944 – Mar. 1950.

Lingnaam agricultural review: see *Lingnan science j.*

Lingnan science j. (LSJ). Canton: Ling-nan ta hsüeh (Lingnan U.). V. 1, no. 1 – v. 23, no. 1/2?, Dec. 1922 – 1950? Title varies: v. 1, no. 1 – v. 4, no. 2, Dec. 1922 – July 1927, issued as *Lingnaam agricultural review.*

Malayan economic review. Singapore: U. of Malaya, Economics Society. V. 1, no. 1 –, June 1956 –.

Mariner's mirror. London: Society for Nautical Research. V. 1, no. 1 –, Jan. 1911 –. Suspended publ. Aug. 1914 – June 1919.

Marriage and family living: see J. of marriage and the family

Materialy po natsional'no-kolonial'nym problemam (MNKP). Moscow: Nauchno-issledovatel'skaia assotsiatsiia po izucheniiu natsional'nykh i kolonial'nykh problem (name changed 1936 to Nauchno-issledovatel'skii institut po izucheniiu natsional'nykh i kolonial'nykh problem). V. 1931, no. 1 – v. 1936, no. 37. Succeeded by *Natsional'no-kolonial'nye problemy.*

Milbank Memorial Fund q. (MMFQ). New York. V. 1, no. 1 –, Oct. 1923 –. Title varies: v. 1, no. 1 – v. 11, no. 4, Oct. 1923 – Oct. 1933, issued as *Milbank Memorial Fund quarterly b.*

Military review. Ft. Leavenworth, Kan.: U.S. Army, General Service Schools; U.S. Army, Command and General Staff School. No. 1–29, Jan. 1922 – June 1928; v. 8, no. 1 –, Sept. 1928 –. Title varies: no. 1–16, Jan. 1922 – Mar. 1925, issued as *Instructors' summary of military articles*; no. 17 – v. 11, no. 1, Apr. 1925 – Sept. 1931, issued as *Review of current military writings*; v. 11, no. 2–4, Dec. 1931 – June 1932, issued as *Review of current military literature.*

Mirovoe khoziaistvo i mirovaia politika (MKhMP). Moscow: Akademiia nauk SSSR, Institut mirovogo khoziaistva i mirovoi politiki. V. 1925–1947. Successor to *Mezhdunarodnaia letopis'.* Succeeded by *Voprosy ekonomiki.*

Missions catholiques. Lyons; Paris. V. 1–, 1868–.

Mitteilungen der Deutschen Gesellschaft für Natur- und Völkerkunde Ostasiens (MDG). Tokyo. V. 1 – v. 32, no. E, 1873/76–1943.

Mitteilungen des Seminars für orientalische Sprachen zu Berlin, Erste Abteilung, Ostasiatische Studien (MSOSB). Berlin: Universität Berlin, Seminar für orientalische Sprachen (from 1936, under the university's Ausland-Hochschule). V. 1–42, 1898–1939. Title varies: v. 39–42, 1936–1939, issued as *Mitteilungen des Seminars für orientalische Sprachen der Ausland-Hochschule, Universität Berlin.*

Modern Asian studies (MAS). Cambridge, Eng. V. 1, no. 1 –, Jan. 1967 –.

Moderne Welt. Cologne: Arbeitskreis für Ost-West-Fragen. V. 1, no. 1 –, 1959/60–. English edition also published. *Modern world.* V. 1960/61–1965/66; v. 5–, 1967–.

Monthly b. on economic China (MBEC). Tientsin: Nan-k'ai ta hsüeh, Ching chi hsüeh yüan (Nankai U., Institute of Economics). V. 7, no. 1–12, Jan. – Dec. 1934. Successor to *Nankai weekly statistical service.* Succeeded by *Nankai social and economic q.*

Monthly information b. of the International Commission Against Concentration Camp Practices: see *Saturne*

Monthly labor review. Washington, D.C.: U.S. Dept. of Labor, Bureau of Labor Statistics. V. 1, no. 1 –, July 1915 –. Title varies: v. 1, no. 1 – v. 6, no. 6, July 1915 – June 1918, issued as *Monthly review of the U.S. Bureau of Labor Statistics.*

Monumenta Serica; j. of Oriental studies (MS). Peiping: Catholic U. of Peking; Tokyo: Society of the Divine Word Research Institute. V. 1, no. 1 –, 1935–.

Na agrarnom fronte. Moscow: Kommunisticheskaia akademiia, Agrarnyi institut. V. 1925, no. 1 – v. 1935, no. 7. Suspended publ. Dec. 1931 – June 1932. Succeeded by *Sotsialisticheskaia rekonstruktsiia sel'skogo khoziaistva.*

Nachrichten der Deutschen Gesellschaft für Natur- und Völkerkunde Ostasiens (NDG). Tokyo; Wiesbaden, No. 1–, Juli 1926 –. Suspended publ. Sept. 1945 – July 1951. Title varies: no. 1–70, 1926 – Sept. 1945, issued as *Nachrichten aus der Deutschen Gesellschaft für Natur- und Völkerkunde Ostasiens.*

Nankai social and economic q. (NSEQ). Tientsin: Nan-k'ai ta hsüeh, Ching chi hsüeh yüan (Nankai U., Institute of Economics). V. 8, no. 1 – v. 11, no. 3/4 / v. 12, no. 1/2?, Apr. 1935 – Jan. 1941? Suspended publ. July 1937 – Jan. 1939. Successor to *Monthly b. on economic China.*

Nankai weekly statistical service (NWSS). Tientsin: Nan-k'ai ta hsüeh, Ching chi hsüeh yüan (Nankai U., Institute of Economics). V. 1, no. 1 – v. 6, no. 52, Jan. 1928 – 25 Dec. 1933. Succeeded by *Monthly b. on economic China.*

Narody Azii i Afriki; istoriia, ekonomika, kul'tura (NAA). Moscow: Akademiia nauk SSSR, Institut narodov Azii *and* Akademiia nauk SSSR, Institut Afriki (issuing agencies vary). V. 1961, no. 2 –.

National geographic magazine (NG). Washington, D.C.: National Geographic Society. V. 1, no. 1 –, 1888–.

New China review (NCR). Shanghai. V. 1, no. 1 – v. 4, no. 6, Mar. 1919 – Dec. 1922.

New York review of books (NYRB). New York. V. 1, no. 1 –, 25 Feb. 1963? –.

Nineteenth century. London. V. 1, no. 1 – v. 158, no. 886, Mar. 1877 – Dec. 1950. Title varies: v. 49, no. 287 – v. 158, no. 886, Jan. 1901 – Dec. 1950, issued as *Nineteenth century and after.* Succeeded by *Twentieth century.*

Notes and queries on China and Japan (NQCJ). Hong Kong. V. 1, no. 1 – v. 4, no. 10, Jan. 1867 – Nov. 1870.

Notes documentaires et études: see *Notes et études documentaires*

Notes et études documentaires (NED). Paris: France, Ministère de l'information; France, Présidence du conseil, Secrétariat général du gouvernement, Direction de la documentation. No. 1–, 10 jan. 1945 –. Title varies: no. 1–1069, 10 jan. 1945 – 3 fév. 1949, issued as *Notes documentaires et études.*

Nouvelle r. Paris. V. 1–120, 1er oct. 1879 – 1er oct. 1899; 2e série, v. 1–49, 15 oct. 1899 – 15 déc. 1907; 3e série, v. 1–26, jan. 1908 – avr. 1912; 4e série, v. 1–, mai 1912 –.

Nouvelles annales des voyages. Paris. No. 1–188, 1819–1865. Successor to *Annales des voyages, de la géographie et de l'histoire.* Succeeded by *Annales des voyages, de la géographie, de l'histoire et de l'archéologie.*

Novyi Vostok (*NV*). Moscow: Nauchnaia assotsiatsiia vostokovedeniia SSSR. No. 1–28, 1922–1930.

Orbis; a quarterly j. of world affairs. Philadelphia: U. of Pennsylvania, Foreign Policy Research Institute. V. 1, no. 1 –, Apr. 1957 –.

Oriens Extremus; Z. für Sprache, Kunst und Kultur der Länder des Fernen Ostens (OE). Wiesbaden. V. 1–, Juli 1954 –.

Orient. Hong Kong. V. 1, no. 1 – v. 6, no. 8, Aug. 1950 – Mar. 1956.

Ostasiatische Lloyd; Organ für die deutschen Interessen im Fernen Osten (OL). Shanghai. V. 1 – v. 31, no. 33, Okt. 1866 – 17 Aug. 1917.

Ostasiatische Rundschau (OR). Berlin: Verband für den Fernen Osten; Deutscher Wirtschaftsdienst. V. 1 – v. 25, no. 5, Feb. 1920 – Sept.-Okt. 1944. Succeeded by *Übersee-Rundschau*.

Ostasiatische Z. Berlin: Gesellschaft für ostasiatische Kunst. V. 1–28, Apr. 1912 – 1942/43.

Osteuropa. Stuttgart: Deutsche Gesellschaft für Osteuropakunde. V. 1, no. 1 –, Okt. 1951 –. Successor to *Osteuropa; Z. für die gesamten Fragen des europäischen Ostens*.

Osteuropa-Recht; Gegenwartsfragen aus den Rechten des Ostens. Stuttgart: Deutsche Gesellschaft für Osteuropakunde. V. 1, no. 1 –, März 1955 –.

Pacific affairs (PA). Honolulu; New York: Institute of Pacific Relations. V. 1, no. 1 –, 26 May 1926 –. Title varies: 26 May 1926 – Apr. 1928 issued as *Institute of Pacific Relations news b*.

Pacific historical review (PHR). Glendale, Calif.: American Historical Assn., Pacific Coast Branch. V. 1, no. 1 –, Mar. 1932 –.

Pacific viewpoint. Wellington, N.Z.: Victoria U. of Wellington, Dept. of Geography. V. 1, no. 1 –, Mar. 1960 –.

Papers of the Michigan Academy of Science, Arts, and Letters. New York; Ann Arbor. V. 1–, 1921–. Successor to *Annual report of the Michigan Academy of Science*.

Papers on China (*PC*). Cambridge: Harvard U., Committee on International and Regional Studies (from 1955 to 1956, Committee on Regional Studies), East Asia Program; Harvard U., Center for East Asian Studies (name changed 1960 to East Asian Research Center). V. 1–24, Dec. 1947 – Dec. 1971.

Papers on Far Eastern history. Canberra: Australian National U., Dept. of Far Eastern History. No. 1–, Mar. 1970 –.

Pays communistes: see *B. du Centre d'étude des pays de l'Est et du Centre national pour l'étude des états de l'Est*

Peking review (PR). Peking. V. 1, no. 1 – v. 9, no. 52, 4 Mar. 1958 – 23 Dec. 1966; v. 1967, no. 1 (1 Jan.) –. Successor to *People's China*.

People's China. Peking: Foreign Languages Press. V. 1, no. 1 – v. 4, no. 12, 1 Jan. 1950 – 16 Dec. 1951; v. 1952, no. 1 (1 Jan.) – v. 1957, no. 24 (16 Dec.). Succeeded by *Peking review*.

People's tribune (*PT*). Peiping. V. 1, no. 1–4, Mar. – June-July 1931; new (2nd) series, v. 1, no. 1 – 30, no. 8?, 19 Dec. 1931 – Apr. 1941?

Petermanns geographische Mitteilungen (*PGM*). Gotha. V. 1–, Feb. 1855 –. Title varies: v. 1 – v. 24, no. 12, 1855–1878, issued as *Mitteilungen aus Justus Perthes' geographischer Anstalt*; v. 25, no. 1 – v. 83, no. 12, 1879–1937, issued as *Dr. A. Petermanns Mitteilungen aus Justus Perthes' geographischer Anstalt*.

Political q. London. V. 1, no. 1 –, Jan. 1930 –.

Political science q. New York: Columbia U., Faculty of Political Science (from 1909, edited by Columbia U., Faculty of Political Science, for Academy of Political Science in the City of New York). V. 1, no. 1 –, Mar. 1886 –.

Politique étrangère. Paris: Centre d'études de politique étrangère. V. 1, no. 1 –, fév. 1936 –.

Population. Paris: Institut national d'études démographiques. V. 1, no. 1 –, jan.-mars 1946 –.

Population index. Princeton: Princeton U., School of Public and International Affairs; Population Assn. of America. V. 1, no. 1 –, Jan. 1935 –. Title varies: v. 1, no. 1, issued as *Review of current research*; v. 1, no. 2 – v. 2, no. 4, Apr. 1935 – Oct. 1936, issued as *Population literature*.

Population studies; a quarterly j. of demography (*PS*). London: Population Investigation Committee. V. 1, no. 1 –, June 1947 –.

Problems of Communism. Washington, D.C.: U.S. International Information Administration, Documentary Studies Section; U.S. Information Agency, Special Materials Section. No. 1–4, 1952; v. 2, no. 1 –, Jan. 1953 –.

Problemy Kitaia (*PK*). Moscow: Nauchno-issledovatel'skii institut po Kitaiu. V. 1–14, 1929–1935. Successor to *Materialy po kitaiskomu voprosu*.

Problemy vostokovedeniia (*PV*). Moscow: Akademiia nauk SSSR, Institut vostokovedeniia *and* Akademiia nauk SSSR, Institut Afriki (issuing agencies vary). V. 1959, no. 1 – v. 1961, no. 1. Successor to *Sovetskoe kitaevedenie* and *Sovetskoe vostokovedenie*. Succeeded by *Narody Azii i Afriki*.

Psychiatry. Baltimore; Washington, D.C.: William A. White Psychiatric Foundation. V. 1, no. 1 –, Feb. 1938 –.

R.I.L.U. magazine: see *Krasnyi internatsional profsoiuzov*

Review; a quarterly j. for the study of Communism and Communist countries. Tokyo. No. 1–, May 1964 –.

R. de géographie. Paris. V. 1–55, jan. 1877 – déc. 1905; nouvelle (2e) série, v. 1, no. 1 – v. 12, no. 2, 1906 – fév. 1924.

R. de Paris. Paris. V. 1, no. 1 –, 1er fév. 1894 –. Suspended publ. with v. 47, no. 11 (1er juin 1940), and resumed with v. 52, no. 1 (1er avr. 1945); v. 48–51 not issued.

R. des deux mondes. Paris; etc. V. 1–2, 1829; 2e série, v. 1–4, 1830; 3e année, v. 1–8, 1831–1832; 2e série, v. 1–4, 1833; 3e série, v. 1–4, 1834; 4e série, v. 1–32, 1835–1842; nouvelle (5e) série, v. 1–24, 1843–1848. Nouvelle période, v. 1–16, 1849–1852; 2e série, v. 1–12, 1853–1855; 2e période, v. 1–108, 1856–1873; 3e période, v. 1–120, 1874–1893; 4e période, v. 121–162, 1893–1900; 5e période, v. 1–60, 1901–1910; 6e période, v. 1–65, 1911 – oct. 1921; 7e période, v. 6–60, nov. 1921 – 15 déc. 1930; 8e période, v. 1–81, 1er jan. 1931 – 15 sept. 1944. Succeeded by *Revue; littérature, histoire, arts et sciences des deux mondes*.

R. du Sud-Est asiatique et de l'Extrême Orient (RSAEO) / J. of South East Asia and the Far East. Brussels: Université libre de Bruxelles, Institut de sociologie Solvay, Centre du Sud-Est asiatique. V. 1962, no. 1 – v. 1970, no. 4. Title varies: v. 1962–1967 issued as *R. du Sud-Est asiatique*. Succeeded by *Asia q*.

R. historique. Paris. V. 1–, 1876–.

R. indo-chinoise (*RI*). Hanoi, V. 1–6, août 1893 – 1903;

nouvelle (2e) série, v. 1–44, 1904–1925. Suspended publ. Nov. 1894 – Jan. 1899. Succeeded by *Extrême-Asie*.

Die Rote Gewerkschafts-Internationale (RGI): see *Krasnyi internatsional profsoiuzov*

Rural sociology. Baton Rouge, La.; etc.: American Sociological Society, Section on Rural Sociology; Rural Sociological Society of America. V. 1, no. 1 –, Mar. 1936 –.

Russkoe bogatstvo. Moscow; St. Petersburg (Petrograd). v. 1876 – v. 1918, no. 4/6; (aprel'-iiun'). Title varies: v. 1914, no. 1 (noiabr') – v. 1917, no. 2/3 (fevral'-mart), issued as *Russkiia zapiski*.

Saeculum; Jahrbuch für Universalgeschichte. Freiburg i.Br. V. 1, no. 1 –, 1950–.

Saturne. Brussels: Commission internationale contre le régime concentrationnaire / International Commission Against Concentration Camp Practices. No. 1–5, déc. 1954 – déc. 1955; v. 2, no. 6 – v. 5, no. 19, jan.-fév. 1956 – jan.-mars 1959. Title varies: no. 1–5, déc. 1954 – déc. 1955, issued as *B. d'information de la Commission internationale contre le régime concentrationnaire*. English edition also published.

Saturn. No. 1–5, Dec. 1954 – Dec. 1955; v. 2, no. 1 – v. 4, no. 1, Jan.-Feb. 1956 – Jan.-Mar. 1958. Title varies: no. 1–5, Dec. 1954 – Dec. 1955, issued as *Monthly information b. of the International Commission Against Concentration Camp Practices*.

Sbornik konsul'skikh donesenii. St. Petersburg: Russia [Imperial], Ministerstvo inostrannykh del (Departamenta vnutrennikh snoshenii), Vtoroi departament. V. 1898, no. 1 – v. 1910.

Schmollers Jahrbuch für Wirtschafts- und Sozialwissenschaften (SJ). Leipzig, Munich; Berlin. V. 1, no. 1 –, 1877–. Suspended publ. 1945–1948. Title varies: v. 1–36, 1877–1912, issued as *Jahrbuch für Gesetzgebung, Verwaltung und Volkswirtschaft im Deutschen Reich*; v. 37–87, 1913–1944, 1949–1967, issued as *Schmollers Jahrbuch für Gesetzgebung, Verwaltung und Volkswirtschaft*.

Scientific monthly. Washington, D.C.: American Assn. for the Advancement of Science. V. 1, no. 1 – v. 85, no. 12, Oct. 1915 – Dec. 1957. Merged into *Science*.

Selections from China Mainland magazines (SCMM). Hong Kong: U.S. Consulate General. No. 213–, 7 June 1960 –. Successor to *Extracts from China Mainland magazines*.

Shanghai market prices report. Shanghai: China [Republic], Ts'ai cheng pu, Chu Hu tiao ch'a huo chia ch'u (Ministry of Finance, [Shanghai] Bureau of Markets); China [Republic], Ts'ai cheng pu, Kuo ting shui tse wei yüan hui (Ministry of Finance, National Tariff Commission). Unnumbered, Jan.-Mar. 1923 – Oct.-Dec. 1933. Bilingual: articles in English and Chinese. Chinese title: *Shang-hai huo chia chi k'an*.

Sinica; Z. für Chinakunde und Chinaforschung. Heidelberg; etc.: China-Institut (Frankfurt a.M.). V. 1 – v. 17, no. 6, 1925/27–1942.

Sinologica. Basel: Sino-Swiss Society. V. 1, no. 1 –, 1947–.

Social forces. Chapel Hill, N.C. V. 1, no. 1 –, Nov. 1922 –. Title varies: v. 1, no. 1 – v. 3, no. 4, Nov. 1922 – May 1925, issued as *J. of social forces*.

Sociology and social research (SSR). Los Angeles. V. 12, no. 1 –, Sept.-Oct. 1928 –. Successor to *J. of applied sociology*.

Sovetskaia etnografiia. Leningrad: Akademiia nauk SSSR (Moscow). V. 1931, no. 1 –. Successor to *Etnografiia*.

Sovetskaia iustitsiia. Moscow: Ministerstvo iustitsii RSFSR. V. 1930, no. 1 – v. 1941; v. 1957, no. 1 –. Successor to *Ezhenedel'nik sovetskoi iustitsii*. Merged into *Sotsialisticheskaia zakonnost'* July 1941 – 1957; resumed independent publ. in 1957.

Sovetskaia pedagogika. Moscow: Akademiia pedagogicheskikh nauk RSFSR. V. 1–, oktiabr' 1937 –. Successor to *Pedagogicheskoe obrazovanie*.

Sovetskoe gosudarstvo i pravo (SGP). Moscow: Akademiia nauk SSSR, Institut gosudarstva i prava. V. 1930–. Suspended publ. May 1941 – Dec. 1945. Successor to *Sovetskoe pravo* and *Revoliutsiia prava*. Title varies: v. 1930–1932 issued as *Sovetskoe gosudarstvo i revoliutsiia prava*; v. 1932–1938 issued as *Sovetskoe gosudarstvo*.

Sovetskoe kitaevedenie (SK). Moscow: Akademiia nauk SSSR, Institut kitaevedeniia. V. 1958, no. 1–4. Merged with *Sovetskoe vostokovedenie* to form *Problemy vostokovedeniia*.

Sovetskoe vostokovedenie (SV). Moscow; Leningrad: Akademiia nauk SSSR, Institut vostokovedeniia. V. 1955, no. 1 – v. 1958. Merged with *Sovetskoe kitaevedenie* to form *Problemy vostokovedeniia*.

Soviet survey: see *Survey; a j. of Soviet and East European studies*

Studies in comparative Communism. Los Angeles: U. of Southern California, School of Politics and International Relations, Research Institute. V. 1, no. 1/2 –, July-Oct. 1968 –.

Studies in family planning (SFP). New York: Population Council. No. 1–60, July 1963 – Dec. 1970; v. 2, no. 1 –, Jan. 1971 –.

Studies in Soviet thought (SST). Dordrecht, The Netherlands: Université de Fribourg, Ost-Europa Institut (1962–). V. 1 –, 1961 –.

Studies on Asia. Lincoln, Neb. V. 1–8, 1960–1967.

Survey; a j. of Soviet and East European studies. London: Congress for Cultural Freedom (Paris). No. 1–, 1956–. Title varies: no. 1–8, 1956, issued as *Soviet culture*; no. 9–19, Nov. 1956 – Sept. 1957, and no. 23–35, Jan.-Mar. 1958 – Jan.-Mar. 1961, issued as *Soviet survey*.

Survey of China Mainland press (SCMP). Hong Kong: U.S. Consulate General. No. 1–, 1 Nov. 1950 –.

T'ien hsia monthly (THM). Shanghai: Chung-shan wen hua chiao yü kuan (Sun Yat-sen Institute for the Advancement of Culture and Education) (Nanking). V. 1, no. 1 – v. 12, no. 1, Aug. 1935 – Aug.-Sept. 1941.

Tijdschrift voor economische en sociale geografie (TESG). The Hague; Rotterdam; etc.: Nederlandsche Vereeniging voor Economische Geographie (from 1950, Nederlandse Vereniging voor Economische en Sociale Geografie). V. 1, no. 1 –, Januari 1910 –. Suspended publ. with v. 35, no. 7 (Juli 1944), and resumed with v. 37, no. 1 (Januari 1946); v. 35, no. 8 – v. 36, no. 12, not issued. Title varies: v. 1, no. 1 – v. 39, no. 2/3, Januari 1910 – Februari-Maart 1948, issued as *Tijdschrift voor economische geographie*.

T'oung pao; archives concernant l'histoire, les langues, la géographie et l'ethnographie de l'Asie orientale (TP). Leiden. V. 1, no. 1 – v. 10, no. 5, 1890–1899; 2e série, v. 1, no. 1 –, 1900–.

Tour du monde. Paris. V. 1, no. 1 – v. 68, no. 26, 1860 – 29 déc.

1894; nouvelle (2e) série, v. 1, no. 1 – v. 20?, 5 jan. 1895 – 1914?

Trade b. of the Hong Kong Dept. of Commerce and Industry (*TBHK*). Hong Kong. Unnumbered, 1953–. Title varies.

Transcultural psychiatric research. Montreal: McGill U., Dept. of Psychiatry *and* McGill U., Dept. of Sociology and Anthropology (to 1962). No. 1–15, May 1956 – Oct. 1963; v. 1–, Apr. 1964 –. Title varies: no. 1–13, May 1956 – Oct. 1962, issued as *Transcultural research in mental health; review and newsletter*.

Tsing Hua j. of Chinese studies (THJ). Peking: Ch'ing hua hsüeh hsiao (Tsing Hua College); Peiping; Kunming: Kuo li ch'ing hua ta hsüeh (National Tsing Hua U.); Taipei: Ch'ing hua hsüeh pao she (Tsing Hua Journal Publication Committee). V. 1 – v. 4, no. 7, 1916 – Jan. 1919; v. 1, no. 1 – v. 15, no. 1, June 1924 – Oct. 1948; new (2nd) series, v. 1, no. 1 –, June 1956 –. Suspended publ. July 1937 – Apr. 1941, Oct. 1941 – Oct. 1947. Bilingual: articles in English or Chinese. Chinese title: *Ch'ing hua hsüeh pao*.

Uchenye zapiski Instituta vostokovedeniia (UZIV). Moscow: Akademiia nauk SSSR, Institut vostokovedeniia (issuing agency varies). No. 1–25, 1950–1960. Title varies: no. 22, 1960, issued as *Uchenye zapiski Instituta narodov Azii*.

Uchenye zapiski Leningradskogo gosudarstvennogo universiteta (*UZLGU*). Leningrad. No. 1–, 1935–.

Union Research service (URS). Hong Kong: Union Research Institute. V. 1, no. 1 –, 16 Sept. 1955 –.

United Asia; international magazine of Asian affairs. Bombay: United Asian Publications. V. 1, no. 1 –, May-June 1948 –.

Vestnik Azii (VA). Harbin: Obshchestvo russkikh orientalistov. No. 1–54?, iiul' 1909 – 1927?

Vestnik Leningradskogo gosudarstvennogo universiteta (*VLGU*). Leningrad. V. 1–, avgust 1946 –.

Vestnik Man'chzhurii (*VM*). Harbin: Upravlenie Kitaiskoi Vostochnoi zheleznoi dorogi. V. 1925, no. 1/2 – v. 1934? Successor to *Ekonomicheskii vestnik Man'chzhurii*. English supplement issued: *Manchuria monitor*. V. 1925, no. 1/2 – v. 1932, no. 11/12.

Vestnik vysshei shkoly. Moscow: U.S.S.R., Ministerstvo vysshego i srednego spetsial'nogo obrazovaniia. V. 1–, 1940–. Successor to *Biulleten' Vsesoiuznogo komiteta po delam vysshei shkoly*.

Voprosy ekonomiki; ezhemesiachnyi zhurnal (VE). Moscow: Akademiia nauk SSSR, Institut ekonomiki. V. 1948, no. 1 (mart) –. Successor to *Mirovoe khoziastvo i mirovaia politika*.

Voprosy istorii (VI). Moscow: Akademiia nauk SSSR, Institut istorii. V. 1945, no. 1 (ianvar') –. Successor to *Istoricheskii zhurnal*.

Vostochnoe obozrenie; obshchestvenno-politicheskii i literaturnyi zhurnal. Harbin: IUzhnaia Man'chzhurskaia zheleznaia doroga. V. 1–20, oktiabr'-dekabr' 1939 – sentiabr' 1944.

Weltwirtschaftliches Archiv; Z. für allgemeine und speziale Weltwirtschaftslehre (WA). Jena: Universität Kiel, Institut für Seeverkehr und Weltwirtschaftslehre; Hamburg: Universität Kiel, Institut für Weltwirtschaft. V. 1, no. 1 –, Jan. 1913 –. Suspended publ. Mar. 1945 – 1949.

Women of China (WC). Peking: Chung-hua jen min kung ho kuo ch'üan kuo fu nü lien ho hui (All-China Democratic Women's Federation). V. 1952, no. 1 –.

World politics; a quarterly j. of international relations (WP). New Haven: Yale U., Institute of International Studies. V. 1, no. 1 –, Oct. 1948 –.

World today. London: Royal Institute of International Affairs, Information Dept. V. 1, no. 1 –, July 1945 –. Successor to *B. of international news*.

Yenching j. of social studies (*YJSS*). Peiping: Yen-ching ta hsüeh (Yenching U.). V. 1, no. 1 – v. 5, no. 1?, June 1938 – July 1950? Suspended publ. Aug. 1942 – Aug. 1948.

Z. der Deutschen morgenländischen Gesellschaft (*ZDMG*). Leipzig. V. 1–, 1847–.

Z. der Gesellschaft für Erdkunde zu Berlin. Berlin. V. 1–36, 1886–1901; v. 1902, no. 1 – v. 1944. Successor to *Z. für allgemeine Erdkunde*. Succeeded by *Die Erde*.

Z. für die gesamte Strafrechtswissenschaft. Berlin; Leipzig; Vienna. V. 1–, 1881–. Suspended publ. 1945–1949.

Z. für Ethnologie (ZE). Berlin; Brunswick: Berliner Gesellschaft für Anthropologie, Ethnologie und Urgeschichte. V. 1–, 1869–. Suspended publ. 1945–1949.

Z. für Geopolitik. Berlin-Grunewald; Bad Godesberg: Institut für Geosoziologie und Politik. V. 1, no. 1 – v. 39, no. 5/6, Jan. 1924 – Sept.-Dez. 1968. Suspended publ. June 1944? – Dec. 1950.

Z. für Missionskunde und Religionswissenschaft. Berlin: Allgemeiner evangelisch-protestantischer Missionsverein. V. 1–54, 1886–1939.

Z. für Politik. Berlin; Cologne. V. 1, no. 1 – v. 35, 1907–1945; neue (2.) Folge, v. 1, no. 1 –, Apr. 1954 –. Suspended publ. 1919–1922.

Z. für vergleichende Rechtswissenschaft (*ZVR*). Stuttgart; Berlin. V. 1–, 1878–. Suspended publ. Sept. 1944 – 1953.

Journal Abbreviations

AA	American anthropologist
AAAG	Annals of the Assn. of American Geographers
AAAPSS	Annals of the American Academy of Political and Social Science
AE	Archiv für Eisenbahnwesen
AF	Asie française
AHMC	Annales d'hygiène et de médecine coloniales
AJCL	American j. of comparative law
AJS	American j. of sociology
AO	Archiv orientálni
APF	Annales de la propagation de la foi
APSR	American political science review
APT	Acta psychologica Taiwanica
AS	Asian survey
ASR	American sociological review
ASTH	Archiv für Schiffs- und Tropen-Hygiene
AUFS-EAS	American Universities Field Staff reports, East Asian series
BAAFC	B. de l'Association amicale franco-chinoise
BCAS	B. of Concerned Asian Scholars
BCE	Bulletins on Chinese education
BEFEO	B. de l'Ecole française d'Extrême-Orient
BEI	B. économique de l'Indochine
BIE	B. of the Institute of Ethnology, Academia Sinica
BIIS	B. de l'Institut international de statistique
BISSA	B. of the International Social Security Assn.
BNI	Biulleten' nauchnoi informatsii
BSB	Bibliograficheskii sbornik Biblioteki Kitaiskoi Vostochnoi zheleznoi dorogi
BSOAS	B. of the School of Oriental and African Studies
BSRB	B. de la Société royale belge d'anthropologie et de préhistoire de Bruxelles
BTLV	Bijdragen tot de taal-, land- en volkenkunde van Nederlandsch-Indië
BUA	B. de l'Université l'Aurore
BVRV	Blätter für vergleichende Rechtwissenschaft und Volkswirtschaftslehre
CB	Current background
CC	Chinese culture
CCA	Chinese Communist affairs
CCJ	Chung Chi j.
CE	Chinese education
CEJ	Chinese economic j. and b.
CEM	Chinese economic monthly
CES	Chinese economic studies
CFC	Cahiers franco-chinois
CH	Current history
CJ	China j.
CJA	Chinese j. of administration
CLR	China law review
CM	China's medicine
CMJ	Chinese medical j. (Peking; etc.)
CMJ-T	Chinese medical j. (Taipei)
CMMJ	China medical missionary j.
CNA	China news analysis
CQ	China q. (London)
CQ-S	China q. (Shanghai)
CR	Chinese recorder
CS	Current scene
CSM	Chinese students' monthly
CSPSR	Chinese social and political science review
CSSH	Comparative studies in society and history
CSWT	Ch'ing-shih wen-t'i
DB	Dokumentacioni bilten Instituta za medjunarodnu politiku i privredu
DCR	Deutsch-chinesische Rechtszeitung
DE	Developing economies
DIRKP	Doneseniia Imperatorskikh rossiiskikh konsul'skikh predstavitelei
EAM	East of Asia magazine
EB	Ekonomicheskii biulleten'
EBAFE	Economic b. for Asia and the Far East
ECMM	Extracts from China Mainland magazines
EDCC	Economic development and cultural change
EF	Economic facts
EG	Economic geography
EH	Eastern horizon
EVM	Ekonomicheskii vestnik Man'chzhurii
FA	Foreign affairs
FEER	Far Eastern economic review
FEQ	Far Eastern q.
FES	Far Eastern survey
FS	Folklore studies
GJ	Geographical j.

GM	Geographical magazine
GR	Geographical review
HJAS	Harvard j. of Asiatic studies
IB	Information b.
IFC	Industry of Free China
ILR	International labour review
IS	Issues and studies
ISR	Internationale syndicale rouge
IVI	Izvestiia Vostochnogo instituta
JA	J. asiatique
JAAA	J. of America Asiatic Assn.
JAAS	J. of Asian and African studies
JAOS	J. of the American Oriental Society
JAS	J. of Asian studies
JCS	J. of the China Society
JOS	J. of Oriental studies
JQ	Japan q.
JRAS	J. of the Royal Asiatic Society
JRAS-CB	J. of the China Branch of the Royal Asiatic Society
JRAS-HKB	J. of the Hong Kong Branch of the Royal Asiatic Society
JRAS-NCB	J. of the North-China Branch of the Royal Asiatic Society
JWCBRS	J. of the West China Border Research Society
KIP	Krasnyi internatsional profsoiuzov
KSINA	Kratkie soobshcheniia Instituta narodov Azii
KSIV	Kratkie soobshcheniia Instituta vostokovedeniia
KUER	Kyoto U. economic review
LSJ	Lingnan science j.
MAS	Modern Asian studies
MBEC	Monthly b. on economic China
MDG	Mitteilungen der Deutschen Gesellschaft für Natur- und Völkerkunde Ostasiens
MKhMP	Mirovoe khoziaistvo i mirovaia politika
MMFQ	Milbank Memorial Fund q.
MNKP	Materialy po natsional'no-kolonial'nym problemam
MS	Monumenta Serica
MSOSB	Mitteilungen des Seminars für orientalische Sprachen zu Berlin
NAA	Narody Azii i Afriki
NCR	New China review
NDG	Nachrichten der Deutschen Gesellschaft für Natur- und Völkerkunde Ostasiens
NED	Notes et études documentaires
NG	National geographic magazine
NQCJ	Notes and queries on China and Japan
NSEQ	Nankai social and economic q.
NV	Novyi Vostok
NWSS	Nankai weekly statistical service
NYRB	New York review of books
OE	Oriens Extremus
OL	Ostasiatische Lloyd
OR	Ostasiatische Rundschau
PA	Pacific affairs
PC	Papers on China
PGM	Petermanns geographische Mitteilungen
PHR	Pacific historical review
PK	Problemy Kitaia
PR	Peking review
PS	Population studies
PT	People's tribune
PV	Problemy vostokovedeniia
RGI	Die Rote Gewerkschafts-Internationale
RI	R. indo-chinoise
RSAEO	R. du Sud-Est asiatique et de l'Extrême Orient
SCMM	Selections from China Mainland magazines
SCMP	Survey of China Mainland press
SFP	Studies in family planning
SGP	Sovetskoe gosudarstvo i pravo
SJ	Schmollers Jahrbuch für Wirtschafts- und Sozialwissenschaften
SK	Sovetskoe kitaevedenie
SSR	Sociology and social research
SST	Studies in Soviet thought
SV	Sovetskoe vostokovedenie
TBHK	Trade b. of the Hong Kong Dept. of Commerce and Industry
TESG	Tijdschrift voor economische en sociale geografie
THJ	Tsing Hua j. of Chinese studies
THM	T'ien hsia monthly
TP	T'oung pao
URS	Union Research Service
UZIV	Uchenye zapiski Instituta vostokovedeniia
UZLGU	Uchenye zapiski Leningradskogo gosudarstvennogo universiteta
VA	Vestnik Azii
VE	Voprosy ekonomiki
VI	Voprosy istorii
VLGU	Vestnik I eningradskogo gosudarstvennogo universiteta
VM	Vestnik Man'chzhurii
WA	Weltwirtschaftliches Archiv
WC	Women of China
WP	World politics
YJSS	Yenching j. of social studies
ZDMG	Z. der Deutschen morgenländischen Gesellschaft
ZE	Z. für Ethnologie
ZVR	Z. für vergleichende Rechtswissenschaft

BIBLIOGRAPHY

Bibliography

書目

文献解題

A bibliography with encoded annotations, arranged by principal subject and historical era

標碼題解書目、依主題及歷史時代排列

主題及び時代別文献解題

Except when they number 15 or fewer, entries within each principal-subject category are grouped into five historical-era subcategories: 1644–1911, 1644–1949, 1911–1949, 1911–1972 (incl. 1644–1972), and 1949–1972. The order with subcategories is alphabetical, with no-author items at the beginning.

10 Chinese Society in General

中國社會通論　　中国社会一般

1644-1911

10001 MCH O P2 G1.1 1644–1895
Allom, Thomas, 1804–1872.
The Chinese empire illustrated: Being a series of views from original sketches displaying the scenery, architecture, social habits . . .
London: London Printing and Publishing, 1858, 1859. 2 vols. 11, 184; 140 p.
Subj 10 13 15 16 16.3 55 ▪ 12.2 14.1 16.1 24.4 31 41 47 57 60

10002 NNC O P2 G1.2 1842–1911
Ball, James Dyer, 1847–1919.
The Chinese at home: or, The man of Tong and his land.
New York: Revell, 1911. 12, 370 p.
Subj 10 17 41 43 55 60 ▪ 12 12.2 14.2 16 23 31 56 62

10003 NNC O P2 G1.2 1842–1911
Ball, James Dyer, 1847–1919.
Things Chinese: or, Notes connected with China, 5th ed., rev., edited by Edward Theodore Chalmers Werner.
Shanghai: Kelly and Walsh, 1925. 766 p. [Reprinted—London: Murray, 1926. 766 p.] [Reprinted—Detroit: Tower Books, 1971. 766 p.]
Subj 10 14 40 55 60 62 ▪ 12.2 14.6 17 29 31 32.2 51 52 56 57

10004 CBU PO P2 G1.1 –1911
Bard, Emile.
Les Chinois chez eux (The Chinese at home), 3rd ed.
Paris: Armand Colin, 1901. 360 p.
Chinese life in town and country. Tr. by Hannah Twitchell. [Rev. in tr.]
New York: Putnam, 1905. 12, 285 p.
Subj 10 11.3 14 16 48 62 ▪ 12 12.2 15 17 18 21.3 22.2 43 47 66

10005 CBU O P2 G1.2 1644–1842
Barrow, John, 1764–1848.
Travels in China: Containing descriptions, observations, and comparisons, made and collected in the course of a short residence at the imperial palace of Yuen-min-yuan [Yüan-ming-yüan, Peking], *and on a subsequent journey through the country from Peking to Canton*, 2nd ed.
London: T. Cadell and W. Davies, 1806. 632 p. [Reprinted—Taipei: Ch'eng-wen, 1972. 632 p.]
Subj 10 12 14.2 47 55 60 ▪ 11 12.1 15 16.1 16.2 46 56 66

10006 DLC S P2 G1.3 1644–1911
Berezin, Nikolai Il'ich, 1866–?
'Kitai' (China). In *Narody zemli* (Peoples of the world), edited by Aleksandr IAkovlevich Ostrogorskii. [Sole entry]
St. Petersburg: Obshchestvennaia pol'za, 1903, vol. 1, 171–220.
Subj 10 24.4 40 43 60 66 ▪ 11.3 12 16.2 16.3 17 22.2 47 50 55 61

10007 NNC O P2 G1.2 –1842
[Bichurin, Nikita Iakovlevich] *Otets* Iakinf, 1777–1853.
Kitai, ego zhiteli, nravy, obychai, prosveshchenie: sochinenie monakha Iakinfa (China, its inhabitants, morals, customs, and education: The works of the monk Iakinf).
St. Petersburg: Tip. imp. Akad. nauk, 1840. 442 p.
Subj 10 14 55 60 ▪ 12 12.2 14.3 15 16.1 17 18 41 57

10008 MCH S P2 G1.1 –1842
[Bichurin, Nikita Iakovlevich] *Otets* Iakinf, 1777–1853.
Statisticheskoe opisanie kitaiskoi imperii (Statistical description of the Chinese empire).
St. Petersburg: Tip. Eduarda Pratsa, 1842. 2 vols. [Reprinted—Peking: Tip. Uspenskago monastyria pri RDM, 1910. 2 vols.]
Subj 10 12 12.2 14 15 17 ▪ 11 13 14.2 14.5

10009 DLC P P2 G1.2 1895–1911
Bogdanovich, Tat'iana.
'Kitai i kitaitsy' (China and the Chinese).
Mir Bozhii 9, 9 (1900), 251–290; 9, 10 (1900), 183–221; 9, 11 (1900), 219–258.
Subj 10 66 ▪ 32.2 41 43 47

10010 CSU P P2 G1.1 –1911
Brinkley, Frank.
China: Its history, arts and literature, Vols. 10–12.
Boston: J. B. Millet, 1902. 273; 285; 292 p.
Subj 10 12 14 60 62 66 ▪ 11 14.2 14.5 15 16 17 25 32.2 33 43

10011 MCH O P2 G1.2 1895–1911
Colquhoun, Archibald Ross, 1848–1914.
The 'overland' to China.
New York: Harper, 1900. 11, 464 p.
Subj 10 12 14.2 20 ▪ 12.1 12.2 14 14.3 14.5 16

10012 GMS P P2 G1.2 –1911
Conrady, August, 1864–1925.
'China' (China). In *Weltgeschichte* (World history), edited by Julius von Pflugk-Harttung. [Sole entry]
Berlin: Ullstein, 1910, vol. 3, 457–567.
Subj 10 12 16 ▪ 13 23 41 47 64 65

10013 NBO O P2 G1.1 1842–1895
Coucheron-Aamot, William, 1868–?
Li Hung-changs fædreland og Østasiens historie efter freden til Shimonoseki (Li Hung-chang's fatherland and the history of East Asia from the peace to Shimonoseki).
Kristiania: Mallingske, 1898. 402 p.
Subj 10 12 15 ▪ 12.1 12.2 14 14.2 14.6 41 47 55

10014 NNC O P2 G1.1 –1895
Courcy, Marie René Roussel de, 1827–1908.
L'Empire du milieu: description géographique, précis historique, institutions sociales, religieuses, politiques, notions sur les sciences, les arts, l'industrie et le commerce (The Middle Kingdom: Geographic description; historical synopsis; social, religious, and political institutions; and a look at advanced learning, the arts, industry, and trade).
Paris: Didier, 1867. 11, 692 p.
Subj 10 12 12.2 13 14.1 14.2 ▪ 14.5 16 17 23 31 41 50 55 62 65

10015 MCH O P1 G1.1 –1842
Dapper, Olfert, 1639–1689.
Gedenkwaerdig bedrijf der Nederlandsche Oost-Indische Maatschappye op de kuste en in het keizerrijk van Taising, of Sina (Memorable trade of the Dutch East India Company along the coast and in the empire of Ta Ch'ing, or China).
Amsterdam: Van Meurs, 1670. 504 p.
Subj 10 14.3 ▪ 12 14 14.2 16 55

10016 CBU O P2 G1.1 –1895
Davis, John Francis, 1795–1890.
China: A general description of that empire and its inhabitants . . ., rev. and enl. ed.
London: Murray, 1857. 2 vols. 20, 480; 428 p.
Subj 10 12 14 55 62 66 ▪ 12.2 14.2 14.5 22.2 31 33 41 42 56 57

10017 NNC O P2 G1.1 1842–1911
Denby, Charles, 1830–1904.
China and her people: Being the observations, reminiscences, and conclusions of an American diplomat.
Boston: Page, 1906. 2 vols. 16, 256; 276 p. [Reprinted—Taipei: Ch'eng-wen, 1968. 2 vols. 16, 256; 276 p.]
Subj 10 12 12.2 14 14.3 66 ▪ 14.1 14.2 14.6 16.3 21 41 47 57 60

10018 DLC PO P2 G1.3 1842–1895
Douglas, Robert Kennaway, 1838–1913.
China. [Memorial ed.]
New York: Collier, 1939. 13, 354 p.
Subj 10 12 41 55 56 65 ▪ 14.1 14.2 16.1 17 23 33 53 57

10019 NNC PO P2 G1.2 1842–1895
Douglas, Robert Kennaway, 1838–1913.
Society in China, rev. and enl. ed.
London: Innes, 1894. 12, 434 p.
Subj 10 12 12.2 16 22 66 ▪ 13 14.3 22.2 34.3 41 47 51 55 56 57

10020 NNC PO P2 G1.2 –1842
Escayrac de Lauture, Pierre-Henri Stanislas d', 1826–1868.
Mémoires sur la Chine (Reports on China).
Paris: Lib. du Magasin pittoresque, 1865. 5 vols. 528 p. [s.p.].
Subj 10 12 15 17 40 60 ▪ 12.2 13 14.2 14.5 23 29 43 57 64 66

10021 NIC O P2 G1.3 1842–1895
Forbes, Frederick Edwyn.
Five years in China, from 1842–1847.
London: Bentley, 1848. 405 p. [Reprinted—Taipei: Ch'eng-wen, 1972. 405 p.]
Subj 10 20 ▪ 12 14 17 22 55

10022 MCH O P2 G1.1 1644–1842
[Forgues, Emile Daurand] Old Nick, pseud., 1813–1883.
La Chine ouverte: aventures d'un Fan-Kouei dans le pays de Tsin (China opened: Adventures of a 'foreign devil' in the land of the Ch'ing).
Paris: Fournier, 1845. 396 p.
Subj 10 12 14.3 16.1 17 60 ▪ 13 15 22.2 23 24.4

10023 MCH O P2 G1.2 1842–1895
Giles, Herbert Allen, 1845–1935.
Chinese sketches.
London: Trübner, 1876. 204 p.
Subj 10 12.2 14.6 16.1 65 ▪ 22.2 34.3 47 56 63

10024 NNC O P2 G1.1 1842–1895
Gordon-Cumming, Constance Frederica, 1837–1924.
Wanderings in China.
Edinburgh: Blackwood, 1900. 528 p.
Subj 10 43 47 55 57 64 ▪ 13 16 17 18 31 34.3 41 51 56 60

10025 CSH O P2 G1.1 1842–1895
Graves, Roswell Hobart, 1833–1912.
Forty years in China: or, China in transition.
Baltimore: R. H. Woodward, 1895. 316 p.
Subj 10 17 22.2 31 55 60 ▪ 12.2 15 33 47 56 63 66

10026 CBU O P2 G1.1 –1842
[Gützlaff, Karl Friedrich August] Charles Gutzlaff, 1803–1851.
China opened: or, A display of the topography, history, customs, manners, arts, manufactures, commerce, literature, religion, jurisprudence, etc. of the Chinese empire, edited by Andrew Reed.
London: Smith, Elder, 1838. 2 vols. 16, 510; 570 p.
Subj 10 12 14.1 14.3 14.4 ▪ 11 13 29 31 41 48 55 60

10027 NNC O P2 G1.3 1644–1842
Guignes, Chrétien Louis Joseph de, 1759–1845.
Voyages à Pékin, Manille, et l'Ile de France, faits dans l'intervalle des années 1784 à 1801 (Journeys to Peking, Manila, and Mauritius from 1784 to 1801).
Paris: Impr. impériale, 1808. 4 vols. 63, 439; 476; 488; 97 p.
Subj 10 15 20 40 60 64 ▪ 12 13 14 16 17 21.3 29 55 57 66

10028 NNC PO P2 G1.5 –1911
Hémon, Félix Louis-Prosper, 1875–1902, et al.
Sur le Yang-tse: journal d'une double exploration pendant la campagne de Chine, 1900–1901 (On the Yangtze: Diary of a dual-purpose expedition during the campaign in China, 1900–1901).
Paris: Ch. Delagrave, 1904. 15, 346 p.
Subj 10 14.2 55 60 66 ▪ 23 29 33 40 50

10029 MCH PO P2 G1.2 –1895
Henningsen, Jakob, 1849–1913.
Det himmelske rige: Skitser fra Kina (The Celestial Kingdom: Sketches from China).
Copenhagen: Høst, 1887. 273 p.
Subj 10 12 13 17 50 53 ▪ 12.2 14.2 15 18 43 47 52 56 57 64

10030 NNC O P2 G1.2 1842–1895
Holcombe, Chester, 1844–1912.
The real Chinaman.
New York: Dodd, Mead, 1895. 20, 350 p.
Subj 10 12 17 41 60 ▪ 12.1 12.2 13 14 16 31 43 47

10031 FPN O P2 G1.5 1842–1895
Huc, Evariste-Régis, 1813–1860.
L'empire chinois, faisant suite à l'ouvrage intitulé 'Souvenirs d'un voyage dans la Tartarie et le Thibet'.
Paris: Gaume Frères, 1853, 1854. 2 vols. n.p. [Reprinted as *Souvenirs d'un voyage dans la Chine* (Recollections of a journey through China). Paris: Club des libraires de France, 1960. 484 p. (CLF, Découverte de la terre, 22)]

A journey through the Chinese empire.
New York: Harper, 1855. 2 vols. 26, 421; 422 p. [Also published as *The Chinese Empire: Forming a sequel to the work entitled 'Recollections of a journey through Tartary and Thibet'*. London: Longman, Brown, Green, and Longmans, 1855. 2 vols. 32, 421; 440 p.] [Reprinted as *The Chinese empire: Forming a sequel to the work entitled 'Recollections of a journey through Tartary and Thibet'*. Port Washington, N.Y.: Kennikat Press, 1971. 2 vols. 32, 421; 440 p.]
Subj 10 12 16.1 33 56 62 ▪ 12.2 13 14 17 22.2 24.4 47 55 57 64

10032 ELB O P2 G1.1 –1842
Kao, Dionyzius.
'Korte beschryving van 't magtig keizerryk China.' In *Driejaarige reize naar China, te lande gedaan, door den Moskovischen Afgezant, E. Ysbrants Ides* (A three-year overland journey to China by the ambassador from Moscow, Evert Ysbrants Ides), by Evert Ysbrants Ides. [Analytic entry]
Amsterdam: François Halma, 1704, 139–243. [For Ides's work, see entry 10580.] [Reprinted in *Driejaarige reize naar China, te lande gedaan, door den Moskovischen Afgezant, E. Ysbrants Ides*, by E. Y. Ides. (Analytic entry.) Amsterdam: Pieter de Coup, 1710, 141–243.]

'A short description of the vast empire of China.' In *Three years of travel from Muscovy overland to China*, by E. Y. Ides. [Selective entry]
London: Freeman, 1706, 115–210.
Subj 10 21.1 29 55 ▪ 13 15 24.1 25 32.2 41 48 57 66

10033 DLC O P2 G1.2 1644–1842
Karnilov, ———.
'Vzgliad na Kitai' (A look at China).
Syn otechestva 1 (1835), 39–59.
Subj 10 12 14 14.5 16 17 ▪ 14.1 14.3 24.4 32.1 63 64

10034 MCH S P2 G1.1 1842–1895
Korostovets, Ivan IAkovlevich.
Kitaitsy i ikh tsivilizatsiia (The Chinese and their civilization).
St. Petersburg: M. M. Lederle, 1896. 625 p. [Reprinted—St. Petersburg: N. Aksarkhanov, 1898. 625 p.]
Subj 10 66 ▪ 12 12.2 14.4 14.5 16 17 33 40 55 64

10035 NNC O P2 G1.2 1842–1895
Kovalevskii, Egor Petrovich, 1811–1868.
Puteshestvie v Kitai (A journey to China).
St. Petersburg: Tip. Koroleva, 1853. 2 vols. 199; 213 p.
Subj 10 11 12 12.2 55 ▪ 14.1 14.3 16.3 18 21 21.1 41

10036 NNC O P2 G1.2 –1842
Le Comte, Louis Daniel, 1655–1728.
Nouveaux mémoires sur l'état présent de la Chine (New observations on the present condition of China).
Paris: Anisson, 1696. 2 vols. n.p.

Memoirs and observations made in a late journey through the Empire of China.
London: Benjamin Tooke and Samuel Buckley, 1697. 527 p. [Reprinted as *Memoirs and remarks made in above ten years travels through the Empire of China.* London: Hughs, 1737. 536 p.]
Subj 10 12 55 60 62 66 ▪ 12.2 13 14 16.1 18 24.4 41 47 56 57

10037 CSU U P2 G1.2 –1911
Liu, James T. C. (Liu Tzu-chien), 1919–.
'Integrative factors through Chinese history: Their interaction.' In *Traditional China*, edited by J. T. C. Liu and Wei-ming Tu. [Selective entry]
Englewood Cliffs, N. J.: Prentice-Hall, 1970, 10–23.
Subj 10 12 14 ▪ 16.1 30 40

10038 CSU O P2 G1.3 1842–1911
Macgowan, John, ?–1922.
Men and manners of modern China, rev. and enl. ed.
New York: Dodd, Mead, 1912. 351 p.
Subj 10 14.5 15 41 48 62 ▪ 12 12.2 14.1 14.2 16 16.1 17 31 43 56

10039 NNC O P2 G1.2 –1842
Magalhães, Gabriel de, 1609?–1677.
Nouvelle relation de la Chine, contenant la description des particularitéz les plus considerables de ce grand empire. Tr. from the Portuguese by ——— Bernou. [Tr. from an unpublished manuscript *Doze excellencias da China* (Twelve outstanding features of China), dated 1668]
Paris: Barbin, 1688. 385 p.

A new history of China, containing a description of the most considerable particulars of that vast empire. Tr. by John Ogilby.
London: Newborough, 1688. 352 p.
Subj 10 12 55 ▪ 11.3 12.2 14.2 14.5 16.1 18 21.3 22 64

10040 MCH O P2 G1.4 1895–1911
Mannnerheim, Carl Gustaf Emil, 1867–1951.
Across Asia from west to east in 1906–1908, Vol. 1, edited by Kaarlo Hildén.
Helsinki: ——, 1940. 741 p. (Suomalais-Ugrilainen Seura, Konsatieteellisiä julkaisuja, 8)
Subj 10 ▪ 12 14 15

10041 CSH U P2 G1.2 1842–1895
Marakuev, V- N-.
Nashi aziatskie sosedy, kitaitsy: narodnaia zhizn', vnutrennee ustroistvo strany, zemledelie, torgovlia, uchenie Konfutsiia, Lao-tche (Lao-tszy), buddizm, rol' Kitaia v budushchem, osnovy kitaiskoi morali (Our Asian neighbors, the Chinese: Their life; the internal structure of the country; agriculture; trade; the teachings of Confucius, Lao-tzu, and Buddhism; China's role in the future; and the principles of Chinese morality).
Odessa: Nar. biblioteka V. A. Marakueva, 1896. 190 p.
Subj 10 12 14 16 40 60 ▪ 12.1 13 14.1 14.2 33 41 50 57 62 63

10042 NNC PO P2 G1.1 1644–1895
Martin, Robert Montgomery, 1803?–1868.
China, political, commercial, and social: In an official report to Her Majesty's government.
London: Madden, 1847. 2 vols. 432; 500 p.
Subj 10 12 14 14.3 60 66 ▪ 11 12.2 13 15 16.2 22 41 48 55 56

10043 NNC O P2 G1.2 1842–1911
Martin, William Alexander Parsons, 1827–1916.
The awakening of China.
New York: Doubleday, Page, 1907. 16, 328 p.
Subj 10 12 13 17 32.2 ▪ 16 16.1 22.2 31 62 65 66

10044 NNC O P2 G1.2 1644–1842
Medhurst, Walter Henry, 1796–1857.
China: Its state and prospects, with especial reference to the spread of the Gospel, containing allusions to the antiquity, extent, population, civilization, literature, and religions of the Chinese.
Boston: Crocker and Brewster, 1838. 15, 542 p.
Subj 10 11 12 12.2 13 14 ▪ 15 16 17 33 47 55 56 57 60 66

10045 DLC O P2 G1.1 1644–1842
Milescu, Nicolae (N. G. Spafarii), 1636–1708.
Opisanie pervyia chasti vselennyia imenuemoi Azii, k nei zhe sostoit kitaiskoe gosudarstvo s prochimi ego gorody i provintsii (A description of the first part of inhabited Asia, which includes the Chinese state and its cities and provinces), edited by N- F- Katanov.
Kazan: Tipo-litogr. Imp. un-ta, 1910. 56, 271 p. [Foreword, index, and description of contents in Russian; text in Church Slavic.]
Subj 10 14 14.2 17 55 ▪ 12 14.1 33 41 56 58 62 66

10046 MCH O P2 G1.5 1644–1895
Milne, William Charles, 1815–1863.
Life in China, 2nd ed.
London: Routledge, 1857. 546 p.
Subj 10 18 32.2 33 60 66 ▪ 14.3 15 23 41 43 47 55 56 57 65

10047 NNC O P2 G1.2 1842–1895
Morrison, George Ernest, 1862–1920.
An Australian in China: Being the narrative of a quiet journey across China to British Burma, 2nd ed.
London: Horace Cox, 1895. 12, 299 p. [Reprinted—Taipei: Ch'eng-wen, 1971. 12, 299 p.]
Subj 10 12 12.2 14 14.2 66 ▪ 15 23 38 41 47 51 55 56 57 60

10048 MCH O P2 G1.1 1842–1911
Navarra, Bruno.
China und die Chinesen (China and the Chinese).
Bremen: Max Nössler, 1901. 16, 1112, 72 p.
Subj 10 12 14 62 ▪ 11 12.1 13 15 22 23 34.3 40 55 65

10049 CSU PO P2 G1.2 1842–1895
Nevius, John Livingston, 1829–1893.
China and the Chinese: A general description of the country and its inhabitants . . ., rev. ed.
Philadelphia: Presbyterian Board of Publication and Sabbath-School Work, 1904. 452 p.
Subj 10 12 23 33 60 62 ▪ 14 17 38 41 43 47 55 57 64 66

10050 DLC O P2 G1.3 –1842
Orlov, Ivan.
Noveishee i podrobneishee istoriko-geograficheskoe opisanie Kitaiskoi imperii (An up-to-date, detailed historical and geographic description of the Chinese empire).
Moscow: Univ. tip., 1820. 2 vols. 415; 491 p.
Subj 10 60 ▪ 11.3 12.2 13 15 16 44 55 57

10051 CSU P P2 G1.2 –1842
Pauthier, Jean-Pierre Guillaume, 1801–1873.
'XXIIième dynastie, la dynastie Ts'ing, actuellement régnant' (The twenty-second dynasty, the reigning Ch'ing dynasty). In *Chine: ou, description historique, géographique et littéraire de ce vaste empire, d'après des documents chinois* (China: or, An historical, geographic, and literary description of that vast empire, based on Chinese documents), by J.-P. G. Pauthier. [Sole entry]
Paris: Firmin-Didot, 1837, 426–474.
Subj 10 15 16.1 60 64 ▪ 12.2 66

10052 MCH P P2 G1.1 1842–1895
Putiata, D- V-.
Kitai: ocherk geografii, ekonomicheskogo sostoianiia, administrativnogo i voennogo ustroistva Sredinnoi imperii i voennogo znacheniia pogranichnoi s Rossiei polosy (China: Survey of the geography, economic condition, and administrative and military structure of the Middle Kingdom and the military significance of the Russian border zone).
St. Petersburg: Voennaia tip., 1895. 265, 83 p. [Reprinted as 'Kitai: geograficheskii ocherk, naselenie, gosudarstvennye biudzhet i vneshniaia torgovlia, vooruzhennyia sily, russko-kitaiskaia granitsa' (China: Geographic sketch, population, state budget and foreign trade, armed forces, and the Sino-Russian border). *Sbornik geograficheskikh, topograficheskikh i statisticheskikh materialov po Azii* 59 (1895), 1–151.]
Subj 10 11.3 14.3 15 ▪ 11 13 14.5 17 43

10053 NIC P P2 G1.1 –1911
Reischauer, Edwin Oldfather, 1910–, and John King Fairbank, 1907–.
East Asia: The great tradition.
Boston: Houghton Mifflin, 1960. 13, 739 p. (History of East Asian civilization, Vol. 1)
Subj 10 12 12.1 14 16.1 64 ▪ 11.4 13 14.5 14.6 15 17 32.2 63 66

10054 NIC O P2 G1.3 1895–1911
Ross, Edward Alsworth, 1866–1951.
The changing Chinese: The conflict of Oriental and Western cultures in China.

New York: Century, 1911. 16, 356 p. [Reprinted—Taipei: Ch'eng-wen, 1972. 16, 356 p.]
SUBJ 10 14.4 17 ▪ 14.2 47 61

10055 MCH O P2 G1.2 1895–1911
Rottach, Edmond.
La Chine moderne (Modern China).
Paris: Roger, 1911. 270 p.
SUBJ 10 14 17 18 66 ▪ 12 14.1 14.4 16.1 19 22.2 23 30

10056 MCH O P2 G1.3 1842–1895
Rousset, Léon.
A travers la Chine (Traveling through China), 2nd ed.
Paris: Hachette, 1886. 431 p.
SUBJ 10 12 16.1 22.2 62 66 ▪ 14 15 18 23 33 40 55 65

10057 NIC O P1 G1.4 1842–1911
Smith, Arthur Henderson, 1845–1932.
Chinese characteristics, rev. and enl. ed.
New York: Revell, 1900. 342 p.
SUBJ 10 23 30 61 ▪ 18 40 50

10058 MCH PO P2 G1.1 –1895
Speer, William, 1822–1904.
The oldest and the newest empire: China and the United States.
Pittsburgh: Davis, 1877. 681 p.
SUBJ 10 12 14 55 66 ▪ 11.2 15 17 22 23 31 34.3 62

10059 NNC O P2 G1.2 1842–1895
Taylor, Charles, 1819–?
Five years in China, with some account of the great rebellion, and a description of St. Helena.
Nashville: McFerrin; New York: Derby and Jackson, 1860. 16, 413 p.
SUBJ 10 12.2 22.2 32.2 57 60 ▪ 13 15 17 23 31 38 41 43 55 56

10060 NNC PO P2 G1.1 –1895
Thomson, John C-.
The land and the people of China: A short account of the geography, history, religion, social life, arts, industries, and government of China and its people.
New York: Pott, Young, 1876. 288 p.
SUBJ 10 11 12 14 16 55 ▪ 11.2 12.2 16.2 21.3 25 33 41 51 57 60

10061 CSH O P2 G1.2 1895–1911
Thomson, John Stuart, 1869–1950.
The Chinese.
Indianapolis: Bobbs-Merrill, 1909. 441 p.
SUBJ 10 14 65 ▪ 14.2 15 22.2 24.4 29 47 55 56 57

10062 CSU PO P2 G1.2 1895–1911
Tuzhilin, Aleksandr Vasil'evich.
Sovremennyi Kitai (Contemporary China).
St. Petersburg: Imp. uch-shche glukhonemykh, 1910. 2 vols. 12, 427; 341 p.
SUBJ 10 11.3 12 14 17 60 ▪ 21.3 22 32.1 33 41 50 52 55 57 72

10063 CSU O P2 G1.2 1895–1911
Webster, Harrie.
'China and her people: Some reflections on their manners and customs, habits, and lives.'
NG 11, 8 (Aug. 1900), 309–319.
SUBJ 10 14 16.3 ▪ 17 60

10064 CBU O P2 G1.4 1842–1895
Williamson, Alexander, 1829–1890.
Journeys in North China, Manchuria, and eastern Mongolia, with some account of Corea.
London: Smith, Elder, 1870. 2 vols. 17, 444; 442 p.
SUBJ 10 14 14.2 20 60 ▪ 12 17 21 22 23 29 33 56 61 66

10065 NIC O P2 G1.2 1842–1911
Wilson, James Harrison, 1837–1925.
China: Travels and investigations in the 'Middle Kingdom', a study of its civilization and possibilities, together with an account of the Boxer war, the relief of the legations, and the re-establishment of peace, 3rd ed., rev. and enl.
New York: Appleton, 1906. 37, 429 p.
SUBJ 10 14 32.2 66 ▪ 11 12 14.2 14.5 14.6 16.1 17 18

10066 NNC S P2 G1.4 –1911
Wittfogel, Karl August, 1896–.
'Die Theorie der orientalischen Gesellschaft' (The theory of Oriental society).
Z. für Sozialforschung 7, 1/2 (1938), 90–122.
SUBJ 10 12 14.1 ▪ 12.1 14.4 16.1 16.3

1644-1949

10067 CSH O P2 G1.2 1644–1928
Baker, John Earl, 1880–1957.
Explaining China.
London: A. M. Philpot, 1927. 18, 312 p.
SUBJ 10 12 14.2 15 32.2 66 ▪ 12.2 14.4 16.1 16.2 18 34.2 37 40 63 64

10068 CSU S P2 G1.2 –1928
Bashford, James Whitford, 1849–1919.
China: An interpretation.
New York: Abingdon Press, 1916. 630 p. [Reprinted—Ann Arbor: University Microfilms, n.d. 630 p.]
SUBJ 10 14 17 62 ▪ 11 12 12.2 14.1 14.3 32.2 34.3 47 59 66

10069 NBO O P2 G1.2 1895–1928
Bugge, Sten, 1885–.
Kina og den hvite fare (China and the white danger).
Kristiania: Norli, 1923. 207 p.
SUBJ 10 13 64 66 ▪ 14.3 17 23 34.2 34.3 41 43 47 52

10070 WSU P P2 G1.1 1842–1949
Cheng, Ch'eng-k'un, 1906–.
China, a folk society in transition.
Unpublished doctoral dissertation in Sociology, U. of Washington, 1946. 218 p.
SUBJ 10 14 19 40 64 ▪ 12 12.1 12.2 41 43 47 61 62

10071 GBT O P2 G1.2 1644–1928
Eichhorn, Werner, 1899–.
China: Gestern, heute, morgen (China: Yesterday, today, and tomorrow).
Leipzig: Hesse und Becker, 1929. 215 p.
SUBJ 10 19 41 ▪ 22.2 23 25 32.2 55 56 61 65

10072 MCH S P2 G1.2 –1928
Gowen, Herbert Henry, 1864–?, and Josef Washington Hall, 1894–.
An outline history of China, with a thorough account of the Republican era interpreted in its historical perspective.
New York: Appleton, 1926. 28, 542 p.
SUBJ 10 12 12.1 ▪ 12.2 14 15 16 19

10073 WSU U P2 G1.1 1644–1928
Kharnskii, Konstantin Andreevich.
'Chast' vtoraia' (Part two). In *Kitai s drevneishikh vremen do nashikh dnei* (China from ancient times to our day), by K. A. Kharnskii. [Sole entry]
Khabarovsk: Knizhnoe delo, 1927, 247–440.
SUBJ 10 12 14 15 19 32.2 ▪ 11 16.1 34.3 39 64 66

10074 MCY P P2 G1.1 –1949
Kiang Kang-hu (Chiang K'ang-hu), 1883–1946.
On Chinese studies.
Shanghai: Commercial Press, 1934. 403 p.
SUBJ 10 14.1 16.1 17 40 ▪ 14 34.2 62 64 66

10075 CSU U P2 G1.1 –1928
Kulp, Daniel Harrison, II, 1888–.
'Chinese continuity.'
AAAPSS 152 (Nov. 1930), 18–29. [Special issue: *China*, edited by Henry F- James]
SUBJ 10 60 ▪ 29

10076 DLC S P2 G1.1 –1928
Mamaev, I-, and Vsevolod Sergeevich Kolokolov.
Kitai: strana, naselenie i istoriia (China: The country, its population, and its history), edited by A- A- Iordanskii.
Moscow: Voengiz, 1924. 266 p.
SUBJ 10 11 14 16.4 66 ▪ 12 15 18 32 32.2 65

10077 MCH O P2 G1.1 –1928
Monroe, Paul, 1869–1947.
China, a nation in evolution.
Chautauqua, N.Y.: Chautauqua Press, 1927. 15, 447 p. [Reprinted—New York: Macmillan, 1928. 15, 447 p.]
SUBJ 10 62 ▪ 12 14 15 16.4 17 18 24.4 66

10078 CSU S P2 G1.2 1644–1949
Moore, Barrington, Jr., 1913–.
'The decay of Imperial China and the origins of the Communist variant.' In *Social origins of dictatorship and democracy: Lord and peasant in the making of the modern world*, by B. Moore, Jr. [Sole entry]
Boston: Beacon Press, 1966, 162–227.
SUBJ 10 12.1 14.1 16.1 16.3 36.3 ▪ 12 14.3 14.5 15 22.2 25 32 32.2 42 45

10079 NNC PO P2 G1.2 –1949
T'ang, Leang-li (T'ang Liang-li), 1901–.
The new social order in China.
Shanghai: China United Press, 1936. 11, 282 p. (China today series, 6)
SUBJ 10 12 18 19 32.2 60 ▪ 12.2 14 15 16 17 36.4 41 47 64 66

10080 NNC U P2 G1.2 1842–1949
Tao, L. K. (T'ao Meng-ho), 1887–1960.
'Social changes.' In *Symposium on Chinese culture*, edited by Sophia H. Chen Zen (Jen Ch'en Heng-che). [Selective entry]
Shanghai: China Institute of Pacific Relations, 1931, 293–304. [Reprinted in *Symposium on Chinese culture*, edited

by S. H. C. Zen. (Selective entry.) New York: Paragon, 1969, 293–304.]
Subj 10 66 ▪ 14 16 40 63

10081 NNC PO P2 G1.2 1895–1928
Tyau, Min-ch'ien T. Z. (Tiao Min-ch'ien), 1888–.
China awakened.
New York: Macmillan, 1922. 16, 475 p.
Subj 10 14.2 17 66 ▪ 12 12.2 14.4 16.4 30 33 41 47 54

10082 NNC PO P2 G1.1 –1928
Werner, Edward Theodore Chalmers, 1864–1954.
China of the Chinese.
New York: Scribner, 1919. 15, 309 p.
Subj 10 12 13 15 41 60 ▪ 12.2 16 22 31 43 45 48 50 55 57

10083 NNC PO P2 G1.2 –1949
Williams, Edward Thomas, 1854–1944.
China yesterday and today, 5th ed., rev.
London: Harrap, 1933. 24, 743 p.
Subj 10 19 20 33 60 ▪ 12 12.2 14 14.1 14.3 16.3 22 23 31 34.3

10084 CSU PO P2 G1.2 –1928
Williams, Edward Thomas, 1854–1944.
'Chinese social institutions as a foundation for republican government.'
Annual report of the American Historical Assn. 1916, 1, 419–443.
Subj 10 12.2 22 30 40 ▪ 16.3 17 34.3 36.2 39 41 42 45 52

10085 CSU PO P2 G1.1 1895–1928
Woodhead, Henry George Wandesforde, 1883–1959.
The truth about the Chinese Republic.
London: Hurst and Blackett, 1925. 287 p.
Subj 10 12 15 32.2 66 ▪ 12.2 14.1 14.2 14.5 16.2 16.4 54

10086 HHU PO P2 G1.2 –1949
Yang, Martin M. C. (Yang Mou-ch'un), 1904–.
Chinese social structure: A historical study.
Taipei: Eurasia, 1969. 412 p.
Subj 10 16 20 30 40 60 ▪ 11.3 24.2 27 32.2 34.3 36.4 39 41 42 44

1911-1949

10087 MCH O P2 G1.3 1911–1949
Arnol'dov, L- V-.
Iz strany belogo solntsa: etiudy o Kitae (From the land of the white sun: Studies on China).
Shanghai: Knigoizd-vo A. P. Malyk i V. P. Kamkina, 1934. 438 p.
Subj 10 12.1 33 64 ▪ 19 23 60 66

10088 MCH O P2 G1.2 1911–1949
Arnol'dov, L- V-.
Kitai, kak on est'. Byt i politika: nabliudeniia, fakty, vyvody (China as it is: Observations, facts, and conclusions on Chinese life and politics).
Shanghai: 'Grafik', 1933. 370 p.
Subj 10 12 16.2 16.3 47 64 ▪ 14.1 23 34.1 41 43 60

10089 MCH O P2 G1.2 1911–1928
Goodnow, Frank Johnson, 1859–1939.
China: An analysis.
Baltimore: Johns Hopkins Press, 1926. 279 p.
Subj 10 12 14.1 16 ▪ 18 33 40 41 64

10090 MCH O P2 G1.2 1911–1949
Gould, Randall.
China in the sun.
Garden City, N.Y.: Doubleday, 1946. 403 p.
Subj 10 12 ▪ 14 32 32.2

10091 CSU O P2 G1.3 1911–1928
High, Stanley Hoflund, 1895–1961.
China's place in the sun.
New York: Macmillan, 1922. 29, 212 p.
Subj 10 16 61 66 ▪ 14.3 14.4 15 16.4 17 36.2 37 47 54 55

10092 MCH O P2 G1.2 1928–1949
Hsiao Ch'ien, 1911–.
China but not Cathay.
London: Pilot Press, 1942. 135 p.
Subj 10 14 15 17 47 ▪ 12 38

10093 MCH O P2 G1.1 1911–1949
Hsu, Francis L. K. (Hsü Lang-kuang), 1909–.
'China.' In *Most of the world*, edited by Ralph Linton. [Sole entry]
New York: Columbia U. Press, 1949, 731–813.
Subj 10 17 40 62 ▪ 11 12.1 14.1 14.4 22.1 64

10094 MCH O P2 G1.2 1911–1928
Legendre, Aimé François, 1867–?
La civilisation chinoise moderne.
Paris: Payot, 1926. 298 p.

Modern Chinese civilization. Tr. by Elsie Martin.
New York: Cape and Smith, 1929. 295 p. [Reprinted—Taipei: Ch'eng-wen, 1971. 295 p.]
Subj 10 14 18 55 60 ▪ 16 16.1 17 24.4 40 54 61 63

10095 NNC O P1 G1.2 1928–1949
Li An-che.
'China: A fundamental approach.'
PA 21, 1 (Mar. 1948), 58–63.
Subj 10 70

10096 MCY O P2 G1.1 1928–1949
Peck, Graham, 1914–.
Two kinds of time.
Boston: Houghton Mifflin, 1950. 725 p.
Subj 10 12.1 16.3 24.4 65 66 ▪ 15 16.1 18 22.2 25 32 32.2 61

10097 CSU O P2 G1.2 1911–1949
Peffer, Nathaniel, 1890–1964.
China: The collapse of a civilization.
New York: Day, 1930. 306 p.
Subj 10 14 16 66 ▪ 12 17 34.3 41

10098 NNC O P2 G1.2 1928–1949
Purcell, Victor William Williams Saunders, 1896–1965.
Chinese evergreen.
London: Michael Joseph, 1938. 286 p.
Subj 10 12 14.2 17 55 66 ▪ 23 29 31 41 48 57 60

10099 MCH O P2 G1.2 1911–1928
Russell, Bertrand Russell, 1872–1970.
The problem of China.
New York: Century, 1922. 276 p.
Subj 10 60 66 ▪ 11 12 14 17

10100 MCH O P2 G1.1 1928–1949
Snow, Edgar, 1905–1972.
Journey to the beginning.
New York: Random House, 1958. 434 p.
Subj 10 32.2 59 66 ▪ 12 15 18 22.2 25 38 54 64

10101 NNC O P2 G1.2 1928–1949
Snow, Edgar, 1905–1972.
Scorched earth.
London: Gollancz, 1941. 2 vols. 188; 386 p.
Subj 10 12 14.4 15 36.4 ▪ 14 14.2 16 17 18 22 24.4 25 32

10102 MCH O P2 G1.3 1911–1949
Townsend, Ralph, 1900–.
Ways that are dark: The truth about China.
New York: Putnam, 1933. 14, 336 p.
Subj 10 17 18 61 63 ▪ 14.3 55 66

10103 MCY PO P2 G1.2 1928–1949
Tyau, Min-ch'ien T. Z. (Tiao Min-ch'ien), 1888–.
Two years of Nationalist China.
Shanghai: Kelly and Walsh, 1930. 523 p.
Subj 10 12 14 15 17 32 ▪ 11 14.4 16.4 22 32.1 32.2 34.2 36.1 36.4 66

10104 NNC O P2 G1.2 1911–1949
Van Dorn, Harold Archer, 1896–.
Twenty years of the Chinese Republic: Two decades of progress.
New York: Knopf, 1932. 14, 309 p.
Subj 10 12 14 17 19 33 ▪ 12.2 18 22.2 31 32.2 38 40 47 56 66

10105 MCH FP P2 G1.2 1928–1949
Winfield, Gerald Freeman, 1908–.
China: The land and the people, rev. ed.
New York: William Sloane Associates, 1950. 431 p.
Subj 10 14 17 55 56 60 ▪ 12 14.1 14.4 15 18 37 51 62 63 64

10106 CSU P P2 G1.1 1911–1928
Woodhead, Henry George Wandesforde, 1883–1959, ed. [H- T- Montague was coeditor of issues for 1912–1921/22.]
The China year book, 1912–1928. [Issues for 1929/30 and 1931–1939 are entered as 10107 and 10108.]
London: Routledge; Tientsin: Tientsin Press. Issued annually, 1912–1929. Average ca. 900 p.
Subj 10 14 14.2 15 32 56 ▪ 11 12 12.2 17 25 33 36.4 55 59 66

10107 CSU P P2 G1.1 1911–1949
Woodhead, Henry George Wandesforde, 1883–1959, ed.
The China year book, 1929/30. [Issues for 1912–1928 and 1931–1939 are entered as 10106 and 10108.]
Tientsin: Tientsin Press, 1929. 23, 1266 p.
Subj 10 14 14.2 15 32 56 ▪ 11 12 12.2 17 25 33 36.4 55 59 66

10108 CSU P P2 G1.1 1928–1949
Woodhead, Henry George Wandesforde, 1883–1959, ed.
The China year book, 1931–1939. [Issues for 1912–1928 and 1929/30 are entered as 10106 and 10107.]
Shanghai: North-China Daily News and Herald. Issued annually, 1931–1939. Average ca. 700 p.
Subj 10 14 14.2 15 33 56 ▪ 11 12 12.2 17 25 32 36.4 38 59 66

1911-1972
(including 1644-1972)

10109 NNC U P1 G1.2 –1972
Balazs, Etienne, 1905–1963.
'Chine historique et Chine nouvelle: continuité et rupture' (Traditional China and modern China: Continuity and discontinuity). In *Aspects de la Chine, vol. 3, époque contemporaine* (Aspects of China, Vol. 3, The modern era), by E. Balazs et al. [Selective entry]
Paris: Presses universitaires, 1962, 636–641.
Subj 10 ▪ 19

10110 NNC PO P2 G1.2 –1972
Cheng, Ch'eng-k'un, 1906–.
The dragon sheds its scales.
New York: New Voices, 1952. 192 p.
Subj 10 40 53 60 66 ▪ 12 13 14 17 22.2 23 56 57

10111 CSU S P2 G1.1 –1972
Eberhard, Wolfram, 1909–.
A history of China, 3rd ed., rev. and enl.
Berkeley, Los Angeles: U. of California Press, 1969. 15, 367 p.
Subj 10 12 14 15 32.2 66 ▪ 11.2 14.3 16.1 33 34.2 64

10112 CSU S P2 G1.2 –1972
Fairbank, John King, 1907–.
New views of China's tradition and modernization.
Washington, D.C.: American Historical Assn., 1968. 59 p.
Subj 10 19 72 ▪ 12 12.1 16.1 32.2 60

10113 NNC U P2 G1.1 –1972
Fairbank, John King, 1907–.
The United States and China, 3rd ed., rev. and enl.
Cambridge: Harvard U. Press, 1971. 16, 500 p.
Subj 10 12 14 16 19 64 ▪ 11 12.1 12.2 13 15 22 32.2 41 62 72

10114 MCH P P2 G1.1 1644–1972
Fairbank, John King, 1907–, Edwin Oldfather Reischauer, 1910–, and Albert Morton Craig, 1927–.
East Asia: The modern transformation.
Boston: Houghton Mifflin, 1965. 16, 955 p. (History of East Asian civilization, Vol. 2)
Subj 10 12 14 14.5 32.2 66 ▪ 12.1 15 16.1 17 22.2 25 36.4 64

10115 MCH O P2 G1.2 1928–1972
Fares, Raimundo, 1922–.
Un inmenso convento sin Dios (A huge convent without God).
Buenos Aires: Ediciones Matepha, 1964. 382 p.
Subj 10 12.1 14.1 14.4 64 ▪ 12 14 16 18 41 47 62

10116 ELB S P1 G1.3 –1972
Frodsham, J- D-.
'Feudalism in China: The comparative approach.'
J. of the Historical Society of the U. of Malaya 2, 1 (1963/64), 88–99.
Subj 10 64 ▪ 71

10117 CSU PO P2 G1.1 –1972
Hsu, Francis L. K. (Hsü Lang-kuang), 1909–.
Americans and Chinese: Purpose and fulfillment in great civilizations, rev. ed.
Garden City, N.Y.: Natural History Press, 1970. 28, 493 p.
Subj 10 16 40 50 60 62 ▪ 22.2 26.1 30 34.2 41 46 47 52 54 55

10118 MCH O P2 G1.1 1911–1972
Keim, Jean Alphonse, 1904–.
Panorama de la Chine (Panorama of China).
Paris: Hachette, 1951. 269 p.
Subj 10 21.3 50 60 ▪ 11.3 14 16.3 31

10119 CSU S P2 G1.1 –1972
Kolb, Albert, 1906–.
'China: The cradle of East Asian culture.' Tr. from the German by C- A- M- Sym. In *East Asia: China, Japan, Korea, Vietnam. Geography of a cultural region*, by A. Kolb. [Selective entry]
London: Methuen, 1971, 25–91. [Rev. ed. of *Ostasien: China, Japan, Korea. Geographie eines Kulturerdteils.* Heidelberg: Quelle und Meyer, 1963.]
Subj 10 11.2 ▪ 11.3 14 16 32 32.2 64

10120 CSH S P2 G1.2 –1972
Latourette, Kenneth Scott, 1884–1968.
The Chinese: Their history and culture, 4th ed., rev.
New York: Macmillan, 1964. 12, 714 p.
Subj 10 12 13 14 32.2 60 ▪ 11 14.1 14.4 15 16 17 31 33 41 47

10121 CSU O P2 G1.2 1928–1972
Lattimore, Owen, 1900–.
History and revolution in China.
Copenhagen: Scandinavian Institute of Asian Studies, 1970. 46 p. (SIAS monographs, 3)
Subj 10 32.2 ▪ 16.3 17 19

10122 CSU S P2 G1.2 1928–1972
Lewis, John Wilson, 1930–.
'Order and modernization in the Chinese city.' In *The city in Communist China*, edited by J. W. Lewis. [Analytic entry]
Stanford: Stanford U. Press, 1971, 1–26.
Subj 10 12 12.1 ▪ 11.1 12.2 14 16.1 16.4 18 64

10123 DLC O P2 G1.2 1928–1972
Neuman, Alois.
Čína a jeji lid (China and its people).
Prague: Orbis, 1954. 330 p.
Subj 10 14 50 ▪ 15 17 25 29 30 47 64

10124 CSU S P2 G1.2 –1972
Pye, Lucian Wilmot, 1921–.
China: An introduction.
Boston: Little, Brown, 1972. 384 p.
Subj 10 16.1 19 32 32.2 64 ▪ 12 13 14 14.1 15 16.3 17 59 60 66

10125 NIC P P2 G1.2 1911–1972
Rostow, Walt Whitman, 1916–.
The prospects for Communist China.
Cambridge: M.I.T. Press; New York: Wiley, 1954. 20, 379 p.
Subj 10 12 14 16 19 64 ▪ 12.1 14.1 14.4 14.5 15 30 32 34.1 60

10126 NNC O P2 G1.2 1928–1972
Snow, Edgar, 1905–1972.
Red China today: The other side of the river, rev. ed.
New York: Random House, 1970. 749 p.
Subj 10 14.1 14.4 15 17 18 ▪ 12 12.1 12.2 13 32 32.2 34.1 41 56 60

10127 CSH U P2 G1.2 –1972
Tao Hsi-sheng (T'ao Hsi-sheng), 1899–.
'Chinese cultural continuity through social changes.' In *Collected documents of the First Sino-American Conference on Mainland China*. [Selective entry]
[Taipei]: Institute of International Relations, Republic of China, 1971, 75–84.
Subj 10 64 ▪ 14 30

10128 CSU O P2 G1.2 1895–1972
White, Theodore Harold, 1915–.
China: The roots of madness.
New York: Norton, 1968. 160 p.
Subj 10 15 66 ▪ 32 32.2 59 64

10129 CSU S P2 G1.1 –1972
Whiting, Kenneth Randolph, 1913–.
Background information on Mainland China.
Maxwell Air Force Base, Ala.: Air U., Aerospace Studies Institute, Documentary Research Division, 1970. 90 p.
Subj 10 12 14 32 32.2 ▪ 11 11.3 12.1 14.1 14.2 14.4 60 66

1949-1972

10130 CBU O P2 G1.2 1949–1972
Álvarez del Vayo, Julio, 1891–.
China vence.
Paris: Ruedo Ibérico, 1964. 208 p.

China triumphs. Tr. by William Rose. [Partial tr.: p. 1–171, 186–208 only]
New York: Monthly Review Press, 1964. 202 p.
Subj 10 14.1 17 18 ▪ 21.3 34.1 55 56 66

10131 CSU F P1 G1.2 1949–1972
Barnett, Arthur Doak, 1921–.
'Some generalizations and hypotheses.' In *Cadres, bureaucracy, and political power in Communist China*, by A. D. Barnett. [Analytic entry]
New York: Columbia U. Press, 1967, 425–446.
Subj 10 12.1 30 ▪ 12 16 32

10132 SSK O P2 G1.2 1949–1972
Blomqvist, Lars-Erik, 1942–.
Östern är röd: En kinarapport (The East is red: A report from China).
Stockholm: Geber, 1967. 139 p.
Subj 10 12 14 18 64 ▪ 12.1 12.2 14.1 14.4 14.6 17 19 31 66

10133 NBU O P2 G1.2 1949–1972
Bredsdorff, Elias, 1912–.
Kinas vej: Samtaler og rejseindtryk (China's way: Talks and impressions from a visit).
Copenhagen: Gyldendal, 1957. 365 p.
Subj 10 12 16 ▪ 12.2 14.1 17 19 47 52 55 56 64 66

10134 MCH O P2 G1.2 1949–1972
Calic, Edouard.
La Chine, grande puissance (China, a great power).
Paris: Bonne, 1960. 268 p.
Subj 10 14 16 19 64 66 ▪ 11 12.1 13 15 32 34.1 40

10135 NNC O P2 G1.2 1949–1972
Cameron, James, 1911–.
Mandarin red: A journey behind the 'Bamboo Curtain'.

New York: Rinehart, 1955. 334 p.
Subj 10 48 55 60 66 ▪ 12 12.1 14.2 16.1 16.2 17 18 22.2 29 64

10136 NNC O P2 G1.2 1949–1972
Chandrasekhar, Sripati, 1917–.
Communist China today.
Bombay: Asia Publishing House, 1964. 235 p. [Rev. and enl. ed. of *Red China: An Asian view*. New York: Praeger, 1961. 230 p.]
Subj 10 11 14.4 19 20 50 ▪ 12.1 14.1 16.1 16.3 17 18 32.1 41 47 58

10137 CSH P P2 G1.5 1949–1972
Chang Min-ch'uan (Chang Ming-ch'üan).
'General conditions in the central south area in Communist China.' Tr. of 'Chung kung k'ung chih hsia ti Chung-nan ti ch'ü kai k'uang' (Conditions in South-central China under Chinese Communist rule); *Tsu kuo chou k'an* 444 (10 July 1961), 10–14; 445 (17 July 1961), 11–14. In *Communist China, 1960*, edited by Union Research Institute. [Selective entry]
Hong Kong: Union Research Institute, 1962, vol. 2, 41–75.
Subj 10 14 ▪ 14.1 14.2 17 18 32 34.1

10138 CSH P P2 G1.3 1949–1972
Chu Tso (Chu Cho).
'East China under the Communist rule.' Tr. of 'Chung kung k'ung chih hsia ti Hua-tung ch'ü'; *Tsu kuo chou k'an* 442 (26 June 1961), 10–14; 443 (3 July 1961), 13–17. In *Communist China, 1960*, edited by Union Research Institute. [Selective entry]
Hong Kong: Union Research Institute, 1962, vol. 2, 1–39.
Subj 10 14 ▪ 14.1 14.2 14.5 17 32.1 34.1

10139 CSH P P2 G1.1 1949–1972
Chu, Valentin.
Ta ta, tan tan (fight fight, talk talk): The inside story of Communist China.
New York: Norton, 1963. 320 p.
Subj 10 12.1 14 14.4 18 61 ▪ 12.2 14.1 14.2 16.1 22.2 41 55 56 59 62

10140 NNC O P2 G1.2 1949–1972
Clark, Gerald.
Impatient giant: Red China today.
New York: McKay, 1959. 12, 212 p.
Subj 10 12.1 14 14.1 ▪ 16.2 16.3 32.1 41 47 55 56 64 66

10141 CSH O P2 G1.3 1949–1972
Davidson, Basil, 1914–.
Daybreak in China.
London: Cape, 1953. 191 p.
Subj 10 16 18 41 47 56 ▪ 12.2 14.1 17 24.4 33 36.4 55 64

10142 MCH P P2 G1.2 1949–1972
Doolin, Dennis James, 1933–, and Robert Carver North, 1914–.
The Chinese People's Republic.
Stanford: Hoover Institution on War, Revolution and Peace, 1966. 68 p. (Hoover Institution studies, 14)
Subj 10 14 64 ▪ 11 12 15 66

10143 CSU O P2 G1.2 1949–1972
Dumas, Roland.
J'ai vu vivre la Chine (I saw the living China).
Paris: Fayard, 1960. 269 p.
Subj 10 14 16 ▪ 17 31 34.1 51 53

10144 CSH O P2 G1.1 1949–1972
Duncan, James Stuart, 1893–.
A businessman looks at Red China.
Princeton: Van Nostrand, 1965. 174 p.
Subj 10 12.1 16 18 55 64 ▪ 14.1 14.2 14.4 17 34.1 41 66

10145 NNC O P2 G1.2 1949–1972
Endicott, Mary Austin.
Five stars over China.
Toronto: The author, 1953. 464 p.
Subj 10 16 18 19 33 63 ▪ 14 31 34.1 34.2 36.4 41 47 55 62 66

10146 CSU S P2 G1.2 1949–1972
Fairbank, John King, 1907–.
'Getting to know you.' [Review of *Report from Red China*, by Frank Tillman Durdin, James Barrett Reston, and Seymour Topping; *China nach dem Sturm* (China after the storm), by Klaus Mehnert; and *The revenge of heaven: Journal of a young Chinese*, by Ken Ling, pseud., edited by Ivan Daniel London, Miriam London, and Ta-ling Lee (Li Ta-ling).] [Mehnert book translated as *China returns*.]
NYRB 18, 3 (24 Feb. 1972), 3–7.
Subj 10 54

10147 CSH P P2 G1.2 1949–1972
Far Eastern Economic Review.
'China.' In *Far Eastern economic review yearbook, 1960–1972*, compiled by the organization cited.
Hong Kong: Far Eastern Economic Review. Issued annually, 1960–1972, average ca. 15 p.
Subj 10 14 14.1 14.4 16 32 ▪ 12 12.1 14.2 17 25 35 54 56 58 64

10148 DLC P P2 G1.2 1949–1972
Gluckstein, Ygael.
Mao's China: Economic and political survey.
Boston: Beacon Press, 1957. 438 p.
Subj 10 12.1 14 14.1 14.4 ▪ 12 16.3 16.4

10149 NNC O P2 G1.2 1949–1972
Greene, Felix, 1909–.
Awakened China: The country Americans don't know.
Garden City, N.Y.: Doubleday, 1961. 425 p. [Reprinted as *The wall has two sides: A portrait of China today*. London: Cape, 1962. 432 p.]
Subj 10 12 14 16 18 60 ▪ 17 24.4 31 41 47 53 55 56 66

10150 MCH O P2 G1.2 1949–1972
Guillain, Robert, 1908–.
600 millions de Chinois sous le drapeau rouge (600 million Chinese under the red flag).
Paris: Juillard, 1956. 290 p.

600 million Chinese. Tr. by M- Savill.
New York: Criterion Books, 1957. 310 p.
Subj 10 12.1 14.1 14.4 19 61 ▪ 13 14 16.1 18 32.1 34.1 34.2 55 60 66

10151 NNC S P2 G1.2 1949–1972
Guillermaz, Jacques, 1911–.
'La République populaire, 1949–1960' (The People's Republic of China, 1949–1960). In *Aspects de la Chine, vol. 3, époque contemporaine* (Aspects of China, Vol. 3, The modern era), by Etienne Balazs et al. [Selective entry]
Paris: Presses universitaires, 1962, 531–585.
Subj 10 14 ▪ 12 15 17 32

10152 CBU O P2 G1.2 1949–1972
Hamm, Harry.
Das Reich der 700 Millionen.
Düsseldorf: Econ-Verlag, 1965. 358 p.

China: Empire of the seven hundred million. Tr. by Victor Andersen.
Garden City, N.Y.: Doubleday, 1966. 21, 310 p.
Subj 10 12.1 ▪ 14 17 18 32 34.1 35 41 46 55

10153 CBU O P2 G1.2 1949–1972
Hassner, Rune, 1928–.
Det nya Kina (New China).
Stockholm: Nordisk Rotogravyr, 1957. 190 p.
Subj 10 12 14 64 ▪ 14.1 14.4 16.3 16.4 17 18 41 46 47 66

10154 CSU P P2 G1.2 1949–1972
Hu, C. T. (Hu Ch'ang-tu), 1920–, et al.
China: Its people, its society, its culture, edited by Hsiao Hsia.
New Haven: Human Relations Area Files Press, 1960. 611 p.
Subj 10 14 16 17 18 60 ▪ 11.4 12 12.1 23 29 30 40 55 62 72

10155 MCH P P2 G1.2 1949–1972
Jomin, Henri.
La Chine (China).
Paris: Flammarion, 1961. 218 p.
Subj 10 12 12.1 16 ▪ 11 13 14 15 17 19 33 40 41 64

10156 CBU O P2 G1.2 1949–1972
Källberg, Sture, 1928–.
Kamrat med 700 miljoner (Comrade of seven hundred million), 2nd ed.
Stockholm: Raben och Sjögren, 1971. 203 p.
Subj 10 12 66 ▪ 14.1 14.4 15 17 18 47 51 55

10157 FPN O P2 G1.2 1949–1972
Karol, K- S-.
La Chine de Mao: l'autre communisme (Mao's China: The other Communism).
Paris: Laffont, 1966. 483 p.

China: The other Communism. Tr. by Tom Baistow.
New York: Hill and Wang, 1967. 352 p.
Subj 10 12.1 14.1 ▪ 11.4 14 14.4 15 16 41

10158 GMS O P2 G1.3 1949–1972
Kempski, Hans Ulrich.
Rote Sonne über gelber Erde: Meine Reise durch China und Japan (Red sun over yellow earth: My trip through China and Japan).
Oldenburg: Stalling, 1958. 167 p.
Subj 10 16 ▪ 12.1 12.2 14.1 14.4 15

10159 DLC O P2 G1.2 1949–1972
Kozhin, Aleksei Ivanovich, 1914–.
Shirokie gorizonty: ocherki i rasskazy o liudiakh novogo Kitaia (Broad horizons: Notes and stories about the people of New China).
Moscow: Molodaia gvardiia, 1955. 200 p.
Subj 10 12.1 14 16 17 47 ▪ 14.1 14.4 15 18 23 34.1 36.3 36.4 62 66

10160 MCH O P2 G1.2 1949–1972
Last, Josephus Carel Franciscus, 1898–.
China, land van de eeuwige omwenteling (China, land of continuous revolution).

Meppel, The Netherlands: Boom en Zoon, 1965. 233 p.
SUBJ 10 64 ▪ 12.1 47 60

10161 CSU O P2 G1.3 1949–1972
Lilli, Virgilio.
Dentro la Cina rossa (Inside Red China).
Milan: Mondadori, 1961. 213 p.
SUBJ 10 14 16 20 61 64 ▪ 12.1 14.1 14.2 14.4 16.1 16.3 19 34.1 47

10162 CBU O P2 G1.1 1949–1972
Lindqvist, Sven, 1932–.
Kina inifrån: En preliminär rapport (Inside China: A preliminary report).
Stockholm: Bonnier, 1963. 178 p.
La Chine familière. Tr. by L- Moltke-Huitfeld.
Paris: Plon, 1965. 272 p.
China in crisis. Tr. by Sylvia Clayton.
London: Faber and Faber, 1965. 125 p.
SUBJ 10 12.1 17 18 66 ▪ 11.2 14 14.1 16.1 28 34.1 48 54 55

10163 CSH P P2 G2.0 1949–1972
Liu Szu (Liu Ssu).
'The northeastern provinces under Chinese Communist control.' Tr. of 'Chung kung k'ung chih hsia ti Tung-pei ch'ü' (Manchuria under Chinese Communist rule); *Tsu kuo chou k'an* 451 (28 Aug. 1961), 12–19; 452 (4 Sept. 1961), 14–20. In *Communist China, 1960*, edited by Union Research Institute. [Selective entry]
Hong Kong: Union Research Institute, 1962, vol. 2, 107–164.
SUBJ 10 12 14 14.4 ▪ 14.1 15 17 32 66

10164 CSU O P2 G1.2 1949–1972
Mackerras, Colin Patrick, 1939–, and Neale Hunter.
China observed.
New York: Praeger, 1968. 194 p.
SUBJ 10 17 19 61 ▪ 12.1 13 21.3 32 33 34.1 41 64 66

10165 CSU O P2 G1.2 1949–1972
Marcuse, Jacques.
The Peking papers.
New York: Dutton, 1967. 351 p.
SUBJ 10 12 12.1 66 ▪ 12.2 14.2 16.1 16.2 34.1 41 46 50 64

10166 CSU O P2 G1.2 1949–1972
Mirsky, Jonathan, 1932–.
'China after Nixon.'
AAAPSS 402 (July 1972), 83–96. [Special issue: *China in the world today*, edited by Richard D- Lambert]
SUBJ 10 47 60 ▪ 16 16.1 24.4 26.1 56

10167 MCH O P2 G1.2 1949–1972
Mukherjee, Sailakumar.
A visit to New China.
Calcutta: Mukherjee, 1956. 147 p.
SUBJ 10 12 14 17 ▪ 12.1 12.2 14.1 14.4 16.3 18 19 32.1 34.1

10168 NBU O P2 G1.2 1949–1972
Munthe-Kaas, Harald.
Med mikrofonen i Maos Kina (With the microphone in Mao's China).
Oslo: Aschehoug, 1965. 167 p.
SUBJ 10 12 14 64 ▪ 11 12.1 13 14.1 14.4 17 18 19 51 66

10169 CSU O P2 G1.2 1949–1972
Myrdal, Jan, 1927–.
Chinese journey.
New York: Pantheon, 1965. 160 p.
SUBJ 10 12.1 55 ▪ 14.1 16 32

10170 GMS O P2 G1.3 1949–1972
Schumacher, Ernst.
Lotosblüten und Turbinen: China zwischen gestern und morgen (Lotus blossoms and turbines: China between yesterday and tomorrow).
Berlin: Verlag der Nation; Düsseldorf: Progress, 1958. 514 p.
SUBJ 10 12.1 14.1 16 ▪ 13 14.4 17 32.2 33 64 66

10171 CSH S P2 G1.2 1949–1972
Schurmann, Herbert Franz, 1926–.
'Introduction.' In *Ideology and organization in Communist China*, 2nd ed., enl., by H. F. Schurmann. [Analytic entry]
Berkeley, Los Angeles: U. of California Press, 1968, 1–16.
SUBJ 10 16.1 ▪ 32 35

10172 NIC PO P2 G1.2 1949–1972
Shapiro, Michael.
Changing China.
London: Lawrence and Wishart, 1958. 182 p.
SUBJ 10 14 14.1 16 24.4 34.2 ▪ 14.3 14.4 16.2 16.3 16.4 18 24.3 34.1 58 66

10173 CSU O P2 G1.2 1949–1972
Snow, Edgar, 1905–1972.
The long revolution.
New York: Random House, 1972. 269 p.
SUBJ 10 13 14 20 32 56 ▪ 11 12 12.1 16 18 35 46 51 58 64

10174 MCH O P2 G1.3 1949–1972
Stucki, Lorenz, 1922–.
Land hinter Mauern: China heute (Land behind walls: China today), rev. ed.
Munich, Zurich: Droemer-Knaur, 1967. 154 p.
Behind the Great Wall: An appraisal of Mao's China. Tr. by Jean Steinberg. [Tr. of 1964 ed.]
New York: Praeger, 1965. 154 p.
SUBJ 10 12.1 ▪ 14.1 14.2 16.1 16.4 17 18 31 66

10175 CSU O P2 G1.3 1949–1972
Terrill, Ross, 1938–.
800,000,000: The real China.
Boston: Little, Brown, 1971. 235 p.
SUBJ 10 12.1 17 31 64 66 ▪ 12 24.2 26.3 26.4 28 29 35 36.1 55 62

10176 CSH P P2 G4.0 1949–1972
Wang Hao-chun (Wang Ho-chün).
'General conditions in Northwest China under Chinese Communist rule.' Tr. of 'Chung kung k'ung chih hsia ti Hsi-pei ti ch'ü kai k'uang'; *Tsu kuo chou k'an* 433 (24 Apr. 1961), 11–18. In *Communist China, 1960*, edited by Union Research Institute. [Selective entry]
Hong Kong: Union Research Institute, 1962, vol. 2, 165–198.
SUBJ 10 14 ▪ 12.1 17 18 21 21.2

10177 CSH O P2 G1.1 1949–1972
[Wilson, Richard Garratt] Dick Wilson, 1928–.
Anatomy of China: An introduction to one quarter of mankind, rev. ed.
New York: Weybright and Talley, 1968. 12, 327 p. [Rev. ed. of *A quarter of mankind: An anatomy of China today*. London: Weidenfeld and Nicholson, 1966. 12, 308 p.]
SUBJ 10 14 16 32 ▪ 12.1 14.1 14.4 17 32.1 34.1 41

10178 CSH P P2 G5.0 1949–1972
Wu Jen-tso.
'General conditions in the North China area under the control of the Chinese Communists.' Tr. of 'Chung kung k'ung chih hsia ti Hua-pei ti ch'ü kai k'uang'; *Tsu kuo chou k'an* 434 (1 May 1961), 9–16. In *Communist China, 1960*, edited by Union Research Institute. [Selective entry]
Hong Kong: Union Research Institute, 1962, vol. 2, 77–106.
SUBJ 10 12 14 ▪ 14.1 14.4 17 18 32.1

10179 CSH P P2 G8.0 1949–1972
Yi Hsiao-hua (I Hsiao-hua).
'General conditions in Communist-controlled Southwest China.' Tr. of 'Chung kung k'ung chih hsia ti Hsi-nan ti ch'ü kai k'uang'; *Tsu kuo chou k'an* 435 (8 May 1961), 10–16. In *Communist China, 1960*, edited by Union Research Institute. [Selective entry]
Hong Kong: Union Research Institute, 1962, vol. 2, 199–229.
SUBJ 10 12 14 66 ▪ 12.1 17 18 21 34.1

10180 CSU O P2 G1.2 1949–1972
Yomiuri Shimbun Staff.
This is Communist China, edited by Robert Trumbull.
New York: McKay, 1968. 12, 274 p.
SUBJ 10 15 32 54 64 ▪ 12.1 14 16 17 18 47 50

11 NATIONAL POPULATION

全國人口　国民総人口

1644-1911

10181 CBU S P1 G1.2 –1895
Köhler, E- M-.
'Kritische Studien zur Bevölkerungsfrage Chinas' (Critical studies of the population question in China).
Deutsche Rundschau für Geographie und Statistik 22, 8 (Mai 1900), 337–347.
SUBJ 11

10182 MCH S P1 G1.2 –1895
Martin, Charles Ernest, 1831–1897.
'Sur la statistique relative au dénombrement de la population en Chine' (About population statistics for China).
B. de la Société de géographie 6e série 4 (juil.–août 1872), 120–132.
SUBJ 11 11.2

10183 NNC S P1 G1.2 –1911
Pritchard, Earl Hampton, 1907–.
'Thoughts on the historical development of the population of China.'
JAS 23, 1 (Nov. 1963), 3–20.
SUBJ 11

10184 MCH P P1 G1.2 –1895
Rockhill, William Woodville, 1854–1914.
'An inquiry into the population of China.'
Smithsonian miscellaneous collections 47, 2, Part 3 (1904), 303–321. [Reprinted—*Annual report of the Board of Regents*

of the Smithsonian Institution 1905, 659–676.] [Reprinted in *Readings in economics for China*, compiled and edited by Charles Frederick Remer. (Selective entry.) Shanghai: Commercial Press, 1922, 463–495.]
Subj 11 ▪ 58

10185 NIC P P2 G1.2 1895–1911
Rockhill, William Woodville, 1854–1914.
'The 1910 census of the population of China.'
TP 2e série 13, 1 (1912), 117–125.
Subj 11 11.1 ▪ 11.2 15 52

10186 NNC P P1 G1.1 1644–1895
Taeuber, Irene Barnes, 1906–, and Nai-chi Wang.
'Population reports in the Ch'ing dynasty.'
JAS 19, 4 (Aug. 1960), 403–417.
Subj 11 ▪ 12 12.1

10187 CSH PO P1 G1.3 1644–1895
Williams, Samuel Wells, 1812–1884.
'Population and statistics.' In *The Middle Kingdom: A survey of the geography, government, literature, social life, arts, and history of the Chinese empire and its inhabitants*, rev. and enl. ed., by S. W. Williams. [Selective entry]
New York: Scribner, 1883, vol. 1, 258–295. [Reprinted in *The Middle Kingdom: A survey of the geography, government, literature, social life, arts, and history of the Chinese empire and its inhabitants*, by S. W. Williams. (Selective entry.) Taipei: Ch'eng-wen, 1965, 258–295 (s.p.)]
Subj 11 ▪ 11.2 14 14.5

10188 NNC P P2 G1.1 –1895
Zakharov, Ivan Il'ich (J. Sacharoff), 1814–1885.
'Istoricheskoe obozrenie narodonaseleniia Kitaia' (Historical survey of China's population). In *Trudy chlenov Rossiiskoi dukhovnoi missii v Pekine* (Works of members of the Russian Orthodox ecclesiastical mission in Peking). [Selective entry]
St. Petersburg: Tip. Shtaba voenno-ucheb. zavedenii, 1852, vol. 1, 247–357. [Reprinted in *Trudy chlenov Rossiiskoi dukhovnoi missii v Pekine*. (Selective entry.) Peking: Tip. Uspenskago monastyria pri RDM, 1909, vol. 1, 141–218.]
'Historische Übersicht der Bevölkerungs-Verhältnisse Chinas.' Tr. by Carl Abel and F- A- Mecklenburg. In *Arbeiten der kaiserlich russischen Gesandtschaft zu Peking über China, sein Volk, seine Religion, seine Institutionen, sozialen Verhältnisse, usw.* (Works of the imperial Russian mission to Peking on China, its people, religion, institutions, social conditions, etc.). [Selective entry]
Berlin: Heinicke, 1858, vol. 2, 127–195.
Subj 11 ▪ 21.1

1644-1949

10189 NIC S P1 G1.3 1895–1928
'The customs' estimate of Chinese population, 1904–1929.'
NWSS 4, 5 (2 Feb. 1931), 25, 28–30.
Subj 11

10190 CSH P P2 G1.2 –1928
'The population of China.' In *The Christian occupation of China*, edited by Milton Theobald Stauffer. [Selective entry]
Shanghai: China Continuation Committee, 1922, 11–14.
Subj 11 ▪ 58

10191 ELE PO P2 G1.2 1895–1949
Balfour, Marshall Coulter, 1896–, et al.
Public health and demography in the Far East: Report of a survey trip, September 13 – December 13, 1948.
New York: Rockefeller Foundation, 1950. 132 p. [Reprinted—Ann Arbor: University Microfilms, n.d. 132 p.]
Subj 11 56 ▪ 18 51 58

10192 NIC S P2 G1.2 1644–1949
Chang, Chih-yi (Chang Chih-i), 1911–.
'China's population problem: A Chinese view.'
PA 22, 4 (Dec. 1949), 339–356.
Subj 11 14.1 16.3 ▪ 12

10193 NIC S P1 G1.2 1895–1949
Chao, Ch'eng-hsin, 1907–.
'Recent population changes in China.'
YJSS 1, 1 (June 1938), 1–48.
Subj 11 58 ▪ 71

10194 MCH P P1 G1.2 1644–1928
Chen, Chang-heng (Ch'en Ch'ang-heng), 1891–.
'Changes in the growth of China's population in the last 182 years.'
CEJ 1, 1 (Jan. 1927), 59–69.
Subj 11 58

10195 CSU P P2 G1.2 –1949
Chen, Chang-heng (Ch'en Ch'ang-heng), 1891–.
'Some phases of China's population problem.'
BIIS 25, 2 (1931), 18–54 [s.p.].
Subj 11 58 71 ▪ 18 21.2 41

10196 CSU P P2 G1.2 –1928
Chen, Chungshen S. (Ch'en Chung-sheng), 1895–.
'The Chinese census of population since 1712.'
BIIS 25, 2, Part 2 (1931), 122–134 [s.p.].
Subj 11 22 ▪ 12 14.5

10197 NNC P P2 G1.1 –1949
Great Britain. Admiralty. Naval Intelligence Division. Geographical Section.
'Growth and distribution of population.' In *China proper, Vol. 2, Modern history and administration*, compiled by the agency cited. [Selective entry]
London: His Majesty's Stationery Office, 1945, 197–302. (NID, Geographical handbook series, BR 530A)
Subj 11 11.3 ▪ 11.1 11.2 58

10198 NIC S P2 G1.2 –1949
Jaffe, Abram J., 1912–.
'A review of the censuses and demographic statistics of China.'
PS 1, 3 (Dec. 1947), 308–337.
Subj 11 12.1 ▪ 14.1 58

10199 CSU P P2 G1.2 1895–1949
Lieu, D. K. (Liu Ta-chün), 1891–1962.
'The 1912 census of China.'
BIIS 26, 2 (1931), 85–109.
Subj 11 41 58 ▪ 62

10200 MCH P P2 G1.1 –1949
Liu, Nanming I. (Liu Nan-ming).
Contribution à l'étude de la population chinoise (A contribution to the study of China's population).
Geneva: Impr. et éditions Union, 1935. 252 p. (Doctoral dissertation, Faculté de droit, Université de Paris)
Subj 11 11.2 ▪ 21 21.1 50 58

10201 NNC S P2 G1.2 1644–1949
Wegener, Georg, 1863–1939.
China: Eine Landes- und Volkskunde (A study of the land and people of China).
Leipzig: Teubner, 1930. 233 p.
Subj 11 11.2 11.3 ▪ 11.1 66 72

10202 CSU S P1 G1.1 1644–1949
Willcox, Walter Francis, 1861–1964.
'A westerner's effort to estimate the population of China, and its increase since 1650.'
J. of the American Statistical Assn. new (2nd) series 25, 171 (Sept. 1930), 255–268.
Subj 11 ▪ 58

1911-1949

10203 NNC P P1 G1.2 1911–1928
'Census of China, 1928.'
NWSS 6, 10 (6 Mar. 1933), 47, 49–50.
Subj 11

10204 NNC S P1 G1.1 1928–1949
Barclay, George Watson, 1923–.
'China's population problem: A closer view.'
PA 23, 2 (June 1950), 184–192.
Subj 11 ▪ 58

10205 ELB P P2 G1.3 1911–1949
Chen Ta (Ch'en Ta), 1892–.
Population in modern China.
Chicago: U. of Chicago Press, 1946. 126 p. [Reprinted—Ann Arbor: University Microfilms, n.d. 126 p.]
Subj 11 11.4 ▪ 41 58

10206 CSU P P2 G1.2 1928–1949
Chen, Warren H. (Ch'en Hua-yin).
'An estimate of the population of China in 1929.'
BIIS 25, 2, Part 2 (1931), 55–87 [s.p.].
Subj 11 21.1 ▪ 41

10207 MCH P P2 G1.1 1911–1928
Hwang, Tsong (Huang Chung), 1904–.
Methode und Ergebnisse der neuesten Bevölkerungsstatistik Chinas (China's latest census: Methods and results).
Leipzig: Teubner, 1933. 77 p. (Deutsches statistisches Zentralblatt, Ergänzungsheft, 13) (Doctoral dissertation, Philosophische Fakultät, Universität Leipzig)
Subj 11 21 ▪ 11.2 21.1

10208 MCH P P8 G1.2 1911–1928
Popov-Tativa, Nikolai Mikhailovich, 1883–.
'K voprosu o kolichestve krest'ianskikh dvorov v Kitae' (The number of peasant households in China).
NV 18 (1927), 91–100.
Subj 11

10209 NNC FP P2 G1.3 1911–1928
Roxby, Percy Maude, 1880–1947.
'The distribution of population in China: Economic and political significance.'
GR 15, 1 (Jan. 1925), 1–24.
Subj 11 11.3 ▪ 12 14 18 29

1911-1972
(including 1644-1972)

10210 CSU P P2 G1.1 1644–1972
Aird, John Shields, 1919–.
'Population growth.' In *Economic trends in Communist China*, edited by Alexander Eckstein, Walter Galenson, and Ta-chung Liu. [Selective entry]
Chicago: Aldine, 1968, 183–327.
Subj 11 58 ▪ 12 12.1

10211 MCH P P1 G1.1 1644–1972
Clark, Colin, 1905–.
'L'accroissement de la population de la Chine' (China's population growth).
Population (Paris) 19, 3 (juin–juil. 1964), 559–568.
Subj 11 58 ▪ 70 71 72

10212 FPN P P1 G1.1 1911–1972
Clark, Colin, 1905–.
'La population de la Chine depuis 1915' (China's population since 1915).
Population (Paris) 21, 6 (nov.–déc. 1966), 1191–1200.
Subj 11 58 ▪ 72

10213 CSU S P1 G1.2 –1972
Durand, John D-.
'The population statistics of China, A.D. 2–1953.'
PS 13, 3 (Mar. 1960), 209–256.
Subj 11

10214 NNC P P2 G1.2 –1972
Ho, Ping-ti, 1917–.
Studies on the population of China, 1368–1953.
Cambridge: Harvard U. Press, 1959. 18, 341, 32 p. (Harvard East Asian series, 4)
Subj 11 11.2 14 14.1 14.5 18 ▪ 14.3 16.2 21 25 41 45 58

10215 CSU P P2 G1.1 1928–1972
Hung, Fu.
'The population of China and present means of subsistence.' In *Proceedings of the International Geographical Union Regional Conference in Japan, 1957.* [Selective entry]
Tokyo: International Geographical Union Regional Conference in Japan, Organizing Committee *with* Science Council of Japan, 1959, 332–340.
Subj 11 ▪ 14.1 58

10216 CSH P P2 G1.1 –1972
Krotevich, S- K-.
'Vsekitaiskaia perepis' naseleniia 1953 g.' (The 1953 pan-Chinese census). In *Poslevoennye perepisi naseleniia (sbornik statei)* (Articles on postwar censuses), compiled by Moskovskii ekonomiko-statisticheskii institut. [Sole entry]
Moscow: Gos. stat. izd-vo, 1957, 80–122.
Subj 11 ▪ 22 41 66 71

10217 DLC S P2 G1.1 1911–1972
Maryański, Andrzej.
'Rozwój ludności Chin w ostatnich 50 latach' (The growth of China's population in the past fifty years).
Czasopismo geograficzne (Wrocław) 28, 1 (1957), 29–47.
Subj 11 11.2 ▪ 11.1 11.3 11.4 14

10218 CSH P P2 G1.2 1928–1972
Orleans, Leo A-, 1924–.
'Population dynamics.' In *Medicine and public health in the People's Republic of China*, edited by Joseph R- Quinn. [Selective entry]
[Washington, D.C.]: U.S. Dept. of Health, Education, and Welfare, Public Health Service, National Institutes of Health, 1972, 191–209.
Subj 11 51 58 ▪ 12.1 56

10219 NNC S P1 G1.2 1911–1972
Orleans, Leo A-, 1924–.
'The 1953 Chinese census in perspective.'
JAS 16, 4 (Aug. 1957), 565–573.
Subj 11

10220 NIC P P2 G1.1 1644–1972
Taeuber, Irene Barnes, 1906–, and Nai-chi Wang.
'Questions on population growth in China.' In *Population trends in eastern Europe, the USSR, and Mainland China*, compiled by Milbank Memorial Fund. [Selective entry]
New York: Milbank Memorial Fund, 1960, 263–302.
Subj 11 12 58 ▪ 12.1 14 18 70

10221 NIC P P2 G1.1 1928–1972
Trewartha, Glenn Thomas, 1896–.
'New maps of China's population.'
GR 47, 2 (Apr. 1957), 234–239.
Subj 11 11.3 ▪ 11.1 11.2 14.1

10222 CSU P P2 G1.1 –1972
Witthauer, Kurt.
'China' (China). In *Verteilung und Dynamik der Erdbevölkerung* (Distribution and dynamics of the world's population), by K. Witthauer. [Sole entry]
Gotha: VEB Hermann Haack, 1969, 251–266. (Petermanns geographische Mitteilungen, Ergänzungsheft, 272)
Subj 11

1949-1972

10223 CSU P P2 G1.2 1949–1972
Aird, John Shields, 1919–.
Estimates and projections of the population of Mainland China: 1953–1986.
Washington, D.C.: U.S. Government Printing Office, 1968. 73 p. (International Population Reports, Series P-91, 17)
Subj 11 58 ▪ 19 51

10224 CSU P P2 G1.2 1949–1972
Aird, John Shields, 1919–.
'Population growth and distribution in Mainland China.' In *An economic profile of Mainland China*, compiled by Joint Economic Committee, U.S. Congress. [Selective entry]
Washington, D.C.: U.S. Government Printing Office, 1967, vol. 2, 341–401. [Reprinted in *An economic profile of Mainland China*, compiled by the agency cited. (Selective entry.) New York: Praeger, 1968, 341–401.]
Subj 11 58 ▪ 11.1 11.2 11.3 12.1

10225 MCH P P2 G1.2 1949–1972
Aird, John Shields, 1919–.
'Population, planning, and economic development in Mainland China in a decade of crisis.'
Population b. 19, 5 (Aug. 1963), 114–135.
Subj 11 12 14 58 ▪ 14.1 14.4 18 51 64

10226 NIC P P2 G1.2 1949–1972
Aird, John Shields, 1919–.
The size, composition, and growth of the population of Mainland China.
Washington, D.C.: U.S. Bureau of the Census, 1961. 100 p. (U.S. Bureau of the Census, International Population Statistics Reports, series P-90, 15) [Reprinted—New York: AMS Press, 1972. 100 p.]
Subj 11 58 ▪ 11.1 11.2 12 12.1 47 50

10227 DLC P P2 G1.2 1949–1972
Berger, IAkov Mikhailovich, 1929–.
'Kitai na karte mira' (China on the world map). In *Kitai segodnia* (China today), compiled by Akademiia nauk SSSR, edited by Lev Petrovich Deliusin and Grigorii Dmitrievich Sukharchuk. [Selective entry]
Moscow: Nauka, Glav. red. vost. lit-ry, 1969, 35–51.
Subj 11 14.1 ▪ 11.3 58

10228 NNC PO P2 G1.2 1949–1972
Chandrasekhar, Sripati, 1917–.
China's population: Census and vital statistics, 2nd ed., rev. and enl.
Hong Kong: Hong Kong U. Press, 1960. 73 p.
Subj 11 58 ▪ 11.3 12 22

10229 CSU P P1 G1.2 1949–1972
Chandrasekhar, Sripati, 1917–.
'Communist China's demographic dilemma.' In *Asia's population problems*, edited by S. Chandrasekhar. [Sole entry]
New York: Praeger, 1967, 48–71.
Subj 11 58 ▪ 41 51 72

10230 CSU P P2 G1.2 1949–1972
Chen, Cheng-siang (Ch'en Cheng-hsiang), 1920–.
'Population growth and urbanization in China, 1953–1970.'
GR 63, 1 (Jan. 1973), 55–72.
Subj 11 11.1 ▪ 11.3 14 21.1 51 58

10231 CSH P P2 G1.2 1949–1972
Chen Ta (Ch'en Ta), 1892–.
'New China's population census of 1953 and its relations to national reconstruction and demographic research.'
B. of International Statistical Institute (Stockholm) 36, 2 (Aug. 1957), 255–271.
Subj 11 11.2 58 ▪ 14 14.1 18

10232 FPN P P2 G1.2 1949–1972
Dumont, René, 1904–.
Chine surpeuplée, tiers monde affamé (China overpopulated, the Third World starving).
Paris: Le Seuil, 1965. 313 p.
Subj 11 14.1 14.3 58 ▪ 12 18 32.1 34.1

10233 CSU P P2 G1.2 1949–1972
Fessler, Loren, 1923–.
'How many hundred million Chinese?'
AUFS-EAS 19, 2 (Dec. 1971), 1–15.
SUBJ 10 11 51 ▪ 17 18 21.2

10234 CSU P P1 G1.2 1949–1972
Field, Robert Michael, 1928–.
'A note on the population of Communist China.'
CQ 38 (Apr.–June 1969), 158–163.
SUBJ 11 58

10235 NIC P P2 G1.2 1949–1972
Krader, Lawrence, 1919–, and John Shields Aird, 1919–.
'Sources of demographic data on Mainland China.'
ASR 24, 5 (Oct. 1959), 623–630.
SUBJ 11 11.1 11.2 ▪ 58 70

10236 MCH P P2 G1.2 1949–1972
[La Dany, Ladislao] ———, 1914–.
'Questions on population.'
CNA 526 (24 July 1964), 1–7; 527 (31 July 1964), 1–7.
SUBJ 11 51 58 ▪ 11.1 11.4 12.1

10237 CSU P P2 G1.2 1949–1972
Lin Chen.
'A study of the Chinese Mainland population.'
IS 5, 2 (Nov. 1968), 17–25.
SUBJ 11

10238 NNC P P2 G1.2 1949–1972
Ma Yin-ch'u, 1882–.
'A new principle of population.' Tr. of 'Hsin jen k'ou lun' (A new population theory); *Jen min jih pao* 5 July 1957, 11–12.
URS 8, 6 (19 July 1957), 86–113.
SUBJ 11 14 ▪ 11.4 18 58

10239 MCH P P2 G1.2 1949–1972
Orleans, Leo A-, 1924–.
'China's population statistics: An illusion?'
CQ 21 (Jan.–Mar. 1965), 168–178.
SUBJ 11 ▪ 12 22

10240 CSU P P2 G1.2 1949–1972
Orleans, Leo A-, 1924–.
Every fifth child: The population of China.
Stanford: Stanford U. Press, 1972. 184 p.
SUBJ 11 11.2 ▪ 11.1 11.4 14.1 17 51 58

10241 MCH PO P2 G1.2 1949–1972
Pressat, Roland.
'La population de la Chine et son économie' (The population and economy of China).
Population (Paris) 13, 4 (oct.–déc. 1958), 569–590.
SUBJ 11 14.1 58 ▪ 14 18 21.1 34.1 51

10242 NIC P P2 G1.2 1949–1972
Pressat, Roland.
'La population de la Chine: structure et évolution récente' (The population of China: Composition and recent developments).
Population (Paris) 16, 4 (oct.–déc. 1961), 649–664.
SUBJ 11 58 ▪ 11.1 47 50 51

10243 MCH P P1 G1.2 1949–1972
Pressat, Roland.
'La révolution démographique en Chine' (The demographic revolution in China). *Economie appliquée* 13, 3 (juil.–sept. 1960), 445–460.
SUBJ 11 58 ▪ 12.1 18 51 64

10244 NNC P P2 G1.2 1949–1972
Sauvy, Alfred, 1898–.
'Les problèmes de population' (Population problems). In *Le régime et les institutions de la République populaire chinoise* (The government and institutions of the People's Republic of China), jointly edited by Centre d'étude des pays de l'Est, Institut de sociologie Solvay, Université libre de Bruxelles *with* Centre national pour l'étude des pays à régime communiste. [Selective entry]
Brussels: Snoeck-Ducaju, 1960, 182–200.
SUBJ 11 58 64 ▪ 14 50

10245 MCH S P2 G1.2 1949–1972
Skibbe, Bruno, 1906–.
'Die Veränderung der Volksdichte in China: Zu einigen Ergebnissen der Volkszählung 1953' (Changes in China's population density: Some results of the census of 1953).
PGM 99, 4 (Dez. 1955), 299–302.
SUBJ 11

10246 MCH P P1 G1.2 1949–1972
Taeuber, Irene Barnes, 1906–, and Leo A- Orleans, 1924–.
'A note on the population statistics of Communist China.'
Population index 22, 4 (Oct. 1956), 274–276.
SUBJ 11 ▪ 11.4

10247 CSH P P2 G1.2 1949–1972
Terent'eva, V- G-, and K- N- Chernozhukov.
'Ob otsenkakh chislennosti naseleniia Kitaia' (Estimates of China's population).
NAA 1970, 4, 169–176.
SUBJ 11 72

10248 CSH P P2 G1.2 1949–1972
T'ung chi kung tso. Tzu liao shih. (Documents Office).
'Data on China's population from 1949 to 1956.' Tr. of '1949–1956 nien wo kuo jen k'ou t'ung chi tzu liao'; *T'ung chi kung tso* 1957, 11 (14 June), 24–25.
ECMM 91 (22 July 1957), 22–25.
SUBJ 11 11.1 ▪ 58

10249 CBU P P2 G1.2 1949–1972
Wang Ya-nan, 1901–.
'The Marxist population theory and China's population problem.' Tr. of *Ma-k'o-ssu chu i ti jen k'ou li lun yü Chung-kuo jen k'ou wen ti*; Peking: K'o hsüeh ch'u pan she, 1956; 45 p.
CES 2, 3/4 (Spring–Summer 1969), 3–91.
SUBJ 11 14 56 ▪ 16 64

10250 MCH PO P2 G1.2 1949–1972
Wertheim, Willem Frederik, 1907–.
'China's bevolkingsvraagstuk' (China's population problem). In *China tussen eergisteren en overmorgen* (China between the day before yesterday and the day after tomorrow), edited by W. F. Wertheim and Erik Zürcher. [Selective entry]
The Hague: Van Hoeve, 1963, 53–69.
SUBJ 11 14.1 ▪ 11.1 18 58

10251 NNC U P2 G1.2 1949–1972
Wu, Ching-chao (Wu Ching-ch'ao), 1901–.
'A new treatise on the problem of China's population.' Tr. of 'Chung-kuo jen k'ou wen t'i hsin lun' (A new discussion of China's population problem); *Hsin chien she* 1957, 3 (Mar.), 1–9.
ECMM 78 (15 Apr. 1957), 1–16.
SUBJ 11 11.4 ▪ 14 14.4 51 58

11.1 NATIONWIDE URBANIZATION

全國性都市化　　全国的都市化

1644-1911

10252 CSU U P2 G1.3 –1911
Mote, Frederick Wade, 1922–.
'The city in traditional Chinese civilization.' In *Traditional China*, edited by James T. C. Liu (Liu Tzu-chien) and Wei-ming Tu. [Selective entry]
Englewood Cliffs, N. J.: Prentice-Hall, 1970, 42–49.
SUBJ 11.1 ▪ 14 16.1 55

1644-1949

10253 NIC P P4 G1.2 –1949
Chang, Sen-dou (Chang Sheng-tao), 1928–.
'The historical trend of Chinese urbanization.'
AAAG 53, 2 (June 1963), 109–143. [For fuller treatment, see entry 10259.]
SUBJ 11.1 11.2 ▪ 12 14 15

10254 NIC P P2 G1.2 1895–1949
Chen Ta (Ch'en Ta), 1892–.
'Factors of urban growth in China.' In *Proceedings of the International Statistical Conference, Vol. 3, 25th session of the International Statistical Institute, Sept. 6–18, 1947, Washington, D.C.*, edited by G- Goudswaard. [Sole entry]
The Hague: International Statistical Institute, 1947, vol. 3, part B, 733–745.
SUBJ 11.1 ▪ 11.2 11.4 14.4

10255 CSU O P2 G1.2 1895–1928
Schmitthenner, Heinrich, 1887–1957.
Chinesische Landschaften und Städte (City and countryside in China).
Stuttgart: Strecker und Schröder, 1925. 304 p.
SUBJ 11.1 14.2 14.4 21.3 ▪ 11.3 13 41

1911-1949

10256 GMS S P3 G1.3 1911–1949
Otte, Friedrich W- K-.
'Vertragshäfen in China als Beispiel für das Wachstum des chinesischen Grosstädte' (China's treaty ports as examples of the growth of large Chinese cities).
Petermanns Mitteilungen 81, 3 (März 1935), 84–86.
SUBJ 11.1

10257 NIC U P4 G1.2 1911–1949
[Torgashev, Boris Pavlovich] Boris P. Torgasheff.
'Town population in China.'

China critic 3, 14 (3 Apr. 1930), 317–322.
SUBJ 11.1 ▪ 11.3 36.2

10258 NNC S P4 G1.3 1911–1949
Trewartha, Glenn Thomas, 1896–.
'Chinese cities: Numbers and distribution.'
AAAG 41, 4 (Dec. 1951), 331–347.
SUBJ 11.1 11.3

1911-1972
(including 1644-1972)

10259 MAM P P4 G1.1 –1972
Chang, Sen-dou (Chang Sheng-tao), 1928–.
The Chinese hsien capital: A study in historical urban geography.
Ann Arbor: University Microfilms (Publ. 61-6629), 1961. 242 p. (Doctoral dissertation in Geography, U. of Washington)
SUBJ 11.1 11.3 14.2 14.3 21.3 ▪ 12 13 39

10260 MCH O P2 G1.2 1928–1972
Keyes, Fenton.
'Urbanism and population distribution in China.'
AJS 56, 6 (May 1951), 519–527.
SUBJ 11 11.1 11.3 ▪ 11.2 11.4 14

10261 CSU S P4 G1.1 –1972
Lee, Rose Hum (T'an Chin-mei), 1893–1964.
'Northern Asian cities: China.' In *The city: Urbanism and urbanization in major world regions*, by R. H. Lee. [Selective entry]
Philadelphia: Lippincott, 1955, 41–72.
SUBJ 11.1 11.3 11.4 14.2 22 ▪ 14.4 16 66

10262 CSU U P3 G1.1 –1972
Mote, Frederick Wade, 1922–.
'Cities in North and South China' [abstract]. In *Symposium on historical, archaeological and linguistic studies on southern China, South-east Asia and the Hong Kong region*, edited by Frederick Seguier Drake. [Selective entry]
Hong Kong: Hong Kong U. Press, 1967, 153–155.
SUBJ 11.1 29 62

1949-1972

10263 NIC P P2 G1.1 1949–1972
Hauser, Philip Morris, 1909–, ed.
Urbanization in Asia and the Far East: Proceedings of the Joint UN/UNESCO Seminar (in co-operation with the International Labour Office) on urbanization in the ECAFE region, Bangkok, 8–18 August, 1956.
Calcutta: UNESCO, Research Centre on the Social Implications of Industrialization in Southern Asia, 1957. 286 p.
SUBJ 11.1 11.2 14 16 58 ▪ 11.3 11.4 12.1 18 22.2 41 47

10264 CSU P P2 G1.2 1949–1972
Onoue, Etsuzō (Onoe Etsuzō).
'Regional distribution of urban population in China.'
DE 8, 1 (Mar. 1970), 93–127.
SUBJ 11 11.1 11.2 21.1 ▪ 11.3 21 58

10265 NIC P P2 G1.2 1949–1972
Orleans, Leo A-, 1924–.
'The recent growth of China's urban population.'
GR 49, 1 (Jan. 1959), 43–57.
SUBJ 11 11.1 ▪ 11.2 12.1 14.4 16.4 18

10266 MCH S P3 G1.2 1949–1972
P. P. and A. S.
'Difficultés en Chine concernant la population urbaine' (Difficulties with the urban population in China).
Population (Paris) 13, 2 (avr.–juin 1958), 309–310.
SUBJ 11.1 ▪ 14

10267 NIC S P4 G1.2 1949–1972
Shabad, Theodore, 1922–.
'The population of China's cities.'
GR 49, 1 (Jan. 1959), 32–42.
SUBJ 11.1 ▪ 21.3

10268 MCY P P4 G1.2 1949–1972
Ullman, Morris Benjamin.
Cities of Mainland China, 1953 and 1958.
Washington, D.C.: U.S. Dept. of Commerce, Bureau of the Census, Foreign Manpower Research Office, 1961. 46 p. (Bureau of the Census, International population statistics reports, series P-95, 59)
SUBJ 11.1 ▪ 21.1

10269 MCY P P4 G1.2 1949–1972
Wu, Yuan-li (Wu Yüan-li), 1920–.
'Principal industrial cities in Communist China: Their regional distribution and ranking.' In *Contemporary China, 1961–1962*, edited by Edward Stuart Kirby. [Selective entry]
Hong Kong: Hong Kong U. Press, 1963, 1–32.
SUBJ 11.1 11.3 14.4 21.1 ▪ 21 21.3

11.2 EXTRANATIONAL MIGRATION & NATIONWIDE GEOGRAPHIC MOBILITY
海外移民及國内大規模遷移
海外移住及び大規模な国内人口移動

1644-1911

10270 CSU U P7 G9.0 –1911
Campbell, George, 1858–?
'Origin and migrations of the Hakkas.'
CR 43, 8 (Aug. 1912), 473–480.
SUBJ 11.2 29

10271 CSH O P4 G9.0 1842–1895
Conwell, Russell Herman, 1843–1925.
Why and how: Why the Chinese emigrate, and the means they adopt for the purpose of reaching America.
Boston: Lee and Shepard; New York: Lee, Shepard, and Dillingham, 1871. 283 p.
SUBJ 11.2 ▪ 12 38 58 65 66

10272 MCH U P3 G1.1 1842–1895
Couturat, Léon.
'L'émigration chinoise' (Chinese emigration).
B. de la Société royale de géographie d'Anvers 5 (1880), 453–482.
SUBJ 11.2 61 ▪ 16.2 16.4 66

10273 CSU P P4 G9.0 1842–1895
Farley, M- Foster.
'The Chinese coolie trade, 1845–1875.'
JAAS 3, 3/4 (July–Oct. 1968), 257–271.
SUBJ 11.2 ▪ 22.2 66

10274 CSU O P3 G6.1 1842–1895
[Gilmore, J-] Hoinos, pseud.
'Chinese emigration.'
CR 14, 1 (Jan.–Feb. 1883), 32–38.
SUBJ 11.2 ▪ 24.2 28 55

10275 MCH P P2 G9.0 1842–1895
Irick, Robert Lee, 1930–.
Ch'ing policy toward the coolie trade, 1847–1878.
Unpublished doctoral dissertation in History and Far Eastern Languages, Harvard U., 1971. 2 vols. 608 p. [c.p.].
SUBJ 11.2 16 66 ▪ 22.2

10276 DLC U P2 G1.1 –1895
Korostovets, Ivan IAkovlevich.
'Dvizhenie naseleniia v Kitae' (Migration in China).
Sibirskii sbornik 9, 3 (1894), 11–22.
SUBJ 11 11.2 ▪ 25 32.2 41 55 56

10277 MCH P P2 G1.1 1644–1895
Ratzel, Friedrich, 1844–1904.
Die chinesische Auswanderung: Ein Beitrag zur Kultur- und Handelsgeographie (A cultural and commercial geography of Chinese emigration).
Breslau: U. Kern, 1876. 12, 272 p.
SUBJ 11.2 14 ▪ 11 11.3 12.1 61

10278 DLC O P2 G9.3 1895–1911
Shuiskii, N-.
'Emigratsiia iz Futsziana: donesenie gen. konsula v Fuchzhou' (Emigration from Fukien: Report of the [Russian] general consul in Foochow).
Sbornik konsul'kikh donesenii 1907, 1, 25–47.
SUBJ 11.2 21.3 ▪ 24.1 26.4 29 55 66

10279 CSH P P1 G1.1 1644–1895
Wang, Sing-wu (Wang Hsing-wu).
'The attitude of the Ch'ing court toward Chinese emigration.'
CC 9, 4 (Dec. 1968), 62–76.
SUBJ 11.2 ▪ 12.2

10280 ACU P P3 G9.0 1842–1895
Wang, Sing-wu (Wang Hsing-wu), 1920–.
The organization of Chinese emigration, 1848–1888, with special reference to Chinese emigration to Australia.
Unpublished masters thesis in History, Australian National U., 1969. 2 vols. 542 p. [c.p.].
SUBJ 11.2

1644-1949

10281 NNC P P2 G1.2 –1928
'History of Chinese migration to Manchuria.'
CEJ 7, 1 (July 1930), 745–769.
SUBJ 11.2

10282 CSU U P3 G9.0 1842–1949
Blue, A- D-.
'Chinese emigration and the deck passenger trade.'
JRAS-HKB 10 (1970), 79–93.
SUBJ 11.2 ▪ 14.2

10283 CSU S P1 G1.1 1842–1949
Chen Han-seng (Ch'en Han-sheng), 1897–.
'The present prospect of Chinese emigration.' In *Limits of land settlement: A preliminary report on present-day possibilities*, edited by Isaiah Bowman. [Selective entry]
New York: American Coördinating Committee for International Studies, 1937, 137–154. [Report to Tenth International Studies Conference, Paris, 28 June – 3 July 1937]
SUBJ 11.2

10284 MCH P P1 G1.1 1644–1928
Chen Ta (Ch'en Ta), 1892–.
'A survey of Chinese migrations: History and scope of Chinese migrations.' In *Chinese migrations, with special reference to labor conditions*, by Chen Ta. [Selective entry]
Washington, D.C.: U.S. Government Printing Office, 1923, 4–21. (U.S. Bureau of Labor Statistics bulletins, Miscellaneous series, 340) (Doctoral dissertation in Sociology, Columbia U., 1923) [Reprinted in *Chinese migrations, with special reference to labor conditions*, by Chen Ta. (Selective entry.) Taipei: Ch'eng-wen, 1967, 4–21.]
SUBJ 11.2 ▪ 11 11.4 18

10285 NNC PO P2 G1.1 –1949
Fochler-Hauke, Gustav, 1906–.
'Chinesische Kolonisation und Kolonialpolitik' (Chinese colonization and colonial policy).
Z. der Gesellschaft für Erdkunde zu Berlin 1933, 3/4, 108–122.
SUBJ 11.2 ▪ 16.3 66

10286 CSU S P1 G1.1 1644–1949
Freeman, T- W-.
'Recent and contemporary Chinese migrations.' In *Comptes rendus du Congrès international de géographie, Amsterdam, 1938, Tome 2, travaux de la section IIIa* (Proceedings of the International Geographical Congress, Amsterdam, 1938, Vol. 2, Papers from Section IIIa). [Sole entry]
Leiden: Brill, 1938, 11–22.
SUBJ 11.2 ▪ 11

10287 CSU P P2 G1.1 –1928
Hsieh T'ing-yu (Hsieh T'ing-yü).
'Origin and migrations of the Hakkas.'
CSPSR 13, 2 (Apr. 1929), 202–227. (Senior thesis, Yenching U., 1928) [Reprinted as 'Origin of the Hakka.' In *The Hakka Chinese: Their origin and folk songs*, by [Hsieh T'ing-yu] Tin-yuke Char. (Sole entry.) San Francisco: Jade Mountain Press, 1969, 1–25.]
SUBJ 11.2 25 ▪ 14 18 29 61

10288 CSU S P1 G1.1 –1949
Lattimore, Owen, 1900–.
'The mainsprings of Asiatic migration.' In *Limits of land settlement: A preliminary report on present-day possibilities*, edited by Isaiah Bowman. [Selective entry]
New York: American Coördinating Committee for International Studies, 1937, 119–135. [Report to Tenth International Studies Conference, Paris, 28 June – 3 July 1937]
SUBJ 11.2 ▪ 14 14.3 66

10289 ELU FP P2 G1.5 –1949
Lin, Chao (Lin Ch'ao), 1909–.
The Nanling–Wu-yi-shan as a geographical divide.
Unpublished doctoral dissertation in Geography, U. of Liverpool, 1938. 517 p.
SUBJ 11.2 11.3 ▪ 11.4 14.3 16.1 16.2 29

10290 CSU P P2 G1.1 1842–1928
MacNair, Harley Farnsworth, 1891–1947.
'Chinese emigration.' In *The Chinese abroad: Their position and protection*, by H. F. MacNair. [Sole entry]
Shanghai: Commercial Press, 1925, 28–55.
SUBJ 11.2 66

10291 MCH P P2 G1.2 –1928
Mosoloff, Hans.
Die chinesische Auswanderung: Ursachen, Wesen und Wirkungen (The causes, nature, and effects of Chinese emigration).
Rostock: Hinstorff, 1932. 518 p. (Hamburger wirtschafts- und sozialwissenschaftliche Schriften, 22–23)
SUBJ 11.2 14.1 16.3 ▪ 11 14.4 14.5 16.4 18 42 45

10292 CSU P P4 G9.0 –1928
Skinner, George William, 1925–.
'Open door and open spaces: Chinese migration and population growth to 1917.' In *Chinese society in Thailand: An analytic history*, by G. W. Skinner. [Sole entry]
Ithaca: Cornell U. Press, 1957, 28–90.
SUBJ 11.2 29 ▪ 21 22.2 26.2 28 34.2

10293 MCH S P2 G1.3 1644–1928
Young, Walter C-.
'Chinese labor migration to Manchuria.'
CEJ 1, 7 (July 1927), 613–633.
SUBJ 11.2 ▪ 16.4 18

1911-1949

10294 MCH P P2 G1.3 1911–1928
Chen Ta (Ch'en Ta), 1892–.
'Home environment of the Chinese emigrants.' In *Chinese migrations, with special reference to labor conditions*, by Chen Ta. [Selective entry]
Washington, D.C.: U.S. Government Printing Office, 1923, 22–36. (U.S. Bureau of Labor Statistics bulletins, Miscellaneous series, 340) (Doctoral dissertation in Sociology, Columbia U., 1923) [Reprinted in *Chinese migrations, with special reference to labor conditions*, by Chen Ta. (Selective entry.) Taipei: Ch'eng-wen, 1967, 22–36.]
SUBJ 11.2 21.3 24 34.3 ▪ 21 24.1 24.4 28 29

10295 MCH PO P2 G1.2 1911–1949
Dennery, Etienne.
'Expansion chinoise.' In *Foules d'Asie: surpopulation japonaise, expansion chinoise, émigration indienne* (Asia's masses: Japanese overpopulation, Chinese expansion, and Indian emigration), by E. Dennery. [Sole entry]
Paris: Armand Colin, 1930, 83–180.
'The expansion of China.' Tr. by John Peile. In *Asia's teeming millions, and its problems for the West*, by E. Dennery. [Sole entry]
London: Cape, 1931, 91–180. [Reprinted in *Asia's teeming millions, and its problems for the West*, by E. Dennery. (Sole entry.) Port Washington, N.Y.: Kennikat Press, 1971, 91–180.]
SUBJ 11.2 14 16 66 ▪ 11 11.4 41 55 61

10296 NNC U P2 G1.2 1928–1949
Farmer, Victor.
'Migrations massives chinoises' (Chinese mass migrations).
R. nationale chinoise 39, 129 (sept. 1940), 231–245.
SUBJ 11.2 12 14 16 18 ▪ 14.2

10297 NIC O P2 G1.2 1928–1949
Fei Hsiao-tung (Fei Hsiao-t'ung), 1910–.
'Relations between city and village in China.'
China economist 3, 7 (15 Nov. 1948), 138–139, 149.
SUBJ 11.1 11.2 ▪ 16.4 18 39 41

10298 NIC S P2 G9.0 1928–1949
Hsu, Francis L. K. (Hsü Lang-kuang), 1909–.
'Influence of South-Seas emigration on certain Chinese provinces.'
FEQ 5, 1 (Nov. 1945), 47–59.
SUBJ 11.2 16 18 ▪ 17 41 55

1911-1972
(including 1644-1972)

10299 CSU P P3 G1.5 –1972
Davis, Sydney George, 1907–.
'Chinese emigration through Hong Kong.'
Economics and finance in Indonesia 8, 1 (Jan. 1955), 25–38.
SUBJ 11.2 ▪ 14.5

10300 CSU S P2 G1.1 –1972
Durand, Maurice M-.
Review of *K'o-chia yüan liu k'ao* (The origins and migrations of the Hakkas), by Lo Hsiang-lin.
BEFEO 52, 1 (1964), 293–299.
SUBJ 11.2 29 ▪ 25

10301 MCH FP P2 G9.5 1928–1972
Hambro, Edvard Isak, 1911–.
The problem of Chinese refugees in Hong Kong.
Leiden: Sijthoff, 1955. 10, 214 p.
SUBJ 11.2 21.1 22.2 26 28 55 ▪ 17 21 21.3 21.4 24 24.1 24.4 24.5 58

10302 MCH P P2 G1.4 –1972
Pan, Chia-lin (P'an Chia-lin), and Irene Barnes Taeuber, 1906–.
'The expansion of the Chinese: North and west.'
Population index 18, 2 (Apr. 1952), 85–107.
SUBJ 11.2 58 ▪ 11.3 11.4

10303 NIC P P1 G1.2 –1972
Wiens, Herold Jacob, 1912–1971.
China's march towards the tropics: A discussion of the southward penetration of China's culture, people, and political control in relation to non–Han-Chinese peoples of South China and in the perspective of historical and cultural geography.

Hamden, Conn.: Shoe String Press, 1954. 15, 441 p. [Reprinted as *Han Chinese expansion in South China*. Hamden, Conn.: Shoe String Press, 1967. 15, 441 p.]
SUBJ 11.2 11.3 12.1 21.3 66 ▪ 11 12 15 24.1 32.2

1949-1972

10304 CSU F P3 G9.5 1949–1972
Barnett, Arthur Doak, 1921–.
'Social osmosis: Refugees in Hong Kong.'
AUFS-EAS 2, 5 (15 Dec. 1953), 1–8.
SUBJ 11.2 38 44 ▪ 21.4 39

10305 CSU P P2 G1.2 1949–1972
Chen, Pi-chao, 1937–.
'Overurbanization, rustication of urban-educated youths, and politics of rural transformation: The case of China.'
Comparative politics 4, 3 (Apr. 1972), 361–386.
SUBJ 11.2 12.1 14 54 ▪ 11 11.1 11.4 16.1 58 64

10306 CSU PO P2 G9.5 1949–1972
Hong Kong. Immigration Dept.
Annual departmental report by the Director of Immigration, 1961/62–1971/72.
Hong Kong: Government Printer. Issued annually, 1963–1972. Average ca. 60 p.
SUBJ 11.2 12.2 22 ▪ 24.2

10307 CSH P P1 G9.4 1949–1972
Kao, Charles H. C. (Kao Hsi-chün).
'A preliminary analysis of the Republic of China's "brain drain" into the United States.'
IFC 32, 3 (Sept. 1969), 22–33.
SUBJ 11.2 16.1

10308 MCH P P2 G1.2 1949–1972
[La Dany, Ladislao] ———, 1914–.
'Manpower distribution and migration.'
CNA 95 (12 Aug. 1955), 1–7.
SUBJ 11.2 11.4

10309 NIC P P2 G1.2 1949–1972
[La Dany, Ladislao] ———, 1914–.
'Movement and immobilization of population.'
CNA 212 (17 Jan. 1958), 1–7.
SUBJ 11.2 12.1

10310 CSU P P1 G1.2 1949–1972
Lal, Amrit.
'Sinification of ethnic minorities in China.'
CS 8, 4 (15 Feb. 1970), 1–25.
SUBJ 11.2 66 ▪ 21

10311 CSU P P2 G1.2 1949–1972
Lieberherr, I- G-.
'Mouvements migratoires et population urbaine en Chine (1953–1957)' (Migration and urban population in China, 1953–1957).
Cahiers de l'Institut de science économique appliqué série G, 24 180 (déc. 1966), 87–118.
SUBJ 11.1 11.2 12.1 ▪ 11 11.4 14.4 19

10312 CSU O P3 G9.5 1949–1972
Link, Eugene Perry, Jr., 1944–.
'Refugees in Hong Kong.'
PC 22B (Dec. 1969), 1–19.
SUBJ 11.2 28 66 ▪ 12.2 38

10313 NIC P P2 G1.2 1949–1972
Orleans, Leo A-, 1924–.
'Population redistribution in Communist China.' In *Population trends in eastern Europe, the USSR, and Mainland China*, compiled by Milbank Memorial Fund. [Selective entry]
New York: Milbank Memorial Fund, 1960, 141–156.
SUBJ 11.1 11.2 ▪ 11 12.1 14.1 19 70

10314 MCH P P2 G1.4 1949–1972
Schwarz, Henry Guenter, 1928–.
'Chinese migration to North-west China and Inner Mongolia, 1949–1959.'
CQ 16 (Oct.–Dec. 1963), 62–74.
SUBJ 11.2 ▪ 12.1

10315 CSU P P2 G1.2 1949–1972
Tien, H. Yuan (T'ien Hsin-yüan), 1926–.
'The demographic significance of organized population transfers in Communist China.'
Demography 1, 1 (1964), 220–226. [Reprinted as 'Internal population migration.' In *Chinese society under Communism: A reader*, edited by William Thomas Liu (Liu Jung). (Selective entry.) New York: Wiley, 1967, 182–189.]
SUBJ 11.2 ▪ 11 11.1 12.1 14.1

10316 CSU P P2 G1.2 1949–1972
Wang Hsueh-wen (Wang Hsüeh-wen).
'A study of the rustication of youth on the Chinese Mainland.'
IS 7, 4 (Jan. 1971), 84–95.
SUBJ 11.2 12.1 54 ▪ 18 35

11.3 MACROECOLOGY AND SETTLEMENT PATTERNS
全域性區位分佈及聚落型態
巨視的社会生態学及び定住様式

1644-1911

10317 MCH O P2 G5.3 1842–1895
Armstrong, Alexander, 1818–1899.
Shantung, China: A general outline of the geography and history of the province.
Shanghai: Shanghai Mercury, 1898. 76 p.
SUBJ 11.3 21 ▪ 21.3 24.2 55 60

10318 ELB O P2 G8.0 1842–1895
Baber, Edward Colborne, 1843–1890.
Travel and researches in western China.
London: Murray, 1882. 201 p. (Royal Geographical Society of London supplementary papers, 1, 1) [Reprinted—Taipei: Ch'eng-wen, 1971. 201 p.]
SUBJ 11.3 14.2 23 29 ▪ 14 14.3

10319 CSH S P2 G5.3 1895–1911
Berensmann, Wilhelm.
'Wirtschaftsgeographie Schantungs, unter besonderer Berücksichtigung des Kiautschou-Gebiets' (An economic geography of Shantung, with special attention to Kiaochow).
Z. für Kolonialpolitik 6 (1904), 570–667.
SUBJ 11.3 21.3 24 24.1 24.2 ▪ 14.3 24.3 24.4

10320 MCH P P2 G1.2 –1842
Biot, Edouard Constant, 1803–1850.
'Mémoire sur les colonies militaires et agricoles des Chinois' (Report on Chinese military and agricultural settlements).
JA 4e série 15 (avr. 1850), 338–370; 15 (mai–juin 1850), 529–595.
SUBJ 11.3 14.1 15 ▪ 12

10321 MCH O P2 G6.3 1842–1911
Carli, Mario.
Il Ce-Kiang: studio geografico-economico con una introduzione storica e una carta (Chekiang: A study in economic geography, with an historical introduction and a map).
Rome: Forzani, 1899. 19, 278 p.
SUBJ 11.3 14.3 24.1 24.2 24.3 ▪ 21.1 24.4 33 66

10322 CSU U P2 G1.3 –1911
Fei Hsiao-tung (Fei Hsiao-t'ung), 1910–.
'Village, town, and city.' In *China's gentry: Essays in rural-urban relations*, rev. ed., by Fei Hsiao-tung, edited by Margaret Park Redfield. [Analytic entry]
Chicago: U. of Chicago Press, 1953, 91–107. [Reprinted in *China's gentry: Essays in rural-urban relations*, by Fei Hsiao-tung, edited by M. P. Redfield. (Analytic entry.) Chicago: U. of Chicago Press, 1968, 91–107.]
SUBJ 11.1 11.3 16.1 ▪ 14.3 24.4

10323 MCH O P2 G1.5 1842–1895
Garnier, Francis, 1839–1873.
'Voyage dans la Chine centrale (vallée de Yang-tzu) fait de mai à août 1873' (Travels in the Yangtze valley from May to August, 1873).
B. de la Société de géographie 6e série 7 (jan. 1874), 5–43.
SUBJ 11.3 14.2 ▪ 14 55

10324 MCH O P2 G7.2 1895–1911
Harfeld, Ferdinand Joseph.
'Contribution à la géographie de Hou Nann' (A contribution to the geography of Hunan). In *Compte rendu des travaux du Neuvième Congrès international de géographie, Genève, 27 juillet – 6 août 1908, Tome troisième, travaux scientifiques* (Proceedings of the Ninth International Geographical Congress, Geneva, 27 July – 6 August 1908, Vol. 3, Scientific papers). [Sole entry]
Geneva: Neuvième Congrès international de géographie, 1911, 181–205.
SUBJ 11.3 24 ▪ 21.1 24.2

10325 CSH PO P2 G9.4 –1895
Imbault-Huart, Camille Clément, 1857–1897.
L'île Formose: histoire et description (History and description of Taiwan).
Paris: Ernest Leroux, 1893. 323 p. [Reprinted—Taipei: Ch'eng-wen, 1968. 323 p.]
SUBJ 11.3 12 14 15 66 72 ▪ 12.1 21.2 21.3 25 29

10326 MCH PO P2 G1.5 1895–1911
Imbault-Huart, Camille Clément, 1857–1897.
'Le Si-Kiang ou fleuve de l'Ouest' (The West River).
B. de la Société de géographie commerciale de Paris 19 (1897), 34–61, 177–199.
SUBJ 11.3 ▪ 22 24 66

10327 NNC P P2 G9.0 1644–1895
Laai, Yi-faai (Lai I-hui), 1906–, Franz Henry Michael, 1907–, and John C-Sherman.
'The use of maps in social research: A case study in South China.'
GR 52, 1 (Jan. 1962), 92–111.
Subj 11.3 20 ▪ 14.3 21 21.2 24.1 24.3 25 29 32.2

10328 MCH O P2 G1.1 1842–1895
Lóczy, Lajos, 1849–1920.
A khínai birodalom természeti viszonyainak és országainak leírása (Description of the physical nature and the lands of the Chinese empire).
Budapest: K. M. Természettudományi Társulat, 1886. 884 p.
Subj 11.3 21.3 24 24.2 28 ▪ 11 21 66

10329 CBU PO P2 G1.1 1644–1895
Matusovskii, Z-.
Geograficheskoe obozrenie Kitaiskoi imperii (Geographic survey of the Chinese empire).
St. Petersburg: Tip. imp. Akad. nauk, 1888. 20, 358, 87 p.
Subj 11 11.3 12 14 15 66 ▪ 11.2 12.1 14.2 25

10330 NNM P P2 G1.2 1895–1911
National Review, comp.
The provinces of China, together with a history of the first year of H.I.M. Hsuan Tung and an account of the government of China.
Shanghai: National Review Office, 1910. 187 p.
Subj 11 11.3 14 14.2 21.3 24.1 ▪ 12 14.3 14.4 21 21.1 24.4

10331 NIC S P2 G1.1 1842–1911
Richard, Louis, 1868–?
Géographie de l'empire de Chine (A geography of the Chinese empire).
Shanghai: Impr. de la Mission catholique, 1905. 18, 564 p.
Comprehensive geography of the Chinese empire and dependencies. Tr. by M-Kennelly. [Rev. and enl. in tr.]
Shanghai: Tou-sè-wè Press, 1908. 18, 713 p.
Subj 10 11.3 14 14.2 ▪ 12 14.5 15 17 21.3 24.4 72

10332 CBU O P2 G4.0 1842–1895
Richthofen, Ferdinand Paul Wilhelm von, 1833–1905.
'China und Central-Asien' (China and Central Asia). In *China: Ergebnisse eigener Reisen und darauf gegründeter Studien* (China: Results of my travels and studies based on them), by F. P. W. von Richthofen. [Sole entry]
Berlin: Reimer, 1877, vol. 1, 1–272. [Reprinted in *China: Ergebnisse eigener Reisen und darauf gegründeter Studien*, by F. P. W. von Richthofen. (Sole entry.) Graz: Akademische Druk, 197?, 1–272.]
Subj 11.3 24.2 ▪ 21.3 24.1 55 66

10333 MAM P P2 G1.3 –1911
Rozman, Gilbert Friedell, 1943–.
Urban networks in Ch'ing China and Tokugawa Japan.
Ann Arbor: University Microfilms (Publ. 72-2743), 1972. 13, 442 p. (Doctoral dissertation in Sociology, Princeton U., 1971)
Subj 11.1 11.3 14 21.1 21.3 ▪ 11 14.2 14.3 16 21 24.3 29 39 72

10334 CSH O P2 G1.2 1842–1895
Williams, Samuel Wells, 1812–1884.
'Geographical description of Manchuria, Mongolia, Ílí, and Tibet.' In *The Middle Kingdom: A survey of the geography, government, literature, social life, arts, and history of the Chinese empire and its inhabitants*, rev. and enl. ed., by S. W. Williams. [Selective entry]
New York: Scribner, 1883, vol. 1, 185–257. [Reprinted in *The Middle Kingdom: A survey of the geography, government, literature, social life, arts, and history of the Chinese empire and its inhabitants*, by S. W. Williams. (Selective entry.) Taipei: Ch'eng-wen, 1965, 185–257 (s.p.)]
Subj 11.3 21.3 66 ▪ 12 12.1 14.1 14.3 14.5 15 24.3 29

10335 CSH O P2 G1.3 1842–1895
Williams, Samuel Wells, 1812–1884.
'Geographical description of the eastern provinces.' In *The Middle Kingdom: A survey of the geography, government, literature, social life, arts, and history of the Chinese empire and its inhabitants*, rev. and enl. ed., by S. W. Williams. [Selective entry]
New York: Scribner, 1883, vol. 1, 49–141. [Reprinted in *The Middle Kingdom: A survey of the geography, government, literature, social life, arts, and history of the Chinese empire and its inhabitants*, by S. W. Williams. (Selective entry.) Taipei: Ch'eng-wen, 1965, 49–141 (s.p.)]
Subj 11.3 21.3 ▪ 29

10336 CSH O P2 G1.1 1842–1895
Williams, Samuel Wells, 1812–1884.
'Geographical description of the western provinces.' In *The Middle Kingdom: A survey of the geography, government, literature, social life, arts, and history of the Chinese empire and its inhabitants*, rev. and enl. ed., by S. W. Williams. [Selective entry]
New York: Scribner, 1883, vol. 1, 142–184. [Reprinted in *The Middle Kingdom: A survey of the geography, government, literature, social life, arts, and history of the Chinese empire and its inhabitants*, by S. W. Williams. (Selective entry.) Taipei: Ch'eng-wen, 1965, 142–184 (s.p.)]
Subj 11.3 21.3 ▪ 29

1644-1949

10337 NNC P P2 G2.0 1895–1949
Anuchin, Vsevolod Aleksandrovich.
Geograficheskie ocherki Man'chzhurii (Geographic notes on Manchuria).
Moscow: Geografgiz, 1948. 298 p.
Subj 11.3 14.1 14.3 21.2 21.3 ▪ 14.2 14.4 21 21.1 21.4 71

10338 MAM P P2 G1.2 1842–1928
Chao, Ch'eng-hsin, 1907–.
An ecological study of China from segmentation to integration.
Ann Arbor: University Microfilms (Publ. 320), 1941. 207 p. (Doctoral dissertation in History, U. of Michigan, 1933)
Subj 11 11.1 11.3 14 14.2 66 ▪ 11.2 11.4 14.3 14.4 21.4 24.4 29 34.1

10339 DLC O P2 G6.3 –1949
Crow, Carl, 1883–1945.
Chekiang highways.
Shanghai: Kelly and Walsh, 1937. 173 p.
Subj 11.3 21.3 65 ▪ 24.2 24.4 33

10340 NNC PO P2 G2.0 1644–1928
Frizendorf, M-.
Severnaia Man'chzhuriia: ocherki ekonomicheskoi geografii (Notes on the economic geography of northern Manchuria).
Khabarovsk: Knizhnoe delo, 1930. 188 p.
Subj 11.3 14 14.4 24.1 24.2 ▪ 21 21.2 25 26.2 26.3 28 47 72

10341 DLC P P2 G2.0 1895–1949
Glushakov, P- I-.
Man'chzhuriia: ekonomiko-geograficheskii ocherk (Survey of the economic geography of Manchuria).
Moscow: Geografgiz, 1948. 261 p.
Subj 11.3 14 14.1 14.2 21 21.4 ▪ 14.3 14.4 16 21.1 21.2

10342 CSU O P2 G1.2 –1928
Goodnow, Frank Johnson, 1859–1939.
'The geography of China: The influence of physical environment on the history and character of the Chinese people.'
NG 51, 6 (June 1927), 651–664.
Subj 10 11.3 14 ▪ 29 30 64

10343 NNC U P4 G1.4 1842–1949
Great Britain. Admiralty. Naval Intelligence Division. Geographical Section.
'The ports of North China.' In *China proper, Vol. 3, Economic geography, ports and communications*, compiled by the agency cited. [Selective entry]
London: His Majesty's Stationery Office, 1945, 383–428. (NID, Geographical handbook series, BR 530B)
Subj 11.3 21.3 24.2 ▪ 14.2 14.3 24.4 72

10344 NNC U P4 G1.5 1842–1949
Great Britain. Admiralty. Naval Intelligence Division. Geographical Section.
'The ports of South China.' In *China proper, Vol. 3, Economic geography, ports and communications*, compiled by the agency cited. [Selective entry]
London: His Majesty's Stationery Office, 1945, 225–295. (NID, Geographical handbook series, BR 530B)
Subj 11.3 14.2 21.3 ▪ 14.3 24.2 24.3 72

10345 NSU FP P2 G9.4 1644–1949
[Hsieh, Chiao-min] James Chiao-min Hsieh, 1918–.
Successive occupance patterns in Taiwan.
Unpublished doctoral dissertation in Geography, Syracuse U., 1953. 417 p.
Subj 11.3 21.2 ▪ 14.4 21 21.3 21.4 24.1 24.2 29 55 58 66

10346 CBU S P2 G1.1 1895–1949
Kazanin, Mark Isaakovich, 1899–.
Ocherk ekonomicheskoi geografii Kitaia (Survey of the economic geography of China), edited by Pavel Aleksandrovich Mif.

Moscow: Sotsekgiz, 1935. 227 p.
SUBJ 11 11.2 11.3 14 16 ▪ 12 14.2 16.4 32 66 72

10347 MCH P P2 G1.2 –1949
Lattimore, Owen, 1900–.
'An inner Asian approach to the historical geography of China.'
GJ 110, 4/6 (Apr. 1948), 180–187.
SUBJ 10 11.3 ▪ 14.1

10348 NNC O P2 G1.3 1895–1928
Otte, Friedrich W- K-.
China: Wirtschaftspolitische Landeskunde (A political and economic geography of China).
Gotha: Justus Perthes, 1927. 111 p. (Petermanns Mitteilungen, Ergänzungsheft, 194)
SUBJ 11.3 14 ▪ 11.2 12 12.1 14.1 14.2 14.4 36.4 41

10349 MCH S P2 G1.2 –1949
Peterson, Alexander Duncan Campbell, 1908–.
The Far East: A social geography, 3rd ed., rev.
London: Duckworth, 1957. 334 p.
SUBJ 10 11.3 14 60 ▪ 17 29 32.2 41

10350 MCH S P2 G1.3 –1949
Roxby, Percy Maude, 1880–1947.
'China as an entity: The comparison with Europe.'
Geography 19, 103 (Mar. 1934), 1–20.
SUBJ 11.3 29 ▪ 11.2

10351 CBU S P7 G1.3 1644–1949
Scholz, Hartmut-Dieter, 1925–.
Die Formen der ländischen Siedlung in China (Patterns of rural settlement in China).
Unpublished doctoral dissertation, Mathematische-Naturwissenschaftliche Fakultät, Universität Bonn, 1949. 184 p.
SUBJ 11.3 55 ▪ 14.1 24.3 62

10352 CSU P P7 G1.2 –1949
Skinner, George William, 1925–.
'Marketing and social structure in rural China, Part II.'
JAS 24, 2 (Feb. 1965), 195–228. [Separately reprinted—Indianapolis: Bobbs-Merrill College Division, 1967. 33 p. (Bobbs-Merrill reprint series in geography, G-627)]
SUBJ 11.3 19 24.2 24.3 ▪ 14.3 21.3

10353 CSU S P2 G1.2 –1949
Spencer, Joseph Earle, 1907–.
'China during fifty centuries.' In *Asia east by south: A cultural geography*, by J. E. Spencer. [Sole entry]
New York: Wiley, 1954, 318–342.
SUBJ 11 11.3 14.1 14.4 ▪ 14.2 14.3 29 56

10354 NNC P P2 G2.0 1644–1928
Tiagin, G-.
'Perspektivy kolonizatsii Man'chzhurii' (The future of the colonization of Manchuria).
Mezhdunarodnaia zhizn' (Moscow: Narodnyi komitet po inostrannym delam) 1929, 7, 73–91; 1929, 9/10, 76–86.
SUBJ 11.3 14.2 21.2 21.4 ▪ 12.1 14.1 14.3 21 45 66

10355 GMU P P2 G1.2 –1928
Wittfogel, Karl August, 1896–.
Die ökonomische Bedeutung der agrikolen und industriellen Produktivkräfte Chinas (The economic significance of China's productivity in agriculture and industry).
Stuttgart: Kohlhammer, 1930. 183 p. (Institut für Sozialforschung an der Universität Frankfurt a.M., Schriften, 3) (Doctoral dissertation, Philosophische Fakultät, Universität Frankfurt a.M.)
SUBJ 11.3 14.1 14.4 ▪ 61

1911-1949

10356 GBS PO P2 G2.1 1911–1949
Beckmann, Johannes, 1901–.
Heilungkiang (Heilungkiang).
Immensee, Switzerland: Verlag des Missionshauses St. Bethlehem, 1932. 96 p.
SUBJ 11.3 20 33 ▪ 17 23 26.3 47 55 56 65

10357 NNC S P2 G9.1 1928–1949
Bobrovskaia, L-.
'Guansi: ekonomiko-geograficheskii ocherk' (Sketch of the economic geography of Kwangsi).
MKhMP 1940, 2 (fevral'), 117–126.
SUBJ 11.3 14 ▪ 17 21

10358 NNC S P2 G8.1 1928–1949
Bobrovskaia, L-.
'Sychuan' i Sikan: ekonomiko-geograficheskii ocherk' (Sketch of the economic geography of Szechwan and Sikang).
MKhMP 1940, 8 (avgust), 141–156.
SUBJ 11.3 14 21.4 24.4 ▪ 14.3 24.2

10359 MCH O P2 G8.1 1911–1928
Bodard, Albert Césaire Auguste, 1883–.
'L'ouest chinois: la province du Setchoan et les marches tibétaines' (West China: Szechwan and the Tibetan border regions).
Géographie 37, 2 (fév. 1922), 196–222.
SUBJ 11.3 55 56 ▪ 21.3 25 66

10360 CSU O P2 G1.2 1911–1928
Buxton, Leonard Halford Dudley, 1889–1939.
China, the land and the people: A human geography.
Oxford: Clarendon Press, 1929. 18, 333 p.
SUBJ 11.3 14.1 ▪ 14.2 14.3 29

10361 MWC S P2 G1.1 1928–1949
Chao Sung-ch'iao, 1919–.
Geographic regions of China: Their component factors and chief characteristics.
Unpublished doctoral dissertation in Geography, Clark U., 1948. 164 p.
SUBJ 11.3 14.1 ▪ 14.2 21

10362 CSH P P1 G6.3 1911–1949
China [Republic]. Shih yeh pu. Kuo chi mao i chü. (Ministry of Industry. Bureau of Foreign Trade), ed.
'Introduction. II, Location and area.' Tr. of 'Tsung shou. 2, Ch'ü yü chi mien chi'; in *Chung-kuo shih yeh chih: Che-chiang sheng* (Chinese economic surveys: Chekiang); Shanghai: Kuo chi mao i chü, 1933, *chia* 4 – *chia* 11 [s.p.] [slightly condensed in tr.]. In *China industrial handbooks: Chekiang*, edited by the agency cited. [Selective entry]
Shanghai: Kuo chi mao i chü, 1935, 6–9. [Reprinted in *China industrial handbooks: Chekiang*, edited by the agency cited. (Selective entry.) Taipei: Ch'eng-wen, 1972, 6–9.]
SUBJ 11.3 21

10363 MCH FP P2 G1.1 1911–1928
Cressey, George Babcock, 1896–1963.
China's geographic foundations: A survey of the land and the people.
New York: McGraw-Hill, 1934. 436 p.
SUBJ 11.3 14.1 14.2 21 29 ▪ 11 14.3 14.4 21.1 21.2 55

10364 MCH FP P2 G2.0 1911–1949
Fochler-Hauke, Gustav, 1906–.
Die Mandschurei: Eine geographisch-geopolitische Landeskunde (A geographic and geopolitical study of Manchuria).
Berlin: Kurt Vowinckel, 1941. 15, 448 p.
SUBJ 11.3 12 14 ▪ 16.3 21.1 21.2 21.3 45

10365 MCH U P2 G1.2 1928–1949
Glushakov, P- I-.
Kitai: ekonomiko-geograficheskii ocherk (Survey of the economic geography of China).
Moscow: Gospolitizdat, 1940. 111 p.
SUBJ 11.3 14 ▪ 11

10366 NNC U P3 G1.5 1911–1949
Great Britain. Admiralty. Naval Intelligence Division. Geographical Section.
'Shanghai and the Yangtze ports.' In *China proper, Vol. 3, Economic geography, ports and communications*, compiled by the agency cited. [Selective entry]
London: His Majesty's Stationery Office, 1945, 296–382. (NID, Geographical handbook series, BR 530B)
SUBJ 11.3 14.2 14.3 21.3 ▪ 21.1 22 24.2 24.4 72

10367 NIC S P2 G1.1 1928–1949
Hsieh, Chiao-min, 1918–.
'A new map of the geographical regions of China.'
CC 4, 4 (Mar. 1963), 79–96.
SUBJ 11 11.3

10368 CSU U P2 G6.1 1928–1949
Hu Huan-yong (Hu Huan-yung), 1901–.
'A geographical sketch of Kiangsu province.'
GR 37, 4 (Oct. 1947), 609–617.
SUBJ 11.3 24.1 24.2 ▪ 18 21 21.1

10369 CSU O P2 G4.3 1911–1928
Lattimore, Owen, 1900–.
'Chinese Turkestan.'
Open court 47, 921 (Mar. 1933), 97–119. [Reprinted in *Studies in frontier history: Collected papers, 1928–1958*, by O. Lattimore. (Selective entry.) London: Oxford U. Press, 1962, 183–199.]
SUBJ 11.3 12 ▪ 14 66

10370 MCH P P2 G1.4 1911–1949
Liu, Dse-ming (Liu Tzu-ming), 1911–.
Die wirtschaftliche Bedeutung der Regulierung des Huang-ho (The economic significance of the regulation of the Yellow River).

Münster: H. Buschmann, 1937. 120 p. (Doctoral dissertation, Rechts- und staatswissenschaftliche Fakultät, Universität Münster)
SUBJ 11.3 11.4 14 18 ▪ 11 11.2 14.1 14.4

10371 CBU F P8 G1.3 1911–1928
Lowdermilk, Walter Clay, 1888–.
'Erosion in the Orient as related to soil conservation in America.'
J. of the American Society of Agronomy 21, 4 (Apr. 1929), 404–414.
SUBJ 11.3 14.1

10372 MCH U P2 G1.2 1911–1928
Schmitthenner, Heinrich, 1887–1957.
'Einheitsstaat und Provinzen in China' (National unity and the provinces in China).
Geographische Z. 31, 1 (1925), 14–26.
SUBJ 11.3 ▪ 14.2 14.3

10373 MCH S P7 G1.3 1928–1949
Scholz, Hartmut-Dieter, 1925–.
'The rural settlements in the eighteen provinces of China.'
Sinologica 3, 1 (1951), 37–49.
SUBJ 11.3 21.3

10374 CSH S P2 G1.2 1911–1928
Serebrennikov, I- I-.
'Ocherk ekonomicheskoi geografii Kitaia' (Survey of the economic geography of China).
VA 53 (1925), 1–113.
SUBJ 11.3 14 ▪ 11 11.1 14.1 14.2 14.3 14.4

10375 NNC P P2 G3.0 1911–1949
Skachkov, Petr Emel'ianovich, 1892–1964.
Vnutrenniaia Mongoliia: ekonomiko-geograficheskii ocherk (Survey of the economic geography of Inner Mongolia).
Moscow: Nauchno-issledov. assots. po izucheniiu nats. i kolon. problem, 1933. 149 p. (Nauchno-issledovatel'skoi assotsiatsii po izucheniiu natsional'nykh i kolonial'nykh problem, Trudy, 10)
SUBJ 11.3 14 ▪ 12 21.1 21.2 32.2

10376 NNC O P2 G1.3 1928–1949
Spencer, Joseph Earle, 1907–.
'On regionalism in China.'
J. of geography 46, 4 (Apr. 1947), 123–136.
SUBJ 11.3 ▪ 55

10377 CSU S P2 G1.1 1928–1949
Stamp, Laurence Dudley, 1898–.
'China.' In *Asia: A regional and economic geography*, 8th ed., by L. D. Stamp. [Selective entry]
New York: Dutton, 1950, 463–539.
SUBJ 11.3 14.1 14.2 ▪ 11 18

10378 CSU S P2 G2.0 1928–1949
Stamp, Laurence Dudley, 1898–.
'Manchuria.' In *Asia: A regional and economic geography*, 8th ed., by L. D. Stamp. [Selective entry]
New York: Dutton, 1950, 540–558.
SUBJ 11.3 14.1 14.2 ▪ 21

10379 MCH P P8 G1.2 1911–1949
Thorp, James, 1896–.
The geography of the soils of China.
Nanking: Shih yeh pu, Te chih tiao ch'a so *with* Academy of Peiping, Institute of Geology, 1936. 16, 552 p. [Reprinted—Ann Arbor: University Microfilms, n.d. 16, 552 p.]
SUBJ 11.3 14.1 ▪ 18

10380 MCH PO P2 G5.0 1911–1928
Tiefensee, Franz Wilhelm, 1880–.
Die Provinz Dschli-li nebst Djing-dschau in wirtschaftsgeographischer Betrachtung (Chihli and the Tsingtao-Kiaochow area: A study in economic geography).
Rastenburg: G. Sack, 1928. 76 p. (Doctoral dissertation, Philosophische Fakultät, Universität Königsberg)
SUBJ 11.3 14 14.5 24.1 ▪ 14.3 21.3

10381 NNU P P2 G2.0 1911–1928
Yü, Tsune-chi (Yü Tsun-chi), 1899–1968.
Economic geographic problems in Manchuria.
New York: American Book–Stratford Press, 1924. 180 p. (Doctoral dissertation in Geography, New York U.)
SUBJ 11.3 14 18 21.3 ▪ 17 21 21.2 23 36.2 66 72

1911-1972
(including 1644-1972)

10382 NNC P P2 G8.1 1895–1972
Afanas'evskii, Evgenii Aleksandrovich (Yevgeniy Aleksandrovich Afanas'yevskiy).
Sychuan': ekonomiko-geograficheskii ocherk (Survey of the economic geography of Szechwan).
Moscow: Izd-vo vost. lit-ry, 1962. 266 p.
Szechwan, mimeo.
Washington, D.C.: U.S. Joint Publications Research Service, 17 Sept. 1962. 404 p. (JPRS 15,308; MC 21,967/1962)
SUBJ 11.3 14 24.1 24.2 ▪ 14.4 17 21 21.1 21.3 21.4 24.4 72

10383 NNC S P2 G1.2 1911–1972
Chang Li-man (Chang Li-men).
'Special features in the changes of administrative areas in China.' Tr. of 'Wo kuo hsing cheng ch'ü hua pien tung ti t'e tien' (Some features of the changes in the units of territorial administration in China); *Cheng fa yen chiu* 1956, 5 (Oct.), 46–52.
ECMM 57 (19 Nov. 1956), 1–14.
SUBJ 11.3 12 ▪ 22 22.1 24 64

10384 CSU P P4 G1.1 –1972
Chang, Sen-dou (Chang Sheng-tao), 1928–.
'Some aspects of the urban geography of the Chinese hsien capital.'
AAAG 51, 1 (Mar. 1961), 23–45. [For fuller treatment, see entry 10259.]
SUBJ 11.1 11.3 21.1 21.3 ▪ 12 17

10385 MCH FP P2 G9.4 1928–1972
Chen, Cheng-siang (Ch'en Cheng-hsiang), 1920–.
Taiwan: An economic and social geography, Vol. 1.
Taipei: Fu-min Geographical Institute of Economic Development, 1963. 653 p. (Fu-min research reports, 96)
SUBJ 11.3 14 24.1 24.2 ▪ 14.4 21 21.1 21.2 21.3

10386 NIC F P2 G1.1 1928–1972
Cressey, George Babcock, 1896–1963.
Land of the 500 million: A geography of China.
New York: McGraw-Hill, 1955. 15, 387 p.
SUBJ 11.3 14 72 ▪ 11 11.2 11.4 14.1 14.4 18 21.1 21.3

10387 MCY S P2 G9.4 –1972
Hsieh, Chiao-min, 1918–.
Taiwan, ilha Formosa: A geography in perspective.
London: Butterworth, 1964. 372 p.
SUBJ 11.3 14 21.1 24.1 24.2 ▪ 14.4 21 21.2 58

10388 GMS FP P2 G5.0 1928–1972
Köhler, Günther, 1909–.
'Siedlungen und verkehrsgeographische Fragen Nordchinas' (Settlement and questions of transport geography in North China). In *Deutsches Geographentag Frankfurt a.M. 12–18/5, 1951: Tagungsbericht und wissenschaftliche Abhandlungen* (Conference of German geographers, Frankfurt a.M., 12–18 May 1951: Report on proceedings and transactions), edited by Herbert Lehmann. [Sole entry]
Remagen: Amt für Landeskunde, 1952, 227–281. (Deutscher Geographentag, Verhandlungen, 28)
SUBJ 11.3 14.2

10389 CSU S P2 G1.1 –1972
Kolb, Albert, 1906–.
'The geographical regions of Chinese and Central Asian culture.' Tr. from the German by C- A- M- Sym. In *East Asia: China, Japan, Korea, Vietnam. Geography of a cultural region*, by A. Kolb. [Selective entry]
London: Methuen, 1971, 196–390. [Rev. ed. of *Ostasien: China, Japan, Korea. Geographie eines Kulturerdteils.* Heidelberg: Quelle und Meyer, 1963.]
SUBJ 11.3 14 14.1 14.4 ▪ 11.1 14.2 18 21.3

10390 CSU S P2 G1.2 1928–1972
Lee, Shu-tang.
'Delimitation of the geographic regions of China.'
AAAG 37, 3 (Sept. 1947), 155–168.
SUBJ 11.3 ▪ 14.1

10391 CSU P P2 G1.2 1928–1972
Lewis, John Wilson, 1930–.
'The study of Chinese political culture.'
WP 18, 3 (Apr. 1966), 503–524.
SUBJ 11.3 16.3 32.2 34.1 ▪ 22 24.3 36.3

10392 CBU P P2 G9.2 –1972
Liang Jen-ts'ai.
Economic geography of Kwangtung, mimeo. Tr. of *Kuang-tung ching chi ti li*; Peking: K'o hsüeh yen chiu she, 1956; 102 p.
New York: U.S. Joint Publications Research Service, 21 Nov. 1958. 114 p. (JPRS 389D; MC 574/1959) [Xerox copyflo available—New York: CCM Information Corp., Research and Microfilm Publications. (Scholarly Book Translation Series, 522)]
SUBJ 11.3 14 14.4 24.1 ▪ 21 21.1 21.3 24.2 24.4

10393 CSU S P2 G1.2 1842–1972
Murphey, William Rhoads, III, 1919–.
'City and countryside as ideological issues: India and China.'

CSSH 14, 3 (June 1972), 250–267.
Subj 11.2 11.3 14 18 21.2 ▪ 14.3 24.3 58 64

10394 MAM FP P2 G9.4 1928–1972
Selya, Roger Mark.
The industrialization of T'aiwan: A geographic analysis.
Ann Arbor: University Microfilms (Publ. 71-28,284), 1971. 332 p. (Doctoral dissertation in Geography, U. of Minnesota)
Subj 11.3 14.4 ▪ 24.2

10395 NNC FP P2 G7.0 1842–1972
Sun Ching-chih, et al., eds.
Economic geography of Central China (Hupeh, Hunan, Kiangsi), mimeo. Tr. of *Hua-chung ti ch'ü ching chi ti li (Hu-pei, Hu-nan, Chiang-hsi)* edited by Chung-hua ti li chih pien chi pu, Chung-kuo k'o hsüeh yüan (Committee for the Compilation of Geographies of China, Chinese Academy of Sciences); Peking: K'o hsüeh ch'u pan she, 1958; 156 p.
Washington, D.C.: U.S. Joint Publications Research Service, 10 Feb. 1960. 522 p. (JPRS 2227N; MC 5457/1960) [Xerox copyflo available—New York: CCM Information Corp., Research and Microfilm Publications. (Scholarly Book Translation Series, 495)]
Subj 11.3 14 14.1 21 ▪ 14.2 14.4 21.1

10396 MMT S P2 G1.1 –1972
Tregear, Thomas Refoy, 1897–.
A geography of China.
Chicago: Aldine, 1965. 17, 342 p.
Subj 11.3 14 14.1 14.4 ▪ 11 11.2 14.2 34.1 58

10397 CSU S P2 G1.1 –1972
Tuan, Yi-fu (Tuan I-fu), 1930–.
China.
Chicago: Aldine, 1969. 11, 225 p.
Subj 11.3 14.1 21.3 ▪ 11 11.1 11.2 14.2 14.4 55 57

10398 CBU FP P2 G2.1 1644–1972
Wu Ch'uan-chün, Kuo Lai-hsi, and Hsieh Hsiang-fang, eds.
Economic geography of the Amur and Ussuri river regions of Heilungkiang province, mimeo. Tr. of *Hei-lung-chiang sheng Hei-lung chiang chi Wu-su-li chiang ti ch'ü ching chi ti li*; Peking: K'o hsüeh ch'u pan she, 1957; 98 p.
Washington, D.C.: U.S. Joint Publications Research Service, 9 Dec. 1958. 161 p. (JPRS 411D; MC 1748/1959)
Subj 11.3 21.2 24 24.2 24.4 ▪ 21 21.1 24.1

1949-1972

10399 MCH P P2 G1.2 1949–1972
Berger, IAkov Mikhailovich (Ya. M. Berger), 1929–.
Kitai: ekonomiko-geograficheskii ocherk (An economic and geographic survey of China).
Moscow: Geografgiz, 1959. 109 p.
China: Economic-geographic sketch, mimeo.
Washington, D.C.: U.S. Joint Publications Research Service, 12 Dec. 1960. 87 p. (JPRS 6394; MC 2256/1961) [Xerox copyflo available—New York: CCM Corp., Research and Microfilm Publications. (Scholarly Book Translation series, 493)]
Subj 11.1 11.3 14 14.1 14.4 ▪ 55 61

10400 CSU U P8 G1.2 1949–1972
Chen, Cheng-siang (Ch'en Cheng-hsiang), 1920–.
The agricultural regions of China, edited by Michael Y. Nuttonson.
Silver Spring, Md.: American Institute of Crop Ecology, 1970. 47 p.
Subj 11.3 14.1

10401 CSH F P2 G4.0 1949–1972
Chou Li-san, et al.
Preliminary research on agricultural regions in the mixed agro-pastoral realm of Kansu and Tsinghai, mimeo. Tr. of *Kan Ch'ing nung mu chiao ts'o ti ch'ü nung yeh ch'ü hua ch'u pu yen chiu* (A preliminary study of agricultural zoning in the mixed agricultural-pastoral area of Kansu and Tsinghai) edited by Ti li yen chiu so, Chung-kuo k'o hsüeh yüan (Institute of Geography, Chinese Academy of Sciences); Peking: K'o hsüeh ch'u pan she, 1958; 80 p.
Washington, D.C.: U.S. Joint Publications Research Service, 1966. 211 p. (JPRS 36,077; MC 12,117/1966)
Subj 11.3 24.1 ▪ 21 21.1 24.2 24.4 28 66

10402 CSU FP P8 G1.4 1949–1972
Chung-kuo k'o hsüeh yüan. Chih sha kung tso tui. (Chinese Academy of Sciences. Sand Control Team).
A report on the coordinated research on the desert regions, Nos. 1 and 2, mimeo. Tr. of *Sha mo ti ch'ü ti tsung ho tiao ch'a yen chiu pao kao*; Peking: K'o hsüeh ch'u pan she, 1958, 1959; 2 vols.
Washington, D.C.: U.S. Joint Publications Research Service, 11 Apr. 1963, 18 Mar. 1963. 351; 222 p. (JPRS 18,658 and 18,178; MC 9017/1963 and 8537/1963) [Xerox copyflo of No. 1 available—New York: CCM Information Corp., Research and Microfilm Publications. (Scholarly Book Translation Series, 520)]
Subj 11.3 14.2 18 ▪ 14.1 21

10403 MCH S P2 G1.2 1949–1972
Cressey, George Babcock, 1896–1963.
'Changing the map of China.'
EG 31, 1 (Jan. 1955), 1–16.
Subj 11.3 14 ▪ 11 11.1 14.1 14.4 19

10404 CSU S P2 G1.4 1949–1972
Cressey, George Babcock, 1896–1963.
'Regions of North China.' In *Asia's lands and peoples: A geography of one-third of the earth and two-thirds of its people*, 3rd ed., by G. B. Cressey. [Selective entry]
New York: McGraw-Hill, 1963, 122–138.
Subj 11.3 ▪ 11.1 14.1 14.2

10405 CSU S P2 G1.2 1949–1972
Cressey, George Babcock, 1896–1963.
'Regions of outer China.' In *Asia's lands and peoples: A geography of one-third of the earth and two-thirds of its people*, 3rd ed., by G. B. Cressey. [Selective entry]
New York: McGraw-Hill, 1963, 160–173.
Subj 11.3 ▪ 11.1 14.1 14.2

10406 CSU S P2 G1.5 1949–1972
Cressey, George Babcock, 1896–1963.
'Regions of South China.' In *Asia's lands and peoples: A geography of one-third of the earth and two-thirds of its people*, 3rd ed., by G. B. Cressey. [Selective entry]
New York: McGraw-Hill, 1963, 139–159.
Subj 11.3 ▪ 11.1 14.1 14.2

10407 CSU P P2 G1.1 1949–1972
De Crespigny, Rafe R. C.
China: The land and its people.
Melbourne: Nelson, 1971. 13, 235 p.
Subj 11.3 14 ▪ 11.4 14.1 14.2 14.4 21.4

10408 NNC P P2 G1.2 1949–1972
Fang Tien-pai (Fang T'ien-pai).
'The new developments in China's urban and rural relations.' Tr. of 'Wo kuo ch'eng hsiang kuan hsi ti hsin fa chan' (New developments in rural-urban interrelations in China); *Hsüeh hsi* 1956, 6 (June), 5–12.
ECMM 46 (7 Aug. 1956), 14–24.
Subj 11.3 14 14.3 16 ▪ 11.2 14.1 14.4

10409 MCH S P2 G1.2 1949–1972
Fochler-Hauke, Gustav, 1906–.
'Geographische Grundzüge der neuen Verwaltungseinteilung Chinas' (Geographic characteristics of China's new administrative divisions).
PGM 97, 2 (1953), 137–139.
Subj 11.3 ▪ 12

10410 CSU S P2 G1.2 1949–1972
Freeberne, John Derek Michael, 1935–.
'The People's Republic of China.' In *The changing map of Asia: A political geography*, 5th ed., rev., edited by W. Gordon East, O. H. K. Spate, and Charles A. Fisher. [Selective entry]
London: Methuen, 1971, 341–447.
Subj 11.3 14.1 14.2 14.4 ▪ 11 12 19 34.1 51 54

10411 MCH P P2 G1.2 1949–1972
Ginsburg, Norton Sydney, 1921–.
'China's changing political geography.'
GR 42, 1 (Jan. 1952), 102–117.
Subj 11.3 12 ▪ 22 66

10412 CSU U P2 G1.2 1949–1972
Ginsburg, Norton Sydney, 1921–.
'The geography of China.' In *Understanding modern China*, edited by Joseph M. Kitagawa (Kitagawa Mitsuo). [Selective entry]
Chicago: Quadrangle, 1969, 42–73.
Subj 11.3 14.1 ▪ 14.2

10413 CSU P P2 G1.2 1949–1972
Hsieh I-yuan.
Legal basis for the delineation of administrative regions throughout the People's Republic of China, mimeo. Tr. of 'Chung-hua jen min kung ho kuo hsing cheng ch'ü yü ti hua fen'; *Ti li hsüeh pao* 1958, 1 (Feb.), 84–97.
Washington, D.C.: U.S. Joint Publications Research Service, 14 Apr. 1959. 30 p. (JPRS 650D; MC 9162/1959)
Subj 11.3 12.2 21

10414 CSU S P2 G1.2 1949–1972
Johnson, Edgar Augustus Jerome, 1900–.
'Efforts at spatial reform in Mainland China.' In *The organization of space in*

developing countries, by E. A. J. Johnson. [Sole entry]
Cambridge: Harvard U. Press, 1970, 326–335.
Subj 11.3 14 ▪ 14.3 14.4 24.3

10415 CSH PO P2 G4.0 1949–1972
Kalmykova, Valentina Grigor'evna, and Ivan Kharitonovich Ovdienko, 1910–.
Severo-Zapadnyi Kitai: geograficheskii ocherk.
Moscow: Geografgiz, 1957. 192 p.
Geographical survey of Northwest China, Parts 1–3, mimeo.
Washington, D.C.: U.S. Joint Publications Research Service, 12 Dec. 1958. 157 p. (JPRS 1025, 1026, and 1027; MC 1843/1959, 1844/1959, and 1845/1959)
Subj 11.3 14 14.1 14.4 ▪ 14.2 17 21 21.2

10416 MCH S P2 G9.4 1949–1972
Kramm, H- J-.
'Taiwan: Eine ökonomisch-geographische Studie' (Taiwan: A study in economic geography).
Geographische Berichte 11, 3 (1966), 161–180.
Subj 11.3 24.1 ▪ 14.4

10417 CSH P P8 G1.4 1949–1972
[La Dany, Ladislao] ———, 1914–.
'The deserts.'
CNA 420 (11 May 1962), 1–7.
Subj 11.3 14.1 ▪ 36.1 62

10418 CSH P P2 G1.2 1949–1972
[La Dany, Ladislao] ———, 1914–.
'Economic issues.'
CNA 880 (12 May 1972), 1–7.
Subj 11.3 14 ▪ 12 35

10419 MCH P P1 G1.2 1949–1972
[La Dany, Ladislao] ———, 1914–.
'Regional administrative division.'
CNA 373 (26 May 1961), 1–7.
Subj 11.3

10420 CSU U P2 G1.2 1949–1972
Lai, Chuen-yün (Li Ch'üan-en), 1937–.
'Chinese written language and geographical names.'
Canadian geographical j. 80, 1 (Jan. 1970), 20–25.
Subj 11.3 29 ▪ 17 62

10421 NNC FP P2 G2.2 1949–1972
Li Chen-ch'uan (Li Chen-ch'üan).
Economic geography of the Yen-pien Korean Autonomous Chou, mimeo. Tr. of *Yen-pien Ch'ao-hsien tsu tzu chih chou ching chi ti li*; Shanghai: Hsin chih shih ch'u pan she, 1957; 84 p.
Washington, D.C.: U.S. Joint Publications Research Service, 1959. 131 p. (JPRS 2019N; MC 909/1960)
Subj 11.3 20 24 24.1 24.4 ▪ 17 21 21.3 24.2 28 55 66

10422 NNC S P2 G1.2 1949–1972
McColl, Robert William, 1938–.
'Development of supra-provincial administrative regions in Communist China, 1949–1960.'
Pacific viewpoint 4, 1 (Mar. 1963), 53–64.
Subj 11.3 12 ▪ 15

10423 NNC P P7 G1.4 1949–1972
Mitchell, William Burton, 1918–.
The prospects for the Chinese Communist Yellow River plan.
Unpublished doctoral dissertation in Geography, Columbia U., 1961. 141 p.
Subj 11.3 11.4 14.1 ▪ 18

10424 NNC P P2 G1.2 1949–1972
Ovdienko, Ivan Kharitonovich, 1910–.
Kitai: ekonomiko-geograficheskii obzor (Survey of the economic geography of China).
Moscow: Uchpedgiz, 1959. 329 p.
Subj 11 11.3 14 14.1 14.2 14.4 ▪ 14.3 21 21.1 72

10425 MCH P P2 G1.2 1949–1972
Shabad, Theodore, 1922–.
China's changing map: National and regional development, 1949–71, rev. ed.
New York: Praeger, 1972. 13, 370 p.
Subj 11 11.3 14 21.3 ▪ 11.1 14.1 14.2 14.4 34.1

10426 CSU FP P2 G9.0 1949–1972
Sun Ching-chih, ed.
Economic geography of South China (Kwangtung, Kwangsi, Fukien), mimeo. Tr. of *Hua-nan ti ch'ü ching chi ti li* (An economic geography of South China) edited by Chung-hua ti li chih pien chi pu, Chung-kuo k'o hsüeh yüan (Committee for the Compilation of Geographies of China, Chinese Academy of Sciences); Peking: K'o hsüeh ch'u pan she, 1959; 147 p.
Washington, D.C.: U.S. Joint Publications Research Service, 24 Aug. 1962. 14, 514 p. (JPRS 14,954; MC 19,715/1962) [Xerox copyflo available—New York: CCM Information Corp., Research and Microfilm Publications. (Scholarly Book Translation Series, 500)]
Subj 11.3 14 ▪ 14.1 14.2 14.4 21 21.1

10427 CBU FP P2 G3.0 1949–1972
Sun Ching-chih.
Excerpts from 'Economic geography of the Inner Mongolia Autonomous Region,' mimeo. Tr. of *Nei Meng-ku tzu chih ch'ü ching chi ti li* (An economic geography of the Inner Mongolian Autonomous Region) edited by Chung-hua ti li chih pien chi pu, Chung-kuo k'o hsüeh yüan (Committee for the Compilation of Geographies of China, Chinese Academy of Sciences); Peking: K'o hsüeh ch'u pan she, 1957; 76 p. [Partial tr.: p. 1–8, 12–76 only]
Washington, D.C.: U.S. Joint Publications Research Service, 7 Nov. 1958. 125 p. (JPRS 368D; MC 17,058/1958) [Xerox copyflo available—New York: CCM Information Corp., Research and Microfilm Publications. (Scholarly Book Translation Series, 498)]
Subj 11.3 14 14.4 21 ▪ 14.1 14.2 21.1 55 66

10428 NNC FP P2 G2.0 1949–1972
Sun Ching-chih, et al.
Economic geography of Northeast China: Liaoning, Kirin, Heilungkiang, mimeo. Tr. of *Tung-pei ti ch'ü ching chi ti li (Liao-ning, Chi-lin, Hei-lung-chiang)* edited by Chung-hua ti li chih pien chi pu, Chung-kuo k'o hsüeh yüan (Committee for the Compilation of Geographies of China, Chinese Academy of Sciences); Peking: K'o hsüeh ch'u pan she, 1959; 211 p.
Washington, D.C.: U.S. Joint Publications Research Service, 21 Sept. 1962. 571 p. (JPRS 15,388; MC 22,026/1962)
Subj 11.3 14 24.1 ▪ 14.2 14.4 21 21.1 21.2 21.4

10429 CSU FP P2 G8.0 1949–1972
Sun Ching-chih, et al.
Economic geography of Southwest China (Szechwan, Kweichow, Yunnan), mimeo. Tr. of *Hsi-nan ti ch'ü ching chi ti li: Ssu-chuan, Kuei-chou, Yün-nan* edited by Chung-hua ti li chih pien chi pu, Chung-kuo k'o hsüeh yüan (Committee for the Compilation of Geographies of China, Chinese Academy of Sciences); Peking: K'o hsüeh ch'u pan she, 1960; 141 p.
Washington, D.C.: U.S. Joint Publications Research Service, 31 Aug. 1962. 737 p. (JPRS 15,069; MC 8438/1963) [Xerox copyflo available—New York: CCM Information Corp., Research and Microfilm Publications. (Scholarly Book Translation Series, 501)]
Subj 11.3 14 14.1 14.4 ▪ 14.2 21 21.1 24.4

10430 CSU FP P2 G6.0 1949–1972
Sun Ching-chih, et al.
Economic geography of the East China Region (Shanghai, Kiangsu, Anhwei, Chekiang), mimeo. Tr. of *Hua-tung ti ch'ü ching chi ti li* (An economic geography of East China) edited by Chung-hua ti li chih pien chi pu, Chung-kuo k'o hsüeh yüan (Committee for the Compilation of Geographies of China, Chinese Academy of Sciences); Peking: K'o hsüeh ch'u pan she, 1959; 153 p.
Washington, D.C.: U.S. Joint Publications Research Service, 7 Dec. 1961. 338 p. (JPRS 11,438; MC 3035/1962) [Xerox copyflo available—New York: CCM Information Corp., Research and Microfilm Publications. (Scholarly Book Translation Series, 496)]
Subj 11.3 14 ▪ 14.1 14.2 14.4 21 21.1

10431 CBU FP P2 G5.0 1949–1972
Sun Ching-chih, et al.
Excerpts from 'Economic geography of North China'. Tr. of *Hua-pei ching chi ti li* (An economic geography of North China) edited by Chung-hua ti li chih pien chi pu, Chung-kuo k'o hsüeh yüan; Peking: K'o hsüeh ch'u pan she, 1957; 183 p. [Partial tr.: p. 1–7, 14–38, 41–88, 90–120, 123–152, 154–183 only]
Washington, D.C.: U.S. Joint Publications Research Service, 23 May 1958. 270 p. (JPRS 144D)
Subj 11.3 14 14.1 14.4 21 ▪ 14.2 21.1 24

10432 CSU P P2 G1.1 1949–1972
Tregear, Thomas Refoy, 1897–.
An economic geography of China.
New York: American Elsevier, 1970. 12, 276 p.
Subj 11.3 14 14.1 14.2 14.4 ▪ 11 11.4 21 21.1 22 34.1 58

10433 CSU S P2 G1.2 1949–1972
Wiens, Herold Jacob, 1912–1971.
'China: The North and Far West.' In *The pattern of Asia*, edited by Norton Sydney Ginsburg. [Selective entry]
Englewood Cliffs, N. J.: Prentice-Hall, 1958, 190–212.
Subj 11.3 14

10434 CSU S P2 G1.5 1949–1972
Wiens, Herold Jacob, 1912–1971.
'China: The South.' In *The pattern of Asia*, edited by Norton Sydney Ginsburg. [Selective entry]
Englewood Cliffs, N. J.: Prentice-Hall, 1958, 213–238.
Subj 11.3 14 ▪ 21.1

10435 CBU FP P2 G1.4 1949–1972
Wu Ch'uan-chün, et al.
Economic geography of the western region of the middle Yellow River. Tr. of *Huang ho chung yu hsi pu ti ch'ü ching chi ti li* edited by Ti li yen chiu so, Chung-kuo k'o hsüeh yüan (Institute of Geography, Chinese Academy of Sciences); Peking: K'o hsüeh ch'u pan she, 1956; 101 p.
Washington, D.C.: U.S. Joint Publications Research Service, 1 Aug. 1958. 200 p. (JPRS 253D) [Xerox copyflo available—New York: CCM Information Corp., Research and Microfilm Publications. (Scholarly Book Translation Series, 502)]
Subj 11.3 14 14.1 14.2 ▪ 14.4 21 21.1 21.3 21.4 34.1

10436 MAM P P2 G9.4 1949–1972
Yuan, D. Y.
The rural-urban continuum: A demographic case study of Taiwan.
Ann Arbor: University Microfilms (Publ. 65-2260), 1965. 297 p. (Doctoral dissertation in Sociology, Brown U., 1964)
Subj 11.3 ▪ 21 21.1 21.4 24.1

11.4 National Labor Force & Occupational Differentiation

全國勞動力及職業分化

国民総労働力及び職業分化

1644-1911

10437 NIC P P2 G1.3 –1911
Chi, Ch'ao-ting, 1903–1963.
Key economic areas in Chinese history, as revealed in the development of public works for water control.
London: Allen and Unwin, 1936. 23, 168 p. (Doctoral dissertation in Economics, Columbia U., 1936) [Reprinted—New York: Paragon, 1963. 23, 168 p.] [Reprinted—New York: Augustus M. Kelley, 1970. 23, 168 p.]
Subj 11.4 14 14.1 14.2 ▪ 12 18

10438 MCH S P7 G1.1 1842–1911
Nepomnin, Oleg Efimovich, 1935–.
'Naem i otkhodnichestvo krest'ian v Kitae vtoroi poloviny XIX – nachala XX v.' (Hired labor and peasant migration in China during the second half of the nineteenth and the beginning of the twentieth centuries). [With English abstract]
PV 1960, 1, 118–128.
Subj 11.2 11.4 ▪ 14.1 16.3

10439 MCH U P1 G1.3 1895–1911
Parker, Edward Harper, 1849–1926.
'Economy of Chinese labor.'
Economic j. 14, 154 (June 1904), 254–258.
Subj 11.4

10440 MCH O P2 G1.2 1842–1895
Simon, G- Eugène, 1829–1896.
'Le travail chez les Chinois' (Labor among the Chinese).
Nouvelle r. 22, 3 (1er juin 1883), 528–567.

'Labour.' In *China: Its social, political, and religious life*, by G. E. Simon. [Analytic entry]
London: Sampson Low, Marston, Searle, and Rivington, 1887, 61–121.
Subj 11.4 16.3 61 62 ▪ 18 24.4 33 34.2

10441 CSU P P2 G1.2 –1911
Yang, Lien-sheng, 1914–.
'Economic aspects of public works in China.' In *Excursions in sinology*, by Lien-sheng Yang. [Selective entry]
Cambridge: Harvard U. Press, 1969, 191–248. (Harvard-Yenching Institute studies, 24)
Subj 11.4 14 14.1 55 62 ▪ 12 14.2 14.5 16.1 22.2 35 47

1644-1949

□

1911-1949

10442 NNC P P2 G1.2 1911–1928
'Census of occupations in China.'
NWSS 4, 2 (12 Jan. 1931), 7, 10–12.
Subj 11.4

10443 NNC P P2 G1.3 1928–1949
'Unemployment in China.'
CEJ 9, 6 (Dec. 1931), 1377–1386.
Subj 11.4 ▪ 14 14.1 14.4 18

10444 NIC O P2 G1.3 1928–1949
Bennett, James William.
'China's perennially unemployed.'
Asia (New York: American Asiatic Assn.) 31, 4 (Apr. 1931), 215–219, 268–269.
Subj 11.4 ▪ 18 34.3

10445 NNC O P2 G1.1 1911–1928
Chen Ta (Ch'en Ta), 1892–.
'Labor conditions in China.'
Monthly labor review 19, 5 (Nov. 1924), 36–49.
Subj 11.4 ▪ 16.3 16.4 18 36.4

10446 NNC O P2 G1.1 1911–1949
Chen Ta (Ch'en Ta), 1892–.
'Labor in China during the civil wars.'
Monthly labor review 31, 1 (July 1930), 1–19.
Subj 11.4 16.3 16.4 ▪ 32.1 34.3 36.3 36.4

10447 MCH U P3 G1.1 1911–1928
Es, Willem Johan Louis van, 1886–1943.
'Waterbouwwerken in China' (Waterworks in China).
Koloniaal tijdschrift 18 (1929), 312–332.
Subj 11.4 14.2 ▪ 14.3

10448 NNC P P2 G1.2 1911–1949
Hsieh, Kia.
The problem of wage protection in China.
Unpublished masters thesis in Economics, Columbia U., 1943. 93 p.
Subj 11.4 18 ▪ 12.2 14.1 14.4

10449 NNC O P2 G1.3 1928–1949
Li ———.
'Bezrabotitsa i bor'ba bezrabotnykh v Kitae' (Unemployment and the struggle of the unemployed in China).
KIP 11, 3 (fevral' 1931), 38–42.

'Arbeitslosigkeit und der Kampf der Arbeitslosen in China.'
RGI 11, 3 (15 Feb. 1931), 89–92.

'Le chômage et la lutte des sans-travail en Chine.'
ISR 2e série 4/5 (15 fév. – 1er mars 1931), 177–180.
Subj 11.4 16.4

10450 GHT FP P2 G1.4 1911–1949
Li, Fu-tu, 1903–.
Die Regelung des Hwangho (The regulation of the Yellow River).
Hanover: Hahnsche Buchhandlung, 1933. 108 p. (Doctoral dissertation, Technische Hochschule Hannover)
Subj 11.3 11.4

10451 NIC S P2 G1.2 1928–1949
Orchard, Dorothy Johnson, 1897–.
'Man-power in China.'
Political science q. 50, 4 (Dec. 1935), 561–583; 51, 1 (Mar. 1936), 1–35.
Subj 11.4 14.1 14.4 16.4 18 ▪ 11.2 14.3 15 16.3 34.3 47 52

10452 WSU S P2 G1.4 1928–1949
Rockwood, Charles Parkman.
The Yellow River Project: A study of aid to an underdeveloped area.
Unpublished masters thesis in Far Eastern and Slavic Languages, U. of Washington, 1950. 153 p.
Subj 11.3 11.4 18 66 ▪ 14 14.1 14.2 25

10453 MCH S P2 G1.2 1911–1949
Shen, Djini (Shen Chin-i).
'Die Faktoren der Lohnbildung in China' (Factors determining the wage structure in China). In *Der Arbeitslohn in China* (Labor wages in China), by Paul Arndt, D. Shen, and Chü-fen Lo. [Analytic entry]
Leipzig: Hans Buske, 1937, 85–195.
Subj 11.4 14 16 18 ▪ 11 64

10454 CSU F P8 G1.4 1928–1949
Todd, Oliver Julian, 1880–, and Sigurd Eliassen, 1884–.
'The Yellow River problem.'
Proceedings of the American Society of Civil Engineers 64, 10 (Dec. 1938), 1921–1991.
Subj 11.3 11.4 18 ▪ 12 14.1 14.2

1911-1972
(including 1644-1972)

10455 CSH O P8 G1.4 1928–1972
Huang Chun.
'Conquering the Yellow River.'
PR 1971, 42 (15 Oct.), 9–14. [Reprinted as 'A new chapter in taming the Yellow River.' In *China tames her rivers*. (Analytic entry.) Peking: Foreign Languages Press, 1972, 1–14.]
Subj 11.3 11.4 14.1 18 ▪ 24.1

10456 CSH P P2 G1.2 1928–1972
Yang Cheng Shih.
'Labor force.' In *A general handbook of China*, compiled by Far Eastern and

Russian Institute, U. of Washington. [Selective entry]
New Haven: Human Relations Area Files, 1956, vol. 1, 751–776. (HRAF subcontractor's monographs, 55; Washington 4)
SUBJ 11.4 16.4 ▪ 11.2 18 35

1949-1972

10457 NNC P P1 G1.2 1949–1972
'Award of pensions to workers and salaried employees.'
BISSA 12, 3 (Mar. 1959), 114–116.
SUBJ 11.4 ▪ 16.2 16.4 18

10458 CSH O P8 G1.4 1949–1972
'The people of three provinces unite to control water.'
China reconstructs 19, 4 (Apr. 1970), 28–32.
SUBJ 11.4

10459 NNC FP P2 G1.2 1949–1972
'Wage revisions in Communist China.'
URS 33, 10 (1 Nov. 1963), 156–173.
SUBJ 11.4 ▪ 15 18

10460 CSH P P8 G1.2 1949–1972
Carin, Robert.
River control in Communist China, mimeo.
Hong Kong: Union Research Institute, 1962. 124, 51 p. (Communist China problem research series, EC31)
SUBJ 11.4 14 18 ▪ 14.1

10461 CSH P P2 G1.2 1949–1972
Chang Ho-wei.
'The worker-peasant labor system in finance and trade departments.' Tr. of 'Lüeh lun ts'ai mao fang mien ti i kung i nung lao tung chih tu' (A brief discussion of the balanced emphasis on industry and agriculture in the finance and trade branches of the government); *Hsin chien she* 1966, 1/2 (20 Feb.), 57–67.
SCMM 534 (25 July 1966), 24–38.
SUBJ 11.4 26.4 ▪ 24.1 24.3 24.4 26.3

10462 MCY FP P7 G1.2 1949–1972
Chao, Kuo-chün, 1918–1962.
'Rural manpower in India and China.'
FEER 35, 2 (11 Jan. 1962), 53–55, 57, 59, 61.
SUBJ 11.4 14.1 16.3 ▪ 34.1 58

10463 CSU P P4 G1.2 1949–1972
Cheng Chu-yuan (Cheng Chu-yüan), 1927–.
'Scientific and engineering manpower in Communist China.' In *An economic profile of Mainland China*, compiled by Joint Economic Committee, U.S. Congress. [Selective entry]
Washington, D.C.: U.S. Government Printing Office, 1967, vol. 2, 519–547. [Reprinted in *An economic profile of Mainland China*, compiled by the agency cited. (Selective entry.) New York: Praeger, 1968, 519–547.]
SUBJ 11.4 16.1 16.2 17 ▪ 14.4 15 36.1

10464 CSH P P4 G1.2 1949–1972
Cheng Chu-yuan (Cheng Chu-yüan), 1927–.
Scientific and engineering manpower in Communist China, 1949–1963.
Washington, D.C.: National Science Foundation, 1966. 588 p. (Revision of *The growth of technical manpower in Communist China, 1949–1962: Training, employment and significance to economic growth*, doctoral dissertation in Economics, Georgetown U., 1964)
SUBJ 11.4 16.1 16.2 17 62 ▪ 14 32.1 36.1 47

10465 CSU P P2 G1.2 1949–1972
Current Scene Editor.
'Sources of labor discontent in China: The worker-peasant system.'
CS 6, 5 (15 Mar. 1968), 1–28.
SUBJ 11.2 11.4 12.1 14.4 16.3 16.4 ▪ 18 22.2 32.1 36.4 54

10466 NNC P P7 G1.2 1949–1972
Doi Akira, 1905–.
Unpaid labor in China, mimeo. Tr. of 'Chūgoku ni okeru mushō rōdo'; *Ajia kenkyū* 1, 1 (Apr. 1954), 119–127.
Washington, D.C.: U.S. Joint Publications Research Service, 4 Nov. 1958. 12 p. (JPRS 350D; MC 17,048/1958)
SUBJ 11.4 12.1 ▪ 18

10467 NIC P P2 G1.2 1949–1972
Emerson, John Philip, 1925–.
'Chinese Communist Party views on labor utilization before and after 1958.'
CS 1, 30 (20 Apr. 1962), 1–10. [Reprinted as 'Party views on labour utilization.' In *This is China: Analyses of Mainland trends and events*, edited by Francis Harper. (Selective entry.) Hong Kong: Dragonfly Books, 1965, 101–114.]
SUBJ 11.4 14 ▪ 16.4 64 70

10468 CSU P P2 G1.2 1949–1972
Emerson, John Philip, 1925–.
'Employment in Mainland China: Problems and prospects.' In *An economic profile of Mainland China*, compiled by Joint Economic Committee, U.S. Congress. [Selective entry]
Washington, D.C.: U.S. Government Printing Office, 1967, vol. 2, 403–470. [Reprinted in *An economic profile of Mainland China*, compiled by the agency cited. (Selective entry.) New York: Praeger, 1968, 403–470.]
SUBJ 11.4 14 14.4 ▪ 11.1 11.2 12.1 17

10469 CSU P P2 G1.2 1949–1972
Emerson, John Philip, 1925–.
'Manpower training and utilization of specialized cadres, 1949–68.' In *The city in Communist China*, edited by John Wilson Lewis. [Analytic entry]
Stanford: Stanford U. Press, 1971, 183–214.
SUBJ 11.4 14 16.1 17 ▪ 11 11.2 12.1 58

10470 MCY P P4 G1.2 1949–1972
Emerson, John Philip, 1925–.
Sex, age, and level of skill of the nonagricultural labor force of Mainland China.
Washington, D.C.: U.S. Bureau of the Census, Foreign Demographic Analysis Division, 1965. 32 p.
SUBJ 11.4 47 ▪ 14.3 14.4 17 50

10471 CSU P P2 G1.4 1949–1972
Freeberne, John Derek Michael, 1935–.
'The Haiho river basin project.'
Geography 57, 3 (July 1972), 217–225.
SUBJ 11.4 18

10472 NNC P P2 G1.2 1949–1972
Gel'bras, Vil' Gdal'evich, 1930–.
'Dostizheniia Kitaiskoi Narodnoi Respubliki v oblasti truda i zarabotnoi platy za desiat' let' (A decade of labor and wage achievements in the People's Republic of China).
Sotsialisticheskii trud 4, 9 (sentiabr' 1959), 27–38.
SUBJ 11.4 16.4 18 ▪ 14.1 14.4 16.3

10473 CSH P P2 G1.2 1949–1972
Gel'bras, Vil' Gdal'evich, 1930–.
'Nekotorye voprosy razvitiia rabochego klassa sovremennogo Kitaia' (Questions on the development of contemporary China's working class).
NAA 1972, 3, 18–34.
SUBJ 11.4 14 ▪ 12.1 36.4

10474 DLC P P2 G1.2 1949–1972
Gel'bras, Vil' Gdal'evich, 1930–.
'Peresmotr tarifno-kvalifikatsionnykh spravochnikov v KNR' (Review of job-classification manuals in the People's Republic of China).
BNI 3, 1 (ianvar' 1960), 64–65.
SUBJ 11.4 ▪ 16.4

10475 ELB P P2 G1.4 1949–1972
Gershman, A- E-.
'Reka Khuankhe i pervoocherednye meropriiatiia po uporiadocheniiu ee rezhima' (The Yellow River and the major steps taken to regulate its course).
Izvestiia Vsesoiuznogo geograficheskogo obshchestva 90, 1 (ianvar'–fevral' 1958), 3–13.
SUBJ 11.4 18

10476 NNC S P2 G1.4 1949–1972
Gortsev, V- I-.
'Vazhneishie meropriiatiia po preobrazovaniiu prirody v Kitaiskoi Narodnoi Respublike' (Serious attempts to modify natural phenomena in the People's Republic of China).
Izvestiia Vsesoiuznogo geograficheskogo obshchestva 86, 1 (ianvar'–fevral' 1954), 50–56.
SUBJ 11.4 14 14.1 18 ▪ 11.3

10477 CSU P P2 G1.2 1949–1972
Hoffmann, Charles, 1921–.
Work incentive practices and policies in the People's Republic of China, 1953–1965.
Albany: State U. of New York Press, 1967. 148 p.
SUBJ 11.4 12.1 16.3 16.4 61 ▪ 14.1 14.4 16 18 34.1 64

10478 CSU P P2 G1.2 1949–1972
Hou, Chi-ming, 1924–.
'Manpower, employment, and unemployment.' In *Economic trends in Communist China*, edited by Alexander Eckstein, Walter Galenson, and Ta-chung Liu. [Selective entry]
Chicago: Aldine, 1968, 329–396.
SUBJ 11.4 ▪ 11 58

10479 MCH P P4 G1.2 1949–1972
Howe, Christopher Barry, 1937–.
Employment and economic growth in urban China, 1949–1957.

Cambridge: Cambridge U. Press, 1971. 170 p. (Revision of *Labour problems in the economic development of urban China, 1949–1957*, doctoral dissertation in Economics, U. of London [School of Oriental and African Studies], 1970)
SUBJ 11.4 21.2 21.4 ▪ 11.2 12.1 14 21.1

10480 DLC P P2 G1.2 1949–1972
Huran, J-, and K- Nan.
'Vodní hospodářství Lidové republiky čínské' (Water conservancy in the People's Republic of China).
Vodní hospodářství (Prague) 10, 1 (1960), 15–22; 10, 2 (1960), 73–77.
SUBJ 11.4 14.1

10481 CSU P P2 G1.2 1949–1972
Iklé, Fred Charles, 1924–.
The growth of China's scientific and technical manpower.
Santa Monica, Calif.: RAND Corp., 1957. 74 p. (RAND memoranda, RM-1893; Astia documents, AD-123,545)
SUBJ 11.4 17 ▪ 14.2 16.1 16.2 36.1 62

10482 CSH P P2 G1.2 1949–1972
[La Dany, Ladislao] ———, 1914–.
'Geopolitical considerations: Redundance or shortage of manpower?'
CNA 844 (11 June 1971), 1–7.
SUBJ 11 11.4 ▪ 11.1 14.1 21.2 51

10483 NNC P P5 G1.2 1949–1972
[La Dany, Ladislao] ———, 1914–.
'Manpower survey: Clerks-and-workers, 1949–1956, manpower in government offices.'
CNA 169 (22 Feb. 1957), 1–7.
SUBJ 11.4 ▪ 12 16.2 22

10484 MCY P P2 G1.2 1949–1972
Lindsay, T- J-.
'Water conservancy and hydro-electric schemes in China.' In *Contemporary China, 1956–1957*, edited by Edward Stuart Kirby. [Selective entry]
Hong Kong: Hong Kong U. Press, 1958, 36–53.
SUBJ 11.4 14.1 14.4

10485 MCY P P2 G1.2 1949–1972
Lindsay, T- J-.
'Water conservancy and hydro-electric schemes in China (II).' In *Contemporary China, 1958–1959*, edited by Edward Stuart Kirby. [Selective entry]
Hong Kong: Hong Kong U. Press, 1960, 163–180.
SUBJ 11.4 14.4 ▪ 14.1

10486 MAM P P2 G1.2 1949–1972
Mesa-Lago, Carmelo, 1934–.
'China.' In *Unemployment in socialist countries: Soviet Union, East Europe, China and Cuba*, by C. Mesa-Lago. [Sole entry]
Ann Arbor: University Microfilms (Publ. 68-11,638), 1968, 278–345. (Doctoral dissertation in Economics, Cornell U.)
SUBJ 11.4 12.1 ▪ 14.1 14.4 16.3 16.4

10487 NNC P P2 G1.2 1949–1972
Mitsuoka Gen, 1928–.
Change in the structure of labor in New China, mimeo. Tr. of 'Shin Chūgoku no rōdō soshiki no hensen'; *Chūgoku shiryō geppō* 137 (July 1959), 1–26.
Washington, D.C.: U.S. Joint Publications Research Service, 7 Dec. 1959. 33 p. (JPRS 2059N; MC 1941/1960)
SUBJ 11.4 14 16.4 ▪ 16.3 34.1 47 58

10488 NNC P P2 G1.2 1949–1972
Ong, Shao-er (Weng Shao-erh), 1917–.
Labor problems in Communist China (to February 1953).
Lackland Air Force Base, San Antonio, Tex.: U.S. Air Force Personnel and Training Research Center, Air Research and Development Command, 1955. 15, 83 p. (U.S. Human Resources Research Institute research memoranda, 42; Studies in Chinese Communism, series 3, 5, 1953)
SUBJ 11.4 12.1 18 36.4 ▪ 12 12.2 14 14.4 16.4 47 72

10489 NIC S P7 G1.2 1949–1972
Orleans, Leo A-, 1924–.
'Problems of manpower absorption in rural China.'
CQ 7 (July–Sept. 1961), 57–68.
SUBJ 11.4 14.1 36.3 ▪ 11.2 14.4 16.3 34.1

10490 MCH P P2 G1.2 1949–1972
Reubens, Edwin Pierce, 1914–.
'The dream and reality of water control in Communist China.'
CS 2, 4 (14 Sept. 1962), 1–14. [Reprinted as 'Water control and labour mobilization.' In *This is China: Analyses of Mainland trends and events*, edited by Francis Harper. (Selective entry.) Hong Kong: Dragonfly Books, 1965, 143–161.]
SUBJ 11.4 14 34.1 ▪ 14.1

10491 MCY P P2 G1.2 1949–1972
Reubens, Edwin Pierce, 1914–.
'Under-employment theory and Chinese Communist experience.'
AS 4, 12 (Dec. 1964), 1191–1204.
SUBJ 11.4 12.1 14 ▪ 18 32.1 47

10492 CSU O P2 G1.2 1949–1972
Robinson, Joan, 1903–.
'For use, not for profit: A report on a recent visit to China.'
EH 11, 4 (1972), 6–15.
SUBJ 11.4 16.3 16.4 ▪ 14.3 14.5 24.4 34.1 34.2

10493 MCH O P2 G1.2 1949–1972
Schoemaker, H- J-.
'Indrukken van het waterbeheer in China' (Impressions of water management in China). In *China tussen eergisteren en overmorgen* (China between the day before yesterday and the day after tomorrow), edited by Willem Frederik Wertheim and Erik Zürcher. [Selective entry]
The Hague: Van Hoeve, 1963, 85–94.
SUBJ 11.4 14 ▪ 14.1 14.2 14.4

10494 DLC U P3 G1.2 1949–1972
Shelekasov, P- V-.
'Pod"em material'nogo blagosostoianiia rabochikh i sluzashchikh KNR' (Improvement in the material welfare of industrial, office, and professional workers in the People's Republic of China).
BNI 3, 5 (mai 1960), 52–55.
SUBJ 11.4 18 ▪ 16.2 16.4

10495 DLC S P4 G1.2 1949–1972
Shelekasov, P- V-.
'Povyshenie kul'turno-tekhnicheskogo urovnia rabochikh i sluzhashchikh KNR' (Raising the cultural and technological level of industrial, office, and professional workers in the People's Republic of China).
BNI 3, 4 (aprel' 1960), 47–49.
SUBJ 11.4 17 ▪ 16.2 16.4

10496 CSH P P2 G1.2 1949–1972
Shirokova, E- A-.
'Sistema organizatsii truda "i rabochii, i krest'ianin" v KNR' (The worker-peasant labor system in the People's Republic of China).
NAA 1969, 4, 15–25.
SUBJ 11.4 12.1 14 16.4 ▪ 11.2 16.3 18 64

10497 NNC P P2 G1.2 1949–1972
Tien, H. Yuan (T'ien Hsin-yüan), 1926–.
'Educational expansion, development of educational personnel and economic development in China.' In *Proceedings of the World Population Conference, 1965*, edited by Dept. of Economic and Social Affairs, United Nations. [Sole entry]
New York: Dept. of Economic and Social Affairs, 1967, vol. 4, 181–183.
SUBJ 11.4 17 ▪ 11.2

10498 NNC P P2 G1.2 1949–1972
Ting, Anna L., 1934–.
The role of population in China's economic development, 1949–1963.
Unpublished masters thesis in Economics, Columbia U., 1964. 116 p.
SUBJ 11 11.4 14 14.6 ▪ 11.2 14.1 14.4 58

10499 NNC P P2 G1.2 1949–1972
T'ung chi kung tso t'ung hsün. Tzu liao shih. (Documents Office).
'The structure and distribution of the national labor force in 1955.' Tr. of '1955 nien ch'üan kuo chih kung jen shu, kou ch'eng yü fen pu ti kai k'uang' (The number, composition, and distribution of employees and workers in China in 1955); *Hsin Hua pan yüeh k'an* 1957, 2 (25 Jan.), 87–89. In *The state of personnel, organizational, and supervisory work in Communist China*, mimeo., compiled by U.S. Joint Publications Research Service. [Sole entry]
Washington, D.C.: JPRS, 18 Jan. 1963, 11–24. (JPRS 17,199; MC 2995/1963) [A different tr.—'China's workers in 1955: Their number, composition, and distribution.' *ECMM* 68 (4 Feb. 1957), 27–34.]
SUBJ 11.4 ▪ 14 16 47

10500 NNC P P4 G1.2 1949–1972
U.S. Central Intelligence Agency.
Average annual money earnings of workers and staff in Communist China, 1949–1960.
Washington, D.C.: U.S. Central Intelligence Agency, 1960. 11 p.
SUBJ 11.4 18 ▪ 16.2 16.4

10501 CSH P P2 G1.2 1949–1972
Wang Chang-ling.
'Peiping's employment of middle school and college graduates.'
CCA 6, 1 (Feb. 1969), 54–59.
SUBJ 11.4 ▪ 16.1 17

10502 MCH PO P 7 G 1.2 1949–1972
Wertheim, Willem Frederik, 1907–.
'La Chine est-elle sous-peuplée? Production agricole et main-d'oeuvre rurale' (Is China underpopulated? Agricultural production and rural manpower).
Population (Paris) 20, 3 (mai–juin 1965), 477–514.
SUBJ 11.4 14 14.1 34.1 58 ▪ 11 16.3 18 22 51

10503 MAM P P 2 G 1.2 1949–1972
Zaccone, June Mary, 1929–.
Some aspects of surplus labor, water control, and planning in China, 1949–1960.
Ann Arbor: University Microfilms (Publ. 64-9448), 1964. 263 p. (Doctoral dissertation in Economics, U. of North Carolina, 1963)
SUBJ 11.4 14 14.1 18 ▪ 14.4 34.1

12 NATIONAL POLITICAL SYSTEM AND BUREAUCRACY

政制及吏治

政治制度及び官僚制

1644-1911

10504 NIC O P 2 G 1.2 1842–1911
Ardsheal, pseud.
'Reminiscences of a Chinese viceroy's secretary.'
JRAS-NCB new (2nd) series 45 (1914), 91–109; 46 (1915), 61–76.
SUBJ 12 16.1 64 ▪ 19 63

10505 MCH P P 3 G 5.1 –1911
Backhouse, Edmund Trelawney, 1873–1944, and John Otway Percy Bland, 1863–1945.
Annals and memoirs of the court of Peking (from the 16th to the 20th century).
Boston: Houghton Mifflin, 1914. 10, 531 p. [Reprinted—Taipei: Ch'eng-wen, 1970. 10, 531 p.] [Reprinted—New York: AMS Press, 1970. 10, 531 p.]
SUBJ 12 16.1 64 ▪ 12.1 13 14.5 17 32.2 62 66

10506 NIC P P 1 G 1.2 –1911
Balazs, Etienne, 1905–1963.
'L'histoire comme guide de la pratique bureaucratique.' In *Historians of China and Japan*, edited by William Gerald Beasley and Edwin George Pulleyblank. [Selective entry]
London: Oxford U. Press, 1961, 78–94. (U. of London, School of Oriental and African Studies, Historical writing on the peoples of Asia, 3).

'History as a guide to bureaucratic practice.' Tr. by Hope M- Wright. In *Chinese civilization and bureaucracy*, by E. Balazs, edited by Arthur Frederick Wright. [Selective entry]
New Haven: Yale U. Press, 1964, 129–149.
SUBJ 12 16.1

10507 MCH P P 2 G 1.3 –1842
Balazs, Etienne, 1905–1963.
Political theory and administrative reality in traditional China.
London: U. of London, School of Oriental and African Studies, 1965. 80 p.
SUBJ 12 16 22 64 ▪ 12.2 17 63

10508 NNC P P 3 G 1.2 1842–1895
Banno, Masataka, 1916–.
China and the West, 1858–1861: The origins of the Tsungli Yamen.
Cambridge: Harvard U. Press, 1964. 10, 367, 14 p. (Harvard East Asian series, 15)
SUBJ 12 16.1 32 ▪ 66

10509 MBA O P 4 G 1.2 1895–1911
Barthélemy, *Marquis* ——— de.
'Lettres de Chine' (Letters from China).
RI nouvelle (2e) série 16, 8 (août 1911), 136–150.
SUBJ 12 13 16.1 ▪ 14

10510 CSU P P 2 G 1.1 1842–1895
Bastid, Marianne, 1940–.
'Le déclin du système impérial (1855–1894)' (The decline of the imperial system, 1885–1894). In *De la guerre franco-chinoise à la fondation du Parti communiste chinois, 1885–1921* (From the Sino-French war to the formation of the Chinese Communist Party, 1885–1921), by M. Bastid, Marie-Claire Bergère, and Jean Chesneaux. [Analytic entry]
Paris: Hatier Université, 1972, 5–47. (HU, Collection d'histoire contemporaine, Histoire de la Chine, 2)
SUBJ 12 14 33 66 ▪ 15 16.1 16.2 22 32 32.2 34.2 64 72

10511 CSU P P 2 G 9.0 1842–1895
Bays, Daniel Henry, 1942–.
'The nature of provincial political authority in late Ch'ing times: Chang Chih-tung in Canton, 1884–1889.'
MAS 4, 4 (Oct. 1970), 325–347.
SUBJ 12 14 59 ▪ 14.4 14.5 25

10512 MCH PO P 2 G 1.2 –1842
Bazin, Antoine Pierre Louis, 1799–1863.
'Recherches sur les institutions administratives et municipales de la Chine: 1er mémoire' (Investigations of China's administrative and municipal institutions: First report).
JA 5e série 3 (jan. 1854), 5–66.
SUBJ 12 22 ▪ 26.1 41 42

10513 MCH PO P 4 G 1.2 1842–1895
Bazin, Antoine Pierre Louis, 1799–1863.
'Recherches sur les institutions administratives et municipales de la Chine: 2e mémoire' (Investigations of China's administrative and municipal institutions: Second report).
JA 5e série 4 (oct.–nov. 1854), 249–348.
SUBJ 12 22 62 ▪ 12.1 12.2 13 22.1 45

10514 NNC P P 2 G 5.1 1895–1911
Betz, Heinrich.
'Die lokale Selbstverwaltung in China' (Local self-government in China).
MSOSB 12 (1909), 49–60.
SUBJ 12 ▪ 22 22.1

10515 NNC P P 3 G 1.2 1895–1911
Betz, Heinrich.
'Die Verwaltungsreformen in China: Die Provinzialbehörden' (Administrative reforms in China: The provincial authorities).
MSOSB 12 (1909), 26–31.
SUBJ 12 ▪ 12.1

10516 MCH PO P 2 G 1.2 1842–1911
Bland, John Otway Percy, 1863–1945.
Recent events and present policies in China.
London: Heinemann, 1912. 12, 482 p. [Reprinted—Westport, Conn.: Hyperion Press, 197? 12, 482 p.]
SUBJ 12 14 54 ▪ 12.1 15 18 19 32.2

10517 MCH O P 4 G 1.2 1842–1895
Bourne, Frederick Samuel Augustus, 1854–1940.
'Historical table of the high officials composing the central and provincial governments of China.'
China review 7, 5 (Mar.–Apr. 1879), 314–329.
SUBJ 12 16.1

10518 NIC P P 4 G 1.2 1842–1911
Brenan, Byron, 1847–1927.
'The office of district magistrate in China.'
JRAS-CB new (2nd) series 32 (1897/98), 36–65. [Separately reprinted—Shanghai: Shanghai Mercury Office, 1899. 14 p.]
SUBJ 12 12.2 16.1 ▪ 14.5 22

10519 DLC P P 4 G 1.2 1895–1911
Brunnert, Ippolit Semenovich (H. S. Brunnert), and V- V- Gagel'strom (V. V. Hagelstrom).
Sovremennaia politicheskaia organizatsiia Kitaia.
Peking: Tip. Uspenskago monastyria pri RDM, 1910. 532 p.

Present day political organization of China, edited by N- Th- Kolessoff. Tr. by A- Beltchenko and E- E- Moran. [Rev. and enl. in tr.]
Shanghai: Kelly and Walsh, 1912. 572, 81 p. [Reprinted—Taipei: Book World, 1960. 572, 81 p.] [Reprinted—New York: Paragon, 1965. 572, 81 p.] [Reprinted—Taipei: Ch'eng-wen, 1970. 572, 81 p.]
SUBJ 12 15 17 22 66 ▪ 12.2 13 14.5

10520 NIC P P 1 G 1.2 –1911
Chang, C. M. (Chang Ch'un-ming), 1904–.
'Chinese standards of good government: Being a study of the 'Biographies of model officials' in dynastic histories.'
NSEQ 8, 2 (July 1935), 219–249. [Separately reprinted—Shanghai: China Institute of Pacific Relations, 1936. 51 p.]
SUBJ 12 16.1 63 64 ▪ 12.2 14.1 14.5 18

10521 CSH S P 4 G 1.2 –1911
Chang, Chin-chien, 1905–.
'Characteristics of Chinese bureaucracy.' Tr. by Joseph P. L. Jiang of 'Chung-kuo wen kuan chih tu chih t'e chih'; in *Chung-kuo wen kuan chih tu shih* (History of China's civil bureaucracy); Taipei: Chung-hua wen hua ch'u pan shih yeh wei yüan hui, 1955, 1–16. In *Chinese bureaucracy and government administration*, edited by T. W. Kwok (Kuo Te-hua). [Selective entry]
Honolulu: East-West Center Press, 1966, 72–90.
SUBJ 12 ▪ 16.1

10522 NIC P P3 G9.0 1644–1842
Chang, Hsin-pao, 1922–.
Commissioner Lin and the Opium War.
Cambridge: Harvard U. Press, 1964. 14, 319 p. (Harvard East Asian series, 18) (Revision of *Lin Tse-hsü and the coming of the Opium War*, doctoral dissertation in History, Harvard U., 1958)
SUBJ 12 16.1 66 ▪ 14.5 14.6 15 34.2 55

10523 NIC U P1 G1.2 1895–1911
Chang, Lau-chi.
'Government and public opinion in China.'
Proceedings of the American Political Science Assn. 6 (1909), 148–154.
SUBJ 12 ▪ 12.1

10524 CSU P P2 G1.2 –1895
Chang Te-ch'ang.
'The economic role of the imperial household in the Ch'ing dynasty.'
JAS 31, 2 (Feb. 1972), 243–273.
SUBJ 12 14.3 14.5 16.1 45

10525 NIC P P2 G1.3 1644–1911
Ch'ü, T'ung-tsu.
Local government in China under the Ch'ing.
Cambridge: Harvard U. Press, 1962. 14, 360, 50 p. (Harvard East Asian series, 9) [Reprinted—Stanford: Stanford U. Press, 1969. 14, 416 p.]
SUBJ 12 14.5 16.1 22 26.1 ▪ 12.1 12.2 14.3 18 30 63

10526 FPN S P2 G1.1 1644–1842
Commeaux, Charles.
De K'ang Hi à Kien Long: l'âge d'or des Ts'ing, 1662–1796 (From the K'ang-hsi reign to the Chien-lung reign: The golden age of the Ch'ing, 1662–1796).
Lyons: Impr. d'Audin; Paris: Belles lettres, 1957. 195 p. (Université de Lyon, annales, 3e série, 29)
SUBJ 12 12.1 15 16.1 17 64 ▪ 11 12.2 16.3 25 29 34.3 66

10527 CSU P P1 G1.2 1644–1842
Corradini, Piero.
'A propos de l'institution du *Nei-ko* sous la dynastie des Ts'ing' (The Grand Secretariat under the Ch'ing).
TP 2e série 48, 4/5 (1960), 416–424.
SUBJ 12 ▪ 66

10528 MCH P P3 G5.1 1644–1842
Corradini, Piero.
'Civil administration at the beginning of the Manchu dynasty: A note on the establishment of the Six Ministries (Liu-pu).'
OE 9, 2 (Dez. 1962), 133–138.
SUBJ 12 ▪ 15 66

10529 MCH P P3 G5.1 1644–1842
Corradini, Piero.
'Riforme nell'amministrazione centrale cinese durante il periodo Yung-Cheng (1723–1736)' (Reforms in the Chinese central administration during the Yung-cheng reign, 1723–1736).
Rivista degli studi orientali 36, 1/2 (giugnio 1961), 135–145.
SUBJ 12 15 ▪ 16.1 22 66

10530 CSU U P2 G1.2 1842–1911
Courant, Maurice Auguste Louis Marie, 1865–1935.
'En Chine: les effets de la crise, intentions de réforme' (Effects of the crisis in China and plans for reform).
Annales des sciences politiques 16, 6 (nov. 1901), 708–717.
SUBJ 12 66 ▪ 12.1 15 16.1 17 32

10531 FPN P P3 G1.2 1842–1911
Courant, Maurice Auguste Louis Marie, 1865–1935.
'La succession au trône de Chine' (The succession to the throne of China).
Annales des sciences politiques 25, 1 (jan. 1910), 56–65.
SUBJ 12 12.2 ▪ 13 41 45 64

10532 NIC U P1 G1.2 –1911
Cress, Paul F-.
'The influence of the literary examination system on the development of Chinese civilization.'
AJS 35, 2 (Sept. 1929), 250–262.
SUBJ 10 12 17 ▪ 16.1

10533 FPN PO P2 G1.3 1644–1842
Domeny de Rienzi, Grégoire Louis.
'Essai de statistique de la Chine' (A statistical essay on China).
R. des deux mondes 3e année, 4 (1831), 239–267.
SUBJ 11 12 14.5 22 ▪ 11.1 11.2 15 16 66 71

10534 MCH O P2 G1.1 1644–1842
Donazolo, Pietro.
'Mons. Eugenio Piloti e le condizioni della Cina nel 1735' (Monseigneur Eugenio Piloti and conditions in China in 1735).
Bollettino della Società geografica italiana 6a serie 5, 5/6 (maggio–giugno 1928), 305–340.
SUBJ 12 ▪ 15

10535 NIC P P1 G1.2 1644–1842
Douglas, Robert Kennaway, 1838–1913.
'A Chinese jubilee.'
Asiatic quarterly review 4 (July–Oct. 1887), 61–84.
SUBJ 12 66 ▪ 13

10536 CSH S P2 G1.2 1842–1911
Duncanson, Dennis J-.
'Modernization under the Manchus: Some recent Harvard studies.' [Review of *Chang Chih-tung and educational reform in China*, by Thomas William Ayers; *The reform and abolition of the traditional Chinese examination system*, by Wolfgang Franke; *Rebellion and its enemies in late Imperial China: Militarization and social structure, 1796–1864*, by Philip Alden Kuhn; *The origin of likin, 1853–1864*, by Edwin George Beal, Jr.; *The modernization of the Chinese salt administration, 1900–1920*, by Samuel Adrian Miles Adshead; *Postal communication in China and its modernization, 1860–1896*, by Ying-wan Cheng (Cheng Ying-huan); and *Communication and imperial control in China: Evolution of the palace memorial system, 1693–1735*, by Silas H. L. Wu (Wu Hsiu-liang).]
Asian affairs (London) 3, 2 (June 1972), 204–211.
SUBJ 12 14 ▪ 14.2 14.5 17 25 32.2 66

10537 NNC P P1 G1.1 1842–1895
Eastman, Lloyd Eric, 1929–.
'Ch'ing-i and Chinese policy formation during the nineteenth century.'
JAS 24, 4 (Aug. 1965), 595–611.
SUBJ 12 16.1 ▪ 32 64

10538 CSU P P1 G1.2 1842–1895
Eastman, Lloyd Eric, 1929–.
'Political reformism in China before the Sino-Japanese War.'
JAS 27, 4 (Aug. 1968), 695–710.
SUBJ 12 16.1 ▪ 14 22 32 66

10539 MCH P P1 G1.1 1842–1895
Eastman, Lloyd Eric, 1929–.
Throne and mandarins: China's search for a policy during the Sino-French controversy, 1880–1885.
Cambridge: Harvard U. Press, 1967. 13, 254 p. (Harvard historical studies, 79)
SUBJ 12 16 ▪ 15 64 66

10540 NIC S P1 G1.2 –1911
Eisenstadt, Shmuel Noah, 1923–.
'Internal contradictions in bureaucratic politics.'
CSSH 1, 1 (Oct. 1958), 58–75.
SUBJ 12 16.1 ▪ 32

10541 NIC S P1 G1.1 –1911
Eisenstadt, Shmuel Noah, 1923–.
The political systems of empires.
New York: Free Press of Glencoe, 1963. 19, 524 p.
SUBJ 12 30 32 ▪ 16 16.1 32.2

10542 DLC P P2 G1.2 –1842
Ermachenko, I- S-.
'K kharakteristike gosudarstvennogo apparata TSinskoi imperii v period zavoevaniia Kitaia' (The nature of the Ch'ing political structure at the time of the conquest of China). In *Man'chzhurskoe vladychestvo v Kitae* (Manchu rule in China), compiled by Institut narodov Azii, Akademiia nauk SSSR, edited by Sergei Leonidovich Tikhvinskii. [Selective entry]
Moscow: Nauka, Glav. red. vost. lit-ry, 1966, 151–168.
SUBJ 12 12.1 14.5 15 ▪ 12.2 13 14.1 16.3 18 66

10543 MCH P P1 G1.2 1842–1895
Fairbank, John King, 1907–.
'The Manchu-Chinese dyarchy in the 1840's and '50's.'
FEQ 12, 3 (May 1953), 265–278.
SUBJ 12 16.1

10544 MCH P P3 G1.3 1842–1895
Fairbank, John King, 1907–.
Trade and diplomacy on the China coast: The opening of the treaty ports, 1842–1854.
Cambridge: Harvard U. Press, 1954. 2 vols. 13, 489; 88 p. (Harvard historical studies, 62–63)
SUBJ 12 14.5 66 ▪ 12.1 14.2 16.1 16.2 25 64

10545 NIC P P1 G1.2 1644–1911
Fairbank, John King, 1907–, and Ssu-yü Teng, 1906–.
'On the types and uses of Ch'ing documents.'
HJAS 5, 1 (Jan. 1940), 1–71. [Reprinted in *Ch'ing administration: Three studies*, by J. K. Fairbank and Ssu-yü Teng. (Analytic entry.) Cambridge: Harvard U. Press, 1960, 36–106. (Harvard-Yenching Institute studies, 19)]
SUBJ 12

10546 MCY P P3 G1.3 1644–1842
Farmer, Edward Lewis, 1935–.
'James Flint versus the Canton interest, 1755–1760.'
PC 17 (Dec. 1963), 38–66.
Subj 12 16.1 ▪ 26.2 34.2

10547 MCH S P3 G5.1 1842–1895
Fauvel, Albert Auguste, 1851–1909.
'L'empereur de Chine Kouang-hsü, son conseiller Kang-yu-wei et l'impératrice douairière Tze-hsi: le coup d'état à Pékin (21–22 septembre 1898)' (The Kuang-hsü Emperor, his counselor K'ang Yu-wei, and the Empress Dowager Tz'u-hsi: The coup d'état in Peking, 21–22 September 1898).
R. de géographie 44, 7 (jan. 1899), 1–10.
Subj 12 32 ▪ 16.1 66

10548 MAM P P2 G1.2 1895–1911
Fincher, John Howard, 1936–.
The Chinese self-government movement, 1900–1912.
Ann Arbor: University Microfilms (Publ. 69-18,287), 1969. 322 p. (Doctoral dissertation in History, U. of Washington)
Subj 12 12.1 16.1 16.2 ▪ 32

10549 CSU S P2 G1.2 1895–1911
Fincher, John Howard, 1936–.
'Political provincialism and the national revolution.' In *China in revolution: The first phase, 1900–1913*, edited by Mary Clabaugh Wright. [Selective entry]
New Haven: Yale U. Press, 1968, 185–226.
Subj 12 29 ▪ 16.1 32.2

10550 NIC P P1 G1.1 –1911
Fitzgerald, Charles Patrick, 1902–.
China: A short cultural history, rev. ed.
New York: Praeger, 1961. 18, 624 p.
Subj 12 13 60 64 ▪ 23 31 55 62

10551 CSU P P4 G1.2 1842–1895
Folsom, Kenneth Everett, 1921–.
Friends, guests, and colleagues: The mu-fu [private secretariats] system in the late Ch'ing period.
Berkeley, Los Angeles: U. of California Press, 1968. 234 p. (Revision of *Li Hung-chang. Friends, guests and colleagues: A study of the mu-fu system in the late Ch'ing period*, doctoral dissertation in History, U. of California, Berkeley, 1964)
Subj 12 16.1 36.1 48 59 63 ▪ 12.1 12.2 15 17 22 30 39 64

10552 NNC P P2 G9.0 1644–1842
Fomina, Nataliia Ivanovna.
'Baza antitsinskoi bor'by na IUgo-Vostoke Kitaia v seredine XVII v.' (The basis of the anti-Ch'ing struggle in Southeast China in the mid-seventeenth century).
KSINA 66 (1963), 38–58.
Subj 12 12.2 14 15 71 ▪ 16.1 17 21.2 24.4 32 32.1 32.2 66 70 72

10553 GMS P P1 G1.1 1895–1911
[Franke, Otto] Sinicus, pseud., 1863–1946.
'Die politische Entwicklung in China seit dem russisch-japanischen Kriege' (Political developments in China since the Russo-Japanese War).
Marine-Rundschau 19, 2 (Feb. 1908), 167–186. [Reprinted in *Ostasiatische Neubildungen: Beiträge zum Verständnis der politischen und kulturellen Entwicklungs-vorgänge im Fernen Osten* (New forms in East Asia: Toward an understanding of political and cultural developmental processes in the Far East), by O. Franke. (Selective entry.) Hamburg: C. Boysen, 1911, 176–199.]
Subj 12 17 19 ▪ 14.2 15 16.2

10554 CSU P P1 G1.2 –1911
Franke, Otto, 1863–1946.
'Die Verfassung und Verwaltung Chinas' (The constitution and government of China). In *Allgemeine Verfassungs- und Verwaltungsgeschichte* (General constitutional and administrative history), by Alfred Vierkandt et al. [Sole entry]
Leipzig: Teubner, 1911, 87–113. (Die Kultur der Gegenwart, Teil 2, Abteilung 2, 1)
Subj 12 12.2 ▪ 12.1 19 62

10555 NNC P P1 G1.2 1895–1911
Franke, Otto, 1863–1946.
'Die wichtigsten chinesischen Reformschriften vom Ende des neunzehnten Jahrhunderts' (The most important Chinese reformist literature from the end of the nineteenth century). In *Aus Kultur und Geschichte Chinas* (Chinese culture and history), by O. Franke. [Selective entry]
Peiping: Deutschland-Institut, 1945, 1–12.
Subj 12 19 32 72 ▪ 16.1 64

10556 CSH P P3 G5.1 1895–1911
Franke, Otto, 1863–1946.
'Zur Beurteilung der pekinger Vorgänge von 1898' (An interpretation of the events of 1898 in Peking).
Marine-Rundschau 17, 11 (Nov. 1906), 1289–1306. [Reprinted in *Ostasiatische Neubildungen: Beiträge zum Verständnis der politischen und kulturellen Entwicklungs-vorgänge im Fernen Osten* (New forms in East Asia: Toward an understanding of political and cultural developmental processes in the Far East), by O. Franke. (Selective entry.) Hamburg: C. Boysen, 1911, 72–95.]
Subj 12 32

10557 NIC P P1 G1.1 1644–1911
Franke, Wolfgang, 1912–.
The reform and abolition of the traditional Chinese examination system.
Cambridge: Harvard U., East Asian Research Center, 1963. 100 p. (Harvard East Asian monographs, 10)
Subj 12 16.1 17 32 ▪ 48 62 64 66

10558 NNC P P1 G1.2 1895–1911
George, Otto Lindemann, 1915–.
The introduction of constitutional government into China, 1905–1911.
Unpublished masters thesis in Chinese, Columbia U., 1940. 226 p.
Subj 12 32 ▪ 12.2

10559 MCH PO P4 G1.2 –1895
Giles, Herbert Allen, 1845–1935.
Historic China, and other sketches.
London: T. de La Rue, 1882. 405 p.
Subj 12 12.2 16.1 17 60 ▪ 22.2 57 62 63

10560 NNC P P2 G1.1 1644–1895
Gorst, Harold Edward, 1868–?
China.
New York: Dutton, 1899. 20, 300 p.
Subj 10 12 14 16 19 66 ▪ 14.1 15 16.1 17 23 34.3 41 47 56 62

10561 MCH O P2 G1.2 1644–1842
Grosier, Jean-Baptiste Gabriel Alexandre, 1743–1823.
'Gouvernement chinois' (The Chinese government). In *De la Chine: description générale de cet empire* (A comprehensive description of the Chinese empire), by J.-B. G. A. Grosier. [Selective entry]
Paris: Pillet, 1819, vol. 5, part 10, 1–269.
Subj 12 12.2 14 14.5 ▪ 12.1 15 16 22 43

10562 MCH P P1 G1.2 1895–1911
Guseo, Marco.
Le riforme cinesi (The reforms in China).
Milan, Turin, Rome: Bocca, 1911. 91, 71 p.
Subj 12 15 ▪ 12.1 12.2 14.5 41

10563 CSU U P3 G1.3 1842–1911
Harris, Richard.
'China under the Empress Dowager.'
History today 7, 10 (Oct. 1957), 662–671.
Subj 12 66 ▪ 15 32.2

10564 CSU P P2 G1.1 1842–1895
Hatano, Yoshihiro, 1908–.
'The response of the Chinese bureaucracy to modern machinery.'
Acta Asiatica (Tokyo) 12 (Mar. 1967), 13–28.
Subj 12 12.1 14 19 ▪ 16 62

10565 NNC P P3 G5.1 1895–1911
Hauer, Erich, 1878–1936.
'Verwaltungsreformen in China: Die pekinger Zentralregierung' (Administrative reforms in China: The central government in Peking).
MSOSB 12 (1909), 1–25.
Subj 12 ▪ 12.1

10566 MAM P P2 G8.1 1842–1911
Hedtke, Charles Herman, 1932–.
Reluctant revolutionaries: Szechwan and the Ch'ing collapse, 1898–1911.
Ann Arbor: University Microfilms (Publ. 69-3609), 1969. 338 p. (Doctoral dissertation in History, U. of California, Berkeley, 1968)
Subj 12 16.1 17 19 32.2 66 ▪ 14.3 15 16.2 24.1 24.2 25 33 34.3

10567 MCH S P4 G1.2 1644–1911
Herson, Lawrence J- R-.
'China's imperial bureaucracy: Its direction and control.'
Public administration review 17, 1 (Winter 1957), 44–53.
Subj 12 ▪ 22

10568 NNC O P4 G1.3 1644–1895
Hirth, Friedrich, 1845–1927.
'Das Beamtenwesen in China' (The bureaucracy in China).
Verhandlungen der Gesellschaft für Erdkunde zu Berlin 9 (1882), 37–51. [Reprinted in *Chinesische Studien*, by F. Hirth. (Selective entry.) Munich: Hirth, 1890, vol. 1, 170–188.]
Subj 12 ▪ 16.1 17 48 55

10569 NIC U P2 G1.3 1895–1911
Hirth, Friedrich, 1845–1927.
'Die chinesische Regierung und ihre Organe' (The Chinese government and its organs).

TP 2e série 2, 1 (mars 1901), 54–67.
SUBJ 12 ▪ 16.1 30 61 66 70

10570 MCY P P3 G5.1 1644–1911
Ho, Alfred Kuo-liang (Ho Kuo-liang), 1919–.
'The Grand Council in the Ch'ing dynasty.'
FEQ 11, 2 (Feb. 1952), 167–182. [Reprinted in *China*, edited by John Armstrong Harrison. (Selective entry.) Tucson: U. of Arizona Press, 1972, 131–146. (Assn. for Asian Studies, Thirtieth Anniversary Commemorative Series, 1)]
SUBJ 12

10571 CSU U P1 G1.2 1644–1911
Ho, Ping-ti, 1917–.
'The significance of the Ch'ing period in Chinese history.'
JAS 26, 2 (Feb. 1967), 189–195.
SUBJ 12 ▪ 39 66

10572 CSU U P2 G1.2 1842–1895
Ho-wei-lin.
'Chinese official ranks.'
NQCJ 2, 12 (Dec. 1868), 184–187.
SUBJ 12 ▪ 15 22

10573 MCH S P1 G1.1 –1911
Houn, Franklin W. (Hou Fu-wu), 1920–.
Chinese political traditions.
Washington, D.C.: Public Affairs Press, 1965. 130 p.
SUBJ 12 16.1 64 ▪ 12.2 13 17 63

10574 NIC P P1 G1.2 1644–1911
Hsieh, Pao Chao (Hsieh Pao-ch'iao), 1896–1959.
The government of China, 1644–1911.
Baltimore: Johns Hopkins Press, 1925. 414 p. (Johns Hopkins studies in historical and political science, new series, 3) (Doctoral dissertation in Political Science, Johns Hopkins U., 1923) [Reprinted—Ann Arbor: University Microfilms, n.d. 414 p.]
SUBJ 12 12.2 14.5 ▪ 12.1 13 15 16.1 17 64 72

10575 CSU P P1 G1.2 1842–1895
Hsü, Immanuel C. Y. (Hsü Chung-yüeh), 1923–.
'Gordon in China, 1880.'
PHR 33, 2 (May 1964), 147–166.
SUBJ 12 15

10576 NNC S P1 G5.0 1644–1895
Hu, C. T. (Hu Ch'ang-tu), 1920–.
'The Yellow River administration in the Ch'ing dynasty.'
FEQ 14, 4 (Aug. 1955), 505–513. [For a fuller version, see entry 10577.]
SUBJ 12 14.2 ▪ 14.5

10577 MAM P P1 G1.4 –1911
Hu, C. T. (Hu Ch'ang-tu), 1920–.
The Yellow River administration in the Ch'ing dynasty.
Ann Arbor: University Microfilms (Publ. 8351), 1954. 287 p. (Doctoral dissertation in History, U. of Washington)
SUBJ 12 14.2 14.5 15 18 ▪ 11.4 14.3

10578 CSU P P3 G1.2 1644–1842
Huang, Pei (Huang P'ei), 1928–.
'Aspects of Ch'ing autocracy: An institutional study, 1644–1735.'
THJ new (2nd) series 6, 1/2 (Dec. 1967), 105–148. [Reprinted in *Readings in modern Chinese history*, edited by Immanuel C. Y. Hsü (Hsü Chung-yüeh). (Selective entry.) New York: Oxford U. Press, 1971, 5–37.]
SUBJ 12

10579 NIC P P1 G1.2 –1644
Hucker, Charles Oscar, 1919–.
'Confucianism and the Chinese censorial system.' In *Confucianism in action*, edited by David Shepherd Nivison and Arthur Frederick Wright. [Selective entry]
Stanford: Stanford U. Press, 1959, 182–208. [Reprinted in *Confucianism and Chinese civilization*, edited by A. F. Wright. (Selective entry.) New York: Atheneum, 1964, 50–77.]
SUBJ 12 ▪ 12.2 64

10580 ELB O P2 G1.4 1644–1842
Ides, Evert Ysbrants, 1660–?
Driejaarige reize naar China, te lande gedaan, door den Moskovischen Afgezant, E. Ysbrants Ides (A three-year overland journey to China by the ambassador from Moscow, Evert Ysbrants Ides).
Amsterdam: François Halma, 1704. 243 p. [Reprinted—Amsterdam: Pieter de Coup, 1710. 28, 243 p.]

Three years of travel from Muscovy overland to China.
London: Freeman, 1706. 10, 210 p.
SUBJ 12 13 14.2 55 66 ▪ 11.3 23 24.3 33 57

10581 MCY P P1 G2.0 1895–1911
Irick, Robert Lee, 1930–.
'The Chinchow-Aigun railroad [Chin-chou–Ai-hui, Sheng-ching] and the Knox Neutralization Plan in Ch'ing diplomacy.'
PC 13 (Dec. 1959), 80–112.
SUBJ 12 14.2 66 ▪ 14.6

10582 NNC PO P2 G2.0 –1895
James, Henry Evan Murchison, 1846–1923.
The long white mountain: or, A journey in Manchuria, with some account of the history, people, administration and religion of that country.
London: Longmans, Green, 1888. 23, 502 p.
SUBJ 12 14 23 ▪ 14.5 14.6 16.1 21.3 22.2 33 34.3 56 57

10583 NIC S P1 G1.2 1644–1911
Jiang, Joseph P. L., 1933–.
'The mo-liao [i.e., mu-liao, private secretariats] system in Ch'ing administration.'
Philippine j. of public administration 7, 4 (Oct. 1963), 258–267.
SUBJ 12 ▪ 16.1 17

10584 NIC O P3 G5.1 1895–1911
Johnston, Reginald Fleming, 1874–1938.
Twilight in the Forbidden City.
London: Gollancz, 1934. 480 p.
SUBJ 12 ▪ 14.5

10585 CSU P P1 G1.1 1644–1842
Kahn, Harold Lionel, 1930–.
'The politics of filiality: Justification for imperial action in eighteenth century China.'
JAS 26, 2 (Feb. 1967), 197–203.
SUBJ 12 41 59 ▪ 63

10586 MCH U P1 G1.1 –1895
Karlgren, Bernhard, 1889–.
Östasien under nittonde århundradet (East Asia in the nineteenth century).
Stockholm: Norstedt, 1920. 88 p.
SUBJ 12 14.3 64 ▪ 11 12.1 13 15 17 32.2 43 66

10587 MCH PO P2 G1.2 1895–1911
Kent, Percy Horace Braund, 1876–.
The passing of the Manchus.
London: Arnold, 1912. 11, 404 p.
SUBJ 12 15 19 32.2 ▪ 14.5 16.1 22.2 64 66

10588 MCH O P3 G9.2 1842–1895
Kerr, John Glasgow, 1824–1901.
'Description of the great examination hall at Canton.'
JRAS-NCB new (2nd) series 3 (Dec. 1866), 63–70.
SUBJ 12

10589 CSU P P1 G1.2 1644–1911
Kessler, Lawrence Devlin, 1936–.
'Ethnic composition of provincial leadership during the Ch'ing dynasty.'
JAS 28, 3 (May 1969), 489–511. [Reprinted in *Readings in modern Chinese history*, edited by Immanuel C. Y. Hsü (Hsü Chung-yüeh). (Selective entry.) New York: Oxford U. Press, 1971, 58–78.] [Reprinted in *China*, edited by John Armstrong Harrison. (Selective entry.) Tucson: U. of Arizona Press, 1972, 107–129. (Assn. for Asian Studies, Thirtieth Anniversary Commemorative Series, 1)]
SUBJ 12 66 ▪ 16.1

10590 CSU P P5 G1.3 1644–1842
Klaproth, Julius Heinrich, 1783–1835.
'L'almanach impérial de la Chine' (The *Ta Ch'ing hui-t'ien*).
Nouvelles annales des voyages 39 (1828), 90–106.
SUBJ 12 15 ▪ 12.2 13 16.1 55

10591 CNY O P3 G5.1 1842–1895
Krone, Rudolf.
'Die chinesischen Mandarinen' (Chinese mandarins).
Berichte der Rheinischen Missionsgesellschaft 1853, 21 (15 Nov.), 321–333.
SUBJ 12 16.1 ▪ 17

10592 NIC P P1 G1.3 –1911
Ku, Tun-jou.
'The evolution of the Chinese hsien government.'
CC 2, 3 (Dec. 1959), 59–75.
SUBJ 12

10593 MCH P P1 G1.5 1644–1842
Kuo, Ping-chia (Kuo Pin-chia), 1908–.
A critical study of the first Anglo-Chinese war, with documents.
Shanghai: Commercial Press, 1935. 315 p. (Doctoral dissertation in History, Harvard U., 1933) [Reprinted—Westport, Conn.: Hyperion Press, 197? 315 p.]
SUBJ 10 12 15 ▪ 66

10594 CSU PO P1 G1.3 1842–1911
Lai, T. C. (Lai T'ien-ch'ang).
A scholar in Imperial China.

Hong Kong: Kelly and Walsh, 1970. 86 p.
Subj 12 ▪ 16.1 17

10595 CSU P P3 G5.1 1644–1911
Lee, Kuo-chi.
'Bemerkungen zum Ch'ing-Dokumentenstil: Eingaben an den Kaiser (tsou)' (Notes on Ch'ing documentary style: Memorials to the emperor).
OE 17, 1/2 (Dez. 1970), 125–135.
Subj 12

10596 NIC S P1 G1.1 –1911
Lee, Shu-ching (Li Shu-ch'ing), 1908–.
'Administration and bureaucracy: The power structure in Chinese society.' In *Transactions of the Second World Congress of Sociology*. [Sole entry]
London: International Sociological Assn., 1954, vol. 2, 3–15.
Subj 12 ▪ 15 16.1

10597 CSU S P1 G1.2 –1911
Levenson, Joseph Richmond, 1920–1969.
'Confucianism and Confucianism: The basic confrontation.' In *Confucian China and its modern fate, Vol. 2, The problem of monarchical decay*, by J. R. Levenson. [Analytic entry]
Berkeley, Los Angeles: U. of California Press, 1964, 51–59.
Subj 12 16.1 64 ▪ 42

10598 NIC O P2 G5.0 1842–1911
[Li Chang] ———.
Reminiscences of a Chinese official: Revelations of official life under the Manchus.
Tientsin: Tientsin Press, 1922. 158 p.
Subj 12 16.1 ▪ 14.2 15 17 34.3 41

10599 NIC P P2 G1.2 1644–1911
Li Chow Chung-cheng (Li Chou Chung-cheng).
L'examen provincial en Chine sous la dynastie des Ts'ing (Provincial examinations in China under the Ch'ing).
Paris: Jouve, 1935. 137 p. (Doctoral dissertation, Faculté des lettres, Université de Paris)
Subj 12 17 ▪ 18

10600 FPN P P4 G1.2 1644–1911
Li Hsiung-fei.
Les censeurs sous la dynastie mandchoue (1616-1911) [i.e., 1644–1911] *en Chine* (The Censorate under the Ch'ing, 1644-1911).
Paris: Presses modernes, 1936. 148 p. (Doctoral dissertation, Faculté des lettres, Université de Paris)
Subj 12 12.2 ▪ 16.1

10601 MCH O P2 G1.2 1842–1895
Lisboa, Henrique Carlos Ribeiro, 1847–?
'Instituições políticas' (Political institutions). In *A China e os Chinos: recordações de viagem* (China and the Chinese: Recollections of a journey), by H. C. R. Lisboa. [Selective entry]
Montevideo: Godel, 1888, 196–224.
Subj 12 12.2 22 ▪ 14.5 15 16.1 45

10602 NIC P P3 G1.3 –1911
Liu, James T. C. (Liu Tzu-chien), 1919–.
'Some classifications of bureaucrats in Chinese historiography.' In *Confucianism in action*, edited by David Shepherd Nivison and Arthur Frederick Wright. [Selective entry]
Stanford: Stanford U. Press, 1959, 165–181.
Subj 12 62

10603 CSU P P2 G1.2 1644–1895
Liu, Kwang-ching (Liu Kuang-ching), 1921–.
'Nineteenth-century China: The disintegration of the old order and the impact of the West' [with comments by Albert Feuerwerker, Philip Alden Kuhn, and Dwight Heald Perkins]. In *China in crisis, Vol. 1, China's heritage and the Communist political system*, edited by Ping-ti Ho and Tang Tsou. [Selective entry]
Chicago: U. of Chicago Press, 1968, 93–202.
Subj 12 22 66 ▪ 16.1 22.2 32.2

10604 CSU P P1 G1.2 1644–1911
Lui, Adam Yuen-chung (Lü Yüan-ch'ung), 1940–.
'The Ch'ing civil service: Promotions, demotions, transfers, leaves, dismissals and retirements.'
JOS 8, 2 (July 1970), 333–356.
Subj 12 16.1 50 ▪ 12.2 57

10605 CSU P P3 G1.2 1644–1842
Lui, Adam Yuen-chung (Lü Yüan-ch'ung), 1940–.
'The practical training of government officials under the early Ch'ing, 1644–1795.'
Asia Major new (3rd) series 16, 1/2 (Jan. 1971), 82–95.
Subj 12 16.1

10606 NNC P P3 G5.1 1895–1911
MacLean, Archibald.
'Die Entwicklung der Selbstverwaltungs-reform in der Provinz Tschili' (The development of reform of self-government in Chihli).
MSOSB 12 (1909), 61–93.
Subj 12 32 ▪ 12.2 22 22.1

10607 WSU P P3 G5.1 1842–1911
Mann, Albert Burwell, 1929–.
The influence of eunuchs in the politics and economy of the Ch'ing court, 1861–1907.
Unpublished masters thesis in Far Eastern and Slavic Languages, U. of Washington, 1957. 141 p.
Subj 12 16.1 ▪ 14 14.5 61 63

10608 NIC P P2 G1.3 1644–1911
Marsh, Robert Mortimer, 1931–.
'Bureaucratic constraints on nepotism in the Ch'ing period.'
JAS 19, 2 (Feb. 1960), 117–133.
Subj 12 15 16.1 ▪ 30 40

10609 NIC P P1 G1.2 1644–1911
Marsh, Robert Mortimer, 1931–.
'The venality of provincial office in China and in comparative perspective.'
CSSH 4, 4 (July 1962), 454–466.
Subj 12 ▪ 14.5 16.1

10610 CSU O P4 G1.2 1842–1911
Martin, William Alexander Parsons, 1827–1916.
'Civil service examinations.' In *The lore of Cathay: or, The intellect of China*, by W. A. P. Martin. [Selective entry]
New York: Revell, 1901, 308–328. [Reprinted in *The lore of Cathay: or, The intellect of China*, by W. A. P. Martin. (Selective entry.) Taipei: Ch'eng-wen, 1971, 308–328.]
Subj 12 17 ▪ 16.1 18 64

10611 CSH O P2 G1.1 1842–1895
Martin, William Alexander Parsons, 1827–1916.
A cycle of Cathay: or, China, South and North, with personal reminiscences, 3rd ed.
New York: Revell, 1900. 464 p. [Reprinted—Taipei: Ch'eng-wen, 1966. 464 p.]
Subj 10 12 13 33 66 ▪ 14.2 14.5 15 16.1 17 31 47 62

10612 NNC O P3 G5.1 1895–1911
Matignon, Jean-Jacques, 1866–?
'Les eunuques de palais impérial à Pékin' (The eunuchs of the imperial palace in Peking). In *La Chine hermétique: superstitions, crime et misère* (China sealed off: Superstition, crime, and poverty), 5th ed., rev., by J.-J. Matignon. [Selective entry]
Paris: Lib. Geuthner, 1936, 201–222.
Subj 12 56 ▪ 16.1 55

10613 NIC P P1 G1.2 1644–1895
Mayers, William Frederick, 1831–1878.
The Chinese government: A manual of Chinese titles categorically arranged and explained, 3rd ed., rev., edited by George Macdonald Home Playfair.
Shanghai: Kelly and Walsh, 1897. 158 p. [Reprinted—Taipei: Ch'eng-wen, 1970. 158 p.]
Subj 12

10614 NIC P P1 G1.1 1842–1911
Meng, Ssu-ming, 1908–.
The Tsungli Yamen: Its organization and functions.
Cambridge: Harvard U., East Asian Research Center, 1962. 146 p. (Harvard East Asian monographs, 13) (Revision of *The organization and functions of the Tsungli Yamen*, doctoral dissertation in Government, Harvard U., 1949)
Subj 12 66 ▪ 14.2 14.3 17 19

10615 MCH P P2 G1.1 1644–1911
Metzger, Thomas Albert, 1933–.
Some legal aspects of bureaucratic organization in China under the Ch'ing.
Unpublished doctoral dissertation in History and Far Eastern Languages, Harvard U., 1967. 16, 572 p.
Subj 12 12.2 16.1 ▪ 12.1 14.5 63 64

10616 CSH U P2 G1.2 1644–1895
Michael, Franz Henry, 1907–.
'Regionalism in nineteenth-century China.' In *Li Hung-chang and the Huai Army: A study in nineteenth-century Chinese regionalism*, by Stanley Spector. [Analytic entry]
Seattle: U. of Washington Press, 1964, 21–43 [s.p.]. [For Spector's work, see entry 13858.] [Reprinted in *Modern China: An interpretive anthology*, edited by Joseph Richmond Levenson. (Selective entry.) London: Macmillan, 1971, 34–52.]
Subj 12 15 16.1 ▪ 22.2 25 26.1 29

10617 CSH P P1 G1.1 1644–1842
Mitchell, Peter MacVicar.
'A further note on the HCCSWP [*Huang-ch'ao ching-shih wen-pien* (Collected Ch'ing essays on benefitting the world)].'
CSWT 2, 3 (July 1970), 40–46.
SUBJ 12 59 ▪ 16.1

10618 NNC P P1 G1.1 1644–1842
Morgan, Evan, 1860–?
'Times and manners in the age of the Emperor K'ang Hsi.'
JRAS-NCB new (2nd) series 69 (1938), 23–45.
SUBJ 12 12.1 48 ▪ 12.2 14 25 32.2

10619 MCH P P1 G1.1 1842–1911
Morrison, Esther, 1915–.
The modernization of the Confucian bureaucracy: An historical study of public administration.
Unpublished doctoral dissertation in History and Far Eastern Languages, Radcliffe College, 1959. 3 vols. 1282 p. [c.p.].
SUBJ 12 64 ▪ 14.5 16.1 32

10620 GMS P P2 G1.2 1895–1911
Müller, Max.
'Örtliche Selbstverwaltung in China' (Local self-government in China).
MSOSB 13 (1910), 119–150.
SUBJ 12

10621 NNC S P4 G1.2 –1895
Murphey, William Rhoads, III, 1919–.
'The city as a center of change: Western Europe and China.'
AAAG 44, 4 (Dec. 1954), 349–362. [Reprinted in *Cultural geography: Selected readings*, edited by Fred E- Dohrs and Lawrence M- Sommers. (Selective entry.) New York: Crowell, 1967, 192–206.]
SUBJ 12 14.3 16.2 ▪ 11.1 22

10622 CSU P P5 G1.2 –1911
Needham, Noël Joseph Terence Montgomery, 1900–.
'Thoughts on the social relations of science and technology in China.'
Centaurus 3 (1953/54), 40–48.
SUBJ 12 16.1 16.2 62

10623 NIC P P3 G1.3 1644–1842
Nivison, David Shepherd, 1923–.
'Ho-shen and his accusers: Ideology and political behavior in the eighteenth century.' In *Confucianism in action*, edited by D. S. Nivison and Arthur Frederick Wright. [Selective entry]
Stanford: Stanford U. Press, 1959, 209–243.
SUBJ 12 16.1 61 ▪ 63 64

10624 NIC P P1 G1.2 –1911
Nivison, David Shepherd, 1923–.
'Protest against conventions and conventions of protest.' In *The Confucian persuasion*, edited by Arthur Frederick Wright. [Selective entry]
Stanford: Stanford U. Press, 1960, 177–201. [Reprinted in *Confucianism and Chinese civilization*, edited by A. F. Wright. (Selective entry.) New York: Atheneum, 1964, 227–251.]
SUBJ 12 61 64 ▪ 17

10625 CSU P P1 G9.0 1644–1895
Nolde, John Jacob, 1919–.
'A plea for a regional approach to Chinese history: The case of the South China coast.'
JRAS-HKB 6 (1966), 9–24.
SUBJ 12 25 ▪ 66

10626 MAM P P2 G1.1 1644–1842
Oxnam, Robert Bromley, 1942–.
Policies and factionalism in the Oboi regency, 1661–1669.
Ann Arbor: University Microfilms (Publ. 70-2784), 1970. 362 p. (Doctoral dissertation in History, Yale U., 1969)
SUBJ 12 15 16.1 25 32 66 ▪ 12.1 12.2 14 14.1 14.5 21.2 22 32.2 59 64

10627 CSU P P2 G1.1 –1842
Pauthier, Jean-Pierre Guillaume, 1801–1873.
'Géographie, organisation politique et administrative de la Chine, langues, philosophie' (Geography, political and administrative organization, languages, and philosophy of China). In *Chine moderne: ou, description historique, géographique et littéraire de ce vaste empire, d'après des documents chinois* (Modern China: or, An historical, geographic, and literary description of that vast empire, based on Chinese documents), by J.-P. G. Pauthier and Antoine Pierre Louis Bazin. [Analytic entry]
Paris: Firmin-Didot, 1853, 1–390. (L'univers. Histoire et description de tous les peuples: Asie, 10)
SUBJ 12 21.3 62 ▪ 14 17 55

10628 CSU S P2 G1.2 –1911
Pelzel, John Campbell, 1914–.
'Notes on the Chinese bureaucracy.'
Proceedings of the Annual Spring Meeting of the American Ethnological Society 1958, 50–57.
SUBJ 12 64 ▪ 22

10629 NNC P P2 G1.2 1895–1911
Pernitzsch, Max Gerhard, 1882–.
'Die örtliche Selbstverwaltung der Präfekturen, Subpräfekturen, Distrikte und Kreise' (Local self-government of prefectures, subprefectures, departments, and counties).
MSOSB 14 (1911), 369–374.
SUBJ 12 ▪ 12.1

10630 NNC PO P3 G1.3 1895–1911
Pernitzsch, Max Gerhard, 1882–.
'Die Provinziallandtage in China' (Provincial assemblies in China).
MSOSB 13 (1910), 151–162.
SUBJ 12 ▪ 32 32.1

10631 WSU P P2 G1.2 1895–1911
Petrov, Arkadii N-.
Kitai za poslednee desiatiletie: sotsial'no-politicheskii ocherk (Sociopolitical survey of China during the past decade).
St. Petersburg: A. D. Popov, 1910. 11, 232 p.
SUBJ 12 32 32.1 32.2 59 66 ▪ 12.2 15 25 33 47 64

10632 NIC P P1 G1.5 1644–1895
Playfair, George Macdonald Home, 1850–1917.
'Hereditary jurisdiction in south-western China.'
JRAS-CB new (2nd) series 20, 2 (1885), 182–184.
SUBJ 12 16.1 45

10633 CSU P P1 G1.2 –1911
Poe, Dison Hsueh-feng (P'u Hsüeh-feng), 1900–.
'Imperial succession and attendant crisis in dynastic China: An analytic-quantitative study through the five-element approach.'
THJ new (2nd) series 8, 1/2 (Aug. 1970), 84–150.
SUBJ 12 59 ▪ 64

10634 MCH O P1 G1.1 1644–1911
Popov, Pavel Stepanovich, 1843–1894.
Gosudarstvennyi stroi Kitaia i organy upravleniia (China's state structure and administrative organs).
St. Petersburg: Tipo-lit. S.-Peterburgskoi tiur'my; St. Petersburg: Elektro-pechatnia I. M. Boraganskago, 1903, 1909. 2 vols. 59; 9 p. [Vol. 1 published by Tipo-lit. S.-Peterburgskoi tiur'my, vol. 2 by Elektro-pechatnia I. M. Boraganskago.] (Imperatorskii Sanktpeterburgskii universitet, Fakul'tet vostochnykh iazykov, Izdaniia, 13)
SUBJ 12 ▪ 16.1 44

10635 CSH P P1 G1.2 1644–1911
Porter, Jonathan, 1938–.
'The "mu-fu" [private secretariats] system: A bibliographical introduction.'
CSWT 2, 8 (May 1972), 56–77.
SUBJ 12 72

10636 CBU P P1 G1.5 1842–1895
Porter, Jonathan, 1938–.
Tseng Kuo-fan's private bureaucracy.
Berkeley: U. of California, Center for Chinese Studies, 1972. 149 p. (CCS, China research monographs, 9) (Revision of doctoral dissertation in History, U. of California, Berkeley, 1971)
SUBJ 12 ▪ 14.5 16.1 48 59

10637 CSU U P3 G1.2 1895–1911
Reinsch, Paul Samuel, 1869–1923.
'A parliament for China.' In *Intellectual and political currents in the Far East*, by P. S. Reinsch. [Selective entry]
Boston: Houghton Mifflin, 1911, 225–271.
SUBJ 12 ▪ 14.5 32

10638 CSU P P1 G9.4 –1895
Riess, Ludwig, 1861–?
'Geschichte der Insel Formosa' (History of Taiwan).
MDG 6, 59 (Apr. 1897), 406–447.
SUBJ 12 ▪ 15 25 66

10639 CSU O P2 G8.2 1895–1911
Rodes, Jean.
'Au Yunnan' (In Yunnan). In *Le Céleste empire avant la révolution* (The Celestial Empire before the Revolution [of 1911]), by J. Rodes. [Selective entry]
Paris: Alcan, 1914, 3–31. (Dix ans de politique chinoise, 3)
SUBJ 12 66 ▪ 15 17 21.3 25 32.2 55

10640 MCH PO P4 G1.2 1895–1911
Rodes, Jean.
La Chine et le mouvement constitutionnel (1910–11) (China and the movement for a constitution, 1910–1911).

Paris: Alcan, 1913. 258 p. (Dix ans de politique chinoise, 2)
Subj 12 12.2 14 16.1 32 ▪ 18 61

10641 CSU O P2 G1.5 1895–1911
Rodes, Jean.
'Dans le bassin du Yangtsé' (In the Yangtze valley). In *Le Céleste empire avant la révolution* (The Celestial Empire before the Revolution [of 1911]), by J. Rodes. [Selective entry]
Paris: Alcan, 1914, 87–111. (Dix ans de politique chinoise, 3)
Subj 12 14 18 31 ▪ 12.2

10642 CSU PO P2 G1.2 1895–1911
Rodes, Jean.
'Pékin et la situation générale' (Peking and the general situation). In *Le Céleste empire avant la révolution* (The Celestial Empire before the Revolution [of 1911]), by J. Rodes. [Selective entry]
Paris: Alcan, 1914, 145–195. (Dix ans de politique chinoise, 3)
Subj 12 14.2 16.1 18 32.2 ▪ 14.6 16.3 54 55

10643 MCH PO P1 G1.2 –1842
Ross, John, 1842–1915.
The Manchus, or the reigning dynasty of China: Their rise and progress.
Paisley, Scotland: J. and R. Parlane, 1880. 32, 751 p. [Reprinted—London: Elliot Stock, 1891. 32, 751 p.] [Reprinted—New York: AMS Press, 1972. 32, 751 p.]
Subj 12 15 16.1 ▪ 11 12.1 12.2 14 14.5 14.6 16

10644 CSH PO P2 G5.3 –1911
Schüler, Wilhelm, 1869–1935.
Abriss der neueren Geschichte Chinas, unter besonderer Berücksichtigung der Provinz Schantung (Summary of modern Chinese history, with special attention to Shantung).
Berlin: Karl Curtius, 1912. 380 p.
Subj 12 15 32.2 66 ▪ 19 33

10645 MAM P P1 G1.1 1895–1911
Schulman, Irwin Jay, 1932–.
China's response to imperialism, 1895–1900.
Ann Arbor: University Microfilms (Publ. 67-14,093), 1967. 323 p. (Doctoral dissertation in Political Science, Columbia U.)
Subj 12 16.1 ▪ 32 66

10646 MCH U P4 G1.1 –1895
Shelgunov, Nikolai Vasil'evich, 1824–1891.
'TSivilizatsiia Kitaia' (Chinese civilization). In *Soch. N. V. Shelgunova* (The works of N. V. Shelgunov), 3rd ed. [Sole entry]
St. Petersburg: Izd-vo O. N. Popovy, 1904, vol. 1, 111–168.
Subj 12 16.1 17 ▪ 12.2 22.1 60

10647 NNC P P1 G2.3 1895–1911
Siebert, F-.
'Geschichtliches und Systematisches über die Entwicklung und Gestaltung des mukdener Provinzialrats' (Historical and structural observations on the development and organization of the provincial council of Fengtien).
MSOSB 13 (1910), 195–209.
Subj 12 ▪ 12.1 16.1

10648 MCH O P4 G1.2 1842–1895
Simon, G- Eugène, 1829–1896.
'L'état et le gouvernement en Chine' (State and government in China).
Nouvelle r. 25, 3 (1er déc. 1883), 521–545.

'The state.' In *China: Its social, political, and religious life*, by G. E. Simon. [Analytic entry]
London: Sampson Low, Marston, Searle, and Rivington, 1887, 122–167.
Subj 12 12.1 ▪ 12.2 22 41

10649 MCH O P4 G1.2 1842–1895
Simon, G- Eugène, 1829–1896.
'Le gouvernement chinois: son rôle dans l'état' (The Chinese government and its role in the state).
Nouvelle r. 27, 4 (15 avr. 1884), 690–719.

'The government.' In *China: Its social, political, and religious life*, by G. E. Simon. [Analytic entry]
London: Sampson Low, Marston, Searle, and Rivington, 1887, 168–208.
Subj 12 63 ▪ 12.1 12.2 17

10650 MCH PO P2 G1.2 1895–1911
[Simpson, Bertram Lenox] B. L. Putnam Weale, pseud., 1877–1930.
'The struggle round China.' In *The coming struggle in Eastern Asia*, 2nd ed., by [B. L. Simpson] B. L. Putnam Weale, pseud. [Sole entry]
London: Macmillan, 1908, 523–640.
Subj 12 14 15 ▪ 14.2 14.4 14.5 14.6 32.2 66

10651 MAM P P2 G8.0 1644–1842
Smith, Kent Clarke, 1937–.
Ch'ing policy and the development of Southwest China: Aspects of Ortai's governor-generalship, 1726–1731.
Ann Arbor: University Microfilms (Publ. 70-26,819), 1970. 360 p. (Doctoral dissertation in History, Yale U.)
Subj 12 14 15 25 59 66 ▪ 17 22

10652 MCH O P3 G5.1 1644–1842
Sofronii, *Arkhimandrit*.
Izvestiia o kitaiskom, nyne man'chzhuro-kitaiskom gosudarstve (Notes on the Chinese, or currently the Manchu-Chinese state).
Moscow: Univ. tip., 1861. 97 p.
Subj 12 12.2 13 14.5 ▪ 16 16.1 26.1 28 41 43 57 63

10653 MAM P P2 G9.4 1842–1895
Speidel, William Miller, 1935–.
Liu Ming-ch'uan in Taiwan, 1884–1891.
Ann Arbor: University Microfilms (Publ. 68-6853), 1968. 460 p. (Doctoral dissertation in History, Yale U.)
Subj 12 15 16.1 66 ▪ 14.5 17 24.2 59

10654 MCH P P3 G1.2 1644–1842
Spence, Jonathan Dermot, 1936–.
Ts'ao Yin and the K'ang-hsi Emperor: Bondservant and master.
New Haven: Yale U. Press, 1966. 14, 329 p. (Revision of *Ts'ao Yin and the Chinese bondservants: Imperial bureaucracy in the early Ch'ing period*, doctoral dissertation in History, Yale U., 1965)
Subj 12 16.1 16.2 ▪ 12.1 14.5 15 17 34.2 41 64

10655 MCH P P1 G1.1 1644–1911
Sun, E-tu Zen (Sun Jen I-tu), 1921–.
'The board of review in nineteenth-century China.'
HJAS 24 (1962/63), 175–228.
Subj 12 14.5 ▪ 14.6

10656 CSU P P2 G1.3 1644–1842
Sun, E-tu Zen (Sun Jen I-tu), 1921–.
'Ch'ing government and the mineral industries before 1800.'
JAS 27, 4 (Aug. 1968), 835–845.
Subj 12 14.4

10657 MCH P P1 G1.1 1644–1911
Tang, Edgar Cha (T'ang Chia), 1902–.
The censorial institution in China, 1644–1911.
Unpublished doctoral dissertation in History, Government and Economics, Harvard U., 1932. 183, 11 p.
Subj 12 16.1 ▪ 12.2 63

10658 MCH O P4 G1.2 1895–1911
Tao, L. K. (T'ao Meng-ho), 1887–1960.
'The town administration.' In *Village and town life in China*, by Y. K. Leong (Liang Yü-kao) and L. K. Tao. [Analytic entry]
London: Allen and Unwin, 1915, 45–155. (London School of Economics and Political Science, Monographs on sociology, 4) [Reprinted in *Village and town life in China*, by Y. K. Leong and L. K. Tao. (Analytic entry.) Westport, Conn.: Hyperion Press, 197?, 45–155.]
Subj 12 14.5 16.1 ▪ 17 22.1 22.2 23

10659 CSH U P4 G1.2 –1911
Tao, Yuan-chen (T'ao Yüan-chen).
'Patterns of changes of Chinese officialism.' Tr. by Joseph P. L. Jiang of 'Chung-kuo li tai kuan chih yen pien chih fang shih' (Historical patterns of change in the Chinese bureaucracy); *Ssu hsiang yü shih tai* 33 (Apr. 1944), 14–19. In *Chinese bureaucracy and government administration*, edited by T. W. Kwok (Kuo Te-hua). [Selective entry]
Honolulu: East-West Center Press, 1966, 19–35.
Subj 12 ▪ 16.1

10660 MCH O P2 G1.2 1842–1911
Thomson, John Stuart, 1869–1950.
China revolutionized.
Indianapolis: Bobbs-Merrill, 1913. 590 p.
Subj 12 12.2 14 14.2 17 32.2 ▪ 14.5 15 18 19 22.2 33 47 64 65 66

10661 CSH S P2 G1.2 1842–1911
Tikhvinskii, Sergei Leonidovich, 1918–.
Review of *Li Hung-chang and the Huai Army: A study in nineteenth-century Chinese regionalism*, by Stanley Spector.
NAA 1965, 6, 180–185.

Review of *Li Hung-chang and the Huai Army: A study in nineteenth-century Chinese regionalism*, by Stanley Spector. Tr. by Myra Ann Lappin.
CSWT 1, 10 (Feb. 1969), 45–65.
Subj 12 16.1 ▪ 15 59

10662 DLC P P2 G1.2 1842–1911
Tikhvinskii, Sergei Leonidovich, 1918–.
'Man'chzhurskoe gospodstvo v Kitae v kontse XIX v. i partiia reform' (Manchu rule in China at the end of the

nineteenth century and the reform party). In *Trudy dvadtsat' piatogo Mezhdunarodnogo kongressa vostokovedov, Moskva, 9–16 avgusta 1960 g.* (Proceedings of the Twenty-fifth International Congress of Orientalists, Moscow, 9–16 August 1960). [Sole entry]
Moscow: Izd-vo vost. lit-ry, 1963, vol. 5, 83–89.
SUBJ 12 16 32 ▪ 14.5 64

10663 ELB P P2 G1.1 1842–1911
Tikhvinskii, Sergei Leonidovich, 1918–.
'Politika "samousileniia" praviashchikh krugov Kitaia (1860–1895 gg.)' (The policy of 'self-strengthening' pursued by China's leaders, 1860–1895).
VI 1969, 4 (aprel'), 78–98.
SUBJ 12 15 66 ▪ 12.1 14.3 16.1 17 64 71

10664 DLC S P2 G1.1 1644–1911
Tikhvinskii, Sergei Leonidovich, 1918–.
'Pravlenie v Kitae man'chzhurskoi dinastii TSin' (Rule of China by the Manchurian Ch'ing dynasty).
VI 1966, 9 (sentiabr' 1966), 71–90. [For an English abstract, see 'Manchus in the Ch'ing dynasty'; *CSWT* 1, 5 (Apr. 1967), 15–19.]
SUBJ 12 12.1 32.2 66 ▪ 14.1 14.2 16.2 16.3 17

10665 WSU P P1 G1.1 1842–1895
Ting, Reuben Tse-Min.
The establishment of Tsungli Yamen and the dispatch of the first Chinese mission to foreign powers.
Unpublished masters thesis in History, U. of Washington, 1949. 93 p.
SUBJ 12 66 ▪ 14.5

10666 MCH P P2 G1.1 –1911
Tschou, Tso-Tschun (Chou Tse-ch'un), 1883–.
'Geschichte der chinesischen Staatsverfassung und Verwaltung bis zu den modernen Reformen' (History of the Chinese constitution and government up to the modern reforms).
ZVR 23, 3 (1910), 382–419.
SUBJ 12 12.2 ▪ 12.1 16.1 22.2 64

10667 NNC P P1 G1.2 –1911
Tsien Tai (Ch'ien T'ai), ?–1962.
Le pouvoir législatif en Chine (Legislative power in China).
Paris: Pedone, 1914. 200 p. (Doctoral dissertation, Faculté de droit, Université de Paris)
SUBJ 12 32 ▪ 12.2 16.1 30 32.2 64 72

10668 CSH P P2 G9.3 1895–1911
Tuzhilin, Aleksandr Vasil'evich.
'Ocherki iz sovremennoi zhizni Kitaia: Futszianskii soveshchatel'nyi komitet, sessiia 1909 g.' (Notes on contemporary life in China: The Fukien consultative committee, 1909 session).
VA 4 (mai 1910), 55–107. [Separately reprinted—Harbin: Yün-tun-pao, 1910. 53 p.]
SUBJ 12 12.2 17 24.1 47 ▪ 24.2 24.5 66

10669 NNC P P1 G1.2 –1911
van der Sprenkel, Otto P- N- Berkelbach, 1906–.
The Chinese civil service.
Canberra: Australian National U., 1958. 23 p. (George Ernest Morrison lectures in ethnology, 19)
SUBJ 12 16.1 ▪ 14.5 17 71

10670 MCH O P4 G1.3 1895–1911
Verraux, H-.
'L'administration publique en Chine' (Public administration in China).
R. française 31 (1906), 65–74, 129–140, 217–226.
SUBJ 12 18 22 ▪ 16.1 61

10671 CSU S P3 G1.2 –1895
Wakeman, Frederic Evans, Jr., 1937–.
'High Ch'ing, 1683–1839.' In *Modern East Asia: Essays in interpretation*, edited by James Buckley Crowley. [Selective entry]
New York: Harcourt, Brace and World, 1970, 1–28.
SUBJ 12 16.1 ▪ 12.1 16.2 62 66

10672 NNC P P2 G1.2 –1842
Watt, John Robertson, 1934–.
The district magistrate in late Imperial China.
New York: Columbia U. Press, 1972. 10, 340 p. (Revision of *Theory and practice in Chinese district administration: The role of the Ch'ing district magistrate in its historical setting*, doctoral dissertation in History, Columbia U., 1967)
SUBJ 12 16.1 62 ▪ 14.5 22 22.1 22.2 59 64

10673 CSU P P3 G5.1 1644–1842
Wilhelm, Hellmut, 1906–.
'The *po-hsüeh hung-ju* examination of 1679.'
JAOS 71 (1951), 60–66.
SUBJ 12 16.1 ▪ 66

10674 CBU S P2 G9.4 –1911
Wirth, Albrecht H-, 1866–?
Geschichte Formosa's bis Anfang 1898 (History of Taiwan to the beginning of 1898).
Bonn: C. Georgi, 1898. 188 p.
SUBJ 12 66 ▪ 15 21.2 21.3 22

10675 MCY P P2 G9.4 1895–1911
Woodside, Alexander Barton, 1938–.
'T'ang Ching-sung and the rise of the 1895 Taiwan Republic.'
PC 17 (Dec. 1963), 160–191.
SUBJ 12 16.1 ▪ 15 26.1 32.2 66

10676 CSU P P2 G1.2 1644–1895
Woodside, Alexander Barton, 1938–.
Vietnam and the Chinese model: A comparative study of Nguyen and Ch'ing civil government in the first half of the nineteenth century.
Cambridge: Harvard U. Press, 1971. 358 p. (Harvard East Asian series, 52)
SUBJ 12 17 ▪ 16.1 22.1

10677 NIC P P2 G1.2 1842–1895
Wright, Mary Clabaugh, 1917–1970.
The last stand of Chinese conservatism: The T'ung-chih Restoration, 1862–1874.
Stanford: Stanford U. Press, 1957. 10, 426 p. (Stanford studies in history, economics, and political science, 13) (Revision of *The Tung-chih Restoration*, doctoral dissertation in History, Radcliffe College, 1951) [Reprinted—New York: Atheneum, 1966. 12, 429 p.]
SUBJ 12 14 16.1 32 64 66 ▪ 12.1 12.2 15 16.2 17 18 22 22.1 22.2 25

10678 CSU P P1 G1.2 1644–1911
Wu, Silas H. L. (Wu Hsiu-liang), 1929–.
'The memorial systems of the Ch'ing dynasty (1644–1911).'
HJAS 27 (1967), 7–75.
SUBJ 12 ▪ 14.2

10679 CSU O P2 G1.4 1895–1911
Wu, Yung.
The flight of an empress, edited by Ida Pruitt. Tr. from the Chinese by Ida Pruitt.
New Haven: Yale U. Press, 1936. 23, 222 p. [Reprinted—London: Faber and Faber, 1937. 294 p.] [Reprinted—Westport, Conn.: Hyperion Press, 197? 23, 222 p.]
SUBJ 12 22 22.2 32.2 ▪ 12.1 12.2 16.1 22.1 26.1 48 63 64 66

10680 NIC P P3 G1.3 1644–1911
Yang, C. K. (Yang Ch'ing-k'un), 1911–.
'Some characteristics of Chinese bureaucratic behavior.' In *Confucianism in action*, edited by David Shepherd Nivison and Arthur Frederick Wright. [Selective entry]
Stanford: Stanford U. Press, 1959, 134–164.
SUBJ 12 16.1 64 ▪ 12.2 30 48 63

10681 MCY P P1 G1.1 –1911
Yang, Lien-sheng, 1914–.
'Toward a study of dynastic configurations in Chinese history.'
HJAS 17, 3/4 (Dec. 1954), 329–345. [Reprinted in *Studies in Chinese institutional history*, by Lien-sheng Yang. (Selective entry.) Cambridge: Harvard U. Press, 1961, 1–17. (Harvard-Yenching Institute studies, 20)]
SUBJ 12 19 62 70 ▪ 64 71

10682 MCH O P2 G1.3 1895–1911
Yen, Kia-lok.
'The bases of democracy in China.'
International j. of ethics 28, 2 (Jan. 1918), 197–219.
SUBJ 12 16 41 64 ▪ 24.6 34.3 42 44 66

10683 NNC U P1 G1.2 1842–1911
Yen, Weiching William (Yen Hui-ch'ing), 1877–1950.
'How China administrates her foreign affairs.'
American j. of international law 3, 3 (July 1909), 537–546. [Reprinted—*JAAA* 9, 10 (Nov. 1909), 306–309.]
SUBJ 12 66 ▪ 12.2

1644-1949

10684 NNC O P2 G1.1 1842–1949
Arlington, Lewis Charles, 1859–1942.
Through the dragon's eyes: Fifty years' experiences of a foreigner in the Chinese government service.
London: Constable, 1931. 57, 348 p.
SUBJ 12 14.2 14.5 15 60 66 ▪ 12.2 16.1 18 29 32.2 55 57 61

10685 CSH P P2 G2.0 1895–1928
Baranov, Ippolit Gavrilovich.
'Administrativnoe ustroistvo severnoi Man'chzhurii' (The administrative structure of northern Manchuria).
VM 1926, 11/12, 5–26.
Subj 12 22

10686 NIC P P1 G1.2 1895–1928
Bau, Mingchien Joshua (Pao Ming-ch'ien), 1894–.
Modern democracy in China.
Shanghai: Commercial Press, 1923. 10, 467 p.
Subj 12 32 ▪ 32.2

10687 NNC P P1 G1.2 1895–1928
Belov, Evgenii Aleksandrovich, 1929–.
'Agressivnaia politika imperialisticheskikh derzhav v Kitae v period revoliutsii 1911–1913 godov' (The aggressive policy of the imperialist powers in China during the Revolution of 1911–1913).
SV 1957, 2, 65–77.
Subj 12 32.2 ▪ 12.1 66

10688 MCH P P2 G1.2 1644–1949
Chan Loi-ming (Ch'en Lai-meng), 1913–.
The development of inter-governmental relations in China, with special reference to Canton (Kwangtung province).
Unpublished doctoral dissertation in Political Science, Harvard U., 1944. 297 p.
Subj 12 15 ▪ 12.2 14.5 14.6 22 59

10689 NNC U P1 G1.2 1842–1949
Chang, Carsun (Chang Chia-sen), 1886–.
'Die staatsrechtliche Krisis der chinesischen Republik' (The constitutional crisis of the Republic of China).
Jahrbuch des öffentlichen Rechts der Gegenwart 19 (1931), 316–355.
Subj 12 12.1 12.2 32 ▪ 32.1 64 66

10690 CSU P P1 G1.2 1895–1949
Chang, Hui Wen, 1907–.
The development of the civil service examination system in China since 1911.
Unpublished doctoral dissertation in Political Science, Stanford U., 1932. 526 p.
Subj 12 16.1 17 64 ▪ 12.2

10691 NIC U P1 G1.2 1644–1928
Chang, Yü-chüan (Chang Yü-ch'üan), 1880–.
'The provincial organs for foreign affairs in China.'
CSPSR 1, 3 (Oct. 1916), 47–70.
Subj 12 66

10692 CSU P P1 G1.2 –1949
Chen En-cheng, 1903–.
The development of supervisory control in China.
Unpublished masters thesis in Political Science, Stanford U., 1932. 166 p.
Subj 12 12.1 12.2

10693 ELS P P1 G1.2 –1949
Chen, Paky (Ch'en Po-chi).
The theory and practice of Chinese democracy.
Unpublished doctoral dissertation in Political Science, U. of London [London School of Economics and Political Science], 1939. 247 p.
Subj 12 32 64 ▪ 19 42

10694 CSU P P2 G1.2 1895–1949
Ch'en, Jerome (Ch'en Chih-jang), 1919–.
'Historical background.' In *Modern China's search for a political form*, edited by Jack Douglas Gray. [Analytic entry]
London: Oxford U. Press, 1969, 1–40.
Subj 12 14 14.5 14.6 15 64 ▪ 12.2 16 16.1 17 32.2 59

10695 MCH P P2 G1.2 1842–1928
Ch'en, Jerome (Ch'en Chih-jang), 1919–.
Yuan Shih-kai, 2nd ed.
Stanford: Stanford U. Press, 1972. 258 p.
Subj 12 15 ▪ 14.5 14.6 22.2 25 32 32.2 64 66 72

10696 NIC P P1 G1.2 1842–1949
Ch'ien, Tuan-sheng, 1900–.
The government and politics of China.
Cambridge: Harvard U. Press, 1950. 18, 526 p. [Reprinted as *The government and politics of China, 1912–1949.* Stanford: Stanford U. Press, 1970. 18, 526 p.]
Subj 12 32 64 ▪ 12.2 14 15 32.1 32.2

10697 NBU S P2 G1.2 1842–1928
Dalland, Olav.
Kina under forvandling (China in transformation).
Oslo: Cappelen, 1927. 150 p.
Subj 12 64 ▪ 11 14.1 14.4 15 16.1 17 25 32 33

10698 MCH P P2 G1.2 1895–1928
Dubarbier, Georges, 1888–.
La Chine contemporaine: politique et économique (Political and economic aspects of contemporary China).
Paris: Lib. Geuthner, 1926. 373 p.
Subj 12 14 14.2 14.3 ▪ 15 17 19 32 60

10699 MCH PO P1 G1.2 1895–1928
Duyvendak, Jan Julius Lodewijk, 1889–1954.
'China's politieke ontwikkeling' (Political development in China).
Onze Eeuw (Haarlem) 22, 1 (1922), 350–379; 22, 2 (1922), 45–67; 22, 3 (1922), 151–182.
Subj 12 19 32.2 ▪ 15 16.1 17 64

10700 NNC PO P2 G1.1 1842–1949
Epstein, Israel, 1915–.
The unfinished revolution in China.
Boston: Little, Brown, 1947. 442 p.
Subj 12 12.1 15 19 32 32.2 ▪ 14 18 24.1 25 32.1 34.1 64 66

10701 NIC P P2 G1.3 1895–1928
Fung, Hing-kwei (Feng Ching-kuei).
'Cotton culture.'
CSPSR 1, 3 (Oct. 1916), 97–112.
Subj 12 14.1

10702 MCY O P2 G1.2 1895–1949
Gale, Esson McDowell, 1884–1964.
Salt for the dragon: A personal history of China, 1908–1945.
East Lansing: Michigan State College Press, 1953. 12, 225 p.
Subj 12 14.5 16.1 66 ▪ 15 22.2 34.2

10703 NNC P P4 G1.2 –1928
Gnien His.
Le régime administratif de la Chine: les rapports juridiques entre le gouvernement central et les gouvernements provinciaux (The administrative system of China: Legal relations between the central government and the provincial governments).
Paris: Jouve, 1923. 163 p. (Doctoral dissertation, Faculté de droit, Université de Paris)
Subj 12 12.2 ▪ 16.1 32 64

10704 NNC S P2 G1.1 –1928
Grosse, Ernst, 1862–1927.
'Die chinesische Staatsidee' (The Chinese concept of the state).
China-Archiv 3, 4 (24 Apr. 1918), 147–153; 3, 5 (24 Mai 1918), 195–201; 3, 6 (24 Juni 1918), 243–247.
Subj 12 12.1 64 ▪ 12.2 41 61

10705 MCH S P1 G1.2 –1949
Han, Yu-shan (Han Yü-shan), 1899–.
'The Chinese civil service, yesterday and today.'
PHR 15, 2 (June 1946), 158–170.
Subj 12 16.1 17

10706 MCH PO P2 G1.2 1895–1949
Hedin, Sven Anders, 1865–1952.
Chiang Kai-shek, marskalk av Kina.
Stockholm: Bonnier, 1939. 392 p.
Chiang Kai-shek, marshal of China. Tr. by Bernard Norbelie.
New York: Day, 1940? 14, 290 p.
Subj 12 15 59 ▪ 11 14 14.1 14.2 14.3 17 25 64 66

10707 ICU P P2 G1.1 1842–1949
Horton, John Ryder.
Hsien government in China: A comparison of local government under the Kuomintang and local government under the Ch'ing dynasty.
Unpublished masters thesis in International Relations, U. of Chicago, 1948. 110 p.
Subj 12 12.2 14.5 22.2 ▪ 12.1 14.6 16.1 22 22.1 24.1 34.3 42 72

10708 MCY P P2 G9.0 1895–1928
Hsieh, Winston (Hsieh Wen-sun), 1935–.
'The ideas and ideals of a warlord: Ch'en Chiung-ming, 1878–1933.'
PC 16 (Dec. 1962), 198–252.
Subj 12 15 16.1 64 ▪ 17 24.2 59

10709 NNC P P4 G1.2 –1928
Hsu, Han-hao (Hsü Han-hao), 1907–.
L'administration provinciale en Chine (Provincial administration in China).
Nancy: Grandville, 1931. 134 p. (Doctoral dissertation, Faculté de droit, Université de Nancy)
Subj 12 ▪ 11.3 12.2 14 19 32 64

10710 CSU S P1 G1.2 –1949
King, Ambrose Yeo-chi (Chin Yao-chi), 1935–.
'Chinese traditional bureaucracy and its culture.'
CJA 7 (July 1966), 26–40 [s.p.].
Subj 12 63 64 ▪ 16 16.1 41

10711 MCH P P4 G1.2 1895–1949
King, Shih-ding (Chin Shih-ting), 1908–.
Le recrutement de la magistrature en Chine (The recruitment of judges in China).
Paris: Lib. sociale et économique, 1940. 194 p. (Doctoral dissertation, Faculté de droit, Université de Paris)
SUBJ 12 12.2 16.1 ▪ 17 22 63

10712 MCH S P2 G1.2 1895–1928
Kiuner, Nikolai Vasil'evich, 1877–1955.
Ocherki noveishei politicheskoi istorii Kitaia (Notes on recent Chinese political history).
Khabarovsk: Knizhnoe delo, 1927. 404 p.
SUBJ 10 12 32.2 66 ▪ 11 14 15 25 32 59 72

10713 MCH P P2 G1.1 1895–1928
Kotenev, Anatol M-, 1882–.
New lamps for old: An interpretation of events in modern China and whither they lead.
Shanghai: North-China Daily News and Herald, 1931. 371 p. [Reprinted—New York: AMS Press, 1971. 371 p.]
SUBJ 12 15 16.1 32 60 ▪ 12.1 13 14.1 14.5 22.2 32.2 33

10714 CBU S P1 G1.1 1842–1949
Laco, Karol.
'Politický a ústavný vývin Číny do vyhlásenia Čínskej l'udovej republiky' (The political and constitutional development of China before the establishment of the People's Republic).
Pravnicke studie (Bratislava) 3, 2 (1955), 185–244.
SUBJ 12 12.2 64 ▪ 12.1 15 19

10715 MMT P P2 G1.2 1842–1949
Li, Chien-nung.
The political history of China, 1840–1928. Tr. by Ssu-yü Teng and Jeremy Ingalls of *Chung-kuo chin pai nien cheng chih shih* (A political history of China in the past century); Shanghai: Shang wu yin shu kuan, 1947; 2 vols. 690 p. [c.p.]. [Abridged tr.]
Princeton: Van Nostrand, 1956. 12, 545 p. [Reprinted—Stanford: Stanford U. Press, 1966. 12, 545 p.]
SUBJ 10 12 15 19 32.2 ▪ 14 14.3 16.1 25 32 64 66

10716 MCH P P1 G1.1 1644–1928
Liang, J'en Kié (Liang Jen-chieh).
Etude sur la juridiction administrative en Chine (A study of administrative jurisdiction in China).
Paris: Jouve, 1920. 178 p. (Doctoral dissertation, Faculté de droit, Université de Paris)
SUBJ 12 12.2 ▪ 16.1 22 64

10717 CSU PO P2 G1.2 1842–1949
Lieu, D. K. (Liu Ta-chün), 1891–1962.
'A brief account of statistical work in China.'
BIIS 25, 2, Part 2 (1931), 88–121 [s.p.].
SUBJ 11 12 14 70 ▪ 12.2 14.1 14.2 14.4 17 24.3 36.1 36.2 56

10718 NNC S P2 G1.2 –1949
Linebarger, Paul Myron Anthony, 1913–1966.
Government in Republican China.
New York: McGraw-Hill, 1938. 15, 203 p. [Reprinted—Ann Arbor: University Microfilms, n.d. 15, 203 p.] [Reprinted—Westport, Conn.: Hyperion Press, 197? 15, 203 p.]
SUBJ 12 15 32 32.2 64 ▪ 12.1 14 16.1 19 25 41 42 62

10719 CSH U P1 G2.0 –1949
Lishin, Artemii.
'Puti gosudarstvennogo i kul'turnogo razvitiia Man'chzhurii' (The course of Manchuria's political and cultural development).
Vostochnoe obozrenie 2 (ianvar'–mart 1940), 36–76.
SUBJ 12 12.2 14 15 66 ▪ 12.1 14.5 14.6 21 21.2 25 32.2

10720 DLC P P1 G1.2 1644–1949
Long Yin (Lung Yin).
Le contrôle du budget en Chine: comparaison avec les systèmes anglais et français (Control of the budget in China: A comparison with the English and French systems).
Lyons: Impr. générale lyonnaise, 1943. 196 p. (Doctoral dissertation, Faculté de droit, Université de Lyon)
SUBJ 12 ▪ 14.5

10721 NIC U P2 G1.2 1644–1949
Lum, Kalfred Dip (Lin Tieh), 1899–.
Chinese government.
Shanghai: Shanghai Mercury Press, 1934. 173 p.
SUBJ 12 14.5

10722 CSU P P3 G1.2 1895–1928
MacKinnon, Stephen Robert, 1940–.
'Liang Shih-i and the communications clique.'
JAS 29, 3 (May 1970), 581–602.
SUBJ 12 14.2 14.6 59 ▪ 12.2 16.1

10723 GMS PO P2 G1.2 1895–1928
Michelsen, Erich.
'Verfassung, Gesetzgebung, Verwaltung und Rechtspflege in China, mit Berücksichtigung der Rechtsstellung der Fremden' (Constitution, legislation, government, and the administration of justice in China, with attention to the legal status of foreigners). In *China: Wirtschaft und Wirtschaftsgrundlagen* (The economy and economic foundations of China), edited by Josef Hellauer. [Selective entry]
Berlin: de Gruyter (Vereinigung wissenschaftlicher Verleger), 1921, 64–94.
SUBJ 12 12.2 ▪ 62

10724 MAM S P4 G1.2 –1949
Mu, Wei-chin, 1913–.
Provincial–central government relations and the problem of national unity in modern China.
Ann Arbor: University Microfilms (Publ. 10,975), 1955. 376, 55 p. (Doctoral dissertation in Politics, Princeton U., 1948)
SUBJ 12 32 ▪ 12.2 14.2 14.5 14.6 15 32.2

10725 MCY P P2 G4.3 –1949
Norins, Martin Richard.
Gateway to Asia: Sinkiang, frontier of the Chinese Far West.
New York: Day, 1944. 200 p.
SUBJ 12 14 16.1 24.2 66 ▪ 14.4 14.5 15 17 21 24.1 32.2 33

10726 NBU U P2 G1.2 1644–1949
Røise, Ernst Gunnar Norgaard, 1901–1948.
Svart og rødt i China (Black and red in China).
Oslo: Tiden, 1947. 148 p.
SUBJ 12 15 64 ▪ 14 14.1 14.4 16.1 16.3 18 66

10727 MCH PO P3 G1.2 1895–1928
Rottach, Edmond.
La Chine en révolution (China in revolution).
Paris: Perrin, 1914. 268 p.
SUBJ 12 15 32.2 ▪ 16.1 16.2 64 66

10728 NNC P P1 G1.2 1895–1928
Rusanov, Nikolai Sergeevich, 1859–?
'Obozrenie inostrannoi zhizni. Chast' 1, Kitaiskii "Napoleon"' (Survey of foreign life. Part 1, The Chinese 'Napoleon').
Russkoe bogatstvo 1914, 2 (fevral'), 293–301.
SUBJ 12 ▪ 12.2 14.5 32.2 66

10729 MCH P P2 G1.2 1842–1949
Soter, Richard Paul, 1927–.
Wu P'ei-fu: Case study of a Chinese warlord.
Unpublished doctoral dissertation in History and Far Eastern Languages, Harvard U., 1958. 266 p.
SUBJ 12 15 19 32.2 59 64 ▪ 12.1 16.1 35 36.4 66

10730 NNC O P3 G5.1 –1949
Starrett, Charles Vincent Emerson, 1886–.
'The passing of the eunuch: Some notes on an old Chinese custom.' In *Oriental encounters: Two essays in bad taste*, by C. V. E. Starrett. [Analytic entry]
Chicago: Normandie House, 1938, 11–31.
SUBJ 12 46 ▪ 16.1

10731 NNC PO P4 G1.2 –1928
Tao, L. K. (T'ao Meng-ho), 1887–1960.
'The Chinese district magistrate.'
CSPSR 1, 1 (Apr. 1916), 56–67; 1, 2 (July 1916), 45–60.
SUBJ 12 16.1 ▪ 12.1 12.2 63 64

10732 MCH P P2 G1.2 –1949
Tung Mong-sheng (T'ung Meng-sheng).
L'administration locale en France et en Chine (Local administration in France and in China).
Nancy: Vagner, 1937. 140 p. (Doctoral dissertation, Faculté de droit, Université de Nancy)
SUBJ 12 14.2 14.5 ▪ 12.1 12.2 14.6 17 18 56

10733 CSU O P2 G1.2 1895–1928
Valentin, Ferdinand.
L'avènement d'une république: luttes intérieures de la Chine de 1911 à 1923 (The birth of a republic: Internal struggles in China from 1911 to 1923).
Paris: Perrin, 1926. 316 p.
SUBJ 12 32.2 ▪ 32

10734 MCH O P2 G1.2 1895–1928
Vaure, Raoul du.
'Yuan-She-Kai, empereur: l'évolution politique de la Chine de 1907 à nos jours' (Yüan Shih-k'ai, Emperor: China's political evolution from 1907 to the present).
Correspondant 263 (25 mai 1916), 577–618.
SUBJ 12 15 32.2 ▪ 14.6 16.1 22.2 25 35 66

10735 CSU S P1 G1.3 1895–1928
Vinacke, Harold Monk, 1893–.
'Military power and constitutional development in China.'
APSR 15, 2 (May 1921), 233–252.
SUBJ 12 12.2 15 ▪ 32 32.2

10736 NNC S P1 G1.1 –1949
Walker, Richard Louis, 1922–.
'The control system of the Chinese government.'
FEQ 7, 1 (Nov. 1947), 2–21.
SUBJ 12 ▪ 12.2 16.1 64

10737 NNC P P1 G1.2 –1949
Wist, Hans, 1904–.
Das chinesische Zensorat (The Chinese censorate).
Hamburg: J. J. Augustin, 1932. 45 p. (Doctoral dissertation, Philosophische Fakultät, Universität Hamburg)
SUBJ 12 ▪ 72

10738 MCH P P1 G1.2 –1949
Wu, John C. H. (Wu Ching-hsiung), 1899–.
'The struggle between government of laws and government of men in the history of China.'
CLR 5, 2 (Feb. 1932), 53–71.
SUBJ 12 12.2 64 ▪ 12.1 22.2

10739 NIC P P1 G1.2 1895–1949
Wu, T. F. (Wu Chih-fang).
Chinese government and politics.
Shanghai: Commercial Press, 1934. 473 p.
SUBJ 12 32 ▪ 14.5 19 32.2

1911-1949

10740 NIC S P1 G1.2 1928–1949
'Educational qualifications of national government employees.'
China critic 3, 1 (2 Jan. 1930), 13.
SUBJ 12 16.1 17

10741 MCH P P1 G1.1 1928–1949
'La situation en Chine' (The situation in China).
Chronique de politique étrangère (Brussels) 1, 5 (sept. 1948), 70–85.
SUBJ 12 16.1 32 ▪ 14.6 64 66

10742 NNC P P1 G1.2 1928–1949
'Statistics on government employees in China.'
NWSS 4, 17 (27 Apr. 1931), 85, 87–88.
SUBJ 12 ▪ 17 32 47

10743 CSH P P2 G1.2 1911–1949
Agapov, Evgenii.
'Rozhdenie novogo Kitaia' (The birth of a new China).
Vostochnoe obozrenie 3 (aprel'–iiun' 1940), 27–53.
SUBJ 12 15 32 66 ▪ 32.2

10744 NNC U P2 G1.2 1911–1928
Al'skii, M-.
'V Kitae' (In China).
Krasnaia nov' 1926, 12 (dekabr'), 207–220.
SUBJ 12 ▪ 14.4 15 16.3 16.4 32.2

10745 MCH PO P2 G2.0 1911–1949
Balet, Jean Cyprien, 1867–?
Le drame de l'Extrême-Orient: la Mandchourie historique, politique, économique, son avenir (Drama in the Far East: The history, politics, and economy of Manchuria and its future).
Paris: Payot, 1932. 222 p.
SUBJ 12 12.2 14 ▪ 14.1 14.4

10746 CSU O P4 G8.2 1928–1949
Barnett, Arthur Doak, 1921–.
'Disunity in the Southwest' [report to Institute of Current World Affairs, October 1949]. In *China on the eve of Communist takeover*, by A. D. Barnett. [Selective entry]
New York: Praeger, 1963, 282–295.
SUBJ 12 32.2 ▪ 12.1 14 14.6 25

10747 CSU O P2 G5.2 1928–1949
Barnett, Arthur Doak, 1921–.
'Old style warlordism' [report to Institute of Current World Affairs, March 1948]. In *China on the eve of Communist takeover*, by A. D. Barnett. [Selective entry]
New York: Praeger, 1963, 157–186.
SUBJ 12 12.1 14 15 ▪ 18 22 22.1 24.3 25 32.2

10748 NNC O P2 G1.2 1928–1949
Bates, Miner Searle, 1897–.
'Toward an understanding of Chinese politics, 1931–1932.'
PA 5, 3 (Mar. 1932), 218–232.
SUBJ 12 32 ▪ 14

10749 CSU U P2 G1.2 1911–1949
Beer, Patrice de, 1942–.
La guerre civile en Chine, 1919–1949 (The civil war in China, 1919–1949).
Tournai, Paris: Casterman, 1968. 298 p.
SUBJ 12 25 32.2 ▪ 14.1 15 16 36.3 36.4

10750 CSU P P2 G1.2 1911–1928
Bergère, Marie-Claire, 1933–.
'De la république à la dictature (1912–1916)' (From republic to dictatorship, 1912–1916). In *De la guerre franco-chinoise à la fondation du Parti communiste chinois, 1885–1921* (From the Sino-French war to the formation of the Chinese Communist Party, 1885–1921), by Marianne Bastid, M.-C. Bergère, and Jean Chesneaux. [Analytic entry]
Paris: Hatier Université, 1972, 126–150. (HU, Collection d'histoire contemporaine, Histoire de la Chine, 2)
SUBJ 12 14 32.2 ▪ 15 16.2 32 32.1 36.2 64 66

10751 CSU P P2 G6.2 1911–1949
Bianco, Lucien, 1930–.
'Fonctionnaires, percepteurs, militaires et brigands en Chine: le Anhui dénonce la mauvaise administration provinciale (1931)' (Government officials, tax collectors, military men, and bandits in China: Anhwei denounces bad provincial administration, 1931).
R. d'histoire moderne et contemporaine 16 (avr.–juin 1969), 300–318.
SUBJ 12 25 ▪ 15 21 24 28

10752 MCH O P3 G1.3 1911–1928
Bland, John Otway Percy, 1863–1945.
China, Japan and Korea.
New York: Scribner, 1921. 327 p.
SUBJ 12 20 ▪ 14.6 15 25 32.2

10753 CSU O P1 G1.2 1911–1928
Bland, John Otway Percy, 1863–1945.
'Civil war as a profession in China.'
Asia (New York: American Asiatic Assn.) 20, 10 (Nov. 1920), 957–967, 1010–1014.
SUBJ 12 15

10754 MCH S P2 G1.2 1928–1949
Bloch, Kurt, 1908–.
'Reflections on the social structure in China.'
Social research 4, 4 (Nov. 1937), 490–508.
SUBJ 12 16 ▪ 12.2 22 22.2

10755 NIC O P1 G1.2 1911–1949
Bloch, Kurt, 1908–.
'Warlordism: A transitory stage in Chinese government.'
AJS 43, 5 (Mar. 1938), 691–703.
SUBJ 12 ▪ 15 32.2

10756 MCH S P2 G9.0 1911–1928
[Böhme, Karl] K. B., 1882–.
'Südchinesische Verwaltungsreform' (Administrative reform in South China).
OR 8, 6 (31 März 1927), 84–87.
SUBJ 12 ▪ 12.2 14.1 14.6

10757 CSH PO P1 G1.2 1911–1928
Borel, Henri, 1869–1933.
De Chineesche Republiek (The Republic of China).
Leiden: Brill, 1913. 51 p.
SUBJ 12 32 64 ▪ 17

10758 CSU P P4 G1.2 1928–1949
Boyle, John Hunter, 1930–.
China and Japan at war, 1937–1945: The politics of collaboration.
Stanford: Stanford U. Press, 1972. 430 p. (Revision of *Japan's puppet regimes in China, 1937–1940*, doctoral dissertation in History, Stanford U., 1968)
SUBJ 12 12.1 59 66 ▪ 14 14.5 14.6 15 16.1 32 32.2 34.2 55 64

10759 MCH P P2 G4.3 1911–1949
Chan, Fook-lam Gilbert (Ch'en Fu-lin), 1938–.
Sinkiang under Sheng Shih-ts'ai, 1933–1944.
Unpublished masters thesis, U. of Hong Kong, 1965. 314 p.
SUBJ 12 12.1 59 66 ▪ 13 14 14.3 15 17 32.2

10760 NIC P P2 G1.3 1928–1949
Chang, C. M. (Chang Ch'un-ming), 1904–.
'A new government for rural China: The political aspect of rural reconstruction.'
NSEQ 9, 2 (July 1936), 239–295.
SUBJ 12 16.1 22 37 ▪ 12.1 14.5 18 19 22.1

10761 NIC O P4 G1.3 1928–1949
Chang, Ray (Chang Jui).
'Trends in Chinese public administration.'
IB 3, 5 (21 Feb. 1937), 99–121.
SUBJ 12 16.1 ▪ 12.1 14 18

10762 MCY P P3 G1.2 1911–1949
Chen, C. M. (Ch'en Chih-mai), 1908–.
'The Chinese executive.'
CSPSR 21, 1 (Apr. 1937), 34–64.
SUBJ 12 12.2 ▪ 12.1 15 16.1 32

10763 CSU P P1 G1.2 1928–1949
Chen, C. M. (Ch'en Chih-mai), 1908–.
'Impeachments of the Control Yuan.'
CSPSR 19, 3 (Oct. 1935), 331–366; 19, 4 (Jan. 1936), 515–542.
SUBJ 12 12.2

10764 MCH O P2 G1.2 1928–1949
Chen, C. M. (Ch'en Chih-mai), 1908–.
'The post-war government of China.'
J. of politics 9, 4 (Nov. 1947), 503–521.
SUBJ 12 12.2 ▪ 12.1 22

10765 MCH S P1 G1.2 1911–1928
Chen, Wan-li (Cheng Wen-li).
Les développements des institutions politiques de la Chine depuis l'établissement de la république (1912) jusqu'à nos jours (1925): étude d'histoire constitutionnelle et de droit comparé (The development of political institutions in China from the establishment of the Republic in 1912 to 1925: A study of constitutional history and comparative law).
Paris: Jouve, 1926. 182 p. (Doctoral dissertation, Faculté de droit, Université de Paris)
SUBJ 12 12.2 ▪ 60

10766 CSU P P2 G1.2 1911–1928
Ch'en, Jerome (Ch'en Chih-jang), 1919–.
'Defining Chinese warlords and their factions.'
BSOAS 31, 3 (Oct. 1968), 563–600.
SUBJ 12 15 25 48 ▪ 16.1 30 32.2 39 59 66

10767 MCH O P2 G8.3 1928–1949
Cheng, Ch'eng-k'un, 1906–.
'Modernization of China's Kweichow province.'
Amerasia 4, 6 (Aug. 1940), 283–288.
SUBJ 12 19 24.1 28 ▪ 17 24.2 24.4 24.6 56

10768 CSH PO P4 G1.2 1911–1928
Cheng, Sih-gung (Ch'eng Hsi-keng).
Modern China: A political study.
Oxford: Clarendon Press, 1919. 380 p. (Doctoral dissertation in Economics, U. of London [London School of Economics], 1921) [Reprinted—Westport, Conn.: Hyperion Press, 197? 380 p.]
SUBJ 12 12.2 66 ▪ 14.2 14.3 14.6 15 22 29 30 32.2 34.3

10769 ICU P P2 G1.2 1911–1928
Chi, Hsi-sheng, 1937–.
The Chinese warlord system.
Unpublished doctoral dissertation in Political Science, U. of Chicago, 1969. 414 p.
SUBJ 12 15 25 30 32.2 35 ▪ 11.1 12.1 14 14.5 16 16.1 18 22 32.1 64

10770 NNC U P3 G6.1 1928–1949
Ch'ien, Tuan-sheng, 1900–.
'The role of the military in Chinese government.'
PA 21, 3 (Sept. 1948), 239–251.
SUBJ 12 15

10771 CSU U P4 G1.2 1928–1949
Ch'ien, Tuan-sheng, 1900–.
'War-time government in China.'
APSR 36, 5 (Oct. 1942), 850–872.
SUBJ 12 12.2 ▪ 32

10772 NIC O P2 G1.2 1928–1949
Ch'ien, Tuan-sheng, 1900–.
'Wartime local government in China.'
PA 16, 4 (Dec. 1943), 441–460.
SUBJ 12

10773 NNC P P1 G1.1 1928–1949
Dickerman, Sherwood Eliot, 1926–.
Li Tsung-jen and the Chinese National Assembly of 1948: A rebellion against authority.
Unpublished masters thesis in History, Columbia U., 1963. 144 p.
SUBJ 12 ▪ 32

10774 CSH PO P2 G1.2 1928–1949
Djang, T. K.
'Factory inspection in China.'
ILR 50, 3 (Sept. 1944), 284–299.
SUBJ 12 12.2 ▪ 22

10775 CSH PO P2 G1.2 1928–1949
Djang, T. K.
'Some problems of labour law enforcement in China.'
ILR 53, 1/2 (Jan.–Feb. 1946), 39–48.
SUBJ 12 12.2 ▪ 16.4 52

10776 WSU PO P2 G5.0 1911–1949
Ellis, Leon Hubbard, 1892–.
The Kuomintang and its government of China.
Unpublished doctoral dissertation in Political Science, U. of Washington, 1939. 2 vols. 19, 634 p. [c.p.].
SUBJ 12 12.1 32 ▪ 14 15 16.1 22 32.2 64

10777 CSH P P1 G1.2 1911–1928
Engel'fel'd, Vladimir Viktorovich, 1891–1937.
'Konstitutsionnye akty gomindana' (Constitutional enactments of the Kuomintang).
VM 1928, 11/12, 87–95.
SUBJ 12 32 ▪ 64

10778 NNC O P2 G1.2 1911–1928
Etherton, Percy Thomas, 1879–.
China: The facts.
London: Benn, 1927. 17, 259 p.
SUBJ 10 12 12.2 32 60 ▪ 14.2 15 16 17 22.2 30 40 50

10779 NIC U P1 G1.2 1911–1928
Eu-yang Kwang.
The political reconstruction of China.
Shanghai: St. John's U., 1922. 190 p. (St. John's U. studies, 1) (Masters thesis in Political Science, St. John's U. [Shanghai])
SUBJ 12 ▪ 32

10780 MAM P P1 G1.2 1928–1949
Gibbons, David Sprague, 1940–.
Dominant political leadership and political integration in a transitional society: China, Chiang Kai-shek and Mao Tse-tung, 1935–1949.
Ann Arbor: University Microfilms (Publ. 69-2739), 1969. 459 p. (Doctoral dissertation in Political Science, Princeton U., 1968)
SUBJ 12 16.1 32 61 ▪ 32.2 59

10781 MCH P P2 G5.2 1911–1949
Gillin, Donald George, 1930–.
Warlord Yen Hsi-shan in Shansi province, 1911–1949.
Princeton: Princeton U. Press, 1967. 334 p.
SUBJ 12 12.1 14 15 17 59 ▪ 14.4 14.5 16.1 23 24.1 25 30 32.2 37

10782 NNC PO P1 G1.2 1911–1949
Hoh, Chih-hsiang (Hao Chih-hsiang), 1904–.
China belongs to the Chinese people.
Shanghai: Commercial Press, 1948. 34, 518 p.
SUBJ 12 12.2 32 60 64 ▪ 15 25 62

10783 NBU O P2 G5.2 1928–1949
Holth, Sverre.
Mellom røde og gule (Among red and yellow).
Oslo: Indremissionsforlaget, 1947. 116 p.
SUBJ 12 15 64 ▪ 17 26.1 28 66

10784 NNC P P1 G1.2 1911–1928
Holzhauer, Fritz.
'Die erste chinesische Parlaments-Gesetzgebung' (The first Chinese parliamentary legislation).
DCR 2 (1912), 1–20.
SUBJ 12 12.1 ▪ 12.2 66

10785 NNC P P1 G1.2 1911–1928
Houn, Franklin W. (Hou Fu-wu), 1920–.
Central government of China, 1912–1928: An institutional study.
Madison: U. of Wisconsin Press, 1957. 246 p. (Revision of doctoral dissertation in Political Science, U. of Wisconsin, 1953)
SUBJ 12 ▪ 12.2 14.5 15 32

10786 NNC P P2 G1.2 1928–1949
Iliushechkin, Vasilii Pavlovich, 1915–.
'Tret'ia revoliutsionnaia grazhdanskaia voina v Kitae, 1945–1949 gg.' (The Third Revolutionary Civil War in China, 1945–1949).
UZIV 11 (1955), 101–154.
SUBJ 12 15 32.2 66 ▪ 12.1 14.1 16 32

10787 NNC P P3 G2.0 1928–1949
Iriye, Akira (Irie Akira), 1934–.
'Chang Hsüeh-liang and the Japanese.'
JAS 20, 1 (Nov. 1960), 33–43.
SUBJ 12 66

10788 NIC U P4 G1.2 1928–1949
Kan Nai-kuang, 1897–1956.
'Problems of public administration in China.'
PT new (2nd) series 7, 8 (16 Oct. 1934), 361–370.
SUBJ 12

10789 NIC P P5 G1.2 1928–1949
Kan Nai-kuang, 1897–1956.
'Recent development of district autonomy in China.'
PT new (2nd) series 3, 10 (16 Dec. 1932), 344–354.
SUBJ 12 12.1 22 ▪ 14.5 32

10790 CSU P P2 G8.1 1911–1949
Kapp, Robert Alexander, 1943–.
'Provincial independence vs. national rule: A case study of Szechwan in the 1920's and 1930's.'
JAS 30, 3 (May 1971), 535–549. [For a fuller version, see entry 10791.]
SUBJ 12 14.5 ▪ 14.6 15 22 32.2

10791 MAM P P2 G8.1 1911–1949
Kapp, Robert Alexander, 1943–.
Szechwanese provincial militarism and central power in Republican China.
Ann Arbor: University Microfilms (Publ. 70-25,289), 1970. 403 p. (Doctoral dissertation in History, Yale U.)
SUBJ 12 12.1 15 16.1 25 35 ▪ 14.5 14.6 16.3 17 21.1 32.2 36.3 36.4 54 59

10792 CSH O P2 G1.4 1928–1949
Ke Han (K'o-han), pseud.
The Shansi-Hopei-Chahar border region: Report 1, 1937–38.
Chungking: New China Information Committee, 1940. 89 p. (NCIC bulletins, 8)
SUBJ 12 14 17 ▪ 15 25 36.3 36.4 47

10793 MCH P P1 G1.2 1911–1949
Kong, Chin Tsong (K'ung Ch'ing-tsung), 1898–.
La constitution des cinq pouvoirs: théorie, application. Etude sur une doctrine nouvelle du droit public chinois et les institutions politiques de la Chine moderne (The five-power constitution in theory and practice: A study of a new doctrine of Chinese public law and the political institutions of modern China).
Paris: Marcel Rivière, 1932. 380 p.
SUBJ 12 12.2 64 ▪ 12.1 16.1 32 72

10794 NIC P P2 G1.2 1928–1949
Ku, Tun-jou.
'Experiments in local government.'
YJSS 2, 1 (July 1939), 70–90.
SUBJ 12 ▪ 12.1 12.2 22

10795 MCH P P4 G1.2 1911–1949
Ku Yen-ju.
Le régime actuel de l'indépendance administrative décentralisée en Chine (The present system of decentralized administrative autonomy in China).
Nancy: Société d'impressions typographiques, 1931. 143 p. (Doctoral dissertation, Faculté de droit, Université de Nancy)
SUBJ 12 ▪ 22

10796 MCH P P2 G2.0 1928–1949
Levine, Steven I., 1941–.
Political integration in Manchuria, 1945–1949.
Unpublished doctoral dissertation in Political Science, Harvard U., 1972. 511 p.
SUBJ 12 12.1 15 16 16.1 32.2 ▪ 14 14.1 16.3 21.2 22 25 32 32.1 34.1 66

10797 CSU F P3 G5.1 1928–1949
Lin, Peter Wei (Lin Wei), 1894–.
'A statistical study of the personnel of Chinese national government.'
BIIS 25, 2, Part 2 (1931), 135–208 [s.p.].
SUBJ 12 16.1 ▪ 32 47

10798 MCH O P2 G1.4 1928–1949
Lindsay, Michael Francis Morris, 1909–.
'Postwar politics and government of Communist China.'
J. of politics 9, 4 (Nov. 1947), 543–564.
SUBJ 12 12.1 32 ▪ 14.1 32.2

10799 MCY PO P2 G1.2 1928–1949
Linebarger, Paul Myron Anthony, 1913–1966.
The China of Chiang K'ai-shek.
Boston: World Peace Foundation, 1941. 11, 449 p. [Reprinted—Ann Arbor: University Microfilms, n.d. 11, 449 p.]
SUBJ 12 12.1 12.2 ▪ 14.4 17 32.1 64

10800 MCY P P1 G1.2 1928–1949
Linebarger, Paul Myron Anthony, 1913–1966, and Robert Ewing Hosack, 1911–.
'The Republic: Phase of resurgence (1928–1946).' In *China*, edited by Harley Farnsworth MacNair. [Selective entry]
Berkeley, Los Angeles: U. of California Press, 1946, 145–165. [Reprinted in *China*, edited by H. F. MacNair. (Selective entry.) Freeport, N.Y.: Books for Libraries, 1970, 145–165.]
SUBJ 12 ▪ 15

10801 CSU U P4 G6.0 1928–1949
Ma, W. H. (Ma Wen-huan), 1900–.
'Hsien government and functions.'
CR 68, 8 (Aug. 1937), 506–512.
SUBJ 12 ▪ 12.1 14.5 18 21.3

10802 CSU U P1 G1.2 1911–1928
McAleavy, Henry.
'China under the war-lords.'
History today 12, 4 (Apr. 1962), 227–233; 12, 5 (May 1962), 303–311.
SUBJ 12 ▪ 15 32.2

10803 MCH P P2 G1.1 1911–1949
MacNair, Harley Farnsworth, 1899–1947.
China in revolution: An analysis of politics and militarism under the Republic.
Chicago: U. of Chicago Press, 1931. 12, 244 p. [Reprinted—New York: Fertig, 1968. 244 p.]
SUBJ 12 32.2 64 ▪ 15 25 32 66

10804 ELB O P3 G1.1 1928–1949
Martin, William, 1888–1934.
Il faut comprendre la Chine.
Paris: Perrin, 1934. 270 p.
Understand the Chinese. Tr. by E- W-Dickes.
New York: Harper, 1934. 249 p. [Reprinted—Taipei: Ch'eng-wen, 1971. 249 p.]
SUBJ 12 20 28 ▪ 15 22.2 32 66

10805 CSU P P2 G1.2 1928–1949
Mast, Herman William, III, 1941–.
'A heavy hand in the examination halls: The earliest attempts of the Kuomintang to staff a modern civil service, 1928–1937.'
Studies on Asia 8 (1967), 87–118.
SUBJ 12 16.1 ▪ 12.2 32

10806 NBU O P2 G1.1 1928–1949
Mohn, Albert Henrik.
China i smeltedigelen (China in the melting pot).
Oslo: Gyldendal, 1950. 229 p.
SUBJ 12 15 ▪ 12.1 14.1 14.4 16.1 16.3 18 33 64 66

10807 CSH P P1 G1.2 1911–1949
Pen Ly-Toan (P'eng Li-tuan).
Etude historique et critique sur l'organisation administrative de la Chine depuis 1912 jusqu'à 1931 (An historical and critical study of China's administrative organization from 1912 to 1931).
Lyons: Bosc et Riou, 1933. 136 p. (Doctoral dissertation, Faculté de droit, Université de Lyon)
SUBJ 12 12.1 12.2 ▪ 14.5 31 64

10808 CBU P P1 G1.2 1928–1949
Pernitzsch, Max Gerhard, 1882–.
'Änderungen in der staatlichen Organisation Chinas' (Changes in the organization of the Chinese state).
MSOSB 42 (1939), 15–20.
SUBJ 12 ▪ 15 17

10809 MCH U P2 G1.2 1928–1949
Pernitzsch, Max Gerhard, 1882–.
'Das Staatswesen des heutigen China' (The state in contemporary China).
MSOSB 39 (1936), 67–138.
SUBJ 12 12.2 ▪ 14.5 15 17

10810 CBU P P1 G1.2 1928–1949
Pernitzsch, Max Gerhard, 1882–.
'Volksvertretungen im China der Kriegszeit' (Representative bodies in wartime China).
MSOSB 42 (1939), 1–14.
SUBJ 12 ▪ 64

10811 CSU P P1 G1.2 1911–1928
Pye, Lucian Wilmot, 1921–.
Warlord politics: Conflict and coalition in the modernization of Republican China.
New York: Praeger, 1972. 313 p. (Revision of *The politics of Tuchunism in North China, 1920–1927: An aspect of political and social change in modern China*, doctoral dissertation in Political Science, Yale U., 1951)
SUBJ 12 15 16 ▪ 25 32

10812 DLC P P2 G1.2 1911–1949
Rajchman, Ludwik J-, 1881–1965.
Report of the technical agent of the Council on his mission in China from the date of appointment until April 1st, 1934.
Geneva: League of Nations, Council, Committee on Technical Co-operation Between the League of Nations and China, 1934. 72 p. (League of Nations publications, General Series, 1934, 1; Official No. C-157.M.66, 1934) [French version also published—Geneva, 1934.] [Reprinted as *Report to the Council of its technical delegate on his mission in China from date of appointment until April 1, 1934.* Nanking: International Relations Committee, 1934. 51 p.]
SUBJ 12 14 14.1 14.2 ▪ 14.5 17 18 34.1 36.3

10813 MCH P P2 G1.2 1928–1949
Rosinger, Lawrence Kaelter, 1915–.
China's crisis.
New York: Knopf, 1945. 12, 259, 13 p.
SUBJ 12 14 15 32 ▪ 12.1 14.1 14.4 14.6 16.1 16.2 19 32.2 66

10814 MCH P P2 G1.2 1928–1949
Rosinger, Lawrence Kaelter, 1915–.
China's wartime politics, 1937–1944.
Princeton: Princeton U. Press, 1944. 133 p.
SUBJ 12 32 ▪ 12.1 12.2 32.2 64 66

10815 CSH U P1 G1.2 1911–1949
Rüdenberg, Ernst.
'Die politischen Mächte Chinas' (Political powers in China).
Z. für Geopoltik 9, 1 (Jan. 1932), 19–34.
SUBJ 12 32 32.2 ▪ 14.6 66

10816 NNC F P2 G5.4 1928–1949
Shang Chen.
'A resumé of Honan administration since the establishment of the national government.'
CQ-S 2, 1 (Winter 1936), 167–200.
SUBJ 12 14 17 ▪ 12.1 14.5 18 24.1

10817 MCH PO P1 G1.2 1928–1949
Shang, Chuan-tao.
'Some problems of hsien government.'

PT new (2nd) series 14, 1 (1 July 1936), 31–41.
Subj 12 12.1 ▪ 14.5 16.1

10818 MCY P P4 G1.2 1928–1949
Shen, Nelson Nai-cheng (Shen Nai-cheng).
'The local government of China.'
CSPSR 20, 2 (July 1936), 163–201.
Subj 12 12.2 ▪ 22

10819 MAM P P2 G1.2 1928–1949
Shyu, Lawrence N. (Hsü Nai-li), 1933–.
The people's political council and China's wartime problems, 1937–1945.
Ann Arbor: University Microfilms (Publ. 72-28,100), 1972. 246 p. (Doctoral dissertation in Political Science, Columbia U., 1971)
Subj 12 32 32.2 ▪ 12.1 12.2 14 14.6 25 64 66

10820 MCH S P1 G1.2 1911–1928
[Simpson, Bertram Lenox] B. L. Putnam Weale, pseud., 1877–1930.
The fight for the Republic in China.
New York: Dodd, Mead, 1917. 13, 490 p.
Subj 12 ▪ 12.1 12.2 14.3 15 64

10821 DCK S P2 G1.2 1928–1949
Sperling, Johannes, 1882–.
Strejflys over det nye Kina (A glimpse of the new China).
Copenhagen: Fremad, 1938. 138 p.
Subj 12 66 ▪ 14.2 16.3 16.4 18 32.1 36.4

10822 NNC U P1 G1.2 1911–1949
Tang, Edgar Cha (T'ang Chia), 1902–.
'Five years of the Control Yuan.'
IB 2, 7 (11 Nov. 1936), 117–131.
Subj 12 ▪ 12.2

10823 NNC P P1 G1.1 1928–1949
Tang, Henry Chenchu.
Chinese examination institutions under the government of the Republic of China, 1930–1948.
Unpublished masters thesis in Political Science, Columbia U., 1958. 123 p.
Subj 12 16 ▪ 12.2 17

10824 MCH O P2 G2.0 1928–1949
Taube, Carl Gunnar, 1885–.
Kriget som inte var något krig (The war that was not a war).
Stockholm: Bonnier, 1932. 131 p.
Subj 12 15 ▪ 14.2 25

10825 NIC O P2 G1.4 1928–1949
Taylor, George Edward, 1905–.
'Administration at Peking.'
Amerasia 4, 12 (Feb. 1941), 574–578.
Subj 12 ▪ 12.1

10826 CSU O P2 G1.2 1928–1949
Taylor, George Edward, 1905–.
'The struggle for government in China.'
International affairs (London) 15, 3 (May–June 1936), 414–432.
Subj 12 16 32 ▪ 12.1 15 16.1 16.2 32.2

10827 MCH PO P2 G1.4 1928–1949
Taylor, George Edward, 1905–.
The struggle for North China.
New York: Institute of Pacific Relations, International Secretariat, 1940. 14, 250 p.
Subj 12 14 16.3 32.2 64 ▪ 12.1 13 14.6 15 16.1 18 21.2 25 66

10828 MCH P P2 G1.1 1911–1949
Tsao, W. Y. (Ts'ao Wen-yen), 1908–.
The constitutional structure of modern China.
Melbourne: Melbourne U. Press, 1947. 17, 304 p. [Reprinted—Westport, Conn.: Hyperion Press, 197? 17, 304 p.]
Subj 12 12.2 14.1 14.6 32 64 ▪ 12.1 14.4 16.3 16.4 22 36.4

10829 NNC P P1 G1.2 1928–1949
Tyau, Min-ch'ien T. Z. (Tiao Min-ch'ien), 1888–.
'The work and organization of the Legislative Yuan.'
CQ-S 2, 1 (Winter 1936), 73–88.
Subj 12 12.2

10830 CSH P P2 G1.4 1928–1949
U.S. Office of Strategic Services. Research and Analysis Branch.
The puppet governmental bodies of occupied North China, mimeo.
[Washington, D.C.]: ——, 1945. 16 p. (R. and A., 3075)
Subj 12 22 ▪ 32

10831 CSH P P3 G1.3 1928–1949
U.S. Office of Strategic Services. Research and Analysis Branch.
Structure and personnel of the Nanking puppet government (and Hong Kong administration), mimeo.
[Washington, D.C.]: ——, 1945. 84 p. (R. and A., 2565)
Subj 12 22 ▪ 24.2 24.6 32 36.2

10832 MCH O P3 G1.5 1928–1949
Utley, Freda, 1898–.
China at war.
London: Faber and Faber, 1939. 306 p.
Subj 12 15 21.1 ▪ 19 25

10833 CSH U P2 G1.2 1911–1928
[Vilenskii, Vladimir Dmitrievich] Vl. Vilenskii-Sibiriakov, pseud., 1888–1942.
Sun' IAt-sen, otets kitaiskoi revoliutsii (Sun Yat-sen, father of the Chinese Revolution).
Moscow: Krasnaia nov', 1924. 183 p. [Reprinted—Moscow: Gosizdat, 1924. 196 p.]
Subj 12 32.2 ▪ 12.1 14.4 19 60

10834 CBU P P2 G1.2 1911–1928
Vissière, Arnold Jacques Antoine, 1858–1930.
'Notes sur la géographie politique et l'administration de la République chinoise' (Notes on the political geography and the administration of the Republic of China).
BAAFC 4, 2 – 7, 2 (avr. 1912 – avr. 1915), 64 p. in all.
Subj 12 15 32 ▪ 12.1 12.2 32.2 62 64

10835 NNC P P4 G1.2 1911–1928
Voitinskii, Grigorii Naumovich, 1893–1956.
'Kitaiskaia burzhuaziia i gomindan' (The Chinese bourgeoisie and the Kuomintang).
MKhMP 1929, 8/9 (avgust–sentiabr'), 51–64. [Reprinted in *KVzhd i politika imperialistov v Kitae* (The Chinese Eastern Railway and imperialist policy in China), by G. N. Voitinskii. (Sole entry.) Moscow: Izd-vo Kom. akad., 1930, 19–36.]
Subj 12 14 16.2 ▪ 32 66

10836 MCH PO P4 G1.2 1928–1949
Wang, Kan-yu (Wang Kan-yü), 1906–.
The hsien (county) government in China.
Unpublished doctoral dissertation in Government, Harvard U., 1947. 350 p.
Subj 12 12.1 ▪ 12.2 14.5 14.6 17 18 22 64

10837 NIC PO P2 G1.2 1928–1949
Wang, Kan-yu (Wang Kan-yü), 1906–.
The local government of China: A study of the administrative nature of local units.
Chungking: China Institute of Pacific Relations, 1945. 50 p. (China Council series, 6)
Subj 12 ▪ 22

10838 MAM P P4 G1.2 1911–1928
Whitaker, Urban George, Jr., 1924–.
Americans and Chinese political problems, 1912–1923.
Ann Arbor: University Microfilms (Publ. 10,018), 1954. 415 p. (Doctoral dissertation in Political Science, U. of Washington)
Subj 12 33 37 64 66 ▪ 14.2 16.1 19 31 32 32.2

10839 NNC O P2 G1.3 1928–1949
White, Theodore Harold, 1915–, and Annalee Jacoby, 1916–.
Thunder out of China.
New York: William Sloane Associates, 1946. 16, 331 p.
Subj 12 15 16.1 16.3 18 32 ▪ 12.1 14.1 14.5 22.2 32.2 66

10840 NNC S P3 G9.2 1911–1928
Wickens, David L–.
Elements and sources of power in the Canton government, 1920–1922.
Unpublished masters thesis in History, Columbia U., 1965. 95 p.
Subj 12 22 22.1 ▪ 26.4 32 36.4

10841 CSU P P3 G6.1 1911–1949
Wiethoff, Bodo, 1931–.
'Zur Anlage und Bearbeitung von Behördenschriftgut im frührepublikanischen China' (The drafting and revision of official documents in early Republican China).
OE 16, 1 (Juni 1969), 1–14.
Subj 12

10842 FPN P P4 G1.2 1928–1949
Yao, Ting-chen (Yao Ting-ch'en).
Le gouvernement central et les gouvernements locaux en Chine (Central and local governments in China).
Paris: Pedone, 1933. 170 p. (Doctoral dissertation, Faculté de droit, Université de Grenoble)
Subj 12 12.2 22 ▪ 64

10843 CSU O P3 G9.2 1928–1949
Yen Chi-chin.
'Administration provinciale de la Chine: le conseil autonome de Kouangtoung' (Provincial administration in China: The Kwangtung autonomous council).
R. internationale des sciences administratives 8, 3 (1935), 397–401.
Subj 12 ▪ 17

10844 MCH P P4 G1.2 1911–1928
Young, Ernest Paddock, 1932–.
Politics in the early Republic: Liang Ch'i-ch'ao and the Yüan Shih-k'ai presidency.
Unpublished doctoral dissertation in History and Far Eastern Languages, Harvard U., 1965. 499 p.
SUBJ 12 12.1 15 32 66 ▪ 14.5 19 32.1 32.2 64

10845 MCH P P1 G1.2 1911–1949
Yü, Wei (Lü Wei).
Le statut des fonctionnaires en Chine depuis la révolution de 1926 à nos jours (The status of civil servants in China from the Revolution of 1926 to the present).
Nancy: Vagner, 1937. 138 p. (Doctoral dissertation, Faculté de droit, Université de Nancy)
SUBJ 12 16.1 ▪ 12.2 22 64

1911-1972
(including 1644-1972)

10846 CSU U P1 G1.2 –1972
Balazs, Etienne, 1905–1963.
'Les aspects significatifs de la société chinoise.'
Etudes asiatiques 6 (1952), 77–87.
'Significant aspects of Chinese society.' Tr. by Hope M- Wright. In *Chinese civilization and bureaucracy*, by E. Balazs, edited by Arthur Frederick Wright. [Selective entry]
New Haven: Yale U. Press, 1964, 3–12.
SUBJ 10 12 16.1 ▪ 12.1 40 64

10847 ²CSU S P1 G1.2 –1972
Balazs, Etienne, 1905–1963.
'La pérennité de la société bureaucratique en Chine.' In *International symposium on history of Eastern and Western cultural contacts: Collection of papers presented*, compiled by Japan National Commission for UNESCO. [Sole entry]
Tokyo: Japan National Commission for UNESCO, 1959, 31–39.
'China as a permanently bureaucratic society.' Tr. by Hope M- Wright. In *Chinese civilization and bureaucracy*, by E. Balazs, edited by Arthur Frederick Wright. [Selective entry]
New Haven: Yale U. Press, 1964, 13–27.
SUBJ 12 12.1 ▪ 16.1 64

10848 CSU P P2 G1.2 1911–1972
Bedeski, Robert Edward, 1937–.
'The formation of national society in Communist China: The convergence of traditions.'
Review of politics 33, 4 (Oct. 1971), 467–488.
SUBJ 12 12.1 16 32 64 ▪ 15 32.1 32.2 47

10849 CSU P P2 G1.2 1928–1972
Chai, Winberg (Chai Wen-po), 1932–.
'The impact of ideology upon public policy in Mainland China.'
IS 6, 9 (June 1970), 32–36.
SUBJ 12 32 64 ▪ 19 32.2

10850 NNC PO P1 G1.1 1911–1972
Chang, Carsun (Chang Chia-sen), 1886–.
The third force in China.
New York: Bookman Associates, 1952. 345 p.
SUBJ 12 32 32.2 64 ▪ 12.2 15 32.1 66

10851 NNC P P2 G1.2 1928–1972
Chao, Kuo-chün, 1918–1962.
Basic level elections and the draft constitution of Communist China, mimeo.
Cambridge: Massachusetts Institute of Technology, Center for International Studies, 1954. 54 p. (Communist bloc program, China project, C/54-12)
SUBJ 12 12.2 22 22.1 ▪ 26.1 30 32 64

10852 NNC P P2 G2.0 1928–1972
Chao, Kuo-chün, 1918–1962.
Northeast China (Manchuria) today, mimeo.
Cambridge: Massachusetts Institute of Technology, Center for International Studies, 1953. 131 p.
SUBJ 12 12.1 14 34.1 ▪ 16.1 17 18 32 32.1 34.2 47 54 62

10853 NNC PO P2 G1.1 1895–1972
Clubb, Oliver Edmund, 1901–.
20th century China, 2nd ed., rev.
New York: Columbia U. Press, 1972. 14, 526 p.
SUBJ 10 12 19 32 32.2 ▪ 12.1 14 15 17 25 34.1 54 64

10854 NNC S P1 G1.1 –1972
Eisenstadt, Shmuel Noah, 1923–.
'The study of Oriental despotisms as systems of total power.' [Review of *Oriental despotism: A comparative study of total power*, by Karl August Wittfogel.]
JAS 17, 3 (May 1958), 435–446.
SUBJ 10 12 12.1 ▪ 14 16 64

10855 MAM FP P2 G9.3 1928–1972
Falkenheim, Victor Carl, 1940–.
Provincial administration in Fukien: 1949–1966.
Ann Arbor: University Microfilms (Publ. 72-20,035), 1972. 383 p. (Doctoral dissertation in Political Science, Columbia U.)
SUBJ 12 14 14.5 16.1 32 32.1 ▪ 15 17 21 21.4 22 22.1 24.1 32.2 34.1 37

10856 MAM S P2 G1.2 1928–1972
Flanders, Steven, 1941–.
'China, 1949–66.' In *Control of movement-regime bureaucracies: A comparative study of Stalinist Russia, Maoist China, and Meiji Japan*, by S. Flanders. [Sole entry]
Ann Arbor: University Microfilms (Publ. 71-6849), 1971, 90–134. (Doctoral dissertation in Political Science, Indiana U., 1970)
SUBJ 12 16.1 32 ▪ 26.1 32.1

10857 MCH O P2 G9.4 –1972
Goddard, William G-.
Formosa: A study in Chinese history.
East Lansing: Michigan State U. Press, 1966. 17, 229 p.
SUBJ 12 16.1 ▪ 12.1 12.2

10858 CSH S P2 G1.2 1644–1972
Harrison, John Armstrong, 1915–.
China since 1800.
New York: Harcourt, Brace and World, 1967. 10, 278 p.
SUBJ 12 19 32.2 ▪ 14 15 16.1 32 66

10859 CSU P P1 G1.2 –1972
Ho, Ping-ti, 1917–.
'Salient aspects of China's heritage' [with comments by Arthur Frederick Wright et al.]. In *China in crisis, Vol. 1, China's heritage and the Communist political system*, edited by Ping-ti Ho and Tang Tsou. [Selective entry]
Chicago: U. of Chicago Press, 1968, 1–92.
SUBJ 12 17 64 ▪ 11 14

10860 NIC P P1 G1.1 –1972
Hucker, Charles Oscar, 1919–.
'The traditional Chinese censorate and the new Peking regime.'
APSR 45, 4 (Dec. 1951), 1041–1057.
SUBJ 12 ▪ 12.1

10861 MCH U P1 G1.2 1911–1972
Hudson, Geoffrey Francis, 1903–.
'Fifteen years after: The Chinese state.'
CQ 21 (Jan.–Mar. 1965), 61–73.
SUBJ 12

10862 MCH P P2 G1.1 –1972
Hulsewé, Anthony François Paulus, 1910–.
Verkenningen in de geschiedenis van de Chinese maatschappij (Research in the history of Chinese society).
Leiden: Brill, 1956. 36 p.
SUBJ 12 70 71 ▪ 14.1 16.1 16.3

10863 CSH P P2 G4.5 1644–1972
Joyaux, François, ed.
'La région autonome du Tibet' (The Tibetan Autonomous Region).
NED 3471 (12 mars 1968), 3–51.
SUBJ 12 14 17 66 ▪ 11.3 15 35

10864 CSU S P1 G1.1 1911–1972
King, Ambrose Yeo-chi (Chin Yao-chi), 1935–.
'Chinese bureaucracy in the transitional society.'
CJA 9 (July 1967), 28–39 [s.p.].
SUBJ 12 16.1 64 ▪ 16 60

10865 MAM P P3 G1.1 –1972
King, Ambrose Yeo-chi (Chin Yao-chi), 1935–.
The Chinese ombudsman institution in an historical and comparative perspective.
Ann Arbor: University Microfilms (Publ. 70-21,938), 1970. 434 p. (Doctoral dissertation in Political Science, U. of Pittsburgh)
SUBJ 12 64 ▪ 12.2 14.2 22.2 32

10866 CSU FP P3 G1.1 1928–1972
Klein, Donald Walker, 1929–.
'The management of foreign affairs in Communist China.' In *China: Management of a revolutionary society*, edited by John Matthew Henry Lindbeck. [Analytic entry]
Seattle: U. of Washington Press, 1971, 305–342. (Social Science Research Council, Studies in Chinese government and politics, 2)
SUBJ 12 16.1 ▪ 17 32

10867 NIC P P2 G1.1 1928–1972
Ku, Tun-jou.
'The hsien government in the Chinese political system.'
CC 1, 2 (Oct. 1957), 15–32.
SUBJ 12

10868 CBU S P1 G1.2 1928–1972
Laco, Karol.
'Politický a ústavný vývin Činskej l'udovej republiky do prijatia ústavy ČL'R z roku 1954' (The political and constitutional development of the People's Republic

of China before the adoption of the constitution in 1954).
Pravnicke studie (Bratislava) 4, 2 (1956), 153–215; 4, 3 (1956), 326–374; 4, 4 (1956), 545–597.
SUBJ 12 12.2 ▪ 12.1 19 64

10869 NNC P P1 G1.2 –1972
Levada, IU- A-.
Review of *Oriental despotism: A comparative study of total power*, by Karl August Wittfogel.
SK 1958, 3, 189–197.
SUBJ 10 12 71

10870 NNC P P2 G1.2 1928–1972
Li, Choh-ming (Li Cho-min), 1912–.
The statistical system of Communist China.
Berkeley, Los Angeles: U. of California Press, 1962. 174 p.
SUBJ 12 16.1 22 ▪ 14 14.1 14.4

10871 MAM P P1 G1.2 1644–1972
Liang, Chi-shad, 1918–.
The civil service in the Republic of China: A critical analysis of its development and character.
Ann Arbor: University Microfilms (Publ. 65-9317), 1965. 343 p. (Doctoral dissertation in Political Science, New York U.)
SUBJ 12 ▪ 16.1 17

10872 CSU P P2 G1.2 1842–1972
Lindsay, Michael Francis Morris, 1909–.
'The public service in China.'
Public administration (Sydney) new (2nd) series 14, 4 (Dec. 1955), 214–228.
SUBJ 12 ▪ 16.1 17 22 26.1

10873 NIC P P2 G1.2 –1972
Linebarger, Paul Myron Anthony, 1913–1966, Chu Djang (Chang Ch'u), and Ardath Walter Burks, 1915–.
Far Eastern governments and politics: China and Japan.
Princeton: Van Nostrand, 1956. 630 p.
SUBJ 12 22 ▪ 12.2 19 32

10874 CSH P P2 G3.0 1895–1972
Lo, J. P. (Lo Jung-pang), 1912–.
'Political dynamics.' In *A regional handbook on the Inner Mongolia Autonomous Region*, compiled by Far Eastern and Russian Institute, U. of Washington. [Selective entry]
New Haven: Human Relations Area Files, 1956, 393–427. (HRAF subcontractor's monographs, 60; Washington 7)
SUBJ 12 12.1 66 ▪ 21 21.2 22 32.1

10875 MCH P P1 G1.1 1928–1972
Ma, Herbert Han-pao.
'The Chinese Control Yuan: An independent supervisory organ of the state.'
Washington U. law q. 1963, 4 (Dec.), 401–426.
SUBJ 12 12.2 ▪ 22

10876 CSH U P1 G3.0 1644–1972
Miller, Robert James, 1923–, and Antoine Mostaert, 1881–.
'Structure of government.' In *A regional handbook on the Inner Mongolia Autonomous Region*, compiled by Far Eastern and Russian Institute, U. of Washington. [Selective entry]
New Haven: Human Relations Area Files, 1956, 367–392. (HRAF subcontractor's monographs, 60; Washington 7)
SUBJ 12 ▪ 22

10877 CSH P P2 G1.2 1928–1972
Molodtsova, L- I-.
'Sud'by kitaiskoi revoliutsii' (The fate of the Chinese revolution).
Voprosy filosofii 1969, 4, 29–40.
SUBJ 12 14 ▪ 19 22 32 32.2 64 66

10878 NNC S P1 G1.2 1842–1972
Monina, A- A-.
Review of *The last stand of Chinese conservatism: The T'ung-chih Restoration, 1862–1874*, by Mary Clabaugh Wright.
SK 1958, 4, 250–254.
SUBJ 12 71 ▪ 66

10879 MCH O P3 G1.2 1928–1972
Panikkar, Kavalam Madhave, 1896–1963.
In two Chinas.
London: Allen and Unwin, 1955. 183 p.
SUBJ 12 ▪ 19 66

10880 MCH P P2 G1.2 1928–1972
Patiulin, V- A-.
'Slom gomindanskogo gosudarstvennogo apparata v Kitae' (Dismantling the Kuomintang state structure in China).
SGP 1959, 10 (oktiabr'), 47–59.
SUBJ 12 32 32.2 34.2 35 ▪ 16.1 22 24.5

10881 NNC P P1 G1.2 1911–1972
Perevertailo, Aleksei Stepanovich, 1897–.
'Kitaiskaia Narodnaia Respublika: gosudarstvo narodnoi demokratii' (The People's Republic of China: A people's democratic government).
UZIV 2 (1951), 95–115.
SUBJ 12 ▪ 14 16 32.2 64

10882 MCH P P2 G9.4 1928–1972
Riggs, Fred Warren, 1917–.
Formosa under Chinese Nationalist rule.
New York: Macmillan, 1952. 195 p. [Reprinted—New York: Octagon Books, 1972. 195 p.]
SUBJ 12 14 15 24.1 32 ▪ 16.1 16.4 17 18 29

10883 CBU S P2 G1.2 1842–1972
[Schulze-Wilde, Harry] H. S. Hegner, pseud., 1899–.
China: Schicksal unserer Kinder (China: The destiny of our children).
Frankfurt a.M.: Frankfurter Bücher, 1963. 503 p.
SUBJ 10 12 32 32.1 32.2 64 ▪ 12.1 14 15 16 18 19 59

10884 MCH O P2 G1.2 1928–1972
Smith, David Howard, 1900–.
'The Chinese enigma.'
Political q. 26, 4 (Oct.–Dec. 1955), 360–370.
SUBJ 12 16 ▪ 16.1 16.3

10885 DLC PO P4 G1.2 1928–1972
Sudarikov, Nikolai Georgievich, 1913–.
Gosudarstvennyi stroi Kitaiskoi Narodnoi Respubliki (The state structure of the People's Republic of China).
Moscow: Znanie, 1956. 48 p.
SUBJ 12 12.1 32 32.1 ▪ 12.2 14 16.2 16.4 47 66

10886 CSH P P1 G2.0 1644–1972
Tang, Peter S. H. (T'ang Sheng-hao), 1919–.
'Structure of government.' In *A regional handbook on Northeast China*, compiled by Far Eastern and Russian Institute, U. of Washington. [Selective entry]
New Haven: Human Relations Area Files, 1956, 322–345. (HRAF subcontractor's monographs, 61; Washington 9)
SUBJ 12 ▪ 22

10887 NIC PO P2 G1.2 1895–1972
Tung, William L. (Tung Lin), 1907–.
The political institutions of modern China.
The Hague: Nijhoff, 1964. 13, 408 p.
SUBJ 12 22 32 64 ▪ 12.2 32.1 32.2 54 66 72

10888 CSU S P2 G1.2 1895–1972
Waller, Derek John, 1937–.
The government and politics of Communist China, 2nd ed.
London: Hutchinson University Press, 1973. 192 p.
SUBJ 12 12.1 14 15 32 32.2 ▪ 12.2 14.1 14.4 16.1 17 22 25 34.1 41 54

10889 CSU S P2 G1.2 –1972
Watanuki, Joji.
'State formation and nation-building in East Asia.'
International social science j. 23, 3 (1971), 421–434.
SUBJ 12

10890 ICU P P2 G1.2 –1972
Whitney, Joseph Bevon Robertson, 1928–.
China: Area, administration, and nation building.
Chicago: U. of Chicago Press, 1970. 13, 198 p. (U. of Chicago, Dept. of Geography research papers, 123) (Revision of doctoral dissertation in Geography, U. of Chicago)
SUBJ 11.1 11.3 12 12.1 14.5 29 ▪ 11 11.2 14.1 14.2 22 32 32.2 66

10891 MCH S P1 G1.1 –1972
Wilhelm, Hellmut, 1906–.
Gesellschaft und Staat in China: Zur Geschichte eines Weltreiches (Society and the state in China: History of an empire), rev. ed.
Hamburg: Rowohlt, 1960. 149 p.
SUBJ 10 12 13 16 64 ▪ 12.1 12.2 14 15 32.2

10892 WSU P P2 G1.1 1895–1972
Williams, Jack Francis, 1939–.
'Mapping activities of China.' In *China in maps, 1890–1960: A selective and annotated cartobibliography*, by J. F. Williams. [Sole entry]
Unpublished masters thesis in Geography, U. of Washington, 1966, 35–48.
SUBJ 12 36.1 70 ▪ 15

10893 NIC S P2 G1.2 –1972
Wittfogel, Karl August, 1896–.
Oriental despotism: A comparative study of total power.
New Haven: Yale U. Press, 1957. 19, 556 p.
SUBJ 10 12 12.1 14.5 15 16 ▪ 14.1 45 64

1949-1972

10894 MCH P P1 G1.2 1949–1972
Handbook on People's China.
Peking: Foreign Languages Press, 1957. 235 p. [Reprinted—New York: AMS Press, 1973. 235 p.]
SUBJ 12 14 17 22 32 ▪ 12.2 18 31 36.4

10895 MCH O P2 G1.2 1949–1972
Álvarez del Vayo, Julio, 1891–.
Reportaje en China (Report on China).
Mexico City: Grijalbo, 1958. 363 p.
SUBJ 12 14 17 18 ▪ 16.1 29 34.1 34.2 36.4 47 52

10896 MCH O P2 G1.2 1949–1972
An Tze-wen (An Tzu-wen).
'Training the people's civil servants.'
People's China 1953, 1 (1 Jan.), 8–11.
SUBJ 12 17 64 ▪ 11.4

10897 DLC P P2 G1.2 1949–1972
Ardant, Philippe.
'L'administration chinoise' (The Chinese administrative system).
B. de l'Institut international d'administration publique 7 (juil–sept. 1968), 19–68.
SUBJ 12 12.2 22 32.1 ▪ 14 14.1 16.1 32 64

10898 CSU FP P3 G5.1 1949–1972
Barnett, Arthur Doak, 1921–.
'A central ministry.' In *Cadres, bureaucracy, and political power in Communist China*, by A. D. Barnett. [Analytic entry]
New York: Columbia U. Press, 1967, 1–103.
SUBJ 12 32.1 ▪ 14 16.1 55

10899 NNC PO P1 G1.2 1949–1972
Barnett, Arthur Doak, 1921–.
'China's "people's democratic dictatorship": Recent political trends in Communist China.'
AUFS-EAS 4, 2 (28 Feb. 1955), 1–19. [Reprinted as 'Party unity and centralization of power.' In *Communist China: The early years, 1949–55*, by A. D. Barnett. (Selective entry.) New York: Praeger, 1964, 303–324.]
SUBJ 12 ▪ 12.1 32 32.1

10900 MCH U P2 G1.2 1949–1972
Barnett, Arthur Doak, 1921–.
'Political power in Communist China.'
J. of international affairs 11, 2 (1957), 102–110.
SUBJ 12 12.1 32 ▪ 15 22 30 32.1 61

10901 NIC S P2 G1.2 1949–1972
Benson, Oliver Earl, 1911–.
'Changing patterns of policy formation and implementation in Communist China.'
Southwestern social science q. 40 (1959), 66–84. [Supplement: *Annual meeting number*] [Reprinted in *Political and social problems of public administration in underdeveloped areas: A symposium*, edited by John Miller Claunch. (Sole entry.) Dallas: Southern Methodist U., Arnold Foundation, 1959, 3–27. (Arnold Foundation monographs, 4)]
SUBJ 12 12.1 14 ▪ 12.2 14.1 15 16 32 32.1

10902 CSU P P2 G1.2 1949–1972
Boyd, R- G-.
'Revolutionary nation-building: The Chinese model.'
International j. 25, 1 (Winter 1969/70), 69–93.
SUBJ 12 12.1 16.1 ▪ 14 35 64

10903 MCY P P1 G1.2 1949–1972
Bridgham, Philip Low, 1921–.
'The National People's Congress.'
CQ 22 (Apr.–June 1965), 62–74.
SUBJ 12 12.1 ▪ 14

10904 MAM F P2 G9.4 1949–1972
Chang, H. C. (Chang Hsi-chih), 1920–.
Functional and structural analysis of scientific farm information development and dissemination in Taiwan.
Ann Arbor: University Microfilms (Publ. 69-3219), 1969. 376 p. (Doctoral dissertation in Sociology, U. of Missouri, 1968)
SUBJ 12 22 24.2 36.3 37 ▪ 24.1 34.1

10905 CSH P P4 G1.2 1949–1972
Chang, Parris H. (Chang Hsü-ch'eng), 1936–.
'Centralization versus decentralization in the Chinese political system, 1949–1971.'
Asian forum 4, 2 (Apr.–June 1972), 14–36.
SUBJ 12 14 32 35 ▪ 11.3 15 54

10906 MAM P P2 G1.2 1949–1972
Chang, Parris H. (Chang Hsü-ch'eng), 1936–.
Pattern and processes of policy-making in Communist China, 1955–1962: Three case studies.
Ann Arbor: University Microfilms (Publ. 72-19,047), 1972. 378 p. (Doctoral dissertation in Public Law and Government, Columbia U., 1969)
SUBJ 12 14.1 ▪ 11.4 12.1 16.1 21.3 22 22.1

10907 CSU P P3 G1.4 1949–1972
Chang, Parris H. (Chang Hsü-ch'eng), 1936–.
'The revolutionary committee in China: Two case studies, Heilungkiang and Honan.'
CS 6, 9 (1 June 1968), 1–37.
SUBJ 12 25 54 ▪ 32 35

10908 NNC P P1 G9.4 1949–1972
Chang, Tien-teh.
The development of a position-classification in the public service in the Republic of China.
Unpublished masters thesis in Political Science, Columbia U., 1955. 90 p.
SUBJ 12 ▪ 16.1 18 21.4

10909 CSU P P1 G1.2 1949–1972
Chang, Yu-nan (Chang Yü-nan), 1920–.
'The Chinese Communist state system under the constitution of 1954.'
J. of politics 18, 3 (Aug. 1956), 520–546.
SUBJ 12 12.2 ▪ 32.1 64

10910 MCH P P1 G1.2 1949–1972
Chang, Yu-nan (Chang Yü-nan), 1920–.
'Industrial administration in Communist China.'
Western political q. 9, 4 (Dec. 1956), 850–872.
SUBJ 12 14 ▪ 22 32 34.2

10911 MMT P P2 G2.0 1949–1972
Chao, Kuo-chün, 1918–1962.
'The government and economy of Manchuria.'
FES 22, 13 (Dec. 1953), 169–175.
SUBJ 12 14 ▪ 16.1 30 64 66

10912 CSH P P2 G1.2 1949–1972
Chen Shen-wen (Ch'en Sen-wen).
'The Peiping regime's administrative organizations.' In *Collected documents of the First Sino-American Conference on Mainland China*. [Selective entry]
[Taipei]: Institute of International Relations, Republic of China, 1971, 601–634.
SUBJ 12 ▪ 12.2 22

10913 NNC P P4 G1.2 1949–1972
Chen, Theodore H. E. (Ch'en Hsi-en), 1902–, and Wen-hui C. Chen (Ch'en Chung Wen-hui), 1913–.
'The "Three-Anti" and "Five-Anti" movements in Communist China.'
PA 26, 1 (Mar. 1953), 3–23.
SUBJ 12 12.1 16 16.1 16.2 32 ▪ 12.2 14 30 34.2

10914 CSH P P1 G9.4 1949–1972
Cheng, Peter P. C., 1930–.
'The Formosa tangle: A Formosan's view.'
AS 7, 11 (Nov. 1967), 791–806.
SUBJ 12 12.1 ▪ 32

10915 CSH P P2 G1.2 1949–1972
Ch'in T'i.
'Communist China's domestic affairs, 1962–1965' [title varies]. Tr. from *Tsu kuo chou k'an* 535 (8 Apr. 1963) *and* from *Tsu kuo* 1–23 (Apr. 1964 – Feb. 1966) [recurring annual feature article]. In *Communist China, 1962–1965*, edited by Union Research Institute.
Hong Kong: Union Research Institute. Issued annually, 1963–1967, average ca. 25 p.
SUBJ 12 14 ▪ 12.1 12.2 18

10916 CSU P P2 G1.2 1949–1972
Ch'in T'i.
'Communist China's internal affairs during 1968.' Tr. of 'I chiu liu pa nien ti Chung kung nei cheng'; *Tsu kuo* 64 (July 1969), 12–24. In *Communist China, 1968*, edited by Union Research Institute. [Selective entry]
Hong Kong: Union Research Institute, 1969, 101–139.
SUBJ 12 16.1 ▪ 12.2 22 35

10917 CSH P P2 G1.2 1949–1972
Ch'in T'i.
'The government system in Mainland China in 1967.' Tr. of '1967 nien ti Chung kung cheng chih' (Politics in Communist China, 1967); *Tsu kuo* 50 (May 1968), 2–21. In *Communist China, 1967*, edited by Union Research Institute. [Selective entry]
Hong Kong: Union Research Institute, 1969, vol. 1, 94–153.
SUBJ 12 12.1 ▪ 22 32.1

10918 NNC P P4 G1.2 1949–1972
Ch'in T'i.
'Political and legal work.' Tr. of 'Shih nien lai ti Chung kung cheng fa kung tso' (Political and judicial activities in Communist China during the past decade); *Tsu kuo chou k'an* 382 (2 May 1960), 10–19. In *Communist China,*

1949–1959, edited by Union Research Institute. [Selective entry]
Hong Kong: Union Research Institute, 1961, vol. 1, 53–90.
SUBJ 12 12.2 ▪ 32 66

10919 NNC P P2 G1.2 1949–1972
Ch'in T'i.
'Politics' [title varies]. Tr. of '1955–1958 nien Chung kung ti cheng chih' (Politics in Communist China, 1955–1958); *Tsu kuo chou k'an* 159–334/335 (16 Jan. 1956 – 8 June 1959) [recurring annual feature article]. In *Communist China, 1955–1958*, edited by Union Research Institute.
Hong Kong: Union Research Institute. Issued annually, 1956–1959, average ca. 10 p.
SUBJ 12 12.1 ▪ 12.2 32 66

10920 CSH P P2 G1.2 1949–1972
Ch'in T'i.
'Politics.' Tr. of '1961 nien ti Chung kung cheng chih' (Politics in Communist China, 1961); *Tsu kuo chou k'an* 483 (9 Apr. 1962), 7–15. In *Communist China, 1961*, edited by Union Research Institute. [Selective entry]
Hong Kong: Union Research Institute, 1962, vol. 2, 1–28.
SUBJ 12 ▪ 12.1 18 32

10921 CSH U P4 G4.0 1949–1972
Chu, Wen-djang (Chu Wen-ch'ang), 1914–.
'Structure of government.' In *A regional handbook on Northwest China*, compiled by Far Eastern and Russian Institute, U. of Washington. [Selective entry]
New Haven: Human Relations Area Files, 1956, vol. 2, 463–483. (HRAF subcontractor's monographs, 59; Washington 5)
SUBJ 12 ▪ 22 66

10922 CSU P P1 G4.5 1949–1972
Chu Wen-lin.
'The Tibet Autonomous Region Revolutionary Committee.'
IS 5, 3 (Dec. 1968), 12–21.
SUBJ 12 ▪ 15 66

10923 CSH F P3 G9.4 1949–1972
Cole, Allan Burnett, 1914–.
'Political roles of Taiwanese enterprisers.'
AS 7, 9 (Sept. 1967), 645–654.
SUBJ 12 16.2 22 ▪ 32 32.1 34.2

10924 CSU P P3 G1.2 1949–1972
Current Scene Editor.
'China's revolutionary committees.'
CS 6, 21 (6 Dec. 1968), 1–18.
SUBJ 12 32 ▪ 16.1 22 35

10925 CSU P P2 G1.2 1949–1972
Current Scene Editor.
'The conflict between Mao Tse-tung and Liu Shao-ch'i over agricultural mechanization in Communist China.'
CS 6, 17 (1 Oct. 1968), 1–20.
SUBJ 12 14.1 ▪ 16.1 32 34.1 64

10926 CSU S P5 G1.2 1949–1972
Current Scene Editor.
'The revolutionary committee and the party in the aftermath of the Cultural Revolution.'
CS 8, 8 (15 Apr. 1970), 1–10.
SUBJ 12 ▪ 22 32 35

10927 CSU U P1 G1.2 1949–1972
Current Scene Editor.
'Revolutionary committee leadership: China's current provincial authorities.'
CS 6, 18 (18 Oct. 1968), 1–28.
SUBJ 12 ▪ 15 16.1 59

10928 MCH P P1 G1.2 1949–1972
Current Scene Editor.
'Who's who in Peking? Leadership and organization in the Chinese party, government, and army.'
CS 4, 15 (8 Aug. 1966), 1–17.
SUBJ 12 32 ▪ 15 16.1

10929 DLC P P2 G1.2 1949–1972
Dapčević-Oreščanin, Sonja, et al.
'Ustavno uredjenje NR Kine' (The constitutional convention in the People's Republic of China).
DB 4, 6/7 (1955), 147–155. [Special issue: *Savremena Kina* (Contemporary China)]
SUBJ 12 12.2 ▪ 22 22.2

10930 DLC P P2 G1.2 1949–1972
Deliusin, Lev Petrovich, 1923–.
'Vnutropoliticheskaia bor'ba v Kitae' (The domestic political struggle in China). In *Kitai segodnia* (China today), compiled by Akademiia nauk SSSR, edited by L. P. Deliusin and Grigorii Dmitrievich Sukharchuk. [Selective entry]
Moscow: Nauka, Glav. red. vost. lit-ry, 1969, 130–207.
SUBJ 12 16 32 35 54 64 ▪ 12.1 14.1 14.4 17 19 22 32.1

10931 GMS P P2 G1.2 1949–1972
Domes, Jürgen Otto, 1932–.
Von der Volkskommune zur Krise in China (From commune to crisis in China).
Duisdorf b. Bonn: Studiengesellschaft für Zeitprobleme, 1964. 85 p. (Staatspolitische Schriftenreihe, 11)
SUBJ 12 19 22 32.1 ▪ 14.1 15 32.2 55 64

10932 MCH P P1 G1.2 1949–1972
Dorrill, William Franklin, 1931–.
'Leadership and succession in Communist China.'
CH 49, 289 (Sept. 1965), 129–135, 179.
SUBJ 12 ▪ 15

10933 CSH P P2 G1.2 1949–1972
Engelborghs-Bertels, Marthe, 1928–.
'La révolution culturelle' (The Cultural Revolution).
B. du Centre d'étude des pays de l'Est 8, 1 (1967), 7–60.
SUBJ 12 14 15 17 32 64 ▪ 16.3 16.4 54

10934 MCH S P1 G1.2 1949–1972
Fabre, Michel-Henry.
'Variations chinoises sur l'unité marxiste du pouvoir d'état' (Chinese variations on the Marxist unity of state authority).
R. du droit public et de la science politique 73, 1 (jan.–fév. 1957), 45–85.
SUBJ 12 64

10935 CSU P P1 G9.3 1949–1972
Falkenheim, Victor Carl, 1940–.
'Peking and the provinces: Continuing central predominance.'
Problems of Communism 21, 4 (July–Aug. 1972), 75–83.
SUBJ 12 32 ▪ 16.1 30

10936 CSU P P3 G1.4 1949–1972
Feurtado, Gardel M-, 1942–.
'The formation of provincial revolutionary committees, 1966–1968: Heilungkiang and Hopei.'
AS 12, 12 (Dec. 1972), 1014–1031.
SUBJ 12 54 ▪ 15 19 26.4 32

10937 NNC PO P2 G1.2 1949–1972
Fitzgerald, Charles Patrick, 1902–.
Flood tide in China.
London: Cresset Press, 1958. 285 p.
SUBJ 12 12.1 16.1 ▪ 14.1 16.3 17 22 23 33 34.1 58 64 66

10938 CBU P P4 G1.2 1949–1972
Freiter, Max.
The eighteen-story pagoda: Bureaucratism in Communist China.
Hong Kong: China Viewpoints, 1957. 50 p.
SUBJ 12 12.1 19 32 64 ▪ 16.1 22.2

10939 CSU P P2 G4.3 1949–1972
Fujino, Susumu.
'Sinkiang today.'
Review (Tokyo) 5 (July 1965), 39–50.
SUBJ 12 14 66 ▪ 12.1 12.2 22 24.1

10940 CSU P P1 G1.2 1949–1972
Gelman, Harry.
'Mao and the permanent purge.'
Problems of Communism 15, 6 (Nov.–Dec. 1966), 2–14.
SUBJ 12 32

10941 MCH P P3 G5.1 1949–1972
Ginsburgs, George, 1932–.
'Theory and practice of parliamentary procedure in Communist China: Organization and institutional principles.'
U. of Toronto law j. 15, 1 (1963), 1–48.
SUBJ 12 12.2 32.1 ▪ 16.1 30 64 66

10942 CSU U P2 G1.2 1949–1972
Goldman, Merle Dorothy, 1931–.
'The aftermath of China's Cultural Revolution.'
CH 61, 361 (Sept. 1971), 165–170, 182.
SUBJ 12 17 ▪ 14 35

10943 MCH PO P2 G1.2 1949–1972
Gudoshnikov, Leonid Moiseevich.
Mestnye organy gosudarstvennoi vlasti i gosudarstvennogo upravleniia Kitaiskoi Narodnoi Respubliki.
Moscow: Izd-vo Akad. nauk SSSR, 1958. 186 p.

Local organs of state authority of the People's Republic of China, mimeo. [Partial tr.: p. 43–67, 82–90, 97–100, 102–107, 133–165, 180–185 only]
New York: U.S. Joint Publications Research Service, 6 Mar. 1959. 66 p. (JPRS 577D; MC 5014/1959)
SUBJ 12 12.1 14 ▪ 22 22.1

10944 NNC P P1 G1.2 1949–1972
Gudoshnikov, Leonid Moiseevich.
Vysshie organy gosudarstvennoi vlasti i gosudarstvennogo upravleniia Kitaiskoi Narodnoi Respubliki (The highest organs of state power and administration in the People's Republic of China).
Moscow: Izd-vo Akad. nauk SSSR, 1960. 108 p.
SUBJ 12 12.2 ▪ 12.1 32.1

10945 DLC P P3 G5.1 1949–1972
Gurtov, Melvin, 1941–.
The Foreign Ministry and foreign affairs in China's 'Cultural Revolution'.
Santa Monica, Calif.: RAND Corp., 1969. 92 p. (RAND memoranda, RM-5934-PR) [Reprinted as 'The Foreign Ministry and foreign affairs in the Chinese Cultural Revolution.' In *The Cultural Revolution in China*, edited by Thomas Webster Robinson. (Selective entry.) Berkeley, Los Angeles: U. of California Press, 1971, 313–366.]
Subj 12 54 ▪ 16.1 22.2

10946 CSH P P3 G1.2 1949–1972
Hai Feng, pseud.
'Communist China's domestic affairs in 1969.' Tr. of '1969 nien ti Chung kung nei cheng' (Governmental affairs in Communist China, 1969); *Tsu kuo* 71 (Feb. 1970), 2–13. In *Communist China, 1969*, edited by Union Research Institute. [Selective entry]
Hong Kong: Union Research Institute, 1970, 81–122.
Subj 12 12.1 16.1 ▪ 15 17 32

10947 GBF P P1 G1.2 1949–1972
Heinzig, Dieter, 1932–.
Mao contra Liu (Mao versus Liu).
Cologne: Bundesinstitut für ostwissenschaftliche und internationale Studien, 1967. 46 p. (BOIS, Berichte, 1967, 48)
Subj 12 ▪ 19

10948 GBF P P1 G1.2 1949–1972
Heinzig, Dieter, 1932–.
Von Lushan zur Kulturrevolution (From Lushan to the Cultural Revolution).
Cologne: Bundesinstitut für ostwissenschaftliche und internationale Studien, 1968. 23 p. (BOIS, Berichte, 1968, 5)
Subj 12

10949 CSH S P1 G1.2 1949–1972
Hinton, Harold Clendenin, 1924–.
'The succession problem in Communist China.'
CS 1, 7 (19 July 1961), 1–7. [Reprinted as 'The succession problem.' In *This is China: Analyses of Mainland trends and events*, edited by Francis Harper. (Selective entry.) Hong Kong: Dragonfly Books, 1965, 57–68.]
Subj 12 ▪ 32

10950 CSU O P2 G9.4 1949–1972
Hough, Richard L-, and Gayl D- Ness.
'The JCRR: A model for internationally induced development.'
International development review 10, 3 (Sept. 1968), 14–17.
Subj 12 36.3 37 ▪ 66

10951 CSU P P3 G1.2 1949–1972
Hsiao, Gene T. (Hsiao Chün), 1922–.
'Communist China's foreign trade organization.'
Vanderbilt law review 20, 2 (Mar. 1967), 303–319.
Subj 12 32.1 34.2 ▪ 14.6 22.2

10952 MCH O P2 G1.2 1949–1972
Hsieh Chueh-tsai.
'How China went to the polls.'
People's China 1954, 15 (1 Aug.), 6–9.
Subj 12 ▪ 32.1

10953 MCH P P2 G1.2 1949–1972
Ignatenko, Gennadii Vladimirovich.
Sistema predstavitel'nykh organov Kitaiskoi Narodnoi Respubliki (The system of representation in the People's Republic of China).
Moscow: Gosiurizdat, 1959. 209 p.
Subj 12 12.1 12.2 22 22.1

10954 MCH P P1 G1.2 1949–1972
Ignatenko, Gennadii Vladimirovich (Gennadiy Wladimirovich Ignatenko).
'Vsekitaiskoe sobranie narodnykh predstavitelei, verkhovnyi organ gosudarstvennoi vlasti Kitaiskoi Narodnoi Respubliki' (The National People's Congress, the supreme organ of state power in the People's Republic of China).
SGP 1957, 2 (fevral'), 61–72.

'Der Nationale Volkskongress, das höchste Organ der Staatsgewalt der Volksrepublik China.'
Sowjetwissenschaft; gesellschaftswissenschaftliche Beiträge 1957, 6 (Juni), 689–702.
Subj 12 12.1 ▪ 12.2

10955 CSH U P1 G9.4 1949–1972
Israel, John Warren, 1935–.
'Politics on Formosa.'
CQ 15 (July–Sept. 1963), 3–11. [Reprinted in *Formosa today*, edited by Mark Mancall. (Selective entry.) New York: Praeger, 1964, 59–67.]
Subj 12 12.1 32 ▪ 12.2 15 22.2 32.1

10956 CSU PO P4 G9.4 1949–1972
Jacobs, J- Bruce.
'Taiwan, 1972: Political season.'
AS 13, 1 (Jan. 1973), 102–112.
Subj 12 ▪ 32

10957 MCY P P1 G4.4 1949–1972
Jones, P- H- M-.
'China hustles Tsinghai.'
FEER 32, 6 (11 May 1961), 250–254.
Subj 12 14 ▪ 21.2 66

10958 MCH P P1 G9.4 1949–1972
Kallgren, Joyce Kislitzin, 1930–.
'Nationalist China: Political inflexibility and economic accommodation.'
AS 4, 1 (Jan. 1964), 638–645.
Subj 12 32 ▪ 14 15 64

10959 CSU S P2 G9.4 1949–1972
Kallgren, Joyce Kislitzin, 1930–.
'Nationalist China: Problems of a modernizing Taiwan.'
AS 5, 1 (Jan. 1965), 12–17.
Subj 12 ▪ 12.1 14 32

10960 MAM FP P2 G1.2 1949–1972
Kau, Ying-mao (Kao Ying-mao), 1934–.
Governmental bureaucracy and cadres in urban China under Communist rule, 1949–1965.
Ann Arbor: University Microfilms (Publ. 69-7391), 1969. 420 p. (Doctoral dissertation in Government, Cornell U., 1968)
Subj 12 16.1 22 22.1 ▪ 11.1 11.2 12.2 17 22.2 32 32.1 35 36.4 64

10961 NNC P P1 G1.2 1949–1972
Keesing, Donald Beaumont.
Use of top-level personnel by the Chinese Communist government, 1949–1953.
Cambridge: Massachusetts Institute of Technology, Center for International Studies, 1954. 73 p.
Subj 12 16.1 ▪ 15 32 32.1

10962 MCH U P4 G1.2 1949–1972
Kondrat'ev, Rem Sergeevich, and L- A- Grachev.
Gosudarstvennyi stroi Kitaiskoi Narodnoi Respubliki (The state structure of the People's Republic of China).
Moscow: Gosiurizdat, 1959. 123 p.
Subj 12 22 22.1 32.1 ▪ 12.1 14 34.2

10963 CSH P P1 G1.2 1949–1972
[La Dany, Ladislao] ———, 1914–.
'Administration: The soldiers, the state, and the rebels.'
CNA 822 (20 Nov. 1970), 1–7.
Subj 12 35

10964 CSH P P2 G1.2 1949–1972
[La Dany, Ladislao] ———, 1914–.
'China goes to the polls.'
CNA 245 (19 Sept. 1958), 2–7.
Subj 12 22

10965 MCH P P2 G1.2 1949–1972
[La Dany, Ladislao] ———, 1914–.
'Emergency administration.'
CNA 465 (26 Apr. 1963), 1–7.
Subj 12 22 32

10966 CSH P P2 G1.2 1949–1972
[La Dany, Ladislao] ———, 1914–.
'Military rule in regional administration.'
CNA 856 (1 Oct. 1971), 1–7.
Subj 12 15 ▪ 32 35

10967 CSH P P2 G1.2 1949–1972
[La Dany, Ladislao] ———, 1914–.
'The political map of China, Parts 1–9.'
CNA 795–805/806 (20 Mar. 1970 – 19 June 1970), 63 p. in all.
Subj 12 12.1 16.1 25 30 ▪ 11.3 14 15 22.1 29 32 35

10968 CSH P P1 G1.2 1949–1972
[La Dany, Ladislao] ———, 1914–.
'The revolutionary committee: Legal aspects of regional administration.'
CNA 699 (8 Mar. 1968), 1–7.
Subj 12 64 ▪ 12.2

10969 ELB P P3 G1.4 1949–1972
Lévy, Roger.
'La grande Révolution culturelle prolétarienne' (The Great Proletarian Cultural Revolution).
Politique étrangère 35, 3 (1970), 303–314.
Subj 12 ▪ 12.1 15 16.4 32 54

10970 CSH P P2 G1.2 1949–1972
Leys, Simon.
Les habits neufs du président Mao: chronique de la 'Révolution culturelle' (Chairman Mao's new clothes: Chronicle of the Cultural Revolution).
Paris: Bibliothèque asiatique, 1971. 310 p.
Subj 12 12.1 32 35 54 64 ▪ 14.1 14.2 16.1 16.3 22 61 62

10971 NIC P P1 G1.2 1949–1972
Li, Chiu-yi.
'Composition of the Chinese Communist Third National People's Congress.'
IS 1, 3 (Dec. 1964), 12–20.
Subj 12 16

10972 MCH P P2 G1.2 1949–1972
Lunev, Aleksandr Efremovich.
'Formy uchastiia narodnykh mass v rabote gosudarstvennykh organov Kitaiskoi Narodnoi Respubliki' (Mass participation in the functioning of state organs in the People's Republic of China).
SGP 1958, 1 (ianvar'), 71–79.
SUBJ 12 ▪ 16.3 16.4

10973 DLC P P7 G1.2 1949–1972
Lunev, Aleksandr Efremovich.
'Mestnye organy narodnoi vlasti v Kitae.'
Sovety deputatov trudiashchikhsia 1957, 6 (dekabr'), 85–90.

Local organs of people's rule in China, mimeo.
Washington, D.C.: U.S. Joint Publications Research Service, 18 Nov. 1958. 8 p. (JPRS 375D; MC 562/1959)
SUBJ 12 22 22.1

10974 CSU P P3 G1.2 1949–1972
Melchior de Molenes, Charles.
'Regards sur les troubles de Chine' (A look at China's problems).
Res publica 10, 1 (1968), 97–113.
SUBJ 12 15 ▪ 64

10975 MAM P P2 G1.2 1949–1972
Mendes, Richard Gerald.
The role of intermediate organizations in a totalitarian society: The case of Communist China, 1949–1964.
Ann Arbor: University Microfilms (Publ. 72-16,479), 1972. 238 p. (Doctoral dissertation in Political Science, Michigan State U., 1971)
SUBJ 12 12.1 30 32 ▪ 24.3 36.1 36.4 47 54

10976 CSU P P1 G1.2 1949–1972
Michael, Franz Henry, 1907–.
'The struggle for power.'
Problems of Communism 16, 3 (May–June 1967), 12–21.
SUBJ 12 19 32

10977 ELB PO P3 G5.1 1949–1972
Monneret, Jean-Léo.
'Aspects de la révolution culturelle en Chine' (Aspects of China's Cultural Revolution).
Politique étrangère 34, 4 (1969), 417–435.
SUBJ 12 24.2 ▪ 32

10978 MCH O P2 G1.2 1949–1972
Musatti, Cesare L-, 1897–.
Paesi del socialismo e problemi della democrazia (Socialist countries and problems of democracy).
Florence: Parenti, 1957. 203 p.
SUBJ 12 13 ▪ 14 14.1 14.4 18 19 66

10979 CSU S P4 G1.2 1949–1972
Nathan, Andrew James, 1943–.
'A factionalism model for CCP politics.'
CQ 53 (Jan.–Mar. 1973), 34–66.
SUBJ 12 19 32 ▪ 15 54

10980 CSH P P2 G1.2 1949–1972
Oksenberg, Michel Charles, 1938–.
'Communist China: A quiet crisis in revolution.'
AS 6, 1 (Jan. 1966), 1–12.
SUBJ 12 32

10981 MCH P P1 G1.2 1949–1972
Oksenberg, Michel Charles, 1938–.
'Paths to leadership in Communist China: A comparison of second echelon positions in 1955 and 1965.'
CS 3, 24 (1 Aug. 1965), 1–11.
SUBJ 12 16 ▪ 15 16.1

10982 CSU U P2 G1.2 1949–1972
Pfeffer, Richard Monroe, 1936–.
'Revolution and rule: Where do we go from here?' [Review of *Canton under Communism: Programs and politics in a provincial capital, 1949–1968*, by Ezra Feivel Vogel.]
BCAS 2, 3 (Apr.–July 1970), 88–95.
SUBJ 12 71 ▪ 12.1

10983 CSU S P2 G9.4 1949–1972
Plummer, Mark Allen, 1929–.
'Taiwan: The "new look" in government.'
AS 9, 1 (Jan. 1969), 18–22.
SUBJ 12 32 ▪ 14 22

10984 CSU O P2 G9.4 1949–1972
Plummer, Mark Allen, 1929–.
'Taiwan's Chinese Nationalist government.'
CH 61, 361 (Sept. 1971), 171–176.
SUBJ 12 14 ▪ 32.2

10985 CSU P P3 G9.4 1949–1972
Po, Ching-Chiu (Po Ch'ing-chiu).
'The general functions of the Ministry of Personnel.'
CJA 17 (July 1971), 29–40 [s.p.].
SUBJ 12 ▪ 28 56

10986 CSU P P2 G1.2 1949–1972
Robinson, Thomas Webster, 1935–.
'China in 1972: Socio-economic progress amidst political uncertainty.'
AS 13, 1 (Jan. 1973), 1–18.
SUBJ 12 ▪ 14 15 17 32 54

10987 MCH P P2 G1.2 1949–1972
Rostow, Walt Whitman, 1916–.
'Russia and China under Communism.'
WP 7, 4 (July 1955), 513–531.
SUBJ 12 14 16 ▪ 12.1 64

10988 CSH FP P2 G1.2 1949–1972
Schurmann, Herbert Franz, 1926–.
'Government.' In *Ideology and organization in Communist China*, 2nd ed., enl., by H. F. Schurmann. [Analytic entry]
Berkeley, Los Angeles: U. of California Press, 1968, 173–219.
SUBJ 12 ▪ 12.1 14.1 14.4 22

10989 NIC P P5 G1.4 1949–1972
Schwarz, Henry Guenter, 1928–.
Leadership patterns in China's frontier regions.
Washington, D.C.: U.S. Dept. of State, Bureau of Intelligence and Research, External Research Staff, 1964. 95 p. (External research papers, 149)
SUBJ 12 16.1 ▪ 32 59 66

10990 MCY P P1 G1.2 1949–1972
Steiner, Harold Arthur, 1905–.
'New regional governments in China.'
FES 19, 11 (31 May 1950), 112–116.
SUBJ 12 ▪ 11.3

10991 MCH P P1 G1.2 1949–1972
Steiner, Harold Arthur, 1905–.
'The people's democratic dictatorship in China.'
Western political q. 3, 1 (Mar. 1950), 38–51.
SUBJ 12 ▪ 12.1 12.2 16

10992 MCH PO P2 G1.2 1949–1972
Sudarikov, Nikolai Georgievich (N. G. Sudarikow), 1913–.
'Izbiratel'naia sistema Kitaiskoi Narodnoi Respubliki' (The electoral system of the People's Republic of China).
SGP 1953, 5 (mai), 114–128.

'Das Wahlsystem der Chinesischen Volksrepublik.'
Rechtswissenschaftlicher Informationsdienst 3, 17 (5 Sept. 1954), 468–482.
SUBJ 12 32 ▪ 22

10993 CSU P P2 G1.2 1949–1972
Teiwes, Frederick Carl, 1939–.
'Provincial politics in China: Themes and variations.' In *China: Management of a revolutionary society*, edited by John Matthew Henry Lindbeck. [Analytic entry]
Seattle: U. of Washington Press, 1971, 116–189. (Social Science Research Council, Studies in Chinese government and politics, 2)
SUBJ 12 14 16.1 ▪ 14.1 14.3 14.4 21 21.1 32 34.1 35

10994 CBU P P2 G1.2 1949–1972
Thomas, Samuel Bernard, 1921–.
Government and administration in Communist China, 2nd ed., mimeo.
New York: Institute of Pacific Relations, International Secretariat, 1955. 196 p. (Revision of *The government and structure of the People's Republic of China*, masters thesis in East Asian Studies, Columbia U., 1951)
SUBJ 12 12.1 16 22 32 64 ▪ 12.2 14 15 17 22.1 22.2 32.1

10995 CSU P P1 G1.2 1949–1972
Thornton, Richard Chester, 1936–.
'The structure of Communist politics.'
WP 24, 4 (July 1972), 498–517.
SUBJ 12 15 ▪ 64

10996 CSU P P3 G5.1 1949–1972
Tretiak, Daniel, 1937–.
'The Chinese Cultural Revolution and foreign policy.'
CS 8, 7 (1 Apr. 1970), 1–26.
SUBJ 12 16.1

10997 ELB P P2 G1.2 1949–1972
Tsien Tche-hao (Ch'ien Chih-hao), 1923–.
La République populaire de Chine: droit constitutionnel et institutions (The People's Republic of China: Constitutional law and institutions).
Paris: Lib. générale de droit et de jurisprudence, 1970. 646 p. (Université de Paris, Institut de droit comparé, systèmes de droit contemporains, 22)
SUBJ 12 12.2 14 17 22 64 ▪ 12.1 15 18 32 36.4 63 66 72

10998 CSU S P1 G1.2 1949–1972
Tsou, Tang, 1918–.
'Western concepts and China's historical experience.' [Review of *Revolutionary immortality: Mao Tse-tung and the Chinese Cultural Revolution*, by Robert Jay Lifton; *The spirit of Chinese politics: A psycho-cultural study of the*

authority crisis in political development, by Lucian Wilmot Pye; and *Political participation in Communist China*, by James Roger Townsend.]
WP 21, 4 (July 1969), 655–691.
SUBJ 12 61 71 ▪ 12.1 19 32.2

10999 NNC U P1 G1.2 1949–1972
U.S. Congress. Senate. Committee on Government Operations. Subcommittee on National Security Staffing and Operations.
Staffing procedures and problems in Communist China.
Washington, D.C.: U.S. Government Printing Office, 1963. 50 p.
SUBJ 12 16.1 32 ▪ 11.4 15 17

11000 MCH S P4 G1.2 1949–1972
Voevodin, Leonid Dmitrievich.
Gosudarstvennyi stroi Kitaiskoi Narodnoi Respubliki (The state structure of the People's Republic of China).
Moscow: Gosiurizdat, 1956. 271 p.
SUBJ 12 12.1 ▪ 16

11001 MCH P P1 G1.2 1949–1972
Vogel, Ezra Feivel, 1930–.
'From revolutionary to semi-bureaucrat: The "regularization" of cadres.'
CQ 29 (Jan.–Mar. 1967), 36–60.
SUBJ 12 16.1 ▪ 12.1 16 17 19

11002 CSU U P2 G1.2 1949–1972
Vogel, Ezra Feivel, 1930–.
'Politicized bureaucracy: Communist China.' In *Frontiers of development administration*, edited by Fred Warren Riggs. [Sole entry]
Durham: Duke U. Press, 1970, 556–568.
SUBJ 12 16.1 ▪ 11.4 12.1 16 22 26.1

11003 NNC P P2 G1.2 1949–1972
Walker, Richard Louis, 1922–.
China under Communism: The first five years.
New Haven: Yale U. Press, 1955. 15, 403 p.
SUBJ 10 12 12.1 16 16.1 16.3 ▪ 12.2 14 16.4 17 19 30 31 32 64 66

11004 MCH P P1 G1.2 1949–1972
Walker, Richard Louis, 1922–.
'Communist China: Power and prospects.'
New leader 41, 38 (20 Oct. 1958), 1–30. [Special issue]
SUBJ 12 ▪ 14

11005 CSH P P2 G1.2 1949–1972
Weggel, Oskar, 1935–.
Die chinesischen Revolutionskomitees: oder, Der Versuch, die Grosse Kulturrevolution durch parzellierung zu retten (Stand: 1. Juli 1968) (Chinese revolutionary committees: The attempt to save the Cultural Revolution by parcelling it out. The situation of 1 July 1968).
Hamburg: Institut für Asienkunde, 1968. 122 p. (IA, Mitteilungen, 25)
SUBJ 12 35 ▪ 15 16.1 16.3 17 32

11006 NIC P P2 G1.2 1949–1972
Wei, Henry (Wei Wen-ch'i), 1909–.
State and government in Communist China: Their ideological basis and statutory pattern to the spring of 1953.
Lackland Air Force Base, San Antonio, Tex.: U.S. Air Force Personnel and Training Research Center, Air Research and Development Command, 1955. 16, 56 p. (U.S. Human Resources Research Institute research memoranda, 38; Studies in Chinese Communism, series 3, 1, 1953)
SUBJ 12 12.1 12.2 22 22.1 30 ▪ 15 16 32 60 64

11007 NNC P P1 G1.2 1949–1972
Whiting, Allen Suess, 1927–.
'China.' In *Modern political systems: Asia*, edited by Robert Edward Ward and Roy Constantine Macridis. [Sole entry]
Englewood Cliffs, N.J.: Prentice-Hall, 1965, 117–216.
SUBJ 12 12.1 64 ▪ 16.1 32 32.1 66

11008 NNC S P1 G1.2 1949–1972
Wright, William.
'Gesetzgebung und Rechtsprechung in der Volksrepublik China' (Legislation and the administration of justice in the People's Republic of China).
Osteuropa-Recht 4, 1 (Juli 1958), 189–197.
SUBJ 12 12.2 ▪ 12.1 32.1

11009 MCY P P1 G1.2 1949–1972
Yu, George T., 1931–.
'The 1962 and 1963 sessions of the National People's Congress of Communist China.'
AS 4, 8 (Aug. 1964), 981–990.
SUBJ 12 14 ▪ 32 64

12.1 STATE CONTROLS OF THE POPULACE

政治控制　　国家の大衆統制

1644-1911

11010 NIC P P2 G1.2 –1842
De Bary, William Theodore, 1918–.
'Chinese despotism and the Confucian ideal: A seventeenth-century view.' In *Chinese thought and institutions*, edited by John King Fairbank. [Selective entry]
Chicago: U. of Chicago Press, 1957, 163–203.
SUBJ 12 12.1 64 ▪ 12.2 14 14.1 15 16.1 17 63

11011 MCY P P1 G1.2 1644–1842
Goodrich, Luther Carrington, 1894–.
The literary inquisition of Ch'ien-lung.
Baltimore: Waverly Press, 1935. 275 p. (American Council of Learned Societies, Studies in Chinese and related civilizations, 1) (Doctoral dissertation in Chinese, Columbia U.) [Reprinted—New York: Paragon, 1966. 26, 275 p.]
SUBJ 12.1 16.1 70 ▪ 64

11012 CSU P P1 G1.2 1644–1842
Goodrich, Luther Carrington, 1894–.
'The ninety-nine ways of destroying the Manchus.'
THM 6, 5 (May 1938), 418–424.
SUBJ 12.1 ▪ 66

11013 NNC PO P2 G1.2 1895–1911
Hosie, Alexander, 1853–1925.
'The inception, organization and methods of the anti-opium crusade in China.' In *On the trail of the opium poppy*, by A. Hosie. [Selective entry]
Boston: Small, Maynard, 1914, vol. 2, 191–231.
SUBJ 12.1 55 66 ▪ 14.1 14.3 14.5 18

11014 CSU P P2 G1.5 1842–1895
Kuo Ting-yee (Kuo T'ing-i), 1903–.
'The totalitarian rule of the Taiping Heavenly Kingdom.' Tr. of 'T'ai-p'ing t'ien kuo ti chi ch'üan t'ung chih'; *Ta lu tsa chih* 10, 2 (31 Jan. 1955), 25–32.
Annals of Academia Sinica 2, 1 (May 1955), 209–230.
SUBJ 12.1 32.2 33 64 ▪ 12 12.2 14.1 14.5 15 47

11015 CSU P P2 G2.0 1644–1911
Lee, Robert H. G. (Li K'ung-chiang), 1922–.
The Manchurian frontier in Ch'ing history.
Cambridge: Harvard U. Press, 1970. 229 p. (Harvard East Asian series, 43) (Revision of *Cultural change and political control on the Manchurian frontier during the Ch'ing dynasty*, doctoral dissertation in History, Columbia U., 1963)
SUBJ 12 12.1 15 25 66 ▪ 12.2 14.1 14.3 14.5 21 21.2 22 22.1

11016 MCY S P2 G1.3 –1911
Mote, Frederick Wade, 1922–.
'The growth of Chinese despotism: A critique of Wittfogel's theory of Oriental despotism as applied to China.'
OE 8, 1 (Aug. 1961), 1–41.
SUBJ 12 12.1 16.1 ▪ 64 71

11017 CSU O P4 G1.5 1895–1911
Rodes, Jean.
'Dans la Chine du Sud' (In South China). In *Le Céleste empire avant la révolution* (The Celestial Empire before the Revolution [of 1911]), by J. Rodes. [Selective entry]
Paris: Alcan, 1914, 35–83. (Dix ans de politique chinoise, 3)
SUBJ 12.1 12.2 15 ▪ 32.2 66

11018 MCH O P1 G1.3 1895–1911
Sibbald, Andrew T-.
'Chinese police.'
Green bag 14, 6 (June 1902), 284–290.
SUBJ 12.1

1644-1949

11019 CSU P P2 G9.4 1895–1949
Chen, Edward I-te (Ch'en I-te), 1930–.
'Japanese colonialism in Korea and Formosa: A comparison of the systems of political control.'
HJAS 30 (1970), 126–158. [For fuller treatment, see entry 22646.]
SUBJ 12 12.1 22 ▪ 12.2 22.1

11020 CSU U P2 G9.4 1895–1949
Kerr, George H-, 1911–.
'Formosa: Colonial laboratory.'
FES 11, 4 (23 Feb. 1942), 50–55.
SUBJ 12.1 17 ▪ 24.2

11021 CBU PO P2 G1.2 1895–1949
[Yee, Frank S. H.] Frank Ki Chun Yee (I Hsiu-hao), 1904–.
Police in modern China.

Unpublished doctoral dissertation in Political Science, U. of California, Berkeley, 1942. 486 p.
Subj 12.1 22.1 ▪ 12.2

1911-1949

11022 MCH P P2 G1.2 1928–1949
'Conditions in enemy occupied and enemy controlled areas in China.'
ILR 49, 3 (Mar. 1944), 362–365.
Subj 12.1 ▪ 11.4 15

11023 NNC O P2 G1.2 1928–1949
'To have and to hold.' [On political aspects of the Japanese occupation of China]
PA 11, 3 (Sept. 1938), 299–310.
Subj 12.1 14.2 66 ▪ 32.2 64

11024 NNC P P4 G1.2 1911–1928
Bereznyi, Lev Abramovich, 1915–.
'Interventsiia SShA v Kitae v period revoliutsii 1924–1927 gg.' (American intervention in China in the period of the Revolution of 1924–1927).
SV 1955, 2, 82–95.
Subj 12 12.1 32.2 66 ▪ 16.2 16.4

11025 MAM P P3 G6.1 1928–1949
Crone, Ruth Beverly, 1919–.
An inquiry into a possible relationship between propaganda and the fall of Shanghai.
Ann Arbor: University Microfilms (Publ. 61-315), 1961. 185 p. (Doctoral dissertation in Political Science, New York U.)
Subj 12.1 24.2

11026 CSH P P2 G1.2 1911–1928
Engel'fel'd, Vladimir Viktorovich, 1891–1937.
'Politsiia v Kitae' (The police in China).
Izvestiia IUridicheskogo fakul'teta v g. Kharbine 6 (1928), 137–228.
Subj 12.1 12.2 22.2 32.1 ▪ 14 17 22.1

11027 FPN S P2 G1.2 1928–1949
Jao Houa-son (Jao Hua-sun).
La police administrative en Chine (The administrative police in China).
Bordeaux: Castera, 1939. 138 p. (Doctoral dissertation, Faculté de droit, Université de Bordeaux)
Subj 12.1 12.2 ▪ 15 22.1

11028 CSU P P2 G1.4 1928–1949
Niijima Atsuyoshi, 1928–.
'The nature of the rectification movement in China.'
DE 4, 1 (Mar. 1966), 55–69.
Subj 12.1 19 32.2 64 ▪ 16.1 17 18 35

11029 MCH P P1 G1.3 1911–1949
Otte, Friedrich W- K-.
'Erziehung der Volkmassen zum nationalen Denken in China als Mittel zur Rettung von Staat und Volk durch das Schrifttum' (Inculcating the Chinese masses with national consciousness: An attempt to save the state and the people through literature).
MSOSB 39 (1936), 33–66.
Subj 12.1 17 32 40 ▪ 63

11030 CSU P P2 G1.2 1928–1949
Tokuda, Noriyuki, 1931–.
'Yenan rectification movement: Mao Tse-tung's big push toward charismatic leadership during 1941–1942.'
DE 9, 1 (Mar. 1971), 83–99.
Subj 12.1 16.1 32.1 ▪ 15 32.2

11031 CBU P P2 G9.5 1928–1949
Ward, Robert Spencer, 1906–.
Hong Kong under Japanese occupation: A case study in the enemy's techniques of control.
Washington, D.C.: U.S. Dept. of Commerce, Bureau of Foreign and Domestic Commerce, Far Eastern Unit, 1943. 105 p.
Subj 12.1 24 24.6 55 66 ▪ 12.2 15 21.2 22 24.2 28 36.2 36.4 39

11032 NNC P P4 G2.0 1928–1949
Warneck, Siegfried.
'Waffen und Methoden des geistigen Kampfes in Mandschukuo' (Weapons and methods of the intellectual struggle in Manchoukuo).
Z. für Geopolitik 16, 8/9 (Aug.–Sept. 1939), 624–630.
Subj 12.1 14.2 16.1 ▪ 62 64

1911-1972
(including 1644-1972)

11033 DLC S P1 G1.2 1911–1972
Boorman, Howard Lyon, 1920–.
'Literature and politics in contemporary China.'
Thought patterns 7 (1960), 101–123.
Subj 12.1 16.1 32.1 64 ▪ 31

11034 FPN P P2 G1.2 1928–1972
Brénier, Henri.
'La victoire du communisme chinois' (The victory of Chinese Communism).
R. des travaux de l'Académie des sciences morales et politiques 4e série 103 (1950), 71–87.
Subj 12.1 14 64 ▪ 14.1 16 17 32.1

11035 CSU O P2 G1.1 1928–1972
Chow Ching-wen (Chou Ching-wen).
Ten years of storm: The true story of the Communist regime in China, edited by Lai Ming. Tr. by Lai Ming of *Feng pao shih nien* (A decade of storm); Hong Kong: Shih tai p'i p'ing she, 1959; 588 p.
New York: Holt, Rinehart and Winston, 1960. 11, 323 p.
Subj 12.1 32 32.1 ▪ 14 14.1 16 18 32.2 34.2 41 55

11036 MCH P P7 G1.2 –1972
Elmquist, Paul Oscar, 1920–.
Rural controls in early modern China.
Unpublished doctoral dissertation in History and Far Eastern Languages, Harvard U., 1963. 445 p.
Subj 12 12.1 12.2 22 22.1 ▪ 14.5 16.1 22.2 25 32.1 41

11037 MCH P P1 G1.2 1928–1972
Goldman, Merle Dorothy, 1931–.
'The fall of Chou Yang.'
CQ 27 (July–Sept. 1966), 132–148.
Subj 12.1 32 ▪ 16.1

11038 MCH P P2 G1.1 1928–1972
Goldman, Merle Dorothy, 1931–.
'Hu Feng's conflict with the Communist literary authorities.'
PC 11 (Dec. 1957), 149–191. [Reprinted—*CQ* 12 (Oct.–Dec. 1962), 102–137.]
Subj 12.1 59 ▪ 16.1 36.1 60 64

11039 CSH S P1 G1.2 1911–1972
Hagemann, Ernst.
'Die proletarische Revolution: Zur Genesis der chinesischen Kulturrevolution' (The proletarian revolution: The genesis of China's Cultural Revolution).
Der Monat 20, 1 (Jan. 1968), 5–21.
Subj 12.1 17 ▪ 19 32

11040 NNC PO P4 G1.2 1928–1972
Ho, Wen-hai.
Chinese Communist exploitation and persecution of the intelligentsia.
Taipei: Asian Peoples' Anti-Communist League, 1963. 60 p. (APACL pamphlets, 79)
Subj 12.1 16.1 ▪ 12.2 16.2 32 32.2

11041 NNC P P2 G1.2 1928–1972
IAkovlev, Aleksandr Grigor'evich, 1928–.
'Politika narodnoi vlasti v skotovodcheskikh raionakh Kitaia' (The policy of the people's government in the pastoral regions of China).
KSIV 25 (1957), 3–17.
Subj 12.1 14.1 66 ▪ 14.3 14.5 34.1

11042 CSH P P2 G1.2 1928–1972
Johnson, Chalmers Ashby, 1931–.
'Building a Communist nation in China.' In *The Communist revolution in Asia: Tactics, goals, and achievements*, edited by Robert Anthony Scalapino. [Sole entry]
Englewood Cliffs, N. J.: Prentice-Hall, 1965, 47–81.
Subj 12.1 14.1 32.1 64 ▪ 14 15 22 32.2 34.1

11043 CSU P P2 G1.2 1928–1972
Johnson, Chalmers Ashby, 1931–.
'Chinese Communist leadership and mass response: The Yenan period and the Socialist Education campaign period' [with comments by Ssu-yü Teng]. In *China in crisis, Vol. 1, China's heritage and the Communist political system*, edited by Ping-ti Ho and Tang Tsou. [Selective entry]
Chicago: U. of Chicago Press, 1968, 397–447.
Subj 12.1 64 ▪ 32.1

11044 CSU PO P2 G9.4 1928–1972
Kerr, George H-, 1911–.
Formosa betrayed.
Boston: Houghton Mifflin, 1965. 22, 514 p.
Subj 12 12.1 14 22.2 66 ▪ 12.2 14.3 14.6 16.1 18 24.2 32 32.2 56

11045 NNC FP P2 G1.1 1928–1972
Labin, Suzanne.
La condition humaine en Chine communiste (The human condition in Communist China).
Paris: Table ronde, 1959. 12, 510 p.
The anthill: The human condition in Communist China. Tr. by E- Fitzgerald.
New York: Praeger, 1960. 10, 442 p.
Subj 12.1 14 16 19 30 64 ▪ 11.4 12.2 17 41 47 50 52 55 60

11046 MAM P P1 G1.2 1928–1972
Lammers, Raymond John, 1926–.
An analysis of a representative sample of plays written and used for propagandistic purposes by the Chinese Communists.
Ann Arbor: University Microfilms (Publ. 63-1225), 1963. 227 p. (Doctoral

dissertation in Speech, U. of Minnesota, 1962)
Subj 12.1 31 64

11047 CSH P P2 G1.1 1928–1972
Lu Yu-sun (Lu Yü-sheng).
Programs of Communist China for overseas Chinese, mimeo.
Hong Kong: Union Research Institute, 1956. 82 p. (Communist China problem research series, EC12)
Subj 12.1 14.1 14.5 54 ▪ 11.2 12 16 34.1

11048 CSH S P2 G1.2 –1972
Mitchison, Lois.
China.
London: Thames and Hudson, 1966. 232 p.
Subj 12 12.1 ▪ 14.4 16.1 32 32.2 34.1

11049 MCH U P1 G1.2 –1972
Pulleyblank, Edwin George, 1922–.
Review of *Oriental despotism: A comparative study of total power*, by Karl August Wittfogel.
BSOAS 21, 3 (Oct. 1958), 657–660.
Subj 10 12.1 71

11050 CSH U P2 G3.0 1928–1972
Shih, Yang Cheng (Shih Yang-ch'eng), 1917–.
'Public order and safety.' In *A regional handbook on the Inner Mongolia Autonomous Region*, compiled by Far Eastern and Russian Institute, U. of Washington. [Selective entry]
New Haven: Human Relations Area Files, 1956, 428–435. (HRAF subcontractor's monographs, 60; Washington 7)
Subj 12.1 12.2

11051 CSH U P2 G2.0 1911–1972
Tang, Peter S. H. (T'ang Sheng-hao), 1919–.
'Public order and safety.' In *A regional handbook on Northeast China*, compiled by Far Eastern and Russian Institute, U. of Washington. [Selective entry]
New Haven: Human Relations Area Files, 1956, 376–396. (HRAF subcontractor's monographs, 61; Washington 9)
Subj 12.1 12.2 ▪ 22.1 22.2

11052 MAM FP P2 G1.2 1928–1972
Teiwes, Frederick Carl, 1939–.
Rectification campaigns and purges in Communist China, 1950–61.
Ann Arbor: University Microfilms (Publ. 72-19,167), 1972. 607 p. (Doctoral dissertation in Political Science, Columbia U., 1971)
Subj 12.1 16.1 19 22 30 32 ▪ 12 14.2 15 21.2 22.1 32.1 36.4 54 59 64

11053 NNC O P2 G1.2 1928–1972
Wang, Tsun-ming (Wang Chün-ming), 1926–.
Wang Tsun-ming, anti-Communist: An autobiographical account of Chinese Communist thought reform.
Washington, D.C.: George Washington U., 1954. 11, 64 p.
Subj 12.1 15 59 61 64 ▪ 25 26 32.1 41 48

11054 NIC P P2 G1.2 –1972
Wittfogel, Karl August, 1896–.
'Chinese society: An historical survey.'
JAS 16, 3 (May 1957), 343–364. [Reprinted as 'Imperial China: A "complex" hydraulic (Oriental) society.' (Slightly rev.) In *The pattern of Chinese history: Cycles, development, or stagnation?*, edited by John Thomas Meskill. (Selective entry.) Boston: Heath, 1965, 85–95.]
Subj 10 12 12.1 14 16 22 ▪ 14.1 14.5 15 16.1 17 19 32.2 64

11055 NIC S P1 G1.2 –1972
Wright, Arthur Frederick, 1913–.
'The Chinese monolith, past and present.'
Problems of Communism 4, 4 (July–Aug. 1955), 1–8.
Subj 12 12.1 ▪ 12.2 32.1 62

1949-1972

11056 CSH O P8 G1.2 1949–1972
'The education of a people's intellectual.'
CS 2, 33 (15 May 1964), 1–11; 2, 34 (1 June 1964), 1–10.
Subj 12.1 16.1 ▪ 16.3 34.1

11057 CSH O P2 G1.2 1949–1972
'Fate of a rightist.'
CS 2, 6 (6 Nov. 1962), 1–12. [Reprinted in *Out of China: A collection of interviews with refugees from China*, edited by Francis Harper. (Analytic entry.) Hong Kong: Dragonfly Books, 1964, 157–183.]
Subj 12.1 59 ▪ 17 54

11058 CSH P P7 G1.2 1949–1972
'Who is our enemy and who is our friend?'
CS 2, 30 (15 Mar. 1964), 1–12. [Reprinted in *This is China: Analyses of Mainland trends and events*, edited by Francis Harper. (Selective entry.) Hong Kong: Dragonfly Books, 1965, 185–201.]
Subj 12.1 ▪ 14.1 16 16.3 32

11059 CSU S P2 G9.4 1949–1972
Appleton, Sheldon Lee, 1933–.
'Taiwan: The year it finally happened.'
AS 12, 1 (Jan. 1972), 32–37.
Subj 12.1 14

11060 ELB P P2 G1.2 1949–1972
Ardant, Philippe.
'Le héros maoïste: modèle du Chinois de demain' (The Maoist hero: Model for the Chinese of tomorrow).
R. française de science politique 19, 6 (déc. 1969), 1145–1171.
Subj 12.1 60 ▪ 41

11061 GMS O P2 G1.3 1949–1972
Barcata, Louis, 1906–.
China geht nicht Russlands Weg: Partner? Konkurrenten? Gegner? (China eschews the Russian road: Are they partners, competitors, or adversaries?).
Stuttgart: Goverts, 1959. 278 p.
Subj 10 12.1 34.2 47 64 ▪ 14 17 19 31 53

11062 NNC PO P2 G1.2 1949–1972
Barnett, Arthur Doak, 1921–.
'Chinese Communist propaganda methods.'
AUFS-EAS 1, 6 (8 Nov. 1952), 1–9. [Reprinted as 'Propaganda.' In *Communist China: The early years, 1949–55*, by A. D. Barnett. (Selective entry.) New York: Praeger, 1964, 71–80.]
Subj 12.1 14.2

11063 MCH PO P3 G1.2 1949–1972
Barnett, Arthur Doak, 1921–.
'The "Five-Anti" campaign' [written in July–August 1952]. In *Communist China: The early years, 1949–55*, by A. D. Barnett. [Selective entry]
New York: Praeger, 1964, 135–171.
Subj 12.1 32.1 34.2 ▪ 12 14 14.3 14.5 16.2

11064 NNC PO P1 G1.2 1949–1972
Barnett, Arthur Doak, 1921–.
'Hsueh Hsi ["study"], a weapon of ideological revolution in China.'
AUFS-EAS 3, 3 (5 Mar. 1954), 1–14. [Reprinted as 'Group indoctrination.' In *Communist China: The early years, 1949–55*, by A. D. Barnett. (Selective entry.) New York: Praeger, 1964, 89–103.] [Reprinted in *Education and Communism: An anthology of commentary and documents*, edited by Stewart Erskine Fraser. (Selective entry.) London: Pall Mall Press, 1971, 281–298.]
Subj 12.1 ▪ 48

11065 MCH PO P1 G1.2 1949–1972
Barnett, Arthur Doak, 1921–.
'The ideological reform campaign' [written in July 1952]. In *Communist China: The early years, 1949–55*, by A. D. Barnett. [Selective entry]
New York: Praeger, 1964, 125–134.
Subj 12.1 16.1 17 ▪ 32.1 61

11066 DLC O P2 G1.2 1949–1972
Barnett, Arthur Doak, 1921–.
'Profile of Red China.'
Foreign policy reports 25, 19 (15 Feb. 1950), 230–243. [Reprinted in *Foundations of national power: Readings on world politics and American security*, edited by Harold Sprout and Margaret Sprout. (Sole entry.) Princeton: Van Nostrand, 1951, 394–411.] [Reprinted as 'New democracy and people's democratic dictatorship.' In *Communist China: The early years, 1949–55*, by A. D. Barnett. (Selective entry.) New York: Praeger, 1964, 3–26.]
Subj 12 12.1 ▪ 14 15

11067 NIC FP P1 G1.2 1949–1972
Barnett, Arthur Doak, 1921–.
'Social controls in Communist China: By mass organization, indoctrination, and police state methods, the Chinese people have been brought under effective Communist discipline.'
FES 22, 5 (22 Apr. 1953), 45–48. [Reprinted as 'Social controls.' In *Communist China: The early years, 1949–55*, by A. D. Barnett. (Selective entry.) New York: Praeger, 1964, 45–51.]
Subj 12.1 32.1 ▪ 30 64

11068 NIC P P1 G1.2 1949–1972
Birch, Cyril, 1925–.
'The literature of the Great Leap Forward.'
CS 1, 31 (5 May 1962), 1–9. [Reprinted in *This is China: Analyses of Mainland trends and events*, edited by Francis Harper. (Selective entry.) Hong Kong: Dragonfly Books, 1965, 33–46.]
Subj 12.1 ▪ 16.1 61 64

11069 NIC O P2 G1.2 1949–1972
Bodard, Lucien, 1916–.
La Chine de la douceur (The gentle aspects of China).
Paris: Gallimard, 1957. 336 p.
SUBJ 12.1 16.2 ▪ 12.2 14.4 16 17

11070 FPN P P2 G1.2 1949–1972
Brénier, Henri.
'Le développement de la "technique de la dictature" en Chine communiste' (The development of the 'technique of dictatorship' in Communist China).
R. des travaux de l'Académie des sciences morales et politiques 4e série 104 (1951), 8–27.
SUBJ 12 12.1 14.1 64 ▪ 16 17 32 32.1 32.2

11071 MMT P P2 G1.2 1949–1972
Chan, Shau Wing (Ch'en Shou-jung), 1906–, and Yuan-li Wu (Wu Yüan-li), 1920–.
'Popular discontent in Communist China.'
Problems of Communism 4, 4 (July–Aug. 1955), 9–17.
SUBJ 12.1 14.5 22.2 ▪ 18 41

11072 NNC P P2 G1.2 1949–1972
Chen Feng (Ch'en Feng).
'Culture.' Tr. of '1958 nien ti Chung kung wen hua kai k'uang' (Cultural affairs in Communist China, 1958); *Tsu kuo chou k'an* 334/335 (8 June 1959), 35–38. In *Communist China, 1958*, edited by Union Research Institute. [Selective entry]
Hong Kong: Union Research Institute, 1959, 106–115.
SUBJ 12.1 16.1 60 ▪ 31 62 64

11073 WSU P P4 G1.2 1949–1972
Chen, S. H. (Ch'en Shih-hsiang), 1912–1971.
'Artificial flowers during a natural thaw.' In *Soviet and Chinese Communism: Similarities and differences*, edited by Donald Warren Treadgold. [Selective entry]
Seattle: U. of Washington Press, 1967, 220–254.
SUBJ 12.1 16.1 36.1 ▪ 31 63 64

11074 CSH P P2 G1.2 1949–1972
Chen, S. H. (Ch'en Shih-hsiang), 1912–1971.
'Multiplicity in uniformity: Poetry and the Great Leap Forward.'
CQ 3 (July–Sept. 1960), 1–15. [Reprinted in *China under Mao: Politics takes command*, edited by Roderick Lemonde MacFarquhar. (Selective entry.) Cambridge: M.I.T. Press, 1966, 392–406.]
SUBJ 12.1 ▪ 44 64

11075 CSH P P1 G1.2 1949–1972
Chen, Theodore H. E. (Ch'en Hsi-en), 1902–, and S. M. Chiu (Chao Shan-ming), 1923–.
'Thought reform in Communist China.'
FES 24, 12 (Dec. 1955), 177–184.
SUBJ 12.1 16.1 ▪ 61

11076 MCH P P2 G1.2 1949–1972
Chen, Wen-hui C. (Ch'en Chung Wen-hui), 1913–.
Wartime 'mass' campaigns in Communist China: Official country-wide 'mass movements' in professed support of the Korean War.
Lackland Air Force Base, San Antonio, Tex.: U.S. Air Force Personnel and Training Research Center, Air Research and Development Command, 1955. 14, 84 p. (U.S. Human Resources Research Institute research memoranda, 43; Studies in Chinese Communism, series 2, 4, 1952)
SUBJ 12.1 14 16 22.2 32 32.1 ▪ 12 12.2 14.5 18 22 30 35 60 64

11077 NNC P P2 G1.2 1949–1972
Cheng Chu-yuan (Cheng Chu-yüan), 1927–.
'The propaganda of Communist China.' Tr. of 'Shih nien lai ti Chung kung hsüan ch'uan kung tso' (Propaganda in Communist China during the past decade); *Tsu kuo chou k'an* 392 (11 July 1960), 13–18. In *Communist China, 1949–1959*, edited by Union Research Institute. [Selective entry]
Hong Kong: Union Research Institute, 1961, vol. 1, 239–264.
SUBJ 12.1 ▪ 14.2 31 32

11078 NNC P P2 G1.2 1949–1972
Chin Ta-kai (Chin Ta-k'ai).
'Cultural activities.' Tr. of '1956 nien Chung kung ti wen hua huo tung' (Cultural activities in Communist China, 1956); *Tsu kuo chou k'an* 214/215 (11 Feb. 1957), 33–37. In *Communist China, 1956*, edited by Union Research Institute. [Selective entry]
Hong Kong: Union Research Institute, 1957, 127–137.
SUBJ 12.1 ▪ 31 62

11079 CSH P P2 G4.0 1949–1972
Chu, Wen-djang (Chu Wen-ch'ang), 1914–.
'Public order and safety.' In *A regional handbook on Northwest China*, compiled by Far Eastern and Russian Institute, U. of Washington. [Selective entry]
New Haven: Human Relations Area Files, 1956, vol. 2, 532–546. (HRAF subcontractor's monographs, 59; Washington 5)
SUBJ 12.1 22.1 ▪ 12.2 32.1

11080 CSU P P3 G5.1 1949–1972
Chuang, H. C. (Chuang Hsin-cheng), 1935–.
'Evening chats at Yenshan': or, The case of Teng T'o.
Berkeley: U. of California, Center for Chinese Studies, 1970. 46 p. (Current Chinese Language Project, Studies in Chinese Communist terminology, 14)
SUBJ 12.1 26.1 ▪ 24.2 59

11081 CSH P P1 G1.2 1949–1972
Chuang, H. C. (Chuang Hsin-cheng), 1935–.
The little red book and current Chinese language.
Berkeley: U. of California, Center for Chinese Studies, 1968. 58 p. (Current Chinese Language Project, Studies in Chinese Communist terminology, 13)
SUBJ 12.1 64

11082 CSU P P1 G1.2 1949–1972
Cohen, Arthur Allen, 1928–.
'What is Maoism? The man and his policies.'
Problems of Communism 15, 5 (Sept.–Oct. 1966), 8–16.
SUBJ 12.1 64

11083 MCH P P1 G1.2 1949–1972
Coillie, Dries van, 1912–.
'Organisationsprinzipien des kommunistischen Regimes in China' (Organizational principles of the Chinese Communist regime). In *Moskau-Peking* (Moscow-Peking), edited by Helmut Reuther. [Sole entry]
Freiburg i. Br.: Walter, 1965, 41–51. (Kontakte der Kontinente, 1)
SUBJ 12.1 30 32 ▪ 16.1 32.1 64

11084 MCH P P1 G1.2 1949–1972
Current Scene Editor.
'In the name of revolution: Peking's campaign to crush the "anti-party" line.'
CS 4, 12 (20 June 1966), 1–15.
SUBJ 12.1 64 ▪ 16.1

11085 CSU P P2 G1.2 1949–1972
Current Scene Editor.
'Peking's program to move human and material resources to the countryside.'
CS 7, 18 (15 Sept. 1969), 1–17.
SUBJ 12.1 14.1 21.2 34.1 ▪ 14.4 14.6 17 64

11086 CSU O P2 G1.2 1949–1972
Duncan, James Stuart, 1893–.
'Communist China today.'
Progressive new (2nd) series 29, 4 (Apr. 1965), 13–23.
SUBJ 12 12.1 ▪ 14.1 14.4 15 17

11087 NNC O P3 G1.2 1949–1972
Dunlap, Albert Menzo, 1884–.
Behind the Bamboo Curtain: The experiences of an American doctor in China.
Washington, D.C.: Public Affairs Press, 1956. 208 p.
SUBJ 12 12.1 14 56 ▪ 16 17 18 55 66

11088 DLC U P4 G1.2 1949–1972
Efimov, Gerontii Valentinovich, 1906–.
Bor'ba Kommunisticheskoi partii Kitaia protiv burzhuaznoi ideologii (The Chinese Communist Party's struggle against bourgeois ideology).
Leningrad: Ob-vo rasprostraneniia polit. i nauch. znanii RSFSR, 1957. 48 p.
SUBJ 12.1 64 ▪ 16.1 16.2

11089 CSH P P2 G1.2 1949–1972
Feng Wen.
'Analysis of the Maoist "purification of class ranks".'
CCA 6, 2 (Apr. 1969), 12–19.
SUBJ 12.1 16 ▪ 22.1

11090 CSU S P1 G9.4 1949–1972
Feng, Yu-kon (Feng Yü-k'un), 1902–.
'Changes in the Chinese police system.'
CJA 3 (July 1964), 36–38 [s.p.]. [See Vol. 2 of this *Bibliography* for Chinese version.]
SUBJ 12.1 ▪ 22.2

11091 CSH P P1 G1.2 1949–1972
Fokkema, Douwe Wessel, 1931–.
'Chinese criticism of humanism: Campaigns against the intellectuals, 1964–1965.'
CQ 26 (Apr.–June 1966), 68–81.
SUBJ 12.1 64 ▪ 16.1 59 62

11092 MAM S P2 G1.2 1949–1972
Frame, William Vermer, 1938–.
Dialectical historicism and the terror in Chinese Communism.
Ann Arbor: University Microfilms (Publ. 70-8454), 1970. 385 p. (Doctoral dissertation in Political Science, U. of Washington, 1969)
SUBJ 12.1 19 64 ▪ 14 16.1 16.3 32 34.1 54

11093 CSH P P1 G1.2 1949–1972
Freedman, Edward H-.
'Power and progress in revolutionizing China.'
JAAS 1, 2 (Apr. 1966), 118–128.
SUBJ 12.1 16.1 ▪ 11.4 14 32

11094 ELS P P2 G1.2 1949–1972
Funnell, Victor Cecil, 1926–.
The cadres: A study of methods of mass control in Communist China.
Unpublished doctoral dissertation in Economics, U. of London [London School of Economics and Political Science], 1969. 514 p.
SUBJ 12 12.1 16.1 22 32 32.1 ▪ 16 19 22.1 26.1 34.1 34.2 36.4 54 64 66

11095 NNC O P2 G1.2 1949–1972
Gale, George Stafford.
No flies in China.
New York: Morrow, 1955. 191 p.
SUBJ 12.1 14.4 ▪ 12.2 18 36.4 50 52 55

11096 CSU P P2 G1.2 1949–1972
Gray, Jack Douglas, 1916–, and Patrick Cavendish, 1937–.
Chinese Communism in crisis: Maoism and the Cultural Revolution.
New York: Praeger, 1968. 279 p.
SUBJ 12.1 16.1 32.1 64 ▪ 14 15 31 34.1 54 60 63

11097 FPN PO P2 G1.2 1949–1972
Guillain, Robert, 1908–.
'Les Chinois à l'épreuve' (The testing of the Chinese).
Le monde 25 sept. – ler oct. 1962.
SUBJ 12.1 14.1 14.4 55 56 ▪ 11.2 14.3 15 16.3 16.4 17 24.4 32 61

11098 CSH P P2 G1.2 1949–1972
Guillermaz, Jacques, 1911–.
'Trois années de Révolution culturelle' (Three years of the Cultural Revolution).
Projet 40 (déc. 1969), 1168–1173. [Special issue: *La Chine s'est levée* (China resurgent)]
SUBJ 12 12.1 32 64 ▪ 15 54

11099 CSU P P2 G3.0 1949–1972
Heaton, William.
'Inner Mongolia: Aftermath of the revolution.'
CS 9, 4 (7 Apr. 1971), 6–16.
SUBJ 12.1 35 66 ▪ 12 14.1 21.2

11100 MCY P P1 G1.2 1949–1972
Hellbeck, Hannspeter.
'The "rightist" movement in 1959.' In *Contemporary China, 1959–1960*, edited by Edward Stuart Kirby. [Selective entry]
Hong Kong: Hong Kong U. Press, 1961, 48–54.
SUBJ 12.1 32.1 ▪ 64

11101 MCM FP P2 G1.2 1949–1972
Hiniker, Paul James, 1938–.
The effects of mass communications in Communist China: The organization and distribution of exposure.
Unpublished doctoral dissertation in Political Science, Massachusetts Institute of Technology, 1966. 525 p.
SUBJ 12.1 14.2 32.1 61 ▪ 11 11.4 12 16 48 64

11102 MCH S P1 G1.2 1949–1972
Hinkle, Lawrence Earle, Jr., 1889–.
'Communist manipulation of behavior: The Russians use confession to convict and condemn, the Chinese to rehabilitate and reform.'
Science 133, 3468 (16 June 1961), 1912–1914.
SUBJ 12.1 61

11103 MCH P P1 G1.2 1949–1972
Hollander, Paul.
'Privacy: A bastion stormed.'
Problems of Communism 12, 6 (Nov.–Dec. 1963), 1–9.
SUBJ 12.1 40 60 ▪ 51

11104 NNC P P2 G1.2 1949–1972
Houn, Franklin W. (Hou Fu-wu), 1920–.
To change a nation: Propaganda and indoctrination in Communist China.
East Lansing: Michigan State U., College of Business and Public Service, Bureau of Social and Political Research; Glencoe, N.Y.: Free Press, 1961. 10, 250 p.
SUBJ 12 12.1 19 64 ▪ 16.1 17 36.1

11105 NIC P P2 G1.2 1949–1972
Hsia, T. A. (Hsia Chi-an), 1916–1965.
Metaphor, myth, ritual and the people's commune.
Berkeley: U. of California, Center for Chinese Studies, 1961. 60 p. (Current Chinese Language Project, Studies in Chinese Communist terminology, 7) [Reprinted—Ann Arbor: University Microfilms, n.d. 60 p.]
SUBJ 12.1 17 60 ▪ 19 21.4 24.1 24.4 31 64 65

11106 MCH O P2 G1.2 1949–1972
Hutheesing, Gunottam Purushottam.
The great peace: An Asian's candid report on Red China.
New York: Harper, 1953. 246 p. [Also published as *Window on China*. London: Derek Verschoyle, 1953. 191 p.]
SUBJ 12.1 14 18 ▪ 12.2 14.1 14.4 16.3 16.4 17 34.1 59 66

11107 NNC P P4 G1.2 1949–1972
Hwang Tien-chien (Huang T'ien-chien).
Analysis of the 'Cultural Revolution' of CCP in 1966.
Taipei: Asian Peoples' Anti-Communist League, 1966. 2 vols. 79; 75 p. (APACL pamphlets, 109–110)
SUBJ 12.1 16.1 ▪ 12 15 17 36.1 64

11108 CSU P P1 G9.4 1949–1972
Jacobs, J- Bruce.
'Recent leadership and political trends in Taiwan.'
CQ 45 (Jan.–Mar. 1971), 129–154.
SUBJ 12.1 16.1 32 ▪ 12 22 50

11109 CSU S P1 G9.4 1949–1972
Kallgren, Joyce Kislitzin, 1930–.
'Nationalist China: The continuing dilemma of the "Mainland" philosophy.'
AS 3, 1 (Jan. 1963), 11–16.
SUBJ 12 12.1 ▪ 14.5 15 32

11110 NNC P P1 G1.2 1949–1972
Kiang, Daniel.
Public security personnel in Mainland China.
Unpublished masters thesis in Political Science, Columbia U., 1969. 51 p. [Certificate essay, East Asian Institute]
SUBJ 12.1 16.1 59 ▪ 12.2 32

11111 NNC P P1 G1.2 1949–1972
King, Vincent V. S.
Propaganda campaigns in Communist China.
Cambridge: Massachusetts Institute of Technology, Center for International Studies, 1966. 89 p.
SUBJ 12.1 30 64 ▪ 12

11112 CSH S P1 G1.2 1949–1972
Kirichenko, V- F- (W. F. Kiritschenko).
'Zakonodatel'nye akty Kitaiskoi Narodnoi Respubliki o bor'be s gosudarstvennymi prestupleniiami' (Legislation in the People's Republic of China concerning the struggle against political crimes).
SGP 1952, 2 (fevral'), 65–69.
'Gesetzgebung der Volksrepublik China über den Kampf gegen die Staatsverbrechen.'
Rechtswissenschaftlicher Informationsdienst 3, 1 (5 Jan. 1954), 24–31.
SUBJ 12.1 12.2 ▪ 14 32 32.2 66

11113 CBU P P4 G1.2 1949–1972
Kiuzadzhian, Liparit Sarkisovich, 1932–.
Ideologicheskie kampanii v KNR (1949–1966).
Moscow: Nauka, Glav. red. vost. lit-ry, 1970. 239 p.
'Ideological campaigns in the People's Republic of China (1949–1966).' [Partial tr.: p. 3–29, 110–151 only]
Chinese sociology and anthropology 3, 1 (Fall 1970), 36–80; 3, 2/3 (Winter–Spring 1971), 83–132.
SUBJ 12.1 14.2 16.1 32 62 64 ▪ 14.3 14.4 16.2 16.4 17 31 54 66 72

11114 DLC S P4 G1.2 1949–1972
Kuznetsova, T- A-.
'Vospitanie Kommunisticheskoi partiei Kitaia sotsialisticheskoi soznatel'nosti u rabochego klassa v gody velikogo pod"ema revoliutsii, 1956–1957' (The Chinese Communist Party's fostering of socialist consciousness among the working class during the great revolutionary upsurge of 1956–1957). [With English abstract]
VLGU 13, 20 (1958), 58–73.
SUBJ 12.1 16.4 32 36.4 ▪ 14.4 17 66

11115 CSH P P2 G1.2 1949–1972
[La Dany, Ladislao] ———, 1914–.
'Civic disobedience.'
CNA 771 (29 Aug. 1969), 1–7.
SUBJ 12.1 ▪ 16 35

11116 CSH P P2 G1.2 1949–1972
[La Dany, Ladislao] ———, 1914–.
'Cleaning up after the Cultural Revolution.'
CNA 858 (15 Oct. 1971), 1–7.
Subj 12.1 64 ▪ 14 16.1 32 35

11117 CSH P P4 G1.2 1949–1972
[La Dany, Ladislao] ———, 1914–.
'Cultural life and death.'
CNA 902 (1 Dec. 1972), 1–7.
Subj 12.1 37 62 ▪ 14.2 36.1

11118 CSH P P2 G1.2 1949–1972
[La Dany, Ladislao] ———, 1914–.
'Police, security, forced labour.'
CNA 742 (31 Jan. 1969), 1–7.
Subj 12.1 ▪ 12.2 21.4 22.2 25

11119 CSH P P1 G1.2 1949–1972
[La Dany, Ladislao] ———, 1914–.
'Praise of dictatorship.'
CNA 879 (5 May 1972), 1–7.
Subj 12.1 64

11120 CSU P P2 G1.2 1949–1972
La Dany, Ladislao, 1914–.
'Problems of administration and control.' In *Communist China, 1949–1969: A twenty-year appraisal*, edited by Frank Newton Trager and William Henderson. [Selective entry]
New York: New York U. Press, 1970, 45–61.
Subj 12.1 12.2 ▪ 30 63

11121 CSH P P2 G6.3 1949–1972
[La Dany, Ladislao] ———, 1914–.
'A province on the eastern coast [Chekiang].'
CNA 731 (1 Nov. 1968), 1–7.
Subj 12.1 32 ▪ 12 22.2 25 32.2

11122 MCH P P1 G1.2 1949–1972
[La Dany, Ladislao] ———, 1914–.
'The purge in action.'
CNA 561 (23 Apr. 1965), 1–7.
Subj 12.1 ▪ 16.1 32

11123 CSH P P1 G1.2 1949–1972
[La Dany, Ladislao] ———, 1914–.
'Socialist culture.'
CNA 613 (27 May 1966), 1–7.
Subj 12.1 16.1

11124 CSH P P7 G1.2 1949–1972
[La Dany, Ladislao] ———, 1914–.
'The Tachai sweat.'
CNA 827 (8 Jan. 1971), 1–7.
Subj 12.1 16.3 ▪ 14.1 22

11125 CSH P P1 G1.2 1949–1972
[Li Hui-min] Li Hwei-min.
'Chinese Communist labor reform policy and measures.'
CCA 2, 1 (Feb. 1965), 19–44.
Subj 12.1 12.2

11126 NNC P P2 G1.2 1949–1972
Li Pai-chen.
'Cultural activities.' Tr. of '1957 nien Chung kung ti wen hua huo tung' (Cultural activities in Communist China, 1957); *Tsu kuo chou k'an* 274/275 (7 Apr. 1958), 30–33. In *Communist China, 1957*, edited by Union Research Institute. [Selective entry]
Hong Kong: Union Research Institute, 1958, 113–127.
Subj 12.1 16.1 ▪ 14.2 32.1 36.1

11127 CSU FP P5 G9.2 1949–1972
Li, Victor H. (Li Hao), 1941–.
'The public security bureau and political-legal work in Hui-yang *hsien* [Kwangtung], 1952–64.' In *The city in Communist China*, edited by John Wilson Lewis. [Analytic entry]
Stanford: Stanford U. Press, 1971, 51–74. [For fuller treatment, see entry 16148.]
Subj 12.1 22.1 ▪ 32.1

11128 CSH P P1 G1.2 1949–1972
Lin Su, Chen Feng (Ch'en Feng), and [Chao Ts'ung] Chung Hua-min, pseud., 1927–. [Authors sequential rather than joint: Lin Su for 1961 and 1962; Chen Feng for 1963–1965; Chao Ts'ung for 1967; Chung Hua-min, pseud., for 1968 and 1969.]
'Communist China's cultural work, 1961–1969' [title varies]. Tr. from *Tsu kuo chou k'an* 488 (14 May 1962); 539 (6 May 1963) *and* from *Tsu kuo* 3–73 (June 1964 – Apr. 1970) [recurring annual feature article]. In *Communist China, 1961–1969*, edited by Union Research Institute.
Hong Kong: Union Research Institute. Issued annually, 1962–1970, average ca. 25 p.
Subj 12.1 16.1 ▪ 14.2 31 64

11129 CSU U P1 G1.2 1949–1972
Lindsay, Michael Francis Morris, 1909–.
'Contradictions in a totalitarian society.'
CQ 39 (July–Sept. 1969), 30–40.
Subj 12.1 32 64 ▪ 12 66

11130 CSH P P2 G4.3 1949–1972
Lo, J. P. (Lo Jung-pang), 1912–.
'Five years of the Sinkiang-Uighur Autonomous Region, 1955–1960.'
CQ 8 (Oct.–Dec. 1961), 92–105.
Subj 12.1 24.1 ▪ 14.4 21.2 34.1

11131 CSH P P1 G3.0 1949–1972
Lo, J. P. (Lo Jung-pang), 1912–.
'Propaganda.' In *A regional handbook on the Inner Mongolia Autonomous Region*, compiled by Far Eastern and Russian Institute, U. of Washington. [Selective entry]
New Haven: Human Relations Area Files, 1956, 466–488. (HRAF subcontractor's monographs, 60; Washington 7)
Subj 12.1 32.1 ▪ 17

11132 CSH U P2 G1.2 1949–1972
MacFarquhar, Emily.
China: Mao's last leap.
London: Economist, 1968. 24 p. (Economist briefs, 6)
Subj 12.1 32 64 ▪ 25 35 54

11133 CSU P P3 G1.2 1949–1972
MacFarquhar, Roderick Lemonde, 1930–.
'Criticism and counter-criticism in China: Effects of the "rectification" movement.'
World today 13, 11 (Nov. 1957), 489–498.
Subj 12.1 16.1

11134 CSU PO P1 G9.4 1949–1972
Mancall, Mark, 1932–.
'Taiwan, island of resignation and despair.' In *Formosa today*, edited by M. Mancall. [Selective entry]
New York: Praeger, 1964, 1–42 [s.p.].
Subj 12 12.1 16 ▪ 14 16.1 22.2

11135 CSH O P3 G5.1 1949–1972
Marsouin, Jacques, and Thérèse Marsouin.
Nous avons enseigné en Chine populaire (We taught in the People's Republic of China).
Paris: Table ronde, 1966. 220 p.
Subj 12.1 17 64 66 ▪ 12.2 13 16 16.1 28 41 55

11136 MCH P P1 G1.2 1949–1972
Mehnert, Klaus, 1906–.
'Pekings Kampf gegen die Rechtsopposition im Sommer 1957' (Peking's struggle against rightist opposition in the summer of 1957).
Osteuropa 7, 11 (Nov. 1957), 800–811.
Subj 12.1 32 ▪ 16.1 64

11137 MCH P P2 G1.2 1949–1972
Mei Ko-wang.
'Police system under the Chinese Communist regime.'
IS 2, 2 (Nov. 1965), 31–41.
Subj 12.1

11138 CSU F P2 G9.4 1949–1972
Mendel, Douglas Heusted, Jr., 1921–.
The politics of Formosan nationalism.
Berkeley, Los Angeles: U. of California Press, 1970. 315 p.
Subj 12.1 14 18 22.2 32.1 32.2 ▪ 12 14.4 15 16.1 17 21 24.1 24.2 32

11139 CSU P P1 G1.2 1949–1972
Meserve, Walter J-, and Ruth I- Meserve.
'China's persecuted playwrights: The theatre in Communist China's current Cultural Revolution.'
JAAS 5, 3 (July 1970), 209–215.
Subj 12.1 16.1 31 ▪ 32.1

11140 MCH O P2 G1.2 1949–1972
Mills, Harriet Cornelia, 1920–.
'Thought reform: Ideological remolding in China.'
Atlantic monthly 204, 6 (Dec. 1959), 71–77. [Special issue: *Red China: The first ten years*]
Subj 12.1 61

11141 MCH S P3 G1.2 1949–1972
Montader, Pierre.
'Les séquelles de la période "libérale" en Chine' (The aftereffects of the 'liberal' period in China).
Saturne 4, 18 (avr.–mai 1958), 11–20.
Subj 12.1 16.1

11142 MCH P P4 G1.2 1949–1972
Montell, Sherwin Theodore, 1929–.
'The San-fan Wu-fan [Three-Anti Five-Anti] movement in Communist China.'
PC 8 (Feb. 1954), 136–196.
Subj 12 12.1 16.2 32.1 34.2 ▪ 36.4 47 54 61

11143 NNC P P2 G9.2 1949–1972
Moss, William W-, III.
Localism in Communist China, with special reference to Kwang-tung province.
Unpublished masters thesis in Political Science, Columbia U., 1965. 112 p.
Subj 12.1 22.1 29 ▪ 22 24 24.1

11144 NNC O P2 G1.2 1949–1972
Nossal, Frederick, 1927–.
Dateline Peking.
New York: Harcourt, Brace and World, 1962. 224 p.
Subj 12.1 18 64 ▪ 14 15 28 30 60 66

11145 MCY P P4 G1.2 1949–1972
Oliver, Adam.
'Perspectives on the intellectual in Communist China: Rectification of Mainland China intellectuals, 1964–65.'
AS 5, 10 (Oct. 1965), 475–490.
SUBJ 12.1 16.1 36.1 ▪ 60

11146 MCY P P1 G1.2 1949–1972
Pak, Hyobom, 1926–.
'Chinese politics: The nature of its "mass image" technique.'
AS 5, 4 (Apr. 1965), 197–206.
SUBJ 12.1 64 ▪ 62

11147 CSH U P2 G4.5 1949–1972
Patterson, George Neilson, 1920–.
'The situation in Tibet.'
CQ 6 (Apr.–June 1961), 81–86.
SUBJ 12.1 18 ▪ 13 32.1 32.2

11148 CSU P P2 G1.2 1949–1972
Powell, Ralph Lorin, 1917–, and Chong-kun Yoon, 1931–.
'Public security and the PLA.'
AS 12, 12 (Dec. 1972), 1082–1100.
SUBJ 12.1 15 ▪ 12.2 19 21.2 32.1 54

11149 CSU O P1 G1.2 1949–1972
Rádvanyi, János, 1922–.
'The Hungarian revolution [of 1956] and the Hundred Flowers campaign.'
CQ 43 (July–Sept. 1970), 121–129.
SUBJ 12.1 16.1 ▪ 32.1 64

11150 CSH P P4 G1.1 1949–1972
Rea, Kenneth W-.
'The Five-Anti campaign in Communist China.'
Asian forum 3, 2 (Apr.–June 1971), 81–94.
SUBJ 12.1 16.2 22.2 34.2 ▪ 14.5 32.1 57

11151 MCH P P1 G1.2 1949–1972
Reinhart, Rainer.
'Das Musikleben in Rotchina' (Musical life in Red China).
Stimmen der Zeit 3. Folge 166, 9 (Juni 1960), 226–232.
SUBJ 12.1 31 ▪ 65

11152 MCH P P1 G1.2 1949–1972
Rich, Doris.
'Who will carry on? The search for red heirs.'
CS 3, 12 (1 Feb. 1965), 1–12.
SUBJ 12.1 17

11153 MCH O P2 G1.2 1949–1972
Ricoeur, Paul, 1913–.
'Certitudes et incertitudes d'une révolution' (Certainties and uncertainties of a revolution).
Esprit 24, 234 (jan. 1956), 5–28.
SUBJ 12 12.1 ▪ 16 23 63 64

11154 NNC P P1 G1.2 1949–1972
Rifkin, Sylvia Beatrice, 1938–.
The 1951 Resist-America–Aid-Korea campaign in Communist China.
Unpublished masters thesis in Public Law and Government, Columbia U., 1963. 120 p. [Certificate essay, East Asian Institute]
SUBJ 12.1 32 66 ▪ 14.5 19 30

11155 NNC P P2 G1.2 1949–1972
Sidikhmenov, Vasilii IAkovlevich, 1912–.
'Bor'ba za sotsialisticheskuiu ideologiiu v Kitae' (The struggle for socialist ideology in China).
SK 1958, 1, 81–91.
SUBJ 12.1 32.1 64 ▪ 14 16 18

11156 CSH P P2 G1.3 1949–1972
Stanford U. China Project.
'Public order and safety.' In *Central South China*, compiled by the organization cited. [Selective entry]
New Haven: Human Relations Area Files, 1956, vol. 2, 495–522. (HRAF subcontractor's monographs, 28; Stanford 2)
SUBJ 12.1 ▪ 12.2

11157 CSH P P2 G1.3 1949–1972
Stanford U. China Project.
'Public order and safety.' In *East China*, compiled by the organization cited. [Selective entry]
New Haven: Human Relations Area Files, 1956, vol. 2, 547–577. (HRAF subcontractor's monographs, 29; Stanford 3)
SUBJ 12.1 ▪ 12.2

11158 CSH P P2 G5.0 1949–1972
Stanford U. China Project.
'Public order and safety.' In *North China*, compiled by the organization cited. [Selective entry]
New Haven: Human Relations Area Files, 1956, vol. 2, 536–565. (HRAF subcontractor's monographs, 27; Stanford 1)
SUBJ 12.1 ▪ 12.2

11159 NNC P P2 G8.0 1949–1972
Stanford U. China Project.
'Public order and safety.' In *Southwest China*, compiled by the organization cited. [Selective entry]
New Haven: Human Relations Area Files, 1956, vol. 2, 539–564. (HRAF subcontractor's monographs, 30; Stanford 4)
SUBJ 12.1 ▪ 12.2

11160 MAM P P2 G1.2 1949–1972
Sung, Chao-sheng, 1935–.
Power politics in Communist China, 1959–1966.
Ann Arbor: University Microfilms (Publ. 70-27,088), 1971. 172 p. (Doctoral dissertation in Political Science, George Washington U.)
SUBJ 12.1 16.1 32 35 ▪ 15 25 64

11161 MSW P P2 G4.3 1949–1972
Tai, Ching-ling.
A study of Communist expansion and policy toward Sinkiang-Uighur.
Unpublished masters thesis in Asian Studies, Washington U., 1967. 117 p.
SUBJ 12.1 14.4 21.2 32.1 ▪ 17 21.4 24.1 34.1 35

11162 CSH P P2 G2.0 1949–1972
Tang, Peter S. H. (T'ang Sheng-hao), 1919–.
'Propaganda.' In *A regional handbook on Northeast China*, compiled by Far Eastern and Russian Institute, U. of Washington. [Selective entry]
New Haven: Human Relations Area Files, 1956, 438–455. (HRAF subcontractor's monographs, 61; Washington 9)
SUBJ 12.1 ▪ 17 22.1

11163 MMT S P1 G1.2 1949–1972
Travert, André.
'The attitude of the Communist Party toward China's cultural legacy.' In *Symposium on economic and social problems of the Far East*, edited by Edward Franciszek Szczepanik. [Selective entry]
Hong Kong: Hong Kong U. Press, 1962, 353–368.
SUBJ 12.1 62 64 ▪ 32.1

11164 MCH F P2 G1.1 1949–1972
Tu Ling.
'A survey of public opinion on the Chinese Mainland.'
CCA 2, 2 (Apr. 1965), 39–55.
SUBJ 12.1 18 ▪ 11.2 21.4 28 56

11165 MCH P P1 G1.2 1949–1972
Uhalley, Stephen, Jr., 1930–.
'The Cultural Revolution and the attack on the "Three family village".'
CQ 27 (July–Sept. 1966), 149–161.
SUBJ 12.1 ▪ 16.1

11166 CSH P P1 G9.4 1949–1972
Uhalley, Stephen, Jr., 1930–.
'Taiwan's response to the Cultural Revolution.'
AS 7, 11 (Nov. 1967), 824–829.
SUBJ 12.1 16.1 ▪ 12

11167 CSU P P2 G1.2 1949–1972
U.S. Congress. House of Representatives. Committee on Un-American Activities.
'Intellectual freedom, Red China style' [testimony of Huang Chi-chou, 24–25 May 1962]. In *Hearings of the 87th Congress, 2nd session*, compiled by the agency cited. [Sole entry]
Washington, D.C.: U.S. Government Printing Office, 1962, 1165–1234.
SUBJ 12.1 32.2

11168 CSU P P2 G1.2 1949–1972
U.S. Congress. Senate. Committee on Foreign Relations.
Tensions in Communist China: An analysis of internal pressures generated since 1949. [Prepared by Legislative Reference Service, U.S. Library of Congress.]
Washington, D.C.: U.S. Government Printing Office, 1960. 73 p. (86th Congress, 1st session, Senate Documents, 66)
SUBJ 12.1 32 ▪ 16.1 17 32.2

11169 MCH U P2 G1.2 1949–1972
Varnai, Ugo.
'La nuova Cina' (New China).
Comunità 13, 67 (febbraio 1959), 25–45.
SUBJ 12.1 ▪ 12 14 14.1 16.1

11170 CSH P P2 G1.2 1949–1972
Wang Hsiao-tang.
'Operation of Chinese Communist security network.'
CCA 3, 1 (Feb. 1966), 19–31.
SUBJ 12.1 12.2 ▪ 11.2 22.1 22.2 32.1

11171 CSH P P2 G1.2 1949–1972
Wang Shao-lan.
'Workers' and peasants' propaganda teams and educational reform on the Mainland.'
CCA 6, 2 (Apr. 1969), 20–28.
SUBJ 12.1 17 ▪ 16

11172 NIC P P2 G1.2 1949–1972
Wittfogel, Karl August, 1896–.
'Forced labor in Communist China.'
Problems of Communism 5, 4 (July–Aug. 1956), 32–42.
SUBJ 11.4 12.1 12.2 ▪ 61

11173 CSH U P2 G5.4 1949–1972
Wu Chih-p'u, 1906–.
'Several experiences in thoroughly implementing the line of taking agriculture as the foundation in developing the national economy.' Tr. of 'Kuan ch'e ch'ih hsing fa chan kuo min ching chi i nung yeh wei chi ch'u ti fang chen ti chi tien ching yen'; *Hung ch'i* 1960, 18 (16 Sept.), 1–6. In *Translations from 'Hung-ch'i' (Red flag) (Peiping, No. 18, 16 September 1960)*, mimeo., compiled by U.S. Joint Publications Research Service. [Selective entry]
Washington, D.C.: JPRS, 31 Oct. 1960, 1–10. (JPRS 6184; MC 18,973/1960)
SUBJ 12.1 21.4 ▪ 14 24.1 24.4 26.4

11174 NNC P P2 G1.2 1949–1972
[Yang] I-fan.
'Cultural activities.' Tr. of '1955 nien Chung kung ti wen hua huo tung' (Cultural activities in Communist China, 1955); *Tsu kuo chou k'an* 159 (16 Jan. 1956), 38–41. In *Communist China, 1955*, edited by Union Research Institute. [Selective entry]
Hong Kong: Union Research Institute, 1956, 157–167.
SUBJ 12.1 16.1 64 ▪ 13 62

11175 MCH P P2 G1.2 1949–1972
Yee, Frank S. H. (I Hsiu-hao), 1904–.
'Chinese Communist police and courts.'
J. of criminal law, criminology and police science 48, 1 (May–June 1957), 83–92.
SUBJ 12.1 12.2

11176 NIC P P2 G1.2 1949–1972
Yu, Frederick T. C. (Yü Te-chi), 1921–.
'Communications and politics in Communist China.' In *Communications and political development*, edited by Lucian Wilmot Pye. [Sole entry]
Princeton: Princeton U. Press, 1963, 259–297. (Princeton studies in political development, 1)
SUBJ 12.1 14.2 64 ▪ 11.4 12 16.3 17 32.1 61

11177 MCH P P1 G1.2 1949–1972
Yu, Frederick T. C. (Yü Te-chi), 1921–.
'How the Chinese Reds transfer mass grievances into power.'
Journalism q. 30, 3 (Summer 1953), 354–364.
SUBJ 12.1 64 ▪ 17 32 32.1

11178 NNC P P2 G1.2 1949–1972
Yu, Frederick T. C. (Yü Te-chi), 1921–.
Mass persuasion in Communist China.
New York: Praeger, 1964. 186 p.
SUBJ 12.1 14.2 64 ▪ 31 32

11179 NNC P P1 G1.2 1949–1972
Yu, Frederick T. C. (Yü Te-chi), 1921–.
The propaganda machine in Communist China, with special reference to ideology, policy and regulations, as of 1952.
Lackland Air Force Base, San Antonio, Tex.: U.S. Air Force Personnel and Training Research Center, Air Research and Development Command, 1955. 18, 79 p. (U.S. Human Resources Research Institute research memoranda, 37; Studies in Chinese Communism, series 1, 3, 1952)
SUBJ 12.1 14.2 32 ▪ 30 54

11180 NNC P P2 G1.2 1949–1972
Yu, Frederick T. C. (Yü Te-chi), 1921–.
The strategy and tactics of Chinese Communist propaganda as of 1952.
Lackland Air Force Base, San Antonio, Tex.: U.S. Air Force Personnel and Training Research Center, Air Research and Development Command, 1955. 15, 70 p. (U.S. Human Resources Research Institute research memoranda, 39; Studies in Chinese Communism, series 2, 3, 1952)
SUBJ 12.1 16 64 ▪ 14.1 14.2 17 32 47

12.2 NATIONAL LEGAL SYSTEM
司法制度 司法制度

1644-1911

11181 CSU F P2 G1.2 1895–1911
'The progress of the anti-opium movement among the Chinese.'
CR 39, 3 (Mar. 1908), 143–153.
SUBJ 12.2 22.2 ▪ 22 24.1 24.3 55 56

11182 MCH P P1 G1.2 1895–1911
'Les travaux de la constitution chinoise' (The [preparatory] work on the Chinese constitution).
AF 8, 84 (mars 1908), 112–116.
SUBJ 12 12.2

11183 ELB P P1 G1.2 1644–1895
Alabaster, Ernest, 1872–?
Notes and commentaries on Chinese criminal law and cognate topics, with special relation to ruling cases.
London: Luzak, 1899. 72, 677 p. [Reprinted—Taipei: Ch'eng-wen, 1968. 72, 677 p.]
SUBJ 12 12.2 ▪ 40 63 64

11184 NIC P P1 G1.2 –1911
Alabaster, Ernest, 1872–?
'Notes on Chinese law and practice preceding revision.'
JRAS-NCB new (2nd) series 37 (1906), 83–149. [Separately reprinted—Shanghai: Shanghai Mercury Press, 1906. 87 p.]
SUBJ 12.2 ▪ 12.1 63

11185 NNC PO P2 G1.3 1895–1911
Betz, Heinrich.
'China, 1907–1908' (China, 1907–1908).
Jahrbuch der Internationalen Vereinigung für vergleichende Rechtswissenschaft 8, 2, Part 4 (1910), 3119–3177.
SUBJ 12 12.2 ▪ 12.1 14.2 14.3 14.6 15 34.2

11186 NNC PO P4 G1.2 1895–1911
Betz, Heinrich.
'China, 1908–1910' (China, 1908–1910).
Jahrbuch der Internationalen Vereinigung für vergleichende Rechtswissenschaft 9, 2, Part 3 (1914), 1223–1327.
SUBJ 12 12.2 14 ▪ 12.1 14.5 14.6 22 22.1 34.2

11187 NNC PO P1 G1.3 1895–1911
Betz, Heinrich.
'Die chinesische Gerichtsverfassung nach dem Edikt vom 7. Febr. 1910' (Chinese judicial organization according to the edict of 7 February 1910).
BVRV 6, 7 (Jan. 1911), 193–202.
SUBJ 12.2 ▪ 12 22.2

11188 MCH P P1 G1.2 1895–1911
Betz, Heinrich.
'Chinesische Strafrechtsfälle' (Chinese criminal law cases).
ZVR 21, 3 (1908), 393–424.
SUBJ 12.2 ▪ 22.2 41 47 63

11189 NNC P P1 G1.2 1895–1911
Betz, Heinrich.
'Ein chinesisches Staatsangehörigkeitsgesetz' (A Chinese citizenship law).
BVRV 5, 5 (Nov. 1909), 129–134.
SUBJ 12.1 12.2 ▪ 12 41 47 66

11190 NNC P P1 G1.2 1895–1911
Betz, Heinrich.
'Neue chinesische Gesetzgebung' (Recent Chinese legislation).
BVRV 4, 2 – 6, 9 (Mai 1908 – März 1910), 37 p. in all.
SUBJ 12.1 12.2 ▪ 12 14.3 22.2 30 34.2

11191 NNC PO P1 G1.2 1895–1911
Betz, Heinrich.
'Die Verfassungsfrage in China' (The constitutional question in China).
BVRV 5, 1 (Apr. 1909), 1–9.
SUBJ 12 12.2 32 ▪ 12.1 14.5 16.1

11192 NNC P P4 G1.2 1895–1911
Betz, Heinrich.
'Die Verwaltungsreformen in China: Die Justizbehörden' (Administrative reforms in China: The judiciary).
MSOSB 12 (1909), 32–48.
SUBJ 12.2 ▪ 22.2

11193 NIC P P1 G1.2 1895–1911
Bevan, L- R- O-.
Constitution building in China.
Shanghai: North-China Daily News and Herald, 1910. 57 p.
SUBJ 12 12.2 ▪ 64

11194 MCH O P2 G1.2 –1895
[Bichurin, Nikita Iakovlevich] *Otets* Iakinf, 1777–1853.
Kitai v grazhdanskom i nravstvennom sostoianii (The civil and moral state of China).
St. Petersburg: Tip. Shtaba voenno-ucheb. zavedenii, 1848. 4 vols. 33, 137; 128, 10; 152; 177 p. [Reprinted—Peking: Rossiiskaia dukhovnaia missiia, 1911–1912. 4 vols. 84; 62; 75; 89 p.] [For a partial tr. by Emmanuel Golitzin (vol. 4, p. 54–67 only), see 'Du chamanisme en Chine' (Shamanism in China); *Nouvelles annales des voyages* 130 (1851), 287–306.]
SUBJ 12 12.2 14 17 18 40 ▪ 13 16.1 23 33 34.2 41 50 53 55 57

11195 CSU P P1 G1.2 –1895
Bodde, Derk, 1909–, and Clarence Morris, 1903–.
Law in Imperial China.

Cambridge: Harvard U. Press, 1967. 615 p. (Harvard studies in East Asian law, 1)
SUBJ 12.1 12.2 63 64 ▪ 16 22.2 41 44 45 46 57

11196 MCH O P4 G1.2 1895–1911
Bone, C-.
'Chinese prisons and the treatment of prisoners.'
EAM 5 (1906), 282–291.
SUBJ 12.2

11197 MCY P P1 G1.2 –1911
Bonnichon, André, 1905–, and François Xavier Yong-tai Tcheng (Cheng Yung-t'ai).
'Le conflit de lois dans le droit chinois ancien' (The conflict of laws in ancient Chinese law).
BUA 3e série 4, 13 (1943), 215–235.
SUBJ 12.2 66 ▪ 22.2 45

11198 CSU P P1 G1.2 –1911
Bünger, Karl A-, 1903–.
'Max Webers Ansichten über Recht und Justiz im kaiserlichen China' (Max Weber's observations on law and justice in Imperial China).
OE 19, 1/2 (Dez. 1972), 9–22.
SUBJ 12.2 64 71 ▪ 12 13

11199 NIC P P1 G1.1 –1911
Bünger, Karl A-, 1903–.
'The punishment of lunatics and negligents according to classical Chinese law.'
Studia Serica 9, Part 2 (1950), 1–16.
SUBJ 12.2 ▪ 16 56 61

11200 CSU S P1 G1.2 –1911
Chen, Fu-mei Chang (Ch'en Chang Fu-mei), 1938–.
Review of *Law in Imperial China*, by Derk Bodde and Clarence Morris.
HJAS 29 (1969), 274–284.
SUBJ 12 12.2

11201 CSU P P1 G1.2 1644–1911
Chen, Fu-mei Chang (Ch'en Chang Fu-mei), 1938–.
'On analogy in Ch'ing law.'
HJAS 30 (1970), 212–224.
SUBJ 12.2

11202 MCH P P1 G1.2 1644–1911
Chen, Fu-mei Chang (Ch'en Chang Fu-mei), 1938–.
Private code commentaries in the development of Ch'ing law (1644–1911).
Unpublished doctoral dissertation in History and Far Eastern Languages, Harvard U., 1970. 272 p.
SUBJ 12.2 50 ▪ 12 16.1 70

11203 NIC P P2 G1.2 –1911
Ch'ü, T'ung-tsu.
Law and society in traditional China. Tr. by T'ung-tsu Ch'ü of *Chung-kuo fa lü yü Chung-kuo she hui* (Law and society in China); Shanghai: Shang wu yin shu kuan, 1947; 259 p. [Rev. and enl. in tr.]
The Hague: Mouton, 1961. 304 p. (Ecole pratique des hautes études de Sorbonne, Sixième section [sciences économiques et sociales], Le monde d'outre-mer, passe et present, Etudes, 1er série, 4) [Reprinted—New York: Humanities Press, 1965. 304 p.]
SUBJ 12.2 16 40 41 45 64 ▪ 12 13 42 55 57 63

11204 MCH P P1 G1.2 1895–1911
Dareste de la Chavanne, Cléophas Madeleine Rudolphe, 1824–1911.
'Le droit en Chine' (Law in China).
J. des savants 66 (sept. 1901), 529–541.
SUBJ 12.2 ▪ 41 45

11205 MCH O P1 G1.2 1895–1911
Enjoy, Paul d', 1866–?
'Pénalités chinoises' (Chinese penalties).
Bulletins et mémoires de la Société d'anthropologie de Paris 5e série 6 (1905), 247–251.
SUBJ 12.2 ▪ 63

11206 MCH O P1 G1.2 1895–1911
Enjoy, Paul d', 1866–?
'Le témoignage en Chine' (Testimony in China).
R. internationale de sociologie 4, 6 (juin 1896), 460–464.
SUBJ 12.2 ▪ 63

11207 MCH S P1 G1.1 –1911
Escarra, Jean, 1885–1955.
'La conception chinoise du droit' (The Chinese concept of law).
Archives de philosophie du droit et de sociologie juridique 1/2 (1935), 7–73.
SUBJ 12.2 62 ▪ 63 64

11208 NIC P P1 G1.2 –1911
Escarra, Jean, 1885–1955.
'Western methods of research into Chinese law.'
CSPSR 8, 1 (Jan. 1924), 227–248.
SUBJ 12.2 ▪ 71

11209 NNC P P1 G1.3 1895–1911
Franke, Otto, 1863–1946.
'Die staatsrechtliche Entwicklung in China seit 1901' (Constitutional development in China since 1901).
Jahrbuch des öffentlichen Rechts der Gegenwart 6 (1912), 503–529.
SUBJ 12.1 12.2 32 ▪ 15 17 64

11210 MCH P P1 G1.1 –1895
Franke, Otto, 1863–1946.
'Zur Geschichte der Exterritorialität in China' (History of extraterritoriality in China).
Sitzungsberichte der Philosophische-historische Klasse der Preussischen Akademie der Wissenschaften 31 (1935), 1–63. [Special issue]
SUBJ 12.2 66 ▪ 14.3 22.2

11211 NNC P P1 G1.2 –1895
Gardner, Christopher Thomas, 1842–1914.
'Chinese laws and customs.'
JRAS new (2nd) series 15, 2 (1883), 221–236.
SUBJ 12.2 ▪ 22.2 40 41 45

11212 NIC U P1 G1.2 –1911
Gen, Lewis.
'Some characteristics of the ancient Chinese law.'
Asiatic review new (4th) series 48, 174 (Apr. 1952), 156–160; 48, 175 (July 1952), 233–240.
SUBJ 12.2 ▪ 16 41

11213 MCH P P2 G1.1 1842–1895
Gundry, Richard Simpson, 1838–?
'Judicial torture in China.'
Fortnightly review 53, 279 (Mar. 1890), 404–420.
SUBJ 12.2 63 ▪ 12.1

11214 NIC P P1 G1.2 1644–1911
Harrison, Judy Feldman.
'Wrongful treatment of prisoners: A case study of Ch'ing legal practice.'
JAS 23, 2 (Feb. 1964), 227–244.
SUBJ 12 12.2

11215 NNC P P4 G1.3 1895–1911
Holzhauer, Fritz.
'Die Personalfrage der höheren Justizbeamten an den neuen chinesischen Gerichten' (The problem of staffing upper-echelon positions in the new Chinese courts).
DCR 1 (1911), 49–57.
SUBJ 12.2 17 ▪ 12

11216 CSU P P1 G1.1 –1911
Hsu Dau-lin (Hsü Tao-lin), 1906–.
'Crime and cosmic order.'
HJAS 30 (1970), 111–125.
SUBJ 12.2 62

11217 CSU P P1 G1.2 –1895
Hsu Dau-lin (Hsü Tao-lin), 1906–.
Review of *Law in Imperial China*, by Derk Bodde and Clarence Morris.
THJ new (2nd) series 8, 1/2 (Aug. 1970), 476–487.
SUBJ 12.2

11218 NNC P P1 G1.2 –1895
Jamieson, George, 1843–1920.
'Cases in Chinese criminal law.'
China review 10, 6 (May–June 1882), 357–365.
SUBJ 12.2 41 ▪ 22.2 44 47 63

11219 CSU P P1 G1.2 –1911
Kennedy, George Alexander, 1901–.
Die Rolle des Geständnisses im chinesischen Gesetz (The role of the confession in Chinese law).
Berlin: The author, 1939. 74 p. (Doctoral dissertation, Philosophische Fakultät, Universität Berlin)
SUBJ 12.2 63 64

11220 NNC P P1 G1.2 –1895
Kohler, Josef, 1848–1919.
'Aus dem chinesischen Civilrecht' (Aspects of Chinese civil law).
ZVR 6, 3 (1886), 351–387.
SUBJ 12.2 41 ▪ 14.1 14.6 45 47 48 52 54

11221 CBU P P1 G1.2 1644–1911
Kohler, Josef, 1848–1919.
'Das chinesische Strafgesetzbuch' (The Chinese penal code).
ZVR 20, 1 (1907), 1–13.
SUBJ 12.2 41

11222 MCH P P1 G1.1 –1895
Kohler, Josef, 1849–1919.
Das chinesische Strafrecht (Chinese criminal law).
Würzburg: Oskar Stahel, 1886. 51 p.
SUBJ 12.2 ▪ 12.1 22.2 41

11223 GBF S P1 G1.2 1842–1895
Kohler, Josef, 1849–1919.
'Über das chinesische Recht' (Chinese law). In *Rechtsvergleichende Studien über islamitisches Recht, das Recht der*

Berber, das chinesische Recht und das Recht auf Ceylon (Comparative studies of Islamic, Berber, Chinese, and Ceylonese law). [Sole entry]
Berlin: Carl Heymann, 1889, 177–208.
SUBJ 12.2 ▪ 34.3 41 43 45

11224 MCH P P1 G1.3 –1911
Kroker, Eduard Josef M-, 1913–.
'Der Revolutionsgedanke im alten chinesischen Recht' (The concept of revolution in traditional Chinese law).
ZDMG 101 (1951), 341–351.
SUBJ 12.2 64 ▪ 12 63

11225 NNC S P2 G1.2 –1911
Lee, Orlan.
'Traditionelle chinesische "Rechtsgebräuche" und der Begriff "Orientalischer Despotismus"' (Traditional Chinese 'legal practices' and the concept of 'Oriental despotism').
ZVR 66, 1 (Jan. 1964), 157–177.
SUBJ 12.1 12.2 71 ▪ 12 62 64

11226 MCH P P1 G1.2 –1911
Lo, Pan-hui.
'A study of Chinese jurisprudence.'
Illinois law review 6, 7 (Feb. 1912), 456–476; 6, 8 (Mar. 1912), 518–533. (Masters thesis in Political Science, U. of Chicago, 1911)
SUBJ 12.2 ▪ 12 14.1 41

11227 NNC P P1 G1.2 –1895
MacGowan, Daniel Jerome, 1814?–1893.
'On the banishment of criminals in China.'
JRAS-NCB 3 (Dec. 1859), 293–301.
SUBJ 12.2 ▪ 11.2 22.2

11228 FPN O P3 G1.1 1842–1895
Martin, Charles Ernest, 1831–1897.
'Le châtiment et les supplices chez les Chinois' (Punishment and torture among the Chinese).
Science moderne 7, 50 (16 déc. 1893), 392–394.
SUBJ 12.2 ▪ 52

11229 CBU O P3 G5.1 1895–1911
Matignon, Jean-Jacques, 1866–?
'La sanction pénale en Chine' (Criminal sanctions in China). In *Dix ans aux pays du dragon* (Ten years in the lands of the dragon), by J.-J. Matignon. [Selective entry]
Paris: Maloine, 1910, 247–272.
SUBJ 12.2

11230 NIC P P1 G1.2 1895–1911
Meijer, Marinus Johan.
The introduction of modern criminal law in China.
Batavia: De Unie, 1950. 214 p. (Sinica Indonesiana, 2) (Doctoral dissertation, Faculteit der Geneeskunde, Universiteit van Indonesie) [Reprinted—Hong Kong: Lung Men, 1967. 214 p.]
SUBJ 12 12.2 41 64 ▪ 40 66

11231 CBU P P1 G9.5 1842–1895
Norton-Kyshe, James William.
The history of the laws and courts of Hong Kong.
Hong Kong: Noronha; London: Unwin, 1898. 2 vols. 28, 740; 637 p. [Reprinted—Hong Kong: Vetch and Lee, 1971. 2 vols. 28, 740; 647 p.]
SUBJ 12.2 61 ▪ 32.2 66

11232 MCH FP P2 G9.4 1895–1911
Okamatsu, Santaro (Okamatsu Santarō), 1871–1921, comp.
Provisional report on investigation of laws and customs in the island of Formosa. Tr. from the Japanese.
Kobe: Kobe Herald, 1900? 155 p.
SUBJ 12.2 24.1 24.5 41 45 ▪ 12 21.1 24.6 42

11233 NIC S P1 G1.2 –1911
Parker, Edward Harper, 1849–1926.
'The principles of Chinese law and equity.'
JRAS-NCB new (2nd) series 40 (1909), 10–43.
SUBJ 12.2 62 ▪ 63 64

11234 MCH P P1 G1.2 –1911
Pelliot, Paul, 1878–1945.
'Notes de bibliographie chinoise: le droit chinois' (Bibliographic notes on China: Chinese law).
BEFEO 9, 1 (1909), 123–152.
SUBJ 12.2 72 ▪ 70 71

11235 MCH P P1 G1.2 1644–1911
Rheinbaden, Rochus Albrecht Krenzwendedich, 1893–.
Chinesische Verfassung 1900–1917 (Constitutional developments in China, 1900–1917).
Berlin: R. v. Decker, 1917. 11, 93 p.
SUBJ 12 12.2 32 64 ▪ 12.1 63

11236 NNC P P1 G1.2 1895–1911
Romberg, ———.
'Die Konkurrenz im chinesischen Strafgesetzbuch' (Concurrent sentences in the Chinese penal code).
DCR 1 (1911), 22–30, 59–63.
SUBJ 12.2

11237 NNC U P1 G2.3 1895–1911
Siebert, F-.
'Justizreform in der Provinz Mukden' (Judicial reform in Fengtien).
MSOSB 12 (1909), 94–109.
SUBJ 12.2

11238 MCH P P3 G1.2 1895–1911
Sun, E-tu Zen (Sun Jen I-tu), 1921–.
'The Chinese constitutional missions of 1905–1906.'
J. of modern history 24, 3 (Sept. 1952), 251–268.
SUBJ 12.2 66 ▪ 12 16.1 59 64

11239 MCY P P1 G1.2 –1911
Tcheng, François Xavier Yong-tai (Cheng Yung-t'ai).
'Obligations naturelles dans les droits français, allemand, suisse et chinois' (Imperfect obligations in French, German, Swiss, and Chinese law).
BUA 3e série 3, 10 (1942), 330–375.
SUBJ 12.2 60 ▪ 14.6 22.2 45 47

11240 MCH P P1 G1.2 1895–1911
Tsai, Chutung.
'Chinese nationality law, 1909.'
American j. of international law 4, 2 (Apr. 1910), 404–411.
SUBJ 12.1 12.2 ▪ 16 66

11241 MCH P P2 G1.1 –1911
Tschou Tso-Tschun (Chou Tse-ch'un), 1883–.
Die Reformen des chinesischen Reiches in Verfassung, Verwaltung und Rechtsprechung (Constitutional, administrative, and judicial reforms in the Chinese empire).
Berlin: Emil Ebering, 1909. 91 p. (Doctoral dissertation, Juristische Fakultät, Universität Berlin)
SUBJ 12 12.2 15 16.1 32 ▪ 12.1 14.5 17 19 64 66 72

11242 CSU P P1 G1.1 –1895
[Valk, Marius Hendrikus van der] Marc H. van der Valk, 1908–.
Review of *Law in Imperial China*, by Derk Bodde and Clarence Morris.
MS 28 (1969), 471–474.
SUBJ 12.2

11243 MCH P P2 G1.2 1644–1911
van der Sprenkel, Sybille Marie, 1919–.
Legal institutions in Manchu China: A sociological analysis.
London: Athlone Press, 1962. 178 p. (London School of Economics, Monographs on Social Anthropology, 24) (Revision of *A sociological analysis of Chinese legal institutions, with special reference to the Ch'ing period, 1644–1911*, masters thesis in Economics, U. of London [London School of Economics and Political Science], 1956)
SUBJ 12 12.1 12.2 22.2 42 64 ▪ 14.5 16.1 17 22 22.1 34.3 40 41 62 63

11244 CSH O P2 G1.2 1842–1895
Williams, Samuel Wells, 1812–1884.
'Administration of the laws.' In *The Middle Kingdom: A survey of the geography, government, literature, social life, arts, and history of the Chinese empire and its inhabitants*, rev. and enl. ed., by S. W. Williams. [Selective entry]
New York: Scribner, 1883, vol. 1, 448–518. [Reprinted in *The Middle Kingdom: A survey of the geography, government, literature, social life, arts, and history of the Chinese empire and its inhabitants*, by S. W. Williams. (Selective entry.) Taipei: Ch'eng-wen, 1965, 448–518 (s.p.)]
SUBJ 12.2 25 ▪ 12 16.1 22.2 32.2 59

11245 CSH PO P1 G1.2 1842–1895
Williams, Samuel Wells, 1812–1884.
'Laws of China, and plan of its government.' In *The Middle Kingdom: A survey of the geography, government, literature, social life, arts, and history of the Chinese empire and its inhabitants*, rev. and enl. ed., by S. W. Williams. [Selective entry]
New York: Scribner, 1883, vol. 1, 380–447. [Reprinted in *The Middle Kingdom: A survey of the geography, government, literature, social life, arts, and history of the Chinese empire and its inhabitants*, by S. W. Williams. (Selective entry.) Taipei: Ch'eng-wen, 1965, 380–447 (s.p.)]
SUBJ 12 12.2 ▪ 12.1 13 14.2 16 66

11246 NNC O P1 G1.3 1644–1911
Wu, Ting-fang, 1842–1922.
'Chinese jurisprudence.'
Proceedings of the New York State Bar Assn. 24 (Jan. 1901), 136–164.
SUBJ 12.2 ▪ 22.2

1644-1949

11247 CBU P P1 G1.2 1895–1928
'Die chinesische Verfassungsfrage 1913' (The Chinese constitutional question of 1913).
Jahrbuch des öffentlichen Rechts der Gegenwart 8 (1914), 513–521.
SUBJ 12 12.2 32 ▪ 13

11248 NNC P P1 G1.2 1644–1928
Betz, Heinrich, and Heinz Lautenschlager.
'China' (China). In *Rechtsvergleichendes Handwörterbuch für das Zivil- und Handelsrecht des In- und Auslandes* (Comparative dictionary of civil and commercial law of Germany and foreign countries), edited by Franz Schlegelberger. [Sole entry]
Berlin: Vahlen, 1927, vol. 1, 328–391.
SUBJ 12.2 14.3 41 ▪ 12 14.6 34.2 45 48 72

11249 NNC P P1 G1.2 1895–1928
Bevan, L- R- O-.
'China's constitutions.'
CSPSR 2, 4 (Dec. 1917), 89–126.
SUBJ 12 12.2 ▪ 12.1

11250 MCH P P1 G1.1 1644–1928
Bryan, Robert Thomas, 1892–.
An outline of Chinese civil law.
Shanghai: Commercial Press, 1925. 92 p.
SUBJ 12 12.2 34.2 40 ▪ 34.3 41 45 47 48

11251 NNC P P1 G1.2 1895–1949
Bünger, Karl A-, 1903–.
'Das neue chinesische BGB: Seine Entstehungsgeschichte und Systematik' (The evolution and structure of the new Chinese civil code).
Blätter für internationales Privatrecht 6, 11 (Nov. 1931), 257–267.
SUBJ 12.2 ▪ 22.2

11252 NNC S P1 G1.2 1895–1949
Bünger, Karl A-, 1903–.
'Die Rezeption des europäischen Rechts in China' (The reception of European law in China). In *Deutsche Landesreferate zum III. Internationalen Kongress für Rechtsvergleichung in London, 1950* (German reports given at the Third International Congress of Comparative Law, London, 1950), edited by Ernst Wolff. [Sole entry]
Berlin: de Gruyter, 1950, 166–189.
SUBJ 12.2 ▪ 22.2 41 66

11253 NNC PO P1 G1.2 1895–1928
Chang, I Pang.
'History of judicial reforms in China.'
CLR 1, 4 (Jan. 1923), 156–166.
SUBJ 12.2

11254 NIC P P1 G1.2 1895–1928
Chang, Yü-chüan (Chang Yü-ch'üan), 1880–.
'The Chinese judiciary.'
CSPSR 2, 4 (Dec. 1917), 68–88; 3, 1 (Mar. 1918), 1–30.
SUBJ 12.2

11255 NIC P P1 G1.2 –1949
Cheng, Chi-yu.
'Chinese theory of criminal law.'
J. of criminal law, criminology and police science 39, 31 (Sept.–Oct. 1948), 461–470.
SUBJ 12.2 22.2 ▪ 63

11256 CSH P P1 G1.2 –1949
Cheng, F. T. (Cheng T'ien-hsi), 1884–.
'A sketch of the history, philosophy, and reform of Chinese law.' In *Studies in the law of the Far East and Southeast Asia*, edited by George Washington U. Law School. [Selective entry]
Washington, D.C.: Washington Foreign Law Society, 1956, 29–45.
SUBJ 12.2

11257 FPN P P1 G1.1 1895–1949
Cheng Yen Cheng (Cheng Yen-ch'eng).
Les principaux mouvements constitutionnels en Chine, de 1887 à 1935 (The major constitutional movements in China from 1887 to 1935).
Lyons: Ferréol, 1936. 156 p. (Doctoral dissertation, Faculté de droit, Université de Dijon)
SUBJ 12.2 32 ▪ 12 12.1

11258 MCH P P1 G1.2 1895–1949
Chiang, Hai-chao (Chiang Hai-ch'ao).
Die Wandlungen im chinesischen Verfassungsrecht seit dem Zusammenbruch der Mandschu-Dynastie, unter besonderer Berücksichtigung der rechtlichen Stellung des Staatshauptes (The changes in Chinese constitutional law since the collapse of the Ch'ing dynasty, with special attention to the legal position of the chief of state).
Berlin: Carl Heymann, 1937. 14, 306 p. (Institut für ausländisches öffentliches Recht und Völkerrecht, Beiträge zum ausländischen öffentlichen Recht und Völkerrecht, 23) (Doctoral dissertation, Rechts- und staatswissenschaftliche Fakultät, Universität Frankfurt a.M.)
SUBJ 12 12.2 ▪ 12.1 13 15 32.2 62 72

11259 NNC PO P1 G1.2 1842–1928
Chin Wen-sze.
'A Chinese view of the foreign consular jurisdiction in China.'
CSPSR 1, 2 (July 1916), 4–20.
SUBJ 12.2 ▪ 66

11260 CSH P P2 G1.2 –1928
Engel'fel'd, Vladimir Viktorovich, 1891–1937.
'Ocherki gosudarstvennago prava Kitaia' (Notes on Chinese constitutional law).
Izvestiia IUridicheskogo fakul'teta v g. Kharbine 2 (1925), 1–254.
SUBJ 12 12.2 32 32.2 66 ▪ 15 22 34.3 41 64

11261 NNC P P1 G1.1 –1928
Escarra, Jean, 1885–1955.
Chinese law and comparative jurisprudence. Tr. from *Annuaire de l'Academie international de droit comparé* 1.
Tientsin: Lib. française, 1926. 35 p.
SUBJ 12.2 22.2 60 ▪ 40 63 64 70

11262 NNC P P1 G1.2 –1949
Escarra, Jean, 1888–1955.
'La codification contemporaine du droit privé chinois' (The contemporary codification of Chinese private law).
B. de la Société de législation comparée 59, 7/9 (juil.–sept. 1930), 407–445.
SUBJ 12.2 22.2 ▪ 41 62 64

11263 NIC PO P1 G1.2 –1949
Escarra, Jean, 1885–1955.
Le droit chinois: conception et évolution, institutions législatives et judiciaires, science et enseignement.
Peiping: Henri Vetch; Paris: Lib. du Recueil Sirey, 1936. 12, 559 p.
Chinese law: Conception and evolution, legislative and judicial institutions, science and teaching. Tr. by Gertrude R- Browne.
Cambridge: Harvard Law School, 1961. 696 p.
SUBJ 12 12.2 17 36.1 41 62 ▪ 14 16.2 32 34.2 45 47 63 64 72

11264 CSU P P1 G1.1 1644–1949
Escarra, Jean, 1885–1955.
'Le droit chinois moderne et son application par les tribunaux' (Modern Chinese law and its application by the courts).
Sinologica 1, 2 (1948), 97–107.
SUBJ 12.2 22.2 ▪ 41 45 63 70

11265 DLC O P2 G1.2 –1949
Escarra, Jean, 1885–1955.
'Loi et coutume en Chine' (Law and custom in China). In *Conférences de la Salle de travail d'ethnologie juridique, Faculté de droit de Paris, 1931*, by Henri Lévy-Bruhl et al. [Sole entry]
Paris: Ed. Domat-Montchrestien, 1931, 27–54. (Université de Paris, Faculté de droit, Salle de travail d'ethnologie juridique, Etudes de sociologie et d'ethnologie juridiques, 4)
SUBJ 12.2 22.2 62 64

11266 MCH P P1 G1.2 1842–1949
Fishel, Wesley Robert, 1919–.
The end of extraterritoriality in China.
Berkeley, Los Angeles: U. of California Press, 1952. 11, 318 p. (Revision of *The abolition of extraterritoriality in China*, doctoral dissertation in International Law and Relations, U. of Chicago, 1949)
SUBJ 12.2 66

11267 MCH S P1 G1.2 1895–1949
Hsia, Chin-lin, 1896–.
'Background and features of the draft constitution of China.'
IB 3, 10 (11 Apr. 1937), 95–237.
SUBJ 12 12.2 60 ▪ 15 17 22 63 66

11268 NNC O P4 G1.2 1895–1928
Hsu Chien (Hsü Ch'ien), 1872–?
'The court system of China.'
CLR 1, 1 (Apr. 1922), 3–8.
SUBJ 12.2 ▪ 12

11269 DLC S P1 G1.2 1895–1928
Kask, L- I-.
'Sun IAt-sen i vremennaia konstitutsiia Kitaiskoi respubliki 1912 g.' (Sun Yat-sen and the 1912 provisional constitution of the Republic of China).
UZLGU 255 (1958), 211–224.
SUBJ 12.2 ▪ 32 32.2

11270 MMT P P4 G1.1 1644–1928
Keeton, George Williams, 1902–.
The development of extraterritoriality in China.

London: Longmans, Green, 1928. 2 vols. 405; 422 p. [Reprinted—New York: Fertig, 1969. 2 vols. 405; 422 p.]
Subj 12.2 14.3 14.5 16.1 66 ▪ 12 12.1 18 22 22.2 33 34.2 55 62 64

11271 NNC PO P1 G1.2 1842–1928
Kiang, Yung (Chiang Yung).
'The development of modern legal institutions and judicial reform in China. Part 1, The fundamental law and its auxiliaries. Part 2, Organization of the central government. Part 3, Organization of the local government. Part 4, Judiciaries and the laws applied therein', edited by Liang Chün-li. Tr. of 'Wu shih nien lai Chung-kuo chih fa chih' (The Chinese legal system during the past fifty years); in *Tsui chin wu shih nien* (The past fifty years), edited by Shen pao kuan; Shanghai: Shen pao kuan, 1923, 1–10 [s.p.].
CLR 2, 1 (July 1924), 19–30; 2, 2 (Oct. 1924), 76–87; 2, 3 (Jan. 1925), 117–134.
Subj 12.2 ▪ 12 22 22.2

11272 NNC P P1 G1.2 –1949
Kuttner, Stephan.
'Altes und neues Strafrecht in China' (Traditional and modern Chinese criminal law).
Sinica 7, 4 (Juli 1932), 135–148.
Subj 12.2 ▪ 22.2

11273 NNC U P1 G1.2 1895–1949
Liang, Lone (Liang Yün-sung), 1894–1967.
'Die Entwicklung des Rechtswesens in China in den letzten 30 Jahren' (The development of the legal system in China in the past thirty years).
Sinica 6, 4 (Juli 1931), 199–211.
Subj 12.2 ▪ 12 22.2

11274 NNU P P4 G1.2 –1949
Lin, Chen-yung, 1906–.
The judicial organization of China.
Unpublished doctoral dissertation in Law, New York U., 1935. 107 p.
Subj 12.2 ▪ 12 17

11275 NNC PO P1 G1.2 –1928
Lobingier, Charles Sumner, 1866–1956.
'A bibliographical introduction to the study of Chinese law.'
JRAS-NCB new (2nd) series 45 (1914), 110–123.
Subj 12.2 72 ▪ 22.2 41 45 71

11276 CSU O P1 G1.3 1895–1928
Lobingier, Charles Sumner, 1866–1956.
'China: Judicial organization.'
American Bar Assn. j. 3 (July 1915), 495–498.
Subj 12.2 ▪ 12.1

11277 NNC PO P1 G1.2 –1928
Loh, Tachuen S. K.
'The administration of criminal justice in China.'
CSPSR 1, 2 (July 1916), 37–44.
Subj 12.2 ▪ 12

11278 MCH P P1 G1.1 –1928
Morse, Hosea Ballou, 1855–1934.
'The new constitution of China.'
J. of comparative legislation and international law 3rd series 1, 3 (1919), 183–195.
Subj 12 12.2 ▪ 12.1

11279 CSU P P1 G1.2 1895–1949
Pan Wei-tung (P'an Wei-tung), 1915–.
The Chinese constitution: A study of forty years of constitution-making in China.
Washington, D.C.: Catholic U. of America Press, 1945. 327 p. (Catholic U. of America studies in politics, government and international law, 3) (Doctoral dissertation in Political Science, Catholic U. of America, 1944) [Reprinted—Washington, D.C.: Institute of Chinese Culture, 1945. 11, 327 p.]
Subj 12 12.2 ▪ 16.1 32 64

11280 NNC P P1 G1.3 1895–1928
Plischke, R-.
'Die Gefängnisreform in China' (Prison reforms in China).
Z. für die gesamte Strafrechtswissenschaft 48 (1928), 572–583.
Subj 12.2 ▪ 22.2

11281 MCH U P1 G1.2 1644–1949
Pound, Roscoe, 1870–1964.
'Comparative law and history as bases for Chinese law.'
Harvard law review 61, 5 (May 1948), 749–762.
Subj 12.2

11282 NNC P P1 G1.2 –1928
Riazanovskii, Valentin Aleksandrovich, 1884–.
Osnovnye nachala zemel'nogo, gornogo i lesnogo prava Kitaia (Fundamentals of Chinese land, mining, and forestry laws).
Harbin: Tip. KVzhd, 1928. 135 p.
Subj 12.2 14.1 14.4

11283 ²CSH S P2 G1.2 1644–1928
Riazanovskii, Valentin Aleksandrovich (Valentin Aleksandrovich Riasanovsky), 1884–.
Sovremennoe grazhdanskoe pravo Kitaia, vol. 2.
Harbin: Zaria, 1927.

The modern civil law of China, Part 2.
Harbin: Harbin Daily News Press, 1928. 141 p.
Subj 12.2

11284 GMU S P1 G1.2 1895–1928
Ruete, Hans-Hellmuth.
'China' (China). In *Der Einfluss des abendländischen Rechtes auf die Rechtsgestaltung in Japan und China* (The influence of Western law on the legal systems of Japan and China), by H.-H. Ruete. [Sole entry]
Bonn: Röhrscheid, 1940, 1–53. (Doctoral dissertation, Rechtswissenschaftliche Fakultät, Universität Marburg)
Subj 12.2 ▪ 12 63 64 66

11285 NNC P P1 G1.2 1895–1928
Schrameier, Wilhelm Ludwig, 1859–1926.
'Chinesische Verfassungsarbeit' (Constitutional developments in China).
China-Archiv 3, 7 (24 Juli 1918), 291–295; 3, 8 (24 Aug. 1918), 331–335; 3, 9 (24 Sept. 1918), 377–381; 3, 10 (24 Okt. 1918), 417–422.
Subj 12.2 32 ▪ 12 12.1

11286 CBU P P1 G1.2 1895–1928
Schüler, Wilhelm, 1869–1935.
'Die chinesische Verfassung vom 10. Oktober 1923' (The Chinese constitution of 10 October 1923).
MSOSB 26/27 (1924), 129–162.
Subj 12.2 ▪ 12 64

11287 MCY P P2 G1.2 1895–1928
Suez, Iuming C.
'Opium suppression.'
CSPSR 1, 1 (Apr. 1916), 118–121.
Subj 12.2 ▪ 14.1

11288 NNC U P1 G1.2 1895–1949
Tang, Edgar Cha (T'ang Chia), 1902–.
'Judicial reforms in China.'
IB 3, 1 (11 Jan. 1937), 1–27.
Subj 12.2 ▪ 66

11289 MCH P P1 G1.2 –1949
Tch'en, Hiong-Fei (Ch'en Hsiung-fei), 1912–.
Essai de droit constitutionnel chinois: les cinq pouvoirs (An essay on Chinese constitutional law: The five powers).
Shanghai: Université l'Aurore, 1933. 186 p. (Doctoral dissertation, Université l'Aurore)
Subj 12 12.2 32 ▪ 12.1 16.1 19 64 72

11290 MCH P P1 G1.2 1842–1949
Tcheng, Chao Yuen (Ch'en Shao-yüan).
L'évolution de la vie constitutionnelle de la Chine sous l'influence de Sun Yat Sen et de sa doctrine, 1885–1937 (The development of constitutionality in China under the influence of Sun Yat-sen and his doctrine, 1885–1937).
Paris: Lib. générale de droit et de jurisprudence, 1937. 190 p. (Doctoral dissertation, Faculté de droit, Université de Dijon)
Subj 12 12.2 64 ▪ 12.1 14 32 32.1 32.2 72

11291 MCH P P2 G1.2 1644–1928
Tchou, Louis Ngaosïang (Chu Ao-hsiang), 1891–.
Le régime des capitulations et la réforme constitutionnelle en Chine (The system of extraterritoriality and constitutional reform in China).
Cambridge: Cambridge U. Press, 1915. 230 p. (Doctoral dissertation, Faculté de droit, Université catholique de Louvain)
Subj 12 12.2 66 ▪ 12.1 16.1 16.2 32 60 72

11292 ELU PO P1 G1.2 1644–1928
Tchou, Ven-fous (Chu Wen-fu), 1888–.
Etude sur la réforme de l'organisation judiciaire en Chine (A study of judicial reform in China).
Paris: Jouve, 1920. 294 p. (Doctoral dissertation, Université de Genève)
Subj 12.2 ▪ 16.1 17 22.2

11293 MCH P P1 G1.1 –1949
Tseng, Ju-Pai.
Entwicklung und Abbau der Exterritorial-Jurisdiktion in China (The development and abolition of extraterritorial jurisdiction in China).
Bonn: Röhrscheid, 1940. 94 p. (Rechtsvergleichende Untersuchungen zur gesamten Strafrechtswissenschaft, 13) (Doctoral dissertation, Rechts- und staatswissenschaftliche Fakultät, Universität Marburg)
Subj 12.2 66 ▪ 14.3 22.2 62

11294 FPN P P1 G1.2 1895–1949
Tsu Djenchow.
Historique de l'évolution des constitutions chinoises, 1905–1931 (History of the

development of the Chinese constitution, 1905–1931).
Paris: Ed. Domat-Montchrestien, 1934. 196 p. (Doctoral dissertation, Faculté de droit, Université de Paris)
SUBJ 12.2

11295 CSU P P1 G1.2 1895–1928
Tyau, Min-ch'ien T. Z. (Tiao Min-ch'ien), 1888–.
'China's new constitution.' In *China's new constitution and international problems*, by Min-ch'ien T. Z. Tyau. [Sole entry]
Shanghai: Commercial Press, 1918, 1–142.
SUBJ 12 12.2 ▪ 22

11296 NNC S P1 G1.1 1644–1949
Valk, Marius Hendrikus van der, 1908–.
'The revolution in Chinese legal thought.'
PA 11, 1 (Mar. 1938), 66–80.
SUBJ 12.2 ▪ 12 64

11297 NIC PO P2 G1.2 1895–1928
Vinacke, Harold Monk, 1893–.
Modern constitutional development in China.
Princeton: Princeton U. Press, 1920. 280 p.
SUBJ 12 12.2 32 ▪ 32.2

11298 CBU P P1 G1.2 –1928
Vogel, Werner, 1902–.
'Die historischen Grundlagen des chinesischen Strafrechts' (The historical foundations of Chinese criminal law).
ZVR 40, 1 (1923), 37–134.
SUBJ 12 12.2 62 64 ▪ 13 63

11299 CBU P P3 G1.1 –1928
Wagner, Wilhelm, 1884–.
Aufenthalt und Niederlassung Fremder in China (Residence and settlement of foreigners in China).
Berlin: Karl Curtius, 1918. 80 p.
SUBJ 12.2 ▪ 45 66

11300 NIC O P1 G1.2 1895–1928
Wang, Chung-hui (Wang Ch'ung-hui), 1881–1958.
Law reform in China.
London: Allen and Unwin, 1919. 16 p.
SUBJ 12.2

11301 FPN P P1 G1.1 1644–1949
Wang, Ming-yang.
La responsibilité civile des fonctionnaires envers les particuliers en droit chinois (The civil liability of government officials toward private persons in Chinese law).
Unpublished doctoral dissertation, Faculté de droit, Université de Paris, 1953. 201 p.
SUBJ 12.2 ▪ 12.1

11302 MCH U P1 G1.2 1895–1928
[Wen Yu Huei Society].
'A brief survey of the Chinese judiciary.'
CSPSR 4, 2 (June 1919), 169–179.
SUBJ 12.2 ▪ 12

11303 CSU S P1 G1.2 –1928
Wigmore, John Henry, 1863–1943.
'The Chinese legal system.' In *A panorama of the world's legal systems*, 2nd ed., by J. H. Wigmore. [Sole entry]
Washington, D.C.: Washington Law Book Co., 1936, 137–206.
SUBJ 12.2 ▪ 22.2

11304 FPN P P1 G1.1 1842–1949
Wu, Chiu-sheng.
La juridiction consulaire en Chine (Consular jurisdiction in China).
Toulouse: Impr. régionale, 1936. 208 p. (Doctoral dissertation, Faculté de droit, Université de Toulouse)
SUBJ 12.2 66

11305 MCH P P1 G1.2 –1928
Wu, John C. H. (Wu Ching-hsiung), 1899–.
Legal systems of old and new China: A comparison.
Chicago: Northwestern U., 1930? 14 p. [Reprinted in *The art of law and other essays, juridical and literary*, by J. C. H. Wu. (Sole entry.) Shanghai: Commercial Press, 1936, 43–62.] [Reprinted in *Essays in jurisprudence and legal philosophy*, edited by J. C. H. Wu and M. C. Liang. (Sole entry.) (Shanghai): Soochow U. Law School, 1937, 1–14 (s.p.)]
SUBJ 12.2 22.2 ▪ 62 63

11306 NNC O P1 G1.2 1895–1949
Yang, Chao Lung, 1904–.
'Powers of Chinese courts.'
Vanderbilt law review 1, 1 (Dec. 1947), 16–46.
SUBJ 12.2 ▪ 12

1911-1949

11307 GBF S P1 G1.2 1928–1949
An, Yü-kun (An Yü-k'un).
Reform von Vermögensverbrechen im deutschen, chinesischen und japanischen Strafrecht (Crimes against property: Reforms in German, Chinese, and Japanese criminal law).
Berlin: Emil Ebering, 1941. 80 p. (Doctoral dissertation, Rechts- und staatswissenschaftliche Fakultät, Universität Berlin)
SUBJ 12.2 ▪ 45

11308 MCH P P1 G1.2 1928–1949
Bünger, Karl A-, 1903–.
'Aus der chinesischen Rechtsprechung' (Examples of Chinese judicial cases).
OR 16, 3 (1 Feb. 1935), 67–69; 16, 5 (1 März 1935), 124–126; 16, 9 (1 Mai 1935), 235–236; 16, 11 (1 Juni 1935), 291–292.
SUBJ 12.2 ▪ 12.1 14.3 41

11309 MCH PO P1 G1.2 1911–1949
Bünger, Karl A-, 1903–.
'Beiträge zum chinesischen Privat- und Prozessrecht, mit vergleichenden Hinweisen auf das japanische und deutsche Recht' (Essays on Chinese private and procedural law, with comparative notes on Japanese and German law).
MSOSB 41 (1938), 95–172.
SUBJ 12.2 ▪ 34.2 45

11310 MCH P P1 G1.2 1928–1949
Bünger, Karl A-, 1903–.
'Gerichtsverfassung und Zivilprozess in China' (Judicial organization and civil procedure in China).
OR 16, 19 (1 Okt. 1935), 506–509.
SUBJ 12.2

11311 NNC U P1 G1.2 1911–1949
Bünger, Karl A-, 1903–.
'Die Quellen des chinesischen Privatrechts' (The sources of Chinese private law).
Blätter für internationales Privatrecht 4, 7 (Juli 1929), 196–202.
SUBJ 12.2 ▪ 22.2

11312 NNC P P1 G1.2 1928–1949
Bünger, Karl A-, 1903–.
'Die Verfassung der chinesischen Nationalregierung von 1947' (The 1947 constitution of the Chinese national government).
Z. für ausländisches öffentliches Recht und Völkerrecht 13, 4 (1951), 808–815.
SUBJ 12.2 ▪ 12.1 64 66

11313 NNC P P1 G1.2 1911–1949
Bünger, Karl A-, 1903–.
Zivil- und Handelsgesetz sowie Wechsel- und Scheckgesetz von China (China's codes on civil and commercial law and on negotiable instruments).
Marburg: Elwert, 1934. 318 p. (Arbeiten zum Handels-, Gewerbe-, und Landwirtschaftsrecht, 73)
SUBJ 12.2 14.3 14.6 34.2 ▪ 45

11314 MCH P P1 G1.2 1928–1949
Chamberlain, Joseph Perkins, 1873–1951.
'Structure of China's constitution.'
FES 16, 9 (7 May 1947), 100–105.
SUBJ 12 12.2 ▪ 12.1

11315 NIC U P1 G1.2 1911–1928
Chan, Y. W. (Ch'en Ying-jung).
'The Chinese supreme court.'
CSPSR 8, 1 (Jan. 1924), 54–67.
SUBJ 12.2

11316 NIC P P1 G1.2 1911–1928
Chang, C. H. (Chang Ching-hui), 1900–, Y. L. Liang (Liang Yün-li), 1900–, and John C. H. Wu (Wu Ching-hsiung), 1899–.
'Persons in Chinese law.'
CLR 2, 6 (Oct. 1925), 257–279.
SUBJ 12.2 ▪ 30 34.2 41 45 47 52

11317 MCH P P1 G1.1 1911–1949
Chang Chu Kuing (Chang Tsu-keng).
Essai sur la nationalité chinoise (An essay on Chinese nationality).
La Varenne Saint-Hilaire (Seine): Durand, 1941. 152 p. (Doctoral dissertation, Faculté de droit, Université de Paris)
SUBJ 12.2 60 66 ▪ 11 11.2 12 29 41 64

11318 GBF P P1 G1.2 1928–1949
Chang, Chung-kong (Chang Chung-chiang), 1908–.
Unrechtsausschliessungsgründe im deutschen und chinesischen Recht (Grounds for the exclusion of illegality in German and Chinese law).
Marburg: Hessischer Verlag K. Euker, 1938. 47 p. (Doctoral dissertation, Rechts- und staatswissenschaftliche Fakultät, Universität Marburg)
SUBJ 12.2

11319 NIC O P1 G1.3 1911–1928
Chang, Yao-tseng.
'The present condition of the Chinese judiciary and its future.'

CLR 2, 7 (Jan. 1926), 311–318.
Subj 12.2 ▪ 12 12.1 16.1

11320 NIC P P1 G1.2 1911–1949
Chang, Yü-chüan (Chang Yü-ch'üan), 1880–.
'The legal practitioner in China.'
CSPSR 22, 2 (July–Sept. 1938), 146–184.
Subj 12.2 16.1

11321 CBU P P1 G1.2 1911–1949
Chen Shu-Chiung (Ch'en Shu-chiung), 1910–.
'Das chinesische Strafrecht' (Chinese criminal law). In *Die Strafzumessung im chinesischen und deutschen Recht: Eine rechtsvergleichende Studie* (Sentencing in Chinese and German law: A study in comparative law), by Chen Shu-Chiung. [Sole entry]
Zeulenroda: Bernhard Sporn, 1937, 28–39. (Doctoral dissertation, Rechts- und staatswissenschaftliche Fakultät, Universität Jena)
Subj 12.1 12.2 ▪ 63

11322 NIC S P1 G1.2 1928–1949
Chen, Ta-chee.
'Observations on the system of judicial supervision in China.'
CQ-S 2, 1 (Winter 1936), 157–166.
Subj 12 12.2

11323 FPN P P1 G1.2 1911–1949
[Chen, Tsen I] Pierre Claver Chen (Shen Tseng-i).
De la responsabilité civile en droit chinois (Civil responsibility in Chinese law).
Paris: Ed. Domat-Montchrestien, 1934. 144 p. (Doctoral dissertation, Faculté de droit, Université de Paris)
Subj 12.2 ▪ 12 63

11324 NNC P P1 G1.2 1911–1928
China [Republic]. Wai chiao pu. Chih wai fa ch'üan wei yüan hui. (Ministry of Foreign Affairs. Commission on Extraterritoriality).
Chinese prisons.
Peking: Chih wai fa ch'üan wei yüan hui, 1925. 130 p.
Subj 12.2 ▪ 22.2

11325 MCH P P1 G1.2 1911–1928
China [Republic]. Wai chiao pu. Chih wai fa ch'üan wei yüan hui. (Ministry of Foreign Affairs. Commission on Extraterritoriality).
A general statement of the present conditions of the Chinese judiciary.
Peking: Chih wai fa ch'üan wei yüan hui, 1925. 19 p.
Subj 12.2

11326 NNC PO P1 G1.2 1928–1949
Chu, Cheng, 1875–1951.
'War-time judicial administration.'
CQ-S 4, 1 (Winter 1938/39), 11–16. [Special issue: *War-time political and social reconstruction*]
Subj 12 12.2 ▪ 22.2

11327 CSU P P1 G1.2 1928–1949
Chu, Yung-hsin, 1922–.
The new constitution and new government of China.
Unpublished masters thesis in Political Science, Stanford U., 1949. 194 p.
Subj 12.2 ▪ 12 32 32.2 64

11328 MCH PO P1 G1.1 1928–1949
Escarra, Jean, 1885–1955.
'Introduction' (Introduction). In *Code pénal de la République de Chine promulgé le 10 mars 1928* (The penal code of the Republic of China promulgated 10 March 1928). [Sole entry]
Paris: Marcel Giard, 1930, 23–74 [s.p.].
Subj 12.1 12.2 ▪ 25 32

11329 FPL P P1 G1.2 1911–1928
Escarra, Jean, 1855–1955.
'Les sources du droit positif actuel de la Chine' (The sources of contemporary positive law in China). In *Travaux de l'Académie internationale de droit comparé: série 1, les sources du droit positif, fascicule 1, Orient (Egypte, Palestine, Chine, Japon)* (Studies of the International Academy of comparative law: Series 1, sources of positive law. Part 1, The Orient: Egypt, Palestine, China, and Japan). [Sole entry]
Haale, Leipzig, Berlin: Académie international de droit comparé, 1929, 53–125.
Subj 12.2 ▪ 12 22.2

11330 MCH P P1 G1.2 1928–1949
Fairlie, John Archibald, 1872–1947.
'Constitutional developments in China.'
APSR 25, 4 (Nov. 1931), 1016–1022.
Subj 12 12.2

11331 NNC P P1 G1.2 1928–1949
Foo, Ping-Sheung (Fu P'ing-hsiung).
'Soziale Gesichtspunkte des bürgerlichen Gesetzbuches der chinesischen Republik' (Social aspects of the civil code of the Republic of China).
Blätter für internationales Privatrecht 6, 11 (Nov. 1931), 267–278.
Subj 12.2 14.6 ▪ 12.1 14.1 22.2 45 47

11332 MCY P P1 G1.2 1928–1949
Gérardin, André.
'L'acte abstrait dans le droit civil chinois' (The abstract act in Chinese civil law).
BUA 3e série 3, 9 (1942), 23–77.
Subj 12.2 45 ▪ 60

11333 MCY P P1 G1.2 1911–1949
Gérardin, André.
'Volonté déclarée et intention réelle en droit chinois' (Stated wish and real intention in Chinese law).
BUA 3e série 5, 18 (1944), 271–305.
Subj 12.2 45 ▪ 22.2

11334 NIC S P4 G1.2 1911–1949
Gilpatrick, Meredith Perry, 1904–.
'The status of law and lawmaking procedure under the Kuomintang, 1925–1946.'
FEQ 10, 1 (Nov. 1950), 38–55.
Subj 12 12.2 ▪ 16.2 41 62

11335 DLC P P1 G2.0 1928–1949
Gins, Georgii Konstantinovich (George Constantine Guins), 1887–, ed.
Novoe grazhdanskoe i torgovoe pravo Man'chzhu-di-go: sbornik statei i obzorov, vyp. 1 (The new civil and commercial law of Manchoukuo: A symposium, Vol. 1).
Harbin: Izd-vo Biuro po delam rossiiskikh emigrantov, 1938. 112 p.
Subj 12.2 14.3 ▪ 14.2 14.6 45

11336 MAM P P2 G1.2 1911–1949
Griffin, Patricia Eileen Peck, 1944–.
The Chinese Communist treatment of counterrevolutionaries, 1924–1949.
Ann Arbor: University Microfilms (Publ. 72-17,363), 1972. 31, 316, 32 p. (Doctoral dissertation in International Relations, U. of Pennsylvania, 1971)
Subj 12.1 12.2 16 22.2 26 66 ▪ 15 16.1 22.1 26.1 32 32.2 36.3 64

11337 CSH P P1 G2.0 1928–1949
Gross, Leo.
'Die Verfassung von Mandschukuo' (The constitution of Manchoukuo).
Z. für Politik 23, 7 (1933), 430–446.
Subj 12 12.2 64 ▪ 12.1 66

11338 CSU P P1 G1.2 1928–1949
Holcombe, Arthur Norman, 1884–.
'Chinese political thought and the proposed new constitution.'
J. of politics 8, 1 (Feb. 1946), 1–23.
Subj 12.2 64 ▪ 32

11339 GMS P P1 G1.3 1911–1928
Holzhauer, Fritz.
Das Justizwesen in China in seiner gegenwärtigen Gestaltung (mit besonderer Berücksichtigung der Provinz Schantung) (The present form of the Chinese judicial system, with special attention to Shantung).
Tsingtao: Deutsch-Chinesische Hochschule, 1912. 151 p. (Enzyklopädischer Grundriss der Rechts- und Staatswissenschaften für Chinesen, B, 1)
Subj 12.2

11340 CSH P P2 G9.5 1928–1949
Hong Kong. Hong Kong and Kowloon Magistracies.
Report, 1946/47–1948/49. [Issues for 1950/51–1971/72 are entered as 11466.]
[Hong Kong]: ——. Issued annually, 1947–1949. Average ca. 15 p.
Subj 12.2 ▪ 22.2

11341 FPN P P1 G1.2 1928–1949
Hou Yong-ling (Hu Yung-ling).
'La vie politique et constitutionnelle en Chine' (Political life and constitutionalism in China).
Politique de Pékin 22, 8 (23 fév. 1935), 194–204; 22, 9 (2 mars 1935), 229–231; 22, 10 (9 mars 1935), 252–254; 22, 11 (16 mars 1935), 284–292; 22, 12 (23 mars 1935), 320–323.
Subj 12 12.2 32 ▪ 64

11342 FPN P P1 G1.2 1911–1928
Hou-Ts'ouei Chou-yen (Hu Ts'ui Shu-yen).
Evolution de la jurisprudence chinoise moderne en matière des obligations (The development of modern Chinese jurisprudence with respect to contract law).
Paris: Lib. technique et économique, 1937. 200 p. (Doctoral dissertation, Faculté de droit, Université de Paris)
Subj 12.2

11343 NNC P P1 G1.2 1928–1949
Hsu Dau-lin (Hsü Tao-lin), 1906–.
'Die Entwicklung des Verfassungsrechts unter der Nationalregierung seit 1927' (The development of constitutional law

under the national government since 1927).
Sinica 8, 1 (Jan. 1933), 17–27; 8, 2 (März 1933), 49–62.
Subj 12 12.2 ▪ 32 32.1

11344 MCH P P1 G1.2 1911–1949
Hung, William S. H. (Hung Shih-hao).
Outlines of modern Chinese law: Legal history, contracts, agency, sales, bailments and carriers, partnership, property, domestic relations, succession, private corporations, negotiable instruments, criminal law, including list of prevailing laws and table of degrees of punishment.
[Shanghai?]: The author, 1934. 25, 317 p.
Subj 12.2 14.6 34.2 41 45

11345 DLC P P2 G2.0 1911–1928
Kitaiskaia Vostochnaia zheleznaia doroga. Ekonomicheskoe biuro.
Osobyi raion Vostochnykh provintsii Kitaiskoi Respubliki: spravochnye svedeniia ob administrativnom i sudebnom ustroistve raiona (Reference information on the administrative and judicial structure of the Special Region of the Eastern Provinces of the Republic of China [i.e., the part of Manchuria controlled by Chang Tso-lin]).
Harbin: T-vo Pechat', 1927. 326 p.
Subj 12.1 12.2 14 66 ▪ 17 34.2 36.2

11346 CSH P P2 G1.3 1928–1949
Leng, Shao-chuan (Leng Shao-ch'üan), 1921–.
'Pre-1949 development of the Communist Chinese system of justice.'
CQ 30 (Apr.–June 1967), 93–114.
Subj 12.2 22.2 ▪ 36.3

11347 NIC S P1 G1.2 1928–1949
Li, Alfred C. T. (Li Chih-t'ai).
'Organization and administration of justice in China.'
CQ-S 2, 1 (Winter 1936), 103–140.
Subj 12.2 ▪ 12

11348 GBS S P1 G1.2 1928–1949
Li, Shih-Tung (Li Shih-t'ung), 1906–.
Die Mängelhaftung im chinesischen Kaufrecht, vergleichend dargestellt mit dem deutschen und schweizerischen Rechte (Warranties for defects in the Chinese law of sales, as compared with German and Swiss law).
Unpublished doctoral dissertation, Rechts- und staatswissenschaftliche Fakultät, Universität Berlin, 1941. 95 p.
Subj 12.2 14.3 ▪ 34.2

11349 CSU P P1 G1.2 1911–1928
Liang, Lone (Liang Yün-sung), 1894–1967.
'China's new constitution.'
CSPSR 10, 1 (Jan. 1926), 145–162.
Subj 12.2 ▪ 32

11350 CSH U P3 G6.1 1928–1949
Liu, Francis S. F. (Liu Shih-fang), 1901–.
'Judicial reforms and the Shanghai Special District Court.'
China critic 5, 35 (1 Sept. 1932), 904–905.
Subj 12.2

11351 NNC P P1 G1.3 1911–1928
Liu, Keetsin (Liu Chi-ch'in).
'Über Urteilsformeln und Rechtsmittel im geltenden chinesischen Strafprozessrecht' (Verdicts and appeals in current Chinese criminal cases).
Z. für die gesamte Strafrechtswissenschaft 46 (1925), 249–259.
Subj 12.2

11352 MCY O P1 G1.2 1911–1928
Lo Wen-kan, 1888–1942.
'The criminal code of the Republic of China.'
CSPSR 4, 3 (Sept. 1919), 213–219.
Subj 12.2 ▪ 12 22.2

11353 NNC P P1 G1.2 1911–1928
Michelsen, Erich.
'Einige strafrechtliche Fragen aus der chinesischen Praxis' (Some problems of criminal law from Chinese legal practice).
DCR 3 (1914), 6–14.
Subj 12.2 ▪ 22.2

11354 NNC PO P1 G1.3 1911–1928
Michelsen, Erich.
'Grundgedanken des neuen chinesischen Strafrechts' (Basic concepts of the new Chinese criminal law).
Z. für die gesamte Strafrechtswissenschaft 35 (1914), 482–493.
Subj 12.2

11355 NNC P P1 G1.2 1911–1928
Michelsen, Erich.
'Wang Tsch'ung-hui's Entwurf einer chinesischen Verfassung' (Wang Ch'ung-hui's draft of a constitution for China).
DCR 2 (1912), 110–119.
Subj 12.2 ▪ 12 12.1

11356 NNP P P1 G1.2 1911–1928
Musso, Giuseppe Domenico.
La Cina ed i Cinesi: loro leggi e costumi (China and the Chinese: Their laws and customs).
Milan: Hoepli, 1927. 1494 p.
Subj 12.2 22.2 60 ▪ 12 12.1 45 57 62 63

11357 MCH U P1 G1.2 1928–1949
Nyi, T. Y.
'The present system of notaries in China.'
CLR 10, 1 (June 1937), 91–99.
Subj 12.2 ▪ 12.1

11358 MCH P P1 G1.2 1911–1928
[Pergament, Mikhail IAkovlevich] M. J. Pergament, 1866–1932.
Questions regarding jurisdiction in China.
Tientsin: Lib. française, 1925.
Subj 12.2 66

11359 NNC PO P1 G1.3 1928–1949
Pound, Roscoe, 1870–1964.
'Progress of the law in China.'
Washington law review 23, 4 (Nov. 1948), 345–362.
Subj 12.2 ▪ 12

11360 CSU P P1 G1.2 1911–1928
Quigley, Harold Scott, 1889–1968.
'The constitution of China.'
APSR 18, 2 (May 1924), 346–350.
Subj 12.2

11361 MCY U P1 G1.2 1928–1949
[Riazanovskii, Valentin Aleksandrovich] V. A. Riasanovsky, 1884–.
'Application and the interpretation of the norms of law.'
CSPSR 22, 3 (Oct.–Dec. 1938), 282–298.
Subj 12.2 ▪ 12 12.1

11362 CSH P P1 G1.2 1928–1949
Riazanovskii, Valentin Aleksandrovich (Valentin Aleksandrovich Riasanovsky), 1884–.
Chinese civil law. Tr. from the Russian by V. A. Riasanovsky and M- N- Lootsky. [Tr. of an unpublished manuscript]
Tientsin: ——, 1938. 310 p.
Subj 12.2 41 45

11363 CSH P P1 G1.2 1911–1928
Riazanovskii, Valentin Aleksandrovich (V. A. Riasanovsky), 1884–.
'Osnovnye instituty kitaiskogo grazhdanskogo prava.'
VM 1926, 5, 18–26; 1926, 6, 19–34.
'Fundamental institutions of Chinese civil law.'
Manchuria monitor 1926, 5, 3–10; 1926, 7, 3–18.
Subj 12.2 ▪ 41 45 57

11364 FPN P P1 G1.2 1911–1928
Sié, Ying-chow (Hsieh Ying-chou), 1894–1972.
Le fédéralisme en Chine: étude sur quelques constitutions provinciales (Federalism in China: A study of several provincial constitutions).
Paris: H. d'Arthez, 1924. 239 p. (Doctoral dissertation, Faculté de droit, Université de Paris)
Subj 12 12.2 22

11365 FPN P P1 G1.2 1911–1928
Siu, Tche Ping (Hsü Chih-p'ing).
L'organisation judiciaire de la Chine (China's judicial system).
Lyons: Bosc et Riou, 1927. 170 p. (Doctoral dissertation, Faculté de droit, Université de Grenoble)
Subj 12.2

11366 CBU P P1 G1.2 1928–1949
Steinwallner, Bruno.
'Chinesische Strafrechtsreform' (The reform of Chinese criminal law).
Monatsschrift für Kriminalpsychologie und Strafrechtsreform 22, 10 (Okt. 1931), 597–604.
Subj 12.2

11367 CSU P P1 G1.2 1928–1949
Sun Keewong.
'A constitution for China.'
Amerasia 4, 4 (June 1940), 175–184.
Subj 12.2 32 ▪ 64

11368 MCH P P2 G1.2 1911–1949
Théry, François, 1890–, ed.
Eléments de droit civil chinois. Livre 1 du code civil: principes généraux (Elements of Chinese civil law. Book 1 of the civil code: General principles).
Tientsin: Hautes études, 1939. 178 p. (Droit chinois moderne, 33, 1)
Subj 12 12.2 60 ▪ 12.1 16 22.2 36.2 38 72

11369 MCH P P2 G1.2 1911–1949
Théry, François, 1890–, ed.
Eléments du droit civil chinois. Livre 2 du code civil: des obligations (Elements of

Chinese civil law. Book 2 of the civil code: Obligations).
Tientsin: Hautes études, 1939? 577 p. (Droit chinois moderne, 33, 2)
SUBJ 12.2 14.3 14.6 22.2

11370 NNC P P1 G1.2 1911–1949
Théry, François, 1890–.
'Sources du droit civil chinois' (Sources of Chinese civil law).
MS 4, 1 (1939), 309–324.
SUBJ 12.2 ▪ 14.2

11371 MCH P P2 G1.2 1928–1949
Théry, François, 1890–, and Hoang Jou-hsiang (Huang Ju-hsiang), eds.
Loi sur l'état-civil, promulguée le 12 décembre 1931, entrée en vigueur le 1 juillet 1934 (The law on civil status, promulgated 12 December 1931 and effective 1 July 1934).
Tientsin: Hautes études, 1934. 32 p. (Droit chinois moderne, 20)
SUBJ 12.2 ▪ 11.2

11372 NIC P P1 G1.2 1928–1949
Valk, Marius Hendrikus van der, 1908–.
'The new Chinese criminal code.'
PA 9, 1 (Mar. 1936), 69–77.
SUBJ 12.2 ▪ 18 38 41 47 54 56

11373 MCH P P1 G1.2 1911–1928
Vogel, Werner, 1902–.
'Moderne Rechtssprechung und Gerichtsbarkeit in China' (Modern administration of justice and jurisdiction in China).
OR 7, 4 (Apr. 1926), 65–68.
SUBJ 12.2 ▪ 12.1 14.3

11374 MCY O P1 G1.2 1911–1928
Wang, Chung-hui (Wang Ch'ung-hui), 1881–1958.
'Reform in criminal procedure.'
CSPSR 4, 1 (Mar. 1919), 1–9.
SUBJ 12.2

11375 FPN P P1 G1.2 1911–1928
[Wei Tao-ming, *Mme*.] Soumé Tcheng (Wei Cheng Yü-hsiu), 1891–1959.
Le mouvement constitutionnel en Chine: étude de droit comparé (The constitutional movement in China: A study in comparative law).
Paris: Tenin, 1925. 157 p. (Doctoral dissertation, Faculté de droit, Université de Paris)
SUBJ 12 12.2 32 ▪ 12.1

11376 MCH P P1 G1.2 1911–1928
Woo, James (Wu K'ai-sheng), 1900–.
Le problème constitutionnel chinoise: la constitution du 10 octobre 1923 (The problem of a Chinese constitution: The constitution of 10 October 1923).
Paris: Marcel Giard, 1925. 150 p. (Bibliothèque de l'Institut de droit comparé de Lyon, Etudes et documents, 11) (Doctoral dissertation, Faculté de droit, Université de Lyon)
SUBJ 12 12.2 ▪ 12.1 32 64

11377 NNC S P1 G1.2 1911–1928
Wu, Friedrich C. (Wu Ch'i).
La nouvelle Chine et le gouvernement national: étude sur la loi organique du 10 octobre 1928 et les organisations des pouvoirs publics dans le gouvernement national (The new China and the national government: A study of the organic law of 10 October 1928 and the organization of public powers in the national government).
Paris: Marcel Rivière, 1929. 216 p. (Doctoral dissertation, Faculté de droit, Université de Paris)
SUBJ 12 12.2 32 ▪ 15 17

11378 CSU O P1 G1.2 1928–1949
Wu, John C. H. (Wu Ching-hsiung), 1899–.
'Notes on the final draft constitution.'
THM 10, 5 (May 1940), 409–426.
SUBJ 12.2 ▪ 64

11379 CBU P P1 G1.2 1911–1949
Wu, John C. H. (Wu Ching-hsiung), 1899–.
'Two forms of tortious liability in the modern Chinese law.' In *The art of law and other essays, juridical and literary*, by J. C. H. Wu. [Selective entry]
Shanghai: Commercial Press, 1936, 63–71.
SUBJ 12.2

11380 MCH O P4 G1.2 1928–1949
Yang, Chao Lung, 1904–.
'Judicial administration in China.'
CLR 6, 1 (Jan. 1933), 6–27.
SUBJ 12 12.2 ▪ 22.2

11381 MCH P P1 G1.2 1928–1949
Yang, Chao Lung, 1904–.
The judicial organization of China: A study of its present conditions and problems with reference to leading foreign systems.
Unpublished doctoral dissertation in Law, Harvard U., 1935. 284 p.
SUBJ 12.2 ▪ 22.2

11382 NNC FP P2 G1.2 1911–1949
Yen, Ching-yueh (Yen Ching-yüeh), 1905–.
'Crime in relation to social change in China.'
AJS 40, 3 (Nov. 1934), 298–308. [For a fuller version, see entry 16123.]
SUBJ 12.2 22.2 ▪ 22.1 25 40 41 50

1911-1972
(including 1644-1972)

11383 NNC P P1 G1.2 1644–1972
Buxbaum, David Charles, 1933–.
'Horizontal and vertical influences upon the substantive criminal law in China: Some preliminary observations.'
Osteuropa-Recht 10, 1 (März 1964), 31–52.
SUBJ 12.1 12.2 ▪ 12 16 22.1 22.2 64

11384 MCH P P2 G1.1 –1972
Caponera, Dante Augusto, 1921–.
'Principi di diritto delle acque nel sistema giuridico cinese.'
Cina 5 (1959), 116–171.

'Water law principles in the Chinese legal system.'
Indian j. of international law 1 (1961), 239–275.
SUBJ 12.2 14.1 14.2 ▪ 11.4 12

11385 FPN S P1 G1.1 1911–1972
Chao, Keh-ming (Chao K'o-ming).
Le ministère public en France et en Chine (The public prosecutor in France and in China).
Unpublished doctoral dissertation, Faculté de droit, Université de Paris, 1957. 296 p.
SUBJ 12.2

11386 NNC P P1 G1.2 1842–1972
Chen, Yuvoon (Ch'en Yü-feng), 1905–.
'Zur Übernahme europäischer Rechte in China' (The reception of European law in China).
Mitteilungen des Instituts für Orientforschung der Deutschen Akademie der Wissenschaften zu Berlin 9 (1963), 392–409.
SUBJ 12 12.2 ▪ 12.1 14.1 22.2 41 45 63 64 66

11387 MCH P P1 G1.1 –1972
Cunha Gonçalves, L- da.
'Evolução das instituições jurídicas da China antes e depois do comunismo' (The evolution of China's judicial institutions before and after Communism).
Boletim da Sociedade de Geografia de Lisboa 73, 7/9 (Julho–Setembro 1955), 349–365.
SUBJ 12.2 41 ▪ 16 44 45 62

11388 CSU P P2 G1.2 –1972
Engelborghs-Bertels, Marthe, 1928–.
'L'assimilation de l'esprit du droit occidental en Chine' (Assimilation of the spirit of Western law in China).
Co-existence 4, 1 (jan. 1967), 77–93.
SUBJ 12.2 22.2 41 64 ▪ 12 12.1 47 63

11389 CSU P P2 G9.5 1842–1972
Evans, David Meurig Emrys, 1938–.
'Some legal aspects of urbanization in Hong Kong.' In *Asian urbanization: A Hong Kong casebook*, edited by Denis John Dwyer. [Analytic entry]
Hong Kong: Hong Kong U. Press, 1971, 20–32. (Centre of Asian Studies series, 3)
SUBJ 12.2 45 ▪ 21.1 21.3

11390 NNC P P2 G1.2 1928–1972
Gudoshnikov, Leonid Moiseevich.
Sudebnye organy Kitaiskoi Narodnoi Respubliki (Judicial organs in the People's Republic of China).
Moscow: Gosiurizdat, 1957. 134 p.

Legal organs of the People's Republic of China, mimeo.
Washington, D.C.: U.S. Joint Publications Research Service, 30 June, 1959. 138 p. (JPRS 1698; MC 10,339/1959)
SUBJ 12.1 12.2 ▪ 12 14.1 22.2 32.1 41

11391 CSH P P2 G1.2 1928–1972
Hazard, John Newbold, 1909–.
Communists and their law: A search for the common core of the legal systems of the Marxian socialist states.
Chicago: U. of Chicago Press, 1969. 16, 560 p.
SUBJ 12.1 12.2 14 22 32.1 64 ▪ 12 14.1 14.4 32 32.2 34.1 36.3 41

11392 MCH P P1 G1.2 1895–1972
Henderson, Dan Fenno, 1922–.
'Japanese influences on Communist Chinese legal language.' In *Contemporary Chinese law: Research problems and perspectives*, edited by Jerome Alan Cohen. [Selective entry]

Cambridge: Harvard U. Press, 1970, 158–187. (Harvard studies in East Asian law, 4)
Subj 12.2 ▪ 66

11393 CSU P P2 G1.2 1895–1972
Jensen, Hermann.
Die Verfassung der Volksrepublik China, mit besonderer Berücksichtigung der Verfassungsgrundsätze und ihrer Anwendung in der Verfassungswirklichkeit (The constitution of the People's Republic of China, with special attention to constitutional principles and their application to constitutional reality).
Marburg: G. Bauknecht, 1964. 171 p.
Subj 12 12.2 14 16 32 64 ▪ 12.1 32.2 34.1 66

11394 DLC S P1 G1.2 1928–1972
Kiesewatter, Zbyněk.
'ČL'R a jeji orgány justice a prokuratury' (The People's Republic of China: Its judicial organs and procuratorate).
Socialisticka zákonnost (Prague) 7, 6 (1959), 317–323.
Subj 12.2

11395 CBU P P1 G1.2 –1972
Kroker, Eduard Josef M-, 1913–.
Der Strafe im chinesischen Recht (Punishment in Chinese law).
Opladen: Westdeutscher Verlag, 1970. 81 p. (Rheinisch-Westfälischen Akademie der Wissenschaften, Veröffentlichungen, 165)
Subj 12.2 62 ▪ 64

11396 MCH P P1 G1.2 –1972
Lee, Luke T. C. (Li Tsung-chou), 1920–.
'Chinese Communist law: Its background and development.'
Michigan law review 60, 4 (Feb. 1962), 439–472.
Subj 12.2 22.2 ▪ 12.1 16.1

11397 CSU P P1 G1.2 –1972
Leng, Shao-chuan (Leng Shao-ch'üan), 1921–.
'Chinese law.' In *Sovereignty within the law*, edited by Arthur Larson et al. [Sole entry]
New York: Oceana, 1965, 242–267.
Subj 12.2 ▪ 63

11398 CSU P P2 G1.2 1928–1972
Leng, Shao-chuan (Leng Shao-ch'üan), 1921–.
Justice in Communist China: A survey of the judicial system of the Chinese People's Republic.
Dobbs Ferry, N.Y.: Oceana, 1967. 196 p.
Subj 12.2 22.2 ▪ 36.1 64

11399 CSH P P1 G1.2 1928–1972
Liang, Lone (Liang Yün-sung), 1894–1967.
'Modern law in China.' In *Studies in the law of the Far East and Southeast Asia*, edited by George Washington U. Law School. [Selective entry]
Washington, D.C.: Washington Foreign Law Society, 1956, 46–69.
Subj 12.2 ▪ 34.2 41 45

11400 NIC P P1 G9.5 –1972
McAleavy, Henry.
'Chinese law in Hong Kong: The choice of sources.' In *Changing law in developing countries*, edited by James Norman Dalrymple Anderson. [Sole entry]
London: Allen and Unwin, 1963, 258–269.
Subj 12.2 41 45 ▪ 47

11401 MCH PO P1 G1.2 1928–1972
McAleavy, Henry.
'The people's courts in Communist China.'
AJCL 11, 1 (Winter 1962), 52–65.
Subj 12.2 ▪ 66

11402 MCH P P1 G1.2 –1972
Michael, Franz Henry, 1907–.
'The role of law in traditional, Nationalist and Communist China.'
CQ 9 (Jan.–Mar. 1962), 124–148.
Subj 12.2 22.2 ▪ 12 12.1 16.1 32 41

11403 CBU PO P1 G1.1 –1972
Middendorf, Wolf.
'Strafgerichtsbarkeit und Kriminalität auf Formosa' (Criminal jurisdiction and criminality in Taiwan).
Z. für die gesamte Strafrechtswissenschaft 78 (1966), 265–301.
Subj 12.2 41 60 ▪ 32.2 47 65

11404 CSU S P1 G1.1 1928–1972
Plummer, Mark Allen, 1929–.
'Chiang K'ai-shek and the National Assembly.'
Studies on Asia 8 (1967), 119–138.
Subj 12.2 16.1 ▪ 32

11405 DLC S P1 G1.2 1928–1972
Plundr, Otakar.
'Organisace soudů a prokuratury v ČL'R' (The organization of the courts and the procuratorate in the People's Republic of China).
Stat a právo (Prague) 6 (1960), 16–50.
Subj 12.2 ▪ 12 15 22.2

11406 CSU PO P2 G1.2 1644–1972
Rickett, Walter Allyn, 1921–.
'Voluntary surrender and confession in Chinese law: The problem of continuity.'
JAS 30, 4 (Aug. 1971), 797–814.
Subj 12.2

11407 CSU S P1 G1.2 –1972
Shiga, Shūzō, 1921–.
'Some remarks on the judicial system in China: Historical development and characteristics.'
JAAS 2, 1/2 (Jan.–Apr. 1967), 44–53. [Reprinted in *Traditional and modern legal institutions in Asia and Africa*, edited by David Charles Buxbaum. (Selective entry.) Leiden: Brill, 1967, 44–53. (International studies in sociology and social anthropology, 5)]
Subj 12.2 22.2

11408 CSU P P1 G1.2 1928–1972
Stahnke, Arthur Allan, 1935–.
'The background and evolution of party policy on the drafting of legal codes in Communist China.'
AJCL 15, 3 (Summer 1966), 506–525.
Subj 12.2 32.1 ▪ 22.2 32 64

11409 CSU S P1 G1.2 –1972
Su, Jyun-hsyong.
'Die Struktur des chinesischen Rechtsdenkens und ihre Wirkung auf das moderne Recht' (The structure of Chinese legal thought and its effect on modern law).
Archiv für Rechts- und Sozialphilosophie 53, 3 (1967), 305–327.
Subj 12.2 60 ▪ 62 63

11410 CSU P P2 G1.2 1644–1972
Tay, Alice Erh-soon (Cheng Ju-chun), 1934–.
'Law in Communist China.'
Sydney law review 6, 2 (Oct. 1969), 153–172; 6, 3 (Aug. 1971), 335–370. [Part 3 of this article was to be published.]
Subj 12.2 ▪ 22.2

11411 GMS S P1 G1.1 1911–1972
Ts'ai Tun-ming.
'Das Bandendelikt im chinesischen Recht' (Gang crime in Chinese law). In *Die Bande als Verbrechensform im deutschen, chinesischen und japanischen Strafrecht* (The gang as a type of criminal activity in German, Chinese, and Japanese criminal law), by Ts'ai Tun-ming. [Sole entry]
Freiburg i. Br.: The author, 1964, 85–99. (Doctoral dissertation, Rechts- und staatswissenschaftliche Fakultät, Universität Freiburg i. Br.)
Subj 12.2 ▪ 25

11412 NIC P P1 G1.2 1644–1972
Valk, Marius Hendrikus van der, 1908–.
'Assimilation and Chinese law.'
U. of Toronto q. 30, 3 (Apr. 1961), 286–298.
Subj 12.2 66 ▪ 22.2 41

11413 MCH P P1 G1.2 1928–1972
Valk, Marius Hendrikus van der, 1908–.
'Konstitutionele ontwikkelingen in het nieuwe China' (Constitutional developments in New China).
Internationale spectator 11, 9 (8 Mei 1957), 251–268.
Subj 12.2 64 ▪ 12.1 16

11414 MCH P P1 G1.2 1895–1972
Valk, Marius Hendrikus van der, 1908–.
'Problemen der rechtshervorming in China' (Problems of legal reform in China).
Indonesië; tijdschrift gewijd aan het Indonesisch cultuurgebied 7, 2 (Oktober 1953), 132–155; 7, 3 (Januari 1954), 199–208.
Subj 12.2 41 47 ▪ 22.2 62 63

11415 MCH PO P1 G1.1 –1972
Wang, Huai Ming, 1894–.
'Chinese and American criminal law: Some comparisons.'
J. of criminal law, criminology and police science 46, 6 (Mar.–Apr. 1956), 796–832.
Subj 12.2 22.2 ▪ 62

11416 DLC U P1 G1.2 1895–1972
Wang, Tze-chién.
'Die Aufnahme des europäischen Rechts in China' (The reception of European law in China).
Archiv für die Civilistische Praxis 166 (1966), 343–351.
Subj 12.2 66 ▪ 63 64

11417 CSU P P1 G9.4 1928–1972
Weggel, Oskar, 1935–.
'Zentralregierung und Provinzverwaltung auf Taiwan' (Central government and provincial administration in Taiwan).
Verfassung und Recht in Übersee 1, 4 (1968), 391–420.
Subj 12 12.2 32 ▪ 12.1 32.2 64

11418 CBU P P1 G1.1 1911–1972
Weng, Yueh-sheng, 1932–.
Die Stellung der Justiz im Verfassungsrecht der Republik China (The position of the judiciary in the constitutional law of the Republic of China).
Heidelberg: The author, 1965. 26, 168 p. (Doctoral dissertation, Juristische Fakultät, Universität Heidelberg) [Reprinted—Taipei: Ch'eng-wen, 1970. 26, 168 p.]
Subj 12 12.2 ▪ 12.1 22.2

1949-1972

11419 FPN P P1 G1.2 1949–1972
'Evénements récents sur le plan juridique en République populaire de Chine.'
B. de la Commission internationale de juristes 8 (déc. 1958), 7–17.
'Recent legal developments in the People's Republic of China.'
B. of the International Commission of Jurists 8 (Dec. 1958), 7–17.
Subj 12.2 ▪ 12.1 16.1 22.2

11420 CSH P P4 G1.2 1949–1972
'Public trial rallies in People's China.'
B. of the International Commission of Jurists 35 (Sept. 1968), 25–29.
Subj 12.2

11421 CSH P P2 G1.2 1949–1972
'Ten years of the Chinese people's constitution.'
B. of the International Commission of Jurists 20 (Sept. 1964), 22–33.
Subj 12.2 ▪ 14.1 41 45

11422 MCH O P1 G1.2 1949–1972
Aparnikova, TS-.
'Predvaritel'naia podgotovka grazhdanskikh del v sudakh Kitaiskoi Narodnoi Respubliki' (Preliminary preparation of civil cases in the courts of the People's Republic of China).
Sovetskaia iustitsiia 1957, 8 (avgust), 59–60.
Subj 12.2 ▪ 22.2

11423 MCH P P1 G1.2 1949–1972
Beliakova, Anna Mikhailovna.
Nekotorye voprosy grazhdanskogo prava Kitaiskoi Narodnoi Respubliki (Problems of civil law in the People's Republic of China).
Moscow: Izd-vo Mosk. un-ta, 1960. 48 p.
Subj 12.2 ▪ 22.2 32.1 34.1 34.2 36.3 36.4 45

11424 MCH O P1 G1.2 1949–1972
Benedek, Jenő.
'A Kínai igazságszolgáltatás rendszeréről.'
Társadalmi szemle 15, 2 (február 1960), 90–102.
The Chinese system of administering justice, mimeo.
Washington, D.C.: U.S. Joint Publications Research Service, 1 Apr. 1960. 15 p. (JPRS 3121; MC 7200/1960)
Subj 12.2 22.2 ▪ 63

11425 CBU PO P1 G1.2 1949–1972
Bernard, Théo.
'Rapport d'instruction.' In *Livre blanc sur le travail forcé et les institutions concentrationnaires dans la République populaire de Chine, II, le dossier*, compiled and edited by Commission internationale contre le régime concentrationnaire. [Selective entry]
Paris: Centre international d'édition et de documentation, 1958, 9–80.
'Report of the investigation.' In *White book on forced labour and concentration camps in the People's Republic of China, Vol. II, The record*, compiled and edited by the organization cited. [Selective entry]
Paris: Centre international d'édition et de documentation, 1958, 3–65.
Subj 12.1 12.2 ▪ 15

11426 CBU P P1 G1.2 1949–1972
Bobbio, Norberto.
'Linee fondamentali della costituzione cinese' (Basic features of the Chinese constitution). In *La Cina d'oggi* (China today), edited by Piero Calamandrei. [Selective entry]
Florence: Nuova Italia editrice, 1956, 220–230. [Supplement to *Il ponte* 12, 4 (aprile 1956)]
Subj 12.2 64 ▪ 12.1

11427 FPN O P1 G1.2 1949–1972
Bonnichon, André, 1905–.
Le droit de la Chine communiste.
The Hague: Commission internationale de juristes, 1955. 28 p.
Law in Communist China.
The Hague: International Commission of Jurists, 1956. 35 p.
Subj 12.2 ▪ 12.1

11428 MCH S P1 G1.2 1949–1972
Bonsdorff, Göran von, 1918–.
'Kinas nya författning' (China's new constitution).
Finsk tidsskrift 156 (1954), 172–181.
Subj 12 12.2

11429 MCH O P2 G1.2 1949–1972
Bratus', S- N-, A- N- Mishutin (A. N. Mischutin), and N- K- Morozov (N. K. Morozow).
'Nekotorye voprosy struktury i form deiatel'nosti organov iustitsii Kitaiskoi Narodnoi Respubliki' (The structure and operation of judicial organs in the People's Republic of China).
SGP 1957, 2 (fevral'), 53–60.
'Zur struktur und zu den Formen der Tätigkeit der Justizorgane in der Volksrepublik China.'
Rechtswissenschaftlicher Informationsdienst 6, 12 (20 Juni 1957), 362–370.
Subj 12 12.2

11430 NNC P P1 G1.2 1949–1972
Bünger, Karl A-, 1903–.
'Die Verfassung der chinesischen Volksrepublik' (The constitution of the People's Republic of China).
Z. für ausländisches öffentliches Recht und Völkerrecht 13 (1950/51), 759–785.
Subj 12 12.2 ▪ 12.1 16 32

11431 CSU P P1 G1.2 1949–1972
Buxbaum, David Charles, 1933–.
'Preliminary trends in the development of the legal institutions of Communist China and the nature of the criminal law.'
International and comparative law q. 4th series 11, 1 (Jan. 1962), 1–30. [For a fuller version, see the author's masters thesis, U. of Washington, 1963.] [Reprinted in *Government of Communist China*, edited by George P. Jan (Jan Po-kung). (Selective entry.) San Francisco: Chandler, 1966, 340–371.]
Subj 12.2 32.1 ▪ 12 12.1 22.2 64

11432 DLC S P1 G1.2 1949–1972
Bystřicky, Rudolf.
'Poznámky o právním životě v ČL'R' (Notes on legal life in the People's Republic of China).
Socialisticka zákonnost (Prague) 8, 2 (1960), 89–99.
Subj 12.1 12.2

11433 CBU PO P1 G1.2 1949–1972
Calamandrei, Piero.
'Rivoluzione pianificata' (Planned revolution). In *La Cina d'oggi* (China today), edited by P. Calamandrei. [Selective entry]
Florence: Nuova Italia editrice, 1956, 231–247. [Supplement to *Il ponte* 12, 4 (aprile 1956)]
Subj 12.1 12.2 ▪ 19 32

11434 CSU P P1 G1.2 1949–1972
Chai, Winberg (Chai Wen-po), 1932–.
'Draft of the new Chinese constitution: Introduction.'
Studies in comparative Communism 4, 1 (Jan. 1971), 97–99.
Subj 12.2

11435 CSH P P2 G1.2 1949–1972
Chang Chen-pang.
'An analysis of the revised draft constitution of the Peiping regime.' In *Collected documents of the First Sino-American Conference on Mainland China*. [Selective entry]
[Taipei]: Institute of International Relations, Republic of China, 1971, 535–548.
Subj 12.2 ▪ 12 14 15 32 32.1

11436 MAM P P1 G1.2 1949–1972
Chen, Phillip Ming, 1935–.
Law and justice: Legal system in Communist China.
Ann Arbor: University Microfilms (Publ. 67-12,011), 1967. 252 p. (Doctoral dissertation in Political Science, U. of Massachusetts)
Subj 12.2 ▪ 64

11437 CSU P P2 G1.2 1949–1972
Chen, Theodore H. E. (Ch'en Hsi-en), 1902–.
The Chinese Communist regime: Documents and commentary.
New York: Praeger, 1967. 344 p.
Subj 12.2 32 32.1 ▪ 14 14.1 34.1 41 64

11438 MCH P P1 G1.2 1949–1972
Chugunov, Vladimir Evgen'evich (V. Ye. Chugunov).
Ugolovnoe sudoproizvodstvo Kitaiskoi Narodnoi Respubliki.
Moscow: Gosiurizdat, 1959. 286 p.
Criminal court procedure in the Chinese People's Republic, mimeo.
Washington, D.C.: U.S. Joint Publications Research Service, 8 May 1961. 241 p. (JPRS 4595; MC 10,757/1961)
Subj 12.2 ▪ 12.1

11439 CSU P P1 G1.2 1949–1972
Chung yang cheng fa kan pu hsüeh hsiao. Hsing fa chiao yen shih. (Central Political-Judicial Cadres School. Institute of Criminal Law Research).
Lectures on the general principles of criminal law in the People's Republic of China, mimeo. Tr. of *Chung-hua jen min kung ho kuo hsing fa tsung tse chiang i*; Peking: Fa lü ch'u pan she, 1957; 266 p.
Washington, D.C.: U.S. Joint Publications Research Service, 1962. 237 p. (JPRS 13,331; MC 10,317/1962) [Xerox copyflo available—New York: CCM Information Corp., Research and Microfilm Publications. (Scholarly Book Translation Series, 463)]
Subj 12.2 ▪ 12.1 22.2 64

11440 NNC P P2 G1.2 1949–1972
Chung yang cheng fa kan pu hsüeh hsiao. Min fa chiao yen shih. (Central Political-Judicial Cadres School. Institute of Civil Law Research), ed.
Basic problems in the civil law of the People's Republic of China, mimeo. Tr. of *Chung-hua jen min kung ho kuo min fa chi pen wen t'i*; Peking: Fa lü ch'u pan she, 1958; 360 p.
Washington, D.C.: U.S. Joint Publications Research Service, 15 Aug. 1961. 358 p. (JPRS 4879; MC 19,500/1961) [Xerox copyflo available—New York: CCM Information Corp., Research and Microfilm Publications. (Scholarly Book Translation Series, 452)]
Subj 12.2 ▪ 12.1 14.2 14.3 14.6 16.2 34.1 45

11441 CSH O P2 G1.2 1949–1972
Cohen, Jerome Alan, 1930–.
'Chinese law: At the crossroads.'
CQ 53 (Jan.–Mar. 1973), 139–143.
Subj 12.2 22.2 ▪ 22 22.1

11442 WSU FP P2 G1.2 1949–1972
Cohen, Jerome Alan, 1930–.
'The criminal process in China.' In *Soviet and Chinese Communism: Similarities and differences*, edited by Donald Warren Treadgold. [Selective entry]
Seattle: U. of Washington Press, 1967, 107–143.
Subj 12.2 22.2 ▪ 63

11443 CSU FP P2 G1.2 1949–1972
Cohen, Jerome Alan, 1930–.
'Introduction.' In *The criminal process in the People's Republic of China, 1949–1963: An introduction*, by J. A. Cohen. [Sole entry]
Cambridge: Harvard U. Press, 1968, 3–53. (Harvard studies in East Asian law, 2)
Subj 12.1 12.2 22.1 22.2 63 ▪ 12 16 32 41 46 64

11444 CSU P P1 G1.2 1949–1972
Cohen, Jerome Alan, 1930–.
'The party and the courts: 1949–1959.'
CQ 38 (Apr.–June 1969), 120–157.
Subj 12.2 32.1 ▪ 32

11445 NNC P P1 G1.2 1949–1972
Corinth, Bernhard.
'Die Organisation der Gerichte in der Volksrepublik China' (The organization of courts of law in the People's Republic of China).
Aussenpolitik 9, 8 (Aug. 1958), 526–531.
Subj 12.2 ▪ 12 12.1 22.2 64

11446 NNC P P1 G1.2 1949–1972
Corinth, Bernhard.
'Die Verfassung der Volksrepublik China' (The constitution of the People's Republic of China).
Aussenpolitik 8, 2 (Feb. 1957), 118–127.
Subj 12.2 ▪ 14 16 64 66

11447 CSU P P1 G1.2 1949–1972
Dekkers, René, 1909–.
'Le droit civil' (Civil law). In *La République populaire de Chine: cadres institutionnels et réalisations. I, l'histoire et le droit* (Institutions and accomplishments of the People's Republic of China, Vol. 1, History and law), by Marthe Engelborghs-Bertels and R. Dekkers. [Selective entry]
Brussels: Université libre de Bruxelles, Institut de sociologie Solvay, Centre d'étude des pays de l'Est *with* Centre national pour l'étude des pays à régime communiste, 1963, 167–199.
Subj 12.2 14 41 45 ▪ 12.1 14.1 14.3 14.4 34.1 64

11448 CSU P P1 G1.2 1949–1972
Dekkers, René, 1909–.
'Le droit pénal' (Criminal law). In *La République populaire de Chine: cadres institutionnels et réalisations. I, l'histoire et le droit* (Institutions and accomplishments of the People's Republic of China, Vol. 1, History and law), by Marthe Engelborghs-Bertels and R. Dekkers. [Selective entry]
Brussels: Université libre de Bruxelles, Institut de sociologie Solvay, Centre d'étude des pays de l'Est *with* Centre national pour l'étude des pays à régime communiste, 1963, 201–207.
Subj 12.2 62

11449 NNC PO P1 G1.2 1949–1972
Dekkers, René, 1909–.
'La vie juridique' (Legal life). In *Le régime et les institutions de la République populaire chinoise* (The government and institutions of the People's Republic of China), jointly edited by Centre d'étude des pays de l'Est, Institut de sociologie Solvay, Université libre de Bruxelles *with* Centre national pour l'étude des pays à régime communiste. [Selective entry]
Brussels: Snoeck-Ducaju, 1960, 56–68.
Subj 12.2

11450 CSU P P1 G1.2 1949–1972
Diwan, Paras.
'Constitutional developments in China.'
Supreme Court j. (Madras) 18 (1955), 293–374.
Subj 12.2 ▪ 12

11451 CSU P P1 G1.2 1949–1972
Engelborghs-Bertels, Marthe, 1928–.
'Le droit public' (Public law). In *La République populaire de Chine: cadres institutionnels et réalisations. I, l'histoire et le droit* (Institutions and accomplishments of the People's Republic of China, Vol. 1, History and law), by M. Engelborghs-Bertels and René Dekkers. [Selective entry]
Brussels: Université libre de Bruxelles, Institut de sociologie Solvay, Centre d'étude des pays de l'Est *with* Centre national pour l'étude des pays à régime communiste, 1963, 113–166.
Subj 12 12.1 12.2 63 64 ▪ 16 32

11452 CSH P P2 G1.2 1949–1972
Engelborghs[-Bertels], Marthe, 1928–.
'Les modifications apportées aux institutions de droit public par la révolution culturelle chinoise' (Public law in China after the Cultural Revolution).
NED 3498/3499 (15 juin 1968), 17–24.
Subj 12 12.2 32 ▪ 12.1 16 35 54 64

11453 FPN P P2 G1.2 1949–1972
Engelborghs-Bertels, Marthe, 1928–.
'Le pluralisme juridique en République populaire de Chine' (Legal pluralism in the People's Republic of China).
R. du Centre d'étude des pays de l'Est et du Centre national pour l'étude des états de l'Est 1968, 125–146.
Subj 12.2 64 ▪ 16.1 16.2 32 32.1 37 66

11454 MCH P P1 G1.2 1949–1972
Finkelstein, David Jacob, 1937–.
'The language of Communist China's criminal law.'
JAS 27, 3 (May 1968), 503–521. [Reprinted in *Contemporary Chinese law: Research problems and perspectives*, edited by Jerome Alan Cohen. (Selective entry.) Cambridge: Harvard U. Press, 1970, 188–209. (Harvard studies in East Asian law, 4)]
Subj 12.2

11455 MCH P P4 G1.2 1949–1972
Ginsburgs, George, 1932–, and Arthur Allan Stahnke, 1935–.
'The genesis of the people's procuratorate in Communist China, 1949–1951.'
CQ 20 (Oct.–Dec. 1964), 1–37.
Subj 12.2 22.2 ▪ 12.1

11456 CSU P P2 G1.2 1949–1972
Ginsburgs, George, 1932–, and Arthur Allan Stahnke, 1935–.
'The people's procuratorate in Communist China: The institution ascendant, 1954–1957.'
CQ 34 (Apr.–June 1968), 82–132.
Subj 12.2 ▪ 12.1 22.2 32

11457 MCH P P1 G1.2 1949–1972
Ginsburgs, George, 1932–, and Arthur Allan Stahnke, 1935–.
'The people's procuratorate in Communist China: The period of maturation, 1951–54.'
CQ 24 (Oct.–Dec. 1965), 53–91.
Subj 12.1 12.2 ▪ 32

11458 CSH P P2 G1.2 1949–1972
Gudoshnikov, Leonid Moiseevich.
'Gosudarstvenno pravovoe stroitel'stvo' (The political and legal structure). In

Kitaiskaia Narodnaia Respublika (The People's Republic of China), compiled by Institut Dal'nego Vostoka, Akademiia nauk SSSR, edited by Mikhail Iosifovich Sladkovskii and Grigorii Dmitrievich Sukharchuk. [Selective entry]
Moscow: Nauka, Glav. red. vost. lit-ry, 1970, 133–168.
SUBJ 12 12.2 22 ▪ 15 32 64

11459 NNC P P1 G1.2 1949–1972
Gudoshnikov, Leonid Moiseevich.
'Kitaiskaia Narodnaia Respublika' (The People's Republic of China). In *Gosudarstvennoe pravo stran narodnoi demokratii* (Public law in the people's democracies), edited by V- F- Kotok. [Sole entry]
Moscow: Gosiurizdat, 1961, 330–372.
SUBJ 10 12 12.2 ▪ 16 32

11460 MCH P P7 G1.2 1949–1972
Gudoshnikov, Leonid Moiseevich.
'Rol' sudebnykh organov Kitaiskoi Narodnoi Respubliki v provedenii zemel'noi reformy' (The role of judicial organs of the People's Republic of China in land reform).
SGP 1953, 2/3 (fevral'–mart), 102–107.
SUBJ 12.2 16 22.2 ▪ 14.1 16.3

11461 CSH P P1 G1.2 1949–1972
Gudoshnikov, Leonid Moiseevich (L. M. Gudoschnikow).
'Sudebnaia reforma 1952–1953 gg. i dal'neishaia demokratizatsiia sudebnoi sistemy Kitaiskoi Narodnoi Respubliki' (The 1952–1953 court reform and further democratization of the court system in the People's Republic of China).
SGP 1954, 8 (avgust), 56–62.
'Die Gerichtsreform in den Jahren 1952–1953 und die weitere Demokratisierung des Gerichtssystems der Volksrepublik China.'
Rechtswissenschaftlicher Informationsdienst 4, 10 (20 Mai 1955), 296–302.
SUBJ 12.2 ▪ 64

11462 NNC P P1 G1.2 1949–1972
Han Shu-chih.
'Several questions concerning procedure in criminal appeal cases.' Tr. of 'Kuan yü hsing shih shang su an chien shen li ch'eng hsü shang ti chi ko wen t'i'; *Fa hsüeh; Hua-tung cheng fa hsüeh pao* 1956, 3 (Dec.), 5–11.
URS 6, 11 (5 Feb. 1957), 158–169.
SUBJ 12.2

11463 DLC P P3 G1.2 1949–1972
Havrylov, I- E-, and A- Kuznetsov.
'Rozhliad kryminal'nykh sprav u narodnykh sudakh Kytaïs'koï Nadornoï Respublyky' (Review of criminal cases in the people's courts of the People's Republic of China).
Radians'ke pravo 1958, 4 (lypen'–serpen'), 124–126.
SUBJ 12.2 ▪ 12

11464 CSU P P1 G1.2 1949–1972
Hazard, John Newbold, 1909–.
'Communist constitutionalism in a new form.'
Studies in comparative Communism 4, 1 (Jan. 1971), 107–116.
SUBJ 12.2 ▪ 12 15 22 45

11465 CBU P P1 G1.2 1949–1972
Heinzig, Dieter, 1932–.
'Die Präambel des neuen Verfassungsentwurfs der Volksrepublik China' (The preamble of the new draft constitution of the People's Republic of China).
Verfassung und Recht in Übersee 5, 1 (1972), 41–56.
SUBJ 12.2 ▪ 64

11466 CSU P P2 G9.5 1949–1972
Hong Kong. Supreme Court.
Annual departmental report by the Registrar, Supreme Court, 1954/55–1971/72. [Issues for 1946/47–1948/49 are entered as 11340.]
Hong Kong: Government Printer. Issued annually, 1951–1972. Average ca. 30 p.
SUBJ 12.2 ▪ 22.2

11467 CSU P P1 G9.5 1949–1972
Hooker, Michael Barry, 1939–.
'The relationship between Chinese law and common law in Malaysia, Singapore, and Hong Kong.'
JAS 28, 4 (Aug. 1969), 723–742.
SUBJ 12.2 22.2 ▪ 38 41 43 45 57

11468 MCH P P1 G1.2 1949–1972
Houn, Franklin W. (Hou Fu-wu), 1920–.
'Communist China's new constitution.'
Western political q. 8, 2 (June 1955), 199–233.
SUBJ 12 12.2 22 ▪ 14

11469 NNC P P1 G1.2 1949–1972
Houn, Franklin W. (Hou Fu-wu), 1920–.
'The draft constitution of Communist China.'
PA 27, 4 (Dec. 1954), 319–337.
SUBJ 12.2 ▪ 12 12.1

11470 MCH P P1 G1.2 1949–1972
Hsia, Tao-tai (Hsia Tao-t'ai), 1915–.
'The constitution of Red China.'
AJCL 4, 3 (Summer 1955), 425–435.
SUBJ 12 12.2

11471 CSU P P1 G1.2 1949–1972
Hsia, Tao-tai (Hsia Tao-t'ai), 1915–, and Deborah Murray.
'Communist Chinese legal development reflected in the country's legal publications.'
Quarterly j. of the Library of Congress 25, 4 (Oct. 1968), 290–298.
SUBJ 12.2 14.2 70

11472 CSU P P1 G1.2 1949–1972
Hsiao, Gene T. (Hsiao Chün), 1922–.
'Communist China: Legal institutions.'
Problems of Communism 14, 2 (Mar.–Apr. 1965), 112–121.
SUBJ 12.2 ▪ 12.1

11473 MCH P P1 G1.2 1949–1972
Hsiao, Gene T. (Hsiao Chün), 1922–.
'The role of contracts in Communist China.'
California law review 53, 4 (Oct. 1964), 1029–1060.
SUBJ 12.2 45 ▪ 14.3

11474 CSU P P1 G1.2 1949–1972
Jain, Hari Mohan.
'Some aspects of the Chinese constitution.'
India q. 14, 4 (Oct.–Dec. 1958), 373–379.
SUBJ 12.2 ▪ 12

11475 CSU S P1 G1.2 1949–1972
Kamenka, Eugene, and Alice Erh-Soon Tay (Cheng Ju-chun), 1934–.
'Beyond the French Revolution: Communist socialism and the concept of law.'
U. of Toronto law j. 21 (1971), 109–140.
SUBJ 12.2

11476 CSH P P4 G1.2 1949–1972
Kim, Chan Jin.
'The procuracy in Communist China.'
Asian forum 2, 1 (Jan.–Mar. 1970), 31–53.
SUBJ 12 12.2 ▪ 32.1

11477 MCH U P1 G1.2 1949–1972
Koldin, Valentin IAkovlevich.
'Nekotorye voprosy ugolovno-pravovoi politiki Kitaiskoi Narodnoi Respubliki' (Criminal-law policy in the People's Republic of China).
Vestnik Moskovskogo universiteta; seriia ekonomiki, filosofii, prava 13, 4 (1958), 153–172.
SUBJ 12.2 22.2 ▪ 63 64

11478 DLC U P1 G1.2 1949–1972
Kolmakov, V- P-.
'Razvitie kriminalistiki i sudebnoi ekspertizy v Kitaiskoi Narodnoi Respublike' (The development of criminal law and legal investigation in the People's Republic of China).
Voprosy kriminalistiki 3 (1962), 112–124.
SUBJ 12.2 ▪ 12 17

11479 CSH P P1 G1.2 1949–1972
[La Dany, Ladislao] — —, 1914–.
'The draft constitution.'
CNA 823 (4 Dec. 1970), 1–7.
SUBJ 12.2

11480 NNC P P1 G1.2 1949–1972
[La Dany, Ladislao] ———, 1914–.
'The judiciary.'
CNA 140 (20 July 1956), 1–7; 141 (27 July 1956), 1–7.
SUBJ 12.2

11481 NIC P P1 G1.2 1949–1972
[La Dany, Ladislao] ———, 1914–.
'Law.'
CNA 255 (28 Nov. 1958), 1–7.
SUBJ 12.2 64

11482 MCH P P1 G1.2 1949–1972
[La Dany, Ladislao] ———, 1914–.
'Law.'
CNA 467 (10 May 1963), 1–7.
SUBJ 12.2 32.1 ▪ 64 70

11483 CSH O P2 G1.2 1949–1972
[La Dany, Ladislao] ———, 1914–.
'A man who knew China.'
CNA 842 (21 May 1971), 1–7.
SUBJ 12.2 32.2 ▪ 18 19 22.2

11484 MMT P P1 G1.2 1949–1972
Lee, Luke T. C. (Li Tsung-chou), 1920–.
'Towards an understanding of law in Communist China.' In *Symposium on economic and social problems of the Far East*, edited by Edward Franciszek Szczepanik. [Selective entry]
Hong Kong: Hong Kong U. Press, 1962, 335–352.
SUBJ 12.1 12.2 16.1 ▪ 12 17 64 66

11485 MCH P P1 G1.2 1949–1972
Leng, Shao-chuan (Leng Shao-ch'üan), 1921–.
'The lawyer in Communist China.'
J. of the International Commission of Jurists 4, 1 (Summer 1962), 33–50.
Subj 12.2 16.1 ▪ 12.1 22.2 32.1

11486 WSU P P2 G1.2 1949–1972
Leng, Shao-chuan (Leng Shao-ch'üan), 1921–.
'Post-constitutional development of "peoples justice" in China.'
J. of the International Commission of Jurists 6, 1 (Summer 1965), 103–128.
Subj 12 12.1 12.2 ▪ 16 22.2 32.2

11487 CSU P P2 G1.2 1949–1972
Li, Victor H. (Li Hao), 1941–.
'The evolution and development of the Chinese legal system.' In *China: Management of a revolutionary society*, edited by John Matthew Henry Lindbeck. [Analytic entry]
Seattle: U. of Washington Press, 1971, 221–255. (Social Science Research Council, Studies in Chinese government and politics, 2)
Subj 12.2 22.2 ▪ 12.1 22.1

11488 CSU P P2 G1.2 1949–1972
Li, Victor H. (Li Hao), 1941–.
'The role of law in Communist China.'
CQ 44 (Oct.–Dec. 1970), 66–111.
Subj 12.2 ▪ 12.1 22 22.2

11489 MCH P P1 G1.2 1949–1972
Lin, Fu-shun, 1929–.
'Communist China's emerging fundamentals of criminal law.'
AJCL 13, 1 (Winter 1964), 80–93.
Subj 12.2

11490 CSH P P1 G1.2 1949–1972
Ling Piao and Ling Feng. [Authors sequential rather than joint: Ling Piao for 1962 and 1964; Ling Feng for 1963.]
'Legal affairs' [title varies]. Tr. from *Tsu kuo chou k'an* 538 (29 Apr. 1963) *and* from *Tsu kuo* 1 (Apr. 1964); 14 (May 1965) [recurring annual feature article]. In *Communist China, 1962–1964*, edited by Union Research Institute.
Hong Kong: Union Research Institute. Issued annually, 1963–1965, average ca. 15 p.
Subj 12.2

11491 CSU P P1 G9.4 1949–1972
Liu, Chin-sui.
'The Chinese Council of Grand Justices.'
AJCL 7, 3 (Summer 1958), 402–408.
Subj 12.2

11492 CSH PO P3 G9.5 1949–1972
Lo, Man Kam (Lo Wen-chin), 1893–196?
Comments on the report of the Committee on Chinese Law and Custom in Hong Kong.
Hong Kong: Government Printer, 1953. 18 p. [For the report, see entry 19878.]
Subj 12.2 43 45

11493 CSU FP P2 G1.2 1949–1972
Lubman, Stanley Bernard, 1934–.
'Form and function in the Chinese criminal process.'
Columbia law review 69, 4 (Apr. 1969), 535–575.
Subj 12.2 22.2 ▪ 12 12.1 16 19 22 26.1 32 32.1 64

11494 MCH P P2 G1.2 1949–1972
Lubman, Stanley Bernard, 1934–.
'Methodological problems in studying Chinese Communist "civil law".' In *Contemporary Chinese law: Research problems and perspectives*, edited by Jerome Alan Cohen. [Selective entry]
Cambridge: Harvard U. Press, 1970, 230–260. (Harvard studies in East Asian law, 4)
Subj 12.2 22.2 34.2

11495 MCH P P1 G1.2 1949–1972
Lunev, Aleksandr Efremovich.
Sud, prokuratura i gosudarstvennyi kontrol' v Kitaiskoi Narodnoi Respublike (The court, the procuratorate, and state control in the People's Republic of China).
Moscow: Gosiurizdat, 1956. 72 p.
Subj 12.1 12.2 ▪ 22.2

11496 NNC P P1 G1.2 1949–1972
Lunev, Aleksandr Efremovich.
Sushchnost' konstitutsii Kitaiskoi Narodnoi Respubliki (Essentials of the constitution of the People's Republic of China).
Moscow: Gosiurizdat, 1958. 158 p.
Subj 12 12.2 22 ▪ 14 17 32 34.1

11497 CSU S P3 G5.1 1949–1972
Matsushita, Teruo.
'The Great Cultural Revolution and principle of law of the proletarian dictatorship.'
Review (Tokyo) 15 (Dec. 1967), 1–48.
Subj 12.2 ▪ 19 64

11498 CSU P P1 G1.2 1949–1972
Melis, Giorgio.
'Il potere statale nella nuova costituzione cinese' (The power of the state in the new Chinese constitution).
L'Est 3 (30 settembre 1971), 7–27.
Subj 12.2

11499 DLC O P2 G1.2 1949–1972
Nathan, Hans, and Gerhard Schüssler.
'Das Gerichtsverfahren in der Volksrepublik China' (Legal procedures in the People's Republic of China).
Neue Justiz 13, 15 (5 Aug. 1959), 511–516.
Subj 12.2 22.2

11500 CSU P P1 G9.4 1949–1972
Ning, Werner Y. F.
'Due process and the Sino-American Status of Forces Agreement.'
AJCL 17, 1 (Winter 1969), 94–115.
Subj 12.2 ▪ 12.1 66

11501 MCH O P4 G1.2 1949–1972
Ostroumov, Georgii Sergeevich.
'Novoe v rabote sudov Kitaiskoi Narodnoi Respubliki' (Developments in court work in the People's Republic of China).
Sovetskaia iustitsiia 1959, 9 (sentiabr'), 64–66.
Subj 12.2 22.2

11502 CSU P P1 G9.4 1949–1972
Peng Ming-min (P'eng Ming-min), 1923–.
'Political offences in Taiwan: Laws and problems.'
CQ 47 (July–Sept. 1971), 471–493.
Subj 12.2 ▪ 12.1

11503 MCH P P2 G1.2 1949–1972
Pfeffer, Richard Monroe, 1936–.
'Contracts in China revisited, with a focus on agriculture, 1949–1963.'
CQ 28 (Oct.–Dec. 1966), 106–129.
Subj 12.2 14.1 14.3 ▪ 12 14 34.1

11504 MCH S P1 G1.2 1949–1972
Pfeffer, Richard Monroe, 1936–.
'Crime and punishment: China and the United States.' In *Contemporary Chinese law: Research problems and perspectives*, edited by Jerome Alan Cohen. [Selective entry]
Cambridge: Harvard U. Press, 1970, 261–281. (Harvard studies in East Asian law, 4)
Subj 12.1 12.2

11505 MCH P P2 G1.2 1949–1972
Pfeffer, Richard Monroe, 1936–.
'The institution of contracts in the Chinese People's Republic.'
Harvard International Law Club j. 4, 1 (Dec. 1962), 1–147. [Reprinted—*CQ* 14 (Apr.–June 1963), 153–177; 15 (July–Sept. 1963), 115–139.]
Subj 12.2 14 ▪ 12 17 34.2

11506 CSU P P3 G9.5 1949–1972
Rear, John.
'The legal regulations of industrial relations in Hong Kong.'
Lawasia 2 (1971), 36–50.
Subj 12.2 36.4

11507 MCH P P1 G1.2 1949–1972
Rech, Ernesto.
'La costituzione cinese del 1954' (The Chinese constitution of 1954).
Cina 1 (1956), 169–186.
Subj 12 12.2 ▪ 12.1

11508 CBU P P1 G1.2 1949–1972
Rosenthal, Gérard.
'Rapport juridique.' In *Livre blanc sur le travail forcé et les institutions concentrationnaires dans la République populaire de Chine, II, le dossier*, compiled and edited by Commission internationale contre le régime concentrationnaire. [Selective entry]
Paris: Centre international d'édition et de documentation, 1958, 83–126.

'Legal report.' In *White book on forced labour and concentration camps in the People's Republic of China, Vol. II, The record*, compiled and edited by the organization cited. [Selective entry]
Paris: Centre international d'édition et de documentation, 1958, 69–104.
Subj 12.1 12.2 64

11509 MCH P P1 G1.2 1949–1972
Sarker, Subhash Chandra.
'Judiciary in China.'
India q. 13, 4 (Oct.–Dec. 1957), 307–325.
Subj 12.2 ▪ 63

11510 NNC P P1 G1.2 1949–1972
Schultz, Lothar.
'Die neue Verfassung der Volksrepublik China' (The new constitution of the People's Republic of China).
Osteuropa-Recht 1, 1 (März 1955), 43–55.
SUBJ 12 12.2 ▪ 12.1 14

11511 NNC P P1 G1.2 1949–1972
Schultz, Lothar.
'Die Verfassungsentwicklung der Volksrepublik China seit 1949' (Constitutional developments in the People's Republic of China since 1949).
Jahrbuch des öffentlichen Rechts der Gegenwart neue (2.) Folge 5 (1956), 329–365.
SUBJ 12.2 64 ▪ 12 12.1 14 16 22

11512 MCH O P2 G1.2 1949–1972
Shi Lian (Shih Liang), 1907?–.
'Organizatsiia i deiatel'nost' sudebnykh organov Kitaiskoi Narodnoi Respubliki' (The organization and operation of judicial organs in the People's Republic of China).
SGP 1955, 8 (avgust), 116–120.
SUBJ 12.2

11513 CSU P P1 G1.2 1949–1972
Spitz, Allan.
'Maoism and the people's courts.'
AS 9, 4 (Apr. 1969), 255–263. [Reprinted as 'The allocation of justice.' In *Communist China: A system-functional reader*, edited by Yung Wei. (Selective entry.) Columbus, Ohio: Merrill, 1972, 359–368.]
SUBJ 12.2 64 ▪ 14.2 32.1

11514 MAM P P2 G1.2 1949–1972
Stahnke, Arthur Allan, 1935–.
The people's procuratorate of Communist China: Problems of organization and development.
Ann Arbor: University Microfilms (Publ. 67-9107), 1967. 331 p. (Doctoral dissertation in Political Science, U. of Iowa)
SUBJ 12.2 22.2 ▪ 12 12.1 16.1 22.1 32

11515 MCH P P1 G1.2 1949–1972
Steiner, Harold Arthur, 1905–.
'Constitutionalism in Communist China.'
APSR 49, 1 (Mar. 1955), 1–21.
SUBJ 12.2 32.1 64 ▪ 12.1 32 34.2

11516 MCH O P3 G1.2 1949–1972
Stepanova, M-, and M- Tulisov.
'Tridtsat' dnei v narodnom Kitae' (Thirty days in the People's Republic of China).
Sovetskaia iustitsiia 1957, 1 (ianvar'), 44–48.
SUBJ 12.2

11517 CBU P P1 G1.2 1949–1972
Su, Jyun-hsyong.
'Zum gegenwärtigen Stand des Strafrechts im kommunistischen China' (The present state of criminal law in Communist China).
Z. für die gesamte Strafrechtswissenschaft 80, 2 (1968), 510–528.
SUBJ 12.2

11518 NNC O P2 G1.2 1949–1972
Sudarikov, Nikolai Georgievich, 1913–.
'Organizatsiia suda i prokuratury KNR' (The organization of courts of law and the procuratorate in the People's Republic of China).
Sotsialisticheskaia zakonnost' 29, 5 (mai 1952), 50–57.
SUBJ 12.2 ▪ 12

11519 NNC O P2 G1.2 1949–1972
Sudarikov, Nikolai Georgievich, 1913–.
'Organy iustitsii Kitaiskoi Narodnoi Respubliki' (Judicial organs in the People's Republic of China).
Sotsialisticheskaia zakonnost' 28, 10 (oktiabr' 1951), 47–54.
SUBJ 12.2 ▪ 12

11520 CSU P P1 G1.2 1949–1972
Tao, Lung-sheng.
'The criminal law of Communist China.'
Cornell law q. 52, 1 (Fall 1966), 43–68.
SUBJ 12.2

11521 CSU P P2 G9.4 1949–1972
Tao, Lung-sheng.
'Reform of the criminal process in Nationalist China.'
AJCL 19, 4 (Fall 1971), 747–765.
SUBJ 12.1 12.2

11522 CSH P P1 G1.2 1949–1972
Tay, Alice Erh-soon (Cheng Ju-chun), 1934–.
'Gemeinschaft, gesellschaft, mobilisation and administration: The future of law in Communist China.'
Asia q. 1971, 3, 257–303.
SUBJ 12.2 ▪ 12.1 32 64

11523 CSU S P1 G1.2 1949–1972
Tay, Alice Erh-soon (Cheng Ju-chun), 1934–.
'Law and society in the People's Republic of China.'
Lawasia 2 (1971), 135–144.
SUBJ 12.2

11524 CSH P P1 G9.4 1949–1972
Too, Horace H. Y. (T'u Huai-ying).
'The legislative process and the legislative staff aids [*sic*] of the Republic of China and their problems: A comparative study.'
CC 7, 2 (June 1966), 39–64.
SUBJ 12 12.2

11525 CSH P P2 G1.2 1949–1972
Tsien Tche-hao (Ch'ien Chih-hao), 1923–.
'Législation nouvelle pour un peuple de civilisation millénaire' (New legislation for the people of an ancient civilization).
Projet 40 (déc. 1969), 1213–1221. [Special issue: *La Chine s'est levée* (China resurgent)]
SUBJ 12.2 64 ▪ 12 14.2 32

11526 CSU P P1 G1.2 1949–1972
Tsien Tche-hao (Ch'ien Chih-hao), 1923–.
'La responsibilité civile délictuelle en Chine populaire' (Tort liability in the People's Republic of China).
R. internationale de droit comparé 19 (oct.–déc. 1967), 875–882.
SUBJ 12.2 ▪ 45

11527 MCH U P1 G1.2 1949–1972
TSzan' TSzi-pyi and Vladimir Evgen'evich Chugunov.
'Osnovnye cherty ugolovnogo protsessa KNR' (Basic features of criminal procedure in the People's Republic of China).
SGP 1957, 2 (fevral'), 73–81.
SUBJ 12.2 ▪ 22.2

11528 CSU P P2 G9.4 1949–1972
United Nations. Secretariat.
'Systems of prison labour in selected countries of Asia and the Far East.'
International review of criminal policy 14 (Apr. 1959), 25–34.
SUBJ 12.2 ▪ 21.4

11529 MCH U P1 G1.2 1949–1972
Van Khou-li (Wang Hou-li).
'Organizatsiia i deiatel'nost' sudebnoi sistemy Kitaiskoi Narodnoi Respubliki' (The organization and operation of the judicial system in the People's Republic of China).
Sovetskaia iustitsiia 1958, 1 (ianvar'), 47–51.
SUBJ 12.1 12.2 ▪ 12 22.2

11530 CSU PO P2 G1.2 1949–1972
van der Sprenkel, Sybille Marie, 1919–.
'The role of law in the changing society.' In *Modern China's search for a political form*, edited by Jack Douglas Gray. [Analytic entry]
London: Oxford U. Press, 1969, 225–267.
SUBJ 12.1 12.2 22.2 ▪ 19 45 61 64

11531 DLC U P1 G1.2 1949–1972
Voevodin, Leonid Dmitrievich.
'Osnovy gosudarstvennogo prava Kitaiskoi Narodnoi Respubliki' (Principles of public law in the People's Republic of China). In *Gosudarstvennoe pravo stran narodnoi demokratii* (Public law in the people's democracies), by L. D. Voevodin. [Sole entry]
Moscow: Izd-vo IMO, 1960, 161–218.
SUBJ 12 12.2 16 ▪ 12.1 14 71

11532 CSU P P1 G1.2 1949–1972
Wang Yun.
'A comparison between the old and new CCP constitutions.'
IS 5, 6 (Mar. 1969), 15–24.
SUBJ 12.2 ▪ 32 64

11533 CSU P P1 G1.2 1949–1972
Weggel, Oskar, 1935–.
'Die Gesetzgebung in der Volksrepublik China' (Legislation in the People's Republic of China).
Verfassung und Recht in Übersee 2 (1970), 139–166.
SUBJ 12.1 12.2 32 64 ▪ 12 16.4 66

11534 MCY P P2 G1.2 1949–1972
Wei, Henry (Wei Wen-ch'i), 1909–.
Courts and police in Communist China to 1952.
Lackland Air Force Base, San Antonio, Tex.: U.S. Air Force Personnel and Training Research Center, Air Research and Development Command, 1955. 11, 63 p. (U.S. Human Resources Research Institute research memoranda, 44; Studies in Chinese Communism, series 1, 1, 1952)
SUBJ 12.1 12.2 22.2 ▪ 14.1 16 32.2 61

11535 CSU PO P1 G1.2 1949–1972
Woodsworth, K- C-.
'The legal system of the Republic of China.'

Canadian Bar j. 4, 4 (Aug. 1961), 299–311.
SUBJ 12.2 ▪ 12

13 ELITE AND OFFICIAL RELIGION
社會領導階層與官定之宗教信仰
国教及び上層階級の宗教

1644-1911

11536 DLC O P3 G1.3 –1842
[Bichurin, Nikita Iakovlevich] *Otets* Iakinf, 1777–1853.
'Obshchestvennaia i chastnaia zhizn' kitaitsev' (The public and private life of the Chinese).
Otechestvennyia zapiski 3-ia seriia 2, 5, Part 10 (1840), 1–36, 63–103.
SUBJ 13 41 57 ▪ 12 21.3 23 44 62

11537 CSU U P3 G5.1 1842–1895
Blodget, Henry, 1825–1903.
'Prayers of the emperor for snow and rain.'
CR 15, 4 (July–Aug. 1884), 249–253.
SUBJ 13

11538 NIC U P3 G5.1 1644–1911
Blodget, Henry, 1825–1903.
'The worship of heaven and earth by the emperor of China.'
JAOS 20, 1 (Jan.–July 1899), 58–69.
SUBJ 13 62 ▪ 64

11539 MCH FP P2 G1.3 –1911
Boerschmann, Ernst, 1873–1949.
Gedächtnistempel (Memorial temples).
Berlin: Reimer, 1914. 21, 286 p.
SUBJ 13 64 ▪ 23 43 62

11540 GBF O P4 G1.2 –1911
Brandt, Max August Scipio von, 1835–1914?
Die chinesische Philosophie und der Staatskonfuzianismus (Chinese philosophy and state Confucianism).
Stuttgart: Strecker und Moser, 1898. 121 p.
SUBJ 13 64

11541 MCH P P2 G5.0 1644–1842
Brucker, Joseph, 1845–1926.
'La mission de Chine de 1722 à 1735' (The mission to China from 1722 to 1735).
R. des questions historiques 29 (1er avr. 1881), 491–532.
SUBJ 13 32.1 33 66 ▪ 12.2 16.1 18

11542 MCH FP P8 G5.3 –1911
Chavannes, Emmanuel Edouard, 1865–1918.
'Le T'ai chan: essai de monographie d'un culte chinois' (T'ai-shan [T'ai-an *hsien*, Shantung]: Treatise on a Chinese cult).
Annales du Musée Guimet, Bibliothèque d'études 21 (1910), 1–591. [Separately reprinted—Taipei: Ch'eng-wen, 1970. 591 p.]
SUBJ 13 21.3 23 33 ▪ 57 58 60

11543 NIC S P1 G1.2 –1911
Coulborn, Rushton.
'The state and religion: Iran, India and China.'
CSSH 1, 1 (Oct. 1958), 44–57.
SUBJ 12 13 66

11544 NIC S P1 G1.1 –1911
Eisenstadt, Shmuel Noah, 1923–.
'Religious organizations and political process in centralized empires.'
JAS 21, 3 (May 1962), 271–294.
SUBJ 12 13 23 ▪ 32.2 33

11545 CBU P P1 G1.2 –1842
Etiemble, René, 1909–.
Les jésuites en Chine (1552–1773): la querelle des rites (The Jesuits in China, 1552–1773: The 'Rites controversy').
Paris: Juillard, 1966. 297 p.
SUBJ 13 33 66

11546 MCH P P4 G1.2 –1911
Farjenel, Fernand, ?–1918.
'Le culte impérial en Chine' (The imperial cult in China).
JA 10e série 8, 1 (juil.–août 1906), 491–516.
SUBJ 13 ▪ 62

11547 CSU O P3 G5.1 1644–1911
Ferguson, John Calvin, 1866–1945.
'The T'ai Miao of Peking [Temple of Ancestors].'
THM 6, 3 (Mar. 1938), 185–190.
SUBJ 13 ▪ 43

11548 NIC O P3 G5.1 1644–1911
Fischer, Emil Sigmund, 1865–1945.
'T'ai Miao: A description of the supreme hall of sacrifices of the Forbidden City.'
JRAS-NCB new (2nd) series 64 (1933), 72–76.
SUBJ 13 ▪ 43

11549 MCH P P1 G1.2 –1911
Groot, Jan Jakob Maria de, 1854–1921.
'Heerscht er in China godsdienstvrijheid?'
Onze Eeuw (Haarlem) 1, 1 (Maart 1901), 268–296; 1, 2 (April 1901), 550–588.

'Is there religious liberty in China?' [Abridged tr.]
MSOSB 5 (1902), 103–151.
SUBJ 13 ▪ 33 64

11550 CBU FP P2 G1.2 –1911
Groot, Jan Jakob Maria de, 1854–1921.
'Die Religionen der Chinesen' (Chinese religions). In *Die Religionen des Orients und die altgermanische Religion* (The religions of the Orient and the old German religion), by Paul Hinneberg et al. [Sole entry]
Leipzig: Teubner, 1923, 162–193. (Die Kultur der Gegenwart, Tiel 1, Abteilung 3, 1)
SUBJ 13 23 62 ▪ 33 43 57 64

11551 MCH O P3 G5.1 1842–1895
Happer, Andrew Patton, 1818–1894.
'A visit to Peking.'
CR 10, 1 (Jan.–Feb. 1879), 23–47. [Separately reprinted as *A visit to Peking, with some notices of the imperial worship at the altars of heaven, earth, sun, moon and the gods of the grain and the land*. Shanghai: American Presbyterian Mission Press, 1879. 27 p.]
SUBJ 13

11552 NIC P P1 G6.2 1644–1911
Huang, Quentin (Huang K'uei-yüan), 1902?–, and John Knight Shryock, 1890–1952.
'A collection of Chinese prayers.'
JAOS 49, 2 (June 1929), 128–155.
SUBJ 12 13 64

11553 CBU O P7 G6.1 1842–1895
Imbault-Huart, Camille Clément, 1857–1897.
'Une visite à l'établissement religieux et scientifique de Si Ka oué près Changhaï' (A visit to the Zikawei [Hsü-chia-hui] religious and scientific establishment near Shanghai).
JA 7e série 16 (oct.–déc. 1880), 538–543.
SUBJ 13 ▪ 21.3

11554 CBU O P3 G6.1 1842–1895
Imbault-Huart, Camille Clément, 1857–1897.
'Une visite au temple de Confucius à Changhaï' (A visit to the temple of Confucius in Shanghai).
JA 7e série 16 (oct.–déc. 1880), 533–538.
SUBJ 13 ▪ 21.3

11555 NNC P P1 G1.1 1644–1842
Legge, James, 1815–1897.
'Imperial Confucianism.'
China review 6, 3 (Nov.–Dec. 1877), 147–158; 6, 4 (Jan.–Feb. 1878), 223–235; 6, 5 (Mar.–Apr. 1878), 299–310; 6, 6 (May–June 1878), 363–374.
SUBJ 12.2 13 ▪ 63 64

11556 MCH P P1 G1.1 –1911
Lyall, Alfred Comyn, 1835–1911.
'On the relations between the state and religion in China.' In *Asiatic studies, religious and social*, 2nd ed., by A. C. Lyall. [Sole entry]
London: Murray, 1907, vol. 2, 101–175.
SUBJ 12 13 33 ▪ 16.1 23 43 62 63 66

11557 NNC P P1 G1.2 1644–1842
Maus, ———.
'Das siebente Edikt des Kaisers Kanghi' (The seventh edict of the K'ang-hsi Emperor).
Allgemeine Missions-Z. 20, 1 (Jan. 1893), 37–41.
SUBJ 13 33 ▪ 32.2 64

11558 NNC PO P4 G1.2 –1895
Mayers, William Frederick, 1831–1878.
'On Wen-ch'ang, the God of Literature: His history and worship.'
JRAS-NCB new (2nd) series 6 (1869/70), 31–44.
SUBJ 13 23 60 ▪ 17

11559 NNC P P4 G1.2 –1911
Messing, Otto.
'Über die chinesische Staatsreligion und ihren Kultus' (The Chinese state religion and its cult).
ZE 43, 2 (1911), 348–375.
SUBJ 13 ▪ 43 62 64

11560 MCH P P2 G1.2 –1911
Morisse, Lucien.
'Les éclipses et les rites chinois' (Eclipses and related Chinese rituals).
AF 2, 17 (août 1902), 367–372.
SUBJ 13 62

11561 NNC PO P3 G6.3 –1911
Moule, George Evans, 1828–1912.
'Notes on the Ting-chi or half-yearly sacrifice to Confucius.'
JRAS-CB new (2nd) series 33 (1899/1900), 120–156.
SUBJ 13 ▪ 62

11562 MCH PO P1 G1.2 –1911
Parker, Edward Harper, 1849–1926.
Studies in Chinese religion.
London: Chapman and Hall, 1910. 11, 308 p.
SUBJ 13 23 33 ▪ 62 63

11563 NNM P P4 G1.2 –1842
Rowbotham, Arnold Horrex, 1888–.
Missionary and mandarin: The Jesuits at the court of China.
Berkeley, Los Angeles: U. of California Press, 1942. 11, 374 p. [Reprinted—New York: Russell and Russell, 1966. 11, 374 p.]
SUBJ 13 60 62 ▪ 33 43 63 64 66 71

11564 NNC S P3 G1.3 –1911
Schmeltz, J- D- E-.
'Das Pflugfest in China' (The plowing festival in China).
Internationales Archiv für Ethnographie 11 (1898), 72–81.
SUBJ 13 ▪ 14.1 64

11565 MCH O P4 G5.0 1842–1911
Schüler, Wilhelm, 1869–1935.
'Die Kultushandlungen der heutigen chinesischen Staatsreligion' (Ritual practices in the contemporary Chinese state religion).
Z. für Missionskunde und Religionswissenschaft 26, 3 (1911), 84–87.
SUBJ 13 ▪ 23

11566 CSU S P4 G1.2 –1911
Smith, David Howard, 1900–.
'The state cult of Confucianism.' In *Chinese religions*, by D. H. Smith. [Selective entry]
New York: Holt, Rinehart and Winston, 1968, 140–147.
SUBJ 13

11567 MCH P P2 G1.3 1842–1911
Tobar, Jérôme, 1855–1917.
La Chine et les religions étrangères (China and foreign religions).
Shanghai: Impr. de la Mission catholique, 1917. 252 p. (Variétés sinologiques, 47)
SUBJ 13 33 64 66 ▪ 12 62

11568 MCH PO P3 G5.1 1644–1911
Wang Ngen-jong (Wang En-jung).
'Cérémonial de la cour et coutumes du peuple de Pékin' (Court ceremony and popular customs in Peking). Tr. from the Chinese by G- Douin.
BAAFC 2, 2 (avr. 1910), 105–138; 2, 3 (juil. 1910), 215–237; 2, 4 (oct. 1910), 347–368; 3, 2 (avr. 1911), 134–155; 3, 3 (juil. 1911), 209–233; 4, 1 (jan. 1912), 66–84.
SUBJ 13 41 55 57 65 ▪ 12 16.1 43 51 62 66

11569 ELO PO P5 G1.2 –1842
Watters, Thomas, 1840–1901.
A guide to the tablets in a temple of Confucius.
Shanghai: American Presbyterian Mission Press, 1879. 20, 259 p.
SUBJ 13 59 64 ▪ 62 63

11570 CSU P P1 G1.3 –1895
Wiethoff, Bodo, 1931–.
'Der staatliche Ma-tsu Kult' (The official cult of Ma-tsu).
ZDMG 116 (1966), 311–357.
SUBJ 13 33 ▪ 23

11571 MCH P P1 G1.3 1644–1842
Willeke, Bernward Henry, 1913–.
Imperial government and Catholic missions in China during the years 1784–1785.
St. Bonaventure, N.Y.: Franciscan Institute, 1948. 14, 227 p. (Doctoral dissertation in History, Columbia U.)
SUBJ 13 66 ▪ 32.2 33

11572 NIC PO P2 G1.2 –1911
Williams, Edward Thomas, 1854–1944.
'Agricultural rites in the religion of old China.'
JRAS-NCB new (2nd) series 67 (1936), 25–49.
SUBJ 13 14.1 60

11573 CSU PO P3 G5.1 1644–1911
Williams, Edward Thomas, 1854–1944.
'The state religion of China during the Manchu dynasty.'
JRAS-NCB new (2nd) series 44 (1913), 11–45.
SUBJ 13 ▪ 55 62

11574 CSH PO P1 G1.2 –1895
Williams, Samuel Wells, 1812–1884.
'Religion of the Chinese.' In *The Middle Kingdom: A survey of the geography, government, literature, social life, arts, and history of the Chinese empire and its inhabitants*, rev. and enl. ed., by S. W. Williams. [Selective entry]
New York: Scribner, 1883, vol. 2, 188–274. [Reprinted in *The Middle Kingdom: A survey of the geography, government, literature, social life, arts, and history of the Chinese empire and its inhabitants*, by S. W. Williams. (Selective entry.) Taipei: Ch'eng-wen, 1965, 188–274 (s.p.)]
SUBJ 13 33 ▪ 23 32.2 38 43 51 57 62

1644-1949

11575 NIC F P3 G5.1 1644–1928
Bouillard, Georges, 1862–1930.
Pékin et ses environs, cinquième série, le Temple de la Terre, les Temples du Soleil et de la Lune, le Temple de l'Agriculture (In and around Peking, Fifth series, The Altar of the Earth, the Altars of the Sun and the Moon, and the Temple of Agriculture).
Peking: Nachbaur, 1923. n.p. [44 p. in all] [Reprinted from *La Chine* 33, 34 (1923).]
SUBJ 13 23

11576 NIC F P8 G5.1 1644–1928
Bouillard, Georges, 1862–1930.
Pékin et ses environs, huitième série, les temples autour du Hsiang Shan: Tien t'ai sze, Wo fo sze (In and around Peking, Eighth series, the temples of T'ien-tai-ssu and Wo-fu-ssu [Wu-ch'ing *hsien*, Hopei]).
Peking: Nachbaur, 1924. n.p. [66 p. in all] [Reprinted from *La Chine* 48, 49, 51 (1923).]
SUBJ 13 65

11577 NIC F P3 G5.1 –1928
Bouillard, Georges, 1862–1930.
Péking et ses environs, quatrième série, le Temple du Ciel (In and around Peking, Fourth series, The Temple of Heaven).
Peking: Nachbaur, 1923. n.p. [100 p. in all] [Reprinted from *La Chine* 27, 28, 31 (1922).]
SUBJ 13 23

11578 NNC P P1 G1.2 –1928
Chang, Daniel Sung-kao.
Position of Chinese Christians in China.
Unpublished masters thesis in Public Law, Columbia U., 1928. 81 p.
SUBJ 13 33 66 ▪ 12.2

11579 NNC P P1 G1.3 –1928
Franke, Otto, 1863–1946.
'Das religiöse Problem in China' (The religious problem in China).
Archiv für Religionswissenschaft 17 (1914), 165–196.
SUBJ 13 62 64 ▪ 16.1 33 66

11580 CBU P P1 G1.2 –1949
Franke, Otto, 1863–1946.
'Die religiöse und politische Bedeutung des Konfuzianismus in Vergangenheit und Gegenwart' (The religious and political significance of Confucianism, past and present).
Z. für systematische Theologie 8, 3 (1930), 579–588.
SUBJ 12 13 64

11581 MCY PO P2 G1.2 –1928
Granet, Marcel, 1884–1940.
La religion des Chinois (Chinese religion), 2nd ed.
Paris: Presses universitaires, 1951. 11, 175 p.
SUBJ 13 23 43 62 65 ▪ 16.1 16.3 41 47 64

11582 MCH PO P3 G3.1 1644–1949
Hedin, Sven Anders, 1865–1952.
Jehol: Kejsarstaden.
Stockholm: L. Hökerberg, 1931. 287 p.
Jehol [i.e., Ch'eng-te], *city of emperors.* Tr. by E- G- Nash.
New York: Dutton, 1933. 14, 278 p. [Reprinted—Ann Arbor: University Microfilms, n.d. 14, 278 p.]
SUBJ 12 13 20 ▪ 65

11583 MCH P P2 G1.2 –1928
Johnston, Reginald Fleming, 1874–1938.
'The cult of military heroes in China.'
NCR 3, 1 (Feb. 1921), 41–64; 3, 2 (Apr. 1921), 79–91.
SUBJ 13 15 ▪ 23 33 63

11584 CSU O P3 G5.1 1895–1928
Meech, Samuel E-.
'The imperial worship at the Altar of Heaven.'
CR 47, 2 (Feb. 1916), 112–117.
SUBJ 13

11585 CSU S P1 G1.2 –1949
Rotours, Robert des.
'Confucianisme et christianisme' (Confucianism and Christianity).
Sinologica 1, 3 (1948), 231–245.
SUBJ 13 33 ▪ 43 64

11586 CNY FP P2 G1.2 1644–1949
Shao, Luther Ching-san (Shao Ching-san), 1901–1958.
Religious liberty and Christian education in China.
Unpublished doctoral dissertation in Religious Studies, Yale U., 1934. 653 p.
SUBJ 12.2 13 17 33 37 66 ▪ 19 32.2 53 63 64

11587 MCH P P4 G1.2 –1928
Shryock, John Knight, 1890–1952.
The origin and development of the state cult of Confucius: An introductory study.
New York: Appleton-Century, 1932. 13, 298 p. [Reprinted—New York: Paragon, 1966. 13, 298 p.]
SUBJ 13 64 ▪ 12 16.1 17 62 66

11588 MCH FP P2 G1.2 –1949
Sirén, Osvald, 1879–1959.
Bilder från Kina (Pictures from China).
Stockholm: Nordisk Rotogravyr, 1936. 127 p.
SUBJ 13 21.3 23 ▪ 24.1 24.2 24.3 55 62

11589 NNC P P1 G1.2 –1928
Werner, Edward Theodore Chalmers, 1864–1954.
'Rebuttal notes: The origin of Chinese religion.' In *Autumn leaves: An autobiography with a sheaf of papers, sociological and sinological, philosophical and metaphysical*, by E. T. C. Werner. [Selective entry]
Shanghai: Kelly and Walsh, 1928, 236–248.
SUBJ 13 71 ▪ 23 43

11590 CSU PO P1 G1.2 1644–1928
Wieger, Léon (Leo Wieger), 1856–1933.
'Temps modernes, sous la dynastie mandchoue Ts'ing. I, tchouhisme officiel. II, culte étatiste du Ciel. III, le culte officiel de Confucius' (Modern times, under the Ch'ing. 1, The official cult of Chou. 2, The state cult of heaven. 3, The official cult of Confucius). In *Histoire des croyances religieuses et des opinions philosophiques en Chine depuis l'origine, jusqu'à nos jours*, 3rd ed., by L. Wieger. [Selective entry]
Hsien-hsien, Hopei: Impr. de Sienhsien, 1927, 715–730.
'Rationalism and indifferentism under the Manchu Ch'ing dynasty.' Tr. by Edward Theodore Chalmers Werner. In *A history of the religious beliefs and philosophical opinions in China from the beginning to the present time*, by L. Wieger. [Selective entry]
Hsien-hsien, Hopei: Hsien-hsien Press, 1927, 715–730. [Reprinted in *A history of the religious beliefs and philosophical opinions in China from the beginning to the present time*, by L. Wieger. (Selective entry.) New York: Paragon, 1969, 715–730.]
SUBJ 13 16.1 62 63 ▪ 12.2 32.2

11591 MCH U P1 G1.2 1895–1928
Williams, Edward Thomas, 1854–1944.
'Confucianism and the new China.'
Harvard theological review 9, 3 (July 1916), 258–285.
SUBJ 13 17 64 ▪ 23 33 37

11592 NNM PO P1 G1.2 –1928
Wright, Harrison King, ?–1923.
'Religious persecution in China: An historical study of the relations between church and state.'
CR 52, 4 (Apr. 1921), 235–249; 52, 5 (May 1921), 341–354; 52, 6 (June 1921), 397–410.
SUBJ 13 33 60 ▪ 32.2 64 66

1911-1949

11593 NIC P P1 G1.2 1911–1949
Bates, Miner Searle, 1897–.
'Religious liberty in China.'
International review of missions 35, 138 (Apr. 1946), 165–173.
SUBJ 13 ▪ 33

11594 MCH O P2 G5.3 1911–1928
Bishop, Carl Whiting, 1881–1942.
'Shantung: China's holy land.'
Museum j. (Philadelphia: U. of Pennsylvania) 12, 2 (June 1921), 85–115.
SUBJ 13 23 ▪ 24.2 33 55

11595 NNC P P1 G1.2 1911–1949
Blackman, Lonnie Elwood, 1892–.
The Kuomintang and non-indigenous religious faiths in China.
Unpublished masters thesis in Chinese, Columbia U., 1931. 64 p.
SUBJ 13 33 ▪ 17 66

11596 ELB P P1 G1.2 1911–1949
Chan, Wing-tsit (Ch'en Jung-chieh), 1901–.
Religious trends in modern China.
New York: Columbia U. Press, 1953. 13, 327 p. (American Council of Learned Societies, Lectures on the history of religions, new series, 3)
SUBJ 13 32.2 33 63 ▪ 62

11597 MCH PO P3 G5.1 1911–1928
Doré, Henri, 1859–1931.
'Le culte de Confucius sous la République chinoise, 1911–1922' (The cult of Confucius in Republican China, 1911–1922).
Etudes 7e série 172, 4 (20 août 1922), 433–448.
SUBJ 12.2 13 64 ▪ 16.1 37 62 66

11598 NNC P P1 G1.2 1911–1949
Grosse-Aschoff, Angelus Francis, 1910–.
Confucianism in China under the Republic.
Unpublished masters thesis in Chinese and Japanese, Columbia U., 1943. 105 p.
SUBJ 13 64 ▪ 60 63

11599 MCH PO P3 G5.1 1911–1928
Perrot, Albert, 1869–?
'Le retour de la vieille Chine: le confucianisme redevenu religion d'état' (Old China's comeback: Confucianism reestablished as the state religion).
Etudes 7e série 139, 4 (20 mai 1914), 461–480.
SUBJ 12.2 13 16.1 64 ▪ 43

11600 MCH P P1 G1.2 1911–1928
Schüler, Wilhelm, 1869–1935.
'Die Gründung des "Amtes zur Regelung der Riten" in Peking' (The establishment of the Board of Rites in Peking).
OR 9, 1 (2 Jan. 1928), 15–17.
SUBJ 12 13 ▪ 64 66

11601 MAM P P2 G1.2 1911–1949
Sovik, Arne, 1918–.
Church and state in Republican China: A survey history of the relations between the Christian churches and the Chinese government, 1911–1945.
Ann Arbor: University Microfilms (Publ. 66-14,280), 1966. 400 p. (Doctoral dissertation in Religion, Yale U., 1952)
SUBJ 13 17 33 66 ▪ 12 32 32.2 37

1911-1972
(including 1644-1972)

11602 MCH P P1 G1.2 1928–1972
'Le mouvement pour une église autonome en Chine' (The movement for an autonomous church in China).
B. des missions St. André de Bruges 25, 1/2 (1952), 76–93.
SUBJ 13 33 64 66 ▪ 12.2 16.1 17 32 62

11603 CBU PO P1 G1.1 1644–1972
Athenoux, André.
Le Christ crucifié au pays de Mao (Christ crucified in the land of Mao).
Paris, Colmar: Ed. Alsatia, 1968. 239 p.
SUBJ 13 33 ▪ 12.2 56 64 66

11604 CSU S P1 G1.2 1928–1972
Bates, Miner Searle, 1897–.
'Christianity in the People's Republic of China.' In *China today*, edited by William Jerome Richardson. [Selective entry]
New York: Maryknoll; New York: Friendship Press, 1969, 85–104.
SUBJ 13 33

11605 CSU O P2 G1.1 1928–1972
Darcourt, Pierre.
Requiem pour l'Eglise de Chine (Requiem for the Church of China).
Paris: Table ronde, 1969. 285 p.
SUBJ 13 22.2 32 33 ▪ 12.2 15 21.3 32.2 64 66

11606 NNR S P1 G1.2 1928–1972
Galligan, David Joseph, 1921–.
American Protestant missions and Communist China, 1947–1950.
Unpublished doctoral dissertation in History, Rutgers U., 1952. 156 p.
SUBJ 13 66 ▪ 17

11607 NNC P P1 G1.2 –1972
Hai, Badruddin W-.
Muslim minority in China.
Unpublished masters thesis in Public Law and Government, Columbia U., 1955. 153 p.
SUBJ 13 33 66 ▪ 12 17 22.2 30 32.2

11608 CSU S P1 G1.1 1895–1972
Kramers, Robert Paul, 1920–.
'Der Konfuzianismus als Religion: Versuche zur Neubelebung eines konfuzianischen Glaubens' (Confucianism as a religion: Attempts to revive a Confucian faith).
Asiatische Studien 18/19 (1965), 143–166.
SUBJ 13 62 64 ▪ 63

11609 NNC P P2 G1.2 1928–1972
[La Dany, Ladislao] ———, 1914–.
'Church-state relations: The Catholic Church, 1948–1957.'
CNA 186 (28 June 1957), 1–7.
SUBJ 13 33

11610 CSU PO P1 G1.2 –1972
Lohmann, Theodor.
'Religion im alten und neuen China' (Religion in traditional and modern China).

Wissenschaftliche Z. der Friedrich-Schiller-Universität Jena; gesellschaft- und sprachwissenschaftliche Reihe 9, 3 (1959/60), 373–383.
Subj 13 33 43 64 ▪ 23 65

11611 NNC PO P 1 G 1.2 1928–1972
Lyall, Leslie Theodore, 1905–.
Come wind, come weather: The present experience of the church in China.
London: Hodder and Stoughton, 1961. 119 p.
Subj 13 33 66 ▪ 63

11612 CSH P P 1 G 1.2 1928–1972
Myers, James Townsend, 1936–.
'The cult of Mao Tse-tung: A preliminary attempt at periodization and description of constructs.' In *Collected documents of the First Sino-American Conference on Mainland China*. [Selective entry]
[Taipei]: Institute of International Relations, Republic of China, 1971, 177–208.
Subj 13 ▪ 16.1 32 32.2 64

11613 CSU P P 1 G 1.2 1928–1972
Myers, James Townsend, 1936–.
'The political dynamics of the cult of Mao Tse-tung.' In *Communist China: A system-functional reader*, edited by Yung Wei. [Selective entry]
Columbus, Ohio: Merrill, 1972, 78–101.
Subj 12.1 13 16.1 60 ▪ 15 32 32.2 35

11614 MAM P P 1 G 1.2 1928–1972
Rinden, Robert Watland, 1914–.
The cult of Mao Tse-tung.
Ann Arbor: University Microfilms (Publ. 69-19,566), 1969. 11, 391 p. (Doctoral dissertation in Political Science, U. of Colorado)
Subj 13 19 32 64 ▪ 15 17 43

11615 MCH P P 1 G 1.2 1928–1972
Schram, Stuart Reynolds, 1924–.
'Mao Tse-tung as a charismatic leader.'
AS 7, 6 (June 1967), 383–388.
Subj 13 61 ▪ 12.1 64

11616 CSU S P 1 G 1.2 1928–1972
Walker, Richard Louis, 1922–.
'Mao as superman.'
J. of international affairs 26, 2 (1972), 160–166.
Subj 13 ▪ 61

1949-1972

11617 NNC PO P 1 G 1.2 1949–1972
Benz, Ernst, 1907–.
'Die Rolle des Buddhismus in der Innen- und Aussenpolitik der chinesischen Volksrepublik.' In *Buddhas Wiederkehr und die Zukunft Asiens* (Buddha's return and the future of Asia), by E. Benz. [Sole entry]
Munich: Nymphenburger Verlagshandlung, 1963, 209–253.

'The role of Buddhism in the domestic and foreign policy of the Chinese People's Republic.' Tr. by Richard Winston and Clara Winston. In *Buddhism or Communism: Which holds the future of Asia?*, by E. Benz. [Sole entry]
Garden City, N.Y.: Doubleday, 1965, 176–215.
Subj 12 13 33 64 ▪ 31

11618 MCH PO P 3 G 1.2 1949–1972
Bonnichon, André, 1905–.
'De la persécution considérée comme l'un des beaux-arts' (Persecution as one of the fine arts).
Etudes 7e série 286 (juil.–août 1955), 36–50.
Subj 13 33 62 ▪ 64

11619 CSU P P 2 G 1.1 1949–1972
Bush, Richard Clarence, Jr., 1923–.
Religion in Communist China.
New York: Abingdon Press, 1970. 432 p.
Subj 13 23 ▪ 17 33 65

11620 CSU O P 1 G 1.2 1949–1972
Chapman, Herbert Owen.
The Second Reformation: A historical study.
Sydney: Times Press, 1968. 32 p.
Subj 13

11621 MCH P P 3 G 1.3 1949–1972
Couturier, Charles.
'Evêques chinois' (Chinese [Catholic] bishops).
Etudes 7e série 305 (mai 1960), 209–221.
Subj 13 33 ▪ 64

11622 MCH P P 1 G 1.2 1949–1972
Hsia, Tao-tai (Hsia Tao-t'ai), 1915–, and Barbara A- Crowell.
Church and state under Communism, Vol. 8, Communist China.
Washington, D.C.: U.S. Government Printing Office, 1965. 50 p. (Senate Judiciary Committee, Subcommittee to Investigate Administration of Internal Security Act and Other Internal Security Laws, Special study)
Subj 12.2 13 ▪ 12 33 64

11623 CSU P P 1 G 1.2 1949–1972
Huang, Lucy Jen (Huang Jen-hua), 1920–.
'The role of religion in Communist Chinese society.'
AS 11, 7 (July 1971), 693–705.
Subj 13 63 64 ▪ 54 61

11624 CSH P P 2 G 1.2 1949–1972
IAkovlev, M- (M. Yakovlev).
'Sotvorenie kumira' (The creation of an idol).
Za rubezhom 1968, 5 (26 ianvaria – 1 fevralia), 19–20.

'A Soviet view of the cult of Mao Tse-tung: The making of an idol.' In *The miracles of Chairman Mao: A compendium of devotional literature, 1966–1970*, edited by George R- Urban. [Selective entry]
Los Angeles: Nash, 1972, 171–178.
Subj 13 64 ▪ 12.1

11625 NNC P P 2 G 1.2 1949–1972
Jones, Francis Price, 1890–.
The church in Communist China: A Protestant appraisal.
New York: Friendship Press, 1962. 180 p.
Subj 13 33 ▪ 64 66

11626 MCH S P 2 G 1.2 1949–1972
Joyaux, François.
'Les minorités musulmanes en Chine populaire' (Muslim minorities in the People's Republic of China).
Afrique et l'Asie 68 (oct.–déc. 1964), 3–12.
Subj 13 22 32.2 33 ▪ 11.2 12 29 32 32.1

11627 MAM F P 2 G 1.2 1949–1972
Lacy, Creighton Boutelle, 1919–.
Protestant missions in Communist China.
Ann Arbor: University Microfilms (Publ. 67-3453), 1967. 704 p. (Doctoral dissertation in Religion, Yale U., 1953)
Subj 13 66 ▪ 32.1 33

11628 MCH P P 2 G 1.2 1949–1972
[La Dany, Ladislao] ———, 1914–.
'Religion.'
CNA 593 (17 Dec. 1965), 1–7.
Subj 13 23 ▪ 64

11629 NIC P P 2 G 1.2 1949–1972
[La Dany, Ladislao] ———, 1914–.
'Religious policy.'
CNA 221 (21 Mar. 1958), 1–7.
Subj 13 23 33

11630 CSH P P 2 G 1.2 1949–1972
[La Dany, Ladislao] ———, 1914–.
'The tortuous history of the cult of Mao.'
CNA 743 (7 Feb. 1969), 1–7.
Subj 13

11631 MCH P P 1 G 1.2 1949–1972
Lee, Rensselaer Wright, III, 1937–.
'General aspects of Chinese Communist religious policy, with Soviet comparisons.'
CQ 19 (July–Sept. 1964), 161–173.
Subj 13 64 ▪ 62

11632 NNC U P 1 G 1.2 1949–1972
Levenson, Joseph Richmond, 1920–1969.
'The Communist attitude towards religion.' In *The Chinese model: A political, economic and social survey*, edited by Werner Klatt. [Selective entry]
Hong Kong: Hong Kong U. Press, 1965, 19–30.
Subj 13 ▪ 16.1 62

11633 CSU P P 1 G 1.2 1949–1972
MacInnis, Donald Earl, 1920–.
'Maoism and religion in China today.' In *The religious situation: 1969*, edited by Donald R- Cutler. [Sole entry]
Boston: Beacon Press, 1969, 3–24.
Subj 13 33 ▪ 25 64

11634 CSU S P 1 G 1.2 1949–1972
MacInnis, Donald Earl, 1920–.
'Maoism: The religious analogy.' In *China today*, edited by William Jerome Richardson. [Selective entry]
New York: Maryknoll; New York: Friendship Press, 1969, 56–71.
Subj 13 19 64 ▪ 16.1 54

11635 IMC PO P 1 G 1.2 1949–1972
Mateos, Fernando.
'La politica religiosa dei Comunisti cinesi' (The religious policy of the Chinese Communists).
Civiltà cattolica 116 (marzo 1965), 445–455.
Subj 13 ▪ 33

11636 NNC O P 1 G 1.2 1949–1972
Matthias, Leo L-, 1893–.
'Religionen im neuen China' (Religions in New China).
Merkur; deutsche Z. für europäisches Denken 11, 2 (Feb. 1957), 168–184.
Subj 13 33 ▪ 23 66

11637 CSU P P1 G1.2 1949–1972
Michael, Franz Henry, 1907–.
'Ideology and the cult of Mao.' In *Communist China, 1949–1969: A twenty-year appraisal*, edited by Frank Newton Trager and William Henderson. [Selective entry]
New York: New York U. Press, 1970, 27–44.
Subj 13 64 ▪ 32 32.1 54

11638 NNC O P2 G1.2 1949–1972
Migot, André, 1892–.
'Situation des religions en Chine populaire: bouddhisme et marxisme' (The position of religion in the People's Republic of China: Buddhism and Marxism). In *Le régime et les institutions de la République populaire chinoise* (The government and institutions of the People's Republic of China), jointly edited by Centre d'étude des pays de l'Est, Institut de sociologie Solvay, Université libre de Bruxelles *with* Centre national pour l'étude des pays à régime communiste. [Selective entry]
Brussels: Snoeck-Ducaju, 1960, 39–55.
Subj 13 62 64 ▪ 23

11639 MAM P P1 G1.2 1949–1972
Myers, James Townsend, 1936–.
The apotheosis of Chairman Mao: Dynamics of the hero cult in the Chinese system, 1949–1967.
Ann Arbor: University Microfilms (Publ. 69-16,707), 1969. 171 p. (Doctoral dissertation in Political Science, George Washington U.)
Subj 13 64 ▪ 16.1 32

11640 CSU P P1 G1.2 1949–1972
Myers, James Townsend, 1936–.
'De-Stalinization and the hero cult of Mao Tse-tung.'
Orbis (Philadelphia) 9, 2 (Summer 1965), 472–493.
Subj 13 ▪ 64

11641 CSH P P1 G1.2 1949–1972
Myers, James Townsend, 1936–.
'Religious aspects of the cult of Mao Tse-tung.'
CS 10, 3 (10 Mar. 1972), 1–11.
Subj 13 60

11642 CBU P P1 G1.2 1949–1972
Myers, James Townsend, 1936–.
'The rise of Lin Piao.'
RSAEO 1969, 2, 215–228.
Subj 13 64 ▪ 12.1 15 16.1

11643 CSU S P2 G1.2 1949–1972
Patterson, George Neilson, 1920–.
Christianity in Communist China.
Waco, Tex.: Word Books, 1969. 174 p.
Subj 13 33

11644 NNC PO P1 G1.2 1949–1972
Ravenholt, Albert, 1919–.
'The new Chinese "red" Catholic church.'
AUFS-EAS 9, 3 (Mar. 1961), 1–8.
Subj 13 33

11645 MCH P P1 G1.2 1949–1972
[Renault-Roulier, Gilbert] Rémy, pseud., 1904–.
'La "triple autonomie": ou, la bataille de Mao Tse-Tung contre Dieu' (The three-autonomies movement: Mao Tse-tung's battle against God).
R. de Paris 60, 5 (mai 1953), 26–48.
Subj 13 64 ▪ 12.2 33 62 66

11646 GMS PO P1 G1.1 1949–1972
Schütte, Johannes.
Die katholische Chinamission im Spiegel der rotchinesischen Presse (The Catholic mission to China as portrayed in the Red Chinese press).
Münster: Aschendorff, 1957. 394 p. (Doctoral dissertation, Theologische Fakultät, Universität Münster)
Subj 12.1 13 64 66

11647 NNC P P1 G1.2 1949–1972
Sohier, A-.
'La religion en Chine populaire' (Religion in the People's Republic of China). In *Le régime et les institutions de la République populaire chinoise* (The government and institutions of the People's Republic of China), jointly edited by Centre d'étude des pays de l'Est, Institut de sociologie Solvay, Université libre de Bruxelles *with* Centre national pour l'étude des pays à régime communiste. [Selective entry]
Brussels: Snoeck-Ducaju, 1960, 138–151.
Subj 13 ▪ 23 33 62

11648 FPN P P3 G1.2 1949–1972
Trivière, Léon, 1915–.
'L'Eglise catholique en Chine continentale' (The Catholic Church in Mainland China).
B. de la Société des missions étrangères de Paris 2e série 105–143 (août-sept. 1957 – fév. 1961), 1037 p. in all.
Subj 13 33 ▪ 12.2 64

11649 CSH PO P2 G1.2 1949–1972
Trivière, Léon, 1915–.
'Le mouvement des "trois autonomies".'
China missionary b. 5 (6), 1 (Jan. 1953), 17–29. [Reprinted in *Livre blanc sur le travail forcé et les institutions concentrationnaires dans la République populaire de Chine, II, le dossier*, compiled and edited by Commission internationale contre le régime concentrationnaire. (Selective entry.) Paris: Centre international d'édition et de documentation, 1958, 427–454.]
'The "three autonomies" movement.' In *White book on forced labour and concentration camps in the People's Republic of China, Vol. II, The record*, compiled and edited by the organization cited. [Selective entry]
Paris: Centre international d'édition et de documentation, 1958, 373–388.
Subj 13 66 ▪ 33

11650 MCH P P1 G1.2 1949–1972
Walker, Richard Louis, 1922–.
'Chairman Mao and the cult of personality.'
Encounter 14, 6 (June 1960), 31–43.
Subj 12 13 61 64 ▪ 32 32.1

11651 CSU FP P2 G1.2 1949–1972
Welch, Holmes Hinkley, 1921–.
Buddhism under Mao.
Cambridge: Harvard U. Press, 1972. 18, 666 p. (Harvard East Asian series, 69)
Subj 13 32.1 33 ▪ 22.1 23 24.1 24.4 34.1

11652 CSU FP P2 G1.2 1949–1972
Welch, Holmes Hinkley, 1921–.
'Facades of religion in China.'
AS 10, 7 (July 1970), 614–626.
Subj 13 33

11653 CSH P P1 G1.2 1949–1972
Whitehead, Raymond L-.
'Religion and social change in China today.' In *Selected seminar papers on contemporary China, I*, edited by Steve S. K. Chin (Chin Ssu-k'ai) and Frank Henry Haviland King. [Analytic entry]
Hong Kong: U. of Hong Kong, Centre of Asian Studies, 1971, 179–198. (CAS occasional papers and monographs, 4)
Subj 13 63

11654 MCH P P2 G1.2 1949–1972
Yang I-fan.
Islam in China.
Hong Kong: Union Press, 1957. 83 p.
Subj 13 33 66 ▪ 17 18 29 63

14 National Economy and Economic Planning

全國經濟及經濟計劃

国家経済及び経済計画

1644-1911

11655 DLC PO P1 G1.3 –1895
'K voprosu o kitaiskoi tsivilizatsii' (Chinese civilization).
Nabliudatel' 7, 11 (noiabr' 1888), 380–410.
Subj 12 14 40 ▪ 12.2 15 18 48 57 63 66

11656 NIC S P2 G1.3 –1911
Balazs, Etienne, 1905–1963.
'The birth of capitalism in China.'
J. of the economic and social history of the Orient 3, 2 (Aug. 1960), 196–216. [Reprinted in *Chinese civilization and bureaucracy*, by E. Balazs, edited by Arthur Frederick Wright. (Selective entry.) New Haven: Yale U. Press, 1964, 34–54.]
Subj 14 14.3 14.4 14.5 ▪ 12 16.2

11657 NNM PO P4 G1.1 1895–1911
Beresford, Charles William De la Poer, 1846–1919.
The break-up of China, with an account of its present commerce, currency, waterways, politics and future prospects.
New York: Harper, 1899. 52, 491 p.
Subj 14 14.2 15 66 ▪ 14.5 14.6 17 21 25

11658 FPN O P2 G1.5 1895–1911
Brenier, Henri, 1867–?
Rapport général sur l'origine, les travaux et les conclusions de la Mission lyonnaise (Report on the origin, works, and conclusions of the Lyons [Trade] Mission [to China]).
Lyons: Rey, 1897. 67 p.
Subj 14 14.3 66 ▪ 14.2 14.6 16.2 17 21 21.1 30 60

11659 NNC P P2 G9.4 1895–1911
Chang Han-yu (Chang Han-yü) and Ramon Hawley Myers, 1929–.
'Japanese colonial development policy in Taiwan, 1895–1906: A case of bureaucratic entrepreneurship.'
JAS 22, 4 (Aug. 1963), 433–449.
Subj 14 14.4 ▪ 17 18 22 24.1 24.2

11660 NIC P P2 G9.4 1842–1895
Chu, Samuel C. (Chu Ch'ang-ling), 1929–.
'Liu Ming-ch'uan and modernization of Taiwan.'
JAS 23, 1 (Nov. 1963), 37–53.
SUBJ 14 14.4 19 24.2

11661 NNC P P4 G1.2 1842–1911
Chudodeev, IUrii Vladimirovich, 1931–.
'Ekonomicheskaia politika TSinov v otnoshenii burzhuazii: k voprosu o krizise "verkhov" nakanune Sin'khaiskoi revoliutsii' (Ch'ing economic policy with regard to the bourgeoisie: Crisis within the elite on the eve of the Revolution of 1911).
KSINA 85 (1964), 85–101.
SUBJ 14 16.2 ▪ 16.1 66

11662 DLC U P2 G1.2 1842–1911
Cunow, Heinrich.
'Die wirtschaftliche Entwicklung Chinas' (The economic development of China).
Die neue Zeit 18, Band 2, 43 (1899/1900), 484–492; 18, Band 2, 44 (1899/1900), 523–530.
SUBJ 12 14 16 40 60 66 ▪ 16.3 16.4 32.2 41 45 47

11663 MCH O P2 G9.4 1644–1911
Davidson, James Wheeler, 1872–1933.
The island of Formosa: Historical view from 1430 to 1900 . . .
New York: Macmillan, 1903. 646, 28 & 46 p. [Reprinted—Taipei: Ch'eng-wen, 1972. 646, 28 & 46 p.]
SUBJ 12 14 ▪ 12.2 14.4 17 24.1

11664 NIC U P2 G1.2 1644–1911
Fairbank, John King, 1907–, Alexander Eckstein, 1915–, and Lien-sheng Yang, 1914–.
'Economic change in early modern China: An analytic framework.'
EDCC 9, 1 (Oct. 1960), 1–26. [Reprinted in *Modern China: An interpretive anthology*, edited by Joseph Richmond Levenson. (Selective entry.) London: Macmillan, 1971, 155–186.]
SUBJ 14 14.1 14.4 ▪ 12 14.5 14.6 16.1 62 64

11665 CSU P P2 G1.1 1842–1911
Feuerwerker, Albert, 1927–.
The Chinese economy, ca. 1870–1911.
Ann Arbor: U. of Michigan, Center for Chinese Studies, 1969. 79 p. (Michigan papers in Chinese studies, 5)
SUBJ 14 14.1 14.3 14.4 24.4 ▪ 11 12 16.1 18 66

11666 NIC P P2 G1.2 1644–1911
Feuerwerker, Albert, 1927–.
'Materials for the study of the economic history of modern China.'
J. of economic history 21, 1 (Mar. 1961), 41–60.
SUBJ 14 72

11667 FPN P P2 G1.3 –1895
Finquel, Edouard.
Eléments pour une histoire économique de la Chine impériale des origines au XIXe siècle (Contributions to an economic history of Imperial China from its origins to the nineteenth century).
Unpublished doctoral dissertation, Faculté de droit, Université de Paris, 1967. 316, 25 p. [Doctorat de l'université]
SUBJ 10 12 14 14.1 14.3 16.2 ▪ 14.5 16.1 64 66

11668 MCH O P2 G9.1 1895–1911
François, Georges Alphonse Florent Octave, 1874–.
'En mission au Kouang-si' (A mission to Kwangsi).
B. de la Société de géographie de Lyon 21, 134/135 (1906), 169–205.
SUBJ 14 25 ▪ 18 32.2 66

11669 MCH U P3 G1.1 1842–1911
Gal'bershtadt, L- I-.
'Dal'nii Vostok: ekonomicheskoe pereustroistvo Kitaia' (The Far East: The economic reconstruction of China).
Russkaia mysl' 30, 9 (1909), 164–180.
SUBJ 14 64 ▪ 14.6 19

11670 NNC P P4 G2.0 1842–1911
Gorelik, S- B-.
'Ekspansiia amerikanskogo kapitala v Man'chzhurii v kontse XIX – nachale XX v.' (The expansion of American capital in Manchuria in the late nineteenth and early twentieth centuries).
KSIV 10 (1953), 35–52.
SUBJ 14 14.6 ▪ 14.2 14.3 14.4

11671 MSE O P2 G2.0 1842–1911
Hosie, Alexander, 1853–1925.
Manchuria: Its people, resources and recent history, 2nd ed.
New York: Scribner, 1904. 11, 293 p.
SUBJ 11.3 14 14.1 14.3 ▪ 12 14.4 25

11672 MCH PO P4 G1.2 –1911
Jernigan, Thomas R-.
China in law and commerce.
New York: Macmillan, 1905. 408 p.
SUBJ 12.2 14 14.5 34.2 34.3 41 ▪ 12 14.2 14.6 16.1 16.2 45 47 66

11673 DLC P P2 G1.1 1842–1895
Liu, Kwang-ching (Liu Kuang-ching), 1921–.
'Li Hung-chang in Chihli: The emergence of a policy, 1870–1875.' In *Approaches to modern Chinese history*, edited by Albert Feuerwerker et al. [Selective entry]
Berkeley, Los Angeles: U. of California Press, 1967, 68–104. [Reprinted in *Readings in modern Chinese history*, edited by Immanuel C. Y. Hsü (Hsü Chung-yüeh). (Selective entry.) New York: Oxford U. Press, 1971, 234–258.]
SUBJ 12 14 14.4 15 ▪ 14.2 14.5 17 18

11674 NNC S P7 G1.2 1895–1911
Nepomnin, Oleg Efimovich, 1935–.
'K voprosu o skladyvanii ekonomicheskikh predposylok revoliutsii 1911 g. v kitaiskoi derevne' (The creation of economic preconditions for the Revolution of 1911 in the Chinese countryside). In *Sin'khaiskaia revoliutsiia v Kitae: sbornik statei* (Articles on the Revolution of 1911 in China), compiled by Institut narodov Azii, Akademiia nauk SSSR. [Selective entry]
Moscow: Izd-vo vost. lit-ry, 1962, 33–40.
SUBJ 14 14.1 ▪ 11.2

11675 MCH O P2 G9.2 1644–1842
Osbeck, Pehr (Peter Osbeck), 1723–1805.
Dagbok öfwer en ostindisk resa åren 1750, 1751, 1752.
Stockholm: Grefing, 1757. 376, 16 p.
Reise nach Ostindien und China. Tr. by Johan Gottlieb Georgi.
Rostock: Koppe, 1765. 24, 552, 26 p.
A voyage to China and the East Indies. Tr. by John Reinhold Forster.
London: White, 1771. 2 vols. 396; 367, 32 p.
SUBJ 12 14 14.3 21.4 ▪ 12.2 13 15 23 24.2 24.4 31 55 56 57

11676 CSU S P2 G1.2 1644–1911
Perkins, Dwight Heald, 1934–.
'Government as an obstacle to industrialization: The case of nineteenth century China.'
J. of economic history 27, 4 (Dec. 1967), 478–492.
SUBJ 12 14 ▪ 14.3 14.4 14.6 16.1 16.2 19

11677 DLC S P2 G2.0 –1911
Russia [Imperial]. Ministerstvo finansov.
Opisanie Man'chzhurii (A description of Manchuria), edited by Dmitrii Matveevich Pozdneev.
St. Petersburg: Tip. IU. N. Erlikh, 1897. 2 vols. s.p. [Vol. 1 has 620 p., vol. 2 s.p.]
SUBJ 10 14 71 ▪ 12 13 15 21 21.2

11678 NNC P P2 G9.4 1895–1911
Taiwan [Sōtokufu] (Japanese Government-General).
The statistical summary of Taiwan.
Tokyo: Japan Times Press, 1912. 15, 457 p.
SUBJ 12 12.2 14 24.1 ▪ 17 21 21.3 22 22.2 56 57 58 66

11679 NNC P P2 G8.2 1895–1911
Weiss, Fritz.
'Die Provinz Yünnan: Ihre Handels- und Verkehrsverhältnisse' (Conditions of trade and transport in Yunnan).
MSOSB 15 (1912), 1–57.
SUBJ 14 14.3 14.5 21 24.2 ▪ 12 24.1 24.3 24.4

11680 NNC P P2 G1.2 –1842
Wittfogel, Karl August, 1896–.
'The foundations and stages of Chinese economic history.'
Z. für Sozialforschung 1 (1935), 26–60.
SUBJ 12 14 ▪ 14.1 14.2 14.5 16.1 16.2 45

11681 MCH O P2 G1.3 1842–1895
Wolff, Eugen, 1850–1912.
Meine Wanderungen im Inneren Chinas (My travels in the interior of China).
Stuttgart: Deutsche Verlags-Anstalt, 1901. 298 p.
SUBJ 14 66 ▪ 12 14.1 14.2 15 21.3 24.4 26.1 28

11682 MCY P P1 G1.1 –1842
Yang, Lien-sheng, 1914–.
'Economic justification for spending: An uncommon idea in traditional China.'
HJAS 20, 1/2 (June 1957), 36–52. [Reprinted in *Studies in Chinese institutional history*, by Lien-sheng Yang. (Selective entry.) Cambridge: Harvard U. Press, 1961, 58–74. (Harvard-Yenching Institute studies, 20)]
SUBJ 14 61 ▪ 19 60 64 70 71

1644-1949

11683 NNM O P2 G9.3 -1928
Anti-Cobweb Club.
Fukien: A study of a province in China.
Shanghai: Presbyterian Mission Press, 1925. 113 p.
Subj 14 14.3 21.4 23 24.4 28 ▪ 12 17 24.1 26.2 26.4 41 47 56 57

11684 CSU P P2 G2.0 1895–1949
Bix, Herbert Philip, 1938–.
'Japanese imperialism and the Manchurian economy, 1900–31.'
CQ 51 (July–Sept. 1972), 425–443.
Subj 14 14.1 14.3 66 ▪ 14.6 16.2 21 21.2 25

11685 MCH S P2 G1.2 -1949
Chang, Chi-yun (Chang Ch'i-yün), 1901–.
The natural resources of China.
New York: Sino-International Economic Research Center, 1945. 71 p. (Sino-International economic pamphlets, 1)
Subj 14 ▪ 14.1 14.4

11686 ELU P P2 G3.0 1644–1928
Chang Yin-t'ang, 1902–.
The economic development and prospects of Inner Mongolia (Chahar, Suiyuan, and Ningsia).
Shanghai: Commercial Press, 1933. 243 p. (Masters thesis in Geography, U. of Liverpool, 1929) [Reprinted—Taipei: Ch'eng-wen, 1970. 243 p.]
Subj 14 14.1 14.4 21 ▪ 11.3 14.2 21.2 21.3 34.1 35

11687 NNP P P2 G1.1 1842–1949
Clark, Grover, 1891–1938.
Economic rivalries in China.
New Haven: Yale U. Press, 1932. 132 p.
Subj 14 14.2 14.6 ▪ 14.4 16.2

11688 CSU S P2 G1.2 1842–1949
Eckstein, Alexander, 1915–.
'The economic heritage.' In *Economic trends in Communist China*, edited by A. Eckstein, Walter Galenson, and Ta-chung Liu. [Selective entry]
Chicago: Aldine, 1968, 33–86.
Subj 14 ▪ 14.1 14.3 14.4

11689 CSU P P2 G1.2 -1949
Elvin, John Mark Dutton, 1938–.
The pattern of the Chinese past.
Stanford: Stanford U. Press, 1973. 346 p.
Subj 10 14 14.1 15 16 45 ▪ 11.1 11.4 14.3 14.5 16.3 24.3 25 34.2 34.3 62

11690 CSH P P2 G9.4 1895–1949
Grajdanzev, Andrew Jonah, 1899–.
Formosa today: An analysis of the economic development and strategic importance of Japan's tropical colony.
New York: Institute of Pacific Relations, International Secretariat, 1942. 193 p. [Reprinted—Ann Arbor: University Microfilms, n.d. 193 p.]
Subj 14 17 18 21 ▪ 12 21.4 22 32 47 58

11691 NNC P P2 G2.0 1644–1928
Hoshino, T., comp.
Economic history of Manchuria, compiled in commemoration of the decennial of the Bank of Chosen.
Seoul: Bank of Chosen, 1921. 10, 303 p.
Subj 14 ▪ 12 14.2 14.3 14.6 16.2 21.2 34.2

11692 MMT P P2 G1.1 1842–1949
Hou, Chi-ming, 1924–.
Foreign investment and economic development in China, 1840–1937.
Cambridge: Harvard U. Press, 1965. 13, 306 p. (Harvard East Asian series, 21) (Revision of *Foreign capital in China's economic development, 1895–1937*, doctoral dissertation in Economics, Columbia U., 1954)
Subj 14 14.2 14.4 ▪ 12 12.2 14.6 16.1 16.2 34.2 62 66

11693 MCH P P2 G1.2 1842–1949
Hou, Chi-ming, 1924–.
'Some reflections on the economic history of modern China (1840–1949).'
J. of economic history 23, 4 (Dec. 1963), 595–605.
Subj 14 ▪ 14.1 14.4 14.5 15 70 71

11694 WSU PO P2 G1.1 1895–1949
IAshnov, Evgenii Evgen'evich.
Osobennosti istorii i khoziaistva Kitaia (Features of China's history and economy).
Harbin: Tip. N. E. Chinareva, 1933. 120 p.
Subj 14 64 ▪ 11.4 14.5 14.6 16.4 32.2

11695 DLC U P1 G2.0 1895–1949
[Kantorovich, Anatolii IAkovlevich] N. Terent'ev, pseud., 1896–1944.
'Bor'ba imperialistov za Man'chzhuriiu' (The imperialists' struggle for Manchuria). In *Okkupatsiia Man'chzhurii i bor'ba imperialistov* (The occupation of Manchuria and the imperialists' struggle), compiled by Kolonial'nyi sektor, Institut mirovogo khoziaistva i mirovoi politiki, Kommunisticheskaia akademiia. [Selective entry]
Moscow: Partizdat, 1932, 68–86.
Subj 14 66 ▪ 15 64

11696 DLC S P2 G2.0 1895–1949
Kantorovich, Anatolii IAkovlevich, 1896–1944.
IAponskii kapital v Man'chzhurii (Japanese capital in Manchuria).
Moscow: Gosfinizdat, 1932. 69 p.
Subj 14 66 ▪ 14.6 15

11697 NNC P P2 G2.0 1895–1928
Kitaiskaia Vostochnaia zheleznaia doroga. Ekonomicheskoe biuro. (Chinese Eastern Railway. Economic Bureau).
Severnaia Man'chzhuriia i Kitaiskaia Vostochnaia zheleznaia doroga.
Harbin: Tip. KVzhd, 1922. 11, 292, 23 p.
North Manchuria and the Chinese Eastern Railway. Tr. by T- L- Lilliestrom and A- G- Skerst, edited by I- A- Mikhailov. [Rev. and enl. in tr.]
Harbin: Chinese Eastern Railway, 1924. 17, 454 p.
Subj 14 14.2 14.3 ▪ 14.1 14.4 21.2

11698 MCH P P2 G1.2 1895–1928
Ko, Siang-feng (K'o Hsiang-feng).
L'organisation de la production, du crédit et de l'échange en Chine de 1894 à 1914 (The organization of production, credit, and exchange in China from 1894 to 1914).
Lyons: Bosc et Riou, 1929. 202 p. (Doctoral dissertation, Faculté des lettres, Université de Lyon)
Subj 14 14.3 14.6 16.3 16.4 34.3 ▪ 24.4 34.2 36.3 38 41 42

11699 MCH S P2 G1.2 1895–1949
Lachin, Maurice.
La Chine capitaliste (Capitalism in China), 5th ed.
Paris: Gallimard, 1938. 303 p.
Subj 12 14 15 16 32 32.2 ▪ 14.4 14.6 18 19 35 36.2 64

11700 CSU S P2 G1.2 1644–1949
Lattimore, Owen, 1900–.
'The industrial impact on China, 1800–1950.' In *First International Conference of Economic History, Stockholm, August 1960.* [Sole entry]
The Hague: Mouton, 1960, 103–113.
Subj 14 14.4 16 66 ▪ 14.1 14.3 16.1 16.2

11701 MCH U P1 G1.2 1842–1928
Lidth de Jeude, O- C- A- van.
'China's economische ontwikkeling' (China's economic development).
China (Amsterdam) 2 (Januari 1927), 68–83.
Subj 14 ▪ 14.6

11702 MCH P P2 G1.2 1842–1928
Lieu, D. K. (Liu Ta-chün), 1891–1962.
Foreign investments in China.
Shanghai: ——, 1929. 131 p. [Cooperative research study made under the joint auspices of Institute of Pacific Relations (Honolulu), Social Science Research Council (New York), Brookings Institute of Economics, and Chinese Government Bureau of Statistics (Nanking).]
Subj 12 14 14.6 ▪ 12.1 12.2 14.3 14.5

11703 MCH P P2 G1.1 1842–1928
Lieu, D. K. (Liu Ta-chün), 1891–1962.
Foreign investments in China.
Shanghai: Institute of Pacific Relations, 1931. 53 p. [Preliminary paper prepared for Fourth Biennial Conference of Institute of Pacific Relations; continuation of entry 11702.]
Subj 14 14.6 ▪ 12 17 34.2 38 66

11704 NNC P P2 G1.1 1895–1949
Mad'iar, Liudvig Ignat'evich, 1891–?
Ocherki po ekonomike Kitaia (Notes on China's economy).
Moscow: Izd-vo Kom. akad., 1930. 306 p.
Subj 14 16 ▪ 14.1 14.3 14.4 14.6 16.3 24.4 32.2

11705 CSH PO P2 G1.2 1644–1928
Morse, Hosea Ballou, 1855–1934.
The trade and administration of China, 3rd ed., rev.
Shanghai: Kelly and Walsh; London: Longmans, Green, 1921. 15, 505 p. [Reprinted—New York: Russell and Russell, 1967. 15, 505 p.]
Subj 12 14 14.5 14.6 66 ▪ 12.2 14.3 22 22.2 32.2 34.2

11706 CSU P P2 G8.1 1644–1949
Myers, Ramon Hawley, 1929–.
'The usefulness of local gazetteers for the study of modern Chinese economic history: Szechuan province during the Ch'ing and Republican periods.'

THJ new (2nd) series 6, 1/2 (Dec. 1967), 72–102.
Subj 14 14.5 24.2 24.3 ▪ 14.3 14.4 21 25 32.2 58

11707 NNC P P2 G1.2 1842–1949
Nagano Akira, 1888–.
The development of capitalism in China. Tr. of *Shina shihonshugi hattatsushi* (History of the development of capitalism in China); Tokyo: Izumi shoten, 1931; 438 p. [Tr. inferred; condensed tr.]
Tokyo: Institute of Pacific Relations, Japan Council, 1931. 139 p.
Subj 14 14.1 14.3 14.4 16 ▪ 14.2 34.2 34.3 64

11708 NNC S P2 G1.1 –1928
Nearing, Scott, 1883–.
Whither China? An economic interpretation of recent events in the Far East.
New York: International Publishers, 1927. 225 p.
Subj 14 19 30 32.2 ▪ 12.1 15 16 32 34.3 36.2 36.3 36.4 66

11709 CSH U P2 G1.1 –1928
Pozdneev, Dmitrii Matveevich, 1865–1942, et al.
Ocherki stran Dal'nego Vostoka (vvedenie v vostokovedenie), vypusk I, sobstvennyi Kitai (Notes on the countries of the Far East: Introduction to Oriental studies. Vol. 1, China proper).
Harbin: Tip. N. A. Frenkelia, 1931. 196 p.
Subj 10 14 16 32.2 66 71 ▪ 11 11.2 12 19 40

11710 CSH U P5 G1.2 –1928
Pozdneev, Dmitrii Matveevich, 1865–1942, et al.
Ocherki stran Dal'nego Vostoka (vvedenie v vostokovedenie), vypusk II, vneshnii Kitai (Man'chzhuriia, Mongoliia, Sin'tszian i Tibet) (Notes on the countries of the Far East: Introduction to Oriental studies. Vol. 2, External China: Manchuria, Mongolia, Sinkiang, and Tibet).
Harbin: Tip. N. A. Frenkelia, 1931. 207 p.
Subj 11.2 14 14.2 ▪ 12 21 21.1 65

11711 CSH S P2 G1.2 1895–1928
Rubinshtein, Modest Iosifovich.
'Ekonomika i sotsial'nye otnosheniia Kitaia' (Economics and social relations in China). In *O Kitae: politiko-ekonomicheskii sbornik* (Articles on China's political economy), edited by [Solomon Abramovich Dridzo] A. Lozovskii, pseud. [Selective entry]
Moscow: Gosizdat, 1928, 28–68.
Subj 14 14.1 14.4 16.1 16.3 18 ▪ 11.2 22 25 36.4

11712 MCH FP P2 G2.0 1895–1949
Sakatani, Yoshiro (Sakatani Yoshirō), 1863–1941.
Manchuria: A survey of its economic development.
[New York]: Carnegie Endowment for International Peace, Division of Economics and History, 1932. 15, 305 p.
Subj 14 ▪ 12 21 21.2 21.4 25 34.2 34.3 36.2 36.4 66

11713 MCH P P2 G1.2 1842–1928
Sié, Tso-tchéou (Hsieh Tso-chou).
La révolution économique dans la Chine contemporaine, 1840–1929 (The economic revolution in modern China, 1840–1929).
Paris: Mechelinck, 1930. 180 p. (Doctoral dissertation, Faculté de droit, Université de Paris)
Subj 14 14.4 ▪ 16.3 16.4 24.4 36.4 64

11714 CSU P P2 G2.0 1644–1949
Sun, Kungtu C., 1895–.
The economic development of Manchuria in the first half of the twentieth century.
Cambridge: Harvard U., East Asian Research Center, 1969. 124 p. (Harvard East Asian monographs, 28)
Subj 14 14.1 14.4 ▪ 12 14.2 14.6 15 21.2 66

11715 MCH P P2 G2.0 1895–1949
Tcheng, Kui-i (Cheng Kuei-i).
La Cie du chemin de fer sud-manchourien et l'emprise japonaise en Mandchourie (The South Manchurian Railway and Japanese ascendancy in Manchuria).
Paris: Bossuet, 1939. 316 p. (Doctoral dissertation, Faculté des lettres, Université de Paris)
Subj 14 14.2 14.3 14.4 ▪ 12 21 21.2 66

11716 DLC P P2 G2.0 1895–1949
Tretchikov, Nikolai G-.
Sovremennaia Man'chzhuriia v faktakh i tsifrakh: ekonomicheskie ocherki, chast' 1-ia (Contemporary Manchuria in facts and figures: Economic notes, Vol. 1).
Shanghai: China Economic Press, 1936. 158 p.
Subj 14 21 34.2 ▪ 14.1 14.3 18 21.2 21.3 21.4 36.4

11717 NNC P P2 G1.2 1644–1928
Veidemiuller, K-.
'Ekonomicheskie predposylki kitaiskoi revoliutsii' (Economic preconditions of the Chinese revolution).
Mezhdunarodnaia letopis' 1925, 8/9 (avgust–sentiabr'), 54–66.
Subj 14 ▪ 11.4 14.1 14.3 14.6 16.4 24.4 66

11718 CSH U P2 G1.2 1895–1928
[Vilenskii, Vladimir Dmitrievich] Vl. Vilenskii-Sibiriakov, pseud., 1888–1942.
Kitai: politiko-ekonomicheskii ocherk (Overview of China's political economy).
Moscow: Mospoligraf, 1923. 97 p.
Subj 12 14 ▪ 14.3 14.4 16.4 32 32.2

11719 MCH O P1 G1.3 1895–1928
Wilhelm, Richard, 1873–1930.
Chinesische Wirtschaftspsychologie.
Leipzig: Deutsche Wissenschaftliche Buchhandlung, 1930. 120 p. (Weltwirtschaftsinstitut der Handels-Hochschule, Leipzig, Schriften, 5).
Chinese economic psychology. Tr. by Bruno Lasker.
New York: Institute of Pacific Relations, International Secretariat, 1947. 64 p.
Subj 14 61 ▪ 40 62

11720 MCY PO P2 G1.1 –1949
Wu, Ching-chao (Wu Ching-ch'ao), 1901–.
'Economic development.' In *China*, edited by Harley Farnsworth MacNair. [Selective entry]
Berkeley, Los Angeles: U. of California Press, 1946, 455–465. [Reprinted in *China*, edited by H. F. MacNair. (Selective entry.) Freeport, N.Y.: Books for Libraries, 1970, 455–465.]
Subj 14 ▪ 14.1 14.4

1911-1949

11721 NIC P P2 G1.2 1911–1949
'China's economic development.' In *Problems of the Pacific, 1931*, edited by Bruno Lasker and William Lancelot Holland. [Selective entry]
Chicago: U. of Chicago Press, 1932, 67–220.
Subj 14 ▪ 16.4

11722 CSU U P2 G3.3 1928–1949
'Economic conditions in Suiyuan province.'
CEJ 13, 4 (Oct. 1933), 385–400.
Subj 14 14.3 14.4 24.1 ▪ 21 24.2 24.4

11723 CSU P P2 G7.2 1928–1949
'Hunan: An economic survey.'
CEJ 18, 1 (Jan. 1936), 23–53; 18, 2 (Feb. 1936), 182–211; 18, 3 (Mar. 1936), 344–367; 18, 4 (Apr. 1936), 559–582; 18, 5 (May 1936), 732–757; 18, 6 (June 1936), 884–913.
Subj 14 14.3 14.4 24.1 24.4 ▪ 14.6 16.3 21 34.2

11724 NNC P P2 G1.2 1928–1949
Reconstruction in China: A record of progress and achievement in facts and figures.
Shanghai: China United Press, 1935. 14, 401 p. (China today series, 3)
Subj 12 14 14.2 14.6 37 56 ▪ 12.1 12.2 14.4 15 18 21.3 27 31 36.1 47

11725 NNC P P2 G1.3 1928–1949
'Wartime economic and social organization in Free China.'
ILR 46, 6 (Dec. 1942), 692–715.
Subj 14 14.4 32.1 ▪ 12 12.2 16.4

11726 CSH S P2 G7.3 1911–1949
Abramson, Manuil Moiseevich, 1898–1941, et al.
'TSiansi: sotsial'no-ekonomicheskii ocherk' (Socioeconomic survey of Kiangsi).
PK 14 (1935), 89–157.
Subj 14 16 ▪ 14.3 14.4 14.5 16.4 21.4 24.1 25 66

11727 CSH U P1 G1.4 1928–1949
Agapov, Evgenii.
'Politiko-ekonomicheskoe stroitel'stvo v Severnom Kitae' (Political and economic reconstruction in North China).
Vostochnoe obozrenie 8 (iiul'–sentiabr' 1941), 30–44.
Subj 12 14

11728 NNC S P2 G1.4 1928–1949
Arens, M-.
'IAponiia v bor'be za syr'evye resursy severnogo Kitaia' (Japan in the struggle for the raw materials of North China).
MKhMP 1936, 4 (aprel'), 46–56.
Subj 14 66 ▪ 14.1 14.2 14.3 14.4

11729 NNC P P2 G1.5 1911–1928
Arkus, R- S-.
'Anglo-iaponskoe sopernichestvo na IAntszy' (Anglo-Japanese competition on the Yangtze).
MKhMP 1927, 7 (iiul'), 73–80.
SUBJ 14 14.3 14.4 ▪ 11.4 14.6

11730 NIC O P2 G1.2 1911–1928
Arnold, Julean Herbert, 1875–1946.
'Changes in the economic life of the Chinese people.'
CSPSR 6, 1 (Feb. 1922), 26–69.
SUBJ 14 14.2 14.4 ▪ 14.1 21.4 24.4 34.2 47

11731 ELB U P4 G1.3 1911–1928
Arnold, Julean Herbert, 1875–1946.
China: A commercial and industrial handbook.
Washington, D.C.: U.S. Government Printing Office, 1926. 16, 818 p. (Bureau of Foreign and Domestic Commerce, Trade promotion series, 38)
SUBJ 11.1 14 14.3 14.4 ▪ 14.6

11732 DLC P P2 G2.0 1928–1949
Avarin, Vladimir IAkovlevich, 1899–.
'Nezavisimaia' Man'chzhuriia ('Independent' Manchuria), 2nd ed., rev. and enl.
Moscow: Partizdat, 1934. 152 p.
SUBJ 12 14 16 32.2 66 ▪ 11.3 21 25 32.1 36.4

11733 NNC P P2 G1.2 1928–1949
Avarin, Vladimir IAkovlevich, 1899–.
'Voprosy voennoi ekonomiki natsional'nogo Kitaia' (The war economy of Nationalist China).
MKhMP 1943, 10/11 (oktiabr'–noiabr'), 50–61.
SUBJ 14 ▪ 14.4 14.5 14.6

11734 CSU P P3 G1.2 1911–1928
Bergère, Marie-Claire, 1933–.
'Le mouvement du 4 mai 1919 en Chine: la conjoncture économique et le rôle de la bourgeoisie nationale' (The May Fourth Movement: The economic situation and the role of the national bourgeoisie).
R. historique 241 (avr.–juin 1969), 309–326.
SUBJ 14 16.2 19 36.2 66 ▪ 24.4

11735 SSK U P2 G1.3 1911–1949
Bielenstein, Hans, 1920–.
'Kinas näringsliv: En aktuell fråga' (Economic life in China: A current question).
Ymer 65 (1945), 257–283.
SUBJ 14 14.1 ▪ 11.3 11.4 14.2 14.4 16.3 16.4 18

11736 CBU P P2 G1.2 1911–1928
Blink, Hendrik, 1852–1931.
'China en de Chineezen in 't verleden en heden' (China and the Chinese, past and present).
TESG 12, 8/9 (Augustus–September 1921), 377–390.
SUBJ 14 14.1 ▪ 12 12.2 14.2 14.4

11737 DLC U P2 G1.4 1911–1928
Burskii, P- D-.
Dal'nevostochnye teatry voennykh deistvii: voenno-geograficheskii ocherk (Survey of the military geography of the Far Eastern theaters of war), edited by I- A- Troitskii.
Moscow: Gos. izd-vo voen. lit-ry, 1928. 200 p.
SUBJ 14 14.2 15 ▪ 14.1 14.4 16

11738 CSU O P2 G1.1 1928–1949
C.
'Economics and politics in China.'
World today 3, 9 (Sept. 1947), 407–417.
SUBJ 14 14.3 14.5 ▪ 14.6 32 32.2

11739 CSU P P2 G6.0 1928–1949
Chang, Bintze T.
'Effects of the silk slump and prospects of revival.'
CEJ 13, 4 (Oct. 1933), 331–355.
SUBJ 14 14.3 14.4 ▪ 14.1 16.4

11740 CSH P P2 G1.2 1928–1949
[Chang Yü-lan] ——— and [Chao Te-hsin] ———.
The development of the people's New Democratic economy, 1937–1945. Tr. by Anthony H. S. Ma of 'Chih min ti pan chih min ti pan feng chien she hui ching chi ti ta p'o huai yü hsin min chu chu i ching chi ti ch'u pu fa chan, 1937–1945' (The collapse of the colonial and the semicolonial, semifeudal socioeconomic structure and the initial development of the New Democratic economy, 1937–1945); in *Chung-kuo chin tai kuo min ching chi shih chiang i* (Lectures on modern Chinese economic history), edited by Cheng chih ching chi hsüeh chiao yen shih, Hu-pei ta hsüeh (Political Economy Research Dept., Hupeh U.); Peking: Kao teng chiao yü ch'u pan she, 1958, 407–485.
Honolulu: East-West Center, Institute of Advanced Projects, Research Publications and Translations, 1969. 137 p. (RPT occasional papers, translation series, 32)
SUBJ 14 14.4 34.2 ▪ 14.5 14.6 16 18 24.3 24.4 34.1 66

11741 CSU P P1 G1.2 1928–1949
Chen, Gideon (Ch'en Ch'i-t'ien), 1893–.
'Chinese government economic planning and reconstruction.' In *Problems of the Pacific, 1933*, edited by Bruno Lasker and William Lancelot Holland. [Selective entry]
Chicago: U. of Chicago Press, 1934, 352–382.
SUBJ 14 ▪ 12 14.2 14.4 34.1

11742 NNC U P2 G1.2 1928–1949
Chen Han-seng (Ch'en Han-sheng), 1897–.
'Economic conditions in China: A brief survey, January to June, 1932.'
PA 5, 9 (Sept. 1932), 769–774.
SUBJ 14 ▪ 14.3 14.5 14.6 18 24.3 24.4

11743 NNC U P2 G1.2 1928–1949
Chen Han-seng (Ch'en Han-sheng), 1897–.
'Economic disintegration in China.'
PA 6, 4/5 (Apr.–May 1933), 173–181.
SUBJ 14 24.4 ▪ 14.1 14.5 14.6 16.3 24.6

11744 MCH O P2 G1.5 1928–1949
[Ch'en Shao-yü] Van-Min (Wang Ming), pseud., 1904–.
'Ekonomicheskaia politika sovetskoi vlasti v Kitae' (The economic policy of the soviet government in China).
Kommunisticheskii Internatsional 1933, 24 (20 avgusta), 19–33. [For a later version in Chinese see Ch'en Shao-yü, *Chung-kuo su wei ai cheng ch'üan ti ching chi cheng ts'e* (Economic policies of the Chinese soviet government); Moscow: Wai kuo kung jen ch'u pan she, 1935; 78 p.]
SUBJ 12 14 ▪ 14.1 14.4 19

11745 CSH P P2 G1.2 1928–1949
Chi, Ch'ao-ting, 1903–1963.
Wartime economic development of China, mimeo.
New York: Institute of Pacific Relations, International Secretariat, 1942. 149 p.
SUBJ 12 14 14.1 14.4 14.6 ▪ 14.2 16.3 21.2 24.4 34.2 34.3

11746 CSH P P2 G6.3 1911–1949
China [Republic]. Shih yeh pu. Kuo chi mao i chü. (Ministry of Industry. Bureau of Foreign Trade), ed.
'Economic conditions.' Tr. of 'Ching chi kai k'uang'; in *Chung-kuo shih yeh chih: Che-chiang sheng* (Chinese economic surveys: Chekiang); Shanghai: Kuo chi mao i chü, 1933, *i* 1 – *i* 134 [s.p.] [slightly condensed in tr.]. In *China industrial handbooks: Chekiang*, edited by the agency cited. [Selective entry]
Shanghai: Kuo chi mao i chü, 1935, 23–74. [Reprinted in *China industrial handbooks: Chekiang*, edited by the agency cited. (Selective entry.) Taipei: Ch'eng-wen, 1972, 23–74.]
SUBJ 14 14.3 24.1 ▪ 24.6 26.3

11747 CSH FP P2 G6.1 1911–1949
China [Republic]. Shih yeh pu. Kuo chi mao i chü. (Ministry of Industry. Bureau of Foreign Trade), ed.
'Economic conditions.' Tr. of 'Ching chi kai k'uang'; in *Chung-kuo shih yeh chih: Chiang-su sheng* (Chinese economic surveys: Kiangsu); Shanghai: Kuo chi mao i chü, 1933, 1–134 [s.p.] [slightly condensed in tr.]. In *China industrial handbooks: Kiangsu*, edited by the agency cited. [Selective entry]
Shanghai: Kuo chi mao i chü, 1933, 19–62. [Reprinted in *China industrial handbooks: Kiangsu*, edited by the agency cited. (Selective entry.) Taipei: Ch'eng-wen, 1972, 19–62.]
SUBJ 14 24.1 ▪ 14.3 24.3 24.6 28 34.1

11748 CSH P P2 G1.2 1928–1949
[Chou Hsiu-luan] ———, [Chao Te-hsin] ———, and [Chang Yü-lan] ———.
The overall victory of the people's New Democratic economy, 1945–1949. Tr. by Anthony H. S. Ma of 'Pan chih min ti pan feng chien she hui ching chi ti tsung peng k'uei ho hsin min chu chu i ching chi ti ch'üan mien sheng li, 1945–1949' (The complete collapse of the semicolonial, semifeudal socioeconomic structure and the total victory of the New Democratic economy, 1945–1949); in *Chung-kuo chin tai kuo min ching chi shih chiang i* (Lectures on modern Chinese economic history), edited by Cheng chih ching chi hsüeh chiao yen shih, Hu-pei ta hsüeh (Political Economy Research Dept., Hupeh U.); Peking: Kao teng chiao yü ch'u pan she, 1958, 486–546.
Honolulu: East-West Center, Institute of Advanced Projects, Research Publications and Translations, 1969. 90

p. (RPT occasional papers, translation series, 33)
SUBJ 14 16 18 ▪ 14.6 15 24.3 24.4 34.2 66

11749 NIC P P2 G2.0 1911–1928
Chu, Hsiao.
'Manchuria: A statistical survey of its resources, industries, trade, railways and immigration.' In *Problems of the Pacific, 1929*, edited by John Bell Condliffe. [Selective entry]
Chicago: U. of Chicago Press, 1930, 380–422.
SUBJ 14 ▪ 14.1 14.2 14.3 21.1 21.2

11750 NIC S P2 G1.2 1928–1949
Condliffe, John Bell, 1891–.
China today: Economic.
Boston: World Peace Foundation, 1932. 214 p.
SUBJ 14 14.1 14.6 58 ▪ 11 12 12.1 14.5 16.3 18 24.4 34.1 36.4

11751 CSU P P3 G1.2 1928–1949
Conolly, Violet.
'Notes on the economic consequences of recent events in Manchuria.' In *Problems of the Pacific, 1933*, edited by Bruno Lasker and William Lancelot Holland. [Selective entry]
Chicago: U. of Chicago Press, 1934, 422–440.
SUBJ 14 ▪ 12

11752 ELO FP P2 G1.2 1928–1949
Coons, Arthur Gardiner, 1900–.
Economic reconstruction in China.
Peiping: California College in China, College of Chinese Studies, 1934. 43 p.
SUBJ 11 11.2 11.4 14 16.3 18 ▪ 15 17 19 41 58 63 64

11753 DLC O P2 G8.1 1928–1949
Crawford, Wallace.
'Recent development in Szechwan.' In *Wartime China, as seen by westerners*. [Selective entry]
Chungking: China Publishing Co., 1942, 95–105.
SUBJ 14 ▪ 14.4 17 24.1 24.2 56

11754 DLC P P2 G1.2 1911–1928
Dal'ne-Vostochnyi krai. Planovaia komissiia. Biuro Tikhookeanskoi kon"iunktury.
Khoziaistvo IAponii i Kitaia v 1927 godu: kon"iunkturnyi obzor (Overview of the Japanese and Chinese economies in 1927).
Khabarovsk: Dal'nevost. kraevaia planovaia komissiia, Biuro soveta tikhookeanskoi kon"iunktury, 1928. 186 p.
SUBJ 14 ▪ 11.2 11.4 14.1 14.3 14.6 16.3 16.4

11755 NNC P P2 G2.0 1928–1949
Fedorov, Nikolai Aleksandrovich.
'Man'chzhuriia: platsdarm voiny na Dal'nem Vostoke' (Manchuria: Springboard for war in the Far East).
MKhMP 1936, 7 (iiul'), 86–105.
SUBJ 14 66 ▪ 21.2

11756 CSU P P2 G1.2 1911–1949
Feuerwerker, Albert, 1927–.
The Chinese economy, 1912–1949.
Ann Arbor: U. of Michigan, Center for Chinese Studies, 1968. 79 p. (Michigan papers in Chinese studies, 1)
SUBJ 14 14.1 24.4 ▪ 11 11.4 14.4 14.6 16 18 34.2

11757 NNC P P2 G1.2 1928–1949
Fong, H. D. (Fang Hsien-t'ing), 1902–.
'A brief survey of economic literature on China during the war.'
NSEQ 12, 1/2 (Jan. 1941), 169–182.
SUBJ 14 72 ▪ 14.2 36.1

11758 NIC S P1 G1.3 1928–1949
Fong, H. D. (Fang Hsien-t'ing), 1902–.
'Toward economic control in China.'
NSEQ 9, 2 (July 1936), 296–397. [Separately reprinted—(Shanghai): China Institute of Pacific Relations, 1936. 91 p.]
SUBJ 14

11759 NIC O P2 G1.3 1928–1949
Fong, H. D. (Fang Hsien-t'ing), 1902–.
'War-time economic reconstruction in China.'
NSEQ 11, 1/2 (Jan. 1940), 101–112.
SUBJ 14

11760 NNC PO P2 G1.2 1928–1949
Freyn, Hubert, 1897–.
Free China's new deal.
New York: Macmillan, 1943. 18, 277 p.
SUBJ 14 14.4 14.5 24.1 24.6 ▪ 12 14.1 18

11761 DLC P P2 G1.2 1928–1949
Gamberg, Viktor.
'Ekonomicheskii krizis v Kitae: itogi 1929 g.' (The effects of the economic crisis in China, 1929).
PK 3 (1930), 21–68.
SUBJ 14 ▪ 14.1 14.4 14.6 16.2 56 66

11762 DLC P P2 G1.2 1928–1949
Gamberg, Viktor.
'Ekonomicheskii krizis v Kitae: itogi 1931–1932 gg.' (The effects of the economic crisis in China, 1931–1932).
PK 12 (1933), 64–127.
SUBJ 14 14.1 14.4 14.6 ▪ 11.2 14.3 16.3 18 32.2 57 66

11763 NNC P P2 G1.2 1928–1949
Gamberg, Viktor.
'Ekonomicheskii krizis v Kitae, pervaia polovina 1933 goda' (The economic crisis in China during the first half of 1933).
MNKP 1934, 1/2, 3–29.
SUBJ 14 ▪ 14.1 14.4 16.3 18

11764 DLC P P2 G1.2 1928–1949
Gamberg, Viktor.
'Uglublenie ekonomicheskogo krizisa v Kitae: itogi 1930 g.' (The effects of the economic crisis in China, 1930).
PK 6/7 (1931), 90–155.
SUBJ 14 14.1 14.4 ▪ 14.5 14.6 55 66

11765 NNC S P1 G5.2 1928–1949
Gillin, Donald George, 1930–.
'China's first five-year plan: Industrialization under the warlords as reflected in the policies of Yen Hsi-shan in Shansi province, 1930–1937.'
JAS 24, 2 (Feb. 1965), 245–259. [For fuller treatment, see entry 10781.]
SUBJ 12.1 14 14.4 17 32 ▪ 12.2 16.1 19 64

11766 CSU PO P2 G1.1 1911–1928
Great Britain. Dept. of Overseas Trade.
Report on the commercial, industrial and economic situation in China, 1919–1928. [Title varies slightly; issues for 1929–1937 are entered as 11767.]
London: His Majesty's Stationery Office. Issued annually, 1920–1928. Average ca. 60 p.
SUBJ 14 14.2 14.4 ▪ 14.5 16.4 22.2 24.4

11767 CSU PO P2 G1.1 1928–1949
Great Britain. Dept. of Overseas Trade.
Trade and economic conditions in China, 1929–1937. [Title varies; issues for 1919–1928 are entered as 11766.]
London: His Majesty's Stationery Office. Issued annually or biennially, 1930–1937. Average ca. 100 p.
SUBJ 14 14.2 14.4 ▪ 14.5 16.4 22.2 24.4

11768 MCH S P2 G1.2 1928–1949
Hanwell, Norman D-.
'The war economy of China's guerrillas.'
FES 7, 23 (23 Nov. 1938), 265–270.
SUBJ 14 14.1 15 ▪ 14.3 24.4 55

11769 NNC PO P2 G6.3 1928–1949
Ho, Franklin L. (Ho Lien), 1897–, and H. D. Fong (Fang Hsien-t'ing), 1902–.
'Report on the economic conditions and problems of Chekiang: Report A of the Report of the economic and financial situation of Chekiang province, 1934.' In *Annexes to the Report to the Council of the League of Nations of its technical delegate on his mission in China from date of appointment until April 1, 1934, Annex 5*. [Selective entry]
Shanghai: North-China Daily News and Herald, 1934, 85–143.
SUBJ 14 14.5 ▪ 24.1 24.2 24.4 34.1

11770 CSU U P2 G1.1 1928–1949
Ho Ping-yin (Ho Ping-hsien), 1903–.
'Industry and commerce during 1932.'
CEJ 12, 1 (Jan. 1933), 1–32.
SUBJ 14 14.3 14.4 ▪ 14.1 24.4

11771 NNC O P1 G1.3 1928–1949
Ho, Yao-tsu, 1889–.
'Chinese economic policy in wartime.'
ILR 47, 5 (May 1943), 555–575.
SUBJ 14

11772 NNC O P2 G1.5 1928–1949
Hoh, Chih-hsiang (Hao Chih-hsiang), 1904–.
'Southwest China: A political, social and economic survey.'
CQ-S 3, 4 (Autumn 1938), 415–430.
SUBJ 14 14.2 14.4 ▪ 11.2 12 15 17

11773 NNC O P2 G1.2 1911–1949
Hsu, Francis L. K. (Hsü Lang-kuang), 1909–.
'A closer view of China's problem.'
FEQ 6, 1 (Nov. 1946), 50–64.
SUBJ 14 14.5 14.6 18 ▪ 12 14.4 16.1 64

11774 CSU U P2 G1.2 1928–1949
Huang, Yi.
'Reconstruction économique de la Chine pendant et après la guerre' (The economic reconstruction of China during and after the war).
Sinologica 1, 1 (1947), 53–64.
SUBJ 14 14.2 14.4

11775 CSH U P2 G1.2 1928–1949
Hui Di-shan.
'China's economy during two years of the War of Resistance.' In *China's resistance, 1937–1939*, by Chou En-lai et al. [Sole entry]

Chungking: New China Information Committee, 1940, 33–41. (NCIC bulletins, 12)
SUBJ 14 ▪ 14.1 14.2 14.4

11776 CSU U P2 G1.3 1911–1949
Hwang, T. H.
'China's cotton trade.'
CEJ 10, 4 (Apr. 1932), 287–303.
SUBJ 14 14.1 14.3 ▪ 14.2 14.4 34.2

11777 MCH P P2 G2.0 1928–1949
Jones, Francis Clifford.
Manchuria since 1931.
London: Royal Institute of International Affairs, 1949. 256 p.
SUBJ 12 14 14.1 14.2 14.4 ▪ 17 18 21.1 21.3 56

11778 CSU P P2 G1.2 1928–1949
Kann, Eduard, 1880–1962.
'China in 1932: An economic review.'
CEJ 12, 3 (Mar. 1933), 284–337.
SUBJ 14 14.5 14.6 ▪ 11 12.2 14.4 24.4

11779 CSU P P2 G1.1 1911–1949
Kann, Eduard, 1880–1962.
'China in 1935: An economic review.'
CEJ 18, 4 (Apr. 1936), 487–544.
SUBJ 14 14.6 ▪ 14.1 14.4 14.5 18

11780 CSU P P2 G1.4 1911–1928
[Karamyshev, V-] W. Karamisheff.
Mongolia and western China: Social and economic study.
Tientsin: Lib. française, 1925. 27, 401 p.
SUBJ 14 14.2 14.3 14.4 ▪ 34.2

11781 CSH S P2 G2.0 1928–1949
Kasai, Taichiroo (Kasai Taichirō).
'Ekonomicheskoe stroitel'stvo Man'chzhugo' (Manchoukuo's economic structure).
Vostochnoe obozrenie 8 (iiul'–sentiabr' 1941), 64–83.
SUBJ 14

11782 NNC O P2 G5.0 1928–1949
Ke Han (K'o-han), pseud.
The Shansi-Hopei-Honan border region: Report for 1937–1939, Part 1.
Chungking: New China Information Committee, 1940. 34 p. (NCIC bulletins, 15)
SUBJ 14 17 ▪ 12 34.2

11783 DLC P P2 G1.2 1911–1928
Khodorov, Abram Evseevich, 1886–1949.
Mirovoi imperializm i Kitai: opyt politiko-ekonomicheskogo issledovaniia (World imperialism and China: Results of a preliminary political and economic study).
Shanghai: Izd-vo Shankhaiskaia zhizn', 1922. 448 p.
SUBJ 11.1 11.4 12.1 14 16.2 ▪ 11 12.2 32.2 37 66

11784 DLC P P2 G1.3 1911–1928
Khodorov, Abram Evseevich, 1886–1949.
Narodnoe khoziaistvo Kitaia (The national economy of China).
Moscow: Prometei, 1925. 12, 420 p.
SUBJ 11.1 11.2 11.3 11.4 14 ▪ 16.3 24.4 32.2 36.2

11785 ELS FP P2 G2.0 1928–1949
Kirby, Edward Stuart, 1909–.
The economic organisation of Manchoukuo, with particular reference to specific features exemplifying the special characteristics of the modern economic system in the Far East.
Unpublished doctoral dissertation in Economics, U. of London [External degree], 1939. 365 p.
SUBJ 14 21.2 ▪ 12 15 16 32.2

11786 CSH P P2 G1.2 1911–1949
Koh, Tso-fan (Ku Ch'un-fan).
'Capital stock in China.' In *Problems of economic reconstruction in China*, by H. D. Fong (Fang Hsien-t'ing), K. Y. Lin, and Tso-fan Koh. [Sole entry]
Chungkung: Institute of Pacific Relations, China Council, 1942, 17–38. (China Council papers, 2)
SUBJ 14 14.2 14.4

11787 CSH O P2 G3.1 1928–1949
Kormazov, V- A-.
'Provintsiia Zhekhe' (Jehol). [With English abstract]
VM 1932, 8, 29–42.
SUBJ 14 ▪ 21 24.2

11788 NNC S P2 G1.2 1928–1949
Krasin, A-.
'Krizis v Kitae' (Crisis in China).
Revoliutsionnyi Vostok 1933, 1, 150–167; 1933, 2, 51–73.
SUBJ 14 ▪ 14.1 14.3 16.3 18 32 32.2

11789 CSU U P2 G8.2 1928–1949
Lattimore, Owen, 1900–.
'Yunnan, pivot of Southeast Asia.'
FA 21, 3 (Apr. 1943), 476–493.
SUBJ 14 ▪ 14.4 24.1 24.2

11790 GMS S P2 G1.2 1911–1928
Li, Banghan (Li Pang-han), 1896–.
Die chinesische Volkswirtschaft unter dem Einfluss der fremden Mächte (China's national economy under the influence of foreign powers).
Leipzig: Robert Noske, 1926. 126 p. (Doctoral dissertation, Wirtschafts- und sozialwissenschaftliche Fakultät, Universität Frankfurt a.M.)
SUBJ 14 14.1 14.3 64 ▪ 11 12 14.2 14.4 16 66

11791 CSU P P2 G1.4 1928–1949
Li, Lincoln.
'Economic control in North China under Japanese occupation, July 1937 to December 1941.'
Papers on Far Eastern history 1 (Mar. 1970), 31–69.
SUBJ 12 14 14.6 ▪ 66

11792 GMS P P2 G1.2 1928–1949
Liang, Ssu-mu (Liang Shih-mu).
'Die Wirtschaftsstruktur Chinas und die Politik der Nanking Regierung' (The economic structure of China and the policy of the Nanking government).
WA 39, 2 (März 1934), 415–444. (Doctoral dissertation, Wirtschafts- und sozialwissenschaftliche Fakultät, Universität Frankfurt a.M.)
SUBJ 14 ▪ 16.3

11793 NIC P P2 G1.2 1928–1949
Lieu, D. K. (Liu Ta-chün), 1891–1962.
China's economic stabilization and reconstruction.
New Brunswick: Rutgers U. Press, 1948. 10, 159 p.
SUBJ 14 14.1 14.4 ▪ 16 34.1 34.2

11794 NNC P P5 G1.2 1911–1928
Lieu, D. K. (Liu Ta-chün), 1891–1962.
China's industries and finance . . .
Peking: Chung-kuo ching chi t'ao lun ch'u, 1927. 14, 238 p.
SUBJ 14 14.4 14.6 34.2 ▪ 14.2 24.4 34.3

11795 CSU O P2 G7.3 1911–1949
Lin, K. C.
'Economic recuperation in Kiangsi province.'
CEJ 15, 1 (July 1934), 27–43.
SUBJ 14 14.3 14.4 ▪ 24.1 24.2 24.4

11796 NNC P P1 G1.2 1928–1949
Liu, Ta-chung, 1914–.
China's national income, 1931–1936: An exploratory study.
Washington, D.C.: Brookings Institution, 1946. 12, 91 p.
SUBJ 14

11797 NNC P P2 G2.0 1928–1949
Lopato, Michael E-, 1907–.
The economic wealth and structure of North Manchuria.
Unpublished masters thesis in Economics, Columbia U., 1931. 82 p.
SUBJ 11.3 14 14.1 ▪ 14.4 21 21.2 21.3

11798 CSU U P2 G1.3 1928–1949
Lowe, Chuan-hua (Lo Ch'uan-hua), 1902–.
'Economic developments in wartime China.'
THM 8, 4 (Apr. 1939), 305–318.
SUBJ 14 ▪ 12 14.1 14.2 14.4 34.1

11799 NNC P P2 G1.2 1928–1949
Maslennikov, Viacheslav Aleksandrovich, 1894–1968.
Kitai: politiko-ekonomicheskii ocherk (Overview of China's political economy).
Moscow: Gospolitizdat, 1946. 263 p.
SUBJ 14 ▪ 11 12 32.2

11800 NNC P P2 G1.2 1928–1949
Maslennikov, Viacheslav Aleksandrovich, 1894–1968.
'Problemy ekonomicheskogo razvitiia Kitaia' (Problems of China's economic development).
MKhMP 1945, 7 (iiul'), 43–55.
SUBJ 14 ▪ 14.3 14.4 16.1 32.2

11801 NNC P P4 G1.2 1911–1949
Maslennikov, Viacheslav Aleksandrovich, 1894–1968.
'Problemy ekonomicheskogo razvitiia poslevoennogo Kitaia' (Problems of economic development in postwar China).
MKhMP 1946, 6 (iiun'), 32–42.
SUBJ 14 14.4

11802 MCH O P2 G1.2 1911–1928
Maynard, Michel de.
'La Chine agricole, industrielle et commerciale' (Agriculture, industry, and trade in China).
B. de la Société de géographie de Lille 1914, 5 (mai–déc.), 278–296.
SUBJ 14 14.1 14.4 ▪ 14.3

11803 CSU O P2 G2.0 1928–1949
Moore, W- Robert.
'In Manchuria now.'
NG 91, 3 (Mar. 1947), 389–414.
SUBJ 14 21.1

11804 MCH P P2 G1.2 1928–1949
Ou, Pao-san (Wu Pao-san), 1905–.
Capital formation and consumers' outlay in China.
Unpublished doctoral dissertation in Economics, Harvard U., 1948. 219 p.
SUBJ 14 ▪ 14.1 14.2 14.4 18

11805 MCY P P2 G1.2 1928–1949
Ou, Pao-san (Wu Pao-san), 1905–.
National income of China, 1933, 1936 and 1946.
Nanking: Academia Sinica, Institute of Social Sciences, 1947. 26 p. (Social sciences study papers, 1) [See Vol. 2 of this *Bibliography* for Chinese version.]
SUBJ 14 ▪ 11 14.1 14.4 18

11806 MCH S P2 G1.2 1928–1949
Paauw, Douglas Seymour, 1921–.
'The Kuomintang and economic stagnation, 1928–1937.'
JAS 16, 2 (Feb. 1957), 213–220. [Reprinted in *Modern China*, edited by Albert Feuerwerker. (Selective entry.) Englewood Cliffs, N. J.: Prentice-Hall, 1964, 126–135.]
SUBJ 14 32 ▪ 14.5 14.6 16.1 18

11807 CBU P P2 G1.2 1928–1949
[P'eng Yü-hsin] ———.
The rise of the new people's democratic economy, 1927–1937. Tr. by William W. L. Wan of 'Pan chih min ti pan feng chien she hui ching chi k'ai shih peng k'uei ho hsin min chu chi i ching chi ti meng ya, 1927–1937' (The beginning of the collapse of the semicolonial, semifeudal socioeconomic structure and the rise of the New Democratic economy, 1927–1937); in *Chung-kuo chin tai kuo min ching chi shih chiang i* (Lectures on modern Chinese economic history), edited by Cheng chih ching chi hsüeh chiao yen shih, Hu-pei ta hsüeh (Political Economy Research Dept., Hupeh U.); Peking: Kao teng chiao yü ch'u pan she, 1958, 355–406.
Honolulu: East-West Center, Institute of Advanced Projects, Research Publications and Translations, 1969. 77 p. (RPT occasional papers, translation series, 31)
SUBJ 14 14.3 14.6 ▪ 14.1 14.4 15 16 18 32.2 34.1 34.2

11808 FPN S P2 G2.0 1928–1949
Peuvergne, Raymond.
Le développement agricole et industriel du Mandchukuo (The agricultural and industrial development of Manchoukuo).
Grenoble: Impr. Boissy Colomb, 1942. 159 p. (Doctoral dissertation, Faculté de droit, Université de Grenoble)
SUBJ 14 14.1 14.4 ▪ 14.2 14.3

11809 MCH P P2 G1.2 1911–1928
Pierre, R- J-.
'La Chine économique' (China's economy).
J. des économistes 6e série 90, 3 (juin 1928), 147–162.
SUBJ 14 14.4 ▪ 11

11810 MCH P P2 G1.2 1911–1949
Pierre, R- J-.
'La Chine économique' (China's economy).
J. des économistes 6e série 100, 2 (oct. 1931), 137–154.
SUBJ 14 ▪ 11 17

11811 MCH P P1 G1.2 1928–1949
Pierre, R- J-.
'La Chine économique' (China's economy).
J. des économistes 6e série 103, 3 (mars 1933), 206–218.
SUBJ 14

11812 CSH P P2 G1.2 1911–1928
Popov-Tativa, Nikolai Mikhailovich, 1883–.
Kitai: ekonomicheskoe opisanie (An economic description of China).
Moscow: Razved. upr-nie shtaba rabochekrest. Krasnoi Armii, 1925. 384 p.
SUBJ 12 14 21 36.4 66 ▪ 11.1 11.2 11.4 12.2

11813 NNC P P2 G1.2 1911–1928
Rubinshtein, Modest Iosifovich.
'K kharakteristike ekonomiki Kitaia' (The nature of China's economy).
Bol'shevik 1927, 9 (1 maia), 64–81; 1927, 10 (31 maia), 68–81. [Reprinted in *Rabochii Kitai v 1927 godu: sbornik statei* (Articles on workers' China in 1927), edited by [Solomon Abramovich Dridzo] A. Lozovskii, pseud. (Selective entry.) Moscow: Profintern, 1928, 77–114.]
SUBJ 14 ▪ 16 45

11814 NNC P P2 G1.2 1911–1928
Rubinshtein, Modest Iosifovich.
'Razvitie kapitalizma v Kitae' (The development of capitalism in China).
MKhMP 1927, 7 (iiul'), 52–68.
SUBJ 14 14.1 14.4 16 ▪ 11.2 11.4 16.1 16.3

11815 NNC S P2 G1.2 1911–1949
Rüdenberg, Ernst.
'Die Wirtschaftsprovinzen Chinas' (An economic characterization of China's provinces).
Z. für Geopolitik 8, 11 (Nov. 1931), 818–824; 8, 12 (Dez. 1934), 880–886.
SUBJ 14 14.1 ▪ 11.2 11.3 11.4 14.2 14.3 14.4

11816 GBS S P2 G1.3 1911–1928
Rüdenberg, Ernst.
Zur Entwicklung von Chinas Wirtschaft und Politik (Economic and political development in China).
Berlin: Kurt Vowinckel, 1932. 50 p.
SUBJ 14 14.1 14.4 ▪ 32

11817 NIC U P2 G1.2 1911–1928
Sakuda, Shoichi.
'Some characteristics of the Chinese national economy.'
KUER 1, 2 (Dec. 1926), 128–154.
SUBJ 14 ▪ 14.3 14.5 63

11818 CSH P P2 G2.1 1928–1949
Shishkanov, V- G- (V. G. Shiskanoff).
'Severnaia Man'chzhuriia v tiskakh ekonomicheskogo krizisa.'
VM 1931, 2, 1–7.
'Northern Manchuria in the grip of an economic crisis.'
Manchuria monitor 1931, 2, 1–7.
SUBJ 14 ▪ 14.3 14.6 24.1

11819 MCY U P1 G1.2 1928–1949
Shtein, Viktor Moritsevich, 1890–1964.
'Ekonomicheskii ocherk Kitaia' (Economic survey of China). In *Kitai: istoriia, ekonomika, kul'tura, geroicheskaia bor'ba za natsional'nuiu nezavisimost'. Sbornik statei* (Articles on the history, economy, and culture of China, and its heroic struggle for national independence), edited by Vasilii Mikhailovich Alekseev et al. [Selective entry]
Moscow: Izd-vo Akad. nauk SSSR, 1940, 63–106.
SUBJ 14 ▪ 24.4

11820 NNC S P2 G1.2 1928–1949
Shtein, Viktor Moritsevich, 1890–1964.
'Ekonomicheskoe polozhenie gomindanovskogo Kitaia' (The economic situation in Kuomintang China).
MKhMP 1936, 3 (mart), 68–90.
SUBJ 14 ▪ 18

11821 NNC S P2 G1.4 1928–1949
Sih, Tien-tsung (Hsüeh Tien-tseng).
'Economic conditions in North China.'
IB 4, 3 (9 June 1937), 47–71.
SUBJ 14 14.1 14.4 ▪ 14.2 14.6 18 66

11822 NNC P P2 G1.2 1928–1949
Siu, Rene K. S., 1923–.
China's domestic capital formation.
Unpublished masters thesis in Business, Columbia U., 1948. 109 p.
SUBJ 14 14.6 ▪ 16.1 16.2

11823 MCH P P2 G2.0 1928–1949
Stewart, John Robert, 1910–.
Manchuria since 1931.
New York: Institute of Pacific Relations, Secretariat, 1936. 53 p. (Secretariat papers, 2)
SUBJ 14 66 ▪ 12 12.2 14.3 14.4 14.6 21

11824 NNC O P2 G1.3 1911–1949
Surányi-Unger, Theo.
'Wirtschaft und Nationalismus im Fernen Osten' (Economics and nationalism in the Far East).
Z. für die gesamte Staatswissenschaft 89, 2 (1930), 278–311.
SUBJ 14 14.1 14.3 36.4 ▪ 14.6 16.4 18 24.4 66 72

11825 CSH PO P2 G2.0 1911–1949
Surin, Vladimir Ivanovich.
Man'chzhuriia i ee perspektivy (Manchuria and its prospects).
Harbin: Tip. KVzhd, 1930. 207 p.
SUBJ 11.3 14 14.1 14.2 14.4 ▪ 12 21.2 21.3

11826 CSH P P2 G2.0 1928–1949
Takakhasi Gen''ichi (Takahashi Gen'ichi).
'Velikaia vostochnoaziatskaia voina i Man'chzhugo' (The great war in East Asia and Manchoukuo).
Vostochnoe obozrenie 20 (iiul'–sentiabr' 1944), 27–47.
SUBJ 12 14 54 66 ▪ 15 16.4

11827 CSU PO P2 G2.0 1928–1949
Tanaka, Tetsujiro (Tanaka Tetsujirō).
'Situation actuelle du Manchoukuo' (The situation in Manchoukuo today).
R. économique internationale 30, 1 (2e quartier) (avr. 1938), 123–153.
SUBJ 14 14.4 14.5 14.6

11828 DLC S P2 G9.0 1911–1928
Tanevitskii, M-.
'Ekonomicheskii ocherk Guandunskoi provintsii' (Overview of the economy of Kwangtung). In *Kantonskaia kommuna:*

sbornik statei i materialov (Articles and documents on the Canton commune), compiled by Nauchno-issledovatel'skii institut po Kitaiu, Kommunisticheskaia akademiia. [Selective entry]
Moscow: Gosizdat, 1929, 101–117.
Subj 11.2 14 ▪ 21 66

11829 MCH P P2 G1.2 1928–1949
Tao Siu (T'ao Hsiu).
L'oeuvre du Conseil national économique chinois (The work of the Chinese National Economic Council).
Nancy: Thomas, 1936. 175 p. (Doctoral dissertation, Faculté de droit, Université de Nancy)
Subj 12 14 18 ▪ 12.2 14.1 14.2 34.1 72

11830 CSH O P2 G1.2 1928–1949
Taylor, George Edward, 1905–.
The reconstruction movement in China, mimeo.
London: Royal Institute of International Affairs, 1936. 35 p. (Institute of Pacific Relations, Sixth Conference, United Kingdom papers, 6)
Subj 12 14 14.1 ▪ 12.1 14.4 14.6 15 16.1 16.2 36.4 64

11831 DLC U P2 G1.2 1911–1928
TSelishchev, M-.
'Obzor ekonomicheskoi zhizni Kitaia za 1925 g.' (Overview of Chinese economic life in 1925).
Ekonomicheskaia zhizn' Dal'nego Vostoka 4, 2 (1926), 133–136.
Subj 14 ▪ 16.4 32.2

11832 CSH S P2 G2.0 1911–1949
Tutaev, A- G-.
'Ekonomicheskii krizis v Man'chzhurii' (The economic crisis in Manchuria).
VM 1931, 5, 1–14.
Subj 14 ▪ 14.1 14.4 14.6

11833 CSH P P1 G1.2 1928–1949
U.S. Office of Strategic Services. Research and Analysis Branch.
Inflation in Free China, mimeo.
[Washington, D.C.]: ——, 1945. 8 p. (R. and A., 33,445; Current intelligence studies, 36)
Subj 14 14.5 14.6 ▪ 14.3

11834 CSH FP P2 G2.0 1928–1949
U.S. Office of Strategic Services. Research and Analysis Branch.
Programs of Japan in Manchukuo, with biographies, mimeo.
[Honolulu]: ——, 1945. 2 vols. 445 p. [c.p.]. (R. and A., 3117)
Subj 12.1 14 14.2 14.4 16.3 16.4 ▪ 14.1 14.3 15 17 52 56 64

11835 CSH U P2 G1.2 1928–1949
Valentinov, M-.
'Kitai na putiakh ekonomicheskogo vosstanovleniia' (China on the road to economic redevelopment). [With English abstract]
VM 1929, 6, 99–107.
Subj 14 ▪ 14.2 14.3 14.6

11836 DLC S P1 G1.2 1911–1949
Vetiukov, N-.
'Put' k nishchete i razvalu: ekonomika Kitaia i ekonomicheskaia politika nankinskogo pravitel'stva v period mirovogo krizisa, 1920–1932 gg.' (The road to poverty and disintegration: China's economy and the economic policy of the Nanking government during the world crisis, 1920–1932).
Problemy marksizma 3, 7/8 (1932), 135–160.
Subj 14 ▪ 12 16.4 66

11837 CSU O P2 G9.1 1911–1949
Wong, Hin.
'On Kwangsi province.'
CEJ 5, 1 (July 1929), 626–635; 5, 2 (Aug. 1929), 703–713.
Subj 14 24.2 ▪ 14.4 14.5 14.6 17 24.1

11838 CSU O P2 G1.2 1928–1949
Wu, Ching-chao (Wu Ching-ch'ao), 1901–.
'Economic reconstruction and planning: Wartime and post-war.' In *Voices from unoccupied China*, edited by Harley Farnsworth MacNair. [Selective entry]
Chicago: U. of Chicago Press, 1944, 65–80.
Subj 14 ▪ 12 14.4 32.1

11839 NNC P P2 G1.1 1911–1949
Wu, Yuan-li (Wu Yüan-li), 1920–.
China's economic policy: Planning or free enterprise?
New York: Sino-International Economic Research Center, 1946. 60 p. (SIERC pamphlets, 4)
Subj 14 14.5 14.6 ▪ 14.4 17 18 34.2

11840 CSH P P3 G1.2 1911–1949
Wu, Yuan-li (Wu Yüan-li), 1920–.
'Industrial development and economic policy' [with comments by Chi-ming Hou]. In *The strenuous decade: China's nation-building efforts, 1927–1937*, edited by Paul K. T. Sih (Hsüeh Kuang-ch'ien). [Selective entry]
Jamaica, N.Y.: St. John's U. Press, 1970, 237–253.
Subj 14 14.4 ▪ 12 14.2 14.3 34.2

11841 CSU PO P2 G1.1 1928–1949
Young, Arthur Nichols, 1890–.
China's nation-building effort, 1927–1937: The financial and economic record.
Stanford: Hoover Institution Press, 1971. 19, 553 p.
Subj 14 14.5 14.6 ▪ 12 14.2 32

1911-1972
(including 1644-1972)

11842 CSH P P2 G1.2 1928–1972
Berger, IAkov Mikhailovich, 1929–, et al.
'Narodnoe khoziaistvo KNR' (The national economy of the People's Republic of China). In *Kitaiskaia Narodnaia Respublika* (The People's Republic of China), compiled by Institut Dal'nego Vostoka, Akademiia nauk SSSR, edited by Mikhail Iosifovich Sladkovskii and Grigorii Dmitrievich Sukharchuk. [Selective entry]
Moscow: Nauka, Glav. red. vost. lit-ry, 1970, 46–112.
Subj 14 16 ▪ 18

11843 CSH P P2 G9.4 1928–1972
Chen, Cheng-siang (Ch'en Cheng-hsiang), 1920–.
'The changing economy of Taiwan.'
IFC 21, 2 (Feb. 1964), 22–31. [Reprinted—*Pacific viewpoint* 6, 2 (Sept. 1965), 179–190.]
Subj 14 24.1 ▪ 14.4 21.4

11844 MCH O P2 G9.4 –1972
Chen, Cheng-siang (Ch'en Cheng-hsiang), 1920–.
'The economic development and geographical changes in Taiwan.' In *Hermann von Wissmann: Festschrift* (Felicitation volume for Hermann von Wissmann), edited by Adolf Leidlmair. [Sole entry]
Tübingen: Universität Tübingen, Geographische Institut, 1962, 238–257.
Subj 14 18 21 ▪ 11.3 16.3 58

11845 CSU P P2 G1.2 1928–1972
Chen, Nai-ruenn (Ch'en Nai-jun), 1927–, and Walter Galenson, 1914–.
The Chinese economy under Communism.
Chicago: Aldine, 1969. 250 p.
Subj 14 14.1 14.4 18 24.4 ▪ 11 11.4 14.2 34.1 36.4 55 58

11846 NNC P P2 G1.2 1928–1972
Cheng Chu-yuan (Cheng Chu-yüan), 1927–.
Communist China's economy, 1949–1962: Structural changes and crisis.
South Orange: Seton Hall U. Press, 1963. 12, 217 p.
Subj 14 14.1 14.4 18 19 20 ▪ 12 14.6 16.2 16.3 34.1 34.2 63 64

11847 CSU S P2 G1.2 1928–1972
Eckstein, Alexander, 1915–, Walter Galenson, 1914–, and Ta-chung Liu, 1914–.
'Introduction.' In *Economic trends in Communist China*, edited by A. Eckstein, W. Galenson, and Ta-chung Liu. [Selective entry]
Chicago: Aldine, 1968, 1–32.
Subj 14 ▪ 11 11.4

11848 MCH PO P2 G1.2 1928–1972
Etienne, Gilbert.
La voie chinoise (The Chinese way).
Paris: Presses universitaires, 1962. 296 p.
Subj 12.1 14 14.1 14.4 19 64 ▪ 11.4 16 18 22 32 34.1 58 62 66

11849 FPN P P2 G1.2 –1972
Finquel, Edouard.
Economie et socialisme en Chine (The economy and socialism in China).
Unpublished doctoral dissertation, Faculté de droit, Université de Paris, 1968. 306, 21 p. [Doctorat d'état]
Subj 12.1 14 14.1 14.4 15 19 ▪ 11 11.4 32.2 34.1 34.2 64

11850 NNC P P2 G1.2 1842–1972
Ganshin, Georgii Aleksandrovich, 1925–.
Ekonomika KNR (The economy of the People's Republic of China).
Moscow: Izd-vo IMO, 1959. 356 p.
Subj 14 14.1 14.3 ▪ 14.2 14.5

11851 MCH P P2 G9.4 1895–1972
Ginsburg, Norton Sydney, 1921–.
'Taiwan: A resource analysis of an Oriental economy.'
EDCC 1, 1 (Mar. 1952), 37–56; 1, 2 (June 1952), 110–131.
Subj 14 14.4 24.1 ▪ 14.6 16.1 18 21.4 34.1 38

11852 MCH P P2 G1.2 1928–1972
Ginsburgh, Victor.
La République populaire de Chine: cadres institutionnels et réalisations. II, la planification et la croissance

économique, 1949–1959 (Institutions and accomplishments in the People's Republic of China, Vol. 2, Economic planning and growth, 1949–1959).
Brussels: Université libre de Bruxelles, Institut de sociologie Solvay, Centre d'étude des pays de l'Est *with* Centre national pour l'étude des pays à régime communiste, 1963. 184 p.
SUBJ 14 14.1 14.4 19 ▪ 11.4 14.6 18 32.1 34.1 34.2 72

11853 CSH S P2 G1.1 1842–1972
Grossmann, Bernhard Paul, 1929–.
'Die Regionen wirtschaftlicher Aktivität im Kommunistischen China' (Natural economic regions in Communist China).
Politische Bildung 2, 2 (1969), 26–32.
SUBJ 11.3 14 14.2

11854 NIC P P2 G1.2 1911–1972
Ishikawa Shigeru, 1918–.
'An analysis of economic growth in China.'
Asian affairs (Tokyo) 2, 1 (Mar. 1957), 21–46.
SUBJ 14 14.4 ▪ 11 11.4 24.4

11855 NIC S P2 G1.2 –1972
Jacobs, Norman Gabriel, 1924–.
The origin of modern capitalism and eastern Asia.
Hong Kong: Hong Kong U. Press, 1958. 10, 243 p.
SUBJ 14 16.1 16.2 64 ▪ 12.2 13 17 34.3 45 62

11856 CSU P P2 G9.4 1928–1972
Kawano, Shigetō.
'Strategic elements in the rapid economic growth of Taiwan.'
DE 5, 3 (Sept. 1967), 486–502.
SUBJ 14 14.4 24.1 ▪ 14.5 58

11857 CSU P P2 G1.1 1842–1972
King, Frank Henry Haviland, 1926–.
A concise economic history of modern China, 1840–1961.
Bombay: Vora, 1968. 244 p. [Reprinted—New York: Praeger, 1969. 244 p.]
SUBJ 14 14.6 16 ▪ 12 14.1 14.4 18 34.1 34.2 64 66

11858 MCH P P2 G1.1 –1972
Kirby, Edward Stuart, 1909–.
Introduction to the economic history of China.
London: Allen and Unwin, 1954. 202 p. [Reprinted—Westport, Conn.: Hyperion Press, 197? 202 p.]
SUBJ 12 14 70 71 ▪ 11.2 14.1 14.4 14.5 32.2

11859 CSU P P2 G1.1 –1972
Kolb, Albert, 1906–.
'Population, society, settlement and economy.' Tr. from the German by C- A- M- Sym. In *East Asia: China, Japan, Korea, Vietnam. Geography of a cultural region*, by A. Kolb. [Selective entry]
London: Methuen, 1971, 92–195. [Rev. ed. of *Ostasien: China, Japan, Korea. Geographie eines Kulturerdteils.* Heidelberg: Quelle und Meyer, 1963.]
SUBJ 11.3 14 14.1 20 ▪ 11 11.1 14.2 14.4 24.3 24.4 34.1 58

11860 DLC P P2 G1.2 1928–1972
Kumachenko, IAkov Stepanovich.
Ekonomicheskii stroi Kitaiskoi Narodnoi Respubliki (The economic structure of the People's Republic of China).
Moscow: Sovetskaia nauka, 1955. 72 p.
SUBJ 14 14.1 14.3 14.4 ▪ 16.2 16.4 24.4 32.2

11861 CSU P P7 G1.2 1928–1972
Lau, Lawrence J. (Liu Tsun-i), 1944–.
'Peasant consumption, saving, and investment in Mainland China' [with comments by Jerzy F- Karcz]. In *Agrarian policies and problems in Communist and non-Communist countries*, edited by William Arthur Douglas Jackson. [Selective entry]
Seattle: U. of Washington Press, 1971, 305–345.
SUBJ 14 16.3 ▪ 34.1

11862 FPN P P2 G1.2 1911–1972
Lavallée, Léon, Paul Noirot, and Victor Dominique.
Economie de la Chine socialiste (The economy of Communist China).
Geneva: Rousseau, 1957. 511 p.
SUBJ 14 16 64 ▪ 11.4 12 18 30 32.1 34.1 36.4 47

11863 MAM P P2 G9.4 1928–1972
Lin, Ching-yuan, 1932–.
The orientation of policy incentives, trade, and industrial development: A case study on Taiwan, 1946–70.
Ann Arbor: University Microfilms (Publ. 72-9003), 1972. 11, 275 p. (Doctoral dissertation in Economics, George Washington U., 1971)
SUBJ 14 14.3 14.4 ▪ 14.5 21.4 24.1

11864 CSU FP P2 G1.2 1928–1972
Liu, Ta-chung, 1914–, and K. C. Yeh (Yeh K'ung-chia), 1924–.
The economy of the Chinese mainland: National income and economic development, 1933–1959.
Princeton: Princeton U. Press, 1965. 16, 771 p.
SUBJ 11.4 14 14.1 14.4 ▪ 12 14.2 18 24.4 34.2 47 55

11865 CSH P P2 G1.2 1928–1972
Mah, Feng-hwa (Ma Feng-hua), 1922–.
'Two approaches to economic development.' In *Realities of Communist China*, edited by Yuan-li Wu (Wu Yüan-li). [Selective entry]
Milwaukee: Marquette U., Institute for Asian Studies *with* Marquette U., Robert A. Johnston College of Business Administration, Center for Business Services, Research Center, 1960, 24–35.
SUBJ 14 14.5 ▪ 14.1 14.6

11866 NNC P P2 G1.2 1928–1972
Maslennikov, Viacheslav Aleksandrovich, 1894–1968.
'Bor'ba kitaiskogo naroda za ukreplenie i nezavisimost' Kitaiskoi Narodnoi Respubliki' (The Chinese people's struggle for the consolidation and independence of the People's Republic of China).
UZIV 2 (1951), 3–35.
SUBJ 12 14 ▪ 12.2 16.3 16.4 17 32 45

11867 NNC P P2 G1.1 1644–1972
Maslennikov, Viacheslav Aleksandrovich, 1894–1968.
'Nekotorye osobennosti ekonomicheskogo razvitiia kolonial'nykh i zavisimykh stran v epokhu imperializma' (Features of economic development in colonial and semicolonial countries in the imperialist era).
SV 1955, 4, 31–42.
SUBJ 14 16

11868 MCH S P2 G1.2 1928–1972
Milenković, Vladislav, 1900–.
'Kina u procesu preobražaja i izgradnje' (China in the process of transformation and development).
Pregled 6, Part 2, 10 (1954), 199–209.
SUBJ 14 19 ▪ 14.1 14.3 14.4

11869 DLC P P2 G1.4 –1972
Muranov, Aleksandr Pavlovich.
Reka Khuankhe (Zheltaia reka) (The Yellow River).
Leningrad: Gidrometeoizdat, 1957. 86 p.
SUBJ 11.3 14 ▪ 38 55 65 71

11870 CSU S P2 G1.2 –1972
Myers, Ramon Hawley, 1929–.
'Studies in modern Chinese economic history.' [Review of *Agricultural development in China, 1368–1968*, by Dwight Heald Perkins; *Industrial development in pre-Communist China: A quantitative analysis*, by John Key Chang (Chang Ch'ang-chi); *The Chinese economy, ca. 1870–1911*, by Albert Feuerwerker; and *The Chinese economy, 1912–1949*, by Albert Feuerwerker.]
JAS 29, 4 (Aug. 1970), 897–905.
SUBJ 14 14.1 14.4

11871 NNC S P2 G1.2 –1972
Parfionovich, IU- M-.
'Kitaiskie istoriki o zarozhdenii kapitalizma v Kitae' (Chinese historians on the origin of capitalism in China). [With English abstract]
SV 1957, 4, 107–116.
SUBJ 14 62 70 ▪ 16 32.2

11872 NNC PO P2 G1.2 1928–1972
Sergiev, Artemii Vladimirovich.
Rol' demokraticheskoi diktatury naroda v stroitel'stve sotsializma v Kitae (The role of the people's democratic dictatorship in socialist construction in China).
Moscow: Gospolitizdat, 1958. 338 p.
SUBJ 12 14 16 19 32 64 ▪ 12.1 14.1 14.3 14.4 25 32.1

11873 CSU P P2 G9.4 1928–1972
United Nations. Economic Commission for Asia and the Far East. Research and Planning Division.
'China: Taiwan.'
EBAFE 4, 4 (Mar. 1954), 50–54. [Special issue: *Economic survey of Asia and the Far East, 1953*]
SUBJ 14 14.4 24.1 ▪ 14.5 14.6

11874 NNC P P2 G1.2 1928–1972
Wu, Yuan-li (Wu Yüan-li), 1920–.
An economic survey of Communist China.
New York: Bookman Associates, 1956. 10, 566 p.
SUBJ 11.4 14 14.1 14.2 14.4 ▪ 11 16.4 18 34.1 34.2 36.3 36.4

11875 CSH P P2 G1.2 1928–1972
Wu, Yuan-li (Wu Yüan-li), 1920–.
'Take-off to sustained economic growth?' In *Realities of Communist China*, edited by Yuan-li Wu. [Selective entry]
Milwaukee: Marquette U., Institute for Asian Studies *with* Marquette U., Robert A. Johnston College of Business Administration, Center for Business Services, Research Center, 1960, 3–13.
SUBJ 14 14.1 14.4 ▪ 24.4

11876 CSH P P2 G1.2 1928–1972
Yeh, K. C. (Yeh K'ung-chia), 1924–.
Capital formation in Communist China.
Santa Monica, Calif.: RAND Corp., 1966. 59 p. (RAND papers, P-3251) [For a fuller version, see entry 11877.] [Reprinted as 'Capital formation.' In *Economic trends in Communist China*, edited by Alexander Eckstein, Walter Galenson, and Ta-chung Liu. (Selective entry.) Chicago: Aldine, 1968, 508–547.]
SUBJ 14 14.1 14.4 ▪ 14.2 24.4

11877 MAM S P2 G1.2 1928–1972
Yeh, K. C. (Yeh K'ung-chia), 1924–.
Capital formation in Mainland China: 1931–36 and 1952–57.
Ann Arbor: University Microfilms (Publ. 65-7411), 1965. 354 p. (Doctoral dissertation in Economics, Columbia U.)
SUBJ 14 14.6 ▪ 14.1 16.2 16.3

11878 NNC S P2 G1.2 1928–1972
Zaichikov, Vladimir Timofeevich, 1909–.
Vostochnyi Kitai: primorskie provintsii (East China: The maritime provinces).
Moscow: Geografgiz, 1955. 310 p.
SUBJ 11.3 14 21 ▪ 14.1 14.2 14.4 21.1 21.3

1949-1972

11879 MCH P P2 G1.2 1949–1972
'Enkele aspekten van de ontwikkeling van het kommunisme in China in 1953–1956' (Aspects of the development of Communism in China, 1953–1956).
Internationale spectator 10, 22 (22 November 1956), 623–668.
SUBJ 14 ▪ 14.1 14.4 64

11880 DLC P P2 G1.2 1949–1972
'Industrijalizacija kineske privrede i sistem planiranja' (Industrialization of the Chinese economy and the system of planning).
Spoljnopolitička dokumentacija 10, 11/12 (1958), 4–17.
SUBJ 11.3 14

11881 CSU S P2 G1.2 1949–1972
'"Plain living and hard struggle": An economic assessment.'
CS 2, 28 (15 Feb. 1964), 1–8.
SUBJ 14 18

11882 MCH P P2 G1.2 1949–1972
'La situation économique de la Chine populaire au début de 1958. A, bilan du premier plan quinquennal et aperçus sur le second plan' (The economic situation in the People's Republic of China at the beginning of 1958. A, Balance sheet of the First Five-Year Plan and glances at the Second [Five-Year] Plan).
NED 2445 (4 août 1958), 1–12.
SUBJ 14 ▪ 18

11883 MCH O P2 G1.2 1949–1972
Abegg, Lily, 1901–.
Im neuen China (In New China).
Zurich: Atlantis, 1957. 285 p.
SUBJ 12.1 14 19 66 ▪ 12 13 16 17 18 32 34.1 47 64

11884 NNC P P2 G1.2 1949–1972
Adler, Solomon.
The Chinese economy.
New York: Monthly Review Press, 1957. 11, 276 p.
SUBJ 14 14.4 ▪ 11 12.2 14.1 16.4 17 18 34.1 58

11885 DLC P P2 G1.2 1949–1972
Adrianovskii, A-, and A- Fomin.
Kitaiskii narod v bor'be za sotsializm (The Chinese people in the struggle for socialism).
Moscow: Gospolitizdat, 1955. 133 p.
SUBJ 12 14 32.1 32.2 ▪ 12.1 12.2 16.2 31 33 34.1 36.4 66

11886 CSH P P2 G1.2 1949–1972
Aoki Shinichi (Aoki Shin'ichi).
'The Chinese economy and Sino-Japanese trade.' Tr. from the Japanese by Alan Wolfe.
CES 5, 2 (Winter 1971/72), 91–121.
SUBJ 14 ▪ 14.1 14.4 18

11887 CSU P P2 G1.2 1949–1972
Ashbrook, Arthur Garwood, Jr., 1921–.
'China: Economic policy and economic results, 1949–71.' In *People's Republic of China: An economic assessment*, compiled by Joint Economic Committee, U.S. Congress. [Selective entry]
Washington, D.C.: U.S. Government Printing Office, 1972, 3–51.
SUBJ 14 14.1 14.4 ▪ 11 18

11888 CSU U P2 G1.2 1949–1972
Ashbrook, Arthur Garwood, Jr., 1921–.
'Main lines of Chinese Communist economic policy.' In *An economic profile of Mainland China*, compiled by Joint Economic Committee, U.S. Congress. [Selective entry]
Washington, D.C.: U.S. Government Printing Office, 1967, vol. 1, 15–44. [Reprinted in *An economic profile of Mainland China*, compiled by the agency cited. (Selective entry.) New York: Praeger, 1968, 15–44.]
SUBJ 14 ▪ 14.1 14.4 34.1

11889 CSH P P2 G1.2 1949–1972
Axilrod, Eric.
The economic theory of the two tendencies in the Cultural Revolution.
Hong Kong: Chinese U. of Hong Kong, Economic Research Centre, 1971. 26 p. (ERC, Mainland China series, occasional papers, 2)
SUBJ 14 ▪ 14.1 14.3 14.4 64

11890 MCH S P2 G1.2 1949–1972
Babić, Blagoje.
'Karakteristike ekonomskog razvitka NR Kine' (Characteristics of China's economic development).
Medjunarodni problemi 17, 3 (1965), 101–122.
SUBJ 14 ▪ 14.1 14.4

11891 NNC P P2 G1.2 1949–1972
Barnett, Arthur Doak, 1921–.
Communist economic strategy: The rise of Mainland China.
Washington, D.C.: National Planning Assn., 1959. 106 p.
SUBJ 14 14.1 14.4 ▪ 11.4 14.3 18 24.4

11892 CSU U P2 G1.1 1949–1972
Barnett, Robert Warren, 1911–.
'China and Taiwan: The economic issues.'
FA 50, 3 (Apr. 1972), 444–458.
SUBJ 14 66 ▪ 11.4 51

11893 NNC PO P1 G1.2 1949–1972
Bayer-Dortmund, Hans, 1914–.
'Geplante Wirtschaftsdynamik in China und Indien' (The dynamics of economic planning in China and India).
SJ 76, 6 (1956), 35–64.
SUBJ 14 14.6 ▪ 14.1 14.4

11894 DLC O P2 G1.2 1949–1972
Berezhkov, Valentin Mikhailovich.
Ot Sungari do tropika Raka (From the Sungari to the Tropic of Cancer).
Moscow: Gospolitizdat, 1958. 149 p.
SUBJ 11.4 12.1 14 16 17 18 ▪ 11.2 14.1 14.4 15 34.1 34.2 47 53 64 66

11895 MCH PO P2 G1.2 1949–1972
Bettelheim, Charles.
'Accumulation et développement économique de la Chine' (Accumulation and economic development in China).
Economie appliquée 13, 3 (juil.–sept. 1960), 347–390.
SUBJ 14 ▪ 11.4 14.1 18 24.4 32.1 34.2

11896 ELB PO P2 G1.2 1949–1972
Bettelheim, Charles.
'Aspects spécifiques de l'économie chinoise contemporaine' (Specific aspects of the contemporary Chinese economy).
R. des travaux de l'Académie des sciences morales et politiques 4e série 119, 1 (1966), 232–244.
SUBJ 14 14.1 14.4 ▪ 18 22

11897 MCH PO P2 G1.2 1949–1972
Bettelheim, Charles, et al.
La construction du socialisme en Chine (Building socialism in China).
Paris: Maspero, 1965. 180 p.
SUBJ 14 14.4 18 19 64 ▪ 12 12.1 14.1 14.3 16.3 24.4 32 34.1 34.2

11898 CSU P P1 G1.2 1949–1972
Biehl, Max, 1902–.
'Die chinesische Volksrepublik am Beginn der dritten Planperiode' (The People's Republic of China at the start of the Third Five-Year Plan).
Wirtschaftsdienst 46, 6 (Juni 1966), 311–317.
SUBJ 14 14.1 14.4

11899 CSU U P1 G1.2 1949–1972
Boorman, Howard Lyon, 1920–.
'The scientific revolution in Communist China.'
China report (New Delhi) 4, 5 (Sept.–Oct. 1968), 10–20.
SUBJ 14 62

11900 DLC S P2 G1.2 1949–1972
Bouc, Alain.
'L'économisme contre le socialisme en Chine populaire' (Economism versus

socialism in the People's Republic of China).
Courrier des pays de l'Est 87 (4 oct. 1967), 19–36.
SUBJ 14 16 32 64 ▪ 12.1 14.1 14.4

11901 NNC O P2 G1.2 1949–1972
Boyd-Orr, John, 1880–1971, and Peter Townsend, 1919–.
What's happening in China?
Garden City, N.Y.: Doubleday, 1959. 159 p.
SUBJ 14 18 ▪ 14.1 14.4 16.2 17 19 31 34.1 47 55

11902 MCH S P2 G1.2 1949–1972
Chambre, Henri, 1908–.
'Développement économique: URSS et Chine' (Economic development: The U.S.S.R. and China).
R. de l'action populaire 138 (mai 1960), 569–593.
SUBJ 14 14.1 14.4 ▪ 11 12 24.4 32.1 63 64

11903 MCH O P2 G1.2 1949–1972
Chand, Gyan, 1893–.
The new economy of China: Factual account, analysis and interpretation.
Bombay: Vora, 1958. 429 p.
SUBJ 14 14.1 14.4 34.2 ▪ 11 14.6 16.3 16.4 24.3 24.4 34.1 58

11904 CSU P P2 G9.4 1949–1972
Chang, David W. (Chang Wen-wei), 1929–.
'U.S. aid and economic progress in Taiwan.'
AS 5, 3 (Mar. 1965), 152–160.
SUBJ 14 ▪ 14.4 24.1

11905 MAM P P2 G9.4 1949–1972
Chang, Lih-yong (Chang Li-jung), 1922–.
Economic development under foreign aid and preparation for war: A case study of Taiwan, 1949–1962.
Ann Arbor: University Microfilms (Publ. 65-6967), 1965. 319 p. (Doctoral dissertation in Economics, Cornell U.)
SUBJ 14 ▪ 14.3 14.4 14.6 24.1

11906 CLU P P2 G1.2 1949–1972
Chang, Tsung-tung, 1931–.
Die chinesische Volkswirtschaft: Grundlagen, Organisation, Planung (The foundations, organization, and planning of China's national economy).
Cologne: Westdeutscher Verlag, 1965. 193 p. (Forschungsinstitut für internationale technische Zusammenarbeit an der Technische Hochschule Aachen, Forschungsberichte des Landes Nordrhein-Westfalen, 1280) (Revision of *Die Grundlagen der chinesischen Volkswirtschaftsplanung* [The bases of China's national economic planning], doctoral dissertation, Wirtschafts- und sozialwissenschaftliche Fakultät, Universität Frankfurt a.M., 1961)
SUBJ 12 14 14.1 14.4 34.1 34.2 ▪ 11.3 11.4 14.3 14.5 17 18

11907 MCH U P2 G1.2 1949–1972
Chang, Wei-ya.
Has the Chinese Communist economy taken a turn for the better? An overall discussion of the Chinese economy in 1964.
Taipei: Asian Peoples' Anti-Communist League, 1965. 70 p. (APACL pamphlets, 95)
SUBJ 14 ▪ 14.1 14.4

11908 MCH P P2 G1.2 1949–1972
Chao, Kang, 1929–.
'Economic aftermath of the Great Leap in Communist China.'
AS 4, 5 (May 1964), 851–858. [Reprinted in *Readings in modern Chinese history*, edited by Immanuel C. Y. Hsü (Hsü Chung-yüeh). (Selective entry.) New York: Oxford U. Press, 1971, 591–597.]
SUBJ 14 ▪ 14.1 14.4 16.4

11909 MCH P P2 G1.2 1949–1972
Chao, Kuo-chün, 1918–1962.
Economic planning and organization in Mainland China: A documentary study, 1949–1957.
Cambridge: Harvard U., Center for East Asian Studies, 1959, 1960. 2 vols. 26, 273; 10, 184 p. (Harvard East Asian monographs, 7)
SUBJ 14 14.1 14.4 ▪ 12 34.1 36.4

11910 CSU S P2 G1.2 1949–1972
Chen, Kuan-i.
'The economic outlook of Mainland China in the 1970's.'
Keio economic studies 7, 2 (1970), 15–32.
SUBJ 14 ▪ 14.1 14.3 14.4

11911 CSU S P2 G1.2 1949–1972
Chen, Kuan-i.
'Prospects for the Chinese economy.' In *Comparative development of India and China*, edited by Kuan-i Chen and Jogindar S- Uppal. [Sole entry]
New York: Free Press, 1971, 372–381.
SUBJ 14 ▪ 14.1 14.4

11912 CSU P P2 G1.2 1949–1972
Chen, Nai-ruenn (Ch'en Nai-jun), 1927–.
Chinese economic statistics: A handbook for Mainland China.
Chicago: Aldine, 1967. 31, 539 p.
SUBJ 11.4 14 14.1 14.4 24.4 ▪ 11 11.1 14.5 14.6 16.3 16.4 18 36.4 58

11913 CSU P P2 G1.2 1949–1972
Chen, Pi-chao, 1937–.
'The political economics of population growth: The case of China.'
WP 23, 2 (Jan. 1971), 245–272.
SUBJ 11 14 14.1 58 ▪ 11.2 11.4 12.1 14.4 50

11914 NNC U P1 G1.2 1949–1972
Cheng Ching-ch'ing.
'On basic contradictions of a socialist society.' Tr. of 'Shih lun she hui chu i ti chi pen mao tun' (A preliminary discussion of the basic contradictions of socialism); *Ching chi yen chiu* (Peking) 1960, 6 (June), 20–35. In *Economic studies in Communist China*, mimeo., compiled by U.S. Joint Publications Research Service. [Sole entry]
Washington, D.C.: JPRS, 27 Nov. 1960, 132–182. (JPRS 5670; MC 2161/1961)
SUBJ 14 ▪ 16 18 64

11915 CSU P P2 G1.2 1949–1972
Cheng Chu-yuan (Cheng Chu-yüan), 1927–.
'The Cultural Revolution and China's economy.'
CH 53, 313 (Sept. 1967), 148–154, 176–177.
SUBJ 14 14.4 19 ▪ 14.1 14.3 16.3 16.4 22.2

11916 CSU S P2 G1.2 1949–1972
Cheng Chu-yuan (Cheng Chu-yüan), 1927–.
'Economy and foreign trade of Mainland China' [with comments by Arthur S. Chen (Ch'en Shu-yüan)]. In *Aspects of modern Communism*, edited by Richard Felix Staar. [Selective entry]
Columbia: U. of South Carolina Press, 1968, 227–258.
SUBJ 14 14.4 ▪ 14.1 14.2 18 36.3

11917 MAU P P2 G1.2 1949–1972
Cheng Chu-yuan (Cheng Chu-yüan), 1927–.
The economy of Communist China, 1949–1969, with a bibliography of selected materials on Chinese economic development.
Ann Arbor: U. of Michigan, Center for Chinese Studies, 1971. 79 p. (Michigan papers in Chinese studies, 9)
SUBJ 14 ▪ 14.1 14.4 72

11918 NNC P P2 G1.2 1949–1972
Cheng Chu-yuan (Cheng Chu-yüan), 1927–.
'Summarizing Communist China's First Five-Year Plan.' Tr. of 'Tsung chieh Chung kung ti i ko wu nien chi hua'; *Tsu kuo chou k'an* 274/275 (7 Apr. 1958), 57–61. In *Communist China, 1957*, edited by Union Research Institute. [Selective entry]
Hong Kong: Union Research Institute, 1958, 216–233.
SUBJ 14 ▪ 14.1 14.2 14.4 18

11919 CBU O P2 G1.2 1949–1972
Chilanti, Felice.
La Cina fa parte del mondo (China is part of the world).
Rome: Editrice di cultura sociale, 1954. 325 p.
SUBJ 14 19 ▪ 32 64

11920 CSH P P2 G1.2 1949–1972
China [People's Republic]. Kuo wu yüan. Kuo chia t'ung chi chü. (State Council. National Statistics Bureau).
Ten great years: Statistics of the economic and cultural achievements of the People's Republic of China. Tr. of *Wei ta ti shih nien: Chung-hua jen min kung ho kuo ching chi ho wen hua chien she ch'eng chiu ti tung chi* (A decade of greatness: Statistics on the economic and cultural achievements of the People's Republic of China); Peking: Jen min ch'u pan she, 1959; 10, 198 p.
Peking: Foreign Languages Press, 1960. 223 p. [Reprinted—New York: AMS Press, 1972. 10, 198 p.]
SUBJ 14 14.1 14.4 16.4 19 ▪ 11 11.4 17 18 34.1 55 64

11921 NNC P P2 G1.1 1949–1972
China [Republic]. Hsing cheng yüan. Ching chi an ting wei yüan hui. (Executive Yüan. Economic Stabilization Board).
An annual review of the economic situation of the Republic of China, July 1955 – June 1956.

Taipei: Ching chi an ting wei yüan hui, 1956. 113 p.
SUBJ 14 14.1 14.4 ▪ 14.2 18

11922 CSU O P2 G1.2 1949–1972
[Chow, Elizabeth K.] Han Suyin, pseud., 1917–.
China in the year 2001.
New York: Basic Books, 1967. 268 p. [Reprinted—New York: Penguin, 1970. 254 p.]
SUBJ 14 64 ▪ 15 17 19 32

11923 MCH O P1 G1.2 1949–1972
Churakov, IU-.
'Voprosy planirovaniia narodnogo khoziaistva v Kitaiskoi Narodnoi Respublike' (Planning the national economy in the People's Republic of China).
Planovoe khoziaistvo 36, 10 (oktiabr' 1959), 92–96.
SUBJ 14 ▪ 14.5

11924 MCH P P2 G1.2 1949–1972
Clark, Colin, 1905–.
'Economic growth in Communist China.'
CQ 21 (Jan.–Mar. 1965), 148–167.
SUBJ 14 18 55 ▪ 14.1 14.4

11925 NNC P P2 G1.4 1949–1972
Clubb, Oliver Edmund, 1901–.
Chinese Communist development programs in Manchuria, with a supplement on Inner Mongolia.
New York: Institute of Pacific Relations, International Secretariat, 1954. 46 p. (IS papers, 3)
SUBJ 14 14.1 14.4 ▪ 14.5

11926 CSU P P2 G4.3 1949–1972
Clubb, Oliver Edmund, 1901–.
'Economic modernization in Sinkiang.'
FES 27, 2 (Feb. 1958), 17–23.
SUBJ 14 14.4 24.1 ▪ 21.2 24.2

11927 CSU S P2 G1.2 1949–1972
Cone, Frederick McGrail, 1910–.
Chinese industrial growth: Investment outlays, 1952–1957.
Santa Monica, Calif.: RAND Corp., 1969. 12, 43 p. (RAND memoranda, RM-5662-PR/ISA)
SUBJ 14 14.4

11928 CSU P P2 G1.2 1949–1972
Cone, Frederick McGrail, 1910–.
Chinese industrial growth: Recent developments and potential growth rate.
Santa Monica, Calif.: RAND Corp., 1969. 12, 79 p. (RAND memoranda, RM-6074-PR/ISA)
SUBJ 14 14.4 ▪ 11.4 14.1 15

11929 CSU S P2 G1.2 1949–1972
Cressey, George Babcock, 1896–1963.
'China's economic potential.' In *Asia's lands and peoples: A geography of one-third of the earth and two-thirds of its people*, 3rd ed., by G. B. Cressey. [Selective entry]
New York: McGraw-Hill, 1963, 105–121.
SUBJ 14 14.1 ▪ 11.3 14.3 14.4

11930 MCH P P2 G1.2 1949–1972
Current Scene Editor.
'And now there are four: A survey of the first year in China's current five-year plan.'
CS 4, 20 (10 Nov. 1966), 1–12.
SUBJ 14 14.4 ▪ 14.1 19

11931 CSU P P2 G1.2 1949–1972
Current Scene Editor.
'China's economy in 1969: Policy, agriculture, industry, foreign trade.'
CS 8, 11 (1 June 1970), 1–17.
SUBJ 14 14.1 14.4

11932 NIC P P2 G1.2 1949–1972
Current Scene Editor.
'Communist China at the crossroads: The dilemma of economic distribution.'
CS 2, 3 (27 Aug. 1962), 1–19.
SUBJ 14 17 18 ▪ 11.4 56

11933 CSU P P2 G1.2 1949–1972
Current Scene Editor.
'Communist China economy at mid-year 1968: Eighteen months of disorder.'
CS 6, 12 (17 July 1968), 1–16.
SUBJ 14 19 ▪ 14.1 14.3 14.4

11934 DLC P P2 G1.3 1949–1972
Dapčević-Oreščanin, Sonja, et al.
'Posleratna obnova privrede' (Postwar restoration of the economy).
DB 4, 6/7 (1955), 91–106. [Special issue: *Savremena Kina* (Contemporary China)]
SUBJ 14 14.4 ▪ 14.1 14.2

11935 CSU S P2 G1.2 1949–1972
Dean, Genevieve Catherine, 1943–.
'Science, technology and development: China as a "case study".'
CQ 51 (July–Sept. 1972), 520–534.
SUBJ 14 14.4 ▪ 62

11936 CSU U P2 G1.2 1949–1972
Dernberger, Robert Franklin, 1929–.
'Economic realities and China's political economics.'
B. of the atomic scientists 25, 2 (Feb. 1969), 34–42. [Special issue: *China after the Cultural Revolution*, edited by (Richard Garratt Wilson) Dick Wilson] [Reprinted in *China after the Cultural Revolution*. (Selective entry.) New York: Random House, 1969, 87–114.]
SUBJ 14 14.1 14.4 ▪ 11 58

11937 NNC U P2 G1.2 1949–1972
[Di Chao-bai] Ti Tschau-bai (Ti Ch'ao-pai).
'Razvitie sotsialisticheskoi ekonomiki i ekonomicheskie zakony v perekhodnyi period v Kitaiskoi Narodnoi Respublike' (Economic laws and the development of the socialist economy during the transitional period in the People's Republic of China).
VE 1957, 1 (ianvar'), 57–72.

'Die Entwicklung der sozialistischen Wirtschaft und die ökonomischen Gesetze in der Übergangsperiode in der chinesische Volksrepublik.' Tr. by W- Busch.
Sowjetwissenschaft; gesellschafts-wissenschaftliche Beiträge 1957, 7 (Juli), 772–790.
SUBJ 14 34.1 64 ▪ 14.1 14.4 16 16.2 32.1 34.2

11938 CSU S P2 G1.2 1949–1972
Dietvorst, A-, 1940–.
'Aspecten van de Chinese economische ontwikkeling na 1960: Een literatuuroverzicht' (Aspects of Chinese economic development since 1960: Survey of the literature).
Geografisch tijdschrift nieuwe (2de) reeks 5, 3 (Junie 1971), 218–227.
SUBJ 14 72

11939 CBU S P2 G1.2 1949–1972
Dietvorst, A-, 1940–.
De Volksrepubliek China (The People's Republic of China).
Roermond: Romen, 1971. 198 p.
SUBJ 14 14.1 14.4 20 ▪ 11 11.1 11.2 21.3 34.1 64

11940 MCH P P2 G1.2 1949–1972
Doi Akira, 1905–.
'Analysis of economic growth in Communist China.' Tr. of 'Chūgoku keizai no seichō to seichōritsu' (Economic growth and the economic growth rate in China); *Ekafe tsūshin* 266 (1 June 1961), 1–25; 271 (21 July 1961), 1–34. In *Analysis of economic growth and industrial indices in Communist China*, mimeo., compiled by U.S. Joint Publications Research Service. [Sole entry]
Washington, D.C.: JPRS, 19 Jan. 1962, 1–56. (JPRS 12,037; MC 5959/1962)
SUBJ 14 ▪ 14.1 14.2 14.4 18

11941 CSU P P2 G1.2 1949–1972
Doi Akira, 1905–.
'Communist China's economy and Sino-Japanese trade under the Cultural Revolution.' Tr. of *Bunkakuka no Chūkyō keizai to Nitchū bōkei*; Tokyo: Tairiku mondai kenkyūjo, 1968; 64 p.
CES 3, 3 (Spring 1970), 224–264.
SUBJ 14 19 32 64 ▪ 11.4 12 16 35

11942 CSU P P2 G1.2 1949–1972
Domes, Jürgen Otto, 1932–.
'Die Entwicklung des Kommunismus in China seit 1949' (The development of Chinese Communism since 1949). In *Kommunismus International, 1950–1965: Probleme einer gespaltenen Welt* (International Communism, 1950–1965: Problems of a divided world), edited by Wolfgang Schneider. [Sole entry]
Cologne: Wissenschaft und Politik, 1965, 189–204.
SUBJ 12.1 14 14.1 14.4 32 64 ▪ 34.1 34.2 66

11943 MCH P P2 G1.2 1949–1972
Dominique, Victor, and B- Couret.
'La Chine populaire au seuil du deuxième quinquennat' (The People's Republic of China on the threshold of the Second Five-Year Plan).
Economie et politique 46 (mai 1958), 55–65.
SUBJ 14 14.4 16.4 ▪ 14.5 16.2 16.3 18 32.1 36.4

11944 MCH P P2 G1.2 1949–1972
Dominique, Victor, and Léon Lavallée.
'L'édification de l'économie socialiste en Chine' (Building a socialist economy in China).
Economie et politique 28 (nov. 1956), 14–27.
SUBJ 14 14.1 14.4 17 ▪ 11.4 19 34.1 34.2

11945 NNC P P2 G1.2 1949–1972
Donnithorne, Audrey Gladys, 1922–.
'Background to the people's communes: Changes in China's economic organization in 1958.'
PA 32, 4 (Dec. 1959), 339–353.
SUBJ 14 ▪ 14.1 34.1

11946 CSH P P2 G1.2 1949–1972
Donnithorne, Audrey Gladys, 1922–.
China's economic system.
London: Allen and Unwin, 1967. 571 p.
SUBJ 14 14.1 14.3 14.4 ▪ 12 24.3 24.4 32.1 34.1 36.1 72

11947 MCH P P2 G1.2 1949–1972
Dresch, Jean.
'Population et ressources de la Chine nouvelle' (New China's population and resources).
Annales de géographie 64, 243 (mai–juin 1955), 177–201.
SUBJ 11 14 ▪ 11.3 11.4 12 16 18 58

11948 GMS P P1 G1.2 1949–1972
Dresdner Bank.
Volksrepublik China: Ein wirtschaftlicher Überblick (Economic survey of the People's Republic of China).
Hamburg: Paul Hartung, 1959. 109 p.
SUBJ 14

11949 MMT P P2 G1.2 1949–1972
Eckstein, Alexander, 1915–.
Communist China's economic growth and foreign trade: Implications for U.S. policy.
New York: McGraw-Hill, 1966. 17, 366 p.
SUBJ 14 14.1 14.4 15 19 ▪ 11.4 12.1 14.3 16.4 18 34.1 64 72

11950 CSU S P1 G1.2 1949–1972
Eckstein, Alexander, 1915–.
'Economic development and political change in Communist systems.'
WP 22, 4 (July 1970), 475–495.
SUBJ 12 14 ▪ 12.1 64

11951 CSU P P1 G1.2 1949–1972
Eckstein, Alexander, 1915–.
'Economic fluctuations in Communist China's domestic development' [with comments by Peter Schran]. In *China in crisis, Vol. 1, China's heritage and the Communist political system*, edited by Ping-ti Ho and Tang Tsou. [Selective entry]
Chicago: U. of Chicago Press, 1968, 691–739.
SUBJ 14 ▪ 19 62

11952 NNC P P1 G1.2 1949–1972
Eckstein, Alexander, 1915–.
The national income of Communist China.
New York: Free Press of Glencoe, 1962. 215 p.
SUBJ 14 ▪ 18

11953 MCH P P2 G1.2 1949–1972
Eckstein, Alexander, 1915–, Yi-chang Yin (Yin I-ch'ang), 1923–, and Helen Yin (Yin Chang Wan-hung), 1928–.
'Communist China's national product in 1952.'
Review of economics and statistics 40, 2 (May 1958), 127–139.
SUBJ 14 14.1 14.4 ▪ 14.3 18

11954 DLC P P2 G1.2 1949–1972
Efimov, Gerontii Valentinovich, 1906–.
'Sovremennyi etap stroitel'stva sotsializma v Kitaiskoi Narodnoi Respublike' (The current stage of socialist construction in the People's Republic of China).
UZLGU 281 (1959), 3–18.
SUBJ 14 14.1 14.4 66 ▪ 16.4 34.1 34.2 64

11955 MCH P P2 G1.2 1949–1972
Etienne, Gilbert.
De Caboul à Pékin: rythmes et perspectives d'expansion économique (From Kabul to Peking: Rhythms and prospects of economic expansion).
Geneva: Droz; Paris: Minard, 1959. 271 p. (Institut universitaire des hautes études internationales, publications, 134)
SUBJ 14 14.1 14.4 ▪ 11 11.2 14.2 24.4 58 64 72

11956 MCH P P1 G1.2 1949–1972
Etienne, Gilbert.
'"Lois objectives" et problèmes de développement dans le contexte Chine-U.R.S.S.' (China and the U.S.S.R.: 'Objective laws' and problems of development).
Tiers-monde 4, 16 (oct.–déc. 1963), 609–627.
SUBJ 14 14.1 14.4 ▪ 17 51

11957 MCH PO P2 G1.2 1949–1972
Etienne, Gilbert.
'Quelques aspects de l'économie chinoise' (Some aspects of China's economy).
Tiers-monde 3, 10 (jan.–juin 1962), 271–282. [Reprinted—*Problèmes économiques* 783 (1er juin 1963), 16–22.]
SUBJ 14 14.4 22 ▪ 18 34.1

11958 DLC O P2 G1.2 1949–1972
Faltán, Michal.
'Rozvoj ekonomiky ČL'R' (The development of the economy in the People's Republic of China).
Naša veda (Bratislava) 6, 5 (1959), 197–208.
SUBJ 14 ▪ 14.1 14.4 41

11959 CSH PO P2 G9.4 1949–1972
Far Eastern Economic Review.
'Taiwan.' In *Far Eastern economic review yearbook, 1960–1972*, compiled by the organization cited.
Hong Kong: Far Eastern Economic Review. Issued annually, 1960–1972, average ca. 7 p.
SUBJ 14 14.4 24.1 24.2 ▪ 14.6 17 18 21 32 51 58

11960 CSH P P2 G1.1 1949–1972
Far Eastern Economic Review.
'Textile survey, China: Poor crop hampers expansion.' In *Far Eastern economic review yearbook, 1961*, compiled by the organization cited. [Selective entry]
Hong Kong: Far Eastern Economic Review, 1961, 179–183.
SUBJ 14 14.1 14.4 ▪ 14.3 24.4

11961 NNC P P2 G1.2 1949–1972
Feng Chi-hsi (Feng Ch'i-hsi).
'The growth of national economy as viewed from the state budget.' Tr. of 'Ts'ung kuo chia yü suan k'an wo kuo kuo min ching chi ti kao chang'; *T'ung chi kung tso* 1957, 12 (29 June), 28–33.
ECMM 96 (26 Aug. 1957), 27–37.
SUBJ 14 14.5 ▪ 17 18

11962 NIC PO P2 G1.2 1949–1972
Ganguli, Birendranath N-, 1902–.
Economic development in New China.
Bombay: Indian Council of World Affairs; London: Oxford U. Press, 1955. 92 p.
SUBJ 14 14.1 14.4 14.6 ▪ 11.4 12.1 16.2 18 34.1

11963 NNC P P2 G1.2 1949–1972
Gel'bras, Vil' Gdal'evich, 1930–, and V- V- Filippovoi.
'Pod"em material'nogo blagosostoianiia i kul'turnogo urovnia trudiashchikhsia v stranakh narodnoi demokratii Azii: statisticheskie materialy, Kitaiskaia Narodnaia Respublika' (The rise in the material and cultural level of workers in the Asian people's democracies: Statistics on the People's Republic of China).
Sotsialisticheskii trud 3, 5 (mai 1958), 127–131.
SUBJ 11.4 14 ▪ 17 18

11964 CSH P P2 G9.4 1949–1972
Glass, Sheppard.
'Some aspects of Formosa's economic growth.'
CQ 15 (July–Sept. 1963), 12–34. [Reprinted in *Formosa today*, edited by Mark Mancall. (Selective entry.) New York: Praeger, 1964, 68–90.]
SUBJ 14 ▪ 14.5 21 24.1

11965 CSH P P2 G1.2 1949–1972
Glunin, Vladimir Ivanovich, 1924–, and B- P- Gurevich.
'Razvertyvanie sotsialisticheskoi industrializatsii i sotsialisticheskikh preobrazovanii (1953–1955)' (The development of socialist industrialization and the socialist transformation, 1953–1955). In *Ocherki istorii Kitaia v noveishee vremia* (Survey of modern Chinese history), compiled by Institut kitaevedeniia, Akademiia nauk SSSR, edited by Aleksei Stepanovich Perevertailo et al. [Selective entry]
Moscow: Izd-vo vost. lit-ry, 1959, 524–562.
SUBJ 14 16 19 32 64 ▪ 14.4 34.1

11966 CSH P P2 G1.2 1949–1972
Goodstadt, Leo F-.
'Great leaps and club feet.'
FEER 66, 51 (18 Dec. 1969), 639–642.
SUBJ 14 ▪ 14.1 14.4 34.2

11967 CSH U P2 G1.2 1949–1972
Goodstadt, Leo F-.
'Wages in command.'
FEER 69, 32 (6 Aug. 1970), 52–54.
SUBJ 11.4 14 ▪ 11.2

11968 CSU S P2 G1.2 1949–1972
Grossmann, Bernhard Paul, 1929–.
'The influence of the war in Vietnam on the economy of Communist China.' In *Vietnam and the Sino-Soviet dispute*, edited by Robert A- Rupen and Robert Farrell. [Sole entry]
New York: Praeger, 1967, 68–73.
SUBJ 14 ▪ 15

11969 GSU P P2 G1.2 1949–1972
Grossmann, Bernhard Paul, 1929–.
'Die Wirtschaft der Volksrepublik China' (The economy of the People's Republic of China). In *China auf zwei Wegen: Gespräch zur politische Bildung* (China on two roads: Discourse on political organization), edited by Martin Schwind. [Sole entry]
Hanover: Jänecke, 1969, 100–128. (Das Gespräch über fremde Staaten, Völker, und Kulturen, 3)
SUBJ 14 14.1 14.4 19 ▪ 11 12.1 14.5

11970 GMS P P2 G1.2 1949–1972
Grossmann, Bernhard Paul, 1929–.
Die wirtschaftliche Entwicklung der Volksrepublik China: Methoden und Probleme kommunistischer Entwicklungspolitik (The economic development of the People's Republic of China: Methods and problems of Communist development policy).
Stuttgart: Gustav Fischer, 1960. 412 p. (Doctoral dissertation, Universität Hamburg)
Subj 14 14.1 14.4 ▪ 12 64

11971 CSH P P2 G1.2 1949–1972
Groupe d'études prospectives sur les échanges internationaux [Paris].
'Tableaux économiques chinois pour les années 1957 et 1964' (Statistics on China's economy in 1957 and 1964).
NED 3448/3449 (26 déc. 1967), 93–100.
Subj 14 ▪ 72

11972 CSU O P2 G1.2 1949–1972
Guillain, Robert, 1908–.
'China revisited.'
World today 21, 3 (Mar. 1965), 101–111.
Subj 12.1 14 ▪ 14.1 14.4 54

11973 CSU P P2 G1.2 1949–1972
Gurley, John Grey, 1920–.
'Capitalist and Maoist economic development.'
BCAS 2, 3 (Apr.–July 1970), 34–50. [Reprinted in *America's Asia: Dissenting essays on Asian-American relations*, edited by Edward Friedman and Mark Selden. (Selective entry.) New York: Pantheon, 1969, 324–356.]
Subj 14 64 ▪ 71

11974 CSU S P2 G1.2 1949–1972
Gurley, John Grey, 1920–.
'Statement of John G. Gurley.' In *Mainland China in the world economy*, compiled by Joint Economic Committee, U.S. Congress. [Selective entry]
Washington, D.C.: U.S. Government Printing Office, 1967, 184–188.
Subj 14 ▪ 14.1 14.4 17

11975 CSH P P2 G9.4 1949–1972
Gurtov, Melvin, 1941–.
Recent developments on Taiwan.
Santa Monica, Calif.: RAND Corp., 1967. 94 p. (RAND papers, P-3537) [Reprinted as 'Recent developments on Formosa.' (Abridged). *CQ* 31 (July–Sept. 1967), 59–95.]
Subj 14 32.1 ▪ 14.4 17 58

11976 DLC O P2 G1.2 1949–1972
Gutt, Józef.
'Twórcze kłopoty Chin Ludowych' (Production problems in the People's Republic of China).
Nowe drogi (Warsaw) 11, 8 (sierpień 1957), 73–92.
Subj 14 16 17 ▪ 12 12.1 16.1 16.2 18 65

11977 MCY P P1 G1.2 1949–1972
Halpern, Abraham Meyer, 1914–.
'Between plenums: A second look at the 1962 National People's Congress in China.'
AS 2, 9 (Nov. 1962), 1–10.
Subj 12 14 ▪ 64

11978 MCH PO P1 G1.2 1949–1972
Handke, Werner.
'China auf dem Wege zum Sozialismus und Kommunismus' (China on the road to socialism and Communism). In *Die Wirtschaftssysteme der Staaten Osteuropas und der Volksrepublik China* (The economic system of Eastern European countries and the People's Republic of China), edited by Georg Jahn. [Sole entry]
Berlin: Duncker und Humblot, 1962, vol. 2, 447–510. (Verein für Sozialpolitik, Gesellschaft für Wirtschafts- und Sozialwissenschaften, Schriften, neue Folge, 23, 2)
Subj 12 14 64 ▪ 14.3 16 19

11979 GBF PO P2 G1.2 1949–1972
Handke, Werner.
'Chinas Wirtschaft und Gesellschaft unter dem Kommunismus' (China's economy and society under Communism).
Aus Politik und Zeitgeschichte 1959, 35/36, 445–456. [Supplement to *Das Parlament*]
Subj 14 64 ▪ 12.1 19

11980 MCH PO P2 G1.2 1949–1972
Handke, Werner.
Die Wirtschaft Chinas: Dogma und Wirklichkeit (China's economy: Dogma and reality).
Frankfurt a.M.: Metzner, 1959. 337 p.
Subj 14 14.1 14.4 ▪ 11 11.4 16 18 32.1 34.1 34.2

11981 CSU P P2 G1.2 1949–1972
Harding, Harry, Jr., 1946–.
'China: Toward revolutionary pragmatism.'
AS 11, 1 (Jan. 1971), 51–67.
Subj 14 32 ▪ 12 17 35

11982 MCH P P1 G1.2 1949–1972
Hidasi, Gábor.
'A Kínai gazdaságfejlesztés problémáiról.'
Közgazdasági szemle 10, 12 (december 1963), 1444–1455.

On the problem of Chinese economic development, mimeo.
Washington, D.C.: U.S. Joint Publications Research Service, 2 Feb. 1964. 13 p. (JPRS 23,424; MC 831/1964)
Subj 14

11983 CSU P P1 G1.2 1949–1972
Hiniker, Paul James, 1938–, and R-Vincent Farace.
'Approaches to national development in China, 1949–1958.'
EDCC 18, 1, Part 1 (Oct. 1969), 51–72.
Subj 14 14.4 ▪ 12 64

11984 MAM P P2 G9.4 1949–1972
Ho, Samuel P. S. (Ho Pao-shan), 1936–.
Development alternatives: The case of Taiwan.
Ann Arbor: University Microfilms (Publ. 65-9684), 1965. 243 p. (Doctoral dissertation in Economics, Yale U.)
Subj 14 ▪ 14.4 24.1

11985 CSU P P2 G9.4 1949–1972
Ho, Yhi-Min, 1934–.
'Development with surplus population: The case of Taiwan. A critique of the classical two-sector model, à la Lewis.'
EDCC 20, 2 (Jan. 1972), 210–234.
Subj 14 24.1 ▪ 14.3 21.2 21.4

11986 CSU P P2 G1.2 1949–1972
Hoffmann, Charles, 1921–.
'The Maoist economic model.'
J. of economic issues 5, 3 (Sept. 1971), 12–27.
Subj 14 64 ▪ 14.1 14.4 16 63

11987 MCH P P2 G1.2 1949–1972
Hollister, William Wallace, 1916–.
'Capital formation in Communist China.'
CQ 17 (Jan.–Mar. 1964), 39–55. [Reprinted in *Industrial development in Communist China*, edited by Choh-ming Li (Li Cho-min). (Selective entry.) New York: Praeger, 1964, 39–55.]
Subj 14 14.4 ▪ 11.4 14.1 14.6 19

11988 CSU P P2 G1.2 1949–1972
Hollister, William Wallace, 1916–.
China's gross national product and social accounts, 1950–1957.
Glencoe, Ill.: Free Press, 1958. 161 p.
Subj 14 14.5 14.6 ▪ 18

11989 CSH P P2 G1.2 1949–1972
Hollister, William Wallace, 1916–.
'Estimates of the gross national product, 1958–1959.' In *Realities of Communist China*, edited by Yuan-li Wu (Wu Yüan-li). [Selective entry]
Milwaukee: Marquette U., Institute for Asian Studies *with* Marquette U., Robert A. Johnston College of Business Administration, Center for Business Services, Research Center, 1960, 14–23.
Subj 14 14.1 14.2 ▪ 11.4 12.2 18

11990 CSU P P2 G1.2 1949–1972
Hollister, William Wallace, 1916–.
'Trends in capital formation in Communist China.' In *An economic profile of Mainland China*, compiled by Joint Economic Committee, U.S. Congress. [Selective entry]
Washington, D.C.: U.S. Government Printing Office, 1967, vol. 1, 121–153. [Reprinted in *An economic profile of Mainland China*, compiled by the agency cited. (Selective entry.) New York: Praeger, 1968, 121–153.]
Subj 14 14.4 ▪ 14.1 14.2 18 19

11991 MCH P P2 G1.2 1949–1972
Holubnychy, Vsevolod.
'Soll und Haben der chinesischen Wirtschaft' (Debit and credit in China's economy).
Ost-Probleme 8, 51/52 (21 Dez. 1956), 1777–1785.
Subj 14 14.6 ▪ 14.1 14.4 14.5

11992 NNC P P2 G1.2 1949–1972
Holubnychy, Vsevolod.
'Zum Verständnis der Vorgänge in China' (Toward a better understanding of the events in China).
Gewerkschaftliche Monatshefte 11 (1960), 138–149.
Subj 11.4 14 14.4 ▪ 12.1 14.1 14.6 22

11993 CSU S P2 G1.2 1949–1972
Howe, Christopher Barry, 1937–.
'The Chinese economy.' [Review of *An economic profile of Mainland China*, compiled by Joint Economic Committee, U.S. Congress; and *Mainland China in the world economy*, compiled by Joint Economic Committee, U.S. Congress.]

CQ 32 (Oct.–Dec. 1967), 136–142.
SUBJ 14 ▪ 11 14.1 14.4

11994 MCH P P2 G1.2 1949–1972
Hsia, Ronald (Hsia Hsiu-yung), 1918–.
'Economic changes in Communist China.'
Political q. 35, 3 (July–Sept. 1964), 298–312.
SUBJ 14 19 ▪ 14.1 14.4

11995 NNC P P2 G1.2 1949–1972
Hsia, Ronald (Hsia Hsiu-yung), 1918–.
Economic planning in Communist China.
New York: Institute of Pacific Relations, International Secretariat, 1955. 89 p.
SUBJ 14 14.4 ▪ 17 34.2

11996 NNC P P2 G1.2 1949–1972
Hsia, Ronald (Hsia Hsiu-yung), 1918–.
The role of labor-intensive investment projects in China's capital formation, mimeo.
Cambridge: Massachusetts Institute of Technology, Center for International Studies, 1954. 103 p. (Communist Bloc Program, China project)
SUBJ 11.4 14 ▪ 14.2 16.3 35

11997 CSH P P2 G1.2 1949–1972
Hsiao Chi-jung, 1892–.
'A survey of the Chinese Communist economy in 1966.'
IS 3, 6 (Mar. 1967), 21–42.
SUBJ 14 14.4 ▪ 14.1

11998 MCY P P2 G1.2 1949–1972
Hsueh Mu-chiao (Hsüeh Mu-ch'iao), 1905?–, Su Hsing, and Lin Tse-li (Lin Tzu-li).
The socialist transformation of the national economy in China. Tr. of *Chung-kuo kuo min ching chi ti she hui chu i kai tsao* (The socialist reform of the national economy of China); Peking: Jen min ch'u pan she, 1959; 190 p.
Peking: Foreign Languages Press, 1960. 287 p. (China knowledge series, 10)
SUBJ 14 34.1 34.2 ▪ 14.4 16 32.1

11999 CSU P P2 G1.2 1949–1972
Hughes, Trevor Jones.
'China's economy: Retrospect and prospect.'
International affairs (London) 46, 1 (Jan. 1970), 63–73.
SUBJ 14 ▪ 12.1 19

12000 NNC P P2 G1.2 1949–1972
Hughes, Trevor Jones, and David Evan Trant Luard, 1926–.
The economic development of Communist China, 1949–1960, 2nd ed.
London: Oxford U. Press, 1961. 229 p.
SUBJ 14 14.1 14.4 16 ▪ 11.4 14.3 34.1 36.4

12001 NNC P P2 G1.2 1949–1972
Hwang Tien-chien (Huang T'ien-chien).
Bitter struggle of Chinese Communists in 1963.
Taipei: Asian Peoples' Anti-Communist League, 1964. 60 p. (APACL pamphlets, 83)
SUBJ 12.1 14 ▪ 12 14.3 15 64

12002 DLC P P2 G1.2 1949–1972
IAremenko, IUrii Vasil'evich.
'Bolshoi skachok' i narodnye kommuny v Kitae (The Great Leap and the communes in China).
Moscow: Politizdat, 1968. 143 p.
SUBJ 14 16 19 22 64 ▪ 34.1 55 66

12003 CSU P P2 G3.0 1949–1972
Inner Mongolian A. R.
Statistics on achievements of the Inner Mongolia Autonomous Region in economic and cultural construction, mimeo. Tr. of *Hui huang ti shih erh nien: Nei Meng-ku tzu chih ch'ü ching chi ho wen hua chien she ch'eng chiu ti t'ung chi* (Twelve years of glory: Statistics on achievements of the Inner Mongolian Autonomous Region in economic and cultural development); Peking: Nei Meng-ku jen min ch'u pan she, 1960; 252 p.
Washington, D.C.: U.S. Joint Publications Research Service, 3 Jan. 1963. 294 p. (JPRS 16,952; MC 2760/1963) [Xerox copyflo available—New York: CCM Information Corp., Research and Microfilm Publications. (Scholarly Book Translation Series, 572)]
SUBJ 14 14.1 14.4 18 34.1 ▪ 11.3 16.4 17 21 21.1 24.4 47 55 56

12004 CSU P P2 G1.2 1949–1972
Ishikawa Shigeru, 1918–.
'Long-term projections of Mainland China's economy: 1957–1982.'
EBAFE 16, 2 (Sept. 1965), 11–56.
SUBJ 14 14.1 14.4 ▪ 11 11.4 14.3 16.3 16.4

12005 MCH P P2 G1.2 1949–1972
Ishikawa Shigeru, 1918–.
National income and capital formation in Mainland China: An examination of official statistics.
Tokyo: Institute of Asian Economic Affairs, 1965. 17, 206 p.
SUBJ 14 14.4 14.6 ▪ 14.1 24.4 72

12006 CSU FP P2 G1.2 1949–1972
Ishikawa Shigeru, 1918–.
'Resource flow between agriculture and industry: The Chinese experience.'
DE 5, 1 (Mar. 1967), 3–31.
SUBJ 14 14.1 14.4 ▪ 14.3 14.5 34.1

12007 NNC P P4 G1.2 1949–1972
Ivanov, A- I-.
'Uluchshenie sistemy upravleniia promyshlennost'iu, torgovlei i finansami v Kitaiskoi Narodnoi Respublike' (The improvement of the system of regulatory control of industry, trade, and finance in the People's Republic of China).
SK 1958, 2, 111–117.
SUBJ 12 14 14.4 ▪ 14.3 14.6

12008 CSU FP P2 G9.4 1949–1972
Jacoby, Neil Herman, 1909–.
U.S. aid to Taiwan: A study of foreign aid, self-help, and development.
New York: Praeger, 1966. 18, 364 p.
SUBJ 14 15 19 66 ▪ 12 17 18 21.1 21.4 32 34.1

12009 CSU P P2 G1.2 1949–1972
Jones, Edwin F-.
'The emerging pattern of China's economic revolution.' In *An economic profile of Mainland China*, compiled by Joint Economic Committee, U.S. Congress. [Selective entry]
Washington, D.C.: U.S. Government Printing Office, 1967, vol. 1, 77–96. [Reprinted in *An economic profile of Mainland China*, compiled by the agency cited. (Selective entry.) New York: Praeger, 1968, 77–96.]
SUBJ 14 19 ▪ 11.4 14.1 14.4 17 54 58 61

12010 CSU P P2 G1.2 1949–1972
Jones, Edwin F-.
'The role of development policies and economic organization in innovation and growth: Communist China.' In *An economic profile of Mainland China*, compiled by Joint Economic Committee, U.S. Congress. [Selective entry]
Washington, D.C.: U.S. Government Printing Office, 1967, vol. 2, 677–684. [Reprinted in *An economic profile of Mainland China*, compiled by the agency cited. (Selective entry.) New York: Praeger, 1968, 677–684.]
SUBJ 11.4 14 ▪ 14.1 14.4 17 34.1 34.2 54 61

12011 MCY P P2 G4.3 1949–1972
Jones, P- H- M-.
'Sinkiang gets to work.'
FEER 35, 12 (22 Mar. 1962), 654–656.
SUBJ 12.1 14 35 66 ▪ 14.4 17 24.1

12012 DLC P P2 G1.2 1949–1972
Kabikov, S- I-.
'Nekotorye osobennosti sotsialisticheskikh preobrazovanii v Kitaiskoi Narodnoi Respublike' (Features of socialist reorganization in the People's Republic of China).
Sbornik trudov Moskovskogo zaochnogo poligraficheskogo instituta 8 (1959), 56–75.
SUBJ 12.1 14 16 18 19 ▪ 11.4 24.3 24.4 30 32.1 34.1 34.2

12013 CSU P P2 G1.2 1949–1972
Kao Hsiang-kao, 1905–.
'The economic outlook of Mainland China.'
IS 5, 9 (June 1969), 14–25.
SUBJ 14 ▪ 14.1 14.3 14.4

12014 NNC U P2 G1.2 1949–1972
Kao Hsiang-kao, 1905–.
Ten years of Chinese Communist economy.
Taipei: Asian Peoples' Anti-Communist League, 1960. 103 p. (APACL pamphlets, 49)
SUBJ 14 ▪ 64

12015 NNC P P2 G1.2 1949–1972
Kapelinskii, IU- N-, et al.
Razvitie ekonomiki i vneshne-ekonomicheskikh sviazei Kitaiskoi Narodnoi Respubliki, compiled by Nauchno-issledovatel'skii kon"iunkturnyi institut, Ministerstvo vneshnei torgovli, U.S.S.R.
Moscow: Vneshtorgizdat, 1959. 559 p.

Development of economy and foreign economic contacts of People's Republic of China, mimeo.
Washington, D.C.: U.S. Joint Publications Research Service, 23 May 1960. 548 p. (JPRS 3234; MC 8641/1960)
SUBJ 14 14.1 14.4 34.1 ▪ 12 14.2 16 17 18 24.4 32

12016 DLC P P2 G1.2 1949–1972
Kautsky, Pravoslav.
'Úspěchy hospodářské politiky Čínské lidové republiky' (Successes of the economic policy of the People's Republic of China).

Politicka ekonomie (Prague) 1, 4 (1953), 237–259.
Subj 14 ▪ 14.1 14.3 14.4

12017 CSU P P2 G9.4 1949–1972
Kawano, Shigetō.
'The reasons for Taiwan's high growth rate.' In *Economic development issues: Greece, Israel, Taiwan, and Thailand*, edited by Committee for Economic Development. [Sole entry]
New York: Praeger, 1968, 121–158. (CED supplementary papers, 25)
Subj 14 ▪ 14.4 14.5 17 21 21.4 24.1 24.2 34.2 58

12018 CSH P P4 G1.2 1949–1972
King, Vincent V. S.
'Industrial enterprise planning process in China.'
China Mainland review 2, 4 (Mar. 1967), 241–256.
Subj 14 34.2 ▪ 12 32.1 36.4

12019 CSU P P2 G1.1 1949–1972
Kirby, Edward Stuart, 1909–.
Economic development in East Asia.
New York: Praeger, 1967. 253 p.
Subj 14 ▪ 11 14.1 14.2 14.4 18 55 58

12020 MCY P P1 G9.4 1949–1972
Kirby, Edward Stuart, 1909–.
'Notes on the economy of Taiwan.' In *Contemporary China, 1956–1957*, edited by E. S. Kirby. [Selective entry]
Hong Kong: Hong Kong U. Press, 1958, 73–84.
Subj 14 ▪ 21 21.4

12021 CSU P P2 G1.2 1949–1972
Klatt, Werner, 1904–.
'China's economy in 1972.'
China report (New Delhi) 8, 1/2 (Jan.–Apr. 1972), 10–18.
Subj 14 ▪ 11 14.1 14.4

12022 CSU S P2 G1.2 1949–1972
Klatt, Werner, 1904–.
'A review of China's economy in 1970.'
CQ 43 (July–Sept. 1970), 100–120.
Subj 14 14.1 14.4 ▪ 11 18

12023 NIC S P2 G1.2 1949–1972
Klein, Sidney, 1923–.
'China's industrialization: Critical sectors.'
CS 1, 32 (20 May 1962), 1–9. [Reprinted as 'Industrialization: Critical sectors.' In *This is China: Analyses of Mainland trends and events*, edited by Francis Harper. (Selective entry.) Hong Kong: Dragonfly Books, 1965, 69–80.]
Subj 14 14.1 14.4 ▪ 11 14.2 18

12024 DLC S P4 G1.2 1949–1972
[Klimko, Nikifor Grigor'evich] N. Klymko.
'Do pytannia pro derzhkapitalizm v umovakh perekhidnoho perioda v Kytaïs'kyi Narodniï Respublitsi ta Nimets'kyi Demokratychniï Respublitsi' (The question of state capitalism under the conditions of the transitional period in the People's Republic of China and in the German Democratic Republic).
Ekonomika Radians'koi Ukraïny 1959, 1 (sichen'–liutyi), 88–96.
Subj 14 64 ▪ 16.2 16.4

12025 MCH P P2 G1.2 1949–1972
König, Johannes.
'Die Volksrepublik China in der Übergangsperiode zum Sozialismus' (The People's Republic of China in the period of transition to socialism).
Einheit; theoretische Z. des wissenschaftlichen Sozialismus 9, 4 (Apr. 1954), 402–413.
Subj 14 64 ▪ 14.1 14.4

12026 CSU P P2 G1.2 1949–1972
Kojima, Reiitsu.
'"Self-sustained national economy" in Mainland China.'
DE 5, 1 (Mar. 1967), 50–67.
Subj 14 ▪ 14.1 14.4

12027 CSH P P2 G1.2 1949–1972
Konovalov, Evgenii Aleksandrovich, 1928–.
Sotsial'no-ekonomicheskie posledstviia 'Bol'shogo skachka' v KNR (Socioeconomic consequences of the Great Leap in the People's Republic of China).
Moscow: Mysl', 1968. 100 p.
Subj 14 14.4 16.3 16.4 24.4 64 ▪ 17 18 32 66

12028 ELB P P4 G1.2 1949–1972
Kurakin, V-.
'Meropriiatiia po uluchsheniiu upravleniia promyshlennost'iu, finansami i torgovlei v KNR' (Measures for improving the administration of industry, finance, and trade in the People's Republic of China).
VE 1958, 6 (iiun'), 120–125.
'Measures for improvement of the management in industry, finances and trade in the CPR.' [Condensed tr.]
Problems of economics 1, 8 (Dec. 1958), 89–90.
Subj 14 32.1 34.2 ▪ 32

12029 MAM P P1 G1.2 1949–1972
Kwak, No Kyoon, 1923–.
A comparative appraisal of developmental planning in India and Communist China under the Second Five Year Plan.
Ann Arbor: University Microfilms (Publ. 65-8914), 1965. 297 p. (Doctoral dissertation in Economics, U. of Southern California)
Subj 14 34.1

12030 IMC PO P2 G1.2 1949–1972
Labini, Paolo Sylos.
'Aspetti dell'economia cinese' (Aspects of China's economy).
Moneta e credito 12 (giugno–agosto 1959), 196–229.
Subj 14 14.1 14.4 ▪ 72

12031 CSH P P2 G1.2 1949–1972
[La Dany, Ladislao] ———, 1914–.
'Assessment of the First Five Year Plan.'
CNA 224 (18 Apr. 1958), 1–7; 227 (9 May 1958), 1–7; 229 (23 May 1958), 1–7; 230 (30 May 1958), 1–7.
Subj 14 14.1 14.4 ▪ 55

12032 NNC P P2 G1.2 1949–1972
[La Dany, Ladislao] ———, 1914–.
'Changes in the economic system.'
CNA 160 (7 Dec. 1956), 1–7.
Subj 14 ▪ 14.3 14.5

12033 NNC P P2 G1.2 1949–1972
[La Dany, Ladislao] ———, 1914–.
'The economic system as related at the Eighth Party Congress.'
CNA 154 (26 Oct. 1956), 1–7.
Subj 14 ▪ 14.3

12034 MCH P P2 G1.2 1949–1972
[La Dany, Ladislao] ———, 1914–.
'Engineering planning.'
CNA 558 (2 Apr. 1965), 1–7.
Subj 14 ▪ 14.4 32.1 34.2

12035 CSH P P2 G1.2 1949–1972
[La Dany, Ladislao] ———, 1914–.
'Mao's vision of economic growth: The 1956–1957 programme in retrospect.'
CNA 734 (22 Nov. 1968), 1–7.
Subj 14

12036 CSH P P2 G1.2 1949–1972
[La Dany, Ladislao] ———, 1914–.
'"Promote production".'
CNA 677 (15 Sept. 1967), 1–7.
Subj 14 ▪ 32.1 34.2

12037 CSH P P2 G4.3 1949–1972
[La Dany, Ladislao] ———, 1914–.
'Sinkiang.'
CNA 103 (7 Oct. 1955), 2–7.
Subj 12 14 32 ▪ 24.1 35

12038 DLC O P2 G6.0 1949–1972
Leszczycki, Stanisław.
'Ostatnie przemiany w rolnictwie i przemyśle w Chinach' (The most recent changes in agriculture and industry in China).
Geografia w szkole (Wrocław) 12, 6 (1959), 281–294.
Subj 14 14.1 14.4 ▪ 14.2 17 18 21.4

12039 NNC P P2 G1.2 1949–1972
Li, Choh-ming (Li Cho-min), 1912–.
Economic development of Communist China: An appraisal of the five years of industrialization.
Berkeley, Los Angeles: U. of California Press, 1959. 16, 284 p.
Subj 14 14.4 14.5 ▪ 11 14.1 14.3 18

12040 CSU P P2 G1.2 1949–1972
Lin Chen.
'Mainland people again resist Communists' economic oppression.'
IS 6, 9 (June 1970), 47–59.
Subj 14 16 18 32.1 34.1 64 ▪ 12 32

12041 CSU S P2 G1.2 1949–1972
Liu, Ta-chung, 1914–.
'Economic development of the Chinese Mainland, 1949–1965' [with comments by Robert Franklin Dernberger, Dwight Heald Perkins, and Anthony M. Tang (T'ang Tsung-ming)]. In *China in crisis, Vol. 1, China's heritage and the Communist political system*, edited by Ping-ti Ho and Tang Tsou. [Selective entry]
Chicago: U. of Chicago Press, 1968, 609–690.
Subj 14 14.1 14.4

12042 CSU P P2 G1.2 1949–1972
Liu, Ta-chung, 1914–.
'Quantitative trends in the economy.' In *Economic trends in Communist China*, edited by Alexander Eckstein, Walter Galenson, and Ta-chung Liu. [Selective entry]
Chicago: Aldine, 1968, 87–182.
Subj 11 14 18 ▪ 11.4 14.1 14.3 14.4 24.4

12043 CSU P P2 G1.2 1949–1972
Liu, Ta-chung, 1914–.
'The tempo of economic development of the Chinese Mainland, 1949–65.' In *An economic profile of Mainland China*, compiled by Joint Economic Committee, U.S. Congress. [Selective entry]
Washington, D.C.: U.S. Government Printing Office, 1967, vol. 1, 45–75. [Reprinted in *An economic profile of Mainland China*, compiled by the agency cited. (Selective entry.) New York: Praeger, 1968, 45–75.]
SUBJ 14 ▪ 14.1 18

12044 MCH P P2 G1.2 1949–1972
Lo IUan'-tszen (Lo Yüan-tseng).
Ekonomicheskie preobrazovaniia v Kitaiskoi Narodnoi Respublike (Economic reorganization in the People's Republic of China).
Leningrad: Izd-vo Leningr. un-ta, 1955. 228 p.
SUBJ 14 14.1 14.4 16 ▪ 11.4 32

12045 CSU P P2 G1.2 1949–1972
[Löwenthal, Richard] Richard Lowenthal, 1908–.
'Development vs. utopia in Communist policy.' In *Change in Communist systems*, edited by Chalmers Ashby Johnson. [Sole entry]
Stanford: Stanford U. Press, 1970, 33–116.
SUBJ 12.1 14 64 ▪ 16.2 16.4 34.2

12046 CSU S P1 G1.2 1949–1972
Luey, Paul (Lü Pao-lo).
'Estimates of Mainland China's national income.' [Review of *The economy of the Chinese mainland: National income and economic development, 1933–1959*, by Ta-chung Liu and K. C. Yeh (Yen K'ung-chia).]
JOS 7, 1 (Jan. 1969), 101–109.
SUBJ 14 71

12047 MCY P P1 G1.2 1949–1972
Luey, Paul (Lü Pao-lo).
'Social accounting in Communist China.' In *Contemporary China, 1959–1960*, edited by Edward Stuart Kirby. [Selective entry]
Hong Kong: Hong Kong U. Press, 1961, 117–129.
SUBJ 14 ▪ 14.5

12048 NNC PO P4 G1.2 1949–1972
Ma Yin-ch'u, 1882–.
'Discussing again the theory of comprehensive balance and law of proportional development in connection with actual conditions in China.' Tr. of 'Lien hsi Chung-kuo shih chi lai tsai t'an t'an tsung ho p'ing heng li lun ho an pi li fa chan kuei lü'; *Jen min jih pao* 11 May 1957, 7; 12 May 1957, 7.
URS 7, 18 (31 May 1957), 228–258.
SUBJ 14 14.4 ▪ 14.2 16.4 24.4

12049 NNC PO P2 G1.2 1949–1972
Ma Yin-ch'u, 1882–.
'Discussing theory of comprehensive balance and law of proportional development in connection with actual conditions in China.' Tr. of 'Lien hsi Chung-kuo shih chi lai t'an t'an tsung ho p'ing heng li lun ho an pi li fa chan kuei lü'; *Jen min jih pao* 28 Dec. 1956, 7; 29 Dec. 1956, 7.
URS 6, 4 (11 Jan. 1957), 45–72.
SUBJ 14 ▪ 14.3 32.1

12050 CBU P P2 G1.2 1949–1972
McFarlane, Bruce.
'Economic policy and economic growth in China.'
J. of contemporary Asia 1, 4 (1971), 19–32.
SUBJ 14 14.1 14.4 ▪ 16.3 19 64

12051 CSU P P1 G1.2 1949–1972
MacFarquhar, Roderick Lemonde, 1930–.
'Communist China's twenty years: A periodization.'
CQ 39 (July–Sept. 1969), 55–63.
SUBJ 14 19

12052 CSU S P2 G1.2 1949–1972
Macrae, John T-.
'Mobilization of the agricultural surplus in China for rapid economic development, 1952–1957.'
DE 8, 1 (Mar. 1970), 79–92.
SUBJ 14 14.5 ▪ 14.1 18

12053 MCH P P2 G1.2 1949–1972
Mah, Feng-hwa (Ma Feng-hua), 1922–.
'The financing of public investment in Communist China.'
JAS 21, 1 (Nov. 1961), 33–48. [For a fuller version, see entry 12054.]
SUBJ 14 14.5 14.6 ▪ 16

12054 MAM P P2 G1.2 1949–1972
Mah, Feng-hwa (Ma Feng-hua), 1922–.
The financing of public investment in Communist China.
Ann Arbor: University Microfilms (Publ. 59-4954), 1959. 248 p. (Doctoral dissertation in Economics, U. of Michigan)
SUBJ 14 14.5 14.6 ▪ 11.4 14.3

12055 MCH P P2 G1.2 1949–1972
Mah, Feng-hwa (Ma Feng-hua), 1922–.
'The First Five-Year Plan and its international aspect.' In *Three essays on the international economics of Communist China*, edited by Charles Frederick Remer. [Sole entry]
Ann Arbor: U. of Michigan Press, 1959, 31–120.
SUBJ 14 ▪ 11 14.1 14.4

12056 NNC P P2 G1.2 1949–1972
Maklakov, A-.
'Ekonomicheskoe razvitie Kitaiskoi Narodnoi Respubliki' (The economic development of the People's Republic of China).
V pomoshch' politicheskomu samoobrazovaniiu 1957, 10 (oktiabr'), 134–141.
SUBJ 14 45 ▪ 18 34.1

12057 ELB P P2 G1.2 1949–1972
Maklakov, A-.
'Iz istorii sotsialisticheskogo planirovaniia narodnogo khoziaistva v KNR.'
VE 1958, 10 (oktiabr'), 139–148.

'From the history of socialist planning in the economy of the Chinese People's Republic.'
Problems of economics 1, 10 (Feb. 1959), 78–84.
SUBJ 14 ▪ 12 32

12058 NIC P P2 G1.2 1949–1972
Malenbaum, Wilfred, 1913–.
'India and China: Contrasts in development performance.'
American economic review 49, 3 (June 1959), 284–309.
SUBJ 14 18 ▪ 12 14.1 14.4 17

12059 MCH P P2 G1.2 1949–1972
Mark, Shelley Muin (Mai Wen-shao), 1922–.
'Chinese economic growth under the five-year plans.'
Malayan economic review 7, 1 (Apr. 1962), 61–76.
SUBJ 14 ▪ 11.4 14.1 14.4 14.6 18

12060 NNC P P2 G1.2 1949–1972
Maslennikov, Viacheslav Aleksandrovich, 1894–1968.
Ekonomicheskii stroi Kitaiskoi Narodnoi Respubliki (The economic structure of the People's Republic of China).
Moscow: Izd-vo Akad. nauk SSSR, 1958. 390 p.
SUBJ 14 14.1 14.4 ▪ 14.6 16.3

12061 NNC P P2 G1.2 1949–1972
Meliksetov, Arlen Vaagovich, 1930–.
'Bol'shoi skachok v ekonomicheskom i kul'turnom razvitii Kitaiskoi Narodnoi Respubliki' (The great leap in the economic and cultural development of the People's Republic of China).
SK 1958, 4, 5–14.
SUBJ 14 14.1 14.4 ▪ 17

12062 MCH S P2 G1.2 1949–1972
Menguy, Marc.
L'économie de la Chine populaire (The economy of the People's Republic of China).
Paris: Presses universitaires, 1965. 126 p.
SUBJ 14

12063 MCY P P2 G1.2 1949–1972
Miyashita, Tadao, 1909–.
'Economic construction of New China.' Tr. of 'Shin Chūgoku no keizai hattan' (Economic development in New China); *Ajia mondai* 46 (Jan. 1957), 22–32. [Slightly rev. in tr.]
Asian affairs (Tokyo) 2, 1 (Mar. 1957), 3–20.
SUBJ 14 14.4 ▪ 12 14.1 16

12064 CSU S P2 G1.2 1949–1972
Miyashita, Tadao, 1909–.
'The Red Chinese and Soviet economies in comparison.'
Kobe U. economic review 7 (1961), 45–66.
SUBJ 14 14.1 ▪ 36.3 64

12065 CSU P P2 G1.2 1949–1972
Motohashi, Atsushi, 1924–.
'Comparison of the socialist economies in China and Korea.'
DE 5, 1 (Mar. 1967), 68–85.
SUBJ 14 ▪ 14.1 14.4

12066 CSU P P2 G1.2 1949–1972
Niwa, Haruki.
'An outline of compilation work for an input-output table for the People's Republic of China, 1956.' Tr. of *1956 nen Chūgoku sangyō renkanhyō suikei no gaiyō* (Overview of an attempt to compute an input-output table for China in 1956); Tokyo: Ajia keizai kenkyūjo, 1970; 197 p.

CES 5, 3/4 (Spring–Summer 1972), 183–432.
Subj 14 14.4 ▪ 14.1 14.3 24.4

12067 MCH U P1 G1.2 1949–1972
Nodiia, L- G-.
'K voprosu ob osobennostiakh gosudarstvennogo kapitalizma v Kitae' (Features of state capitalism in China).
Trudy Instituta ekonomiki AN Gruzinskoi SSR 1961, 12, 285–292.
Subj 14 16.2

12068 MCH P P1 G1.2 1949–1972
North, Robert Carver, 1914–.
'The NEP and the New Democracy.'
PA 24, 1 (Mar. 1951), 52–60.
Subj 14 ▪ 12 64

12069 ICU P P2 G9.2 1949–1972
Osborn, James Franklin, 1942–.
Kwangtung in national development during the ten great years: Area and policy in Communist China, 1949–1959.
Unpublished masters thesis in Geography, U. of Chicago, 1969. 183 p.
Subj 11.3 12.1 14 24.1 ▪ 14.4 21.1 21.4 24.2 24.4 25 29 34.1

12070 MAM P P2 G9.4 1949–1972
Page, Richard S-, 1937–.
Aiding development: The case of Taiwan, 1949–1965.
Ann Arbor: University Microfilms (Publ. 67-13,502), 1967. 282 p. (Doctoral dissertation in Political Science, Princeton U.)
Subj 14 18 66 ▪ 12 16.2 16.3 17 24.1 36.3

12071 NNC P P2 G1.2 1949–1972
Pekshev, IU- A-, and N- I- Shevtsov, comps.
Razvitie narodnogo khoziaistva KNR: statisticheskie pokazateli (Statistical indices of the development of the national economy of the People's Republic of China).
Moscow: Vneshtorgizdat, 1956. 51 p.
Subj 14 ▪ 11 14.1 14.4 17 18 34.1 58

12072 MCH P P1 G1.2 1949–1972
Perkins, Dwight Heald, 1934–.
'Centralization versus decentralization in Mainland China and the Soviet Union.'
AAAPSS 349 (Sept. 1963), 70–80. [Special issue: *Communist China and the Soviet bloc*, edited by Donald S- Zagoria]
Subj 12.1 14 ▪ 12

12073 CSH P P2 G1.2 1949–1972
Perkins, Dwight Heald, 1934–.
'Economic growth in China and the Cultural Revolution (1960 – April 1967).'
CQ 30 (Apr.–June 1967), 33–48.
Subj 14 ▪ 14.1 14.4

12074 CSU S P1 G1.2 1949–1972
Perkins, Dwight Heald, 1934–.
'The international impact on Chinese central planning' [with comments by Ta-chung Liu]. In *International trade and central planning: An analysis of economic interactions*, edited by Alan A- Brown and Egon Neuberger. [Sole entry]
Berkeley, Los Angeles: U. of California Press, 1968, 177–201.
Subj 14 ▪ 14.1 14.4

12075 CSU P P2 G1.2 1949–1972
Perkins, Dwight Heald, 1934–.
'Mao Tse-tung's goals and China's economic performance.'
CS 8, 1 (7 Jan. 1971), 1–15.
Subj 14 64 ▪ 14.1 14.4

12076 MCH P P2 G1.2 1949–1972
Peterson, Joseph.
The Great Leap: China.
Bombay: B. I. Publications, 1966. 387 p.
Subj 14 ▪ 12 16.3 16.4

12077 NNC S P2 G1.2 1949–1972
Pflüger, Gangolf.
'Übergang zum Kommunismus in der UdSSR und in China auf wirtschaftlichem Gebiet' (The economic transition to communism in the U.S.S.R. and China).
Osteuropa-Wirtschaft 4, 1 (Juni 1959), 61–67.
Subj 14 22 ▪ 14.1 45 64

12078 CSU S P1 G9.4 1949–1972
Plummer, Mark Allen, 1929–.
'Taiwan: Toward a second generation of mainland rule.'
AS 10, 1 (Jan. 1970), 18–24.
Subj 14 16.1 32 ▪ 12 12.2 15

12079 CSU P P1 G9.4 1949–1972
Poirer, Joseph Jean Eugène, 1926–.
'Planning economic growth: Capital-labor substitution and foreign aid.'
Yale economic essays 7, 2 (Fall 1967), 5–64. (Doctoral dissertation in Economics, Yale U., 1966)
Subj 14

12080 FPN P P2 G1.2 1949–1972
Polaris, Jean.
'Coup d'oeil sur l'économie chinoise depuis la révolution, 1949–1965' (A glance at China's economy since the Revolution, 1949–1965).
Synthèses 21, 245 (oct. 1966), 14–30.
Subj 14 19 ▪ 14.1 14.3 14.4

12081 CSH P P1 G1.2 1949–1972
Polaris, Jean.
'Revue de l'économie chinoise en 1966' (Review of China's economy in 1966).
B. du Centre d'étude des pays de l'Est 8, 2 (1967), 275–302.
Subj 14

12082 CSU P P2 G1.2 1949–1972
Prybyla, Jan Stanislaw, 1927–.
The political economy of Communist China.
Scranton, Pa.: International Textbook, 1970. 605 p.
Subj 12.1 14 16 17 64 ▪ 12 14.1 14.4 18 22 30 32 34.1 34.2 56

12083 CSU P P2 G1.2 1949–1972
Rawski, Thomas George, 1943–.
'Recent trends in the Chinese economy.'
CQ 53 (Jan.–Mar. 1973), 1–33.
Subj 14 14.1 14.4 ▪ 24.1 24.4

12084 CSH P P2 G1.2 1949–1972
Ray, Dennis Michael, 1939–.
'The future of the Maoist model of development.'
Asian forum 2, 2 (Apr.–June 1970), 123–135.
Subj 11.4 14 ▪ 14.1 14.4 64

12085 CSU PO P2 G1.2 1949–1972
Richman, Barry Martin, 1936–.
'Economic development in China and India: Some conditioning factors.'
PA 45, 1 (Spring 1972), 75–91.
Subj 14 17 ▪ 12.1 34.2 61

12086 MAM U P2 G1.2 1949–1972
Rieman, Barbara K-, 1936–.
'More, faster, better and cheaper': A study of Chinese industrial price, indicator, and reward policies (1950–1965).
Ann Arbor: University Microfilms (Publ. 67-14,132), 1967. 321 p. (Doctoral dissertation, School of Advanced International Studies, Johns Hopkins U.)
Subj 11.4 14 64 ▪ 12 14.3 14.5 32 32.1 34.1

12087 CSU S P2 G1.2 1949–1972
Riskin, Carl Alan, 1938–.
'China's economic growth: Leap or creep?' [Review of *Chinese industrial growth: Overall level of investment and its relation to general growth rate*, by Frederick McGrail Cone.]
BCAS 2, 2 (Jan. 1970), 19–24.
Subj 14 ▪ 14.1 14.4

12088 CSU P P2 G1.2 1949–1972
Riskin, Carl Alan, 1938–.
'The Chinese economy in 1967.' In *The Cultural Revolution: 1967 in review*, by Michel Charles Oksenberg et al. [Selective entry]
Ann Arbor: U. of Michigan, Center for Chinese Studies, 1968, 45–71. (Michigan papers in Chinese studies, 2)
Subj 14 14.1 ▪ 14.3 14.4

12089 CSU P P2 G1.2 1949–1972
Robinson, Joan, 1903–.
'China to-day: Economic organization.'
J. of the Royal Society of Arts 116, 5144 (July 1968), 683–693.
Subj 14 ▪ 14.1 14.4 34.1 34.2

12090 MCH O P2 G1.2 1949–1972
Robinson, Joan, 1903–, and Solomon Adler.
China: An economic perspective.
London: Fabian International Bureau, 1958. 20 p. (Fabian tracts, 314)
Subj 14 18 ▪ 11 41 47 51

12091 CSH S P2 G1.2 1949–1972
Schachter, Gustav.
'Full socialization and uneven economic performance in Communist countries: Romania and Mainland China, 1950–1963.'
Politico 33, 3 (settembre 1968), 630–643.
Subj 14 14.1 19 ▪ 14.3 14.4

12092 CSU P P2 G1.2 1949–1972
Schran, Peter, 1930–.
'Economic management.' In *China: Management of a revolutionary society*, edited by John Matthew Henry Lindbeck. [Analytic entry]
Seattle: U. of Washington Press, 1971, 193–220. (Social Science Research Council, Studies in Chinese government and politics, 2)
Subj 14 34.2 ▪ 12 14.3 14.4 14.5 24.4 34.1

12093 MCY P P1 G1.2 1949–1972
Schran, Peter, 1930–.
'Economic planning in Asia: Communist China.'

AS 2, 10 (Dec. 1962), 29–42.
SUBJ 14 64

12094 NNC P P2 G1.2 1949–1972
Schran, Peter, 1930–.
'The National People's Congress: Some reflections on Chinese Communist economic policy.'
CQ 11 (July–Sept. 1962), 58–77. [Reprinted as 'Some reflections on Chinese Communist economic policy.' In *Modern China*, edited by Albert Feuerwerker. (Selective entry.) Englewood Cliffs, N. J.: Prentice-Hall, 1964, 136–153.]
SUBJ 14 ▪ 11.4 14.1 14.4 16.2

12095 CSU P P2 G1.2 1949–1972
Schran, Peter, 1930–.
'On the rationality of the Great Leap Forward and rural people's communes.'
Ventures 5, 1 (Winter 1965), 31–38. [Reprinted in *Mainland China in the world economy*, compiled by Joint Economic Committee, U.S. Congress. (Selective entry.) Washington, D.C.: U.S. Government Printing Office, 1967, 224–228.]
SUBJ 14 64 ▪ 14.1 14.3 14.4

12096 CBU P P2 G1.2 1949–1972
Schran, Peter, 1930–.
The structure of income in Communist China.
Unpublished doctoral dissertation in Economics, U. of California, Berkeley, 1961. 374 p.
SUBJ 14 14.1 16 ▪ 11.4 14.4 16.3 18

12097 NNC S P2 G1.2 1949–1972
Schulz, Eberhard.
'Langfristige Entwicklungsplanung in China' (Long-range development planning in China).
Osteuropa-Wirtschaft 1, 2 (Mai 1956), 124–134.
SUBJ 14 14.1 14.4 ▪ 14.5 34.1

12098 CSH P P2 G1.2 1949–1972
Schurmann, Herbert Franz, 1926–.
'China's "new economic policy": Transition or beginning?'
CQ 17 (Jan.–Mar. 1964), 65–91. [Reprinted in *Industrial development in Communist China*, edited by Choh-ming Li (Li Cho-min). (Selective entry.) New York: Praeger, 1964, 65–91.] [Reprinted in *China under Mao: Politics takes command*, edited by Roderick Lemonde MacFarquhar. (Selective entry.) Cambridge: M.I.T. Press, 1966, 211–237.]
SUBJ 12 14 14.1 14.4 14.6 ▪ 16.1 18 32.1 64

12099 MCH P P1 G1.2 1949–1972
Schurmann, Herbert Franz, 1926–.
'Economic policy and political power in Communist China.'
AAAPSS 349 (Sept. 1963), 49–69. [Special issue: *Communist China and the Soviet bloc*, edited by Donald S-Zagoria]
SUBJ 12 12.1 14 32 ▪ 16.1 19 34.2

12100 NNC FP P2 G1.2 1949–1972
Schurmann, Herbert Franz, 1926–.
'Peking's recognition of crisis.'
Problems of Communism 10, 5 (Sept.–Oct. 1961), 5–14. [Reprinted in *Modern China*, edited by Albert Feuerwerker. (Selective entry.) Englewood Cliffs, N. J.: Prentice-Hall, 1964, 89–104.]
SUBJ 14 14.1 14.4 ▪ 16.1 18 22 34.1 64

12101 WSU S P2 G1.2 1949–1972
Schurmann, Herbert Franz, 1926–.
'Politics and economics in Russia and China.' In *Soviet and Chinese Communism: Similarities and differences*, edited by Donald Warren Treadgold. [Selective entry]
Seattle: U. of Washington Press, 1967, 297–326.
SUBJ 12 14 14.3 ▪ 14.4 14.6 32.1

12102 MCH O P2 G1.2 1949–1972
Scott, John, 1912–.
Crisis in Communist China: A report on Red China and her neighbors to the publisher of 'Time', the weekly newsmagazine.
New York: Time, 1962. 153 p.
SUBJ 14 14.1 14.4 ▪ 12 15 19

12103 CSU P P2 G1.2 1949–1972
Seth, M- L-.
'Economic planning in China.'
Agra U. j. of research 8, 1 (Jan. 1960), 57–85.
SUBJ 14 14.4 ▪ 14.1 14.2 34.1

12104 NIC P P2 G1.2 1949–1972
Shabad, Theodore, 1922–.
'1, China's year of the "Great Leap Forward". 2, China's Great Leap Forward.'
FES 28, 6 (June 1959), 89–96; 28, 7 (July 1959), 105–109.
SUBJ 14 14.1 14.4

12105 NNC P P1 G1.2 1949–1972
Shcherbakov, I- S-.
'Kitaiskaia Narodnaia Respublika na pod"eme' (The People's Republic of China on the rise).
SK 1958, 3, 5–16.
SUBJ 14 14.1 14.4 ▪ 12.1 64

12106 CBU P P2 G9.4 1949–1972
Shih, Chien-sheng.
'Economic development in Taiwan after the Second World War.'
WA 100, 1 (1968), 113–134.
SUBJ 14 14.4 24.1 ▪ 11.3 14.6 21 21.4

12107 NNC P P2 G1.2 1949–1972
Shih, Joseph Anderson (Shih Ch'eng-chih), 1918–1973.
'The economic tangles in Communist China.' Tr. of 'Shih nien lai ti Chung kung ching chi chiu chieh' (Economic tangles in Communist China during the past decade); *Tsu kuo chou k'an* 385 (23 May 1960), 9–14. In *Communist China, 1949–1959*, edited by Union Research Institute. [Selective entry]
Hong Kong: Union Research Institute, 1961, vol. 1, 117–147.
SUBJ 14 14.1

12108 MCH P P1 G1.2 1949–1972
Shih Yüan-ch'ing.
'Chinese Communist economic planning system: Its function and chronicle.'
IS 1, 8 (May 1965), 10–25.
SUBJ 14 64

12109 DLC P P2 G1.2 1949–1972
Shmyhol', Mykola Mykytovych.
Ekonomichni uspikhy sotsialistychnoho budivnytstva v narodnomu Kytai (The economic success of socialist construction in the People's Republic of China).
Kiev: Derzhavne vydavnytstvo politychnoï literatury RSR, 1960. 147 p.
SUBJ 11.4 14 18 64 66 ▪ 16 17 32 32.1 34.1 34.2 47 54

12110 CSU P P2 G1.2 1949–1972
Shrian, O- N-.
'The Chinese economy since the Great Leap Forward.'
Asian economic review 7, 3 (May 1965), 347–359.
SUBJ 14 14.1 14.4 ▪ 34.1

12111 NNC P P2 G1.2 1949–1972
Sidikhmenov, Vasilii IAkovlevich, 1912–.
'Novyi etap sotsialisticheskikh preobrazovanii v Kitae' (A new stage in the socialist reorganization of China). [With English abstract]
SV 1956, 2, 3–14.
SUBJ 14 14.1 14.4 16.3 34.1 34.2 ▪ 16.2 24.4 32

12112 MCH PO P2 G1.2 1949–1972
Silos-Labini, Paolo.
'Lo sviluppo dell'economia cinese' (The development of China's economy).
Nuovi argomenti 40 (settembre–ottobre 1959), 91–114.
SUBJ 14 14.1 14.4 ▪ 24.4 34.1 56

12113 CBU S P2 G1.2 1949–1972
Silva, Francesco.
'La strategia di sviluppo della Cina comunista: applicazione del modello Von Neumann' (The strategy of development in Communist China: An application of the Von Neumann model).
Rivista di politica economica terza (3a) serie 59, 10 (ottobre 1969), 1287–1323.
SUBJ 14 64 ▪ 14.1 14.4

12114 GBF S P1 G1.2 1949–1972
Simonis, Udo Ernst, 1937–.
Die Entwicklungspolitik der Volksrepublik China, 1949 bis 1962, unter besonderer Berücksichtigung der technologischen Grundlagen (The policies of the People's Republic of China on economic development, 1949–1962, with special attention to the technological bases).
Berlin: Duncker und Humblot, 1968. 196 p.
SUBJ 14 14.4 19

12115 CBU P P2 G1.2 1949–1972
Simonis, Udo Ernst, 1937–.
'Die gesamtwirtschaftliche Entwicklung der Volksrepublik China: Ein Überblick' (The national economic development of the People's Republic of China: An overview).
Gewerkschaftliche Monatshefte 21, 2 (Feb. 1970), 84–97.
SUBJ 14 ▪ 11 14.1 14.3 14.4

12116 ELB P P2 G1.2 1949–1972
Sladkovskii, Mikhail Iosifovich, 1906–.
'Podryv maoistami sotsial'no-ekonomicheskoi struktury KNR' (Maoist subversion of the socioeconomic structure of the People's Republic of China).
VE 1969, 6 (iiun'), 76–87.
SUBJ 12.1 14 16 32 35 ▪ 12 54 64 66

12117 CSH P P2 G1.2 1949–1972
Sladkovskii, Mikhail Iosifovich (M. Sladkovsky), 1906–.
'Ugroza ekonomicheskim osnovam sotsializma v Kitae.'
Kommunist 1967, 12 (avgust), 92–108.
'Threat to the economic foundations of socialism in China.'
Reprints from the Soviet press 6, 4 (23 Feb. 1968), 3–26.
Subj 14 14.4 32 ▪ 12 64 66

12118 NNC P P1 G1.1 1949–1972
Sorich, Richard, 1926–.
Distribution in Communist China: Scope, organization, and procedures of state planning and control.
Unpublished masters thesis in Economics, Columbia U., 1962. 179 p. [Certificate essay, East Asian Institute]
Subj 14 14.3

12119 MCH S P2 G1.2 1949–1972
Spencer, Joseph Earle, 1907–.
'Agriculture and population in relation to economic planning.'
AAAPSS 321 (Jan. 1959), 62–70. [Special issue: *Contemporary China and the Chinese*, edited by Howard Lyon Boorman]
Subj 11.4 14 14.1 ▪ 12.1 18 58 62

12120 MCH P P2 G1.2 1949–1972
Spulber, Nicholas.
'Contrasting economic patterns: Chinese and Soviet development strategies.'
Soviet studies 15, 1 (July 1963), 1–16.
Subj 14 14.1 14.4 ▪ 11.4 34.1

12121 DLC P P2 G1.2 1949–1972
Sukharchuk, Grigorii Dmitrievich, 1927–.
'Vvedenie' (Introduction). In *Kitai segodnia* (China today), compiled by Akademiia nauk SSSR, edited by Lev Petrovich Deliusin and G. D. Sukharchuk. [Selective entry]
Moscow: Nauka, Glav. red. vost. lit-ry, 1969, 3–34.
Subj 14 32 ▪ 12 19 22 34.1 64 66

12122 ELB PO P2 G1.2 1949–1972
Sun' E-fan (Sun Yeh-fang).
'Pod"em ekonomiki Kitaiskoi Narodnoi Respubliki i velikoe znachenie ekonomicheskoi pomoshchi Sovetskogo Soiuza' (Improvement in the economy of the People's Republic of China and the great significance of economic aid from the Soviet Union).
VE 1959, 9 (sentiabr'), 67–74.
Subj 14 14.4 66 ▪ 16.4

12123 DLC P P2 G1.2 1949–1972
Suprunenko, Afanasii Lukich.
Kitai stroit sotsializm (China builds socialism).
Smolensk: Kn. izd-vo, 1959. 331 p.
Subj 14 14.1 14.4 16 17 34.1 ▪ 12 12.1 18 22 32 37 47 56 64 66

12124 MCH O P2 G1.2 1949–1972
Takahashi Kamekichi, 1894–.
'Communist China's economy as I saw it.'
JQ 7, 1 (Jan.–Mar. 1960), 24–31.
Subj 14 ▪ 12 14.4

12125 MCH P P2 G1.2 1949–1972
Tálas, Barna.
'Áttekintés a kínai népgazdaság jelenlegi helyzetéről' (Survey of the present condition of China's national economy).
Társadalmi szemle 13, 1 (január 1958), 22–43.
Subj 14 14.1 ▪ 14.3 14.4 18

12126 MCH P P2 G1.2 1949–1972
Tálas, Barna.
'Kína népgazdasága az ugrásszerű fellendülés szakaszában' (China's national economy during the period of the Great Leap Forward).
Társadalmi szemle 13, 9 (szeptember 1958), 53–74.
Subj 14 ▪ 14.1 14.2 14.3

12127 CSU S P2 G1.2 1949–1972
Tang, Anthony M. (T'ang Tsung-ming), 1924–.
'Agriculture in the industrialization of Communist China and the Soviet Union.'
J. of farm economics 49, 5 (Dec. 1967), 1118–1134.
Subj 14 14.1 ▪ 14.4

12128 MCH S P2 G1.2 1949–1972
Tjoa, Soei Hock.
'De landbouw in industrialiserend China' (Agriculture in industrializing China).
TESG 48, 4/5 (April–Mei 1957), 112–126.
Subj 14 14.1 ▪ 11.1 16.3 34.1 38

12129 MCH P P2 G1.2 1949–1972
Travert, André.
'La première décennie de la Chine populaire. Première partie, de la prise de pouvoir à l'entrée dans le socialisme, 1949–1955. Deuxième partie, de cents fleurs aux communes populaires, 1956–1959' (The first decade of the People's Republic of China. Part 1, From the seizure of power to the transition to socialism, 1949–1955. Part 2, From the Hundred Flowers campaign to the communes, 1956–1959).
NED 2669 (21 mai 1960), 1–22; 2678 (18 juin 1960), 1–23.
Subj 12 12.1 14 16 32 66 ▪ 12.2 15 17 19 22 32.1 33 51 56 64

12130 CSU U P2 G1.2 1949–1972
[Ullerich, Curt] Curtis Ullerich.
'GNP and China's economy.'
EH 10, 5 (1971), 28–37.
Subj 14 14.1 14.4

12131 FPN O P2 G1.2 1949–1972
Ullmann, Bernard.
'La Chine des vaches maigres' (China of the lean cows).
Le monde 26, 27, 28, 31 jan., 1er fév. 1961.
Subj 12.1 14 16.1 47 52 60 ▪ 14.1 14.4 16.3 41 44 50 55 66

12132 DLC P P2 G1.2 1949–1972
U.S.S.R. Ministerstvo vneshnei torgovli. Nauchno-issledovatel'skii kon"iunkturnyi institut.
'Kitaiskaia Narodnaia Respublika' (The People's Republic of China). In *Razvitie ekonomiki stran narodnoi demokratii: obzor za 1953–1959 gg.* (Economic developments in the people's democracies: Overview for 1953–1959), compiled by the agency cited. [Title varies slightly.]
Moscow: Vneshtorgizdat. Issued annually, 1954–1960, average ca. 120 p.
Subj 14 ▪ 14.1 14.4 18

12133 MCH P P2 G1.2 1949–1972
United Nations. Economic Commission for Asia and the Far East. Research and Statistics Division.
'Economic development in Mainland China, 1949–53.'
EBAFE 4, 3 (Nov. 1953), 17–31.
Subj 14 ▪ 14.1 14.3 14.4

12134 CSU P P2 G1.2 1949–1972
United Nations. Economic Commission for Asia and the Far East. Secretariat.
'Case studies of economic growth: Mainland China.'
EBAFE 8, 4 (Mar. 1962), 90–98. [Special issue: *Economic survey of Asia and the Far East, 1961*]
Subj 14 ▪ 14.1 14.4 14.6

12135 CSU P P2 G9.4 1949–1972
United Nations. Economic Commission for Asia and the Far East. Secretariat.
'China. Section 1, Taiwan.'
EBAFE 5, 4 (Mar. 1955), 88–94. [Special issue: *Economic survey of Asia and the Far East, 1954*]
Subj 14 24.1 ▪ 14.4 24.2

12136 CSU P P2 G9.4 1949–1972
United Nations. Economic Commission for Asia and the Far East. Secretariat.
'China. Section 1, Taiwan.'
EBAFE 6, 4 (Mar. 1956), 73–80. [Special issue: *Economic survey of Asia and the Far East, 1955*]
Subj 14 ▪ 14.4 14.5 14.6 21 24.1 24.2 58

12137 CSU P P2 G9.4 1949–1972
United Nations. Economic Commission for Asia and the Far East. Secretariat.
'China. Section 1, Taiwan.'
EBAFE 7, 4 (Mar. 1957), 78–83. [Special issue: *Economic survey of Asia and the Far East, 1956*]
Subj 14 ▪ 24.1

12138 CSU P P2 G1.2 1949–1972
United Nations. Economic Commission for Asia and the Far East. Secretariat.
'China. Section 2, Mainland.'
EBAFE 5, 4 (Mar. 1955), 94–110. [Special issue: *Economic survey of Asia and the Far East, 1954*]
Subj 14 14.2 14.4 ▪ 14.6 18 34.1

12139 CSU P P2 G1.2 1949–1972
United Nations. Economic Commission for Asia and the Far East. Secretariat.
'China. Section 2, Mainland.'
EBAFE 6, 4 (Mar. 1956), 80–99. [Special issue: *Economic survey of Asia and the Far East, 1955*]
Subj 14 14.1 14.4 ▪ 11 14.2 14.3 14.6 34.1

12140 CSU P P2 G1.2 1949–1972
United Nations. Economic Commission for Asia and the Far East. Secretariat.
'China. Section 2, Mainland.'
EBAFE 7, 4 (Mar. 1957), 83–93. [Special issue: *Economic survey of Asia and the Far East, 1956*]
Subj 14 ▪ 14.1 14.2 14.4 34.1

12141 CSU P P2 G1.2 1949–1972
United Nations. Economic Commission for Asia and the Far East. Secretariat.

'Current economic developments and policies: China (Mainland).'
EBAFE 20, 4 (Mar. 1970), 122–130. [Special issue: *Economic survey of Asia and the Far East, 1969*]
SUBJ 14 14.1 14.4 ▪ 11 11.4 14.3 35

12142 CSU P P2 G9.4 1949–1972
United Nations. Economic Commission for Asia and the Far East. Secretariat.
'Current economic developments and policies: China (Taiwan).'
EBAFE 20, 4 (Mar. 1970), 130–136. [Special issue: *Economic survey of Asia and the Far East, 1969*]
SUBJ 14 ▪ 14.4 14.6 21.4

12143 CSU P P2 G9.4 1949–1972
United Nations. Economic Commission for Asia and the Far East. Secretariat.
'Current economic developments in the countries of the ECAFE region: China (Taiwan).'
EBAFE 21, 4 (Mar. 1971), 185–190. [Special issue: *Economic survey of Asia and the Far East, 1970*]
SUBJ 14 14.4 24.1 ▪ 14.6 21.4

12144 CSU P P2 G9.4 1949–1972
United Nations. Economic Commission for Asia and the Far East. Secretariat.
'Economic development and economic policy: China (Taiwan).'
EBAFE 19, 4 (Mar. 1969), 135–141. [Special issue: *Economic survey of Asia and the Far East, 1968*]
SUBJ 14 ▪ 14.4 14.6 21.4 24.1

12145 CSU P P2 G1.2 1949–1972
United Nations. Economic Commission for Asia and the Far East. Secretariat.
'Industrialization in a centrally planned economy (Mainland China).'
EBAFE 8, 4 (Mar. 1958), 86–111. [Special issue: *Economic survey of Asia and the Far East, 1957*]
SUBJ 14 14.1 14.4 ▪ 12 14.3 18

12146 CSU P P2 G9.4 1949–1972
United Nations. Economic Commission for Asia and the Far East *with* United Nations. Food and Agriculture Organization. Agriculture Division.
'Relationship between agricultural and industrial development: A case study in Taiwan, China, 1953–1960.'
EBAFE 14, 1 (June 1963), 29–70.
SUBJ 14 14.4 24.1 ▪ 21 21.2 21.4 41

12147 CSU P P1 G1.1 1949–1972
U.S. Central Intelligence Agency.
'Communist China's balance of payments, 1950–65.' In *An economic profile of Mainland China*, compiled by Joint Economic Committee, U.S. Congress. [Selective entry]
Washington, D.C.: U.S. Government Printing Office, 1967, vol. 2, 621–660. [Reprinted in *An economic profile of Mainland China*, compiled by the agency cited. (Selective entry.) New York: Praeger, 1968, 621–660.]
SUBJ 14 14.3 14.6 ▪ 14.5

12148 NNC P P2 G1.2 1949–1972
U.S. Central Intelligence Agency.
The economy of Communist China, 1958–1962.
Washington, D.C.: U.S. Central Intelligence Agency, 1960. 78 p.
SUBJ 14 14.1 ▪ 11 14.2 14.3 14.4 18

12149 MCY P P2 G9.4 1949–1972
U.S. Mutual Security Mission to China.
Economic development on Taiwan, 1951–1955.
Taipei: International Cooperation Administration, Mutual Security Mission to China, 1956. 87 p.
SUBJ 14 56 ▪ 14.3 14.4 14.6 17 24.1 24.2 55

12150 CSH P P2 G9.4 1949–1972
U.S. Mutual Security Mission to China.
Economic progress of Free China, 1951–1958.
Taipei: International Cooperation Administration, Mutual Security Mission to China, 1958. 83 p. [Reprinted—Westport, Conn.: Greenwood Press, 1970. 83 p.]
SUBJ 14 24.1 24.2 ▪ 14.4 14.6 15 17 18 24.4 35 55

12151 MCH O P2 G1.3 1949–1972
van der Sprenkel, Otto P- N- Berkelbach, 1906–.
'Economic problems and politics.' In *New China: Three views*, by O. P. N. B. van der Sprenkel. [Selective entry]
London: Turnstile Press, 1950, 28–52.
SUBJ 14 ▪ 14.1 14.2 14.6 16.3 18

12152 CBU P P2 G9.4 1949–1972
Verhulst, Michel.
'Taiwan: étude d'expansion économique' (Taiwan: A study of economic expansion).
Actualité économique 42, 4 (jan.–mars 1967), 731–747.
SUBJ 14 24.1 ▪ 18 21 21.1 58

12153 ELB P P2 G1.2 1949–1972
Viatskii, V- (V. Vyatsky), and G- Dmitriev.
'Antinauchnyi, voliuntaristskii kharakter ekonomicheskoi politiki Mao TSze-duna.'
VE 1968, 11 (noiabr'), 76–90.

'The anti-scientific, voluntaristic character of Mao Tse-tung's economic policy.'
Reprints from the Soviet press 8, 4 (21 Feb. 1969), 3–25.
SUBJ 14 64 ▪ 11.4 17 32 35 66

12154 NNC U P2 G1.2 1949–1972
Vladimirova, I- (I. Wladimirova), and V- Zhamin (W. Shamin).
Uspekhi ekonomicheskogo stroitelstva v Kitaiskoi Narodnoi Respublike (Achievements of economic reconstruction in the People's Republic of China).
Moscow: Gospolitizdat, 1953. 99 p.

Erfolge des wirtschaftlichen Aufbaus in der Volksrepublik China.
Berlin: Dietz, 1955. 112 p.
SUBJ 14 14.1 16 19 ▪ 14.2 14.6 18 34.1

12155 CSU O P2 G1.3 1949–1972
Wada Hitoshi.
'A journalist's view of Communist China.'
JQ 3, 1 (Jan.–Mar. 1956), 17–26.
SUBJ 12.1 14 18 55 ▪ 34.1 51

12156 MCH P P2 G1.2 1949–1972
Walker, Kenneth Richard, 1931–.
'A Chinese discussion on planning for balanced growth: A summary of the views of Ma Yin-ch'u and his critics.' In *The economic development of China and Japan*, edited by Charles Donald Cowan. [Selective entry]
New York: Praeger, 1964, 160–191. (U. of London, School of Oriental and African Studies, Studies on modern Asia and Africa, 4)
SUBJ 14 14.1 14.4 ▪ 11 11.4 12 59 64

12157 CSU U P2 G6.1 1949–1972
Wang Wei-p'ing.
Kiangsu, the water country, mimeo. Tr. of *Shui hsiang Chiang-su*; Shanghai: Hsin chih shih ch'u pan she, 1956; 92 p.
Washington, D.C.: U.S. Joint Publications Research Service, 31 Dec. 1962. 98 p. (JPRS 16,910; MC 2718/1963) [Xerox copyflo available—New York: CCM Information Corp., Research and Microfilm Publications. (Scholarly Book Translation Series, 543)]
SUBJ 14 14.4 24.1 24.2 ▪ 11.3 12 18 21 24.4

12158 CSU PO P2 G1.2 1949–1972
Wheelwright, Edward Lawrence, and Bruce McFarlane.
The Chinese road to socialism: Economics of the Cultural Revolution.
New York: Monthly Review Press, 1970. 256 p.
SUBJ 14 14.1 14.4 64 ▪ 16 17 24.4 34.1 34.2 54

12159 CSU S P2 G1.2 1949–1972
Wiens, Herold Jacob, 1912–1971.
'China: Industry and commerce.' In *The pattern of Asia*, edited by Norton Sydney Ginsburg. [Selective entry]
Englewood Cliffs, N. J.: Prentice-Hall, 1958, 239–257.
SUBJ 14 14.2 14.4 ▪ 11.4 14.3

12160 CSU S P2 G1.1 1949–1972
Wiens, Herold Jacob, 1912–1971.
'China: Political organization, population, and prospects.' In *The pattern of Asia*, edited by Norton Sydney Ginsburg. [Selective entry]
Englewood Cliffs, N. J.: Prentice-Hall, 1958, 258–273.
SUBJ 11 14 ▪ 11.3 58

12161 MCH P P2 G1.2 1949–1972
Wu Chi-fang.
'The current economic situation on the Chinese Mainland.'
CCA 4, 1 (Feb. 1967), 1–13.
SUBJ 14 14.4 ▪ 14.1 14.5

12162 NIC P P2 G1.2 1949–1972
Wu Chi-fang.
'A review of the economic conditions on the Chinese Mainland.'
CCA 1, 4 (Dec. 1964), 22–39.
SUBJ 14 14.1 14.4 ▪ 14.3 34.1

12163 MCH P P2 G1.2 1949–1972
Wu, Yuan-li (Wu Yüan-li), 1920–.
Economic development and the use of energy resources in Communist China.
New York: Praeger, 1963. 15, 275 p.
SUBJ 14 14.4 ▪ 16.4

12164 CSU P P2 G1.2 1949–1972
Wu, Yuan-li (Wu Yüan-li), 1920–.
'Economics, ideology and the Cultural Revolution.'
AS 8, 3 (Mar. 1968), 223–235. [Reprinted in *Understanding modern China*, edited by Joseph M. Kitagawa (Kitagawa Mitsuo). (Selective entry.) Chicago: Quadrangle, 1969, 120–138.]
SUBJ 14 64 ▪ 15

12165 CSU P P2 G1.2 1949–1972
Wu, Yuan-li (Wu Yüan-li), 1920–.
'The economy after twenty years.' In *Communist China, 1949–1969: A twenty-year appraisal*, edited by Frank Newton Trager and William Henderson. [Selective entry]
New York: New York U. Press, 1970, 123–151.
SUBJ 14 ▪ 11 14.1 14.4

12166 NNC P P2 G1.2 1949–1972
Wu, Yuan-li (Wu Yüan-li), 1920–.
The economy of Communist China: An introduction.
New York: Praeger, 1965. 225 p.
SUBJ 14 14.1 14.4 ▪ 14.3 34.2 45

12167 NIC S P2 G1.2 1949–1972
Wu, Yuan-li (Wu Yüan-li), 1920–.
'An interpretation of the industrial cutback in Communist China.'
CS 1, 9 (8 Aug. 1961), 1–9.
SUBJ 14 14.1 14.4 ▪ 11.4 41

12168 CSU P P2 G1.2 1949–1972
Wu, Yuan-li (Wu Yüan-li), 1920–.
'Planning, management, and economic development in Communist China.' In *An economic profile of Mainland China*, compiled by Joint Economic Committee, U.S. Congress. [Selective entry]
Washington, D.C.: U.S. Government Printing Office, 1967, vol. 1, 97–120. [Reprinted in *An economic profile of Mainland China*, compiled by the agency cited. (Selective entry.) New York: Praeger, 1968, 97–120.]
SUBJ 12 14 ▪ 34.2

12169 MCH P P1 G1.2 1949–1972
Wu, Yuan-li (Wu Yüan-li), 1920–.
'The Third Five-Year Plan: An economic dilemma.'
CH 51, 301 (Sept. 1966), 159–164.
SUBJ 14 ▪ 14.1 14.4 15

12170 NIC S P4 G1.2 1949–1972
Wu, Yuan-li (Wu Yüan-li), 1920–, and Robert Carver North, 1914–.
'China and India: Two paths to industrialization.'
Problems of Communism 4, 3 (May–June 1955), 13–19.
SUBJ 14 14.4 ▪ 11.4 12 18

12171 NNC P P2 G1.2 1949–1972
Yang Po.
'A study of distribution of China's national income.' Tr. of 'Shih lun wo kuo kuo nien shou ju ti fen p'ei wen t'i'; *Ching chi yen chiu* (Peking) 1957, 6 (Dec.), 1–11.
ECMM 122 (10 Mar. 1958), 12–24.
SUBJ 14 18 ▪ 14.1 14.4 16.3 16.4

12172 CSU P P2 G1.2 1949–1972
Yeh, K. C. (Yeh K'ung-chia), 1924–.
Review of *The rate and pattern of industrial growth in Communist China*, by Kang Chao.
American economic review 56, 3 (June 1966), 571–576.
SUBJ 14 14.4

12173 MCH P P2 G1.2 1949–1972
Yin, Helen (Yin Chang Wan-hung), 1928–, and Yi-chang Yin (Yin I-ch'ang), 1923–.
Economic statistics of Mainland China, 1949–1957.
Cambridge: Harvard U., Center for East Asian Studies, 1960. 106 p. (Harvard East Asian monographs, 9)
SUBJ 11 14 ▪ 11.4 18 34.1 36.3 38

12174 MCH PO P2 G9.4 1949–1972
Yin, K. Y. (Yin Chung-jung), 1903–1963.
Economic development in Taiwan: Record and prospects.
Taipei: Hsing cheng yüan, Mei yüan yün yung wei yüan hui, 1961. 57 p.
SUBJ 14 ▪ 14.4 24.1 24.2

12175 CSH P P2 G9.4 1949–1972
Yum, K. S., 1897–.
Successful economic development of the Republic of China in Taiwan.
New York: Vantage Press, 1968. 60 p.
SUBJ 14 14.4 24.1 ▪ 17 18 51

12176 CSH P P7 G1.2 1949–1972
Zauberman, Alfred.
'Some remarks on the economic aspect.' In *The Chinese communes: A documentary review and analysis of the 'Great Leap Forward'*. [Analytic entry]
London: Soviet Survey, 1959, 62–79.
SUBJ 14 34.1

12177 CSU S P2 G1.2 1949–1972
Zauberman, Alfred.
'Soviet and Chinese strategy for economic growth.'
International affairs (London) 38, 3 (July 1962), 339–352.
SUBJ 14 ▪ 11.4

14.1 AGRARIAN ECONOMY
農業 農業

1644-1911

12178 CSU O P2 G1.2 1895–1911
Anderson, Malcolm P-.
'Notes on the mammals of economic value in China.'
AAAPSS 39 (Jan. 1912), 169–178.
SUBJ 14.1 14.2

12179 CSU S P2 G1.3 –1842
Bazin, Antoine Pierre Louis, 1799–1863.
'Arts, littérature, moeurs, agriculture, histoire naturelle, industrie, etc.' (The arts, literature, customs, agriculture, natural history, industry, etc.). In *Chine moderne: ou, description historique, géographique et littéraire de ce vaste empire, d'après des documents chinois* (Modern China: or, An historical, geographic, and literary description of that vast empire, based on Chinese documents), by Jean-Pierre Guillaume Pauthier and A. P. L. Bazin. [Analytic entry]
Paris: Firmin-Didot, 1853, 391–675. (L'univers. Histoire et description de tous les peuples: Asie, 10)
SUBJ 14.1 14.4 ▪ 13 23 62

12180 NNC PO P2 G2.0 1895–1911
Boloban, Andrei Pavlovich.
Zemledelie i khlebopromyshlennost' severnoi Man'chzhurii (Agriculture and grain production in northern Manchuria).
Harbin: Yuan Tung Pao, 1908. 318, 36 p.
SUBJ 14.1 ▪ 14.2 14.3 21.2 21.3 24.3 34.2 34.3

12181 CSU O P2 G1.5 1842–1895
[Dabry de Thiersant, Claude Philibert] Dabry de Thersant, 1826–1898.
'Ostriculture [i.e., ostreiculture] in China.'
China review 4, 1 (July–Aug. 1875), 38–42.
SUBJ 14.1

12182 NIC O P8 G1.2 1842–1895
Dudgeon, John Hepburn, 1837–1901.
The land question, with lessons to be drawn from peasant proprietorship in China.
Glasgow: Maclehose, 1886. 85 p.
SUBJ 14.1 ▪ 55

12183 MCH P P8 G1.3 –1842
Franke, Otto, 1863–1946.
'Kêng tschi t'u': Ackerbau und Seidengewinnung in China (*Keng chih t'u* [Pictures of tilling and weaving]: Agriculture and sericulture in China).
Hamburg: L. Friedrichsen, 1913. 194 p. (Hamburgisches Kolonialinstitut, Abhandlungen, 11)
SUBJ 14.1 ▪ 24.4 34.1 55

12184 MCH P P8 G1.1 –1842
Hervey Saint-Denys, Marie Jean Léon d', 1823–1892.
Recherches sur l'agriculture et l'horticulture des Chinois (Investigations of Chinese agriculture and horticulture).
Paris: Allouard et Kaeppelin, 1850. 262 p.
SUBJ 14.1 ▪ 62 65

12185 NIC P P8 G1.2 1644–1911
[Hoang, Pierre] Peter Hoang (Huang Po-lu), 1830–1909.
'Law of land tenure in China: A practical treatise on legal ownership.'
CLR 1, 2 (July 1922), 90–96; 1, 5 (Apr. 1923), 232–244.
SUBJ 12.2 14.1 14.5

12186 MCH P P7 G1.5 1842–1895
Iliushechkin, Vasilii Pavlovich, 1915–.
'Agrarnaia politika taipinov' (The agrarian policy of the Taipings).
NAA 1962, 4, 98–106.
SUBJ 14.1 16.3 32.2 ▪ 14.5

12187 NIC O P8 G1.2 1842–1895
Jamieson, George, 1843–1920, et al.
'Tenure of land in China and the condition of the rural population.'
JRAS-CB new (2nd) series 23, 2 (1888), 59–183.
SUBJ 12.2 14.1 14.5 22 45 ▪ 16.3 42

12188 MCH S P2 G1.1 1644–1911
Khodorov, Abram Evseevich, 1886–1949.
'Klassovye korni gospodstva manchzhur v Kitae' (The class roots of Manchu rule in China).
NV 26/27 (1929), 19–42.
SUBJ 14.1 16.3 ▪ 12 16

12189 NNC P P2 G1.2 1644–1842
Khokhlov, Aleksandr Nikolaevich, 1929–.
'Agrarnye otnosheniia v Kitae vo vtoroi polovine XVIII – nachale XIX v.' (Agrarian relations in China in the second half of the eighteenth century and in the early nineteenth century).

KSINA 53 (1962), 95–115.
Subj 14 14.1 16 16.1 45 ▪ 12 13 14.5 15 16.3

12190 CSH P P2 G1.1 1644–1842
Khokhlov, Aleksandr Nikolaevich, 1929–.
'*Da TSin khuidian' shili* kak istochnik po istorii agrarnykh otnoshenii Kitaia (seredina XVII – nachalo XIX v.)' (*Ta Ch'ing hui tien shih li* [Collected statutes of the Ch'ing: Precedents] as a source book for the history of Chinese agrarian relations from the middle of the seventeenth century to the early nineteenth century). In *Strany Dal'nego Vostoka i IUgo-Vostochnoi Azii (problemy istorii i ekonomiki)* (Problems of Far Eastern and Southeast Asian history and economics), compiled by Institut vostokovedeniia, Akademiia nauk SSSR. [Selective entry]
Moscow: Nauka, Glav. red. vost. lit-ry, 1969, 102–114.
Subj 12.2 14.1 16.3 35 72 ▪ 12 16.1 33 70

12191 ELB F P2 G1.5 1895–1911
Klingen, Ivan Nikolaevich, 1851–1922.
'Kitai' (China). In *Sredi patriarkhov zemledeliia narodov Blizhnego i Dal'nego Vostoka* (Among the agricultural patriarchs of the Near and Far Eastern peoples), by I. N. Klingen. [Sole entry]
Moscow: Gossel'khozizdat, 1960, 467–557.
Subj 14.1 ▪ 54 55 66

12192 NNC S P8 G1.2 1895–1911
Kokhanovskii, Nikolai Ivanovich, 1870–?
'Zemlevladenie i zemledelie v Kitae' (Land tenure and agriculture in China).
IVI 23, 2 (1909), 1–126.
Subj 14.1 ▪ 16.3

12193 NNC PO P8 G1.3 –1895
Korrigan, Pol.
Causerie sur la pêche fluviale en Chine (Fishing on China's rivers).
Shanghai: Impr. de la Mission catholique, 1909. 137 p.
Subj 14 14.1 23 40 50 ▪ 14.2 16.3 21.3 22.2 25 60

12194 CSU PO P8 G1.3 –1911
Laufer, Berthold, 1874–1934.
The domestication of the cormorant in China and Japan.
Chicago: Field Museum of Natural History, 1931. 64 p. (Field Museum of Natural History 300; Anthropological series, 18, 3) [Consecutive pagination in Anthropological series: p. 199–262.]
Subj 14.1 ▪ 65

12195 CSU P P2 G1.3 1842–1911
Lecomte, Henri, 1856–?
'La production du coton en Asie: Chine, Corée, Japon' (The production of cotton in Asia: China, Korea, and Japan). In *Le coton: monographie. Culture-histoire* (Treatise on the history of cotton cultivation), by H. Lecomte. [Selective entry]
Paris: Carré et Naud, 1900, 204–220.
Subj 14.1 ▪ 14.3 14.4

12196 MCH S P7 G1.1 –1911
Lewin, Günter.
'Zu einigen Problemen der "asiatischen Produktionsweise" in der gesellschaftlichen Entwicklung Chinas' (Problems presented by the 'Asiatic mode of production' in the social development of China).
Wissenschaftliche Z. der Karl Marx Universität Leipzig; gesellschafts- und sprachwissenschaftliche Reihe 13, 2 (1964), 251–256.
Subj 14.1 ▪ 16.3 34.1

12197 FPN P P7 G1.2 –1911
Loo, Rodolphe van.
'L'agriculture en Chine' (Agriculture in China). In *Premier Congrès international des associations agricoles et de démographie rurale (Bruxelles, 18–22 septembre 1910)* (First International Congress on Agricultural Associations and Rural Demography, Brussels, 18–22 Septmeber 1910). [Sole entry]
Brussels: Goemaere, 1911?, 1–37 [s.p.].
Subj 14.1 16.1 16.3 18 62 ▪ 11.2 12.2 13 14.3 34.2 64

12198 FPN P P8 G1.3 –1842
[Ma Ta] Ma-Ta.
Etude sur les transformations du système de la propriété foncière en Chine (A study of changes in the system of landownership in China).
Paris: Jouve, 1927. 157 p. (Doctoral dissertation, Faculté de droit, Université de Paris)
Subj 12.2 14.1 14.5 45 64 ▪ 16 16.1 16.3 18 41 43 63 72

12199 MCH P P8 G1.2 –1911
Maspero, Henri, 1883–1945.
'Les régimes fonciers en Chine' (Landownership in China).
Recueils de la Société Jean Bodin 2 (1937), 265–314.
Subj 14.1 ▪ 12.2 16.3

12200 CSU P P2 G1.3 –1895
Mayers, William Frederick, 1831–1878.
'Gold fish cultivation.'
NQCJ 2, 8 (Aug. 1868), 123–124.
Subj 14.1

12201 MCH P P7 G1.1 1644–1911
Nepomnin, Oleg Efimovich, 1935–.
Genezis kapitalizma v sel'skom khoziaistve Kitaia (The origin of capitalism in Chinese agriculture).
Moscow: Nauka, 1966. 270 p.
Subj 14 14.1 14.3 16 16.3 24.4 ▪ 11.3 12.2 21.2 72

12202 MCH P P2 G1.1 1895–1911
R. B.
'Le camphre en Extrême-Orient' (Camphor in the Far East).
BEI 3, 30 (déc. 1900), 731–737.
Subj 14.1 ▪ 14.3

12203 CBU P P2 G1.1 1644–1911
Shaw, Norman.
Chinese forest trees and timber supply.
London: Unwin, 1914. 351 p.
Subj 14.1 ▪ 11.2 14.2

12204 MCH O P2 G1.3 1842–1895
Syrski, S-.
'Der Seidenbau in China: Dessen erste Erzeugnisse und Handel mit denselben' (China's silk industry: Its first products and commerce). In *Fachmännische Berichte über die österreichisch-ungarische Expedition nach Siam, China und Japan, 1868–1871* (Expert reports on the Austro-Hungarian expedition to Siam, China, and Japan, 1868–1871), edited by Karl von Scherzer. [Selective entry]
Stuttgart: Julius Maier, 1872, 122–174.
Subj 14.1 14.3

12205 CSH U P8 G1.3 –1911
Wilhelm, Richard, 1873–1930.
'Die Natur in China' (Nature in China).
OL 26, 3 (19 Jan. 1912), 61–64; 26, 22 (31 Mai 1912), 477–481; 26, 44 (1 Nov. 1912), 405–409. [Reprinted from *China: Das Land und die Natur* (China: Countryside and nature). Tsingtao: ——, 1911.]
Subj 14.1 62 ▪ 55

12206 CSH PO P2 G1.2 –1895
Williams, Samuel Wells, 1812–1884.
'Natural history of China.' In *The Middle Kingdom: A survey of the geography, government, literature, social life, arts, and history of the Chinese empire and its inhabitants*, rev. and enl. ed., by S. W. Williams. [Selective entry]
New York: Scribner, 1883, vol. 1, 296–379. [Reprinted in *The Middle Kingdom: A survey of the geography, government, literature, social life, arts, and history of the Chinese empire and its inhabitants*, by S. W. Williams. (Selective entry.) Taipei: Ch'eng-wen, 1965, 296–379 (s.p.)]
Subj 14.1 14.4 ▪ 56 62

12207 NNC PO P2 G1.3 –1842
Zakharov, Ivan Il'ich (J. Sacharoff), 1814–1885.
'Pozemel'naia sobstvennost' v Kitae' (Landed property in China). In *Trudy chlenov Rossiiskoi dukhovnoi missii v Pekine* (Works of members of the Russian Orthodox ecclesiastical mission in Peking). [Selective entry]
St. Petersburg: Tip. Shtaba voenno-ucheb. zavedenii, 1853, vol. 2, no. 1, 1–96. [Reprinted in *Trudy chlenov Rossiiskoi dukhovnoi missii v Pekine*. (Selective entry.) Peking: Tip. Uspenskago monastyria pri RDM, 1910, vol. 2, 1–54.]
'Über das Grundeigenthum in China' (Landownership in China). Tr. by Carl Abel and F- A- Mecklenburg. In *Arbeiten der kaiserlich russischen Gesandtschaft zu Peking über China, sein Volk, seine Religion, seine Institutionen, sozialen Verhältnisse, usw.* (Works of the imperial Russian mission to Peking on China, its people, religion, institutions, social conditions, etc.). [Selective entry]
Berlin: Heinicke, 1858, vol. 2, 1–54.
Subj 14.1 35 ▪ 14.5 16

1644-1949

12208 CSH U P2 G1.3 1895–1928
'A general survey of the raw silk and silkworm industry in China.'
CEM 2, 6 (Mar. 1925), 1–29.
Subj 14.1 14.4 ▪ 14.3 24.3

12209 CSU P P7 G1.2 –1949
Adams, Inez.
'Rice cultivation in Asia.'
AA new (2nd) series 50, 2 (Apr.–June 1948), 256–282.
Subj 14.1

12210 ELE FP P8 G1.3 –1949
Buck, John Lossing, 1890–.
'Fact and theory about China's land.'
FA 28, 1 (Oct. 1949), 92–101.
SUBJ 14.1 14.6 ▪ 14.2

12211 MCH P P8 G2.0 1895–1928
Chen, Chao Shung (Ch'eng Chao-hsiung).
La vie du paysan en Mandchourie, les trois provinces de l'est de la Chine (Peasant life in Manchuria, the three provinces of East China).
Paris: Bossuet, 1937. 158 p. (Doctoral dissertation, Faculté des lettres, Université de Paris)
SUBJ 14.1 16.3 18 36.3 55 ▪ 14.6 21 21.2 21.4 22 41 57

12212 CSU S P2 G1.3 –1949
Elvin, John Mark Dutton, 1938–.
'The last thousand years of Chinese history: Changing patterns in land tenure.'
MAS 4, 2 (Apr. 1970), 97–114.
SUBJ 14.1 16.1 16.3 ▪ 12.2 14.5 14.6 16 25 34.1 45

12213 NIC S P7 G1.2 1895–1949
Gourou, Pierre, 1900–.
'The development of upland areas in China.' In *The development of upland areas in the Far East*, compiled by Institute of Pacific Relations. [Sole entry]
New York: Institute of Pacific Relations, 1949, 1–24.
SUBJ 14.1 ▪ 11 16.3 18

12214 CSH P P2 G1.2 1644–1928
IAshnov, Evgenii Evgen'evich.
'Istochniki poznaniia naseleniia i krest'ianskogo khoziaistva Kitaia' (Sources on China's population and peasant economy). [The title of the second and third installments of this article is 'Istochniki poznaniia naseleniia i sel'skogo khoziaistva Kitaia' (Sources on China's population and agriculture).]
VM 1928, 2, 54–62; 1928, 3, 55–66; 1928, 7, 87–91.
SUBJ 11 14.1 ▪ 18 21 21.1 24.1 59 72

12215 NNC P P2 G1.2 1644–1928
Khokhlov, Aleksandr Nikolaevich, 1929–.
'Zemlevladenie vos'miznamennykh voisk v Kitae i prichiny ego razlozheniia, XVIII–XIX vv.' (The land-tenure system of the Eight Banners troops and the reasons for its decay in the eighteenth and nineteenth centuries).
KSINA 55 (1962), 8–31.
SUBJ 14 14.1 15 16 35 45 ▪ 12 14.5 14.6 18

12216 CSU P P7 G1.2 1644–1928
Lee, Mabel Ping-hua (Li Mei-pu), 1897–.
'Modern China, 1644–1921 A.D.' In *The economic history of China, with special reference to agriculture*, by M. Ping-hua Lee. [Sole entry]
New York: Columbia U., Faculty of Political Science, 1921, 109–133. (Columbia studies in history, economics and public law, 99, 1 [whole no. 225]) (Doctoral dissertation in Economics, Columbia U.) [Reprinted in *The economic history of China, with special reference to agriculture*, by M. Ping-hua Lee. (Sole entry.) New York: AMS Press, 1969, 109–133.]
SUBJ 14.1 18 ▪ 12.1 14.5 32.2

12217 NIC S P2 G1.2 1842–1949
Lee, Shu-ching (Li Shu-ch'ing), 1908–, and Verna Kriesel.
'The rise of agrarian absenteeism and its effect on the traditional society of China.'
Rural sociology 22, 3 (Sept. 1957), 241–249.
SUBJ 14.1 ▪ 16.1 16.3 18

12218 MCH P P2 G1.2 1895–1949
Liang, Ching-chun (Liang Ch'ing-ch'un), 1904–.
The relationship between the population and the food supply of China.
Unpublished doctoral dissertation in Economics, Harvard U., 1933. 346 p.
SUBJ 11 14 14.1 14.3 ▪ 18

12219 CSU S P8 G1.2 1842–1928
Lien, Chan, 1936–.
'Sun Yat-sen on land utilization.'
Agricultural history 42 (Oct. 1968), 297–303.
SUBJ 14.1

12220 MCH P P2 G1.2 –1928
Lieu, D. K. (Liu Ta-chün), 1891–1962.
'Food conservation in China.'
Mid-Pacific magazine 29, 3 (Mar. 1925), 510–519.
SUBJ 14.1 18 ▪ 14.3 14.5 55

12221 MCH P P2 G1.2 –1928
Lieu, D. K. (Liu Ta-chün), 1891–1962, and Chung-min Chen (Ch'en Chung-ming).
'Statistics of farm land in China.'
CEJ 2, 3 (Mar. 1928), 181–213.
SUBJ 14.1 24.1 ▪ 11 14.5 21 71

12222 DLC P P7 G1.2 1644–1928
Mad'iar, Liudvig Ignat'evich, 1891–?
Ekonomika sel'skogo khoziaistva v Kitae (The economics of agriculture in China).
Moscow: Gosizdat, 1931. 360 p.
SUBJ 14 14.1 66 ▪ 14.3 14.6 16 16.1 24.4

12223 CSH P P7 G1.1 1895–1949
Myers, Ramon Hawley, 1929–.
'Agrarian policy and agricultural transformation: Mainland China and Taiwan, 1895–1945.'
J. of the Institute of Chinese Studies of the Chinese U. of Hong Kong 3, 2 (Sept. 1970), 521–542.
SUBJ 14.1 18 ▪ 12 34.1 36.3

12224 NNC S P1 G1.1 1895–1928
Schiffrin, Harold Zvi, 1922–.
'Sun Yat-sen's early land policy: The origin and meaning of "equalization of land rights".'
JAS 16, 4 (Aug. 1957), 549–564.
SUBJ 14.1 64 ▪ 14 14.5

12225 NNC O P8 G1.3 1644–1928
Schrameier, Wilhelm Ludwig, 1859–1926.
'Die Agrarverhältnisse Chinas' (Agrarian conditions in China).
Jahrbuch der Bodenreform 19, 1 (1923), 1–25.
SUBJ 14.1 14.5 45 ▪ 12.2 16.3 41 66

12226 MCH S P2 G1.2 1895–1928
Schultze, Ernst, 1874–?
'Chinas Baumwollanbau und Baumwollindustrie' (Cotton cultivation and the cotton industry in China).
Der neue Orient 7, 2 (Feb. 1923), 60–71.
SUBJ 14.1 ▪ 14 14.3 14.4

12227 MCH P P7 G1.2 –1949
Shao Sui-chu (Shao Hsüeh-ch'u).
La question agraire en Chine (The agrarian problem in China).
Nancy: Grandville, 1934. 172 p. (Doctoral dissertation, Faculté de droit, Université de Nancy)
SUBJ 14.1 16.3 34.1 ▪ 12 14 14.5 14.6 18 36.3 38 64 72

12228 NNC P P2 G1.2 1895–1949
Sun Shao-tsun (Sun Hsiao-ts'un).
'Land ownership and its concentration in China.' Tr. of 'Hsien tai Chung-kuo ti t'u ti wen t'i' (The land problem in modern China); *Chiao yü yü min chung* 8, 3 (28 Nov. 1936), 383–395 [abridged tr.]. In *Agrarian China*, compiled by Institute of Pacific Relations. [Selective entry]
Chicago: U. of Chicago Press, 1939, 1–5.
SUBJ 14.1 ▪ 16.1 16.3 45

12229 NNC P P7 G1.2 –1928
Tang, Chi Yu (T'ang Ch'i-yü), 1895–.
An economic study of Chinese agriculture.
Ithaca?: The author, 1924. 514 p. (Doctoral dissertation in Economics, Cornell U.)
SUBJ 14 14.1 14.5 ▪ 11.2 16.3 17 34.1 45

12230 NIC P P2 G1.2 1895–1949
Tawney, Richard Henry, 1880–1962.
Land and labor in China.
New York: Harcourt, 1932. 207 p. [Reprinted—New York: Octagon Books, 1964. 207 p.]
SUBJ 14.1 14.4 17 ▪ 11 11.2 12 14.6 25 34.1 34.2 41

12231 NNC P P7 G1.3 –1949
Tschang, Wen-hsi (Ch'ang Wen-hsi), 1904–.
Die chinesische Pacht (Land tenancy in China).
Würzburg-Anmühle: Triltsch, 1934. 81 p. (Doctoral dissertation, Philosophische Fakultät, Universität Berlin)
SUBJ 14.1 ▪ 12.2 45 72

12232 MCH PO P7 G1.1 1842–1949
Wilmanns, Wolfgang Otto, 1893–.
Die Landwirtschaft Chinas (The agriculture of China).
Berlin: Parey, 1938. 87 p. (Reichs- und pr. Ministerium für Ernährung und Landwirtschaft, Berichte über Landwirtschaft, neue (2.) Folge, 133, Sonderheft)
SUBJ 14.1 ▪ 11.3 14.2 14.5 16.3 36.3

12233 MCH P P2 G1.1 –1928
Wittfogel, Karl August, 1896–.
Wirtschaft und Gesellschaft Chinas: Versuch der wissenschaftlichen Analyse einer grossen asiatischen Agrargesellschaft. Erster Teil, Produktivkräfte, Produktions- und Zirkulations-prozess (China's economy and society: Toward a scientific analysis of a large-scale Asian agrarian society. Part 1, Productive capacity and processes of production and circulation).

Leipzig: C. L. Hirschfeld, 1931. 24, 767 p. (Institut für Sozialforschung an der Universität Frankfurt a. M., Schriften, 3)
SUBJ 10 12.1 14 14.1 16 ▪ 11.4 16.3 18 34.1 34.2 34.3 36.3 45 60

1911-1949

12234 NIC S P8 G1.4 1911–1928
'Agriculture in Manchuria and Mongolia.'
CEJ 1, 12 (Dec. 1927), 1044–1058.
SUBJ 14.1

12235 CSU U P2 G1.4 1928–1949
'Animal rearing in North Manchuria and Mongolia.'
CEJ 5, 2 (Aug. 1929), 682–695.
SUBJ 14.1 14.3

12236 NNC S P2 G1.2 1911–1928
'Annual production and consumption of food in China.'
NWSS 6, 37 (11 Sept. 1933), 171, 173–174.
SUBJ 14.1 ▪ 14.3 55

12237 NNC S P7 G1.2 1928–1949
'Average percentage of specified farm tenure for different provinces in China.'
NWSS 3, 40 (6 Oct. 1930), 193, 196.
SUBJ 14.1

12238 CSU P P2 G1.1 1928–1949
'China's production and export of groundnuts.'
CEJ 10, 2 (Feb. 1932), 127–140.
SUBJ 14.1 ▪ 14.3

12239 NNC P P7 G1.2 1928–1949
'Farm households, cultivated land and important crops in China.'
NWSS 5, 34 (22 Aug. 1932), 155, 157–160.
SUBJ 14.1 ▪ 16.3

12240 NNC S P7 G1.2 1911–1928
'Farm ownership and tenancy in China.'
NWSS 3, 19 (12 May 1930), 91, 94.
SUBJ 14.1

12241 CSU P P2 G1.2 1911–1949
Lectures in commodities: Vegetable products.
Tientsin: Hautes études; Shanghai: Université l'Aurore, 1936. 172 p. (Institut des hautes études industrielles et commerciales, Faculty of Commerce, Economic studies, 3)
SUBJ 14.1 14.4 ▪ 14.3 55

12242 CSU U P2 G1.3 1928–1949
'The loquat, a special product of China.'
CEJ 5, 1 (July 1929), 621–625.
SUBJ 14.1 14.3

12243 CSU P P2 G1.2 1928–1949
'Production and export of groundnuts.'
CEJ 19, 3 (Sept. 1936), 257–268; 19, 4 (Oct. 1936), 374–395.
SUBJ 14.1 14.3 ▪ 14.5

12244 CSU P P2 G1.2 1928–1949
'Ramie, hemp and jute.'
CEJ 19, 4 (Oct. 1936), 345–361.
SUBJ 14.1 14.3 ▪ 14.2

12245 CSU U P2 G1.5 1928–1949
'Some aspects of China's tea trade.'
CEJ 19, 1 (July 1936), 1–15.
SUBJ 14.1 14.3 ▪ 12 24.3

12246 CSU P P2 G1.1 1928–1949
'Tobacco production and trade.'
CEJ 20, 2 (Feb. 1937), 121–139.
SUBJ 14.1 ▪ 14.3 24.3

12247 NNC S P7 G1.3 1911–1928
'The year's business per farm in China, 1921–1925.'
NWSS 5, 6 (7 Feb. 1932), 23, 25–26.
SUBJ 14.1 ▪ 11.4

12248 NNC P P2 G2.0 1928–1949
B. M.
'Obzor sel'skogo khoziaistva v Man'chzhurii, period ianvar'–avgust 1933 goda' (Overview of agriculture in Manchuria, January–August 1933).
MNKP 1933, 8/9, 190–200.
SUBJ 12 14.1 14.5 16.3 18 ▪ 16.1 21.2 25

12249 CSU P P7 G1.2 1911–1928
Baker, O- E-.
'Agriculture and the future of China.'
FA 6, 3 (Apr. 1928), 483–497.
SUBJ 14.1 ▪ 16.3

12250 NNC S P2 G1.3 1928–1949
Bobrovskaia, L-.
'Nekotorye dannye o krizise sel'skogo khoziaistva v gomindanovskom Kitae' (Data on the agricultural crisis in Kuomintang China).
PK 14 (1935), 332–345.
SUBJ 14.1 18

12251 MCY S P8 G1.2 1911–1949
Brandt, Conrad, 1920–.
'Agrarian reform in Communist China against the background of the Marxist tradition.'
PC 1 (Dec. 1947), 243–288.
SUBJ 14.1 64

12252 NIC S P8 G1.3 1911–1949
Brandt, Vincent Selden Randolph, 1924–.
'Landlord-tenant relations in Republican China.'
PC 17 (Dec. 1963), 192–234.
SUBJ 14.1 16.1 16.3 ▪ 18 48

12253 CSU F P2 G1.3 1911–1928
Buck, John Lossing, 1890–.
'Cost of growing and marketing peanuts in China.'
CEJ 5, 3 (Sept. 1929), 767–788.
SUBJ 14.1 24.3 ▪ 14.3 24.1 34.2

12254 NNM FP P8 G1.2 1911–1928
Buck, John Lossing, 1890–.
Farm ownership and tenancy in China.
Shanghai: National Christian Council, 1927. 34 p.
SUBJ 14.1 ▪ 24.1

12255 CSH FP P7 G1.2 1928–1949
Buck, John Lossing, 1890–.
'Farm tenancy in China.'
EF 33 (June 1944), 455–466; 34 (July 1944), 481–497.
SUBJ 14.1 16.1 16.3 24.1 ▪ 12.2

12256 CSU F P7 G1.2 1928–1949
Buck, John Lossing, 1890–.
Land utilization in China: A study of 16,786 farms in 168 localities, and 32,256 farm families in twenty-two provinces in China, 1929–1933.
Nanking: U. of Nanking, 1937. 3 vols. 32, 494; 12, 146; 15, 473 p. [Reprinted—New York: Paragon, 1964. 32, 494 p. (Reprint of vol. 1 only)]
SUBJ 14.1 16.3 18 58 ▪ 11.2 11.3 17 21 24.1 28 41

12257 NNC FP P7 G1.2 1911–1949
Buck, John Lossing, 1890–.
Some basic agricultural problems of China, mimeo.
New York: Institute of Pacific Relations, International Secretariat, 1947. 62 p. (IS papers, 1)
SUBJ 14 14.1 34.1 ▪ 14.3 14.6 16.3 18 24.4 36.3 38

12258 CSU U P2 G1.5 1928–1949
Chang, Bintze T.
'Timber resources of the southwestern provinces.'
CEJ 5, 6 (Dec. 1929), 1056–1065.
SUBJ 14.1 ▪ 14.3

12259 MCH F P7 G1.2 1911–1949
Chang, C. C. (Chang Hsin-i), 1896–.
'A statistical study of farm tenancy in China.'
China critic 3, 39 (25 Sept. 1930), 917–922.
SUBJ 14.1 ▪ 14.5 16.3 36.3

12260 GGN P P8 G1.1 1928–1949
Chang, Hsün-Yang.
Das chinesische Bodenrecht, unter besonderer Berücksichtigung des deutschen Rechts (China's agricultural-land law, with special attention to German law).
Göttingen: The author, 1949. 264 p. (Doctoral dissertation, Rechts- und staatswissenschaftliche Fakultät, Universität Göttingen)
SUBJ 12.2 14.1

12261 NNC P P7 G1.2 1928–1949
[Chao Mei-sheng] ———.
'Nature of the present land problem in China.' Tr. of 'Chung-kuo t'u ti wen t'i ti pen chih' (The nature of China's land problem); in *Chung-kuo t'u ti wen t'i ho shang yeh kao li tai* (China's land problem and commercial usury), edited by Chung-kuo nung ts'un ching chi yen chiu hui (Research Society for Chinese Agrarian Economy); Shanghai: Li ming shu chü, 1937, 1–8. In *Agrarian China*, compiled by Institute of Pacific Relations. [Selective entry]
Chicago: U. of Chicago Press, 1939, 57–61.
SUBJ 14.1 ▪ 16.1 16.3

12262 MCH F P2 G1.2 1928–1949
Chen Han-seng (Ch'en Han-sheng), 1897–.
'Agrarian reform in China: Kuomintang and Communist achievements.'
FES 17, 4 (25 Feb. 1948), 41–43.
SUBJ 12.1 14.1 ▪ 14.5

12263 CSU U P2 G1.2 1928–1949
Chen Han-seng (Ch'en Han-sheng), 1897–.
'New soul comes to old soil.'
THM 10, 4 (Apr. 1940), 309–323.
SUBJ 14 14.1 ▪ 34.1 66

12264 NNC FP P7 G1.2 1911–1949
Chen Han-seng (Ch'en Han-sheng), 1897–.
The present agrarian problem in China.

Shanghai: China Institute of Pacific Relations, 1933. 32 p.
SUBJ 14.1 16.1 16.3 ▪ 14.5 14.6 18

12265 NNC S P2 G1.5 1928–1949
Chen, Lawrence M. (Ch'en Wen-t'ung).
'The Japanese and the Chinese fishing industry.'
IB 4, 4 (23 June 1937), 73–92.
SUBJ 14.1 66 ▪ 14.3 24.3 34.2

12266 NNC P P2 G1.2 1928–1949
Chen, Lawrence M. (Ch'en Wen-t'ung).
'Rural rehabilitation.'
IB 1, 8 (21 July 1936), 1–19.
SUBJ 14 14.1 ▪ 12.1 19 66

12267 ELO FP P8 G1.2 1911–1949
Chen Po-ta (Ch'en Po-ta), 1904–.
A study of land rent in pre-Liberation China. Tr. of *Chin tai Chung-kuo ti tsu kai shuo*; Peking: Jen min ch'u pan she, 1955.
Peking: Foreign Languages Press, 1958. 101 p. [See Vol. 2 of this *Bibliography* for the more authoritative Chinese ed. of 1948.]
SUBJ 14.1 14.5 16 ▪ 14.6 18

12268 FPN P P8 G1.2 1911–1928
Chen, Yao-tung.
Le régime agraire en Chine (The agricultural system in China).
Lyons: Bosc et Riou, 1933. 222 p. (Doctoral dissertation, Faculté des lettres, Université de Lyon)
SUBJ 14.1 14.5 16.3 64 ▪ 14.6 16 36.3 61

12269 MCY P P8 G1.2 1928–1949
Chiu, Alfred Kaiming (Ch'iu K'ai-ming), 1898–.
'Agriculture.' In *China*, edited by Harley Farnsworth MacNair. [Selective entry]
Berkeley, Los Angeles: U. of California Press, 1946, 466–491. [Reprinted in *China*, edited by H. F. MacNair. (Selective entry.) Freeport, N.Y.: Books for Libraries, 1970, 466–491.]
SUBJ 14 14.1 ▪ 14.6 16.3 27

12270 MCH P P7 G1.2 1911–1949
Chiu, Alfred Kaiming (Ch'iu K'ai-ming), 1898–.
Recent statistical surveys of Chinese rural economy, 1912–1932.
Unpublished doctoral dissertation in Economics, Harvard U., 1933. 651 p.
SUBJ 14 14.1 70 ▪ 14.3 14.6 16.3 18

12271 PPU P P7 G1.2 1911–1949
Chou, Ya-lun, 1922–.
The Chinese agrarian problem and the Communist reform.
Unpublished doctoral dissertation in Economics, U. of Pennsylvania, 1951. s.p.
SUBJ 12.2 14 14.1 16.3 34.1 64 ▪ 12.1 16.1 24.3 24.4 32 32.2 34.2 36.3

12272 NNC S P8 G1.2 1928–1949
Chu Min-chiu (Ch'ü Ming-chou).
'Rent deposit and its tendency to increase.' Tr. of 'Chung-kuo nung t'ien ya tsu ti chin chan' (The collection of land rent payments in advance: Its growing prevalence in China); *Chung-kuo nung ts'un* 1, 4 (Jan. 1935), 19–31 [condensed tr.]. In *Agrarian China*, compiled by Institute of Pacific Relations. [Selective entry]
Chicago: U. of Chicago Press, 1939, 94–101.
SUBJ 14.1 24.1 ▪ 12.2 24.6 26.3

12273 GMU FP P7 G1.2 1911–1928
Chu, Ping (Chu P'ing).
'Bodenreform in China' (Land reform in China).
Jahrbuch der Bodenreform 29, 4 (1933), 145–181. (Doctoral dissertation, Philosophische Fakultät, Universität Leipzig)
SUBJ 14.1 ▪ 12.1 14.5 16.3

12274 NIC O P8 G1.4 1911–1928
Chu, Yu-fen.
'The Chinese peasant: A survey of methods and limitations in soil productivity.'
PA 2, 9 (Sept. 1929), 567–575.
SUBJ 14.1 16.3

12275 NNC P P8 G1.3 1928–1949
Damaschke, Adolf Wilhelm Ferdinand, 1865–?, and Hsiao Cheng.
'Zum Bodengesetz der Republik China vom 30. Juni 1930' (The land law of the Republic of China of 30 June 1930).
Jahrbuch der Bodenreform 27, 1 (1931), 1–33.
SUBJ 12.2 14.1 ▪ 14.5

12276 MCH O P2 G1.2 1928–1949
Dawson, Owen Lafayette, 1892–.
'Agricultural policies in unoccupied China since 1937.'
Foreign agriculture 5, 10 (Oct. 1941), 407–422.
SUBJ 14 14.1 ▪ 14.3

12277 CSU O P2 G1.2 1928–1949
Dawson, Owen Lafayette, 1892–.
'Agricultural reconstruction in China.'
Foreign agriculture 7, 6 (June 1943), 123–134.
SUBJ 14.1 18 ▪ 12 14 14.2 14.5 58

12278 CSU P P1 G1.2 1928–1949
Dawson, Owen Lafayette, 1892–.
'China's food problem.'
Foreign agriculture 8, 5 (May 1944), 99–109.
SUBJ 14.1 14.3 18 ▪ 55

12279 MCH P P8 G1.2 1928–1949
Deliusin, Lev Petrovich, 1923–.
'Agrarnaia politika KPK v gody narodno-osvoboditel'noi voiny' (Chinese Communist Party land policy during the War of National Liberation).
NAA 1961, 5, 124–139.
SUBJ 12.1 14.1 32.2 36.3 ▪ 16 16.3

12280 CSH P P2 G2.0 1911–1928
Engel'fel'd, Vladimir Viktorovich, 1891–1937.
'Kitaiskoe lesnoe pravo v sviazi s lesnym khoziaistvom severnoi Man'chzhurii' (Chinese forestry law relating to the timber industry of northern Manchuria).
Izvestiia IUridicheskogo fakul'teta v g. Kharbine 6 (1928), 229–299.
SUBJ 12.2 14.1 14.4 ▪ 12

12281 MCY P P2 G1.1 1928–1949
Fabel, L- B- A-.
The economic importance of fruit-culture in China.
Peiping: Catholic U. of Peking *with* Chinese Catholic Agricultural Research Assn., 1948. 113 p. (Agricultural Extension Service bulletins, 2)
SUBJ 14.1 ▪ 14.3 55 56

12282 NNC P P8 G1.2 1911–1949
Fedoseev, N- K-.
'Kapital i trud v krest'ianskom khoziaistve Kitaia' (Capital and labor in the Chinese peasant economy).
BSB 2, 5 (1932), 45–60.
SUBJ 14.1 ▪ 16.3

12283 NNC P P8 G1.2 1911–1949
Fong, H. D. (Fang Hsien-t'ing), 1902–.
'Bibliography on the land problems of China.'
NSEQ 8, 2 (July 1935), 325–384.
SUBJ 14.1 72

12284 NNC U P7 G1.2 1911–1928
Freier, B-.
'K kharakteristike agrarnykh otnoshenii v Kitae' (The nature of agrarian relations in China).
Revoliutsionnyi Vostok 1928, 3, 66–82.
SUBJ 14.1 ▪ 14.3

12285 CBU U P2 G2.0 1911–1949
Galitskii, A- M-.
'Mirovoi rynok soevykh bobov i sel'skoe khoziaistvo Man'chzhurii' (The world soybean market and Manchurian agriculture).
VM 1933, 12 (1 iiulia), 1–19.
SUBJ 14.1 14.3 ▪ 14.4

12286 CBU S P8 G2.0 1911–1949
Galitskii, A- M-.
'Proizvoditel'nye sily i proizvodstvennye otnosheniia v man'chzhurskom sel'skom khoziaistve' (Productive forces and production relations in Manchurian agriculture). [With English abstract at end of issue]
VM 1933, 17 (15 sentiabria), 1–17.
SUBJ 14.1 ▪ 16.3 21

12287 CSH P P7 G2.0 1928–1949
Gedin, M-.
'Lesnoi rynok Man'chzhurii' (The Manchurian timber market). [With English abstract]
VM 1931, 10, 37–45.
SUBJ 14.1 14.3

12288 CSU P P8 G1.2 1911–1949
Gibbs, J- Bernard.
'Tobacco in principal producing countries of the Far East.'
Foreign agriculture 4, 5 (May 1940), 287–300.
SUBJ 14.1

12289 MCH S P7 G1.2 1928–1949
Giorgi, Giacomo.
'L'economia agraria cinese e i suoi possibili sviluppi' (The Chinese agricultural economy and its possible development).
Rivista di economia agraria 2, 1 (marzo 1947), 57–83.
SUBJ 14.1 16.3 ▪ 11.2 14.6 24.3

12290 NNC P P8 G1.4 1928–1949
Glunin, Vladimir Ivanovich, 1924–.
'Agrarnaia politika Kommunisticheskoi partii Kitaia v period tret'ei grazhdanskoi revoliutsionnoi voiny, 1946–1949 gg.' (Chinese Communist Party land policy during the Third Revolutionary Civil War, 1946–1949).

KSIV 21 (1956), 15–27.
SUBJ 14 14.1 16 32.2 45 ▪ 16.1 16.3

12291 FPL S P7 G1.2 1928–1949
Gourou, Pierre, 1900–.
La terre et l'homme en Extrême-Orient (Land and man in the Far East), 2nd ed.
Paris: Armand Colin, 1947. 224 p.
SUBJ 14 14.1 16.3 18 41 55 ▪ 14.6 22 24.4 42 43 47 52 53 61

12292 NNC S P2 G2.0 1928–1949
Grajdanzev, Andrew Jonah, 1899–.
'Manchuria as a region of colonization.'
PA 19, 1 (Mar. 1946), 5–19.
SUBJ 14.1 21.2 ▪ 14.2 21

12293 NNC S P8 G1.2 1911–1949
Great Britain. Admiralty. Naval Intelligence Division. Geographical Section.
'Agriculture and forestry.' In *China proper, Vol. 3, Economic geography, ports and communications*, compiled by the agency cited. [Selective entry]
London: His Majesty's Stationery Office, 1945, 1–72. (NID, Geographical handbook series, BR 530B)
SUBJ 14.1 34.1 ▪ 14 14.5 14.6 18 72

12294 NNC U P2 G1.1 1928–1949
Great Britain. Admiralty. Naval Intelligence Division. Geographical Section.
'Fisheries.' In *China proper, Vol. 3, Economic geography, ports and communications*, compiled by the agency cited. [Selective entry]
London: His Majesty's Stationery Office, 1945, 74–83. (NID, Geographical handbook series, BR 530B)
SUBJ 14.1 ▪ 14.2 24.1 72

12295 CBU S P2 G1.2 1911–1949
Grumm-Grzhimai'le, Aleksei Grigor'evich.
Khlopkovodstvo v Kitae (Cotton cultivation in China).
Leningrad: Izd-vo Vses. akad. sel'sko-khoz. nauk im. V. I. Lenina, 1936. 79 p.
SUBJ 11.3 14.1 14.4

12296 NIC P P8 G1.3 1911–1949
Ho, Franklin L. (Ho Lien), 1897–.
'Rural economic reconstruction in China.'
NSEQ 9, 2 (July 1936), 469–535. [Separately reprinted—Shanghai: China Institute of Pacific Relations, 1936. 59 p.]
SUBJ 14.1 ▪ 18 36.3

12297 DLC P P7 G1.5 1911–1949
Hong Fou (Hung Fu), 1908–.
La géographie du thé (The geography of tea), 2nd ed.
Canton: Bibliothèque de l'Institut de géographie de l'Université de Lyon et des 'Etudes rhodaniennes', 1934. 181 p. (Revision of doctoral dissertation, Faculté des lettres, Université de Lyon)
SUBJ 11.3 14.1 14.3 ▪ 18 24.4

12298 WMU P P7 G1.2 1928–1949
Hsiang, C. Y. (Hsiang Ching-yün), 1909–.
Tenure of land in China: A preface to China's land problems and policies.
Unpublished doctoral dissertation in Economics, U. of Wisconsin, 1940. 219 p.
SUBJ 14.1 45 ▪ 16.1 16.3 24.3 24.4 38 41

12299 NNC S P8 G1.2 1928–1949
Hsu, Yung-ying (Hsü Yung-ying), 1902–.
'The revival of the land problem in China.'
PA 15, 1 (Mar. 1942), 96–107.
SUBJ 14.1

12300 CSH P P7 G2.0 1911–1928
IAshnov, Evgenii Evgen'evich, ed.
'Khlebnye zlaki v severnoi Man'chzhurii' (Cereals in northern Manchuria). In *Khlebnaia torgovlia i mukomol'naia promyshlennost' v severnoi Man'chzhurii* (The grain trade and flour-milling industry in northern Manchuria), compiled by Obshchestvo izucheniia Man'chzhurskogo kraia, edited by E. E. IAshnov. [Analytic entry]
Harbin: Tipo-lit. T-va 'Ozo', 1923, vol. 2, 1–8.
SUBJ 14.1 ▪ 14.3

12301 CBU S P7 G2.0 1928–1949
IAshnov, Evgenii Evgen'evich.
'Meropriiatiia v oblasti sel'skogo khoziaistva Man'chzhurii' (Agricultural measures in Manchuria).
VM 1934, 3 (mart), 1–22.
SUBJ 14 14.1 ▪ 16.3

12302 WSU P P2 G1.2 1911–1928
IAshnov, Evgenii Evgen'evich.
Naselenie i krest'ianskoe khoziaistvo Kitaia: obzor istochnikov (China's population and peasant economy: A review of sources).
Harbin: Izd-vo Ob-va izucheniia Man'chzhurskogo kraia, 1928. 119 p. (Obshchestvo izucheniia Man'chzhurskogo kraia, Torgovo-promyshlennaia sektsiia, seriia D, 2)
SUBJ 11.3 14.1 16.3 ▪ 11 36.3

12303 CSH FP P2 G1.2 1911–1949
IAshnov, Evgenii Evgen'evich.
Ocherki kitaiskogo krest'ianskogo khoziaistva (Notes on the Chinese peasant economy).
Harbin: Tip. N. A. Frenkelia, 1935. 15, 231 p.
SUBJ 11 14.1 16.3 58 ▪ 14 14.5 16 22.2 23 41 50

12304 CSH P P2 G1.2 1911–1949
IAshnov, Evgenii Evgen'evich.
'Sel'skoe khoziaistvo Kitaia v tsifrakh' (Chinese agriculture in figures).
VM 1932, 6/7, 79–114; 1932, 8, 58–77; 1932, 9/10, 58–82. [Separately reprinted—Harbin: Tip. KVzhd, 1933. 107 p.]
SUBJ 11 14.1 ▪ 16.3

12305 CSH P P8 G1.3 1911–1949
Kann, Eduard, 1880–1962.
'Baumwolle in China' (Cotton in China).
Das neue China 6, 45 (Okt. 1940), 834–838; 7, 46 (Jan. 1941), 893–906.
SUBJ 14.1

12306 NNP P P8 G1.2 1911–1928
Kantorovich, Anatolii IAkovlevich, 1896–1944.
'Nekotorye dannye ob ekonomike kitaiskoi derevni' (Data on the economy of the Chinese countryside).
Ekonomicheskoe obozrenie 4, 3 (mart 1926), 175–180.
SUBJ 14.1 45 ▪ 16.3 18

12307 CSH P P7 G1.2 1911–1949
Kara-Murza, Georgii Sergeevich, 1906–1945.
'Agrarnyi vopros v Kitae v pervoi polovine 1929 g.' (The land problem in China during the first half of 1929).
PK 2 (1930), 181–197.
SUBJ 14.1 14.5 16.1 16.3 18 32 ▪ 11.2

12308 MAM P P7 G1.2 1911–1949
Keh, Chi-yang (Ko Ch'i-yang), 1909–.
Land utilization in China and in the United States.
Ann Arbor: University Microfilms (Publ. 683), 1944. 121 p. (Doctoral dissertation in Agriculture, Michigan State U.)
SUBJ 14.1

12309 NNC P P8 G2.0 1928–1949
Kehoe, Robert Richard, 1922–.
Agriculture in Manchuria, 1931–1944.
Unpublished masters thesis in Public Law and Government, Columbia U., 1949. 138 p.
SUBJ 14.1 ▪ 21 21.2

12310 FPN P P8 G1.1 1928–1949
Kou, Mei Cheng (Ku Mei-sheng).
La modernisation de l'agriculture chinoise (The modernization of Chinese agriculture).
Unpublished doctoral dissertation, Faculté de droit, Université de Paris, 1950. 278 p.
SUBJ 14.1 14.6 16.3 18 21.2 ▪ 16.1 27 34.1 36.3 56 58

12311 NNC P P7 G1.2 1928–1949
Kovalev, Evgenii Fedorovich, 1907–.
'Agrarnyi krizis v gomindanovskom Kitae' (The land crisis in Kuomintang China).
Uchenye zapiski Tikhookeanskogo instituta 3 (1949), 20–35.
SUBJ 14.1 16.3 18 32.2 36.3 ▪ 14.5 16 25 45 58 66

12312 NNC P P8 G1.2 1928–1949
Kovalev, Evgenii Fedorovich, 1907–.
Arenda i arendnye otnosheniia v Kitae: ocherk (Sketch of rent and tenancy relations in China).
Moscow: Gospolitizdat, 1947. 107 p.
SUBJ 14.1 16.3 ▪ 16.1

12313 NNC P P8 G1.2 1928–1949
Kovalev, Evgenii Fedorovich, 1907–.
'Vliianie voiny na agrarnye otnosheniia v Kitae' (The impact of the war on agrarian relations in China).
MKhMP 1945, 9 (sentiabr'), 64–73.
SUBJ 14.1 14.6 16.3 45 ▪ 16.1 18

12314 DLC P P8 G1.2 1928–1949
Kudrin, V- I-.
'Agrarnaia politika Kommunisticheskoi partii Kitaia v period 1937–1946 gg.' (Chinese Communist Party land policy, 1937–1946).
VLGU 6, 8 (1951), 42–52.
SUBJ 14.1 15 32 ▪ 14.5 14.6 16.3 32.2 34.1

12315 CSU P P2 G2.0 1928–1949
Ladejinsky, Wolf Isaac, 1901–.
'Manchurian agriculture under Japanese control.'
Foreign agriculture 5, 8 (Aug. 1941), 309–340.
SUBJ 14.1 14.3 ▪ 12.2 34.2

12316 CSU P P8 G1.2 1911–1928
La Fleur, Albert, and Edwin J- Foscue.
'Agricultural production in China.'
EG 3, 3 (July 1927), 297–308.
SUBJ 14.1

12317 FPN PO P7 G1.2 1911–1949
Liao, Nan-tse (Liao Nan-ts'ai).
Perspectives de l'économie rurale en Chine (The future of the Chinese rural economy).
Unpublished doctoral dissertation, Faculté de droit, Université de Paris, 1949. 146 p.
SUBJ 14.1 14.6 16.3 55 ▪ 17 34.1 36.3

12318 MCY U P2 G1.2 1928–1949
Lieou, Laurent Li-liang (Liu Li-liang).
'Notes sur l'économie du thé en Chine' (Notes on the tea economy in China).
BUA 3e série 3, 12 (1942), 838–895.
SUBJ 14.1 ▪ 14.3 14.4 34.2

12319 CSU FP P8 G1.2 1911–1928
Lieu, D. K. (Liu Ta-chün), 1891–1962.
'Land tenure systems in China.'
CEJ 2, 6 (June 1928), 457–474.
SUBJ 14.1 24.1

12320 MCH U P7 G1.2 1911–1928
Lin Kho-iuan' (Ling Huo-yüan).
'Agrarnyi vopros v Kitae' (The land problem in China).
Kommunisticheskii Internatsional 1928, 25/26 (29 iiulia), 80–99.
SUBJ 14.1 64 ▪ 18

12321 CSH S P7 G2.0 1928–1949
Liubimov, L- I-.
'Mirovoi krizis i biudzhet man'chzhurskogo krest'ianina' (The worldwide [economic] crisis and the Manchurian peasant's budget). [With English abstract]
VM 1931, 9, 7–15.
SUBJ 14.1 16.3 18 ▪ 14.6 24.3

12322 CSH P P7 G2.0 1911–1949
Liubimov, L- I-.
'Rol' produktov zhivotnovodstva i rybnykh promyslov v khoziaistvennom balanse Man'chzhurii' (The role of livestock and fishery products in the economic balance of Manchuria). [With English abstract]
VM 1930, 7, 1–11.
SUBJ 14.1 ▪ 14.3 16.3 21

12323 CSU O P8 G1.2 1928–1949
Lowdermilk, Walter Clay, 1888–.
'China fights erosion with U.S. aid.'
NG 87, 6 (June 1945), 641–680.
SUBJ 11.3 14.1

12324 CSU S P8 G1.2 1911–1928
Lowdermilk, Walter Clay, 1888–, and T'ien-i Li, 1907–.
'Forestry in denuded China.'
AAAPSS 152 (Nov. 1930), 127–141. [Special issue: *China*, edited by Henry F- James]
SUBJ 14.1 ▪ 11.3 14.2

12325 DLC P P2 G1.2 1911–1949
Mad'iar, Liudvig Ignat'evich, 1891–?
'Dve agrarnye programmy v kitaiskoi revoliutsii' (Two agrarian programs of the Chinese revolution).
PK 4/5 (1930), 60–83.
SUBJ 12.2 14.1 16 32.2 36.3 64 ▪ 12 12.1 14.5 32 33

12326 MCH S P2 G1.2 1928–1949
Mamaeva, R-.
'Agrarnyi krizis v Kitae' (The agrarian crisis in China). In *Agrarnyi krizis* (Agrarian crisis). [Selective entry]
Moscow: Mezhdunar. agrarnyi in-t, 1933, vol. 4, 23–64.
SUBJ 14 14.1 14.3 ▪ 14.5 16.3 64

12327 DLC P P2 G2.0 1911–1928
Marakuev, Aleksandr Vasil'evich, 1891–1955.
Eksport man'chzhurskikh bobov i ego finansirovanie (Financing Manchurian bean exports).
Harbin: Izd-vo Ob-va izucheniia Man'chzhurskogo kraia, 1928. 75 p. (Obshchestvo izucheniia Man'chzhurskogo kraia, Torgovo-promyshlennaia sektsiia, seriia D, 12)
SUBJ 14 14.1 14.6 ▪ 14.3

12328 IUU P P7 G1.1 1911–1949
Meng, Ching Peng (Meng Ch'ing-p'eng), 1919–.
Agricultural progress in China: A study of conditioning factors.
Unpublished doctoral dissertation in Agricultural Economics, U. of Illinois, 1949. 12, 179 p.
SUBJ 14 14.1 ▪ 11.2 14.2 14.5 18 27 34.1 58

12329 CSU P P8 G2.0 1928–1949
Moyer, Raymond Tyson, 1899–.
'The agricultural potentialities of Manchuria.'
Foreign agriculture 8, 8 (Aug. 1944), 171–191.
SUBJ 14.1

12330 MCY O P8 G3.0 1928–1949
Moyer, Raymond Tyson, 1899–.
'Some observations on the agriculture of Inner Mongolia.'
JRAS-NCB new (2nd) series 68 (1937), 19–26.
SUBJ 14.1 ▪ 11.3

12331 CBU P P7 G1.2 1928–1949
Nicolson, John Allen.
Rural problems and reconstruction in Kuomintang China, 1928–1948: A twenty year study of Kuomintang rural problems, policy, and practice.
Unpublished masters thesis in History, U. of California, Berkeley, 1951. 233 p.
SUBJ 14 14.1 32 37 ▪ 14.5 14.6 22 34.1 45

12332 CSU P P2 G1.2 1928–1949
Ojha, Ellen Frost, 1945–.
'Fluctuations in Chinese Communist agrarian policy, 1946–1950.'
PC 22B (Dec. 1969), 20–48.
SUBJ 12.1 14.1 64 ▪ 12.2 16 16.1 32.2

12333 MCY P P7 G1.2 1928–1949
Ostrovskaia, A- I-.
'Agrarnyi vopros v Kitae' (The land problem in China). In *Kitai: istoriia, ekonomika, kul'tura, geroicheskaia bor'ba za natsional'nuiu nezavisimost'. Sbornik statei* (Articles on the history, economy, and culture of China, and its heroic struggle for national independence), edited by Vasilii Mikhailovich Alekseev et al. [Selective entry]
Moscow: Izd-vo Akad. nauk SSSR, 1940, 214–225.
SUBJ 14.1 ▪ 16.3

12334 NNC P P8 G1.2 1911–1949
Ostrovskaia, A- I-.
'Sostoianie sel'skogo khoziaistva Kitaia' (The state of Chinese agriculture).
MKhMP 1940, 8 (avgust), 93–108.
SUBJ 14 14.1 14.6 ▪ 11.2 14.5 16.3 34.1

12335 NNC S P2 G1.3 1911–1949
Otte, Friedrich W- K-.
'Agrarfrage und Kommunismus in China' (The agrarian question and Communism in China).
Z. für Politik 23, 2 (1933), 94–105.
SUBJ 14.1 64 ▪ 16.1 16.3 32.2

12336 DLC P P2 G1.2 1928–1949
Pao, Hung Hsiang.
Wheat problems in China, mimeo.
Tientsin: Hautes études; Shanghai: Université l'Aurore, 1937. 98 p. (Institut des hautes études industrielles et commerciales, Faculty of Commerce, Economic studies, 8)
SUBJ 14.1 ▪ 14.3

12337 CSU P P8 G1.3 1928–1949
Pelzer, Karl Josef, 1909–.
'Land utilization and land tenure: China.' In *An economic survey of the Pacific area, Part 1, Population and land utilization*, by K. J. Pelzer. [Selective entry]
New York: Institute of Pacific Relations, International Secretariat, 1941, 101–111.
SUBJ 14.1

12338 CSU P P8 G2.0 1911–1949
Pelzer, Karl Josef, 1909–.
'Land utilization and land tenure: Manchuria.' In *An economic survey of the Pacific area, Part 1, Population and land utilization*, by K. J. Pelzer. [Selective entry]
New York: Institute of Pacific Relations, International Secretariat, 1941, 98–101.
SUBJ 14.1

12339 CSH PO P2 G1.2 1928–1949
Phillips, Ralph Wesley, 1909–, Ray George Johnson, 1902–, and Raymond Tyson Moyer, 1899–.
The livestock of China.
Washington, D.C.: U.S. Government Printing Office, 1945. 174 p. (U.S. State Dept., Far Eastern series, 9; Publications, 2249)
SUBJ 14.1 ▪ 14.2 14.3 24.3 24.4 72

12340 DLC S P8 G1.3 1911–1928
Poliakov, A- (A. Poljakow).
'Formy arendnykh otnoshenii v Kitae' (Tenancy relations in China).
Agrarnye problemy 2, 4 (1928), 56–83.

'Formen der Pachtverhältnisse in China.'
Agrar-Probleme 1, 4 (1928), 691–721.
SUBJ 14.1 ▪ 16.3 72

12341 NNC O P8 G1.2 1911–1949
Robequain, Charles, 1897–.
'L'agriculture chinoise traditionnelle' (Traditional agriculture in China). In *Aspects de la Chine, vol. 3, époque contemporaine* (Aspects of China, Vol. 3, The modern era), by Etienne Balazs et al. [Selective entry]
Paris: Presses universitaires, 1962, 479–486.
SUBJ 14.1 16.3 ▪ 11.3 18 55

12342 MCH P P8 G1.2 1928–1949
Rossiter, Fred J-.
'Agriculture in China.'
Foreign agriculture 3, 10 (Oct. 1939), 431–498.
SUBJ 14.1 ▪ 14

12343 CSU P P2 G1.2 1928–1949
Rossiter, Fred J-.
'The Sino-Japanese conflict: Effect on Chinese agricultural production and trade.'
Foreign agriculture 2, 4 (Apr. 1938), 199–206.
SUBJ 14.1 14.3

12344 CSU FP P2 G1.2 1911–1949
Rossiter, Fred J-.
'Trends and possibilities of cotton production in China.'
Foreign agriculture 2, 3 (Mar. 1938), 119–146.
SUBJ 14.1 14.3

12345 GBT O P2 G1.3 1928–1949
Schmitz-Mancy, Guido.
Die landwirtschaftliche Produktion Chinas und ihre Bedeutung für den chinesischen Aussenhandel (China's agricultural production and its significance for the Chinese export trade).
Berlin: The author, 1941. 215 p. (Doctoral dissertation, Landwirtschaftliche Fakultät, Universität Berlin)
SUBJ 11.3 14 14.1 14.3 ▪ 11

12346 NNC P P8 G1.3 1911–1928
Schöne, Heinrich.
'Das Landprogramm der chinesischen Nationalregierung und die chinesische Agrarfrage' (The land program of the Chinese national government and the agrarian question in China).
Z. für Politik 17, 8 (1928), 715–730.
SUBJ 14.1 16.3 ▪ 12.2 14.5 14.6 32.1 36.3

12347 CSU P P2 G1.3 1928–1949
Shaw, Earl B-.
'Swine industry of China.'
EG 14, 4 (Oct. 1938), 381–397.
SUBJ 14.1 ▪ 14.3

12348 NNC PO P2 G1.1 1928–1949
Shen, T. H. (Shen Tsung-han), 1895–.
Agricultural resources of China.
Ithaca: Cornell U. Press, 1951. 18, 407 p.
SUBJ 14.1 ▪ 11.2 11.3 14.2 14.3 16.3 18 36.3 55

12349 NIC O P2 G1.2 1911–1928
Sherfesee, William Forsythe.
'The industrial and social importance of forestry in China.'
CSPSR 1, 3 (Oct. 1916), 71–96. [Reprinted in *Readings in economics for China*, compiled and edited by Charles Frederick Remer. (Selective entry.) Shanghai: Commercial Press, 1922, 563–581.]
SUBJ 14 14.1 14.2 ▪ 14.4 18 55

12350 MCY P P8 G1.2 1911–1949
Song, André Kia-hoai (Sung Chia-huai).
'Le régime foncier en Chine' (Landownership in China).
BUA 3e série 8, 29 (1947), 144–169; 8, 32 (1947), 498–515.
SUBJ 14.1 ▪ 14.5 45

12351 CSU P P2 G2.0 1911–1949
Stewart, John Robert, 1910–.
'The resources of Manchuria.'
J. of geography 31, 2 (Feb. 1932), 45–57.
SUBJ 14.1 14.4

12352 NNC P P8 G1.2 1928–1949
Sun Shao-tsun (Sun Hsiao-ts'un) and [Franklin C. H. Lee] Franklin C. H. Li (Li Ching-han), 1895–.
'Characteristic features of farm management in China.' Tr. from *Chiao yü yü min chung* 8, 3 (28 Nov. 1936) *and* from *Shui k'o hsüeh* 1, 3 (Apr. 1936) [abridged tr.]. In *Agrarian China*, compiled by Institute of Pacific Relations. [Selective entry]
Chicago: U. of Chicago Press, 1939, 61–65.
SUBJ 14.1 ▪ 16.1 16.3

12353 GMU S P7 G5.0 1911–1928
Tchang, Pi-kai (Chang P'i-chieh).
Die Bodenzersplitterung in China (The fragmentation of landholdings in China).
Freiburg i. Br.: The author, 1934. 60 p. (Doctoral dissertation, Rechts- und staatswissenschaftliche Fakultät, Universität Freiburg i. Br.)
SUBJ 14.1

12354 CSH O P8 G1.4 1928–1949
Todd, Oliver Julian, 1880–.
'The progress of irrigation in North China.'
Civil engineering 7, 8 (Aug. 1937), 552–556. [Reprinted in *Two decades in China*, by O. J. Todd. (Selective entry.) Peiping: Assn. of Chinese and American Engineers, 1938, 194–202.] [Reprinted in *Two decades in China*, by O. J. Todd. (Selective entry.) Taipei: Ch'eng-wen, 1971, 194–202.]
SUBJ 14.1 24.1

12355 MCH S P2 G1.2 1911–1928
Torgashev, Boris Pavlovich.
China as a tea producer: Area of cultivation, methods of planting and manufacture, export trade, production and consumption, both in China and abroad, with fifty-nine statistical tables.
Shanghai: Commercial Press, 1926. 252 p.
SUBJ 14 14.1 ▪ 12

12356 CSU P P7 G1.2 1928–1949
Trewartha, Glenn Thomas, 1896–.
'Ratio maps of China's farms and crops.'
GR 28, 1 (Jan. 1938), 102–111.
SUBJ 14.1

12357 CSU S P8 G1.5 1911–1928
Trewartha, Glenn Thomas, 1896–.
'The tea crop.'
J. of geography 28, 1 (Jan. 1929), 1–25.
SUBJ 14.1

12358 MMU P P2 G1.2 1928–1949
Tsiang, Chieh (Chiang Chieh), 1909–.
An economic study of some problems of Chinese agriculture.
Unpublished doctoral dissertation in Economics, U. of Minnesota, 1948. 268 p.
SUBJ 14 14.1 14.6 ▪ 11 11.2 11.4 16.3 41 47 55 58

12359 NNC O P2 G1.2 1928–1949
United Nations. Relief and Rehabilitation Administration.
Agricultural rehabilitation in China.
Washington, D.C.: Relief and Rehabilitation Administration, 1948. 46 p. (UNRRA operational analysis papers, 52)
SUBJ 14.1 14.4 18 ▪ 24.4

12360 DLC P P7 G1.2 1928–1949
[Vishniakova-Akimova, Vera Vladimirovna] V. Vishniakova.
'Uglublenie agrarnogo krizisa v Kitae v 1932 g.' (The deepening agrarian crisis in China in 1932).
PK 12 (1933), 232–273.
SUBJ 14 14.1 14.3 16.3 ▪ 14.5 14.6 16.1 18 22.1 32.2

12361 NNC P P7 G1.2 1911–1928
Volin, M-.
'Osnovnye voprosy ekonomiki sel'skogo khoziaistva v Kitae' (Basic questions about agricultural economics in China).
Na agrarnom fronte 1926, 10 (oktiabr'), 57–68; 1926, 11/12 (noiabr'–dekabr'), 89–96.
SUBJ 14.1 16.3 45 ▪ 14 16.1 32.2 71

12362 CSH P P8 G1.2 1911–1928
Volin, M-.
'Struktura sel'skogo khoziaistva v Kitae' (The structure of Chinese agriculture).
VM 1926, 8, 60–66; 1926, 9, 29–37.
SUBJ 14.1 ▪ 11.3 14.6 16 16.3

12363 MCH PO P8 G1.2 1911–1928
Wagner, Wilhelm, 1884–.
Die chinesische Landwirtschaft (Chinese agriculture).
Berlin: Parey, 1926. 15, 668 p.
SUBJ 14.1 14.2 16.3 ▪ 34.1 45 55

12364 DLC P P7 G1.1 1928–1949
Wang, Ping Hsun (Wang Ping-hsün).
Agricultural resources of China and Japan, with a comparative survey, mimeo.
Tientsin: Hautes études; Shanghai: Université l'Aurore, 1938. 254 p. (Institut des hautes études industrielles et commerciales, Faculty of Commerce, Economic studies, 12)
SUBJ 14.1

12365 CSH P P7 G1.2 1928–1949
Wang, Yin-yuen (Wang Yin-yüan).
'China's agricultural production in the war period.'
EF 36 (Sept. 1944), 536–541.
SUBJ 14.1

12366 NNC O P7 G1.3 1911–1928
Warwick, Adam.
'Farmers since the days of Noah: China's remarkable system of agriculture has kept alive the densest population in the world.'
NG 51, 4 (Apr. 1927), 469–500.
SUBJ 14.1 ▪ 16.3 18

12367 CSU P P2 G1.1 1911–1949
Wickizer, Vernon Dale, and Merrill Kelley Bennett.
The rice economy of monsoon Asia.
Stanford: Stanford U., Food Research Institute, 1941. 13, 358 p. (Grain economics series, 3)
SUBJ 14.1 14.3 24.3 ▪ 55

12368 MCH O P8 G3.0 1911–1928
Wilm, Paul W-.
'The agricultural methods of Chinese colonists in Mongolia.'
CEJ 1, 12 (Dec. 1927), 1023–1043.
Subj 14.1 ▪ 16.3 22

12369 CSU FP P2 G1.4 1928–1949
Wilm, Paul W-.
Die Fruchtbarkeit und Ertragsleistung Nordchinas bis 1949 (Agricultural fertility and production in North China to 1949).
Wiesbaden: Harrassowitz, 1968. 258 p. (Institut für Asienkunde, Schriften, 22)
Subj 11.3 14.1

12370 NNC P P7 G1.1 1911–1949
Wong Yin-seng (Wang Yin-sheng), 1902–, Chang Hsi-chang (Chang Hsi-ch'ang), et al.
'Change in land ownership and the fate of permanent tenancy.' Tr. from the Chinese [tr. from an unpublished manuscript on modernization of landownership, dated 1932]. In *Agrarian China*, compiled by Institute of Pacific Relations. [Selective entry]
Chicago: U. of Chicago Press, 1939, 21–26.
Subj 14.1 45 ▪ 12.2 16.1 16.3 22.2

12371 CSU P P2 G1.3 1911–1949
Yang Ch'eng Yu (Yang Ch'eng-yü).
Groundnuts production and trade in China, mimeo.
Tientsin: Hautes études; Shanghai: Université l'Aurore, 1938. 187 p. (Institut des hautes études industrielles et commerciales, Faculty of Commerce, Economic studies, 14)
Subj 14.1 ▪ 14.3 14.4 24.3

12372 MMU P P2 G1.2 1911–1949
Yang Shu-chia, 1907–.
A study of the Chinese economy, with special reference to farm credit.
Unpublished doctoral dissertation in Economics, U. of Minnesota, 1942. 229 p.
Subj 14.1 14.6 34.1 ▪ 14 14.3 14.4 22.2

12373 CSH F P7 G1.3 1928–1949
Yin Lien-ken (Ying Lien-keng), 1904?–.
'Returns on landlord's capital investment in farms.'
EF 2 (Oct. 1936), 122–132. [In Chinese as well as English]
Subj 14.1 16.1 ▪ 14.6

1911-1972
(including 1644-1972)

12374 MCH P P7 G1.2 1928–1972
'Les étapes de la réforme agraire et les conditions sociales de la répression dans la République populaire de Chine.'
B. d'information de la Commission internationale contre le régime concentrationnaire 1, 3 (mai–juil. 1955), 11–27.
'Land reform measures and the social background of repression in the People's Republic of China.'
Monthly information b. of the International Commission Against Concentration Camp Practices 1, 3 (May–July 1955), 11–27.
Subj 14.1 16.3 ▪ 12.1 12.2 34.1 64

12375 MAM P P2 G1.2 1928–1972
Barnett, Irving, 1918–.
UNRRA [United Nations Relief and Rehabilitation Administration] *in China: A case study in financial assistance for economic development, with emphasis on agricultural programs.*
Ann Arbor: University Microfilms (Publ. 16,269), 1956. 357 p. (Doctoral dissertation in Political Science, Columbia U., 1955)
Subj 14 14.1 14.4 16 16.2 34.1 ▪ 12 22 24.4 34.2

12376 CSH S P2 G1.2 1928–1972
Buck, John Lossing, 1890–.
'Food grain production in Mainland China before and during the Communist regime.' In *Food and agriculture in Communist China*, by J. L. Buck et al. [Analytic entry]
New York: Praeger, 1966, 3–72.
Subj 14.1 ▪ 11

12377 CSU PO P8 G1.1 1928–1972
Buck, John Lossing, 1890–.
'Land reform and economic development in Asia: Some general considerations.' In *Land tenure, industrialization and social stability: Experience and prospects in Asia*, edited by Walter Froehlich. [Selective entry]
Milwaukee: Marquette U. Press, 1961, 80–94. (Marquette Asian studies, 2)
Subj 14.1

12378 NIC P P8 G1.2 1911–1972
Carin, Robert.
Agrarian reform movement in Communist China, mimeo.
Kowloon: ——, 1960. 144 p. (China's land problem series, 1)
Subj 12.2 14.1 16 22.2 ▪ 16.1 16.3 22 22.1 36.3

12379 CSH P P7 G1.2 1911–1972
Chao, Kuo-chün, 1918–1962.
Agrarian policy of the Chinese Communist Party, 1921–1959.
Bombay: Asia Publishing House, 1960. 399 p. (Revision of *Land policy of the Chinese Communist Party, 1921–1953*, doctoral dissertation in Government, Cornell U., 1954)
Subj 14.1 22 22.1 34.1 ▪ 14.5 16 16.3 18 32.1 36.3 64

12380 FPL P P7 G1.2 1928–1972
Chen Chi-Yi.
La réforme agraire en Chine populaire (Agrarian reform in the People's Republic of China).
The Hague: Mouton, 1964. 150 p. (Maison des sciences de l'homme, Matériaux pour l'étude de la Chine moderne et contemporaine, 1)
Subj 14 14.1 ▪ 16 22 34.1

12381 CSU U P7 G1.2 –1972
Chen, Nai-ruenn (Ch'en Nai-jun), 1927–.
Review of *Agricultural development in China, 1368–1968*, by Dwight Heald Perkins.
EDCC 20, 2 (Jan. 1972), 359–364.
Subj 14.1

12382 CSU P P8 G2.0 1911–1972
Chen, Nai-ruenn (Ch'en Nai-jun), 1927–.
'Agricultural productivity in a newly settled region: The case of Manchuria.'
EDCC 21, 1 (Oct. 1972), 87–95.
Subj 14.1 ▪ 21.2

12383 CSH P P2 G1.5 1928–1972
Chinese-American Joint Commission on Rural Reconstruction.
Joint Commission on Rural Reconstruction General Reports, No. 1, 1 Oct. 1948 to 15 Feb. 1950. [Issues for 1951–1965 are entered as 16798.]
Taipei: Chinese-American Joint Commission on Rural Reconstruction, 1950. 214 p.
Subj 14.1 ▪ 12 14.6 17 22 24.4 34.1 36.3 56

12384 MAM P P2 G1.2 1928–1972
Currie, Blair Crosby, 1930–.
Agricultural output and consumption in Mainland China, 1929–33 and 1957.
Ann Arbor: University Microfilms (Publ. 70-2856), 1970. 17, 645 p. (Doctoral dissertation in Economics, U. of Rochester, 1969)
Subj 14.1 14.3 ▪ 11 14 14.6 18

12385 DLC P P8 G1.3 1928–1972
Dapčević-Oreščanin, Sonja, et al.
'Agrarna reforma u Kini' (Land reform in China).
DB 4, 6/7 (1955), 43–62. [Special issue: *Savremena Kina* (Contemporary China)]
Subj 14.1 16 16.3 ▪ 12.2 14.5

12386 CSU P P2 G1.2 1928–1972
Dawson, Owen Lafayette, 1892–.
Communist China's agriculture: Its development and future potential.
Washington, D.C.: U.S. Dept. of State, Office of External Research, 1968. 357 p. [Reprinted—New York: Praeger, 1970. 17, 326 p.]
Subj 14.1 ▪ 12 14.4 16.3 18 24.4 36.1 55 62

12387 NNC PO P8 G1.2 1911–1972
Deliusin, Lev Petrovich, 1923–.
Bor'ba Kommunisticheskoi partii Kitaia za razreshenie agrarnogo voprosa (The Chinese Communist Party's struggle to solve the land problem).
Moscow: Nauka, 1964. 183 p.
Subj 14.1 32 ▪ 12.2 16.1 16.3 19 28 32.2 36.3

12388 MCH O P7 G1.2 1928–1972
Dumont, René, 1904–.
'Réforme agraire et collectivisation accélérée' (Agrarian reform and accelerated collectivization).
Esprit 24, 234 (jan. 1956), 32–54.
Subj 14.1 34.1 ▪ 14.5 16.3

12389 CBU P P8 G1.3 1928–1972
Gray, Jack Douglas, 1916–.
'Political aspects of the land reform campaigns in China, 1947–1952.'
Soviet studies 16, 2 (Oct. 1964), 209–231.
Subj 14.1 16.1 16.3 22 ▪ 18

12390 CSU P P2 G1.1 1842–1972
Harler, Campbell R-.
'Tea in China.' In *The culture and marketing of tea*, 3rd ed., by C. R. Harler. [Sole entry]
London: Oxford U. Press, 1964, 95–108.
Subj 14.1 ▪ 14.3 14.4

12391 MCH P P7 G1.2 1928–1972
Harmel, Claude.
'Les révolutions agraires en Chine' (Agrarian revolutions in China).
Est et Ouest nouvelle (2e) série 12, 232/233 (mars 1960), 54–78.
SUBJ 14.1 22 32 34.1 36.3 ▪ 16.1 16.3 32.1 32.2 55 64

12392 NIC P P7 G1.2 1911–1972
Ho, Franklin L. (Ho Lien), 1897–.
'The land problem of China.'
AAAPSS 276 (July 1951), 6–11.
SUBJ 14.1 16.3 ▪ 11.3 16 18

12393 DLC P P8 G1.2 1911–1972
Kautsky, Pravoslav.
'Čínské zemědělstvi na začátku přechodného období' (Chinese agriculture at the beginning of the transitional period).
Politicka ekonomie (Prague) 2, 4 (1954), 238–253.
SUBJ 14.1 16.3 ▪ 34.1

12394 NNC P P7 G1.1 1911–1972
Kindermann, Gottfried-Karl, 1926–.
'Agrarrevolution und Agrarreform als Alternativen der Selbstentwicklung: Die Entwicklungstheorien des Sunyatsenismus und des chinesischen Kommunismus' (Agrarian revolution and agrarian reform as alternative forms of self-development: The developmental theories of Sun Yat-sen and the Chinese Communists). In *Kulturen im Umbruch* (Cultures in upheaval), edited by G.-K. Kindermann. [Sole entry]
Freiburg i. Br.: Rombach, 1962, 65–181.
SUBJ 14.1 34.1 36.3 ▪ 18 19 61 64 72

12395 NNC P P2 G1.2 1928–1972
Klatt, Werner, 1904–.
'The pattern of Communist China's agricultural policy.' In *The Chinese model: A political, economic and social survey*, edited by W. Klatt. [Selective entry]
Hong Kong: Hong Kong U. Press, 1965, 94–116.
SUBJ 14 14.1 ▪ 12.1 16.3 18

12396 CSH P P8 G1.2 1928–1972
Klein, Sidney, 1923–.
'Communist China.' In *The pattern of land tenure reform in East Asia after World War II*, by S. Klein. [Selective entry]
New York: Bookman Associates, 1958, 134–188. (Revision of doctoral dissertation in Economics, Columbia U., 1957)
SUBJ 12.2 14.1 ▪ 12.1 14.5 16.1 16.3 34.1 36.3 72

12397 MCH S P7 G1.2 1928–1972
Kolb, Albert, 1906–.
'Die Landwirtschaft im alten und im neuen China' (Agriculture in traditional China and New China). In *Studien zur Entwicklung in Südost- und Ostasien* (Studies on the development of Southeast and East Asia), by T- H- Silcock et al. [Sole entry]
Frankfurt a.M.: Metzner, 1962, 75–101. (Institut für Asienkunde, Schriften, 11)
SUBJ 14.1 34.1 ▪ 16.3 19

12398 NNC P P8 G1.2 1928–1972
Kovalev, Evgenii Fedorovich, 1907–.
'Agrarnaia politika Kommunisticheskoi partii Kitaia' (The land policy of the Chinese Communist Party).
UZIV 2 (1951), 116–143.
SUBJ 14 14.1 45 ▪ 16.1 16.3 32.2

12399 DLC FP P8 G1.2 –1972
Kovda, Viktor Abramovich.
Ocherki prirody i pochv Kitaia.
Moscow: Izd-vo Akad. nauk SSSR, 1959. 455 p.

Soils and natural environment of China, mimeo.
Washington, D.C.: U.S. Joint Publications Research Service, 1960. 736 p. (JPRS 5967; MC 990/1961) [Xerox copyflo available—New York: CCM Information Corp., Research and Microfilm Publications. (Scholarly Book Translation Series, 510)]
SUBJ 11.3 14.1

12400 NNC P P7 G1.2 1928–1972
[La Dany, Ladislao] ———, 1914–.
'Draught animals.'
CNA 109 (18 Nov. 1955), 2–7.
SUBJ 14.1 24.1 ▪ 14.3 24.3 34.1

12401 ICU P P7 G1.1 1911–1972
Lien, Chan, 1936–.
Agrarian reform in Nationalist China.
Unpublished masters thesis in Political Science, U. of Chicago, 1961. 203 p.
SUBJ 12.1 14.1 16.3 ▪ 11.3 36.3

12402 NIC S P8 G1.2 1928–1972
Liu, Ta-chung, 1914–, Chong Twanmo (Tuan-mu Chung), and K. C. Yeh (Yeh K'ung-chia), 1924–.
Production of food crops on the Chinese mainland: Prewar and postwar.
Santa Monica, Calif.: RAND Corp., 1964. 11, 56 p. (RAND memoranda, RM-3569-PR)
SUBJ 14.1 18 ▪ 55

12403 CBU P P7 G1.2 1911–1972
Marchisio, Hélène.
'Réforme agraire et organisations coopératives en Chine de 1927 à 1952' (Agrarian reform and cooperative organizations in China from 1927 to 1952).
Archives internationales de sociologie de la coopération et du développement 22 (juil.–déc. 1967), 138–193.
SUBJ 14.1 16.3 34.1 36.3 ▪ 27 32.2 37

12404 MCH S P8 G1.2 –1972
Münnich, Horst.
'Die geographischen Auswirkungen der Bodenreform in China' (Geographic effects of the land reform in China).
PGM 98, 4 (1954), 266–268.
SUBJ 14.1 ▪ 45

12405 CSU P P2 G1.2 1895–1972
Muramatsu, Yuji (Muramatsu Yūji), 1911–.
'The land problem in the modernization of China.' Tr. of 'Chūgoku kindaika no tochi mondai'; *Rekishi kyōiku* new (2nd) series 13, 12 (Dec. 1965), 1–12.
Acta Asiatica (Tokyo) 12 (Mar. 1967), 29–41.
SUBJ 14.1 16.1 ▪ 22 22.2 26.1

12406 CSH P P8 G2.0 1928–1972
Myers, Ramon Hawley, 1929–.
'Agriculture.' In *A regional handbook on Northeast China*, compiled by Far Eastern and Russian Institute, U. of Washington. [Selective entry]
New Haven: Human Relations Area Files, 1956, 456–495. (HRAF subcontractor's monographs, 61; Washington 9)
SUBJ 14.1 ▪ 18 34.1

12407 CSH S P8 G3.0 1911–1972
Myers, Ramon Hawley, 1929–.
'Agriculture and animal husbandry.' In *A regional handbook on the Inner Mongolia Autonomous Region*, compiled by Far Eastern and Russian Institute, U. of Washington. [Selective entry]
New Haven: Human Relations Area Files, 1956, 500–529. (HRAF subcontractor's monographs, 60; Washington 7)
SUBJ 14.1 ▪ 34.1

12408 CSU P P2 G1.1 1895–1972
Myers, Ramon Hawley, 1929–.
'The commercialization of agriculture in modern China.' In *Economic organization in Chinese society*, edited by William Earl Willmott. [Selective entry]
Stanford: Stanford U. Press, 1972, 173–191.
SUBJ 14.1 14.3 24.3

12409 CSH P P7 G1.1 1911–1972
Myers, Ramon Hawley, 1929–.
'Rural institutions and their influence upon agricultural development in modern China and Taiwan.'
J. of the Institute of Chinese Studies of the Chinese U. of Hong Kong 2, 2 (Sept. 1969), 349–368.
SUBJ 14.1 45 ▪ 24.6 34.2

12410 WSU S P2 G1.2 1895–1972
Myers, Ramon Hawley, 1929–.
'Theories on modern China's agrarian problem.'
CCJ 6, 2 (May 1967), 210–222.
SUBJ 14 14.1 ▪ 11.1 70 71

12411 MCH P P8 G1.3 1842–1972
Ohanjanian, A-.
'Taiping agrarian policy: Some Chinese and Soviet views.'
PA 39, 1/2 (Spring–Summer 1966), 128–134.
SUBJ 14.1 62 70 71 ▪ 15 32.2

12412 NNC P P7 G1.2 1928–1972
Ong, Shao-er (Weng Shao-erh), 1917–.
Agrarian reform in Communist China to 1952.
Lackland Air Force Base, San Antonio, Tex.: U.S. Air Force Personnel and Training Research Center, Air Research and Development Command, 1955. 18, 61 p. (U.S. Human Resources Research Institute research memoranda, 41; Studies in Chinese Communism, series 1, 2, 1952)
SUBJ 14.1 16.3 ▪ 12.1 14.5 16 19 25 36.3

12413 MCH P P7 G1.2 1911–1972
Overdijkink, Gerrit Willem, 1905–.
'De agrarische revolutie in China' (The agrarian revolution in China).

Internationale spectator 8, 3 (8 Februari 1954), 81–95; 8, 5 (8 Maart 1954), 215–230.
Subj 14.1 36.3 ▪ 16.3 34.1

12414 CSU P P2 G1.2 –1972
Perkins, Dwight Heald, 1934–.
Agricultural development in China, 1368–1968.
Chicago: Aldine, 1969. 15, 395 p.
Subj 11.1 14.1 14.3 ▪ 11 12 14.2 14.4 16.1 18 21 24.3

12415 CSU P P2 G1.2 1928–1972
Phillips, Ralph Wesley, 1909–, and Leslie T. C. Kuo (Kuo Tse-ch'iu), 1914–.
'Agricultural science.' In *Sciences in Communist China*, edited by [Sydney Henry Gould] Sidney H. Gould. [Selective entry]
Washington, D.C.: American Assn. for the Advancement of Science, 1961, 227–296. (AAAS publications, 68)
Subj 11.4 14.1 62 ▪ 11.3 12 17 34.1 36.1

12416 CSU U P2 G1.1 1928–1972
Rawson, Robert Rees.
'China.' In *The monsoon lands of Asia*, by R. R. Rawson. [Sole entry]
London: Hutchinson, 1963, 164–202.
Subj 11.3 14.1 ▪ 11 14.2 14.4

12417 MCH S P2 G1.1 1928–1972
Robinson, H-.
'The Chinese fishing industry.'
Geography 41, 193 (July 1956), 158–166.
Subj 14.1 ▪ 14.3

12418 NNC FP P7 G1.2 1928–1972
Skinner, George William, 1925–.
'Peasant organization in rural China.'
AAAPSS 277 (Sept. 1951), 89–100. [Special issue: *Report on China*, edited by Harold Arthur Steiner]
Subj 14.1 22.1 32.1 36.3 ▪ 22 25 26 34.1

12419 CBU P P7 G1.2 1928–1972
Su Hsing.
'The two-way struggle between socialism and capitalism in China's rural areas after the land reform.' Tr. of 'T'u ti kai ko i hou, wo kuo nung ts'un she hui chu i ho tzu pen chu i liang tiao tao lu ti tou cheng' (The struggle between the two roads of socialism and capitalism in rural China following the land reform); *Ching chi yen chiu* (Peking) 1965, 7 (July), 12–26; 1965, 8 (Aug.), 1–13; 1965, 9 (Sept.), 14–25.
CES 1, 4 (Summer 1968), 3–35; 2, 1 (Fall 1968), 3–31; 2, 2 (Winter 1968/69), 50–80.
Subj 14.1 16.3 18 ▪ 12.1 14.5 14.6 24.4 34.1 55

12420 MAU P P7 G6.0 1911–1972
Sullivan, Joseph James, 1928–.
The Huai river projects: A regional study of economic development in Communist China.
Unpublished masters thesis in Far Eastern Studies, U. of Michigan, 1957. 91 p.
Subj 14 14.1 21.4 ▪ 11.3 14.2 14.6 18

12421 CSU O P7 G1.4 1928–1972
Teng Tse-hui (Teng Tzu-hui), 1895–.
Report on the multiple-purpose plan for permanently controlling the Yellow River and exploiting its water resources.
Peking: Foreign Languages Press, 1955. 49 p.
Subj 11.4 14.1

12422 CSU S P7 G1.2 1928–1972
Wiens, Herold Jacob, 1912–1971.
'China: Agriculture and food supply.' In *The pattern of Asia*, edited by Norton Sydney Ginsburg. [Selective entry]
Englewood Cliffs, N.J.: Prentice-Hall, 1958, 168–189.
Subj 14.1 14.3 ▪ 11.3 24.4 29 34.1

12423 CSU U P7 G1.2 –1972
Wittfogel, Karl August, 1896–.
Agriculture: A key to the understanding of Chinese society, past and present.
Canberra: Australian National U. Press, 1970. 20 p. (George Ernest Morrison lectures in ethnology, 31)
Subj 11.4 14.1 18

12424 ELS P P7 G1.2 1928–1972
Wong, Chiu Hon John.
A study of Communist land reform in post-war China, with special reference to its policy and implementation.
Unpublished doctoral dissertation in Economics, U. of London [University College], 1966. 430 p.
Subj 14.1 16.3 34.1 ▪ 16 18 22 36.3 64

12425 CSU P P8 G1.2 –1972
Yamamoto, Hideo, 1911–.
'On the evolution of the Chinese model of agrarian technology.'
DE 9, 4 (Dec. 1971), 449–474. [Special issue: *On China*]
Subj 14.1 ▪ 11.4 16.3 34.1

12426 MCH P P7 G1.2 1928–1972
Zao, Paul Koé-tseng.
La réforme agraire en Chine communiste (Agrarian reform in Communist China).
Louvian: Ancienne Lib. Desbarax, 1964. 333 p. (Université catholique de Louvain, Faculté des sciences économiques et sociales, Collection de l'Ecole des sciences économiques, 92)
Subj 14 14.1 22 22.1 34.1 ▪ 12.2 14.5 16.3 18 19 32.2 36.3 58 72

1949-1972

12427 MCH P P7 G1.2 1949–1972
'L'agriculture chinoise (1949–1960)' (Agriculture in China, 1949–1960).
NED 2848 (6 jan. 1962), 1–24; 2849 (10 jan. 1962), 1–42; 2850 (13 jan. 1962), 1–46.
Subj 14.1 18 ▪ 14.6 22 24.4 27 40 62

12428 CSU P P2 G9.0 1949–1972
Ajia keizai kenkyūjo (Institute of Asian Economic Affairs).
Intra-regional cooperation and aid in Asian countries.
Tokyo: Institute of Asian Economic Affairs, 1968. 23, 158 p.
Subj 14.1 ▪ 14.4 18

12429 CSH P P7 G1.2 1949–1972
Asakawa Kenji, 1909–.
Four reforms in agriculture, mimeo. Tr. of 'Chūgoku nōgyō no shika' (Four reforms in Chinese agriculture); *Chūgoku kenkyū geppō* 154 (Dec. 1960), 1–34.
Washington, D.C.: U.S. Joint Publications Research Service, 5 May 1961. 97 p. (JPRS 9209; MC 15,380/1961)
Subj 14.1 34.1 ▪ 22.1 24.4 27 62

12430 CSU P P7 G1.2 1949–1972
Bardhan, Pranab K-.
'Chinese and Indian agriculture: A broad comparison of recent policy and performance.'
JAS 29, 3 (May 1970), 515–537.
Subj 14.1 ▪ 14.3 18 34.1

12431 MCH O P2 G1.2 1949–1972
Bartoli, Henri, 1918–.
'Révolution dans l'économie chinoise. 1, les bases d'une civilisation nouvelle. 2, vers quelle civilisation?' (Revolution in China's economy. 1, The bases of a new civilization. 2, Toward what kind of civilization?).
Esprit 27, 269 (jan. 1959), 162–182; 27, 270 (fév. 1959), 246–271.
Subj 11.4 14.1 14.4 18 58 ▪ 17 19 22 55 64 66

12432 CSU S P5 G1.2 1949–1972
Bouchard, Loyal G-.
'Fisheries of Communist China.' In *An economic profile of Mainland China*, compiled by Joint Economic Committee, U.S. Congress. [Selective entry]
Washington, D.C.: U.S. Government Printing Office, 1967, vol. 1, 317–322. [Reprinted in *An economic profile of Mainland China*, compiled by the agency cited. (Selective entry.) New York: Praeger, 1968, 317–322.]
Subj 14.1

12433 DLC O P7 G1.2 1949–1972
Brauner, Ivan.
'Živočíšna výroba v Číné' (Animal production in China).
Naša veda (Bratislava) 3, 12 (1956), 542–548.
Subj 14.1

12434 CSU F P2 G1.2 1949–1972
Buchanan, Keith McPherson, 1919–.
The transformation of the Chinese earth: Aspects of the evaluation of the Chinese earth from earliest times to Mao Tse-tung.
New York: Praeger, 1970. 17, 336 p.
Subj 11.3 14 14.1 18 20 ▪ 11 14.2 14.4 17 21 21.1 21.3 24.4 29

12435 MCH FP P1 G1.2 1949–1972
Buck, John Lossing, 1890–.
'Reliability of Communist China's data on food grain production.'
CS 3, 14 (1 Mar. 1965), 1–13.
Subj 14.1

12436 NIC P P7 G1.2 1949–1972
Carin, Robert.
Irrigation scheme in Communist China, mimeo.
Hong Kong: Union Research Institute, 1963. 266, 65 & 31 p. (Communist China problem research series, EC33)
Subj 14.1 ▪ 12.1 18

12437 CSH U P7 G1.5 1949–1972
Chang Hsin-i.
'Further development of green fertilizer production in the south.' Tr. of 'Chin i pu fa chan wo kuo nan fang ti lü fei sheng ch'an'; *Hung ch'i* 1962, 18,

19–29. In *Translations from 'Hung-ch'i' (Red flag) No. 18, 1962*, mimeo., compiled by U.S. Joint Publications Research Service. [Sole entry]
Washington, D.C.: JPRS, 17 Oct. 1962, 50–78. (JPRS 15,745; MC 22,368/1962)
SUBJ 14.1

12438 CSU P P7 G1.2 1949–1972
Chang, Sen-dou (Chang Sheng-tao), 1928–.
'China's crop-land use, 1957.'
Pacific viewpoint 12, 1 (May 1971), 75–87.
SUBJ 14.1

12439 MCH P P8 G1.1 1949–1972
Chang, Tsung-tung, 1931–.
Die Entwicklung der festland-chinesischen Landwirtschaft aus der Sicht der chinesischen Regierung (The development of Mainland Chinese agriculture from the point of view of the Chinese government).
Cologne: Westdeutscher Verlag, 1961. 118 p. (Forschungsinstitut für internationale technische Zusammenarbeit an der Technische Hochschule Aachen, Forschungsberichte des Landes Nordrhein-Westfalen, 936)
SUBJ 14.1 16.3 34.1 ▪ 12.1 14 14.6 18 64

12440 GBF PO P7 G1.2 1949–1972
Chao, Joseph (Chao Chen-chiang), 1929–.
Die Reorganisation der chinesischen Landwirtschaft (The reorganization of Chinese agriculture).
Cologne: The author, 1962. 226 p. (Doctoral dissertation, Wirtschafts- und sozialwissenschaftliche Fakultät, Universität Köln)
SUBJ 14.1 19 ▪ 12.2 22 34.1

12441 CSU P P2 G1.2 1949–1972
Chao, Kang, 1929–.
Agricultural production in Communist China, 1949–1965.
Madison: U. of Wisconsin Press, 1970. 15, 357 p.
SUBJ 14.1 20 34.1 ▪ 14.4 14.6 17 22 32.1 64

12442 NNC P P7 G1.2 1949–1972
Chao, Kuo-chün, 1918–1962.
Agrarian policies of Mainland China: A documentary study, 1949–1956.
Cambridge: Harvard U., East Asian Research Center, 1957. 13, 276 p. (Harvard East Asian monographs, 4)
SUBJ 14.1 14.3 14.5 24.3 34.2 ▪ 16.1 16.3 22 32.1 36.3 45

12443 MCH P P7 G1.2 1949–1972
Chao, Kuo-chün, 1918–1962.
'Agricultural development and problems in China today.'
India q. 14, 1 (Jan.–Mar. 1958), 3–42.
SUBJ 12.1 14.1 34.1 ▪ 14.5 18

12444 MCY P P7 G1.2 1949–1972
Chao, Kuo-chün, 1918–1962.
'Agricultural production in Mainland China.' In *Contemporary China, 1956–1957*, edited by Edward Stuart Kirby. [Selective entry]
Hong Kong: Hong Kong U. Press, 1958, 11–35.
SUBJ 14 14.1

12445 DLC O P7 G1.2 1949–1972
Chen Shao-diun (Ch'eng Shao-chiung), 1901–, and A- A- Alenkovich.
'Organizatsiia veterinarnoi sluzhby v KNR' (The organization of veterinary service in the People's Republic of China).
Veterinariia 36, 10 (oktiabr' 1959), 70–77.
SUBJ 14 14.1 34.1 ▪ 14.2 17

12446 MCY P P7 G1.2 1949–1972
Cheng Hsueh-chia (Cheng Hsüeh-chia), 1906–.
Hunger in Communist China: An estimate of 1961 food production.
Taipei: Asian Peoples' Anti-Communist League, 1962. 80 p. (APACL pamphlets, 69)
SUBJ 14.1 ▪ 12.1

12447 CSU P P2 G1.2 1949–1972
Cheng, Tien-hsi (Cheng T'ien-hsi), 1912–.
'Zoological sciences since 1949.' In *Sciences in Communist China*, edited by [Sydney Henry Gould] Sidney H. Gould. [Selective entry]
Washington, D.C.: American Assn. for the Advancement of Science, 1961, 197–226. (AAAS publications, 68)
SUBJ 14.1 ▪ 18 36.1 56 62

12448 MCY P P7 G1.2 1949–1972
Chi, Wen-shun (Chi Wen-hsün), 1910–.
'Water conservancy in Communist China.'
CQ 23 (July–Sept. 1965), 37–54.
SUBJ 11.4 14.1 ▪ 18

12449 CSU P P2 G1.2 1949–1972
Chin, Steve S. K. (Chin Ssu-k'ai), 1919–, and William Wing-fai Choa (Ts'ai Yung-hui).
'The mechanization of agriculture.' In *Contemporary China, 1962–1964*, edited by Edward Stuart Kirby. [Selective entry]
Hong Kong: Hong Kong U. Press, 1968, 1–10.
SUBJ 14 14.1 14.4 ▪ 14.2

12450 NNC P P8 G1.2 1949–1972
Chou, Ya-lun, 1922–.
'Chinese agrarian reform and Bolshevik land policy.'
PA 25, 1 (Mar. 1952), 24–39.
SUBJ 14.1 ▪ 16.3

12451 MCH O P7 G1.2 1949–1972
Clairmonte, Frédérick F-.
'The Chinese and Indian land problem: Divergent approaches.'
Malayan economic review 5, 1 (Apr. 1960), 52–65.
SUBJ 14.1 16.3 34.1 ▪ 14 14.5 18

12452 MCH P P7 G1.2 1949–1972
Close, Alexandra.
'Down to earth.'
FEER 54, 10 (8 Dec. 1966), 517–522.
SUBJ 14.1 ▪ 16.3 22

12453 NNC P P7 G1.2 1949–1972
Cook, Richard H-.
Chinese agrarian policy, 1949–1954, in the Chinese and Soviet interpretations.
Unpublished masters thesis in Public Law and Government, Columbia U., 1954. 95 p. [Certificate essay, East Asian Institute]
SUBJ 12.1 14.1 ▪ 16.3 34.1

12454 CSH S P8 G1.2 1949–1972
Dawson, Owen Lafayette, 1892–.
'Fertilizer supply and food requirements.' In *Food and agriculture in Communist China*, by John Lossing Buck et al. [Analytic entry]
New York: Praeger, 1966, 101–148.
SUBJ 14.1 ▪ 14.4

12455 CSH P P8 G1.2 1949–1972
Dawson, Owen Lafayette, 1892–.
'Irrigation developments under the Communist regime.' In *Food and agriculture in Communist China*, by John Lossing Buck et al. [Analytic entry]
New York: Praeger, 1966, 149–168.
SUBJ 14.1

12456 MCH PO P8 G1.2 1949–1972
Deliusin, Lev Petrovich, 1923–.
Zemlia tomu, kto ee obrabatyvaet (Land to the tiller).
Moscow: Izd-vo vost. lit-ry, 1961. 117 p.
SUBJ 14.1 16.3 34.1 ▪ 12.1 16 45

12457 CBU P P2 G1.2 1949–1972
Donnithorne, Audrey Gladys, 1922–.
'China's grain: Output, procurement, transfers and trade.'
RSAEO 1970, 1, 19–57. [Separately reprinted—Hong Kong: Chinese U. of Hong Kong, Economic Research Centre, 1970. 36 p.]
SUBJ 14 14.1 14.3 ▪ 18

12458 MCH O P7 G1.2 1949–1972
Dresch, Jean.
'L'agriculture en Chine' (Agriculture in China).
Confluent nouvelle (2e) série 5 (fév. 1960), 94–107.
SUBJ 14.1 18 34.1 ▪ 16.3 22.1 24.4 36.3 62

12459 NNC PO P7 G1.2 1949–1972
Dumont, René, 1904–.
'Les transformations agraires' (Agricultural transformations). In *Le régime et les institutions de la République populaire chinoise* (The government and institutions of the People's Republic of China), jointly edited by Centre d'étude des pays de l'Est, Institut de sociologie Solvay, Université libre de Bruxelles *with* Centre national pour l'étude des pays à régime communiste. [Selective entry]
Brussels: Snoeck-Ducaju, 1960, 23–38.
SUBJ 14.1 34.1 ▪ 14.5 16.3 22

12460 MMT P P2 G1.2 1949–1972
Emery, Robert Firestone, 1927–.
'Recent economic developments in Communist China.'
AS 6, 6 (June 1966), 303–309.
SUBJ 14 14.1 ▪ 14.4 18

12461 CSU O P7 G1.1 1949–1972
Epstein, Hellmut, 1903–.
Domestic animals of China.
Farnham Royal, Eng.: Commonwealth Agricultural Bureaux, 1969. 17, 166 p.
SUBJ 14.1 ▪ 55

12462 CSU P P7 G1.2 1949–1972
Erisman, Alva Lewis, 1930–.
'China: Agricultural development, 1949–71.' In *People's Republic of China: An economic assessment*, compiled by Joint Economic Committee, U.S. Congress. [Selective entry]

Washington, D.C.: U.S. Government Printing Office, 1972, 112–146.
Subj 14.1 ▪ 14.4 34.1

12463 MAM P P8 G1.4 1949–1972
Erisman, Alva Lewis, 1930–.
Potential costs of and benefits from diverting river flow for irrigation in the North China plain.
Ann Arbor: University Microfilms (Publ. 68-3357), 1968. 282 p. (Doctoral dissertation in Economics, U. of Maryland, 1967)
Subj 14.1 18

12464 GFU P P8 G1.2 1949–1972
Feng, Jordan P., 1927–.
Die Taktik und die Tendenzen der kommunistischen Agrarrevolution in China (The Communist agrarian revolution in China: Tactics and tendencies).
Freiburg i. Br.: The author, 1960. 167 p. (Doctoral dissertation, Philosophische Fakultät, Universität Freiburg i. Br.)
Subj 14.1 34.1 ▪ 12.1 36.3

12465 CSU S P7 G1.2 1949–1972
Field, Robert Michael, 1928–.
'Chinese grain production: Questions raised by the Swamy-Burki series.'
CQ 46 (Apr.–June 1971), 350–353. [See also entry 12545.]
Subj 14.1 18

12466 CSU S P7 G1.2 1949–1972
Field, Robert Michael, 1928–.
'How much grain does Communist China produce?'
CQ 33 (Jan.–Mar. 1968), 98–107.
Subj 14.1

12467 MCH P P7 G1.2 1949–1972
Fukushima Yutaka, 1926–.
Japanese analysis on communes and agricultural mechanization in Communist China, mimeo. Tr. of 'Jimmin kōsha to nōgyō kikaika' (Communes and agricultural mechanization); *Chūgoku shiryō geppō* 144 (Feb. 1960), 1–35.
Washington, D.C.: U.S. Joint Publications Research Service, 17 Aug. 1960. 43 p. (JPRS 3692; MC 15,607/1960)
Subj 14.1 16.3 34.1 ▪ 18 64

12468 CSU P P2 G1.2 1949–1972
Ganguli, Birendranath N-, 1902–.
'An analysis of New China's agrarian reform law.'
Indian economic review 1, 3 (Feb. 1953), 14–32. [Reprinted in *Land reform in New China*, by B. N. Ganguli. (Analytic entry.) Delhi: Ranjit, 1954, 5–35.]
Subj 12.2 14.1 16 ▪ 14.5 16.3

12469 FPN P P8 G1.4 1949–1972
Gentelle, Pierre.
L'irrigation en Chine aride depuis 1949 (Irrigation in China's arid regions since 1949).
Unpublished doctoral dissertation, Faculté des lettres, Université de Paris, 1965. 305 p.
Subj 14.1 ▪ 11.3 14.6 21.4

12470 MCH P P8 G1.2 1949–1972
Giorgi, Giacomo.
'La riforma agraria in Cina' (Land reform in China).
Cina 1 (1956), 149–167.
Subj 14.1 ▪ 12.1 14.6

12471 CSH P P2 G1.2 1949–1972
Ho Chu-fan (Ho Chü-fan).
'Food problem of the Peiping regime.'
IS 2, 12 (Sept. 1966), 25–35.
Subj 14.1 14.3

12472 NNC P P2 G1.2 1949–1972
Hofmann, Werner.
'China und die Sowjetordnung: Zur Frage des "chinesischen Weges"' (China and the Soviet order: The question of the 'Chinese way' [to socialism]).
SJ 76, 2 (1956), 71–84.
Subj 14 14.1 19 ▪ 12.1 14.4 16 34.1 64

12473 CSU P P7 G1.2 1949–1972
Hou, Chi-ming, 1924–.
'Sources of agricultural growth in Communist China.'
JAS 27, 4 (Aug. 1968), 721–737.
Subj 14.1 ▪ 16.3 34.1

12474 CSH P P2 G1.2 1949–1972
Hsiao Chi-jung, 1892–.
'A comprehensive study of food production in Mainland China.'
IS 4, 4 (Jan. 1968), 25–34; 4, 5 (Feb. 1968), 30–36.
Subj 14.1 14.3 ▪ 11 21.1

12475 CSU PO P2 G1.2 1949–1972
India. Ministry of Food and Agriculture.
Report of the Indian delegation to China on agricultural planning and techniques.
Delhi: Manager of Publications, 1956. 199 p.
Subj 12 14 14.1 14.4 34.1 34.2 ▪ 14.5 17 19 22 24.1 24.3 24.4 26.2 28

12476 CSU P P7 G1.2 1949–1972
Ishikawa Shigeru, 1918–.
'Changes in the structure of agricultural production in Mainland China' [with comments by Ernst Hagemann]. In *Agrarian policies and problems in Communist and non-Communist countries*, edited by William Arthur Douglas Jackson. [Selective entry]
Seattle: U. of Washington Press, 1971, 346–380.
Subj 14.1

12477 MCH P P7 G1.2 1949–1972
Khambadkone, M- V-.
'Agrarian reforms and institutional changes in China.'
United Asia 8, 5 (Oct.–Nov. 1956), 362–368.
Subj 14.1 34.1 ▪ 32.1 36.3

12478 CSH P P2 G1.1 1949–1972
King Shu-jen.
'Cotton production in Mainland China.'
IS 3, 8 (May 1967), 24–38.
Subj 14.1 ▪ 14.3 14.4

12479 CSU U P2 G1.2 1949–1972
Kirby, Edward Stuart, 1909–.
'Agrarian problems and the peasantry.' In *Communist China, 1949–1969: A twenty-year appraisal*, edited by Frank Newton Trager and William Henderson. [Selective entry]
New York: New York U. Press, 1970, 153–174.
Subj 14.1 16.3 ▪ 11 12.1 14 18 34.1

12480 CSH P P2 G1.2 1949–1972
[Klatt, Werner?] W. K., 1904–.
'Communist China's agricultural calamities.'
CQ 6 (Apr.–June 1961), 64–75. [Reprinted in *China under Mao: Politics takes command*, edited by Roderick Lemonde MacFarquhar. (Selective entry.) Cambridge: M.I.T. Press, 1966, 163–174.]
Subj 14.1 18 ▪ 14.3 34.1 36.3

12481 MCH S P8 G1.2 1949–1972
Klein, Sidney, 1923–.
'Land problem and economic growth in India and China: Another view.'
Malayan economic review 5, 2 (Oct. 1960), 66–80.
Subj 14.1 ▪ 64

12482 CSU P P2 G1.2 1949–1972
Kojima, Reiitsu.
'Development of the ideas of the Great Leap Forward after the Cultural Revolution.'
DE 9, 4 (Dec. 1971), 577–597. [Special issue: *On China*]
Subj 14.1 24.4 ▪ 14.3 16.3 34.1

12483 NNC P P8 G1.2 1949–1972
Korkunov, Igor' Nikolaevich, 1924–.
'Zemel'nyi fond i ego ispol'zovanie v Kitaiskoi Narodnoi Respublike' (Land resources and their utilization in the People's Republic of China).
KSINA 59 (1962), 3–14.
Subj 14.1 34.1 ▪ 14 16.3

12484 MCH P P8 G1.2 1949–1972
Kung Mien-jen.
'Agricultural production in Communist China.' Tr. of 'Shih nien lai ti Chung kung nung yeh sheng ch'an' (Agricultural production in Communist China during the past decade); *Tsu kuo chou k'an* 383 (9 May 1960), 13–17. In *Communist China, 1949–1959*, edited by Union Research Institute. [Selective entry]
Hong Kong: Union Research Institute, 1961, vol. 1, 91–115.
Subj 14.1 ▪ 14 34.1

12485 CSU P P2 G1.2 1949–1972
Kuo, Leslie T. C. (Kuo Tse-ch'iu), 1914–.
The technical transformation of agriculture in Communist China.
New York: Praeger, 1972. 20, 266 p.
Subj 14.1 ▪ 12 14.4 18 22 24.4 27 32.1 34.1 36.1

12486 NNC P P2 G1.2 1949–1972
Kurbatov, V- P-.
'Nekotorye voprosy mekhanizatsii sel'skogo khoziaistva Kitaia' (The mechanization of Chinese agriculture).
SK 1958, 2, 43–58.
Subj 14.1 14.4 34.1 ▪ 11.3 14.2 14.3

12487 DNA PO P7 G1.2 1949–1972
Kuznetsov, A- V-, and E- N- Sagapovich.
Ovoshchevodstvo v Kitae (Vegetable production in China).
Moscow: Gossel'khozizdat, 1959. 359 p.
Subj 14.1 ▪ 24.3 34.1

12488 CSH P P7 G1.2 1949–1972
[La Dany, Ladislao] ———, 1914–.
'Agricultural performance.'
CNA 898 (20 Oct. 1972), 1–7.
Subj 14.1 16.3

12489 NIC P P7 G1.2 1949–1972
[La Dany, Ladislao] ———, 1914–.
'Agriculture: Causes of decline.'
CNA 413 (23 Mar. 1962), 1–7; 415 (6 Apr. 1962), 1–7.
SUBJ 14.1 ▪ 12.1 16.3

12490 CSH P P7 G1.2 1949–1972
[La Dany, Ladislao] ———, 1914–.
'Agriculture, 1967.'
CNA 691 (12 Jan. 1968), 1–7.
SUBJ 14.1 ▪ 14.3 14.5

12491 CSH P P7 G1.2 1949–1972
[La Dany, Ladislao] ———, 1914–.
'Agriculture, 1968.'
CNA 729 (18 Oct. 1968), 1–7.
SUBJ 14.1 ▪ 18

12492 MCH P P2 G1.2 1949–1972
[La Dany, Ladislao] ———, 1914–.
'Chemical fertilizer.'
CNA 456 (15 Feb. 1963), 1–6.
SUBJ 14.1 14.4

12493 MCH P P7 G1.2 1949–1972
[La Dany, Ladislao] ———, 1914–.
'Draught animals.'
CNA 379 (7 July 1961), 1–7.
SUBJ 14.1 ▪ 34.1

12494 NNC P P2 G1.2 1949–1972
[La Dany, Ladislao] ———, 1914–.
'The fisheries.'
CNA 243 (29 Aug. 1958), 1–7.
SUBJ 14.1 ▪ 34.1

12495 CSH P P2 G1.1 1949–1972
[La Dany, Ladislao] ———, 1914–.
'Fisheries.'
CNA 421 (18 May 1962), 1–7.
SUBJ 14.1 ▪ 14.2

12496 CSH P P7 G1.2 1949–1972
[La Dany, Ladislao] ———, 1914–.
'Good years in agriculture.'
CNA 556 (19 Mar. 1965), 1–7.
SUBJ 14.1 ▪ 16.3 18

12497 CSH P P2 G1.2 1949–1972
[La Dany, Ladislao] ———, 1914–.
'Modernization of agriculture.'
CNA 621 (22 July 1966), 1–7.
SUBJ 14.1 32.1 34.1

12498 CSH P P2 G1.2 1949–1972
[La Dany, Ladislao] ———, 1914–.
'News about the economy: A great leap in 1970?'
CNA 788 (16 Jan. 1970), 1–7.
SUBJ 14.1 ▪ 14.4 24.4

12499 MCH P P7 G1.2 1949–1972
[La Dany, Ladislao] ———, 1914–.
'Pig.'
CNA 122 (2 Mar. 1956), 2–7.
SUBJ 14.1 14.3

12500 CSH P P7 G1.2 1949–1972
[La Dany, Ladislao] ———, 1914–.
'Pigs.'
CNA 778 (17 Oct. 1969), 1–7.
SUBJ 14.1 ▪ 34.1

12501 MCH P P7 G1.2 1949–1972
[La Dany, Ladislao] ———, 1914–.
'Tea.'
CNA 276 (15 May 1959), 1–7.
SUBJ 14.1 34.1

12502 CSH P P2 G1.2 1949–1972
[La Dany, Ladislao] ———, 1914–.
'Timber.'
CNA 442 (19 Oct. 1962), 1–7.
SUBJ 14.1 14.4

12503 CSH P P8 G1.2 1949–1972
[La Dany, Ladislao] ———, 1914–.
'Vicissitudes of cotton.'
CNA 611 (13 May 1966), 1–7.
SUBJ 14.1

12504 MCH P P7 G1.2 1949–1972
[La Dany, Ladislao] ———, 1914–.
'Water conservancy, 1965–1967.'
CNA 673 (18 Aug. 1967), 1–7.
SUBJ 11.4 14.1 ▪ 21.4

12505 CSH P P8 G1.4 1949–1972
[La Dany, Ladislao] ———, 1914–.
'The Yellow River.'
CNA 478 (26 July 1963), 1–7.
SUBJ 14.1 21.4 ▪ 66

12506 CSU P P2 G1.2 1949–1972
Larsen, Marion Rosslyn, 1914–.
'China's agriculture under Communism.' In *An economic profile of Mainland China*, compiled by Joint Economic Committee, U.S. Congress. [Selective entry]
Washington, D.C.: U.S. Government Printing Office, 1967, vol. 1, 197–267. [Reprinted in *An economic profile of Mainland China*, compiled by the agency cited. (Selective entry.) New York: Praeger, 1968, 197–267.]
SUBJ 14.1 34.1 ▪ 14 17 18 55

12507 CSH P P7 G1.2 1949–1972
Li Ch'ang-yen, Lin Hua, Yang Mu-wen, and [Yang] I-fan. [Authors sequential rather than joint: Li Ch'ang-yen for 1961; Lin Hua for 1962–1965; Yang Mu-wen for 1966; Yang I-fan for 1967–1969.]
'Agriculture' [title varies]. Tr. from *Tsu kuo chou k'an* 494 (25 June 1962); 544 (10 June 1963) *and* from *Tsu kuo* 2–72 (May 1964 – Mar. 1970) [recurring annual feature article]. In *Communist China, 1961–1969*, edited by Union Research Institute.
Hong Kong: Union Research Institute. Issued annually, 1962–1970, average ca. 25 p.
SUBJ 14.1 ▪ 16.3 34.1

12508 MCY P P7 G1.2 1949–1972
Li Tien-min (Li T'ien-min).
Can agricultural crises be averted by the Chinese Communists?
Taipei: Asian Peoples' Anti-Communist League, 1963. 78 p. (APACL pamphlets, 73)
SUBJ 14.1 20

12509 WSU P P8 G1.3 1949–1972
Liang, C. S. (Liang Ch'i-shan).
'Three types of agricultural water use in the Yangtze basin.'
CCJ 5, 1 (Nov. 1965), 40–59.
SUBJ 11.3 14.1

12510 CSH P P8 G1.2 1949–1972
Liao Lu-yen, 1908?–.
'Rural class status and land reform.' In *Decisions concerning the differentiation of class status in the countryside adopted by the Government Administrative Council on Aug. 4, 1950*. [Sole entry]
[Peking?]: ——, [1950], 17–20. [Supplement to *People's China* 2, 8 (16 Oct. 1950)]
SUBJ 12.2 14.1 ▪ 16.1 16.3

12511 CBU P P7 G1.2 1949–1972
Lichnowsky, L-.
'Agricultural policy in Mainland China since 1949.'
Monthly b. of agricultural economics and statistics 11, 10 (Oct. 1962), 1–8; 11, 11 (Nov. 1962), 1–7. [Also published in French version of this journal.]
SUBJ 14 14.1 20 34.1 ▪ 14.3 14.5 16.3 24.3 24.6

12512 CSU P P7 G1.2 1949–1972
Lin Chen.
'Chinese Communist food production in 1969.'
IS 6, 8 (May 1970), 51–60.
SUBJ 14.1

12513 CSH P P2 G1.2 1949–1972
Lin Chen.
'Peiping's agricultural production in 1968.'
CCA 6, 2 (Apr. 1969), 48–58.
SUBJ 14.1 24.3 ▪ 21.2 22.1

12514 CSH P P8 G1.2 1949–1972
Lin Ping.
'A study of the food and cotton production on the Chinese Mainland in 1965.'
IS 2, 6 (Mar. 1966), 23–31.
SUBJ 14.1

12515 MAM P P7 G1.2 1949–1972
Lippit, Victor David, 1938–.
Land reform in China: The contribution of institutional change to financing economic development.
Ann Arbor: University Microfilms (Publ. 72-16,672), 1972. 179 p. (Doctoral dissertation in Economics, Yale U., 1971)
SUBJ 14 14.1 14.5 ▪ 14.3 16.1 16.3 34.1

12516 CSH U P7 G1.2 1949–1972
Lu Jui-lung.
'Current tasks on the agricultural front.' Tr. of 'I chiu liu ling nien ti nung yeh chan hsien' (The agricultural front in 1960); *Hung ch'i* 1960, 2 (15 Jan.), 17–27.
ECMM 207 (11 Apr. 1960), 8–21.
SUBJ 14.1 ▪ 34.1

12517 CSU P P2 G1.2 1949–1972
Mah, Feng-hwa (Ma Feng-hua), 1922–.
'Why China imports wheat.'
CQ 45 (Jan.–Mar. 1971), 116–128.
SUBJ 14.1 18

12518 MCH O P2 G1.2 1949–1972
Meso, M- A-.
'El país donde hoy es mañana' (The country where today is tomorrow).
Cuadernos americanos 16, 4 (julio–agosto 1957), 7–38.
SUBJ 14.1 14.4 ▪ 14.2 17 18 31 34.1 36.3 36.4 55

12519 MAM P P8 G1.2 1949–1972
Moore, William Joseph, 1932–.
Ideology and economic development in China and India: A study of contrasting

political approaches to the problem of agricultural development, 1951–1961.
Ann Arbor: University Microfilms (Publ. 63-4208), 1963. 379 p. (Doctoral dissertation in Political Science, U. of Redlands [Redlands, Calif.])
Subj 14 14.1 ▪ 12.1 16.3 34.1 64

12520 DLC U P8 G1.2 1949–1972
Negrul', A- M-, and Liu IUiian (Liu Yü-yen).
'Vinogradarstvo v Kitae' (Grape cultivation in China).
Vinodelie i vinogradarstvo SSSR 1958, 3, 32–36.
Subj 14.1 ▪ 55

12521 DLC P P2 G1.2 1949–1972
Němec, Jaromír.
'Vodní hospodářství Čínské lidové republiky' (Water conservancy in the People's Republic of China).
Vodní hospodářství (Prague) 4, 8 (1954), 253–256; 4, 9 (1954), 275–281.
Subj 11.4 14.1 ▪ 14.4

12522 CBU FP P8 G1.5 1949–1972
Nuttonson, Michael Y-, 1904–.
The physical environment and agriculture of Central and South China, Hong Kong and Taiwan: A study based on field survey data and pertinent records, material and reports.
Washington, D.C.: American Institute of Crop Ecology, 1963. 402 p.
Subj 11.3 14.1 ▪ 21

12523 MAM P P8 G1.2 1949–1972
Oh, Ki-song, 1917–.
Land reform in Communist China and postwar Japan.
Ann Arbor: University Microfilms (Publ. 67-7868), 1967. 448 p. (Doctoral dissertation in Political Science, U. of Pennsylvania, 1966)
Subj 14.1 32.1 ▪ 16.1 16.3 32 64

12524 MAM FP P2 G1.2 1949–1972
Oksenberg, Michel Charles, 1938–.
Policy formulation in Communist China: The case of the Mass Irrigation campaign, 1957–58.
Ann Arbor: University Microfilms (Publ. 70-18,839), 1970. 715 p. (Doctoral dissertation in Political Science, Columbia U., 1969)
Subj 12 12.1 14 14.1 18 22 ▪ 11.3 14.2 14.6 16.1 22.1 32 34.1 59 64

12525 NNC P P2 G1.2 1949–1972
Ong, Shao-er (Weng Shao-erh), 1917–.
Chinese farm economy after agrarian reform.
Lackland Air Force Base, San Antonio, Tex.: U.S. Air Force Personnel and Training Research Center, Air Research and Development Command, 1955. 13, 32 p. (U.S. Human Resources Research Institute technical research reports, 34; Studies in Chinese Communism, series 4, 4, 1953)
Subj 12.1 14 14.1 16.3 ▪ 11.4 12.2 16 45 47 62 64

12526 CSU P P7 G1.2 1949–1972
Onoue, Etsuzō (Onoe Etsuzō).
'Chinese agriculture in the Second Five-Year Plan period.'
DE 1, 2 (July–Dec. 1963), 184–201.
Subj 14.1 ▪ 18 24.4 34.1

12527 MCH P P8 G1.2 1949–1972
Orleans, Leo A-, 1924–.
'The volume of migration in relation to land reclamation in Communist China.'
B. of the Research Group for European Migration Problems 6, 2 (Apr.–June 1958), 25–26.
Subj 11.2 14.1

12528 CSU P P2 G1.2 1949–1972
Ozaki Shotaro (Ozaki Shōtarō), 1906–.
Some characteristics of technical reform movement in Communist China, mimeo. Tr. of 'Chūgoku gijutsu kakushin undō no ikutsuka no tokuchō' (Some noteworthy characteristics of the movement for technological innovation in China); *Ajia keizai jumpō* 434 (10 June 1960), 1–8.
Washington, D.C.: U.S. Joint Publications Research Service, 25 Sept. 1960. 8 p. (JPRS 5620; MC 17,610/1960)
Subj 14.1 ▪ 14.4 27

12529 MCH P P7 G1.2 1949–1972
Perkins, Dwight Heald, 1934–.
'Centralization and decentralization in Mainland China's agriculture, 1949–1962.'
Quarterly j. of economics 78, 2 (May 1964), 208–237.
Subj 14.1 22.1 34.1 ▪ 14.5 16.3 19 32.1 64

12530 CSU P P2 G1.2 1949–1972
Ravenholt, Albert, 1919–.
'Can one billion Chinese feed themselves?'
AUFS-EAS 18, 2 (Apr. 1971), 1–15.
Subj 11 14.1 ▪ 51 58

12531 CSU P P2 G1.2 1949–1972
Ravenholt, Albert, 1919–.
'A note on Communist China: Six hundred million farmers.'
AUFS-EAS 15, 1 (Aug. 1968), 1–16.
Subj 14.1 16.3 22.2 ▪ 12.1 14.3 14.4 16.4

12532 MCH PO P2 G1.2 1949–1972
Richardson, Stanley Dennis, 1925–.
Forestry in Communist China.
Baltimore: Johns Hopkins Press, 1966. 16, 237 p.
Subj 12 14 14.1 17 ▪ 14.4 16.4 24.4

12533 CBU S P1 G1.2 1949–1972
Ruthenberg, H- H-.
'Die Entwicklung der Landwirtschaft in Japan, Indien und China' (The development of agriculture in Japan, India, and China).
Berichte über Landwirtschaft neue (2.) Folge 36, 2 (Juni 1958), 421–458.
Subj 14 14.1 ▪ 24.4

12534 NNC P P2 G1.2 1949–1972
Saburenkov, N- M-.
'Rubovodstvo v Kitaiskoi Narodnoi Respublike' (Fish culture in the People's Republic of China).
Rybnoe khoziaistvo 1961, 9 (sentiabr'), 85–91.
Subj 14.1 ▪ 14.2 16.3 17 62

12535 CSU P P2 G1.2 1949–1972
Schran, Peter, 1930–.
The development of Chinese agriculture, 1950–1959.
Urbana: U. of Illinois Press, 1969. 238 p. (Illinois studies in the social sciences, 56)
Subj 14.1 16.3 18 ▪ 11 11.4 34.1

12536 NNC P P7 G1.2 1949–1972
Shan Mu (Shan Ho), Chen Hsin-hai (Shen Hsing-hai), and Kung Mien-jen. [Authors sequential rather than joint: Shan Mu for 1955; Chen Hsin-hai for 1956; Kung Mien-jen for 1957 and 1958.]
'Agriculture.' Tr. of '1955–1958 nien Chung-kuo ti nung yeh' (Agriculture in Communist China, 1955–1958); *Tsu kuo chou k'an* 159–334/335 (16 Jan. 1956 – 8 June 1959) [recurring annual feature article]. In *Communist China, 1955–1958*, edited by Union Research Institute.
Hong Kong: Union Research Institute. Issued annually, 1956–1959, average ca. 10 p.
Subj 12.1 14.1 34.1 ▪ 16.3 18 45

12537 CSH U P7 G1.2 1949–1972
Shen Ch'i-i.
'The effect of plant protection on the increase of agricultural production.' Tr. of 'Chih wu pao hu tui pao cheng nung yeh tseng ch'an ti tso yung' (The role of the protection of plants in increasing agricultural production); *Hung ch'i* 1962, 22 (16 Nov.), 33–41. In *Translations from 'Hung-ch'i' (Red flag) No. 22, 1962*, mimeo., compiled by U.S. Joint Publications Research Service. [Sole entry]
Washington, D.C.: JPRS, 4 Jan. 1963, 71–103. (JPRS 16,985; MC 2793/1963)
Subj 14.1

12538 CSU P P8 G1.2 1949–1972
Shui li k'o hsüeh yen chiu yüan. Kuan kai yen chiu so. (Institute of Scientific Research on Water Improvements. Laboratory of Irrigation Research).
'Crop irrigation in Communist China.' Tr. of 'Kuan kai'; *Jen min jih pao* 25 Mar. 1959, 7. In *Selected articles on water conservation progress in Communist China*, mimeo., compiled by U.S. Joint Publications Research Service. [Sole entry]
Washington, D.C.: JPRS, 20 Nov. 1959, 1–10. (JPRS 1025D; MC 803/1960)
Subj 14.1 ▪ 18

12539 NNC P P8 G1.2 1949–1972
Stadnichenko, A- I-.
'Razvitie ekonomiki sel'skogo khoziaistva Kitaiskoi Narodnoi Respubliki v 1953–1957 gg.' (The development of the agricultural economy of the People's Republic of China, 1953–1957).
KSINA 49 (1961), 52–58.
Subj 14 14.1

12540 CSH P P7 G1.3 1949–1972
Stanford U. China Project.
'Agriculture.' In *Central South China*, compiled by the organization cited. [Selective entry]
New Haven: Human Relations Area Files, 1956, vol. 2, 642–688. (HRAF subcontractor's monographs, 28; Stanford 2)
Subj 14.1 ▪ 14.3 34.1

12541 CSH P P7 G1.3 1949–1972
Stanford U. China Project.
'Agriculture.' In *East China*, compiled by the organization cited. [Selective entry]
New Haven: Human Relations Area Files, 1956, vol. 2, 738–768. (HRAF

subcontractor's monographs, 29; Stanford 3)
Subj 14.1 ▪ 14.3 34.1

12542 CSH P P7 G5.0 1949–1972
Stanford U. China Project.
'Agriculture.' In *North China*, compiled by the organization cited. [Selective entry]
New Haven: Human Relations Area Files, 1956, vol. 2, 682–717. (HRAF subcontractor's monographs, 27; Stanford 1)
Subj 14.1 ▪ 14.3 34.1

12543 NNC P P7 G8.0 1949–1972
Stanford U. China Project.
'Agriculture.' In *Southwest China*, compiled by the organization cited. [Selective entry]
New Haven: Human Relations Area Files, 1956, vol. 2, 745–773. (HRAF subcontractor's monographs, 30; Stanford 4)
Subj 14.1 ▪ 14.3 34.1

12544 CSH O P2 G1.2 1949–1972
Strong, Anna Louise, 1885–1970.
China's fight for grain.
Peking: New World Press, 1963. 43 p.
Subj 14.1 18 55 ▪ 14.4 34.1

12545 CSU P P8 G1.2 1949–1972
Swamy, Subramanian, and Shahid Javed Burki.
'Foodgrains output in the People's Republic of China, 1958–1965.'
CQ 41 (Jan.–Mar. 1970), 58–63.
Subj 14.1

12546 MCH P P7 G1.2 1949–1972
Tálas, Barna.
'A kínai mezőgazdaság szocialista átalakításának sajátosságai' (Characteristics of the socialist transformation of Chinese agriculture).
Társadalmi szemle 10, 11 (november 1955), 70–81.
Subj 14.1 ▪ 16.3 19

12547 CSU P P7 G1.2 1949–1972
Tang, Anthony M. (T'ang Tsung-ming), 1924–.
'Input-output relations in the agriculture of Communist China, 1952–1965' [with comments by Werner Klatt]. In *Agrarian policies and problems in Communist and non-Communist countries*, edited by William Arthur Douglas Jackson. [Selective entry]
Seattle: U. of Washington Press, 1971, 280–304.
Subj 14.1 ▪ 16.3

12548 CSU P P2 G1.1 1949–1972
Tang, Anthony M. (T'ang Tsung-ming), 1924–.
'Policy and performance in agriculture.' In *Economic trends in Communist China*, edited by Alexander Eckstein, Walter Galenson, and Ta-chung Liu. [Analytic entry]
Chicago: Aldine, 1968, 459–507.
Subj 14.1 14.4 ▪ 14 18

12549 NIC P P8 G1.2 1949–1972
Thomas, Samuel Bernard, 1921–.
'Communist China's agrarian policy, 1954–1956.'
PA 29, 2 (June 1956), 141–160.
Subj 12.1 14.1 34.1 ▪ 11.2 16.3 18 32 36.3 48

12550 GMS PO P8 G1.2 1949–1972
Unger, H-.
'Ertragssteigernde Massnahmen der chinesischen Landwirtschaft' (Measures to increase Chinese agricultural yields).
Berichte über Landwirtschaft neue (2.) Folge 38, 3 (Sept. 1960), 630–634.
Subj 14.1

12551 CSU PO P8 G1.2 1949–1972
Unger, H-.
'Veränderungen und Erfolge der chinesischen Agrarwirtschaft' (Changes and successes in Chinese agriculture).
Berichte über Landwirtschaft neue (2.) Folge 37, 4 (Dez. 1959), 910–931.
Subj 14.1 ▪ 22

12552 NNC P P7 G1.2 1949–1972
Walker, Kenneth Richard, 1931–.
Planning in Chinese agriculture: Socialisation and the private sector, 1956–1962.
Chicago: Aldine, 1965. 18, 109 p.
Subj 14 14.1 16.3 34.1 ▪ 12.1 64

12553 CSU P P7 G1.2 1949–1972
Washenko, Steve.
'Agriculture in China: Priorities and prospects.'
CS 9, 10 (7 Oct. 1971), 1–6.
Subj 14.1

12554 CSU P P8 G1.2 1949–1972
Washenko, Steve.
'Agriculture in Mainland China, 1968.'
CS 7, 6 (31 Mar. 1969), 1–12.
Subj 14.1 ▪ 12.1

12555 CSH P P7 G1.2 1949–1972
Wenmohs, John R-.
'Agriculture in Mainland China, 1967: Cultural Revolution versus favorable weather.'
CS 5, 21 (15 Dec. 1967), 1–12.
Subj 14.1 ▪ 12.1 14.3 18 22 22.2

12556 CSU S P2 G1.2 1949–1972
Wheatley, Paul.
'The ecological transformation of China.' [Review of *The transformation of the Chinese earth: Aspects of the evaluation of the Chinese earth from earliest times to Mao Tse-tung*, by Keith McPherson Buchanan.]
GJ 136, 3 (Sept. 1970), 424–428.
Subj 11.3 14.1

12557 CSH P P8 G1.2 1949–1972
Wu, Yuan-li (Wu Yüan-li), 1920–.
'The economics of Mainland China's agriculture: Some aspects of measurement, interpretation, and evaluation.' In *Food and agriculture in Communist China*, by John Lossing Buck et al. [Analytic entry]
New York: Praeger, 1966, 73–100.
Subj 14.1 ▪ 12.1 34.1

12558 CSU P P2 G1.2 1949–1972
Wu, Yuan-li (Wu Yüan-li), 1920–.
'Food and agriculture in Mainland China.'
CH 61, 361 (Sept. 1971), 160–164.
Subj 14.1 ▪ 14.3 58

12559 CSU P P2 G1.2 1949–1972
Wu, Yuan-li (Wu Yüan-li), 1920–.
'Some economic effects of land "reform", agricultural collectivization and the commune system in China.' In *Land tenure, industrialization and social stability: Experience and prospects in Asia*, edited by Walter Froehlich. [Selective entry]
Milwaukee: Marquette U. Press, 1961, 17–37. (Marquette Asian studies, 2)
Subj 14.1 34.1 ▪ 12.1 12.2 14.4 14.5 16.3

12560 MCH P P8 G1.2 1949–1972
Yang Chien-pai.
'Agricultural mechanization and the question of inheritance and renovation of China's farming system.' Tr. of 'Nung yeh chi hsieh hua ho wo kuo keng tso ti chi ch'eng yü pien ko wen t'i' (Agricultural mechanization and the issue of traditional versus modern methods in Chinese agriculture); *Hsin chien she* 1964, 2 (Feb.), 35–43.
SCMM 421 (15 June 1964), 11–22.
Subj 14.1

12561 NIC O P2 G1.2 1949–1972
Yang Ling.
'Agriculture: Foundation of the national economy.'
PR 3, 42 (18 Oct. 1960), 14–22. [Reprinted—*SCMM* 235 (15 Nov. 1960), 28–42.]
Subj 14 14.1 64 ▪ 14.4

12562 CSU P P7 G1.2 1949–1972
Yeh, K. C. (Yeh K'ung-chia), 1924–.
Agricultural policies and performance.
Santa Monica, Calif.: RAND Corp., 1970. 75 p. (RAND papers, P-4193-1)
Subj 14 14.1 ▪ 14.3 14.5 16.3 34.1 64

12563 NNC P P7 G1.2 1949–1972
Zhamin, Vitalii Alekseevich, 1920–.
Sel'skoe khoziaistvo Kitaia (Agriculture in China).
Moscow: Gossel'khozizdat, 1959. 285 p.
Subj 14.1 34.1 ▪ 19 32.1

12564 DLC P P2 G1.2 1949–1972
Zhamin, Vitalii Alekseevich, 1920–, et al.
Nekotorye voprosy razvitiia sel'skokhoziaistvennoi nauki v KNR.
Moscow: Vysshaia shkola, 1959. 293 p.
Some questions on the development of agricultural sciences in the People's Republic of China, mimeo.
Washington, D.C.: U.S. Joint Publications Research Service, 20 July 1961. 298 p. (JPRS 9717; MC 15,658/1961)
Subj 14.1 34.1 ▪ 14.4 17 18

14.2 Transport and Communications

交通 交通

1644-1911

12565 NIC O P4 G1.2 1842–1895
'Chinese postal service.'
TP 5, 1 (mars 1894), 63–64.
Subj 14.2 16.2 34.2

12566 NNC O P2 G1.2 1842–1911
Barry, Arthur John.
'Railway development in China.'

J. of the Royal Society of Arts 57, 2948 (21 May 1909), 541–558.
SUBJ 14.2 66 ▪ 14.6 34.2 57

12567 MAM P P2 G1.3 1842–1895
Bennett, Adrian Arthur, III, 1941–.
Missionary journalism in nineteenth-century China: Young J. Allen and the early 'Wan-kuo kung-pao' [Globe magazine], *1868–1883*.
Ann Arbor: University Microfilms (Publ. 71-15,519), 1971. 417 p. (Doctoral dissertation in History, U. of California, Davis)
SUBJ 14.2 33 ▪ 17 66

12568 MCH P P2 G1.2 1842–1911
Bidder, Hans.
'Das Seetransportwesen der chinesischen Regierung: Ein Beitrag zur ostasiatischen Schiffahrtsgeschichte aus chinesischen Quellen' (The maritime transport system of the Chinese government: History of East Asian navigation, based on Chinese sources).
SJ 45, 3 (1921), 153–193.
SUBJ 14.2 14.3 ▪ 12 14.6 34.2

12569 CSU O P2 G1.5 1895–1911
[Bishop, Isabella Lucy Bird] *Mrs.* J- F- Bishop, 1831–1904.
The Yangtze valley and beyond.
London: Murray, 1899. 15, 557 p. [Reprinted—Taipei: Ch'eng-wen, 1972. 15, 557 p.]
SUBJ 14.2 38 55 56 57 66 ▪ 14.1 14.3 17 18 21.3 23 25 33

12570 CBU O P2 G1.5 1842–1895
Blakiston, Thomas W-.
Five months on the Yangtze: With a narrative of the exploration of its upper waters and notices of the present rebellions in China.
London: Murray, 1862. 14, 380 p.
SUBJ 14.2 32.2 66 ▪ 14.1 14.4 21.1 22

12571 CSU O P1 G1.4 1895–1911
Bourne, T- Johnstone.
'Railway engineering in China.'
Cassier's magazine 20, 3 (July 1901), 179–193.
SUBJ 14.2 14.4

12572 MCH P P3 G1.2 1644–1911
Britton, Roswell Sessoms, 1897–.
The Chinese periodical press, 1800–1912.
Shanghai: Kelly and Walsh, 1933. 151 p. (Doctoral dissertation in Chinese, Columbia U.) [Reprinted—Taipei: Ch'eng-wen, 1966. 151 p.]
SUBJ 14.2 32.2 33 64 ▪ 12 12.1 24.4 47 66 72

12573 CSH P P2 G1.3 –1911
Canfield, Suzette H. (Kan Hu Hsiao-chao), 1935–.
'Bridge construction and repair in the Ming and Ch'ing.'
PC 24 (Dec. 1971), 19–40.
SUBJ 14.2 ▪ 11.4 12 22

12574 NIC PO P2 G1.3 –1895
Carles, William Richard, 1848–?
'The Grand Canal of China.'
JRAS-CB new (2nd) series 31 (1896/97), 102–115.
SUBJ 14.2 14.5

12575 MCH P P2 G1.1 1842–1895
Cheng, Ying-wan (Cheng Ying-huan), 1915–.
Postal communication in China and its modernization, 1860–1896.
Cambridge: Harvard U., East Asian Research Center, 1970. 10, 152 p. (Harvard East Asian monographs, 34) (Revision of *Modernization of the Chinese postal service (1860–1896)*, doctoral dissertation in History, Radcliffe College, 1960)
SUBJ 14.2 ▪ 12 14.3

12576 DLC PO P4 G1.1 1895–1911
China [Ch'ing]. [Shui wu ch'u]. Hai kuan. ([Board of Customs Control]. [Imperial] Maritime Customs).
Returns of trade and trade reports, Part 1, Report on the working of the Imperial Post Office, 1904–1910. [Title varies slightly.]
Shanghai: Tsung shui wu ssu shu, T'ung chi k'o. Issued annually, 1905–1911. Average ca. 25 p. (Hai kuan statistical series, 3–4)
SUBJ 14.2

12577 MCH P P2 G1.4 1842–1895
Corradini, Piero.
'L'abbandono del "canale imperiale" (Yün-ho) come via di navigazione' (The abandonment of the Grand Canal as a navigation route).
Rivista di studi orientali 37, 1/2 (1962), 115–122.
SUBJ 14.2 ▪ 12 14

12578 MCH O P2 G1.5 –1895
Coucheron-Aamot, William, 1868–?
'2500 kilometer opover Yangtse Kiang' (2500 kilometers up the Yangtze river).
Norske Geografiske Selskabs Aarbok 6 (1894/95), 95–124.
SUBJ 12 14.2 14.3 ▪ 14.1 14.4 15 21.1 65

12579 FPN O P2 G1.5 1895–1911
Courant, Maurice Auguste Louis Marie, 1865–1935.
'Le bassin du Yang-tseu' (The Yangtze valley).
Annales coloniales 4, 22 (15 nov. 1903), 357–364.
SUBJ 14.2 14.3 ▪ 11.2 66

12580 MCH PO P2 G1.5 1895–1911
Dautremer, Joseph, 1860–?
La grande artère de la Chine, le Yangtseu (The great artery of China, the Yangtze).
Paris: Guilmoto, 1911. 304 p.
SUBJ 14.2 14.3 24.3 24.4 ▪ 14 16 21 32.2 41 55 61 62

12581 MCH P P2 G1.5 1842–1895
Dutreuil de Rhins, Jules Léon.
'Routes entre la Chine et l'Inde' (Routes between China and India).
B. de la Société de géographie 7e série 1 (jan.–juin 1881), 5–60.
SUBJ 14.2 ▪ 66

12582 CSU O P2 G1.4 1842–1895
Elias, Ney.
'Notes of a journey to the new course of the Yellow River, in 1868.'
J. of the Royal Geographical Society 40 (1870), 1–33.
SUBJ 14.2 18 ▪ 14.1 14.3 55

12583 MCH P P2 G1.2 1644–1842
Fairbank, John King, 1907–, and Ssu-yü Teng, 1906–.
'On the transmission of Ch'ing documents.'
HJAS 4, 1 (May 1939), 12–46. [Reprinted in *Ch'ing administration: Three studies*, by J. K. Fairbank and Ssu-yü Teng. (Analytic entry.) Cambridge: Harvard U. Press, 1960, 1–35. (Harvard-Yenching Institute studies, 19)]
SUBJ 12 14.2

12584 CSU O P2 G1.3 1842–1895
Fauvel, Albert Auguste, 1851–1909.
'Les phares de la Chine' (Lighthouses in China).
Questions diplomatiques et coloniales 6, 52 (15 avr. 1899), 458–464. [Reprinted in *Les télégraphes, la poste et les phares en Chine* (The telegraph and postal systems and lighthouses in China), by A. A. Fauvel. (Analytic entry.) Paris: Levé, 1899.]
SUBJ 14.2 21.3 66 ▪ 12 25

12585 FPN O P2 G1.1 1842–1895
Fauvel, Albert Auguste, 1851–1909.
'Les télégraphes et la poste en Chine' (The telegraph and postal systems in China).
Questions diplomatiques et coloniales 6, 46 (15 jan. 1899), 83–87; 6, 47 (1er fév. 1899), 164–169. [Reprinted in *Les télégraphes, la poste et les phares en Chine* (The telegraph and postal systems and lighthouses in China), by A. A. Fauvel. (Analytic entry.) Paris: Levé, 1899.]
SUBJ 14.2 ▪ 12 66

12586 NNC P P1 G1.2 1842–1911
Franke, Otto, 1863–1946.
'Eisenbahnbau und Eisenbahnpolitik in China' (Railroad construction and railroad policy in China).
Marine-Rundschau 17, 5 (Mai 1906), 539–560. [Reprinted in *Ostasiatische Neubildungen: Beiträge zum Verständnis der politischen und kulturellen Entwicklungs-vorgänge im Fernen Osten* (New forms in East Asia: Toward an understanding of political and cultural developmental processes in the Far East), by O. Franke. (Selective entry.) Hamburg: C. Boysen, 1911, 328–353.]
SUBJ 14.2

12587 CSH P P2 G1.3 –1895
Gandar, Dominique, 1829–1910.
Le Canal impérial: étude historique et descriptive (An historical and descriptive study of the Grand Canal), 2nd ed.
Shanghai: Impr. de la Mission catholique, 1903. 78 p. (Variétés sinologiques, 4)
SUBJ 14.2 18 ▪ 14.3 14.5

12588 NNC P P1 G1.2 1895–1911
Grigor'ev, Aleksandr Mironovich, 1933–.
'Iz istorii kitaiskoi revoliutsionnoi pressy, 1901–1904' (History of the Chinese revolutionary press, 1901–1904).
KSINA 66 (1963), 94–104.
SUBJ 14.2 32.2 64 ▪ 54

12589 DCK O P2 G1.1 1842–1895
Hoskiær, Valdemar, 1829–1895.
'China' (China). In *Rejse i China, Japan og Indien* (A journey to China, Japan, and India), by V. Hoskiær. [Sole entry]
Copenhagen: Prior, 1880, 3–215.
SUBJ 14.2 66 ▪ 12 15 57 62

12590 CSU P P2 G1.2 1842–1911
Hsu, Mongton Chih (Hsü Ch'ih), 1885–.
Railway problems in China.
New York: Columbia U., Faculty of Political Science, 1915. 184 p. (Columbia studies in history, economics and public law, 66, 2 [whole no. 159]) (Doctoral dissertation in Economics, Columbia U.) [Reprinted—New York: AMS Press, 1969. 184 p.]
SUBJ 14.2 14.6 66 ▪ 12.2 34.2

12591 CSU P P1 G1.2 1644–1842
Huang, Pei (Huang P'ei), 1928–.
Review of *Communication and imperial control in China: Evolution of the palace memorial system, 1693–1735*, by Silas H. L. Wu (Wu Hsiu-liang).
HJAS 31 (1971), 323–332.
SUBJ 12 14.2

12592 NNC O P2 G1.3 1842–1895
[Kafarov, Petr Ivanovich] *Otets* Paladii (O. Palladius), 1817–1878.
'Morskoe soobshchenie mezhdu Gian-tszinem i Shan-khaem' (The sea-route between Tientsin and Shanghai). In *Trudy chlenov Rossiiskoi dukhovnoi missii v Pekine* (Works of members of the Russian Orthodox ecclesiastical mission in Peking). [Selective entry]
St. Petersburg: Tip. Shtaba voenno-ucheb. zavedenii, 1857, vol. 3, 381–392.
'Die See-Verbindung zwischen Thian-zsin und Schang-hai.' Tr. by Carl Abel and F- A- Mecklenburg. In *Arbeiten der kaiserlich russischen Gesandtschaft zu Peking über China, sein Volk, seine Religion, seine Institutionen, sozialen Verhältnisse, usw.* (Works of the imperial Russian mission to Peking on China, its people, religion, institutions, social conditions, etc.). [Selective entry]
Berlin: Heinicke, 1858, vol. 1, 237–245.
SUBJ 14.2

12593 MCH PO P2 G1.1 1842–1911
Kent, Percy Horace Braund, 1876–.
Railway enterprise in China: An account of its origin and development.
London: Arnold, 1907. 304 p.
SUBJ 14 14.2 14.3 34.2 ▪ 12 16.1 16.2 18 22.2 43 66

12594 NNC O P2 G1.2 1842–1895
Kingsmill, Thomas William, 1837–1910, ed.
'Inland communications in China.'
JRAS-CB new (2nd) series 28 (1893/94), 1–213.
SUBJ 14.2 14.3 14.5 ▪ 22.2 55

12595 MCH P P2 G2.0 1895–1911
Kitaiskaia Vostochnaia zheleznaia doroga. Kantseliariia pravleniia obshchestva, comp.
Kitaiskaia Vostochnaia zheleznaia doroga: istoricheskii ocherk, t. I, 1896–1905 gg. (Historical survey of the Chinese Eastern Railway, Vol. 1, 1896–1905).
St. Petersburg: V. F. Kirshbaum, 1914. 303 p.
SUBJ 14.2 ▪ 14.3 22 25 34.2

12596 MCH O P2 G1.2 –1842
Klaproth, Julius Heinrich, 1783–1835.
'Description du Grand canal de la Chine' (A description of China's Grand Canal).
Mémoires relatifs à l'Asie 3 (1828), 312–331.
SUBJ 14.2 ▪ 14.5

12597 CBU O P2 G1.2 1895–1911
Knobel, Fridolin Marinus, 1857–?
Oostersche verpoozingen (Reflections on the East).
Amsterdam: De Bussy, 1902. 434 p.
SUBJ 14.2 ▪ 14.4 17 66

12598 MCH PO P2 G1.1 1895–1911
Laboulaye, Edouard de.
Les chemins de fer de Chine (Railroads in China).
Paris: Emile Larose, 1911. 337 p.
SUBJ 14.2 ▪ 12 66

12599 FPN P P2 G1.2 1842–1911
Lefèvre, Raymond.
Les chemins de fer de pénétration dans la Chine méridionale (Railroads to open up South China).
Paris: Giard et Brière, 1902. 132 p. (Doctoral dissertation, Faculté de droit, Université de Paris)
SUBJ 14.2 ▪ 14.3

12600 MCH P P3 G1.1 1842–1895
Liu, Kwang-ching (Liu Kuang-ching), 1921–.
Anglo-American steamship rivalry in China, 1862–1874.
Cambridge: Harvard U. Press, 1962. 16, 218 p. (Harvard East Asian series, 8) (Revision of *Two steamship companies in China, 1862–1877*, doctoral dissertation in History, Harvard U., 1956)
SUBJ 14.2 34.2 ▪ 26.2 34.3 66

12601 MSE O P2 G8.0 1895–1911
Parsons, William Barclay, 1859–1932.
An American engineer in China.
New York: McClure, Phillips, 1900. 321 p. [Reprinted—Taipei: Ch'eng-wen, 1972. 321 p.]
SUBJ 14 14.2 66 ▪ 12 16.1 25 55

12602 CSU P P2 G1.3 –1895
Playfair, George Macdonald Home, 1850–1917.
'The grain transport system of China: Notes and statistics taken from the *Ta Ch'ing "Hui Tien"* [Collected statutes of the Ch'ing].'
China review 3, 6 (May–June 1875), 354–364.
SUBJ 12.2 14.2 14.5

12603 NNC PO P4 G1.2 1895–1911
Preyer, Otto Ernest, 1881–.
'Das Eisenbahnwesen Chinas' (Railroads in China).
AE 32, 1 (Jan.–Feb. 1909), 84–159.
SUBJ 14.2

12604 NNC PO P4 G1.2 1895–1911
Preyer, Otto Ernest, 1881–.
'Die Entwicklung des chinesischen Eisenbahnwesens in den letzten drei Jahren (1909 bis 1911)' (The development of railroads in China during the past three years, 1909–1911).
AE 36, 4 (Juli–Aug. 1913), 965–1003.
SUBJ 14.2

12605 MCH O P3 G1.2 1842–1895
Rochedragon, L- B-.
'Une compagnie maritime chinoise' (A Chinese shipping company).
B. de la Société de géographie de Lyon 10 (1891), 372–380.
SUBJ 14.2 34.2

12606 MAM P P2 G1.2 1842–1911
Rosenbaum, Arthur Lewis, 1939–.
China's first railway: The imperial railways of North China, 1880–1911.
Ann Arbor: University Microfilms (Publ. 72-17,164), 1972. 581 p. (Doctoral dissertation in History, Yale U.)
SUBJ 14.2 34.2 ▪ 14.3 66

12607 CSH P P1 G1.2 1842–1911
Rosenbaum, Arthur Lewis, 1939–.
'Chinese railway policy and the response to imperialism: The Peking-Mukden railway, 1895–1911.'
CSWT 2, 1 (Oct. 1969), 38–70. [For fuller version, see entry 12606.]
SUBJ 12 14.2 66 ▪ 14.6

12608 NIC U P2 G1.2 1842–1895
Schlegel, Gustaaf, 1840–1903.
'Note sur les moyens et les voies de communication des provinces de la Chine avoisinant le Tong-king' (A note on the ways and means of communication in the Chinese provinces bordering on Tonkin).
TP 3, 2 (1892), 169–180.
SUBJ 14.2 ▪ 21.3

12609 NNC P P1 G1.1 1644–1842
Schlegel, Gustaaf, 1840–1903.
'T'ien-hia Lu-ching [i.e., *T'ien-hsia lu-ch'eng* (The roads of China)], a Chinese "Murray" for 1694.'
TP 2, 2 (1891), 140–148.
SUBJ 14.2

12610 NNC P P4 G1.2 1895–1911
Schumacher, Hermann, 1868–?
'Eisenbahnbau und Eisenbahnpläne in China' (Railroad construction and railroad plans in China).
AE 22, 5 (Sept.–Okt. 1899), 901–978; 22, 6 (Nov.–Dez. 1899), 1194–1226; 23, 1 (Jan.–Feb. 1900), 1–115.
SUBJ 14.2 ▪ 14.3 14.4 66

12611 MCH P P1 G1.1 1895–1911
Sun, E-tu Zen (Sun Jen I-tu), 1921–.
Chinese railways and British interests, 1898–1911.
New York: King's Crown Press, 1954. 230 p. (Revision of *Britain and Chinese railways, 1902–1911*, doctoral dissertation in History, Radcliffe College, 1949) [Reprinted—New York: Russell and Russell, 1971. 230 p.]
SUBJ 14.2 66 ▪ 14.6 16.1 32

12612 CSU P P2 G1.3 1644–1895
Sun, E-tu Zen (Sun Jen I-tu), 1921–.
'The transportation of Yunnan copper to Peking in the Ch'ing period.'
JOS 9, 1 (Jan. 1971), 132–148.
SUBJ 14.2 ▪ 14.4 14.6 22

12613 WSU P P2 G1.5 1895–1911
Sun, Ping Ying.
A short history of the construction of the Szechuan-Hankow-Canton railway on the eve of the Chinese Revolution, 1898–1911.
Unpublished masters thesis in History, U. of Washington, 1949. 103 p.
SUBJ 14.2 ▪ 14.6

12614 CSU P P1 G9.0 1644–1842
Thompson, Laurence Gassius, 1926–.
'The junk passage across the Taiwan strait: Two early Chinese accounts.'
HJAS 28 (1968), 170–194.
SUBJ 14.2

12615 MCH P P3 G1.3 1842–1911
Tikhvinskii, Sergei Leonidovich, 1918–.
'Progressivnaia kitaiskaia publitsistika kontsa XIX veka' (Progressive Chinese publishing in the late nineteenth century).
VI 1958, 8 (avgust'), 160–171.
SUBJ 12 14.2 16.1 16.2 32 64 ▪ 12.1 17

12616 CBU F P2 G1.4 1895–1911
Tret'iak, Pod"esaul.
'Imperatorskaia zheleznaia doroga Pekin-Kalgan-Urga' (The imperial Peking-Kalgan-Urga railroad).
IVI 29, 2 (1909), 15–26.
SUBJ 14.2 ▪ 14 16.4

12617 DLC O P4 G1.2 1842–1895
Veniukov, Mikhail Ivanovich, 1832–1901.
'Puteshestvie v Kitai i IAponiiu' (A journey to China and Japan). In *Puteshestviia po Priamur'iu, Kitaiu i IAponii* (Travels in the Amur region, China, and Japan), by M. I. Veniukov. [Sole entry]
Khabarovsk: Dal'giz, 1952, 187–288.
SUBJ 14.2 14.3 ▪ 15 32.2

12618 MCH S P3 G1.5 1895–1911
Vincent, C-.
'Tchungking, Hangtchéou, Soutchéou et Shatszé: ou, les quatre nouveaux ports chinois ouverts au commerce étranger' (Chungking, Hangchow, Soochow, and Shasi, the four Chinese ports recently opened to foreign trade).
B. de la Société de géographie de Toulouse 15, 7/8 (1896), 350–362.
SUBJ 14.2 14.3 66 ▪ 21.3

12619 MCH P P1 G1.2 1644–1842
Wu, Silas H. L. (Wu Hsiu-liang), 1929–.
Communication and imperial control in China: Evolution of the palace memorial system, 1693–1735.
Cambridge: Harvard U. Press, 1970. 204 p. (Harvard East Asian series, 51) (Revision of *The palace memorial system in China: A description of imperial channels of communication and decision-making in the early Ch'ing government, 1693–1735*, doctoral dissertation in East Asian Languages and Cultures, Columbia U., 1967)
SUBJ 12 14.2 61 ▪ 16.1 63 64

1644-1949

12620 CSH P P2 G1.2 1895–1928
'Communications (railroads, roads, post office).' In *The Christian occupation of China*, edited by Milton Theobald Stauffer. [Selective entry]
Shanghai: China Continuation Committee, 1922, 14–19.
SUBJ 14.2 ▪ 14 21.3

12621 NNC P P1 G1.2 1895–1949
'Progress of Chinese post office since the Republic.'
NWSS 6, 40 (2 Oct. 1933), 183, 185–186.
SUBJ 14.2

12622 NNC P P1 G1.2 1842–1928
'Relative importance of steamers and sailing vessels in China's shipping, 1864–1927.'
NWSS 2, 23 (16 Sept. 1929), 1, 4.
SUBJ 14.2

12623 MCH S P4 G1.2 1842–1949
Altree, Wayne, 1917–.
'A half-century of the administration of the state railways of China.'
PC 3 (May 1949), 78–133.
SUBJ 12 14.2 14.4 ▪ 17 18 30 34.2

12624 CSU PO P2 G1.1 –1928
Audemard, Louis, 1865–1965.
Les jonques chinoises (Chinese junks).
Rotterdam: Museum voor Land- en Volkenkunde *with* Maritiem Museum 'Prins Hendrik', 1957–1963. 5 vols. 396 p. [s.p.].
SUBJ 14.2 15 16.3 21.3 55 65 ▪ 14.3 16.2 25 66

12625 NNC P P1 G1.2 1895–1928
Avenarius, G- G-.
'Vodnyi transport v Kitae (bibliograficheskii ocherk)' (Bibliographic notes on water transport in China).
BSB 2, 5 (1932), 155–179.
SUBJ 14.2 ▪ 72

12626 NNC PO P2 G8.2 1895–1928
Bel'chenko, A- T-.
'Donesenie imperatorskago rossiiskago konsula v Kantone: ocherk Annamo-IUn'nan'skoi zheleznoi dorogi' (Report of the imperial Russian consul in Canton: Overview of the Annam-Yunnan railroad).
DIRKP 44 (1914), 1–58.
SUBJ 14.2 ▪ 14.3 21.4 66

12627 MCH U P1 G1.1 1842–1949
Cantlie, Kenneth.
'Railway construction in China and its effect on recent history.'
Eastern world 4, 5 (May 1950), 35–37; 4, 6 (June 1950), 37–40.
SUBJ 14.2 ▪ 14.5

12628 NIC O P2 G1.5 1895–1949
Carey, H- Foote.
'Transportation on the Yang-tze Kiang.'
CJ 10, 5 (May 1929), 248–255.
SUBJ 14.2

12629 ELO PO P2 G1.1 1842–1949
Chang, Kia-ngau (Chang Chia-ao), 1888–.
China's struggle for railroad development.
New York: Day, 1943. 340 p.
SUBJ 12 14.2 14.5 14.6 ▪ 11.2 11.3 15 66

12630 CBU P P1 G1.4 1895–1949
Chang, Pao-Yüan (Chang Pao-yüan), 1905–.
Die Eisenbahnen in der Mandschurei (The railroads of Manchuria).
Leipzig: The author, 1930. 100 p. (Doctoral dissertation, Philosophische Fakultät, Universität Leipzig)
SUBJ 14.2 66 ▪ 14.6

12631 MCH P P2 G1.2 1644–1949
Chao, Yung-seen (Chao Yung-hsin).
Les chemins de fer chinois: étude historique, politique, économique et financière (An historical, political, economic, and financial study of railroads in China).
Paris: Lib. technique et économique, 1938. 272 p. (Doctoral dissertation, Faculté de droit, Université de Paris)
SUBJ 14 14.2 14.3 34.2 ▪ 12 14.6 16 18 32.2 66 72

12632 MCH PO P1 G1.1 1895–1928
Charignon, Antoine Joseph Henri, 1872–1930.
Les chemins de fer chinois: un programme pour leur développement (A program for the development of railroads in China).
Peking: Impr. des lazaristes au Pe-t'ang, 1914. 222 p.
SUBJ 14.2

12633 GBS S P2 G1.2 –1949
Chen, Chih-Hwa (Ch'en Tse-hua), 1907–.
Verkehrsentwicklung und Verkehrsplanung in China und ihre Auswirkung auf die Volkswirtschaft (The development and planning of transportation in China and its effects on the national economy).
Unpublished doctoral dissertation, Rechts- und staatswissenschaftliche Fakultät, Universität Berlin, 1941. 192 p.
SUBJ 14.2 ▪ 14.3 14.6

12634 CBU P P2 G1.2 1895–1949
Chen, Ho-Sen (Ch'en Ho-sheng).
'Entwicklung und Ausbaumöglichkeiten des chinesischen Transportwesens unter dem Gesichtspunkt der Industrialisierung' (The development of China's transport system and possibilities for its improvement from the standpoint of industrialization).
WA 45, 2 (März 1937), 320–362. (Doctoral dissertation, Rechts- und staatswissenschaftliche Fakultät, Universität Kiel)
SUBJ 14 14.2 ▪ 11 14.4

12635 NNC U P1 G1.2 1895–1949
Chen, Lawrence M. (Ch'en Wen-t'ung).
'Aviation in China.'
IB 3, 12 (1 May 1937), 255–274.
SUBJ 14.2 ▪ 15 34.2

12636 NNC U P1 G1.2 1895–1949
Chen, Lawrence M. (Ch'en Wen-t'ung).
'Highways in China.'
IB 2, 8 (21 Nov. 1936), 133–154.
SUBJ 14.2

12637 CSU PO P1 G1.2 1842–1949
Cheng, Lin, 1901–.
The Chinese railways, past and present.
Shanghai: China United Press, 1937. 332 p. [Rev. and enl. ed. of *The Chinese railways: A historical survey*. Shanghai: China United Press, 1935. 214 p.]
SUBJ 14.2 ▪ 14.3 14.6 66

12638 MCH P P2 G1.2 1842–1949
Cheng, Ming-Ju.
The influence of communications, internal and external, upon the economic future of China.
London: Routledge, 1930. 13, 177 p.
SUBJ 14 14.2 ▪ 12 14.1 14.3 14.4 17

12639 CBU P P2 G1.3 1842–1949
Chiang, Liang-Jën.
'Postwesen und Industrialisierung in China' (The postal service and industrialization in China).
WA 45, 2 (März 1937), 377–392.
SUBJ 14.2 ▪ 14.4 14.6

12640 ELO FP P2 G1.2 1895–1928
China [Republic]. Chiao t'ung pu. Yu cheng kuan li chu. (Ministry of Communications. Directorate General of Posts).
Report on the Chinese post office for the tenth year of Chung-hua min-kuo, 1921, with which is incorporated an historical survey of the quarter-century, 1896–1921.
Shanghai: Yu cheng kuan li chü, 1922. 118 p.
SUBJ 14.2 ▪ 11 14.5

12641 CSU P P2 G2.0 1895–1949
Chou, Shun-hsin, 1915–.
'Railway development and economic growth in Manchuria.'
CQ 45 (Jan.–Mar. 1971), 57–84.
SUBJ 14.2 ▪ 14 34.2

12642 CBU P P2 G1.3 1895–1949
Chun, Y. S.
'Die Bedeutung des Eisenbahnwesens für den Industrialisierungsprozess in China' (The significance of railroads in the industrialization of China).
WA 45, 2 (März 1937), 363–376.
SUBJ 14.2 14.4 ▪ 14.3

12643 MCH S P2 G2.0 1842–1928
Classen, Wilhelm.
'Die verkehrs- und wirtschafts-geographische Situation der Mandschurei vor der Einführung der Eisenbahn' (Manchuria before the introduction of the railroad: An appraisal in terms of commercial and economic geography).
Geographische Z. 43, 6 (1937), 201–214.
SUBJ 14.2 ▪ 11.3 14.1 14.3

12644 NIC PO P4 G1.2 1842–1928
Donovan, John Patrick.
'The press of China.'
Asiatic review new (4th) series 15, 42 (Apr. 1919), 153–167.
SUBJ 14.2 ▪ 12 32

12645 CSH P P2 G2.0 1842–1949
Dorian, Georgii.
'Razvitie sredstv soobshcheniia i elektrifikatsii v Man'chzhurii' (The development of equipment for communications and electrification in Manchuria).
Vostochnoe obozrenie 16 (iiul'–sentiabr' 1943), 46–86.
SUBJ 14.2 14.4

12646 NNC O P2 G1.3 1842–1928
Dorpmüller, J-.
'Vom Eisenbahnbau in China' (Railroad construction in China).
AE 51, 5 (Sept.–Okt. 1928), 1097–1140.
SUBJ 14.2 ▪ 16.4

12647 NNC P P2 G1.5 1895–1949
Dschu, Gwang-tzam (Chu Kuang-tsan).
Die Binnenschiffahrt auf dem Jangtse-Kiang seit 1900 (Inland navigation on the Yangtze river since 1900).
Berlin: Freyhoff, 1933. 95 p. (Doctoral dissertation, Philosophische Fakultät, Universität Berlin)
SUBJ 14.2 14.3 ▪ 14.5 34.2

12648 CSU S P2 G2.0 1895–1949
Ginsburg, Norton Sydney, 1921–.
'Manchurian railway development.'
FEQ 8, 4 (Aug. 1949), 398–411.
SUBJ 14.2 ▪ 14.1 14.4 14.6

12649 NNC U P2 G1.2 1895–1949
Great Britain. Admiralty. Naval Intelligence Division. Geographical Section.
'Posts, telegraphs, and telephones.' In *China proper, Vol. 3, Economic geography, ports and communications,* compiled by the agency cited. [Selective entry]
London: His Majesty's Stationery Office, 1945, 594–601. (NID, Geographical handbook series, BR 530B)
SUBJ 14.2 ▪ 24.2

12650 NNC S P2 G1.2 –1949
Great Britain. Admiralty. Naval Intelligence Division. Geographical Section.
'Roads.' In *China proper, Vol. 3, Economic geography, ports and communications,* compiled by the agency cited. [Selective entry]
London: His Majesty's Stationery Office, 1945, 429–456. (NID, Geographical handbook series, BR 530B)
SUBJ 14.2 ▪ 14 14.6 15 18 72

12651 NNC S P5 G1.2 –1949
Great Britain. Admiralty. Naval Intelligence Division. Geographical Section.
'Shipping.' In *China proper, Vol. 3, Economic geography, ports and communications,* compiled by the agency cited. [Selective entry]
London: His Majesty's Stationery Office, 1945, 578–605. (NID, Geographical handbook series, BR 530B)
SUBJ 14.2 ▪ 16.4 72

12652 DLC U P1 G1.3 –1949
Jack-Hinton, Colin.
'Junks and the Chinese trader.'
Hemisphere 13, 2 (Feb. 1969), 9–14.
SUBJ 14.2

12653 CSH P P1 G1.2 1842–1928
Kantorovich, Anatolii IAkovlevich, 1896–1944.
Inostrannyi kapital na zheleznykh dorogakh Kitaia (Foreign capital in China's railroads).
Harbin: Tip. KVzhd, 1926. 91 p.
SUBJ 14.2 14.6 66

12654 MCH P P4 G1.1 –1928
Kim, Heun-Chun, 1899–.
Die Aufmachung der modernen Zeitung in Ostasien (The make-up of the modern newspaper in East Asia).
Leipzig: A. Twietmeyer, 1928. 61 p. (Doctoral dissertation, Philosophische Fakultät, Universität Leipzig)
SUBJ 14.2 ▪ 12.1 61

12655 ICU S P2 G1.4 1895–1928
Li, Bing Hua (Li Ping-hua), 1893–.
A brief history of the Peking-Hankow railway.
Unpublished masters thesis in Political Economy, U. of Chicago, 1926. 102 p.
SUBJ 14.2 66 ▪ 14 14.3 14.6

12656 NNC U P1 G1.2 1895–1949
Liang, Hubert S. (Liang Shih-ch'un), 1903–.
'Development of modern Chinese press.'
IB 4, 1 (12 May 1937), 1–19.
SUBJ 14.2

12657 MCH PO P4 G1.1 –1949
Lin Yutang (Lin Yü-t'ang), 1895–.
A history of the press and public opinion in China.
Chicago: U. of Chicago Press, 1936. 179 p.
SUBJ 12 14.2 16.1 ▪ 12.2

12658 MCH PO P1 G1.1 1842–1949
Lochow, Hans Juergen von.
China's national railways: Historical survey and postwar planning.
Peiping: The author, 1948. 10, 162 p.
SUBJ 14.2 ▪ 14.5

12659 CSU P P1 G1.2 –1949
Löwenthal, Rudolf, 1904–.
'The copyright in China.'
YJSS 3, 2 (Aug. 1941), 145–173.
SUBJ 12.2 14.2

12660 CSH P P4 G1.1 1895–1949
Löwenthal, Rudolf, 1904–.
The religious periodical press in China.
Peiping: Synodal Commission in China, 1940. 294 p. (Sinological series, 57)
SUBJ 14.2 ▪ 33

12661 NNC S P4 G1.1 –1949
Mayer, Norbert.
'Die Presse in China' (The press in China).
Zeitungswissenschaft 10, 12 (1 Dez. 1935), 589–606.
SUBJ 14.2 ▪ 17 19

12662 CSH S P2 G1.2 1842–1949
Mikhailov, M- IA-.
'K voprosu o transportnoi probleme v Kitae' (The transport problem in China).
VM 1932, 6/7, 1–25.
SUBJ 14.2 ▪ 14 14.3

12663 CSH P P2 G2.0 1895–1928
Nilus, E- Kh-, comp.
Istoricheskii obzor Kitaiskoi Vostochnoi zheleznoi dorogi, 1896–1923, tom I (Historical overview of the Chinese Eastern Railway, 1896–1923, Vol. 1).
Harbin: Tip. KVzhd i T-va 'Ozo', 1923. 18, 690 p.
SUBJ 12 14.2 15 32.2 35 66 ▪ 12.2 14.3 14.6 21.1 24.1 24.4 24.5 25 32.1

12664 NNC PO P1 G1.3 1842–1949
Otte, Friedrich W- K-.
'Die chinesische Reichspost' (The Chinese national postal service).
Sinica 15, 3/6 (Mai–Nov. 1940), 274–305.
SUBJ 14.2 ▪ 12

12665 MCH PO P1 G1.1 –1949
Otte, Friedrich W- K-.
'Schiffahrt in China' (Travel by ship in China).
Sinica 14, 1/2 (Jan.–März 1939), 52–73.
Subj 14.2 ▪ 14.3 14.5 16

12666 MCH P P3 G1.3 1842–1928
Polevoi, S- A-.
'Periodicheskaia pechat' v Kitae' (The periodical press in China).
IVI 47, 7 (15 avgusta 1913), 1–189.
Subj 14.2 32.1 ▪ 12 18 22

12667 NNC S P3 G1.3 –1928
Schultze, Ernst, 1874–?
'Der Schiffsbau in China' (Ship construction in China).
Oesterreichische Monatsschrift für den Orient 44, 7/9 (Juli–Sept. 1918), 228–244.
Subj 14.2 14.4

12668 NIC P P2 G1.2 1644–1949
Sheldon, Charles David, 1918–.
'Some economic reasons for the marked contrast in Japanese and Chinese modernization, as seen in examples from "pre-modern" shipping and trading by water.'
KUER 23, 2 (Oct. 1953), 30–60.
Subj 14.2 14.3 ▪ 16.2 34.2

12669 GMS P P2 G1.2 1842–1928
Siao, Wuisin (Hsiao Wei-hsin), 1898–.
'Die Entwicklung des Eisenbahnwesens in China' (The development of railroads in China).
AE 52, 1 (Jan.–Feb. 1929), 12–46; 52, 2 (März–Apr. 1929), 249–314. (Doctoral dissertation, Philosophische Fakultät, Universität Basel)
Subj 14.2 ▪ 14.4 14.6

12670 NNC U P2 G2.0 1895–1928
Simmersbach, Bruno.
'Von der Ostchinesischen Eisenbahn und ihrem Einflussgebiet' (The Chinese Eastern Railway and its sphere of influence).
AE 43, 2 (März–Apr. 1920), 173–186.
Subj 14.2 ▪ 14.3 21

12671 MCH O P2 G1.2 1895–1928
Sowerby, Arthur de Carle, 1885–1964, et al.
'Transportation.'
CJ 10, 5 (May 1929), 217–284.
Subj 14.2

12672 MCH O P2 G1.5 1895–1949
Spencer, Joseph Earle, 1907–.
'Trade and transshipment in the Yangtze valley.'
GR 28, 1 (Jan. 1938), 112–123.
Subj 14.2 ▪ 14.3

12673 GMS O P3 G1.2 1895–1928
Strewe, M- Th——.
'Das Verkehrswesen in China' (Transport in China). In *China: Wirtschaft und Wirtschaftsgrundlagen* (The economy and economic foundations of China), edited by Josef Hellauer. [Selective entry]
Berlin: de Gruyter (Vereinigung wissenschaftlicher Verleger), 1921, 95–127.
Subj 14.2

12674 CSH P P2 G1.2 1895–1949
Surin, Vladimir Ivanovich.
Zheleznye dorogi v Man'chzhurii i Kitae: materialy k transportnoi probleme v Kitae i Man'chzhurii (Railroads in Manchuria and China: Data on the transport problem in China and Manchuria).
Harbin: Tip. KVzhd, 1932. 58, 393 p.
Subj 14 14.2 ▪ 21.1 21.2 66

12675 MAU PO P2 G1.3 –1949
Tien, Hsing-chih (T'ien Hsing-chih), 1908–.
China's Grand Canal: A study of cultural landscape.
Unpublished doctoral dissertation in Geography, U. of Michigan, 1947. 179 p.
Subj 11.3 12 12.2 14 14.2 14.5 ▪ 14.1 21.3 23 24.4 29 62

12676 ICU S P1 G1.2 1895–1949
Ting, Lee-hsia Hsu, 1923–.
Government control of the press in modern China, 1900–1949: A study of its theories, operations, and effects.
Unpublished doctoral dissertation in Library Science, U. of Chicago, 1969. 448 p.
Subj 12.2 14.2 ▪ 32 32.2 66

12677 GMS P P2 G1.1 1842–1928
Trittel, Walter, 1880–.
'Entwicklung des chinesischen Eisenbahnwesens' (The development of railroads in China).
MSOSB 29 (1926), 43–98.
Subj 14.2

12678 CSU U P2 G1.1 –1949
Tseng, H. P.
'China prior to 1949.' In *The Asian newspapers' reluctant revolution*, edited by John A- Lent. [Selective entry]
Ames: Iowa State U. Press, 1971, 31–42.
Subj 14.2 ▪ 12.1 16.1 32

12679 MCY U P1 G1.1 1842–1928
Wang, Ching-chun (Wang Ching-ch'un), 1883–1956.
'The administration of Chinese government railways.'
CSPSR 1, 1 (Apr. 1916), 68–85.
Subj 12 14.2 ▪ 66

12680 MCH P P2 G1.5 1842–1928
Wang, Chung-chi (Wang Chung-ch'i), 1898–.
La navigation du Yang-tseu (Navigation on the Yangtze).
Paris: Presses modernes, 1932. 315 p. (Doctoral dissertation, Faculté des lettres, Université de Paris)
Subj 11.3 14.2 ▪ 12 14.3

12681 NNC U P2 G1.2 1895–1949
Wang Lien.
'Eisenbahn und Landstrasse in China' (Railroads and highways in China).
AE 59, 5 (Sept.–Okt. 1936), 1103–1130. (Doctoral dissertation, Staatswirtschaftliche Fakultät, Universität München)
Subj 14 14.2 ▪ 14.1 14.4

12682 MAM P P6 G1.3 –1949
Wiens, Herold Jacob, 1912–1971.
The Shu-tao, or the road to Szechuan: A study of the development and significance of Shenshi-Szechuan road communication in West China.
Ann Arbor: University Microfilms (Publ. 1122), 1949. 200 p. (Doctoral dissertation in Geography, U. of Michigan)
Subj 14 14.2 ▪ 12.2 14.5

12683 CSU S P2 G1.3 1644–1949
Worcester, George Raleigh Gray, 1890–1969.
'The coming of the Chinese steamer.'
Mariner's mirror 38, 2 (May 1952), 132–141.
Subj 14.2 ▪ 14.4 15 34.2

12684 CSU FP P2 G1.5 –1949
Worcester, George Raleigh Gray, 1890–1969.
The junks and sampans of the Yangtze.
Annapolis: Naval Institute Press, 1971. 626 p.
Subj 14.2 24.2 ▪ 14.1 14.3 15 18 23 34.3 38 57 65

12685 CSU P P4 G1.2 –1949
Wu, K. T. (Wu Kuang-ch'ing), 1905–.
'The Chinese book: Its evolution and development.'
THM 3, 1 (Aug. 1936), 25–33.
Subj 14.2 ▪ 14.4

12686 CSU P P1 G1.2 –1949
Wu, K. T. (Wu Kuang-ch'ing), 1905–.
'The development of printing in China.'
THM 3, 2 (Sept. 1936), 137–160.
Subj 14.2 ▪ 14.4

12687 CBU S P2 G2.0 1895–1949
Yang, Hung-tu, 1893–.
Das Verkehrswesen der Mandschurei (The transportation system of Manchuria).
Leipzig: The author, 1931. 56 p. (Doctoral dissertation, Philosophische Fakultät, Universität Leipzig)
Subj 14.2 ▪ 11.3 21 21.4

1911-1949

12688 CNY U P3 G1.2 1911–1928
'L'aviation chinoise' (Aviation in China).
La Chine 1 (15 août 1921), 20–25.
Subj 14.2

12689 NNC U P4 G5.0 1928–1949
'Die Bedeutung der Tsang-Shi Eisenbahn für die Wirtschaft Nordchinas' (The significance of the Ts'ang-chou–Shih-chia-chuang railroad [Hopei] to the economy of North China).
AE 59, 6 (Nov.–Dez. 1936), 1449–1451.
Subj 14.2 ▪ 14

12690 CSH P P2 G1.2 1911–1928
'Chinese government railways in 1923.'
CEM 2, 12 (Sept. 1925), 24–37.
Subj 14.2 34.2

12691 CSH P P2 G1.2 1911–1928
'The Chinese government railways, 1922.'
CEM 1, 8 (May 1924), 18–27.
Subj 14.2 34.2

12692 CSU P P3 G1.1 1928–1949
'Chinese shipping companies.'
CEJ 12, 2 (Feb. 1933), 190–199.
Subj 14.2 34.2

12693 NNC U P4 G1.4 1911–1928
'Die Eisenbahnen Nordchinas in den Jahren 1924–1927' (The railroads of North China, 1924–1927).
AE 51, 6 (Nov.–Dez. 1928), 1469–1478.
SUBJ 14.2 ▪ 14.6

12694 CSU U P2 G1.2 1928–1949
'Modern road-construction in China.'
CEJ 13, 2 (Aug. 1933), 169–191; 13, 3 (Sept. 1933), 271–289.
SUBJ 14.2

12695 NNC S P1 G1.2 1911–1949
'Postal statistics in China, 1912–1929.'
NWSS 4, 29 (20 July 1931), 137, 139–142.
SUBJ 14.2 ▪ 14.6

12696 NNC P P4 G1.2 1928–1949
'Postal statistics in China, 1930–1931.'
NWSS 6, 21 (22 May 1933), 97, 99–104.
SUBJ 14.2

12697 NNC P P1 G1.2 1928–1949
'Provincial and national highways in China.'
NWSS 5, 36 (5 Sept. 1932), 167–168.
SUBJ 14.2

12698 CSU P P2 G1.2 1928–1949
'Recent progress in transportation and communication services.'
CEJ 17, 3 (Sept. 1935), 257–274.
SUBJ 14.2

12699 CSU U P3 G1.3 1911–1949
'Shanghai broadcasting activities.'
CEJ 18, 4 (Apr. 1936), 586–590.
SUBJ 14.2 24.2

12700 CSU P P2 G1.2 1928–1949
'A year's progress in transportation and communication services.'
CEJ 15, 1 (July 1934), 44–66.
SUBJ 14.2

12701 GBS S P1 G1.2 1911–1928
An, Yung-Jui.
Das Postwesen in China und seine Entwicklung (China's postal service and its development).
Leipzig: The author, 1931. 80 p. (Doctoral dissertation, Philosophische Fakultät, Universität Leipzig)
SUBJ 14.2

12702 NNC S P2 G1.2 1928–1949
Asiaticus, pseud.
'The new era in Chinese railway construction.'
PA 10, 3 (Sept. 1937), 276–288.
SUBJ 14.2 ▪ 12 14.6 34.2

12703 NIC O P2 G1.2 1928–1949
Baker, John Earl, 1880–1957.
'Transportation in China.'
AAAPSS 152 (Nov. 1930), 160–172. [Special issue: *China*, edited by Henry F- James]
SUBJ 14.2

12704 NNC P P4 G1.3 1911–1928
Baltzer, Franz, 1857–?
'Die chinesischen Eisenbahnen im Kalenderjahr 1922' (Railroads in China in 1922).
AE 48, 2 (März–Apr. 1925), 376–389.
SUBJ 14.2

12705 NNC P P4 G1.3 1911–1928
Baltzer, Franz, 1857–?
'Die chinesischen Staatseisenbahnen im Jahre 1920' (The Chinese government railroads in 1920).
AE 46, 2 (März–Apr. 1923), 328–330.
SUBJ 14.2

12706 NNC P P4 G1.3 1911–1928
Baltzer, Franz, 1857–?
'Die chinesischen Staatseisenbahnen im Kalenderjahr 1921' (The Chinese government railroads in 1921).
AE 47, 2 (März–Apr. 1924), 287–306.
SUBJ 14.2

12707 NNC P P4 G1.2 1911–1928
Baltzer, Franz, 1857–?
'Die Eisenbahnen Chinas während des Bürgerkrieges' (China's railroads during the civil war).
AE 50, 3 (Mai–Juni 1927), 807–814.
SUBJ 14.2 ▪ 14.6

12708 ELS S P2 G1.2 1928–1949
Bao Chiao-ming (Pao Chiao-min).
A geographical study of China, with special reference to the means of transport.
Unpublished doctoral dissertation in Economics, U. of London [London School of Economics and Political Science], 1940. 606, 25 p.
SUBJ 11.3 14 14.1 14.2 14.3 ▪ 11.2 21

12709 CSH P P2 G1.2 1911–1928
Baranov, Ippolit Gavrilovich.
'Kitaiskaia pochta' (China's postal system).
VM 1927, 6, 39–49.
SUBJ 14.2 ▪ 12 14.6

12710 NNC S P3 G1.2 1928–1949
Britton, Roswell Sessoms, 1897–.
'Chinese news interests.'
PA 7, 2 (June 1934), 181–193.
SUBJ 14.2 60

12711 NIC O P2 G1.2 1911–1928
Chatley, Herbert, 1885–.
'River problems in China.'
JRAS-NCB new (2nd) series 49 (1918), 1–12.
SUBJ 14.1 14.2

12712 NNU P P2 G1.2 1928–1949
Chen, Henry H. C. (Ch'en Hsien-chang), 1912–.
A study of the elements of managerial and operating efficiency of motor truck transportation, with special reference to motor transportation in China.
Unpublished doctoral dissertation in Business Administration, New York U., 1942. 283, 10 p.
SUBJ 14.2 34.2 ▪ 12 14.3

12713 MCY P P3 G1.3 1928–1949
Cheng Chu-yuan (Cheng Chu-yüan), 1927–.
'Chinese Communist infiltration of the mainland press, 1927–1949.' In *Communist penetration and exploitation of the free press*, compiled by Judiciary Committee, Senate, U.S. Congress. [Sole entry]
Washington, D.C.: U.S. Government Printing Office, 1962, 22–28.
SUBJ 14.2 32.2

12714 MCH PO P1 G1.2 1911–1949
Chu, Chia-hua, 1893–1963.
China's postal and other communications services.
London: Kegan Paul, Trench, Trübner, 1937. 259 p.
SUBJ 14.2 ▪ 12 12.2 14.3 14.6

12715 CSU O P2 G1.4 1911–1928
Clapp, Frederick G-.
'The Hwang Ho, Yellow River.'
GR 12, 1 (Jan. 1922), 1–18.
SUBJ 14.2

12716 NNC U P4 G2.0 1911–1928
Cremer, Maria.
'Die Ostchinesische Bahn' (The Chinese Eastern Railway).
AE 52, 3 (Mai–Juni 1929), 657–676.
SUBJ 14.2

12717 NNC P P4 G2.0 1911–1928
Cremer, Maria.
'Zur Lage der Ostchinesischen Bahn' (The situation of the Chinese Eastern Railway).
AE 53, 4 (Juli–Aug. 1930), 951–968.
SUBJ 14.2 ▪ 14 21.1

12718 NNC U P2 G1.3 1911–1928
Fitzner, Rudolf.
'Die Wiederherstellung des Grossen Kanals in China' (The reconstruction of China's Grand Canal).
Der neue Orient 1, 1 (7 Apr. 1917), 19–23.
SUBJ 14.2 ▪ 18

12719 NNC U P2 G1.2 1928–1949
Great Britain. Admiralty. Naval Intelligence Division. Geographical Section.
'Railways.' In *China proper, Vol. 3, Economic geography, ports and communications*, compiled by the agency cited. [Selective entry]
London: His Majesty's Stationery Office, 1945, 457–510. (NID, Geographical handbook series, BR 530B)
SUBJ 14.2 ▪ 72

12720 NNC U P2 G1.2 1928–1949
Great Britain. Admiralty. Naval Intelligence Division. Geographical Section.
'Waterways.' In *China proper, Vol. 3, Economic geography, ports and communications*, compiled by the agency cited. [Selective entry]
London: His Majesty's Stationery Office, 1945, 511–556. (NID, Geographical handbook series, BR 530B)
SUBJ 14.2 ▪ 72

12721 GLU S P2 G1.2 1911–1949
Han, Kwei-Chang (Han Kuei-chang), 1909–.
Die Beziehungen zwischen Industrieaufbau und Verkehrsgestaltung im modernen China (The relationship between industrial expansion and the organization of transport in modern China).
Unpublished doctoral dissertation, Philosophische Fakultät, Universität Leipzig, 1941. 192 p.
SUBJ 14.2 ▪ 14.4

12722 MCH O P2 G1.4 1911–1928
Hondelink, E- R-.
'De Lunghai-Spoorweg' (The Lanchow–Hai-tung [Kiangsu] railroad).
China (Amsterdam) 1 (Juli 1926), 316–328.
Subj 14.2 ▪ 14.3

12723 CBU P P2 G1.5 1928–1949
Hu Kwoh-hwa (Hu Kuo-hua) and Yuen-chan Wu.
'Freight rates and their relationship to the general price level in Free China since the war.'
EF 41 (Feb. 1945), 631–640.
Subj 14.2 14.3 14.6

12724 CSU P P4 G1.3 1911–1928
Jen Cho-hsüan, 1896–.
'The introduction of Marxism-Leninism into China: The early years, 1919–1924.' Tr. from the Chinese by Ignatius J. H. Ts'ao and Suny Oneonta.
SST 10, 2 (June 1970), 138–166.
Subj 14.2 32.2 64

12725 NNC U P4 G5.0 1911–1928
K.
'Die Suitschang-Bahn' (The Kuei-sui–Kalgan railroad).
AE 45, 1 (Jan.–Feb. 1922), 137–142.
Subj 14.2 ▪ 14.3 21.1

12726 NNC F P2 G4.0 1928–1949
Köhler, Günther, 1909–.
'Die Bedeutung des Hwang-Ho innerhalb nordwest-chinesischen Verkehrsnetzes' (The significance of the Yellow River in Northwest China's transport network).
PGM 96, 2 (1952), 85–89.
Subj 14.2 ▪ 14.3

12727 CSU S P2 G1.2 1928–1949
Koizumi Teizō, 1905–.
'The operation of Chinese junks.' Tr. by Andrew Watson of 'Shina minsen no keiei ni tsuite' (The management of junks and sampans in China); *Keizai ronsō* 57, 3 (Sept. 1943), 66–92 [greatly condensed in tr.]. In *Transport in transition: The evolution of traditional shipping in China*. [Analytic entry]
Ann Arbor: U. of Michigan, Center for Chinese Studies, 1972, 1–13. (Michigan abstracts of Chinese and Japanese works on Chinese history, 3)
Subj 14.2 14.3 ▪ 34.2 36.2 39

12728 CSU O P2 G1.4 1911–1928
Lattimore, Owen, 1900–.
'Caravan routes of inner Asia.'
GJ 72, 6 (Dec. 1928), 497–531. [Reprinted in *Studies in frontier history: Collected papers, 1928–1958*, by O. Lattimore. (Selective entry.) London: Oxford U. Press, 1962, 37–72.]
Subj 14.2 ▪ 11.2 11.3 14.3 55 65

12729 CSU P P1 G1.2 1928–1949
Lin Yutang (Lin Yü-t'ang), 1895–.
'Contemporary Chinese periodical literature.'
THM 2, 3 (Mar. 1936), 225–244.
Subj 14.2 ▪ 12.1 16.1 63

12730 WSU PO P1 G1.1 1928–1949
Ling, Chuke.
China's railway rolling stock.
Seattle: U. of Washington Press, 1946. 10, 110 p. (Masters thesis in Business Administration, U. of Washington, 1946)
Subj 14.2 14.6 ▪ 12 14 14.3

12731 CSH O P2 G1.2 1911–1949
Ling, H. H. (Ling Hung-hsün), 1929–.
'A decade of Chinese railroad construction (1926–1936)' [with comments by Chiao-min Hsieh]. In *The strenuous decade: China's nation-building efforts, 1927–1937*, edited by Paul K. T. Sih (Hsüeh Kuang-ch'ien). [Selective entry]
New York: St. John's U. Press, 1970, 255–288.
Subj 14.2 ▪ 14.6 66

12732 NNC P P2 G2.0 1911–1928
Liubimov, L- I-.
'Zheleznye dorogi i zhelezhodorozhnoe stroitel'stvo v Man'chzhurii' (Railroads and railroad construction in Manchuria).
BSB 1, 4 (1932), 135–184.
Subj 14.2 ▪ 14 72

12733 MCY P P1 G1.2 1911–1949
Löwenthal, Rudolf, 1904–.
'Public communications in China before July, 1937.'
CSPSR 22, 1 (Apr.–June 1938), 42–58.
Subj 12.1 14.2 ▪ 12 12.2

12734 CSU O P2 G1.4 1928–1949
Moore, W- Robert.
'Raft life on the Hwang Ho [Yellow River].'
NG 61, 6 (June 1932), 743–752.
Subj 14.2

12735 CSU O P2 G8.0 1928–1949
Outram, Frank, and G- E- Fane.
'Burma road, back door to China.'
NG 78, 5 (Nov. 1940), 629–658.
Subj 14.2 ▪ 21.4

12736 NNC U P4 G2.0 1928–1949
Pausin, ———.
'Die Mandschukuo-Staatseisenbahnen' (Government railroads in Manchoukuo).
AE 60, 2 (März–Apr. 1937), 453–466.
Subj 14.2

12737 NNC P P4 G1.4 1911–1928
Preyer, Otto Ernest, 1881–.
'Die Peking-Kalgan Eisenbahn und ihre Verlängerung nach Kweihuacheng' (The Peking-Kalgan railroad and its extension to Kuei-hua-ch'eng [Shansi]).
AE 38, 5 (Sept.–Okt. 1915), 1104–1105.
Subj 14.2

12738 NNC U P4 G1.3 1928–1949
Radermacher, P- P-.
'Die Entwicklung von Schienenweg und Landstrasse in China' (The development of railroads and highways in China).
AE 60, 6 (Nov.–Dez. 1937), 1317–1350.
Subj 14.2 ▪ 14 14.6

12739 CSH S P2 G1.2 1911–1949
Rogov, Vl——.
'Vodnye puti soobshcheniia Kitaia' (Transport and communications via China's waterways).
VM 1932, 5, 51–70.
Subj 14.2 ▪ 14.3

12740 CSU O P2 G1.3 1911–1949
Shaw, Ernest T-.
'Radio broadcasting in China.'
Asia (New York: American Asiatic Assn.) 35, 1 (Jan. 1935), 19–23.
Subj 14.2 ▪ 37

12741 DLC P P3 G5.1 1911–1928
Shneider, Mark Evseevich, 1921–.
'"Sin' Shekhui" i "Zhen'dao": zhurnaly "dvizheniia 4 maia"' (*Hsin she-hui* [The new society] and *Jen-tao yüeh-k'an* [L'humanité]: Periodicals of the May Fourth Movement). In *Dvizhenie '4 maia' 1919 goda v Kitae: sbornik statei* (Articles on the May Fourth Movement in China), compiled by Institut vostokovedeniia, Akademiia nauk SSSR, edited by A- G- Afanas'ev et al. [Selective entry]
Moscow: Nauka, Glav. red. vost. lit-ry, 1971, 176–198.
Subj 14.2 60 66 ▪ 26.1 32 32.1 54

12742 MCH P P1 G1.2 1928–1949
Smith, A- Viola, 1893–, and Anselm Chuh.
Motor roads in China.
Washington, D.C.: U.S. Dept. of Commerce, Bureau of Foreign and Domestic Commerce, 1931. 131 p. (BFDC trade promotion series, 120)
Subj 14.2 ▪ 12 12.2

12743 MCY U P2 G2.0 1928–1949
South Manchuria Railway Co.
South Manchuria Railway, October 1939.
Dairen: South Manchuria Railway Co., 1939. 57 p.
Subj 14.2

12744 NIC O P2 G1.2 1928–1949
Stables, F- H- A-.
'Present conditions of road travel in China.'
J. of the Royal Central Asian Society 35, 2 (Apr. 1948), 144–150.
Subj 14.2

12745 MCH O P2 G1.3 1911–1928
Stringer, Harold.
The Chinese railway system.
Shanghai: Kelly and Walsh, 1922. 216 p.
Subj 14.2 ▪ 12 14

12746 NNC P P2 G2.0 1911–1928
Tarasov, I-.
'Zheleznodorozhnoe stroitel'stvo v Man'chzhurii i politika IAponii' (Railroad construction in Manchuria and Japanese policy).
MKhMP 1927, 10/11 (oktiabr'–noiabr'), 98–104.
Subj 14.2 14.3

12747 CSU O P2 G4.0 1911–1928
Teichman, Eric, 1884–1944.
Travels of a consular officer in North-west China.
Cambridge: Cambridge U. Press, 1921. 219 p. [Reprinted—Ann Arbor: University Microfilms, n.d. 219 p.]
Subj 14.2 66 ▪ 12 14.1 22 22.2 25 32.2 33

12748 NNC P P1 G1.2 1928–1949
Ting, Leonard G. (Ting Chi), 1907–1940, and Rockwood Q. P. Chin (Ch'en Kuo-p'ing), 1911–.
'War and transportation in China.'
NSEQ 12, 1/2 (Jan. 1941), 4–52.
Subj 14.2 ▪ 15

12749 CSH O P2 G1.2 1911–1928
Todd, Oliver Julian, 1880–.
'American engineers in the China field.'
Military engineer 16, 85 (Jan.–Feb. 1924), 1–10. [Reprinted in *Two decades in China*, by O. J. Todd. (Selective entry.) Peiping: Assn. of Chinese and American Engineers, 1938, 19–32.] [Reprinted in *Two decades in China*, by O. J. Todd. (Selective entry.) Taipei: Ch'eng-wen, 1971, 19–32.]
Subj 14.2 ▪ 14.1 18 21.4 24.2

12750 NNC P P1 G1.2 1911–1949
Tung, Samuel C. H.
'The need of coordination in China's transport.'
MBEC 7, 10 (Oct. 1934), 409–420.
Subj 14.2

12751 CSH P P2 G1.2 1928–1949
U.S. Office of Strategic Services. Research and Analysis Branch.
Free China railways: Recent aspects of their construction, operation, and maintenance, mimeo.
[Washington, D.C.]: ——, 1943. 21 p. (R. and A., 1008)
Subj 14.2 ▪ 14.3

12752 NNC P P4 G2.0 1928–1949
Wehde-Textor, O-.
'Die Chinesische Ostbahn im Jahre des russisch-chinesischen Konflikts, 1929' (The Chinese Eastern Railway in 1929, the year of the Russo-Chinese conflict).
AE 54, 5 (Sept.–Okt. 1931), 1203–1230.
Subj 14.2 ▪ 14.3 14.4

12753 NNC P P4 G1.4 1928–1949
Wehde-Textor, O-.
'Jahresbericht 1932 der Peiping-Liaoning Railway' (Annual report of the Peiping-Liaoning railroad for 1932).
AE 58, 1 (Jan.–Feb. 1935), 223–226.
Subj 14.2

12754 NNC P P4 G1.3 1928–1949
Wehde-Textor, O-.
'Der Jahresbericht 1933 über die Chinesischen Staatsbahnen' (Annual report for 1933 on the Chinese national railroads).
AE 59, 2 (März–Apr. 1936), 427–435.
Subj 14.2

12755 NNC P P4 G2.0 1928–1949
Wehde-Textor, O-.
'Die Südmandschurische Eisenbahn im Jahre 1935' (The South Manchurian Railway in 1935).
AE 59, 3 (Mai–Juni 1936), 664–668.
Subj 14.2

12756 CSU O P2 G1.5 1911–1928
Wilton, E- C-.
'Yun-nan and the West River of China.'
GJ 49, 6 (June 1917), 418–440.
Subj 14.2 ▪ 25 66

12757 WSU P P4 G1.2 1911–1949
Wong, Quen Yuen.
The Chinese government railway administration.
Unpublished masters thesis in Business Administration, U. of Washington, 1933. 92 p.
Subj 14.2 ▪ 12 34.2

12758 GMU S P1 G1.3 1911–1928
Wu Dschi-han (Wu Chih-han).
Die wissenschaftlichen Untersuchungen über das chinesische Verkehrswesen (Scientific research on the Chinese transportation system).
Stuttgart: The author, 1935. 135 p. (Doctoral dissertation, Technische Hochschule Stuttgart)
Subj 14.2

12759 ELU S P2 G1.1 1911–1949
Wu, Jullian Chuan-Chun, 1918–.
Rice economy of China.
Unpublished doctoral dissertation in Geography, U. of Liverpool, 1948. 282 p.
Subj 11 14.2 14.3 ▪ 11.2 16.3 18 55

12760 CSU U P3 G1.2 1928–1949
Yu, Chên-ming (Yü Chen-min).
'Press chronicle.' [Recurring feature article: journal issued monthly, article appears annually.]
THM 7, 1 – 12, 1 (Aug. 1938 – Aug.–Sept. 1941), average ca. 4 p.
Subj 14.2

1911-1972
(including 1644-1972)

12761 CSU P P1 G9.5 1928–1972
'The Chinese aircraft in Hong Kong.'
International law q. 4, 2 (Apr. 1951), 159–177.
Subj 12.2 14.2

12762 CSU P P1 G1.2 1895–1972
'L'évolution du réseau ferré chinois depuis dix ans' (The development of China's railroad system in the past ten years).
CFC 3 (oct. 1959), 59–78.
Subj 14.2

12763 CSU P P2 G1.2 –1972
Ajia no yume dōjinkai (Dream of Asia Society), ed.
Canals of China, mimeo. Tr. of *Chūgoku no unga*; Tokyo: Ajia no yume dōjinkai, 1963; 89 p.
Washington, D.C.: U.S. Joint Publications Research Service, 13 May 1965. 94 p. (JPRS 30,079; MC 11,108/1965)
Subj 14.2

12764 WSU S P3 G1.1 1644–1972
Chang Kuo-sin (Chang Kuo-hsing).
A survey of the Chinese language daily press.
Hong Kong: International Press Institute Asian Programme, 1968. 90 p. [s.p.]. [See Vol. 2 of this *Bibliography* for Chinese version.]
Subj 14.2 ▪ 12.2 36.1 36.2

12765 MCH P P4 G1.2 1842–1972
Chesneaux, Jean, 1922–.
'L'évolution du réseau ferroviaire chinois et le nouvel équilibre régional' (The development of China's railroad system and its new regional balance).
Economie appliquée 13, 3 (juil.–sept. 1960), 461–483.
Subj 11.3 14.2 ▪ 14

12766 CSH P P2 G4.0 1928–1972
Chu, Wen-djang (Chu Wen-ch'ang), 1914–.
'Public information.' In *A regional handbook on Northwest China*, compiled by Far Eastern and Russian Institute, U. of Washington. [Selective entry]
New Haven: Human Relations Area Files, 1956, vol. 2, 364–379. (HRAF subcontractor's monographs, 59; Washington 5)
Subj 14.2 ▪ 31

12767 CSH U P2 G1.3 –1972
[Harrington, Evelyn Davis] Lynn Harrington, 1911–.
The Grand Canal of China.
Chicago: Rand McNally, 1967. 110 p.
Subj 14.2 ▪ 14.1 18 25 36.3

12768 CSH U P1 G4.0 1911–1972
Hsü, Paul.
'Communications.' In *A regional handbook on Northwest China*, compiled by Far Eastern and Russian Institute, U. of Washington. [Selective entry]
New Haven: Human Relations Area Files, 1956, vol. 2, 691–704. (HRAF subcontractor's monographs, 59; Washington 5)
Subj 14.2

12769 CSH U P1 G3.0 1911–1972
Hsü, Paul.
'Communications.' In *A regional handbook on the Inner Mongolia Autonomous Region*, compiled by Far Eastern and Russian Institute, U. of Washington. [Selective entry]
New Haven: Human Relations Area Files, 1956, 539–550. (HRAF subcontractor's monographs, 60; Washington 7)
Subj 14.2

12770 DLC S P2 G1.3 1842–1972
Il'in, Aleksei Ivanovich (A. I. Il'yin), and M- P- Voronichev.
Zheleznodorozhnyi transport Kitaiskoi Narodnoi Respubliki.
Moscow: Gos. transp. zhel-dor. izd-vo, 1959. 164 p.
Railroad transport of the Chinese People's Republic, mimeo.
Washington, D.C.: U.S. Joint Publications Research Service, 1960. 151 p. (JPRS 3484; MC 11,481/1960)
Subj 14 14.1 14.2 14.4 ▪ 11 12 16.4 17 66

12771 MCH P P1 G1.2 1928–1972
Lippit, Victor David, 1938–.
'Development of transportation in Communist China.'
CQ 27 (July–Sept. 1966), 101–119. [Reprinted in *An economic profile of Mainland China*, compiled by Joint Economic Committee, U.S. Congress. (Selective entry.) Washington, D.C.: U.S. Government Printing Office, 1967, vol. 2, 661–676.] [Reprinted in *An economic profile of Mainland China*, compiled by the agency cited. (Selective entry.) New York: Praeger, 1968, 661–676.]
Subj 14 14.2

12772 CSU P P2 G1.1 –1972
Markham, James Walter, 1910–.
'China: Confucian and Communist.' In *Voices of the red giants: Communications in Russia and China*, by J. W. Markham. [Sole entry]

Ames: Iowa State U. Press, 1967, 269–442.
Subj 12.1 14.2 16.1 19 ▪ 16 29 31 41 58 64 66

12773 NNC P P1 G1.2 1928–1972
Mordvinov, G- I-.
'Razvitie transporta v Kitaiskoi Narodnoi Respublike' (The development of transportation in the People's Republic of China).
UZIV 11 (1955), 189–219.
Subj 14.2 ▪ 14

12774 NNC PO P2 G1.2 1928–1972
Murphey, William Rhoads, III, 1919–.
'China's transport problem, and Communist planning.'
EG 32, 1 (Jan. 1956), 17–28.
Subj 14.2 ▪ 11.4 14 14.3 14.4

12775 CSU P P2 G1.5 –1972
Nishimura Asahitaro (Nishimura Asahitarō).
'The most primitive means of transportation in Southeast and East Asia.'
Asian folklore studies 28, 2 (1969), 1–93.
Subj 14.1 14.2

12776 CBU P P2 G1.2 1842–1972
Shiriaev, Stepan Lavrent'evich, 1922–.
Zheleznodorozhnyi transport Kitaiskoi Narodnoi Respubliki (Rail transport in the People's Republic of China).
Moscow: Nauka, Glav. red. vost. lit-ry, 1969. 140 p.
Subj 14 14.2 ▪ 11.3

12777 MCY P P1 G1.2 1842–1972
Sun, E-tu Zen (Sun Jen I-tu), 1921–.
'The pattern of railway development in China.'
FEQ 14, 2 (Feb. 1955), 179–199.
Subj 14.2 ▪ 14

12778 FPN P P1 G1.2 1842–1972
Tang, Tsou-peï (T'ang Tsu-p'ei).
Régime de la navigation intérieure en Chine (The regulation of inland navigation in China).
Unpublished doctoral dissertation, Faculté de droit, Université de Paris, 1950. 213 p.
Subj 14.2 66

12779 MCH P P1 G1.2 1842–1972
Watt, John Robertson, 1934–.
'The effect of transportation on famine prevention.'
CQ 6 (Apr.–June 1961), 76–81.
Subj 14.2 18

12780 CSH P P2 G1.2 1928–1972
Weggel, Oskar, 1935–.
Massenkommunikation in der Volksrepublik China, mit besonderer Berücksichtigung des Zustandes seit der Kulturrevolution (Mass communication in the People's Republic of China, with special attention to conditions since the Cultural Revolution).
Hamburg: Institut für Asienkunde, 1970. 88 p. (IA, Mitteilungen, 34)
Subj 12.1 14.2 ▪ 64

12781 NNC P P2 G1.2 1842–1972
Wiens, Herold Jacob, 1912–1971.
'Riverine and coastal junks in China's commerce.'
EG 31, 3 (July 1955), 248–264.
Subj 14.2 ▪ 14.3 14.5

12782 CSH P P2 G1.2 1928–1972
Wong, George H. C. (Huang Tao-chang), 1924–.
'Public information.' In *A general handbook of China*, compiled by Far Eastern and Russian Institute, U. of Washington. [Selective entry]
New Haven: Human Relations Area Files, 1956, vol. 1, 698–750. (HRAF subcontractor's monographs, 55; Washington 4)
Subj 14.2 31 ▪ 12.1

12783 ELB FP P2 G1.2 –1972
Worcester, George Raleigh Gray, 1890–1969.
Sail and sweep in China: The history and development of the Chinese junk as illustrated by the collection of junk models in the Science Museum.
London: Her Majesty's Stationery Office, 1966. 146 p.
Subj 14.1 14.2 15 25 55 ▪ 14.3 16.3 31 62 65

12784 CSU P P2 G1.2 1928–1972
Yao, Ignatius Peng.
'The New China News Agency: How it serves the party.'
Journalism q. 40, 1 (Winter 1963), 83–86.
Subj 14.2 ▪ 12 32.1

12785 NNC S P3 G1.1 1895–1972
Yu, Ping-kuen (Yü Ping-ch'üan), 1925–.
'A note on historical periodicals of twentieth-century China.'
JAS 23, 4 (Aug. 1964), 581–590.
Subj 14.2 70

1949-1972

12786 MCH S P1 G1.2 1949–1972
'La modernisation du réseau navigable chinois' (The modernization of China's network of navigable waterways).
R. de la navigation intérieure et rhénane 33 (10 avr. 1961), 283–286.
Subj 14.2

12787 CSH P P2 G1.2 1949–1972
Ajia no yume dōjinkai (Dream of Asia Society), ed.
Water resources of China (plans and prospects for development), mimeo. Tr. of *Chūgoku no mizu shigen: Kaihatsu kōsō to tembō*; Tokyo: Ajia no yume dōjinkai, 1964; 120, 13 p.
Washington, D.C.: U.S. Joint Publications Research Service, 2 Nov. 1965. 244 p. (JPRS 32,681; MC 889/1966) [Xerox copyflo available—New York: CCM Information Corp., Research and Microfilm Publications. (Scholarly Book Translation Series, 524)]
Subj 11.4 14.1 14.2 ▪ 12 14.4 18

12788 CSU P P2 G1.2 1949–1972
Au, Lewis Li-tang (Ou Li-t'eng), 1914–.
'Civil and hydraulic engineering.' In *Sciences in Communist China*, edited by [Sydney Henry Gould] Sidney H. Gould. [Selective entry]
Washington, D.C.: American Assn. for the Advancement of Science, 1961, 771–804. (AAAS publications, 68)
Subj 14.2 ▪ 12 14.4 17

12789 FPN P P1 G1.2 1949–1972
Bergeron, Régis.
'Les transports en Chine.'
B. des transports 943 (juin 1960), 6–17. [Reprinted—*CFC* 7 (sept. 1960), 41–52.]
Transportation system in China, mimeo.
Washington, D.C.: U.S. Joint Publications Research Service, 24 Mar. 1961. 8 p. (JPRS 4484; MC 7671/1961)
Subj 14.2

12790 MCH P P2 G1.2 1949–1972
Chang, Kuei-sheng, 1921–.
'The changing railroad pattern in Mainland China.'
GR 51, 4 (Oct. 1961), 534–548.
Subj 14.2 ▪ 11.2 14.4

12791 CSU P P1 G1.2 1949–1972
Chang Man.
The 'People's daily' and the 'Red flag magazine' during the Cultural Revolution.
Hong Kong: Union Research Institute, 1969. 126 p. (Communist China problem research series, EC45)
Subj 14.2 19 64 ▪ 16.1 32.1 35 54

12792 NNC P P2 G1.2 1949–1972
Chao Shang-wen, Yao Pi, and Chou Wei-heng. [Authors sequential rather than joint: Chao Shang-wen for 1955; Yao Pi for 1956 and 1957; Chou Wei-heng for 1958.]
'Communications' [title varies]. Tr. of '1955–1958 nien Chung kung ti chiao t'ung chien she yü yün shu k'ai k'uang' (Communications construction and transportation in Communist China, 1955–1958); *Tsu kuo chou k'an* 159–334/335 (16 Jan. 1956 – 8 June 1959) [recurring annual feature article]. In *Communist China, 1955–1958*, edited by Union Research Institute.
Hong Kong: Union Research Institute. Issued annually, 1956–1959, average ca. 10 p.
Subj 14.2

12793 MCH P P2 G1.2 1949–1972
Chao, Yung-seen (Chao Yung-hsin).
Railways in Communist China.
Hong Kong: Union Research Institute, 1955. 101 p. (Communist China problem research series, EC10)
Subj 14.2 ▪ 34.2

12794 CSH O P2 G1.3 1949–1972
Chi Yu-ching.
'Rebuilding the Grand Canal.'
China reconstructs 12, 7 (July 1963), 5–7.
Subj 14.2 ▪ 11.4 14.1

12795 CSU O P5 G1.2 1949–1972
China [People's Republic]. [Kuo wu yüan]. T'ieh tao pu. Yün shu kan pu kung tso hsün lien pan chiang i pien chi wei yüan hui. ([State Council]. Ministry of Railroads. Editorial Committee on Lectures for Transportation Cadres Operational Training Class).
Organizing railway transportation, Communist China, mimeo. Tr. of *T'ieh lu yün shu kung tso tsu chih*; Peking: Jen min t'ieh lu ch'u pan she, 1964; 495 p.

Washington, D.C.: U.S. Joint Publications Research Service, Apr. 1965. 469 p. (JPRS 28,834; MC 6447/1965)
Subj 12 14.2 34.2 ▪ 12.2 14

12796 MCH P P1 G1.2 1949–1972
Current Scene Editor.
'The New China News Agency: Mao's messengers around the world.'
CS 4, 7 (1 Apr. 1966), 1–14.
Subj 12.1 14.2 ▪ 32.1

12797 NNC P P2 G1.2 1949–1972
Grossmann, Bernhard Paul, 1929–.
'Der Ausbau des Verkehrswesens in der Volksrepublik China' (The expansion of the transportation system in the People's Republic of China).
Z. für Geopolitik 28, 1 (Jan. 1957), 16–32.
Subj 14.2 ▪ 14.4 66

12798 MMT P P1 G1.2 1949–1972
Grossmann, Bernhard Paul, 1929–.
'The background of Communist China's transport policy.' In *Symposium on economic and social problems of the Far East*, edited by Edward Franciszek Szczepanik. [Selective entry]
Hong Kong: Hong Kong U. Press, 1962, 46–54.
Subj 14.2 ▪ 14

12799 NNC P P1 G1.2 1949–1972
Howse, Hugh.
'The role of mass media in China.' In *The Chinese model: A political, economic and social survey*, edited by Werner Klatt. [Selective entry]
Hong Kong: Hong Kong U. Press, 1965, 48–64.
Subj 12.1 14.2 ▪ 32.1 62

12800 NIC S P2 G1.2 1949–1972
Howse, Hugh.
'The use of radio in China.'
CQ 2 (Apr.–June 1960), 59–68.
Subj 12.1 14.2

12801 MCH P P2 G1.1 1949–1972
Hsia, Tao-tai (Hsia Tao-t'ai), 1915–.
'Chinese legal publications: An appraisal.' In *Contemporary Chinese law: Research problems and perspectives*, edited by Jerome Alan Cohen. [Selective entry]
Cambridge: Harvard U. Press, 1970, 20–83. (Harvard studies in East Asian Law, 4)
Subj 12.2 14.2 70 ▪ 17 22.2 36.1 72

12802 CSU P P2 G1.2 1949–1972
Hsia, Tao-tai (Hsia Tao-t'ai), 1915–, and Kathryn Haun.
'Communist Chinese legislation on publications and libraries.'
Quarterly j. of the Library of Congress 27, 1 (Jan. 1970), 20–33.
Subj 12.2 14.2 17 32.1

12803 CSH P P2 G1.2 1949–1972
Hsiao Chih, Hsu I (Hsü I), and [Yang] I-fan. [Authors sequential rather than joint: Hsiao Chih for 1963 and 1964; Hsu I for 1965 and 1966; Yang I-fan for 1967–1969.]
'Communist China's communication and transport, 1963–1969' [title varies; article for 1967 covers industry as well as transport and communications]. Tr. from *Tsu kuo* 2–74 (May 1964 – May 1970) [recurring annual feature article]. In *Communist China, 1963–1969*, edited by Union Research Institute.
Hong Kong: Union Research Institute. Issued annually, 1965–1970, average ca. 30 p.
Subj 14.2

12804 MCH S P2 G1.2 1949–1972
Hunter, Holland, 1921–.
'Transport in Soviet and Chinese development.'
EDCC 14, 1 (Oct. 1965), 71–84.
Subj 14.2

12805 FPN F P4 G1.2 1949–1972
Institut international de la presse (International Press Institute).
'République populaire de Chine' (The People's Republic of China). In *La presse dans les états autoritaires*, edited by the organization cited. [Sole entry]
Zurich: Institut international de la presse, 1959, 47–64. (IIP, études, 5).

'The press in Communist China.' In *The press in authoritarian countries*, edited by the organization cited. [Sole entry]
Zurich: International Press Institute, 1959, 45–61.
Subj 14.2 ▪ 12.1

12806 DLC O P4 G1.2 1949–1972
IUi Chzhou (Yü Chou).
'Organizatsiia remonta podvizhnogo sostava na zavodakh zheleznykh dorog KNR' (The organization of shop repair of rolling stock for railroads in the People's Republic of China).
Zheleznodorozhnyi transport 39, 10 (oktiabr' 1957), 59–62.
Subj 14.2 ▪ 14

12807 DLC O P2 G1.2 1949-1972
J. B.
'Urządzenia zabezpieczenia ruchu i łączności na kolejach Chińskiej Republiki Ludowej.'
Przegląd kolejowy elektrotechniczny 9, 7 (lipiec 1957), 158–160.

Traffic safety equipment and communications on railways of Chinese People's Republic, mimeo.
Washington, D.C.: U.S. Joint Publications Research Service, 15 May 1959. 5 p. (JPRS 720D; MC 18,984/1960)
Subj 14.2

12808 MCH P P7 G1.2 1949–1972
Jan, George P. (Jan Po-kung), 1925–.
'Radio propaganda in Chinese villages.'
AS 7, 5 (May 1967), 305–315.
Subj 12.1 14.2 ▪ 22.1 64

12809 NNC O P2 G1.2 1949–1972
Kassell, Bernard M-.
'Chinese waterways.'
J. of the American Society of Naval Engineers 71, 1 (Feb. 1959), 107–112.
Subj 14.2

12810 DLC O P1 G1.2 1949–1972
Ketkov, A-.
'V gostiakh u kitaiskikh druzei' (As guests of Chinese friends).
Sovetskoe radio i televidenie 6, 1 (1957), 23–25.
Subj 14.2 31

12811 CSH O P2 G1.2 1949–1972
Ketlinskaia, Vera Kazimirovna.
Kitai segodnia i zavtra (China today and tomorrow).
Leningrad: Sovetskii pisatel', 1958. 395 p.
Subj 13 14 14.2 16 17 18 ▪ 12 15 19 32 34.1 66

12812 NNC PO P2 G1.2 1949–1972
Kisviantsev, Lev Aleksandrovich.
Transport Kitaiskoi Narodnoi Respubliki.
Moscow: Znanie, 1958. 30 p. (Vsesoiuznoe obshchestvo po rasprostraneniiu politicheskikh i nauchnykh znanii, seriia 3, 35).

Transportation in the People's Republic of China, mimeo.
New York: U.S. Joint Publications Research Service, 17 Aug. 1959. 29 p. (JPRS 854D; MC 12,897/1959)
Subj 14.2

12813 CSU P P2 G1.2 1949–1972
Koschwitz, Hansjürgen, 1933–.
Pressepolitik und Parteijournalismus in der UdSSR und der Volksrepublik China (Press policies and party journalism in the U.S.S.R. and the People's Republic of China).
Düsseldorf: Bertelsmann Universitätsverlag, 1971. 304 p.
Subj 14.2 ▪ 12.1 32 32.1 32.2 64

12814 CSU PO P2 G1.2 1949–1972
Kuo, Leslie T. C. (Kuo Tse-ch'iu), 1914–.
'Communist China: Restoration and expansion.'
Library j. 87, 20 (15 Nov. 1962), 4133–4136. [Special issue: *Libraries in the Far East*, edited by Paul Bixler]
Subj 14.2 17

12815 MCH P P1 G1.2 1949–1972
[La Dany, Ladislao] ———, 1914–.
'Changes in the newspapers.'
CNA 157 (16 Nov. 1956), 1–7.
Subj 14.2 32.1

12816 MCH P P4 G1.2 1949–1972
[La Dany, Ladislao] ———, 1914–.
'Changing bookmarket.'
CNA 170 (1 Mar. 1957), 1–7.
Subj 14.2 34.2 ▪ 12 14.3

12817 CSH P P2 G1.2 1949–1972
[La Dany, Ladislao] ———, 1914–.
'The Chinese New Year, the *People's daily* today, the book.'
CNA 744/745 (14 Feb. 1969), 1–13.
Subj 14.2 ▪ 17 23

12818 MCH P P2 G1.2 1949–1972
[La Dany, Ladislao] ———, 1914–.
'Communications.'
CNA 543 (4 Dec. 1964), 1–7; 553 (26 Feb. 1965), 1–7.
Subj 14.2 14.4

12819 MCH P P3 G1.2 1949–1972
[La Dany, Ladislao] ———, 1914–.
'Communications.'
CNA 651 (10 Mar. 1967), 1–7.
Subj 14.2 36.4

12820 MCH P P4 G1.2 1949–1972
[La Dany, Ladislao] ———, 1914–.
'Journalism.'
CNA 104 (14 Oct. 1955), 2–7.
Subj 14.2

12821 CSH P P2 G1.2 1949–1972
[La Dany, Ladislao] ———, 1914–.
'Literature and publications in 1971.'
CNA 867 (14 Jan. 1972), 1–7.
Subj 14.2 ▪ 16.1 64

12822 CSH P P2 G1.2 1949–1972
[La Dany, Ladislao] ———, 1914–.
'Newspapers and journalism.'
CNA 631 (7 Oct. 1966), 1–7.
Subj 12.1 14.2

12823 CSH P P2 G1.2 1949–1972
[La Dany, Ladislao] ———, 1914–.
'Newspapers and journalism, 1968–1970.'
CNA 828 (15 Jan. 1971), 1–7.
Subj 12.1 14.2

12824 MCH P P2 G1.2 1949–1972
[La Dany, Ladislao] ———, 1914–.
'The post, 1949–1963.'
CNA 514 (1 May 1964), 1–7.
Subj 14.2

12825 CSH P P3 G1.2 1949–1972
[La Dany, Ladislao] ———, 1914–.
'Rail-transport and railway workers.'
CNA 862 (3 Dec. 1971), 1–7.
Subj 14.2 16.4 ▪ 22.2 35

12826 MCH P P4 G1.2 1949–1972
[La Dany, Ladislao] ———, 1914–.
'Readers and reading matter.'
CNA 123 (9 Mar. 1956), 2–7.
Subj 14.2

12827 CSH P P8 G1.3 1949–1972
[La Dany, Ladislao] ———, 1914–.
'Regulation of rivers.'
CNA 807 (10 July 1970), 1–7.
Subj 14.2 ▪ 11.3 11.4 18

12828 MCH P P1 G1.2 1949–1972
[La Dany, Ladislao] ———, 1914–.
'Roads in China.'
CNA 71 (11 Feb. 1955), 2–7.
Subj 14.2

12829 MCH P P1 G1.2 1949–1972
[La Dany, Ladislao] ———, 1914–.
'Sources of the news drying up.'
CNA 570 (2 July 1965), 1–7.
Subj 12.1 14.2

12830 NNC P P1 G1.2 1949–1972
[La Dany, Ladislao] ———, 1914–.
'Transport.'
CNA 213 (24 Jan. 1958), 1–7.
Subj 14.2

12831 CSH P P2 G1.2 1949–1972
[La Dany, Ladislao] ———, 1914–.
'Transport by rail.'
CNA 698 (1 Mar. 1968), 1–7.
Subj 14.2 16.4 ▪ 22.2 35

12832 NIC P P2 G1.2 1949–1972
[La Dany, Ladislao] ———, 1914–.
'Village transport.'
CNA 417 (20 Apr. 1962), 1–7.
Subj 14.2

12833 MCH P P2 G1.2 1949–1972
[La Dany, Ladislao] ———, 1914–.
'Water transport.'
CNA 343 (7 Oct. 1960), 1–6.
Subj 14.2

12834 MCH P P1 G1.2 1949–1972
[La Dany, Ladislao] ———, 1914–.
'What the "Red flag" teaches.'
CNA 440 (5 Oct. 1962), 1–7.
Subj 14.2

12835 CSU P P1 G1.2 1949–1972
Leith, James A-.
'Postage stamps and ideology in Communist China.'
Queen's q. 78, 2 (Summer 1971), 176–186.
Subj 12.1 14.2 ▪ 64

12836 ICU P P4 G1.2 1949–1972
Li, Maria Lien-hui, 1942–.
A study of periodical publishing in Mainland China, 1949–1966.
Unpublished masters thesis in Library Science, U. of Chicago, 1968. 117 p.
Subj 14.2 ▪ 16.1 32.1 36.1

12837 DLC O P2 G1.2 1949–1972
Li Ven' Fan (Li Wen-fang), E TSzia-tsziun (Yeh Chia-chiung), and Sun' Sun-chen (Sun Sung-ch'eng).
'Khoziaistvo puti i sooruzhenii zheleznykh dorog KNR' (Railroad construction and track maintenance in the People's Republic of China).
Zheleznodorozhnyi transport 39, 10 (oktiabr' 1957), 26–30.
Subj 14.2

12838 DLC O P2 G1.2 1949–1972
Lin' Chzhuan (Lin Chuang).
'Organizatsiia ekspluatatsionnoi raboty na zheleznykh dorogakh KNR' (Railroad organization and operation in the People's Republic of China).
Zheleznodorozhnyi transport 39, 10 (oktiabr' 1957), 40–45.
Subj 14.2

12839 CBU FP P2 G1.2 1949–1972
Liu, Alan P. L. (Liu P'ing-lin), 1937–.
Communications and national integration in Communist China.
Berkeley, Los Angeles: U. of California Press, 1971. 18, 225 p. (Michigan studies on China, 2) (Revision of doctoral dissertation in Political Science, Massachusetts Institute of Technology, 1967)
Subj 12.1 14.2 ▪ 16.1 17 30 54 64

12840 CSU P P2 G1.2 1949–1972
Liu, Alan P. L. (Liu P'ing-lin), 1937–.
'Communist China.' In *The Asian newspapers' reluctant revolution*, edited by John A- Lent. [Selective entry]
Ames: Iowa State U. Press, 1971, 43–54.
Subj 14.2 ▪ 64

12841 NNC P P2 G2.0 1949–1972
Lu, David John (Lu K'un-hsi), 1928–.
Railway development in Manchuria, 1931–41.
Unpublished masters thesis in East Asian Studies, Columbia U., 1954. 12, 80 p. [Certificate essay, East Asian Institute]
Subj 14.2 ▪ 14

12842 CSH O P3 G5.1 1949–1972
MacFarquhar, Roderick Lemonde, 1930–.
'A visit to the Chinese press.'
CQ 53 (Jan.–Mar. 1973), 144–152.
Subj 14.2 ▪ 32

12843 DLC S P2 G1.5 1949–1972
Masliakov, Vasilii Nikolaevich.
IAntszy: velikaia reka Kitaia (The Yangtze, China's great river).
Moscow: Rechnoi transport, 1959. 137 p.
Subj 11.3 14.1 14.2 14.4 ▪ 18

12844 CSH P P2 G1.2 1949–1972
[Meng Chan] ———.
'Communist China's transportation work in 1962.' Tr. of '1962 nien ti Chung kung chiao t'ung yün shu chi tui Su-lien chih pi chiao' (Transport and communications in Communist China in 1962, with a comparison to transport and communications in the Soviet Union); *Tsu kuo chou k'an* 546 (24 June 1963), 10–16 [partial tr.]. In *Communist China, 1962*, edited by Union Research Institute. [Selective entry]
Hong Kong: Union Research Institute, 1963, vol. 2, 141–162.
Subj 14.2

12845 CSU P P4 G1.2 1949–1972
Nunn, Godfrey Raymond, 1918–.
Publishing in Mainland China.
Cambridge: M.I.T. Press, 1966. 83 p. (M.I.T. reports, 4)
Subj 14.2 14.4 32.1 ▪ 14.3 17 37

12846 MCH S P1 G1.2 1949–1972
Pankina, Ol'ga Georgievna.
Pechat' Kitaiskoi Narodnoi Respubliki v period sotsialisticheskikh preobrazovanii, 1949–1957 gg. (The press of the People's Republic of China during the period of socialist transformation, 1949–1957).
Moscow: Izd-vo Mosk. un-ta, 1961. 72 p.
Subj 14.2

12847 NNC S P2 G1.2 1949–1972
Pankina, Ol'ga Georgievna.
'Pechat' Kitaiskoi Narodnoi Respubliki v 1944–1957 gg.' (The press of the People's Republic of China, 1944–1957).
Vestnik Moskovskogo universiteta; istoriko-filologicheskaia seriia 14, 1 (1959), 177–192.
Subj 14.2 32.1 ▪ 17

12848 CSU P P1 G1.2 1949–1972
Patterson, George Neilson, 1920–.
'China: The efficient dragon.'
Censorship 2, 1 (Winter 1966), 2–14.
Subj 14.2 ▪ 12 16.1 31 32

12849 CSH P P2 G1.2 1949–1972
Porch, Harriett E-.
Civil aviation in Communist China since 1949.
Santa Monica, Calif.: RAND Corp., 1968. 15, 96 p. (RAND memoranda, RM-4666-1-PR)
Subj 14 14.2 14.4 ▪ 12 12.2 14.1 15 31 32.1 34.2

12850 CSU P P8 G1.2 1949–1972
Porch, Harriett E-.
The use of aviation in agriculture and forestry in Communist China.
Santa Monica, Calif.: RAND Corp., 1967. 14 p. (RAND papers, P-3566)
Subj 14.1 14.2

12851 MCH P P1 G1.2 1949–1972
Schwarz, Henry Guenter, 1928–.
'The *Ts'an-k'ao Hsiao-hsi* [Reference information]: How well informed are Chinese officials about the outside world?'

CQ 27 (July–Sept. 1966), 54–83.
SUBJ 14.2 ▪ 12.1 66

12852 CBU PO P3 G1.2 1949–1972
Sergeenkov, A- A-.
'Izdanie uchebnikov i pedagogicheskoi literatury' (The publication of textbooks and literature on education). In *Shkola i prosveshchenie v Narodnom Kitae: sbornik statei* (Articles on schools and education in the People's Republic of China), compiled by Akademiia pedagogicheskikh nauk RSFSR, edited by Aleksei I- Markushevich, E- I- Monoszon, and M- N- Riakin. [Selective entry]
Moscow: Izd-vo Akad. ped. nauk RSFSR, 1957, 151–156.
SUBJ 14.2 17

12853 DLC O P2 G1.2 1949–1972
Shashkov, Zosima Alekseevich.
Vodnyi transport Kitaiskoi Narodnoi Respubliki.
Moscow: Znanie, 1958. 38 p. (Vsesoiuznoe obshchestvo po rasprostraneniiu politicheskikh i nauchnykh znanii, seriia 4, 11).
Water transportation in the People's Republic of China, mimeo.
Washington, D.C.: U.S. Joint Publications Research Service, 4 Nov. 1958. 28 p. (JPRS 363D; MC 17,057/1958)
SUBJ 14 14.2 ▪ 11.4 18 24.3 24.4

12854 CSU O P2 G1.2 1949–1972
Sherrard, Howard M-.
'Notes on road and bridge engineering in China.'
EH 7, 5 (Sept.–Oct. 1968), 23–31.
SUBJ 14.2 ▪ 16.4

12855 CSH U P1 G1.2 1949–1972
Shih Ming.
'Fifteen years of railway administration under the Chinese Communists.'
CCA 2, 3 (June 1965), 23–44.
SUBJ 14.2 ▪ 12

12856 DLC U P1 G1.2 1949–1972
Shiriaev, Stepan Lavrent'evich, 1922–.
Transport Kitaiskoi Narodnoi Respubliki (Transport in the People's Republic of China).
Moscow: Izd-vo vost. lit-ry, 1962. 108 p.
SUBJ 14.2

12857 NNC O P2 G4.0 1949–1972
Sinitsyn, V- M-.
'Obshchii fiziko-geograficheskii obzor raionov Lan'chzhou-Almaatinskoi zheleznoi dorogi (v predelakh Kitaiskoi Narodnoi Respubliki)' (General physical and geographical survey of the regions of the Lanchow – Alma Ata railroad within the borders of the People's Republic of China).
Izvestiia Vsesoiuznogo geograficheskogo obshchestva 88, 6 (noiabr'–dekabr' 1956), 505–515.
SUBJ 11.3 14.2

12858 CSH P P2 G1.3 1949–1972
Stanford U. China Project.
'Propaganda and public information.' In *Central South China*, compiled by the organization cited. [Selective entry]
New Haven: Human Relations Area Files, 1956, vol. 2, 547–586. (HRAF subcontractor's monographs, 28; Stanford 2)
SUBJ 12.1 14.2 ▪ 31

12859 CSH P P2 G1.3 1949–1972
Stanford U. China Project.
'Propaganda and public information.' In *East China*, compiled by the organization cited. [Selective entry]
New Haven: Human Relations Area Files, 1956, vol. 2, 610–677. (HRAF subcontractor's monographs, 29; Stanford 3)
SUBJ 12.1 14.2 ▪ 31

12860 CSH P P2 G5.0 1949–1972
Stanford U. China Project.
'Propaganda and public information.' In *North China*, compiled by the organization cited. [Selective entry]
New Haven: Human Relations Area Files, 1956, vol. 2, 597–633. (HRAF subcontractor's monographs, 27; Stanford 1)
SUBJ 12.1 14.2 ▪ 31

12861 NNC P P2 G8.0 1949–1972
Stanford U. China Project.
'Propaganda and public information.' In *Southwest China*, compiled by the organization cited. [Selective entry]
New Haven: Human Relations Area Files, 1956, vol. 2, 606–688. (HRAF subcontractor's monographs, 30; Stanford 4)
SUBJ 12.1 14.2 ▪ 31

12862 NNC U P2 G1.2 1949–1972
Stepanenko, Stanislav Ivanovich.
Vodnye puti Kitaiskoi Narodnoi Respubliki (Waterways of the People's Republic of China).
Moscow: Rechnoi transport, 1959. 81 p.
SUBJ 14.2 ▪ 14.3 14.4

12863 CSH P P4 G1.2 1949–1972
Ting Wang, 1942–.
'Communist China's newspapers and periodicals in 1966.' Tr. of '1966 nien Chung kung ti hsin wen ho ch'i k'an chu pan kung tso' (Publication of newspapers and journals in Communist China, 1966); *Tsu kuo* 36 (Mar. 1967), 49–55. In *Communist China, 1966*, edited by Union Research Institute. [Selective entry]
Hong Kong: Union Research Institute, 1968, vol. 2, 171–188.
SUBJ 14.2 32.1 ▪ 24.2

12864 CSU P P1 G1.2 1949–1972
Townsend, James Roger, 1932–.
The revolutionization of 'Chinese youth': A study of 'Chung-kuo ch'ing-nien' [Chinese youth].
Berkeley: U. of California, Center for Chinese Studies, 1967. 71 p. (CCS, China research monographs, 1)
SUBJ 14.2 37 54 ▪ 16.1 17 32 32.1

12865 CSU PO P2 G1.2 1949–1972
United Nations. Educational, Scientific and Cultural Organization.
'Communication facilities, country by country: China (Mainland).' In *World communications: Press, radio, television, film*, 4th ed., compiled by the organization cited. [Selective entry]
New York: UNESCO, 1964, 209–212.
SUBJ 14.2

12866 CSU FP P4 G9.4 1949–1972
United Nations. Educational, Scientific and Cultural Organization.
'Communication facilities, country by country: China (Taiwan).' In *World communications: Press, radio, television, film*, 4th ed., compiled by the organization cited. [Selective entry]
New York: UNESCO, 1964, 206–208.
SUBJ 14.2

12867 CSU FP P3 G9.5 1949–1972
United Nations. Educational, Scientific and Cultural Organization.
'Communication facilities, country by country: Hong Kong.' In *World communications: Press, radio, television, film*, 4th ed., compiled by the organization cited. [Selective entry]
New York: UNESCO, 1964, 212–214.
SUBJ 14.2

12868 CSU P P2 G1.2 1949–1972
Vetterling, Philip W-, and James J- Wagy.
'China: The transportation sector, 1950–71.' In *People's Republic of China: An economic assessment*, compiled by Joint Economic Committee, U.S. Congress. [Selective entry]
Washington, D.C.: U.S. Government Printing Office, 1972, 147–181.
SUBJ 14.2 ▪ 15

12869 NNC P P3 G1.3 1949–1972
Wang, Charles Kilord Athen (Wang Cheng-k'uei), 1904–.
Reactions in Communist China: An analysis of letters to newspaper editors.
Lackland Air Force Base, San Antonio, Tex.: U.S. Air Force Personnel and Training Research Center, Air Research and Development Command, 1955. 11, 115 p. (U.S. Human Resources Research Institute technical research reports, 33; Studies in Chinese Communism, series 3, 7, 1953)
SUBJ 14.2 60 ▪ 12.1 16

12870 CSH U P3 G9.0 1949–1972
Wang, K. (Wang Kuang), 1905–.
'Development and modernization of shipping industry in the Republic of China.'
IFC 31, 1 (Jan. 1969), 2–14.
SUBJ 14.2 14.3

12871 CSH P P2 G1.2 1949–1972
Wang Yü.
'Communications.' Tr. of '1961 nien ti Chung kung chiao t'ung' (Transport and communications in Communist China, 1961); *Tsu kuo chou k'an* 498 (23 July 1962), 9–14. In *Communist China, 1961*, edited by Union Research Institute. [Selective entry]
Hong Kong: Union Research Institute, 1962, vol. 2, 111–130.
SUBJ 14.2

12872 GMS U P2 G1.2 1949–1972
Wehde-Textor, O-.
'Industrialisierung und Verkehr in China' (Industrialization and transport in China).
AE 69, 1 (Jan.–Feb. 1959), 209–224.
SUBJ 14.2 ▪ 14.4

12873 CSH P P1 G1.2 1949–1972
Wu, Eugene W. (Wu Wen-chin), 1922–.
'Recent developments in Chinese publishing.'
CQ 53 (Jan.–Mar. 1973), 134–138.
SUBJ 14.2

12874 NIC S P1 G1.2 1949–1972
Wu, Yuan-li (Wu Yüan-li), 1920–.
'Press regulation in Mao's China.'
Problems of Communism 6, 4 (July–Aug. 1957), 33–40.
SUBJ 14.2 32.1

12875 CSU P P2 G1.2 1949–1972
Yadav, Dharam P-.
'Communist China: Politics above all.' In *National and international systems of broadcasting: Their history, operation and control*, by Walter B- Emery. [Sole entry]
East Lansing: Michigan State U. Press, 1969, 465–479.
SUBJ 14.2 ▪ 17

12876 NNC P P2 G1.2 1949–1972
Yü Ch'ang-ch'in and Yü Hui-yin. [Tr. erroneously gives second author's name as Yu Hui-ing.]
Party control of communication media, mimeo. Tr. of 'Ch'üan tang pan pao ti hsin fa chan' (New developments in party-operated newspapers); *Jen min jih pao* 11 June 1960, 7.
Washington, D.C.: U.S. Joint Publications Research Service, 18 Aug. 1960. 8 p. (JPRS 5260; MC 15,821/1960)
SUBJ 14.2 32.1

12877 MCH U P2 G1.2 1949–1972
Ziman, Lev IAkovlevich, 1900–.
'Transportnoe stroitel'stvo i geograficheskie sdvigi v ekonomike Kitaiskoi Narodnoi Respubliki' (Transport construction and geographic changes in the economy of the People's Republic of China). In *Geografiia Kitaiskoi Narodnoi Respubliki: sbornik statei* (Articles on the geography of the People's Republic of China), edited by Vladimir Timofeevich Zaichikov. [Sole entry]
Moscow: Geografgiz, 1956, 77–95.
SUBJ 14.2 14.4 ▪ 11.3 14

14.3 COMMERCE AND SERVICES

商業 商業

1644-1911

12878 CSU O P2 G1.3 1644–1842
'A dissertation upon the commerce of China' [written in Canton in 1838]. In *Nineteenth century China: Five imperialist perspectives*, edited by William Rhoads Murphey, III. [Sole entry]
Ann Arbor: U. of Michigan, Center for Chinese Studies, 1972, 25–44. (Michigan papers in Chinese studies, 13)
SUBJ 14.3 34.2 ▪ 14.4 14.6 24.4

12879 NNC PO P2 G1.5 1842–1911
'Doneseniia imperatorskago rossiiskago general'nago konsul'stva v Shankhae: kitaiskie porty Ninbo, Fuchzhou i Amoi, ikh ekonomicheskoe polozhenie i torgovlia' (Reports of the imperial Russian consulate general in Shanghai on the Chinese ports of Ningpo, Foochow, and Amoy, their economic situation and trade).
DIRKP 39 (1914), 69–85.
SUBJ 14.2 14.3 14.4 ▪ 24.4 66

12880 DLC P P5 G1.2 1895–1911
'Torgovlia i promyshlennost' Kitaia v 1901 g.' (Trade and industry in China in 1901).
Vestnik finansov, promyshlennosti i torgovli 1902, 30, 187–193.
SUBJ 14 14.3 14.6 ▪ 14.4

12881 NNC PO P3 G9.2 1895–1911
Bel'chenko, A- T-.
'Doneseniia imperatorskago rossiiskago konsula v Kantone: obzor torgovli porta Svatou za 1903–1912' (Reports of the imperial Russian consul in Canton: Survey of the trade at Swatow, 1903–1912).
DIRKP 47 (1915), 137–171.
SUBJ 14.3 20 24.2 ▪ 24

12882 NNC PO P2 G9.5 1842–1911
Bel'chenko, A- T-.
'Doneseniia imperatorskago rossiiskago konsula v Kantone: ocherk torgovli Kouluna za 1887–1912 gody' (Reports of the imperial Russian consul in Canton: Survey of the trade at Kowloon, 1887–1912).
DIRKP 49 (1915), 31–61.
SUBJ 14.3 20 24.2 ▪ 24

12883 NNC PO P2 G9.2 1842–1911
Bel'chenko, A- T-.
'Doneseniia imperatorskago rossiiskago konsula v Kantone: ocherk torgovli Lappa za 1892–1912 g.g.' (Reports of the imperial Russian consul in Canton: Survey of the trade at La-pa shan [Hsiang-shan *hsien*, Kwangtung], 1892–1912).
DIRKP 49 (1915), 1–30.
SUBJ 14.3 ▪ 24 24.2 56

12884 NNC PO P2 G9.2 1842–1911
Bel'chenko, A- T-.
'Doneseniia imperatorskago rossiiskago konsula v Kantone: ocherk torgovli ostrova Hainan za 1882–1912 g.g.' (Reports of the imperial Russian consul in Canton: Survey of the trade in Hainan, 1882–1912).
DIRKP 47 (1915), 172–204.
SUBJ 14.3 20 24.2 ▪ 21.1 24

12885 NNC PO P2 G9.2 1895–1911
Bel'chenko, A- T-.
'Doneseniia imperatorskago rossiiskago konsula v Kantone: ocherk torgovli porta Konmun za 1904–1912 gody' (Reports of the imperial Russian consul in Canton: Survey of the trade at Chiang-men [Hsiang-shan *hsien*, Kwangtung], 1904–1912).
DIRKP 49 (1915), 62–102.
SUBJ 14.3 20 24.2 ▪ 24

12886 NNC PO P2 G9.2 1842–1911
Bel'chenko, A- T-.
'Doneseniia imperatorskago rossiiskago konsula v Kantone: ocherk torgovli porta Pakkhoi za 1882–1912' (Reports of the imperial Russian consul in Canton: Survey of the trade at Pei-hai [Ho-p'u *hsien*, Kwangtung], 1882–1912).
DIRKP 49 (1915), 103–133.
SUBJ 14.3 20 ▪ 24

12887 NNC PO P2 G9.2 1895–1911
Bel'chenko, A- T-.
'Doneseniia imperatorskago rossiiskago konsula v Kantone: ocherk torgovoi deiatel'nosti porta Samshui' (Reports of the imperial Russian consul in Canton: Survey of the trade at San-shui [*hsien* capital, Kwangtung]).
DIRKP 49 (1915), 134–162.
SUBJ 14.3 20 24.2 ▪ 24

12888 GMS PO P2 G1.5 1842–1911
Bernauer, Karl.
Südchina: Wirtschaftliche Verhältnisse (The economic situation of South China).
Vienna: Manz, 1912.
SUBJ 14 14.3 14.4 ▪ 21.1 21.2 55

12889 MCH O P2 G8.1 1895–1911
Betz, Heinrich.
'Eine Reise in Szechuan von Chungking über Land nach Chengtu, Yachou, Chiating und Suifu' (A journey in Szechwan overland from Chungking to Chengtu, Ya-chou-fu, Chia-ting-fu, and Hsü-chou-fu [i.e., I-pin]).
MSOSB 9 (1906), 1–72.
SUBJ 14.3 21.1 24.3 ▪ 24 24.2 24.4 34.3

12890 DLC O P2 G1.3 1644–1842
[Bichurin, Nikita Iakovlevich] *Otets* Iakinf, 1777–1853.
'Mery narodnogo prodovol'stviia v Kitae' (Public food-supply measures in China).
Otechestvennyia zapiski 3-ia seriia 1, 7, Part 2 (1839), 47–56.
SUBJ 14.1 14.3 18 ▪ 11.3 22.1

12891 CSU O P2 G1.5 1842–1895
Bickmore, Albert Smith, 1839–1914.
'Sketch of a journey from Canton to Hankow through the provinces of Kwangtung, Kwangsi, and Hunan, with geological notes.'
JRAS-NCB new (2nd) series 4 (Dec. 1867), 1–20.
SUBJ 14.3 25 ▪ 24.2 24.4 66

12892 MCH O P5 G2.1 1895–1911
Bogoiavlenskii, N- A-.
'Ocherk torgovli Kheiluntszianskoi (TSitsikarskoi) provintsii' (A note on trade in Heilungkiang).
Sbornik konsul'kikh donesenii 1902, 3, 232–240.
SUBJ 14.3 24.2

12893 NNC PO P2 G2.0 1895–1911
Bologovskii, K- F-.
'Donesenie upravliaiushchego imperatorskim rossiiskim konsul'stvom v Dairene: torgovlia v iuzhnoi Man'chzhurii' (Report of the chargé d'affaires of the imperial Russian consulate in Dairen: Trade in southern Manchuria).
DIRKP 13 (1912), 42–76.
SUBJ 14.3 24.3 ▪ 14.2 14.5

12894 CSH O P2 G1.5 1842–1911
Bourne, Frederick Samuel Augustus, 1854–1940.
Trade of central and southern China.

Shanghai: Shanghai Mercury Office, 1898. 68 p.
Subj 14 14.3 ▪ 14.2 14.4 14.5 18 29 34.2 34.3 39 55

12895 FPN P P1 G1.1 1895–1911
Bourret, L-.
'Etude sur le commerce de la Chine en 1906' (A study of China's commerce in 1906).
BEI 10, 65 (juil. 1907), 554–575.
Subj 14.3 ▪ 14.6

12896 MCH P P3 G1.2 1842–1911
Braklo, ———.
'Das Transitsystem in China' (The Chinese system of handling goods in transit).
MSOSB 17 (1914), 18–40.
Subj 14.3 14.5 ▪ 14.2

12897 CSU PO P2 G1.5 1895–1911
[Brenier, Henri] H. B., 1867–?
'Notes sur le commerce de Canton, et sur Pak-hoi et la province du Kouang-si' (Notes on the Canton trade and on Pei-hai [Ho-p'u *hsien*, Kwangtung] and Kwangsi). In *La Mission lyonnaise d'exploration commerciale en Chine, 1895–1897, deuxième partie, rapports commerciaux et notes diverses* (The Lyons Trade Mission to China, 1895–1897, Part 2, Commercial reports and miscellaneous notes), compiled by Chambre de commerce de Lyon. [Selective entry]
Lyons: Rey, 1898, 191–206 [s.p.].
Subj 14.3 21 21.3 ▪ 14.5

12898 NNC O P4 G1.1 1842–1911
Cherevkov, V- D-.
'Po kitaiskomu poberezh'iu' (Along the coast of China).
Istoricheskii vestnik 19 (aprel' 1898 – dekabr' 1898), 207 p. in all.
Subj 14.3 14.4 66 ▪ 12 15 16.1 34.3

12899 NIC O P2 G8.0 1842–1895
Davenport, Arthur.
Report by Mr. Davenport upon the trading capabilities of the country traversed by the Yunnan mission.
London: Harrison, 1877. 35 p.
Subj 14 14.3

12900 DLC P P1 G1.1 1644–1842
Demidova, N- F-, and Vladimir Stepanovich Miasnikov.
Pervye russkie diplomaty v Kitae: 'Rospis' I. Petlina i stateinyi spisok F. I. Baikova (The earliest Russian diplomats in China: I. Petlin's 'Description' and Fedor Isakovich Baikov's report).
Moscow: Nauka, 1966. 156 p.
Subj 14.3 ▪ 55 66

12901 CSU P P2 G1.1 1644–1842
Dermigny, Louis.
La Chine et l'Occident: le commerce à Canton au XVIIIe siècle, 1719–1833 (China and the West: The Canton trade in the eighteenth century, 1719–1833).
Paris: Impr. nationale, 1964. 4 vols. 1627 p. [c.p.]. [Vol. 4 unpaginated] (Ecole pratique des hautes études, VIe section, Centre de recherches historiques: Ports, routes, trafics, 18) (Doctoral dissertation, Faculté des lettres, Université de Paris)
Subj 14 14.3 24.3 34.3 66 ▪ 11.1 12.2 25 36.4 64

12902 MCH O P3 G1.1 1842–1895
Exner, A- H-.
China: Skizzen von Land und Leuten, mit besonderer Berücksichtigung der komerziellen Verhältnisse (Sketches of the land and people of China, with special emphasis on commerce).
Leipzig: Gustav Weigel, 1889. 298 p.
Subj 14.3 20 24.3 ▪ 41 55 57 62 65

12903 MCH O P4 G5.0 1842–1895
Fauvel, Albert Auguste, 1851–1909.
'Le commerce des ports du nord de la Chine' (Trade in the ports of North China).
B. de la Société de géographie commerciale de Paris 17 (1895), 336–352.
Subj 14.3 ▪ 24 24.3 24.5

12904 MCH O P2 G6.3 1842–1895
Fauvel, Albert Auguste, 1851–1909.
'La province du Tché Kiang' (Chekiang).
Questions diplomatiques et coloniales 8, 61 (1er sept. 1899), 22–28.
Subj 14.3 ▪ 24.1

12905 MCH O P2 G5.3 1895–1911
Grosse, V- F-.
'Torgovlia i promyshlennost' Shan'duna: donesenie vitse-konsula v Chifu' (Trade and industry in Shantung: Report of the [Russian] vice-consul in Chefoo).
Sbornik konsul'kikh donesenii 1901, 6, 427–464.
Subj 14 14.3 ▪ 14.4

12906 CBU P P1 G1.2 1842–1895
Gruntzel, Josef L-, 1866–1934.
Die kommerzielle Entwicklung Chinas in den letzten 25 Jahren (The commercial development of China during the past twenty-five years).
Leipzig: W. Friedrich, 1891. 97 p.
Subj 14.3 ▪ 14.5

12907 GBS O P2 G5.3 –1895
Hirth, Friedrich, 1845–1927.
Die Bucht von Kiau-tschau und ihr Hinterland (Kiaochow bay and its hinterland).
Munich: Knorr und Hirth, 1897. 23 p.
Subj 14.3 24 ▪ 21.1 24.1 24.2 24.4

12908 NNC P P2 G9.2 1842–1895
Hirth, Friedrich, 1845–1927.
'Die Handelsprodukte von Kuan-tung' (The commercial products of Kwangtung). In *Chinesische Studien* (Chinese studies), by F. Hirth. [Selective entry]
Munich: Hirth, 1890, vol. 1, 76–101.
Subj 14.3 ▪ 24.1 24.3 24.4

12909 NIC P P2 G1.3 1644–1842
Ho, Ping-ti, 1917–.
'The salt merchants of Yang-chou: A study of commercial capitalists in eighteenth-century China.'
HJAS 17, 1/2 (June 1954), 130–168.
Subj 14.3 14.4 16.2 ▪ 16.1 34.2

12910 MCH P P1 G1.2 1895–1911
Hoang, Pierre (Huang Po-lu), 1830–1909.
Exposé du commerce public du sel (The salt trade).
Shanghai: Impr. de la Mission catholique, 1898. 15 p. (Variétés sinologiques, 15)
Subj 14.3 ▪ 12.2 16.1

12911 MSE P P1 G6.3 1842–1911
Hornbeck, Stanley Kuhl, 1883–1966.
The opium question, legal phases: An elementary study of the rights of Indian opium in China today.
Shanghai: China Press, 1912. 22 p.
Subj 12.1 12.2 14.3 ▪ 14.6 66

12912 CSU S P2 G8.2 1842–1895
Hoskiær, Valdemar, 1829–1895.
'Handelsvejene til Jynnan' (The trade routes to Yunnan).
Geografisk tidskrift 5 (1881), 81–87.

Les routes commerciales du Yunnan, province au nord du Tonkin (Trade routes of Yunnan, the province north of Tonkin).
Paris: Plon-Nourrit, 1883. 32 p.
Subj 14.3 24.2 ▪ 14.4 24.1 66

12913 CSH P P5 G1.4 –1895
Huen, Fook-fai (Hsüan Fu-hui), 1940–.
'The Manchurian fur trade in the early Ch'ing.'
PC 24 (Dec. 1971), 41–73.
Subj 14.3 24.3 ▪ 14.2 14.5 66

12914 MSE P P3 G1.2 1842–1895
Kingsmill, Thomas William, 1837–1910.
Copper cash and the tea trade.
Shanghai: Shanghai Recorder, 1858 [i.e., 1868]. 15 p.
Subj 14.3 14.6 ▪ 66

12915 MCY S P2 G1.2 1842–1911
Kiuner, Nikolai Vasil'evich, 1877–1955.
Kommercheskaia geografiia Kitaia (A commercial geography of China).
Vladivostok: Tipo-lit. Vost. in-ta, 1909. 201 p. (Vostochnyi institut, Lektsii po kommercheskoi geografii stran Dal'nego Vostoka, 1)
Subj 14.2 14.3 ▪ 11 24.4

12916 NNC O P5 G1.2 1895–1911
Ladygin, V- F-.
'Nekotoryia dannyia o polozhenii torgovli v Gan'su, Tibete i Mongolii, sobrannye vo vremia ekspeditsii 1899–1902 gg., snariazhennoi Imp. Russk. Geogr. Ob-vom v TSentral'nuiu Aziiu' (The trade situation in Kansu, Tibet, and Mongolia: Data collected during the 1899–1902 expedition to Central Asia, outfitted by the Imperial Russian Geographic Society).
Izvestiia Imperatorskago russkago geograficheskago obshchestva 38, 4 (1902), 371–466.
Subj 14.3 24.3 ▪ 21.1 24.2 66

12917 DLC PO P4 G5.1 1842–1895
Laptev, Ivan V-.
'Ocherk torgovli v gorodakh Tian'-tszine i Kalgane za 1893 i 1894 gg.' (A note on the trade at Tientsin and Kalgan in 1893 and 1894).
Konsul'skie doneseniia po torgovle i promyshlennosti 1896, 6, 3–80.
Subj 14.3 ▪ 24.2 24.6

12918 CSU P P4 G1.1 1842–1895
LeFevour, Edward Thomas, 1930–.
Western enterprise in late Ch'ing China: A selective survey of Jardine, Matheson and Company's operations, 1842–1895.
Cambridge: Harvard U., East Asian Research Center, 1968. 215 p. (Harvard East Asian monographs, 26) (Revision

of *Western enterprise in China, 1842–1895*, doctoral dissertation in Economics, U. of Cambridge [Peterhouse College], 1962)
SUBJ 14.3 66 ▪ 12 14.2 14.4 14.6

12919 MCH PO P2 G8.2 1895–1911
Lépice, Henri.
'Renseignements commerciaux sur la province du Yunnan, 1910' (Trade notes on Yunnan, 1910).
BEI 14, 88 (mai–juin 1911), 398–421.
SUBJ 14.3 22.1 24.1 24.2 ▪ 21.1 24.3

12920 SSK O P4 G1.5 1842–1895
Liljevalch, C- F-, 1796–1870.
Chinas handel, industri och statsförfattning (China's trade and industry and its constitution).
Stockholm: Beckman, 1848. 374 p.
SUBJ 14 14.3 14.6 ▪ 12 14.4 24.4 34.2 41 66

12921 MCH O P2 G1.2 1842–1911
Little, Archibald John, 1838–1908.
Gleanings from fifty years in China, rev. ed.
London: Sampson Low, Marston, 1910. 16, 335 p.
SUBJ 14.3 18 66 ▪ 12 14 14.1 15 32 32.2 33

12922 MCH P P3 G1.1 1842–1895
Liu, Kwang-ching (Liu Kuang-ching), 1921–.
'British-Chinese steamship rivalry in China, 1873–85.' In *The economic development of China and Japan*, edited by Charles Donald Cowan. [Selective entry]
New York: Praeger, 1964, 49–78. (U. of London, School of Oriental and African Studies, Studies on modern Asia and Africa, 4)
SUBJ 14.3 ▪ 12 14 14.2 16.2

12923 MCH P P2 G1.2 –1911
Lu Lien-tching (Lü Lien-ching).
Les greniers publics de prévoyance sous la dynastie des Ts'ing (Public granaries under the Ch'ing).
Paris: Jouve, 1932. 212 p. (Doctoral dissertation, Faculté des lettres, Université de Paris)
SUBJ 14.1 14.3 14.5 ▪ 12 22.1

12924 MCH O P2 G8.2 1895–1911
Mazzolani, D- A-.
'La provincia dello Yunnan' (Yunnan).
Bollettino della Società geografica italiana 4a serie 12, 4 (aprile 1911), 476–504.
SUBJ 14.3 14.4 24.1 ▪ 12 12.2 15 17 21 24.2

12925 MCH PO P2 G2.1 1895–1911
Meester, Th—— H- de.
'Economische toestand van Noord-Mantsjoerije' (The economic condition of northern Manchuria).
Economische verslagen van Nederlandsche diplomatieke en consulaire ambtenaren 7, 14 (1913/14), 521–546. [Supplement to *Handelsberichten* 345 (23 October 1913)]
SUBJ 14.3 24.4 ▪ 24.1 24.2

12926 NNC O P2 G2.2 1895–1911
Meshcherskii, D- V-.
'Ekonomicheskii obzor Girinskoi provintsii: donesenie imp. ros. konsula v Girine' (Economic survey of Kirin province: Report of the imperial Russian consul in Kirin).
DIRKP 13 (1912), 1–7.
SUBJ 14 14.3

12927 CSH U P1 G1.3 1644–1911
Metzger, Thomas Albert, 1933–.
'Ch'ing commercial policy.'
CSWT 1, 3 (Feb. 1966), 4–10.
SUBJ 14.3 16.2 ▪ 34.2

12928 CSU P P2 G1.3 –1842
Metzger, Thomas Albert, 1933–.
'The organizational capabilities of the Ch'ing state in the field of commerce: The Liang-huai salt monopoly, 1740–1840.' In *Economic organization in Chinese society*, edited by William Earl Willmott. [Selective entry]
Stanford: Stanford U. Press, 1972, 9–45.
SUBJ 14.3 14.4 24.3 ▪ 12 14.5 16.2

12929 CSU P P4 G1.2 –1911
Metzger, Thomas Albert, 1933–.
'The state and commerce in Imperial China.'
Asian and African studies (Jerusalem) 6 (1970), 23–46. [Special issue: *Society and development in Asia*, edited by Martin Rudner]
SUBJ 14.3 16.2 ▪ 14 14.5 16 64

12930 NIC P P2 G1.3 1644–1842
Metzger, Thomas Albert, 1933–.
'T'ao Chu's reform of the Huaipei salt monopoly, 1831–1833.'
PC 16 (Dec. 1962), 1–39.
SUBJ 14.3 ▪ 14.2 14.5 34.2

12931 FPN PO P3 G5.1 –1895
Rondot, Natalis, 1821–1900.
'Pé-King ou Choun-tien-fu (mesures, poids, monnaies et banques)' (Peking, or Shun-t'ien-fu: Measures, weights, currency, and banks). In *Dictionnaire universel théoretique et pratique du commerce et de la navigation* (A general theoretical and practical dictionary of trade and navigation). [Sole entry]
Paris: Guillaumin, 1861, vol. 2, 1050–1061. [Separately reprinted as *Pé-King et la Chine: mesures, monnaies et banques chinoises* (Peking and China: Chinese measures, currency, and banks). Paris: Guillaumin, 1861. 19 p.]
SUBJ 14.3 14.6 62 ▪ 66

12932 NIC P P2 G8.1 –1895
Rosthorn, Arthur von, 1862–1945.
'The salt administration of Ssu-ch'uan.'
JRAS-CB new (2nd) series 27 (1892/93), 1–32.
SUBJ 14.3 14.5

12933 CSU P P2 G1.3 –1911
Saeki Tomi, 1910–.
'Economie et absolutisme dans la Chine moderne: le cas des marchands de sel de Yangchow' (Economy and absolutism in modern China: The case of the Yangchow salt merchants).
R. historique 238 (juil.–sept. 1967), 15–30.
SUBJ 14 14.3 16.2 ▪ 11.4 12.2 14.5 14.6 16.1 32

12934 MCH O P2 G1.1 1842–1895
Scherzer, Karl von, 1821–1903.
'China' (China). In *Fachmännische Berichte über die österreichisch-ungarische Expedition nach Siam, China und Japan, 1868–1871* (Expert reports on the Austro-Hungarian expedition to Siam, China, and Japan, 1868–1871), by K. von Scherzer. [Selective entry]
Stuttgart: Julius Maier, 1872, 215–350.
SUBJ 14 14.3 ▪ 14.1 14.6 66

12935 NNC U P1 G1.3 1644–1911
Schrameier, Wilhelm Ludwig, 1859–1926.
'Opium' (Opium).
China-Archiv 2, 3 (24 März 1917), 129–138; 2, 4 (24 Apr. 1917), 193–199; 2, 5 (24 Mai 1917), 257–262; 2, 6 (24 Juni 1917), 321–328.
SUBJ 14.3 ▪ 22.2 55 66

12936 NNC PO P4 G1.3 1842–1911
Schumacher, Hermann, 1868–?
'Die chinesischen Vertragshäfen: Ihre wirtschaftliche Stellung und Bedeutung' (The economic position and significance of the Chinese treaty ports).
Jahrbücher für Nationalökonomie und Statistik 3. Folge 16, 5 (1898), 577–597; 16, 6 (1898), 721–793; 17, 1 (1899), 55–70; 17, 3 (1899), 289–331.
SUBJ 14.2 14.3 ▪ 21.1 24 24.2 24.4

12937 NNC PO P3 G9.5 1842–1911
Schumacher, Hermann, 1868–?
'Hongkong: Seine Entwicklung und wirtschaftliche Bedeutung' (Hong Kong's development and economic significance).
Jahrbuch der Internationalen Vereinigung für vergleichende Rechtswissenschaft 5 (1899), 315–400.
SUBJ 14.3 24.2 ▪ 21.1 21.2 22.1 22.2 24.4 24.5 66

12938 NNC PO P3 G1.3 1842–1911
Schumacher, Hermann, 1868–?
'Die Organisation des Fremdenhandels in China' (The organization of foreign trade in China).
SJ 23, 2 (1899), 259–293.
SUBJ 14.3 34.2 ▪ 16.2 30 34.3 66

12939 MCH O P3 G5.1 1895–1911
Shuiskii, N-.
'Torgovlia Tian'tszina: donesenie konsula v Tian'tszine' (The trade at Tientsin: Report of the [Russian] consul in Tientsin).
Sbornik konsul'kikh donesenii 1900, 1, 21–36.
SUBJ 14.3 ▪ 24.2

12940 CSU S P1 G1.1 1644–1895
Simkin, Colin George Frederick.
'China eroded.' In *The traditional trade of Asia*, by C. G. F. Simkin. [Sole entry]
London: Oxford U. Press, 1968, 270–284.
SUBJ 14.3 66 ▪ 12 14.2 14.5 25 32.2

12941 NNC PO P2 G1.1 –1895
Sirr, Henry Charles, 1807–1872.
China and the Chinese: Their religion, character, customs, and manufactures; the evils arising from the opium trade; with a glance at our religious, moral, political and commercial intercourse with the country.
London: William S. Orr, 1849. 2 vols. 16, 447; 443 p.
SUBJ 10 14.3 22.2 55 66 ▪ 12.2 13 14.1 23 24.4 43 47 56 60 65

12942 DLC O P3 G7.1 1842–1895
Vakhovich, A-.
'Otchet o torgovle porta Khan'kou za 1894 g.' (Report on the trade at Hankow in 1894).
Konsul'skie doneseniia po torgovle i promyshlennosti 1896, 6, 81–113.
SUBJ 14.3 ▪ 24.2 24.6

12943 CSU PO P2 G7.0 1895–1911
Vial, A-, et al.
'Notes sur le commerce de Han-K'eou' (Notes on trade at Hankow). In *La Mission lyonnaise d'exploration commerciale en Chine, 1895–1897, deuxième partie, rapports commerciaux et notes diverses* (The Lyons Trade Mission to China, 1895–1897, Part 2, Commercial reports and miscellaneous notes), compiled by Chambre de commerce de Lyon. [Selective entry]
Lyons: Rey, 1898, 271–281 [s.p.].
SUBJ 14.3 24.2 ▪ 21.3

12944 MCY PO P2 G1.4 1842–1895
Volosatov, I-.
'Nekotoryia svedeniia o Gui-khua-chene' (Information on Kuei-hua-ch'eng [Shansi]). In *Trudy russkikh torgovykh liudei v Mongolii i Kitae* (Works of Russian merchants in Mongolia and China), compiled by Vostochno-sibirskii otdel, Imperatorskoe russkoe geograficheskoe obshchestvo. [Selective entry]
Irkutsk: Tip. K. I. Vitkovskoi, 1890, 127–137. (Imperatorskoe russkoe geograficheskoe obshchestvo, Vostochno-sibirskii otdel, Zapiski po obshchei geografii, 1, 1)
SUBJ 14.2 14.3 24.3 ▪ 21.3

12945 DLC P P1 G1.2 1895–1911
Wang, Chung-hui (Wang Ch'ung-hui), 1881–1958.
'Das chinesische Beförderungsgesetz vom 24. Januar 1911' (The Chinese forwarding-agent law of 24 January 1911).
BVRV 7, 3 (Juni 1911), 66–74.
SUBJ 12.2 14.3

12946 GBF PO P1 G1.3 1895–1911
Wang, Chung-hui (Wang Ch'ung-hui), 1881–1958, and Alfred Forke, 1867–1944.
'Die Rechtssätze des chinesischen Handels, nebst Bemerkungen über das Gerichtsverfahren und das Prozessrecht' (The legal rules of Chinese commerce, with observations on court proceedings and the law of procedure). In *Die Handelsgesetze des Erdballs* (The commercial laws of the world). [Sole entry]
Berlin: R. v. Decker, 1906, vol. 6, 1–27.
SUBJ 12.2 14.3 22.2 ▪ 34.2 34.3

12947 MCH P P2 G1.1 1644–1911
Whitbeck, Brainerd Hunt, 1943–.
The tea system of the Ch'ing dynasty.
Unpublished senior thesis in History, Harvard U., 1965. 52 p.
SUBJ 14 14.1 14.3 14.5 ▪ 12.2 24.3

12948 MAM P P2 G1.3 –1911
Wilkinson, Endymion Porter, 1941–.
Studies in Chinese price history.
Ann Arbor: University Microfilms (Publ. 71-1644), 1971. 285 p. (Doctoral dissertation in History, Princeton U.)
SUBJ 14 14.2 14.3 14.6 22 24.3 ▪ 12 14.1 21 21.1 62

1644-1949

12949 CSU P P2 G1.2 1842–1928
Adshead, Samuel Adrian Miles, 1932–.
'Commissariat and communications in traditional China.'
Pacific viewpoint 11, 2 (Sept. 1970), 167–180.
SUBJ 14.2 14.3 16.2 ▪ 11.3 14.1 16

12950 MCH P P2 G1.2 1895–1928
Adshead, Samuel Adrian Miles, 1932–.
The modernization of the Chinese salt administration, 1900–1920.
Cambridge: Harvard U. Press, 1970. 280 p. (Harvard East Asian series, 53) (Revision of doctoral dissertation in History and Far Eastern Languages, Harvard U., 1968)
SUBJ 12 14.3 14.4 14.5 ▪ 14.2 16.2 19 34.2 66

12951 NNC PO P2 G8.2 1895–1928
Bel'chenko, A- T-.
'Doneseniia imperatorskago rossiiskago konsula v Kantone: geograficheskii i ekonomicheskii ocherk provintsii IUn'nan' za poslednee desiatiletie' (Reports of the imperial Russian consul in Canton: Overview of the geography and economy of Yunnan during the past decade).
DIRKP 47 (1915), 1–62.
SUBJ 14 14.3 20 ▪ 21.1 24.4

12952 NNC PO P3 G9.2 1895–1928
Bel'chenko, A- T-.
'Doneseniia imperatorskago rossiiskago konsula v Kantone: ocherk torgovli shelkom v Kantone v sezon 1912–1913, 1913–1914 godov' (Reports of the imperial Russian consul in Canton: Survey of the silk trade at Canton in the 1912–1913 and 1913–1914 seasons).
DIRKP 50 (1915), 140–155.
SUBJ 14.3 24.3

12953 NNC PO P2 G9.1 1895–1928
Bel'chenko, A- T-.
'Doneseniia imperatorskago rossiiskago konsula v Kantone: ocherk torgovoi deiatel'nosti provintsii Guan-Si' (Reports of the imperial Russian consul in Canton: Survey of trade in Kwangsi).
DIRKP 47 (1915), 63–136.
SUBJ 14 14.3 24.2 24.3 ▪ 21.1 28

12954 NNC PO P3 G9.2 1842–1928
Bel'chenko, A- T-.
'Doneseniia imperatorskogo rossiiskago konsula v Kantone: ocherk torgovli Kantona za 1882–1912 gody' (Reports of the imperial Russian consul in Canton: Survey of the trade at Canton, 1882–1912).
DIRKP 50 (1915), 1–40.
SUBJ 14.3 24 24.3 ▪ 24.2 24.6 26.2 56 66

12955 CBU PO P3 G6.1 1895–1928
Buchanan, Ralph E-.
The Shanghai raw silk market.
New York: Silk Assn. of America, 1929. 76 p.
SUBJ 14.3 ▪ 12.2 24.3 24.4 24.6 26.2 36.2

12956 CSU P P2 G1.2 1895–1928
Es, Willem Johan Louis van, 1886–1943.
'De ontwikkeling van het handelsverkeer in China, 1900–1923' (The development of trade in China, 1900–1923).
TESG 16, 10 (Oktober 1925), 301–317.
SUBJ 14.3 ▪ 14.4

12957 NBU O P2 G1.1 1842–1928
Hansson, Peder Carl.
Femogtyve år i Midtens rike: Erindringer (Memories of twenty-five years in the Middle Kingdom).
Oslo: Emil Moestoe, 1946. 561 p.
SUBJ 12 14.3 66 ▪ 11 12.1 12.2 14.2 14.5 16.2 53 55 56 62

12958 ICU P P3 G5.1 1895–1928
Hitch, Margaret Armstrong.
The port of Tientsin.
Unpublished masters thesis in Geography, U. of Chicago, 1924. 84 p.
SUBJ 14.3 21.3 24 24.3 ▪ 14.2 24.5

12959 CBU S P2 G1.3 1895–1949
Ko Fuh-ting (Ko Fu-ting).
'Wholesale prices of important farm crops.'
EF 5 (May 1937), 223–224. [In Chinese as well as English]
SUBJ 14.1 14.3

12960 CSU S P1 G1.5 –1949
Kuo Tsung-fei (Ku Ch'un-fan).
'A brief history of the trade routes between Burma, Indochina and Yunnan.'
THM 12, 1 (Aug.–Sept. 1941), 9–32.
SUBJ 14.2 14.3 ▪ 11.2

12961 NNC P P2 G1.2 –1949
Mad'iar, Liudvig Ignat'evich, 1891–?
'Gorod i derevnia v ekonomike Kitaia' (City and countryside in Chinese economics).
MKhMP 1930, 2 (fevral'), 83–93.
SUBJ 14.2 14.3 14.6 ▪ 11.4 16.2 16.3 34.3

12962 NNC S P3 G1.3 1842–1949
Otte, Friedrich W- K-.
'Die Entwicklung der Handelsstatistik in China' (The development of trade statistics in China).
Sinica 9, 3/4 (Mai–Juli 1934), 155–173.
SUBJ 14.3 ▪ 14.6 34.2

12963 CSU PO P2 G1.2 –1928
Parker, Edward Harper, 1849–1926.
China: Her history, diplomacy, and commerce, from the earliest times to the present day, 2nd ed.
London: Murray, 1917. 30, 419 p.
SUBJ 10 12 14.3 14.5 15 66 ▪ 11 14.2 14.6 22.2 23 29 32.2 41 61 62

12964 CBU P P1 G1.2 1842–1949
Raeburn, John R-.
'Changes in China's price level since 1871.'
EF 7 (Oct. 1937), 282–289. [In Chinese as well as English]
SUBJ 14.3 ▪ 14.6

12965 NNC P P4 G1.1 1895–1949
Remer, Charles Frederick, 1889–1972.
A study of Chinese boycotts, with special reference to their economic effectiveness.
Baltimore: Johns Hopkins Press, 1933. 12, 306 p. [Reprinted—Taipei: Ch'eng-wen, 1967. 12, 306 p.]
Subj 14.3 22.1 22.2 36.4 66 ▪ 12 32.2 34.3 36.2 38 54

12966 NNC PO P3 G5.1 1895–1928
Tideman, P- G-.
'Donesenie imperatorskago rossiiskago konsula v Tian'tszine: obzor torgovli gor. Kalgana' (Report of the imperial Russian consul in Tientsin: Survey of the trade at Kalgan).
DIRKP 40 (1914), 112–119.
Subj 14.3 24.2 ▪ 24.4 24.6

12967 ICU P P1 G1.2 –1928
Ting Supao.
A brief history of standard weights and measures in China from the earliest historic times to the present.
Unpublished masters thesis in Physics, U. of Chicago, 1922. 59 p.
Subj 14.3 62

12968 NNC PO P2 G2.1 1895–1928
Trautshol'd, V- V-.
'Donesenie imperatorskago general'nago konsula v Kharbine: torgovlia Kharbinskago raiona za 1914 god' (Report of the imperial [Russian] consul-general in Harbin: Trade in the Harbin region in 1914).
DIRKP 61 (1916), 132–279.
Subj 14.3 ▪ 14.5

12969 NNC PO P2 G2.1 1895–1928
Usatyi, P- K-.
'Donesenie imperatorskago rossiiskago vitse-konsula v Khailare: Barga i ee ekonomicheskoe znachenie' (Report of the imperial Russian vice-consul in Hai-la-erh: Western Heilungkiang and its economic significance).
DIRKP 52 (1915), 1–50.
Subj 14.3 24.3 ▪ 21.1 24 24.2 24.4 66

12970 DLC P P2 G1.2 –1949
Wu, Chenlott C. (Wu Ch'eng-lo).
Unification of weights and measures in China.
Nanking: Shih yeh pu, Ch'üan kuo tu liang heng chü, 1934. 46 p.
Subj 14.3 62 ▪ 12 12.2 29

1911-1949

12971 CSU O P2 G5.0 1928–1949
'Apricot kernels on the Tientsin market.'
CEJ 5, 2 (Aug. 1929), 696–702.
Subj 14.3 55

12972 CSU U P2 G1.4 1928–1949
'China's raw wool trade.'
CEJ 18, 6 (June 1936), 863–877.
Subj 14.1 14.3

12973 NIC U P3 G1.2 1911–1928
'Commerce des cuirs et peaux' (Trade in skins and leather).
La Chine 43 (1er juin 1923), 675–685.
Subj 14.3

12974 NNP P P2 G5.3 1911–1928
'Ekonomicheskoe polozhenie Kiao Chao za 1913, 1914, 1915, 1916 gg.: donesenie rossiiskago vitse-konsula v TSindao' (The economic situation in Kiaochow, 1913–1916: Report of the Russian vice-consul in Tsingtao).
Doneseniia rossiiskikh konsul'skikh predstavitelei za granitsei po torgovo-promyshlennym voprosam 15 (1917), 1–40.
Subj 14.3 24 24.2

12975 NNC PO P2 G7.0 1911–1928
'Iz doneseniia imperatorskago rossiiskago konsul'stva v Khan'kou: kratkii ocherk polozheniia, ekonomicheskago sostoianiia i torgovli Khan'kouskago konsul'skago okruga' (From the report of the imperial Russian consulate in Hankow: Brief sketch of the position, economic condition, and trade of the Hankow consular area).
DIRKP 39 (1914), 54–58.
Subj 14.3 14.4 ▪ 14.2 21

12976 CSU U P2 G1.3 1928–1949
'Ramie and jute fibers on the Hankow market.'
CEJ 5, 2 (Aug. 1929), 729–734.
Subj 14.1 14.3

12977 CSU O P3 G6.1 1928–1949
'Rice market of Wusih.'
CEJ 19, 3 (Sept. 1936), 269–280.
Subj 14.3 24.3 ▪ 24.4 24.6

12978 CSU P P2 G1.3 1928–1949
'Testing and inspection of cotton.'
CEJ 15, 5 (Nov. 1934), 505–538.
Subj 12 14.1 14.3 ▪ 14.4 24.4

12979 CSH O P2 G5.0 1911–1928
'Towns on the Techow [capital of Te *hsien*, Shantung] – Nankung [*hsien* capital, Hopei] motor road.'
CEJ 1, 10 (Oct. 1927), 902–907.
Subj 14.3 24.2 ▪ 24.1 24.4

12980 CSU O P2 G6.1 1928–1949
'Vegetable-tallow and wax trade in Shanghai.'
CEJ 19, 1 (July 1936), 42–50.
Subj 14.3 24.4 ▪ 36.2

12981 CSU U P3 G3.3 1928–1949
'The wool trade in Paotow.'
CEJ 12, 1 (Jan. 1933), 33–42.
Subj 14.3 ▪ 24.4

12982 NIC P P1 G1.2 1911–1928
Allman, Norwood Francis, 1893–.
'Consignment laws in China.'
CLR 2, 4 (Apr. 1925), 167–176.
Subj 12.2 14.3 ▪ 34.2

12983 CSH S P2 G1.2 1928–1949
Avenarius, G- G-.
'Vnutrenniaia torgovlia Kitaia' (Domestic trade in China).
VM 1933, 8/9 (15 maia), 57–71.
Subj 14 14.2 14.3 ▪ 34.3

12984 CBU S P2 G2.0 1928–1949
Avenarius, G- G-.
'Vnutrenniaia torgovlia Man'chzhurii' (Domestic trade in Manchuria).
VM 1933, 21 (15 noiabria), 13–31.
Subj 14.3 ▪ 14.1 14.4

12985 NIC PO P2 G1.2 1911–1928
Baranov, Ippolit Gavrilovich.
Organizatsiia vnutrennei torgovli v Kitae: kratkii ocherk (Brief sketch of the organization of domestic trade in China).
Harbin: Tip. KVzhd, 1917. 40 p.
Subj 14.3 14.6 16.2 34.2 55 63 ▪ 16 23 34.3

12986 CSU O P3 G5.1 1928–1949
Barnett, Arthur Doak, 1921–.
'Business depression' [report to Institute of Current World Affairs, April 1948]. In *China on the eve of Communist takeover*, by A. D. Barnett. [Selective entry]
New York: Praeger, 1963, 52–59.
Subj 14.3 14.4 24.4 ▪ 24

12987 NNC U P3 G1.5 1911–1928
Berliner, Sigfrid, 1884–.
'Technik des einkommenden Frachtengeschäfts in China' (Techniques of handling incoming cargoes in China).
Die Betriebswirtschaft 18, 7 (Juli 1925), 150–151; 18, 8 (Aug. 1925), 178–180; 18, 9 (Sept. 1925), 207–210.
Subj 14.3 ▪ 14.5

12988 NNC PO P2 G2.2 1911–1928
Brattsova, V- A-.
'Donesenie upravliaiushchego imperatorskim rossiiskim konsul'stvom v Girine: torgovyi otchet za 1913 god' (Report of the chargé d'affaires of the imperial Russian consulate in Kirin: An account of trade in 1913).
DIRKP 44 (1914), 73–97.
Subj 14.3 ▪ 14.4 21.1 24.1 24.2 24.3 45

12989 CSU U P2 G1.1 1911–1949
Chang, Bintze T.
'The rapeseed trade.'
CEJ 10, 4 (Apr. 1932), 314–322.
Subj 14.1 14.3 ▪ 24.3

12990 CSU U P2 G1.2 1911–1949
Chang, Bintze T.
'The romance of brick tea.'
CEJ 5, 5 (Nov. 1929), 935–944.
Subj 14.3 14.4

12991 NIC F P2 G5.1 1928–1949
Cheng, Lin-chuang.
'A study of the egg-trade in the Peiping area.'
CSPSR 21, 3 (Oct.–Dec. 1937), 341–390.
Subj 14.3 24 24.3 ▪ 24.1 24.2 34.2

12992 CNY P P2 G1.5 1911–1949
Chi Heng.
The trade in tung oil in China and its prospects.
Tientsin: Hautes études; Shanghai: Université l'Aurore, 1936. 119 p. (Institut des hautes études industrielles et commerciales, Faculty of Commerce, Economic studies, 5)
Subj 14.1 14.3 24.3 34.2 ▪ 24.4 24.5

12993 CSH FP P2 G5.1 1911–1928
Chu, T. S. (Ch'ü Chih-sheng).
Marketing of cotton in Hopei province. Tr. from the Chinese by T. Chin. [Tr. of a report dated 1928]
Peiping: [China Foundation], Institute of Social Research, 1929. 54 p. (ISR bulletins, 3) [For a later, more comprehensive report in Chinese, see Ch'ü Chih-sheng, *Ho-pei mien hua chih*

ch'u ch'an chi fan yün (Cotton production and marketing in Hopei); Shanghai: Shang wu yin shu kuan, 1931; 314 p.]
SUBJ 14.3 24.1 24.3 ▪ 26.2 34.2

12994 NIC U P2 G1.2 1928–1949
Deasy, George F-, 1912–.
'Tung oil production and trade.'
EG 16, 3 (July 1940), 260–274.
SUBJ 14.3 14.4 ▪ 14.1

12995 CSH U P1 G1.2 1911–1949
[Dombrovskii, I- I-?] I. D.
'Torgovlia Man'chzhurii s Kitaem za 10 let, 1922–1931' (A decade of Chinese-Manchurian trade, 1922–1931).
VM 1932, 11/12, 5–10.
SUBJ 14.3 ▪ 14.2 14.4

12996 DLC P P3 G9.0 1911–1928
Dvoretskii, I-.
'Kanton i Gonkong' (Canton and Hong Kong). In *Kantonskaia kommuna: sbornik statei i materialov* (Articles and documents on the Canton commune), compiled by Nauchno-issledovatel'skii institut po Kitaiu, Kommunisticheskaia akademiia. [Selective entry]
Moscow: Gosizdat, 1929, 118–129.
SUBJ 14.3 66

12997 MCH S P1 G1.1 1911–1928
Dvoretskii, I-.
'Tabakovodstvo, tabachnaia promyshlennost' i tabachnyi rynok Kitaia' (Tobacco growing, processing, and marketing in China).
Materialy po kitaiskomu voprosu 11/12 (1928), 120–127.
SUBJ 14.3 ▪ 14.1 14.4 24.3

12998 NNC P P2 G1.4 1911–1949
Fong, H. D. (Fang Hsien-t'ing), 1902–.
'Terminal marketing of Tientsin cotton.'
MBEC 7, 7 (July 1934), 275–321. [Separately reprinted—Tientsin: Chihli Press, 1934. 47 p.] [Separately reprinted—Washington, D.C.: Center for Chinese Research Materials, 1972. 47 p.]
SUBJ 14.3 34.2 ▪ 14.1 14.2 24.3 24.5 24.6 36.2

12999 CSH S P3 G2.0 1911–1949
Gol'fer, L- M-.
'O nekotorykh mestnykh prichinakh zatrudnenii sbyta bobov' (Local causes of difficulties in marketing beans).
VM 1930, 4, 8–10.
'The juncture upon the market for soya beans.'
Manchuria monitor 1930, 4, 1–3.
SUBJ 14.3 ▪ 24.3 24.6

13000 CSH S P2 G1.2 1911–1949
Gol'fer, L- M-.
'Organizatsiia eksporta bobov, zhmykhov i bobovogo masla iz severnoi Man'chzhurii' (Organizing the export of beans, bean cake, and bean oil in northern Manchuria). [With English abstract]
VM 1930, 2, 72–89.
SUBJ 14.3 34.2 ▪ 14.2 14.6 16.2 24.3

13001 CSH O P3 G2.3 1911–1928
Gorshenin, A- I-.
'Itogi gruzovoi raboty porta Dairen za poslednee piatiletie' (Results of freight operations in the port of Dairen in the past five years). [With English abstract]
VM 1930, 3, 25–35.
SUBJ 14.3 24.2 ▪ 24.3

13002 MCH P P3 G5.1 1911–1928
Ho, Franklin L. (Ho Lien), 1897–.
'Prices and price fluctuations in North China, 1913–23.'
CSPSR 13, 3 (July 1929), 349–358.
SUBJ 14.3

13003 CSU P P2 G1.2 1928–1949
Ho Ping-yin (Ho Ping-hsien), 1903–.
'Industry and commerce during 1935.'
CEJ 18, 1 (Jan. 1936), 1–22.
SUBJ 14.3 14.4 ▪ 24.4

13004 MCH P P1 G1.2 1911–1928
Hung, William S. H. (Hung Shih-hao).
Commercial law of China.
[Shanghai?]: ——, 1932. 19, 307 p.
SUBJ 12.2 14.3 34.2

13005 CSH P P5 G2.0 1911–1928
IAgolkovskii, A- F-, ed.
'Khlebnaia torgovlia v severnoi Man'chzhurii' (The grain trade in northern Manchuria). In *Khlebnaia torgovlia i mukomol'naia promyshlennost' v severnoi Man'chzhurii* (The grain trade and flour-milling industry in northern Manchuria), compiled by Obshchestvo izucheniia Man'chzhurskogo kraia, edited by Evgenii Evgen'evich IAshnov. [Analytic entry]
Harbin: Tipo-lit. T-va 'Ozo', 1923, vol. 2, 9–24.
SUBJ 14.3 14.5 ▪ 16.2 34.2

13006 WSU P P2 G1.2 1911–1928
Kitaiskaia Vostochnaia zheleznaia doroga. Ekonomicheskoe biuro.
Ocherki khlebnoi torgovli severnoi Man'chzhurii (Notes on the grain trade of northern Manchuria).
Harbin: Ekon. biuro KVzhd, 1930. 244 p.
SUBJ 11.3 14.1 14.2 14.3 24.3 ▪ 14.6

13007 NNC PO P3 G2.3 1911–1928
Kolokolov, S- A-.
'Doneseniia imperatorskago rossiiskago general'nago konsula v Mukdene' (Reports of the imperial Russian consul-general in Mukden).
DIRKP 61 (1916), 86–124.
SUBJ 14.3 ▪ 24.2

13008 MCH P P3 G1.2 1911–1928
Kries, Wilhelm von, 1886–.
Seezollverwaltung und Handelsstatistik in China (The maritime customs administration and trade statistics in China).
Jena: Gustav Fischer, 1913. 111 p. (Institut für Seeverkehr und Weltwirtschaft an der Universität Kiel, Probleme der Weltwirtschaft, 13) (Doctoral dissertation, Philosophische Fakultät, Universität Kiel)
SUBJ 14.3 14.5

13009 CSU O P3 G6.1 1928–1949
Lin, K. C.
'Shanghai's new fish-market.'
CEJ 15, 6 (Dec. 1934), 599–608.
SUBJ 14.3

13010 MCY P P1 G1.1 1911–1949
Lin, Wei-ying, 1908–.
China under depreciated silver, 1926–1931.
Shanghai: Commercial Press, 1935. 13, 230 p. (Foreign Trade Assn. of China monographs, 1) (Doctoral dissertation in Economics, Columbia U.)
SUBJ 14.3 14.6 ▪ 72

13011 CBU P P2 G2.0 1911–1949
Liubimov, L- I-.
'Man'chzhurskaia derevnia, kak potrebitel' importnykh tovarov' (The Manchurian village as a consumer of import goods).
VM 1933, 12 (1 iiulia), 27–39.
SUBJ 14.2 14.3 ▪ 14.1 16.3 55

13012 CSH P P2 G2.0 1911–1928
Liubimov, L- I- (L. I. Liubimoff).
'Ocherk razvitiia i sovremennogo sostoianiia torgovli v Man'chzhurii' (A note on the development and present state of trade in Manchuria).
VM 1929, 7/8, 25–36.
'Review of contemporary trade conditions in Manchuria.'
Manchuria monitor 1929, 7/8, 12–21.
SUBJ 11.3 14.2 14.3 ▪ 24.3

13013 CSH P P2 G2.0 1928–1949
Liubimov, L- I-.
'Rynok severnoi Man'chzhurii v 1932 g.' (The northern Manchurian market in 1932). [With English abstract]
VM 1933, 1 (ianvar'), 3–18.
SUBJ 14 14.3

13014 CSU P P2 G2.0 1928–1949
Loukashkin, A- S-, and [Vladimir Nikolaevich Zhernakov] V. N. Jernakov, 1909–.
'The fur trade of North Manchuria.'
CJ 21, 5 (Nov. 1934), 227–244; 21, 6 (Dec. 1934), 293–303.
SUBJ 14.3 ▪ 14.1 14.5 24.3

13015 GBS P P4 G1.2 1911–1949
Ma, Tseng-Hsiang (Ma Tseng-hsiang), 1917–.
Die Entwicklung der chinesischen Seehäfen (The development of China's ports).
Unpublished doctoral dissertation, Wirtschaftswissenschaftliche Fakultät, Wirtschafts-Hochschule Berlin, 1944. 209 p.
SUBJ 14.3 24.2 ▪ 21.3

13016 MAM P P3 G9.0 1911–1928
Motz, Earl John.
Great Britain, Hong Kong, and Canton: The Canton – Hong Kong strike and boycott of 1925–26.
Ann Arbor: University Microfilms (Publ. 72-30,014), 1972. 218 p. (Doctoral dissertation in History, Michigan State U.)
SUBJ 14.3 36.4 ▪ 32 66

13017 GBS P P3 G1.1 1911–1949
Otte, Friedrich W- K-.
'Wirtschaftsboykotte und ihre Auswirkungen in China' (Economic boycotts and their effects in China).
Ostasien 1 (1943), 89–120.
SUBJ 14.3 19 ▪ 12.1 60 66

13018 CSU S P7 G1.2 1928–1949
Ou, Pao-san (Wu Pao-san), 1905–.
'Recent discussion on China's food problem.'
PA 15, 3 (Sept. 1942), 345–359.
Subj 14 14.1 14.3 18 70 ▪ 14.5

13019 NNC P P2 G4.3 1911–1949
Paliukaitis, I- I-.
'Otrazhenie mirovogo khoziaistvennogo krizisa na ekonomike Sin'tsziana' (Economic repercussions of the world depression in Sinkiang).
Torgovlia SSSR s Vostokom 1931, 1/2, 29–40.
Subj 14.3 14.6 ▪ 14.4 24.2

13020 CBU FP P2 G1.2 1928–1949
Raeburn, John R-.
'War and China's general price level.'
EF 7 (Oct. 1937), 273–281. [In Chinese as well as English]
Subj 14.3 ▪ 14.6

13021 CBU S P3 G1.4 1911–1949
Raeburn, John R-, and Hu Kwoh-hwa (Hu Kuo-hua).
'China's future price level.'
EF 5 (May 1937), 197–211. [In Chinese as well as English]
Subj 14.3

13022 CBU F P2 G1.3 1928–1949
Raeburn, John R-, and Hu Kwoh-hwa (Hu Kuo-hua).
'The flexibility of prices in China.'
EF 9 (Apr. 1938), 394–405. [In Chinese as well as English]
Subj 14.3 24.3 ▪ 28

13023 CBU P P1 G1.1 1911–1949
Raeburn, John R-, and Wang Lien.
'Wholesale prices in North China, Hong Kong, Manchuria and the United States.'
EF 4 (Feb. 1937), 161–179. [In Chinese as well as English]
Subj 14.3

13024 NNC O P2 G1.4 1928–1949
Rasmussen, Albert Henry.
'The wool trade of North China.'
PA 9, 1 (Mar. 1936), 60–68.
Subj 14.3

13025 GMS PO P4 G1.1 1928–1949
Reichsverband der Deutschen Industrie.
Bericht der China-Studienkommission des Reichsverbandes der Deutschen Industrie (Report by the Study Commission on China of the National Association of German Industries).
Berlin: Reichsverband der Deutschen Industrie, 1930. 191 p. (RDI, Veröffentlichungen, 57)
Subj 14 14.3 ▪ 12.2

13026 MCH PO P2 G1.2 1928–1949
Riemens, H-.
'China in 1936' (China in 1936).
Economische verslagen van Nederlandsche diplomatieke en consulaire ambtenaren 31, 5 (1937), 127–180. [Supplement to *Economische voorlichting* 21 (28 Mei 1937)]
Subj 14.3 ▪ 14.6

13027 CSH P P2 G1.2 1911–1928
Setnitskii, N- A-.
'Raiony torgovli Kitaia zernovymi khlebami i maslichnymi semenami i produktami ikh pererabotki' (Chinese regions of trade in grains and oil seeds and their derivatives).
VM 1929, 1, 8–15.
Subj 14.3 ▪ 14.1

13028 NNC PO P2 G1.1 1928–1949
Stein, Guenther.
'China's price problem.'
PA 14, 3 (Sept. 1941), 322–333.
Subj 14 14.3

13029 ICU S P2 G1.2 1911–1928
Sung, Tsun Hsiang.
Marketing features in China.
Unpublished masters thesis in Commerce and Administration, U. of Chicago, 1925. 102 p.
Subj 14.3 24 24.3 28 34.2 34.3 ▪ 12.2 24.5 24.6 39 41 47

13030 NNC PO P2 G1.5 1928–1949
Sze Ke-kang (Shih K'o-kang).
'Governmental control of tea marketing in Anhwei and Kiangsi.' Tr. of 'Wan Kan ch'a yeh t'ung chih ti chien t'ao' (An examination of supervision of the tea industry in Anhwei and Kiangsi); in *Chung-kuo nung ts'un tung t'ai* (Rural trends in China), edited by Chung-kuo nung ts'un ching chi yen chiu hui (Research Society for Chinese Agrarian Economy); Shanghai: Li ming shu chü, 1937, 42–51 [condensed tr.]. In *Agrarian China*, compiled by Institute of Pacific Relations. [Selective entry]
Chicago: U. of Chicago Press, 1939, 179–183.
Subj 14.3 32.1 34.2 ▪ 14.6 24.3

13031 NNC P P1 G1.2 1911–1949
Torsuev, N- P-.
'Lesnoi rynok Kitaia i severnoi Man'chzhurii' (The timber market of China and northern Manchuria).
Ezhemesiachnik Vsesoiuznoi torgovoi palaty 1932, 2 (fevral'), 32–42.
Subj 14.3

13032 NNP P P2 G2.0 1911–1928
Trautshol'd, V- V-.
'Otchet o torgovle kharbinskogo raiona za 1915 g.' (Trade report for the Harbin region in 1915).
Doneseniia rossiiskikh konsul'skikh predstavitelei za granitsei po torgovo-promyshlennym voprosam 13 (1917), 1–94.
Subj 14.3 14.5 ▪ 14

13033 MCH P P1 G1.1 1928–1949
Tsou, Stanley Szu-yee (Tsou Ssu-i), 1922–.
The world tea industry and China.
Unpublished doctoral dissertation in Economics, Harvard U., 1946. 286 p.
Subj 14.3

13034 NNC PO P2 G5.1 1911–1928
Uspenskii, K- V-.
'Donesenie upravliaiushchego imperatorskim rossiiskim konsul'stvom v Tian'tszine: obzor torgovoi deiatel'nosti porta Tian'tszina i tiagoteiushchikh k nemu raionov za 1914 god' (Report of the chargé d'affaires of the imperial Russian consulate in Tientsin: Survey of the trade at Tientsin and in nearby areas for 1914).
DIRKP 56 (1916), 1–19.
Subj 14.3

13035 CBU U P3 G2.0 1928–1949
Valin, I-.
'Import stroitel'nykh materialov v Man'chzhurii' (The importation of building materials into Manchuria). [With English abstract at end of issue]
VM 1934, 7 (iiul'), 38–43.
Subj 14.3 ▪ 14.2 14.4

13036 CBU P P1 G1.2 1928–1949
Valin, I-.
'Torgovyi balans Man'chzhurii' (Manchuria's balance of trade).
EB 1934, 5 (mai), 15–21.
Subj 14.3 ▪ 14.6

13037 NNC P P2 G1.3 1911–1949
Wang Ting Hsien (Wang T'ing-hsien).
A research on raw cotton and its trade in Tientsin, mimeo.
Tientsin: Hautes études; Shanghai: Université l'Aurore, 1935. 97 p. (Institute des hautes études industrielles et commerciales, Faculty of Commerce, Economic studies, 4)
Subj 14 14.3 24.3 24.4 ▪ 14.1 14.2 34.2 36.2

13038 CSH P P2 G8.1 1928–1949
Wang, Yin-yuen (Wang Yin-yüan).
'Trends of commodity prices and earnings in Szechwan, 1937–1945.'
EF 55 (Apr. 1946), 831–834.
Subj 14.3 ▪ 26 28

13039 MCH O P4 G2.0 1928–1949
Woodhead, Henry George Wandesforde, 1883–1959.
A visit to Manchukuo.
Shanghai: Shanghai Mercury Press, 1932. 112 p.
Subj 14 14.3 25 ▪ 12 12.1 12.2 17 35 47 66

13040 CSH O P4 G1.5 1928–1949
Woodhead, Henry George Wandesforde, 1883–1959.
The Yangtsze and its problems.
Shanghai: Shanghai Mercury Press, 1931. 150 p. [Reprinted from *Shanghai evening post and mercury* 20 May – 16 July 1931.]
Subj 14.2 14.3 14.5 15 ▪ 14.6 22.2 24.4 25 28 32.2

13041 CSU P P2 G1.2 1911–1949
Wu Chao Chang.
Trade in bristles, mimeo.
Tientsin: Hautes études; Shanghai: Université l'Aurore, 1938. 109 p. (Institut des hautes études industrielles et commerciales, Faculty of Commerce, Economic studies, 13)
Subj 14.1 14.3 ▪ 24.3 34.2

13042 MCH S P2 G1.2 1928–1949
Yang, Sueh-chang (Yang Hsüeh-chang), 1918–.
China's depression and subsequent recovery, 1931–1936: An inquiry into the applicability of the modern income-determination theory.
Unpublished doctoral dissertation in Economics, Harvard U., 1950. 265 p.
Subj 14 14.3 14.6 ▪ 14.1 14.4 15 16.3

1911-1972
(including 1644-1972)

13043 MCH P P3 G9.5 1928–1972
Boxer, Baruch, 1932–.
Ocean shipping in the evolution of Hong Kong.
Chicago: U. of Chicago, Dept. of Geography, 1961. 10, 95 p. (DG research papers, 72) (Revision of doctoral dissertation in Geography, U. of Chicago)
Subj 14.2 14.3 ▪ 24.4

13044 CSH S P2 G4.0 1928–1972
Chang, Perry (Chang P'eng), 1921–.
'Trade.' In *A regional handbook on Northwest China*, compiled by Far Eastern and Russian Institute, U. of Washington. [Selective entry]
New Haven: Human Relations Area Files, 1956, vol. 2, 677–690. (HRAF subcontractor's monographs, 59; Washington 5)
Subj 14.3 ▪ 24.3

13045 CSH U P2 G3.0 1911–1972
Chang, Perry (Chang P'eng), 1921–.
'Trade.' In *A regional handbook on the Inner Mongolia Autonomous Region*, compiled by Far Eastern and Russian Institute, U. of Washington. [Selective entry]
New Haven: Human Relations Area Files, 1956, 530–538. (HRAF subcontractor's monographs, 60; Washington 7)
Subj 14.3 ▪ 24.3

13046 MCY P P2 G9.5 1842–1972
Kenrick, Douglas M-.
Price control and its practice in Hong Kong.
Hong Kong: Weiss, 1954. 153 p.
Subj 14.3 24.3 24.6 ▪ 22 24.5

13047 CSH P P1 G1.2 1928–1972
[La Dany, Ladislao] ———, 1914–.
'Weights and measures.'
CNA 427 (6 July 1962), 1–6.
Subj 14.3 62

13048 CSH F P2 G9.5 1928–1972
Maunder, Wynne Frederick, 1920–.
'An examination of demand conditions for rice and related cereals in Hong Kong.' In *Hong Kong economic papers, No. 2*, edited by Edward Stuart Kirby. [Selective entry]
Hong Kong: Hong Kong Economic Assn., 1963, 49–78.
Subj 14.3 24 28 ▪ 26.3 41

13049 CSH P P2 G1.1 1842–1972
Murphey, William Rhoads, III, 1919–.
The treaty ports and China's modernization: What went wrong?
Ann Arbor: U. of Michigan, Center for Chinese Studies, 1970. 73 p. (Michigan papers in Chinese studies, 7)
Subj 11.1 14.3 66 ▪ 14.2 14.4 14.5 16.1 16.2 18 24.3 34.2

13050 NNC P P2 G1.2 1928–1972
[Okazaki Fumiisa] ———, ed.
Analysis of prices in Communist China, mimeo. Tr. of *Shin Chūgoku keizai no bunseki: Bukka hen* (An economic analysis of New China: Prices); Tokyo: Tōa keizai kenkyūkai, 1961; 248 p.
Washington, D.C.: U.S. Joint Publications Research Service, 8 Aug. 1962. 263 p. (JPRS 14,771; MC 18,207/1962) [Xerox copyflo available—New York: CCM Information Corp., Research and Microfilm Publications. (Scholarly Book Translation Series, 400)]
Subj 14 14.3 ▪ 18

13051 NNC P P3 G9.5 1928–1972
Tang, Doris, and Denis John Dwyer, 1933–.
'The port of Hong Kong.' In *Symposium on land use and mineral deposits in Hong Kong, southern China and South-east Asia*, edited by Sydney George Davis. [Selective entry]
Hong Kong: Hong Kong U. Press, 1964, 122–132.
Subj 14.3 ▪ 21.3 24.2

13052 CSU P P2 G9.4 1928–1972
Wu, Hwei Ran.
'Economic effects of rice control policy in postwar Taiwan.'
DE 8, 1 (Mar. 1970), 52–78.
Subj 14.3 ▪ 24.1

13053 NNC FP P2 G9.4 1842–1972
Yeh, S. M. (Yeh Hsin-ming).
Rice marketing in Taiwan.
Taipei: Chinese-American Joint Commission on Rural Reconstruction, 1955. 98 p. (JCRR, Economic digest series, 7)
Subj 14.3 24.1 ▪ 14.6 36.2

13054 CSU P P1 G1.1 1928–1972
Yeung, Patrick.
'Trade ties between Hong Kong and Mainland China.'
AS 10, 9 (Sept. 1970), 820–839.
Subj 14.3

1949-1972

13055 NNC P P2 G1.2 1949–1972
'State procurement of farm produce in Communist China.'
URS 34, 8 (28 Jan. 1964), 121–133.
Subj 14.1 14.3 ▪ 22.1 24.3 34.1

13056 CSU P P7 G1.2 1949–1972
Bandyopadhyaya, Kalyani.
'The Chinese foodgrain crisis: 1959–61.'
China report (New Delhi) 7, 3 (May–June 1971), 16–25.
Subj 14.1 14.3 ▪ 11.4 16.3 34.1

13057 CSU PO P3 G9.5 1949–1972
Barnett, Arthur Doak, 1921–.
'Hong Kong and China trade.'
AUFS-EAS 3, 2 (8 Feb. 1954), 1–34.
Subj 14.3 ▪ 24.6

13058 CSU P P7 G1.2 1949–1972
Bernstein, Thomas Paul, 1937–.
'Cadre and peasant behavior under conditions of insecurity and deprivation: The grain supply crisis of the spring of 1955.' In *Chinese Communist politics in action*, edited by Arthur Doak Barnett. [Selective entry]
Seattle: U. of Washington Press, 1969, 365–399. (Social Science Research Council, Studies in Chinese government and politics, 1)
Subj 14.3 18 22.1 ▪ 14.1 16.1 16.3 22 22.2 32

13059 CSH F P2 G9.4 1949–1972
Chang, Te-tsui (Chang Te-ts'ui), 1904–.
'The guarantee price of sugar in Taiwan.' In *Proceedings of Agricultural Economics Seminar held at the College of Agriculture, National Taiwan University, September 16–20, 1958.* [Selective entry]
Taipei: National Taiwan U., 1959, 105–108.
Subj 14.3 ▪ 24.1 34.2

13060 MCH P P1 G1.2 1949–1972
Chen Chio-shen (Ch'en Chüeh-sheng).
'A quantitative study of food uses under the Chinese Communist regime.'
IS 1, 4 (Jan. 1965), 22–30.
Subj 14.3 18 ▪ 11 55

13061 MCH U P2 G1.2 1949–1972
Chen Chun, 1917–.
'Villages and towns draw closer.'
People's China 3, 4 (16 Feb. 1951), 10–12.
Subj 14.3 ▪ 24.3

13062 CSH U P2 G1.2 1949–1972
Chen Mae Fun (Ch'en Mai-fen).
'Give and take.'
FEER 56, 6 (11 May 1967), 317–319.
Subj 14.3 14.6

13063 MCH P P2 G1.2 1949–1972
Chen, Nai-ruenn (Ch'en Nai-jun), 1927–.
'The theory of price formation in Communist China.'
CQ 27 (July–Sept. 1966), 33–53.
Subj 14 14.3 14.5 64 ▪ 14.1 14.4

13064 CSH P P2 G1.2 1949–1972
Chen Ting-chung (Ch'en Ting-chung).
'Food production on Mainland China as estimated from its food consumption.' In *Collected documents of the First Sino-American Conference on Mainland China*. [Selective entry]
[Taipei]: Institute of International Relations, Republic of China, 1971, 741–772.
Subj 14.1 14.3 ▪ 14.4 24.3

13065 NNC P P1 G1.2 1949–1972
Cheng Chu-yuan (Cheng Chu-yüan), 1927–.
The China Mainland market under Communist control.
Hong Kong: Union Research Institute, 1956. 96 p. (Communist China Problem Research Series, EC14)
Subj 14.3 ▪ 12 14.6

13066 NNC P P2 G1.2 1949–1972
Ch'i Ling.
'Purchase and distribution of grain in Communist China.' Tr. of 'Shih nien lai ti Chung kung liang shih cheng kou yü fen p'ei' (Purchase and distribution of grain in Communist China during the past decade); *Tsu kuo chou k'an* 393 (18 July 1960), 11–25. In *Communist China, 1949–1959*, edited by Union Research Institute. [Selective entry]
Hong Kong: Union Research Institute, 1961, vol. 2, 1–68.
Subj 14.3 18 ▪ 14.1 16.3 34.1

13067 CSU U P2 G1.2 1949–1972
Chiang Huai.
'On simplifying the phases of commodity circulation.' Tr. of 'Lun ching chien shang p'in liu t'ung huan chieh'; *Ching*

chi yen chiu (Peking) 1965, 11 (Nov.), 27–31. In *Translations from 'Ching chi yen chiu' (Economic research) No. 11, 1965*, mimeo., compiled by U.S. Joint Publications Research Service. [Sole entry]
Washington, D.C.: JPRS, 18 Jan. 1966, 57–68. (JPRS 33,768; MC 3587/1966) [A different tr.—'On simplification of the links of commodity circulation.' *SCMM* 508 (24 Jan. 1966), 19–26.]
Subj 14.3

13068 MCH P P2 G1.2 1949–1972
Chou, Shun-hsin, 1915–.
'Prices in Communist China.'
JAS 25, 4 (Aug. 1966), 645–663.
Subj 14 14.3 ▪ 14.5 14.6

13069 DLC P P4 G1.2 1949–1972
Dapčević-Oreščanin, Sonja, et al.
'Državni sektor i politika prema privatnom i zadružnom sektoru' (The state sector and the policy toward private and cooperative sectors).
DB 4, 6/7 (1955), 107–120. [Special issue: *Savremena Kina* (Contemporary China)]
Subj 12.1 14.3 32.1 ▪ 14.4 14.6 16.2 32 32.2

13070 MAM P P2 G1.2 1949–1972
Denny, David Ladd, 1939–.
Rural policies and the distribution of agricultural products in China, 1950–1959.
Ann Arbor: University Microfilms (Publ. 72-29,829), 1972. 414 p. (Doctoral dissertation in Economics, U. of Michigan, 1971)
Subj 14 14.1 14.3 18 ▪ 11.1 12.1 14.5 16.3 24.3 32.1 34.1

13071 NNC P P2 G1.2 1949–1972
Dokukin, V-.
'Sotsialisticheskie preobrazovaniia v torgovle KNR' (Socialist reorganization of trade in the People's Republic of China).
Sovetskaia torgovlia 1959, 7 (iiul'), 54–58.
Subj 14.3 24.3 34.2 ▪ 14 16.2

13072 MMT P P1 G1.2 1949–1972
Donnithorne, Audrey Gladys, 1922–.
'Organizational aspects of the internal trade of the Chinese People's Republic, with special reference to 1958–60.' In *Symposium on economic and social problems of the Far East*, edited by Edward Franciszek Szczepanik. [Selective entry]
Hong Kong: Hong Kong U. Press, 1962, 55–68.
Subj 14.3 ▪ 14

13073 CSU P P2 G1.2 1949–1972
Donnithorne, Audrey Gladys, 1922–.
'State procurement of agricultural produce in China.'
Soviet studies 18, 1 (July 1966), 38–56; 18, 2 (Oct. 1966), 213–224.
Subj 14.1 14.3 14.5 ▪ 16.3 18

13074 CSH P P2 G1.2 1949–1972
Feng Wen.
'Peiping's commercial organizations and its manipulation of marketing.'
CCA 2, 4 (Aug. 1965), 47–61.
Subj 14.3 ▪ 24.3

13075 CSH P P2 G1.2 1949–1972
Gogol', Boris Ionovich (V. Gogol).
'Razvertyvanie tovarooborota v Kitaiskoi Narodnoi Respublike.'
VE 1951, 10 (oktiabr'), 34–45.
'The development of commodity exchange in the Chinese People's Republic.'
Soviet press translations 7, 3 (1 Feb. 1952), 77–85.
Subj 14.3 24.3 34.2 ▪ 14

13076 NNC P P2 G1.2 1949–1972
Gogol', Boris Ionovich.
Razvitie tovarooborota v Kitaiskoi Narodnoi Respublike (The development of commodity circulation in the People's Republic of China).
Moscow: Gospolitizdat, 1954. 142 p.
Subj 14.3

13077 NNP P P2 G1.2 1949–1972
Gogol', Boris Ionovich.
'Vnutrenniaia torgovlia Kitaia v gody sotsialisticheskogo stroitel'stva' (Domestic trade in China during the period of socialist construction).
Sovetskaia torgovlia 1959, 10 (oktiabr'), 31–34.
Subj 14.3 ▪ 14 18

13078 MCH P P1 G1.2 1949–1972
Hsia, Ronald (Hsia Hsiu-yung), 1918–.
Price control in China.
New York: Institute of Pacific Relations, International Secretariat, 1953. 96 p.
Subj 14 14.3 14.6 ▪ 34.2

13079 MCH FP P2 G9.4 1949–1972
Hsieh, S. C. (Hsieh Sen-chung), 1919–, S. M. Yeh (Yeh Hsin-ming), and T. S. Kuo (Kuo Chih-sung), comps.
Food administration in Taiwan.
Taipei: Chinese-American Joint Commission on Rural Reconstruction, 1953. 88 p. (JCRR, Economic digest series, 3)
Subj 14.3 24.1 ▪ 14 24.2 34.1

13080 DLC P P1 G1.2 1949–1972
Hsin Ying, 1915–.
The price problems of Communist China.
Hong Kong: Union Research Institute, 1954. 125 p. (Communist China problem research series, EC3)
Subj 14.3 14.5 14.6 ▪ 14

13081 MAM P P7 G9.4 1949–1972
Hsu, Robert C. (Hsü Ch'ung-ming), 1937–.
A study of the price of fertilizer in Taiwan, 1950–1966: First-best and second-best policies of taxation on traded input.
Ann Arbor: University Microfilms (Publ. 71-15,794), 1971. 155 p. (Doctoral dissertation in Economics, U. of California, Berkeley)
Subj 14.3 14.5 ▪ 24.1

13082 CSH U P2 G2.0 1949–1972
Huang, Cheng Wang.
'Trade.' In *A regional handbook on Northeast China*, compiled by Far Eastern and Russian Institute, U. of Washington. [Selective entry]
New Haven: Human Relations Area Files, 1956, 544–561. (HRAF subcontractor's monographs, 61; Washington 9)
Subj 14.3 ▪ 24.3 34.2

13083 CSH F P2 G9.4 1949–1972
Huang, Shu-min.
'Peasant marketing network in Taiwan.'
BIE 32, 3 (Aug. 1971), 191–215.
Subj 14.3 24 24.3 34.2 ▪ 11.3 24.1 24.2 24.6 26.2 26.3

13084 CSH P P2 G1.2 1949–1972
Huenemann, Ralph William, 1939–.
'Urban rationing in Communist China.'
CQ 26 (Apr.–June 1966), 44–57.
Subj 14 14.3 ▪ 11.2

13085 NNC P P2 G1.2 1949–1972
Hui Hai, pseud.
'Domestic trade.' Tr. of '1955 nien Chung kung ti kuo nei mao i' (Domestic trade in Communist China, 1955); *Tsu kuo chou k'an* 159 (16 Jan. 1956), 28–31. In *Communist China, 1955*, edited by Union Research Institute. [Selective entry]
Hong Kong: Union Research Institute, 1956, 103–115.
Subj 14.3 ▪ 14.6 34.2

13086 MCY S P2 G1.2 1949–1972
Jones, Edwin F-.
'The impact of the food crisis on Peiping's policies.'
AS 2, 10 (Dec. 1962), 1–11.
Subj 14.1 14.3 51 ▪ 12.1 58

13087 CSU P P2 G1.2 1949–1972
Kao Hsiang-kao, 1905–.
'The food problem of Mainland China.'
IS 5, 12 (Sept. 1969), 58–82.
Subj 14.1 14.3 ▪ 11 12 14.5 18

13088 MCY P P2 G1.2 1949–1972
Kojima, Reiitsu.
'Grain acquisition and supply in China.' In *Contemporary China, 1961–1962*, edited by Edward Stuart Kirby. [Selective entry]
Hong Kong: Hong Kong U. Press, 1963, 65–88.
Subj 14.1 14.3 14.5 ▪ 34.1

13089 NNC P P2 G1.2 1949–1972
Konovalov, Evgenii Aleksandrovich, 1928–.
'Razvitie vnutrennei torgovli Kitaiskoi Narodnoi Respubliki' (The development of domestic commerce in the People's Republic of China).
KSINA 49 (1961), 101–110.
Subj 14 14.3 24.3 ▪ 14.1 14.4 16.3

13090 NNC P P2 G1.2 1949–1972
Kuan Ta-t'ung.
'The socialist, unified home market of China.' Tr. of 'Wo kuo she hui chu i t'ung i ti kuo nei shih ch'ang'; *Hung ch'i* 1963, 6 (1 Apr.), 28–35.
SCMM 361 (22 Apr. 1963), 10–19.
Subj 14.3 64

13091 NNC P P2 G1.2 1949–1972
[La Dany, Ladislao] ———, 1914–.
'Cloth and clothes.'
CNA 180 (10 May 1957), 2–7.
Subj 14.3 18 ▪ 14.4 55

13092 NIC P P2 G1.2 1949–1972
[La Dany, Ladislao] ———, 1914–.
'Commerce, 1957–1962.'
CNA 435 (31 Aug. 1962), 1–7.
Subj 14.3 24.3 ▪ 34.2

13093 MCH P P2 G1.2 1949–1972
[La Dany, Ladislao] ———, 1914–.
'The economy: Prospects for state revenue.'
CNA 649 (24 Feb. 1967), 1–7.
Subj 14.3 ▪ 14.5 22 22.2

13094 NNC P P2 G1.2 1949–1972
[La Dany, Ladislao] ———, 1914–.
'Food and famine.'
CNA 84 (20 May 1955), 2–7.
Subj 14.3 ▪ 14.1 18

13095 MCH P P2 G1.2 1949–1972
[La Dany, Ladislao] ———, 1914–.
'The movement of goods.'
CNA 462 (29 Mar. 1963), 1–7.
Subj 14.3 24.3 ▪ 24.2 24.4

13096 NIC P P2 G1.2 1949–1972
[La Dany, Ladislao] ———, 1914–.
'What to eat.'
CNA 411 (9 Mar. 1962), 1–7.
Subj 14.3 18 ▪ 14.1 55

13097 MCY P P2 G1.2 1949–1972
Lee, T. C. (Li T'ai-ch'u).
'The food problem.' In *Contemporary China, 1959–1960*, edited by Edward Stuart Kirby. [Selective entry]
Hong Kong: Hong Kong U. Press, 1961, 1–26.
Subj 14.1 14.3 ▪ 11 11.4 18 32 34.1

13098 CSH P P2 G2.3 1949–1972
Liaoning. T'ung chi chü. (Bureau of Statistics).
Great achievements on the commercial front of Liaoning during the past decade.' Tr. from *Liao-ning shih nien* (Liaoning during the past decade); Shenyang: Jen min ch'u pan she, 196? In *Liao-ning province during the last ten years*, mimeo., compiled by U.S. Joint Publications Research Service. [Selective entry]
Washington, D.C.: JPRS, 17 Jan. 1963, 156–165. (JPRS 17,182; MC 2979/1963) [Xerox copyflo available—New York: CCM Information Corp., Research and Microfilm Publications. (Scholarly Book Translation Series, 545)]
Subj 14.3 18 ▪ 34.2

13099 CSH P P2 G1.2 1949–1972
Liu Yung-hua, Lou Hua, Hsu I (Hsü I), Ju Shih, pseud., and Sung Ying. [Authors sequential rather than joint: Liu Yung-hua for 1961; Lou Hua for 1963–1965; Hsu I for 1966; Ju Shih, pseud., for 1967 and 1968; Sung Ying for 1969.]
'Domestic trade' [title varies]. Tr. from *Tsu kuo chou k'an* 486 (30 Apr. 1962) *and* from *Tsu kuo* 2–74 (May 1964 – May 1970) [recurring annual feature article]. In *Communist China, 1961–1969*, edited by Union Research Institute.
Hong Kong: Union Research Institute. Issued annually, 1962–1970, average ca. 20 p. [Article does not appear in *Communist China, 1962*.]
Subj 14.3 ▪ 14.2 22.2 24.3

13100 NNC P P2 G1.2 1949–1972
Lou Hua. [Tr. erroneously gives author's surname as Liu.]
'Domestic trade.' Tr. of '1956 nien Chung kung ti kuo nei mao i' (Domestic trade in Communist China, 1956); *Tsu kuo chou k'an* 214/215 (11 Feb. 1957), 25–28. In *Communist China, 1956*, edited by Union Research Institute. [Selective entry]
Hong Kong: Union Research Institute, 1957, 96–108.
Subj 14.3 ▪ 24.3 34.2

13101 CSU P P2 G1.2 1949–1972
May, Jacques M-.
'People's Republic of China.' In *The ecology of malnutrition in the Far and Near East: Food resources, habits, and deficiencies*, by J. M. May. [Selective entry]
New York: Hafner, 1961, 9–51. (American Geographical Society, Studies in medical geography, 3)
Subj 14.1 14.3 55 ▪ 18

13102 CSU P P2 G9.4 1949–1972
May, Jacques M-.
'Taiwan.' In *The ecology of malnutrition in the Far and Near East: Food resources, habits, and deficiencies*, by J. M. May. [Selective entry]
New York: Hafner, 1961, 53–77. (American Geographical Society, Studies in medical geography, 3)
Subj 14.3 24.1 ▪ 55 56

13103 CSU P P3 G1.2 1949–1972
Mizoguchi Toshiyuki.
'Statistical analysis of price system in Mainland China.'
DE 3, 3 (Sept. 1965), 305–322.
Subj 14.3 ▪ 18

13104 MCH P P2 G1.2 1949–1972
Perkins, Dwight Heald, 1934–.
Market control and planning in Communist China.
Cambridge: Harvard U. Press, 1966. 303 p. (Harvard economic studies, 128) (Revision of *Price formation in Communist China*, doctoral dissertation in Economics, Harvard U., 1964)
Subj 14 14.3 ▪ 11.4 14.1 14.4 16.3 16.4 32.1 34.1 34.2

13105 MCH P P2 G1.2 1949–1972
Pfeffer, Richard Monroe, 1936–.
Understanding business contracts in Communist China, 1949–1963.
Unpublished doctoral dissertation in Political Science, Harvard U., 1970. 210 p.
Subj 12.2 14 14.3 24.3 32.1 ▪ 14.6 34.1 34.2

13106 CSU O P4 G1.1 1949–1972
Richman, Barry Martin, 1936–.
'China organizes foreign trade to accelerate development.'
Columbia j. of world business 3, 6 (Nov.–Dec. 1968), 27–38.
Subj 14 14.3 14.4 34.2 ▪ 12 22.2 66

13107 CSU O P3 G1.3 1949–1972
Selivankin, S- A-.
Zametki o torgovle v Kitae.
Moscow: Gostorgizdat, 1959. 70 p.
Notes on trade in Communist China, mimeo. [Partial tr.: p. 1–52, 58–70 only]
Washington, D.C.: U.S. Joint Publications Research Service, 8 July 1960. 48 p. (JPRS 3524; MC 14,242/1960)
Subj 14.3 18 34.2 ▪ 12 14.2 55

13108 DLC O P2 G1.2 1949–1972
Shumskii, O- D-.
'Organizatsiia khraneniia i pererabotki zerna v Kitaiskoi Narodnoi Respublike' (The organization of grain storage and processing in the People's Republic of China).
Trudy Moskovskogo tekhnologicheskogo instituta pishchevoi promyshlennosti 7 (1957), 126–141.
Subj 12.1 14 14.3 34.2 ▪ 14.1 14.2

13109 NNC O P2 G1.2 1949–1972
Smirnov, A-.
'Torgovlia v Kitaiskoi Narodnoi Respublike' (Trade in the People's Republic of China).
Sovetskaia torgovlia 1958, 9 (sentiabr'), 47–53.
Subj 14.3 24.3 ▪ 11.4 14 18

13110 CSU P P2 G1.2 1949–1972
Swamy, Subramanian.
'Retail price index in the Peoples' Republic of China.'
Review of economics and statistics 51, 3 (Aug. 1969), 309–319.
Subj 14.3

13111 CSH P P1 G1.1 1949–1972
Szczepanik, Edward Franciszek, 1915–.
'Hong Kong's trade with Mainland China.' In *Hong Kong economic papers, No. 1*, edited by E. F. Szczepanik. [Sole entry]
Hong Kong: Hong Kong Economic Assn., 1961, 65–74.
Subj 14.3

13112 TPY P P2 G9.4 1949–1972
Taiwan. Liang shih chü. (Food Bureau), ed.
Taiwan food statistics book, 1952–1968. [1955 issue covers the years 1953–1955.]
Taipei: Liang shih chü. Issued annually, 1953–1969. Average ca. 200 p. [In Chinese as well as English]
Subj 14.3 24.1 ▪ 24.3 24.5 24.6

13113 MAM FP P2 G9.4 1949–1972
Tseng, Chieh-hsin, 1931–.
The consumption and demand for soybeans in Taiwan, China.
Ann Arbor: University Microfilms (Publ. 72-15,313), 1972. 12, 160 p. (Doctoral dissertation in Agricultural Economics, Ohio State U., 1971)
Subj 14 14.3 55 ▪ 14.4 24.1

13114 NNC O P2 G1.2 1949–1972
Vasil'ev, A-.
'Torgovlia ovoshchami i fruktami v Kitae' (The fruit and vegetable trade in China).
Sovetskaia torgovlia 1960, 8 (avgust), 32–35.
Subj 14.3 24.3

13115 MCH P P2 G1.2 1949–1972
Yang Po.
'New China's price policy.'
PR 7, 47 (20 Nov. 1964), 6–17.
Subj 14 14.3 ▪ 11.4

13116 MCH U P5 G1.2 1949–1972
Yao Kuan.
'Socialist commerce in China.'
PR 7, 8 (21 Feb. 1964), 8–11.
Subj 14.3 ▪ 12 14 14.4

13117 NNC P P2 G1.2 1949–1972
Yonezawa Hideo, 1905–.
Commodity circulation structure and price system in Communist China after communalization, mimeo. Tr. of 'Jimmin kōshakago no shōhin ryūtsū kikō to kakaku seido' (The structure of commodity circulation and the price system after the formation of the communes); *Chūgoku shiryō geppō* 140 (Oct. 1959), 1–30.
Washington, D.C.: U.S. Joint Publications Research Service, 1960. 51 p. (JPRS 2618; MC 9920/1960)
Subj 14.3 24.3 ▪ 14.1 14.4 18 32.1 34.1

13118 NNC P P2 G1.2 1949–1972
Yonezawa Hideo, 1905–.
Communist China's price policy, mimeo. Tr. of 'Chūgoku no kakaku seisaku' (China's pricing policy); *Chūgoku kenkyū geppō* 156 (Feb. 1961), 1–30; 163 (Sept. 1961), 1–31.
Washington, D.C.: U.S. Joint Publications Research Service, 22 Sept. 1961 and 26 Feb. 1962. 33; 51 p. (JPRS 10,241 and 12,670; MC 19,767/1961 and 8200/1962)
Subj 14 14.3 ▪ 14.1 18

13119 CSU P P1 G1.2 1949–1972
Yonezawa Hideo, 1905–.
Japanese analysis on purchase and sale prices in Communist China, mimeo. Tr. of 'Chūgoku shōhin no baibai kakaku no kimekata' (Methods of determining prices for commodities in China); *Ajia keizai jumpō* 436 (1 July 1960), 6–14, 5.
Washington, D.C.: U.S. Joint Publications Research Service, 16 Sept. 1960. 11 p. (JPRS 4042; MC 17,378/1960)
Subj 14.3 34.2 ▪ 14

13120 NNC PO P2 G1.2 1949–1972
Yonezawa Hideo, 1905–.
Supply and demand of durable consumer goods in Communist China, mimeo. Tr. of 'Chūgoku no taikyū shōhizai jukyū'; *Ajia keizai jumpō* 486 (21 Nov. 1961), 1–9.
Washington, D.C.: U.S. Joint Publications Research Service, 19 Feb. 1962. 9 p. (JPRS 12,558; MC 8132/1962)
Subj 14.3 18 ▪ 14.4 55

13121 NNC P P2 G1.2 1949–1972
Yü Heng.
'Domestic trade.' Tr. of '1957 nien Chung kung ti kuo nei mao i' (Domestic trade in Communist China, 1957); *Tsu kuo chou k'an* 274/275 (7 Apr. 1958), 24–26. In *Communist China, 1957*, edited by Union Research Institute. [Selective entry]
Hong Kong: Union Research Institute, 1958, 86–97.
Subj 14.3 ▪ 14

14.4 Industrial Economy

工業 工業

1644-1911

13122 MCH S P4 G1.2 1895–1911
Bellet, Daniel, 1864–?
'L'évolution industrielle de la Chine' (China's industrial development).
R. des sciences politiques 3e série 26, 6 (nov.–déc. 1911), 869–895.
Subj 14.4 36.4 ▪ 14.2 14.3 14.6 24.4 36.2

13123 NNC P P2 G1.5 1895–1911
Bergholz, Leo.
'Machinery in South China.'
JAAA 9, 12 (Jan. 1910), 370–375.
Subj 14.4 24.4 ▪ 34.2

13124 GMS O P2 G1.1 1842–1911
Brandt, Max August Scipio von, 1835–1914?
'China in ethischer, industrieller und politischer Beziehung' (Ethical, industrial, and political aspects of China).
Verhandlungen der Abteilung Berlin-Charlottenburg der Deutschen Kolonialgesellschaft 1, 2 (1896/97), 51–101.
Subj 14.1 14.3 14.4 66 ▪ 63

13125 NNC P P2 G1.2 1842–1895
Chen, Gideon (Ch'en Ch'i-t'ien), 1893–.
Tseng Kuo-fan, pioneer promoter of the steamship in China.
Peiping: Yenching U., [Dept. of Economics], 1935. 98 p. [Reprinted—New York: Paragon, 1961. 98 p.]
Subj 14.4 15 19 ▪ 12 14.2 16.1 17 62

13126 CSU O P2 G5.2 1895–1911
Corbin, Paul L-.
'The industrial future of Shansi province.' In *Recent developments in China*, edited by George Hubbard Blakeslee. [Selective entry]
New York: G. E. Stechert, 1913, 256–271.
Subj 14.4 24.1 24.2

13127 CBU O P2 G1.1 1842–1895
Fauvel, Albert Auguste, 1851–1909.
'La Chine et ses ressources industrielles' (China's industrial resources).
R. des questions scientifiques 26 (20 juil. 1889), 28–78. [Separately reprinted—Brussels: Polleunis, Ceuterick, et de Smet, 1889. 55 p.]
Subj 14.4 24.4

13128 NIC P P2 G1.3 1644–1895
Huard, Pierre Alphonse, 1901–, and Ming Wong.
'Le développement de la technologie dans la Chine du XIXe siècle' (Technological development in nineteenth-century China).
Cahiers d'histoire mondiale 7, 1 (1962), 68–85.
Subj 14.4 ▪ 14.1 14.3 66

13129 MCH P P5 G1.1 1842–1895
Iovchuk, S- M-.
'Ob osobennostiakh razvitiia fabrichno-zavodskoi promyshlennosti v Kitae v 1861–1895 godakh' (Features of the development of factory industry in China, 1861–1895). [With English abstract]
PV 1959, 5, 62–73. [Reprinted in *O genezise kapitalizma v stranakh Vostoka, XV–XIX vv.* (The origin of capitalism in the Orient from the fifteenth through the nineteenth centuries), compiled by Institut narodov Azii, Akademiia nauk SSSR, edited by S- D- Skazkin et al. (Selective entry.) Moscow: Izd-vo vost. lit-ry, 1962, 60–75.]
Subj 14.4 ▪ 11.4 15 16.2

13130 CSU P P2 G1.3 1842–1911
Lecomte, Henri, 1856–?
'Industrie du coton en Chine et au Japon' (The cotton industry in China and Japan). In *Le coton: monographie. Culture-histoire* (Treatise on the history of cotton cultivation), by H. Lecomte. [Selective entry]
Paris: Carré et Naud, 1900, 464–478.
Subj 14.4 24.4 ▪ 16.4 47

13131 MCH O P2 G1.2 1842–1895
Lisboa, Henrique Carlos Ribeiro, 1847–?
'Agricultura e indústria' (Agriculture and industry). In *A China e os Chinos: recordações de viagem* (China and the Chinese: Recollections of a journey), by H. C. R. Lisboa. [Selective entry]
Montevideo: Godel, 1888, 74–102.
Subj 14.1 14.4 ▪ 14.3

13132 MCH P P1 G1.2 –1842
Needham, Noël Joseph Terence Montgomery, 1900–.
The development of iron and steel technology in China.
London: Newcomen Society, 1958. 12, 76 p.
Subj 14.4 62 ▪ 72

13133 NNC P P4 G1.1 1842–1911
Novikov, L- N-.
'Razvitie fabrichno-zavodskoi promyshlennosti v Kitae do Sin'khaiskoi revoliutsii' (The development of factory industry in China before the Revolution of 1911). In *Sin'khaiskaia revoliutsiia v Kitae: sbornik statei* (Articles on the Revolution of 1911 in China), compiled by Institut narodov Azii, Akademiia nauk SSSR. [Selective entry]
Moscow: Izd-vo vost. lit-ry, 1962, 91–120.
Subj 14.4 16.2 ▪ 16.4

13134 DLC S P2 G1.2 –1842
Stuzhina, Emiliia Pavlovna, 1931–.
'Vopros o zarozhdenii kapitalisticheskikh otnoshenii v Kitae v rabotakh sovremennykh kitaiskikh istochnikov' (The origin of capitalistic attitudes in China as exemplified by contemporary Chinese historians).
Srednie veka 17, 12 (1958), 132–137.
Subj 14 14.4 ▪ 34.2

13135 CSH S P4 G1.2 1842–1895
Sung, Shee (Sung Hsi), 1920–.
'Evaluation of the modernization process in China, 1860–1894.'
CC 7, 4 (Dec. 1966), 101–106.
Subj 14.4 19 ▪ 15 17

13136 NNC P P7 G1.2 –1895
TSvetkov, P- (P. Zwehtkoff).
'Zamechaniia o solianom proizvodstve v Kitae.' In *Trudy chlenov Rossiiskoi dukhovnoi missii v Pekine* (Works of members of the Russian Orthodox

ecclesiastical mission in Peking). [Selective entry]
St. Petersburg: Tip. Shtaba voenno-ucheb. zavedenii, 1857, vol. 3, 103–118. [Reprinted in *Trudy chlenov Rossiiskoi dukhovnoi missii v Pekine*. (Selective entry.) Peking: Tip. Uspenskago monastyria pri RDM, 1910, vol. 3, 59–67.]

'Bemerkungen über die Salz-Production in China.' Tr. by Carl Abel and F- A- Mecklenburg. In *Arbeiten der kaiserlich russischen Gesandtschaft zu Peking über China, sein Volk, seine Religion, seine Institutionen, sozialen Verhältnisse, usw.* (Works of the imperial Russian mission to Peking on China, its people, religion, institutions, social conditions, etc.). [Selective entry]
Berlin: Heinicke, 1858, vol. 2, 495–504.

'Remarks on the production of salt in China.' Tr. by William Richard Carles.
JRAS-NCB new (2nd) series 22, 1/2 (1887), 81–89.
SUBJ 14.4 ▪ 14.5

13137 MCH U P2 G9.4 1842–1895
Tyzack, David, and George Alexander Louis Lebour.
'Le nord de Formose et ses mines de charbon' (Northern Taiwan and its coal mines).
Annales de l'Extrême-Orient 7 (1884/85), 225–232.
SUBJ 14.4 ▪ 14.3 21.3 66

1644-1949

13138 CSU U P2 G1.1 1895–1949
'Cement industry in China.'
CEJ 10, 1 (Jan. 1932), 25–36.
SUBJ 14.4 ▪ 14.3 34.2

13139 CSU O P2 G6.1 1895–1949
'Flour industry in Kiangsu.'
CEJ 13, 1 (July 1933), 32–48.
SUBJ 14.3 14.4 ▪ 34.2

13140 CSU U P4 G1.1 1895–1949
'Match industry in China.'
CEJ 10, 3 (Mar. 1932), 197–211.
SUBJ 14.4 ▪ 14.3 36.2

13141 NNC P P3 G1.2 1842–1928
'Power loom weaving in China.'
NWSS 3, 27 (7 July 1930), 129, 132.
SUBJ 14.4

13142 CSU U P3 G1.1 1895–1949
'The soap industry in China.'
CEJ 10, 2 (Feb. 1932), 113–126.
SUBJ 14.4 ▪ 14.3 16.4

13143 CSU P P3 G1.3 1895–1928
Alderfer, Evan B-.
'The textile industry of China.'
AAAPSS 152 (Nov. 1930), 184–190. [Special issue: *China*, edited by Henry F- James]
SUBJ 14.4

13144 MCH P P2 G1.1 1842–1949
Allen, George Cyril, 1900–, and Audrey Gladys Donnithorne, 1922–.
Western enterprise in Far Eastern economic development: China and Japan.
New York: Macmillan, 1954. 291 p.
SUBJ 14.2 14.4 66 ▪ 14.3 14.6 16.2 34.2

13145 NNC P P4 G1.2 1895–1928
Arkus, R- S-.
'Rol' inostrannogo kapitala v osnovnykh otrasliakh kitaiskoi promyshlennosti' (The role of foreign capital in the main branches of Chinese industry).
MKhMP 1929, 8/9 (avgust–sentiabr'), 115–131.
SUBJ 14.4 14.6 ▪ 14.3

13146 DLC P P2 G2.0 1895–1949
Avarin, Vladimir IAkovlevich, 1899–.
'Bor'ba mezhdu iaponskim i tuzemnym kapitalom v kamennougol'noi promyshlennosti Man'chzhurii' (The rivalry between Japanese and domestic capital in the Manchurian coal-mining industry).
Za industrializatsiiu Sovetskogo Vostoka 1933, 2, 195–224.
SUBJ 14.4 14.6 ▪ 14.3 66

13147 NNC P P2 G2.0 1644–1928
Avarin, Vladimir IAkovlevich, 1899–.
Imperializm v Man'chzhurii (Imperialism in Manchuria).
Moscow: Sotsekgiz, 1934. 2 vols. 415; 558 p.
SUBJ 12 14 14.4 14.6 66 ▪ 15 16.3 32.2

13148 NNC P P1 G1.2 1895–1949
Bünger, Karl A-, 1903–.
'Das Bergrecht Chinas' (Mining laws in China).
Z. für Bergrecht 70 (1929), 452–465.
SUBJ 12.2 14.4 ▪ 14.5 66 72

13149 MCH PO P2 G1.2 1895–1928
Chenet, Charles.
'Nouvelles exploitations houillères en Chine' (New coal mines in China).
BEI 23, 144 (sept.–oct. 1920), 614–624.
SUBJ 14.4 34.2 ▪ 11.4 36.4

13150 CSH FP P5 G6.3 1842–1949
China [Republic]. Shih yeh pu. Kuo chi mao i chü. (Ministry of Industry. Bureau of Foreign Trade), ed.
'Manufacturing industries.' Tr. of 'Kung yeh' (Industry); in *Chung-kuo shih yeh chih: Che-chiang sheng* (Chinese economic surveys: Chekiang); Shanghai: Kuo chi mao i chü, 1933, *keng* 1 – *keng* 513 [s.p.] [slightly condensed in tr.]. In *China industrial handbooks: Chekiang*, edited by the agency cited. [Selective entry]
Shanghai: Kuo chi mao i chü, 1935, 471–772. [Reprinted in *China industrial handbooks: Chekiang*, edited by the agency cited. (Selective entry.) Taipei: Ch'eng-wen, 1972, 471–772.]
SUBJ 14.4 24.4 ▪ 24.2 24.3 26.4

13151 NIC P P2 G1.3 1842–1928
Chu, Samuel C. (Chu Ch'ang-ling), 1929–.
Reformer in modern China: Chang Chien, 1853–1926.
New York: Columbia U. Press, 1965. 13, 256 p. (Revision of doctoral dissertation in History, Columbia U., 1958)
SUBJ 12 14.3 14.4 17 19 59 ▪ 14.1 14.6 16.1 18 34.2

13152 CBU PO P2 G1.2 –1928
Collins, William Frederick.
Mineral enterprise in China, rev. ed.
Tientsin: Tientsin Press, 1922. 15, 410 p.
SUBJ 14.4 14.5 62 ▪ 12.2 14.2 14.6 43 64 66

13153 DLC S P2 G1.3 1895–1949
Dapčević-Oreščanin, Sonja, et al.
'Razvitak moderne industrije, rudarstva i transporta u Kini do 1949 g.' (The growth of modern industry, mining, and transport in China before 1949).
DB 4, 6/7 (1955), 75–90. [Special issue: *Savremena Kina* (Contemporary China)]
SUBJ 14 14.4 ▪ 11.4 14.2 14.3

13154 MCH S P2 G1.1 1842–1949
Dernberger, Robert Franklin, 1929–.
Review of *Foreign investment and economic development in China, 1840–1937*, by Chi-ming Hou.
EDCC 15, 3 (Apr. 1967), 361–365.
SUBJ 14 14.4

13155 NIC P P4 G1.3 1842–1928
Feuerwerker, Albert, 1927–.
China's early industrialization: Sheng Hsuan-huai, 1844–1916, and mandarin enterprise.
Cambridge: Harvard U. Press, 1958. 12, 311 p. (Harvard East Asian series, 1) (Revision of *Industrial enterprise in late Ch'ing China: Sheng Hsuan-huai (1844–1916) and the 'Kuan-tu shang-pan system'*, doctoral dissertation in History, Harvard U., 1957)
SUBJ 14.2 14.3 14.4 34.2 ▪ 14.6 16.1 16.2 17 62 66

13156 MCH P P2 G1.2 1895–1949
Feuerwerker, Albert, 1927–.
'China's nineteenth-century industrialization: The case of the Hanyehping Coal and Iron Company, Limited.' In *The economic development of China and Japan*, edited by Charles Donald Cowan. [Selective entry]
New York: Praeger, 1964, 79–110. (U. of London, School of Oriental and African Studies, Studies on modern Asia and Africa, 4)
SUBJ 14.4 34.2 ▪ 14.2 14.6

13157 NNC P P2 G1.2 1842–1949
Fong, H. D. (Fang Hsien-t'ing), 1902–.
'China's silk reeling industry: A survey of its development and distribution.'
MBEC 7, 12 (Dec. 1934), 483–506.
SUBJ 14.4

13158 MCH FP P2 G1.2 1842–1949
Fong, H. D. (Fang Hsien-t'ing), 1902–.
Cotton industry and trade in China.
Tientsin: Chihli Press, 1932. 2 vols. 356; 116 p. (Nankai Institute of Economics, Industry series, 4) [Reprinted—Washington, D.C.: Center for Chinese Research Materials, 1972. 2 vols. 356; 116 p.]
SUBJ 14.3 14.4 ▪ 14.5 16.4 18 36.4

13159 NNC P P2 G1.2 1895–1949
Fong, H. D. (Fang Hsien-t'ing), 1902–.
'Industrial capital in China.'
NSEQ 9, 1 (Apr. 1936), 27–94. [Separately reprinted—Tientsin: Chihli Press, 1936. 68 p. (Nankai Institute of Economics, Industry series, 9)] [Separately reprinted—Washington, D.C.: Center for Chinese Research Materials, 1972. 68 p.]
SUBJ 14.4 ▪ 14.6 16.1 16.2 34.2 66

13160 NIC O P2 G1.3 –1949
Gale, Esson McDowell, 1884–1964.
'Public administration of salt in China: A historical survey.'

AAAPSS 152 (Nov. 1930), 241–251. [Special issue: *China*, edited by Henry F- James]
Subj 14.3 14.4 ▪ 14.5

13161 DLC P P2 G1.2 1842–1928
[Gamberg, Viktor?] V. G.
'Khlopchatobumazhnaia promyshlennost' i rynok tekstil'nykh tovarov v Kitae' (The cotton industry and textile market in China).
PK 3 (1930), 116–147.
Subj 14.4 ▪ 14.3 24.4 66

13162 NNC S P4 G1.2 –1949
Great Britain. Admiralty. Naval Intelligence Division. Geographical Section.
'Industry.' In *China proper, Vol. 3, Economic geography, ports and communications*, compiled by the agency cited. [Selective entry]
London: His Majesty's Stationery Office, 1945, 113–162. (NID, Geographical handbook series, BR 530B)
Subj 14.4 34.2 ▪ 16.4 24.4 36.4 72

13163 CSU S P2 G1.2 1842–1928
Heek, Frederik van, 1907–.
Westersche techniek en maatschappelijk leven in China (Western technology and society in China).
Enschede, The Netherlands: Van der Loeff, 1935. 13, 507 p.
Subj 14 14.1 14.4 16 34.3 66 ▪ 11 14.3 16.3 16.4 22 24.4 41 43 47 62

13164 MCH FP P4 G1.2 1842–1928
Ho, Franklin L. (Ho Lien), 1897–, and H. D. Fong (Fang Hsien-t'ing), 1902–.
Extent and effects of industrialization in China.
Tientsin: [Institute of Pacific Relations], 1929. 34 p. [For a later expanded version in Chinese, see Ho Lien and Fang Hsien-t'ing, *Chung-kuo kung yeh hua chih ch'eng tu chi ch'i ying hsiang*; Shanghai: Kung shang pu, Kung shang fang wen chü, 1930; 91 p.]
Subj 14 14.4 16.4 24.4 ▪ 11.1 14.3 18 36.4 47

13165 MCY U P7 G1.2 1842–1928
Hsieh, C. Y. (Hsieh Chia-jung), 1896–, and M. C. Chu (Chu Mao-ch'eng).
Foreign interest in the mining industry in China.
Shanghai: China Institute of Pacific Relations, 1931. 54 p.
Subj 14.4 ▪ 14.6 66

13166 CSU S P2 G1.3 1842–1949
Hu, Teh-wei.
'The development of the cotton textile industry and Chinese economic development, 1890–1937.'
JAAS 5, 4 (Oct. 1970), 266–273.
Subj 14.4 34.2 ▪ 11.1 14.1

13167 MCH S P4 G1.3 1895–1928
Kantorovich, Anatolii IAkovlevich, 1896–1944.
'Inostrannyi kapital v tiazheloi industrii Kitaia' (Foreign capital in China's heavy industry).
NV 10/11 (1925), 46–77.
Subj 14.4 14.6 ▪ 66

13168 MCH S P4 G1.1 1842–1928
Kantorovich, Anatolii IAkovlevich, 1896–1944.
'Voprosy promyshlennogo razvitiia Kitaia' (The industrial development of China).
Sotsialisticheskoe khoziaistvo 1926, 5, 189–208.
Subj 14 14.4 14.6 ▪ 16.2 16.4 19 34.2

13169 CSH P P3 G1.2 1895–1928
King, S. T. (Chin Hsiu-ch'ing), and D. K. Lieu (Liu Ta-chün), 1890–1962.
China's cotton industry: A statistical study of ownership of capital, output, and labor conditions.
[Shanghai?]: Institute of Pacific Relations, 1929. 51 p. (IPR documents, 4) [Reprinted in *Problems of the Pacific, 1929*, edited by John Bell Condliffe. (Selective entry.) Chicago: U. of Chicago Press, 1930, 262–299.]
Subj 14.4 16.4 34.2 ▪ 36.4

13170 CSU P P2 G1.2 1644–1928
Koh, Sung Jae, 1917–.
'The beginning and growth of the modern cotton industry in China.' In *Stages of industrial development in Asia: A comparative history of the cotton industry in Japan, India, China, and Korea*, by S. J. Koh. [Sole entry]
Philadelphia: U. of Pennsylvania Press, 1966, 181–227.
Subj 14.4 16.2 34.2 ▪ 16.1 24.3

13171 MAM P P2 G1.1 1842–1949
Koo, Shou-eng, 1911–.
Tariff and the development of the cotton industry in China, 1842–1937.
Ann Arbor: University Microfilms (Publ. 61-5471), 1961. 269 p. (Doctoral dissertation in Economics, Columbia U.)
Subj 14.4 14.5 ▪ 14.3 36.2

13172 NNC P P2 G1.2 1895–1928
Krotkov, N- N-, comp.
Russkaia manufaktura i ee konkurenty na kitaiskom rynke, s kratkim ocherkom sovremennogo ekonomicheskogo sostoianiia sobstvennogo Kitaia, Man'chzhurii i Sin'-TSziana (Russian manufactured products and their competitors on the Chinese market, with a brief note on the current economic condition of China proper, Manchuria, and Sinkiang).
St. Petersburg: V. F. Kirshbaum, 1914. 105 p.
Subj 14.4 ▪ 14.1 14.3

13173 CBU PO P4 G1.3 1842–1949
Kung, H. H. (K'ung Hsiang-hsi), 1881–1967.
'Chinas Industriewirtschaft im Aufbau' (The Chinese industrial economy in the process of development).
WA 45, 2 (März 1937), 203–232.
Subj 14 14.4

13174 CSH P P2 G2.0 1842–1949
Lévine, I-.
'L'industrie de l'or en Mandchourie' (The gold industry in Manchuria).
AF 40, 375 (jan. 1940), 16–17.
Subj 14.4

13175 MCH P P2 G1.1 –1949
Li, Ch'iao-p'ing, 1897–.
The chemical arts of old China.
Easton, Pa.: Journal of Chemical Education, 1948. 215 p.
Subj 14.4 ▪ 16.4 62

13176 MAM P P3 G1.2 1895–1949
Liang, Leland S. (Liang Hsün), 1920–.
Problems of the cotton manufacturer in China.
Ann Arbor: University Microfilms (Publ. 13,403), 1955. 228 p. (Doctoral dissertation in Economics, U. of Pennsylvania)
Subj 14 14.4 ▪ 16.2 16.4

13177 MCH P P4 G1.2 1895–1928
Lieu, D. K. (Liu Ta-chün), 1891–1962.
'China's industrial development.'
CEJ 1, 7 (July 1927), 654–674. [Reprinted in *Problems of the Pacific, 1927*, edited by John Bell Condliffe. (Selective entry.) Chicago: U. of Chicago Press, 1928, 392–408.]
Subj 14.4 24.4 ▪ 12 14.2 14.3 34.2

13178 MCH P P3 G1.1 1895–1949
Mangold, Rudolf.
Die elektrotechnische Industrie und der chinesische Markt (The electrical industry and the Chinese market).
Berlin: de Gruyter, 1935. 154 p. (Doctoral dissertation, Technische Hochschule Karlsruhe)
Subj 14.3 14.4

13179 CSH P P2 G9.4 1895–1949
Mitchell, Kate Louise, 1909–.
'Formosa and Korea.' In *Industrialization of the western Pacific*, by K. L. Mitchell. [Selective entry]
New York: Institute of Pacific Relations, International Secretariat, 1942, 49–65.
Subj 14.4 ▪ 16.4 24.1

13180 CSU P P2 G1.2 –1949
Myers, Ramon Hawley, 1929–.
'Cotton textile handicraft and the development of the cotton textile industry in modern China.'
Economic history review 18, 3 (Dec. 1965), 614–632.
Subj 14.3 14.4 24.4 ▪ 14.1 16.4 34.2

13181 CSU PO P4 G1.2 1842–1949
Read, Thomas T-.
'Economic-geographic aspects of China's iron industry.'
GR 33, 1 (Jan. 1943), 42–55.
Subj 14.4 24.4

13182 NNC S P2 G1.2 –1928
Smith, Wilfred, 1903–.
A geographical study of coal and iron in China.
Liverpool: University Press of Liverpool; London: Hodder and Stoughton, 1926. 83 p.
Subj 14.4 ▪ 11.3 14.2

13183 GMS O P3 G1.2 1895–1928
Strewe, M- Th——.
'Industrie und Bergbau Chinas' (Industry and mining in China). In *China: Wirtschaft und Wirtschaftsgrundlagen* (The economy and economic foundations of China), edited by Josef Hellauer. [Selective entry]
Berlin: de Gruyter (Vereinigung wissenschaftlicher Verleger), 1921, 185–217.
Subj 14.4

13184 CSH P P2 G1.2 1842–1949
Tao, L. K. (T'ao Meng-ho), 1887–1960, and Sung-ho Lin.
Industry and labour in China.

The Hague: World Social Economic Congress, 1931. 64 p.
Subj 14.4 16.4 ▪ 18 36.4 47 55

13185 CSU P P2 G1.2 –1928
Tegengren, Felix Reinhold.
'The iron industry of China.' In *The iron ores and iron industry of China*, by F. R. Tegengren. [Sole entry]
Peking: Nung shang pu, Ti tzu tiao ch'a so, 1924, vol. 2, 297–403. (Ti tzu tiao ch'a so memoirs, series A, 2) [Reprinted in *The iron ores and iron industry of China*, by F. R. Tegengren. (Sole entry.) Ann Arbor: University Microfilms, n.d., 297–403.]
Subj 14.4

13186 CSU P P2 G2.0 1895–1949
Tung, C. Y.
'Bean oil industry in Manchuria.'
CEJ 10, 2 (Feb. 1932), 181–190.
Subj 14.4

13187 MCH P P4 G1.2 1895–1928
Vinacke, Harold Monk, 1893–.
Problems of industrial development in China: A preliminary study.
Princeton: Princeton U. Press, 1926. 205 p.
Subj 14 14.4 34.2 ▪ 12 17 32.1 34.3

13188 GMU S P2 G1.3 1842–1928
Wang, Felix Djahung (Wang Chia-hung), 1900–.
Chinas Eisenproduktion und Eiseneinfuhr (China's production and importation of iron).
Berlin: The author, 1933. 69 p. (Doctoral dissertation, Philosophische Fakultät, Universität Berlin)
Subj 14.2 14.3 14.4

13189 CSH P P2 G1.1 1842–1949
Wiens, Herold Jacob, 1912–1971.
'The Japanese role in China's industrialization.' In *East Asian occasional papers, I*, edited by Harry Jerome Lamley. [Selective entry]
Honolulu: U. of Hawaii, Asian Studies Program, 1969, 1–50. (Asian Studies at Hawaii, 3)
Subj 14.2 14.4 ▪ 16.4

13190 CSU P P1 G1.3 1895–1949
Wu, Tao-Kun (Wu Tao-k'un), 1907–.
Mathematisch-statistische Untersuchung zur chinesischen Industrie (Statistical analysis of Chinese industry).
Jena: Neuenhahn, 1937. 63 p. (Doctoral dissertation, Philosophische Fakultät, Universität Berlin)
Subj 14.4

13191 NNC P P3 G1.3 1842–1928
Yen, Chung-ping (Yen Chung-p'ing).
'Zur Geschichte der Baumwollindustrie in China bis zum Ende des ersten Weltkrieges' (History of the cotton industry in China to the end of World War I).
Jahrbuch für Wirtschaftsgeschichte 1961, 2, 199–229.
Subj 14.3 14.4 ▪ 16.2 24.4

1911-1949

13192 CSU P P7 G1.5 1911–1949
'Antimony production in China.'
CEJ 12, 1 (Jan. 1933), 57–64.
Subj 14.4

13193 CSU U P2 G6.1 1928–1949
'Brick and tile industry.'
CEJ 18, 1 (Jan. 1936), 63–75.
Subj 14.4 ▪ 34.2

13194 CSU U P2 G1.1 1928–1949
'China's cotton industry during 1935.'
CEJ 18, 3 (Mar. 1936), 320–329.
Subj 14.3 14.4 24.4 ▪ 14.1

13195 CSU U P2 G1.5 1928–1949
'China's tin production and export.'
CEJ 10, 4 (Apr. 1932), 333–340.
Subj 14.4 ▪ 14.3

13196 CSU O P2 G8.1 1928–1949
'Coal and iron mines of Szechuan.'
CEJ 18, 1 (Jan. 1936), 54–62.
Subj 14.4 ▪ 14.3 24.2

13197 NNC P P3 G1.2 1928–1949
'Cotton mill statistics in China, 1930.'
NWSS 4, 8 (23 Feb. 1931), 41, 43–48.
Subj 14.4 ▪ 11.4 66

13198 CSU P P2 G1.2 1911–1949
'Cotton mill statistics of 1936.'
CEJ 19, 4 (Oct. 1936), 396–409.
Subj 14.1 14.4

13199 NNC P P4 G1.2 1928–1949
'Cotton mills in China, 1931–1933.'
NWSS 6, 50 (11 Dec. 1933), 229, 231–234.
Subj 14.4 ▪ 16.4

13200 NNC P P1 G1.2 1928–1949
'Electric power plants in China, 1929.'
NWSS 6, 46 (13 Nov. 1933), 213, 215–216.
Subj 14.4

13201 CSU U P4 G1.2 1911–1949
'The glass industry in China.'
CEJ 10, 5 (May 1932), 426–433.
Subj 14.4

13202 NNC P P3 G1.2 1911–1928
'The growth of China's industrialization, 1912–1929.'
NWSS 4, 44 (2 Nov. 1931), 201, 203–204.
Subj 14.4 ▪ 14.2 14.3

13203 CSU P P2 G9.2 1928–1949
'Kuangtung government sugar-factory.'
CEJ 18, 2 (Feb. 1936), 152–169.
Subj 14.4 24.1 ▪ 14.6

13204 CSU U P2 G1.2 1911–1949
'Refined-salt industry in China.'
CEJ 13, 1 (July 1933), 65–71.
Subj 14.4 ▪ 14.3 14.5

13205 CSU U P2 G2.0 1911–1949
'Soya beans and bean oil industry in Manchuria.'
CEJ 5, 3 (Sept. 1929), 793–805.
Subj 14.4 ▪ 14.1 24.4

13206 CSU U P2 G1.2 1911–1949
'Tanning industry in China.'
CEJ 10, 5 (May 1932), 376–393.
Subj 14.4 ▪ 14.3

13207 CSU U P2 G1.5 1928–1949
'Tung oil and its trade development in China.'
CEJ 19, 2 (Aug. 1936), 109–123.
Subj 14.3 14.4 ▪ 14.1

13208 CSU U P3 G1.5 1911–1949
'Umbrella manufacturing industry in China.'
CEJ 5, 5 (Nov. 1929), 962–971.
Subj 14.4

13209 MCH O P2 G8.2 1911–1928
'The Yunnan tin industry.'
CEM 3, 4 (Apr. 1926), 154–168.
Subj 14.3 14.4 34.2 ▪ 14.6 16 18 21 36.2 62

13210 MCY O P4 G1.2 1928–1949
Ahlers, John.
'China's cigarette industry.'
China weekly review 93, 3 (15 June 1940), 87–89.
Subj 14.4 ▪ 14.3 14.5

13211 CSU S P2 G1.2 1911–1949
Bain, Harry Foster, 1872–1948.
Ores and industry in the Far East: The influence of key mineral resources on the development of Oriental civilization, rev. ed.
New York: Council on Foreign Relations, 1933. 16, 228 p.
Subj 14.4 ▪ 14.6 16.4

13212 NNC PO P2 G1.3 1911–1949
Barker, Aldred Farrer, 1868–?, and Kenneth Crookes Barker.
The textile industries of China: Their present position and future possibilities.
Shanghai: Chiao-tung U., 1934. 224 p.
Subj 14.4 24.4 34.2 ▪ 14.3 16.4 18 27

13213 GMU S P7 G1.2 1911–1928
Bauer, Heinrich Wilhelm, 1913–.
Der Bergbau in China (Mining in China).
Leipzig: Erich Gürtner, 1938. 127 p. (Doctoral dissertation, Philosophische Fakultät, Universität Berlin)
Subj 14.2 14.4 ▪ 16.4 62

13214 NIC PO P4 G1.2 1911–1949
Blanchard, Fessenden Seaver, 1888–1963.
The textile industries of China and Japan: Post-war opportunities and problems for America.
New York: Textile Research Institute, 1944. 71 p.
Subj 14.4 ▪ 16.4

13215 NNC P P1 G2.0 1928–1949
Bünger, Karl A-, 1903–.
'Die Berggesetze der Mandschurei' (The mining laws of Manchuria [i.e., Manchoukuo]).
Z. für Bergrecht 76 (1935), 416–420.
Subj 12.2 14.4 ▪ 66

13216 CBU P P1 G1.2 1928–1949
Bünger, Karl A-, 1903–.
'Die chinesischen Vorschriften über Patente und Industrieförderung' (Chinese regulations on patents and industrial promotion).
OR 18, 15 (1 Aug. 1937), 407–409.
Subj 12.2 14.4 34.2

13217 MAM P P3 G1.2 1911–1949
Chang, John Key (Chang Ch'ang-chi), 1933–.

Indexes of industrial production of Mainland China, 1912–1949.
Ann Arbor: University Microfilms (Publ. 66-6580), 1966. 163 p. (Doctoral dissertation in Economics, U. of Michigan)
SUBJ 14.3 14.4 ▪ 70 71

13218 CSU P P2 G1.2 1911–1949
Chang, John Key (Chang Ch'ang-chi), 1933–.
Industrial development in pre-Communist China: A quantitative analysis.
Chicago: Aldine, 1969. 148 p.
SUBJ 14.4 ▪ 24.4

13219 GBF P P4 G2.0 1928–1949
Chang, Tian Bin, 1919–.
Industrieplanung in Mandschukuo (Industrial planning in Manchoukuo).
Berlin: The author, 1944. 93 p. (Doctoral dissertation, Rechts- und staatswissenschaftliche Fakultät, Universität Berlin)
SUBJ 14.4

13220 MCH FP P2 G1.2 1911–1928
Chenet, Charles.
'Le mouvement industriel et minier de la Chine en 1917' (The progress of industry and mining in China in 1917).
BEI 22, 134 (jan.–fév. 1919), 402–456.
SUBJ 14.3 14.4 16.2 ▪ 11.1 34.3

13221 MCH O P2 G8.2 1928–1949
Cheng, Ch'eng-k'un, 1906–.
'China's reconstruction in Yunnan province.'
Amerasia 4, 5 (July 1940), 237–242.
SUBJ 14.4 24.2 ▪ 12 17 24.1 34.1

13222 CSU P P2 G1.1 1911–1949
Cheng, Yu-kwei (Cheng Yu-k'uei), 1909–.
Foreign trade and industrial development of China: An historical and integrated analysis through 1948.
Washington, D.C.: University Press of Washington, D.C., 1956. 278 p.
SUBJ 14 14.4 ▪ 14.5 14.6 66

13223 NNC O P2 G1.3 1928–1949
Chin, Rockwood Q. P. (Ch'en Kuo-p'ing), 1911–.
'The Chinese cotton industry under wartime inflation.'
PA 16, 1 (Mar. 1943), 33–46.
SUBJ 14 14.3 14.4 ▪ 14.1 16.4 18 24.3 24.4

13224 CSH FP P4 G6.1 1911–1949
China [Republic]. Shih yeh pu. Kuo chi mao i chü. (Ministry of Industry. Bureau of Foreign Trade), ed.
'Manufacturing industries.' Tr. of 'Kung yeh' (Industry); in *Chung-kuo shih yeh chih: Chiang-su sheng* (Chinese economic surveys: Kiangsu); Shanghai: Kuo chi mao i chü, 1933, 1–1210 [s.p.] [slightly condensed in tr.]. In *China industrial handbooks: Kiangsu*, edited by the agency cited. [Selective entry]
Shanghai: Kuo chi mao i chü, 1933, 309–883. [Reprinted in *China industrial handbooks: Kiangsu*, edited by the agency cited. (Selective entry.) Taipei: Ch'eng-wen, 1972, 309–883.]
SUBJ 14.4 24 24.4 34.2 ▪ 14.3 24.2 26.4 28

13225 CSH FP P2 G6.3 1911–1949
China [Republic]. Shih yeh pu. Kuo chi mao i chü. (Ministry of Industry. Bureau of Foreign Trade), ed.
'Mining.' Tr. of 'K'uang ch'an'; in *Chung-kuo shih yeh chih: Che-chiang sheng* (Chinese economic surveys: Chekiang); Shanghai: Kuo chi mao i chü, 1933, *chi* 1 – *chi* 185 [s.p.] [slightly condensed in tr.]. In *China industrial handbooks: Chekiang*, edited by the agency cited. [Selective entry]
Shanghai: Kuo chi mao i chü, 1935, 393–467. [Reprinted in *China industrial handbooks: Chekiang*, edited by the agency cited. (Selective entry.) Taipei: Ch'eng-wen, 1972, 393–467.]
SUBJ 14.4 24.4 ▪ 14.3

13226 CSH FP P2 G6.1 1911–1949
China [Republic]. Shih yeh pu. Kuo chi mao i chü. (Ministry of Industry. Bureau of Foreign Trade), ed.
'Mining.' Tr. of 'K'uang yeh'; in *Chung-kuo shih yeh chih: Chiang-su sheng* (Chinese economic surveys: Kiangsu); Shanghai: Kuo chi mao i chü, 1933, 1–86 [s.p.] [slightly condensed in tr.]. In *China industrial handbooks: Kiangsu*, edited by the agency cited. [Selective entry]
Shanghai: Kuo chi mao i chü, 1933, 283–305. [Reprinted in *China industrial handbooks: Kiangsu*, edited by the agency cited. (Selective entry.) Taipei: Ch'eng-wen, 1972, 283–305.]
SUBJ 14.4 24.4 ▪ 14.3 34.2

13227 CSU P P2 G7.2 1911–1949
Chu, Johnson.
'Antimony production in Hunan.'
CEJ 17, 3 (Sept. 1935), 291–305.
SUBJ 14.4 ▪ 24.2

13228 MAM P P3 G1.2 1928–1949
Chung, An-min, 1921–.
The development of modern manufacturing industry in China, 1928–1949.
Ann Arbor: University Microfilms (Publ. 4915), 1953. 308 p. (Doctoral dissertation in Economics, U. of Pennsylvania)
SUBJ 14.4 14.6

13229 NNC P P7 G2.0 1928–1949
Dolitskii, IA-.
'IAponskii imperializm i iskopaemye ugli Man'chzhurii i Zhekhe' (Japanese imperialism and the fossil-coals of Manchuria and Jehol).
MNKP 1936, 36, 94–109.
SUBJ 14.3 14.4 ▪ 16.4 21.4

13230 CBU O P3 G2.0 1928–1949
Dombrovskii, I- I-.
'Novoe promyshlennoe stroitel'stvo v Man'chzhurii' (New industrial construction in Manchuria). [With English abstract at end of issue]
VM 1933, 17 (15 sentiabria), 18–43.
SUBJ 14.4 ▪ 14.6 16.4

13231 NNC P P4 G1.2 1911–1949
Fedoseev, N- K-.
'Industrializatsiia Kitaia' (The industrialization of China).
BSB 1, 4 (1932), 29–68.
SUBJ 14.4 ▪ 19 72

13232 NIC P P4 G1.2 1911–1949
Fong, H. D. (Fang Hsien-t'ing), 1902–.
China's industrialization: A statistical study.
Shanghai: China Institute of Pacific Relations, 1931. 46 p. [Reprinted—Washington, D.C.: Center for Chinese Research Materials, 1972. 46 p.]
SUBJ 14.4 ▪ 14

13233 MCH PO P2 G1.2 1911–1949
Fong, H. D. (Fang Hsien-t'ing), 1902–.
'Industrial organization in China.'
NSEQ 9, 4 (Jan. 1937), 919–1006. [Separately reprinted—Tientsin: Chihli Press, 1937. 88 p. (Nankai Institute of Economics, Industry series, 10)] [Separately reprinted—Washington, D.C.: Center for Chinese Research Materials, 1972. 88 p.]
SUBJ 11.4 14.4 34.2 ▪ 14.2 14.3 18 34.3 36.4

13234 NNC P P2 G1.2 1928–1949
Fong, H. D. (Fang Hsien-t'ing), 1902–.
'The prospect for China's industrialization.'
PA 15, 1 (Mar. 1942), 44–60.
SUBJ 14 14.4 ▪ 14.1 14.6

13235 CSU O P2 G9.4 1928–1949
Gage, Eugenia.
'Industrial development in Formosa.'
EG 26, 3 (July 1950), 214–222.
SUBJ 14.4 ▪ 24.2

13236 NNC P P4 G1.2 1928–1949
Gamberg, Viktor.
'Promyshlennost' Kitaia v gody mirovogo ekonomicheskogo krizisa i depressii osobogo roda' (Chinese industry during the worldwide economic crisis: A special type of depression).
MKhMP 1936, 12 (dekabr'), 101–120.
SUBJ 14 14.4 ▪ 14.3 14.6

13237 NNC P P4 G1.2 1928–1949
Gamberg, Viktor.
'Promyshlennost' Kitaia za gody krizisa' (China's industry during the depression years).
MKhMP 1934, 10 (oktiabr'), 99–116.
SUBJ 14.4 ▪ 14.3 14.6

13238 CSH U P3 G1.2 1911–1928
Gerasimov, A- E-.
'Proizvodstvo kitaiskikh kovrov' (Chinese rug production). [With English abstract]
VM 1930, 9, 67–77.
SUBJ 14.4 ▪ 14.3 16.4 24.4

13239 NNC S P5 G1.2 1911–1949
[Grajdanzev, Andrew Jonah?] A- I- Grazhdantsev, 1899–.
'Khlopchatobumazhnaia promyshlennost' dal'nevostochnykh stran' (The cotton industry in the countries of the Far East).
BSB 2, 5 (1932), 275–313.
SUBJ 14.4

13240 NNC P P2 G2.0 1928–1949
Grajdanzev, Andrew Jonah, 1899–.
'Manchuria: An industrial survey.'
PA 18, 4 (Dec. 1945), 321–339.
SUBJ 14.4 ▪ 14.2

13241 NNC S P7 G1.2 1928–1949
Great Britain. Admiralty. Naval Intelligence Division. Geographical Section.
'Mining.' In *China proper, Vol. 3, Economic geography, ports and communications*, compiled by the agency cited. [Selective entry]

London: His Majesty's Stationery Office, 1945, 84–112. (NID, Geographical handbook series, BR 530B)
Subj 14.4 ▪ 24.4

13242 NNC P P5 G1.2 1911–1949
Ho, Franklin L. (Ho Lien), 1897–.
'Industries.' In *Symposium on Chinese culture*, edited by Sophia H. Chen Zen (Jen Ch'en Heng-che). [Selective entry]
Shanghai: China Institute of Pacific Relations, 1931, 237–280. [Reprinted in *Symposium on Chinese culture*, edited by S. H. C. Zen. (Selective entry.) New York: Paragon, 1969, 237–280.]
Subj 14 14.4 24.4 ▪ 12.2 16.4 18 34.2 34.3 36.2 36.4 47 52

13243 CSU P P7 G1.1 1928–1949
Ho Pei Yang (Ho P'i-yang).
The production of tungsten in China, mimeo.
Tientsin: Hautes études; Shanghai: Université l'Aurore, 1941. 26 p. (Institut des hautes études industrielles et commerciales, Faculty of Commerce, Economic studies, 16)
Subj 14.4

13244 CSU PO P2 G1.2 1911–1928
Hosie, Alexander, 1853–1925.
'The salt production and salt revenue of China.'
Nineteenth century and after 75, 447 (May 1914), 1119–1143.
Subj 14.3 14.4 14.5 ▪ 21

13245 MCH U P2 G1.2 1911–1928
Hsueh, K. L.
'The iron and steel industry in China.'
CEJ 2, 1 (Jan. 1928), 1–16.
Subj 14.4

13246 CSU P P7 G1.2 1911–1949
Huang Chin Tao (Huang Chin-t'ao).
'The coal industry in China.'
CEJ 17, 5 (Nov. 1935), 425–438.
Subj 14.4

13247 CSU U P7 G1.2 1911–1949
Hwang, T. H.
'Notes on coal-mining in China.'
CEJ 12, 4 (Apr. 1933), 409–445.
Subj 14.4 ▪ 16.4 18

13248 MCH P P2 G1.2 1911–1928
James, H- P-.
'Industrial China.'
EG 5, 1 (Jan. 1929), 1–21.
Subj 14.4 ▪ 14 14.1

13249 NNC S P2 G2.0 1928–1949
[Kinney, Ann Rasmussen] Ann B- Rasmussen, 1931–.
The development of the Manchurian iron and steel industry, 1931–1945.
Unpublished masters thesis in Economics, Columbia U., 1955. 106 p. [Certificate essay, East Asian Institute]
Subj 14.4 ▪ 14.6

13250 MCH P P2 G1.2 1911–1949
Kraus, Richard Arnold, 1937–.
Cotton and cotton goods in China, 1918–1936: The impact of modernization on the traditional sector.
Unpublished doctoral dissertation in Economics, Harvard U., 1968. 209 p.
Subj 14.1 14.4 24.4 55 ▪ 14.3 16.3 18 34.2 36.2

13251 CNY P P2 G1.2 1911–1949
Lee Chen Tung (Li Chen-tung).
The coal industry of China, mimeo.
Tientsin: Hautes études; Shanghai: Université l'Aurore, 1938. 92 p. (Institut des hautes études industrielles et commerciales, Faculty of Commerce, Economic studies, 11)
Subj 14.2 14.4 ▪ 14.3

13252 CBU S P3 G2.0 1911–1949
Liubimov, L- I-.
'Promyshlennost' khlopchatobumazhnykh izdelii i perspecktivy khlopkovodstva v Man'chzhurii' (The manufacture of cotton products and the future of cotton cultivation in Manchuria).
VM 1933, 14/15 (15 avgusta), 59–71.
Subj 14.4 ▪ 14.1 16.4

13253 CSU P P2 G1.2 1911–1949
Löwenthal, Rudolf, 1904–.
'Printing paper: Its supply and demand in China.'
YJSS 1, 1 (June 1938), 107–121.
Subj 14.3 14.4

13254 CSH P P2 G1.3 1911–1928
M. R.
'The industrialisation of China.'
Pan-Pacific worker 1, 1 (1 July 1927), 13–16.
Subj 14.4 16.4

13255 GMU S P2 G1.3 1911–1949
Ma, Tsie (Ma Chieh), 1916–.
Eine Untersuchung über die Grundlagen der Industrialisierung Chinas (An analysis of the foundations of the industrialization of China).
Munich: The author, 1941. 134 p. (Doctoral dissertation, Staatswirtschaftliche Fakultät, Universität München)
Subj 14 14.4 ▪ 19

13256 CSU O P2 G1.5 1928–1949
McClure, Floyd Alonzo, 1897–.
'Tung oil in the Yangtsze valley.'
LSJ 9, 3 (Sept. 1930), 233–249.
Subj 14.1 14.4 ▪ 14.3

13257 CSH P P2 G1.2 1928–1949
Mitchell, Kate Louise, 1909–.
'China.' In *Industrialization of the western Pacific*, by K. L. Mitchell. [Selective entry]
New York: Institute of Pacific Relations, International Secretariat, 1942, 95–150.
Subj 14.4 ▪ 14 14.1 14.2 34.2

13258 CSH P P2 G2.0 1928–1949
Mitchell, Kate Louise, 1909–.
'Manchukuo.' In *Industrialization of the western Pacific*, by K. L. Mitchell. [Selective entry]
New York: Institute of Pacific Relations, International Secretariat, 1942, 66–94.
Subj 14.4 34.2 ▪ 12 14.1

13259 DLC P P2 G1.2 1911–1949
Naumov, Nikolai Aleksandrovich, 1888–.
'Kitai' (China). In *Promyshlennoe razvitie kolonial'nykh stran* (Industrial development of the colonies), by N. A. Naumov. [Sole entry]
Moscow: Gosizdat, 1930, 48–76.
Subj 14 14.4 64 ▪ 11 11.2 11.4

13260 DLC P P2 G1.2 1911–1928
Nepomnin, Oleg Efimovich, 1935–.
'Razvitie manufakturnogo kapitalizma v Kitae v 1914–1920 gg.' (The development of manufacturing capitalism in China, 1914–1920). In *Dvizhenie '4 maia' 1919 goda v Kitae: sbornik statei* (Articles on the May Fourth Movement in China), compiled by Institut vostokovedeniia, Akademiia nauk SSSR, edited by A- G- Afanas'ev et al. [Selective entry]
Moscow: Nauka, Glav. red. vost. lit-ry, 1971, 76–99.
Subj 14.4 24.4 24.6 34.2 ▪ 24.3 26.3 26.4 32.1 66 72

13261 NNC P P5 G1.2 1911–1949
Nieh, C. L. (Nieh Ch'i-lu).
China's industrial development: Its problems and prospect.
Shanghai: China Institute of Pacific Relations, 1933. 53 p.
Subj 14 14.4 ▪ 16.4 18 34.2 36.4

13262 NIC O P4 G1.2 1928–1949
Orchard, John Ewing, 1893–1962.
'Contrasts in the progress of industrialization in China and Japan.'
Political science q. 52, 1 (Mar. 1937), 18–50.
Subj 14.4 19 ▪ 12.2 14.6

13263 NNC P P2 G1.2 1928–1949
Ostrovskaia, A- I-.
'Rekonstruktsiia kitaiskoi promyshlennosti v usloviiakh antiiaponskoi voiny' (Reconstruction of Chinese industry under the conditions of the Anti-Japanese War).
MKhMP 1939, 9 (sentiabr'), 163–178.
Subj 14 14.4 ▪ 11.2 11.4 14.3 14.6

13264 NIC U P4 G1.2 1928–1949
Ou, Pao-san (Wu Pao-san), 1905–, and Fuh-shen Wang (Wang Fu-sun).
'Industrial production and employment in pre-war China.'
Economic j. 56, 3 (Sept. 1946), 426–434.
Subj 14.4 ▪ 16.4

13265 CSH FP P2 G2.0 1928–1949
Pauley, Edwin Wendell, 1903–.
Report on Japanese assets in Manchuria to the President of the United States, July, 1946.
Washington, D.C.: U.S. Government Printing Office, 1946. 11, 255 p.
Subj 14.2 14.4 ▪ 14

13266 GMU S P2 G1.3 1911–1928
Preusch, Egon Siegfried.
Grundlagen und Probleme der chinesischen Eisenindustrie (The foundations and problems of the Chinese iron industry).
Geneva: The author, 1936. 59 p. (Doctoral dissertation, Rechts- und staatswissenschaftliche Fakultät, Universität Hamburg)
Subj 14.4 ▪ 14.2

13267 GMS FP P3 G1.3 1911–1928
Rische, Berno, 1897–.
Stand und Entwicklung der chinesischen Industrie (China's industry and its development).
Berlin: A. Seydel, 1930. 176 p. (Doctoral dissertation, Technische Hochschule München)
Subj 14.3 14.4 ▪ 14 16.4

13268 CSU S P2 G1.2 1911–1949
Riskin, Carl Alan, 1938–.
Review of *Industrial development in pre-Communist China: A quantitative analysis*, by John Key Chang (Chang Ch'ang-chi).
EDCC 20, 1 (Oct. 1971), 175–178.
Subj 14.4

13269 CSU P P2 G2.0 1911–1949
Rodgers, Allan.
'The Manchurian iron and steel industry and its resource base.'
GR 38, 1 (Jan. 1948), 41–54.
Subj 14.4

13270 CSU P P3 G1.2 1911–1949
Rossiter, Fred J-, and Wolf Isaac Ladejinsky, 1901–.
'The Chinese textile industry and American cotton.'
Foreign agriculture 2, 9 (Sept. 1938), 391–408.
Subj 14.4 ▪ 16.4 34.2

13271 NIC P P2 G2.0 1928–1949
Schumpeter, Elizabeth Boody, 1898–1953, ed.
The industrialization of Japan and Manchukuo.
New York: Macmillan, 1940. 28, 944 p.
Subj 14.1 14.4

13272 MCH P P2 G1.2 1911–1928
Siao, Tsen-Tsan (Hsiao Chen-ch'ang), 1900–.
Die chinesische Seidenindustrie (The Chinese silk industry).
Leipzig: L. A. Klepzig, 1929. 92 p. (Doctoral dissertation, Philosophische Fakultät, Universität Leipzig)
Subj 14.4 ▪ 14.3

13273 MCH O P2 G1.2 1928–1949
Stein, Guenther.
'Free China's industrial production.'
FES 12, 16 (11 Aug. 1943), 161–164.
Subj 14.4

13274 MCH O P2 G1.1 1928–1949
Stepanek, Joseph E-, and Charles H-Prien.
'Small chemical industries for China: An experiment in Point Four technical aid.'
Chemical and engineering news 28, 36 (4 Sept. 1950), 3032–3035.
Subj 14.4 ▪ 14.2 55

13275 NNC P P3 G1.3 1928–1949
Stewart, Maxwell Slutz, 1900–, and Fu-an Fang.
'A statistical study of industry and labor in China.'
CEJ 7, 4 (Oct. 1930), 1081–1121.
Subj 14.4 36.4 ▪ 14.6 16.4 18 34.2

13276 CBU P P3 G2.0 1928–1949
Surin, Vladimir Ivanovich.
'Obrabatyvaiushchaia promyshlennost' Man'chzhurii i tendentsii ee dal'neishego razvitiia' (Manufacturing industry in Manchuria and trends in its further development).
VM 1934, 4 (aprel'), 14–27.
Subj 14.4

13277 MCH F P2 G1.2 1911–1928
Tayler, John Bernard, 1878–.
Farm and factory in China: Aspects of the industrial revolution.
London: Student Christian Movement, 1928. 106 p.
Subj 14.4 24.1 24.4 28 ▪ 14.2 16.4 34.3 36.4 41 52

13278 MCH PO P2 G1.2 1928–1949
Ting, Leonard G. (Ting Chi), 1907–1940.
'The coal industry in China.'
NSEQ 10, 1 (Apr. 1937), 193–277.
Subj 14.4 16.4 ▪ 12.2 14.2

13279 NNC P P2 G1.2 1928–1949
Ting, Leonard G. (Ting Chi), 1907–1940.
'Recent developments in China's cotton industry.'
NSEQ 9, 2 (July 1936), 398–445.
[Separately reprinted—Shanghai: China Institute of Pacific Relations, 1936. 43 p.]
Subj 14 14.4 36.2 ▪ 34.2 34.3 47

13280 NNC P P4 G1.2 1928–1949
Ting, Leonard G. (Ting Chi), 1907–1940.
'War and industry in China.'
NSEQ 11, 1/2 (Jan. 1940), 63–100.
Subj 14 14.4 24.4 ▪ 12 34.2

13281 CBU P P2 G2.0 1911–1949
Tolmachev, V- IA-, and N- A- Setnitskii.
'Man'chzhurskaia pishchevaia promyshlennost'' (The Manchurian food industry).
VM 1933, 14/15 (15 avgusta), 133–146.
Subj 14.3 14.4 55 ▪ 14.1 24.4

13282 WSU PO P7 G1.2 1911–1928
Torgashev, Boris Pavlovich.
Gornaia produktsiia i resursy Dal'nego Vostoka: Kitai, Man'chzhuriia, russkii Dal'nii Vostok, IAponiia, Koreia, Formoza, Indo-Kitai, Filippiny (Mining products and Far Eastern resources: China, Manchuria, the Russian Far East, Japan, Korea, Taiwan, Indochina, and the Philippines).
Harbin: Ekon. biuro KVzhd, 1927. 12, 444 p.

The mineral industry of the Far East.
Shanghai: Chali, 1930. 510 p.
Subj 14.4

13283 CSU P P2 G1.2 1911–1949
[Torgashev, Boris Pavlovich] Boris P. Torgasheff.
'Soda in China, Manchuria and neighboring countries.'
CEJ 5, 2 (Aug. 1929), 662–681.
Subj 14.4 ▪ 14.3

13284 MCH P P2 G1.2 1911–1928
Tsing Tung-chun (Tseng T'ung-ch'un).
De la production et du commerce de la soie en Chine (Silk production and trade in China).
Lyons: Bosc et Riou; Paris: Lib. Geuthner, 1928. 228 p. (Institut franco-chinois de Lyon, Etudes et documents, 4) (Doctoral dissertation, Faculté de droit, Université de Lyon)
Subj 14.1 14.3 14.4 34.2 ▪ 16.2 16.4 36.4 72

13285 NNC O P5 G1.2 1928–1949
United Nations. Relief and Rehabilitation Administration.
Industrial rehabilitation in China.
Washington, D.C.: Relief and Rehabilitation Administration, 1948. 39 p. (UNRRA operational analysis papers, 51)
Subj 14.2 14.4

13286 CSH P P4 G1.4 1928–1949
U.S. Office of Strategic Services. Research and Analysis Branch.
Japanese-controlled firms in occupied China and Inner Mongolia, mimeo.
[Washington, D.C.]: ——, 1945. 32 p. (R. and A., 3109)
Subj 14.4 14.6 ▪ 14

13287 CSU O P2 G8.1 1928–1949
Wan, K.
'Industrial development in Szechuan.'
CEJ 15, 6 (Dec. 1934), 609–620.
[Reprinted as 'Industrial development in Szechuen.' *Far Eastern review* 31, 4 (Apr. 1935), 148–150.]
Subj 14.4 24.4 ▪ 24.1

13288 CSU P P2 G1.3 1911–1949
Wang Chi Tung (Wang Ch'i-tung).
Eggs industry in China, mimeo.
Tientsin: Hautes études; Shanghai: Université l'Aurore, 1937. 107 p. (Institut des hautes études industrielles et commerciales, Faculty of Commerce, Economic studies, 9)
Subj 14.1 14.3 14.4

13289 CSU P P2 G1.2 1928–1949
Wang, K. P. (Wang Kung-pin), 1919–.
Controlling factors in the future development of the Chinese coal industry.
New York: King's Crown Press, 1947. 312 p. (Doctoral dissertation in Economics, Columbia U.)
Subj 14.4 ▪ 14.2 14.3 16.4

13290 MCH P P2 G1.2 1911–1949
Wu, Ching-chao (Wu Ching-ch'ao), 1901–.
Industrial planning in China.
Chungking: China Institute of Pacific Relations, 1945. 41 p. (China Council series, 3)
Subj 12 14 14.4 ▪ 12.2

13291 NNC S P4 G1.2 1911–1949
Wu, Ying-hua.
Causes of the slow progress of industrial revolution in China.
Unpublished masters thesis in Economics, Columbia U., 1930. 65 p.
Subj 14 14.4 19 ▪ 12 16.4 18 34.3

13292 CSH PO P2 G1.1 1911–1949
Yun, C.
'Electrical manufacturing industry in China.'
China economist 2, 12 (20 Sept. 1948), 267–271.
Subj 14.4

1911-1972
(including 1644-1972)

13293 MCH P P4 G1.2 1842–1972
'Industrie sidérurgique chinoise (1890–1959)' (China's iron industry, 1890–1959).
NED 2591 (12 nov. 1959), 1–34.
Subj 14.4 ▪ 14

13294 NNC P P2 G1.2 1928–1972
Astaf'ev, Gennadii Vasil'evich, 1908–.
'Problemy vosstanovleniia i razvitiia promyshlennosti Kitaia' (Problems in restoring and developing industry in China).

UZIV 2 (1951), 144–190.
Subj 14 14.4 32.2 ▪ 14.1 16.4 24.4 45

13295 NNC P P4 G 1.2 1928–1972
Astaf'ev, Gennadii Vasil'evich, 1908–.
'Uspekhi sotsialisticheskoi industrializatsii Kitaia' (Achievements in the socialist industrialization of China).
SK 1958, 1, 62–80.
Subj 11.4 14.4 ▪ 14 17

13296 CSU P P3 G 1.2 1928–1972
Blaker, James R-.
'The production of conventional weapons.' In *The military and political power of China in the 1970s*, edited by William Wallace Whitson. [Selective entry]
New York: Praeger, 1972, 215–227.
Subj 14.4 15

13297 MCH FP P2 G 9.4 1911–1972
Boer, Dirk de.
'De industrialisatie van Taiwan (Formosa) in verband met de spreiding van de bevolking' (The industrialization of Taiwan in connection with the distribution of its population).
TESG 55, 2 (Februari 1964), 29–41; 55, 3 (Maart 1964), 70–77.
Subj 14 14.4 21 ▪ 11.3 21.1 21.3 58

13298 CSU P P2 G 1.2 1928–1972
Chang, Kuei-sheng, 1921–.
'Nuclei-formation of Communist China's iron and steel industry.'
AAAG 60, 2 (June 1970), 257–285.
Subj 11.3 14.4

13299 CSH U P4 G 4.0 1928–1972
Chang, Perry (Chang P'eng), 1921–.
'Industry.' In *A regional handbook on Northwest China*, compiled by Far Eastern and Russian Institute, U. of Washington. [Selective entry]
New Haven: Human Relations Area Files, 1956, vol. 2, 667–676. (HRAF subcontractor's monographs, 59; Washington 5)
Subj 14.4 24.4

13300 CSU P P2 G 1.2 –1972
Chen, Cheng-siang (Ch'en Cheng-hsiang), 1920–.
'The sugar industry of China.'
GJ 137, 1 (Mar. 1971), 29–40.
Subj 14.1 14.4 ▪ 24.1 24.4

13301 CSH FP P2 G 9.4 1911–1972
Chen, Cheng-siang (Ch'en Cheng-hsiang), 1920–.
The sugar industry of Taiwan.
Taipei: Fu-min Institute of Agricultural Geography, 1955. 45 p. (Fu-min research reports, 58)
Subj 14.4 24.1 ▪ 24.2

13302 CSU P P1 G 1.2 1928–1972
Chin, Rockwood Q. P. (Ch'en Kuo-p'ing), 1911–.
'The validity of Mainland China's cotton textile statistics.'
Southern economic j. 34, 3 (Jan. 1968), 319–334.
Subj 14.1 14.4 ▪ 16.4

13303 CSU P P3 G 1.2 1928–1972
ErSelcuk, Muzaffer.
'The iron and steel industry in China.'
EG 32, 4 (Oct. 1956), 347–371.
Subj 14.4 ▪ 14.2 16.4

13304 NNC P P2 G 2.0 1928–1972
Fomicheva, Margarita Vasil'evna, 1924–.
Ocherki ekonomicheskogo stroitel'stva na Severo-Vostoke Kitaia (Notes on the economic development of Manchuria).
Moscow: Izd-vo Akad. nauk SSSR, 1956. 215 p.
Subj 14.1 14.4 ▪ 14.3 19

13305 CSU P P1 G 9.0 1895–1972
Hong, Wontack, 1940–.
'Industrialization and trade in manufactures: The East Asian experience.' In *The open economy: Essays on international trade and finance*, edited by Peter B- Kenen and Roger Lawrence. [Sole entry]
New York: Columbia U. Press, 1968, 213–239. (Columbia studies in economics, 1)
Subj 14.3 14.4 ▪ 14.1

13306 MAM P P4 G 9.4 1895–1972
Hong, Wontack, 1940–.
A study of the changes in the structure of manufacturing industry and in the trade pattern of manufactured products in Korea, Taiwan and Japan.
Ann Arbor: University Microfilms (Publ. 66-12,569), 1966. 277 p. (Doctoral dissertation in Economics, Columbia U.)
Subj 14 14.3 14.4

13307 CSH P P3 G 1.2 1928–1972
Hsia, Ronald (Hsia Hsiu-yung), 1918–.
'Changes in the location of China's steel industry.'
CQ 17 (Jan.–Mar. 1964), 125–133. [Reprinted in *Industrial development in Communist China*, edited by Choh-ming Li (Li Cho-min). (Selective entry) New York: Praeger, 1964, 125–133.]
Subj 14.4 ▪ 11.3

13308 MAM P P2 G 1.2 1928–1972
Hsu, Ih-sen (Hsü I-sheng), 1921–.
A study of possible factors affecting the acceleration of industrial development in China.
Ann Arbor: University Microfilms (Publ. 10,218), 1954. 317 p. (Doctoral dissertation in Economics, State U. of Iowa)
Subj 14 14.4 17 19 34.2 ▪ 11 11.4 14.1 14.6 34.1 58

13309 CSH P P2 G 2.0 1928–1972
Hung, Chia-chun (Hung Chia-chün), 1925–.
'Industry.' In *A regional handbook on Northeast China*, compiled by Far Eastern and Russian Institute, U. of Washington. [Selective entry]
New Haven: Human Relations Area Files, 1956, 521–543. (HRAF subcontractor's monographs, 61; Washington 9)
Subj 14.4

13310 CSH P P7 G 1.2 1911–1972
[La Dany, Ladislao] ———, 1914–.
'Coal in China.'
CNA 47 (13 Aug. 1954), 1–7.
Subj 14.4

13311 ELS P P2 G 1.2 1842–1972
[Lai, Chuen-yan] David C. Y. Lai (Li Ch'üan-en), 1937–.
The cotton spinning and weaving industry of China, c. 1890–1957: A study in industrial geography.
Unpublished doctoral dissertation in Industrial Geography, U. of London [London School of Economics and Political Science], 1967. 459 p.
Subj 11.3 14 14.3 14.4 ▪ 14.1 16.4

13312 CSU P P2 G 9.4 1928–1972
Lin, Ken C. Y.
'Industrial development and changes in the structure of foreign trade: The experience of the Republic of China in Taiwan, 1946–66.'
International Monetary Fund Staff papers 15, 2 (July 1968), 290–318.
Subj 14 14.4 ▪ 24.1 34.2

13313 CSU P P2 G 9.4 1928–1972
Liu, Tchin-ching.
'The process of industrialization in Taiwan.'
DE 7, 1 (Mar. 1969), 63–81.
Subj 14.4 24.1 ▪ 14.3 21 21.4 34.2

13314 MCH P P1 G 1.2 1928–1972
Rawski, Thomas George, 1943–.
The economics of Chinese machine-building, 1931–1967.
Unpublished doctoral dissertation in Economics, Harvard U., 1972. 13, 521 p.
Subj 14 14.4 34.2 ▪ 16.4 32.1

13315 MAM P P2 G 9.4 1928–1972
Tseng, Kuo-cheng, 1937–.
An analysis of the growth of selected export industries in Taiwan, 1952–1969.
Ann Arbor: University Microfilms (Publ. 72-19,394), 1972. 369 p. (Doctoral dissertation in Economics, Pennsylvania State U., 1971)
Subj 14 14.4 24.1 ▪ 14.3 21.4 34.2

13316 NIC P P4 G 1.2 1895–1972
Wu, Yuan-li (Wu Yüan-li), 1920–.
The steel industry in Communist China.
New York: Praeger, 1965. 20, 334 p.
Subj 14.4 ▪ 14

1949-1972

13317 CSU P P1 G 1.2 1949–1972
Japanese appraisal of index numbers of industrial production in Communist China, mimeo. Tr. of 'Chūgoku no kōgyō seisan shisū no gimmi' (An analysis of Chinese industrial production indices); *Ekafe tsūshin* 223 (21 Mar. 1960), 1–22.
Washington, D.C.: U.S. Joint Publications Research Service, 1 Aug. 1960. 15 p. (JPRS 3617; MC 14,318/1960)
Subj 14.4

13318 CSU P P2 G 1.2 1949–1972
Asakawa Kenji, 1909–.
New trends in Communist China's fertilizer industry, mimeo. Tr. of 'Chūgoku hiryō kōgyō no shin keikō'; *Ajia keizai jumpō* 422 (10 Feb. 1960), 1–9.
Washington, D.C.: U.S. Joint Publications Research Service, 25 Aug. 1960. 8 p. (JPRS 3735; MC 15,639/1960)
Subj 14.4 ▪ 14.1

13319 CSU P P2 G 1.2 1949–1972
Ashton, John.
'Development of electric energy resources in Communist China.' In *An economic*

profile of Mainland China, compiled by Joint Economic Committee, U.S. Congress. [Selective entry]
Washington, D.C.: U.S. Government Printing Office, 1967, vol. 1, 297–316. [Reprinted in *An economic profile of Mainland China*, compiled by the agency cited. (Selective entry.) New York: Praeger, 1968, 297–316.]
SUBJ 14.4

13320 NNC P P1 G1.2 1949–1972
Astaf'ev, Gennadii Vasil'evich, 1908–.
'Plan sotsialisticheskoi industrializatsii Kitaiskoi Narodnoi Respubliki' (The plan for the socialist industrialization of the People's Republic of China).
SV 1955, 5, 26–43.
SUBJ 14 14.4 24.4 ▪ 11.4 16.4

13321 NNC P P4 G1.2 1949–1972
Astaf'ev, Gennadii Vasil'evich, 1908–.
'Sotsialisticheskaia industrializatsiia i razvitie promyshlennosti Kitaiskoi Narodnoi Respubliki, v 1953–1957 gg.' (Socialist industrialization and the development of industry in the People's Republic of China, 1953–1957).
KSINA 49 (1961), 3–12.
SUBJ 14 14.4 ▪ 11.4 14.5

13322 NNC P P2 G1.2 1949–1972
Astaf'ev, Gennadii Vasil'evich, 1908–.
'Velikie pobedy Kitaiskogo naroda v stroitel'stve sotsializma' (Great victories of the Chinese people in building socialism).
Vestnik statistiki 1956, 6 (noiabr'–dekabr'), 34–49.
SUBJ 14 14.4 ▪ 14.1 34.1

13323 NNC PO P4 G1.2 1949–1972
Barnett, Arthur Doak, 1921–.
'Economic development in Communist China: The progress of industrialization.'
AUFS-EAS 3, 8 (15 July 1954), 1–45. [Reprinted as 'Industrialization.' In *Communist China: The early years, 1949–55*, by A. D. Barnett. (Selective entry.) New York: Praeger, 1964, 234–267.]
SUBJ 14.4 ▪ 16.4

13324 NNC PO P7 G1.2 1949–1972
Bazhenov, Ivan Ivanovich, Ivan Abramovich Leonenko, and Aleksei Kondrat'evich Kharchenko.
Ugol'naia promyshlennost' Kitaiskoi Narodnoi Respubliki.
Moscow: Gosgortekhizdat, 1959. 479 p.
The coal industry of the People's Republic of China, mimeo. [Partial tr.: p. 23–25, 77–78, 286–289, 313–400, 456–477 only].
Washington, D.C.: U.S. Joint Publications Research Service, 6 Aug. 1962. 150 p. (JPRS 14,738; MC 17,994/1962) [Xerox copyflo available—New York: CCM Information Corp., Research and Microfilm Publications. (Scholarly Book Translation Series, 405)]
SUBJ 14.4 ▪ 17 62

13325 MCH S P2 G1.2 1949–1972
Berezina, IUliia Iosifovna, 1930–.
Toplivno-energeticheskaia baza Kitaiskoi Narodnoi Respubliki.
Moscow: Izd-vo vost. lit-ry, 1959. 139 p.
Fuel and power base of the Chinese People's Republic, mimeo.
Washington, D.C.: U.S. Joint Publications Research Service, 19 Oct. 1960. 114 p. (JPRS 3784; MC 15,665/1960)
SUBJ 14.4 ▪ 14

13326 CSU O P3 G6.1 1949–1972
Bergeron, Régis.
'L'usine de construction mécanique "Edification de Changhai", inventeur de la méthode "les fourmis rongent l'os"' ('Edification of Shanghai', the mechanical engineering factory that originated the [labor-intensive] work method known as 'ants scour the bone').
CFC 12 (déc. 1961), 71–77.
SUBJ 14.4 34.2

13327 NNC PO P1 G1.2 1949–1972
Bettelheim, Charles.
'L'industrialisation de la Chine populaire' (The industrialization of the People's Republic of China). In *Le régime et les institutions de la République populaire chinoise* (The government and institutions of the People's Republic of China), jointly edited by Centre d'étude des pays de l'Est, Institut de sociologie Solvay, Université libre de Bruxelles *with* Centre national pour l'étude des pays à régime communiste. [Selective entry]
Brussels: Snoeck-Ducaju, 1960, 201–227.
SUBJ 14 14.4 ▪ 11.4

13328 CBU O P2 G1.2 1949–1972
Brulé, Jean-Pierre.
La nouvelle révolution de Mao (Mao's new revolution).
Paris: Centurion, 1967. 224 p.
SUBJ 14.1 14.4 15 17 ▪ 11.4 12.1 14.2 18 25 36.4 54

13329 CSU P P2 G1.2 1949–1972
Carin, Robert.
Power industry in Communist China.
Hong Kong: Union Research Institute, 1969. 63 p. (Communist China problem research series, EC44)
SUBJ 14.4

13330 CSU P P2 G1.2 1949–1972
Carin, Robert.
'Rural electrification.' In *Contemporary China, 1962–1964*, edited by Edward Stuart Kirby. [Selective entry]
Hong Kong: Hong Kong U. Press, 1968, 11–21.
SUBJ 14 14.4 ▪ 14.1 14.2

13331 CSH S P2 G1.2 1949–1972
Chang Chün.
'The Soviet evaluation of the industrial development in Mainland China.'
IS 9, 1 (Oct. 1972), 45–53.
SUBJ 14.4

13332 MCM S P2 G4.0 1949–1972
Chang, Kuei-sheng, 1921–.
'Geographical bases for industrial development in northwestern China.'
EG 39, 4 (Oct. 1963), 341–350. [Reprinted in *Cultural geography: Selected readings*, edited by Fred E. Dohrs and Lawrence M. Sommers. (Selective entry.) New York: Crowell, 1967, 375–386.]
SUBJ 11.3 14 14.4 ▪ 14.3 21.1 21.4

13333 NNC P P2 G1.2 1949–1972
Chao I-neng.
'Industries.' Tr. of 'Shih nien lai ti Chung kung kung yeh kai k'uang' (Industries in Communist China during the past decade); *Tsu kuo chou k'an* 387 (6 June 1960), 13–23; 388 (13 June 1960), 18–25. In *Communist China, 1949–1959*, edited by Union Research Institute. [Selective entry]
Hong Kong: Union Research Institute, 1961, vol. 2, 145–219.
SUBJ 14.4 34.2 ▪ 14 14.5 66

13334 NNC P P5 G1.2 1949–1972
Chao I-neng.
'Industry' [title varies]. Tr. of '1955–1958 nien ti Chung kung kung yeh' (Industry in Communist China, 1955–1958); *Tsu kuo chou k'an* 159–334/335 (16 Jan. 1956 – 8 June 1959) [recurring annual feature article]. In *Communist China, 1955–1958*, edited by Union Research Institute.
Hong Kong: Union Research Institute. Issued annually, 1956–1959, average ca. 15 p.
SUBJ 14.4 ▪ 14 24.4

13335 CSH P P2 G1.2 1949–1972
Chao I-neng, Yao Pi, et al. [Authors sequential rather than joint: Chao I-neng for 1961; Yao Pi for 1962; Chao Yung-ch'ing for 1963; Ma Ch'ang-tsung for 1964; Huang Yu-ch'uan (Huang Yü-ch'uan) for 1965; Lin Tzu (Lin Chih) for 1966; I Fan, pseud., for 1967–1969.]
'Communist China's industry, 1961–1969' [title varies; article for 1967 covers transport and communications as well as industry.]. Tr. from *Tsu kuo chou k'an* 499 (30 July 1962) *and* from *Tsu kuo* 2–76 (May 1964 – July 1970) [recurring annual feature article]. In *Communist China, 1961–1969*, edited by Union Research Institute.
Hong Kong: Union Research Institute. Issued annually, 1962–1970, average ca. 35 p.
SUBJ 14.4 ▪ 14 34.2

13336 CSU P P2 G1.2 1949–1972
Chao, Kang, 1929–.
The construction industry in Communist China.
Chicago: Aldine, 1968. 15, 237 p.
SUBJ 11.4 14 14.2 14.4 34.2 ▪ 11.1 11.2 14.6 18 35 55

13337 CSU P P4 G1.2 1949–1972
Chao, Kang, 1929–.
'Policies and performance in industry.' In *Economic trends in Communist China*, edited by Alexander Eckstein, Walter Galenson, and Ta-chung Liu. [Selective entry]
Chicago: Aldine, 1968, 549–595.
SUBJ 14 14.4 ▪ 12

13338 CSU P P2 G1.2 1949–1972
Chao, Kang, 1929–.
The rate and pattern of industrial growth in Communist China.
Ann Arbor: U. of Michigan Press, 1965. 188 p. (Revision of *Indexes of industrial production of Communist China, 1949–1959*, doctoral dissertation in Economics, U. of Michigan, 1962)
SUBJ 14 14.4 ▪ 14.6 16.4 24.4

13339 CSU P P4 G1.2 1949–1972
Cheng Chu-yuan (Cheng Chu-yüan), 1927–.
The machine-building industry in Communist China.
Chicago: Aldine-Atherton, 1971. 13, 339 p.
SUBJ 14 14.4 ▪ 12 16.4 34.2

13340 CSH P P2 G1.2 1949–1972
Chien Yan-heng.
'A study of the electric power industry on the Chinese Mainland.'
CCA 4, 4 (Aug. 1967), 21–31.
SUBJ 14.4

13341 CSH O P4 G1.2 1949–1972
Ch'ien Chih-kuang.
'Essential nature of high speed development of the textile industry.' Tr. of 'Kao su tu fa chan fang chih kung yeh' (Rapidly develop the textile industry); *Hung ch'i* 1959, 8 (6 Apr.), 1–11. In *Translations from 'Hung-ch'i' (Red flag) (No. 5, 1 March 1959 – No. 8, 15 April 1960)*, mimeo., compiled by U.S. Joint Publications Research Service. [Selective entry]
Washington, D.C.: JPRS, 31 July 1961, 37–51. (JPRS 4820; MC 17,376/1961) [A different tr.— 'High speed development of the textile industry.' In *Textile industry in Communist China*, mimeo., compiled by U.S. Joint Publications Research Service. Washington, D.C.: JPRS, Apr. 1961, 98–112. (JPRS 6962; MC 9359/1961)]
SUBJ 14.4 ▪ 34.2

13342 CSU P P7 G1.2 1949–1972
[Chzhen IUei-shen] Cheng Yu-ei-shen.
'Razvitie gornorudnoi promyshlennosti Kitaia.'
Gornyi zhurnal 1960, 4, 19–22.
Development of the mining industry in Communist China, mimeo.
Washington, D.C.: U.S. Joint Publications Research Service, 25 Aug. 1960. 7 p. (JPRS 3754; MC 15,648/1960)
SUBJ 14.4 ▪ 16.4

13343 CSU S P2 G1.2 1949–1972
Cone, Frederick McGrail, 1910–.
Chinese industrial growth: Brief studies of selected investment areas.
Santa Monica, Calif.: RAND Corp., 1969. 16, 101 p. (RAND memoranda, RM-5625-PR/ISA)
SUBJ 14.4 ▪ 14.2 14.3 16.4 24.4

13344 CSU S P2 G1.2 1949–1972
Cone, Frederick McGrail, 1910–.
Chinese industrial growth: Overall level of investment and its relation to general growth rate.
Santa Monica, Calif.: RAND Corp., 1969. 14, 84 p. (RAND memoranda, RM-5841-PR/ISA)
SUBJ 14 14.4 ▪ 14.1 14.3 16.4 24.4

13345 CSH P P7 G1.2 1949–1972
Crosfield [Joseph] and Sons, Ltd.
The Chinese coal industry.
Warrington, Eng.: Crosfield and Sons, 1961–1962. 6 vols. 483 p. [s.p.].
SUBJ 14.4 ▪ 16.4

13346 CSU P P5 G1.2 1949–1972
Current Scene Editor.
'Industrial development in China: A return to decentralization.'
CS 6, 22 (20 Dec. 1968), 1–18.
SUBJ 14.4 32.1 ▪ 12 32 34.2

13347 CSU S P4 G1.2 1949–1972
Dernberger, Robert Franklin, 1929–.
'Another piece of the jigsaw puzzle called Communist China.' [Review of *The construction industry in Communist China*, by Kang Chao.]
EDCC 17, 2 (Jan. 1969), 262–266.
SUBJ 14 14.4 ▪ 55

13348 MCH P P7 G1.2 1949–1972
Dwyer, Denis John, 1933–.
'The coal industry in Mainland China since 1949.'
GJ 129, 3 (Sept. 1963), 329–338.
SUBJ 14.4 ▪ 12 14 14.2

13349 NIC P P2 G1.2 1949–1972
Engelborghs-Bertels, Marthe, 1928–.
'La localisation de l'industrie en Chine populaire' (Localization of industry in the People's Republic of China).
Pays communistes 1, 4 (oct.–déc. 1960), 155–174.
SUBJ 11.3 14 14.4 ▪ 14.1 24.4

13350 DLC O P4 G1.2 1949–1972
Faltus, František.
'Vývoj svařování v Čínské lidové republicé' (The development of welding in the People's Republic of China).
Zváračsky sborník (Bratislava) 9, 4 (1960), 415–423.
SUBJ 14.4

13351 CSU P P1 G1.2 1949–1972
Field, Robert Michael, 1928–.
'Chinese Communist industrial production.' In *An economic profile of Mainland China*, compiled by Joint Economic Committee, U.S. Congress. [Selective entry]
Washington, D.C.: U.S. Government Printing Office, 1967, vol. 1, 269–295. [Reprinted in *An economic profile of Mainland China*, compiled by the agency cited. (Selective entry.) New York: Praeger, 1968, 269–295.]
SUBJ 14.4

13352 CSU P P2 G1.2 1949–1972
Field, Robert Michael, 1928–.
'Chinese industrial development: 1949–70.' In *People's Republic of China: An economic assessment*, compiled by Joint Economic Committee, U.S. Congress. [Selective entry]
Washington, D.C.: U.S. Government Printing Office, 1972, 61–85.
SUBJ 14.4 ▪ 24.4

13353 MCH P P2 G1.2 1949–1972
Field, Robert Michael, 1928–.
The growth of industrial production and productivity in Communist China, 1952–57.
Unpublished doctoral dissertation in Economics, Harvard U., 1966. 15, 221 p.
SUBJ 12 14.4 16.4 ▪ 11.4 14 36.4

13354 CSU P P2 G1.2 1949–1972
Field, Robert Michael, 1928–.
'Industrial production in Communist China: 1957–1968.'
CQ 42 (Apr.–June 1970), 46–64.
SUBJ 14.4 ▪ 14 14.1 22.2 24.4

13355 NNC P P4 G2.0 1949–1972
Fomicheva, Margarita Vasil'evna, 1924–.
'Promyshlennoe stroitel'stvo v Severo-Vostochnom Kitae' (Industrial construction in Manchuria).
KSIV 11 (1954), 3–19.
SUBJ 14 14.4 ▪ 14.5 14.6 16.4 17

13356 CSH P P3 G1.2 1949–1972
Fond, Richard.
'The monoclinic silicon industries of Mainland China.'
IS 7, 6 (Mar. 1971), 52–62.
SUBJ 14.4

13357 CSU S P3 G1.2 1949–1972
Harbron, John D-.
'Communist China as a maritime power.' In *Communist ships and shipping*, by J. D. Harbron. [Sole entry]
London: Adlard Coles, 1962, 249–257.
SUBJ 14.3 14.4 ▪ 14.2 66

13358 MCY S P2 G4.0 1949–1972
Heenan, Brian.
'China's petroleum industry.'
FEER 49, 13 (23 Sept. 1965), 565–567; 50, 2 (14 Oct. 1965), 93–95. [Reprinted as 'The Chinese petroleum industry.' *TESG* 57, 4 (Juli–Augustus 1966), 149–159.]
SUBJ 14 14.4 ▪ 14.2 14.3

13359 CSU P P2 G1.2 1949–1972
Ho Ko-jen.
'Peiping's petroleum industry.'
IS 4, 11 (Aug. 1968), 22–35.
SUBJ 14.4

13360 MCH P P4 G1.2 1949–1972
Hsia, Ronald (Hsia Hsiu-yung), 1918–.
'Les caractéristiques du développement industriel de la Chine continentale' (Characteristics of the industrial development of Mainland China).
Tiers-monde 2, 7 (juil.–sept. 1961), 325–353.
SUBJ 14.4 ▪ 64

13361 CSU P P2 G1.2 1949–1972
Hsia, Ronald (Hsia Hsiu-yung), 1918–.
Steel in China: Its output behavior, productivity and growth pattern.
Wiesbaden: Harrassowitz, 1971. 220 p. (Institut für Asienkunde, Schriften, 29)
SUBJ 14.4 ▪ 16.4

13362 CSH P P4 G2.3 1949–1972
Hu I-min.
'Liaoning's rapid industrial growth is the victory of the party general line.' Tr. from *Liao-ning shih nien* (Liaoning during the past decade); Shenyang: Jen min ch'u pan she, 196? In *Liao-ning province during the last ten years*, mimeo., compiled by U.S. Joint Publications Research Service. [Selective entry]
Washington, D.C.: JPRS, 17 Jan. 1963, 55–69. (JPRS 17,182; MC 2979/1963) [Xerox copyflo available—New York: CCM Information Corp., Research and Microfilm Publications. (Scholarly Book Translation Series, 545)]
SUBJ 14.4

13363 MCH S P1 G1.2 1949–1972
Hung, Fred C., and Yuan-li Wu (Wu Yüan-li), 1920–.
'Conceptual difficulties in measuring China's industrial output.'
CQ 17 (Jan.–Mar. 1964), 56–64. [Reprinted in *Industrial development in Communist China*, edited by Choh-ming Li (Li Cho-min). (Selective entry.) New York: Praeger, 1964, 56–64.]
Subj 14 14.4

13364 CBU P P2 G1.2 1949–1972
Ishikawa Shigeru, 1918–.
'Choice of techniques in Mainland China.'
DE 2, 3 (Sept.–Dec. 1962), 23–56.
Subj 14.4 24.4 34.2 ▪ 14 14.3 16.4

13365 DLC S P2 G1.2 1949–1972
Ivanov, Vladimir Dmitrievich, and Evgenii Pavlovich Kazakevich.
Gidroenergeticheskie resursy Kitaiskoi Narodnoi Respubliki i ikh ispol'zovanie (Hydroelectric power resources in the People's Republic of China and their utilization).
Moscow: Gosenergoizdat, 1960. 47 p.
Subj 11.4 14.4

13366 DLC P P4 G1.2 1949–1972
Kapranov, Ivan Andreevich.
Promyshlennost' Kitaiskoi Narodnoi Respubliki (Industry in the People's Republic of China).
Moscow: Znanie, 1959. 31 p. (Vsesoiuznoe obshchestvo po rasprostraneniiu politicheskikh i nauchnykh znanii, Seriia 3, 12)
Subj 14 14.4 ▪ 16.2 32 34.2 66

13367 MCH U P4 G1.2 1949–1972
Ku Mu.
'New stage in China's mass movement in industry.'
PR 7, 22 (22 May 1964), 11–14.
Subj 14.4

13368 CSH P P2 G1.2 1949–1972
[La Dany, Ladislao] ———, 1914–.
'Coal.'
CNA 697 (23 Feb. 1968), 1–7.
Subj 14.4 ▪ 16.4 25

13369 CSH P P7 G1.2 1949–1972
[La Dany, Ladislao] ———, 1914–.
'Coal mines.'
CNA 266 (27 Feb. 1959), 1–7.
Subj 14.4

13370 MCH P P2 G1.2 1949–1972
[La Dany, Ladislao] ———, 1914–.
'Coal production, 1959–1961.'
CNA 374 (2 June 1961), 1–7.
Subj 14.4 ▪ 16.3 34.2

13371 MCH P P2 G1.2 1949–1972
[La Dany, Ladislao] ———, 1914–.
'Electricity, 1958–1961.'
CNA 405 (26 Jan. 1962), 1–7.
Subj 14.4 ▪ 14.1

13372 CSH P P2 G1.2 1949–1972
[La Dany, Ladislao] ———, 1914–.
'Fuel industry: Petroleum.'
CNA 885 (23 June 1972), 1–7.
Subj 14.4

13373 CSH P P2 G1.2 1949–1972
[La Dany, Ladislao] ———, 1914–.
'Heavy industry.'
CNA 836 (2 Apr. 1971), 1–7.
Subj 14.4 24.4

13374 CSH P P2 G1.2 1949–1972
[La Dany, Ladislao] ———, 1914–.
'Industry: Words and facts.'
CNA 809 (24 July 1970), 1–7.
Subj 14.4 24.4

13375 CSH P P2 G1.2 1949–1972
[La Dany, Ladislao] ———, 1914–.
'Industry.'
CNA 781 (14 Nov. 1969), 1–7.
Subj 14.4 24.4

13376 CSH P P2 G1.2 1949–1972
[La Dany, Ladislao] ———, 1914–.
'Industry.'
CNA 884 (16 June 1972), 1–7.
Subj 14.4

13377 CSH P P2 G1.2 1949–1972
[La Dany, Ladislao] ———, 1914–.
'Iron and steel and capital construction: Efforts to strengthen the military industry.'
CNA 854 (10 Sept. 1971), 1–7.
Subj 14.4 24.4 ▪ 15

13378 MCH P P4 G1.2 1949–1972
[La Dany, Ladislao] ———, 1914–.
'The paper industry.'
CNA 322 (6 May 1960), 1–7.
Subj 14.4 24.4 34.2

13379 MCH P P2 G1.2 1949–1972
[La Dany, Ladislao] ———, 1914–.
'Petroleum industry, 1958–1961.'
CNA 406 (2 Feb. 1962), 1–7.
Subj 14.4 ▪ 14

13380 CSH P P3 G1.2 1949–1972
[La Dany, Ladislao] ———, 1914–.
'Plastics.'
CNA 541 (20 Nov. 1964), 1–7.
Subj 14.4

13381 CSH P P4 G1.2 1949–1972
[La Dany, Ladislao] ———, 1914–.
'Steel industry.'
CNA 603 (11 Mar. 1966), 1–7.
Subj 14.4 ▪ 34.2 36.1

13382 CSH P P2 G1.2 1949–1972
[La Dany, Ladislao] ———, 1914–.
'Textile industry, 1962–1966.'
CNA 619 (8 July 1966), 1–7.
Subj 14.4

13383 MCH P P2 G1.2 1949–1972
[La Dany, Ladislao] ———, 1914–.
'Tractors.'
CNA 396 (10 Nov. 1961), 1–7.
Subj 14.1 14.4

13384 CSU P P2 G1.2 1949–1972
Lau, Lawrence J. (Liu Tsun-i), 1944–.
Economic development and industrialization in Communist China (1949–1968).
Stanford: Stanford U., Research Center in Economic Growth, 1970. 103 p. (RCEG research memoranda, 88)
Subj 14.4 ▪ 11.4 14 24.4 34.2

13385 MCH PO P2 G1.2 1949–1972
Lavallée, Léon.
'Essor de l'industrie chinois' (The progress of Chinese industry).
Economie et politique 66/67 (jan.–fév. 1960), 79–93. [Special issue: *Economie en URSS et en Chine* (The economy of the U.S.S.R. and China)]
Subj 14 14.4

13386 CSU P P4 G1.2 1949–1972
Lee, Rensselaer Wright, III, 1937–.
'Ideology and technical innovation in Chinese industry, 1949–1971.'
AS 12, 8 (Aug. 1972), 647–661.
Subj 14.4 64 ▪ 16.4

13387 CSU P P1 G1.2 1949–1972
Lee Rensselaer Wright, III, 1937–.
'The politics of technology in Communist China.' In *Ideology and politics in contemporary China*, edited by Chalmers Ashby Johnson. [Selective entry]
Seattle: U. of Washington Press, 1973, 301–325. (Social Science Research Council, Studies in Chinese government and politics, 4)
Subj 14.4 64 ▪ 16.1 16.4 34.2 62

13388 MCY P P2 G1.2 1949–1972
Lee, T. C. (Li T'ai-ch'u).
'China's cotton industry.'
FEER 29, 4 (28 July 1960), 151–157.
Subj 14.4 ▪ 14.1

13389 MAM P P2 G1.2 1949–1972
Lee, Yin-po, 1930–.
A statistical test of the validity of the official indexes of industrial production in Communist China, 1949–1958.
Ann Arbor: University Microfilms (Publ. 71-2387), 1971. 195 p. (Doctoral dissertation in Economics, Southern Illinois U., 1970)
Subj 14 14.4

13390 NNC P P2 G1.2 1949–1972
Li Ch'ang-yen.
'Petroleum and electric power industries.' Tr. of 'Shih nien lai ti Chung kung shih yu ho tien li kung yeh' (The petroleum and electric-power industries in Communist China during the past decade); *Tsu kuo chou k'an* 384 (16 May 1960), 12–19. In *Communist China, 1949–1959*, edited by Union Research Institute. [Selective entry]
Hong Kong: Union Research Institute, 1961, vol. 1, 177–212.
Subj 14.4 ▪ 16.4 18

13391 CSH P P2 G1.2 1949–1972
Li, Choh-ming (Li Cho-min), 1912–.
'China's industrial development, 1958–1963.'
CQ 17 (Jan.–Mar. 1964), 3–38. [Reprinted in *Industrial development in Communist China*, edited by Choh-ming Li. (Selective entry.) New York: Praeger, 1964, 3–38.] [Reprinted in *China under Mao: Politics takes command*, edited by Roderick Lemonde MacFarquhar. (Selective entry.) Cambridge: M.I.T. Press, 1966, 175–210.]
Subj 14 14.4 ▪ 12 14.1 14.3 16.4 19 32.1 36.4

13392 CSU O P5 G6.2 1949–1972
Li Jen-chih.
'The continued leap forward in industrial production in Anhwei in 1959.' Tr. of 'I chiu wu chiu nien An-hui sheng kung yeh sheng ch'an chi hsü yao chin ti hsing shih'; *Hung ch'i* 1959, 22 (16 Nov.), 17–23. In *Translations from*

'Hung-ch'i' (Red flag) No. 22, 16 November 1959, Peiping, mimeo., compiled by U.S. Joint Publications Research Service. [Sole entry]
Washington, D.C.: JPRS, 12 Feb. 1960, 17–28. (JPRS 1168D; MC 5639/1960)
Subj 14.4 ▪ 22.1 34.2

13393 CSU U P2 G1.2 1949–1972
Li Jui.
'A discussion of the problem of hydro- and thermo-electricity.' Tr. of 'Kuan yü shui tien ho huo tien wen t'i ti t'ao lun' (A discussion of the issue of hydraulic versus coal generation of electricity); *Hung ch'i* 1959, 10 (16 May), 34–44. In *Articles from the Chinese Communist periodical 'Hung-ch'i' (Red flag) (No. 10, 16 May 1959, Peiping)*, mimeo., compiled by U.S. Joint Publications Research Service. [Sole entry]
Washington, D.C.: JPRS, 29 July 1959, 55–74. (JPRS 844D; MC 12,889/1959)
Subj 14.4 ▪ 11.3 14

13394 CSU P P1 G1.2 1949–1972
Li, Yao Tzu, 1914–, and Way Dong Woo (Ho Hui-t'ang), 1917–.
'Progress in electronics, 1949–1959.' In *Sciences in Communist China*, edited by [Sydney Henry Gould] Sidney H. Gould. [Selective entry]
Washington, D.C.: American Assn. for the Advancement of Science, 1961, 739–746. (AAAS publications, 68)
Subj 14.4 17 ▪ 36.1 62

13395 WSU P P4 G7.0 1949–1972
Liang, C. S. (Liang Ch'i-shan).
'New location pattern of industries in the middle Yangtze provinces, Central China.'
CCJ 5, 2 (May 1966), 167–194.
Subj 11.3 14.4 ▪ 21.1

13396 CSH P P4 G2.3 1949–1972
Liaoning. T'ung chi chü. (Bureau of Statistics).
'Liaoning's great achievements in industrial reconstruction in the past decade.' Tr. from *Liao-ning shih nien* (Liaoning during the past decade); Shenyang: Jen min ch'u pan she, 196? In *Liao-ning province during the last ten years*, mimeo., compiled by U.S. Joint Publications Research Service. [Selective entry]
Washington, D.C.: JPRS, 17 Jan. 1963, 97–110. (JPRS 17,182; MC 2979/1963) [Xerox copyflo available—New York: CCM Information Corp., Research and Microfilm Publications. (Scholarly Book Translation Series, 545)]
Subj 14.4 24.4 ▪ 34.2

13397 NIC P P4 G1.2 1949–1972
Lieu, D. K. (Liu Ta-chün), 1891–1962.
Industrial development in Communist China.
New York: Sino-American Amity, 1955. 37 p.
Subj 14.4 ▪ 14

13398 CSH P P4 G1.2 1949–1972
Lim, E. R.
'The role of profit in China's industrial planning.'
China Mainland review 1, 4 (Mar. 1966), 6–15.
Subj 14.4 34.2 ▪ 14.3

13399 CSU P P2 G1.2 1949–1972
Liu, Jung-chao, 1929–.
China's fertilizer economy.
Chicago: Aldine, 1970. 173 p.
Subj 14 14.1 14.4 34.2 ▪ 14.3 24.3

13400 CSH S P2 G1.2 1949–1972
Liu Kan-chih.
'The sugar industry in Mainland China.'
IS 7, 9 (June 1971), 63–90.
Subj 14.1 14.4

13401 MCH S P2 G1.2 1949–1972
Maquenne, Paul.
'Ressources et perspectives énergétiques de la Chine populaire' (Present and future energy sources of the People's Republic of China).
R. politique et parlementaire 1961, 712 (mai), 35–48.
Subj 14.4 62 ▪ 11 14 14.1 64 66

13402 CSU P P4 G1.2 1949–1972
Nieh, E. K.
'Mechanical engineering.' In *Sciences in Communist China*, edited by [Sydney Henry Gould] Sidney H. Gould. [Selective entry]
Washington, D.C.: American Assn. for the Advancement of Science, 1961, 805–820. (AAAS publications, 68)
Subj 14.4

13403 CSH O P4 G1.5 1949–1972
Nieh Jung-chen, 1899–.
'The new climates in the technical revolutions in the factories.' Tr. of 'Kung ch'ang chi shu ko ming ti hsin ch'i hsiang' (New prospects for technological revolution in factories); *Hung ch'i* 1960, 8 (16 Apr.), 35–41. In *Translations from 'Hung-ch'i' (Red flag) No. 8, 16 April 1960, Peiping*, mimeo., compiled by U.S. Joint Publications Research Service. [Sole entry]
Washington, D.C.: JPRS, 26 July 1960, 1–9. (JPRS 3591; MC 14,295/1960)
Subj 14.4 34.2 ▪ 16.4 24.4

13404 CSU PO P2 G1.1 1949–1972
Nikolayev, S- A-, and L- I- Molodtsova.
'The present state of the Chinese iron and steel industry.' Tr. from *Geografiia i khoziaistvo* 1960, 6, 34–44.
Soviet geography 1, 8 (Oct. 1960), 55–71.
Subj 14.4 24.4

13405 MCH PO P2 G1.2 1949–1972
Noirot, Paul, and Léon Lavallée.
'Resultats, problèmes et méthodes de l'industrialisation chinoise' (The industrialization of China: Achievements, problems, and methods).
Economie appliquée 13, 3 (juil.–sept. 1960), 391–428.
Subj 14.4 ▪ 14 64

13406 MCY P P3 G1.2 1949–1972
Onoue, Etsuzō (Onoe Etsuzō).
'China's cotton industry.'
FEER 33, 1 (6 July 1961), 19–26.
Subj 14.4 ▪ 16.4 17 19

13407 CSU FP P2 G1.2 1949–1972
Orchard, John Ewing, 1893–1962.
'Industrialization in Japan, China mainland, and India: Some world implications.'
AAAG 50, 3 (Sept. 1960), 193–215.
Subj 14 14.4 ▪ 11 14.1

13408 CSU P P4 G1.2 1949–1972
Orleans, Leo A-, 1924–.
'Research and development in Communist China: Mood, management, and measurement.' In *An economic profile of Mainland China*, compiled by Joint Economic Committee, U.S. Congress. [Selective entry]
Washington, D.C.: U.S. Government Printing Office, 1967, vol. 2, 549–578. [Reprinted in *An economic profile of Mainland China*, compiled by the agency cited. (Selective entry.) New York: Praeger, 1968, 549–578.]
Subj 14 14.4 16.1 16.2 36.1 62 ▪ 12 17 32.1 66 70

13409 CSH P P2 G1.2 1949–1972
Ovdienko, Ivan Kharitonovich, 1910–.
'Novaia geografiia promyshlennosti Kitaia' (The new geography of industry in China).
Geografiia v shkole 1959, 6, 28–41.

'The new geography industry of China.'
Soviet geography 1, 4 (Apr. 1960), 63–78.
Subj 14.4 ▪ 24.4

13410 MCH U P3 G1.2 1949–1972
Ovdienko, Ivan Kharitonovich, 1910–.
'Osnovnye sdvigi v strukture i razmeshchenii promyshlennosti v Kitae.'
Vestnik Moskovskogo universiteta; seriia 5, geografiia 15, 2 (mart–aprel' 1960), 28–32.

'Basic shifts in the structure and distribution of China's industry.'
Soviet geography 2, 1 (Jan. 1961), 47–54.
Subj 11.3 14.4 ▪ 14

13411 CSU P P4 G1.2 1949–1972
Pan, L. C. (P'an Lü-chieh), 1897–.
'Chemical engineering.' In *Sciences in Communist China*, edited by [Sydney Henry Gould] Sidney H. Gould. [Selective entry]
Washington, D.C.: American Assn. for the Advancement of Science, 1961, 821–840. (AAAS publications, 68)
Subj 14.4 ▪ 36.1

13412 MCH P P4 G1.2 1949–1972
Perkins, Dwight Heald, 1934–.
'Incentives and profits in Chinese industry: The challenge of economics to ideology's machine.'
CS 4, 10 (15 May 1966), 1–10.
Subj 14.4 16.4 ▪ 34.2

13413 CSU P P4 G1.2 1949–1972
Perkins, Dwight Heald, 1934–.
'Industrial planning and management.' In *Economic trends in Communist China*, edited by Alexander Eckstein, Walter Galenson, and Ta-chung Liu. [Selective entry]
Chicago: Aldine, 1968, 597–635.
Subj 14 14.4 ▪ 32 34.2

13414 MCH S P3 G1.2 1949–1972
Perkins, Dwight Heald, 1934–.
Review of *The rate and pattern of industrial growth in Communist China*, by Kang Chao.
EDCC 15, 2 (Jan. 1967), 242–244.
Subj 14.4 71

13415 DLC P P4 G1.2 1949–1972
Petrichenko, Aleksei Maksimovich, and Elena Alekseevna Sukhodol'skaia.

Sovremennoe liteinoe proizvodstvo Kitaia (Modern foundry production in China).
Kiev: Mashgiz (IUzhnoe otd-nie), 1960. 198 p.
Subj 14.4 16.4 ▪ 27 34.2

13416 CSH U P4 G1.2 1949–1972
Po I-po, 1907–. [Tr. erroneously gives author's name as Po I-pao.]
'New trends in the technological revolution.' Tr. of 'Chi shu ko ming ti hsin hsing shih'; *Hung ch'i* 1960, 10 (16 May), 8–17. In *Translations from 'Hung-ch'i' (Red flag) (Peiping, No. 10, 16 May 1960)*, mimeo., compiled by U.S. Joint Publications Research Service. [Selective entry]
Washington, D.C.: JPRS, 28 Sept. 1960, 3–20. (JPRS 3977; MC 17,236/1960)
Subj 14.4 34.2 ▪ 16.4

13417 CSH O P2 G1.2 1949–1972
Po I-po, 1907–.
'The socialist industrialization of China.' In *Socialist industrialization and agricultural collectivization in China*, by Po I-po and Liao Lu-yen. [Analytic entry]
Peking: Foreign Languages Press, 1964, 1–22.
Subj 14 14.4 ▪ 64

13418 MCH P P7 G1.2 1949–1972
Rech, Ernesto.
'Ricerche petrolifere nella Repubblica popolare cinese' (The search for petroleum in the People's Republic of China).
Cina 4 (1958), 120–125.
Subj 14.4

13419 CSU P P3 G1.2 1949–1972
Reichers, Philip D-.
'The electronics industry of China.' In *People's Republic of China: An economic assessment*, compiled by Joint Economic Committee, U.S. Congress. [Selective entry]
Washington, D.C.: U.S. Government Printing Office, 1972, 86–111.
Subj 14.4 ▪ 16.4 24.4

13420 CSU FP P2 G1.2 1949–1972
Richman, Barry Martin, 1936–.
Industrial society in Communist China.
New York: Random House, 1969. 968 p.
Subj 14 14.4 14.6 17 19 64 ▪ 12 12.2 16 16.2 18 34.2 58 61

13421 CSU P P2 G1.2 1949–1972
Satō, Masumi, 1923–.
'The realities and technological trends of China's heavy and chemical industries.' Tr. by Jason G. B. Choi of *Chūgoku no jūkagaku kōgyō no jittai to gijutsu dōkō*; Tokyo: Tairiku mondai kenkyūjo, 1968; 52 p.
CES 4, 3 (Spring 1971), 161–193.
Subj 14.4

13422 CSU U P4 G1.2 1949–1972
Satō, Masumi, 1923–.
'Technological development in China viewed through the electronics industry: An engineer's view.'
DE 9, 3 (Sept. 1971), 315–331.
Subj 14.4 ▪ 14.2 17

13423 DLC U P4 G1.2 1949–1972
Savinov, A- I-.
'Iz praktiki spetsializatsii i kooperirovaniia v proizvodstve zapasnykh chastei i smennogo oborudovaniia v metallurgicheskoi promyshlennosti Kitaiskoi Narodnoi Respubliki' (Specialization and cooperation in manufacturing spare parts and interchangeable equipment in the Chinese metallurgical industry).
Trudy Leningradskogo inzhenerno-ekonomicheskogo instituta 31 (1960), 133–142.
Subj 14.4 ▪ 34.2

13424 CSU P P2 G1.2 1949–1972
Schüller, Arno.
'Die Bedeutung der Geologie beim Aufbau des neuen China' (The significance of geology in the making of New China).
Z. für angewandte Geologie 4, 12 (Dez. 1958), 545–553.
Subj 14.4 ▪ 14.1

13425 CSU FP P5 G1.2 1949–1972
Shih, Joseph Anderson (Shih Ch'eng-chih), 1918–1973.
'Science and technology in China.'
AS 12, 8 (Aug. 1972), 662–675.
Subj 14 14.4 ▪ 16.1 17 62 64

13426 CSU PO P2 G1.2 1949–1972
Sigurdson, Jon-Sture, 1935–.
'China: Re-cycling that pays.'
Läkartidningen; j. of the Swedish Medical Assn. 69, 23 (31 Maj 1972), 3837–3841.
Subj 14.4 ▪ 11.4 14.1 24.4

13427 CSU PO P2 G1.2 1949–1972
Suga, Eiichi. [Tr. erroneously gives author's name as Sakae Suga.]
'The level of China's industrial technology.' Tr. of *Chūgoku no kōgyō gijutsu*; Tokyo: Tairiku mondai kenkyūjo, 1964; 48 p.
CES 4, 3 (Spring 1971), 132–160.
Subj 14 14.4 ▪ 11.4 14.1 62

13428 MCH P P4 G1.2 1949–1972
Šuljmanac, Nedeljko.
'Industrijalizacija Narodne Republike Kine' (Industrialization in the People's Republic of China).
Pregled 8, Part 2, 7/8 (1956), 421–430.
Subj 14.4 ▪ 14 14.6 19

13429 ELB P P4 G1.2 1949–1972
Trifonov, V-.
'Voprosy industrial'nogo razvitiia KNR v gody pervoi piatiletki.'
VE 1958, 7 (iiul'), 82–93.

'Problems of the industrial development of the Chinese People's Republic during the First Five-Year Plan.'
Problems of economics 1, 8 (Dec. 1958), 38–43.
Subj 14 14.4 ▪ 32

13430 CSU P P2 G1.2 1949–1972
Tsao, T. C.
'Electrical engineering.' In *Sciences in Communist China*, edited by [Sydney Henry Gould] Sidney H. Gould. [Selective entry]
Washington, D.C.: American Assn. for the Advancement of Science, 1961, 747–769. (AAAS publications, 68)
Subj 14.4 ▪ 14 14.2

13431 CSU O P3 G1.2 1949–1972
Tsu, Raphael.
'High technology in China.'
Scientific American 227, 6 (Dec. 1972), 13–17.
Subj 14.4 ▪ 17 62

13432 CBU P P2 G1.2 1949–1972
TSzen Ven'-tszin (Tseng Wen-ching).
Sotsialisticheskaia industrializatsiia Kitaia (The socialist industrialization of China). Tr. by IU- A- Pekshev of *Chung-kuo ti she hui chu i kung yeh hua*, rev. ed.; Peking: Jen min ch'u pan she, 1958; 293 p.
Moscow: Gospolitizdat, 1959. 383 p.

The socialist industrialization of Communist China, mimeo. [Partial tr.: p. 140–381 only]
Washington, D.C.: U.S. Joint Publications Research Service, 31 Aug. 1960. 168 p. (JPRS 3800; MC 15,667/1960) [Xerox copyflo available—New York: CCM Information Corp., Research and Microfilm Publications. (Scholarly Book Translation Series, 467)]
Subj 14 14.4 ▪ 11.3 15 16.4 18 19 34.2

13433 CSU U P2 G1.2 1949–1972
Uchida, Genko (Uchida Genkō).
'Technology in China.'
Scientific American 215, 5 (Nov. 1966), 37–45.
Subj 14 14.4 62 ▪ 11.4 12 14.2

13434 MCH U P2 G1.2 1949–1972
Vigier, A-, and M- Levi.
'Le pétrole en Chine' (Oil in China).
Economie et politique 68 (mai 1960), 76–84.
Subj 14.4

13435 CSU P P2 G1.2 1949–1972
Wang, K. P. (Wang Kung-pin), 1919–.
'The mineral resource base of Communist China.' In *An economic profile of Mainland China*, compiled by Joint Economic Committee, U.S. Congress. [Selective entry]
Washington, D.C.: U.S. Government Printing Office, 1967, vol. 1, 167–195. [Reprinted in *An economic profile of Mainland China*, compiled by the agency cited. (Selective entry.) New York: Praeger, 1968, 167–195.]
Subj 14.4 ▪ 11.4 14 14.2 34.2

13436 CSU P P2 G1.2 1949–1972
Wang, K. P. (Wang Kung-pin), 1919–.
'Mining and metallurgy.' In *Sciences in Communist China*, edited by [Sydney Henry Gould] Sidney H. Gould. [Selective entry]
Washington, D.C.: American Assn. for the Advancement of Science, 1961, 687–738. (AAAS publications, 68)
Subj 14.4 ▪ 17 36.1 62

13437 CSU U P2 G1.2 1949–1972
Wang, K. P. (Wang Kung-pin), 1919–.
Rich mineral resources spur Communist China's bid for industrial power.
Washington, D.C.: U.S. Dept. of the Interior, Bureau of Mines, 1960. 35 p. [Special supplement no. 59 to *Mineral trade notes*]
Subj 14.4 ▪ 34.2

13438 CSU S P2 G1.2 1949–1972
Wang, Kung-lee.
'China's mineral industries in 1967: Victims of the Cultural Revolution.'
AS 9, 6 (June 1969), 425–437.
Subj 14.4 ▪ 14 25 35

13439 NIC P P2 G1.2 1949–1972
Wu, Yuan-li (Wu Yüan-li), 1920–.
'Power crisis in Communist China.'
CS 1, 34 (20 June 1962), 1–14. [Reprinted in *This is China: Analyses of Mainland trends and events*, edited by Francis Harper. (Selective entry.) Hong Kong: Dragonfly Books, 1965, 163–184.]
Subj 14 14.4

13440 CSH P P2 G1.2 1949–1972
Wu, Yuan-li (Wu Yüan-li), 1920–, and Hsien C. Ling.
Spatial economy of Communist China: Railway transportation and industrial location in Communist China.
New York: Praeger, 1967. 367 p.
Subj 11.3 14.2 14.4 ▪ 14 14.3

13441 CSU O P5 G5.4 1949–1972
Yang Wei-p'ing.
'Honan industry maintains the leap forward.' Tr. of 'Ch'ih hsü yao chin chung ti Ho-nan sheng kung yeh' (The sustained leap forward of industry in Honan); *Hung ch'i* 1960, 3 (1 Feb.), 25–29. In *Translations from 'Hung-ch'i' (Red flag) No. 3, 1 February 1960, Peiping*, mimeo., compiled by U.S. Joint Publications Research Service. [Selective entry]
Washington, D.C.: JPRS, 15 Apr. 1960, 22–28. (JPRS 3169; MC 7230/1960)
Subj 14.4 ▪ 24.4

13442 CSU P P7 G1.2 1949–1972
Yeh, K. C. (Yeh K'ung-chia), 1924–.
Communist China's petroleum situation.
Santa Monica, Calif.: RAND Corp., 1962. 69 p. (RAND memoranda, RM-3160-PR)
Subj 14.4 ▪ 14.2 16.4

13443 NIC P P2 G1.2 1949–1972
Yeh, K. C. (Yeh K'ung-chia), 1924–.
Electric power development in Mainland China: Prewar and postwar.
Santa Monica, Calif.: RAND Corp., 1956. 119 p. (RAND memoranda, RM-1821)
Subj 14.4 ▪ 14 14.3 16.4

13444 WSU P P2 G1.2 1949–1972
Yeh, K. C. (Yeh K'ung-chia), 1924–.
'Soviet and Communist Chinese industrialization strategies.' In *Soviet and Chinese Communism: Similarities and differences*, edited by Donald Warren Treadgold. [Selective entry]
Seattle: U. of Washington Press, 1967, 327–363.
Subj 11.4 14 14.4 19 ▪ 14.1 18

13445 CSH P P4 G9.4 1949–1972
Yeh, W. A. (Yeh Wan-an).
'Structure and size of manufacturing industry in Taiwan.'
IFC 31, 4 (Apr. 1969), 13–36.
Subj 14.4 ▪ 16.4 34.2

13446 CSU U P5 G1.2 1949–1972
Yen Chi-tz'u.
Development of technical sciences in China during past decade, mimeo. Tr. of 'Shih nien lai Chung-kuo chi shu k'o hsüeh ti fa chan'; *K'o hsüeh t'ung pao* 1959, 18 (26 Sept.), 607–612.
Washington, D.C.: U.S. Joint Publications Research Service, 27 July 1960. 19 p. (JPRS 5105; MC 14,450/1960)
Subj 14.4 62

13447 MAM P P2 G1.2 1949–1972
Yin, Helen (Yin Chang Wan-hung), 1928–.
The industrial statistics reporting system of Communist China, 1949–1958.
Ann Arbor: University Microfilms (Publ. 67-846), 1967. 301 p. (Doctoral dissertation in Economics, Columbia U., 1966)
Subj 12 14.4

13448 CSU P P4 G1.2 1949–1972
Young, G- B- W-.
Mainland China's chemical industry.
Santa Monica, Calif.: RAND Corp., 1965. 12 p. (RAND, memoranda, RM-4504-PR)
Subj 14.4

13449 NIC P P1 G1.2 1949–1972
Young, G- B- W-.
Some remarks on scientific achievements in Communist China.
Santa Monica, Calif.: RAND Corp., 1962. 28 p. (RAND memoranda, RM-3077-PR)
Subj 14.4 16.1 62 ▪ 14 15 17 36.1

13450 CSH O P2 G9.4 1949–1972
Yu, Johnny H. Y.
'Fertilizer industry in Taiwan.'
IFC 32, 5 (Nov. 1969), 21–28.
Subj 14.4 ▪ 14.3 24.1

14.5 State Revenue and Expenditure

國家財政　国家財政

1644-1911

13451 NNC P P1 G1.2 1644–1895
'Fees paid for the Imperial Academy Scholar title, 1821–1850.'
NWSS 5, 12 (21 Mar. 1932), 49, 51–52.
Subj 14.5 17 ▪ 12 16.1

13452 CSH U P2 G1.2 1842–1911
'Ocherk solianogo dela v Kitae' (A note on the salt monopoly in China).
VA 19/22 (sentiabr'–dekabr' 1913), 151–172.
Subj 14 14.4 14.5 ▪ 14.3

13453 NNC S P1 G1.2 1842–1911
'Revenue and expenditure of the Tsung-li Yamen, 1863–1898.'
NWSS 6, 6 (6 Feb. 1933), 25, 27–29.
Subj 14.5

13454 CSU P P1 G8.1 1842–1911
Adshead, Samuel Adrian Miles, 1932–.
'Viceregal government in Szechwan in the Kuang-hsü period, 1875–1909.'
Papers on Far Eastern history 4 (Sept. 1971), 41–52.
Subj 14.5

13455 ELE P P5 G1.3 1842–1895
Beal, Edwin George, Jr., 1913–.
The origin of likin, 1853–1864.
Cambridge: Harvard U., East Asian Research Center, 1958. 201 p. (Harvard East Asian monographs, 6) (Revision of *The origin of likin*, doctoral dissertation in Chinese and Japanese, Columbia U., 1950)
Subj 12 14.3 14.5 16.2 24.5 ▪ 15 16.1 22 24

13456 ELB P P2 G1.2 1644–1911
Chen, Shao-kwan (Ch'en Chao-k'un), 1886–.
The system of taxation in China during the Tsing dynasty, 1644–1911.
New York: Columbia U., Faculty of Political Science, 1914. 118 p. (Columbia studies in history, economics and public law, 59, 2 [whole no. 143]) (Doctoral dissertation in Economics, Columbia U.) [Reprinted—New York: AMS Press, 1970. 118 p.]
Subj 14.3 14.5 ▪ 12.2 14 16.2 34.2

13457 MBU P P3 G1.1 1644–1911
Chen, Wei Ping (Ch'en Wei-p'ing), 1879–.
The development of the Chinese Maritime Customs under the Ch'ing dynasty, 1644–1911.
Unpublished doctoral dissertation in History, Boston U., 1915.
Subj 14.5 ▪ 12.2 14 14.2 14.3 66

13458 ELS P P2 G1.2 1644–1895
Ch'en, Jerome (Ch'en Chih-jang), 1919–.
The state economic policies of the Ch'ing government, 1840–1895.
Unpublished doctoral dissertation in History, U. of London [School of Oriental and African Studies], 1956. 407, 63 p.
Subj 12 14 14.5 66 ▪ 14.3 14.4 15 17

13459 WSU P P2 G1.5 –1911
Chinn, Grace.
The Grand Canal and the collection of grain tribute revenue in the Ch'ing dynasty (1644–1912).
Unpublished masters thesis in Economics, U. of Washington, 1942. 140 p.
Subj 14.2 14.5 ▪ 14 15

13460 NIC P P3 G1.3 1842–1911
Cordier, Henri, 1849–1925.
'Les douanes impériales maritimes chinoises' (The Chinese Imperial Maritime Customs).
TP 2e série 3, 4 (1902), 222–240; 7, 5 (1906), 515–525.
Subj 14.5 ▪ 14.3 66

13461 MCH P P4 G1.1 1842–1895
Delmas, Philippe.
Les douanes impériales chinoises (The Chinese Imperial [Maritime] Customs).
Paris: Chamion, 1902. 171 p.
Subj 14.2 14.3 14.5 ▪ 16.1 17 66 72

13462 NIC P P1 G1.1 1644–1911
Edkins, Joseph, 1823–1905.
The revenue and taxation of the Chinese empire.
Shanghai: Presbyterian Mission Press, 1903. 240 p.
Subj 14.5

13463 GBF P P5 G1.3 1842–1895
Exner, A- H-.
Die Einnahmequellen und der Credit Chinas, nebst Aphorismen über die Deutsch–ost-asiatischen Handelsbeziehungen (China's sources

of revenue and credit, and German–East-Asian trade relations).
Berlin: Asher, 1887. 71 p.
SUBJ 14.5 14.6 ▪ 16.2 24.5

13464 EOB P P3 G1.2 1842–1895
Fairbank, John King, 1907–.
The origin of the Chinese Maritime Customs Service, 1850–58.
Unpublished doctoral dissertation, Oxford U. [Balliol College], 1936. 809 p.
SUBJ 14.3 14.5 ▪ 14.2 66

13465 MCH P P2 G1.1 1644–1911
Forke, Alfred, 1867–1944.
'Das chinesische Finanz- und Steuerwesen' (China's financial and taxation systems).
MSOSB 3 (1900), 165–191; 4 (1901), 1–75.
SUBJ 14.5 14.6 ▪ 14.1 14.3

13466 NIC P P2 G1.3 1842–1911
Hinton, Harold Clendenin, 1924–.
The grain tribute system of China, 1845–1911.
Cambridge: Harvard U., East Asian Research Center, 1956. 163 p. (Harvard East Asian monographs, 2) (Revision of *The grain tribute system of China, 1845–1911: An aspect of the decline of the Ch'ing dynasty*, doctoral dissertation in History, Harvard U., 1951)
SUBJ 14.2 14.5 ▪ 14.3

13467 CSU P P1 G1.2 1644–1842
Hirth, Friedrich, 1845–1927.
'The Hoppo-Book of 1753.'
JRAS-NCB new (2nd) series 17, 1 (1882), 221–235.
SUBJ 14.5

13468 NNC O P3 G1.3 1842–1895
Hirth, Friedrich, 1845–1927.
'Die Verwaltung der chinesischen Seezölle' (The Chinese maritime customs administration). In *Chinesische Studien* (Chinese studies), by F. Hirth. [Selective entry]
Munich: Hirth, 1890, vol. 1, 189–208. [Reprinted from *Oesterreichische Monatsschrift für den Orient?*]
SUBJ 14.5 ▪ 14.3 66

13469 MAU P P2 G1.3 1644–1842
Hoshi Ayao, 1912–.
'The transition from the Ming to the Ch'ing.' Tr. by Mark Elvin of 'Ketsugen: Shindai sōun e no tenkai' (Conclusion: Developments leading to the Ch'ing tribute-rice system); in *Mindai sōun no kenkyū* (Studies on the Ming tribute-rice system); Tokyo: Nihon gakujutsu shinkōkai, 1963, 401–452 [condensed tr.]. In *The Ming tribute grain system*, by Hoshi Ayao. [Sole entry]
Ann Arbor: U. of Michigan, Center for Chinese Studies, 1969, 86–98. (Michigan abstracts of Chinese and Japanese works on Chinese history, 1)
SUBJ 14.2 14.5 ▪ 12 12.2 14.3 16.4 22.2 35

13470 CNY P P4 G1.2 1842–1911
Hou, Hon-chun (Hu Hung-hsün).
Histoire douanière de la Chine de 1842 à 1911 (History of the Chinese customs administration from 1842 to 1911).
Paris: Presses modernes, 1929. 222 p. (Doctoral dissertation, Faculté des lettres, Université de Paris)
SUBJ 14.3 14.5 66 ▪ 12 19

13471 MMT P P2 G1.5 1842–1895
Hsia Nai.
'The land tax in the Yangtse provinces before and after the Taiping Rebellion.' Tr. by E-tu Zen Sun and John DeFrancis of 'T'ai-p'ing t'ien kuo ch'ien hou Ch'ang chiang ko sheng chih t'ien fu wen t'i'; *Ch'ing hua hsüeh pao* 10, 2 (Apr. 1935), 409–474. In *Chinese social history: Translations of selected studies*, edited by E-tu Zen Sun (Sun Jen I-tu) and John DeFrancis. [Selective entry]
Washington, D.C.: American Council of Learned Societies, 1956, 361–382. (ACLS, Studies in Chinese and related civilizations, 7) [Reprinted in *Chinese social history: Translations of selected studies*, edited by E-tu Zen Sun and J. DeFrancis. (Selective entry.) New York: Octagon Books, 1966, 361–382.]
SUBJ 14.1 14.5 25 ▪ 14.6 15 18 32.2

13472 CSU P P1 G1.2 –1644
Liang Fang-chung.
The single-whip method '(I-t'iao-pien fa)' of taxation in China. Tr. by Wang Yü-ch'uan of 'I t'iao pien fa' (The single whip [taxation] method); *Chung-kuo chin tai ching chi shih yen chiu chi k'an* 4, 1 (May 1936), 1–65.
Cambridge: Harvard U., East Asian Research Center, 1956. 71 p. (Harvard East Asian monographs, 1)
SUBJ 14.5 ▪ 24.5 45

13473 NNC P P1 G1.2 1842–1911
Ma Yin-ch'u, 1882–.
Public revenues in China.
Unpublished masters thesis in Political Economics and Finance, Columbia U., 1911. 60 p.
SUBJ 14.5 ▪ 14.1

13474 GMS P P1 G1.2 –1911
Messing, Otto.
'Steuer und Finanzwesen Chinas an Hand der Geschichte' (China's taxation and fiscal system from an historical perspective).
Verhandlungen der Abteilung Berlin-Charlottenburg der Deutschen Kolonialgesellschaft 6, 5 (1901/02), 110–134.
SUBJ 14.5

13475 NNC P P8 G1.3 –1911
Michelsen, Erich.
'Das Dogma von der unerhöhbaren Grundsteuer' (The dogma of the fixed land tax).
DCR 1 (1911), 39–46.
SUBJ 14.1 14.5

13476 NIC P P1 G1.2 1644–1895
Parker, Edward Harper, 1849–1926.
'The financial capacity of China.'
JRAS-CB new (2nd) series 30 (1895/96), 74–101.
SUBJ 14.5 ▪ 16.1

13477 NIC P P2 G1.2 1644–1895
Parker, Edward Harper, 1849–1926.
'The salt revenue of China.'
JRAS-CB new (2nd) series 22, 1 (1887), 67–80.
SUBJ 14.4 14.5

13478 CSH P P2 G1.3 1895–1911
Petelin, I-.
'Finansy Kitaia' (Fiscal affairs in China).
VA 2 (oktiabr' 1909), 69–95.
SUBJ 14.5 ▪ 14.6

13479 MCH P P1 G7.3 1842–1895
Pong, David Bertram Pak-Tang (P'ang Pai-t'eng), 1938–.
'The income and military expenditure of Kiangsi province in the last years (1860–1864) of the Taiping Rebellion.'
JAS 26, 1 (Nov. 1966), 49–65.
SUBJ 14.5 15

13480 NNP PO P1 G1.2 1842–1895
Putiata, D- V-.
'Kitaiskii biudzhet' (The Chinese budget).
Sbornik geograficheskikh, topograficheskikh i statisticheskikh materialov po Azii 42 (1890), 145–159.
SUBJ 14.5

13481 MCY P P1 G1.1 1842–1911
Stanley, Charles Johnson, 1914–.
'Chinese finance from 1852 to 1908.'
PC 3 (May 1949), 1–23.
SUBJ 14.5 ▪ 14.6

13482 MCH P P2 G1.2 1644–1911
Wang, Yeh-chien, 1930–.
China's land taxation in the late Ch'ing.
Unpublished doctoral dissertation in History and Far Eastern Languages, Harvard U., 1969. 11, 440 p.
SUBJ 14 14.1 14.5 ▪ 11 11.2 14.3 16.1

13483 CSU P P1 G1.2 1644–1911
Wang, Yeh-chien, 1930–.
'The fiscal importance of the land tax during the Ch'ing period.'
JAS 30, 4 (Aug. 1971), 829–842. [For fuller treatment, see entry 13482.]
SUBJ 14.1 14.5

13484 NNC P P2 G1.2 –1911
Wang Yü-ch'üan, 1911–.
'The rise of land tax and the fall of dynasties in Chinese history.'
PA 9, 2 (June 1936), 201–220. [Reprinted in *Modern China: An interpretive anthology*, edited by Joseph Richmond Levenson. (Selective entry.) London: Macmillan, 1971, 130–146.]
SUBJ 14.5 16.1 16.3 ▪ 12 14.1 22.2 45

13485 MCH P P1 G1.1 1842–1911
Wright, Stanley Fowler, 1873–?
Hart and the Chinese customs.
Belfast: William Mullan, 1950. 16, 949 p.
SUBJ 14.5 ▪ 32.2 66

13486 MCH P P1 G1.2 1842–1895
Wu, James T. K.
'The impact of the Taiping Rebellion upon the Manchu fiscal system.'
PHR 19, 3 (Aug. 1950), 265–276.
SUBJ 14.1 14.5 32.2 ▪ 12.1 14 14.6 16.1

1644-1949

13487 NNC P P1 G1.2 1842–1928
Aiaks, ———.
'Tamozhennyi vopros v Kitae' (The customs question in China).
MKhMP 1929, 6 (iiun'), 78–88; 1929, 7 (iiul'), 86–99.
SUBJ 14 14.3 14.5 ▪ 66

13488 MCH U P2 G1.2 1895–1928
Al'skii, M-.
'Gosudarstvennaia sistema priamykh nalogov v Kitae' (The state system of direct taxation in China).
NV 18 (1927), 40–63.
SUBJ 14.5

13489 NNC P P3 G1.2 1644–1928
Buss, Claude Albert, 1903–.
The relation of tariff autonomy to the political situation in China.
Unpublished doctoral dissertation in History, U. of Pennsylvania, 1927. 141 p.
SUBJ 14.5 ▪ 12.2 14.2 15 25 64 66

13490 NNC P P1 G1.2 1842–1928
Chang, Yü-chüan (Chang Yü-ch'üan), 1880–.
'History of tariff revision in China.'
THJ 4, 3 (Feb. 1919), 1–28.
SUBJ 14.5

13491 ICU PO P1 G1.2 –1949
Chau, Yau Pik (Chou Yu-pi), 1905–.
The taxation reforms of the Chinese national government in the decade 1927–1937.
Unpublished doctoral dissertation in Economics, U. of Chicago, 1942. 11, 469 p.
SUBJ 12.2 14.5 ▪ 14 14.3 22.2 45

13492 NNC P P8 G1.2 1644–1949
Chekhutov, Andrei Ivanovich, 1930–.
'Osobennosti pozemel'nogo oblozheniia v Kitae v kontse XIX – nachale XX v.' (Features of the Chinese land tax in the late nineteenth and the early twentieth centuries).
KSINA 55 (1962), 84–93.
SUBJ 14.1 14.5

13493 NNC P P2 G1.2 1842–1928
Chen Han-seng (Ch'en Han-sheng), 1897–.
'The burdens of the Chinese peasantry: A resume of China's finances from 1855 to 1928.' Tr. of 'Chung-kuo nung min tan fu ti fu shui' (The tax burdens borne by the Chinese peasantry); *Tung fang tsa chih* (Shanghai) 25, 19 (10 Oct. 1928), 9–28.
PA 2, 10 (Oct. 1929), 644–658.
SUBJ 14.5 ▪ 14 14.6 15

13494 NNC P P2 G1.1 –1928
Chen, Lucian H.
The tax systems of China.
Unpublished masters thesis in Economics, Columbia U., 1928. 11, 77 p.
SUBJ 14.5 ▪ 14.1

13495 MCH PO P2 G1.2 1895–1928
Denby, Charles, 1830–1904.
'The national debt of China: Its origin and its security.'
AAAPSS 68 (Nov. 1916), 55–70.
SUBJ 14.5 ▪ 14.2

13496 MCH P P1 G1.2 –1949
Dung, Bi (Tung Pi), 1909–.
Eine Studie über die chinesische Finanzwirtschaft, mit besonderer Berücksichtigung ihrer gegenwärtigen Neuordnung (A study of China's fiscal economy, with special attention to present reform).
Hamburg: The author, 1934. 173 p. (Doctoral dissertation, Rechts- und staatswissenschaftliche Fakultät, Universität Hamburg)
SUBJ 14.5 ▪ 45

13497 MCH P P4 G1.1 1842–1928
Es, Willem Johan Louis van, 1886–1943.
'De omwenteling in China: Hare oorzaken en hunne opheffing' (The revolution in China: Its causes and its suppression).
Koloniaal tijdschrift 14, 3 (Mei 1925), 225–252; 14, 4 (Juli 1925), 378–422.
SUBJ 14.2 14.5 14.6 15 ▪ 12 14.4

13498 NNC S P1 G1.2 –1928
Foo, Chuen-poot (Fu Ch'uan-po).
Etude historique et critique sur le régime douanier de la Chine (An historical and critical study of the customs system in China).
Paris: Lib. Geuthner, 1930. 155 p. (Institut franco-chinois de Lyon, Etudes et documents, 8) (Doctoral dissertation, Faculté de droit, Université de Lyon)
SUBJ 14.5 ▪ 14 14.6

13499 GMS P P1 G1.2 1895–1928
Foth, Werner, 1892–.
Der politische Kampf im Fernen Osten und Chinas finanzielle Schwäche (The political struggle in the Far East and China's fiscal weakness).
Gotha: F. A. Perthes, 1919. 118 p. (Doctoral dissertation, Philosophische Fakultät, Universität Berlin)
SUBJ 14.5

13500 CSH PO P2 G2.0 1895–1928
Gerasimov, A- E-.
Kitaiskie nalogi v severnoi Man'chzhurii (Chinese taxes in northern Manchuria).
Harbin: Tip. Doma trudiashchikhsia, 1923. 131 p.
SUBJ 12 12.2 14 14.5 24.5 ▪ 16.2

13501 NNC S P1 G1.2 1895–1949
[Grajdanzev, Andrew Jonah?] A- I- Grazhdantsev, 1899–.
'Finansy Kitaia' (Fiscal affairs in China).
BSB 1, 4 (1932), 69–93.
SUBJ 14.5 14.6 ▪ 12 72

13502 NNC P P1 G1.1 1842–1928
Huang, Feng-hua, 1894–.
Public debts in China.
New York: Columbia U., Faculty of Political Science, 1919. 105 p. (Columbia studies in history, economics and public law, 85, 2 [whole no. 197]) (Doctoral dissertation, Faculty of Political Science, Columbia U.) [Reprinted—New York: AMS Press, 1969. 105 p.]
SUBJ 14.5 ▪ 12 14 14.6 66

13503 NNC P P2 G1.2 –1928
Huang, Han-liang, 1893–.
The land tax in China.
New York: Columbia U., Faculty of Political Science, 1918. 181 p. (Columbia studies in history, economics and public law, 80, 3 [whole no. 187]) (Doctoral dissertation in Economics, Columbia U.) [Reprinted—New York: AMS Press, 1969. 181 p.]
SUBJ 14.1 14.5 ▪ 35

13504 CSH S P4 G1.2 1842–1949
IAkshin, A- A- (A. A. Yakshin).
'Kitaiskie morskie tamozhni i tamozhni Man'chzhu-go.'
VM 1933, 2/3 (15 fevralia), 1–25.
'Chinese maritime customs and the Manchoukuo customs.' [Abridged tr.]
VM 1933, 2/3, 1–8 [s.p.].
SUBJ 14.5 ▪ 12.2 14.2 14.3 24.3

13505 CSU O P4 G1.1 1842–1928
King, Paul Henry, 1853–1938.
In the Chinese customs service: A personal record of forty-seven years.
London: Unwin, 1924. 303 p.
SUBJ 14.5 66 ▪ 14.3 15 32.2

13506 FPL P P3 G1.2 1895–1928
Kou, Cheou-hi (Ku Shou-hsi).
L'impôt sur les propriétés bâties en Chine (The tax on improved properties in China).
Shanghai: Impr. de l'Orphelinat de T'ou-sè-wè, 1920. 78 p. (Doctoral dissertation, Université l'Aurore)
SUBJ 14.5 ▪ 12.2 45

13507 MCH P P1 G1.2 1644–1949
Lee, Chou-ying (Li Ch'ao-ying), 1901–.
The system of Chinese public finance: A comparative study.
London: P. S. King, 1936. 13, 256 p. (Doctoral dissertation, U. of London [London School of Economics and Political Science], 1935)
SUBJ 14.5 ▪ 12.2 14.6

13508 NNC P P2 G1.2 1644–1928
Li, Chuan Shih (Li Ch'üan-shih), 1895–.
Central and local finance in China: A study of the fiscal relations between the central, the provincial, and the local governments.
New York: Columbia U., Faculty of Political Science, 1922. 187 p. (Columbia studies in history, economics and public law, 99, 2 [whole no. 226]) (Doctoral dissertation in Political Science, Columbia U.) [Reprinted—New York: AMS Press, 1969. 187 p.]
SUBJ 14 14.5 ▪ 12.2 24.5 32

13509 CSU P P1 G1.2 1842–1949
Liu, S. Y.
'China's debts and their readjustment.'
CEJ 5, 3 (Sept. 1929), 735–749.
SUBJ 14.5

13510 MCH S P1 G1.2 1842–1928
Long, Chao-kang (Lung Shao-k'ang).
Etude critique sur la dette publique de la Chine (A critical study of China's public debt).
Paris: Jouve, 1918. 135 p. (Doctoral dissertation, Faculté de droit, Université de Paris)
SUBJ 14.5 ▪ 14.6

13511 MCH P P2 G1.2 –1928
Shaw, Kinn-wei (Shou Ching-wei), 1891–.
Democracy and finance in China: A study in the development of fiscal systems and ideas.
New York: Columbia U., Faculty of Political Science, 1926. 217 p. (Columbia studies in history, economics and public law, 282) (Doctoral dissertation in Economics, Columbia U.) [Reprinted—New York: AMS Press, 1971. 217 p.]
SUBJ 12 14 14.5 64 ▪ 12.2 14.1 14.6 62 66

13512 CSU P P2 G2.0 1895–1949
Shiomi, Saburo (Shiomi Saburō), 1895–.
'The Japanese taxation system in south Manchuria.'

KUER 6, 1 (July 1931), 29–57.
Subj 14.5 ▪ 22 24.5

13513 MCH P P4 G 1.2 1644–1928
Siao, Stéphane (Hsiao Tzu-feng).
Les régimes douaniers de la Chine (The Chinese customs administration).
Paris: Bossuet, 1931. 216 p. (Doctoral dissertation in Faculté de droit, Université de Caen)
Subj 14.5 ▪ 66

13514 CSH O P8 G 2.0 1895–1928
Surin, Vladimir Ivanovich.
'Sistema nalogov na les v Man'chzhurii' (The system of taxing timber in Manchuria). [With English abstract]
VM 1930, 6, 54–58.
Subj 14.5 ▪ 14.1

13515 NNC P P1 G 1.2 –1928
T'ang, Chung-tzu, Kuo-shu Wong, Chi-kwang Yen, et al.
'Salt administration in China.'
THJ 4, 7 (June 1919), 33–90; 5, 2 (Feb. 1920), 115–161.
Subj 12 14.5 ▪ 14

13516 MCH PO P2 G 1.2 –1949
Tao, Alfred C. (T'ao Chieh-ch'ing), 1911–1960.
A study of the tax structure in China, with some recommendations for the post-war period.
Unpublished doctoral dissertation in Economics, Harvard U., 1946. 159 p.
Subj 14 14.5 ▪ 14.1 14.6

13517 MCH P P1 G 1.1 1842–1949
Tay, Ming-Chung (Tai Ming-chung), 1914–.
Das Finanz- und Steuerwesen Chinas (Taxation and the fiscal system in China).
Jena: Gustav Fischer, 1940. 96 p. (Wirtschaftshochschule Berlin, Institut für Finanzwesen, Forschungen zur Finanzwissenschaft, 4) (Doctoral dissertation, Rechts- und staatswissenschaftliche Fakultät, Universität Berlin)
Subj 14.5 14.6 ▪ 14

13518 FPN P P1 G 1.2 1644–1928
Tchéou, Jeungens (Chou Hung-chün).
Des dettes publiques chinoises (China's public debts).
Lyons: Bosc et Riou, 1927. 170 p. (Doctoral dissertation, Faculté de droit, Université de Paris)
Subj 14 14.3 14.5 ▪ 14.6

13519 MCH P P1 G 1.2 1644–1928
Ting, Tso-chao (Ting Tso-shao).
La douane chinoise (The Chinese customs).
Paris: Jouve, 1931. 214 p. (Doctoral dissertation, Faculté de droit, Université de Paris)
Subj 14.5 ▪ 66

13520 MCH P P2 G 1.2 1842–1928
Wagel, Srinivas Ram.
Finance in China.
Shanghai: North-China Daily News and Herald, 1914. 503 p.
Subj 14 14.2 14.5 14.6 ▪ 16 18 34.2 34.3 36.4 66

13521 MCH PO P3 G 1.3 1842–1949
Wright, Stanley Fowler, 1873–?
China's struggle for tariff autonomy, 1843–1938.
Shanghai: Kelly and Walsh, 1938. 11, 775 p. [Reprinted—Taipei: Ch'eng-wen, 1966. 11, 775 p.]
Subj 14.5 66 ▪ 12.2 14.3

13522 CSH P P2 G 7.3 1842–1928
Wright, Stanley Fowler, 1873–?
Kiangsi native trade and its taxation.
Shanghai: ——, 1920. 203, 74 & 13 p.
Subj 14.3 14.5 24 24.5 ▪ 22.2 24.2 24.4

13523 MCH P P1 G 1.2 –1928
Yin Wen-ching.
Le système fiscal de la Chine (China's fiscal system).
Paris: Montparnasse et Persan-Beaumont, 1929. 212 p. (Doctoral dissertation, Faculté de droit, Université de Paris)
Subj 14.3 14.5 ▪ 12.2 14.6 66

1911-1949

13524 NNC P P1 G 1.3 1928–1949
'Monthly revenue and expenditure of 12 provinces in China, June, 1932.'
NWSS 6, 23 (5 June 1933), 112, 114–115.
Subj 14.5

13525 NNC P P3 G 5.1 1911–1949
'National and local taxes in Peiping.'
NWSS 5, 47 (21 Nov. 1932), 213, 215–216.
Subj 14.5 24.5

13526 NNC P P1 G 1.2 1911–1928
'Per capita burden of taxation and public debts in China.'
NWSS 2, 3 (1929), 1, 4.
Subj 14.5

13527 NNC P P2 G 1.3 1911–1928
'Provincial debts in China, 1928.'
NWSS 5, 46 (14 Nov. 1932), 209, 211–212.
Subj 14.5

13528 NNC P P1 G 1.2 1928–1949
'Revenue and expenditure of the national government, 1931 and 1932.'
NWSS 6, 15 (10 Apr. 1933), 68, 70–71.
Subj 14.5

13529 CSU P P3 G 1.3 1911–1949
'Special and local public loans.'
CEJ 13, 5 (Nov. 1933), 493–514.
Subj 14.5 24.5

13530 NNC P P1 G 1.2 1911–1928
'Statistics on the expenditures of the Nationalist government, 1927–1928.'
NWSS 2, 7 (27 May 1929), 1, 4.
Subj 14.5 15

13531 NNC P P2 G 1.2 1911–1928
Al'skii, M-.
'Nalogovaia sistema Kitaiskoi Respubliki i ee vliianie na krest'ianstvo' (The taxation system of the Republic of China and its impact on the peasantry).
Na agrarnom fronte 1926, 9 (oktiabr'), 74–80.
Subj 14.5 ▪ 14.1 16.3 18

13532 MCH P P4 G 1.2 1911–1949
Arkus, R- S-.
'Tamozhennaia politika Kitaia' (Chinese customs policy). In *Tamozhennaia politika stran Vostoka* (Customs policy of Oriental countries), compiled by Vsesoiuznaia torgovaia palata. [Sole entry]
Moscow: Vneshtorgizdat, 1933, 7–91.
Subj 12 14.3 14.5 66

13533 NNC P P2 G 1.2 1911–1949
Chang, C. M. (Chang Ch'un-ming), 1904–.
'Local government expenditure in China.'
MBEC 7, 6 (June 1934), 233–247.
Subj 14.5 ▪ 24.6

13534 MCH S P8 G 1.2 1928–1949
Chekhutov, Andrei Ivanovich, 1930–.
'Nalogovoe ograblenie krest'ianstva v gomin'danovskom Kitae (1927–1949 gg.)' (Plunder of the peasantry through taxation in Kuomintang China, 1927–1949). [With English abstract]
PV 1960, 3, 118–128.
Subj 14.5

13535 MCH P P2 G 1.2 1911–1949
Chow, Liang-dong (Chou Liang-tung).
L'impôt du sel en Chine (The salt tax in China).
Nancy: Thomas, 1936. 119 p. (Doctoral dissertation, Faculté de droit, Université de Nancy)
Subj 12.2 14 14.5 ▪ 14.3 14.4 14.6 72

13536 MCH P P1 G 1.2 1911–1928
Chu Pakong (Chu Po-k'ang).
Der Staatshaushalt und das Finanzsystem Chinas (The budget and financial system of China).
Leipzig: Hans Buske, 1937. 133 p. (Frankfurter wirtschaftswissenschaftliche Studien, 2) (Doctoral dissertation, Wirtschafts- und sozialwissenschaftliche Fakultät, Universität Frankfurt a.M.)
Subj 14.5 14.6 ▪ 14 16

13537 CSU FP P4 G 5.1 1911–1949
Feng, H. T. (Feng Hua-te).
'Local government expenditures in Hopei.'
MBEC 7, 12 (Dec. 1934), 507–512. [For a later Chinese version, see Feng Hua-te, 'Ho-pei sheng hsien ts'ai cheng chih ch'u chih fen hsi' (Analysis of the county administration expenditures in Hopei); in *Chung-kuo ching chi yen chiu* (Studies on the Chinese economy), edited by Fang Hsien-t'ing (H. D. Fong); Changsha: Shang wu yin shu kuan, 1938, vol. 2, 1039–1095.]
Subj 14.5 ▪ 17 24 25 28 32.1

13538 DCK O P2 G 8.1 1911–1928
[Gimbel, Carl Wilhelm] Keng Pulu, pseud., 1881–1946.
Røvere og soldater (Robbers and soldiers).
Aarhus, Denmark: Unges forlag, 1931. 160 p.
Subj 12 14 14.3 14.5 15 25 ▪ 24.2

13539 MSW P P3 G 1.2 1911–1928
Grant, Jonathan Stephens.
Financial administration in the early Republic: A perspective on the Yuan Shih-k'ai presidency.

Unpublished masters thesis in Asian Studies, Washington U., 1968. 82 p.
SUBJ 12 14.5 14.6 ▪ 16.1

13540 NNC P P2 G6.3 1928–1949
Ho, Franklin L. (Ho Lien), 1897–.
'Land tax in Chekiang.'
MBEC 7, 1 (Jan. 1934), 1–14.
SUBJ 14.5 ▪ 24.1

13541 CSH P P7 G7.3 1928–1949
Hsü, King-yi.
'Agrarian policies of the PGCSR [Provisional Central Government of the Chinese Soviet Republic]: Extraction of rural resources in the Kiangsi Soviet, 1931–34.'
IS 9, 2 (Nov. 1972), 35–47. [For fuller treatment, see entry 16639.]
SUBJ 14.5 24.1 ▪ 12.1 14.6

13542 NNC PO P2 G1.2 1911–1928
Jacobs, Joseph E-, 1893?–.
Investigation of likin and other forms of internal taxation in China.
Washington, D.C.: U.S. Government Printing Office, 1925. 82 p. (Dept. of State, Division of Publication series D, 82; China, 39)
SUBJ 14.3 14.5

13543 DLC P P1 G1.2 1911–1949
Kann, Eduard, 1880–1962.
The history of China's internal loan issues.
Shanghai: Finance and Commerce, 1934. 104 p.
SUBJ 14.5 ▪ 14.6

13544 NNC PO P2 G6.3 1928–1949
Klepper, Otto, and Kurt Bloch, 1908–.
'Local financial administration in Chekiang: Report B of the Report of the economic and financial situation of Chekiang province, 1934.' In *Annexes to the Report to the Council of the League of Nations of its technical delegate on his mission in China from date of appointment until April 1, 1934, Annex 5.* [Selective entry]
Shanghai: North-China Daily News and Herald, 1934, 143–163.
SUBJ 12 14.5

13545 CBU P P1 G1.2 1928–1949
Kukhtin, K- V-.
'Biudzhet Kitaia' (China's budget).
VM 1933, 18/19 (15 oktiabria), 89–100.
SUBJ 14.5

13546 CSU S P1 G1.2 1911–1949
Li Pao Chen.
Income tax in China, mimeo.
Tientsin: Hautes études; Shanghai: Université l'Aurore, 1937. 105, 15 p. (Institut des hautes études industrielles et commerciales, Faculty of Commerce, Economic studies, 7)
SUBJ 14.5 ▪ 14.6

13547 CSU P P1 G1.2 1911–1928
Lieu, D. K. (Liu Ta-chün), 1891–1962.
'Consolidation of Chinese unsecured loans.'
CSPSR 7, 3 (July 1922 [i.e., 1923]), 125–153.
SUBJ 14.5

13548 CSU P P2 G1.4 1928–1949
Lindsay, Michael Francis Morris, 1909–.
'The taxation system of the Shansi-Chahar-Hopei border region, 1938–1945.'
CQ 42 (Apr.–June 1970), 1–15.
SUBJ 12.2 14.5 ▪ 12.1 14.1 14.6 15 16 45

13549 MAM P P2 G1.2 1928–1949
Mao, Cho-ting (Mao Cho-t'ing), 1926–.
Taxation and accelerated industrialization, with special reference to the Chinese tax system during 1928–1936.
Ann Arbor: University Microfilms (Publ. 10,308), 1954. 347 p. (Doctoral dissertation in Economics, Northwestern U.)
SUBJ 14 14.5 ▪ 14.4

13550 CSU P P2 G1.2 1928–1949
[Mao, Cho-ting] James C. T. Mao (Mao Cho-t'ing), 1926–.
'Taxation in China, 1928–1936.'
Papers of the Michigan Academy of Science, Arts, and Letters 51 (1966), 289–297.
SUBJ 14.5 ▪ 14 14.1

13551 CSH P P1 G1.3 1928–1949
Meng, C. Y. W.
'Chinas Finanzen im Kriege' (Fiscal affairs in wartime China).
Das neue China 6, 45 (Okt. 1940), 812–824.
SUBJ 14.5 14.6

13552 GMS O P4 G1.2 1911–1928
Otte, Friedrich W- K-.
'Die Finanzwirtschaft, mit besonderer Berücksichtigung des Zollwesens' (The fiscal economy, with special attention to the customs system). In *China: Wirtschaft und Wirtschaftsgrundlagen* (The economy and economic foundations of China), edited by Josef Hellauer. [Selective entry]
Berlin: de Gruyter (Vereinigung wissenschaftlicher Verleger), 1921, 128–147.
SUBJ 14.5

13553 CSH PO P2 G1.2 1911–1928
Otte, Friedrich W- K-.
'Notes on the Chinese native customs system.'
CEM 3, 2 (Feb. 1926), 61–71.
SUBJ 14.5

13554 CSU U P3 G1.1 1911–1949
P. A. H.
'The Chinese Maritime Customs: A retrospective survey.'
World today 5, 12 (Dec. 1949), 528–537.
SUBJ 14.5 66

13555 NNC P P1 G1.2 1928–1949
Paauw, Douglas Seymour, 1921–.
'Chinese national expenditure during the Nanking period.'
FEQ 12, 1 (Nov. 1952), 3–26. [For fuller version, see entry 13556.]
SUBJ 14 14.5 15

13556 MCH P P1 G1.2 1928–1949
Paauw, Douglas Seymour, 1921–.
Chinese public finance during the Nanking Government period.
Unpublished doctoral dissertation in Economics, Harvard U., 1950. 389, 21 p.
SUBJ 14 14.5 ▪ 14.6

13557 CSH P P1 G2.0 1911–1949
Pogrebetskii, Aleksandr I-.
'Finansovye meropriiatiia Man'chzhurii' (Fiscal measures in Manchuria). [With English abstract]
VM 1932, 4, 33–43.
SUBJ 14.5 14.6 ▪ 12

13558 CSH P P2 G2.2 1911–1928
Setnitskii, N- A-.
'Mestnye finansy Girinskoi provintsii' (Fiscal affairs of Kirin province).
Izvestiia IUridicheskogo fakul'teta v g. Kharbine 6 (1928), 319–354.
SUBJ 14.5

13559 CBU P P2 G2.0 1928–1949
Setnitskii, N- A-.
'Nalogi i poshliny v Man'chzhurii' (Taxes and customs duties in Manchuria).
VM 1933, 18/19 (15 oktiabria), 52–74.
SUBJ 14 14.5

13560 CBU P P1 G2.0 1928–1949
Setnitskii, N- A-.
'Nalogovaia politika Man'chzhu-go' (Taxation policy in Manchoukuo). [With English abstract at end of issue]
VM 1933, 20 (1 noiabria), 13–22.
SUBJ 14.5 ▪ 14

13561 MCH P P2 G1.2 1911–1949
Shiomi, Saburo (Shiomi Saburō), 1895–.
'The taxation system of China.' Tr. of 'Shina no sozei seido'; *Tōa jimbun gakuhō* 2, 2 (July 1942), 1–25. [Tr. inferred]
KUER 17, 4 (Oct. 1942), 1–26.
SUBJ 14.5 ▪ 12.2 14

13562 MCH PO P4 G1.2 1911–1949
Shtein, Viktor Moritsevich, 1890–1964.
'Finansovoe polozhenie nankinskogo pravitel'stva' (The financial situation of the Nanking government).
Vestnik finansov 1929, 10 (oktiabr'), 85–96.
SUBJ 14.5

13563 NNC PO P1 G1.2 1911–1928
Shtein, Viktor Moritsevich, 1890–1964.
Ocherki finansovogo krizisa v Kitae (Notes on China's fiscal crisis).
Moscow: Gosizdat, 1928. 350 p.
SUBJ 14.5 ▪ 14.6

13564 CBU P P1 G2.0 1928–1949
Siiakin, N- D-.
'Biudzhet Man'chzhu-go' (The budget of Manchoukuo). [With English abstract at end of issue]
VM 1933, 18/19 (15 oktiabria), 15–35.
SUBJ 14.5 ▪ 14

13565 MCH PO P1 G1.2 1928–1949
Soong, T. V. (Sung Tse-wen), 1891–1971.
The financial situation in China and Japan.
Geneva: Press Bureau of the Chinese Delegation [to the League of Nations], 1933. 44 p. [Reprinted from *Manchester guardian.*]
SUBJ 14.5 ▪ 14 14.3 14.6

13566 NNC O P2 G1.3 1928–1949
Spencer, Joseph Earle, 1907–.
'Salt in China.'
GR 25, 3 (July 1935), 353–366.
SUBJ 14.5 ▪ 14.2 14.3 24.4 24.5

13567 NNC U P1 G1.2 1928–1949
Tsao Lien-en (Ts'ao Lien-en).
'The income tax and its introduction into China.'
IB 2, 5 (21 Oct. 1936), 75–96.
SUBJ 14.5 ▪ 16 18

13568 CBU P P1 G2.0 1911–1949
Uzelkov, B- P-.
'Biudzhet man'chzhurskikh provintsial'nykh vlastei do 1931 g.' (The budget of the Manchurian provincial authorities to 1931).
VM 1933, 18/19 (15 oktiabria), 1–14.
SUBJ 14.5

13569 MCY O P4 G1.2 1911–1928
Willoughby, William Franklin, 1867–1945.
'Memorandum on the adjustment of the financial relations between the central government, the provinces and the local governing bodies.'
CSPSR 2, 3 (Sept. 1917), 26–37.
SUBJ 14.5

13570 MCY P P1 G1.2 1911–1949
Wright, Stanley Fowler, 1873–?
China's customs revenue since the Revolution of 1911.
Shanghai: Ts'ai cheng pu kuan wu shu, T'ung chi shih, 1935. 674 p. [Reprinted—New York: AMS Press, 1972. 674 p.]
SUBJ 14.5 14.6 ▪ 14 14.3 66

13571 CSH PO P2 G1.1 1928–1949
Young, Arthur Nichols, 1890–.
'China's fiscal transformation, 1927–1937' [with comments by Ta-chung Liu]. In *The strenuous decade: China's nation-building efforts, 1927–1937*, edited by Paul K. T. Sih (Hsüeh Kuang-ch'ien). [Selective entry]
Jamaica, N.Y.: St. John's U. Press, 1970, 83–128.
SUBJ 14 14.5 14.6 ▪ 12 12.2

13572 CBU P P1 G1.2 1911–1949
Yu Tsung-fan (Yü Tsung-fan).
L'impôt foncier en Chine depuis 1912 (The land tax in China since 1912).
Paris: Delalain, 1939. 104 p. (Doctoral dissertation, Faculté des lettres, Université de Paris)
SUBJ 12.1 14.1 14.5

1911-1972
(including 1644-1972)

13573 FPN S P1 G1.1 1928–1972
Chang-Ho Chen Hwei (Chang Ho Chen-hui).
L'impôt sur le revenu en Chine (Income tax in China).
Unpublished doctoral dissertation, Faculté de droit, Université de Paris, 1958. 202 p.
SUBJ 14.5

13574 WMU P P2 G1.1 –1972
Sun, I-shuan (Sun I-hsüan), 1920–.
Salt taxation in China.
Unpublished doctoral dissertation in Economics, U. of Wisconsin, 1953. 230 p.
SUBJ 14.3 14.4 14.5 ▪ 11.2 34.2

1949-1972

13575 NNC PO P2 G1.2 1949–1972
Barnett, Arthur Doak, 1921–.
'Economic development in Communist China: Finance and capital investment.'
AUFS-EAS 3, 7 (1 July 1954), 1–28. [Reprinted as 'Financing development.' In *Communist China: The early years, 1949–55*, by A. D. Barnett. (Selective entry.) New York: Praeger, 1964, 210–233.]
SUBJ 14 14.5 ▪ 14.3 14.6 18

13576 NNC P P1 G1.2 1949–1972
Borisov, S-.
'Biudzhet i nalogovaia sistema KNR' (The budget and taxation system of the People's Republic of China). In *Finansy i kredit v stranakh narodnoi demokratii* (Finance and credit in the people's democracies), compiled by Nauchno-issledovatel'skii finansovyi institut. [Sole entry]
Moscow: Gosfinizdat, 1954, 119–159.
SUBJ 14.5

13577 NNC P P2 G1.2 1949–1972
Butakov, D- D-, et al.
'Finansy Kitaiskoi Narodnoi Respubliki' (Fiscal administration in the People's Republic of China). In *Finansy stran narodnoi demokratii* (Fiscal administration in the people's democracies), by D. D. Butakov et al. [Sole entry]
Moscow: Gosfinizdat, 1959, 196–283.
SUBJ 14.5

13578 NNC P P1 G1.2 1949–1972
Chekhutov, Andrei Ivanovich, 1930–.
'Biudzhet Kitaiskoi Narodnoi Respubliki za 1950–1957 gg.' (The budgets of the People's Republic of China, 1950–1957).
SK 1958, 1, 124–134.
SUBJ 14.5

13579 NNC P P2 G1.2 1949–1972
Chekhutov, Andrei Ivanovich, 1930–.
Nalogovaia sistema Kitaiskoi Narodnoi Respubliki.
Moscow: Izd-vo vost. lit-ry, 1962. 204 p.
The tax system in the People's Republic of China, mimeo.
Washington, D.C.: U.S. Joint Publications Research Service, 15 Feb. 1963. 204 p. (JPRS 17,675; MC 6758/1963)
SUBJ 14 14.5 ▪ 14.1 14.4 16 16.3

13580 NNC P P1 G1.2 1949–1972
Chekhutov, Andrei Ivanovich, 1930–.
'Rol' gosudarstvennogo biudzheta KNR v finansirovanii sotsialisticheskogo stroitel'stva' (The role of the state budget in financing socialist construction in the People's Republic of China).
KSINA 49 (1961), 69–85.
SUBJ 14 14.5 ▪ 14.4 14.6 17

13581 MAM P P1 G1.2 1949–1972
Chen, Fu Tung (Ch'en Fu-tung), 1931–.
National budgeting in Communist China, 1950–1956.
Ann Arbor: University Microfilms (Publ. 69-13,896), 1969. 198 p. (Doctoral dissertation in Economics, U. of Alabama)
SUBJ 14.5

13582 NNC P P2 G1.2 1949–1972
Chen Yuan-huai (Ch'en Yüan-huai).
'Finance.' Tr. of '1955 nien Chung kung ti ts'ai cheng' (Fiscal administration in Communist China, 1955); *Tsu kuo chou k'an* 159 (16 Jan. 1956), 12–14. In *Communist China, 1955*, edited by Union Research Institute. [Selective entry]
Hong Kong: Union Research Institute, 1956, 71–80.
SUBJ 14.5

13583 NNC P P2 G1.2 1949–1972
Cheng Chu-yuan (Cheng Chu-yüan), 1927–.
'Finance.' Tr. of '1956 nien Chung kung ti ts'ai cheng' (Fiscal administration in Communist China, 1956); *Tsu kuo chou k'an* 214/215 (11 Feb. 1957), 10–14. In *Communist China, 1956*, edited by Union Research Institute. [Selective entry]
Hong Kong: Union Research Institute, 1957, 31–53.
SUBJ 14.5 ▪ 14 14.6

13584 MCH P P2 G1.2 1949–1972
Cheng, Tong-Yung, 1934–.
Finanzpolitik und Kapitalbildung in der Planwirtschaft: Die Finanzierung der Industrialisierung Kontinentalchinas als Beispiel (Fiscal policy and capital formation in the planned economy: Financing the industrialization of Mainland China as an example).
Unpublished doctoral dissertation, Wirtschafts- und sozialwissenschaftliche Fakultät, Universität Köln, 1963. 165 p.
SUBJ 14 14.4 14.5 14.6 ▪ 16 18 34.1 34.2 41 45 58

13585 CSU P P1 G1.2 1949–1972
Chi Ts'ai-ch'eng.
A brief review of comprehensive financial planning, mimeo. Tr. of *Tsung ho ts'ai cheng chi hua chien lun* (Introduction to unified fiscal planning); Peking: Chung-kuo ts'ai cheng ching chi ch'u pan she, 1961; 65 p.
Washington, D.C.: U.S. Joint Publications Research Service, 21 Aug. 1962. 94 p. (JPRS 14,908; MC 19,671/1962) [Xerox copyflo available—New York: CCM Information Corp., Research and Microfilm Publications. (Scholarly Book Translation Series, 401)]
SUBJ 14.5 ▪ 14

13586 MCH P P1 G9.4 1949–1972
Chow, H. T. (Chou Hung-t'ao).
'On income tax administration.'
IFC 24, 4 (Oct. 1965), 2–18.
SUBJ 14.5 ▪ 12.2

13587 MCH P P2 G1.2 1949–1972
Delorme, Henri.
'Budget, monnaie et banques' (Budget, currency, and banks).
Economie et politique 66/67 (jan.–fév. 1960), 103–120. [Special issue: *Economie en URSS et en Chine* (The economy of the U.S.S.R. and China)]
'Budget, money and banks.' In *Articles on Communist China from 'Economie et politique', Paris, January–February, 1960*, mimeo., compiled by U.S. Joint Publications Research Service. [Analytic entry]

Washington, D.C.: JPRS, 29 July 1960, 13–43. (JPRS 3639; MC 14,333/1960)
SUBJ 14.5 14.6 ▪ 14

13588 CSH P P3 G1.2 1949–1972
Donnithorne, Audrey Gladys, 1922–.
The budget and the plan in China: Central-local economic relations.
Canberra: Australian National U. Press, 1972. 19 p. (Contemporary China papers, 3)
SUBJ 14 14.5

13589 MCH P P2 G1.2 1949–1972
Durand, François J-.
Le financement du budget en Chine populaire: un exemple de développement fiscal dans une économie de croissance (Financing the budget in the People's Republic of China: An example of fiscal expansion in a growth economy).
Hong Kong: Ed. Sirey, 1965. 409 p. (Doctoral dissertation, Faculté de droit, Université de Paris, 1962)
SUBJ 14 14.5 ▪ 16

13590 MCH P P2 G1.2 1949–1972
Ecklund, George N-.
Financing the Chinese government budget: Mainland China, 1950–1959.
Chicago: Aldine, 1966. 133 p. (Revision of *Taxation in Communist China, 1950–1959*, doctoral dissertation in Economics, U. of Minnesota, 1963)
SUBJ 14.5 ▪ 14

13591 MCH S P2 G1.2 1949–1972
Froomkin, Joseph, and Ronald Hsia (Hsia Hsiu-yung), 1918–.
'Developments in public finance in Communist China, 1950–1954.'
Public finance 10, 1 (1955), 83–102.
SUBJ 14 14.5 ▪ 15

13592 CSU P P1 G1.2 1949–1972
Fujimoto, Akira, 1928–.
'On taxation system in Communist China.'
Kobe U. economic review 12 (1966), 99–115.
SUBJ 14.5 ▪ 14

13593 DLC P P2 G1.2 1949–1972
Hsia, Ronald (Hsia Hsiu-yung), 1918–.
Government acquisition of agricultural output in Mainland China, 1953–56.
Santa Monica, Calif.: RAND Corp., 1958. 94 p. (RAND memoranda, RM-2207; ASTIA documents, AD-211,940)
SUBJ 14.3 14.5 ▪ 14 14.1

13594 MCH P P2 G1.2 1949–1972
Hsiao Chi-jung, 1892–.
Revenue and disbursement of Communist China, mimeo.
Hong Kong: Union Research Institute, 1954. 118 p. (Communist China problem research series, EC8)
SUBJ 14 14.5

13595 CSU P P1 G9.4 1949–1972
Hsu, L. F. (Hsü Liu-fen).
'Income taxation in China.'
CJA 2 (Jan. 1964), 58–72 [s.p.]. [See Vol. 2 of this *Bibliography* for Chinese version.]
SUBJ 14.5

13596 NIC S P7 G1.2 1949–1972
Klein, Sidney, 1923–.
'Real taxes and real incomes in Communist China.'
CS 1, 19 (29 Nov. 1961), 1–9. [Reprinted as 'Real taxes and real incomes.' In *This is China: Analyses of Mainland trends and events*, edited by Francis Harper. (Selective entry.) Hong Kong: Dragonfly Books, 1965, 115–126.]
SUBJ 14.5 18 ▪ 14.1 16.3 34.1 45

13597 CSU S P1 G1.2 1949–1972
Ko Chih-ta.
China's budget during the transition period, mimeo. Tr. of *Kuo tu shih ch'i ti Chung-kuo yü suan*; Peking: Ts'ai cheng ch'u pan she, 1957; 170 p.
Washington, D.C.: U.S. Joint Publications Research Service, 13 Mar. 1959. 205 p. (JPRS 591D; MC 6357/1959) [Xerox copyflo available—New York: CCM Information Corp., Research and Microfilm Publications. (Scholarly Book Translation Series, 402)]
SUBJ 14 14.5 ▪ 18

13598 CSU P P1 G1.2 1949–1972
Kwang, Ching-wen (K'uang Ching-wen).
'The budgetary system of the People's Republic of China: A preliminary survey.'
Public finance 18, 3/4 (1963), 256–286.
SUBJ 14.5

13599 CSH P P1 G1.2 1949–1972
[La Dany, Ladislao] ———, 1914–.
'The financial status of the state.'
CNA 280 (12 June 1959), 1–7.
SUBJ 14 14.5 ▪ 14.6

13600 MCH P P2 G1.2 1949–1972
[La Dany, Ladislao] ———, 1914–.
'Taxes on industry and commerce, 1949–1959.'
CNA 290 (28 Aug. 1959), 1–7.
SUBJ 14.5

13601 CSH P P2 G1.2 1949–1972
Li Hsien-nien, 1907–.
'The great financial achievements of the People's Republic of China during the past ten years.' Tr. of 'Chung-hua jen min kung ho kuo shih nien ts'ai cheng ti wei to ch'eng chiu' (The great achievements in fiscal administration during the first decade of the People's Republic of China); in *Hui huang ti shih nien* (A decade of glory), edited by *Jen min jih pao* ch'u pan she; [Peking]: Jen min jih pao ch'u pan she, 1959, vol. 1, 342–358. In *Ten glorious years.* [Selective entry]
Peking: Foreign Languages Press, 1960, 166–188.
SUBJ 14 14.5 14.6

13602 MAM P P2 G9.4 1949–1972
Li, Mabel Kwan Wai (Li K'un-wei), 1922–.
The tax system of Taiwan.
Ann Arbor: University Microfilms (Publ. 18,059), 1957. 470 p. (Doctoral dissertation in Economics, New York U., 1956)
SUBJ 14 14.5 ▪ 12.2 14.4 24.1

13603 NNC P P8 G1.2 1949–1972
Li Shu-te.
Agricultural tax work during the last ten years, mimeo. Tr. of 'Shih nien lai ti nung yeh shui kung tso'; *Ts'ai cheng* 1959, 19 (9 Oct.), 1–6.
Washington, D.C.: U.S. Joint Publications Research Service, 7 Nov. 1960. 19 p. (JPRS 4162; MC 814/1961)
SUBJ 14.5 ▪ 14.1

13604 CSH P P2 G1.2 1949–1972
Lin Yün.
'Improvements of our financial management system in 1958.' Tr. of 'Lun wo kuo 1958 nien ts'ai cheng kuan li t'i chih ti kai chin' (Improvements in China's fiscal-management system, 1958); *Ching chi yen chiu* (Peking) 1958, 10 (Oct.), 35–47; 1958, 11 (Nov.), 41–53.
URS 15, 6 (21 Apr. 1959), 76–89; 15, 7 (24 Apr. 1959), 90–110; 15, 9 (1 May 1959), 123–138.
SUBJ 14 14.5 ▪ 14.6

13605 CSH P P2 G1.2 1949–1972
Liu Yung-hua, Richard K. Diao (Tiao K'ai-chih), 1924–, and Huang Yu-chuan (Huang Yü-ch'uan). [Authors sequential rather than joint: Liu Yung-hua for 1961 and 1963; Richard K. Diao for 1964 and 1965; Huang Yu-chuan for 1966.]
'Finance' [title varies]. Tr. from *Tsu kuo chou k'an* 495 (2 July 1962) *and* from *Tsu kuo* 2–37 (May 1964 – Apr. 1967) [recurring annual feature article]. In *Communist China, 1961–1966*, edited by Union Research Institute.
Hong Kong: Union Research Institute. Issued annually, 1962–1968, average ca. 20 p.
SUBJ 14 14.5 ▪ 14.6

13606 NNC P P2 G1.2 1949–1972
Lo Hua.
'Finance.' Tr. of '1957 nien Chung kung ti ts'ai cheng' (Fiscal administration in Communist China, 1957); *Tsu kuo chou k'an* 274/275 (7 Apr. 1958), 10–12. In *Communist China, 1957*, edited by Union Research Institute. [Selective entry]
Hong Kong: Union Research Institute, 1958, 30–40.
SUBJ 14.5

13607 CSU P P1 G1.2 1949–1972
Miyashita, Tadao, 1909–.
'Planned supply of liquid funds to state commercial and industrial enterprises in China.'
Kobe U. economic review 16 (1970), 1–20.
SUBJ 12 14.5 14.6 ▪ 14.3 14.4

13608 CSU P P7 G1.2 1949–1972
Miyashita, Tadao, 1909–.
'State funds and agriculture in China.'
Kobe U. economic review 15 (1969), 1–22.
SUBJ 14.5 14.6 ▪ 14 14.1 18 34.1

13609 NNC PO P1 G1.2 1949–1972
Obolenskii, N-.
'Raspredelenie nakoplenii gosudarstvennykh predpriiatii v Kitae' (The distribution of funds accumulated by state enterprise in China).
Finansy SSSR 22, 4 (aprel' 1961), 70–76.
SUBJ 14.5 14.6 ▪ 14.3 14.4

13610 NNC P P7 G1.2 1949–1972
Ong, Shao-er (Weng Shao-erh), 1917–.
A study of agricultural taxation in Communist China, mimeo.
Los Angeles: U. of Southern California, Dept. of Asiatic Studies, 1952. 105 p. (Studies in Chinese Communism, series 2, 2)
Subj 14.1 14.5

13611 NNC P P1 G1.2 1949–1972
Riumin, S-.
'Biudzhet Kitaiskoi Narodnoi Respubliki na sluzhbe sotsialisticheskogo stroitel'stva' (The budget of the People's Republic of China serving socialist construction).
Finansy SSSR 18, 11 (noiabr' 1957), 73–81.
Subj 14.5 ▪ 14

13612 CSU O P5 G1.2 1949–1972
Shen P'ing.
Industrial and commercial tax revenue work in China during past 10 years, mimeo. Tr. of 'Shih nien lai wo kuo kung shang shui shou kung tso'; *Ts'ai cheng* 1959, 18 (24 Sept.), 27–31.
Washington, D.C.: U.S. Joint Publications Research Service, 18 Oct. 1960. 26 p. (JPRS 5755; MC 18,846/1960)
Subj 14.5 ▪ 12.2 14.3 14.4 34.2

13613 NNC P P2 G1.2 1949–1972
Shih, Joseph Anderson (Shih Ch'eng-chih), 1918–1973.
'Finance and trade.' Tr. of '1958 nien ti Chung kung ts'ai cheng mao i kung tso' (Administration of fiscal affairs and commerce in Communist China, 1958); *Tsu kuo chou k'an* 334/335 (8 June 1959), 11–17. In *Communist China, 1958*, edited by Union Research Institute. [Selective entry]
Hong Kong: Union Research Institute, 1959, 30–49.
Subj 14.3 14.5

13614 MCH P P2 G1.2 1949–1972
Starlight, Lawrence Lee, 1926–.
Monetary and fiscal policies in Communist China, 1949–1954.
Unpublished doctoral dissertation in Economics, Harvard U., 1956. 322 p.
Subj 14 14.5 14.6

13615 MCH P P1 G1.2 1949–1972
Szczepanik, Edward Franciszek, 1915–.
'Four years of fiscal policy in Communist China.'
B. for international fiscal documentation 9, 4 (July–Aug. 1955), 206–226. [Reprinted in *Contemporary China, 1955*, edited by Edward Stuart Kirby. (Selective entry.) Hong Kong: Hong Kong U. Press, 1956, 66–82.]
Subj 14 14.5 ▪ 14.6

13616 CSH P P1 G1.2 1949–1972
Wu Chi-fang.
'A study of Peiping's national income and finance.'
CCA 5, 1 (Feb. 1968), 1–31.
Subj 14 14.5 ▪ 14.3 14.4

13617 CSH F P3 G1.1 1949–1972
Wu, Chun-hsi.
'The institutions and channels of remittances.' In *Dollars, dependents, and dogma: Overseas Chinese remittances to Communist China*, by Chun-hsi Wu. [Sole entry]
Stanford: Hoover Institution on War, Revolution and Peace, 1967, 28–39.
Subj 14.5

13618 CSU P P1 G9.4 1949–1972
Yoingco, Angel Q-, and Ruben F-Trinidad.
Fiscal systems and practices in Asian countries.
New York: Praeger, 1968. 449 p.
Subj 14.5 ▪ 12.2 14

14.6 Financial, Monetary, and Credit Systems
金融、貨幣及信託制度
金融、貨幣及び信用制度

1644-1911

13619 FLO P P2 G1.1 –1911
Bykov, Aleksei Andreevich, 1896–.
Monety Kitaia (China's currency).
Leningrad: Sov. khudozhnik, 1969. 77 p.
Subj 14.6

13620 MCH P P1 G1.2 1644–1895
Ch'en, Jerome (Ch'en Chih-jang), 1919–.
'The Hsien-feng inflation.'
BSOAS 21, 3 (Oct. 1958), 578–586.
Subj 14.6

13621 NNC PO P4 G1.3 1644–1842
Cibot, Pierre-Martial, 1727–1780.
'Mémoire sur l'intérêt de l'argent en Chine' (Report on the interest on money in China). In *Mémoires concernant l'histoire, les sciences, les arts, les moeurs, les usages, etc. des Chinois* (Reports on the history, learning, arts, manners, customs, etc. of the Chinese), by Missionnaires de Pékin. [Selective entry]
Paris: Chez Nyon, 1779, vol. 4, 299–391.
Subj 14.6 ▪ 14 15 16 50 63

13622 MCH P P2 G1.1 –1911
Edkins, Joseph, 1823–1905.
Banking and prices in China.
Shanghai: Presbyterian Mission Press, 1905. 286 p.
Subj 14.3 14.6 ▪ 14.5 15 34.2

13623 NIC P P1 G1.2 –1895
Edkins, Joseph, 1823–1905.
'The relations of copper and silver in China.'
JRAS-CB new (2nd) series 31 (1896/97), 135–145.
Subj 14.6

13624 NNC P P1 G1.2 1842–1911
Heiss, Clemens.
'Die Währungsreform in China, auf den Philippinen, in Panama und anderen Silberwährungsländern' (Currency reform in China, the Philippines, Panama, and other silver-currency countries).
SJ 29, 4 (1905), 365–394.
Subj 14.6 ▪ 14.3 16.2

13625 MCH P P1 G1.1 1644–1842
Hoffmann, Johann Joseph, 1805–1878.
'Iets over Chinesche lombardbriefjes' (A note on Chinese pawn tickets).
BTLV [8] (1862), 145–149.
Subj 14.6

13626 NIC P P1 G1.2 –1911
Hozumi, Fumio, 1902–.
'The characteristics of the history of Chinese money.'
KUER 24, 2 (Oct. 1959), 18–38.
Subj 14.6

13627 CSU P P2 G1.1 1842–1895
King, Frank Henry Haviland, 1926–.
Money and monetary policy in China, 1845–1895.
Cambridge: Harvard U. Press, 1965. 330 p. (Harvard East Asian series, 19) (Revision of *China's monetary system, 1845–1895, and its role in economic development*, doctoral dissertation in Social Studies, Oxford U. [Exeter College], 1959)
Subj 14 14.5 14.6 ▪ 12 14.3

13628 NIC S P8 G1.2 1644–1911
McAleavy, Henry.
'Dien in China and Vietnam.'
JAS 17, 3 (May 1958), 403–415.
Subj 14.6 22.2 ▪ 12.2

13629 NNC PO P2 G1.1 –1895
Morse, Hosea Ballou, 1855–1934, comp.
'Abstract of information on currency and measures in China.'
JRAS-CB new (2nd) series 24, 2 (1889), 46–135.
Subj 14.3 14.5 14.6 ▪ 16.2 24.3 34.3 62 66

13630 MCH S P1 G1.1 –1911
Morse, Hosea Ballou, 1855–1934.
'Currency in China.'
JRAS-NCB new (2nd) series 38 (1907), 1–60.
Subj 14.6

13631 CSH S P1 G1.2 1842–1911
Norman, V-.
'Denezhnoe obrashchenie Kitaia' (Currency circulation in China).
VA 9 (mai 1911), 39–62.
Subj 14.6 ▪ 14 14.3

13632 MCH P P3 G1.2 1644–1842
Peterson, Willard James, 1938–.
'Early nineteenth century monetary ideas on the cash-silver exchange ratio.'
PC 20 (Dec. 1966), 23–48.
Subj 14.6 ▪ 12 62

13633 IMC P P1 G1.1 –1911
Poma, Cesare.
'Il nuovo sistema monetario cinese' (China's new monetary system).
Rivista italiana di numismatica e scienze affini 17 (1904), 99–120.
Subj 14.6

13634 MCH O P2 G2.1 1895–1911
Poppe, N-.
'Denezhnoe obrashchenie v severnoi Man'chzhurii' (Currency circulation in northern Manchuria).
Sbornik konsul'kikh donesenii 1904, 4, 306–321.
Subj 14.6

13635 NNC U P1 G1.3 1895–1911
Schwarzwald, Hermann.
'Das chinesische Geldwesen und seine Neugestaltung' (The Chinese monetary system and its reform).

Jahrbücher für Nationalökonomie und Statistik 3. Folge 48, 1 (1914), 60–85.
SUBJ 14.6

13636 CSU PO P2 G1.1 1895–1911
Sculfort, L-.
'Rapport sur la circulation monétaire en Chine et les conséquences de la baisse de l'argent' (Report on currency circulation in China and on the results of the devaluation of silver). In *La Mission lyonnaise d'exploration commerciale en Chine, 1895–1897, deuxième partie, rapports commerciaux et notes diverses* (The Lyons Trade Mission to China, 1895–1897, Part 2, Commercial reports and miscellaneous notes), compiled by Chambre de commerce de Lyon. [Selective entry]
Lyons: Rey, 1898, 399–416 [s.p.].
SUBJ 14.3 14.6

13637 CSU P P2 G1.3 –1895
Stanley, Charles Johnson, 1914–.
Late Ch'ing finance: Hu Kuang-yung as an innovator.
Cambridge: Harvard U., East Asian Research Center, 1961. 117 p. (Harvard East Asian monographs, 12) (Revision of *Hu Kuang-yung and China's early foreign loans*, doctoral dissertation in History and Far Eastern Languages, Harvard U., 1951)
SUBJ 14.5 14.6 16.2 34.2 ▪ 12 14.3 16.1 66

13638 CSU P P1 G1.1 –1911
Wei, Wen Pin, 1888–1940.
The currency problem in China.
New York: Columbia U., Faculty of Political Science, 1914. 156 p. (Columbia studies in history, economics, and public law, 59, 3 [whole no. 144]) (Doctoral dissertation in Economics, Columbia U.) [Reprinted—New York: AMS Press, 1969. 156 p.] [Reprinted—Taipei: Ch'eng-wen, 1971. 156 p.]
SUBJ 14.6 ▪ 14.5

13639 CSU S P2 G1.2 –1911
Williams, Talcott.
'Silver in China and its relation to Chinese copper coinage.'
AAAPSS 9, 3 (May 1897), 43–63.
SUBJ 14.6

13640 NIC P P5 G5.2 1644–1911
Yang, H. K.
'The rise and decline of the Shansi native banks.'
Central Bank of China b. 3, 4 (Dec. 1937), 301–306.
SUBJ 14.6 ▪ 34.2

13641 NNC P P2 G1.2 –1911
Yang, Lien-sheng, 1914–.
Money and credit in China: A short history.
Cambridge: Harvard U. Press, 1952. 143 p. (Harvard-Yenching Institute monograph series, 12)
SUBJ 14.6 34.2 ▪ 24.6

1644-1949

13642 CSH P P3 G1.1 1895–1928
'Banking institutions in China.'
CEM 3, 1 (Jan. 1926), 21–41.
SUBJ 14.6

13643 NIC O P5 G1.2 1895–1949
Andrew, George Findlay.
'Currency problems in a cycle of Cathay.'
JRAS-HKB 2 (1962), 26–36.
SUBJ 14.6 34.2 ▪ 16.2

13644 CSH P P3 G1.2 1895–1928
Avenarius, G- G-.
'Emissiia kitaiskikh bankov i kontrol' kommercheskikh obshchestv.'
VM 1926, 11/12, 80–92.
'Issue of banknotes by Chinese banks and control exercised by chambers of commerce.'
Manchuria monitor 1926, 11/12, 8–19.
SUBJ 14.6 ▪ 12.2 14.3 36.2

13645 CBU P P4 G1.3 1895–1949
Avenarius, G- G-.
'Menial'nye kontory i ikh rol' v sovremennom denezhnom obrashchenii Kitaia' (Bureaus of exchange and their role in the present currency circulation in China).
VM 1933, 18/19 (15 oktiabria), 101–110.
SUBJ 14.3 14.6

13646 MCY S P3 G1.3 1895–1928
Chafkin, Solomon Herman, 1924–.
'Modern business in China: The Bank of China before 1935.'
PC 2 (May 1948), 103–133.
SUBJ 14.6 ▪ 14 16.2 32.1

13647 NIC U P1 G1.3 1644–1949
Chang, George H.
'A brief survey of Chinese native banks.'
Central Bank of China b. 4, 1 (Mar. 1938), 25–32.
SUBJ 14.6

13648 CSH O P4 G1.2 1895–1928
Chang, Kia-ngau (Chang Chia-ao), 1888–.
'The Bank of China.'
Millard's review 8, 9 (26 Apr. 1919), 330–339. [Reprinted in *Readings in economics for China*, compiled and edited by Charles Frederick Remer. (Selective entry.) Shanghai: Commercial Press, 1922, 358–366.]
SUBJ 14.6 34.2 ▪ 12.2 66

13649 GBS P P2 G1.1 1895–1949
[Chang, Kowie] Kowie Dschang (Chang Kuo-wei), 1901–.
Die chinesische Geldverfassung (The Chinese monetary system).
Berlin: Wilhelm Christian, 1930. 128 p. (Doctoral dissertation, Philosophische Fakultät, Universität Berlin)
SUBJ 14.6 ▪ 12.2 14.3 19

13650 FPN P P5 G1.2 –1949
Chao, Joseph Koei-tsou (Shao Kuei-tsu).
Les banques autochtones chinoises (Native banks in China).
Unpublished doctoral dissertation, Faculté de droit, Université de Paris, 1948. 128 p.
SUBJ 12.2 14.6

13651 CSH P P2 G1.2 –1949
Chen, Chia-Tsün (Ch'en Chia-chün).
Das chinesische Bankwesen, unter besonderer Berücksichtigung der neuen chinesischen Banken (The Chinese banking system, with special attention to modern Chinese banks).
Berlin, Vienna, Zurich: Österreichischer Wirtschaftsverlag, Kommanditgesellschaft Payer und Co., 1938. 104 p. (Doctoral dissertation, Philosophische Fakultät, Universität Berlin)
SUBJ 14.6

13652 ELS P P3 G1.1 1842–1949
Cho, T. L. (Cho Tung-lai).
Joint stock banking in China.
Unpublished masters thesis in Economics, U. of London [London School of Economics and Political Science], 1938. 453 p.
SUBJ 14.6 ▪ 14.5 34.2

13653 GMU P P1 G1.2 1842–1949
Chu, Chi (Chu Ch'i), 1907–.
Hauptprobleme der Finanzreform Chinas (Major problems in the financial reform of China).
Berlin: The author, 1933. 258 p. (Doctoral dissertation, Philosophische Fakultät, Universität Berlin)
SUBJ 14.5 14.6

13654 NNC PO P4 G1.2 1895–1949
Chu, Li-lai.
The Bank of China, 1904–1935.
Unpublished masters thesis in Business, Columbia U., 1937. 66 p.
SUBJ 14.6 ▪ 34.2

13655 CSU O P2 G2.0 1895–1949
Dorfman, Ben David, 1902–.
'Manchurian currencies.'
Asia (New York: American Asiatic Assn.) 34, 5 (May 1934), 304–311.
SUBJ 14.6

13656 CBU P P4 G1.1 1895–1928
Dzen, Tien Yue (Tseng T'ien-yü), 1889–.
Das Bankwesen in China: Ein Beitrag zur Organisation und den Problemen der inländischen und ausländischen Banken in China (Banking in China: The organization and problems of domestic and foreign banks in China).
Berlin: Wilhelm Christian, 1927. 143 p. (Doctoral dissertation, Philosophische Fakultät, Universität Berlin)
SUBJ 14.6

13657 NNC S P1 G1.2 –1949
Great Britain. Admiralty. Naval Intelligence Division. Geographical Section.
'Currency and finance.' In *China proper, Vol. 3, Economic geography, ports and communications*, compiled by the agency cited. [Selective entry]
London: His Majesty's Stationery Office, 1945, 192–224. (NID, Geographical handbook series, BR 530B)
SUBJ 14.6 ▪ 14.5 18

13658 MSE PO P3 G1.1 1895–1928
Hall, Ray Ovid, 1891–1952.
The Chinese national banks, from their founding to the moratorium.
Berlin: The author, 1921. 291 p. (Doctoral dissertation in Political Science, Columbia U.)
SUBJ 14.6 ▪ 12

13659 ELU P P4 G1.2 –1949
Hou, Shutung (Hou Shu-t'ung), 1904–.
The currency and banking problems of China.

Unpublished doctoral dissertation in Economics, U. of Liverpool, 1935. 317 p.
Subj 14.6 ▪ 34.2 66

13660 CSU P P2 G1.2 1895–1928
Kann, Eduard, 1880–1962.
'Copper banknotes in China.'
CEJ 5, 1 (July 1929), 549–577.
Subj 14.6

13661 CSU P P1 G1.1 –1928
Kann, Eduard, 1880–1962.
The currencies of China: An investigation of silver and gold transactions affecting China, with a section on copper, rev. ed.
Shanghai: Kelly and Walsh, 1927. 34, 559 p. [Reprinted—New York: AMS Press, 1972. 34, 559 p.]
Subj 14.3 14.6

13662 GBF P P4 G1.1 1842–1928
Kao, Mong-tsang (Kao Mang-ts'ang).
Die Bedeutung von Schanghai für die chinesische Volkswirtschaft, unter besonderer Berücksichtigung des Bankwesens (The significance of Shanghai in China's national economy, with special attention to the banking system).
Unpublished doctoral dissertation, Philosophische Fakultät, Universität Berlin, 1938. 289 p.
Subj 14 14.6 24.6 ▪ 14.3

13663 NNJ S P4 G1.2 1895–1928
Khodorov, Abram Evseevich, 1886–1949.
'Tuzemnyi i inostrannyi kapital v Kitae' (Domestic and foreign capital in China). In *Rabochii Kitai: sbornik statei* (Articles on workers' China). [Selective entry]
Moscow: Profintern, 1926, 35–68.
Subj 14.6 ▪ 14.2 14.4 14.5

13664 MCH P P1 G1.2 –1928
Ki, Tson-mong (Chi Tsung-meng).
Etude sur la réforme monétaire en Chine (A study of monetary reform in China).
Paris: Jouve, 1920. 160 p. (Doctoral dissertation, Faculté de droit, Université de Paris)
Subj 14.6 ▪ 14.3

13665 GBS P P1 G1.1 –1928
King, Gee-Mai (Chin Ch'i-mei), 1891–.
Das Geldwesen in China (China's monetary system).
Unpublished doctoral dissertation, Rechts- und staatswissenschaftliche Fakultät, Universität Kiel, 1924. 123 p.
Subj 14.6

13666 CBU P P2 G1.2 –1928
Ku, Sui-lu.
Die Form bankmässiger Transaktionen im inneren chinesischen Verkehr, mit besonderer Berücksichtigung des Notengeschäfts (The form of banking transactions in China's domestic trade, with special attention to the use of notes).
Hamburg: Kommissionsverlag L. Friedrichsen, 1926. 77 p. (Seminar für Sprache und Kultur Chinas an der Hamburgischen Universität, Veröffentlichungen, 1) (Doctoral dissertation, Rechts- und staatswissenschaftliche Fakultät, Universität Hamburg, 1924)
Subj 14.3 14.6 34.2 ▪ 12.2

13667 MCH S P1 G1.1 –1928
Lee, Frederic Edward.
Currency, banking and finance in China.
Washington, D.C.: U.S. Government Printing Office, 1926. 10, 220 p. (Dept. of Commerce, Bureau of Foreign and Domestic Commerce, Trade Promotion series, 29)
Subj 14.6 ▪ 14

13668 MCH O P4 G1.2 –1949
Lee, Tuh-yueh (Li Te-yü), 1903–.
The evolution of banking in China.
New Brunswick: ——, 1952. 60 p. [Thesis, Graduate School of Banking, American Bankers Assn.]
Subj 14.6 34.2 ▪ 14.5 16.2 24.6 34.3

13669 MCH P P1 G1.2 1842–1949
Liao Bao-seing (Liao Pao-hsien).
Die Bedeutung des Silberproblems für die Entwicklung der chinesischen Währungsverhältnisse (The significance of the silver problem in the development of the Chinese currency situation).
Berlin: Duncker und Humblot, 1939. 144 p. (Doctoral dissertation, Rechts- und staatswissenschaftliche Fakultät, Universität Frankfurt a.M.)
Subj 14.6 ▪ 14.3

13670 NIC PO P3 G1.2 1895–1928
Lieu, D. K. (Liu Ta-chün), 1891–1962.
'The Chinese financial organization.'
THJ 3, 5 (1918), 19–33; 3, 7 (June 1918), 1–10.
Subj 14.6 34.3 ▪ 24.6

13671 CSU PO P1 G1.3 1842–1949
Masui, Tsuneo, 1907–.
'Silver and China in the 19th century.'
Acta Asiatica (Tokyo) 10 (Feb. 1966), 1–15.
Subj 14.6

13672 MCY P P5 G1.1 1644–1949
Miyashita, Tadao, 1909–.
'The silver tael system in modern China.' [Abstract of *Chūgoku heisei no tokushu kenkyū: Kindai Chūgoku ginyrō seido no kenkyū* (A special study of the Chinese monetary system: The silver-tael system in modern China), 2nd ed.; Tokyo: Nihon gakujutsu shinkōkai, 1952.]
Kobe U. economic review 2 (1956), 11–32.
Subj 14.6 34.3 ▪ 12.2 14.3

13673 WSU P P4 G9.4 1895–1949
Pavlovski, Chester John.
Banking and finance in Taiwan under the Japanese, 1895–1945.
Unpublished masters thesis in Economics, U. of Washington, 1955. 122 p.
Subj 14.6 ▪ 12 14 34.2 38

13674 DLC FP P2 G1.2 –1928
Pogrebetskii, Aleksandr I-.
Denezhnoe obrashchenie i finansy Kitaia (Currency circulation and finance in China).
Harbin: Ekon. biuro KVzhd, 1929. 436 p.
Subj 14.6 ▪ 12.2 14.3 14.5 66

13675 GMS O P1 G1.2 1895–1928
Reiss, August.
'Das Bankwesen in China' (Banking in China). In *China: Wirtschaft und Wirtschaftsgrundlagen* (The economy and economic foundations of China), edited by Josef Hellauer. [Selective entry]
Berlin: de Gruyter (Vereinigung wissenschaftlicher Verleger), 1921, 168–184.
Subj 14.6

13676 CSU P P4 G1.1 1895–1949
Remer, Charles Frederick, 1889–1972.
Foreign investments in China.
New York: Macmillan, 1933. 21, 708 p. [Reprinted—New York: Fertig, 1968. 732 p.]
Subj 14 14.3 14.6 66 ▪ 12.2 34.2 58

13677 NNC P P1 G1.2 1842–1949
Rodin, K-.
'Finansy, denezhnoe obrashchenie i kredit Kitaia' (Finance, currency circulation, and credit in China).
Den'gi i kredit 1939, 7 (iiul'), 21–27.
Subj 14.6

13678 MCY P P5 G1.2 1842–1949
Saquez de Breuvery, Emmanuel.
'Les banques locales et les formes traditionnelles du crédit' (Local banks and traditional forms of credit).
BUA 3e série 1, 2 (1940), 155–192.
Subj 14.6 34.2 ▪ 14.3

13679 MCH S P5 G1.3 –1949
Shen, Ki-fein (Shen Ch'i-fan).
Essai sur l'origine et l'évolution des banques en Chine (The origin and development of banks in China).
Paris: Ed. Domat-Montchrestien, 1936. 261 p. (Doctoral dissertation, Faculté de droit, Université de Caen)
Subj 14.6 ▪ 16.2 36.2 38

13680 MCH P P1 G1.2 –1949
Shen, Lin-Yu (Shen Lin-yü), 1902–.
China's currency reform: A historical survey.
Shanghai: Shanghai Mercury Press, 1941. 14, 184 p.
Subj 12 14.6 ▪ 12.2 14.3

13681 DLC P P3 G1.2 1644–1928
Sou Hi-Suen (Su Hsi-hsün).
Etude sur la Banque de Chine (A study of the Bank of China).
Paris: Jouve, 1920. 281 p. (Doctoral dissertation, Faculté de droit, Université de Paris)
Subj 14 14.6

13682 NNC P P2 G1.2 –1949
T'ang, Leang-li (T'ang Liang-li), 1901–.
China's new currency system.
Shanghai: China United Press; London: Kegan Paul, Trench, Trübner, 1936. 138 p. (China today series, 8)
Subj 14.6 ▪ 14

13683 FPN PO P1 G1.1 –1928
Tchen, Tsou-siang (Cheng Tsu-hsiang).
La circulation fiduciaire et les banques d'émission centrales en Chine (Paper currency and the central issuing banks in China).

Nancy: Thomas, 1931. 159 p. (Doctoral dissertation, Faculté de droit, Université de Nancy)
Subj 14.6 ▪ 66

13684 MCY S P1 G1.2 1842–1949
Tchou Song-sien.
'La monnaie métallique' (Metal currency).
BUA 2e série 32 (1934/35), 36–60.
Subj 14.6

13685 NNC P P4 G1.2 1895–1949
Ting, Leonard G. (Ting Chi), 1907–1940.
'The Chinese modern banks and their finance of government and industry.'
NSEQ 8, 3 (Oct. 1935), 578–616.
Subj 14.5 14.6 ▪ 14.4

13686 MCH P P4 G1.2 1842–1928
Tokunaga, Kiyoyuki, 1904–.
'The Chinese banks in malformed transition, with a special reference to their movement in the early period of the Republican regime.' Tr. of 'Shina ginkō no kikeiteki suii: Toku ni minkoku shoki no dōkō ni tsuite' (Chinese banks in unbalanced transition: Trends in the early Republican period); *Keizai ronsō* 53, 2 (Aug. 1941), 33–49. [Tr. inferred]
KUER 17, 1 (Jan. 1942), 53–69.
Subj 14.6 ▪ 14 16.2

13687 LBU P P1 G1.2 1895–1949
Tseo, Cheng-se (Chou Ch'eng-hsü), 1908–.
The development of China's monetary system.
Unpublished doctoral dissertation in Economics, Louisiana State U., 1942. 266 p.
Subj 14.6 ▪ 12.2 14 14.5

13688 MCH P P2 G1.1 –1928
Wagel, Srinivas Ram.
Chinese currency and banking.
Shanghai: North-China Daily News and Herald, 1915. 457 p.
Subj 14 14.6 16.1 16.2 ▪ 14.3 18 34.2 62 63

13689 CBU S P1 G1.2 1842–1949
Yän Tjing-Hsi, 1910–.
Die Silberentwertung im Rahmen der chinesischen Geldverfassung (The demonetization of silver, with reference to the Chinese monetary system).
Jena: Buchdruck-Werkstätte, 1933. 102 p. (Doctoral dissertation, Rechts- und wirtschaftswissenschaftliche Fakultät, Universität Jena)
Subj 14.3 14.6 ▪ 14.4

13690 NNC O P5 G1.2 1895–1928
Yang, Kweeu-e.
The Chinese native banking system.
Unpublished masters thesis in Political Science, Columbia U., 1913. 14 p.
Subj 14.6 ▪ 34.2

13691 FPN P P2 G1.2 –1949
Yu, Tchen-p'ong (Yü Chen-p'eng).
L'hypothèque dans le droit coutumier chinois (The mortgage in Chinese customary law).
Lyons: Bosc et Riou, 1940. 12, 115 p. (Doctoral dissertation, Faculté de droit, Université de Lyon)
Subj 14.6 22.2 ▪ 12.2

13692 FPN P P4 G1.1 1842–1928
Yuen, Tsé-kien (Yüan Tzu-chien), 1908–.
Etude sur les établissements de crédit en Chine (A study of Chinese credit establishments).
Paris: Au commerce des idées, 1929. 135 p. (Doctoral dissertation, Faculté de droit, Université de Grenoble)
Subj 14.6 24.6 ▪ 14 34.2

1911-1949

13693 CSH P P2 G1.2 1928–1949
'Central Co-operative Bank of China.'
China economist 2, 1 (5 July 1948), 13–15.
Subj 14.6 ▪ 34.2

13694 CSU P P2 G1.2 1911–1949
'Paper currency in China.'
CEJ 18, 4 (Apr. 1936), 545–558.
Subj 14.6

13695 CSU P P2 G1.2 1928–1949
'Pawnbroking business activities.'
CEJ 18, 1 (Jan. 1936), 76–80.
Subj 14.6

13696 NNC P P1 G1.2 1928–1949
'Postal savings bank statistics, 1931.'
NWSS 5, 24 (13 June 1932), 107, 109–110.
Subj 14.6

13697 CSH O P4 G2.0 1911–1928
'Savings societies in Manchuria.'
CEM 2, 8 (May 1925), 1–8.
Subj 14.6

13698 CSU P P3 G1.1 1911–1949
'Shanghai silver movements, 1922–31.'
CEJ 12, 2 (Feb. 1933), 166–189.
Subj 14.3 14.6

13699 CSH PO P3 G2.0 1911–1928
A. K.
'Finansovye zatrudneniia mukdenskogo pravitel'stva' (Fiscal difficulties of the Mukden government).
MKhMP 1927, 2/3 (fevral'–mart), 174–181.
Subj 14.5 14.6 35

13700 CBU U P1 G2.0 1928–1949
Aleksandrov, G- I-.
'TSentral'nyi bank Man'chzhu-go i man'chzhurskii dollar, gobi' (The Central Bank of Manchoukuo and the Manchurian dollar, the *kuo-pi*).
VM 1934, 2 (fevral'), 61–67.
Subj 14.6

13701 MCY S P1 G1.2 1911–1949
Araki, Mitsutaro (Araki Mitsutarō), 1894–1951.
Report on the currency system of China.
Tokyo: Institute of Pacific Relations, Japan Council, 1931. 94 p.
Subj 14 14.2 14.6 ▪ 14.3 14.5

13702 NNC P P1 G1.2 1911–1949
Bloch, Kurt, 1908–.
'On the copper currencies of China.'
NSEQ 8, 3 (Oct. 1935), 617–632.
Subj 14.6

13703 DLC S P2 G1.3 1911–1949
Bregel', Enokh IAkovlevich, 1903–, and A- TSagolov.
'Kreditnaia sistema v Kitae' (The Chinese credit system). In *Kapitalisticheskii kredit* (Capitalist credit), by E. IA. Bregel' and A. TSagolov. [Sole entry]
Moscow: Gosfinizdat, 1939, 417–438.
Subj 14.6 ▪ 12 14.1 34.1

13704 NNP PO P2 G1.1 1928–1949
Chang, Kia-ngau (Chang Chia-ao), 1888–.
The inflationary spiral: The experience in China, 1939–1950.
Cambridge: M.I.T. Press, 1958. 17, 394 p.
Subj 14 14.6 ▪ 14.3 14.5 16.4 18 24.3 34.2

13705 CSH PO P2 G1.1 1928–1949
Chang, Kia-ngau (Chang Chia-ao), 1888–.
'Toward modernization of China's currency and banking, 1927–1937' [with comments by Sho-chieh Tsiang]. In *The strenuous decade: China's nation-building efforts, 1927–1937*, edited by Paul K. T. Sih (Hsüeh Kuang-ch'ien). [Selective entry]
Jamaica, N.Y.: St. John's U. Press, 1970, 129–170.
Subj 14.6 ▪ 12 14

13706 GFS S P1 G1.2 1911–1928
Chen, Homing (Ch'en Ho-ming).
Das chinesische Zinsproblem und seine volks- und weltwirtschaftliche Bedeutung (The problem of interest rates in China and its national and international economic significance).
Unpublished doctoral dissertation, Wirtschafts- und sozialwissenschaftliche Fakultät, Universität Frankfurt a.M., 1924. 87 p.
Subj 14.6

13707 CSH O P3 G1.1 1911–1928
China [Republic]. Ts'ai cheng pu. Kan-mo-erh she chi wei yüan hui. (Ministry of Finance. Kemmerer Commission of Financial Experts).
'Present condition of China's currency.' In *Project of law for the gradual introduction of a gold-standard currency system in China, together with a report in support thereof*, by the agency cited. [Sole entry]
Shanghai: Kan-mo-erh she chi wei yüan hui, 1929, 47–63.
Subj 14.6

13708 NNP PO P2 G1.1 1928–1949
Chou, Shun-hsin, 1915–.
The Chinese inflation, 1937–1949.
New York: Columbia U. Press, 1963. 13, 319 p.
Subj 14 14.3 14.5 14.6 ▪ 18 24.3 34.2

13709 CBU P P4 G1.3 1911–1949
Chu, Chi (Chu Ch'i), 1907–.
'Die allgemeinen kapitalmässigen Voraussetzungen für die Industrialisierung Chinas' (Capital prerequisites for the industrialization of China).
WA 45, 2 (März 1937), 283–297.
Subj 14.4 14.6

13710 NNC P P3 G1.1 1911–1949
Chung-kuo yin hang. Tsung kuan li ch'u. Ching chi yen chiu shih. (Bank of China. [Head Office]. Research Dept.), comp.
An analysis of the accounts of the principal Chinese banks, 1921–31.
Shanghai: Bank of China, 1933. 353 p. [In Chinese as well as English]
Subj 14.6 ▪ 24.6

13711 CLS P P4 G 1.2 1928–1949
Ding, Edwin Hing Ngok (Ch'en Hsing-le), 1902–.
The Central Bank of China.
Unpublished doctoral dissertation in Economics, U. of Southern California, 1937. 278 p.
Subj 14.6 ▪ 14

13712 NNC U P1 G 1.2 1911–1928
Dung, Yien (Teng Hsien), 1905–.
'The present status of life insurance in China.'
CSM 23, 6 (Apr. 1928), 37–43.
Subj 14.6 18

13713 DLC U P2 G 4.3 1911–1928
G. I.
'Denezhnyi rynok Sin'-Dziana' (The Sinkiang money market).
Narodnoe khoziaistvo Srednei Azii 1925, 1, 57–61.
Subj 14.6 ▪ 24.2 24.3

13714 CBU S P2 G 1.2 1928–1949
[Grajdanzev, Andrew Jonah?] A- I- Grazhdantsev, 1899–.
'Tuzemnye banki' (Domestic banks).
VM 1934, 8 (avgust), 27–47.
Subj 14.6 ▪ 14

13715 MCH P P8 G 1.2 1911–1949
Han Wen-ton (Han Wen-t'ung).
Le crédit agricole en Chine et les amendements proposés (Agricultural credit in China and suggested improvements).
Nancy: Thomas, 1936. 152 p. (Doctoral dissertation, Faculté de droit, Université de Nancy)
Subj 14.1 14.6 36.3 ▪ 16.3 18

13716 MCH P P1 G 1.2 1911–1949
Hsia [Chin-hsiung].
La reconstruction monétaire et bancaire de la Chine contemporaine (Reorganizing the monetary and banking systems).
Paris: Lib. économique et scientifique, 1937. 162 p. (Doctoral dissertation, Faculté de droit, Université de Paris)
Subj 14.5 14.6 ▪ 14.3

13717 MCY S P2 G 1.1 1911–1928
Hsu, Chi-lien (Hsü Chi-lien).
'Rural credit in China.'
CSPSR 12, 1 (Jan. 1928), 1–15; 12, 2 (Apr. 1928), 273–286.
Subj 14.6 24.6 34.2 ▪ 12 14.1 14.5 38

13718 ICU P P1 G 1.1 1928–1949
Hu, Ching-hsien.
War financing of China and Japan, 1937–1940.
Unpublished masters thesis in Economics, U. of Chicago, 1941. 187 p.
Subj 14.5 14.6 15 ▪ 14.3

13719 NNC P P4 G 1.2 1928–1949
Johnson, Bonnie Lee, 1945–.
The role of government banks in Chinese finance, 1928–36.
Unpublished masters thesis in East Asian Languages and Cultures, Columbia U., 1969. 65 p. [Certificate essay, East Asian Institute]
Subj 14.6 ▪ 14.4 14.5

13720 MAM P P2 G 2.0 1928–1949
Kinney, Ann Rasmussen, 1931–.
Investment in Manchurian manufacturing, mining and transportation, and communications, 1931–1945.
Ann Arbor: University Microfilms (Publ. 62-5186), 1962. 172 p. (Doctoral dissertation in Economics, Columbia U.)
Subj 14.2 14.4 14.6

13721 CSU P P2 G 6.0 1928–1949
Kojima, Shotaro (Kojima Shōtarō), 1888–.
'Financial circles in Shanghai following the outbreak of the Greater East Asia War.'
KUER 18, 2 (Apr. 1943), 1–26.
Subj 14.6

13722 CBU U P1 G 2.0 1928–1949
Kukhtin, K- V-.
'Denezhnaia reforma Man'chzhu-go' (Currency reform in Manchoukuo).
VM 1933, 13 (15 iiulia), 1–12.
Subj 14.6

13723 CSU O P2 G 1.2 1928–1949
Kung, H. H. (K'ung Hsiang-hsi), 1881–1967.
'China's financial problems.'
FA 23, 2 (Jan. 1945), 222–232.
Subj 14.6 ▪ 14.5

13724 CSU P P3 G 1.3 1911–1949
Kuo Sung Chuan (Kuo Sung-ch'üan).
'Paper currency in China.' In *Paper money*, mimeo., by Kuo Sung Chuan. [Sole entry]
Tientsin: Hautes études; Shanghai: Université l'Aurore, 1938, 48–81. (Institut des hautes études industrielles et commerciales, Faculty of Commerce, Economic studies, 10)
Subj 14.6

13725 MCH P P3 G 1.2 1911–1949
Lai, Kwok-ko (Lai Kuo-kao).
Etudes sur le marché du change de Chang-haï et ses relations avec la balance des comptes de la Chine (Studies of the Shanghai money market and its relation to China's balance of payments).
Lyons: Bosc et Riou, 1935. 191 p. (Doctoral dissertation, Faculté de droit, Université de Lyon)
Subj 14.3 14.6 ▪ 11.2 14 24.6

13726 MCH O P3 G 6.1 1911–1928
Leavens, Dickson Hammond.
'Chinese money and banking.'
AAAPSS 152 (Nov. 1930), 206–213. [Special issue: *China*, edited by Henry F- James]
Subj 14.6 ▪ 12.2

13727 MCH P P1 G 1.2 1911–1949
Lee, Jean (Li Hung-i).
La crise économique et la réforme monétaire en Chine, 1935 (The economic crisis and monetary reform in China, 1935).
Paris: Pedone, 1936. 118 p. (Doctoral dissertation, Faculté de droit, Université de Paris)
Subj 14.6 ▪ 14 18

13728 CSH O P1 G 2.0 1928–1949
Leonidov, I-.
'Denezhnoe obrashchenie i banki Man'chzhurii' (Banks and currency circulation in Manchuria).
VM 1930, 8, 14–26.
Subj 14.6

13729 CBU F P3 G 1.5 1928–1949
Lewis, Ardron B-, and Wang Lien.
'Changes in currency and prices in China.'
EF 1 (Sept. 1936), 1–65. [In Chinese as well as English]
Subj 14.3 14.6

13730 CBU P P1 G 1.1 1911–1949
Lewis, Ardron B-, and Wang Lien.
'Purchasing power of Chinese and Hong Kong currencies, and silver.'
EF 3 (Nov. 1936), 133–141. [In Chinese as well as English]
Subj 14.6

13731 CBU P P2 G 1.3 1911–1949
Liang, Ssu-mu (Liang Shih-mu).
'Spezielle Kapital- und Währungsprobleme im Zusammenhang mit der Industrialisierung Chinas' (Special capital and currency problems affecting the industrialization of China).
WA 45, 2 (März 1937), 298–319.
Subj 14 14.6 ▪ 14.1 14.4 16.3 16.4

13732 NNC U P1 G 1.3 1928–1949
Liao Bao-seing (Liao Pao-hsien).
'Die chinesische Währungsreform vom 4. November 1935 und ihre Auswirkungen' (The Chinese currency reform of 4 November 1935 and its effects).
Sinica 12, 1/2 (Jan.–März 1937), 44–54.
Subj 14.6

13733 MCY PO P4 G 1.1 1911–1928
Lieu, D. K. (Liu Ta-chün), 1891–1962.
'[1] Currency conditions in China. [2] Gold currency scheme.'
CSPSR 3, 2 (June 1918), 187–196; 3, 3 (Sept. 1918), 237–290.
Subj 14.6 ▪ 12 12.2

13734 MCH S P3 G 1.2 1928–1949
Liu, Sien-wei (Liu Hsien-wei).
Les problèmes monétaires et financiers de la Chine avant et depuis les hostilités sino-japonaises (Monetary and financial problems in China before and after the Sino-Japanese hostilities).
Paris: Ed. Domat-Montchrestien, 1940. 200 p. (Doctoral dissertation, Faculté de droit, Université de Paris)
Subj 14.5 14.6

13735 MCH P P1 G 1.2 1928–1949
Liu, Sing-chen (Liu Hsing-ch'en).
La dépréciation actuelle de l'argent en Chine et ses remèdes (The current depreciation of money in China and its remedies).
Nancy: Poncelet, 1931. 146 p. (Doctoral dissertation, Faculté de droit, Université de Nancy)
Subj 14.6 ▪ 14

13736 GMU P P7 G 1.2 1928–1949
Lo Wan-Sen, 1904–.
Probleme der Agrarkreditpolitik in China (Problems of agricultural credit policy in China).

Würzburg-Anmühle: Triltsch, 1941. 142 p. (Doctoral dissertation, Rechts- und staatswissenschaftliche Fakultät, Universität Berlin)
Subj 14.1 14.6

13737 MCY O P3 G1.2 1911–1928
Ma Yin-ch'u, 1882–.
'The fundamental causes of the recent economic crisis in China.'
CSPSR 9, 1 (Jan. 1925), 133–141.
Subj 14 14.6

13738 NNC P P2 G1.2 1911–1928
Mad'iar, Liudvig Ignat'evich, 1891–?
'Torgovo-rostovshchicheskii kapital i krest'ianskoe khoziaistvo Kitaia' (Capital for commerce and usury and the Chinese peasant economy).
Na agrarnom fronte 1928, 8 (avgust), 58–70.
Subj 14 14.1 14.6 16.3 ▪ 14.3 16.2

13739 CSU U P1 G1.2 1928–1949
Matsuoka, Koji.
'The inflation of Chinese legal tender.'
KUER 16, 2 (Apr. 1941), 22–43.
Subj 14.6 ▪ 14.5

13740 MCH P P3 G1.2 1911–1949
Mei Yung-mou (Mei Yüan-mou).
La crise de l'argent en Chine et la réforme monétaire du 4 novembre 1935 (The silver crisis in China and the currency reform of 4 November 1935).
Nancy: Thomas, 1936. 178 p. (Doctoral dissertation, Faculté de droit, Université de Nancy)
Subj 12.2 14.6 34.2 ▪ 14.3 66 72

13741 CSH P P5 G1.2 1911–1928
Pogrebetskii, Aleksandr I-.
'Denezhnyi rynok Kitaia i severnoi Man'chzhurii' (The money market in China and northern Manchuria).
VM 1925, 3/4, 81–91; 1925, 5/7, 99–107.
Subj 14.6 ▪ 14 14.3

13742 MCH P P1 G1.1 1928–1949
Pu, Shou-hai (P'u Shou-hai), 1920–.
Banking reform in China.
Unpublished doctoral dissertation in Economics, Harvard U., 1946. 239 p.
Subj 14.6

13743 MCH PO P2 G1.2 1928–1949
Salter, James Arthur, 1881–1939.
China and silver.
New York: Economic Forum, 1934. 117 p.
Subj 14 14.6 ▪ 12 15 34.2 66

13744 DLC PO P2 G1.2 1928–1949
Salter, James Arthur, 1881–1939.
China and the depression: Impressions of a three months visit.
[Shanghai]: Ch'üan kuo ching chi wei yüan hui, 1934. 149 p. (Ch'üan kuo ching chi wei yüan hui, Special series, 3)
Subj 14 14.6

13745 NNC P P1 G1.2 1911–1928
Schwarzwald, Hermann.
'Das neue chinesische Währungsgesetz' (The new Chinese currency law).
Oesterreichische Monatsschrift für den Orient 40, 3/6 (März–Juni 1914), 112–123.
Subj 12.2 14.6

13746 NNP P P4 G1.2 1911–1928
Shtein, Viktor Moritsevich, 1890–1964.
'Tuzemnyi i inostrannyi kapital v bankovom dele Kitaia' (Domestic and foreign capital in Chinese banking).
Ekonomicheskoe obozrenie 4, 7 (iiul' 1926), 150–164.
Subj 14.6 ▪ 16.2

13747 MCH P P3 G1.1 1911–1949
[Sih, Paul K. T.] Sih Kwang-tsien (Hsüeh Kuang-ch'ien), 1909–.
'Il sistema bancario in Cina' (The banking system in China).
Rivista italiana di scienze economiche 8, 8 (agosto 1936), 567–596.
Subj 14.6 ▪ 12

13748 DLC O P2 G1.1 1928–1949
Simkin, Robert L-.
'Wartime banking services.' In *Wartime China, as seen by westerners.* [Selective entry]
Chungking: China Publishing Co., 1942, 72–82.
Subj 14.6 ▪ 14 38

13749 MCY P P5 G1.2 1911–1949
Siu Siang-fang (Hsü Hsiang-fang).
'Droit de gage et monts-de-piété' (The law on pawnbroking and pawnshops).
BUA 3e série 2, 7 (1941), 403–432. [Reprinted in *Mélanges juridiques de l'Université l'Aurore* (Aurora University legal miscellany). (Selective entry.) Paris: Lib. du Recueil Sirey, 1946, vol. 1, 1–29.]
Subj 12.2 14.6 34.2 ▪ 14.3 22.2 45

13750 NNC FP P2 G1.2 1928–1949
Tamagna, Frank Marius, 1910–.
Banking and finance in China.
New York: Institute of Pacific Relations, International Secretariat, 1942. 21, 400 p. (Revision of *Chinese banking: Structure and policy*, doctoral dissertation in Economics, Yale U., 1937)
Subj 14.6 ▪ 12 14 34.1 34.2 66

13751 MCY P P1 G1.3 1928–1949
Ting, Leonard G. (Ting Chi), 1907–1940.
'The draft labor insurance act in China.'
MBEC 7, 4 (Apr. 1934), 135–148.
Subj 12.2 14.6 16.4 ▪ 14.4

13752 CSU S P4 G1.3 1928–1949
Tokunaga, Kiyoyuki, 1904–.
'Adjustment of the Chinese banking business.'
KUER 18, 4 (Oct. 1943), 42–62.
Subj 14.6

13753 CSU P P4 G1.2 1911–1928
Tokunaga, Kiyoyuki, 1904–.
'The first phase of the Bank of China as a note-issuing bank.'
KUER 16, 1 (Jan. 1941), 32–48.
Subj 14.6

13754 CSU P P2 G5.0 1928–1949
Tokunaga, Kiyoyuki, 1904–.
'Monetary and financial reorganization in North China.'
KUER 15, 2 (Apr. 1940), 71–100.
Subj 14.6

13755 MCH P P4 G1.2 1911–1949
Tson, Hauin-kio (Tseng Huan-chiu).
Le système monétaire en Chine (The Chinese monetary system).
Nancy: Grandville, 1934. 149 p. (Doctoral dissertation, Faculté de droit, Université de Nancy)
Subj 12.2 14 14.6 ▪ 14.5 18 72

13756 WSU P P1 G1.2 1928–1949
Yang, Chi-shi.
China's central banking system, past and future.
Unpublished masters thesis in Economics, U. of Washington, 1951. 152 p.
Subj 14.6 ▪ 12.2 14.5 66

13757 CBU P P3 G1.5 1911–1949
Yang, William Y. (Yang Yü), 1907–, and Hu Kwoh-hwa (Hu Kuo-hua).
'Chinese currency and the price level.'
EF 10 (June 1938), 431–444. [In Chinese as well as English]
Subj 14.3 14.6

13758 DNA F P2 G1.3 1928–1949
Yang, William Y. (Yang Yü), 1907–, and Hu Kwoh-hwa (Hu Kuo-hua).
'Problem of copper dearth.'
EF 12 (June 1939), 561–584. [In Chinese as well as English]
Subj 14.3 14.6

13759 MCH P P3 G1.2 1911–1949
Yen Chi-chin.
Le problème de la monnaie chinoise (China's currency problem).
Paris: Rodstein, 1933. 166 p. (Doctoral dissertation, Faculté de droit, Université de Caen)
Subj 12.2 14.6 ▪ 14.3 14.4 72

13760 MCH PO P2 G1.2 1928–1949
Young, Arthur Nichols, 1890–.
China and the helping hand, 1937–1945.
Cambridge: Harvard U. Press, 1963. 20, 502 p. (Harvard East Asian series, 12)
Subj 14 14.6 ▪ 12 14.3 14.5 15 32.2 66

13761 CSU PO P2 G1.2 1928–1949
Young, Arthur Nichols, 1890–.
China's wartime finance and inflation, 1937–1945.
Cambridge: Harvard U. Press, 1965. 18, 421 p. (Harvard East Asian series, 20)
Subj 14 14.6 ▪ 14.1 14.3 14.5 15 16

1911-1972
(including 1644-1972)

13762 MCH P P1 G1.1 1842–1972
Collis, Maurice, 1889–.
Wayfoong, the Hong Kong and Shanghai Banking Corporation: A study of East Asia's transformation, political, financial, and economic during the last hundred years.
London: Faber and Faber, 1965. 12, 269 p.
Subj 12 14.5 14.6 34.2 ▪ 14.2 14.3 15 32.2 66

13763 CSH PO P2 G1.1 –1972
Kann, Eduard, 1880–1962.
'The history of Chinese paper money, from the middle ages until 1956.' [Title varies.]
FEER 22, 10 – 25, 19 (7 Mar. 1957 – 6 Nov. 1958), 191 p. in all.
Subj 14.6 ▪ 12.2

13764 CSH P P2 G9.4 1928–1972
Liu, Fu-chi (Liu Fu-ch'i), 1936–.
Essays on monetary development in Taiwan.

Taipei: China Committee for Publication Aid and Prize Awards, 1970. 190 p. (Revision of *Supply and demand for money during inflation and stabilization: The case of Taiwan*, doctoral dissertation in Economics, U. of Rochester)
SUBJ 14 14.6

13765 NNC P P1 G1.2 1928–1972
Liu Khun-zhu (Liu Hung-ju).
'O sotsialisticheskom preobrazovanii kreditnoi sistemy v Kitae' (The socialist reorganization of China's credit system).
Den'gi i kredit 1958, 9 (sentiabr'), 45–50.
SUBJ 14 14.6

13766 MCH P P2 G1.2 1911–1972
Miyashita, Tadao, 1909–.
The currency and financial system of Mainland China. Tr. by J- R- McEwan of *Chūgoku no tsūka kin'yū seido* (China's monetary and financial systems); Tokyo: Ajia keizai kenkyūjo, 1965; 203 p.
Seattle: U. of Washington Press, 1966. 278 p.
SUBJ 14.6 34.2 ▪ 14.3 34.1 36.3

13767 HKU P P3 G9.5 1928–1972
Wong, Po-shang (Huang P'u-sheng).
The influx of Chinese capital into Hong Kong since 1937.
Hong Kong: Kai Ming Press, 1958. 12 p.
SUBJ 14.6 24.6

1949-1972

13768 NNC P P1 G1.2 1949–1972
Labour insurance in New China.
Peking: Foreign Languages Press, 1953. 32 p.
SUBJ 14.6 ▪ 16.4 36.4 47 52

13769 MCH P P7 G1.2 1949–1972
Asakawa Kenji, 1909–.
Role of agricultural loans in natural disaster areas in Communist China, mimeo. Tr. of 'Saigai kokufuku to nōgyō kashitsuke shikin no yakuwari' (Natural disasters and the role of agricultural loans); *Ajia keizai jumpō* 471 (21 June 1961), 1–7.
Washington, D.C.: U.S. Joint Publications Research Service, 23 Oct. 1961. 7 p. (JPRS 10,584; MC 1137/1962)
SUBJ 14.1 14.6 18 ▪ 22.1 34.1

13770 CSU P P4 G9.4 1949–1972
Beh, Yu (Pai Yü).
'Commercial credit in Taiwan.'
CJA 3 (July 1964), 30–35 [s.p.]. [See Vol. 2 of this *Bibliography* for Chinese version.]
SUBJ 14.6 ▪ 14.3

13771 CSH P P2 G1.2 1949–1972
Boldyrev, Boris Grigor'evich (B. Boldyriev).
'Finansy, den'gi i kredit na sluzhbe ekonomicheskogo stroitel'stva Kitaiskoi Narodnoi Respubliki' (Finance, money, and credit serving economic development in the People's Republic of China).
VE 1951, 9 (sentiabr'), 33–48.
'Les finances, la monnaie et le crédit au service de l'édification économique de la République populaire de Chine.' *Etudes économiques* 64 (1952), 21–39.
SUBJ 14 14.3 14.6 ▪ 12 14.1 34.2

13772 NNC P P1 G1.2 1949–1972
Boldyrev, Boris Grigor'evich.
Finansy Kitaiskoi Narodnoi Respubliki (Finance in the People's Republic of China), edited by Viacheslav Aleksandrovich Maslennikov.
Moscow: Gosfinizdat, 1953. 197 p.
SUBJ 14.5 14.6 ▪ 18

13773 NNC P P2 G1.2 1949–1972
Cheng Chu-yuan (Cheng Chu-yüan), 1927–.
Monetary affairs of Communist China, mimeo.
Hong Kong: Union Research Institute, 1954. 160 p. (Communist China problem research series, EC5)
SUBJ 14.6 34.2 ▪ 14 14.1 14.3 34.1

13774 MCH O P4 G1.2 1949–1972
Chu Hsueh-fan (Chu Hsüeh-fan), 1906–.
'Labour insurance in New China.' Tr. of 'Hsin Chung-kuo ti lao tung pao hsien chih tu' (The labor-insurance system in New China); *Ching chi chou pao* 12, 11 (15 Mar. 1951), 4–8.
People's China 3, 9 (1 May 1951), 6–8.
SUBJ 14.6 16.4 ▪ 18

13775 MAM P P2 G1.2 1949–1972
Corson, William Raymond, 1925–.
An examination of banking, monetary, and credit practices in Communist China (1949–1957).
Ann Arbor: University Microfilms (Publ. 69-18,804), 1969. 353 p. (Doctoral dissertation in Economics, American U.)
SUBJ 14.6 ▪ 14 32.1

13776 DLC P P4 G1.2 1949–1972
Dapčević-Oreščanin, Sonja.
'Oblici ograničanvanja privatnog kapitala u NR Kini' (Control of private capital in the People's Republic of China).
Pregled 8, Part 1, 5 (1956), 255–260.
SUBJ 14.6 ▪ 14.3 14.5 16.2 34.2

13777 CSU P P1 G9.4 1949–1972
Effros, Robert C-.
'The problem of postdated checks in the Republic of China.'
International Monetary Fund Staff papers 18, 1 (Mar. 1971), 113–133.
SUBJ 12.2 14.6

13778 CSU P P2 G1.2 1949–1972
Hsiao, Katherine Huang, 1923–.
Money and monetary policy in Communist China.
New York: Columbia U. Press, 1971. 16, 308 p. (Revision of *Money in Communist China: An analysis of structure and policy, 1953–1957*, doctoral dissertation in Economics, Columbia U., 1966)
SUBJ 14.6

13779 CSH P P1 G1.2 1949–1972
Hung, Fred C.
'The role of money and credit in Communist China's economic planning.' In *East Asian occasional papers, I*, edited by Harry Jerome Lamley. [Selective entry]
Honolulu: U. of Hawaii, Asian Studies Program, 1969, 51–67. (Asian Studies at Hawaii, 3)
SUBJ 14 14.6

13780 MCY P P2 G1.2 1949–1972
Jones, P- H- M-.
'People's banking.'
FEER 49, 3 (15 July 1965), 137–144.
SUBJ 14.6 ▪ 14 38

13781 DLC O P1 G1.2 1949–1972
Kováčik, Ludovít.
'Čínské banky a ich úloha úseku tuzemskem a zahraničním' (Chinese banks and their role in domestic and foreign affairs).
Finance a úvěr (Prague) 1957, 4 (duben), 172–178.
SUBJ 14.6

13782 CSH P P2 G1.2 1949–1972
[La Dany, Ladislao] ———, 1914–.
'Anti-inflationary efforts.'
CNA 218 (28 Feb. 1958), 1–7.
SUBJ 14 14.6 18

13783 NNC P P2 G1.2 1949–1972
[La Dany, Ladislao] ———, 1914–.
'Banking and finance.'
CNA 135 (8 June 1956), 1–7.
SUBJ 14.6

13784 MCH P P4 G1.2 1949–1972
[La Dany, Ladislao] ———, 1914–.
'Finance in the enterprises.'
CNA 304 (4 Dec. 1959), 1–7.
SUBJ 14 14.6 ▪ 14.4

13785 MCH P P4 G1.2 1949–1972
[La Dany, Ladislao] ———, 1914–.
'Finances. Part 1, Contours of internal financing. Part 2, Bank control of the enterprises.'
CNA 447 (30 Nov. 1962), 1–7; 448 (7 Dec. 1962), 1–7.
SUBJ 14 14.6 ▪ 14.5 34.2

13786 MCH U P1 G1.2 1949–1972
Li Hui-min.
'Money and banking on the Chinese Mainland.'
CCA 4, 1 (Feb. 1967), 34–44.
SUBJ 14.6

13787 CSU O P2 G1.2 1949–1972
Li T'ien-min, ed.
A new course in bank accounting in Communist China, mimeo. Tr. of *Hsin yin hang k'uai chi chiao ch'eng*; Shanghai: Li hsin k'uai chi t'u shu yung p'in she, 1952; 2 vols. 310; 183 p. [Partial tr.: vol. 1 only]
Washington, D.C.: U.S. Joint Publications Research Service, 1 Aug. 1962. 538 p. (JPRS 14,674; MC 17,938/1962) [Xerox copyflo available—New York: CCM Information Corp., Research and Microfilm Publications. (Scholarly Book Translation Series, 409)]
SUBJ 14.6 ▪ 34.2

13788 MAM P P1 G1.2 1949–1972
Ma, James Chao-seng (Ma Ch'ao-sheng), 1920–.
A study of the People's Bank of China.
Ann Arbor: University Microfilms (60-6627), 1960. 182 p. (Doctoral dissertation in Economics, U. of Texas)
SUBJ 14 14.6

13789 CSU P P2 G1.2 1949–1972
Miyashita, Tadao, 1909–.
'Planned extension of credit in China, especially to state-operated enterprises.'

Review (Tokyo) 12 (Mar. 1967), 29–58.
SUBJ 14.6 34.2 ▪ 12 14 14.5 24.3

13790 DLC O P1 G1.2 1949–1972
Obolenskii, N-.
'Organizatsiia oborotnykh sredstv gosudarstvennykh predpriiatii KNR' (The organization of working capital in state enterprises in the People's Republic of China).
Den'gi i kredit 1961, 7 (iiul'), 43–52.
SUBJ 14 14.6 34.2 ▪ 14.3 14.4

13791 NNC P P2 G1.2 1949–1972
Shevel', I- B-.
'Rol' denezhno-kreditnoi sistemy v sotsialisticheskom stroitel'stve v Kitaiskoi Narodnoi Respublike' (The role of the monetary and credit system in socialist construction in the People's Republic of China).
KSINA 49 (1961), 85–100.
SUBJ 14 14.6 ▪ 14.1 14.4

13792 MCH U P2 G1.2 1949–1972
Teng Chia-jung.
'Relationship between the work of various economic departments and the issue of people's currency.' Tr. of 'Ko ching chi pu men kung tso yü jen min pi fa hsing ti kuan hsi'; *Jen min jih pao* 5 July 1964, 5.
SCMP 3266 (27 July 1964), 1–10.
SUBJ 14 14.6

13793 DLC O P2 G1.1 1949–1972
TSao TSziui-zhu (Ts'ao Chu-ju).
'Kredit i denezhnoe obrashchenie KNR' (Credit and currency circulation in the People's Republic of China).
Den'gi i kredit 1960, 4 (aprel'), 48–55.
SUBJ 14.6 ▪ 14 14.3 34.1

13794 CSU P P1 G1.2 1949–1972
Tsiang, S. C.
'Money and banking in Communist China.' In *An economic profile of Mainland China*, compiled by Joint Economic Committee, U.S. Congress. [Selective entry]
Washington, D.C.: U.S. Government Printing Office, 1967, vol. 1, 323–339. [Reprinted in *An economic profile of Mainland China*, compiled by the agency cited. (Selective entry.) New York: Praeger, 1968, 323–340.]
SUBJ 14.6

13795 DLC P P2 G1.2 1949–1972
TSzen Lin (Tseng Ling) and Khan' Lei (Han Lei).
Denezhnoe obrashchenie Kitaiskoi Narodnoi Respubliki, edited by M- N- Sveshnikov. Tr. by E- Grebennikova and L- Novak of *Chung-hua jen min kung ho kuo ti huo pi liu tung*. [Publication data on original not ascertained.]
Moscow: Gosfinizdat, 1959. 182 p.
The circulation of money in the People's Republic of China, mimeo.
Washington, D.C.: U.S. Joint Publications Research Service, 1 June 1960. 133 p. (JPRS 3317; MC 10,076/1960)
SUBJ 14.6 ▪ 14 14.1 14.3 34.1

13796 NNC P P1 G1.2 1949–1972
Valk, Marius Hendrikus van der, 1908–.
'Security [i.e., credit] rights in Communist China.'
Osteuropa-Recht 9, 3 (Sept. 1963), 210–236.
SUBJ 12.2 14.6 ▪ 14.1 45

13797 MCH U P1 G1.2 1949–1972
Yang Pei-hsin (Yang P'ei-hsin).
'China's stable monetary system.'
PR 8, 26 (25 June 1965), 15–19.
SUBJ 14.6

15 THE MILITARY
軍事 軍事

1644-1911

13798 MBA P P3 G9.1 1895–1911
'Les forces militaires de la province du Koang-Si' (Kwangsi's military forces).
RI nouvelle (2e) série 13, 6 (juin 1910), 473–488.
SUBJ 15 16.1 ▪ 12

13799 NNP PO P1 G4.3 1842–1895
'Voennyia, politicheskiia i ekonomicheskia svedeniia o Zapadnom Kitae za 1884 g.' (Military, political and economic information on western China in 1884).
Sbornik geograficheskikh, topograficheskikh i statisticheskikh materialov po Azii 18 (1885), 1–41.
SUBJ 12 15 66 ▪ 14.3 14.6 21.2

13800 NNP S P3 G1.2 1842–1895
'Vooruzhennye sily Kitaia' (The Chinese armed forces).
Sbornik geograficheskikh, topograficheskikh i statisticheskikh materialov po Azii 14 (1885), 95–109.
SUBJ 15 ▪ 66

13801 MCH S P2 G8.2 1895–1911
'Le Yunnan' (Yunnan).
R. maritime et coloniale 147 (nov. 1900), 241–272; 147 (déc. 1900), 449–474, 490.
SUBJ 12 14 14.3 15 ▪ 23 29 32.2

13802 CSU P P2 G6.1 1842–1895
Allen, Bernard M-.
Gordon in China.
London: Macmillan, 1933. 220 p.
SUBJ 15 32.2 ▪ 12 66

13803 CSU PO P2 G5.1 1895–1911
Barnes, Arthur Alison Stuart.
On active service with the Chinese regiment: A record of the operations of the First Chinese Regiment in North China from March to October, 1900.
London: Grant Richards, 1902. 15, 228 p.
SUBJ 15 66 ▪ 35 63

13804 WSU P P2 G1.3 1842–1895
Bell, Mark Sever, 1843–1906.
China: Being a military report on the north-eastern portions of the provinces of Chih-li and Shan-tung, Nanking and its approaches, Canton and its approaches, etc., together with an account of the Chinese civil, naval, and military administrations.
Simla, India: Government Central Press, 1884. 2 vols. 425; 440 p.
SUBJ 14.2 15 21.3 ▪ 11.3 12 13 14.3 14.5 17 55

13805 MCH P P2 G1.3 1842–1895
Borodin, B- A-.
'Nekotorye svedeniia o voennoi organizatsii i voennom iskusstve taipinov' (Information on the Taipings' organizational and military techniques). [With English abstract]
PV 1960, 6, 28–42.
SUBJ 15 32.2 ▪ 14.2 16.3

13806 MCH O P3 G1.2 1842–1895
Boüinais, Albert Marie Aristide, 1851–1895.
'L'armée et la marine chinoises' (The Chinese army and navy). In *De Hanoi à Pékin: notes sur la Chine* (From Hanoi to Peking: Notes on China), by A. M. A. Boüinais. [Selective entry]
Paris: Berger-Levrault, 1892, 235–267.
SUBJ 15

13807 FPN P P1 G1.2 1895–1911
Brissaud-Desmaillet, Georges Henri, 1869–?
Situation de l'armée chinoise au 1er mars 1910 (The situation of the Chinese army as of 1 March 1910).
Paris: Lib. militaire R. Chapelot, 1910. 26 p.
SUBJ 15 ▪ 17 25

13808 NNP P P3 G9.2 1644–1895
Chen, Gideon (Ch'en Ch'i-t'ien), 1893–.
Lin Tse-hsü, pioneer promoter of the adoption of Western means of maritime defense in China.
Peiping: Yenching U., [Dept. of Economics], 1934. 65 p. [Reprinted—New York: Paragon, 1961. 65 p.]
SUBJ 14.2 15 ▪ 12 62 66

13809 NNC P P1 G1.2 1895–1911
Ch'en, Jerome (Ch'en Chih-jang), 1919–.
'A footnote on the Chinese army in 1911–1912.'
TP 2e série 48, 4/5 (1960), 425–446.
SUBJ 15 ▪ 12

13810 CSU P P2 G1.4 1842–1895
Chu, Wen-djang (Chu Wen-ch'ang), 1914–.
'Tso Tsung-t'ang's role in the recovery of Sinkiang.'
THJ new (2nd) series 1, 3 (Sept. 1958), 136–165.
SUBJ 12 15 ▪ 14.2

13811 ELB O P2 G1.1 1842–1895
Cooke, George Wingrove.
China and lower Bengal: Being 'The times' special correspondence from China, 1857–58, 5th ed.
London: Routledge, Warne and Routledge, 1861. 33, 495 p.
SUBJ 14 15 18 55 63 66 ▪ 12.1 12.2 16.2 25 32.2 47

13812 NNC U P2 G1.1 –1842
Dabry de Thiersant, Claude Philibert, 1826–1898.
Organisation militaire des Chinois: ou, la Chine et ses armées, suivi d'un aperçu sur l'administration civile de la Chine (Chinese military organization: or, China and its armies, followed by a look at the civil administration of China).
Paris: Plon, 1859. 19, 428 p.
SUBJ 10 12 15 ▪ 12.2 13 14.2 16 21.2 29 32.1 60 66

13813 DLC P P2 G1.3 –1842
Doronin, B- G-.
'Bor'ba armii Li TSzy Chena protiv ustanovleniia man'chzhurskogo gospodstva v Kitae' (The struggle of Li Tzu-ch'eng's army against the establishment of Manchu rule in China).
UZLGU 281 (1959), 65–81.
Subj 15 32.2 36.3 ▪ 12 66

13814 DLC S P2 G4.3 1644–1842
Duman, Lazar' Isaevich, 1907–.
'Zavoevanie TSinskoi imperiei Dzhungarii i Vostochnogo Turkestana' (The Ch'ing conquest of Dzungaria and eastern Turkestan). In *Man'chzhurskoe vladychestvo v Kitae* (Manchu rule in China), compiled by Institut narodov Azii, Akademiia nauk SSSR, edited by Sergei Leonidovich Tikhvinskii. [Selective entry]
Moscow: Nauka, Glav. red. vost. lit-ry, 1966, 264–288.
Subj 11.2 14.5 15 16.1 16.3 24.1 ▪ 12 12.2 34.1 66

13815 CSH P P2 G1.2 –1842
Dunstheimer, Guillaume Gustave Hubert, 1898–.
'Les guerres chinoises et leurs conjonctures (1628–1831)' (Chinese wars and their circumstances, 1628–1831).
Guerres et paix 1968, 1, 41–61.
Subj 15 25 29

13816 CSU P P4 G7.1 1895–1911
Dutt, Vidya Prakash, 1925–.
'The first week of revolution: The Wuchang Uprising.' In *China in revolution: The first phase, 1900–1913*, edited by Mary Clabaugh Wright. [Selective entry]
New Haven: Yale U. Press, 1968, 383–416.
Subj 15 25 ▪ 32.2

13817 NIC P P1 G1.2 1644–1842
Fang, Chaoying (Fang Chao-ying), 1908–.
'A technique for estimating the numerical strength of the early Manchu military forces.'
HJAS 13, 1/2 (June 1950), 192–215. [Reprinted in *Studies of governmental institutions in Chinese history*, edited by John Lyman Bishop. (Selective entry.) Cambridge: Harvard U. Press, 1968, 243–267. (Harvard-Yenching Institute studies, 23)]
Subj 15

13818 MCH P P1 G1.2 1895–1911
Fass, Josef.
'The role of the new-style army in the 1911 Revolution in China.'
AO 30, 2 (1962), 183–191.
Subj 12 15 ▪ 12.1 16 35 64

13819 MCH PO P1 G1.2 –1911
Frey, Henri Nicolas, 1847–1932.
L'armée chinoise: l'armée ancienne, l'armée nouvelle, l'armée chinoise dans l'avenir (The Chinese army: The old army, the new army, and the army of the future).
Paris: Hachette, 1904. 176 p.
Subj 15 ▪ 61 66

13820 FPN O P2 G7.0 1895–1911
Gadoffre, François.
'Vallée du Yang-tse: les troupes chinoises et leurs instructeurs' (Chinese troops and their instructors in the Yangtze valley).
R. des troupes coloniales 2, 7 (jan. 1903), 1–43.
Subj 15 ▪ 16 17

13821 NNC O P1 G1.2 1842–1895
Gill, William.
'The Chinese army.'
J. of the Royal United Service Institution 24 (1881), 358–377.
Subj 15 60 ▪ 66

13822 MCH P P7 G4.3 1644–1842
Haenisch, Erich, 1880–1966.
'Der chinesische Feldzug in Ili im Jahre 1755' (The Chinese campaign in Ili [Sinkiang] in 1755).
Ostasiatische Z. 7, 1/2 (Apr.–Sept. 1918), 57–86.
Subj 15 62 ▪ 25 66

13823 CSU P P2 G1.2 1895–1911
Hatano, Yoshihiro, 1908–.
'The new armies.' In *China in revolution: The first phase, 1900–1913*, edited by Mary Clabaugh Wright. [Selective entry]
New Haven: Yale U. Press, 1968, 365–382.
Subj 15 ▪ 17 32.2

13824 CSU P P2 G1.1 1644–1895
Holt, Edgar, 1900–.
The opium wars in China.
London: Putnam, 1964. 303 p.
Subj 15 25 66 ▪ 12 55

13825 NNC P P1 G1.1 1842–1895
Hsü, Immanuel C. Y. (Hsü Chung-yüeh), 1923–.
'The great policy debate in China, 1874: Maritime defense vs. frontier defense.'
HJAS 25 (1964/65), 212–228. [Reprinted in *Readings in modern Chinese history*, edited by I. C. Y. Hsü. (Selective entry.) New York: Oxford U. Press, 1971, 258–270.]
Subj 15

13826 CSU P P1 G4.3 1842–1895
Hsü, Immanuel C. Y. (Hsü Chung-yüeh), 1923–.
'The late Ch'ing reconquest of Sinkiang: A reappraisal of Tso Tsung-t'ang's role.'
Central Asiatic j. 12, 1 (1968), 50–63.
Subj 15 25 ▪ 14.6 32.2

13827 CSH P P1 G1.3 1842–1895
Huang, Pei (Huang P'ei), 1928–.
'The Yangtze Navy: An example of Ch'ing innovations.'
J. of Asian history 6, 2 (1972), 97–113.
Subj 15 ▪ 32.2

13828 ICU P P1 G1.1 1842–1911
Hummel, Arthur William, Jr., 1920–.
Yüan Shih-k'ai as an official under the Manchus.
Unpublished masters thesis in Oriental Languages and Literature, U. of Chicago, 1949. 179 p.
Subj 12.1 15 ▪ 12.2 14.5 72

13829 CSH P P1 G1.2 –1842
Jouary, Jean-Paul.
'Contribution à une polémologie des guerres de Chine (1628–1831)' (A contribution to a scientific study of wars in China, 1628–1831).
Guerres et paix 1968, 2, 33–43.
Subj 11 15 61 66

13830 NNC P P2 G1.3 1644–1842
Kaplan, Marshall Ray.
Aspects of the first two years of the White Lotus Rebellion in China, 1796–1797.
Unpublished masters thesis in Political Science, Columbia U., 1970. 56 p. [Certificate essay, East Asian Institute]
Subj 12 15 25 32.2 ▪ 11.2 12.2 14.5

13831 MCH P P2 G1.3 1842–1895
Kara-Murza, Georgii Sergeevich, 1906–1945.
Taipiny: velikaia krest'ianskaia voina i Taipinskoe gosudarstvo v Kitae, 1850–1864 (The Taipings: The great peasant war and the Taiping state in China, 1850–1864), 3rd ed.
Moscow: Uchpedgiz, 1950. 143 p.
Subj 12 14.1 15 16 19 32.2 ▪ 18 36.3 64 66

13832 CSH P P2 G1.4 –1842
Kuznetsov, V- S-.
'Iz istorii zavoevanii Dzhungarii TSinskim Kitaem' (History of the conquest of Dzungaria by Ch'ing China).
NAA 1970, 3, 140–145.
Subj 12 15 66

13833 CSU P P2 G1.5 1842–1895
Laai, Yi-faai (Lai I-hui), 1906–.
'River strategy: A phase of the Taipings' military development.'
Oriens 5 (1952), 302–329.
Subj 14.2 15 ▪ 21.3 29 32.2

13834 CSH P P2 G1.2 –1895
Lin Tsiu-sen (Lin Ch'iu-sheng).
'Neunter Zeitraum, 1603–1867' (The ninth period, 1603–1867). In *China und Japan im Spiegel der Geschichte: Eine Betrachtung anhand des Werdeganges Chinas und Japan* (China and Japan in the mirror of history: A consideration of their respective courses of development), by Lin Tsiu-sen. [Selective entry]
Erlenbach-Zurich: Rentsch, 1946, vol. 2, 155–221.
Subj 15 ▪ 12 32.2 66

13835 CSU P P1 G1.5 –1842
Lo, J. P. (Lo Jung-pang), 1912–.
'China's paddle-wheel boats: Mechanized craft used in the Opium War and their historical background.'
THJ new (2nd) series 2, 1 (May 1960), 189–212.
Subj 14.2 15 66 ▪ 25

13836 CSU O P4 G1.3 –1842
[Martini, Martin] ———, 1614–1661.
'Bellum Tartaricum: or, The history of the warres of the Tartars in China, etc.' Tr. from the Latin. In *The history of that great and renowned monarchy of China*, by F- Alvarez Semedo. [Sole entry]
London: John Crook, 1655, 255–308.
Subj 12 15 16.1 25

13837 DLC P P7 G2.1 1644–1842
Melikhov, G- V-.
'K istorii proniknoveniia man'chzhurov v bassein verkhnego Amura v 80-kh godakh XVII v.' (History of Manchu penetration into the upper Amur basin in the 1680s). In *Man'chzhurskoe vladychestvo v Kitae* (Manchu rule in China), compiled by Institut narodov Azii, Akademiia nauk SSSR, edited by Sergei Leonidovich Tikhvinskii. [Selective entry]
Moscow: Nauka, Glav. red. vost. lit-ry, 1966, 113–127.
SUBJ 15 66

13838 MCH U P2 G1.2 1644–1895
Merruau, Paul.
'La Chine depuis le traité de 1860 et le prince Kong' (China since the treaty of 1860 and Prince Kung).
R. des deux mondes 2e période 88 (1er août 1870), 712–737.
SUBJ 12 15 32.2 66 ▪ 25 32 32.1 33 43

13839 MCH O P2 G1.2 1895–1911
Mury, Francis.
'La Chine en évolution' (China in transition).
B. de la Société de géographie de Marseille 30, 2/4 (mars 1906), 151–178.
SUBJ 12 15 66 ▪ 11.2 14.2 16.1 17 34.3 47

13840 MCH O P2 G1.2 1895–1911
Négrier, François-Oscar de.
'Les forces chinoises en 1910' (The Chinese military forces in 1910).
R. des deux mondes 5e période 58 (1er août 1910), 567–605. [Separately reprinted—Paris: Ch. Delagrave, 1910. 81 p.]
SUBJ 14.2 15 16.1 17 ▪ 11.2 12 14.6 32.2 41 43 63 66

13841 MCH O P4 G1.1 1644–1895
Ouchterlony, John.
The Chinese war, 2nd ed.
London: Saunders and Otley, 1844. 522 p. [Reprinted—New York: Praeger, 1970. 522 p.]
SUBJ 12 15 25 66 ▪ 26.2 55

13842 NIC P P1 G1.2 1644–1895
Parker, Edward Harper, 1849–1926.
'The military organization of China prior to 1842.'
JRAS-CB new (2nd) series 22, 1 (1887), 1–21.
SUBJ 14.5 15

13843 CBU O P4 G1.3 1895–1911
Pfaff, Wilhelm von.
'Heer und Flotte: Das Heerwesen' (Army and navy: Military affairs). In *China: Schilderungen aus Leben und Geschichte, Krieg und Sieg* (China: Portraits from life and history, war and victory), edited by Joseph Kürschner. [Selective entry]
Leipzig: Hermann Zieger, 1901, 188–211 [s.p.].
SUBJ 15 ▪ 25

13844 FPN P P1 G1.1 1644–1895
Picard, Jules.
Etat général des forces militaires et maritimes de la Chine: solde, armes, équipement, etc. (The general condition of military and naval forces in China: Pay, weapons, equipment, etc.).
Paris: J. Corréard, 1860. 534 p.
SUBJ 15 25 ▪ 12 12.2 32.1

13845 CBU O P1 G1.3 1895–1911
Plüddemann, Martin.
'Heer und Flotte: Das chinesische Seekriegswesen' (Army and navy: Chinese naval warfare). In *China: Schilderungen aus Leben und Geschichte, Krieg und Sieg* (China: Portraits from life and history, war and victory), edited by Joseph Kürschner. [Selective entry]
Leipzig: Hermann Zieger, 1901, 211–222 [s.p.].
SUBJ 15 ▪ 55

13846 ELS P P2 G1.1 1644–1895
Pong, David Bertram Pak-Tang (P'ang Pai-t'eng), 1938–.
Modernization and politics in China as seen in the career of Shen Pao-chen (1820–1879).
Unpublished doctoral dissertation in History, U. of London [School of Oriental and African Studies], 1969. 436 p.
SUBJ 15 19 ▪ 12 14.4 66

13847 CSU P P1 G1.2 1895–1911
Powell, Ralph Lorin, 1917–.
The rise of Chinese military power, 1895–1912.
Princeton: Princeton U. Press, 1955. 10, 383 p. (Revision of *The modernization and control of the Chinese armies, 1895–1912*, doctoral dissertation in History, Harvard U., 1953) [Reprinted—Port Washington, N.Y.: Kennikat Press, 1971. 10, 383 p.]
SUBJ 12 15 32.2 ▪ 12.1 14.6 16.1 17 25 66

13848 DLC P P1 G1.1 1842–1895
Rawlinson, John Lang, 1920–.
'China's failure to coordinate her modern fleets in the late nineteenth century.' In *Approaches to modern Chinese history*, edited by Albert Feuerwerker et al. [Selective entry]
Berkeley, Los Angeles: U. of California Press, 1967, 105–132.
SUBJ 15 ▪ 12

13849 MCH P P4 G1.2 1842–1895
Rawlinson, John Lang, 1920–.
China's struggle for naval development, 1839–1895.
Cambridge: Harvard U. Press, 1967. 318 p. (Harvard East Asian series, 25) (Revision of *The Chinese navy, 1839–1895*, doctoral dissertation in History, Harvard U., 1959)
SUBJ 14.4 15 ▪ 12 14.2 64 66

13850 MCY P P1 G1.2 1842–1895
Rawlinson, John Lang, 1920–.
'The Lay-Osborn flotilla: Its development and significance.'
PC 4 (Apr. 1950), 58–93.
SUBJ 15 ▪ 12 66

13851 MCH O P1 G1.2 1842–1895
Rochedragon, L- B-.
'La Chine militaire' (The military in China).
B. de la Société de géographie de Lyon 10 (1891), 507–526; 11 (1892), 62–92, 149–176.
SUBJ 15 32.2 ▪ 12 16.1 66

13852 MCH O P3 G1.2 1895–1911
Rottach, Edmond.
'L'armée dans la révolution chinoise' (The army in the Chinese Revolution [of 1911]).
R. de Paris 19, 4 (15 fév. 1912), 741–754.
SUBJ 15 32.2 ▪ 16.1 35

13853 MCH P P4 G1.2 1895–1911
Rouire, Alphonse Marie Ferdinand, 1855–1917?
'La transformation de la Chine' (The transformation of China).
R. des deux mondes 5e période 56 (1er mars 1910), 180–208.
SUBJ 12 12.2 15 19 25 60 ▪ 13 14.2 14.3 16.1 17 29 32.2 38 66

13854 NNC O P1 G9.0 1842–1895
Scott, James George, 1851–1935.
'The Chinese brave.'
Asiatic quarterly review 1 (Jan.–Apr. 1886), 222–245.
SUBJ 15 ▪ 12 16.1

13855 CSU U P2 G1.1 –1842
Senese, Donald J-.
'Koxinga and a Chinese restoration.'
History today 22, 10 (Oct. 1972), 716–723.
SUBJ 15 25 ▪ 66

13856 MCH U P2 G1.1 –1842
Simonovskaia, Larisa Vasil'evna, 1902–.
'Kitai' (China). In *Novaia istoriia stran zarubezhnogo Vostoka* (Modern history of countries of the non-Soviet Orient), edited by Igor Mikhailovich Reisner and Boris Konstantinovich Rubtsov. [Selective entry]
Moscow: Izd-vo Mosk. un-ta, 1952, vol. 1, 202–238.
SUBJ 12 14.1 15 16 32.2 66 ▪ 11.3 12.1 14.3 14.5 24.4

13857 MBA P P2 G8.2 1895–1911
[Soulié de Morant, Charles Georges?] G. S., 1878–.
'L'armée chinoise du Yunnan' (The Yunnan Army).
RI nouvelle (2e) série 6, 75 (15 fév. 1908), 171–180.
SUBJ 15

13858 MCY P P2 G1.2 1842–1911
Spector, Stanley, 1924–.
Li Hung-chang and the Huai Army: A study in nineteenth-century Chinese regionalism.
Seattle: U. of Washington Press, 1964. 43, 359 p. (Revision of *Li Hung-chang and the Huai-chün*, doctoral dissertation in History, U. of Washington, 1954)
SUBJ 12 15 16.1 ▪ 12.1 22 25 32.2 36.1 61 64 66 70

13859 DLC S P2 G1.2 1644–1911
Tikhvinskii, Sergei Leonidovich, 1918–.
'Man'chzhurskoe vladychestvo v Kitae' (Manchu rule in China). In *Man'chzhurskoe vladychestvo v Kitae* (Manchu rule in China), compiled by Institut narodov Azii, Akademiia nauk SSSR, edited by S. L. Tikhvinskii. [Selective entry]
Moscow: Nauka, Glav. red. vost. lit-ry, 1966, 5–76.
SUBJ 12 12.1 14.1 15 66 ▪ 11.2 14.5 16.1 16.3 19 32.2 70 71

13860 MCH P P2 G1.3 1842–1895
TSzian Di (Chiang Ti) and Nikolai Konstantinovich Chekanov, 1922–1961.
'Osvoboditel'naia bor'ba vostochnykh nian'tsziunei v 1866–1868 godakh' (The liberation struggle of the eastern [band] of the Nien Army, 1866–1868). [With English abstract]
PV 1959, 4, 48–61.
Subj 15 32.2 36.3 ▪ 70 71

13861 NIC S P1 G1.2 1895–1911
U.S. War Dept.
Notes on China.
Washington, D.C.: U.S. Government Printing Office, 1900. 90 p.
Subj 15 ▪ 14.2

13862 MCH P P1 G9.2 1895–1911
Vissière, Arnold Jacques Antoine, 1858–1930.
'La marine chinoise et sa nouvelle nomenclature' (The Chinese navy and its new nomenclature).
JA 11e série 4, 3 (nov.–déc. 1914), 639–649.
Subj 15

13863 CSU P P1 G1.2 1644–1895
Wade, Thomas Francis, 1818–1895.
'The army of the Chinese empire: Its two great divisions, the bannermen, or national guard, and the green standard, or provincial troops, their organization, locations, pay, conditions, etc.'
Chinese repository 20, 5 (May 1851), 250–280; 20, 6 (June 1851), 300–340; 20, 7 (July 1851), 363–422.
Subj 15 ▪ 25 35

13864 MCH P P2 G1.1 1644–1842
[Wei Yüan] ———, 1794–1856.
Chinese account of the Opium War, edited by Edward Harper Parker. Tr. by E. H. Parker from *Sheng wu chi* (Records of the Ch'ing dynasty's military achievements); [Peking?]: ——, 1842, *chüan* 14? [Condensed tr.]
Shanghai: Kelly and Walsh, 1888. 82 p.
Subj 15 25 ▪ 66

13865 CSU P P2 G1.2 –1842
Williams, Frederick Wells, 1857–1928.
'The Manchu conquest of China.' In *Recent developments in China*, edited by George Hubbard Blakeslee. [Selective entry]
New York: G. E. Stechert, 1913, 319–334.
Subj 15 25 66

13866 CSU O P2 G1.3 1842–1895
Wolseley, Garnet Joseph, 1833–1913.
Narrative of the war with China in 1860, to which is added the account of a short residence with the Taiping rebels in Nankin and a voyage from thence to Hankow.
London: Longman, Green, Longman, and Roberts, 1862. 14, 415 p.
Subj 15 32.2 ▪ 12 14.2 18 23 57 66

13867 CSH P P4 G1.1 1644–1895
Wong, George H. C. (Huang Tao-chang), 1924–.
'Sir Henry Pottinger and Hong Kong, 1941–1943.'
CCJ 3, 2 (May 1964), 162–174.
Subj 15 66

13868 MAM P P2 G1.2 –1842
Wu, Wei-ping (Wu Wei-p'ing), 1932–.
The development and decline of the Eight Banners.
Ann Arbor: University Microfilms (Publ. 70-16,231), 1970. 247 p. (Doctoral dissertation in History, U. of Pennsylvania, 1969)
Subj 15 35 ▪ 16 18 25 42 45

13869 MCY P P2 G1.5 1842–1895
Wu, Wei-ping (Wu Wei-p'ing), 1932–.
'The rise of the Anhwei Army.'
PC 14 (Dec. 1960), 30–49.
Subj 12 15 ▪ 14.5 16.1 25 32.2

13870 NNC P P1 G1.2 1842–1895
Zi, Etienne, 1851–?
Pratique des examens militaires en Chine (The military examination system in China).
Shanghai: Impr. de la Mission catholique, 1896. 132 p. (Variétés sinologiques, 9) [Reprinted—Taipei: Ch'eng-wen, 1971. 132 p.]
Subj 15 17

1644-1949

13871 NIC U P2 G1.2 1895–1949
'China's fighting services.'
PT new (2nd) series 7, 1 (1 July 1934), 79–92.
Subj 14.4 15

13872 CSU U P6 G9.3 1842–1928
'The Foochow naval dock yard.'
CEJ 5, 6 (Dec. 1929), 1073–1079.
Subj 15 24.2 24.4

13873 MCH O P2 G1.1 1842–1949
Abegg, Lily, 1901–.
Chinas Erneuerung: Der Raum als Waffe (Space as a weapon in the rebuilding of China).
Frankfurt a.M.: Sozietät, 1940. 481 p.
Subj 15 ▪ 12 12.1 14.2 17 66

13874 CSU P P1 G1.2 1644–1928
Brissaud-Desmaillet, Georges Henri, 1869–?
L'armée chinoise: le problème des troupes en excédent (The problem of excess troops in the Chinese army).
Paris: Henri Charles-Lavauzelle, 1927. 86 p.
Subj 15 ▪ 12.1 14.1 14.4 14.5 35

13875 NIC S P1 G1.2 1644–1949
Fried, Morton Herbert, 1923–.
'Military status in Chinese society.' [With comments by Shu-ch'ing Lee (Li Shu-ch'ing)]
AJS 57, 4 (Jan. 1952), 347–357.
Subj 15 16.1 ▪ 64 65

13876 DLC U P2 G1.1 1895–1928
Khodorov, Abram Evseevich, 1886–1949, and [Mikhail Lazarevich Veltman] Mikhail Pavlovich Pavlovich, pseud., 1871–1927.
Kitai v bor'be za nezavisimost' (China in the struggle for independence).
Moscow: Nauch. assots. vostokoved. pri TsIK SSSR, 1925. 195 p.
Subj 12 15 32.2 ▪ 14.2 14.3 16.2 16.4 66

13877 MCH PO P2 G1.1 –1949
Kotenev, Anatol M-, 1882–.
The Chinese soldier.
Shanghai: Kelly and Walsh, 1937. 16, 173 p.
Subj 15 ▪ 32.2 65

13878 CSH P P2 G1.1 1842–1949
Lin Tsiu-sen (Lin Ch'iu-sheng).
'Zehnter Zeitraum, von 1867 bis zur Gegenwart' (The tenth period, from 1867 to the present). In *China und Japan im Spiegel der Geschichte: Eine Betrachtung anhand des Werdeganges Chinas und Japan* (China and Japan in the mirror of history: A consideration of their respective courses of development), by Lin Tsiu-sen. [Selective entry]
Erlenbach-Zurich: Rentsch, 1946, vol. 2, 223–354.
Subj 12 15 32.2 66 ▪ 14.1 16.1 17 64

13879 NIC P P1 G1.3 1842–1949
Michael, Franz Henry, 1907–.
'Chinese military tradition.'
FES 15, 5 (13 Mar. 1946), 65–69; 15, 6 (27 Mar. 1946), 84–87.
Subj 15 ▪ 12 32.2

13880 NNC PO P2 G1.2 1842–1949
Smedley, Agnes, 1890–1950.
The great road: The life and times of Chu Teh.
New York: Monthly Review Press, 1956. 18, 461 p. [Reprinted—New York: Monthly Review Press, 1972. 20, 460 p.]
Subj 15 16.1 32.2 59 66 ▪ 16.3 17 18 19 32 41 47 52

13881 ECU P P2 G1.5 1895–1928
Sutton, Donald Sinclair, 1938–.
The rise and decline of the Yunnan Army, 1909–1925.
Unpublished doctoral dissertation in Oriental Studies, U. of Cambridge [Downing College], 1970. 262, 18 p.
Subj 15 32.2 ▪ 12 14.5 16.1 17 22 25 59

13882 MCH O P2 G1.2 1842–1928
Tyler, William Ferdinand, 1865–?
Pulling strings in China.
London: Constable, 1929. 10, 310 p.
Subj 12 14.5 15 16.1 22.2 ▪ 14.3 25 29 32.2 33 62 64 66

13883 CSH U P2 G1.2 1895–1928
[Vilenskii, Vladimir Dmitrievich] Vl. Vilenskii-Sibiriakov, pseud., 1888–1942.
Chzan-tszo-lin: man'chzhurskaia problema (Chang Tso-lin: The problem of Manchuria).
Moscow: Gosizdat, 1925. 62 p.
Subj 15 16.1 ▪ 14.2 14.3 32.2 66

13884 CSH PO P2 G1.2 1895–1928
[Vilenskii, Vladimir Dmitrievich] Vl. Vilenskii-Sibiriakov, pseud., 1888–1942.
U Pei-fu: kitaiskii militarizm (Wu P'ei-fu: Chinese militarism).
Moscow: Gosizdat, 1925. 54 p.
Subj 15 16 16.1 ▪ 36.4 66

13885 DLC S P1 G1.2 1895–1928
Vysogorets, V-.
Kitaiskaia armiia: ocherki po osnovnym voprosam vooruzhennykh sil sovremennogo Kitaia (The Chinese army: Notes on the basic problems of the armed forces of contemporary China).

Moscow: Gos. izd-vo, Otdel voen. lit-ry, 1930. 127 p.
SUBJ 15 ▪ 14.2 17 32.2 66

1911-1949

13886 NNC P P4 G1.2 1928–1949
'Military levies in North China, 1929–1930.'
NWSS 6, 13 (27 Mar. 1933), 60, 62–63.
SUBJ 14.5 15

13887 NNC P P2 G1.5 1911–1949
Suppressing Communist-banditry in China.
Shanghai: China United Press, 1934. 110 p. (China today series, 1)
SUBJ 15 25 32 32.2 ▪ 14.1 16.3 16.4 36.4 54 66

13888 MCH O P2 G1.2 1928–1949
Abend, Hallett Edward, 1884–1955, and Anthony J. Billingham.
Can China survive?
New York: Ives Washburn, 1936. 317 p.
SUBJ 15 32 ▪ 12 16.1 17

13889 CSH P P2 G1.5 1911–1928
Akatova, Tat'iana Nikolaevna, 1923–.
'Severnyi pokhod Natsional'no-revoliutsionnoi armii i dal'neishii pod''em revoliutsii (mai 1926 – mart 1927 g.)' (The Northern Expedition of the National Revolutionary Army and the impending revolution, May 1926 – March 1927). In *Ocherki istorii Kitaia v noveishee vremia* (Survey of modern Chinese history), compiled by Institut kitaevedeniia, Akademiia nauk SSSR, edited by Aleksei Stepanovich Perevertailo et al. [Selective entry]
Moscow: Izd-vo vost. lit-ry, 1959, 149–164.
SUBJ 15 32 32.2 ▪ 12 16.2 16.3 66

13890 CSU O P2 G1.3 1928–1949
Asiaticus, pseud.
'New Fourth Army area revisited.'
Amerasia 5, 7 (Sept. 1941), 287–294.
SUBJ 15 ▪ 32.2 66

13891 MCY O P2 G5.0 1928–1949
Band, Claire, and William Band, 1906–.
Dragon fangs: Two years with Chinese guerrillas.
London: Allen and Unwin, 1947. 12, 347 p. [Reprinted as *Two years with the Chinese Communists*. New Haven: Yale U. Press, 1948. 12, 347 p.]
SUBJ 15 22 25 26.3 66 ▪ 17 32.2 54 55 56 62

13892 NNC O P2 G1.5 1928–1949
Belden, Jack, 1910–.
The New Fourth Army.
Shanghai: Shanghai Mercury Press, 1939. 66 p. [Reprinted from *Shanghai evening post and mercury*.]
SUBJ 15 32.2 ▪ 25 61

13893 CSH O P2 G1.2 1928–1949
Bertram, James Munro.
Crisis in China: The story of the Sian mutiny.
London: Macmillan, 1937. 18, 318 p. [Reprinted as *First act in China: The story of the Sian mutiny*. New York: Viking Press, 1938. 18, 284 p.] [Reprinted—Ann Arbor: University Microfilms, n.d. 18, 284 p.] [Reprinted—Westport, Conn.: Hyperion Press, 197? 18, 284 p.]
SUBJ 15 32 59 ▪ 12 16.1 66

13894 CSU O P2 G1.4 1928–1949
Bertram, James Munro.
Unconquered: Journal of a year's adventures among the fighting peasants of North China.
New York: Day, 1939. 340 p. [Also published as *North China front*. London: Macmillan, 1939. 10, 514 p.]
SUBJ 15 64 ▪ 16.1 16.3 32.2 66

13895 FPN P P2 G4.1 1928–1949
Bianco, Lucien, 1930–.
La crise de Sian, décembre 1936 (The Sian Incident, December 1936).
Unpublished doctoral dissertation, Faculté des lettres, Université de Paris, 1968. 403 p.
SUBJ 15 32.2 66 ▪ 64

13896 CSH PO P2 G1.2 1911–1928
Blagodatov, Aleksei Vasil'evich.
Zapiski o kitaiskoi revoliutsii 1925–1927 gg. (Notes on the Chinese revolution of 1925–1927).
Moscow: Nauka, Glav. red. vost. lit-ry, 1970. 250 p.
SUBJ 12 15 32 32.2 35 66 ▪ 16.3 17 21.3 25 36.3 55

13897 CSU P P8 G1.2 1928–1949
Boorman, Howard Lyon, 1920–, and Scott Archer Boorman, 1949–.
'Chinese Communist insurgent warfare, 1935–1949.'
Political science q. 81, 2 (June 1966), 171–195.
SUBJ 15 32.2 ▪ 16.1 64

13898 CSU P P2 G1.2 1928–1949
Boorman, Scott Archer, 1949–.
The protracted game: A wei-ch'i interpretation of Maoist revolutionary strategy.
New York: Oxford U. Press, 1969. 14, 242 p.
SUBJ 15 64 ▪ 32.2 62

13899 CSH S P2 G1.2 1928–1949
Brenier, Henri, 1867–?
'La Guerre sino-nippone' (The Anti-Japanese War).
AF 38, 358 – 39, 374 (mars 1938 – nov.–déc. 1939), 64 p. in all.
SUBJ 15 25 32.2 ▪ 12 18 33 62

13900 CSU O P3 G6.1 1928–1949
Cabot, John Moors, 1901–.
'The last days of Shanghai: 1949.'
Foreign Service j. 44, 5 (May 1967), 28–29.
SUBJ 15 25

13901 NNC O P2 G1.2 1911–1949
Carlson, Evans Fordyce, 1896–1947.
The Chinese army: Its organization and military efficiency.
New York: Institute of Pacific Relations, International Secretariat, 1940. 142 p.
SUBJ 14 15 ▪ 14.2 14.5 16 56 64 66

13902 CSU O P2 G1.1 1928–1949
Carlson, Evans Fordyce, 1896–1947.
Twin stars of China.
New York: Dodd, Mead, 1941. 14, 331 p.
SUBJ 15 25 ▪ 32 32.2 64 66

13903 MCH S P2 G1.2 1928–1949
Chassin, Lionel Max, 1902–.
La conquête de la Chine par Mao Tsé-tung, 1945–1949 (Mao Tse-tung's conquest of China, 1945–1949).
Paris: Payot, 1952. 244 p.
The Communist conquest of China: A history of the civil war, 1945–1949. Tr. by Timothy Osato and Louis Gelas.
Cambridge: Harvard U. Press, 1965. 264 p.
SUBJ 15 32.2 ▪ 14 14.1 64 66

13904 CSH P P2 G1.2 1928–1949
Cheng, James Chester (Cheng Che-hsi), 1926–.
'Commander and commissar: The dynamics of the Chinese Red Army, 1927–49.' In *Collected documents of the First Sino-American Conference on Mainland China*. [Selective entry]
[Taipei]: Institute of International Relations, Republic of China, 1971, 885–893.
SUBJ 15 32.1

13905 CSH PO P2 G1.2 1911–1928
Cherepanov, Aleksandr Ivanovich.
Severnyi pokhod Natsional'no-revoliutsionnoi armii Kitaia (zapiski voennogo sovetnika) (The Northern Expedition: Notes of a military adviser).
Moscow: Nauka, Glav. red. vost. lit-ry, 1968. 303 p.
The Northern Expedition of the National-Revolutionary Army of China: Notes of a military advisor (1926–1927), edited by Lydia Holubnychy. Tr. by Caroline Rogers and Lydia Holubnychy. [Abridged tr.]
[New York]: Columbia U., East Asian Institute, 197? 246 p.
SUBJ 12 15 32 32.2 35 66 ▪ 16.1 16.2 22 36.3

13906 DLC PO P2 G9.0 1911–1928
Cherepanov, Aleksandr Ivanovich.
Zapiski voennogo sovetnika v Kitae: iz istorii pervoi grazhdanskoi revoliutsionnoi voiny (1925–1927) (Notes of a military adviser in China: History of the First Revolutionary Civil War, 1925–1927), 2nd ed.
Moscow: Nauka, 1971. 310 p.
Notes of a military advisor in China, edited by Harry H. Collier and Thomas M. Williamsen. Tr. by Alexandra O. Smith. [Tr. of 1964 ed.]
Taipei: Office of Military History, 1970. 381 p.
SUBJ 12.1 15 32.2 ▪ 17 22.1 24.5 25 32 32.1 36.3 36.4 64

13907 MCH P P4 G2.0 1928–1949
Clubb, Oliver Edmund, 1901–.
'Manchuria in the balance, 1945–1946.'
PHR 26, 4 (Nov. 1957), 377–389.
SUBJ 15 25 ▪ 32 32.2

13908 CSU P P3 G7.2 1928–1949
Cohen, Warren Ira, 1934–.
'Who fought the Japanese in Hunan? Some views of China's war effort.'
JAS 27, 1 (Nov. 1967), 111–115.
SUBJ 15 ▪ 12

13909 NNC O P2 G1.2 1928–1949
Epstein, Israel, 1915–.
The people's war.

London: Gollancz, 1939. 384 p.
SUBJ 15 19 32 ▪ 11.2 12 14 18 22 25 30

13910 MCH O P2 G5.1 1911–1928
Gaudissart, Raphaël, 1854–?
'Scènes de moeurs militaires dans la Chine nouvelle' (Glimpses of military customs in the new China).
Etudes 7e série 161, 4 (20 nov. 1919), 466–479.
SUBJ 15 25 ▪ 12.2 16.1

13911 MAM P P2 G1.3 1911–1949
Gillespie, Richard Eugene.
Whampoa and the Nanking decade (1924–1936).
Ann Arbor: University Microfilms (Publ. 72-1718), 1972. 565 p. (Doctoral dissertation in History, American U., 1971)
SUBJ 15 32 32.2 ▪ 17 32.1

13912 MCH O P2 G1.3 1928–1949
Hanson, Haldore E-, 1912–.
Humane endeavour: The story of the China war.
New York: Farrar and Rinehart, 1939. 10, 390 p.
SUBJ 12 15 ▪ 12.1 14 32

13913 CSU U P4 G9.2 1911–1928
Herzog, James H-.
'The Whampoa Academy.'
Proceedings of the U.S. Naval Institute 94, 4 (Apr. 1968), 46–53.
SUBJ 15 17 ▪ 16.1 32.2 64 66

13914 CSU P P2 G1.2 1928–1949
Hewett, Robert Foster, Jr., 1921–.
The military aspects of the Sino-Japanese War, 1937–1938.
Unpublished masters thesis in History, Stanford U., 1953. 104 p.
SUBJ 15 66

13915 CSU P P1 G1.2 1928–1949
Hsu, Yung-ying (Hsü Yung-ying), 1902–.
'China's war potential.'
Amerasia 7, 7 (25 July 1943), 228–238.
SUBJ 15 ▪ 12

13916 CSH P P2 G1.1 1911–1949
Hu Pu-yu (Hu P'u-yü), comp.
A brief history of the Chinese national revolutionary forces, edited by Yu Po-chuan (Yü Po-ch'üan) et al. Tr. from the Chinese by Wen Ha-hsiung.
Taipei: Chung Wu, 1972. 365 p.
SUBJ 15 25 32 ▪ 12 17 32.2 66

13917 MCH O P2 G2.0 1928–1949
Huang, Ray.
'Some observations on Manchuria in the balance, early 1946.'
PHR 27, 2 (May 1958), 159–169.
SUBJ 15 ▪ 12 25

13918 DLC O P2 G1.4 1911–1928
Impey, Lawrence.
The Chinese army as a military force, 3rd ed., enl.
Tientsin: Tientsin Press, 1926. 56 p.
SUBJ 15

13919 CSH P P2 G1.2 1928–1949
Iolk, Evgenii Sigizmundovich, 1900–1942.
'Piat' let sovetskoi vlasti v Kitae (k piatiletiiu Kantonskoi kommuny)' (Five years of soviet power in China: On the fifth anniversary of the Canton commune).
PK 11 (1933), 27–36.
SUBJ 12 15 32 32.2 66 ▪ 14.4 14.6 19

13920 DLC P P2 G1.2 1911–1949
Iolk, Evgenii Sigizmundovich, 1900–1942.
'Zakhvat Man'chzhurii i revoliutsionnyi pod"em v Kitae' (The seizure of Manchuria and the revolutionary upsurge in China). In *Okkupatsiia Man'chzhurii i bor'ba imperialistov* (The occupation of Manchuria and the imperialists' struggle), compiled by Kolonial'nyi sektor, Institut mirovogo khoziaistva i mirovoi politiki, Kommunisticheskaia akademiia. [Selective entry]
Moscow: Partizdat, 1932, 37–57.
SUBJ 15 16.4 18 32.2 54 ▪ 12 14.5 16.3 19 32 66

13921 DLC S P2 G9.2 1911–1928
IUr'ev, Mikhail Filippovich, 1918–.
'Bor'ba Kommunisticheskoi partii Kitaia za sozdanie kadrov revoliutsionnoi armii (1924–1927)' (The Chinese Communist Party's struggle to form revolutionary army cadres, 1924–1927). In *Sbornik statei po istorii stran Dal'nego Vostoka* (Articles on Far Eastern history), edited by Larisa Vasil'evna Simonovskaia and M. F. IUr'ev. [Selective entry]
Moscow: Izd-vo Mosk. un-ta, 1952, 43–54.
SUBJ 15 17 19 32 32.2 ▪ 64

13922 NNC P P2 G1.3 1911–1928
IUr'ev, Mikhail Filippovich, 1918–.
'K istorii organizatsii Natsional'no-osvoboditel'noi armii Kitaia: 30-letie Nan'chanskogo vosstaniia' (History of the organization of the People's Liberation Army of China: On the thirtieth anniversary of the Nanchang uprising).
SV 1957, 4, 3–8.
SUBJ 15 32.2

13923 NNC P P1 G1.2 1928–1949
IUr'ev, Mikhail Filippovich, 1918–.
Krasnaia armiia Kitaia (The Chinese Red Army).
Moscow: Izd-vo vost. lit-ry, 1958. 193 p.
SUBJ 15 32.1 ▪ 32 32.2

13924 CSH O P3 G6.1 1928–1949
IUzhnyi, A-.
'Voennaia operatsiia v Shankhae' (The military operation in Shanghai).
PK 10 (1932), 104–133.
SUBJ 15 66

13925 CSH P P2 G1.3 1911–1928
[Ivanov, Aleksei Alekseevich] A. Ivin, pseud., 1885–1942.
Ot Khan'kou k Shankhaiu (From Hankow to Shanghai).
Moscow: Moskovskii rabochii, 1927. 139 p.
SUBJ 12 15 16.3 24 35 66 ▪ 11.3 21.3 22 25 26.1 26.3 32.2 36.3

13926 NNC O P7 G1.2 1928–1949
Jones, Albert Tilton.
'Chinese guerrillas. Part 2, Guerrillas today: Their political, military and economic importance.'
CJ 29, 4 (Oct. 1938), 177–183.
SUBJ 15 25 ▪ 32

13927 MAM P P2 G1.2 1911–1928
Jordan, Donald Allan, 1936–.
The Northern Expedition: A military victory.
Ann Arbor: University Microfilms (Publ. 67-12,132), 1967. 2 vols. 463 p. [c.p.]. (Doctoral dissertation in History, U. of Wisconsin)
SUBJ 15 32 32.2 ▪ 25 36.3 36.4 64

13928 DLC O P2 G1.2 1928–1949
Karmen, Roman Lazarevich.
God v Kitae: zapiski kino-zhurnalista (A year in China: Notes of a news cameraman).
Moscow: Sovetskii pisatel', 1941. 155 p.
SUBJ 12 15 21.3 66 ▪ 12.1 14.1 14.4 16 17 23 47 52 55

13929 CSH O P2 G1.5 1911–1928
Konchits, N- I-.
'V riadakh natsional'no-revoliutsionnoi armii Kitaia' (In China's National Revolutionary Army). In *Sovetskie dobrovol'tsy o pervoi grazhdanskoi revoliutsionnoi voine v Kitae: vospominaniia* (Soviet volunteers in China's First Revolutionary Civil War [1924–1927]: Reminiscences), compiled by Institut narodov Azii, Akademiia nauk SSSR, edited by Aleksei Stepanovich Perevertailo. [Analytic entry]
Moscow: Izd-vo vost. lit-ry, 1961, 24–95.
SUBJ 15 17 25 ▪ 16.3 32 32.2 35

13930 NNC P P1 G1.2 1928–1949
Kreisberg, Paul H-.
The New Fourth Army incident and the united front in China.
Unpublished masters thesis in History, Columbia U., 1952. 102 p.
SUBJ 12 15 32.2

13931 MCH O P2 G7.0 1911–1928
Kuo Mo-jo, 1892–.
'A poet with the Northern Expedition.' Tr. by Josiah Whitney Bennett of 'Pei fa t'u tz'u' (Bivouacs on the Northern Expedition); *Yü chou feng* 20–34 (1 July 1936 – 1 Feb. 1937), 52 p. in all.
FEQ 3, 1 (Nov. 1943), 5–36; 3, 2 (Feb. 1944), 144–171; 3, 3 (May 1944), 237–259; 3, 4 (Aug. 1944), 362–380.
SUBJ 15 ▪ 32 32.1

13932 CSU P P2 G1.2 1928–1949
Kuo, Warren (Kuo Hua-lun), 1912–.
'The conference at Lochuan [i.e., the capital of Lo-ch'uan *hsien*, Shensi].'
IS 5, 1 (Oct. 1968), 35–56.
SUBJ 15 32 32.2

13933 CSU P P2 G1.2 1928–1949
Kuo, Warren (Kuo Hua-lun), 1912–.
'Disbandment of the New 4th Army.'
IS 6, 7 (Apr. 1970), 66–79; 6, 8 (May 1970), 93–98.
SUBJ 12 15 32.2 66

13934 CSU P P2 G1.3 1928–1949
Kuo, Warren (Kuo Hua-lun), 1912–.
'Expansion of Communist armed forces in Central China.'
IS 6, 6 (Mar. 1970), 73–88.
SUBJ 15 32.2 66 ▪ 22 32

13935 CSH P P2 G1.4 1928–1949
Kuo Warren (Kuo Hua-lun), 1912–.
'Expansion of Communist armed forces in North China.'

IS 5, 12 (Sept. 1969), 83–93; 6, 1 (Oct. 1969), 83–96.
Subj 15 25 32.2

13936 CSU P P1 G1.2 1928–1949
Kuo, Warren (Kuo Hua-lun), 1912–.
'The zigzag flight of Red Army troops.'
IS 4, 10 (July 1968), 36–56.
Subj 15 ▪ 12.1

13937 MAM P P2 G1.2 1911–1928
Landis, Richard Brian, 1930–.
Institutional trends at the Whampoa Military School: 1924–26.
Ann Arbor: University Microfilms (Publ. 69-20,245), 1969. 251 p. (Doctoral dissertation in History, U. of Washington, 1968)
Subj 15 17 ▪ 14 32 64

13938 CSU P P2 G1.3 1911–1928
Landis, Richard Brian, 1930–.
'The origins of Whampoa graduates who served in the Northern Expedition.'
Studies on Asia 5 (1964), 149–163.
Subj 15 ▪ 12 32

13939 MCY PO P1 G1.2 1928–1949
Lang, Olga.
'The good iron of the new Chinese army.'
PA 12, 1 (Mar. 1939), 20–33.
Subj 15

13940 ELB P P2 G1.2 1911–1949
Larre, Claude.
'L'art militaire de Mao Tse-toung' (The military art of Mao Tse-tung).
Etudes 7e série 333 (oct. 1970), 360–379.
Subj 15 ▪ 32.2 64

13941 CSU P P3 G1.5 1928–1949
Leary, William M-.
'Wings for China: The Jouett mission, 1932–1935.'
PHR 38, 4 (Nov. 1969), 447–462.
Subj 15 66 ▪ 17 25

13942 CSH P P2 G1.2 1928–1949
Lee Ngok (Li O), 1939–.
'Lin Piao's military tactics, 1937–1945.' In *Selected seminar papers on contemporary China, I*, edited by Steve S. K. Chin (Chin Ssu-k'ai) and Frank Henry Haviland King. [Analytic entry]
Hong Kong: U. of Hong Kong, Centre of Asian Studies, 1971, 199–238. (CAS occasional papers and monographs, 4)
Subj 15 25 ▪ 32 32.2

13943 MMT O P2 G1.2 1928–1949
Lindsay, Michael Francis Morris, 1909–.
'Conflict in North China: 1937–1943.'
FES 14, 13 (4 July 1945), 172–176.
Subj 15 ▪ 12 32 32.1 70

13944 CSU O P2 G1.2 1928–1949
Lindsay, Michael Francis Morris, 1909–.
'Who will win the civil war in China?'
Virginia quarterly review 23, 2 (Mar. 1947), 193–208.
Subj 15

13945 NNC P P2 G1.2 1911–1949
Liu, Frederick F. (Liu Fu), 1919–.
A military history of modern China, 1924–1949.
Princeton: Princeton U. Press, 1956. 12, 312 p. (Revision of *The Nationalist Army of China: An administrative study of the period 1924–1946*, doctoral dissertation in Political Science, Princeton U., 1951) [Reprinted—Port Washington, N.Y.: Kennikat Press, 1971. 12, 312 p.]
Subj 12 15 32 32.1 32.2 ▪ 11.4 14.4 17 56 72

13946 CSH O P2 G1.2 1928–1949
Liu Po-cheng (Liu Po-ch'eng), 1892–.
'Looking back on the Long March.' Tr. of 'Hui ku ch'ang cheng'; in *Hsing huo liao yüan* (Sparks set fire to the plain), edited by Chung-kuo jen min chieh fang chün san shih nien cheng wen pien chi wei yüan hui (Committee for the Compilation of the Thirty-year History of the People's Liberation Army); Peking: Jen min wen hsüeh ch'u pan she, 1958, vol. 3, 1–14. In *The Long March: Eyewitness accounts*, edited by the organization cited. [Sole entry]
Peking: Foreign Languages Press, 1963, 202–224.
Subj 15 ▪ 32.2

13947 MCH P P4 G9.2 1911–1928
MacFarquhar, Roderick Lemonde, 1930–.
'The Whampoa Military Academy.'
PC 9 (Aug. 1955), 146–172.
Subj 15 17 32.1 ▪ 64

13948 CSH O P2 G1.2 1911–1949
Mao Tse-tung, 1893–.
'Problems of strategy in China's revolutionary war.' Tr. of 'Chung-kuo ko ming chan cheng ti chan lüeh wen t'i'; in *Mao Tse-tung hsüan chi* (Selected works of Mao Tse-tung), 2nd ed.; Peking: Jen min ch'u pan she, 1960, vol. 2 [originally published in Yenan, 1943]. In *Selected works of Mao Tse-tung*, edited by Mao Tse-tung hsüan chi ch'u pan wei yüan hui (Committee for the Publication of the Selected Works of Mao Tse-tung), Chung yang wei yüan hui (Central Committee), Chung-kuo kung ch'an tang (Chinese Communist Party). [Selective entry]
Peking: Foreign Languages Press, 1965, vol. 1, 179–254.
Subj 15 ▪ 25 32.2

13949 CSH O P2 G1.2 1911–1949
Mao Tse-tung, 1893–.
'Problems of war and strategy.' Tr. of 'Chan cheng ho chan lüeh wen t'i'; in *Mao Tse-tung hsüan chi* (Selected works of Mao Tse-tung), 2nd ed.; Peking: Jen min ch'u pan she, 1960, vol. 2 [originally published in *Chieh fang jih pao* 6 Nov. 1936]. In *Selected works of Mao Tse-tung*, edited by Mao Tse-tung hsüan chi ch'u pan wei yüan hui (Committee for the Publication of the Selected Works of Mao Tse-tung), Chung yang wei yüan hui (Central Committee), Chung-kuo kung ch'an tang (Chinese Communist Party). [Selective entry]
Peking: Foreign Languages Press, 1965, vol. 2, 219–235.
Subj 15 ▪ 32.2

13950 NNC S P2 G1.1 1911–1928
[Mel'nikov, Boris Nikolaevich] B. Semenov, pseud., 1896–1937.
'Nastuplenie reaktsii v Kitae' (The reactionary offensive in China).
MKhMP 1926, 4 (aprel'), 3–14.
Subj 12 15 32.1 35 66 ▪ 16.4 32.2 36.3

13951 CSU O P2 G1.2 1928–1949
Miles, Milton Edward, 1900–1961.
A different kind of war: The little-known story of the combined guerrilla forces created in China by the U.S. Navy and the Chinese during World War II.
Garden City, N.Y.: Doubleday, 1967. 15, 629 p.
Subj 15 66 ▪ 18 25 48 55

13952 MCH O P2 G1.3 1928–1949
Mossdorf, Otto, 1882–.
Der Krieg in Ostasien: Der chinesisch-japanische Konflikt (The war in East Asia: The Sino-Japanese conflict), 3rd ed.
Leipzig: W. Conrad, 1941. 298 p.
Subj 15 66 ▪ 25

13953 CSH O P3 G9.2 1911–1928
Naumov, Samuil Naumovich, 1899–1966.
'Shkola Vampu' (The Whampoa Academy). In *Sovetskie dobrovol'tsy o pervoi grazhdanskoi revoliutsionnoi voine v Kitae: vospominaniia* (Soviet volunteers in China's First Revolutionary Civil War [1924–1927]: Reminiscences), compiled by Institut narodov Azii, Akademiia nauk SSSR, edited by Aleksei Stepanovich Perevertailo. [Analytic entry]
Moscow: Izd-vo vost. lit-ry, 1961, 126–139.
Subj 15 17 ▪ 25 32 32.2 64 66

13954 CSH O P2 G1.4 1928–1949
Peng Teh-huai (P'eng Te-huai), 1898–.
Unity and the defense of North China.
Chungking: New China Information Committee, 1940. 41 p. (NCIC bulletins, 13)
Subj 15 25 ▪ 12 32 32.2

13955 CSH O P2 G1.5 1911–1928
Perevertailo, Aleksei Stepanovich, 1897–.
'Sovetskie dobrovol'tsy v Kitae v 1923–1927 gg. (vstupitel'naia stat'ia)' (Soviet volunteers in China, 1923–1927: Introduction). In *Sovetskie dobrovol'tsy o pervoi grazhdanskoi revoliutsionnoi voine v Kitae: vospominaniia* (Soviet volunteers in China's First Revolutionary Civil War [1924–1927]: Reminiscences), compiled by Institut narodov Azii, Akademiia nauk SSSR, edited by A. S. Perevertailo. [Analytic entry]
Moscow: Izd-vo vost. lit-ry, 1961, 3–23.
Subj 15 17 32 32.2 72 ▪ 25 35 64 66

13956 CSU O P4 G1.3 1911–1928
Rodes, Jean.
Scènes de la vie révolutionnaire en Chine (1911–1914) (Scenes of revolutionary life in China, 1911–1914).
Paris: Plon-Nourrit, 1917. 301 p.
Subj 15 32.2 ▪ 16.1 25 59

13957 CSH PO P2 G1.2 1928–1949
Romanus, Charles F-, and Riley Sunderland.
Stilwell's command problems.
Washington, D.C.: U.S. Dept. of the Army, Office of the Chief of Military History, 1956. 18, 518 p. (U.S. Army in World War II, 9; China, Burma, India Theater, 2)
Subj 15 66 ▪ 12 14.2 14.3 16.1 32.2

13958 CSH PO P2 G1.2 1928–1949
Romanus, Charles F-, and Riley Sunderland.
Stilwell's mission to China.
Washington, D.C.: U.S. Dept. of the Army, Office of the Chief of Military History, 1953. 19, 441 p. (U.S. Army in World War II, 9; China, Burma, India Theater, 1)
Subj 15 66 ▪ 12 12.1 14.3 16.1

13959 CSH PO P2 G1.2 1928–1949
Romanus, Charles F-, and Riley Sunderland.
Time runs out in CBI [the China-Burma-India Theater].
Washington, D.C.: U.S. Dept. of the Army, Office of the Chief of Military History, 1959. 17, 428 p. (U.S. Army in World War II, 9; China, Burma, India Theater, 3)
Subj 15 66 ▪ 12 12.1 14.2 14.3 16.1 17 32.2 55

13960 NNC S P2 G1.2 1928–1949
Rosinger, Lawrence Kaelter, 1915–.
'Politics and strategy of China's mobile war.'
PA 12, 3 (Sept. 1939), 263–277.
Subj 15 ▪ 12.1 14 14.1

13961 NNC S P1 G1.2 1928–1949
Scheindlin, Shira Ann, 1946–.
The political career of Chang Hsüeh-liang, 1928–1936.
Unpublished masters thesis in History, Columbia U., 1969. 74 p. [Certificate essay, East Asian Institute]
Subj 12 15 ▪ 32.2

13962 MCH P P2 G1.4 1911–1928
Sheridan, James Edward, 1922–.
Chinese warlord: The career of Feng Yü-hsiang.
Stanford: Stanford U. Press, 1966. 386 p.
Subj 12 14.5 15 18 32 35 ▪ 14.2 25 64 66

13963 CSH P P2 G1.2 1928–1949
Sikirianskaia, Liia Abramovna, ?–1959.
Velikii pokhod Kitaiskoi Krasnoi Armii, 1934–1936 gg. (The Long March of the Chinese Red Army, 1934–1936).
Moscow: Izd-vo vost. lit-ry, 1962. 91 p. (Revision of doctoral dissertation in History, Moskovskii universitet, 1951. [For sources and documentation of this book, see entry 22941.])
Subj 15 32.2 ▪ 12 66

13964 NNC O P7 G5.0 1928–1949
Smedley, Agnes, 1890–1950.
China fights back: An American woman with the Eighth Route Army.
New York: Vanguard Press, 1938. 22, 282 p.
Subj 15 25 ▪ 26 28 48 55 60 66

13965 NNC O P2 G1.2 1928–1949
Smedley, Agnes, 1890–1950.
China's Red Army marches.
New York: Vanguard Press, 1934. 21, 311 p.
Subj 15 ▪ 22.2 24.1 25 32.1 32.2

13966 DLC P P2 G1.1 1911–1928
Smolov, N-.
'Militaristicheskie armii v istorii Guanduna (ocherk za period 1924–25 g.)' (Survey of militarist armies in the history of Kwangtung in the period 1924–1925). In *Kantonskaia kommuna: sbornik statei i materialov* (Articles and documents on the Canton commune), compiled by Nauchno-issledovatel'skii institut po Kitaiu, Kommunisticheskaia akademiia. [Selective entry]
Moscow: Gosizdat, 1929, 251–276.
Subj 15 25 35 ▪ 26.2 26.4 32 32.2 36.4

13967 CSU O P8 G1.5 1928–1949
Snow, Edgar, 1905–1972.
'China's New Fourth Army.'
Asia (New York: American Asiatic Assn.) 39, 5 (May 1939), 257–260.
Subj 15 25

13968 CSU O P2 G1.5 1911–1949
Snow, Edgar, 1905–1972.
'Han Ying's "lost" Red Army.'
Asia (New York: American Asiatic Assn.) 39, 4 (Apr. 1939), 203–205.
Subj 15 25 ▪ 36.4 59

13969 NNC O P2 G1.2 1928–1949
[Snow, Helen Foster] Nym Wales, pseud., 1907–.
Inside Red China.
New York: Doubleday, Doran, 1939. 24, 356 p.
Subj 15 25 47 54 ▪ 12 16 22 32.2 52 60 64 65 66

13970 MCH O P2 G1.2 1928–1949
Strong, Anna Louise, 1885–1970.
One-fifth of mankind.
New York: Modern Age, 1938. 215 p.
Subj 15 28 ▪ 12 19 21.2 26.3 31 35 36.3 47 54 66

13971 CSH U P2 G1.2 1911–1928
Tarmosin, S-.
'Vooruzhennye sily voenno-politicheskikh gruppirovok v Kitae' (The armed forces of the military-political alignments in China). In *O Kitae: politiko-ekonomicheskii sbornik* (Articles on China's political economy), edited by [Solomon Abramovich Dridzo] A. Lozovskii, pseud. [Selective entry]
Moscow: Gosizdat, 1928, 200–211.
Subj 15 ▪ 32 32.2

13972 CSH O P2 G1.5 1911–1928
Teslenko, E- V-.
'Ot Guanchzhou do Ukhania' (From Canton to Wuhan). In *Sovetskie dobrovol'tsy o pervoi grazhdanskoi revoliutsionnoi voine v Kitae: vospominaniia* (Soviet volunteers in China's First Revolutionary Civil War [1924–1927]: Reminiscences), compiled by Institut narodov Azii, Akademiia nauk SSSR, edited by Aleksei Stepanovich Perevertailo. [Analytic entry]
Moscow: Izd-vo vost. lit-ry, 1961, 96–125.
Subj 15 25 ▪ 17 32 32.2

13973 CSU O P2 G1.5 1928–1949
Tung-li, pseud.
'The founding of the Chinese Red Army.' Tr. by Chün-tu Hsüeh and Robert Carver North of 'Kuan yü Chu Mao hung chün ti li shih chi ch'i chuang k'uang ti pao kao' (History of the Red Army of Chu Te and Mao Tse-tung and a report on its present state); *Chung yang chün shih t'ung hsün* 1 (15 Jan. 1930), 31a–42b. In *Contemporary China, 1962–1964*, edited by Edward Stuart Kirby. [Selective entry]
Hong Kong: Hong Kong U. Press, 1968, 59–83.
Subj 15 ▪ 25

13974 NNC PO P2 G5.3 1928–1949
Wang Yü-ch'üan, 1911–.
'The organization of a typical guerrilla area in south Shantung.' In *The Chinese army: Its organization and military efficiency*, by Evans Fordyce Carlson. [Analytic entry]
New York: Institute of Pacific Relations, International Secretariat, 1940, 84–130. [For Carlson's work, see entry 13901.]
Subj 15 22 22.1 66 ▪ 12 17 24.1 24.2 24.5 26 54 64

13975 CSU PO P2 G1.2 1928–1949
Wedemeyer, Albert Coady, 1896–.
Wedemeyer reports!
New York: Holt, 1958. 12, 497 p.
Subj 15 32 32.2 ▪ 66

13976 MCH P P2 G1.4 1911–1928
Weisshart, Herbert, 1924–.
'Feng Yü-hsiang: His rise as a militarist and his training programs.'
PC 6 (Mar. 1952), 75–111.
Subj 15 28 37 ▪ 24.4 27 61 64

13977 CSU P P2 G1.2 1911–1949
Wilbur, Clarence Martin, 1908–.
'Military separatism and the process of reunification under the Nationalist regime, 1922–1937' [with comments by Wang Gungwu (Wang Keng-wu) and Hsu Dau-lin (Hsü Tao-lin)]. In *China in crisis, Vol. 1, China's heritage and the Communist political system*, edited by Ping-ti Ho and Tang Tsou. [Selective entry]
Chicago: U. of Chicago Press, 1968, 203–276.
Subj 15 22 25 32 ▪ 12 14.5 14.6 16.1 59 64

13978 CSU P P2 G1.4 1928–1949
Wilson, David.
'Leathernecks in North China, 1945.'
BCAS 4, 2 (Summer 1972), 33–37.
Subj 15 32.2

13979 CSU P P2 G1.3 1911–1928
Wou, Odoric Y. K. (Wu Ying-kuang), 1938–.
'A Chinese "warlord" faction: The Chihli clique, 1918–1924.' In *Columbia essays in international affairs, Vol. III, The Dean's papers, 1967*, edited by Andrew Wellington Cordier. [Sole entry]
New York: Columbia U. Press, 1968, 249–273. (Masters thesis in History, Columbia U.)
Subj 15 32 35 ▪ 12 12.1 14.5 22 25 30 48

13980 MAM P P1 G1.2 1911–1949
Wou, Odoric Y. K. (Wu Ying-kuang), 1938–.
Militarism in modern China as exemplified in the career of Wu P'ei-fu.
Ann Arbor: University Microfilms (Publ. 72-10,472), 1972. 358 p. (Doctoral dissertation in History, Columbia U., 1970)
Subj 15 ▪ 12 32.1 32.2

13981 CSU P P1 G4.3 1911–1928
Yang, Richard F. S. (Yang Fu-sen), 1918–.

'Sinkiang under the administration of Governor Yang Tseng-hsin, 1911–1928.'
Central Asiatic j. 6, 4 (Dec. 1961), 270–316.
SUBJ 15 32.2 ▪ 66

13982 MCH O P1 G1.2 1928–1949
Yeh Chien-ying, 1898–.
'Report on the general military situation of the Chinese Communist Party in the War of Resistance' [issued in Yenan in 1944 as a briefing to correspondents]. In *The Chinese Communists*, edited by George Stuart Gelder. [Selective entry]
London: Gollancz, 1946, 73–102.
SUBJ 15 25 ▪ 32.2 64

13983 MAM P P7 G7.3 1928–1949
Yoon, Chong-kun, 1931–.
Mao, the Red Army, and the Chinese Soviet Republic.
Ann Arbor: University Microfilms (Publ. 68-14,578), 1968. 322 p. (Doctoral dissertation in History, American U.)
SUBJ 15 ▪ 16.1 32.2 64

1911-1972
(including 1644-1972)

13984 NNC P P1 G1.2 1911–1972
Asian Peoples' Anti-Communist League.
A research on Mao Tse-tung's thought of military insurrection.
Taipei: Asian Peoples' Anti-Communist League, 1961. 94 p. (APACL pamphlets, 50)
SUBJ 15 32.2 64 ▪ 72

13985 CSU P P1 G1.1 1911–1972
Bedeski, Robert Edward, 1937–.
'Li Tsung-jen and the demise of China's "third force".'
AS 5, 12 (Dec. 1965), 616–628.
SUBJ 12 15 ▪ 59

13986 MCM P P2 G1.2 1842–1972
Bobrow, Davis Bernard, 1936–.
Political and economic role of the military in the Chinese Communist movement, 1927–1959.
Unpublished doctoral dissertation in Political Science, Massachusetts Institute of Technology, 1962. 779 p.
SUBJ 12 15 32.1 32.2 35 60 ▪ 11.4 14 16.1 16.3 17 18 19 30 55 64

13987 CSU P P2 G1.2 –1972
Boorman, Scott Archer, 1949–.
'Deception in Chinese strategy.' In *The military and political power of China in the 1970s*, edited by William Wallace Whitson. [Selective entry]
New York: Praeger, 1972, 313–337.
SUBJ 15 61

13988 CSH F P1 G1.2 1928–1972
Bradbury, William Chapman, 1915–1958, and Jeane J- Kirkpatrick.
'Determinants of loyalty and disaffection in Chinese Communist soldiers during the Korean hostilities: An exploratory study.' In *Mass behavior in battle and captivity: The Communist soldier in the Korean War*, by W. C. Bradbury, edited by Samuel M- Meyers and Albert D- Biderman. [Selective entry]
Chicago: U. of Chicago Press, 1968, 3–105.
SUBJ 15 61 ▪ 32.2

13989 CSU P P1 G1.2 1911–1972
Bueschel, Richard M-.
Communist Chinese air power.
New York: Praeger, 1968. 238 p.
SUBJ 15 32.2 ▪ 14.3 14.4

13990 NIC U P1 G1.3 –1972
Chang, Chi-yun (Chang Ch'i-yün), 1901–.
'Military service and military system in Chinese history.'
CC 4, 1 (Mar. 1962), 38–82.
SUBJ 15 ▪ 14.5

13991 MAM P P1 G1.2 1911–1972
Chiu, S. M. (Chao Shan-ming), 1923–.
A history of the Chinese Communist army.
Ann Arbor: University Microfilms (Publ. 59-864), 1959. 352 p. (Doctoral dissertation in History, U. of Southern California, 1958)
SUBJ 15 32.1 64 ▪ 25 32.2 35 61 66

13992 MCH P P1 G1.2 1928–1972
Chiu, S. M. (Chao Shan-ming), 1923–.
'Political control in the Chinese Communist army.'
Military review 41, 8 (Aug. 1961), 25–35. [For fuller treatment, see entry 13991.]
SUBJ 15 32.1 ▪ 17 64

13993 CSH P P2 G1.2 1928–1972
Chu Wen-lin.
'Personnel changes in the PLA military regions and districts before and after the Cultural Revolution.' In *Collected documents of the First Sino-American Conference on Mainland China.* [Selective entry]
[Taipei]: Institute of International Relations, Republic of China, 1971, 843–884.
SUBJ 15 16.1 ▪ 32.1 35

13994 CSU S P1 G1.2 –1972
Dewenter, John R-.
'China afloat.'
FA 50, 4 (July 1972), 738–751.
SUBJ 15 ▪ 14.2

13995 CSU P P1 G1.2 1928–1972
Domes, Jürgen Otto, 1932–.
'Problems of the Chinese Communist armed forces' [with comments by Kenneth Randolph Whiting]. In *Aspects of modern Communism*, edited by Richard Felix Staar. [Selective entry]
Columbia: U. of South Carolina Press, 1968, 259–285.
SUBJ 12.1 15 ▪ 16.1 25 32

13996 CSU U P2 G1.2 –1972
Dreyer, Edward Leslie.
'Military continuities: The PLA and Imperial China.' In *The military and political power of China in the 1970s*, edited by William Wallace Whitson. [Selective entry]
New York: Praeger, 1972, 3–24.
SUBJ 15 25

13997 CSU U P2 G1.1 1911–1972
Dupuy, Trevor Nevitt, 1916–.
The military history of the Chinese civil war.
New York: Franklin Watts, 1969. 110 p.
SUBJ 15 25 32.2 ▪ 32 64 66

13998 CSU P P1 G1.2 1928–1972
Gillespie, Richard Eugene, and John C- Sims.
'The general rear services department.' In *The military and political power of China in the 1970s*, edited by William Wallace Whitson. [Selective entry]
New York: Praeger, 1972, 185–213.
SUBJ 15 35

13999 CSU P P1 G1.2 1928–1972
Gittings, John, 1938–.
'Army-party relations in the light of the Cultural Revolution.' In *Party leadership and revolutionary power in China*, edited by John Wilson Lewis. [Analytic entry]
Cambridge: Cambridge U. Press, 1970, 373–403.
SUBJ 15 16.1 32 ▪ 25 32.1 35

14000 CSU P P1 G1.2 1644–1972
Gittings, John, 1938–.
'The Chinese army.' In *Modern China's search for a political form*, edited by Jack Douglas Gray. [Analytic entry]
London: Oxford U. Press, 1969, 187–224.
SUBJ 15 32.1 35 ▪ 14.2 16.1 25 64

14001 ELO P P1 G1.2 1928–1972
Gittings, John, 1938–.
The role of the Chinese army.
London: Oxford U. Press, 1967. 19, 331 p.
SUBJ 12 15 25 32.1 35 ▪ 14 19 32 63 64

14002 CSH P P2 G1.2 1928–1972
Griffith, Samuel Blair, II, 1906–.
The Chinese People's Liberation Army.
New York: McGraw-Hill, 1967. 14, 398 p. (Council on Foreign Relations, United States and China in world affairs series, 6)
SUBJ 15 16.1 32 32.2 ▪ 19 25 32.1 59 64

14003 NNC P P1 G1.2 1911–1972
Haffner, Sebastian.
'Der neue Krieg: Zur militärischen Theorie und Praxis Mao Tse-tungs' (The new warfare: The military theory and practice of Mao Tse-tung).
Merkur; deutsche Z. für europäisches Denken 20, 3 (März 1966), 201–219.
SUBJ 15 32.2 ▪ 32.1 64

14004 CSH P P2 G1.2 1644–1972
Joyaux, François.
'Les guerres chinoises et leurs conjonctures (1832–1968)' (Chinese wars and their circumstances, 1832–1968).
Guerres et paix 1969, 12, 39–63.
SUBJ 12 15 32.2 66 ▪ 32 33

14005 MCH P P1 G1.2 1928–1972
Katzenbach, Edward Lawrence, Jr., 1919–, and Gene Z- Hanrahan, 1926–.
'The revolutionary strategy of Mao Tse-tung.'
Political science q. 70, 3 (Sept. 1955), 321–340. [Reprinted in *Modern guerrilla warfare: Fighting Communist guerrilla warfare, 1941–1961*, edited by Franklin Mark Osanka. (Sole entry.) New York: Free Press of Glencoe, 1962, 131–147.]
SUBJ 15 ▪ 32.1 64

14006 CSH P P2 G1.2 1928–1972
Kau, Ying-mao (Kao Ying-mao), 1934–, et al.
The political work system of the Chinese Communist military: Analysis and documents.

Providence: Brown U., East Asia Language and Area Center, 1971. 366 p.
SUBJ 15 32.1 35 ▪ 25 32 32.2

14007 CSU O P1 G1.1 1928–1972
Lee Ping-chai.
'The military legal system of the Republic of China.'
Military law review 14 (1961), 160–170.
SUBJ 12.2 15

14008 CSH P P2 G1.2 1911–1972
Lévy, Roger.
'Armées et armements chinois' (Chinese armies and arms).
Guerres et paix 1969, 12, 29–39.
SUBJ 15 ▪ 32 32.2

14009 ELB P P2 G1.2 –1972
Lévy, Roger.
'La Chine et l'art militaire pendant vingt-cinq siècles' (China and the military arts through twenty-five centuries).
Politique étrangère 34, 4 (1969), 405–415.
SUBJ 15 ▪ 61

14010 NNC S P2 G1.2 1928–1972
Martynov, Aleksandr Aleksandrovich.
Slavnaia narodno-osvoboditel'naia armiia Kitaia (China's glorious People's Liberation Army).
Moscow: Voenizdat, 1957. 157 p.
SUBJ 15 16.1 ▪ 32.1 32.2 72

14011 CSH O P2 G1.2 1928–1972
Meyers, Samuel M-.
'Wang Tsun-ming, anti-Communist: An autobiographical account of Chinese Communist thought reform.' In *Mass behavior in battle and captivity: The Communist soldier in the Korean War*, by William Chapman Bradbury, edited by S. M. Meyers and Albert D- Biderman. [Selective entry]
Chicago: U. of Chicago Press, 1968, 121–159.
SUBJ 15 32.2 61 ▪ 12.1

14012 NNC P P2 G1.2 1911–1972
O'Ballance, Edgar, 1918–.
The Red Army of China: A short history.
New York: Praeger, 1963. 232 p.
SUBJ 15 25 32.2 ▪ 32 47 64

14013 NNC P P1 G1.2 1928–1972
Rifkin, Susan Beth.
The use and development of nuclear energy in the People's Republic of China.
Unpublished masters thesis in Public Law and Government, Columbia U., 1969. 94 p. [Certificate essay, East Asian Institute]
SUBJ 14.4 15 ▪ 12 17

14014 MAM P P1 G1.2 1928–1972
Rigdon, Susan Marie, 1943–.
The Chinese military ethic.
Ann Arbor: University Microfilms (Publ. 72-12,354), 1972. 156 p. (Doctoral dissertation in Political Science, U. of Illinois)
SUBJ 15 64 ▪ 25 32 32.1

14015 MMT O P1 G1.2 1928–1972
Rigg, Robert B-.
Red China's fighting hordes.
Harrisburg, Pa.: Military Service Publishing Co., 1951. 14, 378 p. [Reprinted—Westport, Conn.: Greenwood Press, 1972. 14, 378 p.]
SUBJ 15 16.1 30 ▪ 17 18 32.1 47 64 66

14016 MCH U P1 G1.2 –1972
Sessich, Marcello.
'L'arte della guerra di Sun Zu, il Clausewitz cinese: sua influenza sul pensiero militare di Mao Tse-tung' (The military theory of Sun Tzu, the Chinese Clausewitz, and his influence on Mao Tse-tung's military thought).
Rivista militare 21, 3 (marzo 1965), 357–367.
SUBJ 15 ▪ 64

14017 CSH U P1 G1.2 1928–1972
Tang Ping-chu (T'ang P'ing-chu).
'The democratic tradition of the People's Liberation Army.' Tr. of 'Chung-kuo jen min chieh fang chün ti min chu ch'uan t'ung'; *Hung ch'i* 1959, 8 (16 Apr.), 22–34. In *Translations from 'Hung-ch'i' (Red flag) (No. 5, 1 March 1959 – No. 8, 15 April 1960)*, mimeo., compiled by U.S. Joint Publications Research Service. [Selective entry]
Washington, D.C.: JPRS, 31 July 1961, 62–81. (JPRS 4820; MC 17,376/1961)
SUBJ 15 ▪ 32.1

14018 DLC S P2 G1.2 1842–1972
Whiting, Kenneth Randolph, 1913–.
The Chinese Communist armed forces.
Maxwell Air Force Base, Ala.: Air U., Aerospace Studies Institute, Documentary Research Division, 1967. 85 p.
SUBJ 15 ▪ 17 25 32 32.2 64 66

14019 CSU S P1 G1.2 1911–1972
Whitson, William Wallace, 1926–.
'Introduction.' In *The military and political power of China in the 1970s*, edited by W. W. Whitson. [Selective entry]
New York: Praeger, 1972, 15–34 [s.p.].
SUBJ 15 ▪ 16.1 25

14020 CSU FP P2 G1.2 1911–1972
Whitson, William Wallace, 1926–, and Chen-hsia Huang.
The Chinese high command: A history of Communist military politics, 1927–71.
New York: Praeger, 1973. 25, 638 p.
SUBJ 12 15 25 32.2 ▪ 17 19 32 59 64

1949-1972

14021 CSU U P1 G1.2 1949–1972
[An, Tai Sung] Thomas S. An, 1931–.
'Mao Tse-tung purges military professionalism.'
Military review 48, 8 (Aug. 1968), 88–98.
SUBJ 15 ▪ 35 64

14022 CSU U P1 G1.2 1949–1972
Armbruster, Frank E-.
'China's conventional military capability.' In *China briefing*, by F. E. Armbruster et al. [Sole entry]
Chicago: U. of Chicago Press, 1968, 57–66.
SUBJ 15

14023 CSU P P1 G1.2 1949–1972
Augenstein, Bruno Wilhelm, 1923–.
'The Chinese and French programs for the development of national nuclear forces.'
Orbis (Philadelphia) 11, 3 (Fall 1967), 846–863.
SUBJ 15 ▪ 62

14024 CSH S P1 G1.2 1949–1972
Bielau, Hermann.
'Die "Luftmacht" Rotchinas' (Red China's air power).
Wehrkunde 15, 1 (Jan. 1966), 38–43.
SUBJ 14.2 14.4 15 ▪ 17

14025 CSU P P1 G1.2 1949–1972
Bobrow, Davis Bernard, 1936–.
'The Chinese Communist conflict system.'
Orbis (Philadelphia) 9, 4 (Winter 1966), 930–952.
SUBJ 15

14026 MCH P P1 G1.2 1949–1972
Bobrow, Davis Bernard, 1936–.
'The good officer: Definition and training.'
CQ 18 (Apr.–June 1964), 141–152.
SUBJ 15 ▪ 64

14027 MCH P P1 G1.2 1949–1972
Bobrow, Davis Bernard, 1936–.
'Peking's military calculus.'
WP 16, 1 (Jan. 1964), 287–301.
SUBJ 15

14028 CSU P P1 G1.2 1949–1972
Cheng Chu-yuan (Cheng Chu-yüan), 1927–.
'Progress of nuclear weapons in Communist China.'
Military review 45, 5 (May 1965), 9–15. [Reprinted in *Government of Communist China*, edited by George P. Jan (Jan Po-kung). (Selective entry.) San Francisco: Chandler, 1966, 543–550.]
SUBJ 15 ▪ 11.4 62

14029 MCY P P1 G1.2 1949–1972
Cheng, James Chester (Cheng Che-hsi), 1926–.
'Problems of Chinese Communist leadership as seen in the secret military papers.'
AS 4, 6 (June 1964), 861–872.
SUBJ 15 64 ▪ 12 16.1 32.1

14030 NNC P P2 G1.2 1949–1972
Chiang I-shan.
'Military affairs' [title varies slightly]. Tr. of '1955–1958 nien ti Chung kung chün shih' (Military affairs in Communist China, 1955–1958); *Tsu kuo chou k'an* 159–334/335 (16 Jan. 1956 – 8 June 1959) [recurring annual feature article]. In *Communist China, 1955–1958*, edited by Union Research Institute.
Hong Kong: Union Research Institute. Issued annually, 1956–1959, average ca. 10 p.
SUBJ 15 ▪ 17 25

14031 CSH P P2 G1.2 1949–1972
Chiang I-shan.
'Military affairs in Communist China, 1960–1969' [title varies]. Tr. from *Tsu kuo chou k'an* 450 (21 Aug. 1961); 485 (23 Apr. 1962); 536 (15 Apr. 1963) *and* from *Tsu kuo* 1–71 (Apr. 1964 – Feb. 1970) [recurring annual feature article]. In *Communist China, 1960–1969*, edited by Union Research Institute.

Hong Kong: Union Research Institute. Issued annually, 1962–1970, average ca. 35 p.
SUBJ 15 ▪ 12.1 25 35

14032 NNC P P2 G1.2 1949–1972
Chiang I-shan.
'The military affairs of Communist China.' Tr. of 'Shih nien lai ti Chung kung chün shih' (Military affairs in Communist China during the past decade); *Tsu kuo chou k'an* 391 (4 July 1960), 10–14, 19. In *Communist China, 1949–1959*, edited by Union Research Institute. [Selective entry]
Hong Kong: Union Research Institute, 1961, vol. 1, 213–237.
SUBJ 15 ▪ 12.1 25

14033 CSU P P2 G1.2 1949–1972
Chien Yu-shen.
China's fading revolution: Army dissent and military divisions, 1967–68.
Hong Kong: Centre of Contemporary Chinese Studies, 1969. 405 p.
SUBJ 15 22.2 25 32 35 ▪ 12 16.1 19 54 64

14034 MCY P P1 G1.2 1949–1972
Chiu, S. M. (Chao Shan-ming), 1923–.
'Chinese Communist army in transition.'
FES 27, 11 (Nov. 1958), 168–175. [For fuller treatment, see entry 13991.]
SUBJ 12.1 15

14035 NNC S P1 G1.2 1949–1972
Dahm, Helmut, 1925–.
'Die chinesische Militärdoktrin' (Chinese military doctrine).
Die politische Meinung 10, 109 (Okt. 1965), 25–41.
SUBJ 15 ▪ 64

14036 CSU P P2 G1.2 1949–1972
Domes, Jürgen Otto, 1932–.
'The Cultural Revolution and the army.'
AS 8, 5 (May 1968), 349–363.
SUBJ 12.1 15

14037 CSH P P2 G1.2 1949–1972
Domes, Jürgen Otto, 1932–.
Kulturrevolution und Armee: Die Rolle der Streitkräfte in der chinesischen 'Kulturrevolution' (The Cultural Revolution and the army: The role of the military in the Cultural Revolution).
Bonn: Studiengesellschaft für Zeitprobleme, 1967. 134 p. (Wehrpolitische Schriftenreihe, 19)
SUBJ 15 32 32.1 ▪ 25 35

14038 MCH U P1 G1.2 1949–1972
Fang Chun-kuei (Fan Chün-kuei).
'Factionalism in Peiping's armed forces.'
CCA 4, 2 (Apr. 1967), 3–18.
SUBJ 15 ▪ 16 16.1

14039 MCH P P1 G1.2 1949–1972
Ford, Harald Perry.
'Modern weapons and the Sino-Soviet estrangement.'
CQ 18 (Apr.–June 1964), 160–173.
SUBJ 15 ▪ 12.1 66

14040 NNC FP P1 G1.2 1949–1972
George, Alexander Lawrence, 1920–.
The Chinese Communist Army in action: The Korean War and its aftermath.
New York: Columbia U. Press, 1967. 12, 255 p.
SUBJ 15 32.1 ▪ 12.1 25 30 61

14041 CSU P P2 G1.2 1949–1972
Gittings, John, 1938–.
'The Chinese army's role in the Cultural Revolution.'
PA 39, 3/4 (Fall–Winter 1966/67), 269–289.
SUBJ 15 19 ▪ 32 32.1 35

14042 CSH P P1 G1.2 1949–1972
Gittings, John, 1938–.
'Military control and leadership, 1949–1964.'
CQ 26 (Apr.–June 1966), 82–101.
SUBJ 15 ▪ 32 32.1

14043 CSU P P1 G1.2 1949–1972
Godaire, J- G-.
'Communist China's defense establishment: Some economic implications.' In *An economic profile of Mainland China*, compiled by Joint Economic Committee, U.S. Congress. [Selective entry]
Washington, D.C.: U.S. Government Printing Office, 1967, vol. 1, 155–165. [Reprinted in *An economic profile of Mainland China*, compiled by the agency cited. (Selective entry.) New York: Praeger, 1968, 155–165.]
SUBJ 14 15 ▪ 11.4

14044 CSH P P2 G1.2 1949–1972
Gomane, Jean-Pierre.
'L'Armée populaire de libération' (The People's Liberation Army).
Projet 40 (déc. 1969), 1188–1204. [Special issue: *La Chine s'est levée* (China resurgent)]
SUBJ 12 15 35 66 ▪ 25 32 54

14045 NNC P P1 G1.2 1949–1972
Griffith, Samuel Blair, II, 1906–.
'Communist China's capacity to make war.'
FA 43, 2 (Jan. 1965), 217–236. [Reprinted as 'The military potential of China.' In *China and the peace of Asia*, edited by Alastair Buchan. (Sole entry.) New York: Praeger, 1965, 65–94.]
SUBJ 15 ▪ 32.1

14046 CSU P P1 G1.2 1949–1972
Harding, Harry, Jr., 1946–.
'The making of Chinese military policy.' In *The military and political power of China in the 1970s*, edited by William Wallace Whitson. [Selective entry]
New York: Praeger, 1972, 361–385.
SUBJ 15 64 ▪ 35

14047 CSU P P1 G1.2 1949–1972
Harding, Harry, Jr., 1946–, and Melvin Gurtov, 1941–.
The purge of Lo Jui-ch'ing: The politics of Chinese strategic planning.
Santa Monica, Calif.: RAND Corp., 1971. 11, 63 p. (RAND reports, R-548-PR)
SUBJ 15 16.1 32 32.1 ▪ 35 64

14048 CSU S P1 G1.2 1949–1972
Heinlein, Joseph.
'The ground forces.' In *The military and political power of China in the 1970s*, edited by William Wallace Whitson. [Selective entry]
New York: Praeger, 1972, 153–169.
SUBJ 15 ▪ 35

14049 NNC P P1 G1.2 1949–1972
Hinton, Harold Clendenin, 1924–.
'Political aspects of military power and policy in Communist China.' In *Total war and cold war: Problems in civilian control of the military*, edited by Harry L- Coles. [Sole entry]
Columbus: Ohio State U. Press, 1962, 266–292.
SUBJ 15 ▪ 25 32.1

14050 CSU S P1 G1.2 1949–1972
Horner, Charles.
'The production of nuclear weapons.' In *The military and political power of China in the 1970s*, edited by William Wallace Whitson. [Selective entry]
New York: Praeger, 1972, 229–252.
SUBJ 15

14051 MCH P P1 G1.2 1949–1972
Hsieh, Alice Langley, 1922–.
'China's secret military papers: Military doctrine and strategy.'
CQ 18 (Apr.–June 1964), 79–99.
SUBJ 15

14052 CSH P P1 G1.2 1949–1972
Hsieh, Alice Langley, 1922–.
'Communist China and nuclear warfare.'
CQ 2 (Apr.–June 1960), 1–15.
SUBJ 15 ▪ 32.1

14053 NNC P P1 G1.2 1949–1972
Hwang, William S. C. (Huang Wei-liang), 1925–.
The start of the Cultural Revolution and the unresolved civil-military relationship in Communist China.
Unpublished masters thesis in Political Science, Columbia U., 1969. 104 p. [Certificate essay, East Asian Institute]
SUBJ 12 15 ▪ 32 32.1 35

14054 CSU P P1 G1.2 1949–1972
Joffe, Ellis, 1934–.
'The Chinese army under Lin Piao: Prelude to political intervention.' In *China: Management of a revolutionary society*, edited by John Matthew Henry Lindbeck. [Analytic entry]
Seattle: U. of Washington Press, 1971, 343–374. (Social Science Research Council, Studies in Chinese government and politics, 2)
SUBJ 15 35 ▪ 32 32.1 64

14055 MCH P P1 G1.2 1949–1972
Joffe, Ellis, 1934–.
Party and army: Professionalism and political control in the Chinese officer corps, 1949–1964.
Cambridge: Harvard U., East Asian Research Center, 1965. 12, 198 p. (Harvard East Asian monographs, 19)
SUBJ 15 16.1 32.1 ▪ 25 35 64 72

14056 MCH P P1 G1.2 1949–1972
Johnson, Chalmers Ashby, 1931–.
'Lin Piao's army and its role in Chinese society.'
CS 4, 13 (1 July 1966), 1–10; 4, 14 (15 July 1966), 1–11.
SUBJ 15 35 ▪ 12 12.1

14057 CSU P P1 G1.2 1949–1972
Jordan, James D-.
'The Maoist vs. the professional vision of a people's army.' In *The military and political power of China in the 1970s*,

edited by William Wallace Whitson. [Selective entry]
New York: Praeger, 1972, 25–45.
Subj 15 64 ▪ 25

14058 NNC P P1 G9.4 1949–1972
Kallgren, Joyce Kislitzin, 1930–.
'Nationalist China's armed forces.'
CQ 15 (July–Sept. 1963), 35–44.
Subj 15 ▪ 21.4

14059 CSH F P1 G1.2 1949–1972
Kirkpatrick, Jeane J-, and Pio D- Uliassi.
'Adjustment of Chinese soldiers to the Communist demand for ideological participation.' In *Mass behavior in battle and captivity: The Communist soldier in the Korean War*, by William Chapman Bradbury, edited by Samuel M- Meyers and Albert D- Biderman. [Selective entry]
Chicago: U. of Chicago Press, 1968, 160–206.
Subj 15 61 ▪ 53

14060 CSH P P2 G1.2 1949–1972
[La Dany, Ladislao] ———, 1914–.
'The economy: Military honesty.'
CNA 853 (3 Sept. 1971), 1–7.
Subj 14 15 ▪ 12 35

14061 MCH P P1 G1.2 1949–1972
[La Dany, Ladislao] ———, 1914–.
'The spirit of the army.'
CNA 436 (7 Sept. 1962), 1–7.
Subj 15 32.1 ▪ 35

14062 MCH P P1 G1.2 1949–1972
[La Dany, Ladislao] ———, 1914–.
'The spirit of the army.'
CNA 578 (27 Aug. 1965), 1–7.
Subj 15

14063 MCH P P2 G1.2 1949–1972
[La Dany, Ladislao] ———, 1914–.
'War preparations.'
CNA 566 (28 May 1965), 1–7.
Subj 12.1 15 ▪ 25 54

14064 CSH P P1 G1.2 1949–1972
[La Dany, Ladislao] ———, 1914–.
'Who commands the army?'
CNA 892 (1 Sept. 1972), 1–7.
Subj 15 32.1 ▪ 16.1

14065 MCY P P1 G1.2 1949–1972
Lee, Chin-tsi, 1890–.
What is behind the Chinese Communists' program of military reorganization?
Taipei: Asian Peoples' Anti-Communist League, 1958. 70 p. (APACL pamphlets, 30)
Subj 15 ▪ 32.1 61

14066 MAM FP P2 G1.2 1949–1972
Leocha, Adolph John, 1916–.
The limiting effect of technology on Chinese military strategy.
Ann Arbor: University Microfilms (Publ. 70-26,651), 1970. 264 p. (Doctoral dissertation in Political Science, Georgetown U.)
Subj 14 14.2 15 ▪ 12 12.1 14.4 64

14067 CSH P P1 G1.2 1949–1972
Lewis, John Wilson, 1930–.
'China's secret military papers: "Continuities" and "revelations".'
CQ 18 (Apr.–June 1964), 68–78. [Reprinted in *China under Mao: Politics takes command*, edited by Roderick Lemonde MacFarquhar. (Selective entry.) Cambridge: M.I.T. Press, 1966, 58–68.]
Subj 15 ▪ 32 64

14068 CSH P P2 G1.2 1949–1972
Lu Yung-shu (Lü Yung-shu).
'Preparation for war in Mainland China.' In *Collected documents of the First Sino-American Conference on Mainland China*. [Selective entry]
[Taipei]: Institute of International Relations, Republic of China, 1971, 895–919.
Subj 15 ▪ 12.1 14.2 14.3 25 64

14069 CSU P P1 G1.2 1949–1972
Mogolis, Franz J-.
'The role of the Chinese Communist Air Force in the 1970s.' In *The military and political power of China in the 1970s*, edited by William Wallace Whitson. [Selective entry]
New York: Praeger, 1972, 253–266.
Subj 15

14070 CSU U P1 G1.2 1949–1972
Niu, Sien-chang.
'Troop training in Red China.'
Military review 46, 6 (June 1966), 89–94.
Subj 15

14071 MCH S P1 G1.2 1949–1972
Pool, Ithiel de Sola, 1917–, et al.
'China.' In *Satellite generals: A study of military elites in the Soviet sphere*, by I. de S. Pool et al. [Sole entry]
Stanford: Stanford U. Press, 1955, 123–146. (Hoover Institution studies, series B, 5)
Subj 15

14072 MCY P P1 G1.2 1949–1972
Powell, Ralph Lorin, 1917–.
'Great powers and atomic bombs are "paper tigers".'
CQ 23 (July–Sept. 1965), 55–63.
Subj 15 66

14073 CSU P P1 G1.2 1949–1972
Powell, Ralph Lorin, 1917–.
'The increasing power of Lin Piao and the party-soldiers, 1959–1966.'
CQ 34 (Apr.–June 1968), 38–65.
Subj 15 32 32.1 ▪ 16.1 19 59

14074 CSU P P1 G1.2 1949–1972
Powell, Ralph Lorin, 1917–.
'Maoist military doctrines.'
AS 8, 4 (Apr. 1968), 239–262. [Separately reprinted—New York: American-Asian Educational Exchange, 1968. 25 p.]
Subj 15 64

14075 MCH P P1 G1.2 1949–1972
Powell, Ralph Lorin, 1917–.
'Military affairs of Communist China.'
CH 51, 301 (Sept. 1966), 140–146.
Subj 15 ▪ 12

14076 CSU P P1 G1.2 1949–1972
Powell, Ralph Lorin, 1917–.
'The party, the government and the gun.'
AS 10, 6 (June 1970), 441–471.
Subj 12 15 32 ▪ 12.2 16.1 32.1 64

14077 CSH P P1 G1.2 1949–1972
Powell, Ralph Lorin, 1917–.
Politico-military relationships in Communist China.
Washington, D.C.: U.S. Dept. of State, Bureau of Intelligence and Research, External Research Staff, 1963. 21 p.
Subj 15 32 ▪ 16.1 32.1

14078 CSU P P1 G1.2 1949–1972
Powell, Ralph Lorin, 1917–, and Helena F- Powell.
'Continuity and purge in the PLA.'
Marine Corps gazette 52, 2 (Feb. 1968), 20–30.
Subj 15 35

14079 CSU P P1 G1.2 1949–1972
Ray, Dennis Michael, 1939–.
'The Chinese military and the future of the Maoist vision.'
China report (New Delhi) 6, 5 (Sept.–Oct. 1970), 9–12.
Subj 15

14080 MCH P P1 G4.3 1949–1972
Schwarz, Henry Guenter, 1928–.
'The Chinese Communist Army in Sinkiang.'
Military review 45, 3 (Mar. 1965), 69–79.
Subj 12.1 15

14081 CSU P P1 G1.2 1949–1972
Ting Chu-yuan (Ting Ch'u-yüan).
'An analysis of the purge of Yang Cheng-wu.'
IS 4, 10 (July 1968), 1–12.
Subj 15 32 32.1

14082 CSU P P1 G1.2 1949–1972
Ting Wang, 1942–.
'The emergent military class.' In *The military and political power of China in the 1970s*, edited by William Wallace Whitson. [Selective entry]
New York: Praeger, 1972, 115–132.
Subj 15 16.1 ▪ 12 32 35

14083 CSH P P1 G1.2 1949–1972
Tsao Ching.
'Peiping's struggle between two lines of military strategy.'
IS 3, 3 (Dec. 1966), 35–40.
Subj 15 ▪ 32.1

14084 CBU P P2 G1.2 1949–1972
Weggel, Oskar, 1935–.
'The PLA in the Cultural Revolution.'
RSAEO 1969, 2, 243–254.
Subj 15 35 ▪ 12 30

16 Social Stratification and Mobility

社會階層及社會流動

社会階層及びその流動性

1644-1911

14085 MCH P P1 G1.2 –1842
Biot, Edouard Constant, 1803–1850.
'Mémoire sur la condition des esclaves et des serviteurs gagés en Chine' (Report on the condition of slaves and indentured servants in China).
JA 3e série 3 (mars 1837), 246–299.
Subj 16 ▪ 12.2 41

14086 NIC P P1 G1.3 –1644
Ch'ü, T'ung-tsu.
'Chinese class structure and its ideology.' In *Chinese thought and institutions*,

edited by John King Fairbank. [Selective entry]
Chicago: U. of Chicago Press, 1957, 235–250.
SUBJ 16 64 ▪ 12

14087 CSU S P2 G1.3 1842–1911
Davis, Feiling Blackburn.
'Modes de recrutement et composition sociale des Triades avant 1911' (Methods of recruitment and social composition of the Triads before 1911). In *Mouvements populaires et sociétés secrètes en Chine aux XIXe et XXe siècles* (Popular movements and secret societies in China in the nineteenth and twentieth centuries), edited by Jean Chesneaux, F. B. Davis, and Nguyen Nguyet Ho. [Selective entry]
Paris: Maspero, 1970, 234–247.
SUBJ 16 16.3 16.4 32.2 ▪ 47 54

14088 NIC P P2 G9.0 –1911
Eberhard, Wolfram, 1909–.
Social mobility in traditional China.
Leiden: Brill, 1962. 302 p.
SUBJ 16 16.1 42 ▪ 12.2 14 21 40 58

14089 MCH S P1 G1.1 –1911
Eisenstadt, Shmuel Noah, 1923–.
'Sociological analysis of historical societies.'
CSSH 6, 4 (July 1964), 481–489.
SUBJ 12 16 ▪ 71

14090 NNC P P1 G1.3 –1911
Erkes, Eduard, 1891–1958.
'Ursprung und Bedeutung der Sklaverei in China' (The origin and significance of slavery in China).
Artibus Asiae 6, 3/4 (1937), 294–308.
SUBJ 16 41 48 ▪ 12 12.1 12.2

14091 NNC U P2 G1.3 –1911
Grinevich, Petr Antonovich, 1899–1941.
'K voprosam istorii kitaiskogo feodalizma' (Questions on the history of Chinese feudalism).
PK 14 (1935), 186–271.
SUBJ 16 ▪ 12 12.1 14 16.1

14092 DCK PO P2 G1.3 1842–1895
Henningsen, Jakob, 1849–1913.
Djung rhua dji: Kinesiske typer og skitser (*Chung-hua chi*: Chinese types and sketches).
Copenhagen: Gyldendal, 1894. 224 p.
SUBJ 14.2 14.6 16 47 50 ▪ 12.2 22 60 66

14093 NIC P P2 G1.2 –1911
Ho, Ping-ti, 1917–.
The ladder of success in Imperial China: Aspects of social mobility, 1368–1911.
New York: Columbia U. Press, 1962. 18, 385 p.
SUBJ 12 16 16.1 17 59 ▪ 14.5 16.2 22 25 26 26.1 26.2 42 64 65

14094 CSU U P2 G1.2 1842–1895
McCloy, Thomas.
'Is slavery as practiced among the Chinese immoral?'
CR 22, 12 (Dec. 1891), 567–573.
SUBJ 16 48 ▪ 22.2 41

14095 FPN O P3 G1.1 1842–1895
Martin, Charles Ernest, 1831–1897.
'Les mendiants en Chine' (Beggars in China).
Science moderne 7, 40 (7 oct. 1893), 232–233.
SUBJ 16 56 57 ▪ 18

14096 CSU S P2 G1.2 –1842
Mousnier, Roland.
'Les structures sociales de la Chine dans la première moitié du XVIIe siècle.' In *Fureurs paysannes: les paysans dans les révoltes du XVIIe siècle (France, Russie, Chine)*, by R. Mousnier. [Sole entry]
Paris: Calmann-Lévy, 1967, 237–275.

'The social structures of China in the first half of the seventeenth century.' Tr. by Brian Pearce. In *Peasant uprisings in seventeenth-century France, Russia, and China*, by R. Mousnier. [Sole entry]
New York: Harper and Row, 1970, 233–272.
SUBJ 12 16 16.1 16.3 62 ▪ 12.1 14.1 14.4 17 22 22.1 41

14097 CSU P P2 G1.1 1644–1911
Pan, Quentin (P'an Kuang-tan), 1898–, and Fei Hsiao-tung (Fei Hsiao-t'ung), 1910–.
'City and village: The inequality of opportunity.' Tr. by Johanna M. Menzel, Liu Ming, and Dorothy Shou of 'K'o chü yü she hui liu tung' (The examination system and social mobility); *She hui k'o hsüeh* 4, 1 (Oct. 1947), 1–21. In *The Chinese civil service: Career open to talent?*, edited by [Johanna Menzel Meskill] Johanna Margarete Menzel. [Sole entry]
Boston: Heath, 1963, 9–21.
SUBJ 16 16.1 17 ▪ 12

14098 CSU P P2 G1.1 –1911
[Pippon, Anton] Toni Pippon, 1909–.
'Beitrag zum chinesischen Sklavensystem, nebst einer Übersetzung des "Chung-kuo nu pei chih tu" (Das Sklavensystem Chinas) von Wang Shih-chieh. Teil 1, Beitrag zum chinesischen Sklavensystem' (The Chinese slavery system, including a translation of 'Chung-kuo nu pei chih tu' [The slavery system of China], by Wang Shih-chieh. Part 1, Report on slavery in China).
MDG 29, B (1936), 1–139. (Doctoral dissertation, Philosophische Fakultät, Universität Bonn)
SUBJ 12.2 16 ▪ 11.4 12.1 22.2 41 47 48

14099 NNC P P1 G1.2 –1911
[Pippon, Anton] Toni Pippon, 1909–.
'Die Solidarhaftung im chinesischen Sklavensystem' (Joint liability in the Chinese slavery system).
Archiv für Ostasien 1, 1 (1948), 35–41.
SUBJ 12.2 16 48 ▪ 12.1 41

14100 GBS O P2 G1.3 1842–1895
Rosthorn, Arthur von, 1862–1945.
Das soziale Leben der Chinesen (The social life of the Chinese).
Leipzig: Der Neue Geist, 1919. 24 p.
SUBJ 16 ▪ 14 30

14101 CSU S P2 G1.3 –1911
Skinner, George William, 1925–.
'Chinese peasants and the closed community: An open and shut case.'
CSSH 13, 3 (July 1971), 270–281.
SUBJ 11.3 16 20 21.2 ▪ 16.1 22.1 29

14102 CSU P P2 G1.1 –1911
Wang Shih-chieh, 1891–.
'Das Sklavensystem Chinas' (Slavery in China). Tr. by Toni Pippon of 'Chung-kuo nu pei chih tu'; *She hui k'o hsüeh chi k'an* (Peking: Kuo li Pei-ching ta hsüeh) 3, 3 (Apr.-June 1925), 303–328.
MDG 29, B (1936), 91–139. [Published as Teil II (Part 2) of the translator's doctoral dissertation— 'Beitrag zum chinesischen Sklavensystem, nebst einer Übersetzung des "Chung-kuo nu pei chih tu" (Das Sklavensystem Chinas) von Wang Shih-chieh' (The Chinese slavery system, with a translation of 'Chung-kuo nu pei chih tu' [Slavery in China]), by Wang Shih-chieh. [For Teil I, see entry 14098.]
SUBJ 12.2 16 ▪ 11.4 12.1 15 22.2 41 48

14103 NIC U P1 G1.2 1644–1911
Williams, Edward Thomas, 1854–1944.
'The abolition of slavery in the Chinese empire.'
American j. of international law 4, 4 (Oct. 1910), 794–805.
SUBJ 12.2 16 ▪ 12.1 47

14104 NNC P P1 G1.3 –1911
Wist, Hans, 1904–.
'Sklaverei in China' (Slavery in China).
Artibus Asiae 8, 2/4 (1945), 238–257.
SUBJ 16 48 ▪ 12.1 12.2

1644-1949

14105 CSH S P2 G1.2 –1928
Andreev, M- G-.
'Institut rabstva v Kitae' (The institution of slavery in China).
PK 1 (1929), 206–306.
SUBJ 11 12.2 16 16.3 48 ▪ 12.1 47 64 70 71

14106 CSH U P2 G3.0 1842–1949
Cheney, George Alvin, 1908–, et al.
'Social structure.' In *A regional handbook on the Inner Mongolia Autonomous Region*, compiled by Far Eastern and Russian Institute, U. of Washington. [Selective entry]
New Haven: Human Relations Area Files, 1956, 140–160. (HRAF subcontractor's monographs, 60; Washington 7)
SUBJ 16 ▪ 22 66

14107 NIC P P1 G1.3 1842–1949
Hsu, Francis L. K. (Hsü Lang-kuang), 1909–.
'Social mobility in China.'
ASR 14, 6 (Dec. 1949), 764–771. [Reprinted as 'More evidence on social mobility in China.' In *Under the ancestors' shadow: Kinship, personality and social mobility in village China*, rev. and enl. ed., by F. L. K. Hsu. (Analytic entry.) Garden City, N.Y.: Doubleday, 1967, 337–349.] [Reprinted as 'More evidence on social mobility in China.' In *Under the ancestors' shadow: Kinship, personality and social mobility in village China*, rev. and enl. ed., by F. L. K. Hsu. (Analytic entry.) Stanford: Stanford U. Press, 1971, 337–349. (For the monograph itself, see entry 19729.)]
SUBJ 12 16 16.1

14108 MCH S P1 G1.3 –1928
Kantorovich, Anatolii IAkovlevich, 1896–1944.

'Sistema obshchestvennykh otnoshenii Kitaia dokapitalisticheskoi epokhi' (The system of social relations in precapitalist China).
NV 15 (1926), 67–93.
SUBJ 12 16 ▪ 16.1 32.2

14109 NNC P P2 G1.2 1895–1928
Kuchumov, Vladimir Nikolaevich, 1900–?
Ocherki po istorii kitaiskoi revoliutsii (Notes on the history of the Chinese revolution).
Moscow: Partizdat, 1934. 148 p.
SUBJ 12 14 16 32 36.3 ▪ 15 32.1 64 66

14110 CSU P P2 G1.2 1842–1949
Langlois, Walter G-.
'*The dream of the red chamber*, *The good earth*, and *Man's fate*: Chronicles of social change in China.'
Literature East and West 11, 1 (Mar. 1967), 1–10.
SUBJ 16 ▪ 64

14111 MCH O P2 G1.2 1895–1949
Mortier, Florent.
'De la mendicité en Chine' (Begging in China).
BSRB 59 (1948), 176–187.
SUBJ 16 18 56 ▪ 55 63

14112 DLC P P1 G1.1 –1928
Safarov, Georgii Ivanovich, 1891–1938?
Klassy i klassovaia bor'ba v kitaiskoi istorii (Classes and the class struggle in Chinese history).
Moscow: Gosizdat, 1928. 361 p.
SUBJ 16 19 36.3 ▪ 14.6 32.2 66

14113 MCH P P2 G1.1 –1928
Wittfogel, Karl August, 1896–.
Das erwachende China: Ein Abriss der Geschichte und der gegenwärtigen Probleme Chinas (Awakening China: Sketch of China's history and current problems).
Berlin: Agis, 1926. 173 p.
SUBJ 16 16.4 64 ▪ 12.1 14 32.2 36.4 52

1911-1949

14114 NNP U P2 G1.2 1911–1928
Adzharov, A-.
Klassy i partii sovremennogo Kitaia (Classes and parties of contemporary China).
Moscow: Moskovskii rabochii, 1926. 194 p.
SUBJ 16 32 ▪ 32.2 36.4

14115 MCH P P3 G1.2 1911–1928
Chesneaux, Jean, 1922–.
'Au lendemain de la Première Guerre mondiale: transformations sociales de la Chine' (Social changes in China in the wake of World War I).
Annales; économies, sociétés, civilisations 9, 3 (juil.–sept. 1954), 296–310.
SUBJ 16 16.2 16.4 ▪ 14.4 14.6 34.3

14116 MCH P P2 G1.2 1911–1949
Dapčević-Oreščanin, Sonja.
Istorijske osobenosti kineske revolucije (Historical characteristics of the Chinese revolution).
Beograd, Yugoslavia: Institut za medjunarodnu politiku i privredu, 1964. 235, 18 p.
SUBJ 16 32.2 36.3 ▪ 12 14.1 19 36.4 64

14117 NIC P P2 G1.3 1928–1949
Fei Hsiao-tung (Fei Hsiao-t'ung), 1910–.
'Peasantry and gentry: An interpretation of Chinese social structure and its changes.'
AJS 52, 1 (July 1946), 1–17. [Reprinted in *Class, status and power*, edited by Reinhard Bendix and Seymour Martin Lipset. (Sole entry.) Glencoe, Ill.: Free Press, 1953, 631–650.]
SUBJ 14 16 19 22 66 ▪ 11.3 12 41 42 58

14118 NIC U P4 G1.3 1911–1928
Gee, Nathaniel Gist, 1876–1937.
A class of social outcasts: Notes on the beggars in China.
Peking: Peking Leader Press, 1925. 30 p. (Peking Leader reprints, 1)
SUBJ 16 ▪ 18 34.3

14119 GMS S P2 G1.2 1911–1928
Mänchen-Helfen, Otto, 1894–.
China (China).
Dresden: Kaden, 1931. 232 p.
SUBJ 10 14.4 16 ▪ 15 19 32 32.2 64

14120 CSH U P2 G1.2 1911–1928
Mao Tse-tung, 1893–.
'Analysis of the classes in Chinese society.' Tr. of 'Chung-kuo she hui ko chieh chi ti fen hsi'; in *Mao Tse-tung hsüan chi* (Selected works of Mao Tse-tung), 2nd ed.; Peking: Jen min ch'u pan she, 1960, vol. 1 [originally published in *Chung-kuo nung min* 2 (Feb. 1926)]. In *Selected works of Mao Tse-tung*, edited by Mao Tse-tung hsüan chi ch'u pan wei yüan hui (Committee for the Publication of the Selected Works of Mao Tse-tung), Chung yang wei yüan hui (Central Committee), Chung-kuo kung ch'an tang (Chinese Communist Party). [Selective entry]
Peking: Foreign Languages Press, 1965, vol. 1, 13–21.
SUBJ 16

14121 GMS O P2 G1.3 1928–1949
Tandler, Julius, 1869–1936.
Volk in China: Erlebnisse und Erfahrungen (The people of China: Personal experiences).
Vienna: Thalia, 1935. 47 p.
SUBJ 16 56 ▪ 14.2 14.5 17

14122 DLC O P3 G1.2 1911–1928
[Vilenskii, Vladimir Dmitrievich] Vl. Vilenskii-Sibiriakov, pseud., 1888–1942.
Za kitaiskoi stenoi (Behind the wall of China).
Moscow: Vses. ob-vo politkatorzhan i ssyl'no poselentsev, 1925. 234 p.
SUBJ 14 16 16.2 16.4 ▪ 12.1 15 17 32.2 34.2 36.2 36.4 60

14123 NNC P P2 G1.2 1911–1928
Whiting, Allen Suess, 1927–.
'The Chinese puzzle.' In *Soviet policies in China, 1917–1924*, by A. S. Whiting. [Sole entry]
New York: Columbia U. Press, 1957, 59–71. (Revision of *Soviet policy in China, 1917–1924*, doctoral dissertation in Political Science, Columbia U., 1953)
SUBJ 16 16.3 16.4 ▪ 32.2 36.4

14124 CSU P P7 G1.3 1928–1949
Young, Lung-chang (Yang Lung-chang), 1923–.
'Rural stratification in modern China: The dialectic of images and social reality.'
Social research 37, 4 (Winter 1970), 624–643.
SUBJ 16 26 ▪ 16.1 16.3 18 26.1 26.3

1911-1972
(including 1644-1972)

14125 CSU FP P7 G1.5 –1972
Anderson, Eugene Newton, Jr., 1941–.
'The boat people of South China.'
Anthropos 65, 1/2 (Jan.–Apr. 1970), 248–256. [Reprinted in *Essays on South China's boat people*, by E. N. Anderson, Jr. (Analytic entry.) Taipei: Orient Cultural Service, 1972, 1–9. (Asian Folklore and Social Life monographs, 29)]
SUBJ 16 29 ▪ 72

14126 MCH U P2 G1.1 –1972
Erkes, Eduard, 1891–1958.
'Die Entwicklung der chinesischen Gesellschaft von der Urzeit bis zur Gegenwart' (The development of Chinese society from prehistoric times to the present).
Berichte über die Verhandlungen der philologisch-historischen Klasse der sächsischen Akademie der Wissenschaften zu Leipzig 100, 4 (1953), 1–30.
SUBJ 10 14 16 40 ▪ 12.1 16.3 32.2 41

14127 ICU P P2 G1.2 1911–1972
Lee, Shu-ching (Li Shu-ch'ing), 1908–.
Social implications of farm tenancy in China.
Unpublished doctoral dissertation in Sociology, U. of Chicago, 1950. 268 p.
SUBJ 14.1 16 16.3 ▪ 11 11.3 14.6 36.3 40 63 72

14128 MCH P P2 G1.2 1911–1972
Lewis, John Wilson, 1930–.
'Political aspects of mobility in China's urban development.'
APSR 60, 4 (Dec. 1966), 899–912.
SUBJ 11.1 16 ▪ 11.2 12 12.1

14129 CSH U P2 G2.0 1911–1972
Naff, William Edward, 1924–, and Peter S. H. Tang (T'ang Sheng-hao), 1919–.
'Social structure.' In *A regional handbook on Northeast China*, compiled by Far Eastern and Russian Institute, U. of Washington. [Selective entry]
New Haven: Human Relations Area Files, 1956, 107–141. (HRAF subcontractor's monographs, 61; Washington 9)
SUBJ 16 66 ▪ 14.1 22 32.2 34.1

14130 ELB P P2 G1.2 –1972
Sterbalova, A- A-.
'Traditsionnyi i sovremennyi Kitai: osobennosti sotsial'nogo razvitiia' (Traditional and contemporary China: Special features of social development).
Voprosy filosofii 1969, 8, 37–48.
SUBJ 12 14.1 16 64 ▪ 14.3 14.6 41 45

14131 CSH U P2 G1.2 –1972
Yang, Martin M. C. (Yang Mou-ch'un), 1904–.
'Social structure.' In *A general handbook of China*, compiled by Far Eastern and Russian Institute, U. of Washington. [Selective entry]

New Haven: Human Relations Area Files, 1956, vol. 1, 1–87 [s.p.]. [Pages 1–87 inserted between p. 572 and p. 573.] (HRAF subcontractor's monographs, 55; Washington 4)
SUBJ 16 30 ▪ 11.3 12.1 22 64

1949-1972

14132 CSU P P2 G1.2 1949–1972
Bennett, Gordon Anderson, 1940–.
'Political labels and popular tension.'
CS 7, 4 (26 Feb. 1969), 1–16.
SUBJ 16 ▪ 12.1 32

14133 IMC O P3 G1.2 1949–1972
Bernari, Carlo, 1909–.
Il gigante Cina (China, the giant).
Milan: Feltrinelli, 1957. 343 p.
SUBJ 16 ▪ 14.2 14.5 15 41 43 53 65

14134 NIC FP P2 G9.4 1949–1972
Chen Shao-hsing (Ch'en Shao-hsing), 1906–1966.
'Trends report of studies in social stratification and social mobility in Taiwan.'
East Asian cultural studies 4 (Mar. 1965), 38–51.
SUBJ 16 21 ▪ 17 21.4 58

14135 NNC P P2 G1.2 1949–1972
Chesneaux, Jean, 1922–.
'Les transformations sociales' (Social transformations). In *Le régime et les institutions de la République populaire chinoise* (The government and institutions of the People's Republic of China), jointly edited by Centre d'étude des pays de l'Est, Institut de sociologie Solvay, Université libre de Bruxelles *with* Centre national pour l'étude des pays à régime communiste. [Selective entry]
Brussels: Snoeck-Ducaju, 1960, 97–114.
SUBJ 11.1 16 29 41 ▪ 11.2 22 70

14136 MCH O P2 G1.2 1949–1972
Deelde, M. K. van, pseud.
'"Bevrijding" in China' ('Liberation' in China).
Socialisme en démocratie 1957, 3 (Maart), 154–165.
SUBJ 16 19 ▪ 12.1 32.1

14137 CSU P P2 G1.2 1949–1972
Funnell, Victor Cecil, 1926–.
'The new revolution. 4, Social stratification.'
Problems of Communism 17, 2 (Mar.–Apr. 1968), 14–20.
SUBJ 16 ▪ 12.1

14138 DLC P P2 G1.2 1949–1972
Gel'bras, Vil' Gdal'evich, 1930–.
'Sotsial'no-ekonomicheskii ocherk' (A socioeconomic sketch). In *Kitai segodnia* (China today), compiled by Akademiia nauk SSSR, edited by Lev Petrovich Deliusin and Grigorii Dmitrievich Sukharchuk. [Selective entry]
Moscow: Nauka, Glav. red. vost. lit-ry, 1969, 52–129.

'A socioeconomic essay.' Tr. by Arlo Schultz. [Partial tr.: p. 100–129 only; tr. erroneously cites Ia. M. Berger as author.]
Chinese sociology and anthropology 3, 1 (Fall 1970), 3–35.
SUBJ 14 16 32 34.1 64 ▪ 11.4 12.1 14.4 15 18 22 32.1 34.2 35 36.4

14139 CSU O P2 G1.2 1949–1972
Hinton, William H-, 1919–.
Turning point in China: An essay on the Cultural Revolution.
New York: Monthly Review Press, 1972. 112 p.
SUBJ 16 54 64 ▪ 12 14 16.1 16.3 17 22.2 25 34.1 35

14140 CSU P P1 G1.2 1949–1972
Kikuchi Masanori, 1930–.
'Cultural Revolution in China and the Soviet Union: Two views of class struggle.' Tr. of 'Chūgoku to Sobieto no bunka kakumei: Mō Takutō to Sutārin no kaikyū tōsōkan' (Cultural revolution in China and the Soviet Union: Mao Tse-tung's and Stalin's views on the class struggle); *Ushio* 73 (July 1966), 95–105.
J. of social and political ideas in Japan 5, 1 (Apr. 1967), 91–100.
SUBJ 16 64 ▪ 19

14141 MCH S P2 G1.2 1949–1972
Kosichev, Anatolii Danilovich.
'O likvidatsii ekspluatatorskikh klassov v KNR' (The elimination of exploiting classes in the People's Republic of China).
Vestnik Moskovskogo universiteta; seriia ekonomiki, filosofii, prava 14, 4 (1959), 83–98.
SUBJ 12.1 16 ▪ 11.4 45 64

14142 CSH P P1 G1.2 1949–1972
[La Dany, Ladislao] ———, 1914–.
'The opposition.'
CNA 747 (7 Mar. 1969), 1–7; 749 (21 Mar. 1969), 1–7.
SUBJ 12 16 ▪ 30 35

14143 MCH P P2 G1.2 1949–1972
[La Dany, Ladislao] ———, 1914–.
'Social change: Class struggle.'
CNA 457 (22 Feb. 1963), 1–7.
SUBJ 16 64 ▪ 12.1 17 54

14144 NNC P P1 G1.2 1949–1972
Lieberthal, Kenneth Guy, 1943–.
Mobility in Communist China, 1954–1965: An exploratory survey.
Unpublished masters thesis in Public Law and Government, Columbia U., 1968. 83 p. [Certificate essay, East Asian Institute]
SUBJ 16 ▪ 12 14 15 16.1 17 30 32

14145 PPP FP P2 G1.1 1949–1972
Marsh, Robert Mortimer, 1931–.
'Evolution and revolution: Two types of change in China's system of social stratification.' In *Essays in comparative social stratification*, edited by Leonard Plotnicov and Arthur Tuden. [Sole entry]
Pittsburgh: U. of Pittsburgh Press, 1970, 149–172.
SUBJ 16 ▪ 11.4

14146 CSU F P2 G1.2 1949–1972
Oksenberg, Michel Charles, 1938–.
'Getting ahead and along in Communist China: The ladder of success on the eve of the Cultural Revolution.' In *Party leadership and revolutionary power in China*, edited by John Wilson Lewis. [Analytic entry]
Cambridge: Cambridge U. Press, 1970, 304–347.
SUBJ 16 48 ▪ 12.1 16.1 17 32

14147 CSU P P2 G1.2 1949–1972
Oksenberg, Michel Charles, 1938–.
'Occupational groups in Chinese society and the Cultural Revolution.' In *The Cultural Revolution: 1967 in review*, by M. C. Oksenberg et al. [Selective entry]
Ann Arbor: U. of Michigan, Center for Chinese Studies, 1968, 1–44. (Michigan papers in Chinese studies, 2) [Reprinted as 'Occupational groups and the Cultural Revolution.' In *Communist China: A system-functional reader*, edited by Yung Wei. (Selective entry.) Columbus, Ohio: Merrill, 1972, 215–253.]
SUBJ 11.4 15 16 ▪ 12 22.2 32 54

14148 NNC U P2 G1.2 1949–1972
Pavlov, F- S-.
'Klassovaia bor'ba v Kitae v perekhodnyi period k sotsializmu' (The class struggle in China during the transition to socialism).
Kommunist Ukrainy 1958, 3 (mart), 52–63.
SUBJ 12.1 14 16 64 ▪ 17 34.1 60

14149 CSU P P2 G1.2 1949–1972
Ray, Dennis Michael, 1939–.
'Mao and the classless society.'
Survey (London) 77 (Autumn 1970), 30–50.
SUBJ 14 16 64 ▪ 16.2 16.3 32

14150 MCY P P2 G1.2 1949–1972
Rigby, Thomas Harold.
'The embourgeoisement of the Soviet Union and the proletarianization of Communist China.' In *Unity and contradiction: Major aspects of Sino-Soviet relations*, edited by Kurt London. [Selective entry]
New York: Praeger, 1962, 19–36.
SUBJ 16 16.3 ▪ 19

14151 CSH P P2 G1.2 1949–1972
Schurmann, Herbert Franz, 1926–.
'Supplement: Society.' In *Ideology and organization in Communist China*, 2nd ed., enl., by H. F. Schurmann. [Analytic entry]
Berkeley, Los Angeles: U. of California Press, 1968, 576–592.
SUBJ 16 54 ▪ 12.1 16.1 16.3 17

14152 MCH P P1 G1.2 1949–1972
Sergiev, Artemii Vladimirovich.
'Velikie sotsial'nye preobrazovaniia v Kitaiskoi Narodnoi Respublike' (Massive social reorganization in the People's Republic of China).
Voprosy filosofii 13, 9 (1959), 14–28.
SUBJ 16 ▪ 16.1 18 64

14153 DLC PO P2 G1.2 1949–1972
Sidikhmenov, Vasilii IAkovlevich, 1912–.
Velikaia pobeda (A great victory).
Moscow: Gospolitizdat, 1959. 110 p.
SUBJ 14 14.6 16 24.4 34.1 34.2 ▪ 21.3 22 24.3 24.6 26.3 32 55 64

14154 NNC O P2 G1.2 1949–1972
Siui Di-sin' (Hsü Ti-hsin), 1902–.
'Klassovaia bor'ba v Kitae v perekhodnyi period: osobennosti vzaimootnoshenii

klassov v Kitae v perekhodnyi period' (The class struggle in China: Features of interclass relations during the transitional period).
SK 1958, 3, 17–26.
Subj 16 64 ▪ 14 16.2 16.3

16.1 Elite Strata

社會領導階層　エリート階層

1644-1911

14155 NNC S P2 G1.1 1842–1911
Bland, John Otway Percy, 1863–1945.
Li Hung-chang.
New York: Holt, 1917. 327 p. [Reprinted—Freeport, N.Y.: Books for Libraries, 1971. 327 p.]
Subj 12 16.1 59 66 ▪ 15 17 60 64

14156 FPN O P2 G1.1 1644–1842
Bouvet, Joachim, 1656–1730.
Portrait historique de l'empereur de Chine, presentée au roy par le P. J. Bouvet (An historical portrait of the [K'ang-hsi] Emperor presented to the king by Father Joachim Bouvet).
Paris: E. Michallet, 1697. 264 p. [Another ed.—*Histoire de l'empereur de la Chine, presentée au roy.* The Hague: Utywerf, 1699. 171 p.]
The history of Cang-hy, the present Emperour of China, presented to the Most Christian King, by Father J. Bouvet. [Abridged tr.]
London: F. Coggan, 1699. 111 p.
Subj 12 15 16.1 61 66 ▪ 13 18 32.2 43 46 55 56

14157 NNC O P3 G5.1 1895–1911
Carl, Katherine Augusta, ?–1938.
With the Empress Dowager.
New York: Century, 1905. 25, 306 p.
Subj 16.1 47 48 55 ▪ 12 13 24.2 31 41 45 59

14158 ELB P P2 G1.3 1644–1911
Chang, Chung-li, 1919–.
The Chinese gentry: Studies on their role in nineteenth century Chinese society.
Seattle: U. of Washington Press, 1955. 21, 250 p. (Revision of *The gentry in nineteenth century China: Their economic position as evidenced by their share of the national product,* doctoral dissertation in Economics, U. of Washington, 1953) [Reprinted—Seattle: U. of Washington Press, 1967. 272 p.]
Subj 12 16.1 22 ▪ 17 22.1 26.1

14159 ELB P P1 G1.3 1644–1911
Chang, Chung-li, 1919–.
The income of the Chinese gentry.
Seattle: U. of Washington Press, 1962. 17, 369 p.
Subj 12 14 16.1 ▪ 17 18 30 42 45

14160 MAM P P2 G1.2 1842–1895
Chang, Peter (Chang T'ien-tseng), 1921–.
The power elite: A literary image in late nineteenth century China.
Ann Arbor: University Microfilms (Publ. 66-3951), 1966. 330 p. (Doctoral dissertation in Sociology, New School for Social Research [New York], 1965)
Subj 16.1 64 66 ▪ 12 16.3 22 26.1 62

14161 CSH O P2 G6.0 1842–1911
Ch'en Tu-hsiu, 1879–1942.
'Ch'en Tu-hsiu's unfinished autobiography', edited by Richard Clark Kagan. Tr. by Richard C. Kagan of *Shih-an tzu chuan* (Autobiography of Ch'en Tu-hsiu); Shanghai: Ya tung t'u shu kuan, 1938; 34 p.
CQ 50 (Apr.–June 1972), 295–314.
Subj 12 16.1 ▪ 17 26.1 42 59

14162 NNC P P1 G1.2 1895–1911
Chudodeev, IUrii Vladimirovich, 1931–.
'Bor'ba gruppirovok vnutri gospodstvuiushchego klassa Kitaia nakanune revoliutsii 1911 g.: k voprosu o krizise "verkhov"' (Factional struggle in the ruling class on the eve of the Revolution of 1911: Crisis within the Chinese elite).
KSINA 66 (1963), 105–116.
Subj 12 16.1 ▪ 15 64 66

14163 FPN PO P3 G5.1 1842–1895
Courant, Maurice Auguste Louis Marie, 1865–1935.
'La cour de Péking: notes sur la constitution, la vie et la fonctionnement de cette cour' (Notes on the structure, operations, and life of the court in Peking).
B. de géographie historique et descriptive 1891, 3, 223–330. [Separately reprinted as *La cour de Pékin* (The court in Peking). Paris: Ernest Leroux, 1891. 112 p.]
Subj 12 13 16.1 ▪ 15 17 41 45 46 47 52 57 62

14164 MAM P P2 G1.2 1842–1911
Des Forges, Roger Van Vranken, 1942–.
Hsi-Liang: A portrait of a late Ch'ing patriot.
Ann Arbor: University Microfilms (Publ. 71-28,158), 1971. 484 p. (Doctoral dissertation in History, Yale U., 1971)
Subj 12 14 16.1 59 62 66 ▪ 12.1 14.2 14.4 14.5 15 17 25 34.2 54 55

14165 MCH O P3 G1.2 1644–1895
Douglas, Robert Kennaway, 1838–1913.
'Some Peking politicians.'
Nineteenth century 40, 238 (Dec. 1896), 896–906.
Subj 12 16.1

14166 MCH P P1 G1.1 1644–1842
Eberhard, Wolfram, 1909–.
Die chinesische Novelle des 17.–19. Jahrhunderts: Eine soziologische Untersuchung (A sociological analysis of the Chinese short story from the seventeenth through the nineteenth centuries).
Ascona: Artibus Asiae, 1948. 12, 239 p. [Supplement to *Artibus Asiae* 9 (1946)]
Subj 16 16.1 63 65 ▪ 25 29 46 61

14167 CSU P P2 G1.1 –1895
Faber, Ernst, 1839–1899.
China in the light of history. Tr. from the German by E. M. H.
Shanghai: American Presbyterian Mission Press, 1897. 67 p.
Subj 12 16.1 33 ▪ 13 22 32.2 47 62 64

14168 CSU P P2 G1.3 –1911
Fei Hsiao-tung (Fei Hsiao-t'ung), 1910–.
'The gentry and political power.' In *China's gentry: Essays in rural-urban relations,* rev. ed., by Fei Hsiao-tung, edited by Margaret Park Redfield. [Analytic entry]
Chicago: U. of Chicago Press, 1953, 17–32. [Reprinted in *China's gentry: Essays in rural-urban relations,* by Fei Hsiao-tung, edited by M. P. Redfield. (Analytic entry.) Chicago: U. of Chicago Press, 1968, 17–32.]
Subj 12 16.1 ▪ 42

14169 CSU P P1 G1.3 –1911
Fei Hsiao-tung (Fei Hsiao-t'ung), 1910–.
'The gentry and technical knowledge.' In *China's gentry: Essays in rural-urban relations,* rev. ed., by Fei Hsiao-tung, edited by Margaret Park Redfield. [Analytic entry]
Chicago: U. of Chicago Press, 1953, 59–74. [Reprinted in *China's gentry: Essays in rural-urban relations,* by Fei Hsiao-tung, edited by M. P. Redfield. (Analytic entry.) Chicago: U. of Chicago Press, 1968, 59–74.]
Subj 16.1 62 63

14170 CSU P P1 G1.3 –1911
Fei Hsiao-tung (Fei Hsiao-t'ung), 1910–.
'The scholar becomes the official.' In *China's gentry: Essays in rural-urban relations,* rev. ed., by Fei Hsiao-tung, edited by Margaret Park Redfield. [Analytic entry]
Chicago: U. of Chicago Press, 1953, 33–58. [Reprinted in *China's gentry: Essays in rural-urban relations,* by Fei Hsiao-tung, edited by M. P. Redfield. (Analytic entry.) Chicago: U. of Chicago Press, 1968, 33–58.]
Subj 16.1 64

14171 CSU O P3 G8.1 1895–1911
Fischer, Martin, 1882–1961.
Szetschuan: Diplomatie und Reisen in China während der letzten drei Jahre der Kaiserzeit (Szechwan: Diplomacy and travel in China during the last three years of the Ch'ing period).
Munich: Oldenbourg, 1968. 170 p.
Subj 12 16.1 32.2 ▪ 17 48

14172 NIC P P1 G1.3 1644–1911
Franke, Wolfgang, 1912–.
'Patents for hereditary ranks and honorary titles during the Ch'ing dynasty.'
MS 7, 1/2 (1942), 38–67.
Subj 16.1 ▪ 12

14173 CBU P P1 G1.2 1644–1895
Gardner, Charles.
'Hereditary genius in China.'
China review 2, 4 (Jan.–Feb. 1874), 206–214.
Subj 16 16.1

14174 CSU P P3 G1.1 1895–1911
Gasster, Michael, 1930–.
Chinese intellectuals and the Revolution of 1911: The birth of modern Chinese radicalism.
Seattle: U. of Washington Press, 1969. 29, 288 p. (U. of Washington, Far Eastern Institute, Publications on Asia, 19) (Revision of *Currents of thought in the T'ung-meng Hui,* doctoral dissertation in Far Eastern Studies, U. of Washington, 1962)
Subj 12 16.1 32.2 59 64 ▪ 14.2 36.1 54 66

14175 CSU S P1 G1.1 –1911
Giles, Herbert Allen, 1845–1935.
China and the Manchus.

Cambridge: Cambridge U. Press, 1912. 148 p.
Subj 16.1 32.2 ▪ 12.2 14.5 66

14176 CSU U P2 G1.2 1644–1911
Grousset, René, 1885–1952.
'Les grands empereurs mandchous: K'ang-hi et K'ien-long' (The great Ch'ing rulers: The K'ang-hsi and Ch'ien-lung Emperors). In *Histoire de la Chine* (History of China), by R. Grousset. [Selective entry]
Paris: Fayard, 1943, 335–359.

'The great Manchu emperors.' Tr. by Anthony Watson-Gandy and Terence Gordon. In *The rise and splendour of the Chinese empire*, by R. Grousset. [Selective entry]
Berkeley, Los Angeles: U. of California Press, 1953, 279–302.
Subj 16.1 66 ▪ 11 14.1 15 32.2 62

14177 NNC O P2 G1.2 1895–1911
Grulev, M-.
'Iz poezdki v Man'chzhuriiu' (A trip to Manchuria).
Istoricheskii vestnik 21 (sentiabr' 1900), 945–972.
Subj 12 12.2 16.1 55 ▪ 22 22.2 26.1 48 66

14178 MCH P P2 G1.2 1842–1911
Haldane, Charlotte Franken, 1894–.
The last great empress of China.
London: Constable, 1966. 304 p.
Subj 12 16.1 59 64 66 ▪ 15 32.2 33 41 42 43 47 50

14179 MCH P P1 G1.2 –1911
Hoang, Pierre (Huang Po-lu), 1830–1909.
Mélanges sur l'administration (A miscellany on administration).
Shanghai: Impr. de la Mission catholique, 1902. 233 p. (Variétés sinologiques, 21)
Subj 12 16.1 ▪ 16

14180 CSU S P2 G1.3 1842–1895
Hsüeh, Chün-tu, 1922–.
'The Taiping Rebellion: Editor's introduction.' In *Revolutionary leaders of modern China*, edited by Chün-tu Hsüeh. [Selective entry]
New York: Oxford U. Press, 1971, 3–10.
Subj 16.1 59 ▪ 32.2

14181 MAM P P4 G1.2 1644–1842
Huang, Pei (Huang P'ei), 1928–.
A study of the Yung-cheng period, 1723–1735: The political phase.
Ann Arbor: University Microfilms (Publ. 64-5459), 1964. 392 p. (Doctoral dissertation in History, Indiana U., 1963)
Subj 12 16.1 32.2 ▪ 12.1

14182 MCH FP P3 G5.1 1842–1911
Hussey, Harry, 1881–.
Venerable ancestor: The life and times of Tz'u Hsi, 1835–1908, Empress of China.
Garden City, N.Y.: Doubleday, 1949. 24, 354 p. [Reprinted—Westport, Conn.: Greenwood Press, 1970. 19, 354 p.]
Subj 12 16.1 59 ▪ 41 42 47 66

14183 CSU P P2 G1.2 1644–1842
Kessler, Lawrence Devlin, 1936–.
'Chinese scholars and the early Manchu state.'
HJAS 31 (1971), 179–200.
Subj 12 12.1 16.1 ▪ 14.5 22.2

14184 CSU P P1 G1.1 –1911
King, Ambrose Yeo-chi (Chin Yao-chi), 1935–.
'The behavioral patterns of traditional Confucian bureaucrats.'
CJA 8 (Jan. 1967), 49–55 [s.p.].
Subj 12 16.1 48 ▪ 61 64

14185 MCH U P1 G1.1 –1895
Kracke, Edward Augustus, Jr., 1908–.
'The changing role of the Chinese intellectual: An introductory note.'
CSSH 1, 1 (Oct. 1958), 23–25.
Subj 16.1 ▪ 12

14186 CSU P P4 G7.2 1895–1911
Lewis, Charlton Miner, III, 1930–.
'The Hunanese elite and the reform movement, 1895–1898.'
JAS 29, 1 (Nov. 1969), 35–42. [For fuller treatment, see entry 14187.]
Subj 16.1 32 ▪ 17

14187 MAM P P2 G7.2 1842–1911
Lewis, Charlton Miner, III, 1930–.
The opening of Hunan: Reform and revolution in a Chinese province, 1895–1907.
Ann Arbor: University Microfilms (Publ. 66-3641), 1966. 260 p. (Doctoral dissertation in History, U. of California, Berkeley, 1965)
Subj 16.1 32 32.2 66 ▪ 14.3 14.4 17 24.2 37 64

14188 NIC P P1 G1.3 –1842
Li Chi, 1903–.
'The changing concept of the recluse in Chinese literature.'
HJAS 24 (1962/63), 234–247.
Subj 16.1 ▪ 12

14189 NNC S P4 G1.2 –1911
Lieban, Richard W-, 1921–.
Sociocultural stability of the Chinese intelligentsia: A preliminary analysis.
Unpublished masters thesis in Anthropology, Columbia U., 1951. 72 p.
Subj 16.1 ▪ 12 17 22 32.2 44 60 64

14190 WSU P P1 G1.2 1895–1911
Lust, John, 1918–.
'Introduction.' In *The revolutionary army: A Chinese nationalist tract of 1903*, by Tsou Jung, edited by J. Lust. [Sole entry]
The Hague: Mouton, 1968, 1–47. (Maison des sciences de l'homme, Matériaux pour l'étude de l'Extrême-Orient moderne et contemporaine, 6)
Subj 16.1 66 ▪ 32.2 59 64

14191 MCH PO P5 G5.1 1644–1911
Malone, Carroll Brown, 1886–.
History of the Peking summer palaces under the Ch'ing dynasty.
Urbana: U. of Illinois, 1934. 247 p. (Illinois studies in the social sciences, 19, 1/2) (Doctoral dissertation in History, U. of Illinois, 1928) [Reprinted—New York: Paragon, 1966. 247 p.]
Subj 13 16.1 55 ▪ 17 43

14192 NIC P P1 G1.2 1644–1895
Marsh, Robert Mortimer, 1931–.
'Formal organization and promotion in a pre-industrial society.'
ASR 26, 4 (Aug. 1961), 547–556. [Reprinted as 'Formal organization and promotion in Chinese society.' In *Sociology and history: Theory and research*, edited by Werner Jacob Cahnman and Alvin Boskoff. (Sole entry.) New York: Free Press of Glencoe, 1964, 205–218.]
Subj 12 16.1

14193 NIC P P1 G1.1 1644–1911
Marsh, Robert Mortimer, 1931–.
The mandarins: The circulation of elites in China, 1600–1900.
Glencoe, Ill.: Free Press, 1961. 17, 300 p.
Subj 12 16.1 ▪ 16 17 30

14194 DLC PO P2 G5.0 1842–1895
Martin, William Alexander Parsons, 1827–1916.
'The Duke of K'ung, successor of Confucius.' In *The Chinese: Their education, philosophy and letters*, by W. A. P. Martin. [Selective entry]
New York: Harper, 1881, 307–312. [Reprinted from *Celestial Empire* (Shanghai) 1876?]
Subj 16.1

14195 MCH P P3 G1.4 1842–1911
Maybon, Albert, 1878–.
La vie secrète de la cour de Chine (The secret life of the court of China).
Paris: Juven, 1910. 299 p.
Subj 15 16.1 32.2 66 ▪ 12 17 21.3 22.2 41 43 62 64

14196 NNC P P3 G5.1 1644–1895
Mayers, William Frederick, 1831–1878.
'The Chinese imperial family.'
TP 6, 3 (1895), 333–341. [Reprinted from *North-China herald and supreme court and consular gazette* Jan. 1895.]
Subj 16.1 41

14197 MCH P P3 G5.1 1644–1842
Meskill, John Thomas, 1927–.
'A conferral of the degree of *chin-shih*.'
MS 23 (1964), 351–371.
Subj 12 16.1 ▪ 13 64

14198 CSU S P1 G1.2 1644–1911
Metzger, Thomas Albert, 1933–.
Review of *Friends, guests, and colleagues: The mu-fu system in the late Ch'ing period*, by Kenneth Everett Folsom.
HJAS 29 (1969), 315–320.
Subj 12 16.1 48 ▪ 64

14199 MCH U P2 G1.3 1842–1911
Michael, Franz Henry, 1907–.
'State and society in nineteenth century China.'
WP 7, 3 (Apr. 1955), 419–433. [Reprinted in *Modern China*, edited by Albert Feuerwerker. (Selective entry.) Englewood Cliffs, N. J.: Prentice-Hall, 1964, 57–69.]
Subj 12 16.1 22.1 ▪ 17 22 32.2

14200 MCY P P1 G1.3 1644–1842
Mish, John Leon, 1909–.
'An early Manchu-Chinese patent of nobility.'
Monumenta Nipponica 10, 1/2 (Apr. 1954), 270–276.
Subj 16.1

14201 FPN P P4 G1.2 –1911
[Pouvourville, Eugène-Albert Puyon de] Matgioï, pseud.
La Chine des mandarins (The China of the mandarins).

Paris: Schleicher, 1901. 167 p. (Bibliothèque d'histoire et de géographie universelle, 5)
Subj 12.2 14.5 15 16.1 ▪ 12 12.1 13 14.6 16.2 22 64

14202 CBU S P1 G1.2 1644–1895
Roy, W- T-.
'Sahibs and mandarins: A comparative study of bureaucratic elites in India and China in the nineteenth century.'
Politics (Kensington, N.S.W.) 2, 1 (May 1967), 36–47.
Subj 12 16.1 ▪ 17 64

14203 CSU P P1 G1.1 1895–1911
Schiffrin, Harold Zvi, 1922–.
'The enigma of Sun Yat-sen.' In *China in revolution: The first phase, 1900–1913*, edited by Mary Clabaugh Wright. [Selective entry]
New Haven: Yale U. Press, 1968, 443–474. [Reprinted in *Readings in modern Chinese history*, edited by Immanuel C. Y. Hsü (Hsü Chung-yüeh). (Selective entry.) New York: Oxford U. Press, 1971, 387–409.]
Subj 16.1 59 ▪ 32.2 64 66

14204 MCH PO P3 G5.1 1842–1911
Sergeant, Philip Walsingham, 1872–?
The great Empress Dowager of China . . .
New York: Dodd, Mead, 1911. 344 p.
Subj 12 16.1 19 59 ▪ 15 33 47 66

14205 CSU P P4 G1.2 –1911
Wakeman, Frederic Evans, Jr., 1937–.
'The price of autonomy: Intellectuals in Ming and Ch'ing politics.'
Daedalus 101, 2 (Spring 1972), 35–70.
Subj 12 16.1 36.1 64 ▪ 17 30 32

14206 MAM P P1 G1.2 1644–1911
Wei, Yung, 1937–.
Elite recruitment and political crisis: A study of political leaders of the Ch'ing period, 1644–1911.
Ann Arbor: University Microfilms (Publ. 68-4015), 1968. 366 p. (Doctoral dissertation in Political Science, U. of Oregon, 1967)
Subj 16 16.1 59 ▪ 12 32 32.2

14207 ICU P P2 G1.3 1842–1911
Weiss, Thomas Joel, 1941–.
Hunanese among China's elite, 1851–1911.
Unpublished doctoral dissertation in Political Science, U. of Chicago, 1969. 197 p.
Subj 12 16 16.1 22 29 ▪ 15 25 26 26.1 64

14208 CSU S P2 G1.2 –1911
Wilkinson, Rupert H-.
'Manners and classics in Confucian China.' In *Gentlemanly power: British leadership and the public school tradition. A comparative study in the making of rulers*, by R. H. Wilkinson. [Sole entry]
London: Oxford U. Press, 1964, 125–176.
Subj 12 16.1 17 60 ▪ 16 31 42 55 63

14209 NNC P P1 G1.2 1895–1911
Wonnacott, Donna Elizabeth Cochrane.
Hu Hanmin's articles in the 'Min pao' [People's journal].
Unpublished masters thesis in Political Science, Columbia U., 1960. 88 p. [Certificate essay, East Asian Institute]
Subj 16.1 ▪ 62 66

14210 CSU P P2 G1.4 1644–1842
Wu, Silas H. L. (Wu Hsiu-liang), 1929–.
'Emperors at work: The daily schedules of the K'ang-hsi and Yung-cheng Emperors, 1661–1735.'
THJ new (2nd) series 8, 1/2 (Aug. 1970), 210–226.
Subj 12 16.1 55 ▪ 13 59 64

14211 CSU P P1 G1.1 1644–1911
Yen Ching-hwang.
'Ch'ing's sale of honours and the Chinese leadership in Singapore and Malaya, 1877–1912.'
J. of Southeast Asian studies 1, 2 (Sept. 1970), 20–32.
Subj 12 14.5 16.1

14212 CSU P P1 G1.2 1895–1911
Young, Ernest Paddock, 1932–.
'Yuan Shih-k'ai's rise to the presidency.' In *China in revolution: The first phase, 1900–1913*, edited by Mary Clabaugh Wright. [Analytic entry]
New Haven: Yale U. Press, 1968, 419–442.
Subj 16.1 ▪ 15 32.2

1644-1949

14213 CSU P P1 G1.2 1895–1949
Chisholm, Lawrence Washington, 1929–.
'Lu Hsun and revolution in modern China.'
Yale French studies 39 (Sept. 1967), 226–241.
Subj 16.1 59 ▪ 62

14214 CSU PO P3 G5.1 –1928
Dorn, Frank.
The Forbidden City: The biography of a palace.
New York: Scribner, 1970. 20, 312 p.
Subj 16.1 21.3 31 50 55 62 ▪ 13 14.5 17 21.4 22.2 25 41 43 57 66

14215 MCH S P2 G1.1 –1949
Duboscq, André, 1876–.
L'élite chinoise: ses origines, sa transformation après l'empire (The Chinese elite: Its origins and its transformation after the fall of the empire).
Paris: Nouvelles éditions latines, 1945. 135 p.
Subj 16.1 17 ▪ 12 13 22.1 26.1 32.2 43 47 64

14216 CBU S P1 G1.1 –1928
Eichhorn, Werner, 1899–.
'Die chinesische Intelligenz und der Einbruch Europas' (The Chinese intelligentsia and the European invasion). In *Kulturgeschichte Chinas* (A cultural history of China), by W. Eichhorn. [Sole entry]
Stuttgart: Kohlhammer, 1964, 264–272.

'The Chinese intellectuals and the impact of Europe.' Tr. by Janet Seligman. In *Chinese civilization: An introduction*, by W. Eichhorn. [Sole entry]
New York: Praeger, 1969, 323–332.
Subj 16.1 66 ▪ 47

14217 MAM P P2 G1.3 –1949
Fan, Carol C. (Fan Ch'un), 1935–.
The geographic distribution of leadership in China, 1875–1937.
Ann Arbor: University Microfilms (Publ. 65-6021), 1965. 207 p. (Doctoral dissertation in History, U. of California, Los Angeles)
Subj 11.3 12 16.1 ▪ 15 17 32 32.2 36.1

14218 CSU PO P4 G1.3 –1949
Ferguson, John Calvin, 1866–1945.
'The last of the immortals.'
THM 5, 4 (Nov. 1937), 341–348.
Subj 16.1 36.1 ▪ 12 59

14219 MCH PO P2 G1.2 1842–1949
Hahn, Emily, 1905–.
The Soong sisters.
Garden City, N.Y.: Doubleday, Doran, 1941. 21, 349 p. [Reprinted—Westport, Conn.: Greenwood Press, 1972. 21, 349 p.]
Subj 12 16.1 17 32.2 47 ▪ 15 18 22.2 32 44 61 66

14220 CSU P P1 G1.2 –1949
Hsu, Francis L. K. (Hsü Lang-kuang), 1909–.
'A study of family prominence.' In *Under the ancestors' shadow: Kinship, personality and social mobility in village China*, rev. and enl. ed., by F. L. K. Hsu. [Analytic entry]
Garden City, N.Y.: Doubleday, 1967, 327–336. [Reprinted in *Under the ancestors' shadow: Kinship, personality and social mobility in village China*, rev. and enl. ed., by F. L. K. Hsu. (Selective entry.) Stanford: Stanford U. Press, 1971, 327–336. (For the monograph itself, see entry 19729.)]
Subj 16.1 ▪ 16 41

14221 CSU U P1 G1.2 1895–1928
Hsüeh, Chün-tu, 1922–.
'The republican revolution: Editor's introduction.' In *Revolutionary leaders of modern China*, edited by Chün-tu Hsüeh. [Selective entry]
New York: Oxford U. Press, 1971, 87–101.
Subj 16.1 32.2

14222 CSU S P4 G1.1 1895–1928
Ichiko Chūzō, 1913–.
'The role of the gentry: An hypothesis.' In *China in revolution: The first phase, 1900–1913*, edited by Mary Clabaugh Wright. [Selective entry]
New Haven: Yale U. Press, 1968, 297–317.
Subj 16.1 ▪ 22 32.2

14223 WSU P P2 G1.2 1895–1949
Lamley, Harry Jerome, 1928–.
Liang Shu-ming: The thought and action of a reformer.
Unpublished masters thesis in Far Eastern and Slavic Languages, U. of Washington, 1960. 404 p.
Subj 16.1 22 37 59 60 ▪ 17 19 32 32.2 36.1 64

14224 MAM PO P2 G9.4 1895–1928
Lamley, Harry Jerome, 1928–.
The Taiwan literati and early Japanese rule, 1895–1915: A study of their reactions to the Japanese occupation and subsequent responses to colonial rule and modernization.

Ann Arbor: University Microfilms (Publ. 65-1883), 1965. 530 p. (Doctoral dissertation in History, U. of Washington, 1964)
SUBJ 16.1 66 ▪ 12 17 21.1 21.3 22 25 28 37

14225 NIC O P1 G1.3 –1949
Lee, Shu-ching (Li Shu-ch'ing), 1908–.
'Intelligentsia of China.'
AJS 52, 6 (May 1947), 489–497.
SUBJ 16.1 64 ▪ 12 15 17

14226 CSU P P1 G1.3 1842–1949
Liu Hoh Hsüan (Liu Huo-hsüan).
'Ma Hsiang Po [Ma Liang].'
THM 10, 5 (May 1940), 436–451.
SUBJ 16.1 59 ▪ 12 17 62

14227 CSU P P1 G1.2 1895–1928
Liu, Ts'un-yan (Liu Ts'un-jen), 1917–.
'Ku Hung-ming and his interpretation of Chinese civilization.' In *Symposium on historical, archaeological and linguistic studies on southern China, South-east Asia and the Hong Kong region*, edited by Frederick Seguier Drake. [Selective entry]
Hong Kong: Hong Kong U. Press, 1967, 269–281.
SUBJ 16.1 ▪ 63

14228 NNC O P2 G5.0 1644–1928
Mueller, Herbert, 1885–.
'Denkmalschutz und Denkmalpflege in China' (The protection and preservation of historical monuments in China).
China-Archiv 1, 7 (24 Juli 1916), 331–335; 1, 8 (24 Aug. 1916), 395–399; 1, 9 (24 Sept. 1916), 459–466.
SUBJ 16.1 ▪ 36.1 62 64

14229 CSU U P1 G1.2 1842–1928
T'ang, C. Y. (T'ang Ch'ing-i).
'T'ang Wen-chih, statesman and educator.'
THM 5, 1 (Aug. 1937), 19–26.
SUBJ 16.1 59 ▪ 12 17

14230 MCH P P1 G1.2 1842–1949
Vey Dé Tchao (Wei Te-chao).
Le pouvoir d'examen en Chine (The importance of the examination in China).
Nancy: Thomas, 1935. 140 p. (Doctoral dissertation, Faculté de droit, Université de Nancy)
SUBJ 12 16.1 ▪ 12.1 12.2 17 72

14231 MCY P P4 G1.2 1842–1949
Wang, Y. C. (Wang I-chü; Wang Chi-ch'ien), 1916–.
Chinese intellectuals and the West, 1872–1949.
Chapel Hill: U. of North Carolina Press, 1966. 557 p. (Revision of *Foreign-educated Chinese, 1872–1948*, doctoral dissertation in Sociology, U. of Chicago, 1958)
SUBJ 12 16.1 17 54 59 64 ▪ 14.2 14.5 16.2 32.2 36.1 62 66 70 72

14232 CSU P P1 G1.2 1895–1928
Young, Ernest Paddock, 1932–.
'Nationalism, reform, and republican revolution: China in the early twentieth century.' In *Modern East Asia: Essays in interpretation*, edited by James Buckley Crowley. [Selective entry]
New York: Harcourt, Brace and World, 1970, 151–179.
SUBJ 16 16.1 64 ▪ 12 12.2 17 32 59 66

1911-1949

14233 MCH P P3 G1.2 1928–1949
Bérard, Emile.
'L'agitation universitaire en Chine' (Unrest in Chinese universities).
Afrique et l'Asie 4 (oct.–déc. 1948), 19–28.
SUBJ 16.1 54 ▪ 17 32.2 66

14234 CSU O P3 G5.1 1911–1928
Bland, John Otway Percy, 1863–1945.
'The last imperial Manchu.'
Asia (New York: American Asiatic Assn.) 20, 11 (Dec. 1920), 1047–1053.
SUBJ 16.1

14235 MCH P P1 G1.2 1928–1949
Current Scene Editor.
'Chairman Mao and the heretics: Peking's "great debate".'
CS 3, 13 (15 Feb. 1965), 1–12.
SUBJ 12.1 16.1 ▪ 32 64

14236 CSU P P2 G1.3 1928–1949
Dorrill, William Franklin, 1931–.
'Transfer of legitimacy in the Chinese Communist Party: Origins of the Maoist myth.' In *Party leadership and revolutionary power in China*, edited by John Wilson Lewis. [Analytic entry]
Cambridge: Cambridge U. Press, 1970, 69–113.
SUBJ 16.1 32.2 ▪ 15 64

14237 MCH P P3 G1.3 1911–1928
Duyvendak, Jan Julius Lodewijk, 1889–1954.
'Een letterkundige renaissance in China' (A literary renaissance in China [as seen in the journal *Hsin ch'ing-nien*, La jeunesse]).
De Gids 87, 4 (April 1923), 79–101.
SUBJ 16.1 ▪ 17 64

14238 MAM P P3 G1.3 1911–1949
Gewurtz, Margo Speisman, 1943–.
Tsou T'ao-fen: The 'Sheng-huo' [Life weekly] *years, 1925–1933.*
Ann Arbor: University Microfilms (Publ. 73-345), 1973. 11, 256 p. (Doctoral dissertation in History, Cornell U., 1972)
SUBJ 14.2 16.1 32 59 60 ▪ 12.2 17 27 32.1 37 64

14239 MCY O P7 G1.2 1928–1949
Hanwell, Norman D-.
'Rotten gentry in China.'
Asia (New York: American Asiatic Assn.) 37, 4 (Apr. 1937), 297–300.
SUBJ 16.1 22 ▪ 14.5 32.2

14240 MCH O P1 G1.2 1928–1949
Holcombe, Arthur Norman, 1884–.
'The Chinese road to office: An Occidental view of an Oriental institution.'
American scholar 6, 1 (Winter 1937), 38–45.
SUBJ 12 16.1 17 ▪ 64

14241 CSU P P2 G1.2 1928–1949
Hsia, T. A. (Hsia Chi-an), 1916–1965.
Enigma of the five martyrs: A study of the leftist literary movement in modern China.
Berkeley: U. of California, Center for Chinese Studies, 1962. 150 p. (CCS research series, 2) [Reprinted as 'Enigma of the five martyrs.' In *The gate of darkness: Studies on the leftist literary movement in China*, by T. A. Hsia. (Selective entry.) Seattle: U. of Washington Press, 1968, 163–233. (U. of Washington, Far Eastern and Russian Institute, Publications on Asia, 17)]
SUBJ 16.1 32.2 ▪ 36.1 59 61 64

14242 CSU P P1 G1.2 1911–1949
Hsia, T. A. (Hsia Chi-an), 1916–1965.
'The phenomenon of Chiang Kuang-tz'u.' In *The gate of darkness: Studies on the leftist literary movement in China*, by T. A. Hsia. [Selective entry]
Seattle: U. of Washington Press, 1968, 55–100. (U. of Washington, Far Eastern and Russian Institute, Publications on Asia, 17)
SUBJ 16.1 59 ▪ 32.2 61 64

14243 MCH U P3 G1.2 1911–1928
Kim, R.
'O sovremennoi kitaiskoi intelligentsii' (The contemporary Chinese intelligentsia).
NV 12 (1926), 32–51.
SUBJ 16.1 64 ▪ 17

14244 MCH P P4 G1.1 1928–1949
Lamson, Herbert Day, 1899–.
'The geographical distribution of leaders in China.'
China critic 6, 7 (16 Feb. 1933), 176–181.
SUBJ 16.1 ▪ 16.2 17

14245 CSH U P4 G1.2 1911–1949
Lubot, Eugene Stephen, 1942–.
'The formation of political convictions: Liberalism vs. Communism in modern China.' [Review of *Hu Shih and the Chinese renaissance: Liberalism in the Chinese revolution, 1917–1937*, by Jerome Bailey Grieder; *Kuo Mo-jo: The early years*, by David Tod Roy; and *Ting Wen-chiang: Science and China's new culture*, by Charlotte Davis Furth.]
Asian forum 3, 3 (July–Sept. 1971), 175–182.
SUBJ 16.1 60 61 ▪ 59 64

14246 CSH P P1 G1.2 1911–1949
Mills, Harriet Cornelia, 1920–.
'Lu Hsün and the Communist Party.'
CQ 4 (Oct.–Dec. 1960), 17–27. [For fuller treatment, see entry 14247.]
SUBJ 16.1 32.2 59 ▪ 61 64

14247 MAM P P1 G1.2 1911–1949
Mills, Harriet Cornelia, 1920–.
Lu Hsün, 1927–1936: The years on the left.
Ann Arbor: University Microfilms (Publ. 64-9196), 1964. 368 p. (Doctoral dissertation in Chinese Literature, Columbia U., 1963)
SUBJ 16.1 32.2 59 60 64 ▪ 61

14248 CSU P P2 G1.1 1928–1949
Pepper, Suzanne, 1939–.
'Socialism, democracy, and Chinese Communism: A problem of choice for the intelligentsia, 1945–49.' In *Ideology and politics in contemporary China*, edited by Chalmers Ashby Johnson. [Selective entry]
Seattle: U. of Washington Press, 1973, 161–218. (Social Science Research

Council, Studies in Chinese government and politics, 4)
SUBJ 16.1 32 32.2 64 ▪ 12 12.1 12.2 14 14.2 15 16.3

14249 CSU P P1 G1.2 1928–1949
Schwarz, Henry Guenter, 1928–.
'The nature of leadership: The Chinese Communists, 1930–1945.'
WP 22, 4 (July 1970), 541–581.
SUBJ 12 16.1 32.2 ▪ 12.1 15 30 64

14250 NIC U P1 G1.3 1911–1928
Tao, L. K. (T'ao Meng-ho), 1887–1960.
'Unemployment among intellectual workers in China.'
CSPSR 13, 3 (July 1929), 251–261.
SUBJ 11.4 16.1 17

14251 CSU P P2 G1.2 1911–1928
Wilbur, Clarence Martin, 1908–.
'The influence of the past: How the early years helped to shape the future of the Chinese Communist Party.' In *Party leadership and revolutionary power in China*, edited by John Wilson Lewis. [Analytic entry]
Cambridge: Cambridge U. Press, 1970, 35–68.
SUBJ 16.1 32.2 ▪ 17 36.3 36.4 54

1911-1972
(including 1644-1972)

14252 CSU U P3 G1.2 1928–1972
Bernal, Martin Gardiner, 1937–.
'Mao and the writers.' [Review of *Literary dissent in Communist China*, by Merle Dorothy Goldman; *The gate of darkness: Studies on the leftist literary movement in China*, by T. A. Hsia (Hsia Chi-an); *Literary doctrine in China and Soviet influence, 1956–1960*, by Douwe Wessel Fokkema; *Pa Chin and his writings: Chinese youth between the two revolutions*, by Olga Lang; and *The Hundred Flowers*, by Roderick Lemonde MacFarquhar.]
NYRB 13, 7 (23 Oct. 1969), 32–36.
SUBJ 12.1 16.1 ▪ 36.1 64

14253 CSH P P1 G1.2 1928–1972
Birch, Cyril, 1925–.
'The dragon and the pen: The literary scene.'
Soviet survey 24 (Apr.–June 1958), 22–26. [Special issue on China]
SUBJ 16.1 ▪ 12.1 64

14254 CSU U P1 G1.2 1842–1972
Boorman, Howard Lyon, 1920–.
'Chinese leaders and Chinese politics.' In *Revolutionary leaders of modern China*, edited by Chün-tu Hsüeh. [Selective entry]
New York: Oxford U. Press, 1971, 13–23 [s.p.].
SUBJ 16.1 ▪ 32.2

14255 MMT P P1 G1.2 1911–1972
Brandt, Conrad, 1920–.
'The French-returned elite in the Chinese Communist Party.' In *Symposium on economic and social problems of the Far East*, edited by Edward Franciszek Szczepanik. [Selective entry]
Hong Kong: Hong Kong U. Press, 1962, 229–238.
SUBJ 11.2 16.1 17 32.2 ▪ 37 64

14256 MCH U P2 G1.2 1911–1972
Briessen, Fritz van.
'Chinas "Gentry" und die Revolution: Zur Soziologie des Maoismus' (China's 'gentry' and the revolution: The sociology of Maoism). [Review of *China's gentry: Essays in rural-urban relations*, by Fei Hsiao-tung (Fei Hsiao-t'ung).]
Aussenpolitik 7, 18 (Aug. 1956), 512–521.
SUBJ 16 16.1 30 64 70 ▪ 17 22 36.3 62

14257 MCH S P4 G1.2 1911–1972
Briessen, Fritz van.
'Die Rolle der Gelehrten in der chinesischen Revolution' (The role of scholars in the Chinese revolution).
Aussenpolitik 4, 10 (Okt. 1953), 634–645.
SUBJ 16.1 ▪ 16 17 64

14258 MAU P P2 G1.2 1911–1972
Browning, Charles Hamilton, 1931–.
The Chinese Communist Party and the Chinese intellectuals, 1921–1958.
Unpublished masters thesis in Far Eastern Studies, U. of Michigan, 1958. 99 p.
SUBJ 12.1 16.1 32 64 ▪ 11.4 16 18 19 32.1 32.2 36.4

14259 NNC P P4 G1.2 1928–1972
Chang, Alfred Zee.
'Scientists in Communist China.'
Science 119, 3101 (4 June 1954), 785–789.
SUBJ 11.4 16.1 62 ▪ 17 32.1 36.1

14260 CSU P P2 G1.2 1928–1972
Cheng, Peter P. C., 1930–.
'Liu Shao-ch'i and the Cultural Revolution.'
AS 11, 10 (Oct. 1971), 943–957.
SUBJ 16.1 64 ▪ 32 34.1

14261 CSH P P1 G1.2 1928–1972
Chin, Steve S. K. (Chin Ssu-k'ai), 1919–.
'The Ninth Central Party Committee and Lin Piao's future.' In *Selected seminar papers on contemporary China, I*, edited by S. S. K. Chin and Frank Henry Haviland King. [Analytic entry]
Hong Kong: U. of Hong Kong, Centre of Asian Studies, 1971, 239–276. (CAS occasional papers and monographs, 4)
SUBJ 15 16.1 32

14262 CSU P P2 G1.5 1928–1972
Elmore, Thomas Paul, 1936–.
'The "crimes" of a regional party bureaucrat: Li Ching-ch'üan.'
PC 22B (Dec. 1969), 121–157.
SUBJ 12 16.1 32 59 64 ▪ 14.1 14.2 14.4 17 25

14263 CSU P P1 G1.2 1928–1972
Fokkema, Douwe Wessel, 1931–.
Literary doctrine in China and Soviet influence, 1956–1960.
The Hague: Mouton, 1965. 296 p. (Doctoral dissertation, Faculteit der Wiskunde en Natuurwetenschappen, Rijksuniversiteit te Leiden, 1965)
SUBJ 16.1 32.1 60 ▪ 31 64 66

14264 CSU P P1 G1.2 1928–1972
Goldman, Merle Dorothy, 1931–.
Literary dissent in Communist China.
Cambridge: Harvard U. Press, 1967. 17, 343 p. (Harvard East Asian series, 29) (Revision of *The literati and the Chinese Communist Party*, doctoral dissertation in History and Far Eastern Languages, Harvard U., 1964)
SUBJ 12.1 16.1 31 64 ▪ 32.1 36.1 61

14265 NIC S P1 G1.2 1911–1972
Grieder, Jerome Bailey, 1932–.
'The Communist critique of *Hung lou meng* [Dream of the red chamber].'
PC 10 (Oct. 1956), 142–168.
SUBJ 16.1 64 ▪ 12.1

14266 MCH P P1 G1.1 1644–1972
Hang, Thaddäus.
'Die chinesischen Intellektuellen und das Christentum' (The Chinese intellectuals and Christianity).
Stimmen der Zeit 3. Folge 165, 5 (Feb. 1960), 321–334.
SUBJ 16.1 33 60 66

14267 NIC P P1 G1.2 1911–1972
Hawtin, Faye Elise, 1918–.
'The "Hundred Flowers movement" and the role of the intellectual in China: Fei Hsiao-t'ung, a case history.'
PC 12 (Dec. 1958), 147–198.
SUBJ 12.1 16.1 70 ▪ 64 71

14268 CSH P P3 G1.2 1928–1972
Hsuan Meh (Hsüan Mo).
'A historical study of the Chinese Communist ideological conflict in the literature and arts of the thirties.' In *Collected documents of the First Sino-American Conference on Mainland China*. [Selective entry]
[Taipei]: Institute of International Relations, Republic of China, 1971, 391–411.
SUBJ 16.1 32.1 ▪ 36.1 64

14269 NNC P P4 G1.2 1928–1972
Johnson, Chalmers Ashby, 1931–.
Communist policies toward the intellectual class: Freedom of thought and expression in China, mimeo.
Hong Kong: Union Research Institute, 1959. 130 p. (Communist China problem research series, EC21) [Reprinted—Westport, Conn.: Greenwood Press, 1973. 130 p.]
SUBJ 12.1 16.1 61 64 ▪ 16.2 31 32.1 36.1

14270 NIC P P3 G5.1 1911–1972
Johnson, Chalmers Ashby, 1931–.
'An intellectual weed in the socialist garden: The case of Ch'ien Tuan-sheng.'
CQ 6 (Apr.–June 1961), 29–52.
SUBJ 16.1 32.1 70 ▪ 32 36.1 64

14271 CSH P P2 G1.2 1928–1972
Klein, Donald Walker, 1929–.
'The "next generation" of Chinese Communist leaders.'
CQ 12 (Oct.–Dec. 1962), 57–74. [Reprinted in *China under Mao: Politics takes command*, edited by Roderick Lemonde MacFarquhar. (Selective entry.) Cambridge: M.I.T. Press, 1966, 69–86.]
SUBJ 16.1 36.1 ▪ 12 15 32 32.2 59

14272 MCH P P1 G1.2 1928–1972
[La Dany, Ladislao] ———, 1914–.
'The ruler.'
CNA 272 (17 Apr. 1959), 1–7.
SUBJ 16.1 32 ▪ 13 64

14273 CSH P P3 G1.3 1911–1972
Lee, Robert H. G. (Li K'ung-chiang), 1922–.
'Fung Yu-Lan: A biographical profile.'
CQ 14 (Apr.–June 1963), 141–152.
SUBJ 16.1 59 ▪ 12.1 62 63

14274 CSU P P2 G1.2 1842–1972
Lee, Warner, 1938–.
Intra-intellectual alienation: The case of the Chinese revolution.
Unpublished masters thesis in Political Science, Stanford U., 1962. 189 p.
SUBJ 16.1 19 60 64 66 ▪ 16 32 32.2 54

14275 CSU P P2 G1.2 1928–1972
Lewis, John Wilson, 1930–.
'Introduction: Leadership and power in China.' In *Party leadership and revolutionary power in China*, edited by J. W. Lewis. [Analytic entry]
Cambridge: Cambridge U. Press, 1970, 1–31.
SUBJ 12.1 16.1 19 32 ▪ 15 64

14276 CSH P P1 G1.2 1928–1972
Li Tien-min (Li T'ien-min).
'The Mao-Lin relationship and Lin Piao's future.' In *Collected documents of the First Sino-American Conference on Mainland China*. [Selective entry]
[Taipei]: Institute of International Relations, Republic of China, 1971, 209–234.
SUBJ 16.1 ▪ 15 32 32.2 59

14277 CSH U P3 G1.3 1895–1972
Ling Tou.
'Literary renaissance or intellectual revolution in China?'
Civilisations 1, 1 (jan. 1951), 15–20.
SUBJ 16.1 36.1 60 ▪ 64 66

14278 CSU P P2 G1.2 1911–1972
Purushottam, Prabhakar.
Leadership pattern in China: A study in the emerging leadership.
Delhi: Sterling, 1968. 15, 139 p.
SUBJ 16 16.1 32 32.2 ▪ 15 19 25 36.3 64

14279 CBU PO P2 G1.2 1911–1972
Rice, Edward Earl, 1909–.
Mao's way.
Berkeley, Los Angeles: U. of California Press, 1972. 596 p.
SUBJ 16.1 32 32.2 59 ▪ 15 19 54 64 66

14280 CSU P P2 G1.2 1911–1972
Scalapino, Robert Anthony, 1919–.
'The transition in Chinese party leadership: A comparison of the Eighth and Ninth Central Committees.' In *Elites in the People's Republic of China*, edited by R. A. Scalapino. [Analytic entry]
Seattle: U. of Washington Press, 1972, 67–148. (Social Science Research Council, Studies in Chinese government and politics, 3)
SUBJ 16.1 32 ▪ 50 66

14281 CSU P P1 G1.2 1928–1972
Schapiro, Leonard, and John Wilson Lewis, 1930–.
'The roles of the monolithic party under the totalitarian leader.' In *Party leadership and revolutionary power in China*, edited by J. W. Lewis. [Analytic entry]
Cambridge: Cambridge U. Press, 1970, 114–145.
SUBJ 16.1 32 ▪ 32.2 35 64

14282 CSU S P1 G1.2 1928–1972
Schulman, Irwin Jay, 1932–.
'Mao as prophet.'
CS 8, 13 (7 July 1970), 1–16.
SUBJ 16.1 62 ▪ 32 64

14283 NIC S P1 G1.2 1842–1972
Schwartz, Benjamin Isadore, 1916–.
'The intelligentsia in Communist China: A tentative comparison.'
Daedalus 89, 4 (Summer 1960), 604–621.
SUBJ 16.1 64 ▪ 12 32 63

14284 CSU U P1 G1.1 –1972
Schwartz, Benjamin Isadore, 1916–.
'The limits of "tradition versus modernity" as categories of explanation: The case of the Chinese intellectuals.'
Daedalus 101, 2 (Spring 1972), 71–88.
SUBJ 16.1 60 ▪ 64 66

14285 MMT P P1 G1.2 1895–1972
Scott, Adolphe Clarence, 1909–.
Literature and the arts in twentieth century China.
Garden City, N.Y.: Doubleday, 1963. 212 p.
SUBJ 16.1 31 32.1 64 ▪ 12.1 19 32 32.2 47 50

14286 MCY P P1 G1.2 1928–1972
Shih, Vincent Y. C. (Shih Yu-chung), 1903–.
'Enthusiast and escapist: Writers of the older generation.'
CQ 13 (Jan.–Mar. 1963), 92–112.
SUBJ 12.1 16.1 ▪ 64

14287 CSU S P1 G1.2 1911–1972
Spence, Jonathan Dermot, 1936–.
'On Chinese revolutionary literature.'
Yale French studies 39 (1967), 215–225. [Special issue: *Literature and revolution*, edited by Jacques Ehrmann]
SUBJ 16.1 ▪ 12.1

14288 CSH P P2 G1.2 1928–1972
Tong, T. K. (T'ang Te-kang), 1920–.
'Liu Shao-chi, the Liu Shao-chi faction and Liu-Shao-chi-ism: New lights on the Mao-Liu tangle as revealed by the Red Guard papers.' In *Collected documents of the First Sino-American Conference on Mainland China*. [Selective entry]
[Taipei]: Institute of International Relations, Republic of China, 1971, 235–258.
SUBJ 16.1 32 32.2 59 ▪ 12 15

14289 CSU S P4 G1.2 1911–1972
Walker, Richard Louis, 1922–.
'Students, intellectuals and "the Chinese revolution".' In *The strategy of deception: A study in world-wide Communist tactics*, edited by Jeane J. Kirkpatrick. [Sole entry]
New York: Farrar, Straus, 1963, 87–108.
SUBJ 16.1 19 32.2 ▪ 54 60

14290 CSU P P1 G1.2 1928–1972
Waller, Derek John, 1937–.
'The evolution of the Chinese Communist political elite, 1931–56.' In *Elites in the People's Republic of China*, edited by Robert Anthony Scalapino. [Analytic entry]
Seattle: U. of Washington Press, 1972, 41–66. (Social Science Research Council, Studies in Chinese government and politics, 3)
SUBJ 16.1 ▪ 12 32 32.2 50

14291 CSU P P1 G1.2 1911–1972
Wang Hsueh-wen (Wang Hsüeh-wen).
'The Maoist struggle against former president of Wuhan University.'
IS 4, 10 (July 1968), 13–23.
SUBJ 16.1 32 64 ▪ 17 59

14292 CBU P P2 G1.2 1911–1972
Wong, Paul (Huang Pao-lo), 1944–.
Organizational leadership in Communist China.
Unpublished doctoral dissertation in Sociology, U. of California, Berkeley, 1971. 17, 403 p.
SUBJ 16.1 30 32 ▪ 12 15 32.1 32.2

14293 NIC S P3 G1.2 1928–1972
Yang I-fan.
The case of Hu Feng, mimeo.
Hong Kong: Union Research Institute, 1956. 169 p. (Communist China problem research series, EC16)
SUBJ 12.1 16.1 ▪ 31 36.1 59 60 64

1949-1972

14294 NNC P P1 G1.2 1949–1972
'A new lenient policy towards intellectuals: The use of "red experts".'
URS 2, 25 (30 Mar. 1956), 393–402.
SUBJ 16.1 ▪ 32 64

14295 MCY P P1 G1.2 1949–1972
Arkush, Ralph David, 1940–.
'One of the hundred flowers: Wan Meng's "Young newcomer".'
PC 18 (Dec. 1964), 155–186.
SUBJ 16.1 24 ▪ 12.1 32

14296 CSU P P2 G1.2 1949–1972
Barnett, Arthur Doak, 1921–.
China after Mao.
Princeton: Princeton U. Press, 1967. 287 p.
SUBJ 14 16.1 64 ▪ 12.1 32 59

14297 CSU S P1 G1.2 1949–1972
Bennett, Gordon Anderson, 1940–.
'Elite and society in China: A summary of research and interpretation.' In *Elites in the People's Republic of China*, edited by Robert Anthony Scalapino. [Analytic entry]
Seattle: U. of Washington Press, 1972, 3–37. (Social Science Research Council, Studies in Chinese government and politics, 3)
SUBJ 16.1 30 ▪ 71

14298 IMC PO P1 G1.2 1949–1972
Brunetti, Mino.
'La condizione dell'intellettuale nella Cina di Mao-tse-tung' (The position of the intellectual in Mao Tse-tung's China).
Civitas 10 (ottobre 1965), 61–76.
SUBJ 16.1

14299 MAM P P2 G1.2 1949–1972
Chai, Trong Rong, 1935–.
Professionals in Communist China: Conflict and accommodation.
Ann Arbor: University Microfilms (Publ. 70-344), 1970. 331 p. (Doctoral

dissertation in Public Administration, U. of Southern California, 1969)
SUBJ 12.1 16.1 32.1 36.1 64 ▪ 14.2 32 62 70

14300 CSU P P3 G1.3 1949–1972
Chamberlain, Heath Brosius, 1936–.
'Transition and consolidation in urban China: A study of leaders and organizations in three cities [Tientsin, Shanghai, and Canton], 1949–53.' In *Elites in the People's Republic of China*, edited by Robert Anthony Scalapino. [Analytic entry]
Seattle: U. of Washington Press, 1972, 245–301. (Social Science Research Council, Studies in Chinese government and politics, 3) [For a fuller version, see entry 14301.]
SUBJ 12 16.1 ▪ 22 26.1 59

14301 MAM P P3 G1.3 1949–1972
Chamberlain, Heath Brosius, 1936–.
Transition and consolidation in urban China: A study of leaders and organizations in three cities, 1949–1953.
Ann Arbor: University Microfilms (Publ. 72-5895), 1972. 15, 406 p. (Doctoral dissertation in History, Stanford U., 1971)
SUBJ 12 16.1 ▪ 22 26.1

14302 CSU P P3 G1.2 1949–1972
Chang, Parris H. (Chang Hsü-ch'eng), 1936–.
'Provincial leaders' strategies for survival during the Cultural Revolution.' In *Elites in the People's Republic of China*, edited by Robert Anthony Scalapino. [Analytic entry]
Seattle: U. of Washington Press, 1972, 501–539. (Social Science Research Council, Studies in Chinese government and politics, 3)
SUBJ 12 16.1 22.2 32.1 ▪ 16.4 19 35 54

14303 CSU S P1 G1.2 1949–1972
Chang, Parris H. (Chang Hsü-ch'eng), 1936–.
'The second decade of Maoist rule.'
Problems of Communism 18, 6 (Nov.–Dec. 1969), 1–11. [Reprinted as 'Communist rule in China: A review.' In *Communist China: A system-functional reader*, edited by Yung Wei. (Selective entry.) Columbus, Ohio: Merrill, 1972, 443–460.]
SUBJ 16.1 32 ▪ 14 35 64

14304 CSU P P1 G1.2 1949–1972
Chen, Theodore H. E. (Ch'en Hsi-en), 1902–.
'Science, scientists, and politics.' In *Sciences in Communist China*, edited by [Sydney Henry Gould] Sidney H. Gould. [Selective entry]
Washington, D.C.: American Assn. for the Advancement of Science, 1961, 59–98. (AAAS publications, 68)
SUBJ 16.1 ▪ 12.1 64

14305 NNC P P4 G1.2 1949–1972
Chen, Theodore H. E. (Ch'en Hsi-en), 1902–.
Thought reform of the Chinese intellectuals.
Hong Kong: Hong Kong U. Press; London: Oxford U. Press, 1960. 13, 247 p.
SUBJ 12.1 16.1 61 64 ▪ 16.4 17 32 36.1 66

14306 CSU P P1 G1.2 1949–1972
Ch'en, Jerome (Ch'en Chih-jang), 1919–.
'Writers and artists confer.'
CQ 4 (Oct.–Dec. 1960), 76–81.
SUBJ 16.1 ▪ 12.1 64

14307 CSU P P1 G1.2 1949–1972
Cheng Chu-yuan (Cheng Chu-yüan), 1927–.
'Power struggle in Red China.'
AS 6, 9 (Sept. 1966), 469–484.
SUBJ 16.1 32 ▪ 12 32.1

14308 CSU P P1 G1.2 1949–1972
Cheng Chu-yuan (Cheng Chu-yüan), 1927–.
'The root of China's Cultural Revolution: The feud between Mao Tse-tung and Liu Shao-ch'i.'
Orbis (Philadelphia) 11, 4 (Winter 1968), 1160–1178. [Reprinted in *Readings in modern Chinese history*, edited by Immanuel C. Y. Hsü (Hsü Chung-yüeh). (Selective entry) New York: Oxford U. Press, 1971, 646–659.]
SUBJ 16.1 64 ▪ 32

14309 MAM P P1 G1.2 1949–1972
Chiou, Chwei Liang.
Ideology and political power in Mao Tse-tung's Cultural Revolution, 1965–1968.
Ann Arbor: University Microfilms (Publ. 71-27,073), 1971. 220 p. (Doctoral dissertation in Political Science, U. of California, Riverside)
SUBJ 16.1 19 32 ▪ 12.1 15 54 64

14310 DLC U P5 G1.2 1949–1972
Chou En-lai, 1898–.
Report on the question of intellectuals, delivered on January 14, 1956 at a meeting of the Communist Party of China. Tr. of 'Kuan yü chih shih fen tzu wen t'i ti pai kao (1956 nien 1 yüeh 14 jih tsai Chung-kuo kung ch'an tang chung yang wei yüan hui chao k'ai ti kuan yü chih shih fen tzu wen t'i ti hui i shang)' (Report on the problem of intellectuals: Text of a speech given 14 January 1956 at the Conference on the Problem of Intellectuals called by the Central Committee of the Chinese Communist Party); *Jen min jih pao* 30 Jan. 1956, 1–3.
Peking: Foreign Languages Press, 1956. 44 p.
SUBJ 16.1 ▪ 11.4 19 32.1 60 64

14311 NNC P P1 G1.2 1949–1972
Chu, Richard Yen-yuan.
The underlying causes of the Hundred Flowers campaign.
Unpublished masters thesis in Political Science, Columbia U., 1965. 105 p.
SUBJ 12.1 16.1 ▪ 14 17 64

14312 CSU P P2 G1.2 1949–1972
Chu Wen-lin.
'An analysis of the Peiping regime's important personnel.'
IS 6, 4 (Jan. 1970), 56–66; 6, 5 (Feb. 1970), 46–57; 6, 6 (Mar. 1970), 60–72; 6, 8 (May 1970), 69–80.
SUBJ 12 15 16.1 ▪ 14.2

14313 CSU P P1 G1.2 1949–1972
Collotti Pischel, Enrica, 1930–.
'Il significato della successione di Mao Tse-Tung' (The meaning of Mao Tse-tung's succession).
Comunità internazionale 14, 2/3 (aprile–luglio 1959), 289–300.
SUBJ 16.1 64 ▪ 12 32

14314 CSU P P1 G1.2 1949–1972
Current Scene Editor.
'Lin Piao and the Cultural Revolution.'
CS 8, 14 (1 Aug. 1970), 1–14.
SUBJ 15 16.1 ▪ 35

14315 CSU U P1 G1.2 1949–1972
Diao, Richard K. (Tiao K'ai-chih), 1924–.
'The impact of the Cultural Revolution on China's economic elite.'
CQ 42 (Apr.–June 1970), 65–87.
SUBJ 12 16.1 ▪ 32

14316 NNC S P1 G1.2 1949–1972
Diasio, Matthew Roger.
A study of elites: Comparison of the Central Committees of Communist China and the Soviet Union.
Unpublished masters thesis in Political Science, Columbia U., 1965. 237 p.
SUBJ 16.1 32 ▪ 12

14317 CSU P P1 G1.2 1949–1972
Domes, Jürgen Otto, 1932–.
'Chinas spätmaoistische Führungsgruppe: Die sozio-politische Struktur des IX Zentralkomitees der Kommunistischen Partei Chinas' (The late Maoist leadership group of China: The socio-political structure of the Ninth Central Committee of the Chinese Communist Party).
Politische Vierteljahresschrift 10, 1 (Jan. 1970), 191–219.
SUBJ 16.1 32 ▪ 35

14318 CSU P P1 G1.2 1949–1972
Domes, Jürgen Otto, 1932–.
'The Ninth CCP Central Committee in statistical perspective.'
CS 9, 2 (7 Feb. 1971), 5–14.
SUBJ 16.1 ▪ 32 50

14319 CSU P P1 G1.2 1949–1972
Domes, Jürgen Otto, 1932–.
'Some results of the Cultural Revolution in China.'
AS 11, 9 (Sept. 1971), 932–940.
SUBJ 16.1 32

14320 CSU P P3 G5.1 1949–1972
Domes, Jürgen Otto, 1932–.
'Zentralkomitee der Sieger? Die neue Parteiführung der KP Chinas' (Did the Central Committee win? The new leadership of the Chinese Communist Party).
Moderne Welt 10, 3 (1969), 302–306.
SUBJ 16.1 32 ▪ 35

14321 MCY P P1 G1.2 1949–1972
Doolin, Dennis James, 1933–.
'Both "red and expert": The dilemma of the Chinese intellectual.'
CS 2, 19 (1 Sept. 1963), 1–12.
SUBJ 12.1 16.1 ▪ 64

14322 MAM P P1 G1.2 1949–1972
Doolin, Dennis James, 1933–.
Chinese Communist policies toward the Chinese intelligentsia, 1949–1963.
Ann Arbor: University Microfilms (Publ. 64-13,577), 1964. 249 p. (Doctoral dissertation in History, Literature, and Politics of Communist China, Stanford U., 1964)
SUBJ 12.1 16.1 64 ▪ 14 17 32 32.1

14323 NIC S P1 G1.2 1949–1972
Doolin, Dennis James, 1933–.
'The revival of the "Hundred Flowers" campaign, 1961.'
CQ 8 (Oct.–Dec. 1961), 34–41.
Subj 16.1 ▪ 17 32.1 64

14324 CSU P P1 G1.2 1949–1972
Dreyer, June Teufel, 1939–.
'Traditional minorities elites and the CPR elite engaged in minority nationalities work.' In *Elites in the People's Republic of China*, edited by Robert Anthony Scalapino. [Analytic entry]
Seattle: U. of Washington Press, 1972, 416–450. (Social Science Research Council, Studies in Chinese government and politics, 3)
Subj 16.1 32 ▪ 12 66

14325 CSU P P2 G1.2 1949–1972
Engelborghs-Bertels, Marthe, 1928–.
'Tradition et mutation dans la Révolution culturelle en Chine' (Tradition and change in China's Cultural Revolution). In *Sociologie des mutations* (The sociology of change), edited by Georges Balandier. [Sole entry]
Paris: Ed. Anthropos, 1970, 463–479.
Subj 15 16.1 64 ▪ 12.2 14.1 14.4 32 37

14326 CSU FP P3 G9.3 1949–1972
Falkenheim, Victor Carl, 1940–.
'Provincial leadership in Fukien: 1949–66.' In *Elites in the People's Republic of China*, edited by Robert Anthony Scalapino. [Analytic entry]
Seattle: U. of Washington Press, 1972, 199–244. (Social Science Research Council, Studies in Chinese government and politics, 3) [For a fuller version, see entry 10855.]
Subj 12 16.1 32 ▪ 14 35

14327 CSU P P4 G1.2 1949–1972
Goldman, Merle Dorothy, 1931–.
'Party policies toward the intellectuals: The unique blooming and contending of 1961–2.' In *Party leadership and revolutionary power in China*, edited by John Wilson Lewis. [Analytic entry]
Cambridge: Cambridge U. Press, 1970, 268–303.
Subj 12.1 16.1 64 ▪ 14.2 32.1 36.1 70

14328 CSH P P2 G1.2 1949–1972
Goodstadt, Leo F-.
'The young intellectuals.' In *Youth in China*, edited by Edward Stuart Kirby. [Analytic entry]
Hong Kong: Dragonfly Books, 1965, 191–208.
Subj 12.1 16.1 54 64 ▪ 16

14329 NNC P P2 G1.2 1949–1972
Gourlay, Walter Everett, 1921–.
The Chinese Communist cadre: Key to political control, mimeo.
Cambridge: Harvard U., Russian Research Center, 1952. 122 p.
Subj 12 15 16.1 22 32 64 ▪ 14.1 16 17 22.1 25 30 32.1

14330 CSU FP P3 G5.1 1949–1972
Greenblatt, Sidney Leonard, 1938–.
'Organizational elites and social change at Peking University.' In *Elites in the People's Republic of China*, edited by Robert Anthony Scalapino. [Analytic entry]
Seattle: U. of Washington Press, 1972, 451–497. (Social Science Research Council, Studies in Chinese government and politics, 3)
Subj 16.1 17 ▪ 12.1 32 50

14331 CSU P P2 G1.2 1949–1972
Hah, Chong-Do (Ho Chung-tao), 1937–.
'The dynamics of the Chinese Cultural Revolution: An interpretation based on an analytical framework of political coalitions.'
WP 24, 2 (Jan. 1972), 182–220.
Subj 16 16.1 30 64 ▪ 12.1 32 35 54

14332 CSU P P2 G1.2 1949–1972
Harding, Harry, Jr., 1946–.
'China: The fragmentation of power.'
AS 12, 1 (Jan. 1972), 1–15.
Subj 14 16.1 35 ▪ 12 32

14333 CSU P P1 G1.2 1949–1972
Hinton, Harold Clendenin, 1924–.
'Intra-party politics and economic policy in Communist China.'
WP 12, 4 (July 1960), 509–524.
Subj 14 16.1 32 ▪ 12

14334 NNC P P1 G1.2 1949–1972
Hinton, Harold Clendenin, 1924–.
Leaders of Communist China.
Santa Monica, Calif.: RAND Corp., 1956. 15, 299 p. (RAND memoranda, RM-1845; Astia documents, AD-123522)
Subj 16.1 ▪ 12 15 16 32

14335 CSU S P1 G1.2 1949–1972
Ho, Kikuzo, and Minoru Shibata.
'The dilemma of Mao Tse-tung.'
CQ 35 (July–Sept. 1968), 58–77.
Subj 16.1 ▪ 19 64

14336 CSH P P1 G1.2 1949–1972
Hsiang Nai-kuang.
'An analysis of the personnel of the Ninth Central Committee of the Chinese Communist Party.' In *Collected documents of the First Sino-American Conference on Mainland China.* [Selective entry]
[Taipei]: Institute of International Relations, Republic of China, 1971, 259–306.
Subj 16.1 32 ▪ 16 59

14337 CBU P P2 G1.2 1949–1972
[Hsiao, Gene T.] Tsun Hsiao (Hsiao Chün), 1922–.
The cadre system in Communist China.
Unpublished masters thesis in Political Science, U. of California, Berkeley, 1960. 90 p.
Subj 16.1 22.1 32.1 ▪ 11.4 12 12.2 17 22 30 64

14338 CSU P P1 G1.2 1949–1972
Hsu, Kai-yu (Hsü Chieh-yü), 1922–.
'The Chinese Communist leadership.'
CH 57, 337 (Sept. 1969), 129–134, 178–179.
Subj 16.1 ▪ 15 32

14339 MCH S P1 G1.2 1949–1972
Huck, Arthur.
'The leadership of the Communist Party of China: A critique of the standard picture.'
Australian outlook 16, 3 (Dec. 1962), 260–269.
Subj 12 16.1 ▪ 32 59 71

14340 CSH P P1 G1.2 1949–1972
Johnson, Chalmers Ashby, 1931–.
'Communist China's political turmoil.'
SAIS review 12, 2 (Winter 1968), 5–24.
Subj 16.1 19 ▪ 15 64

14341 CSU P P1 G1.2 1949–1972
Klein, Donald Walker, 1929–.
'Peking's leaders: A study in isolation.'
CQ 7 (July–Sept. 1961), 35–43.
Subj 16.1 ▪ 59

14342 MCH U P1 G1.2 1949–1972
Klein, Donald Walker, 1929–.
'A question of leadership: Problems of mobility, control and policy making in China.'
CS 5, 7 (30 Apr. 1967), 1–8.
Subj 16.1 ▪ 12 32

14343 CSU P P1 G1.2 1949–1972
Klein, Donald Walker, 1929–.
'Sources for elite studies and biographical materials on China.' In *Elites in the People's Republic of China*, edited by Robert Anthony Scalapino. [Analytic entry]
Seattle: U. of Washington Press, 1972, 609–656. (Social Science Research Council, Studies in Chinese government and politics, 3)
Subj 16.1 59 72 ▪ 12 15 17 30 32 70 71

14344 CSU P P1 G1.2 1949–1972
Klein, Donald Walker, 1929–.
'The State Council and the Cultural Revolution.' In *Party leadership and revolutionary power in China*, edited by John Wilson Lewis. [Analytic entry]
Cambridge: Cambridge U. Press, 1970, 351–372.
Subj 12 16.1 ▪ 32 35

14345 CSU S P1 G1.2 1949–1972
Klein, Donald Walker, 1919–, and Lois Bennet Hager.
'The Ninth Central Committee.'
CQ 45 (Jan.–Mar. 1971), 37–56.
Subj 16.1 32 ▪ 12 15 30

14346 MCH P P1 G1.2 1949–1972
[La Dany, Ladislao] ———, 1914–.
'At the summit.'
CNA 148 (14 Sept. 1956), 1–7.
Subj 16.1 32 ▪ 59

14347 CSH P P2 G1.2 1949–1972
[La Dany, Ladislao] ———, 1914–.
'The cadres: The May 7 cadre schools.'
CNA 779 (24 Oct. 1969), 1–7.
Subj 16.1 ▪ 21.2 32.1 37 61

14348 MCH P P1 G1.2 1949–1972
[La Dany, Ladislao] ———, 1914–.
'Chinese experts.'
CNA 458 (1 Mar. 1963), 1–7.
Subj 16.1 ▪ 12.1 62

14349 MCH P P1 G8.3 1949–1972
[La Dany, Ladislao] ———, 1914–.
'Kweichow in the south-west.'
CNA 666 (30 June 1967), 1–7.
Subj 16.1 ▪ 19

14350 MCH P P1 G1.2 1949–1972
[La Dany, Ladislao] ———, 1914–.
'More about Mr. and Mrs. Liu Shao-ch'i.'
CNA 663 (9 June 1967), 1–7.
Subj 16.1 ▪ 12 12.1 19

14351 MCH P P2 G1.2 1949–1972
[La Dany, Ladislao] ———, 1914–.
'Music, 1949–1961.'
CNA 381 (21 July 1961), 1–7; 386 (25 Aug. 1961), 1–7.
SUBJ 12.1 16.1 31 ▪ 17 65

14352 NIC P P1 G1.2 1949–1972
[La Dany, Ladislao] ———, 1914–.
'Political value of art.'
CNA 201 (18 Oct. 1957), 1–7.
SUBJ 12.1 16.1 ▪ 17 32.1 36.1 64

14353 CSH P P1 G1.2 1949–1972
[La Dany, Ladislao] ———, 1914–.
'The post–Lin-Piao period. Part 1, In memoriam.'
CNA 870 (11 Feb. 1972), 1–7.
SUBJ 16.1 64 ▪ 15 32 59

14354 CSH P P2 G1.2 1949–1972
[La Dany, Ladislao] ———, 1914–.
'The post–Lin-Piao period. Part 2, The cadres puzzled.'
CNA 871 (25 Feb. 1972), 1–7.
SUBJ 16.1 64

14355 CSH P P1 G1.2 1949–1972
[La Dany, Ladislao] ———, 1914–.
'The post–Lin-Piao period. Part 3, Who are ruling China?'
CNA 872 (4 Mar. 1972), 1–7.
SUBJ 16.1 32

14356 CSH P P1 G1.2 1949–1972
[La Dany, Ladislao] ———, 1914–.
'The purge of Ch'en Po-ta, the "Liu-type sham Marxist political swindler".'
CNA 851 (13 Aug. 1971), 1–7.
SUBJ 16.1 64

14357 MCH U P1 G1.2 1949–1972
[La Dany, Ladislao] ———, 1914–.
'The rulers.'
CNA 590 (26 Nov. 1965), 1–7.
SUBJ 16.1 32 ▪ 12 15

14358 CSH P P1 G1.2 1949–1972
[La Dany, Ladislao] ———, 1914–.
'Scientists, 1957–1967.'
CNA 696 (16 Feb. 1968), 1–7.
SUBJ 16.1 36.1 ▪ 12 32.1 62

14359 NIC P P2 G1.2 1949–1972
[La Dany, Ladislao] ———, 1914–.
'Signs of freedom.'
CNA 345 (21 Oct. 1960), 1–7; 346 (28 Oct. 1960), 1–7.
SUBJ 16.1 62 ▪ 12.1 37

14360 CSH P P3 G1.2 1949–1972
[La Dany, Ladislao] ———, 1914–.
'University professors.'
CNA 97 (26 Aug. 1955), 2–7.
SUBJ 16.1 17 32.1

14361 CSH P P1 G1.2 1949–1972
[La Dany, Ladislao] ———, 1914–.
'Who is Yang Tzu-jung?'
CNA 787 (9 Jan. 1970), 1–7.
SUBJ 16.1 60

14362 CSU P P2 G1.2 1949–1972
Liu Mao-lan.
'The "May 7 cadre school" and "May 7" movement.'
IS 7, 1 (Oct. 1970), 46–51.
SUBJ 16.1 32.1 37 ▪ 15 35 64

14363 CSU P P2 G1.2 1949–1972
MacDonald, James.
'The performance of the cadres.' In *Modern China's search for a political form*, edited by Jack Douglas Gray. [Analytic entry]
London: Oxford U. Press, 1969, 268–298.
SUBJ 12.1 16.1 26.1 64 ▪ 12 16 17 19 22 22.2 32 32.1 35

14364 MCH P P2 G1.2 1949–1972
MacFarquhar, Roderick Lemonde, 1930–.
The Hundred Flowers campaign and the Chinese intellectuals.
New York: Praeger, 1960. 324 p.
SUBJ 12.1 14.2 16 16.1 54 ▪ 16.2 16.3 32.1 36.1 36.4 64

14365 CSU P P1 G1.2 1949–1972
MacFarquhar, Roderick Lemonde, 1930–.
'On photographs.'
CQ 46 (Apr.–June 1971), 289–307.
SUBJ 16.1 ▪ 12 32

14366 MCY P P1 G1.2 1949–1972
Malden, William.
'A new class structure emerging in China?'
CQ 22 (Apr.–June 1965), 83–88.
SUBJ 12 16.1 ▪ 16

14367 MCH O P1 G9.4 1949–1972
Mancall, Mark, 1932–.
'Succession and myth in Taiwan.'
J. of international affairs 18, 1 (1964), 12–20.
SUBJ 12 16.1 32 ▪ 12.1 15 64 66

14368 CSH O P1 G9.4 1949–1972
Mei, Wen-li.
'The intellectuals on Formosa.'
CQ 15 (July–Sept. 1963), 65–74. [Reprinted in *Formosa today*, edited by Mark Mancall. (Selective entry.) New York: Praeger, 1964, 121–130.]
SUBJ 16.1

14369 NNC O P2 G1.2 1949–1972
Moraes, Francis Robert, 1907–.
Report on Mao's China.
New York: Macmillan, 1953. 212 p.
SUBJ 12.1 16.1 19 47 ▪ 12 12.2 14.1 14.2 16.2 17 31 53 66

14370 CSH O P2 G1.2 1949–1972
Mu Fu-sheng, pseud.
The wilting of the hundred flowers: Free thought in China today.
London: Heinemann, 1962. 12, 324 p. [Reprinted as *The wilting of the hundred flowers: The Chinese intelligentsia under Mao*. New York: Praeger, 1963. 12, 324 p.]
SUBJ 12.1 16 16.1 60 64 ▪ 12.2 13 17 32.1 63

14371 MCH P P1 G1.2 1949–1972
Munro, Donald Jacques, 1931–.
'Dissent in Communist China: The current anti-intellectual campaign in perspective.'
CS 4, 11 (1 June 1966), 1–11.
SUBJ 12.1 16.1 64 ▪ 32

14372 CSU P P1 G1.2 1949–1972
Oksenberg, Michel Charles, 1938–.
'Policy making under Mao, 1949–68: An overview.' In *China: Management of a revolutionary society*, edited by John Matthew Henry Lindbeck. [Analytic entry]
Seattle: U. of Washington Press, 1971, 79–115. (Social Science Research Council, Studies in Chinese government and politics, 2)
SUBJ 12 16.1 ▪ 32

14373 CSU P P2 G1.2 1949–1972
Orleans, Leo A-, 1924–.
'How the Chinese scientist survives.'
Science 177, 4052 (8 Sept. 1972), 864–866.
SUBJ 12.1 16.1

14374 MMT U P1 G1.2 1949–1972
Pye, Lucian Wilmot, 1921–.
'Political leadership and revolutionary power in Communist China.' In *The United States and Communist China*, edited by William Wirt Lockwood. [Sole entry]
Princeton: Princeton U. Conference, 1965, 9–20. (Princeton U. Conference series, 41)
SUBJ 12.1 16.1 ▪ 15 32

14375 CSU P P1 G1.2 1949–1972
Ray, Dennis Michael, 1939–.
'"Red and expert" and China's Cultural Revolution.'
PA 43, 1 (Spring 1970), 22–33.
SUBJ 16.1 ▪ 12 15 32

14376 CSU P P1 G1.2 1949–1972
Robinson, Thomas Webster, 1935–.
'Chou En-lai's political style: Comparisons with Mao Tse-tung and Lin Piao.'
AS 10, 12 (Dec. 1970), 1101–1116.
SUBJ 16.1 61 ▪ 12

14377 CSU U P1 G1.2 1949–1972
Scalapino, Robert Anthony, 1919–.
'Introduction.' In *Elites in the People's Republic of China*, edited by R. A. Scalapino. [Analytic entry]
Seattle: U. of Washington Press, 1972, 5–20 [s.p.]. (Social Science Research Council, Studies in Chinese government and politics, 3)
SUBJ 16.1

14378 MAM P P4 G1.2 1949–1972
Seymour, James Dulles, 1935–.
The policies of the Chinese Communists toward China's intellectuals and professionals.
Ann Arbor: University Microfilms (Publ. 68-16,932), 1968. 318 p. (Doctoral dissertation in Political Science, Columbia U.)
SUBJ 12.1 16.1 70 ▪ 11.4 12 16 16.2 17 32.1 36.1 62

14379 CSU P P1 G1.2 1949–1972
Shih, Vincent Y. C. (Shih Yu-chung), 1903–.
'The state of the intellectuals.' In *Communist China, 1949–1969: A twenty-year appraisal*, edited by Frank Newton Trager and William Henderson. [Selective entry]
New York: New York U. Press, 1970, 221–242.
SUBJ 12.1 16.1

14380 CSU P P1 G1.2 1949–1972
Simmonds, John D-.
'The new gun-barrel elite.' In *The military and political power of China in the 1970s*, edited by William Wallace Whitson. [Selective entry]

New York: Praeger, 1972, 93–113.
Subj 15 16.1 ▪ 12 32 35

14381 CSU P P1 G1.2 1949–1972
Simmonds, John D-.
'P'eng Te-huai: A chronological re-examination.'
CQ 37 (Jan.–Mar. 1969), 120–138.
Subj 16.1 32 ▪ 15 59

14382 MCH P P3 G1.2 1949–1972
Solich, Eduard Jürgen, 1898–.
'Chinas Schriftsteller, Künstler und Wissenschaftler im neu entfachten Klassenkampf.'
Moderne Welt 5, 3 (1964), 307–313.
'China's writers, artists, and scientists in the rekindled class struggle.' Tr. by Rosita Schoenthal and Klaus Schoenthal.
Modern world (Cologne) 1965/66, 80–87.
Subj 12.1 16.1 ▪ 32.1 64

14383 CSU P P1 G1.2 1949–1972
Spitz, Allan.
'Mao's permanent revolution.'
Review of politics 30, 4 (Oct. 1968), 440–454.
Subj 16.1 32 ▪ 64

14384 NNC P P1 G1.2 1949–1972
Tang, Peter S. H. (T'ang Sheng-hao), 1919–.
The training of party cadres in Communist China.
Washington, D.C.: Research Institute on the Sino-Soviet Bloc, 1961. 44 p. (RISSB monographs, 3)
Subj 16.1 17 32 ▪ 64

14385 NNC P P2 G1.2 1949–1972
Teiwes, Frederick Carl, 1939–.
Provincial party personnel in Mainland China, 1956–1966.
New York: Columbia U., East Asian Institute, 1967. 114 p.
Subj 12 16.1 32 ▪ 32.1

14386 CSH P P4 G1.2 1949–1972
Ting Chu-yuan (Ting Ch'u-yüan).
'The problem of revolutionizing the leadership of the county party commissar.'
IS 2, 6 (Mar. 1966), 14–22.
Subj 16.1 32

14387 CSH P P3 G1.2 1949–1972
Ting Chu-yuan (Ting Ch'u-yüan).
Problem of the second generation and successors of Chinese Communist regime.
Taipei: Asian Peoples' Anti-Communist League, 1966. 63 p.
Subj 16.1 32 64 ▪ 12

14388 CSU P P3 G1.3 1949–1972
Ting Wang, 1942–.
'Yao Wen-yuan: Newcomer in China's Politburo.'
CS 7, 14 (15 July 1969), 1–24.
Subj 16.1 59 ▪ 32

14389 CSH P P1 G1.2 1949–1972
Uhalley, Stephen, Jr., 1930–.
'The Wu Han discussion: Act one in a new rectification campaign.'
China Mainland review 1, 4 (Mar. 1966), 24–38.
Subj 16.1 63 ▪ 64

14390 CSU P P1 G1.2 1949–1972
Walker, Robert L-.
'The elusive élan: Problems of political control in Communist China' [with comments by Arthur S. Chen (Ch'en Shu-yüan)]. In *Aspects of modern Communism*, edited by Richard Felix Staar. [Selective entry]
Columbia: U. of South Carolina Press, 1968, 195–225.
Subj 16.1 19 ▪ 12.1 64

14391 CSH P P2 G1.2 1949–1972
Wang Chang-ling.
'The Chinese Communists' policy toward intellectuals.' In *Collected documents of the First Sino-American Conference on Mainland China*. [Selective entry]
[Taipei]: Institute of International Relations, Republic of China, 1971, 427–444.
Subj 16.1 32.1 ▪ 16 21.2

14392 CSH P P3 G1.2 1949–1972
Wang Chang-ling.
'Mainland historians and the "Great Cultural Revolution".'
IS 3, 7 (Apr. 1967), 24–35.
Subj 12.1 16.1 62 ▪ 59 64

14393 CSU O P2 G6.1 1949–1972
Wylie, Raymond Finlay, 1941–.
'Personal notes on the Cultural Revolution.' In *Contemporary China: Papers presented at the University of Guelph Conference, April 1968*. [Selective entry]
Toronto: Canadian Institute of International Affairs, 1968, 34–48.
Subj 12.1 16.1 ▪ 12.2 32 54 66

14394 CSH P P1 G1.2 1949–1972
Yü Heng.
'Changes in party, political and military personnel in 1965.' Tr. of '1965 nien ti Chung kung tang cheng chün jen shih tiao tung'; *Tsu kuo* 23 (Feb. 1966), 43–58. In *Communist China, 1965*, edited by Union Research Institute. [Selective entry]
Hong Kong: Union Research Institute, 1967, vol. 1, 83–167.
Subj 16.1 ▪ 12 15 32

16.2 The Bourgeoisie
商人及市民階級
商人及び市民階級

1644-1911

14395 CSU P P2 G1.1 1895–1911
Bergère, Marie-Claire, 1933–.
'The role of the bourgeoisie.' In *China in revolution: The first phase, 1900–1913*, edited by Mary Clabaugh Wright. [Selective entry]
New Haven: Yale U. Press, 1968, 229–295.
Subj 16.2 32.2 66 ▪ 14.3 14.6 22 22.2

14396 MCH P P2 G1.2 1842–1911
Chan, Wellington K. K. (Ch'en Chin-chiang), 1940–.
Merchants, mandarins and modern enterprise in late Ch'ing China (1872–1911).
Unpublished doctoral dissertation in History, Harvard U., 1972. 378 p.
Subj 12 12.1 16.1 16.2 36.2 ▪ 12.2 14.4 14.6 32.1 34.2 34.3 39 59

14397 CSH P P4 G1.2 1644–1911
Dawson, Francis Lester, Jr., 1922–1962.
'Law and the merchant in traditional China: The Ch'ing code, *Ta-Ch'ing lü-li*, and its implications for the merchant class.'
PC 2 (May 1948), 55–92.
Subj 12 12.1 12.2 14.3 16.2 ▪ 14.5 14.6 34.2 34.3 64

14398 CSU U P3 G1.2 1895–1911
Pao, Kuang Yung.
'The compradore: His position in the foreign trade of China.'
Economic j. 21, 84 (Dec. 1911), 636–641.
Subj 16.2 34.2

14399 CSU P P4 G1.1 1842–1895
Rawski, Thomas George, 1943–.
'Chinese dominance of treaty port commerce and its implications, 1860–1875.'
Explorations in economic history 7, 4 (Summer 1970), 451–473.
Subj 16.2 34.2 ▪ 14.2 14.3 14.6 16.1 66

14400 MCH O P4 G1.1 1895–1911
Weulersse, Georges, 1874–.
'La Chine nouvelle' (Modern China). In *La Chine ancienne et nouvelle: impressions et réflexions* (Ancient and modern China: Impressions and reflections), by G. Weulersse. [Sole entry]
Paris: Armand Colin, 1902, 191–362.
Subj 14 14.4 16.2 17 32.2 ▪ 15 16.4 22.1 23

14401 CBU P P5 G1.3 –1842
Yang, Lien-sheng, 1914–.
'Government control of urban merchants in traditional China.'
THJ new (2nd) series 8, 1/2 (Aug. 1970), 186–206.
Subj 12.1 14.3 16.2 ▪ 12.2 14.5 14.6 16 22.2 34.3 36.2

1644-1949

14402 NNP P P4 G1.2 1895–1928
Avenarius, G- G-.
'Torgovyi klass Kitaia' (China's commercial class).
BSB 1, 4 (1932), 117–134.
Subj 16.2 ▪ 14.3 71 72

14403 CSH P P2 G1.2 1895–1928
Bereznyi, Lev Abramovich, 1915–.
'O nekotorykh problemakh istorii Sin'khaiskoi revoliutsii' (Problems of the history of the Revolution of 1911).
NAA 1971, 5, 56–62.
Subj 16.2 32.2 ▪ 12 15 71

14404 FPN P P3 G1.2 1895–1928
Bergère, Marie-Claire, 1933–.
La bourgeoisie chinoise et la Révolution de 1911 (The Chinese bourgeoisie and the Revolution of 1911).
The Hague: Mouton, 1968. 155 p. (Revision of doctoral dissertation, Faculté des lettres, Université de Paris, 1966)
Subj 16.2 66 ▪ 32.2 36.2

14405 CSH U P4 G1.2 1842–1949
Levy, Marion Joseph, Jr., 1918–.
'The social background of modern business development in China.' In *The rise of the modern Chinese business class: Two introductory essays*, by M. J. Levy, Jr. and Kuo-heng Shih. [Analytic entry]
New York: Institute of Pacific Relations, International Secretariat, 1949, 1–17.
Subj 14.3 16 16.2 ▪ 12 16.1 41

14406 CSH P P4 G1.2 1842–1949
Shih, Kuo-heng.
'The early development of the modern Chinese business class.' In *The rise of the modern Chinese business class: Two introductory essays*, by Marion Joseph Levy, Jr. and Kuo-heng Shih. [Analytic entry]
New York: Institute of Pacific Relations, International Secretariat, 1949, 19–64.
Subj 14.3 14.4 16.2 ▪ 12 16.1 34.2 66

1911-1949

14407 CSH P P3 G1.2 1911–1928
Avenarius, G- G-.
'K kharakteristike torgovogo klassa Kitaia' (The nature of the Chinese merchant class).
VM 1927, 7, 43–51.
Subj 16.2 ▪ 14.3 14.6 22.2 34.3 36.4

14408 CSU P P3 G1.2 1911–1928
Bergère, Marie-Claire, 1933–.
'La bourgeoisie chinoise et les problèmes de développement économique (1917–1923)' (The Chinese bourgeoisie and the problems of economic development, 1917–1923).
R. d'histoire moderne et contemporaine 16 (avr.–juin 1969), 246–267.
Subj 16.2 36.2 60 ▪ 14 34.3 36.4

14409 CSU U P2 G1.4 1911–1949
Nakamura Yoshio.
'Shipping brokers in North China.' Tr. by Andrew Watson from *Senkō* (Shipping); Tsingtao: Kahoku kōgyō sōkōkai, 1943 [greatly condensed in tr.]. In *Transport in transition: The evolution of traditional shipping in China*. [Analytic entry]
Ann Arbor: U. of Michigan, Center for Chinese Studies, 1972, 15–34. (Michigan abstracts of Chinese and Japanese works on Chinese history, 3)
Subj 16.2 34.2 ▪ 14.2 14.3 36.2 39

14410 CSH U P4 G1.2 1911–1928
Panin, I- A-.
'Kitaiskii kupets' (The Chinese merchant).
VM 1926, 6, 86–96; 1926, 7, 109–122; 1926, 8, 51–59.
Subj 14.3 16.2 ▪ 12.2 14 14.2 14.6 34.2

14411 DLC P P4 G1.2 1911–1928
Sukharchuk, Grigorii Dmitrievich, 1927–, and Oleg Efimovich Nepomnin, 1935–.
'Kitaiskaia burzhuaziia i inostrannyi kapital v gody pervoi mirovoi voiny i "dvizhenie 4 maia"' (The Chinese bourgeoisie and foreign capital during World War I and the May Fourth period). In *Dvizhenie '4 maia' 1919 goda v Kitae: sbornik statei* (Articles on the May Fourth Movement in China), compiled by Institut vostokovedeniia, Akademiia nauk SSSR, edited by A- G- Afanas'ev et al. [Selective entry]
Moscow: Nauka, Glav. red. vost. lit-ry, 1971, 52–75.
Subj 14.4 14.6 16.2 66 ▪ 14.2 14.3 72

1911-1972
(including 1644-1972)

14412 CSU S P1 G1.2 1911–1972
Haeger, John Winthrop, 1944–.
'Western words in the Chinese phrase: The significance of irrelevance.' [Review of 'The birth of capitalism in China', by Etienne Balazs.]
Phi Theta papers 10 (May 1967), 20–32.
Subj 16.2 ▪ 12 12.1 16.1 60

14413 NNC P P4 G1.2 1928–1972
Meliksetov, Arlen Vaagovich, 1930–.
'Ideologicheskoe perevospitanie burzhuaznykh elementov v KNR' (Ideological reeducation of bourgeois elements in the People's Republic of China).
SV 1957, 1, 22–35.
Subj 12.1 16.2 32 45 64 ▪ 14 16.4 32.2 34.2 36.2

14414 NNC P P4 G1.2 1928–1972
Okorokov, A-.
'O pravykh burzhuaznykh elementakh v Kitae i bor'be s nimi' (The struggle against right-wing bourgeois elements in China).
V pomoshch' politicheskomu samoobrazovaniiu 1957, 12 (dekabr'), 68–73.
Subj 12.1 16.2 32.2 64 ▪ 14 16 16.1 19 32

14415 NNC P P4 G1.2 1928–1972
Pavlov, F- S-.
'Soiuz i bor'ba rabochego klassa Kitaia s natsional'noi burzhuaziei v period perekhoda k sotsializmu' (The Chinese working class alliance with and struggle against the national bourgeoisie during the transitional period).
Voprosy istorii KPSS 1959, 2, 104–128.
Subj 14.4 16.2 32.2 36.4 64 ▪ 12.1 14.3 16.4 17 32 34.2 36.2 45 61

1949-1972

14416 MCH P P2 G1.2 1949–1972
Deliusin, Lev Petrovich, 1923–.
Bor'ba s pravymi elementami burzhuazii v Kitae, 1957 god (The struggle against right-wing bourgeois elements in China, 1957).
Moscow: Izd-vo vost. lit-ry, 1961. 79 p.
Subj 12.1 14 16.2 32 64 ▪ 12 16.3 54

14417 CSU F P3 G1.2 1949–1972
Richman, Barry Martin, 1936–.
'Capitalists and managers in Communist China.'
Harvard business review 45, 1 (Jan.–Feb. 1967), 57–78.
Subj 14.4 16.2 32.1 34.2 ▪ 14 16.4 24.4 26.2 32

14418 MCH PO P4 G1.2 1949–1972
Shabalin, V- I-.
'K voprosu o kharaktere gosudarstvennogo kapitalizma i "vykupe" sobstvennosti natsional'noi burzhuazii v KNR' (The nature of state capitalism and the 'compensation' paid the national bourgeoisie for their property in the People's Republic of China).
Nauchnye doklady vysshei shkoly; ekonomicheskie nauki 1959, 3, 73–85.
Subj 14.4 16.2 34.2 ▪ 32.1 45

14419 NNC P P2 G1.2 1949–1972
Yonezawa Hideo, 1905–.
Aftermath of the reform of China's capitalists, mimeo. Tr. of 'Chūgoku shihonka no kaizō sonogo'; *Ajia keizai jumpō* 449 (10 Nov. 1960), 1–9.
Washington, D.C.: U.S. Joint Publications Research Service, 24 Jan. 1961. 14 p. (JPRS 7440; MC 10,867/1961)
Subj 12.1 16.2 34.2 ▪ 14.3 14.4 45

16.3 The Peasantry
農民階級 農民階級

1644-1911

14420 CSH P P7 G1.2 1644–1911
Deliusin, Lev Petrovich, 1923–.
'K voprosu ob izuchenii osobennostei razvitiia feodalizma v Kitae' (Features of the development of feudalism in China). [Review of *Genezis kapitalizma v sel'skom khoziaistve Kitaia* (The origin of capitalism in Chinese agriculture), by Oleg Efimovich Nepomnin.]
NAA 1967, 4, 173–180.
Subj 14.1 16.1 16.3 ▪ 14.3

14421 CSH P P8 G1.2 1644–1895
Khokhlov, Aleksandr Nikolaevich, 1929–.
'Kharakter zemledel'cheskogo naima v Kitae v kontse XVIII, pervoi polovine XIX veka' (The nature of hired agricultural labor in China at the end of the eighteenth century and in the first half of the nineteenth century).
NAA 1968, 3, 68–77.
Subj 14.1 16.3

14422 MCH P P8 G1.3 1644–1842
Nepomnin, Oleg Efimovich, 1935–.
'O kharaktere naima v kitaiskoi derevne nachala 19 v.' (The nature of hired agricultural labor in the countryside of early nineteenth-century China). [With English abstract]
PV 1959, 3, 68–73. [Reprinted in *O genezise kapitalizma v stranakh Vostoka, XV–XIX vv.* (The origin of capitalism in the Orient from the fifteenth through the nineteenth centuries), compiled by Institut narodov Azii, Akademiia nauk SSSR, edited by S- D- Skazkin et al. (Selective entry.) Moscow: Izd-vo vost. lit-ry, 1962, 36–43.]
Subj 16.3 48 ▪ 14.1

14423 CSU P P7 G1.2 –1842
Niida Noboru, 1904–1967.
'The state power and serfdom in China.' Tr. of 'Kokka kenryoku to nōdosei'; *Shigaku kenkyū* (Hiroshima) 90 (Apr. 1964), 21–27.
Acta Asiatica (Tokyo) 8 (Mar. 1965), 65–73.
Subj 16.1 16.3 ▪ 12.1 12.2 14.1

1644-1949

14424 NNC P P7 G1.3 1895–1949
Otte, Friedrich W- K-.
'Die Wirtschaft als Umwelts- und Sozialproblem in China' (The economy as an environmental and social problem in China).
MSOSB 37 (1934), 1–31.
Subj 14.1 14.6 16.3 18 ▪ 11.4 17 47 58

1911-1949

14425 NNC P P7 G1.3 1911–1928
'Seasonal fluctuation of farm labor in China, 1922–1924.'
NWSS 6, 36 (4 Sept. 1933), 167, 169–170.
Subj 14.1 16.3

14426 MCH S P8 G1.2 1928–1949
Chun, Chee Kwon (Ch'en Chih-k'un).
'Agrarian unrest and the civil war in China.'
Land economics 26, 1 (Feb. 1950), 17–26.
Subj 14.1 16.1 16.3 ▪ 25 32.2 36.3

14427 NNC P P2 G5.2 1928–1949
Gillin, Donald George, 1930–.
'Peasant nationalism in the history of Chinese Communism.' [Review of *Peasant nationalism and Communist power: The emergence of revolutionary China, 1937–1945*, by Chalmers Ashby Johnson.]
JAS 23, 2 (Feb. 1964), 269–289. [Reprinted in *China*, edited by John Armstrong Harrison. (Selective entry.) Tucson: U. of Arizona Press, 1972, 185–205. (Assn. for Asian Studies, Thirtieth Anniversary Commemorative Series, 1)]
Subj 15 16.1 16.3 32.2 ▪ 14.6 18 24.1 25 64 66

14428 MCH F P7 G1.2 1911–1949
Hsieh, Chiang (Hsieh Ch'iang), 1912–.
'Underemployment in Asia. Part 1, Nature and extent. Part 2, Its relation to investment policy.'
ILR 65, 6 (June 1952), 703–725; 66, 1 (July 1952), 30–39.
Subj 14.1 16.3 ▪ 14

14429 CSH S P8 G1.2 1911–1928
IAshnov, Evgenii Evgen'evich.
'Byt kitaiskoi derevni' (Rural life in China). [With English abstract]
VM 1930, 8, 53–62.
Subj 16.3 ▪ 23 25 27 36.3 41 51 55

14430 CSH S P8 G1.2 1928–1949
IAshnov, Evgenii Evgen'evich.
'Osnovy byta kitaiskoi derevni' (Basic features of rural life in China).
VM 1930, 7, 40–45.
Subj 16.3 40 ▪ 41 42 44

14431 CBU P P7 G2.0 1911–1949
IAshnov, Evgenii Evgen'evich.
'Sovremennoe polozhenie krest'ianstva v severnoi Man'chzhurii' (The current position of the peasantry in northern Manchuria). [With English abstract at end of issue]
VM 1934, 5 (mai), 1–11.
Subj 14.1 14.3 16.3

14432 MCH P P8 G1.3 1911–1928
Khodorov, Abram Evseevich, 1886–1949.
'Sel'skoe khoziaistvo i krest'ianstvo v Kitae' (Agriculture and the peasantry in China).
NV 10/11 (1925), 78–101.
Subj 14.1 16.3 ▪ 14.5

14433 NIC S P8 G1.3 1911–1949
Lee, Shu-ching (Li Shu-ch'ing), 1908–.
'Employment conditions of the agricultural laborer in China and his prospects of social advancement.'
Rural sociology 16, 3 (Sept. 1951), 238–245.
Subj 14.1 16.3 ▪ 18

14434 NNC P P7 G1.2 1911–1928
Shchukar', M-.
'Krest'ianstvo Kitaia' (The Chinese peasantry).
Na agrarnom fronte 1925, 10 (oktiabr'), 135–146; 1925, 11/12 (noiabr'–dekabr'), 145–162.
Subj 14.1 16.3 24.4 45 ▪ 14.6 16 16.1 18

14435 CSU O P2 G1.2 1928–1949
Tawney, Richard Henry, 1880–1962.
'China, 1930–31.' In *'The attack', and other papers*, by R. H. Tawney. [Sole entry]
London: Allen and Unwin, 1953, 35–57.
Subj 14 14.1 16.3 ▪ 12 25

14436 ELS S P7 G1.2 1911–1949
Wu, Wen-hui, 1909?–.
The position of the peasant in modern China.
Unpublished doctoral dissertation in Economics, U. of London [London School of Economics and Political Science], 1939.
Subj 14.1 14.6 16.3 ▪ 14.2 18

1911-1972
(including 1644-1972)

14437 MCY P P2 G1.2 1911–1972
Chesneaux, Jean, 1922–.
'L'alliance ouvrière et paysanne dans la révolution chinoise' (The worker-peasant alliance in the Chinese revolution).
Démocratie nouvelle 17, 3 (mars 1963), 44–48.
Subj 16.3 16.4 ▪ 19

14438 NNC S P2 G1.2 1928–1972
Grottian, Walter, 1909–.
'Die Stellung des Bauern im kommunistischen China' (The position of the peasantry in Communist China).
Z. für Politik neue (2.) Folge 1, 3 (1954), 241–256.
Subj 14.1 16.3 ▪ 12.1 16.4 32 64

14439 MCH P P7 G1.2 1928–1972
Ladejinsky, Wolf Isaac, 1901–.
'Carrot and stick in rural China.'
FA 36, 1 (Oct. 1957), 91–104.
Subj 12.1 14.1 16.3 ▪ 34.1

14440 MCH S P8 G1.2 1928–1972
Šuljmanac, Nedeljko.
'Politika komunističke partiji Kine prema seljaštvu' (Chinese Communist Party policy on the peasantry).
Pregled 7, Part 2 (1955), 265–276.
Subj 14.1 16.3 22.1 34.1 ▪ 14.6

1949-1972

14441 MCH S P7 G1.2 1949–1972
Brénier, Henri.
'La prolétarisation du paysannat chinois et ses conséquences' (The proletarianization of the Chinese peasantry and its effects).
Politique étrangère 19, 2 (avr.–mai 1954), 195–210.
Subj 14.1 16.3 ▪ 12.2 19 32.1

14442 CSH P P7 G1.2 1949–1972
Kataoka, Tetsuya, 1933–.
'Remuneration systems in Chinese agriculture, 1953–1956.' In *Hong Kong economic papers, No. 5*, edited by Ronald Hsia (Hsia Hsiu-yung). [Selective entry]
Hong Kong: Hong Kong Economic Assn., 1970, 49–67.
Subj 16.3 34.1 ▪ 45

14443 CSH P P7 G1.2 1949–1972
[La Dany, Ladislao] ———, 1914–.
'In the countryside.'
CNA 679 (29 Sept. 1967), 1–7.
Subj 16.3 ▪ 14.1 14.5 64

14444 CSH P P7 G1.2 1949–1972
[La Dany, Ladislao] ———, 1914–.
'New agricultural policy and its political meaning.'
CNA 839 (23 Apr. 1971), 1–7.
Subj 14.1 16.3 64

14445 CSH P P7 G1.2 1949–1972
[La Dany, Ladislao] ———, 1914–.
'The post–Lin-Piao period. Part 5, Rural policy.'
CNA 876 (7 Apr. 1972), 1–7.
Subj 16.3 ▪ 18 34.1

14446 CSH P P2 G1.2 1949–1972
Lin Tseng.
'Chinese Communist exploitation of the peasantry.'
IS 3, 1 (Oct. 1966), 33–41.
Subj 12.1 16.3 ▪ 11.4 14.3 18

14447 MCH P P7 G1.2 1949–1972
Mits, F- T-.
'Peking's poor peasants to the front: Communist China organizes lower peasants to lead rural revolution.'
CS 3, 22 (1 July 1965), 1–12.
Subj 16.3 22 ▪ 16 36.3

14448 CSH P P7 G1.2 1949–1972
Moore, William Joseph, 1932–.
'Maoism and incentives in agriculture.' In *East Asian occasional papers, II*, edited by Harry Jerome Lamley. [Selective entry]
Honolulu: U. of Hawaii, Asian Studies Program, 1970, 59–76. (Asian Studies at Hawaii, 4)
Subj 12.1 16.3 34.1 64 ▪ 14.1 32

14449 CSU FP P7 G1.2 1949–1972
Nathan, Andrew James, 1943–.
'China's work-point system: A study in agricultural "splittism".'
CS 2, 31 (15 Apr. 1964), 1–13. [Reprinted as 'Agricultural splittism.' In *Chinese society under Communism: A reader*, edited by William Thomas Liu (Liu Jung). (Selective entry.) New York: Wiley, 1967, 306–319.]
Subj 16.3 34.1 ▪ 14.1

14450 MCY P P7 G1.2 1949–1972
Nathan, Andrew James, 1943–.
'Paying the Chinese farmer.'
FEER 43, 9 (27 Feb. 1964), 457–458.
Subj 14.1 16.3

14451 CSU S P7 G1.2 1949–1972
Potter, Jack Michael, 1936–.
'From peasants to rural proletarians: Social and economic change in rural Communist China.' In *Peasant society: A reader*, edited by J. M. Potter, May Nordquist Diaz, and George McClelland Foster, Jr. [Sole entry]
Boston: Little, Brown, 1967, 407–419.
Subj 14.1 16.3 34.1

14452 FPN P P7 G1.2 1949–1972
Rocquet, J- P-.
'La révolution culturelle et les paysans chinois' (The Cultural Revolution and the Chinese peasantry).
NED 3394/3395 (26 mai 1967), 48–53.
Subj 12.1 14.1 16.3 19 ▪ 17 54

16.4 The Working Class
勞工階級　労働者階級

1644-1911

14453 MCH O P4 G1.2 1842–1911
Barrett, John.
'The plain truth about Asiatic labor.'
North American review 163, 5 (Nov. 1896), 620–632.
Subj 14.4 16.4

14454 DLC P P2 G1.3 1644–1911
Sun, E-tu Zen (Sun Jen I-tu), 1921–.
'Mining labor in the Ch'ing period.' In *Approaches to modern Chinese history*, edited by Albert Feuerwerker et al. [Selective entry]
Berkeley, Los Angeles: U. of California Press, 1967, 45–67.
Subj 14.4 16.4 ▪ 11.2 14 36.4 55

1644-1949

14455 MCH S P4 G1.2 –1949
Arndt, Paul, 1870–?
'Wirtschaftsordnung und Lohngesetz in China' (Economic regulation and the wage law in China). In *Der Arbeitslohn in China* (Labor wages in China), by P. Arndt, Djini Shen (Shen Chin-i), and Chü-fen Lo. [Analytic entry]
Leipzig: Hans Buske, 1937, 3–81.
Subj 12.2 14.4 16.4 34.2 ▪ 14 16 34.3

14456 CBU P P2 G1.3 1895–1949
Cheng, Hai-Fong (Ch'eng Hai-feng).
'Die arbeitsmässigen Voraussetzungen für eine weitere Industrialisierung in China' (Labor prerequisites for the further industrialization of China).
WA 45, 2 (März 1937), 256–282.
Subj 11.4 14.4 16.4 ▪ 11.2 14.1 14.2 16.3 17 18 24.4

14457 NNC P P3 G1.2 1895–1949
Soh Chuan-pao (Shu Ch'üan-pao).
La situation de l'ouvrier industriel en Chine (The position of the industrial worker in China).
Gembloux, Belgium: Duculot, 1937. 207 p. (Doctoral dissertation, Faculté de droit, Université catholique de Louvain)
Subj 16.4 18 ▪ 12.2 14 17 36.4

14458 MCH P P3 G1.2 1842–1928
Vinogradov, Nikolai Pavlovich, 1923–1967.
'O rabochem klasse dorevoliutsionnogo Kitaia' (The working class in prerevolutionary China).
NAA 1965, 4, 60–68.
Subj 16.4 ▪ 14.4 18 36.4 47

1911-1949

14459 NNC P P3 G1.3 1928–1949
'Child and woman labor in China, 1930.'
NWSS 4, 9 (2 Mar. 1931), 49, 51–54.
Subj 16.4 47 52 ▪ 54

14460 NNC S P2 G1.2 1911–1949
'Chinese labour and the contract system.'
PT new (2nd) series 5, 8 (16 Nov. 1933), 407–410.
Subj 16.4 34.2

14461 CSU P P4 G1.3 1928–1949
'An enquiry into the conditions of the workers in China.'
ILR 23, 6 (June 1931), 853–857.
Subj 16.4 18 ▪ 36.4

14462 NNC S P3 G1.3 1911–1928
'Industrial accidents in China, 1928.'
NWSS 5, 51 (19 Dec. 1932), 229, 231–232.
Subj 16.4 18 ▪ 56 58

14463 NNC P P3 G1.3 1911–1949
'Industrial workers in China, 1930.'
NWSS 4, 7 (16 Feb. 1931), 37, 39–40.
Subj 16.4 ▪ 36.4

14464 NNC P P5 G1.2 1928–1949
'Laborers and wages in Chinese government railways, 1930.'
NWSS 5, 43 (24 Oct. 1932), 193, 195–196.
Subj 14.2 16.4 ▪ 18

14465 NNP U P5 G1.1 1911–1928
'Die Lage des Proletariats in China' (The condition of the proletariat in China).
Sozial-ökonomische Arbeiter-Rundschau 2, 4 (Apr. 1927), 1–6.
Subj 16.4 18 ▪ 11.4 14.4

14466 NNC P P3 G1.2 1911–1949
Studies on Chinese labor.
Tientsin: Nankai U., Institute of Economics, 25 July 1932. 7 p. [Supplement to *NWSS* 5 (1932)]
Subj 16.4 ▪ 12.2 18 36.4 47 54

14467 NNC P P3 G1.3 1928–1949
'Wages, hours and family budget of the Chinese laborers, 1930.'
NWSS 4, 38 (21 Sept. 1931), 177, 179–180.
Subj 16.4 18

14468 DLC P P2 G1.1 1911–1928
Akatova, Tat'iana Nikolaevna, 1923–.
'Osobennosti formirovaniia rabochego klassa v Kitae' (Features of the development of the Chinese working class). In *Dvizhenie '4 maia' 1919 goda v Kitae: sbornik statei* (Articles on the May Fourth Movement in China), compiled by Institut vostokovedeniia, Akademiia nauk SSSR, edited by A- G- Afanas'ev et al. [Selective entry]
Moscow: Nauka, Glav. red. vost. lit-ry, 1971, 100–127.
Subj 16.4 36.4 39 66 ▪ 14.4 16.3 24.4 32 32.2 34.2 34.3

14469 DLC S P3 G1.3 1911–1928
Akramovskaia, V-.
'Usloviia truda promyshlennykh rabochikh v Kitae' (Labor conditions of Chinese industrial workers).
Vestnik truda 1926, 2, 112–117.
Subj 16.4 18 ▪ 36.4 47

14470 MCH O P4 G1.2 1911–1928
Arnold, Julean Herbert, 1875–1946, and William Holt Gale, 1864–?
Labor and industrial conditions in China.
Washington, D.C.: U.S. Government Printing Office, 1922. 17 p. (Bureau of Foreign and Domestic Commerce, Trade information bulletins, 75)
Subj 14.1 16.4

14471 MCH P P1 G1.2 1928–1949
Chang, Léon Y. (Chang Lung-yen).
La législation du travail en Chine (Labor legislation in China).
Nancy: Thomas, 1936. 137 p. (Doctoral dissertation, Faculté de droit, Université de Nancy)
Subj 12.2 14.4 16.4 18 ▪ 36.4 47

14472 NIC O P3 G1.3 1928–1949
Chen Ta (Ch'en Ta), 1892–.
'Basic problems of the Chinese working classes.'
AJS 53, 3 (Nov. 1947), 184–191.
Subj 16.4 36.4 ▪ 18 61

14473 MCH O P2 G1.2 1911–1949
Chen Ta (Ch'en Ta), 1892–.
'Chinese labor since 1927.'
China critic 4, 17 (23 Apr. 1931), 391–392.
Subj 16.4 36.4

14474 CSH FP P3 G1.3 1928–1949
Chen Ta (Ch'en Ta), 1892–.
'The labour policy of the Chinese government and its reactions on industry and labour.'
ILR 59, 1 (Jan. 1949), 34–62.
Subj 12.2 16.4 18 ▪ 16.2 27 28 34.2 36.4

14475 MCH FP P2 G1.1 1911–1949
Chesneaux, Jean, 1922–.
'The Chinese labor force in the first part of the twentieth century.' In *The economic development of China and Japan*, edited by Charles Donald Cowan. [Selective entry]
New York: Praeger, 1964, 111–127. (U. of London, School of Oriental and African Studies, Studies on modern Asia and Africa, 4)
Subj 11.4 16.4 ▪ 11.2 34.2 36.4 39

14476 NNC PO P3 G1.1 1911–1928
[Eddy, George Sherwood] Shervud Eddi, 1871–?
'Polozhenie truda v Kitae' (The position of labor in China). In *Voprosy kitaiskoi revoliutsii, tom 1-yi* (Problems of the Chinese revolution, Vol. 1), edited by Karl Radek. [Selective entry]
Moscow: Gosizdat, 1927, 12–31.
Subj 16.4 18 36.4 ▪ 14.4 34.3 47 52 54

14477 CSH P P3 G1.2 1911–1949
Engel'fel'd, Vladimir Viktorovich, 1891–1937.
'Novyi fabrichnyi zakon Kitaia' (China's new factory law).
Vestnik kitaiskogo prava 3 (1931), 35–42.
Subj 12.2 16.4 ▪ 14.4 18

14478 NIC FP P3 G1.2 1928–1949
Epstein, Israel, 1915–.
Notes on labor problems in Nationalist China.
New York: Institute of Pacific Relations, International Secretariat, 1949. 159 p.
Subj 12 14.4 16.4 36.4 47 ▪ 11.2 12.2 15 18 21.4 22.2 26.4 28 32.1 52

14479 NNC PO P2 G1.2 1911–1949
Fang, Fu-an.
Chinese labour: An economic and statistical survey of the labour condition and labour movements in China.
Shanghai: Kelly and Walsh; London: King, 1931. 185 p.
Subj 12.2 16.4 18 36.4 ▪ 11.1 22.2 32 32.1 47 55

14480 NNC P P4 G1.3 1928–1949
Feng, Cheng-hai.
'Labor conditions in China during 1934.'
CEJ 16, 2 (Feb. 1935), 185–199.
Subj 14.4 16.4 18 ▪ 12.1 34.2 36.4

14481 NNC P P2 G1.2 1911–1949
Fong, H. D. (Fang Hsien-t'ing), 1902–
'China's factory act and the cotton industry.'
MBEC 7, 3 (Mar. 1934), 93–104.
Subj 12.2 16.4 18 ▪ 14.4 34.2 47 52

14482 CSH P P1 G1.2 1911–1949
Golianovskii, S- K-.
'Zakonodatel'nye novelly Nankina po rabochemu voprosu' (New labor laws of the Nanking government). [With English abstract]
VM 1930, 6, 74–86.
Subj 12.2 16.4 18 ▪ 14.4 36.4

14483 MCH PO P4 G1.2 1911–1928
Great Britain. Foreign Office.
Memorandum on labour conditions in China.
London: His Majesty's Stationery Office, 1927. 25 p. (Parliament, Papers by command, Cmd. 2846; China, 2, 1927)
Subj 16.4 ▪ 18 36.4 52

14484 DLC U P4 G1.3 1911–1928
[Heller, Leo N-] L. Geller.
'God proletarskoi bor'by v Kitae' (A year of proletarian struggle in China).
Vestnik truda 1927, 9, 119–130.
Subj 16.4 32.2 ▪ 16.2 32.1 36.4

14485 NNC PO P3 G1.3 1911–1928
Henry, P-.
'Some aspects of the labour problem in China.'
ILR 15, 1 (Jan. 1927), 24–50.
Subj 16.4 ▪ 12.2 14.4

14486 ICU P P2 G1.2 1911–1949
Huang, An-li.
Chinese labor.
Unpublished masters thesis in Economics, U. of Chicago, 1942. 122 p.
Subj 16.4 34.3 36.4 ▪ 12.2 14 17 18

14487 NNC S P4 G1.2 1911–1928
IA——n, Genrikh.
'Polozhenie rabochego klassa v Kitae: zametki i materialy k izucheniiu problemy' (Data for the study of the position of the working class in China).
Revoliutsionnyi Vostok 1928, 3, 22–65.
Subj 16.4 18 ▪ 36.4

14488 NNP U P2 G1.2 1911–1928
Kantorovich, Anatolii IAkovlevich, 1896–1944.
'Usloviia truda v Kitae' (Working conditions in China).
Ekonomicheskoe obozrenie 3, 6 (iiun' 1925), 205–208.
Subj 16.4 18 ▪ 16

14489 MCH S P3 G1.3 1911–1928
Khodorov, Abram Evseevich, 1886–1949.
'Klassovaia bor'ba v Kitae' (The class struggle in China).
NV 15 (1926), 94–113.
Subj 16 16.4 ▪ 36.4

14490 CBU P P3 G1.2 1928–1949
Kukhtin, K- V-.
'Fabrichnoe zakonodatel'stvo Kitaia' (Factory legislation in China).
VM 1934, 2 (fevral'), 110–122.
Subj 12.2 16.4 18 ▪ 14.4 16.2

14491 FPN P P3 G1.1 1911–1949
[Le Van Thang] Lê-Van-Thang.
L'oeuvre de l'Organisation internationale du travail en Asie (The work of the International Labour Organisation in Asia).
Aix-en-Provence: E. Fourcine, 1932. 176 p. (Doctoral dissertation, Faculté de droit, Université d'Aix-Marseille)
Subj 14.4 16.4 18 ▪ 36.4 47 52 55

14492 NNC P P3 G1.2 1911–1928
Liau ——.
'Rabochii klass v Kitae' (The working class in China). In *Voprosy kitaiskoi revoliutsii, tom 1-yi* (Problems of the Chinese revolution, Vol. 1), edited by Karl Radek. [Selective entry]
Moscow: Gosizdat, 1927, 1–11.
Subj 16.4 36.4 ▪ 14.2 14.4 18

14493 FPN P P4 G1.3 1911–1928
Lim, Hy-soon (Lin Hsi-ch'un).
La question ouvrière en Chine (The labor question in China).
Nancy: Poncelet, 1931. 160 p. (Doctoral dissertation, Faculté de droit, Université de Nancy)
Subj 11.4 16.4 18 30 ▪ 11.2 14 14.4 16 47 54

14494 NNP P P2 G1.3 1911–1949
Liubimov, L- I-.
'Statistika truda v Kitae' (Labor statistics in China).
Bibliograficheskii biulleten' Kitaiskoi Vostochnoi zheleznoi dorogi 3, 3 (1930), 35–38.
Subj 16.4 ▪ 18

14495 MCH P P5 G1.2 1911–1949
Lo, Chü-fen.
'Die Höhe der Löhne in China' (The level of wages in China). In *Der Arbeitslohn in China* (Labor wages in China), by Paul Arndt, Djini Shen, and Chü-fen Lo. [Analytic entry]
Leipzig: Hans Buske, 1937, 199–352. (Doctoral dissertation, Wirtschafts- und sozialwissenschaftliche Fakultät, Universität Frankfurt a.M.)
Subj 14.3 14.4 16.4 18 ▪ 14 34.2

14496 NNC P P5 G1.2 1911–1949
Lowe, Chuan-hua (Lo Ch'uan-hua), 1902–.
Facing labor issues in China.
Shanghai: China Institute of Pacific Relations; London: Allen and Unwin, 1934. 15, 211 p.
Subj 14.4 16.4 18 34.2 36.4 ▪ 12 12.2 14 27 32 32.1 32.2 34.3

14497 ELB FP P2 G1.2 1911–1928
[Malone, Cecil John L'Estrange] Sesil' Malon, 1890–.
Kak zhivet kitaiskii rabochii (How the Chinese worker lives). Tr. from the English. [Tr. of an unpublished manuscript?]
Moscow: Profintern, 1927. 67 p.
Subj 14.4 16.4 18 36.4 66 ▪ 14.2 34.1 36.3 47

14498 CSH P P3 G1.2 1911–1928
N. G.
'Fabrichnoe zakonodatel'stvo v Kitae' (Factory legislation in China).
VM 1928, 5, 85–88.
Subj 12.2 16.4 ▪ 14.4

14499 NNC S P3 G1.2 1928–1949
Pashkova, M-.
'Kitaiskii proletariat v natsional'no-osvoboditel'noi voine' (The Chinese proletariat in the War of National Liberation).
MKhMP 1939, 5 (mai), 124–130.
Subj 16.4 66 ▪ 14.2 32.2 36.4

14500 NNC P P4 G1.2 1928–1949
Pashkova, M-.
'Polozhenie rabochego klassa v Kitae' (The position of the working class in China).
MKhMP 1936, 6 (iiun'), 113–125.
Subj 14.4 16.4 18 66 ▪ 12.1 14.3 32.2 36.4

14501 MCH P P4 G1.2 1928–1949
P'u, Shou-ch'ang, 1921–.
Labor policy in China.
Unpublished doctoral dissertation in Economics, Harvard U., 1946. 191 p.
Subj 16.4 36.4 ▪ 12.2 14.4 18 32.1

14502 NNC O P2 G1.2 1911–1928
Tayler, John Bernard, 1878–, and W. T. Zung.
'Labour and industry in China.'
ILR 8, 1 (July 1923), 1–20.
Subj 16.4 18 ▪ 14.4 36.4 47

14503 NNP S P2 G1.2 1911–1949
Torgashev, Boris Pavlovich.
'Gornyi trud v Kitae' (Mining labor in China).
Bibliograficheskii biulleten' Kitaiskoi Vostochnoi zheleznoi dorogi 3, 3 (1930), 49–53.
Subj 16.4 36.4 ▪ 14.4 18

14504 MCH S P2 G1.3 1928–1949
[Torgashev, Boris Pavlovich] Boris P. Torgasheff.
'Man power in transportation.'
China critic 4, 25 (18 June 1931), 587–590.
Subj 14.2 16.4

14505 NNC P P2 G1.3 1911–1949
[Torgashev, Boris Pavlovich] Boris P. Torgasheff.
'Mining labor in China.'
CEJ 6, 4 (Apr. 1930), 392–417; 6, 5 (May 1930), 510–541; 6, 6 (June 1930), 652–676; 7, 1 (July 1930), 770–795; 7, 2 (Aug. 1930), 909–927.
Subj 14.4 16.4 18 ▪ 34.2 36.4 55

14506 CSU F P2 G1.2 1928–1949
Tsen Tsonming (Tseng Chung-ming), 1896–1939.
'A statistical review of the conditions of railway workers.'
PT new (2nd) series 5, 5 (1 Oct. 1933), 225–228.
Subj 16.4 ▪ 14.2 17

14507 NNC P P4 G1.3 1911–1928
Tso, S. K. Sheldon (Chu Shih-k'ang), 1901–.
'Present labor conditions in China.'
Monthly labor review 26, 4 (Apr. 1928), 44–55.
Subj 16.4 ▪ 18 47

14508 DLC P P3 G1.2 1911–1949
Vagram, V-.
Kak zhivut i boriutsia rabochie Kitaia (How Chinese workers live and struggle).
Moscow: Profizdat, 1931. 48 p.
Subj 16.4 18 34.3 36.4 64 ▪ 12.2 14.4 14.5 15 24.4 47 55

14509 NIC P P3 G1.2 1911–1949
Wagner, Augusta Bertha, 1895–.
Labor legislation in China.
Peiping: Yenching U., 1938. 301 p. (Doctoral dissertation in Economics, Columbia U.)
Subj 12.2 16.4 18 ▪ 22 36.4 47 52 66

14510 NNC PO P4 G1.2 1911–1949
Wagner, Augusta Bertha, 1895–.
Some aspects of Chinese labor conditions.
Unpublished masters thesis in Economics, Columbia U., 1930. 78 p.
Subj 16.4 18 36.4 ▪ 12.1 14.4 34.3 47 52 66

14511 ²NNC U P2 G1.2 1911–1928
Zung, Tsoong-iung.
'The use of Chinese laborers in the war, and the results for China.'
St. John's echo (Shanghai) 31, 7 (Oct. 1920). [Reprinted in *Readings in economics for China*, compiled and edited by Charles Frederick Remer. (Selective entry.) Shanghai: Commercial Press, 1922, 446–454.]
Subj 16.4 66 ▪ 14.4 18 19 36.4

1911-1972
(including 1644-1972)

14512 DLC P P2 G1.2 1911–1972
Bogatyrev, A- P-.
V ugol'nykh basseinakh Kitaia (In China's coal regions).
Moscow: Ugletekhizdat, 1953. 93 p.
Subj 14.4 16.4 ▪ 15 32.1 32.2 36.4 66

14513 MCH P P2 G1.2 1842–1972
Huang, Sungmo, 1926–.
Das soziale Bewusstsein der Industriearbeiterschaft Chinas: Das Problem der sozialen Dichotomie (The social consciousness of China's industrial workers: The problem of social dichotomy).
Münster: The author, 1960. 152 p. (Doctoral dissertation, Philosophische Fakultät, Universität Münster)
Subj 14 14.4 16 16.4 36.4 60 ▪ 16.1 19 32.2 34.2 47 61 64

14514 MCH U P4 G1.3 1928–1972
Wang Ke-ho.
'The end of gang rule in transport.'
People's China 1, 9 (1 May 1950), 11–12, 27.
Subj 16.4 22.2 ▪ 14.4 32.2 36.4

14515 NNC O P2 G1.2 1928–1972
Zhmykhov, I- N-.
'V novom Kitae' (In New China).
Novyi mir 1951, 7 (iiul'), 153–176; 1951, 8 (avgust), 190–213.
Subj 14.1 14.4 16.3 16.4 34.1 50 ▪ 17 18 22 45

1949-1972

14516 GBF S P4 G1.2 1949–1972
'Die Lage der Arbeiter in Rotchina' (The condition of workers in Red China).
Internationale Arbeitsmitteilungen 11, 6 (1958), 1–11.
Subj 16.4 18 ▪ 22.1 36.4

14517 CSH O P4 G1.2 1949–1972
Ashdown, John.
'China's proletarian problems.'
FEER 47, 10 (12 Mar. 1965), 439–442.
Subj 16.4 ▪ 36.4

14518 MCH P P4 G1.2 1949–1972
Ayers, Thomas William, 1922–.
'Labor policy and factory management in Communist China.'
AAAPSS 277 (Sept. 1951), 124–134. [Special issue: *Report on China*, edited by Harold Arthur Steiner]
Subj 16.4 36.4 ▪ 14.4 32.1

14519 NIC P P3 G1.2 1949–1972
Chao, Kuo-chün, 1918–1962.
'Labour in China today.'
United Asia 12, 3 (1960), 234–240. [Special issue: *Labour in Asia*]
Subj 14.4 16.4 36.4 ▪ 12 12.2 18 28

14520 NIC U P3 G1.2 1949–1972
China [People's Republic]. Lao tung pu. Lao tung pao hu chü. (Ministry of Labor. Office of Labor Protection).
Labour protection in New China.
Peking: Foreign Languages Press, 1960. 94 p.
Subj 16.4 18 ▪ 12.2 14.4 34.2 47 56 58

14521 NIC P P2 G1.2 1949–1972
Eckstein, Alexander, 1915–.
'Manpower and industrialization in Communist China, 1949–1957.' In *Population trends in eastern Europe, the USSR, and Mainland China*, compiled by Milbank Memorial Fund. [Selective entry]
New York: Milbank Memorial Fund, 1960, 157–176.
Subj 14 16.4 ▪ 11.2 14.1 14.4

14522 CSU P P2 G1.2 1949–1972
Emerson, John Philip, 1925–.
Nonagricultural employment in Mainland China, 1949–1958.
Washington, D.C.: U.S. Bureau of the Census, 1965. 240 p. (International population statistics report series, P-90, 21)
Subj 11.4 14 16.4 ▪ 12 14.2 14.3 14.4 17 18 70

14523 CSU P P4 G1.2 1949–1972
Field, Robert Michael, 1928–.
'Labor productivity in industry.' In *Economic trends in Communist China*, edited by Alexander Eckstein, Walter Galenson, and Ta-chung Liu. [Selective entry]
Chicago: Aldine, 1968, 637–670.
Subj 14.4 16.4

14524 NNC P P2 G1.2 1949–1972
Ishikawa Shigeru, 1918–.
Number and wages of industrial workers in Communist China, mimeo. Tr. of 'Chūgoku no shokkōsū chingin tōkei' (Statistics on workers in China: Numbers and wages); *Ekafe tsūshin* 270 (11 July 1961), 1–38.
Washington, D.C.: U.S. Joint Publications Research Service, 15 Dec. 1961. 36 p. (JPRS 11,671; MC 3172/1962)
Subj 16.4 ▪ 18

14525 CSH P P2 G1.2 1949–1972
Kirby, Edward Stuart, 1909–.
'The young worker.' In *Youth in China*, edited by E. S. Kirby. [Analytic entry]
Hong Kong: Dragonfly Books, 1965, 163–189.
Subj 16.3 16.4 18 54 ▪ 12.1

14526 DLC P P3 G1.2 1949–1972
Kuznetsova, T- A-.
'Nekotorye voprosy kul'turno-tekhnicheskogo pod"ema kitaiskogo rabochego klassa' (The cultural and technological rise of the Chinese working class). [With English abstract]
VLGU 14, 20 (1959), 17–29.
Subj 16.4 27 37 ▪ 12.1 14 14.4 32.1 36.4 47

14527 CSH P P4 G1.2 1949–1972
[La Dany, Ladislao] ———, 1914–.
'"Counter-revolutionary economism" among workers.'
CNA 695 (9 Feb. 1968), 1–7.
Subj 16.4 26.4 ▪ 36.4

14528 CSH P P2 G1.2 1949–1972
[La Dany, Ladislao] ———, 1914–.
'Industrial workers, the vanguard of revolution.'
CNA 674 (25 Aug. 1967), 1–7.
Subj 16.4 36.4 ▪ 35

14529 NNC P P4 G1.2 1949–1972
[La Dany, Ladislao] ———, 1914–.
'The Janus-face of labour conditions.'
CNA 128 (20 Apr. 1956), 2–7.
Subj 16.4 18 ▪ 36.4 55

14530 MCH P P4 G1.2 1949–1972
[La Dany, Ladislao] ———, 1914–.
'Wage policy in industry.'
CNA 261 (23 Jan. 1959), 1–6.
Subj 16.4

14531 CSH P P5 G1.2 1949–1972
[La Dany, Ladislao] ———, 1914–.
'Workers and discipline.'
CNA 769 (15 Aug. 1969), 1–7.
Subj 16.4 ▪ 12.1 12.2 22.2 36.4

14532 NNC P P2 G1.2 1949–1972
Lavrent'eva, A- V-, and Margarita Vasil'evna Fomicheva, 1924–.

'Rabochii klass v sotsialisticheskom stroitel'stve Kitaiskoi Narodnoi Respubliki' (The [role of the] working class in socialist construction in the People's Republic of China).
KSINA 49 (1961), 13–23.
Subj 11.4 14.4 16.4 ▪ 14 32

14533 MCH S P4 G1.2 1949–1972
Liu Khou-pu (Liu Hou-p'u).
'K voprosu o metode izmereniia proizvoditel'nosti truda v promyshlennosti Kitaiskoi Narodnoi Respubliki' (Measuring industrial labor productivity in the People's Republic of China).
Voprosy statistiki i ucheta 3 (1961), 100–112.
Subj 14.4 16.4 ▪ 14.6

14534 MCH O P3 G1.2 1949–1972
Liu Tze-chiu.
'Labour emulation among China's working class.'
People's China 1954, 10 (16 May), 6–9.
Subj 12.1 16.4 ▪ 36.4

14535 NIC P P4 G1.2 1949–1972
Priestley, Kenneth Ewart.
Workers of China.
Oxford, Eng.: Holywell Press, 1963. 107 p. [Reprinted—London: Ampersand, 1965. 107 p.]
Subj 12.1 16.4 ▪ 14.4 18 27 36.4

14536 CSH P P3 G1.2 1949–1972
Roux, Alain.
'Le prolétariat chinois et la révolution culturelle' (The Chinese proletariat and the Cultural Revolution).
Nouvelle critique nouvelle (2e) série 16 (sept. 1968), 38–44.
Subj 16 16.4 36.4 ▪ 15 18 19

14537 CSH P P4 G1.2 1949–1972
Rumiantsev, Aleksei Matveevich. (A. Rumjanzew), and A- A- Sterbalova (A. Sterbalowa).
'Sotsial'no-ekonomicheskii kurs gruppy Mao TSze-duna i rabochii klass Kitaia' (The social and economic policy of the Maoists and China's working class).
Mirovaia ekonomika i mezhdunarodnye otnosheniia 1967, 6, 30–44.
'Der sozialökonomische Kurs der Gruppe Mao Tse-tungs und die Arbeiterklasse Chinas.'
Sowjetwissenschaft; gesellschafts-wissenschaftliche Beiträge 1967, 10 (Okt.), 1015–1031.
Subj 12.1 16.4 ▪ 14

14538 NNC S P1 G1.2 1949–1972
Schran, Peter, 1930–.
'Unity and diversity of Russian and Chinese industrial wage policies.'
JAS 23, 2 (Feb. 1964), 245–251.
Subj 14.4 16.4 ▪ 64

14539 CSH P P2 G1.3 1949–1972
Stanford U. China Project.
'Labor.' In *Central South China*, compiled by the organization cited. [Selective entry]
New Haven: Human Relations Area Files, 1956, vol. 2, 802–826. (HRAF subcontractor's monographs, 28; Stanford 2)
Subj 16.4 36.4 ▪ 18

14540 CSH P P2 G1.3 1949–1972
Stanford U. China Project.
'Labor.' In *East China*, compiled by the organization cited. [Selective entry]
New Haven: Human Relations Area Files, 1956, vol. 2, 885–914. (HRAF subcontractor's monographs, 29; Stanford 3)
Subj 16.4 36.4 ▪ 18

14541 CSH P P2 G5.0 1949–1972
Stanford U. China Project.
'Labor.' In *North China*, compiled by the organization cited. [Selective entry]
New Haven: Human Relations Area Files, 1956, vol. 2, 847–869. (HRAF subcontractor's monographs, 27; Stanford 1)
Subj 16.4 36.4 ▪ 18

14542 NNC P P2 G8.0 1949–1972
Stanford U. China Project.
'Labor.' In *Southwest China*, compiled by the organization cited. [Selective entry]
New Haven: Human Relations Area Files, 1956, vol. 2, 899–918. (HRAF subcontractor's monographs, 30; Stanford 4)
Subj 16.4 36.4 ▪ 18

14543 CSU O P2 G1.3 1949–1972
Stewart, Rosemary.
'Inside China's factories and communes.'
GM 39, 12 (Apr. 1967), 967–976.
Subj 16.3 16.4 ▪ 18 55

14544 NNC F P5 G9.4 1949–1972
Taiwan. She hui ch'u. (Dept. of Social Affairs), comp.
Taiwan labor conditions.
Taipei: She hui ch'u, 1957. 106 p. [In Chinese as well as English]
Subj 16.4 18 ▪ 17 47 55 56

14545 CSH P P5 G1.2 1949–1972
Walker, Richard Louis, 1922–.
'The "working class" in Communist China.'
Problems of Communism 2, 3/4 (1953), 42–50.
Subj 16.4 ▪ 32.1 36.4 47

14546 NNC S P1 G1.2 1949–1972
Wang, I-ying.
'Die gewaltigen Erfolge der chinesischen Arbeitsgesetzgebung' (The huge success of Chinese labor legislation).
Rechtswissenschaftlicher Informationsdienst 8, 7/8 (Juli–Aug. 1959), 338–350.
Subj 12.2 16.4 18 ▪ 11.2 14.4 36.4

14547 CSU P P2 G1.2 1949–1972
Wu, Yuan-li (Wu Yüan-li), 1920–.
'Reported increases in labor productivity in Communist China.'
Studies on Asia 1 (1960), 79–87.
Subj 14.4 16.4 ▪ 14.1

14548 MCH P P1 G1.2 1949–1972
Yang, Richard F. S. (Yang Fu-sen), 1918–.
'Industrial workers in Chinese Communist fiction.'
CQ 13 (Jan.–Mar. 1963), 212–225.
Subj 16.4 ▪ 12.1

14549 NNC P P4 G9.4 1949–1972
Zuzik, Michael Benedict, and H- Micocci.
Labor law and practice in Taiwan (Formosa).
Washington, D.C.: U.S. Government Printing Office, 1964. 72 p. (U.S. Bureau of Labor Statistics reports, 268)
Subj 12.2 16.4 18 36.4 ▪ 12 14.4 17 21 34.2 36.2

17 National and Higher Education

全國教育及高等教育

国民教育及び高等教育

1644-1911

14550 NNC P P3 G5.3 1895–1911
'Eine chinesische Hochschule in Tsinanfu' (A Chinese academy in Chi-nan-fu [i.e., Tsinan]).
MSOSB 5 (1902), 163–173.
Subj 17

14551 CSU O P3 G5.1 1895–1911
'L'éducation nouvelle en Chine' (The new educational system in China).
Questions diplomatiques et coloniales 30, 322 (juil.–déc. 1910), 103–116.
Subj 16.1 17 62 ▪ 54 66

14552 NNC O P3 G6.1 1895–1911
'The University of Nanking.'
JAAA 12, 6 (July 1912), 184–185.
Subj 17 ▪ 66

14553 IMN U P1 G1.2 –1911
Agostinoni, Emidio, 1879–1933.
Studi sull'educazione del popolo cinese (Studies on Chinese education).
Milan: Vallardi, 1903. 162 p.
Subj 17

14554 NNM PO P2 G9.4 1895–1911
Arnold, Julean Herbert, 1875–1946.
Education in Formosa.
Washington, D.C.: U.S. Government Printing Office, 1908. 70 p. (Education Bureau bulletins, 5)
Subj 17 ▪ 24.1 24.4 66

14555 MCH P P1 G1.3 1644–1911
Ayers, Thomas William, 1922–.
Chang Chih-tung and educational reform in China.
Cambridge: Harvard U. Press, 1971. 14, 290 p. (Harvard East Asian series, 54) (Revision of *Chang Chih-tung and Chinese educational change*, doctoral dissertation in History, Harvard U., 1959)
Subj 17 32 59 ▪ 15 16.1 32.2 37 62 64 66

14556 CSU P P2 G1.2 1895–1911
Bastid, Marianne, 1940–.
Aspects de la réforme de l'enseignement en Chine au début du 20e siècle (Aspects of educational reform in China at the beginning of the twentieth century).
The Hague: Mouton, 1971. 321 p. (Faculté des lettres et sciences humaines de Paris-Sorbonne, publications, série 'recherches', 64) (Revision of *Quelques aspects de la réforme de l'enseignement en Chine au début du XXe siècle, d'après les écrits de Zhang Jian* [Aspects of educational reform in China at the beginning of the twentieth century, according to the works of Chang Chien], doctoral

dissertation, Faculté des lettres, Université de Paris, 1968)
SUBJ 16.1 17 27 32 37 ▪ 12.1 36.1 63 64

14557 MCH P P1 G1.2 1644–1842
Bazin, Antoine Pierre Louis, 1799–1863.
'Mémoire sur l'organisation intérieure des écoles chinoises' (Report on the internal organization of Chinese schools).
JA 3e série 8 (jan. 1839), 32–80.
SUBJ 17 ▪ 16

14558 MCH P P1 G1.2 –1895
Bazin, Antoine Pierre Louis, 1799–1863.
'Recherches sur l'histoire, l'organisation et les travaux de l'Académie impériale de Pékin' (Investigations of the history, organization, and functions of the Imperial Academy of Peking).
JA 5e série 11 (jan. 1858), 5–105.
SUBJ 17 ▪ 37

14559 DLC O P1 G1.1 1644–1842
[Bichurin, Nikita Iakovlevich] *Otets* Iakinf, 1777–1853.
'Vzgliad na prosveshchenie v Kitae' (A look at education in China).
Zhurnal Ministerstva narodnago prosveshcheniia 16, 4 (1838), 324–366; 16, 5 (1838), 568–595.
SUBJ 17

14560 ELB P P3 G1.1 1842–1895
Biggerstaff, Knight, 1906–.
The earliest modern government schools in China.
Ithaca: Cornell U. Press, 1961. 11, 276 p. [Reprinted—Port Washington, N.Y.: Kennikat Press, 1971. 11, 276 p.]
SUBJ 17 ▪ 15 16.1 66

14561 ELB P P3 G6.1 1842–1911
Biggerstaff, Knight, 1906–.
'Shanghai Polytechnic Institution and reading room: An attempt to introduce Western science and technology to the Chinese.'
PHR 25, 2 (May 1956), 127–149.
SUBJ 17 64 66

14562 MCH P P1 G1.2 –1842
Biot, Edouard Constant, 1803–1850.
'Situation de l'instruction publique et règlement des concours sous la dynastie actuelle des Mandchous' (The place of public education and regulations for competitive examinations under the present Ch'ing dynasty). In *Essai sur l'histoire de l'instruction publique en Chine, et de la corporation des lettrés, depuis les anciens temps jusqu'à nos jours* (An essay on the history of public education in China and the literati from ancient times to the present), by E. C. Biot. [Sole entry]
Paris: Benjamin Duprat, 1847, 491–550. [Reprinted in *Essai sur l'histoire de l'instruction publique en Chine, et de la corporation des lettrés, depuis les anciens temps jusqu'à nos jours*, by E. C. Biot. (Sole entry.) Taipei: Ch'eng-wen, 1969, 491–550.]
SUBJ 12 17 ▪ 15 16.1

14563 CSU U P3 G9.2 1895–1911
Bone, C-.
'The Kwangnga University [i.e., Kuang-ya Academy], Canton.'
EAM 1 (1902), 326–332.
SUBJ 17

14564 MBA O P4 G1.2 1895–1911
Brou, Alexandre, 1862–?
'La discipline dans les établissements scolaires chinois' (Discipline in Chinese educational institutions).
RI nouvelle (2e) série 16, 10 (oct. 1911), 426–431. [Reprinted from *Echo de Chine* 1911?]
SUBJ 17 61 ▪ 16.1

14565 MCH PO P4 G1.2 1895–1911
Brou, Alexandre, 1862–?
'Les missions de Chine et les réformes scolaires' (The missions in China and educational reforms).
Etudes 7e série 129, 3 (5 nov. 1911), 389–410.
SUBJ 17 32.1 33

14566 MCH PO P2 G1.2 1895–1911
Brou, Alexandre, 1862–?
'Les réformes scolaires en Chine' (Educational reforms in China).
Etudes 7e série 127, 4 (20 mai 1911), 461–479; 128, 1 (5 juil. 1911), 25–46.
SUBJ 16.1 17 62 64 ▪ 12.2 13 16 37 47 66

14567 ICU U P1 G1.1 –1911
Bullock, Amasa Archibald.
The old Chinese educational institutions: An estimation of their values with a brief survey of their development.
Unpublished masters thesis in Philosophy, U. of Chicago, 1909. 50 p.
SUBJ 17 ▪ 16.1 64

14568 MCH O P2 G1.3 1895–1911
Chatley, Herbert, 1885–.
'Technical education in China.'
J. of the Royal Society of Arts 61, 3164 (11 July 1913), 817–819.
SUBJ 17

14569 CSH P P2 G1.2 –1911
Chiao, Chien (Ch'iao Chien), 1935–.
'Some aspects in transmission of Confucian tradition.'
BIE 32, 3 (Aug. 1971), 325–342. [For fuller treatment, see entry 20414.]
SUBJ 16.1 17 53 64 ▪ 12 48 63

14570 MCH P P3 G5.1 1644–1842
Chung, A. L. Y.
'The Hanlin Academy in the early Ch'ing period (1644–1795).'
JRAS-HKB 6 (1966), 100–119.
SUBJ 12 16.1 17

14571 MBA P P4 G8.2 1895–1911
Cordier, Charles Georges, 1872–1936.
'Réforme scolaire et instruction publique au Yunnan: situation en 1911' (Educational reform and public education in Yunnan in 1911).
RI nouvelle (2e) série 17, 1 (jan. 1912), 25–61; 17, 2 (fév. 1912), 143–149.
SUBJ 16 17 ▪ 15 16.1 32.1 33 64 66

14572 MCH PO P2 G1.2 1895–1911
Courant, Maurice Auguste Louis Marie, 1865–1935.
'Réforme de l'instruction en Chine' (Educational reform in China).
R. pédagogique nouvelle (2e) série 48, 6 (juin 1906), 548–573.
SUBJ 17 ▪ 12.1 16.1 64

14573 CNY O P3 G5.0 1895–1911
Davrout, Léon, 1875–.
'La réforme scolaire' (Educational reform).
Chine, Ceylan, Madagascar 35 (mai 1911), 292–309.
SUBJ 17 ▪ 66

14574 MCH O P2 G1.2 1842–1911
Edmunds, Charles Keyser, 1876–1949.
Modern education in China.
Washington, D.C.: U.S. Government Printing Office, 1919. 72 p. (U.S. Dept. of Interior, Bureau of Education bulletins, 44, 1919)
SUBJ 17 ▪ 62

14575 CSU P P3 G9.2 1644–1895
Evans, Nancy Jane Frances, 1945–.
'The banner-school background of the Canton T'ung-wen Kuan [Interpreters College].'
PC 22A (May 1969), 89–103.
SUBJ 17 66 ▪ 15

14576 NIC P P1 G1.2 1895–1911
Ferguson, John Calvin, 1866–1945.
'The abolition of the competitive examinations in China.'
JAOS 27, 1 (Jan.–July 1906), 79–87.
SUBJ 12 17

14577 CSU O P3 G7.1 1895–1911
Foster, Arnold, 1846–1919.
'The educational outlook in Wuchang.'
CR 37, 1 (Jan. 1906), 36–42; 37, 4 (Apr. 1906), 208–216; 37, 5 (May 1906), 258–265.
SUBJ 17 ▪ 37 47

14578 CSU S P1 G1.3 1842–1911
Franke, Wolfgang, 1912–.
'Anpassungsprobleme im chinesischen Erziehungswesen des 19. und frühen 20. Jahrhunderts' (Problems of adaptation in the Chinese educational system of the nineteenth and early twentieth centuries).
Saeculum 19, 1 (1968), 67–73.
SUBJ 16.1 17 ▪ 19 66

14579 CSU P P1 G1.2 1895–1911
Franke, Wolfgang, 1912–.
'Kang Yu-wei und die Reform des Prüfungswesens' (K'ang Yu-wei and the reform of the examination system). In *K'ang Yu-wei: A biography and a symposium*, edited by J. P. Lo (Lo Jung-pang). [Selective entry]
Tucson: U. of Arizona Press, 1967, 313–318.
SUBJ 16.1 17

14580 MCH S P1 G1.2 –1842
Fresnel, Fulgence, 1795–1855.
'De l'éducation chez les Chinois' (Education among the Chinese).
JA 3 (nov.–déc. 1823), 257–271, 321–331; 4 (jan. 1824), 3–9.
SUBJ 17 ▪ 63

14581 CSU PO P3 G7.2 1895–1911
Gage, Brownell.
'Government schools in Hunan.'
CR 38, 12 (Dec. 1907), 667–674.
SUBJ 17

14582 NIC PO P3 G5.1 1644–1911
Galt, Howard Spilman, 1872–?
'Kuo tzu chien [the Imperial Academy]: Its historical development and present condition.'
CSPSR 23, 4 (Jan.–Mar. 1940), 442–462.
SUBJ 17 ▪ 55

14583 CSU PO P3 G1.3 1895–1911
Goucher, John Franklin.
'Some recent developments of Christian education in China.' In *Recent developments in China*, edited by George Hubbard Blakeslee. [Selective entry]
New York: G. E. Stechert, 1913, 388–409.
SUBJ 17 ▪ 37

14584 IMC PO P2 G1.2 1895–1911
Gravina di Ramacca, Manfredi.
La Cina dopo il millenovecento (China after 1900).
Milan: Treves, 1907. 482 p.
SUBJ 15 16.1 17 66 ▪ 11.2 12.1 12.2 14.2 14.4 14.5 16 22.2 23 32.2

14585 NNC S P3 G5.1 –1842
Hirth, Friedrich, 1845–1927.
'The Chinese Oriental college [i.e., Ssu-i-kuan, Peking].'
JRAS-CB new (2nd) series 22, 3 (1887), 203–223.
SUBJ 17 ▪ 66

14586 CNY O P4 G9.2 1895–1911
Hötzel, G-.
'Aus dem Schulwesen der Rheinischen Mission in Tungkun' (The schools established by the Rhenish mission in [the capital of] Tung-kuan *hsien* [Kwangtung]).
Berichte der Rheinischen Missionsgesellschaft 1913, 8 (Aug.), 169–175.
SUBJ 17 ▪ 33

14587 CSU P P4 G5.3 1842–1911
Hyatt, Irwin Townsend, Jr., 1935–.
'The missionary as entrepreneur: Calvin Mateer in Shantung.'
J. of Presbyterian history 49, 4 (Winter 1971), 303–327.
SUBJ 17

14588 NIC PO P1 G1.2 1895–1911
King, Harry Edwin.
The educational system of China as recently reconstructed.
Washington, D.C.: U.S. Government Printing Office, 1911. 105 p. (Bureau of Education bulletins, 1911, 15/462)
SUBJ 17

14589 MCH PO P1 G1.2 1895–1911
Kösters, J-.
'Das chinesische Schulwesen' (The Chinese educational system).
Z. für Missionswissenschaft 2 (1912), 49–64.
SUBJ 17

14590 DLC O P2 G1.3 1895–1911
Krasnov, Andrei Nikolaevich, 1862–1914.
'Uchrezhdeniia kitaiskoi derevni: iz kolybeli tsivilizatsii' (From the cradle of civilization: Chinese village institutions).
Knizhki nedeli 1897, 2, 46–69.
SUBJ 17 57 64 ▪ 12 23 27 47 63

14591 CSU PO P2 G1.2 1895–1911
Kuo, Ping-wen, 1880–1969.
'The effect of the revolution upon the educational system of China.' In *Recent developments in China*, edited by George Hubbard Blakeslee. [Selective entry]
New York: G. E. Stechert, 1913, 345–358.
SUBJ 17

14592 NNC P P1 G1.2 1895–1911
Kuo, Ping-wen, 1880–1969.
Teachers for the modern schools of China.
Unpublished masters thesis in Education, Columbia U., 1912. 67 p.
SUBJ 16.1 17 ▪ 32.1 41 66

14593 NNC P P1 G1.2 1842–1895
La Fargue, Thomas Edward, 1900–.
'Chinese Educational Commission to the United States.'
FEQ 1, 1 (Nov. 1941), 59–70.
SUBJ 17 ▪ 32.1 54 66

14594 MCH FP P2 G1.1 –1911
Lewis, Robert Ellsworth, 1869–?
The educational conquest of the Far East.
New York: Revell, 1903. 248 p.
SUBJ 17 ▪ 16.1

14595 NNC S P1 G1.2 1842–1911
Liu, Kwang-ching (Liu Kuang-ching), 1921–.
'Early Christian colleges in China.'
JAS 20, 1 (Nov. 1960), 71–78.
SUBJ 17

14596 WSU P P8 G9.5 –1911
Lo Hsiang-lin, 1905–.
'Li-Ying College in Chin-T'ien (Kam Tin) and other cultural remains of Hong Kong, Kowloon, and the New Territories.' Tr. of 'Chin-t'ien chih Li-ying shu Hsiang-kang Chiu-lung Hsin-chieh teng ti chiu jih wen wu'; in *I pa ssu erh nien i ch'ien chih Hsiang-kang chi ch'i tui wai chiao t'ung: Hsiang-kang ch'ien tai shih*, edited by Lo Hsiang-lin; Hong Kong: Chung-kuo hsüeh she, 1959, 193–220. In *Hong Kong and its external communications before 1842*, edited by Lo Hsiang-lin. [Selective entry]
Hong Kong: Institute of Chinese Culture, 1963, 133–152.
SUBJ 17 26.1 ▪ 63

14597 MSE O P2 G9.5 1842–1895
Lobscheid, William.
A few notices on the extent of Chinese education and the government schools of Hongkong . . .
Hong Kong: China Mail Office, 1859. 48 p.
SUBJ 17 26 ▪ 23 26.1 26.3 33 47 62 64 66

14598 CSU P P1 G1.2 1644–1911
Lui, Adam Yuen-chung (Lü Yüan-ch'ung), 1940–.
'The education of the Manchus, China's ruling race, 1644–1911.'
JAAS 6, 2 (Apr. 1971), 126–133.
SUBJ 17

14599 ELS P P2 G1.2 1644–1842
Lui, Adam Yuen-chung (Lü Yüan-ch'ung), 1940–.
The Han-Lin Academy: A biographical approach to career patterns in the early Ch'ing, 1644–1795.
Unpublished doctoral dissertation in History, U. of London [School of Oriental and African Studies], 1968. 443 p.
SUBJ 12 17 30 ▪ 16 16.1 57

14600 MCH U P1 G1.1 1842–1895
Martello, Tullio, 1841–?
Studio di confronto fra le università tedesche, inglesi e chinesi (A comparative study of the German, English, and Chinese university).
Milan: Valentiner, 1873. 32 p.
SUBJ 17 ▪ 16

14601 CSU O P3 G1.2 1842–1911
Martin, William Alexander Parsons, 1827–1916.
'The Imperial Academy.' In *The lore of Cathay: or, The intellect of China*, by W. A. P. Martin. [Selective entry]
New York: Revell, 1901, 329–370. [Reprinted in *The lore of Cathay: or, The intellect of China*, by W. A. P. Martin. (Selective entry.) Taipei: Ch'eng-wen, 1971, 329–370.]
SUBJ 12 17 36.1 ▪ 13 62

14602 CSU PO P3 G5.1 1644–1911
Martin, William Alexander Parsons, 1827–1916.
'An old university in China [Kuo-tzu chien, Peking].' In *The lore of Cathay: or, The intellect of China*, by W. A. P. Martin. [Selective entry]
New York: Revell, 1901, 371–383. [Reprinted in *The lore of Cathay: or, The intellect of China*, by W. A. P. Martin. (Selective entry.) Taipei: Ch'eng-wen, 1971, 371–383.]
SUBJ 17

14603 CSU O P2 G1.2 1842–1911
Martin, William Alexander Parsons, 1827–1916.
'School and family training.' In *The lore of Cathay: or, The intellect of China*, by W. A. P. Martin. [Selective entry]
New York: Revell, 1901, 281–307. [Reprinted in *The lore of Cathay: or, The intellect of China*, by W. A. P. Martin. (Selective entry.) Taipei: Ch'eng-wen, 1971, 281–307.]
SUBJ 17 ▪ 12 52

14604 CSU O P3 G5.1 1842–1895
Martin, William Alexander Parsons, 1827–1916.
'The Tungwen [Interpreters] College.' In *The international relations of the Chinese empire, Vol. 3, The period of subjection, 1894–1911*, by Hosea Ballou Morse. [Sole entry]
London: Longmans, Green, 1918, 471–478.
SUBJ 17 66

14605 MCH P P1 G1.2 1895–1911
Maybon, Albert, 1878–.
'La réforme scolaire en Chine' (Educational reform in China).
R. mondiale 68 (15 nov. 1907), 228–242.
SUBJ 17 ▪ 58

14606 NNC PO P3 G6.3 1842–1895
Moule, George Evans, 1828–1912.
'Notes on the provincial examination of Chekiang of 1870, with a version of one of the essays.'
JRAS-NCB new (2nd) series 6 (1869/70), 129–138.
SUBJ 17 60 ▪ 12

14607 MCH P P1 G1.2 1895–1911
Ouang Ki-tseng (Wang Chi-tseng).
'La réforme de l'enseignement en Chine: son caractère et ses tendances' (The

nature and direction of educational reform in China).
Annales des sciences politiques 24, 3 (mai 1909), 396–404.
SUBJ 17

14608 NIC P P1 G1.2 1842–1895
Oxenham, Edward Lavington.
'Ages of candidates at Chinese examinations: Tabular statement.'
JRAS-CB new (2nd) series 23, 3 (1888), 286–287.
SUBJ 16.1 17 50

14609 CSU PO P3 G6.1 1842–1895
Parker, Alvin P-, 1850–1924.
'The government colleges of Suchow.'
CR 24, 11 (Nov. 1893), 534–540; 24, 12 (Dec. 1893), 579–584.
SUBJ 17

14610 CSH P P3 G5.1 1842–1911
Paterno, Roberto Montilla, 1936–.
'Devello Z. Sheffield and the founding of the North China College.'
PC 14 (Dec. 1960), 110–160. [Reprinted in *American missionaries in China: Papers from Harvard seminars*, edited by Kwang-ching Liu (Liu Kuang-ching). (Analytic entry.) Cambridge: Harvard U., East Asian Research Center, 1966, 42–92. (Harvard East Asian monographs, 21)]
SUBJ 17 ▪ 66

14611 MCH U P4 G1.2 1895–1911
Pelliot, Paul, 1878–1945.
'La réforme des examens littéraires en Chine' (The reform of the examination system in China).
AF 3, 25 (avr. 1903), 160–165.
SUBJ 12 17

14612 MBA S P2 G1.2 1895–1911
Péri, Noël.
'L'éducation nouvelle en Chine' (The new educational system in China).
R. de Paris 14, 11 (1er juin 1907), 473–494; 14, 12 (15 juin 1907), 873–894. [Reprinted—*RI* nouvelle (2e) série 5, 66 (30 sept. 1907), 1285–1301; 5, 67 (15 oct. 1907), 1382–1398.]
SUBJ 17 ▪ 11.4 15 47 64 66

14613 CSU P P1 G1.2 1842–1895
Pilcher, Leander W-, 1848–1893.
'The new education in China.'
CR 20, 7 (July 1889), 305–310; 20, 8 (Aug. 1889), 343–348; 20, 9 (Sept. 1889), 403–410.
SUBJ 17 66 ▪ 37 62

14614 MCH O P2 G1.2 1895–1911
Pott, Francis Lister Hawks, 1864–1947.
'China's method of revising her educational system.'
AAAPSS 39 (Jan. 1912), 83–96.
SUBJ 17

14615 CSU O P2 G5.0 1895–1911
Smith, Arthur Henderson, 1845–1932.
'The school system of China.'
EAM 3 (1904), 1–10.
SUBJ 17 ▪ 16.1

14616 MBA P P3 G8.2 1895–1911
[Soulié de Morant, Charles Georges?] G. S., 1878–.
'L'instruction publique à Yuannan-fou' (Public education in Yün-nan-fu [i.e., Kunming]).
RI nouvelle (2e) série 10, 85 (15 juil. 1908), 1–10.
SUBJ 17 ▪ 66

14617 CSU P P4 G1.2 1644–1911
Taam, Cheuk-woon (T'an Cho-yüan), 1900–1956.
The development of Chinese libraries under the Ch'ing dynasty, 1644–1911.
Shanghai: The author, 1935. 107 p. (Doctoral dissertation in Library Science, U. of Chicago, 1933)
SUBJ 17 ▪ 16.1 32.1

14618 MCH P P1 G1.2 1895–1911
Tobar, Jérôme, 1855–1917.
'La réforme des études en Chine' (Educational reform in China).
Etudes 7e série 97, 5 (5 déc. 1903), 703–717.
SUBJ 17 ▪ 37

14619 MCY PO P1 G1.2 1895–1911
Wang Feng-gang (Huang Fang-kang), 1901–.
Japanese influence on education reform in China, from 1895 to 1911.
Peiping: Author's Book Store, 1933. 204 p. (Doctoral dissertation in Education, Stanford U., 1931)
SUBJ 17

14620 NNC S P1 G1.1 1842–1911
Wang, Y. C. (Wang I-chü; Wang Chi-ch'ien), 1916–.
'Education, modernization, and profiteering.' [Review of *The earliest modern government schools in China*, by Knight Biggerstaff.]
JAS 24, 2 (Feb. 1965), 299–303.
SUBJ 17

14621 CSH PO P1 G1.1 –1895
Williams, Samuel Wells, 1812–1884.
'Education and literary examinations.' In *The Middle Kingdom: A survey of the geography, government, literature, social life, arts, and history of the Chinese empire and its inhabitants*, rev. and enl. ed., by S. W. Williams. [Selective entry]
New York: Scribner, 1883, vol. 1, 519–577. [Reprinted in *The Middle Kingdom: A survey of the geography, government, literature, social life, arts, and history of the Chinese empire and its inhabitants*, by S. W. Williams. (Selective entry.) Taipei: Ch'eng-wen, 1965, 519–577 (s.p.)]
SUBJ 16.1 17 ▪ 12 47

14622 NNC P P1 G1.2 1895–1911
Wolfe, Alan D-.
The development of modern education in China, 1898–1912.
Unpublished masters thesis in Chinese and Japanese, Columbia U., 1950. 115 p.
SUBJ 17

14623 CSU U P1 G1.2 –1911
Wong, V. L. (Huang Wei-lien).
'Libraries and book-collecting in China from the epoch of the Five Dynasties to the end of Ch'ing.'
THM 8, 4 (Apr. 1939), 327–343.
SUBJ 17 ▪ 14.2

14624 CSU O P3 G9.5 1842–1911
Wright, G- H- Bateson.
'Education.' In *Twentieth century impressions of Hongkong, Shanghai, and other treaty ports of China: Their history, people, commerce, industries and manners*, edited by Arnold Wright and H- A- Cartwright. [Selective entry]
London: Lloyd's Greater Britain Publishing Co., 1908, 121–128.
SUBJ 17

14625 CSU U P3 G5.1 1895–1911
Yen, Weiching William (Yen Hui-ch'ing), 1877–1950.
'The recent imperial metropolitan examinations.'
CR 38, 1 (Jan. 1907), 34–39.
SUBJ 12 17

14626 NNC P P1 G1.2 1895–1911
Young, Samuel Sung.
Chinese education, old and new.
Unpublished masters thesis in Education, Columbia U., 1905. 68 p.
SUBJ 17 ▪ 47

14627 MCH P P1 G1.1 –1895
Zi, Etienne, 1851–?
Pratique des examens littéraires en Chine (The examination system in China).
Shanghai: Impr. de la Mission catholique, 1894. 278 p. (Variétés sinologiques, 5) [Reprinted—Taipei: Ch'eng-wen, 1971. 278 p.]
SUBJ 12 16.1 17 ▪ 12.2 15 60

1644-1949

14628 CSH FP P2 G1.2 1895–1928
'Education.' In *The Christian occupation of China*, edited by Milton Theobald Stauffer. [Selective entry]
Shanghai: China Continuation Committee, 1922, 399–428.
SUBJ 17 ▪ 12.1 14.5 16 37 47

14629 NNM PO P4 G9.0 1644–1949
Anderson, Mary Raleigh, 1878–.
Protestant mission schools for girls in South China (1827 to the Japanese invasion).
Mobile, Alabama: Heiter-Starke, 1943. 365 p. (Doctoral dissertation in Education, Columbia U. [Teachers College], 1943)
SUBJ 17 47 ▪ 27 33

14630 CSH PO P3 G8.1 1895–1949
Beech, Joseph.
'University beginnings: A story of the West China Union University [Chengtu].'
JWCBRS 6 (1933/34), 91–104.
SUBJ 17

14631 NIC O P4 G1.2 1895–1928
Blume, William Wirt, 1893–.
'Legal education in China.'
CLR 1, 7 (Oct. 1923), 305–311.
SUBJ 12.2 17

14632 NNC O P3 G5.1 1895–1928
Bolt, Richard Arthur, 1880–1959.
'The Tsing-hua College, Peking.'
JAAA 15, 4 (May 1915), 108–112.
SUBJ 17 ▪ 66

14633 MCH O P4 G1.2 1895–1928
Borel, Claude.
'L'enseignement en Chine' (Education in China).
B. de la Société de géographie de Marseille 37 (1913), 192–197.
SUBJ 17

14634 WSU F P3 G8.1 1895–1928
Brethorst, Alice Beatrice, 1885?–.
A study of the school system of Chengtu, West China.
Unpublished doctoral dissertation in Education, U. of Washington, 1931. 2 vols. 312 p. [c.p.]
SUBJ 17 20 ▪ 24 28 32 37

14635 ICU O P5 G6.2 1895–1928
Buck, Frank Cornelius, 1884–1950.
The moral value of the Chinese classical educational system, including an estimate of the civil service examinations.
Unpublished masters thesis in Religious Education, U. of Chicago, 1917. 56 p.
SUBJ 17 63 64 ▪ 16.1

14636 NNP U P3 G9.5 1842–1949
Burney, Edmond.
Report on education in Hong Kong.
London: Government of Hong Kong, 1935. 27 p.
SUBJ 17 ▪ 22

14637 FPN P P1 G1.2 1644–1949
Chen Hsien Mei.
Système des examens en Chine de 1911 à 1950 (The Chinese examination system from 1911 to 1950).
Unpublished doctoral dissertation, Faculté des lettres, Université de Paris, 1966. 251 p.
SUBJ 12 17

14638 ICU P P2 G1.2 1895–1928
Cheng, Chi-pao (Ch'eng Ch'i-pao), 1897–.
The training of teachers in China (with special reference to the normal schools).
Unpublished masters thesis in Education, U. of Chicago, 1922. 68 p.
SUBJ 17 ▪ 16.1

14639 NIC S P1 G1.3 1895–1928
Cheng, Chi-pao (Ch'eng Ch'i-pao), 1897–.
'Twenty-five years of modern education in China.'
CSPSR 12, 3 (July 1928), 451–470.
SUBJ 17 62

14640 NNC PO P2 G1.2 1895–1949
Cheng, Ronald Yu-soong (Ch'en Yu-sung), 1903–.
The financing of public education in China: A factual analysis of its major problems of reconstruction.
Shanghai: Commercial Press, 1935. 26, 300 p. (Doctoral dissertation in Education, Columbia U.)
SUBJ 14 14.5 17 ▪ 21 37 64 72

14641 NNC O P3 G5.1 1895–1949
Chiang, Fu-tsung, 1898–.
'Überblick über das moderne chinesische Bibliothekswesen, mit besonderer Berücksichtigung der Nationalbibliothek in Peking' (Survey of modern Chinese libraries, with special attention to the National Library in Peking).
Sinica 7, 2 (März 1932), 49–55.
SUBJ 17 ▪ 70

14642 DLC P P1 G1.2 –1928
Chiang Monlin (Chiang Meng-lin), 1886–1964.
A study in Chinese principles of education.
Shanghai: Commercial Press, 1918. 196 p. (Doctoral dissertation in Education, Columbia U., 1917) [Reprinted—Shanghai: Commercial Press, 1924. 196 p.] [Reprinted as *Chinese culture and education: A historical and comparative survey*. Taipei: World Book Co., 1963. 187, 35 p.]
SUBJ 17 62 ▪ 12.1 63

14643 CSU P P1 G1.2 –1928
Chin, F. (Ch'in Fen), and V. K. Ting (Ting Wen-chiang), 1887–1936.
'Higher education in China.' Tr. from the Chinese [tr. of an unpublished manuscript]. In *Education in China: Papers contributed by the members of committees of the Society for the Study of International Education*, edited by T. Y. Teng (Teng Ts'ui-ying) and Timothy Tingfang Lew (Liu T'ing-fang). [Selective entry]
Peking: Society for the Study of International Education, 1923, 1–21 [s.p.].
SUBJ 17

14644 NIC P P1 G1.2 1895–1928
Chu, Jennings P. (Chu Pin-k'uei), 1895–.
'Normal school education in China.'
BCE 2, 11 (1923), 1–24.
SUBJ 17

14645 NNC P P1 G1.2 1895–1949
Chu, K. (Chu Ching-nun).
'Education.' In *Symposium on Chinese culture*, edited by Sophia H. Chen Zen (Jen Ch'en Heng-che). [Selective entry]
Shanghai: China Institute of Pacific Relations, 1931, 206–223. [Reprinted in *Symposium on Chinese culture*, edited by S. H. C. Zen. (Selective entry.) New York: Paragon, 1969, 206–223.]
SUBJ 17 62 ▪ 47 64 66

14646 MCH P P3 G6.0 1895–1928
Claugherty, Francis Xavier.
'The development of education in China.'
B. of the Catholic U. of Peking 3 (1927), 41–60.
SUBJ 17 ▪ 16.1 60

14647 NIC P P2 G1.2 1895–1949
Djung, Lu-dzai (Chung Lu-chai), 1899–.
A history of democratic education in modern China.
Shanghai: Commercial Press, 1934. 33, 258 p. (Revision of *Democratic tendencies in the development of modern education in China*, doctoral dissertation in Education, Stanford U., 1930)
SUBJ 17 ▪ 37 47

14648 MCH U P1 G1.1 –1949
Duyvendak, Jan Julius Lodewijk, 1889–1954.
'De beteekenis der Chineesche universiteiten' (The importance of Chinese universities).
Het Kouter (Arnhem) 2, 1 (Januari 1937), 430–441. [Reprinted—*China* (Amsterdam) 12, 2 (Maart 1938), 49–59.]
SUBJ 16.1 17 ▪ 62 64

14649 NIC P P3 G1.3 1895–1949
Edwards, Dwight Woodbridge.
Yenching University.
New York: United Board for Christian Higher Education in Asia, 1959. 12, 468 p.
SUBJ 17 ▪ 18 54

14650 DLC S P1 G1.2 1895–1949
Ershov, Matvei Nikolaevich.
Sovremennyi Kitai i evropeiskaia kul'tura (Contemporary China and European culture).
Harbin: ——, 1931. 34 p.
SUBJ 17 47 ▪ 16 40 62 66

14651 NIC S P1 G1.2 –1928
Galt, Howard Spilman, 1872–?
'Oriental and Occidental elements in China's modern educational system.'
CSPSR 12, 3 (July 1928), 405–425; 12, 4 (Oct. 1928), 627–647; 13, 1 (Jan. 1929), 12–29.
SUBJ 16.1 17 62 64

14652 CSH PO P2 G1.2 1644–1949
Gregg, Alice Henrietta, 1893–.
China and educational autonomy: The changing role of the Protestant educational missionary in China, 1807–1937.
Syracuse: Syracuse U. Press, 1946. 283 p. [Reprinted—Ann Arbor: University Microfilms, n.d. 283 p.]
SUBJ 17 19 33 66 ▪ 32.2 34.3 60

14653 NIC O P4 G1.2 1842–1949
Hail, William James, 1877–.
'Education, past and present.'
AAAPSS 152 (Nov. 1930), 47–54. [Special issue: *China*, edited by Henry F. James]
SUBJ 17 ▪ 37 54

14654 ELS P P2 G1.1 –1949
Ho, Tsi-Dsi Irene (Ho Ch'i-tzu).
Ancient and modern educational theory in China.
Unpublished doctoral dissertation in Education, U. of London [Institute of Education], 1936. 470, 131 p.
SUBJ 17 64 ▪ 47

14655 NNM P P1 G1.2 1842–1949
Hockin, Katharine Boehner, 1910–.
Christian and national influences in the development of modern Chinese education . . .
Unpublished masters thesis in Theology, Columbia U., 1947. 112 p.
SUBJ 17 ▪ 32.1 33 47 66

14656 MCH P P2 G1.3 1895–1949
Hsiao, Theodore E. (Hsiao En-ch'eng), 1899–.
The history of modern education in China.
Peiping: Peking U. Press, 1932. 14, 164 p. (Revision of doctoral dissertation in Education, New York U., 1925) [Reprinted—Shanghai: Commercial Press, 1935. 145 p.]
SUBJ 17 37 ▪ 16 32.1 47

14657 CSU P P2 G1.1 1842–1949
Hsü, Stephan Chi-wei, 1924–.
Die Pädagogik von Ts'ai Yüan-p'ei: Die Begegnung zwischen der europäischen und chinesischen Kultur im Bereich der Bildung und Erziehung (The educational theory of Ts'ai Yüan-p'ei:

The meeting of European and Chinese civilization in the field of socialization and education).
[Münster?]: The author, 1969. 119 p. (Doctoral dissertation, Philosophische Fakultät, Universität Münster)
SUBJ 17 63 ▪ 47 62

14658 CSU P P2 G1.2 1842–1928
Hwang, Pu (Huang P'u), 1896–.
The new educational organization of China.
Unpublished masters thesis in Education, Stanford U., 1920. 163 p.
SUBJ 17 ▪ 14.5 16.1

14659 MAM P P2 G1.2 1895–1949
Kiang, Ying-cheng (Chiang Ying-ch'eng), 1913–.
The geography of higher education in China.
Ann Arbor: University Microfilms (Publ. 12,310), 1955. 10, 282 p. (Doctoral dissertation in Education, Columbia U.)
SUBJ 17 ▪ 11.3 47

14660 MCY P P2 G1.3 1895–1949
Kuhn, Philip Alden, 1933–.
'T'ao Hsing-chih, 1891–1946: An educational reformer.'
PC 13 (Dec. 1959), 163–195.
SUBJ 17 59 62 ▪ 14.2 37 66

14661 MCH P P1 G1.2 1842–1928
Kuo, Ping-wen, 1880–1969.
The Chinese system of public education.
New York: Columbia U., Teachers College, 1915. 12, 209 p. (TC contributions to education, 64) (Doctoral dissertation in Education, Columbia U., 1914)
SUBJ 17 60 ▪ 12.1 16.1 66

14662 NIC O P3 G1.2 1895–1928
Kuo, Ping-wen, 1880–1969.
'Higher education in China.'
BCE 2, 10 (1923), 1–24.
SUBJ 17

14663 NNC U P1 G1.2 1842–1949
Kuo, Tze-hsiung.
'Higher education in China.'
IB 3, 2 (21 Jan. 1937), 29–50.
SUBJ 17 ▪ 12.2 62 66

14664 NNC S P1 G1.2 1895–1949
Kuo, Tze-hsiung.
'Secondary education in China.'
IB 4, 2 (26 May 1936), 21–45.
SUBJ 17 ▪ 12.2

14665 CSH PO P3 G6.1 1842–1949
Lamberton, Mary, 1883–.
St. John's University, Shanghai, 1879–1951.
New York: United Board for Christian Colleges in China, 1955. 261 p.
SUBJ 17 ▪ 32.1 38 54 66

14666 NIC P P5 G1.2 1895–1928
[Liao Mou-ju] S. C. Liao (Liao Shih-ch'eng), 1892?–.
'Middle school education in China.'
BCE 2, 12 (1923), 1–14.
SUBJ 17

14667 CSU P P1 G1.2 1895–1928
Lin, Li-Ju, et al.
'Secondary education in China.' Tr. from the Chinese [tr. of an unpublished manuscript]. In *Education in China: Papers contributed by the members of committees of the Society for the Study of International Education*, edited by T. Y. Teng (Teng Ts'ui-ying) and Timothy Tingfang Lew (Liu T'ing-fang). [Selective entry]
Peking: Society for the Study of International Education, 1923, 1–20 [s.p.].
SUBJ 17

14668 WSU O P2 G6.1 1895–1928
Liu, Chi Hung, 1903–.
A study of modern education in Kiangsu province, China.
Unpublished masters thesis in Education, U. of Washington, 1932. 129 p.
SUBJ 17 ▪ 22.1

14669 NNC P P1 G1.2 1895–1949
Liu, Han.
Etude sur la réforme de l'éducation contemporaine en Chine (A study of the reform of contemporary Chinese education).
Paris: E. Muller, 1933. 129 p. (Doctoral dissertation, Faculté des lettres, Université de Paris)
SUBJ 17

14670 MAM P P4 G1.2 –1949
Lund, Renville Clifton, 1923–.
The Imperial University of Peking.
Ann Arbor: University Microfilms (Publ. 21,207), 1957. 363 p. (Doctoral dissertation in History, U. of Washington)
SUBJ 16.1 17 32 66 ▪ 37 62

14671 CSU P P4 G1.3 1842–1949
Lutz, Jessie Gregory, 1925–.
China and the Christian colleges, 1850–1950.
Ithaca: Cornell U. Press, 1971. 13, 575 p.
SUBJ 17 ▪ 54 66

14672 NNC PO P1 G1.1 –1949
Ly, Juwan Usang.
'New and old education in China.'
CJ 32, 5 (May 1940), 174–182; 32, 6 (June 1940), 238–246.
SUBJ 17 60

14673 NNC P P1 G1.2 1842–1928
Monina, A- A-.
'Deiatel'nosti inostrannykh missionerov v oblasti obrazovaniia v Kitae (1901–1920 gg.)' (Foreign missionaries' activities in the field of education in China, 1901–1920).
KSINA 85 (1964), 102–114.
SUBJ 17 ▪ 33 66

14674 MCH O P2 G1.2 1895–1928
Monroe, Paul, 1869–1947.
'Report on education in China, 1922.' In *Essays in comparative education*, by P. Monroe. [Sole entry]
New York: Columbia U., Teachers College, 1927, 50–87.
SUBJ 17 ▪ 37 54 66

14675 CSH PO P3 G6.1 1842–1949
Nance, Walter Buckner, 1868–?
Soochow University.
New York: United Board for Christian Colleges in China, 1956. 163 p.
SUBJ 17 ▪ 25 54

14676 NNC S P3 G1.1 1842–1928
Paragon, Donald.
'Ying Lien-chih (1899–1926) and the rise of Fu Jen, the Catholic University of Peking.'
MS 20 (1961), 165–225. (Revision of masters thesis in Chinese and Japanese, Columbia U., 1958)
SUBJ 17 59 ▪ 26.1 33 63

14677 NNC P P1 G1.2 1842–1949
Peake, Cyrus Henderson, 1900–.
Nationalism and education in modern China.
New York: Columbia U. Press, 1932. 14, 240 p.
SUBJ 17 32.1 62 ▪ 15 37 64

14678 FPN S P3 G1.2 1895–1949
Pélissier, Roger, 1924–1972.
Les bibliothèques en Chine pendant la première partie du XXe siècle (Libraries in China in the early twentieth century).
Unpublished doctoral dissertation, Faculté des lettres, Université de Paris, 1969. 2 vols. 319; 206 p.
SUBJ 17 37 70 72 ▪ 32

14679 ICU P P1 G1.1 1842–1949
Poston, David Gray, 1906–.
The foundation and control of missionary education in China.
Unpublished masters thesis in History, U. of Chicago, 1937. 130 p.
SUBJ 17 32.1 66

14680 MCY O P4 G1.3 1842–1949
Pott, Francis Lister Hawks, 1864–1947.
'Modern education.' In *China*, edited by Harley Farnsworth MacNair. [Selective entry]
Berkeley, Los Angeles: U. of California Press, 1946, 427–440. [Reprinted in *China*, edited by H. F. MacNair. (Selective entry.) Freeport, N.Y.: Books for Libraries, 1970, 427–440.]
SUBJ 17 ▪ 54 64 66

14681 NIC PO P1 G1.2 –1949
Purcell, Victor William Williams Saunders, 1896–1965.
Problems of Chinese education.
London: Kegan Paul, Trench, Trübner, 1936. 261 p. (Revision of *Education in modern China, with special reference to the influence upon it of Western civilization*, doctoral dissertation in Oriental Languages, U. of Cambridge [Trinity College], 1935)
SUBJ 17 64 ▪ 16.1 32.1 37 47 62 66

14682 MCH P P1 G7.2 1895–1928
Reeves, William, Jr., 1934–.
'Sino-American cooperation in medicine: The origins of Hsiang-ya, 1902–1914.'
PC 14 (Dec. 1960), 161–214. [Reprinted in *American missionaries in China: Papers from Harvard seminars*, edited by Kwang-ching Liu (Liu Kuang-ching). (Analytic entry.) Cambridge: Harvard U., East Asian Research Center, 1966, 129–182. (Harvard East Asian monographs, 21)]
SUBJ 17 56 66

14683 WSU S P1 G1.2 1644–1928
Rugh, Arthur Douglas, 1907–.
American influence in China's changing education.

Unpublished doctoral dissertation in Education, U. of Washington, 1940. 207 p.
SUBJ 17 66 ▪ 54

14684 MCH P P1 G1.2 1895–1949
Sakai, Robert Kenjiro (Sakai Kenjirō), 1919–.
Politics and education in modern China.
Unpublished doctoral dissertation in History, Harvard U., 1953. 319 p.
SUBJ 12.1 17 ▪ 12 16.1 19 64 66

14685 NNC O P2 G1.2 1895–1949
Stuart, John Leighton, 1876–1962.
Fifty years in China: The memoirs of John Leighton Stuart, missionary and ambassador.
New York: Random House, 1954. 20, 346 p.
SUBJ 17 54 66 ▪ 15

14686 CBC P P1 G1.2 1895–1949
Sun, Huai Chin, 1904–.
A study of Chinese secondary education, with a suggested program for reorganization.
Unpublished doctoral dissertation in Education, U. of Colorado, 1949. 421 p.
SUBJ 17 ▪ 14 18 32 41 64

14687 NNU PO P2 G1.2 –1949
Taai, Wai-king (Tai Wei-chin), 1898–.
Adolescent education in China.
Unpublished doctoral dissertation in Education, New York U., 1939. 171 p.
SUBJ 17 64 ▪ 12.1 12.2 34.2 41 42 63

14688 PPU P P1 G1.2 1842–1949
Tan, Jen-mei (T'an Jen-mei), 1908–.
History of modern Chinese secondary education.
Unpublished doctoral dissertation in Education, U. of Pennsylvania, 1940. 248 p.
SUBJ 17 ▪ 37 47 66

14689 CSU P P1 G1.2 –1928
Teng, T. Y. (Teng Ts'ui-ying), 1885–1947, W. P. Wang, and C. C. Wu.
'The development of the modern educational system in China.' Tr. from the Chinese [tr. of an unpublished manuscript]. In *Education in China: Papers contributed by the members of committees of the Society for the Study of International Education*, edited by T. Y. Teng and Timothy Tingfang Lew (Liu T'ing-fang). [Selective entry]
Peking: Society for the Study of International Education, 1923, 1–19 [s.p.].
SUBJ 17 ▪ 47

14690 CSU P P1 G1.2 1895–1928
Teng, T. Y. (Teng Ts'ui-ying), 1885–1947, M. T. Wong, and *Mrs.* M. T. Wong.
'Training of teachers in China.' Tr. from the Chinese [tr. of an unpublished manuscript]. In *Education in China: Papers contributed by the members of committees of the Society for the Study of International Education*, edited by T. Y. Teng and Timothy Tingfang Lew (Liu T'ing-fang). [Selective entry]
Peking: Society for the Study of International Education, 1923, 1–27 [s.p.].
SUBJ 17 ▪ 47

14691 NNF P P1 G1.2 1842–1949
Tsai, Mark (Ts'ai Jen-yü), 1908–.
Vital problems in modern Chinese education, 1862–1945.
Unpublished doctoral dissertation in Education, Fordham U., 1951. 161 p.
SUBJ 17 ▪ 12.1 12.2 37

14692 NNC P P1 G1.2 1644–1949
Tsang, Chiu-sam (Tseng Chao-sen), 1901–.
Nationalism in school education in China, 2nd ed.
Hong Kong: Progressive Education Publishers, 1967. 247 p. (Revision of *Nationalism in school education in China since the opening of the twentieth century*, doctoral dissertation in Education, Columbia U., 1933)
SUBJ 17 60 64 66 ▪ 11.2 12.1 32 32.2 62 72

14693 NNC FP P4 G1.2 1842–1928
Twiss, George Ransom, 1863–1944.
Science and education in China: A survey of the present status and a program for progressive improvement.
Shanghai: Commercial Press, 1925. 361 p.
SUBJ 17 62 ▪ 16.2 32 32.1 37

14694 ICU P P4 G1.1 1842–1949
Van Putten, James Dyke, 1899–.
Christian higher education in China: Survey of the historical developments and its contributions to Chinese life.
Unpublished doctoral dissertation in International Relations, U. of Chicago, 1934. 10, 472 p.
SUBJ 14.2 17 33 66 ▪ 12.1 14 18 37 47

14695 WSU S P1 G1.2 1644–1949
Wang, Hsiu-chin.
Popular library movement in China in the last thirty years.
Unpublished masters thesis in Librarianship, U. of Washington, 1952. 84 p.
SUBJ 17 37 ▪ 32.1

14696 MCH P P1 G1.1 1842–1949
Wong Yin-kon.
L'instruction publique de la Chine moderne (Public education in modern China).
Paris: Presses modernes, 1932. 171 p. (Doctoral dissertation, Faculté des lettres, Université de Montpellier)
SUBJ 17 ▪ 37 47 54 62 64 66 72

14697 NIC O P2 G1.2 1842–1928
Wong-Quincey, J. (Wang Wen-hsien), 1886–.
'Modern education in China.'
THJ 2, 7 (May 1917), 155–171. [Reprinted in *Present day impressions of the Far East and prominent and progressive Chinese at home and abroad*, edited by W- Feldwick. (Sole entry.) London: Globe Encyclopedia, 1917, 83–92.]
SUBJ 17 ▪ 37

14698 MAM P P1 G1.1 1895–1949
Wu, Chih-kang, 1915–.
The influence of the YMCA on the development of physical education in China.
Ann Arbor: University Microfilms (Publ. 58-1019), 1958. 211 p. (Doctoral dissertation in Education, U. of Michigan)
SUBJ 17 31 33 38 54 ▪ 30 62

14699 ELS P P1 G1.1 –1949
Yen, Yuen-chang (Yen Yüan-chang), 1909–.
Comparative educational background: A study of historic, geographic, cultural, economic and political factors in the development of Chinese and English education.
Unpublished doctoral dissertation in Educational Administration, U. of London [King's College], 1951. 298 p.
SUBJ 17 60 64 ▪ 19 63

14700 NNC P P2 G1.2 1895–1928
Yin, Chiling (Yin Chih-ling), 1897–.
Reconstruction of modern educational organizations in China.
Shanghai: Commercial Press, 1924. 18, 171 p. (Doctoral dissertation in Education, New York U., 1923)
SUBJ 17 ▪ 14.5

14701 NNC O P3 G5.1 1895–1928
Young, Kwang-sheng.
'A historical sketch of Chinese drama and modern dramatic movement in Tsing-Hua.'
THJ 5, 11 (Feb. 1920), 45–59.
SUBJ 17 31 ▪ 64

14702 CSU U P1 G1.2 1895–1949
Yu, Chên-ming (Yü Chen-min).
'Education chronicle.'
THM 11, 5 (Apr.–May 1941), 476–479.
SUBJ 17

14703 PPU S P2 G1.2 1895–1949
Zen, Wei-ts (Shen Wei-chih), 1896–.
The role of education in postwar China.
Unpublished doctoral dissertation in Education, U. of Pennsylvania, 1945. 199 p. [Extracts from Chaps. 5 and 6 separately published under same title—Philadelphia: The author, 1946. 39 p.]
SUBJ 14 17 32 32.2 ▪ 11 12.1 16 18 36.4 41 66

1911-1949

14704 CSH P P2 G1.2 1911–1928
'Agricultural colleges in China.'
CEM 1, 8 (May 1924), 5–11.
SUBJ 17 36.1

14705 NNC P P3 G6.1 1911–1928
'Stiftung "Deutsche Medizinschule für Chinesen in Schanghai"' (The founding of the German School of Medicine for Chinese in Shanghai).
China-Archiv 2, 11 (24 Nov. 1917), 590–593.
SUBJ 17

14706 NNC O P2 G1.2 1911–1949
Adolph, William Henry.
'Chemistry in China.'
Chemical and engineering news 24, 18 (25 Sept. 1946), 2494–2498.
SUBJ 17 62

14707 MCH PO P2 G1.2 1928–1949
Arens, Richard, 1912–.
'Das Schulwesen in China, mit besonderer Berücksichtigung der Schulverhältnisse in Nordchina' (China's educational system, with special attention to educational conditions in North China).

Missionswissenschaft und Religionswissenschaft 33, 2 (1949), 92–103.
Subj 17 ▪ 32.2

14708 MCH O P3 G1.2 1911–1928
Ariëns Kappers, Cornelis Ubbo, 1877–1946.
'Een en ander over medische scholen in China' (Some remarks about medical schools in China).
China (Amsterdam) 1 (1925), 135–156.
Subj 17 56 ▪ 43

14709 NNC O P2 G1.1 1928–1949
Bates, Miner Searle, 1897–.
'The task of education in China.'
PA 19, 2 (June 1946), 131–145.
Subj 17

14710 MCY P P1 G1.1 1911–1949
Borowitz, Albert Ira, 1930–.
'Chiang Monlin: Theory and practice of Chinese education, 1917–1930.'
PC 8 (Feb. 1954), 107–135.
Subj 17 59 ▪ 16.1 62 64 66

14711 CSH P P3 G9.2 1911–1928
Chan, Wellington K. K. (Ch'en Chin-chiang), 1940–.
'Problems of a Christian missionary college in China: Lingnan College [Canton], 1919–1925.'
CCJ 8, 2 (May 1969), 1–15.
Subj 17 ▪ 32.2 33 54

14712 NIC P P2 G5.1 1928–1949
Chang, Pe Chin (Chang Po-ch'in), 1899–.
The administrative reorganization of the educational system of a county in China, based on the analysis of Cheng Ting hsien [Hopei].
Unpublished doctoral dissertation in Education, Cornell U., 1935. 124 p.
Subj 17 24 ▪ 14.5 21 21.4 24.2

14713 NNC O P2 G1.2 1928–1949
Chang, Pe Chin (Chang Po-ch'in), 1899–.
'Redirecting educational effort in China.'
PA 6, 6/7 (June–July 1933), 281–291.
Subj 17

14714 NNC P P1 G6.1 1911–1928
Chang, Zah-ling.
The administration of public education in Kiangsu province, covering a period of five years from November, 1911, to December, 1916.
Unpublished masters thesis in Education, Columbia U. [Teachers College], 1918. 20 p.
Subj 17 ▪ 14.5

14715 CSH P P2 G1.2 1911–1949
Chen, Theodore H. E. (Ch'en Hsi-en), 1902–.
'Education in China, 1927–1937' [with comments by Chi-pao Cheng]. In *The strenuous decade: China's nation-building efforts, 1927–1937*, edited by Paul K. T. Sih (Hsüeh Kuang-ch'ien). [Selective entry]
Jamaica, N.Y.: St. John's U. Press, 1970, 289–315.
Subj 17 ▪ 32.1 54

14716 NNC P P1 G1.2 1928–1949
Chen, Theodore H. E. (Ch'en Hsi-en), 1902–.
'Educational control in China.'
Hsieh ta j. 3 (Aug. 1935), 1–16 [s.p.].
Subj 17 ▪ 12.1

14717 NIC O P4 G5.1 1928–1949
Ch'en, C. C. (Ch'en Chih-ch'ien).
'An experiment in health education in Chinese county schools.'
MMFQ 12, 3 (July 1934), 232–247.
Subj 17 28 56

14718 DLC PO P1 G1.2 1928–1949
Ch'en, Li-fu, 1899–.
Chinese education during the war (1937–42).
Chungking: Hsing cheng yüan, Chiao yü pu, 1943. 41 p.
Subj 17 ▪ 32.1 47

14719 NNC O P4 G1.2 1911–1949
Chia, Pu-hsia Frederick.
Education for a democratic China.
Unpublished doctoral dissertation in Education, Columbia U. [Teachers College], 1946. 330 p.
Subj 17 37 60 ▪ 12.1 19 23 66

14720 NNM O P2 G1.1 1911–1928
China Educational Commission.
Christian education in China: A study made by an educational commission representing the mission boards and the societies conducting work in China.
New York: Foreign Missions Conference of North America, Committee of Reference and Counsel, 1922. 15, 430 p.
Subj 17 ▪ 33 37 47 54 56

14721 CSH PO P2 G1.2 1928–1949
Chow, Mei-yu.
Development of army nursing school in China, mimeo.
Unpublished masters thesis in Nursing, Massachusetts Institute of Technology, 1944. 56 p. [Certificate of Public Health thesis]
Subj 17 56 ▪ 15 36.1

14722 CSU O P1 G1.2 1911–1949
Chu, Chia-hua, 1893–1963.
'The reform of Chinese education in 1932.'
PT new (2nd) series 9, 6 (16 June 1935), 393–417. [Separately reprinted—Shanghai: China United Press, n.d. 25 p.]
Subj 17

14723 MCH PO P2 G1.2 1911–1949
Chu, Don-chean (Chu Tang-ch'ien), 1914–.
Patterns of education for the developing nations: Tao's work in China, 1917–1946.
Tainan: Kao-chang, 1966. 11, 177 p. (Revision of *Tao Hsing-chih and Chinese education*, doctoral dissertation in Education, Columbia U. [Teachers College], 1953)
Subj 17 37 ▪ 54 64

14724 NNC P P1 G1.2 1911–1928
Chuang, Chai-hsuan (Chuang Tse-hsüan), 1895–.
Tendencies toward a democratic system of education in China, 2nd ed.
Shanghai: Commercial Press, 1922. 16, 176 p. (Revision of doctoral dissertation in Education, Columbia U.)
Subj 17 ▪ 37

14725 NNM P P1 G1.3 1911–1928
Cochrane, Thomas Barnes.
'Medical education in China.'
CMJ 27, 3 (May 1913), 129–143.
Subj 17 56

14726 MBA PO P2 G1.2 1911–1928
Cordier, Charles Georges, 1872–1936.
'L'enseignement en Chine et plus particulièrement au Yunnan' (Education in China, with emphasis on Yunnan).
RI nouvelle (2e) série 44, 11/12 (nov.–déc. 1925), 387–432.
Subj 17 55 ▪ 66

14727 NIC P P3 G1.2 1911–1928
Cressy, Earl Herbert, 1883–.
Christian higher education in China: A study for the year 1925–26.
Shanghai: China Christian Educational Assn., 1928. 320 p. (CCEA bulletins, 20)
Subj 17 ▪ 16.1 47 62

14728 NNC F P4 G6.0 1911–1949
Cressy, Earl Herbert, 1883–, and C. C. Chih.
Middle school standards: Second study.
Shanghai: East China Christian Education Assn., 1929. 111 p. (East China studies in education, 5)
Subj 17 ▪ 66

14729 NNP P P2 G1.2 1911–1949
Ershov, Matvei Nikolaevich.
'Shkola i umstvennye dvizheniia v sovremennom Kitae' (Schools and intellectual movements in contemporary China).
BSB 1, 4 (1932), 191–233.
Subj 17 ▪ 64 72

14730 CSH O P5 G1.2 1928–1949
Faber, Knud Helge, 1862–1956.
Report on medical schools in China.
Geneva: League of Nations, Health Organisation, 1931. 47 p. (League of Nations publications, series 3; Health, 1931 3, 8) [French version also published—Geneva, 1931.]
Subj 17 56

14731 MCH O P3 G5.1 1911–1928
Fabregue, Joseph.
'A survey of higher education in the city of Peking.'
B. of the Catholic U. of Peking 1 (1926), 51–56.
Subj 17 66

14732 IBU P P3 G6.1 1928–1949
Fan, Ih-chi (Fan I-chih), 1914–.
A study of the program of audio-visual education for teacher education in China, 1930–1949.
Unpublished doctoral dissertation in Education, Indiana U., 1952. 465 p.
Subj 17

14733 MCH PO P2 G1.2 1928–1949
Freyn, Hubert, 1897–.
Chinese education in the war.
Shanghai: Kelly and Walsh, 1940. 137 p. (Council of International Affairs, Chungking, Political and economic studies, 9)
Subj 17 ▪ 15 16.1 25 37 54

14734 MCY P P1 G1.2 1911–1949
Gérardin, André.
'L'enseignement du droit civil comparé à l'Université l'Aurore' (The teaching of comparative civil law at Aurora University).
BUA 3e série 8, 29 (1947), 119–135.
SUBJ 12.2 17 ▪ 22.2 45

14735 MCH P P2 G5.2 1911–1928
Gillin, Donald George, 1930–.
'Education and militarism in modern China: Yen Hsi-shan in Shansi province, 1911–1930.'
J. of modern history 34, 2 (June 1962), 161–167.
SUBJ 12.1 17 ▪ 37 54 64

14736 MMU P P4 G1.2 1911–1949
Han, Ch'ing-lien, 1905–.
A comparative study of administration of publicly supported higher education in the United States and China.
Unpublished doctoral dissertation in Education, U. of Minnesota, 1941. 453 p.
SUBJ 17 ▪ 11.4 12.2 14 32.1 54 66

14737 CSU P P2 G9.3 1928–1949
Hinman, George Warren, 1869–1940.
'Education in Fukien.'
CR 67, 7 (July 1936), 414–422.
SUBJ 17

14738 CSU U P2 G1.2 1928–1949
Hinman, George Warren, 1869–1940.
'Who pays for the schools?'
CR 67, 11 (Nov. 1936), 702–707; 67, 12 (Dec. 1936), 771–780.
SUBJ 14.5 17 ▪ 37

14739 NIC F P3 G6.1 1928–1949
Hsia, Lu-i, 1920–.
An ideal teacher from Chinese pupil's viewpoint: A survey of 409 pupils in 6 senior high schools in Shanghai, China.
Unpublished masters thesis in Psychology, Cornell U., 1949. 57 p.
SUBJ 17 ▪ 26.1 60

14740 NIC O P2 G1.2 1911–1949
Hsu, Francis L. K. (Hsü Lang-kuang), 1909–.
'Education: A problem of cultural transition.'
Transactions of the New York Academy of Sciences 2nd series 8, 2 (Dec. 1945), 82–90.
SUBJ 14 16.1 17 54 62

14741 MCH O P3 G1.2 1911–1928
Hsu, Leonard S. (Hsü Shih-lien), 1901–.
'The teaching of sociology in China.'
CSPSR 11, 3 (July 1927), 373–389.
SUBJ 17 70 ▪ 18

14742 CSU FP P1 G1.2 1911–1928
Hsueh, H. T.
'Statistical summaries of Chinese education.'
BCE 2, 16 (1923), 1–54.
SUBJ 17

14743 ICU F P3 G7.3 1911–1928
Hu, I, 1904–.
An experimental study of the reading habits of adult Chinese.
Unpublished doctoral dissertation in Education, U. of Chicago, 1928. 10, 141 p.
SUBJ 17 55 ▪ 24.2

14744 MCH P P1 G1.2 1928–1949
Hu Nan (Hu Lan), 1902–.
Etude comparée des programmes et des méthodes d'enseignement pour les enfants de 6 à 12 ans en Chine et en France (A comparative study of the programs and methods of instruction of six- to twelve-year-old children in China and in France).
Paris: Pedone, 1935. 186 p. (Doctoral dissertation, Faculté des lettres, Université de Paris)
SUBJ 17 ▪ 12.2 64

14745 MSE O P3 G8.1 1911–1928
Hubbard, George David, 1871–1958.
Education in Cheng Tu, Sze Chuan.
Oberlin: ——, 1923. 22 p. (Oberlin College laboratory bulletins, 29)
SUBJ 17

14746 DLC O P3 G1.3 1928–1949
Kilborn, Leslie G-.
'Medical education.' In *Wartime China, as seen by westerners.* [Selective entry]
Chungking: China Publishing Co., 1942, 204–211.
SUBJ 17 56

14747 CSU O P2 G1.2 1928–1949
Lacy, Carleton.
'Immigrant colleges and middle schools.'
CR 71, 9 (Sept. 1940), 557–566.
SUBJ 17 ▪ 11.2

14748 CSU O P3 G6.1 1911–1928
Lanneau, Sophie S-.
'The schools of Soochow: A survey.'
CR 48, 7 (July 1917), 423–434.
SUBJ 17

14749 MCH PO P2 G1.2 1928–1949
League of Nations. Mission of Educational Experts.
The reorganization of education in China.
Paris: League of Nations, Institute of Intellectual Co-operation, 1932. 200 p.
SUBJ 17 ▪ 16.1 32.1 37 62

14750 NIC F P2 G8.1 1928–1949
Li, Mei-yun (Li Mei-yün), 1908–.
An analysis of social, economic and political conditions in Peng-shan hsien, Szechwan, China, looking toward improvement of educational program.
Unpublished doctoral dissertation in Education, Cornell U., 1945. 422 p.
SUBJ 12 17 20 41 55 ▪ 23 24 26 28 31 37 42 43 47

14751 NNC FP P2 G1.4 1911–1949
Liao, T'ai-ch'u.
'School land: A problem of educational finance.'
YJSS 2, 2 (Feb. 1940), 212–233.
SUBJ 14.1 14.5 17 ▪ 12.1

14752 CSU P P1 G1.2 1911–1928
Linden, Allen Bernard, 1931–.
'Politics and education in Nationalist China: The case of the University Council, 1927–1928.'
JAS 27, 4 (Aug. 1968), 763–776. [For fuller treatment, see entry 14753.]
SUBJ 12 17 32.1 ▪ 16.1 32

14753 MAM P P1 G1.2 1911–1949
Linden, Allen Bernard, 1931–.
Politics and higher education in China: The Kuomintang and the university community, 1927–1937.
Ann Arbor: University Microfilms (Publ. 70-7023), 1970. 307 p. (Doctoral dissertation in History, Columbia U., 1969)
SUBJ 12 16.1 17 32 32.1

14754 CSU PO P2 G1.2 1928–1949
Lindsay, Michael Francis Morris, 1909–.
Notes on educational problems in Communist China, 1941–1947, mimeo.
New York: Institute of Pacific Relations, International Secretariat, 1950. 194 p.
SUBJ 12 17 22 22.1 ▪ 16 25 30 31 32.2 37 64

14755 NNC O P3 G1.3 1928–1949
Margouliès, Georges.
'Unterrichtsprobleme und Universitätsleben in China' (Educational problems and university life in China).
Sinica 6, 5 (Sept. 1931), 221–229.
SUBJ 17 ▪ 64 66

14756 CSU U P3 G1.3 1928–1949
Meng, Chih, 1900–.
'Japan's war on Chinese higher education.'
FA 16, 2 (Jan. 1938), 351–354.
SUBJ 17

14757 CSU PO P2 G5.0 1928–1949
Menzies, Marion, and William Paget.
'Communist educational policies in certain North China rural areas, 1948.' In *Notes on educational problems in Communist China, 1941–1947,* mimeo., by Michael Francis Morris Lindsay. [Analytic entry]
New York: Institute of Pacific Relations, International Secretariat, 1950, 146–173. [For Lindsay's work, see entry 14754.]
SUBJ 17 54

14758 NNC PO P2 G9.0 1911–1928
Perkins, Elizabeth Sarah, 1883–.
Mores and education in South China.
Unpublished masters thesis in Sociology, Columbia U., 1922. 47 p.
SUBJ 17 20 65 ▪ 22 23 24 29 40 47 57

14759 MCH O P4 G1.2 1911–1949
Rasmussen, Carl, 1899–.
'Den kinesiske skole i øjeblikket' (The Chinese school at present).
Nordisk missions tidsskrift 41 (1930), 49–61.
SUBJ 17 33 ▪ 14.3 15 66

14760 NNC PO P1 G1.2 1928–1949
Sailer, Thomas Henry Powers, 1868–1962.
'Religious education.' In *China*, edited by Orville Anderson Petty. [Selective entry]
New York: Harper, 1933, 302–353. (Laymans Foreign Missions Inquiry, Factfinders' reports, 5; Supplementary series, part 2)
SUBJ 17 33 61 ▪ 37 54 62 66

14761 CSH O P7 G9.3 1911–1949
Scott, Roderick, 1885–.
Fukien Christian University.

New York: United Board for Christian Colleges in China, 1954. 138 p.
Subj 17 ▪ 32.1 54 66

14762 MCH P P2 G1.4 1928–1949
Seybolt, Peter Jordan, 1934–.
Yenan education and the Chinese revolution, 1937–1945.
Unpublished doctoral dissertation in History and Far Eastern Languages, Harvard U., 1969. 440 p.
Subj 16.1 17 22.1 32.2 64 ▪ 14.2 30 31 32.1 36.1 54

14763 DLC O P3 G1.3 1928–1949
Spooner, Roy L-.
'A new emphasis on chemistry.' In *Wartime China, as seen by westerners.* [Selective entry]
Chungking: China Publishing Co., 1942, 189–203.
Subj 17 62 ▪ 14.4 16.1 36.1

14764 NIC O P5 G4.2 1928–1949
Sung, Ke (Sung Ko), 1905–.
A study of secondary school curriculum in Kansu, China, with a suggested reorganization of the program.
Unpublished doctoral dissertation in Education, Cornell U., 1940. 169 p.
Subj 17 ▪ 21.4 32.1 47

14765 CSU U P3 G1.2 1911–1928
Tai, T. C.
'Library movement in China.'
BCE 2, 3 (1923), 1–20.
Subj 17 ▪ 37

14766 NNM FP P3 G1.1 1928–1949
Tao, S. M.
'Medical education of Chinese women.'
CMJ 47, 10 (Oct. 1933), 1010–1028.
Subj 17 47 56

14767 MCH P P1 G1.2 1911–1928
Tao, W. Tchishin (T'ao Chih-hsing), 1891–1946.
'China.' In *Educational year book of the International Institute of Teachers College, Columbia U., 1924,* edited by I- L- Kandel. [Sole entry]
New York: Macmillan, 1925, 93–145.
Subj 17 ▪ 16.1 18

14768 NNM P P3 G1.2 1928–1949
T'ao, Lee.
'Some statistics on medical schools in China for the year 1933–1934.'
CMJ 49, 9 (Sept. 1935), 894–902.
Subj 17 56

14769 NNM P P3 G1.2 1928–1949
T'ao, Lee.
'Some statistics on medical schools in China for 1932–1933.'
CMJ 47, 10 (Oct. 1933), 1029–1039.
Subj 17

14770 CSH O P3 G1.5 1911–1949
[Thurston, Matilda S- Calder] *Mrs.* Lawrence Thurston, 1875–1958, and Ruth Miriam Chester, 1894–.
Ginling College [Nanking].
New York: United Board for Christian Colleges in China, 1955. 171 p.
Subj 17 ▪ 25 32.1 38 47 54

14771 NNC F P7 G4.2 1928–1949
United Nations. Food and Agriculture Organization.
Training rural leaders: Shantan Bailie School, Kansu province, China.
Washington, D.C.: Food and Agriculture Organization, 1949. 136 p.
Subj 17 24.4 26.1 ▪ 19 24.1 28 32.1 54

14772 MCH U P3 G9.3 1911–1949
Wallace, Lydia Ethel.
Hua Nan College [Foochow], *the woman's college of South China.*
New York: United Board for Christian Colleges in China, 1956. 164 p.
Subj 17 47 ▪ 16 33 37

14773 CSU U P2 G1.2 1911–1949
Wang, Shih-chieh.
'Education in China.' In *The year book of education, 1937.* [Sole entry]
London: Evans, 1938?, 555–601.
Subj 17 ▪ 12.2

14774 MCH FP P3 G1.2 1928–1949
Wee, Kok-an (Huang Kuo-an), 1897–.
Physical education in Protestant Christian colleges and universitics in China.
New York: ——, 1937. 105 p. (Doctoral dissertation in Education, Columbia U.)
Subj 17 ▪ 18 31 37 47 63 72

14775 NIC P P3 G1.2 1911–1928
Whitmore, Ralph D-.
'Engineering education in China.'
THJ 2, 5 (Mar. 1917), 1–25.
Subj 17 ▪ 47

14776 CSU P P1 G1.2 1911–1949
Wong, V. L. (Huang Wei-lien).
'Library chronicle.'
THM 6, 4 (Apr. 1938), 369–376.
Subj 17 ▪ 12.2 37 66

1911-1972
(including 1644-1972)

14777 MCH P P1 G1.2 1842–1972
'L'enseignement dans la Chine contemporaine' (Education in contemporary China).
NED 2066 (27 août 1955), 1–38.
Subj 12.1 16.1 17 32.1 60 ▪ 12 12.2 16 50 64 72

14778 NNC O P2 G1.2 1928–1972
All-China Society of Nurses.
'Uspekhi v dele podgotovki meditsinskikh sester v novom Kitae' (Achievements in nurses training in New China).
Meditsinskaia sestra 19, 6 (iiun' 1960), 33–36.
Subj 17 ▪ 18 56

14779 CSU S P2 G1.3 –1972
Brewer, J- G-.
'Libraries in China: A comparative view.'
Library Assn. record 70, 5 (May 1968), 124–127.
Subj 14.2 17 37 ▪ 66

14780 NIC P P1 G1.2 1928–1972
Cheng, James Chester (Cheng Che-hsi), 1926–.
Basic principles underlying the Chinese Communist approach to education.
Washington, D.C.: U.S. Dept. of Health, Education, and Welfare, Office of Education, 1961. 24 p. (Information on education around the world, 51; OE 14,034-51)
Subj 17 64 ▪ 12.2 16.1 37

14781 MCY P P1 G1.2 –1972
Cheng, James Chester (Cheng Che-hsi), 1926–.
'The education system in modern and contemporary China.' In *Contemporary China, 1958–1959,* edited by Edward Stuart Kirby. [Selective entry]
Hong Kong: Hong Kong U. Press, 1960, 181–199.
Subj 17 ▪ 12.1 16.1 64

14782 CSH P P1 G4.0 1928–1972
Chu, Wen-djang (Chu Wen-ch'ang), 1914–, and Udo Posch.
'Education.' In *A regional handbook on Northwest China,* compiled by Far Eastern and Russian Institute, U. of Washington. [Selective entry]
New Haven: Human Relations Area Files, 1956, vol. 1, 300–323. (HRAF subcontractor's monographs, 59; Washington 5)
Subj 17 ▪ 66

14783 NNC P P2 G1.2 1911–1972
Chung Shih.
Higher education in Communist China, mimeo.
Hong Kong: Union Research Institute, 1953. 97 p. (Communist China problem research series, EC2)
Subj 12.1 17 64 ▪ 14.4 16.1 66

14784 CSU O P3 G1.5 1911–1972
Coe, John L-, 1902–.
Huachung University.
New York: United Board for Christian Higher Education in Asia, 1962. 215 p.
Subj 17 ▪ 32.1 33 37

14785 CSH PO P2 G5.3 1842–1972
Corbett, Charles Hodge, 1881–1963.
Shantung Christian University (Cheeloo) [i.e., Cheeloo University, Tsinan].
New York: United Board for Christian Colleges in China, 1955. 281 p.
Subj 17 ▪ 37 54

14786 CSH PO P3 G6.3 1842–1972
Day, Clarence Burton, 1889–.
Hangchow University.
New York: United Board for Christian Colleges in China, 1955. 183 p.
Subj 17 ▪ 32.1 54 66

14787 CSH P P2 G1.2 1895–1972
Fang Cheng.
'Reform work in the Chinese Communist educational system.' Tr. of 'Chung kung ti hsüeh chih kai ko kung tso' (Chinese Communist reforms of the school system); *Tsu kuo* 20 (Nov. 1965), 2–9.
CE 2, 4 (Winter 1970/71), 228–264.
Subj 17 ▪ 32.1

14788 NNC P P2 G1.2 1928–1972
Fraser, Stewart Erskine, 1929–.
'Education, indoctrination, and ideology in Communist China, 1950–1960.' In *Chinese Communist education: Records of the first decade,* compiled and edited by S. E. Fraser. [Sole entry]
Nashville: Vanderbilt U. Press, 1965, 3–69.
Subj 16.1 17 32.1 ▪ 19 64 72

14789 CSU S P1 G1.2 –1972
Gough, Kathleen, 1925–.
'Implications of literacy in traditional China and India.' In *Literacy in*

traditional societies, edited by John Rankin Goody. [Sole entry]
Cambridge: Cambridge U. Press, 1968, 69–84.
SUBJ 17 62

14790 CSH P P2 G1.2 1928–1972
Hawkins, John N-.
'Commentary.' In *Educational theory in the People's Republic of China: The report of Ch'ien Chün-jui*, edited by J. N. Hawkins. [Sole entry]
Honolulu: U. of Hawaii Press, 1971, 1–62. (Asian Studies at Hawaii, 6) (Masters thesis in Asian Studies, U. of British Columbia, 1969)
SUBJ 17 64 ▪ 12.2 54 59

14791 CSU U P3 G5.1 1911–1972
Ho, Lin, and Mao Tan.
'Métamorphose d'une école supérieure: pour le 50e anniversaire de la fondation de l'Université Tsinghoua' (The metamorphosis of an institution of higher learning: On the fiftieth anniversary of Tsing Hua University).
CFC 12 (déc. 1961), 78–86.
SUBJ 17 ▪ 16

14792 MCH P P3 G7.2 1895–1972
Holden, Reuben Andrus, 1918–.
Yale in China: The mainland, 1901–1951.
New Haven: Yale in China Assn., 1964. 12, 327 p.
SUBJ 17 56 66 ▪ 36.1 37 54

14793 NIC P P1 G1.2 1928–1972
Hsü, Immanuel C. Y. (Hsü Chung-yüeh), 1923–.
Reorganization of higher education in Communist China.
Santa Barbara, Calif.: General Electric Co., Technical Military Planning Operation, 1962. 47 p. (TEMPO reports, RM 62TMP-74)
SUBJ 11.4 17

14794 CSU P P2 G1.2 –1972
Hu, C. T. (Hu Ch'ang-tu), 1920–.
'Tradition and change in Chinese education.' In *Chinese education under Communism*, edited by C. T. Hu. [Selective entry]
New York: Columbia U., Teachers College, Bureau of Publications, 1962, 1–50. (TC classics in education, 7)
SUBJ 17 64 ▪ 12.1 16.1 72

14795 MAM P P2 G1.2 1928–1972
Hu, Shiao Chung.
Education in the People's Republic of China, 1949–1971: Focus on the teaching profession.
Ann Arbor: University Microfilms (Publ. 72-34,195), 1973. 749 p. (Doctoral dissertation in Education, George Peabody College for Teachers, 1972)
SUBJ 16.1 17 64 ▪ 14.4 54

14796 WSU PO P2 G9.4 1928–1972
Lee, Susan Hsun.
A study of education in Taiwan since 1945.
Unpublished masters thesis in Education, U. of Washington, 1963. 85 p.
SUBJ 17 ▪ 12.1

14797 MCH P P1 G1.2 1911–1972
Li, Anthony C. (Li Ching-wen), 1920–.
The history of privately controlled higher education in the Republic of China.
Washington, D.C.: Catholic U. of America Press, 1954. 157 p. (Doctoral dissertation in Education, Catholic U. of America)
SUBJ 17 ▪ 32.1

14798 MAM FP P2 G1.1 1895–1972
Nelson, Wilbur Kenneth, 1929–.
Educational goals in China, with emphasis on the relationship of public and private schools on Taiwan during the period 1949–1962.
Ann Arbor: University Microfilms (Publ. 63-7750), 1963. 213 p. (Doctoral dissertation in Education, Claremont Graduate School and University Center)
SUBJ 17 32.1 33

14799 CSU O P3 G9.4 1928–1972
P'eng, T. M. (P'eng Ta-mou).
'Outstanding problems of medical education, Republic of China.'
CMJ-T 15, 3 (Sept. 1968), 172–176. [See Vol. 2 of this *Bibliography* for Chinese version.]
SUBJ 17 56

14800 CSH P P2 G1.3 1928–1972
Stanford U. China Project.
'Education.' In *Central South China*, compiled by the organization cited. [Selective entry]
New Haven: Human Relations Area Files, 1956, vol. 1, 257–302. (HRAF subcontractor's monographs, 28; Stanford 2)
SUBJ 17 ▪ 12.1 37 64

14801 CSH P P2 G1.3 1928–1972
Stanford U. China Project.
'Education.' In *East China*, compiled by the organization cited. [Selective entry]
New Haven: Human Relations Area Files, 1956, vol. 1, 304–343. (HRAF subcontractor's monographs, 29; Stanford 3)
SUBJ 17 ▪ 12.1 37 64

14802 CSH P P2 G5.0 1928–1972
Stanford U. China Project.
'Education.' In *North China*, compiled by the organization cited. [Selective entry]
New Haven: Human Relations Area Files, 1956, vol. 1, 274–317. (HRAF subcontractor's monographs, 27; Stanford 1)
SUBJ 17 ▪ 12.1 37 64

14803 NNC P P2 G8.0 1928–1972
Stanford U. China Project.
'Education.' In *Southwest China*, compiled by the organization cited. [Selective entry]
New Haven: Human Relations Area Files, 1956, vol. 1, 268–320. (HRAF subcontractor's monographs, 30; Stanford 4)
SUBJ 17 ▪ 12.1 37 64

14804 CSH U P1 G2.0 1911–1972
Tang, Peter S. H. (T'ang Sheng-hao), 1919–.
'Education.' In *A regional handbook on Northeast China*, compiled by Far Eastern and Russian Institute, U. of Washington. [Selective entry]
New Haven: Human Relations Area Files, 1956, 213–226. (HRAF subcontractor's monographs, 61; Washington 9)
SUBJ 17 ▪ 37

14805 CSU S P3 G9.5 1842–1972
To, Cho-yee.
'The development of higher education in Hong Kong.'
Comparative education review 9, 1 (Feb. 1965), 74–80.
SUBJ 17 ▪ 56

14806 MAM P P1 G9.4 1895–1972
Tsai, Pao-tien, 1921–.
Development of a system of teacher education in Taiwan, with emphasis upon the period of 1945–1962.
Ann Arbor: University Microfilms (Publ. 64-5144), 1964. 128 p. (Doctoral dissertation in Education, Indiana U., 1963)
SUBJ 17

14807 NNC O P3 G6.1 1928–1972
Tulaev, A- IA-.
'Shankhaiskii politekhnicheskii institut' (The Shanghai Polytechnic Institute).
Vestnik vysshei shkoly 16, 9 (sentiabr' 1958), 88–89.
SUBJ 17 ▪ 62

14808 CSH P P2 G1.2 1911–1972
Wang, Julia Ju-lie.
A study of the criteria for book selection in Communist China's public libraries, 1949–1964.
Hong Kong: Union Research Institute, 1968. 160 p. (Masters thesis in Library Science, San Jose State College, 1966)
SUBJ 14.2 17 32.1 37 ▪ 31

14809 CSU O P2 G1.2 1928–1972
Wilson, John Tuzo, 1908–.
One Chinese moon.
New York: Hill and Wang, 1959. 274 p.
SUBJ 17 62 ▪ 14.2 15 24.4 26.4 28 31

14810 NNC U P1 G1.2 –1972
Wong, Florence Fung-ye (Huang Feng-i), 1918–.
Music education in modern Chinese schools.
Unpublished doctoral dissertation in Education, Columbia U. [Teachers College], 1952. 189 p.
SUBJ 17 ▪ 54

14811 TPY P P1 G1.1 1928–1972
Yang Hsi-cheng (Yang Hsi-chen).
'The guidance and moral education administrative system in Chinese schools.'
West and East 13, 10 (Oct. 1968), 3–5 [s.p.]; 13, 11 (Nov. 1968), 5–7 [s.p.]. [See Vol. 2 of this *Bibliography* for Chinese version.]
SUBJ 17

14812 TPY P P1 G1.1 1928–1972
Yang Hsi-cheng (Yang Hsi-chen).
'The significant meaning of the students' guidance and moral education in China.'
West and East 14, 1 (Jan. 1969), 5–6 [s.p.]; 14, 2 (Feb. 1969), 5–8 [s.p.]. [See Vol. 2 of this *Bibliography* for Chinese version.]
SUBJ 17 ▪ 54

1949-1972

14813 FPN P P1 G1.2 1949–1972
L'enseignement dans la République populaire de Chine' (Education in the People's Republic of China).
NED 3197 (4 juin 1965), 1–27.
SUBJ 11.4 12.1 17 ▪ 16.1 19 37 72

14814 CSH P P4 G1.2 1949–1972
'La formation des cadres scientifiques et techniques en République populaire de Chine (1949–1963)' (Scientific and technical manpower training in the People's Republic of China, 1949–1963).
NED 3576 (28 mars 1969), 5–50.
SUBJ 11.4 14 16.1 17 66 ▪ 16.2 18 19 32 47 54 62 64

14815 CSH O P7 G9.3 1949–1972
'A network for popularizing socialist education: Report on an investigation conducted in Nanan hsien, Fukien province.' Tr. of 'I ko she hui chu i ti chiao yü p'u chi kang: Fu-chien Nan-an hsien ti tiao ch'a pao kao' (A network for universal socialist education: Report on Nan-an *hsien*, Fukien); *Hung ch'i* 1971, 6 (June), 35–41.
CE 5, 1/2 (Spring–Summer 1972), 66–81.
SUBJ 17 ▪ 24.1

14816 NNC P P3 G5.1 1949–1972
'People's University trains many cadres in seven years.' Tr. of 'Fa hui kao hsiao yu li t'iao chien ta li fa chan han shou chiao yü jen min ta hsüeh ch'i nien lai wei ch'üan kuo ko ti p'ei yang liao ta p'i tsai chih kan pu' (By utilizing the advantages of higher education and developing correspondence courses on a large scale, People's University has completed the in-service training of many cadres throughout the country during the past seven years); *Kuang ming jih pao* (Peking) 24 Mar. 1960, 2. In *Selected articles on education from the 'Kuang ming jih pao' and the 'Pei-ching jih pao', March–April 1960*, mimeo., compiled by U.S. Joint Publications Research Service. [Sole entry]
Washington, D.C.: JPRS, 10 Aug. 1960, 10–15. (JPRS 3680; MC 15,600/1960)
SUBJ 17 ▪ 26.1 32.1

14817 MCY O P2 G7.1 1949–1972
'Politics must always take command.'
CS 1, 26 (5 Mar. 1962), 1–10. [Reprinted in *Out of China: A collection of interviews with refugees from China*, edited by Francis Harper. (Analytic entry.) Hong Kong: Dragonfly Books, 1964, 49–72.]
SUBJ 17 22.1 ▪ 24.2 24.4 28 56

14818 CSH P P2 G1.2 1949–1972
'Recent developments in Chinese education.'
CS 10, 7 (July 1972), 1–6.
SUBJ 17

14819 CSH U P3 G6.1 1949–1972
'The reform in education at colleges of science and engineering as viewed from the struggle between two lines at the Shanghai Institute of Mechanical Engineering.' Tr. of 'Ts'ung Shang-hai chi hsieh hsüeh yüan liang t'iao lu hsien ti tou cheng k'an li kung k'o ta hsüeh ti chiao yü ko ming'; *Hung ch'i* 1958, 3 (10 Sept.), 7–13.
CE 2, 3 (Fall 1969), 3–14. [A different tr.— 'The revolution in education in colleges of science and engineering as reflected in the struggle between the two lines at the Shanghai Institute of Mechanical Engineering.' *SCMM* 627 (16 Sept. 1968), 1–18.]
SUBJ 17 ▪ 26.1 26.4

14820 CSH O P3 G4.2 1949–1972
'Revolution in education in a city middle school [Lanchow No. 5 Middle School].'
China reconstructs 18, 9 (Sept. 1969), 14–17.
SUBJ 17

14821 NNC P P2 G1.2 1949–1972
[Abe Munemitsu] ———.
'Educational program of Communist China.' Tr. of 'Kyōiku' (Education); in *Chūgoku seiji keizai sōran, Shōwa 37 nendoban* (Political and economic overview of China, 1962), edited by Ajia seikai gakkai (Assn. for Asian Political-Economic Studies); Tokyo: Naigai seiji kenkyūjo, 1962, 777–778. In *Education in Communist China*, mimeo., compiled by U.S. Joint Publications Research Service. [Selective entry]
Washington, D.C.: JPRS, 18 Jan. 1963, 1–22. (JPRS 17,188; MC 2985/1963)
SUBJ 17 ▪ 32.1

14822 NNC O P2 G1.2 1949–1972
Abegg, Lily, 1901–.
'Privilegierte und Analphabeten: Das Erziehungswesen in China' (The privileged and the illiterate: The Chinese educational system).
Atlantis 29 (1957), 51–60.
SUBJ 16 17 ▪ 16.1 61

14823 CSU P P2 G1.2 1949–1972
Alitto, Susan Biele.
'The language issue in Communist Chinese education.'
Comparative education review 13, 1 (Feb. 1969), 43–59. [Reprinted in *Aspects of Chinese education*, edited by C. T. Hu (Hu Ch'ang-tu). (Selective entry.) New York: Columbia U., Teachers College, Institute of International Studies, Center for Education in Asia *with* Columbia U., East Asian Institute, 1969, 43–59.]
SUBJ 17 ▪ 37

14824 DLC P P2 G1.2 1949–1972
Anastas'eva, T- N-.
'Bor'ba za novuiu shkolu i marksistskuiu pedagogiku v KNR na sovremennom etape' (The current stage of the struggle for the new school and Marxist education in the People's Republic of China).
Sovetskaia pedagogika 22, 9 (sentiabr' 1958), 126–139.
SUBJ 17 61 64 ▪ 16.2 34.1 52

14825 MAM FP P3 G9.5 1949–1972
Anderson, Maurice John, 1914–.
The survival strategies of a complex western-type educational-religious organization in an eastern culture: A case study of the Hong Kong Baptist College.
Ann Arbor: University Microfilms (Publ. 70-9031), 1970. 19, 263 p. (Doctoral dissertation in Sociology, Louisiana State U., 1969)
SUBJ 17 ▪ 54

14826 MCH O P3 G1.3 1949–1972
Andrew, Geoffrey Clement, 1906–.
'China: An academic appraisal.'
American scholar 32, 3 (Summer 1963), 377–386.
SUBJ 17 ▪ 64 66

14827 NIC P P2 G1.2 1949–1972
Arens, Richard, 1912–.
'Education in Communist China from 1949–1951: The period of policy formation.'
J. of East Asiatic studies 5, 3 (July 1956), 315–325. [For a fuller version, see entry 14828.]
SUBJ 17 ▪ 11.4 18 32.1 37 64

14828 ICU P P2 G1.2 1949–1972
Arens, Richard, 1912–.
The impact of Communism on education in China, 1949–1950.
Unpublished doctoral dissertation in Education, U. of Chicago, 1952. 255 p.
SUBJ 17 64 ▪ 11.4 12.1 16.1 16.3 18 29 32.1 37

14829 DLC O P2 G1.3 1949–1972
Arsent'ev, Aleksandr Ivanovich.
Zvezdy nad Kitaem (Stars over China).
Simferopol, U.S.S.R.: Krymizdat, 1959. 117 p.
SUBJ 14.4 17 21.3 ▪ 18 31 34.2 64 66

14830 ELB P P2 G1.2 1949–1972
Bady, Paul, 1941–.
'La révolution dans l'enseignement en Chine' (The educational revolution in China).
Esprit nouvelle (2e) série 39, 1 (jan. 1971), 73–88.
SUBJ 17 54 ▪ 16.3 16.4 35

14831 CBU PO P3 G1.3 1949–1972
Baranov, M- IA-.
'Obshcheobrazovatel'naia sredniaia shkola' (The comprehensive secondary school). In *Shkola i prosveshchenie v Narodnom Kitae: sbornik statei* (Articles on schools and education in the People's Republic of China), compiled by Akademiia pedagogicheskikh nauk RSFSR, edited by Aleksei I- Markushevich, E- I- Monoszon, and M- N- Riakin. [Selective entry]
Moscow: Izd-vo Akad. ped. nauk RSFSR, 1957, 94–104.
SUBJ 17 52 ▪ 21.3

14832 MMT P P1 G1.2 1949–1972
Barendsen, Robert Dale, 1923–.
'Education in China: A survey.'
Problems of Communism 13, 4 (July–Aug. 1964), 19–27.
SUBJ 17 32.1 ▪ 11.4 12.1 16.1

14833 MCH P P1 G1.2 1949–1972
Barendsen, Robert Dale, 1923–.
Planned reforms in the primary and secondary school system in Communist China.
Washington, D.C.: U.S. Dept. of Health, Education, and Welfare, Office of Education, 1960. 12 p. (Information on education around the world, 45; OE 14,034-45) [Reprinted as 'The 1960 educational reforms.' *CQ* 4 (Oct.–Dec. 1960), 55–65.] [Reprinted in *Education*

and Communism in China: An anthology of commentary and documents, edited by Stewart Erskine Fraser. (Selective entry.) London: Pall Mall Press, 1971, 151–166.]
SUBJ 17 ▪ 11.4 62

14834 CSU P P2 G1.2 1949–1972
Bastid, Marianne, 1940–.
'Economic necessity and political ideals in educational reform during the Cultural Revolution.'
CQ 42 (Apr.–June 1970), 16–45.
SUBJ 17 64 ▪ 16.1 16.3 35

14835 NIC S P2 G1.2 1949–1972
Berberet, John A-.
Science and technology in Communist China.
Santa Barbara, Calif.: General Electric Co., Technical Military Planning Operation, 1960. 13, 157 p. (TEMPO reports, RM 60 TMP-72)
SUBJ 14.4 16.1 17 36.1 62 ▪ 11 12 15 32

14836 NNC PO P2 G9.5 1949–1972
Berrien, Marcia Taff, 1925–, and Robert Dale Barendsen, 1923–.
Education in Hong Kong.
Washington, D.C.: U.S. Dept. of Health, Education, and Welfare, Office of Education, 1960. 40 p. (OE 14,049)
SUBJ 17

14837 DLC O P1 G1.2 1949–1972
Blaskovič, Dionýz.
'Rast vedeckého života v l'udovej Číné' (The growth of scientific life in the People's Republic of China).
Naša veda (Bratislava) 1, 2 (1954), 35–40; 1, 3 (1954), 68–72.
SUBJ 17

14838 CBU PO P3 G1.3 1949–1972
Bortkevich, M- P-.
'Kak gotoviatsia uchitelia nachal'noi shkoly' (Training elementary school teachers). In *Shkola i prosveshchenie v Narodnom Kitae: sbornik statei* (Articles on schools and education in the People's Republic of China), compiled by Akademiia pedagogicheskikh nauk RSFSR, edited by Aleksei I- Markushevich, E- I- Monoszon, and M- N- Riakin. [Selective entry]
Moscow: Izd-vo Akad. ped. nauk RSFSR, 1957, 78–93.
SUBJ 17

14839 NNC F P2 G8.1 1949–1972
Chan Cho.
'The needs and training of agricultural technical cadres.' Tr. of 'Nung yeh chi shu kan pu ti hsü yao ho p'ei yang wen t'i'; *Jen min chiao yü* 1958, 7 (June), 7–9. In *Party and cadre education*, mimeo., compiled by U.S. Joint Publications Research Service. [Selective entry]
Washington, D.C.: JPRS, 17 Jan. 1963, 7–19. (JPRS 17,183; MC 2980/1963)
SUBJ 17 ▪ 24.1 26.1

14840 CSH P P2 G1.2 1949–1972
Chang, Anthony Sherman.
'Education.' In *Youth in China*, edited by Edward Stuart Kirby. [Analytic entry]
Hong Kong: Dragonfly Books, 1965, 67–112.
SUBJ 12.1 17 27 54 ▪ 11

14841 NNC O P1 G9.5 1949–1972
Chang, Chi-yun (Chang Ch'i-yün), 1901–.
'Confucianism and modern education in China.'
CC 3, 1 (Oct. 1960), 101–118.
SUBJ 17 ▪ 64 70

14842 MCH P P3 G1.2 1949–1972
Chang Nai-fan.
'An analysis of universities and colleges on the Chinese Mainland.'
CCA 2, 3 (June 1965), 45–53.
SUBJ 17

14843 CSH P P2 G1.2 1949–1972
Chang Nai-fan. [Author's name erroneously given as Chang Nai-pan.]
'Chinese Communist educational system.'
CCA 3, 1 (Feb. 1966), 32–66.
SUBJ 17

14844 CSH O P2 G4.1 1949–1972
Chao Shou-i.
'Great progress in culture and education.' Tr. of 'Wen chiao chan hsien shang ti ta yao chin' (The great leap forward on the cultural and educational front); *Hung ch'i* 1958, 8 (16 Sept.), 31–37. In *Selected translations from 'Hung ch'i' (Red flag), September 1958*, mimeo., compiled by U.S. Joint Publications Research Service. [Selective entry]
Washington, D.C.: JPRS, 9 May 1961, 19–31. (JPRS 9181; MC 15,357/1961)
SUBJ 17 ▪ 24.2 31 36.1

14845 DLC P P2 G1.2 1949–1972
Chen IU-sin (Ch'eng Yu-hsin).
'Soedinenie obrazovaniia s proizvoditel'nym trudom v shkolakh Kitaiskoi Narodnoi Respubliki' (Combining study with productive work in the schools of the People's Republic of China).
Sovetskaia pedagogika 25, 1 (ianvar' 1961), 116–125.
SUBJ 14.1 14.4 17 ▪ 64

14846 MAM FP P1 G9.4 1949–1972
Chen, John Allen, 1935–.
Higher education in the Republic of China (Taiwan).
Ann Arbor: University Microfilms (Publ. 72-3764), 1972. 158 p. (Doctoral dissertation in Education, U. of Southern California, 1971)
SUBJ 17 ▪ 12.2 21.4 72

14847 NIC S P1 G1.2 1949–1972
Chen, Theodore H. E. (Ch'en Hsi-en), 1902–.
'Chinese Communist education: The three *P*'s.'
FES 29, 6 (June 1960), 86–89.
SUBJ 17 64 ▪ 32.1

14848 CSH P P1 G1.2 1949–1972
Chen, Theodore H. E. (Ch'en Hsi-en), 1902–.
'Collective learning in Communist China's universities.'
FES 26, 1 (Jan. 1957), 8–11.
SUBJ 12.1 17 ▪ 32.1 55

14849 MCH P P1 G1.2 1949–1972
Chen, Theodore H. E. (Ch'en Hsi-en), 1902–.
'Education and propaganda in Communist China.'
AAAPSS 277 (Sept. 1951), 135–145. [Special issue: *Report on China*, edited by Harold Arthur Steiner]
SUBJ 12.1 17 ▪ 32.1 64

14850 CSU P P2 G1.2 1949–1972
Chen, Theodore H. E. (Ch'en Hsi-en), 1902–.
'Education in Communist China.' In *Communist China, 1949–1969: A twenty-year appraisal*, edited by Frank Newton Trager and William Henderson. [Selective entry]
New York: New York U. Press, 1970, 175–198.
SUBJ 12.1 17 ▪ 16 64

14851 CBU P P1 G1.2 1949–1972
Chen, Theodore H. E. (Ch'en Hsi-en), 1902–.
'Government encouragement and control of international education in Communist China.' In *Governmental policy and international education*, edited by Stewart Erskine Fraser. [Sole entry]
New York: Wiley, 1965, 111–133. [Reprinted in *Education and Communism in China: An anthology of commentary and documents*, edited by S. E. Fraser. (Selective entry.) London: Pall Mall Press, 1971, 413–441.]
SUBJ 12.1 17 66 ▪ 11.2

14852 CSH P P4 G1.2 1949–1972
Chen, Theodore H. E. (Ch'en Hsi-en), 1928–.
'Student exchanges in Communist China.' In *Collected documents of the First Sino-American Conference on Mainland China.* [Selective entry]
[Taipei]: Institute of International Relations, Republic of China, 1971, 325–346.
SUBJ 17 66 ▪ 54 55

14853 NIC P P2 G1.2 1949–1972
Chen, Theodore H. E. (Ch'en Hsi-en), 1902–.
Teacher training in Communist China.
Washington, D.C.: U.S. Dept. of Health, Education, and Welfare, Office of Education, 1960. 49 p. (OE 14,058)
SUBJ 17 32.1 64 ▪ 11.4 18 30 36.1

14854 CSU FP P1 G9.5 1949–1972
Cheong, George S. C.
'Attitudes of Chinese parents and pupils towards studying in the Chinese type of high schools in Hong Kong.'
JAAS 5, 3 (July 1970), 202–208.
SUBJ 17

14855 CSU O P2 G1.2 1949–1972
Chi, Cheng.
'Libraries in China today.'
Libri 9, 2 (1959), 105–110.
SUBJ 14.2 17

14856 NNC U P2 G1.2 1949–1972
Chien, Chun-jui (Ch'ien Chün-jui).
'The policy of educational construction in present day China.' In *Culture and education in New China.* [Sole entry]
Peking: Foreign Languages Press, 1951, 21–35.
SUBJ 17 ▪ 16 64

14857 CSH O P2 G1.2 1949–1972
China [People's Republic]. Ministry of Higher Education. Peking Commune.

'Red Rock' Fighting Company *with* China [People's Republic]. Ministry of Higher Education. 'July 1' Fighting Company. [This article has still a third joint author: New Peking U. Commune, 'Torch' Fighting Company.]
'A record of the great events in the struggle between the two lines in the field of higher education.' Tr. from the Chinese by H. Y. Cheng and M. Ch'en.
Chinese sociology and anthropology 2, 1/2 (Fall–Winter 1969/70), 17–76.
SUBJ 17 64 ▪ 32.1

14858 CSU P P4 G9.4 1949–1972
China [Republic]. Chiao yü pu. (Ministry of Education).
'China (Taiwan).' In *World survey of education, Vol. 4, Higher education*, compiled by Educational, Scientific and Cultural Organization, United Nations. [Selective entry]
New York: UNESCO, 1966, 321–335.
SUBJ 17

14859 CSU P P1 G9.4 1949–1972
China [Republic]. Chiao yü pu. (Ministry of Education).
'China (Taiwan).' In *World survey of education, Vol. 5, Educational policy, legislation and administration*, compiled by Educational, Scientific and Cultural Organization, United Nations. [Selective entry]
Paris: UNESCO, 1971, 301–313.
SUBJ 17

14860 NIC P P1 G9.4 1949–1972
China [Republic]. Chiao yü pu. (Ministry of Education).
The present and future roles of the senior colleges of agriculture of Taiwan.
[Taipei?]: ——, 1963. 78 p.
SUBJ 17

14861 NNP O P3 G9.5 1949–1972
Cho, Kevin.
'The Chinese University of Hong Kong.'
Hemisphere 10, 11 (Nov. 1966), 21–23.
SUBJ 17

14862 NIC P P7 G1.2 1949–1972
Chu, Don-chean (Chu Tang-ch'ien), 1914–.
'The communes and their schools in Communist China.'
J. of human relations 9, 2 (Winter 1961), 265–274.
SUBJ 17 20 64 ▪ 34.1 55

14863 CSU P P2 G1.2 1949–1972
Chu, Hung-ti.
'Education in Mainland China.'
CH 59, 349 (Sept. 1970), 165–169, 181–182.
SUBJ 17

14864 CSU PO P1 G1.2 1949–1972
Chu, S. Y. (Ch'ü Shih-ying), 1899–, and Ronald Yu-soong Cheng (Ch'en Yu-sung), 1903–.
'Secondary education in New China.' In *The year book of education, 1958.* [Sole entry]
London: Evans, 1958?, 146–154.
SUBJ 17

14865 CSH PO P1 G9.4 1949–1972
Chu, Ying-shai (Chu Ying-jui).
'Extension of public schooling years in the Republic of China.'
IFC 31, 2 (Feb. 1969), 17–29.
SUBJ 17 ▪ 37

14866 CSH O P3 G6.1 1949–1972
Chung-kuo kung ch'an tang. Fu tan ta hsüeh wei yüan hui. (Chinese Communist Party. Fu-tan U. Committee).
'Reform universities of liberal arts through revolutionary mass criticism: Investigation report on Futan University's "May 7" experimental liberal arts class.' Tr. of 'Yung ko ming ta p'i p'an kai tsao wen k'o ta hsüeh: Fu tan ta hsüeh "wu, ch'i" wen k'o shih tien pan ti tiao ch'a pao kao'; *Hung ch'i* 1971, 6 (June), 67–74.
CE 5, 1/2 (Spring–Summer 1972), 144–160.
SUBJ 17 26.1 ▪ 32.1

14867 DLC S P1 G1.2 1949–1972
Cihak, J-.
'Pedagogická veda l'udovej Číny' (Pedagogy in the People's Republic of China).
Jednotná škola (Bratislava) 12, 6 (1957), 750–756.
SUBJ 17

14868 CSU P P2 G1.2 1949–1972
Current Scene Editor.
'Educational reform and rural resettlement in Communist China.'
CS 8, 17 (7 Nov. 1970), 1–8.
SUBJ 17 ▪ 21.2 35

14869 CSU P P7 G1.2 1949–1972
Current Scene Editor.
'Educational reform in rural China.'
CS 7, 3 (8 Feb. 1969), 1–17.
SUBJ 17 ▪ 64

14870 CSU O P2 G1.2 1949–1972
Dimond, E- Grey.
'Medical education in China.'
Asia (New York: Asia Society) 26 (Summer 1972), 60–73.
SUBJ 17 56

14871 NIC P P2 G1.2 1949–1972
Eitner, Hans-Jürgen.
Erziehung und Wissenschaft in der Volksrepublik China, 1949 bis 1963: Dokumentation und Analyse (Education and science in the People's Republic of China, 1949–1963: Documents and analysis).
Essen-Bredeney: Gesprächskreis Wissenschaft und Wirtschaft BDI/DIHT/SV, 1964. 137 p. (Stifterverband für die deutsche Wissenschaft, Wissenschaft und Wirtschaft, 64)
SUBJ 17 62 64 70 ▪ 16.1 19 32.1 60

14872 MCH PO P2 G1.2 1949–1972
Engelborghs, J-, and Marthe Engelborghs[-Bertels], 1928–.
'Note relative à l'enseignement en République populaire de Chine' (A note on education in the People's Republic of China).
B. du Centre d'étude des pays de l'Est 6, 2 (1965), 73–93.
SUBJ 17 18 60 ▪ 16 30 37 47 55 64

14873 DLC O P4 G1.3 1949–1972
Ershov, V- S-.
'Vysshee veterinarnoe obrazovanie v Kitaiskoi Narodnoi Respublike' (Professional veterinary training in the People's Republic of China).
Veterinariia 35, 12 (dekabr' 1958), 71–73.
SUBJ 14.1 17

14874 MAM FP P2 G9.4 1949–1972
Foster, Donald Murray, 1926–.
Education as an instrument of national policy for economic development in the Republic of China.
Ann Arbor: University Microfilms (Publ. 62-4034), 1962. 337 p. (Doctoral dissertation in Education, Stanford U.)
SUBJ 14.4 16.4 17 21.4 ▪ 14 21 58 64

14875 CSU O P2 G1.3 1949–1972
Frankenberg, Ronald.
'Education in China and China in education.'
EH 10, 6 (1971), 43–49.
SUBJ 17

14876 CSU P P2 G1.2 1949–1972
Fraser, Stewart Erskine, 1929–.
'Educational developments stemming from the Cultural Revolution.' In *Education and Communism in China: An anthology of commentary and documents*, edited by S. E. Fraser. [Selective entry]
London: Pall Mall Press, 1971, 543–553.
SUBJ 17

14877 CSU O P3 G5.1 1949–1972
Frolic, B- Michael.
'A visit to Peking University: What the Cultural Revolution was all about.'
New York times magazine 24 Oct. 1971, 29, 115–129.
SUBJ 17 54 ▪ 26.1 66

14878 NNC PO P3 G1.2 1949–1972
Fukushima Masao, 1906–.
'Legal education and research.' Tr. of 'Hōgaku no kyōiku to kenkyū'; in *Chūgoku no hō to shakai* (Law and society in China), jointly edited by Nihon hōritsuka hō-Chū daihyōdan (Delegation of Japanese lawyers to China) *with* Kokusai hōritsuka renraku kyōkai (International Lawyers Assn.); Tokyo: Shin dokushosha, 1960, 86–93. In *Education in Communist China*, mimeo., compiled by U.S. Joint Publications Research Service. [Selective entry]
Washington, D.C.: JPRS, 18 Jan. 1963, 79–88. (JPRS 17,188; MC 2985/1963)
SUBJ 12.2 17 ▪ 37

14879 CSU O P3 G9.4 1949–1972
Gable, William R-.
'The Center for Public and Business Administration Education at Chengchi University.'
National Chengchi U. j. 6 (Dec. 1962), 1–9.
SUBJ 17 ▪ 36.1 66

14880 NNC PO P2 G1.2 1949–1972
Gerlo, Aloïs.
'L'enseignement en République populaire de Chine' (Education in the People's Republic of China). In *Le régime et les institutions de la République populaire chinoise* (The government and institutions of the People's Republic of China), jointly edited by Centre d'étude des pays de l'Est, Institut de sociologie Solvay, Université libre de Bruxelles *with* Centre national pour l'étude des

pays à régime communiste. [Selective entry]
Brussels: Snoeck-Ducaju, 1960, 163–181.
Subj 17 64 ▪ 11.4 12.1 12.2 14 54

14881 NIC O P3 G5.1 1949–1972
Goldman, René, 1934–.
'Peking University today.'
CQ 7 (July–Sept. 1961), 101–111. [Reprinted as 'Peking University.' In *Education and Communism in China: An anthology of commentary and documents*, edited by Stewart Erskine Fraser. (Selective entry.) London: Pall Mall Press, 1971, 199–234.]
Subj 17 32.1 ▪ 26 28 64

14882 NIC S P2 G1.2 1949–1972
Grushka, Donna Gellis, 1944–.
A case study of manpower development under a revolutionary elite: Productive labor in education programs in the People's Republic of China.
Unpublished masters thesis in Economics, Cornell U., 1968. 251 p.
Subj 11.4 14 17

14883 CSU P P3 G1.2 1949–1972
Gupta, Krishna Prakash.
'Liberal arts education in China.'
China report (New Delhi) 7, 5 (Sept.–Oct. 1971), 18–25.
Subj 17

14884 CSU P P3 G1.2 1949–1972
Gupta, Krishna Prakash.
'Tsinghua experience and higher education in China.'
China report (New Delhi) 7, 1 (Jan.–Feb. 1971), 2–14.
Subj 17 64

14885 MCH P P1 G1.2 1949–1972
Harner, Evelyn L-.
Middle school education as a tool of power in Communist China.
Santa Barbara, Calif.: General Electric Co., Technical Military Planning Operation, 1962. 56 p. (TEMPO reports, RM 62 TMP-79)
Subj 11.4 12.1 16.1 17 32 54 ▪ 12.2 14 14.5 18 32.1 56 64 66 72

14886 MCY P P4 G1.2 1949–1972
Harrison, James Pinckney, 1932–.
'Perspectives on the intellectual in Communist China: The ideological training of intellectuals in Communist China.'
AS 5, 10 (Oct. 1965), 491–502.
Subj 12.1 16.1 17 60 ▪ 36.1 64

14887 CSU F P2 G9.5 1949–1972
Henderson, Norman Keith.
Educational developments and research, with special reference to Hong Kong.
Hong Kong: Hong Kong U. Press, 1963. 44 p. (Hong Kong Council for Educational Research publications, 1)
Subj 17

14888 NNC O P6 G5.4 1949–1972
Honan. Teng-feng hsien cheng fu. Wen chiao chü. (Teng-feng hsien. Cultural and Educational Bureau).
'The San-kuan-miao Hsiang Red and Expert Cadres School.' Tr. of 'San-kuan-miao hsiang ti kan pu hung chuan hsüeh hsiao' (The red-and-expert cadres school in San-kuan-miao *hsiang* [Teng-feng *hsien*, Honan]); *Jen min chiao yü* 1958, 8 (July), 8–10. In *Party and cadre education*, mimeo., compiled by U.S. Joint Publications Research Service. [Selective entry]
Washington, D.C.: JPRS, 17 Jan. 1963, 20–30. (JPRS 17,183; MC 2980/1963)
Subj 17 ▪ 26.1 32

14889 NNC FP P2 G9.5 1949–1972
Hong Kong. Committee on Higher Education.
Report of the Committee on Higher Education in Hong Kong, tabled in the Legislative Council, 17th September, 1952.
Hong Kong: Government Printer, 1952. 74 p.
Subj 17 ▪ 21.4

14890 NIC P P2 G9.5 1949–1972
Hong Kong. Education Dept.
Annual summary, 1955/56–1970/71.
Hong Kong: Government Printer. Issued annually, 1956–1971. Average ca. 60 p.
Subj 17 ▪ 28 37

14891 CSU P P2 G9.5 1949–1972
Hong Kong. Education Dept.
'Hong Kong.' In *World survey of education, Vol. 3, Secondary education*, compiled by Educational, Scientific and Cultural Organization, United Nations. [Selective entry]
New York: International Documents Service, 1961, 1282–1290.
Subj 17

14892 CSU P P2 G9.5 1949–1972
Hong Kong. Education Dept.
'Hong Kong.' In *World survey of education, Vol. 4, Higher education*, compiled by Educational, Scientific and Cultural Organization, United Nations. [Selective entry]
New York: UNESCO, 1966, 1253–1264.
Subj 17

14893 CSU P P2 G9.5 1949–1972
Hong Kong. Education Dept.
'Hong Kong.' In *World survey of education, Vol. 5, Educational policy, legislation and administration*, compiled by Educational, Scientific and Cultural Organization, United Nations. [Selective entry]
Paris: UNESCO, 1971, 1218–1225.
Subj 17

14894 NIC P P2 G9.5 1949–1972
Hong Kong. Education Dept.
Triennial survey, 1955/58–1967/70.
Hong Kong: Government Printer. Issued annually, 1958–1970. Average ca. 100 p.
Subj 17 ▪ 28 37 54

14895 CSU O P2 G9.4 1949–1972
Hsiung, Hsien-chu.
'The present status of curriculum, techniques of teaching and evaluation and textbooks in the Republic of China.' In *Curriculum, methods of teaching, evaluation and textbooks in primary schools in Asia: Report of a working group (Bangkok, 19–23 April 1965)*, edited by Regional Office for Education in Asia, Educational, Scientific and Cultural Organization, United Nations. [Sole entry]
Bangkok: Regional Office for Education in Asia, 1966, 65–72.
Subj 17

14896 CSU F P3 G9.4 1949–1972
Hsu, S. C. (Hsü Shih-chü), 1905–, and K. K. Chang.
'Teaching of fertility regulation in medical schools in Taiwan.'
CMJ-T 13, 4 (Dec. 1966), 319–325.
Subj 17 51 56

14897 CSH P P1 G1.2 1949–1972
Hsü, Immanuel C. Y. (Hsü Chung-yüeh), 1923–.
'The reorganisation of higher education in Communist China, 1949–61.'
CQ 19 (July–Sept. 1964), 128–160. [Reprinted as 'The impact of industrialization on higher education in Communist China.' In *Manpower and education: Country studies in economic development*, edited by Frederick Harbison and Charles A- Meyers. (Sole entry.) New York: McGraw-Hill, 1965, 202–231.] [Reprinted as 'The reorganization of higher education in Communist China, 1949–61.' In *China under Mao: Politics takes command*, edited by Roderick Lemonde MacFarquhar. (Selective entry.) Cambridge: M.I.T. Press, 1966, 271–303.]
Subj 17 ▪ 11.4 16.1 32.1

14898 CSH P P1 G1.2 1949–1972
Hu, C. T. (Hu Ch'ang-tu), 1920–.
'Communist education: Theory and practice.'
CQ 10 (Apr.–June 1962), 84–97. [Reprinted in *China under Mao: Politics takes command*, edited by Roderick Lemonde MacFarquhar. (Selective entry.) Cambridge: M.I.T. Press, 1966, 241–254.]
Subj 12.1 17 64 ▪ 14 16 32.1 60

14899 NNC P P1 G1.2 1949–1972
Hu, C. T. (Hu Ch'ang-tu), 1920–.
Higher education in Mainland China and its implications for world affairs.
New York: Columbia U., Teachers College, 1960. 47 p.
Subj 17 ▪ 32.1 64

14900 CSU P P2 G1.2 1949–1972
Hu, C. T. (Hu Ch'ang-tu), 1920–.
'Orthodoxy over historicity: The teaching of history in Communist China.'
Comparative education review 13, 1 (Feb. 1969), 1–29. [Reprinted in *Aspects of Chinese education*, edited by C. T. Hu. (Selective entry.) New York: Columbia U., Teachers College, Institute of International Studies, Center for Education in Asia *with* Columbia U., East Asian Institute, 1969, 2–19.] [Reprinted as 'The teaching of history in Communist China.' *RSAEO* 1969, 2, 191–213.)
Subj 17 62

14901 NNC P P1 G1.2 1949–1972
Hu, C. T. (Hu Ch'ang-tu), 1920–.
'Politics and economics in Chinese education.' In *The Chinese model: A political, economic and social survey*, edited by Werner Klatt. [Selective entry]

Hong Kong: Hong Kong U. Press, 1965, 31–47.
SUBJ 12.1 17 ▪ 11.4 14

14902 MCH P P1 G1.2 1949–1972
Hu, C. T. (Hu Ch'ang-tu), 1920–.
'Recent trends in Chinese education.'
International review of education 10, 1 (1964), 12–21.
SUBJ 17 64 ▪ 16.1

14903 MAM P P1 G1.1 1949–1972
Hu, Shi Ming, 1927–.
Interrelationship between education and political ideology exemplified in China: A critical analysis of educational policy and curriculum trends in the Chinese People's Republic (Mainland) and in the Republic of China (Taiwan) from 1949 to 1969.
Ann Arbor: University Microfilms (Publ. 72-8823), 1972. 306 p. (Doctoral dissertation in Education, Columbia U. [Teachers College], 1970)
SUBJ 17 64

14904 CSU S P3 G9.5 1949–1972
Huang, Steve S. C.
'The Chinese University of Hong Kong.'
JRAS-HKB 5 (1965), 86–94.
SUBJ 17

14905 NNC P P2 G1.2 1949–1972
I Wo-sheng.
'Education in Communist China.' Tr. of 'Shih nien lai ti Chung kung chiao yü' (Education in Communist China during the past decade); *Tsu kuo chou k'an* 394 (1 Aug. 1960), 17–28. In *Communist China, 1949–1959*, edited by Union Research Institute. [Selective entry]
Hong Kong: Union Research Institute, 1961, vol. 3, 99–152.
SUBJ 17 ▪ 32.1 37 54

14906 CSH P P2 G1.2 1949–1972
I Wo-sheng, Lu Hsu-yin (Lu Hsü-yin), Fang Cheng, and Hsueh Yu (Hsüeh Yu). [Authors sequential rather than joint: I Wo-sheng for 1960–1962; Lu Hsu-yin for 1963; Fang Cheng for 1964–1967; Hsüeh Yu for 1968 and 1969.]
'Education' [title varies]. Tr. from *Tsu kuo chou k'an* 440 (12 June 1961); 489 (21 May 1962) *and from Tsu kuo* 3–73 (June 1964 – Apr. 1970) [recurring annual feature article]. In *Communist China, 1960–1969*, edited by Union Research Institute.
Hong Kong: Union Research Institute. Issued annually, 1962–1970, average ca. 30 p.
SUBJ 17 ▪ 16.1 32.1 37 54 64

14907 NNC O P2 G1.2 1949–1972
Iskhakov, S- I-.
'O sanitarnom prosveshchenii v Kitaiskoi Narodnoi Respublike' (Health education in the People's Republic of China).
Sovetskoe zdravookhranenie 17, 5 (mai 1958), 54–58.
SUBJ 17 56

14908 MAM FP P4 G9.4 1949–1972
Jackson, Malan Robert, 1935–.
The role of higher education in the realization of the national goals of the Republic of China.
Ann Arbor: University Microfilms (Publ. 71-14,431), 1971. 370 p. (Doctoral dissertation in Education, Arizona State U.)
SUBJ 17 ▪ 12.2 16.1 60

14909 NNC P P1 G1.2 1949–1972
Japan. Mombushō. Chōsakyoku. (Ministry of Education. Research Bureau), ed.
Higher education in Communist China, mimeo. Tr. of 'Chūka jimmin kyōwakoku no kōtō kyōiku' (Higher education in the People's Republic of China); in *Kakkoku no kōtō kyōiku* (Higher education in various countries), mimeo., edited by the agency cited; Tokyo: Mombushō, 1958, vol. 4, 95–131.
Washington, D.C.: U.S. Joint Publications Research Service, 1 Aug. 1960. 65 p. (JPRS 5127; MC 15,724/1960)
SUBJ 17 ▪ 32.1 54

14910 CSU P P2 G1.2 1949–1972
Kan, David.
The impact of the Cultural Revolution on Chinese higher education.
Hong Kong: Union Research Institute, 1971. 183 p. (Doctoral dissertation in Education, U. of California, Los Angeles, 1970). [Also published—Ann Arbor: University Microfilms (Publ. 71-16,332), 1971. 183 p.]
SUBJ 16.1 17 54 ▪ 11.2 35 37 64

14911 CSH O P4 G9.4 1949–1972
Kao, Si-chin (Kao Hsi-chin).
'Modern management development in Taiwan today.'
IFC 31, 2 (Feb. 1969), 2–12.
SUBJ 17 34.2

14912 CSH O P4 G1.2 1949–1972
Kirby, Edward Stuart, 1909–.
'Economics in China in the universities.'
Soviet survey 24 (Apr.–June 1958), 37–40. [Special issue on China]
SUBJ 17 70 ▪ 32.1 64

14913 NNC P P2 G1.2 1949–1972
Kirpsha, A- I-.
'Narodnoe obrazovanie v Kitae' (National education in China). In *Voprosy kul'turnoi revoliutsii v Kitaiskoi Narodnoi Respublike: sbornik statei* (Articles on the cultural revolution in the People's Republic of China), compiled by Institut kitaevedeniia, Akademiia nauk SSSR, edited by Nikolai Trofimovich Fedorenko. [Selective entry]
Moscow: Izd-vo vost. lit-ry, 1960, 79–101.
SUBJ 17 32.1 ▪ 37 64

14914 MCH U P1 G1.2 1949–1972
Klepikov, Vladimir Zakharovich, 1932–.
'Iz opyta soedineniia obucheniia s proizvoditel'nym trudom v shkolakh Kitaiskoi Narodnoi Respublike' (The experiment of combining study with productive work in schools of the People's Republic of China).
Politekhnicheskoe obuchenie 1959, 9 (sentiabr'), 83–88.
SUBJ 17 37

14915 NNC P P1 G1.2 1949–1972
Klepikov, Vladimir Zakharovich, 1932–.
'Podgotovka reformy shkoly v Kitae' (Preparations for school reform in China).
Narodnoe obrazovanie 1961, 5 (mai), 99–102.
SUBJ 17

14916 DLC P P2 G1.2 1949–1972
Klepikov, Vladimir Zakharovich, 1932–.
'Soedinenie obucheniia s sel'skokhoziaistvennym trudom v shkolakh Kitaiskoi Narodnoi Respubliki' (Combining farm work with study in the schools of the People's Republic of China).
Biologiia v shkole 1961, 2 (mart–aprel'), 71–76.
SUBJ 17 ▪ 14.1

14917 CSU P P2 G1.2 1949–1972
Kobayashi, Fumio.
'The Great Cultural Revolution and the educational reform: The image of socialist man.'
DE 9, 4 (Dec. 1971), 490–501. [Special issue: *On China*]
SUBJ 12.1 17 19 ▪ 16 54

14918 DLC O P4 G1.2 1949–1972
Kotoc, Jan.
'Zájazd pedagogickej delegácie do l'udovodemokratickej Číny' (Visit by the Slovak educational delegation to the People's Republic of China).
Jednotna škola (Bratislava) 13, 5 (1958), 618–621.
SUBJ 17

14919 DLC S P1 G1.2 1949–1972
Kujal, Bohumír.
'Školství, socialistická výchova a pedagogika v Čínské lidove republice.'
Pedagogika (Prague) 8, 4 (1958), 441–467.

Schools, socialist education, and pedagogy in the People's Republic of China, mimeo.
Washington, D.C.: U.S. Joint Publications Research Service, 30 Jan. 1959. 37 p. (JPRS 512D; MC 4968/1959)
SUBJ 17 ▪ 37

14920 NIC P P1 G1.2 1949–1972
Kun, Joseph C.
'Higher education: Some problems of selection and enrollment.'
CQ 8 (Oct.–Dec. 1961), 135–148. [For a fuller version, see entry 14921.]
SUBJ 16 17 ▪ 11.4 12.1 14 16.1

14921 NNC P P1 G1.2 1949–1972
Kun, Joseph C.
Selection and enrollment of new students in higher educational institutions of Communist China, mimeo.
Cambridge: Massachusetts Institute of Technology, Center for International Studies, 1961. 82 p.
SUBJ 17 54 ▪ 62 64 66 72

14922 CSH O P2 G9.2 1949–1972
Kwangtung. Ko ming wei yüan hui. Tiao ch'a tsu. (Revolutionary Committee. Investigation Team).
'Four new kinds of schools.' Tr. by Akira Odani of 'Ssu chung hsin hsing ti hsüeh hsiao: Kuang-tung sheng ko hsien (shih) ch'uang pan kung yeh, nung yeh, wei sheng shih fan ssu chung tuan ch'i hsüeh hsiao ti tsung ho pao kao' (Four new kinds of schools: Report on the establishment of short-term industrial, agricultural, public-health, and normal

schools in various counties and municipalities of Kwangtung); *Hung ch'i* 1970, 8 (Aug.), 55–57.
CE 4, 2 (Summer 1971), 111–118.
SUBJ 17 ▪ 26.3 26.4

14923 MCH P P1 G1.2 1949–1972
[La Dany, Ladislao] ———, 1914–.
'The anti-academic year of 1966–1967.'
CNA 660 (19 May 1967), 1–7.
SUBJ 17 ▪ 12.1 54

14924 CSH P P2 G1.2 1949–1972
[La Dany, Ladislao] ———, 1914–.
'Education: "Bourgeois" or proletarian?'
CNA 617 (24 June 1966), 1–7.
SUBJ 17

14925 CSH P P3 G6.1 1949–1972
[La Dany, Ladislao] ———, 1914–.
'An episode of the purge: K'uang Ya-ming and Nanking University.'
CNA 623 (5 Aug. 1966), 1–7.
SUBJ 12.1 17

14926 MCH P P2 G1.2 1949–1972
[La Dany, Ladislao] ———, 1914–.
'Higher education.'
CNA 471 (7 June 1963), 1–7; 476 (12 July 1963), 1–7.
SUBJ 17 54

14927 CSH P P4 G1.2 1949–1972
[La Dany, Ladislao] ———, 1914–.
'Higher education.'
CNA 816 (2 Oct. 1970), 1–7.
SUBJ 17 64

14928 MCH P P3 G1.2 1949–1972
[La Dany, Ladislao] ———, 1914–.
'Higher learning.'
CNA 292 (11 Sept. 1959), 1–7.
SUBJ 17

14929 CSH P P2 G1.2 1949–1972
[La Dany, Ladislao] ———, 1914–.
'In the universities.'
CNA 772 (5 Sept. 1969), 1–7.
SUBJ 17 54 ▪ 21.2

14930 CSH P P2 G1.2 1949–1972
[La Dany, Ladislao] ———, 1914–.
'Mao on higher education.'
CNA 723 (30 Aug. 1968), 1–7.
SUBJ 17 64 ▪ 56

14931 NIC P P2 G1.2 1949–1972
[La Dany, Ladislao] ———, 1914–.
'New education.'
CNA 228 (16 May 1958), 1–7.
SUBJ 17 37 ▪ 64

14932 NIC P P2 G1.2 1949–1972
[La Dany, Ladislao] ———, 1914–.
'Reform of education.'
CNA 334 (5 Aug. 1960), 1–7.
SUBJ 17

14933 CSH P P2 G1.2 1949–1972
[La Dany, Ladislao] ———, 1914–.
'Secondary and primary schools.'
CNA 868 (21 Jan. 1972), 1–7.
SUBJ 17

14934 NNC P P1 G1.2 1949–1972
[La Dany, Ladislao] ———, 1914–.
'Secondary education.'
CNA 147 (7 Sept. 1956), 1–7.
SUBJ 17

14935 MCH P P2 G1.2 1949–1972
[La Dany, Ladislao] ———, 1914–.
'Secondary education.'
CNA 554 (5 Mar. 1965), 1–7.
SUBJ 17

14936 MCH P P1 G1.2 1949–1972
[La Dany, Ladislao] ———, 1914–.
'Training in medicine.'
CNA 577 (20 Aug. 1965), 1–7.
SUBJ 17 56

14937 MCH P P1 G1.2 1949–1972
La Dany, Ladislao, 1914–.
'Vita intellettuale in Cina' (Intellectual life in China).
Civiltà cattolica 113, 6 (17 marzo 1962), 556–566.
SUBJ 16.1 17 ▪ 12.1 64

14938 MCH O P3 G5.1 1949–1972
Lary, Diana Cecilia Margaret, 1941–.
'Teaching English in China.'
CQ 24 (Oct.–Dec. 1965), 1–9.
SUBJ 17 ▪ 22.1 26.1 54 66

14939 CSH PO P3 G9.5 1949–1972
Leary, R- H-.
'[1] Principles of opportunism. [2] Regulate, don't operate.'
FEER 41, 5 (1 Aug. 1963), 307–311; 41, 6 (8 Aug. 1963), 357–360.
SUBJ 17 ▪ 21.1 28

14940 MAM P P1 G9.4 1949–1972
Lee, Hwa-wei, 1932–.
Educational development in Taiwan under the Nationalist government, 1945–1962.
Ann Arbor: University Microfilms (Publ. 65-8311), 1965. 347 p. (Doctoral dissertation in Education, U. of Pittsburgh, 1964)
SUBJ 17

14941 CSU P P1 G1.2 1949–1972
Lee, Hwa-wei, 1932–.
'The recent educational reform in Communist China.'
School and society 96, 2311 (9 Nov. 1968), 395–400.
SUBJ 17 ▪ 32.1 64

14942 MAM P P2 G1.2 1949–1972
Lee, Sui Ming, 1923–.
Higher education in Communist China, 1949–1969.
Ann Arbor: University Microfilms (Publ. 71-8002), 1971. 120 p. (Doctoral dissertation in Education, U. of Pittsburgh)
SUBJ 17 ▪ 32.1 64

14943 CBU O P2 G1.2 1949–1972
Leijon, Per Olow, 1938–.
Tre år i Maos Kina (Three years in Mao's China).
Stockholm: Wahlström och Widstrand, 1963. 189 p.
SUBJ 17 64 66 ▪ 12 14.1 16.1 16.4 19 29 46 52

14944 MAM P P1 G9.4 1949–1972
Lew, William Jing Foo, 1925–.
A comparative analysis of current aims of Chinese and American public secondary education.
Ann Arbor: University Microfilms (Publ. 66-1081), 1966. 278 p. (Doctoral dissertation in Education, Southern Illinois U., 1965)
SUBJ 17

14945 NNC P P3 G1.2 1949–1972
Lewis, John Wilson, 1930–.
'Party cadres in Communist China.' In *Education and political development*, edited by James Smoot Coleman. [Sole entry]
Princeton: Princeton U. Press, 1965, 408–436. (Social Science Research Council, Committee on Comparative Politics, Studies in political development, 4)
SUBJ 16.1 17 ▪ 32 61

14946 NNC PO P7 G5.4 1949–1972
Li Kuei-chih. [Tr. erroneously gives author's name as Li K'uang-chih.]
'Survey of red and expert commune universities in Honan.' Tr. of 'Ho-nan Sui-p'ing Wei-hsing jen min kung she hung chuan ta hsüeh ti tiao ch'a pao kao' (Report on the Red and Expert University in Wei-hsing commune, Sui-p'ing *hsien*, Honan); *Pei-ching shih ta hsüeh hsüeh pao; she hui k'o hsüeh* 1959, 1 (Jan.), 37–44. In *Translations from China's political and sociological publications*, mimeo., compiled by U.S. Joint Publications Research Service. [Selective entry]
Washington, D.C.: JPRS, 11 Sept. 1959, 19–30. (JPRS 909D; MC 16,509/1959)
SUBJ 17 ▪ 24.1 26.1 64

14947 CSH O P3 G5.1 1949–1972
Liang Han-ping.
'Work-and-study program is best form of coordination between education and productive labor.' Tr. of 'Pan kung pan tu shih chiao yü ho sheng ch'an lao tung hsiang chieh ho ti tsui hao hsing shih'; *Hung ch'i* 1958, 8 (16 Sept.), 24–27. In *Selected translations from 'Hung ch'i' (Red flag), September 1958*, mimeo., compiled by U.S. Joint Publications Research Service. [Selective entry]
Washington, D.C.: JPRS, 9 May 1961, 43–46. (JPRS 9181; MC 15,357/1961)
SUBJ 17 ▪ 26.4 37

14948 MCH O P1 G1.2 1949–1972
Ling Yang.
'Training medical workers.'
PR 7, 46 (13 Nov. 1964), 23–25.
SUBJ 17 56

14949 CSH O P2 G9.4 1949–1972
Liu, Chen, 1910–.
Education is dedication: A brief account of my personal experience in educational work in Taiwan province, Republic of China. Tr. of 'Pan hsüeh yü ts'ung cheng' (Experiences in education and government administration); in *Pan hsüeh yü ts'ung cheng* (Experiences in education and government administration), by Chen Liu; Taipei: Shang wu yin shu kuan, 1965, 1–112. [Abridged tr.]
Taipei: Student Book Co., 1968. 89 p.
SUBJ 17

14950 MCH O P3 G5.1 1949–1972
Liu Shui Sheng, pseud.
'Life in a Chinese university.'

Atlantic monthly 204, 6 (Dec. 1959), 89–92. [Special issue: *Red China: The first ten years*]
Subj 17 32.1 ▪ 30 64

14951 SEU P P2 G1.1 1949–1972
Liu, William H.
Politico-ideological education in Communist China.
Unpublished doctoral dissertation in Education, U. of Edinburgh, 1969. 217 p.
Subj 15 16 17 32 64 ▪ 12 14.2 37 54

14952 CLU P P2 G1.2 1949–1972
Liu, William H.
'Teacher training in China under the Cultural Revolution.'
Scottish educational studies 3, 2 (Nov. 1971), 88–100.
Subj 17 ▪ 32.1 37

14953 CBU P P1 G1.2 1949–1972
Livshits, E- S- (J. S. Livschiz).
'Uspekhi narodnogo obrazovaniia v novom Kitae' (Achievements in national education in New China).
Sovetskaia pedagogika 17, 11 (dekabr' 1953), 106–112.
'Sowjetisierung des chinesischen Bildungswesens: Schulsystem nach dem Sowjetmodell' (Sovietization of the Chinese educational system: A school system based on the Soviet model).
Ost-Probleme 6, 8 (25 Feb. 1954), 299–304.
Subj 17 ▪ 52

14954 CSU P P2 G1.2 1949–1972
Ma, John T. (Ma Ta-jen), 1920–.
'Libraries in the People's Republic of China since 1949.'
Wilson library b. 45, 10 (June 1971), 970–975.
Subj 17

14955 CBU FP P2 G9.4 1949–1972
McCusker, Henry F-, Jr., and Harry Joseph Robinson, 1909–.
Education and development: The role of educational planning in the economic development of the Republic of China, mimeo.
Menlo Park, Calif.: Stanford Research Institute, 1962. 2 vols. 63; 11, 159 p. (SRI project, IMU-4027)
Subj 17 21.4 ▪ 14 15

14956 CSU P P2 G1.2 1949–1972
McDowell, S- Garrett.
'Educational reform in China as a readjusting country.'
AS 11, 3 (Mar. 1971), 256–270.
Subj 17 ▪ 56

14957 CBU PO P2 G1.2 1949–1972
Monoszon, E- I-.
'Narodnoe obrazovanie v Kitaiskoi Narodnoi Respublike' (Public education in the People's Republic of China). In *Shkola i prosveshchenie v Narodnom Kitae: sbornik statei* (Articles on schools and education in the People's Republic of China), compiled by Akademiia pedagogicheskikh nauk RSFSR, edited by Aleksei I- Markushevich, E- I- Monoszon, and M- N- Riakin. [Selective entry]
Moscow: Izd-vo Akad. ped. nauk RSFSR, 1957, 25–47.
Subj 17 ▪ 27 64

14958 CSU P P2 G1.2 1949–1972
Munro, Donald Jacques, 1931–.
'Egalitarian ideal and educational fact in Communist China.' In *China: Management of a revolutionary society*, edited by John Matthew Henry Lindbeck. [Analytic entry]
Seattle: U. of Washington Press, 1971, 256–301. (Social Science Research Council, Studies in Chinese government and politics, 2)
Subj 16 17 ▪ 54 64

14959 CSU P P2 G1.2 1949–1972
Munro, Donald Jacques, 1931–.
'Maxims and realities in China's educational policy: The half-work, half-study model.'
AS 7, 4 (Apr. 1967), 254–272.
Subj 17 32.1 37 ▪ 11.4 12.1 16 16.1 61 64

14960 CSU O P3 G6.1 1949–1972
Mututantri, Barbara.
'The rebirth of a Chinese university.'
EH 8, 4 (1969), 28–38.
Subj 17 ▪ 24.4 26.1 26.4

14961 CBU PO P3 G9.5 1949–1972
Myers, Ramon Hawley, 1929–.
'Education, technology and the economic development of Hong Kong.'
CCJ 3, 2 (May 1964), 190–201.
Subj 17 21.4 24 ▪ 24.4

14962 CSU P P2 G5.1 1949–1972
Nee, Victor, and Don Layman.
The Cultural Revolution at Peking University.
New York: Monthly Review Press, 1969. 91 p.
Subj 17 19 54 ▪ 26.1 32 32.1 64

14963 NNC O P3 G6.1 1949–1972
Nutting, N-.
'Libraries in Shanghai.'
New Zealand libraries new series 15, 4 (May 1952), 89–90.
Subj 17

14964 MCH O P1 G1.2 1949–1972
Oldham, C- H- G-.
'Science and education in China.' In *Contemporary China*, edited by Ruth Adams. [Selective entry]
New York: Pantheon, 1966, 281–317.
Subj 12.1 16.1 17 36.1 62 ▪ 64

14965 CSU P P2 G1.2 1949–1972
Ong, Ellen K.
'Education in China since the Cultural Revolution.'
Studies in comparative Communism 3, 3/4 (July–Oct. 1970), 158–176.
Subj 12.1 17 37 ▪ 36.3 36.4 64

14966 MCH O P3 G6.1 1949–1972
Ordin, B- M-.
'V odnom iz krupneishikh tekhnikumov Kitaia' (In one of China's largest technical schools).
Srednee spetsial'noe obrazovanie 5, 9 (sentiabr' 1958), 60–63.
Subj 17 ▪ 54

14967 CSU P P2 G1.2 1949–1972
Orleans, Leo A-, 1924–.
'Communist China's education: Policies, problems, and prospects.' In *An economic profile of Mainland China*, compiled by Joint Economic Committee, U.S. Congress. [Selective entry]
Washington, D.C.: U.S. Government Printing Office, 1967, vol. 2, 499–518. [Reprinted in *An economic profile of Mainland China*, compiled by the agency cited. (Selective entry.) New York: Praeger, 1968, 499–518.]
Subj 11.4 12.1 17 ▪ 16 54

14968 CSU P P2 G1.2 1949–1972
Orleans, Leo A-, 1924–.
'Medical education and manpower in Communist China.'
Comparative education review 13, 1 (Feb. 1969), 20–42. [Reprinted in *Aspects of Chinese education*, edited by C. T. Hu (Hu Ch'ang-tu). (Selective entry.) New York: Columbia U., Teachers College, Institute of International Studies, Center for Education in Asia *with* Columbia U., East Asian Institute, 1969, 20–42.]
Subj 17 56 ▪ 16.1

14969 CSU P P2 G1.2 1949–1972
Orleans, Leo A-, 1924–.
Professional manpower and education in Communist China.
Washington, D.C.: National Science Foundation, 1961. 12, 260 p. (NSF 61-3)
Subj 11.4 16.2 17 ▪ 11 16.1 32.1 36.1 37 64

14970 NNC O P3 G9.3 1949–1972
P'an Mou-yuan (P'an Mou-yüan).
'Great accomplishments in educational reform at Amoy University in the last ten years.' Tr. of 'Shih nien lai chiao yü kai ko ti wei ta ch'eng chiu chi chu yao ching yen' (The great achievements and major lessons of experiments in educational reform during the past decade); *Lun t'an* 1959, 5 (Oct.), 17–27. In *Chinese Communist articles on education*, mimeo., compiled by U.S. Joint Publications Research Service. [Sole entry]
Washington, D.C.: JPRS, 12 Feb. 1960, 7–23. (JPRS 1165D; MC 5636/1960)
Subj 17 26.1 ▪ 26 32.1

14971 CSU P P2 G1.2 1949–1972
Pepper, Suzanne, 1939–.
'Education and political development in Communist China.'
Studies in comparative Communism 3, 3/4 (July–Oct. 1970), 132–157.
Subj 17 ▪ 11.2 11.4 12.1 16.1

14972 MCH P P1 G9.4 1949–1972
Pires, Edward Aloysius.
Primary teacher training in Asia.
Bangkok: UNESCO, Regional Office of Education in Asia, 1963. 291 p. (UNESCO studies in Asian education, 1)
Subj 17 ▪ 18

14973 CSU P P2 G1.2 1949–1972
Price, Ronald Francis, 1926–.
'China: In search of an anti-city education.' In *The world year book of education, 1970: Education in cities,*

edited by Joseph Albert Lauwerys and David G- Scanlon. [Sole entry]
London: Evans, 1970, 385–392.
SUBJ 17 ▪ 11.1 11.2

14974 CSU PO P 2 G 1.2 1949–1972
Price, Ronald Francis, 1926–.
Education in Communist China.
New York: Praeger, 1970. 19, 308 p. (Revision of *The Chinese tradition in education and contemporary theory and practice: A survey of education in the People's Republic of China, 1949–1968,* doctoral dissertation, U. of London, 1969)
SUBJ 16.1 17 37 54 64 ▪ 12.1 14 14.2 16 32.1 36.4 50 52 62 66

14975 CSU P P 2 G 1.2 1949–1972
Priestley, Kenneth Ewart.
'China.' In *The year book of education, 1952.* [Sole entry]
London: Evans, 1952?, 490–512. [Reprinted as 'Education in the People's Republic of China: Beginnings.' In *Education and Communism in China: An anthology of commentary and documents,* edited by Stewart Erskine Fraser. (Selective entry.) London: Pall Mall Press, 1971, 49–80.]
SUBJ 17

14976 NNC P P 1 G 1.2 1949–1972
Priestley, Kenneth Ewart.
Education in China.
Hong Kong: Dragonfly Books, 1961. 122 p.
SUBJ 12.1 17 64 ▪ 16.1 62

14977 CBU P P 2 G 1.2 1949–1972
Priestley, Kenneth Ewart.
'The People's Republic of China (Communist China).' In *Comparative educational administration,* edited by Theodore L- Reller and Edgar Leroy Morphet. [Sole entry]
Englewood Cliffs, N. J.: Prentice-Hall, 1962, 275–291. [Reprinted as 'Educational administration in Communist China.' In *Education and Communism in China: An anthology of commentary and documents,* edited by Stewart Erskine Fraser. (Selective entry.) London: Pall Mall Press, 1971, 105–126.]
SUBJ 17 ▪ 32 54

14978 CSH PO P 3 G 9.5 1949–1972
Priestley, Kenneth Ewart.
'The University of Hong Kong.'
Civilisations 5, 3 (1955), 353–361.
SUBJ 17

14979 MCH PO P 3 G 9.4 1949–1972
Purdue–Taiwan Engineering Project.
Comprehensive report of the cooperative project between Purdue University and Cheng Kung University to aid engineering education on Taiwan, 1952–1959.
[Lafayette]: Purdue U., 1959. 164 p.
SUBJ 17 ▪ 16.1

14980 NNC O P 3 G 1.3 1949–1972
Rakovskii, S- N-.
'Rastet podgotovka pedagogov v Narodnom Kitae' (Teacher training in the People's Republic of China is being increased).
Vestnik vysshei shkoly 16, 12 (dekabr' 1958), 80–82.
SUBJ 17 ▪ 62

14981 NIC F P 3 G 9.4 1949–1972
Rodd, William G-.
'A cross-cultural study of Taiwan's schools.'
J. of social psychology 50, 1 (Aug. 1959), 3–36.
SUBJ 17 ▪ 54

14982 CSH O P 3 G 1.3 1949–1972
Ross, D- M-.
'Higher education in China.'
Universities review 26, 2 (Feb. 1954), 64–72.
SUBJ 17

14983 CBU F P 3 G 9.5 1949–1972
Rowe, Elizabeth, et al.
Failure in school: Aspects of the problem in Hong Kong.
Hong Kong: Hong Kong U. Press, 1966. 17, 167 p. (Hong Kong Council for Educational Research publications, 3)
SUBJ 17 41 ▪ 55 58

14984 NNC P P 2 G 1.2 1949–1972
Rytaia, Mariia Nikiforovna.
'Bibliotechnoe delo v Kitaiskoi Narodnoi Respublike' (Libraries in the People's Republic of China).
Bibliotekovedenie i bibliografiia za rubezhom 4 (1959), 4–32.
SUBJ 17 ▪ 32.1 34.1 36.4

14985 CSH O P 3 G 5.3 1949–1972
Shantung Medical College, Tsinan. 'June 26th' Committee. Revolutionary Committee.
'A new approach to medical education.'
CM 1968, 5 (May), 292–296.
SUBJ 17 32.1 56

14986 NNC P P 1 G 1.2 1949–1972
Shelekasov, P- V-.
'Obrazovanie sochetaetsia s proizvoditel'nym trudom: po stranitsam kitaiskoi pechati' (Study combined with productive labor: From the Chinese press).
Vestnik vysshei shkoly 17, 10 (oktiabr' 1959), 22–28.
SUBJ 17 37 ▪ 16 60

14987 CSU PO P 1 G 9.4 1949–1972
Shen, Y. T.
'China (Taiwan).' In *World survey of education, Vol. 3, Secondary education,* compiled by Educational, Scientific and Cultural Organization, United Nations. [Selective entry]
New York: International Documents Service, 1961, 358–367.
SUBJ 17

14988 CSH O P 2 G 2.3 1949–1972
Shen-yang i hsüeh yüan. Kung jen, chieh fang chün Mao Tse-tung ssu hsiang hsüan ch'uan pu. (Shenyang Medical College. Worker – People's Liberation Army Mao Tse-tung Thought Propaganda Team).
'Forever carry forward the revolutionary tradition of the Red Army health school: Report on the educational revolution in the Shenyang Medical College.' Tr. of 'Yung yüan fa yang hung chün wei hsiao ti ko ming ch'uan t'ung: Shen-yang i hsüeh yüan chiao yü ko ming ch'ing k'uang pao kao'; *Hung ch'i* 1971, 6, 98–104.
CE 5, 1/2 (Spring–Summer 1972), 215–231.
SUBJ 17 56

14989 CSH P P 1 G 9.4 1949–1972
Shih, Chien-sheng.
'Reflections on the problems of human resources development in Taiwan.'
IFC 29, 3 (Mar. 1968), 6–12. [Reprinted—*Economic research j.* 15, 2 (Sept. 1968), 69–74.]
SUBJ 17

14990 NNC P P 2 G 1.2 1949–1972
Shih, Joseph Anderson (Shih Ch'eng-chih), 1918–1973.
The status of science and education in Communist China and a comparison with that in USSR, mimeo.
Hong Kong: Union Research Institute, 1962. 13, 76 p. (Communist China problem research series, EC30)
SUBJ 17 36.1 62 64 ▪ 14.1 14.4 16.1 18 41

14991 MCH FP P 2 G 1.2 1949–1972
Sieh, Marie.
'The school teacher, a link to China's future: Notes on professional tensions in the education system.'
CS 3, 18 (1 May 1965), 1–15. [Reprinted in *Education and Communism in China: An anthology of commentary and documents,* edited by Stewart Erskine Fraser. (Selective entry.) London: Pall Mall Press, 1971, 171–192.]
SUBJ 16.1 17 ▪ 12.1 61 63

14992 ELS FP P 3 G 9.5 1949–1972
Simpson, Raymond Frank, 1925–.
The development of education in Hong Kong: Problems and priorities.
Unpublished doctoral dissertation in Education, U. of London [External degree], 1967. 538 p.
SUBJ 17 24 ▪ 21.4 54

14993 MCH P P 1 G 1.2 1949–1972
Simpson, Raymond Frank, 1925–.
'The development of education in Mainland China.'
Phi Delta Kappan 39, 3 (Dec. 1957), 84–93.
SUBJ 17 ▪ 16.1

14994 MCY PO P 2 G 9.4 1949–1972
Simpson, Raymond Frank, 1925–.
'Educational developments in Taiwan.' In *Contemporary China, 1959–1960,* edited by Edward Stuart Kirby. [Selective entry]
Hong Kong: Hong Kong U. Press, 1961, 87–107.
SUBJ 17 ▪ 54

14995 HKU FP P 3 G 9.5 1949–1972
Simpson, Raymond Frank, 1925–.
Graduate employment in Hong Kong and the problems of university expansion.
Hong Kong: Hong Kong U. Press, 1959. 211 p. (Masters thesis in Education, U. of London [External degree], 1959)
SUBJ 17 21.4

14996 NNC O P 7 G 5.4 1949–1972
Smerdov, Aleksandr Ivanovich.
'Volost' poetov i filosofov' (A district of poets and philosophers).
Novyi mir 1959, 10 (oktiabr'), 186–205.
SUBJ 17 23 26.3 65 ▪ 24.1 54

14997 NNC P P2 G1.2 1949–1972
Solich, Eduard Jürgen, 1898–.
'Schule und Stahl: Das chinesische Erziehungswesen.'
Moderne Welt 2, 3 (1960/61), 247–268.
'Schools and steel: Education in China.' Tr. by Kathleen Szasz and Helga Neumann-Jung.
Modern world (Cologne) 1962/63, 110–129.
Subj 17 ▪ 16.1 32.1

14998 MCY P P1 G1.2 1949–1972
Solomon, Richard Harvey, 1937–.
'Educational themes in China's changing culture.'
CQ 22 (Apr.–June 1965), 154–170.
Subj 17 63 ▪ 12.1 47

14999 DLC O P2 G1.2 1949–1972
Stamberger, Walter, 1921–.
Zapisky z Lidové Číny (Notes from a journey to the People's Republic of China).
Prague: Časove otazky, 1951. 105 p.
Subj 17 37 ▪ 14.1 15 16.2 16.3 31 47

15000 CSH P P1 G9.4 1949–1972
Stanford U. China Project.
'Education in Formosa.' In *Taiwan (Formosa)*, compiled by the organization cited. [Selective entry]
New Haven: Human Relations Area Files, 1956, vol. 1, 172–191. (HRAF subcontractor's monographs, 31; Stanford 5)
Subj 17

15001 NNC P P2 G1.2 1949–1972
Sung Jen-chieh, Chi Tung-wei (Ch'i Tung-wei), Hung P'ei-chih, and Ch'en Lei-szu (Ch'en Lei-ssu). [Authors sequential rather than joint: Sung Jen-chieh for 1955; Chi Tung-wei for 1956; Hung P'ei-chih for 1957; Ch'en Lei-szu for 1958.]
'Education.' Tr. of '1955–1958 nien Chung kung ti chiao yü' (Education in Communist China, 1955–1958); *Tsu kuo chou k'an* 159–334/335 (16 Jan. 1956 – 8 June 1959) [recurring annual feature article]. In *Communist China, 1955–1958*, edited by Union Research Institute.
Hong Kong: Union Research Institute. Issued annually, 1956–1959, average ca. 10 p.
Subj 17 ▪ 32.1

15002 MAM FP P2 G9.4 1949–1972
Theummel, William Leslie, 1936–.
High schools and vocational agriculture schools: A comparison of the farmer-performances of their senior graduates in Taiwan.
Ann Arbor: University Microfilms (Publ. 71-2176), 1971. 16, 301 p. (Doctoral dissertation in Education, Michigan State U.)
Subj 17 24.1 ▪ 34.1 36.3 54

15003 MCH O P3 G1.2 1949–1972
Ting, Hao-tschuan (Ting Hao-ch'uan).
'Die pekinger pädagogische Hochschule' (Peking Pedagogical Institute).
Pädagogik 10, 11 (1955), 870–873.
Subj 17 ▪ 16

15004 CBU P P1 G1.2 1949–1972
To, Cho-yee.
'Education and the social ideal in Communist China.'
RSAEO 1970, 1, 85–104.
Subj 17 64

15005 CSH P P1 G1.2 1949–1972
Tsang, Chiu-sam (Tseng Chao-sen), 1901–.
'Social change in China, with special reference to education.' In *Selected seminar papers on contemporary China, I*, edited by Steve S. K. Chin (Chin Ssu-k'ai) and Frank Henry Haviland King. [Analytic entry]
Hong Kong: U. of Hong Kong, Centre of Asian Studies, 1971, 134–148. (CAS occasional papers and monographs, 4)
Subj 17 64

15006 CSU O P2 G1.2 1949–1972
Tsang, Chiu-sam (Tseng Chao-sen), 1901–.
Society, schools and progress in China.
Oxford, Eng.: Pergamon Press, 1968. 20, 333 p.
Subj 10 17 32.1

15007 CSU P P4 G1.2 1949–1972
Tsien Tche-hao (Ch'ien Chih-hao), 1923–.
L'enseignement supérieur et la recherche scientifique en Chine populaire (Higher education and scientific research in the People's Republic of China).
Paris: Lib. générale de droit et de jurisprudence, 1971. 157 p.
Subj 12 17 32.1 36.1 ▪ 54

15008 CSU O P3 G1.2 1949–1972
Tuohy, Frank.
'From a China diary.'
Encounter 27, 6 (Dec. 1966), 7–13.
Subj 17 ▪ 22.1 52 54 66

15009 NNC O P3 G5.1 1949–1972
U Bao-kan (Wu Pao-k'ang).
'Istoriko-arkhivnyi fakul'tet Narodnogo universiteta Kitaia' (The History and Archives Department of the People's University of China).
Istoricheskii arkhiv 1959, 6 (noiabr'–dekabr'), 108–112.
Subj 17 ▪ 64

15010 NNC PO P3 G5.1 1949–1972
U IUi-chzhan (Wu Yü-chang), 1878–1966.
'Narodnyi universitet Kitaia na pod"eme' (The People's University of China on the rise).
Vestnik vysshei shkoly 17, 10 (oktiabr' 1959), 8–13.
Subj 17 ▪ 64

15011 CSU P P1 G1.2 1949–1972
United Nations. Educational, Scientific and Cultural Organization. Secretariat.
'China (Mainland).' In *World survey of education, Vol. 3, Secondary education*, compiled by the organization cited. [Selective entry]
New York: International Documents Service, 1961, 367–371.
Subj 17

15012 CSU U P4 G1.2 1949–1972
United Nations. Educational, Scientific and Cultural Organization. Secretariat.
'China (Mainland).' In *World survey of education, Vol. 4, Higher education*, compiled by the organization cited. [Selective entry]
New York: UNESCO, 1966, 335–340.
Subj 17

15013 CSU U P2 G1.2 1949–1972
United Nations. Educational, Scientific and Cultural Organization. Secretariat.
'China (Mainland).' In *World survey of education, Vol. 5, Educational policy, legislation and administration*, compiled by the organization cited. [Selective entry]
Paris: UNESCO, 1971, 315–320.
Subj 17

15014 MCH O P3 G5.1 1949–1972
van der Sprenkel, Otto P- N- Berkelbach, 1906–.
'The intellectuals and the revolution.' In *New China: Three views*, by O. P. N. B. van der Sprenkel. [Selective entry]
London: Turnstile Press, 1950, 53–70.
Subj 17 26.1 ▪ 15 19 32.1

15015 NNC P P1 G1.2 1949–1972
Vasil'ev, Leonid Sergeevich, and G- V- Melikhov.
'Zhurnal *Lishi tsziaosiue* i problema reformy prepodavaniia istorii v shkolakh Kitaiskoi Narodnoi Respubliki' (The periodical *Li-shih chiao-hsüeh* [Teaching history] and the problem of reforming history teaching in schools of the People's Republic of China).
Prepodavanie istorii v shkole 1960, 1 (ianvar'–fevral'), 107–113.
Subj 16.1 17 ▪ 70

15016 MCH O P3 G1.3 1949–1972
Vasil'eva, V- IA-.
'V nauchnykh uchrezhdeniiakh Kitaia' (In China's scholarly institutions).
PV 1959, 2, 248–252.
Subj 17 36.1 ▪ 70

15017 NNC P P2 G1.2 1949–1972
Wang, Charles Kilord Athen (Wang Cheng-k'uei), 1904–.
The control of teachers in Communist China: A socio-political study.
Lackland Air Force Base, San Antonio, Tex.: U.S. Air Force Personnel and Training Research Center, Air Research and Development Command, 1955. 10, 61 p. (U.S. Human Resources Research Institute technical research reports, 36; Studies in Chinese Communism, series 4, 5, 1953)
Subj 12.1 17 32.1 ▪ 16.1 36.1 37 54 64

15018 CSU P P2 G1.3 1949–1972
Wang Hsueh-wen (Wang Hsüeh-wen).
'Maoist reform of universities of arts.'
IS 6, 9 (June 1970), 37–46.
Subj 16.1 17 64 ▪ 54

15019 CSH P P3 G6.1 1949–1972
Wang Hsueh-wen (Wang Hsüeh-wen).
'The Maoist transformation of science-engineering colleges.'
IS 7, 3 (Dec. 1970), 21–31.
Subj 17 ▪ 64

15020 CSU P P2 G1.2 1949–1972
Wang Hsueh-wen (Wang Hsüeh-wen).
'The problem of the schooling system in the Maoist educational reform.'
IS 6, 6 (Mar. 1970), 42–55.
Subj 17 64 ▪ 14.1 14.4

15021 CSU O P3 G5.1 1949–1972
Whitehead, Raymond L-.
'A revolution in education: Peking University today.'
EH 10, 6 (1971), 36–42.
Subj 17 54 ▪ 26 47

15022 NIC P P1 G1.2 1949–1972
Wong, Jennings L.
Specializations in higher technological education in Communist China.
Washington, D.C.: U.S. Dept. of Health, Education, and Welfare, Office of Education, 1959. 7 p. (Information on education around the world, 13; OE 14,034-13)
Subj 17 ▪ 11.4 16.1 16.2

15023 NIC FP P2 G1.2 1949–1972
World Confederation of Organizations of the Teaching Profession. Asia Office.
Survey of the status of the teaching profession in Asia.
Washington, D.C.: World Confederation of Organizations of the Teaching Profession, 1964? 149 p.
Subj 17 ▪ 16.1

15024 HKU FP P3 G9.5 1949–1972
Wright, Beryl Robina.
Guidance in Hong Kong: A secondary school research project.
Hong Kong: Hong Kong Council for Educational Research, 1967. 54 p.
Subj 17 21.4

15025 MAM P P2 G1.2 1949–1972
Wu, Chien-sung, 1925–.
Ideology, higher education, and professional manpower in Communist China, 1949–1969.
Ann Arbor: University Microfilms (Publ. 71-19,325), 1971. 403 p. (Doctoral dissertation in Education, U. of New Mexico)
Subj 11.4 16.1 16.2 17 64 ▪ 32.1

15026 CSU O P4 G9.4 1949–1972
Wu, Pearl.
'Taiwan: Continuation of new patterns.'
Library j. 87, 20 (15 Nov. 1962), 4129–4132. [Special issue: *Libraries in the Far East*, edited by Paul Bixler]
Subj 17

15027 MAM P P1 G9.4 1949–1972
Wu, Ping-lin, 1926–.
The development of Taiwan education from 1945 to 1962.
Ann Arbor: University Microfilms (Publ. 65-6612), 1965. 188 p. (Doctoral dissertation in Education, New York U., 1964)
Subj 17

15028 MAM P P2 G1.2 1949–1972
Yang, Allency H. Y., 1924–.
Red and expert: Communist China's educational strategies of manpower development.
Ann Arbor: University Microfilms (Publ. 65-13,623), 1965. 270 p. (Doctoral dissertation in Education, U. of California, Berkeley)
Subj 11.4 17 64 ▪ 32.1 37

15029 MAM P P1 G1.2 1949–1972
Yang, Chau-fam Chaucer, 1931–.
A study of the educational policies of the People's Republic of China and the pattern of educational administration, with special reference to the changes in policies and practices in higher education.
Ann Arbor: University Microfilms (Publ. 66-9528), 1966. 233 p. (Doctoral dissertation in Education, New York U., 1965)
Subj 17 64 ▪ 32.1

15030 CSU O P3 G1.3 1949–1972
Yang, Chen Ning.
'Education and scientific research in China.'
Asia (New York: Asia Society) 26 (Summer 1972), 74–84.
Subj 17 36.1

15031 MAM P P1 G9.4 1949–1972
Yang, Edward Chung-chong, 1933–.
High-level manpower policy and process in economic development: The case of Nationalist China, 1949–1965.
Ann Arbor: University Microfilms (Publ. 72-11,487), 1972. 401 p. (Doctoral dissertation in Economics, New York U., 1971)
Subj 17 21.4 ▪ 14 36.1 64

15032 CSU PO P2 G1.2 1949–1972
Yang Hsiu-feng, 1897–.
'Educational revolution and progress: 1949–1959.' Tr. by Lily Tsien of 'Wo kuo chiao yü shih yeh ti ta ko ming ho ta fa chan' (The great revolution and great development of educational programs in China); in *Chien kuo shih nien* (The decade since the founding of the People's Republic of China); Hong Kong: Chi wen ch'u pan she, 1959, vol. 2, 85–102. [Abridged tr.]
School and society 89, 2198 (4 Nov. 1961), 378–381. [Reprinted in *Chinese education under Communism*, edited by C. T. Hu. (Selective entry.) New York: Columbia U., Teachers College, Bureau of Publications, 1962, 146–157. (TC classics in education, 7)]
Subj 17 64

15033 NNC P P1 G1.2 1949–1972
Yao, Katherine York-bing (Yao Jo-ping), 1938–.
Scientific training in institutions of higher learning in Communist China, 1958–1964.
Unpublished masters thesis in Public Law and Government, Columbia U., 1969. 105 p. [Certificate essay, East Asian Institute]
Subj 17 62 ▪ 14 16.1

15034 MAM P P1 G1.2 1949–1972
Yeh, Hsieh-chi.
Political approaches to the achievement of educational goals in secondary education in Mainland China and the United States.
Ann Arbor: University Microfilms (Publ. 67-13,880), 1967. 271 p. (Doctoral dissertation in Education, U. of Missouri)
Subj 17 64 ▪ 12.1 32.1

15035 CBU PO P3 G1.3 1949–1972
Zepalova, T- S-.
'V kitaiskoi srednei shkole' (The Chinese secondary school). In *Shkola i prosveshchenie v Narodnom Kitae: sbornik statei* (Articles on schools and education in the People's Republic of China), compiled by Akademiia pedagogicheskikh nauk RSFSR, edited by Aleksei I- Markushevich, E- I- Monoszon, and M- N- Riakin. [Selective entry]
Moscow: Izd-vo Akad. ped. nauk RSFSR, 1957, 105–133.
Subj 17 27 52

18 National Welfare and Living Standards
全國性福利及生活水準
国民の福祉及び生活水準

1644-1911

15036 CSU O P2 G1.3 1895–1911
'Famine notes.'
CR 43, 2 (Feb. 1912), 91–104.
Subj 18 ▪ 38

15037 MCH P P2 G5.0 –1842
Biot, Edouard Constant, 1803–1850.
'Mémoire sur les changements du cours inférieur du fleuve Jaune' (Report on changes in the lower course of the Yellow River).
JA 4e série 1 (mai 1843), 452–477; 2 (juil.–août 1843), 84–99.
Subj 18 ▪ 12 14.1 14.2 21.4

15038 CSH P P2 G1.3 1842–1895
Bohr, Paul Richard.
Famine in China and the missionary: Timothy Richards as relief administrator and advocate of national reform, 1876–1884.
Cambridge: Harvard U., East Asian Research Center, 1972. 18, 283 p. (Harvard East Asian monographs, 48)
Subj 12 18 66 ▪ 14.1 14.2 14.5 25 33 55 57

15039 NIC P P1 G5.0 1842–1895
China Famine Relief Fund. London Committee, ed.
The famine in China. Tr. from the Chinese by James Legge.
London: Kegan Paul, 1878. 34 p.
Subj 18 56 ▪ 57 58

15040 CSU P P1 G1.2 –1911
Chu, Cochin (Chu K'o-chen), 1890–.
'Climatic pulsations during historic time in China.'
GR 16, 2 (Apr. 1926), 274–282.
Subj 18

15041 CSU P P2 G1.4 1842–1895
Dudgeon, John Hepburn, 1837–1901.
'The famine in North China.'
CR 11, 5 (Sept.–Oct. 1880), 349–357.
Subj 18 ▪ 38 56 58

15042 NNC O P2 G1.5 1895–1911
Ellis, William Thomas, 1873–1950.
'The unspectacular famine.'
JAAA 12, 2 (Mar. 1912), 55–57.
Subj 18 ▪ 66

15043 DLC P P2 G1.2 –1842
Lepeshinskii, K- V-.
'O nekotorykh sotsial'no-ekonomicheskikh posledstviiakh man'chzhurskogo zavoevaniia Kitaia' (Socioeconomic consequences of the Manchu conquest of China). In *Man'chzhurskoe vladychestvo v Kitae* (Manchu rule in China), compiled by Institut narodov Azii, Akademiia nauk SSSR, edited by

Sergei Leonidovich Tikhvinskii. [Selective entry]
Moscow: Nauka, Glav. red. vost. lit-ry, 1966, 128–150.
Subj 12.1 12.2 14.5 15 16 18 ▪ 14.1 16.3

15044 MCH S P2 G1.1 –1911
Martini, G- B- de.
'Le condizioni sociali della Cina' (Social conditions in China).
Rivista italiana di sociologia 6, 1/2 (gennaio–febbraio 1902), 88–102.
Subj 10 18 33 64 ▪ 12 14 14.1 16 41

15045 CSU O P2 G5.0 1842–1895
Morrison, G- James.
'On the breach in the embankment of the Yellow River.'
Engineering 55 (3 Mar. 1893), 263–264; 55 (10 Mar. 1893), 295–297.
Subj 14.2 18 ▪ 16.1 66

15046 CSU P P2 G1.3 –1911
Yao, Shan-yu, 1912–.
'The chronological and seasonal distribution of floods and droughts in Chinese history.'
HJAS 6, 3/4 (Feb. 1942), 273–312.
Subj 18

15047 MCH P P2 G1.3 –1911
Yao, Shan-yu, 1912–.
'The geographical distribution of floods and droughts in Chinese history, 206 B.C. – A.D. 1911.'
FEQ 2, 4 (Aug. 1943), 357–378.
Subj 11.3 18 ▪ 14.1

1644-1949

15048 CSU S P2 G1.1 –1949
Chang, Chi-yun (Chang Ch'i-yün), 1901–.
'Climate and man in China.'
AAAG 36, 1 (Mar. 1946), 44–73.
Subj 14.1 18

15049 CSU U P2 G1.3 –1949
Fei Hsiao-tung (Fei Hsiao-t'ung), 1910–.
'Rural livelihood: Agriculture and handicraft.' In *China's gentry: Essays in rural-urban relations*, rev. ed., by Fei Hsiao-tung, edited by Margaret Park Redfield. [Analytic entry]
Chicago: U. of Chicago Press, 1953, 108–126. [Reprinted in *China's gentry: Essays in rural-urban relations*, by Fei Hsiao-tung, edited by M. P. Redfield. (Analytic entry.) Chicago: U. of Chicago Press, 1968, 108–126.]
Subj 16.1 16.3 18 ▪ 14.1 14.2 24.4

15050 CSU O P2 G1.2 1842–1928
Freeman, John R-.
'Flood problems in China.'
Transactions of the American Society of Civil Engineers 85 (1922), 1405–1460.
Subj 18 62 ▪ 14.1 14.2 66

15051 NNC S P2 G1.3 –1928
Howard, Harry Paxton, 1893–.
'Population pressure and the growth of famine in China.'
CEJ 4, 3 (Mar. 1929), 248–262.
Subj 11 18 ▪ 14.1 58

15052 NIC FP P2 G1.2 1842–1928
Mallory, Walter Hampton, 1892–.
China, land of famine.
New York: American Geographical Society, 1926. 16, 199 p. (AGS special publications, 6) [Reprinted—Ann Arbor: University Microfilms, n.d. 16, 199 p.] [Reprinted—Freeport, N.Y.: Books for Libraries, 1972. 16, 199 p.]
Subj 14.1 18 ▪ 11 11.2 14.2 14.6 25

1911-1949

15053 NNC P P7 G2.0 1928–1949
'The cost of living of Chinese farm labor in Manchuria.'
NWSS 3, 46 (17 Nov. 1930), 217, 220.
Subj 18 ▪ 16.3 21.2

15054 NNC P P7 G1.3 1911–1928
'Cost of living of farmer's family in northern and central eastern China, 1922–1925.'
NWSS 3, 34 (26 Aug. 1930), 161, 164–166.
Subj 18 ▪ 16.3

15055 NNC P P7 G1.3 1928–1949
'Farm losses in the 1931 flood area in the Yang-tze and Hwai river valleys, China.'
NWSS 5, 28 (11 July 1932), 125, 127–128.
Subj 18 ▪ 14.1

15056 CSU P P2 G1.2 1928–1949
'Flood damage in China during 1931.'
CEJ 10, 4 (Apr. 1932), 341–352.
Subj 18

15057 NNC FP P2 G1.2 1911–1928
'Standard of living of working class in China.'
NWSS 3, 10 (10 Mar. 1930), 45, 48.
Subj 18 ▪ 16.4

15058 NNC P P1 G1.3 1928–1949
'Statistics on various calamities in China, 1929–1930.'
NWSS 6, 7 (19 Feb. 1933), 31, 33–34.
Subj 18

15059 NNM FP P2 G1.2 1928–1949
American National Red Cross. Commission to China.
The report of the American Red Cross Commission to China.
Washington, D.C.: American National Red Cross, 1929. 103 p.
Subj 14.2 18 28 ▪ 11 12 14.1

15060 CSU O P2 G1.2 1911–1949
Baker, John Earl, 1880–1957.
'Growth of famine relief and prevention.'
CR 67, 9 (Sept. 1936), 561–569.
Subj 18 38 ▪ 14.1 24.6 34.2

15061 CSU S P3 G1.2 1911–1928
Boone, Wilmot DeSaussure.
'Social problems in China and agencies for relief.'
CR 48, 2 (Feb. 1917), 95–107.
Subj 18 38 ▪ 41 47 50

15062 NIC O P2 G1.3 1911–1928
Browder, Earl Russell, 1891–1973.
'Wages and working conditions in China.'
CSM 23, 1 (Nov. 1927), 9–14.
Subj 16.4 18 ▪ 36.4

15063 MCH S P2 G1.1 1911–1949
Burns, Cecil Delisle, 1879–1942.
The standard of living in China and Japan: An essay on policy.
London: Royal Institute of International Affairs, 1931. 22 p.
Subj 14.3 18 ▪ 14 14.1 16.4 34.1 52 66

15064 NIC S P3 G1.2 1928–1949
Chan, C. S.
'Chinese social legislation and the problem of its enforcement.'
Asiatic review new (4th) series 33, 116 (Oct. 1937), 796–811.
Subj 12.2 18 ▪ 16.4

15065 CSU P P4 G1.1 1911–1928
Chan, C. S.
'Social legislation in China under the Nationalist government.'
ILR 19, 1 (Jan. 1929), 60–75.
Subj 12.2 18 36.4

15066 NIC S P2 G1.2 1911–1928
Chen Ta (Ch'en Ta), 1892–.
'Prices and cost of living in Japan and China since the world war.'
Monthly labor review 13, 6 (Dec. 1921), 1–7.
Subj 14.3 18 ▪ 16.4

15067 NNC PO P2 G1.3 1928–1949
China [Republic]. Chiu chi shui tsai wei yüan hui. (National Flood Relief Commission).
Report of the National Flood Relief Commission, 1931–1932.
Shanghai: Kuo min cheng fu chiu chi shui tsai wei yüan hui, 1933. 304 p.
Subj 12.1 14 18 56 ▪ 16.3 22.1 66

15068 CSU O P2 G1.5 1928–1949
Clubb, Oliver Edmund, 1901–.
'Floods of China: A national disaster.'
J. of geography 31, 5 (May 1932), 199–206.
Subj 18

15069 CSH P P2 G1.2 1928–1949
Gamberg, Viktor.
'Navodnenie v Kitae' (The flood in China).
PK 8/9 (1931), 84–102.
Subj 12.1 14.1 18

15070 NNC O P4 G1.2 1928–1949
Hogg, George Aylwin.
'The cripple in industry.'
CJ 33, 3 (Sept. 1940), 126–130.
Subj 16.4 18 ▪ 14.4 15

15071 NIC P P2 G1.2 1911–1949
Hsu, Leonard S. (Hsü Shih-lien), 1901–.
'Poverty and population in China.' In *Atti del Congresso internazionale per gli studi sulla popolazione (Roma, 7–10 settembre 1931), Vol. IX, sezione di economia* (Proceedings of the International Congress for Studies on Population, Rome, 7–10 September 1931, Vol. 9, Economics), edited by Corrado Gini. [Sole entry]
Rome: Istituto poligrafico dello stato libreria, 1933, 247–264.
Subj 11 18 ▪ 11.4 14 58

15072 NNC FP P8 G1.3 1911–1928
Impey, Lawrence.
'Chinese rural economics and their relation to famines.'
China weekly review 30, 8 (25 Oct. 1924), 245–249. [Reprinted—*CSM* 20, 3 (Jan. 1925), 9–13.]
Subj 14.1 18 ▪ 11.2

15073 CSH P P2 G1.2 1911–1928
Lamb, Jefferson D. H. (Lin Tung-hai), 1895–.

The origin and development of social legislation in China, edited by Maxwell Slutz Stewart.
Peiping: Yenching U., Dept. of Sociology and Social Work, 1930. 73 p. (DSSW, Series C, 24)
SUBJ 12.2 18 36.4 ▪ 16.4 47 50 52 66

15074 CSU F P7 G1.2 1928–1949
Low, H- Brian.
'The standard of living.' In *Land utilization in China: A study of 16,786 farms in 168 localities, and 32,256 farm families in twenty-two provinces in China, 1929–1933*, by John Lossing Buck. [Analytic entry]
Nanking: U. of Nanking, 1937, vol. 1, 437–472. [For Buck's work, see entry 12256.] [Reprinted in *Land utilization in China: A study of 16,786 farms in 168 localities, and 32,256 farm families in twenty-two provinces in China, 1929–1933*, by J. L. Buck. (Analytic entry.) New York: Paragon, 1964, vol. 1, 437–472.]
SUBJ 18 28 55 ▪ 14.6 24.6

15075 MCY O P8 G5.1 1911–1928
MacNair, Harley Farnsworth, 1891–1947.
'Famine relief at work.' In *China's new nationalism and other essays*, by H. F. MacNair. [Sole entry]
Shanghai: Commercial Press, 1925, 347–365.
SUBJ 12 16.1 18 ▪ 17 33 47

15076 CSU S P2 G1.2 1911–1928
Sarvis, Guy W-.
'The standard of living in China and its meaning.'
J. of applied sociology 9, 3 (Jan.–Feb. 1925), 187–195.
SUBJ 18 ▪ 16.3 16.4

15077 NIC FP P2 G5.0 1928–1949
Scott, James Cameron, 1905–.
Health and agriculture in China: A fundamental approach to some of the problems of world hunger.
London: Faber and Faber, 1952. 279 p.
SUBJ 14.1 18 55 56 ▪ 53 58 72

15078 CSU P P2 G1.5 1928–1949
Stroebe, George G-.
'The great Central China flood of 1931.'
CR 63, 11 (Nov. 1932), 667–680.
SUBJ 18 ▪ 14.1 14.2 21.4 38 56

15079 NIC U P2 G1.2 1928–1949
Tao, L. K. (T'ao Meng-ho), 1887–1960.
'Food consumption in the Chinese standard of living.' In *Problems of the Pacific, 1931*, edited by Bruno Lasker and William Lancelot Holland. [Selective entry]
Chicago: U. of Chicago Press, 1932, 52–58.
SUBJ 18 55 ▪ 21.3 29

15080 NIC P P2 G1.3 1911–1949
Tao, L. K. (T'ao Meng-ho), 1887–1960.
The standard of living among Chinese workers.
Shanghai: China Institute of Pacific Relations, 1931. 37 p. [See Vol. 2 of this *Bibliography* for Chinese version.]
SUBJ 11.4 16.4 18 ▪ 55

15081 MCH O P2 G1.4 1911–1949
Todd, Oliver Julian, 1880–.
'Famine prevention and relief projects.'
Far Eastern review 28, 8 (Aug. 1932), 361–373.
SUBJ 14.1 18 ▪ 14.2 66

15082 CSU O P2 G1.4 1911–1949
Todd, Oliver Julian, 1880–.
'Taming "flood dragons" along China's Hwang Ho [Yellow River].'
NG 81, 2 (Feb. 1942), 205–234.
SUBJ 14.2 18 ▪ 14.1 25 55 66

15083 CSU O P2 G5.0 1928–1949
Todd, Oliver Julian, 1880–.
'The Yellow River reharnessed.'
GR 39, 1 (Jan. 1949), 38–56.
SUBJ 18 ▪ 14.1 14.2

15084 CSH U P2 G1.2 1928–1949
Wang, Yin-yuen (Wang Yin-yüan).
'Effect of rising prices on different social classes.'
EF 23 (Aug. 1943), 207–211.
SUBJ 16 18 ▪ 14.3

1911-1972
(including 1644-1972)

15085 NIC P P2 G1.2 1928–1972
Cheng Chu-yuan (Cheng Chu-yüan), 1927–.
Income and standard of living in Mainland China, mimeo.
Hong Kong: Union Research Institute, 1957. 2 vols. 362 p. [c.p.]. (Communist China problem research series, EC19)
SUBJ 11.4 14 16 18 ▪ 11 14.1 14.4 16.3 16.4 24.4 34.1

15086 CSH U P2 G3.0 1911–1972
Hsiung, Helen.
'Public welfare.' In *A regional handbook on the Inner Mongolia Autonomous Region*, compiled by Far Eastern and Russian Institute, U. of Washington. [Selective entry]
New Haven: Human Relations Area Files, 1956, 330–339. (HRAF subcontractor's monographs, 60; Washington 7)
SUBJ 18 38 ▪ 33

15087 CSU P P2 G1.2 1928–1972
Lippit, Victor David, 1938–.
'Economic development and welfare in China.' [Review of *The economy of the Chinese mainland: National income and economic development, 1933–1959*, by Ta-chung Liu and K. C. Yeh (Yeh K'ung-chia); and *Communist China's economic growth and foreign trade: Implications for U.S. policy*, by Alexander Eckstein.]
BCAS 4, 2 (Summer 1972), 76–85.
SUBJ 14 16 18 ▪ 14.3 14.4 16.3 16.4 24.3

15088 NNC P P2 G1.2 1928–1972
Maklakov, A-.
'Rost material'nogo blagosostoianiia trudiashchikhsia Narodnogo Kitaia' (Improvement in the material welfare of workers in the People's Republic of China).
Sotsialisticheskii trud 3, 11 (noiabr' 1958), 33–43.
SUBJ 16.4 18 ▪ 14 14.1 14.4 16.3

15089 MCH S P2 G1.2 1911–1972
Roncy, A-.
'La sécurité sociale en Chine' (Social security in China).
Droit social 27, 5 (mai 1964), 298–311.
SUBJ 18 ▪ 36.4 50 56

15090 MCH O P2 G1.2 1928–1972
Servan-Schreiber, Emile, 1881–1967.
Chine rouge 25 ans après, 1935–1960 (Red China twenty-five years later, 1935–1960).
Paris: Plon, 1960. 217 p.
SUBJ 12.1 14 18 ▪ 16.2 34.1 47 56 58 60

15091 CSH P P2 G9.4 1928–1972
Stanford U. China Project.
'Public welfare.' In *Taiwan (Formosa)*, compiled by the organization cited. [Selective entry]
New Haven: Human Relations Area Files, 1956, vol. 1, 281–291. (HRAF subcontractor's monographs, 31; Stanford 5)
SUBJ 18

1949-1972

15092 NNC P P1 G1.2 1949–1972
'China (People's Republic): Amendment of social insurance system.'
BISSA 7, 5 (May 1954), 177–179.
SUBJ 18

15093 NNC P P1 G9.4 1949–1972
'China (Taiwan): New social insurance legislation.'
BISSA 13, 12 (Dec. 1960), 635–639.
SUBJ 18

15094 NNC P P1 G1.2 1949–1972
'Developments and trends in social security, 1958–60: China (People's Republic).'
BISSA 15, 6/8 (June–Aug. 1962), 172.
SUBJ 18

15095 NNC P P1 G9.4 1949–1972
'Developments and trends in social security, 1958–60: Republic of China (Taiwan).'
BISSA 15, 6/8 (June–Aug. 1962), 171–172.
SUBJ 18

15096 MCH P P1 G1.2 1949–1972
'Social insurance in Mainland China.'
BISSA 10, 6 (June 1957), 240–247.
SUBJ 18 ▪ 12.1 50

15097 CSU P P1 G1.1 1949–1972
'Social security in Asia, I.'
ILR 82, 1 (July 1960), 70–87.
SUBJ 18

15098 MCH PO P7 G1.2 1949–1972
Castro, Josué de.
'Victoire sur la faim.'
Economie et politique 66/67 (jan.–fév. 1960), 94–102. [Special issue: *Economie en URSS et en Chine* (The economy of the U.S.S.R. and China)]
'Victory over hunger.' In *Articles on Communist China from 'Economie et politique', Paris, January–February, 1960*, mimeo., compiled by U.S. Joint Publications Research Service. [Analytic entry]
Washington, D.C.: JPRS, 29 July 1960, 1–12. (JPRS 3639; MC 14,333/1960)
SUBJ 14.1 18 ▪ 14 34.1

15099 CSH P P7 G1.2 1949–1972
Chen Hsüeh-wen (Ch'en Hsüeh-wen).
'Natural calamities in Communist China.' Tr. of '1961 nien ti ta lu tsai huang' (Natural disasters on the Mainland in 1961); *Tsu kuo chou k'an* 496 (9 July 1962), 9–13. In *Communist China, 1961*, edited by Union Research Institute. [Selective entry]
Hong Kong: Union Research Institute, 1962, vol. 2, 171–189.
SUBJ 14.1 18 ▪ 12.1 34.1 63

15100 NIC P P7 G1.2 1949–1972
Cheng Hsueh-chia (Cheng Hsüeh-chia), 1906–.
An unprecedented famine on the Chinese Mainland and the people's communes.
Taipei: Asian Peoples' Anti-Communist League, 1961. 82 p. (APACL pamphlets, 47)
SUBJ 14.1 18 ▪ 22.1 24 24.4 34.1

15101 CSH P P2 G1.2 1949–1972
Dimin, F-.
'Material'nye usloviia i uroven' zhizni kitaiskogo naroda' (Material conditions and the standard of living of the Chinese). In *Kitaiskaia Narodnaia Respublika* (The People's Republic of China), compiled by Institut Dal'nego Vostoka, Akademiia nauk SSSR, edited by Mikhail Iosifovich Sladkovskii and Grigorii Dmitrievich Sukharchuk. [Selective entry]
Moscow: Nauka, Glav. red. vost. lit-ry, 1970, 113–132.
SUBJ 14 16 18 64 ▪ 12 19 32 66

15102 MCH P P2 G1.2 1949–1972
Dwyer, Denis John, 1933–.
'China's natural calamities and their consequences.'
Geography 47, 216 (July 1962), 301–305.
SUBJ 14.1 18

15103 CSU P P2 G1.2 1949–1972
Freeberne, John Derek Michael, 1935–.
'Natural calamities in China, 1949–61: An examination of the reports originating from the mainland.'
Pacific viewpoint 3, 2 (Sept. 1962), 33–72.
SUBJ 18 ▪ 11.2 14.1

15104 CSU P P8 G1.2 1949–1972
Freeberne, John Derek Michael, 1935–.
'The role of natural calamities in Communist China.'
CS 2, 25 (23 Dec. 1963), 1–14.
SUBJ 14.1 18

15105 CSU P P4 G1.2 1949–1972
Kallgren, Joyce Kislitzin, 1930–.
'Social welfare and China's industrial workers.' In *Chinese Communist politics in action*, edited by Arthur Doak Barnett. [Selective entry]
Seattle: U. of Washington Press, 1969, 540–573. (Social Science Research Council, Studies in Chinese government and politics, 1)
SUBJ 12.2 18 ▪ 16.4 36.4 38 50

15106 CSU P P2 G9.4 1949–1972
Ko, Mu-shing.
'Social insurance in the Republic of China.'
International social security review 22, 2 (1969), 258–263.
SUBJ 18

15107 CSH P P2 G1.2 1949–1972
Kung Mien-jen.
'Natural calamities on the Chinese Mainland in 1960.' Tr. of '1960 nien ti ta lu tsai huang'; *Tsu kuo chou k'an* 438 (29 May 1961), 9–12. In *Communist China, 1960*, edited by Union Research Institute. [Selective entry]
Hong Kong: Union Research Institute, 1962, vol. 1, 41–58.
SUBJ 14.1 18 ▪ 22.1 34.1

15108 NNC P P7 G1.2 1949–1972
[La Dany, Ladislao] ———, 1914–.
'Flood, drought, locusts.'
CNA 48 (20 Aug. 1954), 2–7.
SUBJ 18

15109 CSH P P7 G1.2 1949–1972
[La Dany, Ladislao] ———, 1914–.
'Life in the countryside. Part 2, The economic situation of the peasants.'
CNA 819 (23 Oct. 1970), 1–7.
SUBJ 16.3 18 ▪ 14.1 14.6

15110 CSH P P8 G1.2 1949–1972
[La Dany, Ladislao] ———, 1914–.
'Wrestling with nature.'
CNA 283 (3 July 1959), 1–7.
SUBJ 18

15111 CSU O P2 G1.3 1949–1972
Lake, Douglas, and Ruth Lake.
'Back to front.'
EH 9, 4 (1970), 8–25.
SUBJ 18 28 ▪ 12.1 14.2 14.3 56

15112 MCH P P2 G1.2 1949–1972
Mitsuoka Gen, 1928–.
Japanese study on people's livelihood in Communist China, mimeo. Tr. of 'Chūgoku no kokumin seikatsu' (The people's livelihood in China); *Chūgoku kenkyū geppō* 166 (Dec. 1961), 1–30.
Washington, D.C.: U.S. Joint Publications Research Service, 12 July 1962. 47 p. (JPRS 14,441; MC 21,915/1962)
SUBJ 16.4 18 ▪ 11.4 16.3 55

15113 NNC P P2 G1.2 1949–1972
Mitsuoka Gen, 1928–.
Social security in Communist China, mimeo. Tr. of 'Chūgoku no shakai hoshō'; *Chūgoku kenkyū geppō* 161 (July 1961), 1–27.
Washington, D.C.: U.S. Joint Publications Research Service, 29 Dec. 1961. 35 p. (JPRS 11,802; MC 3237/1962)
SUBJ 16.4 18 ▪ 12.2 16.3

15114 NNC PO P2 G1.2 1949–1972
Noirot, Paul.
'Données sur l'évolution du niveau de vie.'
Economie et politique 66/67 (jan.–fév. 1960), 121–145. [Special issue: *Economie en URSS et en Chine* (The economy of the U.S.S.R. and China)]

'Facts of the evolution in the standard of living.' In *Articles on Communist China from 'Economie et politique', Paris, January–February, 1960*, mimeo., compiled by U.S. Joint Publications Research Service. [Analytic entry]
Washington, D.C.: JPRS, 29 July 1960, 44–78. (JPRS 3639; MC 14,333/1960)
SUBJ 16.4 18 ▪ 16.3 58

15115 NIC P P2 G1.2 1949–1972
Okubo Yasushi (Ōkubo Yasushi).
An examination of living standards of workers and farmers in Communist China, mimeo. Tr. of 'Chūgoku ni okeru shokkō (shokuin rōdōsha) to nōmin no seikatsu suijun ni tsuite no kōsatsu' (An examination of living standards of peasants and industrial workers in China); *Ekafe tsūshin* 279 (11 Oct. 1961), 1–52.
Washington, D.C.: U.S. Joint Publications Research Service, 29 Dec. 1961. 64 p. (JPRS 11,756; MC 3219/1962)
SUBJ 16.3 16.4 18 ▪ 14.6 47 55 58

15116 DLC O P1 G1.2 1949–1972
Pavlok, V-.
'Sociální pojištěni v ČL'R' (Social insurance in the People's Republic of China).
Sociální revue (Prague) 4, 1 (1958), 44–47.
SUBJ 18

15117 DLC P P4 G1.2 1949–1972
Shelekasov, P- V-.
'Rost zarabotnoi platy i uluchshenie zhizni rabochikh i sluzhashchikh v KNR.'
BNI 2, 10 (oktiabr' 1959), 59–63.

Wage increase and standard of living improvements for the workers in People's Republic of China, mimeo.
Washington, D.C.: U.S. Joint Publications Research Service, 21 Mar. 1960. 15 p. (JPRS 3088; MC 5618/1960)
SUBJ 16.4 18

15118 CSH P P2 G1.3 1949–1972
Stanford U. China Project.
'Public welfare.' In *Central South China*, compiled by the organization cited. [Selective entry]
New Haven: Human Relations Area Files, 1956, vol. 1, 362–387. (HRAF subcontractor's monographs, 28; Stanford 2)
SUBJ 18 38 ▪ 21.4 52

15119 CSH P P2 G1.3 1949–1972
Stanford U. China Project.
'Public welfare.' In *East China*, compiled by the organization cited. [Selective entry]
New Haven: Human Relations Area Files, 1956, vol. 1, 409–435. (HRAF subcontractor's monographs, 29; Stanford 3)
SUBJ 18 38 ▪ 21.4 52

15120 CSH P P2 G5.0 1949–1972
Stanford U. China Project.
'Public welfare.' In *North China*, compiled by the organization cited. [Selective entry]
New Haven: Human Relations Area Files, 1956, vol. 1, 388–411. (HRAF subcontractor's monographs, 27; Stanford 1)
SUBJ 18 38 ▪ 21.4 52

15121 CSH P P2 G8.0 1949–1972
Stanford U. China Project.
'Public welfare.' In *Southwest China*, compiled by the organization cited. [Selective entry]
New Haven: Human Relations Area Files, 1956, vol. 1, 393–421. (HRAF

subcontractor's monographs, 30; Stanford 4)
SUBJ 18 38 ▪ 21.4 52

15122 CSH P P7 G1.2 1949–1972
T'an Chen-lin.
'A preliminary study of the income and living standard of the peasants of China.' Tr. of 'Kuan yü wo kuo nung min shou ju ch'ing k'uang ho sheng huo shui p'ing ti ch'u pu yen chiu'; *Jen min jih pao* 5 May 1957.
SCMP 1555 (21 June 1957), 25–39.
SUBJ 16.3 18 55 ▪ 14.1 34.1

15123 SSK O P2 G1.2 1949–1972
Vinde, Victor, 1903–.
Rapport från Kina (Report from China).
Stockholm: Bonnier, 1966. 207 p.
SUBJ 12.1 14 18 66 ▪ 14.1 14.4 16.2 16.4 17 34.1 34.2 63

15124 MCH P P1 G1.2 1949–1972
Zöllner, Detlev.
'Die Sozialgesetzgebung in der Volksrepublik China' (Social legislation in the People's Republic of China).
Bundesarbeitsblatt 15, 14 (25 Juli 1964), 467–472.
SUBJ 12.2 18 36.4 ▪ 14.3 14.4

19 MODERNIZATION AND DIRECTED SOCIAL CHANGE
近代化運動及社會改革
近代化及び社会改革

1644-1911

15125 CSH S P1 G1.2 1842–1895
Chu, Samuel C. (Chu Ch'ang-ling), 1929–.
'On the capacity of the Ch'ing government to effect modernization during the early Kuang-hsü period.'
CSWT 1, 10 (Feb. 1969), 23–44.
SUBJ 19 ▪ 12

15126 MCH S P2 G1.1 1842–1895
Hess, Jean, 1862–?
'Les éléments scientifiques de la transformation de la Chine' (Scientific aspects of China's transformation).
R. générale des sciences pures et appliquées 11, 12 (30 juin 1900), 775–787; 11, 13 (15 juil. 1900), 844–855.
SUBJ 14.4 14.6 17 19 62 ▪ 11 12 14 15 32.2 61 66

15127 NIC P P1 G1.3 1842–1895
Leong, Sow-theng, 1939–.
'Wang T'ao and the movement for self-strengthening and reform in the late Ch'ing period.'
PC 17 (Dec. 1963), 101–130.
SUBJ 19 32 66 ▪ 59

15128 MCH S P4 G1.2 1895–1911
Pinon, René, 1870–?
'La japonisation de la Chine' (The Japanization of China).
R. des deux mondes 5e période 28 (15 août 1905), 786–824.
SUBJ 16.1 19 25 62 66 ▪ 12.1 14.3 14.4 15 70

15129 CSU O P2 G7.2 1895–1911
Preston, T- J-.
'Progress and reform in Hunan province.'
EAM 4 (1905), 210–219.
SUBJ 17 19 66 ▪ 14.3 18 24.2

15130 MCH S P2 G1.1 1644–1911
Radek, Karl, 1885–1937?
'Osnovnye voprosy kitaiskoi istorii' (Basic questions of Chinese history).
NV 16/17 (1927), 1–53.
SUBJ 12 14.1 16 19 ▪ 14 18 45 64

15131 MCY U P1 G1.3 1644–1895
Reischauer, Edwin Oldfather, 1910–.
'Modernization in nineteenth-century China and Japan.'
JQ 10, 3 (July–Sept. 1963), 298–307.
SUBJ 19 ▪ 16 60 66

1644-1949

15132 MCH P P2 G1.2 1842–1928
Biggerstaff, Knight, 1906–.
'Modernization—and early modern China.'
JAS 25, 4 (Aug. 1966), 607–619.
SUBJ 10 19 ▪ 11.1 14 14.2 16 17 66

15133 CSU S P2 G1.2 1842–1928
Cole, Allan Burnett, 1914–.
'Factors explaining the disparate pace of modernization in China and Japan.'
Asian studies (Quezon City, Philippines) 4, 1 (Apr. 1966), 1–15.
SUBJ 10 12 16.1 19 60 ▪ 12.1 14 16.2 64

15134 NNC P P4 G1.1 1842–1928
Franke, Wolfgang, 1912–.
Chinas kulturelle Revolution: Die Bewegung vom 4. Mai 1919 (Cultural revolution in China: The May Fourth Movement, 1919).
Munich: Oldenbourg, 1957. 89 p.
SUBJ 16.1 19 64 ▪ 14.2 16 29 32 32.2 47 54 66

15135 CSH U P3 G1.2 1895–1928
Furth, Charlotte Davis, 1926–.
'May Fourth in history.' In *Reflections on the May Fourth Movement: A symposium*, edited by Benjamin Isadore Schwartz. [Analytic entry]
Cambridge: Harvard U., East Asian Research Center, 1972, 59–68. (Harvard East Asian monographs, 44)
SUBJ 19 64 ▪ 54 66

15136 MCH O P2 G1.1 1895–1949
Holcombe, Arthur Norman, 1884–.
The spirit of the Chinese revolution.
New York: Knopf, 1930. 185 p. [Reprinted—Westport, Conn.: Hyperion Press, 197? 185 p.]
SUBJ 19 32.2 ▪ 12 15 59 64 66

15137 NIC U P1 G1.2 1842–1949
Hu Shih, 1891–1962.
'Types of cultural response.'
PT new (2nd) series 6, 2 (16 Jan. 1934), 99–116.
SUBJ 12 19 62 64 66 ▪ 14 15 16.1 17

15138 NIC U P2 G1.2 –1928
Lieu, D. K. (Liu Ta-chün), 1891–1962.
'Social transformation of China.'
CSPSR 2, 3 (Sept. 1917), 78–89.
SUBJ 19 41 ▪ 22.2 42 44 63 66

15139 CSH U P2 G1.2 1842–1949
Schurmann, Herbert Franz, 1926–.
'Prologue.' In *Ideology and organization in Communist China*, 2nd ed., enl., by H. F. Schurmann. [Analytic entry]
Berkeley, Los Angeles: U. of California Press, 1968, 35–52 [s.p.].
SUBJ 19 32 64 ▪ 12 12.1 16.1

15140 NIC O P2 G1.2 1895–1949
T'ang, Leang-li (T'ang Liang-li), 1901–.
The inner history of the Chinese revolution.
London: Routledge, 1930. 15, 391 p.
SUBJ 16.1 19 32 32.1 32.2 64 ▪ 12.1 14.4 16.4 17 18 66

15141 CSH U P1 G1.2 1842–1949
Wilbur, Clarence Martin, 1908–.
'China's transitional century, 1850–1950.' In *China in change: An approach to understanding*, edited by Miner Searle Bates. [Selective entry]
New York: Friendship Press, 1969, 33–62.
SUBJ 19 ▪ 15 32.2

1911-1949

15142 MCH P P2 G1.2 1911–1949
'La révolution chinoise (1911–1947). Première partie, l'évolution politique. Deuxième partie, l'évolution économique' (The Chinese revolution, 1911–1947. Part 1, Political developments. Part 2, Economic developments).
Notes documentaires et études 827 (12 fév. 1948), 1–32; 828 (13 fév. 1948), 1–12.
SUBJ 12 14 19 32.2 ▪ 14.3

15143 CSU P P3 G6.1 1911–1928
Chen, Joseph T. (Ch'en Tseng-tao), 1925–.
The May Fourth Movement in Shanghai: The making of a social movement in modern China.
Leiden: Brill, 1971. 14, 219 p. (*T'oung pao* monographies, 9) (Revision of *The May Fourth Movement in Shanghai*, doctoral dissertation in History, U. of California, Berkeley, 1964)
SUBJ 19 26 30 32 36.4 54 ▪ 17 22.2 24.2 26.1 26.2 26.4 46 47 64 66

15144 CSU P P2 G1.2 1911–1928
Chen, Joseph T. (Ch'en Tseng-tao), 1925–.
'The May Fourth Movement redefined.'
MAS 4, 1 (Jan. 1970), 63–81.
SUBJ 19 60 ▪ 16.1 54 64

15145 NIC PO P4 G1.3 1911–1928
Chow, Tse-tsung (Chou Ts'e-tsung), 1916–.
The May Fourth Movement: Intellectual revolution in modern China.
Cambridge: Harvard U. Press, 1960. 15, 486 p. (Harvard East Asian series, 6) (Revision of *The May Fourth Movement and its influence upon China's socio-political development*, doctoral dissertation in International Law and Relations, U. of Michigan, 1955) [Reprinted—Stanford: Stanford U. Press, 1967. 15, 486 p.]
SUBJ 16.1 17 19 30 54 60 ▪ 12.1 14.2 16.2 32.2 36.4 37 47 63 64 66

15146 CSU PO P1 G1.2 1911–1928
Fass, Josef.
'Sun Yat-sen and the May-4th-Movement.'
AO 36, 4 (1968), 577–584.
SUBJ 19 32.2

15147 DLC P P4 G1.2 1911–1928
Garushiants, IUrii Misakovich.
Dvizhenie 4 maia 1919 goda v Kitae (The May Fourth Movement of 1919 in China).
Moscow: Sotsekgiz, 1959. 48 p.
SUBJ 19 32.2 65 ▪ 16 18 32.1 54

15148 DLC P P4 G1.3 1911–1928
Iliushechkin, Vasilii Pavlovich, 1915–.
'"Dvizhenie 4 maia" i ego istoricheskoe znachenie' (The May Fourth Movement and its historical significance). In *Dvizhenie '4 maia' 1919 goda v Kitae: sbornik statei* (Articles on the May Fourth Movement in China), compiled by Institut vostokovedeniia, Akademiia nauk SSSR, edited by A- G- Afanas'ev et al. [Selective entry]
Moscow: Nauka, Glav. red. vost. lit-ry, 1971, 7–36.
SUBJ 16.2 19 36.4 54 64 66 ▪ 14.2 14.3 14.4 16.1 32.1 35 72

15149 MCH S P1 G1.3 1928–1949
Levenson, Joseph Richmond, 1920–1969.
'The day Confucius died.' [Review of *The May Fourth Movement: Intellectual revolution in modern China*, by Tse-tsung Chow (Chou Ts'e-tsung).]
JAS 20, 2 (Feb. 1961), 221–226.
SUBJ 19 60 ▪ 62 64 66

15150 NNC U P2 G1.2 1928–1949
Levy, Marion Joseph, Jr., 1918–.
Some problems of modernization in China.
New York: Institute of Pacific Relations, International Secretariat, 1949. 35 p.
SUBJ 10 19 48 63 ▪ 12 14 14.4 16 16.2 17 18 40 41

15151 MCY O P2 G1.2 1911–1928
Lo Wen-kan, 1888–1942.
'China's introduction of foreign systems.'
CSPSR 8, 4 (Oct. 1924), 172–182.
SUBJ 12 19 ▪ 15 17 34.2

15152 CSH U P3 G1.2 1911–1928
Meisner, Maurice J-, 1931–.
'Cultural iconoclasm, nationalism, and internationalism in the May Fourth Movement.' In *Reflections on the May Fourth Movement: A symposium*, edited by Benjamin Isadore Schwartz. [Analytic entry]
Cambridge: Harvard U., East Asian Research Center, 1972, 14–22. (Harvard East Asian monographs, 44)
SUBJ 19 ▪ 16.1 54 64

15153 CSH U P3 G1.2 1911–1928
Schwartz, Benjamin Isadore, 1916–.
'Introduction.' In *Reflections on the May Fourth Movement: A symposium*, edited by B. I. Schwartz. [Analytic entry]
Cambridge: Harvard U., East Asian Research Center, 1972, 1–13. (Harvard East Asian monographs, 44)
SUBJ 16.1 19 64 ▪ 37 66

15154 NNC P P2 G1.2 1928–1949
Shevtsov, N- S-.
'Kitai na puti k sotsializmu' (China on the road to socialism).
Uchenye zapiski Moskovskogo gosudarstvennogo universiteta novaia (2-aia) seriia 173 (1955), 225–249.
SUBJ 12 14 14.1 14.4 19 34.1 ▪ 16.3 16.4 32 64

15155 MCH U P2 G7.3 1928–1949
Taylor, George Edward, 1905–.
'Reconstruction after revolution: Kiangsi province and the Chinese nation.'
PA 8, 3 (Sept. 1935), 302–311.
SUBJ 12 12.1 19 ▪ 14 15 17

15156 MCH O P2 G1.2 1911–1949
Vandervelde, Emile, 1866–1938.
A travers la révolution chinoise: soviets et Kuomintang (Through the Chinese revolution: Soviets and the Kuomintang).
Paris: Alcan, 1931. 240 p.
SUBJ 16.1 16.4 19 32 32.2 ▪ 12.1 15 16 36.3 36.4 66

15157 NNC P P4 G1.2 1911–1928
Vinogradov, Nikolai Pavlovich, 1923–1967.
'"Dvizhenie 4 maia" 1919 g. v Kitae' (The May Fourth Movement of 1919 in China).
SV 1955, 6, 46–53.
SUBJ 16.1 19 66 ▪ 12 16.4 64

1911-1972
(including 1644-1972)

15158 NNC S P2 G1.1 1644–1972
Beckmann, George Michael, 1926–.
The modernization of China and Japan.
New York: Harper and Row, 1962. 724 p.
SUBJ 12 14 19 32 32.2 ▪ 12.2 14.1 14.2 14.4 15 17 32.1 64 66

15159 DLC P P1 G1.2 1911–1972
Bereznyi, Lev Abramovich, 1915–.
'O glavnykh etapakh formirovaniia i razvitiia gosudarstva demokraticheskoi diktatury naroda v Kitae' (The principal stages in the development of a people's democratic dictatorship in China).
UZLGU 281 (1959), 19–34.
SUBJ 12 19 32.2 ▪ 14 64 66

15160 MCY P P1 G1.2 1644–1972
Black, Cyril Edwin, 1915–.
'Political modernization in Russia and China.' In *Unity and contradiction: Major aspects of Sino-Soviet relations*, edited by Kurt London. [Selective entry]
New York: Praeger, 1962, 3–18.
SUBJ 12 19 ▪ 32 64

15161 CSU P P2 G1.1 1842–1972
Chai, Winberg (Chai Wen-po), 1932–.
The new politics of Communist China: Modernization process of a developing nation.
Pacific Palisades, Calif.: Goodyear, 1972. 14, 305 p.
SUBJ 12 14 19 32 32.2 ▪ 11 12.1 12.2 14.1 14.4 15 17 54 64 66

15162 CBU P P2 G1.1 1842–1972
Cole, Allan Burnett, 1914–.
'Contrasting modernization in China and Japan.'
CCJ 4, 2 (May 1965), 99–138.
SUBJ 14 19 ▪ 16.1 16.2 64 72

15163 CBU S P2 G1.2 1928–1972
Couturier, Charles.
Chine, où vas-tu? Bilan de la révolution chinoise (1900–1957) (Whither China? Balance sheet of the Chinese revolution, 1900–1957).
Paris: Fleurus, 1958. 268 p.
SUBJ 12 14 19 32 33 ▪ 14.1 14.4 16.1 16.3 17 62 64 66

15164 DLC P P1 G1.2 1911–1972
Domes, Jürgen Otto, 1932–.
'Das Scheitern des "kemalistischen Modells" in China, 1949' (The failure of the 'Kemalist model' in China in 1949). In *Entwicklungsländer zwischen nationaler und kommunistischer Revolution* (Developing nations between nationalist and Communist revolution), by J. O. Domes et al. [Solc entry]
Hanover: Verlag für Literatur und Zeitgeschehen, 1965, 59–79.
SUBJ 19 32 64 ▪ 32.2

15165 CSU S P1 G1.2 1842–1972
Eisenstadt, Shmuel Noah, 1923–.
'Tradition, change, and modernity: Reflections on the Chinese experience.' In *China in crisis, Vol. 1, China's heritage and the Communist political system*, edited by Ping-ti Ho and Tang Tsou. [Selective entry]
Chicago: U. of Chicago Press, 1968, 753–774.
SUBJ 19 ▪ 16.1 32.2

15166 CSU U P2 G1.1 –1972
Fairbank, John King, 1907–.
China, the People's Middle Kingdom, and the U.S.A.
Cambridge: Harvard U. Press, 1967. 11, 145 p.
SUBJ 12 19 64 ▪ 12.1 32 32.2 66 71

15167 NNC S P2 G1.2 1911–1972
Franke, Wolfgang, 1912–.
'Die Stufen der Revolution in China' (Stages in the Chinese Revolution).
Vierteljahreshefte für Zeitgeschichte 1954, 149–176.
SUBJ 19 32.2 ▪ 32 64 72

15168 CSU U P2 G1.2 1895–1972
Gasster, Michael, 1930–.
China's struggle to modernize.
New York: Knopf, 1972. 14, 154 p.
SUBJ 14 19 32 32.2 60 64 ▪ 12 14.2 15 16.1 16.3 36.3 36.4 66

15169 NNC P P2 G1.2 1928–1972
Glunin, Vladimir Ivanovich, 1924–.
Sotsialisticheskaia revoliutsiia v Kitae (The socialist revolution in China).
Moscow: Sotsekgiz, 1960. 247 p.
SUBJ 19 32 ▪ 14 16 32.1 64

15170 CSH U P2 G1.2 1928–1972
Gray, Jack Douglas, 1916–.
'A recapitulation of factors in the Cultural Revolution.' In *Selected seminar papers on contemporary China, I*, edited by Steve S. K. Chin (Chin Ssu-k'ai) and Frank Henry Haviland King. [Analytic entry]
Hong Kong: U. of Hong Kong, Centre of Asian Studies, 1971, 1–43. (CAS occasional papers and monographs, 4)
SUBJ 14 16 16.3 19 60 64 ▪ 12 14.1 15 16.1 32 34.1

15171 MAM FP P2 G1.2 1842–1972
Gregory, Michael Strietmann, 1929–.
Problems of transformation in Communist China.
Ann Arbor: University Microfilms (Publ. 70-13,060), 1970. 446 p. (Doctoral dissertation in Anthropology, U. of California, Berkeley, 1969)
SUBJ 12.1 19 60 62 64 ▪ 14.1 16.1 30 32.2 41 47 50

15172 MCH PO P2 G1.2 –1972
Guardia Mayorga, César A-, 1906–.
De Confucio a Mao Tse-tung: del feudo a la comuna popular (From Confucius to Mao Tse-tung: From the fief to the commune).
Lima: Minerva, 1960. 322 p.
SUBJ 14 17 19 ▪ 14.1 14.4 36.4 64

15173 CSU O P2 G1.2 1928–1972
Hotta Yoshie.
'Impressions of China since the war.'
JQ 5, 3 (July–Sept. 1958), 280–293.
SUBJ 14 19 ▪ 17 18 22.2 24.4 32.2

15174 CSU P P2 G1.1 1644–1972
Hsü, Immanuel C. Y. (Hsü Chung-yüeh), 1923–.
The rise of modern China.
New York: Oxford U. Press, 1970. 23, 830 p.
SUBJ 12 14 19 32.2 60 66 ▪ 12.1 14.1 14.5 15 16 16.1 22 25 32 64

15175 CSU FP P2 G1.1 1928–1972
Karnow, Stanley, 1925–.
Mao and China: From revolution to revolution.
New York: Viking Press, 1972. 15, 592 p.
SUBJ 14 15 16.1 19 32 54 ▪ 12.1 14.1 14.4 18 25 32.2 34.1 35 59 64

15176 CSH O P2 G1.2 1911–1972
Kashin, Alexander, 1927–.
Fünfzehn Jahre Rotchina (Fifteen years of Red China).
Munich: Kopernikus, 1965. 96 p.
SUBJ 12.1 19 32 32.2 ▪ 14.1 14.2 15 16.1 50

15177 CSU S P2 G1.2 –1972
Kierman, Frank Algerton, Jr., 1914–.
'Communist China in the light of Chinese history.' In *Communist China, 1949–1969: A twenty-year appraisal*, edited by Frank Newton Trager and William Henderson. [Selective entry]
New York: New York U. Press, 1970, 1–25.
SUBJ 12.1 16 19 ▪ 12 62 64

15178 CSU U P2 G1.2 1842–1972
Lattimore, Owen, 1900–.
'China to-day: Some social aspects.'
J. of the Royal Society of Arts 116, 5144 (July 1968), 653–665.
SUBJ 19 32.2 64 ▪ 16.3 32 66

15179 CSU S P2 G1.2 1911–1972
Levenson, Joseph Richmond, 1920–1969.
'Communist China in time and space.'
CQ 39 (July–Sept. 1969), 1–11.
SUBJ 19 64 ▪ 16.2 16.3 32.2 66

15180 MMT U P1 G1.2 1644–1972
Levy, Marion Joseph, Jr., 1918–.
'Some structural problems of modernization and "high modernization": China and Japan.' In *Symposium on economic and social problems of the Far East*, edited by Edward Franciszek Szczepanik. [Selective entry]
Hong Kong: Hong Kong U. Press, 1962, 445–458.
SUBJ 14.4 19 41 ▪ 12 14 14.5

15181 NNC P P2 G2.0 1928–1972
Liu IUn-an' (Liu Yung-an).
Demokraticheskoe i sotsialisticheskoe stroitel'stvo v Severo-Vostochnom Kitae (Democratic and socialist construction in Manchuria).
Moscow: Gospolitizdat, 1957. 238 p.

Excerpts from 'Democratic and socialist structure in contemporary [sic] *China'*, mimeo. [Partial tr.: p. 102–230 only].
Washington, D.C.: U.S. Joint Publications Research Service, 12 Nov. 1958. 93 p. (JPRS 367D; MC 557/1959)
SUBJ 12.1 14 14.4 16.4 19 30 ▪ 12 12.2 14.1 16 17 18 25 32 34.1 34.2

15182 NNC P P1 G1.2 1928–1972
Oganian, A- G-.
'Kommunisticheskaia partiia Kitaia v bor'be za pobedu sotsializma: k 10-letiiu Kitaiskoi Narodnoi Respubliki' (The Chinese Communist Party's struggle for the victory of socialism: On the tenth anniversary of the founding of the People's Republic of China).
Voprosy istorii KPSS 1959, 5, 122–134.
SUBJ 12 19 32 32.2 64 ▪ 14 17

15183 CSU PO P1 G1.2 1928–1972
Pye, Lucian Wilmot, 1921–.
'Mass participation in Communist China: Its limitations, and the continuity of culture.' In *China: Management of a revolutionary society*, edited by John Matthew Henry Lindbeck. [Analytic entry]
Seattle: U. of Washington Press, 1971, 3–33. (Social Science Research Council, Studies in Chinese government and politics, 2)
SUBJ 19 30 61 ▪ 12.1 32.1

15184 CSU U P2 G1.2 1911–1972
Saari, Jon.
'China's special modernity.' In *China and ourselves: Explorations and revisions by a new generation*, edited by Bruce Douglass and Ross Terrill. [Selective entry]
Boston: Beacon Press, 1969, 49–68.
SUBJ 19 63 ▪ 32.2

15185 CSU S P2 G1.1 –1972
Schurmann, Herbert Franz, 1926–.
'Chinese society.' In *International encyclopedia of the social sciences*, edited by David L- Sills. [Sole entry]
New York: Macmillan *with* Free Press of Glencoe, 1968, vol. 2, 408–425.
SUBJ 10 12 16 16.1 19 32.2 ▪ 12.1 14.1 22 32 34.1 64

15186 CSU S P1 G1.2 1911–1972
Schwarz, Henry Guenter, 1928–.
'Political leadership and modernization in Communist China.' In *Understanding modern China*, edited by Joseph M. Kitagawa (Kitagawa Mitsuo). [Selective entry]
Chicago: Quadrangle, 1969, 94–119.
SUBJ 12 16.1 19 32 32.2 ▪ 12.1 64 66

15187 CSH S P7 G1.2 1928–1972
Selden, Mark, 1938–.
'Revolution and Third World development: People's war and the transformation of peasant society.' In *National liberation: Revolution in the Third World*, edited by Norman Miller and Roderick Aya. [Selective entry]
New York: Free Press, 1971, 214–248.
SUBJ 16.3 19 32.2 ▪ 14 17 34.2 64

15188 MCH P P2 G1.2 1928–1972
Seton-Watson, Hugh, 1916–.
'The Chinese revolution.' In *The pattern of Communist revolution: A historical analysis*, rev. ed., by H. Seton-Watson. [Sole entry]
London: Methuen, 1961, 271–290.
SUBJ 12.1 14 19 32.2 ▪ 12 14.1 15 32 64 66

15189 CSU O P2 G1.2 1911–1972
Smythe, Lewis Strong Casey, 1901–.
'Recent social changes in China.' In *Societies around the world*, edited by Irwin T- Sanders et al. [Sole entry]
New York: Dryden Press, 1953, vol. 2, 188–194.
SUBJ 14.1 19 41 ▪ 12.1 31 55

15190 CSU U P2 G1.2 1928–1972
Solomon, Richard Harvey, 1937–.
'The pattern of the Chinese revolution.'
CH 55, 325 (Sept. 1968), 129–134, 173–174.
SUBJ 12.1 19 ▪ 16.3 32.2 64

15191 CSU PO P2 G1.1 1928–1972
Topping, Seymour, 1921–.
Journey between two Chinas.
New York: Harper and Row, 1972. 10, 459 p.
SUBJ 15 19 20 25 32 32.2 ▪ 16.1 17 24 24.4 26.3 26.4 28 33 51 66

15192 NNC O P2 G1.2 1928–1972
Townsend, Peter, 1919–.
China phoenix: The revolution in China.
London: Cape, 1955. 406 p.
SUBJ 19 24.1 26 26.3 26.4 28 ▪ 22 22.2 24.3 24.4 32 32.2 34.1 34.2 41 47

15193 NNC S P1 G1.2 –1972
Tsien, Ts'uen-Hsuin (Ch'ien Ts'un-hsün), 1909–.
'Western impact on China through translation.'
FEQ 13, 3 (May 1954), 305–327.
SUBJ 19 62 66 ▪ 17 37

15194 MCH U P2 G1.1 1895–1972
Wright, Mary Clabaugh, 1917–1970.
'Modern China in transition, 1900–1950.'
AAAPSS 321 (Jan. 1959), 1–8. [Special issue: *Contemporary China*, edited by Howard Lyon Boorman] [Reprinted in *Modern China*, edited by Albert Feuerwerker. (Selective entry.) Englewood Cliffs, N. J.: Prentice-Hall, 1964, 5–15.] [Reprinted in *Modern China: An interpretive anthology*, edited by Joseph Richmond Levenson. (Selective entry.) London: Macmillan, 1971, 199–207.]
SUBJ 12 19 66 ▪ 14 15 32.2

15195 MCH P P2 G1.2 1911–1972
Zürcher, Erik, 1928–.
'Het moderne China: Afbraak en vernieuwing' (Modern China: Destruction and reconstruction). In *China tussen eergisteren en*

overmorgen (China between the day before yesterday and the day after tomorrow), edited by Willem Frederik Wertheim and E. Zürcher. [Selective entry]
The Hague: Van Hoeve, 1963, 21–38.
SUBJ 19 64 ▪ 16 18

1949-1972

15196 CSH P P2 G1.2 1949–1972
'Communist China: The Great Proletarian Cultural Revolution, November 1965 – March 1967.'
Current notes on international affairs (Canberra) 38, 3 (Mar. 1967), 87–103.
SUBJ 16.1 19 32 ▪ 15 22.2 54

15197 CSH O P3 G5.1 1949–1972
'Eyewitness of the Cultural Revolution.'
CQ 28 (Oct.–Dec. 1966), 1–7.
SUBJ 19 22.1 ▪ 17 25 32 54

15198 ELB P P2 G1.2 1949–1972
'O kharaktere "kul'turnoi revoliutsii" v Kitae.'
Kommunist 1968, 7 (mai), 103–114.
'On the nature of the "Cultural Revolution" in China.'
Reprints from the Soviet press 7, 3/4 (23 Aug. 1968), 3–20.
SUBJ 16 19 32 ▪ 14 32.1 54

15199 CSU U P2 G1.2 1949–1972
Adie, William Andrew Charles, 1926–.
'China's "second liberation" in perspective.'
B. of the atomic scientists 25, 2 (Feb. 1969), 12–22. [Special issue: *China after the Cultural Revolution*, edited by (Richard Garratt Wilson) Dick Wilson] [Reprinted in *China after the Cultural Revolution*. (Selective entry.) New York: Random House, 1969, 27–56.]
SUBJ 19 64 ▪ 12.1 14 32 35

15200 CSU P P2 G1.2 1949–1972
Ahmad, S- H-.
'China's "Cultural Revolution".'
International studies (New Delhi) 9, 1 (July 1967), 13–54.
SUBJ 16 19 32.1 64 ▪ 12.1 14 15 17 32 54

15201 CSU S P1 G1.2 1949–1972
Albrecht, Dietmar, 1941–.
'Deutschsprachige Literatur zur Grossen Proletarischen Kulturrevolution' (German literature on the Cultural Revolution).
Internationales Asien Forum 1, 2 (Apr. 1970), 292–306.
SUBJ 19 72 ▪ 16.1 32 64

15202 CSU P P2 G1.2 1949–1972
An, Tai Sung, 1931–.
Mao Tse-tung's Cultural Revolution.
Indianapolis: Pegasus, 1972. 12, 211 p.
SUBJ 16.1 19 32 ▪ 12 14 35 54

15203 CSH P P3 G1.3 1949–1972
Ansley, Clive.
'The role of "Hai Jui's dismissal" in China's Cultural Revolution.' In *The heresy of Wu Han: His play 'Hai Jui's dismissal' and its role in China's Cultural Revolution*, by C. Ansley. [Sole entry]
Toronto: U. of Toronto Press, 1972, 83–110.
SUBJ 19 32 64 ▪ 14.2 16.1 32.1

15204 MCH U P1 G1.2 1949–1972
Avarin, Vladimir IAkovlevich (W. Awarin), 1899–.
'Gosudarstvennoe i khoziaistvennoe stroitel'stvo Kitaiskoi Narodnoi Respubliki' (Political and economic development in the People's Republic of China).
VE 1950, 2 (fevral'), 44–64.
'Der staatliche und wirtschaftliche Aufbau der Volksrepublik China.'
Einheit; theoretische Z. des wissenschaftlichen Sozialismus 5, 9 (Sept. 1950), 841–855.
SUBJ 10 12 19 ▪ 14

15205 CSU O P2 G1.5 1949–1972
Barcata, Louis, 1906–.
China in der Kulturrevolution: Ein Augenzeugenbericht.
Vienna: Molden, 1967. 318 p.
China in the throes of the Cultural Revolution: An eyewitness report.
New York: Hart, 1968. 299 p.
SUBJ 12.1 19 20 55 64 66 ▪ 14.2 15 16.1 16.4 18 31 33 46 54

15206 CSH O P2 G1.2 1949–1972
Bastid, Marianne, 1940–.
'Origines et développement de la Révolution culturelle' (Origins and development of the Cultural Revolution).
Politique étrangère 32, 1 (1967), 68–86.
SUBJ 17 19 32 ▪ 16 54

15207 CSU U P2 G1.2 1949–1972
Bastid, Marianne, 1940–.
'A triptych in honor of the Cultural Revolution.' [Review of *The Cultural Revolution in China*, by Joan Robinson; *The Cultural Revolution at Peking University*, by Victor Nee and Don Layman; and *Shanghai journal: An eyewitness account of the Cultural Revolution*, by Neale Hunter.]
BCAS 2, 3 (Apr.–July 1970), 83–87.
SUBJ 19

15208 CSU P P2 G1.2 1949–1972
Baum, Richard Dennis, 1940–.
'China: Year of the mangoes.'
AS 9, 1 (Jan. 1969), 1–17.
SUBJ 19 32 32.1 ▪ 15 16.1

15209 CSU P P7 G1.2 1949–1972
Baum, Richard Dennis, 1940–.
'The Cultural Revolution in the countryside: Anatomy of a limited rebellion.' In *The Cultural Revolution in China*, edited by Thomas Webster Robinson. [Analytic entry]
Berkeley, Los Angeles: U. of California Press, 1971, 367–476.
SUBJ 16.3 19 22.2 25 ▪ 14.1 32.1 35 54

15210 CSU S P2 G1.2 1949–1972
Beckmann, George Michael, 1926–.
'China and the modernization process: Problems of economic development and social reform.' In *American foreign policy and revolutionary change*, edited by Jack B- Gabbert. [Sole entry]
Pullman: Washington State U. Press, 1968, 48–56.
SUBJ 14.1 14.4 19

15211 CSU P P2 G1.2 1949–1972
Bennett, Gordon Anderson, 1940–.
'China's continuing revolution: Will it be permanent?'
AS 10, 1 (Jan. 1970), 2–17.
SUBJ 14 16.1 19 32 35 ▪ 12.2 17 24.3

15212 NIC O P2 G1.2 1949–1972
Bernal, John Desmond, 1901–.
'Some aspects of China's transformation.'
Marxist q. 2, 2 (Apr. 1955), 77–87.
SUBJ 14 16 19 ▪ 17 36.1

15213 CSU O P2 G1.2 1949–1972
Bernal, Martin Gardiner, 1937–.
'North Vietnam and China: Reflections on a visit.'
NYRB 17, 2 (12 Aug. 1971), 16–21.
SUBJ 19 ▪ 16.1 16.3 17

15214 CSU PO P2 G1.2 1949–1972
Blumer, Giovanni.
Die chinesische Kulturrevolution (China's Cultural Revolution).
Frankfurt a.M.: Europäische Verlagsanstalt, 1968. 399 p.
SUBJ 12.1 16.1 19 32 54 64 ▪ 12 15 17 22.2 32.1

15215 CSU U P2 G1.2 1949–1972
Boorman, Howard Lyon, 1920–.
'The social revolution in contemporary China.' In *China today*, edited by William Jerome Richardson. [Selective entry]
New York: Maryknoll; New York: Friendship Press, 1969, 1–19.
SUBJ 18 19 41 ▪ 11 11.1 17 46 47 56

15216 CSU S P2 G1.2 1949–1972
Bornstein, Morris, 1927–.
'Communist Chinese society in Soviet perspective.' [Review of *Ideology and organization in Communist China*, by Herbert Franz Schurmann.]
CSSH 10, 2 (Jan. 1968), 221–229.
SUBJ 19 64 ▪ 12 14 14.1

15217 NIC P P2 G1.2 1949–1972
Bowie, Robert R-, and John King Fairbank, 1907–.
'Domestic policy trends in Communist China, 1955–59.' In *Communist China, 1955–59: Policy documents with analysis*, jointly edited by Center for International Affairs, Harvard U. *with* East Asian Research Center, Harvard U. [Sole entry]
Cambridge: Harvard U. Press, 1962, 1–41. (Harvard East Asian series, 10)
SUBJ 12.1 14 16 19 32.1 34.1 ▪ 14.1 15 17 18 32.2 58 64

15218 CSU P P2 G1.2 1949–1972
Bridgham, Philip Low, 1921–.
'Mao's Cultural Revolution in 1967: The struggle to seize power.'
CQ 34 (Apr.–June 1968), 6–37.
SUBJ 12 19 ▪ 15 32 54

15219 MCH P P2 G1.2 1949–1972
Bridgham, Philip Low, 1921–.
'Mao's "Cultural Revolution": Origin and development.'
CQ 29 (Jan.–Mar. 1967), 1–35.
SUBJ 12 12.1 19 32 ▪ 15 16.1 32.1 54

15220 CSU P P2 G1.2 1949–1972
Bridgham, Philip Low, 1921–.
'Mao's Cultural Revolution: The struggle to consolidate power.'

CQ 41 (Jan.–Mar. 1970), 1–25.
SUBJ 12 19 32 64 ▪ 12.1 14 15 16.1

15221 CSH U P1 G1.2 1949–1972
Briey, Pierre de.
'Technique et développement: La Révolution culturelle chinoise.'
Civilisations 17, 4 (1967), 332–348.
'Technique and development: The Chinese Cultural Revolution.'
Civilisations 17, 4 (1967), 333–347. [English tr. on facing pages.]
SUBJ 19 ▪ 30 63

15222 CSU P P2 G1.2 1949–1972
Chang Man.
'The Great Proletarian Cultural Revolution in 1968.' Tr. of '1968 nien ti wen hua ta ko ming'; *Tsu kuo* 59 (Feb. 1969), 2–19. In *Communist China, 1968*, edited by Union Research Institute. [Selective entry]
Hong Kong: Union Research Institute, 1969, 5–68.
SUBJ 16 19 32 54 ▪ 12 16.1 22.2 35 64

15223 CSH P P2 G1.2 1949–1972
[Chao Ts'ung] Chung Hua-min, pseud., 1927–.
'The Great Proletarian Cultural Revolution in 1967.' Tr. of '1967 nien ti wen hua ta ko ming'; *Tsu kuo* 46 (Jan. 1968), 2–13; 47 (Feb. 1968), 18–31. In *Communist China, 1967*, edited by Union Research Institute. [Selective entry]
Hong Kong: Union Research Institute, 1969, vol. 1, 1–93.
SUBJ 19 32 35 54 ▪ 16.1 25 64

15224 CSH P P2 G1.2 1949–1972
Chin, Steve S. K. (Chin Ssu-k'ai), 1919–.
'The Great Proletarian Cultural Revolution.' Tr. of '1966 nien ti wen hua ta ko ming' (The Cultural Revolution during 1966); *Tsu kuo* 36 (Mar. 1967), 2–11. In *Communist China, 1966*, edited by Union Research Institute. [Selective entry]
Hong Kong: Union Research Institute, 1968, vol. 2, 87–117.
SUBJ 19 32 54 ▪ 16.1 25 32.1

15225 CSU P P2 G1.2 1949–1972
Current Scene Editor.
'Combatting left and right: China's Cultural Revolution in 1968.'
CS 7, 2 (20 Jan. 1969), 1–22.
SUBJ 19 22.2 ▪ 16.1 32

15226 CSU P P2 G1.2 1949–1972
Danrémont, Jean.
'La Révolution culturelle chinoise et les gardes rouges' (China's Cultural Revolution and the Red Guards).
R. de Paris 75, 4 (avr. 1968), 45–56.
SUBJ 15 19 32 54 60 ▪ 64

15227 CBU P P1 G1.2 1949–1972
Dapčević-Oreščanin, Sonja.
'O uzrocima i suštini "kulturne revolucije" u Kini.'
Socijalizam 9, 11 (Novembar 1966), 1406–1425.
'Origin and essence of the "Cultural Revolution" in China.'
International problems (Belgrade) 1967, 163–178.
SUBJ 19 ▪ 12.1 14 16.1 32 64

15228 DLC P P2 G1.2 1949–1972
Dapčević-Oreščanin, Sonja.
'Pogled na savremeni razvitak narodne republike Kine.'
Socijalizam 2, 6 (1959), 123–146.
A look at the modern development of the Chinese People's Republic, mimeo.
Washington, D.C.: U.S. Joint Publications Research Service, 6 May 1960. 24 p. (JPRS 3219; MC 8632/1960)
SUBJ 12 14 19 34.1 ▪ 11 14.1 14.4 16.2 16.4 32.2

15229 CSU P P3 G7.1 1949–1972
Davis, Deborah S-.
'The Cultural Revolution in Wuhan.' In *The Cultural Revolution in the provinces*. [Analytic entry]
Cambridge: Harvard U., East Asian Research Center, 1971, 147–170. (Harvard East Asian monographs, 42)
SUBJ 19 35 54 ▪ 22 25 32

15230 DLC P P2 G1.2 1949–1972
Deliusin, Lev Petrovich (L. P. Delyusin), 1923–.
'Kul'turnaia revoliutsiia' v Kitae.
Moscow: Znanie, 1966. 48 p. (Novoe v zhizni, nauki, tekhnike, seriia: mezhdunarodnaia, 22).
The 'Cultural Revolution' in China.
Moscow: Novosti, 1967. 103 p.
SUBJ 12.1 19 32.1 64 ▪ 14 16.1 17 22.2 32 54

15231 MCH S P2 G1.2 1949–1972
Demarco, Domenico.
'L'opera sociale della Cina popolare (1949–1955)' (Social reform in the People's Republic of China, 1949–1955).
Studi economici 10, 3 (maggio–giugno 1955), 211–230.
SUBJ 16.4 18 19 36.4 ▪ 14.1 16.3 17 47

15232 CSU U P7 G1.2 1949–1972
Diamond, Norma Joyce, 1933–.
'Some aspects of change and continuity in Communist China.'
Papers of the Michigan Academy of Science, Arts, and Letters 51 (1966), 299–306.
SUBJ 19 20 26.3 41 ▪ 34.1 47

15233 GMS P P2 G1.2 1949–1972
Domes, Jürgen Otto, 1932–, and Heinrich Gerhardt.
'Das kommunistische China seit 1949' (Communist China since 1949). In *Chinesische Kommunismus: Zur Geistes- und politischen Geschichte* (An intellectual and political history of Chinese Communism), edited by Gottfried-Karl Kindermann, J. O. Domes, and H. Gerhardt. [Analytic entry]
Bonn: Germany [Federal Republic], Bundeszentrale für politische Bildung, 1966, 87–103. (BzpB, Schriftenreihe, 71)
SUBJ 12.1 14 19 30 32 64 ▪ 12 14.1 14.4 16.4 34.2 35

15234 DLC P P2 G1.2 1949–1972
Dorrill, William Franklin, 1931–.
Power, policy, and ideology in the making of China's 'Cultural Revolution'.
Santa Monica, Calif.: RAND Corp., 1968. 164 p. (RAND memoranda, RM-5731-PR) [Reprinted as 'Power, policy, and ideology in the making of the Chinese Cultural Revolution.' In *The Cultural Revolution in China*, edited by Thomas Webster Robinson. (Analytic entry.) Berkeley, Los Angeles: U. of California Press, 1971, 21–112.]
SUBJ 16.1 19 32 64 ▪ 12.1 14 15

15235 CSH P P2 G1.2 1949–1972
Dutt, Gargi, 1929–, and Vidya Prakash Dutt, 1925–.
China's Cultural Revolution.
New York: Asia Publishing House, 1970. 260 p.
SUBJ 12.1 15 19 32 54 64 ▪ 12 14 16 16.1 25 35

15236 CSH P P2 G1.2 1949–1972
Egashira Kazuma, 1925–. [Tr. erroneously cites Ōa Kyokai (European-Asian Assn.) as author.]
'Courants profonds de la Révolution culturelle chinoise' (Undercurrents of China's Cultural Revolution). Tr. by F-Berthier of 'Chūgoku bunka kakumei no teiryū'; *Kyōsanken no ugoki* 23 (Oct. 1968), 1–23.
NED 3528 (21 oct. 1968), 17–30.
SUBJ 12 12.1 15 19 32 54 ▪ 16 22 64

15237 CSU P P2 G1.2 1949–1972
Elegant, Robert Simpson, 1926–.
Mao's great revolution.
New York: World, 1971. 14, 478 p.
SUBJ 12 12.1 16.1 19 32 59 ▪ 14 15 35 54 64

15238 CSH P P2 G1.2 1949–1972
Etō, Shinkichi, 1923–, and Tatsumi Okabe.
'The current tasks facing the People's Republic of China.' Tr. by Jason G. B. Choi of 'Chūka jimmin kyōwakoku no tōmen suru kadai'; in *Sekai no naka no Chūgoku* (China and the world), by Shinkichi Etō and Tatsumi Okabe; Tokyo: Yomiuri shimbunsha, 1969, 10–53.
Chinese law and government 4, 1/2 (Spring–Summer 1971), 82–114.
SUBJ 19 25 35 64 ▪ 12.1 14 15 32

15239 CSU P P1 G1.5 1949–1972
Falkenheim, Victor Carl, 1940–.
'The Cultural Revolution in Kwangsi, Yunnan, and Fukien.'
AS 9, 8 (Aug. 1969), 580–597.
SUBJ 12 19 32.2 ▪ 25 32 32.1 35

15240 CSU O P3 G1.3 1949–1972
Fattori, Giorgio.
L'ABC della Cina d'oggi (The ABC of today's China).
Milan: Longanesi, 1967. 214 p.
SUBJ 19 ▪ 16.1 32 51 54 64

15241 CSU S P2 G1.2 1949–1972
Faville, Donald David, 1934–.
Forced culture change in Communist China.
Unpublished masters thesis in Anthropology, Stanford U., 1957. 197 p.
SUBJ 10 12 12.1 19 64 ▪ 15 22 23 32 32.1

15242 CSU U P1 G1.2 1949–1972
Fitzgerald, Charles Patrick, 1902–.
'Reflections on the Cultural Revolution in China.'
PA 41, 1 (Spring 1968), 51–59.
SUBJ 19 ▪ 15 32

15243 CSU O P2 G1.3 1949–1972
Fitzgerald, Stephen Arthur, 1938–.
'China visited: A view of the Cultural Revolution.' In *China and ourselves: Explorations and revisions by a new generation*, edited by Bruce Douglass and Ross Terrill. [Selective entry]
Boston: Beacon Press, 1969, 1–29.
SUBJ 19 35 54 ▪ 17 22.2 31 32 64 66

15244 CSH P P2 G1.2 1949–1972
Foa, Lisa, and A- Natoli.
'Origini della Rivoluzione culturale' (Origins of the Cultural Revolution).
Manifesto 2, 5 (maggio 1970), 23–33; 2, 6 (giugno 1970), 31–42; 2, 7/8 (luglio-agosto 1970), 38–49.
SUBJ 14 19 32 ▪ 12.1 14.1 14.4 54 64

15245 DLC PO P2 G1.2 1949–1972
Fokkema, Douwe Wessel, 1931–.
Standplaats in Peking: Verslag van de Culturele Revolutie (Stationed in Peking: Report on the Cultural Revolution).
Amsterdam: Uitgeverij de Arbeiderspers, 1970. 187 p.
Report from Peking: Observations of a Western diplomat on the Cultural Revolution. Tr. by D. W. Fokkema.
London: C. Hurst, 1971. 185 p.
SUBJ 16.1 19 32 54 ▪ 14 14.4 16.4 22.2 35 64

15246 CSU S P2 G1.2 1949–1972
Friedman, Edward, 1937–.
'Cultural limits of the Cultural Revolution.'
AS 9, 3 (Mar. 1969), 188–201.
SUBJ 12.1 19 ▪ 16.3 32 54 64

15247 CSH P P2 G1.2 1949–1972
Germain, Ernest.
'The Cultural Revolution: An attempt at interpretation.'
International socialist review 29, 4 (July–Aug. 1968), 38–64.
SUBJ 14 16 19 64 ▪ 14.1 16.3 16.4 25 35 54

15248 CSU P P2 G1.2 1949–1972
Gunawardhana, Theja.
China's Cultural Revolution.
Colombo: Colombo Apothecaries' Co., 1967. 12, 264 p.
SUBJ 16.1 19 32 64 ▪ 12.1 14 16.2 16.4 17 34.1 54

15249 CSU P P2 G1.2 1949–1972
Harding, Harry, Jr., 1946–.
Modernization and Mao: The logic of the Cultural Revolution and the 1970s.
Santa Monica, Calif.: RAND Corp., 1970. 21 p. (RAND papers, P-4442)
SUBJ 14 19 64 ▪ 12 14.1 17 56

15250 MAM P P3 G1.2 1949–1972
Heaslet, Juliana Pennington, 1942–.
The Cultural Revolution, 1966–1969: The failure of Mao's revolution in China.
Ann Arbor: University Microfilms (Publ. 72-3660), 1972. 11, 221 p. (Doctoral dissertation in History, U. of Colorado, 1971)
SUBJ 19 32 54 ▪ 12 15 35

15251 CSH P P1 G1.2 1949–1972
Heinzig, Dieter, 1932–.
'Neues zur Vorgeschichte der Kulturrevolution in China' (New information on the origins of China's Cultural Revolution).
Aussenpolitik 19, 4 (Apr. 1968), 238–245.
SUBJ 12 19 32 ▪ 12.1 64

15252 NNC O P2 G1.2 1949–1972
Henle, Hans.
'China auf dem Weg zur neuen Gesellschaft' (China on the road to a new society).
Z. für Geopolitik 36, 7/8 (Juli–Aug. 1965), 214–220.
SUBJ 12 17 19 61 ▪ 32 52 53 54

15253 MCH P P2 G1.2 1949–1972
Hsiao, Gene T. (Hsiao Chün), 1922–.
'The background and development of "the Proletarian Cultural Revolution".'
AS 7, 6 (June 1967), 389–404.
[Reprinted in *Readings in modern Chinese history*, edited by Immanuel C. Y. Hsü (Hsü Chung-yüeh). (Selective entry.) New York: Oxford U. Press, 1971, 632–645.]
SUBJ 12 12.1 19 ▪ 14 16 16.1 32 64

15254 CSU O P3 G6.1 1949–1972
Hunter, Neale.
Shanghai journal: An eyewitness account of the Cultural Revolution.
New York: Praeger, 1969. 311 p.
SUBJ 12 19 25 32 64 ▪ 17 22.2 24.2 26.1 26.4 35 54

15255 CSU U P2 G1.2 1949–1972
Jenner, Bill.
'The new Chinese revolution.'
New left review 53 (Jan.–Feb. 1969), 83–96.
SUBJ 16.1 19 32 ▪ 16 17 35

15256 CSU P P1 G1.2 1949–1972
Johnson, Chalmers Ashby, 1931–.
'China: The Cultural Revolution in structural perspective.'
AS 8, 1 (Jan. 1968), 1–15. [Reprinted as 'The Cultural Revolution in structural perspective.' In *Communist China: A system-functional reader*, edited by Yung Wei. (Selective entry.) Columbus, Ohio: Merrill, 1972, 328–344.]
SUBJ 12.1 19 32 ▪ 12 15 25 54

15257 CSU P P1 G1.2 1949–1972
Johnson, Chalmers Ashby, 1931–.
'The two Chinese revolutions.'
CQ 39 (July–Sept. 1969), 12–29.
SUBJ 19 32 64 ▪ 12.1

15258 NIC P P7 G1.2 1949–1972
Johnson, Graham Edwin, 1941–.
Mobilization, growth and diversity: The Chinese case, 1958–1963.
Unpublished masters thesis in Sociology, Cornell U., 1966. 239 p.
SUBJ 14.1 16.1 19 22 30 34.1 ▪ 14 64

15259 CSU U P2 G1.2 1949–1972
Jones, Edwin F-.
'Cultural Revolution: In search of a Maoist model.' In *People's Republic of China: An economic assessment*, compiled by Joint Economic Committee, U.S. Congress. [Selective entry]
Washington, D.C.: U.S. Government Printing Office, 1972, 52–58.
SUBJ 12 14 19

15260 ICU P P2 G1.2 1949–1972
Kataoka, Tetsuya, 1933–.
The Great Leap Forward: A study of Chinese Communism.
Unpublished doctoral dissertation in Political Science, U. of Chicago, 1968. 408 p.
SUBJ 12.1 14 19 32.1 34.1 64 ▪ 16 16.1 18 24.3 32 34.2

15261 CSU P P1 G1.2 1949–1972
Kurai Ryōzō, 1909–.
'Chinese puzzle.'
JQ 16, 1 (Jan.–Mar. 1969), 45–52.
SUBJ 19 ▪ 12 25 32 35 64

15262 CSH U P2 G1.2 1949–1972
[La Dany, Ladislao] ———, 1914–.
'Changes in Chinese society, 1949–1969.'
CNA 774 (19 Sept. 1969), 1–7.
SUBJ 14 16 19

15263 CSH P P2 G9.2 1949–1972
[La Dany, Ladislao] ———, 1914–.
'Cultural Revolution in Kwangtung.'
CNA 724 (6 Sept. 1968), 1–7; 727 (4 Oct. 1968), 1–7; 728 (11 Oct. 1968), 1–7.
SUBJ 19 25 32 54 ▪ 12 15 16.1 24.2 35 36.4

15264 CSH P P2 G1.2 1949–1972
[La Dany, Ladislao] ———, 1914–.
'Cultural Revolution, November 1967.'
CNA 688 (8 Dec. 1967), 1–7.
SUBJ 19 ▪ 12.1 16.1 64

15265 CSU U P2 G1.2 1949–1972
La Dany, Ladislao, 1914–.
'Mao's China: The decline of a dynasty.'
FA 45, 4 (July 1967), 610–623.
SUBJ 12.1 19 ▪ 16.1 32 35

15266 MCH S P1 G1.2 1949–1972
Landheer, Bartholomeus, 1904–.
'De communistische revolutie in China: Een sociologische beschouwing' (The Communist revolution in China: A sociological interpretation).
Oost-West 2, 6 (Januari–Februari 1964), 246–250.
SUBJ 19 64 ▪ 12.1 66

15267 CBU P P2 G1.2 1949–1972
Last, Josephus Carel Franciscus, 1898–.
Vuurwerk achter de Chinese muur (Fireworks behind the Great Wall).
Groningen: Wolters-Noordhoff, 1970. 184 p.
SUBJ 12.1 13 16.1 17 19 54 ▪ 12 14.1 14.4 32 35 64

15268 CSU U P1 G1.2 1949–1972
Leng, Shao-chuan (Lung Shao-ch'üan), 1921–.
'China's internal struggle in perspective.'
Yale review 58, 1 (Autumn 1968), 61–73.
SUBJ 19 64 ▪ 16.1 35

15269 CSH S P1 G1.2 1949–1972
Lie Tektjeng.
'Some Indonesian remarks on modern China studies: The Great Proletarian Cultural Revolution as seen from Jakarta.'
Courrier de l'Extrême-Orient 48 (1971), 123–138.
SUBJ 16.1 19 66

15270 CSU P P2 G8.1 1949–1972
Mathews, Thomas Jay.
'The Cultural Revolution in Szechwan.' In *The Cultural Revolution in the provinces*. [Analytic entry]
Cambridge: Harvard U., East Asian Research Center, 1971, 94–146. (Harvard East Asian monographs, 42)
SUBJ 12 19 25 54 ▪ 15 16.4 35

15271 MCH O P7 G1.2 1949–1972
Myrdal, Jan, 1927–.
'The reshaping of Chinese society.' In *Contemporary China*, edited by Ruth Adams. [Selective entry]
New York: Pantheon, 1966, 65–91.
SUBJ 18 19 41 ▪ 17 46 47 51 61

15272 DLC O P2 G1.3 1949–1972
Neverov, L-.
'Bol'shoi skachok' (The Great Leap).
Ural 1959, 2 (fevral'), 174–189.
SUBJ 19 24.1 ▪ 21.3 24.4

15273 NNC P P2 G1.2 1949–1972
Niijima Atsuyoshi, 1928–. [Tr. erroneously gives author's name as Niijima Junryo.]
China's cultural revolution and technical reforms, mimeo. Tr. of 'Chūgoku no bunka kakumei to gijutsu kakumei' (China's revolutions in culture and technology); *Chūgoku shiryō geppō* 127 (Sept. 1958), 1–40. [Partial tr.: p. 1–25 only]
Washington, D.C.: U.S. Joint Publications Research Service, 23 Apr. 1959. 65 p. (JPRS 673D; MC 17,688/1960)
SUBJ 14.4 17 19 36.1 60 ▪ 14.1 18 62

15274 CSU PO P3 G5.1 1949–1972
Nogami, Tadashi, 1921–.
'Return from Peking.'
JQ 15, 2 (Apr.–June 1968), 187–193.
SUBJ 19 66 ▪ 25 32.1 54

15275 FPN PO P2 G1.2 1949–1972
Noirot, Paul, and Alain Roux.
'Chine: questions et réflexions' (Questions and reflections on China).
Démocratie nouvelle 1966, 12 (déc.), 14–29.
SUBJ 19 64 ▪ 12.1 14 16.3 53 54

15276 MCH P P1 G1.2 1949–1972
Oksenberg, Michel Charles, 1938–.
'China: Forcing the revolution to a new stage.'
AS 7, 1 (Jan. 1967), 1–15.
SUBJ 12 12.1 19 ▪ 15 16.1 54 64

15277 CSU U P2 G1.2 1949–1972
Oksenberg, Michel Charles, 1938–.
'What's going on in China?'
Asia (New York: Asia Society) 13 (Autumn 1968), 13–32.
SUBJ 12.1 16.1 19 ▪ 12 15 32 54 64

15278 CSH U P2 G1.2 1949–1972
Paresce, Gabriele.
'La Rivoluzione culturale in Cina' (China's Cultural Revolution).
Nuova antologia 505, 2017 (gennaio 1969), 69–89.
SUBJ 19 ▪ 32 64

15279 CSU O P2 G1.2 1949–1972
Paron, Charles, 1914–.
La deuxième révolution de Mao Tse-toung: journal quotidien de la Révolution culturelle (Mao's second revolution: A day-by-day account of the Cultural Revolution).
Paris: Ed. de la Francité, 1971? 211 p.
SUBJ 12.1 15 16.2 19 64

15280 CSU S P2 G1.2 1949–1972
Pfeffer, Richard Monroe, 1936–.
'Contradictions and social change in Communist China.' [Review of *Ideology and organization in Communist China*, by Herbert Franz Schurmann.]
PA 39, 3/4 (Fall–Winter 1966/67), 349–360.
SUBJ 19 64 71 ▪ 12 22 30

15281 CSH S P1 G1.2 1949–1972
Pfeffer, Richard Monroe, 1936–.
'Mao Tse-tung and the Cultural Revolution.' In *National liberation: Revolution in the Third World*, edited by Norman Miller and Roderick Aya. [Selective entry]
New York: Free Press, 1971, 249–296.
SUBJ 19 64 ▪ 12 16.1 32

15282 CSU S P1 G1.2 1949–1972
Pfeffer, Richard Monroe, 1936–.
'The pursuit of purity: Mao's Cultural Revolution.'
Problems of Communism 18, 6 (Nov.–Dec. 1969), 12–25.
SUBJ 16.1 19 32 64 ▪ 12 12.2 35 54

15283 CSU O P2 G1.1 1949–1972
[Pincherle, Alberto] Alberto Moravia, pseud., 1907–.
La rivoluzione culturale in Cina (China's Cultural Revolution).
Milan: Valentino Bompiani, 1967. 197 p.
The Red Book and the Great Wall: An impression of Mao's China. Tr. by Ronald Strom.
New York: Farrar, Straus and Giroux, 1968. 170 p.
SUBJ 19 64 ▪ 16 54

15284 CSU P P2 G1.2 1949–1972
Ray, Dennis Michael, 1939–.
'China's unfinished revolution.'
Indian j. of political science 31, 1 (Jan.–Mar. 1970), 21–31.
SUBJ 19 ▪ 12.1 16 64

15285 CSU O P4 G1.2 1949–1972
Robinson, Joan, 1903–.
The Cultural Revolution in China.
Baltimore: Penguin, 1969. 151 p.
SUBJ 15 19 32 ▪ 14.4 17

15286 CSU U P2 G1.2 1949–1972
Robinson, Thomas Webster, 1935–.
'Introduction.' In *The Cultural Revolution in China*, edited by T. W. Robinson. [Analytic entry]
Berkeley, Los Angeles: U. of California Press, 1971, 1–20.
SUBJ 19 ▪ 12 32 64

15287 CSU P P2 G2.1 1949–1972
Sargent, Margie.
'The Cultural Revolution in Heilungkiang.' In *The Cultural Revolution in the provinces*. [Analytic entry]
Cambridge: Harvard U., East Asian Research Center, 1971, 16–65. (Harvard East Asian monographs, 42)
SUBJ 16.1 19 30 32 ▪ 12 12.1 16.4 25 35 54

15288 CSU P P2 G1.2 1949–1972
Schwartz, Benjamin Isadore, 1916–.
'Upheaval in China.'
Commentary 43, 2 (Feb. 1967), 55–62. [Reprinted in *Communism and China: Ideology in flux*, by B. I. Schwartz. (Selective entry.) Cambridge: Harvard U. Press, 1968, 205–227.]
SUBJ 19 ▪ 15 16.1 64

15289 CSU P P2 G1.2 1949–1972
Schwarz, Henry Guenter, 1928–.
'The Great Proletarian Cultural Revolution.'
Orbis (Philadelphia) 10, 3 (Fall 1966), 803–822.
SUBJ 12 19 64 ▪ 16.1 17 32.1

15290 CSH U P2 G1.2 1949–1972
Shibata, Minoru.
'The era of Chou En-lai.' Tr. by Jason G. B. Choi of 'Shu Onrai no jidai'; *Chūō kōron* 85, 11 (Nov. 1970), 109–117.
Chinese law and government 4, 1/2 (Spring–Summer 1971), 115–133. [For an expanded version in Japanese, see Shibata Minoru, *Shu Onrai no jidai*; Tokyo: Chūō kōronsha, 1971; 268 p.]
SUBJ 16.1 19 35 ▪ 12 14 18 32

15291 CSU P P3 G6.1 1949–1972
Shue, Vivienne Bond, 1944–.
'Shanghai after the January storm.' In *The Cultural Revolution in the provinces*. [Analytic entry]
Cambridge: Harvard U., East Asian Research Center, 1971, 66–93. (Harvard East Asian monographs, 42)
SUBJ 12 12.1 19 32 ▪ 17 21.2 22.2 26.1 30 54

15292 CSH P P2 G1.2 1949–1972
Simmonds, John D-.
'Mass modernization: Aspects of the Chinese experience.'
Asia q. 1972, 1, 3–78.
SUBJ 12.1 14.1 14.2 19 21.2 56 ▪ 15 16.1 16.3 24.4 27 50 51 54 64

15293 CSU U P7 G1.2 1949–1972
Skinner, George William, 1925–, and Edwin Arthur Winckler, 1941–.
'Compliance succession in rural Communist China: A cyclical theory.' In *A sociological reader on complex organizations*, 2nd ed., edited by Amitai Etzioni. [Sole entry]
New York: Holt, Rinehart and Winston, 1969, 410–438.
SUBJ 11.4 12.1 19 22.1 ▪ 16.3 32.1

15294 CSU P P2 G1.2 1949–1972
Tang, Peter S. H. (T'ang Sheng-hao), 1919–, and Joan M- Maloney.
Communist China: The domestic scene, 1949–1967.
South Orange: Seton Hall U. Press, 1967. 606 p.
SUBJ 12 12.1 14 19 32 64 ▪ 12.2 15 16 17 18 32.1 32.2 34.1 36.4 47

15295 CSU P P4 G1.2 1949–1972
Tsou, Tang, 1918–.
'The Cultural Revolution and the Chinese political system.'
CQ 38 (Apr.–June 1969), 63–91.
SUBJ 12 12.1 19 32 64 ▪ 15 16.1 16.2 32.1 54 61

15296 CSU P P1 G1.2 1949–1972
Tsou, Tang, 1918–.
'Revolution, reintegration, and crisis in Communist China: A framework for analysis' [with comments by Charles Patrick Fitzgerald and Jerome Alan Cohen]. In *China in crisis, Vol. 1, China's heritage and the Communist political system*, edited by Ping-ti Ho and Tang Tsou. [Selective entry]
Chicago: U. of Chicago Press, 1968, 277–364.
Subj 12 16 16.1 19 32.1 64 ▪ 12.1 22.2 32 62

15297 MCH O P2 G1.2 1949–1972
Ursel, Pierre d'.
La Chine des gardes rouges (The China of the Red Guards).
Tournai, Paris: Casterman, 1968. 205 p.
Subj 19 24 28 47 54 ▪ 15 17 24.4 26.3 34.1 64 66

15298 CSU P P3 G1.2 1949–1972
Vogel, Ezra Feivel, 1930–.
'Introduction.' In *The Cultural Revolution in the provinces*. [Analytic entry]
Cambridge: Harvard U., East Asian Research Center, 1971, 1–15. (Harvard East Asian monographs, 42)
Subj 12 19 54 ▪ 25

15299 CSU P P2 G1.2 1949–1972
Vogel, Ezra Feivel, 1930–.
'The structure of conflict: China in 1967.' In *The Cultural Revolution: 1967 in review*, by Michel Charles Oksenberg et al. [Selective entry]
Ann Arbor: U. of Michigan, Center for Chinese Studies, 1968, 97–125. (Michigan papers in Chinese studies, 2)
Subj 19 32 ▪ 12.1 16.1

15300 CSH U P1 G1.2 1949–1972
Walker, Richard Louis, 1922–.
'Cultural, political and social impacts of the Proletarian Cultural Revolution.'
CC 11, 4 (Dec. 1970), 63–68.
Subj 19

15301 CSU P P1 G1.2 1949–1972
Wang Hsueh-wen (Wang Hsüeh-wen).
'The nature and development of the "Great Cultural Revolution".'
IS 4, 12 (Sept. 1968), 11–21.
Subj 19 ▪ 64

15302 MCH O P3 G4.1 1949–1972
Watson, Andrew John, 1942–.
'[1] Revolution in Sian. [2] Embattled armies. [3] Scarlet and black. [4] Showdown in Sian. [5] Armageddon averted.'
FEER 56, 3 (20 Apr. 1967), 123–126; 56, 4 (27 Apr. 1967), 231–233; 56, 5 (4 May 1967), 266–269; 56, 7 (18 May 1967), 403–406; 56, 8 (25 May 1967), 449–452.
Subj 19 25 54 ▪ 17 24.2 26.4 32 32.1

15303 CSU FP P2 G1.2 1949–1972
Yu, Frederick T. C. (Yü Te-chi), 1921–.
'Campaigns, communications, and development in Communist China.' In *Communication and change in the developing countries*, edited by Daniel Lerner and Wilbur Schramm. [Selective entry]
Honolulu: East-West Center Press, 1967, 195–215.
Subj 12.1 19 30 ▪ 11.4 14 22.1 24.2 26.4 64

15304 FPN O P3 G5.1 1949–1972
Zhelokhovtsev, Aleksei Nikolaevich (A. Jelokhovtsev), 1933–.
La révolution culturelle vue par un Soviétique (A Russian views the Cultural Revolution). Tr. from the Russian by *Mme.* ——— Slodzian and Jacques Michel.
Paris: Laffont, 1968. 240 p.
Subj 19 26.1 32 60 66 ▪ 54 64

20 Local Communities as Total Systems
地方社區整體研究
地方共同体全般

1644-1911

15305 NNC O P2 G9.0 1644–1842
Abeel, David, 1804–1846.
Journal of a residence in China and the neighboring countries, 2nd ed.
New York: J. A. Williamson, 1836. 378 p.
Subj 20 55 ▪ 21.3 23 24.3 26.4 28 29 31

15306 CBU O P2 G1.3 1644–1842
Abel, Clarke, 1780–1826.
Narrative of a journey in the interior of China, and of a voyage to and from that country in the years 1816 and 1817: Containing an account of the most interesting transactions of Lord Amherst's embassy to the court of Pekin . . .
London: Longman, Hurst, Rees, Orme, and Brown, 1818. 16, 420 p. [Reprinted—New York: Arno, 1971. 16, 420 p.]
Subj 20 24.4 28 55 66 ▪ 21.3 23 24.1 24.2 26 56 61

15307 MCH O P3 G6.1 1842–1895
Antonini, Paul, 1851–?
La vie réelle en Chine: Chang-Haï (Everyday life in China: Shanghai).
Paris: Letouzey et Aîné, 1887. 348 p.
Subj 20 22 28 32.2 ▪ 17 21.3 33 43 51 55 66

15308 MCH O P5 G8.2 1895–1911
Aymard, Am——.
'Le long du chemin de fer du Yunnan' (Along the Yunnan railroad).
Tour du monde nouvelle (2e) série 17, 49 (9 déc. 1911), 577–588; 17, 50 (16 déc. 1911), 589–600; 17, 51 (23 déc. 1911), 601–612; 17, 52 (30 déc. 1911), 613–624.
Subj 20 21.1 24.2 55 57 60 ▪ 23 24.1 26 26.2 31 52

15309 MSE O P2 G1.2 1895–1911
Birch, John Grant.
Travels in North and Central China.
London: Hurst and Blackett, 1902. 16, 379 p.
Subj 20 66 ▪ 22 55 61

15310 CSU O P3 G9.2 1644–1842
[Bridgman, Elijah Coleman] E. C. B., 1801–1861.
'Description of the city of Canton and notice of the trade at it.'
Chinese repository 2, 4 (Aug. 1833), 145–160; 2, 5 (Sept. 1833), 193–211; 2, 6 (Oct. 1833), 241–264; 2, 7 (Nov. 1833), 289–308. [Separately reprinted—Canton: Chinese Repository, 1834. 108 p.] [Reprinted as 'Description of the city of Canton.' In *An historical sketch of the Portuguese settlements in China . . .*, by Andrew Ljungstedt. (Sole entry.) Boston: James Munroe, 1836, 221–323.]
Subj 20 22 55 ▪ 15 17 21.1 23 24 28

15311 NNC O P2 G1.1 1895–1911
Chiminelli, Eugenio.
Nel paese dei draghi e delle chimere (In the land of dragons and chimeras).
Castello: Lapi, 1903. 660 p.
Subj 15 20 21.3 ▪ 12.2 19 24.3 26.3 41 43

15312 CSU O P3 G9.2 1895–1911
Clayson, W- W-.
'Canton, 1901–1910.'
CR 42, 7 (July 1911), 387–392.
Subj 20 ▪ 17 21.3 22 24.2 47

15313 CSU PO P2 G6.0 –1911
Cloud, Frederick D-.
Hangchow, the 'City of Heaven', with a brief historical sketch of Soochow.
Shanghai: Presbyterian Mission Press, 1906. 110 p. [Reprinted—Taipei: Ch'eng-wen, 1971. 110 p.]
Subj 20 21.3 65 ▪ 17 21.1 21.4 24.2 24.4 25 28 31 55 56

15314 CSU S P2 G1.2 1842–1911
Cohen, Myron Leon, 1937–.
'Introduction.' In *Village life in China*, by Arthur Henderson Smith. [Analytic entry]
Boston: Little, Brown, 1970, 9–26 [s.p.]. [For Smith's work, see entry 15360.]
Subj 12 17 20 24 26 41 ▪ 21.3 24.1 24.3 42 45 63

15315 MCH O P3 G6.1 1842–1911
Darwent, C- E-.
Shanghai: A handbook for travellers and residents to the chief objects of interest in and around the foreign settlements and native city, 2nd ed., rev. and enl.
Shanghai: Kelly and Walsh, 1920. 204 p.
Subj 17 20 ▪ 24 28

15316 NNP O P2 G8.2 1895–1911
Davies, Henry Rodolph, 1865–?
Yün-nan, the link between India and the Yangtze.
Cambridge: Cambridge U. Press, 1909. 12, 431 p. [Reprinted—Taipei: Ch'eng-wen, 1970. 12, 431 p.]
Subj 20 22 23 60 66 ▪ 22.1 22.2 24 24.2 25 28 55 61 63

15317 MCH O P2 G9.3 1842–1895
Doolittle, Justus, 1824–1880.
Social life of the Chinese: A daguerreotype of daily life in China, rev. ed., edited by Paxton Edwin Hood.
London: Sampson Low, Son, and Marston, 1868. 32, 633 p. [Reprinted—Taipei: Ch'eng-wen, 1966. 32, 633 p.]
Subj 20 23 30 41 50 55 ▪ 13 24.1 26.1 31 34.2 43 47 57 62 65

15318 NNC O P3 G6.1 –1911
Du Bose, Hampden C-.
'Beautiful Soo' [Soochow], *the capital of Kiangsu*.
Shanghai: Kelly and Walsh, 1899. 45 p.
Subj 20 24 26.1 29 ▪ 21.3 22 23 24.2 24.4 25 38 55

15319 NNM O P3 G9.3 1842–1895
Dukes, Edwin Joshua.
Along river and road in Fuh-kien, China, 2nd ed.
London: Religious Tract Society, 1900? 348 p.
SUBJ 20 60 62 ▪ 17 24.2 33 57 63

15320 MCH PO P3 G5.1 –1895
Favier, Alphonse, 1837–1905.
Pékin: histoire et description (Peking: History and description).
Peking: Impr. des lazaristes au Pe-t'ang, 1897. 12, 562 p.
SUBJ 20 24 28 40 55 66 ▪ 15 17 21.3 22.2 23 26.1 32.2 57 62 64

15321 NNC O P2 G9.2 1842–1895
Fielde, Adele Marion, 1839–1916.
A corner of Cathay: Studies from life among the Chinese.
New York: Macmillan, 1894. 11, 286 p.
SUBJ 20 24 41 55 60 ▪ 17 22.2 23 28 43 45 47 50

15322 CBU O P3 G4.2 –1911
Filchner, Wilhelm, 1877–1957.
'Lan-tschóu-fu' (Lan-chou-fu [i.e., Lanchow]). In *Wissenschaftliche Ergebnisse der Expedition Filchner nach China und Tibet, 1903–1905* (Scientific results of the Filchner expedition to China and Tibet, 1903–1905), by W. Filchner. [Selective entry]
Berlin: Mittler, 1912, vol. 2, 1–41.
SUBJ 20 21.3 23 ▪ 14.3 15 17 21.1 22

15323 CBU O P4 G4.2 –1911
Filchner, Wilhelm, 1877–1957.
'Die Stadt Si-ning-fu' (Hsi-ning-fu [Kansu]). In *Wissenschaftliche Ergebnisse der Expedition Filchner nach China und Tibet, 1903–1905* (Scientific results of the Filchner expedition to China and Tibet, 1903–1905), by W. Filchner. [Selective entry]
Berlin: Mittler, 1912, vol. 2, 99–154.
SUBJ 20 21.3 ▪ 14.3 21.1 22 47 65 66

15324 MSE O P2 G1.4 1842–1895
Fleming, George, 1833–1901.
Travels on horseback in Mantchu Tartary: Being a summer's ride beyond the Great Wall of China.
London: Hurst and Blackett, 1863. 14, 579 p.
SUBJ 20 25 26 55 ▪ 12 26.1 26.2 66

15325 NIC O P3 G9.5 1842–1911
França, Bento da, 1859–1906.
Macau e os seus habitantes, relações com Timor (Macau and its inhabitants and its relations with Timor).
Lisbon: Imprensa Nacional, 1897. 296 p.
SUBJ 20 21.1 21.2 24 40 55 ▪ 17 22.1 23 24.4 31 34.2 41 56 57 63

15326 MBA O P7 G8.2 1895–1911
Ganesco, Fernand.
'La campagne chinoise' (The Chinese countryside).
RI nouvelle (2e) série 5, 49 (15 jan. 1907), 18–23.
SUBJ 20 62

15327 NNC PO P3 G1.3 –1911
Geil, William Edgar, 1865–1925.
Eighteen capitals of China.
Philadelphia: Lippincott, 1911. 20, 429 p.
SUBJ 20 21.3 24.4 60 62 ▪ 13 17 21.1 24.2 29 31 33 47 55 56

15328 GMS P P2 G5.3 1895–1911
Germany. Reichsmarineamt.
Denkschrift betreffend die Entwicklung des Kiautschou-Gebiets in der Zeit von 1898 bis 1909 (The development of Kiaochow from 1898 to 1909). [The coverage for each issue, except for the first, runs from October to October; the first issue is entitled *Denkschrift betreffend die Entwicklung von Kiautschou abgeschlossen ende Oktober 1898* (The development of Kiaochow to the end of October 1898).]
Berlin: Reichsdruckerei. Issued annually, 1898–1910. Average ca. 60 p.
SUBJ 20 22.2 24 24.1 ▪ 14.3 17 21 21.4 24.5 28 45 58

15329 NNC O P3 G9.5 1842–1895
Goshkevich, Iosif Antonovich (J. Goschkewitsch), ?–1871.
'Khonkon, iz zapisok russkago puteshestvennika' (Hong Kong, from a Russian traveler's notebook). In *Trudy chlenov Rossiiskoi dukhovnoi missii v Pekine* (Works of members of the Russian Orthodox ecclesiastical mission in Peking). [Selective entry]
St. Petersburg: Tip. Shtaba voenno-ucheb. zavedenii, 1857, vol. 3, 395–409. [Reprinted in *Trudy chlenov Rossiiskoi dukhovnoi missii v Pekine*. (Selective entry.) Peking: Tip. Uspenskago monastyria pri RDM, 1910, vol. 3, 217–225.]

'Hong-Kong, aus dem Tagebuche eines russischen Reisenden.' Tr. by Carl Abel and F- A- Mecklenburg. In *Arbeiten der kaiserlich russischen Gesandtschaft zu Peking über China, sein Volk, seine Religion, seine Institutionen, sozialen Verhältnisse, usw.* (Works of the imperial Russian mission to Peking on China, its people, religion, institutions, social conditions, etc.). [Selective entry]
Berlin: Heinicke, 1858, vol. 1, 247–258.
SUBJ 20 ▪ 21.3 24.3

15330 CSU FP P7 G9.5 1842–1911
Hayes, James William, 1930–.
'A Chinese village on Hong Kong island fifty years ago: Tai Tam Tuk [Ta-t'an-tu], village under the water.' In *Hong Kong: A society in transition*, edited by Ian C- Jarvie and Joseph Agassi. [Analytic entry]
New York: Praeger, 1969, 29–51.
SUBJ 20 24.1 41 ▪ 42 50 56

15331 NIC P P8 G9.5 1644–1911
Hayes, James William, 1930–.
'Peng Chau [i.e., P'ing-chou island, Hong Kong] between 1798–1899.'
JRAS-HKB 4 (1964), 71–96.
SUBJ 20 42 ▪ 22.2 24.4 29

15332 MSE O P2 G1.5 1842–1895
Henry, Benjamin Couch, 1850–1901.
Ling-Nam: or, Interior views of southern China, including explorations into the hitherto untraversed island of Hainan.
London: Partridge, 1886. 511 p.
SUBJ 20 24 ▪ 23 24.2 24.4 29 65 66

15333 DLC O P3 G1.2 1842–1895
Hesse-Wartegg, Ernst von, 1854–1918.
'China' (China). In *China und Japan: Erlebnisse, Studien, Beobachtungen* (Experiences, studies, and observations of China and Japan), rev. and enl. ed., edited by E. von Hesse-Wartegg. [Sole entry]
Leipzig: J. J. Weber, 1900, 3–406.
SUBJ 14.6 20 47 55 ▪ 14.2 32.2 43 60

15334 CBU PO P2 G9.2 1644–1895
Hirth, Friedrich, 1845–1927.
'Über chinesische Quellen zur Geographie von Kuang-tung, mit besonderer Berücksichtigung der Halbinsel Leichou' (Chinese sources on the geography of Kwangtung, with special attention to Lei-chou peninsula).
Mitteilungen des Vereins für Erdkunde zu Leipzig 1881, 1–56. [Reprinted in *Chinesische Studien* (Chinese studies), by F. Hirth. (Selective entry.) Munich: Hirth, 1890, vol. 1, 118–169.]
SUBJ 15 20 22 24.1 ▪ 11.3 12 14.3 21.1 21.3 24.2 24.3 25 55

15335 CSU O P3 G2.3 1895–1911
Inglis, James William.
'Moukden in 1911.'
CR 42, 7 (July 1911), 393–398.
SUBJ 20 ▪ 17 21.3 22 24.2 47

15336 NIC O P2 G5.3 1895–1911
Johnston, Reginald Fleming, 1874–1938.
Lion and dragon in northern China [Weihaiwei].
New York: Dutton, 1910. 14, 461 p.
SUBJ 12.2 20 23 41 ▪ 22 43 45 65

15337 MCH O P5 G9.2 1895–1911
Liang Lan-hsün.
'Pakhoi' (Pei-hai [Ho-p'u *hsien*, Kwangtung]). Tr. from the Chinese by Th—— Metzelthin.
MSOSB 14 (1911), 57–98.
SUBJ 20 24 ▪ 22 43 61

15338 MAM P P7 G5.3 1842–1911
Lindquist, Harry Maurice, 1940–.
North China villages: A comparative analysis of models in the published and unpublished writings of Arthur Henderson Smith, American missionary to China.
Ann Arbor: University Microfilms (Publ. 68-601), 1968. 255 p. (Doctoral dissertation in Anthropology, Kansas State U., 1967)
SUBJ 20 41 48 55 61 66 ▪ 22 22.2 23 26 27 31 42 51 52 62

15339 NIC O P3 G9.0 1895–1911
Lloyd, C- V-.
From Hong Kong to Canton by the Pearl river.
Hong Kong: Daily Press Office, 1902. 80 p.
SUBJ 20 ▪ 24.2 24.3 66

15340 CSU FP P7 G9.5 1895–1911
Lockhart, James Haldane Stewart, 1858–1937.
Report on the New Territory at Hong Kong.
London: Her Majesty's Stationery Office, 1900. 30 p. (Great Britain, Parliament, Papers by command, Cd. 403)
SUBJ 20 22 22.1 24.1 24.5 ▪ 22.2 24.2 25 27

15341 NIC O P2 G5.1 1644–1895
Lockhart, William, 1811–1896.
Notes on Peking and its neighbourhood.
London: Clowes, 1866. 29 p.
SUBJ 20 ▪ 13 22 24.2 57

15342 CSU O P3 G5.1 1895–1911
Lowry, Homer Hiram, 1898–.
'Peking, 1900–1910.'
CR 42, 7 (July 1911), 381–386.
Subj 20 ▪ 21.3 24.2 28

15343 WSU O P4 G9.5 –1842
Lu Hsi-yen, 1631–1704.
'An account of Macao by the Chinese Jesuit Lu Hsi-yen about 1680–90.' Tr. from the Chinese by Earl Hampton Pritchard and Kwan-wai So. [Tr. of an unpublished manuscript, *K'ai-t'ien pao-yao* (Precious keys to heaven), dated 1705 and held at FPN] In *Symposium on Chinese studies: Commemorating the Golden Jubilee of the University of Hong Kong, 1911–1961*, compiled by Dept. of Chinese, U. of Hong Kong. [Selective entry]
Hong Kong: U. of Hong Kong, 1968, vol. 3, 110–122.
Subj 20 ▪ 33

15344 NIC O P3 G0.0 1842–1895
Macgowan, John, ?–1922.
Pictures of southern China.
London: Religious Tract Society, 1897. 320 p.
Subj 20 ▪ 22.2 26.2 26.4 28 33

15345 MCH O P3 G1.1 1842–1895
Mayers, William Frederick, 1831–1878, Nicholas Belfield Dennys, ?–1900, and Charles King.
The treaty ports of China and Japan: A complete guide to the open ports of those countries, together with Peking, Yedo, Hong Kong and Macao.
Hong Kong: Shortrede; London: Trübner, 1867. 668, 48, 26 p.
Subj 20 ▪ 15 22.1 24.2 24.3 28

15346 NNC P P2 G6.1 –1895
Medhurst, Walter Henry, 1796–1857.
General description of Shanghai and its environs, extracted from native authorities.
Shanghai: Mission Press, 1850. 168 p.
Subj 20 24 24.5 26 ▪ 14.3 22.1 24.1 24.2 24.4 28 29 38 62

15347 FPN PO P3 G5.1 1842–1895
Michaux, Alexandre, 1834–?
Pékin et ses habitants (Peking and its inhabitants).
Paris: Ledoyen, 1861. 142 p.
Subj 13 20 24 26 47 57 ▪ 12.2 15 21.3 22 28 50 55 60

15348 CSU O P3 G6.3 1842–1895
Milne, William Charles, 1815–1863.
'Notes of a seven months' residence in the city of Ningpo, from December 7th, 1842, to July 7th, 1843.'
Chinese repository 13, 1 – 16, 3 (Jan. 1844 – Mar. 1847), 134 p. in all.
Subj 20 21.3 33 55 57 66 ▪ 17 22 22.2 23 38 47 50 52 62

15349 NNM O P2 G9.0 1842–1911
Müller, K- F-.
Im Kantonland: Reisen und Studien auf Missionspfaden in China (In the Canton area: Travels and studies of a missionary in China).
Berlin: Buchhandlung der Berliner evangelischen Missionsgesellschaft, 1903. 258 p.
Subj 20 ▪ 24.2 25 27 28 29 33 50 55 65

15350 NNC O P2 G4.1 1895–1911
Nichols, Francis Henry, 1868–1904.
Through hidden Shensi.
New York: Scribner, 1902. 31, 333 p.
Subj 20 55 60 66 ▪ 15 21.3 22 22.1 23 26.1 28 29 52

15351 MCH O P2 G9.4 1842–1895
Pickering, William Alexander, 1840–?
Pioneering in Formosa.
London: Hurst and Blackett, 1898. 16, 283 p.
Subj 12 20 22 66 ▪ 22.2 24.1 25 26.1 34.2 43 51

15352 MCH O P3 G5.3 1895–1911
Pila, Ferdinand, 1874–.
'Une province chinoise en progrès: ce qu'y font les Chinois' (An advancing Chinese province and what the Chinese are doing there).
AF 4, 40 (juil. 1904), 331–336.
Subj 20 24 ▪ 17 22

15353 NNC PO P2 G9.3 1644–1911
Pitcher, Philip Wilson.
In and about Amoy: Some history and other facts connected with one of the first open ports in China, 2nd ed.
Shanghai, Foochow: Methodist Publishing House, 1912. 265 p. [Reprinted—Taipei: Ch'eng-wen, 1972. 265 p.]
Subj 20 24.2 29 43 55 ▪ 21.2 21.3 24.1 26 32.2 57 66

15354 ICU P P2 G6.1 –1911
Poston, David Gray, 1906–.
The city of Soochow (585 B.C. – 1912 A.D.) as portrayed in the 'Wu-Hsien chronicles'.
Unpublished doctoral dissertation in History, U. of Chicago, 1946. 199 p.
Subj 20 24 24.1 24.5 ▪ 21.3 23 25 26 26.1

15355 CSU O P2 G5.1 1842–1895
Rennie, D- F-.
Peking and the Pekingese, during the first year of the British Embassy at Peking.
London: Murray, 1865. 2 vols. 19, 351; 10, 332 p.
Subj 15 20 26.2 55 56 66 ▪ 13 22.2 23 24.1 24.3 24.6 25 28 31 57

15356 MCH O P2 G8.0 1842–1895
Rocher, Emile, 1846–1924.
'Itinéraire de Ch'ung-ch'ing à Yun-nan-fu' (Itinerary from Chungking to Yün-nan-fu [Kunming]).
B. de la Société de géographie 6e série 14 (juil.–déc. 1877), 602–663; 15 (jan.–juin 1878), 247–267.
Subj 20 21 21.3 ▪ 21.1 55

15357 MCH O P3 G6.1 1895–1911
Rottach, Edmond.
'A Nanking' (In Nanking).
R. de Paris 19, 8 (15 avr. 1912), 874–892.
Subj 20 21.3 26.1 32.2 61 ▪ 21.1 22.1 25 28

15358 CSU O P8 G9.3 1842–1895
Simon, G- Eugène, 1829–1896.
'The Ouang-Ming-Tse family.' Tr. from the French. In *China: Its social, political, and religious life*, by G. E. Simon. [Analytic entry]
London: Sampson Low, Marston, Searle, and Rivington, 1887, 209–318. [See also Appendix 1, 319–335.]
Subj 20 24.1 41 55 ▪ 23 26.3 28 66

15359 MCH O P2 G9.0 1842–1895
Skogman, Carl Johan Alfred, 1820–1907.
'Canton och Hongkong' (Canton and Hong Kong). In *Fregatten 'Eugenies' resa omkring jorden åren 1851–1853* (The trip around the world by the frigate *Eugenie*, 1851–1853). [Sole entry]
Stockholm: Bonnier, 1855, vol. 2, 69–117.
Subj 12 14.3 20 66 ▪ 15 21 21.3 22 23 24.3 25 26.2 28 55

15360 NIC O P7 G5.0 1842–1911
Smith, Arthur Henderson, 1845–1932.
Village life in China: A study in sociology.
New York: Revell, 1899. 360 p. [Reprinted—New York: Young People's Missionary Movement, 1907. 360 p.] [Reprinted as *Village life in China*. Boston: Little, Brown, 1970. 278 p.]
Subj 20 22 24 27 30 40 ▪ 23 25 31 34.1 47 54 55 57 65

15361 MCH O P2 G1.5 1842–1895
Smith, George, 1815–1871.
A narrative of an exploratory visit to each of the consular cities of China, and to the islands of Hong Kong and Chusan [i.e., Chou-shan, Ting-hai *hsien*, Chekiang], *in behalf of the Church Missionary Society, in the years 1844, 1845 and 1846.*
New York: Harper, 1847. 15, 467 p. [Reprinted—Taipei: Ch'eng-wen, 1972. 15, 467 p.]
Subj 20 21.3 23 29 55 66 ▪ 12.2 21 22.1 24.3 26.1 28 33 47 52 62

15362 GMS O P7 G5.3 1842–1895
Stenz, Georg Maria, 1869–?
In der Heimat des Konfuzius: Skizzen, Bilder und Erlebnisse aus Schantung (In the homeland of Confucius: Sketches, pictures, and experiences from Shantung).
Kaldenkirchen: Missionsdruckerei, 1902. 288 p.
Subj 20 ▪ 22.2 23 24.2 32.2 47 56 64 65 66

15363 MSE O P2 G1.1 1842–1895
Thomson, John C-.
Through China with a camera, 2nd ed.
New York: Harper, 1899. 15, 269 p.
Subj 20 24 26 33 ▪ 22.2 24.3 24.4 29 31 34.2 47 55

15364 CBU O P3 G9.2 1842–1895
Tiffany, Osmond, Jr.
The Canton Chinese: or, The American's sojourn in the Celestial Empire.
Boston: Munroe, 1849. 271 p.
Subj 20 23 31 34.2 55 66 ▪ 14.3 22.2 24 24.4 26 33 43 47 48 57

15365 NIC O P2 G8.1 1895–1911
Watson, S- C- Haines.
'Journey to Sungp'an [*t'ing*, Szechwan].'
JRAS-CB new (2nd) series 36 (1905), 51–102.
Subj 20 24.3 ▪ 22 23 24.2 24.5 55 56

15366 NNC O P3 G5.1 1842–1895
Werner, Edward Theodore Chalmers, 1864–1954.
'Peking in the eighties.' In *Autumn leaves: An autobiography with a sheaf of papers, sociological and sinological, philosophical and metaphysical*, by E. T. C. Werner. [Selective entry]

Shanghai: Kelly and Walsh, 1928, 165–177.
SUBJ 20 21.3 22.1 ▪ 24.2 28 66

15367 NNC O P2 G5.0 1842–1895
Williamson, Isabelle.
Old highways in China.
New York: American Tract Society, 1884. 227 p.
SUBJ 20 23 24.2 41 47 ▪ 24 24.3 31 53 55 57 62 65 66

15368 MCH FP P7 G6.1 1842–1911
Zi, Etienne, 1851–?
Notice historique sur les T'oan ou cercles du Sui-Tcheou Fou, particulièrement sur ceux du district de Ou-Toan (Historical account of the *t'uan*, or districts, of Hsü-chou *fu* [Kiangsu], with special attention to the Wu-tuan area).
Shanghai: Impr. de la Mission catholique, 1914. 129 p. (Variétés sinologiques, 40)
SUBJ 20 21.2 22 ▪ 22.2 24.1 25

1644-1949

15369 MCH PO P2 G9.4 –1928
Álvarez, José María, 1871–?
Formosa, geográfica e históricamente considerada, Tomo II (A geographic and historical study of Taiwan, Vol. 2).
Barcelona: Librería Católica Internacional, 1930. 530 p.
SUBJ 12 20 24 33 ▪ 24.4 66

15370 NNC O P3 G5.1 1842–1949
Arlington, Lewis Charles, 1859–1942, and William Lewisohn.
In search of old Peking.
Peiping: Henri Vetch, 1935. 382 p. [Reprinted—New York: Paragon, 1967. 382 p.]
SUBJ 20 23 55 ▪ 13 21.3 31 65

15371 NNC PO P2 G9.2 1895–1928
Bel'chenko, A- T-.
'Doneseniia imperatorskago rossiiskago konsula v Kantone: ocherk territorii zaliva Guan-Chzhou (van') i eia torgovli' (Reports of the imperial Russian consul in Canton: Sketch of the Kuang-chou bay area and its trade).
DIRKP 50 (1915), 156–164.
SUBJ 14.3 20 24.3 ▪ 21.3

15372 CSU O P3 G5.1 –1949
Bredon, Juliet.
Peking: A historical and intimate description of its chief places of interest, 3rd ed., rev. and enl.
Shanghai: Kelly and Walsh, 1931. 16, 571 p.
SUBJ 13 20 23 55 65 ▪ 21.3 24.3 24.4 26.1 26.2 28 31 33 41 57

15373 MAM P P3 G5.3 1895–1928
Buck, David Douglas, 1936–.
Tsinan, Shantung: A political and social history of a Chinese city, 1900–1925.
Ann Arbor: University Microfilms (Publ. 72-16,699), 1972. 11, 487 p. (Doctoral dissertation in History, Stanford U., 1972)
SUBJ 12 20 24 26 26.1 66 ▪ 14.3 17 21.1 22 25 28 30 32 32.2 46

15374 NNC F P8 G6.1 1895–1928
Bucklin, Harold S-, et al.
A social survey of Sung-Ka-Hong, China.
Shanghai: ——, 1924. 111 p. (Brown-in-China monographs, 1)
SUBJ 20 22 23 24 27 31 ▪ 26 28 41 42 55 56 57 62 65

15375 NIC O P2 G1.3 1644–1949
Burgess, John Stewart, 1883–1949.
'Community organization in China.'
FES 14, 25 (19 Dec. 1945), 371–373.
SUBJ 20 22.2 42 ▪ 34.3

15376 MCH FP P2 G9.0 1895–1949
Chen Ta (Ch'en Ta), 1892–.
Emigrant communities in South China: A study of overseas migration and its influence on standards of living and social change, edited by Bruno Lasker.
London: Oxford U. Press, 1939. 16, 287 p. [Reprinted—New York: Institute of Pacific Relations, International Secretariat, 1940. 16, 287 p.]
SUBJ 20 21.2 28 34.2 41 66 ▪ 17 23 24 29 42 44 45 55 56 58

15377 MCH P P3 G6.1 1842–1949
Davidson-Houston, James Vivian, 1901–.
Yellow creek: The story of Shanghai.
London: Putnam, 1962. 205 p.
SUBJ 20 24 25 66 ▪ 15 21 21.1 22 22.1 24.2 28 32.2

15378 CNY F P7 G5.2 1895–1928
Garnier, Henri.
Chez les paysans du nord de la Chine (Among the peasants of North China).
Peking: Impr. des lazaristes, 1920. 260 p.
SUBJ 20 23 26.3 41 57 65 ▪ 22.2 27 63

15379 MCH O P3 G8.1 1895–1928
Grainger, Adam.
Studies in Chinese life.
Chengtu: Canadian Methodist Mission Press, 1921. 151 p.
SUBJ 20 23 55 65 ▪ 40 41 51 57

15380 NNC U P2 G9.5 1895–1949
Great Britain. Admiralty. Naval Intelligence Division. Geographical Section.
'Macao.' In *China proper, Vol. 2, Modern history and administration*, compiled by the agency cited. [Selective entry]
London: His Majesty's Stationery Office, 1945, 340–349. (NID, Geographical handbook series, BR 530A)
SUBJ 20 21 24 ▪ 24.2 24.4 24.5 72

15381 CSH P P2 G9.5 1895–1928
Great Britain. Foreign Office. Historical Section.
Macao.
London: His Majesty's Stationery Office, 1920. 26 p.
SUBJ 20 24 ▪ 21 24.2 24.4 56

15382 MAM P P3 G9.5 –1949
Ho, Stanley Dzu-fang (Ho Tso-fan), 1913–.
A hundred years of Hong Kong.
Ann Arbor: University Microfilms (Publ. 2973), 1952. s.p. (Doctoral dissertation in Politics, Princeton U., 1948)
SUBJ 20 21 22 24 24.6 28 ▪ 17 21.1 21.3 24.3 24.5 58 66

15383 NIC O P2 G5.3 1895–1928
Johnston, Reginald Fleming, 1874–1938.
'Weihaiwei.'
J. of the Royal Central Asian Society 18, 2 (Apr. 1931), 175–193.
SUBJ 20 23 25 ▪ 22 24

15384 DLC PO P4 G5.3 1895–1949
Kyi, Alexander Zuh-tsing (Chi Tse-chin).
Tsingtao: A historical, political and economic survey.
Tsingtao: Catholic Mission Press, 1930. 16, 125 p.
SUBJ 20 21.3 22 22.1 24 30 ▪ 17 24.2 24.3 24.4 25 27 28 31 36.4 56

15385 NNC PO P2 G9.2 –1949
Liu, Hans.
'Hainan: The island and the people.'
CJ 29, 5 (Nov. 1938), 236–246; 29, 6 (Dec. 1938), 302–314. [Separately reprinted—Shanghai: China Journal, 1939. 30 p.]
SUBJ 20 24.2 ▪ 22 23 57

15386 CSH U P2 G4.0 1644–1949
Miller, Beatrice Diamond, 1919–, Udo Posch, and Martin M. C. Yang (Yang Mou-ch'un), 1904–.
'Social structure.' In *A regional handbook on Northwest China*, compiled by Far Eastern and Russian Institute, U. of Washington. [Selective entry]
New Haven: Human Relations Area Files, 1956, vol. 1, 183–212. (HRAF subcontractor's monographs, 59; Washington 5)
SUBJ 20 66 ▪ 21.4 23 41

15387 MCH PO P2 G9.5 1842–1949
Mills, Lennox Algernon, 1896–.
'Hong Kong.' In *British rule in eastern Asia*, by L. A. Mills. [Sole entry]
London: Oxford U. Press, 1942, 373–513.
SUBJ 20 22 24 ▪ 14.3 21 22.1 28

15388 MCH S P3 G6.1 1842–1928
Pott, Francis Lister Hawks, 1864–1947.
A short history of Shanghai: Being an account of the growth and development of the International Settlement.
Shanghai: Kelly and Walsh, 1928. 12, 336 p. [Reprinted—New York: AMS Press, 1972. 12, 336 p.]
SUBJ 20 21.3 22 22.2 24 32.2 ▪ 17 22.1 24.5 25 26.1 28 33 66

15389 CSU PO P3 G5.1 1644–1928
Rasmussen, Otto Durham, 1888–.
Tientsin: An illustrated outline history.
Tientsin: Tientsin Press, 1925. 320, 16 p.
SUBJ 20 21.3 22.2 66 ▪ 24 24.2 25 26.1 28

15390 NNC O P3 G5.1 1842–1928
Swallow, Robert William, 1878–.
Sidelights on Peking life.
Peking: China Booksellers, 1927. 18, 135 p.
SUBJ 20 24.3 26 31 ▪ 22 24.6 26.1 26.2 32 41 46 51 55 65

15391 MCH PO P2 G3.0 1895–1949
Verbrugge, Raphaël, 1872–?
'La vie chinoise en Mongolie' (Chinese life in Mongolia).
Anthropos 26, 5/6 (Sept.–Dez. 1931), 783–841; 27, 1/2 (Jan.–Apr. 1932), 95–121; 27, 5/6 (Sept.–Dez. 1932), 855–880; 28, 1/2 (Jan.–Apr. 1933), 55–85; 29, 1/2 (Jan.–Apr. 1934), 149–176.
SUBJ 20 24 55 ▪ 21 22 26.3 28 32.2 66

1911-1949

15392 CSU O P6 G8.1 1928–1949
'A Chinese town [Lung-ch'üan-i, Chien-yang *hsien*, Szechwan]: Little market towns make China unconquerable.'
Life 11, 21 (24 Nov. 1941), 85–91.
SUBJ 20 ▪ 22 24.3

15393 CSH U P2 G3.0 1911–1928
'Paotowchen, the gateway of the Northwest.'
CEM 3, 5 (May 1926), 201–211.
SUBJ 20 21.3 24 ▪ 14.2 14.3 24.4 24.6 28

15394 NNC O P2 G5.1 1928–1949
Bodde, Derk, 1909–.
Peking diary: A year of revolution.
New York: Henry Schuman, 1950. 21, 292 p. [Reprinted—Greenwich, Conn.: Fawcett, 1967. 21, 292 p.]
SUBJ 20 22.2 24 28 54 ▪ 14.6 15 17 22.1 24.2 26.1 31 32 32.2 41

15395 MCH O P3 G5.1 1911–1928
Bonnard, Abel, 1883–1968.
'Dans la Chine d'aujourd'hui. I, Pékin' (In China today. 1, Peking).
R. des deux mondes 7e période 11 (15 oct. 1922), 780–805.
SUBJ 20 21.1 22.1 25 26.1 58 ▪ 21.3 61 62

15396 CSU O P3 G6.1 1928–1949
Boyden, Amanda.
'Changing Shanghai.'
NG 72, 4 (Oct. 1937), 485–508.
SUBJ 20 55 ▪ 66

15397 NIC O P7 G5.1 1911–1928
Bredon, Juliet.
'The altar of a hundred houses: A Chinese village where the peasants are just as illiterate as ever and just as wise.'
Asia (New York: American Asiatic Assn.) 25, 4 (Apr. 1925), 318–323, 346–349.
SUBJ 20 22 ▪ 26 40

15398 MCH O P7 G1.2 1928–1949
Burgess, John Stewart, 1883–1949.
'Some observations on Chinese village-life.'
Social forces 11, 3 (Mar. 1933), 402–409.
SUBJ 20 ▪ 24 24.1 28 47

15399 MCH F P7 G5.1 1928–1949
Chao, Ch'eng-hsin, 1907–.
'P'ing-chiao-tsun as a social laboratory: The process of social cooperation in the solution of similar and common problems of the population of a Peiping suburban village.'
YJSS 4, 1 (Aug. 1948), 121–153.
SUBJ 20 22 23 27 41 ▪ 21 22.1 22.2 40 55 61

15400 NIC F P8 G1.3 1911–1928
Chen Ta (Ch'en Ta), 1892–.
'Socio-economic conditions in two Chinese villages.'
CEM 2, 5 (Feb. 1925), 11–22.
SUBJ 20 21 24 26 ▪ 25 27 55 58

15401 CSU O P2 G8.1 1928–1949
David-Neel, Alexandra, 1874–?
'The new western provinces of China. II, Sikang.'
Asia (New York: American Asiatic Assn.) 42, 6 (June 1942), 367–370.
SUBJ 20 23 ▪ 25 66

15402 NIC F P8 G6.1 1911–1928
Dealey, James Quayle, 1861–1937.
'A Chinese village survey.'
J. of applied sociology 9, 3 (Jan.–Feb. 1925), 174–178.
SUBJ 20

15403 CBU F P8 G5.1 1911–1928
Dickinson, Jean.
Observations on the social life of a North China village (Chien Ying, Wu Ching hsien) [Hopei].
Peking: Yenching U., Dept. of Sociology and Social Work, 1924. 45 p. (DSSW publications, series C, 6)
SUBJ 20 22 24 41 47 55 ▪ 21 21.4 23 26 27 31 51 52 57

15404 CSU O P3 G6.1 1928–1949
Eigner, Julius.
'The rise and fall of Nanking.'
NG 73, 2 (Feb. 1938), 189–224.
SUBJ 20 21.3 24.2 56 ▪ 21.1 24.4 31 47 58

15405 NIC F P7 G6.1 1928–1949
Fei Hsiao-tung (Fei Hsiao-t'ung), 1910–.
Peasant life in China: A field study of country life in the Yangtze valley.
New York: Dutton, 1939. 300 p. (Revision of *Kaihsienkung* [i.e., K'ai-hsien-kung, Wu-chiang *hsien*, Kiangsu]*: Economic life in a Chinese village*, doctoral dissertation in Anthropology, U. of London [London School of Economics and Political Science], 1938) [Reprinted—London: Kegan Paul, 1945. 300 p.] [Reprinted—New York: Oxford U. Press, 1946. 300 p.] [Reprinted—London: Routledge and Kegan Paul, 1962. 300 p.]
SUBJ 20 24 26.3 34.1 41 45 ▪ 22 23 27 28 31 44 65

15406 NIC F P8 G5.0 1928–1949
Gamble, Sidney David, 1890–1968.
North China villages: Social, political and economic activities before 1933.
Berkeley, Los Angeles: U. of California Press, 1963. 10, 352 p.
SUBJ 20 22 24.1 24.5 34.1 35 ▪ 21.3 23 25 26.1 27 28 41 42

15407 NIC FP P3 G5.1 1911–1928
Gamble, Sidney David, 1890–1968.
Peking: A social survey conducted under the auspices of the Princeton University Center in China and the Peking Young Men's Christian Association.
New York: Doran, 1921. 23, 538 p.
SUBJ 17 20 22 28 31 34.3 ▪ 21.1 21.3 22.2 23 24 36.2 38 46 56 66

15408 MCH F P2 G5.1 1911–1949
Gamble, Sidney David, 1890–1968.
Ting hsien [Hopei]*, a North China rural community.*
New York: Institute of Pacific Relations, International Secretariat, 1954. 25, 472 p. [Reprinted—Stanford: Stanford U. Press, 1968. 25, 472 p.]
SUBJ 20 23 24 27 28 41 ▪ 22 24.1 24.4 24.5 31 34.1 37 57 58

15409 CSU P P2 G9.5 1928–1949
Great Britain. Colonial Office.
Annual report on Hong Kong, 1946–1949. [Issues for 1950–1972 are *1949.* [Issues for 1960–1971 are
London: His Majesty's Stationery Office. Issued annually, 1948–1950. Average ca. 150 p.
SUBJ 12.2 20 24 24.1 24.4 28 ▪ 17 21 21.4 22 24.2 24.5 26.4 33 55 56

15410 MCH O P8 G5.1 1928–1949
Hersey, John Richard, 1914–.
'Red Pepper village [Hopei].'
Life 21, 9 (26 Aug. 1946), 93–98, 100, 102, 105.
SUBJ 20 22 24 28 41 55 ▪ 21.3 22.2 25 27 43 47 52 57 61

15411 CSH P P7 G9.5 1928–1949
Hong Kong. District Office, New Territories.
Annual report, 1946/47–1948/49. [Issues for 1950/51–1971/72 are entered as 15520.]
[Hong Kong]: ——. Issued annually, 1947–1949. Average ca. 20 p.
SUBJ 20 22 24 ▪ 21.4 22.2 24.3

15412 NIC O P3 G7.1 1928–1949
Hu, Yung-hwa.
'Shasi under microscope.'
PT new (2nd) series 5, 10 (16 Dec. 1933), 545–550.
SUBJ 20 24 28 ▪ 22 25

15413 NNC O P2 G8.1 1911–1928
Hubbard, George David, 1871–1958.
'The geographical setting of Chengtu.'
B. of the Geographical Society of Philadelphia 21, 4 (Oct. 1923), 109–139.
SUBJ 11.3 20 21.3 24.2 ▪ 14.3 14.4 21.1 24.1 24.3 28

15414 OOC PO P8 G5.1 1928–1949
Hubbard, Mabel Ellis.
An experiment in teaching the Christian religion by life situations in Fan village [Wan-p'ing *hsien*, Hopei]*, China.*
Unpublished masters thesis, Oberlin College, 1938. 87, 23 p.
SUBJ 20 23 27 31 33 47 ▪ 22 24.1 34.1 41 51 52 55 56 57

15415 NNC PO P8 G5.1 1928–1949
[Hubbard, Mabel Ellis] *Mrs.* Hugh W-Hubbard.
New life in Fan village [Wan-p'ing *hsien*, Hopei]*, North China: Description of a missionary project of a newer type.*
New York: Missionary Education Movement, 193? 21 p.
SUBJ 20 27 50 ▪ 24.1 31 33 34.1 47

15416 CSU O P3 G5.1 1928–1949
Kates, George Norbert, 1895–.
The years that were fat: Peking, 1933–1940.
New York: Harper, 1952. 268 p. [Reprinted—Cambridge: M.I.T. Press, 1967. 268 p.]
SUBJ 20 55 62 63 ▪ 13 17 21.3 33 34.2 66

15417 CSU O P3 G5.3 1928–1949
Keith, Ronald A-.
'Tsinan, a Chinese city.'
Canadian geographical j. 12, 3 (Mar. 1936), 153–160.
SUBJ 20 21.3 24.2 24.3 ▪ 21.1 23 26.2 31

15418 NIC F P8 G9.2 1911–1928
Kulp, Daniel Harrison, II, 1888–.
Country life in South China: The sociology of familism. Vol. 1, Phenix

village [i.e., Feng-huang-ts'un, Ch'ao-an *hsien*], *Kwangtung, China*.
New York: Columbia U., Teachers College, Bureau of Publications, 1925. 30, 367 p. [Vol. 2 of this study was never published.] [Reprinted—Taipei: Ch'eng-wen, 1966. 30, 367 p.]
SUBJ 20 22 23 40 ▪ 21.3 24 24.1 26 31 34.1 38 65

15419 CSH O P6 G9.2 1928–1949
Lasker, Bruno.
'Portrait of a Chinese town ["Lao Chen", Kwangtung].'
Asia (New York: American Asiatic Assn.) 38, 2 (Feb. 1938), 79–82.
SUBJ 20 24.3 28 ▪ 26 55 56

15420 MCY PO P3 G9.2 1911–1949
Lee, Edward Bing-shuey (Li Ping-jui), 1903–1956.
Modern Canton.
Shanghai: Shanghai Mercury Press, 1936. 15, 176 p.
SUBJ 20 22 ▪ 21.3 22.1 24 28

15421 NIC O P8 G3.3 1928–1949
Mei, Tuan Ju, and Rewi Alley, 1897–.
'Rural life in Suiyuan province, the scene of present hostilities.'
CJ 27, 4 (Oct. 1937), 181–191.
SUBJ 20 22 23 25 ▪ 24.1 26.3 34.1

15422 CBU O P4 G1.1 1911–1928
Muller, Hendrik P- N-.
'Thans' (The present). In *Azië gespiegeld: Malakka en China, studiën en ervaringen* (Asia reflected: Malaya and China, studies and experiences), by H. P. N. Muller. [Sole entry]
Leiden: Sijthoff, 1918, 174–286.
SUBJ 20 24 24.3 24.4 ▪ 14.2 21.3 24.6 43

15423 CSU U P2 G9.1 1928–1949
Oldfield, Walter Herbert, 1879–.
'Modernized Kwangsi.'
CR 66, 12 (Dec. 1935), 718–724.
SUBJ 20 24 28 ▪ 17 22.2 25

15424 NIC F P7 G8.2 1928–1949
Osgood, Cornelius, 1905–.
Village life in old China: A community study of Kao Yao [K'un-ming *hsien*], *Yunnan*.
New York: Ronald Press, 1963. 12, 401 p.
SUBJ 20 23 28 55 ▪ 22 24 26 27 40 52 57

15425 MCH O P3 G8.2 1911–1928
Patris, Charles.
'Impressions de Yunnan fou' (Impressions of Yün-nan-fu [Kunming]).
RI nouvelle (2e) série 20, 11/12 (nov.–déc. 1913), 563–576.
SUBJ 20 21.1 24 ▪ 22 25 57 63

15426 NNC S P7 G6.1 1928–1949
Pinto, Roger, 1910–.
Review of *Peasant life in China*, by Fei Hsiao-tung (Fei Hsiao-t'ung).
BEFEO 41, 2 (1941), 373–393.
SUBJ 20 24.1 26.3 41 45 ▪ 22.1 24 27 36.3 40 57

15427 MCH O P3 G7.2 1911–1928
Reed, Alfred Cummings, 1884–1951.
'Changsha and the Chinese.'
Scientific monthly 2, 3 (Mar. 1916), 230–259.
SUBJ 20 ▪ 17 24 24.2

15428 MCH O P7 G1.4 1911–1949
Segers, Arthur.
La Chine: le peuple, sa vie quotidienne et ses cérémonies (The people, daily life, and ceremonies of China).
Antwerp: Ed. De Sikkel, 1932. 242 p.
SUBJ 17 20 41 55 57 ▪ 22.2 24 24.3 26 28 47 48 51 56 65

15429 WSU F P3 G6.1 1928–1949
Shang-hai shih ti fang hsieh hui (Shanghai Civic Assn.), ed.
Statistics of Shanghai.
Shanghai: Shanghai Civic Assn., 1933. 2 vols. 297 p. [s.p.]; 112 p. [In Chinese as well as English]
SUBJ 20 24 ▪ 17 21.1 21.4 22 28

15430 CSH P P3 G6.1 1928–1949
Shang-hai shih ti fang hsieh hui (Shanghai Civic Assn.), ed.
Second supplement to the statistics of Shanghai, mimeo.
Shanghai: Shanghai Civic Assn., 1936. 160 p. [In Chinese as well as English]
SUBJ 20 22.2 24 27 28 ▪ 12.2 21.1 24.3 24.4 26.1 26.4 34.2

15431 CSH P P3 G6.1 1928–1949
Shang-hai shih ti fang hsieh hui (Shanghai Civic Assn.), ed.
Supplement to statistics of Shanghai, 1936, mimeo.
Shanghai: Shanghai Civic Assn., 1936. 159 p. [In Chinese as well as English]
SUBJ 20 21.1 22.2 24 ▪ 17 24.4 24.5 28 41 56 57 58

15432 MCH F P2 G6.1 1928–1949
Smythe, Lewis Strong Casey, 1901–.
War damage in the Nanking area, December 1937 to March 1938: Urban and rural surveys.
Shanghai: Shanghai Mercury Press, 1938. 31 p.
SUBJ 20 21.1 21.2 24 28 ▪ 21.4 24.1 24.3 41 58

15433 CSU O P2 G1.4 1928–1949
Stein, Guenther.
'The other China.'
FA 24, 1 (Oct. 1945), 62–74.
SUBJ 20 22 ▪ 25 28 34.1

15434 NNC O P7 G1.2 1928–1949
Strong, Anna Louise, 1885–1970.
The Chinese conquer China.
Garden City, N.Y.: Doubleday, 1949. 12, 275 p.
SUBJ 20 22 25 28 32.2 48 ▪ 11.2 17 22.1 22.2 24.1 24.5 26.3 41 47 55

15435 CSU O P3 G5.1 1928–1949
Thomason, John W-, Jr.
'Approach to Peiping.'
NG 69, 2 (Feb. 1936), 275–308.
SUBJ 20 21.3 ▪ 24.3 55

15436 CSU F P6 G8.1 1928–1949
Treudley, Mary Bosworth.
The men and women of Chung Ho Ch'ang [Hua-yang *hsien*], *(Szechwan)*.
Taipei: Orient Cultural Service, 1971. 274 p. (Asian Folklore and Social Life monographs, 14)
SUBJ 20 24 24.3 26 41 47 ▪ 21.2 22 22.1 23 27 32.2 34.2 34.3 51 56

15437 CSH PO P2 G9.4 1928–1949
U.S. Office of Naval Operations.
Taiwan (Formosa).
[Washington, D.C.]: Office of the Chief of Naval Operations, 1944. 15, 198 p. (OPNAV, 50E-12)
SUBJ 20 22 24 28 55 56 ▪ 12 17 21 21.4 24.2 24.5 26.4 32.2 58

15438 NNC P P2 G9.4 1928–1949
U.S. Office of Naval Operations.
Taiwan (Formosa): Karenko and Taito provinces [i.e., Hua-lien-kang *t'ing* and T'ai-tung *t'ing*].
[Washington, D.C.]: Office of the Chief of Naval Operations, 1944. 10, 101 p. (OPNAV, 13-24)
SUBJ 12 20 22 22.1 24 ▪ 17 19 21.1 28 30 66

15439 NNC P P2 G9.4 1928–1949
U.S. Office of Naval Operations.
Taiwan (Formosa): Shinchiku province [i.e., Hsin-chu *chou*].
[Washington, D.C.]: Office of the Chief of Naval Operations, 1944. 11, 110 p. (OPNAV, 13-25)
SUBJ 12 12.1 20 24 28 ▪ 17 21.1 30 34.1 66

15440 CSH P P2 G9.4 1928–1949
U.S. Office of Naval Operations.
Taiwan (Formosa): Taichu province [i.e., T'ai-chung *chou*].
[Washington, D.C.]: Office of the Chief of Naval Operations, 1944. 13, 235 p. (OPNAV, 13-26)
SUBJ 20 24 ▪ 12.2 17 21 22.1 24.1 30

15441 NNC P P2 G9.4 1928–1949
U.S. Office of Naval Operations.
Taiwan (Formosa): Taihoku province [i.e., T'ai-pei *chou*].
[Washington, D.C.]: Office of the Chief of Naval Operations, 1944. 12, 209 p. (OPNAV, 13-27)
SUBJ 12 20 22 24 ▪ 17 21.1 22.2 28 30 32.1 34.1

15442 CSH P P2 G9.4 1928–1949
U.S. Office of Naval Operations.
Taiwan (Formosa): Tainan province [i.e., T'ai-nan *chou*].
[Washington, D.C.]: Office of the Chief of Naval Operations, 1944. 10, 106 p. (OPNAV, 13-28)
SUBJ 12 20 22.1 24 ▪ 21.1 24.1 24.4

15443 NNC P P2 G9.4 1928–1949
U.S. Office of Naval Operations.
Taiwan (Formosa): Takao province [i.e., Kao-hsiung *chou*].
[Washington, D.C.]: Office of the Chief of Naval Operations, 1944. 10, 136 p. (OPNAV, 13-22)
SUBJ 20 22 24 ▪ 17 22.1 28 30 34.1

15444 NNC P P2 G9.4 1928–1949
U.S. Office of Naval Operations.
Taiwan (Formosa): The Pescadores islands.
[Washington, D.C.]: Office of the Chief of Naval Operations, 1944. 39 p. (OPNAV, 13-21)
SUBJ 20 22 24 ▪ 17 22.1 28

15445 CSU O P3 G7.1 1911–1928
Weil, Elsie F-.
'The Wu-Han cities.'
Asia (New York: American Asiatic Assn.) 17, 3 (May 1917), 183–190.
SUBJ 14.3 20 ▪ 24.4 26.4

15446 ICU P P3 G1.3 1911–1949
Wu, Pek Si (Wu Pai-ssu), 1913–.
Urbanization in China: A study of Shanghai and Peiping.
Unpublished masters thesis in Sociology, U. of Chicago, 1940. 164 p.
SUBJ 20 21.1 21.3 22 24 58 ▪ 17 21.2 21.4 24.4 24.6 31 34.3 36.4 41 50

15447 MCH F P3 G9.2 1928–1949
Wu Yuey-len (Wu Yüeh-lin).
'The boat people of Shanam [i.e., Shanan, Canton municipality]: A statistical study of population and economic conditions.'
NSEQ 9, 3 (Oct. 1936), 613–665.
SUBJ 20 21.1 21.4 41 ▪ 21.3 26 27 28 29 42 58

15448 MCH F P3 G9.2 1928–1949
Wu Yuey-len (Wu Yüeh-lin).
'Life and culture of the Shanam [i.e., Shanan, Canton municipality] boat people.'
NSEQ 9, 4 (Jan. 1937), 807–854.
SUBJ 20 30 41 ▪ 17 23 26 28 29 31 33 38 47 55

15449 NIC O P7 G5.3 1911–1949
Yang, Martin M. C. (Yang Mou-ch'un), 1904–.
A Chinese village: Taitou [i.e., T'ai-t'ou, Chiao *hsien*], *Shantung province.*
New York: Columbia U. Press, 1945. 17, 275 p. [Reprinted—London: Kegan Paul, 1947. 17, 275 p.] [Reprinted—New York: Columbia U. Press, 1965. 17, 275 p.]
SUBJ 20 22 41 59 ▪ 24 42 45 53 55

15450 NIC F P7 G5.1 1911–1928
Yenching U. Dept. of Sociology and Social Work.
Ching Ho [Ch'ing-ho, Peiping municipality]*: A sociological analysis. The report of a preliminary survey of the town of Ching Ho, Hopei, North China.*
Peiping: Yenching U., Dept. of Sociology and Social Work, 1930. 146 p. (Yenching social research series, 1)
SUBJ 20 21 24 24.3 ▪ 17 21.3 21.4 22 22.1 34.1 34.2 36.2 41 45

1911-1972
(including 1644-1972)

15451 CSU FP P7 G9.5 1895–1972
Aijmer, Lars Göran, 1936–.
'Expansion and extension in Hakka society.'
JRAS-HKB 7 (1967), 42–79.
SUBJ 20 21.2 24 40 ▪ 21.3 22 24.1 29 41 42

15452 CSH PO P2 G5.1 –1972
Andō Hikotarō, 1917–.
Peking.
Tokyo: Kodansha, 1968. 150 p.
SUBJ 20 21.3 22.2 55 ▪ 12 17 19 23 24.1 24.2 24.3 28 31 70

15453 CSU U P8 G4.1 1928–1972
Bernal, Martin Gardiner, 1937–.
'Down there on a visit.' [Review of *Rapport från kinesisk by* (Report from a Chinese village), by Jan Myrdal.]
NYRB 4, 10 (17 June 1965), 16–17.
SUBJ 20 26.3 ▪ 59

15454 CSU P P3 G9.5 –1972
Braga, José Maria.
Macau: A short handbook.
Macau: Information and Tourism Dept., 1965. 72 p.
SUBJ 20 33 ▪ 17 21.1 24 38 56

15455 MAM FP P7 G9.5 1895–1972
Brim, John Anthony, 1940–.
Local systems and modernizing change in the New Territories of Hong Kong.
Ann Arbor: University Microfilms (Publ. 71-12,862), 1971. 238 p. (Doctoral dissertation in Anthropology, Stanford U., 1970)
SUBJ 20 22 23 24 42 60 ▪ 21 21.2 21.4 22.2 24.1 24.3 24.6 25 26

15456 CSH P P7 G9.3 1928–1972
Chen, C. S.
'Introductory analysis.' In *Rural people's communes in Lien-chiang: Documents concerning communes in Lien-chiang county, Fukien province*, edited by C. S. Chen. [Sole entry]
Stanford: Hoover Institution Press, 1969, 3–49.
SUBJ 19 20 24 26 34.1 ▪ 21 21.4 22.1 26.1

15457 CSU P P2 G9.4 1928–1972
Chen, Cheng-siang (Ch'en Cheng-hsiang), 1920–.
'The Pescadores.'
GR 43, 1 (Jan. 1953), 77–88.
SUBJ 20 21 24.1 ▪ 21.3 28 57

15458 NNC PO P2 G9.2 1842–1972
China [People's Republic]. [Kuo wu yüan]. Chung-kuo jen min tui wai wen hua hsieh hui. Kuang-chou fen hui. ([State Council]. Chinese People's Assn. for Foreign Cultural Relations. Canton Branch).
Canton, mimeo. Tr. of *Kuang-chou*; Canton: Kuang-chou wen hua ch'u pan she, 1959; 122 p.
Washington, D.C.: U.S. Joint Publications Research Service, 27 Nov. 1962. 86 p. (JPRS 16,369; MC 900/1963) [Xerox copyflo available—New York: CCM Information Corp., Research and Microfilm Publications. (Scholarly Book Translation Series, 540)]
SUBJ 20 21.3 24 24.4 31 ▪ 14.3 17 21.1 21.4 23 25 28 32.2 56 66

15459 MCH PO P7 G5.1 1928–1972
Crook, David, and Isabel Crook.
The first years of Yangyi commune [She *hsien*, Hopei].
New York: Humanities Press, 1966. 14, 288 p.
SUBJ 20 22 22.1 24 24.1 28 ▪ 17 21.3 24.3 24.4 25 26 32 47 54 55

15460 NNC FP P7 G5.1 1928–1972
Crook, Isabel, and David Crook.
Revolution in a Chinese village: Ten Mile Inn [i.e., Shih-li-tien, She *hsien*, Hopei].
London: Routledge and Kegan Paul, 1959. 23, 190 p.
SUBJ 19 20 22 24 25 26 ▪ 23 28 31 32 34.1 36.3 41 44 47 66

15461 CBU P P2 G9.5 1842–1972
Endacott, George Beer, and A. Hinton.
Fragrant harbour: A short history of Hong Kong, 2nd ed.
Hong Kong: Oxford U. Press, 1968. 178 p.
SUBJ 12.2 20 21.3 22.2 24 66 ▪ 14.3 17 21 21.2 22 24.2 25 28 56

15462 CSH FP P7 G9.5 –1972
Hayes, James William, 1930–.
'A mixed community of Hakka and Cantonese on Lantau island [i.e., Ta-yü shan, Hong Kong].' In *Aspects of social organization in the New Territories*, edited by Hong Kong Branch, Royal Asiatic Society. [Selective entry]
Hong Kong: Cathay Press, 1964, 21–26.
SUBJ 20 29 ▪ 42 48

15463 CSU FP P7 G9.5 1895–1972
Hayes, James William, 1930–.
'Old ways of life in Kowloon: The Cheung Sha Wan villages [Ch'ang-sha bay, Hong Kong].'
JOS 8, 1 (Jan. 1970), 154–188.
SUBJ 20 21 24.1 40 41 55 ▪ 21.3 22.2 23 24.3 25 27 29 42 43 45

15464 CSH P P8 G9.5 1644–1972
Hayes, James William, 1930–.
'The settlement and development of a multiple-clan village.' In *Aspects of social organization in the New Territories*, edited by Hong Kong Branch, Royal Asiatic Society. [Selective entry]
Hong Kong: Cathay Press, 1964, 10–15.
SUBJ 20 48 ▪ 21.2 24.1 26.3 29 42

15465 CSU PO P8 G9.5 1842–1972
Hayes, James William, 1930–.
'Visit to old Shau Kei Wan [i.e., the village of Shao-chi-wan, Hong Kong], 24th May 1969.'
JRAS-HKB 10 (1970), 183–188.
SUBJ 20 ▪ 21 23 24.4

15466 MCH O P2 G1.2 1928–1972
Haylen, Leslie Clement.
Chinese journey: The Republic revisited.
Sydney: Angus and Robertson, 1959. 240 p.
SUBJ 20 24.4 28 ▪ 22.1 22.2 26.3 26.4 31 33 34.1 46 56 59

15467 GMS PO P3 G9.5 1842–1972
Hürlimann, Martin, 1897–.
Hongkong.
Zurich: Atlantis, 1962. 122 p.

Hong Kong.
New York: Viking Press, 1962. 139 p.
SUBJ 20 21.1 ▪ 21 21.2 21.3 24.2 24.6 28

15468 CSU O P3 G9.5 1842–1972
Hughes, Richard, 1906?–.
Hong Kong: Borrowed place, borrowed time.
New York: Praeger, 1968. 171 p.
SUBJ 20 24 28 55 66 ▪ 17 21.2 22 22.2 31 32.2 36.4 46

15469 CSU P P2 G7.1 –1972
Hupeh. Local Gazetteer Revision Commission, ed.
Brief gazetteer of Han-ch'uan hsien [Hupeh], mimeo. Tr. of *Han-ch'uan hsien chien chih*; Wuhan: Jen min ch'u pan she, 1959. [Partial tr.: p. 1–105 only]
Washington, D.C.: U.S. Joint Publications Research Service, 20 Nov. 1962. 113 p. (JPRS 16,268; MC 802/1963) [Xerox copyflo available—New York: CCM Information Corp., Research and

Microfilm Publications. (Scholarly Book Translation Series, 539)]
SUBJ 20 24 24.1 24.2 24.4 28 ▪ 12 14.3 17 24.6 31 34.3 56 65

15470 NNC S P7 G1.3 1911–1972
Locker, Marea N-.
The village and the wider community in studies of small Chinese communities.
Unpublished masters thesis in Anthropology, Columbia U., 1966. 269 p.
SUBJ 20 22.1 23 24 24.3 30 ▪ 12.1 21.2 22 22.2 24.1 24.5 27 41 42 48

15471 DLC P P2 G9.4 1928–1972
Lung, Kuan-hai, 1906–.
'Post-war social change in Taiwan, Republic of China, 1945–1969.'
ASPAC q. of cultural and social affairs (Seoul) 2, 4 (Spring 1971), 7–45.
SUBJ 14 16 20 21 21.1 47 ▪ 12 14.4 17 21.2 24.1 41 50 51 54 58

15472 MCH P P2 G9.4 1928–1972
Lung, Kuan-hai, 1906–, ed.
Social statistics of Taiwan, Republic of China.
Taipei: National Taiwan U., [College of Law], Dept. of Sociology, 1968. 136 p. (DS publications, 5) [In Chinese as well as English]
SUBJ 17 20 21 26 28 ▪ 21.1 21.4 24.2 30 41 56 57 58

15473 CSU F P2 G9.5 1895–1972
Potter, Jack Michael, 1936–.
'The structure of rural Chinese society in New Territories.' In *Hong Kong: A society in transition*, edited by Ian C- Jarvie and Joseph Agassi. [Analytic entry]
New York: Praeger, 1969, 3–28.
SUBJ 20 22 24 42 ▪ 21.1 41 60

15474 CSU O P3 G6.1 1928–1972
Tannebaum, Gerald, 1916–.
'Shanghai scenes: The past and the present.'
EH 5, 3 (Mar. 1966), 48–54; 5, 4 (Apr. 1966), 35–42.
SUBJ 19 20 22.1 ▪ 22 22.2 24.4 32.2 34.2 61

15475 NIC O P8 G5.3 1928–1972
Wang Shih Peng and H- W- Spillett.
'A Christian Communist settlement in China [Ma-chuang, T'ai-an *hsien*, Shantung].'
International review of missions 40, 158 (Apr. 1951), 168–178.
SUBJ 20 33 ▪ 24 41 55

15476 NIC F P8 G9.2 1928–1972
Yang, C. K. (Yang Ch'ing-k'un), 1911–.
A Chinese village in early Communist transition.
Cambridge: M.I.T. Press, 1959. 12, 284 p.
SUBJ 19 20 22 24 26 ▪ 25 34.1 41 42 45

1949-1972

15477 MCH O P7 G5.2 1949–1972
'Survey of a commune [Yang-t'an commune, Ch'ü-wo *hsien*, Shansi].'
PR 9, 10 (4 Mar. 1966), 7–11; 9, 11 (11 Mar. 1966), 18–22; 9, 12 (18 Mar. 1966), 7–10; 9, 13 (25 Mar. 1966), 14–18; 9, 14 (1 Apr. 1966), 26–29; 9, 15 (8 Apr. 1966), 26–29.
SUBJ 20 24 24.1 34.1 ▪ 17 21 22.1 24.2 28 55

15478 CBU O P2 G1.3 1949–1972
'Verbali delle riunioni tra i compagni cinesi e i compagni della delegazione italiana' (Official reports from the meetings between the Chinese comrades and comrades of the Italian delegation).
Vento dell'est 6, 21 (marzo 1971), 5–177.
SUBJ 20 24 24.4 26.3 26.4 ▪ 17 24.1 24.2 27 34.1 56 64

15479 CSU O P8 G9.2 1949–1972
Alley, Rewi, 1897–.
'Communes and schools in Kwangtung.'
EH 8, 3 (1969), 8–22.
SUBJ 20 ▪ 24.1 27 28 34.1 52

15480 CSU O P2 G6.3 1949–1972
Alley, Rewi, 1897–.
'Hangchow in 1966, then 1968.'
EH 7, 5 (Sept.–Oct. 1968), 7–22.
SUBJ 20 ▪ 17 24.4 34.1 50

15481 CSH O P2 G7.1 1949–1972
Alley, Rewi, 1897–.
In the spirit of Hunghu: A story of Hupeh today.
Peking: New World Press, 1966. 226 p.
SUBJ 20 22 24 24.1 24.4 61 ▪ 17 22.2 24.2 26 28 31 64

15482 NNC O P2 G1.2 1949–1972
Alley, Rewi, 1897–.
The people have strength.
Peking: The author, 1954. 281 p.
SUBJ 20 24 24.4 26 27 28 ▪ 22.1 24.1 24.2 26.4 31 34.1 36.4 47 54 56

15483 NIC P P7 G1.2 1949–1972
Asian Peoples' Anti-Communist League.
An analytical study of the Chinese Communists' 'people's communes'.
Taipei: Asian Peoples' Anti-Communist League, 1959. 102 p. (APACL pamphlets, 41)
SUBJ 20 21.4 22 24.1 25 34.1 ▪ 17 22.1 24 24.3 24.4 28 41 45 55

15484 CSU F P3 G9.5 1949–1972
Barnett, Arthur Doak, 1921–.
'Who is Hong Kong? Twenty-six people and their part in the life of the colony.'
AUFS-EAS 3, 10 (24 Aug. 1954), 1–26.
SUBJ 20 28

15485 CSU F P2 G9.2 1949–1972
Barnett, Arthur Doak, 1921–, and Ezra Feivel Vogel, 1930–.
'A county.' In *Cadres, bureaucracy, and political power in Communist China*, by A. D. Barnett. [Analytic entry]
New York: Columbia U. Press, 1967, 105–309.
SUBJ 12 12.1 20 24 32 32.1 ▪ 17 21.3 24.3 24.4 25 26.1 56

15486 NNC FP P7 G1.2 1949–1972
Biehl, Max, 1902–.
Die chinesische Volkskommune im "grossen Sprung" und danach (The Chinese commune during and after the Great Leap Forward).
Hamburg: Weltarchiv, 1965. 245, 49 & 18 p.
SUBJ 20 24 ▪ 17 19 24.1 28 35 47 50 53 55

15487 CSU O P2 G9.5 1949–1972
Billard, Jules B-.
'Macao clings to the Bamboo Curtain.'
NG 135, 4 (Apr. 1969), 521–539.
SUBJ 20 24 ▪ 25 28 31

15488 MAM P P7 G1.2 1949–1972
Birrell, Robert James, 1937–.
The structure of the Chinese agricultural communes: 1960–1966.
Ann Arbor: University Microfilms (Publ. 70-23,600), 1970. 426 p. (Doctoral dissertation in Sociology, Princeton U.)
SUBJ 20 22 22.1 26.1 26.3 34.1 ▪ 24.1

15489 MCH P P3 G9.5 1949–1972
Bissing, Wilhelm Moritz, 1891–.
'Das Flüchtlingsproblem in Hong-Kong in seinen wirtschaftlichen und gesellschaftlichen Auswirkungen' (Economic and social effects of the refugee problem in Hong Kong). In *Ostasiatische Studien zur Wirtschaft und Gesellschaft in Thailand, Hong-Kong und Japan* (East Asian studies on economy and society in Thailand, Hong Kong, and Japan), by W. M. Bissing. [Sole entry]
Berlin: Duncker und Humblot, 1962, 71–93.
SUBJ 11.2 20 26 ▪ 36.4 63

15490 CSU O P2 G9.4 1949–1972
Bristol, Horace.
'Pescadores, wind-swept outposts of Formosa.'
NG 109, 2 (Feb. 1956), 265–284.
SUBJ 20 ▪ 23 24.1 25

15491 NIC F P7 G9.4 1949–1972
Burke, Jean T-.
A study of existing social conditions in the eight townships of the Shihmen reservoir area, including a brief analysis of the impact of irrigation and benchmarks for measuring social change.
Lung-t'an, T'ao-yüan, Taiwan: Chinese-American Joint Commission on Rural Reconstruction, 1962. 114 p. (JCRR, Economic digest series, 14)
SUBJ 20 21 28 41 ▪ 17 22 23 24.1 24.3 26.3 36.3 38 58

15492 CSH O P2 G3.0 1949–1972
[Casella, Alexander] Alessandro Casella.
'A visit to Inner Mongolia.'
Royal Central Asian j. 55, 2 (June 1968), 152–157.
SUBJ 20 24 55 ▪ 17 21 24.2

15493 NNC O P7 G6.3 1949–1972
Chen, Jack (Ch'en I-fan).
New earth: How the peasants in one Chinese county [Hsin-teng *hsien* (i.e., Ch'eng-yang *hsien*), Chekiang] solved the problem of poverty.
Peking: New World Press, 1957. 255 p. [Reprinted—Carbondale: Southern Illinois U. Press, 1972. 258 p.]
SUBJ 20 24 24.1 26.3 34.1 ▪ 22 22.2 26 28 31 32 47 55 66

15494 CSH P P7 G1.2 1949–1972
Chen, Vincent (Ch'en Wen-hsing), 1917–.
'The people's commune in Communist China: Exposition and critique.'
CC 9, 1 (Mar. 1968), 52–98.
SUBJ 20 26.3 34.1 ▪ 24 25 55 64

15495 NNC P P2 G1.2 1949–1972
Cheng Chu-yuan (Cheng Chu-yüan), 1927–.
The people's communes, 2nd ed.
Hong Kong: Union Press, 1959. 139 p.
SUBJ 20 22 24.1 25 30 34.1 ▪ 21.4 22.1 45 52 55 63 64

15496 CSH U P7 G1.2 1949–1972
Chi Ch'un-yi (Chi Ch'ün-i).
'The people's commune is a great creation of the popular masses of China.' Tr. of 'Jen min kung she shih wo kuo jen min ch'ün chung ti wei ta ch'uang tsao' (Communes, the greatest achievement of the Chinese masses); *Hung ch'i* 1960, 5 (1 Mar.), 1–15.
ECMM 210 (9 May 1960), 1–20.
SUBJ 20 22 22.1 34.1 ▪ 24.1 26 28 55

15497 CSH P P2 G9.2 1949–1972
Chin Mien-min (Ch'in Mien-min).
'Hainan island under the Chinese Communist rule.' Tr. of 'Chung kung k'ung chih hsia ti Hai-nan tao'; *Tsu kuo chou k'an* 439 (5 June 1961), 7–11. In *Communist China, 1960*, edited by Union Research Institute. [Selective entry]
Hong Kong: Union Research Institute, 1962, vol. 2, 231–251.
SUBJ 12 20 ▪ 15 17 21 22 24 24.2 66

15498 NIC O P2 G7.1 1949–1972
China [People's Republic]. Kuo wu yüan. Chung-kuo jen min tui wai wen hua hsieh hui. Wu-han pan shih ch'u. (State Council. Chinese People's Assn. for Foreign Cultural Relations. Wuhan Branch).
Wuhan in construction.
Peking: Foreign Languages Press, 1959. 24 p.
SUBJ 20 ▪ 22 24.1 24.4 31 38 56

15499 MCH PO P2 G9.3 1949–1972
Chinese-American Joint Commission on Rural Reconstruction.
The invincible island: Ten years of reconstruction on Kinmen [i.e., Chin-men *hsien*, Fukien].
Taipei: Chinese-American Joint Commission on Rural Reconstruction, 1963. 58 p.
SUBJ 20 24.1 28 ▪ 15 17 21.1

15500 CSU O P7 G9.3 1949–1972
Chung-kuo kung ch'an tang. Min-hou hsien wei yüan hui. (Chinese Communist Party. Min-hou Hsien Committee). [Min-hou *hsien* is in Fukien; tr. erroneously gives author as Ming-hou Hsien Committee.]
'Union of laborers, peasants, merchants, intellectuals and soldiers.' Tr. of 'Kung nung shang hsüeh ping chieh wei i t'i' (Each person is a combination of worker, peasant, merchant, soldier, and intellectual); *Hung ch'i* 1958, 10 (16 Oct.), 24–27. In *Selected translations from 'Hung-ch'i' (Red flag), October 1958*, mimeo., compiled by U.S. Joint Publications Research Service. [Sole entry]
Washington, D.C.: JPRS, 9 May 1961, 3–8. (JPRS 9182; MC 15,358/1961)
SUBJ 20 24 ▪ 24.1 24.4 25 26

15501 CSU O P2 G1.3 1949–1972
Committee of Concerned Asian Scholars.
China! Inside the People's Republic.
New York: Bantam Books, 1972. 433 p.
SUBJ 17 19 20 28 47 56 ▪ 22 25 26.3 26.4 31 34.2 35 52 54 55

15502 CSU O P7 G5.1 1949–1972
Courval, Hélène.
'La commune populaire de Guoxiang, district de Changli-Hopei' (Kuo-hsiang commune, Ch'ang-li *hsien*, Hopei).
CFC 8 (déc. 1960), 1–25. [Reprinted as 'La commune populaire de Guoxiang.' *Economie et politique* 79 (fév. 1971), 27–42 (With 'Post-scriptum, novembre 1960' added.)]
SUBJ 20 22 24 24.1 34.1 ▪ 21 21.3 21.4 24.4 26

15503 CSU O P7 G6.1 1949–1972
Davies, Ian Graham.
'The Chinese communes: An Australian student's view.'
EH 8, 1 (Jan.–Feb. 1969), 34–40.
SUBJ 20 24.1 ▪ 24.4 28 55

15504 CSU F P8 G9.4 1949–1972
Diamond, Norma Joyce, 1933–.
K'un Shen [Tainan municipality], *a Taiwan village*.
New York: Holt, Rinehart and Winston, 1969. 10, 110 p. [For a fuller version, see entry 15505.]
SUBJ 20 24.1 26 40 50 55 ▪ 22 23 24.6 33 51 53 56 57 65

15505 MAM F P8 G9.4 1949–1972
Diamond, Norma Joyce, 1933–.
K'un Shen [Tainan municipality]*: A Taiwanese fishing village*.
Ann Arbor: University Microfilms (Publ. 67-1504), 1966. 397 p. (Doctoral dissertation in Anthropology, Cornell U.)
SUBJ 20 24.1 26.3 40 65 ▪ 23 26 41 42 43 47 48 50 57 62

15506 CSU O P2 G1.2 1949–1972
Durdin, Frank Tillman, 1907–, James Barrett Reston, 1909–, and Seymour Topping, 1921–.
Report from Red China, edited by Frank Ching.
New York: Quadrangle, 1971. 367 p.
SUBJ 20 24 26.4 28 56 66 ▪ 17 23 24.3 24.4 25 26.3 34.1 41 55

15507 CSU P P7 G1.2 1949–1972
Dutt, Gargi, 1929–.
Rural communes of China.
Bombay: Asia Publishing House, 1967. 207 p.
SUBJ 20 22 24.1 34.1 64 ▪ 24.3 24.4 26.1 26.3 28 32 32.1 45

15508 CSU O P2 G1.2 1949–1972
Emanuelli, Enrico.
La Cina è vicina (China is near).
Milan: Mondadori, 1957. 272 p.
SUBJ 20 26 29 48 ▪ 14.2 22.1 22.2 24.4 26.3 26.4 27 41 55 56

15509 NNC O P2 G1.2 1949–1972
Eskelund, Karl, 1918–.
De røde mandariner.
Copenhagen: Gyldendal, 1957. 164 p.

The Red mandarins: Travels in Red China.
London: Alvin Redman, 1959. 175 p. [Reprinted—New York: Taplinger, 1961. 175 p.]
SUBJ 10 12.1 18 20 50 55 ▪ 17 19 21.3 30 34.1 41 47 56 62 63

15510 MCH O P7 G5.1 1949–1972
Fairfax-Cholmeley, Elsie.
'A look at the people's communes.'
New world review 27, 2 (Feb. 1959), 20–27.
SUBJ 20 24.1 28 36.3 ▪ 17 25 26.3 55

15511 DLC O P2 G1.3 1949–1972
Fediushov, Nikolai Vasil'evich.
V gostiakh u velikogo druga (As guests of a great friend).
Vladivostok: Primorskoe kn. izd-vo, 1957. 143 p.
SUBJ 20 24.1 24.4 32.1 ▪ 17 26.2 31 34.1 34.2 41 70

15512 MCH O P2 G1.2 1949–1972
Fukász, György.
'A társadalmi ellentmondások megoldásának útjai a Kínai Népköztársaságban.'
Magyar filozófiai szemle 3, 1/2 (1959), 114–126; 3, 3/4 (november 1959), 299–317.

The ways and means of solving social contradictions in the Chinese People's Republic, mimeo. [The title of the second part of this translation is 'Ways of solving social contraditions in the People's Republic of China.']
Washington, D.C.: U.S. Joint Publications Research Service, 12 Nov. 1959, 17 June 1960. 22; 23 p. (JPRS 1992 and 3404; MC 886/1960 and 10,130/1960)
SUBJ 16 19 20 ▪ 17 22.1 24 26.3 64

15513 NNC PO P4 G1.2 1949–1972
Fukushima Yutaka, 1926–.
The urban people's commune, mimeo. Tr. of 'Toshi jimmin kōsha' (Urban communes); *Chūgoku kenkyū geppō* 151 (Sept. 1960), 1–37.
Washington, D.C.: U.S. Joint Publications Research Service, 3 Mar. 1961. 69 p. (JPRS 7323; MC 10,821/1961)
SUBJ 20 22 47 ▪ 24.3 24.4 28 55

15514 CBU O P2 G9.5 1949–1972
Funnell, Victor Cecil, 1926–.
'Hongkong revisited.'
Australian outlook 23, 3 (Dec. 1969), 279–293.
SUBJ 20 22 ▪ 22.2

15515 CSU FP P8 G9.4 1949–1972
Gallin, Bernard, 1929–.
Hsin Hsing [Chang-hua *hsien*], *Taiwan: A Chinese village in change*.
Berkeley, Los Angeles: U. of California Press, 1966. 324 p. (Revision of *Hsin Hsing, a Taiwanese agricultural village*, doctoral dissertation in Anthropology, Cornell U., 1961)
SUBJ 20 23 24.1 40 41 50 ▪ 22 24 24.6 28 34.1 43 44 48 57 62

15516 CSU O P7 G5.1 1949–1972
Galston, Arthur W-.
'Down on the commune [Lu-kou-ch'iao commune, Feng-t'ai *ch'ü*, Peking municipality].'
Natural history 81, 8 (Oct. 1972), 50–59.
SUBJ 20 22.1 28 ▪ 17 24.1 26.3 55 56

15517 NNC F P8 G6.1 1949–1972
Geddes, William Robert, 1916–.
Peasant life in Communist China.

Ithaca: Society for Applied Anthropology, 1963. 66 p. (SAA monographs, 6)
Subj 20 21 22.1 26.3 41 ▪ 22 24.4 27 28 36.3 45 47 51 64 70

15518 CSU P P2 G9.5 1949–1972
Great Britain. Colonial Office.
Annual report on Hong Kong, 1950–1971. [Issues for 1946–1949 are entered as 15409.]
London: Her Majesty's Stationery Office. Issued annually, 1951–1972. Average ca. 350 p.
Subj 12.2 20 24 24.1 24.4 28 ▪ 17 21 21.4 22 24.2 24.5 26.4 33 55 56

15519 MCH O P2 G1.2 1949–1972
Guillain, Robert, 1908–.
Dans trente ans, la Chine (China in thirty years).
Paris: Le Seuil, 1965. 301 p.
When China wakes.
New York: Walker, 1966. 268 p.
Subj 20 24 24.4 28 ▪ 12.1 17 21.3 22 24.1 24.2 34.1 51 54 55

15520 CSU P P2 G9.5 1949–1972
Hong Kong. District Office, New Territories.
Annual departmental report by the District Commissioner, New Territories, 1950/51–1971/72. [Issues for 1946/47–1948/49 are entered as 15411.]
Hong Kong: Government Printer. Issued annually, 1951–1972. Average ca. 50 p.
Subj 20 22 24 ▪ 21 21.3 23 24.1 24.2 24.4 28 56

15521 CSU F P8 G9.4 1949–1972
Hsieh, S. C. (Hsieh Sen-chung), 1919–.
'Socio-economic surveying in China: The experience of rural Taiwan.' In *Social research and problems of rural development in South-east Asia*, edited by Vu Quoc Thue. [Sole entry]
Paris: United Nations, Educational, Scientific and Cultural Organization, 1963, 172–180.
Subj 20 24 ▪ 22.1 23 24.1 27 28

15522 CSH O P3 G8.1 1949–1972
Hua Yi.
'An urban people's commune in Chungking [Ch'i-hsing-kang].'
WC 1960, 4/5, 12–17.
Subj 20 24.4 47 ▪ 27 52 55

15523 NNC FP P7 G7.1 1949–1972
Hua-chung shih fan hsüeh yüan. Kung nung yeh wen hua chiao yü k'ao ch'a t'uan. Li shih hsi fen t'uan. (Hua-chung Normal College. Agricultural, Cultural, and Educational Investigation Group. History Dept. Sub-group).
History of the development of Chien-su commune, mimeo. Tr. of 'Hung-an hsien Chien-su she ti fa chan shih' (The development of Chien-su commune, Hung-an *hsien* [Hupeh]); *Li shih yen chiu* 1959, 1 (Jan.), 45–73.
Washington, D.C.: U.S. Joint Publications Research Service, 5 June 1959. 71 p. (JPRS 1648N; MC 9240/1959)
Subj 17 20 24.1 34.1 ▪ 22 26 28 55

15524 NNC O P7 G1.2 1949–1972
Hughes, Richard, 1906?–.
The Chinese communes: A background book.
Chester Springs, Pa.: Dufour, 1960. 90 p.
Subj 20 22 22.1 24 24.1 25 ▪ 26.3 28 32.1 34.1 55 64 66

15525 CSH O P7 G5.1 1949–1972
Hunt, R- C-.
'Faith in the fields [in Lu-kou-ch'iao tung fang hung commune, Ch'ang-p'ing *hsien*, Peking municipality].'
FEER 59, 6 (8 Feb. 1968), 225–227.
Subj 20 24.1 26.3 ▪ 28 55

15526 NNC O P3 G9.5 1949–1972
Ingrams, William Harold, 1897–.
Hong Kong.
London: Her Majesty's Stationery Office, 1952. 12, 307 p. [Reprinted—New York: AMS Press, 1973. 12, 307 p.]
Subj 20 22 23 24 28 55 ▪ 17 22.2 31 41 47 56 57 62 65 66

15527 NNC O P7 G1.3 1949–1972
Iwamura Michio, 1908–.
People's communes in process of reorganization, mimeo. Tr. of 'Seiton tojō no jimmin kōsha: Pekin Kōshū no kembun o moto ni' (Communes during the process of adjustment: Personal observations of Peking and Canton); *Ajia keizai jumpō* 406 (1 Sept. 1959), 10–18.
Washington, D.C.: U.S. Joint Publications Research Service, 2 Nov. 1959. 11 p. (JPRS 1985N; MC 17,629/1959)
Subj 20 24.1 24.4 ▪ 28 34.1

15528 MCM P P7 G1.2 1949–1972
Jones, Philip P-, and Thomas T- Poleman.
'Communes and the agricultural crisis in Communist China.'
Food Research Institute studies 3, 1 (Feb. 1962), 3–22.
Subj 20 24.1 26.3 ▪ 21.4 22.1 34.1

15529 CSU O P2 G9.5 1949–1972
Judge, Joseph.
'Saturday's child: Hong Kong.'
NG 140, 4 (Oct. 1971), 540–573.
Subj 20 24 55 ▪ 24.1 24.3 28

15530 NIC F P7 G9.4 1949–1972
Kirby, Edward Stuart, 1909–.
Rural progress in Taiwan.
Taipei: Chinese-American Joint Commission on Rural Reconstruction, 1960. 160 p.
Subj 20 22 24 28 ▪ 17 24.1 26 30 34.1 36.3 40

15531 CSU O P2 G1.3 1949–1972
Koningsberger, Hans, 1921–.
'China notes.'
New Yorker unnumbered (23 Apr. 1966), 57–125; unnumbered (30 Apr. 1966), 87–129.
Subj 20 55 ▪ 21.3 22.1 24.3 26.3 26.4 28

15532 NNC O P4 G2.1 1949–1972
Koreniuk, V- I-.
'Nezabyvaemye vstrechi' (Unforgettable encounters). In *V strane druzei: ocherki, stat'i, zametki sovetskikh liudei pobyvavshikh v Narodnom Kitae* (In our friends' country: Notes, articles, and observations of Soviet visitors in the People's Republic of China), edited by K- S- Ovechkin et al. [Selective entry]
Blagoveshchensk: Amurskoe kn. izd-vo, 1959, 53–75.
Subj 20 24.4 ▪ 26.4 36.4

15533 CSH F P7 G9.4 1949–1972
Ku, Tun-jou.
'Hsinchuang village: A study of a Taiwanese village in the context of Lungching township [i.e., Lung-ching *hsiang*, T'ai-chung *hsien*].'
CC 7, 2 (June 1966), 65–106.
Subj 20 ▪ 21 21.4 22 22.1 22.2 24.6 27 28 34.1 56

15534 NNC O P7 G5.4 1949–1972
[La Dany, Ladislao] ———, 1914–.
'A farmer's town: Economic situation, political life, town sociology.'
CNA 36 (21 May 1954), 1–7.
Subj 20 22 24 24.1 ▪ 22.1 22.2 26

15535 CSH P P8 G6.3 1949–1972
[La Dany, Ladislao] ———, 1914–.
'The story of a great brigade [in Chiang-shan *hsien*, Chekiang], 1955–1970.'
CNA 847 (9 July 1971), 1–7.
Subj 20 22.1 ▪ 24.1 34.1 42

15536 CSH O P4 G9.5 1949–1972
Leary, R- H-.
'Rising from the dust.'
FEER 44, 3 (16 Apr. 1964), 179–181.
Subj 20 21.3 24.4 ▪ 55

15537 NNC P P4 G1.2 1949–1972
Lethbridge, Henry James, 1923–.
China's urban communes.
Hong Kong: Dragonfly Books, 1961. 74 p.
Subj 20 22 24 24.4 28 ▪ 21.4 22.1 24.6 26.4 30 52 55

15538 CSU P P2 G5.1 1949–1972
Lewis, John Wilson, 1930–.
'Commerce, education, and political development in Tangshan, 1956–69.' In *The city in Communist China*, edited by J. W. Lewis. [Analytic entry]
Stanford: Stanford U. Press, 1971, 153–179.
Subj 12 14.3 17 20 ▪ 21.1 21.4 26.4 28 54

15539 CSH P P7 G1.1 1949–1972
Liu Hsiu-ching (Liu Hsiu-ch'ing).
'A comparison of the people's commune system on Mainland China and the land-to-the-tiller program on Taiwan.' In *Collected documents of the First Sino-American Conference on Mainland China*. [Selective entry]
[Taipei]: Institute of International Relations, Republic of China, 1971, 693–718.
Subj 20 24.1 34.1 ▪ 21.4 22 45

15540 CSU P P7 G1.2 1949–1972
Liu, Joseph.
'The people's communes and the Paris commune.'
SST 12, 2 (June 1972), 149–165.
Subj 20 30 64 ▪ 22 32

15541 CSU O P2 G9.5 1949–1972
Long, George W-.
'Hong Kong hangs on.'
NG 105, 2 (Feb. 1954), 239–272.
Subj 20 ▪ 24.3

15542 MCH U P7 G1.2 1949–1972
Luard, David Evan Trant, 1926–.
'The Chinese communes.' In *Far Eastern affairs, Number 3*, edited by Geoffrey Francis Hudson. [Sole entry]

London: Chatto and Windus, 1963, 59–79. (St. Antony's papers, 14)
SUBJ 20 22 34.1 ▪ 24 24.1 24.4 28 45

15543 CSU O P2 G1.3 1949–1972
Mehnert, Klaus, 1906–.
China nach dem Sturm (China after the storm).
Stuttgart: Deutsche Verlags-Anstalt, 1971. 349 p.
China returns.
New York: Dutton, 1972. 322 p.
SUBJ 20 24 26.3 28 55 66 ▪ 16.1 17 22 22.1 24.1 24.3 24.4 26.4 34.1 64

15544 NIC O P8 G4.1 1949–1972
Myrdal, Jan, 1927–.
Rapport från kinesisk by.
Stockholm: Norstedt, 1963. 371 p.
Report from a Chinese village. Tr. by Maurice Michael.
New York: Pantheon, 1965. 34, 373 p.
SUBJ 20 22 26.3 27 34.1 41 ▪ 22.1 24.3 25 32 32.1 47 52 54 55 57

15545 DLC O P8 G4.1 1949–1972
Myrdal, Jan, 1927–, and Gun Kessle.
Kina: Revolutionen går vidore.
Stockholm: PAN/Norstedt, 1970. 157 p.
China: The revolution continued. Tr. by Paul Britten Austin.
New York: Pantheon, 1970. 18, 201 p.
SUBJ 20 24 26.3 28 50 64 ▪ 22 24.1 26.1 27 34.1 36.3 47 54 55 56

15546 CSU F P7 G9.5 1949–1972
Ng, Ronald.
'Culture and society of a Hakka community on Lantau island [Ta-yü shan], Hong Kong.' In *Hong Kong: A society in transition*, edited by Ian C- Jarvie and Joseph Agassi. [Analytic entry]
New York: Praeger, 1969, 53–63.
SUBJ 20 22 29 ▪ 21.2 47 57 62

15547 NNC P P3 G9.2 1949–1972
Nikitin, Nikolai Nikolaevich, 1897–.
Kanton (Canton).
Moscow: Geografgiz, 1952. 30 p.
SUBJ 20 ▪ 21.3 24.4

15548 NNC P P3 G5.1 1949–1972
Nikitin, Nikolai Nikolaevich, 1897–, and [Ivan Hnatovych Fedorov] Ivan Ignat'evich Fedorov.
Tian' TSzin' (Tientsin).
Moscow: Geografgiz, 1953. 43 p.
SUBJ 20 ▪ 21.3 24.4

15549 CSH P P7 G1.2 1949–1972
Pang, Thérèse.
Les communes populaires rurales en Chine (Rural communes in China).
Fribourg: Ed. universitaires, 1967. 208 p. (Université de Fribourg, Institut des sciences économiques et sociales, cahiers, 18) (Doctoral dissertation, Faculté de droit et des sciences économiques et sociales, Université de Fribourg)
SUBJ 20 22 24 26 34.1 64 ▪ 11.2 17 22.1 24.1 26.3 28 31 41 47

15550 GMS O P2 G1.2 1949–1972
Portisch, Hugo, 1927–.
So sah ich China: Ein Tatsachen- und Erlebnisbericht aus dem Reich Mao Tse-tungs (The China I saw: Report on facts and experiences from Mao Tse-tung's empire), rev. and enl. ed.
Vienna: Kremayr und Scheriau, 1967. 366 p.
Red China today. Tr. by Heinz von Koschembahr. [Tr. of 1965 ed.]
Chicago: Quadrangle, 1966. 383 p.
SUBJ 20 22.2 24.4 28 56 ▪ 12.1 12.2 14 16 17 31 41 51 54 63

15551 MCH O P7 G1.2 1949–1972
Robinson, Joan, 1903–.
'The Chinese communes.'
Political q. 35, 3 (July–Sept. 1964), 285–297. [Reprinted as 'China, 1963: The communes.' In *Collected economic papers*, by J. Robinson. (Sole entry.) Oxford, Eng.: Basil Blackwell, 1965, vol. 3, 192–206.]
SUBJ 20 22 24 ▪ 22.1 24.1 32.1 34.1

15552 CSU O P2 G6.1 1949–1972
Ronning, Chester.
'Nanking, 1950.'
International j. 22, 3 (Summer 1967), 441–456.
SUBJ 20 ▪ 22.2 26.3 28

15553 CSU PO P2 G1.2 1949–1972
Schickel, Joachim.
Die Mobilisierung der Massen: Chinas ununterbrochene Revolution (The mobilization of the masses: China's continuous revolution).
Munich: Paul List, 1971. 205 p.
SUBJ 16 19 20 28 55 64 ▪ 12 14.3 17 22.1 24.1 24.4 25 32 63

15554 CSU O P2 G9.4 1949–1972
Schreider, Helen, and Frank Schreider.
'Taiwan: The watchful dragon.'
NG 135, 1 (Jan. 1969), 1–45.
SUBJ 20 24 ▪ 15 24.1 28 55

15555 CSU O P2 G9.5 1949–1972
Scofield, John.
'Hong Kong has many faces.'
NG 121, 1 (Jan. 1962), 1–41.
SUBJ 20 24.3 55 ▪ 21.2 24.1 28

15556 CSU O P3 G6.1 1949–1972
Scott, W- A-.
'China revisited by an old China hand.'
EH 5, 6 (June 1966), 34–40.
SUBJ 20 ▪ 26.4 28 55

15557 NNC O P7 G5.4 1949–1972
Shang-hai she hui k'o hsüeh yüan. Wei-hsing jen min kung she ts'an kuan t'uan. (Shanghai College of Social Science. Visiting group to the Wei-hsing commune).
Shanghai Social Science Institute visits Wei-hsing commune, mimeo. Tr. of 'Ta yao chin chung ti Wei-hsing jen min kung she' (Wei-hsing commune [Sui-p'ing *hsien*, Honan] during the Great Leap Forward); *Ts'ai ching yen chiu* 1958, 6 (Sept.), 21–28.
Washington, D.C.: U.S. Joint Publications Research Service, 29 Apr. 1959. 30 p. (JPRS 1525N; MC 9216/1959)
SUBJ 20 22 34.1 50 ▪ 24.1 27 37

15558 CSH P P7 G1.2 1949–1972
Sherman, A- V-.
'The people's commune.' In *The Chinese communes: A documentary review and analysis of the 'Great Leap Forward'*. [Analytic entry]
London: Soviet Survey, 1959, 15–61.
SUBJ 20 26.3 34.1 ▪ 19 41

15559 MCY P P7 G1.2 1949–1972
Shih, Chung Wen, 1922–.
'Co-operatives and communes in Chinese Communist fiction.'
CQ 13 (Jan.–Mar. 1963), 195–211.
SUBJ 20 34.1 ▪ 22 22.1 26.3 61 64

15560 MCM FP P4 G1.2 1949–1972
Shih, Joseph Anderson (Shih Ch'eng-chih), 1918–1973.
Urban commune experiments in Communist China, mimeo.
Hong Kong: Union Research Institute, 1962. 167 p. (Communist China problem research series, EC28)
SUBJ 20 22 24.4 26.4 28 ▪ 22.1 26.1 30 34.2 40 50

15561 NIC U P3 G5.1 1949–1972
[Shu Ch'ing-ch'un] Lao Sheh (Lao She), pseud., 1899–1966.
'Peking after ten years.'
China reconstructs 8, 2 (Feb. 1959), 17–21.
SUBJ 20 24 28 ▪ 47 48

15562 CSU O P2 G9.4 1949–1972
Simpich, Frederick, Jr.
'Changing Formosa: Green island of refuge.'
NG 111, 3 (Mar. 1957), 327–364.
SUBJ 20 24.1 28 ▪ 15 24.4 55

15563 CSH PO P4 G9.5 1949–1972
Smyly, W- J-.
'Tsuen Wan township [i.e., Ch'üan-wan, Hong Kong].'
FEER 33, 9 (31 Aug. 1961), 395–421.
SUBJ 20 21.3 24.4 55 ▪ 17 24.2 30

15564 CSU P P7 G1.2 1949–1972
Sreedhar, Shri.
'Rural communes in China, 1958–62.'
India q. 26, 1 (Jan.–Mar. 1970), 30–45.
SUBJ 20 24.1 34.1 ▪ 22 32.1 45

15565 NNC O P7 G5.1 1949–1972
Steck, Fritz.
Visit to a people's commune in North China, mimeo. Tr. from *Neue Zürcher Zeitung* 15 Nov. 1958, 3–4.
New York: U.S. Joint Publications Research Service, 7 Feb. 1959. 91 p. (JPRS 1117)
SUBJ 20 ▪ 22 24.1 24.4 25 28

15566 CSU O P8 G9.5 1949–1972
Stenton, Jean E-.
'Lantau island [i.e., Ta-yü shan, Hong Kong].'
Canadian geographical j. 84, 3 (Mar. 1972), 98–103.
SUBJ 20 33

15567 MCH O P7 G1.2 1949–1972
Strong, Anna Louise, 1885–1970.
The rise of the Chinese people's communes, and six years after, 2nd ed.
Peking: New World Press, 1964. 227 p.
SUBJ 20 22 24 34.1 ▪ 26.3 28 41 47

15568 TPH P P3 G9.4 1949–1972
Taipei. Chu chi shih. (Office of Accounting and Statistics), ed.
The statistical abstract of Taipei municipality, Nos. 8–23 [1954–1969].
Taipei. T'ai-pei shih cheng fu. Issued annually, 1955–1970. Average ca. 500

p. [In Chinese as well as English; nos. 1–7 are in Chinese only.]
SUBJ 17 20 21.1 22 24 58 ▪ 21.3 21.4 22.2 24.5 28 30 34.2 56

15569 NNC U P3 G2.3 1949–1972
Tambovskii, A- M-.
Mukden (Shen'ian) (Shenyang).
Moscow: Geografgiz, 1954. 55 p.
SUBJ 20 ▪ 21.1 24 26.4

15570 NNC P P2 G1.2 1949–1972
Tang, Peter S. H. (T'ang Sheng-hao), 1919–.
The commune system in Mainland China.
Washington, D.C.: Research Institute on the Sino-Soviet Bloc, 1961. 39 p. (RISSB monographs, 2)
SUBJ 20 32.1 34.1 ▪ 21.4 22 24 25 28 52 55

15571 CBU O P3 G9.5 1949–1972
Tichy, Herbert, 1912–.
Hongkong: Die Laune des Drachen (Hong Kong: The mood of the dragon).
Vienna: Wollzeien Verlag, 1961. 205 p.
SUBJ 20 21.2 ▪ 24 55

15572 CSU FP P2 G9.2 1949–1972
Vogel, Ezra Feivel, 1930–.
Canton under Communism: Programs and politics in a provincial capital, 1949–1968.
Cambridge: Harvard U. Press, 1969. 18, 448 p. (Harvard East Asian series, 41)
SUBJ 12.1 19 20 22 22.1 26.1 ▪ 22.2 24.1 24.4 26 29 32.1 34.1 66

15573 CBU F P8 G9.5 1949–1972
Ward, Barbara Elsie, 1919–.
'Floating villages: Chinese fishermen in Hong Kong.'
Man 59 (Apr. 1959), 44–45.
SUBJ 20 26.3 ▪ 24.1 65

15574 NIC F P8 G9.5 1949–1972
Ward, Barbara Elsie, 1919–.
'A Hong Kong fishing village.'
JOS 1, 1 (Jan. 1954), 195–214.
SUBJ 20 29 55 ▪ 22 23 24.1 24.6 26 41 48

15575 GMS O P4 G1.2 1949–1972
Weisenborn, Günther, 1902–.
Am Yangtse steht ein Riese auf (A giant rises on the Yangtze).
Munich: Paul List, 1961. 257 p.
SUBJ 20 28 55 ▪ 13 17 22.2 24 47 56 64

15576 DLC O P5 G9.2 1949–1972
Weiskopf, Franz Carl, 1900–1955.
Die Reise nach Kanton (Journey to Canton).
Berlin: Dietz, 1953. 149 p.
SUBJ 20 ▪ 47 60

15577 CSU O P7 G6.1 1949–1972
Wertheim, Willem Frederik, 1907–.
'Rainbow Bridge commune [i.e., Hung-ch'iao commune, Shanghai municipality] revisited.'
EH 10, 6 (1971), 7–22; 11, 1 (1972), 31–40.
SUBJ 20 24.1 ▪ 21 27 34.1 58

15578 CSU P P3 G6.1 1949–1972
White, Lynn Townsend, III, 1941–.
'Shanghai's polity in cultural revolution.' In *The city in Communist China*, edited by John Wilson Lewis. [Analytic entry]
Stanford: Stanford U. Press, 1971, 325–370.
SUBJ 20 22 22.1 54 ▪ 17 21.2 25 26.4 35 36.4

15579 MCH O P3 G8.1 1949–1972
Wollaston, Nicholas, 1926–.
'Foreign devil with camera: A visit to Chungking.'
GM 35, 9 (Jan. 1963), 487–498.
SUBJ 17 20 ▪ 22.1 24.2

15580 MCH P P2 G1.2 1949–1972
Zürcher, Erik, 1928–.
'De Chinese volkscommune.'
Rechtsgeleerd magazijn themis (Zwolle) 1961, 498–515.
'The Chinese communes.' [Tr. inferred]
BTLV 118, 1 (1962), 68–90.
SUBJ 20 22 22.1 ▪ 28 34.1 64

21 REGIONAL AND LOCAL POPULATION

地方人口 地方人口

1644-1911

15581 MSE O P2 G8.2 –1895
Clarke, G. W., pseud.
The province of Yun-nan, past, present, and future . . .
Shanghai: Shanghai Mercury Office, 1885. 82 p.
SUBJ 20 21 24 26 ▪ 66

15582 MCH P P2 G9.4 1644–1842
Klaproth, Julius Heinrich, 1783–1835.
'Description de l'île de Formose, extraite de livres chinois' (A description of Taiwan, taken from Chinese books).
Nouvelles annales des voyages 20 (1823), 195–224. [Reprinted in *Mémoires relatifs à l'Asie: contenant des recherches historiques, géographiques et philologiques sur les peuples de l'Orient* (Notes on Asia: Containing historical, geographic, and philological research on the peoples of the Orient), by J. H. Klaproth. (Sole entry.) Paris: Dondey-Dupré, 1826, vol. 1, 321–374.]
SUBJ 12 14 21 22

15583 MCH O P8 G2.0 1842–1895
La Brunière, ——— de.
'Excursion en Mandchourie en 1845' (Travel in Manchuria in 1845).
Nouvelles annales des voyages 114 (1848), 82–115.
SUBJ 21 22.1 23 24 ▪ 24.2 25 26 65 66

15584 MCY P P2 G6.1 1842–1895
Wang, Yeh-chien, 1930–.
'The impact of the Taiping Rebellion on the population in southern Kiangsu.'
PC 19 (Dec. 1965), 120–158.
SUBJ 21 24.1 ▪ 24.5 26

1644-1949

15585 MCH S P2 G2.0 1644–1949
'Manchuria as a demographic frontier.'
Population index 11, 4 (Oct. 1945), 260–274.
SUBJ 21 21.2 21.4 58 ▪ 11.3 14 14.4

15586 NNC P P2 G9.4 1895–1949
Barclay, George Watson, 1923–.
Colonial development and population in Taiwan.
Princeton: Princeton U. Press, 1954. 18, 274 p. (Revision of doctoral dissertation in Economics, Princeton U., 1952) [Reprinted—Port Washington, N.Y.: Kennikat Press, 1971. 18, 274 p.]
SUBJ 21 21.1 21.2 21.4 41 58 ▪ 12.1 14 18 47 56 66

15587 CSH FP P2 G6.1 –1949
China [Republic]. Shih yeh pu. Kuo chi mao i chü. (Ministry of Industry. Bureau of Foreign Trade), ed.
'Introduction. II, Area and population.' Tr. of 'Tsung shuo, 2, mien chi chi jen k'ou'; in *Chung-kuo shih yeh chih: Chiang-su sheng* (Chinese economic surveys: Kiangsu); Shanghai: Kuo chi mao i chü, 1933, 3–19 [s.p.] [slightly condensed in tr.]. In *China industrial handbooks: Kiangsu*, edited by the agency cited. [Selective entry]
Shanghai: Kuo chi mao i chü, 1933, 5–11. [Reprinted in *China industrial handbooks: Kiangsu*, edited by the agency cited. (Selective entry.) Taipei: Ch'eng-wen, 1972, 5–11.]
SUBJ 21 ▪ 21.4

15588 CBU P P2 G2.0 1895–1949
IAshnov, Evgenii Evgen'evich.
'Naselenie i krest'ianstvo Man'chzhu-go: po povodu dannykh ucheta 1933 g.' (The 1933 census data and the population and peasantry of Manchoukuo).
EB 1934, 1 (ianvar'), 1–14.
SUBJ 21 21.1 ▪ 11.3 16.3 21.2 21.3

15589 CNY S P1 G1.2 1895–1949
Pickens, Claude L-, Jr.
'The Moslem population of China.'
Friends of Moslems (Hankow) 10, 2 (Apr. 1936), 25–26. [Reprinted in *Chinese Jews: A compilation of matters relating to the Jews of K'ai-fêng Fu*, 2nd ed., by William Charles White. (Selective entry.) New York: Paragon, 1966, 200–203 (s.p.).]
SUBJ 21

1911-1949

15590 NNC P P8 G2.0 1928–1949
'Population and land utilization in Manchuria, 1929.'
NWSS 4, 43 (26 Oct. 1931), 197, 199–200.
SUBJ 21 ▪ 14.1

15591 NNC P P2 G6.1 1928–1949
'Population census of Kiangsu, 1929.'
NWSS 6, 16 (17 Apr. 1933), 72, 74–75.
SUBJ 21

15592 CSH FP P2 G6.3 1911–1949
China [Republic]. Shih yeh pu. Kuo chi mao i chü. (Ministry of Industry. Bureau of Foreign Trade), ed.
'Population.' Tr. of 'Tsung shuo, 3, jen k'ou chi fen pu' (Introduction. Part 3, Population and population distribution); in *Chung-kuo shih yeh chih: Che-chiang sheng* (Chinese economic surveys: Chekiang); Shanghai: Kuo chi mao i chü, 1933, *chia* 12 – *chia* 25 [s.p.] [abridged tr.]. In *China industrial*

handbooks: Chekiang, edited by the agency cited. [Selective entry]
Shanghai: Kuo chi mao i chü, 1935, 10–14. [Reprinted in *China industrial handbooks: Chekiang*, edited by the agency cited. (Selective entry.) Taipei: Ch'eng-wen, 1972, 10–14.]
SUBJ 21 ▪ 47

15593 MBA PO P2 G8.2 1911–1928
Cordier, Charles Georges, 1872–1936.
'Le Yunnan' (Yunnan).
RI nouvelle (2e) série 24, 11/12 (nov.–déc. 1915), 403–436; 25, 1/2 (jan.–fév. 1916), 99–134; 25, 5/6 (mai–juin 1916), 371–398; 26, 7/8 (juil.–août 1916), 61–102.
SUBJ 21 24 25 ▪ 22 66

15594 MCY F P2 G5.1 1928–1949
Hsu, Leonard S. (Hsü Shih-lien), 1901–.
'Some aspects of the Chinese population problem.'
CSPSR 14, 3 (July 1930), 281–312.
SUBJ 21 21.1 ▪ 21.2 21.4 41 58

15595 CBU S P2 G2.0 1911–1928
Krylov, V- N-.
'Uezdy Man'chzhurii v osveshchenii iaponskoi periodicheskoi pechati: bibliograficheskii obzor' (Overview of Manchurian counties, based on the Japanese periodical press).
VM 1934, 6 (iiun'), 156–159.
SUBJ 21 72 ▪ 21.3 24.1

15596 MCH F P7 G5.1 1928–1949
Lee, Franklin C. H. (Li Ching-han), 1895–.
'An analysis of Chinese rural population.'
CSPSR 19, 1 (Apr. 1935), 22–44. [See Vol. 2 of this *Bibliography* for Chinese version.]
SUBJ 21 41 56 ▪ 21.3 21.4 23 27 42 45 58

15597 CSU P P2 G2.0 1911–1949
Pelzer, Karl Josef, 1909–.
'Population: Manchuria.' In *An economic survey of the Pacific area, Part 1, Population and land utilization*, by K. J. Pelzer. [Selective entry]
New York: Institute of Pacific Relations, International Secretariat, 1941, 23–28.
SUBJ 21 21.2

15598 MCH FP P7 G8.1 1928–1949
Skinner, George William, 1925–.
'A study in miniature of Chinese population [in San-sheng *hsiang*, Hua-yang *hsien*, Szechwan].'
PS 5, 2 (Nov. 1951), 91–103.
SUBJ 21 21.3 41 ▪ 24.1 27 47 50

15599 CSH P P2 G2.2 1911–1949
Sokolov, N- A-.
'Razvitie Mishan'skogo raiona' (Development of the Mi-shan [Kirin] area). [With English abstract]
VM 1931, 7, 24–27.
SUBJ 21 21.2 ▪ 21.3 24.1 24.2 24.4

1911-1972
(including 1644-1972)

15600 CBU P P2 G9.4 1895–1972
Chang, Wei-penn.
Les rapports entre l'accroissement démographique et le développement économique sur l'exemple de Formose (The relationship between population growth and economic development, based on the example of Taiwan).
Munich: F. Frank, 1967. 132 p. (Doctoral dissertation, Faculté de droit et des sciences économiques et sociales, Université de Fribourg, 1966)
SUBJ 14 14.4 21 21.2 21.4 58 ▪ 14.6 21.1 24.1 24.4 51 56

15601 CSH P P2 G9.4 1928–1972
Chang, Yen-tien (Chang Yen-t'ien).
'Population and food supply in Taiwan.' In *Proceedings of Agricultural Economics Seminar held at the College of Agriculture, National Taiwan University, September 16–20, 1958*. [Selective entry]
Taipei: National Taiwan U., 1959, 69–76.
SUBJ 14.3 21 55 ▪ 24.1 58

15602 CSH U P2 G2.0 1911–1972
Chang Yin-t'ang, 1902–.
'Geographical background.' In *A regional handbook on Northeast China*, compiled by Far Eastern and Russian Institute, U. of Washington. [Selective entry]
New Haven: Human Relations Area Files, 1956, 39–57. (HRAF subcontractor's monographs, 61; Washington 9)
SUBJ 21 21.1

15603 CSH P P2 G3.0 1928–1972
Chang Yin-t'ang, 1902–.
'Geographical background.' In *A regional handbook on the Inner Mongolia Autonomous Region*, compiled by Far Eastern and Russian Institute, U. of Washington. [Selective entry]
New Haven: Human Relations Area Files, 1956, 76–101. (HRAF subcontractor's monographs, 60; Washington 7)
SUBJ 11.3 21 ▪ 56 58

15604 CSH P P1 G4.0 1911–1972
Chang Yin-t'ang, 1902–, and Channing Rwen Kao (Kao Chung-jun), 1914–.
'Geographical background.' In *A regional handbook on Northwest China*, compiled by Far Eastern and Russian Institute, U. of Washington. [Selective entry]
New Haven: Human Relations Area Files, 1956, vol. 1, 81–137. (HRAF subcontractor's monographs, 59; Washington 5)
SUBJ 21 ▪ 21.2 58

15605 NIC P P2 G9.4 1895–1972
Chen, Cheng-siang (Ch'en Cheng-hsiang), 1920–.
'Population and settlement in Formosa.'
TESG 45, 9/10 (September–Oktober 1954), 176–181.
SUBJ 21 21.3 ▪ 21.4 58

15606 CSU P P2 G9.4 1928–1972
Chen, Cheng-siang (Ch'en Cheng-hsiang), 1920–.
'Population distribution and change in Taiwan.' In *Proceedings of the International Geographical Union Regional Conference in Japan, 1957*. [Selective entry]
Tokyo: International Geographical Union Regional Conference in Japan, Organizing Committee *with* Science Council of Japan, 1959, 290–295.
SUBJ 21 ▪ 21.1 24 1

15607 NIC P P2 G9.4 1895–1972
Chen Shao-hsing (Ch'en Shao-hsing), 1906–1966.
'Population growth and social change in Taiwan.'
B. of the Dept. of Archaeology and Anthropology, National Taiwan U. 5 (May 1955), 76–103.
SUBJ 21 24 28 58

15608 NIC S P2 G9.0 1842–1972
Davis, Sydney George, 1907–.
'Population growth and pressure in South China and Hong Kong.'
Economics and finance in Indonesia 10, 10 (Oct. 1957), 682–695. [Reprinted in *Proceedings of the International Geographical Union Regional Conference in Japan, 1957*. (Selective entry.) Tokyo: International Geographical Union Regional Conference in Japan, Organizing Committee *with* Science Council of Japan, 1959, 296–302.]
SUBJ 14.1 21 21.1 ▪ 21.2 58

15609 GMS P P2 G4.1 1928–1972
Köhler, Günther, 1909–.
'Karte der Bevölkerungsdichte der Provinz Schensi (Nordchina)' (A map of population density in Shensi).
Wissenschaftliche Veröffentlichungen des Deutschen Instituts für Länderkunde neue (2.) Folge 11 (1952), 120–127. [For maps accompanying this article see *Kartenbeilage* 10 of the journal.]
SUBJ 21 21.1 ▪ 11.3

15610 NNC P P2 G9.5 1842–1972
Ma, Ming-to.
'The 1961 census of Hong Kong.' In *Symposium on land use and mineral deposits in Hong Kong, southern China and South-east Asia*, edited by Sydney George Davis. [Selective entry]
Hong Kong: Hong Kong U. Press, 1964, 115–121.
SUBJ 21 ▪ 21.1 21.2 58

15611 CBU PO P2 G9.5 1842–1972
Podmore, David.
'The population of Hong Kong.' In *Hong Kong: The industrial colony*, edited by Keith Hopkins. [Analytic entry]
Hong Kong: Oxford U. Press, 1971, 21–54.
SUBJ 21 58 ▪ 11.2 17 21.3 41

15612 CSH P P2 G9.4 1911–1972
Stanford U. China Project.
'Population of Formosa.' In *Taiwan (Formosa)*, compiled by the organization cited. [Selective entry]
New Haven: Human Relations Area Files, 1956, vol. 1, 66–88. (HRAF subcontractor's monographs, 31; Stanford 5)
SUBJ 21 ▪ 21.1 21.2 21.4 50 59

15613 TPY P P2 G9.4 1928–1972
Taiwan. Min cheng t'ing. (Dept. of Civil Affairs), ed.
The monthly bulletin of population registration statistics of Taiwan, Vol. 1, No. 1 (Feb. 1966) – Vol. 5, No. 12 (Dec. 1970).
Nan-t'ou, Taiwan: Min cheng t'ing. Issued monthly, Feb. 1966 – Dec. 1970.

Average ca. 90 p. [In Chinese as well as English]
SUBJ 21 21.1 ▪ 17 21.4 22.1 41 50 58

15614 NIC P P2 G2.0 1911–1972
Wynne, Waller, Jr., 1906–.
The population of Manchuria.
Washington, D.C.: U.S. Government Printing Office, 1958. 93 p. (Bureau of the Census, International population statistics reports, series P-90, 7)
SUBJ 14 17 21 21.1 21.2 21.4 ▪ 14.1 14.4 34.1 37 56 58

1949-1972

15615 ELE P P2 G9.4 1949–1972
Barclay, George Watson, 1923–.
A report on Taiwan's population to the Joint Commission on Rural Reconstruction.
Princeton: Princeton U. Press, 1954. 12, 120 p.
SUBJ 21 21.2 ▪ 14 21.3 26 51 58

15616 CSU F P2 G9.5 1949–1972
Barnett, Kenneth Myer Arthur, 1911–.
Hong Kong: Report on the 1966 by-census.
Hong Kong: Government Printer, 1968? 2 vols. 55; 202 p.
SUBJ 21 ▪ 21.1 21.2 21.4 24.2

15617 NIC F P2 G9.5 1949–1972
Barnett, Kenneth Myer Arthur, 1911–.
Report on the 1961 census.
Hong Kong: Government Printer, 1961, 1962, 1962. 3 vols. 41, 39; 69, 89; 211, 80 p.
SUBJ 21 21.1 21.4 47 ▪ 11.2 17 21.2 22.1 24 28 41 50 58

15618 CSU PO P2 G9.5 1949–1972
Fessler, Loren, 1923–.
'Population review 1970: Hong Kong.'
AUFS-EAS 17, 8 (Nov. 1970), 1–11.
SUBJ 21 21.4 24 51 ▪ 11.2 17 50 56 58

15619 CSU P P1 G1.2 1949–1972
Field, Robert Michael, 1928–.
'Chinese provincial population data.'
CQ 44 (Oct.–Dec. 1970), 195–202.
SUBJ 21 ▪ 11 58

15620 CSU P P2 G4.3 1949–1972
Freeberne, John Derek Michael, 1935–.
'Demographic and economic changes in the Sinkiang Uighur Autonomous Region.'
PS 20, 1 (July 1966), 103–124.
SUBJ 14 19 21 21.1 21.2 66 ▪ 12.1 14.3 14.4 17 24.1 24.2 41

15621 HKU F P4 G9.5 1949–1972
Hsu, Chih-ch'eng (Hsü Chih-ch'eng), Wynne Frederick Maunder, 1920–, and J. Tsao.
Hong Kong's resettled squatters: The final report on the 1957 sample survey of resettlement estates.
Hong Kong: The authors, 1959. 128, 24 p.
SUBJ 21 21.3 28 41 55 ▪ 11.2 21.1 21.4 27

15622 CSH P P2 G1.3 1949–1972
Stanford U. China Project.
'Population.' In *Central South China*, compiled by the organization cited. [Selective entry]
New Haven: Human Relations Area Files, 1956, vol. 1, 54–64. (HRAF subcontractor's monographs, 28; Stanford 2)
SUBJ 21 ▪ 21.2 58

15623 CSH P P2 G1.3 1949–1972
Stanford U. China Project.
'Population.' In *East China*, compiled by the organization cited. [Selective entry]
New Haven: Human Relations Area Files, 1956, vol. 1, 75–95. (HRAF subcontractor's monographs, 29; Stanford 3)
SUBJ 21 ▪ 21.1 21.2 21.4

15624 CSH P P2 G5.0 1949–1972
Stanford U. China Project.
'Population.' In *North China*, compiled by the organization cited. [Selective entry]
New Haven: Human Relations Area Files, 1956, vol. 1, 66–78. (HRAF subcontractor's monographs, 27; Stanford 1)
SUBJ 21 ▪ 21.1 21.2 58

15625 NNC P P2 G8.0 1949–1972
Stanford U. China Project.
'Population.' In *Southwest China*, compiled by the organization cited. [Selective entry]
New Haven: Human Relations Area Files, 1956, vol. 1, 54–75. (HRAF subcontractor's monographs, 30; Stanford 4)
SUBJ 21 ▪ 21.2 21.4

21.1 REGIONAL URBANIZATION AND CITY POPULATION
地方性都市化及都市人口
地方の都市化及び都市人口

1644-1911

15626 MCH O P2 G5.0 1644–1895
'Peking und Nord-China' (Peking and North China).
Globus 30, 9 (März 1876), 129–134; 30, 10 (März 1876), 145–150; 30, 11 (März 1876), 161–166; 30, 12 (März 1876), 177–183; 30, 13 (Apr. 1876), 193–198; 30, 14 (Apr. 1876), 209–215.
SUBJ 21.1 26.1 55 ▪ 14.3 22 24.2 24.3 57 62

15627 ELU P P3 G5.1 –1911
Hou, Jen-chih, 1911–.
An historical geography of Peiping.
Unpublished doctoral dissertation in Geography, U. of Liverpool, 1949. 249 p.
SUBJ 21.1 21.3 ▪ 24.2 24.3

15628 NIC P P3 G9.2 1895–1911
Imbault-Huart, Camille Clément, 1857–1897.
'La population de Canton en juin 1895' (The population of Canton in June 1895).
TP 7, 2 (1896), 58–59.
SUBJ 21.1 ▪ 21.3

15629 MCH O P2 G8.0 1895–1911
Labarthe, Emile.
'Dans les provinces du fond de la Chine' (In the inland provinces of China).
Tour du monde nouvelle (2e) série 14, 48 (28 nov. 1908), 565–588; 15, 19 (8 mai 1909), 217–252.
SUBJ 21.1 21.4 23 24 26.4 28 ▪ 17 22.2 26.1 32.2 39 53 55 57

15630 MSE O P3 G9.2 1842–1895
Yvan, Melchior, 1803–1873.
Inside Canton.
London: Henry Vizetelly, 1858. 228 p.
SUBJ 21.1 26 55 ▪ 31

1644-1949

15631 NIC P P3 G1.3 1842–1949
Kung, H. O. (K'ung Tz'u-an).
'The growth of population [in] the six Chinese large cities.' Tr. of 'Tung yüan sheng chung wo kuo liu ta tu shih jen k'ou tseng chien ti ch'ü shih' (Population trends in six large Chinese cities during national mobilization); *Han hsüeh yüeh k'an* 8, 5 (Feb. 1937), 87–94.
CEJ 20, 3 (Mar. 1937), 301–314.
SUBJ 21.1

15632 GBS P P3 G6.1 –1949
Pernitzsch, Max Gerhard, 1882–.
'Shanghai' (Shanghai).
MSOSB 40 (1937), 37–92.
SUBJ 21.1 21.3 22 22.2 ▪ 23 26.1 26.4 66

15633 CSU PO P3 G8.2 –1928
Robequain, Charles, 1897–.
'Yunnanfou en 1926' (Yün-nan-fu [i.e., Kunming] in 1926).
Annales de géographie 26, 203 (15 sept. 1927), 436–450.
SUBJ 21.1 21.2 21.3 21.4 24.2 24.3 ▪ 24 24.4 25 26.2 55

1911-1949

15634 NNC P P3 G6.1 1928–1949
'Population of greater Shanghai, 1930.'
NWSS 5, 41 (10 Oct. 1932), 185, 187–188.
SUBJ 21.1 58

15635 NNC P P3 G6.1 1928–1949
'Population of Shanghai, 1930–1932.'
NWSS 6, 52 (25 Dec. 1933), 243, 245.
SUBJ 21.1

15636 NIC P P3 G5.1 1911–1928
Chow, Ziang-yien.
'The population of the city of Peking.'
CSPSR 1, 3 (Oct. 1916), 121–123.
SUBJ 21.1

15637 CSH P P4 G2.2 1911–1949
Kormazov, V- A-.
'Rost naseleniia v Kharbine i Futsziadiane' (Population growth in Harbin and [its suburb] Fu-chia-tien). [With English abstract]
VM 1930, 7, 25–31.
SUBJ 21.1 ▪ 21.2 58

15638 CSU O P2 G8.2 1911–1949
Lécorché, Maurice.
Vingt-cinq ans d'Indochine et de Yunnan: souvenirs, 1919–1943 (Twenty-five years of Indochina and Yunnan, 1919–1943).
Toulouse: Privat, 1950. 287 p.
SUBJ 20 21.1 ▪ 25 66

15639 CSH O P2 G2.1 1911–1949
N. S.
'Kolonizatsiia uezda Chzhao-chzhou' (The colonization of Chao-chou *hsien* [Heilungkiang]).
EB 1930, 6 (1 aprelia), 14–15.
SUBJ 21.1 ▪ 21.2 24.5

15640 ICU F P2 G8.2 1928–1949
Ni, Ernest (Ni Yin-hsin), 1908–.
Social characteristics of the Chinese population: A study of the population structure and urbanism of a metropolitan community [in the vicinity of Kunming].
Unpublished doctoral dissertation in Sociology, U. of Chicago, 1948. 185 p.
Subj 20 21.1 21.3 ▪ 17 21.4 28 40 41

15641 MCH F P2 G8.2 1928–1949
Ni, Ernest (Ni Yin-hsin), 1908–.
'A study of urbanism and population structure in a metropolitan community in China [in the vicinity of Kunming].' In *Contributions to urban sociology*, edited by Ernest Watson Burgess and Donald J- Bogue. [Sole entry]
Chicago: U. of Chicago Press, 1964, 419–428. [For a fuller version, see entry 15640.]
Subj 21 21.1 21.3 ▪ 41 47 48

15642 ELS FP P2 G7.0 1911–1949
Tregear, Thomas Refoy, 1897–.
Wuhan, its local and wider environment: A port study.
Unpublished doctoral dissertation in Economics, U. of London [External degree], 1934. 155 p.
Subj 21.1 21.3 24 ▪ 14.3 21 21.2 22.1

1911-1972
(including 1644-1972)

15643 CSU FP P2 G9.5 1911–1972
Boxer, Baruch, 1932–.
'Space, change and feng-shui in Tsuen Wan's urbanization [i.e., Ch'üan-wan, Hong Kong].'
JAAS 3, 3/4 (July–Oct. 1968), 226–240.
Subj 21.1 62 ▪ 21.3 22.2 23 24

15644 CSU S P3 G1.2 1911–1972
Chang, Sen-dou (Chang Sheng-tao), 1928–.
'The million city of Mainland China.'
Pacific viewpoint 9, 2 (Sept. 1968), 128–153.
Subj 11.1 21.1 ▪ 14.4

15645 CSU P P3 G1.1 1842–1972
O'Hara, Albert Richard, 1907–.
'Development of urbanization in Asia and in Taiwan.' In *Research on changes of Chinese society*, by A. R. O'Hara. [Selective entry]
Taipei: Orient Cultural Service, 1971, 135–149. (Asian Folklore and Social Life monographs, 20)
Subj 21.1 21.2 ▪ 11.1 11.2 21.4 22.2 41 57

15646 MCH P P3 G9.5 1842–1972
Taeuber, Irene Barnes, 1906–.
'Hong Kong: Migrants and metropolis.'
Population index 29, 1 (Jan. 1963), 3–25.
Subj 21.1 21.2 21.3 21.4 58 ▪ 11.2 17 41

1949-1972

15647 CSH P P3 G9.4 1949–1972
Chen Shao-hsing (Ch'en Shao-hsing), 1906–1966.
'The trend of urbanization and the formation of a metropolitan area in Taiwan during the last decade.' *J. of sociology* (Taipei) 1 (Dec. 1963), 59–79.
Subj 21 21.1 21.3 ▪ 21.2 24.2

15648 CSU P P4 G9.5 1949–1972
Dwyer, Denis John, 1933–.
'Introduction.' In *Asian urbanization: A Hong Kong casebook*, edited by D. J. Dwyer. [Analytic entry]
Hong Kong: Hong Kong U. Press, 1971, 1–10. (Centre of Asian Studies series, 3)
Subj 21.1 ▪ 21.2 55 58

15649 NNC S P3 G9.5 1949–1972
Hughes, R- H-.
'Hong Kong: Far Eastern meeting point.'
GJ 129, 4 (Dec. 1963), 450–465.
Subj 21.1 ▪ 21.3 24.4

15650 CSU P P3 G9.4 1949–1972
Lee, Rose Hum (T'an Chin-mei), 1893–1964.
'Taiwan (Formosa).' In *The city: Urbanism and urbanization in major world regions*, by R. H. Lee. [Selective entry]
Philadelphia: Lippincott, 1955, 86–92.
Subj 21.1 ▪ 21.4 24.2

15651 CSU P P4 G9.1 1949–1972
[Mao Ch'ün] ———.
'A new city built on the Wu-feng-ling (Kiangsi).' Tr. of 'Wu-feng-ling shang chien hsin ch'eng'; *Jen min jih pao* 25 Dec. 1960, 7. In *Economic information on Communist China*, mimeo., compiled by U.S. Joint Publications Research Service. [Sole entry]
Washington, D.C.: JPRS, 11 Aug. 1961, 32–37. (JPRS 8728; MC 15,196/1961)
Subj 21.1 24.2 24.3 24.4 ▪ 26.4

15652 NIC P P2 G1.2 1949–1972
Ni, Ernest (Ni Yin-hsin), 1908–.
Distribution of the urban and rural population of Mainland China, 1953 and 1958.
Washington, D.C.: U.S. Bureau of the Census, Foreign Manpower Research Office, 1960. 22 p. (FMRO, International population statistics reports, Series P-95, 56)
Subj 11 21.1 ▪ 11.1

15653 CSU S P4 G9.5 1949–1972
Prescott, Jon A-.
'Hong Kong: The form and significance of a high density urban development.' In *Asian urbanization: A Hong Kong casebook*, edited by Denis John Dwyer. [Analytic entry]
Hong Kong: Hong Kong U. Press, 1971, 11–19. (Centre of Asian Studies series, 3)
Subj 21.1 21.3 55

15654 CSH FP P2 G9.4 1949–1972
Van Alstyne, Arthur James, Jr., 1928–.
'The role of the city in social change: Some methodological and theoretical problems.'
CCJ 8, 1 (Nov. 1968), 93–106. [For fuller treatment, see entry 15655.]
Subj 21.1 21.3

15655 MAM FP P2 G9.4 1949–1972
Van Alstyne, Arthur James, Jr., 1928–.
Urban influences on rural communities: A Taiwanese example.
Ann Arbor: University Microfilms (Publ. 68-7524), 1968. 230 p. (Doctoral dissertation in Geography, U. of Pittsburgh, 1967)
Subj 21.1 21.3 ▪ 21 21.4 23 24.1 24.2 27 30 51 55 56

21.2 Regional and Local Geographic Mobility
地方性流動遷移
地域間又は地域内人口移動

1644-1911

15656 NNP O P2 G1.4 1842–1911
Boloban, Andrei Pavlovich.
'Kolonizatsionnye problemy Kitaia, v Man'chzhurii i Mongolii' (China's colonization problems in Manchuria and Mongolia).
VA 3 (ianvar' 1910), 85–127.
Subj 21.2 24.1 ▪ 21.4

15657 NIC U P2 G9.4 –1842
Chen Shao-hsing (Ch'en Shao-hsing), 1906–1966.
'How the Chinese came to Taiwan.'
Free China review 13, 2 (Feb. 1963), 31–36.
Subj 14.3 21.2 24.1

15658 MCH P P2 G9.4 –1895
Chen Ta (Ch'en Ta), 1892–.
'Chinese in Formosa (Taiwan).' In *Chinese migrations, with special reference to labor conditions*, by Chen Ta. [Selective entry]
Washington, D.C.: U.S. Government Printing Office, 1923, 37–50. (U.S. Bureau of Labor Statistics bulletins, Miscellaneous series, 340) (Doctoral dissertation in Sociology, Columbia U., 1923) [Reprinted in *Chinese migrations, with special reference to labor conditions*, by Chen Ta. (Selective entry.) Taipei: Ch'eng-wen, 1967, 37–50.]
Subj 14.3 21.2 ▪ 14 24.1

15659 NNP PO P2 G2.2 1644–1911
Davidov, D-.
'Kolonizatsiia Man'chzhurii i s.-v. Mongolii (oblasti Tao-nan'-fu)' (The colonization of Manchuria and northeastern Mongolia: T'ao-nan *fu* [Kirin]).
IVI 37, 1 (1911), 1–172.
Subj 21.2 24.1 ▪ 12 66

15660 NNP U P7 G3.0 –1895
Froze, B-.
'Vostochnaia Mongoliia i ee kolonizatsiia' (The colonization of eastern Mongolia).
VA 10 (oktiabr' 1911), 90–136.
Subj 21.2 24.1 66

15661 CSH S P8 G2.1 –1911
G. N. G.
'Ocherk zaseleniia kitaitsami Priamur'ia' (Sketch of Chinese settlement of the Amur region).
VA 7 (ianvar' 1911), 34–58.
Subj 21.2 24.1 ▪ 21 22.2 24.5 26.3 66

15662 NIC P P2 G1.3 1644–1842
Hsieh, Kuo-ching.
'Removal of coastal population in early Tsing period.'

CSPSR 15, 4 (Jan. 1932), 559–596.
SUBJ 15 21.2 ▪ 12

15663 WSU P P8 G1.5 1644–1842
Hui Kim-bing (Hsü Chien-ping).
'The lion rock and the deserting of the coastal strip and subsequent re-occupation of the region during early Manchu rule.' Tr. of 'Shih-tzu-ling yü Ch'ing ch'u Hsiang-kang Chiu-lung hsin chieh chih ch'ien hai yü fu chieh'; in *I pa ssu erh nien i ch'ien chih Hsiang-kang chi ch'i tui wai chiao t'ung: Hsiang-kang ch'ien tai shih*, edited by Lo Hsiang-lin; Hong Kong: Chung-kuo hsüeh she, 1959, 129–150. In *Hong Kong and its external communications before 1842*, edited by Lo Hsiang-lin. [Selective entry]
Hong Kong: Institute of Chinese Culture, 1963, 89–105.
SUBJ 21.2 24.1 25 ▪ 22.1 29

15664 CBU P P2 G2.0 –1842
Lin, T. C. (Lin T'ung-chi), 1906–.
Chinese expansion to the Northeast: Methods and mechanisms.
Unpublished doctoral dissertation in Political Science, U. of California, Berkeley, 1934. 283 p.
SUBJ 12.1 21.2 ▪ 22 66

15665 MCH P P7 G2.2 1644–1895
Rudakov, Apollinarii Vasil'evich, 1871–?
'Pozemel'nyi vopros v Girinskoi provintsii v sviazi s eia zaseleniem' (The land question in Kirin province and its settlement).
IVI 3, 2 (1902), 1–80.
SUBJ 21.2 21.3 24.1 ▪ 12.1 15 24 66

1644-1949

15666 MCH S P8 G3.0 1842–1949
Cressey, George Babcock, 1896–1963.
'Chinese colonization in Mongolia, 1932.' In *Pioneer settlement: Co-operative studies by twenty-six authors*, edited by Wolfgang Louis Gottfried Joerg. [Selective entry]
New York: American Geographical Society, 1932, 273–287. (AGS special publications, 14)
SUBJ 21.2 ▪ 14.1

15667 CSH S P8 G3.0 1895–1928
Didushok, V- F-.
'Kolonizatsiia Chzherimskogo seima Vnutrennei Mongolii: istoricheskaia spravka' (An historical investigation of the colonization of the Jerim League of Inner Mongolia).
VM 1928, 1, 25–32.
SUBJ 21.2 ▪ 11.3 21 24.1

15668 ELU S P2 G2.0 1895–1949
Gaskell, Arthur, 1907–.
The colonisation and settlement of Manchuria.
Unpublished masters thesis in Geography, U. of Liverpool, 1932. 110 p.
SUBJ 14.1 21 21.2 ▪ 14.2 66

15669 MCY P P2 G2.0 1644–1949
Ho, Franklin L. (Ho Lien), 1897–.
'Population movement to the northeastern provinces in China.'
CSPSR 15, 3 (Oct. 1931), 346–401. [Separately reprinted as *Population movement to the north eastern frontier in China*. Shanghai: China Institute of Pacific Relations, 1931. 51 p.]
SUBJ 11.3 14 14.1 14.2 21.2 21.4 ▪ 14.4 14.6 16.3 16.4 18 21 21.1 25

15670 CSH P P2 G2.0 1842–1928
IAshnov, Evgenii Evgen'evich.
'Kolonizatsiia severnoi Man'chzhurii i K.V. zhel. doroga' (The Chinese Eastern Railway and the colonization of northern Manchuria).
EVM 1923, 21/22 (10 iiunia), 21–26.
SUBJ 21.2 24 24.2 ▪ 12.1 16.3 25

15671 MCH O P7 G3.0 1895–1928
Kolokolov, S- A-.
'O kitaiskoi kolonizatsii mongol'skikh zemel" (Chinese colonization of Mongolian territory).
Izvestiia Ministerstva inostrannykh del 1916, 5/6, 133–143.
SUBJ 21.2 66

15672 NNC O P7 G3.3 1895–1949
Ku Chi-kang.
'Farm settlements north of the Yellow River in western Suiyuan.' Tr. from *Shen pao chou k'an* 2, 16 (25 Apr. 1937). In *Agrarian China*, compiled by Institute of Pacific Relations. [Selective entry]
Chicago: U. of Chicago Press, 1939, 46–50.
SUBJ 21.2 24.1 ▪ 21.3 22 35 38

15673 MCH O P7 G3.0 1644–1928
Lattimore, Owen, 1900–.
'Chinese colonization in Inner Mongolia: Its history and present development.' In *Pioneer settlement: Co-operative studies by twenty-six authors*, edited by Wolfgang Louis Gottfried Joerg. [Selective entry]
New York: American Geographical Society, 1932, 288–312. (AGS special publications, 14)
SUBJ 21.2 21.3 23 24.1 66 ▪ 14.3 22 24 24.2 26 28 55

15674 CBU PO P2 G2.0 –1949
Lattimore, Owen, 1900–.
Manchuria, cradle of conflict, rev. ed.
New York: Macmillan, 1935. 18, 333 p. [Reprinted—New York: AMS Press, 1973. 18, 333 p.]
SUBJ 14 14.1 16 21.2 22 66 ▪ 14.2 15 16.1 16.3 18 25 41 46 47 60

15675 MAM P P2 G9.4 1895–1949
Li, Wen-lang, 1938–.
Interprefectural migration of the native population in Taiwan, 1905–40.
Ann Arbor: University Microfilms (Publ. 68-9217), 1968. 213 p. (Doctoral dissertation in Sociology, U. of Pennsylvania, 1967)
SUBJ 21.2 ▪ 14 47 50

15676 CSH FP P2 G2.0 1842–1949
Liubimov, L- I- (L. I. Liubimoff).
'Puti kolonizatsii severnoi Man'chzhurii.'
VM 1930, 9, 1–10.

'Colonization of north Manchuria.'
Manchuria monitor 1930, 9, 1–10.
SUBJ 11.3 21.2 ▪ 14.2 21 66

15677 NNC P P7 G2.0 1842–1949
Tsao Lien-en (Ts'ao Lien-en).
'The method of Chinese colonization in Manchuria.'
CEJ 7, 2 (Aug. 1930), 831–852.
SUBJ 14.1 21.2 ▪ 16.3 18 21.4

15678 MAM P P2 G2.0 1895–1949
Wang, I-shou, 1937–.
Chinese migration and population change in Manchuria, 1900–1940.
Ann Arbor: University Microfilms (Publ. 72-14,394), 1972. 10, 232 p. (Doctoral dissertation in Geography, U. of Minnesota, 1971)
SUBJ 11.3 21 21.1 21.2 ▪ 14.1 14.4 21.4 50 58

15679 MCH FP P7 G2.0 1644–1949
Young, Carl Walter, 1902–1939.
'Chinese immigration and colonization in Manchuria.' In *Pioneer settlement: Co-operative studies by twenty-six authors*, edited by Wolfgang Louis Gottfried Joerg. [Selective entry]
New York: American Geographical Society, 1932, 330–359. (AGS special publications, 14)
SUBJ 11.3 21.2 21.3 24.1 ▪ 21 24.2 25 34.1 38 40 72

1911-1949

15680 NIC S P2 G2.0 1928–1949
Chang, Chi-hsien.
'Political aspects of the immigration problem in Manchuria.'
IB 1, 4 (11 June 1936), 1–23.
SUBJ 21.2 ▪ 12

15681 CSU U P8 G1.4 1928–1949
Howard, Harry Paxton, 1893–.
'China's economic need of Manchuria.'
CEJ 10, 4 (Apr. 1932), 323–332.
SUBJ 18 21.2 ▪ 14.1

15682 NNC U P2 G1.2 1928–1949
Hu Nai-tsiu (Hu Nai-chiu).
'Internal Chinese migration.' Tr. of 'Tsui chin Chung-kuo nung min ti li ts'un wen t'i' (Recent rural emigration in China); *Chiao yü yü min chung* 8, 3 (28 Nov. 1936), 456–468 [condensed tr.]. In *Agrarian China*, compiled by Institute of Pacific Relations. [Selective entry]
Chicago: U. of Chicago Press, 1939, 255–258.
SUBJ 21.2 ▪ 16.3 18

15683 NNP PO P2 G2.0 1911–1928
I. P.
'Pereselentsy v 1927 godu i KVzhd' (The Chinese Eastern Railway and immigration in 1927).
EB 1927, 11 (20 marta), 5–7; 1927, 36/37, 9–12.
SUBJ 14.2 21.2 ▪ 16.3

15684 CSH P P2 G2.1 1911–1949
Kormazov, V- A-.
'Dvizhenie naseleniia v raione zapadnoi linii KVzhd' (Migration into the area served by the western line of the Chinese Eastern Railway). [With English abstracts]
VM 1930, 4, 51–59; 1930, 5, 29–36.
SUBJ 21.2 ▪ 21 21.1

15685 CSU P P1 G9.4 1911–1949
Li, Wen-lang, 1938–.
'Migration differentials in Taiwan, 1920–40: A comparative study.'

J. of developing areas 6, 2 (Jan. 1972), 227–237.
Subj 21.2 ▪ 21.4 50

15686 CBU P P2 G2.1 1911–1928
Liubimov, L- I-.
'Pereselencheskaia volna i kolonizatsionyi fond v raione zapadnoi linii KVzhd' (The wave of immigration to and lands for colonization in the area served by the western line of the Chinese Eastern Railway).
VM 1929, 3, 37–44.
Subj 21.2 ▪ 21 24.1 26.3

15687 CSU O P2 G2.0 1911–1949
Simpich, Frederick.
'Manchuria, promised land of Asia.'
NG 56, 4 (Oct. 1929), 379–428.
Subj 21.2 ▪ 14.1 14.2

15688 CSH P P2 G2.0 1928–1949
Sokolov, N- A-.
'Pereselencheskoe dvizhenie v severnuiu Man'chzhuriiu v 1931 g.' (Immigration into northern Manchuria in 1931). [With English abstract]
EB 1931, 9/10 (15 maia), 1–2.
Subj 21.2 ▪ 24.2

15689 CSH P P2 G2.0 1911–1949
Sokolov, N- A-.
'Pereselencheskoe dvizhenie v sev[ernuiu] Man'chzhuriiu [v. 1932 g.]' (Immigration into northern Manchuria in 1932).
VM 1932, 3, 55–60.
Subj 21.2 ▪ 21 24.2

15690 CSH P P2 G2.0 1911–1928
Sokolov, N- A-.
'Rasselenie pereselentsev v raionakh severnoi Man'chzhurii' (Regional distribution of immigrants in northern Manchuria). [With English abstract]
VM 1930, 2, 36–45.
Subj 21 21.1 21.2 ▪ 21.4 24.2

15691 CSH P P2 G2.0 1911–1949
Sokolov, N- A-.
'Sokrashchenie pereselencheskogo dvizheniia v sev. Man'chzhurii v 1930 godu' (The slackening of immigration into northern Manchuria in 1930). [With English abstract]
VM 1931, 1, 33–38.
Subj 21.2 ▪ 15 21 24.1 25

15692 NIC P P2 G2.0 1911–1928
Young, Carl Walter, 1902–1939.
Chinese colonization and the development of Manchuria.
Honolulu: Institute of Pacific Relations, 1929. 53 p.
Subj 11.3 14 21.2 ▪ 14.1 14.2

15693 CSH P P2 G2.3 1911–1949
[Zhernakov, Vladimir Nikolaevich] V. Zh., 1909–.
'Kolonizatsiia Taoan'skogo raiona' (The colonization of T'ao-an *hsien* [Liaoning]).
EB 1930, 9 (15 maia), 3.
Subj 21.2 ▪ 21.1 21.3

15694 CSH P P2 G1.4 1911–1928
Zverev, K-.
'Vesennee peredvizhenie rabochikh i pereselentsev (v Man'chzhuriiu)' (The spring movement of workers and migrants into Manchuria)
EVM 1924, 14 (6 aprelia), 12–14.
Subj 21.2 ▪ 14.1 14.2 16.3 16.4

1911-1972
(including 1644-1972)

15695 FGU P P2 G9.4 1928–1972
Chu, Hsien-jen, 1930–.
An exploratory study of internal migration in Taiwan.
Unpublished doctoral dissertation in Sociology, U. of Florida, 1966. 153 p.
Subj 21.2 ▪ 21 21.4 50 58

15696 MCH F P2 G4.0 1928–1972
Köhler, Günther, 1909–.
'Besiedlung und Binnenwanderung in Chinas Nordwesten' (Settlement and internal migration in Northwest China).
PGM 98, 4 (1954), 269–271.
Subj 21.2 ▪ 11.3 21

15697 MAM FP P2 G9.4 1842–1972
Salter, Christopher Lord, 1938–.
The geography of marginality: A study of migration, settlement and agricultural development in the rift valley of eastern Taiwan.
Ann Arbor: University Microfilms (Publ. 71-20,904), 1971. 13, 225 p. (Doctoral dissertation in Geography, U. of California, Berkeley, 1970)
Subj 21.2 21.3 24.1 ▪ 14.4 21 21.1 24.2 26.3 35 55

15698 CSH P P2 G9.4 1895–1972
Wang, Jen-ying.
'Population distribution and internal migration in Taiwan, 1959–1966.'
BIE 32, 3 (Aug. 1971), 111–145.
Subj 21 21.1 21.2 58 ▪ 11.3 14 14.4 21.4 47 56

1949-1972

15699 CSU F P7 G9.5 1949–1972
Berkowitz, Morris Ira, 1931–.
'Plover Cove [Ch'uan-wan] village to Taipo market [i.e., Ta-p'u hsü, Hong Kong]: A study in forced migration.'
JRAS-HKB 8 (1968), 96–108.
Subj 21.2 ▪ 29

15700 CSH O P4 G9.5 1949–1972
Bonavia, David.
'Hongkong's backdoor.'
FEER 49, 10 (2 Sept. 1965), 475–478.
Subj 21.2 28

15701 MAM P P2 G9.4 1949–1972
Chang, Se-moon.
Transformation of dual economies, with special reference to internal migration and marginal product of farm labor.
Ann Arbor: University Microfilms (Publ. 72-10,018), 1972. 204 p. (Doctoral dissertation in Economics, Florida State U., 1971)
Subj 21.2 21.4

15702 NNC S P2 G9.5 1949–1972
Davis, Sydney George, 1907–.
'Rural-urban migration in Hong Kong and the New Territories.' In *Symposium on land use and mineral deposits in Hong Kong, southern China and South-east Asia*, edited by S. G. Davis. [Selective entry]
Hong Kong: Hong Kong U. Press, 1964, 49–54.
Subj 21.2 24 ▪ 21.1 21.3

15703 MAM FP P2 G9.4 1949–1972
Huang, Ta-chou, 1936–.
Rural-urban migration in Taiwan.
Ann Arbor: University Microfilms (Publ. 72-8867), 1972. 88 p. (Doctoral dissertation in Sociology, Cornell U., 1971)
Subj 21.2 21.4

15704 TPU FP P8 G9.4 1949–1972
Huang, Ta-chou, 1936–.
'A study of migration intention differential among the rural youth of Taiwan.'
Memoirs of the College of Agriculture, National Taiwan U. 12, 2 (1968), 170–184.
Subj 21.2 21.4

15705 MCH P P2 G1.2 1949–1972
[La Dany, Ladislao] ———, 1914–.
'Youth to the lead.'
CNA 521 (19 June 1964), 1–7.
Subj 21.2 54

15706 CSU F P2 G9.4 1949–1972
Speare, Alden, Jr., 1939–.
'A cost-benefit model of rural to urban migration in Taiwan.'
PS 25, 1 (Mar. 1971), 117–130.
Subj 21.2

15707 DLC FP P2 G9.4 1949–1972
Speare, Alden, Jr., 1939–.
The determinants of migration to a major city in a developing country: Taichung, Taiwan.
Taipei: Academia Sinica, Institute of Economics, 1972. 22 p.(IE population papers, 4) [For a fuller version, see entry 15708.]
Subj 21.2 ▪ 21.4 28 41

15708 MAM FP P2 G9.4 1949–1972
Speare, Alden, Jr., 1939–.
The determinants of rural to urban migration in Taiwan.
Ann Arbor: University Microfilms (Publ. 70-14,649), 1970. 14, 317 p. (Doctoral dissertation in Sociology, U. of Michigan, 1969)
Subj 21.2 41 ▪ 21 21.1 24 24.2 26 28 58

15709 CSH S P2 G9.4 1949–1972
Wu, T. S. (Wu Tsung-hsien).
'A framework for the study of urban adaptation in the process of rural migration.'
J. of sociology (Taipei) 7 (Apr. 1971), 43–53.
Subj 21.2 ▪ 16 40 50

21.3 Microecology and Particular Settlements
市鎮村舍聚落研究
地域社会生態学及び居住形態

1644-1911

15710 MCH U P2 G5.1 1842–1895
'Peking und Umgebung' (Peking and the surrounding area).
Globus 31, 8 (Feb. 1877), 113–118; 31, 9 (März 1877), 129–133; 31, 10 (März

1877), 145–149; 31, 11 (März 1877), 161–167; 31, 12 (März 1877), 177–180; 31, 13 (Apr. 1877), 193–196.
Subj 13 21.1 21.3 33 ▪ 24.3 43 55

15711 DLC O P3 G9.2 1644–1842
Pis'mo G. Meiera iz Kitaia' (G. Meier's letter from China).
Biblioteka dlia chteniia 39 (1840), 86–97.
Subj 21.3 ▪ 22 47 55

15712 MCH S P3 G7.1 1895–1911
Amaury, E- G-.
'Quelques notes sur le port de Han-Keou' (Notes on the port of Hankow).
AF 2, 15 (juin 1902), 246–253.
Subj 21.3 24.2 ▪ 24.3 34.3

15713 CSH U P2 G5.3 1895–1911
Behme, F-, and M- Krieger.
Guide to Tsingtau and its surroundings, 4th ed.
Wolfenbüttel, Germany: H. Wessel, 1910. 185 p.
Subj 21.3 24.2 ▪ 17 24.4 55 56 57

15714 MCH O P3 G9.2 1842–1895
Boüinais, Albert Marie Aristide, 1851–1895.
'Excursion à Canton' (Excursion to Canton).
B. de la Société normande de géographie 13 (1891), 289–311.
Subj 21.3 ▪ 21.1 66

15715 CSU O P2 G8.2 1895–1911
Brenier, Henri, 1867–?
'De Moung-tse à Yun-nan fou' (From [the capital of] Meng-tzu *hsien* [Yunnan] to Yün-nan-fu [i.e., Kunming]). In *La Mission lyonnaise d'exploration commerciale en Chine, 1895–1897, première partie, récits des voyages* (The Lyons Trade Mission to China, 1895–1897, Part 1, Travel accounts), compiled by Chambre de commerce de Lyon. [Selective entry]
Lyons: Rey, 1898, 33–51 [s.p.].
Subj 21.3 24.2 66 ▪ 24.1 28

15716 CSU O P3 G8.1 1895–1911
Brenier, Henri, 1867–?
'La plus belle ville de Chine: séjour à Tchen-tou' (The most beautiful city in China: A sojourn in Chengtu). In *La Mission lyonnaise d'exploration commerciale en Chine, 1895–1897, première partie, récits des voyages* (The Lyons Trade Mission to China, 1895–1897, Part 1, Travel accounts), compiled by Chambre de commerce de Lyon. [Selective entry]
Lyons: Rey, 1898, 204–216 [s.p.].
Subj 12 21.1 21.3 22 ▪ 29 66

15717 CSU O P2 G8.1 1895–1911
Brenier, Henri, 1867–?
'Une pointe sur la capitale du Se-tchouan: de Soui-fou à Tchen-tou et retour sur Tchoung-king' (To and from the capital of Szechwan: From Hsü-chou-fu to Chengtu and back via Chungking). In *La Mission lyonnaise d'exploration commerciale en Chine, 1895–1897, première partie, récits des voyages* (The Lyons Trade Mission to China, 1895–1897: Part 1, Travel accounts), compiled by Chambre de commerce de Lyon. [Selective entry]
Lyons: Rey, 1898, 119–135 [s.p.].
Subj 21.3 24.2 ▪ 24.1 24.3 28 38 61 66

15718 MBA PO P2 G9.2 1895–1911
Brerault, E-.
'Notice sur l'île de Hainan' (A note on Hainan).
RI nouvelle (2e) série 3, 19 (15 oct. 1905), 1357–1377; 3, 20 (30 oct. 1905), 1464–1480.
Subj 21.3 24.1 24.2 ▪ 14.3 14.4 21 29 56 66

15719 CSU O P2 G9.5 1895–1911
Cartwright, H- A-.
'Hongkong (descriptive).' In *Twentieth century impressions of Hongkong, Shanghai, and other treaty ports of China: Their history, people, commerce, industries and manners*, edited by Arnold Wright and H- A- Cartwright. [Selective entry]
London: Lloyd's Greater Britain Publishing Co., 1908, 145–157.
Subj 21.3

15720 MCH O P2 G6.1 1842–1895
Castano, ———.
'Esquisse topographique de la ville de Shanghai et de ses environs' (Geographic sketch of Shanghai and its environs).
Recueil de mémoires de médecine, de chirurgie et de pharmacie militaires 3e série 4 (oct. 1860), 289–303.
Subj 21.3 28 ▪ 21 24 66

15721 MCH O P2 G1.5 1842–1895
Colquhoun, Archibald Ross, 1848–1914.
Across Chryse: Being the narrative of a journey through the South China borderlands from Canton to Mandalay.
London: Low Marston, Searle, and Rivington, 1883. 2 vols. 30, 420; 16, 408 p. [Reprinted—Taipei: Ch'eng-wen, 1972. 2 vols. 30, 420; 16, 408 p.]
Subj 21.3 22.2 29 33 55 66 ▪ 22 24.2 26 26.1 47 62

15722 CSU O P2 G1.5 1644–1842
Downing, Charles Toogood.
The stranger in China: or, The Fan-qui's visit to the Celestial Empire in 1836–37.
Philadelphia: Lea and Blanchard, 1838. 2 vols. 248; 232 p.
Subj 21.3 22.2 24 55 66 ▪ 24.2 24.3 26.2 29 33 34.2 47 56 57 62

15723 FPN O P3 G1.3 1842–1895
Durand-Fardel, Maxime, 1815–1899.
'Etude sur le climat des côtes de la Chine et les conditions sanitaires des concessions européennes' (A study of the climate of the China coast and the sanitary conditions in the European concessions).
Union médicale 3e série 27, 15 (6 fév. 1879), 178–184; 27, 16 (8 fév. 1879), 189–192; 27, 17 (11 fév. 1879), 207–210. [Separately reprinted—Paris: F. Malteste, 1879. 12 p.]
Subj 21.1 21.3 56 ▪ 21.2 28

15724 CSU P P3 G9.5 1842–1895
Evans, David Meurig Emrys, 1938–.
'Chinatown in Hong Kong: The beginnings of Taipingshan [Victoria Peak].'
JRAS-HKB 10 (1970), 69–78.
Subj 21.3

15725 CSU S P5 G9.0 1644–1842
Fortia d'Urban, Agricole Joseph François Xavier, 1756–1843.
'Quatrième partie de la Chine' (The fourth part of China). In *Description de la Chine et des états tributaires de l'empereur, Tome troisième, contenant la partie méridionale, l'empire d'Annam et l'empire Birman* (A description of China and the emperor's tributary states, Vol. 3, South China, the empire of Annam, and the Burmese empire), by A. J. F. X. Fortia d'Urban. [Sole entry]
Paris: The author, 1840, 15–84.
Subj 12 21.1 21.3

15726 NNC O P2 G1.5 1842–1895
Fortune, Robert, 1813–1880.
Two visits to the tea countries of China and the British tea plantations in the Himalaya, 3rd ed.
London: Murray, 1853. 2 vols. 299; 315 p. [Reprinted—Taipei: Ch'eng-wen, 1970. 2 vols. 299; 315 p.]
Subj 20 21.3 23 24.1 24.3 29 ▪ 14.3 24 24.5 26 55 56 57 65 66

15727 MCH PO P3 G6.1 –1895
Gaillard, Louis, 1850–1900.
Nankin d'alors et d'aujourd'hui: aperçu historique et géographique (Nanking, past and present: Historical and geographic sketch).
Shanghai: Impr. de la Mission catholique, 1903. 350 p. (Variétés sinologiques, 23)
Subj 21.3 ▪ 12 15 24.2 25

15728 FPN O P3 G6.1 1842–1895
Galle, Paul Edouard.
Shanghai au point de vue médical (Shanghai from a medical perspective).
Paris: Delahaye, 1875. 80 p.
Subj 21.3 56 ▪ 21.2 66

15729 DLC PO P2 G4.0 –1911
Grum-Grzhimailo, Grigorii Efimovich, 1860–1936.
Opisanie puteshestviia v zapadnyi Kitai. Tom I, Vdol' vostochnago Tian'-shan'ia. Tom II, Poperek Bei-shania i Nan-shania v dolinu Zheltoi reki. Tom III, Vokrug Kuku-nora, cherez Nan'shan', Bei-shan' i vdol' vostochnago Tian'-shan'ia obratno na rodinu (A description of a journey to western China. Vol. 1, Along the eastern T'ien-shan range. Vol. 2, Across Pei-shan and Nan-shan to the Yellow River valley. Vol. 3, Around Koko Nor, across Nan-shan and Pei-shan, and back home via the eastern T'ien-shan range).
St. Petersburg: Tipo-lit S. M. Nikolaeva; St. Petersburg: V. F. Kirshbaum, 1896, 1899, 1907. 12, 547; 445; 531 p. [Vol. 1 published by Tipo-lit. S. M. Nikolaeva, vols. 2 and 3 by V. F. Kirshbaum.]
Subj 15 21.3 24.2 ▪ 12.2 23 24.3 24.4 47 55 72

15730 MCH O P3 G5.1 1895–1911
Hubert, Charles.
'Pékin en 1908' (Peking in 1908).
B. de la Société de géographie de l'Est 33 (1912), 107–136, 249–274; 34 (1913), 119–147, 219–239; 35 (1914), 5–27.
Subj 21.1 21.3 ▪ 28 55 56

15731 CBU O P2 G6.1 1842–1895
Imbault-Huart, Camille Clément, 1857–1897.

'Une excursion à la ville de Song Kiang' (A visit to Sung-chiang [*fu* capital, Kiangsu]).
JA 7e série 19 (fév.–mars 1882), 522–542.
SUBJ 15 21.3 24.2 33 ▪ 22 32.2 35 55 66

15732 CBU O P2 G6.1 1842–1895
Imbault-Huart, Camille Clément, 1857–1897.
'Fragment d'un voyage dans la province du Kiang-sou' (Part of a journey in Kiangsu).
JA 8e série 2 (août–sept. 1883), 284–303.
SUBJ 21.3 24.2 24.5 33 ▪ 15 24.1

15733 MCH O P2 G1.3 1895–1911
Johnston, Reginald Fleming, 1874–1938.
From Peking to Mandalay: A journey from North China to Burma through Tibetan Ssuch'uan and Yunnan.
London: Murray, 1908. 12, 460 p. [Reprinted—Taipei: Ch'eng-wen, 1972. 12, 460 p.]
SUBJ 21.3 33 66 ▪ 12 22.2 26 26.1 65

15734 DLC O P2 G9.2 1895–1911
Kerr, John Glasgow, 1824–1901.
A guide to the city and suburbs of Canton, rev. and enl. ed.
Hong Kong: Kelly and Walsh, 1904. 93 p.
SUBJ 21.3 24 ▪ 24.2 24.3 24.4 55 57

15735 ECU O P2 G9.2 1842–1895
Krone, Rudolf.
'A notice of the Sanon district [i.e., Hsin-an *hsien*, Kwangtung].'
Transactions of the China Branch of the Royal Asiatic Society 6 (1859), 71–105. [Reprinted—*JRAS-HKB* 7 (1967), 104–137.]
SUBJ 20 21.3 23 24.3 25 38 ▪ 12 15 26.1 27 28 29 42 43 47 62

15736 FPN O P3 G1.3 1842–1895
Labbe, V- E- M-.
Expédition des mers de Chine (An expedition on the seas of China).
Paris: Impr. impériale, 1858. 25 p.
SUBJ 21.3

15737 CSU P P3 G2.3 1895–1911
Leeming, Frank.
'Reconstructing late Ch'ing Fengt'ien (Mukden, Liaoning).'
MAS 4, 4 (Oct. 1970), 305–324.
SUBJ 21.3 21.4 24 24.3 ▪ 21.1 22 24.4 25

15738 MCH F P7 G8.0 1895–1911
Legendre, Aimé François, 1867–?
'Exploration dans la Chine occidentale et les marches thibétaines' (Exploring West China and the Tibetan border regions).
B. de la Société normande de géographie 34 (1912), 196–220.
SUBJ 21 21.3 ▪ 25 66

15739 MCH F P2 G8.1 1895–1911
Legendre, Aimé François, 1867–?
'Explorations dans la Chine occidentale' (Explorations in West China).
Géographie 23, 4 (15 avr. 1911), 249–262.
SUBJ 21.3 ▪ 21 28

15740 WSU O P2 G8.1 1895–1911
Litton, G- J- L-.
China: Report of a journey to North Ssu-Ch'uan.
London: Her Majesty's Stationery Office, 1898. 48 p. (Great Britain, Foreign Office, Diplomatic and consular reports, miscellaneous series, 457)
SUBJ 11.3 21.3 24 ▪ 21 24.2 24.3 66

15741 NSU P P3 G1.2 –1911
Loh, Cheng-shan (Lu Cheng-shan), 1917–.
A descriptive study of selected walled cities in China [Ch'ang-an, Loyang, Nanking, and Peking].
Unpublished doctoral dissertation in Architecture, Syracuse U., 1951. 16, 148 p.
SUBJ 21.3 29 ▪ 11.2 11.3 14.3 24.2

15742 MCH PO P2 G9.2 1644–1911
Madrolle, Claudius, 1870–?
'Etude sur l'île d'Haï-nan' (A study of Hainan).
B. de la Société de géographie 7e série 19 (2e trimestre 1898), 187–228.
SUBJ 12 21.3 66 ▪ 15 21 21.2 29

15743 MCH O P3 G2.3 1644–1911
Matignon, Jean-Jacques, 1866–?
'Moukden et ses tombes' (Mukden and its tombs).
Annales du Musée Guimet, Bibliothèque de vulgarisation 29 (1908), 189–244. [Reprinted in *Dix ans aux pays du dragon* (Ten years in the lands of the dragon), by J.-J. Matignon. (Selective entry.) Paris: Maloine, 1910, 169–230.]
SUBJ 20 21.3 28 55 57 ▪ 13 23 24.3 26.2 62

15744 CSU O P2 G6.0 1842–1911
Moule, Arthur Evans, 1836–1918.
Half a century in China: Recollections and observations.
London: Hodder and Stoughton, 1911. 343 p. [Reprinted—Taipei: Ch'eng-wen, 1972. 343 p. (Reprint of 1903 ed.)]
SUBJ 21.3 23 24 43 62 66 ▪ 12 17 22.2 24.1 24.3 28 41 47 55 63

15745 CSU PO P3 G6.3 –1911
Moule, Arthur Evans, 1836–1918.
'Ningpo, ancient and modern.'
EAM 4 (1905), 128–138.
SUBJ 21.3 ▪ 65

15746 CSU O P3 G5.3 1895–1911
Neal, James Boyd.
'Tsinanfu, capital of Shantung.'
EAM 5 (1906), 324–334.
SUBJ 21.3 ▪ 17 21.1

15747 CSU O P2 G1.2 1842–1895
Poussielgue, Achille.
'Relation de voyage de Shang-hai à Moscou, par Pékin, la Mongolie et la Russie asiatique, rédigée d'après les notes de M. de Bourboulon, ministre de France en Chine, et Mme. de Bourboulon' (An account of a trip from Shanghai to Moscow by way of Peking, Mongolia, and Asiatic Russia, based on the notes of M. de Bourboulon, French Minister to China, and Mme. de Bourboulon).
Tour du monde 5, 1 (1864), 81–128; 5, 2 (1864), 289–336; 6, 1 (1865), 234–272.
SUBJ 21.3 24.3 29 55 ▪ 24.1 24.4 32.2 33 47

15748 NIC O P2 G8.2 1842–1895
Rocher, Emile, 1846–1924.
'Notes sur un voyage au Yun-nan' (Notes on a journey to Yunnan).
TP 1, 1 (1890), 47–55.
SUBJ 21.3 ▪ 14.3 21 24.2

15749 FPN PO P3 G1.5 1842–1895
Roy, Just Jean Etienne, 1794–1870.
Un Français en Chine pendant les années 1850 à 1856 (A Frenchman in China, 1850–1856).
Tours: Alfred Mame, 1857. 188 p.
SUBJ 13 21.3 24 32.2 41 64 ▪ 12 21.1 28 47 55 57 60 66

15750 CSU O P2 G8.0 1895–1911
Sculfort, L-, and Emile Rocher, 1846–1924.
'Vers le Yang-tsé, de Yun-nan fou à Soui-fou' (Toward the Yangtze, from Yün-nan-fu [i.e., Kunming] to Hsü-chou-fu [Szechwan]). In *La Mission lyonnaise d'exploration commerciale en Chine, 1895–1897, première partie, récits des voyages* (The Lyons Trade Mission to China, 1895–1897, Part 1, Travel accounts), compiled by Chambre de commerce de Lyon. [Selective entry]
Lyons: Rey, 1898, 67–82 [s.p.].
SUBJ 21.3 24.1 ▪ 21 24.2 24.4

15751 ELB U P4 G1.3 –1911
Tiessen, Ernst, 1871–?
'Die chinesische Stadt: Eine siedlungskundliche Studie' (The Chinese city: A study of its settlement).
Deutsche geographische Blätter 35 (1912), 1–19.
SUBJ 11.1 21.3 ▪ 12 14.2 24

15752 MCH O P2 G1.4 1644–1842
Timkovskii, Egor Fedorovich, 1790–1875.
Puteshestvie v Kitai cherez Mongoliiu v 1820 i 1821 godakh (A journey to China through Mongolia in 1820 and 1821).
St. Petersburg: Tip. Med. departamenta M-va vnutr. del, 1824. 3 vols. 388; 409; 433, 38 p.
Voyage à Pékin, à travers la Mongolie, en 1820 et 1821, edited by Julius Heinrich Klaproth.
Paris: Dondey-Dupré, 1827. 2 vols. 480; 459 p.
Travels of the Russian mission through Mongolia to China, and residence in Peking, in the years 1820–1821. Tr. by H- E- Lloyd, edited by J. H. Klaproth.
London: Longman, Rees, Orme, Brown and Green, 1827. 2 vols. 468; 496 p.
SUBJ 12.2 14 15 21.3 33 66 ▪ 12 14.3 16.1 22.2 24.6 55 56 57 62 63

15753 MCY O P2 G4.0 1842–1895
Vasenev, A-.
'Dnevnik, vedennyi na puti ot Lan-chzhou-fu do Si-an'-fu i Khan'-chzhun-fu i obratno' (Diary of a journey from Lan-chou-fu [i.e., Lanchow] to Hsi-an-fu [i.e., Sian] and Han-chung-fu [Shensi] and back). In *Trudy russkikh torgovykh liudei v Mongolii i Kitae* (Works of Russian merchants in Mongolia and China), compiled by Vostochno-sibirskii otdel, Imperatorskoe russkoe geograficheskoe obshchestvo. [Selective entry]
Irkutsk: Tip. K. I. Vitkovskoi, 1890, 1 126. (Imperatorskoe russkoe geografischeskoe obshchestvo,

Vostochno-sibirskii otdel, Zapiski po obshchei geografii, 1, 1)
SUBJ 21.3 24 24.2 24.3 55 ▪ 15 23 24.1 24.4 25 28 57 66

15754 DLC O P2 G5.1 1644–1895
Vasil'ev, Vasilii Pavlovich, 1818–1900.
'Vospominaniia o Pekine' (Reminiscences of Peking). In *'Otkrytie Kitaia' i dr. st. akademika V. P. Vasil'eva* ('The opening of China' and other articles by the academician V. P. Vasil'ev). [Selective entry]
St. Petersburg: Stolichnaia tip., 1900, 34–62.
SUBJ 21.3 55 ▪ 21.1 26 57

1644-1949

15755 CBU U P3 G5.1 –1928
Buxton, Leonard Halford Dudley, 1889–1939.
'The historical geography of Peking.'
Geographical teacher 13, 71, Part 1 (Spring 1925), 42–49.
SUBJ 21.3 ▪ 14.2

15756 CBU S P4 G1.2 –1949
Chang, Sen-dou (Chang Sheng-tao), 1928–.
'Some observations on the morphology of Chinese walled cities.'
AAAG 60, 1 (Mar. 1970), 63–91.
SUBJ 11.1 11.3 21.3 29 ▪ 21.1 24.2 55

15757 NIC P P2 G1.2 –1949
Chen, C. Z.
'Some ancient Chinese concepts of town and country.'
Town planning review 19, 3/4 (Summer 1947), 160–163.
SUBJ 21.3 62

15758 MCH PO P3 G9.5 1895–1949
Davis, Sydney George, 1907–.
Hong Kong in its geographical setting.
London: Collins, 1949. 10, 226 p. (Revision of *The geographical growth and development of Hong Kong, 1841–1941*, doctoral dissertation in Geography, U. of London [External degree], 1946) [Reprinted—New York: AMS Press, 1973. 10, 226 p.]
SUBJ 21.3 24 ▪ 21.2 24.2 24.4

15759 NIC P P3 G5.3 1842–1949
Ginsburg, Norton Sydney, 1921–.
'Ch'ing-tao: Development and land utilization.'
EG 24, 3 (July 1948), 181–200.
SUBJ 20 21.3 24 ▪ 24.2 24.4

15760 CSU O P3 G5.1 –1949
Johnson, Nelson T-, and W- Robert Moore.
'Power comes back to Peiping.'
NG 96, 3 (Sept. 1949), 337–368.
SUBJ 21.3 55

15761 ECU P P7 G6.1 –1949
Lee, Shu-tang.
North Kiangsu: A study in regional geography.
Unpublished masters thesis in Geography, U. of Cambridge [Downing College], 1939. 157 p.
SUBJ 20 21.3 24.1 ▪ 21 21.2 24.2 28

15762 MCH P P3 G1.2 1895–1949
Loo, Kon-tung (Lu Kan-tung).
La vie municipale et l'urbanisme en Chine (Municipal life and town planning in China).
Lyons: Bosc et Riou, 1934. 172 p. (Doctoral dissertation, Faculté de droit, Université de Paris)
SUBJ 21.3 22 24.5 28 ▪ 22.1 22.2 24.2 24.4 26.1 45

15763 CSH O P2 G9.2 1895–1949
Madrolle, Claudius, 1870–?, and P- B- de La Brousse.
'Le Japon à Hainan' (Japan in Hainan).
AF 39, 368 (mars 1939), 94–99.
SUBJ 21.3 24.1 24.3 ▪ 15 21 21.2

15764 CSU PO P3 G6.1 1842–1949
Oberhummer, Eugen, 1859–1944.
'Schanghai' (Shanghai).
Mitteilungen der K.u.K. Geographischen Gesellschaft in Wien 75, 1/3 (1932), 5–27.
SUBJ 20 21.1 21.3 24 ▪ 14.3 17

15765 NIC S P3 G6.1 –1949
Orchard, John Ewing, 1893–1962.
'Shanghai.'
GR 26, 1 (Jan. 1936), 1–31.
SUBJ 21.3 24 24.2 24.4 ▪ 14.3 21.1

15766 CSU S P4 G9.4 1644–1949
Pannell, Clifton Wyndham.
'Outlanders on the island: Some historical notes on form and function in the Taiwanese city.'
JCS 6 (1969), 61–78.
SUBJ 21.1 21.3 ▪ 21 21.2 24.2 24.4

15767 CSU O P4 G1.3 –1928
Schmitthenner, Heinrich, 1887–1957.
'Die chinesische Stadt' (The Chinese city). In *Stadtlandschaften der Erde* (Cityscapes of the world), edited by Siegfried Passarge. [Sole entry]
Hamburg: L. Friedrichsen, 1930, 85–108.
SUBJ 11.1 21.3 55 ▪ 21.4 24.2 24.3 62

1911-1949

15768 CSH O P2 G5.1 1911–1928
'Chinwangtao [Ch'in-huang-tao, Lin-yü *hsien*, Hopei].'
CEJ 4, 2 (Feb. 1929), 162–166.
SUBJ 21.1 21.3 ▪ 24 24.1 34.2

15769 CSH O P5 G5.1 1911–1928
'Three towns in southeastern Chihli [Po-t'ou (Nan-p'i *hsien*), Ts'ang-chou (capital of Ts'ang *hsien*), and Tung-kuang (*hsien* capital)].'
CEJ 1, 11 (Nov. 1927), 980–990.
SUBJ 21.3 24 24.3 ▪ 21.1 24.1 24.2 28

15770 CSH O P4 G5.0 1911–1928
'Three towns on the Peking-Hankow railway [Pao-ting, Kao-yang, and Shih-chia-chuang, Hopei].'
CEJ 1, 6 (June 1927), 544–563.
SUBJ 14.2 21.3 24 24.3 24.4 ▪ 21.1 34.2

15771 MCH O P7 G6.1 1911–1928
Chiao, C. M. (Ch'iao Ch'i-ming), 1897–.
'Mapping the rural community.'
CR 55, 12 (Dec. 1924), 805–809.
SUBJ 20 21.3 ▪ 23 27 28 55

15772 NIC O P2 G6.1 1928–1949
Cressey, George Babcock, 1896–1963.
'The Fenghsien landscape [Feng-hsien *hsien*, Kiangsu], a fragment of the Yangtse Delta.'
GR 26, 3 (July 1936), 393–413.
SUBJ 21.3 24.1 24.4 ▪ 24.2 26.3

15773 NIC P P2 G1.1 1928–1949
Crow, Carl, 1883–1945.
Handbook for China, including Hong Kong, 5th ed.
Hong Kong: Kelly and Walsh, 1933. 390 p.
SUBJ 21.3 24 24.2 33 65 ▪ 12 13 14 21 23 24.1 24.4 31 55 62

15774 CSU U P3 G2.2 1928–1949
Ginsburg, Norton Sydney, 1921–.
'Ch'ang-ch'un.'
EG 23, 4 (Oct. 1947), 290–307.
SUBJ 21.3 ▪ 21.1 24.2 24.4

15775 GMS F P2 G1.5 1911–1928
Handel-Mazzetti, Heinrich Raphael Eduard, 1882–1940.
Naturbilder aus Südwest China: Erlebnisse und Eindrücke eines österreichischen Forschers während des Weltkrieges (Nature sketches from Southwest China: Impressions of an Austrian scientist during World War I).
Vienna, Leipzig: Österreichischer Bundesverlag für Unterricht, Wissenschaft und Kunst, 1927. 14, 380 p.
SUBJ 21.3 55 ▪ 24.2 26.3 65

15776 CSH O P2 G2.1 1928–1949
Kormazov, V- A-.
'Severnaia okraina Kheiluntszianskoi provintsii: kitaiskoe Priamur'e' (The outlying northern regions of Heilungkiang: The Chinese Amur region). [With English abstract]
VM 1929, 6, 69–79.
SUBJ 21.3 ▪ 21 21.1 21.2

15777 CSU O P2 G4.2 1928–1949
Liu En-lan.
'The Ho-si [Ho-hsi, Kansu] corridor.'
EG 28, 1 (Jan. 1952), 51–56.
SUBJ 21.3 ▪ 21 24.1 24.4

15778 CSU O P3 G2.1 1928–1949
McCune, Shannon.
'Harbin, Manchoukuo.'
J. of geography 39, 5 (May 1940), 187–196.
SUBJ 21.3 ▪ 21.1 24.2 24.4

15779 NNC O P2 G9.3 1928–1949
Mulder, W- Z-.
'Amoy' (Amoy).
TESG 34, 7 (Juli 1943), 107–112.
SUBJ 21.3 ▪ 21.1 24.1 24.3

15780 MBA O P3 G9.2 1911–1928
Noll, Gabriel.
'Notes et documents: impressions de Canton' (Notes and documents: Impressions of Canton).
RI nouvelle (2e) série 21, 1 (jan. 1914), 99–118.
SUBJ 21.3 ▪ 12 15 21.1 26 32.2 55 66

15781 CSU U P2 G1.3 1911–1928
Roxby, Percy Maude, 1880–1947.
'Wu-han: The heart of China.'

Scottish geographical magazine 32, 6 (June 1916), 266–279.
Subj 11.3 14.2 21.3 ▪ 24.4

15782 MCH O P3 G9.3 1928–1949
Schmitthenner, Heinrich, 1887–1957.
'Fuchau' (Foochow).
OR 15, 17 (1 Sept. 1934), 402–403.
Subj 21.3 ▪ 21.1 26

15783 SSK O P5 G1.4 1911–1928
Sirén, Osvald, 1879–1959.
'Nordkinesiska stadsvyer' (Cityscapes in North China).
Ord och Bild (Stockholm) 1924, 75–90.
Subj 21.3

15784 CSU PO P2 G8.1 1928–1949
Spencer, Joseph Earle, 1907–.
'Changing Chungking: The rebuilding of an old Chinese city.'
GR 29, 1 (Jan. 1939), 46–60.
Subj 21.3 ▪ 21.1 24.2

15785 NIC O P7 G9.4 1928–1949
Tomita, Yoshiro (Tomita Yoshirō), 1895–.
'On the rural settlement forms in Taiwan (Formosa), Japan.' In *Proceedings of the Fifth Pacific Science Congress*. [Sole entry]
Toronto: U. of Toronto Press, 1934, vol. 2, 1391–1395.
Subj 21.3 ▪ 24.1

15786 MCH O P3 G5.1 1911–1928
Van Vorst, Bessie McGinnis, 1873–1928.
'Y a-t-il une Chine moderne?' (Is there a modern China?).
R. hebdomadaire 5/6 (5 mai 1917), 58–86.
Subj 19 21.1 21.3 62 64 ▪ 17 23 53 57

15787 MCH P P3 G1.2 1911–1928
Vissière, Arnold Jacques Antoine, 1858–1930.
'Villes et ports de Chine ouverts au commerce international' (Chinese cities and ports open to international trade).
JA 11e série 4, 1 (juil.–août 1914), 161–183.
Subj 21.3 ▪ 14.3

15788 CBU O P3 G6.1 1928–1949
Yu, Charles Ping-lih.
'Aperçu sur la modernisation des villes de Chine: Wu-Sih d'aujourd'hui et demain' (A look at the modernization of Chinese cities: Wusih today and tomorrow).
Annales franco-chinoises 7, 25 (1er trimestre 1933), 24–43; 7, 26 (2e trimestre 1933), 1–9.
Subj 21.3 ▪ 21.1 24

1911-1972
(including 1644-1972)

15789 DLC U P2 G5.1 –1972
[Bao Chiao-ming] Bao TSziao-min (Pao Chiao-min) and Khe TSzy-tsian (Ho Tzu-ch'iang).
Tian'tszin'. Tr. by V- F- Terent'eva of *T'ien-chin*; Shanghai: Hsin chih shih ch'u pan she, 1958; 78 p.
Moscow: Izd-vo inostr. lit-ry, 1960. 92 p.
Tientsin, mimeo.
Washington, D.C.: U.S. Joint Publications Research Service, 13 July 1962. 127 p. (JPRS 14,466; MC 15,948/1962)
[Xerox copyflo available—New York: CCM Information Corp., Research and Microfilm Publications. (Scholarly Book Translation Series, 537)]
Subj 21.3 24 24.2 24.4 ▪ 14.3 17 21.1 21.2 21.4 28

15790 CSU S P2 G1.2 –1972
Cammann, Schuyler, 1912–.
Review of *Chinese architecture and town planning, 1500 B.C. – A.D. 1911*, by Andrew Charles Hugh Boyd.
HJAS 28 (1968), 221–231.
Subj 21.3 55 ▪ 14.2 29 62

15791 NNC S P3 G5.1 –1972
Chang, Sen-dou (Chang Sheng-tao), 1928–.
'Peking, the growing metropolis of Communist China.'
GR 55, 3 (July 1965), 313–327.
Subj 21.3 24 ▪ 21.1 21.2 22

15792 NIC FP P5 G9.4 1895–1972
Chen, Cheng-siang (Ch'en Cheng-hsiang), 1920–.
Cities and rural towns of Taiwan.
Taipei: Fu-min Geographical Institute of Economic Development, 1953. 40 p. (Fu-min research reports, 48)
Subj 11.3 21.3 24.2 ▪ 24.3

15793 NIC FP P3 G9.4 1644–1972
Chen, Cheng-siang (Ch'en Cheng-hsiang), 1920–.
The city of Taipei.
Taipei: Fu-min Geographical Institute of Economic Development, 1956. 19 p. (Fu-min research reports, 71)
Subj 21.1 21.3 ▪ 24.2 24.3

15794 MCH FP P3 G9.4 1895–1972
Chen, Cheng-siang (Ch'en Cheng-hsiang), 1920–.
Keelung: A study of urban geography.
Keelung: Chi-lung shih cheng fu, 1954. 44 p.
Subj 14.3 21.1 21.3 ▪ 21.4 24.2 24.3 24.4

15795 ELS P P3 G9.5 1842–1972
Chiu Tze Nang (Chao Tzu-neng), 1932–.
Hong Kong: A study in port development.
Unpublished doctoral dissertation in Geography, U. of London [London School of Economics and Political Science], 1963. 299 p.
Subj 14.3 21.3 24 ▪ 21.1 21.2

15796 NIC S P2 G9.5 1842–1972
Clark, Philip Hart, 1938–.
Hong Kong: A survey of residential development from its inception to the present.
Unpublished masters thesis in Regional Planning, Cornell U., 1968. 207 p.
Subj 21.1 21.3 28 ▪ 24 55 57

15797 CSU FP P7 G9.5 –1972
da Silva, Armando Maria.
Tai Yu Shan [Hong Kong]*: Traditional ecological adaptation in a South China island*.
Taipei: Orient Cultural Service, 1972. 102 p. (Asian Folklore and Social Life monographs, 32) (Revision of *Tai Yu Shan: The cultural geography of a South Chinese island*, masters thesis in Geography, U. of California, Berkeley, 1966)
Subj 21.3 24.1 ▪ 24.5 24.6 29 42 62

15798 CSU P P4 G9.5 1928–1972
Dwyer, Denis John, 1933–.
'Problems of urbanization: The example of Hong Kong.' In *Land use and resources: Studies in applied geography*. [Sole entry]
London: Institute of British Geographers, 1968, 169–185. (IBG special publications, 1)
Subj 21.3 55 ▪ 21.1 21.2 58

15799 DLC O P2 G1.2 1911–1972
Glushchenko, Ivan Evdokimovich.
'Velikie preobrazovaniia v velikoi strane' (Great changes in a great country). In *U zarubezhnykh druzei* (With foreign friends), by I. E. Glushchenko. [Sole entry]
Moscow: Izd-vo Akad. nauk SSSR, 1957, 129–208.
Subj 14 17 21.3 26.3 66 ▪ 21.1 32.2 37 47 55 65

15800 CSH O P8 G9.5 1644–1972
Hayes, James William, 1930–.
'Visit to villages in the Sai Kung district [i.e., Hsi-kung, Hong Kong].' In *Aspects of social organization in the New Territories*, edited by Hong Kong Branch, Royal Asiatic Society. [Selective entry]
Hong Kong: Cathay Press, 1964, 41–42.
Subj 21.3 42 43 ▪ 23 24.1

15801 MCH O P3 G5.1 –1972
Heidenreich, Robert.
'Beobachtungen zum Stadtplan von Peking' (Observations on the layout of Peking).
NDG 81 (1957), 32–37.
Subj 21.3 ▪ 62

15802 HKU FP P2 G9.5 1842–1972
Hudson, Brian James.
Land reclamation in Hong Kong.
Unpublished doctoral dissertation, Dept. of Architecture, U. of Hong Kong, 1970. 315 p.
Subj 21.3 24.1 ▪ 21.4 24.2

15803 NNC S P3 G9.5 1842–1972
Hughes, R- H-.
'Hong Kong: An urban study.'
GJ 117, 1 (Mar. 1951), 1–23.
Subj 21.3 ▪ 21.1

15804 NIC U P4 G1.1 –1972
Kuo, Leslie T. C. (Kuo Tse-ch'iu), 1914–.
'Use of urban and suburban land in China.'
THJ new (2nd) series 4, 1 (June 1963), 119–125. [Combined issue with vol. 3, no. 2.]
Subj 21.3

15805 CSU PO P2 G9.5 –1972
Lo, C. P.
'Changing population distribution in the Hong Kong New Territories.'
AAAG 58, 2 (June 1968), 273–284.
Subj 21 21.1 21.3 ▪ 21.2 24.2

15806 DLC P P3 G5.1 –1972
Nikitin, Nikolai Nikolaevich, 1897–.
Pekin, stolitsa Kitaiskoi Narodnoi Respubliki (Peking, capital of the People's Republic of China).
Moscow: Geografgiz, 1950. 69 p.
Subj 17 21.3 32 ▪ 14.4 21.1 24.2 32.2 66

15807 NNC P P3 G1.2 –1972
P'eng, Tso-chih.
'Chinesischer Städtebau, mit besonderer Berücksichtigung der Stadt Peking' (City planning in China, with special attention to Peking).
NDG 89/90 (Juni 1961), 5–80. (Doctoral dissertation, Technische Hochschule Aachen)
SUBJ 21.3 62 ▪ 22 24.2 55 72

15808 NNC U P2 G9.5 1842–1972
So, C. L.
'Land use of Hong Kong island.' In *Symposium on land use and mineral deposits in Hong Kong, southern China and South-east Asia*, edited by Sydney George Davis. [Selective entry]
Hong Kong: Hong Kong U. Press, 1964, 43–48.
SUBJ 21.3 ▪ 21.1 24.1 55

15809 NNP O P8 G9.5 –1972
Tang, Kwong-hon.
'The walled village communities of rural Hong Kong.'
Hemisphere 9, 11 (Nov. 1965), 12–16.
SUBJ 21.3 ▪ 29 55

15810 MCH FP P2 G5.1 1895–1972
Wei Hsin-chen and Chu Yun-ch'eng (Chu Yün-ch'eng).
Economic geography of T'ang-shan, mimeo. Tr. of *T'ang-shan ching chi ti li* (An economic geography of Tangshan); Peking: Shang wu yin shu kuan, 1960; 58 p.
Washington, D.C.: U.S. Joint Publications Research Service, 9 Nov. 1961. 68 p. (JPRS 10,937; MC 1390/1962)
SUBJ 21.1 21.3 24.4 ▪ 14.3 24.1 24.2 26.4 66

15811 CSU P P2 G4.3 –1972
Wiens, Herold Jacob, 1912–1971.
'The historical and geographical role of Urumchi, capital of Chinese Central Asia.'
AAAG 53, 4 (Dec. 1963), 441–464.
SUBJ 21.1 21.3 24.1 24.4 ▪ 12 22 24.2 25

1949-1972

15812 NNC O P5 G5.0 1949–1972
'Construction et reconstruction en Chine' (Construction and redevelopment in China).
Recherches internationales à la lumière du marxisme (Paris) 2, 20/21 (1960), 78–109.
SUBJ 21.3 ▪ 21.1

15813 CSU F P2 G9.5 1949–1972
Anderson, Eugene Newton, Jr., 1941–.
'Changing patterns of land use in rural Hong Kong.'
Pacific viewpoint 9, 1 (May 1968), 33–50.
SUBJ 21.3 24.1 62 ▪ 21.1 21.4 30

15814 CSU O P7 G9.5 1949–1972
Anderson, Eugene Newton, Jr., 1941–.
'Feed the world: A food tract. First of two parts.'
Ecology; the j. of cultural transformation 3 (1970), 5–18.
SUBJ 21.3 24.1 ▪ 26.3 62

15815 CSH O P8 G9.5 1949–1972
Aslett, Michael.
'Lantao [i.e., Ta-yü shan, Hong Kong] in the rain.'
FEER 43, 9 (27 Feb. 1964), 493–496.
SUBJ 21.3 24.4 ▪ 24.1

15816 CSH F P8 G9.4 1949–1972
Chen, Cheng-siang (Ch'en Cheng-hsiang), 1920–.
'Scattered settlements in the Taipei basin.'
Memoirs of the College of Agriculture, National Taiwan U. 3, 1 (Oct. 1953), 35–48. [In Chinese as well as English] [Separately reprinted—Taipei: Fu-min Geographical Institute of Economic Development, 1953. 14 p. (Fu-min research reports, 36)]
SUBJ 21.3

15817 CSU U P3 G5.1 1949–1972
Ch'eng shih chien she. Pien chi pu. (Editorial Dept.).
'Great achievements of the nation's capital in urban reconstruction during the last decade.' Tr. of 'Shou tu shih nien lai ch'eng shih chien she ti wei ta ch'eng chiu' (The great achievements in urban development in Peking during the past decade); *Ch'eng shih chien she* 1959, 10 (Oct.), 14–19. In *Urban construction in Communist China (Part 2)*, mimeo., compiled by U.S. Joint Publications Research Service. [Selective entry]
Washington, D.C.: JPRS, 15 Aug. 1960, 18–29. (JPRS 5258; MC 17,410/1960)
SUBJ 21.3 24.2 28 55 ▪ 17 24.4 31 56

15818 NNC P P8 G9.5 1949–1972
Chiu Tze Nang (Chao Tze-neng), 1932–.
'Agricultural resettlements in the Sai Kung [i.e., Hsi-kung] peninsula, Hong Kong.' In *Symposium on land use and mineral deposits in Hong Kong, southern China and South-east Asia*, edited by Sydney George Davis. [Selective entry]
Hong Kong: Hong Kong U. Press, 1964, 70–74.
SUBJ 21.3 ▪ 24.1

15819 CBU F P7 G9.2 1949–1972
Chung-shan ta hsüeh. Ti li hsi. Jen min kung she kuei hua kung tso tui. Shao-kuan fen tui. (Chung-shan U. Dept. of Geography. Commune Planning Team. Shao-kuan Detachment).
'Relocation of inhabitation spots at Weng-kiang people's commune.' Tr. of 'Kuang-tung Wen-yüan hsien Weng-chiang jen min kung she chü min fen p'ei chih wen t'i' (The distribution of settlements in Weng-chiang commune, Weng-yüan *hsien*, Kwangtung); in *Jen min kung she ching chi kuei hua yü ching chi ti li wen chi* (Collected essays on economic planning and economic geography of the communes); Peking: K'o hsüeh ch'u pan she, 1959, 56–64. In *Economic plans and economic geography of people's communes*, mimeo., jointly edited by Chung-kuo ti li hsüeh hui (Geographical Society of China) *with* Ti li yen chiu so (Institute of Geography), Chung-kuo k'o hsüeh yüan (Chinese Academy of Sciences). [Selective entry]
Washington, D.C.: U.S. Joint Publications Research Service, 25 Feb. 1963, 129–155. (JPRS 17,789; MC 6864/1963) [Xerox copyflo available—New York: CCM Information Corp., Research and Microfilm Publications. (Scholarly Book Translation Series, 421)]
SUBJ 21.3 24.1 ▪ 24

15820 NNC PO P2 G9.5 1949–1972
Clarke, R- C-, and J- E- Jackson.
'Land for industry and factors influencing location in Hong Kong.' In *Symposium on land use and mineral deposits in Hong Kong, southern China and South-east Asia*, edited by Sydney George Davis. [Selective entry]
Hong Kong: Hong Kong U. Press, 1964, 3–19.
SUBJ 21.3 24 24.1 ▪ 21 21.2 45

15821 CSU P P4 G9.5 1949–1972
Dwyer, Denis John, 1933–.
'Urban squatters: The relevance of the Hong Kong experience.'
AS 10, 7 (July 1970), 607–613.
SUBJ 21.3 55 ▪ 21.1 21.2

15822 CSH PO P3 G9.4 1949–1972
Feng, Yu-kon (Feng Yü-k'un), 1902–.
'Urbanization policy and metropolitan planning in Taiwan.'
IFC 25, 5 (May 1966), 20–30; 25, 6 (June 1966), 23–42.
SUBJ 21 21.1 21.2 21.3 ▪ 24.2 24.3 28

15823 MCH F P3 G1.3 1949–1972
Gellert, Johannes Fürchtegott, 1904–.
'Geographische Beobachtungen in chinesischen Grosstädten' (Geographic observations in large Chinese cities).
Geographische Berichte 7, 2 (Okt. 1962), 142–152.
SUBJ 21.3 ▪ 21.1 24

15824 CBU FP P4 G9.5 1949–1972
Golger, Otto Johann.
Squatters and resettlement, symptoms of an urban crisis: Environmental conditions of low-standard housing in Hong Kong.
Wiesbaden: Harrassowitz, 1972. 112 p. (Revision of *An environmental study of squatter and resettlement housing in Hong Kong . . .*, doctoral dissertation, Dept. of Architecture, U. of Hong Kong, 1969)
SUBJ 20 21.1 21.3 55 ▪ 24 28

15825 CBU F P2 G9.4 1949–1972
Huang, Ta-chou, 1936–.
'The process of social differentiation in Taiwanese communities.'
Cornell j. of social relations 5, 1 (1970), 1–9. [For a fuller version, see entry 15826.]
SUBJ 11.3 21.3 ▪ 21.4 60

15826 NIC F P2 G9.4 1949–1972
Huang, Ta-chou, 1936–.
Social differentiation in Taiwanese communities.
Unpublished masters thesis in Rural Sociology, Cornell U., 1966. 35 p.
SUBJ 11.3 21.3 ▪ 21.4 60

15827 MCH P P4 G9.5 1949–1972
Johnson, Sheila K-.
'Hong Kong's resettled squatters: A statistical analysis.'
AS 6, 11 (Nov. 1966), 643–656.
SUBJ 21.1 21.3 55 ▪ 11.2 21.4 22.1 27 41

15828 DLC O P3 G5.1 1949–1972
Kassis, Vadim Borisovich.
Poznakom'tes' s Pekinom (Get acquainted with Peking).
Moscow: Molodaia gvardiia, 1959. 86 p.
Subj 17 21.1 21.3 28 ▪ 24.3 24.4 31 52 55 66

15829 CSU PO P2 G9.5 1949–1972
Küchler, Johannes, and Sum Kong-sut.
'Das räumliche Ungleichgewicht Hong Kongs: Resultat einer liberalischen Wirtschafts- und Raumpolitik' (Regional imbalance in Hong Kong: Result of a liberal economic and land policy).
Die Erde 102, 2/3 (1971), 141–179.
Subj 21 21.3 ▪ 21.4 22 24.1 24.4

15830 DLC O P2 G1.3 1949–1972
Kunaev, Dinmukhamed Akhmetovich, 1912?–.
30 dnei v narodnom Kitae: putevye zametki (Thirty days in the People's Republic of China: Travel notes).
Alma-Ata: Kazgosizdat, 1955. 158 p.
Subj 14.4 16 17 21.3 ▪ 14.1 16.1 66

15831 MCH P P7 G1.2 1949–1972
[La Dany, Ladislao] ———, 1914–.
'The transformation of the communes.'
CNA 358 (3 Feb. 1961), 1–7.
Subj 21.3 34.1 ▪ 21.4 22 32.1 45

15832 CSU O P4 G1.2 1949–1972
Lagneau, Guy.
'Chine en chantier' (Urban planning in China).
CFC 1 (mars 1959), 88–103.
Subj 21.1 21.3 ▪ 24 24.2 24.4

15833 NNC PO P4 G9.5 1949–1972
[Lai, Chuen-yan] David C. Y. Lai (Li Ch'üan-en), 1937–, and Denis John Dwyer, 1933–.
'Kwun Tong [i.e., Kuan-t'ang], Hong Kong: A study of industrial planning.'
Town planning review 35, 4 (Jan. 1965), 299–310.
Subj 21.3 24.4

15834 NNC PO P4 G9.5 1949–1972
[Lai, Chuen-yan] David C. Y. Lai (Li Ch'üan-en), 1937–, and Denis John Dwyer, 1933–.
'Tsuen Wan [i.e., Ch'üan-wan], a new industrial town in Hong Kong.'
GR 54, 2 (Apr. 1964), 151–169.
Subj 21.3 ▪ 21.1 24.4

15835 CSU O P3 G9.5 1949–1972
Leeds, P- F-.
'Housing in Hong Kong: Post war problems.'
J. of administration overseas 5, 3 (July 1966), 184–193.
Subj 21.3 22 55 ▪ 21.1 28 38

15836 CSU U P3 G5.4 1949–1972
Li Ch'eng-hsien.
'The rebirth of Lo-Yang, the ancient capital of nine dynasties.' Tr. of 'Chiu chao ku tu: Lo-yang ti hsin sheng'; *Ch'eng shih chien she* 1959, 10 (Oct.), 34–35. In *Urban construction in Communist China (Part 2)*, mimeo., compiled by U.S. Joint Publications Research Service. [Selective entry]
Washington, D.C.: JPRS, 15 Aug. 1960, 50–56. (JPRS 5258; MC 17,410/1960)
Subj 21.3 24.2 ▪ 24.4 55

15837 CSU O P7 G6.1 1949–1972
Li Teh-hua (Li Te-hua), et al.
'Plan for Ch'ing-p'u hsien and Hung-chi people's commune.' Tr. of 'Ch'ing-p'u hsien chi Hung-ch'i jen min kung she kuei hua' (Ch'ing-p'u *hsien* [Kiangsu] and the planning of Hung-ch'i commune); *Chien chu hsüeh pao* 1958, 10 (Oct.), 1–6. In *Plans and data on four Chinese communes*, mimeo., compiled by U.S. Joint Publications Research Service. [Analytic entry]
Washington, D.C.: JPRS, 10 Mar. 1959, 1–23. (JPRS 564D; MC 6343/1959)
Subj 21.3 55 ▪ 21 28

15838 CSH F P3 G9.5 1949–1972
Liang, C. S. (Liang Ch'i-shan).
'Urban land use in Hong Kong and Kowloon. Part 1, Tsim-Sha-Tsui district. Part 2, The central business district: Its structure and development trend.'
CCJ 6, 1 (Nov. 1966), 1–24; 8, 1 (Nov. 1968), 107–132.
Subj 21.3 45 ▪ 21.1 24.2 24.3 34.2

15839 DLC O P3 G1.3 1949–1972
Prikhod'ko, P-.
'Progressivnye cherty kitaiskogo parkostroeniia' (Progressive features of Chinese park construction).
Stroitel'stvo i arkhitektura 9, 1 (ianvar' 1961), 31–34.
Subj 21.3 ▪ 31

15840 CSU O P7 G9.2 1949–1972
Rose, John.
'Sinjao, a Chinese commune [i.e., Hsin-ts'ao commune, Hua *hsien*, Canton municipality].'
Geography 51, 233 (Nov. 1966), 379–383.
Subj 21.3

15841 CSU O P3 G1.3 1949–1972
Schenk, Hans.
'Notes on urban spatial planning and development in China.'
EH 11, 3 (1972), 34–41.
Subj 21.3 55 ▪ 11.1 24.2

15842 MCH P P2 G9.5 1949–1972
Schmitt, Robert C-.
'Implications of density in Hong Kong.'
J. of the American Institute of Planners 29 (Aug. 1963), 210–217.
Subj 21.3 ▪ 21 21.1 55

15843 CSU O P7 G6.1 1949–1972
Shang-hai shih min yung chien chu she chi yüan. Jen min kung she she chi tsu. (Civil Architectural Designing Institute of Shanghai. [Commune Designing Team]).
'Housing plan and design for Shanghai municipal 1 July people's commune.' Tr. of 'Shang-hai shih "Ch'i i" jen min kung she chü min tien kuei hua she chi' (The planning of residential settlements in 'Ch'i-i' commune, Shanghai municipality); *Chien chu hsüeh pao* 1958, 10 (Oct.), 7–13. In *Plans and data on four Chinese communes*, mimeo., compiled by U.S. Joint Publications Research Service. [Analytic entry]
Washington, D.C.: JPRS, 10 Mar. 1959, 24–47. (JPRS 564D; MC 6343/1959)
Subj 21.3 55 ▪ 21 24.1 41

15844 CSU U P3 G6.1 1949–1972
Shanghai. Ch'eng shih chien she chü. Pan kung shih. (Urban Construction Bureau. [Administrative Office]).
'The new Shanghai in socialist construction.' Tr. of 'Chien she she hui chu i ti hsin Shang-hai' (Developing a new socialist Shanghai); *Ch'eng shih chien she* 1959, 10 (Oct.), 28–31. In *Urban construction in Communist China (Part 2)*, mimeo., compiled by U.S. Joint Publications Research Service. [Selective entry]
Washington, D.C.: JPRS, 15 Aug. 1960, 34–44. (JPRS 5258; MC 17,410/1960)
Subj 21.3 55 ▪ 24.2 24.4 28

15845 CSU P P7 G1.2 1949–1972
Skinner, George William, 1925–.
'Marketing and social structure in rural China, Part III.'
JAS 24, 3 (May 1965), 363–399. [See also Audrey Gladys Donnithorne and G. W. Skinner, 'Communications'; *JAS* 25, 2 (Feb. 1966), 319–324.] [Separately reprinted—Indianapolis: Bobbs-Merrill College Division, 1967. 36 p. (Bobbs-Merrill reprint series in geography, G-628)]
Subj 14.3 19 21.3 24.3 32.1 ▪ 11.3 14 22 22.1 24.1 24.2 30 34.1

15846 MCH F P3 G5.1 1949–1972
Stratil-Sauer, Gustav.
'Zur Stadtgeographie von Peking' (The urban geography of Peking).
PGM 103, 3 (1959), 180–189.
Subj 21.3 ▪ 24

15847 CBU O P2 G2.3 1949–1972
Ta-lien shih fan hsüeh yüan. Ti li hsi. Ching chi ti li chiao yen shih. (Dairen Teachers College. Dept. of Geography. Economic Geography Research Center).
'Experiences on regional planning.' Tr. of 'Chuan ch'ü chi ch'ü yü kuei hua fang fa ch'u pu ching yen' (Preliminary experiences in regional planning for special districts); in *Jen min kung she ching chi kuei hua yü ching chi ti li wen chi* (Collected essays on economic planning and economic geography of the communes); Peking: K'o hsüeh ch'u pan she, 1959, 162–176. In *Economic plans and economic geography of people's communes*, mimeo., jointly edited by Chung-kuo ti li hsüeh hui (Geographical Society of China) *with* Ti li yen chiu so (Institute of Geography), Chung-kuo k'o hsüeh yüan (Chinese Academy of Sciences). [Selective entry]
Washington, D.C.: U.S. Joint Publications Research Service, 25 Feb. 1963, 384–417. (JPRS 17,789; MC 6864/1963) [Xerox copyflo available—New York: CCM Information Corp., Research and Microfilm Publications. (Scholarly Book Translation Series, 421)]
Subj 21.3 24 24.1 24.4 ▪ 14 24.2

15848 NIC P P4 G9.4 1949–1972
Taiwan. Chien she t'ing. Kung kung kung ch'eng chü. (Construction Office. Public Works Bureau), comp.
Chung Hsing village, a new community in Central Taiwan, Republic of China.
Taipei: Kung kung kung ch'eng chü, 1961. 62 p.
Subj 21.3 ▪ 55

15849 CSU O P7 G5.1 1949–1972
T'ien-chin ta hsüeh. Chien chu hsi. Hsiao-chan kuei hua tsu. (Tientsin U. Dept. of Architecture. [Hsiao-chan Planning Group]).
'Preliminary plan and design of Tientsin Hsiao-chan people's commune.' Tr. of 'T'ien-chin shih Hsiao-chan jen min kung she ti ch'u pu kuei hua she chi' (Preliminary planning of Hsiao-chan commune, Tientsin municipality); *Chien chu hsüeh pao* 1958, 10 (Oct.), 14–18. In *Plans and data on four Chinese communes*, mimeo., compiled by U.S. Joint Publications Research Service. [Analytic entry]
Washington, D.C.: JPRS, 10 Mar. 1959, 48–64. (JPRS 564D; MC 6343/1959)
SUBJ 21.3 ▪ 24.1 55

15850 NIC FP P2 G9.5 1949–1972
Tregear, Thomas Refoy, 1897–.
A survey of land use in Hong Kong and the New Territories.
Hong Kong: Hong Kong U. Press, 1958. 75 p. (World Land Use Survey, Regional monographs, 1)
SUBJ 21.3 24.1 ▪ 21 21.2 21.4 24.2 24.4

15851 CSH O P3 G5.1 1949–1972
Tu Tien-feng (T'u T'ien-feng).
'The architectural design of Hungshun alley, Tientsin.' Tr. of 'T'ien-chin shih Hung-shun li she hui chu i ta chia t'ing chien chu she chi chieh shao' (Introduction to architectural designs for socialist living in Hung-shun lane, Tientsin municipality); *Chien chu hsüeh pao* 1958, 10 (Oct.), 34–35. [Abridged tr.]
CB 544 (14 Jan. 1959), 49–52.
SUBJ 21.3 55 ▪ 21.4

15852 CSH FP P2 G9.4 1949–1972
Van Alstyne, Arthur James, Jr., 1928–.
'Urban influences on rural communities: A Taiwanese example.'
CCJ 7, 2 (May 1968), 197–245. [For fuller treatment, see entry 15655.]
SUBJ 21.1 21.3 ▪ 17 21 21.4 23 24.1 24.2 30 51 55 56

15853 CSH O P7 G6.1 1949–1972
Wang Chi-chung.
'The rural planning of the Hsien Feng cooperative in suburban area of Shanghai.' Tr. of 'Shang-hai chiao ch'ü Hsien-feng nung yeh she nung ts'un kuei hua' (Rural planning of Hsien-feng agricultural producers' cooperative [T'ang-nan *hsiang*, Pei-chiao *ch'ü*], Shanghai municipality); *Chien chu hsüeh pao* 1958, 10 (Oct.), 24–33. [Abridged tr.]
CB 544 (14 Jan. 1959), 35–41.
SUBJ 21.3 ▪ 24.1 55

15854 CSU O P7 G6.1 1949–1972
Wang Hua, Wu Hsin-chung, and Wan Kuo-ch'iang. [Tr. erroneously gives second author as Wu Chung-hsin.]
'Scheme and design plan of a Shanghai people's commune new village.' Tr. of 'Shang-hai shih i ko jen min kung she hsin ts'un ti kuei hua she chi fang an' (The planning of a 'new village' in a commune in Shanghai municipality); *Chien chu hsüeh pao* 1958, 10 (Oct.), 19–23. In *Plans and data on four Chinese communes*, mimeo., compiled by U.S. Joint Publications Research Service. [Analytic entry]
Washington, D.C.: JPRS, 10 Mar. 1959, 65–79. (JPRS 564D; MC 6343/1959)
SUBJ 21.3 55 ▪ 24 24.2

15855 CBU O P7 G1.2 1949–1972
Wang Wei-p'ing and Chen Chou-hua (Ch'en Chou-hua).
'Some questions of methodology in commune planning.' Tr. of 'Jen min kung she kuei hua kung tso fang fa ti chi ko wen t'i'; in *Jen min kung she ching chi kuei hua yü ching chi ti li wen chi* (Collected essays on economic planning and economic geography of the communes); Peking: K'o hsüeh ch'u pan she, 1959, 79–82. In *Economic plans and economic geography of people's communes*, mimeo., jointly edited by Chung-kuo ti li hsüeh hui (Geographical Society of China) *with* Ti li yen chiu so (Institute of Geography), Chung-kuo k'o hsüeh yüan (Chinese Academy of Sciences). [Selective entry]
Washington, D.C.: U.S. Joint Publications Research Service, 25 Feb. 1963, 190–198. (JPRS 17,789; MC 6864/1963) [Xerox copyflo available—New York: CCM Information Corp., Research and Microfilm Publications. (Scholarly Book Translation Series, 421)]
SUBJ 21.3 24

15856 [2]DLC O P2 G1.2 1949–1972
Wasilewska, Wanda (Vanda Vasilevskaia), 1905–.
30 dni w Chinach (Thirty days in China).
Warsaw: Ministerstwa obrony narodowej, 1957. 320 p.
Pod nebom Kitaia (Under the sky of China).
Moscow: Gos. izd-vo khudozh. lit-ry, 1958. 310 p.
SUBJ 21.3 32 66 ▪ 14.1 15 16.4 55 56

15857 CSU P P2 G4.3 1949–1972
Wiens, Herold Jacob, 1912–1971.
'The Ili valley as a geographic region of Hsin-chiang.'
CS 7, 15 (1 Aug. 1969), 1–19.
SUBJ 21.3 24 ▪ 24.1 24.2 24.4

15858 CSU P P2 G9.5 1949–1972
Wigglesworth, J- M-.
'The development of new towns.' In *Asian urbanization: A Hong Kong casebook*, edited by Denis John Dwyer. [Analytic entry]
Hong Kong: Hong Kong U. Press, 1971, 48–69. (Centre of Asian Studies series, 3)
SUBJ 21.1 21.3 24 45 ▪ 21.2 21.4

15859 CSU FP P2 G9.5 1949–1972
Wong, Luke S. K.
'The Aplichau [i.e., Ya-li-chou] squatter area: A case study.' In *Asian urbanization: A Hong Kong casebook*, edited by Denis John Dwyer. [Analytic entry]
Hong Kong: Hong Kong U. Press, 1971, 89–110. (Centre of Asian Studies series, 3)
SUBJ 21.3 24 55 ▪ 21 21.4 24.2 24.3 24.4

15860 CSU O P3 G5.3 1949–1972
Yu To (Yü To).
'Tsingtao: A coastal city.' Tr. of 'Pin hai ch'eng shih: Ch'ing-tao'; *Ch'eng shih chien she* 1959, 10 (Oct.), 32–33. In *Urban construction in Communist China (Part 2)*, mimeo., compiled by U.S. Joint Publications Research Service. [Selective entry]
Washington, D.C.: JPRS, 15 Aug. 1960, 45–49. (JPRS 5258; MC 17,410/1960)
SUBJ 21.3 28 55 ▪ 24.2

15861 MCH P P2 G9.4 1949–1972
Yuan, D. Y., and Edward G- Stockwell.
'The rural-urban continuum: A case study of Taiwan.'
Rural sociology 29, 3 (Sept. 1964), 247–260.
SUBJ 21 21.3 ▪ 21.1 21.2 21.4 27 29

21.4 REGIONAL LABOR FORCE AND LOCAL DIVISION OF LABOR

地方勞動力及職業分化

地方労働力及び職業分化

1644-1911

15862 CSU O P2 G8.1 1895–1911
Hutson, James.
'West Szechuan's most remarkable work.'
EAM 4 (1905), 145–161.
SUBJ 21.4 23 24.1 24.2 ▪ 22.2 28

15863 CSU P P2 G7.1 1644–1911
Liu, Ts'ui-jung, 1941–.
'Dike construction in Ching-chou [*fu*, Hupeh]: A study based on the "T'i-fang chih" [Treatise on water conservancy] section of the *Ching-chou fu-chih* [Prefectural gazetteer of Ching-chou].'
PC 23 (July 1970), 1–28.
SUBJ 21.4 22 24.5 24.6 ▪ 22.1 24.1 35 70

1644-1949

15864 NNC P P2 G1.3 1842–1928
Kroker, Eduard Josef M-, 1913–.
'Dienst- und Werkverträge in Chinesischen gewohnheitsrecht' (Service and work contracts in Chinese customary law).
ZDMG 107 (1957), 130–160.
SUBJ 21.4 22.2 26.2 ▪ 12.2 24.1 24.3 24.4 28

1911-1949

15865 NNC P P3 G9.2 1911–1928
'Census of occupation for Canton, 1928.'
NWSS 3, 31 (4 Aug. 1930), 149, 152.
SUBJ 21.4 ▪ 28 47

15866 MCH U P3 G5.1 1911–1949
'The Kailan mining administration and its employees.'
Far Eastern review 27, 6 (June 1931), 359–366.
SUBJ 21.4 28 ▪ 26.4

15867 CSH P P2 G2.3 1911–1928
'Rabochii vopros v iuzhnoi Man'chzhurii' (The labor question in southern Manchuria). Tr. of 'Manshū rōdō mondai sūteki ichi kōsatsu' (A statistical examination of labor problems in

Manchuria); *Keizai shiryō* 13, 5 (May 1927), 1–79. [Condensed tr.]
VM 1928, 4, 39–44.
SUBJ 21.4 ▪ 16.4

15868 NNC P P3 G5.1 1928–1949
'Unemployment in Peiping, 1928–1929.'
NWSS 4, 3 (19 Jan. 1931), 13, 16–18.
SUBJ 21.4 ▪ 26.4 28

15869 NIC F P3 G6.1 1928–1949
Bates, Miner Searle, 1897–.
The Nanking population: Employment, earnings and expenditures.
Nanking: Nanking International Relief Committee; Shanghai: Shanghai Mercury Press, 1939. 32 p.
SUBJ 21.1 21.4 28 ▪ 24 41 47 55

15870 NNC PO P2 G1.5 1928–1949
Pai Yua-yuan (Pai Jo-yüan).
'Labour tax in the building of the Szechwan-Hunan highway.' Tr. of 'Ch'uan Hsiang kung lu fu chin ti min kung men' (Conscripted labor on the Szechwan-Hunan highway); *Chung-kuo nung ts'un* 3, 7 (July 1937), 72–74. In *Agrarian China*, compiled by Institute of Pacific Relations. [Selective entry]
Chicago: U. of Chicago Press, 1939, 110–112.
SUBJ 21.4 ▪ 22.1 24.2 28

15871 CSH F P3 G6.1 1928–1949
Shanghai. She hui chü. (Bureau of Social Affairs).
Wage rates in Shanghai.
Shanghai: She hui chü, 1935. 12, 178 p. [In Chinese as well as English]
SUBJ 21.4 26.4 ▪ 24.4 28 47

15872 NNC O P7 G5.1 1911–1928
Veen, H- van der.
'Conservancy problems in Chih-li.' In *Some aspects of Chinese life and thought*, compiled by College of Chinese Studies, Peking. [Sole entry]
Shanghai: Kwang Hsueh, 1918, 137–154. [Reprinted in *Readings in economics for China*, compiled and edited by Charles Frederick Remer. (Selective entry.) Shanghai: Commercial Press, 1922, 581–599.]
SUBJ 21.4 24.2 28 ▪ 62

1911-1972
(including 1644-1972)

15873 CSH U P2 G2.0 1928–1972
Huang, Cheng Wang.
'Labor force and labor relations.' In *A regional handbook on Northeast China*, compiled by Far Eastern and Russian Institute, U. of Washington. [Selective entry]
New Haven: Human Relations Area Files, 1956, 254–270. (HRAF subcontractor's monographs, 61; Washington 9)
SUBJ 21.4 ▪ 16.3 16.4 18 21.2

15874 MCH P P1 G9.4 1895–1972
Myers, Ramon Hawley, 1929–.
'Economic growth and population change in Taiwan.'
Malayan economic review 8, 2 (Oct. 1963), 104–117.
SUBJ 14 21.4 58 ▪ 12 21

15875 CSH P P2 G9.4 1928–1972
Stanford U. China Project.
'Labor.' In *Taiwan (Formosa)*, compiled by the organization cited. [Selective entry]
New Haven: Human Relations Area Files, 1956, vol. 1, 222–256. (HRAF subcontractor's monographs, 31; Stanford 5)
SUBJ 21.4 ▪ 16.3 16.4 18 36.4

1949-1972

15876 CSU P P3 G9.5 1949–1972
Agassi, Judith Buber, 1924–.
'Social structure and social stratification in Hong Kong.' In *Hong Kong: A society in transition*, edited by Ian C- Jarvie and Joseph Agassi. [Analytic entry]
New York: Praeger, 1969, 65–75.
SUBJ 21.4 26 ▪ 21.2 28

15877 NNC FP P8 G1.1 1949–1972
Barnett, Arthur Doak, 1921–.
'Conscript labor and public works in Communist China.'
AUFS-EAS 1, 5 (15 Oct. 1952), 1–9. [Reprinted as 'Public works.' In *Communist China: The early years, 1949–55*, by A. D. Barnett. (Selective entry.) New York: Praeger, 1964, 199–209.]
SUBJ 21.4 24.2 ▪ 22.1 26.3

15878 CSU F P2 G9.4 1949–1972
Bessac, Francis Bagnall, 1922–.
'The effect of industrialization upon the allocation of labor in a Taiwanese village.'
JCS 6 (1969), 13–51.
SUBJ 21.4 24.1 ▪ 24.4 28 41 47 50

15879 MCH F P2 G9.4 1949–1972
Chang, Kowie (Chang Kuo-wei), 1901–.
'The measurement of employment and unemployment in Taiwan.' Tr. of 'T'ai-wan chiu yeh yü shih yeh ti ts'e liang'; *She hui k'o hsüeh lun ts'ung* (Taipei) 14 (July 1964), 1–46. [Tr. inferred]
IFC 22, 5 (Nov. 1964), 2–33; 22, 6 (Dec. 1964), 27–50.
SUBJ 21.4

15880 NIC O P8 G5.2 1949–1972
Chang Yü-san.
'An investigation of supply-wage system in a people's commune in Shansi.' Tr. of 'Kuan yü jen min kung she shih hsing pan kung chi pan kung tzu ti tiao ch'a' (Survey of the implementation of the half-supply half-wage system in [Hung-ch'i] commune [T'ai-ku *hsien*, Shansi]); *Hung ch'i* 1958, 10 (16 Oct.), 28–32.
ECMM 155 (23 Jan. 1959), 21–26.
SUBJ 21.4 28 ▪ 24.1 26.3

15881 NNC O P3 G6.1 1949–1972
Chao Tsu-kang (Chao Tsu-k'ang).
'Further organize the city people and liberate the housewives.' Tr. of 'Pa ch'eng shih jen min chin i pu tsu chih ch'i lai, pa chia t'ing fu nü chin i pu chieh fang ch'u lai'; *Jen min jih pao* 10 Apr. 1960, 11. In *Speeches given at second session of Second National People's Congress, Communist China*, mimeo., compiled by U.S. Joint Publications Research Service. [Selective entry]
Washington, D.C.: JPRS, 28 Dec. 1960, 41–49. (JPRS 6483; MC 7699/1961)
SUBJ 21.4 47 ▪ 28 55

15882 NNC U P7 G1.2 1949–1972
Ch'en Cheng-jen, 1905–.
'On ownership system and distribution system in people's communes.' Tr. of 'Lun jen min kung she ti so yu chih ho fen p'ei chih tu' (The systems of ownership and income distribution in the communes); *Jen min jih pao* 18 Oct. 1959, 7.
URS 17, 7 (23 Oct. 1959), 90–104.
SUBJ 21.4 34.1 45 ▪ 24.1 24.5 24.6 28

15883 CSU U P8 G5.1 1949–1972
Chien Wen.
'Conquering the Haiho.' In *China tames her rivers.* [Analytic entry]
Peking: Foreign Languages Press, 1972, 32–42.
SUBJ 11.3 21.4 24.1

15884 CSU U P8 G7.1 1949–1972
Chung Chien.
'Water conservancy on the Chianghan plain [Hupeh].' In *China tames her rivers.* [Analytic entry]
Peking: Foreign Languages Press, 1972, 43–51.
SUBJ 21.3 21.4 24.1 28 ▪ 24.2

15885 CSU U P8 G1.3 1949–1972
Chung Wen.
'Three provinces [Honan, Anhwei, and Kiangsu] unite to control the Huai.' In *China tames her rivers.* [Analytic entry]
Peking: Foreign Languages Press, 1972, 22–31.
SUBJ 14.1 21.4 ▪ 18 24.1

15886 NIC S P7 G1.2 1949–1972
Clairmonte, Frédérick F-.
'Labour mobilization in China's communes.'
United Asia 12, 3 (1960), 230–233. [Special issue: *Labour in Asia*]
SUBJ 21.4 24.1 34.1 ▪ 24.4 26.3

15887 CSU F P8 G9.4 1949–1972
Cohen, Myron Leon, 1937–.
'Variations in complexity among Chinese family groups: The impact of modernization.'
Transactions of the New York Academy of Sciences 2nd series 29, 5 (Mar. 1967), 638–644.
SUBJ 21.4 29 41 ▪ 24.1 26.3 45

15888 MAM P P2 G9.4 1949–1972
Fang, Jeffrey Ming-shan.
Investment in human capital in Taiwan, 1952–1965.
Ann Arbor: University Microfilms (Publ. 69-18,286), 1969. 174 p. (Doctoral dissertation in Economics, U. of Washington)
SUBJ 21.4 ▪ 14 17 56

15889 MCY P P2 G9.4 1949–1972
Free China Relief Assn.
Employment services and vocational assistance to Chinese refugees in Taiwan.
Taipei: Free China Relief Assn., 195? 27 p.
SUBJ 21.4 24 34.1 36.4 ▪ 24.5 27

15890 MCH P P2 G9.4 1949–1972
Fung, Kwok-kwan (Feng Kuo-chün), 1938–.
The growth and utilization of the labor force in Taiwan, 1956–1966.
Unpublished doctoral dissertation in Economics, Harvard U., 1970. 201 p.
Subj 21 21.4 50 ▪ 14 14.3 14.4 16.4 17 24.1 34.2 47 58

15891 CSU P P3 G9.5 1949–1972
Hong Kong. Shipbuilding and Ship Repairs Industrial Committee.
Report by the Shipbuilding and Ship Repairs Industrial Committee on the manpower survey of the shipbuilding and ship repairs trades (22nd July 1968 – 27th July 1968).
Hong Kong: Government Printer, 1969. 89 p.
Subj 21.4 26.2 27 ▪ 26.4

15892 CSU P P3 G6.1 1949–1972
Howe, Christopher Barry, 1937–.
'The level and structure of employment and the sources of labor supply in Shanghai, 1949–57.' In *The city in Communist China*, edited by John Wilson Lewis. [Analytic entry]
Stanford: Stanford U. Press, 1971, 215–234.
Subj 21.4 ▪ 21.2

15893 MCY F P2 G9.4 1949–1972
Hsiao Chen-siang (Hsiao Ch'en-hsiang).
'Industrial manpower survey of Taiwan.'
IFC 19, 6 (June 1963), 35–45.
Subj 21.4 ▪ 14 27

15894 CBU O P7 G5.1 1949–1972
Hsieh Kuang-cheng (Hsieh Kuan-cheng).
'Manpower employment and mechanization: Planning at Hsiao-t'ang-shan commune.' Tr. of 'Pei-ching shih Hsiao-t'ang-shan jen min kung she lao tung li ho nung yeh chi hsieh hua kuei hua kung tso ti ch'u pu t'i hui ho ching yen' (Some preliminary lessons and experiences gained in planning for manpower and mechanization in Hsiao-t'ang-shan commune, Peking municipality); in *Jen min kung she ching chi kuei hua yü ching chi ti li wen chi* (Collected essays on economic planning and economic geography of the communes); Peking: K'o hsüeh ch'u pan she, 1959, 152–161. In *Economic plans and economic geography of people's communes*, mimeo., jointly edited by Chung-kuo ti li hsüeh hui (Geographical Society of China) *with* Ti li yen chiu so (Institute of Geography), Chung-kuo k'o hsüeh yüan (Chinese Academy of Sciences). [Selective entry]
Washington, D.C.: U.S. Joint Publications Research Service, 25 Feb. 1963, 365–383. (JPRS 17,789; MC 6864/1963) [Xerox copyflo available—New York: CCM Information Corp., Research and Microfilm Publications. (Scholarly Book Translation Series, 421)]
Subj 21.4 24.1 ▪ 24 26.3

15895 CSU U P8 G1.3 1949–1972
Hung Nung, pseud.?
'Twenty years work on the Huai river.' In *China tames her rivers*. [Analytic entry]
Peking: Foreign Languages Press, 1972, 15–21.
Subj 11.3 14.1 21.4 ▪ 24.1

15896 NIC P P7 G1.2 1949–1972
Ishikawa Shigeru, 1918–.
'Rural communes: A reassessment.'
FEER 29, 13 (29 Sept. 1960), 720–723.
Subj 21.4 24.1 ▪ 22 24 34.1

15897 NNC O P2 G8.1 1949–1972
Jen Pai-ko. [Tr. erroneously gives author's name as Jen Pai-i.]
Utilization of manpower, Communist China, mimeo. Tr. of 'Chieh yüeh lao tung li shih tseng ch'an chieh yüeh yün tung ti chung hsin huan chieh' (Conserving manpower is the key factor in the movement to increase production and practice economy); *Jen min jih pao* 22 Oct. 1960, 2.
Washington, D.C.: U.S. Joint Publications Research Service, 29 Nov. 1960. 20 p. (JPRS 7131; MC 1133/1961)
Subj 21.4 24 ▪ 24.1 24.3 24.4 32.1 34.2

15898 MAM FP P4 G9.4 1949–1972
Juang, Hwai-I, 1935–.
Rates of return to investment in education in Taiwan and their policy implications: A cost-benefit analysis of the academic high school and the vocational high school.
Ann Arbor: University Microfilms (Publ. 72-19,517), 1972. 201 p. (Doctoral dissertation in Education, Columbia U. [Teachers College])
Subj 17 21.4

15899 CSH O P8 G4.2 1949–1972
Ku Lei.
'The Niehho river [Wu-shan *hsien*, Kansu] flows around the mountains.' In *China's big leap in water conservancy*. [Selective entry]
Peking: Foreign Languages Press, 1958, 64–74.
Subj 21.4 24.1

15900 NIC F P7 G5.4 1949–1972
Miao Yueh-sheng (Miao Yüeh-sheng).
'An investigation of conditions of distribution of income in a people's commune in Honan.' Tr. of 'Ch'ang-ko hsien Ho-shang-ch'iao jen min kung she shou i fen p'ei ch'ing k'uang tiao ch'a' (Survey of the distribution of income in Ho-shang-ch'iao commune, Ch'ang-ko *hsien* [Honan]); *T'ung chi kung tso* 1958, 21 (14 Nov.), 6–7.
ECMM 155 (23 Jan. 1959), 36–39.
Subj 21.4 22 24.6 28 50 ▪ 24.1 24.5 26

15901 HKU F P3 G9.5 1949–1972
Mitchell, Robert Edward, 1930–.
The needs of Hong Kong manufacturing industry for higher level manpower.
Hong Kong: Government Printer, 1968. 126 p. (Special Committee on Higher Education, Second Interim Report, 1968)
Subj 21.4 26.2 ▪ 17 24.4

15902 CSU P P2 G9.4 1949–1972
Sabolo, Yves.
'A structural approach to the projection of occupational categories and its application to South Korea and Taiwan.'
ILR 103, 2 (Feb. 1971), 131–155.
Subj 21.4

15903 NIC F P7 G5.4 1949–1972
Shang-hai she hui k'o hsüeh yüan. Jen min kung she tiao ch'a tsu. (Shanghai College of Social Science. Investigation Unit for Communes).
'Wage assessment in the Kuang-ming people's commune.' Tr. of 'Kuang-ming jen min kung she kung tzu p'ing chi chung ti chi ko wen t'i' (Some problems related to wage scales in Kuang-ming commune [Ju-nan *hsien*, Honan]); *Ts'ai ching yen chiu* 1959, 1 (Jan.), 34–36, 40.
ECMM 164 (13 Apr. 1959), 35–43.
Subj 21.4 28 34.1 ▪ 21 26 47

15904 CBU U P8 G5.2 1949–1972
Shih Chi-yen, et al.
'The red, diligent, and skillful emulation movement in the Shansi villages.' Tr. of 'Hung, ch'in, ch'iao ti ching sai yün tung tsai Shan-hsi nung ts'un' (The campaign for contests to increase redness, diligence, and skill in rural Shansi); *Hung ch'i* 1959, 16 (16 Aug.), 20–23. In *Translations from 'Hung-ch'i' (Red flag) (Peiping, No. 16, 16 August 1959)*, mimeo., compiled by U.S. Joint Publications Research Service. [Selective entry]
Washington, D.C.: JPRS, 23 Oct. 1959, 17–24. (JPRS 989D; MC 17,558/1959)
Subj 21.4 ▪ 34.1 61

15905 HKU P P3 G9.5 1949–1972
Simpson, Raymond Frank, 1925–.
Manpower and employment problems, mimeo.
Hong Kong: Hong Kong Council for Educational Research, 1966. 53, 17 p.
Subj 21.4

15906 CSH P P2 G1.3 1949–1972
Stanford U. China Project.
'Forced labor.' In *Central South China*, compiled by the organization cited. [Selective entry]
New Haven: Human Relations Area Files, 1956, vol. 2, 827–842. (HRAF subcontractor's monographs, 28; Stanford 2)
Subj 21.4 ▪ 12.1 12.2 61

15907 CSH P P2 G1.3 1949–1972
Stanford U. China Project.
'Forced labor.' In *East China*, compiled by the organization cited. [Selective entry]
New Haven: Human Relations Area Files, 1956, vol. 2, 915–936. (HRAF subcontractor's monographs, 29; Stanford 3)
Subj 21.4 ▪ 12.1 12.2

15908 CSH P P2 G5.0 1949–1972
Stanford U. China Project.
'Forced labor.' In *North China*, compiled by the organization cited. [Selective entry]
New Haven: Human Relations Area Files, 1956, vol. 2, 870–892. (HRAF subcontractor's monographs, 27; Stanford 1)
Subj 21.4 22.2 ▪ 24.1 37

15909 NNC P P2 G8.0 1949–1972
Stanford U. China Project.
'Forced labor in Southwest China.' In *Southwest China*, compiled by the organization cited. [Selective entry]

New Haven: Human Relations Area Files, 1956, vol. 2, 919–939. (HRAF subcontractor's monographs, 30; Stanford 4)
Subj 21.4 ▪ 12.1 12.2

15910 CSH O P8 G5.1 1949–1972
Sun Li.
'Building a new world' [study of Hsü-shui *hsien*, Hopei]. In *China's big leap in water conservancy*. [Selective entry]
Peking: Foreign Languages Press, 1958, 1–63.
Subj 21.4 24.1 28 ▪ 24

15911 CSH P P2 G2.0 1949–1972
Tang, Peter S. H. (T'ang Sheng-hao), 1919–.
'Forced labor.' In *A regional handbook on Northeast China*, compiled by Far Eastern and Russian Institute, U. of Washington. [Selective entry]
New Haven: Human Relations Area Files, 1956, 271–284. (HRAF subcontractor's monographs, 61; Washington 9)
Subj 21.4 ▪ 12.1 12.2

15912 CSU P P2 G9.4 1949–1972
Tsai, Yung-mei.
'The growth of modern occupations in Taiwan.'
Eastern anthropologist 22, 2 (May–Aug. 1969), 141–160.
Subj 21.4 ▪ 17 30

15913 CSU O P3 G9.5 1949–1972
Tse, N. Q.
'Industrialization and social adjustment in Hong Kong.'
SSR 52, 3 (Apr. 1968), 237–251.
Subj 21.4 24 28 ▪ 19 21.1 26.1 26.4 34.2 39 41 47

15914 NIC F P7 G2.1 1949–1972
Wang Kuang-lieh.
'An investigation of the part-supply and part-wage system as practiced in a people's commune in Heilungkiang.' Tr. of 'Jen min kung she she yüan shih hsing pan kung chi pan kung tzu chih ti tiao ch'a' (Survey of the half-supply half-wage system for commune members [in Pin-hsi commune, Pin *hsien*, Heilungkiang]); *Ts'ai cheng* 1958, 13 (24 Nov.), 12–13.
ECMM 158 (16 Feb. 1959), 37–41.
Subj 21.4 24 28 55 ▪ 22 26 34.1 41

15915 NIC P P2 G1.2 1949–1972
[Wilson, Richard Garratt] Dick Wilson, 1928–.
'The wage problem in China.'
FEER 26, 1 (1 Jan. 1959), 20–22.
Subj 21.4 26.4 ▪ 16.4

15916 CSU O P7 G8.1 1949–1972
Yang Ch'ao.
'A new thing: Experience of Szechwan province in popularizing the "three fixations, one replacement" labor system.' Tr. of 'I chien hsin shih wu: Ssu-ch'uan sheng t'ui hsing "san ting i ting" lao tung chih tu ti ching yen' (A new event: Experiences in implementing the 'three fixed assignments and eventual substitution' system of labor [participation for cadres] in Szechwan); *Hung ch'i* 1965, 2 (27 Feb.), 25–33. In *Translations from 'Hung-ch'i' (Red flag) No. 2, 1965*, mimeo., compiled by U.S. Joint Publications Research Service. [Sole entry]
Washington, D.C.: JPRS, 18 May 1965, 5–18. (JPRS 30,134; MC 11,050-30/1965)
Subj 21.4 26.1 ▪ 26.4 34.2

15917 CSH P P2 G9.4 1949–1972
Yang, Chia-lin.
'An observation on the population and labor force in Taiwan.' In *Proceedings of Agricultural Economics Seminar held at the College of Agriculture, National Taiwan University, September 16–20, 1958*. [Selective entry]
Taipei: National Taiwan U., 1959, 65–68.
Subj 21 21.4 ▪ 11.3 17 18

15918 CSU P P2 G9.4 1949–1972
Yuan, D. Y.
'Relation of type and size of civil divisions to labor force participation rates in Taiwan.'
Population review 9, 1/2 (Jan.–July 1965), 71–81.
Subj 21.3 21.4 ▪ 18 54 58

22 Local Political Systems

地方政治制度　　地方政治制度

1644-1911

15919 MCH PO P3 G7.1 1842–1895
Bazin, Antoine Pierre Louis, 1799–1863.
'Recherches sur les institutions administratives et municipales de la Chine: 3e mémoire' (Investigations of China's administrative and municipal institutions: Third report).
JA 5e série 4 (déc. 1854), 445–481.
Subj 22 ▪ 22.1 25

15920 CSU P P3 G9.5 1842–1895
Endacott, George Beer.
'Proposals for municipal government in early Hong Kong.'
JOS 3, 1 (1956), 75–82.
Subj 22 22.1

15921 NIC P P3 G6.1 1842–1895
Fairbank, John King, 1907–.
'The provisional system at Shanghai in 1853–1854: Foreign consular administration of the Chinese customs.'
CSPSR 18, 4 (Jan. 1935), 455–504; 19, 1 (Apr. 1935), 65–124.
Subj 22 24.5 25 66 ▪ 32.2

15922 CSU O P3 G9.2 1842–1895
[Fried, ———] Fei Li-te.
'Fire brigades in Canton.'
NQCJ 2, 1 (Jan. 1868), 1–3.
Subj 22

15923 MCH O P3 G9.0 1644–1842
Froger, François, 1676–?
Relation du premier voyage des Français à la Chine fait en 1698 et 1700 sur le vaisseau 'L'Amphitrite' (An account of the first French voyage to China, made in 1698 and 1700 on the ship *Amphitrite*), edited by Ernst Arthur Voretzsch.
Leipzig: Asia Major, 1926. 16, 187 p.
Subj 22 24 26.1 33 ▪ 12 14.2 41

15924 MCH PO P2 G6.2 1842–1895
Havret, Henri, 1848–1901.
La province de Ngan-hoei (Anhwei).
Shanghai: Impr. de la Mission catholique, 1893. 130 p. (Variétés sinologiques, 2)
Subj 12 14 14.5 22 ▪ 21 24 26.1

15925 NIC P P7 G9.5 1842–1911
Hayes, James William, 1930–.
'Cheung Chau [i.e., Chang-chou island, Hong Kong], 1850–1898: Information from commemorative tablets.'
JRAS-HKB 3 (1963), 88–106.
Subj 22 22.1 26.1 39 42 ▪ 24.3 25 27

15926 CSU P P7 G9.5 1842–1911
Hayes, James William, 1930–.
'Land and leadership in the Hong Kong region of Kwangtung in the nineteenth century.'
JRAS-HKB 7 (1967), 91–103.
Subj 22 26.1 ▪ 24.1 24.6 26.2 29 59

15927 NIC P P7 G9.5 -1911
Hayes, James William, 1930–.
'The pattern of life in the New Territories in 1898.'
JRAS-HKB 2 (1962), 75–102.
Subj 22 42 50 ▪ 21 23

15928 CSU P P2 G1.5 1842–1895
Kawabata Genji, 1914–.
'Enforcement of Hsiang-kuan chih-tu system of rural officials in the T'ai-p'ing T'ien-kuo and its background.'
Acta Asiatica (Tokyo) 12 (Mar. 1967), 42–69.
Subj 22 22.1 22.2 ▪ 12 24.1 24.5 25 28

15929 MCH O P3 G6.1 1842–1895
Maclellan, J- W-.
The story of Shanghai, from the opening of the port to foreign trade.
Shanghai: North-China Herald, 1889. 124 p.
Subj 21.3 22 24.3 25 32.2 66 ▪ 24.2 24.4 26.1 26.2

15930 MCH P P3 G6.1 1842–1895
Maybon, Charles Batiste, 1872–1926, and Jean Fredet, 1879–1948.
Histoire de la Concession française de Changhaï (History of the French Concession in Shanghai).
Paris: Plon, 1929. 458 p. [Reprinted—New York: AMS Press, 1972. 458 p.]
Subj 22 24 24.5 25 32.2 ▪ 15 21.3 22.2 28 33 66 72

15931 NNC O P4 G1.3 1644–1895
Meadows, Thomas Taylor.
Desultory notes on the government and people of China and on the Chinese language . . .
London: W. H. Allen, 1847. 16, 250 p. [Reprinted—New York: Praeger, 1970. 256 p.]
Subj 16.1 22 22.2 26.1 ▪ 12 12.2 55 60 63 66

15932 MCH O P8 G9.2 1842–1895
Meyners d'Estrey, Guillaume Henri Jean, 1829–?
'Les Hakka et les Hoklo: l'autonomie des villages en Chine' (Hakka and Hoklo: Village autonomy in China).
R. de géographie 27, 1 (juil. 1890), 29–35; 27, 2 (août 1890), 95–103.
Subj 21.2 22 29 ▪ 22.1 28 41 42

15933 CSU P P2 G5.3 1895–1911
Norem, Ralph Augustine, 1897–.
'The administration of Kiaochow.' In *Kiaochow leased territory*, by R. A. Norem. [Sole entry]
Berkeley, Los Angeles: U. of California Press, 1936, 87–127. (U. of California at Los Angeles publications in social sciences, 6, 1)
SUBJ 22 22.2 ▪ 21 24.5 45

15934 CSH P P2 G1.2 1644–1911
Watt, John Robertson, 1934–.
'Leadership criteria in late Imperial China.'
CSWT 2, 3 (July 1970), 17–39.
SUBJ 12 22 ▪ 16.1

15935 CSU P P2 G1.3 –1895
Wiethoff, Bodo, 1931–.
'Bemerkungen zur Bedeutung der Regionalbeschreibungen (fang-chih)' (Observations on the significance of *fang-chih*, local gazetteers).
OE 15, 2 (Dez. 1968), 149–168.
SUBJ 20 22 ▪ 70

15936 MCH P P2 G2.0 1644–1895
Zhelokhovtseva, E- F-.
'Materialy mestnykh uchrezhdenii Severo-Vostochnogo Kitaia XVII–XIX vv. v "Man'chzhurskom arkhive"' (Data from the 'Manchu archives' on local institutions in Manchuria from the seventeenth through the nineteenth centuries). [With English abstract]
PV 1960, 4, 176–185.
SUBJ 12 22 ▪ 21.2

1644-1949

15937 CSU P P3 G1.1 1895–1928
Chan Chung Sing (Ch'en Tsung-ch'eng), 1900–.
Les concessions en Chine (The concessions in China).
Paris: Presses universitaires, 1925. 149 p. (Doctoral dissertation, Faculté de droit, Université de Paris)
SUBJ 22 22.1 66 ▪ 14.3

15938 NNC P P2 G1.2 –1928
Chang, Yu-sing (Chang Yu-hsin).
L'autonomie locale en Chine (Local autonomy in China).
Nancy: Grandville, 1933. 123 p. (Doctoral dissertation, Faculté de droit, Université de Nancy)
SUBJ 12 22 24 32.1 ▪ 12.2 17 28 64 66

15939 ELS P P3 G6.1 1842–1949
Chen, Yao-sheng (Ch'en Yao-sheng).
The International Settlement of Shanghai.
Unpublished doctoral dissertation in Economics, U. of London [London School of Economics and Political Science], 1940. 515 p.
SUBJ 22 ▪ 32.2 66

15940 CSU S P3 G9.5 1842–1949
Cheng, T. C. (Cheng Tung-ts'ai).
'Chinese unofficial members of the legislative and executive councils in Hong Kong up to 1941.'
JRAS-HKB 9 (1969), 7–30.
SUBJ 22 26.1 59 66 ▪ 17 56

15941 CSU P P3 G9.5 1842–1949
Collins, Charles Henry, 1887–.
Public administration in Hong Kong.
London: Royal Institute of International Affairs, 1952. 189 p. [Reprinted—New York: AMS Press, 1973. 189 p.]
SUBJ 22 22.2 66 ▪ 17 22.1 28

15942 NNC P P3 G5.1 1895–1949
Duncan, Robert Moore.
Peiping municipality and the diplomatic quarter.
Peiping: Yenching U., Dept. of Political Science, 1933. 146 p. (Doctoral dissertation, Yenching U.)
SUBJ 22 22.2 ▪ 21.3 22.1 24.5 28

15943 CSU P P3 G6.1 1895–1928
Elvin, John Mark Dutton, 1938–.
'The gentry democracy in Chinese Shanghai, 1905–14.' In *Modern China's search for a political form*, edited by Jack Douglas Gray. [Analytic entry]
London: Oxford U. Press, 1969, 41–65. [For a fuller version, see entry 15944.]
SUBJ 22 25 26.1 ▪ 22.1 22.2 24 24.5 26.2 28

15944 ECU P P3 G6.1 1895–1928
Elvin, John Mark Dutton, 1938–.
The gentry democracy in Shanghai, 1905–1914.
Unpublished doctoral dissertation in Oriental Studies, U. of Cambridge [Clare Hall], 1968. 276 p.
SUBJ 17 22 26 26.1 32 38 ▪ 22.1 22.2 24.2 24.5 26.2 32.1 32.2 36.2 37 39

15945 MCH P P2 G9.5 1644–1949
Endacott, George Beer.
A history of Hong Kong.
London: Oxford U. Press, 1958. 322 p.
SUBJ 20 22 22.2 24 66 ▪ 17 21 21.2 24.5 24.6 25 28 56

15946 CSU FP P3 G6.1 1842–1949
Feetham, Richard, 1874–?
'The foreign settlement and its government: Historical and descriptive.' In *Report of the Hon. Mr. Justice Feetham, C.M.G., to the Shanghai Municipal Council, Vol. 1*, by R. Feetham. [Selective entry]
Shanghai: North-China Daily News and Herald, 1931, 15–251.
SUBJ 12.2 20 21.1 21.3 22 ▪ 22.1 22.2 24.5 28 56 66

15947 CSU O P2 G1.3 –1949
Fei Hsiao-tung (Fei Hsiao-t'ung), 1910–.
'Basic power structure in rural China.' In *China's gentry: Essays in rural-urban relations*, rev. ed., by Fei Hsiao-tung, edited by Margaret Park Redfield. [Analytic entry]
Chicago: U. of Chicago Press, 1953, 75–90. [Reprinted in *China's gentry: Essays in rural-urban relations*, by Fei Hsiao-tung, edited by M. P. Redfield. (Analytic entry.) Chicago: U. of Chicago Press, 1968, 75–90.]
SUBJ 12 16.1 22 26.1

15948 MCH P P3 G6.1 1842–1949
Johnstone, William Crane, 1901–.
The Shanghai problem.
Stanford: Stanford U. Press, 1937. 11, 326 p. [Reprinted—Westport, Conn.: Hyperion Press, 197? 11, 326 p.]
SUBJ 22 22.2 24.6 66 ▪ 21.1 24.4 25 28 34.2

15949 CSU P P3 G9.5 1842–1949
Lethbridge, Henry James, 1923–.
'The District Watch Committee: The Chinese executive council of Hong Kong.'
JRAS-HKB 11 (1971), 116–141.
SUBJ 22 38 ▪ 22.1

15950 CSU S P3 G6.1 1842–1949
Lockwood, William Wirt, 1906–.
'The International Settlement at Shanghai, 1924–34.'
APSR 28, 6 (Dec. 1934), 1030–1046.
SUBJ 22 22.2 66 ▪ 17 24.5 26.4 28

15951 NNC U P3 G1.3 1842–1928
Otte, Friedrich W- K-.
'Niederlassungen, Konzessionen und Pachtgebiete in China' (Settlements, concessions, and leased territories in China).
Z. für Politik 16, 6 (1927), 603–613.
SUBJ 22 ▪ 14.3 14.4 21.1 66

15952 GBF O P2 G5.3 1895–1928
Schrameier, Wilhelm Ludwig, 1859–1926.
Kiautschou: Seine Entwicklung und Bedeutung (The development and significance of Kiaochow).
Berlin: Karl Curtius, 1915. 97 p.
SUBJ 22 66 ▪ 14.3 24 24.6 71

15953 MAM P P3 G6.1 1842–1949
Thomson, John Seabury, 1921–.
The government of the International Settlement at Shanghai: A study in the politics of an international area.
Ann Arbor: University Microfilms (Publ. 6722), 1954. 414 p. (Doctoral dissertation in Political Science, Columbia U., 1953)
SUBJ 22 ▪ 26.1 26.2 54

15954 NNC S P5 G1.3 –1949
Trewartha, Glenn Thomas, 1896–.
'Chinese cities: Origins and functions.'
AAAG 42, 1 (Mar. 1952), 69–93.
SUBJ 21.3 22 ▪ 11.1 11.3 12 14.2 14.3 16.2 24.3

15955 NNC P P8 G1.2 1842–1949
Wilbur, Clarence Martin, 1908–.
Village government in China.
Unpublished masters thesis in Chinese, Columbia U., 1934. 131 p.
SUBJ 22 22.2 41 42 43 63 ▪ 22.1 24.5 29 32 72

15956 FPN P P2 G1.1 –1949
Yen, Ku-wei (Yen K'o-wei).
Le droit administratif local en Chine (Local administrative law in China).
Nancy: Thomas, 1935. 227 p. (Doctoral dissertation, Faculté de droit, Université de Nancy)
SUBJ 12.2 22 ▪ 12 22.1

1911-1949

15957 CSU O P2 G8.1 1928–1949
Barnett, Arthur Doak, 1921–.
'The status quo in the countryside' [report to Institute of Current World Affairs, June 1948]. In *China on the eve of Communist takeover*, by A. D. Barnett. [Selective entry]
New York: Praeger, 1963, 103–154.
SUBJ 20 22 24.1 26.1 26.3 ▪ 12 21.1 21.3 22.2 24 24.5 25 27 32 32.2

15958 CSU O P3 G5.1 1928–1949
Barnett, Arthur Doak, 1921–.
'Uneasy isolation' [report to Institute of Current World Affairs, January 1948]. In *China on the eve of Communist takeover*, by A. D. Barnett. [Selective entry]
New York: Praeger, 1963, 25–39.
Subj 12 22

15959 CSU P P3 G1.2 1911–1949
Chen, Kyi-tsung (Ch'en Chi-chen).
Le système municipal en Chine (The municipal system in China).
Gembloux, Belgium: Duculot, 1937. 178 p. (Doctoral dissertation, Faculté de droit, Université catholique de Louvain)
Subj 22 22.1 ▪ 11.1 22.2 24.5 26 28 58

15960 NNC FP P2 G1.3 1928–1949
Hanwell, Norman D-.
'The dragnet of local government in China.'
PA 10, 1 (Mar. 1937), 43–63.
Subj 22 22.1 22.2 24.5 26 26.1 ▪ 12 24.6 25 26.2

15961 NNC FP P3 G6.1 1911–1949
Hinder, Eleanor M-.
Social and industrial problems of Shanghai, with special reference to the administrative and regulatory work of Shanghai Municipal Council, mimeo.
New York: Institute of Pacific Relations, International Secretariat, 1942. 74 p.
Subj 22 24.4 26.4 28 34.2 ▪ 12.2 24.3 27 52 55

15962 CSU O P3 G9.5 1928–1949
Hong Kong. Wing On Fire Commission.
'Wing On Fire Commission report.' In *Sessional papers laid before the Legislative Council of Hong Kong, 1949*. [Sole entry]
Hong Kong: Government Printer, [1949?], 1–48.
Subj 22 ▪ 24.3

15963 FPN P P3 G1.2 1928–1949
Jao Dain-houa (Jao Tan-hua).
La loi municipale chinoise du 20 mai 1930 (The Chinese municipal law of 20 May 1930).
Bordeaux: Castera, 1939. 146 p. (Doctoral dissertation, Faculté de droit, Université de Bordeaux)
Subj 12.2 22 ▪ 22.1 22.2

15964 CSU P P3 G6.1 1911–1949
Johnstone, William Crane, 1901–.
'The Feetham report: A new plan for Shanghai.'
APSR 25, 4 (Nov. 1931), 1044–1050. [For the report, see entries 15946 and 17052.]
Subj 22 ▪ 66

15965 CSU P P3 G1.3 1928–1949
Jones, Francis Clifford.
Shanghai and Tientsin, with special reference to foreign interests.
New York: Institute of Pacific Relations, American Council, 1940. 10, 182 p. (Studies of the Pacific, 5)
Subj 20 22 24 25 28 66 ▪ 12.2 14.3 17 22.2 24.4 24.5 24.6 26.4 45

15966 ELS FP P3 G1.2 1911–1928
Liu, Nai-chen (Liu Nai-ch'eng), 1902–.
Reform of Chinese city government based on European experience.
Unpublished doctoral dissertation in Economics, U. of London [London School of Economics and Political Science], 1930. 2 vols. 528 p. [c.p.].
Subj 12.2 22 ▪ 12 22.1 22.2 26.1 28

15967 NNC P P2 G1.2 1928–1949
Martynov, K- A-.
'Stroitel'stvo narodno-demokraticheskoi vlasti v osvobozhdennykh raionakh Kitaia v period tret'ei grazhdanskoi revoliutsionnoi voiny' (Building people's-democratic power in the liberated areas of China during the Third Revolutionary Civil War [1946–1949]).
KSINA 55 (1962), 112–135.
Subj 12 22 32.2 ▪ 15 16 32

15968 CSU P P2 G1.2 1928–1949
Meng, C. Y. W.
'Representative government emerges in China.'
FA 22, 3 (Apr. 1944), 484–488.
Subj 12 22 ▪ 30

15969 CSU S P3 G1.3 1911–1928
Quigley, Harold Scott, 1889–1968.
'Foreign concessions in Chinese hands.'
FA 7, 1 (Oct. 1928), 150–155.
Subj 22 ▪ 22.1 66

15970 FPN P P4 G1.2 1928–1949
Tchou, Pao-tien (Chu Pao-t'ien).
Les principes généraux de l'autonomie locale dans la Chine actuelle (General principles of local self-government in contemporary China).
Lyons: Bosc et Riou, 1933. 107 p. (Doctoral dissertation, Faculté de droit, Université de Lyon)
Subj 20 22 ▪ 12 64

15971 IBU P P4 G1.2 1928–1949
Wen, Henry Leonidas (Wen Ling-hsiung), 1917–.
Comparative study of municipal structures and activities in the United States and China.
Unpublished doctoral dissertation in Government, Indiana U., 1942. 291 p.
Subj 21.3 22 22.2 24 28 ▪ 12.2 17 22.1 24.2 24.5 24.6

15972 NNC O P3 G9.2 1911–1928
Wu, S. Y.
'Canton municipal progress.'
Weekly review of the Far East 19, 1 (3 Dec. 1921), 6–10.
Subj 22

1911-1972
(including 1644-1972)

15973 MCH P P2 G9.5 1842–1972
Endacott, George Beer.
Government and people in Hong Kong, 1841–1962: A constitutional history.
Hong Kong: Hong Kong U. Press, 1964. 14, 263 p.
Subj 12.2 22 ▪ 22.1 22.2 26.2 32 39 56

15974 CSH FP P2 G9.5 1895–1972
Freedman, Maurice, 1920–.
'Shifts of power in the Hong Kong New Territories.'
JAAS 1, 1 (Jan. 1966), 3–12.
Subj 22 26.1 ▪ 21 22.1 22.2 24 24.5 42

15975 CSH P P7 G1.2 1928–1972
Hofheinz, Roy Mark, Jr., 1935–.
'Rural administration in Communist China.'
CQ 11 (July–Sept. 1962), 140–159. [Reprinted in *China under Mao: Politics takes command*, edited by Roderick Lemonde MacFarquhar. (Selective entry.) Cambridge: M.I.T. Press, 1966, 99–118.]
Subj 22 24.1 34.1 ▪ 22.1 28 45

15976 MCH PO P2 G9.5 1842–1972
Hsueh, S. S.
Government and administration of Hong Kong.
Hong Kong: University Book Store, 1962. 97 p.
Subj 22 ▪ 12.2 22.1 24.5 66

15977 MCH P P7 G1.2 1911–1972
Lethbridge, Henry James, 1923–.
The peasant and the communes.
Hong Kong: Dragonfly Books, 1963. 202 p.
Subj 20 22 34.1 ▪ 12.1 14.1 25 26.3 64

15978 CSH FP P7 G1.2 1928–1972
Schurmann, Herbert Franz, 1926–.
'Villages.' In *Ideology and organization in Communist China*, 2nd ed., enl., by H. F. Schurmann. [Analytic entry]
Berkeley, Los Angeles: U. of California Press, 1968, 404–500.
Subj 22 22.1 26.3 32.1 34.1 ▪ 24 24.6 26

15979 NIC P P4 G1.2 1928–1972
Steiner, Harold Arthur, 1905–.
'Chinese Communist urban policy.'
APSR 44, 1 (Mar. 1950), 47–63.
Subj 22 32 32.1 35 ▪ 12 15 16.1 22.2

15980 CSU P P2 G1.2 1911–1972
Townsend, James Roger, 1932–.
Political participation in Communist China.
Berkeley, Los Angeles: U. of California Press, 1967. 233 p. (Revision of *Mass political participation in Communist China*, doctoral dissertation in Political Science, U. of California, Berkeley, 1965)
Subj 12.1 22 32 64 ▪ 12 12.2 30 32.1 34.1 36.3

15981 MAM F P3 G9.5 1928–1972
[Wong, Aline K.] Aline Lai-Chung Kan (Huang Chien Li-chung), 1941–.
The kaifong (neighborhood) associations in Hong Kong.
Ann Arbor: University Microfilms (Publ. 71-796), 1971. 540 p. (Doctoral dissertation in Sociology, U. of California, Berkeley, 1970)
Subj 21.3 22 22.1 22.2 26.1 38 ▪ 24.6 26 28 30 31 32.1 56 61

15982 CSU U P2 G1.2 –1972
Yang, C. K. (Yang Ch'ing-k'un), 1911–.
'Power structure and benevolent government: A social-political consideration.' In *Symposium on Chinese culture*, edited by Chi-pao Cheng (Ch'eng Ch'i-pao). [Sole entry]
New York: China Institute in America, 1964, 34–37.
Subj 16 22 ▪ 12 64

1949-1972

15983 CSU O P2 G6.3 1949–1972
Alley, Rewi, 1897–.
'Shaoshing [i.e., Shao-hsing *hsien*, Chekiang] over two years.'
EH 7, 6 (Nov.–Dec. 1968), 6–18.
SUBJ 22 ▪ 24.1 24.4

15984 CSU O P7 G9.2 1949–1972
Alley, Rewi, 1897–.
'Struggle in Polo county [i.e., Po-lo *hsien*], east Kwangtung.'
EH 7, 4 (July–Aug. 1968), 6–21.
SUBJ 20 22 22.1 34.1 ▪ 24.1 26 35 47 54 59 64

15985 CSU O P7 G6.3 1949–1972
Alley, Rewi, 1897–.
'Together with change in Chekiang.'
EH 8, 2 (1969), 23–35.
SUBJ 22 24.1 ▪ 34.1 35 59

15986 CSU O P3 G1.5 1949–1972
Anderson, Dick.
'Street committees in China, 1968.'
EH 7, 6 (Nov.–Dec. 1968), 27–30.
SUBJ 22 22.1 ▪ 28

15987 CSU F P7 G9.2 1949–1972
Barnett, Arthur Doak, 1921–.
'A commune and a brigade.' In *Cadres, bureaucracy, and political power in Communist China*, by A. D. Barnett. [Analytic entry]
New York: Columbia U. Press, 1967, 311–424.
SUBJ 20 22 24 34.1 ▪ 21.3 22.1 22.2 26 32

15988 CSH P P8 G5.1 1949–1972
Baum, Richard Dennis, 1940–.
'A parting of paupers [in Hsi-pu production brigade, Shan-t'ing commune, P'u-t'ien *hsien*, Fukien].'
FEER 59, 1 (4 Jan. 1968), 17–19.
SUBJ 22

15989 CSH F P7 G9.5 1949–1972
Berkowitz, Morris Ira, 1931–, and Eddie K. K. Poon (P'an Kuo-chü).
'Political disintegration of Hakka villages: A study of drastic social change in the New Territories of Hong Kong.'
CCJ 8, 2 (May 1969), 16–31.
SUBJ 22 22.2 26.1 28 ▪ 21.2 24.2 27 29

15990 CSU P P7 G1.2 1949–1972
Birrell, Robert James, 1937–.
'The centralized control of the communes in the post–"Great Leap" period.' In *Chinese Communist politics in action*, edited by Arthur Doak Barnett. [Selective entry]
Seattle: U. of Washington Press, 1969, 400–443. (Social Science Research Council, Studies in Chinese government and politics, 1)
SUBJ 22 22.1 32.1 34.1 ▪ 12 14.3 24.3 26.3 28

15991 NIC P P7 G1.2 1949–1972
Carin, Robert.
Rural communes, September 1, 1958 – August 15, 1959, mimeo.
Kowloon: ——, 1960. 19 & 51, 865 p. (China's land problem series, 3)
SUBJ 22 24.1 26.3 34.1 ▪ 22.1 24.4 28 52 55

15992 NIC P P7 G1.2 1949–1972
Carin, Robert.
Rural communes, (II), August 1959 – March 1960, mimeo.
Kowloon: ——, 1961. 11 & 28, 853 p. (China's land problem series, 4)
SUBJ 22 24.1 26.3 34.1 ▪ 22.1 22.2 26.1 28 55

15993 NNC P P7 G1.2 1949–1972
Carin, Robert.
Rural communes, (III), April–December 1960, mimeo.
Kowloon: ——, 1962. 25, 608 p. (China's land problem series, 5)
SUBJ 22 24.1 26.3 34.1 ▪ 22.1 22.2 24.4 28 52 55 56

15994 CSU P P7 G1.2 1949–1972
Chang, Parris H. (Chang Hsü-ch'eng), 1936–.
'Struggle between the two roads in China's countryside.'
CS 6, 3 (15 Feb. 1968), 1–14.
SUBJ 22 ▪ 32 34.1

15995 NNC O P2 G2.1 1949–1972
Chao Fu-chi.
'The system of one commune for one hsien as seen through the people's commune of Chao-yüan hsien (Heilungkiang).' Tr. of 'Ts'ung Chao-yüan hsien jen min kung she k'an i hsien i she chih' (Chao-yüan *hsien* commune [Heilungkiang]: An example of a county-wide commune); *Ts'ai ching yen chiu* 1958, 9 (Dec.), 11–14, 18.
ECMM 156 (26 Jan. 1959), 15–23.
SUBJ 12 22 24 28 ▪ 21.4 24.4 34.1 45 55

15996 MCY P P7 G1.2 1949–1972
Chao, Kuo-chün, 1918–1962.
'The organization and functions of the people's communes.' In *Contemporary China, 1958–1959*, edited by Edward Stuart Kirby. [Selective entry]
Hong Kong: Hong Kong U. Press, 1960, 131–145.
SUBJ 22 24 34.1 ▪ 26.3 55

15997 NIC O P4 G1.2 1949–1972
Chao, Kuo-chün, 1918–1962.
'Urban communes: A first-hand report.'
FEER 29, 13 (29 Sept. 1960), 715–720.
SUBJ 22 34.2 ▪ 24.4 26.4 28 55

15998 MCH O P7 G7.3 1949–1972
Ch'en Ching-hsing, Tu Shu-ying, and Sun Heng-chi.
'Survey of Chiang-hsiang people's commune, Nan-ch'ang hsien.' Tr. of 'Nan-ch'ang hsien Chiang-hsiang jen min kung she tiao ch'a' (Survey of Chiang-hsiang commune, Nan-ch'ang *hsien* [Kiangsi]); *Chiang-hsi jih pao* 24 Nov. 1959. In *People's communes in Communist China: Their development and accomplishments*, mimeo., compiled by U.S. Joint Publications Research Service. [Sole entry]
Washington, D.C.: JPRS, 29 Aug. 1960, 5–24. (JPRS 3787; MC 15,668/1960)
SUBJ 22 24 28 ▪ 24.1 24.4 24.6 38 55

15999 NIC P P7 G1.2 1949–1972
Cheng Chu-yuan (Cheng Chu-yüan), 1927–.
'The changing pattern of rural communes in Communist China.'
AS 1, 9 (Nov. 1961), 3–9.
SUBJ 22 22.2 34.1 ▪ 24 26.3 28 32.1 55

16000 MCY O P7 G9.2 1949–1972
Davies, Derek.
'A Kwangtung commune [Hua-tung commune, Hua *hsien*].'
FEER 46, 12 (17 Dec. 1964), 564–567.
SUBJ 22 24.1 ▪ 24.4

16001 NNC S P7 G1.2 1949–1972
Delany, Kevin F- X-.
The Soviet communes and the people's communes of Communist China: A comparison.
Unpublished masters thesis in Public Law and Government, Columbia U., 1962. 144 p.
SUBJ 22 22.1 24 34.1 ▪ 24.1 26.3 41

16002 MAM FP P2 G9.5 1949–1972
Dial, Oliver Eugene, 1922–.
An evaluation of the impact of China's refugees in Hong Kong on the structure of the colony's government in the period following World War II.
Ann Arbor: University Microfilms (Publ. 66-3362), 1966. 199 p. (Doctoral dissertation in Political Science, Claremont Graduate School and University Center, 1965)
SUBJ 11.2 22 ▪ 12.2 21.4 22.1 24 28

16003 CSU F P7 G9.4 1949–1972
Gallin, Bernard, 1929–.
'Political factionalism and its impact on Chinese village social organization in Taiwan.' In *Local-level politics: Social and cultural perspectives*, edited by Marc Jerome Swartz. [Sole entry]
Chicago: Aldine, 1968, 377–400.
SUBJ 22 30 41 42 ▪ 21 34.1

16004 CSU O P8 G1.2 1949–1972
Gatti, Armand.
'Notes de voyage dans les communes chinoises' (Notes on a visit to Chinese communes).
CFC 1 (mars 1959), 32–51.
SUBJ 22 24.4 34.1 ▪ 21.4 25 28 47

16005 NNC P P7 G1.2 1949–1972
Glaubitz, Joachim, 1929–.
'Die chinesischen Volkskommunen auf dem Lande: Organisation und Entwicklungstendenzen' (Rural communes in China: Organization and trends in development).
Osteuropa 11, 4/5 (Apr.–Mai 1961), 302–310.
SUBJ 22 24 34.1 55 ▪ 22.1 24.1 28 37

16006 NNC P P3 G1.2 1949–1972
Glaubitz, Joachim, 1929–.
'Die Kommunisierung der chinesischen Stadt: Eine Episode im "Grossen Sprung"' (The communization of the Chinese city: An episode in the Great Leap Forward).
Osteuropa 12, 4/5 (Apr.–Mai 1962), 311–315.
SUBJ 22 ▪ 14.4 19 24.4

16007 MAM FP P3 G9.4 1949–1972
Hoadley, John Stephen, 1937–.
The government and politics of Hong Kong: A descriptive study, with special reference to the analytical framework of Gabriel Almond.
Ann Arbor: University Microfilms (Publ. 71-11,479), 1971. 13, 273 p. (Doctoral dissertation in Political Science, U. of California, Santa Barbara, 1968)
SUBJ 22 30 ▪ 12.2 22.1 22.2 24.2 26 31 53

16008 CSU F P3 G9.5 1949–1972
Hoadley, John Stephen, 1937–.
'"Hong Kong is the lifeboat": Notes on political culture and socialization.'
JOS 8, 1 (Jan. 1970), 206–218. [For fuller treatment, see entry 16007.]
SUBJ 22 66 ▪ 53

16009 MCH P P7 G9.4 1949–1972
Hsieh, S. C. (Hsieh Sen-chung), 1919–.
'The role of local government in rural development.'
IFC 20, 1 (July 1963), 2–7; 20, 2 (Aug. 1963), 10–19.
SUBJ 22 24 37 ▪ 24.1 24.4 24.5 27 56

16010 CBU FP P2 G9.5 1949–1972
Hu, Chia-chien, and Aline K. Wong (Huang Chien Li-chung), 1941–.
'A preliminary report on the kaifong [neighborhood associations] study.'
United College j. (Hong Kong) 7 (1968/69), 27–48 [s.p.].
SUBJ 22 38 ▪ 22.1 28 34.2 54 56

16011 MAM P P7 G1.2 1949–1972
Huang, Mab (Huang Mo), 1935–.
The function and limits of the mass line: A study of the people's commune movement in China, 1958–1966.
Ann Arbor: University Microfilms (Publ. 70-7000), 1970. 435 p. (Doctoral dissertation in Public Law and Government, Columbia U., 1969)
SUBJ 22 34.1 ▪ 22.1 26.3

16012 NNC P P4 G1.2 1949–1972
Ishikawa Shigeru, 1918–.
Chinese urban people's communes, mimeo. Tr. of 'Chūgoku no toshi jimmin kōsha' (Urban communes in China); *Ekafe tsūshin* 237 (11 Aug. 1960), 1–23.
Washington, D.C.: U.S. Joint Publications Research Service, 28 Nov. 1960. 24 p. (JPRS 5850; MC 937/1961)
SUBJ 20 22 24.4 ▪ 21.4 22.1 47 52 55

16013 NNC P P7 G1.2 1949–1972
Jan, George P. (Jan Po-kung), 1925–.
The commune experiment.
Vermillion: U. of South Dakota, 1964. 285 p.
SUBJ 19 22 26.3 32.1 34.1 41 ▪ 17 22.2 23 24.3 24.5 25 28 47 53 72

16014 CBU S P2 G1.2 1949–1972
Jo, Yung-hwan (Ts'ao Ying-huan), 1932–.
'The development of local government in Communist China.'
Public affairs b. (Tempe: Arizona State U., Institute of Public Administration) 6, 2 (1967), 1–6.
SUBJ 11.3 22 22.1 ▪ 12 32

16015 NIC P P4 G1.2 1949–1972
Kuan Ta-t'ung.
'Characteristics and superiorities of urban people's communes.' Tr. of 'Ch'eng shih jen min kung she ti t'e tien ho yu yüeh hsing' (The characteristics and superiorities of urban communes); *Hsin chien she* 1960, 5 (May), 28–35.
SCMM 217 (11 July 1960), 1–12.
SUBJ 22 24.4 28 ▪ 21.3 21.4 26 55

16016 CSU O P3 G5.4 1949–1972
Kuo Jung-hua.
Situation regarding the establishment and development of statistical work in the urban people's communes of Chengchou municipality, mimeo. Tr. of 'Cheng-chou shih ch'eng shih jen min kung she t'ung chi kung tso chien li yü k'ai chan ch'ing k'uang' (The development of statistical work in urban communes in Chengchow); *Chi hua yü t'ung chi* 1960, 5 (May), 20–21.
Washington, D.C.: U.S. Joint Publications Research Service, 29 Sept. 1960. 10 p. (JPRS 4082; MC 18,735/1960)
SUBJ 22 32.1 ▪ 17 24.4 28 34.2

16017 MCH P P2 G9.2 1949–1972
[La Dany, Ladislao] ———, 1914–.
'Life in Kwangtung province.'
CNA 463 (5 Apr. 1963), 1–7.
SUBJ 22 24.1 ▪ 17 31 34.1 56

16018 CSH P P2 G1.2 1949–1972
[La Dany, Ladislao] ———, 1914–.
'Life in the countryside. Part 1, The administration.'
CNA 818 (16 Oct. 1970), 1–7.
SUBJ 12 22 35 ▪ 22.1 26.1 32

16019 NIC P P2 G1.2 1949–1972
[La Dany, Ladislao] ———, 1914–.
'Statistics.'
CNA 424 (8 June 1962), 1–7.
SUBJ 22 62 ▪ 14 24

16020 MCH P P7 G1.2 1949–1972
Lewis, John Wilson, 1930–.
'The leadership doctrine of the Chinese Communist Party: The lesson of the people's commune.'
AS 3, 10 (Oct. 1963), 457–464.
SUBJ 22 26.1 36.1 ▪ 22.1 34.1 64

16021 CSU P P7 G1.2 1949–1972
Li Tien-min (Li T'ien-min).
'The people's commune: Focal point of resistance to the Cultural Revolution.'
IS 6, 1 (Oct. 1969), 43–52.
SUBJ 22

16022 NNC O P2 G9.4 1949–1972
Li, Tsung-huang, 1890–.
Local government in the Republic of China.
Taipei: Chinese-American Joint Commission on Rural Reconstruction, 1961. 50 p.
SUBJ 22

16023 MCH O P3 G5.1 1949–1972
Loboda, Ivan.
'Ulichnyi komitet Chaoiaotsze' (The street committee of Ch'ao-yao chieh).
Sovety deputatov trudiashchikhsia 1960, 3 (mart), 103–106.
SUBJ 22 38 ▪ 22.1

16024 CSU O P3 G9.4 1949–1972
Long Yu-hsien (Lang Yü-hsien).
'The administration of local election in Taipei.'
CJA 12 (Jan. 1969), 20–27 [s.p.].
SUBJ 22

16025 CSU P P2 G9.4 1949–1972
Long Yu-hsien (Lang Yü-hsien).
'Taiwan local elections: An introduction.'
CJA 10 (Jan. 1968), 37–41 [s.p.].
SUBJ 12 22

16026 NIC S P3 G1.2 1949–1972
Luard, David Evan Trant, 1926–.
'The urban communes.'
CQ 3 (July–Sept. 1960), 74–79.
SUBJ 22 24 ▪ 17 21.4 24.6 55

16027 CSH O P2 G1.2 1949–1972
Niijima Atsuyoshi, 1928–.
'The establishment of a new commune state.' Tr. by Jason G. B. Choi of 'Atarashiki komyun kokka no seiritsu'; in *Atarashiki kakumei* (New revolution), by Niijima Atsuyoshi; Tokyo: Keisō shobō, 1969, 149–175.
Chinese law and government 4, 1/2 (Spring–Summer 1971), 38–60.
SUBJ 20 22 26 30 64 ▪ 21.4 22.2 24 28 32

16028 NNC FP P2 G1.2 1949–1972
Oksenberg, Michel Charles, 1938–.
'Local government and politics in China, 1955–1958.' In *Columbia essays in international affairs, Vol. II, The Dean's papers, 1966*, edited by Andrew Wellington Cordier. [Sole entry]
New York: Columbia U. Press, 1967, 223–245. (Revision of *Rural field administration in Communist China, July 1955 – July 1958*, masters thesis in Political Science, Columbia U., 1963)
SUBJ 22 26.1 ▪ 22.1 24 24.5 32.1

16029 WSU S P7 G1.2 1949–1972
Pepper, Suzanne, 1939–.
Rural government in Communist China: The party-state relationship at the local level.
Unpublished masters thesis in Far Eastern and Slavic Languages, U. of Washington, 1963. 126 p.
SUBJ 22 22.1 ▪ 12 26 32 32.1 34.1 64

16030 CSU P P2 G9.5 1949–1972
Podmore, David.
'Localisation in the Hong Kong government service, 1948–1968.'
J. of Commonwealth political studies 9, 1 (Mar. 1971), 36–51.
SUBJ 22 ▪ 12.2 17 22.1 56

16031 NIC P P7 G1.2 1949–1972
Pye, Lucian Wilmot, 1921–.
The communes: A microcosm of Chinese Communism.
Cambridge: Massachusetts Institute of Technology, Center for International Studies, 1964. 92 p.
SUBJ 19 20 22 22.1 26.3 60 ▪ 24.1 28 34.1

16032 CBU PO P2 G9.5 1949–1972
Rear, John.
'The law of the constitution.' In *Hong Kong: The industrial colony*, edited by Keith Hopkins. [Analytic entry]
Hong Kong: Oxford U. Press, 1971, 339–422.
SUBJ 22 22.2 ▪ 12.2 21.3

16033 CBU PO P3 G9.5 1949–1972
Rear, John.
'One brand of politics.' In *Hong Kong: The industrial colony*, edited by Keith Hopkins. [Analytic entry]
Hong Kong: Oxford U. Press, 1971, 55–139.
SUBJ 22 ▪ 22.1 22.2

16034 MCH P P4 G1.2 1949–1972
Salaff, Janet Weitzner, 1940–.
'The urban communes and anti-city experiment in Communist China.'
CQ 29 (Jan.–Mar. 1967), 82–110.
SUBJ 22 22.1 ▪ 21.3 24.4 27 30 52 55

16035 CSU P P4 G1.2 1949–1972
Salaff, Janet Weitzner, 1940–.
'Urban residential communities in the wake of the Cultural Revolution.' In *The city in Communist China*, edited by John Wilson Lewis. [Analytic entry]
Stanford: Stanford U. Press, 1971, 289–323.
Subj 22 22.1 32 ▪ 17 22.2 24.3 32.1 41 56

16036 NIC P P7 G1.2 1949–1972
Sarker, Subhash Chandra.
'The Chinese communes.'
India q. 15, 1 (Jan.–Mar. 1959), 26–52.
Subj 22 28 41 55 ▪ 17 21.4 24 25 32.1 34.1 45 56

16037 CSH FP P3 G1.2 1949–1972
Schurmann, Herbert Franz, 1926–.
'Cities.' In *Ideology and organization in Communist China*, 2nd ed., enl., by H. F. Schurmann. [Analytic entry]
Berkeley, Los Angeles: U. of California Press, 1968, 364–403.
Subj 20 22 22.1 ▪ 11.1 14.3 21.4 26 32.1

16038 CSU P P2 G1.2 1949–1972
Sih, Paul K. T. (Hsüeh Kuang-ch'ien), 1909–.
'The Chinese communes.'
Thought patterns 7 (1960), 125–151.
Subj 20 22 22.1 ▪ 14 16 19 22.2 41 45 55

16039 MCH P P7 G1.2 1949–1972
Siu, K. P. (Hsiu Chia-pei).
'Le régime local en Chine communiste' (Local administration in Communist China).
R. internationale des sciences administratives 24, 3 (mars 1958), 347–354.
Subj 22

16040 MCY P P7 G1.2 1949–1972
Townsend, James Roger, 1932–.
'Democratic management in the rural communes.'
CQ 16 (Oct.–Dec. 1963), 137–150.
Subj 22 ▪ 34.1

16041 MCH P P7 G1.2 1949–1972
Trolliet, Pierre.
'Les communes populaires rurales chinoises' (Rural communes in China).
Tiers-monde 3, 9/10 (jan.–juin 1962), 229–269.
Subj 20 22 24 ▪ 26 28 34.1

16042 CSU F P2 G9.4 1949–1972
Walker, Richard Louis, 1922–.
'Local political development in Taiwan's frontierland.'
CJA 11 (July 1968), 34–43 [s.p.].
Subj 22 ▪ 21 24.2 28 66

16043 CSU U P2 G9.4 1949–1972
Wang, Kuo-chang.
'Local government in Taiwan: An introduction.'
CJA 10 (Jan. 1968), 27–36 [s.p.].
Subj 12 22 ▪ 12.2

16044 CSU F P3 G9.5 1949–1972
Wong, Aline K. (Huang Chien Li-chung), 1941–.
'Chinese community leadership in a colonial setting: The Hong Kong neighbourhood associations.'
AS 12, 7 (July 1972), 587–601. [For a fuller version, see entry 15981.]
Subj 22 26.1 38 ▪ 22.2 26 32.1 61

16045 CBU P P3 G9.5 1949–1972
Wong, Aline K. (Huang Chien Li-chung), 1941–.
'Political apathy and the political system in Hong Kong.'
United College j. (Hong Kong) 8 (1970/71), 1–20 [s.p.].
Subj 22

16046 NNC PO P2 G1.2 1949–1972
Yokogawa Jiro (Yokokawa Jirō).
People's communes in China, mimeo. Tr. of 'Jimmin kōsha: Kyōsanshugi e no ikō no atarashii keitai ni tsuite no ichi kenkyū' (Communes: A study of new forms in the transition to communism); *Chūgoku shiryō geppō* 133 (31 Mar. 1959), 1–44.
Washington, D.C.: U.S. Joint Publications Research Service, 7 Aug. 1959. 60 p. (JPRS 851D; MC 12,895/1959)
Subj 20 22 24.1 34.1 ▪ 22.1 24.4 25 26.3 27 64

22.1 Local Political and Social Controls
地方統治及社會控制
地方の政治的社会的統制

1644-1911

16047 NNC O P4 G5.1 1842–1895
'Razskaz kitaitsa o poezdke sovershennoi im v Zhe-Khe, letniuiu rezidentsiiu kitaiskikh bogdykhanov' (A Chinese traveler's account of his journey to Jehol, summer residence of the Chinese emperors).
Izvestiia Imperatorskago russkago geograficheskago obshchestva 1, 1, Part 2 (1865), 82–88.
Subj 21.3 22.1 ▪ 24.2

16048 NNC PO P2 G1.3 1895–1911
Hosie, Alexander, 1853–1925.
'Summary of opium investigation in the provinces of Shansi, Shensi, Kansu, Szechuan, Yunnan and Kueichou.' In *On the trail of the opium poppy*, by A. Hosie. [Selective entry]
Boston: Small, Maynard, 1914, vol. 2, 232–288.
Subj 22.1 22.2 24.1 55 ▪ 24.3 28

16049 NIC P P2 G1.3 1644–1911
Hsiao, Kung-chuan (Hsiao Kung-ch'üan), 1897–.
Rural China: Imperial control in the nineteenth century.
Seattle: U. of Washington Press, 1960. 14, 783 p.
Subj 22 22.1 22.2 25 26.1 42 ▪ 14.1 16.3 17 23 24.3 24.5 28 33 34.1 36.3

16050 NIC O P3 G6.1 1895–1911
North-China Daily News.
The Shanghai municipal police.
Shanghai: North-China Daily News and Herald, 1910. 27 p.
Subj 22.1

16051 CNY O P6 G5.0 1895–1911
Wetterwald, Albert, 1860–?
'Le réveil de la Chine et les gardes champêtres' (The awakening of China and the rural police).
Chine, Ceylan, Madagascar 24 (juin 1907), 533–537.
Subj 22.1

1644-1949

16052 NIC P P3 G9.2 1895–1928
Gao, Hwei-shung (Kao Wei-hsiung).
'Police administration in Canton.'
CSPSR 10, 2 (Apr. 1926), 332–354; 10, 3 (July 1926), 669–698; 10, 4 (Oct. 1926), 872–890.
Subj 22 22.1 ▪ 30

16053 NIC P P2 G1.2 –1949
Lee, Robert H. G. (Li K'ung-chiang), 1922–.
'The pao-chia system.'
PC 3 (May 1949), 193–224.
Subj 22.1 26.1 26.3 ▪ 22 44

1911-1949

16054 NNC P P7 G1.2 1928–1949
Andors, Stephen Paul, 1938–.
Mass mobilization in Communist controlled areas of China, 1937–1945.
Unpublished masters thesis in Public Law and Government, Columbia U., 1968. 113 p. [Certificate essay, East Asian Institute]
Subj 12.1 22 22.1 32 60 ▪ 14 15 17 37

16055 ELS PO P2 G1.2 1911–1949
Chang, Chung-liang (Chang Tsung-liang).
The English police system and its applicability to rural China.
Unpublished doctoral dissertation in Economics, U. of London [London School of Economics and Political Science], 1937. 1080 p.
Subj 12.1 22.1 ▪ 12.2 15 22.2

16056 NNC F P8 G5.1 1928–1949
Hanson, Haldore E-, 1912–.
'The people behind the Chinese guerillas.'
PA 11, 3 (Sept. 1938), 285–298.
Subj 22.1 32 ▪ 15 24 24.5 27

16057 CSU P P2 G9.5 1928–1949
Hong Kong. Police Dept.
Annual report, 1946/47–1948/49. [Title varies; issues for 1949/50–1971/72 are entered as 16076.]
[Hong Kong]: ——. Issued annually, 1947–1949. Average ca. 30 p.
Subj 22.1 22.2 ▪ 24.2 27 38

16058 NNC P P2 G1.3 1928–1949
[Hsiao San] Siao Emi (Hsiao Ai-mei).
'Kul'turnoe stroitel'stvo v sovetskom Kitae' (Cultural development in soviet China).
PK 14 (1935), 346–363.
Subj 17 22.1 32.2 ▪ 15 31 32.1 33 35 47 54

16059 NNC P P8 G5.0 1928–1949
Maddox, Patrick Gaynor, 1945–.
An analysis of Communist Chinese takeover tactics in the villages of North China, 1935–1949.
Unpublished masters thesis in Public Law and Government, Columbia U., 1970. 54 p. [Certificate essay, East Asian Institute]
Subj 22.1 ▪ 15 25 26.1 26.3

16060 NNC O P3 G6.1 1928–1949
Peters, Ernest William.
Shanghai policeman, edited by Hugh Barnes.
London: Rich and Cowan, 1937. 322 p.
Subj 22.1 22.2 ▪ 22 31 57 63 65

16061 CSH P P2 G1.5 1928–1949
U.S. Office of Strategic Services. Research and Analysis Branch.
Programs of Japan in China, [Part I], Central coastal provinces, with biographies, mimeo.
[Honolulu]: ——, 1945. 222 p. (R. and A., 2896)
Subj 22 22.1 24.1 24.2 24.4 32.1 ▪ 24.6 29

16062 CSH P P2 G9.0 1928–1949
U.S. Office of Strategic Services. Research and Analysis Branch.
Programs of Japan in China, Part II, Southern coast, with biographies, mimeo.
[Washington, D.C.]: ——, 1945. 262 p. (R. and A., 2896.1)
Subj 12 22.1 24.1 24.2 24.4 ▪ 21 24.5 27

16063 CSH P P2 G1.4 1928–1949
U.S. Office of Strategic Services. Research and Analysis Branch.
Programs of Japan in China, Part III, Northern coast, with biographies, mimeo.
[Honolulu]: ——, 1945. 262 p. (R. and A., 3049)
Subj 17 22 22.1 24 26.4 ▪ 24.1 24.2 24.4 28 29 32.2 54

16064 CSH FP P2 G9.0 1928–1949
U.S. Office of Strategic Services. Research and Analysis Branch.
Survey of Hainan, 2nd ed., mimeo.
[Washington, D.C.]: ——, 1943. 13, 49 p. (R. and A., 742)
Subj 15 21 22.1 24 28 32.1 ▪ 22 23 24.2 29 32.2

16065 NNC P P2 G2.0 1928–1949
Yeh Min.
'The Chinese peasantry under the puppet regime of Manchoukuo.' Tr. of 'Tung-pei lao tung ta chung ti wang kuo nu sheng hou' (The life of conquered and enslaved masses of Manchuria); *Chung-kuo nung ts'un* 2, 5 (May 1936), 9–19. In *Agrarian China*, compiled by Institute of Pacific Relations. [Selective entry]
Chicago: U. of Chicago Press, 1939, 216–223.
Subj 22.1 26.3 26.4 ▪ 24.1 28 66

1911-1972
(including 1644-1972)

16066 GBF O P1 G9.4 1644–1972
Middendorf, Wolf.
'Hongkong: Die kriminellen Geheimbünde' (Hong Kong: The criminal secret societies). In *Kriminologische Reisebilder: USA, Mexico, Israel, Hongkong, Taiwan* (A traveler's criminological sketches: The United States, Mexico, Israel, Hong Kong, and Taiwan), by W. Middendorf. [Selective entry]
Hamburg: Kriminalistik Verlag, 1967, 81–98.
Subj 22.1 32.2 ▪ 25

16067 GBF O P1 G9.5 1644–1972
Middendorf, Wolf.
'Taiwan: Der Chinese und sein Staat' (Taiwan: The Chinese and his country). In *Kriminologische Reisebilder: USA, Mexico, Israel, Hongkong, Taiwan* (A traveler's criminological sketches: The United States, Mexico, Israel, Hong Kong, and Taiwan), by W. Middendorf. [Selective entry]
Hamburg: Kriminalistik Verlag, 1967, 99–123.
Subj 22.1 32.2 ▪ 25

16068 CSH O P2 G1.1 1928–1972
Schuman, Julian.
Assignment China.
New York: Whittier Books, 1956. 253 p.
Subj 22.1 22.2 26.2 26.4 34.2 ▪ 12 24.1 24.4 28 32.2 34.1 41 47

1949-1972

16069 MCH O P3 G5.1 1949–1972
'Quatorze mois à Pékin.'
Est et Ouest nouvelle (2e) série 13, 251 (1er–15 fév. 1961), 19–22.
Fourteen months in Peking, Communist China, mimeo.
Washington, D.C.: U.S. Joint Publications Research Service, 17 May 1961. 9 p. (JPRS 8288; MC 13,196/1961)
Subj 17 22.1 ▪ 26.1 55

16070 CBU O P2 G1.2 1949–1972
Averink, Annie, Gerard Maas, and Gerrit de Vries.
China werpt het juk af (China throws off its chains).
Amsterdam: Pegasus, 1958. 135 p.
Subj 22.1 24.1 24.4 26.2 34.1 ▪ 22 26.1 32 32.1 37

16071 MAM FP P2 G1.2 1949–1972
Baum, Richard Dennis, 1940–.
Revolution and reaction in rural China: The struggle between two roads in the socialist education movement (1962–66) and the Great Proletarian Cultural Revolution (1966–1968).
Ann Arbor: University Microfilms (Publ. 71-9762), 1971. 383 p. (Doctoral dissertation in Political Science, U. of California, Berkeley, 1970)
Subj 12 22.1 26 26.1 32 ▪ 15 22.2 26.3 32.1 35 36.3 54 64

16072 CSU P P7 G1.2 1949–1972
Baum, Richard Dennis, 1940–, and Frederick Carl Teiwes, 1939–.
Ssu-ch'ing, the socialist education movement of 1962-1966.
Berkeley: U. of California, Center for Chinese Studies, 1968. 128 p. (CCS, China research monographs, 2)
Subj 22 22.1 26.3 ▪ 21.2 26 32

16073 CSU P P3 G5.1 1949–1972
Current Scene Editor.
'How to wage "revolutionary struggle": "Teaching material" provided by Red Guards of Tsinghua University, Peking.'
CS 6, 6 (15 Apr. 1968), 1–21.
Subj 22.1 54 ▪ 61

16074 CSH O P7 G9.3 1949–1972
Fukien. Chiao yü t'ing. (Dept. of Education).
'Miracle in a Fukien village.' Tr. of 'Fu-chien i ko hsiang ti ch'i chi' (A miracle in a township in Fukien [Wu-shan *hsiang*, Ta-t'ien *hsien*]); *Hung ch'i* 1958, 4 (16 July), 35–37. In *Selected translations from 'Hung-chi' (Red flag), June–August 1958*, mimeo., compiled by U.S. Joint Publications Research Service. [Selective entry]
Washington, D.C.: JPRS, 21 Apr. 1961, 372–382. (JPRS 7837; MC 5498/1962)
Subj 22.1 ▪ 27 29

16075 CSU P P3 G6.1 1949–1972
Gardner, John, 1939–.
'The Wu-fan [Five-Anti] campaign in Shanghai: A study in the consolidation of urban control.' In *Chinese Communist politics in action*, edited by Arthur Doak Barnett. [Selective entry]
Seattle: U. of Washington Press, 1969, 477–539. (Social Science Research Council, Studies in Chinese government and politics, 1)
Subj 22.1 22.2 26.2 32.1 34.2 36.4 ▪ 24.2 24.5 26.1 26.4 32 36.2 50 64

16076 CSU P P2 G9.5 1949–1972
Hong Kong. Police Dept.
Annual departmental report by the Commissioner of Police, 1949/50–1971/72. [Issues for 1946/47–1948/49 are entered as 16057.]
Hong Kong: Government Printer. Issued annually, 1950–1972. Average ca. 70 p.
Subj 22.1 22.2 ▪ 24.2 27 38

16077 NNC O P2 G8.2 1949–1972
Huang, Quentin (Huang K'uei-yüan), 1902?–.
Now I can tell: The story of a Christian bishop under Communist persecution.
New York: Morehouse-Gorham, 1954. 222 p.
Subj 13 22.1 24.1 ▪ 22.2 26 61 64

16078 MCH P P3 G6.1 1949–1972
[La Dany, Ladislao] ———, 1914–.
'Disarray in Shanghai.'
CNA 654 (7 Apr. 1967), 1–7.
Subj 21.2 22.1 ▪ 25 32.2 36.4

16079 CSU P P7 G1.2 1949–1972
Matsuda, Yoshirō.
'Methods of compiling crop statistics in China.'
DE 3, 3 (Sept. 1965), 323–342.
Subj 22 22.1 24.4 ▪ 14.4 34.1

16080 MCH S P3 G5.1 1949–1972
Montader, Pierre.
'Sourd et aveugle, le Bureau politique condamne et réprime' (Deaf and blind, the Political Bureau condemns and represses).
Saturne 3, 15 (oct.–nov. 1957), 114–129.
'The Political Bureau strikes blindly.'
Saturn 3, 5 (Oct.–Nov. 1957), 106–121.
Subj 22.1 26.1 64

16081 MCH P P2 G1.2 1949–1972
Munthe-Kaas, Harald.
'China's "four clean-up's".'
FEER 52, 10 (9 June 1966), 479–484.
Subj 22 22.1 32.1

16082 MCH P P1 G1.2 1949–1972
Ostroumov, Georgii Sergeevich.
'Novaia forma privlecheniia obshchestvennosti k bor'be za sobliudenie pravil sotsialisticheskogo obshchezhitiia v KNR' (A new way of enlisting public cooperation in the

struggle to observe the rules of the socialist community in the People's Republic of China).
SGP 1960, 5 (mai), 73–81.
SUBJ 22.1 22.2 30 32.1 64 ▪ 12 63

16083 NNC F P2 G8.1 1949–1972
Skinner, George William, 1925–.
'Aftermath of Communist liberation in the Chengtu plain.'
PA 24, 1 (Mar. 1951), 61–76.
SUBJ 22.1 24.5 25 26 26.3 32.2 ▪ 21.4 24 24.6 26.2 32.1 35

16084 MCH P P2 G1.2 1949–1972
Tung, Robert.
'The people's policemen.'
FEER 53, 7 (18 Aug. 1966), 319–321.
SUBJ 22.1 ▪ 12.2

16085 CSU FP P4 G1.2 1949–1972
Vogel, Ezra Feivel, 1930–.
'Preserving order in the cities.' In *The city in Communist China*, edited by John Wilson Lewis. [Analytic entry]
Stanford: Stanford U. Press, 1971, 75–93.
SUBJ 22.1 ▪ 12.2 22.2

22.2 CUSTOMARY LAW AND DISPUTE RESOLUTION
習慣法及仲裁解決
慣習法及び紛争の解決

1644-1911

16086 MBA O P3 G6.1 1895–1911
'Une exécution capitale à Changhaï' (An execution at Shanghai).
RI nouvelle (2e) série 5, 60 (30 juin 1907), 888–890.
SUBJ 22.1 22.2

16087 CSU P P3 G5.1 1644–1842
Bodde, Derk, 1909–.
'Prison life in eighteenth century Peking.'
JAOS 89, 2 (Apr.–June 1969), 311–333.
SUBJ 12.2 22.2 ▪ 50 55

16088 CSU P P7 G9.4 1644–1895
Buxbaum, David Charles, 1933–.
'Some aspects of civil procedure and practice at the trial level in Tanshui [T'ai-pei *hsien*, Taiwan] and Hsinchu [Hsin-chu *hsien*, Taiwan] from 1789 to 1895.'
JAS 30, 2 (Feb. 1971), 255–279.
SUBJ 22.2

16089 MCH P P2 G1.2 1895–1911
Cohen, Jerome Alan, 1930–.
'Chinese mediation on the eve of modernization.'
California law review 54, 3 (Aug. 1966), 1201–1226. [Reprinted—*JAAS* 2, 1/2 (Jan.–Apr. 1967), 54–76.] [Reprinted in *Traditional and modern legal institutions in Asia and Africa*, edited by David Charles Buxbaum. (Selective entry.) Leiden: Brill, 1967, 54–76. (International studies in sociology and social anthropology, 5)]
SUBJ 12.2 22.2 ▪ 34.3 36.3 41 42 63

16090 NNC O P2 G7.0 1842–1895
Cornaby, William Arthur, 1860–1921.
A string of Chinese peach-stones.
London: C. H. Kelly, 1895. 15, 479 p. [Reprinted—Detroit: Gale, 1972. 15, 429 p.]
SUBJ 20 22.2 32.2 62 65 ▪ 17 22 23 31 41 55 56

16091 MCY P P3 G6.1 1842–1911
Elvin, John Mark Dutton, 1938–.
'The Mixed Court of the International Settlement at Shanghai (until 1911).'
PC 17 (Dec. 1963), 131–159.
SUBJ 22.2 66 ▪ 22.1

16092 MCY P P4 G1.5 1895–1911
Field, Margaret Hastings, 1934–.
'The Chinese boycott of 1905.'
PC 11 (Dec. 1957), 63–98.
SUBJ 22.2 26.2 66 ▪ 12 24.2 34.3 36.2 54

16093 CSH O P2 G1.3 1842–1895
Giles, Herbert Allen, 1875–1958.
'Democratic China.' In *China and the Chinese*, by H. A. Giles. [Selective entry]
New York: Columbia U. Press, 1912, 75–106. [Reprinted in *China and the Chinese*, by H. A. Giles. (Selective entry.) Taipei: Ch'eng-wen, 1968, 75–106.]
SUBJ 12 22.2 ▪ 14.5 24.5

16094 CSH P P2 G6.1 1895–1911
Ichiko Chūzō, 1913–.
'The gentry and the Ch'uan-sha riot of 1911 [Ch'uan-sha *hsien*, Kiangsu].' In *Kindai Chūgoku no seiji to shakai* (Modern Chinese politics and society), by Ichiko Chūzō. [Selective entry]
Tokyo: Tōkyō daigaku, Shuppankai, 1971, 21–27.
SUBJ 22 22.2 26.1 ▪ 25 26.3

16095 CSU O P3 G9.2 1842–1895
Kerr, John Glasgow, 1824–1901.
'The prisons of Canton.'
China review 4, 2 (Sept.–Oct. 1875), 115–122.
SUBJ 22.2

16096 CSU O P1 G1.2 1842–1895
Mayers, William Frederick, 1831–1878.
'Chinese oaths.'
NQCJ 3, 9 (Sept. 1869), 142–144.
SUBJ 22.2 ▪ 41 48

16097 NNC O P3 G9.2 1842–1895
Meadows, Thomas Taylor.
'Description of an execution at Canton.'
JRAS 16 (1856), 54–58.
SUBJ 22.2

16098 CSH U P7 G1.3 1644–1911
Nagel, August.
'Chinesische Volksjustiz' (Popular adjudication in China).
OL 26, 19 (10 Mai 1912), 411–413; 26, 20 (17 Mai 1912), 435–438.
SUBJ 22.2 ▪ 41 44

16099 WSU P P7 G1.3 1842–1895
Teng, Ssu-yü, 1906–.
'Some new light on the Nien movement and its effect on the fall of the Manchu dynasty.' In *Symposium on Chinese studies: Commemorating the Golden Jubilee of the University of Hong Kong, 1911–1961*, compiled by Dept. of Chinese, U. of Hong Kong. [Selective entry]
Hong Kong: U. of Hong Kong, 1968, vol. 3, 50–69.
SUBJ 22.2 ▪ 32.2

16100 NIC P P1 G1.2 –1842
Tsao, W. Y. (Ts'ao Wen-yen), 1908–.
'Equity in Chinese customary law.'
CC 3, 2 (Dec. 1960), 9–28.
SUBJ 22.2 64 ▪ 12.2 63

1644-1949

16101 CSH O P3 G5.1 1895–1928
The First Peking Prison. Tr. from the Chinese by Chen Chi et al.
Peking: First Peking Prison, 1916. 79 p. [Also available in *China: Questions for readjustment, Appendix 14*; Paris: Paris Peace Conference, 1919.]
SUBJ 22.1 22.2 ▪ 24.4 27 28 55

16102 NIC O P1 G1.3 1842–1928
Baker, John Earl, 1880–1957.
'Chinese views of truth and justice: How taxes and family life have determined the attitude toward law in China.'
Asia (New York: American Asiatic Assn.) 28, 7 (July 1928), 532–539.
SUBJ 12.2 22.2

16103 WSU FP P2 G1.2 1895–1928
China [Republic]. Ssu fa hsing cheng pu. (Ministry of Justice).
Die amtliche Sammlung chinesischer Rechtsgewohnheiten: Untersuchungsbericht über Gewohnheiten in Zivil- und Handelssachen (Min shang shih hsi kuan tiao ch'a pao kao lu) (The official collection of Chinese customary law: A research report on customary law in civil and commercial affairs), edited by Eduard Josef M- Kroker. Tr. by E. J. M. Kroker of *Min shang shih hsi kuan tiao ch'a pao kao lu* (Report on customary practices in civil and commercial affairs); Nanking: Ssu fa hsing cheng pu, 1930; 2 vols. 1822 p. [c.p.].
Bergen-Enkheim: Gerhard Kaffke, 1965. 3 vols. 282; 280; 262 p.
SUBJ 22.2 24.1 41 45 ▪ 23 24.3 24.6 29 38 42 47 57 65

16104 ELS S P7 G1.1 1842–1949
DeGlopper, Donald Robert, 1942–.
The origins and resolution of conflict in traditional Chinese society.
Unpublished masters thesis in Anthropology, U. of London [London School of Economics and Political Science], 1965. 233 p.
SUBJ 22.2 25 41 48 60 63 ▪ 26.1 26.3 30 42 45 47 64

16105 CSU U P2 G1.3 –1949
Fei Hsiao-tung (Fei Hsiao-t'ung), 1910–.
'Social erosion in the rural communities.' In *China's gentry: Essays in rural-urban relations*, rev. ed., by Fei Hsiao-tung, edited by Margaret Park Redfield. [Analytic entry]
Chicago: U. of Chicago Press, 1953, 127–142. [Reprinted in *China's gentry: Essays in rural-urban relations*, by Fei Hsiao-tung, edited by M. P. Redfield. (Analytic entry.) Chicago: U. of Chicago Press, 1968, 127–142.]
SUBJ 22.2 62 ▪ 16.1 16.3 17

16106 GMU P P2 G1.2 1895–1949
Kirfel, Harald Willibald, 1914–.
Das Gewohnheitsrecht bei Kauf und Verkauf von Immobilien in China und Mandschukuo (The customary law on purchase and sale of real estate in China and Manchoukuo).
Bonn: Scheur, 1940. 61 p. (Doctoral dissertation, Philosophische Fakultät, Universität Bonn)
Subj 14.1 22.2 45 ▪ 14.6

16107 NNC P P1 G1.3 –1949
Kirfel, Harald Willibald, 1914–.
'Das Gewohnheitsrecht in China' (Customary law in China).
Sinologica 3, 1 (1951), 52–64.
Subj 22.2 ▪ 41 45

16108 MCH PO P3 G6.1 1842–1928
Kotenev, Anatol M-, 1882–.
Shanghai, its mixed court and council: Material relating to the history of the Shanghai Municipal Council and the history, practice and statistics of the International Mixed Court.
Shanghai: North-China Daily News and Herald, 1925. 26, 588 p. [Reprinted—Taipei: Ch'eng-wen, 1968. 26, 588 p.]
Subj 12.2 22.2 66 ▪ 22 26.2 28 45

16109 MCH PO P3 G6.1 1842–1928
Kotenev, Anatol M-, 1882–.
Shanghai, its municipality and the Chinese: Being the history of the Shanghai Municipal Council and its relations with the Chinese, the practice of the International Mixed Court, and the inauguration and constitution of the Shanghai Provincial Court.
Shanghai: North-China Daily News and Herald, 1927. 17, 548 p.
Subj 20 22.2 66 ▪ 12.2 22

16110 WSU P P2 G1.2 1895–1928
Kroker, Eduard Josef M-, 1913–.
'Einleitung' (Introduction). In *Die amtliche Sammlung chinesischer Rechtsgewohnheiten: Untersuchungsbericht über Gewohnheiten* in Zivil- und Handelssachen *(Min shang shih hsi kuan tiao ch'a pao kao lu)* (The official collection of Chinese customary law: A research report on customary law in civil and commercial affairs), by Ssu fa hsing cheng pu, China [Republic], edited by E. J. M. Kroker. [Analytic entry]
Bergen-Enkheim: Gerhard Kaffke, 1965, vol. 1, 9–78. [For the monograph itself, see entry 16103.]
Subj 22.2 70 ▪ 12 12.2 63

16111 CSU S P1 G5.3 1644–1949
Kroker, Eduard Josef M-, 1913–.
'Rechtsgewohnheiten in der Provinz Shantung nach "Min-shang-shih hsi-kuan tiao-ch'a pao-kao-lu"' (Customary law in Shantung according to the *Report on customary practices in civil and commercial affairs*).
MS 14 (1949/55), 215–302.
Subj 22.2 ▪ 12.2

16112 NIC S P1 G1.2 1842–1949
McAleavy, Henry.
'Certain aspects of Chinese customary law in the light of Japanese scholarship.'
BSOAS 17, 3 (Oct. 1955), 535–547.
Subj 22.2 41 45 71 ▪ 12.2 47

16113 NNU S P3 G6.1 1842–1949
Wang, Shih-yung (Wang Shih-hsiung), 1914–.
The International Settlement of Shanghai.
Unpublished doctoral dissertation in International Law and Relations, New York U., 1939. 108, 55 p.
Subj 12.2 22 22.2 ▪ 12 21.3

1911-1949

16114 NNC P P4 G1.3 1911–1928
Bünger, Karl A-, 1903–.
'Schiedsgerichte in China' (Courts of arbitration in China).
Internationales Jahrbuch für Schiedsgerichtswesen in Zivil- und Handelssachen 2 (1928), 121–124.
Subj 12.2 22.2 ▪ 14.3 34.2 36.2

16115 NNC P P1 G1.3 1911–1949
Haas, Otto.
'Gewohnheitsrechtliche Vertragstypen in China' (Types of contracts in Chinese customary law).
Archiv für Ostasien 1, 1 (1948), 43–59.
Subj 22.2 34.2 ▪ 12.2 14.3 45 72

16116 CSU O P4 G9.2 1928–1949
Hino, Ashihei.
'Reports from Hainan.'
Canton 1, 1 (Apr. 1939), 32–36.
Subj 22.2 55 ▪ 31 46 47

16117 CSU P P2 G9.5 1928–1949
Hong Kong. Prison Dept.
Annual report, 1946/47–1948/49. [Issues for 1950/51–1971/72 are entered as 16141.]
[Hong Kong]: ——. Issued annually, 1947–1949. Average ca. 20 p.
Subj 22.2 ▪ 56

16118 NIC F P2 G8.2 1928–1949
Hsu, Francis L. K. (Hsü Lang-kuang), 1909–.
'Some problems of Chinese law in operation today.'
FEQ 3, 3 (May 1944), 211–221.
Subj 12.2 22.2 41 ▪ 25 26 46

16119 MAM P P2 G1.4 1928–1949
Kehoe, Robert Richard, 1922–.
The cease-fire in China, 1946: The operations of the Peiping executive headquarters and the truce teams during the Marshall mission.
Ann Arbor: University Microfilms (Publ. 70-24,280), 1970. 424 p. (Doctoral dissertation in Far Eastern Studies, American U.)
Subj 12 22.2 66 ▪ 14.2 15 32 32.2

16120 NNC P P2 G2.1 1911–1949
Kroker, Eduard Josef M-, 1913–.
'Rechtsgewohnheiten in Hei-lung-chiang, China' (Customary law in Heilungkiang).
ZVR 66, 1 (Jan. 1964), 29–156.
Subj 22.2 24.1 ▪ 24.6 26.1 26.3 34.2 55

16121 NIC O P3 G5.1 1911–1928
Lynn, Jermyn Chi-hung (Ling Ch'i-hung).
Social life of the Chinese, in Peking.
Peking, Tientsin: China Booksellers, 1928. 182 p.
Subj 22.2 31 55 63 ▪ 24.3 41 47 57

16122 NIC O P3 G6.1 1911–1928
Pollard, Robert Thomas, 1896–1939.
'The economic background of China's Nationalist movement.'
APSR 21, 4 (Nov. 1927), 853–857.
Subj 22.2 24 28 36.4 ▪ 32

16123 ICU FP P2 G1.2 1911–1949
Yen, Ching-yueh (Yen Ching-yüeh), 1905–.
Crime in relation to social change in China.
Unpublished doctoral dissertation in Sociology, U. of Chicago, 1934. 282 p.
Subj 12.2 22.2 25 41 46 ▪ 14.5 22.1 32.2 36.3 47 50 55 59

1911-1972
(including 1644-1972)

16124 CSU FP P2 G1.2 1928–1972
Cohen, Jerome Alan, 1930–.
'Drafting people's mediation rules.' In *The city in Communist China*, edited by John Wilson Lewis. [Analytic entry]
Stanford: Stanford U. Press, 1971, 29–50.
Subj 22.2 ▪ 12.2

16125 CSU P P2 G9.5 1842–1972
Evans, David Meurig Emrys, 1938–.
'Common law in a Chinese setting: The kernel or the nut?'
Hong Kong law j. 1, 1 (Jan. 1971), 9–32.
Subj 12.2 22.2 ▪ 41

16126 MCH S P3 G9.5 1842–1972
Haydon, Edwin Scott.
'The choice of Chinese customary law in Hong Kong.'
International and comparative law q. 4th series 11, 1 (Jan. 1962), 231–250.
Subj 12.2 22.2 ▪ 22.1 29 63

16127 MCH S P2 G1.1 –1972
Kroker, Eduard Josef M-, 1913–.
'Gerechtigkeit im chinesischen Gewohnheitsrecht' (Justice in Chinese customary law).
Archiv für Rechts- und Sozialphilosophie 45 (1959), 321–368.
Subj 22.2 45 ▪ 24.1 41 63

16128 CSU FP P2 G1.1 –1972
Lubman, Stanley Bernard, 1934–.
'Mao and mediation: Politics and dispute resolution in Communist China.'
California law review 55, 5 (Nov. 1967), 1284–1359.
Subj 12.2 22 22.1 22.2 ▪ 12 26.1 30 32 32.1 48 63 64

1949-1972

16129 CSH U P2 G9.4 1949–1972
Chiang Chen-hsin.
'Local shopkeeping.'
FEER 59, 14 (4 Apr. 1968), 29–30.
Subj 12 22.2 ▪ 32

16130 FPN O P2 G5.1 1949–1972
Chomé, Jules.
'Deux procès en République populaire de Chine.'
Droit au service de la paix nouvelle (2e) série 4 (juin 1956), 104–110.

'Two trials in the People's Republic of China.'
Law in the service of peace 4 (June 1956), 102–108. [Reprinted as 'In a Chinese court room.' *New world review* 25, 4 (Apr. 1957), 27–32.]
Subj 12.2 22.2 ▪ 41 47

16131 CSH O P3 G9.5 1949–1972
Close, Alexandra.
'Coming of age.'
FEER 56, 7 (18 May 1967), 421–423.
Subj 22.2 54

16132 CSU O P2 G9.5 1949–1972
Coates, Austin.
Myself a mandarin.
London: Muller, 1968. 250 p.
Subj 22.2 45 60 65 ▪ 12.2 22 41 46 57 66

16133 NIC F P8 G9.4 1949–1972
Gallin, Bernard, 1929–.
'A case for intervention in the field.'
Human organization 18, 3 (Fall 1959), 140–144.
Subj 12.2 22 22.2 48 ▪ 26.1

16134 CSU F P8 G9.4 1949–1972
Gallin, Bernard, 1929–.
'Mediation in changing Chinese society in rural Taiwan.'
JAAS 2, 2 (Apr. 1967), 77–90. [Reprinted in *Traditional and modern legal institutions in Asia and Africa*, edited by David Charles Buxbaum. (Selective entry.) Leiden: Brill, 1967, 77–90. (International studies in sociology and social anthropology, 5)]
Subj 22 22.2 ▪ 21.2 26

16135 CSU O P3 G9.5 1949–1972
Hanna, Willard Anderson, 1911–.
'A trial of two colonies. Part 1, Precarious balance in Portuguese Macao. Part 2, The city of the name of God hails a new messiah. Part 3, Communist challenge to British Hong Kong. Part 4, Paper tiger worsts painted dragon.'
AUFS-EAS 16, 1 (Feb. 1969), 1–14; 16, 2 (Feb. 1969), 1–16; 16, 4 (Mar. 1969), 1–15; 16, 5 (Mar. 1969), 1–11.
Subj 22.2 32.1 32.2 54 66 ▪ 17 22 22.1 24.2 26.2 26.4 31 36.2 36.4

16136 CSU O P3 G5.1 1949–1972
Henle, Hans.
'A prison in China.'
EH 4, 1 (Jan. 1965), 41–44.
Subj 12.2 22.2

16137 MCH PO P3 G9.5 1949–1972
Ho, Portia.
'[1] Delinquency: The background (Hong Kong). [2] The worst policy?'
FEER 50, 6 (11 Nov. 1965), 307–310; 50, 8 (25 Nov. 1965), 387–391.
Subj 22.2 41 54 ▪ 48

16138 CSU P P3 G9.5 1949–1972
Hong Kong.
Reports of the Standing Committee and the Advisory Committee on Corruption.
Hong Kong: Government Printer, 1962. 75 p.
Subj 22.2

16139 CSU O P3 G9.5 1949–1972
Hong Kong. Commission of Inquiry.
Kowloon disturbances, 1966: Report of Commission of Inquiry.
Hong Kong: Government Printer, 1967. 167 p.
Subj 22 22.1 22.2 ▪ 15 24 24.2 25 28 50 54

16140 HKU P P4 G9.5 1949–1972
Hong Kong. Committee to Examine the Law and Practice Relating to Corporal Punishment in Hong Kong.
Report of the Committee to Examine the Law and Practice Relating to Corporal Punishment in Hong Kong.
Hong Kong: Government Printer, 1966. 29 p.
Subj 22.2

16141 CSU P P2 G9.5 1949–1972
Hong Kong. Prison Dept.
Annual report by the Commissioner of Prisons, 1950/51–1971/72. [Issues for 1946/47–1948/49 are entered as 16117.]
Hong Kong: Government Printer. Issued annually, 1951–1972. Average ca. 40 p.
Subj 22.2 ▪ 56

16142 MCH P P3 G5.1 1949–1972
Hsia, Tao-tai (Hsia Tao-t'ai), 1915–.
'Justice in Peking: China's legal system on show.'
CS 5, 1 (16 Jan. 1967), 1–12.
Subj 12.2 22.2 ▪ 12.1 32.1

16143 MCH F P2 G9.2 1949–1972
Karnow, Stanley, 1925–.
'Why they fled: Refugee interviews.'
CS 4, 18 (7 Oct. 1966), 1–9.
Subj 22.1 22.2

16144 MCH P P2 G1.2 1949–1972
[La Dany, Ladislao] ———, 1914–.
'Curious stories: La dolce vita.'
CNA 661 (26 May 1967), 1–7.
Subj 16.1 22.2

16145 MCH P P7 G1.2 1949–1972
[La Dany, Ladislao] ———, 1914–.
'Peasant uprising.'
CNA 645 (27 Jan. 1967), 1–7.
Subj 22.2 25 26.3 ▪ 21.4 22.1 34.1

16146 CSU F P2 G9.5 1949–1972
Lau, M. P.
An epidemiological study of narcotic addiction in Hong Kong, edited by Pow-meng Yap (Yeh Pao-ming).
Hong Kong: Government Printer, 1967. 12, 301 p.
Subj 22.2 55 56

16147 CSU PO P3 G9.5 1949–1972
Lethbridge, Henry James, 1923–.
'Penal policy and crime rates: Comments on the Hong Kong experience.'
Hong Kong law j. 2, 1 (Jan. 1972), 54–68.
Subj 22.2 ▪ 12.2

16148 MCH FP P5 G1.2 1949–1972
Li, Victor H. (Li Hao), 1941–.
Law and social order in the People's Republic of China.
Unpublished doctoral dissertation in Law, Harvard U., 1971. 241, 41 p.
Subj 12 12.2 22 22.2 ▪ 12.1 16.1 22.1 26.1 32

16149 MCH O P3 G1.2 1949–1972
Pollard, Robert Spence Watson, 1907–.
'Prisons in China.'
Criminal law review 1956, 740–750.
Subj 22.2 ▪ 12.2 55

16150 CSU P P3 G7.1 1949–1972
Robinson, Thomas Webster, 1935–.
The Wuhan incident: Local strife and provincial rebellion during the Cultural Revolution.
Santa Monica, Calif.: RAND Corp., 1970. 32 p. (RAND papers, P-4511) [Reprinted—*CQ* 47 (July–Sept. 1971), 413–438.]
Subj 22.2 35 ▪ 32 32.1 54

16151 CSH P P1 G9.4 1949–1972
Snyder, Charles.
'East side story.'
FEER 69, 39 (26 Sept. 1970), 34–39.
Subj 22.2 54 ▪ 12.1

16152 CSU O P3 G9.5 1949–1972
Sung, Kayser.
'China's shadow over Hong Kong.' In *Contemporary China: Papers presented at the University of Guelph Conference, April 1968.* [Selective entry]
Toronto: Canadian Institute of International Affairs, 1968, 98–112.
Subj 22.2 32.2 ▪ 24 26.4 28

16153 MCH P P2 G1.2 1949–1972
Ubukata Naokichi, 1905–. [Tr. erroneously gives author's surname as Yokata.]
'On the regulative organizations in China as the beginning of socialistic autonomy.' Tr. of 'Chūgoku ni okeru shakaishugiteki jichi no tansho to shite no chōsho soshiki ni tsuite'; *Ajia keizai jumpō* 533 (11 Mar. 1963), 1–7.
Translations of political and sociological information on Communist China 101 (30 Sept. 1963), 1–6. (JPRS 21,259; MC 19,561/1963)
Subj 22.1 22.2 ▪ 22

16154 CSU P P2 G1.2 1949–1972
Weiss, Edith Brown.
'The East German social courts: Development and comparison with China.'
AJCL 20, 2 (Spring 1972), 266–289.
Subj 22.2

16155 CSH O P2 G1.3 1949–1972
Yu Hen Mao, pseud.
Fishy winds and bloody rains: The struggle between 'rebels' and 'power holders' in the Chinese Communist camp.
Taipei: World Anti-Communist League, China Chapter, 1970. 89 p. (Asian People's Anti-Communist League pamphlets, 16, 142)
Subj 22.2 54 ▪ 12.1 18 25

23 Folk Religion

民間之宗教信仰　　民間宗教

1644-1911

16156 NNC O P1 G1.3 1895–1911
'Das Stelzenlaufen in China' (Stilt racing in China).
Globus 75, 12 (25 März 1899), 193–194.
Subj 23 31 ▪ 65

16157 CSU O P3 G9.5 1842–1895
A. L.
'The Hongkong dragon feast.'

NQCJ 2, 10 (Oct. 1868), 156–157.
Subj 23

16158 NNC O P2 G1.1 1842–1911
Ball, James Dyer, 1847–1919.
The Celestial and his religions: or, The religious aspect in China.
Hong Kong: Kelly and Walsh, 1906. 240, 18 p.
Subj 23 33

16159 MCH O P2 G1.5 1895–1911
Boerschmann, Ernst, 1873–1949.
'Einige Beispiele für die gegenseitige Durchdringung der drei chinesischen Religionen' (Examples of the interpenetration of China's three religions).
ZE 43, 3/4 (1911), 429–435.
Subj 23 33 62 ▪ 13

16160 NNC F P8 G5.2 1895–1911
Boerschmann, Ernst, 1873–1949.
'Die Kultstätte des T'ien Lung Shan' (Places of worship on T'ien-lung-shan [T'ai-yüan *hsien*, Shansi]).
Artibus Asiae 1, 4 (1926), 262–279.
Subj 23 ▪ 21.3 33 62

16161 MCH PO P2 G1.3 –1911
Boerschmann, Ernst, 1873–1949.
Pagoden (Pagodas).
Berlin: de Gruyter, 1931. 15, 428 p.
Subj 23 62 ▪ 13 33 57

16162 MCH PO P7 G6.3 –1911
Boerschmann, Ernst, 1873–1949.
P'u T'o Shan, die heilige Insel der Kuan Yin (P'u-t'o-shan [Ting-hai *hsien*, Chekiang], the holy island of Kuan-yin [Goddess of Mercy]).
Berlin: Reimer, 1911. 17, 203 p.
Subj 23 ▪ 13 33 65

16163 NNM PO P3 G9.2 –1895
Bone, C-.
'The religious festivals of the Cantonese.'
CR 20, 8 (Aug. 1889), 367–371; 20, 9 (Sept. 1889), 391–403.
Subj 23 60 ▪ 43 47

16164 CBU S P3 G9.3 1842–1911
Booms, A- S- H-, 1841–1915.
De Chineezen: Hun godsdienst, hun jaartelling en hunne feestdagen (The Chinese: Their religion, their calendar, and their festivals).
The Hague: Veenstra, 1900? 93 p.
Subj 23 43 57

16165 MCH O P3 G1.2 1842–1895
Boüinais, Albert Marie Aristide, 1851–1895.
'La religion en Chine' (Religion in China). In *De Hanoi à Pékin: notes sur la Chine* (From Hanoi to Peking: Notes on China), by A. M. A. Boüinais. [Selective entry]
Paris: Berger-Levrault, 1892, 267–288.
Subj 23 ▪ 63

16166 CSU O P2 G8.1 1895–1911
Brenier, Henri, 1867–?
'Sur les frontières du Tibet: de Tchoung-king à Ta-tsien-lou et retour à Tchen-tou' (On the Tibetan frontiers: From Chungking to Ta-ch'ien-lu [i.e., K'ang-ting-fu] and back to Chengtu). In *La Mission lyonnaise d'exploration commerciale en Chine, 1895–1897, première partie, récits des voyages* (The Lyons Trade Mission to China, 1895–1897, Part 1, Travel accounts), compiled by Chambre de commerce de Lyon. [Selective entry]
Lyons: Rey, 1898, 154–170 [s.p.].
Subj 21.3 23 55 ▪ 24.2 26.4 28

16167 MCH O P2 G9.4 1842–1911
Campbell, William, 1841–?
Sketches from Formosa.
London: Marshall, 1915. 394 p.
Subj 23 ▪ 17 41 47 52 55

16168 CSH O P2 G8.2 1895–1911
Cordier, Charles Georges, 1872–1936.
'Prières des musulmans du Yun-nan pour obtenir la pluie' (Prayers for rain by the Muslims of Yunnan).
R. du monde musulman 26 (mars 1914), 84–91.
Subj 23

16169 NNC O P2 G1.4 1842–1895
Culbertson, Michael Simpson, 1819–1862.
Darkness in the flowery land: or, Religious notions and popular superstitions in North China.
New York: Scribner, 1857. 12, 235 p.
Subj 23 33 62 ▪ 13 43 66

16170 FPN O P7 G4.2 1895–1911
Dols, Joseph, 1874–1938.
'Fêtes et usages pendant le courant d'une année dans la province de Kan-sou (Chine)' (The annual round of festivals and customs in Kansu).
Annali lateranensi 1 (1937), 203–274.
Subj 23 43 ▪ 62 65

16171 NIC PO P1 G1.3 1644–1911
Doré, Henri, 1859–1931.
Recherches sur les superstitions en Chine.
Shanghai: Impr. de la Mission catholique, 1911–1938. 18 vols. 8467 p. [s.p.]. (Variétés sinologiques, 32, 34, 36, 39, 41, 42, 44–46, 48, 49, 51, 57, 61, 62, 66).

Researches into Chinese superstitions. Tr. by M- Kennelly, D- J- Finn, and Leo F- McGreal. [Partial tr.: vols. 1–10, 13 only; vols. 1–8 translated by Kennelly, vols. 9–10 by Finn, vol. 13 by McGreal.]
Shanghai: T'usewei Press, 1914–1938. 11 vols. 2341 p. [s.p.]. [Reprinted—Taipei: Ch'eng-wen, 1965–1967. 2341 p. (s.p.)]
Subj 23 56 65 ▪ 33 43 52 57 62 64

16172 CSU O P1 G1.2 1842–1895
Dudgeon, John Hepburn, 1837–1901.
'The worship of the moon.'
CR 13, 2 (Mar.–Apr. 1882), 129–134.
Subj 23 ▪ 62 65

16173 MCH P P4 G1.2 –1911
Eberhard, Wolfram, 1909–.
'Temple building activities in medieval and modern China: An experimental study.'
MS 23 (1964), 264–318. [Reprinted in *Moral and social values of the Chinese: Collected essays*, by W. Eberhard. (Selective entry.) Taipei: Chinese Materials and Research Aids Service Center, 1971, 423–477. (CMRASC occasional series, 6)]
Subj 20 23 ▪ 24 26

16174 CSU O P8 G9.2 1842–1895
Eitel, Ernest John, 1838–1908.
'On dragon-worship.'
NQCJ 3, 3 (Mar. 1869), 34–36.
Subj 23 62

16175 NNC O P7 G9.2 –1895
Eitel, Ernest John, 1838–1908.
'The religion of the Hakkas.'
NQCJ 1, 12 (Dec. 1867), 161–163; 2, 10 (Oct. 1868), 145–147; 2, 11 (Nov. 1868), 167–169; 3, 1 (Jan. 1869), 1–3.
Subj 23 29

16176 CSU O P2 G9.2 1842–1895
Eitel, Ernest John, 1838–1908.
'Somnambulism in China.'
NQCJ 2, 2 (Feb. 1868), 19–20.
Subj 23 ▪ 61

16177 CSU O P1 G1.2 1842–1895
Eitel, Ernest John, 1838–1908.
'Spirit-rapping in China.'
NQCJ 1, 12 (Dec. 1867), 164–165.
Subj 23

16178 CSU O P8 G6.3 1842–1895
Elwin, Arthur.
'A strange scene.' [On exorcism rites]
CR 12, 1 (Jan.–Feb. 1881), 16–19.
Subj 23 62 ▪ 56

16179 MCH O P1 G1.1 –1911
Enjoy, Paul d', 1866–?
'Le spiritisme en Chine' (Spiritism in China).
Bulletins et mémoires de la Société d'anthropologie de Paris 5e série 7 (1906), 87–100.
Subj 23 ▪ 33 62

16180 CSU O P3 G9.2 1842–1895
Ewer, F- H-.
'Some accounts of festivals in Canton.'
CR 3, 7 (Dec. 1870), 185–188.
Subj 23 ▪ 29 43 65

16181 MCH O P2 G9.3 –1895
Francken, J- J- C-.
'Godsdienst en bijgeloof der Chineezen' (Religion and superstition among the Chinese).
Tijdschrift voor Indische taal-, land- en volkenkunde 14 (1864), 38–74.
Subj 23 57 62 65 ▪ 33 43

16182 MCH O P2 G1.5 1842–1895
Galpin, Francis William, 1858–?
'Notes concerning the Chinese belief of evil and evil spirits.'
CR 5, 1 (Jan.–Feb. 1874), 42–50.
Subj 23 62 ▪ 65

16183 CSU O P2 G1.3 1842–1895
Gillespie, William.
The land of Sinim: or, China and Chinese missions.
Edinburgh: MacPhail, 1854. 240 p.
Subj 23 40 60 62 66 ▪ 11 13 33 47 48 65

16184 NNC P P1 G1.2 1644–1895
Goltz, Colmar, 1843–1916.
'Zauberei und Hexenkünste, Spiritismus und Schamanismus in China' (Sorcery and witchcraft, spiritism and shamanism in China).
MDG 6, 51 (1893), 1–36.
Subj 23 56 62 65 ▪ 33 41 47 57 63

16185 NNC P P2 G1.1 –1842
Granet, Marcel, 1884–1940.
Fêtes et chansons anciennes de la Chine (Ancient Chinese festivals and songs).
Paris: Ernest Leroux, 1919. 301 p.
Subj 13 16 23 40 65 ▪ 16.1 16.3 29 30 60

16186 ELO O P2 G1.1 1842–1895
Gray, John Henry, 1828–1890.
China: A history of the laws, manners and customs of the people, edited by William Gow Gregor.
London: Macmillan, 1878. 2 vols. 397; 374 p. [Reprinted—New York: AMS Press, 1972. 2 vols. 397; 374 p.]
Subj 12.1 12.2 13 23 64 ▪ 14 17 33 38 41 43 57 62 65

16187 MCH O P3 G9.2 1842–1895
Gray, John Henry, 1828–1890.
Walks in the city of Canton.
Hong Kong: De Souza, 1875. 695 p.
Subj 21.3 23 24.3 24.4 33 55 ▪ 13 22.2 26.2 28 34.2 34.3 38 39 57 65

16188 MCH P P1 G9.3 –1895
Groot, Jan Jakob Maria de, 1854–1921.
Jaarlijksche feesten en gebruiken van de Emoy-Chineezen (Annual festivals and customs of the Amoy Chinese).
Batavia: W. Bruining, 1881. 2 vols. 13, 644 p. [c.p.]. (Bataviaasch Genootschap van Kunsten en Weetenschappen, Verhandelingen, 42, 1–2).
'Les fêtes annuellement célebrés à Emoui: étude concernant la religion populaire des Chinois' (Annual festivals in Amoy: A study of Chinese folk religion). Tr. by C- G- Chavannes.
Annales du Musée Guimet 11 (1886), 1–399; 12 (1886), 400–830.
Subj 23 43 65 ▪ 41 57 62

16189 NIC FP P2 G1.2 –1911
Groot, Jan Jakob Maria de, 1854–1921.
The religion of the Chinese.
New York: Macmillan, 1910. 230 p.
Subj 23 ▪ 13 33 43 56 57 65

16190 MCH FP P2 G9.0 –1895
Groot, Jan Jakob Maria de, 1854–1921.
The religious system of China: Its ancient forms, evolution, history and present aspect, manners, customs and social institutions connected therewith.
Leiden: Brill, 1892–1910. 6 vols. 2843 p. [s.p.]. [Reprinted—Taipei: Ch'eng-wen, 1969. 2843 p. (s.p.)]
Subj 23 33 57 62 ▪ 13 43 51 56 63 65

16191 NNC U P1 G1.3 –1895
Grube, Wilhelm, 1855–1908.
'Die chinesische Volksreligion und ihre Beeinflussung durch den Buddhismus' (Buddhist influences on Chinese folk religion).
Globus 63, 19 (Mai 1893), 297–303.
Subj 23 ▪ 33 43 62 65

16192 MCH P P1 G1.1 –1911
Grube, Wilhelm, 1855–1908.
Religion und Kultus der Chinesen (The religion and cults of the Chinese).
Leipzig: Johannes Haupt, 1910. 220 p.
Subj 13 23 33 43 62 ▪ 57 63 65

16193 NNC PO P3 G9.3 –1911
Hodous, Lewis, 1872–1949.
'The great summer festival of China as observed in Foochow.'
JRAS-NCB new (2nd) series 43 (1912), 69–80.
Subj 23 ▪ 56 62 65

16194 NIC O P3 G9.3 1644–1911
Hodous, Lewis, 1872–1949.
'The reception of spring observed in Foochow, China.'
JAOS 42 (1922), 53–58.
Subj 13 23 31 65

16195 CSU P P1 G1.3 1842–1895
Hoffmann, Johann Joseph, 1805–1878.
'De Chinesche feestdagen volgens den *Javaanschen Almanak* voor het jaar "Dal" 1783 (J.C. 1854/55)' (The Chinese festivals for the year 'Dal' 1783 [A.D. 1854/55], according to the *Javanese almanac*).
BTLV 4 (1856), 264–277.
Subj 23 ▪ 43 57

16196 CSU P P2 G1.2 –1911
Hsu, Shin-yi (Hsü Hsin-i), 1938–.
'The cultural ecology of the locust cult in traditional China.'
AAAG 59, 4 (Dec. 1969), 731–752. [For fuller treatment, see entry 16335.]
Subj 11.3 18 23 33 65 ▪ 13

16197 CBU O P3 G6.1 1842–1895
Imbault-Huart, Camille Clément, 1857–1897.
'Une cérémonie bouddhiste en Chine: scène de la vie intime chinoise' (A Buddhist ceremony in China: Scene from intimate Chinese life).
JA 7e série 16 (oct.–déc. 1880), 526–533.
Subj 23 57 ▪ 55 62

16198 CBU PO P3 G5.1 1842–1895
Imbault-Huart, Camille Clément, 1857–1897.
'La fête de la mi-automne et du lapin lunaire' (The mid-autumn festival and the rabbit in the moon).
JA 8e série 5 (jan. 1885), 71–73.
Subj 23 65

16199 CBU PO P3 G5.1 1842–1895
Imbault-Huart, Camille Clément, 1857–1897.
'Origine de la fête du Double-Neuf' (The origin of the festival of the double ninth).
JA 8e série 3 (jan. 1884), 84–89.
Subj 23 65

16200 MCH PO P2 G1.3 –1911
Johnston, Reginald Fleming, 1874–1938.
Buddhist China.
New York: Dutton, 1913. 16, 403 p.
Subj 23 33 ▪ 13 62 65

16201 MCH O P6 G5.1 1842–1895
[Kafarov, Petr Ivanovich] *Otets* Palladii, 1817–1878.
'Nedelia v kitaiskoi kumirne v okrestnostiakh Pekina' (A week in a Chinese temple near Peking).
Sovremennik 96 (1863), 403–438.
Subj 20 23 26.1 33 ▪ 62 65

16202 NIC F P2 G2.0 1842–1895
Macintyre, John.
'Roadside religion in Manchuria.'
JRAS-CB new (2nd) series 21, 1 (1886), 43–66.
Subj 23 ▪ 62 65

16203 CSU O P1 G1.2 1842–1911
Martin, William Alexander Parsons, 1827–1916.
'The San Chiao, or three religions of China.' In *The lore of Cathay: or, The intellect of China*, by W. A. P. Martin. [Selective entry]
New York: Revell, 1901, 165–204. [Reprinted in *The lore of Cathay: or, The intellect of China*, by W. A. P. Martin. (Selective entry.) Taipei: Ch'eng-wen, 1971, 165–204.]
Subj 23 62

16204 MCH P P1 G1.3 –1895
Maspero, Henri, 1883–1945, René Grousset, 1885–1952, and Lucien Lion.
Les ivoires religieux et médicaux chinois d'après la collection Lucien Lion (Chinese religious and medical ivories from the collection of Lucien Lion).
Paris: Ed. d'art et d'histoire, 1939. 96 p.
Subj 23 56 ▪ 62 65

16205 NNC U P1 G9.3 1842–1895
Metzger, Emil, 1836–1890.
'Zauber und Zauberjungen bei den Chinesen' (Shamanism and shamans among the Chinese).
Globus 42, 7 (Feb. 1882), 110–112; 42, 8 (Feb. 1882), 119–121.
Subj 23 ▪ 65

16206 NNC PO P2 G5.3 –1911
Moule, Arthur Christopher, 1873–1957.
'T'ai Shan [T'ai-an *hsien*, Shantung].'
JRAS-NCB new (2nd) series 43 (1912), 1–31.
Subj 13 23 33 ▪ 55 62 65

16207 NNC P P1 G1.3 –1911
Mueller, Herbert, 1885–.
'Über das taoistische Pantheon der Chinesen: Seine Grundlagen und seine historische Entwicklung' (The foundations and historical development of the Chinese Taoist pantheon).
ZE 43, 3/4 (1911), 393–428.
Subj 23 62 ▪ 13 65

16208 MCH PO P2 G9.2 –1911
Nagel, August.
'Der chinesische Küchengott (Tsau-kyun)' (The Chinese Kitchen God, Tsao Chün).
Archiv für Religionswissenschaft 11 (1908), 23–43.
Subj 23 ▪ 41 62 65

16209 CSH O P2 G1.2 1895–1911
Nagel, August.
'Die sieben Schwestern' (The festival of the seven sisters [Pleiades]).
OL 25, 46 (17 Nov. 1911), 425–426.
Subj 23

16210 CSU O P2 G1.2 1842–1895
Nevius, John Livingston, 1829–1893.
Demon possession and allied themes: Being an inductive study of phenomena of our own times, 3rd ed.
New York: Revell, n.d. 520 p.
Subj 23 33 60

16211 CSU O P2 G1.3 1895–1911
Otto, Paul, 1873–.
'Some notes on Chinese festivals and their observances.'
EAM 2 (1903), 81–94.
Subj 13 23 ▪ 65

16212 MCH O P1 G1.2 –1895
Richard, Timothy, 1845–1919.
Calendar of the gods in China.
Shanghai: Methodist Publishing House, 1906. 37 p.
Subj 23

16213 GMS S P1 G1.3 –1911
Rousselle, Erwin Arthur, 1890–.
Schiffahrt und Fischerei des chinesischen Volkes (Navigation and fishing among the Chinese).
Darmstadt: Wittich, 1941. 44 p.
Subj 14.1 14.2 23 ▪ 55

16214 CSU P P1 G1.2 1842–1895
Scarborough, William, ?–1894.
'The popular religious literature of the Chinese.'
CR 13, 4 (July–Aug. 1882), 301–307; 13, 5 (Sept.–Oct. 1882), 337–355.
Subj 23 63 ▪ 41 62 65

16215 CBU O P3 G9.3 1842–1895
Schlegel, Gustaaf, 1840–1903.
'La fête de fouler le feu (*tah ho*), célébrée en Chine et par les Chinois à Java, le treize du troisième mois, anniversaire du "Grand Dieu protecteur de la vie (Pao ching Ta Ti)"' (The festival of walking on fire [*t'a huo*] celebrated in China and by the Chinese in Java on the thirteenth day of the third month, the birthday of 'Mighty god, protector of life' [Pao-sheng ta ti]).
Internationales Archiv für Ethnographie 9 (1896), 193–195.
Subj 23

16216 MCH O P3 G5.3 1895–1911
Schüler, Wilhelm, 1869–1935.
'Ein Tempeleinweihungsfest in China' (A temple-consecration ceremony in China).
Z. für Missionskunde und Religionswissenschaft 21, 4 (1906), 110–115.
Subj 23 33 ▪ 62

16217 CSU FP P7 G1.1 1644–1895
Topley, Marjorie Doreen, 1927–.
'Chinese religion and rural cohesion in the nineteenth century.'
JRAS-HKB 8 (1968), 9–43.
Subj 23 33 ▪ 13 26.1 32.2 42 43 48

16218 MCH O P2 G9.2 1644–1842
Torén, Olof (Olof Toreen; Olof Torée), 1718–1753.
'En ostindisk resa til Suratte, China, etc. från 1750 April 1. til 1752 Jun. 26.' In *Dagbok öfwer en ostindisk resa åren 1750, 1751, 1752*, by Pehr Osbeck. [Analytic entry]
Stockholm: Grefing, 1757, 313–376. [Separately reprinted as *En ostindisk resa*. Stockholm: Tiden, 1961. 123 p.]

'Eine ostindische Reise nach Surate, China, etc., von 1750 den 1 April bis 1752 den 26. Juni.' Tr. by Johan Gottlieb Georgi. In *Reise nach Ostindien und China*, by P. Osbeck. [Analytic entry]
Rostock: Koppe, 1765, 431–514.

Voyage de Mons. Olof Torée, aumonier de la Compagnie suedoise des Indes Orientales, fait à Surate, à la Chine etc. depuis le prémier avril 1750 jusqu' au 26. juin 1752. Tr. by Dominique de Blackford.
Milan: Frères Reycends, 1771. 92 p.

'A voyage to Suratte [i.e., Surat], China, etc., from the 1st of April, 1750, to the 26th of June, 1752.' Tr. by John Reinhold Forster. In *A voyage to China and the East Indies*, by P. Osbeck. [Analytic entry]
London: White, 1771, vol. 2, 153–266.
Subj 12.2 14.3 23 31 66 ▪ 12 24.1 24.2 26.2 55 56 57 61

16219 MCH O P3 G5.1 1895–1911
[Tun Li-chen] Fu-ch'a Tun-ch'ung, 1885–1924?
Annual customs and festivals in Peking, as recorded in the 'Yen-ching Sui-shih-chi', 2nd ed. Tr. by Derk Bodde of *Yen-ching sui shih chi* (The annual round of festivities in Peking); Peking: Wen-te-chai, 1906; 70 ab.
Hong Kong: Hong Kong U. Press, 1965. 28, 147 p.
Subj 13 23 31 ▪ 33 62 65

16220 MCH PO P2 G5.3 1895–1911
Volpert, Ant——.
'Chinesische Volksgebräuche beim T'chi ju, Regenbitten' (Chinese folk customs relating to *ch'i-yü*, rain-making rituals).
Anthropos 12/13, 1/2 (Jan.–Apr. 1917/18), 144–151.
Subj 23 65 ▪ 13 24.1 26.1 26.3 28 33

16221 NNC PO P4 G5.3 –1911
Volpert, Ant——.
'Tsch'öng huang, der Schutzgott der Städte in China' (Ch'eng-huang, the Chinese City God).
Anthropos 5, 5/6 (Sept.–Dez. 1910), 991–1026.
Subj 13 23 ▪ 43 64 65

16222 MCH O P8 G5.3 1895–1911
Volpert, Ant——.
'Volksgebräuche bei der Neujahrsfeier in Ost-Schantung' (Folk customs of the New Year's celebration in eastern Shantung).
Anthropos 12/13, 5/6 (Sept.–Dez. 1917/18), 1118–1119.
Subj 23 65 ▪ 24.1 33 43

16223 NIC P P1 G1.2 –1842
Williams, Edward Thomas, 1854–1944.
'Witchcraft in the Chinese penal code.'
JRAS-NCB new (2nd) series 38 (1907), 61–96.
Subj 12.2 23 56 ▪ 62 65

16224 NIC O P1 G1.2 1895–1911
Williams, *Mrs.* Edward Thomas.
'Some popular religious literature of the Chinese.'
JRAS-CB new (2nd) series 33 (1899/1900), 11–29.
Subj 23 62 ▪ 63 65

1644-1949

16225 DLC U P8 G2.0 –1949
Alin, V- N-.
'Verovaniia i suevernye obychai kitaitsev, sviazannye s vrediteliami sel'skogo khoziaistva' (Chinese beliefs and superstitious customs relating to agricultural pests).
Zapiski Kharbinskogo obshchestva estestvoispytatelei i etnografov 1946, 1, 37–39.
Subj 23 65 ▪ 14.1

16226 MCH PO P2 G9.4 –1928
Alvarez, José María, 1871–?
'Los Chinos' (The Chinese). In *Formosa, geográfica e históricamente considerada, Tomo I* (A geographic and historical study of Taiwan, Vol. 1), by J. M. Álvarez. [Sole entry]
Barcelona: Librería Católica Internacional, 1930, 420–502.
Subj 23 40 50 ▪ 29 33 41 55 63

16227 ELO P P4 G6.1 –1928
Ayscough, Florence Wheelock, 1878–1942.
'The cult of the Ch'eng Huang Lao Yeh [city god].'
JRAS-NCB new (2nd) series 55 (1924), 131–155.
Subj 23 33 65 ▪ 22.1

16228 CSU PO P8 G5.3 –1928
Baker, Dwight Condo, 1892–.
T'ai Shan [T'ai-an hsien, Shantung]: An account of the sacred eastern peak of China.
Shanghai: Commercial Press, 1925. 20, 225 p. [Reprinted—Taipei: Ch'eng-wen, 1971. 20, 225 p.]
Subj 23 62 65 ▪ 13 55 57

16229 ELB PO P2 G1.1 –1949
Blofeld, John Eaton Calthorpe, 1913–.
The jewel in the lotus: An outline of present-day Buddhism in China.
London: Sidgwick and Jackson, 1948. 193 p.
Subj 23 33 ▪ 62 65

16230 CNY O P3 G5.1 1895–1928
Bouillard, Georges, 1862–1930.
'La nouvelle anneé chinoise: usage et coutumes. 1, douzième lune. 2, première lune' (Chinese New Year's customs. 1, The twelfth lunar month. 2, The first lunar month).
La Chine 11 (1er fév. 1922), 127–181.
Subj 13 23 ▪ 65

16231 NIC FP P7 G5.1 –1928
Bouillard, Georges, 1862–1930.
Pékin et ses environs, quatorzième série, environs sud-ouest: She King Shan, Yün Kiü Sze, Tung Yü Sze, Si Yü Sze (In and around Peking, Fourteenth series, The area to the southwest: Shih-ching-shan, Yün-chü-ssu, Tung-yü-ssu, Hsi-yü-ssu [Fang-shan *hsien*, Hopei]).
Peking: Nachbaur, 1924. n.p. [74 p. in all] [Reprinted from *La Chine* 1923.]
Subj 23 62 ▪ 33

16232 NIC FP P7 G5.1 –1928
Bouillard, Georges, 1862–1930.
Pékin et ses environs, quinzième série, environs sud-ouest: Tien K'ai Shan, Ku Shan, Shang Fang Shan, Tow Shuai Sze et les grottes de Yun Shui T'ung (In and around Peking, Fifteenth series, The area to the southwest: T'ien-k'ai-shan, Ku-shan, Shang-fang shan, Tou-shuai-ssu, and the grottos of Yün-shui-t'ung [Fang-shan *hsien*, Hopei]).
Peking: Nachbaur, 1924. n.p. [54 p. in all] [Reprinted from *La Chine* 56–59 (1924).]
Subj 13 23 62

16233 NIC F P8 G5.1 1644–1928
Bouillard, Georges, 1862–1930.
Pékin et ses environs, sixième série, le Temple de Pi Yün Sze (In and around

Peking, Sixth series, The Temple of Pi-yün-ssu [Wu-ch'ing *hsien*, Hopei]).
Peking: Nachbaur, 1923. n.p. [22 p. in all] [Reprinted from *La Chine* 44 (1923).]
Subj 23 62

16234 NNC F P7 G5.1 1644–1928
Bouillard, Georges, 1862–1930.
Péking et ses environs, première série, le Yang Shan et ses temples (In and around Peking, First series, Yang-shan and its temples [Wan-p'ing *hsien*, Hopei]).
Peking: Nachbaur, 1921. n.p. [44 p. in all] [Reprinted from *La Chine* 3–6 (1921).]
Subj 23 ▪ 13 62

16235 CNY O P3 G5.1 1895–1928
Bouillard, Georges, 1862–1930.
'Usages et coutumes à Péking durant la huitième lune' (Practices and customs in Peking during the eighth lunar month).
La Chine 26 (15 sept. 1922), 1335–1351.
Subj 13 23 ▪ 65

16236 CNY O P3 G5.1 1895–1928
Bouillard, Georges, 1862–1930.
'Usages et coutumes à Péking durant la 10e lune' (Practices and customs in Peking during the tenth lunar month).
La Chine 30 (15 nov. 1922), 1639–1651.
Subj 13 23 ▪ 65

16237 CNY O P3 G5.1 1895–1928
Bouillard, Georges, 1862–1930.
'Usages et coutumes à Péking durant la 11e lune' (Practices and customs in Peking during the eleventh lunar month).
La Chine 32 (15 déc. 1922), 1791–1796.
Subj 13 23 ▪ 65

16238 CNY O P3 G5.1 1895–1928
Bouillard, Georges, 1862–1930.
'Usages et coutumes à Péking durant la 2e lune' (Practices and customs in Peking during the second lunar month).
La Chine 35 (1er fév. 1923), 117–136.
Subj 13 23 ▪ 65

16239 CNY O P3 G5.1 1895–1928
Bouillard, Georges, 1862–1930.
'Usages et coutumes à Péking durant la 3e lune' (Practices and customs in Peking during the third lunar month).
La Chine 37 (1er mars 1923), 249–264.
Subj 13 23 ▪ 65

16240 CNY O P3 G5.1 1895–1928
Bouillard, Georges, 1862–1930.
'Usages et coutumes à Péking durant la 4e lune' (Practices and customs in Peking during the fourth lunar month).
La Chine 38 (15 mars 1923), 299–311.
Subj 13 23 ▪ 65

16241 CNY O P3 G5.1 1895–1928
Bouillard, Georges, 1862–1930.
'Usages et coutumes à Péking durant la 5e lune' (Practices and customs in Peking during the fifth lunar month).
La Chine 18 (15 mai 1922), 703–720.
Subj 13 23 ▪ 65

16242 CNY O P3 G5.1 1895–1928
Bouillard, Georges, 1862–1930.
'Usages et coutumes à Péking durant la 6e lune' (Practices and customs in Peking during the sixth lunar month).
La Chine 39 (1er avr. 1923), 391–405.
Subj 13 23 ▪ 65

16243 CNY O P3 G5.1 1895–1928
Bouillard, Georges, 1862–1930.
'Usages et coutumes à Péking durant le 7e lune' (Practices and customs in Peking during the seventh lunar month).
La Chine 40 (15 avr. 1923), 469–478.
Subj 13 23 ▪ 65

16244 CNY O P3 G5.1 1895–1928
Bouillard, Georges, 1862–1930.
'Usages et coutumes à Péking pendant la 9e lune' (Practices and customs in Peking during the ninth lunar month).
La Chine 29 (1er nov. 1922), 1573–1582.
Subj 13 23 ▪ 65

16245 NIC O P1 G1.2 1644–1928
Brace, A- J-.
'Spirits and magic in Chinese religion.'
JWCBRS 5 (1932), 133–148.
Subj 23 65 ▪ 56 57

16246 CSU O P1 G1.2 –1928
Bredon, Juliet.
Chinese New Year festivals.
Shanghai: Kelly and Walsh, 1930. 29 p.
Subj 23 31 ▪ 62 65

16247 NNM PO P2 G1.3 –1928
Bredon, Juliet, and Igor Mitrophanow.
The moon year: A record of Chinese customs and festivals.
Shanghai: Kelly and Walsh, 1927. 11, 514, 20 p. [Reprinted—New York: Paragon, 1966. 11, 514 p.] [Reprinted—Taipei: Ch'eng-wen, 1972. 11, 514, 20 p.]
Subj 23 62 65 ▪ 13 64 72

16248 ELS S P1 G1.1 –1949
Chamberlayne, John Henry, 1917–.
The people's religion in China.
Unpublished doctoral dissertation in Theology, U. of London [King's College], 1954. 316 p.
Subj 23 65 ▪ 43 52 57

16249 NIC P P1 G1.2 –1949
Chao Wei-pang.
'The origin and growth of the fu-chi [planchette].'
FS 1 (1942), 9–27.
Subj 23 65

16250 ELB O P3 G5.1 1895–1928
[Cormack, Annie] *Mrs.* James G-Cormack.
Everyday customs in China, 4th ed.
Edinburgh: Moray Press, 1935. 264 p.
Subj 23 41 57 65 ▪ 55

16251 MCH O P8 G1.2 –1949
Day, Clarence Burton, 1889–.
'Current values in peasant religion.'
CR 63, 7 (July 1932), 419–427.
Subj 23 63 ▪ 61

16252 CSU PO P2 G1.3 1895–1928
Doré, Henri, 1859–1931.
Manuel des superstitions chinoises (Handbook of Chinese superstitutions).
Shanghai: Impr. de l'Orphelinat de T'ou-sè-wè, 1926. 219 p.
Subj 23 29 56 57 62 65 ▪ 30 33 41 43 52 55

16253 NIC FP P1 G1.3 –1949
Eberhard, Wolfram, 1909–.
Chinese festivals, rev. ed.
Taipei: Orient Cultural Service, 1972. 160 p. (Asian Folklore and Social Life monographs, 38)
Subj 23 65

16254 NNC P P1 G1.3 –1928
Eberhard, Wolfram, 1909–.
'Chinesischer Bauzauber.'
ZE 71, 1 (1939), 87–99.

'Chinese building magic.' In *Studies in Chinese folklore and related essays*, by W. Eberhard. [Selective entry]
Bloomington: Indiana U., Research Center for the Language Sciences, 1970, 49–65. (Indiana U., Folklore Institute monograph series, 23)
Subj 23 55 65 ▪ 62

16255 CSU S P1 G1.2 –1949
Eberhard, Wolfram, 1909–.
'Neuere Forschungen zur Religion Chinas, 1920–1932' (Recent research on Chinese religion, 1920–1932).
Archiv für Religionswissenschaft 33 (1936), 304–344.

'Studies in Chinese religion: 1920–1932.' Tr. by Alide Eberhard. In *Moral and social values of the Chinese: Collected essays*, by W. Eberhard. [Selective entry]
Taipei: Chinese Materials and Research Aids Service Center, 1971, 335–399. (CMRASC occasional series, 6)
Subj 23 62 72 ▪ 13 70 71

16256 GBS O P3 G5.1 1895–1928
Eckstein, Oskar, 1879–.
Sonne über Peking (Sun over Peking).
Erlenbach-Zurich: Rotapfel, 1942. 197 p.
Subj 23 65 ▪ 19 55 56 66

16257 MCH O P1 G1.2 1895–1928
Edwards, Dwight Woodbridge.
'The syncretic mind in Chinese religions.'
CR 57, 6 (June 1926), 400–413.
Subj 23 ▪ 33 64

16258 MCH S P1 G1.1 –1949
Erkes, Eduard, 1891–1958.
'Gestaltswandel der Götter in China' (The transformation of the gods in China).
Forschungen und Fortschritte 21/23, 25/27 (Dez. 1947), 261–266.
Subj 23 65 ▪ 43

16259 NIC FP P1 G1.2 –1928
Feng, Han-yi (Feng Han-chi), 1902–, and John Knight Shryock, 1890–1952.
'The black magic in China known as *ku*.'
JAOS 55, 1 (Mar. 1935), 1–30.
Subj 23 65

16260 NIC O P2 G8.1 1895–1928
Graham, David Crockett, 1884–.
Religion in Szechwan province, China.
Washington, D.C.: Smithsonian Institution, 1928. 83 p. (Smithsonian miscellaneous collections, 80, 4) (Doctoral dissertation in Religion, U. of Chicago, 1927) [Reprinted—Ann Arbor: University Microfilms, n.d. 83 p.]
Subj 23 65 ▪ 43 52 56 57

16261 NNC S P2 G9.4 1644–1928
Haguenauer, M- C-.
'Formose depuis les origines jusqu'à l'annexion par le Japon' (Taiwan from

its origins to the Japanese annexation). [Review of *Taiwan bunka shi* (Notes on the culture of Taiwan), by Inō Kanori.]
B. de la Maison franco-japonaise 2, 3/4 (1930), 37–92.
Subj 12.1 14 23 47 ▪ 13 14.3 17 18 24.1 65

16262 NIC P P1 G1.2 –1928
Harvey, Edwin Deeks, 1880–1947.
'Shamanism in China.' In *Studies in the science of society*, edited by George Peter Murdock. [Sole entry]
New Haven: Yale U. Press, 1937, 247–266.
Subj 23 ▪ 65

16263 MCY PO P2 G1.2 –1949
Hodous, Lewis, 1872–1949.
'Folk religion.' In *China*, edited by Harley Farnsworth MacNair. [Selective entry]
Berkeley, Los Angeles: U. of California Press, 1946, 231–244. [Reprinted in *China*, edited by H. F. MacNair. (Selective entry.) Freeport, N.Y.: Books for Libraries, 1970, 231–244.]
Subj 23 43 ▪ 57 65

16264 NIC PO P2 G1.3 –1928
Hodous, Lewis, 1872–1949.
Folkways in China.
London: Probsthain, 1929. 248 p. [Reprinted—New York: AMS Press, 1972. 248 p.]
Subj 23 65 ▪ 13 62

16265 NNC O P3 G9.3 –1928
Hodous, Lewis, 1872–1949.
'The kite festival in Foochow, China.'
JRAS-NCB new (2nd) series 49 (1918), 76–81.
Subj 23 ▪ 62 65

16266 NNM O P1 G6.0 1895–1928
Hudson, W- H-.
'Gods and demons: Some current Chinese conceptions.'
CR 51, 8 (Aug. 1920), 550–556.
Subj 23 ▪ 57 65

16267 CSU O P2 G8.1 1895–1928
Hutson, James.
'Chinese life in the Tibetan foothills.'
NCR 1, 3 – 2, 6 (July 1919 – Dec. 1920), 210 p. in all. [Separately reprinted—Shanghai: Far Eastern Geographical Establishment, 1921. 210 p.]
Subj 22.2 23 32.2 41 57 65 ▪ 12.2 14.5 25 30 31 43 45 51 55 56

16268 NNC PO P1 G8.1 –1928
Hutson, James.
'The domestic altar.'
JRAS-NCB new (2nd) series 49 (1918), 93–100.
Subj 23 43 ▪ 62 65

16269 MCH S P1 G1.2 –1928
Krause, Friedrich Ernst August, 1879–.
'Die moderne Volksreligion' (Modern folk religion). In *Ju-Tao-Fo: Die religiösen und philosophischen Systeme Ostasiens* (Confucianism, Taoism, and Buddhism: The religious and philosophical system of East Asia), by F. E. A. Krause. [Sole entry]
Munich: Ernst Reinhardt, 1924, 207–240.
Subj 23 62 ▪ 43 57

16270 CSU O P2 G9.3 1842–1949
Liu, Chiang (Liu Ch'iang), 1895–.
'Fukien folkways and religion.'
CR 64, 11 (Nov. 1933), 701–713. [Reprinted—*Annual of the China Society* (Singapore) 1957, 20–35.]
Subj 23 65 ▪ 29 33 62

16271 MCH PO P2 G1.3 –1949
Maspero, Henri, 1883–1945.
'La religion populaire moderne' (Modern folk religion). In *Mélanges posthumes sur les religions et l'histoire de la Chine, vol. 1, les religions chinoises* (A posthumous miscellany on the religions and history of China, Vol. 1, Chinese religions), by H. Maspero. [Sole entry]
Paris: Civilisations du Sud, 1950, 111–138. (Musée Guimet, Bibliothèque de diffusion, publications, 57)
Subj 23 33 57 65 ▪ 13 41 43 62

16272 MCH PO P2 G1.2 –1949
Miyahara, Mimpei, 1884–.
'Taoism, the popular religion of China.'
Contemporary Japan 9, 9 (Sept. 1940), 1140–1153.
Subj 23 ▪ 13 62 63

16273 MCH O P1 G1.1 –1928
Mortier, Florent.
'Le dragon chinois: son culte et ses fêtes' (The cult and festivals of the dragon in China).
BSRB 59 (1948), 92–99.
Subj 23 ▪ 13 65

16274 MCH O P1 G1.1 –1949
Mortier, Florent.
'La magie en Chine' (Magic in China).
BSRB 47 (1932), 353–360.
Subj 23 65 ▪ 56

16275 ELB O P2 G9.5 1895–1928
Peplow, S- H-, and M- Barker.
Hong Kong around and about, 2nd ed.
Hong Kong: Ye Olde Printerie, 1931. 196 p.
Subj 23 41 47 57 65 ▪ 25 48

16276 NIC O P1 G1.3 1644–1928
Plopper, Clifford Henry, 1885–.
Chinese religion seen through the proverb.
Shanghai: China Press, 1926. 381 p. [Reprinted—New York: Paragon, 1969. 11, 368 p.]
Subj 23 65 ▪ 13 33 57 62

16277 ICU P P2 G1.2 1895–1928
Putnam, Katharine.
Some Chinese customs and their adaptation in Christian practices.
Unpublished masters thesis in Practical Theology, U. of Chicago, 1928. 124 p.
Subj 23 29 43 65 ▪ 41 52 56 57 66

16278 NNC O P1 G1.3 –1949
Rousselle, Erwin Arthur, 1890–.
'Chinesische Neujahrsbräuche' (Chinese New Year's customs).
Sinica 12, 1/2 (Jan.–März 1937), 1–17.
Subj 23 41 ▪ 43 55 65

16279 CBU P P1 G1.3 –1949
Schang, Tscheng-Tsu (Shang Ch'eng-tsu), 1899–.
Der Schamanismus in China: Eine Untersuchung zur Geschichte der chinesischen 'wu' (Shamanism in China: An examination of the history of the Chinese *wu* [shaman]).
Hamburg: The author, 1934. 83 p. (Doctoral dissertation, Philosophische Fakultät, Universität Hamburg)
Subj 23 33 56 62 65 ▪ 12 25 47

16280 CSH U P2 G1.3 –1949
Serebrennikov, I- I-.
'Mif i religioznyi kul't v Kitae' (Myths and religious cults in China). [With English abstract]
VM 1930, 4, 68–76.
Subj 23 ▪ 43 62

16281 DLC P P1 G1.1 –1928
Shkurkin, Pavel Vasil'evich, 1868–1943.
Ocherki daosizma (Notes on Taoism).
Harbin: Izd-vo O-va orientalistov, 1926. 73 p.
Subj 13 23 63 ▪ 62 64

16282 NIC S P1 G1.2 –1949
Smith, David Howard, 1900–.
'Saviour gods in Chinese religion.' In *The saviour god: Comparative studies in the concept of salvation*, edited by Samuel George Frederick Brandon. [Sole entry]
New York: Barnes and Noble, 1963, 174–190.
Subj 23 ▪ 13 33

16283 MCH PO P1 G1.0 –1949
Tao, Pung-fai (T'ao P'eng-fei).
'Blick auf die Welt der Mystik und des Aberglaubens in China' (A look into the world of mysticism and superstition in China).
OR 16, 4 (16 Feb. 1935), 105–108; 16, 5 (1 März 1935), 129–133.
Subj 23 65 ▪ 53 62 63

16284 NIC O P1 G1.2 –1928
Werner, Edward Theodore Chalmers, 1864–1954.
'Chinese composite deities.'
JRAS-NCB new (2nd) series 54 (1923), 250–267.
Subj 23 ▪ 65

1911-1949

16285 CSH U P1 G1.2 1911–1928
Baranov, Ippolit Gavrilovich.
'Kitaiskii novyi god' (The Chinese New Year). [With English abstract]
VM 1927, 1, 1–14 [s.p.]. [Separately reprinted—Harbin: Izd-vo Ob-va izucheniia Man'chzhurskogo kraia, 1927. 18 p. (Obshchestvo izucheniia Man'chzhurskogo kraia, Istoriko-etnograficheskaia sektsiia, seriia A, 16)]
Subj 23 ▪ 13 43 65

16286 MCH P P1 G1.1 1911–1949
Bertuccioli, Giuliano.
'Breve nota sul "maestro del cielo"' (A brief note on the Heavenly Master [T'ien-shih]).
Rivista degli studi orientali 27, 1/4 (1952), 139–140.
Subj 23

16287 NIC O P1 G8.0 1911–1928
Brown, Harold George.
'What the gods say in West China.'
JWCBRS 3 (1926/29), 134–150.
Subj 23 62

16288 NIC S P2 G9.2 1911–1949
Chao Wei-pang.
'Games at the mid-autumn festival in Kuang-tung.'

FS 3, 1 (1944), 1–16.
Subj 23 62 ▪ 65

16289 NNC FP P4 G1.2 1928–1949
Cressy, Earl Herbert, 1883–.
'A study in indigenous religions.' In *China*, edited by Orville Anderson Petty. [Selective entry]
New York: Harper, 1933, 655–716. (Laymans Foreign Missions Inquiry, Factfinders' reports, 5; Supplementary series, part 2)
Subj 23 33 ▪ 41 62 65

16290 MCY O P8 G6.3 1928–1949
Day, Clarence Burton, 1889–.
Chinese peasant cults: Being a study of Chinese paper gods, 2nd ed.
Taipei: Ch'eng-wen, 1969. 243 p.
Subj 23 62 65 ▪ 30 33 43 56 57

16291 NIC O P8 G6.3 1928–1949
Day, Clarence Burton, 1889–.
'The New Year ceremonials of Chow-wang-miao [i.e., Chou-wang-miao village, Ch'ung-te *hsien*, Chekiang].'
CJ 32, 1 (Jan. 1940), 6–12.
Subj 23 65

16292 NIC O P3 G6.1 1911–1928
Day, Clarence Burton, 1889–.
'Shanghai invites the God of Wealth.'
CJ 8, 6 (June 1928), 289–294.
Subj 23 26.2 34.2

16293 CSU O P3 G5.1 1928–1949
Dean, John Anton.
'Consecrated images of China.'
CJ 21, 4 (Oct. 1934), 150–160.
Subj 23 62

16294 MCH O P1 G1.2 1928–1949
Dols, Joseph, 1874–1938.
'L'usage du sang dans les cérémonies chinoises' (The use of blood in Chinese ceremonies).
BSRB 54 (1939), 123–128.
Subj 23 56 65 ▪ 13 48 51

16295 NNC F P3 G5.0 1928–1949
Eder, Matthias, 1902–.
'Spielgeräte und Spiele im chinesischen Neujahrsbrauchtum mit Aufzeigung magischer Bedeutung' (Games and toys in Chinese New Year's customs and their magical significance).
FS 6, 2 (1947), 1–202.
Subj 23 62 65 ▪ 31 51 52

16296 CSU O P2 G5.3 1911–1928
Edmunds, Charles Keyser, 1876–1949.
'Shantung: China's holy land.'
NG 36, 3 (Sept. 1919), 231–252.
Subj 23 ▪ 22.2 28 57

16297 NIC O P3 G6.1 1928–1949
Faulder, H- Crozier.
'The temples of Shanghai.'
CJ 30, 6 (June 1939), 340–345.
Subj 23 ▪ 33 56 57

16298 NIC O P8 G9.5 1911–1949
Finn, Daniel J-, 1886–1936.
'Cult-objects from Aberdeen (Hong Kong, China) in the Lateran Museum.'
Annali lateranensi 1 (1937), 35–68.
Subj 23 43 57 62 65

16299 NNC F P7 G4.2 1911–1949
Frick, Johannes.
'Die Regenprozession in Lungsi, Nord-West China' (The rain procession in Lung-hsi *hsien* [Kansu]). In *Festschrift Paul Schebesta zum 75. Geburtstag* (Felicitation volume for Paul Schebesta on his seventy-fifth birthday). [Sole entry]
Vienna-Mödling: Missionsdruckerei St. Gabriel, 1963, 385–400. (Anthropos-Institut studia, 18)
Subj 23 24.1 26.3 ▪ 25 26.2 41 55 62

16300 NIC O P2 G8.1 1911–1949
Graham, David Crockett, 1884–.
Folk religions in Southwest China.
Washington, D.C.: Smithsonian Institution, 1961. 246 p. (Smithsonian miscellaneous collections, 142, 2)
Subj 23 ▪ 13 33 57 65

16301 CSU F P1 G8.1 1928–1949
Graham, David Crockett, 1884–.
'Religion of the Chinese in Szechwan.'
CR 66, 6 (June 1935), 363–369; 66, 7 (July 1935), 421–428; 66, 8 (Aug. 1935), 484–490; 66, 9 (Sept. 1935), 547–555. [Supplement to entry 16260]
Subj 23 65 ▪ 57 62

16302 MCH F P4 G8.1 1928–1949
Graham, David Crockett, 1884–.
'The temples of Suifu [the capital of I-pin *hsien*, Szechwan].'
CR 61, 2 (Feb. 1930), 108–120.
Subj 23 ▪ 33 62

16303 NIC FP P8 G3.2 1928–1949
Grootaers, Willem A-, 1911–.
'The Hutu god of Wan-ch'üan [*hsien*] (Chahar): A problem of method in folklore.'
Studia Serica 7 (Nov. 1948), 41–53.
Subj 23 65

16304 CBU F P3 G5.1 1928–1949
Grootaers, Willem A-, 1911–.
'Une séance de spiritisme dans une religion secrète à Péking en 1948' (A spiritist seance of a secret religion in Peking in 1948).
Mélanges chinois et bouddhiques 9 (1948/51), 92–98.
Subj 23 33 ▪ 62

16305 CSU F P2 G5.2 1928–1949
Grootaers, Willem A-, 1911–.
'Les temples villageois de la région au sud de Tat'ong (Chansi nord): leurs inscriptions et leur histoire' (Village temples in the area south of Ta-t'ung, northern Shansi: Their inscriptions and history).
FS 4 (1945), 161–212.
Subj 21.3 23 ▪ 33 55

16306 NIC FP P8 G3.2 1928–1949
Grootaers, Willem A-, 1911–, Li Shih-yü, and Chang Chi-wen.
'Temples and history of Wanch'üan [*hsien*] (Chahar): The geographical method applied to folklore.'
MS 13 (1948), 209–316.
Subj 23 ▪ 21.3

16307 NIC F P8 G3.2 1928–1949
Grootaers, Willem A-, 1911–, Li Shih-yü, and Wang Fu-shih.
'Rural temples around Hsüan-hua (south Chahar): Their iconography and their history.'
FS 10, 1 (1951), 1–116.
Subj 23 ▪ 24.2 33 65

16308 NIC O P2 G1.2 1911–1928
Hayes, L- Newton.
'The gods of the Chinese.'
JRAS-NCB new (2nd) series 55 (1924), 84–104.
Subj 23 56 62 65

16309 NIC O P2 G1.2 1911–1949
Hodous, Lewis, 1872–1949.
'The ministry of Chinese religions.'
International review of missions 25, 99 (July 1936), 329–341.
Subj 23 26.3 33 ▪ 18 30 38

16310 NNC F P4 G5.2 1911–1949
Körner, Brunhild.
'Nan-Lao-Ch'üan, eine Flutsage aus West-China, und ihre Auswirkung auf ortliches Brauchtum' (*Nan-lao ch'üan*, a deluge myth from West China, and its effect on local customs).
Ethnos 15, 1/2 (Jan.–Mar. 1950), 46–56.
Subj 23 62 ▪ 41 47 65

16311 MCH F P8 G5.1 1928–1949
Körner, Brunhild.
Die religiöse Welt der Bäuerin in Nordchina (The religious world of the peasant woman of North China [in the village of Huang-ts'un, Ta-hsing *hsien*, Hopei]).
Stockholm: Statens Ethnografiska Museum, 1959. 86 p. (Reports from the Scientific Expedition to the North Western Provinces of China Under the Leadership of Dr. Sven Hedin, publications, 43; Ethnography, 8) (Doctoral dissertation, Freie Universität Berlin)
Subj 23 26.3 47 50 65 ▪ 41 43 51 55 56 57 62

16312 NNC O P2 G8.1 1928–1949
Laprairie, *Père* ———.
'Les religions du Seutchouan' (The religions of Szechwan).
R. nationale chinoise 41, 134 (fév. 1941), 125–142.
Subj 23 62 ▪ 33 43 63 65

16313 CSU O P3 G5.1 1928–1949
Leung, George Kin (Liang She-ch'ien), 1899–.
'Peiping's happy New Year.'
NG 70, 6 (Dec. 1936), 749–792.
Subj 23 24.3 ▪ 31

16314 NIC F P8 G5.1 1928–1949
Li Wei-tsu.
'On the cult of the four sacred animals (Szu Ta Men) in the neighborhood of Peking.'
FS 7 (1948), 1–94.
Subj 23 65 ▪ 33 56 62

16315 CSU O P3 G2.2 1928–1949
Liu, Chiang (Liu Ch'iang), 1895–.
'Religion, funeral rites, sacrifices, and festivals in Kirin.'
CR 65, 4 (Apr. 1934), 227–238.
Subj 23 33 57 ▪ 29 43 62 65

16316 SSK F P3 G5.1 1928–1949
Montell, Gösta, 1899–.
'Hungerandarnas fest' (The 'hungry ghost' festival).
Jorden runt 5, 4 (April 1933), 169–179.
SUBJ 23

16317 GMS O P2 G1.4 1928–1949
Montell, Gösta, 1899–.
Unter Göttern und Menschen: Erinnerungen an glückliche Jahre in Peking (Among gods and men: Memories of happy years in Peking).
Leipzig: Brockhaus, 1948. 202 p.
SUBJ 23 ▪ 26.2 33 41 43 55 65

16318 DLC O P8 G5.1 1911–1949
Murray, A- S-.
'Religion in the villages of North China.'
Religions 16 (July 1936), 18–25.
SUBJ 23 ▪ 65

16319 NIC O P3 G6.1 1911–1928
Ottewill, H- A-.
'Notes on the Tu T'ien Hui, held at Chinkiang on the 31st May, 1917.'
JRAS-NCB new (2nd) series 49 (1918), 86–92.
SUBJ 23 36.2 65

16320 NNM F P2 G1.2 1911–1928
Parker, Albert George, 1863–1937.
'A study of the religious beliefs and practices of the common people of China.'
CR 53, 8 (Aug. 1922), 503–512; 53, 9 (Sept. 1922), 575–585.
SUBJ 23 62 ▪ 43 63 65

16321 NNC O P8 G4.4 1911–1949
Schröder, Dominik.
'Ying-hsi, die Bewillkommnung der Freude' (*Ying-hsi*, the welcoming of joy).
Anthropos 41/44, 1/3 (1946/49), 185–192.
SUBJ 23 ▪ 26.3

16322 NNC F P8 G5.3 1911–1949
Thiel, Josef.
'Stellvertretende Gelübdeerfüllung' (Vow fulfillment by proxy). [A ceremony for redemption of a vow promising a sick child to a god in exchange for a cure]
FS 1 (1942), 28–32.
SUBJ 23 52 ▪ 26.3 65

16323 NNC F P8 G5.3 1911–1949
Thiel, P- I-.
'Der Erdgeist-Tempel als Weiterentwicklung des alten Erdaltars (Aus eigener Feldforschung in Süd-Schantung)' (The earth-god temple as an evolution of the ancient altar to the earth, based on personal field research in southern Shantung).
Sinologica 5, 3 (1957/58), 150–155.
SUBJ 23 ▪ 57 62 65

16324 NIC F P2 G5.2 1911–1928
Vleeschouwer, E- de.
'K'i yu [*ch'i-yü*, rain-making rituals].'
FS 2 (1943), 39–50.
SUBJ 23

16325 NNC O P8 G4.2 1928–1949
Zacher, Joachim.
'Die Tempelanlagen am Südabhang des Richthofengebirges erläutert am Beispiel von Yen-hu-chai-tzu' (The temples on the southern slopes of the Ch'i-lien mountains, as exemplified by Yen-hu-chai-tzu [Chang-yeh *hsien*, Kansu]).
FS 8 (1949), 270–276.
SUBJ 23 ▪ 26.3 33 63

1911-1972
(including 1644-1972)

16326 NIC PO P2 G9.5 –1972
Buck, Samuel, pseud.
'Chinese temples in Hong Kong.'
Orient (Hong Kong) 2, 7 (Feb. 1952), 27–29.
SUBJ 23 56 62

16327 NIC PO P2 G9.5 –1972
Buck, Samuel, pseud.
'Gods and goddesses of navigation.'
Orient (Hong Kong) 2, 9 (Apr. 1952), 25–27.
SUBJ 23 62

16328 ELO O P2 G9.5 –1972
Burkhardt, Valentine Rudolphe, 1884–.
Chinese creeds and customs.
Hong Kong: South China Morning Post, 1953, 1955, 1958. 3 vols. 181; 201; 164 p. [Reprinted—Taipei: Book World, 1958. 181; 201; 164 p.]
SUBJ 23 65 ▪ 29 32.2 33 52 57

16329 CSU S P2 G1.2 –1972
Chamberlayne, John Henry, 1917–.
'The Chinese earth-shrine.'
Numen 12, 1 (Jan. 1965), 164–182.
SUBJ 23 65 ▪ 13 43 62

16330 ICU P P2 G9.4 –1972
Chiu, Ming-chung, 1930–.
Two types of folk piety: A comparative study of two folk religions in Formosa.
Unpublished doctoral dissertation, Divinity School, U. of Chicago, 1970. 340 p.
SUBJ 23 30 65 ▪ 43 57

16331 CSH P P1 G4.0 1644–1972
Coffin, Edna, et al.
'Religion.' In *A regional handbook on Northwest China*, compiled by Far Eastern and Russian Institute, U. of Washington. [Selective entry]
New Haven: Human Relations Area Files, 1956, vol. 1, 324–363. (HRAF subcontractor's monographs, 59; Washington 5)
SUBJ 23 ▪ 13 33 66

16332 NIC P P1 G1.2 –1972
Gomes, Luís G-.
Festividades chinesas (Chinese festivals).
Macau: Notícias de Macau, 1953. 261 p.
SUBJ 23 31 54 65 ▪ 13 29 30 33 42 43 55 57

16333 CSU PO P8 G9.5 1911–1972
Hayes, James William, 1930–.
'A ceremony to propitiate the gods at Tong Fuk, Lantau [i.e., the village of T'ang-fu, Ta-yü shan, Hong Kong], 1958.'
JRAS-HKB 5 (1965), 122–124.
SUBJ 23 62 ▪ 26.1

16334 MAU PO P2 G9.5 1842–1972
Hayes, James William, 1930–.
'Chinese temples in the local setting.' In *Some traditional Chinese ideas and conceptions in Hong Kong social life today*, edited by Marjorie Doreen Topley. [Analytic entry]
Hong Kong: Royal Asiatic Society, Hong Kong Branch, 1967, 86–98.
SUBJ 23 ▪ 22 31 62

16335 MAM P P2 G1.2 –1972
Hsu, Shin-yi (Hsü Hsin-i), 1938–.
A multivariate approach to the analysis of the cultural-geographical factors of the Chinese folk religion.
Ann Arbor: University Microfilms (Publ. 68-3266), 1968. 284 p. (Doctoral dissertation in Geography, U. of California, Los Angeles)
SUBJ 11.3 23 33 65 ▪ 13 14 16 30 38 40

16336 MCH P P1 G1.2 –1972
Kermadec, H- de.
'La religion populaire chinoise actuelle' (Chinese folk religion today).
Rythmes du monde (Bruges) 10, 2 (1962), 13–36.
SUBJ 23 ▪ 13 32.2 43 65

16337 MCH O P1 G1.1 –1972
Koehn, Alfred.
'Harbingers of happiness: The door gods of China.'
Monumenta Nipponica 10, 1/2 (Apr. 1954), 81–106.
SUBJ 23 62 65 ▪ 45 51 56 61

16338 WSU PO P7 G9.0 –1972
Kung Chan-yuen (Kung Ch'un-hsien).
'The development of the islet Fu-T'ang Mên (Fu Tong Mun) and the temples in various parts of the region.' Tr. of 'Fo-t'ang-men yü Hsiang-kang Chiu-lung Hsin-chieh teng ti chih T'ien-hou miao' (Fo-t'ang-men and temples of the Empress of Heaven [Ma-tsu] in Hong Kong, Kowloon, and the New Territories); in *I pa ssu erh nien i ch'ien chih Hsiang-kang chi ch'i tui wai chiao t'ung: Hsiang-kang ch'ien tai shih*, edited by Lo Hsiang-lin; Hong Kong: Chung-kuo hsüeh she, 1959, 171–192. In *Hong Kong and its external communications before 1842*, edited by Lo Hsiang-lin. [Selective entry]
Hong Kong: Institute of Chinese Culture, 1963, 119–132.
SUBJ 23 62 ▪ 65

16339 NNC FP P2 G1.5 –1972
Liu Chi-wan (Liu Chih-wan), 1923–.
'The belief and practice of the Wen-shen [board of gods for cure or prevention of epidemics] cult in South China and Formosa.' In *Proceedings of the Second Biennial Conference of the International Association of Historians of Asia*, edited by Chang Kuei-yung et al. [Selective entry]
Taipei: International Assn. of Historians of Asia, 1962, 715–722.
SUBJ 23 33 56 ▪ 25 65

16340 CSU S P1 G1.1 1644–1972
Smith, David Howard, 1900–.
'The religious situation in modern China.' In *Chinese religions*, by D. H. Smith. [Selective entry]
New York: Holt, Rinehart and Winston, 1968, 170–181
SUBJ 23 ▪ 16.1 62

16341 MCH P P7 G9.2 –1972
Soymié, Michel.
'Le Lo-feou chan: étude de géographie religieuse' (The Lo-fou mountains [Kwangtung]: A study in religious geography).
BEFEO 48, 1 (1956), 1–138.
SUBJ 23 62 ▪ 13 21.3 33 65

16342 MAU PO P3 G9.5 1842–1972
Topley, Marjorie Doreen, 1927–, and James William Hayes, 1930–.
'Notes on temples and shrines of Tai Ping Shan street area [Hong Kong].' In *Some traditional Chinese ideas and conceptions in Hong Kong social life today*, edited by M. D. Topley. [Analytic entry]
Hong Kong: Royal Asiatic Society, Hong Kong Branch, 1967, 123–141.
SUBJ 23 57 62 ▪ 21.1 55

16343 NIC P P2 G1.2 –1972
Yang, C. K. (Yang Ch'ing-k'un), 1911–.
Religion in Chinese society: A study of contemporary social functions of religion and some of their historical factors.
Berkeley, Los Angeles: U. of California Press, 1961. 473 p.
SUBJ 13 23 30 33 62 63 ▪ 22.1 32.2 34.3 41 43 57 64

1949-1972

16344 CSU O P7 G9.5 1949–1972
'Ceremonies of propitiation carried out in connection with road works in the New Territories in 1960.'
JRAS-HKB 11 (1971), 204–209.
SUBJ 23 62

16345 MCH O P3 G6.1 1949–1972
'Spring festival in Shanghai.'
FEER 51, 9 (3 Mar. 1966), 413–415.
SUBJ 22.2 23 ▪ 24.3 33 55

16346 CSU F P6 G9.5 1949–1972
Anderson, Eugene Newton, Jr., 1941–.
'The happy heavenly bureaucracy: Supernaturals and the Hong Kong boat people.' In *Essays on South China's boat people*, by E. N. Anderson, Jr. [Analytic entry]
Taipei: Orient Cultural Service, 1972, 11–19. (Asian Folklore and Social Life monographs, 29)
SUBJ 23 65 ▪ 29

16347 IMC O P2 G9.4 1949–1972
Bellotti, Felice.
Formosa: isola dai due volti (Taiwan: Island of two faces).
Milan: Del Duca, 1958. 220 p.
Formose: l'île aux deux visages. Tr. by Louise Servian.
Paris: Del Duca, 1959. 289 p.
SUBJ 23 29 55 ▪ 11.3 15 19 21.1 22.1 26.1 26.2 32 64

16348 CSU F P7 G9.5 1949–1972
Berkowitz, Morris Ira, 1931–, Frederick Paul Brandauer, 1933–, and John Harland Reed, 1945–.
Folk religion in an urban setting: A study of Hakka villagers in transition.
Hong Kong: Christian Study Centre on Chinese Religion and Culture, 1969. 11, 167 p. [Also published in *Cheng feng; quarterly notes on Christianity and Chinese religion and culture* 12, 3/4 (1969), 1–167.]
SUBJ 23 41 43 50 52 65 ▪ 21 21.3 24.3 27 33 48 55 57 58 62

16349 CSU F P7 G9.5 1949–1972
Berkowitz, Morris Ira, 1931–, and John Harland Reed, 1945–.
'Research into the Chinese little tradition: A progress report.'
JAAS 6, 3/4 (July–Oct. 1971), 233–238.
SUBJ 23 65

16350 CSH O P7 G9.4 1949–1972
Chen Chi-lu (Ch'en Chi-lu).
'An annual procession of Tai-chiou-ya-bio [i.e., Ta-chung-yeh miao], a Taoist temple of Hsin-chuang, Taipei prefecture [i.e., T'ai-pei *hsien*, Taiwan].'
Studia Taiwanica 1 (Summer 1956), 1–4 [s.p.]. [In Chinese as well as English]
SUBJ 23

16351 CSU F P3 G9.4 1949–1972
Eberhard, Wolfram, 1909–.
'Religious activities and religious books in modern China.'
Z. für Missionswissenschaft und Religionswissenschaft 49, 4 (Okt. 1965), 260–269. [Reprinted in *Moral and social values of the Chinese: Collected essays*, by W. Eberhard. (Selective entry.) Taipei: Chinese Materials and Research Aids Service Center, 1971, 161–176. (CMRASC occasional series, 6)]
SUBJ 23 ▪ 62 63

16352 NNC S P8 G1.4 1949–1972
Eitner, Hans-Jürgen.
'"Sie ziehen es vor, sich an Gott zu wenden": Das kommunistische China im Kampf mit der Volksreligion' ('They prefer to turn to God': Communist China's struggle against folk religion).
Zeitwende; die neue Furche 32, 5 (Mai 1961), 320–326.
SUBJ 23 64 ▪ 13 43 62

16353 CSU S P7 G9.5 1949–1972
Johnson, Elizabeth Lominska, 1941–.
Review of *Folk religion in an urban setting: A study of Hakka villagers in transition*, by Morris Ira Berkowitz, Frederick Paul Brandauer, and John Harland Reed.
JRAS-HKB 10 (1970), 204–210.
SUBJ 23 65 ▪ 42 43

16354 CBU F P8 G9.4 1949–1972
Jordan, David Kinsey, 1942–.
Gods, ghosts, and ancestors: The folk religion of a Taiwanese village.
Berkeley, Los Angeles: U. of California Press, 1972. 18, 197 p. (Revision of *Supernatural aspects of family and village in rural southwestern Taiwan*, doctoral dissertation in Anthropology, U. of Chicago, 1969)
SUBJ 20 23 41 42 62 65 ▪ 21 21.2 22 25 30 33 43 57 58

16355 CSH P P2 G1.3 1949–1972
[La Dany, Ladislao] ———, 1914–.
'Life and religion.'
CNA 717 (19 July 1968), 1–7.
SUBJ 23 65 ▪ 22.2 24.3 28

16356 NIC P P1 G1.2 1949–1972
[La Dany, Ladislao] ———, 1914–.
'Popular beliefs: Taoism, Christianity.'
CNA 439 (28 Sept. 1962), 1–7.
SUBJ 13 23 65

16357 CSU F P3 G9.4 1949–1972
O'Hara, Albert Richard, 1907–.
'Attitudes toward religion in the university world of Free China.' In *Research on changes of Chinese society*, by A. R. O'Hara. [Selective entry]
Taipei: Orient Cultural Service, 1971, 111–134. (Asian Folklore and Social Life monographs, 20)
SUBJ 23 54 ▪ 17 33 63 66

16358 CSU F P3 G9.4 1949–1972
O'Hara, Albert Richard, 1907–.
'A factual survey of Taipei's temples and their functions.' In *Research on changes of Chinese society*, by A. R. O'Hara. [Selective entry]
Taipei: Orient Cultural Service, 1971, 91–109. (Asian Folklore and Social Life monographs, 20)
SUBJ 23 ▪ 33

16359 CSU F P2 G9.4 1949–1972
Saso, Michael Raleigh, 1930–.
Taiwan feasts and customs: A handbook of the principal feasts and customs of the lunar calendar on Taiwan.
Hsin-chu, Taiwan: Chabanel Language Institute, 1965. 92 p.
SUBJ 23 62 ▪ 43 55 65

16360 CSU FP P4 G9.4 1949–1972
Saso, Michael Raleigh, 1930–.
Taoism and the rite of cosmic renewal.
Pullman: Washington State U. Press, 1972. 120 p.
SUBJ 23 62 ▪ 33 65

16361 CSU F P8 G9.4 1949–1972
Saso, Michael Raleigh, 1930–.
'The Taoist tradition in Taiwan.'
CQ 41 (Jan.–Mar. 1970), 83–102.
SUBJ 23 33 ▪ 62

16362 CSH PO P1 G9.4 1949–1972
Schipper, Kristofer Marinus.
'The divine jester: Some remarks on the gods of the Chinese marionette theater.'
BIE 21 (Spring 1966), 81–96.
SUBJ 23 ▪ 31 33 65

16363 CSH S P1 G9.4 1949–1972
Stanford U. China Project.
'Religion.' In *Taiwan (Formosa)*, compiled by the organization cited. [Selective entry]
New Haven: Human Relations Area Files, 1956, vol. 1, 193–206. (HRAF subcontractor's monographs, 31; Stanford 5)
SUBJ 23 65 ▪ 33

16364 MCH F P7 G9.4 1949–1972
Thelin, Mark, and Wen-lang Li, 1938–.
'Religion in two Taiwanese villages.'
JCS 3 (1963), 44–57.
SUBJ 23 62

16365 MCH P P2 G9.4 1949–1972
Thompson, Laurence Gassius, 1926–.
'Notes on religious trends in Taiwan.'
MS 23 (1964), 319–350.
SUBJ 23 33 ▪ 29 62

16366 MAU F P3 G9.5 1949–1972
Topley, Marjorie Doreen, 1927–.
'Chinese occasional rites in Hong Kong.' In *Some traditional Chinese ideas and conceptions in Hong Kong social life today*, edited by M. D. Topley. [Analytic entry]
Hong Kong: Royal Asiatic Society, Hong Kong Branch, 1967, 99–117.
SUBJ 23 65

16367 NIC F P3 G1.0 1949–1972
Topley, Marjorie Doreen, 1927–.
'Paper charms and prayer sheets as adjuncts to Chinese worship.'
J. of the Malayan Branch of the Royal Asiatic Society 26, 1 (1953), 63–80.
SUBJ 23 65 ▪ 29

16368 CSM F P8 G9.4 1949–1972
Tseng, Wen-Shing.
'Psychiatric study of shamanism in Taiwan.'
Archives of general psychiatry 26, 6 (June 1972), 561–565.
SUBJ 23 ▪ 56 59 61

24 LOCAL ECONOMIC SYSTEMS
地方經濟　地方経済

1644-1911

16369 FPN O P2 G1.3 1644–1842
Braam Houckgeest, André Everard van, 1739–1801.
Voyage de l'ambassade de la Compagnie des Indes orientales hollandaises, vers l'empereur de la Chine, dans les années 1794, 1795, edited by M- L- E- Moreau de Saint-Méry.
Philadelphia: Chez l'éditeur, 1797, 1798. 2 vols. 80, 437; 12, 520 p.
Journey to Peking: An authentic account of the embassy of the Dutch East-India Company to the court of the Emperor of China, in the years 1794 and 1795.
London: Phillips, 1798. 2 vols. 288; 324 p. [Reprinted—New York: Paragon, 1970. 2 vols. 288; 324 p. (Edited by Barbara B- Stevens.)]
SUBJ 21.3 24 24.1 28 55 ▪ 12 24.4 26.1 26.3 63

16370 CSU PO P2 G8.3 1895–1911
Brenier, Henri, 1867–?
'Rapport sur le Koui-tcheou' (Report on Kweichow). In *La Mission lyonnaise d'exploration commerciale en Chine, 1895–1897, deuxième partie, rapports commerciaux et notes diverses* (The Lyons Trade Mission to China, 1895–1897, Part 2, Commercial reports and miscellaneous notes), compiled by Chambre de commerce de Lyon. [Selective entry]
Lyons: Rey, 1898, 207–230 [s.p.].
SUBJ 14.3 21.1 21.3 24

16371 CSU PO P2 G8.1 1895–1911
Brenier, Henri, 1867–?
'Rapport sur le Se-tchouan' (Report on Szechwan). In *La Mission lyonnaise d'exploration commerciale en Chine, 1895–1897, deuxième partie, rapports commerciaux et notes diverses* (The Lyons Trade Mission to China, 1895–1897, Part 2, Commercial reports and miscellaneous notes), compiled by Chambre de commerce de Lyon. [Selective entry]
Lyons: Rey, 1898, 231–270 [s.p.].
SUBJ 14.3 21 21.3 24 ▪ 14.5 24.2

16372 CSU PO P2 G8.2 1895–1911
[Brenier, Henri] H. B., 1867–?
'Rapport sur le Yun-Nan' (Report on Yunnan). In *La Mission lyonnaise d'exploration commerciale en Chine, 1895–1897, deuxième partie, rapports commerciaux et notes diverses* (The Lyons Trade Mission to China, 1895–1897, Part 2, Commercial reports and miscellaneous notes), compiled by Chambre de commerce de Lyon. [Selective entry]
Lyons: Rey, 1898, 129–156 [s.p.].
SUBJ 14.3 24 ▪ 21

16373 MCH O P3 G5.1 1895–1911
Bure, Pierre.
'Tientsin' (Tientsin).
B. de la Société royale belge de géographie 24 (1900), 312–339.
SUBJ 21.3 24 24.3 ▪ 24.2 24.6

16374 CSU PO P2 G1.1 1895–1911
China [Ch'ing]. [Shui wu ch'u]. Hai kuan. ([Board of Customs Control]. [Imperial] Maritime Customs).
Decennial reports on the trade, industries, etc., of the ports open to foreign commerce, and on the condition and development of the treaty port provinces, 1902–11, 3rd issue. [Issues for 1882–1891, 1892–1901, 1912–1921, and 1922–1931 are entered as 16375, 16376, 16424, and 16423.]
Shanghai: Tsung shui wu ssu shu, T'ung chi k'o, 1913. 2 vols. 435; 367, 42 p. (Hai kuan statistical series, 6)
SUBJ 17 24 24.5 24.6 56 ▪ 21 21.1 21.2 22 22.1 22.2 24.4 25

16375 CBU PO P2 G1.1 1842–1895
China [Ch'ing]. [Tsung li ya men]. Hai kuan. (Tsungli Yamen. [Imperial] Maritime Customs).
Decennial reports on the trade, navigation, industries, etc. of the ports open to foreign commerce in China and Corea, and on the condition and development of the treaty port provinces, 1882–91, 1st issue. [Issues for 1892–1901, 1902–1911, 1912–1921, and 1922–1931 are entered as 16376, 16374, 16424, and 16423.]
Shanghai: Tsung shui wu ssu shu, T'ung chi k'o, 1893. 12, 694, 84 p. (Hai kuan statistical series, 6)
SUBJ 17 24 24.2 24.5 66 ▪ 21 21.1 21.2 22 22.1 22.2 24.6 25 56

16376 CBU PO P2 G1.1 1842–1911
China [Ch'ing]. [Tsung li ya men]. Hai kuan. (Tsungli Yamen. [Imperial] Maritime Customs).
Decennial reports on the trade, navigation, industries, etc., of the ports open to foreign commerce in China, and on the condition and development of the treaty port provinces, 1892–1901, 2nd issue. [Issues for 1882–1891, 1902–1911, 1912–1921, and 1922–1931 are entered as 16375, 16374, 16424, and 16423.]
Shanghai: Tsung shui wu ssu shu, T'ung chi k'o, 1904, 1906. 2 vols. 11, 568; 13, 601, 74 p. (Hai kuan statistical series, 6)
SUBJ 24 24.2 24.5 25 66 ▪ 12 17 21 21.1 21.2 22 22.1 22.2 24.1

16377 FPN O P2 G5.3 1842–1895
Fauvel, Albert Auguste, 1851–1909.
Le théâtre de la guerre au Chan-toung (The theater of war in Shantung).
Paris: Publications périodiques, 1895. 18 p. [Reprinted from *Moniteur universel* 30 jan. – 16 fév. 1895.]
SUBJ 20 24 24.2 25 ▪ 15 21.1 22.2 28

16378 CSU O P2 G1.5 1842–1895
Fortune, Robert, 1813–1880.
A residence among the Chinese, inland, on the coast, and at sea: Being a narrative of a third visit to China, from 1853 to 1856.
London: Murray, 1857. 440 p. [Reprinted—Taipei: Ch'eng-wen, 1971. 440 p.]
SUBJ 23 24 24.3 24.4 32.2 ▪ 24.2 26.1 28 55 56 57 66

16379 NNC PO P2 G5.1 1644–1911
Franke, Otto, 1863–1946.
Beschreibung des Jehol-Gebietes in der Provinz Chihli (A description of the Jehol region of Chihli).
Leipzig: Dieterich'sche Verlagsbuchhandlung, 1902. 15, 103 p.
SUBJ 22 24 ▪ 14.3 21.1 21.2 22.1 25 40

16380 CSU O P7 G1.4 1842–1895
[Gilmore, J-] Hoinos, pseud.
'The Chinese in Mongolia.'
CR 8, 4 (July–Aug. 1877), 273–295.
SUBJ 24 24.3 24.4 28 66 ▪ 24.1 55

16381 GMS O P3 G7.1 1895–1911
Hirsch, Emil.
Wirtschaftliche Verhältnisse in Hankow im Jahre 1907 (The economic situation in Hankow in 1907).
Vienna: Manz, 1908. 14 p. (K. K. österreichisches Handelsmuseum, Kommerzielle Berichte, 9)
SUBJ 14.3 24 ▪ 24.2 24.3 24.4

16382 MBA O P2 G9.2 1895–1911
Jacquet, ———.
'Etude sur le Quang-toung' (Kwangtung).
RI nouvelle (2e) série 2, 4 (31 août 1904), 223–235; 2, 5 (15 sept. 1904), 310–312. [Reprinted—*R. des troupes coloniales* 3, 18 (oct. 1904), 331–367.]
SUBJ 21 24 66

16383 CSH PO P2 G2.0 1895–1911
Kavakami Tosikhiko (Kawakami Toshihiko), comp.
Promyshlennost' v severnoi Man'chzhurii (The productive economy of northern Manchuria). Tr. from the Japanese.
Harbin: Tipo-lit. Shtaba Zaamurskogo okruga pogranichnoi strazhi, 1909. 45, 137, 134 p. [s.p.]. (Materialy po Man'chzhurii, Mongolii, Kitaiu i IAponii, 32–34)
SUBJ 14.3 21.3 24 24.1 24.2 ▪ 11.3 14.5

16384 NNC FP P2 G2.1 1895–1911
Kitaiskaia Vostochnaia zheleznaia doroga.
Severnaia Man'chzhuriia, tom 2-oi, Kheiluntszianskaia provintsiia (Northern Manchuria, Vol. 2, Heilungkiang).
Harbin: Tip. KVzhd, 1918. 646 p.
SUBJ 20 24 24.2 ▪ 21 21.3 22 24.1 24.4 24.6

16385 NNC O P2 G2.3 1842–1911
Kolokolov, S- A-.
'Torgovo-promyshlennyi obzor Mukdenskoi provintsii: doneseniia imp. ros. gen. kons. v Mukdene' (Survey of trade and industry in Fengtien: Reports of the imperial Russian consul-general in Mukden).
DIRKP 13 (1912), 8–21.
SUBJ 24

16386 MCH O P8 G1.5 1895–1911
Leclère, André, ?–1915.
'Géographie générale des provinces chinoises voisines du Tonkin' (Comprehensive geography of the Chinese provinces bordering on Tonkin).
Géographie 1, 4 (15 avr. 1900), 267–288.
SUBJ 11.3 24 ▪ 21 29

16387 NNC O P2 G9.0 1842–1895
Legendre, Charles William, 1829–1899.
Reports on Amoy and the island of Formosa.
Washington, D.C.: U.S. Government Printing Office, 1871. 50 p.
SUBJ 14.3 24 66 ▪ 24.3 24.4 24.5 29

16388 CBU O P2 G1.5 1895–1911
Little, Archibald John, 1838–1908.
Mount Omi and beyond: A record of travel on the Thibetan border.
London: Heinemann, 1901. 14, 272 p.
SUBJ 24 55 66 ▪ 24.1 24.2 24.4 33

16389 FPN PO P2 G9.2 –1911
Madrolle, Claudius, 1870–?
Hai-nan et la côte continentale voisine (Hainan and the neighboring continental coast).
Paris: Augustin Challamel, 1900. 14, 18, 126 p.
SUBJ 12 23 24 66 ▪ 12.1 15 26.1 72

16390 CSU O P2 G5.3 1842–1895
Markham, John.
'Notes on the Shantung province: Being a journey from Chefoo to Tsiuhsien [i.e., Ch'iu-hsien], the city of Mencius.'
JRAS-NCB new (2nd) series 6 (1869/70), 1–29.
SUBJ 24 24.2 24.4 ▪ 21 21.1 24.3 55 57 66

16391 FPN O P2 G9.0 1895–1911
Maybon, Charles Batiste, 1872–1926.
'La vallée du Si-Kiang' (The West River valley).
Annales de la Section indo-chinoise de la Société de géographie commerciale 1898 (sept.), 1–37. [Reprinted—*RI* nouvelle (2e) série 9, 80 (30 avr. 1908), 559–574; 9, 81 (15 mai 1908), 647–668.]
SUBJ 21 24 55 ▪ 11.3 26.1

16392 CSU O P5 G1.5 1842–1895
Merz, Alfred.
'Bericht über seine erste Reise von Amoy nach Kiu-kiang' (Report on my first trip from Amoy to Kiukiang).
Z. der Gesellschaft für Erdkunde zu Berlin 23 (1888), 401–418.
SUBJ 24 24.2 24.3 ▪ 24.4 25 33

16393 MCH PO P2 G7.1 1842–1911
Nadarov, V-.
'Materialy k izucheniiu Khan'kou, ego geograficheskago polozheniia, sviazannykh s nim tranzitnykh putei, ego torgovli i pr.' (Data for the study of Hankow, its geographic position, connecting transportation routes, commerce, etc.).
IVI 2, 4 (1901), 464–522.
SUBJ 11.3 14.3 24 24.4 ▪ 21.4 24.2 24.6

16394 GLU P P2 G6.1 1842–1895
Peters, Helmut.
Die Taiping-Herrschaft in den beiden Kreisen Changshu und Zhaowen, unter besonderer Berücksichtigung ihrer Boden- und Steuerpolitik (Taiping rule in Ch'ang-shu *hsien* and Chao-wen *hsien* [Kiangsu], with special attention to land and fiscal policy).
Unpublished doctoral dissertation, Philosophische Fakultät, Universität Leipzig, 1962. 391 p.
SUBJ 12 24 24.1 24.5 32.2 64 ▪ 14.5 22 25 26.1 26.3

16395 NNC O P2 G1.2 1842–1895
Richthofen, Ferdinand Paul Wilhelm von, 1833–1905.
Baron Richthofen's letters, 1870–1872, 2nd ed.
Shanghai: North-China Herald, 1903. 211 p.
SUBJ 24 24.2 24.4 ▪ 15 22.2 24.3 29 32.2 66

16396 ²CSU O P2 G9.0 1895–1911
Thomas, R- D-.
A trip on the West River.
Canton: China Baptist Publication Society, 1903. 70 p. [Reprinted—Taipei: Ch'eng-wen, 1971. 70 p.]
SUBJ 23 24 65 ▪ 12 24.1 24.2 24.3

16397 MCH O P5 G2.2 1895–1911
Tishenko, Petr S-.
'Poezdka v TSzia-pi-gou' (A trip to Chia-p'i-kou [Hsün-hua *hsien*, Kirin]).
IVI 6 (1903), 1–36.
SUBJ 20 21.4 24 ▪ 26.4

16398 MCH O P2 G9.3 1842–1895
Valencia, Gregorio.
'Xan-fu: o, las tres prefecturas del N. O. de Fu-Kien' (*San-fu*: or, The three prefectures of northwestern Fukien [Chien-ning, Shao-wu, and Ting-ching]).
Correo sino-annamita (Manila) 33 (1905), 186–239.
SUBJ 22 24 ▪ 21 28

16399 MCH O P7 G3.0 1895–1911
Verbrugge, Raphaël, 1872–?
'La vie des pionniers chinois en Mongolie aux prises avec un sol ingrat (étude économique)' (An economic study of the life of Chinese pioneers in Mongolia, grappling with unproductive land).
Anthropos 16/17, 1/3 (1921/22), 265–297, 588–627; 18/19, 1/3 (1923/24), 189–252, 753–770; 20, 1/2 (Jan.–Apr. 1925), 244–275.
SUBJ 24 24.1 24.2 26.3 ▪ 21.2 24.3 26 28 55

1644-1949

16400 HKU P P4 G9.5 1842–1949
Commercial and industrial Hong Kong: A record of 94 years progress of the colony in commerce, trade, industry and shipping, 1841–1935.
Hong Kong: Bedikton Co., 1935. 200 p.
SUBJ 14.3 24 24.3 ▪ 24.2 24.4

16401 CSH FP P4 G6.1 –1949
China [Republic]. Shih yeh pu. Kuo chi mao i chü. (Ministry of Industry. Bureau of Foreign Trade), ed.
'Leading cities.' Tr. of 'Shang pu chi tu hui' (Treaty ports and large cities); in *Chung-kuo shih yeh chih: Chiang-su sheng* (Chinese economic surveys: Kiangsu); Shanghai: Kuo chi mao i chü, 1933, 1–90 [s.p.] [slightly condensed in tr.]. In *China industrial handbooks: Kiangsu*, edited by the agency cited. [Selective entry]
Shanghai: Kuo chi mao i chü, 1933, 99–138. [Reprinted in *China industrial handbooks: Kiangsu*, edited by the agency cited. (Selective entry.) Taipei: Ch'eng-wen, 1972, 99–138.]
SUBJ 24 24.4 ▪ 21.1 21.3 24.2 24.3

16402 CSH FP P3 G6.1 1842–1949
China [Republic]. Shih yeh pu. Kuo chi mao i chü. (Ministry of Industry. Bureau of Foreign Trade), ed.
'Nanking and Shanghai.' Tr. of 'Nan-ching chi Shang-hai'; in *Chung-kuo shih yeh chih: Chiang-su sheng* (Chinese economic surveys: Kiangsu); Shanghai: Kuo chi mao i chü, 1933, 1–50 [s.p.] [slightly condensed in tr.]. In *China industrial handbooks: Kiangsu*, edited by the agency cited. [Selective entry]
Shanghai: Kuo chi mao i chü, 1933, 65–96. [Reprinted in *China industrial handbooks: Kiangsu*, edited by the agency cited. (Selective entry.) Taipei: Ch'eng-wen, 1972, 65–96.]
SUBJ 20 24 ▪ 21.1 21.3 22

16403 CSU P P2 G5.3 1895–1928
Great Britain. Foreign Office. Historical Section.
Kiaochow and Weihaiwei.
London: His Majesty's Stationery Office, 1920. 62 p. (HS handbooks, 71)
SUBJ 24 24.2 ▪ 14.3 21 21.1 24.1 24.5 26.4 34.3 45

16404 NNC O P2 G8.1 1842–1928
Hosie, Alexander, 1853–1925.
Szechwan: Its products, industries and resources.
Shanghai: Kelly and Walsh, 1922. 185 p.
SUBJ 24 24.4 ▪ 14.3 24.1 24.2 55 56

16405 MCH P P3 G7.1 –1949
Li, Teh (Li Te), 1913–.
Hankau und sein Wirtschaftsleben (The economic life of Hankow).
Berlin-Charlottenburg: K. und R. Hoffmann, 1938. 69 p. (Doctoral dissertation, Philosophische Fakultät, Universität Berlin)
SUBJ 24 24.3 24.4 24.6 ▪ 14.3 21.1 21.4 24.2 50 72

16406 MCH P P2 G2.1 1895–1928
Men'shikov, P- N-, P- N- Smol'nikov, and A- I- Chirkov.
Severnaia Man'chzhuriia: otchet po komandirovke agentov kommercheskoi chasti KVzhd, 1914–1915 (Northern Manchuria: Report on a commercial mission by agents of the Commercial Department of the Chinese Eastern Railway, 1914–1915).
Harbin: Izd-vo Komm. chasti KVzhd, 1916, 1918. 2 vols. 652; 646 p.
SUBJ 22 22.1 24 24.1 ▪ 21 24.3 24.4

16407 NIC P P3 G6.1 1842–1949
Murphey, William Rhoads, III, 1919–.
Shanghai, key to modern China.
Cambridge: Harvard U. Press, 1953. 12, 232 p.
SUBJ 14.3 24 24.4 ▪ 14.2 21.1 21.3 22 24.2 66

16408 MCH FP P7 G5.0 1842–1949
Myers, Ramon Hawley, 1929–.
The Chinese peasant economy: Agricultural development in Hopei and Shantung, 1890–1949.
Cambridge: Harvard U. Press, 1970. 20, 396 p. (Harvard East Asian series, 47)
SUBJ 22 24 24.1 24.3 26 ▪ 21.4 24.2 24.5 34.1 65

16409 MCH P P3 G6.1 1842–1949
Penna, José Osvaldo de Meira.
Shanghai: aspectos históricos da China moderna (Shanghai: Historical aspects of modern China).
Rio de Janeiro: Américo-Edit., 1944. 324 p.
SUBJ 24 28 32.2 ▪ 22 33 66

16410 MCH P P8 G1.5 –1949
Rawski, Evelyn Sakakida, 1939–.
Agricultural change and the peasant economy of South China.
Cambridge: Harvard U. Press, 1972. 11, 282 p. (Harvard East Asian series, 66)
SUBJ 24 24.1 24.2 24.3 ▪ 21 22 26.1 26.3

1911-1949

16411 CSU FP P2 G7.3 1928–1949
'Agricultural and industrial conditions in Kiangsi.'
CEJ 17, 4 (Oct. 1935), 345–359; 17, 5 (Nov. 1935), 488–509.
SUBJ 24 24.1 24.4 ▪ 34.2

16412 CSH U P7 G5.1 1911–1928
'Industrial and agricultural conditions in a Chihli circuit [K'ou-pei *tao*].'
CEM 1, 12 (Sept. 1924), 14–21.
SUBJ 24 ▪ 24.1 24.3 24.4

16413 CSH O P4 G5.3 1911–1928
'Tehchow [Te *hsien*], an important town of northern Shantung.'
CEJ 1, 8 (Aug. 1927), 755–761.
SUBJ 24 24.3 ▪ 21.1 21.3 24.2 28

16414 NIC O P8 G6.1 1928–1949
Alley, Rewi, 1897–.
'Rural life in southern Kiangsu.'
CJ 26, 6 (June 1937), 328–333.
SUBJ 24 27

16415 NNC U P2 G7.3 1911–1949
Andreev, M- G-.
'Promyshlennost' TSziansi do sozdaniia sovetskoi vlasti' (Industry in Kiangsi before the establishment of soviet power).
PK 14 (1935), 158–185.
SUBJ 24 24.1 24.4 ▪ 24.3 32.2

16416 CSU O P3 G6.1 1928–1949
Barnett, Arthur Doak, 1921–.
'Riding high for a fall' [report to Institute of Current World Affairs, November 1947]. In *China on the eve of Communist takeover*, by A. D. Barnett. [Selective entry]
New York: Praeger, 1963, 17–24.
SUBJ 24 ▪ 26 32.2

16417 CSH P P3 G6.1 1928–1949
Barnett, Robert Warren, 1911–.
Economic Shanghai: Hostage to politics, 1937–1941.
New York: Institute of Pacific Relations, International Secretariat, 1941. 13, 210 p.
SUBJ 14.6 24 24.4 26.4 ▪ 15 28 36.4 66

16418 NIC F P2 G6.1 1928–1949
Bates, Miner Searle, 1897–.
Crop investigation in the Nanking area and sending economic data.
Shanghai: Shanghai Mercury Press, 1938. 24 p.
SUBJ 24 28 ▪ 24.1 24.2 24.3

16419 CSU O P2 G8.1 1911–1928
Beech, Joseph.
'The Eden of the flowery republic.'
NG 38, 5 (Nov. 1920), 355–390.
SUBJ 24 24.1 24.2 ▪ 24.4

16420 NNC PO P2 G7.3 1928–1949
Brauer, Max, 1887–, E- Briand-Clausen, and A- Stampar.
'Report on a survey of certain localities of Kiangsi: A publication by the National Economic Council, Jan. 1934.' In *Annexes to the Report to the Council of the League of Nations of its technical delegate on his mission in China from date of appointment until April 1, 1934, Annex 4.* [Sole entry]
Shanghai: North-China Daily News and Herald, 1934, 41–69.
SUBJ 17 24 28 34.1 ▪ 22

16421 CSH U P3 G9.2 1911–1949
Canton Advertising and Commission Agency.
Canton: Its port, industries and trade.
Canton: Canton Advertising and Commission Agency, 1932. 10, 250 p. [Reprinted—Taipei: Ch'eng-wen, 1971. 10, 250 p.]
SUBJ 24 24.2 24.6 ▪ 21.1 24.4 55

16422 CSU U P2 G4.1 1928–1949
Chang, Bintze T.
'Natural resources of southern Shensi.'
CEJ 12, 4 (Apr. 1933), 369–385.
SUBJ 21 24 24.1 28 ▪ 11.3 14.3 21.2 24.2 24.4

16423 CSU PO P2 G1.1 1911–1949
China [Republic]. [Yu chuan pu]. Hai kuan tsung shui wu ssu shu. T'ung chi k'o. ([Ministry of Posts and Communications]. Maritime Customs. Statistical Dept.).
Decennial reports on the trade, industries, etc., of the ports open to foreign commerce, and on the condition and development of the treaty port provinces, 1922–31, 5th issue. [Issues for 1882–1891, 1892–1901, 1902–1911, and 1912–1921 are entered as 16375, 16376, 16374, and 16424.]
Shanghai: Tsung shui wu ssu shu, T'ung chi k'o, 1933. 2 vols. 10, 654; 387 p. (Hai kuan tsung shui wu ssu shu statistical series, 6)
SUBJ 17 24 24.5 24.6 56 ▪ 21 21.1 21.2 22 22.1 22.2 24.4 25

16424 CSU PO P2 G1.1 1911–1928
China [Republic]. [Yu chuan pu]. T'ung shang hai kuan. Tsung shui wu ssu shu. ([Ministry of Posts and Communications]. Maritime Customs. Inspectorate General of Customs).
Decennial reports on the trade, industries, etc., of the ports open to foreign commerce, and on the condition and development of the treaty port provinces, 1912–21, 4th issue. [Issues for 1882–1891, 1892–1901, 1902–1911, and 1922–1931 are entered as 16375, 16376, 16374, and 16423]
Shanghai: Tsung shui wu ssu shu, T'ung chi k'o, 1924. 2 vols. 398; 460 p. (T'ung shang hai kuan statistical series, 6)
SUBJ 17 24 24.5 24.6 56 ▪ 21 21.1 21.2 22 22.1 22.2 24.4 25

16425 NIC F P7 G8.2 1928–1949
Fei Hsiao-tung (Fei Hsiao-t'ung), 1910–, and Chih-yi Chang (Chang Chih-i), 1911–.
Earthbound China: A study of rural economy in Yunnan.
Chicago: U. of Chicago Press, 1945. 18, 319 p.
SUBJ 24 24.1 24.4 26 28 ▪ 21.2 21.3 21.4 24.3 24.6 45 55

16426 CSH P P2 G2.2 1911–1928
Gerasimov, A- E-.
'Ocherki ekonomicheskogo sostoianiia raionov verkhov'ev r. Sungari: opyt ucheta kraevoi produktsii i tovarnykh resursov' (Notes on the economic condition of the upper reaches of the Sungari river: An attempt to assess regional products and commodity resources). [With English abstract]
VM 1929, 10, 46–55.
SUBJ 24 ▪ 21 24.1 24.4

16427 CSH O P7 G2.2 1928–1949
Gorlanov, T-.
'Raiony stantsii Siaosuifyn' i Badakhetszy' (The areas served by the train stations at Hsiao-sui-fen [i.e., Sui-yang] and Pa-ta-ho-tzu [Tung-ning *hsien*, Kirin]).
EB 1931, 5 (1 marta), 12–13.
SUBJ 24 ▪ 21 24.1 24.3 24.4

16428 CSH O P2 G2.2 1928–1949
[Gorlanov, T-?] T. G.
'Torgovlia i promyshlennost' uezda Dunnin' (Trade and industry in Tung-ning *hsien* [Kirin]).
EB 1932, 6 (15 marta), 13–14.
SUBJ 24 ▪ 24.3 24.4

16429 NNP P P2 G2.1 1911–1928
Gorlanov, T-.
'Tunkhesianskii uezd' (T'ung-ho *hsien* [Heilungkiang]).
EB 1927, 46 (20 noiabria), 10–12.
SUBJ 24 ▪ 21.2 21.4 45

16430 CSH P P2 G1.4 1928–1949
Hsu, Yung-ying (Hsü Yung-ying), 1902–.
A survey of Shensi-Kansu-Ningsia border region.
New York: Institute of Pacific Relations, International Secretariat, 1945. 2 vols. 97; 159 p.
SUBJ 15 21 22 22.1 22.2 24 ▪ 12 21.1 25 32 32.1 34.1 34.2 36.3

16431 IIU FP P2 G4.2 1928–1949
Kao, Chong-rwen (Kao Chung-jun), 1914–.
Geographic influences upon the economic activities of the Kansu corridor of Northwest China.

Unpublished doctoral dissertation in Geography, State U. of Iowa, 1950. 120 p.
Subj 21.3 21.4 24 24.1 ▪ 14.3 21 24.2 24.4 24.6 34.3 55

16432 MCH PO P2 G7.3 1928–1949
Kapelle, A-.
'Aufbau in Kiangsi' (Reconstruction in Kiangsi).
OR 16, 14 (1 Juli 1935), 375–381.
Subj 17 24 24.1 ▪ 14.3 24.2 28 31 34.1 38

16433 DLC FP P2 G2.1 1911–1928
Kormazov, V- A-.
Barga: ekonomicheskii ocherk (Economic survey of Barga [Hulunbuir League, Heilungkiang]).
Harbin: Tip. KVzhd, 1928. 10, 281, 32 p.
Subj 21 22 24 24.3 ▪ 24.1 24.4 24.6

16434 CSH P P7 G2.0 1911–1928
Kormazov, V- A-.
'Ocherki po ekonomike kitaiskogo Priamur'ia' (Notes on the economy of the Chinese Amur region). [With English abstract]
VM 1929, 11, 59–70.
Subj 11.3 24 ▪ 24.3 24.4

16435 CBU P P7 G2.1 1928–1949
Kormazov, V- A-.
'Torgovlia i promyshlennost' raiona zapadnoi linii Kitaisko-Vostochnoi zheleznoi dorogi' (Trade and industry in the area served by the western line of the Chinese Eastern Railway).
VM 1933, 17 (15 sentiabria), 56–67.
Subj 24 ▪ 21 21.2 24.1 24.3 24.4

16436 CSH PO P3 G2.1 1911–1928
Krestovskii, S- N-.
'Gorod Shuanchensian' i rabota stantsii Shuanchenpu' ([The capital of] Shuang-ch'eng *hsien* and the operation of the Shuang-ch'eng-pao station [Kirin]).
VM 1928, 8, 22–28.
Subj 24 ▪ 21.1 24.1 24.2 24.4

16437 CBU O P2 G2.1 1928–1949
Krylov, V- N-.
'Ekonomicheskie ocherki uezdov severnoi Man'chzhurii' (Economic notes on the counties of northern Manchuria).
VM 1933, 22 (1 dekabria), 43–48.
Subj 24 ▪ 21 24.1 24.3 24.4

16438 MCH P P2 G9.5 1928–1949
Ma, Ronald A. (Ma Jung-li), 1923–, and Edward Franciszek Szczepanik, 1915–.
The national income of Hong Kong, 1947–1950.
Hong Kong: Hong Kong U. Press, 1955. 10, 69 p.
Subj 24 24.5 ▪ 21.1 21.4 24.1 24.3

16439 CSH P P5 G2.2 1928–1949
Nikolaev, Vladimir Ivanovich.
'Sel'skoe khoziaistvo, torgovlia i promyshlennost' uezda Bin'sian'' (Agriculture, commerce, and industry in Pin *hsien* [Kirin]).
EB 1932, 11/12 (15 iiunia), 17–18.
Subj 24 ▪ 21.4 24.3

16440 CSH O P2 G2.1 1928–1949
Nikolaev, Vladimir Ivanovich.
'Torgovlia i promyshlennost' uezda Khailun'' (Trade and industry in Hai-lun *hsien* [Heilungkiang]).
EB 1931, 7 (1 aprelia), 15–16.
Subj 24 ▪ 21.1 24.3 24.4

16441 CSU O P3 G8.2 1928–1949
Passantino, Joseph E-.
'Kunming, southwestern gateway to China.'
NG 90, 2 (Aug. 1946), 137–168.
Subj 24 ▪ 24.2 24.3 24.6

16442 DLC P P2 G2.2 1911–1928
Pavlov, I- V-.
'Khoziaistvennye vozmozhnosti i khlebnaia torgovlia v Tun'binskom uezde Girinskoi prov.' (Economic prospects and the grain trade in T'ung-pin [i.e., Yen-shou] *hsien*, Kirin).
VM 1928, 9, 25–34.
Subj 24 24.3 ▪ 14.3 24.1 26.2 36.2

16443 CSU O P2 G8.1 1928–1949
Richardson, H- L-.
'Szechwan during the war.'
GJ 106, 1/2 (July–Aug. 1945), 1–25.
Subj 24 24.1 24.2 ▪ 11.3 12 17 24.4 28

16444 CSH P P3 G8.1 1928–1949
Tao, Chieh-ching.
'Gegenwärtige Geschäftsverhältnisse in Chungking' (The present situation of commerce in Chungking).
Das neue China 7, 46 (Jan. 1941), 887–892.
Subj 24 24.3 24.4 ▪ 24.6

16445 MCH O P7 G3.0 1911–1928
Verbrugge, Raphaël, 1872–?
'La vie économique au pays de San-Tao-Ho' (Economic life in the San-tao-ho area [Inner Mongolia]).
Anthropos 22, 3/4 (Mai–Aug. 1927), 507–529; 22, 5/6 (Sept.–Dez. 1927), 865–888.
Subj 24 24.1 24.2 55 ▪ 24.3 24.6 26.3 28

16446 CSH P P3 G2.2 1928–1949
Vladimirov, Nikolai Vasil'evich.
'Torgovo-promyshlennye predpriiatiia Kharbina' (Commercial-industrial enterprises in Harbin).
EB 1930, 10 (1 iiunia), 3–4.
Subj 24 34.2 ▪ 24.3 24.4

16447 NNC O P5 G8.1 1911–1928
Weiss, Fritz.
'Wirtschaftliche Verhältnisse des Chienchangtals in Szetschuan' (The economic situation in the Ch'ien-ch'ang valley in Szechwan).
Petermanns Mitteilungen 60, 6 (Juni 1914), 310–315.
Subj 24 ▪ 24.2 24.3 24.4

16448 CSH O P2 G2.1 1928–1949
Zhernakov, Vladimir Nikolaevich, 1909–.
'Ekonomicheskoe sostoianie Khailun'skogo uezda' (Economic conditions in Hai-lun *hsien* [Heilungkiang]).
VM 1933, 10/11 (15 iiunia), 63–70.
Subj 24 ▪ 14.3 21.1 24.1 24.3 24.4

16449 CBU PO P2 G2.1 1911–1949
Zhernakov, Vladimir Nikolaevich, 1909–.
'Keshan'skii uezd: ekonomiko-geograficheskii ocherk' (Survey of the economic geography of K'o-shan *hsien* [Heilungkiang]).
VM 1934, 8 (avgust), 79–96.
Subj 21.3 24 ▪ 21 22 24.1 24.2 24.3

16450 CSH P P7 G2.1 1928–1949
Zhernakov, Vladimir Nikolaevich, 1909–.
'Sel'skoe khoziaistvo i torgovlia uezda Tunkhe' (Agriculture and trade in T'ung-ho *hsien* [Heilungkiang]).
EB 1931, 20 (15 oktiabria), 8–9.
Subj 24 ▪ 24.1 24.3

1911-1972
(including 1644-1972)

16451 CSU U P3 G9.5 1928–1972
'Hong Kong: A survey.'
Economist (London) 229, 6530 (19 Oct. 1968), 1–22.
Subj 24 24.4 24.6 28 ▪ 22 22.2 24.3 26.4 34.2

16452 CSU PO P2 G1.2 1928–1972
Berger, Roland.
'Self-reliance, past and present.'
EH 9, 3 (1970), 8–24.
Subj 24 64 ▪ 24.1 24.4

16453 CSU S P2 G9.5 1928–1972
Dwyer, Denis John, 1933–.
'Size as a factor in economic growth: Some reflections on the case of Hong Kong.'
TESG 56, 5 (September–Oktober 1965), 186–192.
Subj 21.3 24

16454 MCH S P3 G9.5 1842–1972
Emina, Sergio.
'Hong Kong: uno sguardo ai suoi problemi economici e demografici' (A look at Hong Kong's economic and demographic problems).
Universo 41, 4 (luglio–agosto 1961), 635–648.
Subj 21.1 24 ▪ 22 22.2 24.4

16455 MMT S P2 G9.5 1928–1972
Lee, T. C. (Li T'ai-ch'u).
'The economy of Hong Kong since World War II.' In *Symposium on economic and social problems of the Far East*, edited by Edward Franciszek Szczepanik. [Selective entry]
Hong Kong: Hong Kong U. Press, 1962, 166–179.
Subj 24 28 ▪ 24.3 24.4 24.6

16456 CSU F P7 G9.5 1895–1972
Potter, Jack Michael, 1936–.
Capitalism and the Chinese peasant: Social and economic change in a Hong Kong village.
Berkeley, Los Angeles: U. of California Press, 1968. 13, 215 p. (Revision of *P'ing Shan: The changing economy of a Chinese village in Hong Kong*, doctoral dissertation in Anthropology, U. of California, Berkeley, 1964)
Subj 19 20 21.4 24 24.1 45 ▪ 24.3 24.6 26 26.3 34.1 41 42 55

1949-1972

16457 NNC O P2 G1.2 1949–1972
Alley, Rewi, 1897–.
China's hinterland in the Leap Forward.
Peking: New World Press, 1961. 549 p.
Subj 17 20 24 24.1 24.4 34.1 ▪ 22 26 52 54 55

16458 CSU O P2 G6.1 1949–1972
Alley, Rewi, 1897–.
'Nanking.'

EH 10, 2 (1971), 37–48.
Subj 24 24.1 24.4 ▪ 17 21.4 24.2 26.4 50

16459 CSH F P8 G7.1 1949–1972
Chang Chih-ming (Chang Chih-min), Wang En-ming, and Li Cheng-hsien (Li Ch'eng-hsien).
'How state production plan is carried out at the last lap: Hsiang and coops.' Tr. of 'Hsien nung yeh sheng ch'an chi hua t'ung nung yeh sheng ch'an ho tso she sheng ch'an hua ti chieh ho wen t'i' (Problems of coordinating production plans of agricultural producers' cooperatives and counties); *Chi hua ching chi* 1957, 5 (May), 18–19.
ECMM 93 (6 Aug. 1957), 32–34.
Subj 24 24.1 ▪ 32.1 34.1

16460 CSU P P2 G1.2 1949–1972
Chang, Sen-dou (Chang Sheng-tao), 1928–.
'The role of the agricultural geographer in Communist China.'
Professional geographer 18, 3 (May 1966), 125–128.
Subj 24 24.1 ▪ 36.1 62

16461 CBU O P7 G6.3 1949–1972
Chen Ch'iao-yi (Ch'en Ch'iao-i), et al.
'Diversified economy at Chekiang's Li-tu people's commune.' Tr. of 'Che-chiang sheng Shao-hsing hsien Li-chu jen min kung she ti to chung ching ying' (Diversified operations in Li-chu commune, Shao-hsing *hsien*, Chekiang); in *Jen min kung she ching chi kuei hua yü ching chi ti li wen chi* (Collected essays on economic planning and economic geography of the communes); Peking: K'o hsüeh ch'u pan she, 1959, 36–47. In *Economic plans and economic geography of people's communes*, mimeo., jointly edited by Chung-kuo ti li hsüeh hui (Geographical Society of China) *with* Ti li yen chiu so (Institute of Geography), Chung-kuo k'o hsüeh yüan (Chinese Academy of Sciences). [Selective entry]
Washington, D.C.: U.S. Joint Publications Research Service, 25 Feb. 1963, 86–113. (JPRS 17,789; MC 6864/1963) [Xerox copyflo available—New York: CCM Information Corp., Research and Microfilm Publications. (Scholarly Book Translation Series, 421)]
Subj 24 24.1 ▪ 24.4 26.3

16462 CBU O P7 G2.2 1949–1972
Chi-lin shih fan ta hsüeh. Ti li hsi. (Kirin Normal College. Dept. of Geography).
'The principles of planning of Chiang-mi-feng commune, Yung-chi region, Kirin.' Tr. of 'Chi-lin sheng Yung-chi hsien Chiang-mi-feng jen min kung she kuei hua kang yao' (The principles of the planning of Chiang-mi-feng commune, Yung-chi *hsien*, Kirin); in *Jen min kung she ching chi kuei hua yü ching chi ti li wen chi* (Collected essays on economic planning and economic geography of the communes); Peking: K'o hsüeh ch'u pan she, 1959, 177–187. In *Economic plans and economic geography of people's communes*, mimeo., jointly edited by Chung-kuo ti li hsüeh hui (Geographical Society of China) *with* Ti li yen chiu so (Institute of Geography), Chung-kuo k'o hsüeh yüan (Chinese Academy of Sciences). [Selective entry]
Washington, D.C.: U.S. Joint Publications Research Service, 25 Feb. 1963, 418–440. (JPRS 17,789; MC 6864/1963) [Xerox copyflo available—New York: CCM Information Corp., Research and Microfilm Publications. (Scholarly Book Translation Series, 421)]
Subj 24 24.1 ▪ 24.4

16463 CSH P P2 G9.5 1949–1972
Chou, K. R.
The Hong Kong economy: A miracle of growth.
Hong Kong: Academic Publications, 1966. 103 p.
Subj 24 24.6 ▪ 14.3 21 21.2 21.4 24.1 24.4 58

16464 NIC O P4 G9.2 1949–1972
Chung Ming.
'Huicheng [i.e., Hui-ch'eng-chen, Hsin-hui *hsien*, Kwangtung]: A town that rose from the ruins.'
China reconstructs 8, 4 (Apr. 1959), 26–28.
Subj 20 24

16465 CBU O P7 G5.1 1949–1972
Chung-kuo k'o hsüeh yüan. Ti li yen chiu so. Jen min kung she kuei hua kung tso tsu. (Chinese Academy of Sciences. Institute of Geography. Commune Planning Team).
'A general brochure on the principles (draft) of production development of Hsiao-t'ang-shan commune, Peiping [i.e., Peking municipality], 1960–1962.' Tr. of 'Pei-ching shih Hsiao-t'ang-shan jen min kung she 1960–1962 nien sheng ch'an fa chan kang yao (ts'ao an) tsung shuo ming shu'; in *Jen min kung she ching chi kuei hua yü ching chi ti li wen chi* (Collected essays on economic planning and economic geography of the communes); Peking: K'o hsüeh ch'u pan she, 1959, 188–205. In *Economic plans and economic geography of people's communes*, mimeo., jointly edited by Chung-kuo ti li hsüeh hui (Geographical Society of China) *with* Ti li yen chiu so (Institute of Geography), Chung-kuo k'o hsüeh yüan (Chinese Academy of Sciences). [Selective entry]
Washington, D.C.: U.S. Joint Publications Research Service, 25 Feb. 1963, 441–481. (JPRS 17,789; MC 6864/1963) [Xerox copyflo available—New York: CCM Information Corp. (Scholarly Book Translation Series, 421)]
Subj 24 24.1 ▪ 24.4 24.5

16466 CSH O P7 G6.1 1949–1972
Chung-kuo kung ch'an tang. Huai-yin ti fang wei yüan hui. Sheng ch'an ho tso pu. (Chinese Communist Party. Huai-yin Special District Committee. Cooperative Dept.).
'The Yitao township comprehensive plan.' Tr. of 'I-t'ao hsiang ti ch'üan mien kuei hua' (Comprehensive planning in I-t'ao *hsiang* [Shu-yang *hsien*, Kiangsu]); in *Chung-kuo nung ts'un ti she hui chu i kao ch'ao* (The socialist upsurge in rural China); Peking: Jen min ch'u pan she, 1956, vol. 2, 598–610. In *Socialist upsurge in China's countryside*, edited by Pan kung t'ing, Chung yang wei yüan hui, Chung-kuo kung ch'an tang (General Office, Central Committee, Chinese Communist Party). [Selective entry]
Peking: Foreign Languages Press, 1957, 361–377.
Subj 24 24.1 ▪ 26 34.1

16467 CSU O P7 G8.2 1949–1972
Chung-kuo kung ch'an tang. Jung-feng hsien wei yüan hui. (Chinese Communist Party. Jung-feng Hsien Committee).
'Jungfeng county [i.e., Hsüan-wei *hsien*, Yunnan] leaps forward.' In *600 million build industry*. [Selective entry]
Peking: Foreign Languages Press, 1958, 119–130.
Subj 24

16468 CSU P P7 G6.3 1949–1972
Chung-kuo nung yeh k'o hsüeh yüan (China Agricultural Sciences Institute). Nung yeh ching chi yen chiu so (Agricultural Economics Research Office) *and* Chung-kuo jen min ta hsüeh (Chinese People's U.). Nung yeh ching chi hsi (Dept. of Agricultural Economics), *joint sponsors*. Tiao ch'a tsu (Investigation Team), ed.
'Large and public aspect of commune facilitates development of diversified operations: Investigation of the development of diversified economy by the Liu-hsia people's commune, Hanchow municipality, Chekiang province.' Tr. of 'I ta erh kung pien yü fa chan to chung ching chi: Che-chiang sheng Hang-chou shih Liu-hsia jen min kung she fa chan to chung ching chi tiao ch'a' (The 'both large and public' method facilitates the development of economic diversification: Survey of Liu-hsia commune, Hangchow municipality, Chekiang); *Jen min jih pao* 12 Dec. 1959, 7. In *Surveys of diversified operations in communes*, mimeo., compiled by U.S. Joint Publications Research Service. [Analytic entry]
Washington, D.C.: JPRS, 23 May 1960, 1–15. (JPRS 2698; MC 9988/1960)
Subj 21.4 24 24.1 34.1 ▪ 26.3

16469 CSU P P3 G9.5 1949–1972
Davis, Sydney George, 1907–.
'An evaluation of the scope for further expansion of the general economic structure of Hong Kong.'
Economics and finance in Indonesia 8, 5/6 (May–June 1955), 296–322.
Subj 21.4 24 36.4 ▪ 21.1 26.4

16470 CSU P P2 G1.2 1949–1972
Donnithorne, Audrey Gladys, 1922–.
'China's cellular economy: Some economic trends since the Cultural Revolution.'
CQ 52 (Oct.–Dec. 1972), 605–619.
Subj 24 24.4 ▪ 12 24.1 24.3

16471 CSH P P2 G9.5 1949–1972
Far Eastern Economic Review.
'Hongkong.' In *Far Eastern economic review yearbook, 1960–1972*, compiled by the organization cited.
Hong Kong: Far Eastern Economic Review. Issued annually, 1960–1972, average ca. 20 p.
Subj 24 26.4 28 ▪ 22 25 32.2 36.4 55

16472 CSU O P3 G9.5 1949–1972
Fessler, Loren, 1923–.
'Hong Kong revisited: An assessment of the colony's response to the 1967 disturbances.'
AUFS-EAS 16, 6 (Apr. 1969), 1–15.
SUBJ 24 24.2 24.3 ▪ 17 22.2 24.6 55

16473 CSU P P2 G9.5 1949–1972
Hong Kong. Dept. of Commerce and Industry.
Directory of commerce, industry, finance, Hong Kong, 1955–1965. [Title varies slightly.]
Hong Kong: Dept. of Commerce and Industry. Issued annually, 1955–1965. Average ca. 125 p. [Issue for 1956 was not located.]
SUBJ 24 24.3 24.4 ▪ 21.4 22 24.6 36.2

16474 CSU O P7 G5.1 1949–1972
Hsiao Kuang.
'Diversified management in Hochien hsien.' Tr. of 'To chung ching ying tsai Ho-chien hsien' (Diversified operations in Ho-chien *hsien* [Hopei]); *Hung ch'i* 1959, 2 (16 Jan.), 39–41. In *Articles from the Chinese Communist theoretical journal 'Hung ch'i' (Red flag) No. 2, 16 January 1959*, mimeo., compiled by U.S. Joint Publications Research Service. [Selective entry]
Washington, D.C.: JPRS, 25 May 1959, 83–87. (JPRS 1629N; MC 9236/1959)
SUBJ 24 24.1 24.4 ▪ 28 34.1

16475 NNC F P7 G5.4 1949–1972
Huang Chih-ming and Mu Chia-ch'ing.
'Dealing correctly with the relation between accumulation and consumption.' Tr. of 'Ho-nan Sui-p'ing hsien Ch'a-ya-shan jen min kung she tiao ch'a pao kao: Cheng ch'üeh ch'u li chi lei ho hsiao fei ti kuan hsi' (Report on Ch'a-ya-shan commune, Sui-p'ing *hsien*, Honan: Dealing correctly with the relationship between accumulation and consumption); *Ta kung pao* (Peking) 15 June 1959, 3. In *Translations on Communist China's economic services*, mimeo., compiled by U.S. Joint Publications Research Service. [Selective entry]
Washington, D.C.: JPRS, 20 Oct. 1959, 26–40. (JPRS 1956N; MC 17,613/1959)
SUBJ 21.4 24 28 ▪ 34.1

16476 MCH O P2 G5.4 1949–1972
Källberg, Sture, 1928–.
'"Tung fang hung" i Loyang' ('The East is red' in Loyang).
Industria 60, 6 (1964), 1–60.
SUBJ 24 24.1 24.4 ▪ 21.4

16477 MCY P P2 G9.2 1949–1972
Kirk, Donald.
'Unknown Hainan.'
FEER 49, 11 (9 Sept. 1965), 501–503.
SUBJ 24 24.1 24.4 ▪ 15 21.2 24.2

16478 CSU O P2 G1.3 1949–1972
Kraft, Joseph, 1924–.
'A reporter in China: The right road and the wrong road.'
New Yorker unnumbered (6 May 1972), 98–120.
SUBJ 24 26 28 66 ▪ 22.1 24.1 24.4 26.1 26.3 59

16479 CSH P P2 G9.2 1949–1972
[La Dany, Ladislao] ———, 1914–.
'Hainan island.'
CNA 198 (27 Sept. 1957), 1–7.
SUBJ 22 24 ▪ 21.3 34.1

16480 MCH FP P2 G9.2 1949–1972
[La Dany, Ladislao] ———, 1914–.
'Hainan island.'
CNA 434 (24 Aug. 1962), 1–7.
SUBJ 24 24.4 ▪ 24.1 26.4 28

16481 NIC PO P7 G1.2 1949–1972
Li, Choh-ming (Li Cho-min), 1912–.
'Statistics and planning at the hsien level in Communist China.'
CQ 9 (Jan.–Mar. 1962), 112–123. [Reprinted—*CS* 1, 28 (27 Mar. 1962), 1–11.] [Reprinted as 'Statistics and planning at the hsien level.' In *This is China: Analyses of Mainland trends and events*, edited by Francis Harper. (Selective entry.) Hong Kong: Dragonfly Books, 1965, 127–142.]
SUBJ 24 32 ▪ 14.5 17 18 21.4 22.1

16482 NIC O P3 G8.1 1949–1972
Liao Su-hua.
'How is the people's economic life organized in Chungking municipality?' Tr. of 'Ch'ung-ch'ing shih shih tsen yang tsu chih jen min ching chi sheng huo ti'; *Jen min jih pao* 5 Apr. 1960, 10.
CB 625 (6 July 1960), 32–39.
SUBJ 21.4 22 24 28 55 ▪ 22.1 24.3 38 47 52

16483 CSH F P5 G9.5 1949–1972
Lim, E. R.
'Consumer demand in Hong Kong: An econometric analysis.' In *Hong Kong economic papers, No. 4*, edited by Ronald Hsia (Hsia Hsiu-yung). [Selective entry]
Hong Kong: Hong Kong Economic Assn., 1968, 26–44.
SUBJ 24 24.3 24.6 28 ▪ 24.4

16484 CBU PO P7 G6.1 1949–1972
Ma Hsiang-yun (Ma Hsiang-yung).
'Planning for economic production and local conditions in Kiangsu.' Tr. of 'Tsai Chiang-su sheng ti ch'ü yin ti chih i kuei hua jen min kung she ching chi sheng ch'an ti i hsieh jen shih' (Some facts on planning economic production in communes in Kiangsu on the basis of local conditions); in *Jen min kung she ching chi kuei hua yü ching chi ti li wen chi* (Collected essays on economic planning and economic geography of the communes); Peking: K'o hsüeh ch'u pan she, 1959, 100–113. In *Economic plans and economic geography of people's communes*, mimeo., jointly edited by Chung-kuo ti li hsüeh hui (Geographical Society of China) *with* Ti li yen chiu so (Institute of Geography), Chung-kuo k'o hsüeh yüan (Chinese Academy of Sciences). [Selective entry]
Washington, D.C.: U.S. Joint Publications Research Service, 25 Feb. 1963, 240–277. (JPRS 17,789; MC 6864/1963) [Xerox copyflo available—New York: CCM Information Corp., Research and Microfilm Publications. (Scholarly Book Translation Series, 421)]
SUBJ 24 24.1 ▪ 21.3 24.2 24.4

16485 CSH S P4 G9.5 1949–1972
Matveev, M- I-.
'Makao i ego problemy' (Macau and its problems).
NAA 1968, 5, 129–135.
SUBJ 21.2 24 ▪ 17 36.4

16486 GMS P P3 G9.5 1949–1972
Mun, Kin-chok.
Die wirtschaftliche Entwicklung Hongkongs (The economic development of Hong Kong).
Freiburg i. Br.: The author, 1967. 285 p. (Doctoral dissertation, Rechts- und staatswissenschaftliche Fakultät, Universität Freiburg i. Br.)
SUBJ 24 24.3 24.4 ▪ 21.4 26 36.4

16487 CBU PO P2 G9.5 1949–1972
Owen, Nicholas C-.
'Economic policy in Hong Kong.' In *Hong Kong: The industrial colony*, edited by Keith Hopkins. [Analytic entry]
Hong Kong: Oxford U. Press, 1971, 141–206.
SUBJ 24 24.4 26.4 ▪ 21.4 24.5 28

16488 NNC PO P7 G1.2 1949–1972
Ozaki Shotaro (Ozaki Shōtarō), 1906–.
Current situation and problems of managing people's communes, mimeo. Tr. of 'Jimmin kōsha keiei no jitsujō to mondaiten' (Commune management and related problems); *Chūgoku kenkyū geppō* 153 (Nov. 1960), 1–40.
Washington, D.C.: U.S. Joint Publications Research Service, 5 May 1961. 59 p. (JPRS 7754; MC 11,091/1961)
SUBJ 22 24 24.1 34.2 ▪ 24.4 28 34.1 45

16489 CSH O P3 G9.5 1949–1972
Roll, Christian.
'Hong Kong vor dem Bambusvorhang' (Hong Kong in front of the Bamboo Curtain).
Aussenpolitik 18, 3 (März 1967), 180–188.
SUBJ 24 24.6 28 ▪ 24.2 24.4

16490 NNP O P3 G9.5 1949–1972
Saunders, J- A- H-.
'The year in review.'
TBHK Apr. 1967, 84–87.
SUBJ 24 ▪ 24.5 24.6 28

16491 CSU F P3 G9.5 1949–1972
Schöller, Peter.
'Hong Kong: Weltstadt und drittes China' (Hong Kong: A metropolis and a third China).
Geographische Z. 55, 2 (1967), 110–141.
SUBJ 21.1 21.3 24 ▪ 11.2 55

16492 CSU P P2 G9.5 1949–1972
Smith, Henry.
John Stuart Mill's other island: A study of the economic development of Hong Kong.
London: Institute of Economic Affairs, 1966. 32 p. (IEA research monographs, 6)
SUBJ 24 24.6 ▪ 21.1 28 55

16493 NIC P P3 G9.5 1949–1972
Szczepanik, Edward Franciszek, 1915–.
The economic growth of Hong Kong, 2nd ed.
London: Oxford U. Press, 1960. 186 p. (Revision of *The economic growth of Hong Kong, with special reference to*

post-war industrialization, doctoral dissertation in Economics, U. of London [External degree], 1958)
SUBJ 24 24.4 34.2 ▪ 21 21.2 22 36.4

16494 CSU P P3 G9.5 1949–1972
Szczepanik, Edward Franciszek, 1915–.
'Problems of macro-economic programming in Hong Kong.' In *Hong Kong: A society in transition*, edited by Ian C- Jarvie and Joseph Agassi. [Analytic entry]
New York: Praeger, 1969, 231–245.
SUBJ 24 24.4 28 ▪ 24.5

16495 TPH P P2 G9.4 1949–1972
Taiwan. Chu chi ch'u. (Bureau of Accounting and Statistics), ed.
Taiwan statistical abstract, Nos. 14–28 [1953–1969].
Nan-t'ou, Taiwan: Chu chi ch'u. Issued annually, 1953–1969. Average ca. 360 p. [In Chinese as well as English]
SUBJ 20 24 24.1 ▪ 17 21 22 24.2 24.6 28

16496 NIC FP P2 G9.5 1949–1972
Topley, Marjorie Doreen, 1927–.
'Hong Kong.' In *The role of savings and wealth in southern Asia and the West*, edited by Richard D- Lambert and Berthold Frank Hoselitz. [Sole entry]
Paris: United Nations, Educational, Scientific and Cultural Organization, 1963, 126–177. [Reprinted as 'The role of savings and wealth among Hong Kong Chinese.' In *Hong Kong: A society in transition*, edited by Ian C- Jarvie and Joseph Agassi. (Analytic entry.) New York: Praeger, 1969, 167–227.]
SUBJ 22 24 26 ▪ 30 40 60

16497 CSU P P2 G9.5 1949–1972
United Nations. Economic Commission for Asia and the Far East. Research and Planning Division.
'Hong Kong.'
EBAFE 4, 4 (Mar. 1954), 55–57. [Special issue: *Economic survey of Asia and the Far East, 1953*]
SUBJ 14.3 24 24.3 24.4

16498 CSU P P2 G9.5 1949–1972
United Nations. Economic Commission for Asia and the Far East. Secretariat.
'Current economic developments in the countries of the ECAFE region: Hong Kong.'
EBAFE 21, 4 (Mar. 1971), 198–203. [Special issue: *Economic survey of Asia and the Far East, 1970*]
SUBJ 24 ▪ 21.4 24.1 24.4 55

16499 CSU S P2 G9.5 1949–1972
United Nations. Economic Commission for Asia and the Far East. Secretariat.
'Hong Kong.'
EBAFE 5, 4 (Mar. 1955), 111–114. [Special issue: *Economic survey of Asia and the Far East, 1954*]
SUBJ 24 ▪ 14.3 21 24.1 24.3 24.4

16500 CSU U P2 G9.5 1949–1972
United Nations. Economic Commission for Asia and the Far East. Secretariat.
'Hong Kong.'
EBAFE 6, 4 (Mar. 1956), 100–103. [Special issue: *Economic survey of Asia and the Far East, 1955*]
SUBJ 24 ▪ 24.4 24.6

16501 CSU P P2 G9.5 1949–1972
United Nations. Economic Commission for Asia and the Far East. Secretariat.
'Hong Kong.'
EBAFE 7, 4 (Mar. 1957), 94–97. [Special issue: *Economic survey of Asia and the Far East, 1956*]
SUBJ 24 24.4 ▪ 14.3 24.3 24.6 55

16502 NIC O P3 G6.1 1949–1972
Wu Yi-fang (Wu I-fang), 1893–.
'Nanking, a changing city.'
China reconstructs 8, 8 (Aug. 1959), 22–24.
SUBJ 24 ▪ 17

16503 CSH P P7 G1.2 1949–1972
Yu, C. L.
'The local industry and its impact on the agricultural development in China: A report on 23 countries [i.e., counties] in 19 provinces and 1 autonomous region.'
Asia q. 1971, 4, 321–341.
SUBJ 24 24.1 24.4

16504 DLC U P2 G8.0 1949–1972
Zakharova, A- I-.
Review of *Hsi-nan ti ch'ü chi ti li: Ssu-ch'uan, Kuei-chou, Yün-nan* (An economic geography of Southwest China: Szechwan, Kweichow, and Yunnan), edited by Sun Ching-chih.
Sovremennaia kitaiskaia literatura po obshchestvennym naukam 41 (1960), 41–53.
SUBJ 24 24.1 24.4 ▪ 21

24.1 LOCAL AGRARIAN ECONOMIES

地方農業 地方農業

1644-1911

16505 MCH O P2 G9.2 1842–1895
'L'île de Hainan' (Hainan).
R. maritime et coloniale 80 (jan. 1884), 234–242.
SUBJ 14.3 24.1 24.3

16506 MCH O P2 G9.4 1842–1895
Allain, R-.
'L'île Formose' (Taiwan).
R. de géographie 16, 7 (jan. 1885), 44–50.
SUBJ 21.1 24.1 24.4 ▪ 21.3

16507 MCH PO P2 G9.0 –1842
Ball, Samuel, 1781?–1874.
An account of the cultivation and manufacture of tea in China, derived from personal observation during an official residence in that country from 1804 to 1826 . . .
London: Longman, Brown, Green and Longmans, 1848. 19, 382 p.
SUBJ 24.1 24.4 55 ▪ 14.3 22 26.3 28

16508 NNC O P2 G1.3 1895–1911
Boerschmann, Ernst, 1873–1949.
'Beobachtungen über Wassernutzung in China' (Observations on water utilization in China).
Z. der Gesellschaft für Erdkunde zu Berlin 1913, 7, 516–537.
SUBJ 24.1 24.2 ▪ 23 24.4 62

16509 DLC FP P2 G2.0 1895–1911
Boloban, Andrei Pavlovich.
Otchet po obsledovaniiu v 1911 godu raionov Kheiluntszianskoi, Girinskoi i Mukdenskoi provintsii severnoi Man'chzhurii, tiagoteiushchikh k Kitaiskoi Vostochnoi zheleznoi doroge, v zemledel'cheskom i khlebopromyshlennom otnosheniiakh (Report on the 1911 investigation of agriculture and grain production in the areas of Heilungkiang, Kirin, and Fengtien served by the Chinese Eastern Railway).
Harbin: Kommerch. chast' KVzhd, 1912. 352, 21 p.
SUBJ 24.1 24.4 ▪ 26.3

16510 CSH P P2 G2.0 1895–1911
Boloban, Andrei Pavlovich.
'Severo-Vostochnaia Mongoliia i ee khleba: Tao-nan'-fu, Da-lai-tin, Chzhao-chzhou-tin, Gun-e-fu' (Northeastern Mongolia and its livelihood: T'ao-nan *fu* [Kirin], Ta-lai *t'ing* [Heilungkiang], Chao-chou *t'ing* [Heilungkiang], and Kung-yeh *fu* [Sheng-ching province]).
VA 5 (iiun' 1910), 68–94.
SUBJ 20 24.1 ▪ 21 21.3 22 24 24.5

16511 MCH O P7 G8.2 1895–1911
Bons d'Anty, Pierre Remi, 1859–1917.
'Relation d'un voyage dans la région située au sud de Semao' (An account of a journey in the area south of Ssu-mao [*t'ing* capital, Yunnan]).
Annales de géographie 8, 37 (jan. 1899), 49–61.
SUBJ 24.1 66 ▪ 22 24.3 24.6

16512 CSU O P2 G8.0 1895–1911
Brenier, Henri, 1867–?
'De Tchoung-king à Pi-tsié' (From Chungking to [the capital of] Pi-chieh *hsien* [Kweichow]). In *La Mission lyonnaise d'exploration commerciale en Chine, 1895–1897, première partie, récits des voyages* (The Lyons Trade Mission to China, 1895–1897, Part 1, Travel accounts), compiled by Chambre de commerce de Lyon. [Selective entry]
Lyons: Rey, 1898, 229–244 [s.p.].
SUBJ 24.1 24.2 ▪ 21.3 24.4 33 61

16513 FPN O P8 G5.1 1842–1895
Castellani, C- B-.
De l'éducation des vers à soie en Chine, faite et observée sur les lieux (Sericulture in China, based on direct observation).
Paris: Amyot, 1861. 182 p.
SUBJ 24.1 24.4 26.3 ▪ 21.3 21.4 24.3 66

16514 WSU P P2 G9.0 –1842
Chang Yuet-ngo (Chang Yüeh-o).
'Hong Kong ts'un (Hong Kong village) and the cultivation and exportation of incense from Kowloon and the New Territories.' Tr. of 'Hsiang-kang ts'un yü Chiu-lung Hsin-chieh teng ti hsiang p'in chih chung chih yü ch'u k'ou'; in *I pa ssu erh nien i ch'ien chih Hsiang-kang chi ch'i tui wai chiao t'ung: Hsiang-kang ch'ien tai shih*, edited by Lo Hsiang-lin; Hong Kong: Chung-kuo hsüeh she, 1959, 109–128. In *Hong Kong and its external communications before 1842*, edited by Lo Hsiang-lin. [Selective entry]

Hong Kong: Institute of Chinese Culture, 1963, 80–88.
SUBJ 24.1 ▪ 14.3 21.2 24.2 25

16515 FPN P P8 G4.3 1644–1911
Chen, Tsu-Yuen (Ch'en Tsung-ying).
Histoire du défrichement de la province de Sin-Kiang sous la dynastie Ts'ing (History of land reclamation in Sinkiang under the Ch'ing).
Paris: Jouve, 1932. 180 p. (Doctoral dissertation, Faculté des lettres, Université de Paris)
SUBJ 24 24.1 35 ▪ 21

16516 MCH P P7 G1.2 1842–1895
Dabry de Thiersant, Claude Philibert, 1826–1898.
La pisciculture et la pêche en Chine (Fish culture and fishing in China).
Paris: G. Masson, 1872. 195 p.
SUBJ 24.1 55 ▪ 22 22.1 24.3 26.3 34.1

16517 NNC P P2 G4.3 1644–1842
Duman, Lazar' Isaevich, 1907–.
Agrarnaia politika tsinskogo (Man'chzhurskogo) pravitel'stva v Sin'tsziane v kontse 18 veka (Ch'ing land policy in Sinkiang at the end of the eighteenth century).
Moscow: Izd-vo Akad. nauk SSSR, 1936. 254 p. (Institut vostokovedeniia, trudy, 20)
SUBJ 12 15 16 22 24.1 ▪ 14.5 16.1 22.1 25 32.2 72

16518 DLC O P7 G9.3 1644–1842
Ekeberg, Karl Gustaf (Carl Gustav Ekeberg; Charles Gustave Eckeberg), 1716–1784.
Kort berättelse om den chinesiska landthushålningen.
Stockholm: Grefing, 1757. 32 p.

'Kurze Bericht von der chinesischen Landwirtschaft.' Tr. by Johan Gottlieb Georgi. In *Reise nach Ostindien und China*, by [Pehr Osbeck] Peter Osbeck. [Analytic entry]
Rostock: Koppe, 1765, 515–552.

Précis historique de l'économie rurale des Chinois. Tr. by Dominique de Blackford.
Milan: Frères Reycends, 1771. 47 p.

'A short account of the Chinese husbandry.' Tr. by John Reinhold Forster. In *A voyage to China and the East Indies*, by P. Osbeck. [Analytic entry]
London: White, 1771, vol. 2, 267–317.
SUBJ 24.1 ▪ 55

16519 CBU S P2 G5.3 –1895
Fauvel, Albert Auguste, 1851–1909.
'Botanique et agriculture: la flore du Chan-toung' (Botany and agriculture: The flora of Shantung).
R. des questions scientifiques 30 (oct. 1891), 389–427. [Reprinted in *La province chinoise du Chan-toung* (Shantung), by A. A. Fauvel. (Selective entry.) Brussels: Impr. Polleunis et Auterich, 1892.]
SUBJ 24.1 24.4 72

16520 CSU O P2 G1.5 1842–1895
Fortune, Robert, 1813–1880.
Three years' wanderings in the northern provinces of China, including a visit to the tea, silk, and cotton countries: With an account of the agriculture and horticulture of the Chinese, new plants, etc., 2nd ed.
London: Murray, 1847. 24, 420 p.
SUBJ 24.1 55 ▪ 24.4 25 33 66

16521 CSU O P8 G6.0 1842–1895
K.
'The reeds of the Yangtze.'
NQCJ 3, 7 (July 1869), 97–98.
SUBJ 22.2 24.1

16522 DLC O P2 G1.1 1895–1911
King, Franklin Hiram, 1848–1911.
Farmers of forty centuries: or, Permanent agriculture in China, Korea and Japan, 2nd ed., edited by J- P- Bruce.
New York: Harcourt, Brace, 1927. 379 p. [Reprinted—London: Cape, 1949. 379 p.]
SUBJ 24.1 ▪ 21.4 24.3 24.4 26.3 55 57

16523 CBU O P2 G1.2 1644–1911
Köhler, E- M-.
'Das Hausschwein in China' (The domesticated pig in China).
Der zoologische Garten 38, 9 (Sept. 1897), 272–275.
SUBJ 24.1 55

16524 CBU O P2 G1.2 1644–1911
Köhler, E- M-.
'Über die Haustiere des Chinesen' (The domestic animals of the Chinese).
Der zoologische Garten 39, 1 (Jan. 1898), 16–25; 39, 2 (Feb. 1898), 54–60; 40, 2 (Feb. 1899), 45–49; 41, 1 (Jan. 1900), 5–14; 41, 2 (Feb. 1900), 33–47; 41, 3 (März 1900), 65–80.
SUBJ 24.1 55 ▪ 24.2

16525 DLC P P8 G6.0 1842–1895
Koroleva, N- A-.
'K voprosu ob agrarnoi politike Taipin Tian'go' (Taiping land policy). [With English abstract]
VLGU 17, 2 (1962), 60–73.
SUBJ 12 14.5 16.1 16.3 24.1 ▪ 15 64 70

16526 DLC O P2 G7.1 1895–1911
Krasnov, Andrei Nikolaevich, 1862–1914.
'Kitai' (China). In *Chainye okrugi subtropicheskikh oblastei Azii, vypusk II, Kitai, Indiia i TSeilon, Kolkhida* (Tea-producing districts of the subtropical regions of Asia, Vol. 2, China, India and Ceylon, and Colchis), by A. N. Krasnov. [Sole entry]
St. Petersburg: Tip. Glavnago upravleniia udelov, 1898, 247–376.
SUBJ 21.3 23 24.1 40 55 61 ▪ 11.3 17 22.2 24.5 26.3 31 33 39 63

16527 MCH O P8 G8.1 1895–1911
Legendre, Aimé François, 1867–?
'L'élevage des vers à soie dans la vallée du Yalong' (Sericulture in the Ya-lung river valley [Szechwan]).
BEI 16, 100 (jan.–fév. 1913), 80–105.
SUBJ 24.1 ▪ 26.3 55

16528 MCH O P8 G8.1 1895–1911
Legendre, Jean.
'L'agriculture dans la plaine de Tchen-tou (Se-Tchoan), Chine' (Agriculture on the Chengtu plain, Szechwan).
BEI 13, 82 (jan.–fév. 1910), 584–595.
SUBJ 21.3 24.1 ▪ 55

16529 WSU P P7 G9.5 –1842
Lo Hsiang-lin, 1905–.
'A general survey of Hong Kong in former times: Its economic and administrative developments.' Tr. of 'Hsiang-kang chih hai wan yü t'e ch'an chi ch'i ch'ien tai li shu' (The harbor, local products, and administration of Hong Kong prior to 1842); in *I pa ssu erh nien i ch'ien chih Hsiang-kang chi ch'i tui wai chiao t'ung: Hsiang-kang ch'ien tai shih*, edited by Lo Hsiang-lin; Hong Kong: Chung-kuo hsüeh she, 1959, 1–19. In *Hong Kong and its external communications before 1842*, edited by Lo Hsiang-lin. [Selective entry]
Hong Kong: Institute of Chinese Culture, 1963, 1–14.
SUBJ 24.1 24.4 ▪ 22 24.2

16530 MCH P P2 G9.1 1842–1895
Lucas, Alfred, 1867–1945.
'La révolution agraire des Taiping' (The Taiping agrarian revolution).
France-Asie 16, 158/159 (juil.–août 1959), 1047–1062; 16, 160/161 (sept.–oct. 1959), 1153–1174.
SUBJ 14.5 24.1 32.2 36.3 ▪ 12 12.1 16.3 47 66

16531 MCH O P7 G8.3 1842–1895
Perny, Paul Hubert, 1818–1907.
'Monographie du ver à soie du chêne au Kouy-tcheou' (A treatise on the oak silkworm in Kweichow).
B. de la Société zoologique d'acclimatation 5 (1858), 317–322.
SUBJ 24.1 ▪ 24.3 66

16532 NNC O P2 G5.3 1895–1911
Preyer, Otto Ernest, 1881–.
'Aus der Praxis der Landordnung in Kiautschou' (Landholding practices in Kiaochow).
Jahrbuch der Bodenreform 4, 2 (1908), 126–134.
SUBJ 24.1 ▪ 12.2 24.5

16533 CSU O P2 G6.3 1842–1895
Renard, Ed——.
'Aperçu général sur l'archipel de Tchou-san' (A sketch of the Chou-shan archipelago [Ting-hai *hsien*, Chekiang]).
Nouvelles annales des voyages 146 (1855), 163–176.
SUBJ 24 24.1 ▪ 21 31

16534 CSU PO P7 G1.5 1895–1911
Riault, J-, et al.
'Rapport sur le coton et les cotonnades' (Report on cotton and cotton products). In *La Mission lyonnaise d'exploration commerciale en Chine, 1895–1897, deuxième partie, rapports commerciaux et notes diverses* (The Lyons Trade Mission to China, 1895–1897, Part 2, Commercial reports and miscellaneous notes), compiled by Chambre de commerce de Lyon. [Selective entry]
Lyons: Rey, 1898, 351–374 [s.p.].
SUBJ 24.1 24.3 24.4

16535 NNC PO P8 G5.3 1895–1911
Schrameier, Wilhelm Ludwig, 1859–1926.
'Die Landpolitik im Kiautschougebiet' (Land policy in Kiaochow).

Jahrbuch der Bodenreform 7, 1 (1911), 1–62.
SUBJ 24.1 45 ▪ 12.2 24.5

16536 GBF O P2 G5.3 1895–1911
Schrameier, Wilhelm Ludwig, 1859–1926.
Wie die Landordnung von Kiautschou entstand (The origin of the landholding system in Kiaochow).
Berlin: L. Harrwitz, 1902. 24 p.
SUBJ 22.1 24.1 45 66 ▪ 14.3 22 24.5

16537 CSU O P2 G9.3 1895–1911
Smith, Arthur Henderson, 1845–1932.
'Bits of Fukien travel.'
EAM 5 (1906), 390–402.
SUBJ 24.1 ▪ 21.1 42 55

16538 NNC O P8 G5.3 1895–1911
Stenz, Georg Maria, 1869–?
'Der Bauer in Schantung' (The peasant in Shantung).
Anthropos 1, 3/4 (Mai–Aug. 1906), 435–452; 1, 5/6 (Sept.–Dez. 1906), 838–863.
SUBJ 24.1 24.5 26.3 55 ▪ 21 21.3 45 65

16539 MCH O P7 G1.1 1842–1895
Syrski, S-.
'Landwirtschaft, Wasserproduktion und die wichtigsten, zu diesen in näherer Beziehung stehenden mineralischen Erzeugnisse in China' (Chinese agriculture, waterworks, and related mineral products of importance). In *Fachmännische Berichte über die österreichisch-ungarische Expedition nach Siam, China und Japan, 1868–1871* (Expert reports on the Austro-Hungarian expedition to Siam, China, and Japan, 1868–1871), edited by Karl von Scherzer. [Selective entry]
Stuttgart: Julius Maier, 1872, 42–122.
SUBJ 24.1 24.4 ▪ 22.1 24.2 24.3 55

16540 MCH O P2 G8.3 1842–1895
Tch'ang-ngen (Ch'ang En).
'Guide pour l'élevage des vers à soie sauvages (1849)' (An 1849 guide to raising wild silkworms). Tr. by Victor Collen from *Fang yang chan ts'an fa* (Methods of raising silkworms); n.p., n.d.
BAAFC 5, 1 (jan. 1913), 3–29.
SUBJ 24.1 ▪ 22 23 28

16541 CSU P P7 G6.3 1842–1895
Ting, Yueh-hung C.
'Sericulture in Hu-chou as seen in *Hu-chou fu-chih* [Prefectural gazetteer of Hu-chou, Chekiang].'
PC 23 (July 1970), 29–51.
SUBJ 24.1 24.4 ▪ 24.3

16542 NNC PO P8 G8.1 –1911
Vale, Joshua.
'Irrigation of the Ch'eng-tu plain [Szechwan].'
JRAS-CB new (2nd) series 33 (1899/1900), 105–119.
SUBJ 24.1 ▪ 23 28 65

16543 NIC PO P2 G8.1 –1911
Vale, Joshua.
'Irrigation of the Ch'eng-tu plain [Szechwan] and beyond.'
JRAS-CB new (2nd) series 36 (1905), 36–50.
SUBJ 24.1 ▪ 22 24.5 28

16544 CSU P P8 G9.4 1842–1911
Wickberg, Edgar Bernard, 1927–.
'Late nineteenth century land tenure in North Taiwan.' In *Taiwan: Studies in Chinese local history*, edited by Leonard Herman David Gordon. [Selective entry]
New York: Columbia U. Press, 1970, 78–92.
SUBJ 24.1

1644-1949

16545 CBU FP P8 G6.2 –1949
Chen, Chi-yün.
'Über die forstlichen Verhältnisse in der mittelchinesischen Provinz Anhui' (Forestry in Anhwei).
Z. für Weltforstwirtschaft 7, 2 (Nov. 1939), 55–66.
SUBJ 24.1

16546 NNC S P7 G2.1 1895–1928
Chen Han-seng (Ch'en Han-sheng), 1897–, and Wong Yin-seng (Wang Yin-sheng), 1902–.
'Tendencies of farm economics in North-eastern China.' Tr. of *Hei-lung chiang liu yü ti nung min yü ti chu* (Peasants and landlords in the Amur river basin); Shanghai: Kuo li chung yang yen chiu yüan, She hui k'o hsüeh yen chiu so, 1929; 16 p. [condensed tr.]. In *Agrarian China*, compiled by Institute of Pacific Relations. [Selective entry]
Chicago: U. of Chicago Press, 1939, 136–144.
SUBJ 24.1 ▪ 24.5 24.6 26.1 26.3 28

16547 MAM S P7 G1.5 –1949
Drews, Robin Arthur, 1913–.
The cultivation of food fish in China and Japan: A study disclosing contrasting national patterns for rearing fish consistent with the differing cultural histories of China and Japan.
Ann Arbor: University Microfilms (Publ. 3582), 1952. 10, 263 p. (Doctoral dissertation in Anthropology, U. of Michigan)
SUBJ 24.1 24.3 55 ▪ 24 28 65

16548 NIC O P7 G8.1 1895–1928
Dye, Daniel Sheets, 1884–.
'The Szechwanese use of their water resources for agriculture.'
JWCBRS 3 (1926/29), 40–54.
SUBJ 24.1

16549 CSU P P7 G9.4 1895–1949
Ho, Samuel P. S. (Ho Pao-shan), 1936–.
'Agricultural transformation under colonialism: Reply and further observations.'
J. of economic history 31, 3 (Sept. 1971), 682–693. [See also entries 16550 and 16551.]
SUBJ 24.1 ▪ 16.3 18 27

16550 CSU P P8 G9.4 1895–1949
Ho, Samuel P. S. (Ho Pao-shan), 1936–.
'Agricultural transformation under colonialism: The case of Taiwan.'
J. of economic history 28, 3 (Sept. 1968), 313–340.
SUBJ 24.1 36.3 ▪ 12.1 14.5 18 22 34.1 37 55

16551 CSU P P7 G9.4 1895–1949
Ho, Yhi-Min, 1934–.
'On Taiwan's agricultural transformation under colonialism: A critique.' [Review of 'Agricultural transformation under colonialism: The case of Taiwan', by Samuel P. S. Ho (Ho Pao-shan).]
J. of economic history 31, 3 (Sept. 1971), 672–681.
SUBJ 24.1 ▪ 14.5 16.3 24.3

16552 NIC O P2 G9.3 1895–1928
Hurlbut, Floy, 1888–.
The Fukienese: A study in human geography.
Muncie, Ind.: The author, 1939. 23, 143 p. (Revision of doctoral dissertation in Geography, U. of Nebraska, 1930)
SUBJ 11.3 24.1 24.2 55 61 ▪ 21 21.1 23 24.4 26 29 41 57

16553 MCH FP P7 G2.0 1895–1928
IAshnov, Evgenii Evgen'evich.
Kitaiskoe krest'ianskoe khoziaistvo v severnoi Man'chzhurii: ekonomicheskii ocherk (Survey of the Chinese peasant economy in northern Manchuria).
Harbin: Ekon. biuro KVzhd, 1926. 525 p.
SUBJ 21 24.1 24.2 24.6 26.3 ▪ 21.2 25 28 55

16554 NIC P P7 G9.4 1842–1928
Kawada Shiro (Kawada Shirō), 1883–1942.
'The tenant system of Formosa.' Tr. of 'Taiwan no kosaku seido' (Tenancy in Taiwan); *Keizai ronsō* 26, 4 (Apr. 1928), 1–30; 26, 5 (May 1928), 22–44; 26, 6 (June 1928), 19–50. [Tr. inferred]
KUER 3, 2 (Dec. 1928), 86–146.
SUBJ 24.1 ▪ 22.2 24.5 26.3

16555 CSU PO P8 G4.1 –1928
Lowdermilk, Walter Clay, 1888–, and Dean Rockwell Wickes, 1883–.
'Ancient irrigation in China brought up to date.'
Scientific monthly 55, 3 (Sept. 1942), 209–225.
SUBJ 24.1 ▪ 28

16556 CSU FP P8 G5.2 –1949
Lowdermilk, Walter Clay, 1888–, and Dean Rockwell Wickes, 1883–.
'China and America against soil erosion.'
Scientific monthly 56, 5 (May 1943), 393–413; 56, 6 (June 1943), 505–520.
SUBJ 24.1 28 ▪ 21 24.5

16557 MCH FP P8 G5.2 –1949
Lowdermilk, Walter Clay, 1888–, and Dean Rockwell Wickes, 1883–.
History of soil use in the Wu-t'ai shan area [Wu-t'ai *hsien*, Shansi].
Shanghai: Kelly and Walsh, 1938. 31 p.
SUBJ 21.3 24.1 ▪ 21 24.5 28 56 72

16558 CSU F P7 G9.0 1895–1928
Mell, Rudolf, 1878–.
'Südchinesische Landschaftstypen und ihre Nutzung' (Types of landscape in South China and their utilization).
Z. der Gesellschaft für Erdkunde zu Berlin 1927, 1/2, 30–39.
SUBJ 21 24.1 ▪ 11.3

16559 CSU P P2 G6.1 1842–1949
Muramatsu, Yuji (Muramatsu Yūji), 1911–.
'A documentary study of Chinese landlordism in late Ch'ing and early

Republican Kiangnan [southern Kiangsu].'
BSOAS 29, 3 (Oct. 1966), 566–599.
SUBJ 24.1 24.5 34.2 ▪ 12 22 22.1 26.1 42

16560 CSH FP P2 G1.3 1842–1949
Myers, Ramon Hawley, 1929–.
'Land distribution in revolutionary China: 1890–1937.'
CCJ 8, 2 (May 1969), 62–77.
SUBJ 24.1 ▪ 11.1 28 45

16561 MCY S P2 G9.4 1895–1949
Myers, Ramon Hawley, 1929–, and Adrienne Ching.
'Agricultural development in Taiwan under Japanese colonial rule.'
JAS 23, 4 (Aug. 1964), 555–570.
SUBJ 24.1 ▪ 14.5 22 22.1 34.1

16562 CSU S P2 G2.3 1895–1949
Myers, Ramon Hawley, 1929–, and Thomas R- Ulie.
'Foreign influence and agricultural development in Northeast China: A case study of the Liaotung peninsula, 1906–1942.'
JAS 31, 2 (Feb. 1972), 329–350.
SUBJ 24.1 ▪ 21.1 22.1 24.3 26.3

16563 MCY O P8 G5.1 1895–1928
Sherfesee, William Forsythe.
'The vanishing forests of Wei-Chang [i.e., Wei-ch'ang *hsien*, Hopei].'
CSPSR 2, 2 (June 1917), 95–106.
SUBJ 21.3 22 24.1 ▪ 22.2 24.2 24.4

1911-1949

16564 CSU U P7 G9.2 1928–1949
'Agricultural conditions in Kuangtung.'
CEJ 13, 4 (Oct. 1933), 372–384.
SUBJ 24.1

16565 CSU U P7 G5.3 1911–1928
'Agricultural practices in Kiaochow.'
CEJ 1, 11 (Nov. 1927), 991–993.
SUBJ 24.1 ▪ 26.3

16566 CSH U P7 G5.2 1911–1928
'Agricultural practices in Shansi.'
CEM 2, 11 (Aug. 1925), 1–8.
SUBJ 24.1 ▪ 24.3

16567 CSU P P7 G7.1 1928–1949
'Agricultural production in Hupeh during 1934.'
CEJ 17, 2 (Aug. 1935), 164–175.
SUBJ 24.1 ▪ 18

16568 CSH P P2 G5.1 1911–1928
'Animal and agricultural products of Chihli.'
CEM 1, 6 (Mar. 1924), 9–15.
SUBJ 24.1 ▪ 14.3

16569 CSU U P2 G6.3 1928–1949
'Chekiang hams.'
CEJ 5, 2 (Aug. 1929), 643–649.
SUBJ 24.1 24.4 ▪ 14.3

16570 CSU U P8 G6.2 1928–1949
'China-root growth in Tsienshan [Ch'ien-shan *hsien*, Anhwei].'
CEJ 13, 2 (Aug. 1933), 147–156.
SUBJ 24.1

16571 CSU P P2 G6.3 1928–1949
'Cotton production in Chekiang.'
CEJ 13, 3 (Sept. 1933), 258–270.
SUBJ 24.1 ▪ 14.3 24.4

16572 CSU P P2 G7.1 1911–1949
'Cotton production in Hupeh.'
CEJ 13, 4 (Oct. 1933), 356–363.
SUBJ 24.1 ▪ 14.3 24.4

16573 CSU U P7 G5.3 1911–1928
'Farms and orchards at Chefoo, Shantung.'
CEJ 3, 1 (July 1928), 612–615.
SUBJ 24.1 26.3

16574 NNC P P7 G5.1 1928–1949
'Farms in Hopei, 1932.'
NWSS 6, 24 (12 June 1933), 116, 118–119.
SUBJ 24.1 ▪ 34.1

16575 CSU U P2 G5.3 1928–1949
'Fishing industry of Shantung.'
CEJ 18, 1 (Jan. 1936), 81–84.
SUBJ 24.1 ▪ 14.3

16576 CSU U P8 G1.5 1928–1949
'Forestry of Fukien, Kiangsi and Chekiang.'
CEJ 19, 1 (July 1936), 19–35.
SUBJ 24.1

16577 CSU U P2 G9.2 1928–1949
'Fruit cultivation in Kuangtung.'
CEJ 18, 5 (May 1936), 716–725.
SUBJ 24.1 ▪ 14.3

16578 CSH U P2 G5.1 1911–1928
'Hantan [*hsien*], an agricultural center of Chihli.'
CEJ 1, 5 (May 1927), 464–472.
SUBJ 14.3 24.1 ▪ 24.2 26.3

16579 CSU P P8 G9.2 1911–1928
'Kwangtung agricultural statistics.'
CEJ 2, 4 (Apr. 1928), 328–333.
SUBJ 24.1 45

16580 CSU U P7 G9.2 1928–1949
'Kwangtung silk worms.'
CEJ 5, 2 (Aug. 1929), 714–728.
SUBJ 24.1

16581 CSU U P2 G9.3 1911–1949
'Mushroom culture in Fukien.'
CEJ 5, 3 (Sept. 1929), 750–753.
SUBJ 24.1

16582 CSH U P2 G5.1 1911–1928
'Nankung [*hsien*], a cotton producing center of Hopei (Chihli).'
CEJ 3, 4 (Oct. 1928), 859–864.
SUBJ 24.1 ▪ 24.3 24.4

16583 CSU U P2 G7.3 1928–1949
'Ramie and grasscloth of Kiangsi.'
CEJ 19, 6 (Dec. 1936), 646–654.
SUBJ 14.3 24.1 ▪ 24.4

16584 CSU P P2 G9.2 1911–1949
'The silk industry in Kwangtung province.'
CEJ 5, 1 (July 1929), 604–620.
SUBJ 24.1 24.3 ▪ 14.4 24.4

16585 NIC P P8 G1.4 1928–1949
'Statistical abstract of farms, land, and crops.'
China critic 4, 2 (8 Jan. 1931), 39.
SUBJ 24.1

16586 CSU P P2 G7.3 1928–1949
'Sugar production in Kiangsi.'
CEJ 17, 6 (Dec. 1935), 560–582.
SUBJ 14.4 24.1 ▪ 14.3

16587 CSU U P2 G6.3 1928–1949
'Tea crops in Chekiang.'
CEJ 5, 4 (Oct. 1929), 902–907.
SUBJ 24.1 ▪ 14.3 36.2

16588 CSU U P2 G6.3 1928–1949
'Tobacco crops of Chekiang.'
CEJ 5, 3 (Sept. 1929), 806–810.
SUBJ 24.1 ▪ 14.3 24.4

16589 NIC F P8 G8.1 1911–1928
Brown, Harold D-, 1879–1949, and Li Min Liang.
'A survey of fifty farms on the Chengtu plain, Szechwan.'
CEJ 2, 1 (Jan. 1928), 44–73.
SUBJ 24 24.1 28

16590 NIC F P8 G8.1 1911–1928
Brown, Harold D-, 1879–1949, and Li Min Liang.
'A survey of 25 farms on Mt. Omei, Szechwan, China.'
CEJ 1, 12 (Dec. 1927), 1059–1076.
SUBJ 24.1 28 ▪ 23 26.3

16591 ELB F P7 G1.3 1911–1928
Buck, John Lossing, 1890–.
Chinese farm economy: A study of 2866 farms in seventeen localities and seven provinces in China.
Chicago: U. of Chicago Press, 1930. 12, 476 p.
SUBJ 24.1 26.3 ▪ 21 21.4 28 34.1 41 58

16592 CSH F P7 G1.5 1928–1949
Buck, John Lossing, 1890–.
'Costs of crop production.'
EF 32 (May 1944), 433–438.
SUBJ 24.1

16593 NNC F P7 G6.2 1911–1928
Buck, John Lossing, 1890–.
An economic and social survey of 102 farms near Wuhu, Anhwei, China.
Nanking: U. of Nanking, College of Agriculture and Forestry, 1924. 28 p.
SUBJ 24.1 28 41 ▪ 24.3 24.6 27 31 34.1 55

16594 NIC F P8 G5.1 1911–1928
Buck, John Lossing, 1890–.
An economic and social survey of 150 farms, Yenshan county, Chihli province, China.
[Nanking]: U. of Nanking, College of Agriculture and Forestry, 1926. 110 p. (CAF bulletins, 13)
SUBJ 24.1 28 45 ▪ 21 24.2 41

16595 CBU F P7 G6.0 1928–1949
Buck, John Lossing, 1890–.
'Farm implements and machinery for China.'
EF 50 (Nov. 1945), 757–766.
SUBJ 24.1

16596 CBU F P2 G8.1 1928–1949
Buck, John Lossing, 1890–, and Dodge T. Chen (Ch'en Ts'ai-chang).
'Land classification in Hwayang hsien, Szechwan.'
EF 37 (Oct. 1944), 551–565.
SUBJ 24.1 ▪ 21.1

16597 CBU F P8 G8.1 1928–1949
Buck, John Lossing, 1890–, and Dodge T. Chen (Ch'en Ts'ai-chang).
'The most capable use of land in Hwayang hsien, Szechwan.'
EF 38 (Nov. 1944), 575–586.
SUBJ 24.1 ▪ 24.2

16598 NIC F P7 G8.1 1928–1949
Buck, John Lossing, 1890–, and C. M. Chiao (Ch'iao Ch'i-ming), 1897–.
An agricultural survey of Szechwan province, China: A summary and interpretation by John Lossing Buck of a full report in Chinese by the Szechwan Rural Economics Survey Committee of the Farmers' Bank of China.
Chungking: Farmers' Bank of China, 1943. 63 p.
SUBJ 24.1 24.3 26.3 ▪ 24.2 34.1

16599 CSH FP P7 G8.1 1928–1949
Buck, John Lossing, 1890–, and Pan Hong-shen (P'an Hung-sheng).
'The best use of land for the welfare of the people of Penghsien [i.e., P'eng *hsien*], Szechwan.'
EF 27 (Dec. 1943), 314–321; 28 (Jan. 1944), 336–344; 29 (Feb. 1944), 355–364; 30 (Mar. 1944), 381–389; 31 (Apr. 1944), 407–419; 32 (May 1944), 439–445.
SUBJ 24.1 ▪ 21 24.2 28 55

16600 CBU F P8 G8.1 1928–1949
Buck, John Lossing, 1890–, and Tseng-ti Tsui.
'Corn [i.e., maize] production on lower, middle and upper slopes of mountainous areas of Penghsien [i.e., P'eng *hsien*], Szechwan, 1942.'
EF 35 (Aug. 1944), 514–522.
SUBJ 24.1

16601 CSH FP P7 G8.1 1928–1949
Buck, John Lossing, 1890–, and Chong-chan Yien.
'The economic effect of war upon farmers in Penghsien [i.e., P'eng *hsien*], Szechwan.'
EF 19 (Apr. 1943), 106–112.
SUBJ 24.1 26.3 ▪ 24.5 24.6 28

16602 CBU F P8 G1.3 1928–1949
Buck, John Lossing, 1890–, and Yin Lien-ken (Ying Lien-keng), 1904?–.
'Economic conditions of farmers by types of land tenure.'
EF 35 (Aug. 1944), 507–513.
SUBJ 24.1 ▪ 24.6 26.1 26.3 28

16603 CSU P P2 G6.0 1928–1949
Chang, Bintze T.
'The cocoon crops of Chekiang and Kiangsu in 1929.'
CEJ 5, 1 (July 1929), 588–603.
SUBJ 24.1 24.3 ▪ 24.4 34.2

16604 NIC O P8 G6.3 1928–1949
Chang, C. C. (Chang Hsin-i), 1896–.
'Chekiang: Her farms, land, and crops.'
China critic 3, 44 (30 Oct. 1930), 1037–1042.
SUBJ 21 24.1

16605 NIC P P7 G6.1 1911–1949
Chang, C. C. (Chang Hsin-i), 1896–.
'Kiangsu: Her farms, land, and crops.'
China critic 3, 50 (11 Dec. 1930), 1183–1188.
SUBJ 24.1

16606 CSU F P8 G4.3 1928–1949
Chang, Chih-yi (Chang Chih-i), 1911–.
'Land utilization and settlement possibilities in Sinkiang.'
GR 39, 1 (Jan. 1949), 57–75.
SUBJ 24.1 ▪ 21 21.2 21.3 66

16607 NNC O P2 G9.3 1928–1949
Chang Yu-sui.
'The general economic decline in Fuan [i.e., Fu-an *hsien*] in northern Fukien.' Tr. from *Chiao yü yü min chung* 8, 6 (28 Feb. 1937). In *Agrarian China*, compiled by Institute of Pacific Relations. [Selective entry]
Chicago: U. of Chicago Press, 1939, 251–255.
SUBJ 24.1 24.3 24.4 ▪ 21.2 28 38

16608 NIC F P7 G1.2 1928–1949
Chao, Tsai Piao (Chao Ts'ai-piao), 1903–.
A statistical study of crop yields in 12 provinces in China.
Unpublished doctoral dissertation in Economics, Cornell U., 1933. 17, 215 p.
SUBJ 24.1

16609 DNA P P7 G6.3 1928–1949
Chekiang. Chien she t'ing. (Reconstruction Dept.).
Agriculture in the province of Chekiang.
Hangchow: Chien she t'ing, 1946. 16 p.
SUBJ 24.1 ▪ 14.6

16610 CSU P P8 G9.4 1928–1949
Chen, Cheng-siang (Ch'en Cheng-hsiang), 1920–.
'The banana industry in Taiwan.'
Malayan j. of tropical geography 2 (Mar. 1954), 48–55. [Separately reprinted—Taipei: Fu-min Geographical Institute of Economic Development, 1954. 8 p. (Fu-min research reports, 42)]
SUBJ 24.1

16611 CSU P P2 G9.4 1911–1949
Chen, Cheng-siang (Ch'en Cheng-hsiang), 1920–.
'The climate and climatic regions of Taiwan.'
Malayan j. of tropical geography 5 (Mar. 1955), 26–38.
SUBJ 21.3 24.1

16612 CSU FP P7 G1.2 1911–1949
Chen Han-seng (Ch'en Han-sheng), 1897–.
'The agrarian problem of China.' In *Problems of the Pacific, 1933*, edited by Bruno Lasker and William Lancelot Holland. [Selective entry]
Chicago: U. of Chicago Press, 1934, 271–298.
SUBJ 24.1 26.1 26.3 ▪ 22.1 24.5 24.6 28

16613 MCH FP P7 G9.2 1911–1949
Chen Han-seng (Ch'en Han-sheng), 1897–.
Agrarian problems in southernmost China.
Shanghai: Kelly and Walsh, 1936. 144 p. [Reprinted as *Landlord and peasant in China: A study of the agrarian crisis in South China*. New York: International Publishers, 1936. 17, 144 p.] [Reprinted—Ann Arbor: University Microfilms, n.d. 17, 144 p.] [Reprinted—Westport, Conn.: Hyperion Press, 197? 17, 144 p.]
SUBJ 14.5 24 24.1 26.3 45 ▪ 24.3 24.6 26.1

16614 NNC O P8 G5.2 1911–1949
Chen Han-seng (Ch'en Han-sheng), 1897–.
'The good earth of China's model province.'
PA 9, 3 (Sept. 1936), 370–380.
SUBJ 24.1 ▪ 24.5

16615 CSU O P8 G6.3 1928–1949
Chen, T. P. (Ch'en T'ung-pai).
'Notes on cormorant fishing in Chekiang.'
LSJ 16, 3 (1937), 469–471.
SUBJ 24.1

16616 CSU PO P8 G9.2 1928–1949
Chen, T. P. (Ch'en T'ung-pai).
'The oyster industry of Chung-shan [*hsien*, Kwangtung].'
LSJ 14, 1 (1935), 63–72.
SUBJ 24.1 ▪ 55

16617 MCH PO P7 G7.3 1928–1949
China [Republic]. Ch'üan kuo ching chi wei yüan hui. (National Economic Council).
Rural reconstruction in Kiangsi.
Nanchang: Ch'üan kuo ching chi wei yüan hui, 1935. 18 p. (Ch'üan kuo ching chi wei yüan hui special bulletins, 1)
SUBJ 24.1 ▪ 27 28 34.1 37

16618 NNC F P8 G8.2 1928–1949
China [Republic]. Hsing cheng yüan. Nung ts'un fu hsing wei yüan hui. (Executive Yüan. Rural Reconstruction Commission), ed.
'Land ownership and land cultivation in Yunnan.' Tr. from *Yün-nan sheng nung ts'un tiao ch'a* (Rural survey of Yunnan); Shanghai: Shang wu yin shu kuan, 1935 [partial tr.: p. 76 *ff.*, 126 *ff.*, 182 *ff.*, and 254 *ff.* only]. In *Agrarian China*, compiled by Institute of Pacific Relations. [Selective entry]
Chicago: U. of Chicago Press, 1939, 50–56.
SUBJ 24.1 ▪ 21.3 21.4 26.3

16619 NNC F P8 G8.2 1928–1949
China [Republic]. Hsing cheng yüan. Nung ts'un fu hsing wei yüan hui. (Executive Yüan. Rural Reconstruction Commission), ed.
'Poppy growing on the Yunnan plateau.' Tr. of 'Yün-nan ti cheng chih ching chi kai k'uang' (Political and economic conditions in Yunnan); in *Yün-nan sheng nung ts'un tiao ch'a* (Rural survey of Yunnan); Shanghai: Shang wu yin shu kuan, 1935, 28–31. In *Agrarian China*, compiled by Institute of Pacific Relations. [Selective entry]
Chicago: U. of Chicago Press, 1939, 118–122.
SUBJ 22.2 24.1 ▪ 24.5 24.6

16620 CSH FP P2 G6.3 1928–1949
China [Republic]. Shih yeh pu. Kuo chi mao i chü. (Ministry of Industry. Bureau of Foreign Trade), ed.
'Agriculture and forestation.' Tr. of 'Nung lin hsü mu, 1–13, 15' (Agriculture, forestry, and animal husbandry, Chaps. 1–13, 15); in *Chung-kuo shih yeh chih: Che-chiang sheng* (Chinese economic surveys: Chekiang); Shanghai: Kuo chi mao i chü, 1933, *ting* 1 – ting 340, *ting* 397 – *ting* 428 [s.p.] [slightly condensed in tr.]. In *China industrial handbooks: Chekiang*, edited by the agency cited. [Selective entry]
Shanghai: Kuo chi mao i chü, 1935, 167–354. [Reprinted in *China industrial handbooks: Chekiang*, edited by the

agency cited. (Selective entry.) Taipei: Ch'eng-wen, 1972, 167–354.]
SUBJ 24.1 ▪ 14.3 24.3 34.1 34.2

16621 CSH FP P2 G6.1 1911–1949
China [Republic]. Shih yeh pu. Kuo chi mao i chü. (Ministry of Industry. Bureau of Foreign Trade), ed.
'Agriculture and forestation.' Tr. of 'Nung lin hsü mu, 1–13' (Agriculture, forestry, and animal husbandry, Chaps. 1–13); in *Chung-kuo shih yeh chih: Chiang-su sheng* (Chinese economic surveys: Kiangsu); Shanghai: Kuo chi mao i chü, 1933, 1–337 [s.p.] [slightly condensed in tr.]. In *China industrial handbooks: Kiangsu*, edited by the agency cited. [Selective entry]
Shanghai: Kuo chi mao i chü, 1933, 141–243. [Reprinted in *China industrial handbooks: Kiangsu*, edited by the agency cited. (Selective entry.) Taipei: Ch'eng-wen, 1972, 141–243.]
SUBJ 24.1 ▪ 14.3 24.2 24.3 24.4 34.1 34.2

16622 CSH FP P2 G6.3 1928–1949
China [Republic]. Shih yeh pu. Kuo chi mao i chü. (Ministry of Industry. Bureau of Foreign Trade), ed.
'Fishery and stock raising.' Tr. of 'Shui ch'an chi yü yeh' and 'Nung lin hsü mu, 14' (Marine products and the fishing industry *and* Agriculture, forestry, and animal husbandry, Chap. 14); in *Chung-kuo shih yeh chih: Che-chiang sheng* (Chinese economic surveys: Chekiang); Shanghai: Kuo chi mao i chü, 1933, *mao* 1 – *mao* 35, *ting* 341 – *ting* 396 [s.p.] [slightly condensed in tr.]. In *China industrial handbooks: Chekiang*, edited by the agency cited. [Selective entry]
Shanghai: Kuo chi mao i chü, 1935, 357–390. [Reprinted in *China industrial handbooks: Chekiang*, edited by the agency cited. (Selective entry.) Taipei: Ch'eng-wen, 1972, 357–390.]
SUBJ 24.1 ▪ 14.3 24.2 24.3 24.4 34.2

16623 CSH FP P2 G6.1 1928–1949
China [Republic]. Shih yeh pu. Kuo chi mao i chü. (Ministry of Industry. Bureau of Foreign Trade), ed.
'Fishery and stock raising.' Tr. of 'Shui ch'an chi yü yeh' and 'Nung lin hsü mu, 14' (Marine products and the fishing industry *and* Agriculture, forestry, and animal husbandry, Chap. 14); in *Chung-kuo shih yeh chih: Chiang-su sheng* (Chinese economic surveys: Kiangsu); Shanghai: Kuo chi mao i chü, 1933, 1–29, 338–394 [s.p.] [slightly condensed in tr.]. In *China industrial handbooks: Kiangsu*, edited by the agency cited. [Selective entry]
Shanghai: Kuo chi mao i chü, 1933, 247–279. [Reprinted in *China industrial handbooks: Kiangsu*, edited by the agency cited. (Selective entry.) Taipei: Ch'eng-wen, 1972, 247–279.]
SUBJ 24.1 ▪ 14.3 24.3 24.4

16624 CSU FP P7 G6.3 1911–1949
Chung-kuo ching chi t'ung chi yen chiu so (China Institute of Economic and Statistical Research).
A study of the rural economy of Wuhing [i.e., Wu-hsing *hsien*], *Chekiang*.
Shanghai: China Institute of Economic and Statistical Research, 1939. 121 p.
[See Vol. 2 of this *Bibliography* for Chinese version.]
SUBJ 20 24 24.1 26.3 28 55 ▪ 21 21.4 24.4 24.6 26.2 27 41

16625 CSU F P8 G5.0 1928–1949
Dittrich, Scott R-, and Ramon Hawley Myers, 1929–.
'Resource allocation in traditional agriculture: Republican China, 1937–1940.'
J. of political economy 79, 4 (July–Aug. 1971), 887–896.
SUBJ 24.1

16626 NNC PO P7 G1.3 1928–1949
Dragoni, Carlo.
'Report on agriculture reform and development in China.' In *Annexes to the Report to the Council of the League of Nations of its technical delegate on his mission in China from date of appointment until April 1, 1934, Annex 6.* [Sole entry]
Shanghai: North-China Daily News and Herald, 1934, 167–226.
SUBJ 24.1 34.1 ▪ 24.3 24.6 27

16627 CSH O P7 G2.0 1911–1928
Dubovskii, A- (A. Duboffsky).
'K voprosu o krest'ianskom khoziaistve severnoi Man'chzhurii' (The question of the peasant economy in northern Manchuria). [Review of *Kitaiskoe krest'ianskoe khoziastvo v severnoi Man'chzhurii: ekonomicheskii ocherk* (Survey of the Chinese peasant economy in northern Manchuria), by Evgenii Evgen'evich IAshnov.]
VM 1927, 4, 27–42. [See also *VM* 1927, 6, 26–29.]

'Re "Peasants economy in northern Manchuria".'
Manchuria monitor 1927, 4, 10–16.
SUBJ 24.1 ▪ 24.3 28

16628 MMU O P2 G4.1 1928–1949
Eliassen, Sigurd, 1884–.
Gamle Drage Wangs elv: En norsk ingeniörs opplevelser i China (Old Dragon Wang's river: A Norwegian engineer's experiences in China).
Oslo: Gyldendal, 1955. 199 p.

Dragon Wang's river. Tr. by Katherine John.
New York: Day, 1957. 256 p.
SUBJ 24.1 25 28 ▪ 12 15 26.3 33 57 62 66

16629 CSU P P7 G7.3 1928–1949
Elvin, John Mark Dutton, 1938–.
'Early Communist land reform and the Kiangsi rural economy.' [Review of *The land revolution in China, 1930–1934: A study of documents*, by Hsiao Tso-liang.]
MAS 4, 2 (Apr. 1970), 165–169.
SUBJ 24.1 26 26.3

16630 NIC F P8 G9.2 1911–1928
Feng, Rui (Feng Jui), 1899–1936, and Ping-hang Yung.
'A general descriptive survey of the Honan island village community.'
LSJ 10, 2/3 (Aug. 1931), 153–186.
SUBJ 20 24.1 ▪ 24.6 25 26.3 28 38

16631 CSH F P7 G6.1 1928–1949
Fukutake, Tadashi, 1917–.
'Village life in Central China.' Tr. from the Japanese. In *Asian rural society: China, India, Japan*, by Tadashi Fukutake. [Selective entry]
Tokyo: U. of Tokyo Press, 1967, 79–92.
SUBJ 24.1 41 ▪ 26 33 42

16632 NIC F P8 G5.1 1928–1949
Gamble, Sidney David, 1890–1968.
'Four hundred Chinese farms.'
FEQ 4, 4 (Aug. 1945), 341–366.
SUBJ 24.1 26.3 28 41 ▪ 45

16633 NNC FP P2 G4.3 1911–1949
Golomb, Ludwig.
Die Bodenkultur in Ost-Turkestan (Agriculture in eastern Turkestan).
Posieux: Verlag des Anthropos-Instituts, 1959. 12, 160 p. (Anthropos-Institut studia, 14)
SUBJ 24.1 55 ▪ 12 21.1 21.3 24.3 24.4 26.3

16634 CSU O P8 G9.1 1928–1949
Groff, George Weidman, 1884–1955, and T. C. Lau.
'Landscaped Kwangsi, China's province of pictorial art.'
NG 72, 6 (Dec. 1937), 671–710.
SUBJ 24.1

16635 MCH P P7 G8.1 1928–1949
Hsiang, C. Y. (Hsiang Ching-yün), 1909–.
'Mountain economy in Szechuan.'
PA 14, 4 (Dec. 1941), 448–462.
SUBJ 24.1 ▪ 21.2 24.4 25

16636 CSH PO P7 G7.2 1928–1949
Hsiao Ch'ien, 1911–.
How the tillers won back their land.
Peking: Foreign Languages Press, 1951. 148 p.
SUBJ 24.1 26.3 ▪ 24 24.3 24.5 26

16637 CSU P P7 G1.2 1928–1949
Hsiao Tso-liang, 1910–.
The land revolution in China, 1930–1934: A study of documents.
Seattle: U. of Washington Press, 1969. 361 p.
SUBJ 12.2 24.1 26 32.2 64 ▪ 26.3 36.3

16638 NNC PO P2 G6.1 1928–1949
Hsu Fong-ting (Hsü Fang-t'ing).
'Chiehtung, the district of tenants, and the land policy in 1935.' Tr. of 'Ch'ung Ch'i ti tsu tien chiu fen ho "keng che yu t'ien"' (Tenancy disputes in Ch'ung-ming *hsien* and Ch'i-tung *hsien* [Kiangsu] and the idea of 'land to the tiller'); *Chung-kuo nung ts'un* 3, 6 (June 1937), 106–109. In *Agrarian China*, compiled by Institute of Pacific Relations. [Selective entry]
Chicago: U. of Chicago Press, 1939, 26–30.
SUBJ 24.1 ▪ 12 24.5 26.3

16639 MAM P P7 G7.3 1911–1949
Hsü, King-yi.
Agrarian policies of the Chinese Soviet Republic, 1931–1934.
Ann Arbor: University Microfilms (Publ. 72-9980), 1972. 538 p. (Doctoral dissertation in Political Science, Indiana U., 1971)
SUBJ 24.1 32.2 36.3 ▪ 14.5 24.6 26.3 37

16640 ICU PO P2 G8.1 1928–1949
Hu, Charles Y. (Hu Chiao-ju), 1910–.
The agricultural and forestry land-use of the Szechwan basin.

Chicago: ——, 1946. 157 p. (Revision of doctoral dissertation in Geography, U. of Chicago, 1942)
Subj 11.3 24.1 ▪ 24.2

16641 CSU PO P8 G6.1 1928–1949
Hu Huan-yong (Hu Huan-yung), 1901–.
'A new cotton belt in China.'
EG 23, 1 (Jan. 1947), 60–66.
Subj 24.1 ▪ 34.2 45

16642 CSH F P7 G2.0 1911–1928
IAshnov, Evgenii Evgen'evich.
'Dokhody kitaiskogo krest'ianskogo khoziaistva v severnoi Man'chzhurii' (The farm income of Chinese peasants in northern Manchuria).
EVM 1924, 36 (7 sentiabria), 3–8.
Subj 24.1 24.6 26.3 ▪ 24.3

16643 DLC FP P7 G2.0 1911–1928
IAshnov, Evgenii Evgen'evich.
Kitaiskaia kolonizatsiia severnoi Man'chzhurii i ee perspektivy (Chinese colonization of northern Manchuria and its prospects).
Harbin: Tip. KVzhd, 1928. 292 p.
Subj 21 21.2 24.1 ▪ 22 24.2

16644 CSH FP P8 G2.0 1911–1928
IAshnov, Evgenii Evgen'evich (E. E. Yashnoff).
'Kitaiskoe i russkoe krest'ianskoe khoziaistvo na Dal'nem Vostoke: opyt sravnitel'noi kharakteristiki' (A comparison of the Chinese and Russian peasant economies in the Far East).
VM 1926, 9, 1–13.
'Chinese and Russian farming economy in the Far East (An essay on comparative characteristics).'
Manchuria monitor 1926, 9, 1–14.
Subj 24.1 ▪ 21 21.2 24.6 41 45

16645 CSH F P7 G2.0 1911–1928
IAshnov, Evgenii Evgen'evich.
'Raskhody kitaiskogo krest'ianskogo khoziaistva v severnoi Man'chzhurii' (Expenditures of the Chinese peasant economy in northern Manchuria).
EVM 1924, 41/42 (19 oktiabria), 14–18.
Subj 24.1 24.6 26.3 ▪ 24.3 28

16646 CSU F P8 G8.0 1928–1949
Jen, Mei-Ngo (Jen Mei-o).
'Agricultural landscape of southwestern China: A study in land utilization.'
EG 24, 3 (July 1948), 157–169.
Subj 24.1 ▪ 21

16647 CSU O P2 G4.3 1928–1949
Johns Hopkins U. Walter Hines Page School of International Relations. Inner Asian Seminar.
'Sinkiang survey.'
FES 17, 5 (10 Mar. 1948), 53–63.
Subj 12 24.1 ▪ 21 66

16648 MCH O P7 G8.2 1911–1928
Jonery, J-.
'Note sur le thé des états Chans chinois: thé de P'ou-Eul' (A note on the tea of the Chinese Shan states: The tea of the P'u-erh area [Yunnan]).
BEI 18, 114 (juil.–août 1915), 569–576.
Subj 24.1 24.3 ▪ 24.2

16649 CSU O P8 G8.1 1928–1949
Jones, Fred O-.
'Tukiangyien: China's ancient irrigation system [on the Chengtu plain, Szechwan].'
GR 44, 4 (Oct. 1954), 543–559.
Subj 24.1 ▪ 24.2

16650 DNA F P2 G1.5 1928–1949
King, Ogden T. (Chin K'o-tun).
Farm implements in East Central China.
Nanking: U. of Nanking, College of Agriculture and Forestry, 1938. 112 p. (CAF bulletins, new series, 53)
Subj 24.1 ▪ 14.3 24.3 24.4

16651 CSU O P2 G9.4 1911–1928
Kirjassoff, Alice Ballantine.
'Formosa the beautiful.'
NG 37, 3 (Mar. 1920), 247–292.
Subj 24.1 ▪ 24.2 24.4

16652 CBU F P8 G8.1 1928–1949
Ko Fuh-ting (Ko Fu-ting).
'Farm business in two types of land, Hwayang [i.e., Hua-yang *hsien*], Szechwan.'
EF 46 (July 1945), 703–704.
Subj 24.1

16653 CBU FP P2 G8.1 1928–1949
Ko Fuh-ting (Ko Fu-ting).
'Rice production on the Chengtu plain in 1939.'
EF 15 (Apr. 1941), 134–138.
Subj 24.1 24.3 ▪ 26.3

16654 CSH F P7 G8.1 1928–1949
Ko Fuh-ting (Ko Fu-ting).
'A study of profitable types of farming in western Szechwan.'
EF 20 (May 1943), 123–132.
Subj 24.1

16655 CSH FP P7 G8.1 1928–1949
Ko Fuh-ting (Ko Fu-ting) and Rih-hwa Ho.
'Costs and profits of producing rapeseed and other winter crops in Szechwan.'
EF 16 (Jan. 1943), 14–19.
Subj 24.1

16656 CSH FP P7 G4.1 1928–1949
Ko Fuh-ting (Ko Fu-ting) and Yin-yuen Wang (Wang Yin-yüan).
'The production and prices of cotton in Shensi.'
EF 18 (Mar. 1943), 71–80.
Subj 24.1 24.3

16657 CSH P P2 G2.0 1911–1928
Kormazov, V- A-.
'Sel'skokhoziaistvennaia i torgovo-promyshlennaia zhizn' kitaiskogo Priamur'ia: po materialam Ekonomicheskogo biuro KVzhd' (Data from the Economic Bureau of the Chinese Eastern Railway on agricultural, commercial, and industrial life in the Chinese Amur region). [With English abstract]
VM 1929, 9, 39–52.
Subj 14.3 24.1 24.3 24.4 ▪ 12 26.3

16658 NNC O P8 G5.1 1928–1949
Kuo Shih-tze.
'The bankrupt condition of southern Hopei.' Tr. from *I shih pao fu k'an* 31 Aug. 1935. In *Agrarian China*, compiled by Institute of Pacific Relations. [Selective entry]
Chicago: U. of Chicago Press, 1939, 167–171.
Subj 24.1 ▪ 28

16659 NNC PO P7 G1.4 1928–1949
Lee, Frank C.
'Land redistribution in Communist China.'
PA 21, 1 (Mar. 1948), 20–32.
Subj 22.1 24.1 ▪ 26.3 32.1

16660 CSU P P7 G9.2 1911–1949
Lee, Milton Chun.
'The Kwangtung lychee.'
CEJ 5, 5 (Nov. 1929), 945–961.
Subj 24.1

16661 NNC O P7 G5.1 1928–1949
Lee Siao-ming (Li Hsiao-ming).
'Decline of land price and distress of the peasants in Foping [Fou-p'ing *hsien*, Hopei].' Tr. from *I shih pao fu k'an* 30 Nov. 1934. In *Agrarian China*, compiled by Institute of Pacific Relations. [Selective entry]
Chicago: U. of Chicago Press, 1939, 18–21.
Subj 24.1 26.3 28 ▪ 24.6

16662 CBU F P7 G6.1 1928–1949
Li Hwei-chien (Li Te-ch'ien).
'Preliminary note on a study of 533 farms near Molingkwan [Chiang-ning *hsien*], Kiangsu.'
EF 7 (Oct. 1937), 302–311. [In Chinese as well as English]
Subj 24.1 28 ▪ 26.3 27 41

16663 NNC P P7 G6.3 1911–1949
Lin Chu-ching (Lin Chih-ch'ing).
'The Kuomintang policy of rent reduction.' Tr. of 'Che-chiang sheng ti erh wu chien tsu' (The 25 percent farmland-rent reduction in Chekiang); *Hsin ch'uang tsao* 2, 1/2 (July 1932), 191–196. In *Agrarian China*, compiled by Institute of Pacific Relations. [Selective entry]
Chicago: U. of Chicago Press, 1939, 144–149.
Subj 24.1 ▪ 22.2

16664 NNC PO P7 G4.2 1911–1928
Liu, Ju-fan.
A study of the self-sufficing agriculture of the province of Kansu, China.
Unpublished masters thesis in Economics and Financial Economy, Columbia U., 1929. 45 p.
Subj 24.1 24.3 ▪ 12.2 17 24.6 28 41 58

16665 CSH FP P7 G8.1 1928–1949
Liu, R. T.
'Types of farming in Szechwan.'
EF 13 (Sept. 1939), 12–18.
Subj 24.1

16666 NNC F P7 G6.3 1928–1949
Liu Tuan-sheng.
'Oxen and buffaloes in relation to the size of farms' and 'Farm labour in the lower Yangtze region.' Tr. of 'Chia-hsing ssu san i erh hu nung yeh ching ying ti yen chiu' (Agricultural management in 4,312 households of Chia-hsing *hsien* [Chekiang]); *Chung-shan wen hua chiao yü kuan chi k'an* 4, 2 (Summer 1937), 565–576. In *Agrarian China*, compiled by Institute of Pacific Relations. [Selective entry]

Chicago: U. of Chicago Press, 1939, 65–68, 73–79.
SUBJ 24.1 ▪ 26.3 28

16667 CSU F P8 G5.2 1911–1928
Lowdermilk, Walter Clay, 1888–.
'Forest destruction and slope denudation in the province of Shansi.'
China j. of science and arts 4, 3 (Mar. 1926), 127–135.
SUBJ 24.1

16668 NNC P P7 G6.1 1911–1949
Lu, Albert T. (Lu T'ung-p'ing), 1898–.
'Renaissance of rural Kiangsi.'
IB 2, 2 (21 Sept. 1936), 17–38.
SUBJ 24.1 28 34.1 ▪ 24.2 24.4 66

16669 NNC PO P8 G2.0 1911–1928
Meshcherskii, A- S-, and P- N- Men'shikov.
'Sovremennoe sostoianie skotovodstva v Kheiluntszianskoi i Girinskoi provintsiiakh Kitaia' (The current state of cattle raising in Heilungkiang and Kirin provinces). In *Materialy k otchetu o deiatel'nosti s 1915 po 1918 gg.* (Data on activities, 1915–1918), compiled by Mongol'skaia ekspeditsiia po zagotovke miasa dlia deistvuiushchikh armii, Man'chzhursko-Vladivostokskii raion, Ministerstvo prodovol'stviia. [Selective entry]
Harbin: Tip. KVzhd, 1920, vol. 12 (supplement), Part 2, 1–24.
SUBJ 20 24.1 ▪ 21 24.2

16670 CSU O P8 G9.2 1928–1949
Miller, R- C-, and Floyd Alonzo McClure, 1897–.
'The fresh-water clam industry of the Pearl river.'
LSJ 10, 2/3 (Aug. 1931), 307–322.
SUBJ 24.1 55

16671 NNC O P2 G5.4 1911–1949
Min Chi (Ming-chieh), pseud.
'Foreign industrial capital and the peasantry in Honan.' Tr. of 'Ying-Mei yen ts'ao kung ssu ho Yü chung nung min' (The British-American Tobacco Company and the peasants of central Hunan); *Chung-kuo nung ts'un* 2, 7 (July 1936), 69–77 [condensed tr.]. In *Agrarian China*, compiled by Institute of Pacific Relations. [Selective entry]
Chicago: U. of Chicago Press, 1939, 175–179.
SUBJ 24.1 26.3 ▪ 24.3 34.2 66

16672 DLC F P7 G4.3 1928–1949
Monich, ———.
'Novye dannye o tekhnike, ekonomike i klassovom rassloenii krest'ianskikh khoziaistv v Kashgarii' (New data on the equipment, economy, and class stratification of peasant farms in Kashgaria [southwestern Sinkiang]).
MNKP 1935, 2, 35–73; 1935, 3, 116–164; 1935, 4, 95–123.
SUBJ 24 24.1 26.2 26.3 41 ▪ 22.2 24.3 24.4 47 55

16673 CSU O P8 G5.2 1928–1949
Moyer, Raymond Tyson, 1899–.
'Agricultural practices in semi-arid North China.'
Scientific monthly 55, 4 (Oct. 1942), 301–316.
SUBJ 24.1 26.3

16674 CSU P P8 G9.4 1928–1949
Moyer, Raymond Tyson, 1899–.
'Agriculture and foodstuffs in Taiwan (Formosa).'
Foreign agriculture 9, 1 (Jan. 1945), 2–12.
SUBJ 24.1

16675 DLC P P7 G8.1 1911–1949
Mugruzin, Anatolii Sergeevich.
Agrarnye otnosheniia v Kitae v 20–40-kh godakh XX veka (Agrarian relations in China from the 1920s through the 1940s).
Moscow: Nauka, Glav. red. vost. lit-ry, 1970. 236 p.
SUBJ 14.5 24.1 24.3 24.6 26.1 26.3 ▪ 14.3 14.6 21 21.4 45 72

16676 CBU F P8 G1.3 1928–1949
Pan Hong-shen (P'an Hung-sheng).
'A comparative analysis of the economic use of some of the alternative farm implements in East Central China and northern China, 1933–1934 and 1935–1936.'
EF 10 (June 1938), 473–480. [In Chinese as well as English]
SUBJ 24.1

16677 CBU F P7 G1.5 1928–1949
Pan Hong-shen (P'an Hung-sheng) and Ogden T. King (Chin K'o-tun).
'Preliminary note on an economic study of farm implements.'
EF 3 (Nov. 1936), 152–159. [In Chinese as well as English]
SUBJ 24.1

16678 CSH F P2 G8.1 1928–1949
Pan Hong-shen (P'an Hung-sheng) and Cheng Sie.
'Economics of tobacco production and marketing at Pihsien [i.e., P'i *hsien*], Szechwan.'
EF 19 (Apr. 1943), 99–105.
SUBJ 24.1 24.3

16679 CSU O P8 G9.2 1928–1949
Pendleton, Robert Larimore, 1890–.
'Forestry in Kwangtung province, South China.'
LSJ 16, 3 (1937), 473–480.
SUBJ 24.1

16680 NNC O P8 G2.3 1911–1928
Podkopaev, V- P-, and P- N- Men'shikov.
'Sovremennoe sostoianie skotovodstva v Mukdenskoi provintsii Kitaia' (The current state of cattle raising in Fengtien). In *Materialy k otchetu o deiatel'nosti s 1915 po 1918 gg.* (Data on activities, 1915–1918), compiled by Mongol'skaia ekspeditsiia po zagotovke miasa dlia deistvuiushchikh armii, Man'chzhursko-Vladivostokskii raion, Ministerstvo prodovol'stviia. [Selective entry]
Harbin: Tip. KVzhd, 1920, vol. 12 (supplement), Part 2, 27–52.
SUBJ 20 24.1

16681 NNC O P2 G3.3 1928–1949
Pong Zuan-shu (P'ang Shan-shou) and Chen Han-seng (Ch'en Han-sheng), 1897–.
'The agrarian situation in Paotow.' Tr. of 'Sui-yüan Pao-t'ou hsien nung ts'un ti tien tsu ho li hsi' (Tenancy and interest rates in rural Pao-t'ou *hsien*, Suiyuan); *Tung fang tsa chih* (Shanghai) 32, 6 (16 Mar. 1935), 96–97 [unspecified portion translated from unpublished travel notes of Chen Han-seng (Ch'en Han-sheng)]. In *Agrarian China*, compiled by Institute of Pacific Relations. [Selective entry]
Chicago: U. of Chicago Press, 1939, 42–45.
SUBJ 24.1 24.6 ▪ 21.2 24.3

16682 CBU F P7 G6.2 1928–1949
Raeburn, John R-, and Pan Hong-shen (P'an Hung-sheng).
'Ownership and costs of farm implements and work animals in Suhsien [i.e., Su *hsien*], Anhwei.'
EF 7 (Oct. 1937), 296–301. [In Chinese as well as English]
SUBJ 24.1

16683 CSH PO P2 G8.1 1928–1949
Richardson, H- L-, and Y. Wang.
'Observations on the use of night-soil as a manure in Szechwan.'
JWCBRS 13 (1941), 46–59.
SUBJ 24.1 ▪ 24.3 56

16684 NIC O P7 G9.3 1911–1928
Riggs, Charles Henry, 1892–1953.
Agricultural engineering in Chinese agriculture.
Unpublished masters thesis in Agricultural Engineering, Cornell U., 1932. 120 p.
SUBJ 24.1 ▪ 24.3 24.4

16685 NNC P P7 G5.4 1911–1928
S. B.
'Sel'skoe khoziaistvo v Khenani' (Agriculture in Honan).
Na agrarnom fronte 1926, 4 (aprel'), 47–62; 1926, 5/6 (mai–iiun'), 85–92.
SUBJ 24.1 26.3 28 ▪ 24.3 24.5 25 26.1 34.1 45

16686 CSU O P8 G4.3 1928–1949
Schomberg, Reginald Charles Francis, 1880–.
'The habitability of Chinese Turkistan.'
GJ 80, 6 (Dec. 1932), 505–511.
SUBJ 24.1 ▪ 21 28

16687 CSU F P2 G9.2 1911–1928
Shim, Edward.
'Report of a fertilizer survey in the mulberry districts of Kwangtung.'
Lingnaam agricultural review 2, 2 (Feb. 1925), 74–89.
SUBJ 24.1 24.3

16688 NNC O P8 G8.3 1928–1949
Spencer, Joseph Earle, 1907–.
'Kueichou: An internal Chinese colony.'
PA 13, 2 (June 1940), 162–172.
SUBJ 24.1 ▪ 66

16689 GMS O P2 G1.5 1911–1949
Stübel, Hans Bruno, 1885–1961.
'Der Wu-i-schan' (The Wu-i mountain range).
MDG 30, D (1938), 1–41.
SUBJ 11.3 24.1 ▪ 23 33

16690 NNC FP P8 G1.2 1928–1949
[Sun Shao-tsun] Sun Hsiao-tsun (Sun Hsiao-ts'un).
'Forms of farm labour in China.' Tr. of 'Hsien tai Chung-kuo ti nung yeh ching ying wen t'i' (Problems of agricultural management in modern China); *Chung-shan wen hua chiao yü kuan chi k'an* 3, 2 (Summer 1936), 461–474 [condensed

tr.]. In *Agrarian China*, compiled by Institute of Pacific Relations. [Selective entry]
Chicago: U. of Chicago Press, 1939, 69–73.
Subj 24.1 ▪ 21.4 26.3 28

16691 CSH P P7 G2.1 1911–1928
Surin, Vladimir Ivanovich.
'IAlutszianskii lesnoi raion i ego ekonomicheskoe znachenie: po materialam Ekonomicheskogo biuro KVzhd' (Data from the Economic Bureau of the Chinese Eastern Railway on the Yalu river forest region and its economic significance). [With English abstract]
VM 1929, 10, 40–45.
Subj 24.1 24.4 ▪ 14.3 24.2 24.3

16692 NNC F P8 G5.3 1911–1928
Swen, Wen-yuh.
'Types of farming, costs of production, and annual labor distribution in Weihsien county [i.e., Wei *hsien*], Shantung, China.'
CEJ 3, 2 (Aug. 1928), 642–680.
Subj 24.1 26.3 ▪ 21.4 24.4

16693 NNC FP P7 G1.2 1928–1949
[Tang, Hui-sun] Tang Hwei-seng (T'ang Hui-sun), 1899–.
'Comparative economic conditions of tenant and owner-cultivator.' Tr. of 'Chung-kuo hsien shih tzu keng nung yü tien nung chih fen pu chi ch'i ching chi chuang k'uang chih pi chiao' (The distribution of owner-cultivators and tenants in contemporary China and a comparison of their economic conditions); *Ti cheng yüeh k'an* 5, 2/3 (Mar. 1937), 197–220 [condensed tr.]. In *Agrarian China*, compiled by Institute of Pacific Relations. [Selective entry]
Chicago: U. of Chicago Press, 1939, 85–90.
Subj 24.1 26.3 ▪ 28

16694 NNC O P8 G6.2 1928–1949
Tao Shuan (T'ao Jan).
'Attempted rural reforms near Wuhu.' Tr. of 'T'ao-hsin-yü ti hsiang ts'un kai liang kung tso' (Rural-reform work in T'ao-hsin-yü [Wu-hu *hsien*, Anhwei]); *Chung-kuo nung ts'un* 3, 3 (Mar. 1937), 85–89. In *Agrarian China*, compiled by Institute of Pacific Relations. [Selective entry]
Chicago: U. of Chicago Press, 1939, 30–35.
Subj 24.1 37 ▪ 24.6 26.3 28

16695 NIC F P7 G1.4 1911–1928
Tayler, John Bernard, 1878–.
'The study of Chinese rural economy. II, The results of the Famine Commission's investigations.'
CSPSR 8, 1 (Jan. 1924), 196–226; 8, 2 (Apr. 1924), 230–258. [For Part I, see entry 22802.] [Reprinted in *The study of Chinese rural economy*, by Carroll Brown Malone and J. B. Tayler. (Analytic entry.) Peking: China International Famine Relief Commission, 1924, 1–64 (s.p.). (CIFRC, Series B, 10)]
Subj 21 24 24.1 28 ▪ 21.2 21.4 41 55

16696 MCH U P8 G5.3 1928–1949
Thiel, Josef.
'Die wirtschaftliche Ausnutzung des Nan-Yang Sees in Süd-Schantung' (The economic exploitation of Nan-yang lake in southern Shantung).
FS 7 (1948), 116–122.
Subj 24.1 ▪ 21.4 26.3

16697 NNC F P8 G9.2 1928–1949
Trewartha, Glenn Thomas, 1896–.
'Field observations on the Canton delta of South China.'
EG 15, 1 (Jan. 1939), 1–10.
Subj 24.1

16698 CSH F P8 G8.1 1928–1949
Tsui, R. T. (Ts'ui Yü-chün).
'Correlation analysis on factors affecting farm profits.'
EF 53 (Feb. 1946), 801–804.
Subj 24.1

16699 MCH F P7 G5.0 1911–1928
Tsui, R. T. (Ts'ui Yü-chün).
'Farm management study of the eight representative localities in North China.'
CSPSR 24, 3 (Oct.–Dec. 1940), 291–331.
Subj 24.1 24.6 ▪ 26.3

16700 CSH F P8 G6.0 1928–1949
Tsui, R. T. (Ts'ui Yü-chün).
'Feasibility of farming uncultivated land.'
EF 13 (Sept. 1939), 19–31.
Subj 24.1

16701 CBU F P7 G8.1 1928–1949
Tsui, R. T. (Ts'ui Yü-chün).
'Land classification in Shuang-liu *hsien*, Szechwan.'
EF 54 (Mar. 1946), 815–820.
Subj 24.1 ▪ 24.5

16702 CBU F P7 G1.3 1928–1949
Tsui, R. T. (Ts'ui Yü-chün).
'Land classification of 34 hsien in Anhwei, Honan, Hupeh and Kiangsi.'
EF 3 (Nov. 1936), 141–153. [In Chinese as well as English]
Subj 24.1

16703 CBU F P8 G5.4 1928–1949
Tsui, R. T. (Ts'ui Yü-chün).
'Relation of land tenure to size of farm business in Loyang [i.e., Lo-yang *hsien*], Honan.'
EF 10 (June 1938), 445–452. [In Chinese as well as English]
Subj 24.1 ▪ 24.6

16704 CSH F P7 G8.1 1928–1949
Tsui, R. T. (Ts'ui Yü-chün).
'Relation of size of farm to farm efficiency.'
EF 36 (Sept. 1944), 533–535.
Subj 24.1

16705 CBU F P8 G5.4 1928–1949
Tsui, R. T. (Ts'ui Yü-chün).
'Relation of size of farm to utilization of farm land in Kaifeng [i.e., K'ai-feng *hsien*], Honan.'
EF 9 (Apr. 1938), 404–411. [In Chinese as well as English]
Subj 24.1

16706 DNA F P8 G5.1 1928–1949
Tsui, R. T. (Ts'ui Yü-chün).
'Size of farm in relation to the successfulness of a year's business on 93 farms, Tsanghsien [i.e., Ts'ang *hsien*], Hopei, 1936.'
EF 12 (June 1939), 585–594. [In Chinese as well as English]
Subj 24.1 ▪ 26.3

16707 CBU F P8 G8.1 1928–1949
Tsui, R. T. (Ts'ui Yü-chün).
'Summary of a farm business study in Wulung [*hsien*], Szechwan, 1943–44.'
EF 47 (Aug. 1945), 715–718.
Subj 24.1 26.3

16708 CBU F P8 G8.1 1928–1949
Tsui, R. T. (Ts'ui Yü-chün).
'Summary of a farm management survey, Kwanhsien [i.e., Kuan *hsien*], Szechwan, 1943–44.'
EF 44 (May 1945), 677–679.
Subj 24.1 28

16709 NNC U P8 G6.3 1928–1949
Tu Chi-yuan (Tu Chih-yüan).
'Miniature of a representative village in Shangyu.' Tr. of 'Che-chiang Shang-yü nung ts'un shuai lo ti i ko so ying' (Sketch of rural decline in Shang-yü *hsien*, Chekiang); *Chung-kuo nung ts'un* 1, 6 (Mar. 1935), 90–93. In *Agrarian China*, compiled by Institute of Pacific Relations. [Selective entry]
Chicago: U. of Chicago Press, 1939, 90–94.
Subj 24.1 ▪ 21.3 22.1 26.1 26.3 28 55

16710 CSH P P2 G9.4 1928–1949
U.S. Office of Naval Operations.
Agriculture in Taiwan.
[Washington, D.C.]: Office of the Chief of Naval Operations, 1945. 130 p. (OPNAV, 13-32)
Subj 24.1 ▪ 24.3 24.4

16711 CSH P P2 G9.4 1928–1949
U.S. Office of Naval Operations.
The fishing industry in Taiwan (Formosa).
[Washington, D.C.]: Office of the Chief of Naval Operations, 1944. 32 p. (OPNAV, 13-29)
Subj 24.1 ▪ 24.4

16712 DLC F P7 G9.2 1911–1928
[Volin, M-] ———, and [Evgenii Sigizmundovich Iolk] ———, 1900–1942.
'Ocherk agrarnykh otnoshenii provintsii Guandun' (Overview of agrarian relations in Kwangtung). In *Kantonskaia kommuna: sbornik statei i materialov* (Articles and documents on the Canton commune), compiled by Nauchno-issledovatel'skii institut po Kitaiu, Kommunisticheskaia akademiia. [Selective entry]
Moscow: Gosizdat, 1929, 130–163.
Subj 24.1 ▪ 24.3 26 26.3 66

16713 CBU F P7 G8.1 1928–1949
Wang, Yin-yuen (Wang Yin-yüan).
'Price changes and farm business in Szechwan.'
EF 49 (Oct. 1945), 743–746.
Subj 24.1 24.3 ▪ 28

16714 NNC F P7 G6.1 1928–1949
Wong Yin-seng (Wang Yin-sheng), 1902–, et al.
'Land concentration in Wusih, near Shanghai.' Tr. from the Chinese [tr. from an unpublished manuscript on

land distribution and the future of capital, dated 1932]. In *Agrarian China*, compiled by Institute of Pacific Relations. [Selective entry]
Chicago: U. of Chicago Press, 1939, 5–10.
SUBJ 24.1 ▪ 26.1 26.3

16715 CSU O P2 G1.1 1928–1949
Worcester, George Raleigh Gray, 1890–1969.
'Some brief notes on fishing in China.'
Mariner's mirror 44, 1 (Feb. 1958), 49–63.
SUBJ 24.1 ▪ 24.2

16716 NIC F P8 G4.1 1928–1949
Wu, Hwa-pao (Wu Hua-pao), 1909–.
'Agricultural economy of Yung-loh Tien [i.e., Yung-le-tien, Ching-yang *hsien*] in Shensi province.'
NSEQ 9, 1 (Apr. 1936), 164–176.
SUBJ 24.1 ▪ 24.6 38

16717 NIC F P7 G4.1 1928–1949
Wu, Hwa-pao (Wu Hua-pao), 1909–.
An economic study of two areas in Shenshi province, China.
Unpublished masters thesis in Agriculture, Cornell U., 1934. 51 p.
SUBJ 24.1 ▪ 24 28

16718 NNC F P8 G6.1 1928–1949
Wu Sho-peng (Wu Shou-p'eng) and Chang I-pu (Chang I-p'u).
'Land concentration in northern Kiangsu.' Tr. of 'Tou liu yü nung ts'un ching chi shih tai ti Hsü Hai ko shu' (The Hsü-chou–Hai-chou area [Kiangsu] stagnating in an agrarian economic phase); *Tung fang tsa chih* (Shanghai) 27, 6 (27 Mar. 1930), 69–80; 27, 7 (10 Apr. 1930), 59–70 *and* of 'Chiang-su ti t'u ti fen p'ei ho tsu tien chih tu' (Land distribution and tenancy in Kiangsu); *Chung-kuo nung ts'un* 1, 8 (May 1935), 57–67 [greatly condensed in tr.]. In *Agrarian China*, compiled by Institute of Pacific Relations. [Selective entry]
Chicago: U. of Chicago Press, 1939, 11–14.
SUBJ 24 24.1 ▪ 22.1 25 26.1 33

16719 CSH F P7 G7.1 1928–1949
Yang, William Y. (Yang Yü), 1907–.
'Cost of producing cotton in Siangyang [i.e., Hsiang-yang *hsien*], Hupeh.'
EF 13 (Sept. 1939), 1–11.
SUBJ 24.1

16720 CBU F P8 G7.1 1928–1949
Yang, William Y. (Yang Yü), 1907–, and Pan Hong-shen (P'an Hung-sheng).
'Cost of producing cotton in Kwanghwa [i.e., Kuang-hua *hsien*], Hupeh.'
EF 11 (Sept. 1938), 488–520. [In Chinese as well as English]
SUBJ 24.1 28

16721 NNC O P8 G6.1 1928–1949
Yi Ming-shi (I Ming-hsi).
'Experiences of an official in the land tax consolidation bureau.' Tr. of 'Tso liao san ko yüeh ti "t'u ti teng chi" yüan' (Three months as a 'land registration' official); *Chung-kuo nung ts'un* 3, 6 (June 1937), 109–112. In *Agrarian China*, compiled by Institute of Pacific Relations. [Selective entry]
Chicago: U. of Chicago Press, 1939, 149–153.
SUBJ 24.1 24.5 ▪ 26.3 28

16722 CBU F P7 G8.1 1928–1949
Yin Lien-ken (Ying Lien-keng), 1904?–.
'Returns on landlord's capital investment in farms in the localities of Chengtu, Tsingchen, Yunghsien and Kwanhsien [i.e., Ch'eng-tu *hsien*, Ch'ing-shen *hsien*, Jung *hsien*, and Kuan *hsien*], Szechwan.'
EF 45 (June 1945), 689–693.
SUBJ 24.1 26.1 ▪ 24.6

16723 CSH F P8 G8.1 1928–1949
Yin Lien-ken (Ying Lien-keng), 1904?–, and Chao-ling Feng.
'Land classification and taxation in Hwayang hsien, Szechwan province.'
EF 17 (Feb. 1943), 29–42.
SUBJ 24.1 24.5

1911-1972
(including 1644-1972)

16724 MCH U P8 G6.1 1928–1972
'La technique de la réforme agraire dans le nord-Kiangsu.'
B. d'information de la Commission internationale contre le régime concentrationnaire 1, 5 (déc. 1955), 52–55.

'The technique of land reform in northern Kiangsu.'
Monthly information b. of the International Commission Against Concentration Camp Practices 1, 5 (Dec. 1955), 50–53.
SUBJ 24.1 26.3

16725 MAM F P8 G9.4 1928–1972
Chang, Chung-wu, 1937–.
A sociological study of changes in land tenure status in Taiwan: A study of Kwansi community [Kuan-hsi *chen*, Hsin-chu *hsien*].
Ann Arbor: University Microfilms (Publ. 72-17,751), 1972. 98 p. (Doctoral dissertation in Sociology, Louisiana State U., 1971)
SUBJ 24.1 ▪ 26.1 26.3

16726 MCH P P2 G9.4 1895–1972
Chang, Jen-hu (Chang Ching-hu), 1928–.
Agricultural geography of Taiwan.
Taipei: China Cultural Service, 1953. 86 p.
SUBJ 11.3 24.1 ▪ 14.4 21 21.1 72

16727 CSH FP P2 G9.4 1911–1972
Chang, Yen-tien (Chang Yen-t'ien).
Population growth and food production and consumption in Taiwan.
Taipei: National Taiwan U., Research Institute of Rural Socio-economics, 1967. 110 p.
SUBJ 14.3 21 24.1 55 ▪ 21.4 50 58

16728 NIC P P7 G9.4 1895–1972
Chen, Cheng-siang (Ch'en Cheng-hsiang), 1920–.
'Land utilization in Formosa.' Tr. of 'T'ai-wan sheng chih t'u ti li yung' (Land utilization in Taiwan); in *T'ai-wan nung ti chien tsu yen chiu pao* (Reports on farmland-rent reduction), edited by Chung-kuo ti cheng yen chiu so (Research Institute on Chinese Land Administration); Taipei: Chung-kuo ti cheng yen chiu so, 1951, 111–130. [Tr. inferred; condensed tr.]
GR 41, 3 (July 1951), 438–456.
SUBJ 24.1 ▪ 26.3 28

16729 CSU FP P2 G9.4 1911–1972
Christensen, Raymond Peter, 1914–.
Taiwan's agricultural development: Its relevance for developing countries today.
Washington, D.C.: U.S. Dept. of Agriculture, Economic Research Service, Foreign Development and Trade Division, 1968. 92 p.
SUBJ 24 24.1 36.3 ▪ 12 14.3 17 21.1 21.2 21.4 24.3 24.6 28 34.1

16730 MAM U P8 G9.4 1895–1972
Fan, Chwei-lin.
Determination of sugar supply functions in Taiwan.
Ann Arbor: University Microfilms (Publ. 68-11,923), 1968. 251 p. (Doctoral dissertation in Economics, U. of Hawaii, 1967)
SUBJ 24.1

16731 NNC U P2 G9.5 1928–1972
Grant, Charles J-.
'The extension of the arable area in Hong Kong.' In *Symposium on land use and mineral deposits in Hong Kong, southern China and South-east Asia*, edited by Sydney George Davis. [Selective entry]
Hong Kong: Hong Kong U. Press, 1964, 55–59.
SUBJ 24.1 ▪ 21.1 21.2

16732 CSU O P2 G1.4 1928–1972
Hinton, William H-, 1919–.
Iron oxen: A documentary of revolution in Chinese farming.
New York: Monthly Review Press, 1970. 225 p.
SUBJ 24.1 27 34.1 ▪ 24.2 55 66

16733 CSH P P8 G9.4 1895–1972
Ho, Yhi-Min, 1934–.
Agricultural development of Taiwan, 1903–1960.
Nashville: Vanderbilt U. Press, 1966. 12, 172 p. (Revision of *The agricultural development of Taiwan, 1903–1960: Its patterns and sources of productivity increase*, doctoral dissertation in Economics, Vanderbilt U., 1965)
SUBJ 24.1 ▪ 26.3 27

16734 CSU P P7 G9.4 1928–1972
Hsieh, Chiao-min, 1918–.
'Typhoons and rice cultivation in Taiwan.' In *Proceedings of the International Geographical Union Regional Conference in Japan, 1957*. [Selective entry]
Tokyo: International Geographical Union Regional Conference in Japan, Organizing Committee *with* Science Council of Japan, 1959, 326–331.
SUBJ 24.1 ▪ 28

16735 NNC P P8 G4.3 1928–1972
IAkovlev, Aleksandr Grigor'evich, 1928–.
'Agrarnye otnosheniia i agrarnaia reforma v provintsii Sin'tszian (1949–1953 gg.)' (Agrarian relations and land reform in Sinkiang, 1949–1953).
UZIV 11 (1955), 220–262.
SUBJ 24.1 24.6 26.1 26.3 45 66 ▪ 22 24.5 34.1

16736 NNC P P7 G9.2 1928–1972
Iskol'dskii, V- I-.
'Razvitie sel'skogo khoziaistva na ostrove Khainan' (Agricultural development in Hainan).
SK 1958, 2, 117–123.
SUBJ 24.1 34.1 ▪ 21 24.4 26.3 36.3 45

16737 MAM P P8 G9.4 1895–1972
Kao, Charles H. C. (Kao Hsi-chün).
The role of the agricultural sector in Taiwan's economic development.
Ann Arbor: University Microfilms (Publ. 65-1758), 1965. 167 p. (Doctoral dissertation in Economics, Michigan State U., 1964)
SUBJ 14 24.1

16738 GMS FP P2 G4.1 1928–1972
Köhler, Günther, 1909–.
'Wirtschafts- und Landverkehrskarte der Provinz Schensi (Nordchina)' (An economic and land-transport map of Shensi).
Wissenschaftliche Veröffentlichungen des Deutschen Instituts für Länderkunde neue (2.) Folge 12 (1953), 1–3. [For maps accompanying this article see *Kartenbeilagen* 1 and 2 of the journal.]
SUBJ 24.1 24.2

16739 CSU P P8 G9.4 1895–1972
Koo, Anthony Y. C. (Ku Ying-ch'ang), 1918–.
'Agrarian reform, production and employment in Taiwan.'
ILR 104, 1/2 (July–Aug. 1971), 1–22. [Reprinted in *Agrarian reform and employment*, compiled by International Labour Office. (Sole entry.) Geneva: International Labour Office, 1971.]
SUBJ 16.3 21 24.1 ▪ 17 21.2 47

16740 CSU FP P2 G9.4 1895–1972
Koo, Anthony Y. C. (Ku Ying-ch'ang), 1918–.
The role of land reform in economic development: A case study of Taiwan.
New York: Praeger, 1968. 17, 197 p.
SUBJ 14 14.6 16 24.1 ▪ 14.4 14.5 21.2 47

16741 FPN P P8 G9.4 1895–1972
Kouo, Fou-pei (Kuo Fu-p'ei).
La réforme agraire à Taiwan (Agrarian reform in Taiwan).
Unpublished doctoral dissertation, Faculté de droit, Université de Paris, 1956. 395 p.
SUBJ 14 14.5 16.3 24.1

16742 NIC P P2 G9.4 1895–1972
Lee, Teng-hui (Li Teng-hui), 1923–.
Intersectoral capital flows in the economic development of Taiwan, 1895–1960.
Ithaca: Cornell U. Press, 1972. 197 p. (Revision of doctoral dissertation in Economics, Cornell U., 1968)
SUBJ 14 24.1 ▪ 14.5 14.6

16743 CSH U P8 G9.4 1911–1972
Lee, Teng-hui (Li Teng-hui), 1923–, and S. C. Hsieh (Hsieh Sen-chung), 1919–.
'An analytical review of agricultural development in Taiwan: An input-output and productivity approach.' In *Proceedings of Agricultural Economics Seminar held at the College of Agriculture, National Taiwan University, September 16–20, 1958.* [Selective entry]
Taipei: National Taiwan U., 1959, 53–64.
SUBJ 24.1 ▪ 21

16744 CSH P P7 G1.4 1928–1972
Myers, Ramon Hawley, 1929–.
'Agriculture and animal husbandry.' In *A regional handbook on Northwest China*, compiled by Far Eastern and Russian Institute, U. of Washington. [Selective entry]
New Haven: Human Relations Area Files, 1956, vol. 2, 635–666. (HRAF subcontractor's monographs, 59; Washington 5)
SUBJ 24.1 ▪ 34.1

16745 CSU P P8 G9.4 1895–1972
Myers, Ramon Hawley, 1929–.
'Taiwan.' In *Agricultural development in Asia*, edited by R- T- Shand. [Sole entry]
Berkeley, Los Angeles: U. of California Press, 1969, 25–52.
SUBJ 12.1 24.1 ▪ 14.5 16.1 16.3 18 21 58

16746 CSU FP P8 G9.4 1928–1972
Pasternak, Burton, 1933–.
'Some social consequences of land reform in a Taiwanese village.'
Eastern anthropologist 21, 2 (May–Aug. 1968), 135–154.
SUBJ 24.1 26.1 26.3 ▪ 22 27 45

16747 NIC P P2 G9.4 1928–1972
Shen, T. H. (Shen Tsung-han), 1895–.
Agricultural development on Taiwan since World War II. Tr. of *T'ai-wan nung yeh chih fa chan* (The development of agriculture in Taiwan); Taipei: Shang wu yin shu kuan, 1963; 381 p. [Rev. in tr.]
Ithaca: Cornell U. Press, 1964. 29, 399 p.
SUBJ 14 21 24.1 ▪ 24.3 24.6 28 34.1 36.3 58

16748 CSH P P2 G9.4 1928–1972
Sung, T. Y.
Development of seed technology in Taiwan.
Taipei: Chinese-American Joint Commission on Rural Reconstruction, Plant Industry Division, 1965. 41 p. (JCRR, Plant industry series, 27)
SUBJ 24.1 34.1 ▪ 14 62

16749 MCH O P8 G4.2 1928–1972
Trippner, Josef.
'Die Stein-Äcker um Lanchow in Kansu, China' (The 'stone fields' around Lanchow).
Anthropos 53, 5/6 (Sept.–Dez. 1958), 915–924.
SUBJ 24.1 ▪ 21.3 28 55 62

16750 CSU F P8 G4.2 1928–1972
Ulbrich, Joseph.
'Brunnengraben in den T'u-men-tzu-Bergen, Provinz Kansu, Westchina' (Well-digging in the T'u-men-tzu mountains, Kansu).
Anthropos 48, 5/6 (Sept.–Dez. 1953), 837–845.
SUBJ 24.1 65 ▪ 24.4

16751 CSU S P2 G4.3 –1972
Wiens, Herold Jacob, 1912–1971.
'Change in the ethnography and land-use of the Ili valley and region, Chinese Turkestan.'
AAAG 59, 4 (Dec. 1969), 753–775.
SUBJ 11.3 21 24.1 ▪ 21.1 21.2 21.3 24.4 34.1 66

16752 MCH P P2 G4.3 –1972
Wiens, Herold Jacob, 1912–1971.
'Cultivation development and expansion in China's colonial realm in Central Asia.'
JAS 26, 1 (Nov. 1966), 67–88.
SUBJ 11.3 24.1 ▪ 21.1 21.2

16753 NNC PO P2 G9.5 1895–1972
Wong, C. T.
'Changes in agricultural land use in Hong Kong.' In *Symposium on land use and mineral deposits in Hong Kong, southern China and South-east Asia*, edited by Sydney George Davis. [Selective entry]
Hong Kong: Hong Kong U. Press, 1964, 60–69.
SUBJ 24.1 ▪ 21.1 24.4

1949-1972

16754 CSU O P7 G7.1 1949–1972
Alley, Rewi, 1897–.
'Agriculture and industry in two Chinese hinterland counties [Hsin-chou *hsien* and Hsi-shui *hsien*, Hupeh].'
EH 11, 4 (1972), 32–45.
SUBJ 24.1 24.4 ▪ 34.1 56

16755 CSU O P8 G2.1 1949–1972
Alley, Rewi, 1897–.
'Among the forests of Hsingan Ling [Heilungkiang].'
EH 7, 1 (Jan.–Feb. 1968), 14–21.
SUBJ 24.1

16756 MCH O P2 G7.2 1949–1972
Alley, Rewi, 1897–.
Amongst hills and streams of Hunan, in the fall of 1962.
Peking: New World Press, 1963. 129 p.
SUBJ 24.1 24.4 ▪ 63

16757 CSU O P7 G7.2 1949–1972
Alley, Rewi, 1897–.
'Amongst the communes of Mao Tien [i.e., the Mao-t'ien district, Yüeh-yang *hsien*, Hunan].'
EH 6, 3 (Mar. 1967), 33–40.
SUBJ 20 24.1 34.1

16758 CSU O P7 G5.1 1949–1972
Alley, Rewi, 1897–.
'Chinglung county [i.e., Ch'ing-lung *hsien*, Hopei] and the struggle for self-sufficiency.'
EH 10, 5 (1971), 7–16.
SUBJ 24.1 24.4 ▪ 21

16759 CSU O P7 G5.1 1949–1972
Alley, Rewi, 1897–.
'Communes under the Great Wall.'
EH 8, 5 (1969), 24–39.
SUBJ 17 24.1 ▪ 24.4 26.3 28 34.1 56

16760 CSU O P8 G5.1 1949–1972
Alley, Rewi, 1897–.
'Cultural revolution comes to communes on the Pohai bay [Gulf of Chihli].'
EH 8, 1 (Jan.–Feb. 1969), 17–33.
SUBJ 24.1 34.1 ▪ 22 27 36.3

16761 CSU O P2 G5.1 1949–1972
Alley, Rewi, 1897–.
'Hsiao Kuan Chuang [Hsiao-kuan-chuang brigade, Han-erh-chuang commune, Ch'ien-hsi *hsien*, Hopei] and beyond in 1971.'

EH 11, 1 (1972), 6–16.
SUBJ 24.1 24.4 ▪ 28

16762 CSU O P7 G5.1 1949–1972
Alley, Rewi, 1897–.
'Hsintai [i.e., Hsing-t'ai *hsien*, Hopei] after the earthquakes.'
EH 6, 1 (Jan. 1967), 16–26.
SUBJ 20 24.1 28 ▪ 21 34.1

16763 NIC O P2 G7.3 1949–1972
Alley, Rewi, 1897–.
Land and folk in Kiangsi: A Chinese province in 1961.
Peking: New World Press, 1962. 95 p.
SUBJ 20 24.1 ▪ 24.4 26.3 65

16764 CSU O P7 G9.2 1949–1972
Alley, Rewi, 1897–.
'Loting [*hsien*, Kwangtung]: Where the impossible has been achieved.'
EH 11, 3 (1972), 27–33.
SUBJ 24.1 34.1 ▪ 24.4

16765 CSU O P7 G5.3 1949–1972
Alley, Rewi, 1897–.
'Man against nature amongst Shantung hills.'
EH 7, 2 (Mar.–Apr. 1968), 5–19.
SUBJ 24.1 ▪ 24.4 34.1

16766 CSU O P8 G5.1 1949–1972
Alley, Rewi, 1897–.
'Some fighting communes of Chunghua [i.e., Tsun-hua *hsien*, Hopei].'
EH 7, 3 (May–June 1968), 26–41.
SUBJ 24.1 34.1 ▪ 28

16767 CSU F P7 G9.5 1949–1972
Anderson, Eugene Newton, Jr., 1941–.
'Traditional aquaculture in Hong Kong.'
J. of tropical geography 3 (June 1970), 11–16.
SUBJ 24.1 ▪ 24.3

16768 CSU P P7 G1.2 1949–1972
Asakawa Kenji, 1909–.
People's communes and water conservancy in Communist China, mimeo. Tr. of 'Jimmin kōsha to suiri jigyō'; *Ajia keizai jumpō* 433 (1 June 1960), 4–10.
Washington, D.C.: U.S. Joint Publications Research Service, 15 Aug. 1960. 10 p. (JPRS 5224; MC 15,793/1960)
SUBJ 21.4 24.1 28 ▪ 34.1

16769 CSU P P2 G9.2 1949–1972
Bays, Daniel Henry, 1942–.
'Agrarian reform in Kwangtung, 1950–1953.' In *Early Communist China: Two studies*, by Ronald S- Suleski and D. H. Bays. [Analytic entry]
Ann Arbor: U. of Michigan, Center for Chinese Studies, 1969, 28–77. (Michigan papers in Chinese studies, 4)
SUBJ 22 24.1 32 32.1 ▪ 22.1 24.5 36.3

16770 CSU O P7 G1.2 1949–1972
Berger, Roland.
'The mechanisation of Chinese agriculture.'
EH 11, 3 (1972), 7–26.
SUBJ 24.1 34.1 ▪ 24.4

16771 CSU F P8 G9.4 1949–1972
Bessac, Francis Bagnall, 1922–.
An example of social change in Taiwan related to land reform.
Missoula: U. of Montana, Dept. of Anthropology, 1967. 29 p. (U. of Montana, Contributions to Anthropology, 1)
SUBJ 24.1 26 28 ▪ 22 24.4 24.5 26.1 26.3 36.3 47

16772 MCH F P8 G9.4 1949–1972
Bessac, Francis Bagnall, 1922–.
'Some social effects on land reform in a village on the Taichung plain [Taiwan].'
JCS 4 (1964), 15–28.
SUBJ 19 20 24.1 ▪ 41 47 61

16773 DNA PO P7 G9.5 1949–1972
Blackie, W- J-.
Report on agriculture in Hong Kong, with policy recommendations.
Hong Kong: Government Printer, 1955. 93 p.
SUBJ 24.1 ▪ 22 24.3 38

16774 CSU O P7 G9.2 1949–1972
Buchanan, Keith McPherson, 1919–.
'Pearl river, 1964.'
EH 3, 12 (Dec. 1964), 14–22.
SUBJ 24.1 34.1 ▪ 24.4 28

16775 CSU O P7 G9.2 1949–1972
Buchanan, Keith McPherson, 1919–.
'The people's communes after six years: Notes on four communes in Kwangtung province [Shao-chiao commune, Shun-te *hsien*; Hsin-chiao commune, Canton municipality; Chang-ch'a commune, Fo-shan municipality; and Hua-tung commune, Hua *hsien*].'
Pacific viewpoint 6, 1 (May 1965), 52–64.
SUBJ 24.1 ▪ 24.4 28 34.1

16776 MCH P P8 G9.4 1949–1972
Chang, H. T. (Chang Hsien-ch'iu).
Natural environment and crop distribution in Taiwan.
Taipei: Chinese-American Joint Commission on Rural Reconstruction, 1956. 42 p. (JCRR, Plant industry series, 13)
SUBJ 24.1

16777 CSH P P2 G9.4 1949–1972
Chang, H. T. (Chang Hsien-ch'iu).
Problems of tea production in Taiwan.
Taipei: Chinese-American Joint Commission on Rural Reconstruction, 1953. 28 p. (JCRR, Plant industry series, 2)
SUBJ 14.4 24.1 ▪ 14.3

16778 MCH P P8 G9.4 1949–1972
Chang, H. T. (Chang Hsien-ch'iu), et al.
Crop variety improvement and seed multiplication work in Taiwan.
Taipei: Chinese-American Joint Commission on Rural Reconstruction, 1956. 42 p. (JCRR, Plant industry series, 7)
SUBJ 24.1

16779 CSU U P7 G9.2 1949–1972
Chang Han-ch'ing.
'Hua hsien has truly become a "county of flowers".' Tr. of 'Hua hsien chen cheng pien ch'eng liao "hua hsien"' (Hua *hsien* [Kwangtung] becomes a real 'flower county'); *Hung ch'i* 1964, 4 (26 Feb.), 13–17. In *Translations from 'Hung-ch'i' (Red flag) No. 4, 1964*, mimeo., compiled by U.S. Joint Publications Research Service. [Sole entry]
Washington, D.C.: JPRS, 21 Apr. 1964, 1–9. (JPRS 24,292; MC 10,912/1964)
SUBJ 24.1 ▪ 34.1

16780 CSU P P8 G9.4 1949–1972
Chang, Jen-hu (Chang Ching-hu), 1928–.
'Sugar cane in Hawaii and Taiwan: Contrasts in ecology, technology, and economics.'
EG 46, 1 (Jan. 1970), 39–52.
SUBJ 24.1

16781 CSU P P7 G9.2 1949–1972
Chang Ken-sheng.
'Production experiences of some high-production communes and production teams in Kwangtung province.' Tr. of 'Kuang-tung i pu fen shui t'ao kao ch'an she, tui ti tseng ch'an ching yen'; *Jen min jih pao* 1 Apr. 1964, 5.
Translations on Communist China's agriculture, animal husbandry and materials 95 (4 May 1964), 9–18. (JPRS 24,447; MC 11,061/1964)
SUBJ 22.1 24.1 28 34.1

16782 CSH U P8 G5.1 1949–1972
Chang K'o-jang. [Tr. erroneously gives author's surname as Chou.]
The ever expanding agriculture of Hopeh province. Tr. of 'Pu tuan yao chin ti Ho-pei sheng nung yeh' (The continuing leap forward of agriculture in Hopei); *Hung ch'i* 1959, 18 (16 Sept.), 35–41.
Washington, D.C.: U.S. Joint Publications Research Service, 25 May 1962. 19 p. (JPRS 13,889; MC 14,149/1962)
SUBJ 24.1 ▪ 28 34.1

16783 CSH PO P7 G9.4 1949–1972
Chang, Yen-tien (Chang Yen-t'ien).
'Food production in Taiwan: A review of food planning and implementation in the last three four-year plans.'
IFC 32, 3 (Sept. 1969), 6–21.
SUBJ 14 24.1

16784 CSH O P7 G5.1 1949–1972
Ch'ang Yu-min (Ch'ang Yü-min).
'How CCP Tsunhua Hsien Committee leads agricultural production.' Tr. of 'Tsun-hua hsien wei shih tsen yang ling tao nung yeh sheng ch'an ti' (How the party committee in Tsun-hua *hsien* [Hopei] provided leadership in agricultural production); *Ching chi yen chiu* (Peking) 1966, 1 (Jan.), 15–23.
SCMM 516 (21 Mar. 1966), 11–26.
SUBJ 24.1 32.1 ▪ 27

16785 MAM F P8 G9.4 1949–1972
Chao, Ching-yuan (Chao Ch'ing-yüan), 1921–.
Dynamic and nonlinear programming for optimum farm plans in Taiwan.
Ann Arbor: University Microfilms (Publ. 63-5173), 1963. 146 p. (Doctoral dissertation in Economics, Iowa State U.)
SUBJ 24.1

16786 CSU F P2 G3.0 1949–1972
Chao Sung-ch'iao, 1919–, Huang Mien, and Kuo Chien-mou.
Preliminary research on status of agricultural and animal husbandry production in the Inner Mongolian Autonomous Region, mimeo. Tr. of *Nei Meng-ku tzu chih ch'ü nung mu yeh sheng ch'an p'ei chih wen t'i ch'u pu*

yen chiu edited by Ti li yen chiu so, Chung-kuo k'o hsüeh yüan (Institute of Geography, Chinese Academy of Sciences); Peking: K'o hsüeh ch'u pan she, 1958; 84 p.
Washington, D.C.: U.S. Joint Publications Research Service, 1963. 253 p. (JPRS 18,979; MC 10,680/1963) [Xerox copyflo available—New York: CCM Information Corp., Research and Microfilm Publications. (Scholarly Book Translation Series, 422)]
SUBJ 11.3 24.1 ▪ 21 21.4 24 24.2 24.4 34.1 66

16787 CSU FP P2 G8.0 1949–1972
Chao Sung-ch'iao, 1919–, et al.
Geographic survey data on agriculture and livestock industry in parts of Szechwan and Yunnan provinces, mimeo. Tr. of *Ch'uan Tien nung mu chiao ts'o ti ch'ü nung yeh mu yeh ti li tiao ch'a tzu liao* (Geographic data on agriculture and animal husbandry in the mixed agricultural-pastoral area of Szechwan and Yunnan); Peking: K'o hsüeh ch'u pan she, 1959; 72 p.
Washington, D.C.: U.S. Joint Publications Research Service, 27 July 1962. 158 p. (JPRS 14,627; MC 19,623/1962)
SUBJ 11.3 24.1 ▪ 21 21.3 23 24.2 26.3 34.1 66

16788 NNP PO P7 G9.4 1949–1972
Chen, Cheng (Ch'en Ch'eng), 1896–1965.
Land reform in Taiwan.
Taipei: China Publishing Co., 1961. 13, 332 p. [See Vol. 2 of this *Bibliography* for Chinese version.]
SUBJ 24.1 ▪ 12.2 18 22

16789 NIC P P8 G9.4 1949–1972
Chen, Cheng-siang (Ch'en Cheng-hsiang), 1920–.
'Land utilization and its changes in Taiwan.'
Korean affairs 2, 3/4 (Oct. 1963), 304–317.
SUBJ 24.1

16790 MAM P P8 G9.4 1949–1972
Chen, Hsing-yiu (Ch'en Hsin-yu).
Structure and productivity of capital in the agriculture of Taiwan and their policy implications to agricultural finance.
Ann Arbor: University Microfilms (Publ. 67-10,877), 1967. 198 p. (Doctoral dissertation in Economics, Ohio State U.)
SUBJ 24.1 ▪ 24.6 34.2

16791 MCH U P8 G5.2 1949–1972
Chen Hsueh-nung.
'Transforming a poor hill village [Ta-chai brigade, Ta-chai commune, Hsi-yang *hsien*, Shansi].'
PR 7, 25 (19 June 1964), 28–31.
SUBJ 24.1 ▪ 22 34.1

16792 CSU P P7 G9.3 1949–1972
Chen, Pi-chao, 1937–.
'Individual farming after the Great Leap, as revealed by the Lien Kiang [i.e., Lien-chiang *hsien*, Fukien] documents.'
AS 8, 9 (Sept. 1968), 774–791.
SUBJ 22 24.1 26.1 ▪ 22.2 26.3 32 34.1

16793 CSH U P8 G6.1 1949–1972
Ch'en P'ei-hsien (Ch'en P'i-hsien).
'Shanghai's campaign to raise one pig on each mow of land in the countryside.' Tr. of 'Shang-hai nung ts'un ti i mu ti i t'ou chu yün tung'; *Hung ch'i* 1960, 4 (16 Feb.), 11–16.
ECMM 204 (14 Mar. 1960), 9–18.
SUBJ 24.1 ▪ 34.1

16794 MCH F P8 G9.4 1949–1972
Cheng, Chung-fu, 1913–.
Crop improvement and seed distribution of upland food crops in Taiwan.
Taipei: Chinese-American Joint Commission on Rural Reconstruction, 1956. 34 p. (JCRR, Plant industry series, 11)
SUBJ 24.1 ▪ 22 22.1 26.3

16795 CSU P P8 G9.4 1949–1972
Cheung, Steven N. S., 1935–.
The theory of share tenancy, with special application to Asian agriculture and the first phase of Taiwan land reform.
Chicago: U. of Chicago Press, 1969. 15, 188 p. (Revision of *The theory of share tenancy, with special application to the first phase of Taiwan land reform*, doctoral dissertation in Economics, U. of California, Los Angeles, 1967)
SUBJ 12.2 24.1 ▪ 24

16796 MCH U P7 G6.2 1949–1972
Chi Ho-teh.
'Three rivers' irrigation system.'
PR 8, 25 (18 June 1965), 23–25.
SUBJ 24.1 ▪ 24.2

16797 MCH P P7 G9.4 1949–1972
Chinese-American Joint Commission on Rural Reconstruction.
A decade of rural progress, 1948–1958: Tenth anniversary review of the major accomplishments of the Joint Commission on Rural Reconstruction.
Taipei: Chinese-American Joint Commission on Rural Reconstruction, 1958. 68 p.
SUBJ 24 24.1 ▪ 24.3 24.6 26.3 28 34.1

16798 CSH FP P2 G9.0 1949–1972
Chinese-American Joint Commission on Rural Reconstruction.
Joint Commission on Rural Reconstruction General Reports, Nos. 2–16, 1951–1965. [Issue for 1 Oct. 1948 – 15 Feb. 1950 is entered as 12383.]
Taipei: Chinese-American Joint Commission on Rural Reconstruction. Issued annually, 1952–1966. Average ca. 175 p.
SUBJ 24 24.1 34.1 36.3 56 ▪ 17 22 28 36.1 54 55 66

16799 NNC U P8 G9.5 1949–1972
Chiu Tze Nang (Chao Tze-neng), 1932–.
'Land use problems in the extreme east of the New Territories.' In *Symposium on land use and mineral deposits in Hong Kong, southern China and South-east Asia*, edited by Sydney George Davis. [Selective entry]
Hong Kong: Hong Kong U. Press, 1964, 75–80.
SUBJ 24.1 ▪ 24.2

16800 CSU O P7 G4.3 1949–1972
Ch'u An-ping (Ch'u An-p'ing).
The Manass river reclamation district, mimeo. Tr. of *Ma-na-ssu ho k'en ch'ü* (The Ma-na-ssu river reclamation district [Sinkiang]); Peking: Chung-kuo ch'ing nien ch'u pan she, 1956; 147 p.
Washington, D.C.: U.S. Joint Publications Research Service, 8 Jan. 1963. 115 p. (JPRS 17,038; MC 2843/1963) [Xerox copyflo available—New York: CCM Information Corp., Research and Microfilm Publications. (Scholarly Book Translation Series, 544)]
SUBJ 21.3 24.1 28 ▪ 24.2 24.4 35 55

16801 MCH F P8 G2.1 1949–1972
Chung-kuo kung ch'an tang. Hei-lung-chiang sheng wei yüan hui. Tiao ch'a tsu. (Chinese Communist Party. Heilungkiang Provincial Committee. Investigation Team), ed.
'An investigation of economic conditions of five villages in Heilungkiang province.' Tr. of 'Hei-lung-chiang sheng wu ko ts'un ching chi ch'ing k'uang ti tiao ch'a'; *Jen min jih pao* 8 June 1953, 2.
SCMP 602 (3 July 1953), 22–28.
SUBJ 22 24 24.1 26 ▪ 26.3 28 32.1 34.1

16802 CSU U P8 G7.2 1949–1972
Chung-kuo kung ch'an tang. Hsiang-t'an ti fang wei yüan hui. (Chinese Communist Party. Hsiang-t'an Special District Committee).
'The value of revolutionary ardor.' Tr. of 'K'o kuei ti ko ming kan ching' (Invaluable revolutionary ardor); *Hung ch'i* 1963, 10/11 (20 May), 24–28. In *Translations from 'Hung-ch'i' (Red flag) No. 10-11, 1963*, mimeo., compiled by U.S. Joint Publications Research Service. [Sole entry]
Washington, D.C.: JPRS, 25 June 1963, 78–94. (JPRS 19,886; MC 14,238/1963)
SUBJ 24.1 ▪ 34.1

16803 CSU O P7 G4.1 1949–1972
Chung-kuo kung ch'an tang. Lung hsien wei yüan hui. Tiao ch'a tsu. (Chinese Communist Party. Lung Hsien Committee. Investigation Team).
'The experience of a people's commune in undertaking grain production on a large scale.' Tr. of 'I ko jen min kung she ta pan liang shih ti ching yen' (Experiences of [Ho-pei] commune [Lung *hsien*, Shensi] in large-scale grain production); *Hung ch'i* 1961, 7 (1 Apr.), 8–11. In *Translations from 'Hung-ch'i' (Red flag) (Peiping, No. 7, 1 April 1961)*, mimeo., compiled by U.S. Joint Publications Research Service. [Sole entry]
Washington, D.C.: JPRS, 16 Aug. 1961, 27–33. (JPRS 8759; MC 17,450/1961)
SUBJ 24.1 34.1 ▪ 26.3

16804 CBU F P8 G4.1 1949–1972
Chung-kuo nung yeh k'o hsüeh yüan (China Agricultural Sciences Institute). Nung yeh ching chi yen chiu so (Agricultural Economics Research Office) *and* Chung-kuo nung yeh k'o hsüeh yüan (China Agricultural Sciences Institute). Shan-hsi fen yüan (Shensi Sub-institute). Nung ching shih (Office of Agricultural Economics), *joint*

sponsors. Tiao ch'a tsu (Investigation Team), ed.
'Regarding investigations on the economic results of deep plowing, thick planting, fertilizer application, and replanting for wheat.' Tr. of 'Kuan yü hsiao mai shen keng, mi chih, shih fei, fu chung ti ching chi hsiao kuo ti tiao ch'a' (Survey of the economic results of deep plowing, close planting, fertilizer application, and transplanting of wheat); *Hung ch'i* 1959, 16 (16 Aug.), 31–37. In *Translations from 'Hung-ch'i' (Red flag) (Peiping, No. 16, 16 August 1959)*, mimeo., compiled by U.S. Joint Publications Research Service. [Selective entry]
Washington, D.C.: JPRS, 23 Oct. 1959, 31–48. (JPRS 989D; MC 17,558/1959)
SUBJ 24.1 ▪ 26.3 34.1

16805 CSU S P8 G9.5 1949–1972
Dernberger, Robert Franklin, 1929–.
Review of *Capitalism and the Chinese peasant: Social and economic change in a Hong Kong village*, by Jack Michael Potter.
EDCC 18, 1, Part 1 (Oct. 1969), 125–129.
SUBJ 24 24.1 ▪ 26.3 28

16806 DLC F P7 G1.3 1949–1972
Dzhemukhadze, Konstantin Melitonovich.
Kul'tura i proizvodstvo chaia v Kitaiskoi Narodnoi Respublike (Tea cultivation and production in the People's Republic of China).
Moscow: Izd-vo Akad. nauk SSSR, 1961. 150 p.
SUBJ 24.1 24.4 ▪ 17 34.1 66

16807 CSH P P7 G1.2 1949–1972
Feng Wen.
'Rural family sideline production and "self-reserved plot".'
CCA 1, 2 (June 1964), 20–43.
SUBJ 24.1 24.4 34.1 ▪ 24.3 32.1

16808 CBU O P7 G1.2 1949–1972
Fochler-Hauke, Gustav, 1906–.
'Die chinesischen Volkskommunen' (The Chinese communes [Chung-Yüeh yu-hao commune, Ch'ang-p'ing *hsien*, Peking municipality]).
Geographische Rundschau 18, 4 (Apr. 1966), 137–144.
SUBJ 21.3 24.1 34.1 ▪ 19 28 55

16809 CSU P P8 G4.3 1949–1972
Freeberne, John Derek Michael, 1935–.
'Glacial meltwater resources in China.'
GJ 131, 1 (Mar. 1965), 57–60.
SUBJ 24.1

16810 CSU PO P7 G9.4 1949–1972
Freeberne, John Derek Michael, 1935–.
'Lonely Taiwan sows for the future.'
GM 44, 4 (Jan. 1972), 268–274.
SUBJ 24.1 ▪ 34.1 36.3

16811 NIC F P8 G9.4 1949–1972
Gallin, Bernard, 1929–.
'Land reform in Taiwan: Its effect on rural social organization and leadership.'
Human organization 22, 2 (Summer 1963), 109–112.
SUBJ 22 24.1 ▪ 26.1

16812 MCH F P2 G9.4 1949–1972
Gallin, Bernard, 1929–.
'Rural development in Taiwan: The role of the government.'
Rural sociology 29, 3 (Sept. 1964), 313–323.
SUBJ 17 24.1 ▪ 12 22

16813 CSH PO P8 G9.5 1949–1972
Goodstadt, Leo F-.
'[1] Farming finance. [2] Vegetables or rice?'
FEER 43, 6 (6 Feb. 1964), 329–332; 43, 7 (13 Feb. 1964), 397–400.
SUBJ 24.1 26.3 ▪ 21.2

16814 NIC F P8 G9.5 1949–1972
Grant, Charles J-.
The soils and agriculture of Hong Kong.
Hong Kong: Government Printer, 1960? 154 p.
SUBJ 21.3 24.1

16815 CSU O P7 G9.5 1949–1972
Groves, Robert George, 1934–, and Kenneth Richard Walker, 1931–.
'Rice farming in Hong Kong.'
GM 39, 9 (Jan. 1967), 750–763.
SUBJ 24.1 ▪ 26.3

16816 CSU F P2 G9.5 1949–1972
Hong Kong. Dept. of Agriculture, Fisheries and Forestry.
Annual departmental report by the Director of Agriculture, Fisheries and Forestry, 1950/51–1970/71.
Hong Kong: Government Printer. Issued annually, 1951–1972. Average ca. 90 p.
SUBJ 24.1 ▪ 14.3 22 24.3 24.6 56

16817 MCH U P7 G9.4 1949–1972
Hsieh, S. C. (Hsieh Sen-chung), 1919–.
'Agricultural development and small farm system in Taiwan.' Tr. of 'T'ai-wan nung yeh fa chan yü hsiao nung ching ying' (Agricultural development and the management of small farms in Taiwan); *Kuo chi ching chi tzu liao* 8, 5 (May 1962), 12–20.
IFC 18, 5 (Nov. 1962), 7–21.
SUBJ 24.1

16818 CSH F P7 G9.4 1949–1972
Hsieh, S. C. (Hsieh Sen-chung), 1919–.
Application of linear programming to crop competition study in Taiwan (with special reference to rice and sugarcane competition in Central Taiwan).
Taipei: Chinese-American Joint Commission on Rural Reconstruction, 1957. 95 p. (JCRR, Economic digest series, 10)
SUBJ 24.1

16819 NIC F P8 G9.4 1949–1972
Hsieh, S. C. (Hsieh Sen-chung), 1919–.
'Management-decision of small farm in Taiwan.' Tr. of 'T'ai-wan hsiao nung ching ying chih yen chiu' (The management of small farms in Taiwan); *T'ai-wan yin hang chi k'an* 12, 3 (Sept. 1961), 94–118.
J. of agricultural economics (Taichung) 1963, 1 (Jan.), 9–45. [Reprinted—*IFC* 19, 2 (Feb. 1963), 29–36; 19, 3 (Mar. 1963), 36–48; 19, 4 (Apr. 1963), 31–36.] [Separately reprinted—New York: Agricultural Development Council, 1966. 19 p.]
SUBJ 24.1 ▪ 21

16820 MAM F P7 G9.4 1949–1972
Hsieh, S. C. (Hsieh Sen-chung), 1919–.
Rice and sugarcane competition on paddy land in Central Taiwan.
Ann Arbor: University Microfilms (Publ. 22,458), 1957. 113 p. (Doctoral dissertation in Agricultural Economics, U. of Minnesota)
SUBJ 24.1 ▪ 26.3

16821 CSU O P7 G9.4 1949–1972
Hsieh, S. C. (Hsieh Sen-chung), 1919–.
'Taiwan's model of agricultural progress: Potentials of small family farms and their implications for other developing Asian countries' [with comments by George Edward Taylor]. In *Agrarian policies and problems in Communist and non-Communist countries*, edited by William Arthur Douglas Jackson. [Selective entry]
Seattle: U. of Washington Press, 1971, 381–398.
SUBJ 24.1 ▪ 26.3

16822 MCH P P8 G9.4 1949–1972
Hsieh, S. C. (Hsieh Sen-chung), 1919–, and T. H. Lee.
'The effect of population pressure and seasonal labor surplus on the pattern and intensity of agriculture in Taiwan.'
IFC 23, 1 (Jan. 1965), 2–19.
SUBJ 24.1 ▪ 16.3

16823 CSU S P7 G9.4 1949–1972
Hsu, Robert C. (Hsü Ch'ung-ming), 1937–.
'The demand for fertilizer in a developing country: The case of Taiwan, 1950–1966.'
EDCC 20, 2 (Jan. 1972), 299–309. [For fuller treatment, see entry 13081.]
SUBJ 24.1 ▪ 14.3

16824 CSH U P2 G9.4 1949–1972
Hsu, Wan-chun (Hsü Wan-ch'un).
'The promotion of farm mechanization in Taiwan.'
IFC 31, 5 (May 1969), 29–40.
SUBJ 14.4 24.1 ▪ 27 34.1

16825 MAM FP P7 G9.4 1949–1972
Hsu, Wen-fu (Hsü Wen-fu), 1931–.
An economic evaluation of sugar pricing and its influence on sugarcane supply in Taiwan.
Ann Arbor: University Microfilms (Publ. 66-10,466), 1966. 258 p. (Doctoral dissertation in Economics, Pennsylvania State U.)
SUBJ 14.3 24.1

16826 MCH F P7 G9.4 1949–1972
Huang, C., and Howard W- Ream.
Grassland potential and current development on Taiwan.
Taipei: Chinese-American Joint Commission on Rural Reconstruction, 1961. 42 p.
SUBJ 24.1 ▪ 24.3 55

16827 NIC P P7 G9.4 1949–1972
Jensen, Bernhardt M-.
Rice in the economy of Taiwan.
Taipei: U.S. Mutual Security Mission to China *with* United Nations, Food and Agriculture Organization, 1953. 76 p.
SUBJ 24.1 ▪ 21 24.3

16828 CSU P P8 G9.4 1949–1972
Kao, Charles H. C. (Kao Hsi-chün).
'An analysis of agricultural output increase on Taiwan, 1953–1964.'
JAS 26, 4 (Aug. 1967), 611–626.
Subj 24.1 ▪ 34.1

16829 CSU P P7 G9.4 1949–1972
Kao, Charles H. C. (Kao Hsi-chün).
'The factor contribution of agriculture to economic development: A study of Taiwan.'
AS 5, 11 (Nov. 1965), 558–565. [For fuller treatment, see entry 16737.]
Subj 14 14.3 24.1 ▪ 14.5 21.4

16830 CSU U P8 G9.4 1949–1972
Kawano, Shigetō.
Review of *Taiwan's agricultural development: Its relevance for developing countries today*, by Raymond Peter Christensen.
DE 7, 1 (Mar. 1969), 105–108.
Subj 24.1 ▪ 14

16831 MCH O P7 G6.1 1949–1972
Kiang Wen-han (Chiang Wen-han), 1908–.
'Land reform in Shanghai suburbs.'
China monthly review (Shanghai) 122, 1 (Jan. 1953), 18–29.
Subj 24.1 ▪ 12.1 22.1

16832 CSU S P8 G9.4 1949–1972
Kindermann, Gottfried-Karl, 1926–.
'The Taiwan land reform: Its ideological origins and radical features.'
Asian and African studies (Jerusalem) 6 (1970), 149–173. [Special issue: *Society and development in Asia*, edited by Martin Rudner]
Subj 24.1 64 ▪ 12.2 34.1

16833 CSH P P8 G9.4 1949–1972
Klein, Sidney, 1923–.
'Taiwan.' In *The pattern of land tenure reform in East Asia after World War II*, by S. Klein. [Selective entry]
New York: Bookman Associates, 1958, 52–82. (Revision of doctoral dissertation in Economics, Columbia U., 1957)
Subj 24.1 ▪ 22.1 34.1 36.3

16834 CSH O P8 G9.4 1949–1972
Klimley, April.
'The forgotten providers.'
FEER 71, 6 (6 Feb. 1971), 20–22.
Subj 24.1 26.3

16835 CSH P P7 G1.2 1949–1972
[La Dany, Ladislao] ———, 1914–.
'Agriculture at a closer look.'
CNA 899 (3 Nov. 1972), 1–7.
Subj 24.1 34.1 ▪ 22.1 26.1 26.3

16836 MCH P P2 G4.3 1949–1972
[La Dany, Ladislao] ———, 1914–.
'More about Sinkiang.'
CNA 112 (9 Dec. 1955), 1–7.
Subj 24.1 35 ▪ 14.4 24.2 34.1

16837 CSH P P8 G1.2 1949–1972
[La Dany, Ladislao] ———, 1914–.
'Small waterworks and irrigation.'
CNA 837 (9 Apr. 1971), 1–7.
Subj 21.4 24.1 ▪ 24.2

16838 NNC P P7 G9.5 1949–1972
Lai, Chuen-yan (Li Ch'üan-en), 1937–.
'Rice cultivation, distribution and production in Hong Kong.' In *Symposium on land use and mineral deposits in Hong Kong, southern China and South-east Asia*, edited by Sydney George Davis. [Selective entry]
Hong Kong: Hong Kong U. Press, 1964, 81–87.
Subj 24.1 ▪ 24.3

16839 MCH P P2 G9.2 1949–1972
Lee Hwa (Li Hua).
'Hainan island today.'
IS 1, 1 (Oct. 1964), 35–45.
Subj 20 24.1 24.4 ▪ 12 15 17 21 24.2 66

16840 CSH P P8 G9.4 1949–1972
Lee, Teng-hui (Li Teng-hui), 1923–.
'A study on structural change of agricultural production in Taiwan.' In *Proceedings of Agricultural Economics Seminar held at the College of Agriculture, National Taiwan University, September 16–20, 1958*. [Selective entry]
Taipei: National Taiwan U., 1959, 79–89.
Subj 24.1 ▪ 18 21.4

16841 NNC PO P8 G9.3 1949–1972
Lin, Si-dang, and Lin Li.
Land reform on Kinmen [i.e., Chin-men *hsien*, Fukien].
Taipei: Chinese-American Joint Commission on Rural Reconstruction, 1958. 66 p.
Subj 22.2 24.1 ▪ 21 22.1

16842 CSH O P7 G7.3 1949–1972
Liu Kuang-hui and Mei Kuo-pao.
'The victory of Chiangchow people's commune in producing grain.' Tr. of 'Chiang-chou jen min kung she ta pan liang shih ti sheng li' (The victory of Chiang-chou commune [Kiukiang] in large-scale food production); *Hung ch'i* 1961, 2 (16 Jan.), 27–33. In *Translations from 'Hung-ch'i' (Red flag) (Peiping, No. 2, 16 January 1961)*, mimeo., compiled by U.S. Joint Publications Research Service. [Sole entry]
Washington, D.C.: JPRS, 15 Apr. 1961, 44–56. (JPRS 8094; MC 13,055/1961)
Subj 24.1 ▪ 26.3 34.1

16843 CSU S P8 G9.4 1949–1972
Liu, M. Y. (Liu Ming-yüan).
'Administration of land reform in Taiwan.'
CJA 7 (July 1966), 1–8 [s.p.]. [See Vol. 2 of this *Bibliography* for Chinese version.]
Subj 24.1

16844 MAM P P7 G9.4 1949–1972
Liu, Wei-ping, 1924–.
An economic analysis of Taiwanian agricultural development since 1950.
Ann Arbor: University Microfilms (Publ. 61-5854), 1961. 158 p. (Doctoral dissertation in Economics, U. of Minnesota)
Subj 24 24.1 ▪ 18 24.4

16845 CSH F P7 G9.4 1949–1972
Ma, Fengchow C. (Ma Feng-chou), T. Takasaka, and Ching-wen Yang.
A preliminary study of farm implements used in Taiwan province.
Taipei: Chinese-American Joint Commission on Rural Reconstruction, 1955. 331 p. (JCRR, Plant industry series, 4)
Subj 24.1 ▪ 24.4

16846 CSH O P7 G5.1 1949–1972
MacDougall, Colina.
'A Peking commune [Shuang-ch'iao commune, Peking municipality].'
FEER 51, 2 (13 Jan. 1966), 51–52.
Subj 20 24.1 28

16847 MCH O P7 G1.2 1949–1972
MacDougall, Colina.
'The pig and the peasant.'
FEER 52, 3 (21 Apr. 1966), 153–157.
Subj 24.1 24.3 26.3

16848 NNC P P7 G9.5 1949–1972
Mak Shiu Hung.
'The fishing ponds and oyster beds in the Wang Chau [i.e., Heng-chou] area, Hong Kong.' In *Symposium on land use and mineral deposits in Hong Kong, southern China and South-east Asia*, edited by Sydney George Davis. [Selective entry]
Hong Kong: Hong Kong U. Press, 1964, 147–151.
Subj 24.1 ▪ 24.3 62

16849 MAM FP P8 G9.4 1949–1972
Mao, Yu-kang (Mao Yü-kang), 1931–.
A case study of economic effects of land consolidation on farms in Chichow area [i.e., Ch'i-chou *hsiang*], *Chang-hua hsien, Taiwan, 1962–1963*.
Ann Arbor: University Microfilms (Publ. 68-6597), 1968. 316 p. (Doctoral dissertation in Economics, Cornell U.)
Subj 24.1

16850 CBU P P7 G5.2 1949–1972
Marchisio, Hélène.
'La contradiction, moteur de développement dans une commune populaire chinoise: enquête sur la brigade de Dazhai' (Contradiction, the motive force of development in a Chinese commune: An investigation of Ta-chai brigade [Ta-chai commune, Hsi-yang *hsien*, Shansi]).
Archives internationales de sociologie de la coopération et du développement 23 (jan.–juin 1968), 173–214.
Subj 22 22.1 24.1 34.1 60 ▪ 24.3 26.1 26.3 28

16851 MCH P P7 G9.4 1949–1972
Moody, Robert B-.
'Land reform in Taiwan.' In *Hands across frontiers*, edited by Howard Morris Teaf, Jr. and Peter G- Franck. [Sole entry]
Ithaca: Cornell U. Press, 1955, 127–181.
Subj 24.1 ▪ 12.2 22 22.1 24.5 26.1 26.3

16852 NIC O P8 G9.4 1949–1972
Moyer, Raymond Tyson, 1899–.
The JCRR program on Formosa: A summary and evaluation.
Taipei: ——, 1951. 17 p.
Subj 24.1 37 ▪ 26.3 28 34.1 56

16853 NNC O P7 G5.1 1949–1972
Murusidze, D- N-.
'V gosudarstvennom khoziaistve "Nandchzhou"' (On the Nang-chou state farm [Hopei]). In *V strane druzei: ocherki, stat'i, zametki sovetskikh liudei*

pobyvavshikh v Narodnom Kitae (In our friends' country: Notes, articles, and observations of Soviet visitors in the People's Republic of China), edited by K- S- Ovechkin et al. [Selective entry]
Blagoveshchensk: Amurskoe kn. izd-vo, 1959, 45–48.
SUBJ 24.1

16854 MCH S P7 G9.4 1949–1972
Myers, Ramon Hawley, 1929–, and H. C. Hsieh.
'Land reform and agricultural development in Taiwan: A note and a reply.'
Malayan economic review 8, 1 (Apr. 1963), 111–116.
SUBJ 24.1 ▪ 18 22.1 34.1

16855 MCH O P8 G1.5 1949–1972
Pritt, Denis Nowell, 1887–.
'Land reform in the new China.'
New world review 25, 1 (Jan. 1957), 9–27.
SUBJ 22.2 24.1 ▪ 26.3 34.1 47

16856 NNC PO P7 G9.4 1949–1972
Ravenholt, Albert, 1919–.
'Formosa's rural revolution: A unique Chinese and American achievement.'
AUFS-EAS 5, 7 (23 Mar. 1956), 1–25.
SUBJ 24.1 ▪ 19 21 56

16857 CSH F P7 G5.3 1949–1972
Shan-tung sheng ching chi yen chiu so. Nung yeh ching chi tsu. (Shantung Provincial Economic Research Institute. Agro-economic Unit).
'Depending on accumulation of labor to carry out capital construction in farmland irrigation and other fields: A survey of Chang-chia Jung-jen and two other brigades in Ishui hsien.' Tr. of 'I k'ao lao tung chi lei chin hsing nung t'ien shui li teng chi pen chien she: I-shui hsien Chang-chia-jung-jen teng san ko ta tui ti tiao ch'a yen chiu' (Rely on amassing labor to carry out farmland irrigation and other basic construction projects: Survey of Chang-chia-jung-jen and two other brigades in I-shui *hsien* [Shantung]); *Ching chi yen chiu* (Peking) 1965, 9 (Sept.), 1–13.
SCMM 500 (29 Nov. 1965), 18–36.
SUBJ 21.4 24.1 ▪ 24.6 34.1

16858 CSU PO P2 G9.4 1949–1972
Shen, T. H. (Shen Tsung-han), 1895–.
The Sino-American Joint Commission on Rural Reconstruction: Twenty years of cooperation for agricultural development.
Ithaca: Cornell U. Press, 1970. 14, 278 p.
SUBJ 24 24.1 36.3 ▪ 12 17 21.4 24.3 24.6 34.1 36.1 37 51 56

16859 NNC P P8 G4.3 1949–1972
Shevel', I- B-.
'Osushchestvlenie agrarnoi reformy v provintsii KNR: Sin'tsziane' (The implementation of land reform in the provinces of the People's Republic of China: Sinkiang).
SV 1955, 3, 71–81.
SUBJ 24 24.1 45 ▪ 24.5 26.1 26.3 66

16860 CBU O P7 G1.2 1949–1972
Shih-chia-chuang shih fan hsüeh yüan. Ti li hsi. Ching chi ti li chiao yen shih. (Shih-chia-chuang Teachers College. Dept. of Geography. Institute of Economic Geography).
'Experiences regarding planning for sub-urban agriculture.' Tr. of 'Yu kuan chiao ch'ü nung yeh kuei hua ti chi tien t'i hui' (Some lessons regarding agricultural planning in periurban areas); in *Jen min kung she ching chi kuei hua yü ching chi ti li wen chi*; Peking: K'o hsüeh ch'u pan she, 1959, 132–137. In *Economic plans and economic geography of people's communes*, mimeo., jointly edited by Chung-kuo ti li hsüeh hui (Geographical Society of China) *with* Ti li yen chiu so (Institute of Geography), Chung-kuo k'o hsüeh yüan (Chinese Academy of Sciences). [Selective entry]
Washington, D.C.: U.S. Joint Publications Research Service, 25 Feb. 1963, 320–333. (JPRS 17,789; MC 6864/1963) [Xerox copyflo available—New York: CCM Information Corp., Research and Microfilm Publications. (Scholarly Book Translation Series, 421)]
SUBJ 24 24.1 ▪ 26.3

16861 MCH U P7 G1.2 1949–1972
Siui Shu-tsziuan' (Hsü Shu-chuan).
Zemel'naia renta v sel'skokhoziaistvennom kooperative nizshego tipa v Kitaiskoi Narodnoi Respublike' (Land rent in lower-level agricultural producers' cooperatives in the People's Republic of China).
Nauchnye doklady vysshei shkoly; ekonomicheskie nauki 1959, 4, 85–91.
SUBJ 24.1 34.1 ▪ 45

16862 NNC U P7 G9.5 1949–1972
So, C. L.
'The fishing industry of Cheung Chau [i.e., Chang-chou island, Hong Kong].' In *Symposium on land use and mineral deposits in Hong Kong, southern China and South-east Asia*, edited by Sydney George Davis. [Selective entry]
Hong Kong: Hong Kong U. Press, 1964, 142–146.
SUBJ 24.1 24.4 ▪ 21.3 34.2

16863 NNC P P7 G1.2 1949–1972
Sung Ching-hsien and Chia Ch'un-fu.
'The question of production of people's communes: After a study of the resolution of the 6th plenum of 8th CCP Central Committee.' Tr. of 'Jen min kung she ti sheng ch'an wen t'i: Hsüeh hsi pa chieh liu chung ch'üan hui chüeh i ti hsin te chih i' (The question of production in the communes: Implementing the resolution of the eighth session of the Sixth Plenum of the Central Committee); *Jen wen tsa chih* 1959, 1 (Feb.), 10–18.
ECMM 174 (29 June 1959), 14–29.
SUBJ 21.4 24 24.1 34.1 ▪ 24.3 24.4 45

16864 CSU S P2 G9.4 1949–1972
Tai, Hung-chao (Tai Hung-ch'ao), 1929–.
'Land reform and national development: Taiwan.'
Papers of the Michigan Academy of Science, Arts, and Letters 51 (1966), 307–318.
SUBJ 24.1 ▪ 14.4 16.1 16.3 18

16865 NIC F P7 G9.4 1949–1972
Taiwan. Min cheng t'ing. Ti cheng chü. (Dept. of Civil Affairs. Land Bureau), comp.
Statistics on landownership classification in Taiwan, China, 1952.
Taipei: Chinese-American Joint Commission on Rural Reconstruction, 1953. 17, 184 p. [In Chinese as well as English]
SUBJ 24.1 ▪ 26

16866 TPU F P8 G9.4 1949–1972
Taiwan. Nung lin t'ing. (Dept. of Agriculture and Forestry), ed.
Statistical report on costs survey of main crops production in Taiwan [Vols. 1, 2, 4].
Nan-t'ou, Taiwan: Nung lin t'ing, 1954, 1958. 403; 233; 159 p. [In Chinese as well as English; vol. 3 of this study was never published.]
SUBJ 24.1 ▪ 26.3

16867 TPU F P7 G9.4 1949–1972
Taiwan. Nung lin t'ing. (Dept. of Agriculture and Forestry), ed.
Report on agricultural basic survey in Taiwan, 1960.
Nan-t'ou, Taiwan: Nung lin t'ing, 1961. 855 p. [In Chinese as well as English]
SUBJ 24.1 ▪ 24.3 26.3

16868 TPU F P8 G9.4 1949–1972
Taiwan. Nung lin t'ing. (Dept. of Agriculture and Forestry), ed.
Report on production cost survey of major crops in Taiwan, 1966 edition.
Nan-t'ou, Taiwan: Nung lin t'ing, 1966. 227 p. [In Chinese as well as English]
SUBJ 24.1 ▪ 26.3

16869 NIC F P7 G9.4 1949–1972
Taiwan. Nung yeh p'u ch'a wei yüan hui. (Agricultural Census Committee).
General report on the 1961 census of agriculture, Taiwan, Republic of China: Individual farm household.
[Nan-t'ou?], Taiwan: Nung yeh p'u ch'a wei yüan hui, 1963. 18, 723 p. [In Chinese as well as English]
SUBJ 21 24.1 26.3 ▪ 24.3 24.4 28 41 58

16870 CSH F P7 G9.4 1949–1972
Taiwan. Nung yeh p'u ch'a wei yüan hui. (Agricultural Census Committee), ed.
Report on the 1961 census of agriculture, Taiwan, Republic of China: Public and private commercial farm.
Nan-t'ou, Taiwan: Nung yeh p'u ch'a wei yüan hui, 1963. 13, 307 p. [In Chinese as well as English]
SUBJ 21.4 24.1

16871 CSH F P7 G9.4 1949–1972
Taiwan. Nung yeh p'u ch'a wei yüan hui. (Agricultural Census Committee), ed.
Report on the 1961 census of agriculture, Taiwan, Republic of China: 10% sample census.
Nan-t'ou, Taiwan: Nung yeh p'u ch'a wei yüan hui, 1963. 27, 509 p. [In Chinese as well as English]
SUBJ 21.4 24.1 ▪ 21 24.2 26.3 28

16872 NNC FP P7 G9.4 1949–1972
Tang, Hui-sun (T'ang Hui-sun), 1899–.
Land reform in Free China.
Taipei: Chinese-American Joint Commission on Rural Reconstruction,

1954. 336 p. [See Vol. 2 of this *Bibliography* for Chinese version.]
Subj 12.2 24.1 26.3 ▪ 21 22 24.6 26.1 28 45

16873 MCH FP P7 G9.4 1949–1972
Tang, Hui-sun (T'ang Hui-sun), 1899–, and S. C. Hsieh (Hsieh Sen-chung), 1919–.
'Land reform and agricultural development in Taiwan.'
Malayan economic review 6, 1 (Apr. 1961), 49–54. [Reprinted in *Land tenure, industrialization and social stability: Experience and prospects in Asia*, edited by Walter Froehlich. (Selective entry.) Milwaukee: Marquette U. Press, 1961, 114–142. (Marquette Asian studies, 2)]
Subj 24.1 ▪ 24 24.6 26.3 28 34.1 34.2

16874 MCH O P7 G9.2 1949–1972
T'ao Chu, 1906–.
'Survey report on the Humen commune.' Tr. of 'Hu-men kung she tiao ch'a pao kao' (A report on Hu-men commune [Tung-kuan *hsien*, Kwangtung]); *Jen min jih pao* 25 Feb. 1959, 7.
SCMP 1971 (12 Mar. 1959), 26–40.
Subj 21.4 24.1 28 34.1 ▪ 17 22 24 55 64

16875 CSH O P7 G5.2 1949–1972
T'ao Lu-chia.
'The agricultural technical reform of T'ai-ku hsien.' Tr. of 'Lun T'ai-ku hsien ti nung yeh chi shu kai ko' (The technological reform of agriculture in T'ai-ku *hsien* [Shansi]); *Hung ch'i* 1963, 5 (16 Mar.), 19–27. In *Translations from 'Hung-ch'i' (Red flag) No. 5, 1963*, mimeo., compiled by U.S. Joint Publications Research Service. [Sole entry]
Washington, D.C.: JPRS, 23 Apr. 1963, 26–39. (JPRS 18,848; MC 10,549/1963)
Subj 24.1 ▪ 34.1

16876 CSU P P8 G9.5 1949–1972
Taylor, W- A-.
'A note on land measurement and tenant rentals in Hong Kong.'
JRAS-HKB 6 (1966), 165–171.
Subj 24.1

16877 CBU P P7 G1.2 1949–1972
Teng Ching-chung.
'The problems of comprehensive development of commune production.' Tr. of 'Jen min kung she sheng ch'an tsung ho fa chan wen t'i'; in *Jen min kung she ching chi kuei hua yü ching chi ti li wen chi* (Collected essays on economic planning and economic geography of the communes); Peking: K'o hsüeh ch'u pan she, 1959, 5–20. In *Economic plans and economic geography of people's communes*, mimeo., jointly edited by Chung-kuo ti li hsüeh hui (Geographical Society of China) *with* Ti li yen chiu so (Institute of Geography), Chung-kuo k'o hsüeh yüan (Chinese Academy of Sciences). [Selective entry]
Washington, D.C.: U.S. Joint Publications Research Service, 25 Feb. 1963, 10–49. (JPRS 17,789; MC 6864/1963) [Xerox copyflo available—New York: CCM Information Corp., Research and Microfilm Publications. (Scholarly Book Translation Series, 421)]
Subj 24 24.1 ▪ 22 24.3 24.4 26.3

16878 CSU O P3 G9.5 1949–1972
Thompson, J- Charles.
'Traveling the China seas.'
NG 97, 3 (Mar. 1950), 381–395.
Subj 24.1 24.2

16879 MCH F P8 G2.1 1949–1972
Ting Lü-shu. [Tr. erroneously gives author's name as Ting Li-ch'u.]
'Exploration into the rational management of state farms: Investigation and study of the problem of the management of state farms in Heilungkiang province.' Tr. of 'Kuan yü kuo ying nung ch'ang ho li ching ying wen t'i ti t'an t'ao: Tui Hei-lung-chiang sheng kuo ying nung ch'ang ching ying kuan li wen t'i ti tiao ch'a yen chiu' (An examination of the rational management of state farms: A survey of administrative problems of state farms in Heilungkiang); *Ching chi yen chiu* (Peking) 1963, 12 (Dec.), 15–26.
SCMM 403 (10 Feb. 1964), 12–28.
Subj 24.1 34.1 ▪ 22 22.1 24.4 32.1

16880 CSU O P7 G9.5 1949–1972
Trott, Lamarr B-.
'Aspects of Hong Kong marine fauna.'
JRAS-HKB 10 (1970), 57–62.
Subj 21.3 24.1

16881 CBU O P7 G5.1 1949–1972
Tsang Wei-t'ing.
'Planning for animal husbandry at Hsiao-t'ang-shan commune.' Tr. of 'Pei-ching shih Hsiao-t'ang-shan jen min kung she hsü mu yen sheng ch'an kuei hua kung tso ti ch'u pu t'i hui ho ching yen' (Some preliminary lessons and experiences gained in planning livestock production in Hsiao-t'ang-shan commune, Peking municipality); in *Jen min kung she ching chi kuei hua yü ching chi ti li wen chi* (Collected essays on economic planning and economic geography of the communes); Peking: K'o hsüeh ch'u pan she, 1959, 138–145. In *Economic plans and economic geography of people's communes*, mimeo., jointly edited by Chung-kuo ti li hsüeh hui (Geographical Society of China) *with* Ti li yen chiu so (Institute of Geography), Chung-kuo k'o hsüeh yüan (Chinese Academy of Sciences). [Selective entry]
Washington, D.C.: U.S. Joint Publications Research Service, 25 Feb. 1963, 334–350. (JPRS 17,789; MC 6864/1963) [Xerox copyflo available—New York: CCM Information Corp., Research and Microfilm Publications. (Scholarly Book Translation Series, 421)]
Subj 24 24.1 ▪ 26.3

16882 CSH O P7 G7.1 1949–1972
Tsou Wei-tsai and Tan Ai-ching.
'Tienmen county's [T'ien-men *hsien*, Hupeh] double triumph.'
China reconstructs 15, 7 (July 1966), 52–54.
Subj 24.1 26.3

16883 CSH F P7 G9.4 1949–1972
Tsui, Young-chi (Ts'ui Yung-chi), 1908–.
'Current agricultural economics research in Taiwan.' In *Proceedings of Agricultural Economics Seminar held at the College of Agriculture, National Taiwan University, September 16–20, 1958*. [Selective entry]
Taipei: National Taiwan U., 1959, 48–52.
Subj 24.1 ▪ 45 55

16884 CSU S P2 G9.4 1949–1972
Tsui, Young-chi (Ts'ui Yung-chi), 1908–.
'Land-use improvement: A key to the economic development of Taiwan.'
J. of farm economics 44, 2 (May 1962), 363–372.
Subj 14 24.1

16885 MCH P P8 G9.4 1949–1972
Tsui, Young-chi (Ts'ui Yung-chi), 1908–.
'A preliminary assessment of the impact of agrarian reform on Taiwan's agricultural economy.'
IFC 23, 2 (Feb. 1965), 18–37.
Subj 24.1 ▪ 16.3 18

16886 NNC F P7 G9.4 1949–1972
Tsui, Young-chi (Ts'ui Yung-chi), 1908–.
A summary report on farm income of Taiwan in 1957 in comparison with 1952.
Taipei: Chinese-American Joint Commission on Rural Reconstruction, 1959. 67 p.
Subj 24.1 26.3 ▪ 24 28 41

16887 MCH F P8 G9.4 1949–1972
Tsui, Young-chi (Ts'ui Yung-chi), 1908–, and S. C. Hsieh (Hsieh Sen-chung), 1919–, comps.
Farm income of Taiwan in 1952.
Taipei: Chinese-American Joint Commission on Rural Reconstruction, 1954. 181 p. (JCRR, Economic digest series, 4)
Subj 22 24.1 24.5 28 ▪ 22.1 22.2 24.6

16888 CSU O P8 G9.2 1949–1972
Unger, Jonathan.
'[Kuntong village, Kwangtung.] [1] How socialism reshapes a Chinese village. [2] "Revolution" bypassed some Chinese villages.'
Christian Science monitor 25 May 1972, 3; 24 May 1972, 6.
Subj 24.1 28 ▪ 26.1 26.3 34.1

16889 CBU U P7 G9.4 1949–1972
Vedovato, Giuseppe.
'La politica agricola della Repubblica di Cina' (Agrarian policies of the Republic of China).
Rivista di studi politici internazionali 33, 2 (aprile–giugno 1966), 220–240.
Subj 24.1 36.3

16890 MCH FP P7 G1.3 1949–1972
Vinogradov, E- A-.
'O prirode i formakh zemel'noi renty v proizvodstvennykh kooperativakh nizshego tipa Kitaiskoi Narodnoi Respubliki' (The nature and forms of land rent in lower-level agricultural producers' cooperatives in the People's Republic of China).
Uchenye zapiski kafedr obshchestvennykh nauk vuzov goroda Leningrada; politicheskaia ekonomika 1960, 2, 107–131.
Subj 24.1 26.3 34.1 45 ▪ 64

16891 CSH F P8 G9.4 1949–1972
Wang, You-tsao (Wang Yu-chou), 1925–.
'Resource returns and productivity coefficients for selected crop systems in Tainan area.' In *Proceedings of*

Agricultural Economics Seminar held at the College of Agriculture, National Taiwan University, September 16–20, 1958. [Selective entry]
Taipei: National Taiwan U., 1959, 90–98.
SUBJ 24.1

16892 MAM F P8 G9.4 1949–1972
Wang, You-tsao (Wang Yu-chao), 1925–.
Statistical analysis of resource productivity in selected farming regions of Taiwan.
Ann Arbor: University Microfilms (Publ. 65-4654), 1965. 156 p. (Doctoral dissertation in Economics, Iowa State U., 1964)
SUBJ 24.1

16893 CSU F P7 G9.5 1949–1972
Ward, Barbara Elsie, 1919–.
'Chinese fishermen in Hong Kong: Their post-peasant economy.' In *Social organization: Essays presented to Raymond Firth*, edited by Maurice Freedman. [Selective entry]
Chicago: Aldine, 1967, 271–300.
SUBJ 24 24.1 26.3 28 34.2 ▪ 17 24.3 24.6 26 29 41

16894 CSU O P2 G1.3 1949–1972
Watson, Andrew John, 1942–.
'Report from China: The guiders and the guided.'
CQ 49 (Jan.–Mar. 1972), 136–150.
SUBJ 24.1 24.4 34.1 34.2 ▪ 21 21.3 22 26.3 26.4 66

16895 CSH O P7 G6.1 1949–1972
Wei Tung-ping.
'A cotton base brings in rich fruits of the revolution [in Nan-t'ung special district, Kiangsu].'
China reconstructs 18, 2 (Feb. 1969), 43–46.
SUBJ 24.1

16896 CSU P P8 G4.3 1949–1972
Wiens, Herold Jacob, 1912–1971.
'Regional and seasonal water supply in the Tarim basin [Sinkiang] and its relation to cultivated land potentials.'
AAAG 57, 2 (June 1967), 350–366.
SUBJ 11.3 24.1 ▪ 18

16897 MCY O P7 G1.2 1949–1972
[Wilson, Richard Garratt] Dick Wilson, 1928–.
'In the Chinese communes.'
FEER 44, 6 (7 May 1964), 291–293.
SUBJ 20 24.1

16898 CBU S P2 G9.4 1949–1972
Wright, Karl T-, 1901–.
Taiwan's postwar agricultural development.
East Lansing: Michigan State U., Dept. of Agricultural Economics, 1965. 47 p. (Agricultural economics reports, 19)
SUBJ 24.1 ▪ 12 14 14.4 21 21.4 58

16899 MAM P P8 G9.4 1949–1972
Wu, Craig C. (Wu Chih-yen), 1932–.
The contribution of education to farm production in a transitional farm economy.
Ann Arbor: University Microfilms (Publ. 71-29,338), 1971. 156 p. (Doctoral dissertation in Economics, Vanderbilt U.)
SUBJ 24.1 26.3 27

16900 CSH O P8 G5.2 1949–1972
Wu Hsiang, Chang Ch'ang-chen, and Yao Wen-chin.
'Visiting the Hsiao-p'ing-i commune in harvest time.' Tr. of 'Shou huo shih chieh fang Hsiao-p'ing-i kung she' (A visit to Hsiao-p'ing-i commune [Shuo *hsien*, Shansi] during the harvest season); *Hung ch'i* 1963, 19 (1 Oct.), 27–33. In *Translations from 'Hung-ch'i' (Red flag) No. 19, 1963*, mimeo., compiled by U.S. Joint Publications Research Service. [Sole entry]
Washington, D.C.: JPRS, 22 Oct. 1963, 35–44. (JPRS 21,561; MC 20,853/1963)
SUBJ 24.1 ▪ 34.1

16901 MCH F P8 G9.4 1949–1972
Yang, Martin M. C. (Yang Mou-ch'un), 1904–.
'Land reform and community development in Taiwan.'
JCS 3 (1963), 65–75. [Reprinted—*China today* 8, 8 (Aug. 1965), 19–27.]
SUBJ 12.2 24.1 ▪ 28

16902 CSU FP P7 G9.4 1949–1972
Yang, Martin M. C. (Yang Mou-ch'un), 1904–.
Socio-economic results of land reform in Taiwan.
Honolulu: East-West Center Press, 1970. 12, 555 p.
SUBJ 24.1 26 26.1 26.3 36.3 60 ▪ 12.2 17 22 22.1 28 34.2 41 48 55

24.2 LOCAL TRANSPORT AND COMMUNICATIONS
地方交通 地方交通

1644-1911

16903 CSU P P3 G5.1 1842–1895
'The *Peking gazette*.'
China review 3, 1 (July–Aug. 1874), 13–18.
SUBJ 12 24.2

16904 NNC P P5 G5.3 1895–1911
'Die Schantung Eisenbahn' (The Shantung railroad). [Recurring feature article: journal issued bimonthly, article appears irregularly.]
AE 24, 5 – 36, 4 (Sept. 1901 – Aug. 1913), average ca. 3 p.
SUBJ 24.2

16905 NNC P P3 G6.1 1895–1911
'Street railways in China.'
JAAA 8, 10 (Nov. 1908), 300–301.
SUBJ 24.2 ▪ 66

16906 FPN O P2 G5.1 1895–1911
Ballande, Charles Adolphe, 1878–1915.
'Six mois sur les rivières du Pe-Tcheli' (Six months on the rivers of northern Chihli).
B. de la Société de géographie de Rochefort 24, 1 (jan.–mars 1902), 302–323.
SUBJ 21.1 24 24.2 ▪ 28

16907 MCH PO P4 G1.2 1895–1911
Farjenel, Fernand, ?–1918.
'La presse populaire chinoise' (The popular press in China).
AF 7, 80 (nov. 1907), 424–429.
SUBJ 24.2 29 37 46 47 ▪ 16 18

16908 MCH O P2 G6.1 1895–1911
Gadoffre, François.
'Le pays de canaux: essai sur la province du Kiang-sou' (Land of canals: An essay on Kiangsu).
R. de géographie 50, 9 (mars 1902), 218–237.
SUBJ 12 24.2 ▪ 15 21.1 24.4 24.6 39 44

16909 GMS O P2 G5.3 1895–1911
Gaedertz, A-.
'Schantung' (Shantung).
Verhandlungen der Abteilung Berlin-Charlottenburg der Deutschen Kolonialgesellschaft 6, 6 (1901/02), 136–173.
SUBJ 24.2 ▪ 21 21.1 61

16910 CBU PO P4 G1.5 1842–1895
Gaggino, Giovanni.
La vallata del Yang-tse-kiang (The Yangtze valley).
Rome, Bocca: Del Mayno, 1901. 293 p.
SUBJ 24 24.2 66 ▪ 22.2 26.2 28 33 40

16911 FPN O P2 G8.0 1842–1895
Gérard de Rialle, Julien, 1841–1904.
'Voies de communication entre le sud de la Chine et la mer' (Communication routes between South China and the sea).
Réforme économique 4 (1er sept. 1876), 465–479; 4 (15 sept. 1876), 577–591.
SUBJ 24 24.1 24.2 24.4 ▪ 22.2 66

16912 CSU O P2 G4.0 1842–1911
Hedin, Sven Anders, 1865–1952.
En färd genom Asien.
Stockholm: Bonnier, 1898. 2 vols. 565; 537 p.

Through Asia.
London: Methuen, 1898. 2 vols. 18, 649; 12, 606 p. [Reprinted—New York: Harper, 1899. 2 vols. 18, 649; 12, 606 p.]
SUBJ 22 24 24.2 26.1 ▪ 12 21.3 22.2 24.1 24.3 24.4 25 28 33

16913 NNC O P2 G8.0 1842–1895
Hosie, Alexander, 1853–1925.
Three years in western China: A narrative of three journeys in Ssu-ch'uan, Kuei-chow, and Yün-nan, 2nd ed.
London: George Philip, 1897. 27, 302 p. [Reprinted—Taipei: Ch'eng-wen, 1972. 27, 302 p.]
SUBJ 14.3 24.2 24.4 ▪ 24.3 24.6 26.2 28 66

16914 CSU O P2 G1.5 1895–1911
Jack, Robert Logan, 1845–1921.
The back blocks of China.
London: Arnold, 1904. 22, 269 p.
SUBJ 24.2 ▪ 21.3 24.4 66

16915 CSU F P2 G2.0 1895–1911
Japan. Tetsudōin. (Imperial Japanese Government Railways).
'Part II, Manchuria.' In *An official guide to Eastern Asia: Transcontinental connections between Europe and Asia, Vol. I, Manchuria and Chōsen*, compiled by the agency cited. [Sole entry]
Tokyo: Tetsudōin, 1913, 1–208 [s.p.].
SUBJ 20 21.3 24 24.2 ▪ 17 21 21.1 24.1 24.4 28 31 56

16916 NIC O P2 G8.2 1842–1895
Lallemant-Dumoutier, Georges, 1866–1897.
'Routes commerciales de la province de Yun-nan' (Trade routes in Yunnan).
TP 4, 1 (mars 1893), 83–85.
SUBJ 24.2

16917 MCH O P2 G1.5 1842–1895
Little, Archibald John, 1838–1908.
Through the Yang-tse gorges: or, Trade and travel in western China, 3rd ed., rev.
London: Sampson Low, Marston, 1898. 24, 313 p. [Reprinted—Taipei: Ch'eng-wen, 1972. 24, 313 p.]
SUBJ 24.2 24.3 ▪ 24.4 55 62 65

16918 NNC U P4 G9.5 1644–1911
Lo Hsiang-lin, 1905–.
'The role of Hong Kong in China's New Culture Movement.'
CC 1, 2 (Oct. 1957), 86–95.
SUBJ 24.2 36.1 66 ▪ 17 60

16919 FPN O P2 G9.2 1895–1911
Madrolle, Claudius, 1870–?
'L'île d'Hainan' (Hainan).
B. de la Société de géographie commerciale de Paris 20 (jan.–avr. 1898), 361–370.
SUBJ 21.3 24.2 ▪ 29 55 66

16920 CBU O P2 G1.3 1842–1895
Oxenham, E- C-.
'Journey of Mr. Oxenham from Peking to Han-kow, through central Chih-Li, Honan, and the Han river.' In *Journeys in North China, Manchuria, and eastern Mongolia, with some account of Corea*, by Alexander Williamson. [Analytic entry]
London: Smith, Elder, 1870, vol. 2, 393–428. [For Williamson's work, see entry 10064.]
SUBJ 24.2 ▪ 15 24.1 24.3 25 28 66

16921 CSU P P3 G6.1 1895–1911
Parker, Alvin P-, 1850–1924.
'The native press in Shanghai: Our relation to it and how we can utilize it.'
CR 32, 12 (Dec. 1901), 577–589.
SUBJ 24.2 ▪ 19

16922 NIC O P2 G6.3 1842–1895
Parker, Edward Harper, 1849–1926.
'A journey in Chekiang.'
JRAS-CB new (2nd) series 19, 1 (1884), 27–53.
SUBJ 14.3 24.2 24.5 ▪ 24.1

16923 NIC O P2 G9.3 1842–1895
Parker, Edward Harper, 1849–1926.
'A journey in Fukien, with map.'
JRAS-CB new (2nd) series 19, 1 (1884), 54–74.
SUBJ 14.3 24.2 24.5 ▪ 24.1 29

16924 NNC O P2 G9.3 –1895
Phillips, George, 1804–1892.
'Some Fukien bridges.'
TP 5, 1 (mars 1894), 1–11.
SUBJ 24.2 ▪ 62 65

16925 CSU PO P3 G9.5 1895–1911
Rabaud, Louis-M.
'Rapport sur Hong-kong' (Report on Hong Kong). In *La Mission lyonnaise d'exploration commerciale en Chine, 1895–1897, deuxième partie, rapports commerciaux et notes diverses* (The Lyons Trade Mission to China, 1895–1897, Part 2, Commercial reports and miscellaneous notes), compiled by Chambre de commerce de Lyon. [Selective entry]
Lyons: Rey, 1898, 157–189 [s.p.].
SUBJ 14.3 21.3 24.2

16926 CBU O P2 G5.0 1842–1895
Richthofen, Ferdinand Paul Wilhelm von, 1833–1905.
'Das nordöstliche China (Provinzen Shantung, Tshili, Shansi und Honan)' (Northeast China: Shantung, Chihli, Shansi, and Honan). In *China: Ergebnisse eigener Reisen und darauf gegründeter Studien* (China: Results of my travels and studies based on them), by F. P. W. von Richthofen. [Selective entry]
Berlin: Reimer, 1882, vol. 2, 171–538.
SUBJ 24.2 24.3 ▪ 11.3 21 21.3 24.1 24.4 66

16927 CBU O P2 G4.0 1842–1895
Richthofen, Ferdinand Paul Wilhelm von, 1833–1905.
'Das nordwestliche China (Provinzen Shensi und Kansu)' (Northwest China: Shensi and Kansu). In *China: Ergebnisse eigener Reisen und darauf gegründeter Studien* (China: Results of my travels and studies based on them), by F. P. W. von Richthofen. [Selective entry]
Berlin: Reimer, 1882, vol. 2, 539–792.
SUBJ 11.3 21.3 24.2 ▪ 24.3 24.4 25 32.2 66

16928 CSU O P2 G5.3 1842–1911
Richthofen, Ferdinand Paul Wilhelm von, 1833–1905.
Schantung und seine Eingangspforte Kiautschou (Shantung and its gateway, Kiaochow).
Berlin: Reimer, 1898. 27, 324 p.
SUBJ 11.3 24.2 ▪ 21.1 24.1 24.4 55 61

16929 CBU O P2 G2.0 1842–1895
Richthofen, Ferdinand Paul Wilhelm von, 1833–1905.
'Das südliche Mantschurei' (Southern Manchuria). In *China: Ergebnisse eigener Reisen und darauf gegründeter Studien* (China: Results of my travels and studies based on them), by F. P. W. von Richthofen. [Selective entry]
Berlin: Reimer, 1882, vol. 2, 47–170.
SUBJ 11.3 24.2 66 ▪ 21.2 24.1 55

16930 CBU O P2 G1.5 1842–1895
Richthofen, Ferdinand Paul Wilhelm von, 1833–1905.
'Das südöstliche China' (Southeast China). In *China: Ergebnisse eigener Reisen und darauf gegründeter Studien* (China: Results of my travels and studies based on them), by F. P. W. von Richthofen, edited by Ernst Tiessen. [Selective entry]
Berlin: Reimer, 1912, vol. 3, 393–754.
SUBJ 24 24.2 ▪ 11.3 21.3 24.1 29

16931 CBU O P2 G8.0 1842–1895
Richthofen, Ferdinand Paul Wilhelm von, 1833–1905.
'Das südwestliche China (Provinzen Sz'tshwan und Kwéitshou)' (Southwest China: Szechwan and Kweichow). In *China: Ergebnisse eigener Reisen und darauf gegründeter Studien* (China: Results of my travels and studies based on them), by F. P. W. von Richthofen, edited by Ernst Tiessen. [Selective entry]
Berlin: Reimer, 1912, vol. 3, 1–286.
SUBJ 11.3 24 24.2 ▪ 55 71 72

16932 MCH O P2 G8.2 1895–1911
Schmidt, L-.
'Le Yunnan' (Yunnan).
R. de géographie 49, 5 (nov. 1901), 422–437.
SUBJ 11.3 24 24.2 ▪ 21.1 24.1

16933 GBS O P5 G9.1 1842–1895
Schroeter, H-.
Bericht über eine Reise nach Kwang-si (Report on a journey to Kwangsi).
Hong Kong: Kelly and Walsh, 1887. 97 p.
SUBJ 24.2 ▪ 22.1 24.3

16934 MCH O P2 G1.5 1895–1911
Vaulserre, *Vicomte* ——— de.
'A travers le Yun-nan et du Yun-nan au Tonkin, par le Kouei-Tchéou et le Kouang-Si' (Across Yunnan and from Yunnan to Tonkin via Kweichow and Kwangsi).
Tour du monde nouvelle (2e) série 7, 1 (jan.–fév. 1901), 1–72.
SUBJ 21.1 23 24.2 24.3 24.4 55 ▪ 22.1 25 53

16935 CSU O P2 G1.3 1842–1895
Wylie, Alexander, 1815–1887.
'Itinerary of a journey through the provinces of Hoo-pih [i.e., Hupeh], Sze-chuen and Shen-se [i.e., Shensi].'
JRAS-NCB new (2nd) series 5 (Dec. 1868), 153–258.
SUBJ 11.3 24.2 66 ▪ 23 24.1 24.3

1644-1949

16936 NNC P P3 G5.1 1842–1949
Chatley, Herbert, 1885–.
'The port of Tientsin, the shipping center of North China.'
Dock and harbour authority 20, 234 (Apr. 1940), 129–134.
SUBJ 24.2 24.3

16937 CSH FP P5 G6.3 1895–1949
China [Republic]. Shih yeh pu. Kuo chi mao i chü. (Ministry of Industry. Bureau of Foreign Trade), ed.
'Communications and transportation.' Tr. of 'Chiao t'ung' and 'T'e chung shang yeh, 1-3, 5' (Transport and communications *and* Special types of commercial enterprises, Chaps. 1–3, 5); in *Chung-kuo shih yeh chih: Che-chiang sheng* (Chinese economic surveys: Chekiang); Shanghai: Kuo chi mao i chü, 1933, *kuei* 1 – *kuei* 184, *hsin* 1 – *hsin* 21, *hsin* 31 – *hsin* 49 [s.p.] [slightly condensed in tr.]. In *China industrial handbooks: Chekiang*, edited by the agency cited. [Selective entry]
Shanghai: Kuo chi mao i chü, 1935, 831–949. [Reprinted in *China industrial handbooks: Chekiang*, edited by the agency cited. (Selective entry.) Taipei: Ch'eng-wen, 1972, 831–949.]
SUBJ 24.2 24.3 34.2

16938 CSU F P2 G1.1 –1928
Japan. Tetsudōin. (Imperial Japanese Government Railways), comp.
An official guide to eastern Asia: Transcontinental connections between Europe and Asia, Vol IV, China.

Tokyo: Tetsudōin, 1915. 124, 414 p.
SUBJ 21.3 24 24.2 ▪ 17 21 24.4 24.6 28 31 55 59

16939 CSH O P2 G2.0 1895–1949
Liubimov, L- I-.
'Rechnoi transport sev. Man'chzhurii' (River transport in northern Manchuria).
VM 1932, 9/10, 11–25.
SUBJ 24.2 ▪ 24.3 24.4

16940 CSU O P2 G5.3 1895–1949
Sigaut, Etienne.
'A northern type of Chinese junk.'
Mariner's mirror 46, 3 (Aug. 1960), 161–174.
SUBJ 24.2

16941 CSH P P2 G9.5 1842–1949
Tregear, Thomas Refoy, 1897–, and L- Berry.
'The development of Hongkong and Kowloon as told in maps.'
FEER 25, 2 – 25, 11 (10 July 1958 – 11 Sept. 1958), 31 p. in all. [Separately reprinted—Hong Kong: Hong Kong U. Press; London: Macmillan, 1959. 31 p.]
SUBJ 24.2 28 ▪ 21.1 21.2 21.3

16942 CSU PO P2 G9.2 1895–1949
Worcester, George Raleigh Gray, 1890–1969.
'Six craft of Kwangtung.'
Mariner's mirror 45, 2 (1959), 130–144.
SUBJ 24.2 ▪ 25 26.3 57

1911-1949

16943 CSU U P2 G6.3 1911–1949
'Highways of Chekiang.'
CEJ 19, 1 (July 1936), 36–41.
SUBJ 24.2 ▪ 12

16944 CSH P P3 G1.3 1911–1928
'The ricsha in Shanghai and Peking.'
CEM 2, 8 (May 1925), 34–40.
SUBJ 24.2 26.4

16945 MCH O P2 G9.0 1911–1928
Bel, Raymond.
'La vie fluviale dans la région de Canton' (River life in the Canton delta).
Tour du monde nouvelle (2e) série 19, 33 (16 août 1913), 385–396.
SUBJ 21.1 23 24.2 26.2 55 ▪ 24.1 24.4

16946 CSU O P2 G6.3 1928–1949
Chang, Bintze T.
'Modern highways in Chekiang.'
CEJ 12, 3 (Mar. 1933), 231–240.
SUBJ 24.2

16947 CSH FP P2 G6.1 1911–1949
China [Republic]. Shih yeh pu. Kuo chi mao i chü. (Ministry of Industry. Bureau of Foreign Trade), ed.
'Communications and transportation.' Tr. of 'Chiao t'ung' and 'T'e chung shang yeh, 2, 3, 5' (Transport and communications *and* Special types of commercial enterprises, Chaps. 2, 3, 5); in *Chung-kuo shih yeh chih: Chiang-su sheng* (Chinese economic surveys: Kiangsu); Shanghai: Kuo chi mao i chü, 1933, 1–278; 31–60, 73–86 [s.p.] [slightly condensed in tr.]. In *China industrial handbooks: Kiangsu*, edited by the agency cited. [Selective entry]
Shanghai: Kuo chi mao i chü, 1933, 965–1077. [Reprinted in *China industrial handbooks: Kiangsu*, edited by the agency cited. (Selective entry.) Taipei: Ch'eng-wen, 1972, 965–1077.]
SUBJ 24.2 24.3 24.6 ▪ 26.4 34.2

16948 DCK O P2 G1.2 1928–1949
Clausen, Erik Briand, 1901–1945.
'Transportmidler og afsætningsforhold i Kina' (Means of transportation and marketing conditions in China).
Jordbrugs-Teknik 8 (1936), 5–10.
SUBJ 14.3 24.2 ▪ 26.3

16949 CSU O P2 G1.1 1928–1949
Donnelly, Ivon Arthur, 1890–.
Chinese junks and other native craft, 3rd ed.
Shanghai: Kelly and Walsh, 1939. 142 p.
SUBJ 24.2 ▪ 65

16950 NNC O P2 G5.2 1911–1928
Fischer, Emil Sigmund, 1865–1945.
'Modern travel from Tai Yuan Fu [Taiyuan] via Mount Wu Tai [Wu-t'ai *hsien*, Shansi] to the Mongolian frontier.'
JRAS-NCB new (2nd) series 54 (1923), 81–113. [Separately reprinted as *The sacred Wu Tai Shan, in connection with modern travel from Tai Yuan Fu via Mount Wu Tai to the Mongolian border*. Shanghai: Kelly and Walsh, 1925. 37 p.]
SUBJ 23 24.2 ▪ 33

16951 CSH PO P3 G2.2 1911–1949
Gorshenin, A- I-.
'Gruzooborot kharbinskogo uzla' (Freight turnover at the Harbin terminal).
VM 1932, 8, 23–28.

'Goods turnover of the Harbin terminal.'
Manchuria monitor 1932, 8, 1–6.
SUBJ 24.2 ▪ 14.3 24.4

16952 CSU P P1 G9.4 1911–1949
Greene, Katrine R- C-.
'Transportation: Formosa.' In *An economic survey of the Pacific area, Part 2, Transportation*, by K. R. C. Greene. [Sole entry]
New York: Institute of Pacific Relations, International Secretariat, 1942, 37–38.
SUBJ 24.2

16953 CSU P P2 G5.1 1911–1949
Hitch, Margaret Armstrong.
'The port of Tientsin and its problems.'
GR 25, 3 (July 1935), 367–381.
SUBJ 24.2 28

16954 CSH P P2 G9.5 1928–1949
Hong Kong. Kowloon-Canton Railway [British Section].
Annual departmental report by the General Manager, 1946/47–1948/49. [Issues for 1950/51–1971/72 are entered as 17003.]
[Hong Kong]: ——. Issued annually, 1947–1949. Average ca. 30 p.
SUBJ 24.2

16955 CSU P P2 G9.5 1928–1949
Hong Kong. Post Office Dept.
Annual report, 1946/47–1948/49. [Issues for 1949/50–1971/72 are entered as 17004.]
[Hong Kong]: ——. Issued annually, 1947–1949. Average ca. 20 p.
SUBJ 24.2 ▪ 24.5

16956 NNC FP P2 G5.1 1928–1949
Köhler, Günther, 1909–.
'Das Mündungsgebiet des Hwang Ho' (The estuary of the Yellow River). In *Asiatica: Festschrift für Friedrich Weller zum 65. Geburtstag gewidmet von seinen Freunden, Kollegen und Schülern* (Asiatica: Felicitation volume for Friedrich Weller on his sixty-fifth birthday by his friends, colleagues, and students), edited by Johannes Schubert and Ulrich Schneider. [Selective entry]
Leipzig: VEB Otto Harrassowitz, 1954, 355–364.
SUBJ 24.2

16957 NNC F P2 G4.2 1928–1949
Köhler, Günther, 1909–.
'Das Weiho-Einzugsgebiet, unter besonderer Berücksichtigung des Verkehrs' (The headwater region of the Huai river, with special attention to transportation).
PGM 96, 4 (1952), 271–275.
SUBJ 11.3 24.2 ▪ 14.3 24.1

16958 CSU O P3 G9.3 1911–1928
Lacey, Walter N-.
'Road improvements at Foochow, China.'
J. of geography 19, 9 (Dec. 1920), 343–348.
SUBJ 24.2

16959 CSU U P3 G9.2 1911–1949
Lee, Milton Chun.
'Public construction works in Canton.'
CEJ 5, 4 (Oct. 1929), 890–901.
SUBJ 24.2 ▪ 56

16960 CSU S P2 G8.1 1928–1949
Lie Boen Eat.
'Belangrijke toevoerwegen naar Chungking' (Main access roads to Chungking).
TESG 31, 8 (Augustus 1940), 223–225.
SUBJ 24.2

16961 CSH P P2 G2.0 1911–1928
Liubimov, L- I-.
'Sungari' (The Sungari river [basin]).
VM 1927, 2, 33–43; 1927, 3, 28–40.
SUBJ 11.3 24.2 ▪ 14.3 21.2 24.1 24.4

16962 CSU O P3 G1.3 1911–1949
Lu, David Chi-hsin (Lu Ch'i-hsin).
'Gems from the mosquito press.'
THM 6, 1 (Jan. 1938), 7–17.
SUBJ 24.2 ▪ 65

16963 MCH O P4 G8.2 1911–1928
Mazzolani, D- A-.
'In ferrovia da Yunnansen a Lao-cai' (From Yün-nan-sheng [i.e., Kunming] to Laokay [Tonkin] by railroad).
Bollettino della Società geografica italiana 5a serie 1, 4 (aprile 1912), 383–408; 1, 5 (maggio 1912), 505–530.
SUBJ 24.2 ▪ 22.2 24.4 24.5

16964 CSU O P2 G1.5 1928–1949
Moore, W- Robert.
'Along the Yangtze, main street of China.'
NG 93, 3 (Mar. 1948), 325–356.
SUBJ 24.2 ▪ 28

16965 CSH F P7 G8.1 1928–1949
Pan Hong-shen (P'an Hung-sheng).
'Road and water transportation in Hwayang hsien, Szechwan.'
EF 33 (June 1944), 467–470.
SUBJ 24.2

16966 CSU O P2 G5.1 1928–1949
Price, Willard, 1887–.
'Grand Canal panorama.'
NG 71, 4 (Apr. 1937), 487–514.
Subj 24.2 ▪ 23 24.1 66

16967 CBU PO P3 G2.2 1928–1949
Shablinskii, P- A-.
'Gruzooborot kharbinskogo porta za pervyi period navigatsii 1934 goda' (Freight turnover in the port of Harbin for the first navigation period of 1934).
EB 1934, 7 (iiul'), 28–33; 1934, 9 (sentiabr'), 1–7.
Subj 24.2 ▪ 14.3

16968 CSH P P2 G2.2 1911–1928
Sokolov, N- A-.
'Voprosy transporta, kolonizatsii i ekonomiki severnoi Man'chzhurii (raion vostochnoi linii KVzhd)' (The area of northern Manchuria served by the eastern line of the Chinese Eastern Railway: Problems of transport, colonization, and the economy). [With English abstract]
VM 1929, 7/8, 64–70.
Subj 21.2 24 24.1 24.2

16969 NNC O P2 G1.2 1928–1949
Sowerby, Arthur de Carle, 1885–1964.
'China's transport workers, men and beasts.'
CJ 10, 5 (May 1929), 233–243.
Subj 24.2 ▪ 28

16970 CSU O P2 G8.2 1928–1949
Tayman, Nelson Grant.
'Stilwell road: Land route to China.'
NG 87, 6 (June 1945), 681–698.
Subj 24.2

16971 MCH O P2 G8.3 1911–1928
Todd, Oliver Julian, 1880–.
'Highways in a land of barriers: Motor roads, an enterprise for those whose ancestors built the Great Wall.'
Asia (New York: American Asiatic Assn.) 29, 1 (Jan. 1929), 30–37, 62–64. [Reprinted as 'Highways in a land of barriers.' In *Two decades in China*, by O. J. Todd. (Selective entry.) Peiping: Assn. of Chinese and American Engineers, 1938, 239–250.] [Reprinted in *Two decades in China*, by O. J. Todd. (Selective entry.) Taipei: Ch'eng-wen, 1971, 239–250.]
Subj 24.2 ▪ 24.5 25 47 54

16972 CSH FP P2 G3.0 1928–1949
U.S. Office of Strategic Services. Research and Analysis Branch.
Transportation conditions and routes in eastern Suiyuan and southern Chahar, mimeo.
[Washington, D.C.]: ——, 1945. 17 p. (R. and A., 3335)
Subj 24.2 ▪ 22 55 56

16973 CSH FP P2 G1.4 1928–1949
U.S. Office of Strategic Services. Research and Analysis Branch.
Transportation in Northwest China, mimeo.
[Washington, D.C.]: ——, 1945. 40 p. (R. and A., 3088)
Subj 24.2 ▪ 21 21.3

16974 NNP O P4 G2.1 1928–1949
Vagone, V-.
'Po K.-V. zh. d.: ocherk' (Along the Chinese Eastern Railway: A sketch).
Oktiabr'! 1929, 10 (oktiabr'), 163–175.
Subj 24.2 36.4 55 ▪ 17 25 26.4 28

16975 NNC P P4 G5.3 1928–1949
Wehde-Textor, O-.
'Die Shantung-Bahn in den Jahren 1929–1933' (The Shantung railroad in the period 1929–1933).
AE 57, 4 (Juli–Aug. 1934), 961–965.
Subj 24.2

16976 CSU PO P2 G9.3 1911–1949
Worcester, George Raleigh Gray, 1890–1969.
'The Amoy fishing boat.'
Mariner's mirror 40, 4 (1954), 304–308.
Subj 24.2 ▪ 24.1

16977 CSU O P2 G1.1 1911–1949
Worcester, George Raleigh Gray, 1890–1969.
The floating population of China: An illustrated record of the junkmen and their boats on sea and river.
Hong Kong: Vetch and Lee, 1970. 12, 90 p.
Subj 24.2 ▪ 14.3 24.1 26 29 65

16978 CSU O P3 G6.3 1911–1949
Worcester, George Raleigh Gray, 1890–1969.
'The foot-boat of Shaohsing [Chekiang].'
Mariner's mirror 41, 3 (1955), 222–226.
Subj 24.2

16979 NNC O P2 G1.5 1928–1949
Worcester, George Raleigh Gray, 1890–1969.
The junkman smiles.
London: Chatto and Windus, 1959. 254 p.
Subj 24.2 ▪ 25 26.2 26.4 31 48 56 57

16980 FPN P P3 G6.1 1928–1949
Yee, Sau Ug.
Le port de Changhai (The port of Shanghai).
Toulouse: Boisseau, 1935. 216 p. (Doctoral dissertation, Faculté de droit, Université de Toulouse)
Subj 14.3 24.2 24.4 ▪ 21.3 66

1911-1972
(including 1644-1972)

16981 CSU FP P3 G9.5 1842–1972
Atkinson, Robert Llewellyn Peter, and A- K- Williams.
Hongkong Tramways: A history of Hongkong Tramways Limited and predecessor companies.
London: Light Railway Transport League, 1970. 96 p.
Subj 24.2

16982 CSU PO P2 G9.5 1842–1972
Clayton, Charles Curtis, 1902–.
'Hong Kong.' In *The Asian newspapers' reluctant revolution*, edited by John A- Lent. [Selective entry]
Ames: Iowa State U. Press, 1971, 55–64.
Subj 24.2

16983 MAM P P4 G9.4 1895–1972
Jang, John Lun, 1935–.
A history of newspapers in Taiwan.
Ann Arbor: University Microfilms (Publ. 68-18,274), 1968. 165 p. (Doctoral dissertation in Asian Studies, Claremont Graduate School and University Center)
Subj 24.2 ▪ 12.2 34.2

16984 GMS FP P2 G4.1 1895–1972
Köhler, Günther, 1909–.
'Die Provinz Schensi (China): Eine verkehrs-geographische Betrachtung' (A consideration of transport geography in Shensi). In *Geographische Forschungen: Festschrift zum 60. Geburtstag von Hans Kinzl* (Geographic research: Felicitation volume for Hans Kinzl on his sixtieth birthday). [Sole entry]
Innsbruck: Universitätsverlag Wagner, 1958, 115–122.
Subj 11.3 24.2

16985 CSU P P2 G9.5 1842–1972
Leung, C. K. (Liang Chih-ch'iang), 1935–.
'The growth of internal public passenger transport.' In *Asian urbanization: A Hong Kong casebook*, edited by Denis John Dwyer. [Analytic entry]
Hong Kong: Hong Kong U. Press, 1971, 137–154. (Centre of Asian Studies series, 3)
Subj 24.2

16986 CSH FP P7 G9.4 –1972
Ling Shun-sheng (Ling Ch'un-sheng).
'Formosan sea-going raft and its origins in ancient China.'
BIE 1 (Mar. 1956), 25–54. [Chinese version appears in the same issue at pp. 1–23.]
Subj 24.2

16987 CSH S P2 G9.4 1928–1972
Stanford U. China Project.
'Public information.' In *Taiwan (Formosa)*, compiled by the organization cited. [Selective entry]
New Haven: Human Relations Area Files, 1956, vol. 1, 207–221. (HRAF subcontractor's monographs, 31; Stanford 5)
Subj 24.2

1949-1972

16988 CSH O P3 G9.2 1949–1972
'*Yang Cheng Wan Pao* [Canton evening news]: A newspaper in Communist China.'
CS 2, 16 (1 July 1963), 1–14. [Reprinted as 'A journalist and his paper.' In *Out of China: A collection of interviews with refugees from China*, edited by Francis Harper. (Analytic entry.) Hong Kong: Dragonfly Books, 1964, 207–235.]
Subj 24.2 ▪ 34.2

16989 CSU O P3 G9.5 1949–1972
Adam, Kenneth.
'Broadcasting in a colony.'
Listener 75 (16 June 1966), 862–863, 889.
Subj 24.2

16990 NNC P P2 G8.1 1949–1972
Afanas'evskii, Evgenii Aleksandrovich.
'Razvitie sredstv soobshcheniia v Sychuani' (The development of means of communication in Szechwan).
SK 1958, 4, 110–123.
Subj 24.2 ▪ 14

16991 CSU F P4 G9.5 1949–1972
Allen, Charles Laurel, 1902–.
Communication patterns in Hong Kong.
Hong Kong: Chinese U. of Hong Kong, 1970. 125 p.
SUBJ 14.2 24.2 ▪ 26 26.2 26.4 28 41

16992 NNC U P7 G1.2 1949–1972
Chang Chi-tsung.
'Rural transport in China.'
PR 6, 14 (5 Apr. 1963), 22–24.
SUBJ 24.2 ▪ 24.1 24.4

16993 CBU P P7 G1.2 1949–1972
Chang Kuo-wu.
'Principles governing the scheme of communal transportation network.' Tr. of 'P'ei chih jen min kung she yün shu wang ti chi ko yüan tse'; in *Jen min kung she ching chi kuei hua yü ching chi ti li wen chi* (Collected essays on economic planning and economic geography of the communes); Peking: K'o hsüeh ch'u pan she, 1959, 48–55. In *Economic plans and economic geography of people's communes*, mimeo., jointly edited by Chung-kuo ti li hsüeh hui (Geographical Society of China) *with* Ti li yen chiu so (Institute of Geography), Chung-kuo k'o hsüeh yüan (Chinese Academy of Sciences). [Selective entry]
Washington, D.C.: U.S. Joint Publications Research Service, 25 Feb. 1963, 114–128. (JPRS 17,789; MC 6864/1963) [Xerox copyflo available—New York: CCM Information Corp., Research and Microfilm Publications. (Scholarly Book Translation Series, 421)]
SUBJ 24 24.2

16994 CSH O P8 G4.1 1949–1972
Chiang Yen, Ma Hsiung-fan, and Chang Wan-yang.
'Wall newspapers in the rural areas.' Tr. of 'Ta tzu pao tsai nung ts'un chung' ('Large character' bulletins in villages); *Hung ch'i* 1958, 5 (1 Aug.), 4–6. In *Selected translations from 'Hung-chi' (Red flag), June–August 1958*, mimeo., compiled by U.S. Joint Publications Research Service. [Selective entry]
Washington, D.C.: JPRS, 21 Apr. 1961, 93–100. (JPRS 7837; MC 5498/1962)
SUBJ 22.1 24.2 ▪ 34.1

16995 MCY P P1 G9.4 1949–1972
China [Republic]. Chiao t'ung pu. Tien hsin kuan li chü. (Ministry of Communications. Directorate General of Telegraphs).
Telecommunications of Taiwan, China.
Taipei: Tien hsin kuan li chü, 1956. 15 p.
SUBJ 24.2

16996 CSU S P3 G9.4 1949–1972
Chu, Godwin C. (Chu Chien), 1927–.
The press of Nationalist China.
Unpublished masters thesis in Communications and Journalism, Stanford U., 1960. 120 p.
SUBJ 24.2 ▪ 12.2 32.1

16997 CSU U P4 G2.3 1949–1972
Chung-kuo kung ch'an tang. Chin-chou t'ieh lu chü wei yüan hui. (Chinese Communist Party. Chin-chou Railroad Bureau Committee), ed. [Chin-chou is in Chin *hsien*, Liaoning.]
'Raise the quality of equipment uninterruptedly, tap the potentials in railroad transportation.' Tr. of 'Pu tuan t'i kao she pei chih liang wa chüeh t'ieh lu yün shu ch'ien li' (Continue to improve the quality of equipment and realize the potentials in rail transportation); *Hung ch'i* 1960, 22 (16 Nov.), 41–45. In *Translations from 'Hung-ch'i' (Red flag) (Peiping, No. 22, 16 November 1960)*, mimeo., compiled by U.S. Joint Publications Research Service. [Sole entry]
Washington, D.C.: JPRS, 3 Feb. 1961, 62–71. (JPRS 6700; MC 4561/1961)
SUBJ 24.2 34.2 ▪ 22.1 24.4

16998 CSU PO P2 G9.0 1949–1972
Clayton, Charles Curtis, 1902–.
'Taiwan.' In *The Asian newspapers' reluctant revolution*, edited by John A. Lent. [Selective entry]
Ames: Iowa State U. Press, 1971, 105–114.
SUBJ 24.2

16999 MCH O P4 G9.4 1949–1972
Culmsee, Carlton Fordis, 1904–.
'How free is the press in "Free China"?'
Journalism q. 33, 4 (Fall 1956), 493–501.
SUBJ 24.2

17000 CSH P P3 G1.2 1949–1972
Current Scene Editor.
'The handwriting on the wall: Posters and Red Guard papers speak the mind of China.'
CS 5, 9 (31 May 1967), 1–17.
SUBJ 24.2 ▪ 12 22.2 54

17001 CSU F P2 G9.5 1949–1972
Dalby, E-.
Hong Kong passenger transport survey, 1964–66.
Hong Kong: Government Printer, 1967. 19, 214 p.
SUBJ 24.2 ▪ 21 21.1 21.4

17002 CSU FP P2 G9.5 1949–1972
Freeman, Fox, Wilbur Smith and Associates.
Hong Kong mass transport study.
Hong Kong: Government Printer, 1967. 213 p.
SUBJ 24.2 ▪ 21 21.4 24.6 28 34.2

17003 CSU P P2 G9.5 1949–1972
Hong Kong. Kowloon-Canton Railway [British Section].
Annual departmental report by the General Manager, 1950/51–1971/72. [Issues for 1946/47–1948/49 are entered as 16954.]
Hong Kong: Government Printer. Issued annually, 1951–1972. Average ca. 30 p.
SUBJ 24.2

17004 CSU P P2 G9.5 1949–1972
Hong Kong. Post Office Dept.
Annual departmental report by the Postmaster General, 1949/50–1971/72. [Issues for 1946/47–1948/49 are entered as 16955.]
Hong Kong: Government Printer. Issued annually, 1950–1972. Average ca. 25 p.
SUBJ 24.2 ▪ 24.5

17005 NNC O P3 G5.2 1949–1972
I Chih, pseud., and Ai Kang.
'Ten years of the *Shansi jih pao*.' Tr. of '"Shan-hsi jih pao" shih nien' (A decade of *Shan-hsi jih pao* [The Shansi daily]); *Hsin wen chan hsien* 1959, 18 (24 Sept.), 7–12. In *Translations of Chinese Communist articles on newspaper and broadcasting work*, mimeo., compiled by U.S. Joint Publications Research Service. [Sole entry]
Washington, D.C.: JPRS, 14 July 1960, 15–34. (JPRS 3548; MC 14,260/1960)
SUBJ 24.2 34.2 ▪ 32.1

17006 CSU P P4 G9.4 1949–1972
Kaser, David, 1924–.
Book pirating in Taiwan.
Philadelphia: U. of Pennsylvania Press, 1969. 154 p.
SUBJ 17 24.2 ▪ 12.2 22.2 34.2

17007 MCH P P2 G4.3 1949–1972
[La Dany, Ladislao] ———, 1914–.
'The economic situation in Sinkiang.'
CNA 591 (3 Dec. 1965), 1–7.
SUBJ 24.2 ▪ 14.4 24.1

17008 MCH P P2 G1.2 1949–1972
[La Dany, Ladislao] ———, 1914–.
'Newspapers.'
CNA 94 (5 Aug. 1955), 1–7.
SUBJ 22.1 24.2 ▪ 14.2

17009 CSU P P2 G9.5 1949–1972
Leung, C. K. (Liang Chih-ch'iang), 1935–.
'Mass transport in Hong Kong.' In *Asian urbanization: A Hong Kong casebook*, edited by Denis John Dwyer. [Analytic entry]
Hong Kong: Hong Kong U. Press, 1971, 155–166. (Centre of Asian Studies series, 3)
SUBJ 24.2

17010 CSU P P3 G9.5 1949–1972
Mitchell, Robert Edward, 1930–.
'How Hong Kong newspapers have responded to 15 years of rapid social change.'
AS 9, 9 (Sept. 1969), 669–681.
SUBJ 24.2

17011 NIC O P7 G8.1 1949–1972
Mu Tzu-li.
'Local transport networks: "Walking on two legs".'
PR 4, 45 (10 Nov. 1961), 13–15. [Reprinted—*SCMM* 291 (11 Dec. 1961), 31–33.]
SUBJ 24.2

17012 ICU P P3 G9.5 1949–1972
Nissen, Elizabeth Maureen.
Hong Kong: Propaganda crossroads.
Unpublished masters thesis in International Relations, U. of Chicago, 1953. 103 p.
SUBJ 22.1 24.2 32.2 ▪ 21.4 22 24 28 64

17013 CSH P P2 G2.3 1949–1972
Su Chieh.
'The great victory of railway transportation and reconstruction.' Tr. from *Liao-ning shih nien* (Liaoning during the past decade); Shenyang: Jen min ch'u pan she, 196? In *Liao-ning province during the last ten years*, mimeo., compiled by U.S. Joint Publications Research Service. [Selective entry]
Washington, D.C.: JPRS, 17 Jan. 1963, 84–96. (JPRS 17,182; MC 2979/1963) [Xerox copyflo available—New York:

CCM Information Corp., Research and Microfilm Publications. (Scholarly Book Translation Series, 545)]
Subj 24.2

17014 CSU P P4 G1.2 1949–1972
Tong, T. K. (T'ang Te-kang), 1920–.
'Red Guard newspapers.'
Columbia forum 12, 1 (Spring 1969), 38–41.
Subj 24.2 54

17015 NNC O P4 G6.2 1949–1972
Tseng Hsi-ching (Ts'eng Hsi-ch'ing).
On the question of the party press, mimeo. Tr. of 'Kuan yü ch'üan tang pan pao wen t'i'; *Jen min jih pao* 16 June 1960, 7.
Washington, D.C.: U.S. Joint Publications Research Service, 12 July 1960. 11 p. (JPRS 3518; MC 14,237/1960)
Subj 24.2 32.1

17016 MCH O P1 G9.4 1949–1972
Worcester, George Raleigh Gray, 1890–1969.
'Four small craft of T'ai-wan.'
Mariner's mirror 42, 4 (Nov. 1956), 302–312.
Subj 24.2 24.4

17017 MCH O P1 G1.4 1949–1972
Worcester, George Raleigh Gray, 1890–1969.
'The inflated skin rafts of the Huang Ho [Yellow River].'
Mariner's mirror 43, 1 (Feb. 1957), 73–74.
Subj 24.2

24.3 Local Commerce and Services

地方商業　地方商業

1644-1911

17018 CSU PO P6 G1.3 1842–1895
Alabaster, Chaloner.
'Fairs in China.'
NQCJ 3, 7 (July 1869), 109–110.
Subj 24.3

17019 MCH PO P3 G9.5 1842–1911
Clavery, Edouard, 1867–?
Hong Kong: le passé et le présent (Hong Kong, past and present).
Paris: Chevalier et Rivière, 1905. 57 p.
Subj 24.3 ▪ 17 21.1 22 24

17020 CSU O P3 G5.1 1895–1911
Forke, Alfred, 1867–1944.
'Die pekinger Läden und ihre Abzeichen' (The shops of Peking and their signs).
MDG 8 (1899/1902), 1–22.
Subj 24.3 26.2 ▪ 34.2 62

17021 MCH O P3 G9.2 1644–1895
França, Bento da, 1859–1906.
Macau (Macau).
Lisbon: Companhia Nacional Editora, 1890. 62 p.
Subj 24 24.3 ▪ 21.1 21.3 22

17022 MCH PO P3 G9.2 1895–1911
Imbault-Huart, Camille Clément, 1857–1897.
'Notes commerciales sur Canton' (Trade notes on Canton).
B. de la Société de géographie commerciale de Paris 18 (1896), 750–787.
Subj 24.3 ▪ 24.4

17023 NNP O P6 G3.0 1895–1911
Khitrovo, A- D-.
'Ganchzhurskaia iarmarka' (The Kan-chu-erh-miao fair [Inner Mongolia]).
Trudy Troitskosavsko-Kiakhtinskago otdeleniia Priamurskago otdela imperatorskago Russkago geograficheskago obshchestva 13, 2 (1910), 157–171.
Subj 24.3 ▪ 66

17024 MCH O P2 G2.0 1644–1842
Lüdorf, Fr—— Aug——.
'Das Amur-Land' (The Amur region).
Mitteilungen aus Justus Perthes' geographischer Anstalt 14, 9 (Sept. 1868), 325–332.
Subj 11.3 24 24.3 ▪ 21 21.1

17025 MCH O P2 G9.2 1895–1911
Madrolle, Claudius, 1870–?
'La péninsule de Loui-tchéou' (The Lei-chou peninsula [Kwangtung]).
Annales de géographie 7, 32/33 (mars–mai 1898), 177–180.
Subj 11.3 22 24.2 24.3 ▪ 21 21.2 25 29

17026 CBU O P3 G9.5 1842–1895
Nacken, J-.
'Chinese street-cries in Hongkong.'
China review 2, 1 (July–Aug. 1873), 51–55. [Reprinted—*JRAS-HKB* 8 (1968), 128–134.]
Subj 24.3 28

17027 MCY O P4 G5.2 1842–1895
Volosatov, I-.
'O torgovle iziubrevymi rogami' (The trade in tufted deer antlers [in Kuei-hua-ch'eng, Shansi]). In *Trudy russkikh torgovykh liudei v Mongolii i Kitae* (Works of Russian merchants in Mongolia and China), compiled by Vostochno-sibirskii otdel, Imperatorskoe russkoe geograficheskoe obshchestvo. [Selective entry]
Irkutsk: Tip. K. I. Vitkovskoi, 1890, 137–141. (Imperatorskoe russkoe geograficheskoe obshchestvo, Vostochno-sibirskii otdel, Zapiski po obshchei geografii, 1, 1)
Subj 24.3 ▪ 55

17028 CSH P P5 G1.4 –1911
Yamane Yukio, 1921–.
'Periodic markets in North China during the Ming and Ch'ing periods.' Tr. by Mitsugu Matsuda of 'Min shin jidai Kahoku ni okeru teiki ichi'; *Tōkyō joshi daigaku shiron* 8 (Nov. 1960), 493–504. In *Markets in China during the Sung, Ming, and Ch'ing periods*, edited by Research Publications and Translations, Institute of Advanced Projects, East-West Center. [Sole entry]
Honolulu: Research Publications and Translations, 1967, 109–142. (RPT occasional papers, translation series, 23)
Subj 24.3 ▪ 12 21.3 24.2 24.5 26.3 34.2

1644-1949

17029 DLC FP P2 G6.1 1895–1949
Chang, L. L. (Chang Lü-luan).
'Farm prices in Wuchin, Kiangsu, China.' Tr. of 'Chiang-su Wu-chin wu chia chih yen chiu' (Prices in Wu-chin *hsien*, Kiangsu); *Chin-ling hsüeh pao* 3, 1 (May 1933), 153–216.
CEJ 10, 6 (June 1932), 449–512. [Separately reprinted—Shanghai: Shih yeh pu, Kuo chi mao i chü, 1932. 64 p. (Kuo chi mao i chü booklet series, 19)]
Subj 24 24.3 ▪ 24.1 24.5 24.6 28

17030 CSH FP P4 G6.3 –1949
China [Republic]. Shih yeh pu. Kuo chi mao i chü. (Ministry of Industry. Bureau of Foreign Trade), ed.
'Leading cities.' Tr. of 'Shang pu chi tu shih' (Treaty ports and large cities); in *Chung-kuo shih yeh chih: Che-chiang sheng* (Chinese economic surveys: Chekiang); Shanghai: Kuo chi mao i chü, 1933, *ping* 1 – *ping* 112 [s.p.] [slightly condensed in tr.]. In *China industrial handbooks: Chekiang*, edited by the agency cited. [Selective entry]
Shanghai: Kuo chi mao i chü, 1935, 97–163. [Reprinted in *China industrial handbooks: Chekiang*, edited by the agency cited. (Selective entry.) Taipei: Ch'eng-wen, 1972, 97–163.]
Subj 24.3 24.4 ▪ 21.1 21.3 24.2 24.6

17031 CBU FP P5 G8.1 1895–1949
Hu Kwoh-hwa (Hu Kuo-hua).
'Price behavior of rice in Szechwan.'
EF 15 (Apr. 1941), 139–146.
Subj 24.3

17032 CSU F P7 G1.2 1895–1949
Lewis, Ardron B-.
'Prices and taxation.' In *Land utilization in China: A study of 16,786 farms in 168 localities, and 32,256 farm families in twenty-two provinces in China, 1929–1933*, by John Lossing Buck. [Analytic entry]
Nanking: U. of Nanking, 1937, vol. 1, 311–347. [For Buck's work, see entry 12256.] [Reprinted in *Land utilization in China: A study of 16,786 farms in 168 localities, and 32,256 farm families in twenty-two provinces in China, 1929–1933*, by J. L. Buck. (Analytic entry.) New York: Paragon, 1964, vol. 1, 311–347.]
Subj 14.5 24.3 ▪ 14.1 14.6 16.3 24.5

17033 CSH FP P7 G6.1 1895–1949
Lewis, Ardron B-, and Wang Lien.
'Farm prices in Wuchin [*hsien*], Kiangsu.'
EF 2 (Oct. 1936), 73–91. [In Chinese as well as English]
Subj 24.3 24.6 ▪ 28

17034 CBU FP P2 G1.3 1842–1949
Raeburn, John R-, and Hu Kwoh-hwa (Hu Kuo-hua).
'Seasonal variation of prices for farm products and the profitability of storage.'
EF 8 (Jan. 1938), 298–315.
Subj 24.3 ▪ 14.3

17035 CBU FP P2 G6.1 1895–1949
Raeburn, John R-, and Tsu Chwan-hwai (Hsü Chuang-huai).
'Prices paid to farmers for wheat.'

EF 5 (May 1937), 213–217. [In Chinese as well as English]
SUBJ 24.3 ▪ 14.3

17036 CSU FP P7 G1.1 1842–1949
Skinner, George William, 1925–.
'Marketing and social structure in rural China, Part I.'
JAS 24, 1 (Nov. 1964), 3–43. [Separately reprinted—Indianapolis: Bobbs-Merrill College Division, 1967. 41 p. (Bobbs-Merrill reprint series in geography, G-204)] [Reprinted in *Man, space, and environment: Concepts in contemporary human geography*, edited by Paul Ward English and Robert Charles Mayfield. (Sole entry.) New York: Oxford U. Press, 1972, 561–601.]
SUBJ 11.3 20 21.3 24 24.3 26 ▪ 21 22 23 29 30 31 41 42 62

17037 FPN P P3 G6.1 1842–1949
Ts'ien Siang-suen (Ch'ien Hsiang-sun).
Le port de Changhai: étude économique (An economic study of the port of Shanghai).
Lyons: Bosc et Riou, 1934. 164 p. (Doctoral dissertation, Faculté de droit, Université de Grenoble)
SUBJ 24 24.3 ▪ 24.4 24.6

17038 CBU P P2 G1.5 1895–1949
Wang Lien.
'Prices in Szechwan, 1910–1934.' [With a comparison with data from southern Kiangsu]
EF 9 (Apr. 1938), 412–419. [In Chinese as well as English]
SUBJ 14.3 24.3 ▪ 24.6

17039 CBU F P2 G5.1 1895–1949
Yang, William Y. (Yang Yü), 1907–, and Lu Sheng-hwai (Lu Sheng-huai).
'Analysis of prices of farm crops in Chengting [*hsien*], Hopeh, 1907–1937.'
EF 11 (Sept. 1938), 531–542. [In Chinese as well as English]
SUBJ 24.3 ▪ 14.3

1911-1949

17040 NIC O P3 G6.1 1928–1949
'The Bubbling Well Temple basket fair.'
CJ 16, 5 (May 1932), 232–233.
SUBJ 24.3

17041 DLC P P3 G6.1 1911–1928
'Optovyi indeks shankhaiskogo rynka' (Wholesale index of the Shanghai market).
Ekonomicheskaia zhizn' Dal'nego Vostoka 4, 1 (1926), 116–123.
SUBJ 24.3

17042 CSU U P3 G6.1 1928–1949
'Shanghai foodstuff statistics for 1932.'
CEJ 13, 2 (Aug. 1933), 157–168.
SUBJ 24.3

17043 CSU O P2 G3.0 1928–1949
Barnett, Arthur Doak, 1921–.
'Chinese in Inner Mongolia' [report to Institute of Current World Affairs, January 1948]. In *China on the eve of Communist takeover*, by A. D. Barnett. [Selective entry]
New York: Praeger, 1963, 195–204.
SUBJ 24 24.3 ▪ 24.2 25 66

17044 CBU P P3 G8.1 1911–1949
Buck, John Lossing, 1890–, and Hu Kwoh-hwa (Hu Kuo-hua).
'The price of rice and its determining factors in Szechwan.' [Data on Shanghai are also given.]
EF 15 (Apr. 1941), 117–123B.
SUBJ 24.3

17045 CSH F P7 G8.1 1928–1949
Buck, John Lossing, 1890–, and Yin-yuen Wang (Wang Yin-yüan).
'Effect of price relationships on farmers during inflation.'
EF 26 (Nov. 1943), 290–294.
SUBJ 24.3 28 ▪ 26.3

17046 CSU U P2 G5.3 1928–1949
Chen, Chunjen C. (Ch'en Chün-jen).
'Tobacco-growing in Shantung.'
CEJ 10, 1 (Jan. 1932), 37–44.
SUBJ 24.1 24.3 ▪ 14.3 24.6

17047 NNC O P4 G5.3 1928–1949
Cheng, Lin-chuang.
'The Kiaotsi [Kiaochow-Tsinan] Railway Consumers' Co-operative Society: A case study.'
YJSS 1, 1 (June 1938), 87–106.
SUBJ 24.3 28 38 ▪ 32.1 34.2 36.4

17048 CSH P P3 G6.1 1911–1928
China [Republic]. Ts'ai cheng pu. Chu Hu tiao ch'a huo chia ch'u. (Ministry of Finance. [Shanghai] Bureau of Markets), ed.
'Review of the period.' [Recurring feature article: journal issued quarterly, article appears irregularly.]
Shanghai market prices report unnumbered (Jan.–Mar. 1924 – Jan.–Mar. 1928), average ca. 9 p. [See Vol. 2 of this *Bibliography* for Chinese version.]
SUBJ 24.3 ▪ 24.6

17049 CBU F P3 G5.1 1911–1949
Constant, Samuel Victor, 1894–.
Calls, sounds and merchandise of the Peking street peddlers.
Peiping: Camel Bell, 1936. 14, 187 p.
SUBJ 24.3 62 65 ▪ 54 55 56

17050 CBU P P3 G2.2 1911–1949
Dombrovskii, I- I-.
'TSeny kharbinskogo rynka 1920–1930 gg.' (Prices on the Harbin market, 1920–1930).
VM 1931, 2, 8–17; 1931, 3, 37–52; 1932, 2, 18–32; 1932, 6/7, 50–63; 1933, 6 (1 aprelia), 1–20; 1934, 1 (ianvar'), 74–94.
SUBJ 24.1 24.3 ▪ 24.4

17051 MCH P P4 G6.1 1911–1928
Es, Willem Johan Louis van, 1886–1943.
'De plaats van de Lunghaihaven in het handelsverkeer van China' (The port at the terminus of the Lanchow–Hai-tung [Kiangsu] railroad: Its place in China's commerce).
China (Amsterdam) 3 (Mei 1928), 111–131.
SUBJ 24.3 ▪ 24.2

17052 CSU PO P3 G6.1 1911–1949
Feetham, Richard, 1874–?
'Business interests in Shanghai.' In *Report of the Hon. Mr. Justice Feetham, C.M.G., to the Shanghai Municipal Council, Vol. 1*, by R. Feetham. [Selective entry]
Shanghai: North-China Daily News and Herald, 1931, 252–372.
SUBJ 22 24 24.2 24.3 24.6 ▪ 12.2 21.3 66

17053 NIC FP P5 G5.1 1928–1949
Fong, H. D. (Fang Hsien-t'ing), 1902–.
'The cooperative marketing of cotton in Hopei province.'
NSEQ 8, 3 (Oct. 1935), 551–577.
SUBJ 24.3 34.2 ▪ 14.3 24.6

17054 NNC FP P3 G5.1 1911–1949
Fong, H. D. (Fang Hsien-t'ing), 1902–.
'Grain trade and milling in Tientsin.'
CSPSR 17, 3 (Oct. 1933), 367–429; 17, 4 (Jan. 1934), 553–631. [Separately reprinted—Peiping: San Yu Press, 1934. 142 p. (Nankai Institute of Economics, Industry series, 6)] [Separately reprinted—Washington, D.C.: Center for Chinese Research Materials, 1972. 142 p.]
SUBJ 24.3 24.4 26.2 34.2 ▪ 21.4 24.2 24.6 26.4 36.2 36.4 41 47

17055 CSU O P3 G9.2 1911–1928
Funkhouser, W- L-, and L. Hoh.
'Feeding chickens in Canton.'
Lingnaam agricultural review 1, 2 (June 1923), 1–6.
SUBJ 24.3

17056 CSH P P6 G2.0 1928–1949
Gol'fer, L- M-.
'Kontrakty khlebnogo rynka severnoi Man'chzhurii' (Grain-market contracts in northern Manchuria).
VM 1931, 6, 17–22.
SUBJ 24.3 ▪ 24.6

17057 NNC O P7 G5.3 1928–1949
Hsu Yung-sui (Hsü Yung-sui).
'Tobacco marketing in eastern Shantung.' Tr. of 'Lu tung yen shih'; *Shen pao chou k'an* 2, 14 (11 Apr. 1937), 300–301. In *Agrarian China*, compiled by Institute of Pacific Relations. [Selective entry]
Chicago: U. of Chicago Press, 1939, 171–175.
SUBJ 24.1 24.3 ▪ 26.3

17058 CSH P P3 G8.1 1928–1949
Hu Kwoh-hwa (Hu Kuo-hua).
'Wholesale price level in Chengtu, Jan. 1937 – Mar. 1943.'
EF 20 (May 1943), 133–142.
SUBJ 24.3 28

17059 CBU F P4 G1.3 1928–1949
Kao Chi-yu.
'War and farm prices in China.'
EF 14 (Feb. 1940), 107–116.
SUBJ 24.3 ▪ 14.3

17060 CSH P P3 G1.1 1928–1949
Lewis, Ardron B-, and Wang Lien.
'Wholesale prices in different cities in China and in Hong Kong, 1930 to 1936.'
EF 2 (Oct. 1936), 92–106. [In Chinese as well as English]
SUBJ 24.3 ▪ 24.6

17061 CBU F P3 G8.1 1928–1949
Li Teh-hsien (Li Te-hsien) and Wen Hsien-tsuin (Wen Hsien-chün).
'Wholesale prices in Chungking.'

EF 9 (Apr. 1938), 420–429; 10 (June 1937), 481–487. [In Chinese as well as English]
Subj 24.3

17062 NIC F P2 G5.1 1928–1949
Li, Y., and John Bernard Tayler, 1878–.
'Grain marketing in Hopei province: An interim report.'
CSPSR 17, 1 (Apr. 1933), 107–169.
Subj 14.3 24.3 ▪ 22 24.2 24.5 34.2 34.3

17063 CSU F P3 G8.1 1928–1949
Liao, T'ai-ch'u.
'The An Lo Szu market of Chengtu: A field study.'
B. of the Business Historical Society 21, 6 (Dec. 1947), 155–171.
Subj 24.3 26.2 34.2 ▪ 22 24.6

17064 NIC F P2 G8.1 1928–1949
Liao, T'ai-ch'u.
'The rape markets on the Chengtu plain.'
J. of farm economics 28, 4 (Nov. 1946), 1016–1024.
Subj 24.3 ▪ 24.4 32.2 34.2

17065 CSH O P7 G2.0 1911–1949
Liubimov, L- I-.
'Krizis sbyta bobov i poteri man'chzhurskogo krest'ianina' (The crisis in the bean market and losses sustained by the Manchurian peasantry).
VM 1930, 6, 1–11.
Subj 24 24.1 24.3 ▪ 26.3

17066 NNP P P7 G2.1 1911–1928
Liubimov, L- I-.
'Lesnoi rynok pri st. An'da' (The timber market at An-ta station [An-ta *hsien*, Heilungkiang]).
EB 1927, 28 (iiul'), 8–11; 1927, 29/30 (iiul'), 9–11; 1927, 31/32 (avgust), 5–8.
Subj 24.3 ▪ 24.2 24.5

17067 CSH O P7 G2.1 1911–1928
Liubimov, L- I-.
'Ocherki khlebnoi torgovli v raione zapadnoi linii KVzhd' (Notes on the grain trade in the area served by the western line of the Chinese Eastern Railway).
VM 1929, 1, 16–25; 1929, 2, 17–25.
Subj 24 24.1 24.3

17068 NNP P P2 G2.0 1911–1928
Meshcherskii, A- S-.
Polosa otchuzhdeniia Kitaiskoi Vostochnoi zheleznoi dorogi kak raspredelitel'nyi tsentr miasnykh produktov i prilegaiushchie k nei rynki zagotovok skota v Mongolii i v Man'chzhurii (The right-of-way of the Chinese Eastern Railway as a distribution center for meat products and adjacent cattle-supplying markets in Mongolia and Manchuria).
Harbin: Tip. KVzhd, 1920. 91 p. (Ministerstvo prodovol'stviia, Mongol'skaia ekspeditsiia po zagotovke miasa dlia deistvuiushchikh armii, Man'chzhursko-Vladivostokskii raion, Materialy k otchetu o deiatel'nosti s 1915 po 1918 gg., 12)
Subj 24.1 24.3 ▪ 14.3

17069 CSH F P3 G5.1 1911–1949
Nankai U. Committee on Social and Economic Research.
Wholesale prices and price index numbers in North China, 1913 to 1929, compiled by Franklin L. Ho (Ho Lien).
Tientsin: China Press, 1929. 145 p. (CSER bulletins, price series, 1)
Subj 24.3

17070 CSH F P7 G8.1 1928–1949
Pan Hong-shen (P'an Hung-sheng).
'Marketing of agricultural products in Penghsien [i.e., P'eng *hsien*], Szechwan.'
EF 26 (Nov. 1943), 295–298.
Subj 24.3

17071 CBU F P7 G8.1 1928–1949
Pan Hong-shen (P'an Hung-sheng).
'Marketing of cereal grains in Hwayang hsien, Szechwan.'
EF 39 (Dec. 1944), 597–602.
Subj 24.3 26.2 ▪ 34.1

17072 CBU F P5 G8.1 1928–1949
Pan Hong-shen (P'an Hung-sheng).
'A study of marketing of rice in seven hsien on the Chengtu plain.'
EF 15 (Apr. 1941), 147–149.
Subj 24.3 ▪ 24.2

17073 MCH S P4 G9.2 1928–1949
Panzer, Wolfgang, 1896–.
'Der südchinesische Hafen Pakhoi' (The South Chinese port of Pei-hai [Ho-p'u *hsien*, Kwangtung]).
Geographischer Anzeiger 40, 9/10 (5 Mai 1939), 214–220.
Subj 20 24 24.3

17074 CBU F P6 G6.2 1928–1949
Raeburn, John R-, and Hu Kwoh-hwa (Hu Kuo-hua).
'Prices paid and received by farmers in Suhsien [i.e., Su *hsien*], Anhwei.'
EF 7 (Oct. 1937), 290–295. [In Chinese as well as English]
Subj 24.3 24.6 ▪ 28

17075 CBU F P3 G6.1 1911–1949
Raeburn, John R-, and Hu Kwoh-hwa (Hu Kuo-hua).
'"Sauerbeck-Statist" index of prices in Shanghai.'
EF 6 (July 1937), 236–243. [In Chinese as well as English]
Subj 24.3

17076 CBU FP P4 G6.1 1911–1949
Raeburn, John R-, and Hu Kwoh-hwa (Hu Kuo-hua).
'The values of soybean oil, cotton cloth and kerosene in terms of rice.'
EF 5 (May 1937), 218–222. [In Chinese as well as English]
Subj 24 24.3

17077 CBU F P3 G6.1 1928–1949
Raeburn, John R-, Hu Kwoh-hwa (Hu Kuo-hua), and Ko Fuh-ting (Ko Fu-ting).
'Prices in Nanking.'
EF 8 (Jan. 1938), 331–336.
Subj 24.3

17078 CBU F P6 G1.3 1928–1949
Raeburn, John R-, and Ko Fuh-ting (Ko Fu-ting).
'Crop prices.'
EF 6 (July 1937), 262–272. [In Chinese as well as English]
Subj 24.3

17079 CBU FP P7 G6.1 1911–1949
Raeburn, John R-, and Ko Fuh-ting (Ko Fu-ting).
'Prices paid and received by farmers in Wuchin [*hsien*], Kiangsu.'
EF 6 (July 1937), 250–261. [In Chinese as well as English]
Subj 24 24.3 ▪ 24.1

17080 MCH U P7 G1.3 1911–1949
Shen, Chennan.
'Cooperative purchasing of fertilizers.'
China critic 3, 30 (24 July 1930), 703–706.
Subj 24.3 34.2

17081 NIC O P2 G1.2 1928–1949
Sowerby, Arthur de Carle, 1885–1964.
'Fairs in China.'
CJ 27, 2 (Aug. 1937), 96–97.
Subj 24.3

17082 CSU O P7 G8.1 1928–1949
Spencer, Joseph Earle, 1907–.
'The Szechwan village fair.'
EG 16, 1 (Jan. 1940), 48–58.
Subj 24.3 ▪ 24.2 24.5

17083 CBU F P3 G5.1 1911–1949
Tsu Chwan-hwai (Hsü Chuang-huai).
'The effect of production of cotton upon its purchasing power.'
EF 10 (June 1938), 461–474. [In Chinese as well as English]
Subj 24.3

17084 DNA F P3 G6.1 1928–1949
Tsu Chwan-hwai (Hsü Chuang-huai). [Author's name erroneously given as Tsu Chwan-hwa.]
'Retail prices in Nanking since the withdrawal of the Chinese forces.'
EF 12 (June 1939), 607–617. [In Chinese as well as English]
Subj 24.3 ▪ 55

17085 NNP O P2 G2.2 1911–1928
Vlasov, V-.
'Organizatsiia khlebnoi torgovli v Ningutinskom raione' (The organization of the grain trade in Ning-ku-t'ing [i.e., the capital of Ning-an *hsien*, Kirin] and vicinity).
EB 1928, 34 (26 avgust), 5–7.
Subj 24.3 ▪ 24.6

17086 CBU F P7 G8.1 1928–1949
Wang, Yin-yuen (Wang Yin-yüan).
'Index numbers of price and purchasing power of farm products in Szechwan.'
EF 42 (Mar. 1945), 651–652.
Subj 24.3 ▪ 24.6

17087 CSH P P3 G4.1 1928–1949
Wang, Yin-yuen (Wang Yin-yüan).
'Price margins of important raw materials and manufactured goods in Sian, Shensi.'
EF 27 (Dec. 1943), 307–313.
Subj 24.3 ▪ 24.4

17088 CBU P P3 G8.1 1928–1949
Wang, Yin-yuen (Wang Yin-yüan).
'The rate of change of wholesale prices in Chengtu.'
EF 48 (Sept. 1945), 729–732.
Subj 24.3 24.6

17089 CBU FP P2 G8.1 1928–1949
Wang, Yin-yuen.
'The rice control problem in Chengtu.'

EF 15 (Apr. 1941), 124–133.
SUBJ 14.3 24.3 ▪ 28 55

17090 CSH P P3 G8.1 1928–1949
Wang, Yin-yuen.
'A study of price margins of important raw materials and manufactured articles in Chengtu.'
EF 21 (June 1943), 153–162.
SUBJ 24.3

17091 NIC F P7 G8.1 1928–1949
Wen, Gerald Chi-loh, 1916–.
An economic study of the production and marketing of hogs and hog bristles in Yungchang [i.e., Yung-ch'ang *hsien*], *Szechwan, China.*
Unpublished masters thesis in Economics, Cornell U., 1945. 67 p.
SUBJ 24.1 24.3 ▪ 24.2 24.4

17092 NNC P P7 G1.2 1928–1949
Woo, Lillian C., 1938–.
Marketing of agricultural products in rural China during the late 1920's and early 1930's.
Unpublished masters thesis in Economics, Columbia U., 1962. 75 p. [Certificate essay, East Asian Institute]
SUBJ 14.1 24.3 ▪ 34.1

17093 HKU PO P4 G9.5 1928–1949
Wood, A- E-.
Report of the committee regarding marketing of New Territories produce in Hong Kong and Kowloon.
Hong Kong: Government Printer, 1934. 5 p. (Hong Kong Council, Sessional papers, 1)
SUBJ 14.3 24.3

17094 NIC F P6 G5.3 1911–1949
Yang, C. K. (Yang Ch'ing-k'un), 1911–.
A North China local market economy: A summary of a study of periodic markets in Chowping [i.e., Tsou-p'ing] *hsien, Shantung.*
New York: Institute of Pacific Relations, 1944. 41 p.
SUBJ 20 24.2 24.3 ▪ 22 24.4

17095 NIC O P7 G1.2 1911–1949
Yang, Martin M. C. (Yang Mou-ch'un), 1904–.
The market town and rural life in China.
Unpublished doctoral dissertation in Rural Sociology, Cornell U., 1943. 251 p.
SUBJ 22 24.2 24.3 ▪ 17 21.3 24.1 28

17096 NNC P P2 G1.3 1928–1949
Yang, William Y. (Yang Yü), 1907–.
'War-time price movement in China.'
CQ-S 6, 1 (Spring 1941), 22–40.
SUBJ 14.3 24.3 28

17097 DNA F P3 G1.5 1928–1949
Yang, William Y. (Yang Yü), 1907–, and Hu Kwoh-hwa (Hu Kuo-hua).
'Price development in China during the war.'
EF 12 (June 1939), 595–606. [In Chinese as well as English; for an expanded version in Chinese, see Yang Yü, ed., *Chan shih wu chia t'e chi* (Special compilation on wartime prices); Chungking: Chung yang yin hang, Ching chi yen chiu ch'u, 1942; 283 p.]
SUBJ 24.3 28 ▪ 55

17098 CBU F P2 G1.3 1928–1949
Yang, William Y. (Yang Yü), 1907–, and Kao Chi-yu.
'Wartime price movements in different localities in China.'
EF 14 (Feb. 1940), 61–106.
SUBJ 14.3 24.3 28 ▪ 24.6 55

17099 CBU F P6 G1.3 1928–1949
Yang, William Y. (Yang Yü), 1907–, and Lu Sheng-hwai (Lu Sheng-huai). [First author's name erroneously given as Yang Wei.]
'Crop prices.'
EF 7 (Oct. 1937), 312–316. [In Chinese as well as English]
SUBJ 14.3 24.3

17100 CBU F P6 G1.3 1928–1949
Yang, William Y. (Yang Yü), 1907–, and Lu Sheng-hwai (Lu Sheng-huai).
'Price changes in Chinese rural market towns September, 1935 to October, 1937.'
EF 9 (Apr. 1938), 378–393. [In Chinese as well as English]
SUBJ 24.3 ▪ 14.3 28

1911-1972
(including 1644-1972)

17101 CSU FP P7 G9.4 1895–1972
Crissman, Lawrence William, 1940–.
'Marketing on the Changhua plain, Taiwan.' In *Economic organization in Chinese society*, edited by William Earl Willmott. [Selective entry]
Stanford: Stanford U. Press, 1972, 215–259.
SUBJ 21.3 24.3 ▪ 21

17102 CSH FP P7 G9.5 1644–1972
Groves, Robert George, 1934–.
'The origins of two market towns in the New Territories.' In *Aspects of social organization in the New Territories*, edited by Hong Kong Branch, Royal Asiatic Society. [Selective entry]
Hong Kong: Cathay Press, 1964, 16–20.
SUBJ 24.3 42 ▪ 48

17103 PPP FP P7 G9.4 1644–1972
Knapp, Ronald Gary, 1940–.
Spatial aspects of economic and social behavior in T'ai-wan.
Ann Arbor: University Microfilms (Publ. 69-12,513), 1969. 241 p. (Doctoral dissertation in Geography, U. of Pittsburgh, 1968)
SUBJ 21.3 23 24.2 24.3 41 ▪ 21 21.2 29

1949-1972

17104 CSH O P8 G5.4 1949–1972
'A supply and marketing co-op for mountain people.'
China reconstructs 18, 12 (Dec. 1969), 23–27.
SUBJ 24.3

17105 CSH U P3 G8.1 1949–1972
Cheng Yen-shih.
'Rely on masses for rational distribution of commodities.' Tr. of 'I k'ao ch'ün chung, ho li fen p'ei shang p'in: Ch'ung-ch'ing shih ho li fen p'ei shang p'in ti ching yen' (Rely on the masses for rational distribution of commodities: Experiences in Chungking municipality); *Hung ch'i* 1960, 20/21 (1 Nov.), 36–43. In *Translations from 'Hung-ch'i' (Red flag) (Peiping, No. 20-21, 1 November 1960)*, mimeo., compiled by U.S. Joint Publications Research Service. [Sole entry]
Washington, D.C.: JPRS, 22 Dec. 1960, 46–58. (JPRS 6471; MC 2292/1961)
SUBJ 24.3 ▪ 21.4 28

17106 CSU P P3 G8.1 1949–1972
Chow Fu-lin (Chou Fu-lin).
'Refuting the fallacy that the Great Leap Forward causes market tension.' Tr. of 'Po "ta yao chin tsao ch'eng shih ch'ang chin chang" ti miu lun'; *Ssu-ch'uan ta hsüeh hsüeh pao; she hui k'o hsüeh* 1960, 5 (Jan.), 1–7. In *Marx, Malthus, and people's communes*, mimeo., compiled by U.S. Joint Publications Research Service. [Sole entry]
Washington, D.C.: JPRS, 7 Sept. 1960, 58–69. (JPRS 5394; MC 17,486/1960)
SUBJ 14.3 24.3 ▪ 14.4 28

17107 NIC P P7 G1.2 1949–1972
Donnithorne, Audrey Gladys, 1922–.
'The organization of rural trade in China since 1958.'
CQ 8 (Oct.–Dec. 1961), 77–91.
SUBJ 22 24.1 24.3 ▪ 24 24.4 34.1

17108 CSU F P7 G9.5 1949–1972
Drakakis-Smith, David William, 1942–.
'The hinterlands of towns in the New Territories.' In *Asian urbanization: A Hong Kong casebook*, edited by Denis John Dwyer. [Analytic entry]
Hong Kong: Hong Kong U. Press, 1971, 167–181. (Centre of Asian Studies series, 3)
SUBJ 24.3

17109 CSU F P7 G9.5 1949–1972
Drakakis-Smith, David William, 1942–.
'Traditional and modern aspects of urban systems in the Third World: A case study in Hong Kong.'
Pacific viewpoint 12, 1 (May 1971), 21–40.
SUBJ 24.3 ▪ 21

17110 NNC U P7 G1.2 1949–1972
Ho Chiang (Ho Cheng) and Wei Wen.
'Discussion of rural market trade.' Tr. of 'Lun nung ts'un chi shih mao i' (Rural periodic marketing); *Ching chi yen chiu* (Peking) 1962, 4 (Apr.), 11–15. In *Translations from 'Ching chi yen chiu' 4 (1962)*, mimeo., compiled by U.S. Joint Publications Research Service. [Sole entry]
Washington, D.C.: JPRS, 3 July 1962, 21–32. (JPRS 14,371; MC 15,927/1962) [A different tr.—'On rural trade fairs.' *URS* 28, 7 (24 July 1962), 117–126.]
SUBJ 24.3 ▪ 14.3 24.1 34.1 34.2 45

17111 CSH U P6 G1.2 1949–1972
Jen Ching-lü.
'Prices in trading at rural fairs and the role of the law of value.' Tr. of 'Nung ts'un chi shih mao i ti chia ko yü chia chih kuei lü ti tso yung'; *Ta kung pao* (Peking) 12 May 1961, 3.
SCMP 2508 (2 June 1961), 1–5.
SUBJ 24.3

17112 MCH P P7 G1.2 1949–1972
Jones, P- H- M-.
'Get out and sell . . .'

FEER 50, 8 (25 Nov. 1965), 371–375.
SUBJ 22 24.3

17113 MCH P P7 G1.2 1949–1972
Jones, P- H- M-.
'Produce and procure.'
FEER 50, 13 (30 Dec. 1965), 594–601.
SUBJ 24.3 24.4

17114 MCH P P7 G1.2 1949–1972
Jones, P- H- M-.
'Putting a price on it.'
FEER 53, 6 (11 Aug. 1966), 273–277.
SUBJ 24 24.3

17115 MCH P P4 G5.1 1949–1972
Jones, P- H- M-.
'The Tangshan system.'
FEER 52, 1 (1 Apr. 1966), 23–26.
SUBJ 22 24.3

17116 NIC F P8 G9.5 1949–1972
King, Frank Henry Haviland, 1926–.
'Pricing policy in a Chinese fishing village.'
JOS 1, 1 (Jan. 1954), 215–226.
SUBJ 24.3 26.2 34.2 ▪ 24.6

17117 CSU F P2 G9.4 1949–1972
Knapp, Ronald Gary, 1940–.
'Itinerant merchants in T'ai-wan.'
J. of geography 69, 6 (Sept. 1970), 344–347.
SUBJ 24.3

17118 CSU F P7 G9.4 1949–1972
Knapp, Ronald Gary, 1940–.
'Marketing and social patterns in rural Taiwan.'
AAAG 61, 1 (Mar. 1971), 131–155. [For fuller treatment, see entry 17103.]
SUBJ 23 24.3 41

17119 NIC O P7 G1.2 1949–1972
Kuan Ta-t'ung.
'On trade at rural fairs.' Tr. of 'Kuan yü nung ts'un chi shih mao i' (Rural periodic marketing); *Hung ch'i* 1961, 18 (16 Sept.), 16–22.
SCMM 282 (9 Oct. 1961), 9–17.
SUBJ 24.3 64

17120 MCH P P7 G1.2 1949–1972
[La Dany, Ladislao] ———, 1914–.
'Economic freedom of peasants.'
CNA 584 (8 Oct. 1965), 1–7.
SUBJ 24.3 26.3 ▪ 28

17121 MCH P P2 G1.2 1949–1972
[La Dany, Ladislao] ———, 1914–.
'Vicissitudes of state commerce.'
CNA 88 (17 June 1955), 1–7.
SUBJ 14.3 24.3

17122 NNC O P7 G5.1 1949–1972
Li Lien-hsin and Wang Hsi-chih.
'Management methods for the commune trade market at Ho-chien hsien are good.' Tr. of 'Tsu chih sheng ch'an, k'uo ta chiao liu, yu li kuo chia, fang pien ch'ün chung: Ho-chien hsien kuan li kung she mao i shih ch'ang pan fa hao' (Benefit our country and the masses by organizing production and expanding commodity circulation: Good methods of managing commune trade markets in Ho-chien *hsien* [Hopei]); *Ho-pei jih pao* 10 Sept. 1959, 2. In *People's communes in Communist China*, mimeo., compiled by U.S. Joint Publications Research Service. [Sole entry]
Washington, D.C.: JPRS, 10 July 1960, 55–58. (JPRS 2983; MC 14,191/1960)
SUBJ 24.3 34.2 ▪ 24.1 32.1

17123 CSH O P3 G5.1 1949–1972
Ma Hsiu-chung.
'The Kuangfutao store in Tientsin makes steady advance.' Tr. of 'Pu tuan ch'ien chin ti T'ien-chin kuang fu tao shang tien' (The continuing progress of the Kuang-fu-tao Department Store in Tientsin); *Hung ch'i* 1960, 14 (16 July), 27–34.
SCMM 222 (15 Aug. 1960), 27–36.
SUBJ 24.3 ▪ 24.4 34.2

17124 MCH O P2 G9.5 1949–1972
Preston, Lee E-.
'The search for marketing opportunities.'
Hong Kong manager 3, 3 (May–June 1967), 12–16.
SUBJ 24.3 24.6 ▪ 21.4

17125 DLC O P3 G6.1 1949–1972
Selivankin, S- A-.
'Kitaiskie univermagi' (Chinese department stores).
Novosti torgovoi tekhniki 1958, 2, 38–47.
SUBJ 24.3 ▪ 34.2

17126 CSU F P3 G9.5 1949–1972
Silin, Robert Henry, 1940–.
'Marketing and credit in a Hong Kong wholesale market.' In *Economic organization in Chinese society*, edited by William Earl Willmott. [Selective entry]
Stanford: Stanford U. Press, 1972, 327–352.
SUBJ 24.3 34.2 ▪ 24.6 48

17127 CSU P P2 G9.4 1949–1972
Singh, Mohinder.
Co-operatives in Asia.
New York: Praeger, 1970. 17, 489 p.
SUBJ 24.3 24.6 36.3 ▪ 12.2 34.1 34.2

17128 TPU F P7 G9.4 1949–1972
Taiwan. Nung lin t'ing. (Dept. of Agriculture and Forestry), ed.
Report on survey of livestock, fruit and vegetable market in Taiwan, 1965.
Nan-t'ou, Taiwan: Nung lin t'ing, 1965. 247 p. [In Chinese as well as English]
SUBJ 24.1 24.3

17129 MCH P P6 G1.2 1949–1972
Tsung Han.
'Several economic problems concerning market towns.' Tr. of 'Kuan yü chi chen ti chi ko ching chi wen t'i' (Some economic problems of market towns); *Kuang ming jih pao* (Peking) 19 Oct. 1964, 4.
Translations on Communist China's management, trade and finance 18 (16 Nov. 1964), 1–15. (JPRS 27,388; MC 1019/1965)
SUBJ 24.3 ▪ 21.3 21.4 24.4 24.6

17130 MCH PO P7 G1.2 1949–1972
Vidal, Jean-Emile.
'Réorganisation des marchés ruraux en Chine' (The reorganization of rural markets in China).
Economie et politique 87 (oct. 1961), 51–65.
SUBJ 22 24.1 24.3 34.1 ▪ 21.4 22.1 28 32

17131 NNC U P7 G1.2 1949–1972
Yen Ch'iu.
'On the question of establishing supply and marketing department in agricultural co-op.' Tr. of 'Tui nung yeh she chien li kung hsiao pu wen t'i ti shang ch'üeh' (A discussion of the issue of establishing supply-and-marketing departments in agricultural producers' cooperatives); *Ta kung pao* (Peking) 27 Apr. 1958, 1.
URS 11, 18 (30 May 1958), 257–263.
SUBJ 24.3 ▪ 34.1 34.2

24.4 LOCAL INDUSTRY
地方工業　地方工業

1644-1911

17132 CSU U P3 G7.1 1842–1911
'Hankow.' In *Twentieth century impressions of Hongkong, Shanghai, and other treaty ports of China: Their history, people, commerce, industries and manners*, edited by Arnold Wright and H- A- Cartwright. [Selective entry]
London: Lloyd's Greater Britain Publishing Co., 1908, 692–723.
SUBJ 24.4 ▪ 24.6 34.2

17133 CSU U P2 G9.5 1842–1911
'Hongkong industries.' In *Twentieth century impressions of Hongkong, Shanghai, and other treaty ports of China: Their history, people, commerce, industries and manners*, edited by Arnold Wright and H- A- Cartwright. [Selective entry]
London: Lloyd's Greater Britain Publishing Co., 1908, 235–249.
SUBJ 24.4 34.2

17134 CSU U P2 G6.1 1895–1911
'Industries.' In *Twentieth century impressions of Hongkong, Shanghai, and other treaty ports of China: Their history, people, commerce, industries and manners*, edited by Arnold Wright and H- A- Cartwright. [Selective entry]
London: Lloyd's Greater Britain Publishing Co., 1908, 573–598.
SUBJ 24.4

17135 MCH P P1 G1.2 1895–1911
'Note sur la fabrication et sur le commerce des briquettes et des tablettes de thé en Chine' (A note on the manufacture and sale of tea in bricks and bars in China).
BEI 12, 76 (jan.–fév. 1909), 29–44.
SUBJ 14.3 24.4

17136 MBA P P2 G9.2 1895–1911
'Note sur la soie sauvage dans l'île de Hai-nan' (A note on raw silk in Hainan).
RI nouvelle (2e) série 9, 83 (15 juin 1908), 808–812.
SUBJ 24.4

17137 CSU PO P2 G8.0 1895–1911
Antoine, R-, and C- Métral.
'Rapport sur la soie' (Report on silk). In *La Mission lyonnaise d'exploration commerciale en Chine, 1895–1897, deuxième partie, rapports commerciaux et notes diverses* (The Lyons Trade Mission to China, 1895–1897, Part 2,

Commercial reports and miscellaneous notes), compiled by Chambre de commerce de Lyon. [Selective entry]
Lyons: Rey, 1898, 315–347 [s.p.].
Subj 24.1 24.4 ▪ 14.2 14.3 24.3 34.3 65

17138 CSU O P2 G1.5 1895–1911
Brenier, Henri, 1867–?
'De Tchoung-king à Han-k'éou: sur la rivière Yuen et le lac Toung-ting et descente du Yang-tsé' (From Chungking to Hankow: On the Yüan river and Tung-t'ing lake and down the Yangtze). In *La Mission lyonnaise d'exploration commerciale en Chine, 1895–1897, première partie, récits des voyages* (The Lyons Trade Mission to China, 1895–1897, Part 1, Travel accounts), compiled by Chambre de commerce de Lyon. [Selective entry]
Lyons: Rey, 1898, 271–290 [s.p.].
Subj 21.3 24.4 ▪ 55 66

17139 CSU O P2 G8.1 1895–1911
Brenier, Henri, 1867–?
'Le ralliement: retour à Tchoung-king, par Tse-liou-tsin et préparatifs de départ' (The reunion: Return to Chungking via Tzu-liu-ching [Fu-shun *hsien*, Szechwan] and preparations for departure). In *La Mission lyonnaise d'exploration commerciale en Chine, 1895–1897, première partie, récits des voyages* (The Lyons Trade Mission to China, 1895–1897, Part 1, Travel accounts), compiled by Chambre de commerce de Lyon. [Selective entry]
Lyons: Rey, 1898, 217–228 [s.p.].
Subj 24.4 ▪ 22.1 66

17140 MCH PO P2 G1.2 1644–1842
Breton de la Martinière, Jean Baptiste Joseph, ed.
La Chine en miniature: ou, choix de costumes, arts et métiers de cet empire (China in miniature: or, A selection of costumes, arts, and crafts of that empire).
Paris: Nepveu, 1811–1812. 6 vols.
China: Its costumes, arts, manufactures, etc., 3rd ed.
London: Howlett and Brimmer, 1824. 4 vols.
Subj 24.3 24.4 55 ▪ 12 17 24.2

17141 ELE P P5 G5.1 1842–1911
Carlson, Ellsworth Clayton, 1917–.
The Kaiping mines [Luan *hsien*, Hopei], *1877–1912: A case study of early Chinese industrialization*, 2nd ed.
Cambridge: Harvard U., East Asian Research Center, 1971. 235 p. (Harvard East Asian monographs, 3) (Revision of doctoral dissertation in Economics, Harvard U., 1952)
Subj 14.3 24.4 26.2 34.2 ▪ 24.2 26.4 28

17142 MCH O P3 G1.1 1842–1895
Castonnet des Fosses, Henri, 1846–1898.
'La Chine industrielle et commerciale' (Industry and commerce in China).
B. de la Société de géographie de Lyon 7 (1888), 331–365.
Subj 14.3 24.4 55 60 ▪ 66

17143 NNC P P3 G1.3 1842–1895
Chen, Gideon (Ch'en Ch'i-t'ien), 1893–.
Tso Tsung-t'ang, pioneer promoter of the modern dockyard and the woolen mill in China.
Peiping: Yenching U., [Dept. of Economics], 1938. 93 p. [Reprinted—New York: Paragon, 1961. 93 p.]
Subj 15 24.4 26.1 ▪ 17 24.2 26.4 34.2 59

17144 CSU P P2 G1.3 –1842
Dietrich, Craig, 1937–.
'Cotton culture and manufacture in early Ch'ing China.' In *Economic organization in Chinese society*, edited by William Earl Willmott. [Selective entry]
Stanford: Stanford U. Press, 1972, 109–135.
Subj 24.4 ▪ 14.1 14.3 24.3 26.2 34.2

17145 ICU P P2 G1.3 –1842
Dietrich, Craig, 1937–.
Cotton manufacture and trade in China, ca. 1500–1800.
Unpublished doctoral dissertation in Far Eastern Languages and Civilizations, U. of Chicago, 1970. 266 p.
Subj 11.3 14.3 24.4 ▪ 14.1 16.2 34.2 47

17146 CSU PO P7 G8.0 1895–1911
Duclos, P-.
'Rapport sur les mines et la metallurgie' (Report on mines and metallurgy). In *La Mission lyonnaise d'exploration commerciale en Chine, 1895–1897, deuxième partie, rapports commerciaux et notes diverses* (The Lyons Trade Mission to China, 1895–1897, Part 2, Commercial reports and miscellaneous notes), compiled by Chambre de commerce de Lyon. [Selective entry]
Lyons: Rey, 1898, 283–314 [s.p.].
Subj 24.4 ▪ 14.3 24.5 34.2

17147 CSU P P2 G1.2 –1895
Elvin, John Mark Dutton, 1938–.
'The high-level equilibrium trap: The causes of the decline of invention in the traditional Chinese textile industries.' In *Economic organization in Chinese society*, edited by William Earl Willmott. [Selective entry]
Stanford: Stanford U. Press, 1972, 137–172.
Subj 16 24.4 ▪ 16.2 24.3 34.2

17148 CBU PO P2 G5.3 –1895
Fauvel, Albert Auguste, 1851–1909.
'La province chinoise du Chan-toung: géographie et histoire naturelle' (The geography and natural history of Shantung).
R. des questions scientifiques 27 (20 jan. 1890), 169–208; 28 (20 juil. 1890), 123–151; 28 (20 oct. 1890), 517–576; 29 (avr. 1891), 463–512; 30 (juil. 1891), 162–193. [Reprinted in *La province chinoise du Chan-toung* (Shantung), by A. A. Fauvel. (Selective entry.) Brussels: Impr. Polleunis et Auterich, 1892.]
Subj 21.3 24.2 24.4 ▪ 56

17149 CSU P P2 G1.2 1842–1911
Feuerwerker, Albert, 1927–.
'Handicraft and manufactured cotton textiles in China, 1871–1910.'
J. of economic history 30, 2 (June 1970), 338–378.
Subj 14.4 24.4 ▪ 14.1 14.3

17150 NIC F P4 G1.5 1895–1911
Gennep, Arnold van, 1873–?
'Note sur le tissage aux cartons en China' (A note on board-weaving in China).
TP 2e série 13, 4 (1912), 693–698.
Subj 24.4

17151 CBU O P3 G9.3 1842–1895
Giquel, Prosper.
L'Arsenal de Fou-Tcheou, ses résultats.
Shanghai: A. H. de Carvalho, 1874. 53 p.
The Foochow Arsenal, and its results, from the commencement in 1867, to the end of the foreign directorate, on the 16th February, 1874. Tr. by H. Lang.
Shanghai: Shanghai Evening Courier, 1874. 38 p.
Subj 14.4 24.4 34.2 ▪ 12 17 66

17152 CSU PO P2 G1.2 1895–1911
Grosjean, A-.
'Rapport sur les corps gras et leurs dérivés' (Report on natural sources of oil and their derivatives). In *La Mission lyonnaise d'exploration commerciale en Chine, 1895–1897, deuxième partie, rapports commerciaux et notes diverses* (The Lyons Trade Mission to China, 1895–1897, Part 2, Commercial reports and miscellaneous notes), compiled by Chambre de commerce de Lyon. [Selective entry]
Lyons: Rey, 1898, 375–398 [s.p.].
Subj 14.4 24.4 ▪ 24.3

17153 NNC PO P2 G1.3 –1895
Hague, F-.
'On the natural and artificial production of pearls in China.'
JRAS 16 (1856), 280–284.
Subj 24.1 24.4 ▪ 62 65

17154 CSU O P5 G9.2 1842–1895
Hirth, Friedrich, 1845–1927.
'The manufacture of Canton matting.'
China review 1, 4 (Jan.–Feb. 1873), 254–256.
Subj 24.4

17155 CSH FP P3 G6.1 1842–1911
Hsieh Shang.
'A case study in modern Chinese economic history.' Tr. of 'Kuan yü Chung-kuo chin tai ching chi shih chung i ko ts'ai liao ti tiao ch'a: Kuang-hsü chiu nien shang jen Chu Ta-ch'un shih fou tsai Shang-hai ch'uang pan liao "Yüan-ch'ang chi ch'i wu chin ch'ang"' (A study of materials relating to modern Chinese economic history: Did the merchant Chu Ta-ch'un establish the Yüan-ch'ang Machinery Factory in Shanghai in 1883?); *Hung ch'i* 1961, 11 (1 June), 27–30. In *Translations from 'Hung-ch'i' (Red flag) (Peiping, No. 11, 1 June 1961)*, mimeo., compiled by U.S. Joint Publications Research Service. [Sole entry]
Washington, D.C.: JPRS, 29 Sept. 1961, 40–46. (JPRS 8960; MC 19,615/1961)
Subj 24.4 ▪ 26.2

17156 MCH PO P7 G9.2 1895–1911
Imbault-Huart, Camille Clément, 1857–1897.
'Essai sur les gisements minéraux et l'industrie minière de la province du Kouang-toung' (Mineral deposits and mining in Kwangtung).
B. de la Société de géographie commerciale de Paris 19 (1897), 459–476.
Subj 24.4 ▪ 24.1

17157 NNC P P5 G1.2 1842–1911
Iovchuk, S- M-.
'Razvitie kapitalizma v dofabrichnoi promyshlennosti Kitaia nakanune Sin'khaiskoi revoliutsii' (The development of capitalism in Chinese pre-factory industry on the eve of the Revolution of 1911). In *Sin'khaiskaia revoliutsiia v Kitae: sbornik statei* (Articles on the Revolution of 1911 in China), compiled by Institut narodov Azii, Akademiia nauk SSSR. [Selective entry]
Moscow: Izd-vo vost. lit-ry, 1962, 51–90.
Subj 24.4 ▪ 34.2

17158 FPN O P3 G5.1 1842–1895
Jametel, Maurice Louis Marie, 1856–1889.
Emailleurs pékinois (Enamelware craftsmen in Peking).
Geneva: Carey, 1886. 26 p.
Subj 24.3 24.4 26.2 ▪ 21.4 24.2 28 44 54

17159 MCH O P2 G8.2 1895–1911
Jonery, J-.
'Notes sur Ko-Kieou et la région des mines, province chinoise de Yunnan' (Notes on Ko-chiu *t'ing* and the mining area of Yunnan).
B. de la Société de géographie de Lyon 22 (1907), 187–195.
Subj 24.4 ▪ 24.1 24.2

17160 FPN P P2 G1.2 –1842
Julien, Stanislaus, 1797–1873, and Paul Champion.
Industries anciennes et modernes de l'empire chinois (Ancient and modern industries of the Chinese empire).
Paris: Lacroix, 1869. 254 p.
Subj 14.1 14.4 24.4 ▪ 16.2 16.4 18 55 56

17161 MAM P P3 G6.1 1842–1895
Kennedy, Thomas Larew, 1930–.
The establishment and development of the Kiangnan Arsenal, 1860 to 1895.
Ann Arbor: University Microfilms (Publ. 69-9199), 1969. 277 p. (Doctoral dissertation in East Asian Languages and Cultures, Columbia U., 1968)
Subj 14.4 15 24.4 ▪ 12 24 24.2 66

17162 CSH P P3 G6.1 1895–1911
Kennedy, Thomas Larew, 1930–.
'The Kiangnan Arsenal, 1895–1911: The decentralized bureaucracy responds to imperialism.'
CSWT 2, 1 (Oct. 1969), 17–37.
Subj 12 14.4 24.4 34.2 ▪ 15 16.1 22.2

17163 CSU O P8 G8.1 1644–1895
Li Jung.
'An account of the salt industry at Tzu-liu-ching (Szechuan): "Tzu-liu-ching chi", by Li Jung', edited by Lien-che Tu Fang. Tr. by Lien-che Tu Fang of 'Tzu-liu-ching chi' (An account of Tzu-liu-ching [Fu-shun *hsien*, Szechwan]); in *Shih san feng shu wu ch'üan chi: Wen kao* (Complete works of Li Jung: Essays); n.p., 1890, *chüan* ?, 1a–5a.
Isis 39, 118 (Nov. 1948), 228–234.
Subj 24.4 ▪ 34.2

17164 NNC P P3 G9.2 1895–1911
McWade, Robert W-.
'Chinese boots and shoes.'
JAAA 4, 10 (Nov. 1904), 311–312.
Subj 24.4 ▪ 34.2

17165 FPN PO P2 G1.1 –1895
Martin, Charles Ernest, 1831–1897.
'La houille et le chauffage chez les Chinois' (Coal and heating among the Chinese).
J. d'hygiène 16, 753 (26 fév. 1891), 97–102.
Subj 24.4 55 ▪ 28

17166 CBU O P3 G5.1 1895–1911
Matignon, Jean-Jacques, 1866–?
'L'art industriel en Chine: les émaux cloisonnés' (Industrial art in China: Cloisonée). In *Dix ans aux pays du dragon* (Ten years in the lands of the dragon), by J.-J. Matignon. [Selective entry]
Paris: Maloine, 1910, 273–280.
Subj 24.4

17167 CSU P P3 G1.5 1842–1895
Morrell, James, 1944–.
'Two early Chinese cotton mills [the Shanghai cotton cloth mill and the Hupeh cotton mill].'
PC 21 (Feb. 1968), 43–98.
Subj 14.4 24.4 34.2 ▪ 14.6 16.1 24.3 26.2

17168 IMC O P3 G6.1 1895–1911
Nocentini, Lodovico, 1849–1910.
'La città di Succiu e la sua industria serica' (Soochow and its silk industry).
Esplorazione commerciale 13 (1898), 144–155.
Subj 24.4

17169 FPN O P2 G9.4 1842–1895
Raoul, Edouard François Armand, 1845–1898.
Les gages nécessaires (Yun-nan, estuaire du Yang-tse, Hainan, Formose): Première partie, Formose (Necessary pledges: Yunnan, the lower Yangtze, Hainan, and Taiwan. Part 1, Taiwan).
Brest: Gadreau, 1885. 101 p.
Subj 21.3 24.1 24.4 29 56 ▪ 21.1 24.2

17170 CBU O P3 G7.3 1842–1895
Scherzer, Fernand, 1849–1886.
'Fabrication de la porcelaine chinoise' (The manufacture of Chinese porcelain).
BAAFC 6, 4 (oct. 1914), 237–241.
Subj 24.4 ▪ 22 28

17171 CSU P P3 G5.1 1644–1842
Schierlitz, Ernst, 1902–1940.
'Zur Technik der Holztypendrucke aus dem Wu-Ying-Tien in Peking' (The technique of wooden-type printing in Wu-ying imperial hall, Peking).
MS 1, 1 (1935), 17–38.
Subj 24.4

17172 GMS S P3 G7.3 1644–1842
Staehelin, Walter August.
Das Buch vom Porzellan: Herstellung, Transport und Handel von Exportporzellan während des 18. Jahrhunderts, erläutert anhand einer zeitgenössischen Folge chinesischer Aquarelle (The book of porcelain: The manufacture, transport, and marketing of export porcelain in the eighteenth century, illustrated with a contemporary series of Chinese watercolors).
Bern: Benteli, 1965. 88 p.
The book of porcelain: The manufacture, transport, and sale of export porcelain in China during the eighteenth century. Tr. by Michael Bullock.
London: Lund, Humphries, 1966. 87 p.
Subj 24.4 ▪ 14.3 24.2 24.3

17173 DLC P P2 G1.3 –1842
Stuzhina, Emiliia Pavlovna, 1931–.
Kitaiskoe remeslo v XVI–XVIII vekakh (Chinese handicrafts from the sixteenth through the eighteenth centuries).
Moscow: Nauka, Glav. red. vost. lit-ry, 1970. 264 p.
Subj 24.3 24.4 26.2 32.1 39 72 ▪ 14.4 24.1 26.4 34.2 34.3

17174 NNC P P2 G1.2 –1842
Stuzhina, Emiliia Pavlovna, 1931–.
'Tkatskoe proizvodstvo v Kitae so vtoroi poloviny XVI po pervuiu polovinu XVIII veka' (Textile production in China from the second half of the sixteenth century to the first half of the eighteenth century). In *O genezise kapitalizma v stranakh Vostoka, XV–XIX vv.* (The origin of capitalism in the Orient from the fifteenth through the nineteenth centuries), compiled by Institut narodov Azii, Akademiia nauk SSSR, edited by S- D- Skazkin et al. [Selective entry]
Moscow: Izd-vo vost. lit-ry, 1962, 76–97.
Subj 24.4 ▪ 16.4 34.2

17175 CSU P P2 G1.3 1644–1911
Sun, E-tu Zen (Sun Jen I-tu), 1921–.
'Sericulture and silk textile production in Ch'ing China.' In *Economic organization in Chinese society*, edited by William Earl Willmott. [Selective entry]
Stanford: Stanford U. Press, 1972, 79–108.
Subj 24.4 ▪ 24.1 24.3 26.2 34.2 55

17176 CSU PO P2 G6.3 1895–1911
Tsur, Nyok-Ching (Chou I-Ch'ing), 1883–.
Die gewerblichen Betriebsformen der Stadt Ningpo (Industry in Ningpo).
Tübingen: Verlag der H. Laupp'schen Buchhandlungen, 1909. 113 p. (Z. für die gesamte Staatswissenschaft, Ergänzungsheft, 30) (Doctoral dissertation, Philosophische Fakultät, Universität Leipzig)
Subj 21.4 24.4 26.2 26.4 34.2 34.3 ▪ 22 24 24.3 41 55

17177 CSU O P8 G1.5 1842–1911
Wade, H- T-.
'Tea.' In *Twentieth century impressions of Hongkong, Shanghai, and other treaty ports of China: Their history, people, commerce, industries and manners*, edited by Arnold Wright and H- A- Cartwright. [Selective entry]
London: Lloyd's Greater Britain Publishing Co., 1908, 294–301.
Subj 24.4

17178 NNC O P8 G8.1 1895–1911
Weiss, Fritz.
'Die Goldlagerstätten von Wali und Tsai Tse Ti im Chienchangtal' (The gold deposits at Wa-li and Ts'ai-tzu-ti in the Ch'ien-ch'ang valley [Yen-yüan *hsien*, Szechwan]).
Petermanns Mitteilungen 64, 11/12 (Nov.–Dez. 1918), 255–260.
Subj 24.4 ▪ 22 26.4

17179 CSH O P2 G1.5 1842–1895
Williams, Samuel Wells, 1812–1884.
'Industrial arts of the Chinese.' In *The Middle Kingdom: A survey of the geography, government, literature, social life, arts, and history of the Chinese empire and its inhabitants*, rev. and enl. ed., by S. W. Williams. [Selective entry]
New York: Scribner, 1883, vol. 2, 1–64. [Reprinted in *The Middle Kingdom: A survey of the geography, government, literature, social life, arts, and history of the Chinese empire and its inhabitants*, by S. W. Williams. (Selective entry.) Taipei: Ch'eng-wen, 1965, 1–64 (s.p.)]
Subj 14.1 14.4 24.4

17180 CSU O P8 G5.3 1842–1895
[Williams, Samuel Wells?] S. W. W., 1812–1884.
'Tenure of mines.'
NQCJ 2, 7 (July 1868), 97–99.
Subj 24.4

1644-1949

17181 CSU U P2 G5.3 1895–1949
'The salt industry in Tsingtao.'
CEJ 17, 3 (Sept. 1935), 275–290.
Subj 14.3 24.4 ▪ 24.5

17182 NNC PO P7 G8.2 1895–1928
Bel'chenko, A- T-.
'Donesenie imperatorskago rossiiskago konsula v Kantone: svedeniia ob oloviannykh rudnikakh v mestnosti Getsziu' (Report of the imperial Russian consul in Canton: Information on the tin mines in the Ko-chiu area [Yunnan]).
DIRKP 40 (1914), 101–111.
Subj 14.3 24.2 24.4

17183 NIC P P2 G6.1 1842–1928
Chu, Samuel C. (Chu Ch'ang-ling), 1929–.
'Chang Chien and the founding of Dah Sun [Ta-sheng Cotton Mill, Nan-t'ung, Kiangsu].'
THJ new (2nd) series 2, 1 (May 1960), 301–316.
Subj 24.4 ▪ 24.6

17184 MCM FP P3 G5.1 1842–1949
Fong, H. D. (Fang Hsien-t'ing), 1902–.
Hosiery knitting in Tientsin.
Tientsin: Chihli Press, 1930. 76 p. (Nankai U., Committee on Social and Economic Research industry series, 3) [Reprinted—Washington, D.C.: Center for Chinese Research Materials, 1972. 76 p.]
Subj 24.4 ▪ 24.3 24.5 26.4 36.4

17185 MCH FP P3 G5.1 1842–1949
Fong, H. D. (Fang Hsien-t'ing), 1902–.
Rayon and cotton weaving in Tientsin.
Tientsin: Chihli Press, 1930. 79 p. (Nankai U., Committee on Social and Economic Research industry series, 2) [Reprinted—Washington, D.C.: Center for Chinese Research Materials, 1972. 79 p.]
Subj 24.4 ▪ 24.3 24.5 26.4 36.4

17186 NNC FP P2 G5.1 1895–1949
Fong, H. D. (Fang Hsien-t'ing), 1902–.
'Rural weaving and the merchant-employers in a North China district [comprised of An-hsin *hsien*, Ch'ing-yüan *hsien*, Jen-ch'iu *hsien*, Kao-yang *hsien*, and Li *hsien*, Hopei].'
NSEQ 8, 1 (Apr. 1935), 75–120; 8, 2 (July 1935), 274–308. [Separately reprinted—Tientsin: Chihli Press, 1935. 80 p. (Nankai Institute of Economics, Industry series, 7)] [Separately reprinted—Washington, D.C.: Center for Chinese Research Materials, 1972. 80 p.]
Subj 24.3 24.4 24.6 26.2 34.2 ▪ 24.2

17187 NIC FP P7 G5.1 1895–1949
Fong, H. D. (Fang Hsien-t'ing), 1902–, and H. H. Pi (Pi Hsiang-hui).
'The growth and decline of rural industrial enterprise in North China: A case study of the cotton handloom weaving industry in Paoti [i.e., Pao-ti *hsien*, Hopei].'
NSEQ 8, 4 (Jan. 1936), 691–772. [Separately reprinted as *The growth and decline of rural industrial enterprise in North China*. Tientsin: Chihli Press, 1936. 83 p. (Nankai Institute of Economics, Industry series, 8)] [Separately reprinted—Washington, D.C.: Center for Chinese Research Materials, 1972. 83 p.]
Subj 24.3 24.4 34.2 ▪ 21.4 26.2 26.4

17188 CSU O P8 G9.5 1842–1949
Gibbs, L-.
'Kowloon water works: Early history.'
Hong Kong naturalist 2, 1 (Feb. 1931), 65–68.
Subj 24.4

17189 CSU O P2 G1.5 1895–1928
Hayes, James William, 1930–.
'Itinerant Hakka weavers.'
JRAS-HKB 8 (1968), 162–167.
Subj 24.1 24.4 29

17190 MAM PO P5 G1.2 1895–1949
Herman, Theodore, 1913–.
An analysis of China's export handicraft industries to 1930.
Ann Arbor: University Microfilms (Publ. 8348), 1954. 281 p. (Doctoral dissertation in Geography, U. of Washington)
Subj 14.3 24.4 34.2 ▪ 14 16 16.2 34.3 36.4 39

17191 NIC F P2 G9.2 1895–1928
Howard, Charles Walter, 1882–1928, and K- P- Buswell.
A survey of the silk industry of South China.
Hong Kong: Commercial Press, 1925. 208 p. (Lingnan U. agricultural bulletins, 12)
Subj 24.3 24.4 34.2 ▪ 14.3 21.1 24.1 28 42

17192 NNC U P2 G1.2 1895–1949
Lee Tse-tsian (Li Tse-ts'an).
'The decline of Chinese handicrafts.' Tr. from *Chung-shan wen hua chiao yü kuan chi k'an* 4, 3 (Autumn 1937). In *Agrarian China*, compiled by Institute of Pacific Relations. [Selective entry]
Chicago: U. of Chicago Press, 1939, 224–229.
Subj 24.4 34.2 ▪ 24.6 28

17193 NNC FP P3 G6.1 1842–1949
Lieu, D. K. (Liu Ta-chün), 1891–1962.
The growth and industrialization of Shanghai.
Shanghai: China Institute of Pacific Relations, 1936. 473 p.
Subj 24.4 26.4 28 34.2 ▪ 22.2 24 36.4 41 46 47

17194 CSU PO P7 G8.2 1644–1928
Ting, V. K. (Ting Wen-chiang), 1887–1936.
'Tungchwanfu [i.e., Tung-ch'uan *fu*], Yunnan, copper mines.'
Far Eastern review 12, 6 (Nov. 1915), 207–211.
Subj 24.4

1911-1949

17195 CSU P P3 G6.1 1928–1949
'Acid and soda manufacture.'
CEJ 12, 4 (Apr. 1933), 386–393.
Subj 24.4

17196 CSU P P3 G6.1 1928–1949
'Cigar manufacture in Shanghai.'
CEJ 12, 6 (June 1933), 626–634.
Subj 24.4

17197 CSH U P3 G5.1 1911–1928
'Cotton mills and raw cotton supply in Tientsin.'
CEM 1, 7 (Apr. 1924), 1–6.
Subj 14.3 24.4

17198 NIC U P5 G1.3 1928–1949
'Domestic [i.e., cottage] industry in China.'
PT new (2nd) series 4, 12 (16 July 1933), 685–689.
Subj 24.4

17199 CSH P P3 G5.1 1911–1928
'Factories in Peking.'
CEM 2, 7 (Apr. 1925), 24–32.
Subj 24.4 ▪ 26.4 34.2

17200 NNC P P3 G5.1 1911–1949
'Financial statements of cotton mills in Tientsin, 1919–1929.'
NWSS 5, 33 (15 Aug. 1932), 149, 151–154.
Subj 24.4 ▪ 34.2

17201 CSU U P4 G5.3 1911–1949
'Flour-milling industry in Shantung.'
CEJ 15, 3 (Sept. 1934), 328–337.
Subj 24.4

17202 NNC P P4 G5.1 1911–1928
'Home industries in Hopei, 1928.'
NWSS 6, 22 (29 May 1933), 105, 107–111.
Subj 24.4

17203 MCH O P4 G7.3 1911–1928
'Industrial Nantungchow [Nan-t'ung *hsien*, Kiangsi].'
CEM 3, 11 (Nov. 1926), 501–507.
Subj 24.4 ▪ 28 34.2 55

17204 CSU U P3 G5.1 1911–1949
'Industries in Tientsin.'
CEJ 18, 2 (Feb. 1936), 216–225.
Subj 24.4

17205 CSU U P3 G7.1 1928–1949
'Industries of Hankow.'
CEJ 19, 2 (Aug. 1936), 124–143.
Subj 24.4 ▪ 26.4

17206 CSU O P2 G7.2 1911–1949
'The manufacture of firecrackers at Liuyang [*hsien*], Hunan.'

CEJ 5, 4 (Oct. 1929), 837–841.
Subj 24.4 ▪ 14.3

17207 NNC P P4 G6.3 1928–1949
'Native paper mills in Chekiang, 1929.'
NWSS 6, 11 (13 Mar. 1933), 51, 53–55.
Subj 24.4 ▪ 21.4 28

17208 CSU O P2 G6.3 1911–1949
'Production of white alum in Pingyang [P'ing-yang *hsien*, Chekiang].'
CEJ 10, 5 (May 1932), 434–439.
Subj 24.4 ▪ 14.3 24.2

17209 CSU O P2 G9.3 1928–1949
'Salt production in Fukien.'
CEJ 18, 5 (May 1936), 726–731.
Subj 24.4 ▪ 24.3 24.5

17210 CSH U P7 G8.1 1911–1928
'The salt wells of Szechwan.'
CEM 3, 12 (Dec. 1926), 519–526.
Subj 24.4

17211 CSU U P2 G8.1 1928–1949
'Sericulture in Szechuan.'
CEJ 15, 5 (Nov. 1934), 539–546.
Subj 24.1 24.4 ▪ 16.4

17212 CSU O P2 G6.1 1928–1949
'Shanghai seal makers and carvers.'
CEJ 5, 1 (July 1929), 636–642.
Subj 14.3 24.3 24.4

17213 NNC P P2 G6.0 1911–1928
'Shanghai silk filatures.'
CEJ 3, 1 (July 1928), 590–604.
Subj 24.4 34.2 ▪ 14.3 24.1 26.4 47

17214 CSU O P4 G6.3 1928–1949
'Shaohsing [Chekiang] brewing industry.'
CEJ 18, 6 (June 1936), 878–883.
Subj 24.4 ▪ 24.5

17215 NNC P P3 G5.1 1911–1928
'Statistics on factory industries in Tientsin, 1928.'
NWSS 3, 17 (28 Apr. 1930), 81, 85–86.
Subj 24.4 ▪ 26.4

17216 NNC P P3 G6.3 1911–1928
'Statistics on industries in Hangchow, 1928.'
NWSS 3, 23 (9 June 1930), 111, 114.
Subj 24.4 ▪ 26.4

17217 NNC P P3 G6.1 1911–1928
'Statistics on Shanghai industries, 1928.'
NWSS 3, 29 (21 July 1930), 139, 142–144.
Subj 24.4 ▪ 26.4

17218 NNC P P3 G5.1 1911–1928
'Statistics on Tientsin textile industries, 1928.'
NWSS 3, 42 (20 Oct. 1930), 201, 204.
Subj 24.4 ▪ 26.4

17219 NNC P P3 G6.1 1928–1949
'Statistics on Wusih industries, 1929.'
NWSS 3, 50 (15 Dec. 1930), 237, 240–242.
Subj 24.4 ▪ 26.4

17220 CSU U P2 G6.3 1928–1949
'Straw hat industry in Chekiang.'
CEJ 10, 2 (Feb. 1932), 141–146.
Subj 24.4 ▪ 14.3 26.4

17221 CSH U P2 G5.1 1911–1928
'Tangshan, an industrial town on Peking-Mukden railway.'
CEJ 1, 10 (Oct. 1927), 884–893.
Subj 24.3 24.4 ▪ 14.3 21.1 24.6 26.4 28

17222 CSU O P3 G6.1 1911–1949
'Tea baking and processing in Shanghai.'
CEJ 12, 3 (Mar. 1933), 258–264.
Subj 24.4 ▪ 14.3

17223 CSH U P3 G5.3 1911–1928
'Tsingtau today.'
CEJ 1, 1 (Jan. 1927), 48–58.
Subj 14.3 24.4 ▪ 24.3 24.6

17224 CSU O P3 G5.3 1911–1928
Adolph, William Henry, and Wang Yu-Mei.
'The manufacture and distribution of soy bean milk in Shantung.'
LSJ 8 (Dec. 1929), 563–571.
Subj 24.4

17225 CBU PO P2 G1.5 1928–1949
Alley, Rewi, 1897–.
Chinese Industrial Co-operatives, Southeast Headquarters report, July 1939.
Hong Kong: Chinese Industrial Co-operatives, Hongkong Promotion Committee, 1939. 49 p.
Subj 24.4 34.2 ▪ 24.2

17226 NNC PO P2 G1.2 1928–1949
Alley, Rewi, 1897–.
Chinese Industrial Cooperatives general report, May 1939.
Hong Kong: Chinese Industrial Cooperatives, Hongkong Promotion Committee, 1939. 31 p.
Subj 24.4 34.2 ▪ 14.2

17227 NIC O P3 G6.1 1928–1949
Alley, Rewi, 1897–, and C- C- Bojesen, 1897–.
'Rural handicrafts in a new setting.'
CJ 29, 1 (July 1938), 48–54.
Subj 24.4

17228 ICU P P5 G1.2 1928–1949
Armstrong, John Paul, 1910–.
Chinese industrial cooperatives.
Unpublished masters thesis in International Relations, U. of Chicago, 1948. 120 p.
Subj 14 24.4 30 34.2 ▪ 38

17229 NNC P P4 G2.0 1911–1949
Avarin, Vladimir IAkovlevich, 1899–.
'IAponskii kapital v metallurgicheskoi promyshlennosti Man'chzhurii' (Japanese capital in the Manchurian metallurgical industry).
Za industrializatsiiu Sovetskogo Vostoka 1932, 2, 165–175.
Subj 14.4 14.6 24.4 24.6 66 ▪ 14.3

17230 CBU O P3 G2.2 1928–1949
Avenarius, G- G-.
'Promyshlennyia predpriiatiia Kharbina' (Industrial enterprises in Harbin).
VM 1933, 14/15 (15 avgusta), 157–163.
Subj 24.4 ▪ 26.4

17231 CSH O P8 G2.0 1911–1928
Baikov, Nikolai Apollonovich, 1872–1958.
'Ocherki byta obitatelei taigi v s.-v. Kitae' (Notes on the life of the inhabitants of the forest regions of northeastern China).
VM 1928, 3, 31–41.
Subj 24.4 ▪ 21.2 21.3 24 34.1

17232 NNC PO P3 G6.3 1911–1928
Barkman, Charles P-, 1892–.
The industrial revolution in China and its effects as illustrated by the city of Hangchow.
Unpublished masters thesis in History, Columbia U., 1927. 35 p.
Subj 24 24.4 ▪ 24.2 26.4 28

17233 NIC O P7 G1.3 1928–1949
Bojesen, C- C-, 1897–.
'China's rural paper industry.'
CJ 28, 5 (May 1938), 233–243.
Subj 24.4

17234 CSH S P2 G2.3 1911–1949
Borisov, A- B-.
'Uglublenie krizisa v iuzhnoi Man'chzhurii' (The worsening [economic] crisis in southern Manchuria). [With English abstract]
VM 1931, 8, 11–16.
Subj 24.2 24.3 24.4 ▪ 24.1 28

17235 CSH F P5 G4.1 1928–1949
Chen, Ching-fang, and Kwan-yung Hu.
'Comparative business analysis of cooperative cloth-weaving factories and private factories in Hanyang [i.e., Han-yin *hsien*], Shensi.'
EF 31 (Apr. 1944), 420–422.
Subj 24.4 26.4 34.2

17236 MCH PO P2 G1.3 1928–1949
Chen Han-seng (Ch'en Han-sheng), 1897–.
Gung ho! The story of Chinese cooperatives.
New York: Institute of Pacific Relations, 1947. 63 p. (IPR Far Eastern pamphlets, 24)
Subj 24.4 34.2 ▪ 24.6

17237 NNC O P2 G9.0 1911–1949
Chen Nyi-kuan (Ch'en Yeh-k'un) and Chen Han-seng (Ch'en Han-sheng), 1897–.
'Two hand weaving centers in southernmost China.' Tr. of 'Kuang-hsi Yü-lin shou kung mien chih yeh' (The handicraft cotton-industry in Yü-lin *hsien*, Kwangsi); in *Chung-kuo nung ts'un miao hsieh* (Descriptions of rural China), 3rd ed., edited by Chung-kuo nung ts'un ching chi yen chiu hui (Research Society for Chinese Agrarian Economy); Shanghai: Hsin chih shu tien, 1936, 129–134 [condensed tr.; unspecified portion translated from unpublished travel notes of Chen Han-seng]. In *Agrarian China*, compiled by Institute of Pacific Relations. [Selective entry]
Chicago: U. of Chicago Press, 1939, 243–247.
Subj 24.4 ▪ 26.4 28 34.2

17238 CSU P P2 G1.2 1928–1949
Cheng, Shih-min, 1913–.
The industrial cooperative movement in China.
Unpublished masters thesis in Economics, Stanford U., 1943. 176 p.
Subj 14.4 14.6 24.4 34.2 37 47 ▪ 24.3 35 56

17239 NNC U P7 G5.1 1911–1949
Chi Ping.
'The effects of the commercialization of agriculture in southern Hopei.' Tr. from *I shih pao fu k'an* 17 Aug. 1935. In *Agrarian China*, compiled by

Institute of Pacific Relations. [Selective entry]
Chicago: U. of Chicago Press, 1939, 160–167.
Subj 24 24.1 24.4 ▪ 22.1 24.3 28

17240 NIC F P7 G5.1 1928–1949
Chiao, Shu-fan.
The oil pressing industry in Hopei province.
Peiping: Yu Lien Press, 1934. 59 p. (Yenching series on Chinese industry and trade, 3)
Subj 24.4 ▪ 24.5 34.2 34.3

17241 CSH P P2 G1.2 1911–1949
Chin Chien Yin.
Wool industry and trade in China, mimeo.
Tientsin: Hautes études; Shanghai: Université l'Aurore, 1937. 152 p. (Institut des hautes études industrielles et commerciales, Faculty of Commerce, Economic studies, 6)
Subj 14.3 24.1 24.4 34.2 ▪ 24.3

17242 MCY F P3 G6.1 1928–1949
Chung-kuo kung yeh ching chi so (Chinese Institute of Industry and Economics).
'L'état présent de l'industrie à Shanghai (début de 1949)' (The condition of industry in Shanghai at the beginning of 1949). Tr. by Tch'en Ts'iuen-chen from *Kung yeh wen t'i tsung k'an* 7 (Feb. 1949).
BUA 3e série 10, 38 (avr. 1949), 298–315.
Subj 21.4 24.4 ▪ 24.2 26.4

17243 NIC O P2 G8.1 1911–1928
Crawford, Wallace.
'The salt industry of Tzeliutsing [Fu-shun *hsien*, Szechwan].'
CJ 4, 4 (Apr. 1926), 169–175; 4, 5 (May 1926), 281–290; 5, 1 (July 1926), 20–26.
Subj 24.4 ▪ 24.2

17244 CSH O P7 G2.1 1911–1949
Daigorodov, P- M-.
'Rabochii vopros na Chzhalainorskikh burougol'nykh kopiakh KVzhd' (The labor problem at the Chinese Eastern Railway's Cha-lai-no-erh lignite mines [Hsin-pa-erh-hu-cheng-huang-ch'i tribal administrative area, Heilungkiang]). [With English abstract]
VM 1929, 6, 30–38.
Subj 24.4 34.2 ▪ 21.4 26.4 28

17245 MAM P P5 G1.2 1928–1949
Dzung, Kyi-ung (Ch'en Chi-en), 1914–.
The Chinese industrial cooperative movement.
Ann Arbor: University Microfilms (Publ. 2940), 1952. 354 p. (Doctoral dissertation in Economics, Princeton U., 1944)
Subj 16.4 18 24.4 34.2 ▪ 12 14.2 14.3 14.6 27 37

17246 NIC O P3 G6.1 1928–1949
Fang, Frederick.
'Shanghai's cigarette manufacturing industry.'
CJ 32, 6 (June 1940), 269–272.
Subj 14.3 24.4

17247 NIC U P2 G1.2 1928–1949
Fei Hsiao-tung (Fei Hsiao-t'ung), 1910–.
'Problems of rural industrialization.'
China economist 1, 4 (26 Apr. 1948), 102–109.
Subj 14.1 24.4

17248 NNC F P2 G1.3 1911–1949
Fong, H. D. (Fang Hsien-t'ing), 1902–.
'Industrialization and the rural industries in China.'
CQ-S 2, 2 (Spring 1937), 259–279.
Subj 14.4 24.4 ▪ 14 34.2

17249 CSH P P7 G1.2 1928–1949
Fong, H. D. (Fang Hsien-t'ing), 1902–.
Rural industries in China.
Shanghai: Chihli Press, 1933. 68 p. (Nankai Institute of Economics industry series, 5) [Reprinted—Washington, D.C.: Center for Chinese Research Materials, 1972. 68 p.]
Subj 24.4 26 34.2 ▪ 24.3 26.2 26.4

17250 NNC PO P7 G6.3 1928–1949
Fong, H. D. (Fang Hsien-t'ing), 1902–.
'Rural manufacturing industries in Chekiang.'
MBEC 7, 2 (Feb. 1934), 60–71.
Subj 24.4 28 ▪ 24.3 26.3 26.4 34.2

17251 CSH F P3 G5.1 1911–1949
Fong, H. D. (Fang Hsien-t'ing), 1902–.
Tientsin carpet industry.
Tientsin: Chihli Press, 1929. 78 p. (Nankai U., Committee on Social and Economic Research industry series, 1) [Reprinted—Washington, D.C.: Center for Chinese Research Materials, 1972. 78 p.]
Subj 24.4 26.4 34.2 36.4 ▪ 24.5 26.2 36.2

17252 NIC F P3 G5.1 1928–1949
Fong, H. D. (Fang Hsien-t'ing), 1902–, and Y. T. Ku (Ku Yüan-t'ien).
'Shoemaking in a North China port [Tientsin].'
CSPSR 18, 4 (Jan. 1935), 505–538.
Subj 24.3 24.4 34.2

17253 CSH P P5 G2.0 1911–1928
Gerasimov, A- E-.
'Goncharnye izdeliia v severnoi Man'chzhurii' (Pottery in northern Manchuria). [With English abstract; see *Manchuria monitor* 1928, 2, 9–12.]
VM 1928, 1, 32–40. [Separately reprinted—Harbin: Izd-vo Ob-va izucheniia Man'chzhurskogo kraia, 1928. 18 p. (Obshchestvo izucheniia Man'chzhurskogo kraia, Torgovo-promyshlennaia sektsiia, seriia A, 24)]
Subj 24 24.3 24.4 ▪ 24.2 28

17254 MCH P P2 G2.0 1911–1928
Gerasimov, A- E-.
Promyshlennost' raiona Sungari 2-ia (Industry in the upper Sungari river basin).
Harbin: Izd-vo Ob-va izucheniia Man'chzhurskogo kraia, 1928. 11 p. (Obshchestvo izucheniia Man'chzhurskogo kraia, Torgovo-promyshlennaia sektsiia, seriia A, 27)
Subj 24 24.3 24.4

17255 NNC O P7 G1.2 1928–1949
Hader, B- K-, and Rewi Alley, 1897–.
'The rural cotton industry in China.'
CJ 28, 5 (May 1938), 243–250.
Subj 24.4

17256 CSU FP P2 G9.2 1911–1949
Herman, Theodore, 1913–.
'Cultural factors in the location of the Swatow lace and needlework industry.'
AAAG 46, 1 (Mar. 1956), 122–128.
Subj 24.4 ▪ 14.3 24.3 33 34.2 47

17257 CSU O P2 G1.3 1911–1928
[Hobart, Alice Tisdale] Alice Tisdale, 1882–1967.
'The enchantment of the old order.'
GR 7, 1 (Jan. 1919), 11–23.
Subj 24.1 24.4

17258 CSU O P2 G6.1 1928–1949
Hobart, Alice Tisdale, 1882–1967, and Mary A- Nourse.
'How half the world works.'
NG 61, 4 (Apr. 1932), 509–524.
Subj 24.1 24.4

17259 CSU O P7 G9.2 1928–1949
Hoh Shai-kwong.
'Pottery industry in Shek-waan [i.e., Shih-wan, Nan-hai *hsien*], Kwangtung.'
LSJ 12 (1933), 57–64. [Supplement]
Subj 24.4

17260 NNC F P2 G1.2 1911–1949
Hommel, Rudolf P-.
China at work: An illustrated record of the primitive industries of China's masses, whose life is toil, and thus an account of Chinese civilization.
New York: Day, 1937. 10, 366 p. [Reprinted—Cambridge: M.I.T. Press, 1969. 10, 366 p.]
Subj 24 24.4 ▪ 24.1 24.2 29 55 62 65

17261 CSH P P2 G9.5 1928–1949
Hong Kong. Public Works Dept.
Report, 1946/47–1948/49. [Issues for 1950/51–1971/72 are entered as 17362.]
[Hong Kong]: ——. Issued annually, 1947–1949. Average ca. 75 p.
Subj 24.4 55 ▪ 21.3 24.2

17262 ELR O P2 G5.3 1928–1949
[Hsueh Mu-chiao] Muo-Kiao Shueh (Hsüeh Mu-ch'iao), 1905?–.
Industrial cooperative movement in Shantung liberated area, mimeo.
New York: INDUSCO, 1947. 10 p.
Subj 24.4 34.2 ▪ 26.3 26.4 28

17263 CSH O P6 G2.2 1911–1928
I. P.
'Spichechnaia fabrika Min'-ven (st. Ashikhe KVzhd)' (The Min-weng match factory at the A-shih-ho station of the Chinese Eastern Railway [A-ch'eng *hsien*, Kirin]).
VM 1928, 10, 32–34.
Subj 24.4 ▪ 21.4 26.4 28

17264 MCH F P8 G5.2 1928–1949
[Körner, Brunhild] Brunhild Lessing.
'Die Töpferei des Dorfes Mêng-chia-ching in China' (Pottery of Meng-chia-ching village [Yü-tz'u *hsien*, Shansi]).
Ethnos 1, 2 (Mar. 1936), 17–25.
Subj 24.4 ▪ 55

17265 CSH P P3 G2.0 1911–1928
Kovyrkov, P- E-, ed.
'Mukomol'naia promyshlennost' v severnoi Man'chzhurii' (The flour-milling industry in northern Manchuria). In *Khlebnaia torgovlia i mukomol'naia promyshlennost' v*

severnoi Man'chzhurii (The grain trade and flour-milling industry in northern Manchuria), compiled by Obshchestvo izucheniia Man'chzhurskogo kraia, edited by Evgenii Evgen'evich IAshnov. [Analytic entry]
Harbin: Tipo-lit. T-va 'Ozo', 1923, vol. 2, 25–38.
SUBJ 24.4 ▪ 14.3 24.2 24.6

17266 CBU S P2 G2.0 1911–1949
Kukhtin, K- V-.
'Kustarnaia promyshlennost' Man'chzhurii' (Cottage industry in Manchuria). [With English abstract]
VM 1933, 14/15 (15 avgusta), 89–100.
SUBJ 24.4 ▪ 16.4

17267 CSU O P2 G8.2 1928–1949
Lattimore, Owen, 1900–.
'China opens her wild west.'
NG 82, 3 (Sept. 1942), 337–367.
SUBJ 24.4 ▪ 15 24.2

17268 NIC O P3 G9.2 1911–1928
Lau, P. T.
'The story of the jade industry.'
CSPSR 3, 4 (Dec. 1918), 352–360.
SUBJ 24.3 24.4 26.4 34.2 ▪ 36.4 55 66

17269 CSU O P3 G6.1 1928–1949
Lee, B. Y.
'Development and prospects of the dyeing and finishing industry.'
CEJ 17, 5 (Nov. 1935), 439–446.
SUBJ 24.4

17270 CSU F P4 G9.2 1911–1928
Lei Yue Wai (Li Ju-wei) and Lei Hei Kit (Li Hsi-chieh).
'Report on a steam filature in Kwangtung.'
Lingnaam agricultural review 3, 2 (Apr. 1926), 109–150.
SUBJ 24.4 34.2 ▪ 24.3 26.4

17271 CSU O P3 G5.1 1911–1949
Leibbrand, Rose.
'The Peking rug industry.'
CJ 16, 1 (Jan. 1932), 25–29; 16, 2 (Feb. 1932), 82–87.
SUBJ 24.4

17272 NIC P P2 G1.1 1911–1928
Li, Kolu (Li K'o-lu), 1896–.
Die Seidenindustrie in China (The silk industry in China).
Berlin: Wilhelm Christian, 1927. 99 p. (Doctoral dissertation, Philosophische Fakultät, Universität Berlin)
SUBJ 14.4 24.4 ▪ 14 14.2 14.3

17273 CSU F P3 G5.1 1928–1949
Li Pu Lung.
The brick industry in Tientsin and the problem of its modernization, mimeo.
Tientsin: Hautes études; Shanghai: Université l'Aurore, 1940. 42 p. (Institut des hautes études industrielles et commerciales, Faculty of Commerce, Economic studies, 15)
SUBJ 24.4 26.4 ▪ 24.2 24.3

17274 MCH FP P2 G6.0 1911–1949
Lieu, D. K. (Liu Ta-chün), 1891–1962.
The silk industry of China.
Shanghai: Kelly and Walsh, 1941. 28, 266 p.
SUBJ 24 24.1 24.4 26.3 26.4 34.2 ▪ 14.3 28 36.2 36.4 41 47

17275 MCH O P3 G6.1 1928–1949
Lillico, Stuart.
'The rubber manufacturing industry in Shanghai.'
CJ 22, 2 (Feb. 1935), 71–74.
SUBJ 24.4 ▪ 26.4

17276 CSU P P8 G9.5 1911–1949
Lin, Shu-yen.
'Salt manufacture in Hong Kong.'
Hong Kong naturalist 10, 1 (Jan. 1940), 34–38. [Reprinted—*JRAS-HKB* 7 (1967), 138–151.]
SUBJ 24.4 ▪ 34.2

17277 CSU F P3 G5.1 1928–1949
Liu Chin T'ao.
Egg industry in Tientsin, mimeo.
Tientsin: Hautes études; Shanghai: Université l'Aurore, 1941. 46 p. (Institut des hautes études industrielles et commerciales, Faculty of Commerce, Economic studies, 18)
SUBJ 24.4 ▪ 14.3 34.2

17278 NNC P P5 G1.2 1928–1949
Liu, K. P.
'Development of Chinese industrial cooperatives.'
CQ-S 5, 4 (Autumn 1940), 655–679.
SUBJ 24.4 34.2 ▪ 12 15 18 27 37

17279 CBU F P4 G8.1 1928–1949
Liu, R. T.
'Cost of producing silk in Santai [i.e., San-t'ai *hsien*], Szechwan.'
EF 14 (Feb. 1940), 43–59.
SUBJ 24.4 ▪ 24.6

17280 NNC S P2 G1.2 1911–1949
Liubimov, L- I-.
'Domashniaia (kustarnaia) promyshlennost' v Kitae (bibliograficheskii ocherk)' (Bibliographic notes on cottage industry in China).
BSB 2, 5 (1932), 91–131.
SUBJ 24.4

17281 CBU PO P2 G1.3 1928–1949
Lu Kuang-mien, 1906–.
'General report of the Northwest Headquarters for the first year, September, 1938 – September, 1939.' In *Chinese Industrial Cooperatives, Northwest Headquarters, first year reports*, by Lu Kuang-mien et al. [Sole entry]
Hong Kong: Chinese Industrial Cooperatives, Hongkong Promotion Committee, 1940, 7–19.
SUBJ 24.4 ▪ 14.4

17282 NNC U P7 G5.3 1911–1949
Lung An.
'Rural auxiliary occupations in Weihsien [i.e., Wei *hsien*], Shantung.' Tr. from *I shih pao fu k'an* 12 May 1934. In *Agrarian China*, compiled by Institute of Pacific Relations. [Selective entry]
Chicago: U. of Chicago Press, 1939, 229–233.
SUBJ 24.1 24.4 ▪ 28 34.2 66

17283 MCH P P5 G1.2 1911–1949
M. T.
'Sovremennoe polozhenie remesla v Kitae' (The current position of handicraft industry in China).
PK 13 (1934), 200–241.
SUBJ 14.6 16.2 24.4 34.3 ▪ 14.3 16.4 18 34.2

17284 CSU O P7 G9.2 1911–1928
McClure, Floyd Alonzo, 1897–.
'The native paper industry in Kwangtung.'
LSJ 5, 3 (Dec. 1927), 255–268.
SUBJ 24.4 ▪ 26.4

17285 CSU O P8 G9.2 1928–1949
McClure, Floyd Alonzo, 1897–.
'Some Chinese papers made on the ancient "wove" type of screen.'
LSJ 9, 1/2 (June 1930), 115–129.
SUBJ 24.4

17286 CSH O P3 G2.2 1911–1928
Malitskii, V- S-.
'Kustarnaia promyshlennost' Kharbina' (Cottage industry in Harbin).
VM 1929, 2, 11–16.
SUBJ 24.4 ▪ 24 26.2 26.4

17287 NNC O P2 G1.3 1928–1949
Mari, Benito.
'Summary report on an inquiry into the reorganization of Chinese sericulture in the provinces of Chekiang, Kiangsu and Shantung.' In *Annexes to the Report to the Council of the League of Nations of its technical delegate on his mission in China from date of appointment until April 1, 1934, Annex 7.* [Sole entry]
Shanghai: North-China Daily News and Herald, 1934, 227–237.
SUBJ 24.1 24.4 ▪ 27

17288 MCH O P3 G5.1 1928–1949
Montell, Gösta, 1899–.
'The idol factory of Peking.' Tr. from *Hantverk och kultur* 1943.
Ethnos 19, 1/4 (1954), 143–156.
SUBJ 24.4 ▪ 26.2

17289 NIC O P2 G1.2 1928–1949
Pruitt, Ida.
'Small-scale co-operative industries in China.'
J. of geography 41, 5 (May 1942), 161–168.
SUBJ 24 24.4 34.2 ▪ 26.4

17290 CBU P P3 G6.1 1911–1949
Raeburn, John R-, and Hu Kwoh-hwa (Hu Kuo-hua).
'Building construction in Shanghai.'
EF 6 (July 1937), 225–235. [In Chinese as well as English]
SUBJ 24.4 55 ▪ 45

17291 NNC S P2 G1.2 1928–1949
Reynolds, Douglas Robertson, 1944–.
The industrial cooperative movement in wartime China.
Unpublished masters thesis in History, Columbia U., 1968. 108 p. [Certificate essay, East Asian Institute]
SUBJ 24.4 34.2 ▪ 12 36.2

17292 MCH O P2 G5.0 1911–1928
Robinson, H- W-.
'The hairnet industry in North China.'
NG 44, 3 (Sept. 1923), 327–336.
SUBJ 24.4 ▪ 47 66

17293 CSU P P3 G4.2 1928–1949
Selsbee, Elizabeth.
'Cooperatives in Lanchow, China.'
SSR 29, 5 (May–June 1945), 374–381.
SUBJ 24.4 34.2

17294 CSH O P4 G2.3 1911–1928
Shchepin, V- F-.
'Promyshlennost' Inkou' (Industry in [the city of] Ying-k'ou [Liaoning]).
VM 1929, 4, 50–58.
Subj 24.4 ▪ 21.4 26.2 26.4 36.4

17295 NNC O P7 G6.1 1928–1949
Shih Ko.
'The home brewing industry in Tai-hsin [i.e., T'ai-hsing *hsien*], Kiangsu.' Tr. from *Chiao yü yü min chung* 8, 7 (28 Mar. 1937). In *Agrarian China*, compiled by Institute of Pacific Relations. [Selective entry]
Chicago: U. of Chicago Press, 1939, 233–234.
Subj 24.1 24.4 ▪ 24.3

17296 CSU O P3 G7.3 1911–1928
Shryock, John Knight, 1890–1952.
'Kingtehchen [i.e., Ching-te-chen, Kiangsi], the porcelain city.'
Asia (New York: American Asiatic Assn.) 20, 10 (Nov. 1920), 997–1002.
Subj 24.4 ▪ 24.3

17297 MCH PO P2 G1.2 1928–1949
[Snow, Helen Foster] Nym Wales, pseud., 1907–.
China builds for democracy: A story of cooperative industry.
New York: Modern Age, 1941. 15, 310 p. [Reprinted—St. Clair Shores, Mich.: Scholarly Press, 1972. 15, 310 p.]
Subj 24.4 34.2 ▪ 14 18 21.4 47 55

17298 CSH P P2 G2.2 1911–1949
[Sokolov, N- A-?] N. S——v.
'Ocherki ekonomicheskogo sostoianiia pristantsionnykh raionov vostochnoi linii KVzhd: po materialam Ekonomicheskogo biuro KVzhd' (Notes on economic conditions in border districts served by the eastern line of the Chinese Eastern Railway, based on data from the Economic Bureau of the Chinese Eastern Railway). [With English abstract]
VM 1929, 9, 53–59.
Subj 21.2 24 24.1 24.3 24.4 ▪ 26.4

17299 CSU O P7 G7.1 1928–1949
Spencer, Joseph Earle, 1907–.
'Gypsum and salt mining in central Hupeh, China.'
EG 14, 3 (July 1938), 282–286.
Subj 24.4

17300 CSU F P5 G5.1 1928–1949
Tayler, John Bernard, 1878–.
'The Hopei pottery industry and the problem of modernisation.'
CSPSR 14, 4 (Apr. 1930), 184–211. [Separately reprinted—Peiping: Yu Lien Press, 1932. 28 p. (Yenching series on Chinese industry and trade, 1)]
Subj 24.4 34.2 ▪ 24.3 24.6 26.4 36.4

17301 NNC F P7 G1.3 1928–1949
Tayler, John Bernard, 1878–.
'The possibilities of rural industry in China.'
MBEC 7, 2 (Feb. 1934), 47–59.
Subj 24.4 ▪ 21.4 24.3 24.6 34.2

17302 CBU S P2 G2.0 1928–1949
Tesler, E- L-.
'Kozhevennaia promyshlennost' severnoi Man'chzhurii: usloviia proizvodstva i truda' (Production and labor conditions in the leather industry of northern Manchuria). [With English abstract at end of issue]
VM 1934, 10 (oktiabr'), 50–61.
Subj 24.4 ▪ 26.4

17303 CSH S P2 G1.2 1928–1949
Tolmachev, V- IA-.
'Kitaiskaia tekstil'naia promyshlennost' (The Chinese textile industry). [With English abstract]
VM 1931, 5, 69–81.
Subj 24.4 ▪ 14.4

17304 CSH S P2 G1.2 1928–1949
Tolmachev, V- IA-.
'Kitaiskie tkani i syr'e dlia vyrabotki ikh' (Chinese textiles and the raw materials for their production). [With English abstract]
VM 1931, 3, 87–101.
Subj 24.4 ▪ 14.1 24.3

17305 CSH PO P2 G2.0 1928–1949
Tolmachev, V- IA-.
'Kitaiskie tsynovki, ikh raspostranenie i khoziaistvennoe upotreblenie v severnoi Man'chzhurii' (The distribution and economic utilization of Chinese mats in northern Manchuria). [With English abstract]
VM 1930, 6, 43–53.
Subj 24.4 ▪ 14.3 24.3 26.4

17306 DNA FP P2 G6.0 1911–1928
United States Testing Co. Shanghai International Testing House.
A survey of the silk industry of Central China.
Shanghai: Shanghai International Testing House, 1925. 100 p.
Subj 24.1 24.4 ▪ 14.3 26.2 26.4 27 36.2

17307 ELU S P7 G1.4 1911–1949
Valentine, Margaret Shand, 1909–.
A survey of the position and prospects of domestic industries in North China.
Unpublished masters thesis in Geography, U. of Liverpool, 1938. 223 p.
Subj 24.1 24.4 55 ▪ 21.3 24.3 24.6 28

17308 DLC O P2 G1.3 1928–1949
Weiss, Ruth.
'Chinese industrial co-operatives.' In *Wartime China, as seen by westerners.* [Selective entry]
Chungking: China Publishing Co., 1942, 55–71.
Subj 24.4 34.2 ▪ 27 47

17309 NNC F P2 G5.1 1911–1949
Wu, Chih.
'Handloom weaving in Kaoyang [Kao-yang *hsien*, Hopei].' Tr. from *Ching chi chou pao* 8? (24 Jan. 1934); 8? (31 Jan. 1934).
MBEC 7, 6 (June 1934), 248–257. [For an expanded version in Chinese, see Wu Chih, 'Kao-yang chih t'u pu kung yeh' (The native textile industry of Kao-yang *hsien* [Hopei]); in *Chung-kuo ching chi yen chiu* (Studies of the Chinese economy), edited by Fang Hsien-t'ing (H. D. Fong); Changsha: Shang wu yin shu kuan, 1938, vol. 2, 677–700.]
Subj 24.3 24.4 34.2 ▪ 26 28

17310 CSH O P4 G2.0 1928–1949
Zhernakov, Vladimir Nikolaevich (V. N. Jernakov), 1909–.
'Carpet industry in Manchuria.'
B. of the Institute of Scientific Research (Hsin-ching [Changchun]) 6, 1 (Feb. 1942), 46–61.
Subj 24.4 34.2 ▪ 24.3 26.4

1911-1972
(including 1644-1972)

17311 CSH O P2 G1.2 1928–1972
Airey, Willis Thomas Goodwin, 1897–.
A learner in China: A life of Rewi Alley.
Christchurch, N.Z.: Caxton Press *with* Monthly Review Society, 1970. 291 p.
Subj 24.4 26.4 28 34.2 66 ▪ 15 27 32 32.2

17312 CSU O P2 G7.3 1928–1972
Alley, Rewi, 1897–.
'A hinterland city in the Cultural Revolution [Kan-chou, Kiangsi].'
EH 6, 8 (Aug. 1967), 33–43.
Subj 17 24 24.4 ▪ 21.1 24.1 28 34.1

17313 CSH O P2 G1.2 1928–1972
Alley, Rewi, 1897–.
Yo banfa! (We have a way!), 2nd ed., edited by Shirley Barton.
Peking: New World Press, 1955. 216 p.
Subj 20 24 24.4 28 34.2 54 ▪ 15 22.2 24.1 26 27 32.1 47 48 56 63

17314 NNC P P2 G1.2 1928–1972
Chao I-wen.
'Handicraft and industry.' Tr. of 'Ko t'i shou kung yeh' (Individual handicraft industries); in *Hsin Chung-kuo ti kung yeh* (The industry of New China), by Chao I-wen; Peking: T'ung chi ch'u pan she, 1957, 87–114. In *The socialist and handicraft industries of Communist China*, mimeo., compiled by U.S. Joint Publications Research Service. [Sole entry]
Washington, D.C.: JPRS, 20 Dec. 1960, 19–37. (JPRS 6440; MC 2282/1961)
Subj 24.4 ▪ 26.2 34.2

17315 MCH P P3 G2.3 1928–1972
Cheng Chu-yuan (Cheng Chu-yüan), 1927–.
Anshan steel factory in Communist China.
Hong Kong: Union Research Institute, 1956. 88 p. (Communist China problem research series, EC9)
Subj 24.4 34.2 ▪ 14.4 17 32.1

17316 DLC P P2 G1.2 1928–1972
Evseev, P- V- (P. V. Yevseyev).
Sotsialisticheskoe preobrazovanie kustarnoi promyshlennosti Kitaia (The socialist transformation of China's handicraft industry).
Moscow: Vses. koop. izd-vo, 1960. 38 p.

Socialist reorganization of the handicraft industry of Communist China, mimeo.
Washington, D.C.: U.S. Joint Publications Research Service, 10 Apr. 1962. 39 p. (JPRS 13,513; MC 12,146/1962)
Subj 24.4 34.2 ▪ 26.2 26.4

17317 CSH S P2 G1.2 1911–1972
Herman, Theodore, 1913–.
'Handicrafts.' In *A general handbook of China*, compiled by Far Eastern and Russian Institute, U. of Washington. [Selective entry]
New Haven: Human Relations Area Files, 1956, vol. 2, 1554–1566. (HRAF

subcontractor's monographs, 55; Washington 4)
Subj 24.4 ▪ 14.3 34.2

17318 ELS P P3 G9.5 1928–1972
Ho, Henry Chun Yuen (Ho Chen-hüan).
A comparative study of post-war industrial development in Singapore and Hong Kong.
Unpublished masters thesis in Economics, U. of London [London School of Economics and Political Science], 1962. 189 p.
Subj 14.3 21.2 24.4 ▪ 21.1 21.4 26.4 36.4

17319 CSH O P3 G5.1 1911–1972
Hou Teh-pang.
'The Yungli Company: Pioneer of chemical industry in China.'
China reconstructs 4, 3 (Mar. 1955), 21–24.
Subj 24.4 34.2

17320 NNC P P7 G9.5 1895–1972
Knapp, J- H-.
'Mining in Hong Kong.' In *Economic geology of Hong Kong*, edited by Sydney George Davis. [Sole entry]
Hong Kong: Hong Kong U. Press, 1964, 3–10.
Subj 24.4 ▪ 12.2 24.1 62

17321 CSU P P5 G9.5 1928–1972
[Lai, Chuen-yan] David C. Y. Lai (Li Ch'üan-en), 1937–.
'The development and location of the cotton spinning and weaving industry in Hong Kong, 1899–1962.'
Pacific viewpoint 6, 2 (Sept. 1965), 227–228.
Subj 24.4 ▪ 21.3

17322 DLC U P2 G1.3 –1972
Vinogradova, Evgeniia Vladimirova.
Sovremennoe prikladnoe iskusstvo Kitaia (Modern Chinese handicraft arts).
Moscow: Izd-vo vost. lit-ry, 1959. 63 p.
Subj 24.4 ▪ 16.2 17 34.3

17323 CSU P P3 G9.5 1842–1972
Yu, Ta-wei Cheung-lieh, 1930–.
Die Industrialisierung Hongkongs von 1949 bis 1964 (The industrialization of Hong Kong, 1949–1964).
Cologne: The author, 1967. 197 p. (Doctoral dissertation, Wirtschafts- und sozialwissenschaftliche Fakultät, Universität Köln)
Subj 14.3 21.1 24 24.3 24.4 58 ▪ 21.2 24.6

1949-1972

17324 CSH O P3 G6.1 1949–1972
'Develop a variety of metals to achieve greater, faster, and better results under the guidance of Chairman Mao's revolutionary lines: Investigation report on the Shanghai metallurgical industry.' Tr. of 'Tsai Mao chu hsi ko ming lu hsien chih yen hsia to kuai hao hsing ti fa chan yeh chin p'in chung: Shang-hai yeh chin kung yeh tiao ch'a pao kao'; *Jen min jih pao* 9 Aug. 1971, 1, 3.
CES 6, 2 (Winter 1972/73), 64–75.
Subj 24.4 ▪ 32.1

17325 CSH O P7 G5.1 1949–1972
'Firmly adhere to the correct line, achieve high speed in construction: Investigation report on the Peking Petrochemical Main Plant.' Tr. of 'Chien ch'ih cheng ch'üeh lu hsien, ying te chien she kao su tu: Pei-ching shih yu hua kung tsung ch'ang ti tiao ch'a pao kao'; *Hung ch'i* 1972, 2 (Feb.), 13–79.
CES 6, 1 (Fall 1972), 57–71.
Subj 24.4 ▪ 32.1

17326 CSU O P2 G6.3 1949–1972
Alley, Rewi, 1897–.
'From theory to practice in Chekiang.'
EH 9, 4 (1970), 36–45.
Subj 24.4 26.4 ▪ 24.1 26.3 28

17327 CSU O P2 G2.1 1949–1972
Alley, Rewi, 1897–.
'Harbin in the late autumn of 1967.'
EH 6, 12 (Dec. 1967), 22–36.
Subj 24.1 24.4 ▪ 26.4 28

17328 CSU O P2 G7.2 1949–1972
Alley, Rewi, 1897–.
'Hunan revisited.'
EH 6, 4 (Apr. 1967), 6–17.
Subj 24.4 54 ▪ 24

17329 CSU O P2 G9.2 1949–1972
Alley, Rewi, 1897–.
'In and around Canton in November 1970.'
EH 10, 1 (1971), 7–21.
Subj 17 24.1 24.4 ▪ 21.4 26.3 26.4 56

17330 CSU O P2 G6.1 1949–1972
Alley, Rewi, 1897–.
'Life and industrial growth in Wusih.'
EH 10, 4 (1971), 17–26.
Subj 17 24.4 56 ▪ 24.1

17331 CSU O P3 G5.1 1949–1972
Alley, Rewi, 1897–.
'A North China port city [Ch'in-huang-tao, Hopei].'
EH 10, 6 (1971), 23–35.
Subj 24.4 26.4 ▪ 22.1 32.1 47 52 56

17332 CSU O P2 G6.1 1949–1972
Alley, Rewi, 1897–.
'Upsurge in Shanghai.'
EH 9, 2 (1970), 20–38.
Subj 24.4 56 ▪ 17 24.1 26.4

17333 MCH S P3 G9.5 1949–1972
Benham, Frederic Charles, 1900–.
'The growth of manufacturing industry in Hong Kong.'
International affairs (London) 32, 4 (Oct. 1956), 456–463.
Subj 24.4 ▪ 24.3

17334 CSU O P2 G5.1 1949–1972
Berger, Roland.
'Profile of a Chinese county [Tsun-hua *hsien*, Hopei].'
GM 44, 7 (Apr. 1972), 481–486.
Subj 24.4 ▪ 12 24.1 34.1

17335 CSU PO P2 G1.2 1949–1972
Biehl, Max, 1902–.
'Die dezentralisierte Kleinindustrie Chinas im "Grossen Sprung" und heute' (China's decentralized light industry in the Great Leap Forward and today).
Internationales Asien Forum 1, 2 (Apr. 1970), 202–214.
Subj 20 24.4 34.2 ▪ 19 22.1 34.1

17336 CBU P P3 G9.5 1949–1972
Brown, E- Henry Phelps.
'The Hong Kong economy: Achievements and prospects.' In *Hong Kong: The industrial colony*, edited by Keith Hopkins. [Analytic entry]
Hong Kong: Oxford U. Press, 1971, 1–20.
Subj 24.4 ▪ 24.6 26.4 28 34.2 36.4

17337 CSU O P3 G7.1 1949–1972
Carasso, M-.
'A Wouhan' (In Wuhan).
CFC 6 (juin 1960), 13–16.
Subj 24.4 ▪ 21.4 28

17338 CSU O P8 G5.1 1949–1972
Chai Shu-pin and Wang Lin.
'Cement factory in a mountain village [Shan-tuan-cheng, Wu-an *hsien*, Hopei].' In *600 million build industry*. [Selective entry]
Peking: Foreign Languages Press, 1958, 41–47.
Subj 24.4

17339 CSU O P2 G9.3 1949–1972
Chang Kuei-ju.
'Local industry everywhere.' Tr. of 'Shui li ho tien li chieh ho, hsiang she kung yeh p'ien ti k'ai hua' (Hydraulic and electric power are coordinated and industry flourishes in villages and cooperatives); *Hung ch'i* 1958, 2 (16 June 23-26). In *600 million build industry*. [Selective entry]
Peking: Foreign Languages Press, 1958, 140–149. [A different tr.— 'Hydraulic power and electric power promote hsiang and cooperative industry'. In *Selected translations from 'Hung-chi' (Red flag), June–August 1958*, mimeo., compiled by U.S. Joint Publications Research Service. Washington, D.C.: JPRS, 21 Apr. 1961, 548–561. (JPRS 7837; MC 5498/1962)]
Subj 24 24.4

17340 CSH P P7 G2.0 1949–1972
Chao Yu-sheng (Chao Yü-shen).
'The Taching oil field [An-ta *hsien* and Lin-tien *hsien*, Heilungkiang].' In *Collected documents of the First Sino-American Conference on Mainland China*. [Selective entry]
[Taipei]: Institute of International Relations, Republic of China, 1971, 795–820.
Subj 24.4 ▪ 22.1 26.4 28 55 64

17341 CSU O P2 G1.2 1949–1972
China [People's Republic]. Chien chu kung ch'eng pu. Kei shui p'ai shui she chi yüan. (Ministry of Construction and Engineering. Institute of Water Supply and Drainage Design).
'Water supply and drainage engineering designs in China during the last decade.' Tr. of 'Shih nien lai ti kei shui p'ai shui kung ch'eng she chi'; *Ch'eng shih chien she* 1959, 10 (Oct.), 8–11. In *Urban construction in Communist China (Part 2)*, mimeo., compiled by U.S. Joint Publications Research Service. [Selective entry]
Washington, D.C.: JPRS, 15 Aug. 1960, 6–14. (JPRS 5258; MC 17,410/1960)
Subj 24 24.4 ▪ 21.3 21.4

17342 CSH O P2 G5.3 1949–1972
China [People's Republic]. Yeh chin kung yeh pu (Ministry of Metallurgical

Industry). Tiao ch'a tsu (Investigation Team) *with* Shantung. Yen-t'ai ti ch'ü [cheng fu] (Yen-t'ai Special District). Ko ming wei yüan hui (Revolutionary Committee).
'Run small steel mills well: Investigation report on the running of a "small steel complex" in the Yent'ai (Chefoo) area, Shantung.' Tr. of 'Pan hao hsiao tsu kang t'ieh: Shan-tung Yen-t'ai ti ch'ü pan "hsiao kang t'ieh" ti tiao ch'a pao kao'; *Jen min jih pao* 3 Dec. 1970, 1.
CES 6, 2 (Winter 1972/73), 3–13.
SUBJ 24.4 ▪ 32.1

17343 CSU O P7 G7.2 1949–1972
Chu Jung-feng.
'The industry operated by the Nan-yueh people's commune.' Tr. of 'Nan-yüeh jen min kung she ti she pan kung yeh' (Commune-run industries in Nan-yüeh commune [Heng-shan *hsien*, Hunan]); *Hung ch'i* 1960, 3 (1 Feb.), 34–37. In *Translations from 'Hung-ch'i' (Red flag) No. 3, 1 February 1960, Peiping*, mimeo., compiled by U.S. Joint Publications Research Service. [Selective entry]
Washington, D.C.: JPRS, 15 Apr. 1960, 36–42. (JPRS 3169; MC 7230/1960)
SUBJ 24.4 ▪ 21.4 24.1

17344 MMT O P3 G7.3 1949–1972
Chung Ho.
'Chingtehchen [Kiangsi] today.'
PR 2, 26 (30 June 1959), 15–16.
SUBJ 24.4 ▪ 24

17345 CSU O P5 G9.3 1949–1972
Chung-kuo kung ch'an tang. Fu-chien Min-tung ti i ch'a yeh ching chih ch'ang tsung chih wei yüan hui. (Chinese Communist Party. General Party Committee of Tea Plant No. 1, Min-tung, Fukien), ed.
'Realization of the automation of tea processing.' Tr. of 'Shih hsien chih ch'a ch'üan ch'eng tzu tung hua'; *Hung ch'i* 1960, 9 (1 May), 18–20. In *Translations from 'Hung-ch'i' (Red flag) (No. 9, 1 May 1960, Peiping)*, mimeo., compiled by U.S. Joint Publications Research Service. [Sole entry]
Washington, D.C.: JPRS, 13 Sept. 1960, 29–34. (JPRS 3901; MC 17,277/1960)
SUBJ 24.4 ▪ 21.4 32.1

17346 CSU O P3 G2.2 1949–1972
Chung-kuo kung ch'an tang. Ti i ch'i che chih tsao ch'ang wei yüan hui. (Chinese Communist Party. First Automobile Manufacture Plant Committee), ed. [First Automobile Plant is in Changchun.]
'Strive to develop comprehensive utilization of materials and multiple operations.' Tr. of 'Ta kao tsung ho li yung fa chan to chung ching ying' (Strive to develop diversified operations and comprehensive utilization of materials); *Hung ch'i* 1960, 19 (1 Oct.), 36–41. In *Translations from 'Hung-ch'i' (Red flag) (Peiping, No. 19, 1 October 1960)*, mimeo., compiled by U.S. Joint Publications Research Service. [Sole entry]
Washington, D.C.: JPRS, 21 Nov. 1960, 62–71. (JPRS 6276; MC 1067/1961)
SUBJ 24.4 ▪ 34.2

17347 CSH O P2 G5.2 1949–1972
Chung-kuo kung ch'an tang. Yü hsien wei yüan hui. (Chinese Communist Party. Yü Hsien Committee). [Tr. erroneously gives author as Hu-Hsien Committee.]
'Industrialization movement in Hu-Hsien.' Tr. of 'Yü hsien ti kung yeh hua yün tung' (The industrialization movement in Yü *hsien* [Shansi]); *Hung ch'i* 1958, 5 (1 Aug.), 21–26. In *Selected translations from 'Hung-chi' (Red flag), June–August 1958*, mimeo., compiled by U.S. Joint Publications Research Service. [Selective entry]
Washington, D.C.: JPRS, 21 Apr. 1961, 21–38. (JPRS 7837; MC 5498/1962)
SUBJ 24.4 ▪ 24.1

17348 CSU P P8 G2.1 1949–1972
Current Scene Editor.
'China's Taching oilfield [An-ta *hsien* and Lin-tien *hsien*, Heilungkiang]: Eclipse of an industrial model.'
CS 6, 16 (17 Sept. 1968), 1–10.
SUBJ 24.4 ▪ 34.2

17349 CSU FP P2 G9.5 1949–1972
Dwyer, Denis John, 1933–.
'Problems of the small industrial unit.' In *Asian urbanization: A Hong Kong casebook*, edited by D. J. Dwyer. [Analytic entry]
Hong Kong: Hong Kong U. Press, 1971, 123–135. (Centre of Asian Studies series, 3)
SUBJ 24.4 ▪ 34.2

17350 CSU FP P5 G9.5 1949–1972
Dwyer, Denis John, 1933–, and Chuen-yan Lai (Li Ch'üan-en), 1937–.
The small industrial unit in Hong Kong: Patterns and policies.
London: U. of Hull Publications, 1967. 77 p. (U. of Hull occasional papers in geography, 6)
SUBJ 21.1 24.4 28 34.2 ▪ 12.2 14.3 21 21.2 21.3 21.4 55

17351 CSU F P7 G4.4 1949–1972
Eichinger, Franz.
'Die Mühle in den chinesischen Nachbargebieten der tibetanischen Nomaden' (The mill in the Chinese areas bordering on the Tibetan nomadic region).
Sinologica 10, 2/3 (1968), 83–148.
SUBJ 23 24.4 55 ▪ 65

17352 CSU O P3 G1.2 1949–1972
Erroll, F- J-.
'Industrial progress in China.'
GM 31, 6 (Oct. 1958), 265–276.
SUBJ 14.4 24.4

17353 CSU O P2 G9.0 1949–1972
Fairfax-Cholmeley, Elsie.
'Hainan: Awakening paradise.'
EH 2, 14 (Dec. 1963), 35–42.
SUBJ 24 24.4 ▪ 24.1 28

17354 NIC F P7 G9.5 1949–1972
Fan, Winnie, and A- Shepherd.
'Shipbreaking in Hong Kong.' In *Symposium on land use and mineral deposits in Hong Kong, southern China and South-east Asia*, edited by Sydney George Davis. [Selective entry]
Hong Kong: Hong Kong U. Press, 1964, 133–141.
SUBJ 24.4

17355 CBU P P7 G1.2 1949–1972
Fang Wen and Ch'iu Hsin-sheng.
'Industrial development in people's communes.' Tr. of 'Jen min kung she kung yeh fa chan wen t'i'; in *Jen min kung she ching chi kuei hua yü ching chi ti li wen chi* (Collected essays on economic planning and economic geography of the communes); Peking: K'o hsüeh ch'u pan she, 1959, 29–35. In *Economic plans and economic geography of people's communes*, mimeo., jointly edited by Chung-kuo ti li hsüeh hui (Geographical Society of China) *with* Ti li yen chiu so (Institute of Geography), Chung-kuo k'o hsüeh yüan (Chinese Academy of Sciences). [Selective entry]
Washington, D.C.: U.S. Joint Publications Research Service, 25 Feb. 1963, 69–85. (JPRS 17,789; MC 6864/1963) [Xerox copyflo available—New York: CCM Information Corp., Research and Microfilm Publications. (Scholarly Book Translation Series, 421)]
SUBJ 24 24.4 ▪ 24.1

17356 CSH P P4 G9.5 1949–1972
Far Eastern Economic Review.
'Hongkong industry.' In *Far Eastern economic review yearbook, 1960*, compiled by the organization cited. [Selective entry]
Hong Kong: Far Eastern Economic Review, 1960, 87–121.
SUBJ 24.4

17357 CSH P P2 G9.5 1949–1972
Far Eastern Economic Review.
'Textile survey, Hongkong: Lancashire Pact in trouble, garments reach plateau.' In *Far Eastern economic review yearbook, 1961*, compiled by the organization cited. [Selective entry]
Hong Kong: Far Eastern Economic Review, 1961, 183–197.
SUBJ 24.4 ▪ 26.4

17358 CSU O P3 G6.1 1949–1972
Han Che-yi (Han Che-i).
'More extensively and penetratingly unfold the "compare, learn, catch up, and help" movement: Several points of experience concerning the unfolding of the movement on the industrial front in East China.' Tr. of 'Keng kuang fan keng shen ju ti k'ai chan "pi hsüeh kan pang" yün tung: Hua-tung ti ch'ü tsai kung yeh chan hsien shang k'ai chan "pi hsüeh kan pang" yün tung ti chi tien t'i hui' (Broaden and deepen the campaign to compete in learning from and catching up with the experienced and in helping laggards: Some lessons learned from the campaign on the industrial front in the East China region); *Hung ch'i* 1964, 10 (23 May), 39–46. In *Translations from 'Hung ch'i' (Red flag) No. 10, 1964*, mimeo., compiled by U.S. Joint Publications Research Service. [Sole entry]
Washington, D.C.: JPRS, 29 July 1964, 61–75. (JPRS 25,624; MC 16,302/1964)
SUBJ 22.1 24.4 26.4 27

17359 CSU O P7 G9.5 1949–1972
Hayes, James William, 1930–.
'Charcoal burning in Hong Kong.'

JRAS-HKB 11 (1971), 199–203.
Subj 24.4

17360 CSU P P2 G9.5 1949–1972
Hong Kong. Dept. of Commerce and Industry.
Annual departmental report, 1949/50–1971/72. [Issue for 1948/49 is entered as 17419.]
Hong Kong: Government Printer. Issued annually, 1950–1972. Average ca. 80 p.
Subj 24.4 ▪ 12.2 14.3 24.5

17361 CSU P P7 G9.5 1949–1972
Hong Kong. Mines Dept.
Annual departmental report by the Commissioner of Mines, 1958/59–1971/72.
Hong Kong: Government Printer. Issued annually, 1959–1972. Average ca. 25 p.
Subj 24.4 ▪ 26.4

17362 CSU P P2 G9.5 1949–1972
Hong Kong. Public Works Dept.
Annual departmental report by the Director of Public Works, 1950/51–1971/72. [Issues for 1946/47–1948/49 are entered as 17261.]
Hong Kong: Government Printer. Issued annually, 1951–1972. Average ca. 100 p.
Subj 24.4 55 ▪ 21.3 24.2

17363 NNP U P3 G9.5 1949–1972
Hong Kong Trade Development Council.
'Heavy industries in Hong Kong.'
TBHK Apr. 1967, 88–93.
Subj 24.4

17364 NNP U P3 G9.5 1949–1972
Hong Kong Trade Development Council.
'Small-scale industries in Hong Kong.'
TBHK Apr. 1967, 98–103.
Subj 24.4

17365 CSU P P2 G9.2 1949–1972
Hsiang Hsiang.
'The new profile of Canton.' Tr. from *Bao tan Viet hoa* (Hanoi) 5 Oct. 1962, 2. In *Descriptions of Canton and banks of I-li river*, mimeo., compiled by U.S. Joint Publications Research Service. [Sole entry]
Washington, D.C.: JPRS, 22 Mar. 1963, 1–5. (JPRS 18,295; MC 8654/1963)
Subj 24.2 24.4 ▪ 24.1

17366 CSU O P5 G8.1 1949–1972
Ko Jun-sheng, Wei Kuang-ping (Wei Kuang-p'ing), and Tsao Ting-ming (Ts'ao T'ing-ming).
'Nanchung region's good effort.' Tr. of 'Nan-ch'ung chuan ch'ü fa chan ti fang kung yeh ti chi tien ching yen' (Some experiences in developing local industry in Nan-ch'ung special district [Szechwan]); *Hung ch'i* 1958, 4 (16 July), 38–41. In *600 million build industry.* [Selective entry]
Peking: Foreign Languages Press, 1958, 74–84.
Subj 24.4

17367 CSU P P3 G9.5 1949–1972
Koo, Shou-eng, 1911–.
'The role of export expansion in Hong Kong's economic growth.'
AS 8, 6 (June 1968), 499–515.
Subj 24.4 ▪ 24.6 26.4

17368 NNC O P2 G1.2 1949–1972
Kozlaniuk, Petro.
'Kytai bez biznesmeniv i setl'mentiv' (China without 'businessmen' and 'foreign settlements').
Zhovten' 8, 8 (serpen' 1958), 86–107.
Subj 14.4 24.4 55 ▪ 21.1

17369 CSH U P3 G1.2 1949–1972
Kuan Ta-t'ung.
'The progress of street inhabitants' work in cities.' Tr. of 'Ch'eng shih chieh tao chü min kung tso ti yao chin' (The Great Leap Forward of urban residents in streetwork); *Hung ch'i* 1960, 1 (1 Jan.), 27–32.
ECMM 202 (29 Feb. 1960), 29–36.
Subj 24.4 28 ▪ 22.1 24.3 47

17370 CSH P P2 G1.2 1949–1972
[La Dany, Ladislao] ———, 1914–.
'Production of daily commodities: Light industry and handicraft industry.'
CNA 370 (5 May 1961), 1–7.
Subj 24.4 34.2 ▪ 26.2

17371 CSH P P7 G1.2 1949–1972
[La Dany, Ladislao] ———, 1914–.
'Return of pseudo-industry.'
CNA 784 (5 Dec. 1969), 1–7.
Subj 24.4

17372 CSH P P3 G6.1 1949–1972
[La Dany, Ladislao] ———, 1914–.
'Shanghai steel and textile.'
CNA 256 (5 Dec. 1958), 1–7.
Subj 21.2 24.4 ▪ 26.4 34.2

17373 MCH P P7 G1.2 1949–1972
[La Dany, Ladislao] ———, 1914–.
'The small agricultural implements.'
CNA 356 (20 Jan. 1961), 1–7.
Subj 24.1 24.4 ▪ 34.1

17374 CSH P P7 G1.2 1949–1972
[La Dany, Ladislao] ———, 1914–.
'Village side-line production.'
CNA 583 (1 Oct. 1965), 1–7.
Subj 14.3 24.3 24.4

17375 CSU O P3 G5.1 1949–1972
Lake, Douglas.
'A new tide in an old city [Tientsin].'
EH 5, 10 (Oct. 1966), 21–24.
Subj 24.4 ▪ 26.4

17376 CBU O P2 G4.2 1949–1972
Lan-chou ta hsüeh. Ti chih ti li hsi. (Lanchow U. Dept. of Geography and Geology).
'Experiences gained from planning for Lanchow's new industrial center.' Tr. of 'Tsai Lan-chou shih ch'ü hsin kung yeh tien k'ai chan jen min kung she kuei hua kung tso jo kan ching yen ch'u pu tsung chieh' (Preliminary summary of experiences useful for commune planning gained in developing a new industrial center in Lanchow municipality); in *Jen min kung she ching chi kuei hua yü ching chi ti li wen chi* (Collected essays on economic planning and economic geography of the communes); Peking: K'o hsüeh ch'u pan she, 1959, 114–131. In *Economic plans and economic geography of people's communes*, mimeo., jointly edited by Chung-kuo ti li hsüeh hui (Geographical Society of China) *with* Ti li yen chiu so (Institute of Geography), Chung-kuo k'o hsüeh yüan (Chinese Academy of Sciences). [Selective entry]
Washington, D.C.: U.S. Joint Publications Research Service, 25 Feb. 1963, 278–319. (JPRS 17,789; MC 6864/1963) [Xerox copyflo available—New York: CCM Information Corp., Research and Microfilm Publications. (Scholarly Book Translation Series, 421)]
Subj 21.3 24 24.4 ▪ 22 24.1 24.2

17377 CSH O P3 G9.5 1949–1972
Leary, R- H-.
'Aluminum growth.'
FEER 46, 1 (1 Oct. 1964), 49–53.
Subj 24.4

17378 CSU O P8 G6.3 1949–1972
Li Hsing-fa.
'Army veterans run a plant [in Ch'ang-hsing *hsien*, Chekiang].' In *600 million build industry.* [Selective entry]
Peking: Foreign Languages Press, 1958, 12–22.
Subj 24.4 ▪ 35

17379 MCH P P2 G9.5 1949–1972
Lo, K. S.
'Hong Kong small-scale industries.'
Hong Kong manager 3, 1 (Jan.–Feb. 1967), 19–24.
Subj 24.3 24.4 ▪ 24.6

17380 NNC O P3 G6.1 1949–1972
Loboda, Ivan.
'Gorod sadov, shelka i vyshivok' (A city of gardens, silk, and embroidery [Soochow]).
Aziia i Afrika segodnia 1962, 9 (sentiabr'), 46–48.
Subj 20 24.4 ▪ 26.4

17381 WSU P P5 G1.2 1949–1972
Louie, Richard.
Problems of local industry in Communist Chinese economic development.
Unpublished masters thesis in Far Eastern and Slavic Languages, U. of Washington, 1962. 152 p.
Subj 14 24.4 ▪ 12 14.4 32.1

17382 CSU O P8 G5.1 1949–1972
Ma Pao-shan.
'How industry was founded in a farming co-op [Han-chia-wa agricultural producers' cooperative, Ting *hsien*, Hopei].' In *600 million build industry.* [Selective entry]
Peking: Foreign Languages Press, 1958, 54–73.
Subj 24 24.1 24.4 ▪ 27 34.1

17383 CSU O P3 G2.3 1949–1972
Meisner, Mitchell Ralph, 1943–.
'The Shenyang transformer factory: A profile.'
CQ 52 (Oct.–Dec. 1972), 717–737.
Subj 24 24.4 26.4 ▪ 26.1 32 35 36.4 47 55

17384 NIC O P7 G5.3 1949–1972
Pi P'ing-fei.
'The study of some problems in the operation of industrial undertakings by people's communes.' Tr. of 'Jen min kung she pan kung yeh ti jo kan wen t'i ti yen chiu' (Some problems of commune-run industries); *Ching chi yen chiu* (Peking) 1959, 2 (Feb.), 47–51.
ECMM 166 (4 May 1959), 16–27.
Subj 24.4 34.2 ▪ 22 24 28 32.1

17385 CSU FP P3 G9.5 1949–1972
Pryor, E- G-.
'Workshops in domestic premises: A Hong Kong case study.'
Pacific viewpoint 13, 2 (Sept. 1972), 169–186.
Subj 24.4 ▪ 34.2

17386 CSU FP P4 G9.4 1949–1972
Raper, Arthur Franklin, 1899–, Chuan Han-sheng (Ch'üan Han-sheng), 1912–, and Chen Shao-hsing (Ch'en Shao-hsing), 1906–1966.
Urban and industrial Taiwan, crowded and resourceful.
Taipei: Foreign Operations Administration, Mutual Security Mission to China *with* National Taiwan U., 1954. 370 p. [See Vol. 2 of this *Bibliography* for Chinese version.]
Subj 20 21.1 24.4 30 55 ▪ 21.2 24.2 28 34.2 41 47 58

17387 MAM P P2 G9.2 1949–1972
Riskin, Carl Alan, 1938–.
Local industry in Chinese economic development, 1950–1957: The case of Kwangtung province.
Ann Arbor: University Microfilms (Publ. 70-6200), 1970. 237 p. (Doctoral dissertation in Economics, U. of California, Berkeley, 1969)
Subj 24 24.4 32.1 ▪ 21 21.4 24.1 34.2

17388 CSU P P2 G1.2 1949–1972
Riskin, Carl Alan, 1938–.
'Small industry and the Chinese model of development.'
CQ 46 (Apr.–June 1971), 245–273.
Subj 24.4 ▪ 14 14.1 14.4

17389 MCH O P4 G1.2 1949–1972
Roascio, Antonio.
'Le fabbriche cinesi' (Chinese factories).
Rinascita 16, 7/8 (luglio–agosto 1959), 542–545.
Subj 24.4 ▪ 26.4 61

17390 CSU P P2 G9.0 1949–1972
Rose, John.
'Hong Kong's water-supply problem and China's contribution to its solution.'
GR 56, 3 (July 1966), 432–437.
Subj 24 24.4 ▪ 14.3

17391 MCH P P2 G1.2 1949–1972
Schran, Peter, 1930–.
'Handicrafts in Communist China.'
CQ 17 (Jan.–Mar. 1964), 151–173. [Reprinted in *Industrial development in Communist China*, edited by Choh-ming Li (Li Cho-min). (Selective entry.) New York: Praeger, 1964, 151–173.]
Subj 24.4 ▪ 24 34.2

17392 NNC O P3 G5.4 1949–1972
Shmigol', N-.
'Znaete li vy Loian?' (Do you know Loyang?).
Sovremennyi Vostok 1960, 7 (iiul'), 24–25.
Subj 21.1 24.4

17393 CSH O P2 G5.0 1949–1972
Sigurdson, Jon-Sture, 1935–.
'Rural industry: A traveller's tale.'
CQ 50 (Apr.–June 1972), 315–331.
Subj 24.4 ▪ 24.1 26.4 34.2

17394 NNP O P3 G9.5 1949–1972
Sorby, T- D-.
'Hong Kong's economy depends heavily on industry.'
TBHK Dec. 1966, 72–77.
Subj 24.4 ▪ 24.3

17395 NIC P P2 G1.2 1949–1972
Stanford Research Institute. International Industrial Development Center.
Notes on small industry and handicraft development in Mainland China, 1952–1958.
Menlo Park, Calif.: Stanford Research Institute, 1958. 65 p. (Research Program on Small Industry Development miscellaneous papers, 2)
Subj 14 14.4 24.4 ▪ 12 14.1 27 34.2

17396 CSU O P7 G5.3 1949–1972
Sung Nai-te.
'How Kao-t'ang hsien people's communes operate industries.' Tr. of 'Kao-t'ang hsien jen min kung she shih tsen yang ta pan kung yeh ti' (How communes in Kao-t'ang *hsien* [Shantung] promote industries on a large scale); *Hung ch'i* 1959, 3 (1 Feb.), 35–40. In *Articles from the Chinese Communist theoretical journal 'Hung-ch'i' (Red flag) (No. 3, 1 February 1959)*, mimeo., compiled by U.S. Joint Publications Research Service. [Sole entry]
Washington, D.C.: JPRS, 13 Apr. 1959, 28–37. (JPRS 648D; MC 9161/1959)
Subj 24.4 34.2 ▪ 32.1

17397 CSH O P7 G5.1 1949–1972
T'ao Shih.
'A farm implement factory evolved from an ironware produced [i.e., producers] cooperative.' Tr. of 'I ko ts'ung t'ieh yeh sheng ch'an ho tso she fa chan ch'i lai ti nung chü hsiu tsao ch'ang' (A farm-implements factory that grew out of a cooperative iron foundry [in Ch'eng-kuan commune, Fang-shan *hsien*, Peking municipality]); *Hung ch'i* 1961, 3/4 (1 Feb.), 33–37. In *Translations from 'Hung-ch'i' (Red flag) (Peiping, No. 3-4, 1 February 1961)*, mimeo., compiled by U.S. Joint Publications Research Service. [Selective entry]
Washington, D.C.: JPRS, 20 Apr. 1961, 51–58. (JPRS 8123; MC 13,081/1961)
Subj 24.4 ▪ 34.2

17398 CSH P P2 G9.5 1949–1972
Trenerry, Deborah.
'Hongkong's plastic industry.'
FEER 37, 7 (16 Aug. 1962), 301–308.
Subj 24.4

17399 CSH P P2 G9.5 1949–1972
Trenerry, Deborah.
'Ship-breaking in Hongkong.'
FEER 36, 9 (31 May 1962), 465–469.
Subj 24.4

17400 CSH O P2 G5.4 1949–1972
Tseng Chieh.
'The industry of Wen hsien serves agriculture.' Tr. of 'Wei nung yeh fu wu ti Wen hsien kung yeh' (Industry in Wen *hsien* [Honan] serves agriculture); *Hung ch'i* 1960, 18 (16 Sept.), 36–39. In *Translations from 'Hung-ch'i' (Red flag) (Peiping, No. 18, 16 September 1960)*, mimeo., compiled by U.S. Joint Publications Research Service. [Selective entry]
Washington, D.C.: JPRS, 31 Oct. 1960, 58–64. (JPRS 6184; MC 18,973/1960)
Subj 24.4 ▪ 24.1

17401 NNC P P2 G1.2 1949–1972
Voevodin, Stanislav Aleksandrovich.
'Sotsialisticheskoe preobrazovanie kustarnoi promyshlennosti v Kitaiskoi Narodnoi Respublike' (The socialist reorganization of cottage industry in the People's Republic of China).
KSINA 49 (1961), 34–42.
Subj 24.3 24.4 34.2

17402 CSU O P8 G6.1 1949–1972
Wang Hsi-teh.
'Treasures from rice husks' [study of Wu-feng-jun oil pressing plant, Ch'ang-chou municipality, Kiangsu]. In *600 million build industry*. [Selective entry]
Peking: Foreign Languages Press, 1958, 23–40.
Subj 24.4

17403 CSH U P2 G1.2 1949–1972
Wang Yü-lo.
'Industry run by the hsien and communes amidst the big leaps forward.' Tr. of 'Ta yao chin chung ti hsien, she kung yeh' (Industry run by counties and communes during the Great Leap Forward); *Hung ch'i* 1960, 6 (16 Mar.), 29–35.
ECMM 208 (18 Apr. 1960), 15–25.
Subj 14.4 24.4 ▪ 22.1 34.2

17404 CBU P P7 G1.2 1949–1972
Wu Jung-chi, Kao Ling-hsü, and Ch'en Jen-shan.
'Industrial allocation of people's communes.' Tr. of 'Jen min kung she kung yeh p'ei chih' (Industrial allocation in the communes); in *Jen min kung she ching chi kuei hua yü ching chi ti li wen chi* (Collected essays on economic planning and economic geography of the communes); Peking: K'o hsüeh ch'u pan she, 1959, 21–28. In *Economic plans and economic geography of people's communes*, mimeo., jointly edited by Chung-kuo ti li hsüeh hui (Geographical Society of China) *with* Ti li yen chiu so (Institute of Geography), Chung-kuo k'o hsüeh yüan (Chinese Academy of Sciences). [Selective entry]
Washington, D.C.: U.S. Joint Publications Research Service, 25 Feb. 1963, 50–68. (JPRS 17,789; MC 6864/1963) [Xerox copyflo available—New York: CCM Information Corp., Research and Microfilm Publications. (Scholarly Book Translation Series, 421)]
Subj 24 24.4 ▪ 24.3

17405 CSU O P6 G7.2 1949–1972
Yen Ming-jun.
'Birth of a small steel-iron joint enterprise.' Tr. of 'I ko hsiao hsing kang t'ieh lien ho ch'i yeh ti tan sheng' (The birth of a small-scale iron and steel enterprise jointly sponsored [by several communes in Yu *hsien*, Hunan]); *Hung ch'i* 1959, 1 (1 Jan.), 32–34. In *Articles from the Chinese Communist theoretical journal 'Hung-ch'i' (Red flag) No. 1, 1 January 1959*, mimeo., compiled by U.S. Joint

Publications Research Service. [Sole entry]
Washington, D.C.: JPRS, 13 Mar. 1959, 48–55. (JPRS 588D; MC 6354A/1959)
Subj 24.4

17406 CSU O P8 G7.2 1949–1972
Yin Tse-ming (Yin Tzu-ming).
'The strength of the masses is limitless' [study of Shao-yang special district, Hunan]. Tr. of 'Ch'ün chung ti li liang shih wu ch'ung ti'; *Hung ch'i* 1958, 9 (1 Oct.), 29–33. In *600 million build industry*. [Selective entry]
Peking: Foreign Languages Press, 1958, 91–101.
Subj 24.4

24.5 Local Revenue and Expenditure
地方財政 地方財政

1644-1911

17407 CSU PO P8 G5.4 1895–1911
Jamieson, George, 1843–1920.
Report on land taxation in the province of Honan.
London: His Majesty's Stationery Office, 1905. 13 p. (Great Britain, Diplomatic and Consular Reports, miscellaneous series, 641; Cmd., 2683-5)
Subj 24.5 45 ▪ 14.5

17408 CBU PO P3 G9.2 1644–1842
Morrison, John Robert, ?–1834.
A Chinese commercial guide, 3rd ed., rev.
Canton: Chinese Repository, 1848. 311 p.
Subj 24.3 24.5 24.6 26.2 ▪ 12.2 22 22.2 64

17409 CBU FP P2 G5.3 1895–1911
Schrameier, Wilhelm Ludwig, 1859–1926.
Aus Kiautschous Verwaltung: Die Landsteuer und Zollpolitik des Kiautschou (The administration of Kiaochow: Land-tax and customs policy).
Jena: Gustav Fischer, 1914. 255 p.
Subj 22.2 24.5 ▪ 14.3 22 24.1 36.2 45 66

17410 NNC PO P2 G5.3 1895–1911
Schrameier, Wilhelm Ludwig, 1859–1926.
'Die Steuerpolitik im Kiautschougebiet' (Taxation policy in Kiaochow).
Jahrbuch der Bodenreform 8, 1 (1912), 1–68.
Subj 24.5 ▪ 22 24.1 24.2 24.6 31 38

17411 NNC P P2 G6.3 1842–1895
Tomita, Shigeaki, 1937–.
The land-tax revolt of Chinese peasants in Yin hsien, Chekiang, in 1852 and an analysis of its causes.
Unpublished masters thesis in Chinese and Japanese, Columbia U., 1967. 92 p.
Subj 12 22 24.5 24.6 25 32 ▪ 22.1 24.1 26.1 26.3 36.3

1644-1949

17412 NNC P P3 G6.1 1842–1928
'The tax burden of the residents in the foreign settlement in Shanghai, 1870–1925.'
NWSS 4, 37 (14 Sept. 1931), 173, 175–176.
Subj 24.5 ▪ 21.1 66

1911-1949

17413 CSH P P3 G5.1 1911–1928
'The Peking octroi [tax on commodities brought into the city].'
CEM 1, 10 (July 1924), 1–10.
Subj 24.5

17414 MCH FP P4 G5.1 1928–1949
Chang, C. M. (Chang Ch'un-ming), 1904–.
'Tax farming in North China: A case study of the system of auctioned revenue collection made in Ching-hai hsien, Hopei province.' Tr. of 'Ho-pei sheng chih pao shui chih tu' (The tax-farming system in Hopei); *Cheng chih ching chi hsüeh pao* 3, 3 (Apr. 1935), 530–589. [Slightly condensed in tr.; original cites Wang Chih-hsin as author.]
NSEQ 8, 4 (Jan. 1936), 824–852.
Subj 24.5 ▪ 26.2

17415 NNC O P8 G8.1 1928–1949
Chen Von-ko (Ch'en Wang-ku).
'The omnipotence of opium in Fow-chow villages.' Tr. of 'Chien chu tsai ya p'ien yen shang ti Fou-ling nung ts'un' (Villages dependent on opium in Fou-ling *hsien* [Szechwan]); *Chung-kuo nung ts'un* 1, 6 (Mar. 1935), 84–86. In *Agrarian China*, compiled by Institute of Pacific Relations. [Selective entry]
Chicago: U. of Chicago Press, 1939, 122–126.
Subj 24.1 24.5 ▪ 22.2

17416 NNC O P2 G4.2 1928–1949
[Fan Ch'ang-chiang] Chang Kiang, 1907–.
'Opium land tax in central Kansu.' Tr. of 'Ch'i-lien shan pei ti lü hsing' (Travels north of Mount Ch'i-lien); in *Chung-kuo ti hsi pei chiao* (The northwest corner of China), by Fan Ch'ang-chiang; Tientsin: Ta kung pao kuan, 1936, 193–212 [condensed tr.]. In *Agrarian China*, compiled by Institute of Pacific Relations. [Selective entry]
Chicago: U. of Chicago Press, 1939, 126–130.
Subj 22.2 24.5 ▪ 21.2 28

17417 NNC O P2 G3.4 1928–1949
[Fan Ch'ang-chiang] Chang Kiang, 1907–, and Chen Keng-ya (Ch'en Keng-ya).
'How the benefits of irrigation are nullified in Ninghsia.' Tr. from *Chung-kuo ti hsi pei chiao* (The northwest corner of China), by Fan Ch'ang-chiang; Tientsin: Ta kung pao kuan, 1936, 287–325 *and* from *Hsi-pei shih ch'a chi* (Travels in Northwest China), by Ch'en Keng-ya; Shanghai: Shen pao kuan, 1936, vol. 1, 109–138 [condensed tr.]. In *Agrarian China*, compiled by Institute of Pacific Relations. [Selective entry]
Chicago: U. of Chicago Press, 1939, 131–136.
Subj 24.1 24.5 24.6 ▪ 21.2 28

17418 MCH FP P8 G5.1 1928–1949
Feng, H. T. (Feng Hua-te).
'Notes on peasants' tax burden in a Hopei village.' Tr. by Wellington Lee from *Ching chi chou pao* 6 (24 May 1933).
MBEC 7, 3 (Mar. 1934), 105–109. [For an expanded version in Chinese, see Feng Hua-te, 'Nung min t'ien fu fu tan ti i ko shih li' (A concrete example of the burden of land taxes on the peasantry); in *Chung-kuo ching chi yen chiu* (Studies of the Chinese economy), edited by Fang Hsien-t'ing (H. D. Fong); Changsha: Shang wu yin shu kuan, 1938, vol. 2, 1113–1120.]
Subj 24.5 ▪ 24.1 24.6 26.3 28

17419 CSH P P2 G9.5 1928–1949
Hong Kong. Dept. of Commerce and Industry.
Annual report, 1948/49. [Issues for 1949/50–1971/72 are entered as 17360.]
[Hong Kong]: ——, 1949. 29 p.
Subj 24.5 ▪ 12.2

17420 CSH P P1 G9.5 1928–1949
Hong Kong. Inland Revenue Dept.
Report, 1947/48–1948/49. [Issues for 1949/50–1971/72 are entered as 17427.]
[Hong Kong]: ——, 1948, 1949. Average ca. 20 p.
Subj 24.5

17421 CSH P P3 G2.2 1911–1928
Marakulin, V-.
'Finansy goroda Kharbina za 1922 g.' (Public finance in Harbin, 1922).
EVM 1924, 21 (25 maia), 17–18.
Subj 24.5

17422 NNP O P3 G2.2 1911–1928
Tishenko, Petr S-.
'Finansovye problemy kharbinskogo gorodskogo khoziaistva' (Fiscal problems of Harbin's municipal economy).
EB 1927, 17 (1 maia), 6–9.
Subj 24.5

17423 NNC P P7 G1.4 1911–1949
Wong Yin-seng (Wang Yin-sheng), 1902–, Hsieh Pin-hsien (Hsüeh P'in-hsüan), and Shi Kai-fu (Shih K'ai-fu).
'Military requisitions and the peasantry.' Tr. from *Chung-kuo pei pu ti ping ch'ai yü nung min* (Military conscription and the peasantry in North China); Shanghai: Chung yang yen chiu yüan, 1931. In *Agrarian China*, compiled by Institute of Pacific Relations. [Selective entry]
Chicago: U. of Chicago Press, 1939, 101–109.
Subj 24.5 35 ▪ 22.1 25 26.3

1911-1972
(including 1644-1972)

17424 MCY P P8 G9.4 1928–1972
Chinese-American Joint Commission on Rural Reconstruction.
Rural land taxation in Taiwan.
Taipei: Chinese-American Joint Commission on Rural Reconstruction, 1952. 54 p. (JCRR, Econmic digest series, 2)
Subj 24.5 ▪ 24.1 26.3

1949-1972

17425 NNP O P2 G9.5 1949–1972
Cowperthwaite, J- J-.
'The budget report.'
TBHK May 1966, 64–70.
SUBJ 24.5 ▪ 22

17426 NNP O P3 G9.5 1949–1972
Cowperthwaite, J- J-.
'Hong Kong's financial strength.'
TBHK Aug. 1967, 50–53.
SUBJ 24.5 ▪ 24.6

17427 CSU P P1 G9.5 1949–1972
Hong Kong. Inland Revenue Dept.
Annual departmental report by the Commissioner of Internal Revenue, 1949/50–1971/72. [Issues for 1947/48 and 1948/49 are entered as 17420.]
Hong Kong: Government Printer. Issued annually, 1950–1972. Average ca. 30 p.
SUBJ 24.5

17428 CSH O P7 G5.0 1949–1972
Li Hsien-nien, 1907–.
'A glance at the people's communes.' Tr. of 'Jen min kung she so chien'; *Hung ch'i* 1958, 10 (16 Oct.), 4–8.
ECMM 149 (1 Dec. 1958), 34–39.
SUBJ 20 22 24 24.5 ▪ 24.3 28

17429 CBU P P3 G9.5 1949–1972
Stammer, Donald William, 1941–.
'The public finance of Hong Kong.'
Malayan economic review 13, 2 (Oct. 1968), 115–128. [For fuller treatment, see entry 17512.]
SUBJ 24.5 24.6 ▪ 28

17430 CSU PO P3 G9.5 1949–1972
Taxidermist, pseud.
'Evasion of taxation [in Hong Kong].'
Hong Kong law j. 3, 1 (Jan. 1973), 97–107.
SUBJ 12.2 24.5 ▪ 22 22.2

24.6 LOCAL FINANCE, MONEY, AND CREDIT
地方金融、貨幣及信託制度
地方金融、貨幣及び信用制度

1644-1911

17431 MCH P P3 G6.1 1895–1911
Bergère, Marie-Claire, 1933–.
'Introduction' (Introduction). In *Une crise financière à Shanghai à la fin de l'Ancien Régime* (A financial crisis in Shanghai at the end of the ancien régime), compiled and edited by M.-C. Bergère. [Sole entry]
The Hague: Mouton, 1964, 1–11. (Maison des sciences de l'homme, Matériaux pour l'étude de la Chine moderne et contemporaine, 3)
SUBJ 24.6 26.2 ▪ 14.3 24.3 24.4 66

17432 NIC O P3 G6.1 1842–1911
Ferguson, John Calvin, 1866–1945.
'Notes on Chinese banking system in Shanghai.'
JRAS-NCB new (2nd) series 37 (1906), 55–82.
SUBJ 24.6 26.2 34.3

17433 MCH P P7 G9.5 1842–1895
Hayes, James William, 1930–.
'Village credit at Shek Pik [i.e., Shih-pi, Hong Kong], 1879–1895.'
JRAS-HKB 5 (1965), 119–122.
SUBJ 24.6 38

17434 CSU P P2 G6.0 1644–1895
Jones, Susan Mann, 1943–.
'Finance in Ningpo: The "ch'ien chuang", 1750–1880.' In *Economic organization in Chinese society*, edited by William Earl Willmott. [Selective entry]
Stanford: Stanford U. Press, 1972, 47–77.
SUBJ 24.6 34.2 36.2 ▪ 14.3 25 26.2

17435 CSU P P3 G9.5 1842–1895
King, Frank Henry Haviland, 1926–.
'The Bank of China is dead.'
JOS 7, 1 (Jan. 1969), 39–62.
SUBJ 24.6

17436 NIC O P3 G9.3 1842–1895
Parkes, Henry, 1815–1896.
'Account of the paper currency and banking system of Fuchowfoo [i.e., Foochow].'
JRAS 13 (1852), 179–190.
SUBJ 24.6 34.2

17437 CSU PO P3 G8.1 1895–1911
Sculfort, L-.
'Note sur les opérations des banques chinoises de Tchoung-king' (A note on the operations of Chinese banks in Chungking). In *La Mission lyonnaise d'exploration commerciale en Chine, 1895–1897, deuxième partie, rapports commerciaux et notes diverses* (The Lyons Trade Mission to China, 1895–1897, Part 2, Commercial reports and miscellaneous notes), by Chambre de commerce de Lyon. [Selective entry]
Lyons: Rey, 1898, 417–424 [s.p.].
SUBJ 24.6

17438 CSU PO P2 G6.0 1842–1895
Simon, G- Eugène, 1829–1896.
'Note sur les petites sociétés d'argent en Chine' (A note on rotating-credit societies in China).
JRAS-NCB new (2nd) series 5 (Dec. 1868), 1–23.
SUBJ 24.6

17439 CSU O P1 G1.3 1895–1911
Ware, James.
'Chinese provident clubs [i.e., rotating-credit societies].'
EAM 2 (1903), 253–258.
SUBJ 24.6 ▪ 38

1644-1949

17440 MCY S P3 G6.1 1842–1949
Allen, Andrew.
'Le "Shanghai stock exchange"' (The Shanghai stock exchange).
BUA 3e série 3, 9 (1942), 121–178.
SUBJ 24.6 34.2 ▪ 14.3

17441 CSU PO P2 G1.2 –1928
Chang, Wu, 1886–.
Chinesische Kreditvereinigung . . . (Chinese rotating-credit societies).
Berlin: Siegfried Scholem, 1917. 52 p. (Doctoral dissertation, Philosophische Fakultät, Universität Berlin)
SUBJ 24.1 24.6 30 34.2

17442 CSH FP P5 G6.3 1895–1949
China [Republic]. Shih yeh pu. Kuo chi mao i chü. (Ministry of Industry. Bureau of Foreign Trade), ed.
'Financial institutions.' Tr. of 'Chin jung chi kuan' and 'T'e chung shang yeh, 4' (Financial institutions *and* Special types of commercial enterprises, Chap. 4); in *Chung-kuo shih yeh chih: Che-chiang sheng* (Chinese economic surveys: Chekiang); Shanghai: Kuo chi mao i chü, 1933, *jen* 1 – *jen* 100, *hsin* 22 – *hsin* 30 [s.p.] [slightly condensed in tr.]. In *China industrial handbooks: Chekiang*, edited by the agency cited. [Selective entry]
Shanghai: Kuo chi mao i chü, 1935, 775–827. [Reprinted in *China industrial handbooks: Chekiang*, edited by the agency cited. (Selective entry.) Taipei: Ch'eng-wen, 1972, 775–827.]
SUBJ 24.6 34.2

17443 NIC S P2 G1.5 1842–1949
Freedman, Maurice, 1920–.
'The handling of money: A note on the background to the economic sophistication of overseas Chinese.'
Man 59 (Apr. 1959), 64–65.
SUBJ 14.6 24.6 ▪ 34.2 63

17444 MCH FP P8 G5.1 1895–1949
Gamble, Sidney David, 1890–1968.
'Hsin Chuang [Shu-lu *hsien*, Hopei]: A study of Chinese village finance.'
HJAS 8, 1 (Mar. 1944), 1–33.
SUBJ 20 22 24.5 24.6 ▪ 22.1 22.2 24.1 25 27 28 34.1

17445 NIC S P1 G1.3 1895–1949
Geertz, Clifford James, 1926–.
'The rotating credit association: A "middle rung" in development.'
EDCC 10, 3 (Apr. 1962), 241–264.
SUBJ 24.6 ▪ 38

17446 CSU PO P3 G5.1 1842–1949
Li Chien Ming.
The accounting system of native banks in Peking and Tientsin, mimeo.
Tientsin: Hautes études; Shanghai: Université l'Aurore, 1941. 14, 301 p. (Institut des hautes études industrielles et commerciales, Faculty of Commerce, Economic studies, 19)
SUBJ 24.6 26.2 34.2

17447 CSH P P3 G9.5 1842–1949
Tom, C. F. Joseph, 1922–.
'Monetary standard, entrepot trade, and prices: The Hong Kong experience.' In *Hong Kong economic papers, No. 3*, edited by Edward Stuart Kirby. [Analytic entry]
Hong Kong: Hong Kong Economic Assn., 1964, 1–52. (Revision of *Monetary problems of an entrepot: The Hong Kong experience*, doctoral dissertation in Economics, U. of Chicago, 1963)
SUBJ 24.6 ▪ 14.3

17448 NNC P P1 G1.1 –1949
Yang, Lien-sheng, 1914–.
'Buddhist monasteries and four money-raising institutions in Chinese history.'
HJAS 13, 1/2 (June 1950), 174–191. [Reprinted in *Studies in Chinese institutional history*, by Lien-sheng Yang. (Selective entry.) Cambridge: Harvard U. Press, 1961, 198–215.

(Harvard-Yenching Institute studies, 20)]
SUBJ 24.6 33 ▪ 14.6 31

1911-1949

17449 CSH U P3 G5.3 1911–1928
'Banking and currency in Tsinan.'
CEM 2, 2 (Nov. 1924), 5–11.
SUBJ 24.6 ▪ 36.2

17450 NNC U P4 G5.1 1911–1949
'The cooperative credit movement in Hopei, 1923–1930.'
NWSS 4, 42 (19 Oct. 1931), 193, 195–196.
SUBJ 24.6 34.2

17451 NNC P P7 G5.1 1928–1949
'The cooperative credit movement in Hopei, 1931.'
NWSS 5, 49 (5 Dec. 1932), 221, 223–224.
SUBJ 24.6 34.2

17452 MCH O P3 G6.1 1911–1928
'Native banking in Shanghai.'
CEM 3, 4 (Apr. 1926), 168–183.
SUBJ 24.6

17453 CSU O P3 G9.3 1928–1949
'Native banks in Foochow.'
CEJ 10, 5 (May 1932), 440–447.
SUBJ 24.6 ▪ 34.2

17454 NNC O P3 G6.1 1928–1949
Ahlers, John.
'Postwar banking in Shanghai.'
PA 19, 4 (Dec. 1946), 384–393.
SUBJ 24.6

17455 CSH U P4 G2.0 1928–1949
Avdoshchenkov, A- IA-.
'Kitaiskie banki v Girinskoi i Kheiluntszianskoi provintsiiakh' (Chinese banks in Kirin and Heilungkiang). [With English abstract]
VM 1930, 6, 36–42.
SUBJ 24.6

17456 NNC O P7 G1.2 1911–1949
Bloch, Kurt, 1908–, and Chen Han-seng (Ch'en Han-sheng), 1897–.
'Chinese copper currency and the peasantry' [condensed from Kurt Bloch, 'On the copper currencies of China'; *NSEQ* 8, 3 (Oct. 1935), 618–632 *and* from unpublished travel notes by Chen Han-seng (Ch'en Han-sheng), translated from the Chinese]. In *Agrarian China*, compiled by Institute of Pacific Relations. [Selective entry]
Chicago: U. of Chicago Press, 1939, 113–118.
SUBJ 24.6 ▪ 24.1 24.5 26.3

17457 WSU P P3 G6.1 1911–1949
Chao, Ching Hsi.
The Shanghai money market.
Unpublished masters thesis in Economics, U. of Washington, 1948. 182 p.
SUBJ 24.3 24.6 ▪ 24

17458 NIC F P8 G6.2 1928–1949
Chao, Tsai Piao (Chao Ts'ai-piao), 1903–.
A study of the short time loans of 121 farms in Hohsien [i.e., Ho *hsien*], *Anhwei, China, 1930.*
Unpublished masters thesis in Economics, Cornell U., 1932. 34 p.
SUBJ 24.6 ▪ 24.1 26.3 41

17459 MCH P P3 G6.1 1911–1949
Chen Shao-Teh (Ch'eng Shao-te).
Etude sur le marché monétaire de Changhai au début du XXème siècle (The Shanghai money market at the beginning of the twentieth century).
Paris: Rodstein, 1932. 29, 494 p.
SUBJ 24.6 26.2 36.2

17460 FPN FP P7 G1.2 1911–1949
Chiang, Shang-yi (Chiang Shang-i).
Les coopératives de crédit agricole en Chine (Agricultural credit cooperatives in China).
Nancy: Impr. centrale de l'Est, 1931. 132 p. (Doctoral dissertation, Faculté de droit, Université de Nancy)
SUBJ 24.1 24.6 26.3 34.2 ▪ 28 65

17461 CBU F P7 G1.3 1928–1949
Chiao, C. M. (Ch'iao Ch'i-ming), 1897–, and Yin Lien-ken (Ying Lien-keng), 1904?–.
'Farm credit and farm ownership.'
EF 4 (Feb. 1937), 188–196. [In Chinese as well as English]
SUBJ 24.6 ▪ 24.1

17462 NNC O P7 G6.1 1928–1949
Chien Chao-hsuen (Ch'ien Chao-hsiung).
'Trade capital and silk farming in Wusih.' Tr. of 'Shang yeh tzu pen ts'ao tsung hsia ti Wu-hsi ts'an sang' (The dominance of sericulture by commercial capital in Wu-hsi *hsien* [Kiangsu]); *Chung-kuo nung ts'un* 1, 4 (Jan. 1935), 71–74. In *Agrarian China*, compiled by Institute of Pacific Relations. [Selective entry]
Chicago: U. of Chicago Press, 1939, 235–239.
SUBJ 24.1 24.6 34.1 ▪ 24.3 34.2

17463 CSH FP P7 G5.1 1911–1949
China International Famine Relief Commission.
Herr Raiffeisen among Chinese farmers: Experiences gained in rural co-operative credit.
Peiping: China International Famine Relief Commission, 1930. 138 p. (CIFRC, Series B, 37)
SUBJ 24.6 34.2 ▪ 24.3 28 36.3 37

17464 CSH FP P4 G6.1 1911–1949
China [Republic]. Shih yeh pu. Kuo chi mao i chü. (Ministry of Industry. Bureau of Foreign Trade), ed.
'Financial institutions.' Tr. of 'Chin jung chi kuan' and 'T'e chung shang yeh, 1, 4, 6' (Financial institutions *and* Special types of commercial enterprises, Chaps. 1, 4, 6); in *Chung-kuo shih yeh chih: Chiang-su sheng* (Chinese economic surveys: Kiangsu); Shanghai: Kuo chi mao i chü, 1933, 1–94; 1–30, 61–72, 87–98 [s.p.] [slightly condensed in tr.]. In *China industrial handbooks: Kiangsu*, edited by the agency cited. [Selective entry]
Shanghai: Kuo chi mao i chü, 1933, 887–961. [Reprinted in *China industrial handbooks: Kiangsu*, edited by the agency cited. (Selective entry.) Taipei: Ch'eng-wen, 1972, 887–961.]
SUBJ 24.3 24.6 34.2 ▪ 14.6 36.2

17465 CSH O P3 G6.1 1928–1949
China [Republic]. [Ts'ai cheng pu]. Kuo ting shui tse wei yüan hui. ([Ministry of Finance]. National Tariff Commission), ed.
'Commercial and monetary review, 1st quarter 1929 – 4th quarter 1930.' [Recurring feature article: journal issued quarterly, article appears irregularly.]
Shanghai market prices report unnumbered (Jan.–Mar. 1929 – Oct.–Dec. 1930), average ca. 5 p. [See Vol. 2 of this *Bibliography* for Chinese version.]
SUBJ 24.6 ▪ 14.3

17466 CSH O P3 G6.1 1928–1949
China [Republic]. [Ts'ai cheng pu]. Kuo ting shui tse wei yüan hui. ([Ministry of Finance]. National Tariff Commission), ed.
'Review of money market in Shanghai, 1st quarter 1929 – 4th quarter 1930.' [Recurring feature article: journal issued quarterly, article appears irregularly.]
Shanghai market prices report unnumbered (Jan.–Mar. 1929 – Oct.–Dec. 1930), average ca. 2 p. [See Vol. 2 of this *Bibliography* for Chinese version.]
SUBJ 24.6

17467 NIC O P3 G6.1 1911–1949
Chow, C. P.
'Pawnshops in Shanghai.'
Central Bank of China b. 4, 3 (Sept. 1938), 185–203.
SUBJ 24.6 34.2 ▪ 24.3 34.3

17468 NIC O P8 G5.1 1911–1928
Dittmer, Clarence Gus, 1885–.
'Co-operative credit in China.'
THJ 2, 7 (May 1917), 121–125.
SUBJ 24.6 34.2

17469 CSU O P7 G5.1 1911–1928
Djang, Y. S.
'Credit co-operatives in 1,000 villages.'
CSPSR 15, 2 (July 1931), 161–170.
SUBJ 24.6 34.2

17470 NIC F P7 G5.1 1911–1928
Gamble, Sidney David, 1890–1968.
'A Chinese mutual savings society.'
FEQ 4, 1 (Nov. 1944), 41–52.
SUBJ 24.6 ▪ 38

17471 CSH O P5 G2.0 1928–1949
Gerasimov, A- E-.
'Menial'nye lavki i kontory v Man'chzhurii' (Exchange shops and bureaus in Manchuria). [With English abstract]
VM 1932, 2, 37–43.
SUBJ 24.3 24.6 ▪ 34.3

17472 NIC P P8 G1.2 1928–1949
Hsu, Paul C. (Hsü Pao-ch'ien), 1892–1944.
'Rural credit in China.' In *Proceedings of the Second International Conference of Agricultural Economists*. [Sole entry]
Menasha, Wis.: Collegiate Press, 1930, 1006–1011.
SUBJ 24.6 34.2

17473 CBU F P3 G8.1 1928–1949
Hu Kwoh-hwa (Hu Kuo-hua).
'The Sino-Japanese War and the Chungking market.'
EF 11 (Sept. 1938), 519–530. [In Chinese as well as English]
SUBJ 24.6 ▪ 24.2 24.3

17474 DLC P P2 G3.0 1911–1949
Kara-Murza, Georgii Sergeevich, 1906–1945.
'Kitaiskii torgovo-rostovshchicheskii kapital vo Vnutrennei Mongolii' (Chinese capital for commerce and usury in Inner Mongolia).
PK 11 (1933), 155–209.
SUBJ 24.3 24.6 ▪ 24.1 66

17475 CSU P P3 G6.1 1928–1949
Kojima, Shotaro (Kojima Shōtarō), 1888–.
'Special currency system of China: A study on the "Wei Wah" [i.e., wai-hui, credit exchange between banks] system in Shanghai.'
KUER 16, 3 (July 1941), 16–50.
SUBJ 24.6

17476 CSU P P3 G6.1 1928–1949
Kojima, Shotaro (Kojima Shōtarō), 1888–.
'The Wei Wah [i.e., wai-hui, credit exchange between banks] system as a special credit system of China.'
KUER 16, 4 (Oct. 1941), 1–19.
SUBJ 24.6

17477 CBU O P3 G2.0 1928–1949
Kovalevskii, V- N-.
'Kreditno-ssudnye operatsii tuzemnykh bankov' (Credit-loan operations of domestic banks).
VM 1933, 18/19 (15 oktiabria), 43–51.
SUBJ 24.6 ▪ 24.3

17478 CSH P P3 G2.2 1911–1928
Kursel', K- P-.
'Itogi deiatel'nosti Dal'nevostochnogo banka v Kharbine za 1923–1926 gg.' (Results of the activities of the Far Eastern Bank in Harbin, 1923–1926).
VM 1927, 5, 34–44.
'Summary of the activities of the Far Eastern Bank in Harbin (Dalbank) from 1923 to 1926.' [Abridged tr.]
Manchuria monitor 1927, 6, 12–16.
SUBJ 24.6 ▪ 14.3

17479 NNC FP P7 G8.1 1928–1949
Lee Kuo-ch'un (Li Kuo-chen).
'Usury in the rural districts of Szechwan.' Tr. of 'Ssu-ch'uan ti nung ts'un kao li tai' (Usury in rural Szechwan); *Chung-kuo nung ts'un* 2, 11 (Nov. 1936), 67–72. In *Agrarian China*, compiled by Institute of Pacific Relations. [Selective entry]
Chicago: U. of Chicago Press, 1939, 193–199.
SUBJ 24.6 ▪ 24.1 26.3 28

17480 CBU P P2 G8.1 1928–1949
Li Hwei-chien (Li Te-ch'ien).
'Business analysis of cooperative credit societies, Wenkiang [i.e., Wen-chiang *hsien*], Szechwan, 1937–1943.'
EF 40 (Jan. 1945), 613–620.
SUBJ 24.6 34.2

17481 NNC FP P2 G1.2 1928–1949
Lo Kuo-hsian and Chen Han-seng (Ch'en Han-sheng), 1897–.
'Pawnshop and peasantry.' Tr. from *Nung ts'un ho tso* 2, 6 (1937) [condensed tr.; also condensed from Chen Han-seng, *The present agrarian problem of China*, Shanghai: China Institute of Pacific Relations, 1933]. In *Agrarian China*, compiled by Institute of Pacific Relations. [Selective entry]
Chicago: U. of Chicago Press, 1939, 188–193.
SUBJ 24.6 ▪ 26.3

17482 MCH O P7 G1.2 1911–1928
Mallory, Walter Hampton, 1892–.
'Rural cooperative credit in China: A record of seven years of experimentation.'
Quarterly j. of economics 45, 3 (May 1931), 484–498.
SUBJ 24.6 28 34.2 ▪ 24.1

17483 CSH O P3 G2.2 1928–1949
N.
'Torgovlia, promyshlennost' i kredit Kharbina v 1930 godu' (Trade, industry, and credit in Harbin in 1930).
EB 1931, 2 (15 ianvaria), 1–5.
SUBJ 24 24.6 ▪ 24.3 24.4

17484 PPU FP P2 G1.3 1928–1949
Nan, Ping-fang, 1900–.
A practical study of rural credit in four provinces of Central China.
Unpublished doctoral dissertation in Finance, U. of Pennsylvania, 1937. 232 p.
SUBJ 24 24.6 ▪ 14.3 24.1 24.3 25 34.2 38

17485 NNC P P2 G1.2 1911–1949
Peng, Shinwei (P'eng Hsin-wei).
Shanghai money market.
New York: Sino-International Economic Research Center, 1946. 56 p. (SIERC pamphlets, 3)
SUBJ 24.6 ▪ 14.6 34.2

17486 MCH S P8 G1.2 1911–1928
Peo Yu (Pu Yü).
Associations de crédit mutuel rural et associations similaires en Chine (Ts'ing-Houei) (Rural mutual-credit associations and similar associations in China, *ch'ing-hui* [rotating-credit societies]).
Paris: Ed. Domat-Montchrestien, 1936. 157 p. (Doctoral dissertation, Faculté des lettres, Université de Paris)
SUBJ 24.6 ▪ 26.3 36.3 72

17487 CBU F P3 G6.1 1911–1949
Raeburn, John R-, and Hu Kwoh-hwa (Hu Kuo-hua).
'The prices and value of gold.'
EF 6 (July 1937), 244–249. [In Chinese as well as English]
SUBJ 24.6 ▪ 24.3

17488 NNP O P4 G2.3 1911–1928
Shalaev, A-.
'Denezhnyi rynok Inkou' (The money market in [the city of] Ying-k'ou [Fengtien]).
EB 1925, 26, 11–13.
SUBJ 24.6

17489 NNC PO P4 G2.3 1911–1928
Tideman, P- G-.
'Donesenie imperatorskago rossiiskago konsula v Niuchzhuane, k voprosu o neudovletvoritel'nom sostoianii v Niuchzhuane denezhnago obrashcheniia' (Report of the imperial Russian consul in Niu-chuang [Fengtien] on the unsatisfactory state of currency circulation in Niu-chuang).
DIRKP 39 (1914), 49–53.
SUBJ 24.6

17490 CSH O P3 G2.2 1928–1949
Tikhonov, N-.
'Bankovskii i chastnyi kredit v Kharbine' (Bank and private credit in Harbin).
EB 1932, 8 (15 aprelia), 9–11.
SUBJ 24.6

17491 CSU P P3 G6.1 1911–1949
Tokunaga, Kiyoyuki, 1904–.
'Characteristics of the security market in China: Its special relations with Chinese native capital.' Tr. of 'Shina shōken shijō no seikaku: Minzoku shihon to no kanren ni oite' (The nature of stock exchanges in China: Their relation to national capital); *Keizai ronsō* 55, 3 (Sept. 1942), 33–48. [Tr. inferred]
KUER 18, 2 (Apr. 1943), 27–47.
SUBJ 24.6 ▪ 36.2

17492 CSU PO P7 G1.2 1928–1949
Wu, Leonard T. K. (Wu Tsu-kuang).
'Merchant capital and usury capital in rural China.'
FES 5, 7 (25 Mar. 1936), 63–68.
SUBJ 24.6 26.1 26.3 ▪ 24.1 24.3 34.2

1911-1972
(including 1644-1972)

17493 NNC P P1 G9.5 1842–1972
King, Frank Henry Haviland, 1926–.
The monetary system of Hong Kong.
Hong Kong: Weiss, 1953. 151 p. (Far East economic series, 1)
SUBJ 24.6

17494 CSU PO P1 G1.1 –1972
Litton, Henry, and Denis K. L. Chang.
'Chinese money-loan associations [i.e., rotating-credit societies].'
Hong Kong law j. 1, 2 (May 1971), 194–205; 1, 3 (Sept. 1971), 262–273.
SUBJ 12.2 24.6

17495 CSU PO P3 G9.5 1928–1972
Stammer, Donald William, 1941–.
'Financial development and economic growth in underdeveloped countries: Comment [on the Hong Kong case].' [With a reply by Hugh T- Patrick]
EDCC 20, 2 (Jan. 1972), 318–329.
SUBJ 24.6 ▪ 34.2

1949-1972

17496 NNP O P3 G9.5 1949–1972
'Banking in Hong Kong.'
TBHK June 1966, 67–70.
SUBJ 24.6

17497 MCY O P3 G5.1 1949–1972
'How labour insurance works.'
China reconstructs 3, 4 (July–Aug. 1954), 28–32.
SUBJ 24.6 26.4 28 ▪ 36.4 50 56 57

17498 MCH O P7 G7.2 1949–1972
'40 per cent of production teams in Nan hsien have their own production funds: Solution of problems of farm production funds in the spirit of self-reliance.' Tr. of 'Fa yang tzu li keng sheng ko ming ching shen chieh chüeh nung yeh sheng ch'an tzu chin wen t'i: Nan hsien pai fen chih ssu shih sheng ch'an tui sheng ch'an fei yung tzu chi' (Developing the revolutionary spirit of self-reliance to find solutions to the problems of agricultural capital: Forty

percent of production teams in Nan *hsien* [Hunan] are self-supplied); *Ta kung pao* (Peking) 5 July 1964, 1.
SCMP 3267 (28 July 1964), 10–16.
Subj 24.6 ▪ 34.1

17499 NNC F P3 G9.5 1949–1972
Burton, Robert A-, 1922–.
'Self-help, Chinese style [rotating-credit societies].'
AUFS-EAS 6, 9 (15 July 1958), 1–10.
Subj 24.6 34.2

17500 CSH O P3 G2.3 1949–1972
China [People's Republic]. Ts'ai cheng pu (Ministry of Finance) *and* Liaoning. Fu-shun shih [cheng fu] (Fu-shun Municipality). Ko [ming] wei [yüan] hui (Revolutionary Committee), *joint sponsors*. Lien ho tiao ch'a tsu (Joint Investigation Team). [This agency has still a third joint sponsor: Fu-shun chün fen ch'ü (Fu-shun Military Command).]
'Carry out the great principle of "developing the economy and ensuring supplies": Investigation report on the Chien-hsin Service Group of the Fushun Municipal Branch of the People's Bank of China, Liaoning.' Tr. of 'Chih hsing "fa chan ching chi, pao chang kung chi" ti wei ta fang chen: Chung-kuo jen min yin hang Liao-ning Fu-shun shih fen hang chien hsin fu wu pan ti tiao ch'a pao kao'; *Hung ch'i* 1971, 2 (Feb.), 53–58.
CES 6, 2 (Winter 1972/73), 26–39.
Subj 24.6

17501 MCH O P7 G2.3 1949–1972
Chung-kuo kung ch'an tang. Chung yang cheng chih chü. Tung pei chü. Ts'ai cheng wei yüan hui. Kung tso tsu. (Chinese Communist Party. Central Committee. Northeast Bureau. Finance Committee. Work Team), ed.
'A well-operated rural credit cooperative: The work expense of P'aotzuyen credit cooperative of K'uantien hsien, Liaoning province.' Tr. of 'I ko pan te hao ti nung ts'un hsin yung she: Liao-ning sheng K'uan-tien hsien P'ao-tzu-yen hsin yung tso she ti kung tso ching yen' (A well-run rural credit cooperative: Operating experiences of the P'ao-tzu-yen credit cooperative, K'uan-tien *hsien*, Liaoning); *Ta kung pao* (Peking) 20 July 1964, 1–2.
SCMP 3277 (12 Aug. 1964), 7–12.
Subj 24.6 34.2

17502 NNC O P7 G7.1 1949–1972
Chung-kuo kung ch'an tang. Ma-ch'eng hsien wei yüan hui. Pai-kao jen min kung she wei yüan hui. (Chinese Communist Party. Ma-ch'eng Hsien Committee. Pai-kao Commune Committee).
'Conditions of implementation of "two decentralization, three-unification and one-guarantee" in Peikao people's commune of Ma-ch'eng county.' Tr. of 'Ma-ch'eng hsien Pai-kao jen min kung she shih hsing "liang fang, san t'ung, i pao" ti ch'ing k'uang' (Pai-kao commune, Ma-ch'eng *hsien* [Hupeh] and the policy of 'two decentralizations, three unifications and one guarantee'); *Ts'ai cheng* 1958, 15 (24 Dec.), 10–12.
URS 14, 9 (30 Jan. 1959), 125–135.
Subj 22 24.6 ▪ 17 24 32.1 34.1

17503 CSH U P3 G9.5 1949–1972
Jao, Y. C. (Jao Yü-ch'ing).
'Linear programming and banking in Hong Kong.' In *Hong Kong economic papers, No. 6*, edited by Ronald Hsia (Hsia Hsiu-yung). [Sole entry]
Hong Kong: Hong Kong Economic Assn., 1971, 28–32.
Subj 24.6

17504 CSH P P1 G9.5 1949–1972
Jao, Y. C. (Jao Yü-ch'ing).
'Money supply in Hong Kong, 1954–1968.' In *Hong Kong economic papers, No. 5*, edited by Ronald Hsia (Hsia Hsiu-yung). [Selective entry]
Hong Kong: Hong Kong Economic Assn., 1970, 24–48.
Subj 24.6

17505 CSU U P1 G9.4 1949–1972
Jones, Howard L-.
'Chinese mutual savings and loan clubs.'
J. of business (Chicago) 40, 3 (July 1967), 336–338.
Subj 24.6

17506 CSH P P3 G9.5 1949–1972
Jones, P- H- M-.
'Flush with money.'
FEER 64, 16 (17 Apr. 1969), 183–187.
Subj 24.6

17507 MCH F P7 G1.2 1949–1972
[La Dany, Ladislao] ———, 1914–.
'Rural credit.'
CNA 38 (4 June 1954), 2–7.
Subj 24.6 ▪ 34.1

17508 DLC P P1 G9.5 1949–1972
Lin, Tzong-Biau (Lin Ts'ung-piao), 1936–.
Das monetäre System und das Verhallen des Angeboles an und der Nachfrage nach Geld in Hong Kong (The monetary system and the supply of and demand for gold in Hong Kong).
Freibourg i. Br.: Eberhard Albert, 1969. 146 p. (Doctoral dissertation, Rechts- und staatswissenschaftliche Fakultät, Universität Freibourg i. Br.).

Monetary behavior under the sterling exchange standard: Hong Kong as a case study. [Greatly abridged in tr.]
Hong Kong: Chinese U. of Hong Kong, 1971. 51 p. (Economic Research Centre, Hong Kong series, occasional papers, 1)
Subj 24.6

17509 CSU O P3 G9.5 1949–1972
[Litton, Henry] H. L.
'Packing credit facilities: An excercise in faith, hope and charity.'
Hong Kong law j. 1, 1 (Jan. 1971), 57–60.
Subj 24.6

17510 CSU PO P3 G9.5 1949–1972
[Litton, Henry] H. L., and [Denis K. L. Chang] D. C.
'Chit-fund companies or "ngan wuis" [yin-hui].'
Hong Kong law j. 2, 1 (Jan. 1972), 77–83.
Subj 24.6

17511 CSH P P1 G9.5 1949–1972
Moonitz, Maurice.
'Financial reporting in Hong Kong: A preliminary study.' In *Hong Kong economic papers, No. 4*, edited by Ronald Hsia (Hsia Hsiu-yung). [Selective entry]
Hong Kong: Hong Kong Economic Assn., 1968, 1–11.
Subj 24.3 24.6

17512 ACU PO P3 G9.5 1949–1972
Stammer, Donald William, 1941–.
Money and finance in Hong Kong.
Unpublished doctoral dissertation in Economics, Australian National U., 1968. 15, 351 p.
Subj 24 24.5 24.6 ▪ 55

17513 MCY P P3 G9.5 1949–1972
Sutu Hsin (Ssu-t'u Hsin), 1909–, and Derek Davies.
'Finance for industry.'
FEER 40, 8 (23 May 1963), 439, 441, 443.
Subj 24.6 ▪ 24.4

17514 CSH P P1 G9.5 1949–1972
Tang, Anthony M. (T'ang Tsung-ming), 1924–.
'Hong Kong's devaluation and revaluation.' In *Hong Kong economic papers, No. 4*, edited by Ronald Hsia (Hsia Hsiu-yung). [Selective entry]
Hong Kong: Hong Kong Economic Assn., 1968, 45–49.
Subj 24.3 24.6

17515 HKU PO P3 G9.5 1949–1972
Tomkins, H- J-.
Report on the Hong Kong banking system and recommendations for the replacement of the banking ordinance, 1948.
Hong Kong: Government Printer, 1962. 51 p.
Subj 24.6

17516 NIC F P7 G9.5 1949–1972
Ward, Barbara Elsie, 1919–.
'Cash or credit crops? An examination of some implications of peasant commercial production, with special reference to the multiplicity of traders and middlemen.'
EDCC 8, 2 (Jan. 1960), 148–163.
Subj 24.6 34.2 ▪ 24.3 26.2

17517 CSH O P3 G9.5 1949–1972
Whatmore, Richard.
'The Hongkong stock exchange.'
FEER 36, 5 (3 May 1962), 229–231.
Subj 24.6

17518 TPY P P7 G9.4 1949–1972
Wong Wen-cha (Wang Wen-cha) and Lei Chang (Lai Chang).
'The research study of agricultural capital in Taiwan.'
J. of law and commerce (Taipei) 3 (Oct. 1963), 1–54 [s.p.]. [See Vol. 2 of this *Bibliography* for Chinese version.]
Subj 24.1 24.6

17519 NNC U P7 G1.2 1949–1972
Wu Tien-hsi (Wu T'ien-hsi) and I Ming-shen.
'Superiority of the people's communes from the financial standpoint.' Tr. of 'Ts'ung ts'ai wu kung tso k'an jen min kung she ti yu yüeh hsing'; *Ta kung*

pao (Peking) 14 Jan. 1960, 3. In *Translations on Communist China's commune economy*, mimeo., compiled by U.S. Joint Publications Research Service. [Sole entry]
Washington, D.C.: JPRS, 15 June 1960, 9–19. (JPRS 2821; MC 11,385/1960)
SUBJ 24 24.6 34.1 ▪ 22

25 FEUDS, BANDITRY, AND LOCAL PARAMILITARY UNITS

械鬥、盜賊及地方武力

械鬥、匪賊行為及び地方の保安組織

1644-1911

17520 CSU PO P2 G8.2 –1895
Anderson, John, 1833–1900.
'The Mohammedans of Yunnan.' In *Mandalay to Momien: A narrative of the two expeditions to western China of 1868 and 1875 . . .*, by J. Anderson. [Selective entry]
London: Macmillan, 1876, 223–247. [Reprinted in *Mandalay to Momien: A narrative of the two expeditions to western China of 1868 and 1875 . . .*, by J. Anderson. (Selective entry.) Taipei: Ch'eng-wen, 1972, 223–247.]
SUBJ 25 33 66 ▪ 21.2 41

17521 CSU O P7 G9.2 1842–1911
Ashmore, William, 1824–1909.
'A clan feud near Swatow.'
CR 28, 5 (May 1897), 214–223.
SUBJ 22.2 25 ▪ 22.1 66

17522 MCH O P7 G5.1 1895–1911
Becker, Pierre Emile, 1836–1918.
'Une nouvelle insurrection au Tché-li S.-E. en mai 1902' (A new insurrection in southeastern Chihli in May 1902).
Etudes 7e série 94, 1 (20 jan. 1903), 111–119.
SUBJ 22 25 66 ▪ 26

17523 NNC P P3 G9.2 1842–1911
Borokh, Liliia Nikolaevna, 1933–.
'Neudavsheesia vosstanie v Guanchzhou v 1895 g.' (The abortive uprising of 1895 in Canton).
KSINA 66 (1963), 82–93.
SUBJ 25 32.2 ▪ 15 32 32.1 59 64 66

17524 CSU P P3 G9.2 1644–1842
Bowra, E- C-.
'The Manchu conquest of Canton.'
China review 1, 2 (Sept.–Oct. 1872), 86–96; 1, 4 (Jan.–Feb. 1873), 228–237.
SUBJ 15 25 ▪ 12

17525 NNC O P2 G2.0 1895–1911
Budberg, Roger Baron.
'Aus der Mandschurei: Die Chunchudzen' (The Hung Hu-tzu in Manchuria).
Globus 97, 10 (17 März 1910), 149–153; 97, 11 (24 März 1910), 168–173.
SUBJ 22.2 25 32.2 ▪ 12.2 57

17526 CSU P P8 G5.3 1842–1911
Ch'en, Jerome (Ch'en Chih-jang), 1919–.
'The origin of the Boxers.' In *Studies in the social history of China and South-east Asia: Essays in memory of Victor Purcell*, edited by J. Chen and Nicholas Tarling. [Selective entry]
Cambridge: Cambridge U. Press, 1970, 57–84.
SUBJ 25 32.2 ▪ 22 26.1 59 66

17527 CSU P P1 G4.1 1842–1895
Chu, Wen-djang (Chu Wen-ch'ang), 1914–.
'The immediate cause of the Moslem Rebellion in North-west China in 1862.'
Central Asiatic j. 3, 4 (1958), 309–316.
SUBJ 25 ▪ 12 29 32.2

17528 CSU P P8 G9.5 –1842
da Silva, Armando Maria.
'Fan Lau [i.e., Fen-liu, Ta-yü shan, Hong Kong] and its fort: An historical perspective.'
JRAS-HKB 8 (1968), 82–95.
SUBJ 25

17529 MCH P P3 G5.1 1895–1911
Fleming, Peter, 1907–.
The seige at Peking.
London: Rupert Hart-Davis, 1959. 273 p.
SUBJ 15 25 66 ▪ 32.2

17530 NNC P P2 G9.0 1644–1842
Fomina, Nataliia Ivanovna.
'Voennoe iskusstvo antiman'chzhurskogo opolcheniia iugo-vostochnogo Kitaia v seredine XVII v.' (The military technique of the anti-Ch'ing militia of Southeast China in the mid-seventeenth century).
KSINA 85 (1964), 47–59.
SUBJ 15 25 32.2

17531 MCH P P1 G1.1 1644–1895
Fox, Grace Estelle, 1899–.
British admirals and Chinese pirates, 1832–1869.
London: Kegan Paul, Trench, Trübner, 1940. 14, 227 p.
SUBJ 14.3 25 ▪ 12 15

17532 CSU O P2 G5.0 1842–1911
Giles, Lancelot.
The siege of the Peking legations: A diary, edited by Leslie Ronald Marchant.
Nedlands, W.A.: U. of Western Australia Press, 1970. 27, 212 p.
SUBJ 22.2 25 32.2 66 ▪ 15 72

17533 CSU FP P7 G9.0 1895–1911
Groves, Robert George, 1934–.
'Militia, market and lineage: Chinese resistence to the occupation of Hong Kong's New Territories in 1899.'
JRAS-HKB 9 (1969), 31–64.
SUBJ 21.3 24.3 25 32.2 42 66 ▪ 22 22.1 24.2 26.1

17534 MCH O P7 G5.1 1842–1895
Guillon, Joseph, 1830–1869.
'Les brigands dans le Pe-Tche-Ly: les Tchang-mao' (The Ch'ang-mao [Taipings], bandits in northern Chihli).
APF 40 (1868), 348–362.
SUBJ 25 ▪ 32.2

17535 MCH O P4 G8.1 1895–1911
Hourst, E-.
'Le révolte au Se-tchouen' (The revolt in Szechwan [1904]).
Correspondant 216 (25 sept. 1904), 1051–1078.
SUBJ 22.1 23 25 32.2 61 66 ▪ 21.1 35 47 48 57

17536 CSU O P2 G9.3 1842–1895
Hughes, George.
'The capture of Chang-chow-fu [Fukien] by rebels.'
China review 1, 6 (May–June 1873), 348–352.
SUBJ 25 32.2

17537 CSU O P3 G9.3 1842–1895
Hughes, George.
'The Small Knife rebels: An unpublished chapter of Amoy history.'
China review 1, 4 (Jan.–Feb. 1873), 244–248.
SUBJ 25 32.2

17538 MCH O P2 G8.2 1842–1895
Huot, A-, 182?–1864.
'La province de Yunnan envahie par les Lolos' (The Lolo invasion of Yunnan).
APF 35 (1853), 387–399.
SUBJ 25 66

17539 CBU PO P2 G7.1 1842–1895
Imbault-Huart, Camille Clément, 1857–1897.
'Un révolte des troupes chinoises à Vou-tch'ang-fou' (A revolt of Chinese troops in Wu-ch'ang-fu [Hupeh]).
JA 8e série 3 (jan. 1884), 89–94.
SUBJ 12 15 25

17540 NNC O P2 G2.1 1842–1911
IUvachev, I-.
'Bor'ba s khunkhuzami na manchzhurskoi granitse' (The struggle with the Hung Hu-tzu on the Manchurian border).
Istoricheskii vestnik 21 (oktiabr' 1900), 177–206; 21 (noiabr' 1900), 538–564.
SUBJ 25 ▪ 21.2 22.2 32.1 66

17541 MCH P P7 G1.3 1644–1895
Kuhn, Philip Alden, 1933–.
Rebellion and its enemies in late Imperial China: Militarization and social structure, 1796–1864.
Cambridge: Harvard U. Press, 1970. 254 p. (Harvard East Asian series, 49) (Revision of *Militia in China during the Taiping Rebellion*, doctoral dissertation in History and Far Eastern Languages, Harvard U., 1964)
SUBJ 22 25 26 32.1 32.2 ▪ 15 22.1 26.1 26.3 30 35 39 42 64

17542 CSU P P8 G1.3 1644–1895
Kuhn, Philip Alden, 1933–.
'The t'uan-lien local defense system at the time of the Taiping Rebellion.'
HJAS 27 (1967), 218–255.
SUBJ 22.2 25 35 ▪ 22 22.1 26.1

17543 MAM P P2 G1.5 1842–1895
Laffey, Ella Sapira, 1935–.
Relations between Chinese provincial officials and the Black Flag Army, 1883–1885.
Ann Arbor: University Microfilms (Publ. 71-25,165), 1971. 305 p. (Doctoral dissertation in History, Cornell U.)
SUBJ 25 59 ▪ 12 32.2 66

17544 CSU P P2 G9.4 1895–1911
Lamley, Harry Jerome, 1928–.
'The 1895 Taiwan war of resistance: Local Chinese efforts against a foreign power.' In *Taiwan: Studies in Chinese local history*, edited by Leonard Herman David Gordon. [Selective entry]

New York: Columbia U. Press, 1970, 23–77.
SUBJ 22 25 26.1 ▪ 22.1

17545 MBA O P2 G9.1 1842–1911
Lavest, J- M-.
'La situation de Kouang-si depuis 1890' (The condition of Kwangsi since 1890).
RI nouvelle (2e) série 2, 6 (30 sept. 1904), 381–412.
SUBJ 12 15 25 ▪ 32.2 33

17546 MCH O P3 G9.2 1842–1895
Leturdu, *Père* M-.
'Le bombardement de Canton' (The [Taiping] bombardment of Canton).
APF 30 (1858), 249–261.
SUBJ 21.1 25 66

17547 MCY P P2 G9.2 1842–1895
Lo, Winston Wan, 1938–.
'Communal strife in mid-nineteenth century Kwangtung: The establishment of Ch'ih-ch'i [*t'ing*].'
PC 19 (Dec. 1965), 85–119.
SUBJ 22 25 26.1 29 ▪ 11.3 21.2 24.1 32.2 42

17548 CSH O P7 G2.2 1895–1911
Lobza, P-.
'Khunkhuzy v Manchzhurii: ocherki iz puteshestviia po Manchzhurii v 1897–1898 g.g.' (The Hung Hu-tzu in Manchuria: Notes from travels through Manchuria in 1897–1898).
Russkoe bogatstvo 1902, 6 (iiun'), 27–54 [s.p.].
SUBJ 22.2 24.2 25 26.2 63 ▪ 15 21.3 24.1 24.3 24.4

17549 CSU O P2 G6.1 1842–1895
Lyster, Thomas, 1840–1865.
With Gordon in China: Letters from Thomas Lyster, Lieutenant, Royal Engineers, edited by E- A- Lyster.
London: Unwin, 1891. 296 p.
SUBJ 15 25 28 ▪ 32.2

17550 CSU PO P2 G1.2 1842–1895
MacGowan, Daniel Jerome, 1814?–1895.
'Contributions to the history of the [Taiping] insurrection in China.' In *Shanghae almanac for the bissextile or leap year 1856, and miscellany*. [Selective entry]
Shanghai: North-China Herald, 1855, n.p. [31 p. in all.]
SUBJ 14.6 25 32.2 ▪ 12.1 14.5 22.2

17551 CSU S P2 G2.0 1842–1895
Mancall, Mark, 1932–, and Georges G- Jidkoff.
'The Hung Hu-tzu of Northeast China.' In *Popular movements and secret societies in China, 1840–1950*, edited by Jean Chesneaux. [Analytic entry]
Stanford: Stanford U. Press, 1972, 125–134.
SUBJ 20 22 25 32.2 ▪ 21 26 40

17552 CSU O P3 G5.1 1895–1911
Martin, William Alexander Parsons, 1827–1916.
'The causes that led up to the seige of Pekin.'
NG 12, 2 (Feb. 1901), 53–63.
SUBJ 25 66 ▪ 32.2

17553 EOB P P7 G9.2 1842–1895
Roberts, John Anthony George, 1935–.
The Hakka-Punti War.
Unpublished doctoral dissertation in Oriental Studies, Oxford U. [Queen's College], 1968. 273 p.
SUBJ 21.2 25 29 ▪ 22 22.1 26.1 32.2

17554 CSU PO P4 G7.2 1895–1911
Rodes, Jean.
'Au Hounan' (In Hunan). In *Le Céleste empire avant la révolution* (The Celestial Empire before the Revolution [of 1911]), by J. Rodes. [Selective entry]
Paris: Alcan, 1914, 115–141. (Dix ans de politique chinoise, 3)
SUBJ 16.1 24.2 25 66 ▪ 21.3

17555 CSU O P3 G6.1 1644–1842
Wang Hsiu-ch'u.
'A memoir of a ten days' massacre in Yangchow.' Tr. by Lucien Mao of 'Yang-chou shih jih chi' (Diary of ten days in Yangchow); in *Ming chi pai shih hui pien* (Compilation of informal histories of the Ming period), compiled by Liu-yün-chü-shih, pseud.; n.p., n.d., *chüan* 10, 1a–16b [s.p.].
THM 4, 5 (May 1937), 515–537.
SUBJ 25 ▪ 66

17556 CSU U P3 G5.1 1895–1911
Weinert, Richard P-.
'The battle of Tientsin.'
American history illustrated 1, 7 (Nov. 1966), 4–13, 52–55.
SUBJ 15 25 ▪ 66

17557 WSU P P7 G9.5 1644–1842
Woo Kit-yu (Hu Chieh-yü).
'Hsi-Ying-P'an and the end of ravages of the pirate Chang Pao-tsai.' Tr. of 'Hsi-ying-p'an pü Chang Pao-tsai huo luan chih p'ing ting'; in *I pa ssu erh nien i ch'ien chih Hsiang-kang chi ch'i tui wai chiao t'ung: Hsiang-kang ch'ien tai shih*, edited by Lo Hsiang-lin; Hong Kong: Chung-kuo hsüeh she, 1959, 151–170. In *Hong Kong and its external communications before 1842*, edited by Lo Hsiang-lin. [Selective entry]
Hong Kong: Institute of Chinese Culture, 1963, 106–118.
SUBJ 25

17558 CSU O P2 G6.1 1895–1911
Yui, C. Voonping.
'Some experiences at the seige of Nanking during the revolution.' In *Recent developments in China*, edited by George Hubbard Blakeslee. [Selective entry]
New York: G. E. Stechert, 1913, 335–344.
SUBJ 25 ▪ 32.2 56

1644-1949

17559 CSU P P2 G9.2 1895–1928
Friedman, Edward, 1937–.
'Revolution or just another bloody cycle? Swatow and the 1911 Revolution.'
JAS 29, 2 (Feb. 1970), 289–307.
SUBJ 25 26.2 26.3 32.2 ▪ 12 22 22.2 26.1 66

17560 MCH P P2 G9.2 1842–1928
Hsieh, Winston (Hsieh Wen-sun), 1935–.
The Revolution of 1911 in Kwangtung.
Unpublished doctoral dissertation in History and Far Eastern Languages, Harvard U., 1969. 336 p.
SUBJ 21.1 22 24.5 25 32.2 36.3 ▪ 21.3 24.2 24.3 26.1 26.3 42 47 54 64

17561 NOU O P2 G7.2 1895–1949
Vogt, Volrath, 1879–.
Kina i smil og tårer: En laegemisjonaer forteller (China in smiles and tears: A missionary doctor speaks).
Stavanger: Misjonsselskapets forlag, 1948. 192 p.
SUBJ 25 56 ▪ 15 26.3

1911-1949

17562 MBA P P2 G8.0 1911–1928
'Choses militaires de Yunnan' (Military affairs in Yunnan).
RI nouvelle (2e) série 22, 8 (août 1914), 209–215.
SUBJ 15 17 25

17563 CSU O P8 G9.0 1928–1949
Cardwell, Robert.
'Pirate-fighters of the South China Sea.'
NG 89, 6 (June 1946), 787–796.
SUBJ 25

17564 NNC O P2 G1.4 1928–1949
Chu Teh (Chu Te), 1886–.
On the battle fronts of the liberated areas, 2nd ed. Tr. of *Lun chieh fang ch'ü chan ch'ang*; Peking: Jen min ch'u pan she, 1949; 78 p.
Peking: Foreign Languages Press, 1952. 91 p. [The 1952 ed. is cited in preference to the 3rd ed. (1962) because it is more complete.]
SUBJ 25 ▪ 15 22

17565 MCH O P2 G6.0 1928–1949
Clubb, Oliver Edmund, 1901–.
'Chiang Kai-shek's Waterloo: The battle of Hwai-Hai.'
PHR 25, 4 (Nov. 1956), 389–399.
SUBJ 15 25 ▪ 32 32.2

17566 MCH O P8 G2.1 1911–1928
Howard, Harvey James, 1880–1956.
Ten weeks with the Chinese bandits.
New York: Dodd, Mead, 1927. 14, 272 p.
SUBJ 25 ▪ 22 28 55 56 66

17567 CSH O P2 G1.5 1911–1928
Kumanin, M- F-.
'Nan'chanskoe vosstanie' (The Nanchang uprising). In *Sovetskie dobrovol'tsy o pervoi grazhdanskoi revoliutsionnoi voine v Kitae: vospominaniia* (Soviet volunteers in China's First Revolutionary Civil War [1924–1927]: Reminiscences), compiled by Institut narodov Azii, Akademiia nauk SSSR, edited by Aleksei Stepanovich Perevertailo. [Analytic entry]
Moscow: Izd-vo vost. lit-ry, 1961, 140–157.
SUBJ 15 25 32 32.2 ▪ 35

17568 CSH O P7 G2.0 1928–1949
Li Tso-peng.
'Three campaigns to the south of the Sungari river.'
China reconstructs 16, 1 (Jan. 1967), 11–18.
SUBJ 25

17569 CSH U P8 G5.2 1928–1949
Liu, Sydney.
'The battle of Pinghsingkuan [Fan-ching *hsien*, Shansi]: A significant event in Lin Piao's career.'
China Mainland review 2, 3 (Dec. 1966), 161–173.
SUBJ 15 16.1 25 ▪ 32.2 64

17570 CSU O P2 G5.1 1928–1949
Miller, J- Clayton.
'The Chinese still rule North China: Political and military strategy of the Hopei-Shansi-Chahar border government.'
Amerasia 2, 7 (Sept. 1938), 336–345.
SUBJ 12 15 22 25 ▪ 14.5 14.6 30

17571 FPN O P3 G9.2 1911–1928
[Neumann, Heinz] A. Neuberg, pseud., 1902–.
'L'insurrection de Canton' (The Canton uprising). In *L'insurrection armée* (Armed insurrection), by [H. Neumann] A. Neuberg, pseud. [Selective entry]
Paris: Impr. centrale, 1931, 103–129.
SUBJ 25 32.2 36.4 64 ▪ 15

17572 MCH O P3 G1.1 1911–1949
Powell, John Benjamin, 1888–1947.
My twenty-five years in China.
New York: Macmillan, 1945. 436 p.
SUBJ 22 25 ▪ 12 66

17573 MCH O P2 G1.3 1928–1949
Price, Willard, 1887–.
'Bandits of the Grand Canal.'
Blackwood's magazine 241, 1460 (June 1937), 829–843.
SUBJ 22.1 25 ▪ 66

17574 CSH S P2 G1.2 1928–1949
Shinkarev, I-.
'Liaoshen'skaia operatsiia narodno-osvoboditel'noi armii Kitaia' (The Liaoning-Mukden operation of the People's Liberation Army).
Voenno-istoricheskii zhurnal novaia (2-ia) seriia 3, 8 (avgust 1961), 37–49.
SUBJ 25 ▪ 15 32.2

17575 CSH O P2 G1.2 1911–1928
[Simpson, Bertram Lenox] B. L. Putnam Weale, pseud., 1877–1930.
Why China sees red.
London: Macmillan, 1926. 12, 313 p.
SUBJ 25 54 ▪ 14.2 32.2 66

17576 CSH P P2 G7.0 1928–1949
Sommer, Walter.
'Zur Rolle deutscher Berater in den Einkreisungs- und Vernichtungs-feldzügen gegen den südchinesische Sowjetrepublik, 1930–1934' (The role of German advisers in the anti-Communist extermination campaigns against the Kiangsi soviet, 1930–1934).
Z. für Politik neue (2.) Folge 18, 3 (Sept. 1971), 269–304.
SUBJ 25 ▪ 15 35 66

17577 CSH O P2 G1.4 1928–1949
Tipton, Laurance, 1909–.
Chinese escapade.
London: Macmillan, 1949. 247 p.
SUBJ 25 66 ▪ 15 32.2

17578 CSH P P3 G9.2 1911–1928
Wieger, Léon, 1856–1933.
'Sounn-wenn et les Volontaires des marchands de Canton' (Sun Yat-sen and the Canton Merchants Corps). In *Chine moderne, Tome VI, le feu aux poudres (1925)* (Modern China, Vol. 6, The tinderbox, 1925), 2nd ed., by L. Wieger. [Sole entry]
Hsien-hsien, Hopei: Impr. de Sienhsien, 1934, 95–98.
SUBJ 25 32.2 ▪ 22.1

1911-1972
(including 1644-1972)

17579 CSU O P8 G5.1 1928–1972
Alley, Rewi, 1897–.
'China's "Song My" [P'an-chia-yü village, Feng-jun *hsien*, Hopei] thirty years ago and now.'
EH 10, 3 (1971), 29–36.
SUBJ 24.1 25

17580 CSU O P2 G7.3 1911–1972
Alley, Rewi, 1897–.
'Kiangsi.'
EH 9, 6 (1970), 13–33.
SUBJ 25 32.2 59 ▪ 17 24.4 26.3 26.4 36.4

17581 NIC U P1 G1.5 1842–1972
Blue, A- D-.
'Piracy on the China coast.'
JRAS-HKB 5 (1965), 69–85.
SUBJ 22.2 25 ▪ 12.1 66

17582 CSU P P8 G9.3 1928–1972
Fessler, Loren, 1923–.
'The October 1949 battle for Quemoy.'
AUFS-EAS 16, 17 (Dec. 1969), 1–16.
SUBJ 25

17583 CSU P P3 G9.5 1842–1972
Hayes, James William, 1930–.
'A short history of military volunteers in Hong Kong.'
JRAS-HKB 11 (1971), 151–171.
SUBJ 25

17584 MCH P P1 G1.2 1928–1972
[La Dany, Ladislao] ———, 1914–.
'The militia.'
CNA 291 (4 Sept. 1959), 1–7.
SUBJ 25 32.1 ▪ 35

17585 CSU P P2 G1.2 1911–1972
Pak, Hyobom, 1926–.
'China's militia and Mao Tse-tung's "people's war".'
Orbis (Philadelphia) 11, 1 (Spring 1967), 285–294.
SUBJ 25 35 ▪ 15

17586 NNC P P2 G1.2 1928–1972
Ting, Li.
Militia of Communist China, mimeo.
Hong Kong: Union Research Institute, 1954. 145 p. (Communist China problem research series, EC7) [See Vol. 2 of this *Bibliography* for Chinese version.]
SUBJ 25 ▪ 15 22.1 26.3 26.4 32.1

1949-1972

17587 MCH P P1 G1.2 1949–1972
Asian Peoples' Anti-Communist League.
The militia: A thorn in the Peiping regime's side.
Taipei: Asian Peoples' Anti-Communist League, 1963. 21 p.
SUBJ 25 ▪ 12.1 32.1

17588 MSW P P8 G1.2 1949–1972
Behling, Thomas George.
The people's militia of China, 1951–1961.
Unpublished masters thesis in Asian Studies, Washington U., 1969. 107 p.
SUBJ 15 25 26.1 32.1 ▪ 21.4 22.1 24.1 26.3 35

17589 NNC F P2 G9.0 1949–1972
Copp, DeWitt, and Marshall Peck.
The odd day.
New York: Morrow, 1962. 212 p.
SUBJ 12.1 15 20 25 26 ▪ 24.1 28 32.2 52 62 63 66

17590 MCH P P3 G1.2 1949–1972
Current Scene Editor.
'According to Chairman Mao: Rebellion in China as reported by Peking.'
CS 5, 2 (31 Jan. 1967), 1–13.
SUBJ 19 25 ▪ 35 54 64

17591 MCH P P1 G1.2 1949–1972
Gittings, John, 1938–.
'China's militia.'
CQ 18 (Apr.–June 1964), 100–117.
SUBJ 25

17592 CSU P P3 G9.5 1949–1972
Heaton, William.
'Maoist revolutionary strategy and modern colonialism: The Cultural Revolution in Hong Kong.'
AS 10, 9 (Sept. 1970), 840–857.
SUBJ 22.2 25 28 ▪ 12.2 17 21.2

17593 ELB PO P3 G9.5 1949–1972
Hong Kong. Governor.
Report on the riots of Kowloon and Tsuen Wan [i.e., Ch'üan-wan], *October 10th to 12th, together with covering dispatch dated the 23rd December 1956, from the Governor of Hong Kong to the Secretary of State for the Colonies.*
Hong Kong: Government Printer, 1956. 55 p.
SUBJ 22 22.1 25 32.2 ▪ 21.3 22.2 26.4 28

17594 MCH P P7 G1.2 1949–1972
Jan, George P. (Jan Po-kung), 1925–.
'Red China's militia.'
Military review 45, 3 (Mar. 1965), 80–86.
SUBJ 25 ▪ 22.1

17595 CSU P P3 G9.5 1949–1972
Jarvie, Ian C-.
'A postscript on riots and the future of Hong Kong.' In *Hong Kong: A society in transition*, edited by I. C. Jarvie and Joseph Agassi. [Analytic entry]
New York: Praeger, 1969, 361–396.
SUBJ 25 54

17596 CSU P P2 G1.2 1949–1972
Karnow, Stanley, 1925–.
'Letter from Hong Kong.'
Encounter 32, 4 (Apr. 1969), 83–91.
SUBJ 14 25 32 ▪ 54 64 66

17597 CSU P P2 G1.2 1949–1972
Kumano, Shōhei, 1897–.
'The militia system of Communist China.'

Review (Tokyo) 9 (June 1966), 1–17. [See Vol. 3 of this *Bibliography* for Japanese version.]
Subj 22.1 25 35 ▪ 17 32 32.1 34.1 60

17598 MCH P P4 G9.5 1949–1972
[La Dany, Ladislao] ———, 1914–.
'Hong Kong and Macao.'
CNA 662 (2 June 1967), 1–7.
Subj 25 ▪ 32.2

17599 CSU P P1 G1.2 1949–1972
Lu Yung-shu (Lü Yung-shu).
'Peiping's conscription and retirement program.'
IS 5, 2 (Nov. 1968), 1–7.
Subj 25 ▪ 15 35

17600 CSU O P4 G9.5 1949–1972
Mikes, George.
'Letter from Macao.'
Encounter 33, 6 (Dec. 1969), 88–92.
Subj 25 66

17601 CSU P P2 G1.2 1949–1972
Nelsen, Harvey Walter, 1939–.
'Regional and paramilitary ground forces.' In *The military and political power of China in the 1970s*, edited by William Wallace Whitson. [Selective entry]
New York: Praeger, 1972, 135–152.
Subj 25 ▪ 15 35

17602 MCH U P3 G9.5 1949–1972
Pao Chin-an.
'An analysis of the Chinese Communist-led riots in Hong Kong.'
CCA 4, 3 (June 1967), 1–6.
Subj 25 66 ▪ 32.2

17603 MCH P P1 G1.2 1949–1972
Powell, Ralph Lorin, 1917–.
'Communist China's mass militia.'
CS 3, 7 (15 Nov. 1964), 1–8; 3, 8 (1 Dec. 1964), 1–8.
Subj 25 ▪ 15

17604 MCH P P1 G1.2 1949–1972
Powell, Ralph Lorin, 1917–.
'Everyone a soldier: The Communist Chinese militia.'
FA 39, 1 (Oct. 1960), 100–111.
Subj 25

17605 CSH P P1 G1.2 1949–1972
Tai Kao-hsiang.
'Chinese Communist conscription system.'
IS 2, 4 (Jan. 1966), 14–23.
Subj 25

17606 CSH O P7 G6.1 1949–1972
Wylie, Raymond Finlay, 1941–.
'[1] Struggle at Horse Bridge [i.e., Ma-ch'iao commune, Ching-chiang *hsien*, Kiangsu]. [2] Red Guards rebound. [3] The great debate.'
FEER 57, 9 (31 Aug. 1967), 419–420; 57, 10 (7 Sept. 1967), 462–466; 57, 11 (14 Sept. 1967), 509–514.
Subj 25 26.1 26.3 ▪ 22 22.1 54

26 Local Social Stratification and Mobility

地方社會之階層與流動

地方の社会階層及びその流動性

1644-1911

17607 NIC P P2 G9.2 –1911
Eberhard, Wolfram, 1909–.
'Mobility in South Chinese families.'
Sinologica 6, 1 (1959), 16–24.
Subj 26 ▪ 42

17608 ELO U P3 G9.5 1842–1895
Great Britain. Colonial Office.
Correspondence respecting the alleged existence of Chinese slavery in Hong Kong.
London: Her Majesty's Stationery Office, 1882. 124 p.
Subj 22.2 24.3 26 41 ▪ 26.2 38 47

17609 CSU O P3 G5.1 1895–1911
Matignon, Jean-Jacques, 1866–?
'Le mendiant de Pékin' (The beggars of Peking). In *Superstition, crime et misère en Chine* (Superstition, crime, and poverty in China), 4th ed., by J.-J. Matignon. [Selective entry]
Lyons: Storck, 1902, 207–246.
Subj 26 28 ▪ 55

17610 CSU P P8 G9.4 1842–1895
Meskill, Johanna Menzel, 1930–.
'The Lins of Wufeng [Chang-hua *hsien*, Fukien]: The rise of a Taiwanese gentry family.' In *Taiwan: Studies in Chinese local history*, edited by Leonard Herman David Gordon. [Selective entry]
New York: Columbia U. Press, 1970, 6–22.
Subj 25 26 26.1 ▪ 42

1644-1949

□

1911-1949

17611 DLC O P3 G5.1 1911–1928
Andreev, M- G-.
'V Pekine: bytovoi ocherk' (Sketch of life in Peking).
Krasnaia nov' 1927, 5 (mai), 198–213.
Subj 21.3 24.3 26 28 ▪ 21.2 22 23 26.2 26.4 54 55

17612 CSU P P3 G6.1 1911–1928
Chen, Joseph T. (Ch'en Tseng-tao), 1925–.
'Some populist strains in Shanghai during the May Fourth period.'
J. of Asian history 4, 1 (1970), 25–49.
Subj 26 60 ▪ 47 54

17613 NIC F P7 G8.2 1928–1949
Chow, Yung-teh (Chou Jung-te), 1916–.
Social mobility in China: Status careers among the gentry in a Chinese community.
New York: Atherton Press, 1966. 20, 300 p. (Revision of *Status mobility of the Chinese gentry: A field study of social status and social mobility of the gentry in Kunyang* [K'un-yang] *hsien, Yunnan province, Southwest China*, doctoral dissertation in Sociology, U. of Chicago, 1958)
Subj 22 26 26.1 50 59 ▪ 15 17 21.4 22.1 24 25 26.3 32.2 41 42

17614 DLC O P2 G1.3 1911–1928
Tret'iakov, Sergei Mikhailovich, 1892–1939.
Chzhungo: ocherki o Kitae (Chung-kuo: Notes on China), 2nd ed., rev.
Moscow: Gosizdat, 1930. 347 p.
Subj 21.3 24 26 28 32.2 55 ▪ 17 23 25 31 43 47 52 56 57 66

1911-1972
(including 1644-1972)

17615 CSU O P2 G9.0 1928–1972
Rand, Christopher.
Hong Kong: The island between.
New York: Knopf, 1952. 244 p. [Reprinted—New York: AMS Press, 1973. 244 p.]
Subj 21.4 26 29 32.2 66 ▪ 22.1 22.2 26.1 28 31 32 36.4

1949-1972

17616 CSU F P8 G9.4 1949–1972
Chu, Godwin C. (Chu Chien), 1927–.
'Impact of mass media on a gemeinschaft-like social structure.'
Rural sociology 33, 2 (June 1968), 189–199.
Subj 26 48 ▪ 24.2 26.3

17617 CSU F P3 G9.5 1949–1972
Cottle, Thomas J-.
'Comparative evaluation of occupations by English speaking, refugee and local Hong Kong adolescents.'
Sociological review new (2nd) series 15, 1 (Mar. 1967), 21–31.
Subj 21.4 26 54 ▪ 26.2

17618 MCH F P5 G9.4 1949–1972
Eberhard, Wolfram, 1909–.
'Social mobility among businessmen in a Taiwanese town.'
JAS 21, 3 (May 1962), 327–340. [Reprinted in *Settlement and social change in Asia*, by W. Eberhard. (Selective entry.) Hong Kong: Hong Kong U. Press, 1967, 178–193.]
Subj 24.3 24.6 26 ▪ 24.4 42 44

17619 CSH F P2 G9.4 1949–1972
Grichting, Wolfgang Leo.
'Occupational prestige structure in Taiwan.'
J. of sociology (Taipei) 7 (Apr. 1971), 67–78.
Subj 21.4 26

17620 CSU F P7 G5.1 1949–1972
Khan, A- Z- M- Obaidullah, ed.
'Report from China: Class struggle in Yellow Sandhill Commune [Huang-t'u-kang commune, Fang-shan *hsien*, Hopei].'
CQ 51 (July–Sept. 1972), 535–546.
Subj 20 22 26 26.3 ▪ 22.1 24.1 26.1 32 34.1 35

17621 CSU F P3 G9.4 1949–1972
Marsh, Robert Mortimer, 1931–.
'The explanation of occupational prestige hierarchies.'
Social forces 50, 2 (Dec. 1971), 214–222.
Subj 21.4 26

17622 CSU F P3 G9.4 1949–1972
Marsh, Robert Mortimer, 1931–.
'The Taiwanese of Taipei: Some major aspects of their social structure and attitudes.'
JAS 27, 3 (May 1968), 578–584.
SUBJ 26 41 ▪ 44 63

17623 CSU O P2 G9.5 1949–1972
Menard, Wilmon.
'The boat people of Hong Kong.'
Michigan quarterly review 8, 3 (July 1969), 189–193.
SUBJ 26 29 ▪ 22.2 23 24.1 65

17624 DLC O P2 G8.1 1949–1972
Vinar, Jan.
'Reportáž z cesty po provincii S'-čchuan' (Report on a trip in Szechwan).
Mezinárodní politika (Prague) 3, 9 (1959), 573–575.
SUBJ 22 26 26.3

26.1 THE LOCAL ELITE
地方領導階層
地方エリート階層

1644-1911

17625 MCH O P3 G5.1 1895–1911
Carpeaux, Louis.
'Pékin qui s'en va' (The Peking that is slipping away).
Nouvelle r. 4e série 1, 1 – 3, 2 (1er mai 1912 – 15 sept. 1912), 136 p. in all.
SUBJ 21.3 26.1 46 50 53 63 ▪ 12.2 15 29 41 57 66

17626 CSU O P4 G9.5 1842–1895
Ferrière Le Vayer, Théophile de.
'Macao' (Macau). In *Une ambassade française en Chine* (A French embassy in China), by T. de Ferrière Le Vayer. [Selective entry]
Paris: D'Amyot, 1854, 169–234.
SUBJ 23 26.1 ▪ 21.3 21.4 22 33

17627 CSH P P2 G5.3 1644–1911
Myers, Ramon Hawley, 1929–.
'Commercialization, agricultural development, and landlord behavior in Shantung province in the late Ch'ing period.'
CSWT 2, 8 (May 1972), 31–55.
SUBJ 14.3 24 24.1 26.1 45 ▪ 24.2 24.3 26.3

17628 CSU O P3 G5.1 1895–1911
Smith, Arthur Henderson, 1845–1932.
'The new Peking.'
EAM 1 (1902), 3–11.
SUBJ 26.1 ▪ 26

17629 CSU P P3 G9.5 1842–1895
Smith, Carl T-.
'The emergence of a Chinese elite in Hong Kong.'
JRAS-HKB 11 (1971), 74–115.
SUBJ 26.1 26.2 ▪ 38

1644-1949

17630 CBU P P4 G7.0 1895–1928
Esherick, Joseph Wharton, 1942–.
Reform, revolution and reaction: The Chinese Revolution of 1911 in Hunan and Hupeh.
Unpublished doctoral dissertation in History, U. of California, Berkeley, 1971. 642 p.
SUBJ 12 25 26 26.1 32.2 66 ▪ 12.1 14.4 17 22 24.2 26.4 35 64

17631 CSU PO P8 G1.3 –1928
Hughes, Ernest Richard, 1883–1956.
'The village and its scholar.' In *China, body and soul*, edited by E. R. Hughes. [Selective entry]
London: Secker and Warburg, 1938, 44–65. [Reprinted in *China, body and soul*, edited by E. R. Hughes. (Selective entry.) Freeport, N.Y.: Books for Libraries, 1970, 44–65.]
SUBJ 26.1 ▪ 22 27 29 60

1911-1949

17632 NNC O P3 G8.2 1928–1949
Baker, Gilbert.
The changing scene in China.
London: Student Christian Movement Press, 1946. 139 p.
SUBJ 26.1 61 63 ▪ 15 17 28 41

17633 CSH F P3 G8.1 1928–1949
Hu Kwoh-hwa (Hu Kuo-hua).
'The dilemma of salaried classes.'
EF 25 (Oct. 1943), 259–264.
SUBJ 26.1 28

17634 NNC U P7 G5.3 1928–1949
Li Tso-chow (Li Tso-chou).
The big landlords of Wei-hsien [i.e., Wei *hsien*], Shantung. Tr. of 'Shan-tung Wei hsien ti ta ti chu'; *Chung-kuo nung ts'un* 1, 8 (May 1935), 69–70. In *Agrarian China*, compiled by Institute of Pacific Relations. [Selective entry]
Chicago: U. of Chicago Press, 1939, 15–17.
SUBJ 24.1 26.1 ▪ 24.6

1911-1972
(including 1644-1972)

17635 CSU P P3 G9.5 1928–1972
Lethbridge, Henry James, 1923–.
'Hong Kong under Japanese occupation: Changes in social structure.' In *Hong Kong: A society in transition*, edited by Ian C- Jarvie and Joseph Agassi. [Analytic entry]
New York: Praeger, 1969, 77–127.
SUBJ 22 22.1 26.1 66 ▪ 17 21.2 50

1949-1972

17636 NNC O P3 G5.1 1949–1972
'Interview: "Suspicion everywhere".'
CS 1, 33 (5 June 1962), 1–12. [Reprinted in *Out of China: A collection of interviews with refugees from China*, edited by Francis Harper. (Analytic entry.) Hong Kong: Dragonfly Books, 1964, 75–103.]
SUBJ 17 26.1 ▪ 22.1 28 32 56

17637 NIC O P3 G6.1 1949–1972
'Interview with a translator from Shanghai.'
CS 1, 6 (10 July 1961), 1–8. [Reprinted as 'An odd contradiction . . .' In *Out of China: A collection of interviews with refugees from China*, edited by Francis Harper. (Analytic entry.) Hong Kong: Dragonfly Books, 1964, 187–204.]
SUBJ 26.1 28 ▪ 22.1 55

17638 CSU P P2 G1.2 1949–1972
Baum, Richard Dennis, 1940–.
'Elite behavior under conditions of stress: The lesson of the "Tang-ch'üan P'ai" [power-holders] in the Cultural Revolution.' In *Elites in the People's Republic of China*, edited by Robert Anthony Scalapino. [Analytic entry]
Seattle: U. of Washington Press, 1972, 540–574. (Social Science Research Council, Studies in Chinese government and politics, 3)
SUBJ 16.1 22.2 26.1 32 ▪ 12 22 26.3 32.1 54

17639 CSH P P7 G5.1 1949–1972
Baum, Richard Dennis, 1940–.
'Peach garden pestilence.' [On Wang Kuang-mei (*Mme.* Liu Shao-ch'i)]
FEER 58, 7 (16 Nov. 1967), 323–326.
SUBJ 26.1 26.3 32.1 ▪ 22.2 24

17640 CSU P P8 G1.2 1949–1972
Bernstein, Thomas Paul, 1937–.
'Keeping the revolution going: Problems of village leadership after land reform.' In *Party leadership and revolutionary power in China*, edited by John Wilson Lewis. [Analytic entry]
Cambridge: Cambridge U. Press, 1970, 239–267.
SUBJ 22.1 26.1 ▪ 26.3 32 34.1 50 64

17641 DLC O P3 G1.2 1949–1972
Čapek, Abe.
'Deset neděl s čínskými vědci a umělci' (Ten weeks with Chinese scientists and artists).
Literární noviny (Prague) 6, 13 (1957), 8, 6, 15.
SUBJ 26.1 54

17642 CSU P P2 G1.2 1949–1972
Kau, Ying-mao (Kao Ying-mao), 1934–.
'Patterns of recruitment and mobility of urban cadres.' In *The city in Communist China*, edited by John Wilson Lewis. [Analytic entry]
Stanford: Stanford U. Press, 1971, 97–121.
SUBJ 12 16.1 22 26.1 ▪ 11.2 17 21.1 32

17643 CSU P P3 G7.1 1949–1972
Kau, Ying-mao (Kao Ying-mao), 1934–.
'The urban bureaucratic elite in Communist China: A case study of Wuhan, 1949–65.' In *Chinese Communist politics in action*, edited by Arthur Doak Barnett. [Selective entry]
Seattle: U. of Washington Press, 1969, 216–267. (Social Science Research Council, Studies in Chinese government and politics, 1)
SUBJ 22 26.1 32.1 ▪ 26 32 59

17644 CSU F P2 G1.2 1949–1972
Oksenberg, Michel Charles, 1938–.
'Local leaders in rural China, 1962–65: Individual attributes, bureaucratic positions, and political recruitment.' In *Chinese Communist politics in action*, edited by Arthur Doak Barnett. [Selective entry]
Seattle: U. of Washington Press, 1969, 155–215. (Social Science Research

Council, Studies in Chinese government and politics, 1)
SUBJ 12 22 26 26.1 32 32.1 ▪ 16 16.1 22.1 50

17645 CSU O P2 G5.1 1949–1972
Pickowicz, Paul.
'Teaching the teachers: The concept of May 7th cadre school.'
EH 11, 3 (1972), 42–47.
SUBJ 26.1 32.1 37 64 ▪ 21.2 26.3

17646 CSU P P2 G6.1 1949–1972
White, Lynn Townsend, III, 1941–.
'Leadership in Shanghai, 1955–69.' In *Elites in the People's Republic of China*, edited by Robert Anthony Scalapino. [Analytic entry]
Seattle: U. of Washington Press, 1972, 302–377. (Social Science Research Council, Studies in Chinese government and politics, 3)
SUBJ 12 12.1 26.1 26.2 32.1 34.2 ▪ 21.2 24.1 24.3 30 32

17647 NNC P P7 G1.2 1949–1972
Young, Ronald Lee, 1946–.
Commitment among cadres in rural Communist China, 1960–1965.
Unpublished masters thesis in International Affairs, Columbia U., 1970. 70 p. [Certificate essay, East Asian Institute]
SUBJ 22.1 24.1 26.1 ▪ 64

26.2 BUSINESSMEN

商人及市民 商人及び市民

17648 MCH O P3 G6.1 1928–1972
Borovik, G-.
'Shankhaiskie kapitalisty' (The Shanghai capitalists).
Ogonek 50 (1956), 26–28.
SUBJ 26.2 ▪ 17 22.1

17649 NNC O P5 G6.3 1842–1895
Cobbold, Robert Henry.
Pictures of the Chinese drawn by themselves.
London: Murray, 1860. 219 p.
SUBJ 21.4 26.2 65 ▪ 23 28 41 47 61

17650 NIC O P3 G5.1 1911–1928
Dean, Samuel Bridge.
'Singing craftsmen of Peking.'
Asia (New York: American Asiatic Assn.) 21, 8 (Aug. 1921), 669–675.
SUBJ 24.4 26.2

17651 NIC O P3 G6.1 1928–1949
Faulder, H- Crozier.
'Chinese hawkers.'
CJ 21, 6 (Dec. 1934), 271–277.
SUBJ 24.3 26.2

17652 NNC O P3 G5.1 1644–1895
Forke, Alfred, 1867–1944.
'Über den Strassenhandel und das Strassengewerbe in Peking' (Peddlers and street vendors in Peking).
MDG 5, 47 (1892), 295–308.
SUBJ 24.3 26.2 ▪ 21.4

17653 DLC O P3 G6.1 1949–1972
Galin, Boris.
'Soldat i kapitalist' (Soldier and capitalist).
Nash sovremennik 1959, 1, 181–193.
SUBJ 22.1 26.2 ▪ 24.4 34.2 63 66

17654 CSU O P3 G6.1 1949–1972
Guillain, Robert, 1908–.
'Shanghai's repentant capitalists.'
Reporter 34, 7 (7 Apr. 1966), 38–41.
SUBJ 24.4 26.2 34.2 ▪ 22.1

17655 HKU F P3 G9.5 1949–1972
Hong Kong. Urban Council.
Hawkers: A report, with policy recommendations.
Hong Kong: Government Printer, 1957. 30 p.
SUBJ 26.2 ▪ 24.3

17656 NNC O P3 G6.1 1949–1972
Ovchinnikov, V-.
'Ispol'zovat', ogranichit', preobrazovat'' (Use, limit, transform).
Sovremennyi Vostok 1959, 7 (iiul'), 43–45; 1959, 8 (avgust), 38–40; 1959, 9 (sentiabr'), 21–23.
SUBJ 19 26.2 ▪ 24.4

17657 CSU O P3 G9.0 1644–1842
Renouard de Sainte-Croix, Félix.
Voyage commercial et politique aux Indes orientales, aux îles Philippines, à la Chine, avec des notions sur la Cochinchine et le Tonquin, pendant les années 1803, 1804, 1805, 1806 et 1807, Vol. 3 (A commercial and political voyage to the East Indies, the Philippines, and China, with notes on Cochin China and Tonkin, during the period 1803–1807, Vol. 3).
Paris: Clament, 1810. 289 p.
SUBJ 12 24 26.1 26.2 66 ▪ 12.2 21.1 23 25 31 33 55

17658 CSU P P4 G1.4 1644–1842
Rosner, Ehrhard, 1940–.
'Ein Beitrag zur Sozialgeschichte der chinesischen Kaufleute des 18. Jahrhunderts' (A social history of Chinese merchants in the eighteenth century).
OE 14, 1 (Aug. 1967), 27–41.
SUBJ 24.3 26.2 ▪ 14.3 34.2

17659 NNC O P3 G5.1 1949–1972
Sergiev, Artemii Vladimirovich.
'Kak perevospityvaiutsia kitaiskie kapitalisty' (The reeducation of Chinese capitalists).
Sovremennyi Vostok 1958, 10 (oktiabr'), 27–28.
SUBJ 22.1 26.2

17660 MCH P P3 G6.1 1949–1972
Tung, Robert.
'The sins of the capitalists.'
FEER 53, 10 (8 Sept. 1966), 441–442.
SUBJ 22.1 26.2 64 ▪ 22.2

17661 NNC P P2 G1.2 1842–1928
Wu, Chang-chuan.
Cheng Kuan-ying (1844–1923): His business career and mercantile ideas.
Unpublished masters thesis in History, Columbia U., 1969. 104 p. [Certificate essay, East Asian Institute]
SUBJ 24.3 24.4 26.2 34.2 59 64 ▪ 12 24.2 36.2

26.3 PEASANTS

農民 農民

1644-1911

17662 FPN O P7 G6.3 1842–1895
Fauvel, Albert Auguste, 1851–1909.
Promenades d'un naturaliste dans l'archipel des Chusan et sur les côtes du Chekiang (A naturalist's walks through the Chou-shan archipelago [Ting-hai *hsien*, Chekiang] and along the Chekiang coast).
Cherbourg: Impr. Charles Syffert, 1880. 259 p.
SUBJ 23 24.1 24.3 24.4 26.3 65 ▪ 21.3 22 24.2 34.3 47 62

1644-1949

□

1911-1949

17663 CSH F P7 G8.1 1928–1949
Buck, John Lossing, 1890–, and Daniel Shaw.
'The farmer's economic position in relation to other classes of society.'
EF 22 (July 1943), 179–188.
SUBJ 24 26 26.3 28 ▪ 24.1 24.5 24.6

17664 MCH F P8 G8.2 1928–1949
Fei Hsiao-tung (Fei Hsiao-t'ung), 1910–.
'Agricultural labor in a Yunnan village [Lu village, Lu-feng *hsien*].'
NSEQ 12, 1/2 (Jan. 1941), 146–168.
SUBJ 24.1 26.3 ▪ 21.2 26.1 50 58

17665 NNC U P7 G9.1 1928–1949
Hsieh Yu-lin (Hsüeh Yü-lin), Liu Tuan-sheng, et al.
'Agricultural labourers in Kwangsi.' Tr. from *Chung-kuo nung ts'un* 1, 1 (Oct. 1934), 57–74 *and* from *Chung-kuo nung ts'un* 1, 1 (Oct. 1934), 78–80 *and* from *Tung fang tsa chih* (Shanghai) 32, 6 (16 Mar. 1935), 98–99 *and* from *Tung fang tsa chih* (Shanghai) 33, 12 (16 June 1936), 112–114 [greatly condensed in tr.]. In *Agrarian China*, compiled by Institute of Pacific Relations. [Selective entry]
Chicago: U. of Chicago Press, 1939, 80–85.
SUBJ 24.1 26.3 ▪ 28 41 47

17666 CSH FP P8 G1.2 1911–1949
Potepalov, N-.
'Rassloenie kitaiskogo krest'ianstva v svete biudzhetnykh obsledovanii' (The stratification of the Chinese peasantry as indicated by budget studies).
PK 8/9 (1931), 136–180.
SUBJ 24.1 24.6 26.3 28 ▪ 24 24.3

17667 CBU F P7 G6.1 1928–1949
Tsu, François Xavier (Chu Shu-te).
'La vie des pêcheurs du Bas-Yangtsé' (The life of fishermen on the lower Yangtze).
Mémoires et documents du Centre de documentation cartographique et géographique 3 (1952), 59–164. (Doctoral dissertation, Faculté des lettres, Université de Paris)
SUBJ 21.3 24.1 26.3 29 41 55 ▪ 21.4 24.2 24.3 28 34.1 47 56 58

17668 CBU F P2 G8.1 1928–1949
Wang, Yin-yuen (Wang Yin-yüan).
'Changes in farm wages in Szechwan.'
EF 43 (Apr. 1945), 663–666.
SUBJ 24.1 26.3 28

1911-1972
(including 1644-1972)

17669 CSU FP P8 G9.4 1928–1972
Chang Han-yu (Chang Han-yü).
'A study of the living conditions of farmers in Taiwan, 1931–1950.' Tr. of 'T'ai-wan nung min sheng chi chih yen chiu' (The livelihood of Taiwanese peasants); *T'ai-wan yin hang chi k'an* 8, 4 (Dec. 1956), 47–80.
DE 7, 1 (Mar. 1969), 35–62.
SUBJ 26.3 28 55 ▪ 24.1 41

1949-1972

17670 CSU O P7 G6.3 1949–1972
Alley, Rewi, 1897–.
'With poor and middle peasants in northwest Chekiang.'
EH 9, 1 (1970), 12–24.
SUBJ 26.3 27 ▪ 24.1

17671 CSH O P7 G9.2 1949–1972
Chang Yen.
'"The commune gave us wings": Report from Huatung commune [Hua *hsien*, Kwangtung].'
China reconstructs 13, 6 (June 1964), 18–25.
SUBJ 24.1 26.3 ▪ 34.1

17672 CSH F P7 G5.3 1949–1972
Chen Chao (Ch'en Chao).
'A study of the method of grain distribution in the APCs.' Tr. of 'Nung yeh she nei liang shih fen p'ei pan fa ti yen chiu' (Methods of food distribution in agricultural producers' cooperatives); *Liang shih* 1957, 5 (May), 8–10.
ECMM 89 (8 July 1957), 10–15.
SUBJ 26.3 34.1 ▪ 28

17673 MCH P P7 G1.2 1949–1972
Chen Mae Fun (Ch'en Mai-fen).
'Paying the peasant.'
FEER 54, 5 (3 Nov. 1966), 263–264.
SUBJ 22 26.3 34.1

17674 MAM P P7 G1.2 1949–1972
Crook, Frederick William, 1940–.
An analysis of work-payment systems used in Chinese Mainland agriculture, 1956 to 1970.
Ann Arbor: University Microfilms (Publ. 72-2226), 1972. 401 p. (Doctoral dissertation in Economics, Tufts U. [Fletcher School of Law and Diplomacy], 1970)
SUBJ 22.1 26.3 32.1 34.1 ▪ 24.1 24.5 64

17675 NIC F P2 G9.4 1949–1972
Gallin, Bernard, 1929–.
'Chinese peasant values towards the land.'
Proceedings of the Annual Spring Meeting of the American Ethnological Society 1963, 64–71.
SUBJ 24.1 26.3 40 60 65 ▪ 26 42 45

17676 NIC F P8 G9.4 1949–1972
Hsü, Yu-chu, 1930–.
A case study of a farm at Ching-shui, Taichung [i.e., T'ai-chung *hsien*], *Taiwan, the Republic of China.*
New York: Council on Economic and Cultural Affairs, 1962. 10 p.
SUBJ 26.3 28

17677 CSU O P7 G5.1 1949–1972
Kramer, Ione.
'Life on East Wind road: An American in a Chinese village [in Huang-t'u-kang commune, Peking municipality].'
EH 6, 8 (Aug. 1967), 12–23; 6, 9 (Sept. 1967), 55–63.
SUBJ 20 24.1 26.3 34.1 55 ▪ 21.3 22.1

17678 NIC P P7 G1.2 1949–1972
[La Dany, Ladislao] ———, 1914–.
'The party and the peasants.'
CNA 344 (14 Oct. 1960), 1–7.
SUBJ 21.2 26.3 ▪ 22.1 24.1

17679 MCH P P7 G1.2 1949–1972
[La Dany, Ladislao] ———, 1914–.
'People who do no work.'
CNA 487 (27 Sept. 1963), 1–7.
SUBJ 22.1 26.3 ▪ 26.1

17680 NNC F P7 G6.3 1949–1972
Li Pai-kuan.
'On distribution of income in the higher APCs.' Tr. of 'Lun kao chi nung yeh sheng ch'an ho tso she ti shou ju fen p'ei' (Income distribution in higher-level agricultural producers' cooperatives); *Hsin chien she* 1957, 7 (July), 1–5.
ECMM 102 (7 Oct. 1957), 16–27.
SUBJ 26.3 28 34.1 ▪ 21 24 24.1 45

17681 MAM F P8 G9.4 1949–1972
Liu, Su Feng, 1934–.
Disguised unemployment in Taiwan agriculture.
Ann Arbor: University Microfilms (Publ. 66-12,369), 1966. 197 p. (Doctoral dissertation in Economics, U. of Illinois)
SUBJ 24.1 26.3 ▪ 21.4

17682 MCY P P7 G1.2 1949–1972
Schran, Peter, 1930–.
'Rural income policy and the Great Leap Forward.'
AS 4, 7 (July 1964), 958–968.
SUBJ 24 26.3 28 ▪ 24.1 24.5

17683 CSU F P8 G9.5 1949–1972
Topley, Marjorie Doreen, 1927–.
'Capital, saving and credit among indigenous rice farmers and immigrant vegetable farmers in Hong Kong's New Territories.' In *Capital, saving and credit in peasant societies*, edited by Raymond Firth and B- S- Yamey. [Sole entry]
Chicago: Aldine, 1964, 157–186.
SUBJ 24.1 24.6 26.3 36.3 ▪ 22 24.3 29 42 45

17684 NNC P P7 G1.2 1949–1972
T'ung chi yen chiu ch'u pan she. Tzu liao shih. (Documents Office).
'Income and distribution of agricultural producers' cooperatives in 1957.' Tr. of '1957 nien 228 ko nung yeh sheng ch'an ho tso she shou i fen p'ei tien hsing tiao ch'a tzu liao' (Data from a pilot survey of the distribution of profits in 228 agricultural producers' cooperatives in 1957); *T'ung chi yen chiu* 1958, 8 (Aug.), 8–12.
ECMM 148 (17 Nov. 1958), 34–44. [A different tr.—*URS* 13, 1 (3 Oct. 1958), 1–15.]
SUBJ 26.3 28 34.1 ▪ 24 24.5

17685 CSH F P7 G5.3 1949–1972
Wang Shu-ch'ing.
'Who says the peasants now have less food grain than before?' Tr. of 'Shui shuo nung min ti liang shih pi kuo ch'ü chien shao'; *Liang shih* 1957, 5 (May), 10–12.
ECMM 89 (8 July 1957), 6–9.
SUBJ 24.1 26.3 ▪ 21 28 34.1

26.4 WORKERS
劳工　労働者

1644-1911

17686 MCH O P3 G9.2 1895–1911
Anderson, George E-.
'Developments in Chinese labor situation.'
AAAPSS 46 (Mar. 1913), 178–182.
SUBJ 26.4

17687 NIC P P3 G5.1 1644–1911
Gamble, Sidney David, 1890–1968.
'Daily wages of unskilled Chinese laborers, 1807–1902.'
FEQ 3, 1 (Nov. 1943), 41–73.
SUBJ 26.4 28 ▪ 21.4

17688 MCH O P2 G2.0 1895–1911
Gubányi, Károly.
Öt év Mandzsúriában (Five years in Manchuria).
Budapest: Lampel, 1906. 324 p.
SUBJ 26.4 28 ▪ 12.2 22.2 26 32.2 66

17689 DLC P P7 G2.3 1895–1911
Spitsyn, Aleksandr.
'Rabochii vopros na kamennougol'nykh kopiakh Mukdenskoi provintsii' (The labor question in the coal mines of Sheng-ching province).
IVI 9 (1903), 319–382; 10 (1904), 199–248.
SUBJ 21.4 22.1 26.4 34.2 55 56 ▪ 22.2 23 36.2 36.4 39 46 50 53 60

1644-1949

17690 NNC P P3 G5.1 1842–1928
'Wages of handicraft workers in Peiping, 1862–1927.'
NWSS 3, 8 (24 Feb. 1930), 35, 38–40.
SUBJ 26.2 26.4 ▪ 28 34.3

17691 NNC PO P2 G1.1 1842–1928
Anderson, Adelaide Mary, 1863–1936.
Humanity and labour in China: An industrial visit and its sequel, 1923–1926.
London: Student Christian Movement, 1928. 15, 285 p.
SUBJ 24.4 26.4 28 52 ▪ 12.2 22.1 22.2 23 34.2 36.4 38 47

17692 NIC P P3 G5.1 1842–1928
Gamble, Sidney David, 1890–1968.
Peking wages, edited by Maxwell Slutz Stewart.
Peiping: Yenching U., Dept. of Sociology and Social Work, 1929. 14 p.
SUBJ 26.4 34.3 ▪ 24.6

17693 MCH P P3 G6.1 1842–1928
Vetrov, B- V-.
'Polozhenie rabochego klassa i nachalo proletarskogo dvizheniia v Shankhae, 1919–1921 gg.' (The position of the working class and the beginning of the proletarian movement in Shanghai, 1919–1921).
Nauchnye doklady vysshei shkoly; istoricheskie nauki 1959, 4, 137–154.
Subj 26.4 32.2 ▪ 36.4

17694 MCH PO P3 G6.1 1842–1949
Yen, Chung-ping (Yen Chung-p'ing), Jürgen Kuczynski, and Wolfgang Jonas.
Die Lage der Arbeiter in der Baumwollindustrie Shanghais, insbesondere in den englischen Fabriken (The position of workers in the cotton industry of Shanghai, especially in English factories).
Berlin: Akademie, 1964. 255 p.
Subj 24.4 26.4 28 ▪ 22 26 32.2 34.2 36.4 47

1911-1949

17695 CSH O P3 G1.2 1911–1928
'Christian work among ricksha men.' In *The Christian occupation of China*, edited by Milton Theobald Stauffer. [Selective entry]
Shanghai: China Continuation Committee, 1922, 368–369.
Subj 26.4 ▪ 28 37

17696 NNC PO P3 G1.1 1911–1928
'Doneseniia angliiskikh konsulov o polozhenii rabochego klassa v Kitae' (British consular reports on the position of the working class in China). In *Voprosy kitaiskoi revoliutsii, tom 1-yi* (Problems of the Chinese revolution, Vol. 1), edited by Karl Radek. [Selective entry]
Moscow: Gosizdat, 1927, 32–152.
Subj 12.2 24.4 26.4 28 34.3 36.4 ▪ 21.1 21.4 25 32.2 34.2 36.2 47 52

17697 CSH P P3 G5.1 1911–1928
'Economic study of the Peking ricsha puller.'
CEM 3, 6 (June 1926), 253–265.
Subj 26.4 28

17698 NIC O P3 G6.1 1928–1949
'The exploitation of the riksha coolie.'
PT new (2nd) series 5, 1 (1 Aug. 1933), 13–15.
Subj 26.4

17699 NNC P P3 G6.1 1928–1949
'Factory labor in Shanghai, 1929.'
NWSS 6, 39 (25 Sept. 1933), 179, 181–182.
Subj 26.4

17700 NNC P P3 G9.2 1911–1928
'Labor conditions in Canton: A statistical survey.'
CEJ 4, 6 (June 1929), 516–521.
Subj 26.4 36.4

17701 NNC P P3 G6.1 1911–1928
'Labor conditions in Wusih, Kiangsu.'
ILR 20, 5 (Nov. 1929), 709–713.
Subj 26.4

17702 NNC F P3 G5.1 1911–1928
'Statistics on factory workers in Tientsin, 1928.'
NWSS 2, 26 (7 Oct. 1929), 1, 4.
Subj 26.4

17703 NNC F P3 G6.3 1928–1949
'A study of 262 laborers in Hangchow.'
CEJ 8, 3 (Mar. 1931), 309–317.
Subj 26.4 28 ▪ 24.4

17704 NNC P P3 G6.1 1928–1949
'Unemployment of organized labor in Shanghai, 1928–1929.'
NWSS 4, 4 (26 Jan. 1931), 19, 22–24.
Subj 26.4 28 ▪ 36.4

17705 MCH U P3 G5.1 1911–1928
'Wages in Tientsin industries.'
CEM 3, 10 (Oct. 1926), 418–422.
Subj 24.4 26.4 28 ▪ 34.2 47

17706 CSU O P3 G6.1 1928–1949
'Working conditions in Shanghai cotton mills.'
ILR 20, 2 (Aug. 1929), 251–254.
Subj 24.4 26.4

17707 NNC O P3 G6.1 1928–1949
Barr, John S-.
'Shanghai factory conditions.'
CQ-S 1, 4 (Summer 1936), 31–39.
Subj 26.4 28 ▪ 22 24.4 56

17708 HKU P P4 G9.5 1928–1949
Butters, H- R-.
Report on labour and labour conditions in Hong Kong.
Hong Kong: Government Printer, 1939. 62 p.
Subj 26.4 28

17709 MCH F P3 G6.1 1928–1949
Chen Ta (Ch'en Ta), 1892–.
A study of the applicability of the factory act of the Chinese government: A preliminary survey of the Shanghai government.
Shanghai: China Institute of Scientific Management, 1931. 91 p.
Subj 12.2 26.4 28 ▪ 22 24.4 54

17710 NIC F P3 G6.1 1928–1949
Chen Ta (Ch'en Ta), 1892–.
'Toward factory legislation in China.'
CSPSR 15, 4 (Jan. 1932), 506–558.
Subj 12.2 26.4 ▪ 28 36.4

17711 NNC P P3 G1.3 1911–1928
Chen Ta (Ch'en Ta), 1892–.
'Wages and hours of labor in five Chinese cities [Shanghai, Nanking, Peking, Taiyuan, and Amoy], 1917 and 1920.'
Monthly labor review 13, 2 (Aug. 1921), 3–15.
Subj 26.4 ▪ 24

17712 NNC P P3 G1.2 1911–1928
Chesneaux, Jean, 1922–.
'Quelques termes relatifs à la vie ouvrière chinoise vers 1920' (Some terms relating to Chinese working-class life around 1920). In *Mélanges de sinologie offerts à Monsieur Paul Demiéville* (Sinological essays presented to Paul Demiéville). [Sole entry]
Paris: Presses universitaires, 1966, 17–25. (Bibliothèque de l'Institut des hautes études chinoises, 20)
Subj 26.4 36.4 ▪ 28 34.3

17713 NNP FP P3 G5.1 1911–1928
Chu, C. C. (Chu Chi-ch'ien), and Thomas C- Blaisdell, Jr.
Peking rugs and Peking boys: A study of the rug industry in Peking.
Peking: Chinese Social and Political Science Assn., 1924. 47 p. [Supplement to *CSPSR* 8, 2 (Apr. 1924)]
Subj 24.4 26.4 28 34.2 55 ▪ 24.2 24.3 34.3 54

17714 ²NNC O P3 G6.1 1911–1928
Corkery, Kirk J-.
'The Chinese laborer from the point of view of an American manager.'
China press (Shanghai) 12 Dec. 1920. [Reprinted in *Readings in economics for China*, compiled and edited by Charles Frederick Remer. (Selective entry.) Shanghai: Commercial Press, 1922, 455–462.]
Subj 26.4 34.2

17715 NIC P P3 G5.1 1928–1949
Fong, H. D. (Fang Hsien-t'ing), 1902–.
'Industrialization and labor in Hopei, with special reference to Tientsin.'
CSPSR 15, 1 (Apr. 1931), 1–28.
Subj 24.4 26.4 28 ▪ 26.2 32.1 36.4 47

17716 CSH F P5 G2.0 1911–1949
Gerasimov, A- E-.
'Usloviia truda v predpriiatiiakh severnoi Man'chzhurii' (Labor conditions in northern Manchurian enterprises). [With English abstracts]
VM 1931, 2, 18–29; 1931, 3, 59–69; 1931, 4, 70–75. [Reprinted in *Kitaiskii trud (usloviia truda v predpriiatiiakh severnoi Man'chzhurii)* (Chinese labor: Labor conditions in northern Manchurian enterprises), by A. E. Gerasimov. (Analytic entry.) Harbin: Tip. KVzhd, 1931, 9–102.]
Subj 24.4 26.4 34.2 ▪ 47 52

17717 ELO PO P3 G1.2 1911–1928
Great Britain. Foreign Office.
Papers respecting labour conditions in China.
London: His Majesty's Stationery Office, 1925. 130 p. (Parliament, Papers by Command, Cmd. 2442; China, 1, 1925)
Subj 26.4 28 34.3 36.4 ▪ 12.2 21.2 22.1 24.4 34.2 47 52

17718 CSH P P2 G9.5 1928–1949
Hong Kong. Labour Dept.
Annual report by the Commissioner of Labour, 1946/47–1948/49. [Title varies; issues for 1950/51-1971/72 are entered as 17745.]
Hong Kong: ——. Issued annually, 1947–1949. Average ca. 50 p.
Subj 21.4 26.4 28 36.4 ▪ 27 47 54 56

17719 NNC O P3 G6.1 1911–1928
Kuo, Ping-wen, 1880–1969.
'Labour conditions and labour regulations in China.'
ILR 10, 6 (Dec. 1924), 1005–1028.
Subj 12.2 21.4 26.4 28 ▪ 36.4

17720 NNC F P4 G5.1 1911–1928
Lin, Sung-ho.
Factory workers in Tangku [Ning-ho *hsien*, Hopei].
Peiping: China Foundation for the Promotion of Education and Culture, Social Research Dept., 1928. 10, 128 p. [For an expanded version in Chinese,

see Lin Sung-ho, *T'ang-ku kung jen tiao ch'a* (Survey of workers in T'ang-ku); Peiping: Pei-p'ing she hui tiao ch'a so, 1930; 286 p.]
SUBJ 24.4 26.4 38 ▪ 28 31 34.2 36.4 41 55

17721 CSH P P7 G5.3 1911–1949
Liu, Hsin-chuan (Liu Hsin-ch'üan).
Labour conditions in Chunghsing Coal Mine, Shantung. Tr. of 'Shan-tung chung hsing mei k'uang kung jen tiao ch'a' (Survey of workers at the Chung-hsing coal mine [I *hsien*], Shantung); *She hui k'o hsüeh tsa chih* 3, 1 (Mar. 1932), 35–93. [Condensed tr.; Chinese version cites Shih Yü-shou as coauthor.]
Peiping: [China Foundation], Institute of Social Research, 1933. 43 p. (ISR bulletins, 7)
SUBJ 26.4 28 34.2 ▪ 21.2 27 36.4 41 50 55 56

17722 CSU O P3 G6.1 1911–1928
Maitland, Charles Titterton.
'Health and industrial conditions in China.'
CMJ 39, 12 (Dec. 1925), 1089–1099.
SUBJ 26.4 28 56 ▪ 24.4 54

17723 CSH P P3 G2.2 1911–1949
Malitskii, V- S-.
'Prozhitochnyi minimum dlia Kharbina' (The subsistence wage for Harbin).
EB 1930, 3 (15 fevralia), 14–15.
SUBJ 26.4 28 ▪ 24 24.3

17724 NNC P P3 G6.1 1911–1928
Musin, ——— (Mussin; Moussine).
'Promyshlennost' i proletariat Shankhaia' (Industry and the proletariat in Shanghai).
KIP 4, 12 (dekabr' 1924), 94–98.
'Die Industrie und das Proletariat Schanghais.'
RGI 4, 12 (Dez. 1924), 290–291.
'L'industrie et le prolétariat de Chang-Haï.'
ISR 47 (déc. 1924), 939–941.
SUBJ 26.4 ▪ 24.4 47 52

17725 ELO FP P3 G6.1 1928–1949
Pearse, Arno Smith, 1872–?
The cotton industry of Japan and China: Being the report of the journey to Japan and China.
Manchester, Eng.: International Federation of Master Cotton Spinners and Manufacturers, 1929. 254 p.
SUBJ 24.4 26.4 ▪ 21.4 28 34.3 36.4

17726 MCH P P3 G6.1 1928–1949
Riemens, H-.
'De loonen in de industrie te Shanghai' (Industrial wages in Shanghai).
De Economist 86, 9 (September 1937), 628–640.
SUBJ 26.4 ▪ 24.4 28

17727 CSH O P3 G5.3 1911–1928
Rietveld, Harriet.
'Women and children in industry in Chefoo.'
CEM 3, 12 (Dec. 1926), 559–562.
SUBJ 26.4 47 52 ▪ 56

17728 CSH F P3 G6.1 1928–1949
Shanghai. She hui chü. (Bureau of Social Affairs), ed.
Wages and hours of labor, Greater Shanghai, 1929.
Shanghai: Commercial Press, 1931. 15, 153 p. [s.p.]. [See Vol. 2 of this *Bibliography* for Chinese version.]
SUBJ 26.4 28 ▪ 21.4 24.4 36.4

17729 NIC F P3 G8.2 1928–1949
Shih, Kuo-heng.
China enters the machine age: A study of labor in Chinese war industry, edited by Fei Hsiao-tung (Fei Hsiao-t'ung). Tr. from the Chinese by Fei Hsiao-tung and Francis L. K. Hsu. [Tr. of unpublished manuscripts]
Cambridge: Harvard U. Press, 1944. 24, 206 p. [Reprinted—New York: Greenwood Press, 1968. 24, 206 p.]
SUBJ 26.4 ▪ 28 47 55

17730 NNC O P3 G5.1 1928–1949
Starrett, Charles Vincent Emerson, 1886–.
'Old movements in new China: A note on the economy of the East.' In *Oriental encounters: Two essays in bad taste*, by C. V. E. Starrett. [Analytic entry]
Chicago: Normandie House, 1938, 33–45.
SUBJ 26.4 ▪ 24.3 55

17731 MCH O P7 G5.1 1928–1949
Stewart, Maxwell Slutz, 1900–.
'The coolie and the coal pit.'
Asia (New York: American Asiatic Assn.) 33, 1 (Jan. 1933), 49–51.
SUBJ 26.4 ▪ 24.4

17732 CSU F P3 G6.1 1928–1949
Tejima Masaki, 1913–, and Arai Yoshirō. [Tr. erroneously gives second author as Arai Yoshio.]
'Junk crews in Soochow.' Tr. by Andrew Watson of 'Minsen no rōdō' (Workers on junks and sampans); in *Chūshi no minsengyō: Soshū minsen jittai chōsa hōkoku* (Shipping in Central China: Survey of junks and sampans in Soochow), edited by Chōsabu, Mantetsu (Research Division, South Manchurian Railway); Tokyo: Hakubunkan, 1943, 53–148 [greatly condensed in tr.]. In *Transport in transition: The evolution of traditional shipping in China.* [Analytic entry]
Ann Arbor: U. of Michigan, Center for Chinese Studies, 1972, 57–70. (Michigan abstracts of Chinese and Japanese works on Chinese history, 3)
SUBJ 26.4 28 ▪ 14.3 24.2 34.2

17733 MCH P P3 G6.1 1911–1949
Tsha, T. Y. (Ts'ai Cheng-ya).
'Labor legislation, wages and hours in Shanghai.'
China critic 4, 30 (23 July 1931), 705–709.
SUBJ 12.2 26.4 28 ▪ 36.4

17734 NNC FP P3 G6.1 1928–1949
Tsha, T. Y. (Ts'ai Cheng-ya).
'A study of the wage rates in Shanghai, 1930–34.'
NSEQ 8, 3 (Oct. 1935), 459–510.
SUBJ 26.4 70 ▪ 24.4 28 47

17735 CSH P P3 G6.1 1928–1949
[Vladimirova, Tamara Ivanovna] T. V.
'Shankhaiskii proletariat: oborona Shankhaia' (The Shanghai proletariat and the defense of Shanghai).
PK 10 (1932), 195–213.
SUBJ 26.4 32.2 66 ▪ 15 32 36.4

17736 CSH P P3 G5.1 1911–1949
Wang, S. H. (Wang Shu-hsün).
Wages and labor mobility in a flour mill in Tientsin. Tr. by T. H. Chen of 'T'ien-chin mien fen ch'ang kung jen chi kung tzu ti i ko yen chiu' (Workers at a Tientsin flour mill and their wages); *She hui k'o hsüeh tsa chih* 2, 4 (Dec. 1931), 445–472. [Rev. and condensed in tr.]
Peiping: China Foundation, Institute of Social Research, 1932. 30 p. (ISR bulletins, 6)
SUBJ 26.4 34.2 ▪ 24.4 28

17737 MCH O P3 G6.1 1928–1949
Wiegel, John Mason, 1908–.
'In the hold with Shanghai stevedores.'
Asia (New York: American Asiatic Assn.) 29, 3 (Mar. 1929), 188–189, 252–254.
SUBJ 26.4 ▪ 28

1911-1972
(including 1644-1972)

□

1949-1972

17738 NIC O P3 G9.2 1949–1972
'Interview: "A more practical view" . . .'
CS 1, 10 (19 Aug. 1961), 1–9. [Reprinted in *Out of China: A collection of interviews with refugees from China*, edited by Francis Harper. (Analytic entry.) Hong Kong: Dragonfly Books, 1964, 133–154.]
SUBJ 24.4 26.4 28 ▪ 14.3 32.1 55 56

17739 CSU P P3 G9.5 1949–1972
'Notes on the clothing industry in Hong Kong.'
ILR 92, 6 (Dec. 1965), 506–511.
SUBJ 24.4 26.4 ▪ 28

17740 CSH O P7 G5.1 1949–1972
'Peking steelworkers set off nationwide emulation drive.'
China reconstructs 19, 1 (Jan. 1970), 2–9.
SUBJ 24.4 26.4

17741 DLC O P2 G1.3 1949–1972
Burkov, Boris Sergeevich.
Vsiudu druz'ia (Friends everywhere).
Moscow: Gospolitizdat, 1957. 118 p.
SUBJ 24.4 26.4 ▪ 26.3 28

17742 CBU F P3 G9.5 1949–1972
Chaney, D- C-.
'Job satisfaction and unionization: The case of shopworkers.' In *Hong Kong: The industrial colony*, edited by Keith Hopkins. [Analytic entry]
Hong Kong: Oxford U. Press, 1971, 261–270.
SUBJ 26.4 34.2

17743 NIC P P2 G9.4 1949–1972
Eberhard, Wolfram, 1909–.
'Labour mobility in Taiwan.'
AS 2, 3 (May 1962), 38–56. [Reprinted in *Settlement and social change in Asia*, by W. Eberhard. (Selective entry.) Hong Kong: Hong Kong U. Press, 1967, 150–177.]
SUBJ 26 26.4 ▪ 28

17744 CSH O P4 G9.5 1949–1972
Hetherington, R- M-.
'Industrial labour in Hong Kong.' In *Hong Kong economic papers, No. 2*, edited by Edward Stuart Kirby. [Selective entry]
Hong Kong: Hong Kong Economic Assn., 1963, 29–41.
SUBJ 26.4 ▪ 24.4 36.4 50

17745 CSU P P2 G9.5 1949–1972
Hong Kong. Labour Dept.
Annual departmental report by the Commissioner of Labour, 1950/51–1971/72. [Issues for 1946/47–1948/49 are entered as 17718.]
Hong Kong: Government Printer. Issued annually, 1951–1972. Average ca. 150 p.
SUBJ 21.4 26.4 28 36.4 ▪ 27 47 54 56

17746 CSU PO P5 G7.2 1949–1972
Hunan. Lao tung chü. (Labor Bureau).
'A study of the system of piece-work incentive awards.' Tr. of 'Chi chien ch'ao o chiang li chih yen chiu' (The system of incentives for surpassing piecework production quotas); *Lao tung* 1959, 23 (3 Dec.), 24–27. In *Wage system in Communist China*, mimeo., compiled by U.S. Joint Publications Research Service. [Analytic entry]
Washington, D.C.: JPRS, 1 June 1960, 9–16. (JPRS 2640; MC 9937/1960)
SUBJ 26.4 34.2 ▪ 61

17747 CBU U P3 G6.1 1949–1972
K'o Ch'ing-shih. [Tr. erroneously gives author's name as Ko Ch'ing-chih.]
'Continuously raise labor productivity.' Tr. of 'Pu tuan t'i kao lao tung sheng ch'an lü'; *Hung ch'i* 1959, 9 (1 May), 8–17. In *Articles from the Chinese Communist periodical 'Hung-ch'i' (Red flag) (No. 9, 1 May 1959, Peiping)*, mimeo., compiled by U.S. Joint Publications Research Service. [Sole entry]
Washington, D.C.: JPRS, 3 July 1959, 1–16. (JPRS 795D)
SUBJ 24.4 26.4 34.2

17748 MCH O P3 G1.3 1949–1972
Kornilov, IUrii Emmanuilovich.
Pesnia nad stroikoi (A song next to the construction site).
Moscow: Profizdat, 1961. 114 p.
SUBJ 26.4 36.4 ▪ 22.2 27 28 47

17749 DLC O P2 G1.3 1949–1972
Lysenkovskii, A-.
'U shakhterov Kitaia' (Visiting Chinese coal miners).
Sovetskii shakhter 10, 11 (noiabr' 1961), 41–42.
SUBJ 24.4 26.4 ▪ 21.3 24.2 66

17750 CSH U P3 G5.1 1949–1972
MacDougall, Colina.
'Matching the Capital [Iron and Steel Works, Peking] men.'
FEER 66, 48 (27 Nov. 1969), 457–459.
SUBJ 24.4 26.4

17751 CSU O P3 G5.1 1949–1972
Rivière, M-.
'A l'usine de textile de Pékin' (At the Peking textile factory).
CFC 6 (juin 1960), 6–12.
SUBJ 26.4 28 ▪ 24.4 31

17752 TPY F P2 G9.4 1949–1972
Taiwan. Lao tung li tiao ch'a yen chiu so. (Labor Force Survey Research Institute).
Establishment survey on employment, hours, earnings and labor turnover in secondary industries in the Taiwan area (Manpower Requirement Survey, 1).
[Taipei]: Lao tung li tiao ch'a yen chiu so, 1969. 4 vols. 13; 13; 67; 67 p. [In Chinese as well as English]
SUBJ 26.4

27 ELEMENTARY AND VOCATIONAL EDUCATION

初等教育及職業補習教育

初等教育及び補習教育

1644-1911

17753 MCH O P1 G1.2 1644–1842
Biot, Edouard Constant, 1803–1850.
'Détails sur l'état de l'instruction primaire en Chine' (Details on the state of elementary education in China).
J. des savants 2 (mai 1838), 273–287.
SUBJ 27 ▪ 37 63

1644-1949

17754 FPN P P1 G1.2 1895–1949
Chai, Yu Heng (Ch'ai Yu-heng).
Etude sur l'obligation scolaire et l'enseignement primaire en France et en Chine (A study of compulsory schooling and elementary education in France and in China).
Paris: Ed. Domat-Montchrestien, 1935. 296 p. (Doctoral dissertation, Faculté des lettres, Université de Paris)
SUBJ 16.1 27 37 ▪ 15 63

17755 NIC P P2 G1.2 1895–1928
Cheng Tsung-hai.
'Elementary education in China.'
BCE 2, 14 (1923), 1–40.
SUBJ 27

17756 MCH S P7 G1.3 1895–1928
Fugh, Paul Chen (Fu Pao-ch'en), 1895–.
'Reconstruction of the Chinese rural elementary school curriculum to meet rural needs in China.'
CSPSR 9, 1 – 10, 3 (Jan. 1925 – July 1926), 275 p. in all. (Doctoral dissertation in Education, Cornell U., 1924)
SUBJ 27 ▪ 60

17757 ICU P P4 G1.2 1895–1928
Loh, L. S. (Lu Lin-su), 1896–1924.
Organization of vocational education in China.
Unpublished masters thesis in Education, U. of Chicago, 1920. 87 p.
SUBJ 27 ▪ 11.4 14.4 16

17758 ICU P P2 G1.2 1895–1928
Loh, L. S. (Lu Lin-su), 1896–1924.
The status of primary education in China.
Unpublished doctoral dissertation in Education, U. of Chicago, 1922. 224 p.
SUBJ 27 ▪ 14.5 18 22.1

1911-1949

17759 CSU P P2 G1.2 1911–1928
'Vocational education in China.'
ILR 15, 2 (Feb. 1927), 294–298.
SUBJ 27 ▪ 37

17760 NNM O P7 G1.2 1911–1928
Butterfield, Kenyon Leech, 1868–1935.
Education and Chinese agriculture.
Shanghai: China Christian Educational Assn., 1922. 62 p.
SUBJ 14.1 18 27 34.1 37 ▪ 14.2 14.3 16.3 21.4 22 47

17761 ELB O P7 G7.3 1928–1949
Chang, Jen-chi, 1930–.
Pre-Communist China's rural school and community.
Boston: Christopher Publishing House, 1960. 116 p. (Revision of *Certain relationships of the school administration and the rural community in China*, doctoral dissertation in Education, U. of North Dakota, 1951)
SUBJ 21 27 41 ▪ 37

17762 CSU P P1 G1.2 1911–1928
Cheng, C. S., et al.
'The elementary education in China.' Tr. from the Chinese [tr. of an unpublished manuscript]. In *Education in China: Papers contributed by the members of committees of the Society for the Study of International Education*, edited by T. Y. Teng (Teng Ts'ui-ying) and Timothy Tingfang Lew (Liu T'ing-fang). [Selective entry]
Peking: Society for the Study of International Education, 1923, 1–18 [s.p.].
SUBJ 27

17763 MCH PO P2 G1.2 1911–1949
Chin, Kuo-chun.
L'enseignement agricole et rural en Chine (Agricultural and rural education in China).
Paris: Bossuet, 1937. 232 p. (Doctoral dissertation, Faculté des lettres, Université de Paris)
SUBJ 14.1 27 34.1 37 ▪ 12.2 14.3 14.5 36.3 45 62

17764 MCY O P2 G1.2 1911–1928
Huang Yen-pei (Huang Yen-p'ei), 1878–1965.
'Vocational education in China.'
BCE 2, 1 (1923), 1–13.
SUBJ 27

17765 CSU O P3 G6.1 1928–1949
Lewis, Ida Belle, 1887–.
'Neighborhood schools.'
CR 67, 10 (Oct. 1936), 633–644.
SUBJ 27

17766 NNC FP P2 G1.2 1928–1949
Lewis, Ida Belle, 1887–.
'A study of primary schools.' In *China*, edited by Orville Anderson Petty. [Selective entry]
New York: Harper, 1933, 615–654. (Laymans Foreign Missions Inquiry, Factfinders' reports, 5; Supplementary series, Part 2)
SUBJ 27 ▪ 66

17767 NIC F P2 G1.3 1928–1949
Liao, T'ai-ch'u.
'Rural education in transition: A study of old-fashioned Chinese schools (Szu Shu) in Shantung and Szechuan.'
YJSS 4, 2 (Feb. 1949), 19–67.
SUBJ 27 ▪ 32.1 62

17768 NNC P P1 G1.2 1911–1928
Loh, L. S. (Lu Lin-su), 1896–1924.
'Compulsory education in China.'
CSM 17, 4 (Feb. 1922), 313–324.
SUBJ 27

17769 ELS P P7 G1.2 1911–1949
Wang, Cheng-su.
The village school and rural reconstruction in China.
Unpublished masters thesis in Education, U. of London [Institute of Education], 1941. 432 p.
SUBJ 26.3 27 ▪ 24.1 28 34.1 37

17770 ICU P P1 G1.2 1911–1928
Wang, Keh Ren (Wang K'o-jen).
An analysis of the history curriculum in Chinese elementary schools.
Unpublished masters thesis in Education, U. of Chicago, 1924. 68 p.
SUBJ 27 66 ▪ 62

17771 CSU P P1 G1.2 1911–1928
Wang, W. P., and M. T. Wong.
'Vocational education in China.' Tr. from the Chinese [tr. of an unpublished manuscript]. In *Education in China: Papers contributed by the members of committees of the Society for the Study of International Education*, edited by T. Y. Teng (Teng Ts'ui-ying) and Timothy Tingfang Lew (Liu T'ing-fang). [Selective entry]
Peking: Society for the Study of International Education, 1923, 1–21 [s.p.].
SUBJ 27 ▪ 47

1911-1972
(including 1644-1972)

17772 ELO O P7 G4.2 1928–1972
Alley, Rewi, 1897–.
Sandan: An adventure in creative education.
Christchurch, N.Z.: Caxton Press, 1959. 191 p.
SUBJ 24.4 27 28 66 ▪ 22 32.1 37 48 54 64

17773 WSU F P7 G5.1 1928–1972
Crook, David, and Isabel Crook.
'Education and training in Yangyi commune [She *hsien*, Hopei], China.' In *The world year book of education, 1968: Education within industry*, edited by Joseph Albert Lauwerys and David G- Scanlon. [Selective entry]
New York: Harcourt, Brace and World, 1968, 309–316.
SUBJ 27

17774 MAM FP P7 G9.4 1928–1972
Tzeng, John Jenn, 1922–.
Taiwanian vocational education in agriculture, 1945–1963.
Ann Arbor: University Microfilms (Publ. 64-8530), 1964. 193 p. (Doctoral dissertation in Educational Administration, Colorado State College)
SUBJ 24.1 27

1949-1972

17775 NIC O P7 G9.2 1949–1972
'Interview: The cadres nicknamed me "Erh Liu Tzu" (second-rate son).'
CS 1, 18 (18 Nov. 1961), 1–8. [Reprinted in *Out of China: A collection of interviews with refugees from China*, edited by Francis Harper. (Analytic entry.) Hong Kong: Dragonfly Books, 1964, 29–46.]
SUBJ 27 32 ▪ 24.4 28

17776 CSU O P7 G7.3 1949–1972
Alley, Rewi, 1897–.
'Mountain school in Kiangsi.'
EH 6, 6 (June 1967), 35–40; 6, 7 (July 1967), 32–36.
SUBJ 20 27 ▪ 34.1 50

17777 CSU O P2 G1.2 1949–1972
Alley, Rewi, 1897–.
'Some part-work and part-study schools.'
EH 5, 9 (Sept. 1966), 37–44.
SUBJ 27 ▪ 54

17778 CSH P P7 G1.2 1949–1972
Barendsen, Robert Dale, 1923–.
'The agricultural middle school in Communist China.'
CQ 8 (Oct.–Dec. 1961), 106–134. [Reprinted in *China under Mao: Politics takes command*, edited by Roderick Lemonde MacFarquhar. (Selective entry.) Cambridge: M.I.T. Press, 1966, 304–332.]
SUBJ 14.1 27 34.1 ▪ 16.3 32.1 64

17779 NNC P P2 G1.2 1949–1972
Barendsen, Robert Dale, 1923–.
Half-work, half-study schools in Communist China: Recent experiments with self-supporting educational institutions.
Washington, D.C.: U.S. Dept. of Health, Education, and Welfare, Office of Education, 1964. 56 p. (OE bulletins, 1964, 24; OE 14,100)
SUBJ 17 27 ▪ 21.4 24.1 24.4 32

17780 CSU O P3 G5.1 1949–1972
Castillon du Perron, Marguerite.
'En Chine, tous veulent devenir des saints' (In China everyone wants to become a saint).
R. de Paris 74, 7/8 (juil.–août 1967), 84–92.
SUBJ 27 53 ▪ 22.1 51 52 61 66

17781 NIC P P1 G1.2 1949–1972
Chen, Theodore H. E. (Ch'en Hsi-en), 1902–.
'Elementary education in Communist China.'
CQ 10 (Apr.–June 1962), 98–122.
SUBJ 27 ▪ 14 32.1 54 64

17782 NIC P P2 G1.2 1949–1972
Chen, Theodore H. E. (Ch'en Hsi-en), 1902–.
'Worker-peasant education in China.'
Eastern world 6, 7 (July 1952), 19–20; 6, 8 (Aug. 1952), 31–32.
SUBJ 27 ▪ 16.3 16.4

17783 CSH U P2 G6.1 1949–1972
Ch'en Kuang.
'The growth in agricultural middle school (AMS) instruction.' Tr. of 'Nung yeh chung hsüeh chiao shih ti ch'eng chang' (The training of teachers in agricultural middle schools); *Hung ch'i* 1960, 10 (16 May), 37–41. In *Translations from 'Hung-ch'i' (Red flag) (Peiping, No. 10, 16 May 1960)*, mimeo., compiled by U.S. Joint Publications Research Service. [Selective entry]
Washington, D.C.: JPRS, 28 Sept. 1960, 48–55. (JPRS 3977; MC 17,236/1960)
SUBJ 27 ▪ 32.1

17784 CSU U P7 G6.1 1949–1972
Ch'en Kuang.
'Seventh anniversary of founding of agricultural middle schools in Kiangsu.' Tr. of 'Chiang-su sheng nung yeh chung hsüeh ch'uang pan ch'i chou nien'; *Hung ch'i* 1965, 4 (30 Apr.), 36–47. In *Translations from 'Hung-ch'i' (Red flag) No. 4, 1965*, mimeo., compiled by U.S. Joint Publications Research Service. [Sole entry]
Washington, D.C.: JPRS, 16 June 1965, 21–42. (JPRS 30,664; MC 12,585-30/1965)
SUBJ 26 27

17785 NNC P P1 G1.2 1949–1972
Cheng, James Chester (Cheng Che-hsi), 1926–.
'Half-work and half-study in Communist China.'
PA 32, 2 (June 1959), 187–193.
SUBJ 27 ▪ 12.1

17786 CSU P P2 G9.4 1949–1972
China [Republic]. Chiao yü pu. (Ministry of Education).
'Republic of China.' In *World survey of education, Vol. 2, Primary education*, compiled by Educational, Scientific and Cultural Organization, United Nations. [Selective entry]
Paris: UNESCO, 1958, 243–252.
SUBJ 27

17787 CSH O P7 G7.2 1949–1972
Chung-kuo kung ch'an tang. Shao-tung hsien wei yüan hui. (Chinese Communist Party. Shao-tung Hsien Committee). [Shao-tung *hsien* is in Hunan.]
'A red and expert school with half-time farming and half-time study.' Tr. of 'I so pan keng pan tu ti hung chuan hsüeh hsiao'; *Hung ch'i* 1958, 6 (16 Aug.), 31–35. In *Selected translations from 'Hung-chi' (Red flag), June–August 1958*, mimeo., compiled by U.S. Joint Publications Research Service. [Selective entry]
Washington, D.C.: JPRS, 21 Apr. 1961, 144–160. (JPRS 7837; MC 5498/1962)
SUBJ 27 ▪ 24.1

17788 CBU F P3 G9.5 1949–1972
Godman, A-, ed.
The attainment and ability of Hong Kong primary IV pupils: A first study.
Hong Kong: Hong Kong U. Press, 1964. 85 p. (Hong Kong Council for Educational Research publications, 2)
SUBJ 27 52

17789 CSH O P8 G2.1 1949–1972
Heilungkiang. Chao-yüan hsien cheng fu (Chao-yüan Hsien). Ko ming wei yüan hui (Revolutionary Committee) *and* Heilungkiang. Sui-hua ti ch'ü cheng fu (Sui-hua District). Ko ming wei yüan hui (Revolutionary Committee), *joint*

sponsors. Lien ho tiao ch'a tsu (Joint Investigation Group).
'Persist in running schools with diligence and frugality to serve proletarian politics: Report on an investigation in the primary school run by Yuch'ang brigade, Chaoyuan hsien, Heilungkiang province.' Tr. of 'Chien ch'ih ch'in chien pan hsüeh, wei wu ch'an chieh chi cheng chih fu wu: Hei-lung-chiang Chao-yüan hsien Yü-ch'ang ta tui hsiao hsüeh ti tiao ch'a pao kao' (Persist in running schools with diligence and frugality to serve proletarian government: Report on the elementary school run by Yü-ch'ang brigade, Chao-yüan *hsien*, Heilungkiang); *Hung ch'i* 1971, 6 (June), 52–55.
CE 5, 1/2 (Spring–Summer 1972), 96–109.
SUBJ 27 ▪ 24.1

17790 CSH O P8 G5.4 1949–1972
Honan. Hsü-ch'ang ti ch'ü cheng fu (Hsü-ch'ang Special District). Ko ming wei yüan hui (Revolutionary Committee) *and* Honan. Hsü-ch'ang hsien cheng fu (Hsü-ch'ang hsien). Ko ming wei yüan hui (Revolutionary Committee), *joint sponsors*. Tiao ch'a tsu (Investigation Team).
'A middle school serving the three great revolutionary movements: Investigation report of an agricultural middle school in Kuei village, Hsü-ch'ang hsien, Honan.' Tr. by Akira Odani of 'I so wei san ta ko ming yün tung fu wu ti chung hsüeh: Ho-nan Hsü-ch'ang hsien Kuei ts'un nung yeh chung hsüeh ti tiao ch'a pao kao'; *Hung ch'i* 1970, 8 (Aug.), 50–54.
CE 4, 2 (Summer 1971), 101–110.
SUBJ 27 ▪ 26.3

17791 CSU P P1 G9.5 1949–1972
Hong Kong. Education Dept.
'Hong Kong.' In *World survey of education, Vol. 2, Primary education*, compiled by Educational, Scientific and Cultural Organization, United Nations. [Selective entry]
Paris: UNESCO, 1958, 1144–1149.
SUBJ 27

17792 WSU P P2 G1.2 1949–1972
Hook, Brian.
'Education within industry: China.' In *The world year book of education, 1968: Education within industry*, edited by Joseph Albert Lauwerys and David G- Scanlon. [Selective entry]
New York: Harcourt, Brace and World, 1968, 168–181.
SUBJ 27 ▪ 16.4 32.1

17793 CSH O P8 G5.2 1949–1972
Hsin min chu chu i ch'ing nien t'uan. Chin nan ti fang kung tso wei yüan hui. (New Democratic Youth League. South Shansi Regional Work Committee).
'A popular night school for agricultural technique.' Tr. of 'I ko shou huan ying ti nung yeh chi shu yeh hsiao' (A welcomed night school of agricultural technology); in *Chung-kuo nung ts'un ti she hui chu i kao ch'ao* (The socialist upsurge in rural China); Peking: Jen min ch'u pan she, 1956, vol. 1, 165–172. In *Socialist upsurge in China's countryside*, edited by Pan kung t'ing, Chung yang wei yüan hui, Chung-kuo kung ch'an tang (General Office, Central Committee, Chinese Communist Party). [Selective entry]
Peking: Foreign Languages Press, 1957, 415–424.
SUBJ 27 37 ▪ 24.1 26.3 32.1 34.1 61

17794 CSU O P3 G9.4 1949–1972
Hsu, Chen-chin, et al.
'Special education for mentally subnormal children in Taiwan.'
American j. of orthopsychiatry 38, 4 (July 1968), 615–621.
SUBJ 27 ▪ 54 61

17795 CSH O P7 G2.3 1949–1972
Jen min jih pao – Hung ch'i tsa chih tiao ch'a yüan (*People's daily – Red flag* Investigators).
'The revolution in rural education must be dependent upon the poor and lower-middle peasants.' Tr. of 'Nung ts'un ti chiao yü ko ming pi hsü i k'ao p'in hsia chung nung'; *Hung ch'i* 1968, 3 (10 Sept.), 27–31.
CE 2, 1/2 (Spring–Summer 1969), 26–34. [A different tr.—'*Jen min jih pao* and *Hung-ch'i* investigation report on educational revolution in countryside: It is essential to rely on the poor and lower-middle peasants in revolutionizing education in the countryside.' *SCMP* 4261 (19 Sept. 1968), 15–19.]
SUBJ 27 ▪ 26.3 37

17796 CBU PO P2 G1.2 1949–1972
Kashin, M- P-.
'Doshkol'noe obrazovanie' (Preschool education). In *Shkola i prosveshchenie v Narodnom Kitae: sbornik statei* (Articles on schools and education in the People's Republic of China), compiled by Akademiia pedagogicheskikh nauk RSFSR, edited by Aleksei I- Markushevich, E- I- Monoszon, and M- N- Riakin. [Selective entry]
Moscow: Izd-vo Akad. ped. nauk RSFSR, 1957, 57–63.
SUBJ 27 52

17797 CBU PO P3 G1.4 1949–1972
Kashin, M- P-.
'Nachal'noe obrazovanie' (Elementary education). In *Shkola i prosveshchenie v Narodnom Kitae: sbornik statei* (Articles on schools and education in the People's Republic of China), compiled by Akademiia pedagogicheskikh nauk RSFSR, edited by Aleksei I- Markushevich, E- I- Monoszon, and M- N- Riakin. [Selective entry]
Moscow: Izd-vo Akad. ped. nauk RSFSR, 1957, 64–77.
SUBJ 27 ▪ 52

17798 CSH O P6 G7.3 1949–1972
Kiangsi. Wu-yüan hsien [cheng fu] (Wu-yüan Hsien). Ko ming wei yüan hui (Revolutionary Committee). T'ung hsün tsu (Communications Section) *with Chiang-hsi jih pao* (*Kiangsi daily*). Shang-jao chi che chan (Shang-jao Reporter Unit). [This article has still a third joint author: *Hsin Shang-jao pao* chi che (*New Shang-jao daily* Reporter).]
'A new type of school that combines theory with practice: An investigation report on the Wukow Part-Time Tea Growing and Part-Time Study Middle School in Wuyuan county, Kiangsi province.' Tr. of 'I so li lun ho shih chi i chih ti hsin hsing hsüeh hsiao: Chiang-hsi sheng Wu-yüan hsien Wu-k'ou ch'a yeh keng tu chung hsüeh ti tiao ch'a pao kao' (A new type of school that integrates theory and practice: Report on Wu-k'ou Part-Study Part-Tea-Cultivation Middle School, Wu-yüan *hsien*, Kiangsi); *Hung ch'i* 1968, 4 (14 Oct.), 24–31.
CE 2, 3 (Fall 1969), 15–27. [A different tr.—'A new school that integrates theory with practice: A survey report on the Wuk'ou Tea Cultivation and Study Middle School in Wuyuan hsien, Kiangsi province.' *SCMM* 634 (12 Nov. 1968), 8–13.]
SUBJ 27 ▪ 21.4

17799 MAM FP P4 G9.4 1949–1972
Koo, Po-yen (Ku Po-yen), 1916–.
A critical study of vocational-industrial education in Taiwan.
Ann Arbor: University Microfilms (Publ. 69-6747), 1969. 292 p. (Doctoral dissertation in Education, Indiana U.)
SUBJ 17 27 ▪ 21.4

17800 NIC O P2 G2.2 1949–1972
Liang Nien.
'Schools for new-type peasants.'
PR 3, 1 (5 Jan. 1960), 20–21.
SUBJ 27

17801 CSH O P8 G2.3 1949–1972
Liaoning. Ko ming wei yüan hui (Revolutionary Committee) *and* Chung-kuo jen min chieh fang chün (People's Liberation Army). Mo pu ('A Certain Unit'), *joint sponsors*. Lien ho tiao ch'a tsu (Joint Investigation Team).
'A primary school run by the people under the control of the poor and lower-middle peasants.' Tr. of 'I so p'in hsia chung nung chang ch'üan ti min pan hsiao hsüeh: Ts'ung sung shu hsiao hsüeh ti ch'eng chang k'an nung ts'un pan hsüeh ti fang hsiang' (An elementary school run by poor and lower-middle peasants: Trends in rural school management as seen in Sung-shu elementary school [Meng-k'ou *hsien*, Liaoning]); *Hung ch'i* 1968, 5 (Nov.), 46–51.
CE 2, 3 (Fall 1969), 28–36.
SUBJ 27 ▪ 26.3

17802 NNC O P3 G5.1 1949–1972
Lin Chih-wo.
'Report on inspection of Tientsin half-work, half-study schools.' Tr. of 'T'ien-chin shih kung ch'ang chü pan pan kung pan tu hsüeh hsiao ti k'ao ch'a pao kao' (Report of an inspection tour of the half-work half-study schools run by factories in Tientsin); *Pei-ching shih ta hsüeh hsüeh pao; she hui k'o hsüeh* 1959, 1 (Jan.), 19–28. In *Translations from China's political and sociological publications*, mimeo., compiled by U.S. Joint Publications Research Service. [Selective entry]
Washington, D.C.: JPRS, 11 Sept. 1959, 31–45. (JPRS 909D; MC 16,509/1959)
SUBJ 27 ▪ 24.4 26.1 26.4 28 34.2

17803 NNC O P2 G1.2 1949–1972
Naumov, Samuil Naumovich, 1899–1966.
'Vospitanie detei v shkolakh Kitaia' (The education of children in Chinese schools).
Narodnoe obrazovanie 1959, 7 (iiul'), 102–110.
SUBJ 27 ▪ 41 48 54 60

17804 CSU P P1 G1.2 1949–1972
Ridley, Charles Price, 1933–, Paul Herbert Barlow Godwin, 1935–, and Dennis James Doolin, 1933–.
The making of a model citizen in Communist China.
Stanford: Hoover Institution Press, 1971. 404 p.
SUBJ 27 53 ▪ 12.1 60 64

17805 CSH O P3 G6.1 1949–1972
Shang-hai shih Yang-p'u mien fang chih yin jan ch'ang pan kung pan tu chung teng chi shu hsüeh hsiao (Yang P'u Cotton Spinning, Weaving, and Dyeing Factory of Shanghai Work-Study Technical School).
'Part-work, part-study education trains new men.' Tr. of 'Pan kung pan tu yü hsin jen'; *Hung ch'i* 1965, 13 (6 Dec.), 34–40.
SCMM 506 (10 Jan. 1966), 29–37.
SUBJ 26.4 27

17806 CSH O P3 G5.1 1949–1972
Tientsin. Ssu shih erh chung ko ming wei yüan hui. (No. 42 Middle School Revolutionary Committee).
'How did we initiate "industrial study" activities?' Tr. by Akira Odani of 'Wo men shih tsen yang fa chan "hsüeh kung" huo tung ti?'; *Hung ch'i* 1970, 8 (Aug.), 58–60.
CE 4, 2 (Summer 1971), 119–126.
SUBJ 24.4 27 ▪ 26.4

17807 CSU P P2 G1.2 1949–1972
United Nations. Educational, Scientific and Cultural Organization.
'People's Republic of China.' In *World survey of education, Vol. 2, Primary education*, compiled by the organization cited. [Selective entry]
Paris: UNESCO, 1958, 252–260.
SUBJ 27

17808 CBU O P3 G1.3 1949–1972
Vasil'eva, L- V-.
'Na urokakh biologii' (Biology lessons). In *Shkola i prosveshchenie v Narodnom Kitae: sbornik statei* (Articles on schools and education in the People's Republic of China), compiled by Akademiia pedagogicheskikh nauk RSFSR, edited by Aleksei I- Markushevich, E- I- Monoszon, and M- N- Riakin. [Selective entry]
Moscow: Izd-vo Akad. ped. nauk RSFSR, 1957, 134–150.
SUBJ 27 ▪ 17 52 66

17809 NNC O P2 G1.2 1949–1972
Vlasov, G-.
'Novoe v rabote professional'nykh uchilishch KNR' (New work trends in trade schools of the People's Republic of China).
Professional'no-tekhnicheskoe obrazovanie 15, 11 (noiabr' 1958), 30–32.
SUBJ 14.4 27 ▪ 14.1 16.4

17810 MCH O P2 G9.5 1949–1972
Williams, W- D- F-.
'Vocational training in Hong Kong.'
Hong Kong manager 3, 2 (Mar.–Apr. 1967), 22–24, 31.
SUBJ 21.4 24.4 27 ▪ 37

28 LOCAL WELFARE AND LIVING STANDARDS
地方福利及生活水準
地方の福祉及び生活水準

1644-1911

17811 CSU O P7 G5.2 1842–1895
'A record of the famine relief work in Lin Fen Hien [i.e., Lin-fen *hsien*, Shansi]'. Tr. from the Chinese by David Hill.
CR 11, 4 (July–Aug. 1880), 260–269.m
SUBJ 28 ▪ 22.2 25 38

17812 ICU O P7 G6.0 1895–1911
Baird, George Burleigh.
Famine relief and prevention in Central China.
Unpublished masters thesis in Practical Sociology, U. of Chicago, 1915. 92 p.
SUBJ 22.1 28 38 ▪ 22.2 26

17813 MCH O P3 G9.0 1895–1911
Barbedette, F-.
'La Chine méridionale' (South China).
B. de la Société géographique d'Alger et de l'Afrique du Nord 15, 1 (1910), 84–102.
SUBJ 21.3 28 ▪ 43 47

17814 CSU O P3 G9.2 1842–1895
Cantoniensis, pseud.
'Cost of living among the Chinese.'
NQCJ 2, 1 (Jan. 1868), 11–12; 2, 2 (Feb. 1868), 26–27.
SUBJ 28

17815 MCH O P5 G8.2 1895–1911
Delay, *Dr.* ———.
'Notes sur le Yun-Nan' (Notes on Yunnan).
AHMC 3, 2 (avr.–juin 1900), 145–171.
SUBJ 28 55 56

17816 CSU P P7 G6.1 –1895
Havret, Henri, 1848–1901.
L'île de Tsong-ming, à l'embouchure du Yang-tse-kiang (Ch'ung-ming *hsien* [Kiangsu], an island at the mouth of the Yangtze river), 2nd ed.
Shanghai: Impr. de la Mission catholique, 1901. 59 p. (Variétés sinologiques, 1)
SUBJ 20 24.1 28 ▪ 21 22.2 26.3 29 45

17817 CSU O P2 G5.3 1842–1895
Jones, Alfred G-.
'The poverty of Shantung: Its causes and treatment.'
CR 25, 4 (Apr. 1894), 181–187; 25, 5 (May 1894), 214–220.
SUBJ 28 ▪ 24.1 24.2 24.4 62

17818 CSU O P8 G6.0 1895–1911
Junkin, William F-.
'Famine conditions in north Anhui and north Kiangsu.'
CR 43, 2 (Feb. 1912), 75–81.
SUBJ 28 ▪ 41 55 56

17819 DLC O P3 G5.1 1895–1911
Korsakov, Vladimir Viktorovich, 1854–?
'Piat' let v Pekine' (Five years in Peking).
Vestnik obshchestvennoi gigieny, sudebnoi i prakticheskoi meditsiny 1900, 9 (sentiabr'), 1380–1394.
SUBJ 28 56 ▪ 52 53

17820 MCH O P3 G9.2 1644–1842
Malcolm, Howard, 1799–1879.
'Part 3: Travels in Hindustan, Malaya, Siam and China, Chap. 5.' In *Travels in south-eastern Asia, embracing Hindustan, Malaya, Siam and China . . .*, 10th ed., by H. Malcolm. [Sole entry]
Philadelphia: American Baptist Publishing Society, 1857, 218–347.
SUBJ 26.2 28 ▪ 23 24.3

17821 MCH O P7 G6.1 1895–1911
Rodet, Raymond, 1858–?
'Budget de la famille Tcheng' (The Cheng family budget).
Etudes 7e série 84, 3 (5 août 1900), 399–403.
SUBJ 28 41

17822 MCH O P2 G9.4 1644–1842
Vieillard, Ph——.
'Une description inédite de Formose' (An unpublished description of Taiwan), edited by Julien Gérard de Rialle. [Previously unpublished memoir of Ph. Vieillard, French consul in Taiwan, dated 1784]
R. de géographie 16, 10 (avr. 1885), 290–301.
SUBJ 21.1 28 ▪ 24.1 24.3 26.1 26.3 32.1 63

17823 CSH O P2 G5.3 1895–1911
Volpert, Ant——.
'Chinesische Armut' (Poverty in China).
OL 26, 17 (26 Apr. 1912), 367–369.
SUBJ 28

1644-1949

17824 MCY P P3 G5.1 1895–1928
Meng, Tien-pei (Meng T'ien-p'ei), and Sidney David Gamble, 1890–1968.
Prices, wages, and the standard of living in Peking, 1900–1924.
Peking: Peking Express, 1926. 113 p. [Supplement to *CSPSR* 10, 3 (July 1926)]
SUBJ 24.3 26.4 28 ▪ 34.3

1911-1949

17825 NNC P P7 G6.1 1928–1949
'Annual expenditures and receipts of 106 farm households in Shanghai, 1930.'
NWSS 6, 4 (23 Jan. 1933), 15, 17–18.
SUBJ 26.3 28 ▪ 24.1

17826 CSU P P3 G6.1 1928–1949
'Cost of living figures for Shanghai in 1932.'
CEJ 12, 4 (Apr. 1933), 394–408.
SUBJ 24.3 28

17827 NNC P P3 G6.1 1911–1949
'The cost of living index number of laborers, greater Shanghai, 1926–1931.'
NWSS 5, 44 (31 Oct. 1932), 197, 199–202.
SUBJ 26.4 28

17828 CSH F P3 G5.1 1911–1928
'Cost of living of Tsing Hua College employees.'
CEM 2, 1 (Oct. 1924), 5–12.
Subj 26.4 28 55

17829 NNC P P3 G5.1 1911–1928
'Income and expenditure of 283 families in Peiping, 1927.'
NWSS 6, 48 (27 Nov. 1933), 221, 223–224.
Subj 28

17830 NNC P P7 G5.1 1928–1949
'Income and outgo for farmers and landowners in Hopei, 1929.'
NWSS 3, 47 (24 Nov. 1930), 221, 224.
Subj 26.1 26.3 28

17831 NNC F P3 G5.1 1911–1928
'An inquiry into the family budget of the handicraftsmen in Tientsin, 1927–1928.'
NWSS 5, 48 (28 Nov. 1932), 217, 219–220.
Subj 26.2 28 ▪ 55

17832 NIC O P8 G5.2 1911–1949
'Plight of the Shansi peasantry.'
PT new (2nd) series 1, 5 (16 Jan. 1932), 132–136.
Subj 24.1 26.3 28 ▪ 24.5

17833 NNC F P3 G6.1 1928–1949
'Recent family budget enquiries: The Shanghai family budget enquiry of 1929–1930.'
ILR 32, 2 (Aug. 1935), 230–241.
Subj 26.4 28 ▪ 41

17834 CSU F P3 G6.1 1928–1949
'A study of 65 labor families in Nanking.'
CEJ 9, 3 (Sept. 1931), 1002–1007.
Subj 26.4 28 ▪ 41

17835 NNC F P3 G6.1 1911–1928
'The workers' cost of living index in Shanghai.'
NWSS 3, 52 (29 Dec. 1930), 247, 250–251.
Subj 26.4 28

17836 NNC O P3 G6.1 1911–1928
Anderson, Adelaide Mary, 1863–1936.
'The recommendations of the Shanghai Child Labour Commission.'
ILR 11, 5 (May 1925), 665–681.
Subj 26.4 28 52 ▪ 12.2 22.1 24.4

17837 MCH O P2 G4.2 1928–1949
Andrew, George Findlay.
'On the trail of death in Northwest China.'
Asia (New York: American Asiatic Assn.) 32, 1 (Jan. 1932), 42–48, 60–62.
Subj 28 ▪ 55

17838 MCH O P2 G2.0 1928–1949
Arditi, Lazzaro.
'In Manciuria, sulle vie dell'emigrazione cinese' (In Manchuria, along the route of Chinese emigration).
Universo 10, 2 – 16, 7 (febbraio 1929 – luglio 1935), 301 p. in all.
Subj 21.2 24 28 ▪ 12 24.2 25 26.4

17839 NNC U P3 G6.1 1928–1949
Bessmertnyi, B-.
'Zhiznennyi uroven' promyshlennogo proletariata Kitaia' (The standard of living of the Chinese industrial proletariat).
Revoliutsiia i natsional'nosti 1934, 6 (iiun'), 92–95.
Subj 26.4 28 ▪ 52 70

17840 CSH F P7 G8.1 1928–1949
Buck, John Lossing, 1890–.
'The economic position of the Szechwan farmer in 1942–43.'
EF 26 (Nov. 1943), 283–289.
Subj 26.3 28

17841 CSH F P7 G8.1 1928–1949
Buck, John Lossing, 1890–, and Hu Kwoh-hwa (Hu Kuo-hua).
'The economic position of the Szechwan farmer in 1941–42.'
EF 16 (Jan. 1943), 7–13.
Subj 26.3 28

17842 MCH F P2 G1.3 1911–1928
Burgess, John Stewart, 1883–1949.
'China's social challenge. Part 1, An opportunity for American social workers. Part 2, Beginnings of social investigation. Part 3, Social institutions, old and new. Part 4, The Christian movement and social welfare.'
Survey (New York) 38, 23 (8 Sept. 1917), 501–503; 39, 2 (13 Oct. 1917), 41–44; 39, 11 (15 Dec. 1917), 311–316; 40, 23 (7 Sept. 1918), 633–638, 653.
Subj 17 26.4 28 ▪ 12.2 33 37 38 56

17843 CSU O P3 G5.1 1911–1928
Burgess, John Stewart, 1883–1949.
'Peking as a field for social service.'
CR 45, 4 (Apr. 1914), 226–235.
Subj 28 38 ▪ 17 24.4 37 55 56

17844 CSU O P3 G5.1 1911–1928
Burnight, Ralph F-.
'A study of social conditions in Peking, China.'
J. of applied sociology 7, 1 (Sept.–Oct. 1922), 23–30.
Subj 28 ▪ 22.1 46 57

17845 NNC O P8 G5.2 1928–1949
Chang Chiao-fu.
'General living conditions of the peasants in middle Shansi.' Tr. from *I shih pao fu k'an* 13 July 1935. In *Agrarian China*, compiled by Institute of Pacific Relations. [Selective entry]
Chicago: U. of Chicago Press, 1939, 199–204.
Subj 26.3 28 ▪ 24.1 24.6

17846 MCH F P7 G1.4 1928–1949
Chen Han-seng (Ch'en Han-sheng), 1897–.
Industrial capital and Chinese peasants: A study of the livelihood of Chinese tobacco cultivators.
Shanghai: Kelly and Walsh, 1939. 23, 97 p.
Subj 14.5 24.1 26.3 28 34.2 ▪ 24.3 24.4 26.1 66

17847 NIC O P7 G9.2 1928–1949
Chen, Percy Pao.
'Rural rehabilitation in southeastern Kwangtung.'
CQ-S 5, 4 [Supplement] (Winter 1940), 827–835.
Subj 24.1 28

17848 CSU O P2 G1.2 1911–1928
China International Famine Relief Commission.
China International Famine Relief Commission Annual Report, 1922–1927. [Issues for 1928–1935 are entered as 17849.]
Peking: China International Famine Relief Commission. Issued annually, 1923–1928. Average ca. 75 p. (CIFRC, Series A, 5, 12, 16, 19, 23)
Subj 28 38 ▪ 22 24.1 24.2 24.6 56

17849 CSU O P2 G1.2 1928–1949
China International Famine Relief Commission.
China International Famine Relief Commission Annual Report, 1928–1935. [Issues for 1922–1927 are entered as 17848.]
Peiping: China International Famine Relief Commission. Issued annually, 1930–1936. Average ca. 100 p. (CIFRC, Series A, 26, 28, 30, 34, 36, 40, 42, 45)
Subj 28 38 ▪ 22 24.1 24.2 24.6 56

17850 CSH S P3 G6.1 1911–1949
China [Republic]. [Ts'ai cheng pu]. Kuo ting shui tse wei yüan hui. ([Ministry of Finance]. National Tariff Commission), ed.
'Index number of the cost of living in Shanghai, Jan. 1926 – Dec. 1930.'
Shanghai market prices report unnumbered, Part 1 (Oct.–Dec. 1930), 39. [See Vol. 2 of this *Bibliography* for Chinese version.]
Subj 28

17851 CSH S P3 G6.1 1911–1928
China [Republic]. [Ts'ai cheng pu]. Kuo ting shui tse wei yüan hui. ([Ministry of Finance]. National Tariff Commission), ed.
'The "provisional" index number of cost of living in Shanghai (Jan. 1926 – Dec. 1927).'
Shanghai market prices report unnumbered, Part 1 (Jan.–Mar. 1929), 37. [See Vol. 2 of this *Bibliography* for Chinese version.]
Subj 28

17852 CSU O P3 G2.1 1928–1949
Coville, Lilian Grosvenor.
'Here in Manchuria: Many thousand lives were lost and more than half the crops destroyed by the floods of 1932.'
NG 63, 2 (Feb. 1933), 233–256.
Subj 20 28 ▪ 24.3 25 56

17853 NIC F P7 G5.1 1911–1928
Dittmer, Clarence Gus, 1885–1950.
'An estimate of the standard of living in China.'
Quarterly j. of economics 33, 1 (Nov. 1918), 107–128.
Subj 28 55

17854 CSU F P2 G8.2 1928–1949
Fei Hsiao-tung (Fei Hsiao-t'ung), 1910–.
'Some social problems of Free China.' In *Voices from unoccupied China*, edited by Harley Farnsworth MacNair. [Selective entry]
Chicago: U. of Chicago Press, 1944, 46–64.
Subj 20 21.2 21.4 24.1 26 28 ▪ 21.3 26.1 26.3 41 50 61

17855 NNC F P3 G5.1 1911–1928
Gamble, Sidney David, 1890–1968.
The household accounts of two Chinese families.

New York: China Institute in America, 1931. 23 p.
Subj 28 41 55 ▪ 26

17856 CSH F P3 G5.1 1911–1928
Gamble, Sidney David, 1890–1968.
How Chinese families live in Peiping.
New York: Funk and Wagnalls, 1933. 17, 348 p.
Subj 28 41 55 ▪ 17 21.1 21.4 23 24.2 26 57

17857 CSH F P2 G2.0 1911–1949
Gerasimov, A- E-.
'Dzhonochnye arteli na Sungari' (Junk cooperatives on the Sungari). [With English abstract]
VM 1931, 7, 16–20. [Reprinted as 'Dzhonochnye arteli na reke Sungari' (Junk cooperatives on the Sungari river). In *Kitaiskii trud (usloviia truda v predpriiatiiakh severnoi Man'chzhurii)* (Chinese labor: Labor conditions in northern Manchurian enterprises), by A. E. Gerasimov. (Analytic entry.) Harbin: Tip. KVzhd, 1931, 131–157.]
Subj 24.2 28 34.2 ▪ 48 55

17858 CBU O P2 G6.2 1928–1949
Gulbransen, Kaare.
China på naert hold (A close view of China).
Oslo: Aschehoug, 1950. 145 p.
Subj 24.1 28 ▪ 12 14.3 24.2 25 55 66

17859 CSU O P2 G4.2 1911–1928
[Hall, Josef Washington] Upton Close, pseud., 1894–, and Elsie McCormick.
'"Where the mountains walked": An account of the recent earthquake in Kansu province, China, which destroyed 100,000 lives.'
NG 41, 5 (May 1922), 445–464.
Subj 28

17860 NNC O P7 G5.3 1928–1949
Hao P'un-sui (Hao Pen-shui).
'The peasant exodus from western Shantung.' Tr. of 'Yü-ch'eng Ch'eng-nan ti nung ts'un' (The villages of the Ch'eng-nan plain, Yü-ch'eng *hsien* [Shantung]); *Min chien pan yüeh k'an* 3, 19 (10 Feb. 1937), 10–11. In *Agrarian China*, compiled by Institute of Pacific Relations. [Selective entry]
Chicago: U. of Chicago Press, 1939, 247–251.
Subj 21.2 24.1 28 ▪ 24.5 24.6 26.3

17861 CSU O P3 G1.3 1911–1928
Harrison, Agatha, and J- W- Nipps.
'Exhibits A and B. Part 1, Shanghai. Part 2, Chefoo.'
World tomorrow 6, 11 (Nov. 1923), 331–333.
Subj 26.4 28 ▪ 24.4

17862 CSU O P2 G5.3 1911–1928
Heeren, John J-, 1875–1941.
'On the famine front in Shantung.'
Asia (New York: American Asiatic Assn.) 21, 6 (June 1921), 540–544.
Subj 28 38 ▪ 21.4

17863 NIC PO P3 G6.1 1928–1949
Hinder, Eleanor M-.
Life and labour in Shanghai: A decade of labour and social administration in the International Settlement, 2nd ed.
New York: Institute of Pacific Relations, International Secretariat, 1944. 143 p.
Subj 17 26.4 28 ▪ 21.1 22 24 26.2 34.2 36.4 47 52 55

17864 CSH F P3 G8.1 1928–1949
Hu Kwoh-hwa (Hu Kuo-hua).
'A preliminary study of the cost of living of the laborer-peddler class in Chengtu, 1941–42.'
EF 23 (Aug. 1943), 221–226.
Subj 26.2 26.4 28

17865 CSH F P3 G8.1 1928–1949
Hu Kwoh-hwa (Hu Kuo-hua).
'A preliminary study of the cost of living of the merchant-storekeeper class in Chengtu (1941–42).'
EF 22 (July 1943), 189–194.
Subj 26.2 28

17866 CSH F P3 G8.1 1928–1949
Hu Kwoh-hwa (Hu Kuo-hua).
'A preliminary study of the cost of living of the military-official-educational class in Chengtu, 1941–42.'
EF 21 (June 1943), 163–168.
Subj 26.1 28

17867 CSH F P3 G8.1 1928–1949
Hu Kwoh-hwa (Hu Kuo-hua).
'The revision of the cost of living index of the military-official-educational class in Chengtu.'
EF 29 (Feb. 1944), 365–372.
Subj 28 ▪ 26.1

17868 NNC F P7 G6.1 1928–1949
Lamson, Herbert Day, 1899–.
'The effect of industrialization upon village livelihood: A study of fifty families in four villages near the University of Shanghai.'
CEJ 9, 4 (Oct. 1931), 1025–1082. [Separately reprinted—Shanghai: Kung shang pu, Kung shang fang wen chü, 1931. 58 p. (Kung shang fang wen chü, Booklet series, 17)]
Subj 20 26.4 28 41 47 ▪ 17 23 24.1 24.4 26.3 55 61

17869 NNC PO P2 G1.3 1911–1949
Lamson, Herbert Day, 1899–.
Social pathology in China.
Shanghai: Commercial Press, 1935. 18, 607 p.
Subj 26.4 28 37 41 55 56 ▪ 11 12.2 14.1 17 18 24.4 34.2 36.4 47 61

17870 NIC F P3 G6.1 1928–1949
Lamson, Herbert Day, 1899–.
'The standard of living of factory workers.'
CEJ 7, 5 (Nov. 1930), 1240–1256.
Subj 26.4 28

17871 NIC FP P7 G5.1 1911–1928
Lee, Franklin C. H. (Li Ching-han), 1895–.
Village families in the vicinity of Peiping. Tr. by T. Chin of *Pei-p'ing chiao wai chih hsiang ts'un chia t'ing* (Rural households in periurban Peiping); Shanghai: Chung-hua chiao yü wen hua chi chin tung shih hui, She hui tiao ch'a pu, 1929; 151 p. [Rev. and abridged in tr.]
Peiping: China Foundation, Social Research Dept., 1929. 65 p. (Institute of Social Research bulletins, 2)
Subj 20 21 28 55 ▪ 21.4 24.1 26.3 27 41 56 57 58

17872 NNC P P7 G8.1 1928–1949
Owyang, Pearl, 1920–.
A study of rural Szechwan and its reconstruction.
Unpublished masters thesis in Sociology, Columbia U., 1951. 91 p.
Subj 17 24.1 28 37 ▪ 21 24.3 24.4 34.1 41

17873 NNM PO P2 G1.4 1911–1928
Pei-ching kuo chi t'ung i chiu tsai tsung hui (Peking United International Famine Relief Committee).
The North China famine of 1920–1921, with special reference to the West Chihli area.
Peking: Commercial Press, 1922. 175 p. [Reprinted—Taipei: Ch'eng-wen, 1971. 175 p.]
Subj 14.1 18 28 38 56 ▪ 11.4 14.2 16.3 16.4 24.1 52 55 58

17874 CSH S P3 G6.1 1911–1928
S. K.
'Biudzhet kitaiskogo rabochego' (The Chinese worker's budget).
VM 1930, 9, 91–94.
Subj 26.4 28 ▪ 24.4

17875 MCY O P2 G1.5 1928–1949
Saquez de Breuvery, Emmanuel.
'Impressions de voyage au Kwangsi et au Kweichow' (Impressions of Kwangsi and Kweichow).
BUA 3e série 2, 8 (1941), 638–664.
Subj 24.1 28 ▪ 21 24.4

17876 NIC F P3 G5.1 1911–1928
Tao, L. K. (T'ao Meng-ho), 1887–1960.
'Handicraft workers of Peking.'
CSPSR 13, 1 (Jan. 1929), 1–11.
Subj 26.4 28 41 ▪ 24.4 26.2

17877 NNC F P3 G5.1 1911–1928
Tao, L. K. (T'ao Meng-ho), 1887–1960.
Livelihood in Peking: An analysis of the budgets of sixty families.
Peking: China Foundation for the Promotion of Education and Culture, Social Research Dept., 1928. 158, 22 p.
Subj 26.4 28 55 ▪ 21.4 24.3 26.2 34.2 38 41 50

17878 CSH O P8 G5.3 1911–1928
Todd, Oliver Julian, 1880–.
'Famine relief and road building in Shantung.'
J. of the Assn. of Chinese and American Engineers (Peking) 2, 11 (Nov. 1921), 28–40. [Reprinted in *Two decades in China*, by O. J. Todd. (Selective entry.) Peiping: Assn. of Chinese and American Engineers, 1938, 203–215.] [Reprinted in *Two decades in China*, by O. J. Todd. (Selective entry.) Taipei: Ch'eng-wen, 1971, 203–215.]
Subj 21.4 28 ▪ 24.2 56

17879 MCY O P3 G1.2 1911–1928
Tong, Y. L.
'Social conditions and social service endeavor in Peking.'
CSPSR 7, 3 (July 1922 [i.e., 1923]), 75–93.
Subj 28 38 ▪ 14 47 52

17880 MCH P P3 G6.1 1911–1949
Tsha, T. Y. (Ts'ai Cheng-ya).
'Cost of living and labor unrest.'
China critic 4, 31 (30 July 1931), 729–734.
Subj 26.4 28 ▪ 36.4 41

17881 CSH FP P8 G2.3 1911–1928
TSiba, T. (Chiba Toyoharu), 1892–.
'Sravnenie biudzhetov kitaiskikh i iaponskikh krest'ianskikh khoziaistv iuzhnoi Man'chzhurii' (A comparison of Chinese and Japanese peasants' household budgets in southern Manchuria). Tr. of 'Nichi Man nōka seikatsu teido no hikaku' (A comparison of living standards of Chinese and Japanese peasant families); *Shintenchi* 7, 9 (Sept. 1927), 14–26.
VM 1928, 1, 72–77.
Subj 26.3 28

17882 CSU O P8 G5.1 1911–1928
Turner, F- B-.
'Flood and famine in North China.'
JRAS-NCB new (2nd) series 57 (1926), 1–18.
Subj 28 ▪ 21.4

17883 NNC FP P7 G1.5 1928–1949
U. of Nanking. College of Agriculture and Forestry. Dept. of Agricultural Economics *with* China [Republic]. Chiu chi shui tsai wei yüan hui (National Flood Relief Commission), eds.
The 1931 flood in China: An economic survey.
Nanking: College of Agriculture and Forestry, 1932. 74 p. (CAF bulletins, new series, 1)
Subj 24 28 ▪ 21 21.2

17884 NOU O P2 G7.2 1911–1928
Vogt, Volrath, 1879–.
'Hungersnöd i Kina' (Famine in China).
Laegemisionaeren 1921, 73–79.
Subj 28 38

17885 CBU F P3 G8.1 1928–1949
Wang, Yin-yuen (Wang Yin-yüan).
'Inequality of personal income and the tax policy.'
EF 52 (Jan. 1946), 789–790.
Subj 26 28 ▪ 24.5

17886 CSH F P3 G5.1 1911–1928
Yang, Simon (Yang Hsi-meng).
An index of the cost of living in Peiping.
Peiping: China Foundation, Social Research Dept., 1928. 16 p. (Institute of Social Research bulletins, 1)
Subj 28 ▪ 26.4 55

17887 NIC F P3 G6.1 1911–1928
Yang, Simon (Yang Hsi-meng), and L. K. Tao (T'ao Meng-ho), 1887–1960.
A study of the standard of living of working families in Shanghai. Tr. of *Shang-hai kung jen sheng huo ch'eng tu ti i ko yen chiu* (The living standards of workers in Shanghai); Peiping: Pei-p'ing she hui tiao ch'a so, 1930; 100, 58 p. [Tr. inferred; condensed tr.]
Peiping: Institute of Social Research, 1931. 86 p. (ISR monographs, 3)
Subj 26.4 28 ▪ 41 55

17888 CBU F P3 G8.1 1928–1949
Yang, William Y. (Yang Yü), 1907–, and Hu Kwoh-hwa (Hu Kuo-hua).
'A cost of living index for the laborer-pedlar class in Chengtu, Szechwan.'
EF 10 (June 1938), 453–460. [In Chinese as well as English]
Subj 26.4 28 ▪ 21.4 26.2 55

17889 DNA F P3 G8.1 1928–1949
Yang, William Y. (Yang Yü), 1907–, and Hu Kwoh-hwa (Hu Kuo-hua).
'A cost of living index for the M-O-E [military-official-educational] class in Chengtu, Szechwan.'
EF 12 (June 1939), 546–560. [In Chinese as well as English]
Subj 26.1 28 ▪ 55

17890 CSH F P3 G8.1 1928–1949
Yang, William Y. (Yang Yü), 1907–, and Hu Kwoh-hwa (Hu Kuo-hua).
'A cost of living index for the merchant-storekeeper class and for all three classes in Chengtu, Szechwan.'
EF 13 (Sept. 1939), 32–41.
Subj 26.2 28 ▪ 55

17891 NNC O P7 G5.1 1928–1949
Yao, H. S.
Foundation for rural economic reconstruction.
Ting-hsien, Hopei: Chinese National Assn. of the Mass Education Movement, 1936. 38 p.
Subj 24 24.1 28 34.1 37 ▪ 22 27

1911-1972
(including 1644-1972)

17892 CSU P P3 G6.1 1842–1972
A Sheng (A-shen), pseud.
New frontiers in Yang-shu-p'u (eastern Shanghai): From slums to modernity, mimeo. Tr. of 'Chiu Shang-hai p'in min ch'ü Yang-shu-p'u ti pien ch'ien' (Changes in Yang-shu-p'u, an old Shanghai slum area); *Chung-kuo hsin wen* 12 Oct. 1962, 9–10.
Washington, D.C.: U.S. Joint Publications Research Service, 13 Dec. 1962. 4 p. (JPRS 16,671; MC 1136/1963)
Subj 21.3 28 ▪ 24.2 24.3 31

17893 NNC O P2 G9.5 1928–1972
Black, Robert Brown, 1906–.
Immigration and social planning in Hong Kong.
London: China Society, 1965. 12 p. (CS occasional papers, 13)
Subj 28 ▪ 11.2

17894 CSU P P2 G9.5 1928–1972
Hong Kong. Social Welfare Office.
Annual departmental report by the Social Welfare Officer, 1948/54. [Issues for 1955/56–1971/72 are entered as 17909.]
Hong Kong: Government Printer, 1954. 55 p.
Subj 28 38 ▪ 22.1 47 52

17895 DLC O P2 G1.2 1928–1972
Lapwood, Ralph, and Nancy Lapwood.
Through the Chinese revolution.
London: Spalding and Levy, 1954. 216 p. [Reprinted—Westport, Conn.: Hyperion Press, 197? 216 p.]
Subj 17 26.3 28 32.2 54 ▪ 14 14.2 22.1 24.1 24.4 26 31 47 56 66

17896 MCH F P7 G5.1 1911–1972
Lee, Franklin C. H. (Li Ching-han), 1895–.
'Village families in the vicinity of Peking today and yesterday.'
People's China 1957, 6 (16 Mar.), 13–17; 1957, 7 (1 Apr.) 26–30. [See also entry 17871.]
Subj 24 28 ▪ 21.4 24.1 26.3

17897 NIC F P8 G9.4 1928–1972
Raper, Arthur Franklin, 1899–.
Rural Taiwan: Problem and promise.
Taipei: Chinese-American Joint Commission on Rural Reconstruction, 1953. 296 p.
Subj 24 24.1 26.3 28 ▪ 22 23 37 41

17898 CSU O P3 G6.1 1928–1972
Tannebaum, Gerald, 1916–.
'Melon lane.'
EH 5, 9 (Sept. 1966), 48–52.
Subj 28 55 ▪ 21.3

17899 MCH O P2 G9.5 1928–1972
Yueh, Hu.
'The problem of the Hong Kong refugees.'
AS 2, 1 (Mar. 1962), 28–37.
Subj 28 ▪ 11.2 22

1949-1972

17900 NNC P P1 G9.4 1949–1972
'Social insurance in Taiwan in industry, fisheries, and sugar-cane plantations.'
BISSA 11, 3 (Mar. 1958), 87–92.
Subj 24.6 28

17901 CSH O P7 G9.2 1949–1972
'"Who is Mao Tse-tung?" Four answers.'
CS 1, 22 (5 Jan. 1962), 1–10. [Reprinted in *Out of China: A collection of interviews with refugees from China*, edited by Francis Harper. (Analytic entry.) Hong Kong: Dragonfly Books, 1964, 1–25.]
Subj 28 55 ▪ 22.1 24.1

17902 CSU O P3 G1.2 1949–1972
Bastid, Paul.
'Impressions de Chine' (Impressions of China).
Revue; littérature, histoire, arts et sciences des deux mondes 1966, 10 (15 mai), 161–173; 1966, 11 (1er juin), 324–337.
Subj 28 ▪ 24.3 24.4 32 32.2

17903 CSU P P1 G9.4 1949–1972
Chang, Chia-yang.
'The financial problem of government employee's insurance in the past and future.'
CJA 17 (July 1971), 4–14 [s.p.].
Subj 28 ▪ 56

17904 MCH O P3 G2.0 1949–1972
Chow Hsueh-sheng.
'Workers' rising living standards: Three typical workers' budgets from the Northeast.'
People's China 1952, 4 (16 Feb.), 12–14.
Subj 28 ▪ 26.4

17905 CSH P P7 G1.2 1949–1972
Engelborghs-Bertels, Marthe, 1928–.
'Rémunérations et logement des travailleurs dans les communes populaires chinoises' (Remunerations

and housing of workers in Chinese communes).
Pays communistes 1, 2 (1960), 87–92.
Subj 22 26.3 28 ▪ 34.1 55

17906 MCY P P3 G9.5 1949–1972
Evans, Francis.
'Home truths.'
FEER 46, 3 (15 Oct. 1964), 151–154.
Subj 28 ▪ 55

17907 MCH O P7 G9.4 1949–1972
Free China Relief Assn.
Resettlement of war disabled refugees.
Taipei: Free China Relief Assn., 1956. 40 p.
Subj 27 28 ▪ 15 24.4 36.3 55

17908 NNC O P2 G1.3 1949–1972
Henle, Hans.
'Von Kanton nach Peking' (From Canton to Peking).
Z. für Geopolitik 36, 1/2 (Jan.–Feb. 1965), 48–57.
Subj 24 28 ▪ 19 24.1 55

17909 CSU P P2 G9.5 1949–1972
Hong Kong. Social Welfare Dept.
Annual departmental report by the Director of Social Welfare, 1955/56–1971/72. [Issue for 1948/54 is entered as 17894.]
Hong Kong: Government Printer. Issued annually, 1956–1972. Average ca. 70 p.
Subj 28 38 ▪ 22.1 47 52

17910 MAM F P7 G9.4 1949–1972
Hsü, Yu-chu, 1930–.
Income variability and resource productivity of rice farms in Changhwa and Nantou counties [i.e., Chang-hua *hsien* and Nan-t'ou *hsien*], *Taiwan, China: The applicability of farm management analytical methods to a developing area.*
Ann Arbor: University Microfilms (Publ. 66-4119), 1966. 297 p. (Doctoral dissertation in Economics, Cornell U., 1965)
Subj 24.1 28 ▪ 26.3

17911 NIC O P3 G9.5 1949–1972
Jenner, W- F- C-.
A problem of people.
Hong Kong: Government Printer, 1960. 43 p.
Subj 21.1 28 ▪ 11.2 21.3

17912 CSU F P2 G1.3 1949–1972
Karnow, Stanley, 1925–.
'Why they fled: Refugee accounts.'
CS 2, 22 (15 Oct. 1963), 1–12.
Subj 22.1 28 ▪ 22.2 24.3

17913 MCH P P2 G9.3 1949–1972
Li Tien-min (Li T'ien-min).
Crisis of the Chinese Communist regime, as seen from Lienchiang [*hsien*, Fukien] *documents.*
Taipei: Asian Peoples' Anti-Communist League, 1964. 42 p. (APACL pamphlets, 87)
Subj 24.1 28 32 ▪ 12.1 22 24 24.4 26 26.3 34.1

17914 CSH O P7 G5.1 1949–1972
Liu Chia-tse.
'Chinghsing coal mine takes good care of its workers.' Tr. of 'Ching-hsing ssu k'uang shih tsen yang kuan hsin ch'ün chung sheng huo ti' (How Ching-hsing Mine No. 4 [Ching-hsing *hsien*, Hopei] cares for the life of the masses); *Hung ch'i* 1961, 17 (1 Sept.), 30–33. In *Translations from 'Hung-ch'i' (Red Flag) (Peiping, No. 17, 1 September 1961)*, mimeo., compiled by U.S. Joint Publications Research Service. [Sole entry]
Washington, D.C.: JPRS, 10 Nov. 1961, 41–46. (JPRS 11,021; MC 1427/1962)
Subj 26.4 28 ▪ 24.4 32.1 34.2

17915 CSU F P2 G9.4 1949–1972
Reinke, William A-.
'The classification of households by economic level [in Taiwan].'
EDCC 20, 2 (Jan. 1972), 235–242.
Subj 28

17916 CSU O P2 G1.3 1949–1972
Sidel, Ruth, 1933–.
'Social services in China.'
Social work 17, 6 (Nov. 1972), 5–13.
Subj 28 56 ▪ 22 22.1 51 64

17917 MCH P P2 G9.5 1949–1972
Szczepanik, Edward Franciszek, 1915–.
The cost of living in Hong Kong.
Hong Kong: Hong Kong U. Press, 1956. 25 p.
Subj 24.3 28 ▪ 24 55

29 Regional and Subethnic Variation
習俗方言等等地域性差異
習俗方言等の地域的差異

1644-1911

17918 CSU O P8 G5.1 1842–1911
Ament, William S-.
'Strange people in the mountains of Chihli.'
CR 30, 7 (July 1899), 317–328.
Subj 20 29 ▪ 55

17919 CSU O P5 G9.0 1895–1911
Bone, C-.
'The floating population [i.e., boat people] of China.'
EAM 1 (1902), 230–238.
Subj 21.3 24.2 29 ▪ 28 47 55

17920 NNC O P7 G9.2 –1895
Eitel, Ernest John, 1838–1908.
'Character, customs and manners of the Hakkas, compared with those of the other races inhabiting the Canton province.'
NQCJ 1, 7 (July 1867), 81–83; 1, 8 (Aug. 1867), 97–99.
Subj 20 29 50 66 ▪ 21 23 47 51 61

17921 NNC O P2 G9.2 –1895
Eitel, Ernest John, 1838–1908.
'Ethnographical sketches of the Hakka Chinese.'
China review 20, 4 (Jan.–Feb. 1893), 263–267.
Subj 29 ▪ 21 21.2 21.3

17922 MCH O P2 G9.4 1842–1895
Fouque, Prosper.
'L'île de Formose' (Taiwan).
B. de la Société de géographie de Toulouse 4, 6 (1885), 129–135.
Subj 21 29 55 ▪ 21.3

17923 CSH O P2 G1.5 1895–1911
G. K.
'Die Bevölkerung von Nord-Kuangtung und den angrenzenden Gebieten' (The population of northern Kwangtung and the neighboring areas).
OL 26, 4 (26 Jan. 1912), 83–84.
Subj 11.2 29

17924 CSU P P7 G9.5 1842–1911
Hayes, James William, 1930–.
'Old British Kowloon.'
JRAS-HKB 6 (1966), 120–137.
Subj 29 ▪ 21.2 23 25 33 38

17925 NNC O P7 G9.2 1842–1895
Hubrig, ———.
'Über die Hakka-Chinesen' (The Hakka Chinese).
ZE 11 (15 März 1879), 99–105. [Supplement: *Verhandlungen der Berliner Gesellschaft für Anthropologie, Ethnologie und Urgeschichte* (Proceedings of the Berlin Society for Anthropology, Ethnology and Early History)]
Subj 29 ▪ 21.2 23 41 55

17926 MCH O P7 G8.0 1842–1895
Lalanne, J-.
'Une classe de Chinois indépendants' (A class of independent Chinese).
APF 26 (1854), 231–237.
Subj 29 ▪ 21.3 23 55

17927 NNC FP P2 G5.2 –1911
Laufer, Berthold, 1874–1934.
'Zur Kulturhistorischen Stellung der chinesischen Provinz Shansi' (The position of Shansi in China's cultural history).
Anthropos 5, 1 (Jan.–Feb. 1910), 181–203.
Subj 24.2 29 55 ▪ 21.3 26.3 61 71

17928 CSU PO P7 G9.2 1842–1895
Lechler, R-.
'The Hakka Chinese.'
CR 9, 5 (Sept.–Oct. 1878), 352–359.
Subj 29 ▪ 21.2 23 43 55

17929 CSU O P7 G1.5 1842–1895
Piton, Charles, 1835–1905.
'The Hia-k'ah in the Chekiang province, and the Hakka in the Canton province.'
CR 2, 8 (Jan. 1870), 218–220.
Subj 29 ▪ 43 55

17930 MCH O P7 G9.2 1842–1895
Piton, Charles, 1835–1905.
'Une visite au pays des Hakka dans la province de Canton' (A visit to Hakka territory in Kwangtung).
B. de la Société neuchâteloise de géographie 7, 3 (1892), 31–51.
Subj 29 47 ▪ 24.1 55 65

17931 MCH O P7 G1.5 1895–1911
Reynaud, L-.
'Du fleuve Rouge au fleuve Bleu' (From the Red river [Tonkin] to the Yangtze).
BAAFC 3, 4 (oct. 1911), 338–365; 4, 3 (juil. 1912), 229–249.
Subj 20 21.3 29 ▪ 24 55 66

1644-1949

17932 NIC U P1 G1.2 1644–1949
Chao, Y. R. (Chao Yüan-jen), 1892–.
'Languages and dialects in China.'

GJ 102, 2 (Aug. 1943), 63–66.
SUBJ 29

17933 NNC P P1 G1.1 –1949
Demiéville, Paul, 1894–.
'Le chinois vulgaire' (The Chinese vernacular). In *Aspects de la Chine, vol. 1, langue, histoire, religions, philosophie, littérature, arts* (Aspects of China, Vol. 1, Language, history, religions, philosophy, literature, and the arts), by Etienne Balazs et al. [Selective entry]
Paris: Presses universitaires, 1959, 22–26.
SUBJ 29 ▪ 12.1 16.1 16.3

17934 CSU S P2 G9.2 –1928
Fuson, Chester Garfield.
'The peoples of Kwangtung: Their origin, migrations, and present distribution.'
LSJ 7 (June 1929), 5–22.
SUBJ 21.2 29

17935 NNC U P1 G1.2 –1949
Great Britain. Admiralty. Naval Intelligence Division. Geographical Section.
'The peoples of China proper. I, The Chinese.' In *China proper, Vol. 1, Physical geography, history and peoples*, compiled by the agency cited. [Sole entry]
London: His Majesty's Stationery Office, 1944, 366–432. (NID, Geographical handbook series, BR 530)
SUBJ 29 33

17936 CSU U P1 G1.2 –1949
Howard, Harry Paxton, 1893–.
'Language and race in China.'
THM 7, 5 (Dec. 1938), 469–486.
SUBJ 29 ▪ 66

17937 GMS O P2 G1.3 1842–1928
Schmitthenner, Heinrich, 1887–1957.
'Nord und Südchina' (North and South China).
Petermanns Mitteilungen 73, 5/6 (1927), 129–136.
SUBJ 29 ▪ 11.3

1911-1949

17938 CSH U P1 G1.2 1911–1928
'Language areas and language developments in China.' In *The Christian occupation of China*, edited by Milton Theobald Stauffer. [Selective entry]
Shanghai: China Continuation Committee, 1922, 7–11.
SUBJ 29 ▪ 37

17939 NNC O P2 G1.5 1911–1928
Chang, Kingfan.
'The present conditions and the future prospects of the Hakkas.'
CSM 9, 8 (June 1914), 598–601.
SUBJ 29 ▪ 14 47 55

17940 MCH F P7 G5.2 1928–1949
Grootaers, Willem A-, 1911–.
'La géographie linguistique en Chine' (Linguistic geography in China).
MS 8 (1943), 103–166; 11 (1946), 207–231.
SUBJ 20 29

17941 CSU O P2 G1.2 1911–1928
Huntington, Ellsworth.
'North versus south in China.' In *The character of races*, by E. Huntington. [Selective entry]
New York: Scribner, 1925, 158–169.
SUBJ 29 ▪ 16.1 47

17942 CSU O P2 G1.2 1911–1928
Huntington, Ellsworth.
'The selection of the Chinese.' In *The character of races*, by E. Huntington. [Selective entry]
New York: Scribner, 1925, 184–204.
SUBJ 29 61 ▪ 11.2 47

17943 MCH O P3 G6.1 1928–1949
Lamson, Herbert Day, 1899–.
'The Eurasian in Shanghai.'
AJS 41, 5 (Mar. 1936), 642–648.
SUBJ 26 29 58 61 66 ▪ 28 41

17944 CSU P P2 G1.5 1911–1928
Vömel, Johann Heinrich.
'Der Hakkadialekt' (The Hakka dialect).
TP 2e série 14, 5 (déc. 1913), 597–696.
SUBJ 29

17945 GMS O P2 G1.3 1928–1949
Zimmermann, Kurt.
China wie ich es erlebte (China as I experienced it).
Witten: Bundes-Verlag, 1936. 144 p.
SUBJ 29 ▪ 19 23 47 55 56 57 66

1911-1972
(including 1644-1972)

17946 NIC O P2 G9.5 –1972
Barnett, Kenneth Myer Arthur, 1911–.
'The peoples of the New Territories.' In *Hong Kong business symposium*, compiled by José Maria Braga. [Sole entry]
Hong Kong: South China Morning Post, 1957, 261–265.
SUBJ 29 ▪ 21.1 21.3 25

17947 NNC S P2 G1.5 1911–1972
Bartz, Fritz.
'Bevölkerungsgruppen mit besonderer gesellschaftlichen Stellung unter den Küstenbewohnern und Fischern des Fernen Ostens' (Subethnic groups with special social position among coastal inhabitants and fishermen in the Far East).
Erdkunde 13, 4 (Dez. 1959), 381–395.
SUBJ 11.3 16 16.3 29 ▪ 14.1 18 21.3

17948 MAM S P1 G1.2 –1972
Bessac, Francis Bagnall, 1922–.
Culture types of northern and western China.
Ann Arbor: University Microfilms (Publ. 63-2879), 1963. 351 p. (Doctoral dissertation in Anthropology, U. of Wisconsin)
SUBJ 29

17949 NNC P P7 G9.0 1644–1972
Cohen, Myron Leon, 1937–.
'The Hakka or "guest people": Dialect as a socio-cultural variable in southeastern China.'
Ethnohistory 15, 3 (Summer 1968), 237–292. (Revision of masters thesis in Anthropology, Columbia U., 1963)
SUBJ 21.2 25 29 ▪ 12.1 24.1 32.2 41 42

17950 MCH FP P1 G1.3 –1972
Eberhard, Wolfram, 1909–.
'Chinese regional stereotypes.'
AS 5, 12 (Dec. 1965), 596–608. [Reprinted in *Moral and social values of the Chinese: Collected essays*, by W. Eberhard. (Selective entry.) Taipei: Chinese Materials and Research Aids Service Center, 1971, 305–317. (CMRASC occasional series, 6)]
SUBJ 29 61 ▪ 63 65

17951 CSU S P2 G1.1 1928–1972
Egerod, Søren, 1923–.
'Dialectology.' In *Current trends in linguistics, Vol. 2, Linguistics in East Asia and South East Asia*, edited by Thomas A- Sebeok. [Selective entry]
The Hague: Mouton, 1967, 91–129.
SUBJ 29 72 ▪ 70 71

17952 NNC S P2 G1.2 –1972
Forrest, Robert Andrew Dermond, 1893–.
The Chinese language, 2nd ed., rev.
London: Faber and Faber, 1965. 372 p.
SUBJ 29 64 ▪ 62

17953 CBU P P3 G5.4 –1972
Leslie, Donald Daniel, 1922–.
The survival of the Chinese Jews: The Jewish community of Kaifeng.
Leiden: Brill, 1972. 14, 270 p. (*T'oung pao* monographies, 10)
SUBJ 23 29 72 ▪ 22 26.1 33 41 42 59 62 70 71

17954 CSH U P2 G9.4 1928–1972
Salter, Christopher Lord, 1938–.
'The economic uniqueness of eastern Taiwan.'
IFC 31, 6 (June 1969), 31–37.
SUBJ 24.2 29 ▪ 21.2

17955 CSU S P1 G9.4 1928–1972
Uhalley, Stephen, Jr., 1930–.
'The Taiwanese in Taiwan.' In *Understanding modern China*, edited by Joseph M. Kitagawa (Kitagawa Mitsuo). [Selective entry]
Chicago: Quadrangle, 1969, 163–183.
SUBJ 12.1 14 29 32 ▪ 12.2 16.2 25

17956 MAM P P2 G1.5 –1972
Yang, Paul Fu-mien, 1925–.
An ethnolinguistic survey of Hakka.
Ann Arbor: University Microfilms (Publ. 68-1922), 1968. 191 p. (Doctoral dissertation in Language and Linguistics, Georgetown U.)
SUBJ 11.2 29 41 55 ▪ 11 17 21 39 42 65

1949-1972

17957 CSU U P7 G9.5 1949–1972
Anderson, Eugene Newton, Jr., 1941–.
'"Hoklo boat people": Urgent anthropology.'
Current anthropology 11, 1 (Feb. 1970), 82–83.
SUBJ 29

17958 CSU F P7 G9.5 1949–1972
Anderson, Eugene Newton, Jr., 1941–.
'Prejudice and ethnic stereotypes in rural Hong Kong.'
Kroeber Anthropological Society papers 37 (Fall 1967), 90–107.
SUBJ 29 48 66 ▪ 25 53

17959 CSU FP P2 G9.0 1949–1972
Appleton, Sheldon Lee, 1933–.
'Taiwanese and mainlanders on Taiwan: A survey of student attitudes.'
CQ 44 (Oct.–Dec. 1970), 38–65.
Subj 29 60 ▪ 48 54

17960 CSH U P1 G1.2 1949–1972
Chang, Kun (Chang K'un), 1917–.
'Language.' In *A general handbook of China*, compiled by Far Eastern and Russian Institute, U. of Washington. [Selective entry]
New Haven: Human Relations Area Files, 1956, vol. 1, 285–310. (HRAF subcontractor's monographs, 55; Washington 4)
Subj 29

17961 TPY FP P2 G9.4 1949–1972
Chen Shao-hsing (Ch'en Shao-hsing), 1906–1966, and Morton Herbert Fried, 1923–.
The distribution of family names in Taiwan. Vol. I, The data. Vol. II, The maps.
Taipei: National Taiwan U., College of Law, Dept. of Sociology *with* New York: Columbia U., Dept. of Anthropology *and* East Asian Institute, 1968, 1970. 35, 971; 60 p. [In Chinese as well as English; vol. III in preparation.]
Subj 21 29 42 ▪ 21.1 21.2 21.3 26 28 47 58

17962 CSH O P2 G1.3 1949–1972
Fincher, Beverly Hong.
'Impressions of language in China.'
CQ 50 (Apr.–June 1972), 333–340.
Subj 29 ▪ 62

17963 CBU F P2 G9.5 1949–1972
Kani, Hiroaki.
A general survey of the boat people in Hong Kong.
Hong Kong: Chinese U. of Hong Kong, New Asia Research Institute, Southeast Asia Studies Section, 1967. 95, 14 p. (SASS monograph series, 5)
Subj 24.1 26 29 41 55 65 ▪ 21.1 21.2 21.3 23 24.3 24.6 34.2 56

17964 NIC P P1 G1.2 1949–1972
[La Dany, Ladislao] ———, 1914–.
'Provincialism.'
CNA 408 (16 Feb. 1962), 1–7.
Subj 29 62 70

17965 MCH F P2 G9.5 1949–1972
McCoy, William John, Jr., 1924–.
'The dialects of the Hong Kong boat people: Kau Sai.'
JRAS-HKB 5 (1965), 46–64.
Subj 20 29

17966 MCH O P2 G9.5 1949–1972
Menard, Wilmon.
'The sea gypsies of China.'
Natural history 74, 1 (Jan. 1965), 12–21.
Subj 26 29 ▪ 23 24.1 41

17967 CSH P P1 G1.3 1949–1972
Stanford U. China Project.
'Languages.' In *Central South China*, compiled by the organization cited. [Selective entry]
New Haven: Human Relations Area Files, 1956, vol. 1, 85–113. (HRAF subcontractor's monographs, 28; Stanford 2)
Subj 29

17968 CSH P P1 G1.3 1949–1972
Stanford U. China Project.
'Languages.' In *East China*, compiled by the organization cited. [Selective entry]
New Haven: Human Relations Area Files, 1956, vol. 1, 109–138. (HRAF subcontractor's monographs, 29; Stanford 3)
Subj 29

17969 CSH P P1 G5.0 1949–1972
Stanford U. China Project.
'Languages.' In *North China*, compiled by the organization cited. [Selective entry]
New Haven: Human Relations Area Files, 1956, vol. 1, 88–108. (HRAF subcontractor's monographs, 27; Stanford 1)
Subj 29

17970 NNC P P1 G8.0 1949–1972
Stanford U. China Project.
'Languages.' In *Southwest China*, compiled by the organization cited. [Selective entry]
New Haven: Human Relations Area Files, 1956, vol. 1, 92–115. (HRAF subcontractor's monographs, 30; Stanford 4)
Subj 29

17971 CLU F P8 G9.5 1949–1972
Ward, Barbara Elsie, 1919–.
'Varieties of the conscious model: The fishermen of South China.' In *The relevance of models for social anthropology*. [Sole entry]
New York: Praeger, 1965, 113–137. (Assn. of Social Anthropologists monographs, 1)
Subj 22.2 26.3 29 48 64 65 ▪ 22 24.1 41 42

17972 CSU S P2 G1.1 1949–1972
Yang, Paul Fu-mien, 1925–.
'Chinese dialectology, 1955–1965.'
Orbis (Louvain) 15, 1 (1966), 90–159.
Subj 29 70 72 ▪ 36.1 71

30 Voluntary Associations & Formal Organization in General

組織原理及會社團體通論

組織原理及び社会団体一般

1644-1911

17973 MCH PO P2 G1.3 1895–1911
Courant, Maurice Auguste Louis Marie, 1865–1935.
'Les associations en Chine' (Associations in China).
Annales des sciences politiques 14, 1 (jan. 1899), 68–94.
Subj 22 30 33 39 41 42 ▪ 22.2 25 32.1 34.2 61 66

17974 MCH O P3 G1.2 1842–1895
Courant, Maurice Auguste Louis Marie, 1865–1935.
En Chine: moeurs et institutions, hommes et faits (In China: Customs and institutions, men and deeds).
Paris: Alcan, 1901. 275 p.
Subj 12 16 30 ▪ 13 14 32.2 34.2 40 47 52 53 60

17975 FPN O P2 G1.1 –1911
Enjoy, Paul d', 1866–?
'Associations, congrégations et sociétés secrètes chinoises' (Associations, brotherhoods, and secret societies in China).
Bulletins et mémoires de la Société d'anthropologie de Paris 5e série 5 (1904), 373–386. [Reprinted—*RI* nouvelle (2e) série 5, 55 (15 avr. 1907), 440–452.]
Subj 30 32.2 48 ▪ 31 32.1 34.3 38 63

17976 CSU U P2 G1.1 –1911
Holcombe, Chester, 1844–1912.
'Chinese societies.' In *The real Chinese question*, by C. Holcombe. [Sole entry]
New York: Dodd, Mead, 1900, 90–114.
Subj 30 39 ▪ 32.2 34.3 35 38

17977 CSH PO P2 G1.2 –1895
Leboucq, Prosper, 1828–1905.
Associations de la Chine (Associations in China).
Paris: F. Wattelier, 1880. 310 p.
Subj 30 32.2 36.3 ▪ 33 38 57

17978 MCH O P2 G1.2 1895–1911
Ular, Alexandre, 1876–.
'Les principes de la civilisation chinoise.' In *Un empire russo-chinois*, by A. Ular. [Sole entry]
Paris: Juven, 1903, 61–99.

'The principles of Chinese civilization.' In *A Russo-Chinese empire*, by A. Ular. [Sole entry]
Westminster: Archibald Constable, 1904, 38–76.
Subj 30 34.1 63 ▪ 41 45 61 66

1644-1949

17979 CNY P P7 G1.2 –1949
Chen, Francis (Ch'en Hsi-ch'eng), 1905–.
The ethical and economic basis of co-operation in rural China, with special reference to the province of North Fukien.
Unpublished doctoral dissertation in Religion, Yale U., 1934. 296 p.
Subj 16.3 30 34.1 60 63 ▪ 14.1 22 23 38 41 43 45 50 64 66

17980 NIC P P1 G1.1 –1949
Favre, Benoît, 1874–?
'Les sociétés de "frères jurés" en Chine' (Societies of sworn brothers in China).
TP 2e série 19, 1 (1918/19), 1–40.
Subj 30 32.2 33 38 48 ▪ 42 43 53 55 65

17981 NIC P P2 G1.1 1644–1928
Maybon, Pierre Batiste.
Essai sur les associations en Chine (An essay on associations in China).
Paris: Plon-Nourrit, 1925. 205 p.
Subj 30 32.2 33 36.1 38 39 ▪ 12.2 22.2 23 24.3 24.4 32.1 34.3 40 63

1911-1949

17982 CSU P P2 G1.5 1911–1928
Chesneaux, Jean, 1922–.
'Le mouvement fédéraliste en Chine, 1920–3.'
R. historique 236 (oct.–déc. 1966), 347–384.

'The federalist movement in China, 1920–3.' In *Modern China's search for*

a political form, edited by Jack Douglas Gray. [Analytic entry]
London: Oxford U. Press, 1969, 96–137.
SUBJ 12 30 32 ▪ 15 16.1 16.2 64

17983 NNC O P1 G1.0 1911–1928
Werner, Edward Theodore Chalmers, 1864–1954.
'The Chinese group-instinct.' In *Autumn leaves: An autobiography with a sheaf of papers, sociological and sinological, philosophical and metaphysical*, by E. T. C. Werner. [Selective entry]
Shanghai: Kelly and Walsh, 1928, 32–48.
SUBJ 30 48 ▪ 39 61

1911-1972
(including 1644-1972)

17984 NIC O P2 G9.4 1911–1972
Chen Shao-hsing (Ch'en Shao-hsing), 1906–1966.
'Social change in Taiwan.'
Studia Taiwanica 1 (Summer 1956), 1–20.
SUBJ 20 26 30 42 ▪ 21.3 38 39 41 48

17985 MAM FP P2 G9.5 1911–1972
Johnson, Graham Edwin, 1941–.
Natives, migrants and voluntary associations in a colonial Chinese setting.
Ann Arbor: University Microfilms (Publ. 71-18,906), 1971. 17, 429 p. (Doctoral dissertation in Sociology, Cornell U., 1970)
SUBJ 22 26 30 33 39 66 ▪ 21.2 21.3 23 24.4 31 32.1 34.1 34.3 36.4 38

17986 CSH P P1 G1.2 1928–1972
Schurmann, Herbert Franz, 1926–.
'Organisational principles of the Chinese Communists.'
CQ 2 (Apr.–June 1960), 47–58. [Reprinted in *China under Mao: Politics takes command*, edited by Roderick Lemonde MacFarquhar. (Selective entry.) Cambridge: M.I.T. Press, 1966, 87–98.]
SUBJ 30 32.1 64 ▪ 32

17987 MCH P P2 G1.2 1928–1972
Schurmann, Herbert Franz, 1926–.
'The roots of social policy.'
Survey (London) 38 (Oct. 1961), 156–169. [Reprinted in *The future of Communist society*, edited by Walter Z. Laquer and Leopold Labedz. (Selective entry.) New York: Praeger, 1962, 156–169.]
SUBJ 12 22 30 32 ▪ 15 32.1 32.2

17988 CSH S P2 G9.4 1911–1972
Stanford U. China Project.
'General character of society.' In *Taiwan (Formosa)*, compiled by the organization cited. [Selective entry]
New Haven: Human Relations Area Files, 1956, vol. 1, 17–27. (HRAF subcontractor's monographs, 31; Stanford 5)
SUBJ 22 30 42 ▪ 21.2 25

17989 CSH S P2 G9.4 1644–1972
Stanford U. China Project.
'Social structure.' In *Taiwan (Formosa)*, compiled by the organization cited. [Selective entry]
New Haven: Human Relations Area Files, 1956, vol. 1, 95–130. (HRAF subcontractor's monographs, 31; Stanford 5)
SUBJ 16 30 ▪ 24.1 31 34.3 36.3 36.4

1949-1972

17990 NNC P P2 G1.2 1949–1972
Chao, Kuo-chün, 1918–1962.
The mass organizations in Communist China.
Cambridge: Massachusetts Institute of Technology, Center for International Studies, 1953. 157 p.
SUBJ 30 32 32.1 36.4 47 54 ▪ 14.4 17 34.2 36.1 36.2 38

17991 CSU S P2 G1.2 1949–1972
Fairbank, John King, 1907–.
'The state that Mao built.' [Review of *Ideology and organization in Communist China*, by Herbert Franz Schurmann.]
WP 19, 4 (July 1967), 664–677.
SUBJ 30 ▪ 12.1 32

17992 CSU P P2 G1.2 1949–1972
Funnell, Victor Cecil, 1926–.
'Bureaucracy and the Chinese Communist Party.'
CS 9, 5 (7 May 1971), 1–14.
SUBJ 12 30 32 ▪ 16.1 22 64

17993 NIC P P2 G1.2 1949–1972
Hsüeh, Chün-tu, 1922–.
An institutional analysis of the Communist rule in China.
Santa Barbara, Calif.: General Electric Co., Technical Military Planning Operation, 1962. 49 p. (TEMPO reports, RM 62TMP-73)
SUBJ 14 30 32 32.1 ▪ 12 15 16.1

17994 CSU FP P2 G9.5 1949–1972
Johnson, Graham Edwin, 1941–.
'From rural committee to spirit medium cult: Voluntary associations in the development of a Chinese town [Tsuen Wan (Ch'üan-wan), Hong Kong].'
Contributions to Asian studies 1 (Jan. 1971), 123–143.
SUBJ 30 33 38 39 ▪ 21.1 22.1 24.4 26.4 31 32 36.2 36.4 42 47

17995 CBU O P2 G1.3 1949–1972
Macciocchi, Maria Antonietta.
Dalla Cina: dopo la rivoluzione culturale (From China: After the Cultural Revolution).
Milan: Feltrinelli, 1971. 483 p.

Daily life in revolutionary China. Tr. by Kathy Brown et al.
New York: Monthly Review Press, 1972. 506 p.
SUBJ 19 24 30 47 55 64 ▪ 13 17 22.1 24.1 24.3 24.4 26.4 32 54 61

17996 CSU P P2 G1.2 1949–1972
Pfeffer, Richard Monroe, 1936–.
'Serving the people and continuing the revolution.'
CQ 52 (Oct.–Dec. 1972), 620–653.
SUBJ 12.1 19 22.1 30 ▪ 12 16.1 17 22 26.1 32 32.1 35

17997 CSU P P1 G1.2 1949–1972
Schurmann, Herbert Franz, 1926–.
'The attack of the Cultural Revolution on ideology and organization' [with comments by Ezra Feivel Vogel]. In *China in crisis, Vol. 1, China's heritage and the Communist political system*, edited by Ping-ti Ho and Tang Tsou. [Selective entry]
Chicago: U. of Chicago Press, 1968, 525–570.
SUBJ 12 19 30 ▪ 12.1 15 16 32 64

17998 MCH P P1 G1.2 1949–1972
Schurmann, Herbert Franz, 1926–.
'Organization and response in Communist China.'
AAAPSS 321 (Jan. 1959), 51–61. [Special issue: *Contemporary China and the Chinese*, edited by Howard Lyon Boorman]
SUBJ 30 32 ▪ 32.1 61 64

17999 MCY P P2 G1.2 1949–1972
Schurmann, Herbert Franz, 1926–.
'Organizational contrasts between Communist China and the Soviet Union.' In *Unity and contradiction: Major aspects of Sino-Soviet relations*, edited by Kurt London. [Selective entry]
New York: Praeger, 1962, 65–99.
SUBJ 24 30 64 ▪ 22 32.1

18000 CSH P P2 G1.2 1949–1972
Schurmann, Herbert Franz, 1926–.
'Supplement: Organization.' In *Ideology and organization in Communist China*, 2nd ed., enl., by H. F. Schurmann. [Analytic entry]
Berkeley, Los Angeles: U. of California Press, 1968, 532–575.
SUBJ 15 30 32 ▪ 12 16.1 16.3 25 64

18001 CSU O P2 G1.2 1949–1972
Sherrard, Howard M-.
'The Cultural Revolution in China, as an Australian engineer sees it.'
EH 7, 4 (July–Aug. 1968), 41–44.
SUBJ 19 30

18002 CSU P P2 G1.2 1949–1972
Weggel, Oskar, 1935–.
'Aspekte einer zukünftigen chinesischen Gesellschaftsordnung' (Aspects of a future Chinese social order).
Internationales Asien Forum 1, 4 (Okt. 1970), 524–534.
SUBJ 30 64 ▪ 12 17 34.2

18003 MCH FP P2 G1.2 1949–1972
Whyte, Martin King, 1942–.
Small groups and political rituals in Communist China.
Unpublished doctoral dissertation in Sociology, Harvard U., 1970. 515 p.
SUBJ 22.1 26 30 32.1 37 ▪ 12.2 22.2 27 32 34.1 36.4 50 54

18004 MAM F P7 G9.4 1949–1972
Wyeth, Irving Rudolph, 1917–.
Status-role perceptions in the Taiwan extension organization.
Ann Arbor: University Microfilms (Publ. 65-6141), 1965. 177 p. (Doctoral dissertation in Education, Michigan State U., 1964)
SUBJ 26 30 34.1 37

31 SOCIAL ORGANIZATION OF RECREATION
娛樂組織 娯楽組織

1644-1911

18005 NNC U P1 G1.3 1644–1895
'Zeitvertreib der Chinesen' (Chinese pastimes).
Globus 26, 17 (Mai 1874), 261–264.
SUBJ 31 ▪ 55 65

18006 NIC P P1 G1.3 –1895
Adams, George Burton, 1851–1925.
'The Chinese drama.'
Nineteenth century 37, 217 (Mar. 1895), 497–515.
SUBJ 31 63 65

18007 NNC S P1 G1.3 –1911
Cohn-Antenorid, W-.
'Chinesische Artisten' (Chinese performers).
Globus 78, 11 (22 Sept. 1900), 169–173.
SUBJ 31 ▪ 16.2

18008 NNC O P3 G6.1 1842–1911
Goldmann, Paul, 1865–?
'Chinesisches Nachtleben' (Chinese night life). In *Ein Sommer in China* (A summer in China), by P. Goldmann. [Sole entry]
Frankfurt a.M.: Rütten und Loening, 1900, vol. 1, 188–207.
SUBJ 31 ▪ 46 47

18009 NIC O P3 G5.1 1895–1911
Headland, Isaac Taylor, 1859–1942.
'Chinese sports and games.'
Outing 37, 2 (Nov. 1900), 158–162.
SUBJ 31 62 ▪ 52

18010 CSU P P1 G1.3 –1911
Laufer, Berthold, 1874–1934.
'Chinesische Schattenspiele: Einleitung' (Chinese shadow plays: An introduction).
Abhandlungen der Philosophisch-philologischen Klasse der Königlichen Bayerischen Akademie der Wissenschaften 28, 1 (1915), 7–24 [s.p.].
SUBJ 23 31 40 65 ▪ 41 47

18011 CSU P P4 G1.3 –1842
Mackerras, Colin Patrick, 1939–.
'The growth of the Chinese regional drama in the Ming and Ch'ing.'
JOS 9, 1 (Jan. 1971), 58–91.
SUBJ 29 31

18012 ACU P P2 G1.3 –1895
Mackerras, Colin Patrick, 1939–.
The rise of the Peking opera (1760–1860).
Unpublished doctoral dissertation in Far Eastern History, Australian National U., 1970. 431 p.
SUBJ 29 31 59 65 ▪ 12.2 16 16.1 16.2 23 34.3 43 46

18013 CSU P P2 G6.1 1644–1842
Mackerras, Colin Patrick, 1939–.
'The theatre in Yang-chou in the late eighteenth century.'
Papers on Far Eastern history 1 (Mar. 1970), 1–30.
SUBJ 26.2 31 ▪ 21.3 23 26 46

18014 CSU P P7 G1.2 –1842
Tanaka Issei.
'Development of Chinese local plays in the 17th and 18th centuries.'
Acta Asiatica (Tokyo) 23 (Sept. 1972), 42–62.
SUBJ 23 31 42 ▪ 26 26.1 39 65

18015 MCH O P1 G1.3 1644–1911
Tch'ou, Min Yi (Ch'u Min-i), and Louis Laloy, 1874–1944.
'Le volant chinois' (Chinese 'badminton').
BAAFC 2, 4 (oct. 1910), 319–335.
SUBJ 31 52

18016 NNC O P2 G5.3 1895–1911
Volpert, Ant——.
'Das chinesische Schauspielwesen in Südschantung' (Chinese theatre in southern Shantung).
Anthropos 5, 2/3 (März–Juni 1910), 367–380.
SUBJ 31 ▪ 25 26.3 47 65

18017 CSU O P3 G1.3 1895–1911
Voskamp, C- J-.
'The storyteller in China.'
EAM 1 (1902), 12–18.
SUBJ 16.2 31 ▪ 65

1644-1949

18018 NIC O P1 G1.2 1644–1949
Calthorpe, John Eaton.
'The gentle art of tea drinking in China.'
THM 8, 4 (Apr. 1939), 319–326.
SUBJ 31 55 ▪ 16 48

18019 CSH U P2 G9.4 –1949
Chen Shao-hsing (Ch'en Shao-hsing), 1906–1966.
'Diffusion and acceptance of modern Western artistic and intellectual expression in Taiwan.'
Studia Taiwanica 2 (Summer 1957), 1–6.
SUBJ 24.2 31 65 ▪ 66

18020 MCH S P2 G1.2 –1949
Hoffmann, Alfred, 1911–.
'Buffelkämpfe in China' (Buffalo fighting in China).
OR 16, 11 (1 Juni 1935), 295–300.
SUBJ 23 31 ▪ 65

18021 CSU PO P4 G1.2 –1949
Huang de Lopez de la Cámara, Marcelle.
'L'art dramatique en Chine: le théâtre classique' (Drama in China: The classical theatre).
Sinologica 1, 3 (1948), 246–257.
SUBJ 31 ▪ 12.2 16 27 47

18022 NNC O P3 G9.2 –1928
Lemiere, J-.
'Sing-song girl from a throne of glory to a seat of ignominy.'
CJ 1, 2 (Mar. 1923), 126–134.
SUBJ 31 46 47 ▪ 22.1 22.2 34.2 41

18023 ²CSU PO P8 G6.3 –1949
Ts'ao Sung-yeh.
'Der Stierkampf in Chin-hua.'
China-Dienst (Shanghai) 3 (1934), 941–945.

'Bullfighting in Chin-hua (Chekiang province).' In *Studies in Chinese folklore and related essays*, by Wolfram Eberhard. [Selective entry]
Bloomington: Indiana U., Research Center for the Language Sciences, 1970, 73–82. (Indiana U., Folklore Institute monograph series, 23)
SUBJ 23 31

18024 MCH PO P1 G1.1 –1928
Zucker, Adolf Edward, 1890–1971.
The Chinese theatre.
Boston: Little, Brown, 1925. 16, 234 p.
SUBJ 31 65 ▪ 29 34.3 40 41 43 60

1911-1949

18025 CSH U P3 G6.1 1911–1928
'China takes to the motion picture.'
CEM 1, 11 (Aug. 1924), 1–6.
SUBJ 31

18026 DLC P P3 G6.1 1911–1928
Adzhimamudova, V- S-.
'Literaturnoe obshchestvo "Tvorchestvo" na rannem etape (1921–1924)' (The Creation Society in its early period, 1921–1924). In *Dvizhenie '4 maia' 1919 goda v Kitae: sbornik statei* (Articles on the May Fourth Movement in China), compiled by Institut vostokovedeniia, Akademiia nauk SSSR, edited by A- G- Afanas'ev et al. [Selective entry]
Moscow: Nauka, Glav. red. vost. lit-ry, 1971, 199–231.
SUBJ 24.2 31 62 ▪ 64 66 72

18027 NNC P P7 G5.1 1911–1949
Chao Wei-pang.
'Yang-ko, the rural theatre in Ting-hsien, Hopei.'
FS 3, 1 (1944), 17–38.
SUBJ 31 65 ▪ 23

18028 CSH O P3 G6.1 1928–1949
Chen, T. H.
'The Nanking that was.'
Asia (New York: American Asiatic Assn.) 38, 3 (Mar. 1938), 185–187.
SUBJ 31 ▪ 22.2

18029 CSU F P8 G5.1 1911–1949
Gamble, Sidney David, 1890–1968.
'Introduction.' In *Chinese village plays from the Ting hsien region (Yang Ke Hsuan)*, by S. D. Gamble. [Sole entry]
Amsterdam: Philo Press, 1970, 17–29 [s.p.].
SUBJ 31 65 ▪ 23 41 46

18030 MCH O P3 G1.5 1911–1949
Katscher, Leopold, 1853–?
'Einige Zufallsspiele der Chinesen' (Some Chinese games of chance).
Der Erdball 3, 11 (1929), 414–418.
SUBJ 31 62 ▪ 65

18031 CSU O P4 G9.5 1928–1949
Lilius, Aleko E-.
'The Monte Carlo of the Orient: Macao, a Portuguese-Chinese city where gambling-houses thrive.'
Asia (New York: American Asiatic Assn.) 30, 4 (Apr. 1930), 239–245.
SUBJ 31

18032 MCY O P3 G5.1 1928–1949
March, Benjamin, 1899–1934.
Chinese shadow-figure plays and their making.
Detroit: Puppetry Imprints, 1938. 57 p.
SUBJ 26.2 31 65

18033 SSK FP P3 G5.1 1928–1949
Montell, Gösta, 1899–.
'Kinesiska marknadsnöjen' (Chinese market-place amusements).
Jorden runt 5, 9 (September 1933), 459–469.
Subj 31 65 ▪ 24.3

18034 CSU O P3 G1.5 1911–1949
Moorad, George L-, 1908–.
'Chinese talkies.'
Asia (New York: American Asiatic Assn.) 35, 10 (Oct. 1935), 614–619.
Subj 31

18035 NNC O P6 G8.1 1928–1949
Spencer, Joseph Earle, 1907–.
'The Szechwan village tea house.'
J. of geography 41, 2 (Feb. 1942), 52–58.
Subj 26.3 31 ▪ 48

18036 MCY O P3 G5.1 1928–1949
Wimsatt, Genevieve Blanche.
Chinese shadow shows.
Cambridge: Harvard U. Prcss, 1936. 17, 68 p.
Subj 31 65 ▪ 26.2

18037 CSU U P1 G1.3 1928–1949
Yao, Hsin-nung.
'Chinese movies.'
THM 4, 4 (Apr. 1937), 393–400.
Subj 31 ▪ 12.1

1911-1972
(including 1644-1972)

18038 CSU FP P5 G1.4 –1972
Hrdličková, Vencesleva.
'The Chinese storytellers and singers of ballads: Their performances and storytelling techniques.'
Transactions of the Asiatic Society of Japan 3rd series 10 (1968), 97–115.
Subj 31 65 ▪ 16.2

18039 DLC O P1 G1.1 –1972
IAkovlev, Lev Mikhailovich.
'Igra i karty u kitaitsev' (Chinese games and cards).
Zapiski Kharbinskogo obshchestva estestvoispytatelei i etnografov 1946, 1, 24–26.
Subj 31 62 ▪ 53

18040 CSU O P2 G8.1 1644–1972
Kalvodová, D-.
'The origin and character of the Szechwan theatre.'
AO 34, 4 (1966), 505–523.
Subj 31

18041 CSU P P2 G1.2 1895–1972
Kolatch, Jonathan.
Sports, politics, and ideology in China.
Middle Village, N.Y.: Jonathan David, 1972. 19, 254 p. (Revision of *The development of modern sports and physical education in China*, doctoral dissertation in Education, Columbia U. [Teachers College], 1970)
Subj 17 31 ▪ 12.1 15 32.1 64 66

18042 CSU PO P2 G1.1 1895–1972
Leyda, Jay, 1910–.
Dianying [Tien-ying]*: An account of films and the film audience in China.*
Cambridge: M.I.T. Press, 1972. 17, 515 p.
Subj 31 ▪ 14.2 59 66

18043 NNC P P4 G1.2 1928–1972
Men'shikov, Lev Nikolaevich.
'Reforma klassicheskogo teatra i dramy' (The reform of classical theater and drama). In *Voprosy kul'turnoi revoliutsii v Kitaiskoi Narodnoi Respublike: sbornik statei* (Articles on the cultural revolution in the People's Republic of China), compiled by Institut kitaevedeniia, Akademiia nauk SSSR, edited by Nikolai Trofimovich Fedorenko. [Selective entry]
Moscow: Izd-vo vost. lit-ry, 1960, 230–250.
Subj 12.1 31 64 ▪ 29 32.1 36.1

18044 NNC P P1 G1.2 1928–1972
Moy, Clarence, 1916–.
'Communist China's use of the *Yang-ko* [rice-planting song].'
PC 6 (Mar. 1952), 112–148.
Subj 12.1 31 ▪ 32.1 64

18045 NNC U P4 G1.2 1895–1972
Sorokin, V- F-.
'Osnovnye etapy razvitiia dramaticheskogo teatra v Kitae' (Basic stages in the development of the dramatic theater in China). In *Voprosy kul'turnoi revoliutsii v Kitaiskoi Narodnoi Respublike: sbornik statei* (Articles on the cultural revolution in the People's Republic of China), compiled by Institut kitaevedeniia, Akademiia nauk SSSR, edited by Nikolai Trofimovich Fedorenko. [Selective entry]
Moscow: Izd-vo vost. lit-ry, 1960, 251–270.
Subj 31 36.1 64 ▪ 12.1 32.1 32.2

18046 CSH O P2 G6.0 1911–1972
Tai Pu-fan.
'Shaohsing opera.'
People's China 1955, 8 (16 Apr.), 16–23.
Subj 31

1949-1972

18047 NNC PO P1 G1.2 1949–1972
Barnett, Arthur Doak, 1921–.
'Art of mass character: Motion pictures in Communist China.'
AUFS-EAS 3, 6 (12 May 1954), 1–8. [Reprinted as 'Motion pictures.' In *Communist China: The early years, 1949–55*, by A. D. Barnett. (Selective entry.) New York: Praeger, 1964, 81–88.]
Subj 31 ▪ 14.2

18048 CSU F P3 G9.0 1949–1972
Eberhard, Wolfram, 1909–.
The Chinese silver screen: Hong Kong and Taiwanese motion pictures in the 1960's.
Taipei: Orient Cultural Service, 1972. 241 p. (Asian Folklore and Social Life monographs, 23)
Subj 31 40 60 65 ▪ 41 46 48 63

18049 CSU F P3 G9.4 1949–1972
Eberhard, Wolfram, 1909–.
'Notes on Chinese story tellers.'
Fabula 11, 1/2 (1970), 1–31.
Subj 16.2 31 65

18050 CSU O P3 G5.1 1949–1972
Häger, Bengt.
'Music in China today: An eyewitness account of the Cultural Revolution, by the head of the Choreographic Institute of Sweden's Royal Academy of Music.'
High fidelity 17, 10 (Oct. 1967), 93–98.
Subj 31 ▪ 32.1

18051 MCH O P1 G1.2 1949–1972
Hoa, Irène.
'Le "bond en avant" du sport' (The 'leap forward' in sports).
Démocratie nouvelle 15, 6 (mai 1961), 67–74.
Subj 31 ▪ 17 47

18052 CSU P P2 G1.2 1949–1972
Houn, Franklin W. (Hou Fu-wu), 1920–.
'The stage as a medium of propaganda in Communist China.'
Public opinion q. 23, 2 (Summer 1959), 223–235.
Subj 12.1 31 ▪ 12 32.1 64

18053 DLC O P4 G1.2 1949–1972
IUtkevich, Sergei Iosifovich.
V teatrakh i kino svobodnogo Kitaia (In the theaters and cinemas of liberated China).
Moscow: Iskusstvo, 1953. 175 p.
Subj 31 63 ▪ 12.1

18054 NNC P P2 G1.2 1949–1972
[La Dany, Ladislao] ———, 1914–.
'Arts in 1956.'
CNA 166 (1 Feb. 1957), 1–7.
Subj 31 32.1

18055 CSH P P1 G1.2 1949–1972
[La Dany, Ladislao] ———, 1914–.
'The enemy on the screen.'
CNA 614 (3 June 1966), 1–7.
Subj 31

18056 CSH P P3 G1.2 1949–1972
[La Dany, Ladislao] ———, 1914–.
'A film: "Early spring in February".'
CNA 552 (19 Feb. 1965), 1–7.
Subj 31 ▪ 12.1 64

18057 NIC P P2 G1.2 1949–1972
[La Dany, Ladislao] ———, 1914–.
'Films.'
CNA 305 (11 Dec. 1959), 1–7.
Subj 31

18058 MCH P P2 G1.2 1949–1972
[La Dany, Ladislao] ———, 1914–.
'Political recreation.'
CNA 117 (27 Jan. 1956), 2–7.
Subj 12.1 31

18059 MCH P P2 G1.2 1949–1972
[La Dany, Ladislao] ———, 1914–.
'The theatre.'
CNA 253 (14 Nov. 1958), 1–7.
Subj 31 32.1

18060 CSH F P2 G9.5 1949–1972
Lu, Andrew L. C.
Hong Kong workers and their leisure.
Hong Kong: U. of Hong Kong, Centre of Asian Studies, 1970. 44 p.
Subj 26.4 31 ▪ 23 54

18061 DLC O P2 G1.2 1949–1972
Morozov, Georgii.
U nashikh druzei: fizicheskaia kul'tura i sport v Kitaiskoi Narodnoi Respublike (With our friends: Physical culture and sport in the People's Republic of China).
Moscow: Fizkul'tura i sport, 1959. 141 p.
Subj 17 31 32.1 ▪ 18 37 47 52 53 54 62 65

18062 CBU O P2 G1.2 1949–1972
Obraztsov, Sergei Vladimirovich (Sergei Obraszow), 1901–.
Teatr kitaiskogo naroda.
Moscow: Iskusstvo, 1957. 375 p.
Theater in China (The theater in China). Tr. by Wolfgang Pintzka.
Berlin: Henschel, 1963. 236 p.
SUBJ 31 62

18063 CSU O P2 G9.0 1949–1972
Robinson, G- W- S-.
'The recreation geography of South Asia.'
GR 62, 4 (Oct. 1972), 561–572.
SUBJ 21.3 31

18064 DLC O P3 G1.2 1949–1972
Savost'ianov, IU-.
'Na kitaiskikh kinostudiiakh' (Chinese film studios).
Iskusstvo kino 1959, 3 (mart), 140–146.
SUBJ 31 ▪ 16.2 32.1

18065 DLC O P3 G5.1 1949–1972
Serbus, Ladislav.
'Institut tělesné kultury v Pekingu' (The Institute of Physical Culture in Peking).
Teorie a praxe tělesné výchovy a sportu (Prague) 6, 5 (1958), 305–307.
SUBJ 17 31

18066 CSU P P3 G5.1 1949–1972
Swift, Mary Grace.
'Storming the fortress of the Peking opera.'
Modern drama 12, 2 (Sept. 1969), 111–123.
SUBJ 31 32.1 64

18067 CSU O P3 G6.1 1949–1972
Taylor, Lenore.
'A forum with artists from the Shanghai Ballet.'
EH 7, 4 (July–Aug. 1968), 30–36.
SUBJ 31 ▪ 32.1 64

18068 CSU O P3 G5.1 1949–1972
Trillat, Jean-Jacques.
'Premier mai à Pékin' (May 1 in Peking).
Revue; littérature, histoire, arts et sciences des deux mondes 1969, 6 (1er juin), 547–554.
SUBJ 31 33 ▪ 53 54

18069 CSU O P3 G5.1 1949–1972
Vidal, Jean-Emile.
'Choses vues à Pékin' (Seen in Peking).
CFC 10 (juin 1961), 23–39.
SUBJ 31 ▪ 24.3 24.4 47

18070 DLC O P4 G1.3 1949–1972
Vinogradov, Viktor Sergeevich.
Muzyka v Kitaiskoi Narodnoi Respublike (Music in the People's Republic of China).
Moscow: Sovetskii kompozitor, 1959. 85 p.
SUBJ 31 ▪ 26.1 65

18071 CSU P P1 G1.2 1949–1972
Weakland, John Hast, 1919–.
'Themes in Chinese Communist films.'
AA new (2nd) series 68, 2 (Apr. 1966), 477–484.
SUBJ 31 ▪ 41 46 47

18072 NNC P P1 G1.2 1949–1972
Yang, Richard F. S. (Yang Fu-sen), 1918–.
'The reform of Peking opera under the Communists.'
CQ 11 (July–Sept. 1962), 124–139.
SUBJ 31 32.1 ▪ 64

32 POLITICAL PARTIES
政黨　政党

1644-1911

18073 CSU P P2 G1.1 1895–1911
Bastid, Marianne, 1940–.
'Crise, réforme et insurrection' (Crisis, reform, and insurrection). In *De la guerre franco-chinoise à la fondation du Parti communiste chinois, 1885–1921* (From the Sino-French war to the formation of the Chinese Communist Party, 1885–1921), by M. Bastid, Marie-Claire Bergère, and Jean Chesneaux. [Analytic entry]
Paris: Hatier Université, 1972, 48–91. (HU, Collection d'histoire contemporaine, Histoire de la Chine, 2)
SUBJ 12 14 16 32 64 66 ▪ 15 32.1 32.2 33 62 72

18074 MAM P P2 G1.3 1842–1911
Bays, Daniel Henry, 1942–.
Chang Chih-tung and the politics of reform in China, 1895–1905.
Ann Arbor: University Microfilms (Publ. 72-28,997), 1972. 275 p. (Doctoral dissertation in History, U. of Michigan, 1971)
SUBJ 12 14.2 16.1 32 59 ▪ 12.1 17 32.2 64

18075 CSH O P2 G1.2 1895–1911
Borel, Henri, 1869–1933.
'Het daghet in den Oosten' ('It's getting light in the East').
Amsterdam: Veen, 1926. 190 p.
SUBJ 17 20 21.3 32 57 ▪ 12 14.2 16.1 55

18076 WSU P P3 G1.3 1895–1911
Byon, Jae-hyon, 1938–.
The Ch'iang-hsüeh Hui [Society for the Study of National Rejuvenation]*: The initiation of an organized reform movement.*
Unpublished masters thesis in East Asian Studies, U. of Washington, 1970. 167 p.
SUBJ 32 36.1 ▪ 16.1 19 64

18077 NIC P P2 G1.1 1842–1911
Cameron, Meribeth Elliott, 1905–.
The reform movement in China, 1898–1912.
Stanford: Stanford U. Press, 1931. 223 p. (Stanford U. publications in history, economics and political science, 3, 1) (Doctoral dissertation in History, Stanford U., 1929) [Reprinted—New York: Octagon Books, 1963. 223 p.] [Reprinted—New York: AMS Press, 1972. 223 p.]
SUBJ 12 15 17 18 19 32 ▪ 12.2 16.1 47 64 66

18078 CSU P P1 G1.2 1895–1911
Chang, P'eng-yüan, 1929–.
'The constitutionalists.' In *China in revolution: The first phase, 1900–1913*, edited by Mary Clabaugh Wright. [Selective entry]
New Haven: Yale U. Press, 1968, 143–183.
SUBJ 32 ▪ 16.1 32.2

18079 NNC P P1 G1.1 1895–1911
Chudodeev, IUrii Vladimirovich, 1931–.
'Burzhuazno-liberal'nyi lager' nakanune Sin'khaiskoi revoliutsii' (The liberal bourgeois camp on the eve of the Revolution of 1911). In *Sin'khaiskaia revoliutsiia v Kitae: sbornik statei* (Articles on the Revolution of 1911 in China), compiled by Institut narodov Azii, Akademiia nauk SSSR. [Selective entry]
Moscow: Izd-vo vost. lit-ry, 1962, 164–191.
SUBJ 32 32.2 ▪ 12.1 16.1 16.2 19 70 71

18080 GMS P P2 G1.3 1895–1911
Franke, Otto, 1863–1946.
'Der Ursprung der Reformbewegung in China' (The origin of the reform movement in China). In *Ostasiatische Neubildungen: Beiträge zum Verständnis der politischen und kulturellen Entwicklungs-vorgänge im Fernen Osten* (New forms in East Asia: Toward an understanding of political and cultural developmental processes in the Far East), by O. Franke. [Selective entry]
Hamburg: C. Boysen, 1911, 20–35.
SUBJ 12 32 66 ▪ 16.1

18081 CSU S P1 G1.2 1895–1911
Gasster, Michael, 1930–.
'Reform and revolution in China's political modernization.' In *China in revolution: The first phase, 1900–1913*, edited by Mary Clabaugh Wright. [Selective entry]
New Haven: Yale U. Press, 1968, 67–96.
SUBJ 32 ▪ 16.1 32.2 64

18082 MCY S P3 G1.1 1895–1911
Hao, Yen-p'ing, 1934–.
'The abortive cooperation between reformers and revolutionaries, 1895–1900.'
PC 15 (Dec. 1961), 91–114.
SUBJ 16.1 32 32.2 ▪ 64

18083 NIC P P1 G1.3 1842–1895
Hao, Yen-p'ing, 1934–.
'A study of the *Ch'ing-liu tang*: The "disinterested" scholar-official group (1875–1884).'
PC 16 (Dec. 1962), 40–65.
SUBJ 16.1 32 64 66 ▪ 12

18084 MCH P P1 G1.2 1895–1911
Ho, Ping-ti, 1917–.
'Weng T'ung-ho and the "One Hundred Days of Reform".'
FEQ 10, 2 (Feb. 1951), 125–135.
SUBJ 16.1 32 60 ▪ 12

18085 CSU P P4 G1.3 1842–1911
Howard, Richard Campbell, 1925–.
'The Chinese reform movement of the 1890's: A symposium. Introduction.'
JAS 29, 1 (Nov. 1969), 7–14.
SUBJ 16.1 32 ▪ 12

18086 CSU P P1 G1.2 1895–1911
Hsiao, Kung-chuan (Hsiao Kung-ch'üan), 1897–.
'Weng T'ung-ho and the Reform Movement of 1898.'
THJ new (2nd) series 1, 2 (Apr. 1957), 111–243.
SUBJ 12 32 62 ▪ 48 59 63 64 66

18087 MCY P P4 G8.1 1895–1911
Ichiko Chūzō, 1913–.
'The railway protection movement in Szechwan in 1911.'
Memoirs of the Research Dept. of the Toyo Bunko 14 (1955), 47–69. [Reprinted in *Kindai Chūgoku no seiji to shakai* (Modern Chinese politics and society), by Ichiko Chūzō. (Selective entry.) Tokyo: Tōkyō daigaku, Shuppankai, 1971, 1–20.]
SUBJ 24.5 25 32 ▪ 24.2 32.1 66

18088 DLC P P2 G1.2 1895–1911
Iriye, Akira (Irie Akira), 1934–.
'Public opinion and foreign policy: The case of late Ch'ing China.' In *Approaches to modern Chinese history*, edited by Albert Feuerwerker et al. [Selective entry]
Berkeley, Los Angeles: U. of California Press, 1967, 216–238.
SUBJ 12 12.1 32 ▪ 16.2 54 66

18089 MAM P P2 G8.0 1895–1911
Johnson, William Reid, 1929–.
China's 1911 Revolution in the provinces of Yunnan and Kweichow.
Ann Arbor: University Microfilms (Publ. 62-6597), 1962. 217 p. (Doctoral dissertation in History, U. of Washington)
SUBJ 12 12.1 16.1 32 32.2 ▪ 15 16 25 64

18090 MCH O P3 G1.2 1842–1911
Kang Yeu Wei (K'ang Yu-wei), 1858–1927.
'The reform of China and the Revolution of 1898.'
Contemporary review 76, 404 (Aug. 1899), 180–198.
SUBJ 12 16.1 32 ▪ 14 14.5 15 64

18091 MCY P P3 G7.2 1895–1911
Lewis, Charlton Miner, III, 1930–.
'The reform movement in Hunan, 1896–1898.'
PC 15 (Dec. 1961), 62–90. [For fuller treatment, see entry 14187.]
SUBJ 12 32

18092 NNC P P3 G5.1 1895–1911
Ma, Te-chih (Mai Te-chih).
Le mouvement réformiste et les événements de la cour de Pékin en 1898 (The reform movement and the events of 1898 at the court in Peking).
Lyons: Bosc et Riou, 1934. 117 p. (Doctoral dissertation, Faculté des lettres, Université de Lyon)
SUBJ 12 16.1 19 32 64 ▪ 15 17 36.1 59 66 70

18093 MCH P P4 G1.2 1895–1911
Maybon, Albert, 1878–.
'Les étapes du mouvement constitutionnel en Chine' (The stages in the movement for a constitution in China).
AF 11, 121 (avr. 1911), 172–179.
SUBJ 12 12.2 32 ▪ 17

18094 MCH S P3 G1.2 1895–1911
Maybon, Albert, 1878–.
'Les partis politiques en Chine' (Political parties in China).
R. mondiale 68 (15 juin 1907), 523–537.
SUBJ 16.1 32 32.2 64 66 ▪ 15 25

18095 MBA U P3 G1.2 1895–1911
Pelliot, Paul, 1878–1945.
'La politique intérieure de la Chine de 1898 à 1907' (China's domestic policy from 1898 to 1907).
RI nouvelle (2e) série 5, 69 (15 nov. 1907), 1523–1537.
SUBJ 12 32 ▪ 36.1 66

18096 MCH P P3 G5.1 1895–1911
Pusey, James Reeve, 1940–.
'K'ang Yu-wei and *pao-chiao* [preserve our faith]: Confucian reform and reformation.'
PC 20 (Dec. 1966), 144–176.
SUBJ 32 64 ▪ 13 66

18097 MCY P P1 G1.3 1895–1911
Schrecker, John Ernest, 1937–.
'The Pao-kuo Hui, a reform society of 1898.'
PC 14 (Dec. 1960), 50–69.
SUBJ 16.1 32

18098 CSH P P3 G1.2 1644–1911
So, Kwan-wai (Su Chun-wei), 1919–.
Western influence and the Chinese Reform Movement of 1898.
Unpublished doctoral dissertation in History, U. of Wisconsin, 1950. 269 p.
SUBJ 12 15 16.1 32 66 ▪ 14.2 14.4 17 36.1 59 60

18099 NNC P P1 G1.2 1895–1911
Tikhvinskii, Sergei Leonidovich, 1918–.
Dvizhenie za reformy v Kitae v kontse XIX veka i Kan IU-vei (K'ang Yu-wei and the reform movement in China at the end of the nineteenth century).
Moscow: Izd-vo vost. lit-ry, 1959. 418 p.
SUBJ 16.1 32 ▪ 12 64

18100 CSU P P1 G1.2 1895–1911
Wong, Frank Fe (Huang Chin-hui), 1935–.
'The Meiji model and Chinese constitutional reformers.'
Studies on Asia 2nd series 1 (1968), 64–76.
SUBJ 12.2 32 64

1644-1949

18101 CSU P P3 G1.2 1895–1928
Fass, Josef.
'Die Anfänge des Sozialismus in China vor 1921' (The origins of socialism in China before 1921).
Sinologica 12, 1/2 (1971), 109–121.
SUBJ 32 32.2 64

18102 DLC O P2 G1.1 1895–1928
Lo, R. Y. (Lo Yün-yen), 1890–.
China's revolution from the inside.
New York: Abingdon Press, 1930. 307 p.
SUBJ 30 32 33 38 54 64 ▪ 12 14.2 16.1 32.2 36.1 36.3 36.4 37 47 66

18103 MAM P P1 G1.2 1895–1928
Shen, James Cheng-yee (Shen Ch'eng-i), 1920–.
Liang Chi-chao and his times.
Ann Arbor: University Microfilms (Publ. 7589), 1954. 392 p. (Doctoral dissertation in History, U. of Missouri)
SUBJ 14.2 32 64 ▪ 59 62 65

18104 MAM P P2 G1.2 1895–1949
Shirley, James Robert, 1925–.
Political conflict in the Kuomintang: The career of Wang Ching-wei to 1932.
Ann Arbor: University Microfilms (Publ. 64-9113), 1964. 307 p. (Doctoral dissertation in History, U. of California, Berkeley, 1962)
SUBJ 16.1 32 32.2 59 ▪ 15 48 64

18105 DLC U P2 G1.1 1895–1928
[Vilenskii, Vladimir Dmitrievich] Vl. Vilenskii-Sibiriakov, pseud., 1888–1942.
Gomindan, partiia kitaiskoi revoliutsii (The Kuomintang, China's revolutionary party).
Moscow: Molodaia gvardiia, 1926. 108 p.
SUBJ 32 64 ▪ 32.2

18106 CBU P P2 G1.2 1895–1928
Yu, George T., 1931–.
Party politics in Republican China: The Kuomintang, 1912–1924.
Berkeley, Los Angeles: U. of California Press, 1966. 14, 203 p. (Revision of *The party movement in Republican China: The Kuomintang, 1912–1924*, doctoral dissertation in Political Science, U. of California, Berkeley, 1962)
SUBJ 12 32 ▪ 16.1 64

1911-1949

18107 NNC P P2 G1.2 1928–1949
'Gomindan i razdel Kitaia imperialistami' (The Kuomintang and the imperialist partition of China).
MNKP 1934, 1/2, 30–60.
SUBJ 12 15 32 66 ▪ 14.2 14.3

18108 CSU P P1 G1.2 1911–1949
'A review of Kuomintang – Chinese Communist relations, 1921–1944.' In *United States relations with China*, edited by U.S. Dept. of State. [Sole entry]
Washington, D.C.: U.S. Dept. of State, Division of Publications, 1949, 38–58. (USDS, Far Eastern series, 30)
SUBJ 32 32.2

18109 MCH U P3 G1.2 1911–1928
Abramson, Manuil Moiseevich, 1898–1941.
'Politicheskie obshchestva i partii v Kitae' (Political societies and parties in China).
NV 1 (1922), 199–223.
SUBJ 32 64 ▪ 12.1

18110 CSH P P2 G1.2 1911–1928
Akatova, Tat'iana Nikolaevna, 1923–.
'Ot "dvizheniia 30 maia" po podgotovki Severnogo nokhoda (mai 1925 – mai 1926 g.)' (From the May Thirtieth Movement to preparation for the Northern Expedition, May 1925 – May 1926). In *Ocherki istorii Kitaia v noveishee vremia* (Survey of modern Chinese history), compiled by Institut kitaevedeniia, Akademiia nauk SSSR, edited by Aleksei Stepanovich Perevertailo et al. [Selective entry]
Moscow: Izd-vo vost. lit-ry, 1959, 126–148.
SUBJ 16.4 17 32 32.2 66 ▪ 15 16 25 64

18111 CSU P P1 G1.1 1928–1949
Amerasia Staff.
'Democracy vs. one-party rule in Kuomintang China: The "little parties" organize.'
Amerasia 7, 3 (25 Apr. 1943), 97–120.
SUBJ 32 32.1 ▪ 15 16.1 37

18112 CSU O P3 G1.2 1928–1949
Barnett, Arthur Doak, 1921–.
'Clique politics' [report to Institute of Current World Affairs, May 1948]. In *China on the eve of Communist takeover*, by A. D. Barnett. [Selective entry]
New York: Praeger, 1963, 60–70.
SUBJ 12 32 ▪ 32.1

18113 CSU O P3 G1.5 1928–1949
Barnett, Arthur Doak, 1921–.
'Minor parties in opposition' [report to Institute of Current World Affairs, December 1948]. In *China on the eve of Communist takeover*, by A. D. Barnett. [Selective entry]
New York: Praeger, 1963, 83–95.
SUBJ 32 32.2

18114 MAM P P2 G1.2 1928–1949
Bedeski, Robert Edward, 1937–.
The politics of national unification: China, 1928–1936.
Ann Arbor: University Microfilms (Publ. 70-13,015), 1970. 493 p. (Doctoral dissertation in Political Science, U. of California, Berkeley, 1969)
SUBJ 12 14 32 64 ▪ 12.1 14.1 14.6 15 16 25 32.2

18115 ICU P P2 G1.3 1911–1928
Berkenkamp, Elizabeth A-, 1933–.
Rise of the Kuomintang, 1923–27.
Unpublished masters thesis in History, U. of Chicago, 1957. 77 p.
SUBJ 32 ▪ 12.1 15 16.2 17 32.1 36.3 36.4 47 54 64

18116 CSU P P3 G1.2 1928–1949
Boyle, John Hunter, 1930–.
'The road to Sino-Japanese collaboration: The background to the defection of Wang Ching-wei.'
Monumenta Nipponica 25, 3/4 (1970), 267–301.
SUBJ 12 32 66 ▪ 15 32.2

18117 NNC P P4 G1.3 1928–1949
Bünger, Karl A-, 1903–.
'Das Verhältnis zwischen Partei und Staat in China' (The relationship between party and state in China).
Z. für ausländisches öffentliches Recht und Völkerrecht 6, 2 (1936), 286–302.
SUBJ 12 32 ▪ 30 32.1 34.3 36.2 64

18118 ICU P P4 G1.2 1928–1949
Busche, Helen E-.
Minor parties and political groups and their efforts to expand democracy in China, 1927–1947.
Unpublished masters thesis in History, U. of Chicago, 1948. 213 p.
SUBJ 12 30 32 32.2 ▪ 22 32.1 36.4 54

18119 CSU P P2 G1.2 1911–1949
Cavendish, Patrick, 1937–.
'The "new China" of the Kuomintang.' In *Modern China's search for a political form*, edited by Jack Douglas Gray. [Analytic entry]
London: Oxford U. Press, 1969, 138–186.
SUBJ 12 15 32 32.2 ▪ 12.2 14.2 16 22 30 32.1 54 64

18120 ECU P P2 G1.2 1911–1949
Cavendish, Patrick, 1937–.
The rise of the Chinese Nationalist Party and the foundation of the Nanking regime, 1924–1929.
Unpublished doctoral dissertation in Political Science, U. of Cambridge [Trinity College], 1968. 519 p.
SUBJ 12 15 16.1 25 32 32.2 ▪ 12.2 14.2 14.6 17 32.1 36.3 36.4 54 64

18121 CSU P P2 G9.4 1911–1949
Chen, Edward I-te (Ch'en I-te), 1930–.
'Formosan political movements under Japanese colonial rule, 1914–1937.'
JAS 31, 3 (May 1972), 477–497.
SUBJ 32 32.1 66 ▪ 22 36.3 36.4 64

18122 CSU P P1 G1.2 1911–1928
Ch'en, Jerome (Ch'en Chih-jang), 1919–.
'The left wing Kuomintang: A definition.'
BSOAS 25, 3 (Oct. 1962), 557–576.
SUBJ 32 64 ▪ 32.1

18123 GBF P P2 G1.2 1911–1949
Domes, Jürgen Otto, 1932–.
Vertagte Revolution: Die Politik der Kuomintang in China, 1923–1937 (Postponed revolution: The policies of the Kuomintang in China, 1923–1937).
Berlin: de Gruyter, 1969. 795 p. (Beiträge zur auswärtigen und internationalen Politik, 3)
SUBJ 12 32 32.2 ▪ 12.1 14 14.1 15 17 64

18124 CSU FP P2 G1.2 1928–1949
Eastman, Lloyd Eric, 1929–.
'Fascism in Kuomintang China: The Blue Shirts.'
CQ 49 (Jan.–Mar. 1972), 1–31.
SUBJ 12.1 32 64 ▪ 25 32.1

18125 ELO PO P1 G1.1 1928–1949
Escarra, Jean, 1885–1955.
Party government in China.
London: China Institute, 1941. 13 p.
SUBJ 12 32 32.1 ▪ 15 16.1 64

18126 MCH P P3 G1.2 1911–1928
Friedman, Edward, 1937–.
The center cannot hold: The failure of parliamentary democracy in China from the Chinese Revolution of 1911 to the World War in 1914.
Unpublished doctoral dissertation in Political Science, Harvard U., 1968. 620 p.
SUBJ 15 26.2 32 36.2 64 66 ▪ 12 12.2 22 22.2 24 24.6 25 26.1 28 47

18127 MCH S P3 G1.3 1911–1928
Garushiants, IUrii Misakovich.
'O dvizhushchikh silakh antiimperialisticheskoi bor'by 1919 g. v Kitae (k sorokaletiiu dvizheniia "4 maia")' (Motivating forces in the 1919 anti-imperialist struggle in China: On the fortieth anniversary of the May Fourth Movement). [With English abstract]
PV 1959, 3, 16–30.
SUBJ 16.2 19 32 66 ▪ 36.1 36.4 64

18128 MCH P P4 G1.2 1928–1949
Glunin, Vladimir Ivanovich, 1924–.
'Iz istorii edinogo fronta v Kitae' (History of the united front in China). [With English abstract]
VI 1961, 7 (iiul'), 54–69.
SUBJ 12.1 16.2 32 ▪ 32.2 64

18129 MCH FP P3 G1.5 1911–1928
Gourlay, Walter Everett, 1921–.
The Kuomintang and the rise of Chiang Kai-shek, 1920–1924.
Unpublished doctoral dissertation in History, Harvard U., 1966. 2 vols. 307 p. [c.p.].
SUBJ 12 32 66 ▪ 14.5 15 25 36.4 59 64

18130 MCH P P3 G1.2 1928–1949
Grinevich, Petr Antonovich, 1899–1941.
'Krizis gomin'dana' (Crisis in the Kuomintang).
PK 10 (1932), 134–166.
SUBJ 32 32.2 ▪ 16.2 16.4 36.4

18131 ELL P P2 G8.2 1911–1949
Hall, John Christopher Stephen, 1944–.
The provincial warlord faction in Yünnan, 1927–1937.
Unpublished doctoral dissertation in Chinese Studies, U. of Leeds, 1972. 461 p.
SUBJ 12 32 ▪ 14.3 14.5 24.1

18132 NNC S P1 G1.2 1911–1949
Holland, William Lancelot, 1907–.
'Political China today: A review bibliography.'
PA 2, 5 (May 1929), 263–274.
SUBJ 12 32 72

18133 MCY P P1 G1.2 1928–1949
Kennedy, Melville Talbot, Jr., 1917–.
'The Chinese Democratic League.'
PC 7 (Feb. 1953), 136–175.
SUBJ 16.1 32 ▪ 17 18 63

18134 MCH P P2 G1.2 1928–1949
Kennedy, Melville Talbot, Jr., 1917–.
The Kuomintang and Chinese unification, 1928–1931.
Unpublished doctoral dissertation in Government, Harvard U., 1958. 334 p.
SUBJ 12 32 32.1 ▪ 15 16 25 64

18135 MCH S P4 G1.2 1928–1949
Korobov, N- D-.
'Iz istorii demokraticheskogo dvizheniia v gomindanovskom Kitae, v kontse 1945 – nachale 1946 gg.' (History of the democratic movement in Kuomintang China from late 1945 to early 1946).
Nauchnye doklady vysshei shkoly; istoricheskie nauki 1958, 2, 175–189.
SUBJ 32 32.2 64 ▪ 32.1

18136 MCH S P4 G1.2 1928–1949
Kukushkin, Kim Vladimirovich, 1926–.
'Bor'ba Kommunisticheskoi partii Kitaia za edinyi natsional'nyi front, 1935–1937 gg.' (The Chinese Communist Party's struggle for a united national front, 1935–1937).
VI 1956, 2 (fevral'), 53–68.
SUBJ 16.2 19 32 32.2 ▪ 14.3 15 16 16.1

18137 ELS S P1 G1.5 1911–1949
Lary, Diana Cecilia Margaret, 1941–.
The Kwangsi clique in Kuomintang politics, 1921–1936.
Unpublished doctoral dissertation in Oriental and African Languages, U. of

London [School of Oriental and African Studies], 1969. 502 p.
Subj 12 15 32 64 ▪ 16.1 25 32.1 66

18138 WMU P P3 G1.3 1911–1928
Lee, Pei-sen (Li P'ei-sen), 1931–.
Why the Chinese Kuomintang was reorganized in 1924: The development of Sun Yat-sen's policies and their final embodiment in the 1924 reorganization of the National People's Party.
Unpublished masters thesis in History, U. of Wisconsin, 1970. 152 p.
Subj 32 64 ▪ 19 32.2 66

18139 MCH P P1 G1.2 1928–1949
Linebarger, Paul Myron Anthony, 1913–1966.
'Postwar politics of China.'
J. of politics 9, 4 (Nov. 1947), 522–542.
Subj 32 ▪ 32.2

18140 NIC O P4 G1.2 1911–1949
Lynn, Jermyn Chi-hung (Ling Ch'i-hung).
Political parties in China.
Peiping: Henri Vetch, 1930. 255 p.
Subj 12 32 32.2 ▪ 15 19

18141 NNC P P2 G1.2 1928–1949
Maslennikov, Viacheslav Aleksandrovich, 1894–1968.
'Edinyi antiiaponskii natsional'nyi front v Kitae' (The national anti-Japanese united front in China).
MKhMP 1938, 12 (dekabr'), 61–70.
Subj 12 15 32 32.2 66 ▪ 16.4 18

18142 DLC P P2 G1.2 1928–1949
Maslennikov, Viacheslav Aleksandrovich, 1894–1968.
Kitaiskii narod v bor'be za svobodu i nezavisimost' (The Chinese people in the struggle for freedom and independence).
Moscow: Gos. izd-vo kul'turno-prosvetitel'noi lit-ry, 1948. 74 p.
Subj 14 15 16 32 66 ▪ 12 18 32.2

18143 MCH O P2 G1.2 1911–1949
Misselwitz, Henry Francis, 1900–.
The dragon stirs: An intimate sketchbook of China's Kuomintang revolution.
New York: Harbinger House, 1941. 293 p.
Subj 12 15 19 32 ▪ 32.1 32.2 64 66

18144 MCH P P2 G1.2 1911–1928
Nathan, Andrew James, 1943–.
Factionalism in early Republican China: The politics of the Peking government, 1918–1920.
Unpublished doctoral dissertation in Political Science, Harvard U., 1970. 564 p.
Subj 12 16.1 30 32 35 48 ▪ 14.5 14.6 15 16 39 42 44

18145 CSH P P2 G1.2 1928–1949
Nikiforov, Vladimir Nikolaevich, 1920–.
Gomin'danovskie reaktsionery: predateli Kitaia (1937–1945) (The Kuomintang reactionaries: China's traitors, 1937–1945).
Moscow: Izd-vo Mosk. un-ta, 1953. 244 p.
Subj 15 16 32 32.2 66 ▪ 12 35

18146 DLC P P2 G1.4 1928–1949
Nikiforov, Vladimir Nikolaevich, 1920–.
'Pod"em patrioticheskogo dvizheniia v Kitae nakanune Sian'skogo vosstaniia (9 dekabria 1935 g. – 12 dekabria 1936 g.)' (The rise of the Chinese patriotic movement on the eve of the Sian Incident, 9 December 1935 – 12 December 1936). In *Sbornik statei po istorii stran Dal'nego Vostoka* (Articles on Far Eastern history), edited by Larisa Vasil'evna Simonovskaia and Mikhail Filippovich IUr'ev. [Selective entry]
Moscow: Izd-vo Mosk. un-ta, 1952, 23–42.
Subj 15 32 32.2 66 ▪ 12 16.2 16.4

18147 NIC P P1 G1.2 1911–1949
North, Robert Carver, 1914–.
Kuomintang and Chinese Communist elites.
Stanford: Stanford U. Press, 1952. 130 p. [Reprinted in *World revolutionary elites: Studies in coercive ideological movements*, edited by Harold Dwight Lasswell and Daniel Lerner. (Sole entry.) Cambridge: M.I.T. Press, 1965, 319–455.]
Subj 16.1 32 32.2 ▪ 12 15 16 64

18148 MMT P P2 G1.2 1911–1928
North, Robert Carver, 1914–, and Xenia Joukoff Eudin.
M. N. Roy's mission to China: The Communist-Kuomintang split of 1927.
Berkeley, Los Angeles: U. of California Press, 1963. 399 p.
Subj 16.1 32 32.2 ▪ 15 16.3 32.1 64 66 72

18149 NNC P P1 G1.3 1911–1949
Otte, Friedrich W- K-.
'Staat und Partei in China' (State and party in China).
MSOSB 40 (1937), 1–36.
Subj 32 32.1 ▪ 12 12.1 13 30 64

18150 NNC P P1 G1.2 1928–1949
Perlin, B-.
'Edinyi natsional'nyi antiiaponskii front v Kitae' (The national anti-Japanese united front in China).
MKhMP 1937, 12 (dekabr'), 94–100.
Subj 12 32 32.2 66 ▪ 15 17 18 25

18151 CSU U P1 G1.2 1911–1949
Shen, James (Shen Chien-hung).
'Minority parties in China.'
Asia (New York: American Asiatic Assn.) 40, 2 (Feb. 1940), 81–83; 40, 3 (Mar. 1940), 137–139.
Subj 32 ▪ 64

18152 NNC P P1 G1.3 1911–1928
Shirley, James Robert, 1925–.
'Control of the Kuomintang after Sun Yat-sen's death.'
JAS 25, 1 (Nov. 1965), 69–82.
Subj 32 ▪ 15 16.1 32.2 64

18153 CSU P P1 G1.3 1911–1928
Shirley, James Robert, 1925–.
'Factionalism and the left Kuomintang.'
Studies on Asia 6 (1965), 97–104.
Subj 32

18154 CSU P P2 G1.2 1911–1949
Tien, Hung-mao (T'ien Hung-mao), 1938–.
Government and politics in Kuomintang China, 1927–1937.
Stanford: Stanford U. Press, 1972. 14, 226 p. (Revision of *Political development in China, 1927–1937*, doctoral dissertation in Political Science, U. of Wisconsin, 1969)
Subj 12 14.5 16.1 32 ▪ 12.1 14.6 15 16.3 17 25 32.2

18155 NNC P P2 G1.2 1911–1949
Tong, T. K. (T'ang Te-kang), 1920–.
The Kuomintang-Communist relations and the Russian influence, 1924–1927.
Unpublished masters thesis in History, Columbia U., 1952. 236 p.
Subj 32 32.2 ▪ 64

18156 CSU P P1 G9.2 1911–1928
Tsui, Shu-chin (Ts'ui Shu-ch'in), 1906–1957.
'The influence of the Canton-Moscow entente upon Sun Yat-sen's revolutionary tactics.'
CSPSR 20, 1 (Jan. 1936), 101–139. (Doctoral dissertation in History, Government, and Economics, Harvard U., 1934. [The dissertation was published in two parts, of which this is the second. For the first, see entry 22180.])
Subj 32 32.2 ▪ 15 66

18157 NNC P P2 G1.2 1911–1949
Viatkin, Rudol'f Vsevolodovich, 1910–.
'Kitaiskaia revoliutsiia 1925–1927 gg. i angliiskii imperializm' (The Chinese revolution of 1925–1927 and British imperialism).
Uchenye zapiski Tikhookeanskogo instituta 3 (1949), 120–151.
Subj 12 15 16 32 66 ▪ 12.1 14.4 16.4 22 32.2 36.4 64

18158 MAM PO P2 G1.2 1928–1949
Wang, Cheng, 1905–.
The Kuomintang: A sociological study of demoralization.
Ann Arbor: University Microfilms (Publ. 5388), 1953. 185 p. (Doctoral dissertation in Sociology and Anthropology, Stanford U.)
Subj 32 61 ▪ 15 16 60

18159 NNC O P2 G1.2 1928–1949
Wei Meng-pu.
'The Kuomintang in China: Its fabric and future.'
PA 13, 1 (Mar. 1940), 30–44.
Subj 32 ▪ 12 14 15 32.2 64

18160 CSU P P3 G1.4 1911–1928
Wilbur, Clarence Martin, 1908–, and Julie Lien-ying How (Hsia Lien-yin), 1926–.
'Kuomintang and Soviet relations with Feng Yü-hsiang, October, 1924 to September, 1926.' In *Documents on Communism, nationalism, and Soviet advisers in China, 1918–1927*, edited by C. M. Wilbur and J. Lien-ying How. [Selective entry]
New York: Columbia U. Press, 1956, 318–335.
Subj 32 66 ▪ 12 15

18161 MCH O P2 G1.2 1911–1928
Woo, Thomas Tze Chung (Wu Chih-ch'un), 1893–.
The Kuomintang and the future of the Chinese Revolution.
London: Allen and Unwin, 1928. 278 p.
Subj 32 36.3 36.4 64 ▪ 12 16.3 16.4 32.2 66

18162 NNC P P1 G1.2 1911–1949
Wright, Mary Clabaugh, 1917–1970.
'From revolution to restoration: The transformation of Kuomintang ideology.'
FEQ 14, 4 (Aug. 1955), 515–532. [Reprinted in *Modern China: An interpretive anthology*, edited by Joseph Richmond Levenson. (Selective entry.) London: Macmillan, 1971, 99–113.]
SUBJ 32 64 ▪ 16.1 22.1 63

18163 MAM P P1 G1.2 1911–1928
Wu, Ellsworth Tien-wei (Wu T'ien-wei), 1922–.
The Chinese Nationalist and Communist alliance, 1923–1927.
Ann Arbor: University Microfilms (Publ. 66-1369), 1966. 840 p. (Doctoral dissertation in History, U. of Maryland, 1965)
SUBJ 32 32.2

1911-1972
(including 1644-1972)

18164 CSU P P3 G1.2 1911–1972
Bartke, Wolfgang.
Das Politbüro des 8. Zentralkomitees der Kommunistischen Partei Chinas: Persönlicher Hintergrund der Funktionäre und ihre Aktivität in den Jahren 1964–1967 (The Politburo of the Eighth Central Committee of the Chinese Communist Party: Personal background of the officials and their activities, 1964–1967).
Wiesbaden: Harrassowitz, 1969. 165 p.
SUBJ 12 16.1 32 ▪ 32.2 50

18165 MCH P P1 G1.2 1928–1972
Chen, Theodore H. E. (Ch'en Hsi-en), 1902–.
'Deviationism in Chinese Communism.'
World affairs interpreter 25, 4 (Jan. 1955), 414–432.
SUBJ 32 32.2 64

18166 MMT S P1 G1.2 1928–1972
Cole, Allan Burnett, 1914–.
'The united front in the New China.'
AAAPSS 277 (Sept. 1951), 35–45. [Special issue: *Report on China*, edited by Harold Arthur Steiner]
SUBJ 32 32.2 ▪ 12 15 16.1 32.1 64

18167 CSH P P1 G1.2 1911–1972
Doolin, Dennis James, 1933–, and John Emery Rue, 1924–.
'China.' In *World Communism: A handbook, 1918–1965*, edited by Witold Saturnin Sworakowski. [Sole entry]
Stanford: Hoover Institution Press, 1972, 66–74.
SUBJ 32 32.2 ▪ 12.1 16.1

18168 MCH P P1 G1.2 1928–1972
Eitner, Hans-Jürgen.
'Mao Tse-tung und seine Erben: Probleme der Nachfolgeschaft in Peking' (Mao Tse-tung and his heirs: The problem of succession in Peking).
Schweizer Monatshefte 40, 12 (März 1961), 1172–1182.
SUBJ 12 32 ▪ 16 32.2 64

18169 CSU P P1 G1.2 1928–1972
Fessler, Loren, 1923–.
'The party comes of age. Part 1, The Seventh and Eighth Party Congresses of the Chinese Communist Party. Part 2, The Ninth Party Congress of the Chinese Communist Party.'
AUFS-EAS 16, 8 (Sept. 1969), 1–17; 16, 9 (Sept. 1969), 1–12.
SUBJ 32 32.2 ▪ 64

18170 NIC P P2 G1.2 1911–1972
Guillermaz, Jacques, 1911–.
La Chine populaire (The People's Republic of China).
Paris: Presses universitaires, 1959. 126 p.
SUBJ 10 12 14 32 32.2 ▪ 11 15 17 31 34.1 64

18171 NIC P P1 G1.2 1911–1972
Houn, Franklin W. (Hou Fu-wu), 1920–.
'The Eighth Central Committee of the Chinese Communist Party: A study of an elite.'
APSR 51, 2 (June 1957), 392–404.
SUBJ 16.1 32 32.1 ▪ 15 17 47

18172 CSU P P2 G1.2 1911–1972
Houn, Franklin W. (Hou Fu-wu), 1920–.
A short history of Chinese Communism.
Englewood Cliffs, N. J.: Prentice-Hall, 1967. 245 p.
SUBJ 12.1 14 15 32 32.2 64 ▪ 14.1 14.4 16 17 18 32.1 34.1 47 54 66

18173 MCH P P2 G1.2 1928–1972
Klein, Donald Walker, 1929–, and Anne Bolling Clark.
'Li Hsueh-feng: A biographical sketch of P'eng Chen's successor.'
AS 6, 7 (July 1966), 400–405. [A slightly modified version appears in entry 21412, vol. 1, 504–506.]
SUBJ 32 59

18174 MCH P P1 G1.2 1928–1972
[La Dany, Ladislao] ———, 1914–.
'History of small political parties.'
CNA 124 (16 Mar. 1956), 2–7.
SUBJ 32 ▪ 16.1 32.1

18175 CSH P P1 G1.2 1895–1972
[La Dany, Ladislao] ———, 1914–.
'The T'ai-p'ing and the Cultural Revolution.'
CNA 683 (3 Nov. 1967), 1–7.
SUBJ 32 32.2 ▪ 64

18176 NIC P P1 G1.2 1911–1972
Lewis, John Wilson, 1930–.
Chinese Communist Party leadership and the succession to Mao Tse-tung: An appraisal of tensions.
Washington, D.C.: U.S. Dept. of State, Bureau of Intelligence and Research, External Research Staff, 1964. 35 p.
SUBJ 12 16.1 32 ▪ 15 32.1 32.2 64

18177 CSU P P2 G1.2 1928–1972
Lewis, John Wilson, 1930–.
'Leader, commissar, and bureaucrat: The Chinese political system in the last days of the revolution.'
J. of international affairs 24, 1 (1970), 48–74.
SUBJ 32 32.2 64 ▪ 16 16.1

18178 NNC FP P2 G1.2 1928–1972
Lewis, John Wilson, 1930–.
Leadership in Communist China.
Ithaca: Cornell U. Press, 1963. 13, 305 p. (Revision of *Chinese Communist leadership technique*, doctoral dissertation in Political Science, U. of California, Los Angeles, 1962)
SUBJ 12 12.1 16.1 32 64 ▪ 16 17 22 22.1 26 32.1 34.1

18179 CSU P P1 G1.2 1911–1972
Li Tien-min (Li T'ien-min).
'Examination report on Liu Shao-chi's crimes.'
IS 5, 7 (Apr. 1969), 11–17.
SUBJ 32 32.1 ▪ 12.2

18180 WSU P P1 G1.2 1928–1972
Lindbeck, John Matthew Henry, 1915–1971.
'Transformations in the Chinese Communist Party.' In *Soviet and Chinese Communism: Similarities and differences*, edited by Donald Warren Treadgold. [Selective entry]
Seattle: U. of Washington Press, 1967, 73–104.
SUBJ 32 32.2 ▪ 12 15 16 19 32.1

18181 CSH U P1 G2.0 1928–1972
Lo, J. P. (Lo Jung-pang), 1912–, and Peter S. H. Tang (T'ang Sheng-hao), 1919–.
'Political dynamics.' In *A regional handbook on Northeast China*, compiled by Far Eastern and Russian Institute, U. of Washington. [Selective entry]
New Haven: Human Relations Area Files, 1956, 346–375. (HRAF subcontractor's monographs, 61; Washington 9)
SUBJ 32 ▪ 12.1 32.1 32.2

18182 MAM P P2 G1.2 1911–1972
Morrison, James Kent, 1940–.
Political change in a Communist system: Party life in China.
Ann Arbor: University Microfilms (Publ. 71-16,981), 1971. 404 p. (Doctoral dissertation in Political Science, U. of Washington, 1970)
SUBJ 16.1 32 ▪ 19 64

18183 CSH P P1 G1.2 1911–1972
Pringsheim, Klaus Hubert Charl, 1923–.
The Sino-Soviet Friendship Association (October 1949 – October 1951), mimeo.
Unpublished masters thesis in Political Science, Columbia U., 1960? 11, 297 p. [Certificate essay, East Asian Institute]
SUBJ 32 66

18184 CSU F P1 G1.2 1928–1972
Ravenholt, Albert, 1919–.
'Feud among the Red mandarins: How Kao Kang and Jao Shu-shih challenged their comrades.'
AUFS-EAS 11, 2 (Feb. 1964), 1–10.
SUBJ 12.2 16.1 32 ▪ 15

18185 MAM P P2 G1.2 1928–1972
Thomas, Samuel Bernard, 1921–.
Doctrine and strategy of the Chinese Communist Party: Domestic aspects, 1945–1956.
Ann Arbor: University Microfilms (Publ. 65-5868), 1965. 431 p. (Doctoral dissertation in History, Columbia U., 1964)
SUBJ 12.1 14 16 32 32.2 64 ▪ 11.4 14.1 14.4 36.3 36.4

18186 NNC P P1 G1.2 1928–1972
TSzen Siu-fu (Tseng Hsiu-fu).
Kommunisticheskaia partiia Kitaia v bor'be za edinyi front (The Chinese Communist Party in the struggle for a united front).
Moscow: Izd-vo Vysshei partiinei shkoly i AON pri TsK KPSS, 1959. 161 p.
SUBJ 32 32.1 32.2 ▪ 16 19

18187 CSU P P2 G1.2 1911–1972
Van Slyke, Lyman Page, 1929–.
Enemies and friends: The united front in Chinese Communist history.
Stanford: Stanford U. Press, 1967. 330 p. (Revision of *Friends and enemies: The united front and its place in Chinese Communist history*, doctoral dissertation in History, U. of California, Berkeley, 1964)
SUBJ 32 32.1 32.2 ▪ 12.1 14.1 15 16 34.2 36.4 66 72

18188 MCH P P2 G1.2 1928–1972
Wen Shih, pseud.
'Political parties in Communist China.'
AS 3, 3 (Mar. 1963), 157–164.
SUBJ 32 ▪ 12 16.2 32.1 64

1949-1972

18189 CSH P P2 G1.2 1949–1972
'China.' In *Yearbook on international Communist affairs, 1966–1971*, edited by Milorad M- Drachkovitch, Richard V- Allen, and Richard Felix Staar.
Stanford: Hoover Institution Press. Issued annually, 1967–1971, average ca. 25 p. [No issue was published for 1967.]
SUBJ 12.1 16.1 32 ▪ 12 35 64

18190 CSH P P2 G1.2 1949–1972
'Obstanovka v Kitae i polozhenie v KPK na sovremennom etape.'
Kommunist 1969, 4 (mart), 86–114.
'The current situation in China and in the Chinese Communist Party.'
Reprints from the Soviet press 8, 8 (18 Apr. 1969), 14–43.
SUBJ 19 32 64 ▪ 12 12.1 14 16 35

18191 MCH P P1 G1.2 1949–1972
'Über einige Seiten des Parteilebens in der kommunistichen Partei Chinas' (Aspects of party life in the Chinese Communist Party).
Neuer Weg 19, 10 (1964), 441–456.
SUBJ 32 ▪ 12 64

18192 MCH O P2 G1.2 1949–1972
An Tze-wen (An Tzu-wen).
'The consolidation of party organisations.'
People's China 1953, 13 (1 July), 5–10.
SUBJ 32 32.1

18193 NNC PO P1 G1.2 1949–1972
Barnett, Arthur Doak, 1921–.
'Chinese Communist Party: A period of consolidation.'
AUFS-EAS 2, 4 (1 Dec. 1953), 1–8. [Reprinted as 'Party consolidation.' In *Communist China: The early years, 1949–55*, by A. D. Barnett. (Selective entry.) New York: Praeger, 1964, 52–59.]
SUBJ 32

18194 CSU P P1 G1.2 1949–1972
Baum, Richard Dennis, 1940–.
'Ideology redivivus.'
Problems of Communism 16, 3 (May–June 1967), 1–11.
SUBJ 12.1 32 64

18195 CSU P P2 G1.2 1949–1972
Baum, Richard Dennis, 1940–, and Frederick Carl Teiwes, 1939–.
'Liu Shao-ch'i and the cadre question.'
AS 8, 4 (Apr. 1968), 323–345.
SUBJ 19 32 ▪ 16.1 32.1

18196 CSU P P1 G1.2 1949–1972
Bridgham, Philip Low, 1921–.
'Factionalism in the Central Committee.' In *Party leadership and revolutionary power in China*, edited by John Wilson Lewis. [Analytic entry]
Cambridge: Cambridge U. Press, 1970, 203–235.
SUBJ 16.1 32 ▪ 64

18197 CSU P P1 G1.2 1949–1972
Brugger, William Christian, 1941–.
'The Ninth National Congress of the Chinese Communist Party.'
World today 25, 7 (July 1969), 297–305.
SUBJ 32 64 ▪ 12 12.2 54

18198 CSU P P1 G1.2 1949–1972
Burton, Barry.
'The Cultural Revolution's ultraleft conspiracy: The "May 16 group".'
AS 11, 11 (Nov. 1971), 1029–1553.
SUBJ 15 16.1 32 ▪ 14.2 54 64

18199 CSU P P2 G1.2 1949–1972
Chai, Winberg (Chai Wen-po), 1932–.
'The reorganization of the Chinese Communist Party, 1966–1968.'
AS 8, 11 (Nov. 1968), 901–910.
SUBJ 32 ▪ 12 16.1

18200 CSH P P2 G1.2 1949–1972
Chang Chen-pang.
'The present and future situation of the Chinese Communist Party and administration.'
CCA 5, 5 (Oct. 1968), 15–28.
SUBJ 12 32 ▪ 64

18201 NNC P P1 G1.2 1949–1972
Chang Ching-wen.
'Analysis of the 10th Plenary Session of the 8th Central Committee of the Chinese Communist Party.'
Analysis of current Chinese Communist problems (Taipei) 1962 (Dec.), 2–23.
SUBJ 32

18202 CSU P P1 G1.2 1949–1972
Chang, Parris H. (Chang Hsü-ch'eng), 1936–.
'Mao's great purge: A political balance sheet.'
Problems of Communism 18, 2 (Mar.–Apr. 1969), 1–10.
SUBJ 16.1 32 ▪ 15 54

18203 CSU P P1 G1.2 1949–1972
Chang, Parris H. (Chang Hsü-ch'eng), 1936–.
'Research notes on the changing loci of decision in the Chinese Communist Party.'
CQ 44 (Oct.–Dec. 1970), 169–194.
SUBJ 16.1 32

18204 MCH P P2 G1.2 1949–1972
Chao, Kuo-chün, 1918–1962.
'How Communist power is organized in China.'
FA 34, 1 (Oct. 1955), 148–153.
SUBJ 12 32 ▪ 22

18205 MCH P P1 G1.2 1949–1972
Chao, Kuo-chün, 1918–1962.
'Leadership in the Chinese Communist Party.'
AAAPSS 321 (Jan. 1959), 40–50. [Special issue: *Contemporary China and the Chinese*, edited by Howard Lyon Boorman]
SUBJ 32 ▪ 32.1 59 64

18206 CSH P P2 G1.2 1949–1972
[Chao Ts'ung] Chung Hua-min, pseud., 1927–.
'Cultural Revolution in 1969.' Tr. of '1969 nien ti wen hua ta ko ming'; *Tsu kuo* 70 (Jan. 1970), 4–13. In *Communist China, 1969*, edited by Union Research Institute. [Selective entry]
Hong Kong: Union Research Institutc, 1970, 1–36.
SUBJ 16.1 32 64 ▪ 12 25

18207 CSH P P1 G1.2 1949–1972
Charles, David A-.
'The dismissal of Marshal P'eng Teh-huai.'
CQ 8 (Oct.–Dec. 1961), 63–76. [Reprinted in *China under Mao: Politics takes command*, edited by Roderick Lemonde MacFarquhar. (Selective entry.) Cambridge: M.I.T. Press, 1966, 20–33.]
SUBJ 16.1 32 ▪ 15 59 64

18208 NNC P P2 G1.2 1949–1972
Chin, Steve S. K. (Chin Ssu-k'ai), 1919–.
'The party.' Tr. of 'Shih nien lai ti Chung kung tang wu' (Activities of the Chinese Communist Party during the past decade); *Tsu kuo chou k'an* 381 (2 May 1960), 9–17. In *Communist China, 1949–1959*, edited by Union Research Institute. [Selective entry]
Hong Kong: Union Research Institute, 1961, vol. 1, 1–52.
SUBJ 32 32.1 ▪ 12 30 64

18209 CSH P P2 G1.2 1949–1972
Chin, Steve S. K. (Chin Ssu-k'ai), 1919–, Lin Yu-ho (Lin Yü-ho), and Ch'in T'i. [Authors sequential rather than joint: Steve S. K. Chin for 1960–1962; Lin Yu-ho for 1963–1965; Ch'in T'i for 1966–1969.]
'Communist China's party affairs, 1960–1969' [title varies]. Tr. from *Tsu kuo chou k'an* 432 (17 Apr. 1961); 482 (2 Apr. 1962); 534 (1 Apr. 1963) *and* from *Tsu kuo* 1–74 (Apr. 1964 – May 1970) [recurring annual feature article]. In *Communist China, 1960–1969*, edited by Union Research Institute.
Hong Kong: Union Research Institute. Issued annually, 1962–1970, average ca. 35 p.
SUBJ 32 ▪ 12 16.1 32.1 64

18210 CSH P P3 G1.2 1949–1972
Chu Wen-lin.
'An analysis of the 29 new CCP committees at the provincial level.'
IS 8, 2 (Nov. 1971), 47–65; 8, 3 (Dec. 1971), 53–95.
SUBJ 16.1 32

18211 CSU P P4 G1.2 1949–1972
Cocks, Paul Maupin, Jr., 1941–.
'The role of the Party Control Committee in Communist China.'
PC 22B (Dec. 1969), 49–96.
SUBJ 16.1 32 64 ▪ 12

18212 NNC P P1 G1.2 1949–1972
Coillie, Dries van, 1912–.
Rotchina: Die Partei und ihre Führer (Red China: The party and its leaders). Tr. by Georg Hermanowski of *De Chinese communistische Partij en haar leiders*.
Donauwörth, Germany: Ludwig Auer, 1963? 103 p.
SUBJ 16.1 32 32.1 ▪ 12.1 16 64

18213 CBU PO P2 G1.2 1949–1972
Collotti Pischel, Enrica, 1930–.
'Ideologia e strategia rivoluzionaria nelle tesi cinesi.'
Nuovi argomenti 53/54 (novembre 1961 / febbraio 1962), 1–100.

Revolutionary ideology and strategy in the Chinese theses, mimeo.
Washington, D.C.: U.S. Joint Publications Research Service, 11 Apr. 1962. 70 p. (JPRS 13,412; MC 10,355/1962)
SUBJ 32 64 ▪ 12.1 14.1 14.4

18214 NIC S P1 G1.2 1949–1972
Current Scene Editor.
'Blessings in disguise: An effort to sinicize misery.'
CS 1, 12 (12 Sept. 1961), 1–7. [Reprinted in *This is China: Analyses of Mainland trends and events*, edited by Francis Harper. (Selective entry.) Hong Kong: Dragonfly Books, 1965, 47–56.]
SUBJ 18 32 64 ▪ 12.1 16 54

18215 CSU P P1 G1.2 1949–1972
Current Scene Editor.
'China's Communist Party: Orphan of Mao's storm.'
CS 6, 4 (1 Mar. 1968), 1–10.
SUBJ 32 ▪ 15

18216 MCH P P1 G1.2 1949–1972
Current Scene Editor.
'A year of revolution: Mao Tse-tung and the "anti-Party" struggle.'
CS 4, 22 (10 Dec. 1966), 1–9; 4, 23 (26 Dec. 1966), 1–10.
SUBJ 19 32 64 ▪ 15 54

18217 MCH P P4 G1.2 1949–1972
Domes, Jürgen Otto, 1932–.
'Communist China, 1949–1969: Internal party politics and leadership structure.'
RSAEO 1970, 1, 1–18. [Reprinted as 'Basic elements of internal party politics in Communist China, 1949–1969.' *Internationales Asien Forum* 1, 1 (Jan. 1970), 63–75.]
SUBJ 16.1 32 64 ▪ 12 35 54

18218 CSH P P1 G1.2 1949–1972
Domes, Jürgen Otto, 1932–.
'Krise im chinesischen Kommunismus: Zur "Grossen Proletarischen Kulturrevolution".'
Moderne Welt 7, 4 (1966), 368–380.

'The crisis in Chinese Communism: On the "Great Proletarian Cultural Revolution".' Tr. by Michael Glenny.
Modern world (Cologne) 5 (1967), 95–107.
SUBJ 12 32 ▪ 19

18219 CSU P P2 G1.2 1949–1972
Domes, Jürgen Otto, 1932–.
'Party politics and the Cultural Revolution.' In *Communist China, 1949–1969: A twenty-year appraisal*, edited by Frank Newton Trager and William Henderson. [Selective entry]
New York: New York U. Press, 1970, 63–93.
SUBJ 32 ▪ 12 22.2 25 32.1 35 54

18220 CSU P P1 G3.0 1949–1972
Dreyer, June Teufel, 1939–.
'Inner Mongolia: The purge of Ulanfu.'
CS 6, 20 (15 Nov. 1968), 1–14.
SUBJ 32 66 ▪ 16.1 32.2

18221 MCH P P2 G1.2 1949–1972
Dutt, Vidya Prakash, 1925–.
'The rectification campaign in China.'
International studies (New Delhi) 1, 1 (July 1959), 28–50.
SUBJ 12.1 22 32 ▪ 16.1

18222 FPN P P2 G1.2 1949–1972
Engelborghs-Bertels, Marthe, 1928–.
'Les nouveaux statuts du Parti communiste chinois' (The new statutes of the Chinese Communist Party).
R. du Centre d'étude des pays de l'Est et du Centre national pour l'étude des états de l'Est 1970, 2, 93–122.
SUBJ 32 64 ▪ 16.2 16.4 19 66

18223 CSU P P1 G1.2 1949–1972
Fang Chun-kuei (Fang Chün-kuei).
'An analysis of the current status of Chinese Communist Party and government organs.'
IS 6, 4 (Jan. 1970), 50–55.
SUBJ 32 ▪ 12 16.1

18224 NNC P P2 G1.2 1949–1972
Fang Shu.
Campaign of party-expansion of the Chinese Communist Party in 1952, mimeo.
Hong Kong: Union Research Institute, 1953. 43 p. (Communist China problem research series, EC1)
SUBJ 32 ▪ 12.1 32.1

18225 CBU P P2 G1.2 1949–1972
Fletcher, Merton Don, 1938–.
Communist Party leadership and organization in China, 1949–1962.
Unpublished masters thesis in Political Science, U. of California, Berkeley, 1963. 136 p.
SUBJ 12.1 16.1 32 ▪ 11.4 12 12.2 14 14.1 64

18226 CSU P P2 G1.2 1949–1972
Funnell, Victor Cecil, 1926–.
'The metamorphosis of the Chinese Communist Party.'
Studies in comparative Communism 4, 2 (Apr. 1971), 3–29.
SUBJ 16.1 32 32.1 ▪ 12 64

18227 CSH P P2 G1.2 1949–1972
Gel'bras, Vil' Gdal'evich, 1930–.
'Nekotorye cherty politicheskoi bor'by v Kitae' (Features of the political struggle in China).
NAA 1969, 3, 17–31.
SUBJ 15 32 32.1 54 ▪ 12 16.1 35 64

18228 ELB P P2 G1.2 1949–1972
Girard, Georges.
'Sur la situation politique en Chine' (The political situation in China).
Cahiers du communisme 45, 11 (nov. 1969), 84–96.
SUBJ 32 35 ▪ 12 54 66

18229 CSH P P1 G1.2 1949–1972
Gittings, John, 1938–.
'The state of the party.'
FEER 59, 9 (29 Feb. 1968), 375–380.
SUBJ 19 32

18230 NNC P P1 G1.2 1949–1972
Glaser, Hans-Georg.
'Einige Unterschiede im Partei- und Staatsaufbau zwischen der Sowjetunion und der Volksrepublik China' (Differences in the organization of party and state in the Soviet Union and in the People's Republic of China).
Europa-Archiv 15, 1/2 (5–20 Jan. 1960), 1–12.
SUBJ 12 32 ▪ 12.2

18231 CSH P P3 G1.2 1949–1972
Glaubitz, Joachim, 1929–.
'Der Neunte Parteitag der Kommunistischen Partei China' (The Ninth Congress of the Chinese Communist Party).
Europa-Archiv 24, 15 (10 Aug. 1969), 541–552.
SUBJ 32

18232 FPL P P2 G1.2 1949–1972
Grosbois, Charles.
La Chine en nouvelle démocratie (China as a New Democracy).
Rome: Istituto italiano per il Medio ed Estremo Oriente, 1954. 122 p.
SUBJ 12.1 14.1 14.4 32 ▪ 13 14.5 15 16.1 16.4 18 30 64

18233 CSH P P4 G1.2 1949–1972
Hai Feng, pseud.
'The Cultural Revolution and the reconstruction of the Chinese Communist Party.'
Asia q. 1972, 4, 303–320.
SUBJ 15 32 ▪ 12 19

18234 CSU P P2 G1.2 1949–1972
Harding, Harry, Jr., 1946–.
'Political trends in China since the Cultural Revolution.'
AAAPSS 402 (July 1972), 67–82. [Special issue: *China in the world today*, edited by Richard D- Lambert]
SUBJ 12 32 ▪ 14 14.1 15

18235 CBU P P3 G5.1 1949–1972
Heinzig, Dieter, 1932–.
'Die chinesische Kulturrevolution als Machtkampf: Versuch einer Zusammenfassung' (China's Cultural Revolution as a power struggle: Toward a summation).
Politische Studien 22, 199 (Sept.–Okt. 1971), 475–482. [Special issue: *Kommunismus zwischen Bürokratie und Demokratie* (Communism between bureaucracy and democracy)]
SUBJ 12 32 35 ▪ 16.1

18236 DLC P P1 G1.2 1949–1972
Heinzig, Dieter, 1932–.
Die Krise der kommunistischen Partei Chinas in der Kulturrevolution (The crisis of the Chinese Communist Party in the Cultural Revolution).
Cologne: Bundesinstitut für Ostwissenschaftliche und Internationale Studien, 1968. 41 p. (BOI, Berichte,

1968, 68) [Reprinted—Hamburg: Institut für Asienkunde, 1969. 48 p. (IA, Mitteilungen, 27)]
Subj 19 32 ▪ 12.1 12.2 15 16.1 64

18237 CSH P P2 G 1.2 1949–1972
Heinzig, Dieter, 1932–.
'Der Wiederaufbau der kommunistischen Partei Chinas' (The rebuilding of the Chinese Communist Party).
Aussenpolitik 19, 11 (Nov. 1968), 680–690.
Subj 12 19 32 ▪ 12.1 15 64

18238 CSH P P2 G 1.2 1949–1972
Heinzig, Dieter, 1932–.
'Die Zerstörung der kommunistischen Partei Chinas' (The destruction of the Chinese Communist Party).
Aussenpolitik 19, 10 (Okt. 1968), 618–626.
Subj 19 32 ▪ 12.1 16.1 64

18239 CSH P P1 G 1.2 1949–1972
Hinton, Harold Clendenin, 1924–.
'The Eighth Congress of the Chinese Communist Party.'
FES 26, 1 (Jan. 1957), 1–8.
Subj 32

18240 NIC P P1 G 1.2 1949–1972
Hinton, Harold Clendenin, 1924–.
'The minor parties and the "united front".' In *A decade under Mao Tse-tung*, by Sripati Chandrasekhar, H. C. Hinton, Lea E- Williams, et al. [Selective entry]
Hong Kong: Green Pagoda Press, 1959, 19–23. [Reprinted in *A decade of Mao's China: A survey of life and thought in China today*, by S. Chandrasekhar, H. C. Hinton, L. E. Williams, et al. (Selective entry.) Bombay: Perennial Press, 1960, 19–23.]
Subj 32 32.1

18241 NNC P P2 G 1.2 1949–1972
Hsiao Ching and Steve S. K. Chin (Chin Ssu-k'ai), 1919–. [Authors sequential rather than joint: Hsiao Ching for 1955; Steve S. K. Chin for 1956 and 1957.]
'The party.' Tr. of '1955–1958 nien Chung kung ti tang wu' (Activities of the Chinese Communist Party, 1955–1958); *Tsu kuo chou k'an* 159–334/335 (16 Jan. 1956 – 8 June 1959) [recurring annual feature article]. In *Communist China, 1955–1958*, edited by Union Research Institute.
Hong Kong: Union Research Institute. Issued annually, 1956–1959, average ca. 15 p.
Subj 32 32.1 ▪ 16.1 63 64

18242 CSH P P7 G 1.2 1949–1972
Hsu Pang-i (Hsü Pang-i).
'Bring into fuller play the role of rural basic-level party organizations as cores of leadership.' Tr. of 'Keng hao ti fa hui nung ts'un chi ts'eng tang tsu chih ti ling tao ho hsin tso yung' (Improve the function of primary-level rural party organizations as cores of leadership); *Hung ch'i* 1961, 20 (16 Oct.), 21–25. In *Translations from 'Hung-ch'i' (Red flag) (Peiping, No. 20, 16 October 1961)*, mimeo., compiled by U.S. Joint Publications Research Service. [Sole entry]
Washington, D.C.: JPRS, 14 Dec. 1961, 29–37. (JPRS 11,516; MC 3075/1962)
Subj 32 64

18243 CSU P P2 G 1.2 1949–1972
Hsüeh, Chün-tu, 1922–.
'The Cultural Revolution and leadership crisis in Communist China.'
Political science q. 82, 2 (June 1967), 169–190.
Subj 19 32 ▪ 12 12.1 22 54

18244 TPY U P1 G 1.2 1949–1972
Hu Chiu-yuan (Hu Ch'iu-yüan), 1910–.
'New dilemma of the Chinese Communist Party.'
West and East 2, 8 (Aug. 1957), 4–10, 17.
Subj 32

18245 CSU P P2 G 3.0 1949–1972
Hyer, Paul Van, 1926–, and William Heaton.
'The Cultural Revolution in Inner Mongolia.'
CQ 36 (Oct.–Dec. 1968), 114–128.
Subj 12.1 32 66 ▪ 21.2 22.2 32.1

18246 CSU P P2 G 1.2 1949–1972
J. F. A. W.
'The September 1956 Congress of the Chinese Communist Party.'
World today 12, 11 (Nov. 1956), 469–478.
Subj 14 32

18247 CSU P P1 G 1.2 1949–1972
Jan, George P. (Jan Po-kung), 1925–.
'Minor parties in Communist China.'
CH 43, 253 (Sept. 1962), 174–177, 183. [Reprinted in *Government of Communist China*, edited by G. P. Jan. (Selective entry.) San Francisco: Chandler, 1966, 281–288.]
Subj 32 32.1

18248 MCH P P1 G 1.2 1949–1972
Klein, Donald Walker, 1929–.
'Succession and the elite in Peking.'
J. of international affairs 18, 1 (1964), 1–11.
Subj 12 16.1 32

18249 CSU P P1 G 1.2 1949–1972
Kung Te-liang.
'An analysis of the Mao-Lin faction's preparations for the Ninth National Congress, CCP.'
IS 5, 7 (Apr. 1969), 1–10.
Subj 32 ▪ 64

18250 CSU P P1 G 1.2 1949–1972
Kung Te-liang.
'Ideological rectification on the Chinese mainland.'
IS 7, 2 (Nov. 1970), 24–28.
Subj 16.1 32 64

18251 CSH P P1 G 1.2 1949–1972
[La Dany, Ladislao] ———, 1914–.
'After the [Ninth Chinese Communist] Party Congress.'
CNA 764 (11 July 1969), 1–7.
Subj 30 32

18252 CSH P P2 G 1.2 1949–1972
[La Dany, Ladislao] ———, 1914–.
'County leaders: Marxism in theory and in practice.'
CNA 888 (21 July 1972), 1–7.
Subj 32 64 ▪ 12 16.3

18253 NNC P P2 G 1.2 1949–1972
[La Dany, Ladislao] ———, 1914–.
'Growth of the party.'
CNA 146 (31 Aug. 1956), 2–7.
Subj 32 ▪ 16

18254 MCH P P2 G 1.2 1949–1972
[La Dany, Ladislao] ———, 1914–.
'The middle class: The CPPCC [Chinese People's Political Consultative Conference].'
CNA 461 (22 Mar. 1963), 1–7.
Subj 32 32.1 ▪ 16.2 17

18255 NNC P P1 G 1.2 1949–1972
[La Dany, Ladislao] ———, 1914–.
'The new party constitution.'
CNA 153 (19 Oct. 1956), 1–7.
Subj 32 ▪ 12.1 32.1

18256 CSH P P1 G 1.2 1949–1972
[La Dany, Ladislao] ———, 1914–.
'The Party Central Committee today.'
CNA 832 (19 Feb. 1971), 1–7.
Subj 16.1 32

18257 CSH P P1 G 1.2 1949–1972
[La Dany, Ladislao] ——— , 1914–.
'Policy or rivalry? The roots of the Cultural Revolution: The 1959 Lushan meeting.'
CNA 685 (17 Nov. 1967), 1–7.
Subj 16.1 32

18258 CSH P P1 G 1.2 1949–1972
[La Dany, Ladislao] ———, 1914–.
'The Politbureau.'
CNA 758 (23 May 1969), 1–7.
Subj 16.1 32

18259 CSH P P1 G 1.2 1949–1972
[La Dany, Ladislao] ———, 1914–.
'The provincial party committees.'
CNA 859 (22 Oct. 1971), 1–7.
Subj 32 ▪ 16.1 35

18260 CSH P P2 G 1.2 1949–1972
[La Dany, Ladislao] ———, 1914–.
'Provincial party congresses.'
CNA 746 (28 Feb. 1969), 1–7.
Subj 32 ▪ 35

18261 CSH P P4 G 1.2 1949–1972
[La Dany, Ladislao] ———, 1914–.
'Reconstruction of the Communist Party.'
CNA 790 (6 Feb. 1970), 1–7.
Subj 32 ▪ 12 15 22

18262 CSH P P1 G 1.2 1949–1972
[La Dany, Ladislao] ———, 1914–.
'The 9th Party Congress.'
CNA 754 (25 Apr. 1969), 1–7; 756 (9 May 1969), 1–7; 757 (16 May 1969), 1–7.
Subj 32 ▪ 16.1 19 64

18263 NPU FP P2 G 9.4 1949–1972
Lerman, Arthur Jay, 1941–.
Political, traditional, and modern economic groups, and the Taiwan Provincial Assembly.
Unpublished doctoral dissertation in Politics, Princeton U., 1972. 501 p.
Subj 12 16.2 30 32 ▪ 31 36.1 36.3 36.4 42 47 48

18264 CSU P P2 G 1.2 1949–1972
Lewis, John Wilson, 1930–.
Communist China: Crisis and change.

New York: Foreign Policy Assn., 1966. 63 p. (FPA headline series, 179)
Subj 12 16.1 32 32.1 ▪ 12.1 15 22 34.1 35 64

18265 MCH P P1 G1.2 1949–1972
Lewis, John Wilson, 1930–.
'Revolutionary struggle and the second generation in Communist China.'
CQ 21 (Jan.–Mar. 1965), 126–147.
Subj 32 64 ▪ 16.1

18266 MCH P P3 G1.2 1949–1972
Li Shih-fei, pseud.
'The party's middlemen: The role of regional bureaus in the Chinese Communist Party.'
CS 3, 25 (15 Aug. 1965), 1–15.
Subj 16.1 32 59

18267 CSH P P1 G1.2 1949–1972
Li Tien-min (Li T'ien-min).
'Why does the Mao-Lin faction rectify the CCP organization?'
IS 4, 9 (June 1968), 9–16.
Subj 32 ▪ 12 15

18268 NNC P P1 G1.2 1949–1972
MacFarquhar, Roderick Lemonde, 1930–.
'Communist China's intra-party dispute.'
PA 31, 4 (Dec. 1958), 323–335.
Subj 32 64 ▪ 12

18269 NNC P P2 G1.2 1949–1972
Martynov, Aleksandr Aleksandrovich.
'Istoricheskii s"ezd Kommunisticheskoi partii Kitaia' (An historical congress of the Chinese Communist Party).
SV 1956, 6, 3–14.
Subj 12 14 14.1 14.4 32 64 ▪ 34.1

18270 CSH U P1 G1.2 1949–1972
Melis, Giorgio.
'Cina: accenni di ritorno alla normalità. IX Congresso del PCC' (Signs of a return to normal in China: The Ninth Congress of the Chinese Communist Party).
Civiltà cattolica 120, 2855 (7 giugno 1969), 496–506.
Subj 32 ▪ 64

18271 CSU F P3 G9.2 1949–1972
Montaperto, Ronald Nicholas, 1939–.
'The origins of "generational politics": Canton, 1966.'
CS 7, 11 (1 June 1969), 1–16.
Subj 32 32.1 54 ▪ 17

18272 MAM P P1 G1.2 1949–1972
Moody, Peter Richard, Jr., 1943–.
The politics of the Eighth Central Committee of the Communist Party of China.
Ann Arbor: University Microfilms (Publ. 71-29,707), 1971. 439 p. (Doctoral dissertation in Political Science, Yale U.)
Subj 16.1 32 32.1 ▪ 12 13 15 64

18273 CSU P P2 G1.2 1949–1972
Neuhauser, Charles Edward Goode, 1932–.
'The Chinese Communist Party in the 1960s: Prelude to the Cultural Revolution.'
CQ 32 (Oct.–Dec. 1967), 3–36.
Subj 12 12.1 22 32 61 ▪ 14.2 15 19 32.1

18274 CSU P P2 G1.2 1949–1972
Neuhauser, Charles Edward Goode, 1932–.
'The impact of the Cultural Revolution on the Chinese Communist Party machine.'
AS 8, 6 (June 1968), 465–488.
Subj 32

18275 CSU P P1 G1.2 1949–1972
Noumoff, S- J-.
'China's Cultural Revolution as a rectification movement.'
PA 40, 3/4 (Fall–Winter 1967/68), 221–234.
Subj 32 ▪ 64

18276 NNC P P4 G1.2 1949–1972
Ostroumov, Georgii Sergeevich.
'Demokraticheskie partii i bor'ba protiv burzhuaznoi ideologii v Kitae' (Democratic parties and the struggle against bourgeois ideology in China).
SK 1958, 4, 100–110.
Subj 16 32 32.1 64 ▪ 16.1 16.2

18277 MAM P P2 G1.2 1949–1972
Pak, Hyobom, 1926–.
The power structure of the Chinese Communist Party.
Ann Arbor: University Microfilms (Publ. 63-7229), 1963. 301 p. (Doctoral dissertation in Government, New York U.)
Subj 12 22 32 32.1 36.1 64 ▪ 15 16.1 18 22.2 32.2 53

18278 CSU S P1 G1.2 1949–1972
Ray, Dennis Michael, 1939–.
'The Mao-Liu conflict in bureaucratic perspective.'
China report (New Delhi) 5, 6 (Nov.–Dec. 1969), 25–27.
Subj 32 64

18279 NIC S P1 G1.2 1949–1972
Ribner, Susan Caroline, 1940–.
Political control in the Soviet Union and China: A case study of party criticism and self-criticism through party doctrine and contemporary fiction.
Unpublished masters thesis in Government, Cornell U., 1965. 183 p.
Subj 32 ▪ 16.1 32.1 63 64

18280 MCH P P2 G1.2 1949–1972
Scalapino, Robert Anthony, 1919–.
'Communist China: The first fourteen years.' In *Realities of world Communism*, edited by William Petersen. [Sole entry]
Englewood Cliffs, N. J.: Prentice-Hall, 1963, 123–163.
Subj 12.1 13 14.1 16.3 32 ▪ 15 34.1

18281 CSH FP P2 G1.2 1949–1972
Schurmann, Herbert Franz, 1926–.
'Party.' In *Ideology and organization in Communist China*, 2nd ed., enl., by H. F. Schurmann. [Analytic entry]
Berkeley, Los Angeles: U. of California Press, 1968, 105–172.
Subj 32 64 ▪ 16 32.1

18282 CSU P P1 G1.2 1949–1972
Schwartz, Benjamin Isadore, 1916–.
'The reign of virtue: Some broad perspectives on leader and party in the Cultural Revolution.' In *Party leadership and revolutionary power in China*, edited by John Wilson Lewis. [Analytic entry]
Cambridge: Cambridge U. Press, 1970, 149–169.
Subj 16.1 32 64

18283 NNC P P1 G1.2 1949–1972
Seymour, James Dulles, 1935–.
Communist China's bourgeois-democratic parties.
Unpublished masters thesis in Public Law and Government, Columbia U., 1960. 133 p.
Subj 32 ▪ 32.1

18284 CSH P P2 G1.3 1949–1972
Stanford U. China Project.
'Political dynamics.' In *Central South China*, compiled by the organization cited. [Selective entry]
New Haven: Human Relations Area Files, 1956, vol. 2, 442–494. (HRAF subcontractor's monographs, 28; Stanford 2)
Subj 32 32.1 ▪ 12 22 30 54

18285 CSH P P2 G1.3 1949–1972
Stanford U. China Project.
'Political dynamics.' In *East China*, compiled by the organization cited. [Selective entry]
New Haven: Human Relations Area Files, 1956, vol. 2, 489–546. (HRAF subcontractor's monographs, 29; Stanford 3)
Subj 32 32.1 ▪ 12 22 30 54

18286 CSH P P2 G5.0 1949–1972
Stanford U. China Project.
'Political dynamics.' In *North China*, compiled by the organization cited. [Selective entry]
New Haven: Human Relations Area Files, 1956, vol. 2, 478–535. (HRAF subcontractor's monographs, 27; Stanford 1)
Subj 32 32.1 ▪ 12 22 30 54

18287 NNC P P2 G8.0 1949–1972
Stanford U. China Project.
'Political dynamics.' In *Southwest China*, compiled by the organization cited. [Selective entry]
New Haven: Human Relations Area Files, 1956, vol. 2, 476–538. (HRAF subcontractor's monographs, 30; Stanford 4)
Subj 32 32.1 ▪ 12 22 30 54

18288 MCH P P1 G1.2 1949–1972
Steiner, Harold Arthur, 1905–.
'The role of the Chinese Communist Party.'
AAAPSS 277 (Sept. 1951), 56–66. [Special issue: *Report on China*, edited by Harold Arthur Steiner]
Subj 32 ▪ 12 16 32.1

18289 NNC P P7 G1.2 1949–1972
Stiebold, Annette E-.
National integration in Communist China and Guinea: A study of party organization and participation at the grass-roots level.
Unpublished masters thesis in Political Science, Columbia U., 1965. 80 p.
Subj 22.1 32 ▪ 22 24 26.3 61 64

18290 CSU P P2 G9.4 1949–1972
Tai, Hung-chao (Tai Hung-ch'ao), 1929–.
'The Kuomintang and modernization in Taiwan.' In *Authoritarian politics in modern society: The dynamics of*

established one-party systems, edited by Samuel Phillips Huntington and Clement Henry Moore. [Selective entry]
New York: Basic Books, 1970, 406–436.
SUBJ 12 22 32 ▪ 12.1 14 18 21 35

18291 CSH P P1 G1.2 1949–1972
Ting Kuang-hua.
'An analysis of Mao's "Party destruction," "Party rectification," and "Party building".'
CCA 6, 1 (Feb. 1969), 33–53.
SUBJ 32 ▪ 32.1

18292 CSH P P1 G1.2 1949–1972
Ting Wang, 1942–.
'A preliminary appraisal of the personnel of the new CCP Central Committee.' Tr. by Douglas G. Spelman of 'Chung kung chung yang wei yüan hui jen shih wen t'i ch'u t'an'; *Ming pao yüeh k'an* 4, 7 (July 1969), 21–30; 4, 8 (Aug. 1969), 22–30.
Chinese law and government 3, 2/3 (Summer–Fall 1970), 100–133.
SUBJ 16.1 32

18293 CSU P P2 G1.2 1949–1972
Townsend, James Roger, 1932–.
'Chinese Communism.' In *The new Communisms*, edited by Daniel Norman Jacobs. [Sole entry]
New York: Harper and Row, 1969, 131–158.
SUBJ 12 32 ▪ 14 16.1 32.1 34.1 64

18294 CSU S P1 G1.2 1949–1972
Townsend, James Roger, 1932–.
'Intraparty conflict in China: Disintegration in an established one-party system.' In *Authoritarian politics in modern society: The dynamics of established one-party systems*, edited by Samuel Phillips Huntington and Clement Henry Moore. [Selective entry]
New York: Basic Books, 1970, 284–310.
SUBJ 32 ▪ 12 12.1 16.1 32.1 64

18295 CSU P P3 G5.1 1949–1972
Tseng Yung-hsien.
'The Second Plenary Session of the CCP Ninth Central Committee.'
IS 7, 2 (Nov. 1970), 19–23.
SUBJ 32

18296 CSH U P1 G1.2 1949–1972
U.S. Congress. Senate. Committee on Government Operations. Subcommittee on National Policy Machinery.
National policy machinery in Communist China.
Washington, D.C.: U.S. Government Printing Office, 1959. 28 p.
SUBJ 12 32 ▪ 14 16.1

18297 CSU P P2 G9.4 1949–1972
Walker, Richard Louis, 1922–.
'Taiwan's development as Free China.'
AAAPSS 321 (Jan. 1959), 122–135. [Special issue: *Contemporary China and the Chinese*, edited by Howard Lyon Boorman]
SUBJ 14 32 ▪ 12 12.1 15 18 24.1

18298 CSH P P2 G1.2 1949–1972
Weggel, Oskar, 1935–.
Die Partei als Widersacher der Revolutionskomitees: Siegt Lenin oder Rosa Luxembourg in China? (The Party as opponent of the revolutionary committees: Did Lenin or Rosa Luxembourg win in China?).
Hamburg: Institut für Asienkunde, 1970. 152 p. (IA, Mitteilungen, 38)
SUBJ 12 16.1 32 ▪ 32.1 35 64

18299 CSH P P2 G1.1 1949–1972
Zanegin, Boris Nikolaevich, 1912–, Aleksandr Mironovich Mironov, and IAkov Mikhailovich Mikhailov.
K sobytiiam v Kitae, edited by Mikhail Iosifovich Sladkovskii.
Moscow: Politizdat, 1967. 72 p.
Developments in China, edited by M. Sladkovsky.
Moscow: Progress, 1968. 85 p.
SUBJ 14 32 64 ▪ 12.1 22.2 35 54

32.1 STATE OR PARTY CONTROL OF ORGANIZED GROUPS

政府或政黨對於組織團體之控制

政府又は政党による組織団体の統制

1644-1911

18300 MCH O P2 G8.2 1842–1895
Huot, A-, 182?–1864.
'Les partis en présence ou en guerre dans la province du Yun-nan' (Hostile and warring factions in Yunnan).
APF 28 (1856), 130–143.
SUBJ 25 32.1 33 ▪ 28 32.2 66

18301 CBU S P4 G1.1 1842–1895
Paulus, A-.
'Des associations et des corporations de l'Extrême-Orient comparées aux institutions similaires de l'empire romain d'Auguste à Justinien' (Associations and guilds of the Far East compared with similar institutions in the Roman Empire in the period from Augustus to Justinian).
B. de la Section des sciences économiques du Comité des travaux historiques et scientifiques 1892, 1, 116–134. [Separately reprinted—Paris: Ernest Leroux, 1893. 19 p.]
SUBJ 12.2 30 32.1 34.2 34.3 ▪ 16.2 23 33 41 57

1644-1949

□

1911-1949

18302 CSU O P2 G3.0 1928–1949
Bessac, Francis Bagnall, 1922–.
'Revolution and government in Inner Mongolia, 1945–1950.'
Papers of the Michigan Academy of Science, Arts, and Letters 50 (1965), 415–429.
SUBJ 32.1 66

18303 CSU P P2 G1.1 1911–1949
Gillin, Donald George, 1930–.
'Problems of centralization in Republican China: The case of Ch'en Ch'eng and the Kuomintang.'
JAS 29, 4 (Aug. 1970), 835–850.
SUBJ 15 32 32.1 59 ▪ 17 48 54 66

18304 CSH P P2 G1.2 1911–1949
Isaacs, Harold Robert, 1910–, ed.
'Five years of Kuomintang reaction.'
China forum 1, 11–13 (May 1932), 24 p. in all. [Special edition] [Separately reprinted—Shanghai: China Forum, 1932. 136 p.]
SUBJ 12.1 16 25 32 32.1 32.2 ▪ 12.2 14.5 14.6 15 18 22.1 36.1 36.3 36.4

18305 CSU P P7 G7.3 1928–1949
Kim, Ilpyong John (Kim Il-pyong), 1931–.
'Mass mobilization policies and techniques developed in the period of the Chinese Soviet Republic.' In *Chinese Communist politics in action*, edited by Arthur Doak Barnett. [Selective entry]
Seattle: U. of Washington Press, 1969, 78–98. (Social Science Research Council, Studies in Chinese government and politics, 1)
SUBJ 22.1 32.1 32.2 ▪ 22 24.1 26.3 36.3 64

18306 MCH O P2 G1.1 1911–1928
Malone, Cecil John L'Estrange, 1890–.
New China: Report of an investigation. Part 1, The political situation.
London: Independent Labour Party, 1926. 20 p.
SUBJ 32.1 32.2 ▪ 25 66

18307 CSU P P2 G1.4 1928–1949
Selden, Mark, 1938–.
'The Yenan legacy: The mass line.' In *Chinese Communist politics in action*, edited by Arthur Doak Barnett. [Selective entry]
Seattle: U. of Washington Press, 1969, 99–151. (Social Science Research Council, Studies in Chinese government and politics, 1)
SUBJ 12.1 32.1 32.2 64 ▪ 12 14.1 14.4 16.1 16.3 17 22 34.1

18308 CSH P P3 G1.1 1911–1928
Shabsin, IA-.
Belyi terror v Kitae (The White Terror in China).
Moscow: Izd-vo TsK MOPR SSSR, 1927. 53 p.
SUBJ 12.2 32.1 35 36.4 66 ▪ 16.2 16.4 32.2 54

18309 MSW S P3 G1.2 1911–1949
Steele, Allan Thomas, Jr.
Control of the gun: Civilian-military relations in the KMT, 1919–1929.
Unpublished masters thesis in Asian Studies, Washington U., 1971. 189 p.
SUBJ 15 32 32.1 35 ▪ 12 25

18310 CSU P P2 G1.2 1911–1928
Wilbur, Clarence Martin, 1908–, and Julie Lien-ying How (Hsia Lien-yin), 1926–.
'The Chinese Communist Party's policies in the mass movement, July, 1926.' In *Documents on Communism, nationalism, and Soviet advisers in China, 1918–1927*, edited by C. M. Wilbur and J. Lien-ying How. [Selective entry]
New York: Columbia U. Press, 1956, 282–287.
SUBJ 32.1 32.2 64 ▪ 36.2 36.3 36.4 47 54

1911-1972
(including 1644-1972)

18311 MMT PO P 1 G 1.2 1928–1972
Barnett, Arthur Doak, 1921–.
'Mass political organizations in Communist China.'
AAAPSS 277 (Sept. 1951), 76–88. [Special issue: *Report on China*, edited by Harold Arthur Steiner] [Reprinted as 'Mass political organization.' In *Communist China: The early years, 1949–55*, by A. D. Barnett. (Selective entry.) New York: Praeger, 1964, 29–44.]
SUBJ 30 32 32.1 ▪ 16 64

18312 GMS P P2 G 1.2 1911–1972
Domes, Jürgen Otto, 1932–.
Politik und Herrschaft in Rotchina (Politics and power in Red China).
Stuttgart: Kohlhammer, 1965. 183 p.
SUBJ 12 12.1 14 15 32 32.1 ▪ 19 22 32.2 34.1 54 64

18313 NIC P P3 G 5.1 1895–1972
Huang Chieh-shan, 1935–.
Political influences on the Ch'i-hsin Cement Company [Tangshan].
Unpublished masters thesis in Government, Cornell U., 1968. 113 p.
SUBJ 24.4 32.1 34.2 36.4 ▪ 24.2 26.4 30 32 32.2

18314 NNC P P4 G 9.5 1842–1972
Moseley, George Van Horn, III, 1931–.
'New China and old Macao.'
PA 32, 3 (Sept. 1959), 268–276.
SUBJ 24 32.1 ▪ 21.2 66

18315 NNC U P4 G 1.2 1911–1972
[Shen Tuan-hsien] Sia IAn' (Hsia Yen), pseud., 1900–.
'Rol' partiinogo rukovodstva v stanovlenii kitaiskogo kino' (The role of party leadership in the establishment of the Chinese cinema). In *Voprosy kul'turnoi revoliutsii v Kitaiskoi Narodnoi Respublike: sbornik statei* (Articles on the cultural revolution in the People's Republic of China), compiled by Institut kitaevedeniia, Akademiia nauk SSSR, edited by Nikolai Trofimovich Fedorenko. [Selective entry]
Moscow: Izd-vo vost. lit-ry, 1960, 291–301.
SUBJ 31 32.1 ▪ 36.1

1949-1972

18316 MCH P P1 G 1.2 1949–1972
'La "campagna di rettifica"' (The rectification campaign).
Nuovi argomenti 40 (settembre–ottobre 1959), 154–176.
SUBJ 32 32.1 ▪ 12.1 16 64

18317 NIC P P1 G 1.2 1949–1972
'Contradictions between party and armed forces within the Chinese Communist regime.'
Analysis of current Chinese Communist problems (Taipei) 1964 (Aug.), 1–18.
SUBJ 15 32.1 ▪ 12.1 25 64

18318 CSH O P8 G 4.1 1949–1972
Casella, Alexander.
'The Nanniwan May 7th Cadre School [in Nan-ni-wan village, Sian municipality].'
CQ 53 (Jan.–Mar. 1973), 153–157.
SUBJ 16.1 32.1 37

18319 MAM P P1 G 1.2 1949–1972
Chey, Myung, 1940–.
The dynamics of party and army in China: A study of institutions in conflict and consensus.
Ann Arbor: University Microfilms (Publ. 71-5067), 1971. 225 p. (Doctoral dissertation in Political Science, U. of Illinois, 1970)
SUBJ 15 32 32.1 ▪ 35 64

18320 CSU P P1 G 1.2 1949–1972
Chiu, S. M. (Chao Shan-ming), 1923–.
'The PLA and the Party: Recent developments.'
Military review 43, 6 (June 1963), 58–66. [Reprinted in *Government of Communist China*, edited by George P. Jan (Jan Po-kung). (Selective entry.) San Francisco: Chandler, 1966, 550–560.]
SUBJ 15 32.1 ▪ 30

18321 NIC O P3 G 6.2 1949–1972
Chung-ch'ung, pseud.
'For the whole party to run a newspaper is the basic policy on journalistic work.' Tr. of 'Ch'üan tang pan pao shih pao chih kung tso ti ken pen fang chen'; *Jen min jih pao* 12 June 1960, 11.
CB 630 (8 Aug. 1960), 19–28.
SUBJ 24.2 32.1 ▪ 34.2 64

18322 CSH O P7 G 8.3 1949–1972
Chung-kuo kung ch'an tang. Sui-yang hsien wei yüan hui. Hsüan ch'üan pu. (Chinese Communist Party. Sui-yang Hsien Committee. Publicity Dept.). [Sui-yang *hsien* is in Kweichow.]
'Political work in the co-ops.' Tr. of 'Ho tso she ti cheng chih kung tso' (Political work in the cooperatives); in *Chung-kuo nung ts'un ti she hui chu i kao ch'ao* (The socialist upsurge in rural China); Peking: Jen min ch'u pan she, 1956, vol. 3, 1134–1138. In *Socialist upsurge in China's countryside*, edited by Pan kung t'ing, Chung yang wei yüan hui, Chung-kuo kung ch'an tang (General Office, Central Committee, Chinese Communist Party). [Selective entry]
Peking: Foreign Languages Press, 1957, 328–335.
SUBJ 32.1 34.1 ▪ 22

18323 CSU P P2 G 1.2 1949–1972
Current Scene Editor.
'Mass factionalism in Communist China.'
CS 6, 8 (25 May 1968), 1–13.
SUBJ 32.1 ▪ 36.3 36.4 54

18324 CSH PO P2 G 1.2 1949–1972
Daubier, Jean.
Histoire de la Révolution culturelle prolétarienne en Chine (History of China's Cultural Revolution).
Paris: Maspéro, 1970. 306 p.
SUBJ 12 14.2 16.1 32 32.1 54 ▪ 15 16.3 16.4 17 19 36.4 61 64

18325 CSU P P1 G 1.2 1949–1972
Dick, Glenn G-.
'The general political department.' In *The military and political power of China in the 1970s*, edited by William Wallace Whitson. [Selective entry]
New York: Praeger, 1972, 171–183.
SUBJ 15 32.1 ▪ 32

18326 CSU P P1 G 1.2 1949–1972
Donnithorne, Audrey Gladys, 1922–.
'The internal development and external relations of China, with especial reference to the future of Sino-Soviet relations.'
Australian outlook 23, 2 (Aug. 1969), 144–157.
SUBJ 12 12.1 32.1 ▪ 14 14.3 14.6 35

18327 MCY S P2 G 1.2 1949–1972
Ecklund, George N-.
'Protracted expropriation of private business in Communist China.'
PA 36, 3 (Fall 1963), 238–249.
SUBJ 12.1 16.2 32.1 34.2 ▪ 14 14.5 22.1 24.3 26.2

18328 CSU P P1 G 1.2 1949–1972
Gittings, John, 1938–.
'The Cultural Revolution and the Chinese army: A study in escalation.'
World today 23, 4 (Apr. 1967), 166–176.
SUBJ 15 32.1 ▪ 32

18329 CSH P P3 G 5.1 1949–1972
Goldman, René, 1934–.
'The rectification campaign at Peking University, May–June 1957.'
CQ 12 (Oct.–Dec. 1962), 138–153. [For a fuller version, see entry 18330.] [Reprinted in *China under Mao: Politics takes command*, edited by Roderick Lemonde MacFarquhar. (Selective entry.) Cambridge: M.I.T. Press, 1966, 255–270.]
SUBJ 32 32.1 54 62 ▪ 26.1

18330 NNC PO P3 G 5.1 1949–1972
Goldman, René, 1934–.
The rectification campaign of May–June 1957 and the student movement at Peking University.
Unpublished masters thesis in History, Columbia U., 1962. 92 p.
SUBJ 26.1 32.1 54 ▪ 12.1 17

18331 CSU P P1 G 1.2 1949–1972
Halperin, Morton H-, 1938–, and John Wilson Lewis, 1930–.
'New tensions in army-party relations in China, 1965–1966.'
CQ 26 (Apr.–June 1966), 58–67.
SUBJ 15 32.1 ▪ 32

18332 CSH P P2 G 1.2 1949–1972
Hsiang Nai-kuang.
'The Chinese Young Communist League after the "Great Cultural Revolution".'
CCA 6, 2 (Apr. 1969), 29–41.
SUBJ 32.1 54 ▪ 16 21.2

18333 CSH O P3 G 8.1 1949–1972
Jen Pai-ko.
'To organize the economic life of the urban people is an important phase in the building of socialist new cities.' Tr. of 'Tsu chih ch'eng shih jen min ti ching chi sheng huo shih chien she she hui chu i hsin ch'eng shih ti i ko chung yao fang mien'; *Hung ch'i* 1960, 5 (1 Mar.), 35–43.
ECMM 205 (21 Mar. 1960), 5–16.
SUBJ 32.1 ▪ 24 28

18334 MCY P P1 G1.2 1949–1972
Joffe, Ellis, 1934–.
'The Communist Party and the army.' In *Contemporary China, 1959–1960,* edited by Edward Stuart Kirby. [Selective entry]
Hong Kong: Hong Kong U. Press, 1961, 55–69.
SUBJ 32 32.1 ▪ 15

18335 NNC O P2 G1.2 1949–1972
Kravchenko, A-.
'Liniia mass: zametki o partiinoi rabote v Kitae' (The mass line: Notes on party work in China).
Partiinaia zhizn' 1956, 22 (noiabr'), 43–53; 1956, 23 (dekabr'), 26–37; 1956, 24 (dekabr'), 18–29. [Separately reprinted—Moscow: Gospolitizdat, 1957. 104 p.]
SUBJ 22.1 32 32.1 ▪ 24.1 24.4 34.1 64

18336 MCH P P2 G1.2 1949–1972
[La Dany, Ladislao] ———, 1914–.
'Politics in business.'
CNA 581 (17 Sept. 1965), 1–7.
SUBJ 32.1 ▪ 12.2 14.3 35

18337 CSH P P1 G1.2 1949–1972
[La Dany, Ladislao] ———, 1914–.
'The post-Lin-Piao period. Part 4, The party and the army.'
CNA 873 (10 Mar. 1972), 1–7.
SUBJ 32.1 35 ▪ 32 64

18338 MCH P P7 G1.2 1949–1972
[La Dany, Ladislao] ———, 1914–.
'The purge. Part 1, Its general trend. Part 2, In the villages.'
CNA 506 (28 Feb. 1964), 1–7; 507 (6 Mar. 1964), 1–7.
SUBJ 19 32.1 34.1 ▪ 14.2 16.1 16.3 31

18339 MCH P P2 G1.2 1949–1972
Lee, Rensselaer Wright, III, 1937–.
'The hsia fang [downward-transfer] system: Marxism and modernization.'
CQ 28 (Oct.–Dec. 1966), 40–62.
SUBJ 12 16.1 21.2 32.1 64

18340 CSH P P2 G4.0 1949–1972
Lo, J. P. (Lo Jung-pang), 1912–.
'Political dynamics.' In *A regional handbook on Northwest China,* compiled by Far Eastern and Russian Institute, U. of Washington. [Selective entry]
New Haven: Human Relations Area Files, 1956, vol. 2, 483–531. (HRAF subcontractor's monographs, 59; Washington 5)
SUBJ 12 32 32.1 ▪ 12.1 16.1 30 34.1 66

18341 NNC P P3 G1.2 1949–1972
Newcomer, James Roger, 1935–.
On political control of the academies of science in the Soviet Union and China.
Unpublished masters thesis in Public Law and Government, Columbia U., 1964. 164 p.
SUBJ 32.1 36.1 ▪ 16.1 17 62

18342 MCY P P1 G1.2 1949–1972
Powell, Ralph Lorin, 1917–.
'The Military Affairs Committee and party control of the military in China.'
AS 3, 7 (July 1963), 347–356. [Reprinted as 'The structure of military decision-makers.' In *Chinese society under Communism: A reader,* edited by William Thomas Liu (Liu Jung). (Selective entry.) New York: Wiley, 1967, 154–163.]
SUBJ 15 32.1 ▪ 12 35 64

18343 CSH FP P2 G1.2 1949–1972
Schurmann, Herbert Franz, 1926–.
'Control.' In *Ideology and organization in Communist China,* 2nd ed., enl., by H. F. Schurmann. [Analytic entry]
Berkeley, Los Angeles: U. of California Press, 1968, 309–364.
SUBJ 12 12.1 14.6 32 32.1 ▪ 14 14.4

18344 DLC F P3 G5.1 1949–1972
Schurmann, Herbert Franz, 1926–.
'A student from Peking University.' In *The China reader, III, Communist China: Revolutionary reconstruction and international confrontation, 1949 to the present,* edited by H. F. Schurmann and Orville Schell. [Selective entry]
New York: Random House, 1967, 160–165.
SUBJ 17 32 32.1 ▪ 54 64

18345 NNC P P4 G1.2 1949–1972
[*Entry deleted.* In the final proofreading, after the automatic typesetting of the analytical indexes, it was discovered that the entry assigned this number duplicated a later entry in this section.]

18346 CSH P P2 G1.3 1949–1972
Stanford U. China Project.
'Subversive potentialities.' In *Central South China,* compiled by the organization cited. [Selective entry]
New Haven: Human Relations Area Files, 1956, vol. 2, 523–546. (HRAF subcontractor's monographs, 28; Stanford 2)
SUBJ 12.1 32.1 32.2 ▪ 12 15 22.2

18347 CSH P P2 G1.3 1949–1972
Stanford U. China Project.
'Subversive potentialities.' In *East China,* compiled by the organization cited. [Selective entry]
New Haven: Human Relations Area Files, 1956, vol. 2, 578–609. (HRAF subcontractor's monographs, 29; Stanford 3)
SUBJ 12.1 32.1 32.2 ▪ 12 15 22.2

18348 CSH P P2 G5.0 1949–1972
Stanford U. China Project.
'Subversive potentialities.' In *North China,* compiled by the organization cited. [Selective entry]
New Haven: Human Relations Area Files, 1956, vol. 2, 566–596. (HRAF subcontractor's monographs, 27; Stanford 1)
SUBJ 12.1 32.1 32.2 ▪ 12 15 22.2

18349 NNC P P2 G8.0 1949–1972
Stanford U. China Project.
'Subversive potentialities.' In *Southwest China,* compiled by the organization cited. [Selective entry]
New Haven: Human Relations Area Files, 1956, vol. 2, 565–605. (HRAF subcontractor's monographs, 30; Stanford 4)
SUBJ 12.1 32.1 32.2 ▪ 12 15 22.2

18350 NNC P P1 G1.2 1949–1972
Stavis, Benedict Rudy, 1941–.
Politics of science in Communist China.
Unpublished masters thesis in Political Science, Columbia U., 1966. 95 p.
SUBJ 17 32.1 36.1 ▪ 16.1 62

18351 MCH P P2 G1.2 1949–1972
Steiner, Harold Arthur, 1905–.
'Current "mass line" tactics in Communist China.'
APSR 45, 2 (June 1951), 422–436.
SUBJ 12 32.1 ▪ 12.1 22 22.1

18352 MCH P P1 G1.2 1949–1972
Steiner, Harold Arthur, 1905–.
'Ideology and politics in Communist China.'
AAAPSS 321 (Jan. 1959), 29–39. [Special issue: *Contemporary China and the Chinese,* edited by Howard Lyon Boorman]
SUBJ 32.1 64 ▪ 12.1 32 66

18353 CSH P P2 G1.2 1949–1972
Sung, Chao-sheng, 1935–.
'The parallel relationship between the PLA political campaign and the Socialist Education Movement, 1960–1966.'
Asian forum 2, 3 (July–Sept. 1970), 183–200.
SUBJ 15 32 32.1 64

18354 MCH O P3 G6.1 1949–1972
Taire, Lucian.
Shanghai episode: The end of Western commerce in Shanghai.
Hong Kong: Rainbow Press, 1957. 111 p.
SUBJ 12.2 32.1 34.2 66 ▪ 14.3 24 24.3 24.5 26.2 36.4 63

18355 NNC O P3 G5.1 1949–1972
Tang Chu-kuo (T'ang Chu-kuo).
The student anti-Communist movement in Peiping: A participant's report on the movement in May, 1957.
Taipei: Asian Peoples' Anti-Communist League, 1960. 41 p. (APACL pamphlets, 43)
SUBJ 32.1 32.2 54 ▪ 17 26.1

18356 CSH P P2 G2.0 1949–1972
Tang, Peter S. H. (T'ang Sheng-hao), 1919–.
'Subversive potentialities.' In *A regional handbook on Northeast China,* compiled by Far Eastern and Russian Institute, U. of Washington. [Selective entry]
New Haven: Human Relations Area Files, 1956, 426–437. (HRAF subcontractor's monographs, 61; Washington 9)
SUBJ 32.1 32.2 ▪ 15

18357 MCH P P3 G5.1 1949–1972
Trivière, Léon, 1915–.
'Hu Feng, *Le songe du pavillon rouge,* et la dispute des intellectuels à Pékin.'
B. d'information de la Commission internationale contre le régime concentrationnaire 1, 3 (mai–juil. 1955), 37–57.

'Hu Feng, *The dream of the red chamber* and the quarrel of the Peking intellectuals.'
Monthly information b. of the International Commission Against Concentration Camp Practices 1, 3 (May–July 1955), 38–58.
SUBJ 26.1 32.1 ▪ 36.1 64

18358 WSU F P2 G1.2 1949–1972
Vogel, Ezra Feivel, 1930–.
'Voluntarism and social control.' In *Soviet and Chinese Communism: Similarities and differences*, edited by Donald Warren Treadgold. [Selective entry]
Seattle: U. of Washington Press, 1967, 168–184.
Subj 12.1 32.1 63 ▪ 19 34.1 34.2

18359 CSU S P1 G1.2 1949–1972
Waller, Derek John, 1937–.
'China: Red or expert?'
Political q. 38, 2 (Apr.–June 1967), 122–131.
Subj 32.1 34.2 ▪ 15 32

18360 MCH P P2 G1.2 1949–1972
Wang Hsueh-wen (Wang Hsüeh-wen).
'An analysis of Peiping's "send-down" movement.'
IS 1, 6 (Mar. 1965), 58–68.
Subj 21.2 32.1 ▪ 12 32

18361 CSU P P2 G1.2 1949–1972
Wang Hsueh-wen (Wang Hsüeh-wen).
'New developments in Peiping's policy of "sending down" cadres.'
IS 5, 4 (Jan. 1969), 8–18.
Subj 32.1 ▪ 12 21.2 32

18362 NNC O P3 G5.1 1949–1972
[Yen Yün] Maria Yen (Yen Kuei-lai), 1928–.
The umbrella garden: A picture of student life in Red China. Tr. by Maria Yen and Richard M- McCarthy of *Hung ch'i hsia ti ta hsüeh sheng huo* (College life under the red flag); Hong Kong: Yu lien ch'u pan she, 1952; 94 p. [Rev. in tr.]
New York: Macmillan, 1954. 268 p.
Subj 17 32.1 54 ▪ 22.1 26.1 31 47 48 55 61

32.2 Anti-State Associations

反叛集團　反国家的な団体

1644-1911

18363 MCH O P2 G6.1 1842–1895
'Ein Besuch bei den Schangmaos, den chinesischen Rebellen' (A visit with the Ch'ang-mao [Taipings], Chinese rebels).
Das Ausland 34, 4 (20 Jan. 1861), 83–86; 34, 5 (27 Jan. 1861), 112–115.
Subj 25 32.2 64 ▪ 15 55

18364 ELB P P2 G1.3 1842–1895
The Chinese revolution [i.e., Taiping Rebellion]*: The causes which led to it, its rapid progress and anticipated result . . .*
London: Henry Vizetelly, 1853. 179 p.
Subj 14.5 32.2 66 ▪ 12 15 16.1 23

18365 MBA O P3 G8.2 1895–1911
'La révolution au Yunnan: notes journalières' (Daily notes on the Revolution [of 1911] in Yunnan).
RI nouvelle (2e) série 17, 3 (mars 1912), 269–303.
Subj 12 15 19 32.2 ▪ 14.6 57 64 66

18366 NNC P P2 G1.3 1644–1895
Anderson, Flavia Giffard, 1910–.
The rebel emperor [Hung Hsiu-ch'üan].
London: Gollancz, 1958. 356 p. [Reprinted—Garden City, N.Y.: Doubleday, 1959. 352 p.]
Subj 32.2 59 60 ▪ 12.1 15 25 46

18367 NNC U P2 G1.3 –1895
Balfour, Frederic Henry, 1846–1909.
'The secret societies in China.'
J. of the Manchester Geographical Society 7, 1/3 (Jan.–Mar 1891), 40–56.
Subj 32.2 ▪ 34.3 63

18368 DLC P P1 G1.1 1895–1911
Belov, Evgenii Aleksandrovich, 1929–.
'Sin'khaiskaia revoliutsiia i vopros bor'by s man'chzhurami' (The Revolution of 1911 and the question of the struggle against the Ch'ing). In *Man'chzhurskoe vladychestvo v Kitae* (Manchu rule in China), compiled by Institut narodov Azii, Akademiia nauk SSSR, edited by Sergei Leonidovich Tikhvinskii. [Selective entry]
Moscow: Nauka, Glav. red. vost. lit-ry, 1966, 363–374.
Subj 16 32.2 64 66 ▪ 12 12.2

18369 NNC P P1 G1.2 1895–1911
Belov, Evgenii Aleksandrovich, 1929–, and V- I- Danilov.
'Vliianie russkoi revoliutsii 1905–1907 gg. na Kitai' (The impact of the Russian Revolution of 1905–1907 on China).
SV 1955, 6, 14–28.
Subj 12 19 32.2 66 ▪ 12.1 16 64

18370 CSU P P2 G1.2 1895–1911
Bergère, Marie-Claire, 1933–.
'La marche à la révolution (1901–1911)' (The path to revolution, 1901–1911). In *De la guerre franco-chinoise à la fondation du Parti communiste chinois, 1885–1921* (From the Sino-French war to the formation of the Chinese Communist Party, 1885–1921), by Marianne Bastid, M.-C. Bergère, and Jean Chesneaux. [Analytic entry]
Paris: Hatier Université, 1972, 92–125. (HU, Collection d'histoire contemporaine, Histoire de la Chine, 2)
Subj 12 14.2 15 16 32.2 66 ▪ 14.4 14.6 17 32.1 36.3 54 59 64 72

18371 WSU P P2 G1.4 1895–1911
Black, Ruth Marie.
The Boxer uprising as reported by the U.S. consuls in China, 1897–1900.
Unpublished masters thesis in History, U. of Washington, 1961. 380 p.
Subj 32.2 66 ▪ 12.1 15 33

18372 MCH U P4 G4.2 1895–1911
Bonin, Charles Eudes, 1865–1929.
'Les mahométans du Kansou et leur dernière révolte' (The Muslims of Kansu and their latest revolt).
R. du monde musulman 10, 2 (fév. 1910), 210–233.
Subj 32.2 33 ▪ 21.1 25 66

18373 NNC S P1 G1.1 1895–1911
Borokh, Liliia Nikolaevna, 1933–.
'Iz istorii organizatsii "Soiuza vozrozhdeniia Kitaia"' (History of the organization of the Hsing-Chung Hui [Revive China Society]). In *Sin'khaiskaia revoliutsiia v Kitae: sbornik statei* (Articles on the Revolution of 1911 in China), compiled by Institut narodov Azii, Akademiia nauk SSSR. [Selective entry]
Moscow: Izd-vo vost. lit-ry, 1962, 121–143.
Subj 32.2 ▪ 62

18374 DLC P P2 G1.5 1895–1911
Borokh, Liliia Nikolaevna (Lilia N. Borokh), 1933–.
'Pervye kitaiskie revoliutsionery i tainye obshchestva' (The first Chinese revolutionaries and secret societies). In *Tainye obshchestva v starom Kitae* (Secret societies in old China), compiled by Institut vostokovedeniia, Akademiia nauk SSSR, edited by Vasilii Pavlovich Iliushechkin. [Selective entry]
Moscow: Nauka, Glav. red. vost. lit-ry, 1970, 108–122.

'Les débuts du mouvement républicain de Sun Yat-sen et les sociétés secrètes' (The beginnings of Sun Yat-sen's republican movement and the secret societies). In *Mouvements populaires et sociétés secrètes en Chine aux XIXe et XXe siècles* (Popular movements and secret societies in China in the nineteenth and twentieth centuries), edited by Jean Chesneaux, Feiling Blackburn Davis, and Nguyen Nguyet Ho. [Selective entry]
Paris: Maspero, 1970, 344–359.

'Notes on the early role of secret societies in Sun Yat-sen's republican movement' [rev. in tr.]. In *Popular movements and secret societies in China, 1840–1950*, edited by J. Chesneaux. [Analytic entry]
Stanford: Stanford U. Press, 1972, 135–144.
Subj 25 32.2 ▪ 64 65

18375 DLC P P2 G1.1 1842–1911
Borokh, Liliia Nikolaevna, 1933–.
Soiuz vozrozhdeniia Kitaia (The Hsing-Chung Hui [Revive China Society]).
Moscow: Nauka, Glav. red. vost. lit-ry, 1971. 203 p.
Subj 16.1 32.2 59 64 66 72 ▪ 12 15 18 54 70 71

18376 CBU P P2 G1.5 1842–1895
Brine, Lindesay.
The Taeping Rebellion in China: A narrative of its use and progress based upon original documents and information obtained in China.
London: Murray, 1862. 15, 394 p.
Subj 15 25 32.2 ▪ 12 17 60

18377 CSH O P2 G1.5 1842–1895
Broullion, Nicolas.
'Introduction' (Introduction). In *Missions de Chine: mémoire sur l'état actuel de la mission du Kiang-nan, 1842–1855* (Chinese missions: An account of the present state of the Kiangnan mission, 1842–1855), by N. Broullion. [Selective entry]
Paris: Julien, Lanier, 1855, 1–39.
Subj 32.2 33 ▪ 14.3 25

18378 NNC O P2 G1.2 1895–1911
Brown, Arthur Judson, 1856–1963.
The Chinese revolution.
New York: Student Volunteer Movement for Foreign Missions, 1912. 10, 217 p.
Subj 12 14 17 19 32.2 66 ▪ 12.2 13 15 18 22.2 33 47 60

18379 CSH PO P1 G1.1 1842–1895
Callery, Joseph Marie, 1810–1862, and Melchior Yvan, 1803–1873.
L'insurrection en Chine depuis son origine jusqu'à la prise de Nankin (The [Taiping] Rebellion in China from its origin to the capture of Nanking).
Paris: Lib. nouvelle, 1853. 274 p.
History of the insurrection in China, with notices of the Christianity, creed, and proclamations of the insurgents. Tr. by John Oxenford.
London: Smith, Elder, 1853. 328 p. [Reprinted—New York: Paragon, 1969. 301 p.]
SUBJ 32.2 ▪ 12 12.2 14.5 15 23 66

18380 MCH U P1 G1.2 1895–1911
Cerone, Francesco.
'Le associazioni lecite e le società segrete in Cina' (Lawful associations and secret societies in China).
Nuova antologia 172, 686 (16 luglio 1900), 249–272.
SUBJ 30 32.2 33 ▪ 38

18381 MCH P P2 G8.2 1842–1895
Chan, Wellington K. K. (Ch'en Chin-chiang), 1940–.
'Ma Ju-lung, from rebel to turncoat in the Yunnan Rebellion.'
PC 20 (Dec. 1966), 86–118.
SUBJ 12 25 32.2 ▪ 15 59

18382 NNC P P2 G1.3 1842–1895
Chekanov, Nikolai Konstantinovich, 1922–1961.
Vosstanie Nian'tsziunei v Kitae, 1853–1868 gg. (The Nien Rebellion in China, 1853–1868).
Moscow: Izd-vo vost. lit-ry, 1963. 169 p.
SUBJ 22.1 32.2 ▪ 15 16 36.3 66 70 71 72

18383 NIC P P1 G1.4 1895–1911
Ch'en, Jerome (Ch'en Chih-jang), 1919–.
'The nature and characteristics of the Boxer movement: A morphological study.'
BSOAS 23, 2 (June 1960), 287–308.
SUBJ 32.2 ▪ 23 65

18384 CSU P P1 G1.2 1644–1895
Ch'en, Jerome (Ch'en Chih-jang), 1919–.
'Rebels between rebellions: Secret societies in the novel *P'eng-kung an* [The cases of Judge P'eng].'
JAS 29, 4 (Aug. 1970), 807–822.
SUBJ 32.2 ▪ 14.2 22.2 25 63 66

18385 CSH U P1 G1.3 1644–1911
Ch'en, Jerome (Ch'en Chih-jang), 1919–.
'Secret societies.'
CSWT 1, 3 (Feb. 1966), 13–16.
SUBJ 32.2 ▪ 29

18386 MCH P P2 G1.5 1842–1895
Cheng, James Chester (Cheng Che-hsi), 1926–.
Chinese sources for the Taiping Rebellion, 1850–1864.
Hong Kong: Hong Kong U. Press; New York: Oxford U. Press, 1963. 12, 182 p. (Revision of doctoral dissertation in History, U. of Cambridge [Pembroke College], 1950)
SUBJ 32.2 72 ▪ 12 15 62 66

18387 MAM P P2 G1.2 1895–1911
Cheng, Ronald Y. L. (Cheng Yen-ling), 1933–.
A sociological analysis of the Chinese Revolution of 1911.
Ann Arbor: University Microfilms (Publ. 69-18,898), 1969. 270 p. (Doctoral dissertation in Sociology, U. of California, Berkeley)
SUBJ 12 12.1 14 16 32.2 64 ▪ 12.2 15 17 22 33 66

18388 MAM P P2 G1.1 1842–1911
Cheng, Shelley Hsien, 1924–.
The T'ung-meng-hui: Its organization, leadership and finances, 1905–1912.
Ann Arbor: University Microfilms (Publ. 62-6625), 1962. 391 p. (Doctoral dissertation in History, U. of Washington)
SUBJ 14.6 16.1 32.2 ▪ 15 16 16.3 19 25 32 64

18389 NNC P P1 G1.1 1895–1911
Chervova, Nonna Alekseevna.
'O karikature perioda Sin'khaiskoi revoliutsii' (A characterization of the period of the Revolution of 1911). In *Sin'khaiskaia revoliutsiia v Kitae: sbornik statei* (Articles on the Revolution of 1911 in China), compiled by Institut narodov Azii, Akademiia nauk SSSR. [Selective entry]
Moscow: Izd-vo vost. lit-ry, 1962, 302–316.
SUBJ 32.2 ▪ 64

18390 MCH P P2 G1.4 1842–1895
Chiang, Siang-tseh (Chiang Hsiang-tse), 1916–.
The Nien Rebellion.
Seattle: U. of Washington Press, 1954. 16, 159 p. (Revision of *The organization of the Nien Rebellion and the struggle between the Nien and the Loyalists, 1851–1868*, doctoral dissertation in History, U. of Washington, 1951)
SUBJ 15 22.2 25 32.2 ▪ 22.1 26.1 26.3 28 72

18391 MAM P P7 G1.2 –1911
Chu, Yung-deh Richard, 1931–.
An introductory study of the White Lotus Sect in Chinese history, with special reference to peasant movements.
Ann Arbor: University Microfilms (Publ. 67-14,032), 1967. 298 p. (Doctoral dissertation in History, Columbia U.)
SUBJ 32.2 33 36.3 ▪ 32.1 64

18392 DLC P P2 G6.3 1895–1911
Chudodeev, IUrii Vladimirovich, 1931–.
'Sviazi tainykh obshchestv s burzhuaznym revoliutsionnym dvizheniem v provintsii Chzhetszian nakanune Sin'khaiskoi revoliutsii' (Links between the secret societies and the bourgeois revolutionary movement in Chekiang on the eve of the Revolution of 1911). In *Tainye obshchestva v starom Kitae* (Secret societies in old China), compiled by Institut vostokovedeniia, Akademiia nauk SSSR, edited by Vasilii Pavlovich Iliushechkin. [Selective entry]
Moscow: Nauka, Glav. red. vost. lit-ry, 1970, 141–158.
SUBJ 26 32.2 64 ▪ 25 32.1 66 72

18393 MCH O P2 G6.0 1842–1895
Clavelin, *Père* ———.
'L'insurrection victorieuse dans la province du Kiangnan' (The [Taiping] Rebellion succeeds in Anhwei and Kiangsu).
APF 29 (1857), 379–384.
SUBJ 22 25 32.2

18394 MBA PO P2 G8.2 1842–1895
Cordier, Charles Georges, 1872–1936.
'Nouveaux documents sur la révolte musulmanne au Yunnan' (New documents on the Muslim rebellion in Yunnan).
RI nouvelle (2e) série 11, 7 (juil. 1909), 656–675.
SUBJ 22 25 32.2 ▪ 29 33

18395 CSU P P1 G1.2 1895–1911
Cordier, Henri, 1849–1925.
'La révolution en Chine: les origines' (The origins of the [Boxer] Uprising in China).
TP 2e série 1, 5 (déc. 1900), 407–450.
SUBJ 19 32.2 64 ▪ 12 66

18396 MCH S P2 G1.1 1644–1895
Cordier, Henri, 1849–1925.
'Les sociétés secrètes chinoises' (Chinese secret societies).
R. d'ethnographie 7, 1/2 (jan.–avr. 1888), 52–72.
SUBJ 32.2 39 ▪ 33 62 65

18397 MCH S P2 G1.2 1895–1911
Courant, Maurice Auguste Louis Marie, 1865–1935.
'Les débuts de la révolution dans les provinces chinoises' (The beginnings of the Revolution [of 1911] in the Chinese provinces).
R. des sciences politiques 3e série 29, 2 (mars–avr. 1913), 199–220.
SUBJ 32.2 ▪ 12.1 25

18398 MCH P P2 G5.1 1895–1911
Courant, Maurice Auguste Louis Marie, 1865–1935.
'La situation dans le nord de la Chine' (The situation in North China).
Annales des sciences politiques 15, 4 (juil. 1900), 523–539.
SUBJ 12 16.1 32.2 61 ▪ 15 18 41 66

18399 CSU PO P2 G1.3 1842–1895
Courcy, Marie René Roussel de, 1827–1908.
'L'insurrection chinoise: son origine et ses progrès. I, les sociétés secrètes et les premières campagnes des insurgés. II, triomphe de l'insurrection: le nouveau roi et sa doctrine' (The [Taiping] Rebellion in China: Its origins and progress. 1, Secret societies and the insurgents' first campaigns. 2, The rebellion succeeds: The new king and his doctrine).
R. des deux mondes 2e période 34 (1 juil. 1861), 5–35; 34 (15 juil. 1861), 312–360.
SUBJ 12 15 32.2

18400 CSU P P2 G1.5 1842–1895
Curwen, Charles Anthony, 1925–.
'Taiping relations with secret societies and with other rebels.' In *Popular movements and secret societies in China, 1840–1950*, edited by Jean Chesneaux. [Analytic entry]
Stanford: Stanford U. Press, 1972, 65–84.
SUBJ 25 32.2

18401 NNC P P2 G1.2 1895–1911
Danilov, V- I-.
'"Ob"edinennaia liga" v revoliutsii 1911 g.' (The T'ung-meng Hui in the Revolution of 1911).
SK 1958, 2, 39–56.
Subj 12 32.2 ▪ 22 64

18402 CSU P P1 G1.2 1895–1911
Darroch, J-.
'Current events as seen through the medium of the Chinese newspaper.'
CR 43, 1 (Jan. 1912), 23–33.
Subj 14.2 32.2 ▪ 16.1 64

18403 CSU O P2 G5.0 1895–1911
Davies, Llewellyn James.
'The Chinese "Boxers".'
NG 11, 7 (July 1900), 281–287.
Subj 32.2 66 ▪ 25

18404 CSU P P3 G6.1 1842–1895
Dillon, Maureen F-.
'The Triads in Shanghai: The Small Sword Society uprising, 1853–1855.'
PC 23 (July 1970), 67–86.
Subj 25 32.2 ▪ 22 22.1 64 66

18405 DLC S P2 G1.3 1644–1895
Dubinskii, Aleksandr Markovich.
Revoliutsionno-osvoboditel'naia bor'ba v Indii i Kitae v seredine 19 veka: lektsii VPSh pri TsK KPSS (The revolutionary liberation struggle in India and China in the mid-nineteenth century: Lectures delivered at the Higher Party School of the Central Committee of the Communist Party of the U.S.S.R.).
Moscow: ——, 1957. 43 p.
Subj 32.2 66 ▪ 14.1 14.3 22 33

18406 CSU P P1 G1.3 –1911
Dunstheimer, Guillaume Gustave Hubert, 1898–.
'Quelques aspects religieux des sociétés secrètes.' In *Mouvements populaires et sociétés secrètes en Chine aux XIXe et XXe siècles* (Popular movements and secret societies in China in the nineteenth and twentieth centuries), edited by Jean Chesneaux, Feiling Blackburn Davis, and Nguyen Nguyet Ho. [Selective entry]
Paris: Maspero, 1970, 65–73.

'Some religious aspects of secret societies' [rev. in tr.]. In *Popular movements and secret societies in China, 1840–1950*, edited by J. Chesneaux. [Analytic entry]
Stanford: Stanford U. Press, 1972, 23–28.
Subj 32.2 33 65

18407 MCH O P2 G1.1 1895–1911
Enjoy, Paul d', 1866–?
'Congrégations et sociétés secrètes chinoises' (Chinese brotherhoods and secret societies).
R. mondiale 63 (1er nov. 1904), 75–89.
Subj 30 32.1 32.2 38 ▪ 62 66

18408 CSH S P1 G1.2 1895–1911
Erenburg, Grigorii Borisovich, 1902–1967.
Revoliutsiia 1905–1907 godov v Rossii i revoliutsionnoe dvizhenie v Kitae (The Russian Revolution of 1905–1907 and the revolutionary movement in China).
Moscow: Znanie, 1955. 31 p.
Subj 32.2 ▪ 12 14 66

18409 CSH P P2 G1.1 1842–1911
[Fan' Ven'-lan'] Fan Wön-lan (Fan Wen-lan), 1893–1969.
Novaia istoriia Kitaia, tom I, 1840–1901 (Modern Chinese history, Vol. 1, 1840–1901). Tr. by Rudol'f Viatkin et al. of *Chung-kuo chin tai shih, shang pien, ti i fen ts'e* (Modern Chinese history, Vol. 1, Part 1), rev. ed.; Peking: Hsin Hua shu tien, 1949; 543 p.
Moscow: Izd-vo inostr. lit-ry, 1955. 600 p. [Tr. of later Chinese ed.—Peking: Jen min ch'u pan she, 1955.]

Neue Geschichte Chinas, Band 1, 1840–1901. Tr. by Lydia E- Behrsing.
Darmstadt: Fladung, 1958. 576 p.
Subj 10 15 16 32.2 66 ▪ 12 12.2 14.1 16.1 19 36.1

18410 CSU P P3 G6.1 1842–1895
Fass, Josef (Joseph Fass).
'L'insurrection du Xiaodaohui à Shanghai (1853–1855)' (The Small Sword Society uprising in Shanghai, 1853–1855). In *Mouvements populaires et sociétés secrètes en Chine aux XIXe et XXe siècles* (Popular movements and secret societies in China in the nineteenth and twentieth centuries), edited by Jean Chesneaux, Feiling Blackburn Davis, and Nguyen Nguyet Ho. [Selective entry]
Paris: Maspero, 1970, 178–195.
Subj 25 26.4 32.2 ▪ 64

18411 DLC P P3 G7.1 1895–1911
Fass, Josef.
'Revolutionary activity in the province Hu-pei and the Wu-chang Uprising of 1911.'
AO 28, 1 (1960), 127–149.
Subj 32.2 ▪ 15 22.1 25 54

18412 ACU FP P2 G1.5 1895–1911
Fung, Edmund S. K. (Feng Chao-chi), 1943–.
The Hupeh revolutionary movement, 1900–1912: A study of the role of the new-style army.
Unpublished doctoral dissertation in Far Eastern History, Australian National U., 1971. 376 p.
Subj 15 16 25 32.2 54 66 ▪ 12 14.4 16.1 17 59 64

18413 CSU P P2 G1.3 1895–1911
Fung, Edmund S. K. (Feng Chao-chi), 1943–.
'The T'ang Ts'ai-ch'ang revolt.'
Papers on Far Eastern history 1 (Mar. 1970), 70–114.
Subj 32.2 ▪ 59 64

18414 NNC S P1 G1.1 1895–1911
Garushiants, IUrii Misakovich.
'Klassy i klassovaia bor'ba v Sin'khaiskoi revoliutsii' (Classes and the class struggle in the Revolution of 1911). In *Sin'khaiskaia revoliutsiia v Kitae: sbornik statei* (Articles on the Revolution of 1911 in China), compiled by Institut narodov Azii, Akademiia nauk SSSR. [Selective entry]
Moscow: Izd-vo vost. lit-ry, 1962, 17–32.
Subj 16 32.2 ▪ 19 70

18415 CNY O P3 G9.3 1842–1895
Giles, Herbert Allen, 1875–1958.
Freemasonry in China.
Shanghai: ——, 1890. 38 p.
Subj 32.2 ▪ 65

18416 DLC P P4 G1.2 1895–1911
Grigor'ev, Aleksandr Mironovich, 1933–.
Antiimperialisticheskaia programma kitaiskikh burzhuaznykh revoliutsionerov, 1895–1905 (The anti-imperialist program of the Chinese bourgeois revolutionaries, 1895–1905).
Moscow: Nauka, 1966. 100 p.
Subj 32.2 66 ▪ 16.1 16.2 19 64

18417 NNC P P1 G1.1 1895–1911
Grigor'ev, Aleksandr Mironovich, 1933–.
'Sotsial'no-politicheskie idei Chzhan Tai-iania v period podgotovki Sin'khaiskoi revoliutsii' (The social and political ideas of Chang Ping-lin in the period of preparation for the Revolution of 1911). In *Sin'khaiskaia revoliutsiia v Kitae: sbornik statei* (Articles on the Revolution of 1911 in China), compiled by Institut narodov Azii, Akademiia nauk SSSR. [Selective entry]
Moscow: Izd-vo vost. lit-ry, 1962, 144–163.
Subj 32.2 64 ▪ 12.1

18418 CSU U P1 G1.1 –1842
Grousset, René, 1885–1952.
'Le drame de 1644.' In *Histoire de la Chine* (History of China), by R. Grousset. [Selective entry]
Paris: Fayard, 1943, 327–334.

'The drama of 1644.' Tr. by Anthony Watson-Gandy and Terence Gordon. In *The rise and splendour of the Chinese empire*, by R. Grousset. [Selective entry]
Berkeley, Los Angeles: U. of California Press, 1953, 272–278.
Subj 15 32.2 ▪ 25 66

18419 CSU P P1 G1.1 1644–1895
[Gützlaff, Karl Friedrich August] Charles Gutzlaff, 1803–1851.
'On the secret Triad Society of China, chiefly from papers belonging to the Society found at Hong Kong.'
JRAS 8 (1846), 361–367.
Subj 32.2

18420 MCH S P4 G5.3 1644–1842
Gulik, Robert Hans van, 1910–.
'Wang Loen' (Wang Lun).
China (Amsterdam) 5 (December 1930), 268–275.
Subj 32.2 60 ▪ 33

18421 NNC P P2 G1.5 1644–1895
Hail, William James, 1877–.
Tseng Kuo-fan and the Taiping Rebellion, with a short sketch of his later career.
New Haven: Yale U. Press, 1927. 17, 422 p. (Yale historical publications, miscellany, 18) [Reprinted—New York: Paragon, 1964. 17, 422 p.]
Subj 12 13 15 32.2 59 ▪ 12.1 12.2 14 16.1 25 29 41 47 65 72

18422 MCH O P3 G5.1 1895–1911
Hart, Robert, 1835–1911.
'These from the land of Sinim': Essays on the Chinese question, 2nd ed.
London: Chapman and Hall, 1903. 302 p.
Subj 25 32.2 66 ▪ 12 14.5 15

18423 NIC PO P 2 G 1.1 1644–1911
[Hirayama Shū] ———, 1870–1940.
'Chinese secret societies.' Tr. by James Hutson from *Chung-kuo mi mi she hui shih* (History of Chinese secret societies); Shanghai: Shang wu yin shu kuan, 1912. [Greatly condensed in tr.]
CJ 9, 4 (Oct. 1928), 164–170; 9, 5 (Nov. 1928), 215–221; 9, 6 (Dec. 1928), 276–282; 10, 1 (Jan. 1929), 12–16.
Subj 32.2

18424 MCH P P 1 G 1.1 1644–1842
Hoffmann, Johann Joseph, 1805–1878.
'Bijdragen tot de kennis der geheime genootschappen van de Chinezen, bepaaldelijk het T'ien-Tí-Hoeí' (Contributions to the knowledge of Chinese secret societies, specifically the Heaven and Earth Society).
BTLV 2 (1854), 292–329.
Subj 32.2 ▪ 65

18425 MCH P P 1 G 1.3 1644–1842
Hoffmann, Johann Joseph, 1805–1878.
'Het Hemel-Aarde-Verbond, het T'ien-Tí-Hoeí, een geheim genootschap in China en onder de Chineezen in Indië' (The Heaven and Earth Society, a secret society in China and among the Chinese in Indonesia).
BTLV 1 (1853), 260–290.
Subj 32.2 ▪ 32.1 66 71

18426 CSU P P 2 G 1.3 1644–1895
[Hoffmann, Johann Joseph] ———, 1805–1878.
'Oath taken by members of the Triad Society, and notices of its origin.'
Chinese repository 18, 6 (June 1849), 281–295.
Subj 32.2

18427 CSU P P 5 G 9.0 1644–1911
Hsieh, Winston (Hsieh Wen-sun), 1935–.
'Triads, salt smugglers, and local uprisings: Observations on the social and economic background of the Waichow revolution of 1911.' In *Popular movements and secret societies in China, 1840–1950*, edited by Jean Chesneaux. [Analytic entry]
Stanford: Stanford U. Press, 1972, 145–164.
Subj 25 32.2 ▪ 14.3 24.5

18428 MCH P P 3 G 9.2 1842–1895
Huang, Yen-yü, 1903–.
Viceroy Yeh Ming-ch'en and the Canton episode, 1856–1861.
Unpublished doctoral dissertation in Far Eastern Languages, Harvard U., 1940. 215 p.
Subj 32.2 59 66 ▪ 12 22

18429 DLC P P 2 G 1.2 1842–1895
Iliushechkin, Vasilii Pavlovich, 1915–.
'Antiman'chzhurskaia napravlennost' krest'ianskoi voiny taipinov' (The anti-Manchu tendency of the Taiping Rebellion). In *Man'chzhurskoe vladychestvo v Kitae* (Manchu rule in China), compiled by Institut narodov Azii, Akademiia nauk SSSR, edited by Sergei Leonidovich Tikhvinskii. [Selective entry]
Moscow: Nauka, Glav. red. vost. lit-ry, 1966, 289–306.
Subj 15 16.3 32.2 64 66 ▪ 16 18 19

18430 CSH P P 2 G 1.2 1842–1895
Iliushechkin, Vasilii Pavlovich, 1915–.
Krest'ianskaia voina taipinov (The Taiping Rebellion).
Moscow: Nauka, Glav. red. vost. lit-ry, 1967. 394 p.
Subj 12 14 15 32.2 64 66 ▪ 12.1 13 16 18 36.3 72

18431 DLC P P 7 G 1.3 1842–1895
Iliushechkin, Vasilii Pavlovich (Vassili Iliouchetchkine), 1915–.
'Tainye obshchestva i ereticheskie sekty v Kitae v seredine XIX v.' (Secret societies and heretical sects in China in the mid-nineteenth century). In *Tainye obshchestva v starom Kitae* (Secret societies in old China), compiled by Institut vostokovedeniia, Akademiia nauk SSSR, edited by V. P. Iliushechkin. [Selective entry]
Moscow: Nauka, Glav. red. vost. lit-ry, 1970, 54–68.

'Les sociétés secrètes et les sectes hérétiques en Chine au milieu du XIXe siècle' [rev. in tr.]. In *Mouvements populaires et sociétés secrètes en Chine aux XIXe et XXe siècles* (Popular movements and secret societies in China in the nineteenth and twentieth centuries), edited by Jean Chesneaux, Feiling Blackburn Davis, and Nguyen Nguyet Ho. [Selective entry]
Paris: Maspero, 1970, 117–132.
Subj 16.3 32.2 ▪ 16

18432 CSU P P 1 G 1.3 1842–1895
Jen Yu-wen (Chien Yu-wen), 1896–.
'New sidelights on the Taiping Rebellion.'
THM 1, 4 (Nov. 1935), 361–373.
Subj 32.2 ▪ 12 62

18433 DLC P P 2 G 1.4 1895–1911
Kaliuzhnaia, N- M-.
'O kharaktere tainogo soiuza "Ikhetuan"' (The nature of the Boxers). In *Tainye obshchestva v starom Kitae* (Secret societies in old China), compiled by Institut vostokovedeniia, Akademiia nauk SSSR, edited by Vasilii Pavlovich Iliushechkin. [Selective entry]
Moscow: Nauka, Glav. red. vost. lit-ry, 1970, 85–107.
Subj 16 32.2 60 66 ▪ 32.1 35 54 72

18434 NNC P P 1 G 5.3 1842–1911
Kaliuzhnaia, N- M-.
'Vosstanie "Bol'shikh mechei" v Shan'dune v 1896 g.' (The Big Sword Society uprising of 1896 in Shantung).
KSINA 85 (1964), 60–71.
Subj 22.1 22.2 25 32.2 ▪ 66

18435 MCH O P 2 G 1.2 1895–1911
Khorat, Pierre.
'Psychologie de la révolution chinoise' (The psychology of the Chinese Revolution [of 1911]).
R. des deux mondes 6e période 8 (15 mars 1912), 295–330.
Subj 12 16.1 32.2 61 ▪ 15 16.4 25 66

18436 DLC P P 2 G 1.3 1895–1911
Kostiaeva, Aleksandra Sergeevna, 1932–.
Narodnye dvizheniia v Kitae v 1901–1911 gg. (Popular movements in China, 1901–1911).
Moscow: Nauka, Glav. red. vost. lit-ry, 1970. 151 p.
Subj 14.5 16 32.1 32.2 66 72 ▪ 12 14.1 18 33 35 36.3 38 64

18437 DLC P P 2 G 1.3 1895–1911
Kostiaeva, Aleksandra Sergeevna, 1932–.
'Tainye soiuzy nakanune Sin'khaiskoi revoliutsii' (Secret societies on the eve of the Revolution of 1911). In *Tainye obshchestva v starom Kitae* (Secret societies in old China), compiled by Institut vostokovedeniia, Akademiia nauk SSSR, edited by Vasilii Pavlovich Iliushechkin. [Selective entry]
Moscow: Nauka, Glav. red. vost. lit-ry, 1970, 123–140.
Subj 26 26.3 32.2 64 ▪ 32.1 38 72

18438 CBU P P 2 G 9.0 1842–1895
Laai, Yi-faai (Lai I-hui), 1906–.
The part played by the pirates of Kwangtung and Kwangsi provinces in the Taiping insurrection.
Unpublished doctoral dissertation in History, U. of California, Berkeley, 1950. 360 p.
Subj 14.3 21.2 25 32.2 ▪ 15 21 21.4 22.1 26.1 29 33 42 66 72

18439 MCH O P 1 G 1.2 1895–1911
Labadie-Lagrave, G-.
'Les sociétés secrètes en Chine' (Secret societies in China).
A travers le monde 6, 28 (7 juil. 1900), 222–223; 6, 29 (21 juil. 1900), 230.
Subj 32.2 ▪ 33

18440 CSU P P 1 G 9.4 1842–1895
Lamley, Harry Jerome, 1928–.
'The 1895 Taiwan republic.'
JAS 27, 4 (Aug. 1968), 739–762.
Subj 25 32.2 ▪ 16.1 22.2 66

18441 MCH PO P 2 G 1.3 1842–1895
Leboucq, Prosper, 1828–1905.
'Les sociétés secrètes en Chine' (Secret societies in China).
Etudes religieuses 5e série 8 (août 1875), 197–220.
Subj 12 15 32.2 ▪ 33 47 52

18442 CSU P P 4 G 1.1 1895–1911
Lee, Ta-ling (Li Ta-ling), 1934–.
Foundations of the Chinese Revolution, 1905–1912: An historical record of the T'ung-meng Hui.
New York: St. John's U. Press, 1970. 264 p. (Revision of *T'ung-meng Hui and the Chinese revolution, 1905–1912,* doctoral dissertation in History, New York U., 1967)
Subj 32.2 ▪ 15 25 59 64

18443 DLC S P 2 G 1.1 1644–1911
Lennhoff, Eugen, 1891–.
'Zweihundertfünfzig Jahre gegen eine Dynastie: Die Hung-Gesellschaft in China' (Two hundred fifty years against a dynasty: The Triad Society in China). In *Politische Geheimbünde im Völkergeschehen* (Political secret societies in international relations), by E. Lennhoff. [Sole entry]
Berlin: Zsolnay, 1932, 391–455.
Subj 32.2 66 ▪ 12.1

18444 MCH O P2 G5.0 1895–1911
Leroy, Henri Joseph.
'Les causes de l'insurrection en Chine' (The causes of the [Boxer] Uprising in China).
Etudes 7e série 84, 2 (20 juil. 1900), 145–159.
SUBJ 24 28 32.2 ▪ 66

18445 CSU P P2 G1.3 1842–1911
Lewis, Charlton Miner, III, 1930–.
'Some notes on the Kao-lao Hui in late Ch'ing China.' In *Popular movements and secret societies in China, 1840–1950*, edited by Jean Chesneaux. [Analytic entry]
Stanford: Stanford U. Press, 1972, 97–112.
SUBJ 25 32.2 ▪ 15 31

18446 CSU P P1 G1.2 1842–1895
Lewis, Jenny.
'The Gordon papers.'
British Museum q. 28 (1964), 75–81.
SUBJ 15 32.2

18447 CBU O P2 G1.5 1842–1895
[Li Hsiu-ch'eng] ———, ?–1864.
The autobiography of the Chung-wang. Tr. by Walter T- Lay from *Li Hsiu-ch'eng kung chuang* (Autobiography of Li Hsiu-ch'eng). [*Li Hsiu-ch'eng kung chuang*, Li's account of the Taiping Rebellion, was written in 1864 on the order of Tseng Kuo-fan.]
Shanghai: Presbyterian Mission Press, 1865. 104 p. [Reprinted—New York: Praeger, 1970. 104 p.]
SUBJ 32.2 59 ▪ 15 23 28

18448 CSH PO P4 G1.3 1895–1911
Liang, Chin-tung (Liang Ching-tun), 1890–.
The Chinese Revolution of 1911.
Jamaica, N.Y.: St. John's U. Press, 1962. 59 p.
SUBJ 16.1 32.2 ▪ 12 15

18449 MCH O P2 G1.5 1842–1895
[Lindley, Augustus F-] Lin-Le.
Ti-ping tien-kwoh: The history of the Ti-ping Revolution, including a narrative of the author's personal adventures.
London: Day, 1866. 2 vols. 17, 842 p. [c.p.]. [Reprinted—New York: Praeger, 1970. 17, 842 p.]
SUBJ 32.2 62 ▪ 12 14.3 15 18 22 33 41 42 47 66

18450 GMS P P2 G1.1 1895–1911
Ling, Pyau (Lin Piao), 1888–.
Die chinesische Revolution (The Chinese Revolution [of 1911]).
Berlin: The author, 1916. 13, 157 p. (Doctoral dissertation, Rechts- und staatswissenschaftliche Fakultät, Universität Würzburg)
SUBJ 12 14.5 32.2 ▪ 19 66

18451 CSU S P2 G1.3 1842–1895
Lo, H. M. (Lo Hui-min), 1924–.
Review of *The Taiping Rebellion: History and documents. Vol. 1, History*, by Franz Henry Michael and Chung-li Chang.
MS 25 (1966), 440–445.
SUBJ 16.3 32.2 64

18452 CSU P P2 G1.2 1895–1911
Lust, John, 1918–.
'Secret societies, popular movements, and the 1911 Revolution.' In *Popular movements and secret societies in China, 1840–1950*, edited by Jean Chesneaux. [Analytic entry]
Stanford: Stanford U. Press, 1972, 165–200.
SUBJ 16 25 32.2 ▪ 12 14.3 15 18 36.3 65 66

18453 MCH P P3 G6.1 1895–1911
Lust, John, 1918–.
'The Su-pao case: An episode in the early Chinese nationalist movement.'
BSOAS 27, 2 (June 1964), 408–429.
SUBJ 22.2 32.2 54 66 ▪ 24.2 32.1

18454 CSU PO P2 G1.2 1895–1911
McCormick, Frederick, 1870–1951.
The flowery republic.
New York: Appleton, 1913. 17, 447 p.
SUBJ 12 25 32.2 ▪ 15 59 66

18455 CSH S P2 G1.5 1842–1895
MacFarlane, Charles, 1799–1858.
The Chinese revolution [i.e., the Taiping Rebellion].
London: Routledge, 1853. 243 p.
SUBJ 25 32.2 ▪ 12 22.2 23 26.3 66

18456 MCH O P7 G5.1 1895–1911
Mangin, Ignace.
'Les Boxeurs dans le Tché-li sud-est' (The Boxers in southeastern Chihli).
Etudes 7e série 84, 3 (5 août 1900), 366–398; 84, 6 (20 sept. 1900), 836–840; 85, 4 (20 nov. 1900), 544–556.
SUBJ 22.2 25 32.2 ▪ 22 65 66

18457 MCH P P1 G1.2 1895–1911
Maybon, Albert, 1878–.
La politique chinoise: étude sur les doctrines des partis en Chine, 1898–1908 (Chinese politics: A study of party doctrines in China, 1898–1908).
Paris: Giard et Brière, 1908. 268 p.
SUBJ 32 32.2 64 ▪ 12 32.1

18458 MCH P P1 G1.2 1895–1911
Maybon, Albert, 1878–.
La République chinoise (The Republic of China).
Paris: Armand Colin, 1914. 19, 268 p.
SUBJ 12 32.2 ▪ 12.1 16.1 16.2

18459 NIC O P2 G1.5 1644–1895
Meadows, Thomas Taylor.
The Chinese and their rebellions, viewed in connection with their national philosophy, ethics, legislation and administration . . .
London: Smith, Elder, 1856. 60, 656 p. [Reprinted—Stanford: Academic Reprints, 1953. 60, 656 p.]
SUBJ 12.1 32.2 60 66 ▪ 12 12.2 15 17 22.2 25 47 50 62 64

18460 MCH P P2 G1.2 1842–1895
Michael, Franz Henry, 1907–.
'Revolution and renaissance in nineteenth century China: The age of Tseng Kuo-fan.'
PHR 16, 2 (May 1947), 144–151.
SUBJ 32.2 64 ▪ 15 16.1 19

18461 MCH P P2 G1.3 1842–1895
Michael, Franz Henry, 1907–, and Chung-li Chang, 1919–.
The Taiping Rebellion: History and documents. Vol. 1, History.
Seattle: U. of Washington Press, 1966. 12, 244 p.
SUBJ 12 15 25 32.2 63 64 ▪ 11 12.1 14.1 14.5 16.1 16.3 22 46 59 66

18462 MCH U P1 G1.3 –1842
Milne, William Charles, 1785–1822.
'Some account of a secret association in China, entitled the Triad Society.'
Transactions of the Royal Asiatic Society of Great Britain and Ireland 1 (1827), 240–250.
SUBJ 32.2

18463 CSU P P2 G1.5 1842–1895
Miyazaki Ichisada, 1901–.
'The nature of Taiping Rebellion.' Tr. from the Japanese by Charles A- Peterson.
Acta Asiatica (Tokyo) 8 (Mar. 1965), 1–39. [See Vol. 3 of this *Bibliography* for Japanese version.]
SUBJ 14.3 15 25 32.2 36.3 ▪ 11.4 16 47 70

18464 CSU P P3 G6.1 1644–1895
Montalto de Jesus, C- A-.
Historic Shanghai.
Shanghai: Shanghai Mercury, 1909. 28, 257 p.
SUBJ 25 32.2 66 ▪ 21.1 22 22.2 24.5

18465 CSU O P3 G6.3 1842–1895
Moule, Arthur Evans, 1836–1918.
'Ningpo under the Taipings, 1861–1863.'
EAM 5 (1906), 1–15, 114–131.
SUBJ 25 32.2 ▪ 21.3 22.1 66

18466 MCH O P2 G6.0 1842–1895
Moule, Arthur Evans, 1836–1918.
Personal recollections of the T'ai-p'ing Rebellion, 1861–1863.
Shanghai: Shanghai Mercury Office, 1898. 28 p.
SUBJ 32.2 ▪ 12 15 16.1 25 62

18467 MCH O P3 G5.1 1895–1911
Mury, Francis.
'Les sociétés secrètes et le gouvernement chinois' (Secret societies and the Chinese government).
R. des revues 34, 14 (15 juil. 1900), 117–134.
SUBJ 12 16.1 32.1 32.2 ▪ 63

18468 NNC PO P1 G1.1 –1842
Newbold, T- J-, and F- W- Wilson.
'The Chinese secret Triad Society of the Tien-ti-huih.'
JRAS 6 (1841), 120–158.
SUBJ 12.1 32.2 ▪ 22.2 62 65

18469 NNC P P1 G1.2 1842–1911
Nikiforov, Vladimir Nikolaevich, 1920–.
'O dvukh istokakh burzhuazno-revoliutsionnogo dvizheniia v Kitae, po vospominaniiam Chen' Shao-bo' (Two sources of the bourgeois revolutionary movement in China, based on the reminiscences of Ch'en Shao-po).
KSINA 64 (1963), 90–101.
SUBJ 32 32.2 64

18470 DLC P P2 G1.1 1644–1842
Novikov, Boris M-.
'Vosstanie 1787–1788 gg. na Taivane' (The uprising of 1787–1788 in Taiwan). In *Man'chzhurskoe vladychestvo v Kitae* (Manchu rule in China), compiled by Institut narodov Azii, Akademiia nauk

SSSR, edited by Sergei Leonidovich Tikhvinskii. [Selective entry]
Moscow: Nauka, Glav. red. vost. lit-ry, 1966, 197–218.
Subj 12.1 15 32.2 ▪ 14.3 14.5 21.2 24.1 64 66

18471 NNC S P1 G1.5 1842–1895
Oehler, Wilhelm, 1877–.
'Die T'aiping Bewegung: Geschichte eines chinesisch-christlichen Gottesreiches' (The Taiping movement: History of a Chinese-Christian theocracy).
Beiträge zur Förderung christlicher Theologie 28 (1923), 69–244.
Subj 23 32.2 62 ▪ 12 13 15 25 33 64 66

18472 CSU P P4 G1.3 1895–1911
Onogawa, Hidemi, 1909–.
'Liu Shih-p'ei and anarchism.' Tr. of 'Ryū Shibai to museifushugi'; *Tōhō gakuhō* (Kyoto) 36 (Oct. 1964), 695–720. [Tr. inferred]
Acta Asiatica (Tokyo) 12 (Mar. 1967), 70–99.
Subj 16.1 32.2 64 ▪ 14.2 59

18473 MCH O P3 G6.1 1842–1895
Palatre, Gabriel, 1830–1878.
'La magie et le nénuphar blanc au Kiang-nan' (Magic and the White Lotus Society in southern Kiangsu).
Missions catholiques 10 (13 sept. 1878), 434–441, 446–450, 458–465.
Subj 23 32.2 ▪ 33

18474 NIC P P1 G1.3 –1842
Parsons, James Bunyan, 1921–.
'A case history of revolt in China: The late Ming rebellion of Chang Hsien-chung.'
OE 3, 1 (Juli 1956), 81–93.
Subj 32.2

18475 NNC P P2 G8.1 1644–1842
Parsons, James Bunyan, 1921–.
'The culmination of a Chinese peasant rebellion: Chang Hsien-chung in Szechwan, 1644–46.'
JAS 16, 3 (May 1957), 387–400.
Subj 32.2 ▪ 12 15 25

18476 NIC S P1 G1.2 –1842
Parsons, James Bunyan, 1921–.
'Overtones of religion and superstition in the rebellion of Chang Hsien-chung.'
Sinologica 4, 3 (1955), 170–177.
Subj 15 32.2 62 65 ▪ 23

18477 NNC S P2 G1.2 1644–1842
Porshneva, E- B-.
'Narodnoe vosstanie 1796–1803 gg.' (The popular uprising [White Lotus Rebellion] of 1796–1803).
KSINA 53 (1962), 78–94.
Subj 12.1 32.2 ▪ 15 36.3

18478 DLC S P1 G1.1 1644–1842
Porshneva, E- B-.
'Pod"em antiman'chzhurskogo dvizheniia v Kitae pod rukovodstvom tainykh obshchestv (konets XVIII – nachalo XIX v.)' (The upsurge of the anti-Manchu movement in China led by the secret societies from the late eighteenth to the early nineteenth century). In *Man'chzhurskoe vladychestvo v Kitae* (Manchu rule in China), compiled by Institut narodov Azii, Akademiia nauk SSSR, edited by Sergei Leonidovich Tikhvinskii. [Selective entry]
Moscow: Nauka, Glav. red. vost. lit-ry, 1966, 219–233.
Subj 32.2 64 ▪ 15 23 63 66

18479 MCH O P2 G1.2 1895–1911
Pouvourville, Eugène-Albert Puyon de.
'La révolution et les sociétés secrètes en Chine' (The Revolution [of 1911] and secret societies in China).
R. de Paris 19, 5 (1 mars 1912), 119–132.
Subj 32.1 32.2 63 ▪ 11 12.1 14.1 30

18480 FPN P P2 G1.1 –1911
[Pouvourville, Eugène-Albert Puyon de] Matgioï, pseud.
Le taoïsme et les sociétés secrètes chinoises (Taoism and Chinese secret societies).
Paris: Chamuel, 1897. 32 p.
Subj 32.2 33 62 ▪ 64

18481 MCH U P3 G1.3 1895–1911
Pozdneev, Dmitrii Matveevich, 1865–1942.
'Iz istorii revoliutsionnogo dvizheniia v Kitae' (History of the revolutionary movement in China).
NV 2 (1922), 331–340.
Subj 32.2 47

18482 MCH U P2 G1.3 1842–1895
Pozdneev, Dmitrii Matveevich, 1865–1942.
'Taipinskoe vosstanie v Kitae' (The Taiping Rebellion in China).
Zhurnal Ministerstva narodnago prosveshcheniia unnumbered (iiul' 1898), 17–41.
Subj 32.2 64 ▪ 16.3 66

18483 CSH P P2 G9.3 1895–1911
Prisco, Salvatore, III.
'The Vegetarian Society and the Huashan-Kut'ien massacre of 1895.'
Asian forum 3, 1 (Jan.–Mar. 1971), 1–13.
Subj 32.2 66 ▪ 12 25 33

18484 CSH P P1 G1.2 1895–1911
Purcell, Victor William Williams Saunders, 1896–1965.
The Boxer uprising: A background study.
Cambridge: Cambridge U. Press, 1963. 348 p.
Subj 32.2 66

18485 FPN P P4 G1.5 1842–1895
Puyraimond, Guy.
Les événements anti-étrangers du Yangzi, mai–septembre 1891 (Anti-foreign incidents in the Yangtze valley, May–September 1891).
Unpublished doctoral dissertation, Faculté des lettres, Université de Paris, 1969. 2 vols. s.p.
Subj 32.2 66 ▪ 16.1

18486 CSU P P2 G1.5 1842–1895
Puyraimond, Guy.
'Le Gelaohui et les incidents anti-étrangers de 1891.' In *Mouvements populaires et sociétés secrètes en Chine aux XIXe et XXe siècles* (Popular movements and secret societies in China in the nineteenth and twentieth centuries), edited by Jean Chesneaux, Feiling Blackburn Davis, and Nguyen Nguyet Ho. [Selective entry]
Paris: Maspero, 1970, 282–296.
'The Ko-lao Hui and the anti-foreign incidents of 1891' [rev. in tr.]. In *Popular movements and secret societies in China, 1840–1950*, edited by J. Chesneaux. [Analytic entry]
Stanford: Stanford U. Press, 1972, 113–124.
Subj 32.2 66 ▪ 22.2 35

18487 MCH P P2 G6.0 1895–1911
Rankin, Mary Louise Backus, 1934–.
Early Chinese revolutionaries: Radical intellectuals in Shanghai and Chekiang, 1902–1911.
Cambridge: Harvard U. Press, 1971. 342 p. (Harvard East Asian series, 50) (Revision of *Student revolutionaries in Shanghai and Chekiang, 1902–1907*, doctoral dissertation in History, Harvard U., 1966)
Subj 16.1 32.2 54 64 66 ▪ 12.1 14.2 16 17 19 32 37 62

18488 NIC P P5 G9.3 1895–1911
Rankin, Mary Louise Backus, 1934–.
'The Ku-t'ien Incident (1895): Christians versus the Ts'ai-hui.'
PC 15 (Dec. 1961), 30–61.
Subj 25 32.2 66 ▪ 12 22 26

18489 CSU U P1 G1.1 –1911
Rawlinson, Frank Joseph, 1871–1937.
'A study of the rebellions of China.'
CR 36, 3 (Mar. 1905), 107–117.
Subj 32.2 ▪ 12 16 25 62

18490 MCH P P2 G9.0 1895–1911
Rhoads, Edward John Michael, 1938–.
The new Kwangtung: Reform and revolution in China, 1895–1911.
Unpublished doctoral dissertation in History and Far Eastern Languages, Harvard U., 1970. 527 p.
Subj 22.2 25 26.1 26.2 32.2 66 ▪ 15 17 22 24.2 34.3 36.2 37 38 39 54

18491 MCH O P2 G8.2 1842–1895
Rocher, Emile, 1846–1924.
La province chinoise du Yun-nan (Yunnan).
Paris: Ernest Leroux, 1879, 1880. 2 vols. 15, 286; 291 p.
Subj 12 23 24.2 24.4 32.2 66 ▪ 21.3 22 22.2 24 25 26.1 28 33 55 65

18492 CSU PO P2 G1.1 1895–1911
Rodes, Jean.
La fin des Mandchous (The end of the Ch'ing).
Paris: Alcan, 1919. 268 p. (Dix ans de politique chinoise, 4)
Subj 12 15 32.2 ▪ 14.2 16.1 25 66

18493 DLC PO P2 G1.4 –1895
Rudakov, Apollinarii Vasil'evich, 1871–?
'Obshchestvo I-khe-tuan' i ego znachenie v poslednikh sobytiiakh na Dal'nem Vostoke, po ofitsial'nym kitaiskim dannym' (Official Chinese data on the Boxers and its significance in recent developments in the Far East).
IVI 2, 3 (1901), 1–77.
Subj 12 15 23 32.2 33 66 ▪ 12.1 52 62 64

18494 CSU P P2 G1.1 1842–1911
Schiffrin, Harold Zvi, 1922–.
Sun Yat-sen and the origins of the Chinese Revolution.
Berkeley, Los Angeles: U. of California Press, 1968. 15, 412 p.
Subj 16.1 32.2 59 64 ▪ 12 12.2 14.2 15 16.3 17 25 54 56 66

18495 NIC PO P2 G1.1 1644–1895
[Schlegel, Gustaaf] Gustave Schlegel, 1840–1903.
Thian Ti Hwui, the Hung-League, or Heaven-Earth-League: A secret society with the Chinese in China and India.
Batavia: Lange, 1866. 40, 251 p. (Bataviaasch Genootschap van Kunsten en Weetenschappen, Verhandelingen, 32)
Subj 32.2 33 62 ▪ 48

18496 WSU P P2 G1.4 1895–1911
Seki, Massaki.
The 1911 Revolution in Fengt'ien province.
Unpublished masters thesis in East Asian Studies, U. of Washington, 1968. 139 p.
Subj 32.2 ▪ 15 22 25 66

18497 MCH P P2 G1.4 1895–1911
Sheeks, Robert Bruce, 1922–.
'A re-examination of the *I-ho ch'üan* and its role in the Boxer movement.'
PC 1 (Dec. 1947), 74–135.
Subj 16.1 32.2 66 ▪ 25 33

18498 NNC PO P3 G5.1 1842–1895
Skachkov, Konstantin Andreianovich, 1821–1883.
Pekin v dni Taipinskogo vosstaniia: iz zapisok ochevidtsa (Peking in the days of the Taiping Rebellion: From the notes of an eyewitness).
Moscow: Izd-vo vost. lit-ry, 1958. 358 p.
Subj 12.1 32.2 ▪ 12 15 22.1 24.2

18499 MCH S P4 G1.5 1895–1911
Smythe, Ethel Joan, 1934–1963.
'The Tzu-li Hui: Some Chinese and their rebellion.'
PC 12 (Dec. 1958), 51–68.
Subj 32.2

18500 MCH P P2 G1.5 1842–1895
So, Kwan-wai (Su Chun-wei), 1919–, Eugene Powers Boardman, 1910–, and Ch'iu Ping.
'Hung Jen-kan, Taiping prime minister, 1859–1864.'
HJAS 20, 1/2 (June 1957), 262–294. [Reprinted in *Revolutionary leaders of modern China*, edited by Chün-tu Hsüeh. (Selective entry.) New York: Oxford U. Press, 1971, 55–70.]
Subj 16.1 32.2 33 59 ▪ 61 62 66

18501 NIC PO P2 G1.1 1644–1895
Stanton, William.
The Triad Society, or Heaven and Earth Society.
Hong Kong: Kelly and Walsh, 1900. 124 p.
Subj 32.2 62

18502 MCH P P2 G1.3 1895–1911
Steiger, George Nye, 1883–.
China and the Occident: The origin and development of the Boxer movement.
New Haven: Yale U. Press, 1927. 19, 349 p. [Reprinted—New York: Russell and Russell, 1966. 19, 349 p.]
Subj 32.2 66 ▪ 12

18503 CSU U P1 G1.3 1644–1911
T'ang, Leang-li (T'ang Liang-li), 1901–.
'The historical significance of the Chinese secret societies.'
PT new (2nd) series 3, 7 (1 Nov. 1932), 222–228.
Subj 32.2

18504 MCY P P2 G1.2 1842–1895
Taylor, George Edward, 1905–.
'The Taiping Rebellion: Its economic background and social theory.'
CSPSR 16, 4 (Oct. 1933), 545–614.
Subj 12 14 16 32.2 60 ▪ 14.1 14.5 16.1 16.3 18 23 66

18505 MCH P P4 G1.2 1842–1911
Teng, Ssu-yü, 1906–.
'Dr. Sun Yat-sen and Chinese secret societies.'
Studies on Asia 4 (1963), 81–99.
Subj 32.2 ▪ 12 64

18506 MCH P P2 G1.3 1842–1895
Teng, Ssu-yü, 1906–.
Historiography of the Taiping Rebellion.
Cambridge: Harvard U., East Asian Research Center, 1962. 180 p. (Harvard East Asian monographs, 14)
Subj 32.2 72 ▪ 62 70 71

18507 CBU P P3 G1.5 1644–1895
Teng, Ssu-yü, 1906–.
'Hung Jen-kan, prime minister of the Taiping kingdom, and his modernization plans.'
United College j. (Hong Kong) 8 (1970/71), 87–95 [s.p.].
Subj 32.2 59 ▪ 23

18508 MCY P P2 G1.3 1842–1895
Teng, Ssu-yü, 1906–.
New light on the history of the Taiping Rebellion.
Cambridge: Harvard U. Press, 1950. 132 p. [Reprinted—New York: Russell and Russell, 1966. 132 p.]
Subj 19 32.2 72 ▪ 35 47 64

18509 CSU P P2 G1.4 1842–1895
Teng, Ssu-yü, 1906–.
The Nien Army and their guerrilla warfare, 1851–1868.
The Hague: Mouton, 1961. 254 p. (Ecole pratique des hautes études de Sorbonne, Sixième section [sciences économiques et sociales], Le monde d'outre-mer, passé et présent, Etudes, 1er série, 13)
Subj 22.2 25 32.2 ▪ 12.1 15 26.1 59

18510 CSU P P1 G1.2 –1895
Teng, Ssu-yü, 1906–.
'A political interpretation of Chinese rebellions and revolutions.'
THJ new (2nd) series 1, 3 (Sept. 1958), 91–118.
Subj 19 32.2 ▪ 12

18511 CSU P P2 G1.1 1842–1895
Teng, Ssu-yü, 1906–.
The Taiping Rebellion and the western powers: A comprehensive survey.
Oxford: Clarendon Press, 1971. 12, 458 p.
Subj 14 15 25 32.2 64 66 ▪ 12 12.1 12.2 14.5 18 29 41 47 59

18512 NNC P P3 G1.5 1842–1895
Teng, Yuan Chung.
'Reverend Issachar Jacox Roberts and the Taiping Rebellion.'
JAS 23, 1 (Nov. 1963), 55–67.
Subj 32.2 ▪ 61 62 66

18513 CSH O P2 G1.3 1842–1895
Tinguy, *Père* ———, et al.
'Lettres relatives à l'insurrection, 1851–1855' (Letters on the [Taiping] Rebellion, 1851–1855). In *Missions de Chine: mémoire sur l'état actuel de la mission du Kiang-nan, 1842–1855* (Chinese missions: An account of the present state of the Kiangnan mission, 1842–1855), by Nicolas Broullion. [Selective entry]
Paris: Julien, Lanier, 1855, 255–483.
Subj 32.2 33 ▪ 15 25 66

18514 MAM P P2 G1.1 1644–1842
Tsao, Kai-fu, 1921–.
The rebellion of the three feudatories against the Manchu throne in China, 1673–1681: Its setting and significance.
Ann Arbor: University Microfilms (Publ. 65-12,370), 1965. 220 p. (Doctoral dissertation in Political Science, Columbia U.)
Subj 32.2 ▪ 12 12.1

18515 NNC S P2 G1.2 1842–1911
Vaks, L-.
'Kitaiskaia revoliutsiia 1911 g.' (The Revolution of 1911). In *Ocherki istorii natsional'no-burzhuaznykh revoliutsii na Vostoke, 1905–1914: Persiia, Turtsiia, Kitai* (Notes on the history of the national bourgeois revolutions in the Orient, 1905–1914: Persia, Turkey, and China), by L. Vaks. [Sole entry]
Moscow: Moskovskii rabochii, 1931, 78–133.
Subj 12 19 32.2 ▪ 12.1 14 15 16 66

18516 CSU P P2 G1.2 –1911
van der Sprenkel, Sybille Marie, 1919–.
'Les sociétés secrètes et le droit chinois' (Secret societies and Chinese law). In *Mouvements populaires et sociétés secrètes en Chine aux XIXe et XXe siècles* (Popular movements and secret societies in China in the nineteenth and twentieth centuries), edited by Jean Chesneaux, Feiling Blackburn Davis, and Nguyen Nguyet Ho. [Selective entry]
Paris: Maspero, 1970, 74–89.
Subj 12.2 32.2

18517 NNC P P1 G1.2 1895–1911
[Veltman, Mikhail Lazarevich] Mikhail Pavlovich Pavlovich, pseud., 1871–1927.
'Revoliutsionnoe dvizhenie i politicheskie partii v sovremennom Kitae' (The revolutionary movement and political parties in contemporary China).
Vestnik znaniia 1911, 11 (noiabr'), 1006–1013.
Subj 12 32 32.2 ▪ 19 64 66

18518 CSU P P2 G9.2 1644–1895
Wakeman, Frederic Evans, Jr., 1937–.
'The secret societies of Kwangtung, 1800–1856.' In *Popular movements and secret societies in China, 1840–1950*, edited by Jean Chesneaux. [Analytic entry]
Stanford: Stanford U. Press, 1972, 29–47. [Reprinted in *'Nothing concealed': Essays in honor of Liu Yu-yün*, edited by F. E. Wakeman, Jr. (Selective entry.) Taipei: Chinese Materials and Research Aids Service Center, 1970, 127–160. (CMRASC occasional series, 4)]
Subj 25 26 32.2 ▪ 22.1 24.5 50

18519 CBU P P2 G9.2 1644–1895
Wakeman, Frederic Evans, Jr., 1937–.
Strangers at the gate: Social disorder in South China, 1839–1861.
Berkeley, Los Angeles: U. of California Press, 1966. 12, 276 p. (Revision of doctoral dissertation in History, U. of California, Berkeley, 1966)
SUBJ 22 25 32.2 35 66 ▪ 22.1 22.2 26.1 26.2 33 42 64 72

18520 CSH P P1 G1.3 1895–1911
Wang, Teh-chao (Wang Te-chao).
'The role of the Chinese intellectuals in the Revolution of 1911.'
CC 7, 3 (Sept. 1966), 97–116.
SUBJ 16.1 32.2 ▪ 32

18521 CSU S P5 G1.2 1842–1911
Wang Tianjiang (Wang T'ien-chiang).
'L'organisation et l'activité des sociétés secrètes vers 1850–1890' (The organization and activities of secret societies around 1850–1890). Tr. of 'Shih chiu shih chi hsia pan ch'i Chung-kuo ti mi mi hui she' (Secret societies in China during the latter half of the nineteenth century); *Li shih yen chiu* 1963, 2 (Apr.), 83–100 [partial tr.: p. 85–87, 91–92 only]. In *Mouvements populaires et sociétés secrètes en Chine aux XIXe et XXe siècles* (Popular movements and secret societies in China in the nineteenth and twentieth centuries), edited by Jean Chesneaux, Feiling Blackburn Davis, and Nguyen Nguyet Ho. [Selective entry]
Paris: Maspero, 1970, 219–225.
SUBJ 16 32.2 ▪ 11.2 15 32.1 33

18522 CSU P P3 G6.1 1895–1911
Wang, Y. C. (Wang I-chü; Wang Chi-ch'ien), 1916–.
'The Su-Pao case: A study of foreign pressure, intellectual fermentation, and dynastic decline.'
MS 24 (1965), 84–129.
SUBJ 22.2 32.2 ▪ 64 66

18523 CSH U P2 G1.3 1644–1895
Williams, Samuel Wells, 1812–1884.
'The Tai-ping Rebellion.' In *The Middle Kingdom: A survey of the geography, government, literature, social life, arts, and history of the Chinese empire and its inhabitants*, rev. and enl. ed., by S. W. Williams. [Selective entry]
New York: Scribner, 1883, vol. 2, 575–624. [Reprinted in *The Middle Kingdom: A survey of the geography, government, literature, social life, arts, and history of the Chinese empire and its inhabitants*, by S. W. Williams. (Selective entry.) Taipei: Ch'eng-wen, 1965, 575–624 (s.p.)]
SUBJ 15 25 32.2 ▪ 59 66

18524 MCH P P2 G1.5 1842–1895
Wilson, Andrew, 1831–1881.
The 'Ever-Victorious Army': A history of the Chinese campaign under Lt.-Col. C. G. Gordon, and of the suppression of the Tai-ping Rebellion.
Edinburgh: William Blackwood, 1868. 32, 395 p.
SUBJ 15 25 32.2 66 ▪ 24.2 56 63

18525 CSU P P2 G1.1 1895–1911
Wright, Mary Clabaugh, 1917–1970.
'Introduction: The rising tide of change.' In *China in revolution: The first phase, 1900–1913*, edited by M. C. Wright. [Selective entry]
New Haven: Yale U. Press, 1968, 1–63.
SUBJ 16 19 32.2 66 ▪ 15 17 47 54

18526 MAM S P2 G1.2 1644–1895
Wu, Thomas Dong (Wu Tung), 1930–.
A model for revolutions that failed: A case study of the Taiping mass movement in China, 1850–1864.
Ann Arbor: University Microfilms (Publ. 72-10,313), 1972. 160 p. (Doctoral dissertation in Government, Southern Illinois U., 1971)
SUBJ 14 15 16 16.1 32.2 64 ▪ 12.1 14.1 14.5 14.6 18 25 32.1 36.3 66

18527 ²CSU P P2 G1.1 1644–1895
Wylie, Alexander, 1815–1887.
'Secret societies in China.' In *Shanghae almanac for 1854 and miscellany.* [Sole entry]
Shanghai: North-China Herald, 1853. [Reprinted from *North-China herald* Sept. 1853.] [Reprinted in *Chinese researches*, by A. Wylie. (Sole entry.) Shanghai: ——, 1897, 110–146 (s.p.).] [Reprinted in *Chinese researches*, by A. Wylie. (Selective entry.) Taipei: Ch'eng-wen, 1966, 110–146 (s.p.).]
SUBJ 32.2 ▪ 12.2 25

18528 DLC P P1 G1.1 1895–1911
Young, Ernest Paddock, 1932–.
'The reformer as a conspirator: Liang Ch'i-ch'ao and the 1911 Revolution.' In *Approaches to modern Chinese history*, edited by Albert Feuerwerker et al. [Selective entry]
Berkeley, Los Angeles: U. of California Press, 1967, 239–267.
SUBJ 32.2 ▪ 61 64

1644-1949

18529 NIC U P2 G6.0 1644–1949
'The rise and growth of the "Ch'ing Pang" [Green Gang].'
China review (London) 3, 4 (1934), 35–37.
SUBJ 32.2 ▪ 16.4 34.3

18530 NNC P P2 G1.2 1895–1928
Belov, Evgenii Aleksandrovich, 1929–.
Revoliutsiia 1911–1913 godov v Kitae (The Chinese Revolution, 1911–1913).
Moscow: Izd-vo vost. lit-ry, 1958. 112 p.
SUBJ 19 32.2 ▪ 12.1 66

18531 NNC S P2 G7.1 1895–1928
Belov, Evgenii Aleksandrovich, 1929–.
'Uchanskoe vosstanie i sverzhenie man'chzhurskoi vlasti v provintsiiakh' (The Wuchang Uprising and the overthrow of Manchu power in the provinces). In *Sin'khaiskaia revoliutsiia v Kitae: sbornik statei* (Articles on the Revolution of 1911 in China), compiled by Institut narodov Azii, Akademiia nauk SSSR. [Selective entry]
Moscow: Izd-vo vost. lit-ry, 1962, 206–235.
SUBJ 12.1 32.1 32.2

18532 ELO O P2 G8.1 1895–1928
Brace, A- J-.
'Some secret societies of Szechuan.'
JWCBRS 8 (1936), 177–180.
SUBJ 25 32.2 ▪ 23 24

18533 CSU PO P2 G1.2 1895–1928
Challaye, Félicien, 1875–.
'Politique intérieure: la politique intérieure en Chine' (China's domestic policy). In *La Chine et le Japon politiques* (Political aspects of China and Japan), by F. Challaye. [Sole entry]
Paris: Alcan, 1921, 1–54.
SUBJ 12 16.1 32 32.2 59 66 ▪ 15 35 61 64

18534 CSH PO P2 G1.1 1895–1949
Chang Kuo-t'ao, 1897–.
The rise of the Chinese Communist Party: The autobiography of Chang Kuo-t'ao. Vol. 1, 1921–1927. Vol. 2, 1928–1938.
Lawrence: University Press of Kansas, 1971, 1972. 21, 756; 626 p.
SUBJ 15 25 32.2 59 ▪ 12 22.1 24.1 26.3 26.4 32 36.4 54 64 66

18535 NNC P P1 G1.2 1644–1949
Chatterji, Krishnalal K-.
The national movement in modern China.
Calcutta: Mukhopadhyay, 1958. 157 p.
SUBJ 32.2 64 ▪ 12 15 19 25 32 66

18536 NNC P P2 G1.2 1895–1949
Ch'en, Jerome (Ch'en Chih-jang), 1919–.
Mao and the Chinese revolution.
London: Oxford U. Press, 1965. 419 p.
SUBJ 16.1 32.2 ▪ 15 19 22 32 64

18537 FPN S P2 G1.2 1842–1949
Chesneaux, Jean, 1922–.
'La Chine, des guerres de l'opium à 1937' (China from the opium wars to 1937). In *L'Asie orientale aux XIXe et XXe siècles: Chine, Japon, Inde, Sud-Est asiatique* (East Asia in the nineteenth and twentieth centuries: China, Japan, India, and Southeast Asia), by J. Chesneaux. [Sole entry]
Paris: Presses universitaires, 1966, 159–176.
SUBJ 14 16 19 32.2 ▪ 64

18538 CSU P P1 G1.3 1644–1949
Chesneaux, Jean, 1922–.
'The modern relevance of *Shui-hu chuan* [Water margin]: Its influence on rebel movements in nineteenth- and twentieth-century China.'
Papers on Far Eastern history 3 (Mar. 1971), 1–25.
SUBJ 32.2 60

18539 CSU P P2 G1.1 1842–1949
Chesneaux, Jean, 1922–.
'La place des sociétés secrètes dans l'évolution historique de la Chine aux XIXe–XXe siècles' (The place of secret societies in the historical development of China in the nineteenth and twentieth centuries). In *Mouvements populaires et sociétés secrètes en Chine aux XIXe et XXe siècles* (Popular movements and secret societies in China in the nineteenth and twentieth centuries), edited by J. Chesneaux, Feiling Blackburn Davis, and Nguyen Nguyet Ho. [Selective entry]
Paris: Maspero, 1970, 13–43.

'Secret societies in China's historical evolution' [rev. in tr.]. In *Popular movements and secret societies in China, 1840–1950*, edited by J. Chesneaux. [Analytic entry]
Stanford: Stanford U. Press, 1972, 1–21.
SUBJ 16 32.2

18540 CBU U P2 G1.1 1895–1928
Chesneaux, Jean, 1922–.
Sun Yat-sen (Sun Yat-sen).
Paris: Club français du livre, 1959. 266 p.
Subj 12 16.1 25 32.2 59 64 ▪ 12.1 14 14.6 15 16.3 16.4 32 66

18541 CSU S P2 G1.1 –1949
Davis, Feiling Blackburn.
'Le rôle économique et social des sociétés secrètes' (The economic and social role of secret societies). In *Mouvements populaires et sociétés secrètes en Chine aux XIXe et XXe siècles* (Popular movements and secret societies in China in the nineteenth and twentieth centuries), edited by Jean Chesneaux, F. B. Davis, and Nguyen Nguyet Ho. [Selective entry]
Paris: Maspero, 1970, 44–64.
Subj 12.2 16 22.2 32.2

18542 NNC P P2 G1.1 1895–1928
Efimov, Gerontii Valentinovich, 1906–.
Revoliutsiia 1911 goda v Kitae (The Chinese Revolution of 1911).
Moscow: Uchpedgiz, 1959. 129 p.
Subj 12 32 32.2 ▪ 12.1 15 16 64

18543 DLC S P2 G1.2 1895–1949
Erenburg, Grigorii Borisovich, 1902–1967.
Ocherki natsional'no-osvoboditel'noi bor'by kitaiskogo naroda v noveishee vremia (Notes on the national liberation struggle of the Chinese people in the most recent period).
Moscow: Uchpedgiz, 1951. 238 p.
Subj 16 19 32.2 ▪ 14.1 14.2 14.4 16.2 16.4 64

18544 MCH P P1 G1.1 –1949
Favre, Benoît, 1874–?
Les sociétés secrètes en Chine: origine, rôle historique, situation actuelle (The origin, historical role, and present position of secret societies in China).
Paris: Maisonneuve, 1933. 222 p.
Subj 32.2 33 35 48 ▪ 13 23 30 32.1 41 60 72

18545 NIC PO P2 G1.1 1842–1949
Franke, Wolfgang, 1912–.
Das Jahrhundert der chinesischen Revolution, 1851–1949.
Munich: Oldenbourg, 1958? 297 p.

A century of Chinese revolution, 1851–1949. Tr. by Stanley Rudman. [Slightly rev. in tr.]
Columbia: U. of South Carolina Press, 1970. 10, 202 p.
Subj 16 32 32.2 64 ▪ 12 15 16.1 16.3 19 33 36.3 66

18546 MCH PO P2 G1.3 1895–1928
Gain, Léopold, 1852–?
'Dans la Chine nouvelle' (In the new China).
Etudes 7e série 146, 4 (20 fév. 1916), 487–515; 146, 5 (5 mars 1916), 626–641; 147, 1 (5 avr. 1916), 91–114.
Subj 12.2 16.1 25 32.2 64 ▪ 12 17 34.3 66

18547 NNC PO P2 G1.1 –1949
Glick, Carl Cannon, 1890–, and Sheng-hwa Hong (Hung Sheng-hua).
Swords of silence: Chinese secret societies, past and present.
New York: Whittlesey House, 1947. 11, 292 p.
Subj 32.1 32.2 66 ▪ 12.2 25 38 64 65 72

18548 NIC O P1 G8.1 1895–1949
Graham, David Crockett, 1884–.
'Some strange customs in Szechuan province.'
JWCBRS 8 (1936), 141–144.
Subj 22.2 25 32.2 65

18549 CBU PO P3 G1.1 1895–1928
Haenisch, Erich, 1880–1966.
'Vor dreissig Jahren: Ein Rückblick auf den chinesischen Umsturz' (Thirty years ago: The Chinese Revolution [of 1911] in retrospect).
Historische Z. 166, 3 (Sept.–Okt. 1942), 473–506.
Subj 12 32.2 ▪ 15

18550 WSU P P1 G1.2 –1949
Ho, Philip Wen-jen.
A study of historical sources of the Hung Society.
Unpublished masters thesis in Librarianship, U. of Washington, 1953. 40 p.
Subj 22.2 32.2 ▪ 72

18551 NNC PO P2 G1.2 1644–1928
Holcombe, Arthur Norman, 1884–.
The Chinese revolution: A phase in the regeneration of a world power.
Cambridge: Harvard U. Press, 1930. 13, 401 p.
Subj 12 12.1 32 32.2 60 64 ▪ 15 17 19 25 30

18552 NIC P P1 G1.2 1895–1928
Hsüeh, Chün-tu, 1922–.
Huang Hsing and the Chinese revolution.
Stanford: Stanford U. Press, 1961. 11, 260 p. (Stanford studies in history, economics, and political science, 20) (Revision of doctoral dissertation in Political Science, Columbia U., 1958)
Subj 32.2 ▪ 15 16.1 32 66

18553 MCH P P2 G1.1 1895–1928
Jansen, Marius Berthus, 1922–.
The Japanese and Sun Yat-sen.
Cambridge: Harvard U. Press, 1954. 274 p. (Harvard historical monographs, 27) (Revision of *The Japanese and the Chinese revolutionary movement, 1895–1915*, doctoral dissertation in History, Harvard U., 1950)
Subj 32.2 66

18554 CSU P P1 G1.2 1842–1949
Johnson, Chalmers Ashby, 1931–.
Revolution and the social system.
Stanford: Hoover Institution on War, Revolution and Peace, 1964. 68 p. (Hoover Institution studies, 3)
Subj 32.2 ▪ 15

18555 CSU U P2 G1.2 1842–1928
Kara-Murza, Georgii Sergeevich, 1906–1945, and Grigorii Borisovich Erenburg, 1902–1967.
'Kitai' (China). In *Novaia istoriia stran zarubezhnogo Vostoka* (Modern history of countries of the non-Soviet Orient), edited by Igor Mikhailovich Reisner and Boris Konstantinovich Rubtsov. [Sole entry]
Moscow: Izd-vo Mosk. un-ta, 1952, vol. 2, 40–90.
Subj 12 14 16 32.2 66 ▪ 15 32 35 64

18556 MCH U P1 G1.2 1842–1949
Kokin, M-.
'Kitai' (China). In *Ocherki po istorii Vostoka v epokhu imperializma* (Notes on Oriental history in the imperialist era), edited by A- Alimov and M- Godes. [Sole entry]
Moscow: Sotsekgiz, 1934, 260–363.
Subj 10 14 32.2 ▪ 64

18557 MAM P P2 G1.2 1842–1949
Kuo, Thomas C. (Kuo Ch'eng-t'ang), 1929–.
Ch'en Tu-hsiu (1879–1942) and the Chinese Communist movement.
Ann Arbor: University Microfilms (Publ. 70-17,993), 1970. 10, 521 p. (Doctoral dissertation in History, U. of Pittsburgh, 1969)
Subj 16.1 32.2 59 60 64 ▪ 12.2 14.2 15 25 32 36.4 54 66

18558 CSH S P2 G1.1 1895–1949
Léger, François.
'La Chine nouvelle' (New China). In *Les influences occidentales dans la révolution de l'Orient: Inde, Malaisie, Chine, 1850–1950* (Western influences in the revolution in the Orient: India, Malaya, and China, 1850–1950), by F. Léger. [Sole entry]
Paris: Plon, 1955, vol. 2, 3–243.
Subj 12 19 32.2 54 64 66 ▪ 12.2 14.1 14.4 15 16 17 22.2 33 41

18559 MAM P P1 G1.2 1895–1949
[Li Yu-ning] Bernadette Yu-ning Li.
A biography of Ch'ü Chiu-pai: From youth to party leadership (1899–1928).
Ann Arbor: University Microfilms (Publ. 70-17,027), 1970. 301 p. (Doctoral dissertation in History, Columbia U., 1967)
Subj 32.2 59 64 ▪ 19

18560 CSU P P2 G1.1 1895–1928
Liew, K. S. (Liu Chi-hsiang), 1932–.
Struggle for democracy: Sung Chiao-jen and the 1911 Chinese Revolution.
Berkeley, Los Angeles: U. of California Press, 1971. 260 p. (Revision of doctoral dissertation in History, Australian National U., 1967)
Subj 16.1 17 32.2 59 ▪ 12 14.2 15 54

18561 CSH O P2 G1.2 –1949
Mao Tse-tung, 1893–.
'The Chinese Revolution and the Chinese Communist Party.' Tr. of 'Chung-kuo ko ming yü Chung-kuo kung ch'an tang'; in *Mao Tse-tung hsüan chi* (Selected works of Mao Tse-tung), 2nd ed.; Peking: Jen min ch'u pan she, 1960, vol. 2 [written in 1939]. In *Selected works of Mao Tse-tung*, edited by Mao Tse-tung hsüan chi ch'u pan wei yüan hui (Committee for the Publication of the Selected Works of Mao Tse-tung), Chung yang wei yüan hui (Central Committee), Chung-kuo kung ch'an tang (Chinese Communist Party). [Selective entry]
Peking: Foreign Languages Press, 1965, vol. 2, 305–334.
Subj 16 19 32.2 ▪ 14 66

18562 MCH S P2 G1.2 1895–1949
Mende, Tibor, 1915–.
The Chinese revolution.
London: Thames and Hudson, 1961. 190 p.
SUBJ 16.1 32 32.2 ▪ 12 14 14.1 15 64 66

18563 MCH O P4 G1.2 1895–1928
Mullowney, John James, 1878–1952, ed.
A revelation of the Chinese revolution: A retrospect and forecast, by a Chinese patriot.
New York: Revell, 1914. 142 p.
SUBJ 12 15 32.2 59 ▪ 16.1 32

18564 MCH S P1 G1.2 1842–1949
Nikiforov, Vladimir Nikolaevich, 1920–.
'Two lines of interest followed by Wolfgang Franke in his studies on the modern and recent history of China.' [Review of *Das Jahrhundert der chinesischen Revolution, 1851–1949* (The century of the Chinese revolution, 1851–1949), by Wolfgang Franke.]
AO 29, 3 (1961), 455–468.
SUBJ 32.2 ▪ 71

18565 CSU S P2 G1.3 1842–1949
Sakai, Tadao, 1912–.
'Le Hongbang (Band rouge) aux XIXe et XXe siècles' (The Red Gang in the nineteenth and twentieth centuries). In *Mouvements populaires et sociétés secrètes en Chine aux XIXe et XXe siècles* (Popular movements and secret societies in China in the nineteenth and twentieth centuries), edited by Jean Chesneaux, Feiling Blackburn Davis, and Nguyen Nguyet Ho. [Selective entry]
Paris: Maspero, 1970, 316–343.
SUBJ 32 32.2

18566 DLC S P1 G1.1 1895–1928
Simonovskaia, Larisa Vasil'evna, 1902–.
'Soiuz Tunmen v kitaiskoi revoliutsii 1911–1912 gg.' (The T'ung-meng Hui in the Chinese Revolution of 1911–1912). In *Sbornik statei po istorii stran Dal'nego Vostoka* (Articles on Far Eastern history), edited by L. V. Simonovskaia and Mikhail Filippovich IUr'ev. [Selective entry]
Moscow: Izd-vo Mosk. un-ta, 1952, 69–80.
SUBJ 19 32.2 ▪ 15 16 64

18567 NNC O P2 G1.2 1895–1949
[Snow, Helen Foster] Nym Wales, pseud., 1907–.
Red dust: Autobiographies of the Chinese Communists as told to Nym Wales.
Stanford: Stanford U. Press, 1952. 14, 238 p. [Reprinted in *The Chinese Communists: Sketches and autobiographies of the old guard*, by [H. F. Snow] Nym Wales, pseud. (Analytic entry.) Westport, Conn.: Greenwood Press, 1972, 1–224.]
SUBJ 32.2 59 ▪ 15 22 25 64

18568 NNC U P2 G1.3 1895–1928
[Su Chao-pei] Su Tschao-Peh (Su Ch'ao-p'ei).
'Bor'ba za gegemoniiu v kitaiskoi revoliutsii' (The struggle for hegemony in the Chinese revolution).
KIP 8, 7 (iiul' 1928), 14–21.
'Der Kampf um die Hegemonie in der chinesischen Revolution.'
RGI 8, 7 (Juli 1928), 374–378.
'La lutte pour l'hégémonie dans la révolution chinoise.'
ISR 90 (juil. 1928), 428–433.
SUBJ 32.2

18569 ELO PO P3 G9.0 1895–1928
Tse, Tsan-tai (Hsieh Tsuan-t'ai), 1871–193?
The Chinese Republic: Secret history of the revolution.
Hong Kong: South China Morning Post, 1924. 36 p.
SUBJ 32.2 ▪ 16.1 19

18570 NNC P P1 G1.1 1644–1928
Ward, John Sebastian Marlow, 1885–, and William George Stirling.
The Hung Society, or the Society of Heaven and Earth.
London: Baskerville Press, 1925, 1926, 1926. 3 vols. 180; 196; 148 p.
SUBJ 23 32.2 60 ▪ 48 57

18571 CSU S P2 G1.2 –1949
Wolf, Eric Robert, 1923–.
'China.' In *Peasant wars of the twentieth century*, by E. R. Wolf. [Sole entry]
New York: Harper and Row, 1969, 103–155.
SUBJ 12 16 16.1 16.3 32.2 36.3 ▪ 12.1 14 14.1 15 25 26.2 32 42 64

18572 NIC O P2 G1.5 1895–1928
Wu Yu-chang (Wu Yü-chang), 1878–1966.
The Revolution of 1911: A great democratic revolution of China. Tr. of *Hsin hai ko ming* (The Revolution of 1911); Peking: Jen min ch'u pan she, 1961; 172 p.
Peking: Foreign Languages Press, 1962. 145 p.
SUBJ 16.1 32.2 ▪ 25 59

18573 MCH O P3 G8.1 1895–1928
Yang, S. C.
'The revolution in Szechwan, 1911–1912.'
JWCBRS 6 (1933/34), 64–90.
SUBJ 32.2 ▪ 22.1

1911-1949

18574 MCH P P2 G1.2 1911–1949
'Le développement du communisme en Chine' (The growth of Communism in China).
Notes documentaires et études 1153 (28 juin 1949), 1–48; 1154 (29 juin 1949), 1–53.
SUBJ 15 32.2 64 ▪ 12 16 19

18575 NIC U P8 G6.2 1911–1949
'Initiation ceremonies of the "Red Spears".'
PT new (2nd) series 6, 3 (1 Feb. 1934), 147–151.
SUBJ 25 32.2 33

18576 NNC S P2 G2.0 1928–1949
A. D.
'Natsional'no-osvoboditel'noe dvizhenie v Man'chzhurii' (The national liberation movement in Manchuria).
PK 14 (1935), 290–310.
SUBJ 32.2 ▪ 25

18577 MCH O P2 G1.5 1928–1949
Amann, Gustav, 1882–.
Bauernkrieg in China: Chiang Kaisheks Kampf gegen den Aufstand 1932–1935 (Peasant war in China: Chiang Kai-shek's struggle against the rebellion of 1932–1935).
Berlin: Kurt Vowinckel, 1939. 157 p.
SUBJ 32.2 36.3 ▪ 12.1 15 16.3 25

18578 CSH O P2 G1.3 1911–1949
Amann, Gustav, 1882–.
'Kommunismus, Bauernbewegung und die kommunistische Partei in China' (Communism, peasant movements, and the Communist Party in China).
Z. für Geopolitik 8, 8 (Aug. 1931), 618–628.
SUBJ 32.2 ▪ 15 36.3 64

18579 MCH O P2 G1.1 1911–1928
Amann, Gustav, 1882–.
Sun Yatsens Vermächtnis: Geschichte der chinesischen Revolution.
Berlin: Kurt Vowinckel, 1928. 26, 271 p.
The legacy of Sun Yat-sen: A history of the Chinese Revolution. Tr. by Frederick Philip Grove.
New York: Carrier, 1929? 12, 302 p.
SUBJ 12 19 32 32.2 ▪ 12.1 12.2 14 14.5 15 16.1 59 64

18580 NNC P P2 G1.2 1911–1949
Avarin, Vladimir IAkovlevich, 1899–.
'Kitaiskaia kommunisticheskaia partiia, organizator velikikh pobed kitaiskogo naroda' (The Chinese Communist Party, organizer of the great victories of the Chinese people).
UZIV 2 (1951), 36–70.
SUBJ 16.4 32.2 66 ▪ 11.4 14.1 16.3 64

18581 NNC P P2 G2.0 1928–1949
B. M.
'Obzor natsional'no-osvoboditel'nogo dvizheniia v Man'chzhurii, period ianvar'–avgust 1933 goda' (Overview of the national liberation movement in Manchuria, January–August 1933).
MNKP 1933, 8/9, 139–190.
SUBJ 25 32.2 66 ▪ 15 32.1

18582 MCH O P2 G7.0 1911–1928
Bakulin, A- B-.
Zapiski ob ukhanskom periode kitaiskoi revoliutsii: iz istorii kitaiskoi revoliutsii, 1925–1927 (Notes on the Wuhan period of the Chinese Revolution: History of the Chinese Revolution, 1925–1927).
Moscow: Gosizdat, 1930. 288 p.
SUBJ 26.4 32.1 32.2 36.4 ▪ 15 19 24.4 36.3 66

18583 DLC S P2 G1.3 1911–1949
Barandov, G- V-.
Kitaiskaia revoliutsiia i bor'ba kitaiskoi kompartii (The Chinese revolution and the struggle of the Chinese Communist Party).
Moscow: Otdel izd-va Nar. kom. oborony SSSR, 1934. 96 p.
SUBJ 32.2 36.3 36.4 ▪ 12 12.1 64 66

18584 CSH O P4 G4.1 1928–1949
Barrett, David D-.
Dixie mission: The United States Army Observer Group in Yenan, 1944.

Berkeley: U. of California, Center for Chinese Studies, 1970. 92 p. (CCS, China research monographs, 6)
SUBJ 15 32 32.2 66 ▪ 16.1 17 55

18585 NNC O P2 G1.2 1911–1949
Belden, Jack, 1910–.
China shakes the world.
New York: Harper, 1949. 524 p. [Reprinted—New York: Monthly Review Press, 1970. 17, 524 p.]
SUBJ 10 12 15 16.3 32.2 ▪ 12.1 14.1 14.5 14.6 18 22 22.2 25 34.1 47

18586 CSU P P2 G1.3 1911–1928
Bernal, Martin Gardiner, 1937–.
'The Tzu-yu tang [Liberal Party] and Tai Chi-t'ao, 1912–1913.'
MAS 1, 2 (Apr. 1967), 133–154.
SUBJ 32.2 64 ▪ 16.1 32.1 66

18587 CSU S P1 G1.2 1911–1949
Bernal, Martin Gardiner, 1937–.
'Was Chinese Communism inevitable?' [Review of *While China faced West: American reformers in Nationalist China, 1928–1937*, by James Claude Thomson, Jr.]
NYRB 15, 10 (3 Dec. 1970), 43–47.
SUBJ 32.2 ▪ 16.3 32

18588 CBU P P2 G1.2 1911–1949
Bianco, Lucien, 1930–.
Les origines de la Révolution chinoise, 1915–1949.
Paris: Gallimard, 1967. 384 p.

Origins of the Chinese revolution, 1915–1949. Tr. by Muriel Bell.
Stanford: Stanford U. Press, 1971. 13, 223 p.
SUBJ 12 22 32.2 36.3 60 ▪ 14 15 16 18 25

18589 CSU P P8 G1.2 1911–1949
Bianco, Lucien, 1930–.
'Sociétés secrètes et autodéfense paysanne (1921–1933).' In *Mouvements populaires et sociétés secrètes en Chine aux XIXe et XXe siècles* (Popular movements and secret societies in China in the nineteenth and twentieth centuries), edited by Jean Chesneaux, Feiling Blackburn Davis, and Nguyen Nguyet Ho. [Selective entry]
Paris: Maspero, 1970, 407–420.

'Secret societies and peasant self-defense, 1921–1933' [rev. in tr.]. In *Popular movements and secret societies in China, 1840–1950*, edited by J. Chesneaux. [Analytic entry]
Stanford: Stanford U. Press, 1972, 213–224.
SUBJ 25 32.2 ▪ 24.5 26.1 26.3 65

18590 CSU P P3 G1.3 1911–1928
Bing, Dov.
'Sneevliet and the early years of the CCP.'
CQ 48 (Oct.–Dec. 1971), 677–697.
SUBJ 32.2 66 ▪ 16 64

18591 CSU S P2 G1.2 1911–1949
Bisson, Thomas Arthur, 1900–.
'The years of the Kuomintang: Revolution vs. reaction.'
Foreign policy reports 8, 25 (15 Feb. 1933), 292–306.
SUBJ 32.2 ▪ 15 25 32

18592 MCH P P2 G1.3 1911–1928
Brandt, Conrad, 1920–.
Stalin's failure in China, 1924–1927.
Cambridge: Harvard U. Press, 1958. 15, 226 p. (Harvard Russian Research Center studies, 31) (Revision of *Soviet failure in China, 1920–1927*, doctoral dissertation in Government, Harvard U., 1956)
SUBJ 32.2 64 ▪ 16.3 16.4 32.1 36.4

18593 MCY PO P2 G1.2 1911–1949
Brière, O-.
'Les 25 ans du Parti communiste chinois (1921–1946)' (Twenty-five years of the Chinese Communist Party, 1921–1946).
BUA 3e série 7, 27 (1946), 360–393.
SUBJ 12 15 32.2 64 ▪ 66

18594 MCH O P3 G9.2 1911–1928
Buber-Neumann, Margaret, 1901–.
'La rivolta di Canton' (The Canton uprising).
Corrispondenza socialista 4, 10 (ottobre 1963), 549–556.
SUBJ 32.2

18595 CSH P P7 G1.4 1928–1949
Butterfield, Fox, 1939–.
'A missionary view of the Chinese Communists, 1936–1939.'
PC 15 (Dec. 1961), 147–199. [Reprinted in *American missionaries in China: Papers from Harvard seminars*, edited by Kwang-ching Liu (Liu Kuang-ching). (Analytic entry.) Cambridge: Harvard U., East Asian Research Center, 1966, 249–301. (Harvard East Asian monographs, 21)]
SUBJ 25 32.2 33 66 ▪ 24.1 24.5 28 35

18596 NNP PO P2 G1.2 1911–1928
Chapman, Herbert Owen.
The Chinese Revolution, 1926–1927: A record of the period under Communist control as seen from the Nationalist capital, Hankow.
London: Constable, 1928. 17, 310 p.
SUBJ 12 22.1 32 32.2 66 ▪ 12.2 14.4 15 16.4 17 33 36.4 47 56 64

18597 NNC PO P4 G1.2 1911–1928
Chen, Kung Po (Ch'en Kung-po), 1892–1946.
The Communist movement in China, edited by Clarence Martin Wilbur.
New York: Columbia U., East Asian Institute, 1960. 148 p. [For an introduction by C. M. Wilbur, see entry 18773.] (EAI series, 7) (Masters thesis in Economics, Columbia U., 1924)
SUBJ 32.2 64 ▪ 14 16.1 16.4 36.4 47 54 66

18598 NNC O P2 G1.2 1911–1949
Chen Po-ta (Ch'en Po-ta), 1904–.
Notes on ten years of civil war, 1927–1939.
Peking: Foreign Languages Press, 1954. 108 p.
SUBJ 16 25 32.2 ▪ 12 12.1 14.1 14.5 15 16.1 16.4 32 64

18599 CSU P P2 G1.2 1928–1949
Ch'en, Jerome (Ch'en Chih-jang), 1919–.
'Resolutions of the Tsunyi Conference.'
CQ 40 (Oct.–Dec. 1969), 1–38.
SUBJ 15 32.2 ▪ 16.1 64

18600 CSH S P3 G6.1 1911–1928
Cheng Hsueh-chia (Cheng Hsüeh-chia), 1906–.
'Questions concerning the First National Congress of the Chinese Communist Party.' In *Collected documents of the First Sino-American Conference on Mainland China*. [Selective entry]
[Taipei]: Institute of International Relations, Republic of China, 1971, 129–144.
SUBJ 32.2 ▪ 16.1 59

18601 CSU P P2 G1.2 1911–1928
Chesneaux, Jean, 1922–.
'Le "Mouvement du 4 mai" (1919–1921)' (The May Fourth Movement, 1919–1921). In *De la guerre franco-chinoise à la fondation du Parti communiste chinois, 1885–1921* (From the Sino-French war to the formation of the Chinese Communist Party, 1885–1921), by Marianne Bastid, Marie-Claire Bergère, and J. Chesneaux. [Analytic entry]
Paris: Hatier Université, 1972, 179–208. (HU, Collection d'histoire contemporaine, Histoire de la Chine, 2)
SUBJ 12 19 32.2 35 64 66 ▪ 12.1 14.2 14.3 16.1 16.2 18 32 36.4 54 72

18602 DLC P P2 G1.3 1911–1928
[Ch'ü Ch'iu-pai] Tsiui Vei-to (Ch'u Wei-t'o), pseud., 1899–1935.
'Kantonskoe vosstanie i kitaiskaia revoliutsiia' (The Canton uprising and the Chinese Revolution [of 1925–1927]). In *Kantonskaia kommuna: sbornik statei i materialov* (Articles and documents on the Canton commune), compiled by Nauchno-issledovatel'skii institut po Kitaiu, Kommunisticheskaia akademiia. [Selective entry]
Moscow: Gosizdat, 1929, 19–30.
SUBJ 16 32.2 ▪ 32 35 36.3 36.4 64 66

18603 CSU O P2 G1.2 1928–1949
Clubb, Oliver Edmund, 1901–.
Communism in China, as reported from Hankow in 1932.
New York: Columbia U. Press, 1968. 123 p.
SUBJ 15 32 32.2 ▪ 14.1 16.1 36.3 36.4

18604 CSU S P7 G1.3 1928–1949
Cole, George Douglas Howard, 1889–1959.
'Communism in China in the 1930's.' In *A history of socialist thought, Vol. 5, Socialism and fascism, 1931–1939*, by G. D. H. Cole. [Sole entry]
New York: St. Martin's Press, 1960, 264–291.
SUBJ 32.2 36.3 ▪ 15 64

18605 CSU S P2 G1.2 1911–1949
Cole, George Douglas Howard, 1889–1959.
'The rise, fall, and renaissance of Communism in China.' In *A history of socialist thought, Vol. 4, Part 2, Communism and social democracy, 1914–1931*, by G. D. H. Cole. [Sole entry]
New York: St. Martin's Press, 1958, 775–802.
SUBJ 16.3 32.2 64 ▪ 16.4 36.3 36.4 66

18606 WSU P P1 G1.2 1928–1949
Compton, Boyd Ross.
'Introduction.' In *Mao's China: Party reform documents, 1942–44*, edited by B. R. Compton. [Sole entry]
Seattle: U. of Washington Press, 1952, 15–52 [s.p.]. (Revision of *Thought discipline in the Chinese Communist Party*, masters thesis in Far Eastern and

Slavic Languages, U. of Washington, 1951)
SUBJ 32.1 32.2 64 ▪ 12 15 61

18607 MBA O P3 G9.0 1911–1928
Coulon, Jean Philippe.
'Lettre de Hongkong: la question monétaire et le boycottage des tramways' (A letter from Hong Kong: The monetary problem and the tram boycott).
RI nouvelle (2e) série 18, 1 (jan. 1913), 63–70.
SUBJ 24.6 32.2

18608 CSH O P2 G1.2 1928–1949
Cressy-Marcks, Violet Olivia Rutley.
Journey into China.
New York: Dutton, 1942. 324 p.
SUBJ 15 25 32.2 64 66 ▪ 12.1 14.1 14.2 18 47 50 51 55

18609 DLC O P2 G1.3 1911–1928
Dalin, Sergei Alekseevich.
Ocherki revoliutsii v Kitae (Notes on the revolution in China).
Moscow: Moskovskii rabochii, 1927. 282 p.
SUBJ 14.1 15 16 32.2 36.3 ▪ 12 23 34.3 36.2 36.4 66

18610 CSH O P2 G1.2 1911–1928
Dalin, Sergei Alekseevich.
V riadakh kitaiskoi revoliutsii (In the ranks of the Chinese revolution).
Moscow: Moskovskii rabochii, 1926. 144 p.
SUBJ 12 32.2 ▪ 12.1 14 16.1 66

18611 DLC P P2 G9.2 1911–1928
Den Chzhun-sia (Teng Chung-hsia), 1897–1933.
'Kitaiskaia kommunisticheskaia partiia v Kantonskom vosstanii' (The Chinese Communist Party in the Canton uprising). In *Kantonskaia kommuna: sbornik statei i materialov* (Articles and documents on the Canton commune), compiled by Nauchno-issledovatel'skii institut po Kitaiu, Kommunisticheskaia akademiia. [Selective entry]
Moscow: Gosizdat, 1929, 31–45.
SUBJ 15 25 32.2 ▪ 26.3 26.4 36.4

18612 CSH P P2 G1.2 1928–1949
Dorrill, William Franklin, 1931–.
'CCP united front policy after the Manchuria Incident: A critique of the Maoist interpretation.' In *Collected documents of the First Sino-American Conference on Mainland China.* [Selective entry]
[Taipei]: Institute of International Relations, Republic of China, 1971, 569–586.
SUBJ 32.2 66 ▪ 32 64

18613 CSU P P1 G1.5 1928–1949
Dorrill, William Franklin, 1931–.
'The Fukien Rebellion and the CCP: A case of Maoist revisionism.'
CQ 37 (Jan.–Mar. 1969), 31–53.
SUBJ 15 32.2 ▪ 32 64

18614 MCH P P2 G1.5 1911–1949
Dorrill, William Franklin, 1931–.
Mao and the returned students: Issues of policy and power in the Chinese Communist movement, 1930–1932.
Unpublished doctoral dissertation in Political Science, Harvard U., 1970. 332 p.
SUBJ 32.2 64 ▪ 25 54

18615 DLC U P2 G1.2 1911–1928
[Dridzo, Solomon Abramovich] A. Lozovskii, pseud., 1878–.
'Novyi etap kitaiskoi revoliutsii' (A new stage in the Chinese revolution). In *Rabochii Kitai v 1927 godu: sbornik statei* (Articles on workers' China in 1927), edited by [S. A. Dridzo] A. Lozovskii, pseud. [Selective entry]
Moscow: Profintern, 1928, 5–40.
SUBJ 15 16 32.2 64 ▪ 19 32 36.3

18616 CSH U P2 G1.2 1911–1928
[Dridzo, Solomon Abramovich] A. Lozovskii, pseud., 1878–.
'Puti kitaiskoi revoliutsii' (The courses of the Chinese revolution). In *O Kitae: politiko-ekonomicheskii sbornik* (Articles on China's political economy), edited by [S. A. Dridzo] A. Lozovskii, pseud. [Selective entry]
Moscow: Gosizdat, 1928, 1–27.
SUBJ 16 32 32.2 ▪ 15 16.1 25 36.3 54

18617 DLC P P2 G1.2 1911–1928
[Dridzo, Solomon Abramovich] A. Lozovskii, pseud., 1878–.
Revoliutsiia i kontrrevoliutsiia v Kitae (Revolution and counterrevolution in China).
Moscow: Moskovskii rabochii, 1927. 172 p.
SUBJ 16 32.2 64 ▪ 11.4 15 16.3 16.4 22.2 25 36.4 47

18618 DLC P P3 G9.2 1911–1928
[Dridzo, Solomon Abramovich] A. Lozovskii, pseud., 1878–.
'Uroki Kantonskogo vosstaniia' (Lessons of the Canton uprising). In *Kantonskaia kommuna: sbornik statei i materialov* (Articles and documents on the Canton commune), compiled by Nauchno-issledovatel'skii institut po Kitaiu, Kommunisticheskaia akademiia. [Selective entry]
Moscow: Gosizdat, 1929, 12–18.
SUBJ 32.2 ▪ 15 25 26.4 64 66

18619 DLC S P2 G1.2 1911–1949
Erenburg, Grigorii Borisovich, 1902–1967.
Sovetskii Kitai (Soviet China), 2nd ed., rev. and enl.
Moscow: Partizdat, 1934. 141 p.
SUBJ 14.1 15 16 32.2 64 66 ▪ 14 19 30

18620 MAM P P3 G9.2 1911–1928
Esposito, Bruce John, 1941–.
The Comintern and the Canton commune.
Ann Arbor: University Microfilms (Publ. 68-14,965), 1968. 272 p. (Doctoral dissertation in History, American U.)
SUBJ 25 32.2 66 ▪ 32 64

18621 NNC O P3 G1.3 1911–1928
Farjenel, Fernand, ?–1918.
A travers la révolution chinoise, 2nd ed.
Paris: Plon-Nourrit, 1914. 401 p.

Through the Chinese revolution. Tr. by Margaret Vivian.
London: Duckworth, 1915. 360 p.
SUBJ 12 14.5 15 32.2 ▪ 12.2 16.1 22.2 25 30 47 55 66

18622 NNC O P2 G1.4 1911–1949
Forman, Harrison, 1904–.
Report from Red China.
New York: Holt, 1945. 250 p.
SUBJ 25 32.2 66 ▪ 22 22.2 24.1 24.4 26.3 31 34.1 47 59 65

18623 CSH U P3 G1.2 1911–1928
Galkovich, M- (M. Galkowitsch; M. Galkovitch).
'Noveishii fazis natsional'no-osvoboditel'noi bor'by' (The latest phase of the national liberation struggle).
KIP 5, 9 (sentiabr' 1925), 37–43. [Reprinted in *Rabochii Kitai: sbornik statei* (Articles on workers' China). (Selective entry.) Moscow: Profintern, 1926, 131–140.]

'Die neueste Phase des nationalen Befreiungskampfes.'
RGI 5, 9 (Sept. 1925), 126–129. [Reprinted in *Arbeiterbewegung und Revolution in China* (The labor movement and revolution in China), by Karl Radek et al. (Selective entry.) Berlin: Führer, 1925, 103–113.]

'Une nouvelle phase de lutte nationale.'
ISR 56 (sept. 1925), 715–718.
SUBJ 32.2 36.4 ▪ 12.1

18624 MCY P P1 G1.2 1928–1949
Garavente, Anthony.
'The Long March.'
CQ 22 (Apr.–June 1965), 89–124.
SUBJ 15 32.2

18625 MCH P P3 G1.2 1911–1928
Garushiants, IUrii Misakovich.
'Bor'ba kitaiskikh marksistov za sozdanie kompartii Kitaia' (The Chinese Marxists' struggle to form the Chinese Communist Party).
NAA 1961, 3, 81–96.
SUBJ 16.4 32.2 ▪ 14.2 16.1 16.2 36.4

18626 CSU P P2 G1.2 1911–1949
Girling, J- L- S-.
'The model, China: Conditions for success.' In *People's war: Conditions and consequences in China and South East Asia*, by J- L- S- Girling. [Sole entry]
New York: Praeger, 1969, 49–114.
SUBJ 32 32.2 64 ▪ 15 16 36.3 66

18627 CSH P P8 G1.4 1928–1949
Gittings, John, 1938–.
'The party is always right.'
FEER 64, 23 (5 June 1969), 574–575.
SUBJ 14.1 32.2 64

18628 CSH P P2 G1.2 1911–1928
Glunin, Vladimir Ivanovich, 1924–.
'Komintern i stanovlenie kommunisticheskogo dvizheniia v Kitae (1920–1927)' (The Comintern and the development of the Communist movement in China, 1920–1927). In *Komintern i Vostok: bor'ba za leninskuiu strategiiu i taktiku v natsional'no-osvoboditel'nom dvizhenii* (The Comintern and the Orient: The struggle for Leninist strategy and tactics in the national liberation movement), compiled by Institut mezhdunarodnogo rabochego dvizheniia, Akademiia nauk SSSR. [Selective entry]

Moscow: Nauka, Glav. red. vost. lit-ry, 1969, 242–299.
Subj 16.2 16.4 32.2 64 ▪ 66

18629 NNC P P2 G1.2 1928–1949
Glunin, Vladimir Ivanovich, 1924–.
Tret'ia grazhdanskaia revoliutsionnaia voina v Kitae, 1946–1949: ocherk politicheskoi istorii (Survey of the political history of the Third Revolutionary Civil War in China, 1946–1949).
Moscow: Izd-vo vost. lit-ry, 1958. 197 p.
Subj 12 15 32 32.2 ▪ 14 16

18630 DLC P P2 G1.2 1911–1928
Goncharov, Pavel Fedorovich.
Pobeda velikoi oktiabr'skoi sotsialisticheskoi revoliutsii i pod"em natsional'no-osvoboditel'nogo dvizheniia v stranakh Azii v 1917–1923 gg.: na primere Kitaia, Mongolii, Korei (The victory of the October Revolution and the rise of the national liberation movement in Asia, 1917–1923: The examples of China, Mongolia, and Korea).
Moscow: Vses. iurid. zaochnyi in-t, 1960. 55 p.
Subj 16.4 19 32.2 ▪ 16 66

18631 CSU U P2 G1.2 1911–1949
Grieder, Jerome Bailey, 1932–.
'Communism, nationalism, and democracy: The Chinese intelligentsia and the Chinese revolution in the 1920's and 1930's.' In *Modern East Asia: Essays in interpretation*, edited by James Buckley Crowley. [Selective entry]
New York: Harcourt, Brace and World, 1970, 207–234.
Subj 19 32.2 64 ▪ 16.1 54

18632 CSH P P2 G1.2 1928–1949
Grigor'ev, Aleksandr Mironovich, 1933–.
'Komintern i revoliutsionnoe dvizhenie v Kitae pod lozungom sovetov (1928–1930)' (The Comintern and the revolutionary movement in China under the slogan of the soviets, 1928–1930). In *Komintern i Vostok: bor'ba za leninskuiu strategiiu i taktiku v natsional'no-osvoboditel'nom dvizhenii* (The Comintern and the Orient: The struggle for Leninist strategy and tactics in the national liberation movement), compiled by Institut mezhdunarodnogo rabochego dvizheniia, Akademiia nauk SSSR. [Selective entry]
Moscow: Nauka, Glav. red. vost. lit-ry, 1969, 313–349.
Subj 14.1 15 32.2 64 66 ▪ 16.3 16.4

18633 DLC P P2 G1.2 1911–1949
Grigor'ev, Aleksandr Mironovich, 1933–, and Lev Petrovich Deliusin, 1923–.
'Sotsial'no-istoricheskie usloviia razvitiia kitaiskoi revoliutsii: korni kursa gruppy Mao TSze-duna' (Social and historical preconditions for the development of the Chinese revolution: The roots of the policy of the Maoists). In *Kitai segodnia* (China today), compiled by Akademiia nauk SSSR, edited by L. P. Deliusin and Grigorii Dmitrievich Sukharchuk. [Selective entry]
Moscow: Nauka, Glav. red. vost. lit-ry, 1969, 292–335.
Subj 16 32.2 64 ▪ 12 66

18634 MCY P P2 G1.4 1928–1949
Grootaers, Willem A-, 1911–.
'Une société secrète moderne, I-Koan-Tao: bibliographie annotée' (The I-kuan-tao, a modern secret society: An annotated bibliography).
FS 5 (1946), 316–352.
Subj 32.2 62 72 ▪ 70

18635 DLC P P2 G1.2 1911–1949
Guillermaz, Jacques, 1911–.
Histoire du Parti communiste chinois (1921–1949).
Paris: Payot, 1968. 450 p.
A history of the Chinese Communist Party, 1921–1949. Tr. by Anne Destenay.
New York: Random House, 1972. 477 p.
Subj 15 16.1 32.2 64 ▪ 12 12.1 16.3 16.4 32 36.4 66

18636 NNC P P2 G1.2 1911–1949
Hanrahan, Gene Z-, 1926–.
The birth of the Chinese Red Army.
Unpublished masters thesis in Chinese and Japanese, Columbia U., 1953. 286 p.
Subj 15 32.2 ▪ 12.1 14.1 22.2 36.3 36.4 64

18637 CSU U P2 G1.3 1928–1949
Hanwell, Norman D-.
'The Red Spears of China.'
Asia (New York: American Asiatic Assn.) 39, 8 (Aug. 1939), 465–468.
Subj 32.2 ▪ 16.1 16.3

18638 CSH S P2 G1.3 1928–1949
Harrison, James Pinckney, 1932–.
'The Li Li-san line and the CCP in 1930.'
CQ 14 (Apr.–June 1963), 178–194; 15 (July–Sept. 1963), 140–159.
Subj 32.2 ▪ 15 59 64

18639 CSU P P3 G1.3 1911–1928
Heinzig, Dieter, 1932–.
Die Anfänge der kommunistischen Partei Chinas im Lichte der Memoiren Chang Kuo-t'aos (The origins of the Chinese Communist Party in the light of the memoirs of Chang Kuo-t'ao).
Cologne: Bundesinstitut für ostwissenschaftliche und internationale Studien, 1969. 2 vols. 23; 17 p. (BOIS, Berichte, 1969, 60–61)
Subj 32.2 64 ▪ 59

18640 CSU S P4 G8.3 1928–1949
Heinzig, Dieter, 1932–.
'Otto Braun and the Tsunyi Conference [Kweichow].'
CQ 42 (Apr.–June 1970), 131–135.
Subj 16.1 32.2

18641 CSU S P2 G1.5 1928–1949
Heinzig, Dieter, 1932–.
'The Otto Braun memoirs and Mao's rise to power.'
CQ 46 (Apr.–June 1971), 274–288.
Subj 16.1 32.2

18642 NNC U P4 G1.3 1911–1928
[Heller, Leo N-] L. Geller.
'Narodno-revoliutsionnoe dvizhenie i zadachi revoliutsionnykh profsoiuzov v Kitae' (The popular revolutionary movement and tasks of the revolutionary trade unions in China).
KIP 5, 1 (ianvar' 1925), 32–39.
'Die national-revolutionäre Bewegung und die Aufgaben der revolutionären Gewerkschaften in China.'
RGI 5, 1 (Jan. 1925), 20–24.
'Le mouvement révolutionnaire populaire et les tâches des syndicates en Chine.'
ISR 48 (jan. 1925), 24–29.
Subj 16 32.2 36.4 ▪ 16.2 16.4

18643 CSH F P8 G5.2 1928–1949
Hinton, William H-, 1919–.
Fanshen: A documentary of revolution in a Chinese village.
New York: Monthly Review Press, 1966. 17, 637 p.
Subj 22 22.1 22.2 24.1 26 32.2 ▪ 24.5 25 26.1 26.3 32.1 36.3 46 47 50 55

18644 CSU P P2 G7.0 1911–1928
Hofheinz, Roy Mark, Jr., 1935–.
'The Autumn Harvest Insurrection.'
CQ 32 (Oct.–Dec. 1967), 37–87.
Subj 15 32.2 ▪ 25 36.3

18645 CSU S P7 G1.3 1911–1949
Hofheinz, Roy Mark, Jr., 1935–.
'The ecology of Chinese Communist success: Rural influence patterns, 1923–45.' In *Chinese Communist politics in action*, edited by Arthur Doak Barnett. [Selective entry]
Seattle: U. of Washington Press, 1969, 3–77. (Social Science Research Council, Studies in Chinese government and politics, 1)
Subj 11.3 32.1 32.2 36.3 ▪ 14.1 14.2 15 16.3 17 25 32 34.1 66

18646 CSH P P2 G1.5 1911–1928
Hsiao Tso-liang, 1910–.
Chinese Communism in 1927: City vs countryside.
Hong Kong: Chinese U. of Hong Kong, 1970. 197 p.
Subj 25 32.2 64 ▪ 16.3 16.4

18647 MCY P P2 G1.2 1928–1949
Hsiao Tso-liang, 1910–.
Power relations within the Chinese Communist movement, 1930–1934: A study of documents.
Seattle: U. of Washington Press, 1961. 10, 404 p.
Subj 12.1 12.2 15 16.1 32.2 64 ▪ 11.4 12 17 22 30

18648 CSU P P1 G1.2 1928–1949
Hu, Chi-hsi.
'Hua Fu, the fifth encirclement campaign and the Tsunyi Conference.'
CQ 43 (July–Sept. 1970), 31–46.
Subj 15 16.1 32.2 64 ▪ 66

18649 CLS P P1 G1.2 1911–1928
Hughes, Philip Russell, 1937–.
The formation of the Communist-Kuomintang First United Front, 1921–1924.
Unpublished masters thesis in Asian Studies, U. of Southern California, 1965. 88 p.
Subj 32 32.2 66 ▪ 16.1 32.1 64

18650 NNC P P1 G9.4 1911–1949
Hwang, Hsien-chung.
Taiwanese political movement under Japanese rule, 1921–1931.

Unpublished masters thesis in Political Science, Columbia U., 1966. 70 p. [Certificate essay, East Asian Institute]
SUBJ 32.2 ▪ 12 12.1 32.1

18651 MCY S P2 G1.2 1911–1949
Institute of Pacific Relations. American Council.
'Pacific affairs bibliographies. No. 3, Literature on the Chinese soviet movement.'
PA 9, 3 (Sept. 1936), 421–435.
SUBJ 32.2 70 71 72 ▪ 14 32 64

18652 CSU F P3 G1.2 1911–1928
Isaacs, Harold Robert, 1910–.
'Documents on the Comintern and the Chinese Revolution.'
CQ 45 (Jan.–Mar. 1971), 100–115.
SUBJ 32.2 66

18653 NIC P P2 G1.2 1911–1928
Isaacs, Harold Robert, 1910–.
The tragedy of the Chinese revolution, 2nd ed., rev.
Stanford: Stanford U. Press, 1961. 21, 392 p. [Reprinted—Stanford: Stanford U. Press, 1971. 21, 392 p.]
SUBJ 32.2 66 ▪ 14 15 16

18654 CSH P P2 G1.3 1911–1928
IUr'ev, Mikhail Filippovich, 1918–.
Revoliutsiia 1925–1927 gg. v Kitae (The Chinese Revolution of 1925–1927).
Moscow: Nauka, Glav. red. vost. lit-ry, 1968. 518 p.
SUBJ 15 16 32.2 36.3 36.4 66 ▪ 12 14.4 17 18 25 32 32.1 35 54 64

18655 DLC P P2 G1.2 1911–1928
IUr'ev, Mikhail Filippovich, 1918–.
Rol' revoliutsionnoi armii na pervom etape kitaiskoi revoliutsii (The role of the revolutionary army in the first stage of the Chinese revolution).
Moscow: Izd-vo Mosk. un-ta, 1952. 139 p.
SUBJ 15 16 32.1 32.2 36.3 36.4 ▪ 12.1 17 25 35 64 66

18656 NNC P P2 G1.2 1928–1949
[Ivanov, Aleksei Alekseevich] A. Ivin, pseud., 1885–1942.
Bor'ba za vlast' sovetov: ocherki sovetskogo dvizheniia v Kitae (The struggle for soviet power: Notes on the soviet movement in China).
Moscow: Ogiz-Sotsekgiz, 1933. 156 p.
SUBJ 15 32 32.2 ▪ 14.1

18657 MCH O P7 G1.3 1911–1949
[Ivanov, Aleksei Alekseevich] A. Ivin, pseud., 1885–1942.
Ocherki partizanskogo dvizheniia v Kitae, 1927–1930 gg. (Notes on the partisan movement in China, 1927–1930).
Moscow: Gos. izd-vo, Otdel voen. lit-ry, 1930. 106 p.
SUBJ 32.2 ▪ 16.3 25

18658 MCH O P7 G5.1 1928–1949
Jaepher, Raymond de, 1905–.
'Stratégie communiste en Chine du Nord' (Communist strategy in North China).
B. des missions St. André de Bruges 24, 3 (1950), 181–199.
SUBJ 19 22.1 24 32.2 ▪ 15 17 25 28 33 62 64 66

18659 GMS O P2 G1.2 1928–1949
Jensen, Fritz.
China siegt (China victorious).
Berlin: Dietz, 1950. 348 p.
SUBJ 12.1 19 32.2 ▪ 14.5 14.6 15 16.1 16.2 64

18660 MCH P P2 G1.2 1928–1949
Johnson, Chalmers Ashby, 1931–.
Peasant nationalism and Communist power: The emergence of revolutionary China, 1937–1945.
Stanford: Stanford U. Press, 1962. 12, 256 p. (Revision of doctoral dissertation in Political Science, U. of California, Berkeley, 1961)
SUBJ 16.3 25 32.2 36.3 64 ▪ 12 12.1 14.1 15 30 32.1 35 66

18661 MAM P P2 G1.2 1911–1949
Kagan, Richard Clark, 1938–.
The Chinese Trotskyist movement and Ch'en Tu-hsiu: Culture, revolution and polity.
Ann Arbor: University Microfilms (Publ. 70-16,169), 1970. 37, 206 p. (Doctoral dissertation in History, U. of Pennsylvania)
SUBJ 10 32.2 59 64 ▪ 14.2 16 32 36.1

18662 CSH P P3 G1.3 1911–1928
Kartunova, Anastasiia Ivanovna.
'Komintern i nekotorye voprosy reorganizatsii gomin'dana' (The Comintern and certain questions of Kuomintang reorganization). In *Komintern i Vostok: bor'ba za leninskuiu strategiiu i taktiku v natsional'no-osvoboditel'nom dvizhenii* (The Comintern and the Orient: The struggle for Leninist strategy and tactics in the national liberation movement), compiled by Institut mezhdunarodnogo rabochego dvizheniia, Akademiia nauk SSSR. [Selective entry]
Moscow: Nauka, Glav. red. vost. lit-ry, 1969, 300–312.
SUBJ 32.2 ▪ 64 66

18663 CSU P P2 G1.2 1928–1949
Kataoka, Tetsuya, 1933–.
'Communist power in a war of national liberation: The case of China.' [Review of *Peasant nationalism and Communist power*, by Chalmers Ashby Johnson; *Dai Tōa sensō kōkanshi, [17], Hokushi no chiansen* (Publicly recorded history of the Great East Asian War, Vol. 17, The pacification war in China), by Senshishitsu, Bōei kenshūjo, Bōeichō, Sōrifu, Japan (War History Office, Defense Research Institute, Defense Agency, Prime Minister's Office); *Rebellion and its enemies in late Imperial China: Militarization and social structure, 1796–1864*, by Philip Alden Kuhn; *Fanshen: A documentary of revolution in a Chinese village*, by William H. Hinton; and *Revolution in a Chinese village: Ten Mile Inn*, by Isabel Crook and David Crook.]
WP 24, 3 (Apr. 1972), 410–427.
SUBJ 15 20 32.2 36.3 64 ▪ 12.1 16.1 32

18664 CSH O P2 G1.4 1911–1928
Keyte, John Charles, 1875–.
The passing of the dragon: The story of the Shensi revolution and relief expedition.
New York: Hodder and Stoughton, 1913. 12, 311 p.
SUBJ 25 32.2 66 ▪ 15 21.3 47 56

18665 DLC O P3 G9.2 1911–1928
Khuan Pin (Huang P'ing).
'Kantonskoe vosstanie i ego podgotovka' (Laying the groundwork for the Canton uprising). In *Kantonskaia kommuna: sbornik statei i materialov* (Articles and documents on the Canton commune), compiled by Nauchno-issledovatel'skii institut po Kitaiu, Kommunisticheskaia akademiia. [Selective entry]
Moscow: Gosizdat, 1929, 46–62.
SUBJ 15 19 32.2 ▪ 25 36.4

18666 MAM P P1 G1.2 1928–1949
Kim, Hong N. (Kim Hong-nack), 1933–.
The Communist united front movement in China, 1931–1937.
Ann Arbor: University Microfilms (Publ. 65-12,526), 1965. 422 p. (Doctoral dissertation in Political Science, Georgetown U.)
SUBJ 32.2 64 ▪ 15 66

18667 MAM FP P7 G7.0 1928–1949
Kim, Ilpyong John (Kim Il-pyong), 1931–.
Communist politics in China: A study of the development of organizational concepts, behavior, and techniques of the Chinese soviet movement during the Kiangsi period, 1931–1934.
Ann Arbor: University Microfilms (Publ. 71-17,594), 1971. 427 p. (Doctoral dissertation in Public Law and Government, Columbia U., 1968)
SUBJ 12 22 22.1 32.2 ▪ 26.3

18668 DLC S P4 G1.2 1928–1949
Korobov, N- D-.
'Iz istorii stroitel'stva narodnoi demokratii v osvobozhdennykh gorodakh Kitaia nakanune obrazovaniia Kitaiskoi Narodnoi Respubliki' (History of the building of people's democracy in China's liberated cities on the eve of the establishment of the People's Republic of China).
Uchenye zapiski Saratovskogo gosudarstvennogo universiteta 68 (1960), 111–122.
SUBJ 16.4 32.1 32.2 ▪ 36.4 64

18669 DLC P P7 G1.4 1911–1928
Kostiaeva, Aleksandra Sergeevna, 1932–.
'Tainye soiuzy severa v krest'ianskom dvizhenii 1926–1927 gg.' (Northern secret societies in the peasant movement of 1926–1927). In *Tainye obshchestva v starom Kitae* (Secret societies in old China), compiled by Institut vostokovedeniia, Akademiia nauk SSSR, edited by Vasilii Pavlovich Iliushechkin. [Selective entry]
Moscow: Nauka, Glav. red. vost. lit-ry, 1970, 159–173.
SUBJ 26.1 32.1 32.2 35 36.3 ▪ 15 26.3 72

18670 CSH S P2 G1.5 1911–1928
Krymov, A- G-.
'Kontrnastuplenie reaktsionnykh sil i vremennoe porazhenie revoliutsii (mart–iiul' 1927 g.)' (Counterattack of reactionary forces and the temporary setback to the revolution, March–July 1927). In *Ocherki istorii Kitaia v noveishee vremia* (Survey of modern Chinese history), compiled by Institut kitaevedeniia, Akademiia nauk SSSR, edited by Aleksei Stepanovich Perevertailo et al. [Selective entry]

Moscow: Izd-vo vost. lit-ry, 1959, 165–184.
SUBJ 25 32 32.1 32.2 ▪ 16 64 66

18671 CSU O P7 G4.4 1928–1949
Kube, Josef.
'Der Kaiser im Volksdenken' (The role of the emperor in the minds of the people). In *Ethnographische Beiträge aus der Ch'inghai Provinz (China)* (Ethnographic reports from Tsinghai). [Selective entry]
Peking [i.e., Tokyo]: Catholic U. of Peking, Museum of Oriental Ethnology, 1952, 157–166. (MOE, Folklore studies supplements, 1)
SUBJ 22.1 32.2 42 65 ▪ 53

18672 CSH P P2 G1.2 1928–1949
Kukushkin, Kim Vladimirovich, 1926–.
'Komintern i edinyi natsional'nyi antiiaponskii front v Kitae (1935–1943)' (The Comintern and the national anti-Japanese united front in China, 1935–1943). In *Komintern i Vostok: bor'ba za leninskuiu strategiiu i taktiku v natsional'no-osvoboditel'nom dvizhenii* (The Comintern and the Orient: The struggle for Leninist strategy and tactics in the national liberation movement), compiled by Institut mezhdunarodnogo rabochego dvizheniia, Akademiia nauk SSSR. [Selective entry]
Moscow: Nauka, Glav. red. vost. lit-ry, 1969, 350–379.
SUBJ 15 32 32.2 64 66 ▪ 16.3 16.4

18673 NNC P P7 G1.2 1911–1949
Kuo, Evgenii.
'Uglublenie agrarnogo krizisa, pod''em krest'ianskogo revoliutsionnogo dvizheniia v Kitae i zadachi Kitaiskoi kompartii' (The deepening land crisis, the upsurge of the peasant revolutionary movement in China, and the Chinese Communist Party's tasks).
Agrarnye problemy 7, 9/10 (1933), 113–134.
SUBJ 14 14.1 32.2 36.3 ▪ 12.1 14.5 16.3 24.3 57

18674 MCH P P2 G1.2 1911–1949
Kuo, Warren (Kuo Hua-lun), 1912–.
Analytical history of Chinese Communist Party.
Taipei: Institute of International Relations, 1966, 1968. 2 vols. 502; 206 p. [Vols. 3–6 were to be published.]
SUBJ 15 32.2 64 ▪ 12 14 25 36.3 36.4 66

18675 CSU P P2 G1.2 1928–1949
Kuo, Warren (Kuo Hua-lun), 1912–.
'The CCP after the government evacuation of Wuhan.'
IS 5, 8 (May 1969), 34–42; 5, 9 (June 1969), 41–57.
SUBJ 32 32.2 ▪ 16.1 64

18676 CSU P P1 G1.3 1928–1949
Kuo, Warren (Kuo Hua-lun), 1912–.
'The CCP campaign for consolidation of party organizations.'
IS 6, 3 (Dec. 1969), 71–90.
SUBJ 32.2 64 ▪ 14.2 15

18677 CSU P P2 G1.2 1928–1949
Kuo, Warren (Kuo Hua-lun), 1912–.
'The Communist "anti-friction" struggle.'
IS 6, 4 (Jan. 1970), 67–78; 6, 5 (Feb. 1970), 58–80.
SUBJ 16.1 32.2 64 66 ▪ 15 17 32

18678 CSH P P2 G1.4 1928–1949
Kuo, Warren (Kuo Hua-lun), 1912–.
'Communist expansion and clashes with the Kuomintang.'
IS 6, 2 (Nov. 1969), 63–80.
SUBJ 12 25 32.2 ▪ 16.1 22

18679 CSU P P2 G1.3 1928–1949
Kuo, Warren (Kuo Hua-lun), 1912–.
'Communist moves after the incident in southern Anhwei.'
IS 6, 9 (June 1970), 60–71; 6, 10 (July 1970), 52–68.
SUBJ 15 32.2 ▪ 12 16.1 17 59

18680 CSU PO P1 G1.2 1928–1949
Kuo, Warren (Kuo Hua-lun), 1912–.
'The conflict between Chen Shao-yu and Mao Tse-tung.'
IS 5, 2 (Nov. 1968), 35–45; 5, 3 (Dec. 1968), 40–54.
SUBJ 12 15 32.2

18681 CSH P P2 G1.3 1928–1949
Kuo, Warren (Kuo Hua-lun), 1912–.
'The incidents concerning Chen Tu-hsiu and Chang Kuo-tao.'
IS 5, 4 (Jan. 1969), 38–53; 5, 5 (Feb. 1969), 32–49.
SUBJ 16.1 32.2 ▪ 12.1 32

18682 CSU P P2 G1.4 1928–1949
Kuo, Warren (Kuo Hua-lun), 1912–.
'The Shensi-Kansu-Ninghsia border region.'
IS 5, 10 (July 1969), 73–86; 5, 11 (Aug. 1969), 68–86.
SUBJ 12 15 22 32.2 ▪ 14.1 14.5 16.1 22.2 25 64

18683 CSH P P2 G1.3 1928–1949
Kuo, Warren (Kuo Hua-lun), 1912–.
'A study of the "Resolutions of the Tsunyi Conference".' In *Collected documents of the First Sino-American Conference on Mainland China.* [Selective entry]
[Taipei]: Institute of International Relations, Republic of China, 1971, 85–128.
SUBJ 32.2 ▪ 15 16.1

18684 MCY U P2 G1.2 1928–1949
Kusano Fumio, 1915–.
'The economic strength of Chinese Communists.'
Contemporary Japan 18, 4/6 (Apr.–June 1949), 174–187.
SUBJ 14 32.2 ▪ 14.1 14.5 14.6 22 34.2

18685 CSH P P2 G1.2 1911–1949
Kwei, Chung-gi.
The Kuomintang-Communist struggle in China, 1922–1949.
The Hague: Nijhoff, 1970. 131 p.
SUBJ 32 32.2 ▪ 15 25 64 66

18686 CSU P P2 G9.1 1911–1949
Lary, Diana Cecilia Margaret, 1941–.
'Communism and ethnic revolt: Some notes on the Chuang peasant movement in Kwangsi, 1921–31.'
CQ 49 (Jan.–Mar. 1972), 126–135.
SUBJ 25 32.2 66 ▪ 36.3

18687 CSU O P2 G1.1 1928–1949
Lattimore, Owen, 1900–.
The situation in Asia.
Boston: Little, Brown, 1949. 238 p.
SUBJ 12 32.2 ▪ 12.1 15 32

18688 CSU O P2 G1.4 1928–1949
Lattimore, Owen, 1900–.
'Unpublished report from Yenan, 1937.' In *Studies in the social history of China and South-east Asia: Essays in memory of Victor Purcell*, edited by Jerome Ch'en (Ch'en Chih-jang) and Nicholas Tarling. [Selective entry]
Cambridge: Cambridge U. Press, 1970, 153–164.
SUBJ 32.2 ▪ 15 16.1 66

18689 CBU P P1 G1.2 1911–1949
Lee, Ming T.
'The founders of the Chinese Communist Party: A study in revolutionaries.'
Civilisations 18, 1 (1968), 113–127.
SUBJ 16.1 32.2 59

18690 ELS P P7 G1.4 1928–1949
Lee Ngok (Li O), 1939–.
The Chinese Communist bases (ken-chü-ti) in North China, 1938–1943: A study of their growth and anti-Japanese activities, with special reference to administration and mass mobilisation programmes at the village level.
Unpublished doctoral dissertation in History, U. of London [School of Oriental and African Studies], 1968. 331 p.
SUBJ 22 26 32.2 36.3 ▪ 19 24.1 26.3 66

18691 CSU P P7 G1.2 1928–1949
Lee Ngok (Li O), 1939–.
'Liu Shao-ch'i and Communist politics, 1937–1945.'
JOS 7, 2 (July 1969), 347–359.
SUBJ 16.1 32.2 ▪ 64

18692 CBU P P1 G1.2 1928–1949
Lee Ngok (Li O), 1939–.
'The strengthening of party identity in the *cheng feng* [rectification] campaign, 1942–1944.'
CCJ 9, 2 (May 1970), 149–160.
SUBJ 32.1 32.2 64 ▪ 16 63

18693 MCH O P3 G6.1 1928–1949
Li Min (Li Ming).
'Nekotoryi opyt i uroki KPK v organizatsii i rukovodstve stachechnoi bor'boi: litsom k predpriiatiiam' (Experiences and lessons of the Chinese Communist Party in organizing and leading strikes in the struggle against capitalist enterprises).
Kommunisticheskii Internatsional 1934, 11/12 (20 aprelia), 62–65.
SUBJ 32.2 36.4

18694 NIC F P2 G8.1 1928–1949
Liao, T'ai-ch'u.
'The Ko Lao Hui in Szechuan.'
PA 20, 2 (June 1947), 161–173.
SUBJ 22 32.2 ▪ 24.2 24.3 25

18695 CSU O P2 G9.3 1928–1949
Lin, T. L.
'Communism in Fukien.'
CR 66, 5 (May 1935), 272–276.
SUBJ 22.1 32.2 ▪ 24.1 24.5 25 64

18696 CSH O P1 G1.2 1928–1949
Liu Shao-ch'i, 1898–.
On inner-party struggle: A lecture delivered on July 2, 1941 at the party school for Central China. Tr. of *Lun tang nei tou cheng* (On struggle within the party); Hong Kong: Cheng pao she, 1947; 49 p.

Peking: Foreign Languages Press, 1950? 92 p.
SUBJ 32.2 ▪ 64

18697 CSH PO P2 G4.2 1911–1928
Ma TSy-ian' (Ma Tz'u-yen).
'Musul'manskoe vosstanie v Gan'su' (The Muslim rebellion in Kansu).
PK 1 (1929), 380–402.
SUBJ 15 22.2 25 32.2 35 36.3 ▪ 24 28 33

18698 CSU P P2 G1.2 1911–1949
McColl, Robert William, 1938–.
'A political geography of revolution: China, Vietnam, and Thailand.'
J. of conflict resolution 11, 2 (June 1967), 153–167.
SUBJ 32.2 64 ▪ 16 19 32 66

18699 MAM P P2 G1.2 1911–1949
McColl, Robert William, 1938–.
The rise of territorial Communism in China 1921–1934: The geography behind politics.
Ann Arbor: University Microfilms (Publ. 65-5444), 1965. 130 p. (Doctoral dissertation in Geography, U. of Washington, 1964)
SUBJ 11.3 16 32.2 ▪ 11.2 14.2 15 16.2 16.3 32 36.3

18700 MCH O P2 G1.1 1911–1928
Magrini, Luciano, 1885–.
In Cina e in Giappone (In China and Japan).
Milan: La Promotrice, 1927. 305 p.
SUBJ 12 32.2 ▪ 12.1 13 15 33 47 62 64

18701 NNC P P1 G1.2 1928–1949
Mallett, Richard David, 1927–.
Chinese Nationalist and Chinese Communist Party relations, August 1945 to February 1947.
Unpublished masters thesis in History, Columbia U., 1957. 250 p. [Certificate essay, East Asian Institute]
SUBJ 12 32.2 ▪ 14 15 32

18702 MCH O P2 G2.0 1928–1949
Manchuria Daily News.
The Comintern's activity in Manchuria: A general survey.
Changchun: Manchuria Daily News, 1940. 49 p.
SUBJ 32.2 ▪ 12.1

18703 CSH O P2 G7.0 1928–1949
Mao Tse-tung, 1893–.
'The struggle in the Chingkang mountains [Kiangsi-Hunan border region].' Tr. of 'Ching-kang shan ti tou cheng'; in *Mao Tse-tung hsüan chi* (Selected works of Mao Tse-tung), 2nd ed.; Peking: Jen min ch'u pan she, 1960, vol. 1 [report submitted to the Central Committee, Chinese Communist Party, 25 November 1928]. In *Selected works of Mao Tse-tung*, edited by Mao Tse-tung hsüan chi ch'u pan wei yüan hui (Committee for the Publication of the Selected Works of Mao Tse-tung), Chung yang wei yüan hui (Central Committee), Chung-kuo kung ch'an tang (Chinese Communist Party). [Selective entry]
Peking: Foreign Languages Press, 1965, vol. 1, 73–104.)
SUBJ 15 25 26 32.2 ▪ 12 22 22.1 24.1 28 32.1

18704 CSH O P2 G7.0 1911–1928
Mao Tse-tung, 1893–.
'Why is it that red political power can exist in China?' Tr. of 'Chung-kuo ti hung se cheng ch'üan wei shen mo neng kou ts'un tsai?'; in *Mao Tse-tung hsüan chi* (Selected works of Mao Tse-tung), 2nd ed.; Peking: Jen min ch'u pan she, 1960, vol. 1 [from a resolution drafted for the Second Party Congress of the Kiangsi-Hunan border region, 5 October 1928]. In *Selected works of Mao Tse-tung*, edited by Mao Tse-tung hsüan chi ch'u pan wei yüan hui (Committee for the Publication of the Selected Works of Mao Tse-tung), Chung yang wei yüan hui (Central Committee), Chung-kuo kung ch'an tang (Chinese Communist Party). [Selective entry]
Peking: Foreign Languages Press, 1965, vol. 1, 63–72.
SUBJ 16 32.2 ▪ 15

18705 CSU P P2 G1.2 1911–1949
Mark, Max.
'Chinese Communism.'
J. of politics 13, 2 (May 1951), 232–252.
SUBJ 32.2 64 ▪ 16.3 66

18706 MCH O P5 G4.1 1911–1928
Maynard, Michel de.
'Quelques épisodes de la révolution au Chensi' (Some incidents during the Revolution [of 1911] in Shensi).
Missions catholiques 46 (10 avr. – 19 juin 1914), 39 p. in all.
SUBJ 32.2 66 ▪ 15 25 32 61

18707 CSU O P2 G1.1 1928–1949
Melby, John Fremont, 1913–.
The mandate of heaven: Record of a civil war, China, 1945–1949.
Toronto: U. of Toronto Press, 1968. 313 p. [Reprinted—Garden City, N.Y.: Doubleday, 1971. 313 p.]
SUBJ 15 32 32.2 66 ▪ 12 12.1 14 16.1 17 22.2 54

18708 CSH U P2 G1.2 1911–1928
[Mel'nikov, Boris Nikolaevich] B. Semenov, pseud., 1896–1937.
Novyi etap kitaiskoi revoliutsii (A new stage in the Chinese revolution).
Moscow: Gosizdat, 1927. 167 p.
SUBJ 16 16.4 32.2 36.3 36.4 ▪ 11.4 12 19

18709 DLC P P2 G1.2 1911–1928
Mif, Pavel Aleksandrovich, 1865–1935.
Kitaiskaia kommunisticheskaia partiia v kriticheskie dni (The Chinese Communist Party in days of crisis).
Moscow: Gosizdat, 1928. 271 p.
SUBJ 16 32.1 32.2 ▪ 14 14.1 22 36.3 36.4 64 66

18710 NNC P P1 G1.2 1911–1928
Mif, Pavel Aleksandrovich, 1865–1935.
Kitaiskaia revoliutsiia (The Chinese revolution).
Moscow: Partizdat, 1932. 332 p.
SUBJ 32.2 ▪ 14 16 18

18711 DLC O P2 G1.1 1911–1949
Mif, Pavel Aleksandrovich, 1865–1935.
15 let geroicheskoi bor'by: k 15-letiiu Kommunisticheskoi partii Kitaia (Fifteen years of heroic struggle: On the fifteenth anniversary of the Chinese Communist Party).
Moscow: Partizdat, 1936. 118 p.
Pour une Chine forte et libre: quinze années de lutte héroïque du Parti communiste en Chine (For a strong and free China: Fifteen years of the Communist Party's heroic struggle in China).
Paris: Bureau d'éditions, de diffusion et de publicité, 1936. 111 p.
Heroic China: 15 years of the Communist Party of China.
New York: Workers Library, 1937. 96 p. [Also published as *China's struggle for freedom: The 15th anniversary of the Communist Party of China*. London: Modern Books, 1937. 100 p.]
SUBJ 32.2 64 ▪ 14 15 16.3 16.4 36.3 36.4

18712 CSH P P7 G1.4 1928–1949
Mitbreit, Boris Abramovich.
'Preodolenie voennykh i khoziaistvennykh trudnostei v osvobozhdennykh raionakh (iiun' 1941 – iiul' 1943 g.)' (Overcoming military and economic difficulties in the liberated areas, June 1941 – July 1943). In *Ocherki istorii Kitaia v noveishee vremia* (Survey of modern Chinese history), compiled by Institut kitaevedeniia, Akademiia nauk SSSR, edited by Aleksei Stepanovich Perevertailo et al. [Selective entry]
Moscow: Izd-vo vost. lit-ry, 1959, 337–349.
SUBJ 14 16.3 25 32 32.2 66 ▪ 14.3 14.5 15 24.1

18713 CSH O P2 G1.3 1911–1928
Nassunov, Nikolai, N- Fokine, and A- Albrecht.
'The letter from Shanghai.' Tr. from the Russian by Max Schachtman. In *Problems of the Chinese revolution*, 3rd ed., by Leon Trotsky (Lev Trotskii), compiled and edited by Max Schachtman. [Analytic entry]
New York: Paragon, 1966, 397–432. [For Trotsky's work, see entry 18756.]
SUBJ 16 32 32.2 ▪ 15

18714 MCH P P2 G1.2 1911–1949
Nikitine, Basile, 1885–.
'Le communisme en Chine' (Communism in China).
AF 34, 320 (mai 1934), 152–155; 34, 321 (juin 1934), 184–187; 34, 322 (juil.–août 1934), 214–221; 34, 323 (sept.–oct. 1934), 252–262; 34, 324 (nov. 1934), 294–299.
SUBJ 16 19 32.2 ▪ 14.1 14.6 15 32.1 64 66

18715 CSU P P2 G2.0 1911–1949
Pak, Hyobom, 1926–.
'Chinese Communists in the eastern three provinces, 1918–35.'
Contributions to Asian studies 1 (Jan. 1971), 28–48.
SUBJ 32.2 ▪ 15 36.3 36.4 66

18716 CBU O P2 G1.4 1928–1949
Payne, Pierre Stephen Robert, 1911–.
Journey to Red China.
London: Heinemann, 1947. 198 p.
SUBJ 15 32.2 ▪ 17 22.2

18717 CBU P P2 G1.2 1928–1949
Pepper, Suzanne, 1939–.
The politics of civil war: China, 1945–1949.

Unpublished doctoral dissertation in Political Science, U. of California, Berkeley, 1972. 740 p.
SUBJ 12 14 16 25 32.2 54 ▪ 12.1 14.1 14.6 17 18 22.2 32 35 36.4 66

18718 NNC S P2 G1.2 1928–1949
Perevertailo, Aleksei Stepanovich, 1897–.
'Rol' Kommunisticheskoi partii Kitaia na sovremennom etape narodno-osvoboditel'noi bor'by kitaiskogo naroda' (The role of the Chinese Communist Party in the current stage of the Chinese people's liberation struggle).
Uchenye zapiski Tikhookeanskogo instituta 3 (1949), 5–19.
SUBJ 12 32.2 64 ▪ 14.1 14.4 16.2 16.3 32

18719 CSH P P2 G1.1 1911–1928
Persits, M- A-.
'Iz istorii stanovlenii Kommunisticheskoi partii Kitaia (doklad, podgotovlennyi Chzhan Tai-leem dlia III Kongressa Kominterna, kak istoricheskii istochnik)' (History of the formation of the Chinese Communist Party: The report prepared by Chang T'ai-lei for the Third Comintern Congress [1921] as an historical source).
NAA 1971, 4, 47–58.
SUBJ 16 32.2 64 66 ▪ 70

18720 CSH S P2 G1.2 1911–1928
Pokrovskii, S-.
Voprosy kitaiskoi revoliutsii (Problems of the Chinese revolution).
Leningrad: Priboi, 1927. 95 p.
SUBJ 12 16 19 32.2 64 ▪ 11.4 32 36.4

18721 CSU O P8 G1.5 1928–1949
Rittenberg, Sidney Charles, 1914–.
'Rise and fall of a Communist area.'
Amerasia 11, 4 (Apr. 1947), 113–122.
SUBJ 15 32.2

18722 NNC O P2 G1.2 1911–1949
Roy, Manabendra Nath, 1893–1954.
Revolution and counter-revolution in China.
Calcutta: Renaissance Publishers, 1946. 689 p. [Reprinted—Westport, Conn.: Hyperion Press, 197? 689 p.]
SUBJ 10 12 14 16 32.2 45 ▪ 12.1 14.5 19 24.4 32 36.3 36.4 41 64 66

18723 MCH P P1 G1.2 1928–1949
Rue, John Emery, 1924–.
Mao Tse-tung in opposition, 1927–1935.
Stanford: Stanford U. Press, 1966. 387 p. (Revision of *Anti-Stalinist bias in the thought of Mao Tse-tung: A study of the origins of Maoism*, doctoral dissertation in Political Science, U. of Minnesota, 1964)
SUBJ 32.2 61 64 ▪ 15 19

18724 NNC P P1 G1.2 1911–1928
Rusanov, Nikolai Sergeevich, 1859–?
'Obozrenie inostrannoi zhizni. Chast' 3, bor'ba partii v Kitaiskoi respublike' (Survey of foreign life. Part 3, The party struggle in the Republic of China).
Russkoe bogatstvo 1913, 5 (mai), 287–292.
SUBJ 12 32 32.2 ▪ 32.1

18725 DLC P P2 G1.2 1911–1928
Rzhanov, G- A-.
Kitai na putiakh revoliutsii (China on the road to revolution).
Leningrad: Priboi, 1927. 259 p.
SUBJ 12 12.1 16 19 32.2 64 ▪ 14.1 15 32 32.1 36.3 36.4 66

18726 NNC P P2 G7.0 1911–1949
Sapozhnikov, Boris Grigor'evich, 1907–.
'Bor'ba kitaiskoi Krasnoi Armii v raione gor TSzingan' (The Chinese Red Army's struggle in Ching-kang-shan [Kiangsi-Hunan border region]).
SK 1958, 4, 123–136.
SUBJ 15 25 32.2 ▪ 12.1 14.1 22

18727 NNC P P2 G1.3 1911–1928
Sapozhnikov, Boris Grigor'evich, 1907–.
Pervaia grazhdanskaia revoliutsionnaia voina v Kitae, 1924–1927 gg. (The First Revolutionary Civil War in China, 1924–1927).
Moscow: Gospolitizdat, 1954. 99 p.
SUBJ 15 32.2

18728 CSH P P2 G1.2 1911–1949
Schram, Stuart Reynolds, 1924–.
'Mao Tse-tung and secret societies.'
CQ 27 (July–Sept. 1966), 1–13.
SUBJ 32.2 59 ▪ 35 36.3 64

18729 MCH P P1 G1.2 1911–1928
Schram, Stuart Reynolds, 1924–.
'On the nature of Mao Tse-tung's "deviation" in 1927.'
CQ 18 (Apr.–June 1964), 55–66.
SUBJ 32.2 ▪ 15 25

18730 NNC P P2 G1.2 1911–1949
Schwartz, Benjamin Isadore, 1916–.
Chinese Communism and the rise of Mao.
Cambridge: Harvard U. Press, 1951. 258 p. (Harvard Russian Research Center studies, 4) (Revision of *Communism in China until the rise of Mao Tse-tung*, doctoral dissertation in History, Harvard U., 1950)
SUBJ 16 32.2 64 ▪ 12 15 22 32 66

18731 CSH P P2 G1.4 1928–1949
Schwarz, Henry Guenter, 1928–.
'Essay.' In *Liu Shao-ch'i and 'people's war': A report on the creation of base areas in 1938*, by H. G. Schwarz. [Sole entry]
Lawrence: U. of Kansas, Center for East Asian Studies, 1969, 1–30. (CEAS, International Studies, East Asian series, research publications, 3)
SUBJ 15 32.2 64 ▪ 12.1 25 59 66

18732 MCH P P2 G1.4 1911–1949
Selden, Mark, 1938–.
The Yenan way in revolutionary China.
Cambridge: Harvard U. Press, 1971. 311 p. (Harvard East Asian series, 62) (Revision of *Yenan Communism: Revolution in the Shensi-Kansu-Ninghsia border region, 1927–1945*, doctoral dissertation in History, Yale U., 1968)
SUBJ 15 25 26 32.1 32.2 ▪ 12 22 22.1 24.1 24.4 24.5 32 34.1

18733 MCH P P2 G1.2 1911–1928
Seng Sin-fu.
China: A survey of the historical and economic forces behind the revolution.
London: Communist Party of Great Britain, 1927. 104 p.
SUBJ 14.1 14.4 16.3 16.4 19 32.2 ▪ 11 11.4 12 12.1 15 36.4 64

18734 DLC P P2 G9.2 1911–1928
Shao IUi (Shao Yü).
'Kantonskoe vosstanie' (The Canton uprising). In *Kantonskaia kommuna: sbornik statei i materialov* (Articles and documents on the Canton commune), compiled by Nauchno-issledovatel'skii institut po Kitaiu, Kommunisticheskaia akademiia. [Selective entry]
Moscow: Gosizdat, 1929, 63–97.
SUBJ 25 26 32.2 ▪ 15 22 32.1 66

18735 CSH P P4 G1.3 1911–1928
Shen Yün-lung.
Origins of the Chinese Communist Party. Tr. of *Chung-kuo kung ch'an tang chih lai yüan*, rev. ed.; Taipei: Min chu ch'ao she, 1959; 92 p.
Taipei: Wen Hai Press, 1972. 136 p.
SUBJ 32.2 ▪ 32.1 64

18736 CSH PO P2 G1.3 1928–1949
Sheng, Yueh (Sheng Yüeh), 1907–.
Sun Yat-sen University in Moscow and the Chinese Revolution: A personal account.
Lawrence: U. of Kansas, Center for East Asian Studies, 1971. 270 p. (CEAS, International Studies, East Asian series, research publications, 7)
SUBJ 32.2 ▪ 59 64

18737 CSU S P1 G1.2 1928–1949
Shewmaker, Kenneth Earl, 1936–.
'The agrarian reformer myth.'
CQ 34 (Apr.–June 1968), 66–81.
SUBJ 32.2 ▪ 64 66

18738 CSU P P1 G1.4 1928–1949
Shewmaker, Kenneth Earl, 1936–.
'The American liberal dream: Evans F. Carlson and the Chinese Communists, 1937–1947.'
PHR 38, 2 (May 1969), 207–216.
SUBJ 32.2 64 ▪ 15 66

18739 CSH P P2 G2.0 1911–1949
Shishkin, P- P-.
Bol'shevizm v Kitae: obzor deiatel'nosti Severo-man'chzhurskoi Kommunisticheskoi partii (Bolshevism in China: Survey of the activities of the Communist Party of northern Manchuria).
Shanghai: Vremia, 1930. 151 p.
SUBJ 16.4 32.2 36.4 ▪ 12 64 66

18740 MCH S P1 G1.2 1911–1949
Simon, Paul.
Le mouvement communiste en Chine des origines à nos jours (The Communist movement in China from its origins to the present).
Paris: Lib. du Recueil Sirey, 1939. 253 p.
SUBJ 32.2 ▪ 12

18741 DLC PO P2 G1.1 1911–1949
Simonov, Konstantin Mikhailovich.
Srazhaiushchiisia Kitai (China in battle).
Moscow: Sovetskii pisatel', 1950. 251 p.
SUBJ 16 32.2 ▪ 15 64

18742 DLC P P2 G9.2 1911–1928
Skalov, Georgii Borisovich, 1896–.
'20 marta 1926 goda' (20 March 1926). In *Kantonskaia kommuna: sbornik statei i*

materialov (Articles and documents on the Canton commune), compiled by Nauchno-issledovatel'skii institut po Kitaiu, Kommunisticheskaia akademiia. [Selective entry]
Moscow: Gosizdat, 1929, 277–300.
SUBJ 15 26 32 32.2 35 ▪ 12 32.1 36.3 64

18743 CSU P P7 G1.4 1911–1928
Sławiński, Roman, 1931–.
'Les Piques rouges et la révolution chinoise de 1925–1927' (The Red Spears and the Chinese Revolution of 1925–1927). In *Mouvements populaires et sociétés secrètes en Chine aux XIXe et XXe siècles* (Popular movements and secret societies in China in the nineteenth and twentieth centuries), edited by Jean Chesneaux, Feiling Blackburn Davis, and Nguyen Nguyet Ho. [Selective entry]
Paris: Maspero, 1970, 393–406.
'The Red Spears in the late 1920s' [rev. in tr.]. In *Popular movements and secret societies in China, 1840–1950*, edited by J. Chesneaux. [Analytic entry]
Stanford: Stanford U. Press, 1972, 201–211.
SUBJ 25 32.2 36.3 ▪ 14.5 15 18

18744 MCH O P2 G1.2 1928–1949
Smedley, Agnes, 1890–1950.
Battle hymn of China.
New York: Knopf, 1945. 10, 528, 16 p.
SUBJ 15 32.2 ▪ 19 64

18745 MCY O P2 G1.2 1911–1949
Smedley, Agnes, 1890–1950.
'The social revolution.' In *China*, edited by Harley Farnsworth MacNair. [Selective entry]
Berkeley, Los Angeles: U. of California Press, 1946, 166–199. [Reprinted in *China*, edited by H. F. MacNair. (Selective entry.) Freeport, N.Y.: Books for Libraries, 1970, 166–199.]
SUBJ 15 16 19 32.2 64 ▪ 12 12.1 14.5 17 25 30 32 36.3 66

18746 NNC O P2 G1.2 1928–1949
Snow, Edgar, 1905–1972.
Random notes on Red China, 1936–1945.
Cambridge: Harvard U., East Asian Research Center, 1957. 148 p. (Harvard East Asian monographs, 5)
SUBJ 22 22.1 22.2 24.1 25 32.2 ▪ 17 26 26.3 54 55 62 64

18747 MCH PO P1 G1.4 1928–1949
[Snow, Helen Foster] Nym Wales, pseud., 1907–.
Notes on the Sian Incident, 1936.
Madison, Conn.: The author, 1960. 200 p.
SUBJ 12.1 15 32.2 ▪ 16.1 54 64 66

18748 NNC P P3 G9.2 1911–1928
Steffens, Charles Frederick.
The Canton uprising, 11–14 December 1927.
Unpublished masters thesis in History, Columbia U., 1957. 146 p.
SUBJ 25 32.2 ▪ 22.1 32

18749 MMT O P2 G4.1 1928–1949
Stein, Guenther.
The challenge of Red China.
New York: McGraw-Hill, 1945. 10, 490 p.
SUBJ 15 22.1 24 32.2 ▪ 12 22 23 24.1 26.1 26.3 28 64

18750 MCH O P2 G1.4 1928–1949
Strong, Anna Louise, 1885–1970.
Tomorrow's China.
New York: Committee for a Democratic Far Eastern Policy, 1948. 128 p.
SUBJ 19 30 32.2 ▪ 14.1 14.4 15 17 50 61 64

18751 CSU S P7 G7.3 1928–1949
Suleski, Ronald S-, 1942–.
'The Fu-t'ien incident [P'ing-ch'ih *hsien*, Kiangsi], December 1930.' In *Early Communist China: Two studies*, by R. S. Suleski and Daniel Henry Bays. [Analytic entry]
Ann Arbor: U. of Michigan, Center for Chinese Studies, 1969, 1–27. (Michigan papers in Chinese studies, 4)
SUBJ 22 26.1 32.2 ▪ 15 22.2 25

18752 CSH P P2 G1.2 1911–1949
Swarup, Shanti.
A study of the Chinese Communist movement.
Oxford: Clarendon Press, 1966. 289 p.
SUBJ 19 32.2 36.3 36.4 64 ▪ 12.1 14.1 16 32 60 61

18753 MCH O P2 G1.2 1911–1928
Tan Ping-schan (T'an P'ing-shan), 1887–1956.
Entwicklungswege der chinesischen Revolution (Courses of development of the Chinese Revolution).
Hamburg: Carl Hoym, 1927. 36 p.
SUBJ 32.2 64 ▪ 16

18754 NIC S P1 G1.2 1928–1949
Taylor, George Edward, 1905–.
'The hegemony of the Chinese Communists, 1945–1950.'
AAAPSS 277 (Sept. 1951), 13–21. [Special issue: *Report on China*, edited by Harold Arthur Steiner]
SUBJ 12.1 16 32.2 ▪ 15 18 32 64

18755 WSU P P2 G1.2 1928–1949
Thornton, Richard Chester, 1936–.
The Comintern and the Chinese Communists, 1928–1931.
Seattle: U. of Washington Press, 1967. 18, 246 p. (Revision of doctoral dissertation in History, U. of Washington, 1966)
SUBJ 12.1 32.2 64 ▪ 15 32 36.3 36.4

18756 MCH U P1 G1.3 1911–1949
Trotsky, Leon (Lev Trotskii), 1879–1940.
Problems of the Chinese revolution, 3rd ed., compiled by Max Schachtman. Tr. from the Russian by Max Schachtman.
New York: Paragon, 1966. 432 p.
SUBJ 19 32.2 ▪ 12 15 16 32 64

18757 CSH O P2 G1.2 1911–1928
TSai Khe-sen' (Ts'ai Ho-sen), 1890–1931?
'Istoriia opportunizma v Kommunisticheskoi partii Kitaia' (History of opportunism in the Chinese Communist Party).
PK 1 (1929), 1–77.
SUBJ 16 32 32.2 36.3 36.4 64 ▪ 12 12.1 14.1 14.2 15 66

18758 NNC P P1 G1.2 1928–1949
TSzen Siu-fu (Tseng Hsiu-fu).
'Iz istorii politiki Kommunisticheskoi partii Kitaia v edinom antiiaponskom natsional'nom fronte 1937–1945 gg.' (History of Chinese Communist Party policy in the united anti-Japanese national front, 1937–1945). [With English abstract]
SK 1958, 4, 29–41.
SUBJ 12 32.2 66

18759 CSH P P2 G1.2 1911–1949
U.S. War Dept. General Staff. Military Intelligence Division.
The Chinese Communist movement.
Washington, D.C.: Military Intelligence Division, 1945. 2 vols. 12; 279 p. [Reprinted as *The Chinese Communist movement: A report of the United States War Department, 1945* edited by Lyman Page Van Slyke. Stanford: Stanford U. Press, 1968. 274 p.]
SUBJ 14 15 32.2 ▪ 16 17 18 22 25 32 56 64

18760 CSH U P2 G1.2 1911–1928
[Vilenskii, Vladimir Dmitrievich] Vl. Vilenskii-Sibiriakov, pseud., 1888–1942.
Gde korni predatel'stva Chan-kai-shi? O kitaiskoi revoliutsii (The Chinese revolution: Where are the roots of Chiang Kai-shek's betrayal?).
Moscow: Gosizdat, 1927. 60 p.
SUBJ 12 32.2 ▪ 16 64

18761 CSU P P2 G1.2 1928–1949
Vinacke, Harold Monk, 1893–.
'The Communist phase of the Chinese revolution.' In *Far Eastern politics in the postwar period*, by H. M. Vinacke. [Sole entry]
New York: Appleton-Century-Crofts, 1956, 115–151.
SUBJ 32 32.2 ▪ 12 12.1 12.2 14 14.1 15 16 64

18762 NNC P P4 G1.2 1911–1928
Vinogradov, Nikolai Pavlovich, 1923–1967.
'Bor'ba Kommunisticheskoi partii Kitaia za sozdanie edinogo natsional'nogo antiimperialisticheskogo fronta, 1922–1923 gg.' (The Chinese Communist Party's struggle to form a national anti-imperialist united front, 1922–1923).
KSINA 55 (1962), 94–111.
SUBJ 32.2 66 ▪ 16.4 64

18763 CSH S P2 G1.5 1928–1949
Vinogradov, Nikolai Pavlovich, 1923–1967, and Kim Vladimirovich Kukushkin, 1926–.
'Bor'ba Kommunisticheskoi partii Kitaia za sozdanie revoliutsionnykh baz v derevne (1927–1931)' (The struggle of the Chinese Communist Party to establish revolutionary bases in the countryside, 1927–1931). In *Ocherki istorii Kitaia v noveishee vremia* (Survey of modern Chinese history), compiled by Institut kitaevedeniia, Akademiia nauk SSSR, edited by Aleksei Stepanovich Perevertailo et al. [Selective entry]
Moscow: Izd-vo vost. lit-ry, 1959, 187–226.
SUBJ 14 15 16 32.2 ▪ 14.1 16.3 64 66

18764 NNC O P2 G1.1 1911–1928
Vishniakova-Akimova, Vera Vladimirovna.
Dva goda v vosstavshem Kitae, 1925–1927: vospominaniia (Reminiscences of two years in revolutionary China, 1925–27).

Moscow: Nauka, Glav. red. vost. lit-ry, 1965. 389 p.

Two years in revolutionary China, 1925–1927. Tr. by Stephen I. Levine.
Cambridge: Harvard U., East Asian Research Center, 1970. 18, 352 p. (Harvard East Asian monographs, 40)
SUBJ 16 20 32.2 66 ▪ 12 15 18 32 32.1 36.4 55 71

18765 CSH U P1 G1.3 1911–1928
Vuyovitch, Vuyo.
'Speech of Vuyo Vuyovitch.' Tr. from the Russian by Max Schachtman. In *Problems of the Chinese revolution*, 3rd ed., by Leon Trotsky (Lev Trotskii), compiled and edited by Max Schachtman. [Analytic entry]
New York: Paragon, 1966, 382–396. [For Trotsky's work, see entry 18756.]
SUBJ 16 32 32.2 ▪ 15

18766 CBU P P2 G1.5 1928–1949
Waller, Derek John, 1937–.
The Kiangsi Soviet Republic: Mao and the national congresses of 1931 and 1934.
Berkeley: U. of California, Center for Chinese Studies, 1973. 114 p. (CCS, China research monographs, 10) (Revision of *The First and Second National Congresses of the Chinese Soviet Republic, 1931 and 1934*, doctoral dissertation in Economics, U. of London [School of Oriental and African Studies], 1968)
SUBJ 12 32.1 32.2 ▪ 12.1 14.1 15 16.3 32 64

18767 NNC O P2 G1.2 1911–1949
Wan, Yah-kang (Wan Hsia-k'ang), 1909–.
The rise of Communism in China, 1920–1950, edited by C. S. Kwei (Kuei Chung-shu).
Hong Kong: Chung Shu Publishing Co., 1952. 77 p.
SUBJ 32.2 ▪ 12.1 15 25 32

18768 CSU S P2 G1.2 1911–1949
Wang Shih, et al., eds.
Brief history of the Chinese Communist Party, mimeo. Tr. of *Chung-kuo kung ch'an tang li shih chien pien*; Shanghai: Jen min ch'u pan she, 1958; 302 p.
Washington, D.C.: U.S. Joint Publications Research Service, 16 Aug. 1961. 307 p. (JPRS 8756; MC 17,448/1961) [Xerox copyflo available—New York: CCM Information Corp., Research and Microfilm Publications. (Scholarly Book Translation Series, 454)]
SUBJ 16 16.4 32.2 64 ▪ 14 15 16.3 25 32.1

18769 CSU P P3 G1.3 1911–1928
Wei, Carl K.
'The founding of the Chinese Communist Party and its First National Congress, 1920–1921.'
IS 7, 3 (Dec. 1970), 32–57.
SUBJ 32.2 ▪ 66

18770 CSU P P4 G8.3 1928–1949
Wei, Carl K.
'The truth about the CCP Tsunyi Conference.'
IS 5, 4 (Jan. 1969), 29–37; 5, 5 (Feb. 1969), 20–31.
SUBJ 32.2

18771 CSH P P3 G1.5 1911–1928
Wieger, Léon, 1856–1933.
'Ku-klux Klan chinois' (The Chinese Ku Klux Klan). In *Chine moderne, Tome V, nationalisme, xénophobie, antichristianisme* (Modern China, Vol. 5, Nationalism, xenophobia, and antichristianism), 2nd ed., by L. Wieger. [Selective entry]
Hsien-hsien, Hopei: Impr. de Sienhsien, 1934, 100–102.
SUBJ 32.2 ▪ 66

18772 MCH P P2 G1.5 1911–1928
Wilbur, Clarence Martin, 1908–.
'The ashes of defeat.'
CQ 18 (Apr.–June 1964), 3–54.
SUBJ 15 25 32.2 ▪ 14.1

18773 NNC P P2 G1.2 1911–1928
Wilbur, Clarence Martin, 1908–.
'Introduction.' In *The Communist movement in China*, by Kung Po Chen (Ch'en Kung-po), edited by C. M. Wilbur. [Analytic entry]
New York: Columbia U., East Asian Institute, 1960, 1–61. [For Chen's work, see entry 18597.] (EAI series, 7)
SUBJ 32.2 64 ▪ 24.2 54 59

18774 CSU P P2 G1.3 1911–1928
Wilbur, Clarence Martin, 1908–, and Julie Lien-ying How (Hsia Lien-yin), 1926–.
'Conclusions.' In *Documents on Communism, nationalism, and Soviet advisers in China, 1918–1927*, edited by C. M. Wilbur and J. Lien-ying How. [Selective entry]
New York: Columbia U. Press, 1956, 457–467.
SUBJ 32 32.2 ▪ 32.1 66

18775 CSU P P3 G9.2 1911–1928
Wilbur, Clarence Martin, 1908–, and Julie Lien-ying How (Hsia Lien-yin), 1926–.
'Consolidation of the revolutionary base in Kwangtung, 1921–1925.' In *Documents on Communism, nationalism, and Soviet advisers in China, 1918–1927*, edited by C. M. Wilbur and J. Lien-ying How. [Selective entry]
New York: Columbia U. Press, 1956, 138–170.
SUBJ 15 25 32.2 ▪ 12 17 32.1 64 66

18776 CSU P P1 G1.3 1911–1928
Wilbur, Clarence Martin, 1908–, and Julie Lien-ying How (Hsia Lien-yin), 1926–.
'Friction and reconciliation in the revolutionary camp, July, 1925 to July, 1926.' In *Documents on Communism, nationalism, and Soviet advisers in China, 1918–1927*, edited by C. M. Wilbur and J. Lien-ying How. [Selective entry]
New York: Columbia U. Press, 1956, 206–233.
SUBJ 32.2 ▪ 64 66

18777 CSU P P2 G1.3 1911–1928
Wilbur, Clarence Martin, 1908–, and Julie Lien-ying How (Hsia Lien-yin), 1926–.
'Kuomintang-Communist relations during the Northern Expedition, July, 1926 to April 6, 1927.' In *Documents on Communism, nationalism, and Soviet advisers in China, 1918–1927*, edited by C. M. Wilbur and J. Lien-ying How. [Selective entry]
New York: Columbia U. Press, 1956, 367–409.
SUBJ 32 32.2 64 ▪ 12 15 36.3

18778 CSU P P2 G1.3 1911–1928
Wilbur, Clarence Martin, 1908–, and Julie Lien-ying How (Hsia Lien-yin), 1926–.
'The organizational policies of the Chinese Communist Party, 1920 to July, 1926.' In *Documents on Communism, nationalism, and Soviet advisers in China, 1918–1927*, edited by C. M. Wilbur and J. Lien-ying How. [Selective entry]
New York: Columbia U. Press, 1956, 79–99.
SUBJ 32.2 64 ▪ 16.3 16.4 17 36.4 54 66

18779 CSU P P2 G1.5 1911–1928
Wu, Ellsworth Tien-wei (Wu T'ien-wei), 1922–.
'A review of the Wuhan debacle: The Kuomintang-Communist split of 1927.'
JAS 29, 1 (Nov. 1969), 125–143.
SUBJ 32 32.2 64 ▪ 12 15 25 36.3 36.4

18780 MCY P P2 G1.2 1911–1949
Yakhontoff, Victor A-, 1881–.
The Chinese soviets.
New York: Coward-McCann, 1934. 14, 296 p. [Reprinted—Ann Arbor: University Microfilms, n.d. 14, 296 p.] [Reprinted—Westport, Conn.: Greenwood Press, 1972. 14, 296 p.]
SUBJ 14.1 32.2 36.3 ▪ 12 15 16.3 32 36.4 64 66

18781 CSH O P8 G1.5 1928–1949
Yang Shang-kuei (Yang Shang-k'uei).
The red Kiangsi-Kwangtung border region.
Peking: Foreign Languages Press, 1961. 187 p.
SUBJ 15 32.2 ▪ 35

18782 CSU P P2 G1.2 1911–1928
Yeh, K. C. (Yeh K'ung-chia), 1924–.
The Chinese Communist revolutionary strategy and the land problem, 1921–1927.
Santa Monica, Calif.: RAND Corp., 1970. 107 p. (RAND memoranda, RM-6077-ARPA)
SUBJ 14.1 32 32.2 36.3 64 ▪ 15 16.1 16.3

18783 DLC P P2 G1.2 1911–1949
Zhdanov, M- G-.
V boiakh za sovetskii Kitai (In the battles for a soviet China).
Moscow: Molodaia gvardiia, 1932. 96 p.
SUBJ 12.1 16.3 16.4 32.2 54 64 ▪ 14.1 14.4 15 25 34.2 36.4 53

18784 CSH U P2 G1.3 1911–1928
[Zinov'ev, Grigorii] Gregory Zinoviev, 1883–1936.
'Theses on the Chinese revolution.' Tr. from the Russian by Max Schachtman. In *Problems of the Chinese revolution*, 3rd ed., by Leon Trotsky (Lev Trotskii), compiled and edited by Max Schachtman. [Analytic entry]
New York: Paragon, 1966, 313–381. [For Trotsky's work, see entry 18756.]
SUBJ 16 32 32.2 64 ▪ 15 36.3

1911-1972
(including 1644-1972)

18785 NNC P P1 G1.2 1911–1972
Avarin, Vladimir IAkovlevich, 1899–.
'Velikaia oktiabr'skaia sotsialisticheskaia revoliutsiia i Vostok' (The October Revolution and the Orient).
SV 1955, 5, 3–12.
SUBJ 32.2

18786 MCH P P2 G1.1 –1972
Balazs, Etienne, 1905–1963.
'Tradition et révolution en Chine.'
Politique étrangère 19, 3 (juil. 1954), 291–308.
'Tradition and revolution in China.' Tr. by Hope M- Wright. In *Chinese civilization and bureaucracy*, by E. Balazs, edited by Arthur Frederick Wright. [Selective entry]
New Haven: Yale U. Press, 1964, 150–170.
SUBJ 12.1 16 32.2 60 64 ▪ 12 14 34.1 66

18787 MCH S P1 G1.2 1911–1972
Bechtoldt, Heinrich.
'Soziologie und Geschichte des Maoismus: Die Periodisierung des chinesischen Kommunismus' (The sociology and history of Maoism: A periodization of Chinese Communism).
Aussenpolitik 3, 1 (Jan. 1952), 38–47.
SUBJ 32.2 64

18788 MCH O P8 G5.4 1928–1972
Belden, Jack, 1910–.
'The overturning of Sesame Garden village [Honan].'
Reporter 2, 1 (3 Jan. 1950), 8–12.
SUBJ 32.2 ▪ 28

18789 MCH P P2 G1.2 1911–1972
Borchardt, Robert.
'Zur Geschichte des Kommunismus in China' (History of Communism in China).
Internationales Jahrbuch der Politik 1, 1 (Apr. 1954), 100–122.
SUBJ 32 32.2 64 ▪ 15 16 32.1

18790 NNC P P2 G1.2 1911–1972
Butenko, A- P-.
'Kitaiskaia revoliutsiia i ee osobennosti' (Features of the Chinese revolution).
SV 1956, 3, 15–33.
SUBJ 12 14 19 32.2 ▪ 16 64

18791 MCY P P7 G1.2 1842–1972
Butterfield, Fox, 1939–.
'The legend of Sung Ching-shih: An episode in Communist historiography.'
PC 18 (Dec. 1964), 129–154.
SUBJ 12.1 25 26.3 32.2 36.3 ▪ 59 70

18792 NNC P P2 G1.2 1911–1972
Chassin, Lionel Max, 1902–.
L'ascension de Mao Tsé-tung (1921–1945) (The rise of Mao Tse-tung, 1921–1945).
Paris: Payot, 1953. 216 p.
SUBJ 15 32 32.2 ▪ 64

18793 MCH U P1 G1.2 1911–1972
Chesneaux, Jean, 1922–.
'Réflexions d'actualité sur la révolution chinoise' (Reflections of topical interest on the Chinese revolution).
Année politique et économique nouvelle (2e) série 36, 176 (1963), 434–447.
SUBJ 19 32.2 ▪ 60

18794 FPN P P2 G1.1 1842–1972
Chesneaux, Jean, 1922–.
Les sociétés secrètes en Chine (XIXe et XXe siècles).
Paris: Juillard, 1965. 280 p.
Secret societies in China in the nineteenth and twentieth centuries. Tr. by Gillian Nettle.
Ann Arbor: U. of Michigan Press, 1972. 12, 210 p.
SUBJ 25 32.2 65 ▪ 26 36.3 63 66

18795 WMU P P2 G1.2 –1972
Chu, Finley M. (Chu Feng-ming), 1919–.
China's old culture and new order: A study of the Chinese revolutions in the light of the social movement theory.
Unpublished doctoral dissertation in Economics, U. of Wisconsin, 1955. 3 vols. 731 p. [c.p.].
SUBJ 14 16 19 32.2 64 ▪ 30 34.3 36.3 36.4 66

18796 CSH O P2 G1.2 1928–1972
Cordes, Ernst, 1908–.
China: Revolution innerhalb einer Revolution (China: Revolution within a revolution).
Berlin: Safari, 1951. 156 p.
SUBJ 19 32.2 64 ▪ 14.1 15 32 59

18797 MCH S P1 G1.2 1928–1972
Daniels, Robert Vincent.
'The Chinese Revolution in Russian perspective.'
WP 13, 2 (Jan. 1961), 210–230.
SUBJ 19 32.1 32.2 64 ▪ 14 16.1 32 34.1

18798 DLC P P2 G1.2 1911–1972
Deliusin, Lev Petrovich (Lev Delioussine), 1923–.
'Obshchestvo "Iguan'dao"' (The I-kuan Tao). In *Tainye obshchestva v starom Kitae* (Secret societies in old China), compiled by Institut vostokovedeniia, Akademiia nauk SSSR, edited by Vasilii Pavlovich Iliushechkin. [Selective entry]
Moscow: Nauka, Glav. red. vost. lit-ry, 1970, 174–186.
'La société Yiguandao et sa suppression par les autorités de Chine populaire' (The I-kuan Tao and its suppression by the authorities in the People's Republic of China). In *Mouvements populaires et sociétés secrètes en Chine aux XIXe et XXe siècles* (Popular movements and secret societies in China in the nineteenth and twentieth centuries), edited by Jean Chesneaux, Feiling Blackburn Davis, and Nguyen Nguyet Ho. [Selective entry]
Paris: Maspero, 1970, 421–434.
'The I-kuan Tao society' [rev. in tr.]. In *Popular movements and secret societies in China, 1840–1950*, edited by J. Chesneaux. [Analytic entry]
Stanford: Stanford U. Press, 1972, 225–233.
SUBJ 32.1 32.2 ▪ 65

18799 CSU P P2 G1.2 1911–1972
Dunn, John.
'China.' In *Modern revolutions: An introduction to the analysis of a political phenomenon*, by J. Dunn. [Sole entry]
Cambridge: Cambridge U. Press, 1972, 70–95.
SUBJ 12 16 32.2 66 ▪ 11 15 16.1 16.3 18 32 64

18800 MCH P P2 G1.2 1842–1972
Dunstheimer, Guillaume Gustave Hubert, 1898–.
'Le mouvement des Boxeurs: documents et études publiés depuis la Deuxième Guerre mondiale' (The Boxer movement: Documents and studies published since World War II).
R. historique 231 (avr.–juin 1964), 387–416.
SUBJ 32.2 70 71 72 ▪ 12 15 32.1 64

18801 CBU P P2 G1.1 1644–1972
Efimov, Gerontii Valentinovich, 1906–.
Ocherki po novoi i noveishei istorii Kitaia (Notes on modern and recent Chinese history), 2nd ed., rev.
Moscow: Gospolitizdat, 1951. 575 p.
SUBJ 12 14.1 15 16 32.2 66 ▪ 12.1 14.4 14.6 19 35 64 72

18802 CSU P P2 G1.2 1911–1972
Engelborghs-Bertels, Marthe, 1928–.
'La révolution ininterrompue' (The continuous revolution). In *La République populaire de Chine: cadres institutionnels et réalisations. I, l'histoire et le droit* (Institutions and accomplishments of the People's Republic of China, Vol. 1, History and law), by M. Engelborghs-Bertels and René Dekkers. [Selective entry]
Brussels: Université libre de Bruxelles, Institut de sociologie Solvay, Centre d'étude des pays de l'Est *with* Centre national pour l'étude des pays à régime communiste, 1963, 1–34.
SUBJ 12 14.1 16.1 32.2 64 ▪ 14 16 25

18803 CSU U P1 G1.2 1928–1972
Fairbank, John King, 1907–.
'China is far.' [Review of *Marshall in China*, by John Robinson Beal; *China and ourselves: Explorations and revisions by a new generation*, edited by Bruce Douglass and Ross Terrill; *Party leadership and revolutionary power in China*, edited by John Wilson Lewis; and *Revolution and Chinese foreign policy*, by Peter Van Ness.]
NYRB 15, 4 (3 Sept. 1970), 19–23.
SUBJ 32 32.2 ▪ 16.1 66

18804 NNC PO P2 G1.2 1895–1972
Fitzgerald, Charles Patrick, 1902–.
The birth of Communist China.
Baltimore: Penguin, 1964. 288 p. [Rev. ed. of *Revolution in China*. New York: Praeger, 1952. 289 p.]
SUBJ 12 32 32.2 ▪ 12.1 14 16.1 16.3 19 33 64 66

18805 MCH U P1 G1.1 1644–1972
Floris, George A-.
'Chinese secret societies.'
Contemporary review 193, 1110 (June 1958), 319–322.
SUBJ 32.2 ▪ 48 60

18806 ELB P P2 G1.2 1911–1972
Glunin, Vladimir Ivanovich, 1924–, et al.
'Mezhdunarodnoe kommunisticheskoe dvizhenie i Kommunisticheskaia partiia Kitaia (k 50-letiiu so dnia sozdaniia KPK)' (The Chinese Communist Party and the international Communist

movement: On the fiftieth anniversary of the founding of the Chinese Communist Party).
VI 1971, 8 (avgust), 43–58.
Subj 16 32 32.2 64 66

18807 CSU U P2 G1.2 –1972
Gray, Jack Douglas, 1916–.
'Conclusions.' In *Modern China's search for a political form*, edited by J. D. Gray. [Analytic entry]
London: Oxford U. Press, 1969, 330–369.
Subj 19 32.2 64 ▪ 12.1 14 14.1 14.4 16 17

18808 CSH P P2 G1.2 1895–1972
Grigor'ev, Aleksandr Mironovich, 1933–, and Grigorii Dmitrievich Sukharchuk, 1927–.
'Osnovnye etapy sotsial'no-ekonomicheskoi i politicheskoi istorii KNR' (Basic stages in the socioeconomic and political history of the People's Republic of China). In *Kitaiskaia Narodnaia Respublika* (The People's Republic of China), compiled by Institut Dal'nego Vostoka, Akademiia nauk SSSR, edited by Mikhail Iosifovich Sladkovskii and G. D. Sukharchuk. [Selective entry]
Moscow: Nauka, Glav. red. vost. lit-ry, 1970, 11–45.
Subj 16 32 32.2 64 ▪ 12 19 66

18809 CSU S P2 G1.1 1911–1972
Harrison, James Pinckney, 1932–.
The long march to power: A history of the Chinese Communist Party, 1921–72.
New York: Praeger, 1972. 17, 647 p.
Subj 12 12.1 15 16 32 32.2 ▪ 14 14.1 17 19 22 25 30 54 64 72

18810 MCH U P2 G1.1 1911–1972
Ho Kan-chih, ed.
A history of the modern Chinese revolution. Tr. of *Chung-kuo hsien tai ko ming shih* (History of revolution in modern China); Tientsin: Kao teng chiao yü ch'u pan she, 1957; 207 p.
Peking: Foreign Languages Press, 1959. 627 p. (China knowledge series, 6)
Subj 32.2 36.4 ▪ 14 32 32.1 36.3 64

18811 CSU U P2 G1.2 1911–1972
Hsüeh, Chün-tu, 1922–.
'The Communist movement: Editor's introduction.' In *Revolutionary leaders of modern China*, edited by Chün-tu Hsüeh. [Selective entry]
New York: Oxford U. Press, 1971, 321–334.
Subj 16.1 32 32.2

18812 NIC U P2 G1.2 1911–1972
Hu Chiao-mu (Hu Ch'iao-mu), 1905–.
Thirty years of the Communist Party of China, 4th ed.
Peking: Foreign Languages Press, 1959. 113 p.
Subj 32 32.2 64 ▪ 12.1 14 14.1 15 66

18813 CSU P P1 G1.2 1911–1972
Kuo, Warren (Kuo Hua-lun), 1912–.
'The CCP pledge of alliance to the Kuomintang.'
IS 4, 11 (Aug. 1968), 36–50; 4, 12 (Sept. 1968), 31–49.
Subj 12 32.2 ▪ 15 16.1 32

18814 CSU P P1 G1.2 1928–1972
Kuo, Warren (Kuo Hua-lun), 1912–.
'The sixth plenum of the CCP Sixth Central Committee.'
IS 5, 6 (Mar. 1969), 34–48; 5, 7 (Apr. 1969), 29–56.
Subj 32 32.2 ▪ 64

18815 CSH P P2 G1.2 1911–1972
[La Dany, Ladislao] ———, 1914–.
'The fiftieth anniversary of the CCP.'
CNA 846 (25 June 1971), 1–7.
Subj 32 32.2 ▪ 16.1

18816 ELB P P2 G1.2 1911–1972
Larre, Claude.
'Mao Tse-toung, le "campagnard"' (Mao Tse-tung, the country boy).
Etudes 7e série 331 (déc. 1969), 676–684; 332 (jan. 1970), 49–56.
Subj 32.2 59 64 ▪ 15 16.3

18817 MCH PO P2 G1.2 1928–1972
Ljau Gai-lung (Liao Kai-lung).
Kurze Geschichte des chinesischen Volksbefreiungskrieges (Brief history of the Chinese War of National Liberation). Tr. by Liselotte Pötz and Gottfried Spies of *Chung-kuo jen min chieh fang chan cheng chien shih*; Shanghai: Hai yen shu tien, 1952; 134 p.
Berlin: Deutscher Verlag der Wissenschaften, 1957. 198 p.
Subj 12 14 15 32 32.2 64 ▪ 11 12.1 12.2 14.1 14.6 16.1 17 18 32.1 66

18818 CSH P P7 G1.2 1928–1972
Mei Ko-wang.
'An analysis of Chinese Communist guerrilla movements.'
IS 2, 4 (Jan. 1966), 24–32.
Subj 32.2 ▪ 12.1 15

18819 CSH P P2 G1.2 1911–1972
[Miao Chu-khuan] Mjau Tschu-hwang (Miao Ch'u-huang).
Kratkaia istoriia Kommunisticheskoi partii Kitaia (Brief history of the Chinese Communist Party). Tr. by A- Sergeev, R- Kudashev, and O- Rakhmanin of *Chung-kuo kung ch'an tang chien yao li shih*; Peking: Hsüeh hsi tsa chih she, 1956; 182 p.
Moscow: Gospolitizdat, 1958. 225 p.

Kurze Geschichte der Kommunistischen Partei Chinas. Tr. by Erich Salewski.
Berlin: Dietz, 1960. 279 p.
Subj 15 16 32.2 36.3 64 ▪ 12 12.1 14 19 32 36.4 62 66

18820 ELR O P3 G9.5 1842–1972
Morgan, W- P-, 1922–.
Triad societies in Hong Kong.
Hong Kong: Government Printer, 1960. 19, 306 p.
Subj 32.2 65 ▪ 22.2 26.4 36.4 48

18821 NNC S P2 G1.2 1928–1972
Nikhamin, Vladimir Petrovich.
'Kitai posle vtoroi mirovoi voiny, 1945–1957 gg.' (China after World War II, 1945–1957).
Prepodavanie istorii v shkole 1958, 2 (mart–aprel'), 63–77.
Subj 12 14 19 32.2 ▪ 14.1 14.4 34.1 66

18822 MCH P P2 G1.2 1842–1972
North, Robert Carver, 1914–.
Chinese Communism.
New York: McGraw-Hill, 1966. 256 p.
Subj 12.1 32 32.2 64 ▪ 12 15 32.1 66

18823 CSH S P2 G1.2 1911–1972
North, Robert Carver, 1914–.
Moscow and Chinese Communists, 2nd ed.
Stanford: Stanford U. Press, 1963. 302 p.
Subj 32 32.2 ▪ 12.1

18824 CSH U P1 G9.4 1928–1972
Ong Joktik (Wang Yü-te).
'A Formosan's view of the Formosan independence movement.'
CQ 15 (July–Sept. 1963), 107–114. [Reprinted in *Formosa today*, edited by Mark Mancall. (Selective entry.) New York: Praeger, 1964, 163–170.]
Subj 32.2 ▪ 12.1 32.1

18825 CSU P P2 G1.2 1928–1972
Payne, Pierre Stephen Robert, 1911–.
'China: The long wooden ladders.' In *Red storm over Asia*, by P. S. R. Payne. [Sole entry]
New York: Macmillan, 1951, 33–65.
Subj 15 25 32.2 64 ▪ 14.1 16.1 32 61

18826 DLC S P1 G1.2 1895–1972
Semenov, IU- V-.
'Opyt revoliutsii 1905 goda i kitaiskaia revoliutsiia' (Lessons of the Revolution of 1905 and the Chinese revolution).
Uchenye zapiski Saratovskogo gosudarstvennogo universiteta 60 (1957), 64–84.
Subj 16 19 32.2 ▪ 64 66

18827 CSU O P2 G1.2 1928–1972
Snow, Edgar, 1905–1972.
Red star over China, rev. and enl. ed.
New York: Grove Press, 1968. 543 p.
Subj 15 16.1 32.2 59 ▪ 16 18 31 33 34.1 37 54 66

18828 NIC FP P1 G1.1 1644–1972
Topley, Marjorie Doreen, 1927–.
'The Great Way of Former Heaven: A group of Chinese secret religious sects.'
BSOAS 26, 2 (June 1963), 362–392.
Subj 32.2 33 62

18829 ELB S P2 G1.2 1911–1972
Vandermeersch, Léon.
'Le parti et l'armée dans la pratique révolutionnaire maoïste' (Party and army in Maoist revolutionary practice).
Esprit nouvelle (2e) série 38, 12 (déc. 1970), 877–892.
Subj 32.2 ▪ 15 32 32.1 35

18830 CSH P P2 G1.2 1911–1972
Vladimirov, O- (O. Vladimir), and V- Riazantsev (V. Rjazancev).
'O nekotorykh voprosakh istorii kompartii Kitaia' (Questions concerning Chinese Communist Party history).
Kommunist 1968, 9 (iiun'), 83–108.

'Quelques problèmes de l'histoire du P.C.C.' Tr. by L- Albe and C- Béranger.
NED 3579 (8 avr. 1969), 23–31.
Subj 16 32 32.2 64 ▪ 16.1 66

18831 CSH P P1 G1.2 1911–1972
Wang Yun.
'An analytical study of Chinese Communist revisions of party constitution.'
IS 6, 1 (Oct. 1969), 62–82.
Subj 32.2 ▪ 64

18832 CSU U P1 G1.2 –1972
Ward, Barbara Elsie, 1919–.
'Chinese secret societies.' In *Secret societies*, edited by Norman MacKenzie. [Sole entry]
New York: Holt, Rinehart and Winston, 1967, 210–241.
Subj 32.2 65 ▪ 22.2 25 30 66

18833 CSU P P1 G1.2 1911–1972
Weidenbaum, Rhoda Sussman, 1930–.
'The career and writings of Liu Shao-ch'i.' In *Researches in the social sciences on China*, edited by John E- Lane. [Selective entry]
New York: Columbia U., East Asian Institute, 1957, 53–78. (EAI series, 3) (Masters thesis in Chinese and Japanese, Columbia U., 1953)
Subj 32.2 ▪ 32 36.4 64

18834 CSU P P2 G1.3 1928–1972
[Wilson, Richard Garratt] Dick Wilson, 1928–.
The Long March, 1935: The epic of Chinese Communism's survival.
London: Hamish Hamilton, 1971. 20, 331 p.
Subj 15 32.2 59 ▪ 16.1 32 36.3

18835 NNC S P8 G1.2 1928–1972
Wright, Mary Clabaugh, 1917–1970.
'The Chinese peasant and Communism.'
PA 24, 3 (Sept. 1951), 256–265.
Subj 16.3 32.2 ▪ 14.1 36.3

1949-1972

18836 NNC F P3 G9.5 1949–1972
Barnett, Arthur Doak, 1921–.
'New force. Part 1, The idea. Part 2, The people.'
AUFS-EAS 1, 2 (1 Sept. 1952), 1–12; 1, 3 (14 Sept. 1952), 1–10.
Subj 32.2 ▪ 24.2 32.1 59 64

18837 NNC P P2 G1.2 1949–1972
Ho Chen-yun (Ho Chen-yün) and Joseph Anderson Shih (Shih Ch'eng-chih), 1918–1973. [Authors sequential rather than joint: Ho Chen-yun for 1955; J. A. Shih for 1956–1958.]
'People's resistance' [title varies]. Tr. of '1955–1958 nien ta lu jen min ti fan k'ang' (Popular resistance on the Mainland, 1955–1958); *Tsu kuo chou k'an* 159–334/335 (16 Jan. 1956 – 8 June 1959) [recurring annual feature article]. In *Communist China, 1955–1958*, edited by Union Research Institute.
Hong Kong: Union Research Institute. Issued annually, 1956–1959, average ca. 10 p.
Subj 12.1 32.2 ▪ 16.3 54

18838 CSH P P2 G1.2 1949–1972
[La Dany, Ladislao] ———, 1914–.
'Underground anti-CCP trends.'
CNA 705 (26 Apr. 1968), 1–7.
Subj 32.2 ▪ 64

18839 CSU P P2 G1.2 1949–1972
Liu Hsiang.
'Uprisings on the Chinese Mainland during the year of 1965.'
IS 2, 5 (Feb. 1966), 30–36.
Subj 32.2 ▪ 25

18840 MCH U P1 G1.2 1949–1972
Napier, Samuel.
'Can Mao overcome the secret societies?'
Contemporary review 197 (Jan. 1960), 27–28.
Subj 32.2 ▪ 32.1

18841 CBU O P3 G9.5 1949–1972
Shephard, A- J-.
'Communist failure in Hong Kong.'
Commonwealth j. 11, 2 (Apr. 1968), 82–87, 98.
Subj 32.2 ▪ 36.4

18842 NNC P P2 G1.2 1949–1972
Shih, Joseph Anderson (Shih Ch'eng-chih), 1918–1973.
People's resistance in Mainland China, 1950–1955, mimeo.
Hong Kong: Union Research Institute, 1956. 116 p. (Communist China problem research series, EC17)
Subj 12.1 16.3 16.4 32.2 ▪ 13 14.1 14.4 14.5 16.2 25

18843 NNC O P4 G9.2 1949–1972
Wang Tsao-ching.
'The true story of the Lin-kao incident.' Tr. of '"Lin-kao shih chien" chen hsiang'; *Shang yu* (Canton) 1958, 2 (Sept.), 35–38. In *Selected articles on local nationalism in Communist China*, mimeo., compiled by U.S. Joint Publications Research Service. [Sole entry]
Washington, D.C.: JPRS, 10 Apr. 1959, 24–31. (JPRS 1476N; MC 9209/1959)
Subj 32.2 ▪ 22.2

33 Religious Sects and Associations
宗教派別及組織
宗教各派及び組織

1644-1911

18844 CSU O P1 G9.3 1842–1895
'Initiation of Buddhist priests.'
CR 9, 3 (May–June 1878), 181–184.
Subj 33

18845 MCH O P4 G8.1 1895–1911
'Les musulmans de Se-Tchouen' (The Muslims of Szechwan).
R. du monde musulman 5, 5 (mai 1908), 90–94.
Subj 33 ▪ 23 29

18846 MCY P P3 G5.4 –1911
Adler, Marcus Nathan, 1837–1911.
'Chinese Jews.'
Jewish quarterly review 13 (Oct. 1900), 18–41. [Separately reprinted—Oxford: H. Hart, 1900. 24 p.] [Reprinted in *Jews in old China: Some western views*, compiled by Hyman Kublin. (Selective entry.) New York: Paragon, 1971, 94–117.]
Subj 33 ▪ 55

18847 CSU PO P3 G5.4 –1911
Bainbridge, Oliver.
'The Chinese Jews.'
NG 18, 10 (Oct. 1907), 621–632.
Subj 33 ▪ 66

18848 MCH P P2 G1.2 –1895
Bazin, Antoine Pierre Louis, 1799–1863.
'Recherches sur l'origine, l'histoire et la constitution des ordres religieux dans l'empire chinois' (Investigations of the origin, history, and composition of religious orders in the Chinese empire).
JA 5e série 8 (août 1856), 105–174.
Subj 13 33 ▪ 12.1

18849 CSU PO P1 G1.2 –1895
Beal, Samuel, 1825–1889.
Buddhism in China.
New York: E. and J. B. Young, 1884. 263 p. [Reprinted—Freeport, N.Y.: Books for Libraries, 1973. 263 p.]
Subj 23 33 ▪ 62 63

18850 CSH P P3 G1.3 1842–1895
Blatt, Marilyn, 1937–.
'Problems of a China missionary: Justus Doolittle.'
PC 12 (Dec. 1958), 28–50.
Subj 33 66

18851 MCH O P7 G9.1 1842–1895
Bray, Géraud, 1825?–1905.
'Persécution contre les chrétiens' (Persecution of Christians).
APF 48 (1876), 235–253.
Subj 33 66 ▪ 25

18852 NNM PO P2 G1.1 1895–1911
Broomhall, Marshall, 1866–1937, ed.
The Chinese empire: A general and missionary survey . . .
Philadelphia: China Inland Mission, 1907. 24, 472 p.
Subj 11.3 21.1 29 33 ▪ 21 21.3 23 24.4 40 60 66

18853 NIC PO P2 G1.2 –1911
Broomhall, Marshall, 1866–1937.
Islam in China: A neglected problem.
Philadelphia: China Inland Mission, 1910. 20, 332 p. [Reprinted—New York: Paragon, 1966. 332 p.]
Subj 23 29 33 62 ▪ 25 32.2 57

18854 NNM PO P1 G1.2 1895–1911
Broomhall, Marshall, 1866–1937.
Present-day conditions in China: Notes designed to show the moral and spiritual claims of the Chinese empire.
New York: Revell, 1908. 58 p.
Subj 17 33 66 ▪ 16.1 32.2 54 56

18855 CSH O P2 G6.0 1644–1895
Broullion, Nicolas.
'Mémoire sur l'état actuel de la mission du Kiang-nan' (The present state of the Kiangnan mission). In *Missions de Chine: mémoire sur l'état actuel de la mission du Kiang-nan, 1842–1855* (Chinese missions: An account of the present state of the Kiangnan mission, 1842–1855), by N. Broullion. [Selective entry]
Paris: Julien, Lanier, 1855, 41–230.
Subj 33 61 ▪ 43 47

18856 NNM O P3 G5.1 1895–1911
Brown, Frederick, 1860–?
Religion in Tientsin.
Shanghai: Methodist Publishing House, 1908. 61 p.
Subj 23 33 65 ▪ 57 62

18857 MCH O P4 G6.2 1895–1911
Chambeau, Gabriel.
'Une visite aux monastères bouddhiques de Kieou-hoa-chan' (A visit to the Buddhist monastaries of Chiu-hua-shan [Ch'ing-yang *hsien*, Anhwei]).
Etudes 7e série 130, 6 (20 mars 1912), 785–798; 131, 7 (5 avr. 1912), 34–52.
Subj 13 33

18858 CBU P P1 G1.2 1644–1911
Chou, Hsiang-kuang.
'Buddhism in the Ch'ing dynasty.' In *A history of Chinese Buddhism*, by Hsiang-kuang Chou. [Sole entry]
Allahabad: Chou Sinpong, 1955, 199–227.
Subj 33 ▪ 16.1 59

18859 MCH P P2 G1.3 1842–1895
Cohen, Paul Andrew, 1934–.
China and Christianity: The missionary movement and the growth of Chinese antiforeignism, 1860–1870.
Cambridge: Harvard U. Press, 1963. 410 p. (Harvard East Asian series, 11) (Revision of *Chinese hostility to Christianity: A study in intellectual conflict, 1860–1870*, doctoral dissertation in History and Far Eastern Languages, Harvard U., 1961)
Subj 13 33 63 66 ▪ 12.2 16.1 22.1 26.1 64

18860 MAM P P2 G9.0 1644–1895
Coughlin, Margaret Morgan, 1922–.
Strangers in the house: J. Lewis Shuck and Issachar Roberts, first American Baptist missionaries to China.
Ann Arbor: University Microfilms (Publ. 72-22,632), 1972. 332 p. (Doctoral dissertation in History, U. of Virginia)
Subj 33 66

18861 CBU P P4 G8.1 1895–1911
Cunningham, Alfred, 1870–?
A history of the Szechwan riots (May–June, 1895).
Shanghai: Shanghai Mercury Office, 1895. 38, 30 p.
Subj 25 33 66

18862 MCH P P2 G1.2 –1895
Dabry de Thiersant, Claude Philibert, 1826–1898.
Le mahométisme en Chine et dans le Turkestan oriental (Islam in China and in eastern Turkestan).
Paris: Ernest Leroux, 1878. 2 vols. 335; 514 p.
Subj 15 22.2 33 55 62 63 ▪ 11.3 12 13 17 21 25 28 29 41 57

18863 CSU P P1 G9.2 –1842
Dehergne, J-.
'Les origines du Christianisme dans l'île de Hainan (XVIème–XVIIème siècles)' (The origins of Christianity in Hainan in the sixteenth and seventeenth centuries).
MS 5 (1940), 329–348.
Subj 33 66

18864 FPN S P1 G4.0 –1842
Devéria, Jean Gabriel, 1844–1899.
'Musulmans et manichéens chinois' (Chinese Muslims and Manichaeans).
JA 9e série 10 (nov.–déc. 1897), 445–484.
Subj 29 33 ▪ 12 15 23

18865 MCH PO P2 G6.1 –1911
Doré, Henri, 1859–1931.
'Le grand pèlerinage bouddhique de Lang-chan et les cinq montagnes de Tong-tcheou' (The great Buddhist pilgrimage of Lang-shan and the five mountains of T'ung *chou* [Kiangsu]).
NCR 1, 1 (Mar. 1919), 41–56; 1, 2 (May 1919), 120–144; 1, 3 (July 1919), 282–298; 1, 5 (Oct. 1919), 457–479; 1, 6 (Dec. 1919), 580–603; 2, 1 (Feb. 1920), 44–46.
Subj 21.3 23 33 65 ▪ 22 25 26.1 50

18866 CSH P P1 G1.2 1842–1911
Duus, Peter, 1933–.
'Science and salvation in China: The life and work of W. A. P. Martin (1827–1916).'
PC 10 (Oct. 1956), 97–127. [Reprinted in *American missionaries in China: Papers from Harvard seminars*, edited by Kwang-ching Liu (Liu Kuang-ching). (Analytic entry.) Cambridge: Harvard U., East Asian Research Center, 1966, 11–41. (Harvard East Asian monographs, 21)]
Subj 17 33 66 ▪ 62

18867 CSU P P2 G1.2 –1895
Edkins, Joseph, 1823–1905.
Chinese Buddhism: A volume of sketches, historical, descriptive, and critical, 2nd ed.
London: Trübner, 1893. 23, 453 p. [Reprinted—New York: Paragon, 1968. 453 p.]
Subj 23 33 62 ▪ 43 63 65

18868 CSU PO P2 G5.2 1842–1911
Edwards, E- H-.
Fire and sword in Shansi: The story of the martyrdom of foreigners and Chinese Christians.
Edinburgh: Oliphant, Anderson, and Ferrier, 1903. 325 p.
Subj 25 32.2 33 66 ▪ 12 12.2 24.1 26.1 52 57

18869 CSU PO P3 G1.3 –1911
Ezra, Edward Isaac, 1881–.
'Chinese Jews.'
EAM 1 (1902), 278–296. [Reprinted in *Jews in old China: Some western views*, compiled by Hyman Kublin. (Selective entry.) New York: Paragon, 1971, 213–266.]
Subj 33 ▪ 55 62

18870 CSU P P3 G1.3 –1842
Finn, James, 1806–1872.
The Jews in China: Their synagogue, their scriptures, their history, etc.
London: Wertheim, 1843. 86 p. [Reprinted—Taipei: Ch'eng-wen, 1971. 86 p.] [Reprinted in *Jews in old China: Some western views*, compiled by Hyman Kublin. (Selective entry.) New York: Paragon, 1971, 1–92.]
Subj 33 62

18871 ELB PO P2 G1.1 1842–1895
Fishbourne, Edmund Gardiner.
Impressions of China, and the present revolution: Its progress and prospects.
London: Seeley, Jackson and Halliday, 1855. 11, 441 p.
Subj 12 15 32.2 33 50 60 ▪ 12.2 25

18872 CSH P P2 G1.4 1895–1911
Forsythe, Sidney A-, 1920–.
An American missionary community in China, 1895–1905.
Cambridge: Harvard U., East Asian Research Center, 1971. 146 p. (Harvard East Asian monographs, 43) (Revision of *Missionaries and Chinese: A descriptive case study of the responses of American Board missionaries to selected aspects of the setting of their work, 1895–1905*, doctoral dissertation in History and Far Eastern Languages, Harvard U., 1963)
Subj 23 33 60 66 ▪ 16.1 32 32.2

18873 MCH PO P1 G1.2 –1895
Franke, Otto, 1863–1946.
'Eine neue buddhistische Propaganda' (A new outpouring of Buddhist propaganda).
TP 5, 3 (1894), 299–310.
Subj 33 ▪ 13

18874 GMS P P2 G1.3 1895–1911
Franke, Otto, 1863–1946.
'Die Propaganda des japanischen Buddhismus in China' (The proselytizing efforts of Japanese Buddhism in China). In *Ostasiatische Neubildungen: Beiträge zum Verständnis der politischen und kulturellen Entwicklungs-vorgänge im Fernen Osten* (New forms in East Asia: Toward an understanding of political and cultural developmental processes in the Far East), by O. Franke. [Selective entry]
Hamburg: C. Boysen, 1911, 158–165.
Subj 33 66

18875 CSU O P2 G1.5 1895–1911
Geil, William Edgar, 1865–1925.
A Yankee on the Yangtze: Being a narrative of a journey from Shanghai through the Central Kingdom to Burma.
Cincinnati: Jennings and Graham; New York: Eaton and Mains, 1904. 15, 312 p.
Subj 26.1 33 65 66 ▪ 12 22.2 24.1 24.2 24.4 55 56

18876 CNY O P2 G9.2 1644–1895
Giedt, Emmanuel Herman, 1887–.
A history of the planting of Protestant Christianity in the province of Kwangtung, China.
Unpublished doctoral dissertation in Religion, Yale U., 1936. 309 p.
Subj 33 66 ▪ 17 25 29 32.2 56 59

18877 DCK P P2 G9.4 –1842
Ginsel, Willy Abraham.
De Gereformeerde Kerk op Formosa: of, De lotgevallen eener handelskerk onder de Oost-Indische Compagnie, 1627–1662 (The Reformed Church in Taiwan: or, The vicissitudes of a trading church under the [Dutch] East India Company, 1627–1662).
Leiden: Mulder en Zoon, 1931. 138 p.
Subj 24 33 ▪ 16 17

18878 CBU O P2 G9.2 1842–1895
Graves, Roswell Hobart, 1833–1912.
'Persecution in Kwangtung.'
CR 15, 6 (Nov.–Dec. 1884), 445–454.
Subj 33 66 ▪ 22.2

18879 CSU P P1 G1.2 –1895
Groot, Jan Jakob Maria de, 1854–1921.
'Influence du code mahâyâniste sur la vie monacale et sur le monde laïque' (The influence of the Mahayana code on monastic life and the lay world). In *Le code du Mahâyâna en Chine* (The Mahayana code in China), by J. J. M. de Groot. [Sole entry]
Amsterdam: Johannes Müller, 1893, 99–256. (Koninklijke Akademie van Wetenschappen te Amsterdam, Verhandelingen, Afdeeling letterkunde, 1, 2)
SUBJ 33 63 ▪ 23

18880 NIC P P1 G1.3 –1911
Groot, Jan Jakob Maria de, 1854–1921.
Sectarianism and religious persecution in China.
Amsterdam: Johannes Müller, 1903, 1904. 2 vols. 595 p. [c.p.]. (Koniuklijke Akademie van Wetenschappen, Afdeeling letterkunde, Verhandlinger, nieuwe veeks, 4, 1–2) [Reprinted—Taipei: Ch'eng-wen, 1971. 595 p.]
SUBJ 13 32.2 33 ▪ 64

18881 NNC O P2 G1.3 1644–1895
[Gützlaff, Karl Friedrich August] Charles Gutzlaff, 1803–1851.
'Remarks on the present state of Buddhism in China.'
JRAS 16 (1856), 73–92.
SUBJ 23 33 ▪ 57 62 63

18882 NNC O P1 G1.3 –1842
Gurii, *Otets* (O. Gurius).
'Obety buddistov i obriad vozlozheniia ikh u kitaitsev' (Buddhist vows and the vow-taking ceremony among the Chinese). In *Trudy chlenov Rossiiskoi dukhovnoi missii v Pekine* (Works of members of the Russian Orthodox ecclesiastical mission in Peking). [Selective entry]
St. Petersburg: Tip. Shtaba voenno-ucheb. zavedenii, 1853, vol. 2, 195–356. [Reprinted in *Trudy chlenov Rossiiskoi dukhovnoi missii v Pekine*. (Selective entry.) Peking: Tip. Uspenskago monastyria pri RDM, 1910, vol. 2, 117–214.]
'Die Gelübde der Buddhisten und die Ceremonie ihrer Ablegung bei den Chinesen.' Tr. by Carl Abel and F- A- Mecklenburg. In *Arbeiten der kaiserlich russischen Gesandtschaft zu Peking über China, sein Volk, seine Religion, seine Institutionen, sozialen Verhältnisse, usw.* (Works of the imperial Russian mission to Peking on China, its people, religion, institutions, social conditions, etc.). [Selective entry]
Berlin: Heinicke, 1858, vol. 2, 315–419.
SUBJ 33 ▪ 60

18883 CSU O P8 G6.3 1895–1911
Hackmann, Heinrich, 1864–1935.
'Buddhist monastery life in China.'
EAM 1 (1902), 239–261.
SUBJ 33

18884 MCH O P8 G6.3 1895–1911
Hackmann, Heinrich, 1864–1935.
'Das Buddhisten-Kloster Tien-dong in der chinesischen Provinz Chekiang' (The Buddhist monastery T'ien-t'ung in [Yin *hsien*] Chekiang).
Z. für Missionskunde und Religionswissenschaft 17, 5 (1902), 173–178.
SUBJ 33 ▪ 23 62

18885 CBU PO P2 G1.2 –1911
Hackmann, Heinrich, 1864–1935.
'Chinese Buddhism.' Tr. from the German [rev. and enl. in tr.]. In *Buddhism as a religion*, edited by H. Hackmann. [Sole entry]
London: Probsthain, 1910, 200–257.
SUBJ 33 ▪ 57 62

18886 MCH P P1 G1.1 –1911
Hackmann, Heinrich, 1864–1935.
'Ein Heiliger des chinesischen Buddhismus und seine Spuren im heutigen China' (A Chinese Buddhist saint and his traces in contemporary China).
Z. für Missionskunde und Religionswissenschaft 18, 3 (1903), 65–72.
SUBJ 33 ▪ 23

18887 NNC FP P8 G5.3 1644–1911
Hackmann, Heinrich, 1864–1935.
'Die Mönchsregeln des Klostertaoismus' (Rules of conduct for Taoist monks in cloisters).
Ostasiatische Z. 8 (1919/20), 142–170.
SUBJ 33 63 ▪ 62

18888 CBU P P1 G1.1 –1911
Hackmann, Heinrich, 1864–1935.
'Die Schulen des chinesischen Buddhismus' (The schools of Chinese Buddhism).
MSOSB 14 (1911), 232–266.
SUBJ 33

18889 CSU O P2 G8.1 1842–1895
Hart, Virgil Chittenden, 1840–1904.
Western China: A journey to the great Buddhist centre of Mount Omei [Szechwan].
Boston: Ticknor, 1888. 10, 306 p. [Reprinted—Taipei: Ch'eng-wen, 1972. 10, 306 p.]
SUBJ 20 23 24.2 33 66 ▪ 22 24.1 24.3 28 55 62 65

18890 NNC S P2 G4.0 1644–1911
Hartmann, Martin, 1851–1918.
Zur Geschichte des Islams in China (History of Islam in China).
Leipzig: Wilhelm Heims, 1921. 14, 152 p.
SUBJ 32.2 33 ▪ 13 15 16.1 23 25 29 41

18891 MCH P P2 G1.1 1644–1842
Hering, Hollis W-.
'A study of Roman Catholic missions in China, 1692–1744.'
NCR 3, 2 (Apr. 1921), 107–126; 3, 3 (June 1921), 198–212. [Reprinted in *D'Ollone's investigations on Chinese Moslems: A study of Roman Catholic missions in China, 1692–1744*, by G- G- Warren and H. W. Hering. (Analytic entry.) (Peiping): ——, 1940, 41–75.]
SUBJ 33 ▪ 13 16.1 72

18892 MCY P P3 G8.1 1842–1895
Hyatt, Irwin Townsend, Jr., 1935–.
'The Chengtu riots, 1895: Myths and politics.'
PC 18 (Dec. 1964), 26–54.
SUBJ 22.2 33 66 ▪ 12 25

18893 MCH P P2 G1.2 1842–1895
Hyatt, Irwin Townsend, Jr., 1935–.
'Protestant missions in China, 1877–1890: The institutionalization of good works.'
PC 17 (Dec. 1963), 67–100. [Reprinted in *American missionaries in China: Papers from Harvard seminars*, edited by Kwang-ching Liu (Liu Kuang-ching). (Analytic entry.) Cambridge: Harvard U., East Asian Research Center, 1966, 93–128. (Harvard East Asian monographs, 21)]
SUBJ 17 18 33 56 ▪ 66

18894 CBU O P8 G5.1 1842–1895
Imbault-Huart, Camille Clément, 1857–1897.
'Le pèlerinage de la montagne du pic mystérieux près de Péking' (The pilgrimage of the mountain of the mysterious peak near Peking).
JA 8e série 5 (jan. 1885), 62–71.
SUBJ 23 33 ▪ 65

18895 CSU O P4 G7.2 1895–1911
John, Griffith, 1831–1912.
'The situation in Hunan.'
CR 2, 6 (June 1897), 251–265.
SUBJ 33 66 ▪ 24.2

18896 NNC PO P2 G1.2 –1895
[Kafarov, Petr Ivanovich] *Otets* Palladii, 1817–1878.
'O magometanakh v Kitae' (Muslims in China). In *Trudy chlenov Rossiiskoi dukhovnoi missii v Pekine* (Works of members of the Russian Orthodox ecclesiastical mission in Peking). [Selective entry]
St. Petersburg: Tip. Shtaba voenno-ucheb. zavedenii, 1866, vol. 4, 437–460. [Reprinted in *Trudy chlenov Rossiiskoi dukhovnoi missii v Pekine*. (Selective entry.) Peking: Tip. Uspenskago monastyria pri RDM, 1910, vol. 4, 202–211.]
SUBJ 33

18897 MCH P P1 G1.2 –1842
Klaproth, Julius Heinrich, 1783–1835.
'De la religion des Tao-szu en Chine' (Taoism in China).
Nouvelles annales des voyages 58 (1833), 129–150.
SUBJ 33 ▪ 23

18898 CBU PO P8 G1.5 –1895
Kopsch, Henry.
'The Master of Heaven [T'ien-shih].'
China review 2, 4 (Jan.–Feb. 1874), 226–229.
SUBJ 33

18899 CSH P P2 G9.3 1842–1911
Korson, Thomas E-.
'Congregational missionaries in Foochow during the 1911 Revolution.'
CC 8, 2 (June 1967), 44–107.
SUBJ 17 32.2 33 ▪ 56 66

18900 CNY PO P1 G1.1 –1895
Krone, Rudolf.
'Der Buddhismus in China' (Buddhism in China).
Berichte der Rheinischen Missionsgesellschaft 1855, 16, 241–255.
SUBJ 33 ▪ 23 62

18901 CNY PO P2 G9.2 –1895
Krone, Rudolf.
'Die Muhamedaner in China' (Muslims in China).
Berichte der Rheinischen Missionsgesellschaft 1858, 16, 241–244; 1858, 18, 278–285.
Subj 33 ▪ 62 63

18902 CNY PO P1 G1.1 –1895
Krone, Rudolf.
'Der Taoismus in China' (Taoism in China).
Berichte der Rheinischen Missionsgesellschaft 1857, 7, 102–111; 1857, 8, 114–119.
Subj 23 33 ▪ 63 65

18903 MAM P P2 G9.4 1842–1895
Lai, En-tse, 1928–.
The encounter of Christian gospel and Formosan culture, 1865–1895.
Ann Arbor: University Microfilms (Publ. 71-13,710), 1971. 102 p. (Doctoral dissertation in Religion, Claremont Graduate School and University Center)
Subj 23 33 66 ▪ 25 43 57

18904 MCH P P2 G1.1 –1842
La Servière, Joseph de.
Les anciennes missions de la Compagnie de Jésus en Chine, 1552–1814 (The former Jesuit missions in China, 1552–1814).
Shanghai: Impr. de l'Orphelinat de T'ou-sè-wè, 1924. 82 p.
Subj 16.1 33 ▪ 12 13 43 62 66

18905 CSU P P3 G5.4 1644–1842
Laufer, Berthold, 1874–1934.
'A Chinese-Hebrew manuscript: A new source for the history of the Chinese Jews.'
American j. of Semitic languages and literature 46, 3 (Apr. 1930), 189–197. [Reprinted—*FS* 4 (1945), 319–346.] [Reprinted in *Chinese Jews: A compilation of matters relating to the Jews of K'ai-fêng Fu*, 2nd ed., by William Charles White. (Selective entry.) New York: Paragon, 1966, 6–15 (s.p.).] [Reprinted in *Studies of the Chinese Jews: Selections from journals East and West*, compiled by Hyman Kublin. (Selective entry.) New York: Paragon, 1971, 159–169.]
Subj 33 42

18906 ELB O P3 G9.2 1842–1895
Laurie, Peter George.
A reminiscence of Canton.
London: Harrison, 1866. 58 p.
Subj 22.2 33 55 ▪ 21.3 28 57

18907 MCH O P7 G1.3 1842–1895
Leboucq, Prosper, 1828–1905.
'Les sociétés religieuses en Chine' (Religious societies in China).
Etudes religieuses 5e série 8 (août 1875), 641–664.
Subj 33 ▪ 23

18908 NNC O P2 G9.4 1842–1895
MacKay, George Leslie, 1844–1901.
From far Formosa: The island, its people and missions, 4th ed., edited by J- H- Macdonald.
New York: Revell, 1896. 346 p. [Reprinted—Taipei: Ch'eng-wen, 1967. 346 p.]
Subj 33 41 ▪ 12.2 17 23 47 56 66

18909 CSU O P2 G1.3 1842–1895
Martin, William Alexander Parsons, 1827–1916.
'Account of an overland journey from Peking to Shanghai, made in February and March 1866.'
JRAS-NCB new (2nd) series 3 (Dec. 1866), 26–39. [Reprinted as 'Account of a visit to the Jews in Honan, February, 1866.' In *The Chinese: Their education, philosophy and letters*, by W. A. P. Martin. (Selective entry.) New York: Harper, 1881, 287–306.]
Subj 14.2 33

18910 CSU U P1 G5.3 –1895
Mateer, Calvin Wilson, 1836–1908.
'T'ai San [i.e., T'ai-shan, T'ai-an *hsien*, Shantung]: Its temples and worship.'
CR 10, 5 (Sept.–Oct. 1879), 361–369; 10, 6 (Nov.–Dec. 1879), 403–415.
Subj 23 33 ▪ 13 65

18911 MCH O P2 G3.0 1842–1895
Mesnard, *Père* ———.
'Chrétienté et collège de la Bouche des Pins' (Christianity and the seminary in Pine Grove village [Sung-shu-tsui-tzu, Inner Mongolia]).
APF 31 (1859), 209–237.
Subj 13 22.2 33 66 ▪ 64

18912 CSU O P2 G7.1 1895–1911
Miles, George.
'Vegetarian sects.'
CR 33, 1 (Jan. 1902), 1–10.
Subj 33 ▪ 62

18913 CSU P P3 G5.4 –1895
Neubauer, Adolph, 1831–1907.
'Jews in China.'
Jewish quarterly review 8, 29 (Oct. 1895), 123–139. [Reprinted in *Studies of the Chinese Jews: Selections from journals East and West*, compiled by Hyman Kublin. (Selective entry.) New York: Paragon, 1971, 139–157.]
Subj 33

18914 CSU O P2 G1.4 1842–1895
Nevius, Helen Stanford Coan, 1833–1910.
The life of John Livingston Nevius, for forty years a missionary in China.
New York: Revell, 1895. 476 p.
Subj 28 33 66 71 ▪ 17 21.3 48 56 65

18915 NNC FP P2 G1.2 –1911
Ollone, Henri Marie Gustave d', 1868–?, et al.
Recherches sur les musulmans chinois (Investigations of the Chinese Muslims).
Paris: Ernest Leroux, 1911. 12, 470 p. (Mission d'Ollone, Documents scientifiques, 1)
Subj 15 29 33 41 50 57 ▪ 21 21.3 22.2 23 26.1 43 55 66 72

18916 ICU P P2 G1.3 –1842
Overmyer, Daniel Lee, 1935–.
Folk-Buddhist sects: A structure in the history of Chinese religions.
Unpublished doctoral dissertation, Divinity School, U. of Chicago, 1971. 348 p.
Subj 23 33 62 ▪ 12.2 13 32.2

18917 CBU PO P2 G1.3 –1911
Perlmann, Simon Meir.
The history of the Jews in China.
London: Mazin, 1913. 95 p. [Reprinted in *Jews in old China: Some western views*, compiled by Hyman Kublin. (Selective entry.) New York: Paragon, 1971, 119–211.]
Subj 33 ▪ 55 60

18918 CSU O P3 G6.1 1895–1911
Pettus, William Bacon.
'Mohammedanism in Nanking.'
CR 39, 7 (July 1908), 395–402; 39, 8 (Aug. 1908), 448–453.
Subj 33 ▪ 55 57 66

18919 FPN P P1 G1.1 –1911
Piolet, Jean-Baptiste, 1855–1930, and Charles Vadot.
La religion catholique en Chine (Catholicism in China).
Paris: Bloud, 1905. 64 p.
Subj 25 33 66 ▪ 11 16.1 17 61

18920 NNP FP P2 G5.2 –1895
Pokotilov, Dmitrii Dmitrievich, 1865–1908.
U-Tai, ego proshloe i nastoiashchee: otchet o poezdke, sovershennoi v mae 1889 g. (Wu-t'ai-shan [Wu-t'ai *hsien*, Shansi], past and present: Report of a trip in May 1889).
St. Petersburg: Tip. imp. Akad. nauk, 1893. 152 p. (Imperatorskoe Russkoe geograficheskoe obshchestvo, Zapiski po obshchei geografii, 22, 2).
'Der Wu Tai Schan und seine Klöster' (Wu-t'ai-shan and its monasteries). Tr. by W- A- Unkrieg. [Partial tr.: p. 47–116 only]
Sinica 1935, 38–89. [*Sonderausgabe* (Special issue)]
Subj 20 33 ▪ 23 62 72

18921 CSU O P1 G5.3 –1895
Porter, D- H-.
'Secret sects in Shantung.'
CR 17, 1 (Jan. 1886), 1–10; 17, 2 (Feb. 1886), 64–73.
Subj 33 ▪ 32.2 62 63

18922 FPN O P2 G8.2 1842–1895
Pourias, Emile-René, 1843–1884.
La Chine: huit ans au Yun-nan (China: Eight years in Yunnan).
Lille: Société de St. Augustin, 1892. 188 p.
Subj 11.3 22 22.2 33 66 ▪ 12 15 21.3 26.1 28 32.2 50 55

18923 FPN P P1 G1.1 1842–1895
[Pouvourville, Eugène-Albert Puyon de] Matgioï, pseud.
'Le taoïsme contemporain: sa hiérarchie, son enseignement, son rôle' (The hierarchy, teaching, and role of contemporary Taoism).
Mémoires du Comité sinico-japonais 19 (1889), 179–218.
Subj 33 62 ▪ 23

18924 MCH PO P2 G3.0 1842–1895
Pozdneev, Aleksei Matveevich, 1851–1920.
O poslednem kitaiskom vosstanii v iugo-vostochnoi Mongolii i o prichinakh protivokhristianskikh vosstanii v Kitae voobshche (The latest Chinese uprising in southeastern Mongolia and the causes of anti-Christian uprisings in China as a whole).
St. Petersburg: Sviateishii pravitel'stv. sinod, 1896. 26 p.
Subj 25 33 66 ▪ 13

18925 MSE O P2 G8.0 1895–1911
Pruen, *Mrs.* William L-.
The provinces of western China.
London: Alfred Holness, 1906. 231 p.
SUBJ 18 21 33 56 ▪ 16.1 55 66

18926 MCH O P3 G6.1 1842–1895
Ravary, *Père* ——.
'La Chang-hai chrétienne et la Chang-hai païenne' (Christian Shanghai and pagan Shanghai).
Missions catholiques 24 (8 jan. – 6 mai 1892), 58 p. in all.
SUBJ 28 33 ▪ 12.2 13 22.1 23 61

18927 NNM PO P1 G1.2 –1911
Reichelt, Karl Ludvig, 1877–1952.
Kinas religioner: Haandbok i den kinesiske religionshistorie (The religions of China: Handbook on the history of Chinese religions), 2nd ed.
Stavanger: Norske missionsselskap, 1922. 229 p.

Religion in Chinese garment. Tr. by Joseph Tetlie.
New York: Philosophical Library, 1951. 180 p. (Missionary research series, 16)
SUBJ 13 23 33 62 ▪ 32.2 43 57 63

18928 CSU O P2 G1.2 1842–1895
Richard, Timothy, 1845–1919.
'Christian persecutions in China: Their nature, causes, remedies.'
CR 15, 4 (July–Aug. 1884), 237–248.
SUBJ 33 66 ▪ 22.2

18929 NNC O P7 G8.1 1895–1911
Shields, E- T-.
'Omei San [O-mei *hsien*, Szechwan], the sacred mountain of West China.'
JRAS-NCB new (2nd) series 44 (1913), 100–110.
SUBJ 33 ▪ 65

18930 MCH PO P2 G1.3 –1911
Smith, Arthur Henderson, 1845–1932.
Rex Christus: An outline study of China.
New York: Macmillan, 1904. 11, 256 p.
SUBJ 33 64 66 ▪ 12 17 18 19 29 32.2 47 60 72

18931 MSE F P3 G5.4 1842–1895
Smith, George, 1815–1871, ed.
The Jews at K'ae-Fung-foo [i.e., Kaifeng]*: Being a narrative of a mission of enquiry to the Jewish synagogue on behalf of the London Society for Promoting Christianity Among the Jews.*
Shanghai: The author, 1851. 12, 82 p.
SUBJ 33

18932 MCH PO P4 G6.3 1842–1911
Soothill, William Edward, 1861–1935.
A mission in [suburban Wenchow] *China.*
Edinburgh: Oliphant, Anderson, and Ferrier, 1907. 12, 293 p.
SUBJ 23 33 60 ▪ 17 22.2 43 47 66

18933 MCH U P4 G8.2 –1911
Soulié de Morant, Charles Georges, 1878–.
'Les musulmans du Yun-nan' (The Muslims of Yunnan).
R. du monde musulman 9, 10 (oct. 1909), 209–223.
SUBJ 21.1 33 ▪ 41 57 61

18934 NNC O P7 G6.3 1895–1911
Stanley, Arthur.
'Putoshan [i.e., P'u-t'o-shan, Ting-hai *hsien*, Chekiang].'
JRAS-NCB new (2nd) series 46 (1915), 1–18.
SUBJ 33 ▪ 23 62 64

18935 CSU P P2 G4.2 1644–1842
Szcześniak, Boleslaw.
'The description and map of Kansu by Giovanni Battista Maoletti de Serravalle.'
MS 18 (1959), 294–313.
SUBJ 33 ▪ 23

18936 CSU P P2 G1.1 –1842
Thomas, A-.
Histoire de la mission de Pékin, Tome I, depuis les origines à l'arrivée des lazaristes (History of the [Catholic] mission in Peking, Vol. 1, From its origins to the arrival of the Lazarists).
Paris: Louis-Michaud, 1923. 463 p.
SUBJ 12 13 33 60 66 ▪ 21.3 23 43 57

18937 CSU P P2 G1.1 1644–1911
Thomas, A-.
Histoire de la mission de Pékin, Tome II, depuis l'arrivée des lazaristes jusqu'à la révolte des Boxeurs (History of the [Catholic] mission in Peking, Vol. 2, From the arrival of the Lazarists to the Boxer Rebellion).
Paris: Vald. Rasmussen, 1933. 758 p.
SUBJ 12 33 66 ▪ 15 17 47 72

18938 CSU O P1 G1.2 1895–1911
Tong, Kai-son.
'Difficulties of the Chinese clergyman.'
CR 36, 2 (Feb. 1905), 70–75.
SUBJ 33 ▪ 66

18939 MCH PO P7 G5.3 –1911
Tschepe, Albert, 1844–?
Der T'ai-Schan und seine Kultstätten (T'ai-shan [T'ai-an *hsien*, Shantung] and its places of worship).
Chin-chou-fu, Shantung: Katholische Mission, 1906. 124 p. (Studien und Schilderungen aus China, 1)
SUBJ 23 33 62 ▪ 65

18940 ELB P P1 G1.2 –1895
Vasil'ev, Vasilii Pavlovich (Vasilij Pavlovich Vasil'ev), 1818–1900.
O dvizhenii magometanstva v Kitae (The Muslim movement in China).
St. Petersburg: Pechatnia A. Golovina, 1867. 30 p. [Reprinted as 'Magometanstvo v Kitae' (Islam in China). In *'Otkrytie Kitaia' i dr. st. akademika V. P. Vasil'eva* ('The opening of China' and other articles by the academician V. P. Vasil'ev). (Selective entry.) St. Petersburg: Stolichnaia tip., 1900, 106–138.]

Islam in China. Tr. by Rudolf Löwenthal.
Washington, D.C.: Central Asia Collectanea, 1960. 37 p. (CAC, 3)
SUBJ 32.2 33 ▪ 26.1 41 55

18941 MCH FP P2 G1.2 –1911
Warren, G- G-.
'D'Ollone's investigations on Chinese Moslems.'
NCR 2, 3 (June 1920), 267–289; 2, 4 (Aug. 1920), 39–414. [Reprinted in *D'Ollone's investigations on Chinese Moslems: A study of Roman Catholic missions in China, 1692–1744*, by G. G. Warren and Hollis W- Hering. (Analytic entry.) (Peiping): ——, 1940, 1–40.]
SUBJ 33 ▪ 25 29 57

18942 CSU O P5 G2.0 1895–1911
Webster, J-, comp.
'The sifting time in Manchuria: The persecution of the Manchurian church.'
CR 32, 9 (Sept. 1901), 423–435.
SUBJ 33 66

18943 CBU P P1 G1.1 1842–1895
Wei, Louis Tsing-sing (Wei Ching-hsing), 1903–.
La politique missionnaire de la France en Chine, 1842–1856 (French missionary policy in China, 1842–1856).
Paris: Nouvelles éditions latines, 1960. 653 p. (Revision of *L'ouverture des cinq ports au commerce étranger et la liberté religieuse en Chine (1842–1856)* [The opening of the five ports to foreign trade and religious freedom in China, 1842–1856], doctoral dissertation, Faculté des lettres, Université de Paris, 1957)
SUBJ 33 60 66 ▪ 12.2 32.2

18944 CSU PO P1 G1.2 –1911
Wieger, Léon (Leo Wieger), 1856–1933.
'Mahométisme chinois' (Islam in China). In *Histoire des croyances religieuses et des opinions philosophiques en Chine depuis l'origine, jusqu'à nos jours*, 3rd ed., by L. Wieger. [Selective entry]
Hsien-hsien, Hopei: Impr. de Sienhsien, 1927, 705–714.

'Chinese Mohammedanism.' Tr. by Edward Theodore Chalmers Werner. In *A history of the religious beliefs and philosophical opinions in China from the beginning to the present time*, by L. Wieger. [Selective entry]
Hsien-hsien, Hopei: Hsien-hsien Press, 1927, 705–714. [Reprinted in *A history of the religious beliefs and philosophical opinions in China from the beginning to the present time*, by L. Wieger. (Selective entry.) New York: Paragon, 1969, 705–714.]
SUBJ 33 62 ▪ 57 63

18945 WSU P P2 G1.2 –1895
Wiest, Jean-Paul, 1941–.
The Catholic implantation at Canton: French missionary work, 1840–1860.
Unpublished masters thesis in East Asian Studies, U. of Washington, 1972. 188 p.
SUBJ 33 66 ▪ 13 23 26.1

18946 NIC PO P3 G5.1 –1911
Williams, Edward Thomas, 1854–1944.
'The worship of Lei Tsu, patron saint of silk workers.'
JRAS-NCB new (2nd) series 66 (1935), 1–14.
SUBJ 13 16.1 33 47 ▪ 62 65

18947 MCH S P2 G1.1 1842–1911
Wolferstan, Bertram.
The Catholic Church in China, from 1860 to 1907.
St. Louis: Herder, 1909. 37, 470 p.
SUBJ 33 66 ▪ 25 56

18948 MCY P P1 G1.3 –1842
Wong, George H. C. (Huang Tao-chang), 1924–.

'The anti-Christian movement in China: Late Ming and early Ch'ing.'
THJ new (2nd) series 3, 1 (May 1962), 187–220.
SUBJ 13 16.1 33 66 ▪ 64

1644-1949

18949 CSH PO P2 G1.2 1842–1928
'The Chinese [Protestant] church.' In *The Christian occupation of China*, edited by Milton Theobald Stauffer. [Selective entry]
Shanghai: China Continuation Committee, 1922, 379–395.
SUBJ 33 ▪ 17 37 38

18950 CSH O P2 G9.0 –1928
'Christian work among the Hakka.' In *The Christian occupation of China*, edited by Milton Theobald Stauffer. [Selective entry]
Shanghai: China Continuation Committee, 1922, 351–353.
SUBJ 29 33 ▪ 21.2 55

18951 CSH O P2 G1.2 1895–1928
'Christian work among the Moslems in China.' In *The Christian occupation of China*, edited by Milton Theobald Stauffer. [Selective entry]
Shanghai: China Continuation Committee, 1922, 353–358.
SUBJ 20 29 33 ▪ 17 21.3 26.1

18952 ICU P P2 G1.2 1842–1949
Armerding, Hudson Taylor, 1918–.
The China Inland Mission and some aspects of its work.
Unpublished doctoral dissertation in History, U. of Chicago, 1948. 202 p.
SUBJ 17 33 38 56 ▪ 66

18953 IMA O P2 G1.4 1895–1949
Balconi, Lorenzo Maria, 1878–?
Trentatrè anni in Cina: memorie di missione (A missionary's recollections of thirty years in China).
Milan: Pontificio Istituto delle Missioni Estere, 1943. 382 p.
SUBJ 25 33 ▪ 12.2 13 21.1 21.3 22.2 23 28

18954 NIC O P8 G5.1 1644–1949
Blofeld, John Eaton Calthorpe, 1913–.
'Life in a Chinese Buddhist monastery.'
THM 8, 2 (Feb. 1939), 145–154.
SUBJ 33 62 ▪ 55

18955 NNC FP P3 G3.3 –1949
Boerschmann, Ernst, 1873–1949.
'Die Pai t'a von Suiyüan, eine Nebenform der T'ienningpagoden' (The white pagoda of Suiyuan, a form of the *T'ien-ning* pagoda).
Ostasiatische Z. 24, 6 (1938), 185–208.
SUBJ 33 ▪ 62

18956 ELB PO P2 G4.1 1895–1928
Borst-Smith, Ernest Frank, 1882–.
Mandarin and missionary in Cathay: The story of twelve years' strenuous missionary work during stirring times mainly spent in Yenanfu, a prefectural city of Shensi, North China, with a review of its history from the earliest date.
London: Seeley, Service, 1917. 268 p.
SUBJ 22 24.2 25 32.2 33 56 ▪ 15 21.3 24.4 28 47 50 66

18957 CNY O P3 G5.1 1644–1928
Bouillard, Georges, 1862–1930.
'Pèlerinages de la première quinzaine de la 1e lune' (Pilgrimages of the first fortnight of the first lunar month).
La Chine 12 (15 fév. 1922), 193–214.
SUBJ 23 33 ▪ 13

18958 MCH P P3 G5.1 –1928
Bouillard, Georges, 1862–1930.
Le temple des lamas. Temple lamaïste de Yung Ho Kung à Pékin: description, plans, photos, cérémonies (The Temple of the Lamas: Description, diagrams, photographs, and ceremonies of the Lamaist temple Yung-ho Kung in Peking).
Peiping: Nachbaur, 1931. 127 p.
SUBJ 13 21.3 33 ▪ 66

18959 MCH O P2 G1.2 1895–1928
Burkhardt, Martha, 1874–?
Chinesische Kultstätten und Kultgebräuche (Chinese religious customs and places of worship).
Erlenbach-Zurich: Rotapfel, 1920. 176 p.
SUBJ 23 33 57 62 ▪ 13 43 65

18960 WSU PO P2 G1.4 1842–1928
Burt, Ernest Whitby, 1867–?
Fifty years in China: The story of the Baptist mission in Shantung, Shansi and Shensi, 1875–1925.
London: Carey Press, 1925. 127 p.
SUBJ 13 33 66 ▪ 19 25 28

18961 NIC P P1 G1.2 –1928
Cohen, Paul Andrew, 1934–.
'The anti-Christian tradition in China.'
JAS 20, 2 (Feb. 1961), 169–180.
SUBJ 13 33 64 ▪ 66

18962 ELO PO P1 G8.2 –1928
Cordier, Charles Georges, 1872–1936.
Les musulmans du Yunnan (The Muslims of Yunnan).
Hanoi: Impr. tonkinoise, 1927. 328 p.
SUBJ 32.2 33 ▪ 13 62 66

18963 NIC O P1 G1.2 –1949
Day, Clarence Burton, 1889–.
'The cult of Amitabha.'
CJ 33, 6 (Dec. 1940), 235–249.
SUBJ 33 62

18964 MCY P P2 G1.2 –1949
Dehergne, J-.
'L'Eglise de Chine au tournant (1924–49): le milieu, les cadres, les oeuvres, l'histoire' (The [Catholic] Church in China during a period of transition, 1924–1949: Setting, leadership, works, and history).
BUA 3e série 10, 39 (juin 1949), 417–558.
SUBJ 17 33 ▪ 38 56 66 72

18965 CSU O P8 G5.3 –1949
Drake, Frederick Seguier.
'The Taoists of Lao-Shan [Chi-mo *hsien*, Shantung].'
CR 65, 4 (Apr. 1934), 238–245; 65, 5 (May 1934), 308–319.
SUBJ 33

18966 NIC O P8 G6.3 1842–1928
Fitch, Robert Ferris, 1873–?
Pootoo [P'u-t'o-shan, Ting-hai *hsien*, Chekiang] *itineraries: Describing the chief places of interest, with a special trip to Lo-chia shan.*
Shanghai: Kelly and Walsh, 1929. 20, 90 p.
SUBJ 23 33 ▪ 65

18967 CSU O P3 G5.3 1842–1928
Forsyth, R- C-.
'Tsinanfu, the capital of Shantung.'
CR 54, 5 (May 1914), 304–310.
SUBJ 21.3 33 ▪ 21.1 54 66

18968 ICU PO P2 G1.1 1842–1928
Havermale, Lewis Frederick.
The transfer of the functions of Christian missions and the assumption thereof by the Chinese church.
Unpublished masters thesis in Practical Theology, U. of Chicago, 1932. 295 p.
SUBJ 33 62 66 ▪ 23 43

18969 CNY P P2 G1.1 1842–1949
Hobart, Kenneth Gray, 1893–.
A comparative history of the East China and South China Missions of the American Baptist Foreign Mission Society, 1833–1935: A study of the intensive vs. the extensive policy in mission work.
Unpublished doctoral dissertation in Religious Studies, Yale U., 1937. 13, 772 p.
SUBJ 33 66 ▪ 17 29 56

18970 CSU O P4 G1.1 1842–1928
Hutchinson, Paul, 1890–1955.
A guide to important [Protestant] *mission stations in eastern China (lying along the main routes of travel).*
Shanghai: Mission Book Co., 1920. 184 p. [Reprinted—Taipei: Ch'eng-wen, 1971. 184 p.]
SUBJ 33 ▪ 14.2 21.3

18971 CSU S P2 G1.1 1644–1928
Latourette, Kenneth Scott, 1884–1968.
'The Chinese empire.' In *A history of the expansion of Christianity, Vol. 6, The great century in northern Africa and Asia, A.D. 1800 – A.D. 1914*, by K. S. Latourette. [Sole entry]
New York: Harper, 1944, 253–367.
SUBJ 33 66 ▪ 17 18 25 32.2 50 52 56

18972 MCH P P2 G1.1 1644–1928
Latourette, Kenneth Scott, 1884–1968.
A history of Christian missions in China.
New York: Macmillan, 1929. 12, 930 p. [Reprinted—Taipei: Ch'eng-wen, 1966. 12, 930 p.]
SUBJ 33 66

18973 CSU P P3 G1.2 –1949
Löwenthal, Rudolf, 1904–.
'The Jews in China: An annotated bibliography.'
CSPSR 24, 2 (July–Sept. 1940), 113–234.
SUBJ 29 33 72

18974 NIC PO P1 G1.2 1644–1928
Mason, Isaac.
The Mohammedans of China.
London: China Society, 1922? 19 p.
SUBJ 33 ▪ 41 55 62

18975 NNC P P1 G1.1 –1928
Nicholson, John Bradford, 1897–.
The Pure Land Sect of China.
Unpublished masters thesis in Chinese, Columbia U., 1929. 33 p.
SUBJ 33 62

18976 CSU FP P2 G1.1 –1949
Prip-Møller, Johannes, 1889–1943.
Chinese Buddhist monasteries: Their plan and its function as a setting for Buddhist monastic life.
Copenhagen: Gad; London: Oxford U. Press, 1937. 396 p. [Reprinted—Hong Kong: Hong Kong U. Press, 1967. 396 p.]
SUBJ 21.3 23 33 ▪ 28 40 48 55 57 61 62

18977 CSH P P1 G1.2 1895–1928
Rawlinson, Frank Joseph, 1871–1937.
'Change and progress in the Christian movement in China during the last two decades, 1900–1920.' In *The Christian occupation of China*, edited by Milton Theobald Stauffer. [Selective entry]
Shanghai: China Continuation Committee, 1922, 32–39.
SUBJ 33 ▪ 37

18978 CSU PO P1 G1.2 –1928
Reichelt, Karl Ludvig, 1877–1952.
Fra Østens religiøse liv: Et indblik i kinesiske mahayana-buddhisme (Religious life in the Far East: A study of Chinese Mahayana Buddhism).
Copenhagen: Olaus Petri Foundation, 1922. 347 p.

Truth and tradition in Chinese Buddhism: A study of Chinese Mahayana Buddhism. Tr. by Kathrina van Wagenen Bugge. [Rev. and enl. in tr.]
Shanghai: Commercial Press, 1934. 12, 415 p. [Reprinted—New York: Paragon, 1968. 330 p.]
SUBJ 33 63 ▪ 13 23 62 65

18979 NOU PO P2 G1.1 –1949
Reichelt, Karl Ludvig, 1877–1952.
Fromhetstyper og helligdommer i Øst-Asia. 1, En religionspsykologisk undersøkelse. 2, Bak buddhistiske klostermurer. 3, Blant munker og pilegrimer i Øst-Asias helligdommer (Types of piety and meditation in East Asia. Vol. 1, A religious-psychological study. Vol. 2, Behind Buddhist cloister walls. Vol. 3, Among monks and pilgrims in East Asia's shrines).
Oslo, Copenhagen: Dreyer, Gad, 1947, 1948, 1949. 225; 308; 341 p.

Meditation and piety in the Far East: A religious-psychological study. Tr. by Sverre Holth. [Partial tr.: vol. 1 only]
New York: Harper, 1954. 171 p.
SUBJ 33 62 ▪ 23 59 64

18980 MCH O P2 G1.2 1842–1928
Richard, Timothy, 1845–1919.
Forty-five years in China: Reminiscences.
New York: Stokes, 1916. 384 p.
SUBJ 13 16.1 18 19 26.3 33 ▪ 17 32.2 65

18981 MAM P P2 G9.4 1895–1949
Richardson, William Jerome, 1929–.
Christianity in Taiwan under Japanese rule, 1895–1945.
Ann Arbor: University Microfilms (Publ. 72-21,731), 1972. 225 p. (Doctoral dissertation in History, St. John's U., 1971)
SUBJ 12.1 22.1 24 27 33 66 ▪ 12 13 21 22 24.1 24.2 24.4 25 55 56

18982 CBU P P1 G1.1 –1928
Schmitt, Erich, 1893–.
'Taoistische Klöster im Lichte des Universismus' (Taoist monasteries in the light of monist thought).
MSOSB 19 (1916), 76–104.
SUBJ 33 62

18983 NNC FP P3 G6.2 –1928
Shryock, John Knight, 1890–1952.
The temples of Anking [An-ch'ing-fu, Anhwei] *and their cults: A study of modern Chinese religion.*
Paris: Lib. Geuthner, 1931. 206 p. (Doctoral dissertation in History of Religions, U. of Pennsylvania, 1927) [Reprinted—New York: AMS Press, 1972. 206 p.]
SUBJ 13 23 33 60 64 ▪ 22 31 43 56

18984 CSU S P1 G1.1 –1949
Smith, David Howard, 1900–.
'Islam, Christianity and other Western faiths in China.' In *Chinese religions*, by D. H. Smith. [Selective entry]
New York: Holt, Rinehart and Winston, 1968, 148–169.
SUBJ 33 66

18985 CSU PO P3 G1.3 –1928
Sopher, Arthur.
'Appendix.' In *Chinese Jews*, by Edward Isaac Ezra and A. Sopher. [Sole entry]
Shanghai: China Press, 1926, 47–75. [Reprinted in *Jews in old China: Some western views*, compiled by Hyman Kublin. (Selective entry.) New York: Paragon, 1971, 267–295.]
SUBJ 33

18986 CSU U P1 G1.2 –1949
Tsukamoto, Zenryu (Tsukamoto Zenryū), 1898–.
'Buddhism in China and Korea.' Tr. from the Japanese by Leon Hurvitz. In *The path of the Buddha: Buddhism interpreted by Buddhists*, edited by Kenneth W- Morgan. [Sole entry]
New York: Ronald Press, 1956, 182–236.
SUBJ 33 ▪ 23 62

18987 CSH P P2 G1.2 1895–1928
Volokhova, Alena Alekseevna.
Inostrannye missionery v Kitae (1901–1920 gg.) (Foreign missionaries in China, 1901–1920).
Moscow: Nauka, Glav. red. vost. lit-ry, 1969. 144 p.
SUBJ 17 33 56 66 72 ▪ 12 14.3 22 32.2 37

18988 CSU FP P2 G1.2 1895–1949
Welch, Holmes Hinkley, 1921–.
The Buddhist revival in China.
Cambridge: Harvard U. Press, 1968. 385 p. (Harvard East Asian series, 33)
SUBJ 13 33 59 ▪ 12.2 17 18 23 66

18989 MCH FP P2 G1.2 1895–1949
Welch, Holmes Hinkley, 1921–.
The practice of Chinese Buddhism, 1900–1950.
Cambridge: Harvard U. Press, 1967. 22, 568 p. (Harvard East Asian series, 26)
SUBJ 33 63 ▪ 13 23 24.1 46 53 55 57 62 66

18990 CSU PO P3 G5.4 –1949
White, William Charles, 1873–1960.
Chinese Jews: A compilation of matters relating to the Jews of K'ai-fêng Fu, 2nd ed.
New York: Paragon, 1966. s.p.
SUBJ 33 50 55 ▪ 12 16.1 59

18991 MAM P P4 G1.2 1895–1928
Yip, Ka-che (Yeh Chia-chih), 1944–.
The anti-Christian movement in China, 1922–1927, with special reference to the experience of Protestant missions.
Ann Arbor: University Microfilms (Publ. 71-6270), 1971. 358 p. (Doctoral dissertation in History, Columbia U.)
SUBJ 25 32 33 54 66 ▪ 16.1 17 32.2 62 64

1911-1949

18992 CSH FP P2 G1.2 1911–1928
'The Christian occupation of the provinces.' In *The Christian occupation of China*, edited by Milton Theobald Stauffer. [Selective entry]
Shanghai: China Continuation Committee, 1922, 40–260. [See also 'Appendix A: Provincial statistical tables', 1–41 (s.p.).]
SUBJ 17 23 29 33 56 ▪ 11.3 21 24 24.2 28 47 66

18993 CHS PO P2 G4.1 1911–1949
Aske, Sigurd.
The South Shensi Lutheran Mission.
Unpublished doctoral dissertation in Religion, Hartford Seminary Foundation (Hartford, Conn.), 1951. 2 vols. 316 p. [c.p.].
SUBJ 33 66 ▪ 17 21 24 28 47 56

18994 MCH O P3 G5.1 1928–1949
Bertuccioli, Giuliano.
'Note taoiste. II, a proposito di un recente caso di applicazione della pena del rogo nel convento taoista del Pai-yün Kuan' (Notes on Taoism. 2, A recent application of punishment by fire in the Taoist convent Pai-yün Kuan [Peking]).
Rivista degli studi orientali 28, 1/4 (1953), 185–186.
SUBJ 22.2 33

18995 CSU O P2 G1.1 1928–1949
Blofeld, John Eaton Calthorpe, 1913–.
'Lamaism and its influence on Chinese Buddhism.'
THM 7, 2 (Sept. 1938), 151–160.
SUBJ 33 ▪ 62 66

18996 MCH O P2 G4.2 1911–1928
Botham, Mark Edwin, 1892–.
'Islam in Kansu.'
Moslem world 10, 4 (Oct. 1920), 377–390.
SUBJ 16.1 33

18997 MCH PO P3 G9.0 1911–1928
Brou, Alexandre, 1862–?
'La Chine républicaine et le christianisme' (Republican China and Christianity).
Etudes 7e série 135, 1 (5 avr. 1913), 78–104.
SUBJ 13 25 33 64 ▪ 12.2 16.1 17

18998 CSU O P3 G5.4 1928–1949
Brown, David A-.
'Through the eyes of an American Jew.' In *Chinese Jews: A compilation of matters relating to the Jews of K'ai-fêng Fu*, 2nd ed., by William Charles White. [Selective entry]

New York: Paragon, 1966, 150–164 [s.p.]. [Reprinted from *American Hebrew and Jewish tribune* Jan.–Mar. 1933.]
Subj 33

18999 MCH O P3 G1.3 1911–1928
Chang, Neander C. S.
'The anti-religion movement.'
CR 54, 8 (Aug. 1923), 459–467.
Subj 16.1 33 54 ▪ 23

19000 NIC P P1 G1.2 1911–1928
Chow, Tse-tsung (Chou Ts'e-tsung), 1916–.
'The anti-Confucian movement in early Republican China.' In *The Confucian persuasion*, edited by Arthur Frederick Wright. [Selective entry]
Stanford: Stanford U. Press, 1960, 288–312.
Subj 13 19 33 64

19001 NIC PO P2 G1.3 1911–1928
De Korne, John Cornelius, 1888–.
The Fellowship of Goodness (T'ung shan she): A study in contemporary Chinese religion.
Grand Rapids, Mich.: The author, 1941. 109 p. (Doctoral dissertation, Hartford Seminary Foundation [Kennedy School of Missions and College of Missions] (Hartford, Conn.), 1934)
Subj 33 ▪ 13 18 27 62 63

19002 NIC PO P5 G1.3 1911–1928
Drake, Frederick Seguier.
'The Tao Yuan, a new religious and spiritualistic movement.'
CR 54, 3 (Mar. 1923), 133–144.
Subj 33 ▪ 13 16.1 63

19003 NNC FP P2 G1.2 1928–1949
Fisher, Stanley Ross, and Harlan Paul Douglass, 1871–?
'The [Protestant] church and its leadership.' In *China*, edited by Orville Anderson Petty. [Selective entry]
New York: Harper, 1933, 237–301. (Laymans Foreign Missions Inquiry, Factfinders' reports, 5; Supplementary series, part 2)
Subj 17 33 60 ▪ 37 61 63

19004 CSU O P8 G6.3 1928–1949
Fitch, Robert Ferris, 1873–?
'Puto [P'u-t'o-shan, Ting-hai *hsien*, Chekiang], the enchanted island.'
NG 89, 3 (Mar. 1946), 373–384.
Subj 33

19005 CSU O P3 G6.3 1911–1928
Fitch, Robert Ferris, 1873–?
'A study of a Taoist hell.'
CR 45, 10 (Oct. 1914), 603–606.
Subj 23 33 ▪ 62

19006 ELO O P4 G1.5 1911–1949
Foster, John, 1898–.
The Chinese [Protestant] *church in action.*
London: Edinburgh House Press, 1933. 144 p.
Subj 17 32.2 33 36.4 54 ▪ 13 21.1 22 26.4 28 47 50 61 66

19007 NIC O P2 G5.0 1928–1949
Goodrich, Grace.
'Nuns of North China.'
Asia (New York: American Asiatic Assn.) 37, 2 (Feb. 1937), 90–93.
Subj 33 47 62

19008 CSU O P2 G1.3 1911–1949
Goullart, Peter, 1902–.
The monastery of Jade mountain.
London: Murray, 1961. 189 p.
Subj 33 62 ▪ 23 46 66

19009 NIC U P2 G1.2 1911–1928
Hodous, Lewis, 1872–1949.
'The Chinese church of the five religions.'
J. of religion 4, 1 (Jan. 1924), 71–76.
Subj 33 62 63

19010 CSH F P2 G1.2 1911–1928
Hodous, Lewis, 1872–1949.
'Non-Christian religious movements in China.' In *The Christian occupation of China*, edited by Milton Theobald Stauffer. [Selective entry]
Shanghai: China Continuation Committee, 1922, 27–31.
Subj 23 33 ▪ 13 62

19011 NIC F P2 G1.4 1928–1949
Iwamura, Shinobu, 1905–.
'The structure of Moslem society in Inner Mongolia.'
FEQ 8, 1 (Nov. 1948), 34–44.
Subj 22 23 33 62 66 ▪ 21.2 21.3 22.2 41

19012 GMS O P2 G1.3 1911–1928
Knak, Siegfried, 1875–.
Die chinesischen Christen unter den gegenwärtigen Wandlungen in China (Chinese Christians amid the current changes in China).
Berlin: Furche, 1928. 52 p.
Subj 33 ▪ 17 66

19013 MCH O P3 G9.2 1911–1928
Lee, Ying Lam.
'The anti-Christian movement in Canton.'
CR 56, 4 (Apr. 1925), 220–226.
Subj 33 66 ▪ 13 37 54

19014 MCH P P2 G1.2 1911–1949
Ma Chien.
'Notizie d'un musulmano sui musulmani cinesi' (A Muslim's report on Chinese Muslims). Tr. by Virginia Vacca.
Oriente moderno 15, 7 (luglio 1935), 353–364; 15, 8 (agosto 1935), 425–434; 15, 9 (settembre 1935), 483–487.
'The views of a Chinese Moslem.' Tr. by Philip Blackwood.
Moslem world 26, 1 (Jan. 1936), 68–78.
Subj 23 33 ▪ 17 18 21.4 28 41 57 66

19015 CSU O P3 G6.1 1928–1949
Millican, Frank R-.
'Buddhist activities in Shanghai.'
CR 65, 4 (Apr. 1934), 221–227.
Subj 33 ▪ 62 63

19016 MCH O P2 G1.1 1911–1928
Porter, Lucius Chapin, 1880–1958.
'Spiritual quests.' In *China's challenge to Christianity*, by L. C. Porter. [Sole entry]
New York: Missionary Education Movement, 1924, 140–178.
Subj 23 33 60

19017 MCH O P2 G1.3 1911–1928
Pratt, James Bissett, 1875–1944.
The pilgrimage of Buddhism and a Buddhist pilgrimage.
New York: Macmillan, 1928. 11, 758 p. [Chaps. 14–20 treat China.]
Subj 23 33 ▪ 47 62 63

19018 MCH FP P7 G1.3 1928–1949
Price, Frank Wilson, 1895–.
The rural [Protestant] *church in China.*
New York: Agricultural Missions, 1948. 11, 274 p. (Studies in the world missions of Christianity, 9)
Subj 23 33 ▪ 17 22 24 63

19019 CSU O P8 G8.1 1928–1949
Prip-Møller, Johannes, 1889–1943.
'Buddhist meditation ritual.'
CR 66, 12 (Dec. 1935), 713–718.
Subj 33

19020 MCH O P1 G1.2 1911–1928
Reid, Gilbert, 1857–1927.
'New religious movements in China.'
Church missionary review 76, 849 (Mar. 1925), 15–26.
Subj 33 ▪ 23 62

19021 MCH O P2 G1.2 1911–1928
Rhodes, F- H-.
'A survey of Islam in China.'
Moslem world 11, 1 (Jan. 1921), 53–68.
Subj 33 66 ▪ 23 26.1 27

19022 NNC F P2 G8.1 1928–1949
Sarvis, Guy W-.
'Study of missions in Szechwan.' In *China*, edited by Orville Anderson Petty. [Selective entry]
New York: Harper, 1933, 577–614. (Layman's Foreign Missions Inquiry, Factfinders' reports, 5; Supplementary series, Part 2)
Subj 17 33 ▪ 28 56 66

19023 MCH O P3 G6.1 1911–1928
Shen, T. L.
'A study of the anti-Christian movement.'
CR 56, 4 (Apr. 1925), 227–232.
Subj 33 ▪ 30 54 66

19024 MCH O P4 G1.3 1911–1928
Twinem, Paul de Witt.
'Modern syncretic religious societies in China.'
J. of religion 5, 5 (Sept. 1925), 463–482; 5, 6 (Nov. 1925), 595–606.
Subj 33 62 ▪ 13 54 63

19025 NNC PO P1 G1.2 1911–1928
Wang, Chao Hsiang.
'Religious elements in the esoteric societies of China.' Tr. by Frank R- Millican of 'Chung-kuo mi mi hui she chung ti tsung chiao' (Religion in Chinese secret societies); *Wen she yüan k'an* 2, 3 (Jan. 1927), 41–54.
CR 58, 12 (Dec. 1927), 757–766.
Subj 32.2 33

19026 NIC F P2 G8.1 1928–1949
Wood, Chester F-.
'Some studies in the Buddhism of Szechwan.'
JWCBRS 9 (1937), 160–179.
Subj 23 33 ▪ 62

19027 MCH P P2 G1.3 1911–1928
Yamamoto, Tatsuro (Yamamoto Tatsurō), 1910–, and Sumiko Yamamoto, 1914–.
'Anti-Christian movement in China, 1922–1927.'
FEQ 12, 2 (Feb. 1953), 133–147.
Subj 33 ▪ 54 60

19028 MCH O P1 G1.2 1911–1928
Yi, Cheng-ching.
'The Chinese [Protestant] church.' In *China today through Chinese eyes*, by Timothy Tingfang Lew (Liu T'ing-fang) et al. [Selective entry]
London: Student Christian Movement, 1922, 122–144.
Subj 33 ▪ 13

1911-1972
(including 1644-1972)

19029 CSH U P1 G1.2 1895–1972
Bates, Miner Searle, 1897–.
'The church in China in the twentieth century.' In *China and Christian responsibility*, edited by William Jerome Richardson. [Sole entry]
New York: Maryknoll; New York: Friendship Press, 1968, 45–80.
Subj 33 66 ▪ 13

19030 CSU P P4 G1.2 1911–1972
Beckmann, Johannes, 1901–.
'Versuch einer kritischen Rechenschaft über die China-Mission' (A critical account of the [Catholic] mission in China).
Wort und Wahrheit 14, 3 (März 1959), 165–178; 14, 4 (Apr. 1959), 257–272; 14, 5 (Mai 1959), 325–332.
Subj 33 ▪ 12.1 16.2 17

19031 MCY P P2 G1.2 1911–1972
Callahan, Paul Enos, 1920–.
'Christianity and revolution as seen in the National Christian Council of China.'
PC 5 (Apr. 1950 [i.e., May 1951]), 75–106.
Subj 33 ▪ 23 32.1 36.4 37 47

19032 NNC P P1 G1.1 –1972
Chan, Wing-tsit (Ch'en Jung-chieh), 1901–.
'Transformation of Buddhism in China.'
Philosophy, East and West 7, 3/4 (Oct. 1957 / Jan. 1958), 17–116. [Reprinted in *Neo-Confucianism, etc.: Essays by Wing-tsit Chan*, compiled by Charles K. H. Chen (Ch'en Ch'eng-shih). (Sole entry.) Hong Kong: Oriental Society, 1969, 422–437.]
Subj 33 63 ▪ 62 65

19033 NNP P P1 G1.2 –1972
Ch'en, Kenneth K. S. (Ch'en Kuan-sheng), 1907–.
Buddhism in China: A historical survey.
Princeton: Princeton U. Press, 1964. 560 p.
Subj 13 23 33 62 63 ▪ 14.3 14.5 17 18 32.2 45

19034 MCH O P2 G1.2 1928–1972
Colinas Aguirrebengoa, Juan Antonio.
'Labor social de la Iglesia en China' (Social work of the [Catholic] Church in China).
Fomento social 7, 26 (abril–junio 1952), 171–179.
Subj 33 38 ▪ 14.1 17 66

19035 NNC PO P2 G1.2 1842–1972
Geng, George Yuen-hsieh (Keng Yüan-hsüeh), 1905–.
The promotion of the economic welfare of the Chinese people through the Protestant churches in China.
Unpublished doctoral dissertation in Education, Columbia U. [Teachers College], 1951. 11, 244 p.
Subj 18 33 37 63 ▪ 17 19 50 55 64 71

19036 CSH P P2 G1.1 –1972
Hang, Thaddäus.
Die katholische Kirche im chinesischen Raum: Geschichte und Gegenwart (The Catholic Church in Chinese territory, past and present).
Munich: Pustet, 1963. 224 p.
Subj 33 ▪ 11.2 13 16.1 61

19037 WSU P P1 G1.2 –1972
Lessing, Ferdinand Diederich, 1882–.
'Structure and meaning of the rite called The Bath of the Buddha, according to Tibetan and Chinese sources.' In *Studia Serica, Bernhard Karlgren dedicata* (Chinese studies dedicated to Bernhard Karlgren), edited by Søren Egerod and Else Glahn. [Sole entry]
Copenhagen: Munksgaard, 1959, 159–171.
Subj 23 33 ▪ 62

19038 NIC P P1 G1.2 1911–1972
Lu, David John (Lu K'un-hsi), 1928–.
Moslems in China today.
Hong Kong: International Studies Group, 1964. 50 p.
Subj 33 ▪ 13

19039 CSU U P2 G1.1 1842–1972
Lyall, Leslie Theodore, 1905–.
A passion for the impossible: The China Inland Mission, 1865–1965.
Chicago: Moody Press, 1965. 208 p.
Subj 33 66 ▪ 22.2 56

19040 CSH U P2 G1.2 1895–1972
Merwin, Wallace C-.
'Christianity in the life of the Chinese people.' In *China in change: An approach to understanding*, edited by Miner Searle Bates. [Selective entry]
New York: Friendship Press, 1969, 116–142.
Subj 33 66 ▪ 13 17

19041 CSH U P2 G3.0 1928–1972
Miller, Robert James, 1923–, Antoine Mostaert, 1881–, and Martin M. C. Yang (Yang Mou-ch'un), 1904–.
'Religion.' In *A regional handbook on the Inner Mongolia Autonomous Region*, compiled by Far Eastern and Russian Institute, U. of Washington. [Selective entry]
New Haven: Human Relations Area Files, 1956, 281–308. (HRAF subcontractor's monographs, 60; Washington 7)
Subj 33 ▪ 13 23

19042 NNC PO P1 G1.2 1928–1972
Monsterleet, Jean, 1912–.
Les martyrs de Chine parlent: l'empire de Mao Tsé-toung contre l'église du Christ (China's martyrs speak: Mao's empire versus the Christian [i.e., Catholic] church).
Paris: Amiot-Dumont, 1953. 224 p.

Martyrs in China. Tr. by Antonia Pakenham.
Chicago: Regnery, 1956. 288 p.
Subj 12.2 13 22.2 33

19043 CBU P P2 G9.2 1842–1972
Mouly, Dalmas.
Le Père Julliotte, deuxième partie, dans la Chine bouillonnante (Father Julliotte, Part 2, In seething China).
Paris: Lectures missionnaires, 1966. 62 p.
Subj 25 33 66 ▪ 13 32.2 56 57

19044 CSH P P2 G1.1 –1972
Outerbridge, Leonard Mallory.
The lost churches of China.
Philadelphia: Westminster Press, 1952. 237 p. (Revision of *The lost churches of China: A study of the contributing factors in the recurring losses sustained by Christianity in China during the past thirteen hundred years*, doctoral dissertation in Religion, U. of Chicago, 1951)
Subj 33 62 66

19045 NIC P P2 G9.0 1842–1972
Rose, John Richard.
A church born to suffer: Being an account of the first hundred years of the Methodist Church in South China.
London: Cargate Press, 1951. 172 p.
Subj 33 66 ▪ 17 47 56

19046 CSH P P1 G1.3 1928–1972
Stanford U. China Project.
'Religion.' In *Central South China*, compiled by the organization cited. [Selective entry]
New Haven: Human Relations Area Files, 1956, vol. 1, 303–342. (HRAF subcontractor's monographs, 28; Stanford 2)
Subj 13 33 ▪ 23 32.2

19047 CSH P P1 G1.3 1928–1972
Stanford U. China Project.
'Religion.' In *East China*, compiled by the organization cited. [Selective entry]
New Haven: Human Relations Area Files, 1956, vol. 1, 344–387. (HRAF subcontractor's monographs, 29; Stanford 3)
Subj 13 33 ▪ 23 32.2

19048 CSH P P1 G5.0 1928–1972
Stanford U. China Project.
'Religion.' In *North China*, compiled by the organization cited. [Selective entry]
New Haven: Human Relations Area Files, 1956, vol. 1, 318–366. (HRAF subcontractor's monographs, 27; Stanford 1)
Subj 13 33 ▪ 23 32.2

19049 NNC P P1 G8.0 1928–1972
Stanford U. China Project.
'Religion.' In *Southwest China*, compiled by the organization cited. [Selective entry]
New Haven: Human Relations Area Files, 1956, vol. 1, 321–377. (HRAF subcontractor's monographs, 30; Stanford 4)
Subj 13 33 ▪ 23 32.2

19050 CSH U P1 G2.0 1928–1972
Tang, Peter S. H. (T'ang Sheng-hao), 1919–.
'Religion.' In *A regional handbook on Northeast China*, compiled by Far Eastern and Russian Institute, U. of Washington. [Selective entry]

New Haven: Human Relations Area Files, 1956, 227–243. (HRAF subcontractor's monographs, 61; Washington 9)
Subj 33 ▪ 13 23

19051 CSU F P2 G9.5 1895–1972
Topley, Marjorie Doreen, 1927–, and James William Hayes, 1930–.
'Notes on some vegetarian halls in Hong Kong belonging to the sect of *Hsien-t'ien tao* (The Way of Former Heaven).'
JRAS-HKB 8 (1968), 135–148.
Subj 33 ▪ 48 62

19052 NIC P P1 G1.1 1895–1972
Tsukamoto, Zenryu (Tsukamoto Zenryū), 1898–.
'Japanese and Chinese Buddhism in the twentieth century.'
Cahiers d'histoire mondiale 6, 3 (1961), 572–602.
Subj 33 ▪ 13 62

19053 MCY P P2 G1.3 1842–1972
Varg, Paul Albert, 1912–.
Missionaries, Chinese, and diplomats: The American Protestant missionary movement in China, 1890–1952.
Princeton: Princeton U. Press, 1958. 335 p. [Reprinted—Ann Arbor: University Microfilms, n.d. 335 p.]
Subj 33 66 ▪ 17 22.2 32.2 38 56 60

19054 CSU F P2 G1.5 1911–1972
Welch, Holmes Hinkley, 1921–.
'The Chang T'ien Shih and Taoism in China.'
JOS 4, 1/2 (1957/58), 188–212.
Subj 33 62 ▪ 13 25 59

19055 NIC FP P2 G1.1 –1972
Welch, Holmes Hinkley, 1921–.
'Dharma scrolls and the succession of abbots in Chinese monasteries.'
TP 2e série 50, 1/3 (1963), 93–149.
Subj 33 40 ▪ 48

19056 CSU U P1 G1.2 1911–1972
Wright, Arthur Frederick, 1913–.
'Buddhism in modern and contemporary China.' In *Religion and change in contemporary Asia*, edited by Robert F- Spencer. [Sole entry]
Minneapolis: U. of Minnesota Press, 1971, 14–26.
Subj 13 33

1949-1972

19057 MCH P P2 G1.2 1949–1972
'Les musulmans en Chine populaire, 1950–1960' (Muslims in the People's Republic of China, 1950–1960).
NED 2915 (20 août 1962), 1–76.
Subj 13 33 62 ▪ 18 21 22.1 25 32.1 47 72

19058 CSU S P2 G1.2 1949–1972
Bates, Miner Searle, 1897–.
'Churches and Christians in China, 1950–1967: Fragments of understanding.'
PA 41, 2 (Summer 1968), 199–213.
Subj 33 ▪ 13

19059 MCH S P1 G1.2 1949–1972
Bertuccioli, Giuliano.
'Il taoismo nella Cina contemporanea' (Taoism in contemporary China).
Cina 2 (1957), 67–77.
Subj 13 33

19060 CSH U P1 G1.2 1949–1972
Ch'en, Kenneth K. S. (Ch'en Kuan-sheng), 1907–.
'Religious changes in Communist China.'
CC 11, 4 (Dec. 1970), 56–62.
Subj 13 33

19061 CSH S P1 G9.4 1949–1972
Chu Pao-tang (Chu Pao-t'ang).
'Buddhist organizations in Taiwan.'
CC 10, 2 (June 1969), 98–132.
Subj 33 ▪ 12.2 18

19062 MCH O P2 G1.2 1949–1972
Defay, Francis, 1916–, and Douglas Arnold Hyde, 1911–.
Red star versus the cross: The pattern of persecution.
London: Paternoster Publications, 1954. 144 p.
Subj 33 64 66 ▪ 12.1 16 19

19063 NNC PO P2 G1.2 1949–1972
Ferris, Helen.
The Christian church in Communist China to 1952.
Lackland Air Force Base, San Antonio, Tex.: U.S. Air Force Personnel and Training Research Center, Air Research and Development Command, 1956. 11, 76 p. (U.S. Human Resources Research Institute research memoranda, 45; Studies in Chinese Communism, series 2, 5)
Subj 13 33 62 ▪ 12.2 17 32.1 34.1 37 45 66

19064 CSU FP P2 G9.4 1949–1972
Gowing, Peter G-.
'Muslims in Nationalist China.'
Silliman j. 18, 1 (1971), 1–20.
Subj 33

19065 MCH PO P2 G9.4 1949–1972
[Hang, Thaddäus] Thaddeus Hang.
'Le catholicisme à Taiwan' (Catholicism in Taiwan).
Studia missionalia 16 (1967), 37–53.
Subj 22.1 33 ▪ 17 24.2 28

19066 CSU O P3 G9.5 1949–1972
Hayes, James William, 1930–.
'Visit to the Tung Lin Kok Yuen [Tung-lien-chüeh-yüan], Tam Kung [T'ai-kung] temple, Happy Valley, and Tin Hau [T'ien-hou] temple, Causeway Bay [Hong Kong], Saturday, 7th November 1970.'
JRAS-HKB 11 (1971), 194–197.
Subj 33

19067 MCH O P1 G1.2 1949–1972
Høgsgaard, Jens Lind, 1899–.
'Kirken i det kommunistiske Kina' (The [Protestant] church in Communist China).
Nordisk missions tidsskrift 65, 2 (Juni 1954), 107–123; 65, 4 (December 1954), 207–220.
Subj 17 33 64 ▪ 13 66

19068 MCY O P2 G9.4 1949–1972
Kitagawa, Joseph M. (Kitagawa Mitsuo), 1915–.
'Buddhism in Taiwan today.'
France-Asie 18, 174 (juil.–août 1962), 439–444.
Subj 33 62 ▪ 17 66

19069 MCH PO P3 G6.1 1949–1972
Lefeuvre, Jean.
Les enfants dans la ville: chronique de la vie chrétienne à Shanghaï, 1949–1955 (The children in the city: A chronicle of Christian life in Shanghai, 1949–1955), 3rd ed.
Paris: Témoignage chrétien, 1956. 366 p.
Subj 13 33 54 64 ▪ 12 14 15 16 17 32 66

19070 NIC F P3 G9.5 1949–1972
Welch, Holmes Hinkley, 1921–.
'Buddhist organizations in Hong Kong.'
JRAS-HKB 1 (1960/61), 98–114.
Subj 33 ▪ 40 43 48 57 62

34.1 Agricultural Associations and Cooperatives

農業生産組織 農業生產組織

1644-1911

☐

1644-1949

☐

1911-1949

19071 GMU P P7 G1.3 1911–1949
Chen, Yin-Kwong (Ch'en Yen-kuang).
Die landwirtschaftlichen Genossenschaften in China und die Anwendbarkeit der Systeme des deutschen landwirtschaftlichen Genossenschaftswesens auf ihre Fortbildung (Agricultural cooperatives in China and their further development through the application of the German cooperative system).
Leipzig: Hans Buske, 1937. 114 p. (Beiträge zur Genossenschaftskunde, 5) (Doctoral dissertation, Wirtschafts- und sozialwissenschaftliche Fakultät, Universität Halle-Wittenberg)
Subj 34.1 ▪ 14.1 24.6

19072 NIC F P2 G7.0 1911–1949
Chu, T. H. (Chu Tsu-hui).
Tea trade in Central China.
Shanghai: Kelly and Walsh, 1936. 259 p.
Subj 14.3 34.1 34.2 ▪ 14.5 24 34.3

19073 NNC S P8 G1.2 1911–1949
Fedoseev, N- K-.
'Kooperatsiia v kitaiskoi derevne' (Cooperatives in the Chinese countryside).
BSB 2, 5 (1932), 75–89.
Subj 14.1 34.1 ▪ 24.6

19074 NIC O P7 G1.2 1928–1949
Hu, Shih-chi, 1905–.
A study of the farmers' cooperatives in China.
Unpublished masters thesis in Economics, Cornell U., 1949. 83 p.
Subj 34.1 37 ▪ 14.1 36.3 63

19075 NNC PO P2 G6.1 1911–1949
Ku Nung (K'u-nung), pseud.
'Silk filature and silkworm cooperatives in Wusih.' Tr. of 'Yang ts'an ho tso yün tung tsai Wu-hsi' (Sericulture cooperatives in Wu-hsi *hsien* [Kiangsu]); *Chung-kuo nung ts'un* 3, 6

(June 1937), 103–106. In *Agrarian China*, compiled by Institute of Pacific Relations. [Selective entry]
Chicago: U. of Chicago Press, 1939, 184–188.
SUBJ 24.4 34.1 ▪ 14.3 24.6 34.2

1911-1972
(including 1644-1972)

19076 IMC PO P8 G1.2 1928–1972
Berte, Manlio.
'La riforma fondiaria e la cooperazione agricola in Cina' (Land reform and agricultural cooperatives in China).
Rivista della cooperazione 12, 4 (aprile 1958), 277–284.
SUBJ 34.1 ▪ 14.1

19077 NNC P P7 G1.2 1928–1972
Carin, Robert.
Agricultural cooperativization movement, mimeo.
Kowloon: ——, 1960. 11 & 25, 642 p. (China's land problem series, 2)
SUBJ 22.1 22.2 24.1 32.1 34.1 ▪ 21.4 22 26.3 28 36.3

19078 NNC P P8 G1.2 1928–1972
Carin, Robert.
State farms in Communist China, 1947–1961, mimeo.
Kowloon: ——, 1962. 30, 323 p.
SUBJ 14.1 34.1 ▪ 11.2 16.3 18 24.4 62 66

19079 CSU F P8 G9.4 1928–1972
Chow, Lee.
'Development of rotational irrigation in Taiwan.'
J. of the irrigation and drainage division; proceedings of the American Society of Civil Engineers 86, IR3 (Sept. 1960), 1–12.
SUBJ 24.1 34.1 ▪ 26.3 70

19080 CSH F P7 G3.1 1928–1972
Chung-kuo kung ch'an tang. Je-ho sheng wei yüan hui. Pan kung t'ing. (Chinese Communist Party. Jehol Provincial Committee. [General] Office).
'Twelve co-ops give a big boost to stock-raising.' Tr. of 'Weng-niu-ch'ih ch'i chien li liao shih erh ko hsü mu yeh sheng ch'an ho tso she, shih hsü mu ta wei fa chan ch'i lai' (The establishment of twelve livestock cooperatives in Weng-niu-ch'ih *ch'i* [Jehol] and the subsequent increase in livestock production); in *Chung-kuo nung ts'un ti she hui chu i kao ch'ao* (The socialist upsurge in rural China); Peking: Jen min ch'u pan she, 1956, vol. 1, 249–263. In *Socialist upsurge in China's countryside*, edited by Pan kung t'ing, Chung yang wei yüan hui, Chung-kuo kung ch'an tang (General Office, Central Committee, Chinese Communist Party). [Selective entry]
Peking: Foreign Languages Press, 1957, 93–114.
SUBJ 24.1 34.1 ▪ 22 26 26.3 28 32.1

19081 DLC P P8 G1.2 1911–1972
Dapčević-Oreščanin, Sonja.
'Putevi preobraženja kineskog sela' (Ways of transforming the Chinese village).
Medjunarodni problemi 8, 1 (1956), 49–79.

'Transformations in the Chinese village.' *International problems* (Belgrade) 1960, 135–161.
SUBJ 14.1 22.1 34.1 37 ▪ 16.1 16.3 22 36.3

19082 NNC PO P7 G1.2 1911–1972
Dumont, René, 1904–.
Révolution dans les campagnes chinoises (Revolution in the Chinese countryside).
Paris: Le Seuil, 1957. 462 p.
SUBJ 19 20 24.1 26 34.1 ▪ 22 24 28 32.1 47 64 72

19083 NNC P P7 G1.2 1928–1972
Horsey, Susan Sylvia, 1945–.
Mutual aid teams, 1949–1955: The beginning of socialist transformation in China's countryside.
Unpublished masters thesis in Political Science, Columbia U., 1970. 84 p. [Certificate essay, East Asian Institute]
SUBJ 34.1 ▪ 16.3 32.1

19084 NNC P P8 G1.2 1928–1972
[Klimko, Nikifor Grigor'evich] N. Klymko.
'Sotsialisticheskaia perestroika sel'skogo khoziaistva narodnogo Kitaia' (The socialist reconstruction of agriculture in the People's Republic of China).
Kommunist Ukrainy 1959, 8 (avgust), 54–64.
SUBJ 14 14.1 34.1 ▪ 16.3 32.2 45

19085 NNC O P7 G8.2 1928–1972
Kozhin, Aleksei Ivanovich, 1914–.
'Put' millionov' (The path of millions).
Zvezda 1957, 8 (avgust), 160–180.
SUBJ 22 24.1 26.3 34.1 36.3 ▪ 24 32.2 50

19086 DLC P P7 G1.2 1911–1972
Kuo, Ping-chia (Kuo Pin-chia), 1908–.
'Mao Tse-tung and China's "poor peasants".'
Studies on Asia 5 (1964), 13–26.
SUBJ 16.3 34.1 ▪ 14.1 22.1

19087 CSH P P8 G1.2 1928–1972
Stadnichenko, A- I-.
'Agrarnye preobrazovaniia v Kitaiskoi Narodnoi Respublike.' In *Agrarnye preobrazovaniia v narodno-demokraticheskikh stranakh Azii*, edited by Evgenii Fedorovich Kovalev. [Sole entry]
Moscow: Gospolitizdat, 1957, 8–106.

'Agrarian reforms in the People's Republic of China' [partial tr.: p. 43–51 only]. In *Agrarian reforms in the Asiatic people's democracies*, mimeo., edited by E. F. Kovalev. [Sole entry]
Washington, D.C.: U.S. Joint Publications Research Service, 18 Nov. 1958, 1–19. (JPRS 376D; MC 563/1959)
SUBJ 14 14.1 34.1 ▪ 12.2 15 16.1 16.3 19 32.2

19088 CSU F P8 G9.4 1928–1972
Vander Meer, Canute, 1930–.
'Changing water control in a Taiwanese rice-field irrigation system.'
AAAG 58, 4 (Dec. 1968), 720–747.
SUBJ 24.1 34.1

19089 CSU F P8 G9.4 1928–1972
Vander Meer, Canute.
'Water thievery in a rice irrigation system in Taiwan.'
AAAG 61, 1 (Mar. 1971), 156–179.
SUBJ 22.2 24.1 34.1

19090 JTU FP P8 G9.4 1928–1972
Wang, Sung-hsing, 1935–.
Pooling and sharing in a Chinese fishing economy: Kuei-shan Tao [i.e., Kuei-shan island, I-lan *hsien*, Taiwan].
Unpublished doctoral dissertation in Anthropology, Tōkyō daigaku, 1971. 236 p.
SUBJ 20 23 24.1 34.1 41 44 ▪ 21 22 27 33 43 45 50 58 65

19091 CSU S P7 G1.2 1928–1972
Wong, John.
'Peasant economic behavior: The case of traditional agricultural co-operation in China.'
DE 9, 3 (Sept. 1971), 332–349.
SUBJ 14.1 16.3 34.1

19092 NNC P P8 G1.2 1911–1972
Zhamin, Vitalii Alekseevich, 1920–.
Sotsial'no-ekonomicheskie preobrazovaniia v sel'skom khoziaistve KNR (The social and economic transformation of agriculture in the People's Republic of China).
Moscow: Izd-vo IMO, 1958. 278 p.
SUBJ 14 14.1 16.3 32.1 34.1 ▪ 16 16.1 36.3

1949-1972

19093 CSU P P7 G5.1 1949–1972
'Grain is principal, still diversified operations are expanded: The rapidly forward marching T'ang Ho-k'ou people's commune in Huai-jou hsien, Peiping municipality.' Tr. from *Ta kung pao* (Peking) 16 Jan. 1960, 3. In *Surveys of diversified operations in commune*, mimeo., compiled by U.S. Joint Publications Research Service. [Analytic entry]
Washington, D.C.: JPRS, 23 May 1960, 15–27. (JPRS 2698; MC 9988/1960)
SUBJ 24 24.1 24.3 26.3 34.1 ▪ 28

19094 CSH O P8 G5.1 1949–1972
'The party secretary takes the lead and all the party members help run the co-ops.' Tr. of 'Shu chi tung shou, ch'üan tang pan she'; in *Chung-kuo nung ts'un ti she hui chu i kao ch'ao* (The socialist upsurge in rural China); Peking: Jen min ch'u pan she, 1956, vol. 1, 3–15. In *Socialist upsurge in China's countryside*, edited by Pan kung t'ing, Chung yang wei yüan hui, Chung-kuo kung ch'an tang (General Office, Central Committee, Chinese Communist Party). [Selective entry]
Peking: Foreign Languages Press, 1957, 11–26.
SUBJ 32.1 34.1 ▪ 22 24.1

19095 MCH P P7 G1.2 1949–1972
Asian Peoples' Anti-Communist League.
The Communist 'rural people's communes'.
Taipei: Asian Peoples' Anti-Communist League, 1963. 54 p. (APACL pamphlets, 78)
SUBJ 24.1 34.1 ▪ 22 24.4 26.3

19096 MCH P P8 G1.2 1949–1972
Barnett, Arthur Doak, 1921–.
'China's road to collectivization.'
J. of farm economics 35, 2 (May 1953), 188–202.
SUBJ 14.1 34.1

19097 NNC PO P8 G1.2 1949–1972
Barnett, Arthur Doak, 1921–.
'The road to collectivization.'
AUFS-EAS 1, 4 (1 Oct. 1952), 1–14. [Reprinted as 'Collectivization.' In *Communist China: The early years, 1949–55*, by A. D. Barnett. (Selective entry.) New York: Praeger, 1964, 172–188.]
Subj 14.1 34.1

19098 CSU O P7 G1.3 1949–1972
Berger, Roland.
'Reality on the Chinese communes.'
GM 43, 5 (Feb. 1971), 326–332.
Subj 20 24.1 34.1

19099 CSH P P8 G1.2 1949–1972
Bernstein, Thomas Paul, 1937–.
'Leadership and mass mobilization in the Soviet and Chinese collectivization campaigns of 1929–1930 and 1955–1956: A comparison.'
CQ 31 (July–Sept. 1967), 1–47. [For fuller version, see entry 19100.]
Subj 22 22.1 34.1 ▪ 26.3 32 32.1

19100 MAM P P7 G1.2 1949–1972
Bernstein, Thomas Paul, 1937–.
Leadership and mobilization in the collectivization of agriculture in China and Russia: A comparison.
Ann Arbor: University Microfilms (Publ. 71-17,469), 1971. 465 p. (Doctoral dissertation in Political Science, Columbia U., 1970)
Subj 22 22.1 26.1 26.3 34.1 ▪ 24.1 32 32.1

19101 MCH P P7 G1.2 1949–1972
Biehl, Max, 1902–.
'Die Umwälzungen in der Landwirtschaft Chinas' (Revolutionary changes in Chinese agriculture). In *Gegenwartsprobleme der Agrarökonomie: Festschrift für Fritz Baade zum 65. Geburtstag* (Current problems of agrarian economics: Felicitation volume for Fritz Baade on his sixty-fifth birthday). [Sole entry]
Hamburg: Hoffmann und Campe, 1958, 37–82.
Subj 14.1 34.1 ▪ 12.1 18

19102 NNC S P7 G1.2 1949–1972
Bissing, Wilhelm Moritz, 1891–.
'Die Volkskommunen und die chinesische Agrarpolitik' (The communes and Chinese agrarian policy).
SJ 82, 2 (1962), 21–42.
Subj 14.1 34.1 ▪ 19 21.4 22 22.1

19103 MCH O P7 G1.2 1949–1972
Borgojevitch, Georges, and Sripati Chandrasekhar, 1917–.
'Les communes populaires chinoises jugées par un Yougoslave et un Indien' (The Chinese communes evaluated by a Yugoslav and an Indian).
Est et Ouest nouvelle (2e) série 11, 214 (1er–15 avr. 1959), 19–21.
Subj 34.1 ▪ 22.1 28

19104 MCH U P7 G1.2 1949–1972
Bouvier, Charles.
'Le programme de collectivisation en Chine: première étape de réalisation' (The collectivization plan in China: The first stage). In *La collectivisation de l'agriculture: U.R.S.S., Chine, démocraties populaires* (Agricultural collectivization in the USSR, China, and the people's democracies), by C. Bouvier. [Sole entry]
Paris: Armand Colin, 1958, 91–107. (Fondation nationale des sciences politiques, cahiers, 91)
Subj 14.1 16.3 34.1 ▪ 12.1 22 64

19105 CSU FP P7 G1.2 1949–1972
Burki, Shahid Javed.
A study of Chinese communes, 1965.
Cambridge: Harvard U., East Asian Research Center, 1969. 101 p. (Harvard East Asian monographs, 29)
Subj 22 24 24.1 34.1 ▪ 24.3 24.4 28 31

19106 WSU P P8 G5.1 1949–1972
Chao Ming and Tseng Yuan (Tseng Yüan).
'A production brigade which produces grain and raises livestock at the same time.' Tr. of 'I ko shih hsing liang shih sheng ch'an ho hsü mu yeh ping chü ti sheng ch'an ta tui'; *Hung ch'i* 1961, 8 (16 Apr.), 17–19. In *Translations from 'Hung-ch'i' (Red flag) (Peiping, No. 8, 16 April 1961)*, mimeo., compiled by U.S. Joint Publications Research Service. [Selective entry]
Washington, D.C.: JPRS, 7 Sept. 1961, 29–35. (JPRS 8828; MC 19,561/1961)
Subj 34.1 ▪ 24.1

19107 CSU S P7 G1.2 1949–1972
Cheng, C. K.
'Two decades of experiment in communization.'
JAAS 4, 2 (Apr. 1969), 81–106.
Subj 14 14.1 34.1 36.3 ▪ 22 32.1

19108 MCY P P7 G1.2 1949–1972
Cheng, Ronald Y. L. (Cheng Yen-ling), 1933–.
'Changes in the rural people's communes.' In *Contemporary China, 1961–1962*, edited by Edward Stuart Kirby. [Selective entry]
Hong Kong: Hong Kong U. Press, 1963, 89–100.
Subj 20 24 28 34.1 ▪ 22.1

19109 CSH O P8 G9.2 1949–1972
Chung-kuo kung ch'an chu i ch'ing nien t'uan. Yüeh chung ch'ü kung tso wei yüan hui. Kung tso tsu. (New Democratic Youth League. Regional Working Committee of Central Kwangtung. Work Team).
'A youth shock brigade.' Tr. of 'Chung-shan hsien Hsin-p'ing hsiang ti chiu nung yeh sheng ch'an ho tso she ti ch'ing nien t'u chi tui' (The youth shock brigade of the Ninth agricultural producers' cooperative, Hsin-p'ing *hsiang*, Chung-shan *hsien* [Kwangtung]); in *Chung-kuo nung ts'un ti she hui chu i kao ch'ao* (The socialist upsurge in rural China); Peking: Jen min ch'u pan she, 1956, vol. 3, 959–966. In *Socialist upsurge in China's countryside*, edited by Pan kung t'ing, Chung yang wei yüan hui, Chung-kuo kung ch'an tang (General Office, Central Committee, Chinese Communist Party). [Selective entry]
Peking: Foreign Languages Press, 1957, 292–301.
Subj 34.1 54 ▪ 24.1 32.1

19110 NIC O P8 G1.2 1949–1972
Chung-kuo kung ch'an tang (Chinese Communist Party).
Mutual aid and co-operation in China's agricultural production.
Peking: Foreign Languages Press, 1953. 38 p.
Subj 24.1 26.3 34.1 ▪ 21.4 24 32.1 36.3 44 64

19111 CSH O P8 G2.3 1949–1972
Chung-kuo kung ch'an tang. An-shan shih wei yüan hui. (Chinese Communist Party. An-shan Municipal Committee).
'Experience of cadre participation in labor in the Anshan area.' Tr. of 'Pa kan pu ts'an chia lao tung ti chih tu yung yüan chien chih hsia ch'ü: An-shan ti ch'ü tsu chih kan pu ts'an chia chi t'i sheng ch'an lao tung ti ching yen' (Permanently strengthen cadre participation in labor: Experiences of cadre participation in collectivized production in the An-shan area [Liaoning]); *Hung ch'i* 1963, 13/14 (10 July), 66–70. In *Translations from 'Hung-ch'i' (Red flag) No. 13-14, 1963*, mimeo., compiled by U.S. Joint Publications Research Service. [Selective entry]
Washington, D.C.: JPRS, 10 Sept. 1963, 111–119. (JPRS 21,008; MC 17,950/1963)
Subj 26.1 34.1 ▪ 21.4 32

19112 CSH O P8 G5.2 1949–1972
Chung-kuo kung ch'an tang. Chin-chung ti fang wei yüan hui. Nung ts'un kung tso pu. (Chinese Communist Party. Central Shansi District Committee. Rural Work Dept.).
'Great example set by cadre through productive labor in Hsieh-yang hsien.' Tr. of Hsi-yang hsien ssu chi kan pu ts'an chia sheng ch'an lao tung ti wei ta fan li' (The great example set by cadre participation in production in Hsi-yang *hsien* [Shansi]); *Hung ch'i* 1963, 13/14 (10 July), 60–65. In *Translations from 'Hung-ch'i' (Red flag) No. 13-14, 1963*, mimeo., compiled by U.S. Joint Publications Research Service. [Selective entry]
Washington, D.C.: JPRS, 10 Sept. 1963, 101–110. (JPRS 21,008; MC 17,950/1963)c
Subj 26.1 34.1 ▪ 21.4

19113 CSH O P8 G9.2 1949–1972
Chung-kuo kung ch'an tang. Ch'iung-shan hsien wei yüan hui. (Chinese Communist Party. Ch'iung-shan Hsien Committee).
'A co-operative grows strong in the struggle against calamities of nature and capitalist thinking.' Tr. of 'Ch'iung-shan hsien ti i ch'ü Hung-ch'i nung yeh sheng ch'an ho tso she tsai t'ung tzu jan tsai hai ho t'ung tzu pen chu i ssu hsiang tso tou cheng chung kung ku ch'i lai liao' (The consolidation of Hung-ch'i agricultural producers' cooperative, First District, Ch'iung-shan *hsien* [Kwangtung] during struggles with natural disasters and capitalist thinking); in *Chung-kuo nung ts'un ti she hui chu i kao ch'ao* (The socialist upsurge in rural China); Peking: Jen min ch'u pan she, 1956, vol. 3, 976–986. In *Socialist upsurge in China's countryside*, edited by Pan kung t'ing, Chung yang wei yüan hui, Chung-kuo kung ch'an tang (General Office,

Central Committee, Chinese Communist Party). [Selective entry]
Peking: Foreign Languages Press, 1957, 313–327.
Subj 32.1 34.1 ▪ 24.1 54

19114 CSH O P8 G5.4 1949–1972
Chung-kuo kung ch'an tang. Feng-ch'iu hsien wei yüan hui. (Chinese Communist Party. Feng-ch'iu Hsien Committee). [Feng-ch'iu *hsien* is in Honan.]
'A cooperative which changed its face after two years of bitter struggle.' Tr. of 'I ko k'u chan erh nien kai pien liao mien mao ti tso she'; *Hung ch'i* 1958, 1 (1 June), 4–10. In *Selected translations from 'Hung-chi' (Red flag), June–August 1958*, mimeo., compiled by U.S. Joint Publications Research Service. [Selective entry]
Washington, D.C.: JPRS, 21 Apr. 1961, 404–430. (JPRS 7837; MC 5498/1962)
Subj 28 34.1 ▪ 24.1 26.3

19115 WSU F P8 G9.2 1949–1972
Chung-kuo kung ch'an tang (Chinese Communist Party). Hsin-hui hsien wei yüan hui (Hsin-hui Hsien Committee) *and* Chung-kuo kung ch'an tang (Chinese Communist Party). Kuang-tang sheng wei yüan hui (Kwangtung Provincial Committee), *joint sponsors*. Nung ts'un tiao ch'a tsu (Rural Investigation Team), ed.
'Tungjih production brigade develops pig breeding industry: Both public and private breeding promoted.' Tr. of 'Tung-jih sheng ch'an ta tui kung yang ssu yang ping chü fa chan yang chu yeh' (Tung-jih production brigade [Hsin-hui *hsien*, Kwangtung] simultaneously develops public and private pig breeding); *Hung ch'i* 1961, 8 (16 Apr.), 14–16. In *Translations from 'Hung-ch'i' (Red flag) (Peiping, No. 8, 16 April 1961)*, mimeo., compiled by U.S. Joint Publications Research Service. [Selective entry]
Washington, D.C.: JPRS, 7 Sept. 1961, 22–28. (JPRS 8828; MC 19,561/1961)
Subj 24.1 34.1

19116 CSH O P8 G6.1 1949–1972
Chung-kuo kung ch'an tang. K'un-shan hsien wei yüan hui. Sheng ch'an ho tso pu. (Chinese Communist Party. K'un-shan Hsien Committee. Cooperative Production Dept.). [K'un-shan *hsien* is in Kiangsu.]
'This township went co-operative in two years.' Tr. of 'Che ko hsiang liang nien chiu ho tso hua le' (Cooperativization completed in two years in this township); in *Chung-kuo nung ts'un ti she hui chu i kao ch'ao* (The socialist upsurge in rural China); Peking: Jen min ch'u pan she, 1956, vol. 2, 587–597. In *Socialist upsurge in China's countryside*, edited by Pan kung t'ing, Chung yang wei yüan hui, Chung-kuo kung ch'an tang (General Office, Central Committee, Chinese Communist Party). [Selective entry]
Peking: Foreign Languages Press, 1957, 44–59.
Subj 34.1 ▪ 22 24.1 26 26.3 32.1

19117 CSH O P8 G5.1 1949–1972
Chung-kuo kung ch'an tang. Pei-ching shih wei yüan hui. Nung ts'un kung tso pu. (Chinese Communist Party. Peking Municipal Committee. Rural Work Dept.).
'How collective farming came to Paipenyao.' Tr. of 'Pai-p'en-yao nung yeh sheng ch'an ho tso she shih tsen yang pan ch'eng kao chi she ti?' (Formation of a higher-level cooperative by the Pai-p'en-yao agricultural producers' cooperative [Peking municipality]); in *Chung-kuo nung ts'un ti she hui chu i kao ch'ao* (The socialist upsurge in rural China); Peking: Jen min ch'u pan she, 1956, vol. 1, 294–300. In *Socialist upsurge in China's countryside*, edited by Pan kung t'ing, Chung yang wei yüan hui, Chung-kuo kung ch'an tang (General Office, Central Committee, Chinese Communist Party). [Selective entry]
Peking: Foreign Languages Press, 1957, 489–497.
Subj 24.1 34.1 ▪ 26 26.3

19118 CSH O P7 G5.1 1949–1972
Chung-kuo kung ch'an tang (Chinese Communist Party). Pei-ching shih wei yüan hui (Peking Municipal Committee). Nung ts'un kung tso pu (Rural Work Dept.) *with* Peking. Nung lin shui li chü (Bureau of Agriculture, Forestry and Irrigation). Lien ho kuei hua kung tso tsu (Coordinated-Planning Work Team).
'The long-range plan of the Red Star collective farm.' Tr. of 'Hung-hsing chi t'i nung chuang ti yüan ching kuei hua' (The long-range plans of Hung-hsing collective farm [Peking municipality]); in *Chung-kuo nung ts'un ti she hui chu i kao ch'ao* (The socialist upsurge in rural China); Peking: Jen min ch'u pan she, 1956, vol. 1, 311–320. In *Socialist upsurge in China's countryside*, edited by Pan kung t'ing, Chung yang wei yüan hui, Chung-kuo kung ch'an tang (General Office, Central Committee, Chinese Communist Party). [Selective entry]
Peking: Foreign Languages Press, 1957, 402–414.
Subj 24 34.1 ▪ 21.3 24.1

19119 CSH O P8 G4.1 1949–1972
Chung-kuo kung ch'an tang. Shan-hsi sheng wei yüan hui. Nung ts'un kung tso pu. (Chinese Communist Party. Shensi Provincial Committee. Rural Work Dept.).
'How four co-ops in Wangmang village, Changan county, organized a joint management committee.' Tr. of 'Ch'ang-an hsien Wang-mang ts'un ssu ko ho tso she tsu chih lien she ti ching yen' (The merger of four producers' cooperatives to form a joint cooperative in Wang-mang village, Ch'ang-an *hsien* [Shensi]); in *Chung-kuo nung ts'un ti she hui chu i kao ch'ao* (The socialist upsurge in rural China); Peking: Jen min ch'u pan she, 1956, vol. 3, 1197–1203. In *Socialist upsurge in China's countryside*, edited by Pan kung t'ing, Chung yang wei yüan hui, Chung-kuo kung ch'an tang (General Office, Central Committee, Chinese Communist Party). [Selective entry]
Peking: Foreign Languages Press, 1957, 449–459.
Subj 34.1 ▪ 32.1

19120 CSH O P8 G7.1 1949–1972
Chung-kuo kung ch'an tang. Ying-shan hsien wei yüan hui. (Chinese Communist Party. Ying-shan Hsien Committee). [Ying-shan *hsien* is in Hunan.]
'From cadres' experimental plots to the masses' experimental plots.' Tr. of 'Yu kan pu ti shih yen t'ien tao ch'ün chung ti shih yen t'ien'; *Hung ch'i* 1958, 5 (1 Aug.), 32–34. In *Selected translations from 'Hung-chi' (Red flag), June–August 1958*, mimeo., compiled by U.S. Joint Publications Research Service. [Selective entry]
Washington, D.C.: JPRS, 21 Apr. 1961, 108–118. (JPRS 7837; MC 5498/1962)
Subj 34.1

19121 DLC P P7 G1.2 1949–1972
Dapčević-Oreščanin, Sonja, et al.
'Podaci o poljoprivrednom zadrugarstvu u NR Kini' (Data on agricultural producers' cooperatives in the People's Republic of China).
DB 4, 6/7 (1955), 63–74. [Special issue: *Savremena Kina* (Contemporary China)]
Subj 14.1 34.1 ▪ 11.3

19122 DLC P P8 G1.3 1949–1972
Deliusin, Lev Petrovich, 1923–.
Velikie peremeny v kitaiskoi derevne (Great changes in the Chinese countryside).
Moscow: Gospolitizdat, 1957. 176 p.
Subj 14.1 22 34.1 ▪ 14.6 16.3 18 32.1

19123 CSU P P7 G1.2 1949–1972
Doi Akira, 1905–.
'The Chinese communes today.'
JQ 7, 2 (Apr.–June 1960), 161–168.
Subj 22 34.1 ▪ 45

19124 MCH P P8 G1.2 1949–1972
Doi Akira, 1905–.
'The present situation of agricultural collectivization in China.'
Asian affairs (Tokyo) 2, 1 (Mar. 1957), 47–62.
Subj 14.1 34.1 36.3 ▪ 16.3

19125 MCH P P7 G1.2 1949–1972
Dumont, René, 1904–.
'Les communes populaires rurales chinoises' (Rural communes in China).
Politique étrangère 29, 4 (1964), 380–397.
Subj 24.1 34.1 ▪ 21.4 22 22.1 24.2 24.4

19126 CSH P P7 G1.2 1949–1972
Dutt, Gargi, 1929–.
'Some problems of China's rural communes.'
CQ 16 (Oct.–Dec. 1963), 112–136. [Reprinted in *China under Mao: Politics takes command*, edited by Roderick Lemonde MacFarquhar. (Selective entry.) Cambridge: M.I.T. Press, 1966, 119–143.]
Subj 22 24.1 34.1 ▪ 24.4

19127 CSH O P8 G7.1 1949–1972
Fang Ti and Lo Chung-chang.
'Murmuring water everywhere: Introducing the "automatic melon-vine" irrigation system of the Hsiangyang Special Administrative Region [Hsiang-yang special district], Hupeh.' In *China's big leap in water conservancy*. [Selective entry]

Peking: Foreign Languages Press, 1958, 118–123.
Subj 24.1 34.1

19128 CSU O P7 G1.2 1949–1972
Ganguli, Birendranath N-, 1902–.
'Reorganization of Chinese agriculture after land reform.'
Indian economic review 1, 4 (Aug. 1953), 22–44. [Reprinted in *Land reform in New China*, by B. N. Ganguli. (Analytic entry.) Delhi: Ranjit, 1954, 36–74.]
Subj 14.1 16.3 34.1 ▪ 14.2 14.3

19129 CSU P P8 G1.2 1949–1972
Gray, Jack Douglas, 1916–.
'The high tide of socialism in the Chinese countryside.' In *Studies in the social history of China and South-east Asia: Essays in memory of Victor Purcell*, edited by Jerome Ch'en (Ch'en Chih-jang) and Nicholas Tarling. [Selective entry]
Cambridge: Cambridge U. Press, 1970, 85–134.
Subj 14.1 34.1 ▪ 14.6 16.1 16.3 45 64

19130 MCH P P7 G1.2 1949–1972
Hinton, Harold Clendenin, 1924–.
'Métodos chinos y soviéticos en la colectivización de la agricultura' (Chinese and Soviet methods of collectivizing agriculture).
Estudios sobre el comunismo 5, 15 (enero–marzo 1957), 48–64.
Subj 14.1 34.1 ▪ 12.1 64

19131 MCH P P7 G1.2 1949–1972
Hsia, T. A. (Hsia Chi-an), 1916–1965.
The commune in retreat as evidenced in terminology and semantics.
Berkeley: U. of California, Center for Chinese Studies, 1964. 91 p. (Current Chinese Language Project, Studies in Chinese Communist terminology, 11) [Reprinted—Ann Arbor: University Microfilms, n.d. 91 p.]
Subj 22 22.1 24.1 34.1 62 ▪ 24.4 26.1 32.1 64

19132 CSH P P7 G1.2 1949–1972
Jo, Yung-hwan (Ts'ao Ying-huan), 1932–.
Agricultural collectivization as the developmental model for Communist China.
Tempe: Arizona State U., Center for Asian Studies, 1967. 46 p. (CAS occasional papers, 1)
Subj 14.1 16 34.1 ▪ 12.1 25 41

19133 MCH PO P7 G1.2 1949–1972
Kaminskii, Aleksandr Evgen'evich.
Kooperirovanie sel'skogo khoziaistva Kitaia (The cooperativization of agriculture in China).
Moscow: Gossel'khozizdat, 1959. 166 p.
Subj 14.1 34.1 ▪ 16.3 32.1 36.3

19134 MCH P P8 G1.2 1949–1972
Kokarev, Nikolai Aleksandrovich.
Sotsialisticheskoe preobrazovanie sel'skogo khoziaistva v Kitaiskoi Narodnoi Respublike (The socialist transformation of agriculture in the People's Republic of China).
Moscow: Gospolitizdat, 1958. 251 p.
Socialist reorganization of agriculture in the Chinese People's Republic, mimeo. [Partial tr.: p. 186–228 only].
Washington, D.C.: U.S. Joint Publications Research Service, 13 July 1959. 33 p. (JPRS 808D; MC 12,856/1959) [Xerox copyflo available—New York: CCM Information Corp., Research and Microfilm Publications (Scholarly Book Translation Series, 468)]
Subj 14.1 34.1 ▪ 36.3

19135 NNC P P7 G1.2 1949–1972
Korkunov, Igor' Nikolaevich, 1924–, et al.
Sotsialisticheskoe preobrazovanie sel'skogo khoziaistva v Kitaiskoi Narodnoi Respublike (1949–1957).
Moscow: Izd-vo vost. lit-ry, 1960. 206 p.
Socialist transformation of agriculture in the Chinese People's Republic, 1949–1957, mimeo.
Washington, D.C.: U.S. Joint Publications Research Service, 9 Dec. 1960. 188 p. (JPRS 4255; MC 2135/1961)
Subj 14.1 16.3 34.1 ▪ 14 14.6 16 18 22 32 32.1 36.3 64 72

19136 DLC O P7 G1.2 1949–1972
Krutikov, P-.
'Goskhozy Kitaia za 10 let' (State farms in China during the past decade).
Sel'skoe khoziaistvo Sibiri 1959, 10 (oktiabr'), 84–88.
Subj 14.1 34.1 ▪ 11.2

19137 MCH P P7 G1.2 1949–1972
Kurbatov, V- P-.
'Rol' goskhozov v razvitii sel'skokhoziaistvennogo proizvodstva KNR' (The role of state farms in the development of agricultural production in the People's Republic of China).
NAA 1961, 3, 26–36.
Subj 14.1 16.3 34.1 ▪ 12.1 18

19138 MCY P P7 G1.2 1949–1972
Kwan, Rebecca S.
'The commune, the family, and the emancipation of women.' In *Contemporary China, 1958–1959*, edited by Edward Stuart Kirby. [Selective entry]
Hong Kong: Hong Kong U. Press, 1960, 146–151.
Subj 20 28 34.1 ▪ 26.3 41 47 55

19139 MCH P P7 G1.2 1949–1972
[La Dany, Ladislao] ———, 1914–.
'Collective farms.'
CNA 130 (4 May 1956), 2–7.
Subj 34.1 ▪ 32 35

19140 NNC P P7 G1.2 1949–1972
[La Dany, Ladislao] ———, 1914–.
'The collective farms.'
CNA 162 (4 Jan. 1957), 1–7; 164 (18 Jan. 1957), 1–7.
Subj 26.3 28 34.1 ▪ 22 24.1 24.6

19141 NNC P P7 G1.2 1949–1972
[La Dany, Ladislao] ———, 1914–.
'Collectivization drive.'
CNA 78 (8 Apr. 1955), 2–7.
Subj 16.3 34.1

19142 NIC P P7 G1.2 1949–1972
[La Dany, Ladislao] ———, 1914–.
'Commune, great brigade, brigade.'
CNA 429 (20 July 1962), 1–7.
Subj 22 34.1 ▪ 26.1 26.3

19143 MCH P P7 G1.2 1949–1972
[La Dany, Ladislao] ———, 1914–.
'Farmers in collectivization.'
CNA 79 (15 Apr. 1955), 2–7.
Subj 34.1 ▪ 12.1

19144 NIC P P7 G1.2 1949–1972
[La Dany, Ladislao] ———, 1914–.
'Reshaping the villages: The people's communes.'
CNA 246 (26 Sept. 1958), 1–7.
Subj 22 34.1 ▪ 26.3 55

19145 MCH P P7 G1.2 1949–1972
[La Dany, Ladislao] ———, 1914–.
'Why communes? The purpose behind the present movement.'
CNA 257 (12 Dec. 1958), 1–7.
Subj 34.1 41 ▪ 11.4 14.1

19146 CSH P P7 G1.2 1949–1972
Lei Ta-hua.
'Agricultural cooperativization in Communist China during 1962.' Tr. of '1962 nien ti Chung kung nung yeh chi t'i hua chi tui Su-lien chih pi chiao' (Agricultural collectivization in Communist China during 1962, with a comparison to agricultural collectivization in the Soviet Union); *Tsu kuo chou k'an* 545 (17 June 1963), 7–10. In *Communist China, 1962*, edited by Union Research Institute. [Selective entry]
Hong Kong: Union Research Institute, 1963, vol. 2, 128–140.
Subj 34.1 ▪ 14.1

19147 CSH O P8 G5.1 1949–1972
Li Kai (Li K'ai) and Ching Shen (Ch'ing Ch'en), pseud.
'The road for five hundred million peasants.' Tr. of 'Wu i nung min ti fang hsiang' (The orientation of five hundred million peasants); in *Chung-kuo nung ts'un ti she hui chu i kao ch'ao* (The socialist upsurge in rural China); Peking: Jen min ch'u pan she, 1956, vol. 1, 27–36. In *Socialist upsurge in China's countryside*, edited by Pan kung t'ing, Chung yang wei yüan hui, Chung-kuo kung ch'an tang (General Office, Central Committee, Chinese Communist Party). [Selective entry]
Peking: Foreign Languages Press, 1957, 115–127.
Subj 34.1 ▪ 24.1 26.3

19148 CSH O P7 G9.2 1949–1972
Liang Hsiang-sheng.
'My experience as chairman of a large co-operative.' Tr. of 'Wo tang ta she chu jen ti ching yen' (My experiences as director of a large cooperative [Ch'ün-chung ti i agricultural producers' cooperative, Chung-shan *hsien*, Kwangtung]); in *Chung-kuo nung ts'un ti she hui chu i kao ch'ao* (The socialist upsurge in rural China); Peking: Jen min ch'u pan she, 1956, vol. 3, 951–958. In *Socialist upsurge in China's countryside*, edited by Pan kung t'ing, Chung yang wei yüan hui, Chung-kuo kung ch'an tang (General Office, Central Committee, Chinese Communist Party). [Selective entry]
Peking: Foreign Languages Press, 1957, 187–197.
Subj 22 34.1 ▪ 21.4 24.1 26.3

19149 CSH O P7 G1.2 1949–1972
Liao Lu-yen, 1908?–.
'Agricultural collectivization in China.' In *Socialist industrialization and agricultural collectivization in China*, by Po I-po and Liao Lu-yen. [Analytic entry]
Peking: Foreign Languages Press, 1964, 23–51.
SUBJ 14.1 34.1 ▪ 12.1 16.3

19150 CSU P P2 G1.2 1949–1972
Lin Chen.
'Peiping again raises the question of the "road of socialist agriculture".'
IS 6, 10 (July 1970), 42–51.
SUBJ 14.1 16.3 34.1 64 ▪ 32

19151 CSH P P7 G1.2 1949–1972
Lin Chen.
'The present status of Chinese Communist rural communes.'
IS 3, 12 (Sept. 1967), 30–39.
SUBJ 20 24.1 34.1 ▪ 22 26.3

19152 NNC O P7 G5.1 1949–1972
Lin Tieh (Lin T'ieh), 1904–.
'The people's commune movement in Hopei.' Tr. of 'Ho-pei sheng ti jen min kung she yün tung'; *Hung ch'i* 1958, 9 (1 Oct.), 16–21. In *People's communes in China*. [Selective entry]
Peking: Foreign Languages Press, 1959, 47–60.
SUBJ 20 34.1 ▪ 22.1 24.1 28

19153 DLC F P8 G5.1 1949–1972
Liu Tzu-li, et al.
A report of an investigation of the Kuang-huei agricultural producer cooperative in T'ien-chia-fu ts'un, mimeo. Tr. of 'T'ien-chia-fu ts'un Kuang-hui nung yeh sheng ch'an ho tso she tiao ch'a pao kao' (Report on Kuang-hui agricultural producers' cooperative, T'ien-chia-fu village, Hsi-hsia-ying *hsiang*, T'ung *hsien*, Peking municipality); *Ching chi yen chiu* (Peking) 1955, 4 (Oct.), 83–104.
Washington, D.C.: U.S. Joint Publications Research Service, 25 Apr. 1958. 39 p. (JPRS 106D)
SUBJ 22 24.1 34.1 ▪ 21 24.5 26 28 47 55

19154 MCH P P8 G1.2 1949–1972
Luard, David Evan Trant, 1926–.
'The Chinese co-operative farm.' In *Far Eastern affairs, Number 2*, edited by Geoffrey Francis Hudson. [Sole entry]
London: Chatto and Windus, 1963, 37–50. (St. Antony's papers, 7)
SUBJ 22 22.1 24.1 26.3 28 34.1

19155 MCH P P7 G1.2 1949–1972
Lunev, Aleksandr Efremovich.
'Pravo kooperativnoi sobstvennosti v Kitaiskoi Narodnoi Respublike' (Cooperative property law in the People's Republic of China).
SGP 1955, 8 (avgust), 74–81.
SUBJ 12.2 34.1 45 ▪ 24.6 34.2

19156 NIC P P7 G1.2 1949–1972
Lü Ch'ang, et al.
'More on Chinese Communist Party policy relating to rural people's communes.' Tr. of 'Jen chen hsüeh hsi tang ti cheng ts'e chi chi chih yüan nung yeh chieh she' (Understanding and practicing party policy on maximum aid for agricultural development); *Kung jen jih pao* 7 Nov. – 9 Dec. 1961.
CB 677 (26 Feb. 1962), 1–34.
SUBJ 20 34.1 34.2 ▪ 14.1 22 24 26.3 28 32.1

19157 CSU P P8 G1.2 1949–1972
MacDougall, Colina.
'The Cultural Revolution in the communes: Back to 1958?'
CS 7, 7 (11 Apr. 1969), 1–11.
SUBJ 22.1 34.1 ▪ 22 24 28

19158 CBU P P7 G1.2 1949–1972
Marchisio, Hélène.
'Communes populaires et organismes coopératives dans les campagnes chinoises' (Communes and cooperative organizations in the Chinese countryside).
Archives internationales de sociologie de la coopération 20 (juil.–déc. 1966), 76–132.
SUBJ 22 24 24.1 34.1 ▪ 17 21.4 28 31

19159 CSU P P7 G1.2 1949–1972
[Melis, Giorgio] George Melis.
'Special report: China's communes, what the Chinese say.'
Philippine studies 16, 2 (Apr. 1968), 348–370.
SUBJ 24.1 34.1 64 ▪ 19 22.1 24.3 24.4 32.1 45

19160 CSU P P7 G1.2 1949–1972
Miyashita, Tadao, 1909–.
'Problems of the rural people's communes in China.'
Review (Tokyo) 1 (May 1964), 1–21.
SUBJ 24.3 34.1 45 ▪ 22 24.1 32.1

19161 CSH O P7 G5.1 1949–1972
Mo Chan-lin.
'Good example for commune members, guide for youths.' Tr. of 'She yüan ti hao pang yang, ch'ing nien ti tai lu jen'; *Hung ch'i* 1963, 13/14 (10 July), 35–39. In *Translations from 'Hung-ch'i' (Red flag) No. 13-14, 1963*, mimeo., compiled by U.S. Joint Publications Research Service. [Selective entry]
Washington, D.C.: JPRS, 10 Sept. 1963, 57–64. (JPRS 21,008; MC 17,950/1963)
SUBJ 26.1 34.1 ▪ 26.3

19162 MMT U P7 G1.2 1949–1972
Nove, Alec.
'Collectivization of agriculture in Russia and China.' In *Symposium on economic and social problems of the Far East*, edited by Edward Franciszek Szczepanik. [Selective entry]
Hong Kong: Hong Kong U. Press, 1962, 16–24.
SUBJ 14.1 34.1 ▪ 32.1 64

19163 CSU FP P8 G9.4 1949–1972
Pasternak, Burton, 1933–.
'Social consequences of equalizing irrigation access.'
Human organization 27, 4 (Winter 1968), 332–343.
SUBJ 24.1 34.1 ▪ 21.4 28 42

19164 MCH PO P7 G1.2 1949–1972
Pavlov, I- V-.
'Nekotorye voprosy pravovogo polozheniia sel'skokhoziaistvennykh proizvodstvennykh kooperativov Kitaiskoi Narodnoi Respubliki' (The legal status of agricultural producers' cooperatives in the People's Republic of China).
SGP 1957, 7 (iiul'), 32–42.
SUBJ 12.2 24.1 34.1 ▪ 32.1 45 55

19165 CSU F P8 G9.2 1949–1972
Pelzel, John Campbell, 1914–.
'Economic management of a production brigade in post-Leap China.' In *Economic organization in Chinese society*, edited by William Earl Willmott. [Selective entry]
Stanford: Stanford U. Press, 1972, 387–414.
SUBJ 24 24.1 34.1 ▪ 22 26.1 26.3 28 32

19166 MAM P P2 G1.2 1949–1972
Ray, Dennis Michael, 1939–.
The people's communes in Communist China, 1958–1962.
Ann Arbor: University Microfilms (Publ. 68-6820), 1968. 880 p. (Doctoral dissertation in Economics, U. of Denver, 1967)
SUBJ 12.1 14 32.1 34.1 ▪ 14.1 14.4 16.1 19

19167 MCH O P7 G1.2 1949–1972
Robinson, Joan, 1903–.
'Organization of agriculture.' In *Contemporary China*, edited by Ruth Adams. [Selective entry]
New York: Pantheon, 1966, 221–234.
SUBJ 24.1 24.3 26.3 34.1 ▪ 24.5 28

19168 MCH PO P2 G1.2 1949–1972
[Rousset, David] D. R., 1912–.
'Réflexions à propos de la crise des structures économiques en Chine continentale.'
Saturne 3, 11 (jan.–fév. 1957), 67–79.
'Reflections on the crisis in the economic structures of the People's Republic of China.'
Saturn 3, 1 (Jan.–Feb. 1957), 67–78.
SUBJ 16.1 16.3 32.1 34.1 ▪ 12 14.1 64

19169 MCH PO P2 G1.2 1949–1972
Rousset, David, 1912–.
'Vers une seconde révolution en Chine?' (Toward a second revolution in China?).
Saturne 5, 19 (jan.–mars 1959), 47–94.
SUBJ 14.1 16.3 32 32.1 34.1 ▪ 12 14.4 18 22 22.1

19170 MCY S P7 G1.2 1949–1972
Schiller, Otto, 1901–.
'The agrarian systems in the Soviet Union and Communist China: A comparison.' In *Unity and contradiction: Major aspects of Sino-Soviet relations*, edited by Kurt London. [Selective entry]
New York: Praeger, 1962, 331–350.
SUBJ 14.1 34.1 ▪ 16.3 18 19 22

19171 NNC P P7 G5.4 1949–1972
Shih Hsiang-sheng.
'Several problems concerning the consolidation and development of people's communes.' Tr. of 'Kuan yü kung ku ho fa chan jen min kung she ti chi ko wen t'i'; *Jen min jih pao* 14 Mar. 1960, 7.
URS 19, 2 (5 Apr. 1960), 18–33.
SUBJ 20 34.1 ▪ 34.2 45

19172 CSH O P7 G5.4 1949–1972
Shih Shao-chu (Shih Shao-chü).
'Glorious labor, blessed old age.' Tr. of 'Kuang jung ti lao tung, hsing fu ti wan nien: Huai-pin hsien Teng-t'a-shih-she

tsu chih "Wu-pao" she yüan ts'an chia sheng ch'an ti ching yen' (Glorious labor, happy old age: Experiences in organizing members of 'Wu-pao' cooperative to join Teng-t'a No. 10 cooperative in production in Huai-pin *hsien* [Honan]); *Hung ch'i* 1958, 6 (16 Aug.), 35–37. In *Selected translations from 'Hung-chi' (Red flag), June–August 1958*, mimeo., compiled by U.S. Joint Publications Research Service. [Selective entry]
Washington, D.C.: JPRS, 21 Apr. 1961, 119–124. (JPRS 7837; MC 5498/1962)
SUBJ 34.1 ▪ 24.4 26.3 28

19173 CSU S P7 G9.4 1949–1972
Spaeth, David Hollingsworth, 1924–.
'Quasi-cooperative arrangements: The Japanese and Taiwanese experience.' In *Agricultural cooperatives and markets in developing countries*, edited by Kurt R- Anschel, Russell H- Brannon, and Eldon D- Smith. [Sole entry]
New York: Praeger, 1969, 291–307.
SUBJ 34.1 ▪ 22

19174 CSU P P7 G1.2 1949–1972
Sreedhar, Shri.
'Co-operation in China's agriculture (1953–57).'
India q. 25, 2 (Apr.–June 1969), 122–138.
SUBJ 14.1 34.1

19175 NNC P P8 G1.2 1949–1972
Stadnichenko, A- I-.
'Nekotorye voprosy razvitiia sel'skogo khoziaistva v Kitaiskoi Narodnoi Respublike' (Agricultural development in the People's Republic of China).
SK 1958, 2, 11–22.
SUBJ 14.1 34.1 ▪ 14.6 18

19176 CSH P P8 G1.2 1949–1972
Sukharchuk, Grigorii Dmitrievich, 1927–.
'Formy organizatsii truda i proizvodstva v kitaiskoi derevne (1950–1955)' (Labor and production organization in the Chinese countryside, 1950–1955).
NAA 1968, 4, 71–79.
SUBJ 16.3 34.1 ▪ 14.1

19177 NNC P P8 G1.2 1949–1972
Sukharchuk, Grigorii Dmitrievich, 1927–.
'Organizatsiia truda v gruppakh trudovoi vzaimopomoshchi Kitaia' (Labor organization in the mutual-aid teams of China).
KSIV 25 (1957), 18–28.
SUBJ 24.1 26.3 34.1 45 ▪ 36.3

19178 MCH O P8 G5.2 1949–1972
Sun Tan-wei.
A village moves to socialism [Hsi-kou, P'ing-shun *hsien*, Shansi].
Shanghai: China Reconstructs, 1956. 47 p. [Supplement to *China reconstructs* 5, 10 (Oct. 1956)]
SUBJ 34.1 ▪ 28 36.3

19179 NNC P P7 G9.2 1949–1972
T'ao Chu, 1906–.
'The people's communes are making progress: A preliminary summary of the five years' experience of the rural people's communes in Kwangtung province.' Tr. of 'Jen min kung she tsai ch'ien chin: Kuang-tung nung ts'un jen min kung she wu nien ching yen ti chi pen tsung chieh' (The communes advance: Basic conclusions on experiences of rural communes in Kwangtung during the past five years); *Hung ch'i* 1964, 4 (26 Feb.), 1–12.
SCMM 410 (31 Mar. 1964), 1–16.
SUBJ 20 34.1 ▪ 22 22.1 24.1 28 45

19180 CSU O P8 G5.2 1949–1972
T'ao Lu-chia.
'Let the spirit of Tachai blossom and bear fruit throughout our land.' Tr. of 'Jang Ta-chai ching shen p'ien ti k'ai hua chieh kuo: Shan-hsi nung ts'un k'ai chan hsüeh Ta-chai yün tung ti ch'u pu tsung chieh' (Results of letting the spirit of 'Ta-chai' flourish: Preliminary conclusions on implementing the campaign to follow the example of Ta-chai brigade [Ta-chai commune, Hsi-yang *hsien*] in rural Shansi); *Hung ch'i* 1965, 11 (1 Oct.), 4–14. In *Translations from 'Hung-ch'i' (Red flag) No. 11, 1965*, mimeo., compiled by U.S. Joint Publications Research Service. [Selective entry]
Washington, D.C.: JPRS, 3 Nov. 1965, 5–24. (JPRS 32,698; MC 875-33/1966)
SUBJ 21.4 34.1 ▪ 24.1

19181 NNC P P8 G1.2 1949–1972
Telegin, IAroslav Ivanovich, and Vladimir Ivanovich Potapov.
Sel'skoe khoziaistvo Kitaiskoi Narodnoi Respubliki.
Moscow: Znanie, 1958. 31 p. (Vsesoiuznoe obshchestvo po rasprostraneniiu politicheskikh i nauchnykh znanii, seriia 3, 34).

Agriculture in the People's Republic of China, mimeo.
Washington, D.C.: U.S. Joint Publications Research Service, 20 May 1959. 33 p. (JPRS 731D; MC 9188/1959)
SUBJ 14.1 34.1

19182 CSH U P7 G1.2 1949–1972
Teng Tse-hui (Teng Tzu-hui), 1895–.
'The socialist transformation of agriculture in China.' Tr. of 'Chung-kuo nung yeh ti she hui chu i kai tsao' (The socialist reform of Chinese agriculture); in *Hui huang ti shih nien* (A decade of glory), edited by *Jen min jih pao* ch'u pan she; [Peking]: Jen min jih pao ch'u pan she, 1959, vol. 2, 531–551. In *Ten glorious years*. [Selective entry]
Peking: Foreign Languages Press, 1960, 298–327.
SUBJ 14.1 34.1 ▪ 16.3 22

19183 MCH P P2 G1.2 1949–1972
Trivière, Léon, 1915–.
'La politique pré-kolkhozienne en Chine de 1951 au tournant de juillet 1955 et la crise du Parti communiste chinois' (The pre-cooperativization policy in China from 1951 to the turning point of July 1955, and the crisis in the Chinese Communist Party).
Saturne 2, 6 (jan.–fév. 1956), 55–88.

'The 1951 pre-kolkhoze policy in China at the turning-point in July 1955, and the crisis in the Chinese Communist Party.'
Saturn 2, 1 (Jan.–Feb. 1956), 52–82.
SUBJ 14.1 16.3 32 34.1 ▪ 12.2 14.3 14.4 64

19184 NIC PO P8 G1.2 1949–1972
Tung, Ta-lin.
Agricultural cooperation in China, 2nd ed.
Peking: Foreign Languages Press, 1959. 179 p.
SUBJ 24.1 26.3 32.1 34.1 ▪ 21.4 24 24.4 25 28 36.3

19185 CSH U P7 G1.2 1949–1972
Ullerich, Curt.
'Die chinesische Volkskommune: Eine Institution von beispielhafter Bedeutung Entwicklungsländer' (The Chinese commune: An institution of exemplary significance for developing nations).
Z. für Geopolitik 15, 2 (Apr.–Juni 1967), 98–116.
SUBJ 24.1 34.1 ▪ 22 24 24.4

19186 CSU P P8 G5.2 1949–1972
Unger, Jonathan.
'"Learn from Tachai": China's agricultural model.'
CS 9, 9 (7 Sept. 1971), 1–11.
SUBJ 22.1 24.1 34.1

19187 DLC S P8 G1.2 1949–1972
Vladimirskii, E- A-.
'Razvitie sel'skokhoziastvennoi proizvodstvennoi kooperatsii v Kitaiskoi Narodnoi Respublike' (The development of agricultural producers' cooperatives in the People's Republic of China).
UZLGU 241 (1957), 150–182.
SUBJ 14.1 34.1 ▪ 12.1 16.3 66

19188 CSU S P7 G1.2 1949–1972
Vogel, Ezra Feivel, 1930–.
'Agriculture as the foundation.' [Review of *Rapport från kinesisk by* (Report from a Chinese village), by Jan Myrdal; *Planning in Chinese agriculture: Socialisation and the private sector, 1956–1962*, by Kenneth Richard Walker; and *A Chinese village in early Communist transition*, by C. K. Yang (Yang Ch'ing-k'un).]
WP 18, 4 (July 1966), 761–779.
SUBJ 34.1 ▪ 14 14.1 22

19189 CSU P P7 G1.2 1949–1972
Walker, Kenneth Richard, 1931–.
'Collectivisation in retrospect: The "socialist high tide" of Autumn 1955 – Spring 1956.'
CQ 26 (Apr.–June 1966), 1–43.
SUBJ 14.1 34.1 36.3 ▪ 12.1 16.3 64

19190 CSU P P7 G1.2 1949–1972
Walker, Kenneth Richard, 1931–.
'Organization of agricultural production.' In *Economic trends in Communist China*, edited by Alexander Eckstein, Walter Galenson, and Ta-chung Liu. [Selective entry]
Chicago: Aldine, 1968, 397–458.
SUBJ 14.1 34.1 ▪ 12.1 16.3 22

19191 CSH O P7 G7.3 1949–1972
Wan Shao-ho.
'Five years of the "Eight-One" commune.' Tr. of '"Pai-i" kung she wu nien chien' (Five years of Pa-i commune [Nan-ch'ang *hsien*, Kiangsi]); *Hung ch'i* 1963, 21 (7 Nov.), 23–27. In *Translations from 'Hung-ch'i' (Red flag) No. 21, 1963*, mimeo., compiled by U.S. Joint

Publications Research Service. [Sole entry]
Washington, D.C.: JPRS, 6 Dec. 1963, 34–40. (JPRS 22,117; MC 2545/1964)
SUBJ 28 34.1 ▪ 22 24.1

19192 CSH O P7 G5.1 1949–1972
Wang Chih-chi (Wang Chih-ch'i).
'A whole village goes co-operative in a little over a month.' Tr. of 'Chih hua i ko to yüeh shih chien chiu shih ch'üan ts'un ho tso hua' (Village cooperativization completed in one month); in *Chung-kuo nung ts'un ti she hui chu i kao ch'ao* (The socialist upsurge in rural China); Peking: Jen min ch'u pan she, 1956, vol. 1, 44–55. In *Socialist upsurge in China's countryside*, edited by Pan kung t'ing, Chung yang wei yüan hui, Chung-kuo kung ch'an tang (General Office, Central Committee, Chinese Communist Party). [Selective entry]
Peking: Foreign Languages Press, 1957, 27–43.
SUBJ 34.1 ▪ 21.4 22 22.1 24.1 28

19193 CSH O P7 G5.1 1949–1972
Wang Lin.
'Diligent and frugal co-op operation.' Tr. of 'Ch'in chien pan she' (Diligent and frugal operation of cooperatives); in *Chung-kuo nung ts'un ti she hui chu i kao ch'ao* (The socialist upsurge in rural China); Peking: Jen min ch'u pan she, 1956, vol. 1, 16–26. In *Socialist upsurge in China's countryside*, edited by Pan kung t'ing, Chung yang wei yüan hui, Chung-kuo kung ch'an tang (General Office, Central Committee, Chinese Communist Party). [Selective entry]
Peking: Foreign Languages Press, 1957, 67–81.
SUBJ 34.1 ▪ 24.1 28 32.1 45

19194 MAM P P8 G1.2 1949–1972
Wang, Tong-eng, 1933–.
Structural change and development in Chinese agriculture.
Ann Arbor: University Microfilms (Publ. 67-2101), 1967. 399 p. (Doctoral dissertation in Economics, Iowa State U., 1966)
SUBJ 14.1 34.1 ▪ 12.1 36.3

19195 NNC F P7 G2.3 1949–1972
Wang Yen-li, et al.
'An investigation and study of the problem of transition from higher cooperatives to people's communes.' Tr. of 'Kuan yü kao chi nung yeh she hsiang ch'üan min so yu chih kuo tu wen t'i ti tiao ch'a yen chiu' (An investigation of the problem of transition from higher-level agricultural producers' cooperatives to group ownership); *Hsin chien she* 1958, 9 (Sept.), 1–7.
ECMM 145 (13 Oct. 1958), 1–15.
SUBJ 34.1 ▪ 21.4 24.1 24.6 26.3 28 45 64

19196 MCY U P7 G2.2 1949–1972
Wei Chuang.
'Notes from a rural people's commune [Lo-tzu-kou commune, Wang-ch'ing *hsien*, Kirin].'
PR 6, 5 (1 Feb. 1963), 16–18.
SUBJ 24.1 34.1 ▪ 24.4

19197 CSU F P8 G9.2 1949–1972
Whyte, Martin King, 1942–.
'The Tachai brigade [Ta-chai commune, Hsi-yang *hsien*, Shansi] and incentives for the peasant.'
CS 7, 16 (15 Aug. 1969), 1–13.
SUBJ 26.3 34.1 ▪ 22 26.1

19198 CSU P P2 G1.2 1949–1972
Wittfogel, Karl August, 1896–.
'Communist and non-Communist agrarian systems, with special reference to the U.S.S.R. and Communist China: A comparative approach' [with comments by R- P- Rochlin and Werner Klatt]. In *Agrarian policies and problems in Communist and non-Communist countries*, edited by William Arthur Douglas Jackson. [Selective entry]
Seattle: U. of Washington Press, 1971, 3–68.
SUBJ 14.1 16.3 20 34.1 ▪ 11.2 11.4

19199 CSH P P7 G1.2 1949–1972
Wong, John.
'Economic organization of the collectives in China.' In *Selected seminar papers on contemporary China, I*, edited by Steve S. K. Chin (Chin Ssu-k'ai) and Frank Henry Haviland King. [Analytic entry]
Hong Kong: U. of Hong Kong, Centre of Asian Studies, 1971, 91–133. (CAS occasional papers and monographs, 4)
SUBJ 34.1 ▪ 14.1 14.5 16.3

19200 NNC O P7 G5.4 1949–1972
Wu Chih-p'u, 1906–.
'From agricultural producers' cooperatives to people's communes.' Tr. of 'Yu nung yeh sheng ch'an ho tso she tao jen min kung she' (From agricultural producers' cooperatives to communes); *Hung ch'i* 1958, 8 (16 Sept.), 5–11. In *People's communes in China*. [Selective entry]
Peking: Foreign Languages Press, 1959, 26–46.
SUBJ 20 24.1 34.1 ▪ 22.1 24.4 26.1 28 32.1

19201 MCY P P7 G1.2 1949–1972
Yamamoto, Hideo, 1911–.
Development of agricultural collectivization in China.
Tokyo: Japan, National Research Institute of Agriculture, 1961. 50 p. (NRIA bulletins, 5)
SUBJ 34.1 ▪ 26 36.3

19202 NNC P P7 G1.2 1949–1972
Yang Mu-wen.
'Socialist transformation of agriculture in Communist China.' Tr. of 'Shih nien lai ti Chung kung nung yeh she hui chu i kai tsao' (The socialist reform of agriculture in Communist China during the past decade); *Tsu kuo chou k'an* 385 (23 May 1960), 15–20. In *Communist China, 1949–1959*, edited by Union Research Institute. [Selective entry]
Hong Kong: Union Research Institute, 1961, vol. 1, 149–176.
SUBJ 14.1 34.1 ▪ 16.3 18 22.1

19203 MAM P P7 G1.2 1949–1972
Yin, Yi-chang (Yin I-ch'ang), 1923–.
Agricultural reorganization of Mainland China, 1949–1957: Its process and effects on agricultural performance.
Ann Arbor: University Microfilms (Publ. 67-816), 1967. 318 p. (Doctoral dissertation in Economics, Columbia U., 1966)
SUBJ 14.1 34.1 ▪ 12.1

34.2 Business Organization

商業組織 商業組織

1644-1911

19204 NIC O P4 G1.2 1842–1895
'Chinese partnerships: Liability of the individual members.'
JRAS-CB new (2nd) series 22, 1 (1887), 39–52.
SUBJ 12.2 16.2 34.2 ▪ 14.3

19205 NIC P P3 G9.2 1644–1842
The Chinese security merchants in Canton and their debts.
Canton: Canton Press Office, 1838. 33 p.
SUBJ 24.6 34.2 34.3 ▪ 24.3 24.5 66

19206 DLC PO P4 G6.0 1895–1911
'La classe marchande et le commerce indigène en Chine' (The merchant class and the native trade in China).
B. de la Société de géographie commerciale du Havre 17 (3e trimestre 1900), 133–157.
SUBJ 14.3 16.2 34.2 ▪ 14.6 34.3

19207 CSU O P3 G9.5 1842–1911
'The Oriental mercantile community, Hongkong.' In *Twentieth century impressions of Hongkong, Shanghai, and other treaty ports of China: Their history, people, commerce, industries and manners*, edited by Arnold Wright and H- A- Cartwright. [Selective entry]
London: Lloyd's Greater Britain Publishing Co., 1908, 224–234.
SUBJ 34.2 ▪ 24.3 24.6

19208 NNC P P1 G1.2 1895–1911
Dove, Heinrich W-, 1853–?
'Das chinesische Konkursgesetz vom 26. April 1906' (The Chinese bankruptcy law of 26 April 1906).
BVRV 3, 6 (Dez. 1907), 161–165.
SUBJ 12.2 34.2 ▪ 22.2 36.2

19209 NNC O P3 G9.2 1644–1895
Hunter, William C-, 1812–1891.
The 'fan kwae' at Canton before treaty days, 1825–1844, 2nd ed.
Shanghai: Kelly and Walsh, 1911. 157 p. [Reprinted—Taipei: Ch'eng-wen, 1970. 157 p.]
SUBJ 24.3 34.2 36.2 66 ▪ 12.2 14.3 22.2 24.6 62

19210 MCY U P2 G1.3 1644–1895
Jernigan, Thomas R-.
China's business methods and policy.
Shanghai: Kelly and Walsh; London: Unwin, 1904. 439 p.
SUBJ 14 34.2 34.3 ▪ 12.2 17 22.2

19211 CSU P P7 G5.1 –1842
Teng T'o, 1911?–.
'En Chine, du XVIe au XVIIIe siècle: les mines de charbon de Men-t'ou-kou' (The coal mines of Men-t'ou-kou [Wan-p'ing *hsien*, Chihli] from the sixteenth to the eighteenth century). Tr. of 'Ts'ung Wan-li tao Ch'ien-lung: Kuan yü Chung-kuo tzu pen chu i meng ya shih ch'i ti i ko lun cheng' (From the

Wan-li reign to the Ch'ien-lung reign: A documentary essay on the period of the emergence of capitalism in China); *Li shih yen chiu* 1956, 10 (Oct.), 1–31. [Abridged tr.]
Annales; économies, sociétés, civilisations 22, 1 (jan.–fév. 1967), 50–87.
SUBJ 24.4 34.2 ▪ 21.4 24.6 26.1 26.2

19212 NNC P P4 G1.3 1895–1911
Wang, Chung-hui (Wang Ch'ung-hui), 1881–1958.
'Wie ist nach dem neuen chinesischen Handelsgestz eine Handelsgesellschaft zu gründen?' (The founding of a trading company according to the new Chinese commercial code).
BVRV 2, 1 (Apr. 1906), 12–15.
SUBJ 12.2 34.2 ▪ 14.3

1644-1949

19213 NNC P P7 G6.1 1895–1949
Chen Hung-tsin (Ch'en Hung-chin).
'Land division through the land development companies in northern Kiangsu.' Tr. of 'Chiang-su yen k'en ch'ü yen k'en kung ssu chih ku tung fen ti chih' (The system whereby reclaimed salt lands in Kiangsu are subdivided by shareholders of salt-production companies); *Chung-shan wen hua chiao yü kuan chi k'an* 4, 1 (Spring 1937), 61–79 [condensed tr.]. In *Agrarian China*, compiled by Institute of Pacific Relations. [Selective entry]
Chicago: U. of Chicago Press, 1939, 35–42.
SUBJ 24.1 34.2

19214 CSU P P1 G1.2 1895–1949
Chi, Chung-Jui (Ch'i Tsung-sui).
'Points of Chinese trade-mark law.'
CEJ 12, 2 (Feb. 1933), 160–165.
SUBJ 12.2 34.2

19215 NNC O P5 G1.2 1895–1928
Child, Richard Washburn, 1881–1935.
'The ways of Chinese business.'
Asia (New York: American Asiatic Assn.) 17, 5 (July 1917), 341–349.
SUBJ 34.2 ▪ 14 16 22.2 32.1 63

19216 DLC P P2 G1.2 1895–1949
Feuerwerker, Albert, 1927–.
'Industrial enterprise in twentieth-century China: The Chee Hsin Cement Co. [Tangshan].' In *Approaches to modern Chinese history*, edited by A. Feuerwerker et al. [Selective entry]
Berkeley, Los Angeles: U. of California Press, 1967, 304–341.
SUBJ 24.4 34.2 ▪ 24.5 26.4 32.1

19217 MCH P P3 G1.1 1842–1949
Hao, Yen-p'ing, 1934–.
The comprador in nineteenth-century China: Bridge between East and West.
Cambridge: Harvard U. Press, 1970. 315 p. (Harvard East Asian series, 45) (Revision of *Cantonese comprador-merchants: A study of their functions and influences, 1842–1884*, doctoral dissertation in History and Far Eastern Languages, Harvard U., 1966)
SUBJ 14.3 24.6 26.2 34.2 66 ▪ 24.4 63

19218 CSU U P1 G1.2 1842–1949
Levy, Marion Joseph, Jr., 1918–.
'Contrasting factors in the modernization of China and Japan.'
EDCC 2, 1 (Oct. 1953), 161–197. [Reprinted in *Economic growth: Brazil, India, Japan*, edited by Simon Kuznets, Wilbert E- Moore, and Joseph John Spengler. (Sole entry.) Durham: Duke U. Press, 1955, 496–536.]
SUBJ 16 19 34.2 40 ▪ 12.1 14 16.2 30 48

19219 CSH S P2 G1.1 1895–1928
Liu Tai-ban (Liu T'ai-pang).
'Kitaiskaia kompradorskaia burzhuaziia' (The Chinese comprador). Tr. from the English by M- I- Kazanin. [Tr. of an unpublished manuscript]
PK 1 (1929), 161–205; 2 (1930), 140–156.
SUBJ 14.3 14.6 16.2 34.2 ▪ 11.2 14.4 16.4 22 24.2 33 66

19220 CSH P P4 G6.1 1895–1928
McCall, Davy H-.
'Chang Chien: Mandarin turned manufacturer.'
PC 2 (May 1948), 93–102.
SUBJ 24.4 34.2 ▪ 26.4 27 59

19221 NNC U P3 G1.2 1895–1949
Sih, Tien-tsung (Hsüeh Tien-tseng).
'Factory inspection in China.'
IB 2, 6 (1 Nov. 1936), 97–116.
SUBJ 14.4 34.2 ▪ 12.2 18 66

19222 FPN P P4 G1.2 1895–1928
Yei, Kwang Yee.
Du régime des sociétés commerciales en Chine (The regulation of trading companies in China).
Paris: Jouve, 1927. 214 p. (Doctoral dissertation, Faculté de droit, Université de Paris)
SUBJ 12.2 14.3 34.2

1911-1949

19223 CSH F P3 G1.3 1911–1928
'An analytical study of advertisements in Chinese newspapers.'
CEM 3, 4 (Apr. 1926), 139–143.
SUBJ 34.2

19224 NIC O P7 G1.2 1928–1949
'The contract system in Chinese mining.'
PT new (2nd) series 1, 6 (23 Jan. 1932), 152–158.
SUBJ 14.4 16.4 34.2

19225 CSH U P4 G1.4 1911–1928
'Metody torgovli v Kitae: torgovlia sherst'iu' (Methods of commerce in China: The wool trade).
EVM 1924, 49/50 (14 dekabria), 11–15.
SUBJ 14.3 34.2 ▪ 14.6 16.2

19226 NNC P P2 G1.2 1928–1949
'Registered companies in China, 1929–1932.'
NWSS 6, 30 (24 July 1933), 141, 143–145.
SUBJ 14.4 34.2

19227 CSU U P7 G5.3 1928–1949
'Rural co-operative societies in Shantung.'
CEJ 17, 2 (Aug. 1935), 176–181.
SUBJ 34.2 ▪ 24.3 24.6 34.1

19228 CSU F P3 G1.3 1911–1949
Bacon, C- A-.
'Advertising in China.'
CEJ 5, 3 (Sept. 1929), 754–766.
SUBJ 24.2 34.2

19229 NIC O P5 G1.2 1911–1928
Baker, John Earl, 1880–1957.
'Why Chinese business is not business: Ways in which Confucian etiquette hinders the industrialization of China.'
Asia (New York: American Asiatic Assn.) 28, 5 (May 1928), 390–397, 426–427.
SUBJ 14 34.2 ▪ 19 48

19230 CSH S P1 G1.2 1928–1949
Baranov, Ippolit Gavrilovich.
'Kommercheskaia reklama v kitaiskikh gazetakh' (Commercial advertising in Chinese newspapers). [With English abstract]
VM 1930, 1, 90–103.
SUBJ 34.2 ▪ 14.2

19231 CSH O P3 G1.4 1911–1928
Baranov, Ippolit Gavrilovich.
'Ocherk torgovogo byta v Kitae' (Sketch of commercial life in China).
EVM 1924, 22 (1 iiunia), 3–11.
SUBJ 24.3 26.2 34.2 ▪ 24 24.6 26

19232 MCH P P3 G1.2 1911–1928
Berliner, Sigfrid, 1884–.
Organisation und Betrieb des Export-Geschäfts in China (The organization and operation of the export business in China).
Hanover: Hahnsche Buchhandlung, 1920. 131 p.
SUBJ 14.3 34.2

19233 NNC F P7 G4.1 1911–1949
Brauer, Max, 1887–, and Gaines Liu.
Rural conditions and co-operative movement in central Shensi, mimeo.
n.p., China: Ch'üan kuo ching chi wei yüan hui, 1934. 129, 10 p.
SUBJ 24 24.4 34.1 34.2 ▪ 26 27 28 38

19234 CBU P P1 G1.2 1928–1949
Bünger, Karl A-, 1903–.
'Die Haftung der Gesellschafter einer offenen Handelsgesellschaft nach japanischem und chinesischem Recht' (The liability of members of a trading partnership in Japanese and Chinese law).
OR 16, 5 (1 März 1935), 127–128.
SUBJ 12.2 34.2 ▪ 14.3

19235 MCH P P1 G1.2 1911–1949
Bünger, Karl A-, 1903–.
'Das neue chinesische Warenzeichenrecht' (The new Chinese trademark law).
OR 16, 1 (1 Jan. 1935), 14–16; 16, 3 (1 Feb. 1935), 69–70.
SUBJ 12.2 34.2 ▪ 14.3 14.4

19236 NNC P P1 G1.2 1911–1949
Bünger, Karl A-, 1903–.
'Das Recht der Handelsgesellschaften in China' (Trading-company law in China).
Z. für das gesamte Handelsrecht 98, 3 (Nov. 1932), 285–297.
SUBJ 12.2 14.3 34.2 ▪ 66

19237 CBU P P1 G2.0 1928–1949
Bünger, Karl A-, 1903–.
'Der Schutz von Warenzeichen in der Mandschurei' (The protection of

trademarks in Manchuria [i.e., Manchoukuo]).
OR 16, 7 (1 Apr. 1935), 183–185.
Subj 12.2 34.2 ▪ 14.2

19238 CSU O P3 G1.5 1928–1949
Chang, Bintze T.
'Timber dealers in Shanghai.'
CEJ 5, 6 (Dec. 1929), 1138–1147.
Subj 34.2 ▪ 14.3 36.2

19239 CSH F P5 G1.3 1928–1949
Chang, L. L. (Chang Lü-luan).
'Some principles governing the success and failure of merchants and cotton wholesalers.'
EF 2 (Oct. 1936), 107–121. [In Chinese as well as English]
Subj 14.3 34.2

19240 MMU PO P2 G1.2 1911–1949
Chen, Kuo-fu (Ch'en Kuo-fu), 1892–1951.
The Chinese cooperative movement, rev. and enl. ed.
Nanking: China Co-operators' Union, 1947. 48 p.
Subj 34.2 ▪ 14 18 24.3 24.6 25 34.1

19241 NIC U P2 G1.3 1911–1949
Chen, Lawrence M. (Ch'en Wen-t'ung).
'The co-operative movement in China.'
IB 1, 12 (Sept. 1936), 1–26.
Subj 34.2 ▪ 14

19242 NNC O P3 G1.2 1911–1928
Child, Richard Washburn, 1881–1935.
'China's efforts in modern industry.'
Asia (New York: American Asiatic Assn.) 18, 11 (Nov. 1918), 962–967.
Subj 14.4 34.2 ▪ 14 16.4 62

19243 NNC P P7 G1.3 1928–1949
Colby, Scott Dearborn, 1944–.
The Oyüwan [Hupeh-Honan-Anhwei] *soviet: An early Chinese Communist rural base.*
Unpublished masters thesis in History, Columbia U., 1969. 81 p. [Certificate essay, East Asian Institute]
Subj 22 34.1 ▪ 15 24.3
[Editor's note: This entry belongs under subject heading 34.1]

19244 CSU U P7 G1.3 1928–1949
Coons, Arthur Gardiner, 1900–.
'Chinese farmers learn to cooperate.'
Asia (New York: American Asiatic Assn.) 34, 12 (Dec. 1934), 751–755.
Subj 34.2 ▪ 24.6 34.1

19245 NIC O P2 G1.3 1911–1949
Crow, Carl, 1883–1945.
The Chinese are like that.
New York: Harper, 1938. 328 p. [Also published as *My friends, the Chinese*. London: Hamilton, 1938. 277 p.]
Subj 10 14.2 34.2 60 61 ▪ 14.3 18 22.2 25 31 34.3 57

19246 MCH O P5 G1.2 1911–1949
Crow, Carl, 1883–1945.
Four hundred million customers: The experiences, some happy, some sad, of an American in China, and what they taught him, 8th ed.
New York: Harper, 1937. 316 p.
Subj 24.3 34.2 47 66 ▪ 14.6 23 41 61 63

19247 NIC P P3 G9.4 1911–1949
Eberhard, Wolfram, 1909–.
'The business activities of a small Chinese merchant.'
MS 21 (1962), 345–356. [Reprinted in *Settlement and social change in Asia*, by W. Eberhard. (Selective entry.) Hong Kong: Hong Kong U. Press, 1967, 194–203.]
Subj 24.3 34.2

19248 NNC O P4 G1.2 1911–1928
Eldridge, Frank Reed, 1889–.
Oriental trade methods.
New York: Appleton, 1923. 441 p.
Subj 14 14.3 34.2 34.3 ▪ 24.3 26.2 55 60

19249 FPN PO P3 G1.2 1911–1928
Escarra, Jean, 1885–1955.
'Sur le régime juridique d'une société anonyme qui établit son siège social dans une concession étrangère en Chine' (The legal position of a corporation that sets up headquarters in a foreign concession in China).
Annales de droit commercial et industriel, français, étranger et international 33, 2 (1924), 114–120.
Subj 12.2 34.2 66

19250 NNC P P1 G1.2 1928–1949
Fong, H. D. (Fang Hsien-t'ing), 1902–.
'Cooperative literature in China.'
NSEQ 8, 1 (Apr. 1935), 131–155.
Subj 34.2 72

19251 NNC P P2 G1.2 1911–1928
Fong, H. D. (Fang Hsien-t'ing), 1902–.
'The cooperative movement in China.'
MBEC 7, 5 (May 1934), 179–208.
Subj 24.6 34.2 ▪ 24.3 34.1 38

19252 MCH PO P1 G1.2 1911–1928
Gil'cher, M- E-.
Ocherki kitaiskogo aktsionernogo prava (Notes on Chinese corporation law).
Harbin: Tip. KVzhd, 1925. 22 p.
Subj 12.2 34.2

19253 CSH PO P4 G1.2 1928–1949
Gins, Georgii Konstantinovich (George Constantine Guins), 1887–.
'Novyi aktsionernyi zakon Kitaia' (The new Chinese law on joint-stock companies). [With English abstract]
VM 1930, 5, 60–67. [Reprinted as 'Aktsionernye kompanii' (Joint-stock companies). In *Ocherki torgovogo prava Kitaia, vypusk 1-i, torgovye tovarishchestva* (Notes on Chinese commercial law, Vol. 1, Trading companies), by G. K. Gins. (Selective entry.) Harbin: Tip. L. M. Abramovicha, 1930, 44–64.]
Subj 12.2 34.2

19254 CSH PO P4 G1.2 1928–1949
Gins, Georgii Konstantinovich (George Constantine Guins), 1887–.
'Registratsiia torgovykh tovarishchestv i predpriiatii po novym zakonam Kitaiskoi respubliki' (The registration of trading companies and business enterprises according to the new laws of the Republic of China).
EB 1930, 12 (1 iiulia), 19–22. [Reprinted as 'Registratsiia torgovykh tovarishchestv i predpriiatii' (The registration of trading companies and enterprises). In *Ocherki torgovogo prava Kitaia, vypusk 1-i, torgovye tovarishchestva* (Notes on Chinese commercial law, Vol. 1, Trading companies), by G. K. Gins. (Selective entry.) Harbin: Tip. L. M. Abramovicha, 1930, 88–100.]
Subj 12.2 34.2

19255 CSH PO P4 G1.2 1911–1928
Gins, Georgii Konstantinovich (George Constantine Guins), 1887–.
'Torgovoe tovarishchestvo po kitaiskomu pravu' (The trading company in Chinese law). [With English abstract]
VM 1930, 3, 59–70. [Reprinted as 'Torgovye tovarishchestva: vvedenie. Prostoe tovarishchestvo, polnoe tovarishchestvo, tovarishchestvo na vere' (Introduction to trading companies: The simple partnership, the joint-stock company, and the no-contract partnership). In *Ocherki torgovogo prava Kitaia, vypusk 1-i, torgovye tovarishchestva* (Notes on Chinese commercial law, Vol. 1, Trading companies), by G. K. Gins. (Selective entry.) Harbin: Tip. L. M. Abramovicha, 1930, 5–40.]
Subj 12.2 34.2 ▪ 14.6 41

19256 CSH O P3 G1.2 1911–1928
Harrison, Agatha.
'The coming of the factory system to China.' In *The Christian occupation of China*, edited by Milton Theobald Stauffer. [Selective entry]
Shanghai: China Continuation Committee, 1922, 25–27.
Subj 14.4 16.4 18 34.2 ▪ 30 38 52

19257 NNC P P7 G1.2 1911–1949
Hatch, Nancy M- S-, 1927–.
The rural cooperative movement in China, 1919–1945.
Unpublished masters thesis in Chinese and Japanese, Columbia U., 1955. 150 p.
Subj 24.6 34.1 34.2 ▪ 22 24.3 24.4 27 37

19258 CSU U P3 G6.1 1928–1949
Hayashi Tokumura.
'The shipping brokers and transport companies of Soochow.' Tr. by Andrew Watson of 'Senkō, un'yu kōshi, sonota' (Shipping brokers and transport companies); in *Chūshi no minsengyō: Soshū minsen jittai chōsa hōkoku* (Shipping in Central China: Survey of junks and sampans in Soochow), edited by Chōsabu, Mantetsu (Research Division, South Manchurian Railway); Tokyo: Hakubunkan, 1943, 293–396 [greatly condensed in tr.]. In *Transport in transition: The evolution of traditional shipping in China*. [Analytic entry]
Ann Arbor: U. of Michigan, Center for Chinese Studies, 1972, 35–52. (Michigan abstracts of Chinese and Japanese works on Chinese history, 3)
Subj 26.2 34.2 ▪ 14.3 24.2 36.2

19259 NNC P P7 G1.3 1911–1928
Hsu, Paul C. (Hsü Pao-ch'ien), 1892–1944.
'Rural cooperatives in China.'
PA 2, 10 (Oct. 1929), 611–624. [Separately reprinted—Honolulu: Institute of Pacific Relations, 1929. 16 p. (IPR documents, 4)]
Subj 24.6 34.1 34.2 ▪ 24.1 24.3 36.3 38

19260 CSU P P2 G1.4 1928–1949
Kōsaka Torizō, 1888–, and Nakamura Yoshio.

'Junk ownership and operation in North China.' Tr. by Andrew Watson from *Chūgoku kōeki kikō no kenkyū* (The structure of Chinese commerce); Tokyo: Waseda daigaku, Shuppambu, 1949, 55–61 [also tr. from *Kahoku kōgyō* 11 (Sept. 1941), 34–38; greatly condensed in tr.]. In *Transport in transition: The evolution of traditional shipping in China*. [Analytic entry]
Ann Arbor: U. of Michigan, Center for Chinese Studies, 1972, 53–56. (Michigan abstracts of Chinese and Japanese works on Chinese history, 3)
SUBJ 14.2 14.3 34.2

19261 MCH F P3 G8.1 1928–1949
Liao, T'ai-ch'u.
'The apprentices in Chengtu during and after the war.'
YJSS 4, 1 (Aug. 1948), 89–106.
SUBJ 24.4 26.2 34.2 ▪ 48 54 55 61 65

19262 NNC PO P1 G1.3 1928–1949
Lorentz, Hendrik Antoon, 1853–1928.
'Bemerkungen zum Entwurf einer chinesischen Konkursordnung' (Observations on a draft of a Chinese bankruptcy law).
Mecklenburgishe Z. für Rechtspflege, Rechtswissenschaft und Verwaltung 51 (1935), 439–448.
SUBJ 12.2 34.2 ▪ 14.6

19263 GMU S P4 G1.2 1928–1949
Ma, Tsie (Ma Chieh), 1916–.
Die Werbung in der chinesischen Presse (Advertising in the Chinese press).
Unpublished doctoral dissertation, Philosophische Fakultät, Universität München, 1944. 148, 11 p.
SUBJ 14.2 34.2

19264 CSU F P3 G6.1 1928–1949
Nagasaka Hajime.
'Junk transport in Soochow.' Tr. by Andrew Watson of 'Minsen no shoyū kankei' (Ownership of junks and sampans); in *Chūshi no minsengyō: Soshū minsen jittai chōsa hōkoku* (Shipping in Central China: Survey of junks and sampans in Soochow), edited by Chōsabu, Mantetsu (Research Division, South Manchurian Railway); Tokyo: Hakubunkan, 1943, 149–182 [greatly condensed in tr.]. In *Transport in transition: The evolution of traditional shipping in China*. [Analytic entry]
Ann Arbor: U. of Michigan, Center for Chinese Studies, 1972, 71–77. (Michigan abstracts of Chinese and Japanese works on Chinese history, 3)
SUBJ 34.2 ▪ 14.3 24.2

19265 NNC O P3 G1.3 1911–1928
Otte, Friedrich W- K-.
'The evolution of bookkeeping and accounting in China.'
Annalen der Betriebswirtschaft 2, 1 (1928), 166–180.
SUBJ 34.2 ▪ 12.2 14.3 14.6 36.1

19266 CSH P P2 G2.0 1911–1928
Panin, I- A-.
'Kitaiskaia torgovlia: ee osnovy i praktika' (Chinese commerce: Principles and practice).
VM 1925, 1/2, 69–81.
SUBJ 14.3 24 24.3 34.2

19267 CSH P P3 G6.1 1928–1949
Shanghai. She hui chü. (Bureau of Social Affairs).
'Industrial disputes in Shanghai since 1928.' In *Industrial disputes in Shanghai since 1928*, edited by the agency cited. [Sole entry]
Shanghai: Chung Hwa, 1934, 17–78 [s.p.]. [In Chinese as well as English]
SUBJ 22.2 26.4 34.2 36.4 ▪ 12.2 24.4 36.2

19268 CBU F P3 G6.1 1928–1949
Shanghai. She hui chü. (Bureau of Social Affairs).
Industrial disputes (not including strikes and lockouts) in Greater Shanghai, 1929.
Shanghai: Commercial Press, 1931. 164 p. [s.p.]. [See Vol. 2 of this *Bibliography* for Chinese version.]
SUBJ 26 34.2 36.4 ▪ 24.4 26.4

19269 JTT FP P3 G6.1 1928–1949
Shanghai. She hui chü. (Bureau of Social Affairs).
Industrial disputes (not including strikes and lockouts) in Greater Shanghai, 1930.
Shanghai: China Bookstore, 1932. 124 p. [s.p.]. [See Vol. 2 of this *Bibliography* for Chinese version.]
SUBJ 26.4 34.2

19270 MCH O P2 G8.2 1928–1949
Shih, Kuo-heng.
'Social implications of tin-mining in Yunnan.'
PA 20, 1 (Mar. 1947), 53–61.
SUBJ 24.4 26 32.1 34.2 ▪ 12.2 14.3 21.1 26.4 30 39

19271 MCY P P4 G1.2 1911–1949
Song, André Kia-hoai (Sung Chia-huai).
'La responsabilité des administrateurs de sociétés anonymes en droit chinois' (The responsibility of administrators of corporations in Chinese law).
BUA 3e série 3, 9 (1942), 78–121. [Reprinted in *Mélanges juridiques de l'Université l'Aurore* (Aurora University legal miscellany). (Selective entry.) Paris: Lib. du Recueil Sirey, 1946, vol. 1, 114–156.]
SUBJ 12.2 34.2 ▪ 14.6 45 61 63

19272 CSH P P1 G1.2 1928–1949
Stevens, Wayne Mackenzie, 1893–.
'Critique of the Chinese cooperative law.'
NSEQ 8, 4 (Jan. 1936), 773–823.
SUBJ 12.2 34.2 ▪ 36.2

19273 NNC O P2 G1.2 1911–1949
Tayler, John Bernard, 1878–.
'Potentialities of the co-operative movement in China.'
CSPSR 21, 1 (Apr. 1937), 1–33.
SUBJ 24.6 34.2 ▪ 24.3 24.4

19274 MCH P P1 G1.3 1928–1949
Teesdale, J- H-.
'A short analysis of the new Chinese company and partnership law.'
J. of comparative legislation and international law 3rd series 14, 4 (Nov. 1932), 247–254.
SUBJ 12.2 34.2

19275 MCH P P1 G1.2 1911–1949
Théry, François, 1890–, ed.
La loi du 26 décembre 1929 sur les sociétés commerciales (The law of 26 December 1929 on trading companies).
Peiping: Impr. de la 'Politique de Pékin', 1930. 47 p.
'The company law of 1929.' In *Chinese laws*, compiled by China-America Council of Commerce and Industry. [Sole entry]
New York: China-America Council of Commerce and Industry, 1943, 3–17. (CACCI legal series, 3)
SUBJ 12.2 34.2 ▪ 24.3

19276 MCH P P1 G1.2 1928–1949
Théry, François, 1890–, ed.
Loi sur la faillite, promulguée le 17 juillet 1935, entrée en vigueur le 1 octobre 1935 (The bankruptcy law promulgated 17 July 1935 and effective 1 October 1935).
Tientsin: Hautes études, 1935. 31 p. (Droit chinois moderne, 24)
SUBJ 12.2 34.2 ▪ 14.6

19277 MCH P P4 G1.2 1911–1928
Théry, François, 1890–.
Les sociétés de commerce en Chine (Trading companies in China).
Tientsin: Société française de librairie et d'édition, 1929. 437 p. (Doctoral dissertation in Commercial Sciences, Université catholique de Louvain)
SUBJ 12.2 14.3 34.2 66 ▪ 41 45 72

19278 MCH P P1 G1.2 1911–1928
Utescher, ———.
'Warenzeichen und Patentschutz in China' (Trademarks and patent protection in China).
OR 7, 5 (Mai 1926), 78–80.
SUBJ 12.2 34.2 ▪ 14.3 14.4 14.5

19279 MCH F P4 G1.2 1911–1949
Ware, Edith Ellen, 1882–.
'Business contractual relationships in China: Their bearing upon the abolition of extraterritoriality.' In *Business and politics in the Far East*, by E. E. Ware. [Sole entry]
New Haven: Yale U. Press, 1932, 5–128.
SUBJ 12.2 34.2 66 ▪ 12 14.3

19280 NNC O P2 G1.2 1928–1949
Wong Li-jen (Wang Li-jen).
'The experiences of a district director of cooperatives.' Tr. of 'Tso liao san ko yüeh ti ho tso chih tao yüan' (Three months as a director of cooperatives); *Chung-kuo nung ts'un* 3, 4 (Apr. 1937), 75–78. In *Agrarian China*, compiled by Institute of Pacific Relations. [Selective entry]
Chicago: U. of Chicago Press, 1939, 211–216.
SUBJ 24.3 24.6 34.1 34.2 ▪ 12 22 28 32.1

19281 NNC U P5 G1.2 1911–1928
Woo, Tonzoo Choh.
China's business methods and policy.
Unpublished masters thesis in Political Science, Columbia U., 1921. 51 p.
SUBJ 14.3 16.2 34.2 ▪ 14.6 16.4 34.3 36.2 39 47 61 63

19282 NNC P P2 G1.3 1911–1949
Yang, H. K.
'The cooperative movement in China.'

Central Bank of China b. 3, 2 (June 1937), 111–125.
Subj 24.6 34.2 ▪ 12.2 34.1 38

1911-1972
(including 1644-1972)

19283 MCH F P3 G9.5 1928–1972
Espy, John Lee, 1922–.
The strategies of Chinese industrial enterprises in Hong Kong.
Unpublished doctoral dissertation in Business Administration, Harvard U., 1970. 237 p.
Subj 24.4 34.2

19284 CSH P P2 G1.2 1911–1972
Herman, Theodore, 1913–.
'Cooperatives in China.' In *A general handbook of China*, compiled by Far Eastern and Russian Institute, U. of Washington. [Selective entry]
New Haven: Human Relations Area Files, 1956, vol. 2, 1567–1585. (HRAF subcontractor's monographs, 55; Washington 4)
Subj 30 34.1 34.2 ▪ 24.3 24.4 24.6

19285 NIC P P5 G1.2 1928–1972
Kuan Ta-t'ung, et al.
The socialist transformation of capitalist industry and commerce in China.
Peking: Foreign Languages Press, 1960. 133 p. (China knowledge series, 8)
Subj 14 14.3 14.4 16.2 34.2 ▪ 32.1 64

19286 NNC O P5 G1.2 1928–1972
Loh, Robert, 1924–.
Businessmen in China, 2nd ed.
Hong Kong: China Viewpoints, 1960. 92 p.
Subj 14.3 16.2 32.1 34.2 ▪ 14.5 14.6 36.2 64

19287 MCH P P3 G1.5 1895–1972
Wang, Y. C. (Wang I-chü; Wang Chi-ch'ien), 1916–.
'Free enterprise in China: The case of a cigarette concern, 1905–1953.'
PHR 29, 4 (Nov. 1960), 395–414.
Subj 34.2 ▪ 32.1

1949-1972

19288 NNC U P3 G5.1 1949–1972
A shop takes root among the masses, mimeo. Tr. of 'Kuang fu tao shang tien tsai ch'ün chung chung cha hsia shen ken' (Kuang-fu-tao Department Store [Tientsin] takes root among the masses); *Ta kung pao* (Peking) 9 Aug. 1960, 2.
Washington, D.C.: U.S. Joint Publications Research Service, 7 Oct. 1960. 14 p. (JPRS 5663; MC 18,819/1960)
Subj 24.3 34.2 ▪ 32.1

19289 DLC S P4 G1.2 1949–1972
Aleksandrenko, G-.
'Perebudova upravlinnia promyslovosty v krainakh narodnoï demokratii' (The reorganization of industrial management in the people's democracies).
Radians'ke pravo 1958, 6 (lystopad-hruden'), 97–106.
Subj 12 14.4 34.2 ▪ 14.2

19290 CSU P P4 G1.2 1949–1972
Andors, Stephen Paul, 1938–.
'Revolution and modernization. Man and machine in industrializing society: The Chinese case.' In *America's Asia: Dissenting essays on Asian-American relations*, edited by Edward Friedman and Mark Selden. [Selective entry]
New York: Pantheon, 1969, 393–444.
Subj 14 32.1 34.2 64 ▪ 16.1 16.4 32

19291 ELS P P2 G1.2 1949–1972
Brugger, William Christian, 1941–.
Political organisation of the industrial enterprise in China during the new democratic period, 1949–53.
Unpublished doctoral dissertation in Political Science, U. of London [School of Oriental and African Studies], 1971. 440 p.
Subj 14.4 16.4 34.2 36.4 ▪ 12.1 14 22.1 24 24.4 26.4 32.1

19292 MAM F P3 G9.4 1949–1972
Carter, Richard Duane.
An empirical study of selected management practices in the Taiwan metal industries.
Ann Arbor: University Microfilms (Publ. 68-12,460), 1968. 349 p. (Doctoral dissertation in Business Administration, U. of California, Los Angeles)
Subj 17 34.2 ▪ 24.4 26.2

19293 WSU O P3 G2.3 1949–1972
Chao Min.
'One result of the labor competitions: Introducing experiences of competition in technical demonstrations at Anshan.' Tr. of 'Lao tung ching sai ti i hsiang ch'uang ch'ü: An kang chi shu piao yen ching sai ching yen chieh shao' (A momentous event in labor contests: Our experience with technological performance competitions in the Anshan Iron and Steel Company); *Hung ch'i* 1959, 23 (1 Dec.), 17–23. In *Translations from 'Hung-ch'i' (Red flag) No. 23, 1 December 1959, Peiping*, mimeo., compiled by U.S. Joint Publications Research Service. [Sole entry]
Washington, D.C.: JPRS, 4 Mar. 1960, 22–33. (JPRS 3046; MC 5592/1960)
Subj 26.4 34.2

19294 MCY P P5 G1.2 1949–1972
Chen, Theodore H. E. (Ch'en Hsi-en), 1902–.
'The liquidation of private business in Communist China.'
FES 24, 6 (June 1955), 81–89.
Subj 16.2 34.2 ▪ 24.3 32 32.1

19295 CSU O P3 G6.3 1949–1972
Chen Wang-hui (Ch'en Wang-hui). [Jointly authored with Hangchow, Lao tung chü (Labor Bureau).]
'Wage and award system for promoting quality and quantity in production.' Tr. of 'Ch'an chih liang hsiang chieh ho ti kung tzu chia chiang li chih'; *Lao tung* 1959, 23 (3 Dec.), 27–28. In *Wage system in Communist China*, mimeo., compiled by U.S. Joint Publications Research Service. [Analytic entry]
Washington, D.C.: JPRS, 1 June 1960, 17–20. (JPRS 2640; MC 9937/1960)
Subj 26.4 34.2 ▪ 32.1

19296 NNC O P3 G1.5 1949–1972
China [People's Republic]. Kuo wu yüan. Ts'ai mao pan kung shih. Kung tso tsu. (State Council. Trade and Finance Office. Work Team).
Mass economic auditing movement in state-operated enterprises, mimeo. Tr. of 'Ch'ün chung hsing chih ching chi ho suan yün tung tsai kuo ying ch'i yeh: Cheng-tu, Ch'ung-ch'ing, Wu-han ch'i yeh ts'ai wu ta kao ch'ün chung yün tung chien wen tu' (The mass movement for auditing in state-run enterprises: Observations on the mass campaign for financial [reforms] in enterprises in Chengtu, Chungking, and Wuhan); *Ta kung pao* (Peking) 17 Feb. 1960, 2–3.
Washington, D.C.: U.S. Joint Publications Research Service, 15 June 1960. 29 p. (JPRS 2721; MC 14,074/1960)
Subj 24.6 34.2 ▪ 14.4 32.1

19297 NNP O P3 G9.5 1949–1972
Chung, S. Y.
'Our labour management relations.'
TBHK July 1967, 72–77.
Subj 26.4 34.2 ▪ 24.4 36.4

19298 CSU O P4 G2.1 1949–1972
Chung-kuo kung ch'an tang. A-ch'eng chi tien ch'i ch'ang wei yüan hui. (Chinese Communist Party. A-ch'eng Relay Instrument Factory Committee), ed. [A-ch'eng Relay Instrument Factory is in A-ch'eng *hsien*, Heilungkiang; tr. erroneously gives author as Ai-cheng Relay Instrument Factory Committee.]
'The yearlong technical innovation and technical revolution campaign.' Tr. of 'Chi shu ko hsin ho chi shu ko ming yün tung i nien chien' (The year-long campaign for technological innovation and technological revolution); *Hung ch'i* 1960, 23 (1 Dec.), 37–41. In *Translations from 'Hung-ch'i' (Red flag) (Peiping, No. 23, 1 December 1960)*, mimeo., compiled by U.S. Joint Publications Research Service. [Sole entry]
Washington, D.C.: JPRS, 6 Mar. 1961, 59–68. (JPRS 6848; MC 7834/1961)
Subj 24.4 34.2 ▪ 32.1

19299 NNC O P3 G8.1 1949–1972
Chung-kuo kung ch'an tang (Chinese Communist Party). Chung yang cheng chih chü (Central Committee). Ts'ai mao pu (Finance and Trade Dept.). Cheng ts'e yen chiu shih (Policy Research Office) *with* Chung-kuo kung ch'an tang (Chinese Communist Party). Ch'ung-ch'ing shih wei yüan hui (Chungking Municipal Committee). Ts'ai mao pu (Finance and Trade Dept.). Kung tso tsu (Work Team).
'Area general store: A good form of basic-level commercial organization.' Tr. of 'Ti ch'ü tsung ho shang tien: Chi ts'eng shang yeh tsu chih ti i chung hao hsing shih'; *Ta kung pao* (Peking) 9 Oct. 1960, 3. In *Selected translations on economic topics in Communist China*, mimeo., compiled by U.S. Joint Publications Research Service. [Sole entry]
Washington, D.C.: JPRS, 31 Jan. 1961, 1–9. (JPRS 6664; MC 4544/1961)
Subj 24.3 34.2 ▪ 32.1 55

19300 NNC PO P3 G6.1 1949–1972
Chung-kuo kung ch'an tang. Nan-ching shih wei yüan hui. Kung yeh pu. (Chinese Communist Party. Nanking Municipal Committee. Dept. of Industry).
'Investigation report on new management of Pu-chen Rolling Stock Plant in Nanking.' Tr. of 'Tsai ch'i yeh kuan li ti ko ko fang mien chien li ch'ün chung yün tung ti ch'ang kuei: Nan-ching p'u chen ch'e liang kung ch'ang ch'i yeh kuan li kai ko ti tiao ch'a pao kao' (Establishing regulations for mass campaigns in various aspects of business management: A report on managerial reforms in P'u-chen Rolling Stock Plant, Nanking); *Jen min jih pao* 29 May 1960, 7. In *Reports on developments in education, industry and medicine in Communist China*, mimeo., compiled by U.S. Joint Publications Research Service. [Sole entry]
Washington, D.C.: JPRS, 14 July 1960, 30–34. (JPRS 5044; MC 14,403/1960)
Subj 34.2 ▪ 32.1

19301 CSU P P2 G1.3 1949–1972
Ecklund, George N-.
'Communist China tries linear programming.'
AS 1, 7 (Sept. 1961), 27–31.
Subj 14 34.2

19302 CBU P P5 G1.2 1949–1972
Gatterdam, Dwain Roger.
The socialization of private industry in Communist China, 1949–1956.
Unpublished masters thesis in Economics, U. of California, Berkeley, 1960. 126 p.
Subj 14 14.4 34.2 66 ▪ 14.3 14.6 16.2 24.3 24.4 36.2 64

19303 DLC P P7 G1.2 1949–1972
Gel'bras, Vil' Gdal'evich, 1930–.
'Izmenenie rezhima rabochego dnia v ugol'noi promyshlennosti Kitaiskoi Narodnoi Respubliki' (A change in the workday schedule in the coal-mining industry of the People's Republic of China).
BNI 3, 3 (mart 1960), 52–54.
Subj 34.2 ▪ 14.4

19304 DLC P P1 G1.2 1949–1972
Gel'bras, Vil' Gdal'evich, 1930–.
'Novaia sistema premirovaniia na predpriiatiiakh Kitaiskoi Narodnoi Respubliki' (The new bonus system in enterprises in the People's Republic of China).
BNI 2, 12 (dekabr' 1959), 54–56.
Subj 34.2 ▪ 14.4

19305 CSH P P3 G1.2 1949–1972
Gittings, John, 1938–.
'The millers' tale.'
FEER 65, 31 (31 July 1969), 283–286.
Subj 24.4 34.2 ▪ 26.4 32

19306 MCH O P2 G9.5 1949–1972
Grant, Ian.
'Industrial training in Hong Kong: Apprenticeship.'
Hong Kong manager 4, 1 (Jan.–Feb. 1968), 30–32.
Subj 26.4 34.2 ▪ 24.4

19307 CSU FP P2 G1.2 1949–1972
Harper, Paul Frederick, 1929–.
'Workers' participation in management in Communist China.'
Studies in comparative Communism 4, 3/4 (July–Oct. 1971), 111–140.
Subj 34.2 36.4 ▪ 16.4 32.1

19308 NNC P P3 G6.1 1949–1972
Ho Chun (Ho Chün).
'On state-private joint operation of all trades as viewed from seven trades of private industry in Shanghai.' Tr. of 'Lun ch'üan yeh ho ying: Ts'ung Shang-hai ssu ying kung yeh ti ch'i ko hang yeh ti ch'ing k'uang k'an shih hsing ch'üan yeh ho ying ti tso yung' (Unified state-private management of all businesses in a given trade: Experiences in seven types of private industry in Shanghai); *Hsüeh hsi* 1956, 3 (2 Mar.), 19–25.
ECMM 31 (16 Apr. 1956), 26–36.
Subj 24.4 34.2 ▪ 26.4 64

19309 CSU P P2 G9.5 1949–1972
Hong Kong. Co-operative and Marketing Dept.
Annual departmental report by the Registrar of Co-operative Societies and Director of Marketing, 1950/51–1963/64.
Hong Kong: Government Printer. Issued annually, 1951–1964. Average ca. 50 p.
Subj 24.3 24.6 34.2 ▪ 24.1 27 34.1 36.1

19310 NNC P P3 G1.2 1949–1972
Hsia, Ronald (Hsia Hsiu-yung), 1918–.
'Private enterprise in Communist China.'
PA 26, 4 (Dec. 1953), 329–335.
Subj 14.4 32.1 34.2 ▪ 14.3 14.6

19311 CSH U P3 G2.2 1949–1972
Jao Pin.
'Changchun Motor-Car Works strives for an annual output of 150,000 motor-cars.' Tr. of 'Ch'ang-ch'un ch'i ch'e ch'ang wei cheng ch'ü nien ch'an shih wu wan liang ch'i ch'e erh fen tou'; *Hung ch'i* 1958, 12 (16 Nov.), 7–12.
ECMM 156 (26 Jan. 1959), 43–48.
Subj 14.4 34.2 ▪ 32.1

19312 NNC P P4 G1.2 1949–1972
Kruglov, A- M-.
'Sotsialisticheskoe preobrazovanie kapitalisticheskoi promyshlennosti v Kitaiskoi Narodnoi Respublike' (The socialist reorganization of capitalist industry in the People's Republic of China).
KSINA 49 (1961), 24–33.
Subj 14 14.4 34.2 ▪ 16.2 32.1

19313 CSH F P2 G9.4 1949–1972
Kuo, Kuo-shao.
'A survey of the financial position and operating results of some principal private enterprises in Taiwan.'
IFC 32, 6 (Dec. 1969), 27–42.
Subj 24.4 34.2

19314 CSU P P1 G1.2 1949–1972
Kwang, Ching-wen (K'uang Ching-wen).
'The economic accounting system of state enterprises in Mainland China.'
International j. of accounting 1, 2 (Spring 1966), 61–99.
Subj 14 34.2 ▪ 14.6

19315 MCH P P4 G1.2 1949–1972
[La Dany, Ladislao] ———, 1914–.
'Factory administration.'
CNA 387 (1 Sept. 1961), 1–7.
Subj 14.4 34.2 ▪ 16.4 32.1

19316 CSH P P4 G1.2 1949–1972
[La Dany, Ladislao] ———, 1914–.
'Industrial management in 1964–67.'
CNA 694 (2 Feb. 1968), 1–7.
Subj 14 34.2 ▪ 14.4 35

19317 CSH P P2 G1.2 1949–1972
[La Dany, Ladislao] ———, 1914–.
'Industrial management in 1968.'
CNA 735 (29 Nov. 1968), 1–7.
Subj 14.4 34.2 ▪ 16.4 32.1 35

19318 CSH O P3 G2.3 1949–1972
Liaoning. Fu-shun shih [cheng fu] (Fu-shun Municipality). Ko ming wei yüan hui (Revolutionary Committee). Hsieh tso hsiao tsu (Write-up Team) *with* China [People's Republic]. Kuo chia chi [hua] wei [yüan hui] (State Planning Commission). Hsieh tso hsiao tsu (Write-up Team).
'Industrial and mining enterprises can increase production without increasing manpower: Investigation report on the tapping of labor potentials in Fushun municipality.' Tr. of 'Kung k'uang ch'i yeh neng kou tso tao tseng ch'an pu tseng jen: Fu-shun shih wa chüeh lao tung ch'ien li ti tiao ch'a pao kao'; *Jen min jih pao* 16 Jan. 1971, 1, 4.
CES 6, 2 (Winter 1972/73), 14–25.
Subj 34.2 ▪ 24.4 26.4 32.1

19319 CSH U P3 G6.1 1949–1972
Ma T'ien-shui.
'1958 technical revolution on the Shanghai industrial front.' Tr. of 'I chiu wu pa nien Shang-hai kung yeh chan hsien shang ti chi shu ko ming yün tung' (The campaign to revolutionize technology waged on the industrial front in Shanghai during 1958); *Hung ch'i* 1959, 7 (1 Apr.), 23–33. In *Articles from the Chinese Communist theoretical journal 'Hung-ch'i' (Red flag) No. 7, 1 April 1959*, mimeo., compiled by U.S. Joint Publications Research Service. [Sole entry]
Washington, D.C.: JPRS, 4 June 1959, 30–47. (JPRS 745D; MC 9193/1959)
Subj 34.2 ▪ 22.1 24.4

19320 CSH F P4 G9.4 1949–1972
Negandhi, Anant R-.
'Management of industrial enterprises in Taiwan.'
IFC 31, 1 (Jan. 1969), 27–35.
Subj 34.2

19321 MCH P P4 G1.2 1949–1972
Nikol'skii, M- M-.
'Osnovnye printsipy i metody upravleniia gosudarstvennym sektorom ekonomiki KNR v vosstanovitel'nyi period' (Basic management principles and methods in the state sector of the economy of the People's Republic of China during the period of reconstruction).
Uchenye zapiski Kafedry geografii i ekonomiki stran Vostoka Instituta mezhdunarodnykh otnoshenii 2 (1958), 5–23.
Subj 14 14.4 34.2 ▪ 14.2 16.4 36.4

19322 CBU P P1 G1.2 1949–1972
Reyneri, Emilio.
'La lotta per la produzione e l'organizzazione del lavoro nelle fabbriche cinesi' (The struggle for production and the organization of work in Chinese factories).
Vento dell'est 6, 23 (settembre 1971), 85–99.
Subj 34.2 64 ▪ 26.4

19323 NIC P P2 G1.2 1949–1972
Schurmann, Herbert Franz, 1926–.
'The dialectic in action: Vicissitudes in industrial management in China.'
AS 1, 3 (May 1961), 3–18.
Subj 14.4 34.2 64 ▪ 14 32.1

19324 CSH FP P4 G1.2 1949–1972
Schurmann, Herbert Franz, 1926–.
'Management.' In *Ideology and organization in Communist China*, 2nd ed., enl., by H. F. Schurmann. [Analytic entry]
Berkeley, Los Angeles: U. of California Press, 1968, 220–308.
Subj 12 14.4 32.1 34.2 ▪ 12.1 32

19325 NNP O P3 G9.5 1949–1972
Sedgwick, P- C- M-.
'Promoting good labour relations.'
TBHK Aug. 1965, 91–97.
Subj 26.4 34.2 ▪ 22 24.2 28

19326 MCH PO P4 G1.2 1949–1972
Shabalin, V- I-.
'O prirode smeshannykh predpriiatii v KNR' (The nature of mixed enterprises in the People's Republic of China).
Vestnik Moskovskogo universiteta; seriia 8, ekonomika, filosofiia 15, 3 (mai–iiun' 1960), 26–37.
Subj 14.4 16.2 34.2 ▪ 14

19327 NNC P P3 G1.2 1949–1972
Shelekasov, P- V-.
'Beztsekhovaia struktura upravleniia na promyshlennykh predpriatiiakh Kitaia' (The unbureaucratized structure of management in Chinese industrial enterprises).
Sotsialisticheskii trud 4, 7 (iiul' 1959), 36–41.
Subj 14.4 34.2 ▪ 16.4

19328 DLC P P4 G1.2 1949–1972
Shelekasov, P- V-.
'Meropriiatiia po sokrashcheniiu i uluchsheniiu raboty upravlencheskogo apparata v promyshlennosti KNR' (Measures for the improvement of industrial administration in the People's Republic of China).
BNI 2, 6 (iiun' 1959), 57–60.
Subj 12 34.2 ▪ 14.4 32.1

19329 CSH O P3 G2.1 1949–1972
Shen Chung. [Tr. erroneously gives author's surname as Sh'en.]
'Movement to innovate supervisory tools in Mu-tan-chiang city.' Tr. of 'Mu-tan-chiang shih ti kuan li kung chü kai ko yün tung' (The campaign to reform managerial procedures in Mu-tan-chiang municipality [Heilungkiang]); *Hung ch'i* 1960, 12 (16 June), 30–33. In *Translations from 'Hung-ch'i' (Red flag) (Peiping, No. 12, 16 June 1960)*, mimeo., compiled by U.S. Joint Publications Research Service. [Sole entry]
Washington, D.C.: JPRS, 27 Sept. 1960, 13–19. (JPRS 6010; MC 17,639/1960)
Subj 34.2

19330 NNC U P3 G1.2 1949–1972
[Siui Di-sin'] Ssü Di-ssin (Hsü Ti-hsin), 1902–.
'Sotsialisticheskoe preobrazovanie kapitalisticheskoi promyshlennosti i torgovli v Kitae' (Socialist reorganization of capitalist industry and trade in China).
Kommunist 1956, 6 (aprel'), 72–84.

'Die sozialistische Umgestaltung der kapitalistischen Industrie und des Handels in China.' Tr. by W- Fickenscher.
Sowjetwissenschaft; gesellschafts-wissenschaftliche Beiträge 1956, 9 (Sept.), 1101–1116.
Subj 14.3 14.4 32.1 34.2 ▪ 16.2

19331 CSH P P2 G5.0 1949–1972
Stanford U. China Project.
'Socialist transformation of private commerce and industry.' In *North China*, compiled by the organization cited. [Selective entry]
New Haven: Human Relations Area Files, 1956, vol. 2, 838–846. (HRAF subcontractor's monographs, 27; Stanford 1)
Subj 32.1 34.2 ▪ 14.3 14.4

19332 CSH P P2 G1.2 1949–1972
Stanford U. China Project.
'Socialist transformation of private industry and commerce.' In *Central South China*, compiled by the organization cited. [Selective entry]
New Haven: Human Relations Area Files, 1956, vol. 2, 795–801. (HRAF subcontractor's monographs, 28; Stanford 2)
Subj 32.1 34.2 ▪ 14.3 14.4

19333 CSH P P3 G1.2 1949–1972
Stanford U. China Project.
'Socialist transformation of private industry and commerce in East China.' In *East China*, compiled by the organization cited. [Selective entry]
New Haven: Human Relations Area Files, 1956, vol. 2, 876–884. (HRAF subcontractor's monographs, 29; Stanford 3)
Subj 32.1 34.2 ▪ 14.3 14.4

19334 CSH P P2 G8.0 1949–1972
Stanford U. China Project.
'Socialist transformation of private industry and commerce.' In *Southwest China*, compiled by the organization cited. [Selective entry]
New Haven: Human Relations Area Files, 1956, vol. 2, 891–898. (HRAF subcontractor's monographs, 30; Stanford 4)
Subj 32.1 34.2 ▪ 14.3 14.4

19335 CSH P P2 G9.5 1949–1972
Sutu, Hsin (Ssu-t'u Hsin), 1909–.
'The small man's problem.'
FEER 44, 5 (30 Apr. 1964), 271–273.
Subj 24.4 34.2

19336 CSU O P2 G2.3 1949–1972
Ts'ao Yang-ko.
'Wage fund control in Liaoning province.' Tr. of 'Liao-ning sheng ti kung tzu chi chin kuan li kung tso'; *Lao tung* 1959, 23 (3 Dec.), 19–22. In *Wage system in Communist China*, mimeo., compiled by U.S. Joint Publications Research Service. [Analytic entry]
Washington, D.C.: JPRS, 1 June 1960, 1–8. (JPRS 2640; MC 9937/1960)
Subj 26.4 34.2 ▪ 24 32.1

19337 NNC O P3 G5.1 1949–1972
Tseng Kien (Tseng Chien).
'La société textile Houasin, société mixte à capital privé et d'état' (The Hua-hsin Textile Company [Tangshan], a joint public-private enterprise). In *L'économie chinoise sur la voie du socialisme* (China's economy on the road to socialism). [Sole entry]
Peking: Editions en langues étrangères, 1954, 70–80.
Subj 34.2 ▪ 24.4

19338 NNC P P5 G1.2 1949–1972
Voevodin, Stanislav Aleksandrovich, and A- M- Kruglov.
Sotsialisticheskoe preobrazovanie kapitalisticheskoi promyshlennosti i torgovli v Kitaiskoi Narodnoi Respublike (The socialist transformation of capitalist industry and trade in the People's Republic of China).
Moscow: Izd-vo vost. lit-ry, 1959. 164 p.
Subj 14.3 14.4 16.2 32.1 34.2 ▪ 16.4 32

19339 CSH O P7 G5.1 1949–1972
Wang Cheng.
'Experience of the Chinghsi coal mines in continued leaps forward of production.' Tr. of 'Ching-hsi mei k'uang sheng ch'an chih hsü yao chin ti ching yen' (Experiences of coal mines managed by the West Peking Bureau of Mines with a continuing leap forward in production); *Hung ch'i* 1961, 3/4 (1 Feb.), 51–57. In *Translations from 'Hung-ch'i' (Red flag) (Peiping, No. 3-4, 1 February 1961)*, mimeo., compiled by U.S. Joint Publications Research Service. [Selective entry]
Washington, D.C.: JPRS, 20 Apr. 1961, 79–90. (JPRS 8123; MC 13,081/1961)
Subj 24.4 34.2 ▪ 26.4

19340 NIC O P3 G5.4 1949–1972
Wang Li-chih.
'Some questions concerning urban people's communes.' Tr. of 'Kuan yü ch'eng shih jen min kung she ti chi ko wen t'i'; *Ts'ai ching yen chiu* 1959, 2 (Feb.), 10–13.
ECMM 164 (13 Apr. 1959), 19–26.
Subj 20 21.3 24 26 34.2 ▪ 21.4 22 22.1 28 45

19341 CSU F P3 G9.5 1949–1972
Ward, Barbara Elsie, 1919–.
'A small factory in Hong Kong: Some aspects of its internal organization.' In *Economic organization in Chinese society*, edited by William Earl Willmott. [Selective entry]
Stanford: Stanford U. Press, 1972, 353–385.
Subj 24.4 34.2 ▪ 26.2 26.4

19342 CSU O P3 G9.2 1949–1972
Waters, Joseph.
'Department store, Cantonese style.'
EH 6, 10 (Oct. 1967), 36–40.
Subj 34.2

34.3 Guilds
舊式行會　ギルド

1644-1911

19343 FPN S P4 G1.2 1842–1895
Fromageot, Henri.
'L'organisation et le rôle des associations ouvrières et marchandes en Chine' (The organization and role of workers and merchants associations in China).
B. de la Section des sciences économiques et sociales du Comité des travaux historiques et scientifiques 1897, 320–337.
Subj 30 34.3 39 ▪ 23 24.3 24.5 24.6 32.1 36.2 38

19344 MCH S P5 G1.2 1895–1911
Hauchecorne, A-.
'Le commerce chinois et son organisation' (China's commerce and its organization).
BAAFC 1, 3 (jan. 1909), 166–189.
Subj 14.3 14.6 34.2 34.3 38 ▪ 16.2 22.2 25 33

19345 NIC P P4 G1.3 –1911
Kato, Shigeshi (Katō Shigeshi), 1880–1946.
'On the Hang or the association of merchants in China, with especial reference to the institution in the T'ang and Sung periods.'
Memoirs of the Research Dept. of the Toyo Bunko 8 (1936), 45–83.
Subj 34.2 34.3 ▪ 14.3 36.2

19346 NNC P P4 G9.2 –1895
[Kopsch, Henry?] K.
'Guilds, Chinese, and their rules.'
China review 12, 1 (July–Aug. 1883), 5–9.
Subj 34.3 ▪ 22.2 24.3

19347 CSU PO P3 G1.3 1644–1895
MacGowan, Daniel Jerome, 1814?–1893.
'Chinese guilds, or chambers of commerce, and trades unions.'
JRAS-CB new (2nd) series 21, 3 (1886), 133–192.
Subj 34.3 36.2 39 ▪ 14.5 14.6 36.4 38

19348 CSH O P3 G9.2 1895–1911
Mell, Richard.
'Die Bettlegilde von Canton' (The beggars guild of Canton).
OL 25, 37 (15 Sept. 1911), 227–228.
Subj 26 34.3

19349 NIC P P3 G1.3 1895–1911
Morse, Hosea Ballou, 1855–1934.
The gilds of China: With an account of the gild merchant, or Co-hong, of Canton, 2nd ed.
London: Longmans, Green, 1932. 111 p. [Reprinted—Taipei: Ch'eng-wen, 1966. 111 p.] [Reprinted—New York: Russell and Russell, 1967. 111 p.]
Subj 34.2 34.3 39 ▪ 16 32.1 32.2 36.2

19350 MCH P P4 G1.3 1644–1842
Stuzhina, Emiliia Pavlovna, 1931–.
'O kharaktere tsekhovoi organizatsii v Kitae v XVII – pervoi polovine XIX v.' (The nature of guild organization in China from the seventeenth century to the first half of the nineteenth century). [With English abstract]
PV 1961, 1, 35–53.
Subj 11.4 34.3 ▪ 16.2 32.1

19351 NNC P P4 G1.2 1644–1895
Williams, Frederick Wells, 1857–1928.
'Chinese and mediaeval gilds.'
Yale review 1, 2 (Aug. 1892), 200–217; 1, 3 (Nov. 1892), 275–290.
Subj 34.2 34.3 ▪ 24.3 26.2 39

1644-1949

19352 NNC O P2 G1.2 1895–1928
Child, Richard Washburn, 1881–1935.
'Trade unions in China: The gilds or "tongs" into which all trades and businesses are organized.'
Asia (New York: American Asiatic Assn.) 17, 6 (Aug. 1917), 466–468.
Subj 34.3 ▪ 34.2 39 66

19353 MCH S P2 G1.1 –1949
Heek, Frederik van, 1907–.
'De Chineesche handwerkersgilden' (Chinese craft guilds).
Mensch en maatschappij 12, 3 (Mei 1936), 200–216.
Subj 16.2 34.3 ▪ 16 41

19354 NNC P P4 G1.3 –1949
[Hrdličková, Vencesleva] Vena Hrdlickova.
'The professional training of Chinese storytellers and the storytellers' guilds.'
AO 33, 2 (1965), 225–248.
Subj 16.2 31 34.3 ▪ 53 65

19355 CSU FP P2 G3.3 1644–1949
Imahori, Seizi (Imahori Seiji), 1914–.
'Chinese feudal society: An intensive investigation of social groups in Kuei-Sui since 1644.' [Abstract of *Chūgoku hōken shakai no kikō (Fufuhoto) ni okeru shakai shūdan no jittai chōsa* (The structure of feudal society in China: A field survey of social groups in [the capital of] Kuei-suei *hsien* [Huhehot], Suiyuan); Tokyo, 1955.]
Japan science review; literature, philosophy and history 8 (1957), 71–75.
Subj 22 34.3 ▪ 30 36.3

19356 NNC U P4 G1.3 –1949
Liang, Ssu-mu (Liang Shih-mu).
'Handwerk und Handwerksorganisation in China' (Crafts and their organization in China).
Sinica 9, 2 (März 1934), 77–81.
Subj 24.4 34.2 34.3 ▪ 16.2 36.4

19357 NIC FP P3 G5.1 1644–1949
Niida Noboru, 1904–1967.
'The industrial and commercial guilds of Peking and religion and fellow-countrymanship as elements of their coherence.' Tr. of 'Pekin kōshō girudo skūkyō oyobi dōkyōteki ketsugō' (Religious and regional bonds in merchant and craft guilds in Peking); in *Kindai Chūgoku kenkyū* (Studies of modern China), edited by Gakujutsu kenkyū kaigi, Gendai Chūgoku kenkyū tokubetsu iinkai; Tokyo: Kōgakusha, 1948, 55–88.
FS 9 (1950), 179–206.
Subj 30 34.3 39 ▪ 34.2 40

19358 NIC P P3 G1.2 1895–1949
Wou Monpeng (Wu Meng-pan).
L'évolution des corporations ouvrières et commerciales dans la Chine contemporaine (The development of labor unions and trade associations in contemporary China).
Paris: Lib. Geuthner, 1931. 299 p. (Doctoral dissertation, Faculté des lettres, Université de Paris)
Subj 34.3 36.4 ▪ 12.2 16.4 18 30 32.1 36.2

1911-1949

19359 CSH S P3 G1.2 1911–1928
Avenarius, G- G-.
'Kitaiskie tsekhi' (Chinese guilds). [With English abstract; see *Manchuria monitor* 1927, 12, 3–7.]
VM 1927, 11, 49–59; 1927, 12, 49–56.
The Chinese guilds: Brief sketch of their history.
Harbin: Manchuria Research Society, 1928? 78, 19 p.
Subj 14.3 34.3 ▪ 16.2 24.3

19360 ELB F P3 G5.1 1911–1928
Burgess, John Stewart, 1883–1949.
The guilds of Peking.
New York: Columbia U., Faculty of Political Science, 1928. 270 p. (Columbia studies in history, economics and public law, 308) (Doctoral dissertation in Sociology, Columbia U.) [Reprinted—Ann Arbor: University Microfilms, 1965. 270 p.] [Reprinted—Taipei: Ch'eng-wen, 1966. 270 p.] [Reprinted—New York: AMS Press, 1970. 270 p. (Columbia studies in the social sciences, 308)]
Subj 24.3 24.4 34.3 39 ▪ 22.2 26.2

19361 NIC U P3 G1.2 1911–1928
Fong, H. D. (Fang Hsien-t'ing), 1902–.
'Chinese guilds, old and new.'
CSM 23, 6 (Apr. 1928), 14–19.
Subj 34.3

19362 NIC F P6 G8.2 1928–1949
Hsu, Francis L. K. (Hsü Lang-kuang), 1909–, and J. H. Hu.
'Guild and kinship among the butchers in West Town [i.e., Hsi-chou, Ta-li *hsien*, Yunnan].'
ASR 10, 3 (June 1945), 357–364.
Subj 34.3 44 ▪ 24.3 30 41

19363 NIC U P3 G1.2 1911–1928
Peffer, Nathaniel, 1890–1964.
'Guilds and government in China.'
Transpacific 5, 1 (July 1921), 67–69.
Subj 22 34.3 ▪ 39

19364 MCH O P4 G1.2 1911–1928
Stott, Amelia O-.
'Chinese knights of the open palm.'
Asia (New York: American Asiatic Assn.) 27, 10 (Oct. 1927), 830–833.
Subj 26 34.3 ▪ 25 28

1911-1972
(including 1644-1972)

□

1949-1972

□

35 Veterans Associations and the Military in Society
退伍軍人組織及軍人之社會活動
在郷軍人会及び軍人の社会活動

1644-1911

19365 CSU P P2 G1.2 1895–1911
Chesneaux, Jean, 1922–.
'La république des seigneurs de la guerre (1916–1919)' (The warlord republic, 1916–1919). In *De la guerre franco-chinoise à la fondation du Parti communiste chinois, 1885–1921* (From the Sino-French war to the formation of the Chinese Communist Party, 1885–1921), by Marianne Bastid, Marie-Claire Bergère, and J. Chesneaux. [Analytic entry]
Paris: Hatier Université, 1972, 151–178. (HU, Collection d'histoire contemporaine, Histoire de la Chine, 2)
Subj 12 14.2 16 32 35 66 ▪ 14.4 14.6 15 17 36.2 54 64 72

1644-1949

☐

1911-1949

☐

1911-1972
(including 1644-1972)

☐

1949-1972

19366 CSH S P1 G1.2 1949–1972
Adie, William Andrew Charles, 1926–.
'Uneasy riders: The role of military and paramilitary elites in China and some other "developing" countries.'
Asia q. 1972, 2, 167–188.
Subj 15 16.1 35 ▪ 16 17 61 64

19367 NNC P P2 G1.2 1949–1972
Asian Peoples' Anti-Communist League.
An analysis of the Communist 'Learning from the Liberation Army' movement.
Taipei: Asian Peoples' Anti-Communist League, 1964. 64 p. (APACL pamphlets, 85)
Subj 35 64 ▪ 32.1

19368 MCH S P1 G1.2 1949–1972
Brunetti, Mino.
'La militarizzazione nella vita pubblica cinese' (The militarization of Chinese public life).
Civitas 17, 1/2 (gennaio–febbraio 1966), 49–64.
Subj 12.1 15 35 ▪ 17 19

19369 CSU P P1 G1.2 1949–1972
Chang, Parris H. (Chang Hsü-ch'eng), 1936–.
'Changing patterns of military roles in Chinese politics.' In *The military and political power of China in the 1970s*, edited by William Wallace Whitson. [Selective entry]
New York: Praeger, 1972, 47–70.
Subj 32 35 ▪ 15 32.1 54

19370 CSU P P1 G1.2 1949–1972
Chang, Parris H. (Chang Hsü-ch'eng), 1936–.
'Regional military power: The aftermath of the Cultural Revolution.'
AS 12, 12 (Dec. 1972), 999–1013.
Subj 12 32 35 ▪ 15 16.1 32.1

19371 CSH P P2 G9.2 1949–1972
Domes, Jürgen Otto, 1932–.
'Generals and Red Guards: The role of Huang Yung-sheng and the Canton Military Area Command in the Kuangtung Cultural Revolution.'
Asia q. 1971, 1, 3–31; 1971, 2, 123–159.
Subj 25 35 54 ▪ 12 15 32 59

19372 CSU P P3 G1.2 1949–1972
Domes, Jürgen Otto, 1932–.
'The role of the military in the formation of revolutionary committees, 1967–68.'
CQ 44 (Oct.–Dec. 1970), 112–145.
Subj 12 35 ▪ 25

19373 CSU P P1 G1.2 1949–1972
Elmquist, Paul Oscar, 1920–.
'The internal role of the military.' In *The military and political power of China in the 1970s*, edited by William Wallace Whitson. [Selective entry]
New York: Praeger, 1972, 269–290.
Subj 15 35 ▪ 12 32 32.1

19374 CBU P P2 G1.2 1949–1972
Grossmann, Bernhard Paul, 1929–.
'The P.L.A.: Economic aspects.'
RSAEO 1969, 2, 229–241.
Subj 14 35 ▪ 14.5 15

19375 NNC P P2 G4.3 1949–1972
IAkovlev, Aleksandr Grigor'evich, 1928–.
'Rol' Narodno-osvoboditel'noi armii v ekonomicheskom stroitel'stve na okrainakh Kitaiskoi Narodnoi Respubliki v 1950–1955 godakh, na primere Sin'tsziana' (The role of the People's Liberation Army in economic construction in the outlying areas of the People's Republic of China from 1950 to 1955: The example of Sinkiang).
KSIV 21 (1956), 54–70.
Subj 14 15 24.1 35 ▪ 14.4 16.3 34.1 45

19376 CSU P P3 G1.2 1949–1972
Joffe, Ellis, 1934–.
'The Chinese army in the Cultural Revolution: The politics of intervention.'
CS 8, 18 (7 Dec. 1970), 1–25.
Subj 15 35 ▪ 12 32 54

19377 CSH P P2 G1.2 1949–1972
[La Dany, Ladislao] ———, 1914–.
'Army rule.'
CNA 707 (10 May 1968), 1–7; 708 (17 May 1968), 1–7; 710 (31 May 1968), 1–7; 711 (7 June 1968), 1–7; 712 (14 June 1968), 1–7; 715 (5 July 1968), 1–7.
Subj 15 16 35 ▪ 12 14.4 16.1 16.4 17 25

19378 MCH P P1 G1.2 1949–1972
[La Dany, Ladislao] ———, 1914–.
'Decline in the prestige of the PLA.'
CNA 664 (16 June 1967), 1–7.
Subj 15 35 ▪ 16.1 32

19379 CSH P P2 G1.2 1949–1972
[La Dany, Ladislao] ———, 1914–.
'Military imprint on the nation.'
CNA 732 (8 Nov. 1968), 1–7.
Subj 32 35 ▪ 12 25

19380 MCH P P2 G1.2 1949–1972
[La Dany, Ladislao] ———, 1914–.
'Military rule.'
CNA 655 (14 Apr. 1967), 1–7.
Subj 15 25 35

19381 CSH P P2 G1.2 1949–1972
[La Dany, Ladislao] ———, 1914–.
'PLA soldiers in politics.'
CNA 751 (4 Apr. 1969), 1–7.
Subj 15 35

19382 CSH P P1 G1.2 1949–1972
[La Dany, Ladislao] ———, 1914–.
'Soldiers in civilian administration.'
CNA 893 (8 Sept. 1972), 1–7.
Subj 15 35 ▪ 12 32 32.1

19383 CSH P P2 G1.2 1949–1972
[La Dany, Ladislao] ———, 1914–.
'The sugar-coated shells. The Army: Honeyed temptations.'
CNA 755 (2 May 1969), 1–7.
Subj 12.2 15 22.2 35

19384 CSU P P2 G1.2 1949–1972
Nelsen, Harvey Walter, 1939–.
'Military forces in the Cultural Revolution.'
CQ 51 (July–Sept. 1972), 444–474.
Subj 15 35 ▪ 25

19385 MCY P P1 G1.2 1949–1972
Powell, Ralph Lorin, 1917–.
'Commissars in the economy: "Learn from the PLA" movement in China.'
AS 5, 3 (Mar. 1965), 125–138.
Subj 12.1 15 35 ▪ 32.1

19386 CSU P P3 G1.2 1949–1972
Powell, Ralph Lorin, 1917–.
'The military and the struggle for power in China.'
CH 63, 373 (Sept. 1972), 97–102, 134.
Subj 15 32.1 35 ▪ 12 16.1 32

19387 CSU P P1 G1.2 1949–1972
Powell, Ralph Lorin, 1917–.
'The power of the Chinese military.'
CH 59, 349 (Sept. 1970), 129–133, 175–178.
Subj 35 ▪ 15 32

19388 CSU P P2 G1.2 1949–1972
Powell, Ralph Lorin, 1917–.
'Soldiers in the Chinese economy.'
AS 11, 8 (Aug. 1971), 742–760.
Subj 35 ▪ 14.1 14.4

19389 NNC P P1 G1.2 1949–1972
Tryon, Carol Gillespie.
The role of demobilized soldiers in the People's Republic of China, 1955–1965.
Unpublished masters thesis in Public Law and Government, Columbia U., 1969. 61 p. [Certificate essay, East Asian Institute]
Subj 11.4 15 35 ▪ 12.2 32.1

19390 MAM P P2 G1.2 1949–1972
Wang, James C. F. (Wang Chia-fan), 1927–.
The People's Liberation Army in Communist China's political development: A contingency analysis of the military's perception and verbal

symbolization during the Cultural Revolution, 1966–1969.
Ann Arbor: University Microfilms (Publ. 72-10,161), 1972. 282 p. (Doctoral dissertation in Political Science, U. of Hawaii, 1971)
SUBJ 12 15 35 ▪ 14.2 16.1 25 32

19391 CSU P P1 G1.2 1949–1972
Wilson, D- C-.
'The role of the People's Liberation Army in the Cultural Revolution.'
Papers on Far Eastern history 3 (Mar. 1971), 27–59.
SUBJ 15 35 ▪ 12 14.2 25

19392 CSU P P2 G1.2 1949–1972
Wu Chao.
'A study of the Chinese Communist buildup of "production and construction corps" along the Sino-Soviet frontiers.'
IS 6, 2 (Nov. 1969), 56–62.
SUBJ 14.1 15 35 ▪ 11.2 12 12.1 66

36.1 ELITE AND PROFESSIONAL ASSOCIATIONS

社會領導階層與專門職業之會社

エリート及び専門職業者の団体

1644-1911

□

1644-1949

19393 NNC P P1 G1.2 –1949
Hummel, Arthur William, 1884–.
'The New-Culture movement in China.'
AAAPSS 152 (Nov. 1930), 55–62. [Special issue: *China*, edited by Henry F- James]
SUBJ 36.1 60 ▪ 16.1 70

1911-1949

19394 MCY P P3 G5.1 1911–1949
Ayers, Thomas William, 1922–.
'The Society for Literary Studies, 1921–1930.'
PC 7 (Feb. 1953), 34–79.
SUBJ 36.1 60 ▪ 24.2

19395 NIC S P4 G1.3 1911–1949
Chang, Yü-chüan (Chang Yü-ch'üan), 1880–.
'The bar association in China.'
CSPSR 22, 3 (Oct.–Dec. 1938), 235–281.
SUBJ 12.2 36.1

19396 CSH P P2 G1.2 1928–1949
Chao Tzu-fan.
'Left-wing Chinese literary and art movement in the 1930's.'
IS 3, 1 (Oct. 1966), 20–32; 3, 2 (Nov. 1966), 24–35.
SUBJ 36.1 ▪ 14.2 31 32.1 59

19397 MCH O P2 G1.3 1911–1949
Hsu, Leonard S. (Hsü Shih-lien), 1901–.
'The sociological movement in China.'
PA 4, 4 (Apr. 1931), 283–307.
SUBJ 17 36.1 70 ▪ 14.2 18

19398 CSU S P1 G1.2 1911–1949
Lee, Leo Ou-fan (Li Ou-fan), 1939–.
Review of *The gate of darkness: Studies on the leftist literary movement in China*, by T. A. Hsia (Hsia Chi-an).
HJAS 29 (1969), 309–314.
SUBJ 36.1 ▪ 32.1 61

19399 DLC O P2 G1.5 1928–1949
Richardson, H- L-.
'Research on the earth and its products.' In *Wartime China, as seen by westerners*. [Selective entry]
Chungking: China Publishing Co., 1942, 173–188.
SUBJ 36.1 62 70 ▪ 14.1 71

19400 CSU O P2 G1.2 1911–1949
Ting, V. K. (Ting Wen-chiang), 1887–1936.
'Modern science in China.'
Asia (New York: American Asiatic Assn.) 36, 2 (Feb. 1936), 131–134.
SUBJ 36.1 62

19401 CSU O P3 G1.3 1928–1949
Ting, V. K. (Ting Wen-chiang), 1887–1936.
'Scientific research in China: The Academia Sinica.'
Nature 136, 3432 (10 Aug. 1935), 208–211.
SUBJ 36.1 ▪ 70

19402 CSU S P4 G1.2 1911–1928
Uberoi, Patricia Robyn, 1942–.
'Nationalism and internationalism: Conflicting values of the Chinese New Culture Movement.'
China report (New Delhi) 8, 1/2 (Jan.–Apr. 1972), 54–62.
SUBJ 19 36.1 60 64 ▪ 14.2 37 62

1911-1972
(including 1644-1972)

19403 CSH U P2 G1.1 1928–1972
Academia Sinica.
Taiwan's Academia Sinica: Research in Free China, 1927–1961.
Taipei: Heritage Press, 1961. 28 p.
SUBJ 36.1 ▪ 62 70

19404 CSU P P3 G1.2 1928–1972
Hsia, T. A. (Hsia Chi-an), 1916–1965.
'Lu Hsün and the dissolution of the League of Leftist Writers.' In *The gate of darkness: Studies on the leftist literary movement in China*, by T. A. Hsia. [Selective entry]
Seattle: U. of Washington Press, 1968, 101–145. (U. of Washington, Far Eastern and Russian Institute, Publications on Asia, 17)
SUBJ 16.1 36.1 ▪ 32.2 59 64

19405 MAM P P3 G1.2 1895–1972
Rosen, Richard Barry, 1934–.
The national heritage opposition to the new literature and New Culture movements of China in the 1920's.
Ann Arbor: University Microfilms (Publ. 70-13,154), 1970. 161 p. (Doctoral dissertation in History, U. of California, Berkeley, 1969)
SUBJ 16.1 36.1 60 ▪ 14.2 59

1949-1972

19406 CSU O P3 G5.1 1949–1972
Andō Hikotarō, 1917–.
'My two years in Peking.'
JQ 14, 1 (Jan.–Mar. 1967), 26–32.
SUBJ 36.1 ▪ 19 28 55

19407 CSU P P1 G1.2 1949–1972
Beyer, Robert Thomas, 1920–.
'Solid state physics.' In *Sciences in Communist China*, edited by [Sydney Henry Gould] Sidney H. Gould. [Selective entry]
Washington, D.C.: American Assn. for the Advancement of Science, 1961, 645–658. (AAAS publications, 68)
SUBJ 36.1 62 ▪ 16.1 17

19408 CSU PO P2 G9.2 1949–1972
Chang Ch'ang-hai and Ch'iu T'ing.
South China Subtropical Products Research Institute has found new approach toward integration of research, education, and production, mimeo. Tr. of 'Hua-nan ya je tai wu yen chiu so tao sheng ch'an chi ti cha ken li yeh chao tao yen chiu, chiao yü, sheng ch'an san chieh ho ti hsin t'u ching shih hsing "i t'ung ssu pao san chieh ho" fang fa shih ko hsiang kung tso hu hsiang ts'u chin' (The South China Subtropical Products Research Institute has taken root in the field and discovered a new method of integrating research, education, and production, and by practicing the 'i t'ung, ssu pao, san chieh ho' method has stimulated activities on all fronts); *Kuang ming jih pao* (Peking) 15 May 1960, 2.
Washington, D.C.: U.S. Joint Publications Research Service, 21 Sept. 1960. 7 p. (JPRS 3939; MC 17,302/1960)
SUBJ 34.1 36.1 ▪ 17 32.1 62

19409 CSU P P1 G1.2 1949–1972
Chao, Edward C. T. (Chao Ching-te), 1919–.
'Progress and outlook of geology.' In *Sciences in Communist China*, edited by [Sydney Henry Gould] Sidney H. Gould. [Selective entry]
Washington, D.C.: American Assn. for the Advancement of Science, 1961, 497–522. (AAAS publications, 68)
SUBJ 36.1 62 ▪ 11.4 17

19410 FPN P P4 G1.2 1949–1972
Eyraud, Henri.
'Organisation et développement de la science en République populaire de Chine' (The organization and development of science in the People's Republic of China).
NED 3255 (18 jan. 1966), 1–38.
SUBJ 16.1 17 32.1 36.1 62 ▪ 14.4 18

19411 ELB O P3 G5.1 1949–1972
Kuan Zhi-an' (Kuang Jih-an).
'V Institute ekonomiki Akademii nauk Kitaiskoi Narodnoi Respubliki' (The Institute of Economics of the Chinese Academy of Sciences).
VE 1959, 9 (sentiabr'), 150–152.
SUBJ 36.1 70

19412 CSH P P2 G1.2 1949–1972
[La Dany, Ladislao] ———, 1914–.
'Life in the Academy of Science.'
CNA 843 (4 June 1971), 1–7.
SUBJ 36.1 ▪ 32.1 35

19413 CSU P P1 G1.2 1949–1972
Li Hui-lin, 1912–.
'Botanical sciences.' In *Sciences in Communist China*, edited by [Gould Sydney Henry] Sidney H. Gould. [Selective entry]
Washington, D.C.: American Assn. for the Advancement of Science, 1961, 161–195. (AAAS publications, 68)
Subj 36.1 ▪ 17 62

19414 CSH P P4 G1.2 1949–1972
Lindbeck, John Matthew Henry, 1915–1971.
'The organization and development of science.'
CQ 6 (Apr.–June 1961), 98–132. [Reprinted in *Sciences in Communist China*, edited by [Sydney Henry Gould] Sidney H. Gould. (Selective entry.) Washington, D.C.: American Assn. for the Advancement of Science, 1961, 3–58. (AAAS publications, 68)] [Reprinted in *China under Mao: Politics takes command*, edited by Roderick Lemonde MacFarquhar. (Selective entry.) Cambridge: M.I.T. Press, 1966, 333–367.]
Subj 12 17 36.1 ▪ 14 16.1 32.1 62 64 70

19415 NNC O P3 G1.2 1949–1972
Luzhnaia, N- P-.
'Nauchnye uchrezhdeniia Kitaiskoi Narodnoi Respubliki' (Scientific institutions in the People's Republic of China).
Zhurnal neorganicheskoi khimii 3, 2 (fevral' 1958), 542–545.
Subj 36.1 62

19416 CSH O P3 G9.5 1949–1972
Mitchell, Robert Edward, 1930–.
'Research centers: The Social Science Research Centre of the Chinese University of Hong Kong.'
Social sciences information (Paris) 5, 4 (Dec. 1966), 117–118.
Subj 36.1 ▪ 70 71

19417 MCH O P2 G1.2 1949–1972
Needham, Noël Joseph Terence Montgomery, 1900–.
'Chinese science revisited.'
Nature 171, 4345 (7 Feb. 1953), 237–239; 171, 4346 (14 Feb. 1953), 283–285.
Subj 36.1 ▪ 17 56

19418 CSU P P1 G1.2 1949–1972
Rigby, Malcolm.
'Meteorology, hydrology, and oceanography, 1949–1960.' In *Sciences in Communist China*, edited by [Sydney Henry Gould] Sidney H. Gould. [Selective entry]
Washington, D.C.: American Assn. for the Advancement of Science, 1961, 523–614. (AAAS publications, 68)
Subj 36.1 ▪ 17 18 62

19419 NNC U P1 G9.4 1949–1972
Schwind, Martin, 1906–.
'Academia Sinica, Stätte chinesischer Forschung' (The Academia Sinica, a Chinese research center).
Universitas; Z. für Wissenschaft, Kunst und Literatur 13, 6 (Juni 1958), 656–657.
Subj 36.1

19420 DLC U P4 G1.2 1949–1972
Siue IUi (Hsüeh Yu).
'Vo Vsesoiuznom nauchnom farmatsevticheskom obshchestve' (The All-Union Pharmaceutical Society).
Aptechnoe delo 6, 3 (mai–iiun' 1957), 67–69.
Subj 30 36.1 ▪ 32.1

19421 CSH P P4 G1.2 1949–1972
Suttmeier, Richard Peter, 1942–.
'The Academy of Medical Sciences.' In *Medicine and public health in the People's Republic of China*, edited by Joseph R- Quinn. [Selective entry]
[Washington, D.C.]: U.S. Dept. of Health, Education, and Welfare, Public Health Service, National Institutes of Health, 1972, 173–188.
Subj 36.1 56 ▪ 17

19422 MAM P P3 G1.2 1949–1972
Suttmeier, Richard Peter, 1942–.
The Chinese Academy of Sciences: Institutional change in a research-oriented organization.
Ann Arbor: University Microfilms (Publ. 70-7510), 1970. 274 p. (Doctoral dissertation in Government, Indiana U., 1969)
Subj 32.1 36.1 62 ▪ 12 16.1 17 64 66

19423 CSU O P3 G1.3 1949–1972
Wilson, John Tuzo, 1908–.
'Geophysics.' In *Sciences in Communist China*, edited by [Sydney Henry Gould] Sidney H. Gould. [Selective entry]
Washington, D.C.: American Assn. for the Advancement of Science, 1961, 483–496. (AAAS publications, 68)
Subj 36.1 ▪ 17

19424 CSU P P1 G1.2 1949–1972
Wood, Frank Bradshaw.
'Astronomy.' In *Sciences in Communist China*, edited by [Sydney Henry Gould] Sidney H. Gould. [Selective entry]
Washington, D.C.: American Assn. for the Advancement of Science, 1961, 671–683. (AAAS publications, 68)
Subj 36.1 62 ▪ 17

19425 CSU P P1 G1.2 1949–1972
Yu, Arthur J. (Yu Jun-shen), 1930–.
'Chemistry.' In *Sciences in Communist China*, edited by [Sydney Henry Gould] Sidney H. Gould. [Selective entry]
Washington, D.C.: American Assn. for the Advancement of Science, 1961, 659–670. (AAAS publications, 68)
Subj 36.1 62 ▪ 56

36.2 Employers Associations

商業雇主之社團　　雇用者団体

19426 CSU U P3 G6.1 1911–1949
'Exchanges in Shanghai.'
CEJ 12, 1 (Jan. 1933), 43–56.
Subj 24.3 24.6 36.2

19427 CSH P P3 G1.2 1911–1928
Baranov, Ippolit Gavrilovich.
'Kommercheskie obshchestva v Kitae' (Chambers of commerce in China).
EVM 1924, 27 (6 iiulia), 18–21.
Subj 36.2 ▪ 12.2 26.2 32.1

19428 NIC P P3 G9.5 1949–1972
Chen, Francis (Ch'en Hsi-ch'eng), 1905–.
The Jaycee movement in Hong Kong.
Hong Kong: Hong Kong Junior Chamber of Commerce, 1954. 97 p.
Subj 36.2 ▪ 38

19429 NIC P P3 G9.2 1644–1842
Cordier, Henri, 1849–1925.
'Les marchands hanistes de Canton' (The hong merchants of Canton).
TP 2e série 3, 5 (1902), 281–315.
Subj 14.3 24.5 26.2 34.2 36.2 ▪ 21.1 22.2 66

19430 CSH U P4 G1.2 1911–1928
Gladkii, Pavel.
'Torgovye palaty v Kitae' (Chambers of commerce in China).
VA 33 (ianvar' 1915), 43–49.
Subj 36.2 ▪ 14.6 16.2 34.2 34.3

19431 NNP O P3 G9.5 1949–1972
Hong Kong Trade Development Council.
'Hong Kong industry's formidable vanguard.'
TBHK June 1967, 84–88.
Subj 24.3 36.2 ▪ 24.4

19432 NNC P P4 G1.3 1895–1949
Otte, Friedrich W- K-.
'Handels- und Gewerbekammern in China als Fortbildung des Gildenwesens' (Chambers of commerce in China as the successors of the guilds).
MSOSB 36 (1933), 91–112.
Subj 12.2 36.2 ▪ 14.3 14.4 16.2 34.3

19433 HKU P P3 G9.5 1842–1972
Pennell, Wilfrid Victor.
History of Hong Kong General Chamber of Commerce, 1861–1961.
Hong Kong: General Chamber of Commerce, 1961. 84 p.
Subj 24 36.2

19434 ICU P P3 G9.2 1644–1895
Sung, Ann Yun, 1918–.
A study of the thirteen hongs of Kuangtung: A translation of parts of the 'Kuang-tung shih san hang k'ao' of Liang Chia-pin. Tr. by Ann Yun Sung from *Kuang-tung shih san hang k'ao: Ya p'ien chan ch'ien Kuang-tung kuo chi mao i chiao t'ung shih k'ao* (The thirteen hong merchants of Canton: An historical study of foreign trade and transportation in Canton prior to the Opium War); Shanghai: Shang wu yin shu kuan, 1937. [Greatly condensed in tr.]
Unpublished masters thesis in History, U. of Chicago, 1958. 112 p.
Subj 34.2 36.2 ▪ 14.3 26.2 66

19435 MCY P P4 G1.2 1911–1949
Tchen, Ngan-min (Ch'en An-min), and R- H- Mankiewicz.
'Le registre de commerce en Chine' (The commercial register in China).
BUA 3e série 4, 16 (1943), 798–828. [Reprinted in *Mélanges juridiques de l'Université l'Aurore* (Aurora University legal miscellany). (Selective entry.) Paris: Lib. du Recueil Sirey, 1946, vol. 1, 299–263.]
Subj 12.2 14.3 36.2 ▪ 32.1 34.2

19436 MCY P P3 G9.2 1644–1842
Tsiang, Tingfu Fuller (Chiang T'ing-fu), 1895–1965.

'The government and the Co-hong of Canton, 1839.'
CSPSR 15, 4 (Jan. 1932), 602–607.
SUBJ 24.5 34.2 36.2 ▪ 26.2

19437 MAM P P3 G9.2 1644–1895
White, Ann Bolbach, 1939–.
The hong merchants of Canton.
Ann Arbor: University Microfilms (Publ. 68-9249), 1968. 217 p. (Doctoral dissertation in History, U. of Pennsylvania, 1967)
SUBJ 26.2 34.2 36.2 ▪ 32.1 66

36.3 PEASANT ASSOCIATIONS AND MOVEMENTS

農民協會及農民運動

農民団体及び農民運動

1644-1911

19438 NNC P P7 G5.3 1842–1895
Behrsing, Siegfried.
'Chinesische Arbeiten zum Bauernaufstand des Sung Ching-shih' (Chinese works on the peasant uprising of Sung Ching-shih).
Mitteilungen des Instituts für Orientforschung der Deutschen Akademie der Wissenschaften zu Berlin 4 (1956), 128–160.
SUBJ 32.2 36.3 70 ▪ 15 25 32.1 71

19439 CSU S P1 G1.3 –1842
Chan, Hok-lam (Ch'en Hsüeh-lin), 1938–.
'The White Lotus – Maitreya doctrine and popular uprisings in Ming and Ch'ing China.'
Sinologica 10, 4 (1969), 211–233.
SUBJ 32.2 33 36.3 62 ▪ 64 65

19440 DLC P P2 G1.2 –1842
Doronin, B- G-.
'Arkhivnye dokumenty kak istochnik po istorii Velikoi krest'ianskoi voiny v Kitae 1627–1646 godov' (Archival material as a source for the history of the great Chinese peasant uprising of 1627–1646). [With English abstract]
VLGU 15, 14 (1960), 38–50.
SUBJ 32.2 36.3 70 ▪ 15 16.1 16.3 25

19441 CSU P P2 G1.3 –1842
Parsons, James Bunyan, 1921–.
The peasant rebellions of the late Ming dynasty.
Tucson: U. of Arizona Press, 1970. 15, 292 p.
SUBJ 15 25 32.2 36.3 ▪ 12 16.1 65

1644-1949

□

1911-1949

19442 CSH PO P8 G5.4 1911–1928
'Khenanskie "Krasnye piki"' (The Red Spears of Honan).
Materialy po kitaiskomu voprosu 10 (1928), 167–175.
SUBJ 24.1 24.5 25 32.2 36.3 ▪ 12 15 22 23 55

19443 CSH U P8 G7.0 1911–1928
'O sotsial'nom sostave krest'ianskikh soiuzov' (The social structure of peasant associations).
Materialy po kitaiskomu voprosu 10 (1928), 187–188.
SUBJ 36.3 ▪ 16.3

19444 DLC P P7 G1.2 1911–1949
Akhmatov, Iv——.
'K voprosu ob organizatsii sel'skokhoziaistvennykh rabochikh Kitaia: Lilisanevshchina v voprose ob organizatsii sel'skokhoziaistvennykh rabochikh' (Organizing agricultural laborers in China: The Li Li-san line and the question of farm-labor organization).
PK 6/7 (1931), 74–89.
SUBJ 14.1 16.3 36.3 ▪ 16.1 21.2 32.1

19445 NNC P P7 G1.2 1911–1928
Andrews, Carol Corder, 1938–.
The relationship between the Chinese Communist Party and the peasant movement, 1921–1927: Ideological and organizational aspects.
Unpublished masters thesis in Public Law and Government, Columbia U., 1964. 167 p. [Certificate essay, East Asian Institute]
SUBJ 16.3 32.2 36.3 ▪ 14.1 19 64

19446 MCH P P2 G1.3 1911–1928
Belov, Evgenii Aleksandrovich, 1929–.
'Krest'ianskoe vosstanie v Kitae pod rukovodstvom Bai Lana, 1912–1914 gg.' (The peasant uprising in China led by Pai Lang, 1912–1914).
VI 1960, 2 (fevral'), 167–180.
SUBJ 32.2 36.3 ▪ 16

19447 CSH U P7 G1.2 1911–1949
Bianco, Lucien, 1930–.
'Les paysans et la révolution: Chine, 1919–1949' (Peasants and revolution: China, 1919–1949).
Politique étrangère 33, 2/3 (1968), 117–141.
SUBJ 16.3 25 32.2 36.3 61 ▪ 15 19

19448 DLC P P2 G1.5 1911–1928
Chubarov, IUrii Nikolaevich.
'Organizatorskaia rabota kitaiskikh kommunistov sredi krest'ianstva nakanune severnogo pokhoda, 1921–1926' (Chinese Communist organizational work among the peasantry on the eve of the Northern Expedition, 1921–1926).
Uchenye zapiski Akademii obshchestvennykh nauk 42 (1958), 3–32.
SUBJ 15 16.3 32.1 32.2 36.3 ▪ 14.1 64

19449 CSU P P2 G9.2 1911–1928
Etō, Shinkichi, 1923–.
'Hai-lu-feng: The first Chinese soviet government.' Tr. of 'Chūgoku saisho no kyōsan seiken: Kai- Riku-hō sobieto shi' (The first Communist government in China: History of the Hai- Lu-feng soviet [Hai-feng *hsien* and Lu-feng *hsien*, Kwangtung]); in *Kindai Chūgoku kenkyū* (Studies of modern China), edited by Kindai Chūgoku kenkyū iinkai, Tōyō bunko; Tokyo: Tōkyō daigaku, Shuppankai, 1958, vol. 2, 1–98. [Rev. in tr.]
CQ 8 (Oct.–Dec. 1961), 160–183; 9 (Jan.–Mar. 1962), 149–181.
SUBJ 22 25 26.3 32.2 36.3 ▪ 22.1 24.1 26.1 64

19450 NNC P P7 G7.0 1911–1928
Freier, B-.
'Noveishie etapy krest'ianskogo dvizheniia v Kitae' (The latest stages in the peasant movement in China).
Agrarnye problemy 1, 2 (noiabr' 1927), 33–61.

'Die neuesten Etappen der Bauernbewegung in China.'
Agrar-Probleme 1, 1 (1928), 110–148.
SUBJ 14.1 32.2 36.3 ▪ 14.6 16.3 22.2 32

19451 MCH O P7 G5.4 1911–1928
G. S.
'Krest'ianskoe vosstanie v Khenani' (The peasant uprising in Honan).
NV 13/14 (1926), 1–16.
SUBJ 35 36.3 ▪ 26.3 32.2

19452 NNC S P2 G5.0 1911–1928
Hegel, Charlotte Beahan.
The White Wolf: The career of a Chinese bandit [Pai Lang], *1912–1914.*
Unpublished masters thesis in History, Columbia U., 1969. 55 p. [Certificate essay, East Asian Institute]
SUBJ 25 36.3 ▪ 12 32.2

19453 MCH P P2 G1.2 1911–1928
Hofheinz, Roy Mark, Jr., 1935–.
The peasant movement and rural revolution: Chinese Communists in the countryside, 1923–7.
Unpublished doctoral dissertation in Political Science, Harvard U., 1967. 11, 426 p.
SUBJ 11.3 12 22.1 32.2 36.3 ▪ 14.1 16.3 19 64

19454 DLC FP P7 G9.2 1911–1928
Iolk, Evgenii Sigizmundovich, 1900–1942.
'Krest'ianskoe dvizhenie v Guandune' (The peasant movement in Kwangtung). In *Kantonskaia kommuna: sbornik statei i materialov* (Articles and documents on the Canton commune), compiled by Nauchno-issledovatel'skii institut po Kitaiu, Kommunisticheskaia akademiia. [Selective entry]
Moscow: Gosizdat, 1929, 201–250.
SUBJ 20 26.3 36.3 ▪ 15 26.1 28 32.1 32.2 66

19455 CSH P P8 G1.2 1911–1928
[Ivanov, Aleksei Alekseevich] A. Ivin, pseud., 1885–1942.
Krasnye piki: krest'ianskoe dvizhenie v Kitae (The Red Spears: The peasant movement in China).
Moscow: Moskovskii rabochii, 1927. 157 p.
SUBJ 14.1 16.3 32.1 32.2 36.3 54 ▪ 24.1 26.3 28 34.1 35 66

19456 CSH P P2 G5.4 1911–1928
Kostiaeva, Aleksandra Sergeevna, 1932–.
'Vosstanie "Krasnykh pik" v Khenani zimoi 1926 g.' (The Red Spears uprising in Honan during the winter of 1926). In *Strany Dal'nego Vostoka i IUgo-Vostochnoi Azii (problemy istorii i ekonomiki)* (Problems of Far Eastern and Southeast Asian history and economics), compiled by Institut vostokovedeniia, Akademiia nauk SSSR. [Selective entry]

Moscow: Nauka, Glav. red. vost. lit-ry, 1969, 34–41.
Subj 15 32.2 36.3 ▪ 25 26.3

19457 NNC P P7 G1.2 1911–1949
Lamb, Jefferson D. H. (Lin Tung-hai), 1895–.
The development of the agrarian movement and agrarian legislation in China, 1912–1930.
Shanghai: Commercial Press, 1934. 228 p.
Subj 12.2 14.1 36.3 ▪ 12.1 16.3 32 34.1

19458 CBU U P8 G1.3 1911–1949
Mänchen-Helfen, Otto, 1894–.
'Die Bauernbewegung in China' (The peasant movement in China).
Der Kampf 23, 8 (Aug. 1930), 317–330; 23, 9 (Sept. 1930), 371–390.
Subj 14.1 16.3 32.2 36.3 ▪ 14.5 14.6 15 16.1 18 24.4 25

19459 CSH U P7 G1.2 1911–1928
Mamaev, I-.
'Krest'ianskoe dvizhenie' (The peasant movement). In *O Kitae: politiko-ekonomicheskii sbornik* (Articles on China's political economy), edited by [Solomon Abramovich Dridzo] A. Lozovskii, pseud. [Selective entry]
Moscow: Gosizdat, 1928, 115–140.
Subj 16.3 32.2 36.3 ▪ 14.1 16.1 32

19460 CSH F P8 G7.2 1911–1928
Mao Tse-tung, 1893–.
'Report on an investigation of the peasant movement in Hunan.' Tr. of 'Hu-nan nung min yün tung k'ao ch'a pao kao'; in *Mao Tse-tung hsüan chi* (Selected works of Mao Tse-tung), 2nd ed.; Peking: Jen min ch'u pan she, 1960, vol. 1 [originally published in *Hsiang tao chou pao* 191 (12 Mar. 1927)]. In *Selected works of Mao Tse-tung*, edited by Mao Tse-tung hsüan chi ch'u pan wei yüan hui (Committee for the Publication of the Selected Works of Mao Tse-tung), Chung yang wei yüan hui (Central Committee), Chung-kuo kung ch'an tang (Chinese Communist Party). [Selective entry]
Peking: Foreign Languages Press, 1965, vol. 1, 23–59.
Subj 26.3 32.2 36.3 ▪ 22.2 25 26.1 42

19461 NNP P P8 G1.2 1911–1928
Shchukar', M-.
'Krest'ianskie soiuzy v Kitae' (Chinese peasant unions).
Sputnik agitatora 1927, 10 (30 maia), 25–30.
Subj 16.3 32.2 34.1 36.3

19462 NNC U P7 G1.2 1911–1928
Val'den, V-.
'Krest'ianskoe dvizhenie v Kitae' (The peasant movement in China).
Agrarnye problemy 1, 1 (iiul' 1927), 31–43.
Subj 14.1 32.2 36.3 ▪ 14 16.3 25

19463 CSH P P2 G1.2 1911–1949
[Vishniakova-Akimova, Vera Vladimirovna] V. Vishniakova.
'Krest'ianskoe dvizhenie v Kitae za leto 1929 g.' (The peasant movement in China in the summer of 1929).
PK 2 (1930), 157–180.
Subj 15 32.2 36.3 ▪ 12.1 14.1 16.1 16.3 18 32 42

19464 CSH P P7 G1.2 1928–1949
[Vishniakova-Akimova, Vera Vladimirovna] V. Vishniakova.
'Krest'ianskoe dvizhenie v Kitae za leto 1930 g.' (The peasant movement in China in the summer of 1930).
PK 4/5 (1930), 160–171.
Subj 15 32 32.2 36.3 ▪ 16.3

19465 CSH F P7 G8.1 1928–1949
Yin Lien-ken (Ying Lien-keng), 1904?–, and Yu-choh Wang.
'Farmers association in Szechwan.'
EF 30 (Mar. 1944), 390–397.
Subj 36.3

1911-1972
(including 1644-1972)

19466 NNC F P7 G9.4 1928–1972
Anderson, Walfred Albin, 1892–.
Farmers' associations in Taiwan: A report to the Joint Commission on Rural Reconstruction, Economic Cooperation Mission to China, mimeo.
Taipei: Chinese-American Joint Commission on Rural Reconstruction, 1950. 70 p.
Subj 24.1 34.1 36.3 ▪ 27 32.1 54 55

19467 MCH S P7 G1.2 1911–1972
Gillin, Donald George, 1930–.
'Peasant and Communist in modern China: Reflections on the origins of the Communist-led peasant movement.'
South Atlantic q. 60, 4 (Autumn 1961), 434–446.
Subj 32.2 36.3 ▪ 15 19 64

19468 NIC F P7 G9.4 1928–1972
Kwoh, Min-hsioh (Kuo Min-hsüeh).
The farmers' associations movement of Taiwan (Formosa).
Unpublished masters thesis in Sociology, Cornell U., 1957. 88 p.
Subj 36.3 ▪ 32.1 34.1

19469 CSU O P2 G1.2 1911–1972
Lin, Yi-Chou.
'La révolution paysanne dans la révolution démocratique' (The peasant revolution in the democratic revolution).
CFC 10 (juin 1961), 1–22.
Subj 14.1 32.2 36.3 64 ▪ 16.3

1949-1972

19470 NIC S P8 G1.2 1949–1972
Lee, Shu-ching (Li Shu-ch'ing), 1908–.
'Agrarianism and social upheaval in China.'
AJS 56, 6 (May 1951), 511–518.
Subj 14.1 36.3 ▪ 12.1 14 14.5

19471 MCH P P7 G1.2 1949–1972
Li Ming-hua.
'"Peasants' association" and "class struggle" in rural areas in China Mainland.'
IS 1, 7 (Apr. 1965), 46–52.
Subj 36.3 ▪ 16 16.3 22.1 32.1

36.4 Labor Unions and the Labor Movement
工會及勞工運動
労働組合及び労働運動

1644-1911

□

1644-1949

19472 CSU U P5 G9.0 1895–1928
C. H. L.
'The Kwangtung Mechanics' Union.'
PT new (2nd) series 2, 7 (30 Apr. 1932), 171–176.
Subj 36.4 ▪ 36.2

19473 CBU S P4 G1.2 1895–1949
Eichhorn, Werner, 1899–.
'Zur Vorgeschichte der chinesischen Arbeiterbewegung' (Antecedents of the Chinese labor movement).
Saeculum 12, 1 (1961), 30–60.
Subj 16.4 36.4 ▪ 11.2 11.4 14.4 32.2 34.2 34.3

19474 GMS U P4 G1.2 1895–1928
[Heller, Leo N-] L. Geller.
'Natsional'noe dvizhenie i rabochii klass' (The nationalist movement and the working class).
KIP 5, 9 (sentiabr' 1925), 5–18.

'Nationale Bewegung und Arbeiterklasse.'
RGI 5, 9 (Sept. 1925), 106–116. [Reprinted in *Arbeiterbewegung und Revolution in China* (The labor movement and revolution in China), by Karl Radek et al. (Selective entry.) Berlin: Führer, 1925, 40–72.]

'Le mouvement national et la classe ouvrière en Chine.'
ISR 56 (sept. 1925), 679–689.
Subj 16.4 36.4 ▪ 32

19475 CSH U P4 G1.1 1842–1928
[Heller, Leo N-] L. Geller.
'Rabochee dvizhenie' (The labor movement). In *O Kitae: politiko-ekonomicheskii sbornik* (Articles on China's political economy), edited by [Solomon Abramovich Dridzo] A. Lozovskii, pseud. [Selective entry]
Moscow: Gosizdat, 1928, 69–114.
Subj 16.4 32.2 36.4 ▪ 14.4 25 32 47 66

19476 NNC P P2 G1.2 1895–1949
Lamb, Jefferson D. H. (Lin Tung-hai), 1895–.
The labour movement and labour legislation in China.
Shanghai: China United Press, 1933. 12, 252 p.
Subj 12.2 16.4 36.4 ▪ 14.4 18 32 32.1 32.2 34.2 47 52

19477 MCH PO P4 G1.2 1895–1928
Ma, Chao-chun (Ma Ch'ao-chün), 1885–.
History of the labor movement in China. Tr. by Peter Min Chi Liang of *Chung-kuo lao kung wen t'i* (Chinese labor problems); Shanghai: Min chih shu chü, 1927; 114 p.
Taipei: China Cultural Service, 1955. 169 p.
Subj 16.4 18 36.4 ▪ 12.2 22.2 32 32.1 32.2 34.3 39 47

19478 DLC U P4 G1.1 1895–1928
Mandalian, T-.
Rabochee dvizhenie Kitaia (The labor movement in China).
Moscow: Moskovskii rabochii, 1928. 224 p.
SUBJ 14.4 16.4 36.4 ▪ 16.2 18 32.2 34.3

19479 GMS U P2 G1.3 1895–1928
Mstislavskii, S- (S. Mstislawski).
'Rabochee dvizhenie v Kitae' (The labor movement in China).
KIP 5, 9 (sentiabr' 1925), 19–36.
'Die Arbeiterbewegung in China.'
RGI 5, 9 (Sept. 1925), 116–126. [Reprinted in *Arbeiterbewegung und Revolution in China* (The labor movement and revolution in China), by Karl Radek et al. (Selective entry.) Berlin: Führer, 1925, 73–102.]
'Le mouvement ouvrier en Chine.'
ISR 56 (sept. 1925), 703–714.
SUBJ 32.2 36.4 ▪ 18 32.1

19480 NNC P P3 G1.2 1895–1928
Tsing, Chin-chun (Tseng Chin-ch'un).
Le mouvement ouvrier en Chine (The labor movement in China).
Paris: Lib. Geuthner, 1929. 176 p. (Institut franco-chinois de Lyon, Etudes et documents, 7) (Doctoral dissertation, Faculté de droit, Université de Lyon)
SUBJ 16.4 18 34.2 36.4 ▪ 30 47

19481 NIC P P3 G1.1 1842–1928
Tso, S. K. Sheldon (Chu Shih-k'ang), 1901–.
The labor movement in China.
Shanghai: Commercial Press, 1928. 230 p. (Doctoral dissertation, Indiana U., 1928)
SUBJ 16.4 36.4 ▪ 12.2 14.4 18 34.2 34.3 47 64

1911-1949

19482 NNP P P3 G1.1 1911–1928
'Anderthalbjahre Streiks in China' (A year and a half of strikes in China).
Sozial-ökonomische Arbeiter-Rundschau 2, 9 (Sept. 1927), 1–6.
SUBJ 36.4

19483 NNC U P4 G1.3 1911–1928
'Kitai: rabochee dvizhenie' (The labor movement in China).
KIP 1, 11 (dekabr' 1921), 572–577.
'Die chinesische Arbeiterbewegung.'
RGI 1, 11 (31 Dez. 1921), 54–58.
'Chine: le mouvement ouvrier.'
ISR 11 (déc. 1921), 684–690.
SUBJ 36.4 ▪ 16.4 34.3

19484 NIC O P3 G1.2 1928–1949
'Labor and trade union organizations.'
CEJ 7, 4 (Oct. 1930), 1099–1121.
SUBJ 16.4 18 36.4 ▪ 14.4

19485 NNC P P3 G1.2 1928–1949
'Labor disputes and strikes in China, 1932.'
NWSS 6, 44 (30 Oct. 1933), 199, 201–206.
SUBJ 36.4 ▪ 16.4

19486 NNC P P3 G6.1 1911–1949
'Labor strikes in Shanghai cotton mills, 1918–1929.'
NWSS 5, 32 (8 Aug. 1932), 143, 145–148.
SUBJ 26.4 36.4 ▪ 24.4

19487 NNC P P3 G1.3 1928–1949
'Labor unions in China, 1932.'
NWSS 6, 29 (17 July 1933), 137, 139–141.
SUBJ 36.4 ▪ 16.4

19488 NNC P P3 G1.3 1928–1949
'Organized labor in China, 1930.'
NWSS 4, 10 (9 Mar. 1931), 55, 58.
SUBJ 36.4 ▪ 16.4

19489 NNC O P4 G1.3 1911–1928
'Otchet II Kongressu Profinterna o rabochem dvizhenii v Kitae' (Report to the Second Profintern Congress on the labor movement in China).
KIP 3, 1 (ianvar' 1923), 132–137.
'Berichte an den zweiten Kongress der RGI: Die Arbeiterbewegung in China.'
RGI 3, 1 (Jan. 1923), 71–74.
'Rapports présentés au IIe Congrès de l'I.S.R.: rapport sur le mouvement ouvrier chinois.'
ISR 24 (mai 1923), 78–81.
SUBJ 36.4 ▪ 14.4

19490 DLC PO P2 G1.1 1911–1928
Rabochii Kitai v bor'be protiv imperializma: otchet pervoi profsoiuznoi delegatsii SSSR v Kitai (Workers' China in the struggle against imperialism: Report of the first U.S.S.R. trade-union delegation to China).
Moscow: Profizdat, 1927. 175 p.
SUBJ 22.1 26.4 28 36.4 54 66 ▪ 24.4 25 26.2 26.3 32.2 64

19491 NNC U P4 G1.3 1911–1928
'Stachechnoe dvizhenie v Kitae' (The strike movement in China).
KIP 3, 2 (fevral' 1923), 294–299.
'China: Die Streikbewegung.'
RGI 3, 2 (Feb. 1923), 164–166.
'Chine: le mouvement de grèves.'
ISR 25 (juin 1923), 60–63.
SUBJ 36.4 ▪ 24.4

19492 NNC P P3 G5.1 1911–1949
'Statistics on labor disputes in the province of Hopei and the municipalities of Peiping and Tientsin.'
NWSS 3, 12 (24 Mar. 1930), 57, 60.
SUBJ 16.4 36.4 ▪ 26.4

19493 NNC P P4 G9.2 1928–1949
'Statistics on trade unions in Kwangtung, 1929.'
NWSS 3, 20 (19 May 1930), 95, 98–100.
SUBJ 36.4 ▪ 32.1

19494 CSU P P4 G1.2 1928–1949
'Trade unionism in China since 1929.'
ILR 28, 5 (Nov. 1933), 688–694.
SUBJ 36.4 ▪ 12.2 32.1

19495 NNC F P3 G9.2 1911–1928
'Trade unions in Canton, 1927.'
NWSS 3, 15 (4 Apr. 1930), 71, 74.
SUBJ 36.4 ▪ 26.4

19496 NNC P P4 G1.2 1911–1928
'Trade unions in China, 1928.'
NWSS 3, 48 (1 Dec. 1930), 225, 228–230.
SUBJ 36.4 ▪ 14.4 16.4

19497 NNC F P3 G5.1 1928–1949
'Trade unions in Tientsin.'
NWSS 3, 18 (5 May 1930), 87, 90.
SUBJ 36.4 ▪ 21.4 26.4

19498 CSH P P3 G6.1 1911–1928
A. A.
'Tri shankhaiskikh vosstaniia' (Three Shanghai uprisings).
PK 2 (1930), 63–86.
SUBJ 25 32.2 36.4 ▪ 22.1 26.2 26.4

19499 NNC P P3 G9.2 1911–1928
Akatova, Tat'iana Nikolaevna, 1923–.
'Antiimperialisticheskaia bor'ba rabochego klassa Guanduna v period pervoi grazhdanskoi revoliutsionnoi voiny v Kitae, 1924–1927' (The anti-imperialist struggle of the Kwangtung working class during the First Revolutionary Civil War in China, 1924–1927).
KSIV 16 (1955), 1–17.
SUBJ 26.4 36.4 66 ▪ 22.1 32.2

19500 DLC P P4 G1.1 1911–1928
Akatova, Tat'iana Nikolaevna, 1923–.
'Predislovie' (Foreword). In *Rabochee dvizhenie v Kitae: revoliutsiia 1924–1927 gg.* (The labor movement in China: The Revolution of 1924–1927), compiled by Institut narodov Azii, Akademiia nauk SSSR. [Sole entry]
Moscow: Nauka, Glav. red. vost. lit-ry, 1966, 3–15.
SUBJ 16.4 32 32.2 36.4 ▪ 64 71

19501 NNC P P3 G9.0 1911–1928
Akatova, Tat'iana Nikolaevna, 1923–.
'Shamian'skii rasstrel 23 iiunia 1925 g.' (The Shameen massacre [i.e., Shakee Road Incident] of 23 June 1925).
KSIV 11 (1954), 72–81.
SUBJ 32.1 32.2 36.4 66

19502 NNC P P3 G9.0 1911–1928
Akatova, Tat'iana Nikolaevna, 1923–.
Siangan-Guanchzhouskaia (Gonkong-Kantonskaia) zabastovka (The Canton – Hong Kong strike).
Moscow: Izd-vo vost. lit-ry, 1959. 149 p.
SUBJ 32.2 36.4 ▪ 16.4 32 32.1

19503 CSH FP P2 G1.1 1911–1928
Al'skii, M-.
Kanton pobezhdaet (Canton will triumph).
Moscow: Izd-vo Kom. akad., 1927. 152 p.
SUBJ 12 24 26 36.3 36.4 64 ▪ 12.2 15 17 21.3 25 32 32.1 32.2

19504 DLC P P2 G7.0 1911–1928
Andreichik, A-.
'IV Vsekitaiskii S"ezd Profsoiuzov' (The Fourth Pan-Chinese Trade Union Congress). In *Rabochii Kitai v 1927 godu: sbornik statei* (Articles on workers' China in 1927), edited by [Solomon Abramovich Dridzo] A. Lozovskii, pseud. [Selective entry]
Moscow: Profintern, 1928, 250–257.
SUBJ 18 36.3 36.4 ▪ 16.4 32.1

19505 CSH P P3 G2.3 1928–1949
Avdoshchenkov, A- IA-.
'Rabochie konflikty v iuzhnoi Man'chzhurii v 1929 g.' (Labor conflicts in southern Manchuria in 1929).
VM 1930, 9, 31–43.
SUBJ 26.4 36.4 ▪ 32.2

19506 MCH P P3 G9.0 1911–1928
Ayers, Thomas William, 1922–.
'The Hong Kong strikes, 1920–1926.'
PC 4 (Apr. 1950), 94–130.
Subj 26.4 36.4 ▪ 32.1 34.2 34.3 47 54

19507 NIC P P3 G6.1 1911–1928
Ayers, Thomas William, 1922–.
'Shanghai labor and the May 30th movement.'
PC 5 (Apr. 1950 [i.e., May 1951]), 1–38.
Subj 36.4 ▪ 26.2 26.4 32.2

19508 CSU O P3 G6.1 1928–1949
Barnett, Arthur Doak, 1921–.
'Pressures on labor' [report to Institute of Current World Affairs, October 1948]. In *China on the eve of Communist takeover*, by A. D. Barnett. [Selective entry]
New York: Praeger, 1963, 71–82.
Subj 36.4 ▪ 24.6 32.1

19509 NNC P P3 G6.1 1911–1928
Bereznyi, Lev Abramovich, 1915–.
'Geroicheskoe vosstanie shankhaiskogo proletariata v marte 1927 g.' (The heroic uprising of the Shanghai proletariat in March 1927).
SK 1958, 3, 97–107.
Subj 22.1 26.4 32.2 36.4 ▪ 22.2 66

19510 DLC P P3 G6.1 1911–1928
Bereznyi, Lev Abramovich, 1915–.
'Pod"em zabastovochnogo dvizheniia v Shankhae letom 1926 g.' (The upsurge in the strike movement in Shanghai in the summer of 1926).
UZLGU 282 (1959), 66–79.
Subj 26.4 36.4 ▪ 32.1 32.2

19511 DLC O P3 G6.1 1911–1928
[Chen Po-ta?] TSzen'-Fo-ta (Ch'en Po-ta), 1904–.
'Shankhaiskoe rabochee dvizhenie: doklad TSzen' Fo-ta (predstavitelia Shankhaiskogo soveta profsoiuzov) na Tikhookeanskoi konferentsii profsoiuzov' (The Shanghai labor movement: Report by Ch'en Po-ta, Shanghai Trade Union Council representative, at the Pan-Pacific Trade Union Congress). In *Rabochii Kitai v 1927 godu: sbornik statei* (Articles on workers' China in 1927), edited by [Solomon Abramovich Dridzo] A. Lozovskii, pseud. [Selective entry]
Moscow: Profintern, 1928, 220–244.
Subj 15 26.2 26.4 28 36.4 ▪ 24.2 66

19512 NIC P P4 G1.2 1911–1928
Chen Ta (Ch'en Ta), 1892–.
'Analysis of strikes in China, from 1918 to 1926.' Tr. of 'Chin pa nien lai kuo nei pa kung ti fen hsi'; *Ch'ing hua hsüeh pao* 3, 1 (June 1926), 803–863.
CEJ 1, 10 (Oct. 1927), 843–865; 1, 11 (Nov. 1927), 945–962; 1, 12 (Dec. 1927), 1077–1088.
Subj 14 14.4 16.4 32 36.4 ▪ 16.2 18 36.2 66

19513 NIC U P3 G1.3 1911–1949
Chen Ta (Ch'en Ta), 1892–.
'Fundamentals of the Chinese labor movement.'
AAAPSS 152 (Nov. 1930), 196–205. [Special issue: *China*, edited by Henry F. James]
Subj 36.4

19514 NNC P P2 G1.3 1911–1928
Chen Ta (Ch'en Ta), 1892–.
'Labor unrest in China.'
Monthly labor review 13, 2 (Aug. 1921), 16–30.
Subj 18 22.2 36.4 ▪ 34.3

19515 NNC O P3 G1.3 1911–1928
Chen Ta (Ch'en Ta), 1892–.
'The labour movement in China.'
ILR 15, 3 (Mar. 1927), 339–363. [Reprinted in *Problems of the Pacific, 1927*, edited by John Bell Condliffe. (Selective entry.) Chicago: U. of Chicago Press, 1928, 409–435.]
Subj 36.4 ▪ 12.2 14.4 16.4 47

19516 NNC S P3 G9.5 1911–1928
Chen Ta (Ch'en Ta), 1892–.
'Shipping strike in Hong Kong.'
Monthly labor review 14, 5 (May 1922), 9–15.
Subj 36.4 ▪ 24.2 28

19517 NNC FP P3 G1.2 1911–1928
Chesneaux, Jean, 1922–.
Le mouvement ouvrier chinois de 1919 à 1927.
The Hague: Mouton, 1962. 652 p. (Ecole pratique des hautes études de Sorbonne, Sixième section [sciences économiques et sociales], Le monde d'outre-mer passé et présent, Etudes, 1er série, 17) (Revision of *Recherches sur l'histoire du mouvement ouvrier chinois de 1919 à 1927* [Investigations on the history of the Chinese labor movement, 1919–1927], doctoral dissertation, Faculté de droit, Université de Paris).
The Chinese labor movement, 1919–1927. Tr. by Hope M- Wright.
Stanford: Stanford U. Press, 1968. 11, 574 p.
Subj 14.4 16.4 18 32.2 34.2 36.4 ▪ 16 29 34.3 47 56 66 72

19518 NNC O P4 G1.3 1911–1928
[Den Chzhun-sia] Dunchunshia (Teng Chung-hsia), 1897–1933.
'Profdvizhenie v Kitae za 1928 g.' (The trade-union movement in China in 1928).
KIP 9, 4 (aprel' 1929), 308–314.
'Die Gewerkschaftsbewegung im Jahre 1928.'
RGI 9, 4 (Apr. 1929), 196–199.
Subj 36.4 ▪ 32.2

19519 NNC O P3 G6.1 1911–1949
[Den Chzhun-sia] Tsenhungsiang (Teng Chung-hsia), 1897–1933.
'Zheltye proforganizatsii v Shankhae.'
KIP 9, 1 (ianvar' 1929), 64–68.
'Die gelben Gewerkschaften in Schanghai.'
RGI 9, 1 (Jan. 1929), 43–45.
'Les organisations jaunes à Shangaï.'
ISR 96 (jan. 1929), 60–63.
'The yellow trade unions in Shanghai.'
R.I.L.U. magazine 1, 4 (Jan. 1929), 183–185.
Subj 36.4 ▪ 32.1

19520 NNC O P3 G1.2 1911–1928
[Dridzo, Solomon Abramovich] A. Lozovskii, pseud., 1878–.
Besedy o profdvizhenii provedennye v Profshkole Vsekitaiskoi federatsii profsoiuzov v Khan'kou, 1–18 iiunia 1927 g. (Discussions on the trade-union movement conducted at the Trade Union School of the All-China Federation of Labor in Hankow, 1–18 June 1927).
Moscow: Profintern, 1927. 106 p.
Subj 36.4 ▪ 16.4 32.2

19521 CSH U P3 G1.2 1928–1949
E Sun-tsziun' (O Sung-chun).
'Zakon o rabochikh soiuzakh i rabochee dvizhenie v Kitae' (The law on labor unions and the labor movement in China).
Vestnik kitaiskogo prava 3 (1931), 43–50.
Subj 12.2 36.4

19522 NNC U P3 G6.1 1911–1928
Galkovich, M- (M. Galkowitsch; M. Galkovitch).
'Razgon shankhaiskogo profsoveta' (The dispersal of the Shanghai General Union).
KIP 5, 11 (noiabr' 1925), 82–88.
'Die Zerstörung des Schanghaier Gewerkschaftsrates.'
RGI 5, 11 (Nov. 1925), 290–293.
'La dissolution violente du Conseil syndical de Shanghaï.'
ISR 58 (nov. 1925), 924–927.
Subj 32.2 36.4

19523 CSH F P2 G2.0 1911–1949
Gerasimov, A- E-.
'Pogruzochnye arteli v severnoi Man'chzhurii' (Loading cooperatives in northern Manchuria).
VM 1931, 6, 29–36. [Reprinted as 'Rabochie arteli' (Workers' cooperatives). In *Kitaiskii trud (usloviia truda v predpriiatiiakh severnoi Man'chzhurii)* (Chinese labor: Labor conditions in northern Manchurian enterprises), by A. E. Gerasimov. (Analytic entry.) Harbin: Tip. KVzhd, 1931, 105–128.]
Subj 24.2 24.4 26.4 34.2 36.4 ▪ 28

19524 NNC P P3 G1.1 1911–1928
Glick, Gary Wallace, 1946–.
The Chinese Seamen's Union and the Hong Kong seamen's strike of 1922.
Unpublished masters thesis in History, Columbia U., 1969. 108 p. [Certificate essay, East Asian Institute]
Subj 24 36.4 ▪ 22 26.4

19525 MCY S P3 G1.2 1928–1949
Gourlay, Walter Everett, 1921–.
"Yellow" unionism in Shanghai: A study of Kuomintang technique in labor control, 1927–1937.'
PC 7 (Feb. 1953), 103–135.
Subj 32.1 36.4 ▪ 16.4

19526 DLC U P3 G1.2 1911–1928
Gun-Zhen (Kung Jeng).
'Chernye profsoiuzy v Kitae v 1927 godu' (Black [right-wing] trade unions in China in 1927). In *Rabochii Kitai v 1927 godu: sbornik statei* (Articles on workers' China in 1927), edited by [Solomon Abramovich Dridzo] A. Lozovskii, pseud. [Selective entry]
Moscow: Profintern, 1928, 296–307.
Subj 36.4 ▪ 16.2 16.4 32 64

19527 DLC U P4 G1.3 1911–1928
[Heller, Leo N-] L. Geller.
'Natsional'noe i rabochee dvizhenie v Kitae' (The nationalist and labor movements in China).
Vestnik truda 1927, 3, 120–130.
Subj 16.4 34.2 36.4 ▪ 16.2 32.2

19528 NNC U P2 G1.3 1911–1928
[Heller, Leo N-] L. Geller.
'Novyi etap kitaiskoi revoliutsii' (A new stage in the Chinese revolution).
KIP 7, 2 (fevral' 1927), 115–126. [Reprinted in *Rabochii Kitai v 1927 godu: sbornik statei* (Articles on workers' China in 1927), edited by [Solomon Abramovich Dridzo] A. Lozovskii, pseud. (Selective entry.) Moscow: Profintern, 1928, 41–56.]
'Die neue Etappe der chinesischen Revolution.'
RGI 7, 2 (Feb. 1927), 73–79.
'Une nouvelle étape dans le développement de la révolution chinoise.'
ISR 73 (fév. 1927), 99–108.
Subj 36.4 ▪ 16 32.2

19529 NNC U P3 G6.1 1911–1928
[Heller, Leo N-] L. Geller.
'Shankhaiskaia zabastovka tekstil'shchikov' (The Shanghai textile-workers' strike).
KIP 5, 4 (aprel' 1925), 92–96.
'Der Textilarbeiterstreik in Schanghai.'
RGI 5, 4 (Apr. 1925), 237–239.
'La grève des textiles à Shanghaï.'
ISR 51 (avr. 1925), 318–321.
Subj 36.4

19530 NNC U P4 G1.3 1911–1928
[Heller, Leo N-] L. Geller.
'Zheltye soiuzy i zadachi revoliutsionnogo profdvizheniia v Kitae' ('Yellow' unions and the tasks of the Chinese revolutionary trade-union movement).
KIP 8, 8 (avgust 1928), 138–146.
'Die gelben Verbände und die Aufgaben der revolutionären, Gewerkschafts-bewegung in China.'
RGI 8, 8 (Aug. 1928), 447–451.
'Les syndicats jaunes et les objectifs du mouvement révolutionnaire en Chine.'
ISR 91 (août 1928), 520–526.
Subj 32.1 36.4

19531 MCH O P4 G1.2 1911–1928
Hinder, Eleanor M-.
'Some facts and factors in the labor movement in China.'
CR 59, 1 (Jan. 1928), 27–34. [Reprinted as 'Some facts regarding the Chinese labor movement.' *China weekly review* 43, 1 (11 Feb. 1928), 261–263.]
Subj 36.4 ▪ 16.4

19532 DCK U P4 G1.2 1911–1949
Holmberg, Johannes, 1877–1939.
'Den kinesiske arbejderbevægelse' (The Chinese working-class movement).
Udenrigsministeriets tidsskrift 12 (1931), 183–186; 12 (1931), 389–391.
Subj 16.4 36.4 ▪ 18 32.1 32.2

19533 NNC P P3 G6.1 1911–1928
Horovitz, Herbert Eugene, 1930–.
The policy of the Kuomintang toward labor, 1927–1932, with special reference to Shanghai.
Unpublished masters thesis in Political Science, Columbia U., 1964. 130 p. [Certificate essay, East Asian Institute]
Subj 22.1 32.1 36.4 ▪ 22.2 26.4

19534 WMU P P2 G1.1 1911–1928
Huang, Khai-loo (Huang K'ai-lu), 1909–.
A theory of the 1927 Chinese labor movement.
Unpublished doctoral dissertation in Economics, U. of Wisconsin, 1938. 750, 15 p.
Subj 16 16.4 32 32.2 36.4 64 ▪ 14 14.1 14.4 25 34.2 66

19535 MCH P P3 G6.1 1911–1928
Kartunova, Anastasiia Ivanovna.
'Deiatel'nost' Shankhaiskogo soveta profsoiuzov v iiune–avguste 1925 goda' (Activities of the Shanghai Trade Union Council, June–August 1925). [With English abstract]
PV 1960, 2, 91–104.
Subj 36.4

19536 NNC U P4 G1.3 1911–1928
[Kataiama, Sen] Sen-Kataiama (Katayama Sen), 1859–1933.
'Grazhdanskaia voina v Kitae i rabochii klass' (The civil war in China and the working class).
KIP 4, 12 (dekabr' 1924), 91–94.
'Der Bürgerkreig in China und die Arbeiterklasse.'
RGI 4, 12 (Dez. 1924), 288–290.
'La guerre civile en Chine et la classe ouvrière.'
ISR 47 (déc. 1924), 937–939.
Subj 36.4 ▪ 16.4 32.2

19537 NNC U P2 G1.3 1928–1949
Kennedy, ———.
'Situation and tasks of the red trade unions in China.'
R.I.L.U. magazine new (2nd) series 16 (15 Sept. 1931), 16–23.
Subj 32.2 36.4 ▪ 32.1

19538 CSH O P2 G2.0 1911–1928
Kudrevatov, V-.
'Polozhenie sluzhashchikh i rabochikh na Kitaiskoi Vostochnoi zheleznoi doroge' (The position of industrial, office, and professional workers of the Chinese Eastern Railway).
EVM 1923, 6/7 (4 marta), 40–42.
Subj 21.4 28 36.4 ▪ 26.2 26.4

19539 CBU P P3 G1.2 1911–1949
Kukhtin, K- V-.
'Trudovye assotsiatsii i trudovye konflikty v svete kitaiskogo zakonodatel'stva' (Labor associations and labor conflicts in the light of Chinese legislation).
VM 1933, 21 (15 noiabria), 89–99.
Subj 12.2 36.4 ▪ 16.4

19540 NNC U P2 G1.3 1928–1949
Li Min (Li Ming).
'Profsoiuzy v bor'be za sovetskuiu vlast' v Kitae' (Trade unions in the struggle for soviet control in China).
KIP 14, 1/2 (ianvar' 1934), 54–60.
Subj 36.4 ▪ 32.1 32.2

19541 MCH O P3 G9.2 1911–1928
Lockwood, Edward.
'Labor unions in Canton.'
CR 58, 7 (July 1927), 399–403.
Subj 36.4

19542 NNC U P4 G1.2 1911–1949
Lowe, Chuan-hua (Lo Ch'uan-hua), 1902–.
'China's labor movement.'
CEJ 6, 5 (May 1930), 487–509. [Separately reprinted—Shanghai: Kung shang pu, Kung shang fang wen chü, n.d. 23 p. (Kung shang fang wen chü, Booklet series, 14)]
Subj 16.4 36.4 ▪ 12.2 18 32 32.1 32.2 34.3

19543 MCH O P3 G1.1 1911–1928
Lowe, Chuan-hua (Lo Ch'uan-hua), 1902–.
'The Chinese Seamen's Union: Its history and organization.'
Chinese nation 1, 6 (23 July 1930), 85, 93.
Subj 36.4

19544 NNC P P2 G1.2 1928–1949
Lowe, Chuan-hua (Lo Ch'uan-hua), 1902–.
'Labor conditions in China.'
IB 4, 5 (7 July 1937), 93–116.
Subj 16.4 18 36.4 ▪ 12.2

19545 MCH P P4 G1.3 1911–1928
Musin, ———.
'Kitaiskoe rabochee dvizhenie i fevral'skaia zheleznodorozhnaia zabastovka' (The Chinese labor movement and the February [1923] rail strike).
NV 4 (1923), 129–150.
Subj 36.4 ▪ 14.2 16.4 32.1

19546 NNC P P3 G1.1 1911–1928
Musin, ———.
'Ocherki rabochego dvizheniia v Kitae' (Notes on the labor movement in China). In *Voprosy kitaiskoi revoliutsii, tom 1-yi* (Problems of the Chinese revolution, Vol. 1), edited by Karl Radek. [Selective entry]
Moscow: Gosizdat, 1927, 153–232.
Subj 16.4 22.2 32.2 36.4 ▪ 11.4 12.1 18 32.1 34.2 47 52 54

19547 CSU PO P4 G2.0 1911–1928
Nagano, G. (Nagano Gasei).
'Review over labour movements in Manchuria.' Tr. of 'Manshū rōdō undō tembō' (A look at the labor movement in Manchuria); *Shintenchi* 10, 6 (June 1930), 220–232. [Condensed tr.]
Manchurian daily news monthly supplement 81 (1 July 1930), 9–10; 84 (1 Oct. 1930), 12–13.
Subj 36.4 ▪ 18 22 24.4 32.2 34.2

19548 CSH P P3 G2.0 1911–1928
Nakazawa Hironori. [Tr. erroneously gives author's surname as Nikadzimo.]
'Rabochee dvizhenie v iuzhnoi Man'chzhurii' (The labor movement in southern Manchuria). Tr. of 'Manshū ni okeru rōdōsha undō no sūsei' (Trends in the labor movement in Manchuria); *Mammō* 8, 1 (Jan. 1927), 27–37.
VM 1927, 8, 24–29.
Subj 36.4 ▪ 16.4 32.1 32.2

19549 NNC U P3 G6.1 1911–1928
[Nassunov, Nikolai?] Nikolai N. (Nikolas N.), pseud.
'Zabastovochnaia volna v Shankhae' (The wave of strikes in Shanghai).
KIP 6, 9/10 (sentiabr'–oktiabr' 1926), 372–377.

'Die Streikbewegung in Shanghai.'
RGI 6, 9/10 (Sept.–Okt. 1926), 677–680.

'La vague des grèves à Shanghai.'
ISR 68/69 (sept.–oct. 1926), 911–914.
Subj 36.4 ▪ 34.3

19550 FPN O P3 G6.1 1911–1928
[Neumann, Heinz] A. Neuberg, pseud., 1902–.
'Les insurrections de Changhaï' (The Shanghai uprisings). In *L'insurrection armée* (Armed insurrection), by [H. Neumann] A. Neuberg, pseud. [Selective entry]
Paris: Impr. centrale, 1931, 130–147.
Subj 25 32.2 36.4 64 ▪ 15

19551 ELB P P2 G1.2 1911–1949
Pashkova, M-.
V bor'be za raskreposhchenie kitaiskogo naroda: ocherki rabochego dvizheniia v Kitae, 1925–1939 gg. (The struggle to liberate the Chinese people: Notes on the Chinese labor movement, 1925–1939).
Moscow: Sotsekgiz, 1939. 144 p.
Subj 16.4 36.4 ▪ 11.4 14.4 15 18 25 32.2 47 66

19552 MCH U P3 G6.1 1911–1928
Rafes, M-.
'Shankhaiskoe dvizhenie i ego itogi' (The Shanghai [labor] movement and its results).
NV 12 (1926), 1–17.
Subj 36.4 ▪ 16.4 64

19553 MCH U P3 G9.5 1911–1928
Robert, L-.
'La grève maritime de Hongkong' (The maritime strike in Hong Kong).
R. du Pacifique 1, 6 (oct. 1922), 10–19.
Subj 24.6 36.4 ▪ 36.2 66

19554 CBU P P3 G1.1 1911–1928
Schwarz, Rainer.
'A Chinese labour organization of 1919, the Chung-hua Ch'üan-kuo Kung-chieh Hsieh-chin-hui [All-China Labor Association for Common Progress].'
Mitteilungen des Instituts für Orientforschung der Deutschen Akademie der Wissenschaften zu Berlin 15, 3 (1969), 517–523.
Subj 32.2 36.4 ▪ 16.4

19555 CSH FP P3 G6.1 1928–1949
Shanghai. She hui chü. (Bureau of Social Affairs).
Strikes and lockouts, Greater Shanghai, 1929. Tr. from *Shang-hai t'e pieh shih pa kung t'ing yeh t'ung chi, min kuo 18 nien* (Statistics on strikes and lockouts in Shanghai special municipality, 1929); Shanghai: She hui chü, 1929. [Tr. inferred; abridged tr.]
Shanghai: She hui chü, 1929. 70 p. [s.p.].
Subj 26.4 34.2 36.4 ▪ 22 22.2 24.2 24.3 24.4 28 34.3 36.2

19556 MCH P P3 G6.1 1911–1949
Shanghai. She hui chü. (Bureau of Social Affairs).
Strikes and lockouts in Shanghai since 1918.
Shanghai: Chung Hwa, 1933. 180 p. [See Vol. 2 of this *Bibliography* for Chinese version.]
Subj 26.4 36.4 ▪ 21.4 22.2 24.4 61

19557 DLC P P4 G9.0 1911–1928
Skalov, Georgii Borisovich, 1896–.
'Rabochii vopros i rabochee dvizhenie v Guandune' (The labor question and the labor movement in Kwangtung). In *Kantonskaia kommuna: sbornik statei i materialov* (Articles and documents on the Canton commune), compiled by Nauchno-issledovatel'skii institut po Kitaiu, Kommunisticheskaia akademiia. [Selective entry]
Moscow: Gosizdat, 1929, 164–200.
Subj 26.4 36.4 ▪ 32.2 66

19558 NNP U P2 G1.2 1911–1928
Smurgis, IU-.
Kitai i ego rabochee dvizhenie (The labor movement in China).
Moscow: Profintern, 1922. 55 p.
Subj 14.4 16.4 34.3 36.4 ▪ 14.1 14.2 18 22 22.2 24.4 32 32.1 48

19559 NNC PO P5 G1.1 1911–1949
[Snow, Helen Foster] Nym Wales, pseud., 1907–.
The Chinese labor movement.
New York: Day, 1945. 11, 235 p. [Reprinted—New York: Paragon, 1970. 11, 235 p.]
Subj 16.4 18 36.4 ▪ 14.4 32.1 34.2 72

19560 NNP P P2 G2.0 1911–1928
[Sokolov, N- A-?] N. S——ov.
'Kooperativ sluzhashchikh, masterovykh i rabochikh KVzhd' (The Chinese Eastern Railway cooperative of employees, artisans, and workers).
EB 1927, 3/4 (30 ianvaria), 16–18; 1928, 1 (8 ianvaria), 7–10.
Subj 36.4 ▪ 14.2 24.3

19561 DLC P P3 G1.2 1911–1949
Strakhov, V-.
'Voprosy kitaiskogo professional'nogo dvizheniia' (The Chinese trade-union movement).
PK 2 (1930), 28–62.
Subj 16 16.4 32.1 32.2 36.4 ▪ 14.4 21.2 34.3 35 36.2 39 66

19562 DLC O P4 G1.2 1911–1928
Su Chzhao-zhen (Su Chao-cheng), 1885–1929.
'Rabochee dvizhenie Kitaia: doklad Su Chzhao-zhena (predsedatelia Vsekitaiskoi federatsii profsoiuzov) na Tikhookeanskoi konferentsii profsoiuzov' (The Chinese labor movement: Report by Su Chao-cheng, president of the All-China Federation of Labor, at the Pan-Pacific Trade Union Congress). In *Rabochii Kitai v 1927 godu: sbornik statei* (Articles on workers' China in 1927), edited by [Solomon Abramovich Dridzo] A. Lozovskii, pseud. [Selective entry]
Moscow: Profintern, 1928, 191–219.
Subj 14.4 16.4 36.4 ▪ 14.2 16.2 18 66

19563 DLC U P5 G1.2 1911–1928
T. M.
'Krasnye profsoiuzy v podpol'e v 1927 g.' (Underground red trade unions in 1927). In *Rabochii Kitai v 1927 godu: sbornik statei* (Articles on workers' China in 1927), edited by [Solomon Abramovich Dridzo] A. Lozovskii, pseud. [Selective entry]
Moscow: Profintern, 1928, 308–321.
Subj 16.4 36.4

19564 NNC U P2 G1.3 1928–1949
[Tailan'-shen] Tai-lan-shen (T'ai Lan-sheng).
'Profsoiuzy v sovetskom Kitae.'
KIP 11, 19 (oktiabr' 1931), 26–29.

'Les syndicats en Chine soviétique.'
ISR 2e série 20 (15 oct. 1931), 991–994.

'Trade unions in soviet China.'
R.I.L.U. magazine new (2nd) series 19 (1 Nov. 1931), 23–26.
Subj 36.4 ▪ 26.4 32.2

19565 NNC O P3 G1.2 1928–1949
Teng, Tsung-hsia (Teng Chung-hsia), 1897–1933.
'The Chinese trade unions after the past revolutionary wave.'
CSM 24, 7 (May 1929), 315–323.
Subj 36.4 ▪ 16.2 16.4 32.1

19566 MCH P P3 G6.1 1911–1949
Tsha, T. Y. (Ts'ai Cheng-ya).
'Labor organization in Shanghai.'
China critic 4, 29 (16 July 1931), 679–682.
Subj 36.4 ▪ 12 24.4 26.4

19567 NNC U P4 G1.1 1911–1928
[Van Chen-min] Wan Chen-Myn (Wang Ch'eng-ming).
'Stachechnoe dvizhenie v Kitae' (The strike movement in China).
KIP 8, 7 (iiul' 1928), 22–27.

'Die Streikbewegung in China.'
RGI 8, 7 (Juli 1928), 378–381.
Subj 36.4 ▪ 18

19568 DLC S P3 G1.2 1928–1949
Venis-Chen.
'Obshchii itog stachechnogo dvizheniia za 1933 g. v gomindanovskom Kitae' (General result for 1933 of the strike movement in Kuomintang China).
MNKP 1934, 8, 37–57.
Subj 14 16.4 32.2 36.4 ▪ 14.4 64

19569 NNC U P4 G1.3 1911–1928
[Vilenskii, Vladimir Dmitrievich] Vl. Vilenskii-Sibiriakov (W. Wilenski-Sibirjakoff; V. Vilensky-Sibiriakov), pseud., 1888–1942.
'Puti rabochego dvizheniia v Kitae' (The course of the labor movement in China).
KIP 5, 7/8 (iiul'–avgust 1925), 40–45.

'Die Wege der Arbeiterbewegung in China.'
RGI 5, 7/8 (Juli–Aug. 1925), 27–29.

'Les voies du mouvement ouvrier en Chine.'
ISR 54/55 (juil.–août 1925), 589–592.
Subj 36.4

19570 NNC P P2 G1.3 1911–1928
Vinogradov, Nikolai Pavlovich, 1923–1967.
'Zabastovka zheleznodorozhnikov Pekin-Khan'kouskoi zheleznoi dorogi 7 fevralia 1923 g. i ee znachenie dlia razvitiia natsional'no-osvoboditel'nogo dvizheniia v Kitae' (The strike of the Peking-Hankow railroad workers on 7 February 1923 and its significance in the development of the national liberation movement in China).
KSIV 7 (1952), 20–31.
Subj 32.2 36.4 ▪ 14.2 16.4 32.1 64

19571 CSH P P3 G1.2 1928–1949
Vladimirova, Tamara Ivanovna.
'Bor'ba kitaiskogo proletariata v 1930 g.' (The struggle of the Chinese proletariat in 1930).
PK 3 (1930), 92–98.
Subj 16.4 32.2 36.4 ▪ 32

19572 DLC P P2 G1.2 1928–1949
[Vladimirova, Tamara Ivanovna] T. V.
'Pered novymi boiami: itogi rabochego dvizheniia v Kitae v 1932 g.' (Confronting new battles: Results of the labor movement in China in 1932).
PK 12 (1933), 203–231.
Subj 16.4 18 32.1 36.4 ▪ 12.2 14.2 14.4 32.2 34.2 47 66

19573 DLC P P3 G1.2 1928–1949
[Vladimirova, Tamara Ivanovna] T. V.
'Rabochee dvizhenie v Kitae v 1931–1932 gg.' (The labor movement in China, 1931–1932).
PK 11 (1933), 210–233.
Subj 18 32.1 36.4 66 ▪ 12.2 14.4 16.2 16.4 32 32.2

19574 DLC P P3 G1.2 1928–1949
Vladimirova, Tamara Ivanovna.
'Rabochee dvizhenie v Kitae za 1928–1929 g.' (The labor movement in China, 1928–1929).
PK 2 (1930), 198–212.
Subj 32.1 32.2 36.4 ▪ 16.2 16.4 18 34.3 66

19575 NNC U P2 G1.3 1911–1928
Voitinskii, Grigorii Naumovich (G. Woitinski; G. Voitinsky), 1893–1956.
'Politicheskoe polozhenie v Kitae i kitaiskii proletariat' (The political situation in China and the Chinese proletariat).
KIP 6, 3 (mart 1925), 344–349.

'Die politische Lage in China und das chinesische Proletariat.'
RGI 6, 3 (März 1926), 184–186.

'La situation politique en Chine et le prolétariat chinois.'
ISR 62 (mars 1926), 253–256.
Subj 16.4 36.4

19576 NNC P P3 G1.2 1911–1949
Wagner, Augusta Bertha, 1895–.
'The International Labor Organization and the regulation of labor conditions in China.'
YJSS 2, 1 (July 1939), 1–38.
Subj 14.4 16.4 18 36.4 ▪ 12.2 22 66

19577 NNC P P3 G1.3 1911–1949
Wittfogel, Karl August, 1896–.
'Die Grundlagen der chinesischen Arbeiterbewegung' (The foundations of the Chinese labor movement).
Archiv für die Geschichte des Sozialismus und der Arbeiterbewegung 15, 2 (1930), 238–269.
Subj 14.4 16.4 18 36.4 ▪ 22.2 34.2 47 52 55

19578 NNC S P7 G7.3 1911–1928
Womack, Lynda Norene.
Anyuan [coal mines, An-yüan *hsien*, Kiangsi]*: The cradle of the Chinese workers' revolutionary movement, 1921–1922.*
Unpublished masters thesis in History, Columbia U., 1970. 55 p. [Certificate essay, East Asian Institute]
Subj 26.4 36.4 ▪ 24.4 32.2

19579 CSH P P2 G5.1 1911–1949
Wu, Leonard T. K. (Wu Tsu-kuang).
An analysis of labour disputes in Hopei province and the cities of Peiping and Tientsin, January 1927 – June 1929. Tr. of *Ho-pei sheng chi P'ing Chin liang shih lao tzu cheng i ti fen hsi, shih liu nien i yüeh – shih pa nien liu yüeh*; Peiping: She hui tiao ch'a so, 1930; 72 p. [Rev. and condensed in tr.]
Peiping: [China Foundation], Institute of Social Research, 1930. 21 p. (ISR bulletins, 4)
Subj 36.4 ▪ 26.4 34.2

19580 CSH P P3 G1.4 1911–1928
Zabarko, B- M-, and IU- A- L'vunin.
'Iz istorii pomoshchi Mezhrabpoma bor'be trudiashchikhsia Kitaia (1925 g.)' (An account of the aid provided by Workers' International Relief to the workers' struggle in China, 1925).
NAA 1969, 5, 148–155.
Subj 36.4 66

1911-1972
(including 1644-1972)

19581 MCH U P4 G1.2 1928–1972
'China's trade unions.'
PR 8, 18 (30 Apr. 1965), 22–25.
Subj 36.4 ▪ 17 18

19582 FPN P P3 G1.2 1911–1972
Engelborghs-Bertels, Marthe, 1928–.
'Les syndicats en République populaire de Chine' (Labor unions in the People's Republic of China).
B. du Centre d'étude des pays de l'Est 7, 2 (1966), 213–226.
Subj 14 16.4 36.4 ▪ 12.2 14.4 18 32.1

19583 MAM P P4 G1.2 1911–1972
Fletcher, Merton Don, 1938–.
Trade unions in Communist China.
Ann Arbor: University Microfilms (Publ. 69-14,882), 1969. 328 p. (Doctoral dissertation in Political Science, U. of California, Berkeley, 1968)
Subj 14.4 18 36.4 ▪ 11.4 17 32 32.1 32.2 34.3

19584 CSH P P3 G1.1 1911–1972
Kartunova, Anastasiia Ivanovna.
'Profintern i profsoiuznoe dvizhenie v Kitae (iz istorii ikh vzaimootnoshenii)' (The Profintern and the labor-union movement in China: History of their interrelationship).
NAA 1972, 1, 48–59.
Subj 36.4 66

19585 CSH P P4 G1.2 1911–1972
Yang Cheng Shih.
'Labor relations and organization.' In *A general handbook of China*, compiled by Far Eastern and Russian Institute, U. of Washington. [Selective entry]
New Haven: Human Relations Area Files, 1956, vol. 1, 817–882. (HRAF subcontractor's monographs, 55; Washington 4)
Subj 16.4 36.4 ▪ 12.2 14.6 18 32.2

1949-1972

19586 MCH O P3 G5.1 1949–1972
Cheng Kuo-tai.
'The trade union in our plant [Shih-ching-shan power plant, Peking municipality].'
People's China 1954, 10 (16 May), 14–17.
Subj 36.4 ▪ 21.4 24.4 26.4

19587 CSH O P4 G9.4 1949–1972
Cheng, Tracy T. S.
'Experience in the settlement of labor problems in the course of industrialization.' In *Labor relations in the Asian countries: Proceedings of the Second International Conference on Industrial Relations, Tokyo, 1967*. [Sole entry]
Tokyo: Japan Institute of Labour, 1967, 145–161.
Subj 34.2 36.4 37 38 ▪ 18

19588 CSH P P4 G1.2 1949–1972
Chin I-hua (Ch'in I-hua).
'The labour movement.' Tr. of '1961 nien ti Chung kung kung yün' (The labor movement in Communist China, 1961); *Tsu kuo chou k'an* 493 (18 June 1962), 11–19. In *Communist China, 1961*, edited by Union Research Institute. [Selective entry]
Hong Kong: Union Research Institute, 1962, vol. 1, 127–158.
Subj 36.4 ▪ 16.4 32.1

19589 NNC P P4 G1.2 1949–1972
Ching Ming-sze (Ch'eng Ming-chih) and Chiang Hui-ch'uan. [Authors sequential rather than joint: Ching Ming-sze for 1955; Chiang Hui-ch'uan for 1956–1958.]
'Labor movement' [title varies]. Tr. of '1955–1958 nien Chung kung ti kung yün' (The labor movement in Communist China, 1955–1958); *Tsu kuo chou k'an* 159–334/335 (16 Jan. 1956 – 8 June 1959) [recurring annual feature article]. In *Communist China, 1955–1958*, edited by Union Research Institute.
Hong Kong: Union Research Institute. Issued annually, 1956–1959, average ca. 10 p.
Subj 36.4 ▪ 16.4 18 32.1

19590 [2]NNC P P4 G1.2 1949–1972
Chung-hua ch'üan kuo tsung kung hui (All-China Federation of Trade Unions).
Les syndicats chinois.
Peking: Fédération des syndicats chinois, 1961. 60 p.

Chinese trade unions, mimeo.
Washington, D.C.: U.S. Joint Publications Research Service, 1963. 67 p. (JPRS 21,209; MC 19,511/1963)
Subj 16.4 36.4 ▪ 12.2 17 18 31 32.1 38 55

19591 CSH O P2 G9.5 1949–1972
Cooper, John, 1936–.
Colony in conflict: The Hong Kong disturbances, May 1967 – January 1968.
Hong Kong: Swindon Book Co., 1970. 315 p.
Subj 22.1 36.4 ▪ 22.2 25 32.2 66

19592 MCH P P3 G1.2 1949–1972
Current Scene Editor.
'Trouble on the tracks: Railway labour unrest in China's Cultural Revolution.'
CS 5, 8 (19 May 1967), 1–12.
SUBJ 14.2 36.4 ▪ 16.4 25 32.1 54

19593 CBU PO P2 G9.5 1949–1972
England, Joe.
'Industrial relations in Hong Kong.' In *Hong Kong: The industrial colony*, edited by Keith Hopkins. [Analytic entry]
Hong Kong: Oxford U. Press, 1971, 207–259.
SUBJ 21.4 34.2 36.4 ▪ 12.2 22 26.4 36.2

19594 NNC U P4 G1.2 1949–1972
Evstratov, M- P-.
Profsoiuzy narodnogo Kitaia v bor'be za novuiu zhizn' (Trade unions of the People's Republic of China in the struggle for a new life).
Moscow: Profizdat, 1953. 93 p.
SUBJ 32.1 36.4 ▪ 14.4 16.1 16.4 17 18 31 34.2

19595 CBU S P4 G1.2 1949–1972
Francis, Albert Allen, 1932–.
Control of labor in Communist China.
Unpublished masters thesis in Political Science, U. of California, Berkeley, 1958. 198 p.
SUBJ 14.4 32.1 36.4 ▪ 16.1 16.4 18 30 31 32 47

19596 CSU P P4 G1.2 1949–1972
Harper, Paul Frederick, 1929–.
'The party and the unions in Communist China.'
CQ 37 (Jan.–Mar. 1969), 84–119.
SUBJ 32 32.1 36.4 ▪ 16.1 16.4 64

19597 MAM FP P2 G1.2 1949–1972
Harper, Paul Frederick, 1929–.
Political roles of trade unions in Communist China.
Ann Arbor: University Microfilms (Publ. 69-13,022), 1969. 442 p. (Doctoral dissertation in Government, Cornell U.)
SUBJ 16.4 18 27 32.1 36.4 ▪ 12.2 16 16.1 25 32 50

19598 CSU FP P4 G1.2 1949–1972
Harper, Paul Frederick, 1929–.
'Trade union cultivation of workers for leadership.' In *The city in Communist China*, edited by John Wilson Lewis. [Analytic entry]
Stanford: Stanford U. Press, 1971, 123–152.
SUBJ 16.4 36.4 ▪ 17 32.1

19599 ELB P P4 G1.2 1949–1972
Kholodkovskaia, A-.
'Razgrom profsoiuzov v Kitae' (The destruction of trade unions in China).
Kommunist 1968, 10 (iiul'), 90–99.
SUBJ 32.1 36.4 ▪ 16.4 18 19 32 35 64 66

19600 NIC P P3 G1.2 1949–1972
[La Dany, Ladislao] ———, 1914–.
'Industrial labour and trade unions, 1957–1960.'
CNA 355 (13 Jan. 1961), 1–7; 359 (10 Feb. 1961), 1–7; 361 (24 Feb. 1961), 1–7.
SUBJ 16.4 32.1 36.4 ▪ 12.1 18

19601 NNC P P4 G1.2 1949–1972
[La Dany, Ladislao] ———, 1914–.
'Labour unions. Part 1, 1948–1950. Part 2, 1951–1952.'
CNA 26 (5 Mar. 1954), 2–5; 31 (9 Apr. 1954), 2–5.
SUBJ 14.4 36.4 ▪ 16.4 32.1

19602 MCH P P4 G1.2 1949–1972
[La Dany, Ladislao] ———, 1914–.
'Trade unions and industrial workers.'
CNA 482 (23 Aug. 1963), 1–7.
SUBJ 16.4 36.4

19603 CSH P P4 G1.2 1949–1972
Lin Mu-sen.
'Communist China's trade union movement in 1965.' Tr. of '1965 nien ti Chung kung kung yün kung tso'; *Tsu kuo* 26 (May 1966), 2–12. In *Communist China, 1965*, edited by Union Research Institute. [Selective entry]
Hong Kong: Union Research Institute, 1967, vol. 1, 168–192.
SUBJ 36.4 ▪ 32.1

19604 CSH O P3 G9.5 1949–1972
Lutz, Hans, and Robert Snow.
'Hard labour for life.'
FEER 71, 3 (16 Jan. 1971), 17–19.
SUBJ 36.4

19605 CSU O P3 G6.1 1949–1972
Shih Hsi-min, 1897–, and Lan Ying.
'Questions in developing a mass movement in factories.' Tr. of 'Tsai kung ch'ang chung k'ai chan ch'ün chung yün tung ti chi ko wen t'i'; *Hung ch'i* 1959, 6 (16 Mar.), 25–33. In *Articles from the Chinese Communist theoretical journal 'Hung ch'i' No. 6, 14 May* [i.e., 16 March] *1959*, mimeo., compiled by U.S. Joint Publications Research Service. [Sole entry]
Washington, D.C.: JPRS, 14 May 1959, 20–32. (JPRS 715D; MC 9180/1959)
SUBJ 32.1 34.2 36.4 ▪ 24.4 26.4

19606 MCH P P3 G1.2 1949–1972
Shurcliff, Alice Warburton, 1915–.
'The control of industrial labor in Communist China.'
Monthly labor review 76, 8 (Aug. 1953), 821–825.
SUBJ 16.4 32.1 36.4 ▪ 14.4 18 47

19607 NIC P P3 G1.2 1949–1972
Steiner, Harold Arthur, 1905–.
'Trade unions in Mao's China.'
Problems of Communism 5, 2 (Mar.–Apr. 1956), 27–33.
SUBJ 32.1 36.4 ▪ 12.2 30 64

19608 NNC P P4 G1.2 1949–1972
T'an Hsin-wen.
'Labour union movement.' Tr. of 'Shih nien lai ti Chung kung kung yün' (The labor movement in Communist China during the past decade); *Tsu kuo chou k'an* 389 (20 June 1960), 14–23. In *Communist China, 1949–1959*, edited by Union Research Institute. [Selective entry]
Hong Kong: Union Research Institute, 1961, vol. 3, 57–98.
SUBJ 32.1 36.4 ▪ 16.4 18

19609 CBU P P1 G1.2 1949–1972
Tsien, Josiane, 1934–, and Tsien Tche-hao (Ch'ien Chih-hao), 1923–.
'Les syndicats et la loi sur les syndicats en Chine populaire' (The labor unions and the Trade Union Law [of 1950] in the People's Republic of China).
Rivista di diritto internazionale e comparato del lavoro (Padua) nuova (2a) serie 2, 3 (settembre–dicembre 1962), 288–299.
SUBJ 12.2 36.4 ▪ 16.4 32.1

19610 FPN P P3 G1.2 1949–1972
Vercruyse-Bousson, J-.
'Les statuts des syndicats en République populaire de Chine' (Statutes on labor unions in the People's Republic of China).
B. du Centre d'étude des pays de l'Est 7, 2 (1966), 226–234.
SUBJ 12.2 36.4 ▪ 14.4 16.4 32

19611 NNC P P4 G1.2 1949–1972
Wang, Minta C. H. C. (Wang Chou Ming-te), 1917–.
A study of the All China Federation of Labor.
Unpublished masters thesis in Public Law and Government, Columbia U., 1953. 117 p.
SUBJ 16.4 36.4 ▪ 12.2 32.1

37 EDUCATIONAL ASSOCIATIONS AND MOVEMENTS

教育團體及教育運動

教育団体及び教育運動

1644-1911

19612 MCH U P4 G7.2 1895–1911
'L'effort scolaire au Hounan' (The movement for education in Hunan).
AF 10, 113 (août 1910), 340–344.
SUBJ 27 37

19613 NIC U P1 G1.2 1842–1911
Broomhall, Marshall, 1866–1937.
'The present position of the anti-opium movement.'
Imperial and Asiatic quarterly review 3rd series 27, 53 (Jan. 1909), 85–99.
SUBJ 12.1 18 37 ▪ 14.3

19614 CSU O P3 G1.1 1842–1895
Yung Shang Him (Jung Shang-chien).
'The Chinese educational mission and its influence.'
THM 9, 3 (Oct. 1939), 225–256.
SUBJ 37 66 ▪ 11.2 16.1 59

1644-1949

19615 NNU PO P2 G1.2 –1949
Chen, Weilun (Ch'en Wei-lun), 1897–.
A sociological foundation of adult education in China.
Unpublished doctoral dissertation in Education, New York U., 1935. 100 p.
SUBJ 37 ▪ 27 50

19616 MCH S P1 G1.2 1895–1928
Chuang, Chai-hsuan (Chuang Tse-hsüan), 1895–.
'Movement for educating illiterates in China.'
BCE 2, 2 (1923), 1–22.
SUBJ 37 ▪ 27

19617 NNC P P2 G1.2 1842–1949
DeFrancis, John, 1911–.
Nationalism and language reform in China.
Princeton: Princeton U. Press, 1950. 11, 306 p. (Doctoral dissertation in Chinese and Japanese, Columbia U.) [Reprinted—New York: Octagon Books, 1972. 11, 306 p.]
SUBJ 37 64 ▪ 16.1 17 32.2

1911-1949

19618 MCH P P7 G1.3 1911–1949
Brown, William Andreas, 1930–.
'The Protestant rural movement in China, 1920–1937.'
PC 9 (Aug. 1955), 173–202. [Reprinted in *American missionaries in China: Papers from Harvard seminars*, edited by Kwang-ching Liu (Liu Kuang-ching). (Analytic entry.) Cambridge: Harvard U., East Asian Research Center, 1966, 217–248. (Harvard East Asian monographs, 21)]
SUBJ 33 37 ▪ 17 24.1 66

19619 NNC O P7 G5.1 1911–1949
Buck, Pearl Sydenstricker, 1892–1973.
Tell the people: Talks with James Yen about the Mass Education Movement.
New York: Day, 1945. 84 p.
SUBJ 26.3 27 28 37 ▪ 22 24 24.1 26.1 56

19620 PPP FP P2 G5.3 1911–1949
Chandler, Horace Edward, 1884–.
The work of the American Presbyterian Mission from 1918 to 1941 toward the lessening of adult illiteracy in Shantung province.
Unpublished doctoral dissertation in Religion, U. of Pittsburgh, 1943. 192 p.
SUBJ 27 37 ▪ 24.2 33 59 66

19621 NIC O P7 G7.3 1928–1949
Chang, Fu-liang.
'Rural reconstruction in Kiangsi.'
CQ-S 5, 2 (Spring 1940), 215–226.
SUBJ 28 37 ▪ 24 27 38

19622 NNC S P7 G1.2 1928–1949
Chang, Jen-chi, 1930–.
'Rural reconstruction in pre-Communist China.'
Rural sociology 20, 2 (June 1955), 156–160.
SUBJ 37 ▪ 17 28

19623 NIC PO P4 G1.2 1928–1949
Chen, Walter Hanming (Ch'en Han-ming).
'The New Life Movement.'
IB 2, 11 (21 Dec. 1936), 189–230.
SUBJ 12.1 18 37 ▪ 32 34.3 64

19624 MCH O P7 G5.1 1928–1949
Ch'en, C. C. (Ch'en Chih-ch'ien).
'The development of systematic training in rural public health work in China.'
MMFQ 14, 4 (Oct. 1936), 370–387.
SUBJ 37 56 ▪ 28 58

19625 NNC S P1 G1.2 1928–1949
Chiu, Cheng-ho (Ch'iu Cheng-ou).
Le mouvement de la vie nouvelle en Chine (The New Life Movement in China).
Paris: Foulon, 1941. 139 p. (Doctoral dissertation, Faculté des lettres, Université de Paris)
SUBJ 19 37 48 60 64 ▪ 12.1 32.1 63

19626 CSU P P2 G1.2 1928–1949
Chu, Samuel C. (Chu Ch'ang-ling), 1929–.
'The New Life Movement, 1934–1937.' In *Researches in the social sciences on China*, edited by John E- Lane. [Selective entry]
New York: Columbia U., East Asian Institute, 1957, 1–17. (EAI studies, 3) (Masters thesis in History, Columbia U., 1953)
SUBJ 12.1 32 37 60 ▪ 32.1 35 56

19627 MCH O P2 G1.2 1911–1928
De Vargas, Philippe.
'The fight against illiteracy in China.'
New mandarin 1, 1 (Jan. 1926), 5–9.
SUBJ 37

19628 CSH P P2 G1.2 1911–1949
Goldman, Merle Dorothy, 1931–.
'Left-wing criticism of the *Pai Hua* movement.' In *Reflections on the May Fourth Movement: A symposium*, edited by Benjamin Isadore Schwartz. [Analytic entry]
Cambridge: Harvard U., East Asian Research Center, 1972, 85–94. (Harvard East Asian monographs, 44)
SUBJ 37 64

19629 NNC P P2 G1.2 1928–1949
Hsu, Leonard S. (Hsü Shih-lien), 1901–.
'Rural reconstruction in China.'
PA 10, 3 (Sept. 1937), 249–265.
SUBJ 12 14 14.1 37 ▪ 17 18 22 22.1 34.2 38 56

19630 CSH P P2 G1.3 1911–1949
Lamley, Harry Jerome, 1928–.
'Liang Shu-ming, rural reconstruction, and the Rural Work Discussion Society, 1933–1935.'
CCJ 8, 2 (May 1969), 50–61.
SUBJ 22 36.1 37 ▪ 32.1 59

19631 MAM P P2 G1.3 1911–1949
Lee, Hsiang-po, 1919–.
Rural-mass education movement in China, 1923–1937.
Ann Arbor: University Microfilms (Publ. 18,041), 1970. 331 p. (Doctoral dissertation in Education, Ohio State U.)
SUBJ 27 37 ▪ 59

19632 MCY S P7 G1.3 1911–1949
Lee, Robert H. G. (Li K'ung-chiang), 1922–.
'The rural reconstruction movement.'
PC 4 (Apr. 1950), 160–198.
SUBJ 22 26.3 28 37 ▪ 24.1 24.6 25 27 36.3 56

19633 NNC O P7 G5.3 1928–1949
[Liang Shu-ming] ———, 1893–.
Rural reconstruction in Tsouping [i.e., Tsou-p'ing *hsien*, Shantung].
Tsou-p'ing, Shantung: Shantung Institute of Rural Reconstruction, 1935. 16 p. (Rural reconstruction series, 1)
SUBJ 27 37 ▪ 24.1 26.3 28

19634 MCH O P2 G1.2 1928–1949
Ling, Betty Wang.
'The New Life Movement of China.'
SSR 21, 6 (July–Aug. 1937), 534–537.
SUBJ 37 63 ▪ 64

19635 CSU O P7 G1.2 1928–1949
Moyer, Raymond Tyson, 1899–.
'China's agricultural-improvement program.'
Foreign agriculture 11, 10 (Oct. 1947), 130–140.
SUBJ 14.1 37 ▪ 34.1 34.2 36.1

19636 MCH O P7 G1.2 1928–1949
Neumeyer, Martin Henry, 1892–.
'Rural reconstruction in China.'
SSR 19, 6 (July–Aug. 1935), 527–539.
SUBJ 18 19 37 ▪ 14.1

19637 CSH O P2 G1.3 1911–1949
Shen, T. H. (Shen Tsung-han), 1895–.
'First attempts to transform Chinese agriculture, 1927–1937' [with comments by Franklin L. Ho (Ho Lien)]. In *The strenuous decade: China's nation-building efforts, 1927–1937*, edited by Paul K. T. Sih (Hsüeh Kuang-ch'ien). [Selective entry]
Jamaica, N.Y.: St. John's U. Press, 1970, 205–236.
SUBJ 14.1 17 37 70 71 ▪ 12 18

19638 NIC S P7 G1.2 1928–1949
Sun, Tien Hsi, 1901–.
A study of the rural reconstruction movement in China.
Unpublished masters thesis in Sociology, Cornell U., 1936. 168 p.
SUBJ 16.3 18 19 27 34.1 37 ▪ 14.1 14.6 22 22.1 24.4 25 31 33 38 58

19639 NNC P P1 G1.2 1911–1928
Tai, Chen-hua (T'ai Chen-hua), 1914–.
A critical study of the Chinese Federation of Educational Associations.
Unpublished doctoral dissertation in Education, Columbia U. [Teachers College], 1954. 206 p.
SUBJ 17 37 ▪ 32.1 60 66

19640 NNC P P7 G1.2 1928–1949
Tan, Lynette P. C., 1926–.
The contribution of private agencies in rural reconstruction in China.
Unpublished masters thesis in Sociology, Columbia U., 1952. 136 p.
SUBJ 17 30 37 38 ▪ 14.1 24.3 24.4 34.2 41 58

19641 MCH U P8 G1.2 1911–1928
Tao, W. Tchishin (T'ao Chih-hsing), 1891–1946.
'The village education movement in China.'
Educational review 20, 1 (Jan. 1928), 25–35.
SUBJ 27 37 ▪ 28 34.1

19642 NNC S P7 G5.3 1928–1949
Van Slyke, Lyman Page, 1929–.
'Liang Sou-ming and the rural reconstruction movement.'
JAS 18, 4 (Aug. 1959), 457–474.
SUBJ 37 64 ▪ 22 24 25 34.2 59

19643 NNC P P2 G1.2 1911–1949
Vee, Ling-nyi.
Mass education in China.
Unpublished masters thesis in Education, Columbia U. [Teachers College], 1931. 32 p.
SUBJ 37 ▪ 19 27 47

19644 CLS PO P2 G1.2 1911–1949
Wong, Pearl Hui (Huang Hui-chu), 1918–.
A comparative study of four social movements in China, 1912–1942.
Unpublished doctoral dissertation in Sociology, U. of Southern California, 1946. 430 p.
SUBJ 34.3 37 47 63 ▪ 18 24.3 24.4 25 27 28 34.2 59

19645 NIC P P1 G1.2 1911–1928
World Assn. for Adult Education.
Adult education in China.
London: Allen and Unwin, 1921. 31 p. (WAAE bulletins, 8)
SUBJ 37 ▪ 27

19646 NIC O P2 G1.3 1911–1928
Yen, Y. C. James (Yen Yang-ch'u), 1894–.
The Mass Education Movement in China.
Shanghai: Commercial Press, 1925. 25 p.
SUBJ 27 37

19647 CSH O P2 G1.2 1911–1928
Yen, Y. C. James (Yen Yang-ch'u), 1894–.
'New citizens for China.'
Yale review new (2nd) series 18, 2 (Dec. 1928), 262–276. [Separately reprinted—Ting-hsien, Hopei: Chinese National Assn. of the Mass Education Movement, 1929. 15 p.]
SUBJ 37 ▪ 16

19648 CSH O P7 G5.1 1928–1949
Yen, Y. C. James (Yen Yang-ch'u), 1894–.
The Ting hsien experiment in 1934.
Peiping: Chinese National Assn. of the Mass Education Movement, 1934? 46 p.
SUBJ 27 28 34.1 37 ▪ 22 24.2 24.4

19649 CSH O P7 G1.2 1928–1949
Yen, Y. C. James (Yen Yang-ch'u), 1894–.
Ting hsien experiment, 1930–1931.
Ting-hsien, Hopei: Chinese National Assn. of the Mass Education Movement, 1931. 37 p.
SUBJ 37 ▪ 26.1 26.3 27 28 33 34.1 38

1911-1972
(including 1644-1972)

19650 MAM PO P2 G1.1 1911–1972
Atterbury, Marguerite, 1896–.
A study of some phases of Chinese-American co-operation in promoting China's agricultural extension.
Ann Arbor: University Microfilms (Publ. 8600), 1954. 401 p. (Doctoral dissertation in Sociology, Columbia U.)
SUBJ 14.1 37 ▪ 14.2 16.3 22 24.3 30 56 66

19651 MCH S P1 G1.2 –1972
Brémond, René.
'La réforme de l'écriture et la langue chinoises et l'opinion confucéenne' (The reform of Chinese writing and language and Confucian opinion). [With English abstract]
Civilisations 6, 2 (1956), 221–232.
SUBJ 37 64 ▪ 17

19652 MAM P P2 G1.2 1928–1972
Bruckner, Lee Ira, 1927–.
Spare-time higher education in Communist China, with emphasis on higher correspondence education.
Ann Arbor: University Microfilms (Publ. 70-14,694), 1970. 273 p. (Doctoral dissertation in Education, Montana State U.)
SUBJ 17 37 ▪ 14.2

19653 CSU P P1 G1.1 1911–1972
Chu, Yu-kuang, 1902–, and Nishimoto Noji.
'A comparative study of language reforms in China and Japan.'
Skidmore College b. 55, 2 (Dec. 1969), 3–36.
SUBJ 37 ▪ 66

19654 CSU PO P7 G1.1 1928–1972
Ladejinsky, Wolf Isaac, 1901–.
'Rural reconstruction under the China Aid Act.'
Foreign agriculture 14, 8 (Aug. 1950), 167–174.
SUBJ 14.1 37

19655 MAM P P2 G1.2 1911–1972
Lin, Vincent Tsing Ching, 1916–.
Adult education in People's Republic of China, 1950–1958.
Ann Arbor: University Microfilms (Publ. 64-2092), 1964. 472 p. (Doctoral dissertation in Education, U. of California, Berkeley, 1963)
SUBJ 16 27 37 ▪ 11 11.4 12.1 19 64

19656 NIC P P1 G1.2 1928–1972
Mills, Harriet Cornelia, 1920–.
'Language reform in China: Some recent developments.'
FEQ 15, 4 (Aug. 1956), 517–540.
SUBJ 37 62 64 ▪ 17 29

19657 MMT P P1 G1.2 1911–1972
Serruys, Paul Leo Mary, 1912–.
Survey of the Chinese language reform and the anti-illiteracy movement in Communist China.
Berkeley: U. of California, Center for Chinese Studies, 1962. 208 p. (Current Chinese Language Project, Studies in Chinese Communist terminology, 8) [Reprinted—Ann Arbor: University Microfilms, n.d. 208 p.]
SUBJ 29 37 62 ▪ 12.1 14.2 64 70 72

19658 CSU P P2 G1.2 1928–1972
Seybolt, Peter Jordan, 1934–.
'The Yenan revolution in mass education.'
CQ 48 (Oct.–Dec. 1971), 641–669.
SUBJ 27 37 64 ▪ 12.1

19659 CSH P P2 G1.2 1928–1972
Volzhanin, V-.
'Politika kitaiskogo rukovodstva v oblasti kul'tury' (The cultural policy of China's leaders). In *Kitaiskaia Narodnaia Respublika* (The People's Republic of China), compiled by Institut Dal'nego Vostoka, Akademiia nauk SSSR, edited by Mikhail Iosifovich Sladkovskii and Grigorii Dmitrievich Sukharchuk. [Selective entry]
Moscow: Nauka, Glav. red. vost. lit-ry, 1970, 189–227.
SUBJ 17 31 37 64 ▪ 16.1

1949-1972

19660 NIC P P2 G1.2 1949–1972
Abe Munemitsu.
'Spare-time education in Communist China.'
CQ 8 (Oct.–Dec. 1961), 149–159. [Reprinted as 'Spare-time education in Communist China: A general survey.' In *Education and Communism in China: An anthology of commentary and documents*, edited by Stewart Erskine Fraser. London: Pall Mall Press, 1971, 239–253.]
SUBJ 17 37

19661 CSH O P7 G4.2 1949–1972
Che Hung-chang (Ch'e Hung-chang) and Huang Hsin-teh (Huang Hsin-te).
'How Yinta township started spare-time education for peasants.' Tr. of 'Chiu-ch'üan hsien Yin-ta hsiang shih tsen yang chin hsing nung min yeh yü wen hua chiao yü ti?' (Promoting part-time education for the peasantry in Yin-ta *hsiang*, Chiu-ch'üan *hsien* [Kansu]); in *Chung-kuo nung ts'un ti she hui chu i kao ch'ao* (The socialist upsurge in rural China); Peking: Jen min ch'u pan she, 1956, vol. 3, 1262–1270. In *Socialist upsurge in China's countryside*, edited by Pan kung t'ing, Chung yang wei yüan hui, Chung-kuo kung ch'an tang (General Office, Central Committee, Chinese Communist Party). [Selective entry]
Peking: Foreign Languages Press, 1957, 433–442.
SUBJ 34.1 37 ▪ 22.1 26.3

19662 NNC P P2 G1.2 1949–1972
Chi Tung-wei.
Education for the proletariat in Communist China, mimeo.
Hong Kong: Union Research Institute, 1954. 73 p. (Communist China problem research series, EC6)
SUBJ 27 37 ▪ 12.1 16.3 16.4 64

19663 NNC PO P7 G9.4 1949–1972
Chinese-American Joint Commission on Rural Reconstruction.
Intensive village improvement in Taiwan.
Taipei: Chinese-American Joint Commission on Rural Reconstruction, 1960. 63, 54 p.
SUBJ 20 24.1 28 37 ▪ 31 56

19664 CSH O P8 G5.3 1949–1972
Chung-kuo kung ch'an tang (Chinese Communist Party). Shan-tung sheng wei yüan hui (Shantung Provincial Committee) *and* Shantung. Lin-i ti ch'ü cheng fu (Lin-i District). Ko ming wei yüan hui (Revolutionary Committee), *joint sponsors*. Lien ho tiao ch'a tsu (Joint Investigation Team). [This agency has still a third joint sponsor: Shantung, Chü-nan hsien cheng fu, Ko ming wei yüan hui (Chü-nan Hsien, Revolutionary Committee).]
'Run spare-time education well according to Chairman Mao's directive: Report on an investigation of Kaochialiukou production brigade of Chünan hsien, Shantúng.' Tr. of 'An Mao chu hsi chih shih pan hao yeh yü chiao yü: Shan-tung Chü-nan hsien Kao-chia-liu-kou ta tui ti tiao ch'a pao kao' (Manage sparetime education according to Mao

Tse-tung's directive: Report on Kao-chia-liu-kou brigade, Chü-nan *hsien*, Shantung); *Hung ch'i* 1971, 6 (June), 26–34.
CE 5, 1/2 (Spring–Summer 1972), 47–65.
Subj 37 ▪ 26.3

19665 MCH P P1 G1.2 1949–1972
Collotti Pischel, Enrica, 1930–.
'Riflessi politici della riforma della lingua in Cina' (Political consequences of the language reform in China).
Politico 21, 3 (dicembre 1956), 598–607.
Subj 17 37 ▪ 12.1 29

19666 CSU P P1 G1.2 1949–1972
DeFrancis, John, 1911–.
'Language and script reform.' In *Current trends in linguistics, Vol. 2, Linguistics in East Asia and South East Asia*, edited by Thomas A. Sebeok. [Selective entry]
The Hague: Mouton, 1967, 130–150.
Subj 37 ▪ 14.2 29 36.1

19667 MCH P P3 G1.2 1949–1972
Harper, Paul Frederick, 1929–.
'Closing the education gap: Problems of industrial spare-time schools.'
CS 3, 15 (15 Mar. 1965), 1–16. [Reprinted as 'Problems of industrial spare-time schools.' In *Education and Communism: An anthology of commentary and documents*, edited by Stewart Erskine Fraser. (Selective entry.) London: Pall Mall Press, 1971, 255–274.]
Subj 14.4 37 ▪ 12.1 16.4 27 36.4

19668 MCH P P5 G1.2 1949–1972
Harper, Paul Frederick, 1929–.
Spare-time education for workers in Communist China.
Washington, D.C.: U.S. Dept. of Health, Education, and Welfare, Office of Education, 1964. 29 p. (OE bulletins, 1964, 30; OE 14,102)
Subj 16.4 27 32.1 37 ▪ 11.4 14.4 34.2

19669 CSH O P7 G2.1 1949–1972
Heilungkiang. Yen-shou Hsien. Revolutionary Committee *and* Mu-tan-chiang Health School, *joint sponsors*. Culture, Education, and Health Section.
'Resolutely implement Chairman Mao's great "June 26" directive by training medical workers to serve the vast rural population.'
CM 1968, 6 (June), 323–330.
Subj 37 56

19670 CSU P P1 G1.2 1949–1972
Hsia, Tao-tai (Hsia Tao-t'ai), 1915–.
China's language reforms.
New Haven: Yale U., Far Eastern Publications, 1956. 200 p.
Subj 17 37

19671 MCY P P7 G1.2 1949–1972
Jan, George P. (Jan Po-kung), 1925–.
'Mass education in the Chinese communes.'
AS 4, 10 (Oct. 1964), 1102–1114. [Reprinted in *Education and Communism in China: An anthology of commentary and documents*, edited by Stewart Erskine Fraser. (Selective entry.) London: Pall Mall Press, 1971, 127–145.]
Subj 27 37 ▪ 22.1 24.2

19672 CSH O P8 G4.2 1949–1972
Kansu. Lin-t'ao hsien cheng fu. Ko ming wei yüan hui. (Lin-t'ao Hsien. Revolutionary Committee).
'The poor and lower-middle peasants have acquired socialist culture: Investigation report on the rural educational revolution by the Niu-t'ou-kou brigade, Lin-t'ao *hsien*, Kansu.' Tr. by Akira Odani of 'P'in hsia chung nung yu liao she hui chu i wen hua: Kan-su Lin-t'ao hsien Niu-t'ou-kou ta tui kuan yü nung ts'un chiao yü ko ming ti tiao ch'a pao kao'; *Hung ch'i* 1970, 8 (Aug.), 35–39.
CE 4, 1 (Spring 1971), 64–73.
Subj 37 ▪ 24.1 26.3

19673 DLC P P2 G1.2 1949–1972
Klepikov, Vladimir Zakharovich, 1932–.
'Narodnoe obrazovanie v Kitaiskoi Narodnoi Respublike za 10 let' (A decade of national education in the People's Republic of China).
Sovetskaia pedagogika 23, 11 (noiabr' 1959), 119–131.
Subj 14 37 ▪ 14.1 14.4 19 27 34.1 52 54

19674 NNC O P2 G1.2 1949–1972
Kuraishi Takeshiro (Kuraishi Takeshirō), 1897–.
Spot report on Communist China's language reform, mimeo. Tr. of 'Genchi de mita moji kaikaku' (Personal observations of the reform of Chinese characters); *Ajia keizai jumpō* 439 (1 Aug. 1960), 1–9.
Washington, D.C.: U.S. Joint Publications Research Service, 5 Dec. 1960. 9 p. (JPRS 6280; MC 1071/1961)
Subj 37

19675 CSH O P8 G9.1 1949–1972
Kwangsi. Yü-lin chuan ch'ü cheng fu (Yü-lin Special District). Ko ming wei yüan hui (Revolutionary Committee) *and* Kwangsi. Kuei-p'ing hsien cheng fu (Kuei-p'ing Hsien). Ko ming wei yüan hui (Revolutionary Committee), *joint sponsors*. Tiao ch'a tsu (Investigation Team).
'Train workers to have socialist consciousness and culture: Investigation report on the "May 7" labor school in Kuei-p'ing *hsien*, Kwangsi.' Tr. by Akira Odani of 'P'ei yang yu she hui chu i chüeh wu ti yu wen hua ti lao tung che: Kuang-hsi Kuei-p'ing hsien "wu, ch'i" lao tung hsüeh hsiao ti tiao ch'a pao kao'; *Hung ch'i* 1970, 8 (Aug.), 40–45.
CE 4, 1 (Spring 1971), 74–85.
Subj 26.1 37 ▪ 32.1

19676 NNC P P2 G1.2 1949–1972
[La Dany, Ladislao] ———, 1914–.
'Facing illiteracy.'
CNA 115 (13 Jan. 1956), 2–7.
Subj 37

19677 NIC P P2 G1.2 1949–1972
[La Dany, Ladislao] ———, 1914–.
'The writing reform.'
CNA 315 (11 Mar. 1960), 1–7.
Subj 37

19678 MCH P P1 G1.2 1949–1972
Lin, Vincent Tsing Ching, 1916–.
'Adult education in Red China.'
Adult education 14, 4 (Summer 1964), 240–252. [For fuller treatment, see entry 19655.]
Subj 37 ▪ 27 64

19679 CSU FP P7 G9.4 1949–1972
Lionberger, Herbert Frederick, 1912–, and H. C. Chang (Chang Hsi-chih), 1920–.
Farm information for modernizing agriculture: The Taiwan system.
New York: Praeger, 1970. 26, 425 p.
Subj 24.2 26.3 27 37 ▪ 22 24.1 26.1 28 34.1 41 62

19680 CSH O P3 G6.1 1949–1972
Ma Fei-hai.
'New trends in the after-hours education of the workers of Shanghai.' Tr. of 'Shang-hai shih chih kung yeh yü chiao yü ti hsin hsing shih'; *Hung ch'i* 1960, 16 (16 Aug.), 31–36. In *Translations from 'Hung-ch'i' (Red flag) (Peiping, No. 16, 16 August 1960)*, mimeo., compiled by U.S. Joint Publications Research Service. [Sole entry]
Washington, D.C.: JPRS, 12 Oct. 1960, 49–60. (JPRS 6077; MC 18,911/1960)
Subj 26.4 37

19681 CSU P P2 G1.2 1949–1972
Milsky, Constantin.
'New developments in language reform.'
CQ 53 (Jan.–Mar. 1973), 98–133.
Subj 37

19682 MCH P P1 G1.2 1949–1972
Scholze, F- Th——.
'Probleme der Volksbildung und der Pädagogik in der Volksrepublik China' (Problems of mass education and educational theory in the People's Republic of China).
Pädagogik 12, 7 (1957), 550–557.
Subj 17 37 ▪ 64

19683 NNC F P3 G9.5 1949–1972
Styler, W- E-.
'Adult education in Hong Kong.'
Oversea education 34, 3 (Oct. 1962), 112–118.
Subj 37 ▪ 17 50

19684 CSH P P1 G1.2 1949–1972
Wang Hsueh-wen (Wang Hsüeh-wen).
'New trend of the Chinese Communist characters reform movement.'
IS 9, 3 (Dec. 1972), 26–38.
Subj 37

38 Organized Philanthropy and Mutual-Aid Societies

慈善團體及互助組織

慈善団体及び共済組合

1644-1911

19685 CSU O P2 G9.5 1842–1895
Aborigine, pseud.
'On the mode of raising and administering public subscriptions in China.'
NQCJ 3, 9 (Sept. 1869), 134–137.
Subj 38

19686 CSU O P3 G1.3 1895–1911
Edwards, Dwight Woodbridge.
'The Chinese Young Men's Christian Association.'

AAAPSS 39 (Jan. 1912), 109–123.
SUBJ 17 33 38 54 ▪ 14.2 31

19687 NNC P P1 G1.1 –1911
Garrett, Frank.
Chinese charitable institutions as mentioned in Chinese literature.
Unpublished masters thesis in Chinese, Columbia U., 1904. 27 p.
SUBJ 18 38 ▪ 63 64

19688 GMS P P2 G1.3 –1911
Hirth, Friedrich, 1845–1927.
'Über gemeinnützige Anstalten in China' (Public institutions in China).
Beiträge zur Kenntnis des Orients 1 (1902/03), 1–25. [Separately reprinted—Leipzig: Harrassowitz, 1903. 25 p.]
SUBJ 28 38 50 ▪ 42 52 56 57

19689 CBU O P7 G6.1 1842–1895
Imbault-Huart, Camille Clément, 1857–1897.
'Une visite à un établissement charitable indigène près Changhaï' (A visit to a native charitable institution near Shanghai).
JA 7e série 18 (oct.–déc. 1881), 255–263.
SUBJ 38

19690 CSU O P3 G6.1 1842–1895
K.
'Life boats in China.'
NQCJ 2, 12 (Dec. 1868), 190.
SUBJ 38 ▪ 57

19691 NNM O P3 G9.2 1842–1895
Kerr, John Glasgow, 1824–1901.
'A Chinese benevolent association.'
CMMJ 3, 4 (Dec. 1889), 152–155.
SUBJ 38 ▪ 28

19692 MCH PO P3 G9.0 1644–1895
Kerr, John Glasgow, 1824–1901.
'The native benevolent institutions of Canton.'
China review 2, 2 (Sept.–Oct. 1873), 88–95; 3, 2 (Sept.–Oct. 1874), 108–114.
SUBJ 28 38 50 56 ▪ 27 52 57

19693 CSU P P3 G9.5 1842–1911
Lethbridge, Henry James, 1923–.
'A Chinese association in Hong Kong: The Tung Wah [i.e., Tung-hua].'
Contributions to Asian studies 1 (Jan. 1971), 144–158.
SUBJ 38 66 ▪ 26.2 32.2 56

19694 CSU O P3 G7.2 1895–1911
Preston, T- J-.
'Chinese benevolent institutions in theory and practice.'
CR 38, 5 (May 1907), 245–253.
SUBJ 38 ▪ 22.2 28 50 52 56

19695 CSU P P2 G1.3 1644–1911
Tsu, Y. Y. (Chu Yu-yü), 1886–.
The spirit of Chinese philanthropy: A study in mutual aid.
New York: Columbia U., Faculty of Political Science, 1912. 122 p. (Columbia studies in history, economics and public law, 50, 1 [whole no. 125]) (Doctoral dissertation in Sociology, Columbia U.) [Reprinted—New York: AMS Press, 1969. 122 p.]
SUBJ 18 34.3 38 42 ▪ 12.2 17 33 37 39 47 50 57 63

19696 NNC O P3 G9.5 1842–1895
Wedepohl, ———.
'Das Findelhaus Bethesda auf Hongkong' (The Bethesda foundling-home in Hong Kong).
Allgemeine Missions-Z. 13, 11 (Nov. 1886), 529–545.
SUBJ 38 52 ▪ 33 47 56

1644-1949

19697 MCH P P3 G1.2 1895–1928
Garrett, Shirley Stone, 1924–.
Social reformers in urban China: The Chinese Y.M.C.A., 1895–1926.
Cambridge: Harvard U. Press, 1970. 224 p. (Harvard East Asian series, 56) (Revision of *The salvation of China: Urban reform and the Chinese Y.M.C.A.*, doctoral dissertation in History, Harvard U., 1966)
SUBJ 31 37 38 54 64 ▪ 17 32.1 62 66

19698 CSU O P4 G1.3 1895–1928
Rawlinson, Frank Joseph, 1871–1937.
'The Young Men's Christian Association in China.'
CR 51, 5 (May 1920), 342–348.
SUBJ 38 54

1911-1949

19699 CSH O P3 G1.1 1911–1928
'The Young Men's Christian Associations of China.' In *The Christian occupation of China*, edited by Milton Theobald Stauffer. [Selective entry]
Shanghai: China Continuation Committee, 1922, 371–375.
SUBJ 33 37 38 54 ▪ 17

19700 CSU O P2 G1.2 1928–1949
Barr, John S-, comp.
'Christian activities in war-torn China.'
CR 69, 9 – 72, 9 (Sept. 1938 – Sept. 1941), 195 p. in all.
SUBJ 28 38 ▪ 11.2 17 33 54

19701 MCY P P1 G1.2 1911–1949
Gérardin, André, and Chen Tsai-k'i (Shen Tsai-ch'i).
'La fondation en droit chinois moderne' (Endowed institutions in modern Chinese law).
BUA 3e série 6, 24 (1945), 726–754.
SUBJ 12.2 22.2 38

19702 CSH P P2 G9.5 1928–1949
Hong Kong. Secretariat for Chinese Affairs.
Report, 1946/47–1947/48. [Issues for 1950/51–1966/67 are entered as 19713.]
[Hong Kong]: ——, 1947, 1948. Average ca. 30 p.
SUBJ 22.2 30 38 ▪ 22.1 24.5 27 31 52 57

19703 MCH O P3 G6.1 1928–1949
Liu, Frances W.
'Woman's fight against beggary.'
CQ-S 1, 4 (Summer 1936), 99–104.
SUBJ 26 28 38 47 ▪ 34.3

19704 MCH P P3 G1.2 1928–1949
Lou, Yee-wen (Lu Yü-wen).
Les oeuvres sociales dans les chemins de fer chinois (Social welfare in the Chinese railroads).
Paris: Bossuet, 1937. 135 p. (Doctoral dissertation, Faculté des lettres, Université de Paris)
SUBJ 16.4 18 36.4 37 38 ▪ 12.2 14.2 39 47

19705 MCH P P2 G1.2 1911–1949
Nathan, Andrew James, 1943–.
A history of the China International Famine Relief Commission.
Cambridge: Harvard U., East Asian Research Center, 1965. 106 p. (Harvard East Asian monographs, 17) (Revision of senior thesis in History, Harvard U., 1963)
SUBJ 14.6 18 34.1 38 ▪ 14.2 66

19706 NNC O P3 G6.1 1928–1949
Tsao, Y. S. (Ts'ao Yün-hsiang), 1881–.
'The Red Cross Society in China.'
CQ-S 1, 4 (Summer 1936), 55–63.
SUBJ 38 ▪ 12

19707 NNC O P7 G1.2 1928–1949
United Nations. Relief and Rehabilitation Administration.
UNRRA in China, 1945–1947.
Washington, D.C.: Relief and Rehabilitation Administration, 1948. 375 p. (UNRRA operational analysis papers, 53)
SUBJ 14.1 18 38 ▪ 24.4 34.2 62

19708 NNC O P8 G5.3 1928–1949
Wong Yo-yui.
'"The Filial Mourning Headdress Society" in the villages of Chang-i [i.e., Ch'ang-i *hsien*], Shantung.' Tr. from *I shih pao fu k'an* 23 Mar. 1935. In *Agrarian China*, compiled by Institute of Pacific Relations. [Selective entry]
Chicago: U. of Chicago Press, 1939, 204–207.
SUBJ 38 57

1911-1972
(including 1644-1972)

19709 CSH P P3 G1.2 1895–1972
Latourette, Kenneth Scott, 1884–1968.
'Serving in revolutionary China.' In *World service: A history of the foreign work and world service of the Young Men's Christian Associations of the United States and Canada*, by K. S. Latourette. [Sole entry]
New York: Association Press, 1957, 245–314.
SUBJ 33 38 ▪ 16.1 17 37 54 66

19710 CSU P P3 G9.5 1842–1972
Lethbridge, Henry James, 1923–.
'The evolution of a Chinese voluntary association in Hong Kong: The Po Leung Kuk [i.e., Pao-liang Chü, Society for the Protection of Women and Girls].'
JOS 10, 1 (Jan. 1972), 33–50.
SUBJ 38 46 47 ▪ 22.2 26 52 66

1949-1972

19711 MCY FP P2 G9.4 1949–1972
China [Republic]. Nei cheng pu. (Ministry of Interior).
Social welfare services in the Republic of China.
Taipei: Nei cheng pu, 1958. 38 p.
SUBJ 28 38 ▪ 52 56

19712 MCH O P3 G9.5 1949–1972
Gamarekian, Edward.
'Hong Kong's forgotten girls.'
United Asia 15, 6 (June 1963), 432–435.
SUBJ 38 47 54 ▪ 24.4 28

19713 CSU P P2 G9.5 1949–1972
Hong Kong. Secretariat for Chinese Affairs.
Annual departmental report of the Secretary for Chinese Affairs for the financial year 1950/51–1966/67. [Issues for 1946/47–1947/48 are entered as 19702.]
Hong Kong: Government Printer. Issued annually, 1951–1967. Average ca. 50 p.
SUBJ 22.2 30 38 ▪ 22.1 24.5 27 31 52 57

19714 HKU P P4 G9.5 1949–1972
Hong Kong Council of Social Service, comp.
Working together: A survey of the work of voluntary and governmental social service organizations in Hong Kong.
Hong Kong: Government Printer, 1958. 149 p.
SUBJ 28 30 38 ▪ 31

39 ASSOCIATIONS BASED ON COMMON PLACE OF ORIGIN
鄉誼組織　同鄉組織

19715 CSH U P2 G1.2 –1928
Avenarius, G- G-.
'Zemliachestva i tsekhovye ob"edineniia v Kitae' (Native-place associations and guilds in China).
VM 1926, 5, 92–98.
SUBJ 34.3 39 ▪ 22.2 34.1 34.2 36.1 36.2 66

19716 NNC P P4 G9.2 1842–1911
Bach, A- H-, and Alfred Forke, 1867–1944.
'Regeln der kantoner Kaufmannsgilde in Pakhoi' (Statutes of the guild for Cantonese merchants at Pei-hai [Ho-p'u *hsien*, Kwangtung]).
MSOSB 8 (1905), 263–268.
SUBJ 34.3 39 ▪ 26.2

19717 MAM P P2 G1.1 1842–1911
Chang, Perry (Chang P'eng), 1921–.
The distribution and relative strength of the provincial merchant groups in China, 1842–1911.
Ann Arbor: University Microfilms (Publ. 58-2134), 1958. 217 p. (Doctoral dissertation in Economics, U. of Washington)
SUBJ 14.3 16.2 34.3 39 ▪ 30 34.2 36.2

19718 CSU P P2 G1.5 –1911
Ho, Ping-ti, 1917–.
'The geographic distribution of *hui-kuan* (landsmannschaften) in central and upper Yangtze provinces.'
THJ new (2nd) series 5, 2 (Dec. 1966), 120–152.
SUBJ 21.2 39 ▪ 24.1 31

40 KINSHIP SYSTEMS IN GENERAL
親屬制度通論　親族制度一般

1644-1911

19719 FPL P P2 G1.2 1895–1911
Farjenel, Fernand, ?–1918.
Le peuple chinois: ses moeurs et ses institutions (The Chinese people: Their customs and institutions).
Paris: Chevalier et Rivière, 1901. 11, 426 p.
SUBJ 12 12.2 13 40 41 45 ▪ 16 18 21.1 23 42 43 50 62 65 66

19720 MCH O P8 G1.2 1895–1911
Leong, Y. K. (Liang Yü-kao), 1888–.
'The internal working of a Chinese village.' In *Village and town life in China*, by Y. K. Leong and L. K. Tao (T'ao Meng-ho). [Analytic entry]
London: Allen and Unwin, 1915, 3–41. (London School of Economics and Political Science, Monographs on sociology, 4) [Reprinted in *Village and town life in China*, by Y. K. Leong and L. K. Tao. (Analytic entry.) Westport, Conn.: Hyperion Press, 197?, 3–41.]
SUBJ 22.1 40 41 43 ▪ 23 42 44

19721 MCH PO P2 G1.2 1842–1895
Macgowan, John, ?–1922.
'Social life and religious ideas of the Chinese.' In *Narrative of the mission to China of the English Presbyterian Church . . .*, 2nd ed., by Donald Matheson. [Analytic entry]
London: Nisbet, 1866, 81–144.
SUBJ 40 41 52 57 62 63 ▪ 17 22 43 47 51 55

19722 CSU P P1 G1.2 –1895
Medhurst, Walter Henry, 1796–1857.
'Marriage, affinity, and inheritance in China.'
Transactions of the China Branch of the Royal Asiatic Society 4 (1853/54), 1–32.
SUBJ 40 41 44 45 ▪ 12.2 16 46 57

19723 NNC F P4 G5.3 –1911
Volpert, Ant——.
'Die Ehrenpforten in China' (Memorial gates in China).
Orientalisches Archiv 1, 3 (1910/11), 140–148; 1, 4 (1910/11), 190–195.
SUBJ 40 41 47 ▪ 43 57 63

1644-1949

19724 NIC U P1 G1.2 –1949
Ariga, Kizaemon.
'Introduction to the family system in Japan, China and Korea.' In *Transactions of the Third World Congress of Sociology, Vol. 4, Changes in the family.* [Selective entry]
London: International Sociological Assn., 1956, 199–207.
SUBJ 40 41 ▪ 43 45

19725 CSU P P1 G1.0 –1949
Cheng, Ch'eng-k'un, 1906–.
'Familism, the foundation of Chinese social organization.'
Social forces 23, 1 (Oct. 1944), 50–59.
SUBJ 40 63 ▪ 43 47 57

19726 NNC O P7 G7.3 1895–1928
Chiang, Yee (Chiang I), 1903–.
A Chinese childhood.
New York: Norton, 1963. 304 p.
SUBJ 27 40 41 55 64 ▪ 21.3 24.1 26.1 29 30 53 56 66

19727 NIC S P1 G1.1 –1949
Tao, L. K. (T'ao Meng-ho), 1887–1960.
'Some Chinese characteristics in the light of the Chinese family.' In *Essays presented to C. G. Seligman*, edited by Edward Evan Evans-Pritchard et al. [Sole entry]
London: Kegan Paul, Trench, Trübner, 1934, 335–344.
SUBJ 40 41 61 ▪ 22.2 42

1911-1949

19728 CSH F P8 G1.2 1928–1949
Fukutake, Tadashi, 1917–.
'Chinese village and Japanese village.' Tr. from the Japanese. In *Asian rural society: China, India, Japan*, by Tadashi Fukutake. [Selective entry]
Tokyo: U. of Tokyo Press, 1967, 13–25.
SUBJ 40 ▪ 24.1 26

19729 CSU F P6 G8.2 1928–1949
Hsu, Francis L. K. (Hsü Lang-kuang), 1909–.
Under the ancestors' shadow: Kinship, personality and social mobility in village China, rev. and enl. ed.
Garden City, N.Y.: Doubleday, 1967. 13, 370 p. [Reprinted—Stanford: Stanford U. Press, 1971. 12, 370 p.]
SUBJ 26 40 41 43 57 61 ▪ 23 45 46 47 50 53 55 62 65

1911-1972
(including 1644-1972)

19730 CSU S P1 G1.1 –1972
Cheung, Steven N. S., 1935–.
'Enforcement of property rights in children, and the marriage contract.'
Economic j. 82, 326 (June 1972), 641–657.
SUBJ 40 41 52 ▪ 44 45 47

19731 CSU S P1 G1.2 –1972
Choi, Jai-seuk.
'Comparative study on the traditional families in Korea, Japan and China.' In *Families in East and West: Socialization process and kinship ties*, edited by Reuben Hill and René König. [Selective entry]
The Hague: Mouton, 1970, 202–210.
SUBJ 40 41 45 ▪ 43 44

19732 ICU P P2 G1.2 1928–1972
Dittmer, Lowell, 1941–.
The Chinese marriage law of 1950: A study of elite control and social change.
Unpublished masters thesis in Political Science, U. of Chicago, 1967. 309 p.
SUBJ 12.1 12.2 40 41 47 50 ▪ 14.2 42 46 52 53 57 61 64

19733 CSU S P1 G1.1 –1972
Freedman, Maurice, 1920–.
'Ritual aspects of Chinese kinship and marriage.' In *Family and kinship in Chinese society*, edited by M. Freedman. [Selective entry]

Stanford: Stanford U. Press, 1970, 163–187.
SUBJ 40 41 43 ▪ 45 47

19734 CSU O P1 G1.0 –1972
Hsu, Francis L. K. (Hsü Lang-kuang), 1909–.
'Chinese kinship and Chinese behavior.' In *China in crisis, Vol. 1, China's heritage and the Communist political system*, edited by Ping-ti Ho and Tang Tsou. [Selective entry]
Chicago: U. of Chicago Press, 1968, 579–608.
SUBJ 40 41 46 ▪ 30 47 48

19735 CBU S P1 G1.1 –1972
Hsu, Francis L. K. (Hsü Lang-kuang), 1909–.
'Filial piety in Japan and China: Borrowing, variation and significance.'
J. of comparative family studies 2, 1 (Spring 1971), 67–74.
SUBJ 40 43 ▪ 41 42 63

19736 CSU S P1 G1.2 –1972
Rohlen, Thomas P-.
'Father-son dominance: Tikopia and China.' In *Kinship and culture*, edited by Francis L. K. Hsu (Hsü Lang-kuang). [Selective entry]
Chicago: Aldine, 1971, 144–157.
SUBJ 40 41 ▪ 42 43 46

1949-1972

19737 CSU FP P8 G9.4 1949–1972
Pasternak, Burton, 1933–.
Kinship and community in two Chinese villages [Ta-t'ieh, P'ing-tung *hsien*, and Chung-she, T'ai-nan *hsien*, Taiwan].
Stanford: Stanford U. Press, 1972. 174 p.
SUBJ 20 24 24.1 30 40 42 ▪ 22 22.2 23 25 26 29 34.1 41 44 45

19738 CSU F P7 G9.4 1949–1972
Wolf, Margery, 1933–.
The house of Lim: A study of a Chinese farm family.
New York: Appleton-Century-Crofts, 1968. 16, 147 p.
SUBJ 40 41 47 48 55 ▪ 22.2 23 24.3 31 42 46 50 61 65

41 MARRIAGE AND THE FAMILY
婚姻與家庭 婚姻と家庭

1644-1911

19739 NIC O P1 G5.2 1895–1911
'A posthumous marriage.'
TP 10, 1 (1899), 114.
SUBJ 41 57 ▪ 43

19740 NIC O P3 G5.1 1842–1895
Bismark, Karl.
'The marriage of the emperor of China.'
Galaxy 19 (Jan.–June 1875), 182–193.
SUBJ 41 ▪ 13

19741 MCH O P1 G1.2 1644–1842
Bohet, M-.
'Solemnités des mariages chez les Chinois' (Chinese wedding ceremonies).
Nouvelles annales des voyages 63 (1834), 152–161.
SUBJ 41

19742 CSU O P2 G8.1 1895–1911
Brenier, Henri, 1867–?
'Une tournée dans l'est du Se-tchouan: de Tchoung-king à Tchen-tou par Su-tin fou' (A trip through eastern Szechwan, from Chungking to Chengtu via Sui-ting-fu). In *La Mission lyonnaise d'exploration commerciale en Chine, 1895–1897, première partie, récits des voyages* (The Lyons Trade Mission to China, 1895–1897, Part 1, Travel accounts), compiled by Chambre de commerce de Lyon. [Selective entry]
Lyons: Rey, 1898, 189–203 [s.p.].
SUBJ 41 55 ▪ 21.3 22.2 26.2 47 56

19743 IMN PO P1 G1.1 –1895
Cerone, Francesco.
Il matrimonio in Cina (Marriage in China), 2nd ed.
Naples: Tocco, 1900. 126 p.
SUBJ 41 ▪ 47 65

19744 CBU U P1 G1.3 –1911
Chiu, Vermier Yantak (Chao P'ing), 1890–1964.
'Some notes on Chinese customary marriage.' In *Family law and customary law in Asia: A contemporary legal perspective*, edited by David Charles Buxbaum. [Sole entry]
The Hague: Nijhoff, 1968, 45–49.
SUBJ 22.2 41

19745 MCH U P1 G1.2 1842–1895
Cordier, Henri, 1849–1925.
'Le divorce en Chine' (Divorce in China).
R. de l'Extrême-Orient 1, 2 (1882), 329–331.
SUBJ 41 ▪ 47

19746 MCH PO P8 G6.3 1842–1895
Donnat, Léon, 1832–1893.
'Paysans en communauté du Ning-po-fou' (An extended family of peasants in Ning-po *fu* [Chekiang]).
Ouvriers des deux mondes 4, 30 (1862), 83–158.
SUBJ 24 26.3 41 55 ▪ 23 24.1 43 47 62

19747 NNC P P2 G1.3 –1895
Eberhard, Wolfram, 1909–.
'Research on the Chinese family.'
Sociologus neue (2.) Folge 9, 1 (1959), 1–11. [Reprinted in *Settlement and social change in Asia*, by W. Eberhard. (Selective entry.) Hong Kong: Hong Kong U. Press, 1967, 28–42.]
SUBJ 41 58 ▪ 11 11.2 14.1 42

19748 MCH PO P2 G6.1 –1895
Entrecolles, François-Xavier d', 1662–1741.
'Moeurs chinoises au Kiang-sou' (Chinese customs in Kiangsu).
Missions catholiques 4 (2 fév. – 24 mai 1872), 23 p. in all.
SUBJ 22.2 41 43 57 ▪ 23 40 55 63

19749 MCH O P7 G9.2 1842–1895
Fielde, Adele Marion, 1839–1916.
'Chinese marriage customs.'
Popular science monthly 34, 2 (Dec. 1888), 241–246.
SUBJ 41

19750 ELO FP P1 G1.1 1644–1911
Groot, Jan Jakob Maria de, 1854–1921.
'Adoption (Chinese).' In *Encyclopedia of religion and ethics*, edited by James Hastings. [Sole entry]
New York: Scribner, 1908, vol. 1, 107.
SUBJ 41 ▪ 43

19751 NNC O P2 G1.2 1842–1911
Headland, Isaac Taylor, 1859–1942.
Home life in China.
New York: Macmillan, 1914. 12, 319 p. [Reprinted—Detroit: Grand River Books, 1971. 12, 319 p.]
SUBJ 41 47 50 53 55 ▪ 14.1 16.3 17 31 33 43 48 62 65

19752 MCH P P1 G1.1 –1895
Hoang, Pierre (Huang Po-lu), 1830–1909.
Le mariage chinois au point de vue légal (Chinese marriage from a legal viewpoint), 2nd ed.
Shanghai: Impr. de la Mission catholique, 1915. 259, 86 p. (Variétés sinologiques, 14)
SUBJ 12.2 16.1 41 57 66 ▪ 12.1 33 44 47 60

19753 MCH P P1 G1.2 1842–1911
Huberich, Charles Henry, 1877–1945.
'The paternal power in Chinese law.'
Juridical review; a j. of legal and political science 14, 4 (Dec. 1902), 378–385.
SUBJ 12.2 41 ▪ 12

19754 NNC PO P1 G1.3 –1895
Jamieson, George, 1843–1920.
'The history of adoption and its relation to modern wills.'
China review 18, 3 (Nov.–Dec. 1889), 137–146.
SUBJ 22.2 41 45 ▪ 57

19755 NNC PO P1 G1.1 –1895
Kul'chitskii, Aleksandr.
Brak u kitaitsev (Marriage among the Chinese).
Peking: Tip. Uspenskago monastyria pri RDM, 1908. 67 p.
SUBJ 41 62 65 ▪ 12.2 22.2 23 47 55

19756 NNC O P2 G9.2 1644–1895
Lechler, R-.
'Das Volks- und Familienleben' (The family life and daily existence of the common people). In *Acht Vorträge über China* (Eight essays on China), by R. Lechler. [Sole entry]
Basel: Evangelische Missionsgesellschaft, 1861, 146–173.
SUBJ 41 55 ▪ 57

19757 NNC U P1 G1.2 –1911
Liao Bao-seing (Liao Pao-hsien).
'Die chinesischen Hochzeitsbräuche vor der Revolution 1911' (Chinese wedding customs before the Revolution of 1911).
Sinica 15, 3/6 (Mai–Nov. 1940), 173–180.
SUBJ 41

19758 MCH O P3 G5.1 1842–1895
Lockhart, James Haldane Stewart, 1858–1937.
'The marriage ceremonies of the Manchus.'
Folk-lore 1, 4 (Dec. 1890), 481–492.
SUBJ 41

19759 FPN PO P1 G1.1 1842–1895
Martin, Charles Ernest, 1831–1897.
'Consanguinité et mariage chez les Chinois' (Consanguinity and marriage among the Chinese).
J. d'hygiène 16, 746 (8 jan. 1891), 13–16.
SUBJ 41 44 ▪ 22.2 23

19760 FPN PO P1 G1.2 1842–1895
Martin, Charles Ernest, 1831–1897.
'Le mariage en Chine dans ses rapports avec l'hygiène' (Marriage in China in relation to hygiene).
J. d'hygiène 17, 806 (3 mars 1892), 99–103.
SUBJ 12.2 41 ▪ 22.2 56

19761 MCH O P7 G9.3 1895–1911
Masip, Jaime P-.
'Del matrimonio chino' (Chinese marriage).
Anthropos 2, 4/5 (Juli–Sept. 1907), 715–721.
SUBJ 41 ▪ 47 61 63

19762 MCH S P1 G1.1 1842–1895
Meyners d'Estrey, Guillaume Henri Jean, 1829–?
Review of 'Het huwelijk en de wetgeving dienaangaande in China' (Marriage legislation in China), by J- W- Young.
Anthropologie 6, 4 (juil.–août 1895), 463–467.
SUBJ 12.2 41 ▪ 22.2

19763 MCH P P1 G1.1 –1895
Möllendorff, Paul Georg von, 1848–1901.
Das chinesische Familienrecht.
Leipzig: Harrassowitz, 1895. 67 p.
The family law of the Chinese.
Shanghai: Kelly and Walsh, 1896. 60 p. [A different tr.—*The family law of the Chinese*. Tr. by *Mrs*. S- M- Broadbent. Rangoon: Supdt. Government Printing and Stationery of Burma, 1925. 43 p.]
SUBJ 12.2 40 41 47 ▪ 43 44 57

19764 CSH O P2 G1.5 1895–1911
Nagel, August.
'Südchinesische Hochzeitsgebräuche' (Wedding customs of South China).
OL 26, 28 (12 Juli 1912), 39–42; 26, 29 (19 Juli 1912), 61–64.
SUBJ 41

19765 NIC O P2 G1.3 1842–1895
Parker, Edward Harper, 1849–1926.
Chinese customs.
Shanghai: Kelly and Walsh, 1899. 48 p.
SUBJ 22.2 41 57 ▪ 47 55

19766 NIC O P1 G1.2 –1895
Parker, Edward Harper, 1849–1926.
'Comparative Chinese family law.'
China review 8, 2 (Sept.–Oct. 1879), 67–107.
SUBJ 12.2 41 47 ▪ 42 44

19767 MCH PO P1 G1.2 –1911
Piton, Charles, 1835–1905.
'La famille en Chine' (The family in China). In *La Chine: sa religion, ses moeurs, ses missions* (China: Religion, customs, and missions), by C. Piton. [Sole entry]
Lausanne: Bridel; Basel: Lib. des Missions; Paris: Lib. Fishbacher, 1902, 61–122.
SUBJ 41 51 ▪ 12.1 43

19768 CBU P P2 G1.2 –1895
Plath, J- Heinrich.
'Über die häuslichen Verhältnisse der alten Chinesen' (The domestic relations of the traditional Chinese).
Sitzungsberichte der Königlichen Bayerischen Akademie der Wissenschaften 2, 4 (1862), 201–248.
SUBJ 41 47 ▪ 16.1 52 53

19769 NNC P P2 G9.4 1644–1895
Plaut, Hermann, ?–1909.
'Beiträge zur Kenntnis der Insel Formosa' (Features of Taiwan).
MSOSB 6 (1903), 28–62.
SUBJ 12 12.2 41 ▪ 12.1 22.2 42 45 52 66

19770 NIC S P1 G1.0 –1911
Queen, Stuart Alfred, 1890–, Robert Wesley Habenstein, 1914–, and John B- Adams.
'The Chinese system of familism.' In *The family in various cultures*, by S. A. Queen, R. W. Habenstein, and J. B. Adams. [Sole entry]
Philadelphia: Lippincott, 1961, 88–115.
SUBJ 41 ▪ 43 45 47

19771 MCH S P1 G1.1 1644–1911
Rivetta, Pietro Silvio, 1886–1952.
'Il matrimonio nel diritto cinese' (Marriage in Chinese law).
Rivista italiana di sociologia 16, 2 (marzo–aprile 1912), 175–214.
SUBJ 12.2 41 ▪ 63

19772 MCH P P1 G1.1 1644–1895
Scherzer, Fernand, 1849–1886.
La puissance paternelle en Chine: étude de droit chinois (Paternal authority in China: A study of Chinese law).
Paris: Ernest Leroux, 1878. 80 p.
SUBJ 12.2 41 47 57 ▪ 22.2 40 45 46 51

19773 MCH PO P1 G9.3 1842–1895
Schlegel, Gustaaf, 1840–1903.
'Wettelijke bepalingen omtrent de huwelijken in China en beschrijving der daartoe gebruikelijke plegtigheden' (Legal provisions concerning marriage in China and a description of the ceremonies usually connected with it).
Het Regt in Nederlandsch-Indië (Batavia) 20 (November 1862), 394–408.
SUBJ 12.2 22.2 41 ▪ 46

19774 GMS P P1 G1.1 –1911
Schmitt, Erich, 1893–.
Die Grundlagen der chinesischen Ehe (The foundations of marriage in China).
Leipzig: Brockhaus, 1927. 223 p.
SUBJ 12.2 41 ▪ 22.2 44 46 66

19775 MCH O P2 G1.2 1842–1895
Simon, G- Eugène, 1829–1896.
'La famille chinoise' (The Chinese family).
Nouvelle r. 21, 2 (15 mars 1883), 375–415.
'The family.' In *China: Its social, political, and religious life*, by G. E. Simon. [Analytic entry]
London: Sampson Low, Marston, Searle, and Rivington, 1887, 1–60.
SUBJ 14.5 41 ▪ 12.1 14.1 33 45 47 51

19776 NNC FP P2 G5.3 –1911
Stenz, Georg Maria, 1869–?
Beiträge zur Volkskunde Süd-Schantungs (The folklore of southern Shantung), edited by August Conrady.
Leipzig: R. Voigtländer, 1907. 116 p. (Städtisches Museum für Völkerkunde zu Leipzig, Veröffentlichungen, 1)
SUBJ 23 41 51 57 65 ▪ 43 55 62

19777 CSU O P1 G1.2 1895–1911
Tao, P. L. K.
'The family system in China.'
Sociological review 6, 1 (Jan. 1913), 47–54.
SUBJ 41 42 43 ▪ 22.2 57

19778 MCH PO P3 G9.3 1842–1895
Wettum, B- A- J- van.
'A pair of Chinese marriage contracts.'
TP 5, 5 (déc. 1894), 371–385.
SUBJ 22.2 41 ▪ 47 65

19779 NNC P P3 G5.1 1842–1895
Wilkinson, William Henry, 1858–1930.
'The marriage of the Chinese emperor.'
Asiatic quarterly review 8 (July–Oct. 1889), 82–93.
SUBJ 13 41 ▪ 12 12.2 16.1

19780 MCH P P1 G1.2 1842–1895
Young, J- W-, 1855–1898.
'Het huwelijk en de wetgeving dienaangaande in China' (Marriage legislation in China).
Tijdschrift voor Indische taal-, land- en volkenkunde 38 (1895), 1–190.
SUBJ 12.2 41 ▪ 47

1644-1949

19781 NNC U P1 G1.3 1644–1949
Carl, Wilhelm.
'Kindesadoption bei den Chinesen' (Adoption of children among the Chinese).
Anthropos 26, 1/2 (Jan.–Apr. 1931), 258–260.
SUBJ 41 ▪ 48 52 62

19782 NIC P P2 G9.4 –1949
Chen, Chiyen (Ch'en Chi-yen).
'The foster daughter-in-law system in Formosa.'
AJCL 6, 3 (Summer 1957), 302–314.
SUBJ 22.2 41

19783 MCH S P1 G1.2 1895–1949
Chiu, H. P. (Ch'iu Han-p'ing), 1904–.
'Part 1, Requisites of adoption in Roman, Hindu and Chinese law. Part 2, The effect of adoption in Roman, Hindu and Chinese law.'
CLR 4, 5 (July 1930), 133–149; 4, 7 (Jan. 1931), 277–287.
SUBJ 12.2 41

19784 GMS P P1 G1.2 1644–1928
Engelmann, Herbert.
'Das chinesische Eherecht' (Chinese marriage law).
ZVR 43, 1/2 (1927), 161–247; 43, 3 (1928), 321–415. (Doctoral dissertation, Rechts- und staatswissenschaftliche Fakultät, Universität Breslau)
SUBJ 12.2 41 ▪ 44 47 57

19785 NNC P P1 G1.2 –1949
Escarra, Jean, 1885–1955.
'Das chinesische Familienrecht in der alten Gesetzgebung und in der neuen Kodifikation' (Chinese family law in traditional legislation and in the recent codification).
Sinica 8, 3 (Mai 1933), 97–109.
SUBJ 12.2 40 41 42 ▪ 22.2 45 52

19786 CSU U P1 G1.0 1842–1949
Freedman, Maurice, 1920–.
'The Chinese domestic family: Models.' In *VIe Congrès international des sciences anthropologiques et ethnologiques, Paris, 30 juillet – 6 août 1960* (Sixth International Congress of Anthropological and Ethnological Sciences, Paris, 30 July – 6 August 1960). [Sole entry]
Paris: Musée de l'homme, 1963, vol. 2, part 1, 97–100.
Subj 41

19787 MCH U P1 G1.0 1842–1949
Freedman, Maurice, 1920–.
'Problems in the analysis of the Chinese family.'
Philadelphia Anthropological Society b. 14, 2 (Mar. 1961), 21–23.
Subj 41 ▪ 16 45

19788 CSU FP P1 G1.2 –1949
Hsu, Francis L. K. (Hsü Lang-kuang), 1909–.
'The family in China: The classical form.' In *The family: Its function and destiny*, rev. ed., edited by Ruth Nanda Anshen. [Selective entry]
New York: Harper, 1959, 123–145.
Subj 41 ▪ 12.2 47

19789 NIC P P2 G1.2 1644–1928
Jamieson, George, 1843–1920.
Chinese family and commercial law.
Shanghai: Kelly and Walsh, 1921. 188 p. [Reprinted—Taipei: Ch'eng-wen, 1968. 188 p.]
Subj 12.2 34.2 41 45 ▪ 14.3 14.5 16.2 18 22 47

19790 NNC PO P1 G1.2 –1928
Kuo Yun-kuan.
'A critical exposition of the essence of Chinese family law.'
CSPSR 1, 2 (July 1916), 21–36.
Subj 12.2 41 ▪ 43 44

19791 MCH P P1 G1.2 –1928
Lo, Tung Fan (Lo Tung-hsün), ?–1943.
'The institution of marriage in China: A historical study.'
Hong Kong U. law j. 1, 2 (Jan. 1927), 131–149.
Subj 41 ▪ 12.1 12.2 46 47

19792 NNC P P1 G1.2 1644–1949
Pernitzsch, Max Gerhard, 1882–.
'Einige Sonderfälle des chinesischen Eherechts' (Some special cases in Chinese marriage law).
MSOSB 41 (1938), 1–8.
Subj 12.2 41 ▪ 22.2 45 47

19793 FPN P P1 G1.2 –1928
Scié Ton-fa (Hsieh Tung-fa).
'L'évolution psychologique et sociale de la famille en Chine' (The psychological and social development of the family in China).
Fascicules des séances du Comité national d'études sociales et politiques (Boulogne-sur-Seine) 11 (26 avr. 1926), 1–30.
Subj 12.2 41 ▪ 13 42 43 47

19794 FPN P P1 G1.2 –1928
Shu, Mien André (Hsü Mien).
L'évolution de la notion de fiançailles dans le droit matrimonial chinois (The evolution of the concept of betrothal in Chinese marriage law).
Unpublished doctoral dissertation, Faculté de droit, Université de Paris, 1954. 195, 36 p.
Subj 41

19795 NNC P P1 G1.2 –1928
Su, Sing Ging (Hsü Sheng-chin), 1892–.
The Chinese family system.
New York: International Press, 1922. 109 p. (Doctoral dissertation in Sociology, Columbia U.)
Subj 40 41 ▪ 12.2 42 45 52 63 65

19796 FPN P P1 G1.2 –1949
Sun, Georges Si-fong (Sun Hsi-feng).
Du rôle des décisions d'interprétation (Kiai che li) comme sources du droit chinois, principalement en matière de fiançailles (The role of interpretive decisions [*chieh shih li*] as sources of Chinese law, primarily in matters of betrothal).
Paris: Jouve, 1932. 180 p. (Doctoral dissertation, Faculté de droit, Université de Paris)
Subj 12.2 41 ▪ 47

19797 DLC PO P2 G1.3 –1928
Tch'en Si-tan (Ch'en Hsi-t'an).
L'adoption en droit chinois (Adoption in Chinese law).
Shanghai: Impr. de l'Orphelinat de T'ou-sè-wè, 1924. 84 p. (Doctoral dissertation, Université l'Aurore)
Subj 12.2 41 48 ▪ 44 56

19798 MCY P P1 G1.2 –1949
Théry, François, 1890–.
'L'ancien régime légal du mariage et son évolution par voie de jurisprudence pendant les 20 années qui ont précédé le code civil' (The old marriage law and its development through court decisions in the twenty years preceding the adoption of the civil code).
BUA 3e série 10, 39 (juin 1949), 367–416; 10, 40 (oct. 1949), 779–816.
Subj 12.2 41 47 ▪ 45 46 57

19799 MCY P P1 G1.2 –1949
Théry, François, 1890–.
'Les coutumes chinoises relatives au mariage' (Chinese customs relating to marriage).
BUA 3e série 9, 36 (oct. 1948), 367–400; 10, 37 (jan. 1949), 21–62; 10, 38 (avr. 1949), 255–297.
Subj 22.2 41 47 ▪ 12.2 29 45 46 57

19800 NIC P P1 G1.1 1644–1949
Titiev, Mischa, 1901–, and Hsing-chih Tien (T'ien Hsing-chih), 1908–.
'A primer of filial piety.'
Papers of the Michigan Academy of Science, Arts, and Letters 33 (1947), 259–267.
Subj 41 63

19801 MCH P P1 G1.2 –1949
Valk, Marius Hendrikus van der, 1908–.
Aantekeningen omtrent intergentiel huwelijksrecht in China (Notes on Chinese law respecting marriage with foreigners).
Leiden: Brill, 1952. 61 p. (Uitgaven vanwege de Stichting voor Niet-Westers Recht, 5)
Subj 12.2 41 66 ▪ 22.2 71

19802 IMA PO P2 G1.1 –1949
Vannicelli, Luigi.
La famiglia cinese: studio etnologico (An ethnological study of the Chinese family).
Milan: Vita e pensiero, 1943. 479 p.
Subj 40 41 ▪ 51 52 72

19803 CSU PO P2 G1.2 –1928
Wang, Cheng, 1905–.
A preliminary study of the disintegration of the Chinese family under the impact of Western ideologies.
Unpublished masters thesis in Sociology, Stanford U., 1930. 173 p.
Subj 41 47 ▪ 46 57

19804 NIC P P1 G1.2 –1949
Wang Tse-sin (Wang Tsu-hsin).
Le divorce en Chine (Divorce in China).
Paris: Ed. Domat-Montchrestien, 1932. 267 p. (Institut de droit comparé, Etudes de sociologie et d'ethnologie juridiques, 15) (Doctoral dissertation, Faculté de droit, Université de Paris)
Subj 12.2 41 47 ▪ 45

19805 NNC U P1 G1.3 –1928
Wilhelm, Richard, 1873–1930.
'Die chinesische Ehe.' In *Das Ehebuch*, edited by Hermann Alexander Keyserling. [Sole entry]
Freiburg i. Br.: Niels Kampmann, 1925, 111–123.

'The Chinese conception of marriage.' Tr. by W- H- Hilton-Brown. In *The book of marriage*, edited by H. A. Keyserling. [Sole entry]
New York: Harcourt, Brace, 1926, 123–137.
Subj 41 63 ▪ 42 43 47 52

19806 ELS P P1 G1.2 1644–1949
Woo, Pak Chuen (Wu Pai-ch'üan), 1910–.
A comparative study of the family law in the Chinese and English legal systems.
Unpublished doctoral dissertation in Law, U. of London [King's College], 1940. 357 p.
Subj 12.2 40 41 ▪ 64

1911-1949

19807 NIC O P3 G6.1 1928–1949
'Divorce statistics in Shanghai, 1929–1930.'
China critic 4, 11 (12 Mar. 1931), 257.
Subj 41

19808 NNC P P2 G1.3 1928–1949
'Latest statistics on the size of urban and rural families in China.'
NWSS 2, 2 (1929), 1, 4.
Subj 41 ▪ 11 11.1

19809 NIC U P1 G1.2 1911–1949
'Marriage beyond the grave.'
CJ 35, 2 (Aug. 1941), 45–46.
Subj 41 57

19810 NIC P P1 G1.2 1928–1949
Brown, Carrie Chu, 1938–.
The position of a wife in late traditional China.
Unpublished masters thesis in Anthropology, Cornell U., 1966. 58 p.
Subj 40 41 ▪ 12.2 45 47

19811 MCY P P1 G1.2 1911–1928
Bryan, Robert Thomas, 1892–.
'Divorce law of China.'
CSPSR 4, 2 (June 1919), 126–132.
SUBJ 12.2 41 ▪ 47 52

19812 NIC O P3 G1.3 1911–1928
Buck, Pearl Sydenstricker, 1892–1973.
'New modes of Chinese marriage.'
Asia (New York: American Asiatic Assn.) 27, 8 (Aug. 1927), 650–653.
SUBJ 41 47 54

19813 NNC P P1 G1.2 1928–1949
Bünger, Karl A-, 1903–.
'Die Familie in der chinesischen Rechtssprechung' (The family in the Chinese administration of justice).
Sinica 10, 1 (Jan. 1935), 22–31.
SUBJ 12.2 40 41 ▪ 22.2 52

19814 CBU P P1 G1.2 1928–1949
Bünger, Karl A-, 1903–.
'Statistik der chinesischen Ehescheidungen' (Statistics on divorce in China).
OR 17, 9 (1 Mai 1936), 238.
SUBJ 41

19815 MCH P P3 G1.3 1928–1949
Chang, Shao-wei.
'Divorce plague in China.'
China critic 6, 17 (27 Apr. 1933), 426–429. [See Vol. 2 of this *Bibliography* for Chinese version.]
SUBJ 41

19816 ICU FP P2 G1.2 1911–1949
Chen, Ifu.
The old Chinese family: A study in familial control.
Unpublished masters thesis in Sociology, U. of Chicago, 1934. 212 p.
SUBJ 40 41 50 53 63 ▪ 43 44 47 52 54 57

19817 NIC O P3 G8.1 1928–1949
Cheng, Hawthorne (Cheng Chün).
'Marriage in Chungking.'
Asia and the Americas 44, 7 (July 1944), 308–311.
SUBJ 41 55

19818 MCH FP P7 G4.2 1911–1928
Dols, Joseph, 1874–1938.
'La vie chinoise dans la province de Kan-sou' (Chinese life in Kansu).
Anthropos 10/11, 1/2 (Jan.–Apr. 1915/16), 68–74; 10/11, 3/4 (Mai–Aug. 1915/16), 466–503; 10/11, 5/6 (Sept.–Dez. 1915/16), 726–757; 12/13, 1/2 (Jan.–Apr. 1917/18), 236–262; 12/13, 5/6 (Sept.–Dez. 1917/18), 958–1013.
SUBJ 41 51 55 57 ▪ 21.3 23 43 46 50 62 65

19819 MCH P P1 G1.2 1911–1949
Escarra, Jean, 1885–1955.
La codification du droit de la famille et du droit des successions (livres IV et V du code civil de la République chinoise) (The codification of family law and the law of inheritance: Books 4 and 5 of the civil code of the Republic of China).
Shanghai: Impr. de l'Orphelinat de T'ou-sè-wè, 1931. 87 p.
SUBJ 12.2 41 45 ▪ 47

19820 NIC F P8 G7.1 1928–1949
Feng, Han-yi (Feng Han-chi), 1902–, and John Knight Shryock, 1890–1952.
'Marriage customs in the vicinity of I-ch'ang [Hupeh].'
HJAS 13, 3/4 (Dec. 1950), 362–430.
SUBJ 41 ▪ 65

19821 MCY P P1 G1.2 1911–1949
Fou, J- Pang (Fu Pang).
'De la situation juridique de l'héritier institué dans le nouveau droit civil chinois' (The legal position of the heir in the new Chinese civil law).
BUA 3e série 2, 8 (1941), 610–637. [Reprinted in *Mélanges juridiques de l'Université l'Aurore* (Aurora University legal miscellany). (Selective entry.) Paris: Lib. du Recueil Sirey, 1946, vol. 1, 31–57.]
SUBJ 12.2 41 45 ▪ 48

19822 CSU F P2 G4.4 1928–1949
Frick, Johannes.
'Hochzeitssitten von Hei-tsuei-tzu in der Provinz Ch'ing-hai (China)' (Wedding customs in the village of Hei-tsui-tzu [Hsi-ning *hsien*], Tsinghai). In *Ethnographische Beiträge aus der Ch'inghai Provinz (China)* (Ethnographic reports from Tsinghai). [Selective entry]
Peking [i.e., Tokyo]: Catholic U. of Peking, Museum of Oriental Ethnology, 1952, 1–102. (MOE, Folklore studies supplements, 1)
SUBJ 41 ▪ 47 65

19823 DLC O P7 G1.3 1928–1949
Highbaugh, Irma, 1891–.
'Effects of the war on rural homes.' In *Wartime China, as seen by westerners.* [Selective entry]
Chungking: China Publishing Co., 1942, 140–151.
SUBJ 41 47 55 ▪ 11.2 17 24.1 24.4 42

19824 CSU PO P2 G9.5 1911–1949
Hong Kong. Mui-tsai Committee.
Mui-tsai in Hong Kong: Report of the Committee appointed by His Excellency the Governor, Sir William Peel.
London: His Majesty's Stationery Office, 1936. 83 p. (Great Britain, Reports from Commissioners, Inspectors, and Others, Vol. 7, 1935–36; Cmd. 5121)
SUBJ 41 47 ▪ 12.2 52

19825 NNC O P3 G5.0 1911–1928
Hosie, Dorothea Soothill, 1885–.
Two gentlemen of China: An intimate description of the private life of two patrician Chinese families . . .
London: Seeley, Service, 1924. 316 p.
SUBJ 41 55 59 ▪ 12 12.2 15 17 23 26 31 47 63 66

19826 FPN P P1 G1.2 1911–1928
Houx, Koung-ou (Wu K'un-wu; Wu Kun-wu).
La famille et l'institution du mariage et du divorce en Chine (The family and the institutions of marriage and divorce in China).
Geneva: Richter, 1919. 166 p. (Doctoral dissertation, Faculté de droit, Université de Genève)
SUBJ 12.2 40 41 ▪ 44 45 48 52 54

19827 NIC F P6 G8.1 1928–1949
Hsiung, Yana, 1919–.
A study of the family life of preschool children in a Chinese rural town.
Unpublished masters thesis in Sociology, Cornell U., 1947. 229 p.
SUBJ 28 41 50 52 55 ▪ 21.4 46 53 56 63 65

19828 ELS PO P8 G2.3 1911–1949
Hsu, Francis L. K. (Hsü Lang-kuang), 1909–.
The functioning of a North China family [in Mu-erh-shan-li, Ta-ku-shan *chen*, Chuang-ho *hsien*, Liaoning].
Unpublished doctoral dissertation in Anthropology, U. of London [London School of Economics and Political Science], 1940. 373 p.
SUBJ 41 42 43 44 45 ▪ 23 26 48 52 53 54 61

19829 NIC S P1 G1.3 1911–1949
Hsu, Francis L. K. (Hsü Lang-kuang), 1909–.
'The myth of Chinese family size.'
AJS 48, 5 (Mar. 1943), 555–562.
SUBJ 41 ▪ 26 43 63

19830 NIC F P8 G8.2 1928–1949
Hsu, Francis L. K. (Hsü Lang-kuang), 1909–.
'Observations on cross-cousin marriage in China.'
AA new (2nd) series 47, 1 (Jan.–Mar. 1945), 83–103.
SUBJ 41 ▪ 62 65

19831 NIC P P1 G1.2 1928–1949
Hu, Henry Yü-chieh (Hu Yü-chieh).
'Marriage and divorce in Chinese civil code, with reference to the rules of conflict of laws.'
CSPSR 22, 4 (Jan.–Mar. 1939), 400–427.
SUBJ 12.2 41 45

19832 MCY P P1 G1.2 1911–1949
La Dany, Ladislao, 1914–.
'Annulation du mariage en droit chinois' (Annulment of marriage in Chinese law).
BUA 3e série 6, 23 (1945), 517–545.
SUBJ 12.2 41 ▪ 47

19833 NIC FP P2 G1.3 1911–1949
Lamson, Herbert Day, 1899–.
'Differential reproduction in China.'
Quarterly review of biology 10, 3 (Sept. 1935), 308–321.
SUBJ 41 ▪ 17 47 58

19834 NNC F P4 G6.0 1928–1949
Lamson, Herbert Day, 1899–.
'Population studies: Size of the Chinese family in relation to occupation, age, and education.'
CEJ 11, 6 (Dec. 1932), 478–496.
SUBJ 41 58 ▪ 21.1 21.4 28 50

19835 MCH F P3 G1.3 1911–1949
Lamson, Herbert Day, 1899–.
'A study of the relation of education to family size.'
China critic 3, 34 (21 Aug. 1930), 799–802.
SUBJ 16.1 17 41

19836 NIC F P2 G1.3 1911–1949
Lang, Olga.
Chinese family and society.
New Haven: Yale U. Press, 1946. 15, 395 p. [Reprinted—Hamden, Conn.: Archon Books, 1968. 15, 395 p.]
SUBJ 41 44 47 ▪ 42 48 50 52 54 63

19837 NIC S P8 G1.0 1911–1949
Lee, Shu-ching (Li Shu-ch'ing), 1908–.
'China's traditional family: Its characteristics and disintegration.'

ASR 18, 3 (June 1953), 272–280.
SUBJ 41 ▪ 42 47

19838 NIC S P1 G1.3 1928–1949
Levi, Werner, 1912–.
'The family in modern Chinese law.'
FEQ 4, 3 (May 1945), 263–273.
SUBJ 12.2 41 42 47

19839 NIC PO P1 G1.3 1911–1949
Levy, Marion Joseph, Jr., 1918–.
The family revolution in modern China.
Cambridge: Harvard U. Press, 1949. 16, 390 p. (Revision of *Some aspects of family structure and the problem of industrialization in China*, doctoral dissertation in Sociology, Harvard U., 1947) [Reprinted—New York: Octagon Books, 1963. 16, 390 p.]
SUBJ 41 44 47 50 ▪ 16 45 46 52 53 54

19840 NIC O P2 G9.3 1911–1949
Lin Yueh-hwa (Lin Yüeh-hua), 1910–.
The golden wing: A sociological study of Chinese familism.
New York: Oxford U. Press, 1948. 15, 234 p.
SUBJ 24 34.2 41 ▪ 22.2 26 36.2 48 50

19841 MCH O P1 G1.0 1911–1928
Liu, Chiang (Liu Ch'iang), 1895–.
'Chinese versus American ideas concerning the family.'
J. of applied sociology 10, 3 (Jan.–Feb. 1926), 243–248.
SUBJ 40 41 ▪ 22.2 55

19842 NNC P P1 G1.2 1911–1928
Michelsen, Erich.
'Das chinesische Familienrecht und das neue Strafgesetzbuch' (Chinese family law and the new penal code).
DCR 2 (1912), 33–38.
SUBJ 12.2 41 ▪ 22.2 47

19843 CSU S P8 G1.3 1911–1949
Morioka, Kiyomi.
'Life cycle patterns in Japan, China, and the United States.'
J. of marriage and the family 29, 3 (Aug. 1967), 595–606.
SUBJ 41 ▪ 50

19844 CSU O P3 G6.1 1928–1949
Mossman, Mereb E–.
'The changing marriage customs in China.'
SSR 29, 2 (Nov.–Dec. 1944), 105–112.
SUBJ 41

19845 MCH S P2 G1.3 1928–1949
Newell, Jane I–.
'The Chinese family: An arena of conflicting cultures.'
Social forces 9, 4 (June 1931), 564–571.
SUBJ 41 ▪ 12.2 47

19846 ICU P P3 G8.2 1928–1949
Ni, Ernest (Ni Yin-hsin), 1908–.
Marital status and family size in China.
Unpublished masters thesis in Sociology, U. of Chicago, 1945. 76 p.
SUBJ 21.1 21.3 41 ▪ 21 28 43 58

19847 CSU FP P7 G5.2 1928–1949
Serruys, Paul Leo Mary, 1912–.
'Les cérémonies du mariage: usages populaires et textes dialectaux du sud de la préfecture de Ta-t'oung (Chansi)' (Wedding ceremonies: Popular customs and dialect texts from the southern part of Ta-t'ung *hsien*, Shansi).
FS 3, 1 (1944), 73–154; 3, 2 (1944), 77–129.
SUBJ 23 40 41 43 ▪ 29 65

19848 NIC F P2 G1.3 1911–1949
Smythe, Lewis Strong Casey, 1901–.
'The composition of the Chinese family.'
Nanking j. 5, 2 (1935), 371–393.
SUBJ 41 ▪ 45

19849 NIC F P2 G8.1 1928–1949
Smythe, Lewis Strong Casey, 1901–.
'Factors associated with success of Chinese families as families.'
Marriage and family living 14, 4 (Nov. 1952), 286–294.
SUBJ 41

19850 CSU F P8 G1.2 1928–1949
Taeuber, Irene Barnes, 1906–.
'The families of Chinese farmers.' In *Family and kinship in Chinese society*, edited by Maurice Freedman. [Selective entry]
Stanford: Stanford U. Press, 1970, 63–85.
SUBJ 21 29 41 58 ▪ 21.2 26.3 47

19851 NNC O P2 G5.3 1911–1928
Tremanns, Johann M–.
'Gebräuche und Zeremonien bei Verlobungen und Hochzeiten in China' (Customs and ceremonies of betrothal and marriage in China).
Baessler-Archiv 10 (1926), 37–44.
SUBJ 41 ▪ 47 55 62 65

19852 NNC P P1 G1.2 1911–1928
Tsai, Tsong Wang (Ts'ai Tsung-huang).
'The principles of the law of succession in China.' Tr. by R. C. W. Sheng of 'Li ssu ch'eng hsü'; in *Ssu hsü fa chen ch'üan* (An explanation of the law of succession), by Ts'ai Tsung-huang; Shanghai: Shang wu yin shu kuan, 1922, 1–16.
CLR 1, 6 (June 1923), 276–286; 1, 7 (Oct. 1923), 312–321.
SUBJ 12.2 41 45 ▪ 43

19853 NNC P P1 G1.2 1911–1949
Valk, Marius Hendrikus van der, 1908–.
'Freedom of marriage in modern Chinese law.'
MS 3, 1 (1938), 1–34.
SUBJ 12.2 41 ▪ 47

19854 NIC P P1 G1.2 1911–1949
Valk, Marius Hendrikus van der, 1908–.
An outline of modern Chinese family law.
Peiping: Henri Vetch, 1939. 219 p. (Monumenta serica monograph series, 2) [Reprinted—Taipei: Ch'eng-wen, 1969. 219 p.]
SUBJ 12.2 41 ▪ 44 45 47

19855 GMS S P1 G1.2 1928–1949
Vogel, Werner, 1902–.
'Das neue chinesische Familienrecht' (The new Chinese family law). In *Jubiläumsband der Deutschen Gesellschaft für Natur- und Völkerkunde Ostasiens* (Anniversary volume of the German Society for East Asian Natural History and Ethnology). [Sole entry]
Tokyo: Deutsche Gesellschaft für Natur- und Völkerkunde Ostasiens, 1933, vol. 2, 20–33.
SUBJ 41

19856 NNC O P1 G1.0 1911–1928
Wu, Ching-chao (Wu Ching-ch'ao), 1901–.
'The Chinese family: Organization, names, and kinship terms.'
AA new (2nd) series 29, 3 (July–Sept. 1927), 316–325.
SUBJ 41 44 ▪ 43

1911-1972
(including 1644-1972)

19857 NNC O P3 G5.1 1928–1972
Berezhkov, Valentin Mikhailovich.
'V kitaiskikh sem'iakh' (In Chinese families).
Novoe vremia 15, 43 (24 oktiabria 1957), 22–24.
SUBJ 26 41 ▪ 17 38

19858 MCH F P7 G9.5 1928–1972
Bracey, Dorothy Heid, 1941–.
The effects of emigration on a Hakka village.
Unpublished doctoral dissertation in Social Anthropology, Harvard U., 1967. 143 p.
SUBJ 21.2 41 42 ▪ 24.3 29 47 66

19859 MAM FP P2 G1.1 1895–1972
Buxbaum, David Charles, 1933–.
Some aspects of substantive family law and social change in rural China (1896–1967), with a case study of a North Taiwan village.
Ann Arbor: University Microfilms (Publ. 69-1148), 1969. 357 p. (Doctoral dissertation in Political Science, U. of Washington, 1968)
SUBJ 12.2 22.2 41 ▪ 22.1 44 45 47 48 65

19860 NNC U P1 G1.2 –1972
Chao, J.
'Sozialer Wandel und Familie in China' (Social change and the family in China).
Kölner Z. für Soziologie und Sozialpsychologie 14, 4 (1962), 645–672.
SUBJ 41 ▪ 12.2 14 47 50

19861 CSU P P1 G1.1 1911–1972
Chin, Ai-li Sung (Ch'en Shen Ai-li), 1919–.
'Family relations in modern Chinese fiction.' In *Family and kinship in Chinese society*, edited by Maurice Freedman. [Selective entry]
Stanford: Stanford U. Press, 1970, 87–120.
SUBJ 41 63 ▪ 14.2 44 46 48

19862 NIC P P1 G1.2 –1972
Chiu, Vermier Yantak (Chao P'ing), 1890–1964.
Marriage laws and customs of China.
Hong Kong: Chinese U. of Hong Kong, New Asia College, Institute of Advanced Chinese Studies and Research, 1966. 238 p.
SUBJ 12.2 40 41 ▪ 42 45 47

19863 CSU F P2 G9.4 1928–1972
Cohen, Myron Leon, 1937–.
'Developmental process in the Chinese domestic group.' In *Family and kinship*

in Chinese society, edited by Maurice Freedman. [Selective entry]
Stanford: Stanford U. Press, 1970, 21–36.
SUBJ 41 ▪ 21.2 45

19864 MAM FP P8 G9.4 1911–1972
Cohen, Myron Leon, 1937–.
Family economy and development in Yen-liao [Mei-nung *chen*, Kao-hsiung *hsien*], *Taiwan*.
Ann Arbor: University Microfilms (Publ. 68-8573), 1968. 296 p. (Doctoral dissertation in Anthropology, Columbia U., 1967)
SUBJ 24.1 41 ▪ 42 44

19865 NIC P P1 G9.0 1644–1972
Eberhard, Wolfram, 1909–.
'Auspicious marriages: A statistical study of a Chinese custom.'
Sociologus neue (2.) Folge 13, 1 (1963), 49–55. [Reprinted in *Studies in Chinese folklore and related essays*, by W. Eberhard. (Selective entry.) Bloomington: Indiana U., Research Center for the Language Sciences, 1970, 201–207. (Indiana U., Folklore Institute monograph series, 23)]
SUBJ 41 65 ▪ 23 62

19866 FPN P P2 G1.2 –1972
Engelborghs-Bertels, Marthe, 1928–.
'Evolution de la famille en Chine' (Evolution of the family in China). In *Les rôles familiaux dans les civilisations différentes* (Familial roles in various civilizations). [Sole entry]
Brussels: Université libre de Bruxelles, Institut de sociologie Solvay, 1971, 13–29.
SUBJ 12.2 41 47 ▪ 42 51 62 63 64

19867 CSH P P1 G1.2 –1972
Fan Jo-yu (Fan Jo-yü).
'Why we have abolished the feudal patriarchal system.' Tr. of 'Wo men wei shen mo fei ch'u liao feng chien chia ch'ang chih'; *Hung ch'i* 1960, 5 (1 Mar.), 19–27. In *Translations from selected issues of 'Hung-ch'i' (Red flag) (Communist China)*, mimeo., compiled by U.S. Joint Publications Research Service. [Selective entry]
Washington, D.C.: JPRS, 19 June 1961, 31–45. (JPRS 8476; MC 13,335/1961)
SUBJ 41 63 ▪ 12.2 45 47

19868 MCH S P1 G1.2 1644–1972
Freedman, Maurice, 1920–.
'The family in China, past and present.'
PA 34, 4 (Winter 1961/62), 323–336. [Reprinted in *Modern China*, edited by Albert Feuerwerker. (Selective entry.) Englewood Cliffs, N.J.: Prentice-Hall, 1964, 27–40.]
SUBJ 12.2 40 41 42 ▪ 12 12.1 16 64

19869 MCH S P2 G1.2 1928–1972
Freedman, Maurice, 1920–.
'The family under Chinese Communism.'
Political q. 35, 3 (July–Sept. 1964), 342–350.
SUBJ 40 41 47 ▪ 12.2 42 44

19870 ELE U P1 G1.1 1644–1972
Freedman, Maurice, 1920–.
Rites and duties: or, Chinese marriage.
London: Bell, 1967. 24 p.
SUBJ 41 45 47 ▪ 44 62 65

19871 MMT S P1 G1.1 1842–1972
Fried, Morton Herbert, 1923–.
'Trends in Chinese domestic organization.' In *Symposium on economic and social problems of the Far East*, edited by Edward Franciszek Szczepanik. [Selective entry]
Hong Kong: Hong Kong U. Press, 1962, 405–414.
SUBJ 40 41 ▪ 12.2 64

19872 CSU P P1 G1.2 1928–1972
Gales, Robert Robinson.
'Marriage and the family: Chinese law.'
J. of family law (Louisville, Kentucky) 6 (1966), 36–60.
SUBJ 12.2 41 ▪ 12.1 40 46 47 50 51 52

19873 NIC S P2 G1.2 1911–1972
Goode, William Josiah, 1917–.
'China.' In *World revolution and family patterns*, by W. J. Goode. [Sole entry]
New York: Free Press of Glencoe, 1963, 270–320.
SUBJ 12.2 41 47 50 58 ▪ 22 22.2 42 46 52 57 64

19874 CSU P P2 G9.5 1842–1972
Greenfield, D- E-.
'Marriage by Chinese law and custom in Hongkong.'
International and comparative law q. 4th series 7, 3 (July 1958), 437–451.
SUBJ 22.2 41 ▪ 12.2

19875 MCH P P2 G1.2 –1972
Hellstrom, Inger.
'The Chinese family in the Communist Revolution.'
Acta sociologica 6, 4 (1962), 256–277.
SUBJ 12.2 41 47 ▪ 12.1 42 43 53 54 64

19876 CSH U P2 G2.0 1911–1972
Hirabayashi, Jo Anne, and Peter S. H. Tang (T'ang Sheng-hao), 1919–.
'Family.' In *A regional handbook on Northeast China*, compiled by Far Eastern and Russian Institute, U. of Washington. [Selective entry]
New Haven: Human Relations Area Files, 1956, 142–156. (HRAF subcontractor's monographs, 61; Washington 9)
SUBJ 41 ▪ 12.1

19877 CSU P P1 G1.2 –1972
Ho, Ping-ti, 1917–.
'An historian's view of the Chinese family system.' In *Man and civilization: The family's search for survival*, edited by Seymour M- Farber, Piero Mustacchi, and Roger H- L- Wilson. [Sole entry]
New York: McGraw-Hill, 1965, 15–30.
SUBJ 41 42 ▪ 45 47 52

19878 ELE PO P1 G9.5 1842–1972
Hong Kong. Committee on Chinese Law and Custom.
Chinese law and custom in Hong Kong: Report of a committee appointed by the governor in October 1948.
Hong Kong: Government Printer, 1953. 315 p.
SUBJ 22.2 41 45 ▪ 12.2

19879 MCH P P1 G1.1 1644–1972
Kirfel, Harald Willibald, 1914–.
'Die Ehe im chinesischen Recht' (Marriage in Chinese law).
Sinologica 2, 2 (1949/50), 155–162.
SUBJ 12.2 41

19880 CSU S P2 G1.2 –1972
Leslie, Gerald R-.
'The family system of China.' In *The family in social context*, by G. R. Leslie. [Sole entry]
New York: Oxford U. Press, 1967, 81–124.
SUBJ 41 42 44 46 ▪ 12.1 12.2 16.1 16.3 50

19881 NNC PO P1 G1.1 –1972
Mace, David Robert, 1907–, and Vera Mace.
Marriage, East and West.
Garden City, N.Y.: Doubleday, 1960. 359 p.
SUBJ 41 ▪ 46 47 53

19882 NIC U P1 G1.0 1644–1972
Makino, Tatsumi, 1905–.
'The family system in China.' In *Transactions of the Third World Congress of Sociology, Vol. 4, Changes in the family*. [Selective entry]
London: International Sociological Assn., 1956, 208–214.
SUBJ 40 41 ▪ 42 43 45

19883 CSU P P2 G1.2 1928–1972
Meijer, Marinus Johan.
Marriage law and policy in the Chinese People's Republic.
Hong Kong: Hong Kong U. Press, 1971. 369 p.
SUBJ 12.2 41 ▪ 12.1 45 47

19884 MCH P P1 G1.2 1928–1972
Meijer, Marinus Johan.
'Problems of translating the marriage law.' In *Contemporary Chinese law: Research problems and perspectives*, edited by Jerome Alan Cohen. [Selective entry]
Cambridge: Harvard U. Press, 1970, 210–229. (Harvard studies in East Asian law, 4)
SUBJ 12.2 41

19885 NIC P P2 G8.2 1911–1972
Ni, Ernest (Ni Yin-hsin), 1908–.
'The family in China.'
Marriage and family living 16, 4 (Nov. 1954), 315–318.
SUBJ 21.1 41 ▪ 47 58

19886 MAM S P1 G1.2 1644–1972
Reber, Calvin H-, Jr., 1915–.
Protestant Christianity and marriage in China.
Ann Arbor: University Microfilms (Publ. 58-2600), 1958. 403 p. (Doctoral dissertation in Religion, Columbia U.)
SUBJ 41 ▪ 12.2 33 47 72

19887 CSU P P1 G9.5 1928–1972
Ridehalgh, A-, and J- C- McDouall.
Chinese marriages in Hong Kong.
Hong Kong: Government Printer, 1960. 34 p.
SUBJ 41 ▪ 12.2 22.2

19888 MCH S P2 G1.1 –1972
Ruey Yih-fu (Jui I-fu).
'Changing structure of the Chinese family.'
B. of the Dept. of Archaeology and Anthropology, National Taiwan U. 17/18 (Nov. 1961), 1–15.
SUBJ 40 41 ▪ 42 44

19889 NNC F P8 G4.4 1928–1972
Schröder, Dominik.
'Bemerkungen zur "Scheffel-Zeremonie" bei der Hochzeit der Tsinghai-Chinesen' (Observations on the 'bushel ceremony' at weddings of the Tsinghai Chinese).
Anthropos 51, 5/6 (Sept.–Dez. 1956), 1086–1093.
SUBJ 23 41 65 ▪ 26.3 46 47 51 54 62

19890 CSH S P2 G9.4 1644–1972
Stanford U. China Project.
'Family.' In *Taiwan (Formosa)*, compiled by the organization cited. [Selective entry]
New Haven: Human Relations Area Files, 1956, vol. 1, 131–148. (HRAF subcontractor's monographs, 31; Stanford 5)
SUBJ 41 ▪ 45 47

19891 CSU P P1 G1.2 –1972
Tsao, W. Y. (Ts'ao Wen-yen), 1908–.
'The Chinese family from customary law to positive law.'
Hastings law j. 17 (May 1966), 727–765.
SUBJ 12.2 22.2 41 ▪ 42 47 64

19892 MCY P P1 G1.2 1928–1972
Valk, Marius Hendrikus van der, 1908–.
Conservatism in modern Chinese family law.
Leiden: Brill, 1956. 90 p. (Studia et documenta ad iura orientis antiqui pertinentia, 4)
SUBJ 12.2 40 41 ▪ 22.2 45 47 57

19893 MCH P P1 G1.2 1928–1972
Valk, Marius Hendrikus van der, 1908–.
'Familie- en erfrecht in communistisch China' (Family law and hereditary law in Communist China). In *China tussen eergisteren en overmorgen* (China between the day before yesterday and the day after tomorrow), edited by Willem Frederik Wertheim and Erik Zürcher. [Selective entry]
The Hague: Van Hoeve, 1963, 142–153.
SUBJ 12.2 41 45

19894 CSU FP P2 G1.5 1842–1972
Wolf, Arthur Paul, 1932–.
'Adopt a daughter-in-law, marry a sister: A Chinese solution to the problem of the incest taboo.'
AA new (2nd) series 70, 5 (Oct. 1968), 864–874.
SUBJ 41 46 61 ▪ 22.2 47 53 63

19895 MCH FP P8 G9.4 1911–1972
Wolf, Arthur Paul, 1932–.
'Childhood association, sexual attraction and the incest taboo: A Chinese case.'
AA new (2nd) series 68, 4 (Aug. 1966), 883–898.
SUBJ 41 46 53 ▪ 52

19896 MAM FP P8 G9.4 1895–1972
Wolf, Arthur Paul, 1932–.
Marriage and adoption in a Hokkien village [Hsia-chi-chou, T'ai-pei *hsien*, Taiwan].
Ann Arbor: University Microfilms (Publ. 65-4171), 1965. 300 p. (Doctoral dissertation in Anthropology, Cornell U., 1964)
SUBJ 41 46 47 50 ▪ 43 51 52 55 57 65

19897 NIC P P1 G1.1 –1972
Wong, C. M. (Wang Mei-ch'ih).
'The ancient custom of Cantonese marriage.'
Annual of the China Society (Singapore) 1960/61, 60–65.
SUBJ 41 ▪ 22.2

19898 NIC O P3 G9.5 1928–1972
Wright, Beryl Robina.
'Social aspects of change in the Chinese family pattern in Hong Kong.'
J. of social psychology 63, 1 (June 1964), 31–39.
SUBJ 41 ▪ 17 26

19899 NNC P P2 G1.2 1644–1972
Yang, C. K. (Yang Ch'ing-k'un), 1911–.
The Chinese family in the Communist Revolution.
Cambridge, Mass.: Technology Press, 1959. 246 p.
SUBJ 12.1 40 41 47 54 ▪ 32 44 45 50 60 64

1949-1972

19900 MCH O P3 G1.3 1949–1972
Auclair, Marcelle, 1899–.
'La femme chinoise' (The Chinese woman).
Annales conferencia 71, 163 (mai 1964), 18–30.
SUBJ 41 47 ▪ 12.2 52 61

19901 CSH F P7 G9.5 1949–1972
Baker, Hugh David Roberts, 1937–.
'Marriage and the family.' In *Aspects of social organization in the New Territories*, edited by Hong Kong Branch, Royal Asiatic Society. [Selective entry]
Hong Kong: Cathay Press, 1964, 27–31.
SUBJ 41 47

19902 MCH O P3 G1.3 1949–1972
Bender, Peter L-.
'Niemand will, was er nicht soll, chinesische Parole: Erziehung zum neuen Menschen' (The Chinese proverb 'Nobody wants to do what he shouldn't do': Education creates the new man).
Die Zeit; Wochenschrift für Politik, Wirtschaft und Kultur 20, 10 (12 März 1965), 4–5.

'Divorce Chinese style.'
Atlas 9, 6 (June 1965), 348–352.
SUBJ 12.1 41 ▪ 12.2 17

19903 NNC P P1 G1.2 1949–1972
Bünger, Karl A-, 1903–.
'Das Ehegesetz der Volksrepublik von 1950' (The 1950 marriage law of the People's Republic of China).
Z. für ausländisches und internationales Privatrecht 16, 1 (1951), 112–126.
SUBJ 12.2 41 ▪ 52

19904 CSU PO P1 G9.5 1949–1972
Chang, Denis K. L.
'The new law of divorce in Hong Kong.'
Hong Kong law j. 3, 1 (Jan. 1973), 51–66. [Further installments were to be published.]
SUBJ 12.2 41

19905 MAM P P2 G1.2 1949–1972
Chao, Paul Kwang-yi, 1919–.
Analysis of Marxist doctrine on the family, with testing its validity in Soviet Russia and Communist China: A study of the relationship between evolutionary theories of family development and Marxist doctrine of the family.
Ann Arbor: University Microfilms (Publ. 66-5650), 1966. 252 p. (Doctoral dissertation in Political Science, New York U., 1963)
SUBJ 12.1 12.2 40 41 63 64 ▪ 47 51 55 58

19906 CSU P P2 G1.2 1949–1972
Chao, Paul Kwang-yi, 1919–.
'The Marxist doctrine and the recent development of the Chinese family in Communist China.'
JAAS 2, 3/4 (July–Oct. 1967), 161–173. [For fuller treatment, see entry 19905.]
SUBJ 12.1 12.2 41 63 ▪ 47 51 55 64

19907 NIC O P8 G5.1 1949–1972
Chen Hsiu-cheng.
'A family in a people's commune [Yung-feng commune, Hai-ting *ch'ü*, Peking municipality].'
China reconstructs 8, 5 (May 1959), 14–16.
SUBJ 41 55

19908 MCH P P1 G1.2 1949–1972
Chen, Theodore H. E. (Ch'en Hsi-en), 1902–, and Wen-hui C. Chen (Ch'en Chung Wen-hui), 1913–.
'Changing attitudes towards parents in Communist China.'
SSR 43, 3 (Jan.–Feb. 1959), 175–182.
SUBJ 41 47 63 ▪ 12.1 16 50 64

19909 CSH P P2 G1.2 1949–1972
Chen, Theodore H. E. (Ch'en Hsi-en), 1902–, and Wen-hui C. Chen (Ch'en Chung Wen-hui), 1913–.
The Chinese family under Communist rule, Part I, mimeo.
Los Angeles: U. of Southern California, East Asian Studies Center, 1967. 74 p.
SUBJ 41 47 ▪ 12.1 12.2 46 63

19910 MAM F P3 G9.4 1949–1972
Chu, Solomon S. P., 1937–.
Family structure and extended kinship in a Chinese community [Taichung].
Ann Arbor: University Microfilms (Publ. 70-4047), 1970. 232 p. (Doctoral dissertation in Sociology, U. of Michigan, 1969)
SUBJ 21.2 26 41 44 ▪ 28 45 58

19911 CSU P P2 G9.4 1949–1972
Eberhard, Wolfram, 1909–.
'Aspirations concerning marriage and married life among contemporary Taiwanese.' In *Moral and social values of the Chinese: Collected essays*, by W. Eberhard. [Selective entry]
Taipei: Chinese Materials and Research Aids Service Center, 1971, 235–269. (CMRASC occasional series, 6)
SUBJ 41 46 61 ▪ 47 48

19912 CSH P P2 G9.5 1949–1972
Evans, David Meurig Emrys, 1938–.
'The new law of succession in Hong Kong.'
Hong Kong law j. 3, 1 (Jan. 1973), 7–50.
SUBJ 12.2 22.2 41 45 ▪ 47

19913 CSU S P2 G1.1 1949–1972
Freedman, Maurice, 1920–.
'Introduction.' In *Family and kinship in Chinese society*, edited by M. Freedman. [Selective entry]

Stanford: Stanford U. Press, 1970, 1–19.
SUBJ 41 ▪ 29 42 43 44 57

19914 CSU S P1 G1.2 1949–1972
Fried, Morton Herbert, 1923–.
'The family in China: The People's Republic.' In *The family: Its function and destiny*, rev. ed., edited by Ruth Nanda Anshen. [Selective entry]
New York: Harper, 1959, 146–166.
SUBJ 41 ▪ 12.2 46 47 51

19915 NNC P P1 G1.2 1949–1972
Fu, S. L. (Fu Shang-lin).
'The new marriage law of Communist China.' In *Contemporary China, 1955*, edited by Edward Stuart Kirby. [Selective entry]
Hong Kong: Hong Kong U. Press, 1956, 115–138.
SUBJ 12.2 41 ▪ 12 12.1 47 52 64

19916 NIC F P8 G9.4 1949–1972
Gallin, Bernard, 1929–.
'Cousin marriage in China.'
Ethnology 2, 1 (Jan. 1963), 104–108.
SUBJ 41 44

19917 CSU P P3 G9.5 1949–1972
[Hong Kong Bar Assn. Sub-committee on Chinese Marriages].
Chinese marriages in Hong Kong: A report by the Sub-Committee of the H. K. Bar Association on Chinese marriages.
Hong Kong: Hong Kong Bar Assn., 1967. 52 p.
SUBJ 41 ▪ 22.2 47

19918 MAM F P3 G9.5 1949–1972
Hong, Lawrence K., 1941–.
The Chinese family in a modern industrial setting [Hong Kong]*: Its structure and functions*.
Ann Arbor: University Microfilms (Publ. 71-5540), 1971. 217 p. (Doctoral dissertation in Sociology and Anthropology, U. of Notre Dame, 1970)
SUBJ 41 45 47 ▪ 21.4 26 43 53

19919 MMT P P1 G1.2 1949–1972
Hsieh, Frances Mei-huei Yang (Hsieh Yang Mei-hui), 1938–.
The normative pattern of family life in Chinese Communist society: A content analysis of 120 magazine short stories.
Unpublished masters thesis in Sociology, Tufts U., 1965. 99 p.
SUBJ 41 60 64 ▪ 12.1 19 47 63

19920 CSH U P2 G1.4 1949–1972
Hu Sheng.
The collectivization and socialization of domestic labor, mimeo. Tr. of 'Chia wu lao tung ti chi t'i hua, she hui hua'; *Hung ch'i* 1958, 7 (1 Sept.), 24–30.
Washington, D.C.: U.S. Joint Publications Research Service, 18 Nov. 1958. 9 p. (JPRS 383D; MC 569/1959)
SUBJ 41 47 ▪ 28 55 64

19921 NNC P P2 G1.2 1949–1972
Huang, Lucy Jen (Huang Jen-hua), 1920–.
'The Communist Chinese attitude towards interclass marriage.'
CQ 12 (Oct.–Dec. 1962), 183–190. [Also published as 'Attitude of the Communist Chinese toward inter-class marriage.' *Marriage and family living* 24, 4 (Nov. 1962), 389–392.]
SUBJ 16 41 ▪ 12.1 47 63

19922 MCH P P7 G1.2 1949–1972
Huang, Lucy Jen (Huang Jen-hua), 1920–.
The impact of the commune on the Chinese family.
Santa Barbara, Calif.: General Electric Co., Technical Military Planning Operation, 1962. 56 p. (TEMPO reports, RM 62TMP-78)
SUBJ 22 22.1 41 47 54 ▪ 12.2 24.4 26.3 28 32 34.1 55 64 70

19923 MCH P P1 G1.2 1949–1972
Huang, Lucy Jen (Huang Jen-hua), 1920–.
'Some changing patterns in the Communist Chinese family.'
Marriage and family living 23, 2 (May 1961), 137–146.
SUBJ 41 ▪ 12.1 47

19924 DLC U P1 G1.2 1949–1972
IAn IUi-tsai (Yang Yü-ts'ai).
'Nekotorye voprosy brachnosemeinykh otnoshenii v KNR' (Marital and family relations in the People's Republic of China).
Sbornik studencheskikh nauchnykh rabot Leningradskogo Universiteta 3, 4 (1963), 81–88.
SUBJ 41 ▪ 12.1 12.2 44 47

19925 CSU F P8 G9.4 1949–1972
Jordan, David Kinsey, 1942–.
'Two forms of spirit marriage in rural Taiwan.'
BTLV 127, 1 (1971), 181–189.
SUBJ 22.2 41 47 62 ▪ 43 44 56 57

19926 MCH P P1 G1.2 1949–1972
[La Dany, Ladislao] ———, 1914–.
'Drawing the line: Family reform.'
CNA 571 (9 July 1965), 1–7.
SUBJ 12.1 16 41 ▪ 47 54 64

19927 CSH P P2 G1.2 1949–1972
[La Dany, Ladislao] ———, 1914–.
'The family.'
CNA 776 (3 Oct. 1969), 1–7.
SUBJ 12.1 41 ▪ 16 42

19928 CSH P P2 G1.2 1949–1972
Lethbridge, Henry James, 1923–.
'Youth, society, and the family in China.' In *Youth in China*, edited by Edward Stuart Kirby. [Analytic entry]
Hong Kong: Dragonfly Books, 1965, 31–65.
SUBJ 12.1 41 54 64 ▪ 46

19929 CSU F P2 G9.5 1949–1972
Liu, William Thomas (Liu Jung), 1930–.
'Family interactions among local and refugee Chinese families in Hong Kong.'
J. of marriage and the family 28, 3 (Aug. 1966), 314–323.
SUBJ 41 ▪ 11.2

19930 CSU P P2 G1.2 1949–1972
McAleavy, Henry.
'Some aspects of marriage and divorce in Communist China.' In *Family law in Asia and Africa*, edited by James Norman Dalrymple Anderson. [Sole entry]
New York: Praeger, 1968, 73–89.
SUBJ 12.2 41

19931 NNC P P1 G1.2 1949–1972
Madian, Marcia Dunn, 1936–.
The marriage law of Communist China, 1950–1953: A means of disrupting the traditional Chinese family system.
Unpublished masters thesis in Public Law and Government, Columbia U., 1962. 102 p. [Certificate essay, East Asian Institute]
SUBJ 12.1 12.2 41 47 ▪ 30 45

19932 CSU F P3 G9.5 1949–1972
Mitchell, Robert Edward, 1930–.
'Changes in fertility rates and family size [in Hong Kong] in response to changes in age at marriage, the trend away from arranged marriages, and increasing urbanization.'
PS 25, 3 (Nov. 1971), 481–489.
SUBJ 41 58 ▪ 21.1 51

19933 CSU FP P3 G9.5 1949–1972
Mitchell, Robert Edward, 1930–.
Family life in urban Hong Kong.
Taipei: Orient Cultural Service, 1972. 2 vols. 25, 571 p. [c.p.]. (Asian Folklore and Social Life monographs, 24–25)
SUBJ 41 47 50 ▪ 21.1 23 26 28 42 51 55 58 61

19934 MCY P P1 G1.2 1949–1972
Niida Noboru, 1904–1967.
'Land reform and new marriage law in China.'
DE 2, 1 (Mar. 1964), 3–15.
SUBJ 12.2 41 ▪ 14.1 45 47

19935 CSU F P3 G9.4 1949–1972
O'Hara, Albert Richard, 1907–.
'Changing attitudes of university students toward marriage and the family in Taiwan.' In *Research on changes of Chinese society*, by A. R. O'Hara. [Selective entry]
Taipei: Orient Cultural Service, 1971, 21–26. (Asian Folklore and Social Life monographs, 20)
SUBJ 41 54 60

19936 MCH F P3 G9.4 1949–1972
O'Hara, Albert Richard, 1907–.
'Changing attitudes toward marriage and the family in Free China.'
JCS 2 (1962), 57–79. [Reprinted in *Research on changes of Chinese society*, by A. R. O'Hara. (Selective entry.) Taipei: Orient Cultural Service, 1971, 9–19. (Asian Folklore and Social Life monographs, 20)]
SUBJ 41 61 63 ▪ 12.2 17 47 54

19937 CBU F P3 G9.4 1949–1972
O'Hara, Albert Richard, 1907–.
'Comparative values of American and Chinese university students in choosing a mate.'
JCS 5 (1967), 93–100. [Reprinted in *Research on changes of Chinese society*, by A. R. O'Hara. (Selective entry.) Taipei: Orient Cultural Service, 1971, 27–34. (Asian Folklore and Social Life monographs, 20)]
SUBJ 41 60 ▪ 54 61

19938 CBU F P2 G9.4 1949–1972
O'Hara, Albert Richard, 1907–.
'Some indications of changes in functions of the family in China.'

J. of sociology (Taipei) 3 (Apr. 1967), 59–76. [Reprinted in *Research on changes of Chinese society*, by A. R. O'Hara. (Selective entry.) Taipei: Orient Cultural Service, 1971, 35–52. (Asian Folklore and Social Life monographs, 20)]
Subj 41 ▪ 16 23 31 63

19939 MAM F P2 G9.4 1949–1972
Parish, William Lucious, Jr., 1939–.
Kinship and modernization in Taiwan.
Ann Arbor: University Microfilms (Publ. 70-14,398), 1970. 332 p. (Doctoral dissertation in Sociology, Cornell U.)
Subj 19 21.2 41 42 44 ▪ 21.4 26 34.2 45 50

19940 CSU PO P1 G1.1 1949–1972
Pegg, Leonard.
'Legitimacy ordinance and affiliation proceedings ordinance (Nos. 29 and 28 of 1971).'
Hong Kong law j. 2, 3 (Sept. 1972), 348–360.
Subj 12.2 41

19941 MCH S P1 G1.2 1949–1972
Petrov, N- A-.
'Voprosy braka i sem'i v novom Kitae' (Marriage and the family in New China).
Sovetskaia etnografiia 1954, 1, 85–96.
Subj 12.1 41 ▪ 12.2 64

19942 MCH O P2 G1.3 1949–1972
Pollard, Robert Spence Watson, 1907–.
'Marriage and divorce in China now.'
Plain view 11, 2 (Nov. 1956), 54–64.
Subj 12.2 41 47 ▪ 22.2 45

19943 NIC F P8 G9.5 1949–1972
Pratt, Jean A-.
'Emigration and unilineal descent groups: A study of marriage in a Hakka village in the New Territories, Hong Kong.'
Eastern anthropologist 13, 4 (June–Aug. 1960), 147–158.
Subj 41 ▪ 24 29 42 43 45 47

19944 MCH P P1 G1.2 1949–1972
Regis, Maria Arena.
'La nuova famiglia nella Cina popolare' (The new family in the People's Republic of China).
Problemi di Ulisse 51 (dicembre 1963), 86–93.
Subj 12.1 41 ▪ 42 47 51

19945 CSH FP P2 G1.2 1949–1972
Salaff, Janet Weitzner, 1940–.
'The role of the family in health care.' In *Medicine and public health in the People's Republic of China*, edited by Joseph R- Quinn. [Selective entry]
[Washington, D.C.]: U.S. Dept. of Health, Education, and Welfare, Public Health Service, National Institutes of Health, 1972, 23–53.
Subj 28 41 56 ▪ 22 50 52 53 54

19946 CVB FP P2 G9.5 1949–1972
Salaff, Janet Weitzner, 1940–.
Social and demographic determinants of marriage age in Hong Kong.
Vancouver: U. of British Columbia, Institute of Asian and Slavonic Research, 1972. 40 p. (IASR working papers, 2)
Subj 41 47 ▪ 21.4 26 48 50

19947 CSU F P3 G9.5 1949–1972
Stoodley, Bartlett H-, 1907–.
'Normative family orientations of Chinese college students in Hong Kong.'
J. of marriage and the family 29, 4 (Nov. 1967), 773–782.
Subj 41 ▪ 43 46 54

19948 CSU P P2 G1.2 1949–1972
Tien, H. Yuan (T'ien Hsin-yüan), 1926–.
'Marital moratorium and fertility control in China.'
PS 24, 3 (Nov. 1970), 311–323.
Subj 41 50 51 ▪ 12.1

19949 MCH P P1 G1.2 1949–1972
U Chan-chzhen' (Wu Ch'ang-chen) and M- IA- Kirillova.
'Osnovaniia i poriadok rastorzheniia braka v Kitaiskoi Narodnoi Respublike' (Legal grounds and procedure for divorce in the People's Republic of China).
Izvestiia vysshikh uchebnykh zavedenii; pravovedenie 3, 2 (1959), 142–150.
Subj 12.2 41 47 ▪ 12.1 45

19950 NIC P P1 G1.2 1949–1972
Valk, Marius Hendrikus van der, 1908–.
'The registration of marriage in Communist China.'
MS 16, 1/2 (1957), 347–359.
Subj 12.2 22.2 41 ▪ 12.1 29 56 65

19951 CSU FP P3 G1.2 1949–1972
Vogel, Ezra Feivel, 1930–.
'A preliminary view of family and mental health in urban Communist China.' In *Mental health research in Asia and the Pacific*, edited by William A- Caudill and Tsung-yi Lin (Lin Tsung-i). [Selective entry]
Honolulu: East-West Center Press, 1969, 393–404.
Subj 12.1 41 48 61 ▪ 46 47 52 53 55 63

19952 CSH P P2 G1.2 1949–1972
Wong, Aline K. (Huang Chien Li-chung), 1941–.
'Changes in the marriage and family institutions in China, 1949–1969.' In *Selected seminar papers on contemporary China, I*, edited by Steve S. K. Chin (Chin Ssu-k'ai) and Frank Henry Haviland King. [Analytic entry]
Hong Kong: U. of Hong Kong, Centre of Asian Studies, 1971, 149–178. (CAS occasional papers and monographs, 4)
Subj 41 ▪ 12.1 12.2 47 54

19953 MAM F P3 G9.5 1949–1972
Wong, Fai-Ming, 1936–.
Modern ideology, industrialization, and the middle-class Chinese family in Hong Kong.
Ann Arbor: University Microfilms (Publ. 71-11,496), 1971. 360 p. (Doctoral dissertation in Sociology, U. of California, Santa Barbara, 1969)
Subj 19 26 41 60 ▪ 21.4 24.4 44 47 55

19954 CSU O P2 G1.3 1949–1972
Woodsworth, K- C-.
'Family law and resolution of domestic disputes in the People's Republic of China.'
McGill law j. 13, 1 (1967), 169–177.
Subj 12.2 22.2 41 ▪ 45 47

19955 NIC F P7 G9.4 1949–1972
Yang, Martin M. C. (Yang Mou-ch'un), 1904–.
'Changes in family life in rural Taiwan.'
JCS 2 (1962), 68–79. [See Vol. 2 of this *Bibliography* for Chinese version.]
Subj 41 ▪ 28 47 55

19956 CSU P P2 G9.4 1949–1972
Yuan, D. Y.
'Marital characteristics in relation to the rural-urban continuum in Taiwan.'
Demography 5, 1 (1968), 93–103.
Subj 41 ▪ 47 50

42 Lineages and Clanship

氏族及譜系　　氏族及び系譜

1644-1911

19957 NIC O P7 G1.5 1842–1895
'Chinese clans and their customs.'
Chinese and Japanese repository 3, 23 (1 June 1865), 281–284.
Subj 25 29 42 ▪ 18 65

19958 CSU O P7 G9.2 1644–1842
'Clanship among the Chinese.'
Chinese repository 4, 9 (Jan. 1836), 411–415.
Subj 25 42 ▪ 22 22.2

19959 NIC P P7 G9.5 –1842
Balfour, S- F-.
'Hong Kong before the British.'
THM 11, 4 (Feb.–Mar. 1941), 330–352; 1, 5 (Apr.–May 1941), 440–464. [Reprinted—*JRAS-HKB* 10 (1970), 134–179.]
Subj 29 42 ▪ 21.2 21.3 25

19960 MCH PO P1 G1.4 –1911
Bernhardi, Anna.
'Stammtafeln und Geschlechterkunde in China' (Genealogical charts and genealogy in China).
ZE 50, 2/3 (1918), 154–165.
Subj 42 44 ▪ 41 43

19961 MCH PO P1 G1.2 –1911
Schüler, Wilhelm, 1869–1935.
'Der chinesischen Familiennamen' (Chinese surnames).
Z. für Missionskunde und Religionswissenschaft 23, 1 (1908), 1–11; 23, 2 (1908), 33–39.
Subj 42 62 ▪ 11.2

1644-1949

19962 NIC S P7 G9.0 1842–1949
Freedman, Maurice, 1920–.
Lineage organization in southeastern China.
London: Athlone Press, 1958. 151 p. (London School of Economics, Monographs on Social Anthropology, 18)
Subj 22 41 42 43 57 ▪ 24.1 24.6 25 26 27 30 32.2 44 45 47

19963 NIC P P2 G1.3 1644–1949
Hu, Hsien-chin, 1910–.
The common descent group in China and its functions.
New York: Viking Fund, 1948. 204 p. (Viking Fund publications in anthropology, 10) (Doctoral dissertation in Anthropology, Columbia U.)
Subj 40 42 43 45 ▪ 22 24 25 26 27

19964 MCH P P1 G1.3 –1949
Liu, Hui-chen Wang (Liu Wang Hui-chen), 1919–.
The traditional Chinese clan rules.
Locust Valley, N.Y.: J. J. Augustin, 1959. 10, 264 p. (Assn. for Asian Studies monographs, 7) (Revision of *An analysis of Chinese clan rules: A study of social control*, doctoral dissertation in Sociology, U. of Pittsburgh, 1956)
SUBJ 41 42 45 53 63 64 ▪ 12 12.2 13 16.1 17 22.2 38 40 50 72

19965 CBU P P2 G1.2 –1949
Lo Hsiang-lin, 1905–.
'The history and arrangement of Chinese genealogies.' In *Studies in Asian genealogy*, edited by Spencer John Palmer. [Selective entry]
Provo: Brigham Young U. Press, 1972, 13–26.
SUBJ 42 ▪ 11.2 12 17 41

1911-1949

19966 MCH O P2 G7.3 1911–1928
Brown, Fred R-.
'Clan customs in Kiangsi province.'
CR 53, 8 (Aug. 1922), 518–522.
SUBJ 22.2 42 ▪ 43

19967 MCY P P1 G1.2 1911–1949
Gérardin, André.
'Le conseil de famille en droit chinois' (The lineage council [to consider the interests of a minor] in Chinese law).
BUA 3e série 2, 5 (1941), 59–83.
SUBJ 12.2 42 ▪ 41 45

19968 NIC O P8 G9.2 1911–1949
Spencer, Robert F-, 1917–, and S- A- Barnett.
'Notes on a bachelor house in the South China area.'
AA new (2nd) series 50, 3 (July–Sept. 1948), 463–478.
SUBJ 42 54 ▪ 43 46

1911-1972
(including 1644-1972)

19969 CSH O P8 G9.5 1644–1972
Akers-Jones, David.
'Visit to San Tin village complex [i.e., Hsin-t'ien, Hong Kong].' In *Aspects of social organization in the New Territories*, edited by Hong Kong Branch, Royal Asiatic Society. [Selective entry]
Hong Kong: Cathay Press, 1964, 43–44.
SUBJ 21.3 26.1 42 43 ▪ 21.4

19970 CSU FP P7 G9.5 –1972
Baker, Hugh David Roberts, 1937–.
A Chinese lineage village: Sheung Shui [i.e., Shang-shui, Hong Kong].
Stanford: Stanford U. Press, 1968. 237 p. (Revision of *A lineage village in the New Territories of Hong Kong*, doctoral dissertation in Anthropology, U. of London [School of Oriental and African Studies], 1967)
SUBJ 21.3 22 24.1 26.1 42 45 ▪ 22.1 24.3 25 26.3 27 41 43 57

19971 CSH U P8 G9.5 –1972
Baker, Hugh David Roberts, 1937–.
'Clan organization and its role in village affairs: Some differences between single-clan and multiple-clan villages.' In *Aspects of social organization in the New Territories*, edited by Hong Kong Branch, Royal Asiatic Society. [Selective entry]
Hong Kong: Cathay Press, 1964, 4–9.
SUBJ 22 42 ▪ 40

19972 CSU FP P7 G9.5 –1972
Baker, Hugh David Roberts, 1937–.
'The five great clans of the New Territories.'
JRAS-HKB 6 (1966), 25–48.
SUBJ 20 26 42 ▪ 21.2 21.3 25 40 43

19973 CSU FP P8 G9.4 1644–1972
Cohen, Myron Leon, 1937–.
'Agnatic kinship in south Taiwan.'
Ethnology 8, 2 (Apr. 1969), 167–182.
SUBJ 21.3 40 42 43 44 ▪ 25 29 41

19974 CBU P P2 G1.2 –1972
Eberhard, Wolfram, 1909–.
'Chinese genealogies as a source for the study of Chinese society.' In *Studies in Asian genealogy*, edited by Spencer John Palmer. [Selective entry]
Provo: Brigham Young U. Press, 1972, 27–37.
SUBJ 42 58 ▪ 11.2 16 41 51

19975 CSU FP P7 G9.0 –1972
Freedman, Maurice, 1920–.
Chinese lineage and society: Fukien and Kwangtung.
New York: Humanities Press, 1966. 10, 207 p. (London School of Economics, Monographs on Social Anthropology, 33)
SUBJ 26 40 41 42 43 62 ▪ 21 21.3 22 22.1 22.2 25 27 45 47

19976 CSH S P8 G1.5 1644–1972
Fried, Morton Herbert, 1923–.
'Clans and lineages: How to tell them apart and why, with special reference to Chinese society.'
BIE 29 (Spring 1970), 11–36.
SUBJ 42 ▪ 43 45

19977 CSU S P1 G1.5 1895–1972
Fried, Morton Herbert, 1923–.
'The classification of corporate unilineal descent groups.'
J. of the Royal Anthropological Institute 87, 1 (Jan.–June 1957), 1–29.
SUBJ 42

19978 NIC FP P2 G1.1 1842–1972
Hsu, Francis L. K. (Hsü Lang-kuang), 1909–.
Clan, caste, and club: A comparative study of Chinese, Hindu, and American ways of life.
Princeton: Van Nostrand, 1963. 11, 335 p.
SUBJ 41 42 61 63 ▪ 25 30 40 43 48 62

19979 CSU P P1 G1.1 –1972
Meskill, Johanna Menzel, 1930–.
'The Chinese genealogy as a research source.' In *Family and kinship in Chinese society*, edited by Maurice Freedman. [Selective entry]
Stanford: Stanford U. Press, 1970, 139–161.
SUBJ 42 ▪ 41 44 45 47

19980 CSU FP P8 G9.4 1895–1972
Pasternak, Burton, 1933–.
'Atrophy of patrilineal bonds in a Chinese village in historical perspective.'
Ethnohistory 15, 3 (Summer 1968), 293–327.
SUBJ 40 42 44 ▪ 21 24.1 29 41 45 48

19981 CSU FP P7 G9.0 –1972
Pasternak, Burton, 1933–.
Review of *Chinese lineage and society: Fukien and Kwangtung*, by Maurice Freedman.
AA new (2nd) series 70, 3 (June 1968), 597–598.
SUBJ 29 42

19982 CSU S P8 G1.1 –1972
Pasternak, Burton, 1933–.
'The role of the frontier in Chinese lineage development.'
JAS 28, 3 (May 1969), 551–561.
SUBJ 42 ▪ 11.2 14.1 25 29 44

19983 CSU F P7 G1.1 –1972
Potter, Jack Michael, 1936–.
'Land and lineage in traditional China.' In *Family and kinship in Chinese society*, edited by Maurice Freedman. [Selective entry]
Stanford: Stanford U. Press, 1970, 121–138.
SUBJ 42 45 ▪ 21.3 29 43

19984 CSU S P1 G1.5 –1972
Sharma, Satya P-.
'Structural and functional characteristics of lineages in societies with unilineal descent groups and centralized government: A comparative exploration.'
JAAS 6, 3/4 (July–Oct. 1971), 226–232.
SUBJ 12 42

19985 CSU O P7 G9.5 1644–1972
Williams, Bernard V-.
'The Chan [Ch'en] family of Tseung Kwan O [i.e., Chiang-chün-ao], New Territories [Hong Kong].'
JRAS-HKB 7 (1967), 158–160.
SUBJ 26.1 42 ▪ 21.3 41 59

19986 CSH O P8 G9.5 1644–1972
Williams, Bernard V-.
'Visit to Ho Chung and Sheung Yeung villages in the Sai Kung area [i.e., Hao-t'ung and Shang-yüan villages in the Hsi-kung area, Hong Kong].' In *Aspects of social organization in the New Territories*, edited by Hong Kong Branch, Royal Asiatic Society. [Selective entry]
Hong Kong: Cathay Press, 1964, 46–47.
SUBJ 26.1 42 43

1949-1972

19987 CSU F P8 G9.0 1949–1972
Anderson, Eugene Newton, Jr., 1941–.
'Lineage atrophy in Chinese society.'
AA new (2nd) series 72, 2 (Apr. 1970), 363–365.
SUBJ 42

19988 CSU S P8 G9.5 1949–1972
Berkowitz, Morris Ira, 1931–.
'Sheung Shui: A review article. Problems relating to social research in the New Territories of Hong Kong.' [Review of *A Chinese lineage village: Sheung Shui*, by Hugh David Roberts Baker.]
JRAS-HKB 9 (1969), 165–170.
SUBJ 42 ▪ 71

19989 CSU F P3 G9.4 1949–1972
Fried, Morton Herbert, 1923–.
'Some political aspects of clanship in a modern Chinese city' [Taipei]. In *Political anthropology*, edited by Marc Jerome Swartz, Victor W- Turner, and Arthur Tuden. [Selective entry]
Chicago: Aldine, 1966, 285–300.
SUBJ 22 42 ▪ 29 43

19990 MAM FP P8 G9.5 1949–1972
Watson, James Lee, 1943–.
A Chinese emigrant community: The Man [i.e., Wen] *lineage in Hong Kong and London*.
Ann Arbor: University Microfilms (Publ. 72-27,149), 1972. 326 p. (Doctoral dissertation in Anthropology, U. of California, Berkeley)
SUBJ 11.2 20 24 40 42 50 ▪ 24.5 24.6 27 28 31 41 43 46 53 55

43 ANCESTOR WORSHIP

祖先崇祀 祖先崇拜

1644-1911

19991 ELB U P1 G1.3 1644–1895
'The worship of ancestors among the Chinese.'
Chinese repository 18, 7 (July 1849), 363–384.
SUBJ 43 57 ▪ 65

19992 MCH S P1 G1.2 –1895
Boüinais, Albert Marie Aristide, 1851–1895, and A- Paulus.
'Le culte des morts dans le Céleste empire et l'Annam comparé au culte des ancêtres dans l'antiquité occidentale' (A comparison of the cult of the dead in the Celestial Empire and Annam with the ancestral cult in Western antiquity).
Annales du Musée Guimet, Bibliothèque de vulgarisation 16 (1893), 1–267 [s.p.].
SUBJ 41 43 57 ▪ 12 13 23 40 50 51 56 60

19993 MCH P P1 G1.1 –1911
Cordier, Henri, 1849–1925.
'La piété filiale et le culte des ancêtres en Chine' (Filial piety and the ancestral cult in China).
Annales du Musée Guimet, Bibliothèque de vulgarisation 35 (1910), 67–101.
SUBJ 43 63 ▪ 57 62

19994 MCH O P1 G1.2 1895–1911
Enjoy, Paul d', 1866–?
'Le culte des morts en Chine' (The cult of the dead in China).
R. internationale de sociologie 5, 3 (mars 1897), 210–214.
SUBJ 43 47 ▪ 41

19995 MCH P P1 G1.1 –1911
Farjenel, Fernand, ?–1918.
'Quelques particularités du culte des ancêtres en Chine' (Some characteristics of the ancestral cult in China).
JA 10e série 2, 1 (juil.–août 1903), 85–96.
SUBJ 43

19996 MCH PO P2 G1.1 1895–1911
Hoogers, Joseph.
'Théorie et pratique de la piété filiale chez les Chinois' (Chinese filial piety in theory and practice).
Anthropos 5, 1 (Jan.–Feb. 1910), 1–15; 5, 4 (Juli–Aug. 1910), 688–702.
SUBJ 41 43 63 ▪ 47 51 56 57 62

19997 CSU U P1 G1.3 –1911
Laufer, Berthold, 1874–1934.
'The development of ancestral images in China.'
J. of religious psychology 6, 2 (Apr. 1913), 111–123.
SUBJ 43 ▪ 57

19998 FPN PO P1 G1.1 –1895
Martin, Charles Ernest, 1831–1897.
'Le culte des ancêtres, le culte des morts et le culte des funérailles chez les Chinois' (The ancestral cult, the cult of the dead, and funeral cults among the Chinese).
J. d'hygiène 16, 772 (2 juil. 1891), 313–320; 16, 773 (9 juil. 1891), 325–332.
SUBJ 43 57 64 ▪ 66

19999 CSU PO P1 G1.2 –1911
Martin, William Alexander Parsons, 1827–1916.
'The worship of ancestors in China.' In *The lore of Cathay: or, The intellect of China*, by W. A. P. Martin. [Selective entry]
New York: Revell, 1901, 264–278. [Reprinted in *The lore of Cathay: or, The intellect of China*, by W. A. P. Martin. (Selective entry.) Taipei: Ch'eng-wen, 1971, 264–278.]
SUBJ 43 ▪ 12.1 62

20000 NNC PO P1 G1.2 1895–1911
Matignon, Jean-Jacques, 1866–?
'Les morts qui gouvernent' (The dead who rule). In *La Chine hermétique: superstitions, crime et misère* (China sealed off: Superstition, crime, and poverty), 5th ed., rev., by J.-J. Matignon. [Selective entry]
Paris: Lib. Geuthner, 1936, 319–353.
SUBJ 43 57 60 ▪ 56

20001 MCH PO P2 G1.2 1842–1895
Ravary, *Père* ———.
'Les tablettes des ancêtres et leurs registres de la famille en Chine' (Ancestral tablets and their family registers in China).
Etudes religieuses 5e série 6 (nov. 1874), 762–768.
SUBJ 43 ▪ 62 63

20002 NNC P P1 G1.3 –1895
Ritschkowsky, ———.
'Der chinesische Ahnenkultus' (Chinese ancestral cults).
Allgemeine Missions-Z. 22, 7 (Juli 1895), 289–301; 22, 8 (Aug. 1895), 360–374; 22, 9 (Sept. 1895), 385–390.
SUBJ 43 57 ▪ 13 41 62

20003 NIC O P5 G6.1 1842–1895
Yates, Matthew Tyson, 1819–1888.
Ancestral worship.
Shanghai: American Presbyterian Mission Press, 1877. 48 p.
SUBJ 43 57 ▪ 12.2 23 62 65

1644-1949

20004 ELO S P1 G1.3 –1928
Addison, James Thayer, 1887–1953.
Chinese ancestor worship: A study of its meaning and its relations with Christianity.
Shanghai, Tokyo: Chung Hua Sheng Kung Hui, 1925. 85 p.
SUBJ 43 64 65 66 ▪ 57

20005 ICU S P1 G1.1 –1928
Chen, Arthur S. (Ch'en Shu-yüan), 1905–.
Religion in the Chinese family.
Unpublished masters thesis in Christian Theology and Ethics, U. of Chicago, 1930. 54 p.
SUBJ 23 40 41 43 63 ▪ 17 42 52 53 64

20006 NIC PO P8 G9.3 1895–1928
Lin, Peter Wei (Lin Wei), 1894–.
The social effects of ancestor worship in a South China town.
Unpublished masters thesis in Sociology, Columbia U., 1922. 33 p.
SUBJ 42 43 45 ▪ 22 23 24 26 27 28 34.1

20007 MCH O P1 G1.2 –1928
Munn, William.
'Ancestor-worship: Its origins and results.'
Church missionary review 71, 832 (Dec. 1920), 319–328.
SUBJ 43 ▪ 23

20008 NIC S P1 G1.2 –1928
Rydh, Hanna Albertina, 1891–.
'Seasonal fertility rites and the death cult in Scandinavia and China.'
B. of the Museum of Far Eastern Antiquities (Stockholm) 3 (1931), 69–98.
SUBJ 43 57 ▪ 23 46

20009 ELS S P1 G1.1 1644–1949
Scheinfeld, Daniel R-.
A comparative study of ancestor worship, with special reference to social structure.
Unpublished masters thesis in Anthropology, U. of London [London School of Economics and Political Science], 1960. 193 p.
SUBJ 16 43 ▪ 16.1 16.3 22.2 40 42 62

20010 GBF P P2 G1.1 –1949
Tiberi, Fortunato.
'Der Ahnenkult in China nach den kanonischen Schriften' (The ancestral cult in China according to classical works).
Annali lateranensi 27 (1963), 283–475.
SUBJ 16 23 43 ▪ 22.2 29 41 47 57 72

20011 MCY P P2 G1.2 –1949
Waong, L. (Wang Jen-sheng).
'Les tablettes des ancêtres' (Ancestral tablets).
BUA 3e série 2, 6 (1941), 243–272.
SUBJ 43 57

20012 NIC PO P2 G5.1 1895–1949
Williams, Edward Thomas, 1854–1944.
'Worshipping imperial ancestors in Peking.'
JRAS-NCB new (2nd) series 70 (1939), 46–65.
SUBJ 16.1 43 ▪ 13 62

20013 MCH P P1 G1.2 –1949
Yang, Kun (Yang K'un), 1901–.
Recherches sur le culte des ancêtres comme principe ordonnateur de la famille chinoise: la succession au culte, la succession au patrimoine (Investigations of the ancestral cult as the organizing principle of the Chinese family: Ritual succession and property inheritance).
Lyons: Bosc et Riou, 1934. 174 p. (Doctoral dissertation, Faculté des lettres, Université de Lyon)
SUBJ 40 41 43 45 ▪ 12.2 22.2 42 57 63

1911-1949

20014 NNC O P3 G9.3 1911–1928
Hodous, Lewis, 1872–1949.
'The Ch'ing Ming festival.'
JRAS-NCB new (2nd) series 46 (1915), 58–60.
SUBJ 43 ▪ 23 62

20015 NNC F P3 G5.1 1928–1949
Körner, Brunhild.
'Der Ahnenkult der Mandschu in Peking' (The ancestral cult of the Manchus in Peking).
Baessler-Archiv neue (2.) Folge 3 (1955), 175–193.
SUBJ 43 ▪ 29 41 42 62

1911-1972
(including 1644-1972)

20016 CSU P P1 G1.1 –1972
Aijmer, Lars Göran, 1936–.
'A structural approach to Chinese ancestor worship.'
BTLV 124, 1 (1968), 91–98.
SUBJ 23 43 ▪ 57 62

20017 CSU F P1 G1.1 –1972
Freedman, Maurice, 1920–.
'Ancestor worship: Two facets of the Chinese case.' In *Social organization: Essays presented to Raymond Firth*, edited by M. Freedman. [Selective entry]
Chicago: Aldine, 1967, 85–103.
SUBJ 40 43 57 62 ▪ 41 42 45 63

1949-1972

20018 MAM F P8 G9.4 1949–1972
Ahern, Emily Martin, 1944–.
The cult of the dead in a Chinese village.
Stanford: Stanford U. Press, 1973. 15, 280 p. (Revision of *The cult of the dead in Ch'inan* [T'ai-pei *hsien*], *Taiwan: A study of ancestor worship in a four-lineage community*, doctoral dissertation in Anthropology, Cornell U., 1971)
SUBJ 20 23 24 42 43 62 ▪ 21 22 24.2 25 28 45 56 57 65

44 KIN TERMS AND RELATIONSHIPS
親屬關係及稱呼
親属関係及び称呼

20019 NIC O P1 G1.0 1911–1972
Chao, Y. R. (Chao Yüan-jen), 1892–.
'Chinese terms of address.'
Language 32, 1 (Jan.–Mar. 1956), 217–241.
SUBJ 44 48 ▪ 63

20020 NIC P P1 G1.0 –1911
Chen Ta (Ch'en Ta), 1892–, and John Knight Shryock, 1890–1952.
'Chinese relationship terms.'
AA new (2nd) series 34, 4 (Oct.–Dec. 1932), 623–669.
SUBJ 44 ▪ 41

20021 NIC F P4 G1.3 1928–1949
Fei Hsiao-tung (Fei Hsiao-t'ung), 1910–.
'The problem of Chinese relationship system.'
MS 2, 1 (1936), 125–148.
SUBJ 44

20022 NIC P P1 G1.3 –1911
Feng, Han-yi (Feng Han-chi), 1902–.
'The Chinese kinship system.'
HJAS 2, 2 (July 1937), 141–276. (Doctoral dissertation in Anthropology, U. of Pennsylvania) [Separately reprinted—Cambridge: Harvard U. Press, 1948. 135 p.] [Separately reprinted—Cambridge: Harvard U. Press, 1967. 135 p. (Harvard-Yenching Institute studies, 22)]
SUBJ 40 44 ▪ 41 42 43 57 59

20023 CSU P P1 G1.0 –1949
Feng, Han-yi (Feng Han-chi), 1902–.
'Teknonymy as a formative factor in the Chinese kinship system.'
AA new (2nd) series 38, 1 (Jan.–Mar. 1936), 59–66.
SUBJ 44

20024 NIC F P8 G9.4 1949–1972
Gallin, Bernard, 1929–.
'Matrilineal and affinal relationships of a Taiwanese village [Hsin-hsing, Chang-hua *hsien*].'
AA new (2nd) series 62, 4 (Aug. 1960), 632–642. [For fuller treatment, see entry 15515.]
SUBJ 42 44 ▪ 22 24

20025 NIC P P1 G1.1 –1949
Hou You-ing (Hu Yü-yin).
Etude sur la parenté en droit chinois (A study of kinship in Chinese law).
Paris: Ed. Domat-Montchrestien, 1933. 254 p. (Doctoral dissertation, Faculté de droit, Université de Paris)
SUBJ 12.2 40 44 ▪ 41 57

20026 NIC O P1 G1.0 1911–1949
Hsu, Francis L. K. (Hsü Lang-kuang), 1909–.
'The differential functions of relationship terms.'
AA new (2nd) series 44, 2 (Apr.–June 1942), 248–256.
SUBJ 44

20027 NIC S P1 G1.3 1911–1949
Hsu, Francis L. K. (Hsü Lang-kuang), 1909–.
'On a technique for studying relationship terms.'
AA new (2nd) series 49, 4 (Oct.–Dec. 1947), 618–624.
SUBJ 44

20028 CSU S P1 G1.0 –1949
Kroeber, Alfred Louis, 1876–1960.
'Process in the Chinese kinship system.'
AA new (2nd) series 35, 1 (Jan.–Mar. 1933), 151–157.
SUBJ 41 44

20029 CSU F P1 G9.0 1949–1972
McCoy, William John, Jr., 1924–.
'Chinese kin terms of reference and address.' In *Family and kinship in Chinese society*, edited by Maurice Freedman. [Selective entry]
Stanford: Stanford U. Press, 1970, 209–226.
SUBJ 44

20030 NNC O P1 G1.0 –1895
May, Alfred J-.
'Chinese relationships.'
China review 21, 1 (July–Aug. 1894), 15–39.
SUBJ 44

20031 MCH S P1 G1.1 –1972
Rygaloff, Alexis, 1922–.
'Deux points de nomenclature dans le système chinois de parenté' (Two points on Chinese kinship terminology).
L'homme 2, 3 (sept.–déc. 1962), 53–74.
SUBJ 44

20032 CSU P P1 G1.0 1842–1895
Scarborough, William, ?–1894.
'Chinese modes of address: A chapter in native etiquette.'
CR 10, 3 (May–June 1879), 187–197; 10, 4 (July–Aug. 1879), 261–269; 10, 5 (Sept.–Oct. 1879), 337–348.
SUBJ 44 48 ▪ 63

45 PROPERTY AND INHERITANCE
財產及繼承　財産及び相続

1644-1911

20033 NNC P P3 G9.2 1644–1895
Eitel, Ernest John, 1838–1908.
'The law of testamentary succession as popularly understood and applied in China.'
China review 15, 3 (Nov.–Dec. 1886), 150–155.
SUBJ 12.2 45 ▪ 22.2 44

20034 CBU PO P2 G1.2 1895–1911
Franke, Otto, 1863–1946.
Die Rechtsverhältnisse am Grundeigentum in China (Legal aspects of landownership in China).
Leipzig: Dieterich'sche Verlagsbuchhandlung, 1903. 104 p.
SUBJ 12.2 14.1 14.5 45 ▪ 66

20035 CSU P P1 G1.3 –1842
Gans, Eduard, 1798–1839.
'Chinesisches Erbrecht' (Chinese inheritance law). In *Das Erbrecht in weltgeschichtlicher Entwicklung* (The development of inheritance law in world history), by E. Gans. [Sole entry]
Berlin: Maurersche Buchhandlung, 1824, vol. 1, 98–123. [Reprinted in *Das Erbrecht in weltgeschichtlicher Entwicklung*, by E. Gans. (Sole entry.) Aalen: Scientia, 1963, vol. 1, 98–123.]
SUBJ 22.2 41 45

20036 MCH P P2 G1.2 1842–1895
Hoang, Pierre (Huang Po-lu), 1830–1909.
Notions techniques sur la propriété en Chine, avec un choix d'actes et de documents officiels (Technical notions of property in China, with selected deeds and official documents).
Shanghai: Impr. de la Mission catholique, 1897. 200 p. (Variétés sinologiques, 11)
SUBJ 12.2 14.1 43 45 ▪ 14 14.5 16.1 63

20037 NNC PO P1 G1.3 –1895
Jamieson, George, 1843–1920, et al.
'Chinese wills.'
China review 4, 4 (Jan.–Feb. 1876), 268; 4, 5 (Mar.–Apr. 1876), 331–332; 4, 6 (May–June 1876), 399; 5, 1 (July–Aug. 1876), 69.
SUBJ 45 ▪ 22.2 63

20038 CSU P P7 G1.2 1644–1895
Meadows, Thomas Taylor.
'Land tenure in China: Remarks on the acquisition, common-tenure, and alienation of real property in China, accompanied by a facsimile and translation of a deed of sale.'
Transactions of the China Branch of the Royal Asiatic Society 1 (1847), 1–15. [Reprinted as 'Remarks on the acquisition, tenure, and alienation of real property in China, accompanied by a deed of sale.' *Chinese repository* 18, 11 (Nov. 1849), 561–573.]
SUBJ 12.2 14.1 45 ▪ 14.5 22.2

20039 MCH O P1 G9.3 1842–1895
Schlegel, Gustaaf, 1840–1903.
'Iets over Chineesche testamenten, donatiën en erfopvolging' (A note on Chinese wills, inheritances, and rules of succession).
Het Regt in Nederlandsch-Indië (Batavia) 20 (September 1862), 369–374.
SUBJ 22.2 45

20040 NIC S P8 G1.2 –1842
Schurmann, Herbert Franz, 1926–.
'Traditional property concepts in China.'
FEQ 15, 4 (Aug. 1956), 507–516.
SUBJ 12.2 45 ▪ 41

20041 MCH O P1 G1.2 –1895
Simon, G- Eugène, 1829–1896.
'La propriété en Chine' (Property in China).
Annales de l'Extrême-Orient 4 (1881/82), 257–269.
SUBJ 45 ▪ 12.1 14.5

20042 NNC P P1 G1.2 –1911
Sternberg, Theodor.
'Der Geist des chinesischen Vermögensrechts' (The spirit of Chinese property law).
ZVR 26 (1912), 143–153.
SUBJ 12.2 30 45 ▪ 14.6 34.2 44 48 63

20043 NIC P P8 G6.1 –1842
Twitchett, Denis Crispin, 1925–.
'The Fan clan's charitable estate, 1050–1760.' In *Confucianism in action*, edited by David Shepherd Nivison and Arthur Frederick Wright. [Selective entry]
Stanford: Stanford U. Press, 1959, 97–133.
SUBJ 38 42 45 ▪ 26.1 27 28 63

20044 MCH P P1 G1.1 1644–1895
Young, J- W-, 1855–1898.
'Versterfrecht, adoptie en pleegkinderen bij de Chineezen: Behandeling der betrekkelijke artikelen van het wetboek "Tai tshing loet le"' (Inheritance law, adoption, and foster children among the Chinese: A treatment of the relevant articles in the *Ta Ch'ing lü-li* [Statutes and sub-statutes of the great Ch'ing]).
Tijdschrift voor Indische taal-, land- en volkenkunde 31 (1886), 214–239.
SUBJ 12.2 41 45 ▪ 44 47 52

1644-1949

20045 NNC P P1 G1.2 1644–1949
Bünger, Karl A-, 1903–.
'Alte chinesische Rechtsgedanken im modernen chinesischen Grundstücksrecht' (Traditional legal concepts in modern Chinese real-estate law).
Sinica 8, 5/6 (Sept.–Nov. 1933), 176–182.
SUBJ 12.2 45 ▪ 14.1 22.2

20046 MCY P P1 G1.2 –1949
Chao, Joseph Koei-tsou (Shao Kuei-tsu).
'Les pactes sur succession future' (Agreements on future inheritance).
BUA 3e série 1, 3 (1940), 233–271.
SUBJ 12.2 45 ▪ 22.2 43 44

20047 NNC P P2 G2.3 1895–1928
Kroker, Eduard Josef M-, 1913–.
'Sachenrechtliche Gewohnheiten in der Provinz Feng-t'ien, China' (Customary property law in Fengtien).
ZVR 62 (1960), 1–84.
SUBJ 22.2 24.1 45 ▪ 12.2 63 70

20048 NNC P P8 G4.2 1842–1928
Kroker, Eduard Josef M-, 1913–.
'Sachenrechtliche Gewohnheiten in der Provinz Kansu' (Customary property law in Kansu).
FS 19 (1960), 273–362.
SUBJ 22.2 24.1 45 ▪ 22.1

20049 MCH P P2 G1.2 –1928
Kuo, Shien-yen (Kuo Hsien-yen), 1905–.
Kapitalismus und Grundeigentum in China (Capitalism and landownership in China).
Gelnhausen, Germany: Wettig, 1930. 83 p. (Doctoral dissertation, Wirtschafts- und sozialwissenschaftliche Fakultät, Universität Frankfurt a.M.)
SUBJ 14.1 14.4 45 ▪ 11 16.3 16.4 18

20050 ELS S P2 G1.1 –1949
Nelson, Howard George Horatio, 1942–.
An anthropological study of inheritance and succession in traditional China.
Unpublished masters thesis in Anthropology, U. of London [London School of Economics and Political Science], 1966. 279 p.
SUBJ 16 41 43 45 ▪ 12 12.2 42 63 64

20051 NIC P P1 G1.1 1644–1928
Siao, T'ong (Hsiao T'ung).
De la succession et de l'adoption en droit Chinois (Inheritance and adoption in Chinese law).
Shanghai: Impr. de l'Orphelinat de T'ou-sè-wè, 1927. 112 p. (Doctoral dissertation, Université l'Aurore)
SUBJ 12.2 41 45

20052 MCY P P1 G1.2 –1949
Siu Chen-tai (Hsü Shen-t'ai).
'Du rapport successoral et de la réserve en droit Chinois' (Inclusion of inter vivos gifts in the estate and the non-barrable share in Chinese law).
BUA 3e série 4, 15 (1943), 579–650.
SUBJ 12.2 45

20053 MCH P P1 G1.1 –1949
Suen, Peng-hien (Sun P'eng-hsien).
Les principes généraux du droit de succession en Chine, jusqu'à la fin du 1er quart du XXème siècle (General principles of rights of inheritance in China to the end of the first quarter of the twentieth century).
Nancy: Société d'impressions typographiques, 1929. 147 p. (Doctoral dissertation, Faculté de droit, Université de Nancy)
SUBJ 12.2 40 45 48 ▪ 41 44 57 62 64

20054 MCM P P1 G1.2 –1949
Tchou Kao-yong (Chu Kao-jung).
'L'indivision en droit chinois' (Joint ownership in Chinese law).
BUA 2e série 28 (1933/34), 1–31. [Reprinted in *De l'indivision sous ses deux principales formes en droit chinois comparé avec le droit étranger* (The two main forms of joint ownership in Chinese law as compared with foreign law), by Tchou Kao-yong. (Sole entry.) Shanghai: Université l'Aurore; Paris: Lib. du Recueil Sirey, 1934, 30–62. (Doctoral dissertation, Université l'Aurore). (Also published—Tientsin: Hautes études, 1934.)]
SUBJ 12.2 34.2 45 ▪ 14.3 66

20055 MCY P P1 G1.2 1644–1949
Yang Fong-siang (Yang Feng-hsiang).
'La représentation successorale en droit civil chinois' (Inheritance by right of representation in Chinese civil law).
BUA 3e série 1, 4 (1940), 351–379.
SUBJ 12.2 45 ▪ 41

1911-1949

20056 CSH U P3 G7.1 1911–1928
'Real estate in Hankow.'
CEM 2, 10 (July 1925), 1–5.
SUBJ 21.3 45 ▪ 55

20057 NNC P P7 G1.3 1911–1949
Boehling, Hans Bruno Horst.
'Das Dien, ein altes chinesisches Rechtsgebilde' (Tien, a traditional Chinese legal institution).
Sinologica 2, 1 (1949/50), 56–64.
SUBJ 12.2 45 ▪ 14.1 14.6 40 72

20058 NIC P P1 G1.2 1928–1949
Bonnichon, André, 1905–.
'La clause de prélèvement du fonds de commerce par le conjoint survivant, en droit chinois moderne' (The clause in modern Chinese law that treats appropriation of the family business by the surviving spouse).
BUA 3e série 1, 4 (1940), 436–455.
SUBJ 12.2 45 ▪ 34.2

20059 MCH S P1 G1.3 1928–1949
Chang, Tao Hsing, 1908–.
'Inheritance in China.'

Iowa law review 20, 2 (Jan. 1935), 411–415.
Subj 12.2 45

20060 NNC P P3 G5.3 1911–1928
Crusen, ———.
'Die Rechtsverhältnisse an den Pachtgrundstücken in der Fremdenniederlassung zu Tsinanfu' (The legal position of leased land in the foreign settlement in Chi-nan-fu [i.e., Tsinan]).
DCR 3 (1914), 14–22.
Subj 12.2 45 ▪ 66

20061 MCY P P1 G1.2 1911–1949
Gérardin, André, and André Kia-hoai Song (Sung Chia-huai).
'Révision des contrats et conditions d'existence du droit de dien' (The revision of contracts and the conditions in which *tien* obtains).
BUA 3e série 5, 18 (1944), 306–332.
Subj 12.2 22.2 45

20062 CSH P P2 G9.5 1928–1949
Hong Kong. Land Office.
Annual departmental report by the Land Officer and Registrar of Marriages, 1946/47–1948/49. [Issues for 1949/50–1971/72 are entered as 20075.]
[Hong Kong]: ——. Issued annually, 1947–1949. Average ca. 15 p.
Subj 45 ▪ 24.5 41

20063 NIC P P8 G1.3 1911–1949
Kroker, Eduard Josef M-, 1913–.
'The concept of property in Chinese customary law.'
Transactions of the Asiatic Society of Japan 3rd series 7 (Nov. 1959), 123–146.
Subj 14.1 22.2 45 ▪ 22 44 47

20064 CSH P P2 G1.2 1928–1949
Liubimov, L- I-.
'Zemel'nyi kodeks Kitaia' (The Chinese land code).
VM 1931, 8, 60–74.
Subj 12.2 14.1 14.5 45 ▪ 21.3 55

20065 FPN P P1 G1.2 1928–1949
Lo, Che-tsi (Lo Shih-chi).
La succession 'ab intestat' dans le code civil chinois (Intestate succession in the Chinese civil code).
Toulouse: Impr. Toulouse, 1932. 116 p. (Doctoral dissertation, Faculté de droit, Université de Nancy)
Subj 12.2 45

20066 NNC P P1 G1.2 1928–1949
Shih, Hung-shun (Shih Hung-hsün).
Le testament dans le nouveau code civil chinois (Wills under the new Chinese civil code).
Nancy: Thomas, 1936. 115 p. (Doctoral dissertation, Faculté de droit, Université de Nancy)
Subj 12.2 40 45 ▪ 41 63

20067 CSH P P2 G1.2 1911–1949
Théry, François, 1890–, ed.
Eléments du droit civil chinois. Livre 3 du code civil: des droits réels, chapitres 1 à 5 (Elements of Chinese civil law. Book 3 of the civil code: Property rights, chapts. 1–5).
Tientsin: Hautes études, 1942. 156 p.
Subj 12.2 14.1 22.2 45 ▪ 14.3 14.6 18 48

20068 CSH P P2 G1.2 1911–1949
Théry, François, 1890–, ed.
Eléments du droit civil chinois. Livre 3 du code civil: des droits réels, chapitres 6 à 10 (Elements of Chinese civil law. Book 3 of the civil code: Property rights, chapts. 6–10).
Tientsin: Hautes études, 1942. 320 p.
Subj 12.2 14.6 22.2 45 ▪ 14.1 14.3

1911-1972
(including 1644-1972)

20069 GMS PO P1 G9.0 1895–1972
Mäding, Klaus.
Chinesisches traditionelles Erbrecht, unter besonderer Berücksichtigung südost-chinesischen Gewohnheitsrechts vom Ende des 19. Jahrhunderts (Traditional Chinese inheritance law, with special attention to customary law in Southeast China since the end of the nineteenth century).
Berlin: de Gruyter, 1966. 11, 110 p. (Rechtswissenschaftliche Fakultät der Universität Köln, Neue kölner rechtswissenschaftliche Abhandlungen, 40) (Doctoral dissertation, Rechtswissenschaftliche Fakultät, Universität Köln, 1963)
Subj 12.2 22.2 40 45 ▪ 41

20070 CSU FP P8 G9.5 1895–1972
Nelson, Howard George Horatio, 1942–.
'The Chinese descent system and the occupancy level of village houses.'
JRAS-HKB 9 (1969), 113–123.
Subj 41 45 ▪ 43 55

20071 NIC P P1 G1.2 1895–1972
Valk, Marius Hendrikus van der, 1908–.
'Movables and immovables and connected subjects in Chinese law.' In *Miscellanea, articles and texts*, edited by Z- Szirmai. [Sole entry]
Leiden: Sythoff, 1963, 167–206. (U. of Leiden, Documentation Office for Eastern European Law, Law in Eastern Europe, 7)
Subj 12.2 45 ▪ 22.2

1949-1972

20072 CSU F P7 G9.4 1949–1972
Cohen, Myron Leon, 1937–.
'A case study of Chinese family economy and development.'
JAAS 3, 3/4 (July–Oct. 1968), 161–180.
Subj 24.1 41 45 ▪ 24.6 26.3 29 47 55 57

20073 NNC P P1 G1.2 1949–1972
Corinth, Bernhard.
'Das Erbrecht der Volksrepublik China.'
Z. für ausländisches und internationales Privatrecht 24, 4 (1959), 719–728.

'The law of succession of the People's Republic of China.' Tr. by Wiebke Lorenzen. In *Preliminary materials on the law of Communist China*, edited by Jerome Alan Cohen. [Sole entry]
Berkeley, Los Angeles: U. of California Press, 1961, 235–242.
Subj 45 ▪ 12.2 41

20074 MAM FP P2 G9.4 1949–1972
Freedman, Deborah Selin, 1918–.
The role of consumption of modern durables in a developing economy: The case of Taiwan.
Ann Arbor: University Microfilms (Publ. 68-7597), 1968. 196 p. (Doctoral dissertation in Economics, U. of Michigan, 1967)
Subj 28 45 ▪ 24 24.4 24.6 26 41 51

20075 CSU P P2 G9.5 1949–1972
Hong Kong. Registrar General's Dept.
Annual departmental report by the Registrar General, 1949/50–1971/72. [Issues for 1946/47–1948/49 are entered as 20062.]
Hong Kong: Government Printer. Issued annually, 1950–1972. Average ca. 75 p.
Subj 34.2 45 ▪ 21.3 24.5 41 58

20076 MCH U P1 G1.2 1949–1972
Kirillova, M- IA-, and Chzhan D'e.
'Voprosy nasledovaniia v Kitaiskoi Narodnoi Respublike' (Inheritance in the People's Republic of China).
Sovetskaia iustitsiia 1959, 6 (iiun'), 31–34.
Subj 12.2 45 ▪ 44

20077 NNC P P1 G1.2 1949–1972
Loeber, Dietrich A-.
'Das Erbrecht in der Volksrepublik China' (Inheritance law in the People's Republic of China).
Osteuropa-Recht 5, 2 (Okt. 1959), 122–126.
Subj 12.2 45 ▪ 41 52

20078 MCH P P2 G1.2 1949–1972
Lunev, Aleksandr Efremovich.
'Nekotorye voprosy prava gosudarstvennoi sotsialisticheskoi sobstvennosti v Kitaiskoi Narodnoi Respublike' (Legal questions concerning state socialist property in the People's Republic of China).
SGP 1954, 7 (iiul'), 27–32.
Subj 12.2 45

20079 NNC P P7 G1.2 1949–1972
Titus, Kaoru M-, 1937–.
The changes in ownership system of the people's communes, Aug. 1958 to Aug. 1960.
Unpublished masters thesis in Public Law and Government, Columbia U., 1963. 71 p.
Subj 22 34.1 45 ▪ 24.1 26.3 32.1 64

20080 NNC P P7 G1.2 1949–1972
Tu, Yuan-li.
The nature and evolution of the ownership system of the rural peoples commune in Communist China.
Unpublished masters thesis in Political Science, Columbia U., 1965. 141 p.
Subj 24 24.1 26.3 34.1 45 ▪ 19 28 61

20081 CSH P P2 G1.2 1949–1972
Valk, Marius Hendrikus van der, 1908–.
'China.' In *The law of inheritance in Eastern Europe and in the People's Republic of China*, edited by Z- Szirmai. [Sole entry]
Leiden: Sythoff, 1961, 297–364. (U. of Leiden, Documentation Office for Eastern European Law, Law in Eastern Europe, 5)
Subj 12.2 45 ▪ 14.1 22.2 34.1 41 47 48 50 52 64 66

20082 NNC O P7 G9.2 1949–1972
Wang Shao-fei.
'The change in the system of collective ownership as viewed from the federation of cooperatives in one

hsiang.' Tr. of 'Ts'ung i ko hsiang lien she k'an chi t'i so yu chih ti pien hua' (Changes in the collective ownership system as seen in the federation of cooperatives in one township [Chang-shih *hsiang*, Ch'ü-chiang *hsien*, Kwangtung]); *Ching chi yen chiu* (Peking) 1958, 8 (Aug.), 38–43.
ECMM 150 (8 Dec. 1958), 14–23.
Subj 34.1 45 ▪ 22 24.1

46 Sex
性 性

1644-1911

20083 MCH P P1 G1.1 –1911
Cheng, Wou-chan, pseud.
Erotologie de la Chine: tradition chinoise de l'érotisme (Erotology in China: The Chinese tradition of eroticism). Tr. from the Chinese by F- Albertini. [Tr. of an unpublished manuscript]
Paris: J.-J. Pauvert, 1963. 234 p. (Bibliothèque internationale d'érotologie, 11)
Subj 46 62 ▪ 12 23 41 47 51

20084 CSU O P1 G5.1 1842–1895
[Dudgeon, John Hepburn?] J. D., 1837–1901.
'Jottings about the Chinese. No. 1, Summary revenge for adultery.'
CR 1, 3 (July 1868), 49–50.
Subj 22.2 46

20085 FPN P P2 G1.1 1842–1895
Durand-Fardel, Maxime, 1815–1899.
'La prostitution et la condition des femmes en Chine' (Prostitution and the condition of women in China).
Union médicale 3e série 21, 60 (23 mai 1876), 809–812; 21, 64 (1er juin 1876), 869–874; 21, 67 (8 juin 1876), 905–910; 21, 73 (22 juin 1876), 992–998. [Separately reprinted as *La vie irrégulière et la condition des femmes en Chine* (The irregular life and the condition of women in China). Paris: Gernier-Baillière, 1876. 16 p.]
Subj 41 46 47 51 ▪ 12.2 16 52 54 63

20086 CBU S P1 G1.1 –1911
Ehrenfels, Christian, 1859–1932.
'Die sadistischen Liebesopfer des Abendlandes und des Morgenlandes' (Sadistic love sacrifices of East and West).
Sexual-Probleme 4 (Juni 1908), 299–320.
Subj 46 47 ▪ 54

20087 MSE O P3 G6.1 1842–1895
Henderson, Edward.
A report on prostitution in Shanghai.
Shanghai: North-China Herald, 1871. 28 p.
Subj 46 ▪ 47 56

20088 DLC F P3 G1.1 1895–1911
Korsakov, Vladimir Viktorovich, 1854–?
'Prostitutsiia v Kitae' (Prostitution in China).
Vestnik obshchestvennoi gigieny, sudebnoi i prakticheskoi meditsiny 1900, 3 (mart), 343–360.
Subj 40 46 47 ▪ 41 48 55 56 60 63 65

20089 NIC P P1 G1.1 –1911
Levy, Howard Seymour, 1923–.
Chinese footbinding: The history of a curious erotic custom.
New York: W. Rawls, 1966. 352 p.
Subj 46 47 ▪ 22.2 41

20090 CSU PO P3 G1.3 –1895
Martin, Charles Ernest, 1831–1897.
'Etude sur la prostitution en Chine' (Prostitution in China).
Gazette hebdomadaire de médecine et de chirurgie 19, 25 (21 juin 1872), 401–408; 19, 29 (19 juil. 1872), 465–474. [Separately reprinted as *Etude historique et médicale sur la prostitution dans l'empire chinois* (An historical and medical study of prostitution in the Chinese empire). Paris: Masson, 1872. 15 p.]
Subj 46 47 56 ▪ 12 12.2 21.3 22.1 26 63

20091 CSU O P3 G5.1 1895–1911
Matignon, Jean-Jacques, 1866–?
'Deux mots sur la pédérastie' (A word or two on pederasty). In *Superstitition, crime et misère en Chine* (Superstition, crime, and poverty in China), 4th ed., by J.-J. Matignon. [Selective entry]
Lyons: Storck, 1902, 185–205.
Subj 46 50 ▪ 54

20092 CSU P P2 G1.3 –1911
Mitamura, Taisuke, 1909–.
Chinese eunuchs: The structure of intimate politics. Tr. by Charles A- Pomeroy of *Kangan: Sokkin seiji no kōzō*; Tokyo: Chūō kōronsha, 1963; 221 p.
Rutland, Vt.: Charles E. Tuttle, 1970. 176 p.
Subj 12 16 46 ▪ 41 61 63

20093 NNC O P3 G9.2 1842–1895
Schlegel, Gustaaf, 1840–1903.
'A Canton flower-boat.'
Internationales Archiv für Ethnographie 7 (1894), 1–9.
Subj 31 46 ▪ 26.1

20094 NIC U P3 G1.3 1842–1895
Schlegel, Gustaaf (Gustave Schlegel), 1840–1903.
Iets over de prostitutie in China (A note on prostitution in China).
Batavia: Lange, 1866. 25 p. (Bataviaasch Genootschap van Kunsten en Weetenschappen, Verhandelingen, 32, 3).

Histoire de la prostitution en Chine (History of prostitution in China).
Rouen: J. Lemonnyer, 1880. 47 p.
Subj 46 ▪ 47

20095 GMS PO P3 G1.3 –1911
Stent, George Carter, 1833–1884.
Chinesische Eunuchen: oder, Der Ursprung, Charakter, Habitus, Obliegenheiten und Zurichtung der Hämmlinge Chinas (Chinese eunuchs: The origin, character, habits, duties, and surgical preparation of eunuchs in China).
Leipzig: Otto Schulze Verlag, 1879? 47 p.
Subj 46 ▪ 47 63

20096 MCH P P2 G1.1 –1911
Vannicelli, Luigi.
'Le fête des fiançailles et l'amour des fiancés chez les peuples de l'Extrême-Orient' (The betrothal celebration and love between the betrothed among the peoples of the Far East).
Internationales Archiv für Ethnographie 47 (1955), 160–203.
Subj 29 41 46

1644-1949

20097 CSU P P1 G1.3 –1928
Beurdeley, Michel, et al.
Chinese erotic art. Tr. from the French by Diana Imber.
Rutland, Vt.: Charles E. Tuttle, 1969. 13, 209 p.
Subj 46 62 ▪ 61 63

20098 CSU O P3 G1.3 1895–1949
Drew, Dennis, and Jonathan Drake.
'China.' In *Boys for sale: A sociological study of boy prostitution*, by D. Drew and J. Drake. [Sole entry]
New York: Brown, 1969, 97–107.
Subj 46 54 ▪ 28 52

20099 NIC P P1 G1.0 –1928
Heyer, Virginia.
'Relations between men and women in Chinese stories.' In *The study of culture at a distance*, edited by Margaret Mead and Rhoda Metraux. [Selective entry]
Chicago: U. of Chicago Press, 1953, 221–234.
Subj 46 62 ▪ 48 61 65

20100 NNC U P1 G1.3 –1928
Hsu Dau-lin (Hsü Tao-lin), 1906–.
'Die chinesische Liebe' (Chinese love).
Sinica 4, 6 (Nov. 1929), 241–251.
Subj 46 ▪ 41 48 63

20101 CSU S P1 G1.1 –1949
Podach, Eric Friedrich, 1894–.
'Gin-lien: Ein aktualistischer Beitrag zur Ethnologie des Hässlichen' (*Chin-lien* [foot-binding]: Toward an up-to-date ethnology of an offensive custom).
Jahrbuch des Linden-Museums 1 (1951), 160–171.
Subj 16 46 47 65 ▪ 53

1911-1949

20102 CSH PO P5 G1.2 1911–1928
'Commercialized vice in China.' In *The Christian occupation of China*, edited by Milton Theobald Stauffer. [Selective entry]
Shanghai: China Continuation Committee, 1922, 396–397.
Subj 46

20103 NNM O P3 G6.1 1911–1928
'The demi-monde of Shanghai.'
CMJ 37, 9 (Sept. 1923), 782–788.
Subj 46 47 ▪ 26 28 31 55

20104 NIC O P8 G2.3 1911–1949
Hsu, Francis L. K. (Hsü Lang-kuang), 1909–.
'The problem of incest tabu in a North China village [Mu-erh-shan-li, Ta-ku-shan *chen*, Chuang-ho *hsien*, Liaoning].'
AA new (2nd) series 42, 1 (Jan.–Mar. 1940), 122–135.
Subj 41 46

20105 MCH U P1 G1.2 1928–1949
Liu, Francis S. F. (Liu Shih-fang), 1901–.
'Adultery as crime in China.'
CLR 7, 3/4 (Feb. 1935), 144–147.
SUBJ 12.2 46 ▪ 12.1

20106 MCH O P3 G9.2 1911–1949
Shên, Fu.
'Le barche dei fiori' (The flower boats). Tr. from the Chinese by Lionello Lanciotti and Tao-lu Tsui.
Cina 1 (1956), 141–148.
SUBJ 31 46 ▪ 28 47

20107 ICU S P2 G1.2 1911–1928
Wiley, James Hundley.
A study of Chinese prostitution.
Unpublished masters thesis in Sociology and Anthropology, U. of Chicago, 1928. 114 p.
SUBJ 12.2 41 46 47 ▪ 15 31 33 40 56 65

20108 NNC PO P3 G1.1 1911–1928
Wong, K. Chimin (Wang Chi-min).
'The social evil in China.'
CMJ 34, 6 (Nov. 1920), 630–634.
SUBJ 46 63 ▪ 12.2 47

1911-1972
(including 1644-1972)

20109 CSU P P2 G1.1 –1972
Chou, Eric, 1915–.
The dragon and the phoenix: Love, sex and the Chinese.
London: Michael Joseph, 1971. 222 p.
SUBJ 46 47 ▪ 16 16.1 29 41 55 59 65

20110 CSU PO P1 G1.2 1895–1972
Edwardes, Allen, and R- E- L- Masters.
The cradle of erotica.
New York: Julian Press, 1962. 362 p.
SUBJ 46 53

20111 NNC S P2 G1.1 –1972
Henriques, Fernando.
'The prostitutes of China.' In *Prostitution and society: A survey*, by F. Henriques. [Sole entry]
London: MacGibbon and Kee, 1962, vol. 1, 241–277.
SUBJ 34.2 46 ▪ 12.1 41 47 66

20112 CSH O P3 G6.1 1928–1972
Hsiao Wen.
'Shanghai prostitutes begin their lives anew.'
WC 1957, 2 (Mar.–Apr.), 24–27.
SUBJ 46 ▪ 47 59

20113 CSU O P4 G9.5 1842–1972
O'Callaghan, Sean.
'Macao: "The cesspool of the Far East".' In *The yellow slave trade: A survey of the traffic in women and children in the East*, by S. O'Callaghan. [Selective entry]
London: Blond, 1968, 51–59.
SUBJ 46 ▪ 22.2

20114 CSU O P3 G9.5 1842–1972
O'Callaghan, Sean.
'The mui-tsai: The child slaves of Hong Kong.' In *The yellow slave trade: A survey of the traffic in women and children in the East*, by S. O'Callaghan. [Selective entry]
London: Blond, 1968, 17–28.
SUBJ 46 47 52 ▪ 12.2 22.2

20115 CSU S P2 G1.2 –1972
O'Callaghan, Sean.
'The traffic in women and children in China.' In *The yellow slave trade: A survey of the traffic in women and children in the East*, by S. O'Callaghan. [Selective entry]
London: Blond, 1968, 7–16.
SUBJ 46 47 ▪ 12.2 22.2

1949-1972

20116 MCH O P3 G5.1 1949–1972
Hsiao Kan.
'The return to daylight: The reformation of Peking prostitutes.'
People's China 1, 6 (16 Mar. 1950), 12, 22–26.
SUBJ 46 47 59

20117 CSH FP P4 G9.5 1949–1972
Lethbridge, Henry James, 1923–.
'Girls in danger.'
FEER 53, 12 (22 Sept. 1966), 583–587.
SUBJ 22.1 46

20118 CSU O P3 G9.5 1949–1972
O'Callaghan, Sean.
'Hong Kong: Clearing house of the Far East vice trade.' In *The yellow slave trade: A survey of the traffic in women and children in the East*, by S. O'Callaghan. [Selective entry]
London: Blond, 1968, 40–50.
SUBJ 46 ▪ 12.2

20119 CSU O P3 G9.4 1949–1972
O'Callaghan, Sean.
'The room girls of Taiwan.' In *The yellow slave trade: A survey of the traffic in women and children in the East*, by S. O'Callaghan. [Selective entry]
London: Blond, 1968, 60–65.
SUBJ 46 ▪ 21.2

20120 CSU O P3 G9.5 1949–1972
O'Callaghan, Sean.
'The world of Suzie Wong.' In *The yellow slave trade: A survey of the traffic in women and children in the East*, by S. O'Callaghan. [Selective entry]
London: Blond, 1968, 29–39.
SUBJ 11.2 46 ▪ 12.2 22.2 25

20121 CSU P P2 G1.2 1949–1972
Stafford, Peter.
'China.' In *Sexual behavior in the Communist world*, by P. Stafford. [Sole entry]
New York: Julian Press, 1967, 13–57.
SUBJ 12.1 41 46 ▪ 16.1 47 51 54

20122 CSU F P3 G9.5 1949–1972
Yap, Pow-meng (Yeh Pao-ming).
'Koro, a culture-bound depersonalization syndrome.'
British j. of psychiatry 111, 470 (Jan. 1965), 43–50.
SUBJ 46 56 61

47 Female Roles and Male-Female Differences
婦女地位及男女分別
女性の地位及び男女の区別

1644-1911

20123 DLC U P2 G1.2 1644–1895
'Kitaiskie zhenshchiny' (Chinese women).
Biblioteka dlia chteniia 117 (1853), 48–56.
SUBJ 47 ▪ 41

20124 NNM PO P4 G1.2 –1911
Boggs, Lucinda Pearl.
Chinese womanhood.
Cincinnati: Jennings and Graham; New York: Eaton and Mains, 1913. 129 p.
SUBJ 47 ▪ 17 33 41 50 60

20125 NNC O P2 G1.3 1842–1895
Brandt, Max August Scipio von, 1835–1914?
Sittenbilder aus China, Mädchen und Frauen: Ein Beitrag zur Kenntnis des chinesischen Volkes (Genre sketches of Chinese girls and women: An insight into the Chinese people).
Stuttgart: Strecker und Schröder, 1895. 87 p.
SUBJ 41 47 ▪ 46 51 52 55 63

20126 ELB S P5 G1.3 1842–1911
Burton, Margaret Ernestine, 1885–.
The education of women in China.
New York: Revell, 1911. 232 p.
SUBJ 17 47 ▪ 66

20127 NNC P P2 G1.1 1842–1911
Chau, Virginia Chi-tin.
The anti-footbinding movement in China (1850–1912).
Unpublished masters thesis in History, Columbia U., 1966. 170 p.
SUBJ 47 ▪ 61

20128 CSU O P3 G5.1 1895–1911
Conger, Sarah Pike.
Letters from China, with particular reference to the Empress Dowager and the women of China.
Chicago: McClurg, 1909. 392 p.
SUBJ 12 25 47 60 66 ▪ 17 23 43 57

20129 CSU O P6 G7.1 1895–1911
Cornaby, William Arthur, 1860–1921.
'The Chinese maiden at home.'
EAM 3 (1904), 137–147.
SUBJ 47 ▪ 41 54 55

20130 MCH O P2 G1.2 1895–1911
Courant, Maurice Auguste Louis Marie, 1865–1935.
'La femme chinoise dans la famille et dans la société' (The Chinese woman in the family and in society).
R. des deux mondes 4e période 141 (1er mai 1897), 171–204.
SUBJ 40 41 47 50 55 ▪ 17 22.2 46 51 53 57 58 61 63

20131 MCH PO P2 G1.2 –1895
Dudgeon, John Hepburn, 1837–1901.
'The small feet of Chinese women.'
CR 2, 4 (Sept. 1869), 93–96; 2, 5 (Oct. 1869), 130–133.
SUBJ 47 ▪ 41

20132 CSU P P1 G1.0 1644–1842
Eberhard, Wolfram, 1909–.
'Ideas about social reforms in the novel *Ching-hua yüan* [Flowers in the mirror].' In *Festschrift für Ad. E. Jensen* (Felicitation volume for Adolf Ellegard Jensen), edited by Eike Haberland. [Sole entry]
Munich: K. Renner, 1964, vol. 1, 113–121. [Reprinted in *Moral and social values of the Chinese: Collected essays*, by W. Eberhard. (Selective entry.) Taipei: Chinese Materials and Research Aids Service Center, 1971, 413–421. (CMRASC occasional series, 6)]
Subj 47 ▪ 62 64

20133 CSU P P1 G1.2 1644–1842
Evans, Nancy Jane Frances, 1945–.
'Social criticism in the Ch'ing: The novel *Ching-hua yuan* [Flowers in the mirror].'
PC 23 (July 1970), 52–66.
Subj 47 ▪ 46

20134 CSU P P2 G1.2 –1895
Faber, Ernst, 1839–1899.
The famous women of China.
Shanghai: Society for the Diffusion of Christian and General Knowledge Among the Chinese, 1890. 62 p.
Subj 47 63 ▪ 59 65

20135 NIC PO P1 G1.2 –1895
Faber, Ernst, 1839–1899.
The status of women in China, 2nd ed.
Shanghai: American Presbyterian Mission Press, 1897. 19 p. [Reprinted—*CR* 48, 9 (Sept. 1917), 590–602.]
Subj 41 47 ▪ 22.2 42 46 52 53 63

20136 CSH O P4 G6.0 1895–1911
Fan Wen-lan, 1893–1969.
'Chiu Chin: A woman revolutionary.'
WC 1956, 4 (Oct.–Dec.), 31–33.
Subj 32.2 47

20137 NIC O P2 G1.2 1842–1895
Fielde, Adele Marion, 1839–1916.
Pagoda shadows: Studies from life in China.
Boston: Corthell, 1884. 14, 285 p.
Subj 41 47 50 ▪ 17 23 25 33 43 51 52 55 57 63

20138 ELB O P2 G7.1 1895–1911
[Foster, Amy] *Mrs.* Arnold Foster.
Chinese schoolgirls in the valley of the Yangtse.
London: London Missionary Society, 1909. 93 p.
Subj 27 47 50 52 55 ▪ 33 41 48 57

20139 NNC U P1 G1.3 1895–1911
Giles, Lionel, 1875–1958.
'Ch'iu Chin, a Chinese heroine.'
Asiatic review new (4th) series 12, 34 (Aug. 1917), 125–146.
Subj 47 59 ▪ 12.1 16.1 32.2 41

20140 NIC O P3 G5.1 1895–1911
Headland, Isaac Taylor, 1859–1942.
Court life in China: The capital, its officials and people.
New York: Revell, 1909. 372 p.
Subj 16.1 47 59 ▪ 26 55

20141 CSH O P4 G2.2 1895–1911
Lobza, P-.
'Sem'ia i zhenshchina v Man'chzhurii' (The family and the role of women in Manchuria).
Mir Bozhii 10, 4 (1901), 250–263.
Subj 47 ▪ 40 41 46

20142 CSU O P2 G5.1 1842–1895
M. F. C.
'The Chinese daughter-in-law.'
CR 5, 4 (July–Aug. 1874), 207–214.
Subj 41 47

20143 MCH U P1 G1.1 1842–1895
Martin, Charles Ernest, 1831–1897.
'Considérations sur la valeur ethnique de la mutilation des pieds de la femme chinoise' (Reflections on the significance of foot-binding to the Chinese).
Bulletins de la Société d'anthropologie de Paris 2e série 6 (nov. 1871), 304–313.
Subj 47 ▪ 56 61 63

20144 FPN P P1 G1.3 –1895
Martin, Louis Auguste, 1811–1875.
La femme en Chine (Women in China).
Paris: Sandoz et Fischbacher, 1876. 11, 204 p.
Subj 12.2 40 41 47 60 ▪ 11.4 16 51 53 57

20145 MBA P P3 G1.2 1895–1911
Maybon, Albert, 1878–.
'Le féminisme en Chine' (The feminist movement in China).
RI nouvelle (2e) série 11, 5 (mai 1909), 472–485.
Subj 16.1 47

20146 MCH O P2 G1.3 1842–1895
Morache, Georges.
'Note sur la déformation du pied chez les femmes chinoises' (A note on foot-binding among Chinese women).
Recueil de mémoires de médecine, de chirurgie et de pharmacie militaires 3e série 11 (mars 1864), 177–189.
Subj 47 55 ▪ 29

20147 NIC P P1 G1.3 –1911
O'Hara, Albert Richard, 1907–.
The position of women in early China according to the 'Lieh nü chuan', 'The biographies of eminent Chinese women'.
Washington, D.C.: Catholic U. of America Press, 1945. 12, 301 p. (Catholic U. of America studies in sociology, 16) (Doctoral dissertation in Sociology, Catholic U. of America)
Subj 47 63 ▪ 59

20148 NNC O P2 G1.2 1842–1895
Potanina, Aleksandra Viktorovna.
'O kitaiskoi zhenshchine: iz puteshestviia po Kitaiu' (The Chinese woman: Observations based on a journey through China).
Russkoe bogatstvo 1887, 7 (iiul'), 57–89.
Subj 47 55 66 ▪ 16 52 57

20149 NIC S P1 G1.3 –1911
Rousselle, Erwin Arthur, 1890–.
'Die Frau im Gesellschaft und Mythos der Chinesen' (The woman in Chinese society and mythology).
Sinica 16 (1941), 130–151.
Subj 13 41 47 62 ▪ 23 43 61 65

20150 NNC U P1 G1.3 –1911
Rousselle, Erwin Arthur, 1890–.
'Die Frauentypen in der Geschichte der chinesischen Gesellschaft' (Types of women in Chinese social history).
NDG 49 (Feb. 1939), 13–24.
Subj 47 ▪ 41 46 62

20151 CSU O P1 G9.2 1842–1895
Sampson, Theos, ?–1897.
'Anti-marriage associations.'
NQCJ 2, 9 (Sept. 1868), 142–143.
Subj 47

20152 MCH O P2 G1.1 1644–1895
Schaalje, M-.
'De kleine voeten der vrouwen in China: Een bijdrage tot de kennis van Chinesche gewoonten' (The small feet of Chinese women: A contribution to our knowledge of Chinese customs).
Tijdschrift voor Indische taal-, land- en volkenkunde 20 (1873), 33–57.
Subj 16 47 ▪ 16.1 29

20153 NNC O P3 G9.2 1644–1895
Schlegel, Gustaaf, 1840–1903.
'Chinesische Bootführerinnen' (Chinese boatwomen). In *Ethnographische Beiträge: Dem Altmeister der ethnologischen Wissenschaft, Prof. Adolph Bastian zum seinen 70sten. Geburtstage* (Ethnographic reports in honor of the old master of ethnology Professor Adolph Bastian on his seventieth birthday), by Franz Boas et al. [Sole entry]
Leiden: Brill, 1896, 10–12. [Supplement to *Internationales Archiv für Ethnographie* 9 (1896)]
Subj 47 ▪ 24.2

20154 NNC P P1 G1.2 –1911
Sié, Kang (Hsieh K'ang), 1901–.
L'amour maternel dans la littérature féminine en Chine (Maternal love in women's literature in China).
Paris: Pedone, 1937. 187 p. (Doctoral dissertation, Faculté des lettres, Université de Paris)
Subj 40 46 47 51 53 ▪ 41 50 52 61 63 65 70

20155 MCH O P2 G1.1 1895–1911
Tsao, Li Yieni.
'The life of a girl in China.'
AAAPSS 39 (Jan. 1912), 62–70.
Subj 47 59 ▪ 40 50 52 54

20156 NNC P P1 G1.3 –1895
Welcker, Hermann, 1822–1897.
'Die Füsse der Chinesinnen' (The feet of Chinese women).
Archiv für Anthropologie 5, 2 (1872), 133–152.
Subj 47 55 ▪ 46

20157 CSU O P1 G1.2 –1895
Williams, Samuel Wells, 1812–1884.
'Education of women in China.'
CR 11, 1 (Jan.–Feb. 1880), 40–53.
Subj 27 47 ▪ 12.2 41 53

20158 CSU P P1 G1.2 –1911
Yang, Lien-sheng, 1914–.
'Female rulers in Imperial China.'
HJAS 23 (1960/61), 47–61. [Reprinted in *Studies of governmental institutions in Chinese history*, edited by John Lyman Bishop. (Selective entry.) Cambridge: Harvard U. Press, 1968, 153–169.

(Harvard-Yenching Institute studies, 23)]
SUBJ 47 ▪ 12.2

1644-1949

20159 ELB PO P2 G1.2 –1949
Ayscough, Florence Wheelock, 1878–1942.
Chinese women, yesterday and today.
Boston: Houghton Mifflin, 1937. 14, 324 p.
SUBJ 41 46 47 60 ▪ 59 72

20160 MAU PO P2 G1.1 1895–1949
Callis, Maud Eva, 1911–.
Tradition and change in the status of Chinese women.
Unpublished doctoral dissertation in Oriental Civilizations, U. of Michigan, 1946. 422, 25 p.
SUBJ 11.4 12.2 38 41 47 ▪ 11.1 15 17 40 44 45 72

20161 NNC P P3 G1.2 –1949
Chen, Kuan-chin.
Emancipation of women in China.
Unpublished masters thesis in Social Science, Columbia U., 1933. 55 p.
SUBJ 19 47 ▪ 12.2 16.4 17 41 64

20162 MCH P P1 G1.1 –1949
Cheng Hsiu (Ch'eng Hsiu), 1904–.
La situation en droit privé de la femme chinoise envisagée dans son évolution historique (The historical evolution of the Chinese woman's status in private law).
Nancy: Bailly et Wettstein, 1935. 195 p. (Doctoral dissertation, Faculté de droit, Université de Nancy)
SUBJ 12.2 41 47 ▪ 17 45 63

20163 CSH P P1 G1.2 –1928
Chiao, Chien (Ch'iao Chien), 1935–.
'Female chastity in Chinese culture.'
BIE 31 (Spring 1971), 205–211.
SUBJ 47 63 ▪ 41

20164 MCY FP P1 G1.1 –1949
Chippaux, C-.
'Du petit pied de la Chinoise' (The small feet of the Chinese woman).
B. de la Société des études indo-chinoises de Saigon nouvelle (2e) série 25, 1 (1950), 51–84.
SUBJ 47 ▪ 53 60 61

20165 NIC F P8 G5.1 1842–1928
Gamble, Sidney David, 1890–1968.
'The disappearance of foot-binding in Tinghsien [i.e., Ting *hsien*, Hopei].'
AJS 49, 2 (Sept. 1943), 181–183.
SUBJ 47

20166 NNC O P2 G1.2 1895–1949
Hosie, Dorothea Soothill, 1885–.
Portrait of a Chinese lady and certain of her contemporaries.
New York: Morrow, 1930. 15, 404 p.
SUBJ 26 28 41 47 59 60 ▪ 12 13 15 17 52 66

20167 CBU S P1 G1.2 –1928
Krische, Paul.
'Die Frau im vaterrechtlichen Orient. II. (d), Die Chinesen' (The woman in the patriarchal societies of East Asia. 2d, The Chinese).
Archiv für Frauenkunde und Konstitutionsforschung 15, 5 (1929), 414–426.
SUBJ 47 64 ▪ 55

20168 CSU U P1 G1.2 1895–1949
L. C. C.
'The women's movement in China during the last thirty years.'
CR 72, 10 (Oct. 1941), 560–575.
SUBJ 47 ▪ 12.2 17 41

20169 NNC FP P2 G1.2 1842–1928
Lewis, Ida Belle, 1887–.
The education of girls in China.
New York: Columbia U., Teachers College, 1919. 92 p. (TC contributions to education, 104) (Doctoral dissertation in Education, Columbia U. [Teachers College])
SUBJ 17 47 ▪ 16 41 64

20170 NNC P P1 G1.2 1895–1928
Lin, Paotchin (Lin Pao-chüan).
L'instruction féminine en Chine (après la Révolution de 1911) (Education of women in China after the Revolution of 1911).
Paris: Jouve, 1926. 188 p. (Doctoral dissertation, Faculté des lettres, Université de Paris)
SUBJ 17 47

20171 CSH F P2 G1.3 1895–1949
Lund, Caroline.
'Women in the Chinese revolution.'
International socialist review 31, 4 (June 1970), 10–13, 39.
SUBJ 47 59

20172 SEU F P1 G1.1 –1949
McDougall, Colin.
Chinese footbinding.
Unpublished doctoral dissertation in Medicine, U. of Edinburgh, 1958. 102 p.
SUBJ 46 47 ▪ 53 56 61

20173 WSU S P1 G1.1 1842–1949
Newcomb, Holly Ellen.
Western influence and the transition of Chinese upperclass women, 1830's–1930's.
Unpublished masters thesis in Far Eastern and Slavic Languages, U. of Washington, 1967. 174 p.
SUBJ 47 59 66 ▪ 17 41

20174 MCH P P1 G1.2 –1928
Tang, Chindon Yiu.
'Woman's education in China.'
BCE 2, 9 (1923), 1–36.
SUBJ 17 47

20175 FPN P P1 G1.2 1895–1928
Tchang, Ting-tchang (Chang Ting-chang).
Le mariage et la situation de la femme mariée en Chine au premier quart du XXe siècle (Marriage and the position of the married woman in China in the first quarter of the twentieth century).
Paris: Rousseau, 1930. 130 p. (Collection d'études théoriques et pratiques de droit étranger, de droit comparé et de droit international, 19) (Doctoral dissertation, Faculté de droit, Université de Paris)
SUBJ 12.2 41 47 ▪ 22.2 44 45 57

20176 NNC U P1 G1.2 –1949
Tseng, P. S. (Tseng Pao-sun).
'The Chinese woman, past and present.' In *Symposium on Chinese culture*, edited by Sophia H. Chen Zen (Jen Ch'en Heng-che). [Selective entry]
Shanghai: China Institute of Pacific Relations, 1931, 281–292. [Reprinted in *Symposium on Chinese culture*, edited by S. H. C. Zen. (Selective entry.) New York: Paragon, 1969, 281–292.]
SUBJ 47 ▪ 17 41 63 65

20177 ACU P P2 G1.2 1895–1928
Twanmoh, Chien-ming.
Hu Shih and female emancipation in China.
Unpublished masters thesis in Oriental Studies, Australian National U., 1966. 167 p.
SUBJ 16.1 41 47 ▪ 17 52

20178 NIC PO P2 G1.3 1895–1949
Wang, Tsang-pao (Wang Ch'ang-pao).
La femme dans la société chinoise: sa situation sociale, civile et politique (The social, civil, and political status of women in Chinese society).
Paris: Pedone, 1933. 11, 252 p. (Doctoral dissertation, Faculté de droit, Université de Bruxelles)
SUBJ 11.4 41 47 ▪ 12.2 16.4 18 46

20179 CSU P P1 G1.2 1644–1928
Wei, Wilson Shih-sheng (Wei Shih-sheng), 1901–.
The education of women in modern China.
Unpublished masters thesis in Education, Stanford U., 1927. 166 p.
SUBJ 17 47 ▪ 12.2 33 41 63

20180 CNY PO P1 G1.1 –1928
Wilhelm, Richard, 1873–1930.
'Chinesische Frauenschönheit' (The Chinese conception of feminine beauty).
Chinesisch-Deutscher Almanach 1931, 19–32.
SUBJ 47 ▪ 46 55 62

20181 MCH P P1 G1.1 –1928
Wilhelm, Richard, 1873–1930.
'Die Frau in der chinesischen Kunst' (The woman in Chinese art).
OR 10, 6 (16 März 1929), 165–169.
SUBJ 47 62 ▪ 41 44 46 63

20182 MAM P P2 G1.2 1842–1928
Witke, Roxane Heater, 1938–.
Transformation of attitudes towards women during the May Fourth era of modern China.
Ann Arbor: University Microfilms (Publ. 71-868), 1971. 338 p. (Doctoral dissertation in History, U. of California, Berkeley, 1970)
SUBJ 17 37 41 46 47 57 ▪ 12.2 14.2 25 32.2 38 48 50 54 63 66

20183 NNC P P2 G9.2 1842–1928
Young, Ludvig J-.
The emancipation of women in China before 1920, with special reference to Kwangtung.
Unpublished masters thesis in History, Columbia U., 1965. 134 p.
SUBJ 47 ▪ 17

1911-1949

20184 NIC U P1 G1.2 1928–1949
'The feminist movement in China.'
PT new (2nd) series 9, 5 (1 June 1935), 301–314.
SUBJ 32 47 ▪ 38 41

20185 MCH O P2 G9.2 1911–1928
'Women's work in Kwangtung province.'
CEJ 1, 6 (June 1927), 564–578.
SUBJ 47 ▪ 21.4 26.3 26.4

20186 CSH O P3 G1.1 1911–1928
'The Young Women's Christian Association in China.' In *The Christian occupation of China*, edited by Milton Theobald Stauffer. [Selective entry]
Shanghai: China Continuation Committee, 1922, 375–377.
SUBJ 47 ▪ 38

20187 NNC P P2 G1.2 1911–1949
Anna, pseud.
'Zhizn' i bor'ba zhenshchiny v dvukh Kitaiakh' (The life and struggle of women in two Chinas).
Revoliutsiia i natsional'nosti 1934, 3 (mart), 44–49.
SUBJ 16.4 47 ▪ 18 32.2 52

20188 NNC O P1 G1.2 1928–1949
Buck, Pearl Sydenstricker, 1892–1973.
'Chinese women: Their predicament in the China of today.'
PA 4, 10 (Oct. 1931), 905–909.
SUBJ 47 ▪ 41

20189 NNC P P1 G1.2 1928–1949
Budd, Josephine E-.
'Education for women.' In *China*, edited by Orville Anderson Petty. [Selective entry]
New York: Harper, 1933, 535–576. (Layman's Foreign Missions Inquiry, Factfinders' reports, 5; Supplementary series, part 2)
SUBJ 17 37 47 ▪ 61 63

20190 CSH P P2 G1.3 1928–1949
Bulle, Mil'da Ottovna.
Chinese toiling women: How they are helping the Chinese soviets. Tr. of *Zhizn' i borba kitaiskikh rabotnii i krest'ianok*.
Moscow: Co-operative Publishing Society of Foreign Workers in the USSR, 1933. 31 p. [Originally published—London, Modern Books; neither Russian original nor first ed. in English was located.]
SUBJ 16.3 16.4 32.2 36.4 47 ▪ 12.2 18 41 52

20191 MCH PO P2 G1.2 1911–1949
Chang, Shao-wei.
'Feminist movement in China.'
China critic 5, 50 (15 Dec. 1932), 1324–1327.
SUBJ 47 ▪ 12.2

20192 NIC O P3 G1.3 1911–1949
Chao, Chi-chen.
'Being an old maid in China.'
Asia (New York: American Asiatic Assn.) 41, 9 (Sept. 1941), 492–496.
SUBJ 17 41 47 54

20193 DLC P P2 G1.3 1911–1928
Chen Ta (Ch'en Ta), 1892–.
'Working women in China.'
Monthly labor review 15, 6 (Dec. 1922), 142–149.
SUBJ 11.4 47 ▪ 16 19

20194 CSU O P3 G9.5 1911–1949
Cheng, Irene (Cheng Ho Ai-ling).
'Women students and graduates.' In *University of Hong Kong: The first fifty years, 1911–1961*, edited by Brian Harrison. [Sole entry]
Hong Kong: Hong Kong U. Press, 1962, 148–158.
SUBJ 17 47 54

20195 NNM FP P3 G6.1 1928–1949
Ching, Chung Shou, and May Bagwell.
Women in industry in the Chapei, Hongkew and Pootung [i.e., Cha-pei, Hung-k'ou, and P'u-tung] *districts of Shanghai*.
Shanghai: Y.W.C.A. of China, National Committee, 1931. 28 p.
SUBJ 26.4 36.4 47 ▪ 24.4 27 28 52 55

20196 CSH O P1 G1.2 1911–1928
Ershov, Matvei Nikolaevich.
'K kharakteristike zhenskogo voprosa v sovremennom Kitae' (The nature of feminism in contemporary China).
VM 1927, 11, 60–70.
SUBJ 16 47 ▪ 17

20197 CSH O P2 G1.2 1911–1928
Ershov, Matvei Nikolaevich.
'Zhenshchina i trud v sovremennom Kitae' (Women and labor in contemporary China).
VM 1928, 2, 62–73.
SUBJ 16 47 ▪ 12.2 16.3 16.4

20198 CSU F P8 G4.4 1928–1949
Frick, Johannes.
'Lohnverhältnisse der Landarbeiterinnen in Ch'inghai' (Wages of female agricultural laborers in Tsinghai). In *Ethnographische Beiträge aus der Ch'inghai Provinz (China)* (Ethnographic reports from Tsinghai). [Selective entry]
Peking [i.e., Tokyo]: Catholic U. of Peking, Museum of Oriental Ethnology, 1952, 148–156. (MOE, Folklore studies supplements, 1)
SUBJ 26.3 47 ▪ 24.1 28 55

20199 ELO O P7 G7.2 1928–1949
Galbraith, Winifred.
Willow pattern: A picture of China today.
London: Edinburgh House Press, 1933. 63 p.
SUBJ 24.4 27 41 47 55 ▪ 23 25 26 28 43 52 65 66

20200 DLC O P2 G1.1 1928–1949
Haass, Lily K-.
'Chinese women's organizations.' In *Wartime China, as seen by westerners*. [Selective entry]
Chungking: China Publishing Co., 1942, 83–94.
SUBJ 47 ▪ 24.4 27 37 52

20201 CSU P P4 G1.2 1928–1949
Hinder, Eleanor M-.
'China's new factory law as affecting women and children.'
CR 62, 3 (Mar. 1931), 149–155.
SUBJ 12.2 16.4 47 52 ▪ 34.2

20202 CSU U P4 G1.2 1911–1928
Hsu, Shou Shang, Hsiao Lan Ou-Yang, and Yoehngoo Tsohsang Wu Lew.
'Education of women in China.' Tr. from the Chinese [tr. of an unpublished manuscript]. In *Education in China: Papers contributed by the members of committees of the Society for the Study of International Education*, edited by T. Y. Teng (Teng Ts'ui-ying) and Timothy Tingfang Lew (Liu T'ing-fang). [Selective entry]
Peking: Society for the Study of International Education, 1923, 1–35 [s.p.].
SUBJ 17 47

20203 MCH O P1 G1.0 1928–1949
Kalff, Lambert.
'Die Frau im chinesischen Sprichwort' (The woman in Chinese proverbs).
OR 11, 6 (16 März 1930), 194.
SUBJ 47 65 ▪ 41

20204 DLC P P2 G1.2 1911–1949
Koz'mina, A-.
Zhenshchiny Kitaia (Women of China).
Moscow: Gospolitizdat, 1940. 72 p.
SUBJ 17 32.2 41 47 52 64 ▪ 16.3 16.4 18 25 36.4 55 61 63 66

20205 MCH O P2 G5.3 1911–1949
Marquart, Jakob.
Die Frau in Schantung: Bilder aus Vergangenheit und Gegenwart (The woman in Shantung: Sketches from the past and the present).
Tsingtao: Missionsdruckerei Tsingtao, 1932. 93 p.
SUBJ 41 47 ▪ 33 46 51 52 54 57

20206 MCY O P3 G5.1 1928–1949
Miller, I- L-.
The Chinese girl. Tr. from the Russian by E- de Laberbis. [Tr. from an unpublished manuscript]
Tientsin: Peiyang Press, 1932. 108 p.
SUBJ 46 47 63 ▪ 41 60 66

20207 MCH O P3 G6.1 1911–1928
Morrison, Elizabeth.
'Helping increase the literacy of Chinese women.'
CR 54, 10 (Oct. 1923), 595–600.
SUBJ 37 47 ▪ 27

20208 GMS O P2 G1.5 1911–1949
Oehler-Heimerdinger, Elisabeth, 1884–.
Die Chinesin: Das Leben der Frau im Osten (The life of women in China).
Elmshorn: Bramstedt, 1939. 238 p.
SUBJ 41 47 50 55 56 ▪ 17 23 33 44 46 52 53 57 65

20209 NNC P P3 G1.1 1911–1928
Ostrofsky, Diane Betty.
The role of women in the Chinese labor movement, 1919–1927.
Unpublished masters thesis in History, Columbia U., 1967. 139 p.
SUBJ 36.4 47 ▪ 14.4 16.4 18

20210 WSU P P2 G7.0 1911–1949
Pearson, Margaret Jean, 1944–.
Hsieh Ping-ying: Participant in the family revolution in China.
Unpublished masters thesis in East Asian Studies, U. of Washington, 1970. 106 p.
SUBJ 41 47 59 ▪ 15 26.1 26.3 27 34.2 36.3 64

20211 NIC O P4 G1.2 1911–1928
Pye, Edith M-.
'The woman's movement in China.'
Asiatic review new (4th) series 25, 82 (Apr. 1929), 204–219.
SUBJ 32 47 ▪ 17 18

20212 NNC P P2 G1.2 1928–1949
Seesholtz, Ann Groh, 1883–.
'Distinctive activities and interests of Chinese women.' In *China*, edited by Orville Anderson Petty. [Selective entry]
New York: Harper, 1933, 502–534. (Laymans Foreign Missions Inquiry, Factfinders' reports, 5; Supplementary series, part 2)
SUBJ 17 41 47 ▪ 18 50 55 61 63

20213 MCH O P3 G1.1 1911–1928
Seton, Grace Thompson, 1872–1959.
Chinese lanterns.
New York: Dodd, Mead, 1924. 15, 373 p.
SUBJ 41 47 ▪ 12.1 17 22.2 23 30

20214 CSU O P2 G1.2 1911–1949
Soong Ching Ling (Sung Ch'ing-ling), 1892–.
'The Chinese woman's fight for freedom.'
Asia (New York: American Asiatic Assn.) 42, 7 (July 1942), 391–393; 42, 8 (Aug. 1942), 470–472.
SUBJ 47 ▪ 30 34.2

20215 MCH O P3 G9.2 1911–1928
Strong, Anna Louise, 1885–1970.
'New women of old Canton.'
Asia (New York: American Asiatic Assn.) 26, 6 (June 1926), 493–495, 555–557.
SUBJ 47 ▪ 40 41

20216 NIC F P3 G5.1 1911–1928
T'ao, Ling, and Lydia Johnson.
Women in Tientsin industries: A study of the working conditions of women and girls.
Peking: Peking Leader Press, 1928. 11 p.
SUBJ 26.4 47 ▪ 28

20217 CSU F P3 G8.2 1928–1949
T'ien, Ju-k'ang, 1917–.
'Female labor in a cotton mill [in Kunming].' Tr. from the Chinese by Francis L. K. Hsu [tr. of an unpublished manuscript]. In *China enters the machine age: A study of labor in Chinese war industry*, by Kuo-heng Shih, edited by Fei Hsiao-tung (Fei Hsiao-t'ung). [Analytic entry]
Cambridge: Harvard U. Press, 1944, 178–195. [For Shih's work, see entry 17729.] [Reprinted in *China enters the machine age: A study of labor in Chinese war industry*, by Kuo-heng Shih, edited by Fei Hsiao-tung. (Analytic entry.) New York: Greenwood Press, 1968, 178–195.]
SUBJ 26.4 47 ▪ 41 48

20218 NNM O P3 G5.2 1911–1928
Walton, Cara May.
'Women's work in Fenchow [i.e., Feng-chou, Feng-yang *hsien*, Shansi].'
CR 53, 9 (Sept. 1922), 595–598.
SUBJ 47 ▪ 27

20219 NNC P P3 G1.2 1928–1949
Wang, Simine (Wang Hsi-min).
Le travail industriel des femmes et des enfants en Chine (Female and child industrial labor in China).
Paris: Pedone, 1933. 298 p. (Doctoral dissertation, Faculté de droit, Université de Bruxelles)
SUBJ 16.4 18 47 52 ▪ 12.2 14.4

20220 CSH P P3 G7.2 1911–1928
Witke, Roxane Heater, 1938–.
'Mao Tse-tung, women and suicide in the May Fourth era.'
CQ 31 (July–Sept. 1967), 128–147.
SUBJ 47 54 57 ▪ 41 64

20221 MCH O P2 G1.2 1928–1949
Woodsmall, Ruth Frances, 1883–1963.
Eastern women today and tomorrow.
Boston: Central Committee on the United Study of Foreign Missions, 1933. 18, 221 p.
SUBJ 23 27 33 41 47 ▪ 28 52 54

20222 NNM S P3 G1.1 1911–1928
Y.W.C.A. United States National Board. Education and Research Division *with* Y.W.C.A. Industrial Dept.
'China.' In *Women in industry in the Orient: A sourcebook*, compiled by the organization cited. [Sole entry]
New York: Women's Press, 1926, 75–165.
SUBJ 11.4 16.4 18 47 52 ▪ 12.2 14.4 17 19 36.4 56 58

1911-1972
(including 1644-1972)

20223 CSH O P2 G1.3 1928–1972
Chang Hsiang-yu (Chang Hsiang-yü).
'My rebirth.' In *Chinese women in the Great Leap Forward*. [Sole entry]
Peking: Foreign Languages Press, 1960, 50–56.
SUBJ 47 59 ▪ 16 31

20224 MCH O P2 G1.2 1911–1972
Cusak, Dymphna.
Chinese women speak.
Sydney: Angus and Robertson, 1959. 262 p.
SUBJ 47 ▪ 28 31 41 53 55 59

20225 CSU P P1 G1.1 1644–1972
Eberhard, Wolfram, 1909–.
'What is beautiful in a Chinese woman?' In *Moral and social values of the Chinese: Collected essays*, by W. Eberhard. [Selective entry]
Taipei: Chinese Materials and Research Aids Service Center, 1971, 271–304. (CMRASC occasional series, 6)
SUBJ 46 47 60

20226 NIC PO P2 G1.2 –1972
Grisar, Elisabeth.
La femme en Chine (Women in China).
Paris: Buchet/Chastel (Corrêa), 1957. 247 p.
SUBJ 12.2 18 41 47 50 60 ▪ 12.1 15 16.3 16.4 52 54 55 57

20227 MCY P P1 G1.2 1928–1972
Hsia, C. T. (Hsia Chih-ch'ing), 1921–.
'Residual femininity: Women in Chinese Communist fiction.'
CQ 13 (Jan.–Mar. 1963), 158–179.
SUBJ 47 ▪ 12.1 40 41 63 64

20228 NNC P P2 G1.2 1911–1972
Kaltenmark-Ghéquier, Odile.
'L'émancipation de la femme' (The emancipation of women). In *Aspects de la Chine, vol. 3, époque contemporaine* (Aspects of China, Vol. 3, The modern era), by Etienne Balazs et al. [Selective entry]
Paris: Presses universitaires, 1962, 589–599.
SUBJ 12.2 47 ▪ 11.4 41

20229 FPN P P1 G1.2 1928–1972
Maurizi, Madeleine.
La condition juridique de la femme en Chine (The legal status of women in China).
Unpublished doctoral dissertation, Faculté de droit, Université de Paris, 1964. 446 p.
SUBJ 41 47 51 ▪ 12.2 17 46 63

20230 CSU S P2 G1.2 1842–1972
Salaff, Janet Weitzner, 1940–, and Judith Merkle, 1942–.
'Women in revolution: The lessons of the Soviet Union and China.'
Berkeley j. of sociology 15 (1970), 166–191.
SUBJ 47 ▪ 12.1 25 41

20231 CSU PO P2 G1.1 1911–1972
Snow, Helen Foster, 1907–.
Women in modern China.
The Hague: Mouton, 1967. 16, 264 p.
SUBJ 32.2 41 47 50 ▪ 12.2 17 22.2 32 33 40 46 55

20232 MCH O P1 G1.2 1928–1972
Sudarikov, Nikolai Georgievich, 1928–.
'Demokratizatsiia semeino-brachnogo zakonodatel'stva Kitaiskoi Narodnoi Respubliki' (The democratization of marriage and family legislation in the People's Republic of China).
SGP 1954, 7 (iiul'), 33–40.
SUBJ 12.2 41 47

20233 MCH S P2 G1.2 1928–1972
Tricht-Kessing, E- E- van.
'Emancipatie voor de Chinese vrouwen' (Emancipation for Chinese women). In *China tussen eergisteren en overmorgen* (China between the day before yesterday and the day after tomorrow), edited by Willem Frederik Wertheim and Erik Zürcher. [Selective entry]
The Hague: Van Hoeve, 1963, 154–166.
SUBJ 47 ▪ 41

20234 NIC PO P2 G9.0 –1972
Tsung, Tien.
'Women who do not marry.'
Orient (Hong Kong) 2, 12 (July 1952), 41–43.
SUBJ 41 47 ▪ 40 57

20235 CSU O P2 G1.1 –1972
Ward, Barbara Elsie, 1919–.
'Men, women and change: An essay in understanding social roles in South and Southeast Asia.' In *Women in the new Asia*, by B. E. Ward. [Sole entry]
Paris: United Nations, Educational, Scientific and Cultural Organization, 1963, 25–99.
SUBJ 41 47 ▪ 11.1 42 44 52

1949-1972

20236 MAM F P8 G9.4 1949–1972
Barnett, William Kester, 1930–.
An ethnographic description of Sanlei Ts'un, Taiwan, with emphasis on women's roles: Overcoming research

problems caused by the presence of a great tradition.
Ann Arbor: University Microfilms (Publ. 71-2026), 1971. 15, 565 p. (Doctoral dissertation in Anthropology, Michigan State U., 1970)
Subj 20 30 40 41 47 55 ▪ 21.4 22 22.2 23 24.1 36.3 42 48 50 65

20237 CSU O P2 G1.2 1949–1972
Brugger, William Christian, 1941–.
'The male (and female) in Chinese society.'
Impact of science on society 21, 1 (Jan.–Mar. 1971), 5–19.
Subj 41 46 47 ▪ 12.1 16.1 16.3 52

20238 NNC O P3 G5.1 1949–1972
Chang Hsiao-mei, 1906–.
'The women in the capital are completely liberated and are leaping forward.' Tr. of 'Shou tu fu nü tsai ch'e ti chieh fang ti tao lu shang fei yao ch'ien chin'; *Jen min jih pao* 10 Apr. 1960, 10. In *Speeches given at second session of Second National People's Congress, Communist China*, mimeo., compiled by U.S. Joint Publications Research Service. [Selective entry]
Washington, D.C.: JPRS, 28 Dec. 1960, 20–29. (JPRS 6483; MC 7699/1961)
Subj 47 ▪ 21.4 24.4 28 52 55

20239 CBU O P3 G9.5 1949–1972
Chau, Chong Kim Yin.
'Hongkong women and society: A study.'
Philippine educational forum 16, 3 (Nov. 1967), 32–38.
Subj 47 ▪ 17 41

20240 MCH P P1 G1.2 1949–1972
Huang, Lucy Jen (Huang Jen-hua), 1920–.
'A re-evaluation of the primary role of the Communist Chinese woman: The homemaker or the worker.'
Marriage and family living 25, 2 (May 1963), 162–166.
Subj 47 ▪ 41 63

20241 NIC O P8 G7.3 1949–1972
Jui-chin hsien min chu fu nü lien ho hui. Kung tso tsu. (Jui-chin Hsien Women's Federation. Work Section).
'Same pay for same work to men and women in the Ch'ing-hsi production brigade.' Tr. of 'Ch'ing-hsi ta tui nan nü t'ung kung t'ung ch'ou kuan ch'e ti hao' (Equal pay for equal work for both men and women in Ch'ing-hsi brigade [Jui-chin *hsien*, Kiangsi]); *Chung-kuo fu nü* 1961, 11 (Nov.), 4–5.
SCMM 291 (11 Dec. 1961), 13–15.
Subj 26.3 47 ▪ 28 34.1

20242 NIC P P2 G1.2 1949–1972
[La Dany, Ladislao] ———, 1914–.
'Chinese women.'
CNA 215 (7 Feb. 1958), 1–7.
Subj 41 47 ▪ 52

20243 MCH P P2 G1.2 1949–1972
[La Dany, Ladislao] ———, 1914–.
'Housewives' problems.'
CNA 121 (24 Feb. 1956), 2–7.
Subj 18 47 55

20244 CSH P P2 G1.2 1949–1972
Lucas, Christopher.
Women of China.
Hong Kong: Dragonfly Books, 1965. 331 p.
Subj 12.1 41 47 55 ▪ 12.2 16.1 16.4 22.2

20245 CSH O P2 G5.2 1949–1972
Nan Ts'ai-ying.
'The dexterous girls movement.' Tr. of '"Ch'iao ku niang" yün tung'; *Hung ch'i* 1958, 7 (1 Sept.), 30–32. In *Selected translations from 'Hung ch'i' (Red flag), September 1958*, mimeo., compiled by U.S. Joint Publications Research Service. [Selective entry]
Washington, D.C.: JPRS, 9 May 1961, 91–95. (JPRS 9181; MC 15,357/1961)
Subj 47

20246 CSH O P1 G9.4 1949–1972
O'Hara, Albert Richard, 1907–.
'The position of women in modern China.'
Chinese j. of sociology (Taipei) 1 (Oct. 1971), 61–68. [Reprinted in *Research on changes of Chinese society*, by A. R. O'Hara. (Selective entry.) Taipei: Orient Cultural Service, 1971, 159–165. (Asian Folklore and Social Life monographs, 20)]
Subj 47

20247 NNC P P7 G1.2 1949–1972
Rossabi, Morris, 1941–.
Chinese Communists and the peasant women, 1949–1962.
Unpublished masters thesis in History, Columbia U., 1964. 154 p.
Subj 16.3 47 ▪ 12.1 18 41 52 64

20248 MCH O P2 G1.2 1949–1972
Tsao Meng-chun.
'The status of women in the world of today: China.'
Review of contemporary law 7, 1 (June 1960), 54–60.
Subj 12.2 18 47 ▪ 12.1 40 64

20249 CSU F P7 G9.4 1949–1972
Wolf, Margery, 1933–.
Women and the family in rural Taiwan.
Stanford: Stanford U. Press, 1972. 10, 235 p.
Subj 40 41 47 50 51 52 ▪ 27 31 46 48 53 55 57 59 65

20250 NNC U P3 G1.2 1949–1972
Yang Hui-chin.
'The life of our women textile workers.'
WC 1953 (June), 17–26.
Subj 14.4 16.4 18 47 ▪ 17 52 56

20251 CSH O P3 G6.1 1949–1972
Yin Hsiang.
'Protestant women in Shanghai.'
WC 1957, 6, 29–31.
Subj 33 47

48 Non-Kin Interpersonal Relationships

非親屬關係　　非親族関係

1644-1911

20252 NIC P P4 G9.3 1842–1895
Borel, Henri, 1869–1933.
'Serment d'amitié chinois' (A Chinese oath of friendship).
TP 4, 5 (déc. 1893), 420–426.
Subj 48 ▪ 60 63

20253 NNP O P1 G2.0 1895–1911
D. I.
'Pobratimstvo u kitaitsev' (Sworn brotherhood among the Chinese).
VA 4 (mai 1910), 186–187.
Subj 48

20254 CSH P P2 G1.2 1895–1911
Ivanov, L-.
'TSin-lan'-pu: pobratimstvo v Kitae' (*Ch'ing lan p'u*: Sworn brotherhood in China).
VA 30 (oktiabr' 1914), 5–18.
Subj 22.2 30 48 ▪ 23 24.1 31 32 33 34.1

20255 MCH PO P1 G1.2 1895–1911
Kiong, Simon (Kung Ku-yü).
Quelques mots sur la politesse chinoise (Notes on Chinese courtesy).
Shanghai: Impr. de la Mission catholique, 1906. 119 p. (Variétés sinologiques, 25)
Subj 48 53 55 63 ▪ 16.1 57 72

20256 NNC U P1 G1.3 –1911
Lederer, Emil, 1882–1939.
'Die Bedeutung der konventionellen Formen im Osten' (The significance of conventional forms of behavior in the East).
Sinica 3, 2 (1928), 61–73; 3, 3 (1928), 148–155.
Subj 48 61 63 ▪ 16 64

20257 NIC U P1 G1.3 –1911
Levy, Marion Joseph, Jr., 1918–.
'Some aspects of "individualism" and the problem of modernization of China and Japan.'
EDCC 10, 3 (Apr. 1962), 225–241.
Subj 14 48 ▪ 12

20258 NNC O P2 G1.2 1895–1911
Walshe, William Gilbert.
'Ways that are dark': Some chapters on Chinese etiquette and social procedure.
Shanghai: Kelly and Walsh, 1906? 276 p.
Subj 16 18 31 48 55 63 ▪ 13 22.2 27 38 41 47 50 53 56 57

20259 CSH O P1 G1.2 1842–1895
Williams, Samuel Wells, 1812–1884.
'Social life among the Chinese.' In *The Middle Kingdom: A survey of the geography, government, literature, social life, arts, and history of the Chinese empire and its inhabitants*, rev. and enl. ed., by S. W. Williams. [Selective entry]
New York: Scribner, 1883, vol. 1, 782–836. [Reprinted in *The Middle Kingdom: A survey of the geography, government, literature, social life, arts, and history of the Chinese empire and its inhabitants*, by S. W. Williams. (Selective entry.) Taipei: Ch'eng-wen, 1965, 782–836 (s.p.)]
Subj 31 41 48 ▪ 47 52 61

1644-1949

20260 MCH O P8 G5.1 1895–1928
Liu, John.
'The social relationships of the villagers in China.'
SSR 14, 5 (May–June 1930), 462–468.
Subj 20 22 48 ▪ 42

1911-1949

20261 NIC S P1 G9.0 1911–1949
'The Mui Tsai system in China, Hong Kong and Malaya.'
ILR 34, 5 (Nov. 1936), 663–676.
Subj 47 48 52 54 55 ▪ 18

20262 NIC F P2 G6.2 1928–1949
Fried, Morton Herbert, 1923–.
Fabric of Chinese society: A study of the social life of a Chinese county seat.
New York: Praeger, 1953. 243 p. (Revision of *Kin and non-kin in Chinese society: An analysis of extra-kin relationships in Chinese society, with special reference to a selected community, Ch'u Hsien* [i.e., Ch'u-hsien, Anhwei], doctoral dissertation in Anthropology, Columbia U., 1951) [Reprinted—New York: Octagon Books, 1969. 243 p.]
Subj 20 26 34.2 41 48 ▪ 24 24.1 24.3 26.1 26.2 27 34.3 40 42 44

20263 MCH U P1 G1.0 1911–1928
Hermant, Paul.
'La face chinoise' ('Face' in China).
B. de la Société royale belge de géographie 48, 2 (1924), 84–92.
Subj 48 61 ▪ 63

20264 NIC O P1 G1.0 1911–1949
Hu, Hsien-chin, 1910–.
'The Chinese concept of face.'
AA new (2nd) series 46, 1 (Jan.–Mar. 1944), 45–65.
Subj 48 63 ▪ 22.2 27 34.2 53 61

20265 NNC O P1 G1.3 1911–1949
Plopper, Clifford Henry, 1885–.
'The relationship of friends as brought out by the proverbs.' In *Chinese proverbs*, by C. H. Plopper. [Analytic entry]
Peiping: North China Union Language School, 1932, 1–23.
Subj 22.2 48 65 ▪ 61 63

20266 CSU PO P1 G1.0 1911–1928
Tiefensee, Franz Wilhelm, 1880–.
'Wegweiser durch die chinesischen Höflichkeitsformen' (A guide to Chinese etiquette).
MDG 18 (1924), 1–224.
Subj 48 63 ▪ 41 57

1911-1972
(including 1644-1972)

□

1949-1972

20267 CSU F P3 G9.5 1949–1972
Agassi, Joseph, and Ian C- Jarvie.
'A study of westernization.' In *Hong Kong: A society in transition*, edited by I. C. Jarvie and J. Agassi. [Analytic entry]
New York: Praeger, 1969, 129–163.
Subj 48 63 66 ▪ 41 61

20268 CSU F P6 G9.4 1949–1972
DeGlopper, Donald Robert, 1942–.
'Doing business in Lukang [Chang-hua *hsien*, Taiwan].' In *Economic organization in Chinese society*, edited by William Earl Willmott. [Selective entry]
Stanford: Stanford U. Press, 1972, 297–326.
Subj 24.3 24.6 34.2 48 ▪ 30 45

20269 CSU F P1 G9.4 1949–1972
Eberhard, Wolfram, 1909–.
'A note on modern Chinese nicknames.' In *Studies in Chinese folklore and related essays*, by W. Eberhard. [Selective entry]
Bloomington: Indiana U., Research Center for the Language Sciences, 1970, 217–222. (Indiana U., Folklore Institute monograph series, 23)
Subj 48 52 ▪ 47

20270 DLC O P1 G1.2 1949–1972
Jabłoński, Witold.
'Etykieta chińska' (Chinese etiquette).
Przegląd orientalistyczny (Warsaw) 1957, 3, 271–286.
Subj 48 60 63

20271 CSH F P1 G1.2 1949–1972
Vogel, Ezra Feivel, 1930–.
'From friendship to comradeship: The change in personal relations in Communist China.'
CQ 21 (Jan.–Mar. 1965), 46–60. [Reprinted in *China under Mao: Politics takes command*, edited by Roderick Lemonde MacFarquhar. (Selective entry.) Cambridge: M.I.T. Press, 1966, 407–421.]
Subj 12.1 48 61 ▪ 16 63

20272 MAM FP P7 G9.5 1949–1972
Young, John Aubrey, 1941–.
Interpersonal networks and economic behavior in a Chinese market town [Yuen Long (i.e., Yüan-lang), Hong Kong].
Ann Arbor: University Microfilms (Publ. 71-23,574), 1971. 259 p. (Doctoral dissertation in Anthropology, Stanford U.)
Subj 24.3 26.2 30 31 38 48 ▪ 22 24.6 34.2 36.1 36.2 39 44 66

50 Life Cycle and Age Grading
生命周期及年齡
生命周期及び年齡

20273 NNC O P3 G5.1 1911–1928
Bogan, *Mrs.* M- L- C-.
Manchu customs and superstitions.
Tientsin, Peking: China Booksellers, 1928. 13, 140 p.
Subj 23 50 55 62 65 ▪ 29 31 43 51 52 57 63

20274 NNM O P3 G1.5 1842–1895
Bridgman, Eliza Jane Gillett, 1805–1871.
Daughters of China: or, Sketches of domestic life in the Celestial Empire.
New York: Carter, 1853. 10, 234 p.
Subj 47 50 55 65 ▪ 41 43 51 52 57 61 62 66

20275 NNM O P4 G7.1 1842–1895
Bryson, Mary Isabella.
Home-life in China.
New York: American Tract Society, 1886. 314 p.
Subj 27 47 50 54 55 65 ▪ 21.3 23 41 51 52 53 57 66

20276 DCK O P4 G2.3 1911–1949
Christensen, Robert, 1885–1945.
Kineseren i sit rige (The Chinese in his kingdom).
Copenhagen: Danske forlag, 1945. 184 p.
Subj 41 47 50 55 61 65 ▪ 23 24.4 24.6 44 51 56 57 66

20277 CSH O P7 G5.1 1949–1972
Lu Chiang.
'Home of respect for the aged.'
WC 1959, 1, 23–25.
Subj 50

20278 CSU S P1 G1.0 –1972
Saw, Swee-Hock.
'Errors in Chinese age statistics.'
Demography 4, 2 (1967), 859–875.
Subj 50

20279 CSU O P1 G9.5 1895–1911
Tso, S. W.
'Ceremonies and customs of the Chinese.' In *Twentieth century impressions of Hongkong, Shanghai, and other treaty ports of China: Their history, people, commerce, industries and manners*, edited by Arnold Wright and H- A- Cartwright. [Selective entry]
London: Lloyd's Greater Britain Publishing Co., 1908, 307–318.
Subj 31 50 52 55 ▪ 23 41 45 56 57

20280 CSH P P1 G1.2 –1972
Wilhelm, Hellmut, 1906–.
'The image of youth and age in Chinese Communist literature.'
CQ 13 (Jan.–Mar. 1963), 180–194.
Subj 50 ▪ 12.1 16.1

51 Reproduction
生殖　　生殖

1644-1911

20281 FPN O P5 G5.0 1895–1911
'L'infanticide en Chine' (Infanticide in China).
Relations de Chine 20, 4 (oct. 1922), 195–203; 21, 1 (jan.–avr. 1923), 25–31.
Subj 28 51 58 ▪ 22 66

20282 NIC O P2 G1.2 1842–1895
'The prevalence of infanticide in China.'
JRAS-CB new (2nd) series 20, 1 (1885), 25–68. [Reprinted from *North-China herald*.]
Subj 28 41 47 51 ▪ 38

20283 CBU O P3 G9.3 1842–1895
A. C. D.
'Female infanticide, from an unpublished history of Amoy.'
China review 2, 1 (July–Aug. 1873), 55–58.
Subj 51 ▪ 52

20284 FPN P P1 G1.3 1644–1895
Hureau de Villeneuve, Abel.
De l'accouchement dans la race jaune (Childbirth among Orientals).
Paris: Benjamin Duprat, 1863. 39 p.
Subj 51 56 62 ▪ 12.2 16 23 46 47 53

20285 FPN P P1 G1.1 –1895
Largent, Augustin.
L'infanticide en Chine (Infanticide in China).

Paris: Société de Sainte-Enfance, 1885. 72 p.
Subj 18 22.2 38 47 51 ▪ 12.2 23 52 65

20286 MCH P P2 G1.2 –1911
Laufer, Berthold, 1874–1934.
'Multiple births among the Chinese.'
NCR 2, 2 (Apr. 1920), 109–136.
Subj 51 ▪ 58

20287 FPN P P1 G1.3 1842–1895
Martin, Charles Ernest, 1831–1897.
Etude médico-légal sur l'infanticide et l'avortement dans l'empire chinois (A medical and legal study of infanticide and abortion in the Chinese empire).
Paris: G. Masson, 1872. 15 p.
Subj 12.2 40 50 51 56 ▪ 16 22.2 60

20288 NNC PO P1 G1.2 1895–1911
Matignon, Jean-Jacques, 1866–?
'Infanticide et avortement' (Infanticide and abortion). In *La Chine hermétique: superstitions, crime et misère* (China sealed off: Superstition, crime, and poverty), 5th ed., rev., by J.-J. Matignon. [Selective entry]
Paris: Lib. Geuthner, 1936, 237–262.
Subj 51 65 ▪ 47

20289 CSH O P2 G1.5 1895–1911
Nagel, August.
'Chinesische Geburtsgebräuche' (Chinese childbirth customs).
OL 25, 38 (22 Sept. 1911), 247–250; 25, 39 (29 Sept. 1911), 269–272.
Subj 51 52

20290 MCH O P2 G1.3 1842–1895
Rondot, Natalis, 1821–1900.
'Note sur l'infanticide en Chine' (A note on infanticide in China).
J. des économistes 26, 111 (15 juin 1850), 258–286.
Subj 51 ▪ 22.2 47

1644-1949

20291 NNM O P1 G1.1 –1928
Best, A- E-.
'Chinese folklore, relating to conception and maternity.'
CMJ 40, 6 (June 1926), 564–574.
Subj 51 65 ▪ 23

20292 MCH S P2 G1.2 1842–1949
Falcone, Pompeo.
'L'infanticidio in Cina' (Infanticide in China). In *Atti del Congresso internazionale per gli studi sulla popolazione (Roma, 7–10 settembre 1931), Vol. VII, sezione de demografia* (Proceedings of the International Congress for Studies on Population, Rome, 7–10 September 1931, Vol. 7, Demography), edited by Corrado Gini. [Sole entry]
Rome: Istituto poligrafico dell stato libreria, 1934, 213–232.
Subj 12.2 51 63 ▪ 29 41 47 50

20293 NIC P P1 G5.0 1644–1928
Johnston, Reginald Fleming, 1874–1938.
'A note on multiple births in China.'
NCR 2, 4 (Aug. 1920), 415–418.
Subj 51

20294 IMA PO P2 G1.2 1842–1928
Tragella, G- B-.
L'infanticidio e la S. Infanzia, con particolare riguardo alla Cina (Infanticide and St. Infance, with special attention to China).
Milan: Istituto delle Missioni Estere, 1920. 172 p.
Subj 51 66 ▪ 18 38 62

20295 NNC O P1 G1.1 –1928
Tsay, Queenie.
'Chinese superstitions relating to child birth.'
CMJ 32, 6 (Nov. 1918), 533–536.
Subj 51 65

1911-1949

20296 MCH O P2 G9.3 1911–1928
Aguirre, ———.
'L'infanticide au Fo-kien' (Infanticide in Fukien).
APF 89 (1917), 207–214.
Subj 47 51 ▪ 28

20297 MCY O P2 G9.0 1911–1949
Baudrit, A-.
'La femme et l'enfant dans l'Indochine française et dans la Chine du Sud' (Women and children in French Indochina and South China).
B. de la Société des études indo-chinoises de Saigon nouvelle (2e) série 16, 3 (1941), 83–152.
Subj 47 51 52 ▪ 25 63

20298 CSU F P7 G4.4 1911–1949
Eichinger, Franz.
'Kinderlosigkeit und ihre Bekämpfung in der Volksmedizin' (Barrenness and its treatment in folk medicine). In *Ethnographische Beiträge aus der Ch'inghai Provinz (China)* (Ethnographic reports from Tsinghai). [Selective entry]
Peking [i.e., Tokyo]: Catholic U. of Peking, Museum of Oriental Ethnology, 1952, 167–201. (MOE, Folklore studies supplements, 1)
Subj 41 51 56 65 ▪ 23 46 47 52 57 62

20299 NNC F P8 G4.4 1911–1949
Frick, Johannes.
'Magische Schutzmittel für Kinder aus dem Westtal von Sining' (Magic for the protection of children, as practiced in the western valley of Hsi-ning [Tsinghai]).
Anthropos 45, 4/6 (Juli-Dez. 1950), 787–800.
Subj 23 51 65 ▪ 52 56 57

20300 NNC F P3 G1.3 1928–1949
Lamson, Herbert Day, 1899–.
'Educated women and birth control in China.'
CMJ 44, 11 (Nov. 1930), 1100–1109.
Subj 47 51 ▪ 18 58

20301 NNM F P1 G1.3 1928–1949
Lamson, Herbert Day, 1899–.
'Family limitation among educated Chinese married women: A study of the practice and attitudes of 120 women.'
CMJ 47, 5 (May 1933), 493–503.
Subj 47 51

20302 ICU FP P2 G1.2 1911–1949
Su, Ru-chiang.
Birth control in China.
Unpublished masters thesis in Sociology, U. of Chicago, 1946. 232 p.
Subj 11 18 43 50 51 58 ▪ 11.3 38 41 61 63

1911-1972
(including 1644-1972)

20303 MMT P P2 G1.2 1911–1972
Coughlin, Richard James, 1917–.
'Population controls in China.' In *Symposium on economic and social problems of the Far East*, edited by Edward Franciszek Szczepanik. [Selective entry]
Hong Kong: Hong Kong U. Press, 1962, 389–399.
Subj 11 51 58 ▪ 41 47

20304 NNC F P2 G4.4 1911–1972
Frick, Johannes.
'Mutter und Kind bei den Chinesen in Tsinghai' (Mother and child among the Chinese in Tsinghai).
Anthropos 50, 1/3 (Jan.–Juni 1955), 337–374; 50, 4/6 (Juli–Dez. 1955), 659–701; 51, 3/4 (Mai–Aug. 1956), 513–550; 51, 5/6 (Sept.–Dez. 1956), 1055–1063.
Subj 51 52 57 62 ▪ 23 41 46 47 55 56 63 65

20305 CSU P P1 G1.2 1911–1972
Varma, Asha.
'Birth control and planned parenthood in China.'
China report (New Delhi) 7, 2 (Mar.–Apr. 1971), 41–48.
Subj 51

1949-1972

20306 CSU P P2 G1.1 1949–1972
Aird, John Shields, 1919–.
'Population policy and demographic prospects in the People's Republic of China.' In *People's Republic of China: An economic assessment*, compiled by Joint Economic Committee, U.S. Congress. [Selective entry]
Washington, D.C.: U.S. Government Printing Office, 1972, 220–331.
Subj 12.1 51 ▪ 11 11.1 14.1 14.3 34.1 41 58 64

20307 CSU F P2 G9.4 1949–1972
Cernada, George Peter, 1938–, and L. P. Chow (Chou Lien-pin), 1924–.
'The coupon system in an ongoing family planning program.'
American j. of public health 59, 12 (Dec. 1969), 2199–2208.
Subj 51

20308 CSU F P3 G9.4 1949–1972
Cernada, George Peter, 1938–, and Laura P. Lu.
'The Kaoshiung study.'
SFP 3, 8 (Aug. 1972), 198–203.
Subj 24.2 51

20309 CSU F P2 G9.5 1949–1972
Chan, K. C.
'Hong Kong: Oral contraceptive follow-up study.'
SFP 2, 3 (Mar. 1971), 70–74.
Subj 51 ▪ 50

20310 CSU F P2 G9.5 1949–1972
Chan, K. C.
'Hong Kong: Report of the IUD reassurance project.'
SFP 2, 11 (Nov. 1971), 225–233.
Subj 51

20311 CSU F P2 G9.4 1949–1972
Chang, M. C., George Peter Cernada, 1938–, and T. H. Sun (Sun Te-hsiung), 1930–.
'A field-worker incentive experimental study.'
SFP 3, 11 (Nov. 1972), 270–272.
Subj 51

20312 CSU F P2 G9.4 1949–1972
Chen, F. L., et al.
'Taiwan: First island-wide pill acceptor follow-up survey.'
SFP 60 (Dec. 1970), 18–23.
Subj 51 ▪ 50

20313 CSU P P2 G1.2 1949–1972
Chen, Pi-chao, 1937–.
'China's birth control action programme, 1956–1964.'
PS 24, 2 (July 1970), 141–158.
Subj 51 ▪ 41

20314 MAM P P2 G1.2 1949–1972
Chen, Pi-chao, 1937–.
The politics of population in Communist China: A case study of birth control policy, 1949–1965.
Ann Arbor: University Microfilms (Publ. 67-12,014), 1967. 319 p. (Doctoral dissertation in Political Science, Princeton U., 1966)
Subj 32 51 58 64 ▪ 11.2 11.4 12 12.1 14 16.1

20315 CSU PO P3 G5.1 1949–1972
Ch'en Wen-chen.
'A clinical analysis of 8063 cases of painless labor by the psychoprophylactic method.'
CMJ 75, 5 (May 1957), 337–343.
Subj 51

20316 CSU F P2 G9.4 1949–1972
Chi, I. C. (Ch'i I-cheng), L. P. Chow (Chou Lien-pin), 1924–, and Rowland V- Rider.
'The randomized response technique as used in the Taiwan outcome of pregnancy study.'
SFP 3, 11 (Nov. 1972), 265–269.
Subj 51

20317 CSU F P7 G9.4 1949–1972
Chi, I. C. (Ch'i I-cheng), and W. P. Mao (Mao Wen-ping).
'Male attitude toward birth control in Musa, Taipei county [Mu-shan *hsiang*, T'ai-pei *hsien*], Taiwan.'
CMJ-T 14, 1 (Mar. 1967), 71–86. [Follow-up of study conducted in 1962; for earlier study, see Ch'i I-cheng and Mao Wen-ping, 'Nan hsing hu chang tui chia t'ing chi hua chih i chien: T'ai-wan sheng T'ai-pei hsien Mu-shan hsiang tiao ch'a pao kao' (Attitudes of male family heads on family planning: Report on Mu-shan *hsiang*, T'ai-pei *hsien*, Taiwan); *Chung-hua i hsüeh tsa chih* 10, 2 (June 1963), 89–95.]
Subj 46 51 ▪ 41 58

20318 CSU O P2 G1.2 1949–1972
[Chow, Elizabeth K.] Han Suyin, pseud., 1917–.
'Family planning in China.'
JQ 17, 4 (Oct.–Dec. 1970), 433–442.
Subj 51 ▪ 41 47 56 58

20319 CSU F P2 G9.4 1949–1972
Chow, L. P. (Chou Lien-pin), 1924–.
'Evaluation procedures for a family planning program.' In *Family planning and population programs: A review of world developments*, edited by Bernard Berelson et al. [Selective entry]
Chicago: U. of Chicago Press, 1966, 675–689. [Proceedings of International Conference on Family Planning Programs, Geneva, 1965]
Subj 51 ▪ 58 70

20320 CSU FP P2 G9.4 1949–1972
Chow, L. P. (Chou Lien-pin), 1924–.
'Family planning in Taiwan, Republic of China: Progress and prospects.'
PS 24, 3 (Nov. 1970), 339–352.
Subj 51 ▪ 21 50 58

20321 CSU F P1 G9.4 1949–1972
Chow, L. P. (Chou Lien-pin), 1924–, and S. C. Hsu (Hsü Shih-chü), 1905–.
'A Chinese view of family planning in the developing world.' In *Fertility and family planning: A world view*, edited by S- J- Behrman, Leslie Corsa, and Ronald Freedman. [Sole entry]
Ann Arbor: U. of Michigan Press, 1969, 451–466.
Subj 51 ▪ 41 58

20322 CSU F P2 G9.4 1949–1972
Chow, L. P. (Chou Lien-pin), 1924–, et al.
'Correlates of IUD termination in a mass family planning program: The first Taiwan IUD follow-up survey.'
MMFQ 46, 2, Part 1 (Apr. 1968), 215–235.
Subj 51

20323 CSU O P2 G9.5 1949–1972
Chun, Daphne (Ch'in Hui-chen).
'National programs: Achievements and problems, Hong Kong.' In *Family planning and population programs: A review of world developments*, by Bernard Berelson et al. [Selective entry]
Chicago: U. of Chicago Press, 1966, 71–84. [Proceedings of International Conference on Family Planning Programs, Geneva, 1965]
Subj 51 ▪ 24.2 58

20324 NIC F P3 G9.5 1949–1972
Coughlin, Richard James, 1917–, and Margaret Morgan Coughlin, 1922–.
'Fertility and birth control among low income Chinese families in Hong Kong.'
Marriage and family living 25, 2 (May 1963), 171–177.
Subj 51 58 ▪ 28 47

20325 CSU S P2 G1.2 1949–1972
Dreijmanis, John.
'The politics of birth prevention: A comparison of the Chinese and Japanese approaches.'
Population review 12, 1/2 (Jan.–Dec. 1968), 23–32.
Subj 51 ▪ 58

20326 MCH F P4 G9.4 1949–1972
Eberhard, Wolfram, 1909–, and Alide Eberhard.
'Family planning in a Taiwan town [the capital of T'ao-yüan *hsien*].' In *Settlement and social change in Asia*, by W. Eberhard. [Selective entry]
Hong Kong: Hong Kong U. Press, 1967, 204–254.
Subj 41 51 ▪ 26 47 58

20327 MCH P P1 G1.2 1949–1972
Eitner, Hans-Jürgen.
'Wechselnde Bevölkerungspolitik in China.'
Aussenpolitik 11, 12 (Dez. 1960), 826–834.
Changing population policy in Communist China, mimeo.
Washington, D.C.: U.S. Joint Publications Research Service, 19 Apr. 1961. 10 p. (JPRS 8130; MC 13,086/1961)
Subj 51 ▪ 11 58 64

20328 NNC P P2 G1.2 1949–1972
Falkenheim, Victor Carl, 1940–.
Communist China's population policy.
Unpublished masters thesis in Public Law and Government, Columbia U., 1964. 129 p.
Subj 11 12 12.1 32 51 58 ▪ 14 18 41 47 64 72

20329 CSU O P2 G1.3 1949–1972
Faundes, Anibal, and Tapani Luukkainen.
'Health and family planning services in the Chinese People's Republic.'
SFP 3, 7 (July 1972), 165–176. [Supplement]
Subj 51 ▪ 18 41 56

20330 CSU F P2 G9.4 1949–1972
Finnigan, O- D-, and Spurgeon Milton Keeny, 1893–.
'Taiwan, 1970: Report on the national family planning programs.'
SFP 2, 3 (Mar. 1971), 63–69.
Subj 51 ▪ 24.2 58

20331 CSH P P2 G1.2 1949–1972
Freeberne, John Derek Michael, 1935–.
'The spectre of Malthus: Birth control in Communist China.'
CS 2, 18 (15 Aug. 1963), 1–14. [Reprinted as 'Birth control in China.' *PS* 18, 1 (July 1964), 5–16.] [Reprinted as 'Birth control in China.' In *This is China: Analyses of Mainland trends and events*, edited by Francis Harper. (Selective entry.) Hong Kong: Dragonfly Books, 1965, 1–18.]
Subj 46 51 ▪ 12.1 41

20332 CSU F P3 G9.4 1949–1972
Freedman, Deborah Selin, 1918–.
'The relationship of family planning to savings and consumption in Taiwan.'
Demography 9, 3 (Aug. 1972), 499–505.
Subj 24 51

20333 CSU FP P3 G9.4 1949–1972
Freedman, Ronald, 1917–.
'Sample surveys for family planning research in Taiwan.'
Public opinion q. 28, 3 (Fall 1964), 373–382.
Subj 51 ▪ 70 71

20334 CSU FP P2 G9.4 1949–1972
Freedman, Ronald, 1917–, Yuzuru John Takeshita, 1926–, et al.
Family planning in Taiwan: An experiment in social change.
Princeton: Princeton U. Press, 1969. 501 p.
Subj 51 58 ▪ 12 14 16 21.1 21.4 41 46

20335 DLC P P1 G9.4 1949–1972
Gillespie, Robert W-.
Family planning on Taiwan, 1964–1965.
Taichung: ——, 1965. 91 p.
Subj 46 51 ▪ 12.1 17 18

20336 CSU F P2 G9.4 1949–1972
Heidt, Sarajane.
'Knowledge and its consequences: The impact of information on a family planning program.'
American behavioral scientist 12, 2 (Nov.–Dec. 1968), 43–48.
Subj 51

20337 CSU O P2 G9.4 1949–1972
Hsu, S. C. (Hsü Shih-chü), 1905–.
'Personnel problems in family planning programs.' In *Family planning and population programs: A review of world developments*, edited by Bernard Berelson et al. [Selective entry]
Chicago: U. of Chicago Press, 1966, 335–343. [Proceedings of International Conference on Family Planning Programs, Geneva, 1965]
Subj 51

20338 CSU F P1 G9.0 1949–1972
Hsu, S. C. (Hsü Shih-chü), 1905–.
'Summary report of present status of family planning programs in East Asia.'
CMJ-T 15, 2 (June 1968), 89–118.
Subj 51 ▪ 21 50 58

20339 CSU O P2 G9.4 1949–1972
Hsu, T. C., and L. P. Chow (Chou Lien-pin), 1924–.
'National programs: Achievements and problems, Taiwan, Republic of China.' In *Family planning and population programs: A review of world developments*, by Bernard Berelson et al. [Selective entry]
Chicago: U. of Chicago Press, 1966, 55–70. [Proceedings of International Conference on Family Planning Programs, Geneva, 1965]
Subj 51 ▪ 56 58

20340 CSU F P3 G9.4 1949–1972
Jain, Anrudh Kumar, 1938–.
'Fecundability and its relation to age in a sample of Taiwanese women.'
PS 23, 1 (Mar. 1969), 69–85. [For fuller treatment, see entry 20341.]
Subj 51 ▪ 50 58

20341 MAM F P3 G9.4 1949–1972
Jain, Anrudh Kumar, 1938–.
Fecundity components in Taiwan: Application of a stochastic model of human reproduction.
Ann Arbor: University Microfilms (Publ. 68-13,335), 1968. 239 p. (Doctoral dissertation in Sociology, U. of Michigan)
Subj 51 58 ▪ 50

20342 CSU F P3 G9.4 1949–1972
Jain, Anrudh Kumar, 1938–.
'Fetal wastage in a sample of Taiwanese women.'
MMFQ 47, 3, Part 1 (July 1969), 297–306. [For fuller treatment, see entry 20341.]
Subj 51 ▪ 50

20343 CSU F P3 G9.4 1949–1972
Jain, Anrudh Kumar, 1938–.
'Pregnancy outcome and the time required for next conception.'
PS 23, 3 (Nov. 1969), 421–433. [For fuller treatment, see entry 20341.]
Subj 51 ▪ 50

20344 CSU F P3 G9.4 1949–1972
Jain, Anrudh Kumar, 1938–.
'Socio-economic correlates of fecundability in a sample of Taiwanese women.'
Demography 6, 1 (Feb. 1969), 75–90.
Subj 26 51

20345 CSU F P2 G9.4 1949–1972
Keeny, Spurgeon Milton, 1893–.
'Country profiles: Taiwan.'
SFP 50 (Feb. 1970), 1–15. [Supplement]
Subj 51 ▪ 21.4 41 58

20346 CSU F P2 G9.4 1949–1972
Keeny, Spurgeon Milton, 1893–, and George Peter Cernada, 1938–.
'Taiwan, 1969: Report on the national family planning programs.'
SFP 54 (June 1970), 8–16.
Subj 51 ▪ 24.2 58

20347 MAM F P1 G9.4 1949–1972
Kindermann, Charles Robert, 1939–.
Perception and source of information: Their effect on contraceptive use in Taiwan.
Ann Arbor: University Microfilms (Publ. 69-18,036), 1969. 162 p. (Doctoral dissertation in Sociology, U. of Michigan)
Subj 24.2 51

20348 NIC P P2 G1.2 1949–1972
[La Dany, Ladislao] ———, 1914–.
'Limitation of births and Ma Yin-ch'u.'
CNA 313 (26 Feb. 1960), 1–7.
Subj 51 64 ▪ 58

20349 CSU S P1 G1.2 1949–1972
Lal, Amrit.
'Fertility management and concern with overpopulation in Mainland China.'
Eugenics q. 11, 3 (Sept. 1964), 170–174.
Subj 51 64

20350 CSU O P2 G9.5 1949–1972
Lam, Peggy.
'East Asia review, 1971: Hong Kong.'
SFP 3, 7 (July 1972), 125–127.
Subj 51

20351 CSU F P2 G9.4 1949–1972
Lee, T. M. (Li Tung-ming), and L. P. Chow (Chou Lien-pin), 1924–.
'Mailing to the recent postpartum women to encourage loop acceptance.'
CMJ-T 16, 3 (Sept. 1969), 206–214.
Subj 51 ▪ 24.2 50

20352 CSU F P2 G9.4 1949–1972
Lee T. Y.
'East Asia review, 1971: Taiwan.'
SFP 3, 7 (July 1972), 145–150.
Subj 51 ▪ 24.2 58

20353 NNC O P3 G5.1 1949–1972
Lin Chiao-chih.
'A doctor looks around her.'
WC 1959, 5, 24–27.
Subj 51 56 ▪ 52

20354 CSU S P1 G9.4 1949–1972
Liu, P. T., and L. P. Chow (Chou Lien-pin), 1924–.
'A stochastic approach to the estimation of the prevalence of IUD: Example of Taiwan, Republic of China.'
Demography 8, 3 (Aug. 1971), 341–352.
Subj 51

20355 CSU F P8 G9.4 1949–1972
Lu, Laura P., H. C. Chen, and L. P. Chow (Chou Lien-pin), 1924–.
'An experimental study of the effect of group meetings on the acceptance of family planning in Taiwan.'
J. of social issues 23, 4 (Oct. 1967), 171–177.
Subj 48 51

20356 NIC P P2 G1.2 1949–1972
Mauldin, Wayman Parker.
'Fertility control in Communist countries: Policy and practice.' In *Population trends in eastern Europe, the USSR, and Mainland China*, compiled by Milbank Memorial Fund. [Selective entry]
New York: Milbank Memorial Fund, 1960, 179–223.
Subj 51

20357 CSU S P2 G9.0 1949–1972
Mauldin, Wayman Parker, Dorothy Nortman, and Frederick F- Stephan.
'Retention of IUDs: An international comparison.'
SFP 18 (Apr. 1967), 1–12.
Subj 51 ▪ 58

20358 CSU F P2 G9.5 1949–1972
Mitchell, Robert Edward, 1930–.
'Hong Kong: An evaluation of field workers and decision making in family planning programs.'
SFP 30 (May 1968), 7–12.
Subj 51 ▪ 41

20359 CSU F P3 G9.5 1949–1972
Mitchell, Robert Edward, 1930–.
'Husband-wife relations and family-planning practices in urban Hong Kong.'
J. of marriage and the family 34, 1 (Feb. 1972), 139–146.
Subj 41 51 ▪ 26

20360 MAM F P3 G9.4 1949–1972
Mohapatra, Partha Sarathi, 1933–.
The effect of age at marriage and birth control practices on fertility differentials in Taiwan.
Ann Arbor: University Microfilms (Publ. 67-8313), 1967. 249 p. (Doctoral dissertation in Sociology, U. of Michigan, 1966)
Subj 41 51 58 ▪ 26

20361 NIC P P2 G1.2 1949–1972
Orleans, Leo A-, 1924–.
'Birth control: Reversal or postponement?'
CQ 3 (July–Sept. 1960), 59–73.
Subj 12.1 51 58 ▪ 41 70

20362 CSU P P2 G1.2 1949–1972
Orleans, Leo A-, 1924–.
'Evidence from Chinese medical journals on current population policy.'
CQ 40 (Oct.–Dec. 1969), 137–146.
Subj 18 51 ▪ 12.1 56 58

20363 NNC P P2 G1.2 1949–1972
Orleans, Leo A-, 1924–.
'A new birth control campaign?'
CQ 12 (Oct.–Dec. 1962), 207–210.
Subj 41 51 ▪ 11 58

20364 CSU F P3 G9.4 1949–1972
Peng, J. Y., L. P. Chow (Chou Lien-pin), 1924–, and Leslie Corsa.
'Medical correlates of termination of use of intrauterine contraceptive devices in Taichung.'
International j. of fertility 15, 2 (June 1970), 120–126. [Reprinted as 'Taiwan: Medical correlates of termination of use of intrauterine devices.' *SFP* 60 (Dec. 1970), 24–27.]
Subj 51 56 ▪ 50

20365 CSU P P2 G1.2 1949–1972
Sarker, Subhash Chandra.
'Population planning in China.'
Population review 2, 2 (July 1958), 49–58.
Subj 11 51 ▪ 12.1

20366 CSU P P1 G9.4 1949–1972
Schultz, T- Paul.
Evaluation of population policies: A framework for analysis and its application to Taiwan's family planning program.
Santa Monica, Calif.: RAND Corp., 1971. 18, 82 p. (RAND reports, R-643-AID)
Subj 51 58 ▪ 50

20367 MAM F P3 G9.4 1949–1972
Srikantan, Kodaganallur Sivaswamy, 1930–.
Effects of neighborhood and individual factors on family planning in Taichung.
Ann Arbor: University Microfilms (Publ. 68-7734), 1968. 238 p. (Doctoral dissertation in Sociology, U. of Michigan, 1967)
Subj 20 51 ▪ 61

20368 MAM F P2 G9.4 1949–1972
Sun, T. H. (Sun Te-hsiung), 1930–.
Socio-structural analysis of fertility differentials in Taiwan.
Ann Arbor: University Microfilms (Publ. 69-12,249), 1969. 273 p. (Doctoral dissertation in Sociology, U. of Michigan, 1968)
Subj 26 41 51 58 ▪ 17 24.2 28 45 50

20369 CSU U P2 G9.4 1949–1972
Taeuber, Irene Barnes, 1906–.
Review of *Family planning in Taiwan: An experiment in social change*, by Ronald Freedman, Yuzuru John Takeshita et al.
EDCC 19, 4 (July 1971), 682–688.
Subj 51 ▪ 58

20370 MCH P P2 G1.2 1949–1972
Taeuber, Irene Barnes, 1906–.
'Population policies in Communist China.'
Population index 22, 4 (Oct. 1956), 261–274.
Subj 11 51 ▪ 18 41 58 64

20371 CSU P P2 G1.2 1949–1972
Taeuber, Irene Barnes, 1906–, and Leo A- Orleans, 1924–.
'National programs: Achievements and problems, Mainland China.' In *Family planning and population programs: A review of world developments*, by Bernard Berelson et al. [Selective entry]
Chicago: U. of Chicago Press, 1966, 31–54. [Proceedings of International Conference on Family Planning Programs, Geneva, 1965]
Subj 11 51 56 ▪ 11.4 12.1 54 58

20372 CSU F P3 G9.4 1949–1972
Takeshita, Yuzuru John, 1926–.
'Lessons learned from family planning studies in Taiwan and Korea.' In *Family planning and population programs: A review of world developments*, edited by Bernard Berelson et al. [Selective entry]
Chicago: U. of Chicago Press, 1966, 691–710. [Proceedings of International Conference on Family Planning Programs, Geneva, 1965]
Subj 51 ▪ 70

20373 MCY P P1 G1.2 1949–1972
Tien, H. Yuan (T'ien Hsin-yüan), 1926–.
'"Birth control in Communist China".' [With a reply by Leo A- Orleans]
CQ 14 (Apr.–June 1963), 218–229.
Subj 51 ▪ 11

20374 CSU P P1 G1.2 1949–1972
Tien, H. Yuan (T'ien Hsin-yüan), 1926–.
'Birth control in Mainland China: Ideology and politics.'
MMFQ 41, 3 (July 1963), 269–290.
Subj 32 51 ▪ 12.1 14 64

20375 MCH P P2 G1.2 1949–1972
Tien, H. Yuan (T'ien Hsin-yüan), 1926–.
'Induced abortion and population control in Mainland China.'
Marriage and family living 25, 1 (Feb. 1963), 35–43.
Subj 51 ▪ 11 58

20376 MCH P P1 G1.2 1949–1972
Tien, H. Yuan (T'ien Hsin-yüan), 1926–.
'Sterilization, oral contraception, and population control in China.'
PS 18, 3 (Mar. 1965), 215–235.
Subj 51 ▪ 12.1 41

20377 CSU F P8 G9.4 1949–1972
Tuan, Chi-hsien.
'Reproductive histories of Chinese women in rural Taiwan.'
PS 12, 1 (July 1958), 40–50.
Subj 51 58 ▪ 41 47

20378 CSU F P3 G9.4 1949–1972
Wang, Yi-chang.
'The medical practitioners' points of view on birth control: A survey of selected practitioners on OBG, non-OBG and midwives in Taipei City.'
CMJ-T 16, 1 (Mar. 1969), 43–54.
Subj 51 56 ▪ 41

52 Infancy and Childhood

嬰兒及童年　　嬰児及び幼年

1644-1911

20379 NNC O P4 G7.1 1842–1895
Bryson, Mary Isabella.
Child life in Chinese homes.
London: Religious Tract Society, 1885. 208 p.
Subj 41 51 52 53 54 55 ▪ 23 26 27 31 47 60 66

20380 MCH O P7 G4.2 1895–1911
Dols, Joseph, 1874–1938.
'L'enfance chez les Chinois de la province de Kan-Sou' (Childhood among the Chinese in Kansu).
Anthropos 3, 4 (Juli–Aug. 1908), 761–770.
Subj 51 52 ▪ 27 46 47 53 56

20381 NNM O P2 G5.1 1895–1911
Headland, Isaac Taylor, 1859–1942.
The Chinese boy and girl.
New York: Revell, 1901. 176 p.
Subj 52 62 ▪ 31 53 65

20382 NNC O P1 G1.2 1895–1911
Headland, Isaac Taylor, 1859–1942.
'Chinese children's games.'
JRAS-NCB new (2nd) series 37 (1906), 150–184.
Subj 31 52 62 ▪ 53 54 65

20383 CSU O P1 G1.2 1895–1911
Headland, Isaac Taylor, 1859–1942.
'Chinese nursery rhymes.'
CR 31, 1 (Jan. 1900), 1–10.
Subj 52 65 ▪ 53

20384 MCH O P3 G5.1 1895–1911
Korsakov, Vladimir Viktorovich, 1854–?
'Detskii mir v Kitae' (A child's world in China).
Vestnik Evropy 36, 3 (mart 1901), 217–226.
Subj 23 52

20385 NNC O P5 G9.0 1842–1895
Lee, Yan Phou (Li Yen-fu), 1861–?
When I was a boy in China.
Boston: Lothrop, 1903. 111 p.
Subj 41 52 54 55 ▪ 27 31 33 47 53

20386 CNY O P7 G9.0 1842–1895
Pritzsche, ———.
'Sitten und Gebräuche der Hakka-Chinesen' (Habits and customs of the Hakka Chinese).
Berichte der Rheinischen Missionsgesellschaft 1877, 8 (Aug.), 230–243.
Subj 50 52 ▪ 29 53

20387 NNC F P4 G1.5 1895–1911
Wood, Edith Elmer, 1871–1945.
'Notes on Oriental babies.'
AA new (2nd) series 5, 4 (Oct.–Dec. 1903), 659–666.
Subj 52

1644-1949

20388 NIC U P1 G1.3 1644–1928
Arlington, Lewis Charles, 1859–1942.
'The Chinese female names.'
CJ 1, 4 (July 1923), 316–325; 1, 5 (Sept. 1923), 454–462; 1, 6 (Nov. 1923), 561–571.
Subj 47 52 62

20389 NNC PO P3 G9.5 1842–1928
Haslewood, Hugh Lyttleton, 1886–.
Child slavery in Hong Kong.
London: Sheldon Press, 1930. 130 p.
Subj 41 47 52 ▪ 22 22.1 22.2 38

20390 CSH S P3 G1.2 1895–1949
Nadezhdin, A- G-.
'Detskii trud v tekstil'noi promyshlennosti Kitaia' (Child labor in the Chinese textile industry). [With English abstract]

VM 1931, 4, 97–103.
SUBJ 16.4 52 ▪ 14.4 24.4

20391 NNC P P1 G1.2 –1928
Werner, Edward Theodore Chalmers, 1864–1954.
'A note on head-flattening.' In *Autumn leaves: An autobiography with a sheaf of papers, sociological and sinological, philosophical and metaphysical*, by E. T. C. Werner. [Selective entry]
Shanghai: Kelly and Walsh, 1928, 119–123.
SUBJ 52 ▪ 65

1911-1949

20392 NNM S P3 G6.1 1911–1928
'Child labour in China.'
CMJ 38, 11 (Nov. 1924), 923–929.
SUBJ 26.4 52 ▪ 24.4 28

20393 NIC O P2 G1.3 1928–1949
Chen Chi-yi.
'Three years of child welfare work.'
CQ-S 5, 4 (Autumn 1940), 688–694.
SUBJ 18 52 ▪ 38

20394 MCH P P3 G6.1 1911–1928
Finch, Percival.
'Battle against child labor in China.'
Current history and forum 22, 5 (Aug. 1925), 759–765.
SUBJ 26.4 52 ▪ 28

20395 NNC F P3 G5.1 1911–1949
Grimm, Irmgard.
'Chinesische Kinderreime' (Chinese children's rhymes).
Sinica 8, 4 (Juli 1933), 138–144.
SUBJ 52 65 ▪ 53

20396 NIC O P8 G8.1 1928–1949
Highbaugh, Irma, 1891–.
Family life in West China.
New York: Agricultural Missions, 1948. 11, 240 p.
SUBJ 52 53 ▪ 27 28

20397 MCY F P7 G5.2 1928–1949
Serruys, Paul Leo Mary, 1912–.
'Children's riddles and ditties from the south of Tatung [Ta-t'ung *hsien*] (Shansi).'
FS 4 (1945), 213–290.
SUBJ 52 65

20398 CBU PO P1 G1.2 1928–1949
Siao King-fang (Hsiao Chin-fang), 1902–.
'La situation actuelle des enfants réfugiés en Chine' (The present situation of refugee children in China). In *Report of the 1st International Congress for the Education of Exceptional Children, Genève, 24–26 VII (July) 1939*, edited by Secretariat, International Gesellschaft für Heilpädagogik. [Sole entry]
Zurich: Leemann, 1940, 133–136.
SUBJ 18 38 52

20399 CSU F P7 G4.4 1928–1949
Trippner, Josef.
'Die "*shao nien*" – Lieder in Ch'inghai' (Children's songs in Tsinghai). In *Ethnographische Beiträge aus der Ch'inghai Provinz (China)* (Ethnographic reports from Tsinghai). [Selective entry]
Peking [i.e., Tokyo]: Catholic U. of Peking, Museum of Oriental Ethnology, 1952, 264–305. (MOE, Folklore studies supplements, 1)
SUBJ 52 65

20400 CSH O P8 G5.3 1928–1949
Wang Hsueh-li.
'The children's league in the Anti-Japanese War.'
WC 1961, 3, 40–41.
SUBJ 52

1911-1972
(including 1644-1972)

20401 ELB P P1 G1.0 –1972
Bauer, Wolfgang, 1930–.
Der chinesische Personenname: Die Bildungsgesetze und hauptsächlichsten Bedeutungsinhalte von Ming, Tzu und Hsiao-Ming (Chinese personal names: The rules for constructing and primary signification of given names, courtesy names, and childhood names).
Wiesbaden: Harrassowitz, 1959. 406 p. (Universität Bonn, Asiatische Forschungen, 4) (Doctoral dissertation, Philosophische Fakultät, Universität München)
SUBJ 50 52 62 ▪ 23 44 65

20402 DLC S P2 G1.2 1911–1972
Klepikov, Vladimir Zakharovich, 1932–.
'Pionerskaia organizatsiia Kitaia' (China's Young Pioneers).
Sovetskaia pedagogika 26, 10 (oktiabr' 1962), 100–108.
SUBJ 37 52 ▪ 34.1

20403 NIC P P2 G1.2 1928–1972
Li Shen.
'Maternity and child welfare in people's communes.'
CMJ 78, 6 (June 1959), 576–579.
SUBJ 28 51 52 56 ▪ 47 58

1949-1972

20404 NIC F P3 G9.5 1949–1972
Chang, K. S. F., et al.
'Height and weight of southern Chinese children.'
American j. of physical anthropology new (2nd) series 21, 4 (Dec. 1963), 479–509.
SUBJ 52

20405 MCH O P1 G1.2 1949–1972
Chu Fu-t'ang.
'Progress of pediatric work in China in the past eight years.'
CMJ 83, 12 (Dec. 1964), 795–802.
SUBJ 52 56 ▪ 18 51

20406 CSH O P3 G5.1 1949–1972
Huang Ying.
'A nursery run well, and thriftily too.'
WC 1961, 3, 11–13.
SUBJ 52

20407 NIC P P2 G1.2 1949–1972
[La Dany, Ladislao] ———, 1914–.
'From cradle to manhood.'
CNA 332 (15 July 1960), 1–5.
SUBJ 27 52 ▪ 41 47

20408 HKU F P4 G9.5 1949–1972
Low, Weng-djin (Liu Yung-cheng).
Physical growth and development of southern Chinese children in Hong Kong.
Unpublished doctoral dissertation, Dept. of Anatomy, U. of Hong Kong, 1969. 367 p.
SUBJ 52

20409 CSU O P2 G9.5 1949–1972
Nye, Patricia.
'The special needs of young children in shantytowns in Hong Kong.' In *Urban development: Its implications for social welfare*. [Sole entry]
New York: Columbia U. Press, 1967, 358–364.
SUBJ 28 52 55 ▪ 21 21.1 21.2

20410 NNC F P7 G2.3 1949–1972
Shen-yang shih wei sheng fang i chan (Mukden Health and Epidemic Control Station) *with* Shen-yang i hsüeh yüan (Mukden Medical School). Wei sheng chiao yen tsu (Study Group for Public Health Education).
'Report on a survey of day nurseries and kindergartens in the Liao-shen people's commune.' Tr. of 'Liao-shen jen min kung she t'o erh so yu erh yüan tiao ch'a pao kao' (Report on child-care centers and kindergartens in Liao-shan commune [Shenyang municipality, Liaoning]); *Jen min pao chien* 1959, 7 (July), 668–669. In *Organization of health services under Communist China's commune system (2)*, mimeo., compiled by U.S. Joint Publications Research Service. [Selective entry]
Washington, D.C.: JPRS, 27 July 1960, 1–7. (JPRS 5104; MC 14,449/1960)
SUBJ 27 52 ▪ 28 55

20411 CSU O P2 G1.3 1949–1972
Sidel, Ruth, 1933–.
Woman and child care in China.
New York: Hill and Wang, 1972. 14, 207 p.
SUBJ 20 47 51 52 ▪ 41 46 53 55 56

20412 CSH F P1 G9.4 1949–1972
Su, Chien-Wen.
'A study of concept formation in children.'
Psychology and education (Taipei) 1 (Apr. 1967), 85–95.
SUBJ 52

20413 CSH O P3 G5.1 1949–1972
Yen Wen-ching.
'A home for the homeless.'
WC 1957, 3, 1–5.
SUBJ 52

53 SOCIALIZATION

教養化育　　社会化

20414 MAM P P1 G1.2 –1911
Chiao, Chien (Ch'iao Chien), 1935–.
The continuation of tradition: Navaho and Chinese models.
Ann Arbor: University Microfilms (Publ. 69-20,970), 1969. 11, 216 p. (Doctoral dissertation in Anthropology, Cornell U.)
SUBJ 16.1 17 53 64 ▪ 12 48 63

20415 CSU F P1 G9.4 1949–1972
Chu, Cheng-ping (Ch'u Cheng-p'ing).
'A study of the effects of maternal employment for the preschool children in Taiwan.'

APT 12 (Mar. 1970), 80–100.
Subj 52 53

20416 CSU U P2 G2.2 1949–1972
Chung-kuo kung ch'an tang. Chi-lin sheng wei yüan hui. (Chinese Communist Party. Kirin Provincial Committee).
'Labor-study program can be carried out in the elementary schools.' Tr. of 'Hsiao hsüeh yeh neng shih hsing ch'in kung chien hsüeh' (The dilligent-work and assiduous-study program can be implemented in elementary schools); *Hung ch'i* 1958, 11 (1 Nov.), 31–33. In *Selected translations from 'Hung-chi' (Red flag), November–December 1958*, mimeo., compiled by U.S. Joint Publications Research Service. [Sole entry]
Washington, D.C.: JPRS, 17 May 1961, 105–109. (JPRS 7836; MC 11,159/1961)
Subj 27 53 ▪ 24.4 28 52

20417 DLC O P2 G5.0 1928–1972
Jabłoński, Witold.
'Z chińskiego notatnika' (From a Chinese notebook).
Wiedza i życie 7 (1958), 400–407.
Subj 53 55 ▪ 30 60

20418 DLC P P1 G1.1 1644–1842
Kahn, Harold Lionel, 1930–.
'The education of a prince: The emperor learns his roles.' In *Approaches to modern Chinese history*, edited by Albert Feuerwerker et al. [Selective entry]
Berkeley, Los Angeles: U. of California Press, 1967, 15–44. [Reprinted in *Readings in modern Chinese history*, edited by Immanuel C. Y. Hsü (Hsü Chung-yüeh). (Selective entry.) New York: Oxford U. Press, 1971, 38–57.]
Subj 12 53 60 61 ▪ 12.1 27 64

20419 CSU O P3 G9.5 1949–1972
Kvan, Erik, 1917–.
'Problems of bilingual milieu in Hong Kong: Strain of the two-language system.' In *Hong Kong: A society in transition*, edited by Ian C- Jarvie and Joseph Agassi. [Analytic entry]
New York: Praeger, 1969, 327–343.
Subj 27 53

20420 NIC O P1 G1.3 1895–1911
Monroe, Harriet.
'The training of Chinese children.'
Century magazine 83, 5 (Mar. 1912), 643–652.
Subj 52 53

20421 MAM F P2 G9.4 1949–1972
Olsen, Nancy Johnston, 1939–.
The effect of household composition on the child rearing practices of Taiwanese families.
Ann Arbor: University Microfilms (Publ. 71-22,993), 1971. 204 p. (Doctoral dissertation in Human Development and Family Studies, Cornell U.)
Subj 26 41 53 ▪ 50 52 61

20422 NIC F P8 G9.4 1949–1972
Olsen, Nancy Johnston, 1939–.
Family structure, child training, and achievement motivation: The Chinese case.
Unpublished masters thesis in Child Development and Family Relations, Cornell U., 1967. 101 p.
Subj 41 47 53 ▪ 52 61

20423 CSU F P8 G9.4 1949–1972
Olsen, Nancy Johnston, 1939–.
'Sex differences in child training antecedents of achievement motivation among Chinese children.'
J. of social psychology 83, 2 (Apr. 1971), 303–304. [For fuller treatment, see entry 20422.]
Subj 47 53

20424 CSU F P3 G9.4 1949–1972
Olsen, Stephen Milton, 1940–.
'The inculcation of economic values in Taipei business families.' In *Economic organization in Chinese society*, edited by William Earl Willmott. [Selective entry]
Stanford: Stanford U. Press, 1972, 261–295.
Subj 34.2 53 54

20425 CSU F P3 G9.4 1949–1972
Schak, David C-.
'Determinants of children's play patterns in a Chinese city [Taipei]: The interplay of space and values.'
Urban anthropology 1, 2 (Fall 1972), 195–204.
Subj 52 53 ▪ 26 27 48

20426 CSU FP P2 G9.5 1949–1972
Wilson, Richard Whittingham, 1933–.
Learning to be Chinese: The political socialization of children in Taiwan.
Cambridge: M.I.T. Press, 1970. 203 p. (Revision of *Childhood political socialization on Taiwan*, doctoral dissertation in Political Science, Princeton U., 1967)
Subj 27 53 63 64 ▪ 30 41 61

20427 CSU F P2 G9.4 1949–1972
Wolf, Margery, 1933–.
'Child training and the Chinese family.' In *Family and kinship in Chinese society*, edited by Maurice Freedman. [Selective entry]
Stanford: Stanford U. Press, 1970, 37–62.
Subj 41 52 53 ▪ 44 47 50

20428 CSU O P3 G9.5 1928–1972
Wong Shau-lam.
'Social change and parent-child relations in Hong Kong.' In *Families in East and West: Socialization process and kinship ties*, edited by Reuben Hill and René König. [Selective entry]
The Hague: Mouton, 1970, 167–174.
Subj 41 53 ▪ 27

54 Adolescence and Youth

青春期及青年　　青春期及び青年

1644-1911

20429 CSU O P3 G1.3 1895–1911
Tsao, Y. S. (Ts'ao Yün-hsiang), 1881–.
'The relation of the returned students to the Chinese revolution.' In *Recent developments in China*, edited by George Hubbard Blakeslee. [Selective entry]
New York: G. E. Stechert, 1913, 162–175.
Subj 32.2 54

1644-1949

20430 DLC P P2 G1.2 1842–1928
Dalin, Sergei Alekseevich.
Molodezh' v revoliutsionnom dvizhenii Kitaia (Youth in the Chinese revolutionary movement).
Moscow: Novaia Moskva, 1925. 143 p.
Subj 17 32.2 54 ▪ 16.3 16.4 19 41 47 66

20431 NIC P P4 G1.2 1842–1949
Kiang Wen-han (Chiang Wen-han), 1908–.
The Chinese student movement.
New York: King's Crown Press, 1948. 10, 176 p. (Doctoral dissertation in History, Columbia U.)
Subj 19 54 ▪ 16.1 17 32 32.2 62 64 66

20432 CSU P P2 G1.2 1895–1949
Lang, Olga.
Pa Chin and his writings: Chinese youth between the two revolutions.
Cambridge: Harvard U. Press, 1967. 402 p. (Harvard East Asian series, 28) (Revision of *Writer Pa Chin and his time: Chinese youth of the transitional period*, doctoral dissertation in Philosophy, Columbia U., 1962)
Subj 19 41 54 59 60 ▪ 16.1 32.2 61 64 66

20433 CSH P P3 G1.2 1842–1928
Mou Jun-sun.
'Tradition and revolution: The clash of old and new in China.' In *Youth in China*, edited by Edward Stuart Kirby. [Analytic entry]
Hong Kong: Dragonfly Books, 1965, 1–29.
Subj 32.2 54 ▪ 19 66

1911-1949

20434 CSH O P2 G1.2 1911–1928
'Christian work among boys in China.' In *The Christian occupation of China*, edited by Milton Theobald Stauffer. [Selective entry]
Shanghai: China Continuation Committee, 1922, 369–370.
Subj 54 ▪ 26.4 31 33

20435 CSU O P3 G5.1 1928–1949
Barnett, Arthur Doak, 1921–.
'Student disaffection' [report to Institute of Current World Affairs, March 1948]. In *China on the eve of Communist takeover*, by A. D. Barnett. [Selective entry]
New York: Praeger, 1963, 40–51.
Subj 54 ▪ 12.1 18 66

20436 FPN O P3 G5.1 1928–1949
Bonningue, A-.
Etudiants chinois: silhouettes et tendances (Chinese students: Profiles and orientations).
Paris: Ed. Alsatia, 1948. 129 p.
Subj 33 41 47 54 60 62 ▪ 12.2 15 17 26.1 28 61 66

20437 MCH O P3 G1.2 1928–1949
Borg, Dorothy, 1902–.
'Students in Kuomintang China.'
FES 17, 1 (14 Jan. 1948), 4–7.
Subj 17 54 ▪ 32 32.1

20438 MCH F P1 G1.2 1911–1928
Bullock, Amasa Archibald.
'What do students in Christian schools really think?'
CR 54, 1 (Jan. 1923), 9–14.
Subj 17 54 ▪ 60

20439 NIC P P4 G1.2 1928–1949
Chin, Ai-li Sung (Ch'en Shen Ai-li), 1919–.
'Some problems of Chinese youth in transition.'
AJS 54, 1 (July 1948), 1–9.
Subj 41 47 54 63

20440 DLC O P3 G5.1 1928–1949
Freyn, Hubert, 1897–.
Prelude to war: The Chinese student rebellion of 1935–36.
Shanghai: China Journal, 1939. 122 p.
Subj 17 32 54 ▪ 19

20441 NNC P P2 G1.2 1928–1949
Iliushechkin, Vasilii Pavlovich, 1915–.
'Studencheskoe dvizhenie 9 dekabria 1935 g. v Kitae' (The Chinese student movement of 9 December 1935).
KSIV 7 (1952), 3–19.
Subj 12 32.2 54 66 ▪ 12.1 16 17

20442 CSH P P3 G1.2 1911–1949
Israel, John Warren, 1935–.
The Chinese student movement, 1927–1937: A bibliographical essay based on the resources of the Hoover Institution.
Stanford: Hoover Institution on War, Revolution and Peace, 1959. 29 p. (HI bibliographical series, 6) [Reprinted—Ann Arbor: University Microfilms, n.d. 29 p.]
Subj 54 72 ▪ 32

20443 DLC P P1 G1.2 1928–1949
Israel, John Warren, 1935–.
'Kuomintang policy and student politics, 1927–1937.' In *Approaches to modern Chinese history*, edited by Albert Feuerwerker et al. [Selective entry]
Berkeley, Los Angeles: U. of California Press, 1967, 289–303.
Subj 32 32.1 54 ▪ 17 37

20444 MCH P P2 G1.2 1928–1949
Israel, John Warren, 1935–.
Student nationalism in China, 1927–1937.
Stanford: Stanford U. Press, 1966. 253 p. (Revision of *The Chinese student movement, 1927–1937*, doctoral dissertation in History, Harvard U., 1963)
Subj 32 32.2 37 54 64 ▪ 12 15 17 32.1 66

20445 NNC O P2 G1.1 1928–1949
Kiang Wen-han (Chiang Wen-han), 1908–.
'Student life in war-time China.'
CQ-S 5, 1 (Winter 1939), 47–55.
Subj 17 54 ▪ 18

20446 NNC P P1 G1.2 1928–1949
Linfo (Ling Fo).
'Molodye zashchitniki Kitaia' (China's young defenders).
Internatsional molodezhi 1938, 10 (oktiabr'), 47–50.
Subj 54 66 ▪ 15 32.2

20447 ICU F P3 G8.1 1928–1949
Liu, Sao-dsi.
Extra-class activities of pupils in a junior high school in China.
Unpublished masters thesis in Education, U. of Chicago, 1930. 81 p.
Subj 54 ▪ 17 31

20448 CSH P P3 G5.1 1911–1928
Lubot, Eugene Stephen, 1942–.
'Ts'ai Yuan-p'ei and the May Fourth incident: One liberal's attitude toward student activism.'
CC 13, 2 (June 1972), 73–82.
Subj 19 54 64

20449 CSU P P4 G1.3 1928–1949
Lutz, Jessie Gregory, 1925–.
'The Chinese student movement of 1945–1949.'
JAS 31, 1 (Nov. 1971), 89–110.
Subj 54 66 ▪ 16.1 32 32.2 50

20450 CSU P P2 G1.3 1928–1949
Lutz, Jessie Gregory, 1925–.
'December 9, 1935: Student nationalism and the Chinese Christian colleges.'
JAS 26, 4 (Aug. 1967), 627–648.
Subj 26.1 32 54 66 ▪ 17 36.1 37

20451 MCH O P7 G9.3 1928–1949
MacInnis, Donald Earl, 1920–.
'China in transition.'
Amerasia 5, 10 (Dec. 1941), 456–463.
Subj 28 54 ▪ 21.2 27 37 55 60

20452 NNC P P1 G1.2 1911–1928
[Nassunov, Nikolai?] N. N.
'U istokov kitaiskogo Komsomola' (Origins of the Young Communist League of China).
Internatsional molodezhi 1929, 9 (sentiabr'), 60–65.
Subj 32.2 54 ▪ 66

20453 CSU P P3 G1.2 1928–1949
Pepper, Suzanne, 1939–.
'The student movement and the Chinese civil war, 1945–49.'
CQ 48 (Oct.–Dec. 1971), 698–735.
Subj 22.2 54 ▪ 32.2 66

20454 NNC P P1 G1.2 1911–1949
Pringsheim, Klaus Hubert Charl, 1923–.
'The functions of the Chinese Communist youth leagues (1920–1949).'
CQ 12 (Oct.–Dec. 1962), 75–91.
Subj 32.2 54 ▪ 32 52

20455 DLC U P2 G1.2 1911–1928
Sediakin, Semen M-.
Kratkii ocherk istorii kitaiskogo komsomola (Brief historical sketch of the Young Communist League of China).
Moscow: Molodaia gvardiia, 1929. 128 p.
Subj 14.4 16.3 32.2 54 ▪ 16.4 18 36.3 47 55 56

20456 WSU O P3 G8.1 1928–1949
Sewell, William Gawan.
China through a college window.
New York: Friendship Press, 1938. 183 p.
Subj 17 54 66 ▪ 47 48

20457 NNC O P2 G1.2 1911–1928
Shumiatskii, Boris.
'Iz istorii komsomola i kompartii v Kitae: pamiati odnogo iz organizatorov komsomola i kompartii Kitaia tovarishcha Chzhan T'a-laia' (History of the Young Communist League and Communist Party of China: In memory of Comrade Chang T'ai-lai, one of the organizers).
Revoliutsionnyi Vostok 1928, 4/5, 194–230.
Subj 32.2 54 ▪ 36.4 64

20458 MCH O P3 G5.1 1928–1949
[Snow, Helen Foster] Nym Wales, pseud., 1907–.
Notes on the Chinese student movement, 1935–1936.
Madison, Conn.: The author, 1959. 201 p. (Historical notes on China, 2)
Subj 17 32.2 54 ▪ 26.1 32.1 37 66

20459 CSU O P2 G1.3 1928–1949
Tao, Frank (T'ao Ch'i-hsiang).
'Student life in war-time China.'
Asia and the Americas 44, 11 (Nov. 1944), 493–496.
Subj 17 54

20460 CSU O P3 G5.1 1928–1949
Timperley, Harold John, 1898–.
'The North China Federation of Students.'
School and society 43, 1098 (11 Jan. 1936), 67–68.
Subj 32.1 54

20461 NNC P P1 G1.2 1928–1949
Van, Amber Lurraine.
The development of indigenous leadership for youth work in China.
Unpublished masters thesis, Columbia U. [Union Theological Seminary], 1946. 79 p.
Subj 38 54 ▪ 16.1 31 33

20462 MCH FP P2 G1.2 1911–1928
Wang, Tsi C. (Wang Chü-chang), 1899–.
The youth movement in China.
New York: New Republic, 1927. 15, 245 p. (Doctoral dissertation in Sociology, U. of Chicago, 1925)
Subj 19 22.2 54 64 ▪ 16.1 17 33 38 41 47 62 66

20463 NNC F P3 G1.1 1911–1928
Webster, James Benjamin, 1879–1929.
Interests of Chinese students.
Shanghai: U. of Shanghai, Bureau of Publications, 1932. 166 p. (Studies in education and psychology, 1)
Subj 17 54 61 62 63 ▪ 11.4 14.6 16 23 31 41 45 47 48 66

20464 CSH P P3 G5.1 1911–1928
Wieger, Léon, 1856–1933.
'Grève des étudiants de l'Ecole Pei-yang à Tientsin: historique' (Historical account of the student strike at Peiyang University, Tientsin). In *Chine moderne, Tome V, nationalisme, xénophobie, antichristianisme* (Modern China, Vol. 5, Nationalism, xenophobia, and antichristianism), 2nd ed., by L. Wieger. [Selective entry]
Hsien-hsien, Hopei: Impr. de Sienhsien, 1934, 119–122.
Subj 12 17 54 ▪ 12.1

20465 ICU P P3 G1.2 1911–1928
Williston, Frank Goodman, 1899–.
The Chinese student movement.
Unpublished masters thesis in History, U. of Chicago, 1926. 149 p.
Subj 19 32.2 54 ▪ 17 32.1

20466 MCH U P4 G1.2 1911–1928
Wong-Quincey, J. (Wang Wen-hsien), 1886–.
'Some reflections on the Chinese student movement.'
CSM 18, 7 (May 1923), 5–17.
SUBJ 16.1 32.2 54 ▪ 12 32.1 63

20467 NNC P P3 G5.1 1911–1928
Woo, Doreen Hsiao-ying.
Chinese student attitudes in Peking, 1925: A case study.
Unpublished masters thesis in History, Columbia U., 1970. 99 p. [Certificate essay, East Asian Institute]
SUBJ 17 54 ▪ 63

20468 MCH U P2 G1.2 1911–1928
Wu, Y. T. (Wu Yao-tsung), 1893?–.
'Modern student life.'
CR 54, 8 (Aug. 1923), 473–478.
SUBJ 31 54 ▪ 17 28 55

20469 MCH F P4 G1.2 1911–1928
Wu, Y. T. (Wu Yao-tsung), 1893?–.
'Student life problems.'
CR 55, 8 (Aug. 1923), 478–484.
SUBJ 33 54 61

20470 NNC U P4 G1.2 1928–1949
Zhdanov, M- G-.
'Komsomol Kitaia v boiakh mezhdu trudom i kapitalom' (The Young Communist League of China in the battles between labor and capital).
Internatsional molodezhi 1930, 9 (sentiabr'), 29–33.
SUBJ 32.2 54 ▪ 36.4

1911-1972
(including 1644-1972)

20471 CSU S P1 G1.2 1895–1972
Israel, John Warren, 1935–.
'Reflections on the modern Chinese student movement.'
Daedalus 97, 1 (Winter 1968), 229–253.
SUBJ 16.1 54 ▪ 17 32.2

20472 CSU P P3 G1.2 1911–1972
Larkin, Bruce Drummond, 1936–.
'China.' In *Students and politics in developing nations*, edited by Donald K- Emmerson. [Sole entry]
New York: Praeger, 1968, 146–179.
SUBJ 17 32.2 54 ▪ 19 25 32 32.1 41 64

20473 NNC P P2 G1.2 1911–1972
Mitbreit, Boris Abramovich.
Ocherki istorii Kommunisticheskogo soiuza molodezhi Kitaia (Outline history of the Young Communist League of China).
Moscow: Izd-vo vost. lit-ry, 1961. 189 p.
SUBJ 32 54 ▪ 16.1 19 32.1 32.2 64 66

20474 CSU P P2 G1.2 1928–1972
Ravenholt, Albert, 1919–.
'The Red Guards.'
AUFS-EAS 14, 3 (Apr. 1967), 1–23.
SUBJ 14 32 54 ▪ 25 35 50

20475 CSH O P4 G8.1 1928–1972
Sewell, William Gawan.
I stayed in China.
London: Allen and Unwin, 1966. 221 p.
SUBJ 17 22.1 28 54 61 66 ▪ 14.6 22 26.1 32.1 35 41 47 48 60

1949-1972

20476 CSH P P2 G1.2 1949–1972
Albrecht, Dietmar, 1941–.
'Die roten Garden' (The Red Guards).
Aus Politik und Zeitgeschichte 1969, 46 (15 Nov.), 1–46. [Supplement to *Das Parlament*]
SUBJ 15 16 19 32 54 64 ▪ 12 12.1 17 32.1

20477 CSU O P2 G5.1 1949–1972
Alley, Rewi, 1897–.
'Factories and students in Peking.'
EH 8, 6 (1969), 16–28.
SUBJ 24.4 54 ▪ 26.4

20478 CSU F P2 G1.3 1949–1972
Bennett, Gordon Anderson, 1940–, and Ronald Nicholas Montaperto, 1939–.
Red Guard: The political biography of Dai Hsiao-ai.
Garden City, N.Y.: Doubleday, 1971. 20, 267 p.
SUBJ 16 54 59 ▪ 17 22.2 32 35 55 64

20479 CSH O P3 G5.1 1949–1972
Billeter, Jean-François.
'Chine: de la révolte des étudients à la Révolution culturelle' (From student revolt to Cultural Revolution in China).
Croissance des jeunes nations 79 (juil.–août 1968), 19–26.
SUBJ 17 26 54 ▪ 12 15 22.1 25 32

20480 CSH P P2 G1.2 1949–1972
Chang, Anthony Sherman, and Wen Shih, pseud.
'The political role of youth.' In *Youth in China*, edited by Edward Stuart Kirby. [Analytic entry]
Hong Kong: Dragonfly Books, 1965, 113–162.
SUBJ 12.1 54 64 ▪ 16 41

20481 MCH P P1 G1.2 1949–1972
Chang Ching-wen.
'An analysis of Peiping's program of cultivating revolutionary successors.'
IS 1, 3 (Dec. 1964), 21–26.
SUBJ 12.1 54 ▪ 64

20482 MCH U P2 G1.2 1949–1972
Chang Ching-wen.
'Movement of teen-agers and children on the Chinese Mainland.'
IS 2, 3 (Dec. 1965), 17–24.
SUBJ 52 54 ▪ 32.1

20483 CSH P P1 G1.2 1949–1972
Chang Ching-wen.
'The youth problem on the Chinese Mainland.'
IS 2, 7 (Apr. 1966), 21–29.
SUBJ 54

20484 NNC P P2 G1.2 1949–1972
[Chao Ts'ung] Chao Chung, 1927–, and Yang I-fan.
Students in Mainland China, mimeo.
Hong Kong: Union Research Institute, 1956. 139 p. (Communist China problem research series, EC13)
SUBJ 17 54 64 ▪ 11.4 12.1 30 31 32.1

20485 CSU O P4 G1.2 1949–1972
Chen, Peter, 1934–.
'Betrachtungen zu den Rotgardisten in der Kulturrevolution' (The Red Guards in the Cultural Revolution).
Internationales Asien Forum 1, 2 (Apr. 1970), 271–279.
SUBJ 19 54 ▪ 16 25 32 64

20486 CSH P P2 G1.2 1949–1972
Ch'in T'i and Li Meng-ch'uan. [Authors sequential rather than joint: Ch'in T'i for 1962, 1963, and 1966; Li Meng-ch'uan for 1964 and 1965.]
'Youth movements.' Tr. from *Tsu kuo chou k'an* 547 (1 July 1963) *and* from *Tsu kuo* 3–38 (June 1964 – May 1967) [recurring annual feature article]. In *Communist China, 1962–1966*, edited by Union Research Institute.
Hong Kong: Union Research Institute. Issued annually, 1963–1967, average ca. 20 p.
SUBJ 54 ▪ 32.1 37

20487 CSU P P2 G1.2 1949–1972
Current Scene Editor.
'The revival of the Communist Youth League.'
CS 8, 5 (1 Mar. 1970), 1–7.
SUBJ 54

20488 CSH P P2 G1.2 1949–1972
Current Scene Editor.
'Youth to the countryside, and back again.'
CS 5, 16 (2 Oct. 1967), 1–8.
SUBJ 21.2 54 ▪ 12.1 17 22.2 61

20489 CSU O P3 G1.3 1949–1972
Dellinger, Dave.
'Report from revolutionary China.'
Liberation 11, 10 (Jan. 1967), 4–10.
SUBJ 19 54 ▪ 14.2 15 17 32

20490 CSU P P2 G1.2 1949–1972
Funnell, Victor Cecil, 1926–.
'The Chinese Communist youth movement, 1949–1966.'
CQ 42 (Apr.–June 1970), 105–130.
SUBJ 16.1 32.1 54 ▪ 14.2 16 17 32

20491 CSU P P2 G1.2 1949–1972
Gardner, John, 1939–.
'Educated youth and urban-rural inequalities, 1958–66.' In *The city in Communist China*, edited by John Wilson Lewis. [Analytic entry]
Stanford: Stanford U. Press, 1971, 235–286.
SUBJ 17 21.2 54 ▪ 16.1 16.3 64

20492 CSU P P3 G1.2 1949–1972
Gigon, Fernand, 1908–.
Vie et mort de la révolution culturelle (The life and death of the Cultural Revolution).
Paris: Flammarion, 1969. 290 p.
SUBJ 12 14.2 16 17 22 54 ▪ 12.1 15 19 32 61 64

20493 CSH P P3 G9.2 1949–1972
Gittings, John, 1938–.
'A Red Guard repents.'
FEER 65, 28 (10 July 1969), 123–126.
SUBJ 54 ▪ 15

20494 CSH P P4 G7.2 1949–1972
Gittings, John, 1938–.
'Student power in China.'
FEER 60, 26 (27 June 1968), 648–650.
SUBJ 32.2 54 ▪ 15 64

20495 CSH P P2 G1.2 1949–1972
Goodstadt, Leo F-.
'Prospects and frustrations of young people.' In *Youth in China*, edited by Edward Stuart Kirby. [Analytic entry]
Hong Kong: Dragonfly Books, 1965, 209–226.
SUBJ 12.1 18 54 ▪ 17 41

20496 DLC PO P2 G1.2 1949–1972
Granqvist, Hans, 1924–.
Kinas Röda Garde.
Stockholm: Bonnier, 1967. 153 p.
The Red Guard: A report on Mao's revolution. Tr. by Erik J- Friis.
New York: Praeger, 1967. 159 p.
SUBJ 12.1 15 17 19 54 64 ▪ 14 16 16.1 22 22.1 32

20497 CSU F P2 G5.1 1949–1972
Hinton, William H-, 1919–.
'Hundred day war: The Cultural Revolution at Tsinghua University [Peking].'
Monthly review 24 (July 1972), 1–288. [Special issue]
SUBJ 17 26 32.1 54 ▪ 22 26.1 26.4 64

20498 MCH P P2 G1.2 1949–1972
Hsiang Nai-kuang.
'A look at Peiping's "Red Guards".'
CCA 3, 6 (Dec. 1966), 33–39.
SUBJ 54 ▪ 18

20499 MCH P P2 G1.2 1949–1972
Huang, Lucy Jen (Huang Jen-hua), 1920–.
'The problem child and delinquent youth in the Communist Chinese family.'
Marriage and family living 25, 4 (Nov. 1963), 459–465.
SUBJ 22.2 54 ▪ 12.1 52 53

20500 MCY P P1 G1.2 1949–1972
[Huang, Lucy Jen] Lucy Jen Huang Hickrod (Huang Jen-hua), 1920–, and George Alan Hickrod, 1930–.
'The Communist Chinese and the American adolescent subcultures.'
CQ 22 (Apr.–June 1965), 171–180.
SUBJ 54 ▪ 61 63

20501 CSH P P2 G1.2 1949–1972
Israel, John Warren, 1935–.
'The Red Guards in historical perspective: Continuity and change in the Chinese youth movement.'
CQ 30 (Apr.–June 1967), 1–32.
SUBJ 17 32 54 ▪ 16 32.1 61

20502 DLC O P2 G1.2 1949–1972
Kapitsa, Mikhail Stepanovich.
Molodezh' velikogo Kitaia (The youth of great China).
Moscow: Molodaia gvardiia, 1953. 160 p.
SUBJ 14.1 14.4 16.4 18 54 ▪ 14.2 16.3 17 31 32.2 66

20503 CSU O P2 G1.3 1949–1972
Ken Ling, pseud.
The revenge of heaven: Journal of a young Chinese, edited by Ivan Daniel London, Miriam London, and Ta-ling Lee (Li Ta-ling).
New York: Putnam, 1972. 413 p.
SUBJ 19 22.1 25 26 54 59 ▪ 17 22 22.2 23 26.3 26.4 28 41 46 47

20504 CSH P P2 G1.2 1949–1972
Kirby, Edward Stuart, 1909–.
'Conclusions: Young China today and tomorrow.' In *Youth in China*, edited by E. S. Kirby. [Analytic entry]
Hong Kong: Dragonfly Books, 1965, 227–251.
SUBJ 16 18 54 ▪ 47

20505 CSH PO P3 G5.1 1949–1972
Kosiukov, IUrii L-.
Pekinskii dnevnik (Peking diary).
Moscow: Molodaia gvardiia, 1968. 80 p.
SUBJ 12 22.1 26 32 54 66 ▪ 15 24.4 28 55 64

20506 NNC P P1 G1.2 1949–1972
Kraus, Richard Curt, 1944–.
The People's Liberation Army and the Chinese Communist Youth League, 1949–1966.
Unpublished masters thesis in Public Law and Government, Columbia U., 1969. 116 p. [Certificate essay, East Asian Institute]
SUBJ 15 54 ▪ 32.1 35

20507 NNC P P3 G5.1 1949–1972
Kwong, Peter.
The Red Guards in Peking, December, 1965 – March, 1967: The dialectic of participation and control.
Unpublished masters thesis in Political Science, Columbia U., 1970. 124 p. [Certificate essay, East Asian Institute]
SUBJ 32.1 54 ▪ 17 35

20508 CSH F P2 G1.2 1949–1972
[La Dany, Ladislao] ———, 1914–.
'An essay on the typology of youths in China.'
CNA 808 (17 July 1970), 1–7.
SUBJ 54 59 ▪ 61

20509 CSH P P3 G1.3 1949–1972
[La Dany, Ladislao] ———, 1914–.
'The fighting youth: The history of Red Guards.'
CNA 682 (27 Oct. 1967), 1–7.
SUBJ 25 54

20510 CSH P P2 G1.2 1949–1972
[La Dany, Ladislao] ———, 1914–.
'Labour day and youth day.'
CNA 881 (19 May 1972), 1–7.
SUBJ 11.2 54

20511 NIC P P2 G1.2 1949–1972
[La Dany, Ladislao] ———, 1914–.
'Model youngsters.'
CNA 264 (13 Feb. 1959), 1–7.
SUBJ 54 ▪ 17 59

20512 CSH P P2 G1.2 1949–1972
[La Dany, Ladislao] ———, 1914–.
'Redundant youths.'
CNA 835 (19 Mar. 1971), 1–7.
SUBJ 21.2 54

20513 MCH P P3 G1.3 1949–1972
[La Dany, Ladislao] ———, 1914–.
'The storm.'
CNA 195 (6 Sept. 1957), 1–7.
SUBJ 17 54 ▪ 32.1

20514 CSH P P2 G1.2 1949–1972
[La Dany, Ladislao] ———, 1914–.
'What has happened to the Youth Corps.'
CNA 633 (21 Oct. 1966), 1–7; 634 (28 Oct. 1966), 1–7.
SUBJ 32.1 54 ▪ 15 17 32

20515 NIC P P2 G1.2 1949–1972
[La Dany, Ladislao] ———, 1914–.
'Youth and the classics.'
CNA 233 (20 June 1958), 1–7.
SUBJ 17 54 62

20516 CSH P P4 G9.5 1949–1972
Lethbridge, Henry James, 1923–.
'Delinquency: Fact or myth?'
FEER 52, 7 (19 May 1966), 345–347.
SUBJ 22.2 54 ▪ 22.1

20517 NIC F P4 G9.4 1949–1972
Lin, Tsung-yi (Lin Tsung-i), 1920–.
'Tai-pau [t'ai-pao] and Liu-mang: Two types of delinquent youths in Chinese society.'
British j. of delinquency 8, 4 (Apr. 1958), 244–256. [Reprinted as 'Two types of delinquent youths in Chinese society.' In *Culture and mental health*, edited by Marvin Kaufmann Opler. (Selective entry.) New York: Macmillan, 1959, 257–271.]
SUBJ 22.2 54 ▪ 48 50

20518 CSH F P2 G1.2 1949–1972
London, Ivan Daniel, 1913–, and Miriam London, 1923–.
'Attitudes of Mainland youth toward traditional Chinese customs and beliefs.'
CC 11, 4 (Dec. 1970), 46–55.
SUBJ 25 54 65 ▪ 61

20519 CSU F P3 G9.5 1949–1972
Meade, Robert D-.
'Leadership studies of Chinese and Chinese-Americans.'
J. of cross-cultural psychology 1, 4 (Dec. 1970), 325–332.
SUBJ 47 54 61 ▪ 53

20520 ELB P P2 G1.2 1949–1972
Milsky, Constantin.
'Révolution culturelle et jeunesse chinoise' (The Cultural Revolution and Chinese youth).
Etudes 7e série 329 (nov. 1968), 554–571.
SUBJ 32.1 54 ▪ 12 17 18 32 35 41 64 66

20521 NNC P P2 G1.2 1949–1972
Mitbreit, Boris Abramovich.
'Novo-demokraticheskii soiuz molodezhi Kitaia: aktivnyi pomoshchnik Kommunisticheskoi partii v bor'be za zavershenie demokraticheskikh preobrazovanii i postroenie osnov sotsializma' (The New Democratic Youth League of China: An active helper of the Communist Party in the struggle to complete the democratic reorganization and build a base for socialism).
UZIV 11 (1955), 263–302.
SUBJ 15 16.4 17 32 54 60 ▪ 14.1 16.3 34.1 36.4 37 61 64 66

20522 CSU FP P3 G9.5 1949–1972
Mitchell, Robert Edward, 1930–.
Pupil, parent and school: A Hong Kong study.
Taipei: Orient Cultural Service, 1972. 24, 400 p. (Asian Folklore and Social Life monographs, 26)
SUBJ 17 26 41 54 60 61 ▪ 21.4 22.2 31 47 50

20523 CSH P P2 G1.2 1949–1972
Mits, F- T-.
'Mao's revolutionary successors. Part 1, The wanderers.'
CS 5, 13 (15 Aug. 1967), 1–7.
SUBJ 54 61 ▪ 12 12.1 22.2

20524 CSU FP P3 G9.2 1949–1972
Montaperto, Ronald Nicholas, 1939–.
'From revolutionary successors to revolutionaries: Chinese students in the early stages of the Cultural Revolution.' In *Elites in the People's Republic of China*, edited by Robert Anthony Scalapino. [Analytic entry]
Seattle: U. of Washington Press, 1972, 575–605. (Social Science Research Council, Studies in Chinese government and politics, 3)
SUBJ 32 54 ▪ 26 26.1

20525 CSH F P2 G9.2 1949–1972
Raddock, David.
'Innocents in limbo.'
FEER 76, 18 (29 Apr. 1972), 18–20. [Reprinted as 'Innocents in limbo: China's youth recall.' *CS* 10, 6 (10 June 1972), 12–16.]
SUBJ 12.1 54 ▪ 61

20526 MAU P P2 G1.2 1949–1972
Singer, Martin.
Educated youth and the Cultural Revolution in China.
Ann Arbor: U. of Michigan, Center for Chinese Studies, 1971. 114 p. (Michigan papers in Chinese studies, 10)
SUBJ 17 54 ▪ 25 32.1 35 64

20527 MCH O P3 G5.1 1949–1972
[Soo, Chin-yee] Sansan, pseud., 1945–.
Eighth moon: The true story of a young girl's life in Communist China, edited by Betty Lord.
New York: Harper and Row, 1964. 213 p.
SUBJ 17 22.1 28 54 ▪ 41 47 55 59 63

20528 NIC P P1 G1.2 1949–1972
Stefansson, Nils.
'Youth and the family.' In *A decade under Mao Tse-tung*, by Sripati Chandrasekhar, Harold Clendenin Hinton, Lea E- Williams, et al. [Selective entry]
Hong Kong: Green Pagoda Press, 1959, 51–57. [Reprinted in *A decade of Mao's China: A survey of life and thought in China today*, by S. Chandrasekhar, H. C. Hinton, L. E. Williams, et al. (Selective entry.) Bombay: Perennial Press, 1960, 50–57.]
SUBJ 54 ▪ 17

20529 WSU F P3 G9.5 1949–1972
Stoodley, Bartlett H-, 1907–.
'Christian preference and Western cultural influence among Chinese college youth in Hong Kong.'
CCJ 5, 1 (Nov. 1965), 21–30.
SUBJ 33 54 ▪ 41 64 66

20530 NNC P P1 G1.2 1949–1972
Tan Chang-hung (T'an Ch'ang-hung) and T'an Hsin-wen. [Authors sequential rather than joint: Tan Chang-hung for 1955; T'an Hsin-wen for 1956–1958.]
'Youth League and youth movements' [title varies slightly]. Tr. of '1955–1958 nien Chung kung ti t'uan wu yü ch'ing yün' (The Youth League and youth movements in Communist China, 1955–1958); *Tsu kuo chou k'an* 159–334/335 (16 Jan. 1956 – 8 June 1959) [recurring annual feature article]. In *Communist China, 1955–1958*, edited by Union Research Institute.
Hong Kong: Union Research Institute. Issued annually, 1956–1959, average ca. 10 p.
SUBJ 54 ▪ 17 32 32.1 37 63

20531 CSU PO P3 G1.2 1949–1972
Vandermeersch, Léon.
'La révolte de la jeunesse dans la révolution culturelle chinoise' (The revolt of the young in China's Cultural Revolution).
Esprit nouvelle (2e) série 37, 381 (mai 1969), 764–775.
SUBJ 16 17 54 ▪ 15 19

20532 MCH P P2 G1.2 1949–1972
Wang Hsiao-lan.
'Brutalities and future of the "Red Guards".'
CCA 3, 6 (Dec. 1966), 52–63.
SUBJ 22.2 54 ▪ 12.1

20533 CSU P P2 G1.2 1949–1972
Wang Hsueh-wen (Wang Hsüeh-wen).
'Maoist rectification of the Young Communist League.'
IS 7, 2 (Nov. 1970), 29–38.
SUBJ 32.1 54 ▪ 12 64

20534 CSU P P4 G1.2 1949–1972
Wilson, Richard Whittingham, 1933–, and Amy Auerbacher Wilson, 1934–.
'The Red Guards and the world student movement.'
CQ 42 (Apr.–June 1970), 88–104.
SUBJ 54 ▪ 53 61

55 LIVING ROUTINES

生活起居　　日常生活

1644-1911

20535 NNC O P3 G6.3 1842–1895
'Ob ustroistve lednikov v Severnoi Amerike i Kitae' (The structure of ice-houses in North America and China).
Trudy Vol'nago ekonomicheskago obshchestva 1849, 2, 42–47.
SUBJ 55 ▪ 24.3 62

20536 CSU O P3 G5.1 –1842
'Serres chinoises' (Chinese greenhouses). In *Mémoires concernant l'histoire, les sciences, les arts, les moeurs, les usages, etc. des Chinois* (Reports on the history, learning, arts, manners, customs, etc. of the Chinese), by Missionnaires de Pékin. [Sole entry]
Paris: Chez Nyon, 1778, vol. 3, 423–437.
SUBJ 55 ▪ 24.1

20537 CSU P P2 G8.1 1842–1911
Adshead, Samuel Adrian Miles, 1932–.
'The opium trade in Szechwan, 1881 to 1911.'
J. of South-east Asian history 7, 2 (Sept. 1966), 93–99.
SUBJ 55 ▪ 14.3 24.1 24.5

20538 CBU S P3 G1.5 1842–1895
Allen, Nathan, 1813–1889.
The opium trade: Including a sketch of its history, extent, effects, etc., as carried on in India and China, 2nd ed.
Lowell, Mass.: James P. Walker, 1853. 80 p.
SUBJ 24.3 55 ▪ 14.3

20539 CBU O P4 G1.4 1842–1895
Arendt, Carl, 1838–1902.
Bilder aus dem Häuslichen- und Familienleben der Chinesen (Sketches of Chinese home and family life).
Berlin: H. Reuther, 1888. 48 p.
SUBJ 41 55 ▪ 16 65

20540 FPN O P2 G1.1 1842–1895
Armand, Adolphe, 1818–?
Lettres de l'expédition de Chine et Cochinchine (Letters from the expedition to China and Cochin China), 2nd ed.
Paris: Rozier, 1864. 368 p.
SUBJ 24.3 55 56 64 66 ▪ 12.2 13 14.1 14.2 16 16.1 21.3 47 51 57

20541 MCH O P2 G1.4 1842–1895
Baret, L-.
'Un hivernage dans la Chine du Nord (1890–91)' (A winter's layover in North China, 1890–1891).
Archives de la médecine navale 58 (1892), 241–257, 342–358, 401–423.
SUBJ 55 ▪ 21.3 24.2 28 41 51 57

20542 MCH O P2 G9.3 1895–1911
Behayhel, G-.
'Eine Reise in der chinesischen Provinz Fukien' (A journey in Fukien).
Globus 94, 16 (22 Okt. 1908), 245–252; 94, 17 (29 Okt. 1908), 265–269; 94, 18 (5 Nov. 1908), 277–283.
SUBJ 24.2 55 ▪ 21.1 21.2 23 24.1 28 57

20543 MCH O P1 G1.1 1895–1911
Betteloni, Vittorio.
'Modo di mangiare e di vestire dei Cinesi' (The Chinese way of eating and dressing).
Bollettino della Società geografica italiana 4a serie 11, 1 (gennaio 1910), 38–63.
SUBJ 55 ▪ 16

20544 MCH F P2 G1.3 1895–1911
Boerschmann, Ernst, 1873–1949.
'Architektur- und Kulturstudien in China' (Architectural and cultural studies in China).
ZE 42, 3/4 (1910), 390–426.
SUBJ 13 33 55 62 ▪ 16.1 23 43 57 60

20545 NNC FP P2 G1.2 –1911
Boerschmann, Ernst, 1873–1949.
'Baukunst und Landschaft in China' (Architecture and landscape in China).
Z. der Gesellschaft für Erdkunde zu Berlin 1912, 5, 321–365.
SUBJ 21.3 23 43 55 62 ▪ 13 16.1 57

20546 DLC F P2 G1.2 1895–1911
Boerschmann, Ernst, 1873–1949.
Baukunst und Landschaft in China: Eine Reise durch zwölf Provinzen (Architecture and landscape in China: A journey through twelve provinces).
Berlin: Wasmuth, 1923. 25, 288 p.

Picturesque China: Architecture and landscape. A journey through twelve provinces. Tr. by Louis Hamilton.

New York: Brentano's, 1923. 26, 288 p.
Subj 55 62 ▪ 21.3 57

20547 NNC FP P2 G1.3 –1911
Boerschmann, Ernst, 1873–1949.
'Eisen- und Bronzepagoden in China' (Iron and bronze pagodas in China).
Jahrbuch der asiatischen Kunst 1 (1924), 223–235.
Subj 33 55 ▪ 62

20548 NIC S P2 G1.3 –1911
Boyd, Andrew Charles Hugh.
Chinese architecture and town planning, 1500 B.C. – A.D. 1911.
Chicago: U. of Chicago Press, 1962. 166 p.
Subj 21.3 29 55 ▪ 24.2 33 40 57 62 64

20549 ELB O P2 G1.4 1644–1842
Brand, Adam.
Beschreibung der chinesischen Reise, welche vermittelst einer Zaaris. Gesandschaft durch dero Ambassadeur Herrn Isbrand Ao. 1693, 94 und 95. von Moscau über Gross-Ustiga, Siberien, Dauren und durch die Mongolische Tartarey verrichtet worden (A description of the trip to China made by ambassador [Evert] Ysbrants [Ides], in the name of the tsar, in the years 1693, 1694, and 1695 from Moscow via Gross Ustiga, Siberia, Dauri, and Manchuria).
Hamburg: Schiller, 1698. 215, 16 p.
A journal of the embassy from their majesties John and Peter Alexievitz, emperors of Muscovy, etc. over land into China, through the provinces of Ustiugha, Siberia, Dauri, and the Great Tartary, to Peking, the capital city of the Chinese empire, by Everard Isbrand, their ambassador in the years 1693, 1694, and 1695.
London: Brown, 1698. 134 p.
Subj 12 14.2 55 ▪ 21.1 57

20550 CSU O P3 G8.2 1895–1911
Brenier, Henri, 1867–?
'La capitale du Yun-nan: séjour à Yun-nan fou' (The capital of Yunnan: A sojourn in Yün-nan-fu [Kunming]). In *La Mission lyonnaise d'exploration commerciale en Chine, 1895–1897, première partie, récits des voyages* (The Lyons Trade Mission to China, 1895–1897, Part 1, Travel accounts), compiled by Chambre de commerce de Lyon. [Selective entry]
Lyons: Rey, 1898, 52–66 [s.p.].
Subj 22 55 ▪ 24.3 26.1

20551 CSU O P3 G8.1 1895–1911
Brenier, Henri, 1867–?
'La métropole commerciale du Se-tchouan: séjour à Tchoung-king' (Szechwan's commercial metropolis: A sojourn in Chungking). In *La Mission lyonnaise d'exploration commerciale en Chine, 1895–1897, première partie, récits des voyages* (The Lyons Trade Mission to China, 1895–1897, Part 1, Travel accounts), compiled by Chambre de commerce de Lyon. [Selective entry]
Lyons: Rey, 1898, 136–153 [s.p.].
Subj 21.3 55 ▪ 21 24.2 24.4 66

20552 MSE O P3 G9.5 1842–1895
Brereton, William H-.
The truth about opium: Being the substance of three lectures delivered at St. James' Hall.
London: Allen, 1882. 275 p.
Subj 55 66

20553 CSU O P5 G1.2 1895–1911
Budberg, Roger Baron.
'Einige hygienische Prinzipien im Volksleben der Chinesen' (Principles of hygiene in Chinese life).
Deutsche medizinische Wochenschrift 37, 27 (11 Sept. 1911), 1707–1708.
Subj 55 56 ▪ 65

20554 NNC P P1 G1.2 1644–1911
Cammann, Schuyler, 1912–.
'Origins of the court and official robes of the Ch'ing dynasty.'
Artibus Asiae 12, 3 (1949), 189–201.
Subj 55 ▪ 12 16.1

20555 MCH O P3 G9.2 1644–1842
Chambers, William, 1726–1796.
Designs of Chinese buildings, furniture, dresses, machines and utensils.
London: The author, 1757. 19 p.
Subj 55 ▪ 66

20556 CSU O P2 G1.2 1842–1895
China [Ch'ing]. [Tsung li ya men]. Hai kuan. (Tsungli Yamen. Imperial Maritime Customs).
Opium.
Shanghai: Tsung shui wu ssu shu, T'ung chi k'o, 1881. 80 p. (Hai kuan, Special series, 4)
Subj 55 ▪ 24.1 24.3 24.5

20557 CSU O P3 G5.1 1842–1895
Choutzé, T.
'Pékin et le nord de la Chine' (Peking and North China).
Tour du monde 16, 1 (1876), 305–368; 16, 2 (1876), 193–256.
Subj 12 24.3 28 33 55 ▪ 13 21.3 26.1 31 50 57

20558 CSH S P2 G1.2 1644–1842
Commeaux, Charles.
La vie quotidienne en Chine sous les Mandchous (Daily life in China in the Ch'ing period).
Paris: Hachette, 1970. 320 p.
Subj 15 16.1 17 41 55 ▪ 12 23 26.3 28 47 48

20559 NNC O P3 G5.1 1895–1911
Der Ling (Te-ling), ?–1944.
Two years in the Forbidden City.
New York: Moffat, Yard, 1911. 383 p. [Reprinted—New York: Dodd, Mead, 1924. 383 p.]
Subj 47 50 55 66 ▪ 12 13 16.1 17 31 61 62

20560 NIC P P1 G1.1 –1895
Edkins, Joseph, 1823–1905.
Opium: Historical note. Or, The poppy in China.
Shanghai: Presbyterian Mission Press, 1889. 50 p.
Subj 55 ▪ 12.1 14.3 18

20561 CSH O P2 G1.5 1895–1911
Endemann, Gottfried.
'Hausbau und Hausweihe bei den Hak-ka' (The construction and consecration of houses among the Hakkas).
OL 25, 30 (28 Juli 1911), 79–80.
Subj 55 ▪ 29 65

20562 MCH O P1 G1.2 1895–1911
Enjoy, Paul d', 1866–?
'Le repas chinois' (The Chinese meal).
R. scientifique 4e série 20, 25 (19 déc. 1903), 779–783.
Subj 55

20563 FPN S P2 G1.1 –1842
[Ferrario, Giulio] Jules Ferrario, 1767–1847.
'Costume ancien et moderne des Chinois' (Ancient and modern Chinese customs). In *Le costume ancien et moderne: ou, histoire du gouvernement, de la milice, de la religion, des arts, sciences et usages de tous les peuples anciens et modernes, tome 1, Asie* (Modern and ancient customs: or, History of the government, military, religion, arts, learning, and customs of all ancient and modern peoples, Vol. 1, Asia), by G. Ferrario. [Sole entry]
Milan: Impr. de l'éditeur, 1815, 35–366.
Subj 14 15 21.3 33 55 60 ▪ 11.3 12 13 16.1 17 23 41 47 57

20564 CSU O P8 G9.5 1842–1895
Ferrière Le Vayer, Théophile de.
'Ki-yng' (Ch'i Ying). In *Une ambassade française en Chine* (A French embassy in China), by T. de Ferrière Le Vayer. [Selective entry]
Paris: D'Amyot, 1854, 235–270.
Subj 55 66 ▪ 16.1 41

20565 ELO PO P2 G1.3 1842–1895
Fisher, George Battye.
Personal narrative of three years' service in China.
London: Richard Bentley, 1863. 420 p.
Subj 15 55 66 ▪ 21.3 24.2 28 48 51

20566 MCH PO P4 G1.2 1842–1911
Gaillard, Louis, 1850–1900.
'L'opium' (Opium).
Etudes 7e série 82, 5 (5 mars 1900), 652–668.
Subj 14.3 55 ▪ 12.1 32.2

20567 MCH O P3 G9.2 1895–1911
Gauducheau, *Dr.* ———.
'Observation sur l'hygiène des Chinois à Canton' (Observation on the hygiene of the Chinese in Canton).
AHMC 14, 1 (jan–mars 1911), 5–26.
Subj 55 ▪ 28 56

20568 NIC P P1 G1.3 –1911
Giles, Herbert Allen, 1845–1935.
'The opium edict and alcohol in China.'
Nineteenth century and after 62, 370 (Dec. 1907), 987–1002.
Subj 55 ▪ 65

20569 NIC O P3 G9.2 1842–1895
Gordon-Cumming, William Gordon, 1829–1908, and Constance Frederica Gordon-Cumming, 1837–1924.
'New Year's Day in Canton.'
Lusine hour 7 (Jan. 1880), 8–13.
Subj 23 55

20570 NNC O P1 G9.3 –1895
Groot, Jan Jakob Maria de, 1854–1921.
'The wedding garments of a Chinese woman.'

Internationales Archiv für Ethnographie 4 (1891), 182–184.
Subj 41 55 ▪ 57 65

20571 MCH O P1 G1.2 1644–1842
Grosier, Jean-Baptiste Gabriel Alexandre, 1743–1823.
'Vie privée des Chinois: leur caractère, leurs usages, moeurs des deux sexes' (The private life of the Chinese: Their character and customs, and the manners of both sexes). In *De la Chine: description générale de cet empire* (A comprehensive description of the Chinese empire), by J.-B. G. A. Grosier. [Selective entry]
Paris: Pillet, 1819, vol. 5, part 11, 270–465.
Subj 48 55 57 ▪ 17 41 47 61

20572 WSU F P1 G1.2 1842–1911
Hansen, Henny Harald, 1900–.
'Kinesiske dragter' (Chinese costumes).
Fra Nationalmuseets arbejdsmark 1947, 80–90.
Subj 48 55

20573 MBA O P7 G8.2 1895–1911
Hautefeuille, Léon.
'La Chine abordable' (Accessible China).
RI nouvelle (2e) série 16, 2 (fév. 1911), 101–110.
Subj 20 24.1 55 ▪ 26

20574 MSE PO P2 G8.1 –1911
Hutson, James.
Mythical and practical in Szechwan.
Shanghai: National Review Office, 1915. 70 p.
Subj 24 55 65 ▪ 66

20575 NNC O P4 G2.1 1895–1911
IAstremskii, F- P-.
'Ocherk byta i nravov severnoi Man'chzhurii' (Sketch of the life and customs of northern Manchuria).
Istoricheskii vestnik 25 (aprel' 1904), 223–234.
Subj 55 ▪ 56 57

20576 NNC PO P2 G1.1 1842–1895
Irisson, Maurice d', 1839–1898.
Journal d'un interprète en Chine (Diary of an interpreter in China), 8th ed.
Paris: Ollendorff, 1886. 442 p.
Subj 15 32.2 55 ▪ 14.3 21.3 41 47 66

20577 NNC O P3 G2.3 1895–1911
Ivanov, I- E-.
'Mukdenskii dvorets' (Mukden palace).
Istoricheskii vestnik 24 (iiun' 1903), 987–1006.
Subj 55 ▪ 21.3 62

20578 CSH O P2 G1.4 1842–1895
Jametel, Maurice Louis Marie, 1856–1889.
Pékin: souvenirs de l'Empire du milieu (Peking: Reminiscences of the Middle Kingdom).
Paris: Plon, 1887. 305 p.
Subj 15 21.3 24.2 33 55 ▪ 22.2 24.6 26.1 31 62

20579 DLC O P3 G5.1 1895–1911
Korsakov, Vladimir Viktorovich, 1854–?
V starom Pekine: ocherki iz zhizni v Kitae (In old Peking: Notes on Chinese life).
St. Petersburg: Trud, 1904. 360 p.
Subj 12 17 31 52 55 66 ▪ 13 21.3 23 24.2 26.1 26.2 28 57

20580 NNC O P4 G5.3 1895–1911
Krebs, Wilhelm.
'Eine chinesische Badeanstalt in Kiautschou' (A Chinese public bath in Kiaochow).
Globus 88, 2 (13 Juli 1905), 27–29.
Subj 55 ▪ 24.3

20581 NIC O P3 G6.2 1895–1911
Laufer, Berthold, 1874–1934.
'Anneaux nasaux en Chine' (Nasal rings in China).
TP 2e série 6, 3 (1905), 321–323.
Subj 55 ▪ 47 56 65

20582 NNC P P2 G1.2 –1842
Laufer, Berthold, 1874–1934.
Tobacco and its use in Asia.
Chicago: Field Museum of Natural History, 1924. 39 p. (FMNH, Anthropology leaflets, 18)
Subj 55 56 ▪ 12.2 14.1 14.3 24.4

20583 NIC O P2 G8.1 1895–1911
Legendre, Aimé François, 1867–?
Le Far-West chinois: deux années au Setchouen (China's 'Far West': Two years in Szechwan).
Paris: Plon-Nourrit, 1905. 16, 546 p.
Subj 26 28 55 ▪ 21 24 24.1 47 60 66

20584 MCH O P4 G8.1 1895–1911
Legendre, Jean.
'Etude d'hygiène chinoise: l'habitation' (A study of Chinese hygiene: Housing).
AHMC 10, 4 (oct.–déc. 1907), 615–620.
Subj 55 56 ▪ 21.3

20585 NIC O P2 G5.1 1842–1895
Martin, Charles Ernest, 1831–1897.
'Notes sur les principales fourrures qu'on trouve actuellement à Pékin et à Tien-tsin' (Notes on the most important furs now to be had in Peking and Tientsin).
TP 4, 3 (1893), 298–302.
Subj 24.3 26 55

20586 CSU PO P4 G1.2 –1842
Mayers, William Frederick, 1831–1878.
'The Buddhist rosary and its place in Chinese official costume.'
NQCJ 3, 2 (Feb. 1869), 26–28.
Subj 55 66

20587 CSU P P1 G1.2 –1842
Mayers, William Frederick, 1831–1878.
'The "button" in Chinese official uniform.'
NQCJ 3, 3 (Mar. 1869), 44.
Subj 55 ▪ 16.1

20588 MCH O P2 G1.1 1895–1911
Mazzolani, D- A-.
'La casa cinese' (The Chinese house).
Bollettino della Società geografica italiana 4a serie 10, 6 (giugno 1909), 634–645.
Subj 55 ▪ 15 16

20589 CSU P P2 G1.2 1644–1911
Messing, Otto.
'Gebrauch des Opiums bei den Chinesen' (Opium use among the Chinese).
ZE 38 (1906), 205–219.
Subj 55 ▪ 14.3

20590 IMA PO P3 G1.1 1842–1895
Nocentini, Lodovico, 1849–1910.
Nell'Asia Orientale (In East Asia).
Florence: Le Monnier, 1894. 312 p.
Subj 21.1 40 55 60 ▪ 12.2 14.2 22.2 24.4 26 28

20591 CSU PO P3 G1.1 –1911
Olpp, Gottlieb, 1872–?
'Die chronische Opiumvergiftung der Chinesen' (Chronic opium-poisoning among the Chinese).
Münchener medizinische Wochenschrift 53, 9 (27 Feb. 1906), 428–432; 53, 10 (6 März 1906), 474–477; 53, 11 (13 März 1906), 524–526.
Subj 18 22.2 55 56 ▪ 14.3 57

20592 GBF U P1 G1.1 1895–1911
Pfeiffer, M-.
'Fleischgenuss der Chinesen' (Consumption of meat among the Chinese).
Z. für Veterinärkunde 17 (1905), 488–493.
Subj 23 55 ▪ 29

20593 MCH O P1 G1.2 1895–1911
Regnault, Jules Emile Joseph, 1873–?
'L'hygiène chez les Chinois' (Hygiene among the Chinese).
R. scientifique 5e série 2, 19 (5 nov. 1904), 582–585; 2, 20 (12 nov. 1904), 617–620; 2, 21 (19 nov. 1904), 651–654.
Subj 55 56 ▪ 51 57

20594 FPN PO P3 G1.1 1644–1895
Rondot, Natalis, 1821–1900.
'Observations générales sur le commerce, la consommation et la convenance des étoffes de laine en Chine' (General observations on the trade in woolens and on their consumption in and suitability for China). In *Etude pratique des tissus de laine convenables pour la Chine, le Japon, la Cochinchine et l'archipel indien* (A practical study of woolens suitable for China, Japan, Cochin China, and the Indian archipelago), by N. Rondot. [Selective entry]
Paris: Guillaumin, 1847, 1–38.
Subj 55 ▪ 14.3 66

20595 FPN PO P3 G1.1 1644–1895
Rondot, Natalis, 1821–1900.
'Renseignements pratiques sur les étoffes de laine importées et consommées en Chine' (Practical information on the woolens brought into and consumed in China). In *Etude pratique des tissus de laine convenables pour la Chine, le Japon, la Cochinchine et l'archipel indien* (A practical study of woolens suitable for China, Japan, Cochin China, and the Indian archipelago), by N. Rondot. [Selective entry]
Paris: Guillaumin, 1847, 39–205.
Subj 24.4 55 ▪ 14.2 14.3 14.5

20596 NNC O P2 G2.0 1895–1911
Runich, Sergei.
'V Manchzhurii' (In Manchuria).
Istoricheskii vestnik 25 (fevral' 1904), 608–632; 25 (mart 1904), 952–982; 25 (aprel' 1904), 235–271.
Subj 14.2 55 66 ▪ 14 21.3 25 33 60

20597 MCH P P1 G1.2 –1895
Schlegel, Gustaaf, 1840–1903.
'The Chinese bean-curd and soy and the soya-bread of Mr. Lecerf.'
TP 5, 2 (mai 1894), 135–146.
Subj 55

20598 MCH O P3 G1.4 1842–1895
Skachkov, Konstantin Andreianovich, 1821–1883.
'Natsional'naia kitaiskaia kukhnia' (National Chinese cuisine).
Vestnik Evropy 18, 7 (iiul' 1883), 69–94.
Subj 55

20599 CSU S P3 G5.1 –1911
Soper, Alexander Coburn, 1904–.
'Architecture: Ming and Ch'ing.' In *The art and architecture of China*, 2nd ed., by Laurence Chalfont Stevens Sickman and A. C. Soper. [Sole entry]
Baltimore: Penguin, 1960, 283–288.
Subj 55

20600 MSE O P2 G6.0 1842–1895
Tarrant, William, pseud.
Ningpo to Shanghai in 1857.
Canton: Friend of China, 1862. 112 p.
Subj 21 55 66 ▪ 24.2

20601 NNC O P2 G4.3 1842–1895
Valikhanov, Chokan Chingisovich, 1837–1865.
'Zapadnyi krai Kitaiskoi imperii i gorod Kul'dzha: dnevnik puteshestviia 1856 goda' (The western territory of the Chinese empire and the city of Kuldja [i.e., I-ning]: Diary of a journey, 1856).
Druzhba narodov 1958, 12 (dekabr'), 160–183.
Subj 21.3 55 ▪ 12 24.3 26.2 47 62 71

20602 NNC O P3 G5.3 1895–1911
Völling, A-.
'Die Haartracht der Chinesen' (Chinese hair styles).
Anthropos 1, 1 (Jan.–Feb. 1906), 60–65.
Subj 55 ▪ 47 53 54

20603 CSU O P1 G1.3 1895–1911
von Poseck, Helena.
'How John Chinaman builds his house.'
EAM 4 (1905), 348–355.
Subj 55 62 ▪ 65

20604 CSU O P2 G1.3 –1911
Wada, Tsunashirō, 1856–1920.
'Die Schmuck- und Edelsteine bei den Chinesen' (Precious stones and jewelry among the Chinese).
MDG 10, 1 (1904), 1–16.
Subj 55 ▪ 16 62

20605 CSH O P2 G1.2 1842–1895
Williams, Samuel Wells, 1812–1884.
'Architecture, dress, and diet of the Chinese.' In *The Middle Kingdom: A survey of the geography, government, literature, social life, arts, and history of the Chinese empire and its inhabitants*, rev. and enl. ed., by S. W. Williams. [Selective entry]
New York: Scribner, 1883, vol. 1, 724–781. [Reprinted in *The Middle Kingdom: A survey of the geography, government, literature, social life, arts, and history of the Chinese empire and its inhabitants*, by S. W. Williams. (Selective entry.) Taipei: Ch'eng-wen, 1965, 724–781 (s.p.)]
Subj 55 ▪ 14.2 47

20606 NIC P P2 G1.3 –1911
Yang, Lien-sheng, 1914–.
'Schedules of work and rest in Imperial China.'
HJAS 18, 3/4 (Dec. 1955), 301–325. [Reprinted in *Studies in Chinese institutional history*, by Lien-sheng Yang. (Selective entry.) Cambridge: Harvard U. Press, 1961, 18–42. (Harvard-Yenching Institute studies, 20)]
Subj 12 16 55 ▪ 11.4 16.1 16.2 16.3

1644-1949

20607 NIC O P1 G1.3 –1928
Arlington, Lewis Charles, 1859–1942.
'Chinese women's coiffure.'
CJ 11, 1 (July 1929), 4–10; 11, 2 (Aug. 1929), 69–76; 11, 3 (Sept. 1929), 119–126.
Subj 47 55 ▪ 29

20608 NIC P P3 G5.1 –1928
Ayscough, Florence Wheelock, 1878–1942.
'Notes on the symbolism of the purple Forbidden City.'
JRAS-NCB new (2nd) series 52 (1921), 51–78.
Subj 55 62 ▪ 12 16.1 21.3 64

20609 NIC PO P1 G1.3 –1949
Blofeld, John Eaton Calthorpe, 1913–.
'Tea drinking in China.'
J. of the Royal Central Asian Society 32, 2 (May 1945), 193–198.
Subj 31 55

20610 MCH P P1 G1.2 –1928
Dols, Joseph, 1874–1938.
'Het bouwen in China' (Architecture in China).
China (Amsterdam) 5 (December 1930), 284–294.
Subj 55 ▪ 43 62

20611 DCK S P2 G1.2 1895–1949
Glahn, Else, 1921–.
'Boligen i Kina' (Housing in China).
Arkitekten 56 (1954), 149–155.
Subj 21.3 55 ▪ 43 62 65

20612 NNC FP P2 G1.3 –1949
Hoffmann, Alfred, 1911–.
'Vogel und Mensch in China' (Man and bird in China).
NDG 88 (Dez. 1960), 45–77.
Subj 55 65 ▪ 24.1 24.3 31 62

20613 CSU FP P3 G5.1 –1928
Kates, George Norbert, 1895–.
Chinese household furniture.
New York: Harper, 1948. 13, 125 p. [Reprinted—Ann Arbor: University Microfilms, n.d. 13, 125 p.]
Subj 55

20614 CBU P P2 G1.2 –1949
Kelling, Rudolf.
Das chinesische Wohnhaus (The Chinese dwelling).
Tokyo: Deutsche Gesellschaft für Natur- und Völkerkunde Ostasiens, 1935. 128 p. (MDG, Supplementband, 13)
Subj 55 62 65 ▪ 18 21.3 41 43 45

20615 CSU O P2 G1.1 –1949
Laloy, Louis, 1874–1944.
Miroir de la Chine (Images of China).
Paris: Desclée de Brouwer, 1933. 337 p.
Subj 12 41 55 64 ▪ 13 16.1 17 25 31 32.2 54

20616 CSU O P2 G1.2 1895–1928
McCormick, Frederick, 1870–1951.
'China's treasures.'
NG 23, 10 (Oct. 1912), 996–1040.
Subj 55 ▪ 14.2 57

20617 NNC FP P3 G5.1 –1949
Martin, Ilse.
'Über die Ho-pao und ihre Technik' (*Ho-pao* [belt pouches] and the techniques [of manufacturing them]).
FS 4 (1945), 291–318.
Subj 24.4 55 ▪ 65

20618 MCH PO P2 G1.2 –1928
Moule, Arthur Evans, 1836–1918.
The Chinese people: A handbook on China.
London: Society for Promoting Christian Knowledge, 1914. 14, 469 p.
Subj 14 14.2 29 50 55 ▪ 13 14.1 14.3 23 24.4 33 43 52 57 60

20619 CSU O P2 G1.1 1895–1928
Perzyński, Friedrich.
Von Chinas Göttern: Reisen in China (China's gods: Travels in China).
Munich: Wolff, 1920. 259 p.
Subj 33 55 62 ▪ 13 16.1 23 43 65

20620 CSU PO P2 G1.1 –1949
Ukers, William Harrison, 1873–1954.
All about tea.
New York: Tea and Coffee Trade Journal Co., 1935. 2 vols. 14, 559; 568 p.
Subj 14 14.3 24.3 55 ▪ 14.1 24.4 34.2

20621 CSH U P1 G4.0 1644–1949
Wang, Frances.
'Social values and patterns of living.' In *A regional handbook on Northwest China*, compiled by Far Eastern and Russian Institute, U. of Washington. [Selective entry]
New Haven: Human Relations Area Files, 1956, vol. 1, 231–276. (HRAF subcontractor's monographs, 59; Washington 5)
Subj 23 55 ▪ 41 57 60 66

20622 CSU P P2 G9.5 1842–1949
Wong, Luke S. K.
'Squatters in pre-war Hong Kong.'
JOS 8, 1 (Jan. 1970), 189–205.
Subj 21.3 55 ▪ 21 21.1 26.4 28 50 56

20623 NNC PO P2 G1.2 –1949
Yuan, L. Z.
Through a moon gate, rev. ed.
Shanghai: Shanghai Mercury Press, 1948. 162 p.
Subj 23 41 50 55 57 ▪ 31 43 46 47 52 56

1911-1949

20624 CSU O P2 G5.0 1928–1949
'Opium profits in North China.'
Asia (New York: American Asiatic Assn.) 40, 10 (Oct. 1940), 551–554.
Subj 24.3 55 ▪ 14.1

20625 NIC FP P1 G1.3 1911–1949
Adolph, William Henry.
'Aspects of nutrition and metabolism in China.'
Scientific monthly 29, 1 (July 1929), 39–43.
Subj 55 ▪ 56

20626 NNM F P8 G5.3 1911–1928
Adolph, William Henry.
'Diet studies in Shantung.'
CMJ 37, 12 (Dec. 1923), 1013–1019.
Subj 55 ▪ 28

20627 NIC F P2 G8.1 1911–1928
Agnew, Mary Caldwell, 1899–.
'Dietary studies in Szechwan.'
JWCBRS 3 (1926/29), 55–60.
SUBJ 28 55

20628 CSU O P3 G5.1 1911–1928
Anderson, Luther.
'The splendor of Chinese architecture.'
Asia (New York: American Asiatic Assn.) 17, 4 (June 1917), 278–285.
SUBJ 55

20629 NNC O P8 G6.1 1911–1949
Boehling, Hans Bruno Horst.
'Chinesische Stampfbauten' (Pisé [tamped-earth wall] construction in China).
Sinologica 3, 1 (1951), 16–22.
SUBJ 55 ▪ 26.3

20630 CSU O P2 G1.4 1911–1928
Clapp, Frederick G-.
'Along and across the Great Wall of China.'
GR 9, 4 (Apr. 1920), 221–249.
SUBJ 55

20631 NIC O P3 G5.1 1911–1928
Crane, Louise.
China in sign and symbol: A panorama of Chinese life, past and present.
London: Batsford; Shanghai: Kelly and Walsh, 1927. 20, 227 p.
SUBJ 24.3 26.2 55 62 ▪ 23 24.6 34.3 56 57 65

20632 CSU F P3 G5.0 1928–1949
Eder, Matthias, 1902–.
'Hausfrontdekorationen in Peking, mit parallelen aus Shantung und Nord-Honan' (Decorative house facades in Peking, compared to those in Shantung and northern Honan).
FS 2 (1943), 51–78.
SUBJ 29 55 65

20633 CSU O P2 G1.5 1911–1928
Fitch, Robert Ferris, 1873–?
'Life afloat in China.'
NG 51, 6 (June 1927), 665–686.
SUBJ 24.2 55 ▪ 41

20634 NIC O P8 G4.1 1911–1928
Fuller, Myron Leslie, 1873–?, and Frederick G- Clapp.
'Loess and rock dwellings of Shensi, China.'
GR 14, 2 (Apr. 1924), 215–226.
SUBJ 55

20635 CSH PO P2 G1.1 1911–1928
Giles, Herbert Allen, 1845–1935.
Some truths about opium.
Cambridge, Eng.: Heffer, 1923. 40 p.
SUBJ 55 56 ▪ 18 24.3 24.5

20636 NNC S P1 G1.2 1928–1949
Great Britain. Admiralty. Naval Intelligence Division. Geographical Section.
'Note on diet and nutrition.' In *China proper, Vol. 3, Economic geography, ports and communications*, compiled by the agency cited. [Selective entry]
London: His Majesty's Stationery Office, 1945, 575–577. (NID, Geographical handbook series, BR 530B)
SUBJ 55 ▪ 72

20637 NNM F P3 G5.1 1928–1949
Guy, R- A-.
'The diet of nursing mothers and young children in Peiping.'
CMJ 50, 4 (Apr. 1936), 434–442.
SUBJ 51 55 ▪ 28 52

20638 GMS O P7 G1.3 1928–1949
Helfritz, Hans, 1902–.
Ewigkeit und Wandel im Fernen Osten (Eternity and change in the Far East).
Berlin: Deutsche Verlagsgesellschaft, 1936. 111 p.
SUBJ 55

20639 NIC S P2 G1.2 1928–1949
Holmes, Maybel Marion, 1904–.
A source book of Chinese food habits.
Unpublished doctoral dissertation in Home Economics, Cornell U., 1948. 520 p.
SUBJ 10 23 41 55 ▪ 12.1 13 14 14.1 18 43 53 56 57 65

20640 MCH O P8 G1.2 1911–1928
Horning, Emma.
'Chinese village life.'
CR 61, 4 (Apr. 1930), 234–238.
SUBJ 55 ▪ 65

20641 CSH F P7 G2.0 1911–1928
IAshnov, Evgenii Evgen'evich.
'Pitanie krest'ian v severnoi Man'chzhurii' (Peasant nutrition in northern Manchuria).
EVM 1924, 45 (9 noiabria), 15–18.
SUBJ 24.1 26.3 55 ▪ 24.3 24.6

20642 NNC F P2 G1.3 1928–1949
Lamson, Herbert Day, 1899–.
'The problem of housing for workers in China.'
CEJ 11, 2 (Aug. 1932), 139–162.
SUBJ 26.4 28 55 ▪ 12.2 21.3 41 61

20643 CSU P P2 G1.1 1911–1949
Lee Hsien-wei (Li Hsien-wei).
The tobacco in China, mimeo.
Tientsin: Hautes études; Shanghai: Université l'Aurore, 1941. 59 p. (Institut des hautes études industrielles et commerciales, Faculty of Commerce, Economic studies, 1)
SUBJ 14.1 14.4 55 ▪ 14.3 16.4 24.3

20644 NNC F P3 G6.1 1928–1949
Lee, Wei-yung, Eric Reid, and Bernard Emms Read, 1887–1949.
Industrial health in Shanghai, China, III, Shanghai factory diets compared with those of institutional workers.
Shanghai: Chinese Medical Assn., 1936. 37 p. (CMA, Special report series, 7)
SUBJ 28 55 ▪ 26.2 26.4 56

20645 MCH F P7 G8.2 1911–1928
Legendre, Aimé François, 1867–?
'Voyage d'exploration au Yunnan central et septentrional: populations chinois et aborigènes' (An exploratory trip in central and northern Yunnan: Chinese and indigenous populations).
Bulletins et mémoires de la Société d'anthropologie de Paris 6e série 4 (1913), 447–457.
SUBJ 55 ▪ 21.3 24.1 28 56

20646 NNC S P2 G1.3 1911–1949
Lindstedt, H-.
'Food consumption habits in China.'
International review of agriculture 30, 8 (Aug. 1939), 363–389.
SUBJ 55

20647 CSU F P7 G1.2 1928–1949
Maynard, Leonard A-, and Wen-yuh Swen.
'Nutrition.' In *Land utilization in China: A study of 16,786 farms in 168 localities, and 32,256 farm families in twenty-two provinces in China, 1929–1933*, by John Lossing Buck. [Analytic entry]
Nanking: U. of Nanking, 1937, vol. 1, 400–436. [For Buck's work, see entry 12256.] [Reprinted in *Land utilization in China: A study of 16,786 farms in 168 localities, and 32,256 farm families in twenty-two provinces in China, 1929–1933*, by J. L. Buck. (Analytic entry.) New York: Paragon, 1964, vol. 1, 400–436.]
SUBJ 55 ▪ 14.1 18

20648 NIC F P2 G1.2 1911–1928
Milam, Ava Bertha, 1884–.
A study of the student homes of China.
New York: Columbia U., Teachers College, 1930. 98 p. (Teachers College, International Institute studies, 10)
SUBJ 41 55 ▪ 45 47 52 56

20649 CSU O P2 G1.3 1911–1928
Murphy, Henry Killam.
'An architectural renaissance in China.'
Asia (New York: American Asiatic Assn.) 28, 6 (June 1928), 468–475, 507–509.
SUBJ 55

20650 CSU O P7 G9.5 1928–1949
Schofield, Walter, 1888–1968.
'Pile houses at Tai O, Lantau island [i.e., the village of Ta-ao, Ta-yü shan], Hong Kong, 10th January 1937.'
JRAS-HKB 10 (1970), 197–200.
SUBJ 55

20651 CSU S P4 G1.2 1928–1949
Spencer, Joseph Earle, 1907–.
'The houses of the Chinese.'
GR 37, 2 (Apr. 1947), 254–273.
SUBJ 21.3 29 55

20652 CSU F P2 G1.2 1928–1949
Tsai Chiao (Ts'ai Ch'iao), 1898–.
'Problems of nutrition in present-day China.' In *Voices from unoccupied China*, edited by Harley Farnsworth MacNair. [Selective entry]
Chicago: U. of Chicago Press, 1944, 16–25.
SUBJ 18 55 56

20653 CSU O P2 G1.1 1911–1949
Waln, Nora, 1895–1964.
The house of exile.
Boston: Little, Brown, 1933. 337 p.
SUBJ 41 55 ▪ 32 57

20654 CSH U P2 G2.0 1911–1949
Wang, Frances.
'Social values and patterns of living.' In *A regional handbook on Northeast China*, compiled by Far Eastern and Russian Institute, U. of Washington. [Selective entry]
New Haven: Human Relations Area Files, 1956, 157–181. (HRAF subcontractor's monographs, 61; Washington 9)
SUBJ 55 65 ▪ 21.4 23 41 47

20655 MCH F P2 G1.4 1911–1928
Wu, Hsien, 1839–1959.
'Chinese diet in the light of modern knowledge of nutrition.'
CSPSR 11, 1 (Jan. 1927), 56–81.
Subj 55 58

1911-1972
(including 1644-1972)

20656 DLC P P1 G1.1 –1972
Bogoiavlenskii, N- A-.
'U istokov sanitarnoi kul'tury kitaiskogo naroda' (Origins of the hygienic practices of the Chinese people).
Fel'dsher i akusherka 26, 12 (dekabr' 1961), 31–35.
Subj 55 65 ▪ 53 56

20657 CSU PO P3 G9.5 1928–1972
Goodstadt, Leo F-.
'Urban housing in Hong Kong, 1945–63.' In *Hong Kong: A society in transition*, edited by Ian C- Jarvie and Joseph Agassi. [Analytic entry]
New York: Praeger, 1969, 257–298.
Subj 28 55 ▪ 21.3 22.1 24 45 47 61 63

20658 CSU F P3 G9.5 1928–1972
Maunder, Wynne Frederick, 1920–.
Hong Kong urban rents and housing.
Hong Kong: Hong Kong U. Press, 1969. 14, 192 p. (Centre of Asian Studies series, 1)
Subj 55 ▪ 12.2 21.1 28 41

20659 MCH O P4 G1.1 1644–1972
Scott, Adolphe Clarence, 1909–.
Chinese costume in transition.
Singapore: Moore, 1958. 110 p. [Reprinted—New York: Theatre Arts Books, 1960. 110 p.]
Subj 55 ▪ 12 47

20660 CSU F P2 G4.4 1928–1972
Trippner, Josef.
'Das "Röstmehl" bei den Ackerbauern in Tsinghai, China' (The 'roasted flour' of farmers in Tsinghai).
Anthropos 52, 3/4 (Mai–Aug. 1957), 603–616.
Subj 55

20661 CSH U P1 G1.2 –1972
Wang, Frances.
'Social values and patterns of living.' In *A general handbook of China*, compiled by Far Eastern and Russian Institute, U. of Washington. [Selective entry]
New Haven: Human Relations Area Files, 1956, vol. 1, 342–396. (HRAF subcontractor's monographs, 55; Washington 4)
Subj 23 55 60 ▪ 31 41 48 51 58 63 65

20662 MAU S P1 G1.1 1644–1972
Ward, David A-.
Narcotic drugs and addiction in China and Japan.
Unpublished masters thesis in Far Eastern Studies, U. of Michigan, 1963. 148 p.
Subj 14.3 22.2 55 56 ▪ 12.1 18 61

20663 CSU P P3 G9.5 1928–1972
Whisson, Michael G-.
'Some sociological aspects of the illegal use of narcotics in Hong Kong.' In *Hong Kong: A society in transition*, edited by Ian C- Jarvie and Joseph Agassi. [Analytic entry]
New York: Praeger, 1969, 299–316.
Subj 28 55 ▪ 22.2 24.3 26 34.2

1949-1972

20664 CSH P P3 G9.5 1949–1972
Agassi, Judith Buber, 1924–.
'Hong Kong's housing problems.'
FEER 36, 10 (7 June 1962), 515–522. [Reprinted as 'Housing the needy.' In *Hong Kong: A society in transition*, edited by Ian C- Jarvie and Joseph Agassi. (Analytic entry.) New York: Praeger, 1969, 247–256.]
Subj 28 38 55

20665 CSU F P7 G9.5 1949–1972
Anderson, Eugene Newton, Jr., 1941–, and Marja Lisa Anderson, 1943–.
'Cantonese ethnohoptology.'
Ethnos 34 (1969), 107–117.
Subj 55

20666 CSU U P3 G1.2 1949–1972
Biener, Kurt.
'Jugendhygiene in China' (Adolescent hygiene in China).
Z. für ärztliche Fortbildung 51, 21/22 (15 Nov. 1957), 1014–1017.
Subj 17 55 ▪ 54 56

20667 CSU P P4 G9.5 1949–1972
Bishop, P-.
'Some aspects of the Hong Kong resettlement programme.' In *Asian urbanization: A Hong Kong casebook*, edited by Denis John Dwyer. [Analytic entry]
Hong Kong: Hong Kong U. Press, 1971, 111–122. (Centre of Asian Studies series, 3)
Subj 55 ▪ 21.3 21.4 22.1 28 38

20668 DLC O P2 G1.3 1949–1972
Borovikov, Grigorii.
'Po gorodam Kitaia' (In the cities of China).
Novaia Volga 26 (1957), 160–240.
Subj 21.3 24.2 24.4 31 55 ▪ 13 17 23 24.3 34.1 56 57 61 66

20669 NIC P P4 G1.2 1949–1972
Chao, Kang, 1929–.
'Industrialization and urban housing in Communist China.'
JAS 25, 3 (May 1966), 381–396.
Subj 11.1 11.2 55 ▪ 14.4

20670 MAU O P1 G9.5 1949–1972
Choa, Gerald.
'Some ideas concerning food and diet among Hong Kong Chinese: The constitution and food therapy.' In *Some traditional Chinese ideas and conceptions in Hong Kong social life today*, edited by Marjorie Doreen Topley. [Analytic entry]
Hong Kong: Royal Asiatic Society, Hong Kong Branch, 1967, 54–59.
Subj 55 56 62

20671 CSU O P8 G5.1 1949–1972
Christiansen, S- A-.
'Letters from a people's commune [in periurban Peking].'
EH 7, 3 (May–June 1968), 42–48.
Subj 24.1 55

20672 NIC O P7 G2.3 1949–1972
Chung-kuo kung ch'an tang. Liao-ning sheng wei yüan hui. Kung tso tsu. (Chinese Communist Party. Liaoning Provincial Central Committee. Work Team).
'Report on conditions in rural community mess halls: Liaoning.' Tr. of 'Kuan yü nung ts'un kung kung shih t'ang ch'ing k'uang ti tiao ch'a pao kao' (Report on communal mess halls in rural areas); *Liao-ning jih pao* 24 May 1960, 2.
SCMP 2289 (5 July 1960), 1–7.
Subj 28 55 ▪ 32.1 34.1

20673 CSU P P2 G9.4 1949–1972
Djang, T. K.
'Aided self-help housing programmes for workers in Taiwan.'
ILR 73, 1 (Jan. 1956), 37–57.
Subj 26.4 55 ▪ 24.4 36.4

20674 CSU F P3 G9.5 1949–1972
Drakakis-Smith, David William, 1942–.
'Tenement slum renewal: Hong Kong.'
Pacific viewpoint 13, 2 (Sept. 1972), 155–168.
Subj 55 ▪ 21.3 22 28 56

20675 CSU P P4 G9.5 1949–1972
Dwyer, Denis John, 1933–.
'Housing provision in Hong Kong.' In *Asian urbanization: A Hong Kong casebook*, edited by D. J. Dwyer. [Analytic entry]
Hong Kong: Hong Kong U. Press, 1971, 33–47. (Centre of Asian Studies series, 3)
Subj 55

20676 CSU P P3 G9.5 1949–1972
Dwyer, Denis John, 1933–.
'The problem of in-migration and squatter settlement in Asian cities: Two case studies, Manila and Victoria-Kowloon.'
Asian studies (Quezon City, Philippines) 2, 2 (Aug. 1964), 145–169.
Subj 55 ▪ 21.1 21.2

20677 CSU O P3 G9.5 1949–1972
Firth, J- R-.
'The work of the Hong Kong Housing Authority.'
J. of the Royal Society of Arts 113, 5103 (Feb. 1965), 175–195.
Subj 21.1 21.3 55 ▪ 22

20678 CSU O P3 G9.5 1949–1972
Grantham, Alexander.
'Housing Hong Kong's 600,000 homeless.'
GM 31, 12 (Apr. 1959), 573–586.
Subj 28 55 ▪ 17 21.1

20679 CSU O P3 G4.1 1949–1972
Hanbury-Tenison, Euphan.
'In China today: Sian.'
GM 39, 2 (June 1966), 139–148.
Subj 55 ▪ 24.4 26.4

20680 MCY F P3 G9.5 1949–1972
Hess, Albert G-.
Chasing the dragon: A report on drug addiction in Hong Kong.
New York: Free Press of Glencoe, 1965. 182 p.
Subj 28 55 ▪ 21.4 22.2 56

20681 CSU F P2 G9.5 1949–1972
Hong Kong. Housing Authority.
Annual report, 1954/55–1971/72.

Hong Kong: Government Printer. Issued annually, 1955–1972. Average ca. 50 p.
SUBJ 22 55 ▪ 21 24.3 24.6

20682 CSU P P2 G9.5 1949–1972
Hong Kong. Resettlement Dept.
Annual departmental report by the Commissioner for Resettlement, 1954/55–1971/72.
Hong Kong: Government Printer. Issued annually, 1955–1972. Average ca. 50 p.
SUBJ 55 ▪ 21 22.1 28

20683 CBU FP P3 G9.5 1949–1972
Hopkins, Keith.
'Housing the poor.' In *Hong Kong: The industrial colony*, edited by K. Hopkins. [Analytic entry]
Hong Kong: Oxford U. Press, 1971, 271–335.
SUBJ 22 28 55 ▪ 11.2 41 45 58

20684 CSU P P3 G9.5 1949–1972
Hopkins, Keith.
'Public and private housing in Hong Kong.' In *The city as a centre of change in Asia*, edited by Denis John Dwyer. [Sole entry]
Hong Kong: Hong Kong U. Press, 1972, 200–215. (Centre of Asian Studies series, 4)
SUBJ 55 ▪ 45

20685 CSU P P3 G6.1 1949–1972
Howe, Christopher Barry, 1937–.
'The supply and administration of urban housing in Mainland China: The case of Shanghai.'
CQ 33 (Jan.–Mar. 1968), 73–97.
SUBJ 55 ▪ 21.1 21.3

20686 NNC FP P2 G9.4 1949–1972
Hsu, S. C. (Hsü Shih-chü), 1905–.
'Report on the nutrition program in Taiwan, Republic of China.'
CMJ-T 11, 1 (Mar. 1964), 72–94.
SUBJ 28 55 56 ▪ 24.1

20687 DLC S P1 G1.2 1949–1972
IAn' En-fu.
'Otsenka diety s vysokim soderzhaniem zlakov' (An evaluation of a diet with a high cereal content).
Usloviia zhizni i zdorov'e 1, 5 (1959), 21–26.
SUBJ 55 ▪ 52 54 56

20688 FPN O P2 G9.5 1949–1972
Kessel, Joseph, 1898–.
Hong Kong et Macao (Hong Kong and Macau).
Paris: Gallimard, 1957. 276 p.
SUBJ 12.2 21.3 24.3 28 46 55 ▪ 15 21.2 24.2 31 47 52 66

20689 MCH P P1 G1.2 1949–1972
[Klatt, Werner?] W. K., 1904–.
'The state of nutrition in Communist China.'
CQ 7 (July–Sept. 1961), 121–127.
SUBJ 55

20690 NNC P P3 G1.2 1949–1972
Kwok, Reginald Yin-wang.
Urban housing development in Mainland China, 1949–1966: An exploratory study of diverse materials and an interpretation of housing and planning trends in a developing socialist nation.
Unpublished doctoral dissertation in Urban Planning, Columbia U., 1969. 222 p.
SUBJ 11.1 21.3 55 ▪ 11.2 11.3 12 12.2 18

20691 CSH P P3 G5.1 1949–1972
[La Dany, Ladislao] ———, 1914–.
'Architecture.'
CNA 87 (10 June 1955), 2–7.
SUBJ 55

20692 NNC P P4 G1.2 1949–1972
[La Dany, Ladislao] ———, 1914–.
'Housing.'
CNA 161 (14 Dec. 1956), 1–7.
SUBJ 55 ▪ 21.3 28

20693 NNC O P2 G5.1 1949–1972
Liu Tzu-hou.
'Organize the people's life comprehensively with the messhall as the center.' Tr. of 'I shih t'ang wei chung hsin ch'üan mien tsu chih jen min sheng huo'; *Jen min jih pao* 11 Apr. 1960, 13. In *Translations of 'Jen min jih pao' articles on sociological and economic subjects*, mimeo., compiled by U.S. Joint Publications Research Service. [Sole entry]
Washington, D.C.: JPRS, 23 June 1960, 247–261. (JPRS 2908; MC 14,138/1960)
SUBJ 28 55 ▪ 21.4 32.1 52

20694 CSU F P3 G9.5 1949–1972
Mitchell, Robert Edward, 1930–.
Housing, urban growth and economic development [in Hong Kong, with comparison data from other Southeast Asian cities].
Taipei: Orient Cultural Service, 1972. 304 p. (Asian Folklore and Social Life monographs, 31)
SUBJ 28 55 ▪ 21.3 22 24.4 24.5 26.4 41 61

20695 MCH PO P3 G9.5 1949–1972
Nelissen-Jakobs, H- M-.
'Het woningvraagstuk in Hong Kong' (The housing problem in Hong Kong).
Tijdschrift van het Koninklijk Nederlandsch Aardrijkskundig Genootschap 2e serie 78, 1 (Januari 1961), 35–52.
SUBJ 21.3 28 55 ▪ 21.1 21.2 58

20696 DLC O P4 G1.3 1949–1972
Prikhod'ko, P-.
'Zhilishchnoe stroitel'stvo v Kitae' (Housing construction in China).
Stroitel'stvo i arkhitektura 10, 11 (noiabr' 1962), 36–37.
SUBJ 21.3 55 ▪ 18

20697 CSU P P3 G9.5 1949–1972
Pryor, E- G-.
'The delineation of blighted areas in urban Hong Kong.' In *Asian urbanization: A Hong Kong casebook*, edited by Denis John Dwyer. [Analytic entry]
Hong Kong: Hong Kong U. Press, 1971, 70–88. (Centre of Asian Studies series, 3)
SUBJ 45 55 ▪ 21.3 24.2 28

20698 CSH O P2 G1.2 1949–1972
Starobin, Joseph Robert, 1913–.
'Peking, the unbelievable.' In *Paris to Peking*, by J. R. Starobin. [Sole entry]
New York: Cameron Associates, 1955, 98–223.
SUBJ 12.1 32 55 ▪ 14 15 16 64

20699 CSU O P2 G1.3 1949–1972
Ting, Jan C.
An American in China.
New York: Paperback Library, 1972. 190 p.
SUBJ 20 24 24.3 28 55 66 ▪ 14.2 24.2 24.4 26.3 26.4 27 31 52 56

20700 NNC P P2 G1.2 1949–1972
Wang Ch'eng-fa, Fang Yun-chung (Fang Yün-chung), and Lu I (Lü I).
New China's research achievements in nutrition in the past decade, mimeo. Tr. of 'Shih nien lai hsin Chung-kuo ti ying yang yen chiu ch'eng chiu'; *Jen min pao chien* 1959, 10 (Oct.), 907–916.
Washington, D.C.: U.S. Joint Publications Research Service, 7 July 1960. 40 p. (JPRS 2968; MC 14,178/1960)
SUBJ 55 ▪ 18

20701 CSU F P7 G5.1 1949–1972
Yu Hsi-hsuan (Yü Hsi-hsüan), et al.
'On the caloric consumption of farmers.' Tr. of 'Nung min je neng hsiao hao wen t'i'; *Jen min pao chien* 1960, 3 (Mar.), 148–151. In *Public health in Communist China*, mimeo., compiled by U.S. Joint Publications Research Service. [Selective entry]
Washington, D.C.: JPRS, 15 July 1960, 89–107. (JPRS 2976; MC 14,181/1960)
SUBJ 26.3 55 ▪ 47

56 ILLNESS AND MEDICINE
疾病及醫療 疾病及び医療

1644-1911

20702 NNM O P3 G9.4 1895–1911
'Formosa under the Japanese, with special reference to the treatment of plague on that island.'
CMMJ 19, 6 (Nov. 1905), 231–235.
SUBJ 22.1 56 ▪ 28

20703 NNC O P1 G1.1 1644–1842
'Notice du Cong-Fou des bonzes Tao-sée' (A note on *kung fu* [medical gymnastics] as practiced by Taoist monks). In *Mémoires concernant l'histoire, les sciences, les arts, les moeurs, les usages, etc. des Chinois* (Reports on the history, learning, arts, manners, customs, etc. of the Chinese), by Missionnaires de Pékin. [Selective entry]
Paris: Chez Nyon, 1779, vol. 4, 441–451.
SUBJ 56 ▪ 62

20704 NIC O P3 G8.1 1842–1895
'La police des épidémies en Chine' (Sanitary controls during epidemics in China).
TP 4, 5 (déc. 1893), 432–433.
SUBJ 28 56

20705 MCH O P4 G9.2 1895–1911
Abbatucci, *Dr.* ———.
'Les épidémies pesteuses en Chine et à Pak-hoi en particulier' (Plague epidemics in China, in particular at Pei-hai [Ho-p'u *hsien*, Kwangtung]).

AHMC 14, 4 (oct.–déc. 1911), 691–714.
SUBJ 28 55 56

20706 MCH O P4 G9.2 1895–1911
Attatucci, *Dr.* ———.
'Les épidémies pesteuses du foyer chinois de Pak-hoi' (The plague epidemics in the Chinese quarter of Pei-hai [Ho-p'u *hsien*, Kwangtung]).
AHMC 6, 2 (avr.–juin 1903), 272–289.
SUBJ 21.3 56 ▪ 21.1

20707 MCH O P2 G8.2 1895–1911
Ayraud, *Dr.* ———.
'Notes succinctes sur le paludisme à Mongtzeu' (Notes on malaria in Meng-tzu *hsien* [Yunnan]).
AHMC 10, 2 (avr.–juin 1907), 281–285.
SUBJ 28 56

20708 MCY U P1 G1.0 –1911
Behrens, ———.
'Der Kannibalismus der Chinesen' (Chinese cannibalism).
Globus 81, 6 (6 Feb. 1902), 96–97.
SUBJ 56 ▪ 62 65

20709 MCH O P2 G5.0 1842–1911
Besenbruch, Peter.
'Zur Epidemiologie der Pocken in Nordchina' (Smallpox epidemiology in North China).
ASTH 16, 2 (Feb. 1912), 48–53.
SUBJ 56 ▪ 55

20710 FPN O P2 G1.1 1895–1911
Bizeul, Sévère, 1848–1912.
'La tuberculose en Chine' (Tuberculosis in China).
Relations de Chine 4 (oct. 1908), 179–184.
SUBJ 52 55 56 58 ▪ 18 21.3

20711 MCH O P3 G8.1 1895–1911
Bouffard, G-.
'Notes médicales recueillies à Tchen-tou' (Medical notes collected in Chengtu).
AHMC 3, 2 (avr.–juin 1900), 172–183.
SUBJ 28 55 56 ▪ 66

20712 CSU O P3 G9.2 1895–1911
Cadbury, William Warder, 1877–1959.
'Medicine as practised by the Chinese.'
AAAPSS 39 (Jan. 1912), 124–129. [Reprinted—*CMJ* 28, 6 (Nov. 1914), 375–380.]
SUBJ 56 ▪ 62

20713 NIC O P2 G9.5 1842–1895
Cantlie, James, 1851–1926.
Leprosy in Hong Kong.
Hong Kong: Kelly and Walsh, 1890. 99 p.
SUBJ 56 ▪ 28 58

20714 MCH O P2 G1.4 1895–1911
Chabaneix, *Dr.* ———.
'La défense contre la peste pulmonaire dans la province du Petchile' (The fight against tuberculosis in northern Chihli).
AHMC 15, 1 (jan.–mars 1912), 85–103.
SUBJ 56 ▪ 18

20715 NNC O P3 G2.3 1842–1895
Christie, Dugald, 1855–1936.
Ten years in Manchuria: A story of medical mission work in Moukden, 1883–1893.
Paisley, Scotland: J. and R. Parlane, 1895. 100 p.
SUBJ 47 56 ▪ 22.2 62 65 66

20716 CBU O P2 G1.4 1842–1895
Coltman, Robert, Jr.
The Chinese: Their present and future, medical, political, and social.
Philadelphia: Davis, 1891. 212 p.
SUBJ 16 56 66 ▪ 16.1 33 41 46 47 55 61

20717 NNM P P1 G1.1 –1911
Cormack, James G-.
'Treatment of mad dog bites.'
CMMJ 20, 5 (Sept. 1906), 209–211.
SUBJ 56

20718 MCH O P4 G5.1 1895–1911
Creignon, *Dr.* ———.
'Service de santé de la direction du port de Ching-wan tao' (Health services of the port administration of Ch'in-huang-tao [Lin-yü *hsien*, Hopei]).
Archives de la médecine navale 78 (1902), 5–33.
SUBJ 56

20719 NNC PO P1 G1.1 –1842
Dabry de Thiersant, Claude Philibert, 1826–1898.
La médecine chez les Chinois (Medicine in China).
Paris: Plon, 1863. 12, 580 p.
SUBJ 55 56 65 ▪ 46 51 62

20720 MCH PO P1 G1.2 –1895
Dudgeon, John Hepburn, 1837–1901.
'Chinese arts of healing.'
CR 2, 6 – 4, 11 (Nov. 1869 – Apr. 1872), 43 p. in all.
SUBJ 56 60 62 ▪ 23 41 51 65

20721 NNC O P2 G1.2 1842–1895
Dudgeon, John Hepburn, 1837–1901.
Diseases of China: Their causes, conditions, and prevalence, contrasted with those of Europe.
Glasgow: Dunn and Wright, 1877. 64 p.
SUBJ 55 56 ▪ 18 57

20722 FPN P P4 G9.0 1842–1895
Durand-Fardel, Maxime, 1815–1899.
'La lèpre en Chine' (Leprosy in China).
Gazette médicale de Paris 4e série 6, 26 (30 juin 1877), 318–319; 6, 28 (14 juil. 1877), 341–343; 6, 30 (28 juil. 1877), 367–368; 6, 33 (18 août 1877), 414–415. [Separately reprinted—Paris: G. Baillière, 1877. 33 p.]
SUBJ 56 62 ▪ 14.2 16 57 63

20723 MCH O P4 G1.2 1842–1895
Faust, Ernest Carroll, 1890–.
'Social diseases in China.'
Social pathology 1, 6 (1925), 274–277.
SUBJ 56 ▪ 46 63

20724 MCH PO P2 G1.5 1895–1911
Féray, *Dr.* ———.
'Historique et pratique de la vaccine en Chine' (History and practice of vaccination in China).
AHMC 10, 4 (oct.–déc. 1907), 498–517.
SUBJ 56

20725 NNC PO P2 G1.2 –1911
Fest, Francis T- B-.
'Die Ärzte Chinas' (Chinese doctors).
MDG 7, 1 (1898), 94–109.
SUBJ 16.2 56 ▪ 62 65

20726 GMS F P2 G1.3 1842–1895
Friedel, C-.
Beiträge zur Kenntnis des Klimas und der Krankheiten Ost-Asiens (The climate and diseases of East Asia).
Berlin: Reimer, 1863. 183 p.
SUBJ 18 21.3 56

20727 MCH O P4 G5.3 1895–1911
Fürth, *Dr.* ———.
'Eine Scharlachepidemie im Schantung: Ein Beitrag zur Kenntnis des chinesischen Arznei- und Seuchenwesens' (A scarlet-fever epidemic in Shantung: Chinese medicine and methods of handling epidemics).
ASTH 14, 1 (1910), 12–20.
SUBJ 56 ▪ 62 66

20728 MCH O P4 G1.3 1842–1895
Fuzier, ———.
'De l'usage de la déformation des pieds chez les femmes chinoises, principalemant au point de vue médico-chirurgical' (The practice of foot-binding among Chinese women, primarily from a medical-surgical viewpoint).
Recueil de mémoires de médecine, de chirurgie et de pharmacie militaires 3e série 7 (jan. 1862), 28–52.
SUBJ 47 55 56 ▪ 16

20729 CSU O P2 G1.3 1895–1911
Gaide, *Dr.* ———.
'Notes médicales sur la Chine' (Medical notes on China).
AHMC 3, 4 (oct.–déc. 1900), 492–505.
SUBJ 18 56 58 ▪ 46

20730 MCH P P1 G1.3 1644–1911
Gaupp, Hans.
'Über die Geburtshilfe der Chinesen' (Midwifery among the Chinese).
ZE 39, 4/5 (1907), 729–745.
SUBJ 51 56 62 ▪ 46 47 52 55 65

20731 MCH O P3 G2.0 1895–1911
Gothein, Wolfgang.
Die Lungenpest in Ostasien, auf Grund persönlicher Erfahrungen (Pulmonary plague in East Asia, on the basis of personal experience).
Leipzig: Johann Ambrosius Barth, 1912. 8 p. (Archiv für Schiffs- und Tropenhygiene, Beiheft, 16, 1) [Consecutive pagination in Beiheft: pp. 184–191]
SUBJ 56 ▪ 66

20732 MCH P P1 G1.2 –1911
Grünhagen, ———.
'Die Grundlagen der chinesischen Medizin' (The foundations of Chinese medicine).
Janus; archives internationales pour l'histoire de la médecine et la géographie médicale 13, 1 (Jan. 1908), 1–14; 13, 3 (März 1908), 121–137; 13, 4 (Apr. 1908), 191–205; 13, 5 (Mai 1908), 268–278; 13, 6 (Juni 1908), 328–337.
SUBJ 56 62 ▪ 52 55

20733 NNC PO P1 G1.2 –1842
[Gützlaff, Karl Friedrich August] Charles Gutzlaff, 1803–1851.
'The medical art amongst the Chinese.'
JRAS 4 (1837), 154–171.
SUBJ 56 ▪ 62

20734 MCH O P2 G1.5 1895–1911
Guillemet, *Dr.* ———.
'La médecine et les médecins en Chine' (Medicine and doctors in China).
AHMC 15, 1 (jan.–mars 1912), 152–175; 15, 2 (avr.–juin 1912), 234–254.
SUBJ 56 ▪ 62

20735 MCH O P3 G8.1 1895–1911
Guillemet, *Dr.* ———.
'Tch'ong-k'ing: description, population, climatologie, maladies les plus fréquemment observées' (Chungking: Description, population, climate, and most common diseases).
AHMC 13, 4 (oct.–déc. 1910), 561–599.
SUBJ 21.3 56 58 ▪ 21.1

20736 MCH P P1 G1.2 –1895
Harlez, Charles Joseph de, 1832–1899.
'Miscellanées chinoises' (A miscellany on China).
Giornale della Società asiatica italiana 7 (1893), 173–194.
SUBJ 56

20737 MCH P P1 G1.1 1644–1895
Harlez, Charles Joseph de, 1832–1899.
'Quelques traits de l'art médical chez les Chinois' (Some features of Chinese medical practice).
Archives de biologie 7 (1887), 411–431.
SUBJ 56 ▪ 62

20738 NNC PO P1 G1.2 –1895
Henderson, James, 1830–1865.
'The medicine and medical practice of the Chinese.'
JRAS-NCB new (2nd) series 1 (Dec. 1864), 21–69.
SUBJ 56 ▪ 62

20739 NNC O P1 G1.3 –1911
Hoeppli, Reinhard J- C-, 1893–.
'Malaria in Chinese medicine.'
Sinologica 4, 2 (1955), 91–100.
SUBJ 56 ▪ 62 65

20740 NNM P P1 G1.1 –1842
Hoeppli, Reinhard J- C-, 1893–, and I-hung Ch'iang.
'The louse, crab-louse and bed bug in old Chinese medical literature, with special consideration of phthiriasis.'
CMJ 58, 3 (Sept. 1940), 338–362.
SUBJ 56

20741 CSU P P1 G1.2 –1911
Huard, Pierre Alphonse, 1901–.
'La médecine du monde chinois et sinisé' (Medicine in China and the sinicized world).
La nef nouvelle (2e) série 23 (juil.–sept. 1965), 61–108.
SUBJ 56 62 ▪ 23 46 50 72

20742 CSU O P2 G1.3 1644–1842
Huard, Pierre Alphonse, 1901–, J-Sonolet, and Ming Wong.
'Mesmer en Chine: trois lettres médicales du R. P. Amiot, rédigées à Pékin de 1783 à 1790' (Mesmer in China: Three medical letters from Father Amiot, written in Peking from 1783 to 1790).
R. de synthèse 81, 17/18 (jan.–juin 1960), 61–98.
SUBJ 56 62

20743 MCH PO P1 G1.2 –1911
Hübotter, Franz, 1881–.
Die chinesische Medizin zu Beginn des 20. Jahrhunderts und ihr historischer Entwicklungsgang (Chinese medicine at the beginning of the twentieth century and its historical development).
Leipzig: Asia Major, 1929. 356 p.
SUBJ 56 ▪ 62

20744 CSU S P3 G9.2 1644–1895
Hume, Edward Hicks, 1876–1957.
'Peter Parker and the introduction of anesthesia into China.'
J. of the history of medicine and allied sciences 1, 4 (Oct. 1946), 670–674.
SUBJ 56

20745 CSU O P2 G1.2 –1895
Kerr, John J-.
'Medicine in China.'
North American medico-chirurgical review 3, 2 (Mar. 1859), 282–297.
SUBJ 18 56 ▪ 51

20746 NNM O P3 G9.3 1895–1911
Kinnear, ———.
'Propitiating the plague spirits.'
CMMJ 16, 4 (Oct. 1902), 204–206.
SUBJ 56 ▪ 23 57

20747 NNC U P4 G1.5 1842–1911
Krebs, Wilhelm.
'Die Beulenpest Shu-yi' (*Shu i*: Bubonic plague).
Globus 71, 12 (20 März 1897), 181–183.
SUBJ 56 ▪ 55

20748 MCH O P2 G1.4 1842–1895
Libermann, Henri, ?–1890.
'Recherches sur l'usage de la fumée d'opium en Chine' (Investigations on the custom of smoking opium in China).
Recueil de mémoires de médecine, de chirurgie et de pharmacie militaires 3e série 8 (oct. 1862), 287–310; 8 (nov. 1862), 352–373; 8 (déc. 1862), 440–455.
SUBJ 22.2 55 56 ▪ 26 28 53

20749 NNC O P2 G1.2 1842–1895
Lockhart, William, 1811–1896.
The medical missionary in China: A narrative of twenty years' experience.
London: Hurst and Blackett, 1861. 11, 404 p.
SUBJ 15 17 18 56 ▪ 12.2 31 32.2 57 62 65 66

20750 NNC PO P1 G1.2 –1895
MacGowan, Daniel Jerome, 1814?–1893.
'Chinese use of shad in consumption and iodine plants in scrofula.'
JRAS-NCB new (2nd) series 7 (1871/72), 235–236.
SUBJ 56

20751 NNC PO P1 G1.2 –1895
MacGowan, Daniel Jerome, 1814?–1893.
'Notes on Chinese toxicology. 1, Arsenic.'
JRAS-NCB new (2nd) series 9 (1875), 173–182.
SUBJ 56 ▪ 12.2 65

20752 NNC PO P1 G1.2 –1895
MacGowan, Daniel Jerome, 1814?–1893.
'On the "mutton wine" of the Mongols and analogous preparations of the Chinese.'
JRAS-NCB new (2nd) series 7 (1871/72), 237–240.
SUBJ 56

20753 CSU O P1 G9.4 1842–1895
MacKay, George Leslie, 1844–1901.
'Ignorant and superstitious methods of curing disease in North Formosa.'
CR 23, 11 (Nov. 1892), 524–529.
SUBJ 56 ▪ 62 65

20754 FPN O P3 G5.1 1842–1895
Martin, Charles Ernest, 1831–1897.
'L'hygiène de Pékin' (Hygiene in Peking).
Science moderne 7, 28 (15 juil. 1893), 57–59.
SUBJ 28 55 56 ▪ 57

20755 FPN PO P2 G9.0 1842–1895
Martin, Charles Ernest, 1831–1897.
'La morphinomanie en Extrême-Orient' (Morphine addiction in the Far East).
J. d'hygiène 18, 894 (9 nov. 1893), 529–532.
SUBJ 12.2 56

20756 MCH O P2 G1.1 1842–1895
Martin, Charles Ernest, 1831–1897.
'La tuberculose dans la race jaune' (Tuberculosis among Orientals).
R. scientifique 4e série 2, 20 (17 nov. 1894), 623–627.
SUBJ 56 ▪ 55

20757 MCH O P3 G9.2 1895–1911
Mas, *Dr.* ———.
'Rapport sur l'état sanitaire de Canton du 30 oct. 1900, au 1er oct. 1901' (Report on sanitary conditions in Canton, 30 October 1900 – 1 October 1901).
AHMC 5, 3 (juil.–sept. 1902), 380–384.
SUBJ 21.3 56

20758 FPN O P3 G5.1 1842–1895
Matignon, Jean-Jacques, 1866–?
'Les instruments de chirurgie des Chinois' (Chinese surgical instruments).
Archives cliniques de Bordeaux 6 (nov. 1897), 525–532.
SUBJ 28 56 ▪ 26.1 62

20759 MCH O P1 G1.1 1842–1895
Matignon, Jean-Jacques, 1866–?
'Quelques superstitions médicales du Chinois' (Some Chinese medical superstitions).
Bulletins de la Société d'anthropologie de Paris 4e série 9 (1898), 408–413.
SUBJ 56 ▪ 62 65

20760 GMS F P2 G1.3 1895–1911
Mayer, Georg, 1848–?
Hygienische Studien in China (Studies of sanitation in China).
Leipzig: Johann Ambrosius Barth, 1904. 167 p.
SUBJ 21.3 24.4 56 ▪ 28 46

20761 MCH P P1 G1.2 –1895
Meyners d'Estrey, Guillaume Henri Jean, 1829–?
'L'art médical en Chine' (Medical practice in China).
Annales de l'Extrême-Orient 5 (1882/83), 129–145, 161–174. [Separately reprinted—Paris: Challamel aîné, 1882. 31 p.]
SUBJ 56 ▪ 18 46 50 51 62

20762 MCH O P3 G5.1 1644–1895
Morache, Georges.
Pékin et ses habitants: étude d'hygiène (Peking and its inhabitants: A study of hygienic conditions).
Paris: J.-B. Baillière et fils, 1869. 164 p.
SUBJ 20 28 47 55 56 57 ▪ 15 21.1 21.3 22.2 24 26 43 51 63

20763 NNC PO P1 G1.2 –1911
Morse, William Reginald, 1874–1939.
Chinese medicine.
New York: Hoeber, 1934. 23, 185 p.
SUBJ 56 ▪ 62

20764 NNM O P3 G5.1 1895–1911
Mullowney, John James, 1878–1952.
'Modern hospitals for Chinese by Chinese.'
CMJ 26, 1 (Jan. 1912), 34–43.
SUBJ 56 ▪ 28

20765 MCH O P2 G1.2 1895–1911
Ortholan, *Dr.* ———.
'Quelques notes sur Ssé-Mao' (Notes on Ssu-mao *t'ing* [Yunnan]).
AHMC 4, 2 (avr.–juin 1901), 205–210.
SUBJ 56 ▪ 28

20766 MSE P P2 G1.1 1895–1911
Park, William Hector, comp.
Opinions of over 100 physicians on the use of opium in China.
Shanghai: American Presbyterian Mission Press, 1899. 14, 95 p.
SUBJ 18 55 56 ▪ 14.1 16.3 57 61 63

20767 MCH P P1 G1.2 1895–1911
Portengen, J- A-.
'Une théorie chinoise sur l'étiologie et la thérapie de la peste' (A Chinese theory on the causes and treatment of plague).
Janus; archives internationales pour l'histoire de la médecine et la géographie médicale 1, 5 (1896/97), 461–468.
SUBJ 56 ▪ 62

20768 MCH O P1 G9.0 1895–1911
Prahl, *Dr.* ———.
'Eine "Borstenkrankheit" in Südchina' (A disease of the hair in South China).
ASTH 13, 4 (1909), 116–119.
SUBJ 56

20769 NNC PO P4 G1.1 –1911
Regnault, Jules Emile Joseph, 1873–?
Médecine et pharmacie chez les Chinois et chez les Annamites (Medicine and pharmacology among the Chinese and the Annamese).
Paris: Augustin Challamel, 1902. 10, 233 p.
SUBJ 22.2 56 62 65 ▪ 16.1 17 18 23 36.1 46 51 55 57

20770 MCH O P3 G9.3 1895–1911
Rouffiandis, V-.
'Note sur l'épidémie de peste de Foutcheou' (A note on the plague epidemic in Foochow).
AHMC 7, 3 (juil.–sept. 1904), 417–433.
SUBJ 56 ▪ 21.3 55

20771 MCH O P7 G8.2 1895–1911
Sautarel, *Dr.* ———.
'Quelques notes médicales sur Ssé-mar' (Medical notes on Ssu-mao *t'ing* [Yunnan]).
AHMC 5, 2 (avr.–juin 1902), 179–184.
SUBJ 28 56

20772 NNC P P1 G1.3 –1911
Schramm, Gottfried.
'Über chinesische Moxibustion' (Chinese moxibustion).
Forschungen und Fortschritte 30, 1 (Jan. 1956), 11–12.
SUBJ 56

20773 CBU F P2 G9.5 1842–1911
Simpson, William John Ritchie, 1855–?
Report of the causes and continuance of plague in Hong Kong and suggestions as to remedial measures.
London: Waterlow, 1903. 115 p.
SUBJ 21.3 28 55 56 ▪ 12.2 21.1

20774 MCH U P1 G1.1 –1895
Soubeiran, Jean Léon, 1827–1892, and Claude Philibert Dabry de Thiersant, 1826–1898.
La matière médicale chez les Chinois (Materia medica among the Chinese).
Paris: G. Masson, 1874. 10, 373 p.
SUBJ 56 62 ▪ 65

20775 NNC O P7 G5.3 1842–1911
Stenz, Georg Maria, 1869–?
'Arzt und Apotheker in China' (Doctor and apothecary in China).
Globus 81, 24 (26 Juni 1902), 383–386.
SUBJ 56 ▪ 26.2 62

20776 NNC PO P2 G1.3 –1895
Tatarinov, Aleksandr Alekseevich (A. Tartarinoff), 1817–1886.
'Kitaiskaia meditsina' (Chinese medicine). In *Trudy chlenov Rossiiskoi dukhovnoi missii v Pekine* (Works of members of the Russian Orthodox ecclesiastical mission in Peking). [Selective entry]
St. Petersburg: Tip. Shtaba voenno-ucheb. zavedenii, 1853, vol. 2, 357–441. [Reprinted in *Trudy chlenov Rossiiskoi dukhovnoi missii v Pekine.* (Selective entry.) Peking: Tip. Uspenskago monastyria pri RDM, 1910, vol. 2, 215–258.]
'Die chinesische Medicin.' Tr. by Carl Abel and F- A- Mecklenburg. In *Arbeiten der kaiserlich russischen Gesandtschaft zu Peking über China, sein Volk, seine Religion, seine Institutionen, sozialen Verhältnisse, usw.* (Works of the imperial Russian mission to Peking on China, its people, religion, institutions, social conditions, etc.). [Selective entry]
Berlin: Heinicke, 1858, vol. 2, 421–464.
SUBJ 56 ▪ 16.1 62 72

20777 NNM O P1 G1.1 1842–1895
Thomson, John C-.
'The heavenly flowers [smallpox].'
CMMJ 1, 4 (Dec. 1887), 157–161.
SUBJ 56 ▪ 23 65

20778 NNM O P3 G9.2 1842–1895
Thomson, John C-.
'Native practice and practitioners.'
CMMJ 4, 3 (Sept. 1890), 175–196.
SUBJ 56 ▪ 51 65

20779 NNM O P4 G1.1 1842–1895
Thomson, John C-.
'Surgery in China.'
CMMJ 6, 4 (Dec. 1892), 219–228; 7, 1 (Mar. 1893), 1–9; 7, 2 (June 1893), 69–79.
SUBJ 56

20780 MCH O P2 G1.4 1895–1911
Tsuzuki, J.
'Bericht über meine epidemiologischen Beobachtungen und Forschungen während der Choleraepedemie im Nordchina im Jahre 1902 und über die im Verlaufe derselben von mir durchgeführten prophylaktischen Massregeln, mit besonderer Berücksichtigung der Choleraschutzimpfung' (Report on my epidemiological observations and researches during the cholera epidemic of 1902 in North China and on the preventive measures that I took, with special attention to vaccination against cholera).
ASTH 8, 2 (Feb. 1904), 71–81.
SUBJ 56 66 ▪ 55

20781 MCH O P2 G5.3 1895–1911
Uthemann, *Dr.* ———, and *Dr.* ——— Fürth.
Tsingtau: Ein kolonialhygienischer Rückblick auf die Entwicklung des deutschen Kiautschougebietes (Tsingtao: A retrospective view of hygienic development in German Kiaochow).
Leipzig: Johann Ambrosius Barth, 1911. 39 p. (Archiv für Schiffs- und Tropenhygiene, Beiheft, 15, 4)
SUBJ 56 ▪ 55 57 66

20782 NNC S P1 G1.2 1895–1911
Vincent, Eugène.
La médecine en Chine au XXe siècle (Medicine in China in the twentieth century).
Paris: Steinheil, 1915. 316 p.
SUBJ 50 56 62 65 ▪ 18 22.2 23 46 51 55 57 72

20783 MCH O P4 G9.2 1895–1911
Vortisch–van Vloten, H-.
'Statistik einer chinesischen Poliklinik' (Statistics of a Chinese polyclinic).
ASTH 17, 8 (Aug. 1913), 253–262.
SUBJ 56 ▪ 51

20784 MCH O P5 G9.2 1895–1911
Wittenberg, *Dr.* ———.
'Ärztliche Erfahrungen aus Süd-China' (Medical experiences in South China).
ASTH 4, 1 (Jan.–Feb. 1900), 1–12.
SUBJ 56 ▪ 55

20785 CSU P P4 G1.1 –1895
Wu Lien-teh (Wu Lien-te), 1879–1960.
'Early days of Western medicine in China.'
JRAS-NCB new (2nd) series 62 (1931), 1–31.
SUBJ 56 66

20786 CSU PO P2 G1.1 1842–1911
Young, Charles W-.
'The westernizing of Chinese medical practice.' In *Recent developments in China*, edited by George Hubbard Blakeslee. [Selective entry]
New York: G. E. Stechert, 1913, 199–222.
SUBJ 56 ▪ 17

20787 NNM P P1 G1.1 1644–1911
Yu Yün Hsiü (Yu Yün-hsiu).
'Scarlet fever in Chinese indigenous medicine.' Tr. from the Chinese by Peter G. Mar.
CMJ 58, 3 (Sept. 1940), 284–301.
SUBJ 56 ▪ 62

20788 CSU S P1 G1.2 –1911
Zaremba, R- W- von.
'Die Heilkunst in China (Eine geschichtliche Skizze)' (Historical sketch of medicine in China).
Janus; archives internationales pour l'histoire de la médecine et la géographie médicale 9, 2 (Feb. 1904), 103–116; 9, 3 (März 1904), 158–169; 9, 4 (Apr. 1904), 201–211; 9, 5 (Mai 1904), 257–269.
Subj 56 62 ▪ 18 51

1644-1949

20789 NIC P P1 G1.3 –1928
Arlington, Lewis Charles, 1859–1942.
'The mystic art of pulse feeling in China.'
CJ 2, 5 (Sept. 1924), 400–411.
Subj 56 62

20790 NNC PO P4 G1.1 1644–1928
Balme, Harold, 1878–1953.
China and modern medicine: A study in medical missionary development.
London: United Council for Missionary Education, 1921. 224 p.
Subj 17 56 66 ▪ 18 36.1 47 62 65

20791 CSU P P3 G9.2 1842–1949
Cadbury, William Warder, 1877–1959, and Mary Hoxie Jones.
At the point of a lancet: One hundred years of the Canton Hospital, 1835–1935.
Shanghai: Kelly and Walsh, 1935. 17, 304 p.
Subj 56 66 ▪ 17 28 33

20792 NNM PO P1 G1.1 –1949
Chao, C. S. (Chao Ching-shen), 1902–.
'Chinese anthelmintic prescriptions: Examples from the Han period to the present time.'
CMJ 57, 3 (Mar. 1940), 251–289.
Subj 56 ▪ 65

20793 NIC O P5 G1.3 1644–1928
Chen, K. K. (Ch'en K'o-hui), 1896–.
'Chinese drug stores.'
Annals of medical history 7, 2 (Summer 1925), 103–109.
Subj 34.2 56 ▪ 16.2 62

20794 NIC P P1 G1.2 1644–1949
Ch'en Hsiang-ch'un.
'Examples of charms against epidemics, with short explanations.'
FS 1 (1942), 37–54.
Subj 56 62 65

20795 NNC O P2 G2.0 1842–1928
Christie, Dugald, 1855–1936.
Thirty years in the Manchu capital, in and around Moukden, in peace and war: Being the recollections of Dugald Christie, C.M.G., edited by Iza Inglis Christie.
New York: McBride, Nast, 1914. 14, 303 p.
Subj 25 28 56 62 66 ▪ 12 12.2 15 17 23 24.2 48 55 63

20796 NIC O P1 G1.2 –1949
Dittrick, Howard, 1877–1954.
'Chinese medicine dolls.'
B. of the history of medicine 26, 5 (1952), 422–429.
Subj 46 47 56

20797 MCH P P1 G1.2 –1949
Eckardht, P- A-.
'Ginseng, die Wunderwurzel des Fernen Ostens' (Ginseng, the miracle root of the Far East).
OR 12, 21 (1 Nov. 1931), 538–541.
Subj 56 ▪ 62 65

20798 NNC O P2 G1.2 1895–1928
Gamewell, Mary Louise Ninde, 1858–1947.
New life currents in China.
New York: Interchurch Press, 1919. 12, 232 p.
Subj 17 18 19 56 ▪ 41 47 62 65 66

20799 CSU O P3 G1.2 1895–1949
Grant, John Black, 1890–1962.
'Western medicine in pre-Communist China.'
American j. of public health 50, 6 (June 1960), 36–39. [Supplement: *Public health is one world*]
Subj 56

20800 NNC O P3 G1.3 1895–1928
Greene, Roger S-.
'The Rockefeller Foundation in China.'
Asia (New York: American Asiatic Assn.) 19, 11 (Nov. 1919), 1117–1124.
Subj 56 ▪ 17 18 38

20801 NNC P P1 G1.2 –1949
Hume, Edward Hicks, 1876–1957.
The Chinese way in medicine.
Baltimore: Johns Hopkins Press, 1940. 189 p. (Johns Hopkins U., Institute of the History of Medicine, Hideyo Noguchi lectures, 4)
Subj 56 62 ▪ 50 51 64 65 72

20802 MCY PO P3 G7.2 1895–1928
Hume, Edward Hicks, 1876–1957.
Doctors east, doctors west: An American physician's life in China.
New York: Norton, 1946. 278 p.
Subj 56 66 ▪ 22 23 28

20803 NNC P P2 G1.1 1644–1949
Kho Guan-tin (Huo Kuang-t'ing) and Gnien Shou-min.
'K voprosu ob endemichnosti i periodichnosti kholery v Kitae' (Endemic and cyclical cholera in China).
Zhurnal mikrobiologii, epidemologii i immunobiologii 29, 7 (iiul' 1958), 85–90.
Subj 56 ▪ 58

20804 NNC PO P3 G8.1 –1949
Lindsay, Ashley W-, 1884–1968.
'Dentistry in China.'
JWCBRS 4 (1930/31), 127–142.
Subj 56 ▪ 17 62 65

20805 NIC O P1 G1.1 1895–1928
Maxwell, James Laidlaw.
The diseases of China, 2nd ed.
Shanghai: A.B.C. Press, 1929. 530 p.
Subj 56

20806 NIC PO P1 G1.2 1842–1949
Maxwell, James Laidlaw.
Leprosy: A practical textbook for use in China.
Shanghai: ——, 1937. 109 p.
Subj 56 ▪ 18

20807 MCH S P1 G1.1 –1928
[Möller, Heinz] Asiaticus, pseud.
'Chinesische Arzneimittel' (Chinese medicines).
Der Erdball 2, 1 (1928), 4–10.
Subj 56 ▪ 62 65

20808 NNC PO P2 G8.1 –1949
Morse, William Reginald, 1874–1939.
'A memorandum on the Chinese procedure of acupuncture.'
JWCBRS 5 (1932), 153–220.
Subj 56 ▪ 62

20809 NNC PO P2 G8.1 –1928
Morse, William Reginald, 1874–1939.
'The practices and principles of Chinese medicine.'
JWCBRS 3 (1926/29), 82–104.
Subj 56 ▪ 62

20810 MCH O P1 G1.2 –1949
Mortier, Florent.
'Les animaux dans la divination et la médecine populaire chinoise' (Animals in divination and in Chinese folk medicine).
BSRB 51 (1936), 268–275.
Subj 56 62 65

20811 MCH S P1 G1.1 –1928
Müller, Reinhold F- E-.
'Über Skelettdarstellungen in Asia Major' (The depiction of the skeleton in East Asia).
Asia Major 2, 3/4 (July–Oct. 1925), 531–563.
Subj 56 ▪ 57 62

20812 MCH P P1 G1.0 –1949
Nakayama, T.
Acupuncture et médecine chinoises vérifiées au Japon (Chinese acupuncture and medicine examined in Japan). Tr. from the Japanese by T. Sakurazawa and Georges Soulié.
Paris: Ed. Hippocrate, 1934. 85 p.
Subj 56 62 ▪ 51 55

20813 CSU P P2 G2.0 1895–1949
Nathan, Carl F-.
Plague prevention and politics in Manchuria, 1910–1931.
Cambridge: Harvard U., East Asian Research Center, 1967. 106 p. (Harvard East Asian monographs, 23)
Subj 12 18 56 ▪ 12.1 57 66

20814 MCH S P1 G1.2 –1928
Olpp, Gottlieb, 1872–?
'Medizin und Naturwissenschaften in China' (Medicine and the natural sciences in China). In *Das Licht des Ostens* (The light from the East), edited by Maximilian Kern. [Selective entry]
Stuttgart: Union deutsche Verlagsgesellschaft, 1922, 489–504.
Subj 56 ▪ 62

20815 IMA PO P4 G1.1 –1949
Piaggio, Manlio.
La medicina cinese (Chinese medicine).
Turin: Minerva medica, 1939. 79 p.
Subj 56 ▪ 62

20816 CSU P P1 G1.2 –1949
Read, Bernard Emms, 1887–1949.
'Ancient Chinese medicine and its modern interpretation.'

THM 8, 3 (Mar. 1939), 221–234.
SUBJ 56

20817 CSU P P1 G1.2 -1949
Read, Bernard Emms, 1887–1949.
'Animal preparations used in Chinese medicine.'
THM 8, 2 (Feb. 1939), 128–144.
SUBJ 56

20818 NNC PO P2 G1.3 -1949
Read, Bernard Emms, 1887–1949.
'The dragon in Chinese medicine.'
JRAS-NCB new (2nd) series 70 (1939), 21–29.
SUBJ 56 ▪ 62 65

20819 CBU O P1 G1.2 1895–1949
Tsu Min-yi.
'Le problème médico-pharmaceutique d'hier et d'aujourd'hui en Chine' (Medical and pharmaceutical problems in China, past and present).
Annales franco-chinoises 4, 16 (4e trimestre 1930), 2–13.
SUBJ 17 56 62

20820 NBO O P2 G7.2 1895–1949
Vogt, Volrath, 1879–.
Blandt syke i Kina (Among the sick in China).
Stavanger: Norske missionsselskap, 1931. 135 p.
SUBJ 56 ▪ 12 15 23 33 53 55 64

20821 MCH O P2 G1.5 1895–1928
Vortisch-van Vloten, H-.
'Die Aussätzigen in China' (Lepers in China).
ASTH 20, 6 (1916), 141–147.
SUBJ 56 ▪ 26 55 57

20822 CLS PO P4 G1.3 -1949
Whitmore, Clara Belle, 1882–.
An historical sketch of medicine and obstetrics in China.
Unpublished masters thesis in History, U. of Southern California, 1931. 107 p.
SUBJ 51 56 ▪ 18 23 52 66

20823 CLS PO P4 G1.2 -1949
Whitmore, Clara Belle, 1882–.
A history of the development of Western medicine in China.
Unpublished doctoral dissertation in History, U. of Southern California, 1934. 368 p.
SUBJ 17 56 66 ▪ 18 33 36.1 47 63 64

20824 CSU P P1 G1.1 -1928
Wong, K. Chimin (Wang Chi-min).
'Chinese medical sayings and proverbs.'
CMJ 39, 12 (Dec. 1925), 1099–1101; 40, 1 (Jan. 1926), 25–27; 40, 2 (Feb. 1926), 150–153; 40, 4 (Apr. 1926), 350–353.
SUBJ 56 65

20825 CSU U P3 G1.3 1895–1949
Wong, K. Chimin (Wang Chi-min).
'A short history of psychiatry and mental hygiene in China.'
CMJ 68, 1/2 (Jan.–Feb. 1950), 44–48.
SUBJ 56 61 ▪ 17

20826 NNC P P2 G1.1 -1949
Wong, K. Chimin (Wang Chi-min), and Wu Lien-teh (Wu Lien-te), 1879–1960.
History of Chinese medicine: Being a chronicle of medical happenings in China from ancient times to the present period, 2nd ed.
Shanghai: Wei sheng pu, Ch'üan kuo hai kang chien i kuan li ch'u, 1936. 28, 906 p. [Reprinted—New York: AMS Press, 1972. 28, 906 p.]
SUBJ 17 18 56 62 ▪ 16.1 16.2 36.1 47 51 64 65 66 72

20827 NNC PO P3 G1.1 -1949
Wu Lien-teh (Wu Lien-te), 1879–1960.
'Public hospitals in China.'
CQ-S 1, 4 (Summer 1936), 1–11.
SUBJ 17 18 56 ▪ 38 62

1911-1949

20828 NNM O P3 G9.1 1928–1949
'Health in Wuchow [Kwangsi].'
CMJ 46, 7 (July 1932), 732–733.
SUBJ 56

20829 NNC O P7 G7.3 1928–1949
'Health work in Kiangsi.'
CMJ 51, 1 (Jan. 1937), 102–104.
SUBJ 56 ▪ 51

20830 CSU O P3 G6.1 1928–1949
'Hospital reports: Lester Chinese Hospital, Shanghai, 1929; Soochow Hospital, M.E.S., 1929.'
CMJ 44, 10 (Oct. 1930), 1140–1142.
SUBJ 56

20831 NNM P P1 G1.2 1928–1949
'Hygiene and public health: Public health reconstruction under the national government.'
CMJ 46, 8 (Aug. 1932), 826–834.
SUBJ 18 56 ▪ 17

20832 CSH FP P2 G1.1 1911–1928
'Medical work.' In *The Christian occupation of China*, edited by Milton Theobald Stauffer. [Selective entry]
Shanghai: China Continuation Committee, 1922, 429–442.
SUBJ 38 55 56 ▪ 14.3 17 18

20833 NNC P P4 G1.2 1928–1949
'National health administration.'
CMJ 61, 1 (Jan.–Mar. 1943), 75–84.
SUBJ 38 56 ▪ 12

20834 NNC P P2 G1.2 1928–1949
'Report of the National Health Administration on the three year plan, 1931–34.' In *Annexes to the Report to the Council of the League of Nations of its technical delegate on his mission in China from date of appointment until April 1, 1934, Annex 8.* [Sole entry]
Shanghai: North-China Daily News and Herald, 1934, 241–277.
SUBJ 18 56

20835 NNC O P2 G1.4 1928–1949
Adolph, Paul Ernest, 1901–.
Surgery speaks to China: The experiences of a medical missionary to China in peace and in war.
Philadelphia: China Inland Mission, 1945. 195 p.
SUBJ 56 ▪ 51 65 66

20836 NNC O P7 G2.1 1911–1949
[Arsen'ev, Vladimir Klavdievich] W. Arssenjew, 1872–1930, and Friedrich Dorbeck.
'Die chinesische Allheilwurzel (Jen-Schen) und ihre Sammler im Amurlande' (Ginseng root, the Chinese panacea, and its collectors in the Amur region).
NDG 82 (1957), 66–72.
SUBJ 56 ▪ 24.3 65

20837 MCH PO P2 G1.2 1911–1928
Assn. for the Advancement of Public Health in China.
Memorandum on the need of a public health organization in China.
Peking: Assn. for the Advancement of Public Health in China, 1926. 108 p.
SUBJ 18 51 56 ▪ 11.4 12.1 16 55

20838 CSU O P3 G6.1 1928–1949
Bacon, C- A-.
'Pharmacy in Shanghai.'
CEJ 5, 2 (Aug. 1929), 650–661.
SUBJ 56 ▪ 34.2

20839 NNM O P3 G8.1 1928–1949
Basil, George Chester, 1902–.
Test tubes and dragon scales.
Philadelphia: Winston, 1940? 11, 316 p.
SUBJ 51 56 62 63 ▪ 65 66

20840 NNC F P8 G8.1 1928–1949
Chang, K. (Chang Kuei), 1906–, et al.
'The epidemiology and importance of hookworm diseases in Szechuan province.'
CMJ (Chengtu) 61A, 1 (Oct. 1942), 1–8.
SUBJ 56 ▪ 24.1 28

20841 NNC U P1 G1.2 1928–1949
Chen, Lawrence M. (Ch'en Wen-t'ung).
'Public health in national reconstruction.'
IB 3, 3 (1 Feb. 1937), 51–82.
SUBJ 17 18 56 ▪ 12.1 37

20842 NNM F P7 G5.1 1928–1949
Ch'en, C. C. (Ch'en Chih-ch'ien).
'A practical survey of rural health.'
CMJ 47, 7 (July 1933), 680–688.
SUBJ 56 58

20843 MCH F P7 G5.1 1928–1949
Ch'en, C. C. (Ch'en Chih-ch'ien).
'Public health in rural reconstruction at Ting hsien [Hopei]: Fourth annual report of the public health experiment in China.'
MMFQ 12, 4 (Oct. 1934), 370–378.
SUBJ 28 56 ▪ 27 37

20844 NIC F P2 G5.1 1928–1949
Ch'en, C. C. (Ch'en Chih-ch'ien).
'The rural public health experiment in Ting hsien [Hopei], China.'
MMFQ 14, 1 (Jan. 1936), 66–80.
SUBJ 28 56 58 ▪ 22 27 37 38

20845 NIC F P7 G5.1 1911–1949
Ch'en, C. C. (Ch'en Chih-ch'ien).
'Scientific medicine as applied in Ting hsien [Hopei]: Third annual report of the rural public health experiment in China.'
MMFQ 11, 2 (Apr. 1933), 97–129.
SUBJ 56 ▪ 27 28 37

20846 NIC O P2 G5.1 1928–1949
Ch'en, C. C. (Ch'en Chih-ch'ien).
'Ting hsien [Hopei] and the public health movement in China.'
MMFQ 15, 4 (Oct. 1937), 380–390.
SUBJ 28 56 58

20847 NNM PO P7 G5.1 1928–1949
Ch'en, C. C. (Ch'en Chih-ch'ien), and F. J. Li.

'Controlling smallpox under Chinese rural conditions.'
CMJ 48, 2 (Feb. 1934), 153–157.
Subj 56

20848 CSU U P2 G1.5 1928–1949
Chu, C. K., 1901–.
'The modern public health movement in China.' In *Voices from unoccupied China*, edited by Harley Farnsworth MacNair. [Selective entry]
Chicago: U. of Chicago Press, 1944, 26–35.
Subj 18 56

20849 NNM P P2 G1.2 1928–1949
Chu, Hsi-ju, and Daniel G. Lai.
'Distribution of modern-trained physicians in China.'
CMJ 49, 6 (June 1935), 542–552.
Subj 56 ▪ 16.1

20850 NNM F P3 G6.1 1911–1928
Decker, H- W-.
'Industrial Hospital, Shanghai: Review of 880 cases from the cotton mills.'
CMJ 38, 3 (Mar. 1924), 226–233.
Subj 56 ▪ 26.4

20851 DCK S P3 G6.1 1928–1949
Faber, Knud Helge, 1862–1956.
'Nanking som lægevidenskabeligt centrum i Kina' (Nanking as a scientific-medical center in China).
Ugeskrift for læger 98 (1936), 144–146.
Subj 56 ▪ 28

20852 NIC O P2 G1.2 1911–1928
Faust, Ernest Carroll, 1890–.
'Some facts regarding the relation between nightsoil disposal in China and the propagation of helminthic diseases.'
American j. of tropical medicine 4, 6 (Nov. 1924), 487–505.
Subj 55 56

20853 NNM F P8 G9.1 1928–1949
Feng, Lan-chou.
'Malaria and its transmission in Kwangsi, China.'
CMJ 50, 12 (Dec. 1936), 1799–1814.
Subj 56

20854 NNM F P3 G7.2 1911–1928
Foster, John Harold, 1880–.
'Physical examination of Chinese students.'
CMJ 37, 8 (Aug. 1923), 643–649.
Subj 56

20855 GMS O P2 G1.5 1928–1949
Freudmann, W-.
Tschi-lai! Erhebt Euch! Erlebnisse eines Arztes in China und Burma, 1939–45 (Ch'i-lai! Rise up! A doctor's experiences in China and Burma, 1939–1945).
Linz-Urfahr: Neue Zeit, 1947. 220 p.
Subj 56 ▪ 19 47 55

20856 NIC O P1 G4.4 1928–1949
Frick, Johannes.
'How blood is used in magic and medicine in Ch'inghai province.'
Anthropos 46, 5/6 (Sept.–Dez. 1951), 964–979.
Subj 23 56 65 ▪ 47

20857 NNC O P1 G4.0 1911–1949
Frick, Johannes.
'Körpergeruch als Krankheit' (Body odor as an illness).
Anthropos 58, 3/4 (Mai–Aug. 1963), 477–484.
Subj 56 ▪ 41 65

20858 CSU F P8 G4.4 1928–1949
Frick, Johannes.
'Magic remedies used on sick children in the western valley of Sining.' Tr. from the German by James E- Mertz.
Anthropos 46, 1/2 (Jan.–Apr. 1951), 175–186.
Subj 23 52 56 ▪ 57 62 65

20859 CSU F P8 G4.4 1928–1949
Frick, Johannes.
'Medicinal uses of substances derived from the animal organism (in Tsinghai).' Tr. from the German by James E- Mertz.
Anthropos 52, 1/2 (Jan.–Apr. 1957), 177–198.
Subj 56

20860 NNM P P3 G1.2 1928–1949
Gear, Harry Sutherland, 1903–.
'Disease incidence in China: An analysis of hospital records for 1934.'
CMJ 50, 7 (July 1936), 947–972.
Subj 56

20861 NNM P P4 G1.1 1928–1949
Gear, Harry Sutherland, 1903–.
'The incidence of venereal diseases in hospital patients in China.'
CMJ 49, 10 (Oct. 1935), 1122–1135.
Subj 56 ▪ 47

20862 NNC F P3 G6.1 1928–1949
Gear, Harry Sutherland, 1903–, et al.
Industrial health in Shanghai, China, [I], An investigation of printing works.
Shanghai: Chinese Medical Assn., 1935. 26 p. (CMA, Special report series, 4)
Subj 26.4 56 ▪ 24.4 28 55

20863 NNC O P2 G8.1 1928–1949
Gervais, Albert, 1892–.
Æsculape en Chine.
Paris: Gallimard, 1933. 255 p.

Medicine man in China. Tr. by Vincent Sheean.
New York: Stokes, 1934. 336 p. [Also published as *A surgeon's China.* London: Hamilton, 1934. 302 p.]
Subj 25 28 56 ▪ 17 24.2 41 61 66

20864 NNM F P3 G1.3 1911–1949
Grant, John Black, 1890–1962, and T. M. P'eng (P'eng Ta-mou).
'Survey of urban public health practice in China.'
CMJ 48, 10 (Oct. 1934), 1074–1079.
Subj 56

20865 MCH O P2 G1.2 1911–1928
Greene, Roger S-.
'Public health and the training of doctors and nurses in China.'
International review of missions 14, 56 (Oct. 1925), 481–498.
Subj 17 56 66 ▪ 18 47 55

20866 MCH O P4 G1.2 1911–1928
Heath, F- J-.
'Venereal diseases in relation to prostitution in China.'
Social pathology 1, 6 (1925), 278–284.
Subj 46 47 56 ▪ 18

20867 NNM P P1 G1.2 1911–1928
Hedblom, Carl Arthur, 1879–1934.
'On disease incidence in China.'
CMJ 31, 4 (July 1917), 271–283.
Subj 56

20868 NNM F P3 G5.3 1911–1928
Heimburger, L- F-.
'The incidence of syphilis at the Shantung Christian University dispensary.'
CMJ 41, 6 (June 1927), 541–550.
Subj 56 ▪ 28

20869 CSH P P2 G9.5 1928–1949
Hong Kong. Dept. of Medical Sciences.
Annual report, 1947, 1948/49. [Issues for 1949/50–1971/72 are entered as 21061.]
[Hong Kong]: ——, 1947, 1949. Average ca. 140 p.
Subj 56 ▪ 17 51 58

20870 CSU P P2 G9.5 1928–1949
Hong Kong. Urban Council *with* Hong Kong. Sanitary Dept.
Annual departmental report by the Chairman, Urban Council, 1947, 1948, 1948/49. [Issues for 1949/50–1971/72 are entered as 21063.]
[Hong Kong]: ——. Issued annually, 1947–1949. Average ca. 30 p.
Subj 56 ▪ 24.3 24.5 57

20871 CSH P P2 G2.0 1928–1949
Hsiao, Tsai-yu (Hsiao Ts'ai-yü), 1905–.
Epidemiology of the diseases of naval importance in Manchuria.
Washington, D.C.: U.S. Dept. of the Navy, Bureau of Medicine and Surgery, 1946. 54 p. (Nav Med, 958)
Subj 56 ▪ 18 58

20872 NIC F P6 G8.2 1928–1949
Hsu, Francis L. K. (Hsü Lang-kuang), 1909–.
'A cholera epidemic in a Chinese town [Hsi-chou, Ta-li *hsien*, Yunnan].' In *Health, culture and community*, edited by Benjamin David Paul. [Sole entry]
New York: Russel Sage Foundation, 1955, 135–154.
Subj 23 56 ▪ 28 60 62

20873 MCH FP P7 G8.2 1928–1949
Hsu, Francis L. K. (Hsü Lang-kuang), 1909–.
Religion, science, and human crisis: A study of China in transition and its implications for the west. [Study of Hsi-chou, Ta-li *hsien*, Yunnan]
London: Routledge and Kegan Paul, 1952. 10, 142 p.
Subj 20 23 28 56 62 65 ▪ 21.4 29 30 33 55 57 61 71

20874 NNC F P3 G8.1 1928–1949
Hsu, Kuo Chin (Hsü Kuo-ch'ing).
'A survey of human intestinal parasites in Chengtu.'
CMJ 65, 3/4 (Mar.–Apr. 1947), 85–90.
Subj 56

20875 NNM O P3 G6.1 1911–1928
Hu, Hou-ki.
'The new Department of Health, Port of Shanghai and Woosung.'
CMJ 41, 5 (May 1927), 429–438.
Subj 56 ▪ 22

20876 NNM PO P2 G6.1 1928–1949
Huang, H. H., and T. H. Wang.
'A survey of the maternity and child health work in Nanking [municipality].'
CMJ 50, 4 (Apr. 1936), 554–561.
Subj 51 56 ▪ 22 52 58

20877 CSU P P2 G1.2 1911–1928
Huang, Tse-fang (Huang Tzu-fang).
'Public health in China: A proposed program.' Tr. of 'Chung-kuo wei sheng ch'u i' (Proposals on public health and sanitation in China); *She hui hsüeh chieh* 1 (June 1927), 187–203.
Special b. of the National Epidemic Prevention Bureau 3 (1927), 1–26.
Subj 18 56 ▪ 58

20878 NNM F P2 G7.2 1911–1928
Hume, Edward Hicks, 1876–1957.
'Hookworm control in South China.'
CMJ 31, 6 (Nov. 1917), 471–482.
Subj 56 ▪ 28

20879 FPN P P3 G6.1 1911–1949
Jen, Huei-chia (Jen Hui-chia), 1909–.
Le choléra à Changhai dans les dix dernières années (1926–1935) (Cholera in Shanghai during the past ten years, 1926–1935).
Paris: M. Vigné, 1937. 48 p. (Doctoral dissertation, Faculté de médecine, Université de Paris)
Subj 56

20880 NNC PO P2 G5.0 1928–1949
K'ai-luan k'uang wu tsung chü (Kailan Mining Administration, North China).
Annual report of the medical service, 1st July 1930 – 30th June 1931.
[Tientsin?]: ——, 1932. 17 p.
Subj 56 ▪ 18

20881 NNC P P2 G8.3 1928–1949
Kao, Yung-en.
'Incidence of various diseases among children in Kweichow.'
CMJ 66, 9 (Sept. 1948), 487–493.
Subj 52 56

20882 NNM F P2 G6.1 1928–1949
Khaw, O. K. (Hsü Yü-chieh), and H. C. Kan.
'Some observations on the prevalence of malaria in Nanking and its vicinity.'
CMJ 48, 2 (Feb. 1934), 109–123.
Subj 56 ▪ 28

20883 NNC S P3 G6.1 1911–1928
Kim, C. S.
'A brief survey of the public health activities in Shanghai.'
CMJ 42, 3 (Mar. 1928), 162–180.
Subj 22 28 56 ▪ 21.1 58

20884 NNC O P3 G6.1 1911–1928
King, Gerald.
'A Chinese chemist's shop.'
CMJ 33, 2 (Mar. 1919), 155–159.
Subj 56 ▪ 34.2 65

20885 NNC P P3 G6.1 1928–1949
King, P. Z. (Chin Pao-shan), 1893–, Y. Y. Ying, and Y. T. Yao.
'Health survey of Nanking.'
CMJ 43, 11 (Nov. 1929), 1128–1141.
Subj 28 56 ▪ 21.1 58

20886 CSU O P3 G6.1 1911–1949
King-Salmon, Frances W-.
House of a thousand babies: Experiences of an American woman physician in China (1922–1940).
New York: Exposition Press, 1968. 168 p.
Subj 56 66 ▪ 14.6 17 41 51 62 63

20887 DLC O P7 G8.1 1928–1949
Knights, F-.
'A rural hospital at work.' In *Wartime China, as seen by westerners.* [Selective entry]
Chungking: China Publishing Co., 1942, 157–162.
Subj 56 ▪ 28

20888 CSU F P2 G5.1 1911–1928
Korns, John H-.
'Incidence of tuberculous infection in China.'
CMJ 39, 1 (Jan. 1925), 10–19.
Subj 56

20889 NNM F P3 G5.1 1911–1928
Korns, John H-.
'Incidence of vaccination and smallpox in North China.'
CMJ 35, 6 (Nov. 1921), 561–563.
Subj 28 56

20890 NNM PO P4 G8.2 1928–1949
Lai, Daniel G., and C. M. Chu.
'The Kutsing [i.e., the capital of Ch'ü-ching *hsien*] (Yunnan) Health Demonstration Centre: A review for 1939–40.'
CMJ 59, 5 (May 1941), 468–475.
Subj 28 56 ▪ 21.1 58

20891 NNC O P5 G9.2 1911–1928
Lai, Daniel G., and Yuan Kai Huang.
'Notes on diseases of the Hakkas.'
CMJ 43, 2 (Feb. 1929), 104–110.
Subj 56 ▪ 28 29

20892 NNC F P3 G9.2 1928–1949
Lai, Daniel G., and Suchen Wang Lai.
'Incidence of syphilis among Chinese civilian patients in Swatow district.'
CMJ 43, 1 (Jan. 1929), 22–27.
Subj 56

20893 NNC F P3 G9.2 1911–1928
Lai, Daniel G., and Suchen Wang Lai.
'Incidence of syphilis among the Chinese soldiers at Swatow.'
CMJ 42, 8 (Aug. 1928), 557–567.
Subj 56 ▪ 15

20894 CSH O P2 G9.1 1928–1949
Lasnet, ———.
'Dix mois de mission sanitaire dans le Sud de la Chine' (Ten months on a hospital mission in South China).
AF 39, 371 (juin 1939), 203–207; 39, 372 (juil.–août 1939), 241–247; 39, 373 (sept.–oct. 1939), 296–300.
Subj 12 28 56 ▪ 15 21.3 25 32.2 55

20895 NNC F P3 G1.3 1928–1949
Lennox, William Gordon, 1884–1960.
'The distribution of medical school graduates in China.'
CMJ 46, 4 (Apr. 1932), 404–411.
Subj 56 ▪ 16.1 17

20896 NNC FP P2 G1.2 1928–1949
Lennox, William Gordon, 1884–1960.
'Medical missions.' In *China*, edited by Orville Anderson Petty. [Selective entry]
New York: Harper, 1933, 425–501. (Layman's Foreign Missions Inquiry, Factfinders' reports, 5; Supplementary series, part 2)
Subj 33 55 56 ▪ 17 18 37

20897 NNM O P3 G9.2 1911–1928
Li Shu-fan (Li Shu-fen), 1887–1966.
'Sanitation in South China.'
CMJ 27, 4 (July 1913), 226–231.
Subj 56 ▪ 22 28

20898 NNM PO P3 G6.1 1928–1949
Li, T. A. (Li T'ing-an), 1899–.
'Activities of the Bureau of Public Health, city government of Greater Shanghai.' Tr. of 'Shang-hai shih chih kung kung wei sheng hsing cheng' (Public-health administration in Shanghai municipality); *Wei sheng yüeh k'an* 4, 1 (Jan. 1934), 20–25. [Tr. inferred]
CMJ 49, 9 (Sept. 1935), 990–992.
Subj 22 56 ▪ 28 58

20899 NNM F P8 G1.3 1928–1949
Li, T. A. (Li T'ing-an), 1899–.
'Summary report on rural public health practice in China.'
CMJ 48, 10 (Oct. 1934), 1086–1090.
Subj 56

20900 NNC PO P3 G1.3 1928–1949
Liu, J. Heng (Liu Jui-heng), 1890–1961.
'The Ministry of Health.'
CMJ 43, 4 (Apr. 1929), 319–331.
Subj 12 56 ▪ 17

20901 CSU O P2 G1.5 1928–1949
Liu, J. Heng (Liu Jui-heng), 1890–1961.
'The origin and development of the Public Health Service in China.' In *Voices from unoccupied China*, edited by Harley Farnsworth MacNair. [Selective entry]
Chicago: U. of Chicago Press, 1944, 36–45.
Subj 56 ▪ 17

20902 CSU PO P3 G1.2 1911–1928
McCartney, James Lincoln, 1898–.
'Neuropsychiatry in China: A preliminary observation.'
CMJ 40, 7 (July 1926), 617–626.
Subj 18 56 61 ▪ 62

20903 CSU PO P3 G1.2 1911–1928
McCartney, James Lincoln, 1898–.
'Neuropsychiatry in China: A retrospect of diagnosis.'
CMJ 40, 9 (Sept. 1926), 831–842.
Subj 56 61 ▪ 62

20904 NNC FP P3 G1.2 1911–1928
Maitland, Charles Titterton.
'Phosphorous poisoning in match factories in China, with brief observations on the general conditions of labour found.'
CJ 3, 2 (Feb. 1925), 103–113; 3, 3 (Mar. 1925), 169–178.
Subj 14.4 16.4 56 ▪ 34.2 58

20905 NNM O P8 G9.3 1911–1928
Maxwell, J- Preston.
'Intestinal parasitism in south Fukien.'

CMJ 35, 4 (July 1921), 377–382.
Subj 52 56

20906 CSU F P4 G9.2 1928–1949
Meister, H-.
'Ärztliches Arbeiten in China 1937–1949' (Medical work in China, 1937–1949).
Schweizerische medizinische Wochenschrift 80, 46 (18 Nov. 1950), 1238–1340.
Subj 56

20907 NNC O P4 G1.3 1911–1928
Merrins, Edward M-.
'Medical ethics in China.'
CMJ 38, 8 (Aug. 1924), 679–694.
Subj 56 63

20908 DLC O P3 G1.3 1928–1949
Meuser, E- N-.
'Native medical supplies.' In *Wartime China, as seen by westerners*. [Selective entry]
Chungking: China Publishing Co., 1942, 217–224.
Subj 56 ▪ 17

20909 NIC O P2 G5.1 1911–1949
Milbank Memorial Fund.
'A rural health experiment in China.'
MMFQ 8, 4 (Oct. 1930), 97–107.
Subj 56 ▪ 37

20910 NNC O P7 G8.1 1928–1949
Nutting, Clara A-.
'Health department.' In *The healthy village: An experiment in visual education in West China*, edited by Educational, Scientific and Cultural Organization, United Nations. [Sole entry]
Paris: UNESCO, 1951, 34–40. (Monographs on fundamental education, 5)
Subj 28 56 ▪ 37 38 55

20911 NNC P P3 G9.2 1911–1928
Oldt, Frank.
'Purity campaign, Canton.'
CMJ 37, 9 (Sept. 1923), 776–782.
Subj 46 56 ▪ 47

20912 NNM P P1 G9.2 1911–1949
Oldt, Frank.
'Tuberculosis in Kwangtung, according to age, sex, occupation and economic condition.'
CMJ 47, 2 (Feb. 1933), 111–127.
Subj 56 ▪ 28 47 50

20913 CSU F P3 G5.1 1928–1949
Pei, T. (Pai Tuan).
'The post-withdrawal care of Chinese drug addicts.' In *Social and psychological studies in neuropsychiatry in China*, edited by Richard Sherman Lyman, V- Maeker, and P. Liang (Liang Meng-chüan). [Selective entry]
Peiping: Peking Union Medical College, Division of Neuropsychiatry, 1939, 231–247.
Subj 56

20914 CSU O P2 G1.2 1911–1928
Peter, William Wesley, 1882–.
'Field and methods of public health work in missionary enterprise.'
CMJ 40, 3 (Mar. 1926), 185–239. [Separately reprinted as *Broadcasting health in China: The field and methods of public health work in the missionary enterprise*. Shanghai: Presbyterian Mission Press, 1926. 89 p.]
Subj 24.2 56 ▪ 28 66

20915 CSH F P3 G6.1 1928–1949
Platt, B- S-, and Rewi Alley, 1897–.
Industrial health in Shanghai, China, IV, Lead and antimony in Shanghai industries.
Shanghai: Chinese Medical Assn., 1937. 33 p. (CMA, Special report series, 9)
Subj 26.4 56 ▪ 24.4

20916 NNM P P3 G8.2 1928–1949
Pollitzer, R-, et al.
'The 1939 cholera epidemic in Yunnan province, with special reference to Kunming city.'
CMJ 59, 5 (May 1941), 457–467.
Subj 56 ▪ 28

20917 NNM O P4 G9.3 1911–1928
Poulter, Mabel C-.
'Obstetrical experiences in Futsing city [i.e., Fu-ch'ing *hsien*], Fukien, China.'
CMJ 35, 4 (July 1921), 331–347.
Subj 51 56

20918 NNC O P3 G6.1 1911–1949
Rasmussen, Otto Durham, 1888–.
'Chinesische Brillen' (Chinese eyeglasses).
Atlantis 2 (1930), 12–15.
Subj 56 ▪ 62

20919 NNC F P3 G6.1 1928–1949
Read, Bernard Emms, 1887–1949, et al.
Industrial health in Shanghai, China, II, A study of the chromium plating and polishing trade.
Shanghai: Chinese Medical Assn., 1936. 47 p. (CMA, Special report series, 6)
Subj 26.4 55 56 ▪ 24.4 28

20920 NNM F P3 G7.2 1911–1928
Reed, Alfred Cummings, 1884–1951.
'Prevalence of hookworm at Changsha.'
CMJ 28, 4 (July 1914), 263–266.
Subj 56

20921 CSU F P3 G5.1 1928–1949
Schaltenbrand, Georg.
'Psychiatrie in Peking' (Psychiatry in Peking).
Z. für die gesamte Neurologie und Psychiatrie 137 (1931), 168–232.
Subj 28 56 61 ▪ 41 46

20922 NNM F P3 G5.1 1911–1928
Sia, Richard H. P.
'Routine Wasserman test on 502 in-patients.'
CMJ 35, 1 (Jan. 1921), 39–42.
Subj 56

20923 MCH PO P3 G5.4 1928–1949
Snapper, Isidore, 1889–.
Chinese lessons to Western medicine.
New York: Interscience Publishers, 1941. 10, 380 p. [Reprinted—New York: Grune and Stratton, 1965. 416 p.]
Subj 56 ▪ 17 28 57

20924 NNM F P3 G6.1 1911–1928
Snell, John A-, and P. Y. Chang.
'Report of routine Wasserman test at Soochow hospital for one year.'
CMJ 35, 1 (Jan. 1921), 36–39.
Subj 56

20925 NNM F P7 G6.1 1928–1949
Su, T. L., and T. F. Huang.
'Malaria as a rural social problem in the south-western suburbs of Shanghai.'
CMJ 51, 6 (June 1937), 963–970.
Subj 56 ▪ 28

20926 NNC PO P2 G1.2 1928–1949
Sze, Szeming (Shih Ssu-ming), 1908–.
China's health problems.
New York: China Institute in America, 1942. 46 p. [Reprinted—Washington, D.C.: Chinese Medical Assn., 1943. 60 p.]
Subj 12.1 18 56 ▪ 15 17 36.1 38 58 66

20927 NNC F P7 G4.4 1928–1949
Trippner, Josef.
'Der wandernde Medizingott' (The itinerant Medicine God [Yao-wang]).
Anthropos 46, 5/6 (Sept.–Dez. 1951), 801–807.
Subj 23 56 ▪ 62

20928 CSU F P3 G5.1 1928–1949
Ts'ai, Ju-sheng.
'The study of annual tuberculin conversion in Peking.'
CMJ 69, 9/10 (Sept.–Oct. 1951), 392–399.
Subj 56

20929 NNC O P1 G1.2 1928–1949
Tsao Lien-en (Ts'ao Lien-en).
'Quarantine service in China.'
IB 3, 7 (11 Mar. 1937), 139–156.
Subj 56

20930 NNM O P3 G5.1 1928–1949
Tseng, Lily.
'Midwifery.'
CMJ 44, 5 (May 1930), 431–445.
Subj 51 56 ▪ 22 27

20931 NNC O P3 G5.1 1911–1928
Tso, Ernest.
'Statistics of communicable diseases among hospital employees.'
CMJ 37, 3/4 (Mar.–Apr. 1923), 226–231.
Subj 56

20932 CBU O P3 G1.2 1911–1928
Tsu Min-yi.
'La réorganisation sanitaire et le développement de l'éducation physique en Chine' (The reorganization of public health and the development of physical education in China).
Annales franco-chinoises 4, 15 (3e trimestre 1930), 1–18.
Subj 18 56 ▪ 12 17

20933 MCH O P2 G8.2 1911–1928
Vadon, *Dr.* ———.
'Un poste médical consulaire en Chine, Yunnanfou' (Yün-nan-fu [i.e., Kunming], a consular medical post in China).
AHMC 17, 2 (avr.–juin 1914), 501–525.
Subj 56

20934 MCH P P3 G1.1 1911–1949
Wang, Adine (Wang Ya-cheng).
La Chine et le problème de l'opium (China and the opium problem).
Paris: Pedone, 1933. 244 p. (Doctoral dissertation, Faculté de droit, Université de Bruxelles)
Subj 12.1 12.2 38 55 56 66 ▪ 14.3 14.5 19 32.2 72

20935 CSU O P3 G6.1 1928–1949
Wang, L. S., and M. P. Young.
'Psychopathic department, Elizabeth Blake Hospital, Soochow: Summary of inpatients, Jan. 1 to July 1, 1930.'
CMJ 44, 9 (Sept. 1930), 946–947.
Subj 56 61

20936 NNM F P3 G6.1 1928–1949
Wang, T. H., James Y. Shen, and C. C. Chung.
'An inquiry into the prevalence of syphilis in Nanking.'
CMJ 51, 6 (June 1937), 983–988.
Subj 56 ▪ 58

20937 NNM F P2 G5.3 1928–1949
Winfield, Gerald Freeman, 1908–. [Part 4 coauthored by Tzu-ming Yao; part 5 coauthored by C. H. Meng.]
'Studies on the control of fecal borne diseases in North China.'
CMJ 51, 2 (Feb. 1937), 217–236; 51, 4 (Apr. 1937), 502–518; 51, 5 (May 1937), 643–658; 51, 6 (June 1937), 919–926; Supplement 2 (Mar. 1938), 463–486; 54, 3 (Sept. 1938), 233–254.
Subj 56 ▪ 28 55 58

20938 CSH P P3 G5.1 1911–1928
Woo, Toh (Wu To).
An analysis of 2,330 case work records of the Social Service Department, Peiping Union Medical College. Tr. of 'Pei-p'ing hsieh i she hui shih yeh pu ko an ti fen hsi' (An analysis of cases handled by the Department of Social Work, Peiping Union Medical College Hospital); *She hui k'o hsüeh tsa chih* 2, 1 (Mar. 1931), 23–50. [Rev. and condensed in tr.]
Peiping: China Foundation, Institute of Social Research, 1931. 20 p. (ISR bulletins, 5)
Subj 28 56 ▪ 26 41 50 55

20939 MCH O P3 G1.2 1911–1949
Woods, A- H-.
'The nervous diseases of the Chinese.'
Archives of neurology and psychiatry 21 (1929), 542–570.
Subj 56 ▪ 18 46 47 51 61

20940 NNC S P2 G1.2 1928–1949
Wu, Anna I. C., 1923–.
Some social aspects of the leprosy problem in China.
Unpublished masters thesis in Sociology, Columbia U., 1948. 66 p.
Subj 22.2 56 ▪ 12.2 18

20941 NNM O P1 G1.3 1928–1949
Wu, C. Y.
'The National Quarantine Service.'
CMJ 49, 9 (Sept. 1935), 969–972.
Subj 56

20942 NNC O P3 G1.2 1911–1928
Wu Lien-teh (Wu Lien-te), 1879–1960.
'The practice of hygiene in China.'
CSM 9, 5 (Mar. 1914), 389–398.
Subj 18 56 ▪ 55

20943 CSU O P2 G1.2 1928–1949
Wu Lien-teh (Wu Lien-te), 1879–1960.
'Present status of medical practice in China.'
CR 67, 8 (Aug. 1936), 472–480.
Subj 56 ▪ 17

20944 CSU PO P1 G1.5 1928–1949
Wu, T. C.
'Leprosy in Southwest China.'
CR 70, 11 (Nov. 1939), 631–638.
Subj 18 56 ▪ 28

20945 NNM O P2 G9.3 1928–1949
Yang, Y. N., et al.
'Plague work in Fukien, China, December 1935 to November 1936.'
CMJ 55, 1 (Jan. 1939), 55–73; 55, 2 (Feb. 1939), 162–173; 55, 3 (Mar. 1939), 262–275; 55, 4 (Apr. 1939), 383–390; 55, 5 (May 1939), 479–487.
Subj 28 56

20946 NIC F P7 G5.1 1911–1949
Yao, H. Y. (Yao Hsün-yüan).
'The first year of the rural health experiment in Ting hsien [Hopei], China.'
MMFQ 9, 3 (July 1931), 61–77.
Subj 56 ▪ 27 28 37

20947 NNC O P3 G5.1 1911–1928
Yao, H. Y. (Yao Hsün-yüan).
'Industrial health work in the Peiping special health area.'
CMJ 43, 4 (Apr. 1929), 379–387.
Subj 28 56 ▪ 24.4 27

20948 NNM O P3 G8.2 1928–1949
Yao, H. Y. (Yao Hsün-yüan).
'The Provincial Health Administration of Yunnan: A brief report of its activities since its establishment, July 1, 1936 – December 31, 1937.'
CMJ 53, 6 (June 1938), 577–583.
Subj 56

20949 NIC F P7 G5.1 1911–1949
Yao, H. Y. (Yao Hsün-yüan).
'The second year of the rural health experiment in Ting hsien [Hopei], China.'
MMFQ 10, 1 (Jan. 1932), 55–66.
Subj 56 ▪ 27 28 37

20950 NNC F P3 G8.1 1928–1949
Yui, H. W. (Yü Huan-wen), and K. W. Li (Li K'o-wen).
'Diphtheria immunity in Chengtu students.'
CMJ (Chengtu) 62A, 1 (Oct. 1943), 1–5.
Subj 56

20951 NNC O P3 G6.1 1928–1949
Yui, John (Yü Hsin-en).
'Industrial health work in Shanghai.'
CMJ 65, 7/8 (July–Aug. 1947), 233–240.
Subj 56 ▪ 26.4 28

20952 NNM PO P3 G5.1 1928–1949
Yung, W. W.
'Child health work in Peiping first health area.'
CMJ 50, 4 (Apr. 1936), 562–572.
Subj 52 56 ▪ 51 58

1911-1972
(including 1644-1972)

20953 NNC PO P1 G1.2 –1972
Alekseenko, Ivan Pimenovich.
Ocherki o kitaiskoi narodnoi meditsine (Notes on Chinese folk medicine).
Kiev: Gos. med. izd-vo USSR, 1959. 210 p.
Subj 56 62 ▪ 18 23 65

20954 NNC FP P1 G1.1 –1972
Bolocan, Alice Kwong (K'uang Ch'iao-ch'ien), 1933–.
The physician in the practice of traditional Chinese medicine in China and the U.S., contrasted and compared with the practice of Western medicine.
Unpublished masters thesis in Anthropology, Columbia U., 1957. 28, 168 p. [Certificate essay, East Asian Institute]
Subj 56 ▪ 12.1 17 36.1

20955 CSU P P2 G1.1 1911–1972
Cerny, Jan.
'Chinese psychiatry.' [With comments by Ezra Feivel Vogel, Denis Lazure, and Pow-meng Yap (Yeh Pao-ming)]
International j. of psychiatry 1, 2 (Apr. 1965), 229–247.
Subj 56 61 ▪ 52 63 72

20956 MCY P P1 G1.1 –1972
Chamfrault, A-.
'Vérités révolutionnaires sur la médecine chinoise' (Revolutionary truths about Chinese medicine).
France-Asie 12, 112 (sept. 1955), 127–135.
Subj 56 ▪ 62

20957 CSH P P2 G1.2 –1972
Chen, James Y. P. (Ch'en Yen-ping), 1900–.
'Pharmacology.' In *Medicine and public health in the People's Republic of China*, edited by Joseph R- Quinn. [Selective entry]
[Washington, D.C.]: U.S. Dept. of Health, Education, and Welfare, Public Health Service, National Institutes of Health, 1972, 91–106.
Subj 56 ▪ 14.1 14.4 36.1

20958 CSH U P1 G4.0 1911–1972
Coffin, Edna, and Beatrice Diamond Miller, 1919–.
'Health and sanitation.' In *A regional handbook on Northwest China*, compiled by Far Eastern and Russian Institute, U. of Washington. [Selective entry]
New Haven: Human Relations Area Files, 1956, vol. 2, 386–400. (HRAF subcontractor's monographs, 59; Washington 5)
Subj 56 ▪ 55

20959 CSU P P1 G1.2 1911–1972
Croizier, Ralph Charles, 1935–.
'Medicine, modernization, and cultural crisis in China and India.'
CSSH 12, 3 (July 1970), 275–291. [Reprinted as 'Medicine, modernization, and cultural crisis: Chung I and Ayurveda in the twentieth century.' In *'Nothing concealed': Essays in honor of Liu Yu-yün*, edited by Frederic Evans Wakeman, Jr. (Selective entry.) Taipei: Chinese Materials and Research Aids Service Center, 1970, 193–219. (CMRASC occasional series, 4)]
Subj 56 60 ▪ 36.1

20960 CSU P P2 G1.1 –1972
Croizier, Ralph Charles, 1935–.
Traditional medicine in modern China: Science, nationalism, and the tensions of cultural change.
Cambridge: Harvard U. Press, 1968. 16, 325 p. (Harvard East Asian series, 34)

(Revision of *Chinese medicine in the twentieth century intellectual revolution: The tensions of cultural choice*, doctoral dissertation in History, U. of California, Berkeley, 1965)
Subj 16.1 32.1 36.1 56 64 ▪ 12 12.1 17 18 62 66

20961 MCH PO P2 G1.2 1928–1972
Eloesser, Leo.
'Assembly line for country midwives.'
Pacific spectator 7, 2 (Spring 1953), 232–242.
Subj 51 56 ▪ 12.1 37

20962 DLC FP P2 G1.2 1928–1972
Fedorov, Ivan Hnatovych.
Narodna medytsyna Kytaiu (Nationalized medicine in China).
Kiev: Tovarystvo dlia poshyrennia politychnykh i naukovykh znan' Ukraïns'koï RSR, 1958. 35 p. (TPPNZ URSR, series 5, 6)
Subj 17 56 ▪ 18 65 66

20963 NNC P P1 G1.1 –1972
[Fedorov, Ivan Hnatovych] Ivan Ignat'evich Fedorov.
Ocherki po narodnoi kitaiskoi meditsine (Notes on Chinese folk medicine).
Moscow: Medgiz, 1960. 76 p.
Subj 56 ▪ 17 62

20964 MCH PO P2 G1.4 1928–1972
Feniuk, B- K-.
'Zametki o prirodnykh ochagakh chumy i protivochumnoi rabote v Kitaiskoi Narodnoi Respublike (po putevym vpechatleniiam)' (Notes on natural breeding grounds for plague and on plague control in the People's Republic of China: Impressions from a trip).
Zhurnal mikrobiologii, epidemologii i immunobiologii 30, 10 (oktiabr' 1959), 8–16.
Subj 56 ▪ 28 72

20965 GBF O P3 G1.2 –1972
Fischer, Walther, 1882–.
'Die Medizin im alten und neuen China' (Medicine in traditional and modern China).
Münchener medizinische Wochenschrift 100, 42 (17 Okt. 1958), 1597–1602.
Subj 56 ▪ 57 62 65

20966 CSH O P2 G1.2 1928–1972
Horn, Joshua Samuel.
Away with all pests . . .: An English surgeon in People's China.
New York: Paul Hamlyn, 1969. 192 p. [Reprinted—New York: Monthly Review Press, 1971. 192 p.]
Subj 56 ▪ 18 52

20967 CSH P P2 G2.0 1911–1972
Hsiung, Helen.
'Health and sanitation.' In *A regional handbook on Northeast China*, compiled by Far Eastern and Russian Institute, U. of Washington. [Selective entry]
New Haven: Human Relations Area Files, 1956, 285–302. (HRAF subcontractor's monographs, 61; Washington 9)
Subj 56 ▪ 18

20968 CSH P P7 G3.0 1928–1972
Hsiung, Helen.
'Health and sanitation.' In *A regional handbook on the Inner Mongolia Autonomous Region*, compiled by Far Eastern and Russian Institute, U. of Washington. [Selective entry]
New Haven: Human Relations Area Files, 1956, 318–329. (HRAF subcontractor's monographs, 60; Washington 7)
Subj 56

20969 MCY P P1 G1.1 –1972
Huard, Pierre Alphonse, 1901–.
'Structure de la médecine chinoise' (The integration of Chinese medicine).
B. de la Société des études indo-chinoises de Saigon nouvelle (2e) série 33, 4 (1957), 299–376. [Also published under same title—Paris: Université de Paris, 1957. 88 p. (Université de Paris, Conférences du Palais de la Découverte, Série D, 49)]
Subj 56 ▪ 46 51 62 72

20970 MCY P P1 G1.2 –1972
Huard, Pierre Alphonse, 1901–, and Ming Wong.
'Bio-bibliographie de la médecine chinoise' (Bio-bibliography of Chinese medicine).
B. de la Société des études indo-chinoises de Saigon nouvelle (2e) série 31, 3 (1956), 181–246.
Subj 56 70 72

20971 FPN P P1 G1.2 –1972
Huard, Pierre Alphonse, 1901–, and Ming Wong.
'Le bouddhisme et la médecine chinoise' (Buddhism and Chinese medicine).
Histoire de la médecine 8, 1 (jan. 1958), 5–51.
Subj 56 62 ▪ 63

20972 FPN P P1 G1.2 –1972
Huard, Pierre Alphonse, 1901–, and Ming Wong.
'Cautérisation ignée et moxas en Chine, au Japon, dans le Proche et Moyen-Orient, en Europe' (Cauterization by fire and moxabustion in China, Japan, the Near and Middle East, and Europe).
Histoire de la médecine 8, 7 (juil. 1958), 7–41.
Subj 56

20973 CSU P P1 G1.2 –1972
Huard, Pierre Alphonse, 1901–, and Ming Wong.
Chinese medicine. Tr. from the French by Bernard Fielding.
New York: McGraw-Hill, 1968. 253 p.
Subj 16.1 17 56 66 ▪ 14.4 18 62 65

20974 MCY P P1 G1.1 –1972
Huard, Pierre Alphonse, 1901–, and Ming Wong.
'Histoire de l'acupuncture chinoise' (History of Chinese acupuncture).
B. de la Société des études indo-chinoises de Saigon nouvelle (2e) série 34, 4 (1959), 403–424.
Subj 56

20975 MBM P P1 G1.2 –1972
Huard, Pierre Alphonse, 1901–, and Ming Wong.
'La médecine de la Chine moderne' (Medicine in modern China). In *La médecine chinoise* (Chinese medicine), 2nd ed., by P. A. Huard and Ming Wong. [Sole entry]
Paris: Presses universitaires, 1969, 89–121.
Subj 56 ▪ 17 66

20976 NNC PO P1 G1.3 –1972
Ibragimov, Fatikh Ibragimovich, and Valentina Semenova Ibragimova.
Osnovnye lekarstvennye sredstva kitaiskoi meditsiny (Basic Chinese medicinal remedies).
Moscow: Medgiz, 1960. 410 p.
Subj 56 62 ▪ 24.4

20977 DLC PO P2 G1.4 1895–1972
Kamnev, P- I-.
'K voprosu o prirodnoi ochagovosti chumy na iugo-zapade severo-vostochnogo Kitaia v raionakh intensivnogo zemledeliia' (Natural breeding grounds for plague in the intensively cultivated regions of southwestern Manchuria and eastern Inner Mongolia).
Izvestiia Irkutskogo gosudarstvennogo nauchno-issledovatel'skogo protivochumnogo instituta Sibiri i Dal'nego Vostoka 15 (1957), 57–77.
Subj 56 ▪ 21.3 72

20978 DLC O P2 G1.3 1928–1972
Kochergin, Ivan Georgievich, 1903–.
'Desiat' let kitaiskogo zdravookhraneniia' (A decade of Chinese public-health services).
Zdravookhranenie Rossiiskoi Federatsii 3, 9 (sentiabr' 1959), 35–40.
Subj 17 56 ▪ 12.1 16.4 18

20979 DLC S P1 G1.3 –1972
Kraminskii, V- A-.
'K istorii kholernykh epidemii v Kitaie' (History of cholera epidemics in China).
Izvestiia Irkutskogo gosudarstvennogo nauchno-issledovatel'skogo protivochumnogo instituta Sibiri i Dal'nego Vostoka 19 (1959), 3–18.
Subj 56 ▪ 18 54 55

20980 CSH P P1 G1.3 –1972
Li Huan-hsin, 1901–.
'Chinese medicine.'
CC 10, 1 (Mar. 1969), 67–79.
Subj 56

20981 CSU P P2 G1.1 –1972
Lim, Robert K. S. (Lin K'o-sheng), 1897–, and G. H. Wang (Wang Ching-hsi), 1897–.
'Physiological sciences.' In *Sciences in Communist China*, edited by [Sydney Henry Gould] Sidney H. Gould. [Selective entry]
Washington, D.C.: American Assn. for the Advancement of Science, 1961, 323–362. (AAAS publications, 68)
Subj 17 56 ▪ 14.1 36.1 62 66

20982 MCH O P3 G5.4 1928–1972
Lippa, Ernest M-.
Captive surgeon: Adventures and misadventures of a doctor in Red China.
New York: Morrow, 1953. 280 p.
Subj 28 56 ▪ 22.1 55 62

20983 MBM PO P1 G1.2 1928–1972
Mann, Felix.
The treatment of disease by acupuncture, 2nd ed.

London: Heinemann Medical Books, 1971. 11, 226 p.
Subj 56 ▪ 51

20984 CSU P P1 G1.2 -1972
Needham, Noël Joseph Terence Montgomery, 1900–, and Lu Gwei Djen.
'Medicine and Chinese culture.' In *Clerks and craftsmen in China and the West*, by N. J. T. M. Needham. [Selective entry]
Cambridge: Cambridge U. Press, 1970, 263–293.
Subj 56 ▪ 60

20985 MCH P P1 G1.0 -1972
Pálos, István (Stephen Pálos), 1922–.
Chinesische Heilkunst: Rückbesinnung auf eine grosse Tradition (Chinese medicine: A great tradition in retrospect). Tr. by Wilhelm Kronfuss of *Á hagyományos kínai gyógyitás*.
Munich: Delp'sche Verlagsbuchhandlung, 1966. 205 p.
The Chinese art of healing.
New York: Herder and Herder, 1971. 15, 235 p.
Subj 56 62

20986 NNC S P1 G1.3 -1972
Schramm, Gottfried.
'Heilpflanzen und Drogen der altchinesischen Materia Medica' (Medicinal herbs and drugs in China's traditional materia medica substances).
Forschungen und Fortschritte 30, 8 (Aug. 1956), 235–238; 31, 2 (Feb. 1957), 40–44.
Subj 56

20987 MCH P P1 G1.0 -1972
Schramm, Gottfried.
Schriftzeichenanalysen medizinischer termini technici in der chinesischen Sprache (An analysis of the characters for technical medical terms in the Chinese language).
Leipzig: VEB Otto Harrassowitz, 1958. 11, 107 p.
Subj 56 62 ▪ 65

20988 CSH O P2 G1.2 1928–1972
Sidel, Victor W-, 1931–.
'Medical personnel and their training.' In *Medicine and public health in the People's Republic of China*, edited by Joseph R- Quinn. [Selective entry]
[Washington, D.C.]: U.S. Dept. of Health, Education, and Welfare, Public Health Service, National Institutes of Health, 1972, 151–171.
Subj 17 56

20989 CSH P P2 G9.4 1928–1972
Stanford U. China Project.
'Health and sanitation in Formosa.' In *Taiwan (Formosa)*, compiled by the organization cited. [Selective entry]
New Haven: Human Relations Area Files, 1956, vol. 1, 258–280. (HRAF subcontractor's monographs, 31; Stanford 5)
Subj 55 56

20990 DLC U P1 G1.2 -1972
TSan IU-chuan (Ts'ang Yu-ch'uang).
'Ocherk istorii anatomii v Kitae' (A note on the history of anatomy in China).
Arkhiv anatomii, gistologii i embriologii 37, 10 (oktiabr' 1959), 3–16.
Subj 56 62 ▪ 17 18 36.1

20991 DLC PO P2 G1.2 1842–1972
TSzin' Sin'-chzhun (Chin Hsin-chung) and Ivan Georgievich Kochergin, 1903–.
Zdravookhranenie i meditsina v Kitaiskoi Narodnoi Respubliki (Public health and medicine in the People's Republic of China).
Moscow: Medgiz, 1959. 267 p.
Subj 18 56 62 ▪ 51 52 53 58

20992 NNC U P1 G1.1 -1972
Wallnöfer, Heinrich, and Anna von Rottauscher.
Der goldene Schatz der chinesischen Medizin (The golden treasury of Chinese medicine).
Stuttgart: Schuler, 1959. 173 p.
Chinese folk medicine. Tr. by Marion Palmedo.
New York: Crown, 1965. 184 p.
Subj 56 65 ▪ 62

20993 CSU S P8 G1.2 1928–1972
Worth, Robert McAlpine, 1924–.
'Health in rural China: From village to commune.'
American j. of hygiene 77, 3 (May 1963), 228–239.
Subj 18 56 ▪ 16.3

20994 NNC O P5 G1.1 1842–1972
Wu Lien-teh (Wu Lien-te), 1879–1960.
Plague fighter: The autobiography of a modern Chinese physician.
Cambridge, Eng.: Heffer, 1959. 10, 667 p.
Subj 26.1 28 56 58 59 ▪ 13 14.2 26.2 32.2 41 47 48 55 66

20995 CSU FP P2 G9.4 1928–1972
Yeh, Eng-kung (Yeh Ying-k'un).
'Social psychiatry in Taiwan (Formosa).' In *Progress in psychotherapy, Vol. 4, Social psychotherapy*, edited by Jules H- Masserman and J- L- Moreno. [Sole entry]
New York, London: Grune and Stratton, 1959, 306–309.
Subj 56 61 ▪ 41 52

1949-1972

20996 CSU FP P2 G1.2 1949–1972
Collection of theses on achievements in medical sciences in commemoration of the Tenth National Foundation Day of China, mimeo. Tr. from *Ch'ing chu chien kuo shih chou nien i hsüeh k'o hsüeh ch'eng chiu lun wen chi hsia chüan*; Peking: ——, 1959. [Partial tr.: vol. 2, p. 131–137, 144–206, 373–484, 521–585, 587–643, 683–813 only]
Washington, D.C.: U.S. Joint Publications Research Service, 13 July, 10 Aug., 14 Aug. 1962. 395; 152; 699 p. (JPRS 14,460, 14,900, and 14,829; MC 17,783/1962, 19,665/1962, and 18,081/1962) [Xerox copyflo available—New York: CCM Information Corp., Research and Microfilm Publications. (Scholarly Book Translation Series, 531)]
Subj 51 52 56 62 ▪ 14.2 18 36.1 58 61

20997 NIC O P2 G9.2 1949–1972
'Interview with Chinese medical doctor.'
CS 1, 3 (12 June 1961), 1–12.
Subj 28 32.1 56 ▪ 32 48

20998 NIC O P2 G9.2 1949–1972
'Interview: "Years of constant caution".'
CS 1, 14 (3 Oct. 1961), 1–10. [Reprinted in *Out of China: A collection of interviews with refugees from China*, edited by Francis Harper. (Analytic entry.) Hong Kong: Dragonfly Books, 1964, 107–129.]
Subj 26.1 28 56 ▪ 24.4 32

20999 CSU P P1 G1.2 1949–1972
'New China's progress in internal medicine.' Tr. of 'Hsin Chung-kuo tsai nei k'o hsüeh fang mien ti chin chan'; *Chung-hua nei k'o tsa chih* 1959, 9 (Sept.), 816–836. In *New China's progress in internal medicine*, mimeo., compiled by U.S. Joint Publications Research Service. [Analytic entry]
Washington, D.C.: JPRS, 13 Sept. 1960, 11–60. (JPRS 3899; MC 17,276/1960)
Subj 56 ▪ 18 58

21000 CSH U P7 G6.1 1949–1972
'The orientation of revolution in medical education as seen in the growth of "barefoot doctors": Report of an investigation from Shanghai.' Tr. of 'Ts'ung "chih chiao i sheng" ti ch'eng chang k'an i hsüeh chiao yü ko ming ti fang hsiang' (Trends in the revolution in medical education: The 'barefoot doctors'); *Hung ch'i* 1968, 3 (10 Sept.), 20–26.
CM 1968, 10 (Oct.), 574–581. [A different tr.— 'The orientation of revolution in medical education as seen from the "barefoot doctors": An investigation report.' *SCMM* 628 (23 Sept. 1968), 3–10.]
Subj 17 56

21001 NNC O P8 G9.3 1949–1972
'Report on the prevention and treatment of hookworm disease in the Hsi-pu production brigade of Shan-t'ing people's commune, P'u-t'ien hsien, Fukien province.' Tr. of 'Fu-chien sheng P'u-t'ien hsien Shan-t'ing jen min kung she Hsi-pu ta tui fang chih kou ch'ung ping kung tso tsung chieh' (Results of the prevention of hookworm in Hsi-pu brigade, Shan-t'ing commune, P'u-t'ien *hsien*, Fukien); *Jen min pao chien* 1959, 7 (July), 665–667. In *Organization of health services under Communist China's commune system (2)*, mimeo., compiled by U.S. Joint Publications Research Service. [Selective entry]
Washington, D.C.: JPRS, 27 July 1960, 13–21. (JPRS 5104; MC 14,449/1960)
Subj 28 56

21002 CSH O P7 G7.1 1949–1972
'Rural cooperative medical service.'
China reconstructs 18, 6 (June 1969), 15–18.
Subj 56

21003 NNC P P7 G1.2 1949–1972
Allen, Edwin Joseph, Jr., 1938–.
Disease control in China: An investigation into the ways in which public health propaganda effects changes in medicine

and hygiene, with emphasis on schistosomiosis control.
Unpublished masters thesis in Public Law and Government, Columbia U., 1965. 89 p. [Certificate essay, East Asian Institute]
SUBJ 12.1 56 ▪ 65 72

21004 CSU U P6 G2.2 1949–1972
An Hsüan-hung. [Tr. erroneously gives Hsuan-hung as author's full name.]
'A hospital that is at the service of peasants.' Tr. of 'I so wei nung min fu wu ti i yüan' (A hospital that serves peasants); *Hung ch'i* 1965, 11 (1 Oct.), 29–34. In *Translations from 'Hung-ch'i' (Red flag) No. 11, 1965*, mimeo., compiled by U.S. Joint Publications Research Service. [Selective entry]
Washington, D.C.: JPRS, 3 Nov. 1965, 52–62. (JPRS 32,698; MC 875-33/1966)
SUBJ 56

21005 CBU F P7 G9.5 1949–1972
Anderson, Eugene Newton, Jr., 1941–, and Marja Lisa Anderson, 1943–.
'Folk medicine in rural Hong Kong.'
Etnoiatria 2, 1 (1968), 22–28.
SUBJ 56 65 ▪ 28 62

21006 NNC O P3 G1.2 1949–1972
Antelava, N- V-.
'Vpechatleniia o khirurgii Narodnogo Kitaia' (Impressions of surgery in the People's Republic of China).
Khirurgiia 33, 6 (iiun' 1957), 146–149.
SUBJ 56 ▪ 62

21007 NNC O P2 G1.2 1949–1972
Antituberculosis Assn. of China.
'Prevention and treatment of tuberculosis in China.'
CMJ 80, 1 (Jan. 1960), 62–67.
SUBJ 56 ▪ 18

21008 CSU F P2 G9.4 1949–1972
Baker, Timothy Danforth, 1925–.
'Problems in measuring the influence of economic levels on morbidity.'
American j. of public health 56, 3 (Mar. 1966), 499–507.
SUBJ 16 56 ▪ 18 50

21009 CSU FP P2 G9.4 1949–1972
Baker, Timothy Danforth, 1925–, and Mark Perlman.
Health manpower in a developing economy: Taiwan, a case study in planning.
Baltimore: Johns Hopkins Press, 1967. 203 p.
SUBJ 17 21.4 28 51 56 58 ▪ 12 16.1 21.2 22 34.2 47 70

21010 CSU PO P2 G1.2 1949–1972
Biener, Kurt.
'Chinesische Gesundheitsfürsorge.'
Das deutsche Gesundheitswesen 12, 38 (19 Sept. 1957), 1178–1182.

Health care in China, mimeo. Tr. by E- Benes. [Tr. from *Československa zdravotictvi* 6, 2 (1958), 90–95.]
Washington, D.C.: U.S. Joint Publications Research Service, 23 Mar. 1959. 10 p. (JPRS 1386; MC 6500/1959)
SUBJ 52 56 ▪ 31 51 55 58

21011 DLC O P4 G1.2 1949–1972
Blagovidova, IU- A-.
'Aptechnoe delo i farmatsevticheskoe obrazovanie v Kitaiskoi Narodnoi Respublike' (Pharmacy and pharmaceutical training in the People's Republic of China).
Aptechnoe delo 6, 5 (sentiabr'–oktiabr' 1957), 81–85.
SUBJ 17 56

21012 NNC O P2 G1.2 1949–1972
Boldyrev, T- E-.
'Patrioticheskoe dvizhenie za okhranu zdorov'ia naroda v Kitaiskoi Narodnoi Respublike' (The patriotic movement for the protection of public health in the People's Republic of China).
Gigiena i sanitariia 22, 4 (aprel' 1957), 48–52.
SUBJ 56 ▪ 18 30

21013 CSU P P2 G1.2 1949–1972
Bowers, John Zimmerman, 1913–.
'Medicine in Mainland China: Red and rural.'
CS 8, 12 (15 June 1970), 1–11.
SUBJ 56 ▪ 17 51

21014 NNC U P2 G1.2 1949–1972
Bridgman, R- F-.
'La Chine populaire devant les problèmes de sa santé publique.'
Comptes rendus mensuels des séances de l'Académie des sciences d'outre-mer 21 (juil.–oct. 1961), 383–386.

'The People's Republic of China faces public health problems.' In *Information on public health and national education in Communist China*, mimeo., compiled by U.S. Joint Publications Research Service. [Selective entry]
Washington, D.C.: JPRS, 19 Feb. 1962, 1–3. (JPRS 12,572; MC 8143/1962)
SUBJ 18 56 ▪ 38 51

21015 DLC O P2 G1.2 1949–1972
Burnashev, E- IU-.
'Zdravookhranenie v Narodnom Kitae' (Public-health services in the People's Republic of China).
Zdravookhranenie Rossiiskoi Federatsii 2, 11 (noiabr' 1958), 35–41.
SUBJ 11.2 17 56 ▪ 12 16.3 16.4 36.4

21016 CSU F P1 G9.4 1949–1972
Cameron, Richard R-, and Fernando G- Torgerson.
'Cultural considerations in the teaching of American psychiatry to the Chinese.'
Mental hygiene 46, 3 (July 1962), 351–360.
SUBJ 56 61

21017 CSU F P.7 G9.4 1949–1972
Chang, Chung-yung (Chang Tsung-yin).
'Health needs and health perceptions of older peasants.'
CMJ-T 13, 1 (Mar. 1966), 81–86.
SUBJ 56 ▪ 26.3

21018 CSU F P3 G5.1 1949–1972
Chang, Hsioh-teh (Chang Hsüeh-te), and Yu-tu Chiang (Chiang Yü-t'u).
'Studies on an epidemic of influenza in Peking.'
CMJ 68, 7/8 (July–Aug. 1950), 185–192.
SUBJ 56

21019 NNC O P7 G5.1 1949–1972
Chang Kuo-chung. [Tr. erroneously gives author's name as Chang Kuo-chün.]
'The people's communes have great power: Hsin An, the water town (Shui Hsiang) has no mosquitoes.' Tr. of 'Jen min kung she wei li chü ta shui hsiang Hsin-an chi pen wu wen' (The great power of the communes: Hsin-an, the watery township [Hsü-shui *hsien*, Hopei], has no mosquitoes); *Jen min jih pao* 8 Apr. 1960, 10. In *Speeches given at second session of Second National People's Congress, Communist China*, mimeo., compiled by U.S. Joint Publications Research Service. [Sole entry]
Washington, D.C.: JPRS, 16 Dec. 1960, 26–34. (JPRS 6397; MC 2259/1961)
SUBJ 56 ▪ 22.1

21020 CSU F P2 G9.4 1949–1972
Chao, C. W.
'A survey on the practicability of mass domiciliary chemotherapy of tuberculosis patients in Taiwan.'
CMJ-T 15, 3 (Sept. 1968), 189–199.
SUBJ 56 ▪ 24.2 50

21021 CSU S P1 G1.2 1949–1972
Chao Yi-ch'eng (Chao I-ch'eng).
'Neurology, neurosurgery and psychiatry in New China.'
CMJ 84, 11 (Nov. 1965), 714–742.
SUBJ 56 ▪ 61

21022 CSH O P7 G6.3 1949–1972
Chekiang. Chia-shan Hsien Antiepidemic Station. Revolutionary Leading Group.
'As Chairman Mao directs, we follow: How schistosomiasis in Jiashan county was wiped out by "people's war".'
CM 1968, 10 (Oct.), 603–609.
SUBJ 56

21023 CSH P P2 G1.2 1949–1972
Chen, James Y. P. (Ch'en Yen-ping), 1900–.
'Acupuncture.' In *Medicine and public health in the People's Republic of China*, edited by Joseph R- Quinn. [Selective entry]
[Washington, D.C.]: U.S. Dept. of Health, Education, and Welfare, Public Health Service, National Institutes of Health, 1972, 65–90.
SUBJ 56

21024 CSU F P3 G9.4 1949–1972
Chen, Joseph S. (Ch'en Shang-ch'iu), and Jing-chuen Liu.
'Nutritional anemias and serum protein pattern in Chinese.'
CMJ-T 13, 2 (June 1966), 131–145.
SUBJ 56 ▪ 55

21025 CSU P P2 G1.2 1949–1972
Chen, William Y. (Ch'en Yüan-lung), 1896–.
'Medicine and public health.' In *Sciences in Communist China*, edited by [Sydney Henry Gould] Sidney H. Gould. [Selective entry]
Washington, D.C.: American Assn. for the Advancement of Science, 1961, 383–408. (AAAS publications, 68)
SUBJ 56 ▪ 17 18 36.1

21026 NNC O P3 G6.3 1949–1972
Ch'en Li-chieh.
'Hsiao Ying Hsiang in forefront in struggle against disease.' Tr. of 'Hsiao-ying hsiang hsien chin chung tzu sa p'ien Hang-chou shih' (Hsiao-ying lane leads the struggle against disease in Hangchow); *Jen min jih pao* 8 Apr. 1960, 20. In *Speeches given at second session of Second National People's Congress, Communist China*, mimeo., compiled by U.S. Joint Publications Research Service. [Sole entry]
Washington, D.C.: JPRS, 20 Jan. 1961, 39–45. (JPRS 6623; MC 4523/1961)
SUBJ 28 56 ▪ 22.1

21027 CSH O P1 G1.2 1949–1972
Ch'en Tse-lin and Ch'en Mei-fang.
'Tongue inspection: A diagnostic method in traditional Chinese medicine.'
CM 1966, 1 (Oct.), 69–75.
SUBJ 56

21028 CSU P P2 G1.2 1949–1972
Cheng, Tien-hsi (Cheng T'ien-hsi), 1912–.
'Disease control and prevention in China.'
Asia (New York: Asia Society) 26 (Summer 1972), 31–59.
SUBJ 56

21029 CSU FP P2 G1.5 1949–1972
Cheng, Tien-hsi (Cheng T'ien-hsi), 1912–.
'Schistosomiasis in Mainland China: A review of research and control programs since 1949.'
American j. of tropical medicine and hygiene 20, 1 (Jan. 1971), 26–53.
SUBJ 56 ▪ 14.1 24.1

21030 CSU F P7 G9.4 1949–1972
Chi, I. C. (Ch'i I-cheng), et al.
'Health status, medical care, and their relationship with socio-economic condition in Musa, Taipei county [Mu-shan *hsiang*, T'ai-pei *hsien*], Taiwan, Republic of China.'
CMJ-T 17, 3 (Sept. 1970), 146–156.
SUBJ 26 56 ▪ 50 51

21031 NNC F P8 G5.4 1949–1972
Chia Shan-fu, Liu Tzu-t'ai, and Chang Wen-t'ung. [Tr. erroneously gives second author's name as Liu Tzu-ch'in.]
'The prevalence of measles and epidemic control measures in the Huang-chuang brigade of Tung-chiao people's commune, Cheng-chou city.' Tr. of 'Cheng-chou shih Tung-chiao jen min kung she Huang-chuang ta tui ma chen liu hsing ch'ing k'uang chi ch'i fang i ts'o shih' (The prevalence of measles and epidemic control measures in Huang-chiang brigade, Tung-chiao commune, Chengchow municipality); *Jen min pao chien* 1959, 9 (Sept.), 855–857. In *Organization of health services under Communist China's commune system (2)*, mimeo., compiled by U.S. Joint Publications Research Service. [Selective entry]
Washington, D.C.: JPRS, 27 July 1960, 31–39. (JPRS 5104; MC 14,449/1960)
SUBJ 56 ▪ 28

21032 CSU F P1 G9.4 1949–1972
Chiang, B. N. (Chiang Pi-ning), et al.
'Maximal exercise responses in middle aged hypertensive and normotensive Chinese males: A preliminary report.'
CMJ-T 14, 3 (Sept. 1967), 239–249.
SUBJ 56

21033 CSU U P3 G9.2 1949–1972
Chiang Lin.
'A health red-flag city: Fo-shan in Kwangtung.' Tr. of 'Wei sheng hung ch'i ch'eng shih: Kuang-tung Fo-shan' (The city that earned a red flag for hygiene: Fo-shan, Kwangtung); *Hung ch'i* 1960, 6 (16 Mar.), 16–22. In *Translations from 'Hung-ch'i' (Red flag) No. 6, 16 March 1960, Peiping*, mimeo., compiled by U.S. Joint Publications Research Service. [Sole entry]
Washington, D.C.: JPRS, 18 Aug. 1960, 14–23. (JPRS 3730; MC 15,634/ 1960)
SUBJ 28 56 ▪ 21.3

21034 CSH O P2 G1.2 1949–1972
Ch'ien Hsin-chung.
'Chinese medicine: Progress and achievements.'
PR 7, 9 (28 Feb. 1964), 16–19.
SUBJ 56

21035 NIC O P2 G1.2 1949–1972
Ch'ien Hsin-chung.
'Research in labor hygiene and occupational diseases: Its achievements and perspectives in socialist construction.'
CMJ 80, 3 (Mar. 1960), 197–207.
SUBJ 26.4 56 ▪ 28 62

21036 NNC U P2 G1.2 1949–1972
Ch'ien Hsin-chung.
Summary of Communist China's achievements in the medical sciences in the past decade, mimeo. Tr. of 'Chien kuo shih nien lai wo kuo i hsüeh k'o hsüeh ch'eng chiu tsung shu' (Achievements in medical sciences in the decade since the founding of the People's Republic of China); *Jen min pao chien* 1959, 12 (Dec.), 1092–1099.
Washington, D.C.: U.S. Joint Publications Research Service, 26 Apr. 1960. 12 p. (JPRS 3200; MC 8618/1960)
SUBJ 56

21037 NNC F P3 G6.1 1949–1972
Chin P'ei-huan (Chin P'i-huan) and Hsueh Chi-jen (Hsüeh Chi-jen).
A study on health conditions in workers' residential area in Jih-Hui Hsin-Ts'un, Shanghai, mimeo. Tr. of 'Shang-hai shih Jih-hui hsin ts'un kung jen chu chai ch'ü chü min chien k'ang chuang k'uang ti tiao ch'a yen chiu' (A study of conditions in workers residential areas in Jih-hui 'new village', Shanghai); *Jen min pao chien* 1959, 3 (Mar.), 281–287.
Washington, D.C.: U.S. Joint Publications Research Service, 15 July 1960. 23 p. (JPRS 5046; MC 14,405/1960)
SUBJ 28 41 56 ▪ 17 26.4 50 58

21038 MAU F P3 G9.5 1949–1972
Choa, Gerald.
'Chinese traditional medicine and contemporary Hong Kong.' In *Some traditional Chinese ideas and conceptions in Hong Kong social life today*, edited by Marjorie Doreen Topley. [Analytic entry]
Hong Kong: Royal Asiatic Society, Hong Kong Branch, 1967, 31–35.
SUBJ 56 ▪ 17 62

21039 CSH P P1 G9.4 1949–1972
Chow, H. C. (Chou Hsüeh-chung).
'Pharmaceutical industry in the Republic of China.'
IFC 31, 6 (June 1969), 19–25.
SUBJ 14.4 56

21040 NNC PO P1 G1.2 1949–1972
Chu Fu-t'ang.
'Accomplishments in child health since liberation.'
CMJ 79, 5 (Nov. 1959), 384–397.
SUBJ 52 56 ▪ 18

21041 CSH O P3 G7.1 1949–1972
Chung-kuo jen min chieh fang chün. Wu-han pu tui. Mo shih. Chih yao ch'ang. (People's Liberation Army. Wuhan Unit. 'A Certain Division'. Pharmaceutical Plant).
'Operate the pharmaceutical plant for preparedness against war.' Tr. of 'Wei chan lüeh pan yao ch'ang'; *Hung ch'i* 1971, 6 (June), 52–55.
CE 5, 1/2 (Spring–Summer 1972), 110–118.
SUBJ 56 ▪ 15 24.4

21042 CSU O P7 G5.4 1949–1972
Chung-kuo kung ch'an tang. Ho-nan sheng wei yüan hui. Wen chiao kung tso tsu. (Chinese Communist Party. Honan Provincial Committee. Cultural and Educational Work Team).
'The public health system and network of Hung-ch'i commune, Yu-hsien, Honan.' Tr. of 'Ho-nan Yü hsien Hung-ch'i jen min kung she ti wei sheng t'i chih ho wei sheng pao chien wang' (The public-health system and public-health network of Hung-ch'i commune, Yü *hsien*, Honan); *Jen min pao chien* 1959, 4 (Apr.), 373–375. In *Organization of health services under Communist China's commune system (1)*, mimeo., compiled by U.S. Joint Publications Research Service. [Selective entry]
Washington, D.C.: JPRS, 15 July 1960, 69–81. (JPRS 5045; MC 14,404/1960)
SUBJ 56 ▪ 52

21043 CSU P P2 G1.2 1949–1972
Current Scene Editor.
'The Mao-Liu controversy over rural public health.'
CS 7, 12 (15 June 1969), 1–18.
SUBJ 18 56 ▪ 14.2 17 32.1

21044 CSU P P2 G1.2 1949–1972
Current Scene Editor.
'Mao's revolution in public health.'
CS 6, 7 (1 May 1968), 1–10.
SUBJ 56 ▪ 12.1

21045 CSU P P2 G1.2 1949–1972
Current Scene Editor.
'Public health developments: Continued focus on the farms.'
CS 7, 24 (15 Dec. 1969), 1–12.
SUBJ 18 34.1 56 ▪ 35 51 65

21046 CSU O P8 G9.5 1949–1972
da Silva, Armando Maria.
'Some notes on ethno-botany in the New Territories of Hong Kong.'
JRAS-HKB 9 (1969), 124–130.
SUBJ 24.1 56

21047 NIC P P1 G1.2 1949–1972
Davidoff, Georges.
'De la médecine et de la sécurité sociale en Chine' (Medicine and social security in China).
Population (Paris) 12, 4 (oct.–déc. 1957), 679–694.
Subj 18 56 ▪ 11.4 17 58

21048 CSU PO P2 G1.3 1949–1972
Dimond, E- Grey.
'Medical education and care in the People's Republic of China.'
J. of the American Medical Assn. 218, 10 (6 Dec. 1971), 1552–1557.
Subj 17 56 ▪ 21.2 32.1 36.1

21049 CSU F P3 G9.4 1949–1972
Fan, P. C. (Fan Ping-chen), T. K. Chiu (Ch'iu T'ing-kuang), and V. Y: Wu (Wu Wang-yü).
'Studies on "oxyuriasis". 5, Epidemiology of "oxyuriasis" among children in I-kuang orphanage in Taipei City, northern Taiwan.'
CMJ-T 15, 2 (June 1968), 148–156.
Subj 56 ▪ 52

21050 CBU PO P3 G1.2 1949–1972
Favilli, Giovanni.
'Panorama della scienza medica in Cina' (Overview of medical science in China). In *La Cina d'oggi* (China today), edited by Piero Calamandrei. [Selective entry]
Florence: Nuova Italia editrice, 1956, 590–604. [Supplement to *Il ponte* 12, 4 (aprile 1956)]
Subj 17 56 ▪ 36.1 52

21051 NNC F P3 G9.4 1949–1972
Fay, Hsiao-dsung (Fei Hsiao-tsung).
'The effects of oral prophylaxis and oral health education on reduction of periodontal disease: An epidemiological study.'
CMJ-T 10, 3 (Sept. 1963), 243–247.
Subj 56 ▪ 28

21052 CSU O P2 G1.2 1949–1972
Fox, T- F-.
'Medical care in China today.'
American j. of public health 50, 6 (June 1960), 28–35. [Supplement: *Public health is one world*]
Subj 56

21053 CSU O P2 G1.2 1949–1972
Fu Lien-chang.
'A decade's achievements of the Chinese Medical Association.' Tr. of 'Chung-hua i hsüeh hui shih nien lai kung tso ti ch'eng chiu'; *Chung-hua nei k'o tsa chih* 1959, 9 (Sept.), 813–815. In *New China's progress in internal medicine*, mimeo., compiled by U.S. Joint Publications Research Service. [Analytic entry]
Washington, D.C.: JPRS, 13 Sept. 1960, 1–10. (JPRS 3899; MC 17,276/1960)
Subj 36.1 56

21054 CSH O P8 G2.1 1949–1972
Heilungkiang Provincial Hospital for Mental Diseases, Pei-an. Fu-yü Medical Team.
'How we operated a small hospital in the countryside [in Hsiang-yang production brigade, Fu-yü *hsien*, Heilungkiang].'
CM 1968, 6 (June), 347–350.
Subj 56 ▪ 21.2

21055 CSU O P7 G2.1 1949–1972
Heilungkiang Provincial Revolutionary Committee. Dept. of Culture and Education.
'Experience in organizing health work teams for the countryside during the Great Proletarian Cultural Revolution.'
CM 1968, 3 (Mar.), 142–147.
Subj 56 ▪ 21.2 64

21056 CSH O P2 G2.1 1949–1972
Heilungkiang Provincial Revolutionary Committee. Dept. of Health Protection.
'Experiences in health work and disease prevention in Heilungkiang province in the past year.'
CM 1968, 3 (Mar.), 148–153.
Subj 56 ▪ 21.2 22.1 64

21057 MCH S P2 G1.2 1949–1972
Ho Ch'i.
'Studies on malaria in New China.'
CMJ 84, 8 (Aug. 1965), 491–497.
Subj 56 ▪ 18

21058 NNC PO P1 G1.2 1949–1972
Ho Piao.
'Development of hygiene and health work during the First Five-Year Plan.'
CMJ 75, 12 (Dec. 1957), 953–957.
Subj 18 56 ▪ 17

21059 CSH S P3 G9.5 1949–1972
Ho, Portia.
'[1] The struggle for air. [2] In search of health.'
FEER 46, 4 (22 Oct. 1964), 225–228; 46, 5 (29 Oct. 1964), 275–278. [Reprinted as 'The struggle for air.' In *Hong Kong: A society in transition*, edited by Ian C- Jarvie and Joseph Agassi. (Analytic entry.) New York: Praeger, 1969, 317–326.]
Subj 28 56 ▪ 55

21060 CSU O P7 G5.4 1949–1972
Honan. Sui-p'ing hsien cheng fu. Wei-hsing jen min kung she. Wen chiao wei sheng pu. Wei sheng ch'u. (Sui-p'ing Hsien. Wei-hsing Commune. Dept. of Culture, Education, and Health. Public Health Office).
'How is free medical service realized by Wei-hsing commune, Sui-p'ing (Honan).' Tr. of 'Sui-p'ing hsien Wei-hsing jen min kung she shih tsen yang shih hsing ch'üan min hsing kung fei i liao ti' (How free medical service is realized by Wei-hsing commune, Sui-p'ing *hsien* [Honan]); *Jen min pao chien* 1959, 5 (May), 472. In *Organization of health services under Communist China's commune system (1)*, mimeo., compiled by U.S. Joint Publications Research Service. [Selective entry]
Washington, D.C.: JPRS, 15 July 1960, 82–85. (JPRS 5045; MC 14,404/1960)
Subj 56

21061 CSU P P2 G9.5 1949–1972
Hong Kong. Dept. of Medical and Health Services.
Annual departmental report by the Director of Medical and Health Services, 1949/50–1971/72. [Issues for 1947 and 1948/49 are entered as 20869.]
Hong Kong: Government Printer. Issued annually, 1952–1972. Average ca. 150 p.
Subj 56 ▪ 17 51 58

21062 CSU P P3 G9.5 1949–1972
[Hong Kong. Dept. of Medical and Health Services].
Development of medical services in Hong Kong.
Hong Kong: Government Printer, 1963. 47 p.
Subj 56

21063 CSU P P2 G9.5 1949–1972
Hong Kong. Urban Council *with* Hong Kong. Urban Services Dept.
Annual departmental report, 1949/50–1971/72. [Issues for 1947, 1948, and 1948/49 are entered as 20870.]
Hong Kong: Government Printer. Issued annually, 1950–1972. Average ca. 100 p.
Subj 55 56 57 ▪ 24.3 24.5 31

21064 NNC O P7 G5.1 1949–1972
Hopei. Chiao-ho hsien cheng fu. Wang-ssu jen min kung she. (Chiao-ho Hsien. Wang-ssu commune).
'Report on our commune's system of medical treatment at public expense provided by the people during the past year.' Tr. of 'Wo she "min pan kung fei i liao chih tu" i nien lai ti ch'ing k'uang chieh shao' (Introduction to the experiences of Wang-ssu commune [Chiao-ho *hsien*, Hopei] during the past year with a popularly managed system of free medical care); *Jen min pao chien* 1960, 5 (May), 278–280. In *Health services in an urban commune and in a rural commune*, mimeo., compiled by U.S. Joint Publications Research Service. [Sole entry]
Washington, D.C.: JPRS, 17 Jan. 1961, 15–21. (JPRS 4340; MC 4400/1961)
Subj 28 56 ▪ 32.1

21065 CSU O P7 G5.1 1949–1972
Hopei. Hsin-li ts'un jen min kung she. Wei sheng kung tso shih tien kung tso tsu. (Hsin-li-ts'un Commune. Health Work Experimental Group).
'A preliminary report on the health organization and work of Hsin-li-ts'un commune in Ho-tung ch'u.' Tr. of 'Ho-tung ch'ü Hsin-li-ts'un jen min kung she wei sheng pao chien tsu chih kung tso ch'u pu tsung chieh' (Preliminary conclusions concerning the organization of public-health programs in Hsin-li-ts'un commune, Ho-tung *ch'ü* [Tientsin municipality]); *Jen min pao chien* 1959, 3 (Mar.), 272–275. In *Organization of health services under Communist China's commune system (1)*, mimeo., compiled by U.S. Joint Publications Research Service. [Selective entry]
Washington, D.C.: JPRS, 15 July 1960, 34–58. (JPRS 5045; MC 14,404/1960)
Subj 56 ▪ 22 28 51 55

21066 CSH P P2 G1.2 1949–1972
Hsia, Tao-tai (Hsia Tao-t'ai), 1915–.
'Laws on public health.' In *Medicine and public health in the People's Republic of China*, edited by Joseph R- Quinn. [Selective entry]
[Washington, D.C.]: U.S. Dept. of Health, Education, and Welfare, Public Health

Service, National Institutes of Health, 1972, 109–135.
SUBJ 12.2 56 ▪ 12 14.1 14.3 17

21067 CSU F P8 G1.2 1949–1972
Hsu Chih-hui (Hsü Chih-hui).
'The influence of sewage-irrigated farms on the occurrence of dermatosis and infectious enteric diseases.' Tr. of 'Wu shui kuan kai nung t'ien tui p'i ju ping chi ch'ang tao ch'uan jan ping ti ying hsiang' (The connection between irrigation of farms with sewage and the occurrence of dermatosis and infectious enteric diseases); *Jen min pao chien* 1960, 3 (Mar.), 121–124. In *Public health in Communist China*, mimeo., compiled by U.S. Joint Publications Research Service. [Selective entry]
Washington, D.C.: JPRS, 15 July 1960, 16–29. (JPRS 2976; MC 14,181/1960)
SUBJ 56 ▪ 14.1

21068 NNC O P2 G9.4 1949–1972
Hsu, S. C. (Hsü Shih-chü), 1905–.
'Family planning health program in Taiwan: Development, organization and accomplishments.'
CMJ-T 12, 4 (Nov. 1965), 374–380.
SUBJ 56 ▪ 22 51

21069 CSU F P3 G5.1 1949–1972
Hsüeh Ch'in-ping, et al.
'An experimental study on the organization of urban child health services.'
CMJ 84, 9 (Sept. 1965), 563–570.
SUBJ 52 56

21070 CSH P P2 G1.2 1949–1972
Huang, Kun-yen (Huang K'un-yen), 1933–.
'Infectious and parasitic diseases.' In *Medicine and public health in the People's Republic of China*, edited by Joseph R- Quinn. [Selective entry]
[Washington, D.C.]: U.S. Dept. of Health, Education, and Welfare, Public Health Service, National Institutes of Health, 1972, 239–262.
SUBJ 56

21071 NNC S P1 G9.4 1949–1972
Hwang, T. S. (Huang T'ien-ssu), and T. C. Chen (Ch'en Tien-chang).
'Incidence of leukemia in Chinese.'
CMJ-T 9, 3 (Sept. 1962), 215–222.
SUBJ 56

21072 CSH O P7 G7.3 1949–1972
Kiangsi. Yü-chiang Hsien. Revolutionary Committee. Culture, Education, Health, and Antischistosomiasis Section *with* Yü-chiang Antischistosomiasis Station.
'A great victory of Mao Tse-tung's thought in the battle against schistosomiasis: The 10 years since the eradication of schistosomiasis in Yukiang county in 1958.'
CM 1968, 10 (Oct.), 588–602.
SUBJ 56

21073 CSH P P2 G1.2 1949–1972
King, Haitung (Chin Hai-tung), 1917–.
'Cancer research organization and preventive programs.' In *Medicine and public health in the People's Republic of China*, edited by Joseph R- Quinn. [Selective entry]
[Washington, D.C.]: U.S. Dept. of Health, Education, and Welfare, Public Health Service, National Institutes of Health, 1972, 263–288.
SUBJ 56 ▪ 17 36.1

21074 CSU O P3 G9.4 1949–1972
King, Hwa-kou (Chin Hua-kao).
'Design, organization and function of intensive care unit at the Tri-Service General Hospital [Taipei].'
CMJ-T 17, 3 (Sept. 1970), 184–189.
SUBJ 56

21075 CSU O P2 G1.2 1949–1972
Klotz, H- P-.
'Les médecins chinois vus à travers mon carnet de voyage' (Chinese doctors: Notes from my travel notebook).
CFC 2 (juin 1959), 53–71.
SUBJ 16.1 56 ▪ 17 18

21076 MCH P P2 G1.2 1949–1972
[La Dany, Ladislao] ———, 1914–.
'Health.'
CNA 365 (24 Mar. 1961), 1–7.
SUBJ 56

21077 CSH P P2 G1.2 1949–1972
[La Dany, Ladislao] ———, 1914–.
'Health for the millions.'
CNA 738 (3 Jan. 1969), 1–7.
SUBJ 56 ▪ 17 35

21078 MCH P P5 G1.2 1949–1972
[La Dany, Ladislao] ———, 1914–.
'Medicine in China.'
CNA 98 (2 Nov. 1955), 1–7.
SUBJ 56

21079 CSH P P7 G1.2 1949–1972
[La Dany, Ladislao] ———, 1914–.
'Medicine to the villages.'
CNA 602 (4 Mar. 1966), 1–7.
SUBJ 56

21080 CSH P P2 G1.2 1949–1972
[La Dany, Ladislao] ———, 1914–.
'Public health.'
CNA 889 (4 Aug. 1972), 1–7.
SUBJ 56

21081 MCH P P1 G1.2 1949–1972
[La Dany, Ladislao] ———, 1914–.
'Towards a new science of medicine?'
CNA 269 (20 Mar. 1959), 1–7.
SUBJ 56 ▪ 17

21082 CSU P P2 G1.2 1949–1972
Lambin, Denis A-.
'La Chine propre' ('Clean' China).
CFC 3 (oct. 1959), 104–115.
SUBJ 18 56

21083 MCH F P2 G5.0 1949–1972
Li Kuang-heng, Kao Jun-ch'üan, and Wu Ying-k'ai.
'A survey of the prevalence of carcinoma of the esophagus in North China.'
CMJ 81, 8 (Aug. 1962), 489–494.
SUBJ 28 56 ▪ 58

21084 CSU O P2 G9.4 1949–1972
Li, S. F., and H- W- Brown.
'Public health nursing in Taiwan, Republic of China.'
American j. of public health 56, 3 (Mar. 1966), 492–498.
SUBJ 17 18 56 ▪ 51 58

21085 NIC S P2 G1.2 1949–1972
Li Teh-chuan (Li Te-ch'üan).
'Ten years of public health work in New China.'
CMJ 79, 6 (Dec. 1959), 483–488.
SUBJ 56 ▪ 18 36.4

21086 NNC P P1 G1.2 1949–1972
Lin Chiao-chih.
Achievements of obstetrics in China, mimeo. Tr. from *Ch'ing chu chien kuo shih chou nien i hsüeh k'o hsüeh ch'eng chiu lun wen chi, hsia chuan* (Collected articles on medical achievements in commemoration of the tenth anniversary of the founding of the People's Republic of China, Vol. 2); Peking: Jen min ch'u pan she, 1959?, 1–11.
Washington, D.C.: U.S. Joint Publications Research Service, 21 June 1962. 17 p. (JPRS 14,211; MC 15,801/1962)
SUBJ 47 51 56

21087 NNC O P7 G5.2 1949–1972
Lin Chiao-ya (Lin Ch'iao-ya) and Huang Ting-ch'en.
'New trends in rural sanitation and health work.' Tr. of 'Nung ts'un wei sheng pao chien kung tso ti hsin mien mao'; *Jen min jih pao* 6 Apr. 1960, 16. In *Speeches given at second session of Second National People's Congress, Communist China*, mimeo., compiled by U.S. Joint Publications Research Service. [Sole entry]
Washington, D.C.: JPRS, 1 Mar. 1961, 109–114. (JPRS 6825; MC 7820/1961)
SUBJ 56

21088 CSH O P3 G9.5 1949–1972
Lindsay, T- J-.
'Medical assistance fund of Butterfield and Swire Ltd. (Hong Kong).' In *Hong Kong economic papers, No. 2*, edited by Edward Stuart Kirby. [Selective entry]
Hong Kong: Hong Kong Economic Assn., 1963, 42–48.
SUBJ 56

21089 CSU F P8 G9.4 1949–1972
Liu, J. C. (Liu Jui-chung), O. K. Khaw (Hsü Yü-chieh), and P. C. Fan (Fan Ping-chen).
'Paragonimiasis among school children in Shenkeng hsiang, Taipei hsieng [i.e., T'ai-pei *hsien*], northern Taiwan.'
CMJ-T 15, 1 (Mar. 1968), 44–53.
SUBJ 56 ▪ 52

21090 MCH U P4 G1.2 1949–1972
Liu Shih-chieh, Wu Chih-chung, and Wang Wen-yen.
'Industrial health and prevention of occupational diseases in New China.'
CMJ 81, 1 (Jan. 1962), 1–8.
SUBJ 14.4 56 ▪ 18

21091 CSU F P8 G1.2 1949–1972
Lu, C. C. (Lu Chih-chün), et al.
'New China's achievements in the treatment and prevention of kala-azar.'
CMJ 73, 2 (Mar.–Apr. 1955), 91–99.
SUBJ 56

21092 CSH FP P2 G1.2 1949–1972
Ma Hai-teh (Ma Hai-te).
'With Mao Tse-tung's thought as the compass for action in the control of venereal diseases in China.'

CM 1966, 1 (Oct.), 52–67.
Subj 56 ▪ 12.1 36.1 46 47 64

21093 CSU O P2 G9.5 1949–1972
MacKenzie, D- J- M-.
Report on the outbreak of cholera in Hong Kong, covering the period 11th August to 12 October, 1961.
Hong Kong: Government Printer, 1961. 48 p.
Subj 56

21094 MCY O P1 G1.2 1949–1972
Mann, Felix.
'Chinese traditional medicine: A practitioner's view.'
CQ 23 (July–Sept. 1965), 28–36.
Subj 56 ▪ 18 62

21095 CSU O P3 G9.2 1949–1972
Morris, G- E-.
'Chinese hospitals.'
EH 6, 4 (Apr. 1967), 31–33.
Subj 56

21096 DLC O P4 G1.3 1949–1972
Nagnibeda, N- I-.
'Organizatsiia khirurgicheskoi raboty v Kitaiskoi Narodnoi Respublike: lichnoe vpechatlenie' (A personal impression of the organization of surgical work in the People's Republic of China).
Vestnik khirurgii 1957, 9 (sentiabr'), 140–147.
Subj 17 36.1 56 ▪ 16.1 18 66

21097 CSU P P2 G1.2 1949–1972
Orleans, Leo A-, 1924–, and Richard Peter Suttmeier, 1942–.
'The Mao ethic and environmental quality.'
Science 170, 3963 (11 Dec. 1970), 1173–1176.
Subj 14.4 56 64

21098 GMU P P1 G1.2 1949–1972
Pálos, István, 1922–.
Atem und Meditation. Moderne chinesische Atemtherapie als Vorschule der Meditation: Theorie, Praxis, Originaltexte (Breathing and meditation: Theory, practice, and original texts on modern Chinese breathing therapy as preparation for meditation).
Weilheim: Barth, 1968. 225 p.
Subj 56

21099 CSU F P4 G5.1 1949–1972
Pei-ching i hsüeh yüan (Peking Medical College). Wei sheng hsi (Dept. of Hygiene). Hsüeh hsiao wei sheng chiao yen tsu (School Hygiene Teaching Unit) *with* Peking. Wei sheng fang i chan (Hygiene and Disease Prevention Station). Hsüeh hsiao wei sheng tsu (School Hygiene Unit). [This article has still a third joint author: Peking, Hsi-ch'eng ch'ü wei sheng fang i chan, Hsüeh hsiao wei sheng tsu (Peking, Hsi-ch'eng *ch'ü* Hygiene and Disease-Prevention Station, School Hygiene Unit).]
'Health survey of middle school students participating in productive labor.' Tr. of 'Chung hsüeh sheng ts'an chia sheng ch'an lao tung ti wei sheng hsüeh tiao ch'a'; *Jen min pao chien* 1960, 3 (Mar.), 142–145. In *Public health in Communist China,* mimeo., compiled by U.S. Joint Publications Research Service. [Selective entry]
Washington, D.C.: JPRS, 15 July 1960, 108–123. (JPRS 2976; MC 14,181/1960)
Subj 56 ▪ 17 28 47 54

21100 MCY U P1 G1.2 1949–1972
Peking Academy of Traditional Chinese Medicine. Research Institute of Acupuncture and Moxibustion.
Chinese therapeutical methods of acupuncture and moxibustion.
Peking: Foreign Languages Press, 1964. 18 p.
Subj 56 ▪ 62

21101 MCY PO P3 G9.5 1949–1972
Pillai, K- S- C-.
'Return to living.'
FEER 42, 12 (19 Dec. 1963), 625–627, 629–631.
Subj 56 ▪ 28

21102 MCH O P3 G1.2 1949–1972
Popov, Evgenii Aleksandrovich.
'Psikhiatriia v Kitaiskoi Narodnoi Respublike: po lichnym vpechatleniiam' (Personal impressions of psychiatry in the People's Republic of China).
Zhurnal nevropatologii i psikhiatrii 59, 10 (1959), 1179–1183.
Subj 56 61 70 ▪ 18

21103 NIC O P2 G1.2 1949–1972
Quijada Cerda, Osvaldo A-.
Medicina en China (Medicine in China).
Santiago: Soc. Impresora Horizonte, 1962. 180 p.
Subj 17 18 56 ▪ 16 23 28 60

21104 NNC O P1 G1.2 1949–1972
Ravenholt, Albert, 1919–.
'The human price of China's disastrous food shortage.'
AUFS-EAS 10, 4 (May 1962), 1–12.
Subj 18 51 56 ▪ 12.1 14.3

21105 CSH P P2 G1.2 1949–1972
Rifkin, Susan Beth.
'Health care for rural areas.' In *Medicine and public health in the People's Republic of China,* edited by Joseph R-Quinn. [Selective entry]
[Washington, D.C.]: U.S. Dept. of Health, Education, and Welfare, Public Health Service, National Institutes of Health, 1972, 137–149.
Subj 56 ▪ 17 22

21106 CSU O P2 G1.2 1949–1972
Rocholl, Horst.
'Von einer Studienreise in die Volksrepublik China vom 21.2. bis 21.3. 1960' (A field trip to the People's Republic of China from 21 February to 21 March 1960).
Das deutsche Gesundheitswesen 15, 41/42 (20 Okt. 1960), 2088–2092.
Subj 56 ▪ 17 18 55

21107 NNC O P2 G1.2 1949–1972
Rogozin, I- I-, and I- F- Mikhailov.
'Uspekhi epidemiologii v Kitaiskoi Narodnoi Respublike' (Achievements in epidemiology in the People's Republic of China).
Zhurnal mikrobiologii, epidemologii i immunobiologii 30, 10 (oktiabr' 1959), 3–8.
Subj 18 56

21108 MAM FP P7 G9.4 1949–1972
Rossman, John Charles, 1931–.
An approach toward applying cost-benefit analysis to an industrial health problem in a developing country: An economic analysis of direct loss from occupational accidents in the coal mining industry of Taiwan, Republic of China.
Ann Arbor: University Microfilms (Publ. 71-9250), 1971. 199 p. (Doctoral dissertation in Public Health, U. of California, Los Angeles)
Subj 16.4 56 ▪ 12.2 14.4 50

21109 DLC O P4 G1.4 1949–1972
Rusakovich, A-.
'Obshchestvennost' Kitaia v bor'be za sanitarnuiu kul'turu' (Chinese society in the struggle for hygienic practices).
Sovetskii krasnyi krest 8, 3 (mai–iiun' 1958), 28–29.
Subj 12.1 56 ▪ 21.3

21110 CSU P P1 G1.2 1949–1972
Sakka, Michel.
'La chirurgie cardiaque et vasculaire en Chine' (Cardiovascular surgery in China).
CFC 10 (juin 1961), 73–83.
Subj 56

21111 CSU U P2 G1.2 1949–1972
Sakka, Michel.
'Hygiène de masse en Chine.'
CFC 7 (sept. 1960), 70, 72–79.

Public health in China, mimeo.
Washington, D.C.: U.S. Joint Publications Research Service, 24 Mar. 1961. 7 p. (JPRS 4485; MC 7672/1961)
Subj 56

21112 MCH F P3 G9.5 1949–1972
Scarpa, António, 1752–1832.
'A medicina tradicional chinesa em Macau' (Chinese traditional medicine in Macau).
Boletim da Sociedade de Geografia de Lisboa 83, 1/3 (Janeiro–Março 1965), 35–42.
Subj 56 ▪ 17

21113 CSU O P3 G1.2 1949–1972
Schmaus, Albert K-.
'Das Gesundheitswesen und der Stand der Chirurgie in der VR China' (Public health and surgery in the People's Republic of China).
Z. für ärztliche Fortbildung 54, 22 (15 Nov. 1960), 1290–1295; 55, 7 (1 Apr. 1961), 361–365; 55, 9 (1 Mai 1961), 577–581; 55, 16 (15 Aug. 1961), 953–959.
Subj 17 18 56 62

21114 CSH O P7 G8.3 1949–1972
Shanghai First Medical College. Revolutionary Committee. Politics and Education Section.
'The "spearhead" squad [in Kweichow]: Young medical workers nurtured by Mao Tse-tung's thought.'
CM 1968, 12 (Dec.), 724–734.
Subj 56 ▪ 22.1 64

21115 CSH O P8 G6.2 1949–1972
Shanghai Hua-shan Hospital. Medical Team to Anhwei.
'A brilliant example in implementing Chairman Mao's "June 26" directive.'

CM 1968, 9 (Sept.), 529–536.
Subj 22.1 56 ▪ 21.2 64

21116 CSH O P7 G6.1 1949–1972
Shanghai. Ch'ing-pu Hsien. Lien-sheng Commune.
'Struggle against schistosomiasis.'
CM 1968, 11 (Nov.), 669–672.
Subj 56

21117 NNC PO P2 G1.5 1949–1972
Shen Ch'i-chen.
'Report on prevention of schistosomiasis.' Tr. of 'Wan min huan t'eng sung wen shen' (The millions celebrate the demise of the god of plague); *Jen min jih pao* 10 Apr. 1960, 13. In *Speeches given at second session of Second National People's Congress, Communist China*, mimeo., compiled by U.S. Joint Publications Research Service. [Sole entry]
Washington, D.C.: JPRS, 9 Jan. 1961, 1–6. (JPRS 6526; MC 2311/1961)
Subj 56 ▪ 12.1

21118 CSH U P4 G2.2 1949–1972
Shih Liu and Szu Chi (Ssu Chi).
'Using Mao Tse-tung's thought to open up a "forbidden zone", curing deaf-mutes: Achievement of a Mao Tse-tung's thought propaganda team of medical workers from the PLA 3016 unit's health section.'
CM 1968, 11 (Nov.), 641–646.
Subj 56 ▪ 27

21119 CSH O P4 G1.2 1949–1972
Sidel, Ruth, 1933–.
'Mental diseases and their treatment.' In *Medicine and public health in the People's Republic of China*, edited by Joseph R- Quinn. [Selective entry]
[Washington, D.C.]: U.S. Dept. of Health, Education, and Welfare, Public Health Service, National Institutes of Health, 1972, 289–305.
Subj 56 61

21120 CSU O P2 G1.3 1949–1972
Sidel, Victor W-, 1931–.
'The barefoot doctors of the People's Republic of China.'
New England j. of medicine 286, 24 (15 June 1972), 1292–1299.
Subj 56

21121 CSU O P2 G1.3 1949–1972
Sidel, Victor W-, 1931–.
'Serve the people! Medical care in the People's Republic of China.'
Asia (New York: Asia Society) 26 (Summer 1972), 3–30.
Subj 56 ▪ 51 58

21122 CSU O P2 G1.3 1949–1972
Sidel, Victor W-, 1931–, and Ruth Sidel, 1933–.
'The human services in China.'
Social policy 2, 6 (Mar.–Apr. 1972), 25–34.
Subj 52 56 ▪ 17 22 27 58 61

21123 CSH O P2 G1.2 1949–1972
Sieh, Marie.
'Medicine in China: Wealth for the state.'
CS 3, 5 (15 Oct. 1964), 1–12; 3, 6 (1 Nov. 1964), 1–15.
Subj 17 56 ▪ 18

21124 DLC PO P3 G1.2 1949–1972
Smirnov-Kamenskii, Evgenii Arsen'evich.
Dva goda v Kitae: zapiski sovetskogo vracha (Two years in China: A Soviet physician's notes).
Stavropol: Kn. izd-vo, 1959. 196 p.
Subj 17 18 37 53 56 64 ▪ 14 31 47 58

21125 CSH P P2 G1.3 1949–1972
Stanford U. China Project.
'Health and sanitation.' In *Central South China*, compiled by the organization cited. [Selective entry]
New Haven: Human Relations Area Files, 1956, vol. 1, 345–361. (HRAF subcontractor's monographs, 28; Stanford 2)
Subj 56 ▪ 18

21126 CSH P P2 G1.3 1949–1972
Stanford U. China Project.
'Health and sanitation.' In *East China*, compiled by the organization cited. [Selective entry]
New Haven: Human Relations Area Files, 1956, vol. 1, 388–408. (HRAF subcontractor's monographs, 29; Stanford 3)
Subj 56

21127 CSH P P2 G5.0 1949–1972
Stanford U. China Project.
'Health and sanitation.' In *North China*, compiled by the organization cited. [Selective entry]
New Haven: Human Relations Area Files, 1956, vol. 1, 367–387. (HRAF subcontractor's monographs, 27; Stanford 1)
Subj 56 ▪ 58

21128 NNC P P2 G8.0 1949–1972
Stanford U. China Project.
'Health and sanitation.' In *Southwest China*, compiled by the organization cited. [Selective entry]
New Haven: Human Relations Area Files, 1956, vol. 1, 378–392. (HRAF subcontractor's monographs, 30; Stanford 4)
Subj 56

21129 CSU F P8 G1.3 1949–1972
Sun Mien-ling.
'Sanitary survey of underground water, soil, and vegetables in areas irrigated with sewage.' Tr. of 'Wu shui kuan kai ch'ü ti hsia shui, tu jang chi su ts'ai ti wei sheng tiao ch'a' (Sanitation survey of underground water, soil, and vegetables in areas irrigated with sewage); *Jen min pao chien* 1960, 3 (Mar.), 124–126. In *Public health in Communist China*, mimeo., compiled by U.S. Joint Publications Research Service. [Selective entry]
Washington, D.C.: JPRS, 15 July 1960, 30–42. (JPRS 2976; MC 14,181/1960)
Subj 14.1 56

21130 CSU F P2 G9.3 1949–1972
Sun, T. S., Y. S. Chang, and S. C. Hsu (Hsü Shih-chü), 1905–.
'Epidemiology and control of plague on Kinmen [i.e., Chin-men *hsien*, Fukien].'
CMJ-T 13, 2 (June 1966), 153–160.
Subj 56

21131 CSU FP P2 G9.4 1949–1972
Taiwan. Wei sheng ch'u. (Dept. of Health).
Taiwan's health, 1968 and 1969, 4th ed.
Taichung: Wei sheng ch'u, 1970. 147 p.
Subj 56 ▪ 51 58 61

21132 CSU P P1 G9.4 1949–1972
Takeshita, Yuzuru John, 1926–, J. Y. Peng, and Paul K. C. Liu (Liu K'o-chih), 1930–.
'A study of the effectiveness of the prepregnancy health program in Taiwan.'
Eugenics q. 11, 4 (Dec. 1964), 222–233.
Subj 51 56 ▪ 58

21133 CSU F P3 G6.2 1949–1972
Tan, Alfred Y. S. (T'an Yüan-sheng).
'An outbreak of smallpox in Wuhu: Analysis of 108 cases.'
CMJ 69, 1/2 (Jan.–Feb. 1951), 69–75.
Subj 56

21134 DLC O P3 G5.1 1949–1972
Tan Guan (T'ang Kuang).
'Nasha apteka idet vpered' (Our drugstore is improving).
Aptechnoe delo 8, 3 (mai–iiun' 1959), 87–88.
Subj 56 ▪ 28 66

21135 NNC F P2 G9.4 1949–1972
Tao, Jung-chin.
'BCG vaccination program in Taiwan.'
CMJ-T 1, 1 (Jan. 1954), 61–70.
Subj 56

21136 CSU F P3 G6.1 1949–1972
T'ao Jen, et al.
'Prevention of postpartum hemorrhage with ergonovine: An analysis of 19,510 cases.'
CMJ 84, 9 (Sept. 1965), 585–590.
Subj 51 56

21137 DLC U P1 G1.2 1949–1972
Tatarinov, A- L-.
'Okhrana materinstva i detstva v narodnom Kitae' (Protection of maternal and child health in the People's Republic of China).
Fel'dsher i akusherka 22, 7 (iiul' 1957), 56–61.
Subj 47 51 56 ▪ 41 52 58

21138 CSU F P3 G9.5 1949–1972
Topley, Marjorie Doreen, 1927–.
'Chinese traditional ideas and the treatment of disease: Two examples from Hong Kong.'
Man new (2nd) series 5, 3 (Sept. 1970), 421–437.
Subj 56 65 ▪ 46 52

21139 CSH O P7 G5.1 1949–1972
Tsao Ting-chüan (Ts'ao Ting-chüan).
'Mao Tse-tung's thought restores vision to the blind: Traditional cataractopiesis in the countryside.'
CM 1968, 1 (Jan.), 65–70.
Subj 56 ▪ 21.2

21140 CSH PO P3 G5.3 1949–1972
Tsingtao Medical College Hospital. Dept. of General Surgery.
'How we upgraded the quality and lowered the cost of our surgical treatment.'
CMJ 85, 7 (July 1966), 457–462.
Subj 56

21141 MCH O P7 G9.1 1949–1972
Tsou Yu-ning.
'The basic experience of eradication of pestilence and disease in Yü-lin special district.' Tr. of 'Yü-lin chuan ch'ü ch'u hai mieh ping kung tso ti chi pen ching yen' (Basic results of the elimination of pestilence and disease in Yü-lin special district [Kwangsi]); *Jen min pao chien* 1960, 6 (June), 332–335. In *Selected translations from 'Jen min pao chien' (People's health) on disease control*, mimeo., compiled by U.S. Joint Publications Research Service. [Sole entry]
Washington, D.C.: JPRS, Jan. 1961, 21–38. (JPRS 7280; MC 10,809/1961)
Subj 28 56 ▪ 22.1 24.1

21142 NNC O P2 G1.2 1949–1972
TSzin' Sin'-chzhun (Chin Hsin-chung).
'Bor'ba s infektsionnymi i parazitarnymi bolezniami v Kitaiskoi Narodnoi Respublike' (The struggle against infectious and parasitic diseases in the People's Republic of China).
Sovetskoe zdravookhranenie 21, 1 (ianvar' 1962), 63–72.
Subj 18 56 ▪ 28

21143 NNC O P2 G1.2 1949–1972
Vashkov, V- I-.
'Nekotorye dannye o rabote sanitarno-protivoepidemicheskoi sluzhby v Kitaiskoi Narodnoi Respublike' (Data on the work of the sanitary and anti-epidemic service in the People's Republic of China).
Zhurnal mikrobiologii, epidemologii i immunobiologii 32, 12 (dekabr' 1961), 24–29.
Subj 56 ▪ 18

21144 CSH O P6 G7.3 1949–1972
Wang Chao-lin.
'Medicine town revived [Chang-shu-chen, Ch'ing-chiang *hsien*, Kiangsi].'
PR 6, 7 (15 Feb. 1963), 17–18.
Subj 24.3 56

21145 CSU F P2 G9.3 1949–1972
Wang, Shu-yon (Wang Shu-jung), and Khang-lee Liu. [Part 1 authored by Wang only; part 2 coauthored by Liu and Wang.]
'Epidemiologic study of dental caries in the Pescadores (Penghu), Taiwan.'
CMJ-T 15, 3 (Sept. 1968), 224–231; 16, 1 (Mar. 1969), 56–61.
Subj 56 ▪ 50

21146 CSU P P1 G1.2 1949–1972
Way, Edward Leong (Liang Tung-ts'ai), 1916–.
'Pharmacology.' In *Sciences in Communist China*, edited by [Sydney Henry Gould] Sidney H. Gould. [Selective entry]
Washington, D.C.: American Assn. for the Advancement of Science, 1961, 363–382. (AAAS publications, 68)
Subj 56 ▪ 14.4 18 32.1 36.1

21147 CSH U P8 G1.5 1949–1972
Wei Wen-po.
'The land of 600 million banishes the god of plague.' Tr. of 'Liu i Shen-chou sung wen shen'; *Hung ch'i* 1960, 2 (16 Jan.), 28–32. In *Translations from selected issues of 'Hung-ch'i' (Red flag) (Communist China)*, mimeo., compiled by U.S. Joint Publications Research Service. [Selective entry]
Washington, D.C.: JPRS, 19 June 1961, 11–18. (JPRS 8476; MC 13,335/1961)
Subj 56 ▪ 18

21148 MCH O P3 G1.2 1949–1972
Willox, G- L-.
'Contemporary Chinese health, medical practice and philosophy.' In *Contemporary China*, edited by Ruth Adams. [Selective entry]
New York: Pantheon, 1966, 105–120.
Subj 18 56 ▪ 17

21149 MCH F P2 G9.2 1949–1972
Worth, Robert McAlpine, 1924–.
'Health trends in China since the "Great Leap Forward".'
American j. of hygiene 78, 3 (Nov. 1963), 349–357.
Subj 56 ▪ 28 55

21150 CSU F P2 G1.2 1949–1972
Worth, Robert McAlpine, 1924–.
'Strategy of change in the People's Republic of China: The rural health center.' In *Communication and change in the developing countries*, edited by Daniel Lerner and Wilbur Schramm. [Selective entry]
Honolulu: East-West Center Press, 1967, 216–230.
Subj 28 56 ▪ 22 37 58

21151 CSH O P8 G2.1 1949–1972
Wu Tse-min.
'How I have studied and applied Chairman Mao's teachings in my work as a rural doctor [in Hung-ch'i production brigade, Hsing-hua commune, Ning-an *hsien*, Heilungkiang].'
CM 1968, 5 (May), 276–284.
Subj 56 64 ▪ 21.2 61

21152 NNC O P2 G6.2 1949–1972
Wu Yen-chiu (Wu Yen-ch'iu), Chiao Ming-lan (Chiao Ming-lüan), and Chu Sui.
'Anhwei bids farewell to the plagues.' Tr. of 'An-hui ch'u ch'u sung wen shen' (Anhwei celebrates the demise of the god of plague); *Jen min jih pao* 11 Apr. 1960, 22. In *Translations of 'Jen min jih pao' articles on health, people's communes and physical culture*, mimeo., compiled by U.S. Joint Publications Research Service. [Selective entry]
Washington, D.C.: JPRS, 27 June 1960, 43–51. (JPRS 2949; MC 14,165/1960)
Subj 28 56 ▪ 24.1

21153 CSH S P2 G1.2 1949–1972
Yeh, Samuel D. J. (Yeh Ta-chu), 1926–, and Bacon Field Chow (Chou T'ien), 1909–.
'Nutrition.' In *Medicine and public health in the People's Republic of China*, edited by Joseph R- Quinn. [Selective entry]
[Washington, D.C.]: U.S. Dept. of Health, Education, and Welfare, Public Health Service, National Institutes of Health, 1972, 211–237.
Subj 56 ▪ 18

21154 NNC O P3 G6.1 1949–1972
Yen Fu-ch'ing, 1882–, et al.
'The sustained big leap forward in medical and health enterprises.' Tr. of 'I yao wei sheng shih yeh ti ch'ih hsü ta yao chin'; *Jen min jih pao* 11 Apr. 1960, 22. In *Translations of 'Jen min jih pao' articles on health, people's communes and physical culture*, mimeo., compiled by U.S. Joint Publications Research Service. [Selective entry]
Washington, D.C.: JPRS, 27 June 1960, 25–42. (JPRS 2949; MC 14,165/1960)
Subj 28 56 ▪ 17

21155 ELU F P2 G9.4 1949–1972
Yen, Y. T. (Yen Yü-t'ing), and Timothy Danforth Baker, 1925–.
'A study on the quality of medical care in health stations.'
J. of the Formosan Medical Assn. 70 (28 Jan. 1971), 21–27.
Subj 56

21156 CSU F P1 G9.4 1949–1972
Yen, Y. T. (Yen Yü-t'ing), and S. H. Chao (Chao Hsiu-hsiung).
'Administrative functions at health stations in Taiwan.'
CMJ-T 17, 3 (Sept. 1970), 190–197.
Subj 56

21157 CSH O P3 G5.1 1949–1972
Yueh Sung-sheng.
'A traditional medicine shop [i.e., Tung-jen T'ang, Peking].'
China reconstructs 11, 3 (Mar. 1962), 41–43.
Subj 24.3 56

21158 MCH U P7 G1.2 1949–1972
Zakharov, A- V-.
'Organizatsiia zdravookhraneniia v narodnykh kommunakh Kitaia.'
Sovetskoe zdravookhranenie 19, 2 (fevral' 1960), 82–87.

Organization of public health in the people's communes of China, mimeo.
Washington, D.C.: U.S. Joint Publications Research Service, 23 Jan. 1961. 10 p. (JPRS 7611; MC 10,975/1961)
Subj 56 ▪ 18 52

57 Death Practices

死亡及喪葬　死亡及び葬祭

1644-1911

21159 NIC P P1 G1.3 1842–1895
'Chinese coroners' inquests.'
Popular science monthly 25, 5 (Sept. 1884), 690–692.
Subj 12.2 57

21160 MCH PO P1 G1.2 1842–1895
'Chinesische Witwenopfer' (The sacrifice of widows in China).
Das Ausland 34, 44 (27 Okt. 1861), 1051–1053.
Subj 57 ▪ 41 47 65

21161 MCH O P2 G5.1 1895–1911
'Les funérailles de Kuang-Su, empereur des Chinois' (The funeral rites of the Kuang-hsü Emperor).

A travers le monde 15, 24 (12 juin 1909), 190–191.
Subj 57

21162 MCH O P2 G1.3 1895–1911
Aingreville, Pacifique-Marie d'.
'Funérailles païennes en Chine' (Pagan funerals in China).
Missions catholiques 36 (19 août 1904), 406–418; 36 (26 août 1904), 417–419; 36 (2 sept. 1904), 429–431; 36 (9 sept. 1904), 442–444.
Subj 57 ▪ 23 43

21163 MCY FP P7 G1.2 –1911
Bouillard, Georges, 1862–1930.
Les tombeaux impériaux Ming et Tsing (The Ming and Ch'ing imperial tombs).
Peiping: Nachbaur, 1931. 225 p.
Subj 13 57 62 ▪ 41 43 47 64

21164 CSU O P2 G1.2 1842–1895
Dudgeon, John Hepburn, 1837–1901.
'Chinese inquests.'
NQCJ 3, 8 (Aug. 1869), 127–128.
Subj 57

21165 CSU PO P1 G1.2 –1842
Fedele, Benedetto.
'Di alcune sopravvienze arcaiche nei riti funebri cinesi' (Archaic survivals in Chinese funeral rites). In *Die Wiener Schule der Völkerkunde: Festschrift anlässlich des 25-jährigen Bestandes des Instituts für Völkerkunde der Universität Wien (1929–1954)* (The Vienna School of Anthropology: Felicitation volume in honor of the twenty-fifth anniversary of the founding of the Institute for Ethnology of the University of Vienna, 1929–1954), edited by J- Haekel, A- Hohenwart-Gerlachstein, A- Slawik, et al. [Sole entry]
Horn-Vienna: Berger, 1956, 434–447.
Subj 43 57

21166 NNC O P2 G1.3 1842–1895
Galpin, Francis William, 1858–?
'China's tribute to the dead.'
J. of the Manchester Geographical Society 11, 7/9 (July–Sept. 1895), 209–216.
Subj 57 ▪ 43 62

21167 CSU FP P3 G9.3 –1895
Groot, Jan Jakob Maria de, 1854–1921.
'Buddhist masses for the dead at Amoy.' In *Actes du Sixième Congrès international des orientalistes, tenu en 1883 à Leide, section 4, de l'Extrême-Orient* (Transactions of the Sixth International Congress of Orientalists, Leiden, 1883, Section 4, The Far East). [Sole entry]
Leiden: Brill, 1885, 1–120.
Subj 43 57 ▪ 62 65

21168 MCH O P3 G9.3 1842–1895
Groot, Jan Jakob Maria de, 1854–1921.
'De lijkbezorging der Emoy-Chineezen' (The funeral practices of the Amoy Chinese).
BTLV 41 (1892), 1–114.
Subj 57 ▪ 26.1 41

21169 CBU PO P3 G5.1 1842–1895
Imbault-Huart, Camille Clément, 1857–1897.
'La mort d'une impératrice régente en Chine (coutumes chinoises et page d'histoire contemporaine)' (The death of an empress dowager in China [Hsiao Chen]: Chinese customs and a page from contemporary history).
JA 7e série 19 (fév.–mars 1882), 252–265.
Subj 12 57 ▪ 16.1

21170 CSU P P1 G1.2 –1895
MacGowan, Daniel Jerome, 1814?–1893.
'Self-immolation by fire in China.'
CR 19, 10 (Oct. 1888), 445–451; 19, 11 (Nov. 1888), 508–521.
Subj 33 57 ▪ 62

21171 FPN O P3 G1.1 1842–1895
Martin, Charles Ernest, 1831–1897.
'Le culte des morts et les sépultures chez les Chinois' (The cult of the dead and burials in China).
Science moderne 7, 44 (14 oct. 1893), 248–250.
Subj 57 ▪ 23 43

21172 NNC P P2 G1.2 –1895
Martin, Charles Ernest, 1831–1897.
Exposé des principaux passages contenus dans le 'Si-yuen-lu' (An analysis of the most important passages in *Hsi-yüan lu* [Instructions to coroners]).
Paris: Ernest Leroux, 1884. 78 p.
Subj 12.2 57 ▪ 38 41 43 46 47 51 63 65

21173 MCH O P2 G1.1 –1895
Martin, Charles Ernest, 1831–1897.
'Les sépultures dans l'Extrême-Orient' (Burials in the Far East).
R. scientifique 3e série 52, 24 (9 déc. 1893), 753–756.
Subj 57 ▪ 13 43

21174 NNC O P3 G5.1 1895–1911
Matignon, Jean-Jacques, 1866–?
'Le suicide' (Suicide). In *La Chine hermétique: superstitions, crime et misère* (China sealed off: Superstition, crime, and poverty), 5th ed., rev., by J.-J. Matignon. [Selective entry]
Paris: Lib. Geuthner, 1936, 97–173.
Subj 57 ▪ 47 63

21175 CSH O P2 G1.5 1895–1911
Nagel, August.
'Goldheben und Goldschau in Südchina' (The ritual disinterment and display of 'gold' [bones] in South China).
OL 27, 2 (10 Jan. 1913), 47–78.
Subj 43 57

21176 CSU P P1 G5.1 1842–1895
Perkins, H- P-.
'Chinese epitaphs.'
CR 19, 6 (June 1888), 245–250.
Subj 57 65 ▪ 43

21177 MCH O P7 G5.0 1842–1895
Piton, Charles, 1835–1905.
'Les ensevelissements de personnes vivantes et le loess dans le nord de la Chine' (Live burials and loess soil in North China).
B. de la Société neuchâteloise de géographie 7, 3 (1892), 52–62.
Subj 22.2 57

21178 MCH O P2 G5.3 1895–1911
Prahl, *Dr.* ———.
'Über Selbstmorde bei den Chinesen, unter besonderer Berücksichtigung des deutschen Schutzgebiets Kiautschou und der Provinz Schantung' (Suicide among the Chinese, with special attention to the German protectorate of Kiaochow and to Shantung).
Archiv für Rassen- und Gesellschafts-Biologie 5, 5/6 (Sept.–Dez. 1908), 669–706.
Subj 47 56 57 ▪ 60 62

21179 CSU O P2 G9.2 1842–1895
Sampson, Theos, ?–1897.
'Urn-burial in China.'
NQCJ 2, 7 (July 1868), 108–111.
Subj 57 ▪ 62

21180 NIC O P1 G6.3 1895–1911
Walshe, William Gilbert.
'Some Chinese funeral customs.'
JRAS-CB new (2nd) series 35 (1903/04), 26–64.
Subj 57 ▪ 62

21181 NNC O P2 G5.3 1842–1911
Wilhelm, Richard, 1873–1930.
'Totenbräuche in Schantung' (Funeral customs in Shantung).
MDG 11, 1 (1907/09), 33–45.
Subj 57 ▪ 41 62

21182 CSU U P1 G1.2 1842–1895
Yates, Matthew Tyson, 1819–1888.
'Ancestral worship and fung-shuy.'
CR 1, 2 (June 1868), 23–28; 1, 3 (July 1868), 37–43.
Subj 43 57 62 ▪ 23 65

21183 NIC PO P2 G1.2 –1911
Yetts, Walter Perceval, 1878–1958.
'Notes on the disposal of Buddhist dead in China.'
JRAS 3rd series 1911, 3 (July), 699–725.
Subj 57 ▪ 23 62

1644-1949

21184 CNY P P5 G9.3 1644–1928
'Description de tombes et de mausolées' (A description of tombs and mausoleums).
La Chine 2 (1er sept. 1921), 118–126.
Subj 57 ▪ 16.1 62

21185 CSH P P1 G1.2 –1949
Chao, P. (Chao Kuang-i).
'The mourning ritual within the Chinese kinship system.'
CC 13, 2 (June 1972), 49–71.
Subj 44 57

21186 NNC S P2 G1.3 –1928
Fischer, Otto, 1886–1948.
'Chuan-chou: Die Magie der Umkreisung' (*Chuan-chou*: The magic of encirclement).
Artibus Asiae 4, 4 (1931), 213–220.
Subj 23 57 ▪ 62

21187 MCH O P2 G5.3 1895–1928
Kalff, Lambert.
Der Totenkult in Südschantung: Ein Beitrag zur Volkskunde des Landes (The cult of the dead in southern Shantung: A contribution to the folklore of the area).
Yen-chou-fu, Shantung: Katholische Mission, 1932. 109 p.
Subj 57 ▪ 43 62 65

21188 NNC F P3 G5.3 1644–1949
Thiel, P- I-.
'Doppelsprüche auf den Torsäulen der Grabhaine' (Couplets on the gateposts of burial groves).
Sinologica 6, 1 (1959), 25–56.
Subj 57 65 ▪ 23 62

21189 NNC PO P2 G1.2 –1928
Werner, Edward Theodore Chalmers, 1864–1954.
'The spirit that clears the way.' In *Autumn leaves: An autobiography with a sheaf of papers, sociological and sinological, philosophical and metaphysical*, by E. T. C. Werner. [Selective entry]
Shanghai: Kelly and Walsh, 1928, 49–68.
Subj 57 65 ▪ 23 41

1911-1949

21190 MCH O P2 G1.2 1928–1949
Carl, Wilhelm.
'Friedhofswahl in China' (Cemetery selection in China).
Der Erdball 4, 10 (1930), 365–369.
Subj 57 ▪ 43 62 65

21191 CSU O P2 G5.1 1928–1949
Gilbert, Rodney Yonkers, 1889–.
'China's shadow land.'
Asia (New York: American Asiatic Assn.) 31, 5 (May 1931), 310–317, 331–334.
Subj 57 ▪ 23 43

21192 NNC U P1 G8.3 1911–1949
Körner, Theo.
'Das Zurückrufen der Seele in Kuei-chou' (Recalling the souls of the dead in Kweichow).
Ethnos 3, 4/5 (July–Sept. 1938), 108–112.
Subj 57 ▪ 23 62

21193 NNC O P3 G1.3 1928–1949
[Serebrennikov, I- I-] J. J. Serebrennikov.
'Funeral money in China.'
CJ 18, 4 (Apr. 1933), 191–193.
Subj 57

21194 NNM O P4 G8.2 1928–1949
Ts'ai, Yung-ch'un.
Tali funeral rites [Ta-li *hsien*, Yunnan]*: A study in 'ancestor worship'*.
Unpublished masters thesis in Religion, Columbia U., 1947. 54 p.
Subj 57 ▪ 23 43 64

21195 MCH PO P2 G1.2 1911–1928
Werner, Edward Theodore Chalmers, 1864–1954.
'Reform in Chinese mourning rites.'
NCR 2, 3 (June 1920), 223–247. [Reprinted in *Autumn leaves: An autobiography with a sheaf of papers, sociological and sinological, philosophical and metaphysical*, by E. T. C. Werner. (Selective entry.) Shanghai: Kelly and Walsh, 1928, 69–95.]
Subj 57 ▪ 43 55 61

1911-1972
(including 1644-1972)

21196 CSU F P2 G4.4 1911–1972
Ternay, Johannes.
'Familienjustiz im Trauerhaus' (Family justice in a household in mourning). In *Ethnographische Beiträge aus der Ch'inghai Provinz (China)* (Ethnographic reports from Tsinghai). [Selective entry]
Peking [i.e., Tokyo]: Catholic U. of Peking, Museum of Oriental Ethnology, 1952, 103–124. (MOE, Folklore studies supplements, 1)
Subj 22.2 57 ▪ 41 44 45

21197 NNC FP P2 G9.5 1928–1972
Yap, Pow-meng (Yeh Pao-ming).
Suicide in Hong Kong, with special reference to attempted suicide.
Hong Kong: Hong Kong U. Press, 1958. 101 p. (Revision of doctoral dissertation in Medicine, U. of Cambridge [Sidney Sussex College], 1957)
Subj 56 57 ▪ 26 47 63

1949-1972

21198 CSH F P8 G9.5 1949–1972
Baker, Hugh David Roberts, 1937–.
'Burial, geomancy and ancestor worship.' In *Aspects of social organization in the New Territories*, edited by Hong Kong Branch, Royal Asiatic Society. [Selective entry]
Hong Kong: Cathay Press, 1964, 36–39.
Subj 57 ▪ 43 62

21199 CSU P P7 G1.3 1949–1972
Ravenholt, Albert, 1919–.
'The gods must go!'
AUFS-EAS 6, 16 (22 Nov. 1958), 1–7.
Subj 23 33 57 ▪ 62

21200 NIC O P2 G9.5 1949–1972
Wilson, B- D-.
'Chinese burial customs in Hong Kong.'
JRAS-HKB 1 (1960/61), 115–123.
Subj 57

21201 CSU O P8 G9.4 1949–1972
Wolf, Arthur Paul, 1932–.
'Chinese kinship and mourning dress.' In *Family and kinship in Chinese society*, edited by Maurice Freedman. [Selective entry]
Stanford: Stanford U. Press, 1970, 189–207.
Subj 40 57 ▪ 44

21202 NIC O P3 G9.5 1949–1972
Yap, Pow-meng (Yeh Pao-ming).
'Hypereridism and attempted suicide in Chinese.'
J. of nervous and mental diseases 127, 1 (July 1958), 34–41.
Subj 47 56 57 ▪ 41

58 Fertility and Mortality
繁殖率及死亡率
出生率及び死亡率

1644-1911

21203 NNC P P1 G9.2 –1895
'Life tables for a southern Chinese family from 1365–1849.'
NWSS 5, 17 (25 Apr. 1932), 75, 77–78.
Subj 42 58

1644-1949

21204 NIC P P2 G1.1 1895–1949
Taeuber, Irene Barnes, 1906–.
'Manpower utilization and demographic transition: Japan, Manchuria, Taiwan.'
AS 1, 3 (May 1961), 19–25.
Subj 21 21.4 58 ▪ 21.1 21.2

1911-1949

21205 NNC P P3 G1.3 1928–1949
'Birth-rate and death-rate in Chinese cities, 1929.'
NWSS 3, 28 (14 July 1930), 133, 136–138.
Subj 58 ▪ 21.1

21206 NNC P P1 G5.2 1911–1928
'Population statistics in Shansi, 1923.'
NWSS 4, 28 (13 July 1931), 131, 133–135.
Subj 21 58 ▪ 50

21207 NNC F P8 G1.3 1911–1928
'Rural population of China, 1924–1925.'
NWSS 3, 11 (17 Mar. 1930), 53, 56.
Subj 58 ▪ 41 50

21208 NIC F P8 G1.3 1911–1928
Buck, John Lossing, 1890–, and C. M. Chiao (Ch'iao Ch'i-ming), 1897–.
'The composition and growth of rural population groups in China.'
CEJ 2, 3 (Mar. 1928), 219–235.
Subj 21 41 58 ▪ 16.3

21209 NIC S P1 G1.2 1911–1949
Chao, Ch'eng-hsin, 1907–.
'Familism as a factor in the Chinese population balance.'
YJSS 3, 1 (Oct. 1940), 1–21.
Subj 41 58 ▪ 11

21210 MCH FP P7 G6.1 1928–1949
[Chen, Dodge T.] Chen Tsai-chang (Ch'en Ts'ai-chang), and C. M. Chiao (Ch'iao Ch'i-ming), 1897–.
'Birth and death rates in Kiangyin registration area [Ch'iao-ch'i *chen*, Chiang-yin *hsien*, Kiangsu].'
EF 1 (Sept. 1936), 66–71. [In Chinese as well as English]
Subj 21 58 ▪ 26 28 56

21211 NIC P P2 G1.2 1911–1949
Chen, Warren H. (Ch'en Hua-yin).
'Differential fertility according to social class.' In *Atti del Congresso internazionale per gli studi sulla popolazione (Roma, 7–10 settembre 1931), Vol. VIII, sezione di sociologia* (Proceedings of the International Congress for Studies on Population, Rome, 7–10 September 1931, Vol. 8, Sociology), edited by Corrado Gini. [Sole entry]
Rome: Istituto poligrafico dello stato libreria, 1933, 95–103.
Subj 16 58 ▪ 47

21212 NNC F P3 G8.1 1928–1949
Cheng Mei Yu (Ch'eng Mei-yü).
'Report of an investigation on infant mortality and its causes in Chengtu.'
CMJ (Chengtu) 62A, 1 (Oct. 1943), 19–25. [Reprinted—*CMJ* 62, 1 (Jan.–Mar. 1944), 47–54.]
Subj 51 52 58 ▪ 28

21213 NNC FP P2 G1.3 1928–1949
Chiao, C. M. (Ch'iao Ch'i-ming), 1897–.
'Rural population and vital statistics for selected areas of China, 1929–1931.'
CEJ 14, 3 (Mar. 1934), 304–336; 14, 4 (Apr. 1934), 391–425. (Masters thesis in Sociology, Cornell U., 1933)
Subj 41 58 ▪ 21 29 47 50

21214 NIC F P7 G1.3 1928–1949
Chiao, C. M. (Ch'iao Ch'i-ming), 1897–.
'A study of the Chinese population.'
MMFQ 11, 4 (Oct. 1933), 325–341; 12, 1 (Jan. 1934), 85–96; 12, 2 (Apr. 1934), 171–183; 12, 3 (July 1934), 270–282.
Subj 41 58 ▪ 47

21215 CBU FP P7 G6.1 1928–1949
Chiao, C. M. (Ch'iao Ch'i-ming), 1897–, and [Dodge T. Chen] Chen Tsai-cheng (Ch'en Ts'ai-chang).
'Factors affecting the birth rate in China.'
EF 4 (Feb. 1937), 180–189. [In Chinese as well as English]
Subj 41 58 ▪ 22.1 47 51

21216 MCH F P7 G6.1 1928–1949
Chiao, C. M. (Ch'iao Ch'i-ming), 1897–, Warren Simpson Thompson, 1887–, and Dodge T. Chen (Ch'en Ts'ai-chang).
An experiment in the registration of vital statistics in China [in Ch'iao-ch'i *chen*, Chiang-yin *hsien*, Kiangsu], mimeo.
Oxford, Ohio: Scripps Foundation for Research in Population Problems, 1938. 115 p.
Subj 21 58 ▪ 21.2 26 51 56 62 65

21217 NNM P P3 G5.3 1928–1949
Fan, P. L.
'Chinese infants and children: A study of the infant and child mortality, size of the family, and sex ratio, on 2500 cases.'
CMJ 47, 7 (July 1933), 652–661.
Subj 41 51 58 ▪ 47 52

21218 NIC F P2 G1.3 1911–1928
Griffing, John B-.
'Size of the family in China.'
SSR 13, 1 (Sept.–Oct. 1928), 63–72.
Subj 41 58 ▪ 17

21219 NNC F P3 G5.1 1911–1928
Hammond, John, and Kang-liang Hsu.
'A note on infant and child mortality in North China.'
CMJ 41, 12 (Dec. 1927), 1006–1010.
Subj 51 58

21220 NIC F P3 G5.1 1911–1949
Hsu, Kang-liang, and Chu Fu-t'ang.
'Statistics concerning births and deaths in the children of 2,168 Chinese families.'
National medical j. of China 16, 6 (Dec. 1930), 744–755.
Subj 51 58

21221 NNM FP P3 G5.1 1928–1949
Hsu, S. C. (Hsü Shih-chü), 1905–, and T. H. Wang.
'A study of infant mortality in Nanking.'
CMJ 50, 4 (Apr. 1936), 573–580.
Subj 51 58 ▪ 52

21222 NIC S P1 G1.2 1928–1949
Jaffe, Abram J., 1912–.
'Notes on the rate of growth of the Chinese population.'
Human biology 19 (Feb. 1947), 1–11. [Reprinted in *Demographic analysis: Selected readings*, edited by Joseph John Spengler and Otis Dudley Duncan. (Sole entry.) Glencoe, Ill.: Free Press, 1956, 704–713.]
Subj 11 58

21223 NNC F P3 G5.1 1911–1928
Lennox, William Gordon, 1884–1960.
'Some vital statistics based on the histories of 4,000 Chinese families.'
CMJ 33, 4 (July 1919), 325–345.
Subj 58 ▪ 41 56

21224 NIC F P3 G5.1 1928–1949
Maxwell, J- Preston, and Amos I. H. Wong.
'On puerperal mortality and morbidity.'
National medical j. of China 16, 6 (Dec. 1930), 684–703.
Subj 51 56 58

21225 CSU F P7 G1.3 1928–1949
Notestein, Frank Wallace, 1902–, and C. M. Chiao (Ch'iao Ch'i-ming), 1897–.
'Population.' In *Land utilization in China: A study of 16,786 farms in 168 localities, and 32,256 farm families in twenty-two provinces in China, 1929–1933*, by John Lossing Buck. [Analytic entry]
Nanking: U. of Nanking, 1937, vol. 1, 358–399. [For Buck's work, see entry 12256.] [Reprinted in *Land utilization in China: A study of 16,786 farms in 168 localities, and 32,256 farm families in twenty-two provinces in China, 1929–1933*, by J. L. Buck. (Analytic entry.) New York: Paragon, 1964, vol. 1, 358–399.]
Subj 58 ▪ 11.2 11.4 14.1 17 41 47

21226 NNC F P3 G1.3 1911–1928
Oppenheim, F-.
'Birth and death ratios of the Chinese.'
CJ 2, 5 (Sept. 1924), 466–477.
Subj 58 ▪ 41

21227 CSU S P8 G1.2 1928–1949
Pan, Chia-lin (P'an Chia-lin).
'An estimate of the long-term crude birth rate of the agricultural population of China.'
Demography 3, 1 (1966), 204–208.
Subj 58 ▪ 16.3

21228 NIC F P8 G1.3 1928–1949
Seifert, Harry E-.
'Life tables for Chinese farmers.'
MMFQ 13, 3 (July 1935), 223–236.
Subj 58 ▪ 16.3

21229 CBU P P2 G2.0 1928–1949
Taeuber, Irene Barnes, 1906–, and Karl Ernst Taeuber, 1936–.
'The fertility of the Chinese in Northeast China.' In *Proceedings of the International Population Conference, Wien, 1959*, compiled by International Union for the Scientific Study of Population. [Sole entry]
Vienna: International Union for the Scientific Study of Population, 1959, 348–354.
Subj 58 ▪ 21.2 41 47 50 51

21230 NNM F P3 G5.1 1928–1949
Yang, Marion, and I-chin Yuan.
'Report of an investigation on infant mortality and its causes in Peiping.'
CMJ 47, 6 (June 1933), 597–604.
Subj 51 58 ▪ 28

1911-1972
(including 1644-1972)

21231 NIC P P2 G9.4 1895–1972
Chen Shao-hsing (Ch'en Shao-hsing), 1906–1966.
'Population change in Taiwan.'
B. of the Dept. of Archaeology and Anthropology, National Taiwan U. 6 (Nov. 1955), 86–119.
Subj 21 28 56 58 ▪ 21.4

21232 MBJ FP P2 G9.4 1895–1972
Chow, L. P. (Chou Lien-pin), 1924–.
Studies on the registration of births and infant deaths in Taiwan.
Unpublished doctoral dissertation in Hygiene and Public Health, Johns Hopkins U., 1963. 292 p.
Subj 58 ▪ 21 21.1 21.2 50

21233 MCH FP P2 G9.4 1928–1972
Chow, L. P. (Chou Lien-pin), 1924–, and S. C. Hsu (Hsü Shih-chü), 1905–.
'Taiwan's population problem.'
Population review 4, 2 (July 1960), 17–36.
Subj 21 58 ▪ 11.3 21.2 21.4 50 51

21234 CSU P P2 G9.5 1911–1972
Taeuber, Irene Barnes, 1906–.
'Chinese populations in transition: The city-states.'
Population index 38, 1 (Jan.–Mar. 1972), 3–34.
Subj 21 21.1 58 ▪ 21.2 21.4 47 50 51

21235 MCH P P2 G9.4 1644–1972
Taeuber, Irene Barnes, 1906–.
'Population growth in a Chinese microcosm: Taiwan.'
Population index 27, 2 (Apr. 1961), 101–126.
Subj 21 21.1 58 ▪ 21.2

1949-1972

21236 CSU F P8 G9.4 1949–1972
Chang, M. C., T. H. Liu, and L. P. Chow (Chou Lien-pin), 1924–.
'Study by matching of the demographic impact of an IUD program: A preliminary report.'
MMFQ 47, 2 (Apr. 1969), 137–157.
Subj 51 58 ▪ 21.2

21237 CSH FP P2 G9.4 1949–1972
Chen Shao-hsing (Ch'en Shao-hsing), 1906–1966, Yao-tung Wang, and Frederick Joseph Foley.
'Pattern of fertility in Taiwan: Report of a survey made in 1957.'
J. of social science (Taipei) 13 (1963), 209–294.
Subj 41 58 ▪ 29 47 51 65 72

21238 CSH P P2 G9.4 1949–1972
Chow, L. P. (Chou Lien-pin), 1924–.
'Current fertility in Taiwan.'
IFC 32, 6 (Dec. 1969), 12–26.
Subj 51 58 ▪ 41 50

21239 NNC F P2 G9.4 1949–1972
Chow, L. P. (Chou Lien-pin), 1924–, et al.
'A fertility survey of Taiwan.'

CMJ-T 12, 3 (Sept. 1965), 177–194.
SUBJ 58

21240 CSU P P2 G9.4 1949–1972
Collver, Andrew, Alden Speare, Jr., 1939–, and Paul K. C. Liu (Liu K'o-chih), 1930–.
'Local variations of fertility in Taiwan.'
PS 20, 3 (Mar. 1967), 329–342.
SUBJ 58 ▪ 41 50

21241 CSU P P2 G1.2 1949–1972
Current Scene Editor.
'The food and population balance: China's modernization dilemma.'
CS 9, 6 (7 June 1971), 1–7.
SUBJ 14.1 58 ▪ 11 51

21242 CSU FP P3 G9.5 1949–1972
Freedman, Ronald, 1917–, and Arjun L-Adlakha.
'Recent fertility declines in Hong Kong: The role of the changing age structure.'
PS 22, 2 (July 1968), 181–198.
SUBJ 50 58

21243 CSU FP P2 G9.4 1949–1972
Freedman, Ronald, 1917–, and T. H. Sun (Sun Te-hsiung), 1930–.
'Fertility trends in Taiwan, 1961–1970.'
Population index 38, 2 (Apr.–June 1972), 141–166.
SUBJ 41 58 ▪ 51

21244 CSU FP P2 G9.5 1949–1972
Freedman, Ronald, 1917–, et al.
'Hong Kong's fertility decline, 1961–68.'
Population b. 36, 1 (Jan.–Mar. 1970), 3–18.
SUBJ 50 51 58 ▪ 21.2 41

21245 MCH P P1 G9.4 1949–1972
Liu, Paul K. C. (Liu K'o-chih), 1930–.
'Socio-economic development and fertility levels in Taiwan.'
IFC 24, 2 (Aug. 1965), 2–17.
SUBJ 58 ▪ 18

21246 CSU P P3 G2.2 1949–1972
Lu Shou-tseng and Wang Kuang-i.
'1955 vs. 1958 life-tables for men and women in Ch'ang-ch'un.' Tr. of 'Ch'ang-ch'un shih 1955 nien ho 1958 nien nan nü hsing jen k'ou chien lüeh shou ming piao' (Abridged life-tables for males and females in Changchun, 1955 and 1958); *Jen min pao chien* 1960, 3 (Mar.), 160–166. In *Public health in Communist China*, mimeo., compiled by U.S. Joint Publications Research Service. [Selective entry]
Washington, D.C.: JPRS, 15 July 1960, 124–145. (JPRS 2976; MC 14,181/1960)
SUBJ 58 ▪ 47 56

21247 NNC P P2 G9.4 1949–1972
Ma, Chia-chi.
'Infant mortality in Taoyuan [i.e., T'ao-yüan *hsien*], Taiwan, 1948–1951.'
CMJ-T 1, 2 (Apr. 1954), 210–214.
SUBJ 51 58 ▪ 52

21248 CSU P P2 G1.2 1949–1972
Orleans, Leo A-, 1924–.
'Propheteering: The population of Communist China.'
CS 7, 24 (15 Dec. 1969), 13–19.
SUBJ 11 58 ▪ 18 51

21249 MAM FP P1 G9.4 1949–1972
Rutstein, Shea Oscar, 1945–.
The influence of child mortality on fertility in Taiwan: A study based on sample surveys conducted in 1967 and 1969.
Ann Arbor: University Microfilms (Publ. 72-29,186), 1972. 12, 226 p. (Doctoral dissertation in Economics, U. of Michigan, 1971)
SUBJ 51 58 ▪ 41 50

21250 CSU P P2 G1.2 1949–1972
Salaff, Janet Weitzner, 1940–.
'Institutionalized motivation for fertility limitation in China.'
PS 26, 2 (July 1972), 233–262.
SUBJ 11.4 41 47 51 52 58 ▪ 17 42 43 50

21251 CSU P P1 G1.2 1949–1972
Sauvy, Alfred, 1898–.
'La Chine.' In *De Malthus à Mao Tsé-Toung: le problème de la population dans le monde* (From Malthus to Mao Tse-tung: The world population problem), by A. Sauvy. [Sole entry]
Paris: Denoël, 1958, 241–247.
'China.' Tr. by Christine Brooke-Rose. In *Fertility and survival: Population problems from Malthus to Mao Tse-tung*, by A. Sauvy. [Sole entry]
New York: Criterion Books, 1961, 189–194.
SUBJ 58 ▪ 12.1 41 51

21252 CSH PO P3 G6.1 1949–1972
Shih Shu-chung, Chiang Ti-hsien, and Sung Chieh.
'Endeavors to reduce perinatal mortality in a maternity hospital.'
CMJ 85, 5 (May 1966), 288–290.
SUBJ 51 56 58

21253 NNC P P1 G1.2 1949–1972
T'ien Feng-tiao.
'China's planned births and population increase.' Tr. of 'Wo kuo chi hua sheng yü ho jen k'ou tseng chih wen t'i' (Birth control and the problem of population growth in China); *Jen min pao chien* 1959, 5 (May), 459–466. In *Translations on Communist China's economic services*, mimeo., compiled by U.S. Joint Publications Research Service. [Selective entry]
Washington, D.C.: JPRS, 20 Oct. 1959, 1–25. (JPRS 1956N; MC 17,613/1959)
SUBJ 51 58 ▪ 11

21254 CSU P P2 G9.5 1949–1972
Vaughan, T- D-, and Denis John Dwyer, 1933–.
'Some aspects of postwar population growth in Hong Kong.'
EG 42, 1 (Jan. 1966), 37–51.
SUBJ 11.2 21 21.1 58 ▪ 21.3 24.1 24.4 28 55

21255 NNC F P3 G2.1 1949–1972
Yang Chien-po.
'The influence of winter upon the mortality rate of infants in Harbin.' Tr. of 'Ha-erh-pin tung chi tui yü ying erh ssu wang lü ti ying hsiang'; *Jen min pao chien* 1959, 11 (Nov.), 1063–1066. In *Reports on health and sanitation and related subjects in Communist China*, mimeo., compiled by U.S. Joint Publications Research Service. [Sole entry]
Washington, D.C.: JPRS, 3 Oct. 1960, 42–50. (JPRS 6051; MC 17,666/1960)
SUBJ 58 ▪ 52

21256 NNC P P3 G5.1 1949–1972
Yen Ching-ch'ing and Liu Ch'ung-hsüeh.
'Death rates in the city districts of Peking.'
CMJ 78, 1 (Jan. 1959), 27–30.
SUBJ 58

59 LIFE HISTORIES AND BIOGRAPHIES

生活史及傳記　　生活史及び伝記

1644-1911

21257 CSU U P3 G9.5 1842–1911
'Oriental social and professional biographies.' In *Twentieth century impressions of Hongkong, Shanghai, and other treaty ports of China: Their history, people, commerce, industries and manners*, edited by Arnold Wright and H- A- Cartwright. [Selective entry]
London: Lloyd's Greater Britain Publishing Co., 1908, 174–187.
SUBJ 26.2 59

21258 CSU U P3 G6.1 1842–1911
'Prominent Chinese residents.' In *Twentieth century impressions of Hongkong, Shanghai, and other treaty ports of China: Their history, people, commerce, industries and manners*, edited by Arnold Wright and H- A- Cartwright. [Selective entry]
London: Lloyd's Greater Britain Publishing Co., 1908, 525–572.
SUBJ 59 ▪ 26.1 26.2

21259 CSU P P2 G1.2 1644–1895
Bales, William Leslie, 1893–.
Tso Tsungt'ang: Soldier and statesman of old China.
Shanghai: Kelly and Walsh, 1937. 436 p. (Revision of *Tso Tsungt'ang and the suppression of the Mohammedan rebellion*, doctoral dissertation, College of Chinese Studies [Peiping]) [Reprinted—Ann Arbor: University Microfilms, n.d. 436 p.]
SUBJ 15 25 32.2 59 ▪ 12 14.5 14.6 16.1 33 66

21260 CSU PO P2 G1.2 1842–1911
Bland, John Otway Percy, 1863–1945, and Edmund Trelawney Backhouse, 1873–1944.
China under the Empress Dowager: Being the life and times of Tz'u Hsi.
Philadelphia: Lippincott, 1910. 15, 525 p. [A rev. ed. was published in 1939—Peiping: Henri Vetch. 23, 470 p.] [Reprinted—Taipei: Ch'eng-wen, 1962. 15, 525 p.]
SUBJ 12 13 59 61 ▪ 16.1 17 32 32.1 43 47 48 62 66

21261 CSU P P2 G1.3 1842–1911
Cameron, Meribeth Elliott, 1905–.
'The public career of Chang Chih-tung, 1837–1909.'
PHR 7, 3 (Sept. 1938), 187–210.
SUBJ 12 59 ▪ 14 16.1 17 25

21262 CSU O P2 G1.1 1842–1911
Cantlie, James, 1851–1926, and Charles Sheridan Jones, 1876–1938.
Sun Yat-sen and the awakening of China.
New York: Revell, 1912. 252 p.
Subj 12 32.2 59 ▪ 17 47 55 56 66

21263 CSU P P2 G1.2 1644–1895
Chen, Gideon (Ch'en Ch'i-t'ien), 1893–.
'Tso Tsung-t'ang: The farmer of Hsiangshang.'
YJSS 1, 2 (Jan. 1939), 211–225.
Subj 14 14.1 35 59 ▪ 14.6 18 24.4

21264 CSU O P3 G5.1 1842–1911
Der Ling (Te-ling), ?–1944.
Son of Heaven. [Biography of the Kuang-hsü Emperor]
New York: Appleton-Century, 1935. 248 p.
Subj 16.1 41 59 62 ▪ 13 15 17 32 51 55 66

21265 NNC P P2 G1.2 1842–1895
Douglas, Robert Kennaway, 1838–1913.
Li Hungchang.
London: Bliss, Sands and Foster, 1895. 16, 251 p.
Subj 12 15 16.1 32 59 66 ▪ 14.2 17 18 22 25 29 30 40 47 61

21266 CSH O P2 G1.3 1842–1895
Feng Yu-hsiang (Feng Yü-hsiang), 1882–1948.
'Autobiography of General Feng Yu-hsiang.' Tr. by George Kao from *Wo ti sheng huo* (My life); n.p.: San hu t'u shu she, 1944.
China magazine 16, 6 (Oct. 1946), 37–47; 16, 7 (Nov. 1946), 37–44; 16, 8 (Dec. 1946), 37–43.
Subj 52 59 ▪ 24.6 28 41 55

21267 GHU P P2 G1.3 1842–1911
Franke, Otto, 1863–1946.
'Li Hung-tschang' (Li Hung-chang). In *Meister der Politik* (Masters of politics), edited by Erich Marcks and Karl Alexander von Müller. [Selective entry]
Stuttgart: Deutsche Verlags-Anstalt, 1923, 487–517.
Subj 12 15 59 61 ▪ 16.1 19 64

21268 CSU P P3 G9.2 1644–1895
Greenbie, Sydney, 1889–.
'Houqua of Canton: A Chinese Croesus.'
Asia (New York: American Asiatic Assn.) 25, 10 (Oct. 1925), 823–827, 892–895.
Subj 34.2 59

21269 CSU U P2 G1.1 1644–1895
[Gützlaff, Karl Friedrich August] Charles Gutzlaff, 1803–1851.
The life of Taou-Kwang, late Emperor of China, with memoirs of the Court of Peking.
London: Smith, Elder, 1852. 16, 279 p.
Subj 59 ▪ 12 13 15 18 25 66

21270
[*Entry deleted.* In the final proofreading, after the automatic typesetting of the analytical indexes, it was discovered that the entry assigned this number duplicated a later entry in this section.]

21271 CBU O P2 G9.0 1644–1895
Hamberg, Theodore, 1819–1854.
The visions of Hung Siu-tshuen [Hung Hsiu-ch'üan], *and the origin of the Kwang-si insurrection.*
Hong Kong: China Mail, 1854. 63 p. [Reprinted in *Shanghae almanac for the bissextile or leap year 1856, and miscellany.* (Selective entry.) Shanghai: North-China Herald, 1855, n.p.] [Reprinted—Peiping: Yenching U. Library, 1935. 63 p.] [Reprinted—New York: Praeger, 1969. 63 p.]
Subj 25 59 ▪ 12 32.2 33

21272 CSU P P2 G1.3 1842–1895
Howard, Richard Campbell, 1925–.
The early life and thought of K'ang Yu-wei, 1858–1895.
Ann Arbor: University Microfilms (Publ. 72-20,045), 1972. 672 p. (Doctoral dissertation in History, Columbia U., 1971)
Subj 16.1 32 59 ▪ 17 64

21273 CSU U P2 G5.3 1842–1895
Hsu Ti-shan (Hsü Ti-shan).
'Wuu Shiunn [Wu Hsün], the great beggar and promoter of free education.'
THM 7, 3 (Oct. 1938), 235–255.
Subj 27 59 ▪ 26 65

21274 CSU P P1 G9.0 1895–1911
Hsüeh, Chün-tu, 1922–.
'Sun Yat-sen, Yang Ch'ü-yün, and the early revolutionary movement in China.' In *Revolutionary leaders of modern China,* edited by Chün-tu Hsüeh. [Selective entry]
New York: Oxford U. Press, 1971, 102–122.
Subj 32.2 59 ▪ 16.1

21275 CSU P P1 G1.5 1842–1911
Hsüeh, Chün-tu, 1922–, and Geraldine R-Schiff.
'The life and writings of Tsou Jung.' In *Revolutionary leaders of modern China,* edited by Chün-tu Hsüeh. [Selective entry]
New York: Oxford U. Press, 1971, 153–209.
Subj 59 64

21276 MCY P P2 G1.1 –1911
Hummel, Arthur William, 1884–, ed.
Eminent Chinese of the Ch'ing period (1644–1912), compiled by Orientalia Division, U.S. Library of Congress.
Washington, D.C.: U.S. Government Printing Office, 1943, 1944. 2 vols. 1104 p. [c.p.]. [Reprinted—Taipei: Ch'eng-wen, 1970. 1104 p.]
Subj 14 16 16.1 59 70 ▪ 12 15 16.2 17 25 31 32.2 47

21277 MAM P P2 G1.3 1644–1842
Jones, Susan Mann, 1943–.
Hung Liang-chi (1746–1809): The perception and articulation of political problems in late eighteenth century China.
Ann Arbor: University Microfilms (Publ. 72-16,731), 1972. 228 p. (Doctoral dissertation in Asian Languages, Stanford U., 1971)
Subj 12 16.1 59 60 ▪ 17 25 32.2 66

21278 MCH P P3 G5.1 1644–1842
Kahn, Harold Lionel, 1930–.
Monarchy in the emperor's eyes: Image and reality in the Ch'ien-lung reign.
Cambridge: Harvard U. Press, 1971. 314 p. (Harvard East Asian series, 59) (Revision of *Monarchy in the emperor's eyes: A study of image and reality in eighteenth-century China,* doctoral dissertation in History and Far Eastern Languages, Harvard U., 1966)
Subj 17 50 53 54 59 60 ▪ 12 15 16.1 41 43 61 62 64 66

21279 ICU P P2 G1.1 1644–1842
Kessler, Lawrence Devlin, 1936–.
The apprenticeship of the K'ang-Hsi Emperor, 1661–1684.
Unpublished doctoral dissertation in History, U. of Chicago, 1969. 293 p.
Subj 12 12.1 15 16.1 59 66 ▪ 12.2 14.5 21.2 25 27 32.2 45 53 62 63

21280 DLC O P5 G8.1 1895–1911
Kuo Mo-jo, 1892–.
Autobiographie: mes années d'enfance (Autobiography: My childhood). Tr. by P- Rykmans of 'Wo ti t'ung nien' (My childhood); in *Mo-jo tzu chuan: Shao nien shih tai* (Autobiography of Kuo Mo-jo: Youth); Shanghai: Hai yen shu tien, 1947, vol. 1, 1–170.
Paris: Gallimard, 1970. 197 p.
Subj 54 59 ▪ 25 41 53

21281 CSU P P1 G9.0 1842–1895
Laffey, Ella Sapira, 1935–.
'The making of a rebel: Liu Yung-fu and the formation of the Black Flag Army.' In *Popular movements and secret societies in China, 1840–1950,* edited by Jean Chesneaux. [Analytic entry]
Stanford: Stanford U. Press, 1972, 85–96.
Subj 25 32.2 59

21282 CSU P P3 G1.3 –1842
Leslie, Donald Daniel, 1922–.
'The K'aifeng Jew Chao Ying-ch'eng and his family.'
TP 2e série 53, 1/3 (1967), 147–179. [Reprinted in *Studies of the Chinese Jews: Selections from journals East and West,* compiled by Hyman Kublin. (Selective entry.) New York: Paragon, 1971, 101–137.]
Subj 59 ▪ 12

21283 CSU P P2 G1.2 1644–1895
Liu, Kwang-ching (Liu Kuang-ching), 1921–.
'The Confucian as patriot and pragmatist: Li Hung-chang's formative years, 1823–1866.'
HJAS 30 (1970), 5–45.
Subj 12 15 59 66 ▪ 14.5 16.1 18

21284 NNC P P2 G1.2 1644–1842
Liu Ta-nien.
'On (Emperor) Kang Hsi.' Tr. of 'Lun K'ang-hsi' (The K'ang-hsi Emperor); *Li shih yen chiu* 1961, 3 (15 Feb.), 5–21.
URS 24, 23 (19 Sept. 1961), 351–365; 24, 24 (22 Sept. 1961), 367–378.
Subj 12 14 16 59 ▪ 16.1 18 33 66

21285 CSH P P3 G1.1 1644–1895
McAleavy, Henry.
Wang T'ao (1828–1890): The life and writings of a displaced person.

London: China Society, 1953. 48 p. (CS occasional papers, 7)
SUBJ 59 66

21286 MCH P P1 G1.2 1842–1895
Mackie, John Milton, 1813–1894.
Life of Tai-ping-wang [Hung Hsiu-ch'üan], *chief of the Chinese insurrection.*
New York: Dix, Edwards, 1857. 10, 370 p.
SUBJ 32.2 59 61 ▪ 15 23 29 33 64 66

21287 MAM P P2 G1.4 1895–1911
MacKinnon, Stephen Robert, 1940–.
Yüan Shih-k'ai in Tientsin and Peking: The sources and structure of his power, 1901–1908.
Ann Arbor: University Microfilms (Publ. 71-9902), 1972. 269 p. (Doctoral dissertation in History, U. of California, Davis, 1971)
SUBJ 12 14 15 16.1 25 59 ▪ 14.2 14.4 14.5 17 32.2

21288 MAM P P1 G1.2 1644–1895
Mitchell, Peter MacVicar.
Wei Yüan (1794–1857) and the early modernization movement in China and Japan.
Ann Arbor: University Microfilms (Publ. 70-21,548), 1970. 327 p. (Doctoral dissertation in History, Indiana U.)
SUBJ 16.1 59 66 ▪ 14 32 64

21289 NNC P P1 G1.2 –1895
Nivison, David Shepherd, 1923–.
'Aspects of traditional Chinese biography.'
JAS 21, 4 (Aug. 1962), 457–463.
SUBJ 59 70

21290 CSU P P1 G1.2 –1911
Olbricht, Peter, 1909–.
'Die Biographie in China' (Biography in China).
Saeculum 8, 2/3 (1957), 224–235.
SUBJ 50 59 62 ▪ 16.1 43

21291 NIC P P2 G1.1 1644–1895
Overdijkink, Gerrit Willem, 1905–.
Lin Tsê-hsü: Een biographische schets (Lin Tse-hsü: A biographical sketch).
Leiden: Brill, 1938. 173 p. (Institutum sinologicum Lugduno-Batavum, Sinica leidensia, 4) (Doctoral dissertation in Philosophy, Rijksuniversiteit te Leiden)
SUBJ 14.3 14.5 59 ▪ 12 14 14.6

21292 CSU S P2 G1.4 –1842
Reid, John Gilbert, 1899–.
'Peking's first Manchu emperor.'
PHR 5, 2 (May 1936), 130–146.
SUBJ 59 ▪ 12 16.1 66

21293 CSU P P3 G5.1 1644–1895
Shen, Han-yin Chen.
'Tseng Kuo-fan in Peking, 1840–1852: His ideas on statecraft and reform.'
JAS 27, 1 (Nov. 1967), 61–80.
SUBJ 12 59 63 64 ▪ 14.5 15 16.1

21294 CSH P P1 G1.5 1644–1842
Smith, Kent Clarke, 1937–.
'O-erh-t'ai and the Yung-cheng Emperor.'
CSWT 1, 8 (May 1968), 10–15.
SUBJ 12 59 ▪ 16.1 66

21295 CSH U P1 G1.3 1644–1842
Spence, Jonathan Dermot, 1936–.
'Chang Po-hsing and the K'ang-hsi Emperor.'
CSWT 1, 8 (May 1968), 3–9.
SUBJ 16.1 59 ▪ 12 61

21296 CSU P P1 G1.1 1644–1842
Spence, Jonathan Dermot, 1936–.
'The seven ages of K'ang-hsi, 1654–1722.'
JAS 26, 2 (Feb. 1967), 205–211.
SUBJ 12 59

21297 CSU P P2 G1.3 1644–1895
Sun, E-tu Zen (Sun Jen I-tu), 1921–.
'Wu Ch'i-chun: Profile of a Chinese scholar-technologist.'
Technology and culture 6, 3 (Summer 1965), 394–406.
SUBJ 16.1 59 62 ▪ 14.4

21298 NNM O P2 G5.0 1842–1895
[Taylor, Mary Geraldine Guinness] *Mrs.* Howard Taylor, 1862–1949.
Pastor Hsi, Confucian scholar and Christian. [20th ed., rev.]
London: China Inland Mission, 1949. 16, 293 p.
SUBJ 33 56 59 ▪ 55 66

21299 CSU P P2 G1.5 1842–1895
Uhalley, Stephen, Jr., 1930–.
'Li Hsiu-ch'eng: Taiping hero.' In *Revolutionary leaders of modern China*, edited by Chün-tu Hsüeh. [Selective entry]
New York: Oxford U. Press, 1971, 71–86.
SUBJ 59 ▪ 15 32.2 66 70

21300 CSU S P2 G1.2 1644–1911
Warner, Marina, 1946–.
The Dragon Empress: The life and times of Tz'u-hsi, Empress Dowager of China, 1835–1908.
New York: Macmillan, 1972. 271 p.
SUBJ 16.1 32.2 47 59 66 ▪ 12 13 15 32 33 46 48 55 64

21301 CSU P P1 G1.3 1895–1911
Young, Ernest Paddock, 1932–.
'Problems of a late Ch'ing revolutionary: Ch'en T'ien-hua.' In *Revolutionary leaders of modern China*, edited by Chün-tu Hsüeh. [Selective entry]
New York: Oxford U. Press, 1971, 210–247.
SUBJ 59 64 ▪ 32.2 57 66

21302 CSU O P2 G1.1 1842–1911
Yung Wing (Jung Hung), 1828–1912.
My life in China and America.
New York: Holt, 1909. 286 p.
SUBJ 12 16.1 59 ▪ 14.4 14.6 17 25 32.2 37 66

1644-1949

21303 CSU P P2 G1.2 1895–1949
Boorman, Howard Lyon, 1920–.
'Wang Ching-wei: A political profile.' In *Revolutionary leaders of modern China*, edited by Chün-tu Hsüeh. [Selective entry]
New York: Oxford U. Press, 1971, 295–319.
SUBJ 32.2 59 ▪ 12 16.1 32 66

21304 CSU P P2 G1.1 1842–1928
Bruce, Robert.
Sun Yat-sen.
London: Oxford U. Press, 1969. 62 p.
SUBJ 32.2 59 ▪ 32 64 66

21305 NIC O P4 G1.3 1895–1928
Chao, Pu-wei Yang (Chao Yang Pu-wei), 1889–.
Autobiography of a Chinese woman. Tr. from the Chinese by Yuenren Chao. [Tr. of an unpublished manuscript]
New York: Day, 1947. 16, 327 p. [For a later ed. in Chinese, see Chao Yang Pu-wei, *I ko nü jen ti tsu chuan* (Autobiography of a woman); Taipei: Chuan chi wen hsüeh ch'u pan she, 1967; 216 p.] [Reprinted—Westport, Conn.: Greenwood Press, 1970. 16, 327 p.]
SUBJ 26.1 41 59 ▪ 17 47 52 53 55

21306 CSU P P2 G1.1 1842–1928
Chen, Stephen (Ch'eng Hsi-fan), and Pierre Stephen Robert Payne, 1911–.
Sun Yat-sen: A portrait.
New York: Day, 1946. 242 p.
SUBJ 32.2 59 64 ▪ 12 16.1 25 32

21307 FPN O P2 G1.2 1895–1928
[Cheng Tcheng] Sheng-Cheng (Sheng Ch'eng), 1899–.
Vers l'unité. 1, ma mère. 2, ma mère et moi à travers la Révolution chinoise (Toward unity. Vol. 1, My mother. Vol. 2, My mother and I through the Chinese revolution).
Paris: Victor Attinger, 1928, 1929. 2 vols. 191; 239 p. (Orient, 1, 2).
A son of China. Tr. by Marvin McCord Lowes.
New York: Norton, 1930. 286 p.
SUBJ 19 32.2 41 59 ▪ 12 23 25 47 52 65 66

21308 ELO O P2 G1.2 1842–1949
Chiang Monlin (Chiang Meng-lin), 1886–1964.
Tides from the West: A Chinese autobiography.
New Haven: Yale U. Press, 1947. 282 p.
SUBJ 17 26.1 59 ▪ 12 22.2 23 25 32.2 40 60 63

21309 CSU P P2 G1.3 1895–1949
Chih, Yü-ju.
'Ch'en Tu-hsiu: His career and political ideas.' In *Revolutionary leaders of modern China*, edited by Chün-tu Hsüeh. [Selective entry]
New York: Oxford U. Press, 1971, 335–366.
SUBJ 32.2 59 64 ▪ 16.1 32 63 72

21310 CSU P P1 G1.3 1895–1928
Chin Ch'ung-chi and Hu Sheng-wu.
'Huang Hsing, co-founder of the Republic of China.' Tr. by Chün-tu Hsüeh of 'Lun Huang Hsing' (A discussion of Huang Hsing); *Li shih yen chiu* 1962, 3 (Mar.), 11–26. In *Revolutionary leaders of modern China*, edited by Chün-tu Hsüeh. [Selective entry]
New York: Oxford U. Press, 1971, 123–152.
SUBJ 32.2 59 ▪ 16.1

21311 CSU O P2 G1.2 1842–1928
[Chow, Elizabeth K.] Han Suyin, pseud., 1917–.
The crippled tree.
New York: Putnam, 1965. 461 p.
SUBJ 19 41 59 66 ▪ 14.2 16.1 22.2 25 29 32.2

21312 CSU F P4 G8.2 1895–1949
Chow, Yung-teh (Chou Jung-te), 1916–.
'Life histories: The bureaucrat, Head Chang.' In *China's gentry: Essays in rural-urban relations*, rev. ed., by Fei Hsiao-tung (Fei Hsiao-t'ung), edited by Margaret Park Redfield. [Analytic entry]
Chicago: U. of Chicago Press, 1953, 203–224. [Reprinted in *China's gentry: Essays in rural-urban relations*, by Fei Hsiao-tung, edited by M. P. Redfield. (Analytic entry.) Chicago: U. of Chicago Press, 1968, 203–224.]
SUBJ 22 26.1 59 ▪ 22.2

21313 CSU F P2 G8.2 1895–1949
Chow, Yung-teh (Chou Jung-te), 1916–.
'Life histories: The gangster, Captain Yang.' In *China's gentry: Essays in rural-urban relations*, rev. ed., by Fei Hsiao-tung (Fei Hsiao-t'ung), edited by Margaret Park Redfield. [Analytic entry]
Chicago: U. of Chicago Press, 1953, 242–268. [Reprinted in *China's gentry: Essays in rural-urban relations*, by Fei Hsiao-tung, edited by M. P. Redfield. (Analytic entry.) Chicago: U. of Chicago Press, 1968, 242–268.]
SUBJ 22.2 25 59 ▪ 22 26.1

21314 CSU F P4 G8.2 1895–1949
Chow, Yung-teh (Chou Jung-te), 1916–.
'Life histories: The merchant, Head Ting.' In *China's gentry: Essays in rural-urban relations*, rev. ed., by Fei Hsiao-tung (Fei Hsiao-t'ung), edited by Margaret Park Redfield. [Analytic entry]
Chicago: U. of Chicago Press, 1953, 225–241. [Reprinted in *China's gentry: Essays in rural-urban relations*, by Fei Hsiao-tung, edited by M. P. Redfield. (Analytic entry.) Chicago: U. of Chicago Press, 1968, 225–241.]
SUBJ 26.2 59 ▪ 22 22.2 24.3

21315 CSU F P2 G8.2 1895–1949
Chow, Yung-teh (Chou Jung-te), 1916–.
'Life histories: The military man, Commander Chu.' In *China's gentry: Essays in rural-urban relations*, rev. ed., by Fei Hsiao-tung (Fei Hsiao-t'ung), edited by Margaret Park Redfield. [Analytic entry]
Chicago: U. of Chicago Press, 1953, 173–202. [Reprinted in *China's gentry: Essays in rural-urban relations*, by Fei Hsiao-tung, edited by M. P. Redfield. (Analytic entry.) Chicago: U. of Chicago Press, 1968, 173–202.]
SUBJ 25 26.1 59 ▪ 22 22.2 24.5 26.2 57

21316 CSU F P2 G8.2 1895–1949
Chow, Yung-teh (Chou Jung-te), 1916–.
'Life histories: The scholar, Chairman Wang.' In *China's gentry: Essays in rural-urban relations*, rev. ed., by Fei Hsiao-tung (Fei Hsiao-t'ung), edited by Margaret Park Redfield. [Analytic entry]
Chicago: U. of Chicago Press, 1953, 149–172. [Reprinted in *China's gentry: Essays in rural-urban relations*, by Fei Hsiao-tung, edited by M. P. Redfield. (Analytic entry.) Chicago: U. of Chicago Press, 1968, 149–172.]
SUBJ 26.1 59 ▪ 17

21317 MCH P P1 G1.1 1895–1928
[Elia, Pasquale M- d'] Pascal M- d'Elia (Paschal M- d'Elia), 1890–.
'Introduction.' In *Le triple demisme de Suen Wen* (The Three People's Principles of Sun Yat-sen), by [Sun Yat-sen] Suen Wen (Sun Chung-shan), compiled and edited by P. M. d'Elia. [Sole entry]
Shanghai: Bureau sinologique de Zi-ka-wei, Imp. de T'ou-sè-wè, 1930, 3–45.

'Introduction.' In *The triple demism of Sun Yat-sen*, by Sun Yat-sen, compiled and edited by P. M. d'Elia. [Sole entry]
Wuchang: Franciscan Press, 1931, 3–49. [Reprinted in *The triple demism of Sun Yat-sen*, by Sun Yat-sen, compiled and edited by P. M. d'Elia. (Sole entry.) New York: AMS Press, 1973, 3–49.]
SUBJ 59 64 ▪ 32.2 66

21318 NIC P P1 G1.1 1842–1928
[Elia, Pasquale M- d'] Pascal M. d'Elia, 1890–.
'Un maître de la jeune Chine, Liang K'i-Tchao' (Liang Ch'i-ch'ao, a leader of young China).
TP 2e série 18, 3 (1917), 247–294.
SUBJ 17 59 60 ▪ 16.1 19 43 62 64 66 70

21319 GHU P P2 G1.3 1842–1928
Franke, Otto, 1863–1946.
'Yuan Schi-kai' (Yüan Shih-k'ai). In *Meister der Politik* (Masters of politics), edited by Erich Marcks and Karl Alexander von Müller. [Selective entry]
Stuttgart: Deutsche Verlags-Anstalt, 1923, 521–551.
SUBJ 15 19 59 ▪ 16.1 61 64

21320 CSH U P2 G1.2 1895–1949
Fromentin, Pierre.
Mao Tse-toung: le dragon rouge (Mao Tse-tung: The red dragon).
Paris: Ed. Médicis, 1949. 211 p.
SUBJ 15 25 32.2 36.3 59 ▪ 16.3 26

21321 CSU P P2 G1.2 1895–1949
Furth, Charlotte Davis, 1934–.
Ting Wen-chiang: Science and China's new culture.
Cambridge: Harvard U. Press, 1970. 307 p. (Harvard East Asian series, 42) (Revision of *Ting Wen-chiang: An intellectual under the Chinese Republic*, doctoral dissertation in History, Stanford U., 1965)
SUBJ 14.2 16.1 59 62 ▪ 12 15 17 32 36.1 37 64 66

21322 CSU S P1 G1.2 1895–1949
Howard, Richard Campbell, 1925–.
'Modern Chinese biographical writing.'
JAS 21, 4 (Aug. 1962), 465–475.
SUBJ 59 ▪ 14.2 16.1

21323 CSU P P1 G1.3 1895–1949
Hsia, T. A. (Hsia Chi-an), 1916–1965.
'Ch'ü Ch'iu-pai's autobiographical writings: The making and destruction of a "tender-hearted" Communist.'
CQ 25 (Jan.–Mar. 1966), 176–212. [Reprinted as 'Ch'ü Ch'iu-po: The making and destruction of a tenderhearted Communist.' In *The gate of darkness: Studies on the leftist literary movement in China*, by T. A. Hsia. (Selective entry.) Seattle: U. of Washington Press, 1968, 3–54. (U. of Washington, Far Eastern and Russian Institute, Publications on Asia, 17)] [Reprinted as 'Ch'ü Ch'iu-pai's autobiographical writings: The making and destruction of a "tender-hearted" Communist.' In *Revolutionary leaders of modern China*, by Chün-tu Hsüeh. (Selective entry.) New York: Oxford U. Press, 1971, 471–516.]
SUBJ 59 ▪ 32.2 61

21324 CSU P P2 G1.2 1895–1949
Hsiung, Shih-i, 1902–.
The life of Chiang Kai-shek.
London: Davies, 1948. 17, 398 p.
SUBJ 15 32 59 ▪ 12 19 32.2 64

21325 MAM P P2 G1.2 1895–1949
Hsu, Kai-yu (Hsü Chieh-yü), 1922–.
The intellectual biography of a modern Chinese poet: Wen I-To (1899–1946).
Ann Arbor: University Microfilms (Publ. 59-6894), 1959. 208 p. (Doctoral dissertation in Modern Chinese Literature and Thought, Stanford U.)
SUBJ 16.1 17 59 66 ▪ 16 18 31 32 41 60

21326 CSU P P2 G1.2 1895–1949
Hsüeh, Chün-tu, 1922–.
'Chang Kuo-t'ao and the Chinese Communist movement.' In *Revolutionary leaders of modern China*, edited by Chün-tu Hsüeh. [Selective entry]
New York: Oxford U. Press, 1971, 422–454.
SUBJ 32.2 59 ▪ 16.1 32 66

21327 CBU P P2 G1.1 1895–1928
Hsüeh, Chün-tu, 1922–.
'A Chinese democrat: The life of Sung Chiao-jen.'
RSAEO 1969, 1, 115–136. [Reprinted in *Revolutionary leaders of modern China*, edited by Chün-tu Hsüeh. (Selective entry.) New York: Oxford U. Press, 1971, 248–270.]
SUBJ 32.2 59 ▪ 12 14.2 64

21328 CSH P P2 G1.1 1895–1928
Hsüeh, Chün-tu, 1922–.
'The life and political thought of Huang Hsing.'
CC 7, 3 (Sept. 1966), 79–96. [A slightly modified version appears in entry 21392, vol. 2, 192–197.] [Reprinted as 'The life and political thought of Huang Hsing, co-founder of the Republic of China.' *Australian j. of politics and history* 13, 1 (Apr. 1967), 21–33.]
SUBJ 32.2 59 ▪ 15

21329 CSU O P1 G6.0 1895–1928
Hu Shih, 1891–1962.
'Hu Shih.' In *Living philosophies*, by Albert Einstein et al. [Sole entry]
New York: Simon and Schuster, 1931, 235–263.
SUBJ 59 ▪ 62 63

21330 CSU O P7 G5.4 1842–1949
Hwang Tsu-Yü (Huang Tsu-yü), 1911–.
Der blühende Granatapfelbaum: Eine einfache Geschichte einer chinesischen Familie (The blossoming pomegranate trees: A plain story of a Chinese family), edited by Hanna Hindbeck. Tr. from the English by Hanna Hindbeck. [Tr. of an unpublished manuscript, 'The blossoming pomegranate trees: Plain tale of a Chinese family']
Munich: Winkler, 1948. 259 p.
SUBJ 40 41 47 52 59 63 ▪ 19 26 27 46 48 55 62 65

21331 NIC O P1 G6.3 1842–1928
Johnston, Reginald Fleming, 1874–1938.
'A poet-monk of modern China [Ching An].'
JRAS-NCB new (2nd) series 63 (1932), 14–30.
SUBJ 33 59 62 63 ▪ 31

21332 CSU P P1 G1.1 1895–1949
Kennedy, Melville Talbot, Jr., 1917–.
'Hu Han-min: His career and thought.' In *Revolutionary leaders of modern China*, edited by Chün-tu Hsüeh. [Selective entry]
New York: Oxford U. Press, 1971, 271–294.
SUBJ 32.2 59 ▪ 16.1 32 64

21333 CSU O P2 G1.1 1895–1949
Koo, Hui-lan (Ku Huang Hui-lan).
Hui-lan Koo (Madame Wellington Koo): An autobiography, as told to Mary van Rensselaer Thayer.
New York: Dial, 1943. 364 p.
SUBJ 59 ▪ 16.2 41 43 48 66

21334 CSH O P2 G1.3 1895–1928
Kuo Mo-jo, 1892–.
'The spring and autumn of revolution.' Tr. from *Ko ming ch'un ch'iu: Mo-jo tzu chuan ti erh chüan* (The revolutionary years: Part two of Kuo Mo-jo's autobiography); Shanghai: Hsin wen i ch'u pan she, 1951. [Greatly abridged tr.]
CE 3, 2/3 (Summer–Fall 1970), 116–138.
SUBJ 59 ▪ 17

21335 MCH P P1 G1.2 1842–1928
La Fargue, Thomas Edward, 1900–.
China's first hundred.
Pullman: State College of Washington Press, 1942. 14, 176 p.
SUBJ 12.1 17 59 ▪ 37 50 54 66

21336 NIC P P1 G1.2 1842–1928
Levenson, Joseph Richmond, 1920–1969.
Liang Ch'i-ch'ao and the mind of modern China.
Cambridge: Harvard U. Press, 1953. 12, 256 p. (Harvard historical monographs, 26) (Revision of *Crisis of the mind in China: The life and writings of Liang Ch'i-ch'ao, down to the fall of the empire*, doctoral dissertation in History, Harvard U., 1949) [Reprinted—Berkeley, Los Angeles: U. of California Press, 1970. 12, 257 p.]
SUBJ 59 64 66

21337 MCH PO P2 G1.1 1842–1928
Linebarger, Paul Myron Wentworth, 1871–1939.
Sun Yat Sen and the Chinese Republic.
New York: Century, 1925. 18, 371 p. [Reprinted—New York: AMS Press, 1970. 18, 371 p.]
SUBJ 16.1 59 60 61 ▪ 17 25 32 32.2 41 66

21338 CSU P P1 G1.1 1895–1928
Lo, J. P. (Lo Jung-pang), 1912–.
'Sequel to the chronological autobiography.' In *K'ang Yu-wei: A biography and a symposium*, edited by J. P. Lo. [Selective entry]
Tucson: U. of Arizona Press, 1967, 175–278.
SUBJ 59 63 ▪ 16.1 32

21339 CSU P P2 G1.5 1842–1928
Loh, Pichon P. Y. (Lu P'ei-yung), 1928–.
The early Chiang Kai-shek: A study of his personality and politics, 1887–1924.
New York: Columbia U. Press, 1971. 216 p.
SUBJ 59 61 ▪ 32.2 72

21340 MAM P P3 G1.3 1842–1928
Lubot, Eugene Stephen, 1942–.
Ts'ai Yuan-p'ei from Confucian scholar to chancellor of Peking University, 1868–1923: The evolution of a patient reformer.
Ann Arbor: University Microfilms (Publ. 70-19,335), 1970. 176 p. (Doctoral dissertation in History, Ohio State U., 1970)
SUBJ 16.1 59 60 62 63 ▪ 12 14.2 17 32.2 37

21341 MCH P P2 G1.2 1895–1949
McAleavy, Henry.
'Sai-chin-hua, 1874–1936: The fortunes of a Chinese singing girl.'
History today 7, 3 (Mar. 1957), 191–199.
SUBJ 59 ▪ 47

21342 CBU P P2 G1.1 1842–1928
Martin, Bernard, 1897–.
Strange vigour: A biography of Sun Yat-sen.
London: Heinemann, 1944. 12, 248 p. [Reprinted—Port Washington, N.Y.: Kennikat Press, 1970. 12, 248 p.] [Reprinted—Clifton, N.J.: Augustus M. Kelley, 1970. 12, 248 p.]
SUBJ 32.2 59 64 66 ▪ 12 17 27 52 56

21343 CSU P P2 G1.3 1895–1928
Meisner, Maurice J-, 1931–.
'Li Ta-chao and the intellectual prerequisites for the Maoist strategy of revolution.' In *Revolutionary leaders of modern China*, edited by Chün-tu Hsüeh. [Selective entry]
New York: Oxford U. Press, 1971, 367–394.
SUBJ 59 64 ▪ 32 32.2 36.1

21344 CSU O P2 G5.0 1842–1949
Pruitt, Ida.
A daughter of Han: The autobiography of a Chinese working woman.
New Haven: Yale U. Press, 1945. 249 p. [Reprinted—Stanford: Stanford U. Press, 1967. 254 p.]
SUBJ 40 55 56 59 62 65 ▪ 26.1 26.3 47 51 52 54 57 66

21345 CSU P P2 G1.2 1895–1949
Robinson, Thomas Webster, 1935–.
A politico-military biography of Lin Piao, Part 1, 1907–1949.
Santa Monica, Calif.: RAND Corp., 1971. 14, 217 p. (RAND reports, R-526-PR)
SUBJ 15 59 64 ▪ 25 32.2

21346 MCH P P2 G1.2 1895–1928
Roy, David Tod, 1933–.
Kuo Mo-jo: The early years.
Cambridge: Harvard U. Press, 1971. 244 p. (Harvard East Asian series, 55) (Revision of doctoral dissertation in History and Far Eastern Languages, Harvard U., 1965)
SUBJ 31 59 ▪ 16.1 17 32.2 46 54 61 64 66

21347 CSH P P2 G1.1 1842–1928
Saggitarius, pseud.
The strange apotheosis of Sun Yat-sen.
London: Heath Cranton, 1939. 189 p.
SUBJ 32.2 59 ▪ 12 14.5 22 25 64

21348 MCY O P3 G1.4 1895–1949
Scott, Adolphe Clarence, 1909–.
Mei Lan-fang, leader of the pear garden.
Hong Kong: Hong Kong U. Press, 1959. 139 p. [Reprinted as *The life and times of a Peking actor*. Hong Kong: Hong Kong U. Press, 1971. 139 p.]
SUBJ 16.2 31 59 ▪ 34.3

21349 MCY PO P1 G1.1 1842–1928
Sharman, Lyon, 1872–1937.
Sun Yat-sen: His life and its meaning.
New York: Day, 1934. 418 p. [Reprinted—Stanford: Stanford U. Press, 1968. 21, 420 p.]
SUBJ 32.2 59 64 ▪ 12 61 66

21350 MAM P P3 G1.1 1842–1928
Shin, Linda Pomerantz, 1938–.
China in transition: The role of Wu T'ing-fang (1842–1922).
Ann Arbor: University Microfilms (Publ. 70-19,893), 1970. 521 p. (Doctoral dissertation in History, U. of California, Los Angeles)
SUBJ 12 16.1 59 ▪ 12.2 14.2 32.2 60 66

21351 NNC P P1 G1.2 1895–1949
Shneider, Mark Evseevich, 1921–.
'TSiui TSiu-bo: k shestidesiatiletiiu so dnia rozhdeniia' (On the sixtieth anniversary of the birth of Ch'ü Ch'iu-pai).
SK 1958, 4, 51–70.
SUBJ 32.2 59 64 ▪ 12.1 31

21352 MCH O P2 G7.2 1895–1928
Siao-yü (Hsiao Yü).
Mao Tse-tung and I were beggars.
Syracuse: Syracuse U. Press, 1959. 18, 266 p.
SUBJ 59 64 ▪ 17 32.2

21353 CSU O P2 G1.2 1895–1949
[Snow, Helen Foster] Nym Wales, pseud., 1907–.
'Autobiographical profiles and biographical sketches.' In *The Chinese Communists: Sketches and autobiographies of the old guard*, by [H. F. Snow] Nym Wales, pseud. [Analytic entry]
Westport, Conn.: Greenwood Press, 1972, 228–363.
SUBJ 59 ▪ 32.2

21354 CSH PO P2 G1.2 1895–1949
T'ang, Leang-li (T'ang Liang-li), 1901–.
Wang Ching-wei: A political biography.
Peiping: China United Press, 1931. 223 p.
SUBJ 32 32.2 59 ▪ 15 16.1 64

21355 NNP O P2 G1.2 1895–1928
Tret'iakov, Sergei Mikhailovich (Sergej Tretjakow), 1892–1939.
Den Shi-khua: bio-interv'iu (Teng Hsi-hua: A biographical interview).
Moscow: Molodaia gvardiia, 1930. 391 p. [Later Russian editions—Moscow: Molodaia gvardiia, 1931, 399 p.; Moscow: Khudozhestvennaia literatura, 1935, 455 p.]

Den Schi-chua, ein junger Chinese, erzählt sein Leben: Bio-Interview (Teng Hsi-hua, a young Chinese, relates his life story: A biographical interview).
Berlin: Malik-Verlag, 1932. 507 p. [A different tr.—*Deng Schi-hua, ein*

chinesischer Student, erzählt sein Leben (Teng Hsi-hua, a Chinese student, relates his life). Tr. by Alfred Kurella. Berlin: Neues Leben, 1948. 421 p.]

A Chinese testament: The autobiography of Tan Shih-hua, as told to S. Tretiakov.
New York: Simon and Schuster, 1934. 316 p.
SUBJ 16.1 17 32.2 41 54 59 ▪ 15 22 33 46 57 66

21356 CSU P P2 G1.3 1842–1928
Tu, Ching-I.
'Conservatism in a constructive form: The case of Wang Kuo-wei (1877–1927).'
MS 28 (1969), 188–214.
SUBJ 59 62 63

21357 NIC P P1 G1.2 –1949
Twitchett, Denis Crispin, 1925–.
'Chinese biographical writing.' In *Historians of China and Japan*, edited by William Gerald Beasley and Edwin George Pulleyblank. [Selective entry]
London: Oxford U. Press, 1961, 95–114. (U. of London, School of Oriental and African Studies, Historical writing on the peoples of Asia, 3)
SUBJ 16.1 59 60 70 ▪ 12 62 63

21358 MCH O P1 G1.2 1895–1928
Van Vorst, Bessie McGinnis, 1873–1928.
A girl from China, Soumay Tcheng [Mme. Wei Tao-ming].
New York: Stokes, 1926. 11, 249 p.
SUBJ 59 ▪ 47

21359 MCH P P3 G5.0 1895–1949
Vohra, Ranbir, 1928–.
The Chinese world of Lao She: Dealing with Lao She's life and fiction up to 1937.
Unpublished doctoral dissertation in History and Far Eastern Languages, Harvard U., 1969. 330 p.
SUBJ 16.1 17 59 63 ▪ 15 16 31 32 32.2 41 47 48 61 66

21360 CSH P P2 G1.2 1842–1949
Wang, Chêng-ju (Wang Ch'eng-ju).
Lu Hsün, sein Leben und sein Werk: Ein Beitrag zur chinesischen Revolution (The life and work of Lu Hsün: A contribution to the Chinese revolution).
Berlin: Reichsdruckerei, 1940. 67 p. (Doctoral dissertation, Philosophische Fakultät, Universität Bonn)
SUBJ 59 64 ▪ 19 66

21361 CSU P P1 G1.2 1842–1928
Wang, Chester Chen-i.
Wang Kuo-wei (1877–1927): His life and scholarship.
Unpublished doctoral dissertation in History, U. of Chicago, 1962. 207 p.
SUBJ 16.1 59 60 64 66 70 ▪ 17 32 57

21362 CSU O P3 G1.3 1895–1949
[Wei Tao-ming, *Mme.*] Soumé Tcheng (Wei Cheng Yü-hsiu), 1891–1959.
My revolutionary years: The autobiography of Madame Wei Tao-ming.
New York: Scribner, 1943. 238 p.
SUBJ 32.2 59 ▪ 12 12.2 16.1 25 32 41 47

21363 NNC U P4 G1.2 1895–1949
Yu Liang (Yü-liang), pseud.
K'ung Hsiang-hsi: The biography of a former premier of Nationalist China.
Tr. of *K'ung Hsiang-hsi* ([The life of] K'ung Hsiang-hsi); Hong Kong: K'ai yüan shu tien, 1955; 307 p.
n.p.: Alumni Club of Oberlin Shansi Memorial College, 1957. 17, 248 p.
SUBJ 12 14.5 14.6 59 ▪ 13 16.1 16.2 17 33

1911-1949

21364 CSU P P2 G4.3 1928–1949
Chan, Fook-lam Gilbert (Ch'en Fu-lin), 1938–.
'The road to power: Sheng Shih-ts'ai's early years in Sinkiang, 1930–1934.'
JOS 7, 2 (July 1969), 224–260.
SUBJ 59 ▪ 12 25 66

21365 MCH O P3 G1.3 1911–1928
Chow, Chung-cheng (Chou Chung-cheng).
Kleine Sampan (Little sampan).
Aarau, Switzerland: Sauerländer, 1957. 314 p.

The lotus-pool of memory. Tr. by Joyce Emerson.
New York: Appleton-Century-Crofts, 1961. 272 p.
SUBJ 16.1 47 59 61 ▪ 27 41 43 52 53 54 55 63

21366 CSU O P2 G1.1 1928–1949
[Chow, Elizabeth K.] Han Suyin, pseud., 1917–.
Birdless summer.
New York: Putnam, 1968. 347 p.
SUBJ 19 41 47 59 ▪ 15 17 25 46 51 55 66

21367 CSU O P2 G1.2 1911–1949
[Chow, Elizabeth K.] Han Suyin, pseud., 1917–.
Destination Chungking.
Boston: Little, Brown, 1942. 367 p.
SUBJ 15 19 59 ▪ 14.2 23 32.2 41 44 48

21368 CSU O P2 G1.1 1911–1949
[Chow, Elizabeth K.] Han Suyin, pseud., 1917–.
A mortal flower.
New York: Putnam, 1965. 413 p.
SUBJ 15 19 32.2 59 ▪ 14.5 14.6 16 16.3 17 22.2 41 64 66

21369 CSU F P2 G8.2 1911–1949
Chow, Yung-teh (Chou Jung-te), 1916–.
'Life histories: The reformer, Liu Tsung-tao.' In *China's gentry: Essays in rural-urban relations*, rev. ed., by Fei Hsiao-tung (Fei Hsiao-t'ung), edited by Margaret Park Redfield. [Analytic entry]
Chicago: U. of Chicago Press, 1953, 269–287. [Reprinted in *China's gentry: Essays in rural-urban relations*, by Fei Hsiao-tung, edited by M. P. Redfield. (Analytic entry.) Chicago: U. of Chicago Press, 1968, 269–287.]
SUBJ 26.1 59 ▪ 22 25

21370 MCH O P2 G1.3 1911–1949
Hsieh Ping-ying, 1906–.
Girl rebel: The autobiography of Hsieh Pingying, with extracts from her 'New war diaries'. Tr. by Adet Lin and Anor Lin of *I ko nü ping ti tzu chuan* (Autobiography of a female soldier); Shanghai: Liang yu t'u shu yin shua kung ssu, 1936; 388 p.
New York: Day, 1940. 18, 270 p. [A different tr.—*Autobiography of a Chinese girl.* Tr. by Tsui Chi. London: Allen and Unwin, 1948. 216 p.]
SUBJ 17 47 59 ▪ 16.1 41 46 53 54 65

21371 CSH O P3 G5.1 1928–1949
Hu Hung-hsia.
'Chi Hung-chang: Unbending hero in resisting Japanese aggression.'
China reconstructs 20, 11 (Nov. 1971), 43–48.
SUBJ 59 ▪ 32 32.2

21372 CSU O P2 G1.2 1928–1949
Isaacs, Harold Robert, 1910–.
'China: The long travail.' In *No peace for Asia*, by H. R. Isaacs. [Sole entry]
New York: Macmillan, 1947, 43–80. [Reprinted in *No peace for Asia*, by H. R. Isaacs. (Sole entry.) Cambridge: M.I.T. Press, 1967, 43–80.]
SUBJ 32 32.2 59 ▪ 15 64 66

21373 MAM P P1 G1.2 1911–1949
Lin, Han-sheng, 1930–.
Wang Ching-wei and the Japanese peace efforts.
Ann Arbor: University Microfilms (Publ. 67-12,773), 1967. 607 p. (Doctoral dissertation in History, U. of Pennsylvania)
SUBJ 12 32 59 66 ▪ 15 25 32.2

21374 CSH O P3 G1.1 1928–1949
Loo, Pin-fei.
It is dark underground.
New York: Putnam, 1946. 200 p.
SUBJ 25 54 59 66

21375 *NIC O P3 G5.1 1911–1949
Lowe, H. Y. (Lu Hsing-yüan).
The adventures of Wu: The life cycle of a Peking man.
Peiping: Peking Chronicle Press, 1941. 2 vols. [*Vol. 2 held at NIC; vol. 1 was not located.]
SUBJ 23 50 59 65 ▪ 41 48 56 57

21376 CSH O P2 G1.5 1928–1949
Ma Shih-tu.
'In memory of the martyr Liu Hui-hsin: A revolutionary fighter, a courageous mother.'
WC 1962, 3, 22–27.
SUBJ 47 59 ▪ 32.2

21377 ELB O P2 G1.1 1911–1928
Ma Sian (Ma Hsiang).
'Desiat' let s Sun' IAt-senom' (A decade with Sun Yat-sen).
VI 1966, 11 (noiabr'), 134–150; 1966, 2 (dekabr'), 125–138.
SUBJ 12 15 59 ▪ 32.2

21378 CSU O P2 G1.2 1911–1928
Reinsch, Paul Samuel, 1869–1923.
'The rise and fall of Yuan Shih-kai.'
Asia (New York: American Asiatic Assn.) 21, 12 (Dec. 1921), 1000–1005, 1045–1047.
SUBJ 12 16.1 59 ▪ 13 32.2 58

21379 NIC O P2 G1.2 1928–1949
[Snow, Helen Foster] Nym Wales, pseud., 1907–.
My Yenan notebooks.
Madison, Conn.: The author, 1961. 221 p.
SUBJ 32.2 59 ▪ 36.4 47 63 64 66

21380 CSH O P2 G1.3 1911–1949
Tao Cheng.
My family.
Peking: Foreign Languages Press, 1960. 134 p.
Subj 59 ▪ 32.2 41

21381 MAM P P1 G1.2 1911–1949
Wang, Chi, 1930–.
Young Marshall Chang Hsueh-liang and Manchuria, 1928–1931.
Ann Arbor: University Microfilms (Publ. 70-5926), 1970. 230 p. (Doctoral dissertation in History, Georgetown U., 1969)
Subj 15 25 59 ▪ 12 66

21382 CSH O P2 G1.5 1911–1928
Wang Yi-chih.
'Comrade Hsiang Ching-yu, beloved teacher and friend: On the 35th anniversary of her martyrdom.'
WC 1963, 2, 22–25, 33.
Subj 47 59 ▪ 32.2

21383 MCH F P2 G1.1 1911–1949
Welch, Holmes Hinkley, 1921–.
'Case histories of motivation: Two modern Chinese monks.'
Z. für Missionswissenschaft und Religionswissenschaft 54, 2 (1970), 112–123.
Subj 33 59

21384 NNC O P2 G1.5 1911–1949
Wong, Su-ling (Wang Shu-ling), pseud., 1918– and Earl Herbert Cressy, 1883–.
Daughter of Confucius: A personal history.
New York: Farrar, Straus and Young, 1952. 381 p.
Subj 41 42 59 ▪ 23 26.2 27 44 47 48 52 55 57

21385 CSH U P2 G9.2 1911–1928
Wu Wen.
'A staunch revolutionary fighter [Ch'en Tieh-chun].'
WC 1965, 2, 28–32.
Subj 47 59 ▪ 32.2

1911-1972
(including 1644-1972)

21386 NNC F P3 G1.3 1928–1972
Barnett, Arthur Doak, 1921–.
'The evolution of an anti-Communist Chinese youth: A case study.'
AUFS-EAS 2, 1 (Mar. 1953), 1–7.
Subj 59 61 ▪ 54 66

21387 CSU S P2 G1.2 1644–1972
Bernal, Martin Gardiner, 1937–.
'Who's who in China.' [Review of *In search of wealth and power: Yen Fu and the West*, by Benjamin Isadore Schwartz; *Hu Shih and the Chinese renaissance: Liberalism in the Chinese revolution, 1917–1937*, by Jerome Bailey Grieder; *Ting Wen-chiang: Science and China's new culture*, by Charlotte Davis Furth; *Kuo Mo-jo: The early years*, by David Tod Roy; *Eminent Chinese of the Ch'ing period*, edited by Arthur William Hummel; *Biographical dictionary of Republican China*, edited by Howard Lyon Boorman and Richard Campbell Howard; *Ku Chieh-kang and China's new history: Nationalism and the quest for alternative traditions*, by Laurence Allen Schneider; *Biographic dictionary of Chinese Communism, 1921–1965*, by Donald Walker Klein and Anne Bolling Clark; and *Who's who in Communist China*, compiled by Union Research Institute.]
NYRB 18, 5 (23 Mar. 1972), 31–36.
Subj 16.1 59

21388 CSU P P2 G1.2 1895–1972
Boorman, Howard Lyon, 1920–.
'Liu Shao-ch'i: The man and the iceberg.' In *Revolutionary leaders of modern China*, edited by Chün-tu Hsüeh. [Selective entry]
New York: Oxford U. Press, 1971, 535–560.
Subj 32.2 59 ▪ 12 16.1 36.4 64

21389 CSH P P2 G1.3 1911–1972
Boorman, Howard Lyon, 1920–.
'Mao Tse-tung: The lacquered image.'
CQ 16 (Oct.–Dec. 1963), 1–55. [A condensed version appears in entry 21392, vol. 3, 2–22.] [Separately reprinted—New Delhi: China Study Centre, 1965. 75 p. (Slightly rev.)]
Subj 32.2 59 ▪ 15 36.3

21390 CSH P P2 G1.2 1928–1972
Boorman, Howard Lyon, 1920–.
'Teng Hsiao-p'ing: A political profile.'
CQ 21 (Jan.–Mar. 1965), 108–125. [A condensed version appears in entry 21392, vol. 3, 252–254.]
Subj 32 59 ▪ 15 32.2

21391 CSH S P1 G1.3 1895–1972
Boorman, Howard Lyon, 1920–.
'Tung Pi-wu: A political profile.'
CQ 19 (July–Sept. 1964), 66–83. [A condensed version appears in entry 21392, vol. 3, 341–344.]
Subj 59 ▪ 18 32.2

21392 CSH PO P2 G1.1 1842–1972
Boorman, Howard Lyon, 1920–, and Richard Campbell Howard, 1925–, eds.
Biographical dictionary of Republican China.
New York: Columbia U. Press, 1967, 1968, 1970, 1971. 4 vols. 20, 484; 12, 482; 12, 472; 11, 418 p.
Subj 14 16 16.1 32.2 59 70 ▪ 12 14.2 15 16.2 17 32 33 36.1 47

21393 NIC O P2 G9.2 1911–1972
Burton, Robert A-, 1922–.
'A Chinese craftsman under three regimes: National characteristics and attitudes as revealed in the life story of a refugee.'
AUFS-EAS 8, 1 (Jan. 1960), 1–47.
Subj 26.2 41 59 ▪ 24.1 26 28 36.3

21394 CSU O P1 G1.2 1911–1972
Chang Kuo-t'ao, 1897–.
'Introduction.' In *Collected works of Liu Shao-ch'i, 1958–1967*, compiled by Union Research Institute. [Sole entry]
Hong Kong: Union Research Institute, 1968, 1–9 [s.p.].
Subj 32.2 59 ▪ 16.1 64

21395 CSU PO P2 G1.2 1911–1972
[Chao Ts'ung] Chung Hua-min, pseud., 1927– and Arthur C- Miller.
Madame Mao: A profile of Chiang Ch'ing.
Hong Kong: Union Research Institute, 1968. 314 p.
Subj 14.2 19 31 59 ▪ 32 32.1 32.2 46 47 64

21396 CSU S P1 G1.2 1911–1972
Ch'en, Jerome (Ch'en Chih-jang), 1919–.
'The last emperor of China.' [Review of *From emperor to citizen: The autobiography of Aisin-Gioro Pu Yi*, by Pu Yi Aisin-Gioro (P'u I).]
BSOAS 28, 2 (June 1965), 336–355.
Subj 59

21397 CSH P P2 G1.2 1928–1972
Cheng, Peter P. C., 1930–.
'An analysis of the 1965–68 attacks on Liu Shao-chi's early career.'
IS 7, 12 (Sept. 1971), 55–77.
Subj 32.2 59 64 ▪ 32 36.4

21398 CSU P P1 G1.2 1895–1972
Current Scene Editor.
'Lin Piao: A political profile.'
CS 7, 5 (10 Mar. 1969), 1–16.
Subj 15 59 ▪ 16.1

21399 MAM P P2 G1.1 1895–1972
Eber, Irene, 1929–.
Hu Shih (1891–1962): A sketch of his life and his role in the intellectual and political dialogue of modern China.
Ann Arbor: University Microfilms (Publ. 67-9542), 1967. 421 p. (Doctoral dissertation in History, Claremont Graduate School and University Center, 1965)
Subj 59 62 ▪ 14.2 36.1

21400 CSU P P2 G1.2 1911–1972
Ebon, Martin.
Lin Piao: The life and writings of China's new ruler.
New York: Stein and Day, 1970. 378 p.
Subj 32 32.2 59 64 ▪ 12.2 15 16.1 25 35

21401 ICU P P3 G1.2 1911–1972
Edmunds, Clifford Galloway, Jr., 1938–.
Bureaucracy, historiography, and ideology in Communist China: The case of Chien Po-tsan, 1949–1958.
Unpublished masters thesis in Far Eastern Civilizations, U. of Chicago, 1968. 194 p.
Subj 16.1 59 62 64 ▪ 12 12.1 66

21402 CSU U P1 G1.1 –1972
Garraty, John Arthur, 1920–.
'Chinese and Western biography: A comparison.'
JAS 21, 4 (Aug. 1962), 487–489.
Subj 59 70

21403 CSU S P1 G1.2 1911–1972
Goldman, René, 1934–.
'Mao, Maoism and Mao-ology: A review article.'
PA 41, 4 (Winter 1968/69), 560–574.
Subj 59 64 71 ▪ 16.1 32.2

21404 MCH P P1 G1.1 1842–1972
Grieder, Jerome Bailey, 1932–.
Hu Shih and the Chinese renaissance: Liberalism in the Chinese revolution, 1917–1937.
Cambridge: Harvard U. Press, 1970. 42, 420 p. (Harvard East Asian series, 46) (Revision of *Hu Shih and liberalism: A chapter in the intellectual modernization of China, 1917–1930,*

doctoral dissertation in History and Far Eastern Languages, Harvard U., 1963)
Subj 16.1 17 59 60 64 66 ▪ 12 16 19 37 62 63

21405 CSU P P1 G1.2 1895–1972
Grimm, Tilemann, 1922–.
Mao Tse-tung, in Selbstzeugnissen und Bilddokumenten (Mao Tse-tung: A personal and pictorial documentary).
Hamburg: Rowohlt, 1968. 179 p.
Subj 32 32.2 59 64 ▪ 15

21406 CBU P P2 G1.2 1911–1972
Guarnotta, Donatelle.
Mao Tsetung: la vita, il pensiero i testi esemplari (Mao Tse-tung: His life, thought and exemplary texts).
Milan: Accademia-Sansoni, 1970. 239 p.
Subj 32.2 59 64 ▪ 14.2 19 32

21407 NNC S P3 G1.2 1895–1972
Harrell, Paula S- Johnson.
Yeh Sheng-t'ao: His life and literary works, 1894–1963.
Unpublished masters thesis in East Asian Languages and Cultures, Columbia U., 1964. 112 p. [Certificate essay, East Asian Institute]
Subj 16.1 59 ▪ 12.1 17 63 64

21408 CSU P P2 G1.1 1842–1972
Hsieh, Winston (Hsieh Wen-sun), 1935–.
'An unfinished pyramid in the field of twentieth century Chinese studies.' [Review of *Biographical dictionary of Republican China*, edited by Howard Lyon Boorman and Richard Campbell Howard.]
JAS 31, 3 (May 1972), 615–631.
Subj 16.1 59 ▪ 15 32 32.2

21409 CSU U P2 G1.2 1895–1972
Hsu, Kai-yu (Hsü Chieh-yü), 1922–.
'Chou En-lai.' In *Revolutionary leaders of modern China*, edited by Chün-tu Hsüeh. [Selective entry]
New York: Oxford U. Press, 1971, 517–534.
Subj 59 ▪ 12 16.1 32.2

21410 CSU FP P2 G1.2 1895–1972
Hsu, Kai-yu (Hsü Chieh-yü), 1922–.
Chou En-lai, China's gray eminence.
Garden City, N.Y.: Doubleday, 1968. 294 p.
Subj 16.1 59 ▪ 12 15 22 22.2 32 32.2 64 66

21411 CSU S P2 G1.1 1842–1972
Johnson, Chalmers Ashby, 1931–.
'A choreography of the Chinese Communist movement.' [Review of *Biographic dictionary of Chinese Communism, 1921–1965*, by Donald Walker Klein and Anne Bolling Clark; and *Biographical dictionary of Republican China*, edited by Howard Lyon Boorman and Richard Campbell Howard.]
CQ 48 (Oct.–Dec. 1971), 741–748.
Subj 16 59

21412 CSH P P2 G1.1 1911–1972
Klein, Donald Walker, 1929–, and Anne Bolling Clark.
Biographic dictionary of Chinese Communism, 1921–1965.
Cambridge: Harvard U. Press, 1971. 2 vols. 16, 1190 p. [c.p.]. (Harvard East Asian series, 57)
Subj 16 16.1 32 32.2 59 ▪ 12 13 14.2 15 17 36.1 36.4 47 64

21413 CSU O P3 G9.0 1911–1972
Li Shu-fan (Li Shu-fen), 1887–1966.
Hong Kong surgeon.
New York: Dutton, 1964. 16, 240 p.
Subj 17 18 56 59 ▪ 32.2 41 55 62

21414 CSH FP P2 G1.2 1911–1972
Li Tien-min (Li T'ien-min).
Chou En-lai.
Taipei: Institute of International Relations, Republic of China, 1970. 10, 425 p.
Subj 15 16.1 32 32.2 59 ▪ 12 14 25 32.1 36.4 66

21415 CSU P P1 G1.2 1911–1972
Liu, Yuen-sun.
The current and the past of Lin Piao. Tr. by Robert Liang of 'Lin Piao ti kuo ch'ü hsien tsai'; *Fei ch'ing ycn chiu yüeh k'an* 1, 1 (31 Jan. 1967), 61–77.
Santa Monica, Calif.: RAND Corp., 1967. 58 p. (RAND papers, P-3671)
Subj 15 59 ▪ 12 16.1 35 64

21416 NNC O P2 G1.2 1928–1972
Loh, Robert, 1924–.
Escape from Red China.
New York: Coward-McCann, 1962. 378 p.
Subj 12.1 14.4 16.2 59 ▪ 12.2 16.1 22.2 32.1 34.1 34.2 41 46 66

21417 CBU P P2 G1.2 1842–1972
McAleavy, Henry.
A dream of Tartary: The origins and misfortunes of Henry P'u Yi.
London: Allen and Unwin, 1963. 292 p.
Subj 16.1 47 59 ▪ 15 27 55 66

21418 MCH O P2 G1.2 1911–1972
Martinson, Harold H-, 1905–.
Red dragon over China.
Minneapolis: Augsburg, 1956. 328 p.
Subj 59 ▪ 12.1 15 19 32.2

21419 MAM P P2 G1.2 1911–1972
O'Keefe, Thomas Emmett, 1930–.
Liu Shao-ch'i: A political biography.
Ann Arbor: University Microfilms (Publ. 69-4126), 1969. 245 p. (Doctoral dissertation in History, St. John's U., 1968)
Subj 32 59 64 ▪ 16.1 32.2

21420 CSU PO P2 G1.2 1842–1972
Payne, Pierre Stephen Robert, 1911–.
Mao Tse-tung, rev. and enl. ed.
New York: Weybright and Talley, 1969. 343 p.
Subj 15 19 32.2 59 64 ▪ 14.2 16.1 16.3 25 32 36.3 54

21421 CSU O P3 G9.4 1928–1972
Peng Ming-min (P'eng Ming-min), 1923–.
A taste of freedom: Memoirs of a Formosan independence leader.
New York: Holt, Rinehart and Winston, 1972. 16, 270 p.
Subj 17 22.1 59 ▪ 13 22.2 25 64 66

21422 NNC O P2 G1.2 1895–1972
Pu Yi Aisin-Gioro (P'u-i Aisin Gioro), 1906–1967.
From emperor to citizen: The autobiography of Aisin-Gioro Pu Yi. Tr. by W- J- F- Jenner of *Wo ti ch'ien pan sheng* (The first half of my life); Hong Kong: Wen t'ung shu tien, 1964; 3 vols. 542 p. [c.p.].
Peking: Foreign Languages Press, 1964, 1965. 2 vols. 496 p. [c.p.]. [A different tr.—*The last Manchu: The autobiography of Henry Pu Yi, last Emperor of China*, edited by Paul Kramer. Tr. by Kuo Ying Paul Tsai. New York: Putnam, 1967. 318 p.]
Subj 12 16.1 59 ▪ 32 32.2 41 48 55 64 66

21423 CSU P P2 G1.2 1928–1972
Robinson, Thomas Webster, 1935–.
Lin Piao as an elite type.
Santa Monica, Calif.: RAND Corp., 1971. 56 p. (RAND papers, P-4639) [Reprinted in *Elites in the People's Republic of China*, edited by Robert Anthony Scalapino. (Analytic entry.) Seattle: U. of Washington Press, 1972, 149–195. (Social Science Research Council, Studies in Chinese government and politics, 3)]
Subj 16.1 59 ▪ 48 64

21424 CSU P P2 G1.2 1895–1972
Schram, Stuart Reynolds, 1924–.
Mao Tse-tung.
New York: Simon and Schuster, 1966. 351 p.
Subj 32.2 59 64 ▪ 15 16.1 32 66

21425 CSH P P5 G1.1 1895–1972
Tong, Hollington K. (Tung Hsien-kuang), 1887–1970.
Chiang Kai-shek, rev. ed.
Taipei: China Publishing Co., 1953. 21, 562 p. [See Vol. 2 of this *Bibliography* for Chinese version.]
Subj 15 32 32.2 59 ▪ 12 12.2 25 64 66

21426 CSU P P3 G1.5 1895–1972
Wang, Y. C. (Wang I-chü; Wang Chi-ch'ien), 1916–.
'Ta Yueh-Sheng, 1888–1951: A tentative political biography.'
JAS 26, 3 (May 1967), 433–455.
Subj 22 22.2 59 ▪ 14.3 22.1 24.6 26.1 32 34.2

21427 CSH PO P1 G1.1 1895–1972
[Yaukey, Grace Sydenstricker] Cornelia Spencer, pseud., 1899–.
Chiang Kai-shek, Generalissimo of Nationalist China.
New York: Day, 1968. 253 p.
Subj 15 32 59 ▪ 12

21428 CSH O P2 G9.0 1928–1972
Ying, Lai, pseud.?, 1937–.
The thirty-sixth way: A personal account of imprisonment and escape from Red China, edited by Edward Behr and Sydney Liu.
Garden City, N.Y.: Doubleday, 1969. 204 p.
Subj 22.1 55 59 ▪ 13 24.1 31 46

1949-1972

21429 NNC P P1 G1.2 1949–1972
Ayers, Thomas William, 1922–.
'Current biography in Communist China.'
JAS 21, 4 (Aug. 1962), 477–485.
Subj 12.1 59 ▪ 64

21430 MCH F P2 G1.2 1949–1972
[La Dany, Ladislao] ———, 1914–.
'In the spider's web.'
CNA 454 (1 Feb. 1963), 1–7.
SUBJ 12.1 59 ▪ 12.2

21431 MCH F P2 G5.1 1949–1972
[La Dany, Ladislao] ———, 1914–.
'The story of a Youth Corps member.'
CNA 259 (9 Jan. 1959), 1–7.
SUBJ 32.1 59 ▪ 26.1 54

21432 CSU P P3 G1.2 1949–1972
Robinson, Thomas Webster, 1935–.
'Chou En-lai and the Cultural Revolution in China.' In *The Cultural Revolution in China*, edited by T. W. Robinson. [Analytic entry]
Berkeley, Los Angeles: U. of California Press, 1971, 165–312.
SUBJ 12 22.2 59 ▪ 16.1 25 35 54 64

21433 CSH O P2 G6.0 1949–1972
Tung, Chi-ping, 1940–, and Humphrey Evans.
The thought revolution.
New York: Coward-McCann, 1966. 254 p.
SUBJ 17 22.1 32.1 59 61 ▪ 26 28 32 47 54 63

21434 CSH O P2 G1.1 1949–1972
Wang Chao-tien.
A Red Guard tells his own story.
Taipei: Asian Peoples' Anti-Communist League, 1967. 69 p. (APACL pamphlets, 111)
SUBJ 25 54 59 ▪ 12.1 17 35

21435 CSU O P2 G1.1 1949–1972
Yuan, Nathan S. Y.
Crossing the Rubicon.
Taipei: The author, 1967. 101 p. [Reprinted from *Free China review* 4, 4 – 5, 8 (Apr. 1954 – Aug. 1955).]
SUBJ 59 ▪ 12 12.1 12.2 32.1

60 IDEA SYSTEMS AND VALUES IN GENERAL
觀念及價值體系通論
観念及び価値体系一般

1644-1911

21436 NNC P P1 G1.2 1895–1911
Franke, Otto, 1863–1946.
'Geistige Strömungen im heutigen China' (Intellectual trends in contemporary China). In *Ostasiatische Neubildungen: Beiträge zum Verständnis der politischen und kulturellen Entwicklungs-vorgänge im Fernen Osten* (New forms in East Asia: Toward an understanding of political and cultural developmental processes in the Far East), by O. Franke. [Selective entry]
Hamburg: C. Boysen, 1911, 36–55.
SUBJ 60 66 ▪ 32 32.2 64

21437 MCH P P1 G1.2 –1911
Granet, Marcel, 1884–1940.
La pensée chinoise (Chinese thought).
Paris: Renaissance du livre, 1934. 23, 614 p. [Reprinted—Paris: Michel, 1968. 569 p.]
SUBJ 13 60 62 ▪ 23 43 63

21438 NNC PO P3 G5.1 1895–1911
Krebs, E-.
'Die politische Karikatur in China' (Political cartoons in China).
Ostasiatische Z. 8 (1919/20), 268–274.
SUBJ 24.2 60 ▪ 12.1 12.2 22 66

21439 CSU P P2 G1.2 –1911
Wang, Y. C. (Wang I-chü; Wang Chi-ch'ien), 1916–.
'Ideas and men in traditional China.'
MS 19 (1960), 210–275.
SUBJ 12 16.1 60 ▪ 16.3 17

21440 NNC O P1 G1.3 –1911
Wilhelm, Richard, 1873–1930.
'Die weltanschaulichen Grundlagen der Liebe in Europa und China' (The ideological bases of love in Europe and China).
Sinica 4, 6 (Nov. 1929), 251–258.
SUBJ 46 60 ▪ 41 47 63

21441 CSH S P1 G1.2 1644–1911
Wu, Silas H. L. (Wu Hsiu-liang), 1929–.
'Value demands and value fulfillment: An approach to the study of the Ch'ing emperor-official relationship.'
CSWT 1, 8 (May 1968), 27–37.
SUBJ 12 60 61 64 ▪ 16.1 71

1644-1949

21442 MCH P P1 G1.0 –1949
Bodde, Derk, 1909–.
'Dominant ideas in the formation of Chinese culture.'
JAOS 62, 4 (Dec. 1942), 293–299.
SUBJ 60 62 ▪ 63 64

21443 NNC F P1 G1.0 –1949
Bunzel, Ruth Leah, 1898–.
Explorations in Chinese culture, mimeo.
New York: Columbia U., Research in Contemporary Cultures, 1950. 231, 12 p.
SUBJ 52 53 60 61 63 ▪ 41 46 47 55 62

21444 ICU P P1 G1.2 1895–1949
Chen, Pearl Hsia (Ch'en Hsia Lu-jung), 1919–.
The social thought of Lusin, 1881–1936.
Unpublished doctoral dissertation in History, U. of Chicago, 1953. 381 p.
SUBJ 59 60 62 64 ▪ 16.1 17 41 47 61 66

21445 NNC O P1 G1.2 1895–1928
Dewey, John, 1859–1952.
'Transforming the mind of China.'
Asia (New York: American Asiatic Assn.) 19, 11 (Nov. 1919), 1103–1108.
SUBJ 60

21446 MCY P P1 G1.0 –1928
Grousset, René, 1885–1952.
'La pensée chinoise' (Chinese thought). In *Histoire de la philosophie orientale* (History of Oriental philosophy), by R. Grousset. [Sole entry]
Paris: Nouvelle lib. nationale, 1923, 296–359.
SUBJ 60 62 64 ▪ 63

21447 NIC PO P2 G1.2 –1949
Hu Shih, 1891–1962.
The Chinese renaissance.
Chicago: U. of Chicago Press, 1934. 11, 110 p. (Haskell Lectures in Comparative Religion, 1933) [Reprinted—New York: Paragon, 1963. 110 p.]
SUBJ 60 ▪ 13 16.1 17 64 66

21448 CSU P P1 G1.2 1842–1928
Hummel, William Frederick.
'K'ang Yu-wei: Historical critic and social philosopher, 1858–1927.'
PHR 4, 4 (Nov. 1935), 343–355.
SUBJ 59 60

21449 CSU U P2 G1.0 –1949
Lin, T. C. (Lin T'ung-chi), 1906–.
'The Chinese mind: Its Taoist substratum.'
J. of the history of ideas 8, 3 (June 1947), 259–272.
SUBJ 60 61

21450 NNC P P2 G1.2 1842–1928
Muir, Robert F-.
Hu Shih: A biographical sketch, 1891–1917, with emphasis on his intellectual development.
Unpublished masters thesis in History, Columbia U., 1959. 136 p. [Certificate essay, East Asian Institute]
SUBJ 59 60 63 ▪ 64 66

21451 CSH P P1 G1.2 –1928
Roy, Andrew Tod.
'Attacks upon Confucianism in the 1911–1927 period. Parts 2 and 3, From a Taoist lawyer: Wu Yü.'
CCJ 4, 2 (May 1965), 149–163; 5, 1 (Nov. 1965), 69–78.
SUBJ 60 64 ▪ 63

21452 CBU P P1 G1.2 –1949
Roy, Andrew Tod.
'The background of the Confucian dilemma in the period 1927–47.'
CCJ 9, 2 (May 1970), 182–201.
SUBJ 60 64 ▪ 63

21453 NIC O P1 G1.3 1895–1928
Shen, Nelson Nai-cheng (Shen Nai-cheng).
'The changing Chinese social mind.'
CSPSR 8, 1 (Jan. 1924), 68–87; 8, 2 (Apr. 1924), 125–166.
SUBJ 19 41 54 60 64 ▪ 17 43 47

21454 CSH U P1 G1.0 –1949
TSuda, Sookichi (Tsuda Sōkichi).
'Obshchii obzor techenii kitaiskoi mysli' (Overview of the currents of Chinese thought).
Vostochnoe obozrenie 1 (oktiabr'–dekabr' 1939), 138–158.
SUBJ 60

1911-1949

21455 NIC O P5 G1.3 1911–1928
Ayscough, Florence Wheelock, 1878–1942.
A Chinese mirror: Being reflections of the reality behind appearances.
Boston: Houghton Mifflin, 1925. 464 p.
SUBJ 13 60 62 ▪ 16.1 23 55 65

21456 MCH O P2 G1.3 1911–1928
Bonnard, Abel, 1883–1968.
En Chine, 1920–1921.
Paris: Fayard, 1924. 362 p.
In China, 1920–1921. Tr. by Veronica Lucas.

London: Routledge, 1926. 361 p.
SUBJ 48 60 61 62 ▪ 15 16.1 16.3 18 23 33 47 52 65 66

21457 MAM P P1 G1.2 1911–1949
Chen, William Juntung (Ch'en Chen-tung), 1915–.
Some controversies on Chinese culture and education.
Ann Arbor: University Microfilms (Publ. 2526), 1951. 345 p. (Doctoral dissertation in Educational Research, Columbia U.)
SUBJ 17 60 63 64 ▪ 19 41 47 66

21458 CSH P P1 G1.2 1911–1949
Eber, Irene, 1929–.
'Hu Shih and the controversy on Chinese culture and western civilization.' In *East Asian occasional papers, II*, edited by Harry Jerome Lamley. [Selective entry]
Honolulu: U. of Hawaii, Asian Studies Program, 1970, 29–45. (Asian Studies at Hawaii, 4)
SUBJ 60

21459 NNC P P4 G1.2 1911–1949
Huang, Sung-k'ang.
Lu Hsün and the New Culture Movement of modern China.
Amsterdam: Djambatan, 1957. 10, 158 p. (Doctoral dissertation, Rijksuniversiteit te Leiden)
SUBJ 16.1 31 36.1 60 64 ▪ 12 12.1 16 18 19 32 32.2 63 66

21460 CSH P P3 G1.2 1911–1928
Lee, Leo Ou-fan (Li Ou-fan), 1939–.
'The romantic temper of May Fourth writers.' In *Reflections on the May Fourth Movement: A symposium*, edited by Benjamin Isadore Schwartz. [Analytic entry]
Cambridge: Harvard U., East Asian Research Center, 1972, 69–84. (Harvard East Asian monographs, 44)
SUBJ 16.1 60

21461 ICU P P1 G1.2 1911–1928
Lin Yu-sheng (Lin Yü-sheng), 1934–.
The crisis of Chinese consciousness: Iconoclasm in the May Fourth era.
Unpublished doctoral dissertation in Social Thought, U. of Chicago, 1970. 287 p.
SUBJ 16.1 60

21462 NNM O P1 G1.2 1911–1928
Lo, R. Y. (Lo Yün-yen), 1890–, and Paul Hutchinson, 1890–.
'What the Chinese are thinking about Christianity: Modern radical thought among Chinese students.'
CR 52, 4 (Apr. 1921), 157–167.
SUBJ 17 33 60 ▪ 47 54

21463 NIC F P1 G1.3 1928–1949
Morris, Charles William, 1901–.
Varieties of human value.
Chicago: U. of Chicago Press, 1956. 15, 208 p.
SUBJ 60 61 ▪ 62 63

21464 CSU P P1 G1.2 1911–1928
Saywell, William George Gabriel, 1936–.
'Modernization without modernity: Tai Chi-t'ao, a conservative nationalist.'
JAAS 5, 4 (Oct. 1970), 256–265.
SUBJ 19 60

21465 MCH O P2 G1.2 1928–1949
Schmitthenner, Heinrich, 1887–1957.
China im Profil (China in profile).
Leipzig: Bibliographisches Institut, 1934. 129 p.
SUBJ 14.2 18 60 ▪ 11.3 14.6 21.3

1911-1972
(including 1644-1972)

21466 CSU P P1 G1.2 –1972
Bauer, Wolfgang, 1930–.
China und die Hoffnung auf Glück: Paradiese, Utopien, Idealvorstellungen (China and the search for prosperity: Paradise, utopia, and the concept of the ideal).
Munich: C. Hanser, 1971. 703 p.
SUBJ 60 62 64 ▪ 12 32 32.2 40 47

21467 NNC S P1 G1.1 –1972
Bodde, Derk, 1909–.
China's cultural tradition: What and whither?
New York: Rinehart, 1957. 90 p.
SUBJ 12 13 16 40 60 62 ▪ 12.2 15 16.1 17 48 63 64 66

21468 CSU U P1 G1.2 –1972
Chan, Wing-tsit (Ch'en Jung-chieh), 1901–.
'Modern trends in Chinese philosophy and religion.' In *Modern trends in world religions*, edited by Joseph M. Kitagawa (Kitagawa Mitsuo). [Sole entry]
Chicago: Open Court, 1959, 193–216.
SUBJ 60 62 ▪ 33 63 64

21469 CSU U P2 G1.1 –1972
Fairbank, John King, 1907–.
'How to deal with the Chinese revolution.'
NYRB 6, 2 (17 Feb. 1966), 10–15.
SUBJ 60 ▪ 30 66

21470 NNC S P1 G1.0 –1972
Franke, Wolfgang, 1912–.
'Some investigation in the structure, concepts and ideals of Chinese culture.' In *The cultural problems of Malaysia in the context of Southeast Asia*, edited by Sutan Takdir Alisjabana et al. [Sole entry]
Kuala Lumpur: Malaysian Society of Orientalists, 1968?, 139–163.
SUBJ 60 63 ▪ 16.1 44

21471 ICU P P1 G1.2 1895–1972
Lien, Chan, 1936–.
The criticism of Hu Shih's thought in Communist China.
Unpublished doctoral dissertation in Political Science, U. of Chicago, 1965. 481 p.
SUBJ 16.1 59 60 64 ▪ 12.1 14.2 36.1 62

21472 CSU S P1 G1.1 –1972
Mote, Frederick Wade, 1922–.
'China's past in the study of China today: Some comments on the recent work of Richard Solomon.' [Review of *Mao's revolution and the Chinese political culture*, by Richard Harvey Solomon.]
JAS 32, 1 (Nov. 1972), 107–120.
SUBJ 17 60 61 64 ▪ 41 53 63

21473 CSU PO P2 G1.3 –1972
Needham, Noël Joseph Terence Montgomery, 1900–.
'The past in China's present: A cultural, social, and philosophic background for contemporary China.'
Centennial review 4, 2 (Spring 1960), 145–178; 4, 3 (Summer 1960), 281–308. [Reprinted in *The grand titration: Science and society in East and West*, by N. J. T. M. Needham. (Selective entry.) Toronto: U. of Toronto Press, 1969, 177–189.]
SUBJ 16 16.1 60 62 ▪ 12 12.2 14.4 15 19 32.2 34.3 41 66

21474 CSH P P2 G1.2 –1972
Oort, H- A- van.
'Chinese culture values, past and present.'
CC 11, 1 (Mar. 1970), 34–44.
SUBJ 10 60

21475 CSU P P1 G1.0 –1972
Pye, Lucian Wilmot, 1921–, and Nathan Leites.
Nuances in Chinese political culture.
Santa Monica, Calif.: RAND Corp., 1970. 22 p. (RAND papers, P-4504)
SUBJ 60 61 ▪ 57 62

21476 NNC S P2 G1.2 –1972
Riencourt, Amaury de, 1918–.
The soul of China.
New York: Coward-McCann, 1958. 298 p.
SUBJ 10 60 62 64 ▪ 12 13 14 16 16.1 30 32.2

21477 NIC S P2 G1.1 –1972
Wright, Arthur Frederick, 1913–.
'Buddhism and Chinese culture.'
JAS 17, 1 (Nov. 1957), 17–42.
SUBJ 33 60 ▪ 13 23

1949-1972

21478 CSU F P2 G9.4 1949–1972
Appleton, Sheldon Lee, 1933–.
'Silent students and the future of Taiwan.'
PA 43, 2 (Summer 1970), 227–239. [Reprinted as 'The political socialization of Taiwan's college students.' *AS* 10, 10 (Oct. 1970), 910–923.]
SUBJ 17 54 60 61 ▪ 21.2

21479 CSH F P2 G9.0 1949–1972
Appleton, Sheldon Lee, 1933–.
'Surveying the values of Chinese college students.'
Asian forum 2, 2 (Apr.–June 1970), 75–88.
SUBJ 54 60

21480 CSU O P2 G9.0 1949–1972
Bennett, Gordon Anderson, 1940–.
'Student attitudes in Taiwan.' [Review of 'Taiwanese and mainlanders on Taiwan: A survey of student attitudes', by Sheldon Lee Appleton.] [With a reply by Appleton]
CQ 46 (Apr.–June 1971), 353–357.
SUBJ 60 ▪ 29 48 54

21481 CSH F P3 G9.4 1949–1972
Chin, Robert (Ch'en Yü-li), 1918–, and Ai-li Sung Chin (Ch'en Shen Ai-li), 1919–.
'Comparative evaluations of aspects of contemporary Chinese culture by college students in Taiwan.'
J. of sociology (Taipei) 1 (Dec. 1963), 41–55.
SUBJ 54 60 66 ▪ 41 48 63

21482 MAM F P4 G 1.3 1949–1972
Covin, David Leroy, 1940–.
Political culture as an analytical instrument: An examination of refugees in Hong Kong.
Ann Arbor: University Microfilms (Publ. 71-4390), 1971. 192 p. (Doctoral dissertation in Political Science, Washington State U., 1970)
SUBJ 16 60 ▪ 16.2 16.4 50

21483 CBU FP P2 G 9.4 1949–1972
Eberhard, Wolfram, 1909–.
'Social interaction and social values in Chinese dreams.'
J. of sociology (Taipei) 4 (Apr. 1968), 21–43; 5 (Apr. 1969), 61–105.
[Reprinted in *Moral and social values of the Chinese: Collected essays*, by W. Eberhard. (Selective entry.) Taipei: Chinese Materials and Research Aids Service Center, 1971, 27–96. (CMRASC occasional series, 6)]
SUBJ 40 60 61 ▪ 41 46 47 48 57 65

21484 CSU F P2 G 9.4 1949–1972
Grichting, Wolfgang Leo.
The value system in Taiwan, 1970: A preliminary report.
Taipei: The author, 1971. 30, 588 p.
SUBJ 29 41 60 63 ▪ 16 18 31 43 46 48 55

21485 CSH P P1 G 1.2 1949–1972
[La Dany, Ladislao] ———, 1914–.
'Criticisms of Prof. Liang Shu-ming.'
CNA 111 (2 Dec. 1955), 1–7.
SUBJ 60 62 ▪ 72

21486 DLC O P2 G 1.2 1949–1972
Shepelev, Aleksandr Grigor'evich, Evgenii Andreevich Ashchepkov, and Savva Elizarovich Kozhevnikov, 1903–.
'Kitai' (China). In *U nashikh druzei: vpechatleniia sibiriakov, pobyvavshikh v stranakh narodnoi demokratii* (With our friends: Impressions of Siberian visitors to the people's democracies), edited by A. G. Shepelev. [Sole entry]
Novosibirsk: Kn. izd-vo, 1957, 3–57.
SUBJ 14 34.1 36.3 36.4 60 ▪ 16.3 16.4 17 18 31 34.2 66

21487 MCY U P1 G 9.4 1949–1972
Starr, Kenneth, 1922–.
'Cultural problems on Nationalist Taiwan.'
France-Asie 18, 175/176 (sept.–déc. 1962), 539–560.
SUBJ 19 60 ▪ 29 41 66

21488 CSU P P1 G 9.4 1949–1972
Tozer, Warren Wilson, 1933–.
'Taiwan's "Cultural Renaissance": A preliminary view.'
CQ 43 (July–Sept. 1970), 81–99.
SUBJ 12.1 60 64 ▪ 54

21489 MCH O P2 G 1.3 1949–1972
Zalygin, Sergei Pavlovich, 1913–.
V strane druzei: ocherki (In our friends' country: Notes).
Moscow: Molodaia gvardiia, 1958. 318 p.
SUBJ 23 24 26 60 ▪ 28 34.1 50 62 65

61 PERSONALITY AND BEHAVIORAL PROCESSES
人格及行爲
パーソナリティ及び行為

1644-1911

21490 NNM O P3 G 9.2 1895–1911
Selden, C- C-.
'Work among the Chinese insane and some of its results.'
CMMJ 19 (1905), 1–17.
SUBJ 56 61 ▪ 63

21491 NNC S P1 G 1.1 1842–1895
Yap, Pow-meng (Yeh Pao-ming).
'The mental illness of Hung Hsiu-ch'uan, leader of the Taiping Rebellion.'
FEQ 13, 3 (May 1954), 287–304.
[Reprinted in *Revolutionary leaders of modern China*, edited by Chün-tu Hsüeh. (Selective entry.) New York: Oxford U. Press, 1971, 32–54.]
SUBJ 59 61 ▪ 32.2 62 63

1644-1949

21492 CSU P P1 G 1.2 –1949
Chen, Theodore H. E. (Ch'en Hsi-en), 1902–.
'Racial characteristics of the Chinese.'
SSR 24, 3 (Jan.–Feb. 1940), 216–230.
SUBJ 60 61

21493 NDD P P1 G 1.0 –1949
Chen, William Y. (Ch'en Yüan-lung), 1896–.
A psychological interpretation of Chinese culture, with special reference to its stability.
Unpublished doctoral dissertation in Religion, Duke U., 1930. 270 p.
SUBJ 60 61 63 ▪ 62

21494 CSU P P1 G 1.0 –1949
Cheng, Ch'eng-k'un, 1906–.
'Characteristic traits of the Chinese people.'
Social forces 25, 2 (Dec. 1946), 146–155.
SUBJ 60 61 63 ▪ 62 66

21495 MAM S P1 G 1.2 1895–1949
Cummins, Howard Wallace, 1937–.
Mao Tse-tung: A value analysis.
Ann Arbor: University Microfilms (Publ. 73-7876), 1973. 100 p. (Doctoral dissertation in Political Science, U. of Oregon, 1972)
SUBJ 59 61

21496 GMS S P1 G 1.0 –1949
Hang, Thaddäus.
Grundzüge des chinesischen Volkscharakters (Basic features of the Chinese national character).
Würzburg: Echter, 1964. 134 p. (Institut für missionswissenschaftliche Forschung, Münster, Veröffentlichungen)
SUBJ 61 62

21497 NIC P P1 G 1.0 –1949
Klineberg, Otto, 1899–.
'Emotional expression in Chinese literature.'
J. of abnormal and social psychology 33, 4 (Oct. 1938), 517–520.
SUBJ 61

21498 CSU U P1 G 1.0 –1949
Lin, T. C. (Lin T'ung-chi), 1906–.
'The Taoist in every Chinese.'
THM 11, 3 (Dec.–Jan. 1940/41), 211–225.
SUBJ 61 62 ▪ 63

21499 CSU S P1 G 1.2 –1949
Veith, Ilza, 1915–.
'Psychiatric thought in Chinese medicine.'
J. of the history of medicine and allied sciences 10, 3 (July 1955), 261–268.
SUBJ 56 61 62 ▪ 43 63

21500 NIC S P1 G 1.2 –1949
Veith, Ilza, 1915–.
'The supernatural in Far Eastern concepts of mental disease.'
B. of the history of medicine 37, 2 (Mar.–Apr. 1963), 139–159.
SUBJ 46 61 65 ▪ 47 56 62

21501 NIC S P2 G 1.2 1895–1949
Weakland, John Hast, 1919–.
'Lusin's "Ah Q": A rejected image of Chinese character.'
Pacific spectator 10, 2 (Spring 1956), 137–146.
SUBJ 26 61 ▪ 22.2

21502 NNC U P8 G 1.3 1644–1928
Wilhelm, Richard, 1873–1930.
'Die chinesische Landwirtschaft in ihren psychologischen Wirkungen' (Psychological phenomena related to agricultural work in China).
Sinica 4, 2 (März 1929), 49–61.
SUBJ 14.1 61 ▪ 16.3 23 41 43 55 62 63

21503 MCH P P1 G 1.0 –1928
Wilhelm, Richard, 1873–1930.
'Einige Probleme der buddhistischen Psychologie' (Problems of Buddhist psychology).
Sinica 4, 3 (Mai 1929), 120–130.
SUBJ 61 ▪ 62 63

21504 DLC O P2 G 1.2 1895–1928
Wilhelm, Richard, 1873–1930.
Die Seele Chinas.
Berlin: Reimar Hobbing, 1926. 356 p.
The soul of China. Tr. by John Holroyd Reece and Arthur Waley.
New York: Harcourt, Brace, 1928. 382 p. [Reprinted—Ann Arbor: University Microfilms, n.d. 382 p.]
SUBJ 18 55 60 61 62 ▪ 16.1 17 22.2 23 31 32.2 41 64 66

1911-1949

21505 NIC F P1 G 1.0 1928–1949
Abel, Theodora Mead, 1899–, and Francis L. K. Hsu (Hsü Lang-kuang), 1909–.
'Some aspects of personality of Chinese as revealed by the Rorschach test.'
J. of projective techniques 13, 3 (Sept. 1949), 285–301.
SUBJ 61

21506 MCH O P3 G 1.2 1911–1928
Bouchot, Jean.
'La Chine souveraine' (Sovereign China).
Mercure de France 156 (15 juin 1922), 577–599.
SUBJ 16.1 61 ▪ 12 18

21507 CSU F P3 G5.1 1928–1949
Chao, W. H. (Chao Wan-ho).
'Handwriting of Chinese mental patients.' In *Social and psychological studies in neuropsychiatry in China*, edited by Richard Sherman Lyman, V- Maeker, and P. Liang (Liang Meng-chüan). [Selective entry]
Peiping: Peking Union Medical College, Division of Neuropsychiatry, 1939, 279–314.
SUBJ 56 61

21508 CSU F P3 G5.1 1928–1949
Chou, L. C. (Chou Li-ch'iu), and Y. C. Lu (Lu I-chuang).
'A sociological study of Chinese mental patients.' In *Social and psychological studies in neuropsychiatry in China*, edited by Richard Sherman Lyman, V- Maeker, and P. Liang (Liang Meng-chüan). [Selective entry]
Peiping: Peking Union Medical College, Division of Neuropsychiatry, 1939, 31–116.
SUBJ 56 61 ▪ 17 21.4 41 46 47

21509 NIC F P3 G5.0 1928–1949
Chou, Siegen K. (Chou Hsien-keng), 1903–, and Ching-yuan Mi.
'Relative neurotic tendency of Chinese and American students.'
J. of social psychology 8, 2 (May 1937), 155–184.
SUBJ 61 ▪ 54

21510 CSU F P3 G5.1 1928–1949
Chu, Liang-wei, and Mei-chen Liu.
'Mental diseases in Peking between 1933 and 1943.'
J. of mental science 106, 442 (Jan. 1960), 274–280.
SUBJ 56 61 ▪ 28

21511 MCH F P3 G5.1 1928–1949
Dai, Bingham (Tai Ping-heng), 1899–.
'Culture and delusional systems of some Chinese patients.'
International j. of social psychiatry 11, 1 (Winter 1965), 59–69.
SUBJ 56 61 62 ▪ 41 46 65

21512 NIC F P3 G5.1 1928–1949
Dai, Bingham (Tai Ping-heng), 1899–.
'Obsessive-compulsive disorders in Chinese culture.'
Social problems 4, 4 (Apr. 1957), 313–321. [Reprinted in *Culture and mental health*, edited by Marvin Kaufmann Opler. (Selective entry.) New York: Macmillan, 1959, 243–255.]
SUBJ 56 61 ▪ 41 46 53

21513 NIC F P3 G5.1 1928–1949
Dai, Bingham (Tai Ping-heng), 1899–.
'Personality problems in Chinese culture.'
ASR 6, 5 (Oct. 1941), 688–696.
SUBJ 61 ▪ 41 46 47 56

21514 NIC S P1 G1.0 1911–1928
Hsiao, Hsiao Hung, 1898–.
'Mentality of the Chinese and Japanese.'
J. of applied psychology 13, 1 (Feb. 1929), 9–31.
SUBJ 61

21515 CSU F P3 G5.1 1928–1949
Hsu, Francis L. K. (Hsü Lang-kuang), 1909–.
'A brief report on the police co-operation in connection with mental cases in Peiping.' In *Social and psychological studies in neuropsychiatry in China*, edited by Richard Sherman Lyman, V- Maeker, and P. Liang (Liang Meng-chüan). [Selective entry]
Peiping: Peking Union Medical College, Division of Neuropsychiatry, 1939, 199–230.
SUBJ 22.1 56 61

21516 NIC O P1 G1.0 1911–1949
Hsu, Francis L. K. (Hsü Lang-kuang), 1909–.
'Suppression versus repression: A limited psychological interpretation of four cultures.'
Psychiatry 12, 3 (Aug. 1949), 223–242.
SUBJ 61 ▪ 46 53 60

21517 NIC O P3 G5.1 1911–1928
Ingram, J- H-.
'The pitiable condition of the insane in North China.'
CMJ 32, 2 (Mar. 1918), 153–154.
SUBJ 28 61

21518 MCH P P3 G9.4 1928–1949
Jacobs, Norman Gabriel, 1924–.
'The phantom slasher of Taipei: Mass hysteria in a non-Western society.'
Social problems 12, 3 (Winter 1965), 318–328.
SUBJ 61

21519 NIC O P1 G1.3 1928–1949
LaBarre, Weston, 1911–.
'Some observations on character structure in the Orient. 2, The Chinese.'
Psychiatry 9, 3 (Aug. 1946), 215–237; 9, 4 (Nov. 1946), 375–395.
SUBJ 61 ▪ 46 52 53 62 65

21520 NIC O P2 G9.4 1928–1949
Lin, Tsung-yi (Lin Tsung-i), 1920–.
'A study of the incidence of mental disorder in Chinese and other cultures.'
Psychiatry 16, 4 (Nov. 1953), 313–336.
SUBJ 56 61 ▪ 21 43 50 57 65

21521 NNC F P1 G1.0 1928–1949
May, Helen Selma.
A study of emotional expression among Chinese and Americans.
Unpublished masters thesis in Psychology, Columbia U., 1938. 59 p.
SUBJ 61

21522 NIC O P1 G9.0 1928–1949
Muensterberger, Warner, 1913–.
'Orality and dependence: Characteristics of southern Chinese.'
Psychoanalysis and the social sciences 3 (1951), 37–69.
SUBJ 46 53 61 ▪ 41 47 50

21523 NIC F P3 G5.1 1928–1949
Pai, T. (Pai Tuan), S. M. Sung (Sung Ssu-ming), and E. H. Hsu (Hsü En-hsi), 1911–.
'The application of Thurstone's personality schedule to Chinese subjects.'
J. of social psychology 8, 1 (Feb. 1937), 47–72.
SUBJ 61

21524 CSU F P1 G9.4 1928–1949
Rin, Hsien, and Tsung-yi Lin (Lin Tsung-i), 1920–.
'Mental illness among Formosan aborigines as compared with the Chinese in Taiwan.'
J. of mental science 108, 453 (Mar. 1962), 134–146.
SUBJ 56 61

21525 CSU O P1 G1.3 1911–1928
Ross, Robert M-.
'The insane in China: Examination hints.'
CMJ 34, 5 (Sept. 1920), 514–518.
SUBJ 56 61 ▪ 41 62

21526 CSU F P3 G5.1 1928–1949
Sung, S. M. (Sung Ssu-ming).
'Prediction on Chinese mental patients.' In *Social and psychological studies in neuropsychiatry in China*, edited by Richard Sherman Lyman, V- Maeker, and P. Liang (Liang Meng-chüan). [Selective entry]
Peiping: Peking Union Medical College, Division of Neuropsychiatry, 1939, 167–198.
SUBJ 56 61

21527 NIC F P1 G9.2 1928–1949
Weakland, John Hast, 1919–.
'An analysis of seven Cantonese films.' In *The study of culture at a distance*, edited by Margaret Mead and Rhoda Metraux. [Selective entry]
Chicago: U. of Chicago Press, 1953, 292–295.
SUBJ 31 61 ▪ 41 47

21528 NIC F P3 G6.1 1928–1949
Westbrook, Charles Hart, and Hsien-hwei Yao.
'Emotional stability of Chinese adolescents as measured by the Woodworth-Cady-Matthews questionnaire.'
J. of social psychology 8, 4 (Nov. 1937), 401–409.
SUBJ 61 ▪ 47 54

1911-1972
(including 1644-1972)

21529 CSU PO P3 G1.2 –1972
Bermann, Gregorio, 1894–.
'Mental health in China.' In *Psychiatry in the Communist world*, edited by Ari Kiev. [Sole entry]
New York: Science House, 1968, 223–261.
SUBJ 17 18 22.2 56 60 61 ▪ 12.1 12.2 38 46 50 52 55

21530 CSU FP P1 G1.0 –1972
Eberhard, Wolfram, 1909–.
'Chinesische Träume als soziologisches Quellenmaterial' (Chinese dreams as sociological source material).
Sociologus neue (2.) Folge 17, 1 (1967), 71–91. [Reprinted in *Moral and social values of the Chinese: Collected essays*, by W. Eberhard. (Selective entry.) Taipei: Chinese Materials and Research Aids Service Center, 1971, 97–134. (CMRASC occasional series, 6)]
SUBJ 61 62

21531 NIC F P3 G5.0 1928–1972
Hsu, E. H. (Hsü En-hsi), 1911–.
'The neurotic score as a function of culture.'

J. of social psychology 34, 1 (Aug. 1951), 3–30.
SUBJ 61

21532 NIC O P1 G1.0 –1972
Hsu, Francis L. K. (Hsü Lang-kuang), 1909–.
American and Chinese: Two ways of life.
New York: Henry Schuman, 1953. 457 p. [Reprinted—London: Cresset Press, 1955. 457 p.]
SUBJ 61 62 ▪ 17 40 55 64 65

21533 CSU S P1 G1.0 –1972
Hsu, Francis L. K. (Hsü Lang-kuang), 1909–.
'Psychosocial homeostasis and jen: Conceptual tools for advancing psychological anthropology.'
AA new (2nd) series 73, 1 (Feb. 1971), 23–44.
SUBJ 44 48 61 ▪ 41

21534 CSU F P2 G9.4 1928–1972
Lin, Tsung-yi (Lin Tsung-i), 1920–, et al.
'Mental disorders in Taiwan, fifteen years later: A preliminary report.' In *Mental health research in Asia and the Pacific*, edited by William A- Caudill and Tsung-yi Lin. [Selective entry]
Honolulu: East-West Center Press, 1969, 66–91.
SUBJ 56 61 ▪ 21.2 59

21535 NIC P P1 G1.0 –1972
McClelland, David Clarence, 1917–.
'Motivational patterns in Southeast Asia, with special reference to the Chinese case.'
J. of social issues 19, 1 (Jan. 1963), 6–19.
SUBJ 61 ▪ 53 64

21536 CSU U P1 G1.2 –1972
Metzger, Thomas Albert, 1933–.
'On Chinese political culture.' [Review of *Mao's revolution and the Chinese political culture*, by Richard Harvey Solomon.]
JAS 32, 1 (Nov. 1972), 101–105.
SUBJ 60 61 64 ▪ 12.1 17 53

21537 CSM P P2 G1.5 1928–1972
Rin, Hsien.
'Koro: A consideration on Chinese concepts of illness and case illustrations.'
Transcultural psychiatric research 15 (Oct. 1963), 23–30.
SUBJ 46 61 ▪ 56 59

21538 CSH FP P2 G1.1 –1972
Solomon, Richard Harvey, 1937–.
Mao's revolution and the Chinese political culture.
Berkeley, Los Angeles: U. of California Press, 1971. 19, 604 p. (Revision of *The Chinese Revolution and the politics of dependency: The struggle for change in a traditional political culture*, doctoral dissertation in Political Science, Massachusetts Institute of Technology, 1966)
SUBJ 32 41 48 53 60 61 ▪ 12 12.1 16 17 22 22.1 22.2 32.1 32.2 62

21539 MAM F P3 G1.0 1895–1972
Stover, Leon Eugene, 1929–.
'Face' and verbal analogues of interaction in Chinese culture: A theory of formalized social behavior based upon participant-observation of an upper class Chinese household, together with a biographical study of the primary informant.
Ann Arbor: University Microfilms (Publ. 62-5199), 1962. 404 p. (Doctoral dissertation in Anthropology, Columbia U.)
SUBJ 61 ▪ 63 64

21540 CSU S P1 G1.2 1928–1972
Taylor, Norman W-.
'Freudian theory and economic behavior in China and Japan.'
JCS 6 (1969), 107–115.
SUBJ 53 61 ▪ 34.2 63

21541 NIC P P1 G1.2 1928–1972
Weakland, John Hast, 1919–.
'Family imagery in a passage by Mao Tse-tung: An essay in psycho-cultural method.'
WP 10, 3 (Apr. 1958), 387–407.
SUBJ 61 62 64 ▪ 41 44 59

21542 NIC S P1 G1.0 –1972
Weakland, John Hast, 1919–.
'Orality in Chinese conceptions of male genital sexuality.'
Psychiatry 19, 3 (Aug. 1956), 237–247.
SUBJ 46 47 61 62 ▪ 52 53

21543 CSU O P1 G1.0 –1972
Weakland, John Hast, 1919–.
'The organization of action in Chinese culture.'
Psychiatry 13, 3 (Aug. 1950), 361–370.
SUBJ 48 61 ▪ 41 53

21544 CSU S P2 G1.1 1928–1972
Yap, Pow-meng (Yeh Pao-ming).
'Mental diseases peculiar to certain cultures: A survey of comparative psychiatry.'
J. of mental science 97, 407 (Apr. 1951), 313–327.
SUBJ 56 61 ▪ 46

21545 CSM O P1 G9.4 1928–1972
Yeh, Eng-kung (Yeh Ying-k'un).
'Case histories. Case 4, Taiwan.'
Transcultural research in mental health problems; review and newsletter 9 (Dec. 1960), 62–66.
SUBJ 56 61 ▪ 41 59

1949-1972

21546 CSU F P3 G1.0 1949–1972
Abbott, Kenneth Albert, 1927–.
Harmony and individualism: Changing Chinese psychosocial functioning in Taipei and San Francisco.
Taipei: Orient Cultural Service, 1970. 15, 374 p. (Asian Folklore and Social Life monographs, 12) (Doctoral dissertation; Dept of Social Work, U. of California, Berkeley) [Title of dissertation: *Cultural change, psychosocial functioning, and the family: A case study in the Chinese-American community of San Francisco*]
SUBJ 40 61 63 ▪ 41 42 48 53 62

21547 CSU O P3 G9.5 1949–1972
Anderson, Eugene Newton, Jr., 1941–.
'Some Chinese methods of dealing with crowding.'
Urban anthropology 1, 2 (Fall 1972), 141–150.
SUBJ 61 ▪ 41 48

21548 MCH O P2 G1.2 1949–1972
Arnault, Jacques, et al.
'Pourquoi, comment . . .' (Why and how).
Nouvelle critique 150 (nov. 1963), 39–82. [Special issue: *Chine où vas-tu?* (Whither China?)]
SUBJ 12.1 14.1 19 34.1 61 64 ▪ 14.4 32 47 66

21549 CSU O P3 G9.5 1949–1972
Cansdale, J. S., pseud.
'Cultural problems of Chinese students in a Western-type university.' In *Hong Kong: A society in transition*, edited by Ian C- Jarvie and Joseph Agassi. [Analytic entry]
New York: Praeger, 1969, 345–360.
SUBJ 17 54 61 66 ▪ 60

21550 NNC F P3 G9.5 1949–1972
Cheng, Irene (Cheng Ho Ai-ling).
'The development of the mental health movement in Hong Kong.'
Oversea education 34, 2 (July 1962), 63–70.
SUBJ 28 56 61 ▪ 17 38

21551 CSU F P1 G9.4 1949–1972
Chu, Cheng-ping (Ch'u Cheng-p'ing).
'The remodification of TAT [Thematic Apperception Test] adapted to Chinese primary school children. Part 1, Remodification of the pictures and setting up the objective scoring methods. Part 2, The application and evaluation of pictures.'
APT 10 (Mar. 1968), 59–89.
SUBJ 52 61

21552 MAM F P3 G9.4 1949–1972
Chu, Godwin C. (Chu Chien), 1927–.
Culture, personality and persuasibility.
Ann Arbor: University Microfilms (Publ. 64-7629), 1964. 178 p. (Doctoral dissertation in Mass Communications Research, Stanford U.)
SUBJ 61 ▪ 24.2 53 54

21553 CSU F P1 G9.4 1949–1972
Chu, Godwin C. (Chu Chien), 1927–.
'Fear arousal, efficacy, and imminency.'
J. of personality and social psychology 4, 5 (Nov. 1966), 517–524.
SUBJ 61

21554 [2]MCH O P3 G5.1 1949–1972
Coillie, Dries van, 1912–.
De enthousiaste zelfmoord (The enthusiastic suicide).
Antwerp: De Vlijt, 1958. 397 p.

J'ai subi le lavage de cerveau (I was brainwashed). Tr. by Catherine Michel and Pierre Grenaud.
Paris: Desclée de Brouwer, 1964. 325 p.

I was brainwashed in Peking.
's-Hertogenbosch, The Netherlands: Nederlandse Boekdruk Industrie, n.v., 1969. 320 p.
SUBJ 12.1 61 ▪ 33

21555 CSU F P2 G9.5 1949–1972
Dawson, John L-, et al.
'Scaling Chinese traditional-modern attitudes and the GSR measurement of "important" vs. "un-important" Chinese concepts.'

J. of cross-cultural psychology 2, 1 (Mar. 1971), 1–27.
SUBJ 53 61 62 ▪ 29

21556 CSU F P2 G9.4 1949–1972
Eberhard, Wolfram, 1909–.
'A comparison of dreams of San Francisco Chinese-Americans with dreams of Taiwanese.' In *Moral and social values of the Chinese: Collected essays*, by W. Eberhard. [Selective entry]
Taipei: Chinese Materials and Research Aids Service Center, 1971, 135–159. (CMRASC occasional series, 6)
SUBJ 40 60 61 ▪ 41 46 47 48 57 65

21557 CSU U P2 G1.1 1949–1972
Gittings, John, 1938–.
'Bringing up the Red Guards.' [Review of *Mao's revolution and the Chinese political culture*, by Richard Harvey Solomon.]
NYRB 17, 10 (16 Dec. 1971), 13–17.
SUBJ 61 64 ▪ 16.3 53 54

21558 CSM F P3 G9.5 1949–1972
Goodnow, Robert E-.
'Study of Chinese personality.'
Transcultural research in mental health problems; review and newsletter 12 (Apr. 1962), 22–24.
SUBJ 61

21559 CSU F P1 G1.0 1949–1972
Hiniker, Paul James, 1938–.
'Chinese reactions to forced compliance: Dissonance reduction or national character.'
J. of social psychology 77, 2 (Apr. 1969), 157–176.
SUBJ 61

21560 MCH S P1 G1.2 1949–1972
Hinkle, Lawrence Earle, Jr., 1889–, and Harold George Wolff, 1898–.
'Communist interrogation and indoctrination of "enemies of the states": Analysis of methods used by the Communist state police.'
American Medical Assn. archives of neurology and psychiatry 76, 2 (Aug. 1956), 115–174.
SUBJ 12.1 53 61 ▪ 12 12.2 32 55 56 64 66

21561 MBM F P2 G9.4 1949–1972
Hsu, Chen-chin.
'Child psychiatric service.'
Acta paediatrica Sinica 9, 2 (1968), 71–79.
SUBJ 54 56 61 ▪ 17 28

21562 CSU O P3 G9.4 1949–1972
Hsu, Chen-chin, and Tsung-yi Lin (Lin Tsung-i), 1920–.
'A mental health program at the elementary school level in Taiwan: A six-year review of the East-Gate Project [East-Gate Elementary School, Taipei].' In *Mental health research in Asia and the Pacific*, edited by William A- Caudill and Tsung-yi Lin. [Selective entry]
Honolulu: East-West Center Press, 1969, 178–194.
SUBJ 27 37 61

21563 NNC PO P1 G1.2 1949–1972
Hunter, Edward, 1902–.
Brainwashing in Red China: The calculated destruction of men's minds, enl. ed.
New York: Vanguard Press, 1953. 341 p.
SUBJ 12.1 17 60 61 64 ▪ 13 14.5 15 41 46 47 50 53 54 66

21564 CSH F P3 G9.4 1949–1972
Hwang, Chien-hou (Huang Chien-hou).
'Parent-child resemblance in psychological characteristics.'
Psychology and education (Taipei) 3 (Dec. 1969), 29–36.
SUBJ 41 61 ▪ 47

21565 CSH F P3 G9.4 1949–1972
Hwang, Chien-hou (Huang Chien-hou).
'Reactions of Chinese university students in Rosenzweig's picture-frustration study.'
Psychology and education (Taipei) 2 (Dec. 1968), 37–48.
SUBJ 61 ▪ 47 54

21566 CSH F P3 G9.4 1949–1972
Hwang, Chien-hou (Huang Chien-hou).
'A study of the personal preferences of Chinese university students by Edwards Personal Preference Schedule.'
Psychology and education (Taipei) 1 (Apr. 1967), 52–67.
SUBJ 61 ▪ 47 54

21567 CSU F P2 G9.4 1949–1972
Ko, Yung-ho (K'o Yung-ho), and Li-huei Lin.
'The relationships between personality and ordinal positions among university students.'
APT 8 (Mar. 1966), 29–37.
SUBJ 41 54 61

21568 CSU F P3 G9.4 1949–1972
Ko, Yung-ho (K'o Yung-ho), and Long-chu Sun (Sun Lung-chu).
'Ordinal position and the behavior of [patients] visiting the child guidance clinic.'
APT 7 (Mar. 1965), 10–16; 8 (Mar. 1966), 92–95.
SUBJ 41 61 ▪ 52

21569 CSU P P1 G1.2 1949–1972
Lifton, Robert Jay, 1926–.
Revolutionary immortality: Mao Tse-tung and the Chinese Cultural Revolution.
New York: Random House, 1968. 178 p.
SUBJ 61 62 64 ▪ 12.1 15 16.1 19 22.2 54 59

21570 NNC FP P1 G1.2 1949–1972
Lifton, Robert Jay, 1926–.
Thought reform and the psychology of totalism: A study of 'brainwashing' in China.
New York: Norton, 1961. 10, 510 p.
SUBJ 12.1 48 53 61 62 63 ▪ 14 16.1 17 50 66

21571 CSU F P3 G9.4 1949–1972
Lin, Pi-fong (Lin Pi-feng), and Fang Yen.
'A study of psychological after-effect of the contraceptive operation of tubal ligation.'
APT 10 (Mar. 1968), 90–104.
SUBJ 51 61 ▪ 47 56

21572 NIC O P1 G9.4 1949–1972
Lin, Tsung-yi (Lin Tsung-i), 1920–.
'Evolution of mental health programme in Taiwan.'
American j. of psychiatry 117, 11 (May 1961), 961–971.
SUBJ 56 61 ▪ 17 28

21573 CSU F P3 G9.0 1949–1972
Liu, Phyllis Y. H. (Liu Yung-ho), and Gerald M- Meredith.
'Personality structure of Chinese college students in Taiwan and Hong Kong.'
J. of social psychology 70, 1 (Oct. 1966), 165–166.
SUBJ 16.1 61 ▪ 54

21574 GMS FP P3 G9.5 1949–1972
Mäding, Klaus.
Wirtschaftswachstum und Kulturwandel in Hongkong: Ein Beitrag zur Wirtschafts- und Sozialpsychologie der Hongkong-Chinesen (Economic growth and cultural change in Hong Kong: The economic and social psychology of the Hong Kong Chinese).
Cologne: Westdeutscher Verlag, 1964. 76 p. (Das Land Nordrhein-Westfalen, Forschungsberichte, 1326)
SUBJ 21.4 26.4 40 61 66 ▪ 17 21.3 24.2 24.3 24.4 28 72

21575 CSU FP P3 G9.0 1949–1972
Mitchell, Robert Edward, 1930–.
Levels of emotional strain in Southeast Asian cities: A study of individual responses to the stresses of urbanization and industrialization [in Hong Kong, with comparison data from Taipei and other Southeast Asian cities].
Taipei: Orient Cultural Service, 1972. 2 vols. 30, 605 p. [c.p.]. (Asian Folklore and Social Life monographs, 27–28)
SUBJ 21.1 21.2 26 48 61 ▪ 21.4 23 28 34.2 41 42 47 50 55 60

21576 CSU F P3 G9.5 1949–1972
Mitchell, Robert Edward, 1930–, and Irene Lo.
'Implications of changes in family authority relations for the development of independence and assertiveness in Hong Kong children.'
AS 8, 4 (Apr. 1968), 309–322.
SUBJ 53 61 ▪ 41 52

21577 MAM FP P3 G9.4 1949–1972
Olsen, Stephen Milton, 1940–.
Family, occupation and values in a Chinese urban community [Taipei].
Ann Arbor: University Microfilms (Publ. 72-8982), 1972. 13, 273 p. (Doctoral dissertation in Sociology, Cornell U., 1971)
SUBJ 21.4 26 60 61 ▪ 41

21578 NIC O P3 G9.5 1949–1972
Priestley, Kenneth Ewart, and Beryl Robina Wright.
Mental health and education in Hong Kong.
Hong Kong: Hong Kong U. Press, 1956. 97 p.
SUBJ 17 28 56 61 ▪ 22.2 41 66

21579 CSU PO P2 G1.1 1949–1972
Pye, Lucian Wilmot, 1921–.
The spirit of Chinese politics: A psycho-cultural study of the authority crisis in political development.
Cambridge: M.I.T. Press, 1968. 22, 255 p.
SUBJ 30 41 53 60, 61 63 ▪ 12 12.1 16.1 44 48 56 64

21580 CSM F P3 G9.4 1949–1972
Rin, Hsien.
'Family study of Chinese schizophrenic patients: Loss of parents, sibling rank,

parental attitude and short-term prognosis.'
Transcultural psychiatric research 2 (Apr. 1965), 24–27.
SUBJ 41 61 ▪ 56

21581 CSU FP P3 G9.4 1949–1972
Rin, Hsien.
'Sibling rank, culture, and mental disorders.' In *Mental health research in Asia and the Pacific*, edited by William A- Caudill and Tsung-yi Lin (Lin Tsung-i). [Selective entry]
Honolulu: East-West Center Press, 1969, 105–113.
SUBJ 41 61 ▪ 53

21582 CSM P P3 G9.4 1949–1972
Rin, Hsien.
'Two forms of vital deficiency syndrome among Chinese male mental patients.'
Transcultural psychiatric research 3 (Apr. 1966), 19–21.
SUBJ 61 ▪ 46 56 59

21583 CSM F P8 G9.4 1949–1972
Rin, Hsien, Hung-ming Chu, and Tsung-yi Lin (Lin Tsung-i), 1920–.
'Psychophysiological reactions of a rural and suburban population in Taiwan.'
Transcultural psychiatric research 3 (Oct. 1966), 98–101.
SUBJ 56 61 ▪ 26 47

21584 NIC O P3 G9.4 1949–1972
Rin, Hsien, Chen-chin Hsu, and Sau-lien Liu.
'The characteristics of paranoid reaction in present-day Taiwan.'
Memoirs of the College of Medicine, National Taiwan U. 5, 1/2 (Jan. 1958), 1–15.
SUBJ 41 56 61 ▪ 21.2 46 47

21585 NNC O P2 G1.2 1949–1972
Schein, Edgar Henry, Inge Schneier, and Curtis H- Barker.
Coercive persuasion: A socio-psychological analysis of the 'brainwashing' of American civilian prisoners by the Chinese Communists.
New York: Norton, 1961. 320 p. [Reprinted—Bombay: Asia Publishing House, 1962. 320 p.]
SUBJ 12.1 12.2 61 ▪ 12 32 48 60 64 66

21586 MAM F P3 G9.5 1949–1972
Scilligo, Pio Felix, 1928–.
The persuasibility of upper elementary parochial school children in several cultural groups.
Ann Arbor: University Microfilms (Publ. 68-11,347), 1968. 170 p. (Doctoral dissertation in Education, Stanford U.)
SUBJ 52 61 ▪ 41 48

21587 CSU P P1 G1.2 1949–1972
Sheridan, Mary, 1938–.
'The emulation of heroes.'
CQ 33 (Jan.–Mar. 1968), 47–72.
SUBJ 12.1 61 ▪ 54

21588 NIC F P3 G9.4 1949–1972
Su, Hsiang-yu (Su Hsiang-yü), and Kuo-shu Yang, 1932–.
'Self-concept congruence in relation to juvenile delinquency.'
APT 6 (Mar. 1964), 1–9.
SUBJ 22.2 54 61

21589 NNC P P5 G1.2 1949–1972
Ts'ao Jih-ch'ang and Li Chia-chih.
'Industrial psychology in China.' Tr. from *Hsin li hsüeh pao* 4 (Sept. 1959), 204–213. In *Articles on psychology in Communist China*, mimeo., compiled by U.S. Joint Publications Research Service. [Sole entry]
Washington, D.C.: JPRS, 21 June 1960, 18–37. (JPRS 3424; MC 11,441/1960)
SUBJ 61 ▪ 16.4

21590 CSM P P3 G9.4 1949–1972
Tseng, Wen-Shing, and Jing Hsu.
'Chinese culture, personality formation and mental illness.'
Transcultural psychiatric research 6 (Oct. 1969), 139–141.
SUBJ 52 61 ▪ 41 46 56

21591 CSU P P2 G1.2 1949–1972
Tung, Constantine.
'The Communist anxiety: A study of two Chinese plays.'
Modern drama 12, 2 (Sept. 1969), 124–134.
SUBJ 60 61 64 ▪ 31 32.1

21592 CSU F P3 G9.4 1949–1972
Wang, May-Jane (Wang Mei-chen).
'Report on the revision of the Thematic Apperception Test.'
APT 11 (Mar. 1969), 24–41.
SUBJ 61

21593 CSU PO P1 G1.2 1949–1972
Welch, Holmes Hinkley, 1921–.
'The Chinese art of make-believe.'
Encounter 30, 5 (May 1968), 8–13.
SUBJ 61 ▪ 33 54

21594 MAM S P1 G1.2 1949–1972
Windemiller, Duane Arlo, 1918–.
The psychodynamics of change in religious conversion and Communist brainwashing, with particular reference to the 18th century evangelical revival and the Chinese thought control movement.
Ann Arbor: University Microfilms (Publ. 60-3492), 1960. 186 p. (Doctoral dissertation in Religion, Boston U.)
SUBJ 12.1 16.1 53 61 ▪ 17 32 55 63 64

21595 NIC F P2 G9.4 1949–1972
Yang, Kuo-shu, 1932–, et al.
'Wo kuo cheng ch'ang ch'eng jen tsai Lo-hsia mo chih ts'e yen shang fan ying. [1], Mo chih ch'ü wei chih hua fen' (Rorschach responses of normal Chinese adults. Part 1, The normal details). [In Chinese]
APT 4 (Mar. 1962), 78–103.
'Part 2, The popular responses.'
J. of social psychology 60, 2 (Aug. 1963), 175–186.
'[3] Fan ying shu liang yü hui chüeh shu liang' (Part 3, The number of responses and number of refusals). [In Chinese]
Psychological testing 10 (1963), 127–136.
'Part 4, The speed of production.'
APT 7 (Mar. 1965), 34–51.
SUBJ 61 ▪ 63

21596 MAU O P1 G9.5 1949–1972
Yap, Pow-meng (Yeh Pao-ming).
'Ideas of mental health and disorder in Hong Kong and their practical influence.' In *Some traditional Chinese ideas and conceptions in Hong Kong social life today*, edited by Marjorie Doreen Topley. [Analytic entry]
Hong Kong: Royal Asiatic Society, Hong Kong Branch, 1967, 73–85.
SUBJ 61 62 65

21597 CSU F P3 G9.5 1949–1972
Yap, Pow-meng (Yeh Pao-ming).
'Phenomenology of affective disorder in Chinese and other cultures.' In *Transcultural psychiatry*, edited by Anthony V- S- de Reuck and Ruth Porter. [Sole entry]
Boston: Little, Brown, 1965, 84–107.
SUBJ 61 ▪ 47 57

21598 CSU F P3 G9.5 1949–1972
Yap, Pow-meng (Yeh Pao-ming).
'The possession syndrome: A comparison of Hong Kong and French findings.'
J. of mental science 106, 442 (Jan. 1960), 114–137.
SUBJ 23 61 65 ▪ 26 47

21599 CSM F P2 G9.4 1949–1972
Yeh, Eng-kung (Yeh Ying-k'un), et al.
'Some psychiatric findings of the college students in Taiwan.'
Transcultural psychiatric research 6 (Oct. 1969), 142–145.
SUBJ 54 61 ▪ 56

21600 CSU F P3 G9.4 1949–1972
Yeh, Eng-kung (Yeh Ying-k'un), et al.
'Student mental health: An epidemiological study in Taiwan.'
APT 14 (Mar. 1972), 1–25.
SUBJ 54 56 61

62 COGNITION

認知 認知

1644-1911

21601 MCH P P1 G1.0 –1895
Review of 'Die Arithmetik der Chinesen' (Chinese arithmetic), by Karl L- Biernatzki.
Nouvelles annales de mathématiques 2e série 8 (1862), 35–44; 2 (1863), 529–540.
SUBJ 62 ▪ 66

21602 CBU S P2 G1.1 –1895
'Feng Shui: A review.' [Review of *Feng-shui: or, The rudiments of natural science in China*, by Ernest John Eitel.]
China review 2, 1 (July–Aug. 1873), 34–40.
SUBJ 62

21603 MCH P P3 G1.1 1842–1911
Bennett, Adrian Arthur, III, 1941–.
John Fryer: The introduction of Western science and technology into nineteenth-century China.
Cambridge: Harvard U., East Asian Research Center, 1967. 157 p. (Harvard East Asian monographs, 24)
SUBJ 37 62 ▪ 17 66

21604 CSU P P1 G1.2 –1842
Bernard, Henri, 1897–.
'Les étapes de la cartographie scientifique pour la Chine et les pays voisins depuis le XVIe siècle jusqu'à la fin du XVIIIe siècle' (The stages in the scientific mapping of China and neighboring

countries from the sixteenth century to the end of the eighteenth century).
MS 1, 2 (1935), 425–477.
Subj 62 ▪ 66

21605 CSU P P1 G1.0 –1895
Biernatzki, Karl L-.
'Die Arithmetik der Chinesen' (Chinese arithmetic).
J. für die reine und angewandte Mathematik 52, 1 (1856), 59–94.
Subj 62

21606 NNC P P1 G1.2 1842–1895
Boardman, Eugene Powers, 1910–.
'Millenary aspects of the Taiping Rebellion, 1851–64.' In *Millenial dreams in action*, edited by Sylvia Lettice Thrupp. [Sole entry]
The Hague: Mouton, 1962, 70–79.
Subj 23 32.2 62 ▪ 19 64

21607 NNC P P1 G1.0 –1911
Bodde, Derk, 1909–.
'Evidence for "laws of nature" in Chinese thought.' [Review of *Science and civilisation in China, Vol. 2, History of scientific thought*, by Noël Joseph Terence Montgomery Needham.] [With a reply by Needham]
HJAS 20, 3/4 (Dec. 1957), 709–727.
Subj 62

21608 NNC P P1 G1.0 –1911
Bodde, Derk, 1909–.
'Harmony and conflict in Chinese philosophy.' In *Studies in Chinese thought*, edited by Arthur Frederick Wright. [Selective entry]
Chicago: U. of Chicago Press, 1953, 19–80. (American Anthropological Assn. memoirs, 75)
Subj 62 63 ▪ 64

21609 NIC P P1 G1.2 –1911
Bodde, Derk, 1909–.
'Types of Chinese categorical thinking.'
JAOS 59, 2 (June 1939), 200–219.
Subj 12 59 62 63 ▪ 16.1

21610 NNC F P2 G1.3 1644–1911
Boerschmann, Ernst, 1873–1949.
'K'ueising-Türme und Fengshui-Säulen' (*K'uei-hsing* towers and *feng-shui* pillars).
Asia Major 2, 3/4 (July–Oct. 1925), 503–530.
Subj 23 55 62 ▪ 13 21.3

21611 NNC FP P2 G1.3 –1911
Boerschmann, Ernst, 1873–1949.
'Steinlöwen in China' (Stone lions in China).
Sinica 13, 5/6 (Aug.–Nov. 1938), 217–224.
Subj 62 ▪ 65

21612 NNC P P1 G1.3 –1911
Cammann, Schuyler, 1912–.
'Types of symbols in Chinese art.' In *Studies in Chinese thought*, edited by Arthur Frederick Wright. [Selective entry]
Chicago: U. of Chicago Press, 1953, 195–231. (American Anthropological Assn. memoirs, 75)
Subj 62 65 ▪ 13 23

21613 ELO U P1 G1.1 –1911
Carus, Paul, 1852–1919.
Chinese thought: An exposition of the main characteristic features of the Chinese world conception.
Chicago: Open Court, 1907. 195 p.
Subj 23 62 65 ▪ 61

21614 CSU P P1 G1.0 –1911
Chan, Wing-tsit (Ch'en Jung-chieh), 1901–.
'The evolution of the Neo-Confucian concept "li" as principle.'
THJ new (2nd) series 4, 2 (Feb. 1964), 123–148.
Subj 62

21615 MCH S P1 G1.3 1842–1895
Chesneaux, Jean, 1922–.
'Le millénarisme des Taiping' (The millenarianism of the Taipings). [Review of 'Millenary aspects of the Taiping Rebellion, 1851–64', by Eugene Powers Boardman.]
Archives de sociologie des religions 16 (juil.–déc. 1963), 122–124.
Subj 62 ▪ 32.2 66

21616 GHU P P1 G1.0 –1911
Cho, Kah Kyung, 1927–.
Die Bedeutung der Natur in der chinesischen Gedankenwelt (The significance of nature in traditional Chinese thought).
Unpublished doctoral dissertation, Philosophische Fakultät, Universität Heidelberg, 1956. 118 p.
Subj 62 ▪ 63

21617 FPN P P1 G1.2 –1895
Chochod, Louis Simon Fortuné Frédéric, 1877–.
Occultisme et magie en Extrême-Orient (Occultism and magic in the Far East).
Paris: Payot, 1945. 404 p.
Subj 23 60 62 ▪ 65

21618 MBA P P7 G8.2 –1911
Cordier, Charles Georges, 1872–1936.
'La divination chinoise' (Chinese divination).
RI nouvelle (2e) série 11, 10 (oct. 1909), 1033–1041; 11, 11 (nov. 1909), 1135–1140; 11, 12 (déc. 1909), 1241–1243; 16, 12 (déc. 1911), 638–653; 17, 5 (mai 1912), 484–491.
Subj 62

21619 FPN P P1 G1.1 –1911
Demiéville, Paul, 1894–.
'Les premiers contacts philosophiques entre la Chine et l'Europe.'
Diogène 58 (avr.–juin 1967), 81–110.

'The first philosophic contacts between Europe and China.' Tr. by Martin Faigel.
Diogenes 58 (Summer 1967), 75–103.
Subj 62 66 ▪ 16.1 64 70

21620 CSU P P1 G1.2 1644–1895
Drake, Fred William, 1939–.
'A mid-nineteenth-century discovery of the non-Chinese world [*Ying-huan chih-lüeh* (Brief survey of the maritime circuit), by Hsü Chi-yü].'
MAS 6, 2 (Apr. 1972), 205–224.
Subj 62 66 ▪ 59 64

21621 ELO O P1 G6.1 1842–1895
Du Bose, Hampden C-.
The dragon, image and demon: or, The three religions of China, Confucianism, Buddhism and Taoism . . .
New York: A. C. Armstrong, 1887. 468 p.
Subj 62 65 ▪ 13 33 43 56 57

21622 CSU P P1 G1.4 1842–1895
Edkins, Joseph, 1823–1905.
'The books of the modern religious sects in North China.'
CR 19, 6 (June 1888), 261–268; 19, 7 (July 1888), 302–310.
Subj 33 62 63

21623 MCH O P2 G1.3 1842–1895
Edkins, Joseph, 1823–1905.
'Feng shui.'
CR 4, 10 (Mar. 1872), 274–277; 4, 11 (Apr. 1872), 291–298; 4, 12 (May 1872), 316–320.
Subj 62 ▪ 57

21624 NNC O P2 G1.2 1842–1895
Edkins, Joseph, 1823–1905.
Religion in China, 4th ed.
London: Kegan Paul, Trench, Trübner, 1893. 20, 260 p.
Subj 33 43 60 62 ▪ 13 23 57 66

21625 NIC S P1 G1.0 1644–1911
Edmunds, Charles Keyser, 1876–1949.
Science among the Chinese: Some aspects of the Chinese conception of the universe as compared with modern scientific knowledge.
Shanghai: ——, 1911. 33 p.
Subj 62 ▪ 16.1 17

21626 NIC PO P2 G1.1 –1895
Eitel, Ernest John, 1838–1908.
Feng-shui: or, The rudiments of natural science in China.
Hong Kong: Lane, Crawford, 1873. 84 p.
Subj 62 ▪ 63

21627 NNC U P1 G1.3 –1895
Feigl, Hermann.
'Die Religion der Chinesen' (Chinese religion).
Oesterreichische Monatsschrift für den Orient 21 (1895), 41–51, 74–84, 101–112; 22 (1896), 1–12.
Subj 13 23 62 ▪ 33 43 63

21628 CSU O P7 G6.1 1895–1911
Fink, Carl.
'The Sicawei [i.e., Zikawei] Observatory [Hsü-chia-hui, Shanghai].'
EAM 1 (1902), 350–377.
Subj 17 62 ▪ 33 47

21629 CSU P P2 G1.3 1644–1895
Foster, John, 1898–.
'The Christian origins of the Taiping Rebellion.'
International review of missions 40, 158 (Apr. 1951), 156–167.
Subj 62 ▪ 32.2

21630 NNC P P1 G1.3 –1911
Franke, Otto, 1863–1946.
'Der kosmische Gedanke in Philosophie und im Staat der Chinesen' (The cosmos as conceptualized in Chinese philosophy and political thought). In *Aus Kultur und Geschichte Chinas* (Chinese culture and history), by O. Franke. [Selective entry]

Peiping: Deutschland-Institut, 1945, 271–312.
SUBJ 62 64 ▪ 12 13

21631 CSU P P8 G5.1 –1842
Freeman, Mansfield.
'Yen Hsi Chai, a 17th century philosopher.'
JRAS-NCB new (2nd) series 57 (1926), 70–91.
SUBJ 59 62

21632 CSU P P1 G1.2 –1911
Gardner, Charles Sidney, 1900–.
Chinese traditional historiography.
Cambridge: Harvard U. Press, 1938. 124 p. (Harvard historical monographs, 1) [Reprinted—Cambridge: Harvard U. Press, 1961. 11, 124 p. (Slightly rev.)]
SUBJ 62 70 ▪ 12

21633 MCH P P1 G1.2 –1911
Gieseler, ———.
'Le mythe du dragon en Chine' (The dragon myth in China).
R. archéologique 5e série 6 (juil.–oct. 1917), 104–170.
SUBJ 62 ▪ 43

21634 MSE P P2 G1.1 –1911
Giles, Herbert Allen, 1845–1935.
Adversaria Sinica.
Shanghai: Kelly and Walsh, 1914. 438 p.
SUBJ 62 ▪ 47 55 56

21635 NIC O P1 G1.3 –1911
Giles, Herbert Allen, 1845–1935.
'Palmistry in China.'
Nineteenth century and after 56, 334 (Dec. 1904), 985–988.
SUBJ 62

21636 CSU P P1 G1.1 –1842
Goodrich, Luther Carrington, 1894–.
'China's first knowledge of the Americas.'
GR 28, 3 (July 1938), 400–411.
SUBJ 62

21637 MCH P P1 G1.0 –1911
Granet, Marcel, 1884–1940.
'La droite et la gauche en Chine' (Right and left in China).
B. de l'Institut français de sociologie 3, 3 (juin 1933), 87–116. [Reprinted in *Etudes sociologiques sur la Chine* (Sociological studies on China), by M. Granet. (Selective entry.) Paris: Presses universitaires, 1953, 261–278.]
SUBJ 62

21638 FPN P P1 G1.0 –1644
Granet, Marcel, 1884–1940.
'Quelques particularités de la langue et de la pensée chinoises' (Special characteristics of Chinese language and thought).
R. philosophique 89 (mars–avr. 1920), 98–128, 161–195. [Reprinted in *Etudes sociologiques sur la Chine* (Sociological studies on China), by M. Granet. (Selective entry.) Paris: Presses universitaires, 1953, 95–157.]
SUBJ 62

21639 NIC P P1 G1.1 –1895
Groot, Jan Jakob Maria de, 1854–1921.
'Miséricorde envers les animaux dans le bouddhisme chinois' (Compassion for animals in Chinese Buddhism).
TP 3, 5 (1892), 466–489.
SUBJ 62 63 ▪ 33 55

21640 NIC PO P1 G1.2 –1895
Groot, Jan Jakob Maria de, 1854–1921.
'On Chinese divination by dissecting written characters.'
TP 1, 3 (oct. 1890), 239–247.
SUBJ 62 65

21641 NIC FP P1 G1.1 –1911
Groot, Jan Jakob Maria de, 1854–1921.
Religion in China: Universism, a key to the study of Taoism and Confucianism.
New York: Putnam, 1912. 15, 327 p.
SUBJ 62 63 ▪ 13 23 33

21642 NNC FP P1 G1.3 –1911
Groot, Jan Jakob Maria de, 1854–1921.
Universismus, die Grundlage der Religion und Ethik, des Staatswesens und der Wissenschaften Chinas (Monism, the basis of religion and ethics, state affairs, and sciences in China).
Berlin: Reimer, 1918. 404 p.
SUBJ 13 33 62 63 64 ▪ 23 43

21643 MCH PO P1 G1.2 –1842
Grosier, Jean-Baptiste Gabriel Alexandre, 1743–1823.
'De la religion des Chinois' (Chinese religion). In *De la Chine: description générale de cet empire* (A comprehensive description of the Chinese empire), by J.-B. G. A. Grosier. [Sole entry]
Paris: Pillet, 1819, vol. 4, part 9, 366–508.
SUBJ 62 ▪ 13 66

21644 FPN P P2 G1.2 –1842
Halde, Jean Baptiste du, 1674–1743.
Description géographique, historique, chronologique, politique, et physique de l'empire de la Chine (A geographic, historical, chronological, political, and physical description of the Chinese empire).
Paris: P. G. Lemercier, 1735. 4 vols.

A description of the Empire of China.
London: E. Cave, 1738. 2 vols. 11 & 12, 678; 388 p. [A different tr.—*The general history of China.* Tr. by R- Brookes. London: J. Watts, 1741. 4 vols. 509; 438; 496; 464 p.] [Reprinted—New York: AMS Press, 1972. 2 vols. 11 & 12, 678; 388 p.]
SUBJ 12 16.1 29 56 62 ▪ 13 14.1 14.3 15 41 57

21645 FPN P P1 G1.3 –1895
Harlez, Charles Joseph de, 1832–1899.
'Shēn-Siēn-Shū', le livre des esprits et des immortels: essai de mythologie chinoise (*Shen hsien shu*, the book of spirits and immortals: An essay on Chinese mythology).
Brussels: Hayez, 1893. 492 p.
SUBJ 23 62 ▪ 13 65

21646 CSU S P1 G1.2 –1842
Hiortdahl, T-.
'Chinesische Alchemie' (Chinese alchemy). In *Beiträge aus der Geschichte der Chemie dem Gedächtnis von Georg W. A. Kahlbaum gewidmet* (History of chemistry, dedicated to the memory of Georg Wilhelm August Kahlbaum), edited by Paul Diergart. [Sole entry]
Vienna: Franz Deuticke, 1909, 215–226.
SUBJ 62 ▪ 56

21647 CSU P P1 G1.2 –1911
Ho Peng-yoke and Ang Tian-se.
'Chinese astronomical records on comets and "guest stars" in the official histories of Ming and Ch'ing and other supplementary sources.'
OE 17, 1/2 (Dez. 1970), 63–99.
SUBJ 62

21648 CSU P P1 G1.3 1842–1911
Howard, Richard Campbell, 1925–.
'K'ang Yu-wei (1858–1927): His intellectual background and early thought.' In *Confucian personalities*, edited by Arthur Frederick Wright and Denis Crispin Twitchett. [Sole entry]
Stanford: Stanford U. Press, 1962, 294–316. [For fuller treatment, see entry 21272.]
SUBJ 59 62 64 ▪ 44 57 61 66

21649 CSU P P1 G1.1 1842–1911
Hsiao, Kung-chuan (Hsiao Kung-ch'üan), 1897–.
'The philosophical thought of K'ang Yu-wei: An attempt at a new synthesis.'
MS 21 (1962), 129–193.
SUBJ 62 ▪ 63

21650 NIC P P1 G1.0 –1911
Hu Shih, 1891–1962.
'The scientific spirit and method in Chinese philosophy.' In *Philosophy and culture, East and West*, edited by Charles Alexander Moore. [Selective entry]
Honolulu: U. of Hawaii Press, 1962, 199–222. [Reprinted in *The Chinese mind*, edited by C. A. Moore. (Selective entry.) Honolulu: U. of Hawaii Press, 1967, 104–131.]
SUBJ 62

21651 NNC O P1 G1.3 –1895
Hubrig, ———.
'Fung Schui, oder chinesische Geomantie' (Feng-shui, or Chinese geomancy).
ZE 11 (18 Jan. 1879), 34–43. [Supplement: *Verhandlungen der Berliner Gesellschaft für Anthropologie, Ethnologie und Urgeschichte* (Proceedings of the Berlin Society for Anthropology, Ethnology and Early History)] [Reprinted—*Allgemeine Missions-Z.* 7, 1 (Jan. 1880), 16–28.]
SUBJ 62 ▪ 23 55

21652 NNP O P2 G1.2 1842–1895
Ivanova, Elisaveta.
'Kitai' (China).
Russkaia rech' 1881, 8 (avgust), 175–202; 1881, 9 (sentiabr'), 128–147; 1881, 10 (oktiabr'), 51–87; 1881, 11 (noiabr'), 50–78; 1881, 12 (dekabr'), 59–75.
SUBJ 12.2 33 41 55 57 62 ▪ 14 16.1 17 47 61

21653 NNC P P1 G1.2 1644–1842
Kahn, Harold Lionel, 1930–.
'Some mid-Ch'ing views of the monarchy.'
JAS 24, 2 (Feb. 1965), 229–243.
SUBJ 62 ▪ 16.1

21654 NIC P P1 G1.0 –1895
Kühnert, Franz.
'Der chinesische Kalender' (The Chinese calendar).
TP 2, 1 (avr. 1891), 49–80.
SUBJ 62

21655 CSU O P5 G1.3 1842–1895
La Gravière, Jurien de, 1812–1892.
Voyage en Chine et dans les mers et archipels de cet empire pendant les années 1847–1850, Vol. 1 (A journey in China and through the seas and archipelagos of that empire from 1847 to 1850, Vol. 1).
Paris: Charpentier, 1854. 396 p.
SUBJ 12 14.3 24.3 33 62 ▪ 25 26.1 26.4 64

21656 MCH P P1 G1.1 –1895
Legge, James, 1815–1897.
The notions of the Chinese concerning God and spirits.
Hong Kong: Hong Kong Register, 1852. 161 p.
SUBJ 13 43 62 ▪ 23

21657 NNC P P1 G1.2 –1895
Legge, James, 1815–1897.
The religions of China: Confucianism and Taoism described and compared with Christianity.
New York: Scribner, 1881. 11, 308 p. [Reprinted—New York: Paragon, 1972. 11, 308 p.]
SUBJ 13 33 62 63 ▪ 16.1 41 43 47 48 64

21658 CSU P P1 G1.1 1644–1895
Leonard, Jane Kate, 1939–.
'Chinese overlordship and western penetration in maritime Asia: A late Ch'ing reappraisal of Chinese maritime relations [*Hai-kuo t'u-chih* (Illustrated treatise on overseas kingdoms), by Wei Yüan].'
MAS 6, 2 (Apr. 1972), 151–174. [For fuller treatment, see entry 21659.]
SUBJ 62 66

21659 MAM P P1 G1.1 1644–1895
Leonard, Jane Kate, 1939–.
Wei Yüan and the 'Hai-kuo t'u-chih' [Illustrated treatise on overseas kingdoms]*: A geopolitical analysis of western expansion in maritime Asia.*
Ann Arbor: University Microfilms (Publ. 71-24,517), 1971. 215 p. (Doctoral dissertation in History, Cornell U.)
SUBJ 62 66 ▪ 59 64 72

21660 CSU S P1 G1.1 1644–1911
Levenson, Joseph Richmond, 1920–1969.
'The abortiveness of empiricism in early Ch'ing thought.' In *Confucian China and its modern fate, Vol. 1, The problem of intellectual continuity*, by J. R. Levenson. [Analytic entry]
Berkeley, Los Angeles: U. of California Press, 1966, 3–14. [Revision of article with same title in *FEQ* 13, 2 (Feb. 1954), 155–165.]
SUBJ 62 ▪ 60

21661 FPN PO P1 G6.0 1644–1842
Longobardi, Nicolas.
Traité sur quelques points de la religion des Chinois (A treatise on some aspects of Chinese religion).
Paris: Guérin, 1701. 100 p.
SUBJ 13 62 66 ▪ 16.1 17 23 64

21662 CSU P P1 G1.3 –1911
Martin, William Alexander Parsons, 1827–1916.
'Alchemy in China, the source of chemistry.' In *The lore of Cathay: or, The intellect of China*, by W. A. P. Martin. [Selective entry]
New York: Revell, 1901, 44–71. [Reprinted in *The lore of Cathay: or, The intellect of China*, by W. A. P. Martin. (Selective entry.) Taipei: Ch'eng-wen, 1971, 44–71.]
SUBJ 62

21663 CSU P P1 G1.2 –1911
Martin, William Alexander Parsons, 1827–1916.
'The study of Chinese history.' In *The lore of Cathay: or, The intellect of China*, by W. A. P. Martin. [Selective entry]
New York: Revell, 1901, 387–408. [Reprinted in *The lore of Cathay: or, The intellect of China*, by W. A. P. Martin. (Selective entry.) Taipei: Ch'eng-wen, 1971, 387–408.]
SUBJ 62 ▪ 12

21664 NNC O P3 G5.1 1895–1911
Matignon, Jean-Jacques, 1866–?
'De quelques superstitions' (Some superstitions). In *La Chine hermétique: superstitions, crime et misère* (China sealed off: Superstition, crime, and poverty), 5th ed., rev., by J.-J. Matignon. [Selective entry]
Paris: Lib. Geuthner, 1936, 1–87.
SUBJ 62 65 ▪ 41 51 56 57

21665 CSU P P1 G1.2 –1895
Mayers, William Frederick, 1831–1878.
'On the legends relating to Nu Kwa [i.e., Nü-wa, patron goddess of marriage brokers].'
NQCJ 2, 7 (July 1868), 99–101.
SUBJ 62

21666 NIC S P1 G1.0 –1911
Mei, Yi-pao (Mei I-pao), 1900–.
'Man and nature in Chinese philosophy.' In *Indiana University Conference on Oriental-Western Literary Relations*, edited by Horst Frenz and G- L- Anderson. [Sole entry]
Chapel Hill: U. of North Carolina Press, 1955, 151–160. (U. of North Carolina studies in comparative literature, 13)
SUBJ 62 63 ▪ 64

21667 MCH P P1 G1.0 –1895
Mély, Fernand de, 1851–1935.
'Le "De monstris" chinois et les bestiaires occidentaux' (The Chinese 'De monstris' and Western bestiaries).
R. archéologique 3e série 31 (nov.–déc. 1897), 353–373.
SUBJ 62 ▪ 65

21668 NIC P P1 G1.0 –1911
Nakamura Hajime, 1912–.
'China.' Tr. by Philip Paul Wiener of 'Shinajin no shii hōhō' (Thought patterns of the Chinese people); in *Tōyōjin no shii hōhō* (Thought patterns of Asian peoples), by Nakamura Hajime; Tokyo: Misuzu shobō, 1948, vol. 1, 291–554. In *Ways of thinking of Eastern peoples: India, China, Tibet, Japan*, rev. ed., by Nakamura Hajime, edited by Philip Paul Wiener. [Sole entry]
Honolulu: East-West Center Press, 1964, 175–294.
SUBJ 60 62 ▪ 33 63 65

21669 CSU S P1 G1.2 –1911
Nakayama, Shigeru.
'Characteristics of Chinese astrology.'
Isis 57, 190 (Winter 1966), 442–454.
SUBJ 62 ▪ 13

21670 CSU P P3 G6.1 –1842
Needham, Noël Joseph Terence Montgomery, 1900–.
'The optick artists of Chiangsu.' In *Studies in the social history of China and South-east Asia: Essays in memory of Victor Purcell*, edited by Jerome Ch'en (Ch'en Chih-jang) and Nicholas Tarling. [Selective entry]
Cambridge: Cambridge U. Press, 1970, 197–226.
SUBJ 59 62

21671 CSU P P1 G1.2 –1895
Needham, Noël Joseph Terence Montgomery, 1900–.
'The roles of Europe and China in the evolution of oecumenical science.'
J. of Asian history 1, 1 (1967), 3–32. [Reprinted in *Clerks and craftsmen in China and the West*, by N. J. T. M. Needham. (Selective entry.) Cambridge: Cambridge U. Press, 1970, 396–418.]
SUBJ 56 62 ▪ 66

21672 CSU P P1 G1.3 –1644
Needham, Noël Joseph Terence Montgomery, 1900–.
Science and civilisation in China, Vol. 1, Introductory orientations.
Cambridge: Cambridge U. Press, 1954. 38, 318 p.
SUBJ 62 ▪ 14.3 66

21673 CSU P P1 G1.3 –1644
Needham, Noël Joseph Terence Montgomery, 1900–.
Science and civilisation in China, Vol. 2, History of scientific thought.
Cambridge: Cambridge U. Press, 1956. 22, 696 p.
SUBJ 60 62 ▪ 64

21674 CSU P P1 G1.0 –1842
Needham, Noël Joseph Terence Montgomery, 1900–.
Science and civilisation in China, Vol. 3, Mathematics and the science of the heavens and the earth.
Cambridge: Cambridge U. Press, 1959. 36, 877 p.
SUBJ 62

21675 CSU P P1 G1.3 –1842
Needham, Noël Joseph Terence Montgomery, 1900–.
Science and civilisation in China, Vol. 4, Physics and physical technology. Part 1, Physics.
Cambridge: Cambridge U. Press, 1962. 34, 434 p.
SUBJ 62 ▪ 14.2 24.4

21676 CSU P P2 G1.3 –1842
Needham, Noël Joseph Terence Montgomery, 1900–.
Science and civilisation in China, Vol. 4, Physics and physical technology. Part 2, Mechanical engineering.
Cambridge: Cambridge U. Press, 1965. 34, 579 p.
SUBJ 14.2 62 ▪ 14.1 16.2

21677 CSU FP P2 G1.2 –1911
Needham, Noël Joseph Terence Montgomery, 1900–.

Science and civilisation in China, Vol. 4, Physics and physical technology. Part 3, Civil engineering and nautics.
Cambridge: Cambridge U. Press, 1971. 57, 931 p.
SUBJ 14.2 21.3 55 60 62 ▪ 11.3 11.4 12 24.4 65

21678 CSU P P2 G1.3 –1895
Needham, Noël Joseph Terence Montgomery, 1900–.
'Science and society in East and West.'
Centaurus 10, 3 (1964), 174–197. [Reprinted in *Society and science*, edited by Maurice Goldsmith and Alan Mackay. (Sole entry.) New York: Simon and Schuster, 1964, 127–149.] [Reprinted in *The grand titration: Science and society in East and West*, by N. J. T. M. Needham. (Selective entry.) Toronto: U. of Toronto Press, 1969, 190–217.]
SUBJ 62 64 70 71 ▪ 12 16

21679 MCH P P4 G1.3 1644–1842
Nivison, David Shepherd, 1923–.
The life and thought of Chang Hsüeh-ch'eng (1738–1801).
Stanford: Stanford U. Press, 1966. 336 p. (Revision of *The literary and historical thought of Chang Hsüeh-ch'eng (1738–1801): A study of his life and writing, with translations of six essays from the 'Wen-shih t'ung-i'* [The general principles of literature and history], doctoral dissertation in Oriental literature, Harvard U., 1953)
SUBJ 16.1 59 62 64 ▪ 17 70

21680 MCY P P1 G1.2 1842–1911
Oka, Takashi, 1924–.
'The philosophy of T'an Ssu-t'ung.'
PC 9 (Aug. 1955), 1–47.
SUBJ 32 62 64 ▪ 59 66

21681 MCH S P1 G1.2 –1842
Olfers, Ignaz Franz Maria von, 1793–1872.
Die Überreste vorweltlicher Riesentiere in Beziehung zu ostasiatischen Sagen und chinesischen Schriften (The remains of prehistoric monsters and their relation to East Asian legends and Chinese writings).
Berlin: Nicolaische Buchhandlung Borstell und Reimarus, 1840. 31 p.
SUBJ 62 ▪ 65

21682 CSU P P2 G1.2 –1911
Ou Tsuin-chen.
'Some facts and ideas about talent and genius in Chinese history.' In *The year book of education, 1961*. [Sole entry]
London: Evans, 1961, 54–61.
SUBJ 17 62 ▪ 52 54

21683 CSU P P1 G1.2 1842–1895
Parker, Alvin P-, 1850–1924.
'The Chinese almanac.'
CR 19, 2 (Feb. 1888), 61–74.
SUBJ 62 ▪ 65

21684 CSU P P1 G1.2 1644–1895
Parker, Alvin P-, 1850–1924.
'A review of the imperial guide to astrology.'
CR 19, 11 (Nov. 1888), 493–499; 19, 12 (Dec. 1888), 547–554.
SUBJ 62

21685 MCH P P2 G1.3 –1842
Peterson, Willard James, 1938–.
Fang I-chih's response to Western knowledge.
Unpublished doctoral dissertation in History and Far Eastern Languages, Harvard U., 1970. 246 p.
SUBJ 59 62 66 ▪ 12 16.1 25 36.1 63

21686 DLC P P2 G1.3 –1842
Porshneva, E- B-.
'Verovaniia "Bailian'tsziao" kak ideologiia vosstavshego krest'ianstva' (Beliefs of the White Lotus Sect as an ideology for a rebellious peasantry). In *Tainye obshchestva v starom Kitae* (Secret societies in old China), compiled by Institut vostokovedeniia, Akademiia nauk SSSR, edited by Vasilii Pavlovich Iliushechkin. [Selective entry]
Moscow: Nauka, Glav. red. vost. lit-ry, 1970, 6–27.
SUBJ 32.2 33 36.3 62 64 ▪ 47 72

21687 NIC P P1 G1.2 –1911
Průšek, Jaroslav, 1904–.
'History and epics in China and in the West: A study of the differences in conception of the history.'
New Orient 3, 1 (Feb. 1962), 1–8. [Reprinted—*Diogenes* 42 (1963), 20–43.] [Reprinted as 'History and epics in China and the West.' In *Chinese history and literature: Collection of studies*, by J. Průšek. (Selective entry.) Dordrecht: Reidel, 1970, 17–34.]
SUBJ 62

21688 MCH P P1 G1.1 –1911
Puini, Carlo, 1839–1924.
'L'uomo e la società secondo la dottrina di Confucio' (Man and society according to Confucian doctrine).
Rivista italiana di sociologia 14, 5/6 (settembre–dicembre 1910), 510–528.
SUBJ 60 62 ▪ 63

21689 MCH O P2 G1.1 1842–1911
Regnault, Jules Emile Joseph, 1873–?
'Rôle du Foung-chouei et de la sorcellerie dans la vie privée et publique des jaunes' (The role of feng-shui and sorcery in the private and public life of Orientals).
R. politique et parlementaire 46, 137 (nov. 1905), 353–373.
SUBJ 23 56 62 65 ▪ 32.2 43 57 66

21690 NIC PO P1 G1.2 –1911
Reymond, Du Bois.
'Notes on Chinese archery.'
JRAS-NCB new (2nd) series 43 (1912), 32–43.
SUBJ 15 62

21691 CSU PO P2 G1.2 –1911
[Richard, Mary Martin] *Mrs.* Timothy Richard, 1843–1903.
Paper on Chinese music, 4th ed.
Shanghai: American Presbyterian Mission Press, 1923. 40 p.
SUBJ 62 ▪ 31 65

21692 MCH S P1 G1.0 –1895
Rodet, Léon, 1850–1895.
'Le souan-pan des Chinois et la banque des argentiers' (The Chinese abacus and the [medieval European] money-changer's table).
B. de la Société mathématique de France 8 (1879/80), 158–168.
SUBJ 62

21693 FPN S P1 G1.2 –1895
Rosny, Léon Louis Lucien Prunol de, 1837–1914.
'L'idée de Dieu dans la philosophie religieuse de la Chine' (The concept of God in Chinese religious philosophy).
B. de la Ligue nationale contre l'athéisme 12 (mars 1899), 165–186.
SUBJ 62 ▪ 43 64

21694 NNC S P1 G1.0 –1911
Saussure, Léopold de, 1866–1925.
L'horométrie et le système cosmologique des Chinois (Chinese cosmology and measurement of time).
Neuchâtel: Victor Attinger, 1919. 18 p.
SUBJ 62 ▪ 60

21695 CSU S P2 G1.1 –1911
Sivin, Nathan, 1931–.
Review of *Science and civilisation in China, Vol. 4, Physics and physical technology. Part 3, Civil engineering and nautics*, by Noël Joseph Terence Montgomery Needham.
TP 2e série 57, 5 (1971), 306–320.
SUBJ 62 ▪ 14.2 21.3

21696 CSU P P1 G1.2 –1911
Smith, Huston.
'Transcendence in traditional China.'
Religious studies 2, 2 (Apr. 1967), 185–196. [Reprinted in *Traditional China*, edited by James T. C. Liu (Liu Tzu-chien) and Wei-ming Tu. (Selective entry.) Englewood Cliffs, N. J.: Prentice-Hall, 1970, 109–122.]
SUBJ 62 ▪ 13 65

21697 NIC PO P1 G1.3 –1911
Soothill, William Edward, 1861–1935.
The three religions of China.
London: Oxford U. Press, 1930. 271 p. [Reprinted—Westport, Conn.: Hyperion Press, 197? 271 p.]
SUBJ 13 33 62 63 ▪ 23

21698 GBF P P1 G1.1 –1911
Su, Jyun-hsyong.
Das chinesische Rechtsdenken im Licht der Naturrechtslehre (Chinese legal thought in the light of natural law).
Freiburg i. Br.: The author, 1966. 229 p. (Doctoral dissertation, Rechts- und staatswissenschaftliche Fakultät, Universität Freiburg i. Br.)
SUBJ 12.2 60 62

21699 CSU P P1 G1.2 –1895
Szcześniak, Boleslaw.
'Notes on the penetration of the Copernican theory into China (seventeenth–nineteenth centuries).'
JRAS 3rd series 1945, 30–38.
SUBJ 62 66

21700 CSU S P1 G1.3 1644–1842
Teng, Ssu-yü, 1906–.
'Wang Fu-chih's views on history and historical writing.'
JAS 28, 1 (Nov. 1968), 111–123.
SUBJ 62 70 ▪ 16.1 72

21701 MCH S P1 G1.0 –1911
Vanhée, Louis.
'Algèbre chinoise' (Chinese algebra).

TP 2e série 13, 2 (mai 1912), 291–300.
SUBJ 62

21702 MCH S P1 G1.1 –1911
Vanhée, Louis.
'Les cent volailles: ou, l'analyse indéterminée en Chine' (The hundred fowls: Indeterminate analysis in China).
TP 2e série 14, 2 (mai 1913), 203–210; 14, 4 (oct. 1913), 435–450.
SUBJ 62 70

21703 DLC U P1 G1.1 –1895
Vasil'ev, Vasilii Pavlovich, 1818–1900.
Religii Vostoka: konfutsianstvo, buddizm i daosizm (The religions of the Orient: Confucianism, Buddhism, and Taoism).
St. Petersburg: Tip. V. S. Balasheva, 1873. 183 p.
SUBJ 13 62 63 ▪ 33 41

21704 MCY P P1 G1.0 –1911
Visser, Marinus Willem de, 1876–1930.
The dragon in China and Japan.
Amsterdam: Johannes Müller, 1913. 243 p.
SUBJ 62

21705 NNC PO P1 G1.2 –1911
Vuilleumier, Bernard.
The art of silk weaving in China: Symbolism of Chinese imperial ritual robes.
London: China Institute, 1939. 10, 37 p.
SUBJ 55 62 ▪ 12 16 24.4

21706 CSU P P1 G1.0 –1895
Wagner, G-.
'Bemerkungen über die Theorie der chinesischen Musik und ihren Zusammenhang mit der Philosophie' (Observations on the theory of Chinese music and its relation to philosophy).
MDG 2, 11 (1876), 42–61.
SUBJ 62

21707 NNC P P3 G6.1 1842–1895
Wang Ping.
'Alexander Wylie's influence on Chinese mathematics.' In *Proceedings of the Second Biennial Conference of the International Association of Historians of Asia*, edited by Chang Kuei-yung et al. [Selective entry]
Taipei: International Assn. of Historians of Asia, 1962, 777–786.
SUBJ 62 66 ▪ 26.1

21708 NIC U P1 G1.0 –1895
Watters, Thomas, 1840–1901.
'Chinese notions about pigeons and doves.'
JRAS-NCB new (2nd) series 4 (Dec. 1867), 225–242.
SUBJ 62

21709 MCH P P2 G1.2 –1895
Weber, Max, 1864–1920.
'Die Wirtschaftsethik der Weltreligionen: Konfuzianismus und Taoismus' (The economic ethic of world religions: Confucianism and Taoism). In *Gesammelte Aufsätze zur Religionssoziologie* (Collected essays on the sociology of religion), by M. Weber. [Sole entry]
Tübingen: Mohr, 1922, vol. 1, 276–536.

The religion of China: Confucianism and Taoism, edited by Hans Heinrich Gerth. Tr. by Hans H. Gerth.
Glencoe, Ill.: Free Press, 1951. 11, 308 p. [Reprinted—New York: Macmillan, 1964. 43, 308 p.]
SUBJ 13 16.1 33 62 63 ▪ 12 12.2 14 16.3 22 34.3 42 45

21710 CSU P P1 G1.0 –1911
Wei, Francis C. M. (Wei Cho-min), 1888–.
'Religious beliefs of the ancient Chinese and their influence on the national character of the Chinese people.'
CR 42, 6 (June 1911), 319–328; 42, 7 (July 1911), 403–415.
SUBJ 43 60 62 ▪ 63 64

21711 CBU P P1 G1.2 –1842
Wells, Henry Willis, 1895–.
Traditional Chinese humor: A study in art and literature.
Bloomington: Indiana U. Press, 1971. 242 p.
SUBJ 60 62 ▪ 65

21712 CSU P P2 G1.1 –1842
Wiethoff, Bodo, 1931–.
'Ermittlung' (An inquiry). In *Chinas dritte Grenze: Der traditionelle chinesische Staat und der küstennahe Seeraum* (China's third border: The traditional Chinese state and its offshore waters), by B. Wiethoff. [Sole entry]
Wiesbaden: Harrassowitz, 1969, 12–93.
SUBJ 12 12.1 62 66 ▪ 12.2 15 16 25

21713 CSH PO P1 G1.0 –1895
Williams, Samuel Wells, 1812–1884.
'Science among the Chinese.' In *The Middle Kingdom: A survey of the geography, government, literature, social life, arts, and history of the Chinese empire and its inhabitants*, rev. and enl. ed., by S. W. Williams. [Selective entry]
New York: Scribner, 1883, vol. 2, 65–134. [Reprinted in *The Middle Kingdom: A survey of the geography, government, literature, social life, arts, and history of the Chinese empire and its inhabitants*, by S. W. Williams. (Selective entry.) Taipei: Ch'eng-wen, 1965, 65–134 (s.p.)]
SUBJ 62 ▪ 15 56

21714 CBU P P1 G1.2 1644–1895
Wong, George H. C. (Huang Tao-chang), 1924–.
'Wang Jen-tsün, a late nineteenth century obstructor to the introduction of western thought.'
CCJ 9, 2 (May 1970), 210–215.
SUBJ 62 66

21715 MAM P P1 G1.3 –1842
Wu, Pei-yi (Wu P'ei-i), 1927–.
'The white snake': The evolution of a myth in China.
Ann Arbor: University Microfilms (Publ. 70-7096), 1970. 225 p. (Doctoral dissertation in Language and Literature, Columbia U., 1969)
SUBJ 62

21716 CSH U P1 G1.2 1644–1911
Yabuuti, Kiyosi (Yabuuchi Kiyoshi).
'Comparative aspects of the introduction of Western astronomy into China and Japan, sixteenth to nineteenth centuries.'
CCJ 7, 2 (May 1968), 151–154.
SUBJ 33 62 70 ▪ 66

21717 NIC P P1 G1.0 –1911
Yetts, Walter Perceval, 1878–1958.
Symbolism in Chinese art.
Leiden: Brill, 1912. 28 p.
SUBJ 62

1644-1949

21718 MCH O P1 G1.1 –1949
Abegg, Lily, 1901–.
Ostasien denkt anders: Versuch einer Analyse des west-östlichen Gegensatzes (East Asia thinks differently: Toward an analysis of East-West antagonism).
Zurich: Atlantis, 1949. 425 p.

The mind of East Asia. Tr. by A- I- Crick and E- E- Thomas.
London: Thames and Hudson, 1952. 344 p.
SUBJ 60 62 ▪ 13 16 43 61 66

21719 NIC P P1 G1.0 –1928
[Alekseev, Vasilii Mikhailovich] Basil M. Alexeiev, 1880–1951.
The Chinese gods of wealth.
[London]: U. of London, School of Oriental Studies *with* China Society, 1928. 36 p.
SUBJ 23 62 ▪ 65

21720 NIC O P1 G1.3 –1928
Arlington, Lewis Charles, 1859–1942.
'Chinese versus Western chiromancy.'
CJ 7, 4 (Oct. 1927), 170–175; 7, 5 (Nov. 1927), 228–235; 8, 2 (Feb. 1928), 67–76.
SUBJ 62 65

21721 NIC O P4 G1.3 1895–1928
Arlington, Lewis Charles, 1859–1942.
'Symbolism of Chinese sign-boards.'
CJ 11, 5 (Nov. 1929), 222–232.
SUBJ 56 62

21722 NNC O P1 G1.2 –1949
Bassett, Beulah E-.
'Lecture on Chinese mythology.'
JWCBRS 5 (1932), 92–101.
SUBJ 62 65 ▪ 63

21723 NNC PO P1 G1.2 –1928
Bernard, Henri, 1897–.
Sagesse chinoise et philosophie chrétienne: essai sur leurs relations historiques (A study of the historical relationships between Chinese wisdom and Christian philosophy).
Tientsin: Hautes études, 1935. 277 p. [Reprinted—Paris: Cathasia, 1950. 277 p.]
SUBJ 13 23 62 63 ▪ 15 16.1 19 43 65 66 70

21724 MCH P P1 G1.2 –1949
Berthelot, René.
'L'astrobiologie et l'état chinois' (Cosmological integration and the Chinese state).
R. de métaphysique et de morale 40, 1 (jan.–mars 1933), 41–64.
SUBJ 13 62 64 ▪ 12

21725 NNC P P1 G1.2 1895–1949
Brière, O-.
'Les courants philosophiques en Chine depuis 50 ans, 1898–1950' (Philosophical trends in China during the past fifty years, 1898–1950).
BUA 3e série 10, 40 (oct. 1949), 561–650.

Fifty years of Chinese philosophy, 1898–1950. Tr. by Laurence Gassius Thompson.
New York: Macmillan, 1956. 159 p. [Reprinted as *Fifty years of Chinese philosophy, 1898–1948* edited by Dennis James Doolin. New York: Praeger, 1965. 10, 159 p.]
SUBJ 62 64 ▪ 16.1 63 72

21726 NIC U P1 G1.0 –1949
Buck, Samuel, pseud.
'The Chinese spirit world.'
Orient (Hong Kong) 2, 1 – 2, 12 (Aug. 1951 – July 1952), 47 p. in all.
SUBJ 23 62 65

21727 NIC P P1 G1.0 –1949
Cammann, Schuyler, 1912–.
'Old Chinese magic squares.'
Sinologica 7, 1 (1962), 14–53.
SUBJ 62

21728 NIC U P1 G1.2 1644–1949
Chang, Chung-yuan (Chang Chung-yüan), 1907–.
'Law and reason in Chinese culture.'
United Asia 7, 4 (Aug. 1955), 225–227.
SUBJ 62 ▪ 22.2 63

21729 NIC P P7 G5.0 1644–1949
Chang, Hsueh-yen (Chang Hsüeh-yen), 1904–.
The lunar calendar as a social control mechanism in Chinese rural life.
Unpublished doctoral dissertation in Sociology, Cornell U., 1940. 230 p.
SUBJ 22.1 23 62 ▪ 41 52 57

21730 NIC P P1 G1.0 –1949
Chang, Tung-sun, 1886–.
'A Chinese philosopher's theory of knowledge.' Tr. by Li An-che of 'Ssu hsiang yen yü yü wen hua' (Thought, language, and culture); *She hui hsüeh chieh* 10 (June 1938), 17–54.
YJSS 1, 2 (Jan. 1939), 155–191.
SUBJ 62

21731 NIC P P1 G1.0 –1949
Chao Wei-pang.
'The Chinese science of fate calculation.'
FS 5 (1946), 279–315.
SUBJ 62 ▪ 23 65

21732 NIC P P1 G1.2 –1949
Chatley, Herbert, 1885–.
'The cycles of Cathay.'
JRAS-NCB new (2nd) series 65 (1934), 36–54.
SUBJ 62

21733 CSU P P1 G1.0 –1949
Chiao Wei.
'Die Raumbegriffe *shang*, *chung*, *hsia* und ihr Bedeutungswandel' (The spatial concepts 'shang', 'chung,' 'hsia' and their transformations in meaning).
OE 18, 2 (Dez. 1971), 217–236.
SUBJ 62 ▪ 65

21734 CSU P P2 G1.2 –1949
Danielli, Mary.
'The geomancer in China, with some reference to geomancy as observed in Madagascar.'
Folk-lore 63, 4 (Dec. 1952), 204–226.
SUBJ 62

21735 MCH PO P1 G1.2 –1928
Dols, Joseph, 1874–1938.
'Chineesche cosmogonie: Eene studie over de verklaring van het wereldsysteem' (Chinese cosmogony: A study of the exploration of the cosmic system).
China (Amsterdam) 4 (December 1929), 293–305; 5 (April 1930), 51–57; 5 (Oktober 1930), 231–236; 6 (Augustus 1931), 123–132; 6 (Oktober–November 1931), 196–212.
SUBJ 13 62 ▪ 23 65

21736 MCH PO P1 G1.2 –1928
Duyvendak, Jan Julius Lodewijk, 1889–1954.
'Een herleefd Chinees wijsgeer' (A Chinese philosopher revived [Wang Yang-ming]).
De Gids 86, 3 (Maart 1922), 445–477.
SUBJ 60 62 ▪ 19 63 64

21737 CSU P P1 G1.0 –1949
Eberhard, Wolfram, 1909–.
'Fatalism in the life of the common man in non-Communist China.'
Anthropological q. 39, 3 (July 1966), 148–160. [Reprinted in *Moral and social values of the Chinese: Collected essays*, by W. Eberhard. (Selective entry.) Taipei: Chinese Materials and Research Aids Service Center, 1971, 177–189. (CMRASC occasional series, 6)]
SUBJ 60 62 ▪ 64 65

21738 GMS O P2 G1.3 1895–1928
Esterer, Maximilian.
Chinas natürliche Ordnung und die Maschine (China's natural order and the machine).
Stuttgart: Cotta, 1929. 175 p.
SUBJ 62 ▪ 34.1 64

21739 MCY P P1 G1.2 –1928
Ferguson, John Calvin, 1866–1945.
'Chinese mythology.' In *The mythology of all races*, edited by John Arnott MacCulloch and George Foot Moore. [Sole entry]
Boston: George A. Jones, 1928, vol. 8, 3–203.
SUBJ 62 ▪ 23 65

21740 ELS P P1 G1.1 1842–1949
Feuchtwang, Stephan David Raphael, 1937–.
An anthropological analysis of Chinese geomancy.
Unpublished masters thesis in Anthropology, U. of London [London School of Economics and Political Science], 1965. 467 p.
SUBJ 62 65 ▪ 13 23 40 57 64 72

21741 CSU P P1 G1.2 –1928
Forke, Alfred, 1867–1944.
Die Gedankenwelt des chinesischen Kulturkreises (The intellectual milieu of the Chinese cultural sphere).
Munich: Oldenbourg, 1927. 215 p.
SUBJ 60 62

21742 CBU S P1 G1.1 –1928
Franke, Otto, 1863–1946.
'Die religionswissenschaftliche Literatur über China seit 1909' (Scholarly literature on religion in China since 1909).
Archiv für Religionswissenschaft 18 (1915), 394–479.
SUBJ 13 23 62 71 72 ▪ 33

21743 ²CBU P P1 G1.1 –1949
Franke, Otto, 1863–1946.
'Der Sinn der chinesischen Geschichtschreibung.'
Sinologische Arbeiten (Peiping) 3 (1945), 96–113.
'The meaning of Chinese historiography.' Tr. by Ulrich Mammitzsch.
East-West Center review 2, 1 (June 1965), 6–22.
SUBJ 62 70

21744 NIC P P1 G1.2 –1949
Fung, Yu-lan (Feng Yu-lan), 1895–.
'The Confucianist theory of mourning, sacrificial and wedding rites.'
CSPSR 15, 3 (Oct. 1931), 335–345.
SUBJ 41 43 57 62

21745 CSH U P1 G1.0 –1949
Goraiskii, I- I-.
'Kitaiskii kalendar' i ego sviaz' s kul'turno-bytovymi usloviiami zhizni naroda' (The Chinese calendar and its connection with popular culture and customs). [With English abstract]
VM 1930, 5, 51–58.
SUBJ 62 ▪ 23 55 65

21746 MCH U P1 G1.1 –1949
Granet, Marcel, 1884–1940.
'L'esprit de la religion chinoise' (The spirit of Chinese religion).
Scientia 45, 205 (1 maggio 1929), 329–337. [Reprinted in *Etudes sociologiques sur la Chine* (Sociological studies on China), by M. Granet. (Selective entry.) Paris: Presses universitaires, 1953, 251–260.]
SUBJ 13 62 ▪ 63

21747 NIC P P1 G1.2 1644–1949
Gray, Jack Douglas, 1916–.
'Historical writing in twentieth-century China: Notes on its background and development.' In *Historians of China and Japan*, edited by William Gerald Beasley and Edwin George Pulleyblank. [Selective entry]
London: Oxford U. Press, 1961, 186–212. (U. of London, School of Oriental and African Studies, Historical writing on the peoples of Asia, 3)
SUBJ 62 70 ▪ 16.1 64

21748 CSU S P1 G1.2 –1949
Grimm, Tilemann, 1922–.
'Idee und Wirklichkeit in der chinesischen Geschichte' (Idea and reality in Chinese history).
Saeculum 10, 2 (1959), 186–195.
SUBJ 62 64

21749 MCY P P1 G1.2 –1928
Han, Yu-shan (Han Yü-shan), 1899–.
Elements of Chinese historiography.
Hollywood: Hawley, 1955. 246 p.
SUBJ 60 62

21750 NNC PO P1 G1.1 –1949
Harvey, Edwin Deeks, 1880–1947.
The mind of China.
New Haven: Yale U. Press, 1933. 10, 321 p. [Reprinted—Westport, Conn.: Hyperion Press, 197? 10, 321 p.]
SUBJ 13 23 62 65 ▪ 33 43 55 56 57 63 72

21751 MSE O P1 G1.1 –1928
Hayes, L. Newton.
The Chinese dragon.
Shanghai: Commercial Press, 1923. 15, 66 p.
SUBJ 62 ▪ 65

21752 NNC PO P1 G1.2 –1928
Hodous, Lewis, 1872–1949.
'The dragon.'
JRAS-NCB new (2nd) series 48 (1917), 29–41.
SUBJ 13 62 ▪ 23 56 65

21753 CSU P P1 G1.2 1895–1928
Hsiao, Kung-chuan (Hsiao Kung-ch'üan), 1897–.
'K'ang Yu-wei's excursion into science: "Lectures on the heavens".' In *K'ang Yu-wei: A biography and a symposium*, edited by J. P. Lo (Lo Jung-pang). [Selective entry]
Tucson: U. of Arizona Press, 1967, 375–407.
SUBJ 62

21754 CSU P P1 G1.1 –1928
Hsü, Ti-shan.
'Taoism.' In *Religions of the empire*, edited by William Loftus Hare. [Sole entry]
London: Duckworth, 1925, 245–271.
SUBJ 33 60 62 ▪ 23

21755 NIC P P1 G1.2 –1928
Hu Shih, 1891–1962.
'Buddhistic influence on Chinese religious life.'
CSPSR 9, 1 (Jan. 1925), 142–150.
SUBJ 23 62

21756 MCH P P1 G1.0 –1928
Hu, Tao-wei, 1900–.
'The Chinese version of the law of nature.'
International j. of ethics 38, 1 (Oct. 1927), 27–43.
SUBJ 62

21757 CSU S P1 G1.2 –1928
Hummel, Arthur William, 1884–.
'What Chinese historians are doing in their own history.'
American historical review 34, 4 (July 1929), 715–724.
SUBJ 62 ▪ 70

21758 CLS P P1 G1.2 –1949
Hummel, William Frederick.
The role of historical criticism in the Chinese renaissance of today.
Unpublished doctoral dissertation in History, U. of Southern California, 1931. 155 p.
SUBJ 16.1 62 64 ▪ 66

21759 DLC O P2 G1.2 –1949
IAkovlev, Lev Mikhailovich.
'Drakon (etnograficheskii ocherk)' (The dragon: An ethnographic sketch).
Zapiski Kharbinskogo obshchestva estestvoispytatelei i etnografov 1946, 1, 17–24.
SUBJ 23 62 ▪ 65

21760 MCH P P1 G1.1 –1928
Johnson, Obed Simon, 1881–.
A study of Chinese alchemy.
Shanghai: Commercial Press, 1928. 11, 156 p. (Doctoral dissertation, U. of California, Berkeley, 1925)
SUBJ 62 65 ▪ 33 55 56 72

21761 FPN P P1 G1.3 –1949
Kaltenmark-Ghéquier, Odile.
Littérature religieuse: la Chine (Religious literature: China).
Paris: Armand Colin, 1949. 843 p.
SUBJ 13 16 40 60 62 ▪ 16.1 41 43 47 63

21762 MCY U P1 G1.0 –1949
Koehn, Alfred.
Chinese flower symbolism.
Tokyo: At the Lotus Court, 1954. 26 p.
SUBJ 62 ▪ 65

21763 NNC U P1 G1.0 –1949
Körner, Brunhild.
'Die Brautkrone der Chinesen' (The Chinese bridal crown).
Baessler-Archiv neue (2.) Folge 6, 1 (1958), 81–98.
SUBJ 41 62 ▪ 23 65

21764 CSU P P1 G1.2 1895–1949
Krebsová, Berta.
'Lu Hsun's contribution to modern Chinese thought and literature.'
New Orient 7, 1 (Feb. 1968), 9–13.
SUBJ 16.1 62

21765 CSU PO P1 G1.3 1895–1928
Ku Chieh-kang, 1895–.
The autobiography of a Chinese historian: Being the preface to 'A symposium on ancient Chinese history' (Ku Shih Pien). Tr. by Arthur William Hummel of 'Tzu hsü' (Preface); in *Ku shih pien* (Symposium of arguments on ancient Chinese history), by Ku Chieh-kang; Peking: P'u she, 1926, vol. 1, 1–103.
Leiden: Brill, 1931. 42, 199 p. (Doctoral dissertation, Rijksuniversiteit te Leiden) [Reprinted—Taipei: Ch'eng-wen, 1966. 42, 199 p.]
SUBJ 59 62 64 70 ▪ 16.1 17 23 65

21766 MCH P P1 G1.2 1842–1949
Kwok, Daniel W. Y. (Kuo Ying-i), 1932–.
Scientism in Chinese thought, 1900–1950.
New Haven: Yale U. Press, 1965. 12, 231 p. (Yale historical publications, miscellany, 82) (Revision of *Scientism in Chinese thought, 1900–1930: A study of doctrinal impact as revealed by Wu Chih-hui, Ch'en Tu-hsiu, Hu Shih and as seen in the debate of 1923*, doctoral dissertation in History, Yale U., 1959) [Reprinted—New York: Biblo and Tannen, 1971. 12, 231 p.]
SUBJ 60 62 ▪ 14.2 16.1 59 72

21767 CSU P P1 G1.2 –1949
Lee, Robert H. G. (Li K'ung-chiang), 1922–.
'The study of history: Some contemporary Chinese views.' In *Researches in the social sciences on China*, edited by John E. Lane. [Selective entry]
New York: Columbia U., East Asian Institute, 1957, 18–52. (EAI studies, 3) (Masters thesis in East Asian Studies, Columbia U., 1953)
SUBJ 16 62 64 ▪ 66

21768 CBU S P1 G1.3 1842–1928
Levenson, Joseph Richmond, 1920–1969.
Review of *In search of wealth and power: Yen Fu and the West*, by Benjamin Isadore Schwartz.
JAOS 85, 3 (July–Sept. 1965), 437–441.
SUBJ 62 ▪ 19

21769 CSU U P3 G9.2 –1928
Lo Hsiang-lin, 1905–.
'The southward expansion of Chinese civilization and the advancement of learning in Kwangtung province.' In *Symposium on historical, archaeological and linguistic studies on southern China, South-east Asia and the Hong Kong region*, edited by Frederick Seguier Drake. [Selective entry]
Hong Kong: Hong Kong U. Press, 1967, 139–149.
SUBJ 11.2 62 70 ▪ 16.1 66

21770 CSU P P3 G5.4 –1949
Löwenthal, Rudolf, 1904–.
'The nomenclature of Jews in China.'
MS 12 (1947), 97–126. [Reprinted in *Studies of the Chinese Jews: Selections from journals East and West*, compiled by Hyman Kublin. (Selective entry.) New York: Paragon, 1971, 55–84.]
SUBJ 33 62 ▪ 42

21771 DLC PO P1 G1.2 –1949
Lübke, Anton, 1890–.
Der Himmel der Chinesen (The Chinese heavens).
Leipzig: R. Voigtländer, 1931. 141 p.
SUBJ 60 62 ▪ 13 23 55

21772 MCH S P1 G1.2 –1928
MacKenzie, Donald Alexander, 1873–1936.
Myths of China and Japan.
London: Gresham Publishing Co., 1923. 16, 404 p.
SUBJ 23 62 ▪ 65

21773 CSU P P1 G1.3 –1949
March, Andrew Lee, 1932–.
'An appreciation of Chinese geomancy.'
JAS 27, 2 (Feb. 1968), 253–267.
SUBJ 62 ▪ 43 57 65

21774 MCH U P2 G1.2 –1928
Maspero, Henri, 1883–1945.
'Mythologie de la Chine moderne.' In *Mythologie asiatique illustrée* (An illustrated mythology of Asia), by Joseph Hackin et al. [Sole entry]
Paris: Lib. de France, 1928, 227–362.

'The mythology of modern China.' Tr. by F. M. Atkinson. In *Asiatic mythology*, by J. Hackin et al. [Sole entry]
New York: Crowell, 1932, 252–284. [Reprinted in *Asiatic mythology*, by J. Hackin et al. (Sole entry.) New York: Crowell, 1963, 252–284.]
SUBJ 13 23 62 65 ▪ 17 34.3

21775 MCH U P1 G1.2 –1928
Mauger, Georges Edouard Marie Jean, 1870–?
'Quelques considérations sur les jeux en Chine et leur développement synchronique avec celui de l'empire chinois' (Reflections on the parallel development of games and empire in China).

Bulletins et mémoires de la Société d'anthropologie de Paris 6e série 6 (1915), 238–281.
Subj 60 62 ▪ 12 15 53

21776 MCH P P1 G1.0 –1949
Meurs, H- van.
'De vleermuis als Chineesch gelukssymbool: Geen vraagstuk van mythologie of magie, doch van taalbouw' (The bat as Chinese good luck symbol: A problem of language structure rather than of mythology or magic).
Studia Catholica (Nijmegen) 17, 6 (November 1941), 445–457.
Subj 62 ▪ 71

21777 NNC O P1 G1.2 –1949
Nance, Florence Rush.
'Chinese symbolism.'
CJ 20, 1 (Jan. 1934), 5–24.
Subj 62 65 ▪ 23

21778 NIC S P1 G1.3 1644–1949
Peake, Cyrus Henderson, 1900–.
'Some aspects of the introduction of modern science into China.'
Isis 22, 63 (Dec. 1934), 173–219.
Subj 62 66

21779 NNM O P1 G1.2 –1928
Porter, Lucius Chapin, 1880–1958.
'Feng shui: or, How the Chinese keep in tune with nature.'
CR 51, 12 (Dec. 1920), 837–850.
Subj 60 62 ▪ 23 43

21780 DCK FP P2 G1.2 –1949
Prip-Møller, Johannes, 1889–1943.
'Vind og vand' (Feng-shui: Wind and water). In *Kina før og nu* (China, past and present), by J. Prip-Møller. [Sole entry]
Copenhagen: Gad, 1944, 109–120.
Subj 23 62

21781 NIC S P1 G9.0 –1928
Przyluski, Jean.
'La divination par l'aiguille flottante et par l'araignée dans la Chine méridionale' (Divination by floating needle and by spider in South China).
TP 2e série 15, 2 (mai 1914), 214–224.
Subj 47 62 65 ▪ 23 29 41 51 56

21782 MCY P P1 G1.0 –1928
Rawlinson, Frank Joseph, 1871–1937.
Chinese ideas of the Supreme Being.
Shanghai: Presbyterian Mission Press, 1927. 57 p.
Subj 23 60 62 ▪ 33 63

21783 MCH P P1 G1.0 –1928
Rawlinson, Frank Joseph, 1871–1937.
'A prevalent Chinese theory of the universe.'
CR 57, 9 (Sept. 1926), 644–658.
Subj 62 ▪ 64

21784 NNC FP P7 G1.4 –1928
Rousselle, Erwin Arthur, 1890–.
'Die typischen Bildwerke eines buddhistischen Tempels in China' (The typical iconography of a Buddhist temple in China).
Sinica 6, 2 – 10, 4 (März 1931 – Juli 1935), 148 p. in all.
Subj 62 ▪ 23 33 65

21785 CSH P P1 G1.2 1895–1928
Sakai, Robert Kenjiro (Sakai Kenjirō), 1919–.
'Ts'ai Yuan-p'ei as a synthesizer of Western and Chinese thought.'
PC 3 (May 1949), 170–192.
Subj 16.1 62 66 ▪ 17 59

21786 CSU P P1 G1.3 1842–1928
Schwartz, Benjamin Isadore, 1916–.
In search of wealth and power: Yen Fu and the West.
Cambridge: Harvard U. Press, 1964. 20, 298 p. (Harvard East Asian series, 16)
Subj 10 60 62 ▪ 12 59 66

21787 MCY PO P3 G1.4 1644–1949
Sirén, Osvald, 1879–1959.
Gardens of China.
New York: Ronald Press, 1949. 141 p.
Subj 16.1 55 62

21788 ICU P P1 G1.1 1842–1928
Smythe, Lewis Strong Casey, 1901–.
Changes in the Christian message for China by Protestant missionaries.
Unpublished doctoral dissertation in Christian Theology and Ethics, U. of Chicago, 1928. 298 p.
Subj 33 43 62 ▪ 12.2 13 64 66

21789 CSU P P1 G1.2 –1928
Solger, Friedrich, 1877–.
'Astronomische Anmerkungen zu chinesischen Märchen' (Astronomical footnotes to Chinese tales).
MDG 17 (1922), 133–201.
Subj 62 65

21790 FPN PO P1 G1.2 –1928
Soulié de Morant, Charles Georges, 1878–.
Sciences occultes en Chine: la main (The occult sciences in China: The hand).
Paris: Nilsson, 1932. 143 p.
Subj 62 ▪ 56

21791 MCH PO P1 G1.3 –1928
Stewart, James Livingstone.
Chinese culture and Christianity: A review of China's religions and related systems from the Christian standpoint.
New York: Revell, 1926. 316 p.
Subj 13 23 60 62 ▪ 43 56 57 63 65 66

21792 CSU S P1 G1.2 –1949
Teng, Ssu-yü, 1906–.
'Chinese historiography in the last fifty years.'
FEQ 8, 2 (Feb. 1949), 131–156.
Subj 62 70 ▪ 16.1

21793 CSU P P1 G1.2 1842–1928
Thompson, Laurence Gassius, 1926–.
'Introduction.' In *Ta T'ung Shu*, the one-world philosophy of K'ang Yu-wei, by L. G. Thompson. [Sole entry]
London: Allen and Unwin, 1958, 11–57. (Revision of doctoral dissertation in Oriental Literature, Claremont Graduate School and University Center, 1954)
Subj 59 62 ▪ 16.1 63 70

21794 CSU O P1 G1.2 –1928
Tsu, Y. Y. (Chu Yu-yü), 1886–.
'The Chinese idea of worship.'
CR 45, 10 (Oct. 1914), 615–625.
Subj 13 62 ▪ 23 33

21795 NNM P P1 G1.2 –1928
Tsu, Y. Y. (Chu Yu-yü), 1886–.
'The Confucian God-idea.'
CR 50, 5 (May 1919), 294–306.
Subj 62 ▪ 64

21796 NIC S P1 G1.3 –1949
Wei, Francis C. M. (Wei Cho-min), 1888–.
The spirit of Chinese culture.
New York: Scribner, 1947. 186 p.
Subj 23 62 63 ▪ 60 66

21797 NIC P P1 G1.2 –1949
Welch, Holmes Hinkley, 1921–.
The parting of the way: Lao Tsu and the Taoist movement.
Boston: Beacon Press, 1957. 204 p.
Subj 33 62 ▪ 23

21798 MCH P P1 G1.2 –1928
Werner, Edward Theodore Chalmers, 1864–1954.
Myths and legends of China.
New York: Brentano's, 1922. 453 p. [Reprinted—New York: B. Blom, 1971. 453 p.]
Subj 13 23 40 41 62 65 ▪ 11.2 15 31 45 50 57 60

21799 NNC O P1 G1.0 –1928
Wilhelm, Richard, 1873–1930.
'Chinesische Schicksalsbeherrschung' (Chinese methods of predicting fate).
Sinica 1, 3 (1925/27), 88–103.
Subj 23 62 ▪ 65

21800 NNC U P1 G1.0 –1928
Wilhelm, Richard, 1873–1930.
'Die Einordnung des Menschenlebens in dem kosmischen Verlauf im chinesischen Kulturgebiet' (The place of man in the Chinese cosmic order).
Jahrbuch für kosmo-biologische Forschung 1 (1928), 11–20.
Subj 62

21801 MCY P P1 G1.0 –1928
Williams, Charles Alfred Speed, 1884–.
A manual of Chinese metaphor: Being a selection of typical Chinese metaphors with explanatory notes and indices.
Shanghai: Commercial Press, 1920. 14, 320 p.
Subj 60 62 65

21802 MCH P P1 G1.2 –1928
Woitsch, L-.
'Die Astronomie der Chinesen' (Chinese astronomy). In *Das Licht des Ostens* (The light of the East), edited by Maximilian Kern. [Selective entry]
Stuttgart: Union deutsche Verlagsgesellschaft, 1922, 505–512.
Subj 62

21803 NNC P P1 G1.1 –1949
Yampolsky, Philip B-.
'Modern Chinese historiography.' In *The development of historiography*, edited by Matthew A- Fitzsimons, Alfred G- Pundt, and Charles E- Nowell. [Sole entry]
Harrisburg, Pa.: Stackpole, 1954, 391–439.
Subj 62 70

21804 NIC P P1 G1.2 –1949
Yang, C. K. (Yang Ch'ing-k'un), 1911–.
'The functional relationship between Confucian thought and Chinese

religion.' In *Chinese thought and institutions*, edited by John King Fairbank. [Selective entry]
Chicago: U. of Chicago Press, 1957, 269–290.
Subj 62 ▪ 13 33 43 64

21805 MCY P P1 G1.2 –1949
Yang, Lien-sheng, 1914–.
'Numbers and units in Chinese economic history.'
HJAS 12, 1/2 (June 1949), 216–225. [Reprinted in *Studies in Chinese institutional history*, by Lien-sheng Yang. (Selective entry.) Cambridge: Harvard U. Press, 1961, 75–84. (Harvard-Yenching Institute studies, 20)]
Subj 62 ▪ 14.5

1911-1949

21806 MCH S P1 G1.2 1911–1949
Boorman, Howard Lyon, 1920–, and Scott Archer Boorman, 1949–.
'Strategy and national psychology in China.'
AAAPSS 370 (Mar. 1967), 143–155.
Subj 61 62 ▪ 12 15 48 63

21807 CSH O P4 G1.3 1911–1928
Chang, Carsun (Chang Chia-sen), 1886–.
'Reflections on the philosophical controversy in 1923.'
CCJ 3, 1 (Nov. 1963), 19–22.
Subj 16.1 62

21808 NNC F P8 G4.4 1911–1949
Frick, Johannes.
'Der Traum und seine Deutung bei den Chinesen in Ch'ing-hai' (Dreams and their interpretation among the Chinese in Tsinghai).
Anthropos 49, 1/2 (Jan.–Apr. 1954), 311–313.
Subj 62 ▪ 51 61 65

21809 CSU P P1 G1.2 1911–1928
Gálik, Marián.
'From Chuang-tzu to Lenin: Mao Tun's intellectual development.'
Asian and African studies 3 (1967), 98–109.
Subj 16.1 62 ▪ 59 66

21810 CSU O P2 G8.1 1928–1949
Graham, David Crockett, 1884–.
'Chinese yinyang and fengshui conceptions.'
CR 67, 1 (Jan. 1936), 34–38; 67, 3 (Mar. 1936), 166–172.
Subj 62 65

21811 NNC O P3 G9.3 1911–1928
Harding, H- L-.
'On a method of divination practised at Foochow.'
JRAS-NCB new (2nd) series 49 (1918), 82–85.
Subj 23 62 ▪ 65

21812 CSU U P1 G1.2 1928–1949
Hu, H. H. (Hu Hsien-su).
'Chronicle of the biological sciences in China.'
THM 4, 5 (May 1937), 484–497.
Subj 62 ▪ 16.1 17

21813 DLC P P1 G1.0 1928–1949
IAkovlev, Lev Mikhailovich.
'Kitaiskii lunnyi kalendar' na 1943 god.' (The Chinese lunar calendar for 1943).
Zapiski Kharbinskogo obshchestva estestvoispytatelei i etnografov 1946, 1, 6–17.
Subj 62 65

21814 NNC O P1 G1.2 1928–1949
Kwei, Chi-ting (Kuei Chih-t'ung).
'The status of physics in China.'
American j. of physics 12, 1 (Feb. 1944), 13–18.
Subj 17 62

21815 CSU P P1 G1.2 1911–1928
Levenson, Joseph Richmond, 1920–1969.
'Theory and history.' In *Confucian China and its modern fate, Vol. 3, The problem of historical significance*, by J. R. Levenson. [Analytic entry]
Berkeley, Los Angeles: U. of California Press, 1965, 85–109.
Subj 62 ▪ 64 66

21816 CSU P P2 G1.3 1911–1928
Millican, Frank R-.
'Tai Hsü and modern Buddhism.'
CR 54, 6 (June 1923), 326–334.
Subj 33 62 ▪ 24.2 27

21817 CSU P P1 G1.2 1911–1949
Munro, Donald Jacques, 1931–.
'Humanism in modern China: Fung Yu-lan and Hsiung Shih-li.' In *'Nothing concealed': Essays in honor of Liu Yu-yün*, edited by Frederic Evans Wakeman, Jr. [Selective entry]
Taipei: Chinese Materials and Research Aids Service Center, 1970, 177–192. (CMRASC occasional series, 4)
Subj 62

21818 NNC O P2 G1.2 1928–1949
Needham, Noël Joseph Terence Montgomery, 1900–.
Chinese science.
London: Pilot Press, 1945. 71 p.
Subj 36.1 62 ▪ 12 14.4 17

21819 CBU O P2 G1.2 1928–1949
Needham, Noël Joseph Terence Montgomery, 1900–, and Dorothy Needham, eds.
Science outpost: Papers of the Sino-British Science Cooperation Office (British Council Scientific Office in China), 1942–1946.
London: Pilot Press, 1948. 313 p.
Subj 17 62 ▪ 14.2 14.4 36.1

21820 CSU S P1 G1.2 1928–1949
Ouang Te-tchao (Huang Te-chao).
'La recherche scientifique en Chine pendant la guerre' (Scientific research in China during the [Anti-Japanese] War).
Sinologica 1, 2 (1948), 87–95.
Subj 17 62

21821 FPN O P2 G1.2 1911–1949
Porak, René.
L'âme chinoise (The mind of China).
Paris: Flammarion, 1950. 284 p.
Subj 16 21.1 41 55 62 ▪ 11.1 13 23 43 47 60

21822 NNC P P1 G1.3 1911–1949
Rousselle, Erwin Arthur, 1890–.
'Der lebendige Taoismus im heutigen China' (Living Taoism in contemporary China).
Sinica 8, 4 (Juli 1933), 122–131.
Subj 33 62 ▪ 23

21823 CSH P P1 G1.2 1928–1949
Roy, Andrew Tod.
'Confucian thought in China in the nineteen thirties. Part 1, Ch'en Li-fu's theory of the universe and of the significance of man. Part 2, Application of his theory to social, cultural, and political questions.'
CCJ 7, 1 (Nov. 1967), 72–89; 8, 1 (Nov. 1968), 63–92.
Subj 62 64 ▪ 63

21824 CSH P P1 G1.2 1911–1928
Roy, Andrew Tod.
'Liberal re-evaluations of Confucianism in the 1911–1927 period.'
CCJ 6, 1 (Nov. 1966), 79–100.
Subj 62 64 ▪ 32.2

21825 NNC P P1 G1.2 1911–1928
Wycott, William A-, Jr.
Chang Tung-sun: Interpretation of the 1923 science-philosophy controversy.
Unpublished masters thesis in History, Columbia U., 1960. 70 p. [Certificate essay, East Asian Institute]
Subj 16.1 62 ▪ 63 66

21826 MAM P P2 G1.2 1911–1949
Young, Lung-chang (Yang Lung-chang), 1923–.
Literary reflections of social change in China, 1919–1949.
Ann Arbor: University Microfilms (Publ. 65-2455), 1965. 247 p. (Doctoral dissertation in Sociology, New School for Social Research [New York], 1964)
Subj 19 62 ▪ 16 16.1

1911-1972
(including 1644-1972)

21827 CSU FP P7 G9.5 1895–1972
Aijmer, Lars Göran, 1936–.
'Being caught by a fishnet: On fengshui in southeastern China.'
JRAS-HKB 8 (1968), 74–81.
Subj 24 24.1 62 ▪ 21 21.2 26 29

21828 MAU P P1 G1.0 –1972
Barnett, Kenneth Myer Arthur, 1911–.
'The measurement of elapsed time in Hong Kong: The Chinese calendar, its uses and value.' In *Some traditional Chinese ideas and conceptions in Hong Kong social life today*, edited by Marjorie Doreen Topley. [Analytic entry]
Hong Kong: Royal Asiatic Society, Hong Kong Branch, 1967, 36–53.
Subj 62

21829 FPN P P1 G1.2 –1972
Bauer, Wolfgang, 1930–.
'The encyclopaedia in China.'
Cahiers d'histoire mondiale 9, 3 (1966), 665–691.
Subj 62 ▪ 16.1 17

21830 MCH S P2 G1.2 1895–1972
Bergère, Marie-Claire, 1933–.
'La révolution de 1911 jugée par les historiens de la République populaire de Chine: thèmes et controverses' (Historians of the People's Republic of China on the Revolution of 1911: Themes and controversies).
R. historique 230 (oct.–déc. 1963), 403–436.
SUBJ 15 32.2 62 70 ▪ 16.1 16.2 30 64

21831 CSU P P1 G1.2 1911–1972
Boorman, Howard Lyon, 1920–.
'Mao Tse-tung as historian.' In *History in Communist China*, edited by Albert Feuerwerker. [Selective entry]
Cambridge: M.I.T. Press, 1968, 306–330.
SUBJ 62 64 70 ▪ 32.2

21832 CSH U P1 G1.2 1895–1972
Cartier, Michel, 1934–.
'La réévaluation du passé dans la Chine contemporaine' (The reevaluation of the past in contemporary China).
NED 3498/3499 (15 juin 1968), 53–59.
SUBJ 60 62

21833 NIC O P1 G1.0 1911–1972
Chao, Y. R. (Chao Yüan-jen), 1892–.
'How Chinese logic operates.'
Anthropological linguistics 1, 1 (Jan. 1959), 1–8.
SUBJ 62

21834 CSU P P1 G1.2 –1972
Cheng, Chung-ying.
'Chinese philosophy: A characterization.'
Inquiry 14, 1/2 (Summer 1971), 113–137.
SUBJ 62

21835 FPN S P1 G1.1 1842–1972
Chesneaux, Jean, 1922–.
'Pour une histoire asiocentrique de l'Asie moderne.'
Diogène 55 (juil.–sept. 1966), 110–126.

'For an Asian history of modern Asia.' Tr. by Alessandro Ferace and Nelda Cantarella.
Diogenes 55 (Fall 1966), 104–119.
SUBJ 60 62 ▪ 19 64 66

21836 CSU U P1 G1.2 –1972
Chien Po-tsan, 1898–.
'Problems in the Communist periodization of Chinese history.' Tr. by John T. Meskill of 'Kuan yü Chung-kuo li shih fen ch'i ti wen t'i' (The periodization of Chinese history); *Tōyōshi kenkyū* 14, 4 (Mar. 1956), 93–102. In *The pattern of Chinese history: Cycles, development, or stagnation?*, edited by John Thomas Meskill. [Selective entry]
Boston: Heath, 1965, 76–84.
SUBJ 19 62 ▪ 64

21837 CSU P P2 G1.2 1928–1972
Chin, Steve S. K. (Chin Ssu-k'ai), 1919–.
'Changes in the meaning of the term "the people" (jen-min): An example of conceptual revolution as reflected in semantic evolution.'
SST 12, 2 (June 1972), 124–148.
SUBJ 62 64 ▪ 16

21838 CSU P P2 G1.2 –1972
Christie, Anthony.
Chinese mythology.
Middlesex, Eng.: Hamlyn, 1968. 141 p.
SUBJ 62 ▪ 65

21839 CSH S P1 G1.2 1644–1972
Cranmer-Byng, John, 1919–.
'The Chinese view of their place in the world: An historical perspective.'
CQ 53 (Jan.–Mar. 1973), 67–79.
SUBJ 62 66

21840 CSH S P2 G1.2 –1972
Doronin, B- G-.
'Krest'ianskaia voina 1627–1646 gg. v sovremennoi kitaiskoi istoriografii' (The peasant wars of 1627–1646 in contemporary Chinese historiography). In *Istoricheskaia nauka v KNR* (Historiography in the People's Republic of China), compiled by Institut vostokovedeniia, Akademiia nauk SSSR, edited by Rudol'f Vsevolodovich Viatkin and Nataliia Pavlovna Svistunova. [Selective entry]
Moscow: Nauka, Glav. red. vost. lit-ry, 1971, 131–145.
SUBJ 32.2 36.3 62 70 ▪ 18 64 72

21841 CSU P P1 G1.2 –1972
Eber, Irene, 1929–.
'Hu Shih and Chinese history: The problem of "cheng-li kuo-ku" [reorganization of the national past].'
MS 27 (1968), 169–207.
SUBJ 62 64 70

21842 MCH P P1 G1.2 –1972
Eberhard, Wolfram, 1909–.
'Das Problem des Kulturverfalls in China' (The problem of cultural decay in China). In *Klassizismus und Kulturverfall* (Classicism and cultural decline), edited by Gustav Edmund von Grunebaum and Willy Hartner. [Sole entry]
Frankfurt a.M.: Klostermann, 1960, 217–236.
SUBJ 62 ▪ 32.2 71

21843 DCK PO P1 G1.2 –1972
Egerod, Søren, 1923–.
'De kinesiske religioner' (The religions of China). In *Verdens religioner* (The religions of the world), edited by Johannes Aagaard and Stephan Kehler. [Sole entry]
Copenhagen: Politikens, 1964, 315–334.
SUBJ 62 ▪ 13 23

21844 CSU P P2 G1.1 1842–1972
Fairbank, John King, 1907–, et al.
'The influence of modern Western science and technology on Japan and China.'
Explorations in entrepreneurial history 7 (Apr. 1955), 189–204.
SUBJ 14.4 60 62 66 ▪ 19

21845 CSU P P1 G1.2 –1972
Feuerwerker, Albert, 1927–.
'China's history in Marxian dress.' In *History in Communist China*, edited by A. Feuerwerker. [Selective entry]
Cambridge: M.I.T. Press, 1968, 14–44.
SUBJ 62 70 ▪ 12

21846 NIC P P1 G1.2 –1972
Feuerwerker, Albert, 1927–.
'Rewriting Chinese history: Interpreting the past in the People's Republic of China.'
U. of Toronto q. 30, 3 (Apr. 1961), 273–285.
SUBJ 62 64 70 ▪ 16.1 32.2 66

21847 CSH P P2 G1.1 –1972
Feuerwerker, Albert, 1927–, and Sally Cheng.
Chinese Communist studies of modern Chinese history.
Cambridge: Harvard U., East Asian Research Center, 1961. 25, 287 p. (Harvard East Asian monographs, 11)
SUBJ 62 70 72 ▪ 12 14 16 17 19 32 32.2 64 66

21848 CSH S P2 G1.2 1644–1972
Fomina, Nataliia Ivanovna.
'Izuchenie v KNR osnovnikh voprosov istorii antitsinskoi bor'by XVII v.' (Research in the People's Republic of China on basic historical questions relating to the anti-Ch'ing struggle in the seventeenth century). In *Istoricheskaia nauka v KNR* (Historiography in the People's Republic of China), compiled by Institut vostokovedeniia, Akademiia nauk SSSR, edited by Rudol'f Vsevolodovich Viatkin and Nataliia Pavlovna Svistunova. [Selective entry]
Moscow: Nauka, Glav. red. vost. lit-ry, 1971, 146–157.
SUBJ 32.2 62 64 ▪ 12.1 16 66 70 72

21849 MCH S P1 G1.2 1644–1972
Franke, Herbert, 1914–.
'Zur Frage der einheimischen Voraussetzungen des chinesischen Kommunismus' (The question of the indigenous preconditions of Chinese Communism).
Z. für Politik neue (2.) Folge 7, 2 (1960), 134–138.
SUBJ 32.2 62 64 ▪ 16.1

21850 CSU F P2 G1.1 –1972
Freedman, Maurice, 1920–.
'Geomancy.'
Proceedings of the Royal Anthropological Institute of Great Britain and Ireland 1968, 5–15.
SUBJ 57 62 ▪ 44

21851 CSH O P8 G4.1 1928–1972
Gittings, John, 1938–.
'The spirit of Yenan.'
FEER 72, 23 (5 June 1971), 59–62.
SUBJ 13 62 ▪ 32.2 64

21852 CSU P P1 G1.0 –1972
Graham, Angus Charles, 1919–.
'"Being" in Western philosophy compared with *shih/fei* and *yu/wu* in Chinese philosophy.'
Asia Major new (3rd) series 7, 1/2 (Jan. 1959), 79–112.
SUBJ 62

21853 CSU P P2 G1.1 –1972
Harrison, James Pinckney, 1932–.
The Communists and Chinese peasant rebellions: A study in the rewriting of Chinese history.
New York: Atheneum, 1969. 363 p. (Revision of *The Communist treatment of Chinese peasant wars: A case study in the reinterpretation of history according to the theory of class struggle*, doctoral dissertation in Political Science, Columbia U., 1965) [Reprinted—London: Gollancz, 1970. 25, 363 p.]
SUBJ 16 32.2 36.3 62 64 70 ▪ 16.1 16.3 22.2 25 32.1 65 66

21854 MAU PO P8 G9.5 1911–1972
Hayes, James William, 1930–.
'Geomancy and the village.' In *Some traditional Chinese ideas and conceptions in Hong Kong social life today*, edited by Marjorie Doreen Topley. [Analytic entry]
Hong Kong: Royal Asiatic Society, Hong Kong Branch, 1967, 22–30.
Subj 62 ▪ 21 21.3

21855 NIC S P2 G1.1 1842–1972
Herman, Theodore, 1913–.
'Group values toward the national space: The case of China.'
GR 49, 2 (Apr. 1959), 164–182.
Subj 10 11.3 60 62 ▪ 12 14 15 18 29 66

21856 CSU U P1 G1.2 –1972
Hu Shih, 1891–1962.
'The natural law in the Chinese tradition.' In *U. of Notre Dame Natural Law Institute Proceedings*, edited by Edward F- Barrett. [Sole entry]
Notre Dame: U. of Notre Dame Press, 1953, vol. 5, 119–153.
Subj 62 63 ▪ 12.2 64

21857 MCH P P1 G1.1 –1972
Huard, Pierre Alphonse, 1901–.
'Panorama de la science chinoise et de quelques-unes de ses disciplines' (Overview of Chinese science and some scientific disciplines).
R. de synthèse 77, 4 (oct.–déc. 1956), 419–518.
Subj 62 64 70 ▪ 72

21858 CSU P P1 G1.2 1928–1972
Israel, John Warren, 1935–.
'The December 9th movement: A case study in Chinese Communist historiography.' In *History in Communist China*, edited by Albert Feuerwerker. [Selective entry]
Cambridge: M.I.T. Press, 1968, 247–276.
Subj 16.1 62 70 ▪ 32 32.2 54

21859 NNC P P1 G1.2 1842–1972
Jen Yu-wen (Chien Yu-wen), 1896–.
'The Marxian interpretation of Taiping Tienkuo (TPTK).' In *Proceedings of the Second Biennial Conference of the International Association of Historians of Asia*, edited by Chang Kuei-yung et al. [Selective entry]
Taipei: International Assn. of Historians of Asia, 1962, 745–776.
Subj 16 16.3 62 ▪ 32.2 64 70 71

21860 MCH O P1 G1.2 1928–1972
Jones, Francis Price, 1890–.
'Theological thinking in the Chinese Protestant church under Communism.'
Religion in life 32, 4 (Autumn 1963), 534–546.
Subj 13 33 62

21861 CSU P P1 G1.0 –1972
Köster, Hermann.
'Gibt es ein *chinesisches* Denken?' (Is there a *Chinese* philosophy?).
Sinologica 12, 1/2 (1971), 14–29.
Subj 62 66

21862 CSU S P1 G1.2 –1972
Köster, Hermann.
Symbolik des chinesischen Universismus (Symbolism within Chinese monism).
Stuttgart: Hiersemann, 1958. 104 p.
Subj 62 64 ▪ 41 43 65

21863 CNY S P1 G1.0 –1972
Köster, Hermann.
Über eine Grundidee der chinesischen Kultur (A fundamental idea in Chinese culture).
Kaldenkirchen: Steyler Verlagsbuchhandlung, 1957. 28 p. (Missionspriesterseminars St. Augustin, Siegburg, Veröffentlichungen, 1)
Subj 62 ▪ 61

21864 NNC S P1 G1.2 1644–1972
Kovalev, Evgenii Fedorovich, 1907–.
'Voprosy periodizatsii novoi i noveishei istorii Kitaia' (The periodization of modern and recent Chinese history).
SV 1956, 6, 106–112.
Subj 19 32.2 62 ▪ 70 71

21865 CSU P P2 G1.5 1842–1972
[Kuliang, Jonas] John S. Koe.
'Chinese Communist views on the Taiping Revolution.'
France-Asie 21, 4 (août 1967), 533–548.
Subj 32.2 62 64 70 ▪ 16 66

21866 CSH P P1 G1.2 1895–1972
[La Dany, Ladislao] ———, 1914–.
'The two Ch'en historians.'
CNA 529 (21 Aug. 1964), 1–7.
Subj 62 70

21867 CSH P P1 G1.2 –1972
Lancashire, Douglas.
'A Confucian interpretation of history.'
J. of the Oriental Society of Australia 3, 1 (Jan. 1965), 76–87.
Subj 62 64 ▪ 63

21868 ELB P P1 G1.2 –1972
Larre, Claude.
'Mao Tse-toung, héritier de la vieille Chine?' (Mao Tse-tung, heir to ancient China?).
Etudes 7e série 329 (déc. 1968), 666–681.
Subj 13 62 64 ▪ 41 43

21869 CSU S P1 G1.2 –1972
Lessa, William Armand, 1908–.
Chinese body divination: Its forms, affinities, and functions.
Los Angeles: United World Academy and Fellowship, 1968. 13, 220 p.
Subj 62 65 ▪ 16 46

21870 CSU S P1 G1.2 1911–1972
Levenson, Joseph Richmond, 1920–1969.
'Conclusion.' In *Confucian China and its modern fate, Vol. 3, The problem of historical significance*, by J. R. Levenson. [Analytic entry]
Berkeley, Los Angeles: U. of California Press, 1965, 110–125.
Subj 12.1 16.1 62 ▪ 64

21871 CSU P P1 G1.2 –1972
Levenson, Joseph Richmond, 1920–1969.
'Part 2, Chinese culture in its modern metamorphoses: The tensions of intellectual choice.' In *Confucian China and its modern fate, Vol. 1, The problem of intellectual continuity*, by J. R. Levenson. [Analytic entry]
Berkeley, Los Angeles: U. of California Press, 1966, 47–163. [Revision of "History" and "value": The tensions of intellectual choice in modern China'; in *Studies in Chinese thought*, edited by Arthur Frederick Wright; Chicago: U. of Chicago Press, 1953, 146–194; except that chap. 4 incorporates 'The attenuation of a Chinese philosophical concept: "T'i-yung" in the 19th century'; *Asiatische Studien* 9 (1955), 95–102 and chap. 9 incorporates 'Western religion and the decay of traditional China: The intrusion of history on judgments of value'; *Sinologica* 4, 1 (1954), 14–20.]
Subj 16.1 62 64 ▪ 12 16 19 63 66 71

21872 CSU P P1 G1.2 –1972
Levenson, Joseph Richmond, 1920–1969.
'The placing of the Chinese Communists by their studies of the past.' In *Confucian China and its modern fate, Vol. 3, The problem of historical significance*, by J. R. Levenson. [Analytic entry]
Berkeley, Los Angeles: U. of California Press, 1965, 47–60. [Slight revision of 'History under Chairman Mao'; *Soviet survey* 24 (Apr.–June 1958), 32–37.]
Subj 62 70 ▪ 16 64

21873 CSU P P3 G1.2 1842–1972
Levenson, Joseph Richmond, 1920–1969.
Revolution and cosmopolitanism: The Western stage and the Chinese stages.
Berkeley, Los Angeles: U. of California Press, 1971. 31, 64 p.
Subj 62 ▪ 16.1 64 66

21874 NNC P P2 G1.2 1911–1972
Li Chi, 1903–.
General trends of Chinese linguistic changes under Communist rule.
Berkeley: U. of California, Center for Chinese Studies, 1956. 42 p. (Current Chinese Language Project, Studies in Chinese Communist terminology, 1) [Reprinted—Ann Arbor: University Microfilms, n.d. 42 p.]
Subj 12.1 17 62 ▪ 29 31 37 64

21875 CSU P P1 G1.1 1895–1972
Liu, Shu-hsien.
'The contemporary development of a Neo-Confucian epistomology.'
Inquiry 14, 1/2 (Summer 1971), 19–40.
Subj 62

21876 CSU P P1 G1.2 1911–1972
Meisner, Maurice J-, 1931–.
'Li Ta-chao and the Chinese Communist treatment of the materialist conception of history.' In *History in Communist China*, edited by Albert Feuerwerker. [Selective entry]
Cambridge: M.I.T. Press, 1968, 277–305.
Subj 62 64 70

21877 CSH S P3 G1.2 1928–1972
Meliksetov, Arlen Vaagovich, 1930–.
'Sovremennaia kitaiskaia kontseptsiia sotsial'no-ekonomicheskogo razvitiia gomin'danovskogo Kitaia' (Contemporary Chinese conceptions of socioeconomic development in Kuomintang China). In *Istoricheskaia nauka v KNR* (Historiography in the People's Republic of China), compiled by Institut vostokovedeniia, Akademiia nauk SSSR, edited by Rudol'f Vsevolodovich Viatkin and Nataliia Pavlovna Svistunova. [Selective entry]
Moscow: Nauka, Glav. red. vost. lit-ry, 1971, 170–179.
Subj 14.6 32 62 70 ▪ 14.5 16.1 16.2 64 72

21878 CSU S P1 G1.2 –1972
Meskill, John Thomas, 1927–.
'Introduction.' In *The pattern of Chinese history: Cycles, development, or stagnation?*, edited by J. T. Meskill. [Selective entry]
Boston: Heath, 1965, 7–17 [s.p.].
Subj 62 70 71 ▪ 19

21879 NNC P P1 G1.2 1928–1972
Morrison, Esther, 1915–.
'A comparison of Kuomintang and Communist modern history textbooks.'
PC 6 (Mar. 1952), 3–44.
Subj 12.1 17 62 64

21880 MCH P P1 G1.2 –1972
Needham, Noël Joseph Terence Montgomery, 1900–.
'Poverties and triumphs of the Chinese scientific tradition' [with comments by Willy Hartner, Pierre Huard, and Wong Chu-ming]. In *Scientific change*, edited by Alistair Cameron Crombie. [Sole entry]
New York: Basic Books, 1963, 117–153. [Reprinted in *The grand titration: Science and society in East and West*, by N. J. T. M. Needham. (Selective entry.) Toronto: U. of Toronto Press, 1969, 14–54.]
Subj 16.1 60 62

21881 NNC P P1 G1.2 –1972
Nivison, David Shepherd, 1923–.
'The problem of "knowledge" and "action" in Chinese thought since Wang Yang-ming.' In *Studies in Chinese thought*, edited by Arthur Frederick Wright. [Selective entry]
Chicago: U. of Chicago Press, 1953, 112–143. (American Anthropological Assn. memoirs, 75)
Subj 60 62 63 64

21882 NNC P P1 G1.2 1842–1972
Novikov, L- N-.
'Izuchenie v Kitaiskoi Narodnoi Respublike ekonomicheskoi istorii Kitaia v novoe i noveishee vremia' (Chinese economic history in modern and recent times and its study in the People's Republic of China). In *Sovremennaia istoriografiia stran zarubezhnogo Vostoka, vyp. 1, Kitai* (Current historiography of countries of the non-Soviet Orient, Vol. 1, China), edited by Boris Nikolaevich Zanegin et al. [Selective entry]
Moscow: Izd-vo vost. lit-ry, 1963, 88–101.
Subj 62 70 ▪ 12 14 72

21883 NIC P P1 G1.3 –1972
Parsons, James Bunyan, 1921–.
'Attitudes toward the late Ming rebellions.'
OE 6, 2 (Dez. 1959), 177–209.
Subj 32.2 62 64 ▪ 12 15

21884 MCH P P1 G1.2 –1972
Porkert, Manfred, 1933–.
'Farbemblematik in China' (Color symbolism in China).
Antaios; Z. für eine freie Welt 4, 2 (Juli 1962), 154–167.
Subj 62 ▪ 56

21885 CSH S P2 G1.2 –1972
Porshneva, E- B-.
'Diskussiia o krest'ianskikh voinakh v Kitae pri feodalizme (1964–1965)' (The 1964–1965 debate on peasant wars in feudal China). In *Istoricheskaia nauka v KNR* (Historiography in the People's Republic of China), compiled by Institut vostokovedeniia, Akademiia nauk SSSR, edited by Rudol'f Vsevolodovich Viatkin and Nataliia Pavlovna Svistunova. [Selective entry]
Moscow: Nauka, Glav. red. vost. lit-ry, 1971, 101–110.
Subj 36.3 62 64 ▪ 16 18 32.2 70 72

21886 CSU P P1 G1.2 1928–1972
Sabattini, Mario.
'"Crocianism" in Chu Kuang-ch'ien's "Wen-i hsin-li-hsueh" [Psychology of aesthetics].'
East and West (Rome) 20, 1/2 (Mar.–June 1970), 179–197.
Subj 62

21887 CBU P P2 G1.2 –1972
Schneider, Laurence Allen.
Ku Chieh-kang and China's new history: Nationalism and the quest for alternative traditions.
Berkeley, Los Angeles: U. of California Press, 1971. 14, 337 p. (Revision of *Reorganizing the past: Ku Chieh-kang and China's new history*, doctoral dissertation in History, U. of California, Berkeley, 1968)
Subj 16.1 60 62 70 ▪ 14.2 36.1 64 65 66

21888 CSU U P1 G1.0 –1972
Sivin, Nathan, 1931–.
'Chinese conceptions of time.'
Earlham review 1, 2 (Fall 1966), 82–92.
Subj 62

21889 MCH P P1 G1.2 –1972
Soymié, Michel.
'La lune dans les religions chinoises' (The moon in Chinese religion). In *La lune: mythes et rites* (The moon: Myths and rites), by Philippe Derchain et al., edited by Denise Bernot et al. [Sole entry]
Paris: Le Seuil, 1962, 289–321.
Subj 62 65 ▪ 23

21890 MCH P P1 G1.1 –1972
Soymié, Michel.
'Sources et sourciers en Chine' (Springs and water-diviners in China).
B. de la Maison franco-japonaise nouvelle (2e) série 7, 1 (1961), 1–56.
Subj 62

21891 CBU P P1 G1.2 –1972
Staiger, Brunhild, 1938–.
Das Konfuzius-Bild im kommunistischen China: Die Neubewertung von Konfuzius in der chinesisch-marxischen Geschichtsschreibung (The image of Confucius in Communist China: The reevaluation of Confucius in Chinese-Marxist historical writings).
Wiesbaden: Harrassowitz, 1969. 143 p. (Institut für Asienkunde, Schriften, 23) (Doctoral dissertation, Universität Hamburg)
Subj 16 62 64 70 ▪ 63

21892 CSH S P2 G8.0 1842–1972
Stuzhina, Emiliia Pavlovna, 1931–.
'Antiman'chzhurskie i antifeodal'nie natsional'nie dvizheniia vtoroi polovini XIX v. v IUgo-zapadnom Kitae i sovremennaia kitaiskaia istoriografiia' (Contemporary Chinese historiography on the anti-Manchu and antifeudal national movement in the second half of the nineteenth century in Southwest China). In *Istoricheskaia nauka v KNR* (Historiography in the People's Republic of China), compiled by Institut vostokovedeniia, Akademiia nauk SSSR, edited by Rudol'f Vsevolodovich Viatkin and Nataliia Pavlovna Svistunova. [Selective entry]
Moscow: Nauka, Glav. red. vost. lit-ry, 1971, 158–169.
Subj 62 66 70 ▪ 16 29 32.2 33 72

21893 CSH P P2 G1.2 1928–1972
Svistunova, Nataliia Pavlovna.
'Ob istoricheskikh vzgliadakh TSzian' Botszania i ikh kritike v KNR' (Chien Potsan's historical views and their critique in the People's Republic of China). In *Istoricheskaia nauka v KNR* (Historiography in the People's Republic of China), compiled by Institut vostokovedeniia, Akademiia nauk SSSR, edited by Rudol'f Vsevolodovich Viatkin and N. P. Svistunova. [Selective entry]
Moscow: Nauka, Glav. red. vost. lit-ry, 1971, 217–231.
Subj 62 64 70 ▪ 14.1 16 32 32.2 72

21894 CSH S P2 G1.2 –1972
Svistunova, Nataliia Pavlovna.
'Obzor diskussii o formakh zemel'noi sobstvennosti v feodal'nom Kitae' (Summary of the debate on forms of agrarian property in feudal China). In *Istoricheskaia nauka v KNR* (Historiography in the People's Republic of China), compiled by Institut vostokovedeniia, Akademiia nauk SSSR, edited by Rudol'f Vsevolodovich Viatkin and N. P. Svistunova. [Selective entry]
Moscow: Nauka, Glav. red. vost. lit-ry, 1971, 82–100.
Subj 14.1 62 70 ▪ 12.1 16 18 64 72

21895 CSU U P1 G1.0 –1972
Ting, Su.
'Fortune telling.'
Asia (Saigon) 3, 11 (Dec. 1953), 428–437.
Subj 62

21896 CSU P P1 G1.0 –1972
Tong, Paul K. K.
'Understanding Confucianism.'
International philosophical q. 9, 4 (Dec. 1969), 518–532.
Subj 62 63

21897 CSU S P2 G1.3 –1972
Tuan, Yi-fu (Tuan I-fu), 1930–.
'Discrepancies between environmental attitude and behavior: Examples from Europe and China.'
Canadian geographer 12, 3 (1968), 176–191.
Subj 11.3 62

21898 CSH PO P1 G1.2 1911–1972
Viatkin, Rudol'f Vsevolodovich, 1910–.
'Istoricheskaia nauka v KNR' (Historiography in the People's Republic of China). In *Istoricheskaia nauka v KNR* (Historiography in the People's Republic of China), compiled by Institut vostokovedeniia, Akademiia nauk SSSR, edited by R. V. Viatkin and Nataliia Pavlovna Svistunova. [Selective entry]

Moscow: Nauka, Glav. red. vost. lit-ry, 1971, 3–63.
SUBJ 16.1 62 64 ▪ 17 32 70 72

21899 CSU U P1 G1.2 –1972
Wang Gungwu (Wang Keng-wu), 1930–.
'The inside and outside of Chinese history: A perspective on China's relations with the world.'
Round table (London) 247 (July 1972), 283–295.
SUBJ 62 66

21900 NIC P P2 G1.2 –1972
Wright, Arthur Frederick, 1913–.
Buddhism in Chinese history.
Stanford: Stanford U. Press, 1959. 14, 144 p.
SUBJ 23 33 62 ▪ 17 32.2 47 60 63

21901 NNC S P1 G1.2 –1972
Wright, Arthur Frederick, 1913–.
'The Chinese language and foreign ideas.' In *Studies in Chinese thought*, edited by A. F. Wright. [Selective entry]
Chicago: U. of Chicago Press, 1953, 286–303. (American Anthropological Assn. memoirs, 75)
SUBJ 62 66 ▪ 63 64 71 72

21902 CSU P P2 G1.1 –1972
Wright, Arthur Frederick, 1913–.
'Historiography. Part 3, Chinese historiography.' In *International encyclopedia of the social sciences*, edited by David L- Sills. [Selective entry]
New York: Macmillan *with* Free Press of Glencoe, 1968, vol. 6, 400–407.
SUBJ 62 70 ▪ 14.2 36.1

21903 CSU S P1 G1.1 –1972
Wright, Arthur Frederick, 1913–, and John Whitney Hall, 1916–.
'Chinese and Japanese historiography: Some trends, 1961–1966.'
AAAPSS 371 (May 1967), 178–193.
SUBJ 62 70 71 72

21904 CSU FP P2 G1.1 1928–1972
Wu, Yuan-li (Wu Yüan-li), 1920–, and Robert Bruce Sheeks, 1922–.
The organization and support of scientific research and development in Mainland China.
New York: Praeger, 1970. 22, 592 p.
SUBJ 14 36.1 62 ▪ 11.4 12 14.1 14.2 14.4 17

1949-1972

21905 CSU F P8 G9.5 1949–1972
Anderson, Eugene Newton, Jr., 1941–.
'The ethnoichthyology of the Hong Kong boat people.' In *Essays on South China's boat people*, by E. N. Anderson, Jr. [Analytic entry]
Taipei: Orient Cultural Service, 1972, 41–146. (Asian Folklore and Social Life monographs, 29) (Doctoral dissertation in Anthropology, U. of California, Berkeley, 1967)
SUBJ 62 65 ▪ 24.1

21906 CSU F P8 G9.5 1949–1972
Anderson, Eugene Newton, Jr., 1941–.
'Sacred fish.'
Man new (2nd) series 4, 3 (Sept. 1969), 443–449. [Reprinted in *Essays on South China's boat people*, by E. N. Anderson, Jr. (Analytic entry.) Taipei: Orient Cultural Service, 1972, 33–39. (Asian Folklore and Social Life monographs, 29)]
SUBJ 62 65 ▪ 23 24.1

21907 CSH P P1 G1.2 1949–1972
Borokh, Liliia Nikolaevna, 1933–.
'Kitaiskie istoriki o printsipakh istoricheskogo issledovaniia' (Chinese historians on the principles of historical research). In *Istoricheskaia nauka v KNR* (Historiography in the People's Republic of China), compiled by Institut vostokovedeniia, Akademiia nauk SSSR, edited by Rudol'f Vsevolodovich Viatkin and Nataliia Pavlovna Svistunova. [Selective entry]
Moscow: Nauka, Glav. red. vost. lit-ry, 1971, 180–191.
SUBJ 62 64 ▪ 16 32.2 36.3 70 72

21908 NIC O P3 G9.5 1949–1972
Buck, Samuel, pseud.
'Chinese fortune telling.'
Orient (Hong Kong) 2, 10 (May 1952), 39–42.
SUBJ 23 62 ▪ 65

21909 CSU P P1 G1.2 1949–1972
Chan, Wing-tsit (Ch'en Jung-chieh), 1901–.
'Chinese philosophy in Mainland China, 1949–1963.'
Philosophy, East and West 14, 1 (Apr. 1964), 25–38.
SUBJ 36.1 62 ▪ 32.1 63 64

21910 CSU P P1 G1.2 1949–1972
Ch'en, Kenneth K. S. (Ch'en Kuan-sheng), 1907–.
'Chinese Communist attitudes towards Buddhism in Chinese history.' In *History in Communist China*, edited by Albert Feuerwerker. [Selective entry]
Cambridge: M.I.T. Press, 1968, 158–174.
SUBJ 33 62 70

21911 CSH P P1 G1.2 1949–1972
Ch'iu Shih-chih.
'Communist China's science work in 1966.' Tr. of '1966 nien ta lu ti k'o hsüeh kung tso'; *Tsu kuo* 36 (Mar. 1967), 42–48. In *Communist China, 1966*, edited by Union Research Institute. [Selective entry]
Hong Kong: Union Research Institute, 1968, vol. 2, 151–170.
SUBJ 16.1 62 ▪ 14.1 32.1 36.1

21912 CSH P P2 G1.2 1949–1972
Ch'iu Shih-chih.
'Communist China's work of scientific research in 1965.' Tr. of '1965 nien ta lu ti tzu jan k'o hsüeh kung tso' (Activities in the natural sciences on the Mainland, 1965); *Tsu kuo* 25 (Apr. 1966), 15–25. In *Communist China, 1965*, edited by Union Research Institute. [Selective entry]
Hong Kong: Union Research Institute, 1967, vol. 2, 208–229.
SUBJ 17 62 ▪ 36.1

21913 CSH P P1 G1.2 1949–1972
Ch'iu Shih-chih.
'Scientific and technological development.' Tr. of '1964 nien ta lu ti k'o hsüeh chi shu kung tso' (Science and technology in Mainland China, 1964); *Tsu kuo* 14 (May 1965), 23–33. In *Communist China, 1964*, edited by Union Research Institute. [Selective entry]
Hong Kong: Union Research Institute, 1965, vol. 1, 172–210.
SUBJ 17 36.1 62 ▪ 16.1 32.1

21914 WSU U P1 G1.2 1949–1972
Chu, Cochin (Chu K'o-chen), 1890–.
'The development of science and technology in New China.'
Scientific world 4, 3/4 (1960), 16–22.
SUBJ 14.4 62 ▪ 11.4 16.1

21915 CSU S P1 G1.2 1949–1972
Chzhao TSziu-chzhan (Chao Chiu-chang).
'Meteorologiia i seismologiia v Kitae' (Meteorology and seismology in China).
Priroda 1959, 10 (oktiabr'), 27–34.
SUBJ 62

21916 CSH P P2 G1.2 1949–1972
Dobrinin, K- A-.
'Kritika kitaiskikh istorikov na stranitsakh kitaiskoi pechati v period "Kul'turnoi revoliutsie"' (Criticisms of Chinese historians in the Chinese press during the Cultural Revolution). In *Istoricheskaia nauka v KNR* (Historiography in the People's Republic of China), compiled by Institut vostokovedeniia, Akademiia nauk SSSR, edited by Rudol'f Vsevolodovich Viatkin and Nataliia Pavlovna Svistunova. [Selective entry]
Moscow: Nauka, Glav. red. vost. lit-ry, 1971, 232–243.
SUBJ 32.1 62 64 70 ▪ 16 32

21917 CSU P P2 G1.2 1949–1972
Du Ruen-sheng.
'Great progress made in the natural sciences in China during the last decade.'
Scientia sinica 8, 11 (Nov. 1959), 1196–1217. [Reprinted as 'Communist Chinese claims regarding scientific progress in the last decade.' *Science news letter* 78, 24 (10 Dec. 1960), 379–392.]
SUBJ 14.4 62 ▪ 14.1 56 72

21918 CSH P P2 G1.2 1949–1972
Esposito, Bruce John, 1941–.
'The Cultural Revolution and science policy and development in Mainland China.'
Courrier de l'Extrême-Orient 48 (1971), 114–122.
SUBJ 16.1 36.1 62 ▪ 17 32.1

21919 CSU P P2 G1.2 1949–1972
Fann, K. T. (Fan Kuang-t'i), 1937–.
'Philosophy in the Chinese Cultural Revolution.'
International philosophical q. 9, 3 (Sept. 1969), 449–459.
SUBJ 60 62 64 ▪ 12.1 16.1 17

21920 CSU S P1 G1.2 1949–1972
Farquhar, David Miller, 1927–.
'Chinese Communist assessments of a foreign conquest dynasty.' In *History in Communist China*, edited by Albert Feuerwerker. [Selective entry]
Cambridge: M.I.T. Press, 1968, 175–188.
SUBJ 62 70 ▪ 66

21921 CSU P P1 G1.2 1949–1972
Feuerwerker, Albert, 1927–.
'China's modern economic history in Communist Chinese historiography.' In

History in Communist China, edited by A. Feuerwerker. [Selective entry]
Cambridge: M.I.T. Press, 1968, 216–246.
Subj 14 62 70

21922 NNC P P1 G1.2 1949–1972
Feuerwerker, Albert, 1927–.
'From "feudalism" to "capitalism" in recent historical writing from Mainland China.'
JAS 18, 1 (Nov. 1958), 107–116.
Subj 14 62

21923 CSU P P1 G1.2 1949–1972
Fitzgerald, Charles Patrick, 1902–.
'The Chinese middle ages in Communist historiography.' In *History in Communist China*, edited by Albert Feuerwerker. [Selective entry]
Cambridge: M.I.T. Press, 1968, 124–139.
Subj 62 70

21924 MCH S P1 G1.2 1949–1972
Grootaers, Willem A-, 1911–.
'Language study in China (1951–1952).'
Orbis (Louvain) 2, 1 (1953), 165–175.
Subj 62 ▪ 17 29

21925 MCH F P3 G9.4 1949–1972
[Hang, Thaddäus] Thaddeus Hang, and J- Masson.
'Une enquête religieuse chez des étudiants de Tainan' (A religious investigation among students in Tainan).
Studia missionalia 16 (1967), 99–115.
Subj 62 63 ▪ 33 54

21926 CSH O P1 G1.2 1949–1972
Harris, Richard.
'Confucian Asia and democratic Asia.'
Asian affairs (London) 1, 3 (Oct. 1970), 265–274.
Subj 62

21927 NIC F P1 G1.0 1949–1972
Hellersberg, Elisabeth F-.
'Visual perception and spatial organization: A study of performance on the Horn-Hellersberg test by Chinese subjects.' In *The study of culture at a distance*, edited by Margaret Mead and Rhoda Metraux. [Selective entry]
Chicago: U. of Chicago Press, 1953, 320–328.
Subj 61 62 ▪ 63

21928 NIC P P2 G1.2 1949–1972
Hsia, T. A. (Hsia Chi-an), 1916–1965.
A terminological study of the Hsia-fang [downward-transfer] *movement.*
Berkeley: U. of California, Center for Chinese Studies, 1963. 68 p. (Current Chinese Language Project, Studies in Chinese Communist terminology, 10) [Reprinted—Ann Arbor: University Microfilms, n.d. 68 p.]
Subj 32.1 62 ▪ 21.2 61

21929 CSU P P1 G1.2 1949–1972
Hulsewé, Anthony François Paulus, 1910–.
'Chinese Communist treatment of the origins and foundation of the Chinese empire.' In *History in Communist China*, edited by Albert Feuerwerker. [Selective entry]
Cambridge: M.I.T. Press, 1968, 96–123.
Subj 62 70

21930 CSU O P2 G1.2 1949–1972
Hunter, Neale.
'The good earth and the good society.' In *China and ourselves: Explorations and revisions by a new generation*, edited by Bruce Douglass and Ross Terrill. [Selective entry]
Boston: Beacon Press, 1969, 174–188.
Subj 10 62

21931 CSU P P1 G1.2 1949–1972
Kahn, Harold Lionel, 1930–, and Albert Feuerwerker, 1927–.
'The ideology of scholarship: China's new historiography.' In *History in Communist China*, edited by A. Feuerwerker. [Selective entry]
Cambridge: M.I.T. Press, 1968, 1–13.
Subj 62 64 70

21932 MAM F P1 G9.4 1949–1972
Kao, Yung-huo Liu (Kao Liu Yung-huo), 1913–.
A comparison of semantic structure in Chinese and English.
Ann Arbor: University Microfilms (Publ. 58-7736), 1958. 143 p. (Doctoral dissertation in Psychology, U. of Michigan)
Subj 60 62 ▪ 29 43 61

21933 CSU F P1 G1.0 1949–1972
Kehl, Frank, 1940–.
'Chinese nicknaming behavior: A sociolinguistic pilot study.'
JOS 9, 1 (Jan. 1971), 149–172.
Subj 48 52 62 ▪ 63

21934 MMT P P1 G1.2 1949–1972
Kirby, Edward Stuart, 1909–.
'The perspective of Chinese economic history in the light of recent studies in Communist China.' In *Symposium on economic and social problems of the Far East*, edited by Edward Franciszek Szczepanik. [Selective entry]
Hong Kong: Hong Kong U. Press, 1962, 3–10.
Subj 62 ▪ 14 17 66 70

21935 WSU P P1 G1.2 1949–1972
Kiuzadzhian, Liparit Sarkisovich, 1932–.
'Obsuzhdenie kitaiskimi istorikami vzgliadov burzhuaznogo ideologa Khu Shi' (Chinese historians discuss the views of Hu Shih, a bourgeois ideologue).
VI 1955, 6 (iiun'), 186–190.
Subj 62 70 ▪ 64

21936 CSH O P3 G1.2 1949–1972
Klochko, Mikhail Antonovich, 1902–.
Un Russe en Chine (A Russian in China). Tr. from the Russian by Stefan Chripounoff. [Tr. from an unpublished manuscript]
Paris: Gallimard, 1964. 289 p.

Soviet scientist in China. Tr. by Andrew MacAndrew.
New York: Praeger, 1964. 192 p.
Subj 12.1 36.1 62 ▪ 14.4 16.1 17 55 66

21937 CSU P P2 G1.2 1949–1972
Kusano Fumio, 1915–. [Tr. erroneously gives author's name as Kusano Fumiko.]
Evaluation of comprehensive study of Chinese Communist science and technology, mimeo. Tr. of *Chūkyō no kagaku gijutsu ippan ni kansuru sōgōteki kenkyū* (A general study of science and technology in Communist China); Tokyo: [Kōjimachi kenkyūjo], 1964; 116 p.
Washington, D.C.: U.S. Joint Publications Research Service, 26 Sept. 1966. 76 p. (JPRS 37,828; MC 16,460/1966)
Subj 17 62 ▪ 36.1 66

21938 CSH P P1 G1.2 1949–1972
[La Dany, Ladislao] ———, 1914–.
'Dialectical materialism: The state of philosophy.'
CNA 191 (2 Aug. 1957), 1–7.
Subj 62 64

21939 NIC P P1 G1.2 1949–1972
[La Dany, Ladislao] ———, 1914–.
'Fung Yu-lan.'
CNA 336 (19 Aug. 1960), 1–7.
Subj 16.1 62 ▪ 12.1

21940 CSH P P1 G1.2 1949–1972
[La Dany, Ladislao] ———, 1914–.
'Fung Yu-lan. Part One, 1949–1957. Part Two, 1958.'
CNA 241 (15 Aug. 1958), 1–7; 244 (12 Sept. 1958), 1–7.
Subj 16.1 62 64 ▪ 12.1 17

21941 CSH P P1 G1.2 1949–1972
[La Dany, Ladislao] ———, 1914–.
'Of K'ung Tzu (Confucius), Fung Yu-lan and others.'
CNA 398 (24 Nov. 1961), 1–7.
Subj 62 64

21942 CSH P P1 G1.2 1949–1972
[La Dany, Ladislao] ———, 1914–.
'Psychology, 1959–1961.'
CNA 388 (8 Sept. 1961), 1–7.
Subj 62 64 ▪ 70

21943 CSH P P3 G1.2 1949–1972
[La Dany, Ladislao] ———, 1914–.
'Tools for research.'
CNA 504 (12 Feb. 1964), 1–7.
Subj 17 62

21944 MAM F P3 G9.4 1949–1972
Lee, Chang Kuei, 1932–.
Major dimensions of non-Christian religious orientations in Formosa: Cultural analysis and interpretation of non-Christian students.
Ann Arbor: University Microfilms (Publ. 66-8144), 1966. 187 p. (Doctoral dissertation in Religion, U. of Pittsburgh, 1965)
Subj 54 62 ▪ 23 61 63

21945 [2]CSU U P1 G1.2 1949–1972
Levenson, Joseph Richmond, 1920–1969.
'Marxism and the Middle Kingdom.'
Diplomat 17, 196 (Sept. 1966), 48–51. [Reprinted in *Modern China: An interpretive anthology*, edited by J. R. Levenson. (Selective entry.) London: Macmillan, 1971, 229–236.]
Subj 62 ▪ 64

21946 CSU O P7 G9.4 1949–1972
Lévesque, Léonard.
Hakka beliefs and customs [as observed in Kuan-hsi *chen*, Hsin-chu *hsien*, Taiwan]. Tr. from the French by J- Maynard Murphy. [Tr. of an unpublished manuscript, *Croyances et coutumes Hakka*]
Taichung: Kuang Chi Press, 1969. 113 p.
Subj 23 41 62 ▪ 29 43 57 65

21947 CSU P P2 G1.2 1949–1972
Li, C. C. (Li Ching-chün), 1912–.
'Genetics and animal and plant breeding.' In *Sciences in Communist China*, edited by [Sydney Henry Gould] Sidney H. Gould. [Selective entry]
Washington, D.C.: American Assn. for the Advancement of Science, 1961, 297–321. (AAAS publications, 68)
SUBJ 14.1 62 64 ▪ 16.1 32.1 36.1

21948 NIC P P2 G1.2 1949–1972
Li Chi, 1903–.
I, Literacy and colloquial terms in new usage. II, Terms topped by numerals.
Berkeley: U. of California, Center for Chinese Studies, 1957. 51 p. (Current Chinese Language Project, Studies in Chinese Communist terminology, 3) [Reprinted—Ann Arbor: University Microfilms, n.d. 51 p.]
SUBJ 29 48 62 64 ▪ 12.2 14.1 16.3 19 65 72

21949 NIC P P1 G1.2 1949–1972
Li Chi, 1903–.
I, The Communist term 'the common language' and related terms. II, Dialectical terms in common usage. III, Literary and colloquial terms in common usage.
Berkeley: U. of California, Center for Chinese Studies, 1957. 88 p. (Current Chinese Language Project, Studies in Chinese Communist terminology, 4) [Reprinted—Ann Arbor: University Microfilms, n.d. 88 p.]
SUBJ 62 65 ▪ 29 64

21950 NIC P P1 G1.2 1949–1972
Li Chi, 1903–.
Preliminary study of selected terms.
Berkeley: U. of California, Center for Chinese Studies, 1956. 24 p. (Current Chinese Language Project, Studies in Chinese Communist terminology, 2) [Reprinted—Ann Arbor: University Microfilms, n.d. 24 p.]
SUBJ 62 65 ▪ 64

21951 NIC P P1 G1.2 1949–1972
Li Chi, 1903–.
The use of figurative language in Communist China.
Berkeley: U. of California, Center for Chinese Studies, 1958. 85 p. (Current Chinese Language Project, Studies in Chinese Communist terminology, 5) [Reprinted—Ann Arbor: University Microfilms, n.d. 25 p.]
SUBJ 12.1 62 ▪ 16.1 60

21952 CSH P P1 G1.2 1949–1972
Li Yu-ning.
'Wu Han's view of history.' In *Collected documents of the First Sino-American Conference on Mainland China.* [Selective entry]
[Taipei]: Institute of International Relations, Republic of China, 1971, 413–426.
SUBJ 62

21953 CSU P P1 G1.2 1949–1972
Lindbeck, John Matthew Henry, 1915–1971.
'An isolationist science policy.'
B. of the atomic scientists 25, 2 (Feb. 1969), 66–72. [Special issue: *China after the Cultural Revolution*, edited by (Richard Garratt Wilson) Dick Wilson] [Reprinted in *China after the Cultural Revolution*. (Selective entry.) New York: Random House, 1969, 181–197.]
SUBJ 62 ▪ 16.1

21954 MCY P P1 G1.2 1949–1972
Lu Yau-tung.
'An analysis of Chinese Communist interpretation of history.'
CC 6, 1 (Oct. 1964), 47–54.
SUBJ 62 70

21955 CSU P P1 G1.2 1949–1972
Luey, Paul (Lü Pao-lo).
'The yün-ch'ou-hsüeh movement [maximization of manpower and material resources through application of methods of mathematics and economics].' In *Contemporary China, 1962–1964*, edited by Edward Stuart Kirby. [Selective entry]
Hong Kong: Hong Kong U. Press, 1968, 37–41.
SUBJ 14 62 ▪ 12.1 19

21956 MCH P P1 G1.2 1949–1972
Marchisio, Joseph.
'L'orientation actuelle des études historiques: les études historiques en Chine populaire' (Present trends in historiography: History in the People's Republic of China).
R. historique 229 (jan.–mars 1963), 159–169.
SUBJ 62 70 72 ▪ 12.1 16.1 17

21957 CSU O P3 G1.2 1949–1972
Mendelssohn, Kurt.
'Science in China.'
Nature 215, 5096 (1 July 1967), 10–12.
SUBJ 62 ▪ 14.4 17

21958 CSU P P1 G1.2 1949–1972
Modelski, George Alexander.
'Communist China prepares for nuclear expansion.' In *Atomic energy in the Communist bloc*, by G. A. Modelski. [Sole entry]
Carlton: Melbourne U. Press, 1959, 181–195. (Australian National U., Social Science Monographs, 15)
SUBJ 16.1 62 ▪ 14.4 15 17 66

21959 CSU P P1 G1.2 1949–1972
Munro, Donald Jacques, 1931–.
'Chinese Communist treatment of the thinkers of the Hundred Schools period.' In *History in Communist China*, edited by Albert Feuerwerker. [Selective entry]
Cambridge: M.I.T. Press, 1968, 74–95.
SUBJ 62 70 ▪ 16.1 64

21960 CSH S P2 G1.2 1949–1972
Murphey, William Rhoads, III, 1919–.
'Man and nature in China.'
MAS 1, 4 (Oct. 1967), 313–333.
SUBJ 12.1 61 62 ▪ 14 14.1 19

21961 CBU P P2 G1.2 1949–1972
Oldham, C- H- G-.
'China today: Science.'
J. of the Royal Society of Arts 116, 5144 (July 1968), 666–682.
SUBJ 62 64 ▪ 16.1 17 36.1

21962 CSU P P3 G1.2 1949–1972
Oldham, C- H- G-.
'Science and technology in China's future.' In *Contemporary China: Papers presented at the University of Guelph Conference, April 1968.* [Selective entry]
Toronto: Canadian Institute of International Affairs, 1968, 113–129.
SUBJ 16.1 62 ▪ 32.1 36.1

21963 CSU O P4 G1.2 1949–1972
Oldham, C- H- G-.
'Science in China's development.'
Advancement of science 24, 122 (June 1968), 481–487.
SUBJ 62 ▪ 17 36.1

21964 CSU P P2 G1.2 1949–1972
Orleans, Leo A-, 1924–.
'China's science and technology: Continuity and innovation.' In *People's Republic of China: An economic assessment*, compiled by Joint Economic Committee, U.S. Congress. [Selective entry]
Washington, D.C.: U.S. Government Printing Office, 1972, 185–219.
SUBJ 12.1 16.1 17 62 ▪ 14.2 14.4 36.1

21965 CSH P P2 G1.2 1949–1972
Pai Chen.
'Scientific work.' Tr. of '1961 nien ti Chung kung k'o hsüeh kung tso' (Activities in the sciences in Communist China, 1961); *Tsu kuo chou k'an* 492 (11 June 1962), 7–13. In *Communist China, 1961*, edited by Union Research Institute. [Selective entry]
Hong Kong: Union Research Institute, 1962, vol. 1, 199–224.
SUBJ 17 62 ▪ 32.1

21966 CSU F P8 G9.5 1949–1972
Potter, Jack Michael, 1936–.
'Wind, water, bones and souls: The religious world of the Cantonese peasant.'
JOS 8, 1 (Jan. 1970), 139–153.
SUBJ 43 62 ▪ 23 42 57

21967 CSU O P1 G1.2 1949–1972
Shiraishi Bon.
'The Chinese way of thinking.'
JQ 12, 1 (Jan.–Mar. 1965), 87–92.
SUBJ 60 62 ▪ 66

21968 CSH P P3 G1.2 1949–1972
Sung, Shee (Sung Hsi), 1920–.
'The study of history in Communist China.'
CC 10, 4 (Dec. 1969), 15–51.
SUBJ 32.1 62 70 ▪ 16.1 36.1 64

21969 CSU P P1 G1.2 1949–1972
Suttmeier, Richard Peter, 1942–.
'Party views of science: The record from the first decade.'
CQ 44 (Oct.–Dec. 1970), 146–168.
SUBJ 62 ▪ 32.1 64

21970 CSU P P1 G1.2 1949–1972
Ts'ao, Ignatius J. H.
'A decade of philosophical issues in Mainland China, 1956–1965.'
SST 8, 4 (Dec. 1968), 306–314.
SUBJ 62 64

21971 MAU O P1 G9.5 1949–1972
Tseung, F. I.
'Some aspects of fortune-telling in Hong Kong.' In *Some traditional Chinese ideas and conceptions in Hong Kong social life today*, edited by Marjorie Doreen Topley. [Analytic entry]

Hong Kong: Royal Asiatic Society, Hong Kong Branch, 1967, 60–72.
SUBJ 62

21972 MCH P P1 G1.2 1949–1972
Uhalley, Stephen, Jr., 1930–.
'The "Four-histories" movement: A revolution in writing China's past.'
CS 4, 2 (15 Jan. 1966), 1–11.
SUBJ 12.1 62 70

21973 MCH P P1 G1.2 1949–1972
Viatkin, Rudol'f Vsevolodovich, 1910–, and Sergei Leonidovich Tikhvinskii (S. L. Tikhvinsky), 1918–.
'O nekotorykh voprosakh istoricheskoi nauki v KNR.'
VI 1963, 10 (oktiabr'), 3–20.
'Some questions of historical science in the Chinese People's Republic.'
Current digest of the Soviet press 16, 4 (19 Feb. 1964), 3–10. [A different tr.—'Some problems of historical scholarship in the Chinese People's Republic.' *Soviet studies in history* 2, 4 (Spring 1964), 44–60.] [Reprinted in *History in Communist China*, edited by Albert Feuerwerker. (Selective entry.) Cambridge: M.I.T. Press, 1968, 331–355.]
SUBJ 62 70 ▪ 64 66

21974 CSU O P1 G1.2 1949–1972
Waddington, C- H-.
'Biology in China.'
Arts and sciences in China 1, 3 (July–Sept. 1963), 2–5.
SUBJ 62

21975 MCH PO P3 G1.2 1949–1972
[Wilson, Richard Garratt] Dick Wilson, 1928–.
'Technology in China.'
FEER 50, 6 (11 Nov. 1965), 289–291.
SUBJ 14.4 62 ▪ 66

21976 CSU U P1 G1.2 1949–1972
Wright, Mary Clabaugh, 1917–1970.
'China reassesses its past: Historical writing in the People's Republic.'
Ventures 5, 1 (Winter 1965), 24–30.
SUBJ 62 70

21977 CSH P P2 G1.2 1949–1972
[Wu Leng] ———.
'Communist China's natural science work in 1962.' Tr. of '1962 nien ti Chung kung tzu jan k'o hsüeh kung tso'; *Tsu kuo chou k'an* 542 (27 May 1963), 8–14. In *Communist China, 1962*, edited by Union Research Institute. [Selective entry]
Hong Kong: Union Research Institute, 1963, vol. 2, 55–83.
SUBJ 62 ▪ 14.2 17 36.1

21978 CSH P P2 G1.2 1949–1972
Wu Leng.
'Scientific development.' Tr. of '1963 nien ti Chung kung k'o hsüeh kung tso' (Activities in the sciences in Communist China, 1963); *Tsu kuo* 3 (June 1964), 18–25. In *Communist China, 1963*, edited by Union Research Institute. [Selective entry]
Hong Kong: Union Research Institute, 1965, vol. 1, 127–150.
SUBJ 17 62 ▪ 14.2 32.1 36.1

21979 CSU P P4 G1.2 1949–1972
Yamada, Keiji, 1932–.
'The development of science and technology in China: 1949–65.'
DE 9, 4 (Dec. 1971), 502–537. [Special issue: *On China*]
SUBJ 14.4 16.1 17 36.1 62 ▪ 70

63 ETHICS
倫理 倫理

1644-1911

21980 NNC O P4 G1.2 1895–1911
Brandt, Max August Scipio von, 1835–1914?
Der Chinese in der Öffentlichkeit und der Familie, wie er sich selbst sieht und schildert (The Chinese as he views and portrays himself in public and at home).
Berlin: Reimer, 1911. 165 p.
SUBJ 40 63 ▪ 13 23 31 33 51 57 60

21981 MCH O P1 G1.2 –1911
Farjenel, Fernand, ?–1918.
La morale chinoise, fondement des sociétés d'Extrême-Orient (Chinese ethics, the basis of Far Eastern societies).
Paris: Giard et Brière, 1906. 258 p.
SUBJ 62 63 ▪ 41 43 47

21982 NNC P P2 G1.2 –1895
Georgievskii, Sergei.
Printsipy zhizni Kitaia (Principles of Chinese life).
St. Petersburg: I. N. Skorokhodov, 1888. 22, 494, 16 p.
SUBJ 40 41 63 64 ▪ 43 47 65

21983 NNC P P1 G1.3 –1911
Haenisch, Erich, 1880–1966.
'Die Heiligung des Vater- und Fürstennamens in China: Ihre ethische Begründung und ihre Bedeutung in Leben und Schrifttum' (The consecration of the father's and ruler's name in China: Its moral basis and its significance in life and literature).
Berichte über die Verhandlungen der philologisch-historischen Klasse der sächsischen Akademie der Wissenschaften zu Leipzig 84, 4 (1932), 1–20.
SUBJ 12 62 63 ▪ 41 43 64

21984 NNC U P1 G1.0 –1911
Haenisch, Erich, 1880–1966.
'Der Treubegriff in der konfuzianischen Ethik' (The concept of loyalty in the Confucian ethic).
Forschungen und Fortschritte 9, 17 (10 Juni 1933), 251–252.
SUBJ 63 ▪ 16.1 64

21985 FPN P P1 G1.0 1644–1842
Le Gobien, Charles.
'Eclaircissement sur les honneurs que les Chinois rendent à Confucius et aux morts' (An explanation of the respect paid by the Chinese to Confucius and to the dead). In *Affaires de la Chine* (Affairs of China), by C. Le Gobien. [Sole entry]
Paris: Anisson, 1700, vol. 3, 217–332.
SUBJ 43 63 ▪ 57 64

21986 CSU P P1 G1.2 –1911
Martin, William Alexander Parsons, 1827–1916.
'The ethical philosophy of the Chinese.' In *The lore of Cathay: or, The intellect of China*, by W. A. P. Martin. [Selective entry]
New York: Revell, 1901, 205–233. [Reprinted in *The lore of Cathay: or, The intellect of China*, by W. A. P. Martin. (Selective entry.) Taipei: Ch'eng-wen, 1971, 205–233.]
SUBJ 63 64 ▪ 62

21987 CSU O P3 G5.1 1895–1911
Martin, William Alexander Parsons, 1827–1916.
'Native tracts of China.' In *The lore of Cathay: or, The intellect of China*, by W. A. P. Martin. [Selective entry]
New York: Revell, 1901, 148–162. [Reprinted in *The lore of Cathay: or, The intellect of China*, by W. A. P. Martin. (Selective entry.) Taipei: Ch'eng-wen, 1971, 148–162.]
SUBJ 63 65

21988 MCH P P1 G1.1 –1895
Schlegel, Gustaaf, 1840–1903.
'De Chineesche eed' (Chinese oaths).
Het Regt in Nederlandsch-Indië (Batavia) 21 (Mei 1863), 247–259.
SUBJ 22.2 63 ▪ 32.2 48

21989 CSU P P1 G1.2 1842–1911
Thompson, Laurence Gassius, 1926–.
'*Ta-t'ung shu* [Book of the Great Unity] and "The Communist manifesto": Some comparisons.' In *K'ang Yu-wei: A biography and a symposium*, edited by J. P. Lo (Lo Jung-pang). [Selective entry]
Tucson: U. of Arizona Press, 1967, 341–354.
SUBJ 63

21990 NIC O P1 G8.1 1895–1911
Vale, Joshua.
Chinese superstitions.
London: China Inland Mission, 1906. 48 p.
SUBJ 23 63 ▪ 41 51 57 65

1644-1949

21991 NIC PO P1 G1.2 –1928
Beach, Harlan Page, 1854–1933.
'The ethics of Confucianism.' In *The evolution of ethics*, edited by Elias Hershey Sneath. [Sole entry]
New Haven: Yale U. Press, 1927, 39–74.
SUBJ 63 ▪ 12 62

21992 CSU P P1 G1.2 –1949
Berthelot, René.
'L'astrobiologie et les moralistes chinois' (Cosmological integration and Chinese moralists).
R. de métaphysique et de morale 40, 4 (oct.–déc. 1933), 457–479.
SUBJ 62 63 ▪ 13 64

21993 MCH P P1 G1.2 –1928
Chavannes, Emmanuel Edouard, 1865–1918.
'De quelques idées morales des Chinois' (Some Chinese moral concepts).

AF 17, 169 (avr.–juin 1917), 85–88. [Reprinted—*R. franco-étrangère* 4, 7/9 (juil–sept. 1917), 230–235.]
SUBJ 63 ▪ 12 64 65

21994 ELB U P1 G1.0 –1949
Cheng, F. T. (Cheng T'ien-hsi), 1884–.
China moulded by Confucius: The Chinese way in Western light.
London: Stevens, 1947. 264 p.
SUBJ 22.2 41 63 64 ▪ 43 47 48

21995 FPN P P1 G1.0 –1928
Duyvendak, Jan Julius Lodewijk, 1889–1954.
'De philosophie van Woe Wéi' (The philosophy of *wu-wei* [non-action]). In *Jaarboek der Nederlandsche Akademie van Wettenschappen, Letterkunde en Schoone Kunsten* (Yearbook of the Dutch Academy of Sciences, Letters, and Arts). [Sole entry]
Amsterdam: Nederlandsche Akademie van Weetenschappen, Letterkunde en Schoone Kunsten, 1941/42, 163–184.
SUBJ 62 63 ▪ 64

21996 NNC P P1 G1.3 –1928
Haenisch, Erich, 1880–1966.
'Die Rachepflicht: Ein Widerstreit zwischen konfuzianischer Ethik und chinesischem Staatsgefühl' (The duty of blood vengeance: A conflict between Confucian ethics and Chinese nationalism).
ZDMG 85 (1931), 69–92.
SUBJ 22.2 25 63 64 ▪ 12 12.1 41 44 48 61

21997 NIC P P1 G1.0 –1949
Hsieh Yu-wei.
'Filial piety and Chinese culture.' In *Philosophy and culture, East and West*, edited by Charles Alexander Moore. [Selective entry]
Honolulu: U. of Hawaii Press, 1962, 411–427. [Reprinted as 'Filial piety and Chinese society.' In *The Chinese mind*, edited by C. A. Moore. (Selective entry.) Honolulu: U. of Hawaii Press, 1967, 167–187.]
SUBJ 43 63 ▪ 40

21998 MCY P P1 G1.2 –1928
Lin Yutang (Lin Yü-t'ang), 1895–.
'Li, the Chinese principle of social control and organization.'
CSPSR 2, 1 (Mar. 1917), 106–118.
SUBJ 48 63 ▪ 22.1 23 26 30 40 41

21999 CSU P P1 G1.0 –1949
Rawlinson, Frank Joseph, 1871–1937.
'The Chinese sense of evil.'
CR 63, 7 (July 1932), 428–434.
SUBJ 62 63

22000 NIC P P1 G1.2 –1949
Ruhlmann, Robert.
'Traditional heroes in Chinese popular fiction.' In *The Confucian persuasion*, edited by Arthur Frederick Wright. [Selective entry]
Stanford: Stanford U. Press, 1960, 141–176. [Reprinted in *Confucianism and Chinese civilization*, edited by A. F. Wright. (Selective entry.) New York: Atheneum, 1964, 122–157.]
SUBJ 60 63 ▪ 12 15 16.1 65

22001 CBU P P1 G1.1 –1928
Vannicelli, Luigi.
La religione e la morale dei Cinesi (The religion and ethics of the Chinese).
Naples: Istituto Superiore di Scienze e Lettere S. Chiara, 1955. 720 p.
SUBJ 33 62 63 ▪ 13 22.2 23 43 53 57 72

22002 MCH P P1 G1.1 –1928
Wilhelm, Richard, 1873–1930.
Chinesische Lebensweisheit (The practical wisdom of the Chinese).
Darmstadt: Otto Reichl, 1922. 107 p.
SUBJ 63 64 ▪ 12.1 17 41 48 62

22003 NIC P P1 G1.0 –1949
Yang, Lien-sheng, 1914–.
'The concept of "pao" as a basis for social relations in China.' In *Chinese thought and institutions*, edited by John King Fairbank. [Selective entry]
Chicago: U. of Chicago Press, 1957, 291–309. [Reprinted in *Excursions in sinology*, by Lien-sheng Yang. (Selective entry.) Cambridge: Harvard U. Press, 1969, 3–26. (Harvard-Yenching Institute studies, 24)]
SUBJ 48 63

1911-1949

22004 MCH P P1 G1.3 1911–1949
Chin, Ai-li Sung (Ch'en Shen Ai-li), 1919–.
Interdependence of roles in transitional China: A structural analysis of attitudes in contemporary Chinese literature.
Unpublished doctoral dissertation in Sociology, Radcliffe College, 1951. 310 p.
SUBJ 40 60 61 63 ▪ 16 31 41 46 47 48 50

22005 CSH U P1 G4.0 1911–1949
Coffin, Edna, Udo Posch, and Martin M. C. Yang (Yang Mou-ch'un), 1904–.
'Attitudes and reactions of the people.' In *A regional handbook on Northwest China*, compiled by Far Eastern and Russian Institute, U. of Washington. [Selective entry]
New Haven: Human Relations Area Files, 1956, vol. 2, 410–435. (HRAF subcontractor's monographs, 59; Washington 5)
SUBJ 23 60 63 ▪ 43 61 66

22006 NNC S P1 G1.2 1911–1949
Durfee, Mary Elizabeth, 1883–.
The conflict between Chinese mores and Western industry.
Unpublished masters thesis in Social Science, Columbia U., 1930. 68 p.
SUBJ 34.2 48 60 63 ▪ 12 13 14 17 19 34.3 40 61

22007 NNC S P1 G1.2 1911–1928
Gins, Georgii Konstantinovich (George Constantine Guins), 1887–.
'Eticheskie problemy sovremennogo Kitaia' (Ethical problems in contemporary China).
Izvestiia IUridicheskogo fakul'teta v g. Kharbine 4 (1927), 1–80.
SUBJ 60 63 ▪ 12.2 62

22008 MCH O P1 G1.0 1911–1928
Liu, Chiang (Liu Ch'iang), 1895–.
'Contrasts between Chinese and American social codes.'
J. of applied sociology 10, 1 (Sept.–Oct. 1925), 41–45.
SUBJ 61 63

22009 MAM P P2 G1.3 1911–1949
Ng, Lee Ming, 1936–.
Christianity and social change: The case in China, 1920–1950.
Ann Arbor: University Microfilms (Publ. 71-29,245), 1971. 279 p. (Doctoral dissertation in Religion, Princeton Theological Seminary)
SUBJ 59 60 63 ▪ 16 33 54 66

22010 NNC P P1 G1.2 1928–1949
Nivison, David Shepherd, 1923–.
'Communist ethics and Chinese tradition.'
JAS 16, 1 (Nov. 1956), 51–74. [Reprinted in *China*, edited by John Armstrong Harrison. (Selective entry.) Tucson: U. of Arizona Press, 1972, 207–230. (Assn. for Asian Studies, Thirtieth Anniversary Commemorative Series, 1)]
SUBJ 13 60 63 ▪ 32.2 64

22011 MCH O P1 G1.2 1911–1928
Rawlinson, Frank Joseph, 1871–1937.
'Some of China's life-sets.'
CR 57, 5 (May 1926), 344–357.
SUBJ 60 63

1911-1972
(including 1644-1972)

22012 MCH P P1 G1.2 1928–1972
Boorman, Howard Lyon, 1920–.
'How to be a good Communist: The political ethics of Liu Shao-ch'i.'
AS 3, 8 (Aug. 1963), 372–383.
SUBJ 60 63 64

22013 NIC P P1 G1.1 –1972
Chan, Wing-tsit (Ch'en Jung-chieh), 1901–.
'Chinese theory and practice, with special reference to humanism.' In *Philosophy and culture, East and West*, edited by Charles Alexander Moore. [Selective entry]
Honolulu: U. of Hawaii Press, 1962, 81–95. [Reprinted in *The Chinese mind*, edited by C. A. Moore. (Selective entry.) Honolulu: U. of Hawaii Press, 1967, 11–30.]
SUBJ 60 63 ▪ 62

22014 CSH U P1 G1.1 –1972
Eberhard, Wolfram, 1909–.
'On three principles in Chinese social structure.'
J. of sociology (Taipei) 6 (Apr. 1970), 13–26. [Reprinted—*CC* 11, 1 (Mar. 1970), 21–33.] [Reprinted in *Moral and social values of the Chinese: Collected essays*, by W. Eberhard. (Selective entry.) Taipei: Chinese Materials and Research Aids Service Center, 1971, 1–14. (CMRASC occasional series, 6)]
SUBJ 63 ▪ 12.1 16.1 41 48

22015 MCH P P1 G1.1 –1972
Hsiao, Paul S. Y.
'Dschündz, das Menschenideal der Chinesen: Der Edle in seinem Privatleben und in der Familie' (*Chün-tzu*, the gentleman of the Chinese: The noble in his private and family life).

Z. für Missionswissenschaft und Religionswissenschaft 39, 4 (1955), 269–283.
Subj 63 ▪ 13 41 62

22016 CSU S P1 G1.1 –1972
Hsu, Francis L. K. (Hsü Lang-kuang), 1909–.
'Eros, affect, and pao.' In *Kinship and culture*, edited by F. L. K. Hsu. [Selective entry]
Chicago: Aldine, 1971, 439–475.
Subj 30 46 48 63 ▪ 41 62

22017 NIC S P1 G1.0 –1972
Hummel, Arthur William, 1884–.
'The art of social relations in China.'
Philosophy, East and West 10, 1/2 (Apr.–July 1960), 13–22.
Subj 63 ▪ 48

1949-1972

22018 MAM F P4 G9.4 1949–1972
Huang, Sophia Chang.
A comparison of selected values among Formosan and American adolescents.
Ann Arbor: University Microfilms (Publ. 63-56), 1963. 198 p. (Doctoral dissertation in Psychology, Ohio State U., 1962)
Subj 61 63 ▪ 41 48 54

22019 CSH P P1 G1.2 1949–1972
[La Dany, Ladislao] ———, 1914–.
'Morality.'
CNA 505 (21 Feb. 1964), 1–7.
Subj 63

22020 NIC P P1 G1.2 1949–1972
[La Dany, Ladislao] ———, 1914–.
'Morality in practice.'
CNA 416 (13 Apr. 1962), 1–7.
Subj 48 63 ▪ 12.1 46

22021 CSH P P2 G1.2 1949–1972
[La Dany, Ladislao] ———, 1914–.
'Two sources of morality.'
CNA 864 (10 Dec. 1971), 1–7.
Subj 22.2 63 ▪ 30 42

22022 CBU P P1 G9.0 1949–1972
Lefeuvre, J- A-.
'Confucian and scientific humanisms in modern China.'
JCS 5 (1967), 63–76.
Subj 62 63 ▪ 16.1

22023 CSH F P3 G9.4 1949–1972
O'Hara, Albert Richard, 1907–.
'Some problems and results of attitude testing among university students.'
J. of sociology (Taipei) 2 (Nov. 1965), 61–69. [Reprinted in *Research on changes of Chinese society*, by A. R. O'Hara. (Selective entry.) Taipei: Orient Cultural Service, 1971, 61–69. (Asian Folklore and Social Life monographs, 20)]
Subj 54 60 63 ▪ 17 55 62 66

64 Ideology and the Great Tradition
正統思想及意識型態
正統思想及びイデオロギー

1644-1911

22024 CSH P P1 G1.1 –1911
Avenarius, G- G-.
'Kratkii ocherk istorii Kitaia v sviazi s ucheniem Konfutsiia o sushchestve gosudarstvennoi vlasti' (Brief overview of Chinese history in connection with Confucian teachings on the nature of state power).
VA 19/22 (sentiabr'–dekabr' 1913), 1–149.
Subj 12 64 ▪ 12.1 13 43 60

22025 CSU P P1 G1.2 1895–1911
Bernal, Martin Gardiner, 1937–.
'The triumph of anarchism over Marxism, 1906–1907.' In *China in revolution: The first phase, 1900–1913*, edited by Mary Clabaugh Wright. [Selective entry]
New Haven: Yale U. Press, 1968, 97–142.
Subj 32 64 ▪ 14.2 16.1 32.2

22026 CSU P P1 G1.5 1842–1895
Boardman, Eugene Powers, 1910–.
Christian influence upon the ideology of the Taiping Rebellion, 1851–1864.
Madison: U. of Wisconsin Press, 1952. 11, 188 p. (Revision of *Biblical influence upon the ideology of the T'ai-p'ing Rebellion*, doctoral dissertation in History, Harvard U., 1947) [Reprinted—New York: Octagon Books, 1971. 11, 188 p.]
Subj 32.2 64 66 ▪ 23 62 63

22027 CSH P P4 G1.1 1842–1911
Chang, Hao, 1936–.
Liang Ch'i-ch'ao and intellectual transition in China, 1890–1907.
Cambridge: Harvard U. Press, 1971. 342 p. (Harvard East Asian series, 64) (Revision of *Liang Ch'i-ch'ao's early intellectual life (1873–1903)*, doctoral dissertation in History and Far Eastern Languages, Harvard U., 1967)
Subj 16.1 64 ▪ 14.2 17 32 59 66

22028 NNC P P1 G1.2 1895–1911
Chang, Yu-fa (Chang Yü-fa), 1936–.
The effects of western socialism on the 1911 Revolution in China.
Unpublished masters thesis in History, Columbia U., 1970. 166 p.
Subj 64 ▪ 16.1 32.2

22029 MCY P P3 G1.3 1842–1911
Chen, Chi-yun, 1913–.
'Liang Ch'i-ch'ao's "missionary education": A case study of missionary influence on the reformers.'
PC 16 (Dec. 1962), 66–125.
Subj 16.1 32 33 64 66 ▪ 17 36.1 59

22030 DLC P P1 G1.1 1842–1895
Cohen, Paul Andrew, 1934–.
'Wang T'ao's perspective on a changing world.' In *Approaches to modern Chinese history*, edited by Albert Feuerwerker et al. [Selective entry]
Berkeley, Los Angeles: U. of California Press, 1967, 133–162.
Subj 64

22031 MAM P P1 G1.2 1842–1911
Fan, Winston Ping, 1925–.
The political philosophy of K'ang Yu-wei: A sociological study of religious syncretism.
Ann Arbor: University Microfilms (Publ. 67-1622), 1967. 168 p. (Doctoral dissertation in Political Science, Michigan State U., 1966)
Subj 16.1 64 ▪ 62

22032 CSU P P1 G1.1 1895–1911
Fass, Josef.
'A few notes on the birth of nationalism in China.'
AO 32, 3 (1964), 376–382.
Subj 64 66

22033 DLC P P1 G1.2 1644–1842
Fishman, Ol'ga Lazarevna, 1919–.
'O politike TSinov v oblasti ideologii' (Ch'ing policy regarding ideology). In *Man'chzhurskoe vladychestvo v Kitae* (Manchu rule in China), compiled by Institut narodov Azii, Akademiia nauk SSSR, edited by Sergei Leonidovich Tikhvinskii. [Selective entry]
Moscow: Nauka, Glav. red. vost. lit-ry, 1966, 169–184.
Subj 12 12.1 16.1 64 ▪ 13 17

22034 DLC P P2 G1.2 –1842
Fishman, Ol'ga Lazarevna, 1919–.
'Razvitie prosvetitel'skoi ideologii v Kitae (XVII – nachalo XIX v.).' In *Kitaiskii satiricheskii roman (epokha prosveshcheniia)* (The Chinese satirical novel: The age of enlightenment). [Sole entry]
Moscow: Nauka, Glav. red. vost. lit-ry, 1966, 7–39.

'The development of the ideology of enlightenment in China (from the seventeenth to the early nineteenth century).' Tr. by Arlo Schultz.
Chinese sociology and anthropology 3, 2/3 (Winter–Spring 1971), 133–189.
Subj 62 64 ▪ 12 12.1 12.2 14.1 14.5 16 17 66

22035 CBU S P1 G1.2 –1911
Franke, Herbert, 1914–.
'Das Begriffsfeld des Staatlichen im chinesischen Kulturbereich' (The range of concepts of the state in the Chinese cultural sphere).
Saeculum 4, 2 (1953), 231–239.
Subj 62 64

22036 NNC P P1 G1.3 –1911
Franke, Otto, 1863–1946.
'Das Konfuzianische System und sein Ende' (The Confucian system and its demise). In *Aus Kultur und Geschichte Chinas* (Chinese culture and history), by O. Franke. [Selective entry]
Peiping: Deutschland-Institut, 1945, 331–348.
Subj 12 64 ▪ 13 16.1

22037 MCY P P1 G1.2 1842–1911
Franke, Wolfgang, 1912–.
'Die staatspolitischen Reformsversuche K'ang Yu-weis und seiner Schule: Ein Beitrag zur geistigen Auseinandersetzung Chinas mit dem Abendlande' (The attempts at political reform by K'ang Yu-wei and his school: China's intellectual confrontation with the West).

MSOSB 38 (1935), 1–84.
Subj 12 19 32 64 ▪ 12.2 13 16.1 17

22038 MCH PO P 1 G 1.2 1842–1911
Giles, Herbert Allen, 1845–1935.
'Le confucianisme au XIXème siècle' (Confucianism in the nineteenth century).
Chine et Sibérie 1, 23 (déc. 1900), 536–540; 1, 24 (déc. 1900), 555–559.
Subj 64 ▪ 17 43

22039 NNC P P 1 G 1.2 1895–1911
Grigor'ev, Aleksandr Mironovich, 1933–.
'K voprosu o formirovanii natsional'nykh trebovanii revoliutsionnogo kryla kitaiskoi burzhuazii, 1895–1900 gg.' (The development of nationalist demands by the revolutionary wing of the Chinese bourgeoisie, 1895–1900).
KSINA 55 (1962), 45–66.
Subj 64 66 ▪ 32 32.2

22040 CSU P P 1 G 1.2 1644–1842
Hozumi, Fumio, 1902–.
'Paper currency theory of Wang Liu.'
KUER 34, 2 (Oct. 1964), 1–34.
Subj 14.6 64

22041 CSU P P 2 G 1.2 1895–1911
Hsiao, Kung-chuan (Hsiao Kung-ch'üan), 1897–.
'Administrative modernization: K'ang Yu-wei's proposals and their historical meaning.'
THJ new (2nd) series 8, 1/2 (Aug. 1970), 1–34.
Subj 12 64 ▪ 17 22

22042 WSU P P 1 G 1.2 1842–1911
Hsiao, Kung-chuan (Hsiao Kung-ch'üan), 1897–.
'In and out of utopia: K'ang Yu-wei's social thought. I, Path finding in two worlds. II, Road to utopia. III, Detour to industrial society.'
CCJ 7, 1 (Nov. 1967), 1–18; 7, 2 (May 1968), 101–149; 8, 1 (Nov. 1968), 1–52.
Subj 60 64 66 ▪ 19 62

22043 NNC P P 1 G 1.1 1842–1911
Hsiao, Kung-chuan (Hsiao Kung-ch'üan), 1897–.
'K'ang Yu-wei and Confucianism.'
MS 18 (1959), 96–212.
Subj 64 ▪ 61 63

22044 MCY P P 1 G 1.3 –1911
Hsiao, Kung-chuan (Hsiao Kung-ch'üan), 1897–.
'Legalism and autocracy in traditional China.'
THJ new (2nd) series 4, 2 (Feb. 1964), 108–122.
Subj 12.1 64 ▪ 12 12.2

22045 NNC U P 1 G 1.3 –1911
Hsu Dau-lin (Hsü Tao-lin), 1906–.
'Wissenschaft und Politik in China' (Science and politics in China).
Sinica 7, 2 (März 1932), 41–49.
Subj 64 ▪ 12 16.1 17 62 63

22046 MAM P P 1 G 1.2 1895–1911
Huang, Joe C. (Huang Chou), 1929–.
The political theories of K'ang Liang School and their application to the reform movement in China, 1895–1911.
Ann Arbor: University Microfilms (Publ. 64-4471), 1964. 234 p. (Doctoral dissertation in Political Science, Southern Illinois U., 1963)
Subj 16.1 32 64 ▪ 62

22047 CSH P P 2 G 1.2 1842–1895
Iliushechkin, Vasilii Pavlovich, 1915–.
'"Krest'ianskii kommunism" taipinov' (The Taipings' 'peasant communism').
NAA 1972, 3, 57–66.
Subj 16 22.1 64 ▪ 14.1 14.5 24.3 25 41 47 63 72

22048 CSU P P 1 G 1.2 –1842
Levenson, Joseph Richmond, 1920–1969.
'The amateur ideal in Ming and early Ch'ing society: Evidence from painting.' In *Confucian China and its modern fate, Vol. 1, The problem of intellectual continuity*, by J. R. Levenson. [Analytic entry]
Berkeley, Los Angeles: U. of California Press, 1966, 15–43. [Slight revision of chap. with same title in *Chinese thought and institutions*, edited by John King Fairbank; Chicago: U. of Chicago Press, 1957, 320–341.]
Subj 60 64 ▪ 16.1 17

22049 MCH P P 1 G 1.2 1842–1911
Levenson, Joseph Richmond, 1920–1969.
'The breakdown of Confucianism: Liang Ch'i-ch'ao before exile, 1873–1898.'
J. of the history of ideas 11, 4 (Oct. 1950), 448–485.
Subj 64 66 ▪ 12 16.1 32

22050 CSU S P 1 G 1.2 –1842
Levenson, Joseph Richmond, 1920–1969.
'Confucianism and monarchy: The limits of despotic control.' In *Confucian China and its modern fate, Vol. 2, The problem of monarchical decay*, by J. R. Levenson. [Analytic entry]
Berkeley, Los Angeles: U. of California Press, 1964, 60–73.
Subj 12.1 64 ▪ 16.1

22051 CSU P P 1 G 1.2 1842–1895
Levenson, Joseph Richmond, 1920–1969.
'Part 3, The break in the line of tension.' In *Confucian China and its modern fate, Vol. 2, The problem of monarchical decay*, by J. R. Levenson. [Analytic entry]
Berkeley, Los Angeles: U. of California Press, 1964, 75–116. [Revision of 'Confucian and Taiping "heaven": The political implications of clashing religious concepts'; *CSSH* 4, 4 (July 1962), 436–453.]
Subj 64 ▪ 13 62

22052 CSU P P 4 G 1.2 1895–1911
Li Yu-ning.
The introduction of socialism into China.
New York: Columbia U. Press, 1971. 138 p.
Subj 64 ▪ 14.2 16.1

22053 NIC P P 1 G 1.2 1644–1911
Liang Chi-chao (Liang Ch'i-ch'ao), 1873–1929.
Intellectual trends in the Ch'ing period. Tr. by Immanuel C. Y. Hsü of *Ch'ing tai hsüeh shu kai lun*; Shanghai: Shang wu yin shu kuan, 1927; 183 p.
Cambridge: Harvard U. Press, 1959. 22, 147, 52 p. (Harvard East Asian series, 2)
Subj 64 70 ▪ 16.1 17 19

22054 MCH P P 1 G 1.2 –1911
Liau Schang Kuo (Liao Shang-kuo).
'Von chinesischen Rechts- und Staatstheorien: Ein Beitrag zu den Grundlagen und Grundbegriffen des chinesischen Staatsrechts' (Chinese legal and political theories: Toward an understanding of the foundations and basic concepts of Chinese constitutional law).
ZVR 40, 1 (1923), 135–173. (Doctoral dissertation, Rechts- und Staatswissenschaftliche Fakultät, Universität Hamburg)
Subj 12.2 64 ▪ 12.1 13 62 63

22055 CSU P P 1 G 1.2 –1842
Liu Hsien-mei.
'A brief discourse on Wang Ch'uan-shan's political ideology.' Tr. of 'Ch'uan-shan cheng chih ssu hsiang lun lüeh'; in *Wang Ch'uan-shan hsüeh shu t'ao lun chi* (Collected essays on Wang Fu-chih's scholarship and philosophy), jointly edited by Hu-nan sheng che hsüeh she hui k'o hsüeh hsüeh hui lien ho hui (Hunan Provincial Joint Philosophical and Social Sciences Study Assn.) *with* Hu-pei sheng che hsüeh she hui k'o hsüeh hsüeh hui lien ho hui (Hupeh Provincial Joint Philosophical and Social Sciences Study Assn.); Peking: Chung-hua shu chü, 1965, vol. 2, 387–429.
Chinese studies in history and philosophy 1, 3 (Spring 1968), 39–52.
Subj 64 ▪ 12 62

22056 ICU P P 1 G 1.1 –1911
Liu, Su-i.
The reign of Confucianism in China, with emphasis on the resistance to social change by vested interests.
Unpublished masters thesis in Sociology, U. of Chicago, 1947. 256 p.
Subj 16.1 64 ▪ 12.2 13 16 17 63

22057 EOB P P 2 G 1.3 –1842
McMorran, C- Ian.
Wang Fu-chih and his political thought.
Unpublished doctoral dissertation in Oriental Studies, Oxford U., 1968. 328 p.
Subj 12 14.1 14.5 58 60 64 ▪ 14.3 15 16.1

22058 CSU P P 1 G 1.2 1644–1895
Mitchell, Peter MacVicar.
'The limits of reformism: Wei Yüan's reaction to western intrusion.'
MAS 6, 2 (Apr. 1972), 175–204.
Subj 59 64 66 ▪ 12 14 15 32

22059 NIC P P 1 G 1.1 –1911
Muramatsu, Yuji (Muramatsu Yūji), 1911–.
'Some themes in Chinese rebel ideologies.' In *The Confucian persuasion*, edited by Arthur Frederick Wright. [Selective entry]
Stanford: Stanford U. Press, 1960, 241–267.
Subj 32.2 64 ▪ 23 63 65 66

22060 CSU P P 1 G 1.2 1895–1911
Robel, Ronald R-.
'T'an Ssu-t'ung on Hsueh Hui or "study associations".' In *'Nothing concealed': Essays in honor of Liu Yu-yün*, edited by Frederic Evans Wakeman, Jr. [Selective entry]

Taipei: Chinese Materials and Research Aids Service Center, 1970, 161–176. (CMRASC occasional series, 4)
SUBJ 32 64

22061 NNC P P1 G1.2 –1911
Rousselle, Erwin Arthur, 1890–.
'Zur Würdigung des konfuzianischen Staatsgedankens' (An appraisal of the Confucian concept of the state).
Sinica 9, 1 (Jan. 1934), 1–8.
SUBJ 12 64 ▪ 12.1 13

22062 MCH P P1 G1.1 1895–1911
Scalapino, Robert Anthony, 1919–, and Harold Zvi Schiffrin, 1922–.
'Early socialist currents in the Chinese revolutionary movement: Sun Yat-sen versus Liang Ch'i-ch'ao.'
JAS 18, 3 (May 1959), 321–342.
SUBJ 32.2 64

22063 CSU P P1 G1.2 1895–1911
Schiffrin, Harold Zvi, 1922–.
'The "great leap" image in early Chinese nationalism.'
Asian and African studies (Jerusalem) 3 (1967), 101–119.
SUBJ 64 ▪ 16.1

22064 NIC P P1 G1.3 –1842
Schwartz, Benjamin Isadore, 1916–.
'Some polarities in Confucian thought.' In *Confucianism in action*, edited by David Shepherd Nivison and Arthur Frederick Wright. [Selective entry]
Stanford: Stanford U. Press, 1959, 50–62. [Reprinted in *Confucianism and Chinese civilization*, edited by A. F. Wright. (Selective entry.) New York: Atheneum, 1964, 3–15.]
SUBJ 60 64 ▪ 12

22065 NNC P P1 G1.1 1895–1911
Semanov, Vladimir Ivanovich.
'Literatura perioda Sin'khaiskoi revoliutsii' (The literature of the period of the Revolution of 1911). In *Sin'khaiskaia revoliutsiia v Kitae: sbornik statei* (Articles on the Revolution of 1911 in China), compiled by Institut narodov Azii, Akademiia nauk SSSR. [Selective entry]
Moscow: Izd-vo vost. lit-ry, 1962, 272–301.
SUBJ 32.2 64 ▪ 16.1

22066 CSU P P2 G1.2 1842–1895
Shih, Vincent Y. C. (Shih Yu-chung), 1903–.
The Taiping ideology: Its sources, interpretations, and influences.
Seattle: U. of Washington Press, 1967. 19, 442 p. (U. of Washington, Far Eastern and Russian Institute publications on Asia, 15)
SUBJ 32.2 63 64 ▪ 12 14.1 16 29 41 47

22067 CSU O P2 G1.3 1842–1895
Simon, G- Eugène, 1829–1896.
La cité chinoise (The Chinese city).
Paris: Nouvelle revue, 1885. 389 p.
SUBJ 11.4 12 16.3 41 55 64 ▪ 11 15 16.1 22 23 31 51 61 63

22068 MAM P P1 G1.2 –1911
Talbott, Nathan McKee, 1917–.
Intellectual origins and aspects of political thought in the 'Jen hsüeh' [A study of benevolence] *of T'an Ssu-t'ung, martyr of the 1898 reform.*
Ann Arbor: University Microfilms (Publ. 16,542), 1956. 398 p. (Doctoral dissertation in Political Science, U. of Washington)
SUBJ 60 62 64 ▪ 32 33

22069 NNC P P2 G1.2 1842–1911
Tikhvinskii, Sergei Leonidovich, 1918–.
'Tan' Sy-tun, ideolog levogo kryla dvizheniia za reformy v kontse XIX v.' (T'an Ssu-t'ung, left-wing ideologue of the reform movement at the end of the nineteenth century).
SK 1958, 3, 59–71.
SUBJ 12 32 64 ▪ 59 66

22070 NNC U P1 G1.2 1644–1911
Ting, W. Y.
'Der Anteil der Mandschu und der Chinesen an der chinesischen Kulturarbeit der letzten Jahrhunderte' (Manchu and Chinese participation in China's cultural development of recent centuries).
Sinica 4, 4 (Juli 1929), 157–166.
SUBJ 64 ▪ 12 62

22071 CSU P P1 G1.2 1644–1842
Vierheller, Ernstjoachim, 1933–.
National und Elite im Denken von Wang Fu-chih (1619–1692) (Nation and elite in the philosophy of Wang Fu-chih, 1619–1692).
Unpublished doctoral dissertation, Philosophische Fakultet, Universität Hamburg, 1968. 137, 30 p.
SUBJ 12 16.1 64 66 ▪ 59 62

22072 CSU U P1 G1.3 1842–1895
Wilhelm, Hellmut, 1906–.
'The background of Tseng Kuo-fan's ideology.'
Asiatische Studien 3 (1949), 90–100.
SUBJ 64 ▪ 59 63

22073 MAM P P1 G1.2 1895–1911
Wong, Frank Fe (Huang Chin-hui), 1935–.
Liang Ch'i-ch'ao and the conflict of Confucian and constitutional politics.
Ann Arbor: University Microfilms (Publ. 65-10,677), 1965. 265 p. (Doctoral dissertation in History, U. of Wisconsin)
SUBJ 32 62 64 ▪ 12

22074 MAM P P2 G1.1 1842–1911
Wong, Young-tsu (Wang Yung-tsu), 1940–.
Remolders of tradition: Reformist thought in nineteenth century China.
Ann Arbor: University Microfilms (Publ. 71-28,496), 1971. 370 p. (Doctoral dissertation in History, U. of Washington)
SUBJ 16.1 32 59 64 66 ▪ 12 14 17 22 72

22075 NIC P P1 G1.2 –1842
Wu, John C. H. (Wu Ching-hsiung), 1899–.
'Chinese legal philosophy: A brief historical survey.'
CC 1, 4 (Apr. 1958), 7–48.
SUBJ 12.2 64

1644-1949

22076 DLC S P1 G1.3 1842–1928
Antonov, Konstantin Vladimirovich.
Suniatsenizm i kitaiskaia revoliutsiia (Sun Yat-sen-ism and the Chinese revolution).
Moscow: Izd-vo Kom. akad., 1931. 136 p.
SUBJ 14 19 32 32.2 64 ▪ 12 16 66

22077 MCY P P2 G1.2 1842–1928
Arkush, Ralph David, 1940–.
'Ku Hung-ming, 1857–1928.'
PC 19 (Dec. 1965), 194–238.
SUBJ 12 16.1 59 64 66 ▪ 33

22078 CSU P P2 G1.2 1895–1928
Bernal, Martin Gardiner, 1937–.
'Chinese socialism before 1913.' In *Modern China's search for a political form*, edited by Jack Douglas Gray. [Analytic entry]
London: Oxford U. Press, 1969, 66–95. [For a fuller version, see entry 22079.]
SUBJ 32.2 64 ▪ 16 16.1

22079 ECU P P2 G1.2 1895–1928
Bernal, Martin Gardiner, 1937–.
Chinese socialism to 1913.
Unpublished doctoral dissertation in Oriental Studies, U. of Cambridge [King's College], 1966. 434 p.
SUBJ 32 32.2 36.1 64 ▪ 14 14.1 16 16.1 19

22080 NNC P P1 G1.1 –1949
Chai, Winberg (Chai Wen-po), 1932–.
'The evolution of Chinese constitutionalism.'
CC 4, 2 (June 1962), 86–103.
SUBJ 12 12.2 32 64 ▪ 63

22081 MCY S P1 G1.1 1842–1949
Chan, Wing-tsit (Ch'en Jung-chieh), 1901–.
'Trends in contemporary philosophy.' In *China*, edited by Harley Farnsworth MacNair. [Selective entry]
Berkeley, Los Angeles: U. of California Press, 1946, 312–330. [Reprinted in *China*, edited by H. F. MacNair. (Selective entry.) Freeport, N.Y.: Books for Libraries, 1970, 312–330.]
SUBJ 64 ▪ 66

22082 MCH P P1 G1.1 –1928
Chang, Carsun (Chang Chia-sen), 1886–.
The development of neo-Confucian thought.
New York: Bookman Associates, 1957, 1962. 2 vols. 376; 521 p.
SUBJ 60 63 64 ▪ 12 16.1 62 66

22083 NNC P P1 G1.3 1842–1928
Chang, Carsun (Chang Chia-sen), 1886–.
'Die Stellung der kanonischen Literatur im modernen Geistesleben Chinas' (The position of classical literature in the intellectual life of modern China).
Sinica 6, 1 (Jan. 1931), 13–26; 6, 3 (Mai 1931), 97–108.
SUBJ 16.1 62 64 ▪ 13 17 19

22084 CSH P P1 G1.2 1895–1949
Chen, Vincent (Ch'en Wen-hsing), 1917–.
'An evaluation of Mao Tse-tung's analysis of the nature of Chinese society.'
CC 9, 2 (June 1968), 55–72.
SUBJ 64 ▪ 16

22085 CBU P P1 G1.1 –1928
Ching, Dao Wang.
'Die Staatsidee des Konfuzius und ihre Beziehung zu konstitutioneller Verfassung' (The Confucian concept of the state and its relation to the constitution).
MSOSB 16 (1913), 1–49.
Subj 12 12.2 64 ▪ 13

22086 CSU S P1 G1.3 1842–1928
Chong, Key Ray, 1933–.
'Cheng Kuan-ying (1841–1920): A source of Sun Yat-sen's nationalist ideology?'
JAS 28, 2 (Feb. 1969), 247–267.
Subj 16.1 64 66 ▪ 32.2 59 62

22087 MAM P P1 G1.2 1842–1928
Chong, Key Ray, 1933–.
The sources and development of Sun Yat-sen's nationalistic ideology as expressed in his 'San Min Chu I'.
Ann Arbor: University Microfilms (Publ. 68-10,501), 1968. 297 p. (Doctoral dissertation in Political Science, Claremont Graduate School and University Center, 1967)
Subj 64 66

22088 MCH P P1 G1.1 1842–1949
Collotti Pischel, Enrica, 1930–.
Le origini ideologiche della rivoluzione cinese (The ideological origins of the Chinese revolution).
Turin: Einaudi, 1958. 289 p.
Subj 19 32.2 64 ▪ 16 66

22089 CSH P P2 G1.2 1895–1928
Deliusin, Lev Petrovich, 1923–.
Spor o sotsializme: iz istorii obshchestvenno-politicheskoi mysli Kitaia v nachale 20-kh godov (The controversy on socialism: History of sociopolitical thought in China in the early 1920s).
Moscow: Nauka, Glav. red. vost. lit-ry, 1970. 92 p.
Subj 14.2 16 64 66 ▪ 14.4

22090 CSU P P3 G1.3 1895–1949
Duiker, William John, 1932–.
'Ts'ai Yuan-p'ei and the Confucian heritage.'
MAS 5, 3 (July 1971), 207–226. [For fuller treatment, see entry 22091.]
Subj 59 62 64

22091 MAM P P1 G1.2 1842–1949
Duiker, William John, 1932–.
Ts'ai Yuan-p'ei and the intellectual revolution in modern China.
Ann Arbor: University Microfilms (Publ. 68-11,117), 1968. 463 p. (Doctoral dissertation in History, Georgetown U.)
Subj 59 62 64 ▪ 16.1 32 36.1

22092 DLC P P3 G1.3 1895–1928
Evgen'ev, A- G-.
'Nachalo rasprostraneniia marksizma v Kitae i bor'ba pervykh kitaiskikh marksistov s anarkhistami' (The beginning of the dissemination of Marxism in China and the early Chinese Marxists' struggle with the anarchists). In *Dvizhenie '4 maia' 1919 goda v Kitae: sbornik statei* (Articles on the May Fourth Movement in China), compiled by Institut vostokovedeniia, Akademiia nauk SSSR, edited by A- G-Afanas'ev et al. [Selective entry]
Moscow: Nauka, Glav. red. vost. lit-ry, 1971, 150–175.
Subj 14.2 32.2 64 ▪ 16.1 36.4 66 72

22093 MCH P P1 G1.2 1644–1928
Hamilton, David, 1936–.
'Kuo Sung-tao: A maverick Confucian.'
PC 15 (Dec. 1961), 1–29.
Subj 64 ▪ 59 66

22094 GMS S P2 G1.3 1842–1928
Herrfahrdt, Heinrich, 1890–.
Sun Yatsen, der Vater des neuen China: Ein Beispiel west-östlicher Begegnung (Sun Yat-sen, father of modern China: An example of the meeting of East and West).
Hamburg: Drei-Türme, 1948. 239 p.
Subj 19 64 ▪ 12 32.2 59

22095 MCH P P2 G1.1 –1949
Ho, Owen (Ho Shih).
L'évolution du socialisme en Chine (The evolution of socialism in China).
Nancy: Thomas, 1935. 151 p. (Doctoral dissertation, Faculté de droit, Université de Nancy)
Subj 19 32 32.2 64 ▪ 12 14 16 18 60

22096 NNC S P1 G1.2 1895–1949
Holland, William Lancelot, 1907–.
'New trends in Asian nationalism: Chinese nationalism.' In *Asian nationalism and the West*, edited by W. L. Holland. [Sole entry]
New York: Macmillan, 1953, 38–51.
Subj 64 ▪ 12.1 19 66

22097 CSU P P1 G1.2 1895–1928
Hsiao, Kung-chuan (Hsiao Kung-ch'üan), 1897–.
'The case for constitutional monarchy: K'ang Yu-wei's plan for the democratization of China.'
MS 24 (1965), 1–83.
Subj 64 ▪ 16.1 32 66

22098 CSU P P2 G1.2 1842–1949
Hsiao, Kung-chuan (Hsiao Kung-ch'üan), 1897–.
'Economic modernization: K'ang Yu-wei's ideas in historical perspective.'
MS 27 (1968), 1–90.
Subj 12 14 14.4 64 ▪ 14.1 14.6 16.1 18 34.2 66

22099 WSU P P2 G1.2 1895–1928
Huang, Philip C. (Huang Tsung-chih), 1940–.
Liang Ch'i-ch'ao and modern Chinese liberalism.
Seattle: U. of Washington Press, 1972. 231 p. (Revision of *A Confucian liberal: Liang Ch'i-ch'ao in action and thought*, doctoral dissertation in History, U. of Washington, 1966)
Subj 16.1 64 ▪ 59 62

22100 NNM S P1 G1.1 –1928
Hummel, Arthur William, 1884–.
'Force in Chinese philosophy.'
World tomorrow 9, 1 (Jan. 1926), 15–17. [Special issue: *The spirit of new China: Interpretations by Chinese writers*]
Subj 63 64

22101 FPN P P1 G1.1 1842–1928
Hung, Jair.
Les idées économiques de Sun Yat Sen (The economic concepts of Sun Yat-sen).
Toulouse: Boisseau, 1934. 200 p. (Doctoral dissertation, Faculté de droit, Université de Toulouse)
Subj 64 ▪ 12 14

22102 ELR PO P2 G1.1 1895–1949
Johnston, Reginald Fleming, 1874–1938.
Confucianism and modern China.
New York: Appleton-Century, 1935. 272 p.
Subj 13 63 64 ▪ 16.1 17 19 32.2 33 43

22103 CSU U P1 G1.2 –1928
Krause, Friedrich Ernst August, 1879–.
'Kulturform und Staatsgedanke in Ostasien und Europa' (Cultural patterns and concepts of the state in East Asia and Europe).
Historische Z. 131, 2 (März–Apr. 1925), 197–239.
Subj 60 64 ▪ 12.1 61

22104 NNC P P1 G1.2 1842–1928
Kuo Shao-tan (Kuo Shao-t'ang), 1905–.
'Sun' IAt-sen, velikii kitaiskii revoliutsioner-demokrat: k 90-letiiu so dnia rozhdeniia' (Sun Yat-sen, a great Chinese revolutionary democrat: On the ninetieth anniversary of his birth).
SV 1956, 6, 15–28.
Subj 12 32.2 64 ▪ 59

22105 NNC O P2 G1.2 1895–1949
Lee, John, pseud.
'The Chinese struggle for democracy.'
AAAPSS 258 (July 1948), 31–52.
Subj 12 17 19 64 ▪ 12.1 15 16 18 32.2 62 66

22106 ICU U P1 G1.2 1895–1928
Lenin, Vladimir Il'ich, 1870–1923.
O Kitae (China), compiled by P- M-Tashkarov.
Moscow: Gosizdat, 1926. 49 p.
Subj 64 66 ▪ 16 19

22107 CSU P P1 G1.3 1842–1949
Levenson, Joseph Richmond, 1920–1969.
'A little life: Liao P'ing and the Confucian departure from history.' In *Confucian China and its modern fate, Vol. 3, The problem of historical significance*, by J. R. Levenson. [Selective entry]
Berkeley, Los Angeles: U. of California Press, 1965, 3–15. [Slight revision of 'Liao P'ing and the Confucian departure from history'; in *Confucian personalities*, edited by Arthur Frederick Wright and Denis Crispin Twitchett; Stanford: Stanford U. Press, 1962, 317–325.]
Subj 59 64 ▪ 60

22108 NIC P P1 G1.2 –1928
Levenson, Joseph Richmond, 1920–1969.
'The suggestiveness of vestiges: Confucianism and monarchy at the last.' In *Confucianism in action*, edited by David Shepherd Nivison and Arthur Frederick Wright. [Selective entry]
Stanford: Stanford U. Press, 1959, 244–267. [Reprinted in *Confucianism and Chinese civilization*, edited by A. F. Wright. (Selective entry.) New York: Atheneum, 1964, 291–314. (For a revised version of this chap., see 'Part 1, The suggestiveness of vestiges: Confucianism and monarchy at the last (I)'; 'Confucianism and monarchy: The basic confrontation'; 'The evolution of the Confucian bureaucratic personality';

and 'Part 4, The vestige of suggestiveness: Confucianism and the monarchy at the last (II)'; in *Confucian China and its modern fate, Vol. 2, The problem of monarchical decay*, by J. R. Levenson; Berkeley, Los Angeles: U. of California Press, 1964, 3–50, 117–139.)]
Subj 12 62 64 ▪ 13 16.1

22109 GMS S P2 G1.1 –1949
Liang, Chiang (Liang Ch'iang).
Die chinesische Wirtschafts- und Sozialverfassung zwischen Freiheit und Bindung: Ein Überblick bis zum jahre 1937 (China's economy and society between freedom and constraint: Overview to 1937).
Würzburg-Anmühle: Triltsch, 1938. 121 p. (Doctoral dissertation, Rechts- und wirtschaftswissenschaftliche Fakultät, Universität Jena)
Subj 14 14.4 16 64 ▪ 19 34.3 41

22110 MAM P P1 G1.3 –1928
Lien, Channing, 1909–.
The influence of Western political thought upon China.
Ann Arbor: University Microfilms (Publ. 2997), 1952. 229 p. (Doctoral dissertation in Political Science, Princeton U., 1946)
Subj 12 17 59 60 64 66 ▪ 15 33 37

22111 MAM P P1 G1.2 1895–1928
Lin, Jing-min, 1936–.
The economic ideas of Sun Yat-sen.
Ann Arbor: University Microfilms (Publ. 64-6838), 1964. 147 p. (Doctoral dissertation in Economics, Kansas State U., 1963)
Subj 64 70

22112 CSU P P2 G1.2 –1928
Lin Mousheng (Lin Mou-sheng), 1906–.
Men and ideas: An informal history of Chinese political thought.
New York: Day, 1942. 14, 256 p.
Subj 59 62 64 ▪ 12 13 14.1 16.1 17 66

22113 CSH P P1 G1.2 –1928
Lin, Yu-sheng (Lin Yü-sheng), 1934–.
'Radical iconoclasm in the May Fourth period and the future of Chinese liberalism.' In *Reflections on the May Fourth Movement: A symposium*, edited by Benjamin Isadore Schwartz. [Analytic entry]
Cambridge: Harvard U., East Asian Research Center, 1972, 23–58. (Harvard East Asian monographs, 44)
Subj 64

22114 NNC P P1 G1.1 1895–1928
Linebarger, Paul Myron Anthony, 1913–1966.
The political doctrines of Sun Yat-sen: An exposition of the 'San min chu i'.
Baltimore: Johns Hopkins Press, 1937. 14, 278 p. (Johns Hopkins studies in historical and political science, new series, 24) (Doctoral dissertation in Political Science, Johns Hopkins U.) [Reprinted—Westport, Conn.: Hyperion Press, 197? 14, 278 p.]
Subj 64

22115 CSU P P1 G1.1 1895–1928
Liu, Shia-ling.
'A new concept of law: A study of Dr. Sun Yat-sen's political philosophy.' *Asian studies* (Quezon City, Philippines) 4, 1 (Apr. 1966), 29–39.
Subj 64

22116 CSH P P4 G1.3 1895–1928
Lubot, Eugene Stephen, 1942–.
'Ts'ai Yuan-p'ei from Confucian scholar to Chancellor of Peking University, 1898–1923: The evolution of a patient reformer.'
Asian forum 2, 3 (July–Sept. 1970), 139–151. [For a fuller version, see entry 21340.]
Subj 64 ▪ 17 62

22117 MAM P P2 G1.2 1895–1928
Mast, Herman William, III, 1941–.
An intellectual biography of Tai Chi-t'ao from 1891 to 1928.
Ann Arbor: University Microfilms (Publ. 71-5172), 1971. 424 p. (Doctoral dissertation in History, U. of Illinois, 1970)
Subj 14.2 59 64 ▪ 16.4 32 54 66

22118 MCH P P1 G1.2 1895–1928
Meisner, Maurice J-, 1931–.
Li Ta-chao and the origins of Chinese Marxism.
Cambridge: Harvard U. Press, 1967. 326 p. (Harvard East Asian series, 27) (Revision of doctoral dissertation in History, U. of Chicago, 1963) [Reprinted—New York: Atheneum, 1970. 326 p.]
Subj 59 60 64 66 ▪ 16.1 17 19 32 32.2 63

22119 CSH U P2 G1.2 1842–1949
Muramatsu, Yuji (Muramatsu Yūji), 1911–.
'Nationalism and Communism in China.'
Asian affairs (Tokyo) 1, 4 (Dec. 1956), 379–391.
Subj 32.2 64 66 ▪ 15

22120 MCY S P1 G1.2 1895–1949
O'Bryant, Albert Henry, 1917–.
'Liang Sou-ming: His response to the West.'
PC 7 (Feb. 1953), 1–33.
Subj 64 ▪ 16 16.1 59 62 66

22121 CSU P P1 G1.2 1895–1928
Pokora, Timoteus.
'Nationalism versus Marxism?' [Review of *Li Ta-chao and the origins of Chinese Marxism*, by Maurice J- Meisner.]
AO 37, 1 (1969), 87–93.
Subj 64 ▪ 16.1 32.2

22122 CSH P P1 G1.2 1895–1928
Richter, Melvin.
'Sun Yat-sen's doctrine of Min Ch'uan [democracy].'
PC 1 (Dec. 1947), 136–174.
Subj 64

22123 CSH P P1 G1.2 –1928
Roy, Andrew Tod.
'Attacks upon Confucianism in the 1911–1927 period. Part 1, From the left: Ch'en Tu-hsiu.'
CCJ 4, 1 (Nov. 1964), 10–26.
Subj 60 64 ▪ 13 47 63

22124 CBU P P1 G1.2 –1949
Roy, Andrew Tod.
'Confucianism and social change.'
CCJ 3, 1 (Nov. 1963), 88–104.
Subj 64

22125 MAM P P1 G1.2 1644–1949
Roy, Andrew Tod.
Modern Confucian social theory and its concept of change.
Ann Arbor: University Microfilms (Publ. 11,014), 1955. 538 p. (Doctoral dissertation in Philosophy, Princeton U., 1948)
Subj 64

22126 MCY P P1 G1.1 1644–1949
Sakai, Robert Kenjiro (Sakai Kenjirō), 1919–.
'A study of *China's destiny* and its adaptation of Confucianism.'
PC 2 (May 1948), 198–224.
Subj 63 64

22127 MCH P P1 G1.1 1895–1928
Scalapino, Robert Anthony, 1919–, and George T. Yu, 1931–.
The Chinese anarchist movement.
Berkeley: U. of California, Center for Chinese Studies, 1961. 81 p. [Reprinted—Ann Arbor: University Microfilms, n.d. 81 p.]
Subj 32 64 ▪ 14.2 32.2

22128 CSH P P1 G1.2 1842–1928
Senin, Nikolai Gerasimovich.
Obshchestvenno-politicheskie i filosofskie vzgliady Sun' IAt-sena (The sociopolitical and philosophical views of Sun Yat-sen).
Moscow: Izd-vo Akad. nauk SSSR, 1956. 216 p.
Subj 32 60 64 ▪ 12 16 16.1 19 32.2

22129 MCY P P1 G1.2 –1949
Shryock, John Knight, 1890–1952.
'Confucianism.' In *China*, edited by Harley Farnsworth MacNair. [Selective entry]
Berkeley, Los Angeles: U. of California Press, 1946, 245–253. [Reprinted in *China*, edited by H. F. MacNair. (Selective entry.) Freeport, N.Y.: Books for Libraries, 1970, 245–253.]
Subj 13 60 64 ▪ 12

22130 CSU P P2 G1.2 1842–1949
Sumiya, Kazuhiko, 1925–.
'The Long March and the Exodus: "The thought of Mao Tse-tung" and the contemporary significance of "emissary prophecy".' Tr. by Pharis Harvey, Hiroshi Shinmi, and Tadashi Miyabe of 'Chōsei to shutsu Ejiputo' (The Long March and the Exodus); *Tembō* 102 (June 1967), 33–61 [slightly abridged in tr.]. In *China and ourselves: Explorations and revisions by a new generation*, edited by Bruce Douglass and Ross Terrill. [Selective entry]
Boston: Beacon Press, 1969, 189–223.
Subj 64 ▪ 15 32.2 60

22131 NNC PO P2 G1.2 –1928
T'ang, Leang-li (T'ang Liang-li), 1901–.
The foundations of modern China.
London: Noel Douglas, 1928. 10, 290 p.
Subj 12 19 32.2 64 66 ▪ 12.2 14 15 16 17 36.2 36.4 41 54 62

22132 MCY P P1 G1.3 –1949
Tseng Yu-hao, 1900–.
Modern Chinese legal and political philosophy.
Shanghai: Commercial Press, 1934. 320 p.
Subj 12.2 64 ▪ 12 17 63 66

22133 MCH PO P2 G1.1 –1949
Tsiang, Kuen.
Les origines économiques et politiques du socialisme de Sun Yat Sen (The economic and political origins of Sun Yat-sen's socialism).
Paris: Ed. Domat-Montchrestien, 1933. 204 p.
Subj 64 66 ▪ 14.2 14.3 14.4 16.2 18 19 45 72

22134 NNC P P2 G1.2 1895–1928
TSzian Chun-fan (Chiang Ch'un-fang).
'Iz istorii rasprostraneniia marksizma v Kitae.'
VI 1958, 5 (mai), 43–64.
'History of the dissemination of Marxism in China.' In *Selected political translations from Soviet journals*, mimeo., compiled by U.S. Joint Publications Research Service. [Analytic entry]
Washington, D.C.: JPRS, 26 Sept. 1958, 1–51. (JPRS 295D; MC 16,112/1958)
Subj 64 ▪ 14.2 14.4 32.2

22135 MAM P P2 G1.2 1895–1949
Wang Jan-chih, 1925–.
General Chiang Pai-li and his military thought.
Ann Arbor: University Microfilms (Publ. 72-21,738), 1972. 210 p. (Doctoral dissertation in History, St. John's U., 1971)
Subj 15 59 64 ▪ 12 16.1 17 32

22136 CSU P P1 G1.1 1895–1928
Wang, Y. C. (Wang I-chü; Wang Chi-ch'ien), 1916–.
'The influence of Yen Fu and Liang Ch'i-ch'ao on the San Min Chu I.'
PHR 34, 2 (May 1965), 163–184.
Subj 62 64 ▪ 59 60

22137 NNC S P2 G1.3 1842–1928
Wittfogel, Karl August, 1896–.
'Die Entwicklung Sun Yat Sens und des Sun-Yat-Senismus: Versuch einer politischen Biographie' (The development of Sun Yat-sen and Sun-yat-sen-ism: Toward a political biography). In *Sun Yat Sen: Aufzeichnungen eines chinesischen Revolutionärs* (Sun Yat-sen: Memoirs of a Chinese revolutionary), edited by K. A. Wittfogel. [Sole entry]
Berlin: Agis, 1928, 7–150.
Subj 16 32.2 59 64 ▪ 14.3 32.1

22138 CSH P P1 G1.2 1895–1928
Wu, John C. H. (Wu Ching-hsiung), 1899–.
'The philosophy of "Min-Sheng" [people's livelihood].'
CC 11, 3 (Sept. 1970), 1–16.
Subj 64

22139 CSH U P1 G1.1 1895–1928
Wu, John C. H. (Wu Ching-hsiung), 1899–.
'Sun Yat-sen's philosophy of nationalism.'
CC 11, 1 (Mar. 1970), 1–20. [Reprinted—*ASPAC q. of cultural and social affairs* (Seoul) 2, 1 (Summer 1970), 27–41.]
Subj 64 ▪ 66

22140 MCH P P1 G1.2 –1928
Zia, Z. K. (Hsieh Sung-kao), 1895–.
'The Confucian civilization: The Confucian theory of moral and religious education.'
CR 54, 10 – 55, 4 (Oct. 1923 – Apr. 1924), 57 p. in all.
Subj 17 60 62 63 64 ▪ 33

1911-1949

22141 DLC P P3 G1.4 1911–1928
Afanas'ev, A- G-.
'Li Da-chzhao i "dvizhenie 4 maia"' (Li Ta-chao and the May Fourth Movement). In *Dvizhenie '4 maia' 1919 goda v Kitae: sbornik statei* (Articles on the May Fourth Movement in China), compiled by Institut vostokovedeniia, Akademiia nauk SSSR, edited by A- G- Afanas'ev et al. [Selective entry]
Moscow: Nauka, Glav. red. vost. lit-ry, 1971, 132–149.
Subj 16 59 64 66 ▪ 14.2 32.2 54 72

22142 MCH P P1 G1.2 1911–1928
Alekseev, Vasilii Mikhailovich, 1880–1951.
'Uchenie Konfutsiia v kitaiskom sinteze' (Confucian teaching in its Chinese synthesis).
Vostok 3 (1923), 126–149.
Subj 64 ▪ 70

22143 CSU P P1 G1.2 1928–1949
Bedeski, Robert Edward, 1937–.
'The tutelary state and national revolution in Kuomintang ideology, 1928–31.'
CQ 46 (Apr.–June 1971), 308–330.
Subj 64 ▪ 32

22144 NNC P P2 G1.2 1911–1949
Brandt, Conrad, 1920–, Benjamin Isadore Schwartz, 1916–, and John King Fairbank, 1907–.
A documentary history of Chinese Communism.
Cambridge: Harvard U. Press, 1952. 552 p. (Harvard Russian Research Center studies, 6) [Reprinted—Cambridge: Harvard U. Press, 1959. 552 p.] [Reprinted—New York: Atheneum, 1966. 552 p.]
Subj 16 64 ▪ 14.1 16.1 32 32.2 72

22145 MCY P P1 G1.2 1911–1949
Brière, O-.
'L'effort de la philosophie marxiste en Chine' (The reach of Marxist philosophy in China).
BUA 3e série 8, 31 (1947), 309–347.
Subj 64 ▪ 19

22146 CSU P P2 G1.2 1928–1949
Ch'en, Jerome (Ch'en Chih-jang), 1919–.
'The development and logic of Mao Tse-tung's thought, 1928–49.' In *Ideology and politics in contemporary China*, edited by Chalmers Ashby Johnson. [Selective entry]
Seattle: U. of Washington Press, 1973, 78–114. (Social Science Research Council, Studies in Chinese government and politics, 4)
Subj 16 32.2 64 ▪ 14.1 15 16.1

22147 MAM P P1 G1.2 1911–1928
Chu, Chi-hsien (Chu Ch'i-hsien), 1911–.
A study of the development of Sun Yat-sen's philosophical ideas.
Ann Arbor: University Microfilms (Publ. 1837), 1950. 256 p. (Doctoral dissertation in Philosophy, Columbia U.)
Subj 62 64 ▪ 63

22148 CBU S P2 G1.2 1911–1928
[Deliusin, Lev Petrovich] L. P. Delyusin, 1923–.
'Influence of the Great October Revolution on the development of revolutionary democratic ideas in China.' Tr. from the Russian by G- Kasanina et al. In *Asia in Soviet studies*, compiled by Institut narodov Azii, Akademiia nauk SSSR (Institute of the Peoples of Asia, U.S.S.R. Academy of Sciences). [Sole entry]
Moscow: Nauka, Central Dept. of Oriental Literature, 1969, 18–50.
Subj 60 64 66 ▪ 16 32.2

22149 CSH S P2 G1.2 1911–1928
Deliusin, Lev Petrovich, 1923–.
'Oktiabr'skaia revoliutsiia i Kitai (otkliki nachala 20-kh godov)' (The October Revolution and China: Reactions of the early 1920s). [With English abstract]
NAA 1967, 6, 32–39.
Subj 16 64 66 ▪ 32.2 54

22150 CSH S P5 G1.2 1911–1949
Ershov, Matvei Nikolaevich.
'Natsionalisticheskoe dvizhenie v Kitae (obzor literatury)' (Survey of the literature on the nationalist movement in China). [With English abstract]
VM 1929, 6, 91–98.
Subj 17 32 64 66 72 ▪ 32.2

22151 MAM P P1 G1.2 1911–1949
Fan, Kuang-huan, 1922–.
A study of Hu Shih's thought.
Ann Arbor: University Microfilms (Publ. 64-6462), 1964. 325 p. (Doctoral dissertation in Philosophy, New York U.)
Subj 62 64

22152 CSH P P8 G1.2 1911–1949
Fuller, Francis F-.
'Mao Tse-tung: Military thinker.'
Military affairs 22, 3 (Fall 1958), 139–145.
Subj 15 25 64

22153 NNC P P1 G1.2 1911–1928
Garushiants, IUrii Misakovich.
'Ideinaia bor'ba sredi kitaiskoi intelligentsii v kontse 1918 – nachale 1919 goda' (The ideological struggle within the Chinese intelligentsia from late 1918 to early 1919).
SK 1958, 1, 49–61.
Subj 16.1 64 ▪ 32.2 36.1

22154 CSH U P3 G1.2 1911–1928
Grieder, Jerome Bailey, 1932–.
'The question of "politics" in the May Fourth era.' In *Reflections on the May Fourth Movement: A symposium*, edited by Benjamin Isadore Schwartz. [Analytic entry]
Cambridge: Harvard U., East Asian Research Center, 1972, 95–101. (Harvard East Asian monographs, 44)
Subj 64

22155 CSU P P1 G1.2 1911–1928
Huang, P. C., and W. P. Yuen.
'The alleged influence of Maurice William on Sun Yat-sen.'

THM 5, 4 (Nov. 1937), 349–376.
Subj 64 ▪ 59 66

22156 WSU P P1 G1.2 1911–1928
Huang, Sung-k'ang.
Li Ta-chao and the impact of Marxism on modern Chinese thinking.
The Hague: Mouton, 1965. 91 p.
Subj 64 ▪ 16.1 54 60

22157 NNC P P1 G1.2 1928–1949
IAn Khin-shun (Yang Hsing-shun).
'Sotsiologicheskie vzgliady Chen' Li-fu kak ideologicheskaia osnova reaktsionnoi politiki gomindana' (Ch'en Li-fu's sociological views as the ideological basis of reactionary Kuomintang policy).
Filosofskie zapiski 2 (1948), 187–195.
Subj 32 62 64 ▪ 12.1 59

22158 CNY P P2 G1.2 1928–1949
[Jobez, Robert] Robert Magnenoz, pseud.
De Confucius à Lénine: la montée au pouvoir du Parti communiste chinois (From Confucius to Lenin: The Chinese Communist Party's rise to power).
Saigon: Ed. France-Asie, 1951. 221 p.
Subj 32.2 64 ▪ 16

22159 NNC P P2 G1.2 1911–1928
Kapitsa, Mikhail Stepanovich.
'Iz istorii rasprostraneniia idei marksizma-leninizma v Kitae, 1917–1924 gg.' (History of the dissemination of Marxist-Leninist ideas in China, 1917–1924).
SV 1956, 2, 34–44.
Subj 32.2 64 ▪ 16.1 16.4 36.4

22160 CSU P P1 G1.1 1911–1928
Kriegel, Annie.
'Aux origines françaises du communisme chinois' (French origins of Chinese Communism).
Preuves 209/210 (août–sept. 1968), 24–41.
Subj 16.1 16.4 37 64 ▪ 30 32.2 54

22161 CSU P P4 G1.2 1928–1949
Lieberthal, Kenneth Guy, 1943–.
'Mao versus Liu? Policy towards industry and commerce, 1946–49.'
CQ 47 (July–Sept. 1971), 494–520.
Subj 16.4 36.4 64 ▪ 14.3 14.4 16 16.2 22 34.2

22162 ICU P P2 G1.2 1911–1928
Loh, Pichon P. Y. (Lu P'ei-yung), 1928–.
The popular upsurge in China: Nationalism and westernization, 1919–1927.
Unpublished doctoral dissertation in International Relations, U. of Chicago, 1955. 362 p.
Subj 16.3 16.4 19 32.2 64 ▪ 14.3 14.4 16 17 32.1 36.3 36.4 72

22163 MCH P P1 G1.2 1911–1928
Lucardie, W- G-.
'Het communisme in China' (Communism in China).
De Indische Gids (Amsterdam) 53, 3 (Maart 1931), 193–213.
Subj 32.2 64 ▪ 66

22164 CSU P P3 G6.1 1911–1928
Mast, Herman William, III, 1941–.
'Tai Chi-t'ao: Sunism and Marxism during the May Fourth Movement in Shanghai.'
MAS 5, 3 (July 1971), 227–249. [For fuller treatment, see entry 22117.]
Subj 59 64 ▪ 19 26.4 54

22165 CSH FP P1 G1.2 1911–1928
Mast, Herman William, III, 1941–, and William George Gabriel Saywell, 1936–.
'The culturalism of political despair: Tai Chi-t'aoism and Chiang Kai-shek.'
Asia q. 1972, 3, 227–244.
Subj 64 ▪ 32 32.2 54 59

22166 CSU P P2 G1.2 1928–1949
Meisner, Maurice J-, 1931–.
'Yenan Communism and the rise of the Chinese People's Republic.' In *Modern East Asia: Essays in interpretation*, edited by James Buckley Crowley. [Selective entry]
New York: Harcourt, Brace and World, 1970, 265–297.
Subj 32.2 64 ▪ 15 16.3 61

22167 CSH P P2 G1.2 1911–1949
Meliksetov, Arlen Vaagovich, 1930–.
'K otsenke vzgliadov Sun' IAt-sena' (An evaluation of Sun Yat-sen's views).
NAA 1969, 5, 80–91.
Subj 12 14 32.2 64

22168 CSU P P2 G1.2 1911–1949
Nomura Kōichi, 1930–.
'Mao Tse-tung's thought and the Chinese Revolution.' Tr. of 'Mō Takutō no shisō to Chūgoku kakumei'; *Tembō* 91 (July 1966), 17–37.
J. of social and political ideas in Japan 5, 1 (Apr. 1967), 67–90.
Subj 32.2 64 ▪ 15 16.3 16.4 59

22169 CSH P P2 G1.2 1928–1949
Poe, Dison Hsueh-feng (P'u Hsüeh-feng), 1900–.
'Political reconstruction, 1927–1937' [with comments by Franz Michael]. In *The strenuous decade: China's nation-building efforts, 1927–1937*, edited by Paul K. T. Sih (Hsüeh Kuang-ch'ien). [Selective entry]
Jamaica, N.Y.: St. John's U. Press, 1970, 33–81.
Subj 15 32 64 ▪ 12 12.2 14 22

22170 MCY P P1 G1.3 1911–1949
Roy, Andrew Tod.
'Liang Shu-ming and Hu Shih on the intuitional interpretation of Confucianism.'
CCJ 1, 2 (July 1962), 139–157.
Subj 60 64 ▪ 13 16.1 62

22171 CSH S P2 G1.2 1911–1949
Safarov, Georgii Ivanovich, 1891–1938?
'Revoliutsiia i kontrrevoliutsiia v Kitae' (Revolution and counterrevolution in China).
PK 4/5 (1930), 3–32.
Subj 14.1 14.4 32.2 64 ▪ 15 16.2 16.3 18 32 66

22172 CTU P P2 G1.2 1911–1928
Saywell, William George Gabriel, 1936–.
The thought of Tai Chi-t'ao, 1912–1928.
Unpublished doctoral dissertation in History, U. of Toronto, 1968. 487 p.
Subj 59 64 ▪ 32.2 66

22173 GMS P P2 G1.2 1911–1949
Schmitz, Peter.
Der Bolschewismus in China (Bolshevism in China).
Vienna-Mödling: Missionsdruckerei St. Gabriel, 1932. 84 p. (Akademischer Missionsverein, Wien, Veröffentlichungen, 6)
Subj 32.2 36.3 64 ▪ 12.1 19

22174 MCY P P1 G1.2 1911–1928
Schwartz, Benjamin Isadore, 1916–.
'Ch'en Tu-hsiu: Pre-Communist phase.'
PC 2 (May 1948), 167–197.
Subj 16.1 64 ▪ 59 61

22175 MCY P P1 G1.2 1911–1949
Schwartz, Benjamin Isadore, 1916–.
'Marxist doctrine in the Chinese Communist movement.'
PC 1 (Dec. 1947), 209–242.
Subj 32.2 64

22176 CSU P P1 G1.2 1928–1949
Stevens, Charles R-.
'A content analysis of the wartime writings of Chiang Kai-shek and Mao Tse-tung.'
AS 4, 6 (June 1964), 890–903.
Subj 64 ▪ 32 32.2

22177 CSU P P3 G1.3 1911–1928
Sullivan, Lawrence, and Richard Harvey Solomon, 1937–.
'The formation of Chinese Communist ideology in the May Fourth era: A content analysis of "Hsin ch'ing-nien" [La jeunesse].' In *Ideology and politics in contemporary China*, edited by Chalmers Ashby Johnson. [Selective entry]
Seattle: U. of Washington Press, 1973, 117–160. (Social Science Research Council, Studies in Chinese government and politics, 4)
Subj 62 64 ▪ 14.2 16.1 32.2

22178 NNC P P1 G1.1 1911–1949
Tan, Chester C. (T'an Ch'un-lin).
'Tradition and the new culture.'
THJ new (2nd) series 2, 1 (May 1960), 287–300.
Subj 60 64

22179 MCH O P1 G1.2 1911–1928
Tsiang, Tingfu Fuller (Chiang T'ing-fu), 1895–1965.
Das kämpfende China: Die störenden und fördernden Kräfte im Einigungsproblem Chinas (Struggling China: The positive and negative forces affecting Chinese unification).
Berlin: Gerlt, 1936. 40 p.
Subj 16 64 ▪ 13 61 63 66

22180 CSU P P2 G1.2 1911–1928
Tsui, Shu-chin (Ts'ui Shu-ch'in), 1906–1957.
'The influence of the Canton-Moscow entente upon Sun Yat-sen's political philosophy.'
CSPSR 18, 1 (Apr. 1934), 96–145; 18, 2 (July 1934), 177–209; 18, 3 (Oct. 1934), 341–388. (Doctoral dissertation in History, Government, and Economics, Harvard U., 1934. [The dissertation was published in two parts, of which this item is the first. For the second, see entry 18156.])
Subj 64 ▪ 12 32 32.2 66

22181 CSU FP P3 G1.3 1911–1928
Wei, Carl K.
'The founding of the Chinese Communist Party and its first national congress (1920–1921).'
IS 7, 2 (Nov. 1970), 39–50.
SUBJ 14.2 32.2 64 66 ▪ 17 54 59

1911-1972
(including 1644-1972)

22182 CSH P P2 G1.2 1911–1972
Axilrod, Eric.
Mao, Lenin and the two revolutions.
Hong Kong: Chinese U. of Hong Kong, Economic Research Centre, 1972. 47 p. (ERC, Mainland China series, occasional papers, 3)
SUBJ 64 ▪ 16 32.2

22183 FPN P P1 G1.2 –1972
Banu, Ion.
'La formation sociale "asiatique" dans la perspective de la philosophie orientale antique' (The relation between 'Asiatic' social structure and ancient Oriental philosophy).
La pensée nouvelle (2e) série 132 (mars–avr. 1967), 53–70.
SUBJ 12.1 16 64 ▪ 14 14.1

22184 CSH P P1 G1.2 1928–1972
Bartsch, Günter.
'Die Philosophie Mao Tse-tungs' (The philosophy of Mao Tse-tung).
Die neue Gesellschaft 14, 3 (Mai–Juni 1967), 180–189.
SUBJ 64

22185 CBU S P1 G1.2 –1972
Bauer, Wolfgang, 1930–.
Chinas Vergangenheit als Trauma und Vorbild (China's past as trauma and example).
Stuttgart: Kohlhammer, 1968. 100 p.
SUBJ 64 ▪ 12 62 66

22186 CSU U P2 G1.2 1928–1972
Bernal, Martin Gardiner, 1937–.
'A Mao for all seasons.' [Review of *Revolutionary immortality: Mao Tse-tung and the Chinese Cultural Revolution*, by Robert Jay Lifton; *La rivoluzione culturale in Cina* (China's Cultural Revolution), by [Alberto Pincherle] Alberto Moravia, pseud.; *Communism and China: Ideology in flux*, by Benjamin Isadore Schwartz; *Red star over China*, rev. and enl. ed., by Edgar Snow; and *Selected readings from the works of Mao Tse-tung*.] [Pincherle book translated as *The red book and the Great Wall*.]
NYRB 12, 1 (16 Jan. 1969), 5–10.
SUBJ 19 64 ▪ 16

22187 NIC S P1 G1.2 –1972
Boles, Donald Edward, 1926–.
'Chinese Confucianism and Communist power.'
World affairs q. 30, 3 (Oct. 1959), 226–240.
SUBJ 63 64 ▪ 40

22188 CSH P P1 G1.2 1911–1972
Boorman, Howard Lyon, 1920–.
'The literary world of Mao Tse-tung.'
CQ 13 (Jan.–Mar. 1963), 15–38.
[Reprinted in *China under Mao: Politics takes command*, edited by Roderick Lemonde MacFarquhar. (Selective entry.) Cambridge: M.I.T. Press, 1966, 368–391.]
SUBJ 12.1 64 ▪ 32.1 36.1

22189 MCH U P1 G1.1 1911–1972
Borsa, Giorgio, 1912–.
'Lo sviluppo del nazionalismo in Cina' (The development of Chinese nationalism).
Civiltà cinese 1, 1 (luglio 1960), 7–26.
SUBJ 32.2 60 64 66 ▪ 14 16 17 19 32

22190 CSH P P2 G1.2 1928–1972
Bulatov, B-.
Maoism versus culture. Tr. of *Maoizm protiv kul'tury.*
Moscow: Novosti, 1970. 77 p.
SUBJ 64 ▪ 12.1 16.1 32.1

22191 CSU P P2 G1.2 1928–1972
Carrère d'Encausse, Hélène, and Stuart Reynolds Schram, 1924–.
'Les caractères généraux de la révolution en Russie et en Chine' (General characteristics of revolution in Russia and China). In *L'U.R.S.S. et la Chine devant les révolutions dans les sociétés pré-industrielles* (The U.S.S.R. and China confronting revolutions in pre-industrial societies), by H. Carrère d'Encausse and S. R. Schram. [Sole entry]
Paris: Armand Colin, 1970, 11–38. (Fondation nationale des sciences politiques, Travaux et recherches de science politique, 8)
SUBJ 12 32.2 64 ▪ 12.1 15 19

22192 MCH P P2 G1.2 1911–1972
Carrère d'Encausse, Hélène, and Stuart Reynolds Schram, 1924–.
'Présentation.' In *Le marxisme et l'Asie, 1853–1964* (Marxism and Asia, 1853–1964), edited by H. Carrère d'Encausse and S. R. Schram. [Sole entry]
Paris: Armand Colin, 1965, 7–135.

'Introduction.' Tr. by Stuart R. Schram. [Slightly rev. in tr.] In *Marxism and Asia*, edited by H. Carrère d'Encausse and S. R. Schram. [Sole entry]
London: Allen Lane, 1969, 1–112.
SUBJ 12 32.2 64 66 ▪ 16 62

22193 NNC U P1 G1.3 1842–1972
Chang, Carsun (Chang Chia-sen), 1886–.
'Konfuzianismus und chinesischer Kommunismus' (Confucianism and Chinese Communism).
Osteuropa 10, 4 (Apr. 1960), 228–237.
SUBJ 13 64 ▪ 19 70

22194 MAM P P1 G1.2 –1972
Chen, David Hsiao-hsin, 1929–.
The thought of Mao in the light of Chinese tradition and revolutionary development.
Ann Arbor: University Microfilms (Publ. 70-14,439), 1970. 206 p. (Doctoral dissertation in Political Science, U. of Utah)
SUBJ 64

22195 MCH P P1 G1.2 1928–1972
Chen, Theodore H. E. (Ch'en Hsi-en), 1902–.
'Chinese Communism.' In *Contemporary political ideologies*, edited by Joseph Slabey Roucek. [Sole entry]
Paterson, N. J.: Littlefield, Adams, 1961, 47–64.
SUBJ 64

22196 NNC P P1 G1.2 1911–1972
Chen, Yung Ping (Ch'en Yung-p'ing), 1928–.
Chinese political thought: Mao Tse-tung and Liu Shao-chi, 2nd ed., rev.
The Hague: Nijhoff, 1971. 131 p. (Revision of doctoral dissertation in Political Science, U. of Maryland, 1959)
SUBJ 32 64 ▪ 16 32.2 62

22197 CSU P P2 G1.2 1911–1972
Ch'en, Jerome (Ch'en Chih-jang), 1919–.
'Introduction.' In *Mao*, edited by Jerome Ch'en. [Sole entry]
Englewood Cliffs, N. J.: Prentice-Hall, 1969, 1–45.
SUBJ 32.2 59 64 ▪ 12.1 16.1 16.3 32

22198 ELO O P2 G1.2 1842–1972
Cheng, F. T. (Cheng T'ien-hsi), 1884–.
East and West: Episodes in a sixty-years' journey.
London: Hutchinson, 1951. 247 p.
SUBJ 17 53 64 ▪ 16.1 22.2 40

22199 FPN P P1 G1.2 –1972
Chesneaux, Jean, 1922–.
'Les traditions égalitaires et utopiques en Orient.'
Diogène 62 (avr.–juin 1968), 87–115.

'Egalitarian and utopian traditions in the Orient.'
Diogenes 62 (Summer 1968), 76–102.
SUBJ 63 64 ▪ 16 30 32.2 45

22200 CSU P P2 G1.2 1911–1972
Chi, Wen-shun (Chi Wen-hsün), 1910–.
'Liang Shu-ming and Chinese Communism.'
CQ 41 (Jan.–Mar. 1970), 64–82.
SUBJ 64 ▪ 59

22201 CSU P P1 G1.2 1928–1972
Chin, Steve S. K. (Chin Ssu-k'ai), 1919–.
'Identity and contradiction: An explanation of the Mao-Liu struggle from an ideological point of view.'
SST 10, 3 (Sept. 1970), 227–254.
SUBJ 64 ▪ 32 32.2

22202 NNC P P1 G1.2 –1972
Chou, Hsiang-kuang.
Political thought of China.
Delhi: Chand, 1954. 244 p.
SUBJ 12 60 64 ▪ 16.1 62

22203 NNC P P2 G1.2 1928–1972
Cohen, Arthur Allen, 1928–.
The Communism of Mao Tse-tung.
Chicago: U. of Chicago Press, 1964. 210 p.
SUBJ 64 ▪ 12 12.1 15 16 19 25 32 32.2 36.3

22204 MCH P P2 G1.2 1928–1972
Collotti Pischel, Enrica, 1930–.
La rivoluzione ininterrotta: sviluppi interni e prospettive internazionali della rivoluzione cinese (The continuous revolution: Internal developments and international prospects of the Chinese Revolution).
Turin: Einaudi, 1962. 198 p.

La révolution ininterrompue. Tr. by Anne Marchand.
Paris: Julliard, 1964. 312 p.
SUBJ 32.2 64 ▪ 14.1

22205 CSU S P1 G1.2 -1972
Corwin, Charles.
'China.' In *East to Eden? Religion and the dynamics of social change.* [Sole entry]
Grand Rapids, Mich.: Eerdmans, 1972, 51–93.
Subj 33 60 64 ▪ 32 32.2 66

22206 NNC P P1 G1.1 1644–1972
Creel, Herrlee Glessner, 1905–.
Chinese thought from Confucius to Mao Tse-tung.
Chicago: U. of Chicago Press, 1953. 293 p.
Subj 60 64 ▪ 16.1 66 72

22207 MAM P P1 G1.2 -1972
Dai, Shen-yu (Tai Sheng-yü), 1921–.
Mao Tse-tung and Confucianism.
Ann Arbor: University Microfilms (Publ. 5307), 1953. 456 p. (Doctoral dissertation in Political Science, U. of Pennsylvania)
Subj 60 64

22208 ELB P P1 G1.2 1895–1972
Deliusin, Lev Petrovich, 1923–.
'"Diskussiia o sotsializme" v Kitae i sovremennost" (The 'discussion on socialism' in China and the present). [With English abstract]
Voprosy filosofii 1969, 1, 87–98.
Subj 64 66 ▪ 12 32.2

22209 CSU S P1 G1.2 1842–1972
Dernberger, Robert Franklin, 1929–.
'The role of nationalism in the rise and development of Communist China.' In *Economic nationalism in old and new states*, edited by Harry G- Johnson. [Sole entry]
Chicago: U. of Chicago Press, 1967, 48–70.
Subj 14.3 32.2 64 66 ▪ 12 14 32

22210 CBU P P2 G1.2 1895–1972
Devillers, Philippe, 1920–.
Ce que Mao a vraiment dit (What Mao really said).
Paris: Stock, 1968. 295 p.

Mao. Tr. by Tony White.
New York: Schocken, 1969. 317 p.
Subj 59 64 66 ▪ 15 16 16.1 32.2 34.1

22211 MCH P P1 G1.2 1928–1972
Doolin, Dennis James, 1933–, and Peter John Golas.
'"On contradiction" in the light of Mao Tse-tung's essay on "dialectical materialism".'
CQ 19 (July–Sept. 1964), 38–46.
Subj 64

22212 CSU P P2 G1.2 1911–1972
Douglass, Bruce.
'The socialist tradition and China's new socialism.' In *China and ourselves: Explorations and revisions by a new generation*, edited by B. Douglass and Ross Terrill. [Selective entry]
Boston: Beacon Press, 1969, 224–248.
Subj 64 ▪ 14 19

22213 MCH P P2 G1.2 1911–1972
Fetscher, Irving, 1922–.
'Die ideologische Eigenart des chinesischen Kommunismus' (The ideological uniqueness of Chinese Communism).
Civitas (Mannheim) 4 (1965), 63–87.
Subj 15 16.4 19 32.2 64 ▪ 12.1 16 32

22214 MCH U P1 G1.1 -1972
Franke, Herbert, 1914–.
'Geschichtliche Grundlagen des chinesischen Kommunismus' (Historical foundations of Chinese Communism).
Hochland 57, 1 (Okt. 1964), 41–55.
Subj 64 ▪ 16 66

22215 CSU S P2 G1.2 1911–1972
Franke, Wolfgang, 1912–.
'Revolutionslehre und Revolutionspraxis Mao Tse-tungs.'
Moderne Welt 1, 1 (1959/60), 44–49.

'The revolutionary theory and practice of Mao Tse-tung.' Tr. by Kathleen Szasz.
Modern world (Cologne) 1960/61, 48–53.
Subj 32.2 64

22216 NNC S P1 G1.2 -1972
Franke, Wolfgang, 1912–.
'Die Rolle der Tradition im heutigen China.'
Moderne Welt 3, 2 (1961/62), 146–164.

'The role of tradition in present-day China.' Tr. by Rosita Schoenthal and Klaus Schoenthal.
Modern world (Cologne) 1963/64, 75–92.
Subj 12 61 64 ▪ 12.2 13 16 16.1 66

22217 NNC P P2 G1.2 1928–1972
Garvey, James Emmett, 1917–.
Marxist-Leninist China: Military and social doctrine.
New York: Exposition Press, 1960. 447 p.
Subj 15 64 ▪ 12 25 32.1 62

22218 CSU S P1 G1.3 1911–1972
Gasster, Michael, 1930–.
'The death and transfiguration of Confucianism.' [Review of *Confucian China and its modern fate, Vol. 3, The problem of historical significance*, by Joseph Richmond Levenson.]
Philosophy, East and West 18, 3 (July 1968), 205–213.
Subj 19 64 ▪ 12 16.1 66

22219 CSH P P2 G1.2 1911–1972
Gel'bras, Vil' Gdal'evich, 1930–.
Mao's pseudo-socialism.
Moscow: Novosti, 1968? 156 p.
Subj 14 16 64 ▪ 12 12.1 35

22220 CSU P P1 G1.2 1911–1972
Glaberman, Martin.
'Mao as a dialectician.'
International philosophical q. 8, 1 (Mar. 1968), 94–112.
Subj 64 ▪ 16 32.2

22221 MCH S P2 G1.2 1911–1972
Go Shao-tan (Kuo Shao-t'ang), 1905–, and Nikolai Pavlovich Vinogradov, 1923–1967.
'V. I. Lenin i Kitai' (V. I. Lenin and China). In *Lenin i Vostok: sbornik statei* (Articles on Lenin and the Orient), jointly edited by Institut kitaevedeniia, Akademiia nauk SSSR *with* Institut vostokovedeniia, Akademiia nauk SSSR. [Sole entry]
Moscow: Izd-vo vost. lit-ry, 1960, 90–146.
Subj 12.1 14 16 64 ▪ 16.2 16.3 17 32.2 34.1

22222 CSU S P1 G1.2 -1972
Grimm, Tilemann, 1922–.
'Tradition und Revolution in China' (Tradition and revolution in China).
Historische Z. 204, 1 (Feb.–März 1967), 79–103.
Subj 19 62 64

22223 CSU P P2 G1.2 1928–1972
Gupta, Krishna Prakash.
'"Society as a factory": Maoist approach to social sciences.'
China report (New Delhi) 8, 3 (May–June 1972), 36–57.
Subj 62 64 ▪ 12.1 17 61 70

22224 MAM P P2 G1.2 1911–1972
Harman, Richard Snyder, 1942–.
The Maoist case against Liu Shao-ch'i (1967): A leadership crisis in the Chinese People's Republic.
Ann Arbor: University Microfilms (Publ. 70-4796), 1970. 298 p. (Doctoral dissertation in Political Science, U. of Virginia)
Subj 59 64 ▪ 14 16.4 17 32 32.2 36.4

22225 NNC S P2 G1.1 1644–1972
Harrison, James Pinckney, 1932–.
Modern Chinese nationalism.
New York: Hunter College of the City U. of New York, 1970. 61 p.
Subj 19 60 64 66 ▪ 11.1 16 16.1 32 32.2

22226 NNC P P1 G1.2 1928–1972
Holubnychy, Vsevolod.
'Der dialektische Materialismus Mao Tse-tungs im Vergleich mit den Klassikern des Marxismus-Leninismus, untersucht als Faktor zur Beurteilung der chinesisch-sowjetischen Beziehung' (Interpreting Sino-Soviet relations: Mao Tse-tung's dialectical materialism and that of classical Marxism-Leninism).
Ostblock und Entwicklungsländer; Vierteljahresbericht der Friedrich-Ebert-Stiftung 8/9 (Sept. 1962), 15–59.

'Mao Tse-tung's materialistic dialectics' [Condensed tr.].
CQ 19 (July–Sept. 1964), 3–37.
Subj 64

22227 MCH S P1 G1.2 -1972
Houn, Franklin W. (Hou Fu-wu), 1920–.
'The Communist monolith versus the Chinese tradition.'
Orbis (Philadelphia) 8, 4 (Winter 1965), 894–921.
Subj 12 12.1 64 ▪ 16.1 22 62

22228 MCY P P1 G1.2 1928–1972
Hsia, T. A. (Hsia Chi-an), 1916–1965.
'Twenty years after the Yenan forum.'
CQ 13 (Jan.–Mar. 1963), 226–253. [Reprinted in *The gate of darkness: Studies on the leftist literary movement in China*, by T. A. Hsia. (Selective entry.) Seattle: U. of Washington Press, 1968, 234–262. (U. of Washington, Far Eastern and Russian Institute, Publications on Asia, 17)]
Subj 64 ▪ 12 12.1 32

22229 CSU P P2 G1.2 1911–1972
Hsiung, James Chieh (Hsiung Chieh), 1935–.
Ideology and practice: The evolution of Chinese Communism.
New York: Praeger, 1970. 359 p.
Subj 32 32.2 64 ▪ 12 14 16 17 35 54 62

22230 MCY P P1 G1.2 1928–1972
Inoki, Masamichi, 1914–.
'Leninism and Mao Tse-tung's ideology.' In *Unity and contradiction: Major aspects of Sino-Soviet relations*, edited by Kurt London. [Selective entry]
New York: Praeger, 1962, 103–121.
Subj 64

22231 CSU P P1 G1.2 –1972
Israel, John Warren, 1935–.
'Continuities and discontinuities in the ideology of the Great Proletarian Cultural Revolution.' In *Ideology and politics in contemporary China*, edited by Chalmers Ashby Johnson. [Selective entry]
Seattle: U. of Washington Press, 1973, 3–46. (Social Science Research Council, Studies in Chinese government and politics, 4)
Subj 19 64 ▪ 13

22232 CSH P P1 G1.2 1928–1972
Jen Cho-hsüan, 1896–.
'An analysis of the thought of Mao Tse-tung.' In *Collected documents of the First Sino-American Conference on Mainland China*. [Selective entry]
[Taipei]: Institute of International Relations, Republic of China, 1971, 307–323.
Subj 64

22233 FPN PO P2 G1.2 1911–1972
[Jobez, Robert] Robert Magnenoz, pseud.
L'expérience communiste en Chine: de Confucius à la nouvelle démocratie (The Communist experiment in China: From Confucius to New Democracy).
Paris: Isles d'or, 1954. 307 p.
Subj 12.1 14.1 64 ▪ 12 14 32.1 61 66

22234 CSU P P2 G1.2 1928–1972
Johnson, Chalmers Ashby, 1931–.
'The changing nature and locus of authority in Communist China.' In *China: Management of a revolutionary society*, edited by John Matthew Henry Lindbeck. [Analytic entry]
Seattle: U. of Washington Press, 1971, 34–76. (Social Science Research Council, Studies in Chinese government and politics, 2)
Subj 12.1 32.2 64 ▪ 12.2 13 32

22235 CSU P P2 G1.2 1928–1972
Kent, A- E-.
Indictment without trial: The case of Liu Shao-ch'i.
Canberra: Australian National U., Institute of Advanced Studies, Research School of Pacific Studies, Dept. of International Relations, 1969. 68 p. (DIR working papers, 11)
Subj 32 59 64 ▪ 16 32.2

22236 NNC P P1 G1.2 1644–1972
Khou Vai-lu (Hou Wai-lu), 1912–.
'Kul'turnaia revoliutsiia i ideologicheskaia bor'ba v Kitae' (Cultural revolution and ideological struggle in China). In *Voprosy kul'turnoi revoliutsii v Kitaiskoi Narodnoi Respublike: sbornik statei* (Articles on the cultural revolution in the People's Republic of China), compiled by Institut kitaevedeniia, Akademiia nauk SSSR, edited by Nikolai Trofimovich Fedorenko. [Selective entry]
Moscow: Izd-vo vost. lit-ry, 1960, 33–78.
Subj 12.1 32.2 64 ▪ 32 32.1 62

22237 NNC S P1 G1.1 1895–1972
Kindermann, Gottfried-Karl, 1926–.
'Einleitung' (Introduction). In *Konfuzianismus, Sunyatsenismus und chinesischer Kommunismus* (Confucianism, Sun Yat-sen-ism, and Chinese Communism), edited by G.-K. Kindermann. [Sole entry]
Freiburg i. Br.: Rombach, 1962, 13–71.
Subj 64 ▪ 19 72

22238 GMS P P4 G1.2 1911–1972
Kindermann, Gottfried-Karl, 1926–.
'Schicksalstunden in der politischen Geistesgeschichte des chinesischen Kommunismus, 1919–1966' (Fateful moments in the political and intellectual development of Chinese Communism, 1919–1966). In *Chinesische Kommunismus: Zur Geistes- und politischen Geschichte* (An intellectual and political history of Chinese Communism), edited by G.-K. Kindermann, Jürgen Otto Domes, and Heinrich Gerhardt. [Analytic entry]
Bonn: Germany [Federal Republic], Bundeszentrale für politische Bildung, 1966, 1–84. (BzpB, Schriftenreihe, 71)
Subj 16 16.1 16.4 19 32.2 64 ▪ 12.1 14 22.2 30 54 66

22239 NIC S P2 G1.2 1928–1972
Klein, Sidney, 1923–.
'Capitalism, socialism, and the economic theories of Mao Tse-tung.'
Political science q. 73, 1 (Mar. 1958), 28–46.
Subj 14 64 ▪ 11.4 14.1 34.1 34.2 36.4

22240 CSU P P1 G1.2 1895–1972
Krivtsov, V- A-.
'Maoism: An ideological-political anachronism in the twentieth century.' Tr. from *Problemy Dal'nego Vostoka* 1972, 1.
Reprints from the Soviet press 15, 6 (22 Sept. 1972), 39–57.
Subj 64

22241 MCH P P1 G1.2 –1972
Kwee, Swan-liat, 1922–.
'Het neo-Confuciaanse mensen wereldbeeld' (The neo-Confucian world view).
Wijsgerig perspectief op maatschappij en wetenschap (Amsterdam) 3, 2 (November 1962), 69–83.
Subj 64 ▪ 62

22242 CSH P P1 G1.2 –1972
[La Dany, Ladislao] ———, 1914–.
'Historical references in Mao's selected works.'
CNA 829 (22 Jan. 1971), 1–7.
Subj 64

22243 MCH P P1 G1.2 1895–1972
Leng, Shao-chuan (Leng Shao-ch'üan), 1921–, and Norman Dunbar Palmer.
Sun Yat-sen and Communism.
New York: Praeger, 1961. 234 p.
Subj 64 ▪ 66

22244 CSU P P1 G1.2 –1972
Levenson, Joseph Richmond, 1920–1969.
'Ill wind in the well-field: The erosion of the Confucian ground of controversy.' In *Confucian China and its modern fate, Vol. 3, The problem of historical significance*, by J. R. Levenson. [Selective entry]
Berkeley, Los Angeles: U. of California Press, 1965, 16–43. [Slight revision of chap. with same title in *The Confucian persuasion*, edited by Arthur Frederick Wright; Stanford: Stanford U. Press, 1960, 268–287.]
Subj 64 ▪ 70

22245 MCH U P1 G1.2 1842–1972
Levenson, Joseph Richmond, 1920–1969.
'The intellectual revolution in China.'
U. of Toronto q. 30, 3 (Apr. 1961), 258–272. [Reprinted in *Modern China*, edited by Albert Feuerwerker. (Selective entry.) Englewood Cliffs, N. J.: Prentice-Hall, 1964, 154–168.]
Subj 16.1 19 60 64 66 ▪ 12 12.1 32 32.2

22246 CSU S P2 G1.2 –1972
Levenson, Joseph Richmond, 1920–1969.
'The past and future of nationalism in China.'
Survey (London) 67 (Apr. 1968), 28–40. [Reprinted in *Modern China: An interpretive anthology*, edited by J. R. Levenson. (Selective entry.) London: Macmillan, 1971, 3–16.]
Subj 10 62 64 ▪ 16 66

22247 MMT O P1 G1.2 1928–1972
Lindsay, Michael Francis Morris, 1909–.
'Changes in Chinese Communist thought, 1937–1960.' In *Symposium on economic and social problems of the Far East*, edited by Edward Franciszek Szczepanik. [Selective entry]
Hong Kong: Hong Kong U. Press, 1962, 215–228.
Subj 32 32.2 64 ▪ 16 32.1 63

22248 CSU P P1 G1.2 1928–1972
Liu, Joseph.
'Mao's "On contradition".'
SST 11, 2 (June 1971), 71–89.
Subj 64 ▪ 15 32.2

22249 MCH P P1 G1.2 1644–1972
Lowe, Donald M. (Lo Ming-ta), 1928–.
The function of 'China' in Marx, Lenin, and Mao.
Berkeley, Los Angeles: U. of California Press, 1966. 200 p. (Revision of *The idea of China in Marx, Lenin, and Mao: A study in Marxist ideological persistence and transformation*, doctoral dissertation in History, U. of California, Berkeley, 1963)
Subj 60 64 ▪ 12 19

22250 ICU P P2 G1.2 1911–1972
[Marsh, Susan Han] Susan Han (Han Su-shan), 1926–.
The concept of the proletariat in Chinese Communism.
Unpublished doctoral dissertation in Political Science, U. of Chicago, 1955. 156 p.
Subj 16 16.4 64 ▪ 16.3 32 32.1 32.2 36.4

22251 CSU P P2 G1.2 1911–1972
Masi, Edoarda.
La contestazione cinese: note per una strategia socialista (The Chinese challenge: Notes on a socialist strategy), 2nd ed., enl.
Turin: Einaudi, 1968. 230 p.
Subj 32 32.2 64 ▪ 12 15 16.1 16.2 19 36.3 54

22252 CSU P P2 G1.2 1911–1972
Meisner, Maurice J-, 1931–.
'Leninism and Maoism: Some populist perspectives on Marxism-Leninism in China.'
CQ 45 (Jan.–Mar. 1971), 2–36.
SUBJ 64

22253 CSH P P1 G1.2 1928–1972
Meisner, Maurice J-, 1931–.
'Maoist utopianism and the future of Chinese society.'
International j. 26, 3 (Summer 1971), 535–555.
SUBJ 64

22254 CSU S P1 G1.2 –1972
Meisner, Maurice J-, 1931–.
'Sinological determinism.' [Review of *Confucian China and its modern fate, Vol. 3, The problem of historical significance*, by Joseph Richmond Levenson.]
CQ 30 (Apr.–June 1967), 175–183.
SUBJ 64

22255 CSH P P2 G1.2 1928–1972
Nakanishi, Tsutomu, 1910–.
'The Chinese revolution and Mao Tsetung thought.' Tr. by Jason G. B. Choi from *Chūgoku kakumei to Mō Takutō shisō* (The Chinese revolution and the thought of Mao Tse-tung); Tokyo: Aoki shoten, 1969, 76–102.
Chinese law and government 4, 1/2 (Spring–Summer 1971), 5–37.
SUBJ 16 64 ▪ 14 32.2

22256 NNC P P1 G1.2 1928–1972
North, Robert Carver, 1914–.
'Two revolutionary models: Russian and Chinese.' In *Communist strategies in Asia*, edited by Arthur Doak Barnett. [Selective entry]
New York: Praeger, 1963, 34–60.
SUBJ 16 32.2 64 ▪ 15 19

22257 NNC P P1 G1.2 1911–1972
Ostrowska, Nina von.
'Der gelbe Kommunismus.'
Politische Studien 10, 106 (Feb. 1959), 102–110.

Yellow Communism, mimeo.
Washington, D.C.: U.S. Joint Publications Research Service, 17 Apr. 1959. 10 p. (JPRS 660D; MC 10,216/1959)
SUBJ 64 ▪ 32.2

22258 CSH P P1 G1.2 1928–1972
Palandri, Angela Jung.
'The political significance of Mao Tse-tung's poetry: Certain contradictions between theory and practice.' In *East Asian occasional papers, II*, edited by Harry Jerome Lamley. [Selective entry]
Honolulu: U. of Hawaii, Asian Studies Program, 1970, 46–58. (Asian Studies at Hawaii, 4)
SUBJ 64

22259 CSU P P2 G1.2 1911–1972
Rejai, Mostafa, 1931–.
'Redefinition of "Maoism".'
JAAS 2, 3/4 (July–Oct. 1967), 186–191.
SUBJ 64

22260 MAM P P1 G1.2 1911–1972
Rejai, Mostafa, 1931–.
The theory of revolution in Mao Tse-tung.
Ann Arbor: University Microfilms (Publ. 65-2180), 1965. 306 p. (Doctoral dissertation in Political Science, U. of California, Los Angeles, 1964)
SUBJ 12 16 64 ▪ 15 32 32.2 66

22261 ELB P P1 G1.2 1911–1972
Rumiantsev, Aleksei Matveevich.
'Maoizm i antimarksistskaia sushchnost' ego "filosofii".'
Kommunist 1969, 2 (ianvar'), 91–106.

'Maoism and the anti-Marxist nature of Maoist philosophy.'
Chinese studies in history and philosophy 2 (Summer 1969), 76–102.
SUBJ 64 ▪ 32.2

22262 CSU P P2 G1.2 1911–1972
Schram, Stuart Reynolds, 1924–.
'From the "Great Union of the Popular Masses" to the "Great Alliance".'
CQ 49 (Jan.–Mar. 1972), 88–105.
SUBJ 64

22263 CSH P P7 G1.2 1928–1972
Schram, Stuart Reynolds, 1924–.
'Introduction.' In *Basic tactics*, by Mao Tse-tung, compiled and edited by S. R. Schram. [Sole entry]
New York: Praeger, 1966, 13–48.
SUBJ 32.2 64 ▪ 15

22264 FPN P P1 G1.2 1928–1972
Schram, Stuart Reynolds, 1924–.
'Introduction' (Introduction). In *Documents sur la théorie de la 'révolution permanente' en Chine: idéologie dialectique et dialectique du réel* (Documents on the theory of permanent revolution in China: Dialectical ideology and dialectic of reality), compiled and edited by S. R. Schram. [Sole entry]
The Hague: Mouton, 1963, 1–49 [s.p.]. (Maison des sciences de l'homme, Matériaux pour l'étude de la Chine moderne et contemporaine, 4)
SUBJ 19 64 ▪ 12.2 16 22.2

22265 CSU P P2 G1.1 1928–1972
Schram, Stuart Reynolds, 1924–.
'Mao Tse-tung and Liu Shao-ch'i, 1939–1969.'
AS 12, 4 (Apr. 1972), 275–293.
SUBJ 16 64 ▪ 16.3 16.4 32 32.2

22266 MCH P P1 G1.2 1928–1972
Schram, Stuart Reynolds, 1924–.
'Mao Tse-tung as Marxist dialectician.' [Review of *The Communism of Mao Tse-tung*, by Arthur Allen Cohen.]
CQ 29 (Jan.–Mar. 1967), 155–165.
SUBJ 64 ▪ 61

22267 CSU P P1 G1.2 1928–1972
Schram, Stuart Reynolds, 1924–.
'The party in Chinese Communist ideology.' In *Party leadership and revolutionary power in China*, edited by John Wilson Lewis. [Analytic entry]
Cambridge: Cambridge U. Press, 1970, 170–202.
SUBJ 16.1 32 32.2 64

22268 CSU P P1 G1.2 1911–1972
Schram, Stuart Reynolds, 1924–.
The political thought of Mao Tse-tung, rev. and enl. ed.
New York: Praeger, 1969. 479 p.
SUBJ 59 64 ▪ 15 16 16.1 19 32.2

22269 NNC P P1 G1.2 1928–1972
Schwartz, Benjamin Isadore, 1916–.
China and the Soviet theory of 'peoples democracy'.
Cambridge: Massachusetts Institute of Technology, Center for International Studies, 1954. 17 p. [Reprinted in *Communism and China: Ideology in flux*, by B. I. Schwartz. (Selective entry.) Cambridge: Harvard U. Press, 1968, 47–65.]
SUBJ 12 64

22270 MCH P P1 G1.2 1911–1972
Schwartz, Benjamin Isadore, 1916–.
'The legend of the "legend of Maoism".'
CQ 2 (Apr.–June 1960), 35–42.
SUBJ 64

22271 MAM P P1 G1.2 1928–1972
Sherman, James Charles, 1941–.
Mao Tse-tung's concept of higher education.
Ann Arbor: University Microfilms (Publ. 72-31,657), 1972. 177 p. (Doctoral dissertation in Education, U. of Denver)
SUBJ 17 64

22272 CSU P P1 G1.2 1911–1972
Solomon, Richard Harvey, 1937–.
'From commitment to cant: The evolving functions of ideology in the revolutionary process.' In *Ideology and politics in contemporary China*, edited by Chalmers Ashby Johnson. [Selective entry]
Seattle: U. of Washington Press, 1973, 47–77. (Social Science Research Council, Studies in Chinese government and politics, 4)
SUBJ 32.2 64 ▪ 16.1 32

22273 CSU P P2 G1.2 1911–1972
Tan, Chester C. (T'an Ch'un-lin).
Chinese political thought in the twentieth century.
Garden City, N.Y.: Doubleday, 1971. 390 p.
SUBJ 64 ▪ 14.2 32 32.2 59 63

22274 CSU S P1 G1.2 1928–1972
Townsend, James Roger, 1932–.
'Mao and Maoism.' [Review of *The Communism of Mao Tse-tung*, by Arthur Allen Cohen; *The political thought of Mao Tse-tung*, by Stuart Reynolds Schram; *Mao and the Chinese Revolution*, by Jerome Ch'en (Ch'en Chih-jang); *Major doctrines of Communist China*, edited by John Wilson Lewis; and *Communist China's crusade*, by Guy Wint.]
Problems of Communism 15, 1 (Jan.–Feb. 1966), 35–39.
SUBJ 59 64 ▪ 32 32.2

22275 GMS P P1 G1.2 1644–1972
Traut-Welser, Ludwig, 1919–.
Die geistigen und ideologischen Strömungen im chinesischen Kommunismus (Spiritual and ideological currents in Chinese Communism).
Hanover: Niedersächsische Landeszentrale für politische Bildung, 1961. 50 p.
SUBJ 19 64 ▪ 12.1

22276 CSU P P2 G1.2 1928–1972
Ts'ao, Ignatius J. H.
'Ai Ssu-ch'i, the apostle of Chinese Communism. Part one, His life and works.'
SST 12, 1 (Apr. 1972), 2–36. [Further installments were to be published.]
SUBJ 59 64 ▪ 14.2 16.1 32.2

22277 MAM P P1 G1.2 –1972
Tseng, Edward C. (Tseng Chao-yang), 1934–.
Democratic and authoritarian elements in twentieth-century Chinese political thought.
Ann Arbor: University Microfilms (Publ. 70-16,911), 1970. 203 p. (Doctoral dissertation in Political Science, New York U., 1968)
SUBJ 12.1 64 ▪ 12

22278 CSH S P1 G1.2 1911–1972
Ullerich, Curt.
'Kultur als Element der Revolution in China' (Culture as an element in the Chinese revolution).
Z. für Geopolitik 38, 1 (Jan.–März 1967), 25–40.
SUBJ 64 ▪ 12.1 16.1 19

22279 MCH P P1 G1.2 1911–1972
van der Kroef, Justus Maria, 1925–.
'Lenin, Mao and Aidit.'
CQ 10 (Apr.–June 1962), 23–44.
SUBJ 64

22280 MCH P P1 G1.2 1911–1972
Wittfogel, Karl August, 1896–.
'The legend of "Maoism".'
CQ 1 (Jan.–Mar. 1960), 72–86.
SUBJ 64 ▪ 32 32.2

22281 CSU P P2 G1.2 1928–1972
Wittfogel, Karl August, 1896–.
'Some remarks on Mao's handling of concepts and problems of dialectics.'
SST 3, 4 (Dec. 1963), 251–269.
SUBJ 64 ▪ 32.2

22282 FPN P P2 G1.2 1928–1972
Wou, Saofong (Wu Hsiu-feng), 1898–.
'Application pratique du marxisme-léninisme en Chine nouvelle, et ses raisons historiques' (The practical application of Marxism-Leninism in New China and its historical bases). In *Influence des expériences communistes sur les doctrines* (The influence of Communist experiences on doctrine), edited by Centre d'étude des pays de l'Est, Institut de sociologie Solvay, Université libre de Bruxelles. [Sole entry]
Brussels: Centre d'étude des pays de l'Est, 1959, 95–113.
SUBJ 14.1 16 64 ▪ 12 14 34.1

22283 NIC P P1 G1.2 –1972
Wright, Arthur Frederick, 1913–.
'From creed to ideology to rhetoric: Confucianism in the politics of modern China.' In *The ethic of power: The interplay of religion, philosophy and politics*, edited by Harold Dwight Lasswell and Harlan Cleveland. [Sole entry]
New York: Conference on Science, Philosophy and Religion in Their Relation to the Democratic Way of Life, 1962, vol. 1, 71–84.
SUBJ 64

22284 MCH S P1 G1.1 –1972
Wright, Arthur Frederick, 1913–.
'Struggle versus harmony: Symbols of competing values in modern China.'
WP 6, 1 (Oct. 1953), 31–44.
SUBJ 60 64 ▪ 12.1 63

22285 CSU P P1 G1.2 1928–1972
Yin Ching-yao.
'From Leninism to Trotskyism: A study of Mao Tse-tung's change in tactics.'
IS 6, 4 (Jan. 1970), 17–31.
SUBJ 64

22286 CSU P P1 G1.3 –1972
Yu, Anthony C.
'The Confucian concept of order.'
Thought 43, 169 (Summer 1968), 249–272.
SUBJ 63 64 ▪ 16.1 62

22287 NNC P P1 G1.2 1928–1972
Zagoria, Donald S-, 1928–.
'Some comparisons between the Russian and Chinese models.' In *Communist strategies in Asia*, edited by Arthur Doak Barnett. [Selective entry]
New York: Praeger, 1963, 11–33.
SUBJ 10 14 64 ▪ 62

22288 MCH P P1 G1.2 1911–1972
Zürcher, Erik, 1928–.
'De reïnterpretatie van de oude kultuur in het huidige China' (The reinterpretation of traditional culture in today's China).
Internationale spectator 17, 5 (8 Maart 1963), 115–126.
SUBJ 60 64 70 ▪ 62 66

1949-1972

22289 MCH P P1 G1.2 1949–1972
'Protiv dogmatizma i vul'garizatsii v literature i iskusstve' (In opposition to dogmatism and vulgarization in literature and art).
Kommunist 1964, 9 (iiun'), 9–26.
SUBJ 12.1 64 ▪ 16.1

22290 CSU P P2 G1.2 1949–1972
Ahn, Byung-joon, 1936–.
'Adjustments in the Great Leap Forward and their ideological legacy, 1959–62.' In *Ideology and politics in contemporary China*, edited by Chalmers Ashby Johnson. [Selective entry]
Seattle: U. of Washington Press, 1973, 257–300. (Social Science Research Council, Studies in Chinese government and politics, 4)
SUBJ 14 19 32 64 ▪ 12.1 15 16.1 17 22 32.1 34.1

22291 MAM P P2 G1.2 1949–1972
Ahn, Byung-joon, 1936–.
Ideology, policy and power in Chinese politics and the evolution of the Cultural Revolution, 1959–1965.
Ann Arbor: University Microfilms (Publ. 72-19,096), 1972. 534 p. (Doctoral dissertation in Political Science, Columbia U., 1972)
SUBJ 12.1 14 19 20 32 64 ▪ 12 15 16.1 16.3 17 22 26.1 32.1 34.1 56

22292 ELB P P2 G1.2 1949–1972
Bady, Paul, 1941–.
'La révolution culturelle en Chine. 2, le degré zéro de la culture bourgeoise' (China's Cultural Revolution. 2, The nadir of bourgeois culture).
Esprit nouvelle (2e) série 39, 3 (mars 1971), 505–523.
SUBJ 12.1 16 19 64 ▪ 14.2 17 31 35

22293 CBU S P2 G1.2 1949–1972
Baum, Richard Dennis, 1940–.
The nature and function of ideological and political 'superstructure' in Communist China.
Unpublished masters thesis in Political Science, U. of California, Berkeley, 1963. 153 p.
SUBJ 11.4 14.1 64 ▪ 12.1 14 16 16.1 16.3 17

22294 MCY P P1 G1.2 1949–1972
Baum, Richard Dennis, 1940–.
'"Red and expert": The politico-ideological foundations of China's Great Leap Forward.'
AS 4, 9 (Sept. 1964), 1048–1057.
SUBJ 12.1 64 ▪ 12 14 19

22295 CSU U P2 G1.2 1949–1972
Bernal, Martin Gardiner, 1937–.
'Contradictions.' [Review of *Ideology and organization in Communist China*, by Herbert Franz Schurmann.]
NYRB 6, 12 (7 July 1966), 10–13.
SUBJ 64

22296 NNU P P2 G1.2 1949–1972
Bietz, Gary R-, 1943–.
The politics of educational reform in the People's Republic of China: Revolutionary destruction, 1966–68.
Unpublished doctoral dissertation in History, New York U., 1972. 334 p.
SUBJ 17 64 ▪ 15 16.1 27 32.1 54

22297 CSU P P2 G1.2 1949–1972
Boyd, R- G-.
'The new Chinese polity.'
International j. 24, 1 (Winter 1968/69), 86–108.
SUBJ 35 64 ▪ 12 12.1

22298 CSH P P2 G1.2 1949–1972
Burlatskii, Fedor Mikhailovich.
Maoizm ili marksizm? (Maoism or Marxism?).
Moscow: Izd-vo polit. lit-ry, 1967. 126 p.

The true face of Maoism. [Partial tr.: p. 1–19, 36–126 only]
Moscow: Novosti, 1968? 109 p.
SUBJ 32 64 ▪ 14 16.3 16.4

22299 DLC P P2 G1.2 1949–1972
Burlatskii, Fedor Mikhailovich.
Maoizm: ugroza sotsializmu v Kitae.
Moscow: Gospolitizdat, 1968. 192 p.

Maoism, the threat to socialism in China, mimeo. [Abridged tr.]
Washington, D.C.: U.S. Joint Publications Research Service, 6 May 1969. 79 p. (JPRS 47,958; MC 8515/1969)
SUBJ 19 32 64 ▪ 12.1 16 16.1 35 45 54

22300 CSU P P1 G1.2 1949–1972
Chi, Wen-shun (Chi Wen-hsün), 1910–.
'The Great Proletarian Cultural Revolution in ideological perspective.'
AS 9, 8 (Aug. 1969), 563–579.
SUBJ 64 ▪ 12 14 14.2 17 63

22301 CSU P P2 G1.2 1949–1972
Chi, Wen-shun (Chi Wen-hsün), 1910–.
'The ideological source of the people's communes in Communist China.'
Pacific coast philology 2 (Apr. 1967), 62–78. [Reprinted in *Readings in modern Chinese history*, edited by Immanuel C. Y. Hsü (Hsü Chung-yüeh). (Selective entry.) New York: Oxford U. Press, 1971, 598–613.]
Subj 64 ▪ 24.1 28 34.1 41 47

22302 CSU P P1 G1.2 1949–1972
Chi, Wen-shun (Chi Wen-hsün), 1910–.
'Sun Yeh-fang and his revisionist economics.'
AS 12, 10 (Oct. 1972), 887–900.
Subj 14 64

22303 CSU P P1 G1.2 1949–1972
[Chin, Ai-li Sung] A. S. Chen (Ch'en Shen Ai-li), 1919–.
'The ideal local party secretary and the "model" man.'
CQ 17 (Jan.–Mar. 1964), 229–240.
Subj 26.1 32 64 ▪ 22.1 48

22304 NIC P P1 G1.2 1949–1972
Chiu, S. M. (Chao Shan-ming), 1923–.
Some basic conceptions and rules of conduct of Chinese Communism: Initial collation towards the conceptual and operational code of Chinese Communist leaders.
Lackland Air Force Base, San Antonio, Tex.: U.S. Air Force Personnel and Training Research Center, Air Research and Development Command, 1955. 39 p. (U.S. Human Resources Research Institute research memoranda, 34; Studies in Chinese Communism, series 4, 2, 1953)
Subj 64 ▪ 12 15 16.1 30 32 62

22305 CSH P P1 G1.2 1949–1972
Chuang, H. C. (Chuang Hsin-cheng), 1935–.
The Great Proletarian Cultural Revolution: A terminological study.
Berkeley: U. of California, Center for Chinese Studies, 1967. 72 p. (Current Chinese Language Project, Studies in Chinese Communist terminology, 12) [Reprinted—Ann Arbor: University Microfilms, n.d. 72 p.]
Subj 62 64 ▪ 16.1 19

22306 MCH P P1 G1.2 1949–1972
Collotti Pischel, Enrica, 1930–.
'Appunti per una analisi della "via cinese"' (Notes toward an analysis of the 'Chinese way').
Nuovi argomenti 40 (settembre–ottobre 1959), 1–77.
Subj 12 19 34.1 64 ▪ 14 16 61 66

22307 IMC PO P1 G1.2 1949–1972
Costa Massucco, Angiola.
'Principi teorici dell'organizzazione sociale cinese' (Theoretical principles of Chinese social organization).
Rivista di psicologia sociale 28, 1 (gennaio–marzo 1961), 77–86.
Subj 30 64

22308 CSH P P1 G1.2 1949–1972
Damien, George D-.
'The dialectical structure of the Chinese Great Proletarian Cultural Revolution.'
Orbis (Philadelphia) 14, 1 (Spring 1970), 192–217.
Subj 64 ▪ 15 25 54

22309 CSU P P1 G1.2 1949–1972
Doi Akira, 1905–.
'The Chinese Marxists' way of thinking: Their recognition of man and machinery, labor and capital.'
Review (Tokyo) 1 (May 1964), 22–34.
Subj 64 ▪ 12.1 14.1 14.4 16.4

22310 CSU P P1 G1.2 1949–1972
Eastman, Lloyd Eric, 1929–.
'Mao, Marx, and the future society.'
Problems of Communism 18, 3 (May–June 1969), 21–26.
Subj 64 ▪ 61 62

22311 CBU U P1 G1.2 1949–1972
Ellegiers, Daniël.
'Ideology and education in Communist China.'
RSAEO 1969, 2, 149–158.
Subj 17 64 ▪ 12.1

22312 CSH U P1 G1.2 1949–1972
Engelborghs-Bertels, Marthe, 1928–.
'La grande révolution prolétarienne chinoise' (China's Great Proletarian Cultural Revolution). [With English summary]
Civilisations 17, 4 (1967), 349–379.
Subj 19 64 ▪ 12 12.2 14 15 16

22313 CSU P P1 G1.2 1949–1972
Etō, Shinkichi, 1923–.
'Communist China: Moderation and reform in the Chinese Revolution.' In *Modern East Asia: Essays in interpretation*, edited by James Buckley Crowley. [Selective entry]
New York: Harcourt, Brace and World, 1970, 337–373.
Subj 19 32 64 ▪ 12 15 16.1

22314 CSU P P2 G1.2 1949–1972
Fann, K. T. (Fan Kuang-t'i), 1937–.
'Mao and the Chinese revolution in philosophy.'
SST 12, 2 (June 1972), 111–123.
Subj 16.1 64 ▪ 12.1 17 19

22315 DLC U P1 G1.2 1949–1972
Fibich, Jindřich.
'Diskuse o otázkach vědeckého komunismu v Čině' (A discussion of scientific Communism in China).
Filosofický časopis 5, 6 (1957), 941–949.
Subj 64

22316 NNC P P1 G1.2 1949–1972
Fokkema, Douwe Wessel, 1931–.
'Die jüngste chinesische Humanismus-Kritik und ihre Beziehung zum chinesisch-sowjetischen Konflikt' (The latest Chinese critique of humanism and its relation to the Sino-Soviet conflict).
Osteuropa 16, 5/6 (Mai–Juni 1966), 364–377.
Subj 62 64 ▪ 12.1 16.1 66

22317 MCH P P1 G1.2 1949–1972
Fokkema, Douwe Wessel, 1931–.
'Sinocentrisme in wetenschap, literatuur en moraal' (Sinocentrism in science, literature, and morality).
Oost-West 2, 6 (Januari–Februari 1964), 265–269.
Subj 64 66 ▪ 62 63

22318 CSH P P2 G1.2 1949–1972
Garaudy, Roger.
Le problème chinois, avec des textes essentiels de Mao Tsé-Toung (The problem of China, with some basic writings of Mao Tse-tung).
Paris: Seghers, 1967. 300 p.
Subj 14 14.1 16 64 ▪ 12.1 19 22 32.2 34.1 36.3 36.4

22319 FPN P P1 G1.2 1949–1972
Glucksmann, André.
'Autour d'une pensée de Mao Tsé-toung' (One aspect of the thought of Mao Tse-tung). In *Les discours de la guerre: théorie et strategie* (Discussions of war: Theory and strategy), by A. Glucksmann. [Sole entry]
Paris: L'Herne, 1967, 285–351.
'Politics and war in the thought of Mao Tse-tung.' Tr. by Ben Brewster. [Condensed tr.]
New left review 49 (May–June 1968), 41–57.
Subj 15 64

22320 MCH P P1 G1.2 1949–1972
Go Shao-tan (Kuo Shao-t'ang), 1905–.
'Kritika nekotorykh filosofskikh i sotsiologicheskikh vzgliadov burzhuaznykh pravykh elementov i revizionistov v Kitae, 1957–1958 gg.' (Criticism of some philosophical and sociological views of right-wing bourgeois elements and revisionists in China, 1957–1958). [With English abstract]
PV 1959, 5, 83–92.
Subj 64 ▪ 12.1 62

22321 CSU P P3 G1.2 1949–1972
Goldman, Merle Dorothy, 1931–.
'The Chinese Communist Party's "cultural revolution" of 1962–64.' In *Ideology and politics in contemporary China*, edited by Chalmers Ashby Johnson. [Selective entry]
Seattle: U. of Washington Press, 1973, 219–254. (Social Science Research Council, Studies in Chinese government and politics, 4)
Subj 16.1 32 64 ▪ 12.1 16 62

22322 CSU P P2 G1.2 1949–1972
Goodstadt, Leo F-.
China's search for plenty: The economics of Mao Tse-tung.
New York: Weatherhill, 1973. 11, 266 p.
Subj 14 64 ▪ 12 14.1 14.4 16 18 22 34.1 34.2

22323 CSU P P7 G1.2 1949–1972
Gray, Jack Douglas, 1916–.
'The economics of Maoism.'
B. of the atomic scientists 25, 2 (Feb. 1969), 42–51. [Special issue: *China after the Cultural Revolution*, edited by (Richard Garratt Wilson) Dick Wilson] [Reprinted in *China after the Cultural Revolution*. (Selective entry.) New York: Random House, 1969, 115–142.]
Subj 14 64 ▪ 34.1

22324 CSU P P2 G1.2 1949–1972
Harding, Harry, Jr., 1946–.
Maoist theories of policy-making and organization: Lessons from the Cultural Revolution.
Santa Monica, Calif.: RAND Corp., 1969. 39 p. (RAND reports, R-487-PR)

[Reprinted as 'Maoist theories of policy-making and organization.' In *The Cultural Revolution in China*, edited by Thomas Webster Robinson. (Analytic entry.) Berkeley, Los Angeles: U. of California Press, 1971, 113–164.]
SUBJ 32 64 ▪ 12 16.1

22325 SSK P P2 G1.2 1949–1972
Hart, Thomas George, 1936–.
The dynamics of revolution: A cybernetic theory of the dynamics of modern social revolution, with a study of ideological change and organizational dynamics in the Chinese revolution.
Stockholm: Stockholms Universitet, Statsvetenskapliga Institutionen, 1971. 13, 203 p. (Stockholm studies in politics, 1) (Doctoral dissertation in Political Science, Stockholms Universitet)
SUBJ 19 64 ▪ 11.2 32 35 54

22326 CSU S P1 G1.2 1949–1972
Holz, Hans Heinz.
Widerspruch in China: Politisch-philosophische Erläuterungen zu Mao Tse-tung (Contradiction in China: Political and philosophical insights into Mao Tse-tung).
Munich: C. Hanser, 1970? 119 p.
SUBJ 64 ▪ 12 16 19 32

22327 CSU P P1 G1.2 1949–1972
Jao, Y. C. (Jao Yü-ch'ing).
'Trends of economic thinking in China.' In *Contemporary China, 1962–1964*, edited by Edward Stuart Kirby. [Selective entry]
Hong Kong: Hong Kong U. Press, 1968, 42–57.
SUBJ 64 70 ▪ 14 36.1

22328 CSU P P2 G1.2 1949–1972
Kataoka, Tetsuya, 1933–.
'Political theory of the Great Leap Forward.'
Social research 36, 1 (Spring 1969), 93–122.
SUBJ 14 19 64 ▪ 32 32.1

22329 CSU P P2 G1.2 1949–1972
Kawachi, Jūzō, 1928–.
'Mao Tse-tung's view of the Chinese economy.'
Review (Tokyo) 19 (Dec. 1968), 26–56.
SUBJ 64 ▪ 12 14

22330 CSU P P1 G1.2 1949–1972
Kroker, Eduard Josef M-, 1913–.
'Mao Tse-tung und die Veränderung des Bewusstseins' (Mao Tse-tung and the transformation of consciousness).
Stimmen der Zeit 3 (März 1972), 147–164.
SUBJ 16 62 64 ▪ 12 12.1 32 63

22331 CSH P P1 G1.2 1949–1972
[La Dany, Ladislao] ———, 1914–.
'Anti-humanism.'
CNA 849 (23 July 1971), 1–7.
SUBJ 16 63 64

22332 CSH P P1 G1.2 1949–1972
La Dany, Ladislao, 1914–.
'Marxism in China: Ideological history of the People's Republic.'
Pacific community 3, 2 (Jan. 1972), 277–285.
SUBJ 16 64 ▪ 12.1

22333 CSH P P2 G1.2 1949–1972
[La Dany, Ladislao] ———, 1914–.
'The voice and the response: Mao and the nation.'
CNA 739 (10 Jan. 1969), 1–7.
SUBJ 16 64

22334 CSH P P1 G1.2 1949–1972
[La Dany, Ladislao] ———, 1914–.
'Who are the sham Marxists?'
CNA 841 (14 May 1971), 1–7.
SUBJ 12.1 64

22335 CSU P P1 G1.2 1949–1972
Levenson, Joseph Richmond, 1920–1969.
'The place of Confucius in Communist China.' In *Confucian China and its modern fate, Vol. 3, The problem of historical significance*, by J. R. Levenson. [Analytic entry]
Berkeley, Los Angeles: U. of California Press, 1965, 61–82. [Slight revision of 'The place of Confucius in Communist China'; in *History in Communist China*, edited by Albert Feuerwerker; Cambridge: M.I.T. Press, 1968, 56–73.]
SUBJ 62 64 70 ▪ 13

22336 CSU P P1 G1.2 1949–1972
MacDonald, James.
'The use of slogans and "uninterrupted revolution" in China in the early part of 1964.' In *Studies in the social history of China and South-east Asia: Essays in memory of Victor Purcell*, edited by Jerome Ch'en (Ch'en Chih-jang) and Nicholas Tarling. [Selective entry]
Cambridge: Cambridge U. Press, 1970, 165–196.
SUBJ 12.1 19 64 ▪ 14 14.2 16.1 35

22337 CSU U P1 G1.2 1949–1972
Madian, A- L-.
'The organization of ideology: Variations on a revolutionary Chinese theme.' [Review of *Ideology and organization in Communist China*, by Herbert Franz Schurmann.]
British j. of sociology 18, 1 (Mar. 1967), 99–108.
SUBJ 62 64 ▪ 12.1 30 32 63

22338 CSH P P1 G1.2 1949–1972
Mateos, Fernando.
'Il comunismo in Cina: una controversia sulla natura della religione' (Communism in China: A controversy on the nature of religion).
Civiltà cattolica 117, 2775 (5 febbraio 1966), 255–262.
SUBJ 62 64

22339 CSU P P2 G1.2 1949–1972
Mehnert, Klaus, 1906–.
Peking and the new left, at home and abroad.
Berkeley: U. of California, Center for Chinese Studies, 1969. 156 p. (CCS China research monographs, 4)
SUBJ 16.1 54 64 ▪ 12.1 17 32 35 36.4

22340 CSU P P2 G1.2 1949–1972
Meisner, Maurice J-, 1931–.
'Images of the Paris commune in contemporary Chinese Marxist thought.'
Massachusetts review 12, 3 (Summer 1971), 479–497.
SUBJ 20 22 64

22341 CSU P P1 G1.2 1949–1972
Meisner, Maurice J-, 1931–.
'Utopian goals and ascetic values in Chinese Communist ideology.'
JAS 28, 1 (Nov. 1968), 101–110.
SUBJ 64 ▪ 63

22342 CSH P P1 G1.2 1949–1972
Meisner, Mitchell Ralph, 1943–.
'From theory to practice, science, and revolution: The "three great revolutionary movements" in China, 1963–1966.' In *Selected seminar papers on contemporary China, I*, edited by Steve S. K. Chin (Chin Ssu-k'ai) and Frank Henry Haviland King. [Analytic entry]
Hong Kong: U. of Hong Kong, Centre of Asian Studies, 1971, 44–90. (CAS occasional papers and monographs, 4)
SUBJ 19 64 ▪ 12.1 62

22343 CBU P P7 G1.2 1949–1972
Meissner, Boris, 1915–.
'Die Volkskommunenkonzeption als Ausdruck der ideologischen Differenz zwischen Peking und Moskau' (The conception of the commune as an expression of the ideological differences between Peking and Moscow).
Moderne Welt 2, 4 (1960/61), 339–352.

'The people's commune: A manifestation of Sino-Soviet differences.' Tr. by Kathleen Szasz and Helga Neumann-Jang.
Modern world (Cologne) 1962/63, 95–109. [Reprinted in *Unity and contradiction: Major aspects of Sino-Soviet relations*, edited by Kurt London. (Selective entry.) New York: Praeger, 1962, 122–141.]
SUBJ 20 64

22344 CSH P P2 G1.2 1949–1972
Melis, Giorgio.
'Il comunismo cinese alla vigilia della "Rivoluzione culturale"' (Chinese communism on the eve of the Cultural Revolution).
Civiltà cattolica 118, 2802 (18 marzo 1967), 539–552.
SUBJ 32 64 ▪ 11.2 12.1 14.2 16.1 54

22345 CSU O P2 G1.1 1949–1972
Mori Kyōzō.
'The "two Chinas".'
JQ 13, 3 (July–Sept. 1966), 301–319.
SUBJ 12 64 ▪ 14 14.1 14.3 15 32

22346 CSU P P2 G1.2 1949–1972
Munro, Donald Jacques, 1931–.
'The malleability of man in Chinese Marxism.'
CQ 48 (Oct.–Dec. 1971), 609–640.
SUBJ 17 64 ▪ 16

22347 CSU P P1 G1.2 1949–1972
Munro, Donald Jacques, 1931–.
'The Yang Hsien-chen affair.'
CQ 22 (Apr.–June 1965), 75–82.
SUBJ 16.1 64 ▪ 12.1 62

22348 CSH P P1 G1.2 1949–1972
Nakajima, Mineo, 1936–.
'The commune concept in Mao Tsetung thought.' Tr. from the Japanese by Jason G. B. Choi. [Tr. of an unpublished manuscript, 'Mō Takutō shisō ni okeru komyunteki hassō']

Chinese law and government 4, 1/2 (Spring–Summer 1971), 61–81.
Subj 64

22349 CSH P P2 G1.2 1949–1972
Ostroumov, Georgii Sergeevich.
'Politiko-pravovaia ideologiia i krizis politicheskoi vlasti v Kitae.'
SGP 1967, 6 (iiun'), 59–66.
'Politico-judicial ideology and the crisis of political power in China.'
Chinese law and government 1, 3 (Fall 1968), 4–22.
Subj 12.2 64 ▪ 12 12.1

22350 CSU P P1 G1.2 1949–1972
Pusey, James Reeve, 1940–.
Wu Han: Attacking the present through the past.
Cambridge: Harvard U., East Asian Research Center, 1969. 10, 84 p. (Harvard East Asian monographs, 33)
Subj 12.1 64 ▪ 14.2 16.1 19 61 70

22351 CSU P P2 G1.2 1949–1972
Ramachandran, K- N-.
'Maoism.'
International studies (New Delhi) 8, 4 (Apr. 1967), 422–443.
Subj 64

22352 CBU S P2 G1.2 1949–1972
Ray, Dennis Michael, 1939–.
'Mao Tse-tung: The tragic perspective.'
Political science review (Jaipur, India) 8, 3/4 (July–Dec. 1969), 347–360.
Subj 14 64

22353 MCH U P1 G1.2 1949–1972
Rumiantsev, Aleksei Matveevich.
'"Kitaizirovannyi marksizm": natsionalisticheskoe soderzhanie v psevdomarksistskoi obolochke' ('Sinicized Marxism': Nationalist content in pseudo-Marxist garb).
Kommunist 1964, 12 (avgust), 34–43.
Subj 64

22354 MCY P P1 G1.2 1949–1972
Schram, Stuart Reynolds, 1924–.
'Chinese and Leninist components in the personality of Mao Tse-tung.'
AS 3, 6 (June 1963), 259–273.
Subj 60 61 64

22355 CSU P P1 G1.2 1949–1972
Schram, Stuart Reynolds, 1924–.
'Mao Tse-tung and the theory of the permanent revolution, 1958–69.'
CQ 46 (Apr.–June 1971), 221–244.
Subj 64

22356 CSU P P1 G1.2 1949–1972
Schran, Peter, 1930–.
'On the Marxism-Leninism of Chinese Communist development strategy.' In *Mainland China in the world economy*, compiled by Joint Economic Committee, U.S. Congress. [Selective entry]
Washington, D.C.: U.S. Government Printing Office, 1967, 215–223.
Subj 14 64

22357 CSH FP P2 G1.2 1949–1972
Schurmann, Herbert Franz, 1926–.
'Ideology.' In *Ideology and organization in Communist China*, 2nd ed., enl., by H. F. Schurmann. [Analytic entry]
Berkeley, Los Angeles: U. of California Press, 1968, 17–104.
Subj 12.1 61 64 ▪ 12 14.2 14.4 16 22.1 32.1

22358 CSH P P1 G1.2 1949–1972
Schurmann, Herbert Franz, 1926–.
'Supplement: Ideology.' In *Ideology and organization in Communist China*, 2nd ed., enl., by H. F. Schurmann. [Analytic entry]
Berkeley, Los Angeles: U. of California Press, 1968, 506–531.
Subj 64 ▪ 16 32

22359 CSU U P1 G1.2 1949–1972
Schwartz, Benjamin Isadore, 1916–.
'China and the West in the "thought of Mao Tse-tung"' [with comments by Stuart Reynolds Schram and Donald Jacques Munro]. In *China in crisis, Vol. 1, China's heritage and the Communist political system*, edited by Ping-ti Ho and Tang Tsou. [Selective entry]
Chicago: U. of Chicago Press, 1968, 365–396.
Subj 64

22360 CSU U P1 G1.2 1949–1972
Schwartz, Benjamin Isadore, 1916–.
'Communism and China: Ideology in flux.' In *Communism and China: Ideology in flux*, by B. I. Schwartz. [Selective entry]
Cambridge: Harvard U. Press, 1968, 1–46.
Subj 64

22361 CSH P P1 G1.2 1949–1972
Schwartz, Benjamin Isadore, 1916–.
'Modernization and the Maoist vision: Some reflections on Chinese Communist goals.'
CQ 21 (Jan.–Mar. 1965), 3–19. [Reprinted in *China under Mao: Politics takes command*, edited by Roderick Lemonde MacFarquhar. (Selective entry.) Cambridge: M.I.T. Press, 1966, 3–19.] [Reprinted in *Communism and China: Ideology in flux*, by B. I. Schwartz. (Selective entry.) Cambridge: Harvard U. Press, 1968, 162–185.]
Subj 12.1 19 64 ▪ 14 30 32 62

22362 MCH P P1 G1.2 1949–1972
Schwartz, Benjamin Isadore, 1916–.
'New trends in Maoism?'
Problems of Communism 6, 4 (July–Aug. 1957), 1–8. [Reprinted as 'Let the hundred flowers bloom.' In *Communism and China: Ideology in flux*, by B. I. Schwartz. (Selective entry.) Cambridge: Harvard U. Press, 1968, 99–116.]
Subj 64 ▪ 12.1 16

22363 CSU P P2 G1.2 1949–1972
Schwartz, Benjamin Isadore, 1916–.
'A personal view of some thoughts of Mao Tse-tung.' In *Ideology and politics in contemporary China*, edited by Chalmers Ashby Johnson. [Selective entry]
Seattle: U. of Washington Press, 1973, 352–372. (Social Science Research Council, Studies in Chinese government and politics, 4)
Subj 64 ▪ 12 16 62

22364 CSU P P1 G1.2 1949–1972
Solomon, Richard Harvey, 1937–.
'Mao's linking of foreign relations with China's domestic political process.' In *China in crisis, Vol. 1, China's heritage and the Communist political system*, edited by Ping-ti Ho and Tang Tsou. [Selective entry]
Chicago: U. of Chicago Press, 1968, 570–578.
Subj 19 64

22365 MCH O P2 G1.2 1949–1972
Spirito, Ugo, 1896–.
'Il comunismo cinese' (Chinese Communism).
Rassegna italiana di sociologia 2, 1 (gennaio–marzo 1961), 11–42.
Subj 62 64 ▪ 12.1 17 66

22366 CSU P P1 G1.2 1949–1972
Starr, John Bryan, 1939–.
'Conceptual foundations of Mao Tse-tung's theory of continuous revolution.'
AS 11, 6 (June 1971), 610–628. [For fuller treatment, see entry 22367.]
Subj 64 ▪ 16

22367 CBU P P1 G1.2 1949–1972
Starr, John Bryan, 1939–.
Mao Tse-tung's theory of continuing the revolution under the dictatorship of the proletariat: Its origins, development, and practical consequences.
Unpublished doctoral dissertation in Political Science, U. of California, Berkeley, 1971. 604 p.
Subj 64 ▪ 16 19

22368 CSU P P3 G1.2 1949–1972
Starr, John Bryan, 1939–.
'Revolution in retrospect: The Paris commune through Chinese eyes.'
CQ 49 (Jan.–Mar. 1972), 106–125.
Subj 64 ▪ 12 22

22369 NIC P P1 G1.2 1949–1972
Steiner, Harold Arthur, 1905–.
'The curriculum in Chinese socialist education: An official bibliography of "Maoism".'
PA 31, 3 (Sept. 1958), 285–299.
Subj 17 32.1 64 ▪ 72

22370 MCY P P1 G1.2 1949–1972
Townsend, James Roger, 1932–.
'Communist China: The new protracted war.'
AS 5, 1 (Jan. 1965), 1–11.
Subj 64 ▪ 32 35

22371 CSU P P1 G1.2 1949–1972
Ts'ao, Ignatius J. H.
'Remoulding world outlook and the "Red flag".'
SST 11, 2 (June 1971), 113–117.
Subj 14.2 64

22372 NNC P P1 G1.2 1949–1972
Uhalley, Stephen, Jr., 1930–.
'The controversy over Li Hsiu-ch'eng: An ill-timed centenary.'
JAS 25, 2 (Feb. 1966), 305–317.
Subj 64 ▪ 12

22373 CSH U P1 G1.2 1949–1972
Urban, George R-.
'Introduction.' In *The miracles of Chairman Mao: A compendium of devotional literature, 1966–1970*, edited by G. R. Urban. [Selective entry]
Los Angeles: Nash, 1972, 11–16.
Subj 64 ▪ 12.1 61

22374 ELB P P3 G5.1 1949–1972
Vandermeersch, Léon.
'La Chine à l'heure du IXe Congrès' (China at the time of the Ninth Congress [of the Chinese Communist Party]).
Esprit nouvelle (2e) série 37, 9 (sept. 1969), 346–361.
Subj 32 64 ▪ 12.1 35 66

22375 FPN PO P2 G1.2 1949–1972
Vidal, Jean-Emile.
Où va la Chine? (Whither China?).
Paris: Editions sociales, 1967. 284 p.
Subj 16 22 32 54 64 66 ▪ 12 12.1 14.1 14.4 17 25 34.1 35

22376 CSU P P1 G1.2 1949–1972
Wang Chang-ling.
'A comparison of the ideologies of Mao Tse-tung and Liu Shao-chi.'
IS 4, 12 (Sept. 1968), 22–30; 5, 1 (Oct. 1968), 19–30.
Subj 64 ▪ 14 17

22377 CSU P P1 G1.2 1949–1972
Wang Hsueh-wen (Wang Hsüeh-wen).
'Maoists resume purge of Confucianism.'
IS 6, 3 (Dec. 1969), 61–70.
Subj 64 ▪ 16.1

22378 CSU P P1 G1.2 1949–1972
Wilhelm, Hellmut, 1906–.
'The reappraisal of Neo-Confucianism.' In *History in Communist China*, edited by Albert Feuerwerker. [Selective entry]
Cambridge: M.I.T. Press, 1968, 140–157.
Subj 64 70 ▪ 63

22379 CSU O P2 G1.2 1949–1972
Wylie, Raymond Finlay, 1941–.
'The meaning of the Cultural Revolution.' In *China and ourselves: Explorations and revisions by a new generation*, edited by Bruce Douglass and Ross Terrill. [Selective entry]
Boston: Beacon Press, 1969, 30–48.
Subj 15 56 64 ▪ 17

22380 CSU P P1 G1.2 1949–1972
Yang, C. K. (Yang Ch'ing-k'un), 1911–.
'Cultural Revolution and revisionism.' In *China in crisis, Vol. 1, China's heritage and the Communist political system*, edited by Ping-ti Ho and Tang Tsou. [Selective entry]
Chicago: U. of Chicago Press, 1968, 501–524.
Subj 64 ▪ 16.1 32

22381 CSU P P1 G1.2 1949–1972
Yin Ching-yao.
'The ideological origin of Mao Tse-tung's theory of "permanent revolution".'
IS 6, 3 (Dec. 1969), 39–51.
Subj 64

22382 CSU S P2 G1.2 1949–1972
Zinn, Howard, 1922–.
'Another look at the Chinese Communists.'
Antioch review 22, 1 (Spring 1962), 39–60.
Subj 12.1 64 ▪ 14 19 32

65 Folklore and Little Traditions
民俗　民間伝承

1644-1911

22383 NNC PO P2 G5.0 1895–1911
Alekseev, Vasilii Mikhailovich, 1880–1951.
V starom Kitae: dnevniki puteshestviia 1907 g. (In old China: Diaries of a journey of 1907).
Moscow: Izd-vo vost. lit-ry, 1958. 310 p.
Subj 23 65 ▪ 33 43

22384 NIC O P2 G6.0 1842–1911
Box, Ernest.
'Shanghai folklore.'
JRAS-CB new (2nd) series 34 (1901/02), 101–135; 36 (1905), 130–156.
Subj 57 65 ▪ 23 52 56

22385 MCH O P1 G9.2 1895–1911
Callado Crespo, Joaquim Heliodoro.
'Costumes e crenças da China: amuletos, e objectos e expressões de bom e mau agouro' (Customs and beliefs of China: Amulets and objects and expressions of good and bad luck).
Ta-ssi-yang-kuo; archivos e annaes do Extremo-Oriente portuguez 2 (1899/1901), 675–681.
Subj 55 65 ▪ 62

22386 MCH P P1 G1.0 –1911
Chavannes, Emmanuel Edouard, 1865–1918.
De l'expression des voeux dans l'art populaire chinois (The expression of wishes in Chinese folk art).
Paris: Bossard, 1922. 43 p.

The five happinesses: Symbolism in Chinese popular art. Tr. by Elaine Spalding Atwood, edited by Elaine Spalding Atwood.
New York: Wetherhill, 1973.
Subj 43 62 65 ▪ 23

22387 MCH P P1 G1.2 –1842
Cibot, Pierre-Martial, 1727–1780.
'Pensées, maximes et proverbes' (Thoughts, maxims, and proverbs). In *Mémoires concernant l'histoire, les sciences, les arts, les moeurs, les usages, etc. des Chinois* (Reports on the history, learning, arts, manners, customs, etc. of the Chinese), by Missionnaires de Pékin. [Sole entry]
Paris: Chez Nyon, 1784, vol. 10, 144–178.
Subj 65 ▪ 63

22388 MBA O P7 G8.2 1895–1911
Cordier, Charles Georges, 1872–1936.
'Croyances populaires au Yunnan' (Folk beliefs in Yunnan).
RI nouvelle (2e) série 11, 6 (juin 1909), 597–601.
Subj 65 ▪ 55

22389 CSU O P1 G1.3 1895–1911
Cornaby, William Arthur, 1860–1921.
'Demon-scare-demon.'
EAM 3 (1904), 363–370.
Subj 65 ▪ 66

22390 CSU P P2 G1.3 –1895
Dennys, Nicholas Belfield, ?–1900.
'The folklore of China.'
China review 3, 5 – 5, 2 (Mar.–Apr. 1875 – Sept.–Oct. 1876), 135 p. in all. [Separately reprinted as *The folklore of China, and its affinities with that of the Aryan and Semitic races*. Hong Kong: China Mail Office; London: Trübner, 1876. 156 p.] [Separately reprinted as *The folklore of China, and its affinities with that of the Aryan and Semitic races*. Chicago: Argonaut, 1968. 156 p.] [Separately reprinted—Detroit: Tower Books, 1971. 156 p.]
Subj 65 ▪ 41 51 57 62 63

22391 NNC P P1 G1.5 –1842
Eberhard, Wolfram, 1909–.
'The girl that became a bird: A comparative study.' In *Semitic and Oriental studies*, edited by Walter J. Fischel. [Sole entry]
Berkeley, Los Angeles: U. of California Press, 1951, 79–86. (U. of California publications in Semitic philology, 11) [Reprinted in *Studies in Chinese folklore and related essays*, by Wolfram Eberhard. (Selective entry.) Bloomington: Indiana U., Research Center for the Language Sciences, 1970, 247–253. (Indiana U., Folklore Institute monograph series, 23)]
Subj 65

22392 NNC O P7 G9.2 –1895
Eitel, Ernest John, 1838–1908.
'Popular songs of the Hakkas.'
NQCJ 1, 9 (Sept. 1867), 113–114; 1, 10 (Oct. 1867), 129–130; 1, 11 (Nov. 1867), 145–146.
Subj 29 65

22393 MCH O P1 G1.2 1842–1895
Fielde, Adele Marion, 1839–1916.
'The character of Chinese folk-tales.'
J. of American folklore 8 (July–Sept. 1895), 185–191.
Subj 65

22394 MSE PO P2 G1.4 –1911
Geil, William Edgar, 1865–1925.
The Great Wall of China.
New York: Sturgis and Walton, 1909. 16, 373 p.
Subj 23 65 ▪ 13 15 16.1 57 62 64 66

22395 CSH O P2 G1.3 1842–1895
Giles, Herbert Allen, 1875–1958.
'Some Chinese manners and customs.' In *China and the Chinese*, by H. A. Giles. [Selective entry]
New York: Columbia U. Press, 1912, 177–211. [Reprinted in *China and the Chinese*, by H. A. Giles. (Selective entry.) Taipei: Ch'eng-wen, 1968, 177–211.]
Subj 47 65 ▪ 48 51 55

22396 MCH P P1 G1.2 –1895
Groot, Jan Jakob Maria de, 1854–1921.
'Iets naders omtrent het bijgeloof der haarwervels op het paard in Oost-Asië' (A further note on the superstition concerning horses' manes in East Asia).
BTLV 50 (1899), 201–212.
Subj 65 ▪ 62

22397 NNC FP P3 G5.1 1842–1911
Grube, Wilhelm, 1855–1908.
'Zur pekinger Volkskunde' (The folklore of Peking).
Veröffentlichungen aus dem königlichen Museum für Völkerkunde 7, 1/4 (1901), 1–160.
Subj 31 41 52 57 65 ▪ 23 43 51

22398 NNC O P4 G9.0 1644–1842
Hunter, William C-, 1812–1891.
Bits of old China.
London: Kegan Paul, Trench, 1885. 280 p. [Reprinted—Taipei: Ch'eng-wen, 1966. 280 p.]
Subj 13 16 62 65 66 ▪ 12 12.2 17 25 31 34.2 55 56

22399 CSU S P2 G1.3 1842–1895
Jenner, William John Francis, 1940–.
'Les Nian et le Laoniuhui: les rebelles et leurs adversaires dans la tradition populaire' (The Nien and the Lao-niu Hui: The rebels and their adversaries in popular tradition). In *Mouvements populaires et sociétés secrètes en Chine aux XIXe et XXe siècles* (Popular movements and secret societies in China in the nineteenth and twentieth centuries), edited by Jean Chesneaux, Feiling Blackburn Davis, and Nguyen Nguyet Ho. [Selective entry]
Paris: Maspero, 1970, 205–218.
Subj 32.2 65 70 ▪ 16.1 16.3 25

22400 CSU O P2 G1.2 1895–1911
Junor, Kenneth F-.
'Curious and characteristic customs of China.'
NG 21, 9 (Sept. 1910), 791–806.
Subj 23 65 ▪ 16.1 22.2 48 55 57

22401 CBU O P2 G6.1 1895–1911
Kahler, William R-.
Rambles round Shanghai, 2nd ed.
Shanghai: Shanghai Mercury Press, 1905. 206 p. [Reprinted from *The union*.]
Subj 65

22402 CSU U P1 G1.0 –1895
Lister, Alfred.
'Chinese proverbs and their lessons.'
China review 3, 3 (Nov.–Dec. 1874), 129–138.
Subj 65

22403 MCH P P1 G9.0 1842–1895
Lockhart, James Haldane Stewart, 1858–1937.
'Notes on Chinese folk-lore.'
Folk-lore 1, 3 (Sept. 1890), 359–368.
Subj 65 ▪ 41 62

22404 CBU O P2 G1.3 1842–1895
MacGowan, Daniel Jerome, 1814?–1893.
'Alleged avenging habits of the cobra in India and China folklore.'
China review 17, 3 (Nov.–Dec. 1888), 145–151.
Subj 65

22405 NNP O P1 G1.3 1644–1842
Morrison, John Robert, ?–1834.
'Some account of charms, talismans, and felicitous appendages worn about the person, or hung up in houses, etc., used by the Chinese.'
Transactions of the Royal Asiatic Society of Great Britain and Ireland 3 (1835), 285–290.
Subj 23 65

22406 CSU O P1 G1.2 1842–1895
Moule, Arthur Evans, 1836–1918.
'Chinese proverbial philosophy.'
CR 5, 2 (Mar.–Apr. 1874), 72–77.
Subj 65

22407 NIC O P1 G9.3 1895–1911
Ohlinger, F- W-.
'Hsing-hua [*fu*] (Fuh-kien, China) proverbs and sayings.'
TP 2e série 2, 3 (1901), 269–273.
Subj 65

22408 CSU O P1 G1.2 1842–1895
Owen, G-.
'Animal worship among the Chinese.'
CR 18, 7 (July 1887), 249–255; 18, 9 (Sept. 1887), 334–346.
Subj 23 65 ▪ 62

22409 CSU P P2 G6.1 –1911
Parker, Alvin P-, 1850–1924.
'Some notes on the history and folklore of old Shanghai.'
JRAS-NCB new (2nd) series 47 (1916), 85–102.
Subj 23 65 ▪ 21.3 47 50

22410 MCH PO P1 G1.0 –1895
Perny, Paul Hubert, 1818–1907, comp.
Proverbes chinois, recueillis et mis en ordre (A collection of Chinese proverbs).
Paris: Firmin-Didot, 1869. 135 p.
Subj 65

22411 CBU O P1 G1.3 –1895
Preston, John.
'Charms and spells in use amongst the Chinese.'
China review 2, 3 (Nov.–Dec. 1873), 164–169.
Subj 65

22412 CSU O P2 G2.3 1842–1895
Ross, John, 1842–1915.
'Superstitions of Manchuria.'
CR 8, 6 (Nov.–Dec. 1877), 516–519.
Subj 23 65 ▪ 57 62

22413 CSU P P1 G1.0 1842–1895
Selby, T- G-.
'Yan Kwo [conduct and consequences], Yuk Lik [spirit-world memorials]: or, The purgatories of popular Budhism.'
China review 1, 5 (Mar.–Apr. 1873), 301–311.
Subj 65

22414 NNC S P1 G1.3 –1911
Sternberg, Leo, 1876–.
'Der Zwillingskult in China und die indischen Einflüsse' (The twin cult in China and its Indian influences).
Baessler-Archiv 13 (1929), 31–46.
Subj 23 65 ▪ 13 52 62

22415 CSU O P2 G9.0 1895–1911
Tope, S- G-.
'The bondage of fear, as illustrated among the Chinese.'
CR 30, 12 (Dec. 1899), 590–598.
Subj 62 65 ▪ 55 56 57

22416 CSU O P1 G1.0 1895–1911
von Poseck, Helena.
'John Chinaman as a humorist.'
EAM 2 (1903), 61–66.
Subj 65

22417 NIC PO P1 G1.2 –1895
Watters, Thomas, 1840–1901.
'Chinese fox-myths.'
JRAS-NCB new (2nd) series 8 (1874), 45–66.
Subj 65 ▪ 56 62

22418 MCH P P1 G1.3 –1911
Wieger, Léon, 1856–1933.
Folk-lore chinois moderne (Modern Chinese folklore).
Hsien-hsien, Hopei: Impr. de la Mission catholique, 1909. 422 p.
Subj 65 ▪ 62

22419 NIC O P1 G1.3 –1911
Williams, Frederick Wells, 1857–1928.
'Chinese folklore and some western analogies.'
Annual report of the Board of Regents of the Smithsonian Institution 1900, 575–600.
Subj 65 ▪ 47 62

22420 MCH P P1 G1.0 –1644
Yen, Alsace (Yen Chün-ch'iang), 1934–.
Demon tales in early vernacular Chinese: A folkloristic view.
Unpublished doctoral dissertation in Folklore and Mythology, Harvard U., 1971. 346 p.
Subj 23 62 65 ▪ 57

1644-1949

22421 DLC S P1 G1.1 –1928
'Kitaiskie pover'ia o ptitsakh: sobraniia I. V. Lareva' (Chinese beliefs relating to birds, from the collection of I. V. Larev). Tr. from the Chinese by Ippolit Gavrilovich Baranov. [Tr. of unpublished materials]
VA 48 (1922), 146–148.
Subj 65

22422 CNY FP P1 G1.2 –1928
Alekseev, Vasilii Mikhailovich, 1880–1951.
Bezsmertnye dvoiniki i daos s zolotoi zhaboi v svite boga bogatstva (The Two Immortals [Ho-ho] and the genius with the golden toad [Liu-hai] in the retinue of the God of Wealth [Ts'ai-shen]).
Petrograd: Tip. rossiiskoi Akad. nauk, 1918. 65 p.
Subj 23 65

22423 CSU PO P7 G1.2 –1928
Alekseev, Vasilii Mikhailovich, 1880–1951.
Kitaiskaia narodnaia kartina (Chinese folk art), edited by L- Z- Eidlin.
Moscow: Nauka, 1966. 260 p.
Subj 23 60 65 71 ▪ 26.2 26.3 27 47 66

22424 CSU U P1 G1.2 –1949
Chen, S. H. (Ch'en Shih-hsiang), 1912–1971.
'Chinese poetry and its popular sources.'
THJ new (2nd) series 2, 2 (June 1961), 320–325.
Subj 65

22425 CSU P P1 G1.3 –1949
Eberhard, Wolfram, 1909–.
'Chinese toggles.'
Palacio 49, 5 (May 1942), 91–104. [Reprinted in *Studies in Chinese folklore and related essays*, by W. Eberhard. (Selective entry.) Bloomington: Indiana U., Research Center for the Language Sciences, 1970, 209–216. (Indiana U., Folklore Institute monograph series, 23)]
Subj 55 65

22426 CSU P P3 G5.1 –1949
Eberhard, Wolfram, 1909–.
'Pekinger Stampferlieder' (Earth-tamping songs of Peking).
ZE 67, 2 (1936), 202–248.
'Pounding songs from Peking.' In *Studies in Chinese folklore and related essays*, by W. Eberhard. [Selective entry]
Bloomington: Indiana U., Research Center for the Language Sciences, 1970, 147–171. (Indiana U., Folklore Institute monograph series, 23)
Subj 65

22427 CSU S P1 G1.5 –1949
Eberhard, Wolfram, 1909–.
'Studies of Near Eastern and Chinese folktales.'
Sinologica 1, 1 (1947), 144–151. [Reprinted in *Studies in Chinese folklore and related essays*, by W. Eberhard. (Selective entry.) Bloomington: Indiana U., Research Center for the Language Sciences, 1970, 241–246. (Indiana U., Folklore Institute monograph series, 23)]
Subj 65

22428 NNC FP P2 G6.3 –1949
Feng Hui-t'ien, Wolfram Eberhard, 1909–, and Ts'ao Sung-yeh.
'Zur Volkskunde von Chekiang.'
ZE 67, 1 (1935), 248–265.
'On the folklore of Chekiang.' In *Studies in Chinese folklore and related essays*, by W. Eberhard. [Selective entry]
Bloomington: Indiana U., Research Center for the Language Sciences, 1970, 19–36. (Indiana U., Folklore Institute monograph series, 23)
Subj 23 65

22429 NIC PO P8 G3.2 –1949
Grootaers, Willem A-, 1911–.
'The hagiography of the Chinese god Chen-wu: The transmission of rural traditions in Chahar.'
FS 11, 2 (1952), 139–181.
Subj 23 65 ▪ 62

22430 NNC O P8 G4.1 –1949
Ho Chi-fang (Ho Ch'i-fang).
'Chinese folk songs.'
Chinese literature 1954, 1, 126–142.
Subj 26.3 65 ▪ 32.2 41 47

22431 NNM S P1 G1.3 –1949
Huizenga, Lee Sjords, 1881–1945.
'Lu Tsu, and his relation to the other medicine gods in Chinese medical lore.'
CMJ 58, 3 (Sept. 1940), 275–283.
Subj 56 65 ▪ 23 62

22432 NNC P P1 G1.2 –1949
Jameson, Raymond De Loy, 1896–.
Three lectures on Chinese folklore, delivered before the convocation of the North China Union Language School, March and April 1932.
Peiping: North China Union Language School *with* California College in China, 1932. 164 p.
Subj 62 65 ▪ 29 41 47 61 70 72

22433 NNC S P1 G1.3 –1949
Kühn, Alfred, 1885–.
'Das Schwanenjungfrau-Motiv in Ost- und Südostasien' (The swan-maiden motif in East and Southeast Asia).
Artibus Asiae 6, 3/4 (1937), 256–264.
Subj 65 ▪ 62

22434 NIC O P1 G1.5 1842–1949
Li, Lienfung, 1923–.
Chinese folklore of the lower Yangtze region.
Unpublished masters thesis in Literature, Cornell U., 1946. 171 p.
Subj 65

22435 MCH O P1 G1.2 –1949
Mortier, Florent.
'Les vampires en Chine' (Vampires in China).
BSRB 54 (1939), 61–65.
Subj 65 ▪ 23 56 57 62

22436 NIC U P1 G1.2 –1949
Okuno, Mitsunori.
'Chinese superstition in fiction and folklore.'
Contemporary Japan 9, 12 (Dec. 1940), 1567–1577.
Subj 62 65

22437 MCH F P2 G3.0 1895–1928
Oost, Josephus van, 1877–.
Dictons et proverbes des Chinois habitant la Mongolie sud-ouest (Maxims and proverbs of the Chinese living in southwestern Mongolia).
Shanghai: Impr. de l'Orphelinat de T'ou-sè-wè, 1918. 356 p. (Variétés sinologiques, 50)
Subj 50 63 65

22438 NIC O P1 G1.3 –1928
Scarborough, William, ?–1894.
A collection of Chinese proverbs, edited by Charles Wilfrid Allan.
Shanghai: Presbyterian Mission Press, 1927. 381, 14 p. [Reprinted—New York: Paragon, 1964. 381 p.]
Subj 65

22439 CSU O P1 G1.3 –1928
Smith, Arthur Henderson, 1845–1932.
Proverbs and common sayings from the Chinese, rev. ed.
Shanghai: American Presbyterian Mission Press, 1914. 374, 29 p. [Reprinted—New York: Paragon, 1965. 374, 29 p.]
Subj 65

22440 NNC O P1 G1.2 –1949
Sowerby, Arthur de Carle, 1885–1964.
'Some Chinese animal myths and legends.'
JRAS-NCB new (2nd) series 70 (1939), 3–21.
Subj 62 65

22441 CSU P P7 G9.5 –1949
Sung, Hok-p'ang.
'Legends and stories of the New Territories.'
Hong Kong naturalist 6, 1 – 8, 3/4 (May 1935 – Mar. 1938), 46 p. in all.
Subj 43 65 ▪ 24.3 25 33 42 57

22442 CSU PO P1 G1.2 –1928
Wieger, Léon (Leo Wieger), 1856–1933.
'Influence du roman et du théâtre sur les croyances et le moeurs populaires, depuis les *Yuan* (triezième siècle).' In *Histoire des croyances religieuses et des opinions philosophiques en Chine depuis l'origine, jusqu'à nos jours*, 3rd ed., by L. Wieger. [Selective entry]
Hsien-hsien, Hopei: Impr. de Sienhsien, 1927, 731–752.
'Influence of the novel and play on popular beliefs and morals since the Yüan (thirteenth century).' Tr. by Edward Theodore Chalmers Werner. In *A history of the religious beliefs and philosophical opinions in China from the beginning to the present time*, by L. Wieger. [Selective entry]
Hsien-hsien, Hopei: Hsien-hsien Press, 1927, 731–752. [Reprinted in *A history of the religious beliefs and philosophical opinions in China from the beginning to the present time*, by L. Wieger. (Selective entry.) New York: Paragon, 1969, 731–752.]
Subj 65

22443 MCH P P1 G1.0 –1928
Willoughby-Meade, Gerald.
Chinese ghouls and goblins.
London: Constable, 1928. 15, 431 p.
Subj 23 65 ▪ 43 57

1911-1949

22444 MCH O P2 G1.5 1928–1949
Ayscough, Florence Wheelock, 1878–1942.
'Der Yangtse Kiang, Chinas grosser Strom: Seine Legende und Poesie' (The Yangtze, China's great river: Its legends and poetry).
MDG 29, E (1937), 1–18.
Subj 65

22445 NIC O P1 G7.3 1911–1928
Brown, Fred R-.
'Superstitions common in Kiangsi province.'
NCR 4, 6 (Dec. 1922), 493–504.
Subj 23 65 ▪ 24.2 33 41 56 57

22446 CSU O P2 G1.2 1911–1949
Cammann, Schuyler, 1912–.
Substance and symbol in Chinese toggles: Chinese belt toggles from the C. F. Bieber collection.
Philadelphia: U. of Pennsylvania Press, 1962. 256 p.
Subj 55 65

22447 CNY O P7 G8.2 1911–1928
Cordier, Charles Georges, 1872–1936.
'Croyances populaires au Yunnan' (Folk beliefs in Yunnan).
La Chine 36 (15 fév. 1923), 203–208.
Subj 65

22448 NNC O P8 G8.2 1911–1928
Cordier, Charles Georges, 1872–1936.
'Folklore du Yunnan: jeux d'enfants et chansons diverses' (The folklore of Yunnan: Children's games and assorted songs).
BEFEO 28, 3/4 (1928), 349–440.
Subj 52 62 65

22449 CSU F P3 G5.1 1928–1949
Eberhard, Wolfram, 1909–.
'Notes on Chinese proverbs: Notes on the structure of Pekinese proverbs.' In *Studies in Chinese folklore and related essays*, by W. Eberhard. [Selective entry]
Bloomington: Indiana U., Research Center for the Language Sciences,

1970, 173–176. (Indiana U., Folklore Institute monograph series, 23)
Subj 65

22450 NIC F P2 G6.3 1928–1949
Eberhard, Wolfram, 1909–.
'The supernatural in Chinese folktales from Chekiang.' In *Humaniora: Essays in literature, folklore, and bibliography*, edited by Wayland D- Hand and Gustave O- Arlt. [Sole entry]
Locust Valley, N.Y.: J. J. Augustin, 1960, 335–341. [Reprinted in *Studies in Chinese folklore and related essays*, by W. Eberhard. (Selective entry.) Bloomington: Indiana U., Research Center for the Language Sciences, 1970, 67–72. (Indiana U., Folklore Institute monograph series, 23)]
Subj 65

22451 NNC F P7 G1.3 1928–1949
Eberhard, Wolfram, 1909–.
'Volkspoesie an Tempelwänden' (Folk poetry on temple walls).
Sinica 11, 3/4 (Mai–Juli 1936), 127–130. [Reprinted in *Studies in Chinese folklore and related essays*, by W. Eberhard. (Selective entry.) Bloomington: Indiana U., Research Center for the Language Sciences, 1970, 97–112. (Indiana U., Folklore Institute monograph series, 23)]
Subj 65 ▪ 23

22452 NNC FP P2 G1.2 1911–1949
Eder, Matthias, 1902–.
'Das Jahr im chinesischen Volkslied' (The year in Chinese folk songs).
FS 4 (1945), 1–160.
Subj 23 65 ▪ 24.1 26.3 31 52 55

22453 CSU F P8 G4.4 1928–1949
Frick, Johannes, and Franz Eichinger.
'Tiere im Volksleben' (The role of animals in the life of the people). In *Ethnographische Beiträge aus der Ch'inghai Provinz (China)* (Ethnographic reports from Tsinghai). [Selective entry]
Peking [i.e., Tokyo]: Catholic U. of Peking, Museum of Oriental Ethnology, 1952, 125–147. (MOE, Folklore studies supplements, 1)
Subj 62 65 ▪ 23 24.1 26.3 55 56

22454 MCY F P7 G5.0 1928–1949
Grootaers, Willem A-, 1911–.
'La méthode géographique et linguistique en folklore' (The geographic and linguistic method in folklore).
BUA 3e série 9, 35 (juil. 1948), 221–233.
Subj 20 21.3 29 65

22455 NNC F P2 G9.2 1928–1949
Herrmann, Ferdinand.
'Zur Volkskunde der Hakka in Kuangtung' (The folklore of the Hakkas in Kwangtung).
Sinica 12, 1/2 (Jan.–März 1937), 18–38.
Subj 50 65 ▪ 23 29 31 41 51 55 57

22456 NNC U P1 G5.1 1911–1949
Herrmann, Ferdinand, and K'o-kun Yao.
'Chinesischer Schutz-und Glückszauber' (Chinese talismans and good-luck charms).
Sinica 1935, 24–38. [*Sonderausgabe* (Special issue)]
Subj 62 65 ▪ 23 41 53 57

22457 CSU F P3 G5.1 1911–1949
Ho Feng-ju and Wolfram Eberhard, 1909–.
'Pekinger Sprichwörter' (Proverbs of Peking).
Baessler-Archiv 24, 1 (1941), 1–43.
Subj 65 ▪ 22.2 23 24 26.2 28 40 48 50 55 60

22458 NNC F P8 G5.3 1911–1949
[Körner, Brunhild] Brunhild Lessing.
'Fünf chinesische Volksmärchen aus Schantung' (Five Chinese folk tales from Shantung).
Sinica 10, 3 (Mai 1935), 108–120.
Subj 65 ▪ 53

22459 CSU F P3 G5.1 1911–1949
Kroll, J- L-.
'A tentative classification and description of the structure of Peking common sayings (*hsieh-hou-yü* [synecdochic proverbs]).'
JAOS 86, 3 (July–Sept. 1966), 267–276.
Subj 65

22460 NNC O P7 G8.1 1928–1949
Manly, Grace Edna, 1899–1943.
'A study of the roadcalls of chair carriers.'
JWCBRS 13 (1941), 13–41.
Subj 24.2 26.4 65

22461 MCY F P3 G5.1 1928–1949
Martin, Ilse.
'Frühlingsdoppelsprüche von 1942 an pekinger Haustüren' (Spring couplets on doors of houses in Peking, 1942).
FS 2 (1943), 89–174.
Subj 23 65 ▪ 53

22462 CSU F P7 G4.4 1911–1949
Oberle, A-.
'Der Hundertkopfdämon im Volksglauben des Westtales und des chinesisch-tibetanischen Kontaktgebietes im Osttale von Kuei-te in der Provinz Ch'ing-hai' (The hundred-headed demon in the popular beliefs of the west valley and of the area of Sino-Tibetan contact in the east valley of the Kuei-te region, Tsinghai). In *Ethnographische Beiträge aus der Ch'inghai Provinz (China)* (Ethnographic reports from Tsinghai). [Selective entry]
Peking [i.e., Tokyo]: Catholic U. of Peking, Museum of Oriental Ethnology, 1952, 222–233. (MOE, Folklore studies supplements, 1)
Subj 23 29 65 ▪ 24.3 56 66

22463 NNC O P1 G1.3 1911–1949
Plopper, Clifford Henry, 1885–.
'Economics as seen through the proverbs.' In *Chinese proverbs*, by C. H. Plopper. [Analytic entry]
Peiping: North China Union Language School, 1932, 25–47.
Subj 24.6 62 65 ▪ 24.3 34.2 48 61 63

22464 NNC F P3 G5.1 1911–1949
Schmitt, Erich, 1893–.
'Pekinger Hsieh-hou-yü' (*Hsieh hou-yü* [synecdochic proverbs] of Peking).
Archiv für Ostasien 1, 1 (1948), 13–19.
Subj 65

22465 MCY F P7 G5.2 1928–1949
Serruys, Paul Leo Mary, 1912–.
'Fifteen popular tales from the south of Tatung [Ta-t'ung *hsien*] (Shansi).'
FS 5 (1946), 191–278.
Subj 65

22466 NIC O P8 G3.1 1911–1949
Serruys, Paul Leo Mary, 1912–.
'Folklore contributions in *Sino-Mongolica*: Notes on customs, legends, proverbs and riddles of the province of Jehol.'
FS 6, 2 (1947), 1–128. [Special issue]
Subj 65 ▪ 23 24.1

22467 MCH F P8 G4.4 1928–1949
Trippner, Josef.
'Rätsel aus der Provinz Chinghai, NW China' (Riddles of Tsinghai).
Sinologica 9, 1 (1966), 29–62.
Subj 65 ▪ 62 63

22468 MCH P P1 G1.3 1911–1928
Werner, Edward Theodore Chalmers, 1864–1954.
'Chinese ditties.'
NCR 3, 4 (Aug. 1921), 259–272; 3, 5 (Oct. 1921), 368–375; 3, 6 (Dec. 1921), 442–450; 4, 1 (Feb. 1922), 23–31; 4, 2 (Apr. 1922), 106–113.
Subj 65

22469 MCH O P1 G1.2 1911–1928
Whymant, A- Neville John, 1894–.
'Chinese coolie songs.'
B. of the School of Oriental Studies, London Institution 1, 4 (Oct. 1920), 145–166.
Subj 55 65 ▪ 43 48

1911-1972
(including 1644-1972)

22470 SSK S P1 G1.0 –1972
Aspberg, Johan.
'Lao Tien, ett poplärt gudsnamn i Kina' (Lao Tien, a popular religious name in China).
Svensk missionstidskrift 1950, 152–162.
Subj 62 65

22471 CSU F P1 G1.1 –1972
Cammann, Schuyler, 1912–.
'On the decoration of modern temples in Taiwan and Hongkong.' [Review of 'Topics and moral values in Chinese temple decorations', by Wolfram Eberhard.] [With a reply by Eberhard]
JAOS 88, 4 (Oct.–Dec. 1968), 785–792.
Subj 62 65 ▪ 23

22472 CSU S P1 G1.0 –1972
Chiang, Alpha C. (Chiang Chung-i), 1927–.
'Religion, proverbs, and economic mentality.'
American j. of economics and sociology 20, 3 (Apr. 1961), 253–264.
Subj 63 65 ▪ 19 23

22473 CSU S P2 G1.2 1911–1972
Dorson, Richard Mercer, 1916–.
'Foreword.' In *Folktales of China*, edited by Wolfram Eberhard. [Selective entry]
Chicago: U. of Chicago Press, 1965, 5–31 [s.p.].
Subj 65 ▪ 31 70

22474 CBU P P1 G1.1 –1972
Eberhard, Wolfram, 1909–.
Guilt and sin in traditional China.

Berkeley, Los Angeles: U. of California Press, 1967. 141 p.
SUBJ 23 46 60 62 65 ▪ 17 45 61 63 66

22475 CSU P P1 G1.2 1911–1972
Eberhard, Wolfram, 1909–.
'Introduction.' In *Folktales of China*, edited by W. Eberhard. [Selective entry]
Chicago: U. of Chicago Press, 1965, 33–38 [s.p.].
SUBJ 65 ▪ 70

22476 CSU P P2 G1.1 –1972
Eberhard, Wolfram, 1909–.
'Introduction: Observations on Chinese fables.' In *Chinese fables and parables: A catalogus*, by W. Eberhard. [Sole entry]
Taipei: Orient Cultural Service, 1971, 1–25 [s.p.].
SUBJ 65 ▪ 16 41

22477 CSU P P1 G1.1 1911–1972
Eberhard, Wolfram, 1909–.
'Introduction: The use of folklore in China.' In *Studies in Chinese folklore and related essays*, by W. Eberhard. [Selective entry]
Bloomington: Indiana U., Research Center for the Language Sciences, 1970, 1–16. (Indiana U., Folklore Institute monograph series, 23)
SUBJ 65 70 ▪ 12.1

22478 CSU FP P2 G1.1 –1972
Eberhard, Wolfram, 1909–.
'Orakel und Theater in China.'
Asiatische Studien 18/19 (1965), 11–18.

'Oracle and theater in China.' In *Studies in Chinese folklore and related essays*, by W. Eberhard. [Selective entry]
Bloomington: Indiana U., Research Center for the Language Sciences, 1970, 191–199. (Indiana U., Folklore Institute monograph series, 23)
SUBJ 65

22479 CSU P P8 G9.0 –1972
Eberhard, Wolfram, 1909–.
'Die soziale Welt der südchinesischen Volksballaden' (The social context of South Chinese folk ballads). In *Volksüberlieferung: Festschrift für Kurt Ranke zur Vollendung des 60. Lebensjahres* (Folk traditions: Felicitation volume for Kurt Ranke on his sixtieth year), edited by Fritz Harkort, Karel C- Peeters, and Robert Wildhaber. [Sole entry]
Göttingen: O. Schwartz, 1968, 429–444.

'South Chinese folk ballads and their moral values' [rev. in tr.]. In *Moral and social values of the Chinese: Collected essays*, by W. Eberhard. [Selective entry]
Taipei: Chinese Materials and Research Aids Service Center, 1971, 191–234. (CMRASC occasional series, 6)
SUBJ 46 63 65 ▪ 41 47

22480 CSU F P1 G9.0 1928–1972
Eberhard, Wolfram, 1909–.
'Topics and moral values in Chinese temple decorations.'
JAOS 87, 1 (Jan.–Mar. 1967), 22–32. [Reprinted in *Moral and social values of the Chinese: Collected essays*, by W. Eberhard. (Selective entry.) Taipei: Chinese Materials and Research Aids Service Center, 1971, 15–25. (CMRASC occasional series, 6)]
SUBJ 23 65 ▪ 31 63

22481 MCH O P8 G4.4 1911–1972
Frick, Johannes.
'Bäuerliches Sprachgut aus Tsinghai' (Peasant sayings from Tsinghai).
Sinologica 8, 1 (1964), 13–33; 8, 4 (1965), 211–240; 9, 2 (1966/67), 108–131; 11, 3/4 (1970), 145–170.
SUBJ 65 ▪ 26.3

22482 CSU P P1 G1.1 –1972
Fujino Iwatomo, 1898–.
'On Chinese soul-inviting and firefly-catching songs: A study on Chinese folklore.'
Acta Asiatica (Tokyo) 19 (Dec. 1970), 40–57.
SUBJ 65

22483 NNC S P8 G8.3 –1972
Its, Rudol'f Fernandovich.
'Ob odnom fol'klornom zhanre kitaitsev Guichzhou' (A folklore genre of the Chinese in Kweichow).
Kratkie soobshcheniia Instituta etnogrofii im. N. Miklukho-Maklaia Akademii nauk SSSR 32 (1959), 130–133.
SUBJ 65 ▪ 66

22484 CSH S P1 G1.2 –1972
Petrov, N- A-.
'Nekotorye izdaniia kitaiskogo fol'klora XIX veka v kollektsii ksilografov Leningradskogo otdeleniia Instituta narodov Azii Akademii nauk SSSR' (Nineteenth-century Chinese folklore publications in the xylographic collection of the Leningrad Branch of the Institute of Asian Peoples, USSR Academy of Sciences). In *Strany i narody Vostoka: geografiia, etnografiia, istoriia* (Countries and peoples of the Orient: Geography, ethnography, and history), edited by Vostochnaia komissiia, Geograficheskoe obshchestvo SSSR, Akademiia nauk SSSR. [Selective entry]
Moscow: Izd-vo vost. lit-ry, 1961, vol. 2, 266–269.
SUBJ 65 72

22485 NNC S P2 G5.4 1644–1972
Průšek, Jaroslav, 1904–.
'Die *chui-tsi-shu*, erzählende Volksgesänge aus Ho-nan' (*Chui tzu shu*, folk ballads from Honan). In *Asiatica: Festschrift für Friedrich Weller zum 65. Geburtstag gewidmet von seinen Freunden, Kollegen und Schülern* (Asiatica: Felicitation volume for Friedrich Weller on his sixty-fifth birthday by his friends, colleagues, and students), edited by Johannes Schubert and Ulrich Schneider. [Selective entry]
Leipzig: VEB Otto Harrassowitz, 1954, 453–483.

'Chui-tzu-shu: Folk songs from Ho-nan.' In *Chinese history and literature: Collection of studies*, by J. Průšek. [Selective entry]
Dordrecht: Reidel, 1970, 170–198.
SUBJ 65 ▪ 31 47

22486 DLC PO P8 G1.2 1928–1972
Průšek, Jaroslav, 1904–.
Literatura osvobozené Číny a její lidové tradice (The literature of liberated China and its popular traditions).
Prague: Ceskoslovenské Akademie Ved, 1953. 559 p.

Die Literatur des befreiten Chinas und ihre Volkstraditionen. Tr. by Pavel Eisner and Wilhelm Gampert.
Prague: Artia, 1955. 736 p.
SUBJ 16.1 64 65 ▪ 32.2 50 62 66

22487 MCH U P7 G1.2 1911–1972
Riftin, Boris L'vovich, 1932–.
'Kitaiskie poslovitsy kak material dlia izucheniia narodnogo mirovozzreniia' (The world view of the common people in China, as expressed in proverbs). [With English abstract]
Sovetskaia etnografiia 1960, 4, 105–120.
SUBJ 62 65 ▪ 70

22488 NNC S P1 G1.2 –1972
Riftin, Boris L'vovich, 1932–.
Skazanie o Velikoi stene i problema zhanra v kitaiskom fol'klore (The legend of the Great Wall and the problem of genre in Chinese folklore).
Moscow: Izd-vo vost. lit-ry, 1961. 245 p.
SUBJ 65 ▪ 47

22489 MCH S P1 G1.2 1911–1972
Riftin, Boris L'vovich, 1932–.
'Sovremennaia kitaiskaia fol'kloristika' (Current research on Chinese folklore). [With English abstract]
Sovetskaia etnografiia 1960, 1, 38–59.
SUBJ 65 70

22490 CSH S P2 G9.4 1928–1972
Stanford U. China Project.
'Social values, patterns of living, and folk beliefs.' In *Taiwan (Formosa)*, compiled by the organization cited. [Selective entry]
New Haven: Human Relations Area Files, 1956, vol. 1, 149–162. (HRAF subcontractor's monographs, 31; Stanford 5)
SUBJ 23 55 65 ▪ 18 41

22491 CSU P P2 G1.1 –1972
Ting, Nai-tung.
'AT type 301 in China and some countries adjacent to China: A study of a regional group and its significance in world tradition.'
Fabula 11, 1/2 (1970), 54–125.
SUBJ 65

22492 CSU P P1 G1.2 –1972
Ting, Nai-tung.
'More Chinese versions of AT 301.'
Fabula 12, 1 (1971), 65–76.
SUBJ 65

22493 CSU S P2 G1.2 1928–1972
Yen, Chun-chiang.
'Folklore research in Communist China.'
Asian folklore studies 26, 2 (1967), 1–62.
SUBJ 23 65 70 ▪ 12.1 31 71

1949-1972

22494 CSU F P2 G9.5 1949–1972
Anderson, Eugene Newton, Jr., 1941–.
'The folksongs of the Hong Kong boat people.'

J. of American folklore 80, 317 (July–Sept. 1967), 285–296. [Reprinted in *Essays on South China's boat people*, by E. N. Anderson, Jr. (Analytic entry.) Taipei: Orient Cultural Service, 1972, 21–32. (Asian Folklore and Social Life monographs, 29)]
Subj 46 65 ▪ 29 41 57

22495 ²CSU F P1 G9.0 1949–1972
Eberhard, Wolfram, 1909–.
'Chinesische Volksliteratur in chinesischen Volkstempeln.' In *IV International Congress for Folk-Narrative Research: Lectures and reports*, edited by Geōrgios A- Megas. [Sole entry]
Athens: ——, 1965, 100–105.

'Chinese folk literature in Chinese folk temples.' In *Studies in Chinese folklore and related essays*, by W. Eberhard. [Selective entry]
Bloomington: Indiana U., Research Center for the Language Sciences, 1970, 183–189. (Indiana U., Folklore Institute monograph series, 23)
Subj 65

22496 CSU F P1 G9.4 1949–1972
Eberhard, Wolfram, 1909–.
'On some Chinese terms of abuse.'
Asian folklore studies 27, 1 (1968), 25–40. [Reprinted in *Moral and social values of the Chinese: Collected essays*, by W. Eberhard. (Selective entry.) Taipei: Chinese Materials and Research Aids Service Center, 1971, 319–334. (CMRASC occasional series, 6)]
Subj 62 65 ▪ 22.2 61

22497 CSH F P3 G9.4 1949–1972
Eberhard, Wolfram, 1909–.
Studies in Taiwanese folktales.
Taipei: Orient Cultural Service, 1970. 193 p. (Asian folklore and social life monographs, 1)
Subj 65

22498 CSU F P2 G9.5 1949–1972
Eberhard, Wolfram, 1909–.
'A study of ghost stories from Taiwan and San Francisco.'
Asian folklore studies 30, 2 (1971), 1–26.
Subj 65

22499 DLC P P1 G1.2 1949–1972
Evans, Humphrey.
The adventures of Li Chi: A modern Chinese legend.
New York: Dutton, 1967. 222 p.
Subj 65

22500 CSU O P3 G9.5 1949–1972
[Gleason, Eugene Franklin] Gene Gleason, 1914–.
Tales of Hong Kong.
New York: Roy, 1967. 190 p.
Subj 23 46 47 55 65 66 ▪ 22.2 24 24.2 31 34.2 43 52 56 62

22501 CSU O P1 G9.4 1949–1972
Hwang Teh-shih (Huang Te-shih).
'An important characteristic of Taiwan folk belief.'
JCS 6 (1969), 79–85.
Subj 65

22502 CSH P P1 G1.2 1949–1972
[La Dany, Ladislao] ———, 1914–.
'Folk songs and folk tales.'
CNA 353 (16 Dec. 1960), 1–7.
Subj 62 65

22503 MAU S P1 G9.5 1949–1972
Topley, Marjorie Doreen, 1927–.
'Some basic conceptions and their traditional relationship to society.' In *Some traditional Chinese ideas and conceptions in Hong Kong social life today*, edited by M. D. Topley. [Analytic entry]
Hong Kong: Royal Asiatic Society, Hong Kong Branch, 1967, 7–21.
Subj 62 65

22504 MAM P P1 G9.4 1949–1972
Young, Conrad. C. S. (Yang Chün-shih), 1920–.
The morphology of Chinese folk stories, derived from shadow plays of Taiwan.
Ann Arbor: University Microfilms (Publ. 71-21,344), 1971. 15, 864 p. (Doctoral dissertation in Anthropology, U. of California, Los Angeles)
Subj 31 65

66 Self-Conception in Relation to Outsiders

「華夷」「中外」之分辨及對異族之觀念

「華夷」「中外」等異民族に対する観念

1644-1911

22505 CBU P P1 G1.2 –1842
'O pervykh Rossiiskikh puteshestviiakh i posol'stvakh v Kitai' (The first Russian expeditions and embassies to China).
Ezhemesiachnyia sochineniia k pol'ze i uveseleniiu sluzhashchikh 2 (iiul' 1755), 15–57.
Subj 12 66 ▪ 55

22506 NNC O P2 G2.1 1842–1895
A. I.
'Poslednie dni v Man'chzhurii: iz lichnykh vospominanii' (Personal reminiscences of recent days in Manchuria).
Russkoe bogatstvo 1900, 10 (oktiabr'), 143–168.
Subj 66 ▪ 12.1 15 24.2

22507 CSU S P1 G1.2 –1911
Adshead, Samuel Adrian Miles, 1932–.
'China and Central Asia.' In *China and its place in the world*, edited by Nicholas Tarling. [Sole entry]
Auckland, N.Z.: Blackwood and Paul, 1967, 11–25.
Subj 66 ▪ 14.3 15

22508 CSU O P2 G8.2 1842–1895
Anderson, John, 1833–1900.
'Momien [T'eng-yüeh-chou, Yunnan].' In *Mandalay to Momien: A narrative of the two expeditions to western China of 1868 and 1875 . . .*, by J. Anderson. [Selective entry]
London: Macmillan, 1876, 189–222. [Reprinted in *Mandalay to Momien: A narrative of the two expeditions to western China of 1868 and 1875 . . .*, by J. Anderson. (Selective entry.) Taipei: Ch'eng-wen, 1972, 189–222.]
Subj 24.3 56 66 ▪ 14.3 21.3 25 47

22509 IMN O P7 G5.4 1842–1911
Anelli, Emilio.
Cenni storici sulla missione dell'Ho-nan in Cina nell'ultimo trentennio (1870–1900) (Historical notes on the [Catholic] mission in Honan in the past thirty years, 1870–1900).
Milan: Tipografia Pontificia S. Giuseppe, 1900. 42 p.
Subj 66

22510 MBA P P2 G9.1 –1895
Beauvais, Jean Joseph, 1867–1924.
'Documents géographiques, historiques, et linguistiques sur la ville et la région de Long-tcheou' (Geographic, historical, and linguistic documents on the capital of Lung-chou *t'ing* and the surrounding area [Kwangsi]).
RI nouvelle (2e) série 10, 88 – 11, 2 (31 août 1908 – fév. 1909), 118 p. in all.
Subj 21 21.3 22 66 ▪ 29

22511 CBU O P2 G1.4 1644–1842
Bell, John, 1691–1780.
'A journey from St. Petersburg in Russia, to Pekin in China, with an embassy from His Imperial Majesty Peter the First, to Kamhi, Emperor of China [the K'ang-hsi Emperor], in the year 1719.' In *Travels from St. Petersburg in Russia to diverse parts of Asia*, by J. Bell. [Sole entry]
Glasgow: Robert and Andrew Foulis, 1763, vol. 1, 155–357; vol. 2, 1–168. [Reprinted in *A general collection of the best and most interesting voyages and travels in all parts of the world . . .*, edited by John Pinkerton. (Sole entry.) London: Longman, Hurst, Rees, Orme, and Brown, 1811, vol. 7, 318–434.] [Separately reprinted as *A journey from St. Petersburg to Pekin, 1719–22* edited by J- L- Stevenson. Edinburgh: Edinburgh U. Press, 1965. 248 p.]
Subj 31 55 66 ▪ 15 24.3 47

22512 CSU P P1 G1.1 –1842
Bernard, Henri, 1897–.
'Notes on the introduction of the natural sciences into the Chinese empire.'
YJSS 3, 2 (Aug. 1941), 220–241.
Subj 62 66 ▪ 56

22513 CSU PO P2 G1.5 1842–1895
Bernard, William Dallas.
The 'Nemesis' in China: Comprising a history of the late war in that country, with an account of the colony of Hong Kong, 4th ed.
London: Colburn, 1848. 2, 399 p. [Reprinted—New York: Praeger, 1969. 29, 399 p.]
Subj 66 ▪ 15 16.1 25

22514 CSU P P1 G1.3 1842–1895
Biggerstaff, Knight, 1906–.
'The official Chinese attitude toward the Burlingame mission.'
American historical review 41, 4 (July 1936), 682–707.
Subj 66 ▪ 12 32.1

22515 MCH P P3 G1.1 1842–1895
Biggerstaff, Knight, 1906–.
'The secret correspondence of 1867–1868: Views of leading Chinese statesmen regarding the further opening of China to Western influence.'

J. of modern history 22, 2 (June 1950), 122–136.
SUBJ 12.2 16.1 66 ▪ 12 12.1 14.3

22516 CSU U P1 G1.2 –1911
Boardman, Eugene Powers, 1910–.
'Chinese mandarins and Western traders: The effect of the frontier in Chinese history.' In *The frontier in perspective*, edited by Walker D- Wyman and Clifton B- Kroeber. [Sole entry]
Madison: U. of Wisconsin Press, 1957, 95–110.
SUBJ 66 ▪ 15

22517 MCH O P2 G8.1 1842–1895
Bonnet, ———.
'La persécution en Chine' (Persecution in China).
APF 59 (1887), 149–175.
SUBJ 33 66 ▪ 22 25 26

22518 DLC P P1 G1.1 1842–1911
Borokh, Liliia Nikolaevna, 1933–.
'Antiman'chzhurskie idei pervykh kitaiskikh burzhuaznykh revoliutsionerov (o "Pokazaniiakh Lu Khao-duna")' (The anti-Manchu ideas of the early Chinese bourgeois revolutionaries: 'The testimony of Lu Hao-tung'). In *Man'chzhurskoe vladychestvo v Kitae* (Manchu rule in China), compiled by Institut narodov Azii, Akademiia nauk SSSR, edited by Sergei Leonidovich Tikhvinskii. [Selective entry]
Moscow: Nauka, Glav. red. vost. lit-ry, 1966, 333–349.
SUBJ 64 66 70 ▪ 32.2 59

22519 CSU S P1 G1.3 1644–1842
Boxer, Charles Ralph, 1904–.
'Isaac Titsingh's embassy to the court of Ch'ien Lung (1794–1795).'
THM 8, 1 (Jan. 1939), 9–33.
SUBJ 66

22520 MCH P P3 G5.1 –1842
Boxer, Charles Ralph, 1904–.
'Jesuits at the court of Peking, 1601–1775.'
History today 7, 9 (7 Sept. 1957), 580–589.
SUBJ 13 66 ▪ 33 43 64

22521 CSU S P1 G1.5 –1842
Boxer, Charles Ralph, 1904–.
'Portuguese military expeditions in aid of the Mings against the Manchus, 1621–1647.'
THM 7, 1 (Aug. 1938), 24–36.
SUBJ 66 ▪ 15 32.2

22522 CSU O P2 G1.5 1895–1911
Brenier, Henri, 1867–?
'Un détour imprévu: de Hin-y fou à Canton par Koui-yang' (An unforeseen detour: From Hsing-i-fu [Kweichow] to Canton via Kweiyang). In *La Mission lyonnaise d'exploration commerciale en Chine, 1895–1897, première partie, récits des voyages* (The Lyons Trade Mission to China, 1895–1897, Part 1, Travel accounts), compiled by Chambre de commerce de Lyon. [Selective entry]
Lyons: Rey, 1898, 328–347 [s.p.].
SUBJ 21.3 22 66 ▪ 15 24.1 25 55 58

22523 CSU O P2 G8.0 1895–1911
Brenier, Henri, 1867–?
'Du Koui-tcheou au Se-tchoan: séjour à Koui-yang et voyage de Koui-yang à Tchoung-king' (From Kweichow to Szechwan: A sojourn in Kweiyang and the journey from Kweiyang to Chungking). In *La Mission lyonnaise d'exploration commerciale en Chine, 1895–1897, première partie, récits des voyages* (The Lyons Trade Mission to China, 1895–1897, Part 1, Travel accounts), compiled by Chambre de commerce de Lyon. [Selective entry]
Lyons: Rey, 1898, 100–118 [s.p.].
SUBJ 33 66 ▪ 22 24.2 28 38 47

22524 CSU P P1 G1.2 –1911
Cammann, Schuyler, 1912–.
'Presentation of dragon robes by the Ming and Ch'ing court for diplomatic purposes.'
Sinologica 3, 3 (1951/53), 193–202.
SUBJ 66 ▪ 62 64

22525 CSU O P2 G1.2 1895–1911
Capen, Edward W-.
'The Western influence in China.' In *Recent developments in China*, edited by George Hubbard Blakeslee. [Selective entry]
New York: G. E. Stechert, 1913, 93–118.
SUBJ 14.2 17 33 66 ▪ 12.2 47 56

22526 CSU P P3 G9.3 1842–1895
Carlson, Ellsworth Clayton, 1917–.
'Obstacles to missionary success in nineteenth century China.'
Asian studies (Quezon City, Philippines) 4, 1 (Apr. 1966), 16–28.
SUBJ 33 66

22527 IMC O P3 G1.3 1842–1895
Catellani, Enrico Levi, 1856–?
'I "Settlements" europei e i privilegi degli stranieri nell'Estremo Oriente' (The European settlements and foreigners' privileges in the Far East).
Atti del Reale istituto veneto di scienze, lettere, ed arti 5 (1902), 859–913; 6 (1903), 395–559.
SUBJ 66 ▪ 22.2

22528 MCH P P1 G1.2 1644–1895
Chang, Hao, 1936–.
'The anti-foreignist role of Wo-jen, 1804–1871.'
PC 14 (Dec. 1960), 1–29.
SUBJ 60 61 64 66 ▪ 16.1 17

22529 CSU P P3 G1.2 1644–1895
Chang Hsi-t'ung.
'The earliest phase of the introduction of Western political science into China.'
YJSS 5, 1 (July 1950), 1–29.
SUBJ 16.1 66 ▪ 12

22530 FPN P P1 G1.2 1842–1911
Chih, André (Ch'ih Feng-t'ung).
L'Occident 'chrétien' vu par les Chinois vers la fin du XIXe siècle (1870–1900) (The 'Christian' West as seen by the Chinese toward the end of the nineteenth century, 1870–1900).
Paris: Presses universitaires, 1962. 273 p. (Université de Paris, Faculté des lettres et des sciences humaines publications, série 'Textes et Documents', 2) (Doctoral dissertation, Pontificia Universitas Gregoriana [Vatican City])
SUBJ 16.1 17 33 64 66 ▪ 12 13 55 63

22531 CSU P P2 G4.0 1644–1895
Chu, Wen-djang (Chu Wen-ch'ang), 1914–.
The Moslem rebellion in Northwest China, 1862–1878: A study of government minority policy.
The Hague: Mouton, 1966. 232 p. (Central Asiatic studies, 5) (Revision of *The policy of the Manchu government in the suppression of the Moslem rebellion in Shensi, Kansu, and Sinkiang from 1862 to 1878*, doctoral dissertation in History, U. of Washington, 1955)
SUBJ 12 15 25 32.2 66 ▪ 14.5 16.1 18 21.2 22 59

22532 NIC P P2 G1.4 1895–1911
Clements, Paul Henry, 1884–.
The Boxer Rebellion: A political and diplomatic review.
New York: Columbia U., Faculty of Political Science, 1915. 243 p. (Columbia studies in history, economics and public law, 66, 3 [whole no. 160]) (Doctoral dissertation in International Law, Columbia U.)
SUBJ 22.2 32.2 66 ▪ 12 25

22533 CSU S P1 G1.2 1842–1895
Cohen, Paul Andrew, 1934–.
'Ch'ing China: Confrontation with the West, 1850–1900.' In *Modern East Asia: Essays in interpretation*, edited by James Buckley Crowley. [Selective entry]
New York: Harcourt, Brace and World, 1970, 29–61.
SUBJ 66 ▪ 32.2 64

22534 CSH P P1 G1.3 1842–1911
Cohen, Paul Andrew, 1934–.
'Missionary approaches: Hudson Taylor and Timothy Richard.'
PC 11 (Dec. 1957), 29–62.
SUBJ 66 ▪ 18 33 56

22535 CSU P P3 G1.5 1842–1895
Cohen, Paul Andrew, 1934–.
'Wang T'ao and incipient Chinese nationalism.'
JAS 26, 4 (Aug. 1967), 559–574.
SUBJ 64 66 ▪ 59 60

22536 MCH P P3 G6.0 1842–1895
Cordier, Henri, 1849–1925.
Les origines de deux établissements français dans l'Extrême-Orient: Chang-hai, Ning-po (The origins of two French settlements in the Far East, Shanghai and Ningpo).
Paris: The author, 1896. 39, 76 p.
SUBJ 66 ▪ 12 14.3

22537 CSU P P1 G1.3 1644–1842
Cranmer-Byng, John, 1919–.
'Lord Macartney's embassy to Peking in 1793.'
JOS 4, 1/2 (1957/58), 117–187.
SUBJ 12 66 ▪ 13 14.3

22538 CSU P P3 G6.1 1842–1895
Cranston, Earl M-, 1895–.
'Shanghai in the Táiping period.'
PHR 5, 2 (May 1936), 147–160.
SUBJ 25 32.2 66

22539 MCH P P2 G6.1 1842–1895
Currie, Blair Crosby, 1930–.
'The Woosung railroad (1872–1877).'

PC 20 (Dec. 1966), 49–85.
SUBJ 12 24.2 66

22540 NIC P P1 G1.2 1842–1911
Curti, Merle Eugene, 1897–, and John Stalker.
'"The Flowery Flag Devils": The American image in China, 1840–1900.'
Proceedings of the American Philosophical Society 96, 6 (20 Dec. 1952), 663–690.
SUBJ 66 ▪ 14.3 33

22541 MCH O P3 G5.1 1895–1911
Delines, Michel.
'Les dames européennes chez l'impératrice de Chine' (The reception of European ladies by the Empress of China).
A travers le monde 9, 19 (9 mai 1903), 145–148; 9, 32 (8 août 1903), 249–251.
SUBJ 48 55 66 ▪ 41 47

22542 CSU O P2 G8.0 1895–1911
Dingle, Edwin John.
Across China on foot: Life in the interior and the reform movement.
New York: Holt, 1911. 16, 446 p. [Reprinted—Taipei: Ch'eng-wen, 1972. 16, 446 p.]
SUBJ 24.2 66 ▪ 22.2 24.6 28 32 47 56 62

22543 MCH P P1 G1.2 1842–1895
Drake, Fred William, 1939–.
'A nineteenth-century view of the United States from Hsü Chi-yü's *Ying-huan chih-lüeh* [Brief survey of the maritime circuit].'
PC 19 (Dec. 1965), 30–54.
SUBJ 66 ▪ 64 70

22544 MCH P P3 G1.2 1644–1842
Duyvendak, Jan Julius Lodewijk, 1889–1954.
'The last Dutch embassy to the Chinese court (1794–95).'
TP 2e série 34, 1/2 (1938), 1–137.
SUBJ 66

22545 MCY P P4 G9.2 1842–1895
Eastman, Lloyd Eric, 1929–.
'The Kwangtung anti-foreign disturbances during the Sino-French War.'
PC 13 (Dec. 1959), 1–31.
SUBJ 25 33 66 ▪ 22.2 26

22546 NIC P P3 G5.1 1842–1895
Fairbank, John King, 1907–.
'Patterns behind the Tientsin Massacre.'
HJAS 20, 3/4 (Dec. 1957), 480–511.
SUBJ 66 ▪ 22

22547 CSU U P1 G1.2 –1911
Fairbank, John King, 1907–.
'A preliminary framework.' In *The Chinese world order: Traditional China's foreign relations*, edited by J. K. Fairbank. [Selective entry]
Cambridge: Harvard U. Press, 1968, 1–19.
SUBJ 66

22548 NIC S P1 G1.2 –1895
Fairbank, John King, 1907–.
'Synarchy under the treaties.' In *Chinese thought and institutions*, edited by J. K. Fairbank. [Selective entry]
Chicago: U. of Chicago Press, 1957, 205–231. [Reprinted in *Readings in modern Chinese history*, edited by Immanuel C. Y. Hsü (Hsü Chung-yüeh). (Selective entry.) New York: Oxford U. Press, 1971, 211–233.]
SUBJ 12 62 66 ▪ 12.1 14.3 14.5 16.1 64

22549 MCH P P1 G1.2 1842–1911
Fairbank, John King, 1907–, and Ssu-yü Teng, 1906–.
'On the Ch'ing tributary system.'
HJAS 6, 2 (June 1941), 135–242. [Reprinted in *Ch'ing administration: Three studies*, by J. K. Fairbank and Ssu-yü Teng. (Analytic entry.) Cambridge: Harvard U. Press, 1960, 107–218. (Harvard-Yenching Institute studies, 19)]
SUBJ 12 66 ▪ 12.2 14.5

22550 CSU P P4 G9.0 1644–1842
Fay, Peter W-.
'The Protestant Mission and the Opium War.'
PHR 40, 2 (May 1971), 145–161.
SUBJ 66 ▪ 33

22551 NNC P P1 G1.2 1644–1911
Franke, Otto, 1863–1946.
'Der chinesische Staatsgedanke und seine Bedeutung für die abendländisch-chinesischen Beziehungen' (The Chinese concept of the state and its significance for relations between China and the West).
Marine-Rundschau 15, 5 (Mai 1904), 515–530. [Reprinted in *Ostasiatische Neubildungen: Beiträge zum Verständnis der politischen und kulturellen Entwicklungs-vorgänge im Fernen Osten* (New forms in East Asia: Toward an understanding of political and cultural developmental processes in the Far East), by O. Franke. (Selective entry.) Hamburg: C. Boysen, 1911, 1–19.]
SUBJ 64 66 ▪ 12 13

22552 NNC S P8 G8.0 –1842
Fried, Morton Herbert, 1923–.
'Land tenure, geography and ecology in the contact of cultures.'
American j. of economics and sociology 11, 4 (July 1952), 391–412.
SUBJ 66 ▪ 11.3 12.1 14.1 14.5

22553 CSU O P2 G1.3 1895–1911
Garnett, W- J-.
Journey through the provinces of Shantung and Kiangsu.
London: His Majesty's Stationery Office, 1907. 26 p. [Report submitted to Parliament: China, 1 (1907)]
SUBJ 24.2 66 ▪ 24.1 24.4 33 55

22554 NNC P P1 G1.2 1842–1895
Gracey, John Talbot, 1831–1912.
'On some causes of the Chinese anti-foreign riots of 1892–1893.'
JAOS 16, 2 (1896), 134–135.
SUBJ 25 66 ▪ 15 32.2 33

22555 CSU O P2 G1.1 –1842
[Gützlaff, Karl Friedrich August] Charles Gutzlaff, 1803–1851.
Journal of three voyages along the coast of China, in 1831, 1832, and 1833, with notices of Siam, Corea, and the Loo-Choo islands.
London: Westley and Davis, 1834. 450 p. [Reprinted—Taipei: Ch'eng-wen, 1968. 450 p.]
SUBJ 14.3 33 66 ▪ 12 15 22 23 29 56 64

22556 MCH PO P2 G1.2 1895–1911
Harfeld, Ferdinand Joseph.
Opinions chinoises sur les barbares d'Occident (Chinese opinions of the barbarians of the West).
Paris: Plon-Nourrit, 1909. 308 p.
SUBJ 32.2 33 50 57 60 66 ▪ 12 14 18 25 43 48 51 55 56

22557 CSU O P3 G9.3 1842–1895
Hartwell, Charles, 1825–1905.
'War and its effects at Foochow.'
CR 16, 2 (Mar. 1885), 88–95.
SUBJ 66 ▪ 22.1 22.2 25

22558 NNC P P2 G1.3 1644–1895
Ho, Pauline Pao-lin.
Kuo Sung-tao, 1818–1891: One Chinese scholar-official's response to the West.
Unpublished masters thesis in Philosophy, Columbia U., 1966. 220 p.
SUBJ 12 16.1 59 60 66 ▪ 14.5 25 32

22559 CBU O P2 G1.1 1644–1842
Holmes, Samuel.
The journal of Mr. Samuel Holmes, serjeant-major of the 11th light dragoons, during his attendance, as one of the guard on Lord Macartney's embassy to China and Tartary, 1792–3.
London: Bulmer, 1798. 256 p.
SUBJ 15 66 ▪ 14.1 16.1 47 55

22560 CSU S P1 G1.1 –1842
Hudson, Geoffrey Francis, 1903–.
'The Jesuits in Peking.' In *Europe and China: A survey of their relations from the earliest times to 1800*, by G. F. Hudson. [Sole entry]
London: Arnold, 1931, 291–329. [Reprinted in *Europe and China: A survey of their relations from the earliest times to 1800*, by G. F. Hudson. (Sole entry.) Boston: Beacon Press, 1961, 291–329.]
SUBJ 66 ▪ 33 64

22561 CSU P P1 G1.1 1842–1895
Hurd, Douglas, 1930–.
The Arrow War: An Anglo-Chinese confusion, 1856–60.
New York: Macmillan, 1967. 254 p.
SUBJ 66 ▪ 14.3 15

22562 DLC O P3 G1.4 1895–1911
IAnchevetskii, Dmitrii Grigor'evich.
U sten nedvizhimago Kitaia: dnevnik korrespondenta 'Novogo kraia' na teatre voennykh deistvii v Kitae v 1900 g. (At the walls of immovable China: Diary of the *Novyi krai* correspondent in the theater of war in China, 1900), 4th ed., rev. and enl.
St. Petersburg: Izd-vo A. Artem'eva, 1903. 12, 619, 12 p.
SUBJ 12 32.2 66 ▪ 13 15 17 23

22563 NNC P P2 G9.2 1644–1842
Ipatova, A- S-.
'Iz istorii osvoboditel'noi bor'by kitaiskogo naroda protiv angliiskikh kolonizatorov v gody pervoi "opiumnoi" voiny' (History of the Chinese people's liberation struggle against the English colonizers during the First Opium War).
KSINA 66 (1963), 59–68.
SUBJ 25 66 ▪ 16.3

22564 NNC P P2 G1.2 1842–1895
Kaliuzhnaia, N- M-.
'Antimissionerskie vystupleniia v Kitae, 1886–1893' (Anti-missionary movements in China, 1886–1893).
KSINA 66 (1963), 69–81.
Subj 22.2 33 66 ▪ 13 63

22565 CSU U P2 G1.2 1644–1895
Kara-Murza, Georgii Sergeevich, 1906–1945, and Grigorii Borisovich Erenburg, 1902–1967.
'Kitai' (China). In *Novaia istoriia stran zarubezhnogo Vostoka* (Modern history of countries of the non-Soviet Orient), edited by Igor Mikhailovich Reisner and Boris Konstantinovich Rubtsov. [Selective entry]
Moscow: Izd-vo Mosk. un-ta, 1952, vol. 1, 473–512.
Subj 15 32.2 66 ▪ 12 16.3 64

22566 MCH P P3 G9.3 1842–1895
Kirby, James Edmund, Jr., 1933–.
'The Foochow anti-missionary riot, August 30, 1878.'
JAS 25, 4 (Aug. 1966), 665–679.
Subj 25 33 66 ▪ 12.2 22.2 62

22567 CSU P P1 G1.1 1644–1911
Koo, Vi Kyuin Wellington (Ku Wei-yüeh), 1888–.
The status of aliens in China.
New York: Columbia U., Faculty of Political Science, 1912. 359 p. (Columbia studies in history, economics and public law, 50, 2 [whole no. 126]) (Doctoral dissertation in International Law, Columbia U.) [Reprinted—New York: AMS Press, 1969. 359 p.]
Subj 12.2 66 ▪ 14.3 14.5

22568 CSB P P3 G1.2 1895–1911
Lee, En-han (Li En-han), 1930–.
China's quest for the recovery of her railway rights, 1904–1911: Economic nationalism in action.
Unpublished doctoral dissertation in History, U. of California, Santa Barbara, 1971. 13, 378 p.
Subj 14 14.2 66 ▪ 12.2 16.1 16.2 34.2

22569 CSU P P2 G1.2 1895–1911
Lee, En-han (Li En-han), 1930–.
'China's response to foreign investment in her mining industry (1902–1911).'
JAS 28, 1 (Nov. 1968), 55–76.
Subj 12 14.4 66 ▪ 16.1

22570 CSU P P3 G8.1 1842–1895
Levering, Miriam Lindsey, 1945–.
'The Chungking riot of 1886: Justice and ideological diversity.'
PC 22A (May 1969), 158–183.
Subj 25 66 ▪ 22 22.2 26.1

22571 CSU P P2 G6.0 1842–1895
Li, Lillian M. (Li Ming-chu), 1943–.
'The Ever-Victorious Army: Sino-Western cooperation in the defense of Shanghai against the Taiping rebels.'
PC 21 (Feb. 1968), 1–42.
Subj 15 32 66 ▪ 25 32.1 32.2

22572 CSU O P2 G1.2 1842–1911
[Lim Boon Keng (Lin Wen-ch'ing)] Wen Ching, pseud., 1869–1957.
The Chinese crisis from within, edited by George M- Reith.
London: Grant Richards, 1901. 354 p. [Reprinted from *Singapore free press* 1900.]
Subj 12 16.1 32.2 60 66 ▪ 13 14.4 15 17 33 64

22573 CSU P P1 G1.2 1842–1895
Litzinger, Charles Albert, 1941–.
'Patterns of missionary cases following the Tientsin Massacre, 1870–1875.'
PC 23 (July 1970), 87–108.
Subj 66 ▪ 22.2 45 52 62

22574 MCH P P2 G1.3 1895–1911
Livshits, S- G-.
'Iz istorii antiimperialisticheskogo dvizheniia v TSentral'nom i IUzhnom Kitae v 1900 godu' (History of the anti-imperialist movement in Central and South China in 1900). [With English abstract]
PV 1960, 4, 93–104.
Subj 12.1 66 ▪ 19

22575 ECU P P1 G1.2 1895–1911
Lo, H. M. (Lo Hui-min), 1924–.
The battle of concessions in China, 1895–1900.
Unpublished doctoral dissertation in History, U. of Cambridge [Emmanuel College], 1957. 390 p.
Subj 14.2 66 ▪ 14.3 14.5 19

22576 CSU O P2 G5.1 1842–1895
Loch, Henry Brougham.
Personal narrative of occurrences during Lord Elgin's second embassy to China in 1860, 3rd ed.
London: Murray, 1900. 12, 185 p.
Subj 15 66

22577 MMT P P2 G5.0 1644–1842
Ma Feng-ch'en.
'Manchu-Chinese social and economic conflicts in early Ch'ing.' Tr. by E-tu Zen Sun and John DeFrancis of 'Ching ch'u Man Han she hui ching chi ch'ung t'u chih i pan'; *Shih huo* (Shanghai) 4, 6 (16 Aug. 1936), 32–39; 4, 8 (16 Sept. 1936), 27–34; 4, 9 (1 Oct. 1936), 16–34. In *Chinese social history: Translations of selected studies*, edited by E-tu Zen Sun (Sun Jen I-tu) and John DeFrancis. [Selective entry]
Washington, D.C.: American Council of Learned Societies, 1956, 333–351. (ACLS, Studies in Chinese and related civilizations, 7) [Reprinted in *Chinese social history: Translations of selected studies*, edited by E-tu Zen Sun and J. DeFrancis. (Selective entry.) New York: Octagon Books, 1966, 333–351.]
Subj 12.1 14.1 16 66 ▪ 12.2 14.3 15 18 21.2 22.2

22578 DLC O P2 G1.1 1644–1842
Macartney, George, 1737–1806.
'A journal of an embassy from the King of Great Britain to the Emperor of China, in the years 1792, 1793, and 1794.' In *Some account of the public life, and a selection from the unpublished writings, of the Earl of Macartney*, by John Barrow. [Sole entry]
London: Cadell and Davies, 1807, vol. 2, 163–531. [Separately reprinted as *An embassy to China: Being the journal kept by Lord Macartney during his embassy to the Emperor Ch'ien-lung, 1793–1794* edited by John Cranmer-Byng. Hamden, Conn.: Archon Books, 1963. 16, 421 p.] [Separately reprinted—St. Clair Shores, Mich.: Scholarly Press, 1972. 16, 421 p.]
Subj 12 13 14.5 16.1 48 66 ▪ 11 12.2 14.2 14.3 15 18 41 47 55 62

22579 CSU S P4 G1.1 1644–1895
McCutcheon, James M-.
'"Tremblingly obey": British and other Western responses to China and the Chinese kowtow.'
Historian 33, 4 (Aug. 1971), 557–577.
Subj 66

22580 FPN PO P2 G1.1 1842–1895
Maison, Emile.
Expédition de Chine (An expedition to China).
Paris: Benjamin Duprat, 1861. 12, 208 p.
Subj 15 60 66 ▪ 12.2 13 14.1 16 16.1 21.3 29 41 47

22581 CSU P P1 G1.2 –1911
Mancall, Mark, 1932–.
'The Ch'ing tribute system: An interpretive essay.' In *The Chinese world order: Traditional China's foreign relations*, edited by John King Fairbank. [Selective entry]
Cambridge: Harvard U. Press, 1968, 63–89.
Subj 66 ▪ 14.3 14.5 64

22582 MCH O P3 G6.1 1842–1895
Maresca, François-Xavier.
'La ville de Changhai au pouvoir des insurgés' (Shanghai under the [Taiping] insurgents).
APF 27 (1855), 278–285.
Subj 21.1 25 66 ▪ 23

22583 MCH PO P4 G5.0 1842–1895
Martin, Charles Ernest, 1831–1897.
'Notes sur le massacre de Tien-tsin' (Notes on the Tientsin Massacre).
R. de l'Extrême-Orient 2 (1887), 89–138.
Subj 33 66 ▪ 25 65

22584 CSU S P2 G1.4 1895–1911
Martin, Christopher.
The Boxer Rebellion.
New York: Abelard Schuman, 1968. 175 p.
Subj 15 25 32.2 66 ▪ 12

22585 NIC P P1 G1.2 –1842
Michael, Franz Henry, 1907–.
The origin of Manchu rule in China: Frontier and bureaucracy as interacting forces in the Chinese empire.
Baltimore: Johns Hopkins Press, 1942. 127 p. [Reprinted—New York: Octagon Books, 1965. 127 p.]
Subj 66 ▪ 12 15 30 64

22586 CSU P P3 G1.1 1842–1895
Michie, Alexander, 1833–1902.
The Englishman in China during the Victorian era, as illustrated in the career of Sir Rutherford Alcock, K.C.B., D.C.L., many years consul and minister in China and Japan.
Edinburgh: William Blackwood, 1900. 2 vols. 12, 442; 510 p. [Reprinted—Taipei: Ch'eng-wen, 1966. 2 vols. 12, 442; 510 p.]
Subj 12 14.3 16.1 66 ▪ 11.2 12.2 14.5 22.2 25

22587 NNC P P3 G1.2 1842–1895
Monina, A- A-.
'Iz istorii Tian'tszin'skikh sobytii 1870 g.' (History of the Tientsin Massacre of 1870).
KSINA 55 (1962), 32–44.
Subj 22.2 66 ▪ 22.1

22588 DLC P P1 G1.1 1842–1895
Monina, A- A-.
'"Missionerskii vopros" v politike tsinskogo pravitel'stva (o memorandume TSunliiamynia ot 9 fevralia 1871 g.)' (The 'missionary question' in Ch'ing government policy: The Tsungli Yamen memorandum of 9 February 1871). In *Man'chzhurskoe vladychestvo v Kitae* (Manchu rule in China), compiled by Institut narodov Azii, Akademiia nauk SSSR, edited by Sergei Leonidovich Tikhvinskii. [Selective entry]
Moscow: Nauka, Glav. red. vost. lit-ry, 1966, 307–318.
Subj 12 13 66 ▪ 16 33

22589 CSH P P2 G6.1 1842–1895
Morse, Hosea Ballou, 1855–1934.
In the days of the Taipings.
Salem, Mass.: Essex Institute, 1927. 12, 434 p.
Subj 25 32.2 66 ▪ 24.6 26.1 26.2 41 59

22590 CSH O P3 G1.3 –1842
Navarrete, Domingo Fernández, 1618–1686.
'Tratado VI' (Book VI). In *Tratados historicos, politicos, ethicos, y religiosos de la monarchia de China* (Historical, political, ethical, and religious works on the Chinese monarchy), by D. F. Navarrete. [Sole entry]
Madrid: Imprenta Real, 1676, 329–429.
'Book VI, The author's travels (1646–1674).' Tr. by J- S- Cummins. [Partial tr.: p. 329–411, 420–429 only; materials from Navarrete's other works added.] In *The 'Travels' and 'Controversies' of Friar Domingo Navarrete, 1618–1686*, edited by J- S- Cummins. [Analytic entry]
Cambridge, Eng.: Hakluyt Society, 1962, vol. 1, 1–163 [s.p.]; vol. 2, 165–475. (HS works, series 2, 118–119) [For an introduction by J- S- Cummins, see entry 22865; an earlier but less accurate English tr. appeared in the 1704, 1732, 1744, and 1752 editions of *A collection of voyages and travels*, compiled and edited by Awnsham Churchill.]
Subj 12.2 14.2 15 21.1 55 66 ▪ 13 14.5 18 32.1 43 47 60

22591 ELO PO P1 G1.2 1842–1895
North-China Daily News with North-China Herald, comps.
Anti-foreign riots in China in 1891.
Shanghai: North-China Herald, 1892. 304 p.
Subj 12.1 25 66 ▪ 32.2 33 64

22592 DLC P P1 G1.5 1644–1895
Novikov, Boris M-.
'Antiman'chzhurskaia propaganda tainykh obshchestv v Kitae v pervoi polovine XIX v.' (Anti-Manchu propaganda of Chinese secret societies in the first half of the nineteenth century). In *Tainye obshchestva v starom Kitae* (Secret societies in old China), compiled by Institut vostokovedeniia, Akademiia nauk SSSR, edited by Vasilii Pavlovich Iliushechkin. [Selective entry]
Moscow: Nauka, Glav. red. vost. lit-ry, 1970, 38–53.
'La propagande antimandchoue de la Triade en Chine pendant la première moitié du XIXe siècle.' In *Mouvements populaires et sociétés secrètes en Chine aux XIXe et XXe siècles* (Popular movements and secret societies in China in the nineteenth and twentieth centuries), edited by Jean Chesneaux, Feiling Blackburn Davis, and Nguyen Nguyet Ho. [Selective entry]
Paris: Maspero, 1970, 133–150.
'The anti-Manchu propaganda of the Triads, ca. 1800–1860' [rev. in tr.]. In *Popular movements and secret societies in China, 1840–1950*, edited by J. Chesneaux. [Analytic entry]
Stanford: Stanford U. Press, 1972, 49–63.
Subj 32.2 65 66 ▪ 25

22593 DCK O P2 G1.1 1842–1895
Nyholm, Johannes, 1863–1936.
'Om aarsagerne til urolighederne i Kina' (The reasons for the riots in China).
Nordisk missions tidsskrift 5 (1894), 135–192.
Subj 32.2 66 ▪ 25 33

22594 CSU O P2 G1.1 1842–1895
Oliphant, Laurence.
Narrative of the Earl of Elgin's mission to China and Japan in the years 1857, '58, '59.
Edinburgh: Blackwood, 1859. 2 vols. 13, 492; 11, 496 p.
Subj 15 25 66 ▪ 12 12.2 14.2 14.3 14.5 16.1 32.2 33 55 57

22595 MCH P P5 G1.2 1842–1895
Paterno, Roberto Montilla, 1936–.
The Yangtze valley anti-missionary riots of 1891.
Unpublished doctoral dissertation in History and Far Eastern Languages, Harvard U., 1967. 2 vols. 712 p. [c.p.].
Subj 22.2 25 32.2 33 66 ▪ 12 12.1 12.2 22 22.1

22596 CSU P P3 G6.0 1842–1895
Paulsen, George Edward, 1923–.
'Machinery for the mills of China, 1882–1896.'
MS 27 (1968), 320–342.
Subj 14.4 66

22597 CSU P P3 G8.1 1842–1895
Paulsen, George Edward, 1923–.
'The Szechwan riots of 1895 and American "missionary diplomacy".'
JAS 28, 2 (Feb. 1969), 285–298.
Subj 66 ▪ 12 22.2 25 33

22598 CSU P P4 G4.5 1644–1842
Petech, Luciano, 1914–.
China and Tibet in the early eighteenth century: History of the establishment of the Chinese protectorate in Tibet, 2nd ed., rev.
Leiden: Brill, 1972. 309 p. (*T'oung pao* monographies, 1)
Subj 12 66

22599 CSU O P2 G1.2 1842–1895
Piasetskii, Pavel IAkovlevich, 1843–?
Puteshestvie po Kitaiu v 1874–1875 cherez Sibir, Mongoliiu, Vostochnyi, Srednii i Severo-Zapadnyi Kitai (A journey to China in 1874–1875, through Siberia, Mongolia, and East, Central, and Northwest China).
St. Petersburg: Tip. M. Stasiulevicha, 1880. 2 vols. 1122 p. [c.p.].
Voyage à travers la Mongolie et la Chine (A journey through Mongolia and China). Tr. by A- Kuscinski. [Abridged tr.]
Paris: Hachette, 1883. 563 p.
Russian travellers in Mongolia and China. Tr. by J- Gordon-Cumming.
London: Chapman and Hall, 1884. 2 vols. 321; 315 p.
Subj 14.2 16.1 29 55 66 ▪ 12.2 14.1 17 22.2 23 24.4 31 47 56 63

22600 ICU P P2 G9.4 1842–1895
Pletcher, Charles Hutchinson.
The Formosan uprisings of 1868.
Unpublished masters thesis in International Relations, U. of Chicago, 1949. 61 p.
Subj 22.2 25 66

22601 CBU O P2 G1.5 1842–1895
Power, William James Tyrone, 1819–?
Recollections of a three years' residence in China . . .
London: Bentley, 1853. 15, 380 p.
Subj 25 31 66 ▪ 22.2 24 26 33 47 55 61 62

22602 MCH P P1 G1.2 1895–1911
Price, Don Cravens, 1937–.
The Chinese intelligentsia's image of Russia, 1896–1911.
Unpublished doctoral dissertation in History, Harvard U., 1967. 526 p.
Subj 14.2 62 66 ▪ 16.1 32.2 59

22603 CSU P P1 G1.3 1644–1842
Pritchard, Earl Hampton, 1907–.
'The kotow in the Macartney embassy to China in 1793.'
FEQ 2, 2 (Feb. 1943), 163–203.
Subj 60 66 ▪ 12

22604 CSH P P3 G1.1 1895–1911
Rankin, Mary Louise Backus, 1934–.
'The Manchurian crisis and radical student nationalism, 1903.'
CSWT 2, 1 (Oct. 1969), 87–106.
Subj 54 64 66 ▪ 17 24.2 32.2

22605 NIC P P2 G1.2 1842–1895
Reid, Gilbert, 1857–1927.
The source of the anti-foreign disturbances in China, with a supplementary account of the uprising of 1900.
Shanghai: North-China Herald, 1903. 155 p.
Subj 32.2 60 66 ▪ 16.1 16.3 22.2 62

22606 CSH P P3 G9.0 1895–1911
Rhoads, Edward John Michael, 1938–.
'Late Ch'ing response to imperialism: The case of Canton.'
CSWT 2, 1 (Oct. 1969), 71–86.
Subj 66 ▪ 36.1 36.2 54

22607 MCH P P2 G9.2 1895–1911
Rhoads, Edward John Michael, 1938–.
'Nationalism and xenophobia in Kwangtung (1905–1906): The Canton anti-American boycott and the Lienchow anti-missionary uprising.'
PC 16 (Dec. 1962), 154–197.
Subj 25 33 66 ▪ 32 34.3 64

22608 CSU P P1 G1.2 1842–1895
Ring, Martin Robert, 1919–.
'The Burgevine case and extrality in China, 1863–1866.'
PC 22A (May 1969), 134–157.
Subj 12.2 66 ▪ 15

22609 ²CSU O P3 G1.2 1644–1842
Ripa, Matteo.
Storia della fondazione della congregazione e del collegio dei Cinesi . . . (An account of the foundation of the Chinese congregation and college).
Naples: ——, 1832. 3 vols.
Memoirs of Father Ripa during 13 years' residence at the court of Peking in the service of the Emperor of China, edited by Fortunato Prandi. Tr. by Fortunato Prandi. [Abridged tr.]
London: Murray, 1844. 160 p.
Subj 66 ▪ 16.1 57

22610 CSU S P3 G5.1 1644–1895
Rockhill, William Woodville, 1854–1914.
'Diplomatic missions to the court of China.'
American historical review 2, 3 (Apr. 1897), 427–442; 2, 4 (July 1897), 627–643.
Subj 66

22611 CSU P P1 G1.1 1644–1842
Rouleau, Francis A-.
'Maillard de Tournon, papal legate at the court of Peking: The first imperial audience (31 December 1705).'
Archivum historicum Societatis Iesu 31 (July.–Dec. 1962), 264–323.
Subj 66

22612 MCH P P2 G5.3 1895–1911
Schrecker, John Ernest, 1937–.
Imperialism and Chinese nationalism: Germany in Shantung.
Cambridge: Harvard U. Press, 1971. 14, 322 p. (Harvard East Asian series, 58) (Revision of *Imperialism contained: German colonialism and Chinese nationalism in Shantung, 1897–1907*, doctoral dissertation in History and Far Eastern Languages, Harvard U., 1968)
Subj 22 24 24.2 24.4 25 66 ▪ 12 17 21.3 22.2 28 34.2

22613 CSH S P1 G1.2 1842–1911
Schrecker, John Ernest, 1937–.
'Late Ch'ing responses to imperialism: Discussants' remarks.'
CSWT 2, 1 (Oct. 1969), 5–16.
Subj 12 66 ▪ 16.2 54

22614 CSU U P3 G1.1 1842–1895
Selby, John.
The paper dragon: An account of the China wars, 1840–1900.
New York: Praeger, 1968. 214 p.
Subj 14.3 66 ▪ 15 32.2

22615 ²CSU O P2 G1.3 1895–1911
Shanghai Mercury, comp.
The Boxer rising: A history of the Boxer trouble in China.
Shanghai: Shanghai Mercury, 1901. 15, 118 p. [Reprinted from *Shanghai mercury* 1900.] [Reprinted—New York: Paragon, 1967. 15, 118 p.]
Subj 32.2 33 66 ▪ 12.2 15 22.2 23 25

22616 MCH P P1 G4.5 1895–1911
Sigel, Louis Tepperman, 1943–.
'Ch'ing Tibetan policy, 1906–1910.'
PC 20 (Dec. 1966), 177–201.
Subj 12 66

22617 CSU PO P2 G5.0 1842–1911
Smith, Arthur Henderson, 1845–1932.
China in convulsion.
Edinburgh: Oliphant, Anderson, and Ferrier, 1901. 2 vols. 770 p. [c.p.]. [Reprinted—New York: AMS Press, 1972. 2 vols. 770 p. (c.p.).]
Subj 25 32.2 66 ▪ 12 14.2 15 56

22618 DLC O P2 G1.1 1842–1895
Spiess, Gustav.
'China, die Philippinen, Siam, Java und Rückreise über Bombay nach Europa' (China, the Philippines, Siam, Java, and the return trip to Europe via Bombay). In *Die preussische Expedition nach Ostasien während der Jahre 1860–62* (The Prussian expedition to East Asia, 1860–1862), by G. Spiess. [Sole entry]
Leipzig: Spamer, 1864, 217–428.
Subj 66 ▪ 14.3 23 24.1 24.2 24.4 25 32.2 33 55 59

22619 CSU PO P2 G1.2 1644–1842
Staunton, George Thomas, 1781–1859.
An authentic account of an embassy from the King of Great Britain to the Emperor of China, Vols. 2–3.
London: Nicol, 1797. 15, 383; 17, 490 p. [Reprinted—New York: AMS Press, 1972. 15, 383; 17, 490 p.]
Subj 14 14.2 16 40 55 66 ▪ 13 14.1 14.6 15 21 21.3 47 56 57 62

22620 DLC U P1 G1.1 –1911
Stolpovskaia, Anna.
Snosheniia kitaitsev s inostrantsami i ikh posledstviia v Kitae (Chinese relations with foreigners and their consequences in China).
Moscow: Pechatnia A. I. Snegirevoi, 1903. 61 p.
Subj 66 ▪ 14.3 17 32.2 63

22621 MCH P P1 G1.2 1644–1911
Swisher, Earl, 1902–.
'Chinese intellectuals and the western impact, 1838–1900.'
CSSH 1, 1 (Oct. 1958), 26–37.
Subj 16.1 62 66 ▪ 12 59

22622 NNC P P3 G9.2 1842–1895
Szcześniak, Boleslaw.
'Pictorials of contempt: A note on the British in mid-nineteenth century Canton.'
MS 15, 2 (1956), 512–515.
Subj 66

22623 NIC P P2 G1.4 1842–1911
Tan, Chester C. (T'an Ch'un-lin).
The Boxer catastrophe.
New York: Columbia U., Faculty of Political Science, 1955. 276 p. (Columbia studies in the social sciences, 583) (Doctoral dissertation in Political Science, Columbia U., 1952) [Reprinted—New York: Octagon Books, 1967. 276 p.]
Subj 22.2 32.2 66 ▪ 12 14 15 18 19 23 33

22624 CSU P P1 G1.1 1842–1895
Tang, E.
'The status in China of Chinese British subjects from the Straits Settlements, 1844–1900.'
Papers on Far Eastern history 3 (Mar. 1971), 189–209.
Subj 66 ▪ 12.2

22625 MCH P P2 G1.2 1895–1911
Tikhvinskii, Sergei Leonidovich, 1918–.
'Dva razlichnykh podkhoda k voprosu o tseliakh reform v Kitae v kontse XIX veka' (Two approaches to the question of the goals of reform in China at the end of the nineteenth century). [With English abstract]
PV 1960, 3, 55–66.
Subj 12 14.5 32 66 ▪ 14.2

22626 CSU P P2 G1.1 1644–1842
Treutlein, Theodore E-.
'Jesuit missions in China during the last years of K'ang Hsi.'
PHR 10, 4 (Dec. 1941), 435–446.
Subj 62 66

22627 CSU S P7 G9.4 –1842
Ts'ao, Yung-ho.
'The acceptance of Western civilization in China: A brief observation in the case of Taiwan, with special emphasis on its interrelation in the settlement of Chinese in Taiwan.'
East Asian cultural studies 6 (Mar. 1967), 55–72.
Subj 24.3 66 ▪ 21.2 24.1

22628 CSU U P3 G1.3 1644–1895
Wakeman, Frederic Evans, Jr., 1937–.
'The opening of China.' In *Modern China: An interpretive anthology*, edited by Joseph Richmond Levenson. [Selective entry]
London: Macmillan, 1971, 147–154.
Subj 62 66 ▪ 16.2 34.2

22629 NIC P P2 G1.1 1644–1842
Waley, Arthur David, 1889–1966.
The Opium War through Chinese eyes.
London: Allen and Unwin, 1958. 257 p. [Reprinted—Stanford: Stanford U. Press, 1968. 257 p.]
Subj 15 66 ▪ 12 12.1 12.2 14.3

22630 MCH P P2 G1.3 1842–1911
Wehrle, Edmund S-, 1930–.
Britain, China and the anti-missionary riots, 1891–1900.
Minneapolis: U. of Minnesota Press, 1966. 12, 223 p.
Subj 33 66

22631 GMS S P1 G1.1 1842–1911
Wertheimer, Fritz.
Deutsche Leistungen und deutsche Aufgaben in China (German accomplishments and projects in China).
Berlin: Springer, 1913. 136 p.
Subj 14 66 ▪ 12 19

22632 MCH P P3 G5.3 1842–1895
West, Philip, 1938–.
'The Tsinan property disputes (1887–1891): Gentry loss and missionary "victory".'
PC 20 (Dec. 1966), 119–143.
Subj 22 26.1 66

22633 CSU P P1 G1.2 –1911
Wiens, Mi Chu (Chü Mi), 1944–.
'Anti-Manchu thought during the early Ch'ing.'
PC 22A (May 1969), 1–24.
Subj 64 66 ▪ 12.1 16.1 32.2

22634 NIC P P1 G1.1 1842–1911
Wilhelm, Hellmut, 1906–.
'The problem of within and without: A Confucian attempt in syncretism.'
J. of the history of ideas 12, 1 (Jan. 1951), 48–60.
Subj 16.1 64 66 ▪ 12 62 70

22635 CSH P P1 G9.0 1644–1842
Williams, Samuel Wells, 1812–1884.
'Origin of the first war with England.' In *The Middle Kingdom: A survey of the geography, government, literature, social life, arts, and history of the Chinese empire and its inhabitants*, rev. and enl. ed., by S. W. Williams. [Selective entry]
New York: Scribner, 1883, vol. 2, 463–513. [Reprinted in *The Middle Kingdom: A survey of the geography, government, literature, social life, arts, and history of the Chinese empire and its inhabitants*, by S. W. Williams. (Selective entry.) Taipei: Ch'eng-wen, 1965, 463–513 (s.p.)]
Subj 66 ▪ 22.2 25

22636 CSU P P1 G1.2 –1842
Wong, George H. C. (Huang Tao-chang), 1924–.
'China's opposition to western science during late Ming and early Ch'ing.'
Isis 54, 175 (Mar. 1963), 29–49. [For a fuller version, see entry 22637.]
Subj 62 66 ▪ 16.1

22637 MAM P P1 G1.1 –1842
Wong, George H. C. (Huang Tao-chang), 1924–.
China's oppositions to western religion and science during late Ming and early Ch'ing.
Ann Arbor: University Microfilms (Publ. 58-7381), 1958. 223 p. (Doctoral dissertation in History, U. of Washington)
Subj 13 16.1 62 66 ▪ 33 64 70

22638 MCH O P1 G1.1 1644–1895
Wu, Ting-fang, 1842–1922.
'The causes of the unpopularity of the foreigner in China.'
AAAPSS 17, 1 (Jan. 1901), 1–14.
Subj 66

22639 CSU P P1 G1.2 –1911
Yang, Lien-sheng, 1914–.
'Historical notes on the Chinese world order.' In *The Chinese world order: Traditional China's foreign relations*, edited by John King Fairbank. [Selective entry]
Cambridge: Harvard U. Press, 1968, 20–33.
Subj 66 ▪ 15 40 64

22640 MCY P P1 G1.1 –1842
Yang, Lien-sheng, 1914–.
'Hostages in Chinese history.'
HJAS 15, 3/4 (Dec. 1952), 507–521. [Reprinted in *Studies in Chinese institutional history*, by Lien-sheng Yang. (Selective entry.) Cambridge: Harvard U. Press, 1961, 43–57. (Harvard-Yenching Institute studies, 20)]
Subj 16 66 ▪ 12 64

22641 CSU P P2 G1.3 1842–1895
Yuan Chung Teng.
'American China-trade, American-Chinese relations and the Taiping Rebellion, 1853–1858.'
J. of Asian history 3, 2 (1969), 93–117.
Subj 32.2 66 ▪ 14.5 14.6 15 25

22642 CSU P P4 G4.3 1842–1895
Yuan, Tsing.
'Yakub Beg (1820–1877) and the Moslem rebellion in Chinese Turkestan.'
Central Asiatic j. 6, 2 (1961), 134–167.
Subj 15 25 66 ▪ 12

1644-1949

22643 CSH S P1 G1.2 1895–1928
Arkus, R- S-.
'Inostrannye kapitaly' (Foreign capital). In *O Kitae: politiko-ekonomicheskii sbornik* (Articles on China's political economy), edited by [Solomon Abramovich Dridzo] A. Lozovskii, pseud. [Selective entry]
Moscow: Gosizdat, 1928, 177–199.
Subj 14.3 14.6 66 ▪ 14.2 14.4

22644 NNC O P2 G1.2 1895–1928
Barnes, George G-.
Enter China! A study in race contacts.
London: Edinburgh House Press, 1928. 168 p.
Subj 10 12 14 17 40 66 ▪ 16 19 32.2 54 55 56 60

22645 ICU S P1 G1.1 –1949
Brown, Bernice, 1903–.
The policy of the Chinese government toward the Mongols.
Unpublished masters thesis in International Relations, U. of Chicago, 1938. 59 p.
Subj 12.1 66

22646 MAM P P2 G9.4 1895–1949
Chen, Edward I-te (Chen I-te), 1930–.
Japanese colonialism in Korea and Formosa: A comparison of its effects upon the development of nationalism.
Ann Arbor: University Microfilms (Publ. 69-76), 1969. 376 p. (Doctoral dissertation in Political Science, U. of Pennsylvania, 1968)
Subj 12.1 66 ▪ 12 14 32.2 64

22647 MAM P P1 G9.1 –1949
Cushman, Richard David.
Rebel haunts and lotus huts: Problems in the ethnohistory of the Yao.
Ann Arbor: University Microfilms (Publ. 71-1051), 1971. 567 p. (Doctoral dissertation in Anthropology, Cornell U., 1970)
Subj 66 ▪ 72

22648 CSU PO P2 G1.2 1895–1949
Davies, John Paton, 1908–.
Dragon by the tail: American, British, Japanese, and Russian encounters with China and one another.
New York: Norton, 1972. 448 p.
Subj 10 32.2 66 ▪ 12 15 16 32 59 64

22649 MCH P P1 G1.2 –1949
Dubs, Homer Hasenpflug, 1892–1969.
'The concept of unity in China.' In *The quest for political unity in world history*, edited by Stanley Pargellis. [Sole entry]
Washington, D.C.: U.S. Government Printing Office, 1944, 3–19. (American Historical Assn. annual reports, 1942)
Subj 29 64 66 ▪ 12 62

22650 MCH P P3 G1.1 1842–1928
Escarra, Jean, 1885–1955.
Droits et intérêts étrangers en Chine (Foreign rights and interests in China).
Paris: Lib. du Recueil Sirey, 1928. 88 p.
Subj 12.2 14 14.4 14.6 66 ▪ 12 14.3 15

22651 CSH S P2 G1.1 1842–1949
Esherick, Joseph Wharton, 1942–.
'Harvard on China: The apologetics of imperialism.'
BCAS 4, 4 (Dec. 1972), 9–16.
Subj 14 66 71 ▪ 12 14.4 19 24.4

22652 MCH P P3 G1.1 1842–1928
Ferguson, Jan Willem Helenus.
De rechtspositie van Nederlanders in China (The legal status of the Dutch in China).
The Hague: ——, 1925. 14, 298 p.
Subj 12.2 66 ▪ 14.3 14.5 14.6 72

22653 CSU S P1 G1.2 –1949
Franke, Wolfgang, 1912–.
China und das Abendland.
Göttingen: Vandenhoeck und Ruprecht, 1962. 140 p.

China and the West. Tr. by R- A- Wilson.
Columbia: U. of South Carolina Press, 1967. 165 p.
Subj 66 ▪ 19

22654 CSU P P2 G2.0 1842–1949
Fulton, Austin.
Through earthquake, wind and fire: Church and mission in Manchuria, 1867–1950.
Edinburgh: St. Andrew Press, 1967. 22, 416 p.
Subj 32.1 33 66 ▪ 17 22.2 28

22655 ELO O P3 G1.2 1895–1949
Hewlett, William Meyrick, 1876–1944.
Forty years in China.
London: Macmillan, 1943. 261 p.
Subj 12 16 25 32.2 66 ▪ 15 18 21.2 23 38 61 63

22656 CSU U P1 G1.2 –1949
Howard, Harry Paxton, 1893–.
'Chinese cosmopolitanism and modern nationalism.'
THM 6, 5 (May 1938), 425–439.
Subj 29 64 66 ▪ 14.2 32 32.2

22657 MCH S P1 G1.1 1842–1928
Hu Sheng.
Imperialism and Chinese politics, 1840–1925. Tr. of *Ti kuo chu i yü Chung-kuo cheng chih*, rev. ed.; Peking: Jen min ch'u pan she, 1952; 222 p.
Peking: Foreign Languages Press, 1955. 308 p. [Reprinted—Westport, Conn.: Hyperion Press, 197? 308 p.]
Subj 12 66 ▪ 15 16.1 32 54

22658 MCH S P1 G1.2 1644–1928
Hughes, Ernest Richard, 1883–1956.
The invasion of China by the western world.
London: A. and C. Black, 1937. 16, 323 p. [Reprinted—New York: Macmillan, 1938. 16, 323 p.] [Reprinted—New York: Barnes and Noble, 1967. 16, 318 p.]
SUBJ 12 66 ▪ 12.1 16 16.1 23

22659 MCH U P1 G1.2 –1949
Lattimore, Owen, 1900–.
'China and the barbarians.' In *Empire in the East*, edited by Joseph Barnes. [Sole entry]
New York: Doubleday, Doran, 1934, 3–36.
SUBJ 66

22660 NIC PO P2 G1.4 –1949
Lattimore, Owen, 1900–.
Inner Asian frontiers of China, 2nd ed.
New York: American Geographical Society, 1951. 61, 585 p. (AGS research series, 21)
SUBJ 11.2 11.3 12.1 14 29 66 ▪ 15 16 21 70 71

22661 DLC U P2 G1.2 1895–1928
Levenson, Joseph Richmond, 1920–1969.
'The province, the nation and the world: The problem of Chinese identity.' In *Approaches to modern Chinese history*, edited by Albert Feuerwerker et al. [Selective entry]
Berkeley, Los Angeles: U. of California Press, 1967, 268–288. [Reprinted in *Modern China: An interpretive anthology*, edited by J. R. Levenson. (Selective entry.) London: Macmillan, 1971, 53–68.]
SUBJ 29 62 66 ▪ 65

22662 CSH U P1 G3.0 –1949
Lo, J. P. (Lo Jung-pang), 1912–, and Robert James Miller, 1923–.
'Historical setting.' In *A regional handbook on the Inner Mongolia Autonomous Region*, compiled by Far Eastern and Russian Institute, U. of Washington. [Selective entry]
New Haven: Human Relations Area Files, 1956, 32–75. (HRAF subcontractor's monographs, 60; Washington 7)
SUBJ 32.2 66 ▪ 12.1 21.2

22663 CSU S P2 G1.2 1842–1928
Lockwood, William Wirt, 1906–.
'Japan's response to the West: The contrast with China.'
WP 9, 1 (Oct. 1956), 37–54.
SUBJ 10 66 ▪ 16.1 16.2

22664 ELS P P4 G1.5 1895–1928
Marchant, Leslie Ronald, 1924–.
Anglo-Chinese relations in the provinces of the West River and the Yangtze river basins, 1889–1900.
Unpublished masters thesis in History, U. of London [School of Oriental and African Studies], 1965. 265 p.
SUBJ 12 66 ▪ 14.3 25

22665 CSH S P2 G1.1 1842–1949
Nathan, Andrew James, 1943–.
'Imperialism's effects on China.'
BCAS 4, 4 (Dec. 1972), 3–8.
SUBJ 14 32.2 66 ▪ 14.4 18 24.4

22666 CBU S P2 G1.1 1644–1949
Pélissier, Roger, 1924–1972.
La Chine entre en scène (de 1839 à nos jours) (China enters the scene, 1839 to the present).
Paris: Juillard, 1963. 411 p.
The awakening of China, 1793–1949. Tr. by Martin Kieffer, edited by Martin Kieffer.
London: Secker and Warburg, 1967. 532 p.
SUBJ 15 32.2 61 66 ▪ 12.2 14.3 16.1 18 32 47

22667 MAM P P1 G1.2 1895–1949
Quale, Gladys Robina, 1931–.
The mission compound in modern China: The role of the United States Protestant Mission as an asylum in the civil and international strife of China, 1900–1941.
Ann Arbor: University Microfilms (Publ. 58-2453), 1958. 311 p. (Doctoral dissertation in History, U. of Michigan)
SUBJ 12.1 22.2 33 66 ▪ 12.2 32.2 61

22668 CSU P P1 G1.2 1895–1949
Schwartz, Benjamin Isadore, 1916–.
'Ch'en Tu-hsiu and the acceptance of the modern West.'
J. of the history of ideas 12, 1 (Jan. 1951), 61–72.
SUBJ 16.1 66 ▪ 59 62 64

22669 MCH S P1 G1.2 –1928
Soothill, William Edward, 1861–1935.
China and the West: A sketch of their intercourse.
London: Oxford U. Press, 1925. 216 p.
SUBJ 66 ▪ 12 14.3 15 22.2 25

22670 CSU U P1 G9.5 1842–1928
Su, Chung-jen.
'China's assimilation of Western cultures through Hong Kong.'
East Asian cultural studies 6 (Mar. 1967), 73–81.
SUBJ 66 ▪ 14.2 16.1 17

22671 TPY U P1 G1.2 1644–1949
Tang Chun-I (T'ang Chün-i).
'On the mental attitude of China and the West in seeking mutual understanding.'
West and East 1, 2 (Nov. 1956), 4–9; 1, 3 (Dec. 1956), 9–13.
SUBJ 66

22672 MAM P P1 G1.1 1895–1949
Tao, Chia-lin Pao, 1939–.
The role of Wang Ching-wei during the Sino-Japanese War.
Ann Arbor: University Microfilms (Publ. 72-13,139), 1972. 212 p. (Doctoral dissertation in History, Indiana U., 1971)
SUBJ 12 32 59 66 ▪ 16.1 32.2

22673 MBJ P P4 G1.2 1895–1928
Tsü, Kwoh-mo (Hsü Kuo-mou), 1905–.
Leased areas and concessions in China, with special reference to their retrocession.
Unpublished doctoral dissertation in Political Science, Johns Hopkins U., 1932. 191 p.
SUBJ 22 66 ▪ 22.2 24 24.2 24.4 24.5

22674 ELS P P1 G1.2 1842–1949
Wu, Hei Tak (Hu Hsing-te).
The treatment of Europe in Chinese school text-books.
Unpublished masters thesis in Education, U. of London [Institute of Education], 1949. 259 p.
SUBJ 66 ▪ 17 62

22675 MCY P P1 G1.2 1644–1928
Wu, Hung-chu.
'China's attitude towards foreign nations and nationals historically considered.'
CSPSR 10, 1 (Jan. 1926), 13–45.
SUBJ 66 ▪ 12 17 19 60 72

22676 NNM O P1 G1.2 1895–1928
Wu Lien-teh (Wu Lien-te), 1879–1960.
'A Chinese view of the missionaries.'
CR 51, 1 (Jan. 1920), 9–12.
SUBJ 66 ▪ 17

1911-1949

22677 CSU O P2 G8.1 1928–1949
Barnett, Arthur Doak, 1921–.
'Tibetan border region' [report to Institute of Current World Affairs, July 1948]. In *China on the eve of Communist takeover*, by A. D. Barnett. [Selective entry]
New York: Praeger, 1963, 215–229.
SUBJ 22 66 ▪ 24 25

22678 MCH O P3 G9.2 1911–1928
Bell, Francis Hayley.
'The Canton tragedy.'
Blackwood's magazine 238, 1438 (Aug. 1935), 145–167.
SUBJ 22.2 66 ▪ 14.3 15 32 36.4

22679 CSH S P2 G1.2 1911–1949
Bland, John Otway Percy, 1863–1945.
China: The pity of it.
London: Heinemann, 1932. 358 p.
SUBJ 16.1 17 60 66 ▪ 32.2 64 65 70 71

22680 CSH O P3 G1.3 1911–1928
Borodina, Fania S-.
V zastenkakh kitaiskikh satrapov: moi vospominaniia (In the prisons of the Chinese satraps: My reminiscences).
Moscow: Gosizdat, 1928. 216 p.
SUBJ 12 66 ▪ 12.1 15 16.1 22 22.2

22681 MCH FP P3 G1.1 1928–1949
Bunker, Gerald Edward, 1938–.
The peace conspiracy: Wang Ching-wei and the China War, 1937–1941.
Cambridge: Harvard U. Press, 1972. 327 p. (Harvard East Asian series, 67) (Revision of *A political tragedy: The story of Wang Ching-wei's peace movement*, doctoral dissertation in History and Far Eastern Languages, Harvard U., 1969)
SUBJ 12 32 66 ▪ 14.6 15 22 22.2 32.2 59

22682 MCH O P2 G4.0 1911–1949
Ekvall, Robert Brainerd, 1898–.
Cultural relations on the Kansu-Tibetan border.
Chicago: U. of Chicago Press, 1939. 13, 87 p. (U. of Chicago, Publications in Anthropology, occasional papers, 1)
SUBJ 23 33 40 44 66 ▪ 21.2 21.4 22 34.2 55 58

22683 CSU S P2 G1.3 1928–1949
Engelhardt, Tom.
'Long day's journey: American observers in China, 1948–50.' In *China and ourselves: Explorations and revisions by a new generation*, edited by Bruce Douglass and Ross Terrill. [Selective entry]
Boston: Beacon Press, 1969, 90–121.
Subj 19 66 ▪ 32 32.2

22684 CSU P P1 G1.3 1911–1928
Fass, Josef.
'Sun Yat-sen and the World War I.'
AO 35, 1 (1967), 111–120.
Subj 16.1 66 ▪ 32

22685 MCH P P1 G1.2 1911–1928
Ferguson, Thomas T- H-.
'Het moderne Chineesche nationalisme, echt en onecht' (Modern Chinese nationalism, genuine and artificial).
China (Amsterdam) 3 (Augustus–September 1928), 187–202.
Subj 66 ▪ 64

22686 CSU U P1 G1.2 1911–1949
Gillin, Donald George, 1930–.
'China and the foreigner, 1911–1950.'
South Atlantic q. 68, 2 (Spring 1969), 208–219.
Subj 66 ▪ 15 32.2

22687 CSH PO P4 G1.2 1928–1949
Gins, Georgii Konstantinovich (George Constantine Guins), 1887–.
'Inostrannye tovarishchestva v Kitae' (Foreign companies in China). [With English abstract]
VM 1930, 6, 67–73. [Reprinted in *Ocherki torgovogo prava Kitaia, vypusk 1-i, torgovye tovarishchestva* (Notes on Chinese commercial law, Vol. 1, Trading companies), by G. K. Gins. (Selective entry.) Harbin: Tip. L. M. Abramovicha, 1930, 69–87.]
Subj 12.2 66

22688 NNC S P1 G1.2 1928–1949
Griggs, David Thurston, 1916–.
Americans in China: Some Chinese views.
Washington, D.C.: Foundation for Foreign Affairs, 1948. 59 p. (FFA pamphlets, 5)
Subj 66 ▪ 12.1 19 32

22689 MCH P P1 G1.2 1911–1928
Griggs, David Thurston, 1916–.
The anti-imperialist theme in Chinese nationalism, 1919–1926.
Unpublished doctoral dissertation in History, Harvard U., 1952. 510, 35 p.
Subj 12 32 64 66 ▪ 12.1 16.1 32.2 60

22690 CSU P P3 G1.1 1911–1928
Hay, Stephen Northrup, 1925–.
'Chinese views of Tagore's message.' In *Asian ideas of East and West: Tagore and his critics in Japan, China, and India*, by S. N. Hay. [Selective entry]
Cambridge: Harvard U. Press, 1970, 186–245. (Harvard East Asian series, 40)
Subj 16.1 60 66 ▪ 14.2 32.2 54 64

22691 CSU P P3 G1.3 1911–1928
Hay, Stephen Northrup, 1925–.
'"The representative of Asia" visits China.' In *Asian ideas of East and West: Tagore and his critics in Japan, China, and India*, by S. N. Hay. [Selective entry]
Cambridge: Harvard U. Press, 1970, 146–185. (Harvard East Asian series, 40)
Subj 66 ▪ 16.1 60

22692 NNC O P1 G1.2 1911–1949
Herald of Asia, comp.
The origin and history of the anti-Japanese movement in China.
Tokyo: Herald Press, 1932. 102 p. (Herald of Asia library of contemporary history, 7)
Subj 66

22693 DCK O P2 G2.0 1928–1949
Høgsgaard, Jens Lind, 1899–.
'Manchuriet under besættelse og borgerkrig' (Manchuria during the occupation and civil war).
Nordisk missions tidsskrift 67 (1956), 5–18.
Subj 61 66 ▪ 12 15 17 21.2 24.1 25

22694 CSH O P3 G1.1 1911–1949
Hussey, Harry, 1881–.
My pleasures and palaces: An informal memoir of forty years in modern China.
Garden City, N.Y.: Doubleday, 1968. 384 p.
Subj 16.1 50 55 66 ▪ 14.2 14.4 15 18 25 32.2 33 48 57

22695 NNC P P2 G1.4 1928–1949
Iliushechkin, Vasilii Pavlovich, 1915–.
'Sian'skie sobytiia 12 dekabria 1936 g.' (The Sian Incident, 12 December 1936).
KSIV 11 (1954), 44–56.
Subj 15 32 32.2 54 66 ▪ 12

22696 DLC O P3 G6.1 1911–1928
İlkul, Ahmet Kemal.
Şanghay hatıraları (Memoirs of Shanghai).
Istanbul: Kadar Basımevi, 1939. 116 p.
Subj 33 66 ▪ 14.3 26.1 29 32.2

22697 NNC U P2 G1.2 1928–1949
Lasswell, Harold Dwight, 1902–.
'Chinese resistance to Japanese invasion: The predictive value of precrisis symbols.'
AJS 43, 5 (Mar. 1938), 704–716.
Subj 15 66

22698 NIC O P2 G4.3 1911–1928
Lattimore, Owen, 1900–.
'The Chinese as a dominant race.'
J. of the Royal Central Asian Society 15, 3 (1928), 278–300.
Subj 12.1 14 66 ▪ 12 12.2 14.6

22699 CSU P P3 G1.2 1928–1949
Liang, Chin-tung (Liang Ching-tun), 1890–.
The sinister face of the Mukden Incident.
New York: St. John's U. Press, 1969. 11, 188 p.
Subj 32 32.2 66 ▪ 15 54

22700 NNC P P3 G1.2 1911–1928
Monina, A- A-.
'Kampaniia boikota iaponskikh tovarov v 1915 g.' (The campaign to boycott Japanese goods in 1915).
KSINA 66 (1963), 117–125.
Subj 22.2 66 ▪ 14.3 22.1

22701 DLC U P2 G4.3 1928–1949
Nemchenko, M-.
'Kolonial'nyi rezhim i agrarnye otnosheniia v Sin'tsziane' (China's colonial regime in Sinkiang and agrarian relations).
PK 8/9 (1931), 181–190.
Subj 14.5 21.3 66 ▪ 24.1 29

22702 NNC P P1 G1.2 1928–1949
Nikiforov, Vladimir Nikolaevich, 1920–.
'IAponskaia agressiia v Kitae v 1931–1935 gg. i predatel'skaia politika Gomin'dana, 18 sentiabria 1931 – 9 dekabria 1935 g.' (Japanese aggression in China, 1931–1935, and the treacherous policies of the Kuomintang, 18 September 1931 – 9 December 1935).
KSIV 5 (1952), 17–36.
Subj 12 32.2 66 ▪ 12.1 15 32

22703 NNC PO P1 G1.2 1928–1949
Nikiforov, Vladimir Nikolaevich, 1920–.
'Predatel'skaia politika kliki Chan Kai-shi na pervom etape antiiaponskoi voiny (1937–1938)' (The treacherous policy of the Chiang Kai-shek clique during the first stage of the Anti-Japanese War, 1937–1938).
UZIV 3 (1951), 32–61.
Subj 12 32.2 66 ▪ 12.1

22704 CSU O P3 G5.1 1928–1949
Oliver, Frank.
'Unconquerable Peking.'
Asia (New York: American Asiatic Assn.) 40, 5 (May 1940), 235–237.
Subj 20 66 ▪ 22 24.3 47

22705 MCH U P1 G1.1 1911–1928
Orchard, Dorothy Johnson, 1897–.
'China's use of the boycott as a political weapon.'
AAAPSS 152 (Nov. 1930), 252–261. [Special issue: *China*, edited by Henry F- James]
Subj 14.3 66

22706 ICU O P6 G5.1 1911–1949
Regier, Marie Joanna.
Cultural interpenetration in a local community in China.
Unpublished masters thesis in Divinity, U. of Chicago, 1936. 128 p.
Subj 20 23 66 ▪ 17 33 50 53 55

22707 MCH P P3 G9.2 1911–1928
Rhoads, Edward John Michael, 1938–.
'Lingnan's response to the rise of Chinese nationalism: The Shakee Incident (1925).'
PC 15 (Dec. 1961), 115–146. [Reprinted in *American missionaries in China: Papers from Harvard seminars*, edited by Kwang-ching Liu (Liu Kuang-ching). (Analytic entry.) Cambridge: Harvard U., East Asian Research Center, 1966, 183–216. (Harvard East Asian monographs, 21)]
Subj 17 33 66 ▪ 64

22708 MCH O P3 G1.3 1911–1928
Rodes, Jean.
A travers la Chine actuelle (Through China today).
Paris: Eugène Fasquelle, 1932. 194 p.
Subj 12 19 32.2 64 66 ▪ 14.5 15 17 25 47 53 59

22709 CSU P P1 G1.2 1928–1949
Shewmaker, Kenneth Earl, 1936–.
'The Mandate of Heaven vs. U.S. newsmen in China, 1941–45.'
Journalism q. 46, 2 (Summer 1969), 274–280.
SUBJ 66

22710 CSU O P2 G1.2 1928–1949
Snow, Edgar, 1905–1972.
Far Eastern front.
New York: Smith and Haas, 1933. 336 p.
SUBJ 15 66 ▪ 11.2 16.1 18 22.2 25 32 32.2 59

22711 ELO P P1 G1.2 1928–1949
[Sokokusha].
Anti-foreign teachings in new text-books of China.
Tokyo: Sokokusha, 1931. 109, 72 p.
SUBJ 17 66 ▪ 19 54

22712 CSH O P7 G5.4 1928–1949
Suigo, Carlo.
Nella terra di Mao-Tse-tung.
Rome: L'Arnia, 1951. 574 p.

In the land of Mao Tse-tung, edited by Clifford Witting. Tr. by Muriel Currey.
London: Allen and Unwin, 1953. 312 p.
SUBJ 12.1 32.2 66 ▪ 12.2 15 47 54

22713 MCH F P5 G3.1 1928–1949
Sun, E-tu Zen (Sun Jen I-tu), 1921–.
'Results of culture contact in two Mongol-Chinese communities.'
Southwestern j. of anthropology 8, 2 (Summer 1952), 182–210.
SUBJ 20 40 66 ▪ 24 50

22714 CSU P P2 G1.2 1928–1949
Thomson, James Claude, Jr., 1931–.
While China faced West: American reformers in Nationalist China, 1928–1937.
Cambridge: Harvard U. Press, 1969. 15, 310 p. (Harvard East Asian series, 38) (Revision of *Americans as reformers in Kuomintang China, 1928–1937*, doctoral dissertation in History, Harvard U., 1961)
SUBJ 12 18 33 37 38 66 ▪ 14 14.1 16.1 17 19 32 32.1 32.2 64

22715 CSU S P2 G1.4 1928–1949
Tozer, Warren Wilson, 1933–.
'The foreign correspondents' visit to Yenan in 1944: A reassessment.'
PHR 41, 2 (May 1972), 207–224.
SUBJ 14 18 32.2 66 ▪ 15 22 64

22716 CSU P P3 G6.1 1928–1949
Treat, Payson Jackson, 1879–.
'Shanghai, January 28, 1932.'
PHR 9, 3 (Sept. 1940), 337–343.
SUBJ 25 66

22717 CSU P P2 G1.2 1911–1949
Vincent, John Carter.
The extraterritorial system in China: Final phase.
Cambridge: Harvard U., East Asian Research Center, 1970. 119 p. (Harvard East Asian monographs, 30)
SUBJ 66 ▪ 12 12.2 14.5 17 32.2

22718 DLC U P1 G2.0 1928–1949
Voitinskii, Grigorii Naumovich, 1893–1956, ed.
Okkupatsiia Man'chzhurii i bor'ba kitaiskogo naroda (The occupation of Manchuria and the struggle of the Chinese people).
Moscow: Sotsekgiz, 1937. 148 p.
SUBJ 14 32.2 66 ▪ 12 15 18 21.2

22719 CSH O P3 G2.0 1928–1949
Zalesskii, B-.
Manchzhurskie zapiski (Notes from Manchuria).
Leningrad: Izd-vo pisatelei v Leningrade, 1932. 123 p.
SUBJ 66 ▪ 15 33 60

22720 DLC PO P3 G1.1 1928–1949
Zaporozhskii, F-.
IAnki v Kitae: putevye ocherki (Yankees in China: Travel notes).
Moscow: Sovetskii pisatel', 1949. 149 p.
SUBJ 18 21.3 66 ▪ 12.2 14.2 14.4 14.6 15 17 32 33

22721 NNC P P2 G1.2 1928–1949
Ziuzin, A-.
'Osvoboditel'naia bor'ba kitaiskogo naroda v tylu iaponskikh zakhvatchikov' (The liberation struggle of the Chinese people behind the Japanese lines).
MKhMP 1939, 2 (fevral'), 88–104.
SUBJ 15 20 25 66 ▪ 12 32.2

22722 NNC P P2 G1.2 1928–1949
Ziuzin, A-.
'Polozhenie v okkupirovannykh raionakh Kitaia' (The situation in the occupied regions of China).
MKhMP 1938, 6 (iiun'), 52–70.
SUBJ 12 15 66 ▪ 12.1 14

1911-1972
(including 1644-1972)

22723 CSU O P4 G9.5 1644–1972
Banks, Mike.
'Europe's side-door to China [Macau].'
GM 39, 11 (Mar. 1967), 887–898.
SUBJ 14.3 66 ▪ 11.2

22724 MCH P P2 G9.5 1928–1972
Catron, Gary Wayne, 1944–.
China and Hong Kong, 1945–1967.
Unpublished doctoral dissertation in Political Science, Harvard U., 1971. 353 p.
SUBJ 14.3 24.2 25 32.2 36.4 66 ▪ 17 21.2 22 22.1 24.1 24.6 26.1 26.2 27 54

22725 MCH P P1 G1.2 1895–1972
Ch'en, Jerome (Ch'en Chih-jang), 1919–.
'China's conception of her place in the world.'
Political q. 35, 3 (July–Sept. 1964), 260–269.
SUBJ 66 ▪ 12

22726 CSU S P3 G1.2 1644–1972
Cranmer-Byng, John, 1919–.
'The Chinese attitude towards external relations.'
International j. 21, 1 (Winter 1965/66), 57–77.
SUBJ 60 66 ▪ 62 64

22727 MCH P P1 G1.2 1842–1972
Franke, Wolfgang, 1912–.
'Zur anti-imperialistischen Bewegung in China' (The anti-imperialist movement in China).
Saeculum 5, 4 (1954), 337–358. [Reprinted—*Aus Politik und Zeitgeschichte* 1955, 20, 311–320. (Supplement to *Das Parlament*)]
SUBJ 66 ▪ 33 61 64

22728 CSU O P2 G1.1 1928–1972
Frillman, Paul, 1911–, and Graham Peck, 1914–.
China: The remembered life.
Boston: Houghton Mifflin, 1968. 17, 291 p.
SUBJ 15 66 ▪ 14.2 16.1 22.2 32.2

22729 CSU P P1 G1.2 1928–1972
Gittings, John, 1938–.
'A shameful tale.' [Review of *Dragon by the tail: American, British, Japanese, and Russian encounters with China and one another*, by John Paton Davies.]
NYRB 19, 8 (16 Nov. 1972), 7–12.
SUBJ 32.2 66

22730 GMS P P1 G1.1 1842–1972
Kuo, Heng-yü, 1930–.
China und die "Barbaren" (China and the 'barbarians').
Pfullingen: Neske, 1967. 247 p.
SUBJ 66 ▪ 19

22731 CSU S P1 G1.2 –1972
Lamb, Alastair, 1930–.
Asian frontiers: Studies in a continuing problem.
New York: Praeger, 1968. 246 p.
SUBJ 66

22732 MCY FP P2 G4.3 –1972
Lattimore, Owen, 1900–.
Pivot of Asia: Sinkiang and the Inner Asian frontiers of China and Russia.
Boston: Little, Brown, 1950. 12, 288 p. [Reprinted—New York: AMS Press, 1973. 12, 288 p.]
SUBJ 11.3 12 14.6 66 ▪ 12.1 14.3 15 21 22.2 24.1

22733 CSH P P3 G9.5 1842–1972
Lo Hsiang-lin, 1905–.
Hong Kong and Western cultures. Tr. of *Hsiang-kang yü Chung hsi wen hua chih chiao liu* (The role of Hong Kong in cultural exchange between China and the West); Hong Kong: Chung-kuo hsüeh she, 1961; 266 p.
Tokyo: Centre for East Asian Cultural Studies; Honolulu: East-West Center Press, 1964. 289, 56 p. [Also published as *The role of Hong Kong in the cultural interchange between East and West*; Tokyo: Centre for East Asian Cultural Studies, 1963; 2 vols; 289, 50 p. (c.p.).]
SUBJ 26.1 50 66 ▪ 17 33 57 62 71

22734 NNC O P2 G1.2 1911–1972
Mehnert, Klaus, 1906–.
Peking und Moskau.
Stuttgart: Deutsche Verlags-Anstalt, 1962. 605 p.

Peking and Moscow. Tr. by Leila Vennewitz.
New York: Putnam, 1963. 14, 522 p.
SUBJ 10 12 16 32.2 66 ▪ 32 64

22735 CSH S P2 G9.4 1644–1972
Meisner, Maurice J-, 1931–.
'The development of Formosan nationalism.'
CQ 15 (July–Sept. 1963), 91–106. [Reprinted in *Formosa today*, edited by

Mark Mancall. (Selective entry.) New York: Praeger, 1964, 147–162.]
SUBJ 16 64 66 ▪ 12.1 22.2 29

22736 CSU PO P2 G9.5 1842–1972
Pope-Hennessy, James.
Half-crown colony: A historical profile of Hong Kong.
Boston: Little, Brown, 1969. 150 p.
SUBJ 22.2 28 66 ▪ 17 23 25 55 56 57

22737 CSU U P1 G1.2 –1972
Pulleyblank, Edwin George, 1922–.
'The unity of China.' In *Understanding modern China*, edited by Joseph M. Kitagawa (Kitagawa Mitsuo). [Selective entry]
Chicago: Quadrangle, 1969, 74–93.
SUBJ 64 66 ▪ 29

22738 CSU P P2 G3.0 1928–1972
Sakamoto, Koretada, 1918–.
'Inner Mongolia: A tragic nation and its tragic leaders.' Tr. of 'Uchimōko: Higeki no minzoku, higeki no shidōsha'; *Kyōsanken mondai* 12, 5 (May 1968), 47–66.
Review (Tokyo) 17 (June 1968), 1–32.
SUBJ 32.1 66 ▪ 11.3 34.1

22739 CSU P P1 G1.2 –1972
Schwartz, Benjamin Isadore, 1916–.
'The Chinese perception of world order, past and present.' In *The Chinese world order: Traditional China's foreign relations*, edited by John King Fairbank. [Selective entry]
Cambridge: Harvard U. Press, 1968, 276–288.
SUBJ 62 66 ▪ 64

22740 CSU P P2 G1.1 –1972
Spence, Jonathan Dermot, 1936–.
To change China: Western advisers in China, 1620–1960.
Boston: Little, Brown, 1969. 16, 335 p.
SUBJ 12 14 15 17 62 66 ▪ 14.2 14.3 14.5 16.1 18 19 22.2 32.2 56 64

22741 CSH U P2 G9.4 1644–1972
Tang, Mei-chun (T'ang Mei-chün), 1927–.
'Han and non-Han in Taiwan: A case of acculturation.'
BIE 30 (Autumn 1970), 99–109.
SUBJ 66 ▪ 12 12.1 25

22742 CSU P P1 G1.1 1928–1972
Tao, Lung-sheng.
'Communist China's criminal jurisdiction over aliens.'
International and comparative law q. 4th series 19, 4 (Oct. 1970), 599–625.
SUBJ 12.2 66

22743 NIC P P1 G1.2 1928–1972
Weakland, John Hast, 1919–.
'Chinese family images in international affairs.' In *The study of culture at a distance*, edited by Margaret Mead and Rhoda Metraux. [Selective entry]
Chicago: U. of Chicago Press, 1953, 421–426.
SUBJ 66 ▪ 60 63

1949-1972

22744 CSU O P3 G6.1 1949–1972
Barrymaine, Norman.
The time bomb: A veteran journalist assesses today's China from the inside.
New York: Taplinger, 1971. 16, 213 p.
SUBJ 22.2 66

22745 CSU O P2 G1.2 1949–1972
Bisch, Jørgen.
'This is the China I saw.'
NG 126, 5 (Nov. 1964), 591–639.
SUBJ 18 66 ▪ 12.1

22746 NNC P P1 G1.2 1949–1972
Chen, Wen-hui C. (Ch'en Chung Wen-hui), 1913–.
Chinese Communist anti-Americanism and the Resist-America Aid-Korea campaign.
Lackland Air Force Base, San Antonio, Tex.: U.S. Air Force Personnel and Training Research Center, Air Research and Development Command, 1955. 22 p. (U.S. Human Resources Research Institute research memoranda, 36; Studies in Chinese Communism, series 1, 4, 1952)
SUBJ 12.1 66 ▪ 30 62 64

22747 CSU O P2 G5.1 1949–1972
Ciantar, Maurice.
Mille jours à Pekin (A thousand days in Peking).
Paris: Gallimard, 1969. 467 p.
SUBJ 12 22.1 26 54 55 66 ▪ 15 21.4 22.2 24.2 32 34.1 47 56 64

22748 CSU P P1 G1.2 1949–1972
Edelstein, Alex S-, and Alan P. L. Liu (Liu P'ing-lin), 1937–.
'Anti-Americanism in Red China's *People's daily*: A functional analysis, 1959.'
Journalism q. 40, 2 (Spring 1963), 187–195.
SUBJ 14.2 66 ▪ 64

22749 NNC P P2 G4.5 1949–1972
Ginsburgs, George, 1932–, and Michael Mathos, 1933–.
Communist China and Tibet: The first dozen years.
The Hague: Nijhoff, 1964. 218 p.
SUBJ 12 12.1 13 66 ▪ 17 18 24.1 24.4

22750 CSU O P3 G5.1 1949–1972
Gordon, Eric.
Freedom is a word.
New York: Morrow, 1972. 350 p.
SUBJ 19 22.1 66 ▪ 14.2 25 31 54 55 64

22751 CSU O P3 G5.1 1949–1972
Grey, Anthony, 1938–.
Hostage in Peking.
Garden City, N.Y.: Doubleday, 1971. 17, 365 p.
SUBJ 66 ▪ 22.2 54

22752 CSU O P5 G9.4 1949–1972
Hanna, Willard Anderson, 1911–.
'Vestiges of Japanese colonialism in Taiwan.'
AUFS-EAS 5, 5 (3 Feb. 1956), 1–8.
SUBJ 66

22753 NNC O P3 G5.1 1949–1972
Hevi, Emmanuel John, 1932–.
An African student in China.
New York: Praeger, 1963. 220 p.
SUBJ 17 66 ▪ 26 28 32.1 54 64

22754 CSH P P2 G3.0 1949–1972
Hyer, Paul Van, 1926–.
'The China-Mongol frontier: The Cultural Revolution and after.' In *Collected documents of the First Sino-American Conference on Mainland China.* [Selective entry]
[Taipei]: Institute of International Relations, Republic of China, 1971, 635–650.
SUBJ 12 19 66 ▪ 11.3 14.2 21.2 32.1 35 54

22755 CSU O P3 G6.1 1949–1972
Knight, Sophia.
Window on Shanghai: Letters from China, 1965–1967.
London: Deutsch, 1967. 256 p.
SUBJ 27 28 53 54 55 66 ▪ 22.1 24.2 24.4 26.2 31 50 56 61 63

22756 NNC P P1 G1.2 1949–1972
Kurgantsev, M-.
'Pravdivye predki i fal'sifikatory-potomki' (True ancestors and false descendants).
Aziia i Afrika segodnia 1963, 11 (noiabr'), 36–37.
SUBJ 66 70

22757 CSH P P1 G1.2 1949–1972
McCarthy, J- P-.
'The Soviet model and Chinese culture.'
Soviet survey 24 (Apr.–June 1958), 16–21. [Special issue on China]
SUBJ 16.1 66 ▪ 12.1 17

22758 CSU F P3 G9.5 1949–1972
Morland, John Kenneth, 1916–.
'Race awareness among American and Hong Kong Chinese children.'
AJS 75, 3 (Nov. 1969), 360–374.
SUBJ 52 66 ▪ 26

22759 MCH U P1 G9.4 1949–1972
Müller, Wolfgang Dietrich, 1916–.
'Formosa: Völkerrechtliche Fiktion und politische Realität' (Taiwan: Legal fiction and political reality).
Aussenpolitik 4, 11 (Nov. 1953), 726–732.
SUBJ 66 ▪ 12 32

22760 CBU O P3 G1.3 1949–1972
Parise, Goffredo.
Cara Cina (Dear China).
Milan: Longanesi, 1966. 235 p.
SUBJ 14 16 66 ▪ 14.2 16.2 16.4 33 47 54

22761 CSU O P3 G1.3 1949–1972
Preston, E- C-.
'No love from China.'
Blackwood's magazine 302, 1825 (Nov. 1967), 429–441.
SUBJ 14.3 66 ▪ 12 12.2 16.4

22762 CSH S P2 G9.5 1949–1972
Priestley, Kenneth Ewart.
'Ethnic and cultural pluralism in Hong Kong.' In *Ethnic and cultural pluralism in intertropical communities*, compiled by International Institute of Differing Civilizations. [Sole entry]
Brussels: International Institute of Differing Civilizations, 1957, 427–438.
SUBJ 17 41 66 ▪ 22 61

22763 NNC O P3 G5.1 1949–1972
Rickett, Walter Allyn, 1921–, and Adele Austin Rickett.
Prisoners of liberation.
New York: Cameron Associates, 1957. 288 p.
SUBJ 12.2 22.1 60 66 ▪ 47 61

22764 CSH O P3 G6.1 1949–1972
Rossi, Paolo Alberto, 1887–1969.
The Communist conquest of Shanghai: A warning to the West.
Arlington, Va.: Twin Circle *with* Crestwood Books, 1970. 170 p.
SUBJ 22.1 32.1 66 ▪ 17 24.3 24.6 33 36.2 45

22765 MCH P P2 G4.3 1949–1972
Shevel', I- B-.
'Natsional'noe stroitel'stvo v Sin'tszianskom uigurskom avtonomnom raione KNR' (National construction in the Sinkiang Uighur Autonomous Region of the People's Republic of China).
Sovetskaia etnografiia 1956, 2, 95–105.
SUBJ 12 66

22766 CSU P P1 G1.2 1949–1972
Tao, Cheng.
'Communist China and the law of the sea.'
American j. of international law 63, 1 (Jan. 1969), 47–73.
SUBJ 12.2 66 ▪ 14.1 14.2 14.4

22767 CBU O P2 G1.2 1949–1972
Topping, Audrey.
'Return to changing China.'
NG 140, 6 (Dec. 1971), 801–833.
SUBJ 20 66 ▪ 26.3 28

22768 CSU P P2 G4.3 1949–1972
Tretiak, Daniel, 1937–.
'Peking's policy towards Sinkiang: Trouble on the "new frontier".'
CS 2, 24 (15 Nov. 1963), 1–13.
SUBJ 14 21.2 66 ▪ 32.1 35

22769 CSU O P2 G1.2 1949–1972
Wills, Morris R-, 1933–, and J- Robert Moskin.
Turncoat: An American's twelve years in Communist China.
Englewood Cliffs, N.J.: Prentice-Hall, 1968. 186 p.
SUBJ 12.1 66 ▪ 14.2 17 18 19 41 46 55 61 64

22770 NIC F P3 G9.4 1949–1972
Yang, Kuo-shu, 1932–, Pen-hua Lee (Li Pen-hua), and Ching-fang Yu (Yü Chin-fang).
'The social distance attitudes of Chinese students towards twenty-five national and ethnic groups.'
APT 5 (Mar. 1963), 37–51.
SUBJ 66 ▪ 47 54

70 CHINESE SCHOLARS OF CHINESE SOCIETY

華人硏究中國社會

中国人学者による中国社会研究

1644-1911

22771 MCH P P2 G1.2 1842–1895
Chesneaux, Jean, 1922–.
'La révolution Taiping d'après quelques travaux recents' (Recent works on the Taiping Rebellion).
R. historique 209 (jan.–mars 1953), 33–57.
SUBJ 32.2 62 70 71 72 ▪ 12 14 14.1 14.5 15 16.1 19 29 66

22772 MAM P P2 G1.2 1644–1842
Chu Shih-chia, 1905–.
Chang Hsüeh-ch'êng: His contributions to Chinese local historiography.
Ann Arbor: University Microfilms (Publ. 1644), 1950. 231 p. (Doctoral dissertation in History, Columbia U.)
SUBJ 59 62 70

22773 NIC P P2 G1.3 1644–1842
Demiéville, Paul, 1894–.
'Chang Hsüeh-ch'eng and his historiography.' In *Historians of China and Japan*, edited by William Gerald Beasley and Edwin George Pulleyblank. [Selective entry]
London: Oxford U. Press, 1961, 167–185. (U. of London, School of Oriental and African Studies, Historical writing on the peoples of Asia, 3)
SUBJ 62 70 ▪ 16.1 71

22774 MCH P P1 G1.2 1895–1911
Fass, Josef, and L- Stupski.
'New materials on Chinese political and cultural history during the last year of the Ch'ing dynasty.'
AO 30, 3 (1962), 654–659.
SUBJ 32.2 70 ▪ 62

22775 MCH S P1 G1.2 1895–1911
Garushiants, IUrii Misakovich.
'Publikatsiia v KNR istochnikov po istorii revoliutsii 1911 goda' (Publications in the People's Republic of China of source materials on the history of the Revolution of 1911).
NAA 1961, 4, 106–121.
SUBJ 70 72 ▪ 32.2

22776 CSU P P2 G1.3 –1842
Peterson, Willard James, 1938–.
'The life of Ku Yen-wu (1613–1682).'
HJAS 28 (1968), 114–156; 29 (1969), 201–247. (Revision of *Ku Yen-wu, 1613–1682: A short biography*, masters thesis in History, U. of London [School of Oriental and African Studies], 1964)
SUBJ 16.1 59 63 70 ▪ 12 12.2 25 36.1 48

22777 CSU P P1 G1.1 –1911
Pritchard, Earl Hampton, 1907–.
'Traditional Chinese historiography and local histories.' In *The uses of history: Essays in intellectual and social history presented to William J. Bossenbrook*, compiled and edited by Hayden V- White. [Sole entry]
Detroit: Wayne State U. Press, 1968, 187–219.
SUBJ 62 70

22778 MCH U P1 G1.1 1842–1895
Senin, Nikolai Gerasimovich.
'Vvedenie' (Introduction). In *Izbrannye proizvedeniia progressivnykh kitaiskikh myslitelei novogo vremeni, 1840–1898* (Selected works of progressive Chinese thinkers of modern times, 1840–1898). [Sole entry]
Moscow: Izd-vo Akad. nauk SSSR, 1961, 1–25.
SUBJ 62 70

22779 NNC P P1 G1.1 –1842
Stuzhina, Emiliia Pavlovna, 1931–.
'Sovremenaia kitaiskaia istoricheskaia nauka o problemakh sotsial'no-ekonomicheskoi istorii Kitaia v pozdnee srednevekov'e (XVI–XVIII vv.)' (Contemporary Chinese historical scholarship on problems of China's social and economic history in the late middle ages, from the sixteenth through the eighteenth centuries). In *Sovremennaia istoriografiia stran zarubezhnogo Vostoka, vyp. 1, Kitai* (Current historiography of countries of the non-Soviet Orient, Vol. 1, China), edited by Boris Nikolaevich Zanegin et al. [Selective entry]
Moscow: Izd-vo vost. lit-ry, 1963, 102–121.
SUBJ 62 70 ▪ 12 14 16 72

22780 NNC P P1 G1.1 1644–1911
Twitchett, Denis Crispin, 1925–.
'A critique of some recent studies of modern Chinese social-economic history.' In *Transactions of the International Conference of Orientalists in Japan*. [Sole entry]
Tokyo: Tōhō gakkai, 1965, vol. 10, 28–41.
SUBJ 62 70 ▪ 16 19 42

22781 CSU P P1 G1.2 1644–1911
Wei, Ying-pang.
'Les historiens chinois sous la dynastie Ts'ing (1644–1911): leurs oeuvres et leurs méthodes' (Chinese historians in the Ch'ing period, 1644–1911: Their works and their methods).
Sinologica 1, 4 (1948), 292–315.
SUBJ 62 70 ▪ 72

1644-1949

22782 CSU P P3 G1.2 –1949
Chiu, Alfred Kaiming (Ch'iu K'ai-ming), 1898–.
'Chinese historical documents of the Ch'ing dynasty, 1644–1911.'
PHR 1, 3 (July 1932), 324–336.
SUBJ 62 70 ▪ 12

22783 NIC S P1 G1.2 1895–1949
Hsü, I-t'ang.
'Ethnological research in China.'
Quarterly b. of Chinese bibliography new (2nd) series 4, 1/4 (Mar.–Dec. 1944), 27–33.
SUBJ 62 70 ▪ 72

22784 NNP P P2 G1.2 1895–1949
IAshnov, Evgenii Evgen'evich.
'Obzor osnovnoi literatury po sel'skomu khoziaistvu i naseleniiu Kitaia' (Review of the basic literature on China's agriculture and population).
BSB 1, 4 (1932), 1–28.
SUBJ 14.1 70 71 ▪ 11 72

22785 CBU S P1 G1.2 1842–1949
Otte, Friedrich W- K-.
'Bemerkungen zur angewandten Wirtschaftswissenschaft in China' (Observations on applied economics in China).
MSOSB 33 (1930), 137–154.
SUBJ 70 ▪ 14 14.5 14.6 71

22786 CSU P P1 G1.2 –1949
Schneider, Laurence Allen.
'From textual criticism to social criticism: The historiography of Ku Chieh-kang.'
JAS 28, 4 (Aug. 1969), 771–788. [Reprinted in *China*, edited by John Armstrong Harrison. (Selective entry.) Tucson: U. of Arizona Press, 1972, 167–184. (Assn. for Asian Studies,

Thirtieth Anniversary Commemorative Series, 1)]
Subj 62 70 ▪ 16.1 64

22787 WMU S P2 G1.2 –1949
Shao, Bing-kun (Shao Ping-k'un).
Methodology in the development of agricultural economics in China.
Unpublished doctoral dissertation in Agricultural Economics, U. of Wisconsin, 1950. 145 p.
Subj 14.1 64 70 ▪ 14 62 71

22788 MCH S P1 G1.2 1895–1949
Sun, Pen-wen, 1892–.
'La sociologie en Chine.'
Cahiers internationaux de sociologie 5 (1948), 151–157.
'Sociology in China.'
Social forces 27, 3 (Mar. 1949), 247–251.
Subj 70 71 ▪ 62 64

22789 MCH S P1 G1.2 1842–1949
Wang Yü-ch'üan, 1911–.
'Pacific affairs bibliographies. No. 5, The development of modern social science in China.'
PA 11, 3 (Sept. 1938), 345–362.
Subj 70 ▪ 14.2

1911-1949

22790 NNC O P1 G1.2 1928–1949
'Research notes.'
NSEQ 8, 1 (Apr. 1935), 163–177; 8, 2 (July 1935), 385–396.
Subj 70

22791 NIC S P2 G1.2 1911–1949
Chang, Chi-yun (Chang Ch'i-yün), 1901–.
'Geographic research in China.'
AAAG 34, 1 (Mar. 1944), 47–62.
Subj 70 ▪ 11 11.3 14.1 14.2

22792 NIC S P1 G1.2 1911–1949
Chao Wei-pang.
'Modern Chinese folklore investigation.'
FS 1 (1942), 55–76; 2 (1943), 79–88.
Subj 65 70 ▪ 72

22793 NIC O P1 G1.2 1911–1949
Chen Ta (Ch'en Ta), 1892–.
'The need of population research in China.'
PS 1, 4 (Mar. 1948), 342–352.
Subj 11 58 70 71

22794 CSU U P1 G1.2 1911–1949
Fong, H. D. (Fang Hsien-t'ing), 1902–.
'Recollections of early research on Chinese economy.'
THJ new (2nd) series 4, 1 (June 1963), 69–84. [Combined issue with vol. 3, no. 2.]
Subj 70 ▪ 72

22795 NIC O P1 G1.2 1911–1949
Ho Lien-kwei (Ho Lien-k'uei), 1902–.
'Dr. Tsai Yuan-pei's contribution to ethnology.'
BIE 9 (Spring 1960), 13–17. [See Vol. 2 of this *Bibliography* for Chinese version.]
Subj 70

22796 NIC S P1 G1.2 1911–1949
Hsu Chu-yeh (Hsü Tsu-i).
'Anthropology chronicle.'
THM 10, 1 (Jan. 1940), 61–65.
Subj 70

22797 CSU O P2 G1.2 1928–1949
Hsu, Francis L. K. (Hsü Lang-kuang), 1909–.
'Sociological research in China.'
Quarterly b. of Chinese bibliography new (2nd) series 4, 1/4 (Mar.–Dec. 1944), 12–26.
Subj 70 71 ▪ 17 36.1 72

22798 NNC O P1 G1.2 1928–1949
Li An-che.
'Notes on the necessity of field research in social science in China.'
YJSS 1, 1 (June 1938), 122–127.
Subj 70 ▪ 17

22799 NNC O P1 G1.1 1928–1949
Li Chi, 1896–.
'Some anthropological problems of China reconsidered.' In *Proceedings of the Second Biennial Conference of the International Association of Historians of Asia*, edited by Chang Kuei-yung et al. [Selective entry]
Taipei: International Assn. of Historians of Asia, 1962, 1–12.
Subj 70 ▪ 71

22800 NNC O P2 G1.3 1928–1949
Li, Choh-ming (Li Cho-min), 1912–.
'Economic and social research in wartime China.'
PA 17, 2 (June 1944), 209–216.
Subj 70

22801 CSU O P3 G1.3 1911–1949
Lou Tse-k'uang (Lou Tzu-k'uang).
'Früherer und jetziger Stand der Volkskundebewegung Chinas.'
ZE 65 (1933), 316–325.
'The past and present state of the folklore movement in China.' Tr. by Wolfram Eberhard. In *Studies in Chinese folklore and related essays*, by Wolfram Eberhard. [Selective entry]
Bloomington: Indiana U., Research Center for the Language Sciences, 1970, 113–127. (Indiana U., Folklore Institute monograph series, 23)
Subj 36.1 65 70 ▪ 24.2 72

22802 NNC FP P7 G5.1 1911–1928
Malone, Carroll Brown, 1886–.
'The study of Chinese rural economy. I, Work and experiences of the Tsing Hua survey team in T'ang hsien (Chihli).'
CSPSR 7, 4 (Oct. 1923), 88–101. [For Part II, see entry 16695.] [Reprinted in *The study of Chinese rural economy*, by C. B. Malone and John Bernard Tayler. (Analytic entry.) Peking: China International Famine Relief Commission, 1924, 1–14 (s.p.). (CIFRC, Series B, 10)]
Subj 70 ▪ 22 28

22803 ELO S P1 G1.2 1911–1949
Newell, William Hare, 1922–.
'Modern Chinese sociologists.'
Sociological b. (Bombay) 1, 2 (1952), 89–94.
Subj 70

22804 MCH S P4 G1.2 1911–1928
Stupski, L-, and Timoteus Pokora.
'New opinions on the May Fourth Movement in China.'
AO 28, 2 (1960), 308–322.
Subj 16.1 19 70 71 ▪ 64

22805 DNA O P2 G1.2 1911–1949
Yin Lien-ken (Ying Lien-keng), 1904?–.
Twenty-two years of agricultural economics: A review of the work of the Department of Agricultural Economics, College of Agriculture and Forestry, University of Nanking (1920–42).
Nanking: U. of Nanking, College of Agriculture and Forestry, Dept. of Agricultural Economics, 1942. 23 p.
Subj 17 70 71 ▪ 14.1 18 24.6 34.2 36.3 55

1911-1972
(including 1644-1972)

22806 DLC P P1 G1.2 –1972
Akademiia nauk SSSR. Institut geografii.
Puteshestvenniki drevnego Kitaia i geograficheskie issledovaniia v Kitaiskoi Narodnoi Respublike (Travelers in ancient China and geographic studies in the People's Republic of China).
Moscow: Geografgiz, 1955. 86 p.
Subj 70 ▪ 17 36.1 62

22807 MCH S P1 G1.2 –1972
Cheboksarov, N- N-.
'Osnovnye etapy razvitiia etnografii v Kitae' (Basic stages in the development of ethnography in China). [With English abstract]
Sovetskaia etnografiia 1959, 6, 123–149.
Subj 66 70

22808 CSH O P1 G9.4 1928–1972
Chen Shao-hsing (Ch'en Shao-hsing), 1906–1966.
'Taiwan as a laboratory for the study of Chinese society and culture.'
BIE 22 (Autumn 1966), 1–8.
Subj 70

22809 ASU P P1 G1.1 –1972
Chey, Jocelyn Valerie, 1938–.
The search for a native ancestry for modern Chinese materialism.
Unpublished doctoral dissertation in Oriental Studies, U. of Sydney, 1970. s.p.
Subj 62 64 70 ▪ 59

22810 NNC S P1 G1.2 1928–1972
Efimov, Gerontii Valentinovich, 1906–.
Review of *Chung-kuo chin tai shih* (Modern Chinese history), by Fan Wen-lan.
SV 1956, 3, 158–165.
Subj 70

22811 NNC U P1 G1.2 1895–1972
Fedorenko, Nikolai Trofimovich, 1912–.
Laureat mezhdunarodnoi Stalinskoi premii mira Go Mo-zho (International Stalin Peace Prize laureate Kuo Mo-jo).
Moscow: Znanie, 1952. 31 p.
Subj 59 70

22812 MCH S P1 G1.1 1928–1972
Freedman, Maurice, 1920–.
'Sociology in and of China.'
British j. of sociology 13, 2 (June 1962), 106–116.
Subj 70 71 ▪ 17

22813 NNC P P1 G1.1 1895–1972
Fried, Morton Herbert, 1923–.
'China.' In *Contemporary sociology*, edited by Joseph Slabey Roucek. [Sole entry]

New York: Philosophical Library, 1958, 993–1012.
SUBJ 70 71 ▪ 12.1

22814 NNC S P1 G1.2 1911–1972
Goodrich, Luther Carrington, 1894–.
'Archaeology in China: The first decades.'
JAS 17, 1 (Nov. 1957), 5–15.
SUBJ 70 ▪ 17

22815 NIC P P1 G1.2 1911–1972
Hsia, Ronald (Hsia Hsiu-yung), 1918–.
'The intellectual and public life of Ma Yin-ch'u.'
CQ 6 (Apr.–June 1961), 53–63.
SUBJ 16.1 70 ▪ 14

22816 NIC P P1 G1.1 1928–1972
Hsu, Francis L. K. (Hsü Lang-kuang), 1909–.
'China.' In *International directory of anthropological institutions*, edited by William Leroy Thomas, Jr. and Anna M- Pikelis. [Sole entry]
New York: Wenner-Gren Foundation for Anthropological Research, 1953, 55–57.
SUBJ 70 ▪ 17 36.1

22817 NIC O P2 G1.1 1895–1972
Huang Wen-shan, 1901–, and Ho Lien-kwei (Ho Lien-k'uei), 1902–.
'Recent developments and trends in ethnological studies in China.' In *Men and cultures: Selected papers of the Fifth International Congress of Anthropological and Ethnological Sciences, Philadelphia, September 1–9, 1956*, edited by Anthony F- C- Wallace et al. [Sole entry]
Philadelphia: U. of Pennsylvania Press, 1960, 54–58.
SUBJ 70 ▪ 36.1 66

22818 CSU S P1 G1.2 1911–1972
Huard, Pierre Alphonse, 1901–, and Ming Wong.
'Le Professeur Li T'ao (1901–1959)' (Professor Li T'ao, 1901–1959).
BEFEO 52, 1 (1964), 307–309.
SUBJ 70 ▪ 56

22819 WSU S P1 G1.1 1895–1972
Krader, Ruth.
Sinological periodicals in Chinese and Japanese.
Unpublished masters thesis in Far Eastern and Slavic Languages, U. of Washington, 1955. 56 p.
SUBJ 70 71 ▪ 14.2

22820 CSU P P1 G9.4 1928–1972
Lo, C. T.
'Chinese studies in Taiwan.' In *Symposium on historical, archaeological and linguistic studies on southern China, South-east Asia and the Hong Kong region*, edited by Frederick Seguier Drake. [Selective entry]
Hong Kong: Hong Kong U. Press, 1967, 306–309.
SUBJ 70 ▪ 17 36.1

22821 NIC O P1 G1.1 1928–1972
O'Hara, Albert Richard, 1907–.
'Recent development of sociology in China.'
ASR 26, 6 (Dec. 1961), 928–929.
SUBJ 70

22822 CSU O P1 G1.1 1928–1972
O'Hara, Albert Richard, 1907–.
'Sociology in China again.'
ASR 28, 1 (Feb. 1963), 134.
SUBJ 70

22823 CSU S P1 G1.2 1895–1972
Scholz, Hartmut-Dieter, 1925–.
'Die geographische Wissenschaft in China' (The study of geography in China).
Geographica helvetica 5, 1 (1950), 40–46.
SUBJ 70

22824 CSU S P1 G1.2 1644–1972
Silberman, Leo.
'Hung Liang-chi: A Chinese Malthus.'
PS 13, 3 (Mar. 1960), 257–265.
SUBJ 62 70 ▪ 11

1949-1972

22825 MCH U P1 G1.2 1949–1972
Anan'eva, M- I-, and Liparit Sarkisovich Kiuzadzhian, 1932–.
'Bor'ba protiv burzhuaznoi sotsiologii v Kitae v 1957 g.' (The struggle against bourgeois sociology in China in 1957).
Vestnik istorii mirovoi kul'tury 1961, 3 (mai–iiun'), 115–126.
SUBJ 32.1 70 ▪ 62 64

22826 NNC U P1 G1.1 1949–1972
Astaf'ev, Gennadii Vasil'evich, 1908–.
'Nauchno-issledovatel'skaia rabota v oblasti istorii i ekonomiki Kitaia v Kitaiskoi Narodnoi Respublike' (Research on Chinese history and economics in the People's Republic of China).
SV 1956, 1, 176–180.
SUBJ 70

22827 CSH P P1 G1.2 1949–1972
[Chao Ts'ung] Chung Hua-min, pseud., 1927–.
'Criticism of academic theories in Communist China, 1966.' Tr. of '1966 nien Chung kung ti hsüeh shu ssu hsiang p'i p'an'; *Tsu kuo* 36 (Mar. 1967), 15–27. In *Communist China, 1966*, edited by Union Research Institute. [Selective entry]
Hong Kong: Union Research Institute, 1968, vol. 2, 118–150.
SUBJ 16.1 64 70 ▪ 12.1 62

22828 MCM S P1 G1.2 1949–1972
Ch'en, C. J.
'Chinese social scientists.'
Twentieth century 163, 976 (June 1958), 511–522.
SUBJ 17 70 ▪ 12.1 64 66

22829 CSU P P1 G1.2 1949–1972
Cheng, Te-k'un, 1908–.
'Archeology in Communist China.' In *History in Communist China*, edited by Albert Feuerwerker. [Selective entry]
Cambridge: M.I.T. Press, 1968, 45–55.
SUBJ 62 70

22830 MCH S P1 G1.2 1949–1972
Chesneaux, Jean, 1922–.
'Les travaux d'histoire moderne et contemporaine en Chine populaire' (Works on modern and contemporary history in the People's Republic of China).
R. historique 215 (avr.–juin 1956), 274–282.
SUBJ 62 70 ▪ 72

22831 CSU P P2 G1.2 1949–1972
Chin, Robert (Ch'en Yü-li), 1918–, and Ai-li Sung Chin (Ch'en Shen Ai-li), 1919–.
Psychological research in Communist China, 1949–1966.
Cambridge: M.I.T. Press, 1969. 274 p.
SUBJ 17 61 62 70 ▪ 12.1 32.1 36.1 53 56 64

22832 CSU S P1 G1.2 1949–1972
Gellert, Johannes Fürchtegott, 1904–.
'Die Entwicklung der geographischen Wissenschaften in der Volkrepublik China' (The development of geographical sciences in the People's Republic of China).
PGM 105, 1 (1961), 25–29.
SUBJ 70

22833 MCH P P1 G1.2 1949–1972
Gentelle, Pierre.
'Recherche et enseignement géographiques en République populaire de Chine' (Geographic research and teaching in the People's Republic of China).
Annales de géographie 74, 403 (mai–juin 1965), 354–358.
SUBJ 17 70

22834 NIC PO P1 G1.2 1949–1972
Gjessing, Gutorm, 1906–.
'Chinese anthropology and New China's policy toward her minorities.'
Acta sociologica 2, 1 (1956), 45–68.
SUBJ 70 ▪ 66

22835 CSU P P1 G9.4 1949–1972
Gordon, Leonard Herman David, 1928–, and Sidney Chang.
'John K. Fairbank and his critics in the Republic of China.'
JAS 30, 1 (Nov. 1970), 137–149.
SUBJ 70 71

22836 MCH S P2 G1.2 1949–1972
Hsieh, Chiao-min, 1918–.
'The status of geography in Communist China.'
GR 49, 4 (Oct. 1959), 535–551.
SUBJ 14.2 17 70 ▪ 16.1 36.1

22837 CSU S P1 G1.2 1949–1972
Hsu, Francis L. K. (Hsü Lang-kuang), 1909–.
'Anthropological sciences.' In *Sciences in Communist China*, edited by [Sydney Henry Gould] Sidney H. Gould. [Selective entry]
Washington, D.C.: American Assn. for the Advancement of Science, 1961, 129–157. (AAAS publications, 68)
SUBJ 70 ▪ 62 64

22838 MCH S P2 G1.2 1949–1972
Karymov, V-.
'Bor'ba s pravymi v oblasti ekonomicheskoi náuki v Kitae' (The struggle against right-wing economists in China).
VE 1958, 2 (fevral'), 94–101.
SUBJ 64 70 ▪ 14.1 14.4 16.2 32

22839 CSU P P2 G1.2 1949–1972
Kikolski, Bohdan.
'Contemporary research in physical geography in the Chinese People's Republic.'
AAAG 54, 2 (June 1964), 181–189.
Subj 70 ▪ 11.4 14.1 36.1 62

22840 CSH O P3 G9.4 1949–1972
Kuo, Warren (Kuo Hua-lun), 1912–.
'Research on Chinese Communist affairs in the Republic of China.' In *Collected documents of the First Sino-American Conference on Mainland China*. [Selective entry]
[Taipei]: Institute of International Relations, Republic of China, 1971, 21–27.
Subj 36.1 70

22841 MCH P P1 G1.2 1949–1972
[La Dany, Ladislao] ———, 1914–.
'Psychology.'
CNA 260 (16 Jan. 1959), 1–7.
Subj 56 70 ▪ 61

22842 CSH P P1 G1.2 1949–1972
[La Dany, Ladislao] ———, 1914–.
'Ten years' study of history.'
CNA 326 (3 June 1960), 1–7.
Subj 62 70

22843 NNC P P1 G1.2 1949–1972
[La Dany, Ladislao] ———, 1914–.
'A year of history studies.'
CNA 237 (18 July 1958), 1–7.
Subj 62 70 ▪ 12.1 16.1

22844 MCY P P7 G1.2 1949–1972
Lethbridge, Henry James, 1923–.
'Classes in class.'
FEER 41, 6 (8 Aug. 1963), 333–334.
Subj 16 54 70 ▪ 12.1 64

22845 CSU S P1 G1.2 1949–1972
Li, S. K.
'Social sciences in Communist China.'
American behavioral scientist 9, 8 (Apr. 1966), 3–7.
Subj 70 ▪ 17

22846 MCH U P3 G1.2 1949–1972
M. K.
'IUridicheskaia nauka za rubezhom v Kitaiskoi Narodnoi Respublike' (The study of law in the People's Republic of China).
SGP 1957, 2 (fevral'), 142–143.
Subj 70 ▪ 12.2

22847 MCH O P1 G1.2 1949–1972
Pan' Shu (P'an Shu).
'Razvitie psikhologii v Kitae' (The development of psychology in China).
Voprosy psikhologii 4, 6 (noiabr'–dekabr' 1958), 166–168.
Subj 61 70 ▪ 64

22848 MCH O P1 G1.2 1949–1972
Petrushevskii, S- A-.
'O sovremennom sostoianii psikhologicheskoi nauki v Kitae i o razvitii nauchnogo kontakta s kitaiskimi psikhologami' (The current state of psychology in China and the development of scientific contacts with Chinese psychologists).
Voprosy psikhologii 2 (1956), 102–108.
Subj 62 70 ▪ 64

22849 NNC P P1 G1.2 1949–1972
Riftin, Boris L'vovich, 1932–.
'Sobiranie i izuchenie fol'klora v Kitae' (The collection and study of folklore in China).
Voprosy literatury 1957, 5, 207–210.
Subj 65 70

22850 MCH O P3 G1.3 1949–1972
Shabalin, V- I-.
'Nad chem rabotaiut uchenye-ekonomisti Narodnogo Kitaia' (Research projects carried out by economists in the People's Republic of China).
VE 1958, 3 (mart), 158–160.
Subj 36.1 70 ▪ 64 72

22851 MCH S P4 G1.2 1949–1972
Siui Lian'-tsan (Hsü Lien-ts'ang).
'Psikhologiia truda v Kitae' (The psychology of labor in China).
Voprosy psikhologii 6, 3 (mai 1960), 179–183.
Subj 70 ▪ 16.4 61

22852 NNC FP P1 G1.2 1949–1972
Skinner, George William, 1925–.
'The new sociology in China.'
FEQ 10, 4 (Aug. 1951), 365–371.
Subj 17 64 70 ▪ 66

22853 MCH U P1 G1.2 1949–1972
Tien, H. Yuan (T'ien Hsin-yüan), 1926–.
'Is sociology dead in Communist China?'
ASR 27, 3 (June 1962), 413–414.
Subj 70 ▪ 12.1

22854 NNC O P1 G1.2 1949–1972
TSzen San' (Tseng San) and Pei Tun (P'ei T'ung).
'Uchastie arkhivov v sotsialisticheskom stroitel'stve narodnogo Kitaia' (The role of archives in socialist construction in the People's Republic of China).
Istoricheskii arkhiv 1959, 5 (sentiabr'–oktiabr'), 179–185.
Subj 70 ▪ 17 64

22855 DLC O P1 G1.2 1949–1972
U Zhu-kan (Wu Ju-k'ang).
'Antropologiia v Kitae' (Anthropology in China).
Sovetskaia antropologiia 3, 1 (1959), 107–112.
Subj 70 ▪ 17 32.1

22856 NNC U P3 G1.2 1949–1972
Volchenkov, G- I-.
'Arkhivnoe delo v Kitaiskoi Narodnoi Respublike' (Archival work in the People's Republic of China).
SK 1958, 4, 149–155.
Subj 70 ▪ 17

22857 CSU S P2 G1.2 1949–1972
Wiens, Herold Jacob, 1912–1971.
'Development of geographical science, 1949–1960.' In *Sciences in Communist China*, edited by [Sydney Henry Gould] Sidney H. Gould. [Selective entry]
Washington, D.C.: American Assn. for the Advancement of Science, 1961, 411–481. (AAAS publications, 68)
Subj 17 32.1 36.1 70 ▪ 16.1 62 64

22858 CSU O P1 G9.4 1949–1972
Wu Chen-tsai.
'Mainland China studies in Free China since June 1966.'
IS 5, 10 (July 1969), 2–4.
Subj 70

71 Non-Chinese Scholars of Chinese Society
外人研究中國社會
外国人学者による中国社会研究

1644-1911

22859 NNC O P1 G1.2 1895–1911
'The Department of Chinese at Columbia.'
JAAA 2, 10 (Nov. 1902), 285–288.
Subj 71 ▪ 17

22860 NIC PO P1 G1.1 1842–1895
Cordier, Henri, 1849–1925.
'Les études chinoises (1891–1894)' (Chinese studies, 1891–1894).
TP 5, 6 (1894), 420–457; 6, 2 (1895), 99–147.
Subj 70 71 ▪ 72

22861 CSU O P1 G1.1 1842–1911
Cordier, Henri, 1849–1925.
Les études chinoises (1895–1898).
Leiden: Brill, 1898. 141 p. [Supplement to *TP* 9 (1898)]
Subj 71

22862 NIC S P1 G1.1 1842–1911
Cordier, Henri, 1849–1925.
'Les études chinoises (1899–1902)' (Chinese studies, 1899–1902).
TP 2e série 4 (1903), 23–52, 146–162, 324–342, 371–384.
Subj 71 72

22863 NIC O P1 G1.2 1842–1895
Cordier, Henri, 1849–1925.
'Half a decade of Chinese studies, 1886–1891.'
TP 3, 5 (1892), 532–563.
Subj 71

22864 CSU S P1 G1.1 –1895
Cranmer-Byng, John, 1919–.
'The first English sinologists, Sir George Staunton and the Reverend Robert Morrison.' In *Symposium on historical, archaeological and linguistic studies on southern China, South-east Asia and the Hong Kong region*, edited by Frederick Seguier Drake. [Selective entry]
Hong Kong: Hong Kong U. Press, 1967, 247–260.
Subj 71 ▪ 66

22865 CSU S P3 G1.3 –1842
Cummins, J- S-.
'Introduction.' In *The 'Travels' and 'Controversies' of Friar Domingo Navarrete, 1618–1686*, edited by J. S. Cummins. [Analytic entry]
Cambridge, Eng.: Hakluyt Society, 1962, vol. 1, 17–120 [s.p.]. (HS works, series 2, 118) [For Navarrete's work, see entry 22590.]
Subj 71 ▪ 13 33 66

22866 CBU P P2 G1.1 1644–1911
Efimov, Gerontii Valentinovich, 1906–.
Istoriko-bibliograficheskii obzor istochnikov i literatury po novoi istorii Kitaia. Chast' pervaia, Vvedenie, obzor istochnikov. Chast' vtoraia, Russkaia i sovetskaia literatura po novoi istorii Kitaia (An historical-bibliographic survey of sources and literature on modern Chinese history. Vol. 1,

Introduction and survey of sources. Vol. 2, Russian and Soviet literature on modern Chinese history).
Leningrad: Izd-vo Leningr. un-ta, 1965, 1968. 2 vols. 177; 91 p.
Subj 12 32.2 33 70 71 72 ▪ 12.2 14.2 14.3 15 32.1 35 36.3 59 64 66

22867 MCH S P1 G1.2 1842–1895
Fairbank, John King, 1907–.
'Meadows on China: A centennial review.'
FEQ 14, 3 (May 1955), 365–371.
Subj 71

22868 WSU S P1 G1.2 1842–1911
Fei, Anne Hsiu-ai.
China: A study of travel narratives as research sources, 1842–1911, with selected, annotated bibliography.
Unpublished masters thesis in Librarianship, U. of Washington, 1955. 42 p.
Subj 71 72 ▪ 66

22869 CSU S P1 G1.2 –1911
Franke, Adolf.
'Die sinologischen Studien und Professor Hirth' (Sinological studies and Professor Friedrich Hirth).
TP 7, 4 (1896), 241–250.
Subj 71

22870 NNC S P1 G1.2 –1911
Franke, Otto, 1863–1946.
'Friedrich Hirth' (Friedrich Hirth).
Ostasiatische Z. 13 (1926), 197–207.
Subj 71

22871 NNC S P1 G1.1 1644–1911
Gorbacheva, Zoia Ivanovna, 1907–, and D- I- Tikhonov.
'Iz istorii izucheniia Kitaia v Rossii' (History of Chinese studies in Russia).
SV 1955, 2, 140–147.
Subj 71

22872 CSU P P1 G1.1 –1842
Henderson, Dan Fenno, 1922–.
'Chinese legal studies in early 18th century Japan: Scholars and sources.'
JAS 30, 1 (Nov. 1970), 21–56.
Subj 71

22873 NIC O P1 G1.1 1842–1895
Hirth, Friedrich, 1845–1927.
'Über sinologische Studien' (Sinological studies).
TP 6, 5 (1895), 364–368.
Subj 71

22874 CSU P P1 G1.2 –1842
Huard, Pierre Alphonse, 1901–, and Ming Wong.
'Les enquêtes françaises sur la science et la technologie chinoises au 18e siècle' (French research on Chinese science and technology in the eighteenth century).
BEFEO 53, 1 (1966), 137–226.
Subj 14 56 62 71 ▪ 29 66

22875 CSH P P2 G1.2 1644–1842
Kazanin, Mark Isaakovich, 1899–.
'Spafarii i Martini' (Spafarii [Nicolae Milescu] and Martinius Martini).
NAA 1971, 6, 106–112.
Subj 71 72

22876 MCH S P1 G1.2 1644–1842
Lutfalla, Michel.
'La Chine vue par quelques économistes du XVIIIe siècle' (China as seen by eighteenth-century economists).
Population (Paris) 17, 2 (avr.-juin 1962), 289–296.
Subj 71 ▪ 14

22877 CSU P P1 G1.1 1842–1895
Meisner, Maurice J-, 1931–.
'The despotism of concepts: Wittfogel and Marx on China.'
CQ 16 (Oct.–Dec. 1963), 99–111.
Subj 10 71

22878 DLC P P1 G1.2 –1842
Miasnikov, Vladimir Stepanovich.
'Russkie arkhivnye istochniki o zavoevanii Kitaia man'chzhurami (1618–1690 gg.)' (Russian archival sources on the Manchu conquest of China, 1618–1690). In *Man'chzhurskoe vladychestvo v Kitae* (Manchu rule in China), compiled by Institut narodov Azii, Akademiia nauk SSSR, edited by Sergei Leonidovich Tikhvinskii. [Selective entry]
Moscow: Nauka, Glav. red. vost. lit-ry, 1966, 98–112.
Subj 15 66 71 ▪ 16.1

22879 CSH S P8 G1.2 1842–1911
Nepomnin, Oleg Efimovich, 1935–.
'O metodike izucheniia perekhodnogo perioda v Kitae (XIX – nachalo XX veka)' (Methods of studying the period of transition in China, from the nineteenth century to the early twentieth century).
NAA 1968, 4, 98–107.
Subj 71 ▪ 14.1 16.3

22880 NNC U P1 G1.3 1644–1842
Neumann, Karl Friedrich, 1793–1870.
'Die Sinologen und ihre Werke: Robert Morrison' (Sinologists and their works: Robert Morrison).
ZDMG 1 (1847), 91–128, 217–237.
Subj 71 ▪ 13 64

22881 CSH S P1 G1.2 1842–1911
Setnitskii, N- A-.
'Russkie mysliteli o Kitae (V. S. Solov'ev i N. F. Fedorov)' (Russian thinkers on China: V. S. Solov'ev and N. F. Fedorov).
Izvestiia IUridicheskogo fakul'teta v g. Kharbine 3 (1926), 191–222.
Subj 71

22882 NNC P P1 G1.2 1644–1895
Skachkov, Petr Emel'ianovich, 1892–1964.
'Russkie vrachi pri Rossiiskoi dukhovnoi missii v Pekine' (Russian doctors connected with the Russian Orthodox ecclesiastical mission in Peking). [With English abstract]
SK 1958, 4, 136–148.
Subj 56 71

22883 NNC U P1 G9.2 1644–1842
Strumpfel, ———.
'Robert Morrison' (Robert Morrison).
Allgemeine Missions-Z. 32, 1 (Jan. 1905), 1–15.
Subj 71

22884 NNC S P1 G1.1 1895–1911
Tikhvinskii, Sergei Leonidovich, 1918–.
'Burzhuaznaia istoriografiia o bor'be Sun' IAt-sena za natsional'nuiu nezavisimost' Kitaia' (Bourgeois historiography of Sun Yat-sen's struggle for Chinese national independence). In *Sovremennaia istoriografiia stran zarubezhnogo Vostoka, vyp. 1, Kitai* (Current historiography of countries of the non-Soviet Orient, Vol. 1, China), edited by Boris Nikolaevich Zanegin et al. [Selective entry]
Moscow: Izd-vo vost. lit-ry, 1963, 138–155.
Subj 32.2 71

22885 CSU S P2 G1.3 –1842
Trauzettel, Rolf, 1930–.
'Stabilität und Kontinuität der chinesischen Gesellschaft: Bemerkungen zum Werk des Sinologen Etienne Balazs, 1905–1963' (Stability and continuity of Chinese society: Observations on the work of the sinologist Etienne Balazs, 1905–1963).
Saeculum 18, 3 (1967), 264–277.
Subj 12 16 71 ▪ 16.2 64

22886 MCH S P1 G1.1 –1911
van der Sprenkel, Otto P- N- Berkelbach, 1906–.
'Max Weber on China.'
History and theory 3, 3 (1964), 348–370.
Subj 10 16 71 ▪ 12 16.1 30 42

22887 MCH S P3 G9.2 1644–1895
Vargas, Philippe de, 1888–1956.
'William C. Hunter's books on the old Canton factories.' [Review of *The 'fan kwae' at Canton before treaty days, 1825–1844*, by William C- Hunter; and *Bits of old China*, by William C- Hunter.]
YJSS 2, 1 (July 1939), 91–117.
Subj 71 ▪ 34.2 66

22888 CSH S P1 G1.2 1644–1911
Widmer, Eric George, 1940–.
'Recent Soviet studies of the Ch'ing.'
CSWT 1, 7 (Nov. 1967), 3–7.
Subj 71

1644-1949

22889 NNC U P1 G1.3 –1928
'Otto Franke und sein sinologisches Werk' (Otto Franke and his sinological work).
Sinologica 1, 4 (1948), 352–354.
Subj 71

22890 NNC U P1 G1.3 1842–1949
Auboyer, Jeannine, 1912–.
'Paul Pelliot, 1878–1945' (Paul Pelliot, 1878–1945).
Artibus Asiae 9, 1/3 (1946), 141–143.
Subj 71

22891 NNC U P1 G1.3 1895–1949
Chang, Carsun (Chang Chia-sen), 1886–.
'Richard Wilhelm, der Weltbürger' (Richard Wilhelm, citizen of the world).
Sinica 5, 2 (März 1930), 71–73.
Subj 71

22892 CSU S P1 G1.3 –1949
Demiéville, Paul, 1894–.
'Aperçu historique des études sinologiques en France' (Historical sketch of sinological studies in France).
Acta Asiatica (Tokyo) 11 (Sept. 1966), 56–110.
SUBJ 71

22893 CSU O P1 G1.2 –1949
Demiéville, Paul, 1894–.
'Henri Maspero et l'avenir des études chinoises' (Henri Maspero and the future of Chinese studies).
TP 2e série 38, 1 (1947), 16–42.
SUBJ 71 ▪ 13 23

22894 MCH S P1 G1.1 –1949
Duyvendak, Jan Julius Lodewijk, 1889–1954.
'China in de Nederlandse letterkunde' (China in Dutch literature). In *Jaarboek der Maatschappij der Nederlandse Letterkunde* (Yearbook of the Society of Dutch Literature). [Sole entry]
Leiden: Brill, 1938, 3–14.
SUBJ 71 72

22895 FPN S P1 G1.1 1895–1928
Duyvendak, Jan Julius Lodewijk, 1889–1954.
'Herdenking van Paul Pelliot (28 Mei 1878 – 26 Oktober 1945)' (Paul Pelliot, 28 May 1878 – 26 October 1945). In *Jaarboek der Koninklijke Nederlandse Akademie van Wetenschappen* (Yearbook of the Royal Dutch Academy of Sciences). [Sole entry]
Amsterdam: Koninklijke Nederlandse Akademie van Wetenschappen, 1946, 238–243.
SUBJ 71

22896 FPN S P1 G1.1 1895–1928
Duyvendak, Jan Julius Lodewijk, 1889–1954.
'Levensbericht van Heinrich Hackmann (31 Augustus 1864 – 18 Juli 1935)' (Biography of Heinrich Hackmann, 31 August 1864 – 18 July 1935). In *Jaarboek der Koninklijke Akademie van Weetenschappen* (Yearbook of the Royal Academy of Sciences). [Sole entry]
Amsterdam: Koninklijke Akademie van Wettenschappen, 1933/36, 239–249.
SUBJ 71 ▪ 62

22897 NNC U P1 G1.2 1842–1949
Eberhard, Wolfram, 1909–.
'Otto Franke, 1863–1946: In Memoriam' (In memory of Otto Franke, 1863–1946).
Artibus Asiae 9, 4 (1946), 353–354.
SUBJ 71

22898 NNC S P1 G1.3 1644–1928
Erkes, Eduard, 1891–1958, and Bruno Schindler, 1882–.
'Zur Geschichte der europäischen Sinologie' (Toward a history of European sinology).
Ostasiatische Z. 5 (1916/17), 105–115.
SUBJ 71

22899 CSH S P2 G1.1 1644–1949
Fairbank, John King, 1907–, and Masataka Banno, 1916–.
Japanese studies of modern China: A bibliographical guide to historical and social-science research on the 19th and 20th centuries.
Rutland, Vt.: Charles E. Tuttle, 1955. 28, 331 p. [Reprinted—Cambridge: Harvard U. Press, 1971. 28, 331 p. (Harvard-Yenching Institute studies, 26) (Slightly rev.)]
SUBJ 71 72

22900 NNC U P1 G1.2 –1949
Finsterbusch, Barbara Käte, 1924–.
'In Memoriam: Eduard Erkes, 23 Juli 1891 – 2 April 1958' (In memory of Eduard Erkes, 23 July 1891 – 2 April 1958).
Artibus Asiae 21, 2 (1958), 167–170.
SUBJ 71

22901 NNC U P1 G1.0 –1949
Forke, Alfred, 1867–1944.
'De Groots Lebenswerk' (The lifework of Jan Jakob Maria de Groot).
Ostasiatische Z. 9 (1920/22), 266–275.
SUBJ 71

22902 NNC S P1 G1.2 –1928
Franke, Otto, 1863–1946.
'China' (China). In *Aus Kultur und Geschichte Chinas* (Chinese culture and history), by O. Franke. [Selective entry]
Peiping: Deutschland-Institut, 1945, 358–373.
SUBJ 12.1 71 ▪ 12 19 61 64

22903 NNC S P1 G1.2 –1949
Franke, Otto, 1863–1946.
'Die Chinakunde in Deutschland' (Chinese studies in Germany). In *Aus Kultur und Geschichte Chinas* (Chinese culture and history), by O. Franke. [Selective entry]
Peiping: Deutschland-Institut, 1945, 385–394.
SUBJ 71 ▪ 72

22904 NNC S P1 G1.2 1842–1928
Franke, Otto, 1863–1946.
'Edouard Chavannes' (Edouard Chavannes).
Ostasiatische Z. 6, 1/2 (1917), 87–94.
SUBJ 71

22905 CBU O P3 G1.1 1842–1949
Franke, Otto, 1863–1946.
Erinnerungen aus zwei Welten: Randglossen zur eigenem Lebensgeschichte (Memories from two worlds: Marginalia on my life).
Berlin: de Gruyter, 1954. 185 p.
SUBJ 71 ▪ 66

22906 NNC S P1 G1.2 –1949
Franke, Wolfgang, 1912–.
'Die Entwicklung der Chinakunde in den letzen 50 Jahren' (The development of China studies in the past fifty years).
NDG 72 (Juni 1952), 8–18.
SUBJ 71

22907 DLC S P1 G1.1 –1928
Godes, M-, et al.
Diskussiia ob aziatskom sposobe proizvodstva po dokladu M. Godesa (A discussion of the Asiatic mode of production: Report by M. Godes).
Moscow: Sotsekgiz, 1931. 180 p.
SUBJ 71 ▪ 14 64

22908 CSU U P2 G1.2 1644–1949
Hao Wu-Teh.
'The history of a social myth.'
PT new (2nd) series 5, 1 (1 Aug. 1933), 33–39.
SUBJ 11 71

22909 NNC U P1 G1.2 1895–1949
Hummel, Arthur William, 1884–.
'Berthold Laufer, 1874–1934.'
AA new (2nd) series 38, 1 (Jan.–Mar. 1936), 101–111.
SUBJ 71

22910 CSU S P1 G1.1 1842–1949
Kublin, Hyman, 1919–.
'Introduction.' In *Jews in old China: Some western views*, compiled by H. Kublin. [Selective entry]
New York: Paragon, 1971, 11–22 [s.p.].
SUBJ 71

22911 NNC O P1 G1.1 1842–1928
Latourette, Kenneth Scott, 1884–1968.
'American scholarship and Chinese history.'
JAOS 38, 2 (Apr. 1918), 97–106.
SUBJ 71

22912 NNC O P1 G1.1 –1928
Latourette, Kenneth Scott, 1884–1968.
'A survey of the work by western students of Chinese history.'
JRAS-NCB new (2nd) series 47 (1916), 103–115.
SUBJ 71 ▪ 62

22913 CSU S P1 G1.2 –1949
Merkel, Rudolf Franz, 1870–?
'Heinrich Hackmann: Zum 70. Geburtstag am 31. August 1934' (In honor of Heinrich Hackmann on his seventieth birthday, 31 August 1934).
Sinica 9, 3/4 (Mai–Juli 1934), 175–176.
SUBJ 71

22914 MCH P P1 G1.1 –1949
Minderaa, Pieter, 1893–.
'Jan Julius Lodewijk Duyvendak (1889–1954)' (Jan Julius Lodewijk Duyvendak, 1889–1954). In *Jaarboek van de Maatschappij der Nederlandse Letterkunde te Leiden* (Yearbook of the Society of Dutch Literature of Leiden). [Sole entry]
Leiden: Maatschappij der Nederlandse Letterkunde te Leiden, 1956, 68–81.
SUBJ 71

22915 CSH S P1 G9.4 1895–1928
Myers, Ramon Hawley, 1929–.
'The research of the "Commission for the Investigation of Traditional Customs in Taiwan".'
CSWT 2, 6 (June 1971), 24–54.
SUBJ 71

22916 NIC S P1 G1.2 1644–1949
Peake, Cyrus Henderson, 1900–.
'Recent studies on Chinese law.'
Political science q. 52, 1 (Mar. 1937), 117–138.
SUBJ 12.2 70 71 72

22917 CSU S P1 G1.1 1842–1949
Reid, John Gilbert, 1899–.
'A brief survey of German works on modern Chinese history.'
PHR 2, 3 (July 1933), 329–335.
SUBJ 71 ▪ 62

22918 NNC U P1 G1.3 1895–1949
Schüler, Wilhelm, 1869–1935.
'Richard Wilhelm's wissenschaftliche Arbeit' (The scholarly work of Richard Wilhelm).
Sinica 5, 2 (März 1930), 57–71.
SUBJ 71 ▪ 72

22919 CSH S P1 G1.1 1644–1928
Skachkov, Petr Emel'ianovich, 1892–1964.
'Vedomost' o kitaiskoi zemle' (Information on China). In *Strany i narody Vostoka: geografiia, etnografiia, istoriia* (Countries and peoples of the Orient: Geography, ethnography, and history), edited by Vostochnaia komissiia, Geograficheskoe obshchestvo SSSR, Akademiia nauk SSSR. [Selective entry]
Moscow: Izd-vo vost. lit-ry, 1961, vol. 2, 206–219.
SUBJ 71 ▪ 12 72

22920 NNC S P1 G1.1 1842–1928
Thompson, Laurence Gassius, 1926–.
'American sinology, 1830–1920: A bibliographical survey.'
THJ new (2nd) series 2, 2 (June 1961), 244–285.
SUBJ 71 72

22921 MCH U P1 G1.1 1842–1949
Tscharner, Eduard Horst von, 1901–1962.
Die Chinakunde als Wissenschaft (Chinese studies as a science).
St. Gallen: Tschudy, 1940. 24 p.
SUBJ 71

22922 DLC S P1 G1.1 1842–1928
Vostochnyi, pseud.
'Ekonomicheskaia kharakteristika Kitaia v sovremennoi russkoi literature: kriticheskii obzor' (Critical overview of the nature of China's economy as reflected in contemporary Russian literature).
Ekonomicheskaia zhizn' Dal'nego Vostoka 6, 4/5 (1928), 163–174.
SUBJ 14 71 ▪ 11 16

22923 NIC FP P2 G1.3 –1949
Wittfogel, Karl August, 1896–.
New light on Chinese society: An investigation of China's socio-economic structure.
New York: Institute of Pacific Relations, International Secretariat, 1938. 41 p.
SUBJ 10 71 ▪ 12 14 16 40

22924 NIC P P1 G1.2 –1949
Wright, Arthur Frederick, 1913–.
'On the uses of generalization in the study of Chinese history.' In *Generalization in the writing of history*, edited by Louis Gottschalk. [Sole entry]
Chicago: U. of Chicago Press, 1963, 36–58.
SUBJ 71 ▪ 16.1 62 66

22925 MCH S P1 G1.2 1895–1949
Yang, Kun (Yang K'un), 1901–.
'Marcel Granet: An appreciation.'
YJSS 1, 2 (Jan. 1939), 226–241.
SUBJ 71

22926 CSH P P2 G1.2 1895–1949
Young, John (Yang Chüeh-yung), 1920–.
The research activities of the South Manchurian Railway Company, 1907–1945: A history and bibliography.
New York: Columbia U., East Asian Institute, 1966. 678 p.
SUBJ 71 72

1911-1949

22927 MCH S P1 G1.2 1911–1928
Bereznyi, Lev Abramovich, 1915–.
'Protiv burzhuaznykh kontseptsii nachal'nogo etapa noveishei istorii Kitaia, 1917–1927' (In opposition to the bourgeois conception of the initial stage of China's recent history, 1917–1927). In *Problemy istorii natsional'no-osvoboditel'nogo dvizheniia v stranakh Azii* (Historical problems of the national liberation movement in Asian countries), edited by Gerontii Valentinovich Efimov. [Selective entry]
Leningrad: Izd-vo Leningr. un-ta, 1963, 36–65.
SUBJ 64 71

22928 CSH O P2 G1.3 1928–1949
Buck, John Lossing, 1890–.
'The agricultural economy of China, 1927–1937, as exemplified by the work at the University of Nanking' [with comments by Franklin L. Ho (Ho Lien)]. In *The strenuous decade: China's nation-building efforts, 1927–1937*, edited by Paul K. T. Sih (Hsüeh Kuang-ch'ien). [Selective entry]
Jamaica, N.Y.: St. John's U. Press, 1970, 171–203.
SUBJ 14.1 17 70 71 ▪ 12 14.6 36.1

22929 NNC S P1 G1.3 1911–1928
Dostoyewski, Milius.
'China und seine Probleme im Lichte der Literatur der Sowjet-Union' (China and its problems, from the perspective of Soviet literature).
Sinica 2, 4/5 (1927), 79–87.
SUBJ 71

22930 NNC S P1 G1.3 1911–1928
Dostoyewski, Milius.
'Das moderne China in russischer Darstellung' (Modern China in Russian literature).
Sinica 3, 1 (1928), 46–49; 3, 2 (1928), 92–95; 3, 3/4 (1928), 168–170.
SUBJ 71

22931 MCH S P1 G1.1 1911–1928
Efimov, Gerontii Valentinovich, 1906–.
'K istoriografii dvizheniia 4 maia' (Historiography of the May Fourth Movement). In *Problemy istorii natsional'no-osvoboditel'nogo dvizheniia v stranakh Azii* (Historical problems of the national liberation movement in Asian countries), edited by G. V. Efimov. [Selective entry]
Leningrad: Izd-vo Leningr. un-ta, 1963, 66–75.
SUBJ 62 71 ▪ 19 32.2 64

22932 NIC S P2 G1.2 1911–1949
Fried, Morton Herbert, 1923–.
'Community studies in China.'
FEQ 14, 1 (Nov. 1954), 11–36.
SUBJ 70 71 ▪ 16 55 61 72

22933 CSU S P1 G1.2 1911–1949
Jabłoński, Witold.
'Marcel Granet and his work.'
YJSS 1, 2 (Jan. 1939), 242–255.
SUBJ 71

22934 CSU S P1 G1.2 1911–1928
Jacobs, Daniel Norman, 1925–.
'Recent Russian material on Soviet advisers in China: 1923–1927.'
CQ 41 (Jan.–Mar. 1970), 103–112.
SUBJ 71 ▪ 32 32.2 66

22935 CSU P P1 G1.2 1928–1949
Levine, Steven I., 1941–.
'Trotsky on China: The exile period.'
PC 18 (Dec. 1964), 90–128.
SUBJ 71 ▪ 64

22936 CSU S P1 G1.2 1911–1949
Levy, Marion Joseph, Jr., 1918–.
'Granet, Marcel.' In *International encyclopedia of the social sciences*, edited by David L. Sills. [Selective entry]
New York: Macmillan *with* Free Press of Glencoe, 1968, vol. 6, 241–243.
SUBJ 71

22937 NNC O P1 G1.2 1911–1949
Otte, W. F.
'Richard Wilhelm: Ein Bild seiner Persönlichkeit' (Richard Wilhelm: A personality sketch).
Sinica 5, 2 (März 1930), 49–57.
SUBJ 71

22938 CSU P P1 G1.2 1928–1949
Schwartz, Benjamin Isadore, 1916–.
'A Marxist controversy on China.'
FEQ 13, 2 (Feb. 1954), 143–153.
SUBJ 71 ▪ 64

22939 CSU P P2 G1.2 1911–1949
Shewmaker, Kenneth Earl, 1936–.
Americans and Chinese Communists, 1927–1945: A persuading encounter.
Ithaca: Cornell U. Press, 1971. 10, 387 p. (Revision of *Persuading encounter: American reporters and Chinese Communists, 1927–1945*, doctoral dissertation in History, Northwestern U., 1966)
SUBJ 71 ▪ 12 15 16.1 30 32 32.2 66 72

22940 MCY O P2 G1.2 1928–1949
[Shirokogorov, Sergei Mikhailovich] S. M. Shirokogoroff, 1887–1939.
'Ethnographic investigation of China.'
FS 1 (1942), 1–8.
SUBJ 71 ▪ 70

22941 NNC P P2 G1.2 1928–1949
Sikirianskaia, Liia Abramovna, ?–1959.
'Velikii pokhod Kitaiskoi Krasnoi Armii, 1934–1936 gg.' (The Long March of the Chinese Red Army, 1934–1936).
KSIV 3 (1952), 33–39. [For a fuller version, see entry 13963.]
SUBJ 15 32.2 71 ▪ 64 72

22942 CSU S P1 G1.2 1928–1949
Ubukata Naokichi, 1905–.
'Profile of Asian minded man. 1, Tadao Yanaihara: His colonial studies and religious faith.'
DE 4, 1 (Mar. 1966), 90–105.
SUBJ 71 ▪ 32 32.2 72

22943 CSU S P1 G1.2 1911–1949
Yamamoto, Hideo, 1911–.
'Profile of Asian minded man. 3, Shiraki Tachibana.'
DE 4, 3 (Sept. 1966), 381–403.
SUBJ 71 ▪ 64 72

22944 NNC O P1 G1.2 1911–1928
Zach, Erwin von, 1872–1942.
'Sinologische Seminare und Bibliotheken' (Sinological institutes and libraries).
Ostasiatische Z. 7 (1918/19), 238–241.
SUBJ 71

1911-1972
(including 1644-1972)

22945 NNC S P4 G1.1 1911–1972
Akatova, Tat'iana Nikolaevna, 1923–.
'Izuchenie v SSSR istorii kitaiskogo rabochego dvizheniia' (Study in the U.S.S.R. of the history of the Chinese labor movement). In *Sovremennaia istoriografiia stran zarubezhnogo Vostoka, vyp. 1, Kitai* (Current historiography of countries of the non-Soviet Orient, Vol. 1, China), edited by Boris Nikolaevich Zanegin et al. [Selective entry]
Moscow: Izd-vo vost. lit-ry, 1963, 122–137.
SUBJ 71 ▪ 36.4 72

22946 NNC O P1 G1.2 1895–1972
Alekseeva, N- M-.
'Arkhiv akademika V. M. Alekseeva' (Archives of the academician Vasilii Mikhailovich Alekseev).
SK 1958, 2, 198–204.
SUBJ 71 72

22947 NNC P P1 G1.2 1928–1972
Arturov, O- A-, Vil' Gdal'evich Gel'bras, 1930–, and T- G- Maiorova.
'Protiv poverkhnostnogo osveshcheniia ekonomiki Narodnogo Kitaia' (In opposition to superficial treatment of the economics of the People's Republic of China). [Review of a lecture by A. M. Kosolapov, 'The economic system of the People's Republic of China'.]
Vestnik vysshei shkoly 16, 1 (ianvar' 1958), 82–87.
SUBJ 14 71 ▪ 14.4 16 24.4 32.2

22948 CBU S P1 G1.1 1911–1972
Banno, Masataka, 1916–, et al.
'Development of Chinese studies in postwar Japan.'
DE 2, 3 (Sept.–Dec. 1962), 57–98.
SUBJ 71 ▪ 72

22949 CSU U P1 G1.2 1895–1972
Bates, Miner Searle, 1897–.
'Christian historian, doer of Christian history: In memory of Kenneth Scott Latourette, 1884–1968.'
International review of missions 58, 231 (July 1969), 317–326.
SUBJ 71 ▪ 62

22950 CSH S P2 G1.2 –1972
Bereznyi, Lev Abramovich, 1915–.
Kritika metodologii amerikanskoi burzhuaznoi istoriografii Kitaia (problem y obshchestvennogo razvitiia v 19 – pervoi polovine 20 veka.
Leningrad: Izd-vo Leningr. un-ta, 1968. 262 p.
An unauthorized digest of L. A. Bereznii, 'A critique of American bourgeois historiography on China: Problems of social development in the nineteenth and early twentieth centuries'. Tr. by Ellen Widmer. [Greatly abridged in tr.]
Cambridge: Harvard U., East Asian Research Center, 1969. 46 p.
SUBJ 10 71 ▪ 14 16 32 32.2

22951 CSU S P1 G1.2 –1972
Chesneaux, Jean, 1922–.
'Où en est la discussion sur le mode de production asiatique (III)' (The debate on the Asiatic mode of production, Part 3).
La pensée nouvelle (2e) série 138 (mars–avr. 1968), 47–55.
SUBJ 71 ▪ 70

22952 MCY O P1 G1.2 1911–1972
Chesneaux, Jean, 1922–.
'Perspectives des études d'histoire contemporaine chinoise' (Prospects for the study of contemporary Chinese history).
AO 31, 2 (1963), 310–320.
SUBJ 71

22953 CSU S P1 G1.3 1842–1972
Chesneaux, Jean, 1922–.
'Les recherches sur l'histoire moderne et contemporaine de Chine à Paris' (Research in Paris on the history of modern and contemporary China).
R. historique 235 (avr.–juin 1966), 413–422.
SUBJ 71

22954 FPN P P1 G1.2 1895–1972
Chesneaux, Jean, 1922–, and John Lust, 1918–.
Introduction aux études d'histoire contemporaine de Chine, 1898–1949 (Introduction to studies of modern Chinese history, 1898–1949).
The Hague: Mouton, 1964. 148 p. (Maison des sciences de l'homme, Matériaux pour l'étude de l'Extrême-Orient moderne et contemporain, 2)
SUBJ 70 71 72 ▪ 12 14 15 16 32 32.2 59 60

22955 CSH P P2 G1.2 –1972
Chudodeev, IUrii Vladimirovich, 1931–.
'Obshchestvo i gosudarstvo v Kitae' (Society and state in China).
NAA 1971, 6, 220–223.
SUBJ 16 71 ▪ 12 15

22956 MCH S P1 G1.2 1928–1972
Cohen, Jerome Alan, 1930–.
'Introduction.' In *Contemporary Chinese law: Research problems and perspectives*, edited by J. A. Cohen. [Selective entry]
Cambridge: Harvard U. Press, 1970, 1–19. (Harvard studies in East Asian law, 4)
SUBJ 71 ▪ 12.2 72

22957 CSU S P1 G1.2 –1972
Cohen, Jerome Alan, 1930–.
'New developments in western studies of Chinese law: A symposium (Introduction).'
JAS 27, 3 (May 1968), 475–483.
SUBJ 12.2 71

22958 NIC P P1 G1.1 1895–1972
Demiéville, Paul, 1894–.
'Etienne Balazs (1905–1963)' (Etienne Balazs, 1905–1963).
TP 2e série 51, 2/3 (1964), 247–261.
SUBJ 71 ▪ 72

22959 NNC S P1 G1.2 1842–1972
Eder, Matthias, 1902–.
'Gedanken zur Methode der chinesischen Volkskundeforschung' (Toward a methodology of folklore research in China).
FS 9 (1950), 207–212.
SUBJ 71 ▪ 72

22960 CSU S P1 G1.1 1842–1972
Fairbank, John King, 1907–.
'Assignment for the '70's.'
American historical review 74, 3 (Feb. 1969), 861–879.
SUBJ 71

22961 MCH S P1 G1.2 1842–1972
Franke, Herbert, 1914–.
Sinologie (Sinology).
Bern: A. Francke, 1953. 216 p. (Wissenschaftliche Forschungsberichte, Geisteswissenschaftliche Reihe, 19; Orientalistik, Teil 1)
SUBJ 70 71 ▪ 72

22962 CBU S P1 G1.2 –1972
Franke, Herbert, 1914–.
Sinologie an deutschen Universitäten, mit einem Anhang über die Mandschustudien.
Wiesbaden: Steiner, 1968. 58 p.
Sinology at German universities, with a supplement on Manchu studies.
Wiesbaden: Steiner, 1968. 59 p.
SUBJ 71

22963 MCH S P1 G1.1 1644–1972
Franke, Wolfgang, 1912–.
'Probleme und heutiger Stand der Chinaforschung in Deutschland' (Problems and current status of China studies in Germany).
Moderne Welt 1, 3/4 (1959/60), 409–428.
SUBJ 71 72

22964 NIC S P2 G1.1 1911–1972
Freedman, Maurice, 1920–.
'A Chinese phase in social anthropology.'
British j. of sociology 14, 1 (Mar. 1963), 1–19.
SUBJ 70 71

22965 NIC S P1 G1.0 1911–1972
Freedman, Maurice, 1920–.
'What social science can do for Chinese studies.'
JAS 23, 4 (Aug. 1964), 523–529.
SUBJ 71

22966 CSU U P1 G1.1 1928–1972
Fujieda, Akira, and Wilma Fairbank, 1909–.
'Current trends in Japanese studies of China and adjacent areas.'
FEQ 13, 1 (Nov. 1953), 37–47.
SUBJ 71

22967 CSU S P1 G1.2 –1972
Fukushima Masao, 1906–.
'Profile of Asian minded man. 6, Noboru Niida.'
DE 5, 1 (Mar. 1967), 173–190.
SUBJ 71 ▪ 72

22968 CSU S P1 G1.1 1911–1972
Goodpasture, H- McKennie.
'China in an American, Frank Wilson Price: A bibliographical essay.'

J. of Presbyterian history 49, 4 (Winter 1971), 352–364.
Subj 71 72

22969 CSU U P1 G1.2 1895–1972
Goodrich, Luther Carrington, 1894–.
'Homer Dubs (1892–1969).'
JAS 29, 4 (Aug. 1970), 889–891.
Subj 71

22970 CSU S P1 G1.1 1644–1972
Goodrich, Luther Carrington, 1894–.
'Recent developments in Chinese studies.'
JAOS 85, 2 (Apr.–June 1965), 117–121.
Subj 71 ▪ 70

22971 NNC S P1 G1.1 1911–1972
Gorbacheva, Zoia Ivanovna, 1907–, Lev Nikolaevich Men'shikov, and N- A- Petrov.
'Kitaevedenie v Leningrade za sorok let' (Forty years of Chinese studies in Leningrad).
UZIV 25 (1960), 82–101.
Subj 71 ▪ 72

22972 NIC P P1 G1.1 –1972
Gotō, Kimpei, 1926–.
'Studies on Chinese religion in postwar Japan.'
MS 15, 2 (1956), 463–511.
Subj 33 71 72

22973 NNC S P1 G1.3 –1972
Grimm, Tilemann, 1922–.
'Bemerkungen zum Studium der Sinologie in Japan' (Observations on sinological studies in Japan).
NDG 83 (1958), 61–70.
Subj 71

22974 GMS S P1 G1.1 1911–1972
Grossmann, Bernhard Paul, 1929–.
Die Asienkunde in den USA (Asian studies in the United States).
Hamburg: Institut für Asienkunde, 1966. 96 p. (IA, Mitteilungen, 16)
Subj 71

22975 MCH U P1 G1.2 1928–1972
Halpern, Abraham Meyer, 1914–.
'Contemporary China as a problem for political science.'
WP 15, 3 (Apr. 1963), 361–376.
Subj 71 ▪ 12

22976 NNC S P1 G1.1 –1972
Honda, Minobu, and Eric B- Ceadel.
'Postwar Japanese research on the Far East (excluding Japan).'
Asia Major new (3rd) series 4, 1 (July 1954), 103–149.
Subj 71

22977 CSU S P1 G1.2 1911–1972
Horowitz, David.
'Politics and knowledge: An unorthodox history of modern China studies.'
BCAS 3, 3/4 (Summer–Fall 1971), 139–168.
Subj 71

22978 CSU S P1 G1.2 –1972
Hucker, Charles Oscar, 1919–.
Chinese history: A bibliographic review.
Washington, D.C.: American Historical Assn., 1958. 42 p. (AHA, Service Center for Teachers of History publications, 15)
Subj 71 72 ▪ 70

22979 CSH S P1 G1.1 1842–1972
Hulsewé, Anthony François Paulus, 1910–.
'Chinese and Japanese studies in Holland.'
CC 10, 3 (Sept. 1969), 67–75.
Subj 71

22980 MCH S P1 G1.1 –1972
Jäger, Fritz, 1886–1957.
'Otto Franke (1863–1946)' (Otto Franke, 1863–1946).
ZDMG 100 (1950), 19–36.
Subj 71

22981 NNC S P1 G1.1 1928–1972
Kovalev, Evgenii Fedorovich, 1907–.
'Izuchenie Kitaia v Sovetskom Soiuze' (Chinese studies in the Soviet Union).
SV 1955, 3, 158–162.
Subj 71 ▪ 72

22982 DLC P P1 G1.1 1911–1972
Kuznetsova, Nina Alekseevna, 1924–, and Liudmila Mikhailovna Kulagina, 1927–.
Iz istorii sovetskogo vostokovedeniia, 1917–1967 (History of Oriental studies in the Soviet Union, 1917–1967).
Moscow: Nauka, Glav. red. vost. lit-ry, 1970. 251 p.
Subj 71

22983 DLC U P1 G1.1 –1972
Levenson, Joseph Richmond, 1920–1969.
'The humanistic disciplines: Will sinology do?'
JAS 23, 4 (Aug. 1964), 507–512.
Subj 71

22984 MCH S P1 G1.1 –1972
Levy, Marion Joseph, Jr., 1918–.
'Some light on the Far East.' [Review of *Oriental despotism: A comparative study of total power,* by Karl August Wittfogel; and *Science and civilisation in China. Vol. 1, Introductory orientations. Vol. 2, History of scientific thought,* by Noël Joseph Terence Montgomery Needham.]
WP 10, 3 (Apr. 1958), 462–474.
Subj 10 62 71 ▪ 12 12.1 64

22985 CSU O P1 G1.1 1928–1972
Lindbeck, John Matthew Henry, 1915–1971.
Understanding China: An assessment of scholarly resources.
New York: Praeger, 1971. 159 p.
Subj 71

22986 NNC U P1 G1.2 1928–1972
Liu, Ts'un-yan (Liu Ts'un-jen), 1917–.
Chinese scholarship in Australia.
Canberra: Australian National U., 1967. 20 p.
Subj 71

22987 CSU S P1 G1.1 1842–1972
Löwenthal, Rudolf, 1904–.
'Russian contributions to the history of Islam in China.'
Central Asiatic j. 7, 4 (Dec. 1962), 312–315.
Subj 71 ▪ 72

22988 CSU S P1 G1.2 –1972
Masubuchi, Tatsuo, 1916–.
'Wittfogel's theory of Oriental society (or hydraulic society) and the development of studies of Chinese social and economic history in Japan.'
DE 4, 3 (Sept. 1966), 316–333.
Subj 71 ▪ 12 14 16

22989 NNC U P1 G1.1 –1972
Mote, Frederick Wade, 1922–.
'The case for the integrity of sinology.'
JAS 23, 4 (Aug. 1964), 531–534.
Subj 71

22990 ELB S P1 G1.2 1895–1972
Nikiforov, Vladimir Nikolaevich, 1920–.
'Izuchenie istorii Kitaia v SSSR.'
VI 1969, 6 (iiun'), 158–168.
'The study of Chinese history in the U.S.S.R.'
Soviet studies in history 8, 2 (Fall 1969), 143–166. [Reprinted—*Soviet review* 11, 3 (Fall 1970), 258–281.]
Subj 71 72 ▪ 62

22991 CBU S P2 G1.2 –1972
Nikiforov, Vladimir Nikolaevich, 1920–.
Sovetskie istoriki o problemakh Kitaia (Soviet historians on the problems of China).
Moscow: Nauka, Glav. red. vost. lit-ry, 1970. 416 p.
Subj 12 16 32.2 64 71 72 ▪ 14.1 24.4 33 35 36.4 66

22992 CSU P P1 G1.3 1928–1972
Palát, Augustin.
'Jaroslav Průšek, sexagenarian.'
AO 34, 4 (1966), 481–493.
Subj 71

22993 NNC S P1 G1.1 1928–1972
Parfionovich, IU- M-.
'Obzor dissertatsii po istorii i ekonomike Kitaia, zashchishchennykh v 1946–1956 gg.' (Review of dissertations on Chinese history and economics defended between 1946 and 1956).
SK 1958, 1, 198–201.
Subj 71 ▪ 72

22994 CBU S P1 G1.2 –1972
Pecirka, Jan.
'Die sowjetischen Diskussionen über die asiatische Produktionsweise und über die Sklavenhalterformation' (Soviet discussions of the Asiatic mode of production and the formation of a slave-owning class).
Eirene 3 (1964), 147–169.
Subj 64 71 ▪ 12 14.1 16

22995 CSU S P2 G1.1 –1972
Schwartz, Benjamin Isadore, 1916–.
'A brief defense of political and intellectual history, with particular reference to non-western cultures.'
Daedalus 100, 1 (Winter 1971), 98–112.
Subj 10 71 ▪ 16 62 65

22996 NNC U P2 G1.1 –1972
Skinner, George William, 1925–.
'What the study of China can do for social science.'
JAS 23, 4 (Aug. 1964), 517–522.
Subj 10 71

22997 CSU S P1 G1.2 1644–1972
Sung, Shee (Sung Hsi), 1920–.
'Sinological study in the United States of America.' Tr. by T. W. Kwok of 'Mei-kuo ti han hsüeh yen chiu' (Sinology in the United States); in *Shih chieh ko kuo han hsüeh yen chiu lun wen chi* (Sinology in various countries), by T'ao Chen-yü et al.; Taipei: Kuo fang yen

chiu yüan, 1962, 137–184. In *Sinology in Japan and the United States*, compiled and edited by T. W. Kwok (Kuo Te-hua). [Sole entry]
Honolulu: U. of Hawaii, East-West Center, Institute of Advanced Projects, 1966, 76–127. (IAP translation series, 11) [Reprinted—*CC* 8, 2 (June 1967), 133–170.]
Subj 71

22998 CSU S P1 G1.1 1911–1972
Thornton, Richard Chester, 1936–.
'Soviet historians and China's past.'
Problems of Communism 17, 2 (Mar.–Apr. 1968), 71–75.
Subj 62 71

22999 NNC U P1 G1.1 –1972
Twitchett, Denis Crispin, 1925–.
'A lone cheer for sinology.'
JAS 24, 1 (Nov. 1964), 109–112.
Subj 71

23000 CSU S P1 G1.1 –1972
Twitchett, Denis Crispin, 1925–.
'Niida Noboru and Chinese legal history.'
Asia Major new (3rd) series 13, 1/2 (Jan. 1967), 218–228.
Subj 12.2 71 ▪ 72

23001 NNC S P1 G1.2 1911–1972
V. N.
'K semidesiatiletiiu Petra Emel'ianovicha Skachkova' (On the seventieth birthday of Petr Emel'ianovich Skachkov).
KSINA 55 (1962), 3–7.
Subj 71

23002 CSU P P1 G1.0 1895–1972
van der Sprenkel, Sybille Marie, 1919–.
'V. W. W. S. Purcell: A memoir.' In *Studies in the social history of China and South-east Asia: Essays in memory of Victor Purcell*, edited by Jerome Ch'en (Ch'en Chih-jang) and Nicholas Tarling. [Selective entry]
Cambridge: Cambridge U. Press, 1970, 1–20.
Subj 71

23003 CSU S P2 G1.2 –1972
Viatkin, Rudol'f Vsevolodovich, 1910–.
Sinology: Fifty years of Soviet Oriental studies (brief reviews).
Moscow: Nauka, Central Dept. of Oriental Literature, 1968. 31 p.
Subj 71

23004 NNC S P1 G1.1 1842–1972
Vinogradov, T- V-.
'Organizatsiia kitaevedeniia v IAponii' (The organization of Chinese studies in Japan).
KSINA 66 (1963), 126–139.
Subj 71

23005 CSH S P1 G1.2 –1972
Wheeler, Geoffrey.
'A new look at Oriental studies.'
Royal Central Asian j. 55, 1 (Feb. 1968), 12–19.
Subj 71

23006 CSU S P1 G1.0 –1972
Wilson, Richard Whittingham, 1933–.
'Chinese studies in crisis.' [Review of *China in crisis, Vol. 1, China's heritage and the Communist political system*, edited by Ping-ti Ho and Tang Tsou.]
WP 23, 2 (Jan. 1971), 295–317.
Subj 10 71

23007 NNC P P1 G1.2 1842–1972
Wittfogel, Karl August, 1896–.
'The Marxist view of China.'
CQ 11 (July–Sept. 1962), 1–20; 12 (Oct.–Dec. 1962), 154–169.
Subj 10 14 70 71 ▪ 14.1 19 45 62 64

23008 NIC S P1 G1.2 1644–1972
Wright, Arthur Frederick, 1913–.
'The study of Chinese civilization.'
J. of the history of ideas 21, 2 (Apr.–June 1960), 233–255.
Subj 64 71

23009 CSU O P1 G1.0 1928–1972
Wu, Eugene W. (Wu Wen-chin), 1922–.
'Mary Clabaugh Wright: A memorial.'
CQ 43 (July–Sept. 1970), 134–135.
Subj 71

1949-1972

23010 NNC S P1 G1.1 1949–1972
'An analysis of Chinese studies in American colleges and universities, 1955–1956: A summary.'
CC 1, 1 (July 1957), 201–252.
Subj 71 ▪ 72

23011 CBU O P1 G1.1 1949–1972
'Kitaevedenie za rubezhom' (Sinology abroad).
SK 1958, 1, 218–238; 1958, 2, 220–238; 1958, 3, 213–227; 1958, 4, 291–303.
Subj 71 ▪ 70

23012 CSU S P1 G1.2 1949–1972
Almond, Gabriel Abraham, 1911–.
'Some thoughts on Chinese political studies.' In *China: Management of a revolutionary society*, edited by John Matthew Henry Lindbeck. [Analytic entry]
Seattle: U. of Washington Press, 1971, 377–384. (Social Science Research Council, Studies in Chinese government and politics, 2)
Subj 71

23013 CSU U P1 G1.1 1949–1972
Barnett, Arthur Doak, 1921–.
'John Lindbeck: A memorial.'
CQ 45 (Jan.–Mar. 1971), 155–156.
Subj 71

23014 MCH S P1 G1.2 1949–1972
Berman, Harold Joseph, 1918–.
'Soviet perspectives on Chinese law.' In *Contemporary Chinese law: Research problems and perspectives*, edited by Jerome Alan Cohen. [Selective entry]
Cambridge: Harvard U. Press, 1970, 313–327. (Harvard studies in East Asian law, 4)
Subj 71 ▪ 12.2

23015 CSU S P1 G1.1 1949–1972
Boorman, Howard Lyon, 1920–.
'The study of contemporary Chinese politics: Some remarks on retarded development.'
WP 12, 4 (July 1960), 585–599.
Subj 71

23016 NNC O P1 G1.2 1949–1972
Bushev, P- P-.
'Rabota Instituta vostokovedeniia Akademii nauk SSSR v 1954 g. i plan 1955 g.' (The work of the Institute of Oriental Studies of the USSR Academy of Sciences in 1954 and its plan for 1955).
SV 1955, 2, 158–164.
Subj 71 ▪ 72

23017 CSU U P1 G1.1 1949–1972
Chesneaux, Jean, 1922–.
'Approaches to the study of China.'
BCAS 4 (May 1969), 32–35.
Subj 71

23018 MCH S P1 G1.2 1949–1972
Chesneaux, Jean, 1922–.
'La Chine contemporaine: état des travaux' (Contemporary China: Survey of the field).
R. française de science politique 8, 2 (juin 1958), 384–411.
Subj 10 71 72

23019 MCH O P1 G1.2 1949–1972
Chesneaux, Jean, 1922–.
'Quel Orient faut-il étudier?' (Which Orient should one study?).
La pensée nouvelle (2e) série 48/49 (1953), 175–184.
Subj 71

23020 MCH U P1 G1.2 1949–1972
Chesneaux, Jean, 1922–.
'La recherche marxiste et le réveil contemporain de l'Asie et de l'Afrique' (Marxist research and the current awakening of Asia and Africa).
La pensée nouvelle (2e) série 95 (jan.–fév. 1961), 15–28.
Subj 71

23021 CSU F P2 G1.1 1949–1972
Cohen, Jerome Alan, 1930–.
'Interviewing Chinese refugees: Indispensable aid to legal research on China.'
J. of legal education 20, 4 (1967), 33–62. [Reprinted in *Contemporary Chinese law: Research problems and perspectives*, edited by J. A. Cohen. (Selective entry.) Cambridge: Harvard U. Press, 1970, 84–117. (Harvard studies in East Asian law, 4)]
Subj 12.2 71 ▪ 14.2 16.1 22.2 32.1

23022 CSU S P1 G1.2 1949–1972
Committee of Concerned Asian Scholars. Columbia U. Committee.
'The American Asian studies establishment.' [With comments by John King Fairbank]
BCAS 3, 3/4 (Summer–Fall 1971), 92–111.
Subj 71

23023 NNC S P1 G1.1 1949–1972
Dorrill, William Franklin, 1931–.
Political research on contemporary China: Some problems and opportunities.
Santa Monica, Calif.: RAND Corp., 1964. 26 p. (RAND papers, P-2896)
Subj 71

23024 NNC S P1 G1.1 1949–1972
Duman, Lazar' Isaevich, 1907–.
Review of *Sbornik statei po istorii stran Dal'nego Vostoka* (Articles on Far Eastern history), edited by Larisa Vasil'evna Simonovskaia and Mikhail Filippovich IUr'ev.
KSIV 11 (1954), 92–97.
Subj 71

23025 CSU O P1 G1.1 1949–1972
Eide, Elling O-.
'Methods in sinology: Problems of teaching and learning.'
JAS 31, 1 (Nov. 1971), 131–141.
Subj 71

23026 MCH S P1 G1.2 1949–1972
Faminskii, Igor' Pavlovich.
'Izuchenie ekonomiki Kitaia na ekonomicheskom fakul'tete' (The study of China's economy in the Economics Department [of Moscow University]).
Vestnik Moskovskogo universiteta; seriia ekonomiki, filosofii, prava 14, 4 (1959), 219–222.
Subj 71 ▪ 72

23027 CSU O P2 G9.4 1949–1972
Fessler, Loren, 1923–.
'More "ways" than one: Taoist studies in Taiwan.'
AUFS-EAS 16, 10 (Sept. 1969), 1–20.
Subj 71 ▪ 23 33

23028 CSU S P2 G1.2 1949–1972
Galenson, Walter, 1914–.
'The current state of Chinese economic studies.' In *An economic profile of Mainland China*, compiled by Joint Economic Committee, U.S. Congress. [Selective entry]
Washington, D.C.: U.S. Government Printing Office, 1967, vol. 1, 1–13. [Reprinted in *An economic profile of Mainland China*, compiled by the agency cited. (Selective entry.) New York: Praeger, 1968, 1–13.]
Subj 71 ▪ 14 72

23029 CSU S P1 G1.2 1949–1972
Ginsburgs, George, 1932–.
'Soviet sources on the law of the Chinese People's Republic.'
U. of Toronto law j. 18, 2 (1968), 179–197. [Reprinted in *Contemporary Chinese law: Research problems and perspectives*, edited by Jerome Alan Cohen. (Selective entry.) Cambridge: Harvard U. Press, 1970, 328–355. (Harvard studies in East Asian law, 4)]
Subj 12.2 71 ▪ 72

23030 CSH O P1 G1.2 1949–1972
Grossmann, Bernhard Paul, 1929–.
'China research in Germany today.'
Aussenpolitik 23, 2 (1972), 225–233.
Subj 71

23031 MCH S P1 G1.2 1949–1972
Grossmann, Bernhard Paul, 1929–.
'Die Volksrepublik China im Spiegel der Literatur' (The People's Republic of China as reflected in literature).
Hamburger Jahrbuch für Wirtschafts- und Gesellschaftspolitik 2 (1957), 206–234.
Subj 71 ▪ 72

23032 MCH S P1 G1.2 1949–1972
Il'ichev, L-.
'Sovetskaia iuridicheskaia literatura v KNR, kitaiskaia iuridicheskaia literatura v SSSR' (Soviet legal studies published in the People's Republic of China and Chinese legal studies published in the U.S.S.R.).
SGP 1959, 9 (sentiabr'), 132–135.
Subj 12.2 71 ▪ 70 72

23033 CSU S P1 G1.2 1949–1972
Johnson, Chalmers Ashby, 1931–.
'The role of social science in China scholarship.'
WP 17, 2 (Jan. 1965), 256–271.
Subj 71

23034 CSU O P2 G9.5 1949–1972
Johnson, Elizabeth Lominska, 1941–.
'Study of family organization in an industrial setting.' In *Anthropology and sociology in Hong Kong: Field projects and problems of overseas scholars*, compiled by Marjorie Doreen Topley. [Analytic entry]
Hong Kong: U. of Hong Kong, Centre of Asian Studies, 1969, 97–114.
Subj 41 71 ▪ 51 66

23035 CSU O P2 G9.5 1949–1972
Johnson, Graham Edwin, 1941–.
'Research in industrializing society.' In *Anthropology and sociology in Hong Kong: Field projects and problems of overseas scholars*, compiled by Marjorie Doreen Topley. [Analytic entry]
Hong Kong: U. of Hong Kong, Centre of Asian Studies, 1969, 28–51.
Subj 71 ▪ 19 22 30

23036 CSU O P3 G9.5 1949–1972
Kehl, Frank, 1940–.
'Anthropology and the interests of society: A field worker's point of view.' In *Anthropology and sociology in Hong Kong: Field projects and problems of overseas scholars*, compiled by Marjorie Doreen Topley. [Analytic entry]
Hong Kong: U. of Hong Kong, Centre of Asian Studies, 1969, 60–79.
Subj 71 ▪ 22

23037 NNC U P1 G1.2 1949–1972
Kukushkin, Kim Vladimirovich, 1926–, and Arlen Vaagovich Meliksetov, 1930–.
'Nauchnaia rabota na Otdelenii Vostoka Moskovskogo gosudarstvennogo universiteta' (Research work of the Department of Oriental Studies of Moscow State University).
SV 1955, 2, 166–168.
Subj 71 ▪ 72

23038 CSH O P1 G1.2 1949–1972
[La Dany, Ladislao] ———, 1914–.
'Japanese studies on contemporary China.'
CNA 517 (22 May 1964), 1–7.
Subj 71

23039 NNC P P1 G1.2 1949–1972
Levada, IU- A-.
'Sotsialisticheskaia revoliutsiia v Kitae i ee burzhuaznye kritiki' (The socialist revolution in China and its bourgeois critics).
SK 1958, 1, 153–160.
Subj 71 ▪ 12.1 14 19

23040 MCH F P3 G9.5 1949–1972
Li, Victor H. (Li Hao), 1941–.
'The use of survey interviewing in research on Communist Chinese law.' In *Contemporary Chinese law: Research problems and perspectives*, edited by Jerome Alan Cohen. [Selective entry]
Cambridge: Harvard U. Press, 1970, 118–138. (Harvard studies in East Asian law, 4)
Subj 71

23041 MCH O P1 G1.2 1949–1972
Lindbeck, John Matthew Henry, 1915–1971.
Scholarship and the image of China in East Asia: The place of Chinese studies.
Cambridge: Harvard U., East Asian Research Center, 1963. 45 p.
Subj 71

23042 CSH PO P1 G1.1 1949–1972
Ma, John T. (Ma Ta-jen), 1920–.
'Collecting research materials on post-1949 Mainland China.' In *Collected documents of the First Sino-American Conference on Mainland China*. [Selective entry]
[Taipei]: Institute of International Relations, Republic of China, 1971, 47–61.
Subj 14.2 70 71

23043 CSU S P1 G1.1 1949–1972
McDonald, Angus.
'The historian's quest: Joseph R. Levenson.'
BCAS 2, 3 (Apr.–July 1970), 71–82.
Subj 62 71

23044 CSU S P1 G1.2 1949–1972
Mehnert, Klaus, 1906–.
'Mao and Maoism: Some Soviet views.'
CS 8, 15 (1 Sept. 1970), 1–17.
Subj 13 64 71 ▪ 72

23045 MCH O P2 G9.5 1949–1972
Mitchell, Robert Edward, 1930–.
'Perspectives on consumer research in the West and in Hong Kong.'
Hong Kong manager 4, 3 (May–June 1968), 25–26.
Subj 24.3 71

23046 CSU P P1 G1.2 1949–1972
Oksenberg, Michel Charles, 1938–.
'Sources and methodological problems in the study of contemporary China.' In *Chinese Communist politics in action*, edited by Arthur Doak Barnett. [Selective entry]
Seattle: U. of Washington Press, 1969, 577–606. (Social Science Research Council, Studies in Chinese government and politics, 1)
Subj 71 ▪ 11.2 14.2 26.1

23047 CSU U P1 G1.2 1949–1972
Orleans, Leo A-, 1924–.
'Basic resources for social science research on Communist China.' In *Mainland China in the world economy*, compiled by Joint Economic Committee, U.S. Congress. [Selective entry]
Washington, D.C.: U.S. Government Printing Office, 1967, 229–234.
Subj 71

23048 CSU S P1 G1.2 1949–1972
Roberts, Moss.
'Some problems concerning the structure and direction of contemporary China studies: A reply to Professor Fairbank.'
BCAS 3, 3/4 (Summer–Fall 1971), 113–137.
Subj 71

23049 NNC U P1 G1.1 1949–1972
Sukharchuk, Grigorii Dmitrievich, 1927–.
'Institut kitaevedeniia Akademii nauk SSSR' (The Institute of Chinese Studies of the USSR Academy of Sciences).
SK 1958, 1, 201–202.
SUBJ 71 ▪ 72

23050 MCH S P1 G1.2 1949–1972
Taniguchi, Yasuhei.
'Some characteristics of Japanese studies on contemporary Chinese law.' In *Contemporary Chinese law: Research problems and perspectives*, edited by Jerome Alan Cohen. [Selective entry]
Cambridge: Harvard U. Press, 1970, 294–312. (Harvard studies in East Asian law, 4)
SUBJ 12.2 71

23051 CSU O P1 G9.5 1949–1972
Topley, Kenneth.
'Anthropology, practicality and policy in Hong Kong: A governmental point of view.' In *Anthropology and sociology in Hong Kong: Field projects and problems of overseas scholars*, compiled by Marjorie Doreen Topley. [Analytic entry]
Hong Kong: U. of Hong Kong, Centre of Asian Studies, 1969, 52–59.
SUBJ 71 ▪ 19 22 30

23052 CSU O P2 G9.5 1949–1972
Topley, Marjorie Doreen, 1927–.
'Anthropology and field work in Hong Kong.' In *Anthropology and sociology in Hong Kong: Field projects and problems of overseas scholars*, compiled by M. D. Topley. [Analytic entry]
Hong Kong: U. of Hong Kong, Centre of Asian Studies, 1969, 1–27.
SUBJ 71

23053 CSU O P1 G9.5 1949–1972
Topley, Marjorie Doreen, 1927–.
'Commentary on the symposium.' In *Anthropology and sociology in Hong Kong: Field projects and problems of overseas scholars*, compiled by M. D. Topley. [Analytic entry]
Hong Kong: U. of Hong Kong, Centre of Asian Studies, 1969, 115–125.
SUBJ 71 ▪ 17 22

23054 CSU S P3 G9.5 1949–1972
Weakland, John Hast, 1919–.
'Real and reel life in Hong Kong: Film studies of cultural adaptation?'
JAAS 6, 3/4 (July–Oct. 1971), 238–243.
SUBJ 31 71

23055 CSU U P1 G1.2 1949–1972
Williams, Jack Francis, 1939–.
'American geographers and China.'
Professional geographer 21, 5 (Sept. 1969), 354–357.
SUBJ 71

23056 CSU P P1 G1.2 1949–1972
Wong, Paul (Huang Pao-lo), 1944–.
'Coding and analysis of documentary materials from Communist China.'
AS 7, 3 (Mar. 1967), 198–211.
SUBJ 71 ▪ 12.1 64

23057 DLC U P1 G1.1 1949–1972
Wright, Arthur Frederick, 1913–.
'Chinese studies today.'
Newsletter of the Assn. for Asian studies 10, 3 (Feb. 1965), 2–12.
SUBJ 71

23058 CSU O P1 G1.1 1949–1972
Wu, Eugene W. (Wu Wen-chin), 1922–.
'Studies of contemporary China outside the United States.'
Harvard library b. 18, 2 (Apr. 1970), 141–154.
SUBJ 70 71 ▪ 17

23059 CSH O P1 G1.2 1949–1972
Wu, Eugene W. (Wu Wen-chin), 1922–.
'Studies of Mainland China in the United States.' In *Collected documents of the First Sino-American Conference on Mainland China*. [Selective entry]
[Taipei]: Institute of International Relations, Republic of China, 1971, 29–46.
SUBJ 71

ANALYTICAL INDEXES

Historical Index

歷史索引

歴史索引

A subject index to entries, arranged by historical period and showing nature of sources

款目內容索引、依時期先後排列、並示資料性質

時期別並びに資料の来源を示す解題索引

"Primary" and "Secondary" (or "Second.") refer to the relative usefulness of the entry for the subject in question. Open squares indicate that the Bibliography lacks entries so classified. Letter suffixes are Sources codes (see p. xxxiv or the back endpapers); numbers with no suffix indicate entries that are "unsupported or poorly documented." The structure of this index is described fully on p. xl.

10 Chinese Society in General

中國社會通論　　中国社会一般

1644-1842

Primary 10015 o 10027 o 10039 o 10051 p
10005 o 10020 po 10032 o 10044 o 10593 p
10007 o 10022 o 10033 o 10045 o 13812
10008 s 10026 o 10036 o 10050 o

Secondary: *Not used*

1644-1911

Primary 10012 p 10037 10060 po 11677 s
10001 o 10014 o 10042 po 10066 s 12941 po
10004 po 10016 o 10046 o 10532 15044 s
10006 s 10028 po 10053 p 10560 p 22886 s
10010 p 10029 po 10058 po 11667 p

Secondary: *Not used*

1842-1911

Primary 10019 po 10035 o 10052 p 10063 o
10002 o 10021 o 10038 o 10054 o 10064 o
10003 o 10023 o 10040 o 10055 o 10065 o
10009 p 10024 o 10041 10056 o 10331 s
10011 o 10025 o 10043 o 10057 o 10611 o
10013 o 10030 o 10047 o 10059 o 18409 p
10017 o 10031 o 10048 o 10061 o 22877 p
10018 po 10034 s 10049 po 10062 po

Secondary: *Not used*

1842-1928
(including 1644-1928)

Primary 10072 s 10081 po 10712 s 15133 s
10067 o 10073 10082 po 11709 21786 p
10068 s 10075 10084 po 12233 p 22644 o
10069 o 10076 s 10085 po 12963 po 22663 s
10071 o 10077 o 10342 o 15132 p

Secondary: *Not used*

1911-1928

Primary 10091 o 10099 o 10778 o 14119 s
10089 o 10094 o 10106 p

Secondary: *Not used*

1911-1949
(including 1644-1949, 1842-1949)

Primary 10078 s 10083 po 10088 o 10097 o
10070 p 10079 po 10086 po 10090 o 10102 o
10074 p 10080 10087 o 10093 o 10104 o
10107 p 10715 p 18585 o 18722 o 22648 po
10347 p 11689 p 18661 p 19245 o 22923 fp
10349 s 18556

Secondary: *Not used*

1928-1949

Primary 10096 o 10101 o 10105 fp 15150
10092 o 10098 o 10103 po 10108 p 20639 s
10095 o 10100 o

Secondary: *Not used*

1928-1972
(incl. 1644-1972, 1842-1972, 1911-1972)

Primary 10118 o 10127 10893 s 22246 s
10109 10119 s 10128 o 11049 22287 p
10110 po 10120 s 10129 s 11054 p 22734 o
10111 s 10121 o 10846 14126 22950 s
10112 s 10122 s 10853 po 15185 s 22984 s
10113 10123 o 10854 s 18170 p 22995 s
10114 p 10124 s 10869 p 21474 p 22996
10115 o 10125 p 10883 s 21476 s 23006 s
10116 s 10126 o 10891 s 21855 s 23007 p
10117 po

Secondary: *Not used*

1949-1972

Primary 10142 p 10155 p 10167 o 10179 p
10130 o 10143 o 10156 o 10168 o 10180 o
10131 f 10144 o 10157 o 10169 o 10233 p
10132 o 10145 o 10158 o 10170 o 11003 p
10133 o 10146 s 10159 o 10171 s 11061 o
10134 o 10147 p 10160 o 10172 po 11459 p
10135 o 10148 p 10161 o 10173 o 15006 o
10136 o 10149 o 10162 o 10174 o 15204
10137 p 10150 o 10163 p 10175 o 15241 s
10138 p 10151 s 10164 o 10176 p 15509 o
10139 p 10152 o 10165 o 10177 o 21930 o
10140 o 10153 o 10166 o 10178 p 23018 s
10141 o 10154 p

Secondary: *Not used*

11 National Population

全國人口　　国民総人口

1644-1842

Primary 10044 o 10533 po 13829 p

Second. 10005 o 10008 s 10026 o 10526 s
10643 po 22578 o

1644-1911

Primary 10182 s 10184 p 10187 po 10276
10060 po 10183 s 10186 p 10188 p 10329 po
10181 s

Second. 10042 po 10333 p 13482 p 18919 p
10010 p 10277 p 10586 14176 19747 p

1842-1911

Primary 10035 o 10185 p 10330 p

Second. 10065 o 12915 s 16183 o 18479 o
10048 o 10328 o 15126 s 18461 p 22067 o
10052 p 11665 p

1842-1928
(including 1644-1928)

Primary 10189 s 10194 p 10338 p 14105 s
10076 s 10190 p 10196 p 12214 p 15051 s

Second. 10291 p 11709 12957 o 15052 fp
10068 s 10697 s 12221 p 12963 po 20049 p
10073 10712 s 12640 fp 13163 s 22922 s
10284 p

1911-1928

Primary 10203 p 10207 p 10208 p 10209 fp

Second. 10106 p 10374 s 11790 s 12302 p
10099 o 10363 fp 11783 p 11809 p 18733 p

1911-1949
(including 1644-1949, 1842-1949)

Primary 10197 p 10202 s 12218 p 15071 p
10191 po 10198 s 10205 p 12303 fp 20302 fp
10192 s 10199 p 10346 s 12304 p 22793 o
10193 s 10200 p 10353 s 12759 s 22908
10195 p 10201 s 10717 po

Second. 10295 po 11317 p 12230 p 17869 po
10093 o 10370 p 11756 p 12634 p 21209 s
10107 p 10453 s 11810 p 13259 p 22784 p
10286 s 10706 po 12213 s 14703 s 22791 s

1928-1949

Primary 10204 s 10206 p 10367 s 11752 fp
21222 s

Second. 10365 11778 p 12345 o 15059 fp
10103 po 10377 s 11799 p 12358 p 19808 p
10108 p 11750 s 11805 p

1928-1972
(incl. 1644-1972, 1842-1972, 1911-1972)

Primary 10213 s 10216 P 10219 s 10222 P
10210 P 10214 P 10217 s 10220 P 10260 O
10211 P 10215 P 10218 P 10221 P 20303 P
10212 P

Second. 10397 s 11854 P 12416 17956 P
10113 10859 P 11859 P 12770 s 18170 P
10120 s 10890 P 11874 P 13308 P 18799 P
10129 s 11845 P 12376 s 14127 P 18817 PO
10303 P 11847 s 12384 P 15085 P 19655 P
10386 F 11849 P 12414 P 15161 P 22824 s
10396 s

1949-1972

Primary 10231 P 10241 PO 10251 12160 s
10136 O 10232 P 10242 P 10264 P 12173 P
10223 P 10233 P 10243 P 10265 P 12530 P
10224 P 10234 P 10244 P 10424 P 15652 P
10225 P 10235 P 10245 s 10425 P 20328 P
10226 P 10236 P 10246 P 10482 P 20365 P
10227 P 10237 P 10247 P 10498 P 20370 P
10228 PO 10238 P 10248 P 11913 P 20371 P
10229 P 10239 P 10249 P 11947 P 21248 P
10230 P 10240 P 10250 PO 12042 P

Second. 10478 P 11980 PO 12141 P 14835 s
10134 O 10502 PO 11993 s 12148 P 14840 P
10142 P 11101 FP 12004 P 12156 P 14969 P
10155 P 11884 P 12019 P 12165 P 15215
10168 O 11887 P 12021 P 12434 F 15228 P
10173 O 11902 s 12022 s 12474 P 15619 P
10305 P 11903 O 12023 s 12479 20306 P
10311 P 11912 P 12039 P 12535 P 20327 P
10313 P 11920 P 12055 P 13060 P 20363 P
10315 P 11936 12071 P 13087 P 20373 P
10403 s 11939 s 12090 O 13097 P 20375 P
10410 s 11955 P 12115 P 13401 s 21241 P
10432 P 11969 P 12139 P 13407 FP 21253 P
10469 P

11.1 Nationwide Urbanization
全國性都市化 全国的都市化

1644-1842

Primary □

Second. 10533 PO 12901 P

1644-1911

Primary 10252 10322 10333 P 15751

Second. 10621 s

1842-1911

Primary 10185 P

Second. □

1842-1928
(including 1644-1928)

Primary 10255 O 10338 P 15767 O

Second. 13164 FP 15132 P

1911-1928

Primary 11731 11783 P 11784 P

Second. 10374 s 10769 P 11812 P 13220 FP

1911-1949
(including 1644-1949, 1842-1949)

Primary 10253 P 10254 P 10256 s 10257
10258 s 15756 s

Second. 11689 P 14479 PO 15959 P 20160 PO
10197 P 13166 s 15954 s 16560 FP 21821 O
10201 s

1928-1949

Primary 10297 O

Second. 19808 P

1928-1972
(incl. 1644-1972, 1842-1972, 1911-1972)

Primary 10261 s 10384 P 12414 P 14128 P
10259 P 10262 10890 P 13049 P 15644 s
10260 O

Second. 10221 P 10397 s 12410 s 20235 O
10122 s 10389 s 11859 P 15645 P 22225 s
10217 s

1949-1972

Primary 10263 P 10267 s 10311 P 14135 P
10230 P 10264 P 10268 P 10313 P 20669 P
10235 P 10265 P 10269 P 10399 P 20690 P
10248 P 10266 s

Second. 10250 PO 10406 s 11939 s 15215
10224 P 10305 P 10425 P 12128 s 15652 P
10226 P 10315 P 10468 P 13070 P 15841 O
10236 P 10403 s 10482 P 13336 P 16037 FP
10240 P 10404 s 10960 FP 14973 P 20306 P
10242 P 10405 s 11912 P

11.2 Extranational Migration & Nationwide Geographic Mobility
海外移民及國內大規模遷移
海外移住及び大規模な国内人口移動

1644-1842

Primary 13814 s

Second. 10533 PO 13830 P

1644-1911

Primary 10182 s 10270 10276 10277 P
10279 P

Second. 10187 PO 12197 P 13859 s 19747 P
10058 PO 10329 PO 12203 P 14454 P 19961 PO
10060 PO 11227 P 13482 P 15741 P

1842-1911

Primary 10272 10274 O 10278 O 10438 s
10271 O 10273 P 10275 P 10280 P 17923 O

Second. 11674 s 13839 O 14584 PO 19614 O
10185 P 12579 O 13840 O 18521 s 22586 P

1842-1928
(including 1644-1928)

Primary 10284 P 10290 P 10292 P 11710
10281 P 10287 P 10291 P 10293 s 21769

Second. 10348 O 11711 s 15052 FP 21798 P
10338 P 11709 12229 P 19219 s

1911-1928

Primary 10294 P 11784 P 11828 s

Second. 11754 P 11814 P 14493 P 17942 O
10207 P 11812 P 12728 O 15072 FP

1911-1949
(including 1644-1949, 1842-1949)

Primary 10253 P 10285 PO 10289 FP 10346 s
10200 P 10282 10286 s 10295 PO 22660 PO
10201 s 10283 s 10288 s

Second. 11317 P 12334 P 13259 P 14692 P
10197 P 11815 s 12629 PO 13725 P 18699 P
10254 P 12230 P 12759 s 14456 P 19473 s
10350 s 12307 P 12960 s 14475 FP 19965 P
10370 P 12328 P

1928-1949

Primary 10296 10297 O 10298 s 11752 FP

Second. 11772 O 12358 P 14478 FP 19823 O
10451 s 12256 F 12708 s 14747 O 21225 F
11371 P 12289 s 13263 P 15434 O 22710 O
11762 P 12348 PO 13909 O 19700 O

1928-1972
(incl. 1644-1972, 1842-1972, 1911-1972)

Primary 10217 s 10301 FP 10303 P 14255 P
10119 s 10299 P 10302 P 10393 s 17956 P
10214 P 10300 s

Second. 10396 s 11858 P 15646 P 19078 P
10111 s 10397 s 14128 P 17893 O 19974 P
10221 P 10456 P 15611 PO 17899 O 19982 s
10260 O 10890 P 15645 P 19036 P 22723 O
10386 F 11047 P

1949-1972

Primary 10304 F 10310 P 10316 P 20120 O
10231 P 10305 P 10311 P 10465 P 20510 P
10235 P 10306 PO 10312 O 12527 P 20669 P
10240 P 10307 P 10313 P 15489 P 21015 O
10263 P 10308 P 10314 P 16002 FP 21254 P
10264 P 10309 P 10315 P 19990 FP

Second. 10497 P 11967 14973 P 19136 O
10162 O 10498 P 12549 P 15103 P 19198 P
10224 P 10960 FP 12790 P 15549 P 19392 P
10226 P 11097 PO 13084 P 15617 F 19929 F
10265 P 11164 F 13336 P 15618 PO 20314 P
10408 P 11170 P 14135 P 15621 F 20683 FP
10468 P 11626 s 14521 P 15827 P 20690 P
10469 P 11894 O 14546 s 16491 F 22325 P
10479 P 11913 P 14851 P 17642 P 22344 P
10489 s 11939 s 14910 P 17911 O 23046 P
10496 P 11955 P 14971 P

11.3 Macroecology and Settlement Patterns
全域性區位分佈及聚落型態
巨視的社会生態学及び定住様式

1644-1842

Primary 10320 P 17024 O 17145 P

Second. 10050 O 12890 O 20563 s 22552 s
10039 O 10580 O 13856

1644-1911

Primary 10322 10327 P 10333 P 15047 P
10004 PO 10325 PO 10329 PO 14101 s 16196 P

Second. 10277 P 15334 PO 18862 P 21677 FP
10006 s 12201 P 15741 P

1842-1911

Primary 10321 O 10331 s 15740 O 16931 O
10052 P 10323 O 10332 O 16386 O 16932 O
10062 PO 10324 O 10334 O 16393 PO 16935 O
10317 O 10326 PO 10335 O 16927 O 17025 O
10318 O 10328 O 10336 O 16928 O 18852 PO
10319 s 10330 P 11671 O 16929 O 18922 O

Second. 16383 PO 16526 O 16930 O 17547 P
13804 P 16391 O 16926 O

1842-1928
(including 1644-1928)

Primary 10340 PO 10348 O 10355 P 16552 O
10338 P 10342 O 10354 P 12680 P

Second. 10709 P 12643 s 13182 s 16558 F
10255 O 11686 P 12949 P 15667 s 17937 O

1911-1928

Primary 10359 O 10363 FP 10371 F 10374 s
10209 FP 10360 O 10369 O 10372 10380 PO

10381 P 13006 P 15413 O 15781 16961 P
11784 P 13012 P 15692 P 16434 P 19453 P
12302 P

SECOND. 12324 S 12362 P 12728 O 13925 P
18992 FP

1911-1949
(including 1644-1949, 1842-1949)

PRIMARY 10344 10353 S 10450 FP 15678 P
10197 P 10345 FP 10356 PO 11825 PO 15679 FP
10201 S 10346 S 10362 P 12295 S 15756 S
10258 S 10347 P 10364 FP 12297 P 16689 O
10289 FP 10349 S 10366 12675 PO 17036 FP
10337 P 10350 S 10370 P 14217 P 18645 S
10339 O 10351 S 10375 P 15669 P 18699 P
10341 P 10352 P 10379 P 15676 FP 22660 PO
10343

SECOND. 11735 12341 O 14659 P 15954 S
10086 PO 11815 S 12629 PO 15585 S 20302 FP
10257 12232 PO 12687 S 15588 P 22791 S

1928-1949

PRIMARY 10365 10376 O 10454 F 12369 FP
10357 S 10367 S 10377 S 11797 P 12708 S
10358 S 10368 10378 S 12323 O 16640 PO
10361 S 10373 S 10452 S 12345 O 16957 F

SECOND. 12256 F 12348 PO 16422 21465 O
11732 P 12330 O 14117 P 16443 O

1928-1972
(incl. 1644-1972, 1842-1972, 1911-1972)

PRIMARY 10385 FP 10394 FP 11869 P 16335 P
10221 P 10386 F 10395 FP 11878 S 16726 P
10259 P 10387 S 10396 S 12399 FP 16751 S
10260 O 10388 FP 10397 S 12416 16752 P
10261 S 10389 S 10398 FP 12765 P 16984 FP
10303 P 10390 S 10455 O 13298 P 17947 S
10382 P 10391 P 10890 P 13311 P 21855 S
10383 S 10392 P 11853 S 15603 P 21897 S
10384 P 10393 S 11859 P 15792 FP 22732 FP

SECOND. 10302 P 12415 P 13307 P 15696 F
10118 O 10863 P 12420 P 14127 P 15698 P
10119 S 11844 O 12422 S 14131 21233 FP
10129 S 12392 P 12776 P 15609 P 22738 P
10217 S 12401 P 13297 FP

1949-1972

PRIMARY 10410 S 10422 S 10434 S 13349 P
10269 P 10411 P 10423 P 10435 FP 13395 P
10399 P 10412 10424 P 10436 P 13410
10400 10413 P 10425 P 11880 P 13440 P
10401 F 10414 S 10426 FP 12069 P 15825 F
10402 FP 10415 PO 10427 FP 12434 F 15826 F
10403 S 10416 S 10428 FP 12509 P 15883
10404 S 10417 P 10429 FP 12522 FP 15895
10405 S 10418 P 10430 FP 12556 S 16014 S
10406 S 10419 P 10431 FP 12843 S 16786 F
10407 P 10420 10432 P 12857 O 16787 FP
10408 P 10421 FP 10433 S 13332 S 16896 P
10409 S

SECOND. 10476 S 12003 P 12524 FP 15845 P
10224 P 10905 P 12106 P 12827 P 15917 P
10227 P 10967 P 12157 12877 16347 O
10228 PO 10990 P 12160 S 13083 F 19121 P
10230 P 11906 P 12469 P 13393 20690 P
10263 P 11929 S 12486 P 13432 P 22754 P
10264 P 11947 P

11.4 National Labor Force & Occupational Differentiation
全國勞動力及職業分化
国民総労働力及び職業分化

1644-1842

PRIMARY 19350 P

SECOND. □

1644-1911

PRIMARY 10437 P 10441 P

SECOND. 10577 P 12933 P 14102 P 20606 P
10053 P 12573 P 14098 P 20144 P 21677 FP

1842-1911

PRIMARY 10438 S 10439 10440 O 22067 O

SECOND. 13129 P 14612 S 18463 P

1842-1928
(including 1644-1928)

PRIMARY □

SECOND. 10284 P 10338 P 11717 P 12233 P
13149 PO 17757 P

1911-1928

PRIMARY 10445 O 11783 P 14250 20193 P
10442 P 10447 11784 P 14493 P 20222 S

SECOND. 11812 P 14465 18708 19546 P
11729 P 11814 P 17873 PO 18720 S 20463 F
11754 P 12247 S 18617 P 18733 P 20837 PO

1911-1949
(including 1644-1949, 1842-1949)

PRIMARY 10446 O 10453 S 14475 FP 20160 PO
10205 P 10448 P 13233 PO 15080 P 20178 PO
10370 P 10450 FP 14456 P

SECOND. 11689 P 11815 S 13945 P 18580 P
10254 P 11694 PO 12961 P 14424 P 19473 S
10289 FP 11735 13153 S 14736 P 19551 P
10295 PO 11756 P 13259 P 15071 P

1928-1949

PRIMARY 10444 O 10451 S 10454 F 11752 FP
10443 P 10449 O 10452 S

SECOND. 11022 P 12358 P 13197 P 13263 P
18647 P 21225 F

1928-1972
(incl. 1644-1972, 1842-1972, 1911-1972)

PRIMARY 10456 P 12415 P 13295 P 14793 P
10261 S 11864 FP 12421 O 14259 P 15085 P
10455 O 11874 P 12423

SECOND. 11045 FP 11849 P 12774 PO 19583 P
10217 S 11384 P 11852 P 13308 P 19655 P
10260 O 11845 P 11854 P 13986 P 20228 P
10302 P 11847 S 11862 P 14258 P 21904 FP
10386 F 11848 PO 12425 P 18185 P 22239 S

1949-1972

PRIMARY: MONOGRAPHS
10423 P 10479 P 10503 P 12787 P 14969 P
10460 P 10481 P 11894 O 13336 P 15025 P
10464 P 10487 P 11912 P 13365 S 15028 P
10466 P 10488 P 11996 P 14522 P 19389 P
10470 P 10498 P 12086 14882 S 22293 S
10477 P 10500 P 12109 P 14885 P

PRIMARY: INCLUSIONS
10463 P 10478 P 10486 P 10499 P 14147 P
10468 P 10484 P 10493 O 12010 P 14967 P
10469 P 10485 P 10497 P 13444 P 15293

PRIMARY: JOURNAL ARTICLES
10251 10471 P 10483 P 10501 P 12431 O
10308 P 10472 P 10489 S 10502 PO 12448 P
10457 P 10473 P 10490 P 11172 P 12504 P
10458 O 10474 P 10491 P 11963 P 12521 P
10459 FP 10475 P 10492 O 11967 14532 P
10461 P 10476 S 10494 11992 P 14813 P
10462 FP 10480 P 10495 S 12084 P 14814 P
10465 P 10482 P 10496 P 12119 S 21250 P
10467 P

SECONDARY: MONOGRAPHS
10154 P 11101 FP 12000 P 13104 P 14833 P
10157 O 11891 P 12044 P 13328 O 14853 P
10240 P 11906 P 12054 P 13353 P 15022 P
10263 P 11920 P 12096 P 13384 P 15112 P
10407 P 11928 P 12173 P 14310 18225 P
10432 P 11949 P 12525 P 14337 P 19668 P
10906 P 11962 PO 12535 P 14378 P 20314 P
10999 11980 PO 12853 O 14828 P 20484 P

SECONDARY: INCLUSIONS
11002 12042 P 13327 PO 14145 FP 19198 P
11176 P 12156 P 13435 P 14880 PO 19409 P
11989 P 12159 S 14043 P 14901 P 20371 P
12009 P 13097 P 14138 P 15303 FP

SECONDARY: JOURNAL ARTICLES
10236 P 11932 P 12141 P 13320 P 14832 P
10238 P 11941 P 12153 P 13321 P 14897 P
10246 P 11944 P 12167 S 13426 PO 14920 P
10305 P 11947 P 12170 S 13427 PO 14959 P
10311 P 11987 P 12177 S 13433 14971 P
10896 O 12004 P 12794 O 14028 P 19145 P
11093 P 12012 P 12827 P 14141 S 21047 P
11892 12059 P 13056 P 14446 P 21914
11895 PO 12094 P 13109 O 14827 P 22839 P
11913 P 12120 P 13115 P

12 National Political System and Bureaucracy
政制及吏治
政治制度及び官僚制

1644-1842

PRIMARY: MONOGRAPHS
10005 O 10507 P 10651 P 13830 P 20549 O
10008 S 10522 P 10652 O 14156 O 21277 P
10020 PO 10526 S 10654 P 14181 P 21279 P
10022 O 10580 O 10672 P 14599 P 21644 P
10026 O 10593 P 11675 O 16517 P 22057 P
10036 O 10626 P 12619 P 17657 O 22071 P
10039 O 10643 PO 13812 18936 P 22598 P
10044 O

PRIMARY: INCLUSIONS
10542 P 10623 P 13836 O 14562 P 21712 P
10561 O 10627 P 13856 15725 S 22033 P
10579 P 11010 P 14096 S 20418 P 22578 O

PRIMARY: JOURNAL ARTICLES
10033 O 10535 P 10617 P 13832 P 21284 P
10512 PO 10546 P 10618 P 14183 P 21294 P
10527 P 10552 P 10656 P 14197 P 21296 P
10528 P 10578 P 10673 P 14210 P 22505 P
10529 P 10585 P 11680 P 14570 P 22537 P
10533 PO 10590 P 12583 P 15582 P 22885 S
10534 O 10605 P 12591 P

SECOND. 13469 P 16218 O 20558 S 22064 P
10007 O 13632 P 16369 O 20563 S 22398 O
10015 O 13813 P 17140 PO 21278 P 22555 O
10027 O 13814 S 17524 P 21282 P 22585 P
10045 O 14086 P 18475 P 21292 S 22603 P
10320 P 14188 P 18514 P 21295 22629 P
11536 O 15037 P 18864 S 21685 P 22640 P
12189 P 15662 P 18904 P 22034 P 22776 P
12190 P 15752 O 19441 P 22055 P 22779 P
12928 P 15923 O

1644-1911

PRIMARY: MONOGRAPHS
10010 P 10016 O 10042 PO 10058 PO 10325 PO
10014 O 10029 PO 10053 P 10060 PO 10329 PO

10505 p 10582 po 10669 p 11667 p 14627 p
10525 p 10586 10674 s 13458 p 16389 po
10541 s 10599 p 10676 p 13841 o 18098 p
10550 p 10600 p 11015 p 14093 p 18421 p
10557 p 10613 p 11183 p 14158 p 18937 p
10559 po 10615 p 11194 o 14159 p 20092 p
10560 p 10634 o 11235 p 14167 p 22531 p
10573 s 10644 po 11241 p 14179 p 22558 p
10574 p 10657 p 11243 p 14193 p 22866 p
10577 p 10667 p 11663 o

Primary: Inclusions
10012 p 10596 s 10616 10671 s 14168 p
10037 10597 s 10624 p 10680 p 14208 s
10506 p 10602 p 10646 11556 p 22036 p
10521 s 10603 p 10659 13859 s 22548 s
10554 p

Primary: Journal Articles
10066 s 10592 p 10655 p 12578 o 15934 p
10520 p 10595 p 10664 s 13838 15936 p
10524 p 10604 p 10666 p 14089 s 18493 po
10532 10608 p 10678 p 14165 o 19769 p
10540 s 10609 p 10681 p 14184 p 20606 p
10545 p 10621 s 11016 s 14192 p 21283 p
10567 s 10622 p 11200 s 14198 s 21293 p
10568 o 10625 p 11214 p 14202 s 21439 p
10570 p 10628 s 11543 s 14205 p 21441 s
10571 10632 p 11544 s 14211 p 21609 p
10576 s 10633 p 11552 p 14397 p 21983 p
10583 s 10635 p 11655 po 15130 s 22024 p
10589 p 10638 p 11676 s 15742 po 22061 p

Secondary: Monographs
10004 po 12923 p 14189 s 18862 p 21276 p
10437 p 12948 p 14201 p 18930 po 21291 p
11202 p 13637 p 14206 p 20083 p 21300 s
11203 p 13808 p 15727 po 20414 p 21632 p
11672 po 13824 p 15931 o 21259 p 21677 fp
11677 s 13844 p 17531 p 21269 21705 po
12572 p 13846 p 18459 o 21271 o

Secondary: Inclusions
10006 s 13834 p 14621 po 21630 p 21709 p
10441 p 14097 p 17028 p 21663 p 22565
12940 s

Secondary: Journal Articles
10186 p 12188 s 14185 18510 p 22045
11198 p 12573 p 14569 p 19992 s 22058 p
11224 p 13451 p 15044 s 20090 po 22070
11225 s 13484 p 15334 po 20257 22529 p
11226 p 14090 p 15659 po 20554 p 22551 p
11568 po 14091 15751 21678 p 22621 p
11656 s 14172 p 18489 22044 p 22886 s
11664

1842-1911

Primary: Monographs
10011 o 10544 p 10653 p 14204 po 18458 p
10013 o 10548 p 10660 o 14207 p 18461 p
10017 o 10551 p 10665 p 14396 p 18491 o
10018 po 10558 p 10677 p 15038 p 18492 po
10019 po 10562 p 10679 o 15351 o 18871 po
10030 o 10566 p 11193 p 15924 po 19719 p
10031 o 10584 o 11230 p 16394 p 20128 o
10035 o 10587 po 11678 p 17411 p 20579 o
10041 10594 po 13455 p 17974 o 21260 po
10043 o 10598 o 13831 p 18074 p 21262 o
10047 o 10607 p 13847 p 18077 p 21265 p
10048 o 10611 o 13858 p 18089 p 21287 p
10049 po 10614 p 14155 s 18092 p 21302 o
10056 o 10619 p 14164 p 18378 o 21655 o
10062 po 10631 p 14171 o 18387 p 22067 o
10508 p 10636 p 14174 p 18430 p 22562 o
10516 po 10640 po 14178 p 18450 p 22572 o
10519 p 10645 p 14182 fp 18454 po 22586 p
10539 p

Primary: Inclusions
10510 p 10637 10662 p 15716 o 18370 p
10549 s 10639 o 11245 po 16093 o 18515 s
10555 p 10641 o 11673 p 18073 p 19365 p
10601 o 10642 po 14601 o 18080 p 21267 p
10610 o 10650 po 15314 s 18088 p 22588 p
10612 o 10658 o 15359 o

Primary: Journal Articles
10504 o 10565 p 10683 14199 18399 po
10509 o 10569 11182 p 14576 p 18401 p
10511 p 10572 11185 po 14611 18435 o
10513 po 10575 p 11186 po 14625 18441 po
10514 p 10581 p 11191 po 16525 p 18467 o
10515 p 10588 o 11662 16903 p 18504 p
10517 o 10591 o 12607 p 16908 o 18517 p
10518 p 10606 p 12615 p 17162 p 20557 o
10523 10620 p 13799 po 17539 po 21169 po
10530 10629 p 13801 s 17545 o 21261 p
10531 p 10630 po 13810 p 18086 p 22037 p
10536 s 10647 p 13818 p 18090 o 22041 p
10537 p 10648 o 13839 o 18091 p 22069 p
10538 p 10649 o 13853 p 18093 p 22539 p
10543 p 10661 s 13869 p 18095 22549 p
10547 s 10663 p 14161 o 18365 o 22569 p
10553 p 10668 p 14162 p 18369 p 22613 s
10556 p 10670 o 14163 po 18381 p 22616 p
10563 10675 p 14177 o 18398 p 22625 p
10564 p 10682 o

Secondary: Monographs
10002 o 12593 po 15733 o 18409 p 18922 o
10021 o 12598 po 15744 o 18412 fp 20559 o
10034 s 12601 o 15749 po 18422 o 22066 p
10038 o 12918 p 16376 po 18428 p 22073 p
10040 o 12920 o 16396 o 18436 p 22074 p
10055 o 12921 o 16912 o 18448 po 22530 p
10064 o 13125 p 17151 o 18449 o 22532 p
10065 o 13470 p 17161 p 18455 s 22536 p
10271 o 13627 p 17543 p 18457 p 22556 po
10330 p 13802 p 18075 o 18466 o 22584 s
10331 s 13804 p 18099 p 18494 p 22594 o
11232 fp 13849 p 18364 p 18498 po 22595 p
11567 p 13866 o 18375 p 18502 p 22612 p
11665 p 14157 o 18376 p 18511 p 22617 po
11671 o 14160 p 18379 po 18868 po 22623 p
11681 o 14195 p 18386 p 18875 o 22631 s
12575 p 15324 o 18408 s

Secondary: Inclusions
10334 o 12589 o 13848 p 18368 p 18452 p
11244 o 12922 p 14603 o

Secondary: Journal Articles
11014 p 12585 o 14606 po 18085 p 19779 p
11187 po 12898 o 15125 s 18395 p 20601 o
11189 p 12924 o 15126 s 18432 p 22049 p
11190 p 13798 p 15735 o 18471 s 22514 p
11215 p 13809 p 15928 p 18483 p 22515 p
11238 p 13840 o 16092 p 18488 p 22597 p
11679 p 13850 p 16530 p 18505 p 22634 p
12568 p 13851 o 17527 p 18892 p 22642 p
12577 p 13854 o 18083 p 19753 p 22771 p
12584 o 14590 o 18084 p

1842-1928
(including 1644-1928)

Primary: Monographs
10067 o 10712 s 11718 13882 o 18551 po
10072 s 10713 p 12663 p 14109 p 18563 o
10082 po 10716 p 12950 p 15369 po 21350 p
10085 po 10727 po 12957 o 15373 p 22110 p
10686 p 10733 o 12963 po 15938 p 22131 po
10695 p 11250 p 13147 p 17630 p 22644 o
10697 s 11291 p 13151 p 18106 p 22657 s
10698 p 11297 po 13500 po 18540 22658 s
10703 p 11702 p 13511 p 18542 p 22664 p
10709 p 11705 po 13876

Primary: Inclusions
10073 10723 po 11295 p 18533 po 18555
22108 p

Primary: Journal Articles
10685 p 10704 s 10734 o 11278 p 15133 s
10687 p 10708 p 10735 s 11298 p 18549 po
10691 10722 p 11247 p 12679 22077 p
10699 po 10728 p 11249 p 13515 p 22085 p
10701 p 10731 po 11260 p 14108 s 22104 p

Second. 10348 o 11284 s 11691 p 12666 p
10068 s 11248 p 11285 p 11703 p 12680 p
10076 s 11268 o 11286 p 11709 13177 p
10077 o 11270 p 11302 11710 13187 p
10081 po 11271 po 11587 p 12215 p 13497 p
10196 p 11277 po 11683 o 12644 po 13502 p

13658 po 17661 p 21307 o 21991 po 22112 p
13881 p 18102 o 21327 p 21993 p 22128 p
14224 po 18546 po 21340 p 21996 p 22650 p
14229 18560 p 21342 p 22076 s 22669 s
14232 p 18987 p 21347 p 22082 p 22675 p
14403 p 20608 p 21349 po 22094 s 22902 s
16110 p 20795 o 21775 22101 p 22919 s
17559 p 21306 p 21786 p

1911-1928

Primary 10777 p 10844 p 13950 s 18700 o
10089 o 10778 o 11024 p 13962 p 18720 s
10369 o 10779 11364 p 14752 p 18724 p
10744 10784 p 11375 p 15075 o 18725 p
10750 p 10785 p 11376 p 15151 o 18760
10752 o 10802 11377 s 17982 p 19453 p
10753 o 10811 p 11600 p 18129 fp 19503 fp
10756 s 10820 s 11812 p 18144 p 20464 p
10757 po 10833 13538 o 18579 o 21377 o
10765 s 10834 p 13539 p 18596 po 21378 o
10766 p 10835 p 13896 po 18601 p 22680 o
10768 po 10838 p 13905 po 18610 o 22689 p
10769 p 10840 s 13925 p 18621 o 22708 o

Second. 11790 s 13938 p 18609 o 18779 p
10099 o 12280 p 13979 p 18654 p 19442 po
10106 p 12355 s 15157 p 18708 19452 s
10209 fp 12709 p 15780 o 18733 p 19825 o
11319 o 12745 o 15966 fp 18742 p 20466
11329 p 12747 o 16657 p 18757 o 20932 o
11352 o 13717 s 18126 p 18764 o 21506 o
11355 p 13733 po 18160 p 18775 p 22180 p
11356 p 13889 p 18161 o 18777 p 22698 o
11736 p

1911-1949
(including 1644-1949, 1842-1949)

Primary: Monographs
10079 po 10715 p 10782 po 11582 po 18123 p
10088 o 10718 s 10791 p 11699 s 18131 p
10090 o 10720 p 10793 p 12629 po 18137 s
10104 o 10721 10795 p 12657 po 18140 o
10364 fp 10724 s 10803 p 12675 po 18143 o
10684 o 10725 p 10807 p 13290 p 18154 p
10688 p 10726 10812 p 13680 p 18585 o
10690 p 10729 p 10828 p 13945 p 18588 p
10692 p 10732 p 10845 p 14217 p 18722 o
10693 p 10737 p 11258 p 14219 po 20615 o
10696 p 10739 p 11263 po 14230 p 20813 p
10700 po 10745 po 11279 p 14231 p 21363
10702 o 10749 11289 p 14637 p 21373 p
10706 po 10759 p 11290 p 14753 p 22655 o
10707 p 10776 po 11368 p 18120 p 22672 p
10711 p 10781 p

Primary: Inclusions
10694 p 13532 p 15947 o 18558 s 18571 s
10730 o 13878 p 18119 p

Primary: Journal Articles
10689 10738 p 10815 11580 p 18157 p
10705 s 10743 p 10822 12623 s 18593 po
10710 s 10751 p 10841 p 14107 p 22080 p
10714 s 10755 o 11019 p 15137 22098 p
10717 po 10762 p 11267 s 15142 p 22105 o
10719 10790 p 11334 s 18132 s 22167 p
10736 s

Secondary: Monographs
10070 p 11825 po 14496 p 18635 p 21308 o
10083 po 12227 p 14684 p 18650 p 21321 p
10097 o 12230 p 15136 o 18674 p 21324 p
10107 p 12631 p 15956 p 18730 p 21362 o
10346 s 12638 p 16113 s 18732 p 21381 p
10375 p 12714 po 16279 p 18739 p 21459 p
11257 p 12757 p 16633 fp 18740 s 22006 s
11274 p 12965 p 17572 o 18756 22095 p
11317 p 12970 p 18147 p 18780 p 22132 p
11323 p 13291 s 18309 s 18981 p 22135 p
11601 p 13673 p 18534 po 18990 po 22646 p
11690 p 13873 o 18535 p 19964 p 22648 po
11692 p 13916 p 18545 po 20050 s 22717 p
11712 fp 13980 p 18562 s 20166 o 22923 fp
11714 p 14116 p 18583 s 20820 o 22939 p
11715 p 14215 s 18598 o

19376 P 19391 P 20523 P 22297 P 22349 P
19377 P 19392 P 20533 P 22300 P 22368 P
19379 P 20476 P 21015 O 22312 22372 P
19382 P 20479 O 21560 S 22329 P 22759
19386 P 20520 P 22294 P 22330 P 22761 O

12.1 State Controls of the Populace

政治控制 国家の大衆統制

1644-1842

Primary 11010 P 14401 P 18470 P 22033 P
10526 S 11011 P 15043 P 18477 S 22050 S
10542 P 11012 P 15664 P 21279 P 22577 P
10618 P 14183 P 18468 PO 21712 P

Second. 10626 P 13856 14423 P 22034 P
10005 O 10643 PO 14096 S 18514 P 22552 S
10561 O 10654 P 14181 P 20418 P 22629 P

1644-1911

Primary 11015 P 11225 S 13859 S 18459 O
10053 P 11016 S 11243 P 14397 P 22044 P
10664 S 11195 P

Second. 10586 14090 P 16389 PO 19769 P
10066 S 10615 P 14091 18366 P 19999 PO
10186 P 10666 P 14098 P 18421 P 20041 O
10277 P 10671 S 14099 P 18443 S 20560 P
10325 PO 11184 P 14102 P 18493 PO 22024 P
10329 PO 11222 P 14103 18526 S 22054 P
10505 P 11235 P 14104 P 18848 P 22061 P
10525 P 11241 P 14201 P 19752 P 22548 S
10554 P 12572 P 15665 P 19767 PO 22633 P
10574 P

1842-1911

Primary 11014 P 11209 P 16186 O 18498 PO
10548 P 11017 O 11240 P 18088 P 19613
10564 P 11018 O 12911 P 18089 P 22574 P
10648 O 11189 P 13828 P 18387 P 22591 PO
11013 PO 11190 P 14396 P

Second. 10551 P 11213 P 15128 S 18479 O
10011 O 10562 P 11245 PO 16530 P 18487 P
10013 O 10565 P 12615 P 17550 PO 18509 P
10030 O 10629 P 13486 P 18074 P 18511 P
10041 10647 P 13811 O 18079 P 18515 S
10048 O 10649 O 13818 P 18369 P 19775 O
10334 O 10663 P 13847 P 18371 P 20139
10513 PO 10677 P 13858 P 18397 S 20566 PO
10515 P 10679 O 14164 P 18417 P 21438 PO
10516 PO 11185 PO 14556 P 18430 P 22506 O
10523 11186 PO 14572 PO 18458 P 22515 P
10530 11191 PO 14584 PO 18461 P 22595 P
10544 P

1842-1928
(including 1644-1928)

Primary 10704 S 16261 S 18551 PO 22902 S
10072 S 12233 P 18531 S 21335 P

Second. 11270 P 12216 P 14642 P 18542 P
10348 O 11276 O 12654 P 14661 P 19791 P
10354 P 11278 P 12957 O 15133 S 21996 P
10687 P 11285 P 13874 P 15670 P 22002 P
10713 P 11291 P 14105 S 17630 P 22103
10731 PO 11702 P 14113 P 18530 P 22658 S
11249 P 11708 S 14628 FP 18540

1911-1928

Primary 11024 P 11345 P 13906 PO 18725 P
10784 P 11026 P 11783 P 14735 P 22698 O
10844 P

Second. 10834 P 11373 P 13979 P 18115 P
10769 P 11319 O 11375 P 14122 O 18579 O
10820 S 11355 P 11376 P 15145 PO 18601 P
10833 11356 P 12273 FP 18109 18610 O

18623 18733 P 19546 P 20464 P 22680 O
18655 P 18757 O 20213 O 20837 PO 22689 P
18700 O

1911-1949
(including 1644-1949, 1842-1949)

Primary 10700 PO 11019 P 12733 P 18981 P
10078 S 10759 P 11020 13572 P 20934 P
10087 O 10776 PO 11021 PO 14684 P 22645 S
10198 S 10781 P 11029 P 16055 PO 22646 P
10689 10791 P 11321 P 18304 P 22660 PO
10692 P 10807 P 11336 P 18783 P 22667 P

Second. 11258 P 14691 P 18149 P 18745 O
10070 P 11289 P 14692 P 18154 P 18752 P
10093 O 11290 P 14694 P 18157 P 18767 O
10707 P 11301 P 14703 S 18571 S 19218
10714 S 11368 P 14719 O 18583 S 19457 P
10718 S 12271 P 14751 FP 18585 O 19463 P
10719 12325 P 15139 18598 O 20813 P
10729 P 12678 15140 O 18635 P 21351 P
10732 P 13017 P 15156 O 18636 P 21459 P
10738 P 13873 O 15586 P 18650 P 22096 S
10762 P 14230 P 16550 P 18673 P 22105 O
10793 P 14510 PO 17933 P 18722 O 22173 P
10828 P 14687 PO 18123 P 18726 P 22662
11257 P

1928-1949

Primary 10836 PO 11328 PO 15069 P 18659 O
10096 O 11022 P 11765 S 15155 18747 PO
10747 O 11023 O 11834 FP 15439 P 18754 S
10758 P 11025 P 12262 F 16054 P 18755 P
10789 P 11027 S 12279 P 18124 FP 19623 PO
10796 P 11028 P 12332 P 18128 P 19626 P
10798 O 11030 P 14235 P 18307 P 20926 PO
10799 PO 11031 P 15067 PO 18647 P 22712 O
10817 PO 11032 P

Second. 10826 O 12729 P 14716 P 18761 P
10746 O 10827 PO 13039 O 18037 18766 P
10760 P 10839 O 13541 P 18114 P 19625 S
10761 O 11308 P 13548 P 18577 O 20105
10764 O 11312 P 13912 O 18608 O 20435 O
10786 P 11314 P 13928 O 18660 P 20441 P
10794 P 11331 P 13936 P 18663 P 20639 S
10801 11337 P 13958 PO 18681 P 20841
10806 O 11357 13959 PO 18687 O 22157 P
10813 P 11361 13960 S 18702 O 22688 S
10814 P 11724 P 14248 P 18707 O 22702 P
10816 F 11750 S 14249 P 18717 P 22703 PO
10819 P 11830 O 14480 P 18731 P 22722 P
10825 O 12266 P 14500 P

1928-1972
(incl. 1644-1972, 1842-1972, 1911-1972)

Primary: Monographs
10115 O 11040 PO 11391 P 14783 P 18312 P
10303 P 11044 PO 11848 PO 15090 O 18809 S
10852 P 11045 FP 11849 P 15171 FP 18822 P
10885 PO 11046 P 12401 P 15176 O 19732 P
10888 S 11047 P 12780 P 15181 P 19899 P
10890 P 11048 S 14258 P 15980 P 21416 O
10893 S 11052 FP 14264 P 18172 P 21874 P
11035 O 11053 O 14269 P 18178 FP 22233 PO
11036 P 11390 P 14293 S 18185 P 22277 P

Primary: Inclusions
10122 S 11043 P 12772 P 15188 P 21870 S
10847 S 11050 13995 P 16745 P 22221 S
10874 P 11051 14275 P 17955 S 22234 P
11042 P 11613 P 15177 S 18043 P 22236 P

Primary: Journal Articles
10848 P 11039 S 14252 14439 P 18791 P
10854 S 11041 P 14267 P 14777 P 21879 P
11033 S 11049 14286 P 15190 22183 P
11034 P 11054 P 14413 P 18044 P 22188 P
11037 P 11055 S 14414 P 18786 P 22227 S
11038 P 11383 P

Secondary: Monographs
10112 S 10126 O 10883 S 11872 PO 15161 P
10113 10129 S 10891 S 12412 P 15166
10114 P 10853 PO 11393 P 14285 P 15174 P
10125 P 10857 O 11418 P 14796 PO 15175 FP

15470 S 18812 19883 P 21401 P 22190 P
15977 P 18817 PO 20226 PO 21407 S 22203 P
18041 P 18819 P 20662 S 21418 O 22219 P
18187 P 18823 S 20954 FP 21471 P 22275 P
18801 P 19655 P 20960 P 21538 FP 22732 FP
18804 PO 19657 P

Secondary: Inclusions
10210 P 14131 15183 PO 18807 21894 S
10218 P 14781 P 15185 S 19876 22191 P
10220 P 14794 P 15186 S 19880 S 22197 P
12395 P 14800 P 15189 O 20111 S 22238 P
12396 P 14801 P 18045 21529 PO 22477 P
12782 P 14802 P 18167 P 21848 S 22813 P
14011 O 14803 P 18181

Secondary: Journal Articles
10846 12374 P 14438 S 19875 P 22223 P
10860 P 12419 P 17581 20227 P 22228 P
10868 S 14126 17949 P 20230 S 22245
11386 P 14128 P 18818 P 20280 P 22278 S
11388 P 14253 P 18824 20961 PO 22284 S
11396 P 14265 S 19030 P 20978 O 22493 S
11402 P 14273 P 19658 P 21536 22735 S
11413 P 14287 S 19868 S 22014 22741
11417 P 14412 S 19872 P 22213 P 22984 S
11615 P 14415 P

1949-1972

Primary: Monographs
10139 P 11000 S 11138 F 14311 P 15572 FP
10140 O 11003 P 11143 P 14322 P 17589 F
10144 O 11006 P 11144 O 14364 P 18225 P
10148 P 11061 O 11154 P 14369 O 18232 P
10150 O 11069 O 11160 P 14370 O 18842 P
10152 O 11076 P 11161 P 14378 P 19166 P
10155 P 11080 P 11168 P 14416 P 19905 P
10157 O 11081 P 11178 P 14419 P 19931 P
10159 O 11087 O 11179 P 14535 P 20244 P
10162 O 11088 11180 P 14885 P 20328 P
10165 O 11092 S 11495 P 14976 P 20496 PO
10169 O 11094 P 11534 P 15017 P 21003 P
10170 O 11095 O 11646 PO 15123 O 21554 O
10174 O 11096 P 11883 O 15205 O 21563 PO
10175 O 11101 FP 11894 O 15214 PO 21570 FP
10466 P 11104 P 12001 P 15230 P 21585 O
10477 P 11105 P 12069 P 15235 P 21594 S
10488 P 11106 O 12082 P 15237 P 21936 O
10937 PO 11107 P 12453 P 15241 S 21951 P
10938 P 11110 P 12524 FP 15260 P 22291 P
10943 PO 11111 P 12525 P 15267 P 22350 P
10953 P 11113 P 12839 FP 15279 O 22746 P
10970 P 11132 14299 P 15294 P 22749 P
10975 P 11135 O 14305 P 15509 O 22769 O
10994 P

Primary: Inclusions
10131 F 11128 P 11484 P 14393 O 18343 FP
10486 P 11131 P 11504 S 14448 P 18346 P
10917 P 11134 PO 11508 P 14840 P 18347 P
10919 P 11156 P 11530 PO 14850 P 18348 P
10946 P 11157 P 11942 P 14851 P 18349 P
11007 P 11158 P 12045 P 14901 P 18358 F
11063 PO 11159 P 12536 P 14964 O 18837 P
11065 PO 11162 P 12799 P 14967 P 19928 P
11072 P 11163 S 12858 P 15217 P 19951 FP
11073 P 11167 P 12859 P 15233 P 20121 P
11077 P 11173 12860 P 15291 P 20306 P
11078 P 11174 P 12861 P 15293 20480 P
11079 P 11176 P 14327 P 15303 FP 20495 P
11083 P 11425 PO 14328 P 15485 F 20698 O
11100 P 11433 PO 14363 P 17646 P 21964 P
11120 P 11443 FP 14374 18189 P 22336 P
11126 P 11451 P 14379 P 18280 P 22357 FP
11127 FP

Primary: Journal Articles
10305 P 10903 P 11060 P 11082 P 11099 P
10309 P 10913 P 11062 PO 11084 P 11102 S
10311 P 10914 P 11064 PO 11085 P 11103 P
10316 P 10954 P 11066 O 11086 O 11108 P
10465 P 10955 11067 FP 11089 P 11109 S
10491 P 10967 P 11068 P 11090 S 11112 S
10496 P 11056 O 11070 P 11091 P 11114 S
10900 11057 O 11071 P 11093 P 11115 P
10901 S 11058 P 11074 P 11097 PO 11116 P
10902 P 11059 S 11075 P 11098 P 11117 P

11118 P 11165 P 12808 P 14849 P 19385 P
11119 P 11166 P 12822 P 14886 P 19902 O
11121 P 11169 12823 P 14898 P 19906 P
11122 P 11170 P 12829 P 14917 P 19926 P
11123 P 11171 P 12835 P 14925 P 19927 P
11124 P 11172 P 13069 P 14965 P 19941 S
11125 P 11175 P 13108 O 15219 P 19944 P
11129 11177 P 14034 P 15236 P 20271 F
11130 P 11432 S 14036 P 15246 S 20361 P
11133 P 11457 P 14063 P 15253 P 20481 P
11136 P 11486 P 14080 P 15256 P 20525 F
11137 P 11521 P 14141 S 15265 21109 O
11139 P 11529 14148 15276 P 21429 P
11140 O 11533 P 14321 P 15277 21430 F
11141 S 11972 O 14351 P 15292 P 21488 P
11142 P 12011 P 14352 P 15295 P 21548 O
11145 P 12012 P 14371 P 17996 P 21560 S
11146 P 12072 P 14373 P 18052 P 21587 P
11147 12099 P 14382 P 18058 P 21960 S
11148 P 12116 P 14392 P 18194 P 21972 P
11149 O 12129 P 14446 P 18221 P 22289 P
11150 P 12131 O 14452 P 18245 P 22292 P
11151 P 12155 O 14534 O 18273 P 22294 P
11152 P 12443 P 14537 P 18326 P 22334 P
11153 O 12549 P 14813 P 18327 S 22361 P
11155 P 12796 P 14848 P 19368 S 22382 S
11164 F 12800 S

Secondary: Monographs
10132 O 10944 P 12519 P 16155 O 19909 P
10134 O 10962 12552 P 17587 P 19919 P
10135 O 10997 P 12813 P 17804 P 20247 P
10136 O 11427 O 12869 P 17913 P 20314 P
10154 P 11438 P 13070 P 18053 O 20335 P
10158 O 11439 P 13328 O 18212 P 20484 P
10160 O 11440 P 14040 FP 18224 P 20492 P
10161 O 11514 P 14066 FP 18236 P 21434 O
10164 O 11885 P 14296 P 18264 P 21435 O
10167 O 11897 PO 14309 P 18299 P 21569 P
10168 O 11949 P 14828 P 18330 PO 21579 PO
10173 O 11962 PO 14974 PO 19062 O 22293 S
10177 O 12123 P 15034 P 19132 P 22299 P
10180 O 12436 P 15234 P 19194 P 22318 P
10226 P 12439 P 15248 P 19203 P 22339 P
10263 P 12446 P 15519 O 19291 P 22375 PO
10479 P 12456 PO 15550 O 19662 P 22831 P
10906 P 12464 P 16148 FP

Secondary: Inclusions
10147 P 11426 P 14138 P 15906 P 19324 FP
10176 P 11447 P 14146 F 15907 P 19915 P
10179 P 11487 P 14151 P 15909 P 19952 P
10224 P 11531 14304 P 15911 P 20371 P
10313 P 11969 P 14330 FP 17997 P 21117 PO
10468 P 12479 14390 P 18290 P 21251 P
10469 P 12557 P 14525 P 18294 S 21955 P
10915 P 12559 P 14880 PO 18340 P 22290 P
10920 P 12805 F 15099 P 19101 P 22321 P
10930 P 14031 P 15287 P 19104 22342 P
10988 FP 14032 P 15296 P 19149 O 22373
11002 14068 P 15299 P 19190 P 22827 P

Secondary: Journal Articles
10236 P 11472 P 12472 P 14920 P 16831 O
10243 P 11485 P 12489 P 14923 P 17785 P
10265 P 11488 P 12531 P 14937 P 17991 S
10314 P 11493 FP 12554 P 14959 P 18056 P
10315 P 11500 P 12555 P 14971 P 18190 P
10473 P 11502 P 12851 P 14991 FP 18213 PO
10899 PO 11507 P 13086 S 14998 P 18214 S
10939 P 11510 P 14039 P 15096 P 18237 P
10959 S 11511 P 14056 P 15111 O 18238 P
10969 P 11515 P 14132 P 15199 18243 P
10982 11522 P 14136 O 15200 P 18255 P
10987 P 11624 P 14137 P 15220 P 18297 P
10991 P 11642 P 14143 P 15227 P 18316 P
10998 S 11900 S 14295 P 15238 P 18317 P
11001 P 11913 P 14306 P 15244 P 18351 P
11008 S 11950 S 14331 P 15251 P 18352 P
11419 P 11976 O 14348 P 15257 P 19130 P
11430 P 11979 PO 14350 P 15264 P 19137 P
11431 P 11992 P 14359 P 15266 S 19143 P
11445 P 11999 P 14367 O 15275 PO 19187 S
11452 P 12085 PO 14526 P 15284 P 19189 P
11455 P 12105 P 14531 P 15620 P 19392 P
11456 P 12119 S 14548 P 16142 P 19470 S
11469 P 12470 P 14832 P 16151 P 19600 P
19665 P 20331 P 21092 FP 22314 P 22365 O
19667 P 20362 P 21104 O 22316 P 22374 P
19908 P 20365 P 21919 P 22320 P 22745 O
19921 P 20374 P 21939 P 22330 P 22757 P
19923 P 20376 P 21940 P 22332 P 22828 S
19924 20476 P 21956 P 22337 22843 P
19948 P 20488 P 22020 P 22344 P 22844 P
19949 P 20499 P 22297 P 22347 P 22853
19950 P 20523 P 22309 P 22349 P 23039 P
20237 O 20532 P 22311 22362 P 23056 P
20248 O 21044 P

12.2 National Legal System

司法制度 司法制度

1644-1842

Primary 10561 O 12198 P 16087 P 20040 S
10008 S 10652 O 15043 P 16218 O 22075 P
10044 O 11555 P 15752 O 16223 P 22590 O
10552 P 12190 P

Second. 10526 S 11541 P 14401 P 21712 P
10007 O 10542 P 11675 O 14423 P 22034 P
10020 PO 10579 P 12901 P 16100 P 22398 O
10036 O 10590 P 13469 P 17408 PO 22577 P
10039 O 10618 P 13812 17657 O 22578 O
10050 O 10626 P 13814 S 18916 P 22629 P
10051 P 10643 PO 13830 P 20582 P 22776 P
10507 P 11010 P 14085 P 21279 P

1644-1911

Primary 11199 P 11219 P 11243 P 19766 O
10014 O 11200 S 11220 P 11246 O 19769 P
10554 P 11201 P 11221 P 11672 PO 19771 S
10559 PO 11202 P 11222 P 12185 P 19772 P
10574 P 11203 P 11224 P 12602 P 19774 P
10600 P 11207 S 11225 S 14098 P 20033 P
10615 P 11208 P 11226 P 14099 P 20038 P
10666 P 11210 P 11227 P 14102 P 20042 P
11183 P 11211 P 11233 S 14103 20044 P
11184 P 11212 11234 P 14201 P 20144 P
11194 O 11214 P 11235 P 14397 P 21172 P
11195 P 11216 P 11239 P 18516 P 21698 P
11197 P 11217 P 11241 P 19752 P 22054 P
11198 P 11218 P 11242 P 19763 P 22567 P

Second. 10604 P 12933 P 14627 P 19755 PO
10001 O 10646 12941 PO 15729 PO 20090 PO
10004 PO 10657 P 12947 P 15931 O 20157 O
10016 O 10667 P 13456 P 18012 P 20158 P
10029 PO 10680 P 13457 P 18421 P 20284 P
10042 PO 11015 P 13628 S 18459 O 20285 P
10060 PO 11655 PO 13844 P 18527 P 20751 PO
10279 P 11663 O 14088 P 19209 O 21709 P
10520 P 12197 P 14090 P 19210 22044 P
10525 P 12199 P 14104 P 19695 P 22056 P
10573 S 12201 P 14175 S 19722 P 22866 P

1842-1911

Primary 11182 P 11213 P 12187 O 19719 P
10017 O 11185 PO 11215 P 12911 P 19753 P
10019 PO 11186 PO 11223 S 12945 P 19760 PO
10023 O 11187 PO 11228 O 12946 PO 19762 S
10035 O 11188 P 11229 O 13853 P 19773 PO
10047 O 11189 P 11230 P 14177 O 19780 P
10059 O 11190 P 11231 P 15336 O 20034 PO
10518 P 11191 PO 11232 FP 16089 P 20036 P
10531 P 11192 P 11236 P 16186 O 20287 P
10601 O 11193 P 11237 18093 P 20755 PO
10640 PO 11196 O 11238 P 18100 P 21159 P
10660 O 11204 P 11240 P 18301 S 21652 O
10668 P 11205 O 11244 O 19204 O 22515 P
11017 O 11206 O 11245 PO 19208 P 22608 P
11181 F 11209 P 11678 P 19212 P

Second. 10031 O 10562 P 10679 O 13828 P
10002 O 10034 S 10606 P 10683 14092 PO
10003 O 10038 O 10631 P 11014 P 14396 P
10011 O 10513 PO 10641 O 12590 P 14566 PO
10013 O 10519 P 10648 O 12910 P 14584 PO
10025 O 10551 P 10649 O 12924 O 15311 O
10030 O 10558 P 10677 P 13811 O 15347 PO
15361 O 18378 O 18871 PO 20590 PO 22568 P
16532 O 18379 PO 18908 O 20749 O 22580 PO
16535 PO 18387 P 18926 O 20773 F 22586 P
17525 O 18409 P 18943 P 21438 PO 22594 O
17625 O 18494 P 19779 P 22037 P 22595 P
17688 O 18511 P 20003 O 22525 O 22599 O
18077 P 18859 P 20085 P 22549 P 22615 O
18368 P 18868 PO 20540 O 22566 P 22624 P

1842-1928

(including 1644-1928)

Primary 11259 PO 11282 P 11299 P 19222 P
10084 PO 11260 P 11283 S 11300 O 19784 P
10703 P 11261 P 11284 S 11302 19789 P
10716 P 11268 O 11285 P 11303 S 19790 PO
10723 PO 11269 S 11286 P 11305 P 19793 P
10735 S 11270 P 11287 P 13500 PO 19797 PO
11247 P 11271 PO 11291 P 14105 S 20051 P
11248 P 11275 PO 11292 PO 14631 O 20175 P
11249 P 11276 O 11295 P 16102 O 22085 P
11250 P 11277 PO 11297 PO 16108 PO 22650 P
11253 PO 11278 P 11298 P 18546 PO 22652 P
11254 P 11280 P

Second. 10728 P 13152 PO 14232 P 19791 P
10067 O 10731 PO 13489 P 15864 P 19795 P
10068 S 11578 P 13506 P 15938 P 20047 P
10072 S 11590 PO 13508 P 16109 PO 20179 P
10081 PO 11702 P 13511 P 16110 P 20182 P
10082 PO 11705 PO 13523 P 16267 O 20795 O
10085 PO 12225 O 13644 P 17691 PO 21350 P
10704 S 12663 P 13648 O 17981 P 21788 P
10709 P 12955 PO 13666 P 19477 PO 22131 PO
10722 P 12957 O 13674 FP 19481 P

1911-1928

Primary 11342 P 11363 P 12982 P 19249 PO
10765 S 11345 P 11364 P 13004 P 19252 PO
10768 PO 11349 P 11365 P 13745 P 19255 PO
10778 O 11351 P 11373 P 14498 P 19277 P
11026 P 11352 O 11374 O 15065 P 19278 P
11315 11353 P 11375 P 15073 P 19811 P
11316 P 11354 PO 11376 P 15966 FP 19826 P
11319 O 11355 P 11377 S 16114 P 19842 P
11324 P 11356 P 11597 PO 17696 PO 19852 P
11325 P 11358 P 11599 PO 17719 O 20060 P
11329 P 11360 P 12280 P 18308 P 20107 S
11339 P

Second. 11783 P 14410 18579 O 19515 O
10106 P 11812 P 14485 PO 18596 PO 19825 O
10756 S 12346 P 16664 PO 18621 O 20108 PO
10784 P 13029 S 17717 PO 18997 PO 20197 O
10785 P 13726 O 17836 O 19265 O 20222 S
10820 S 13733 PO 17842 F 19427 P 22007 S
10834 P 13910 O 18126 P 19503 FP 22698 O
11736 P

1911-1949

(including 1644-1949, 1842-1949)

Primary: Monographs
10692 P 11274 P 11344 P 13759 P 19806 P
10707 P 11279 P 11368 P 14479 PO 19819 P
10711 P 11289 P 11369 P 14509 P 19854 P
10745 PO 11290 P 11586 FP 15956 P 20025 P
10782 PO 11293 P 12271 P 16113 S 20053 P
10793 P 11294 P 12675 PO 16123 FP 20067 P
10807 P 11301 P 12676 S 19275 P 20068 P
10828 P 11304 P 13491 PO 19457 P 20160 PO
11257 P 11313 P 13535 P 19476 P 20162 P
11258 P 11317 P 13650 P 19796 P 20934 P
11263 PO 11323 P 13740 P 19801 P 22132 P
11266 P 11336 P 13755 P 19804 P

Primary: Inclusions
11252 S 11265 O 11379 P 15946 FP 19279 F
11256 P 11321 P 14455 S 18541 S 20292 S

Primary: Journal Articles
10689 11255 P 11281 11320 P 12659 P
10714 S 11262 P 11288 11333 P 13148 P
10719 11264 P 11296 S 11334 S 13749 P
10738 P 11267 S 11306 O 11370 P 14477 P
10762 P 11272 P 11309 PO 11382 FP 14481 P
11251 P 11273 11311 12325 P 14482 P

14734 P 19395 S 19785 P 19967 P 20055 P
17733 P 19432 P 19792 P 20045 P 20057 P
19214 P 19435 P 19798 P 20046 P 20061 P
19235 P 19539 P 19821 P 20052 P 22080 P
19236 P 19701 P 19832 P 20054 P 22916 S
19271 P 19783 S 19853 P

Secondary: Monographs
10070 P 10845 P 13676 P 14691 P 19358 P
10079 PO 11021 PO 13680 P 14736 P 19824 PO
10083 PO 11692 P 13687 P 15961 FP 19964 P
10104 O 12231 P 13691 P 16055 PO 20013 P
10107 P 12657 PO 14230 P 17763 PO 20050 S
10448 P 12682 P 14238 P 17869 PO 20161 P
10684 O 12714 PO 14457 P 18120 P 20178 PO
10688 P 12970 P 14466 P 18547 PO 21362 O
10690 P 13290 P 14486 P 18557 P 22666 S
10696 P 13507 P 14496 P 18953 O 22667 P
10724 S 13521 PO 14508 P 18988 FP 22717 P
10732 P 13649 P 14687 PO

Secondary: Inclusions
10694 P 13242 P 17052 PO 18558 S 19788 FP
12370 P 14773 18119 P

Secondary: Journal Articles
10717 PO 12733 P 14664 S 18021 PO 19576 P
10736 S 13504 S 14776 P 18304 P 19799 P
10822 13561 P 16111 S 19221 20168
11019 P 13672 P 16112 S 19282 P 20191 PO
12212 S 14663 16115 P 19542

1928-1949

Primary: Monographs
10799 PO 11327 P 11371 P 15409 P 18647 P
10842 P 11335 P 11381 P 15963 P 19276 P
11027 S 11340 P 12260 P 16637 P 20065 P
11307 S 11348 S 14471 P 17709 F 20066 P
11318 P 11362 P

Primary: Inclusions
11328 PO

Primary: Journal Articles
10763 P 11322 S 11357 13751 P 19274 P
10764 O 11326 PO 11359 PO 14474 FP 19521
10771 11330 P 11361 14490 P 19813 P
10774 PO 11331 P 11366 P 15064 S 19831 P
10775 PO 11332 P 11367 P 16118 F 19838 S
10809 11337 P 11372 P 17710 F 20058 P
10818 P 11338 P 11378 O 19234 P 20059 S
10829 P 11341 P 11380 O 19237 P 20064 P
11308 P 11343 P 12275 P 19253 PO 20105
11310 P 11346 P 13215 P 19254 PO 20201 P
11312 P 11347 S 13216 P 19262 PO 22687 PO
11314 P 11350 13548 P 19272 P

Second. 11725 P 13039 O 15965 P 19810 P
10108 P 11765 S 13262 O 15971 P 19845 S
10754 S 11778 P 13278 PO 17419 P 20190 P
10794 P 11823 P 13571 PO 18761 P 20219 P
10805 P 11829 P 13756 P 19267 P 20436 O
10814 P 12255 FP 14248 P 19270 O 20642 F
10819 P 12272 S 14478 FP 19494 P 20940 S
10823 P 12315 P 14501 P 19544 P 22169 P
10836 PO 12332 P 14744 P 19572 P 22712 O
11031 P 12742 P 15430 P 19573 P 22720 PO
11724 P 13025 PO 15440 P 19704 P

1928-1972
(incl. 1644-1972, 1842-1972, 1911-1972)

Primary: Monographs
10851 P 11391 P 11418 P 19042 PO 19883 P
11036 P 11393 P 12378 P 19732 P 19892 P
11385 S 11395 P 15461 P 19859 FP 20069 PO
11390 P 11398 P 15973 P 19862 P 20226 PO

Primary: Inclusions
11050 11392 P 11400 P 19866 P 19893 P
11051 11397 P 11411 S 19873 S 20071 P
11389 P 11399 P 12396 P 19884 P 20228 P

Primary: Journal Articles
10868 S 11388 P 11404 S 11410 P 11417 P
10875 P 11394 S 11405 S 11412 P 12761 P
11383 P 11396 P 11406 PO 11413 P 14007 O
11384 P 11401 PO 11407 S 11414 P 16125 P
11386 P 11402 P 11408 P 11415 PO 16126 S
11387 P 11403 PO 11409 S 11416 16128 FP
17494 PO 19872 P 19879 P 20232 O 22957 S
18184 F 19875 P 19891 P 22742 P 23000 S
19868 S

Second. 11045 FP 14780 P 19582 P 20231 PO
10113 11055 S 14790 P 19585 P 20658 F
10122 S 11602 P 15158 S 19860 21400 P
10126 O 11603 PO 15161 P 19867 P 21416 O
10850 PO 11605 O 15181 P 19869 S 21425 P
10857 O 11855 S 15976 PO 19871 S 21467 S
10865 P 11866 P 15980 P 19874 P 21473 PO
10873 P 12374 P 16124 FP 19878 PO 21529 PO
10885 PO 12385 P 16983 P 19880 S 21856
10887 PO 12387 PO 17320 P 19886 S 22216 S
10888 S 12426 P 17955 S 19887 P 22234 P
10891 S 12764 S 18179 P 20114 O 22264 P
11040 PO 13763 PO 18817 PO 20115 S 22956 S
11044 PO 14777 P 19087 P 20229 P

1949-1972

Primary: Monographs
10306 PO 11427 O 11492 PO 13105 P 18354 O
10413 P 11436 P 11495 P 14549 P 19905 P
10944 P 11437 P 11496 P 15518 P 19931 P
10953 P 11438 P 11514 P 16148 FP 20688 O
10997 P 11439 P 11534 P 16795 P 21585 O
11006 P 11440 P 11622 P 16872 FP 22763 O
11423 P 11466 P

Primary: Inclusions
10918 P 11443 FP 11459 P 11508 P 15105 P
11120 P 11447 P 11484 P 11530 PO 19915 P
11425 PO 11448 P 11487 P 11531 19930 P
11426 P 11449 PO 11490 P 12510 P 20081 P
11433 PO 11451 P 11494 P 12801 P 21066 P
11435 P 11458 P 11504 S 14878 PO 23050 S
11442 FP

Primary: Journal Articles
10897 P 11452 P 11481 P 11517 P 16901 F
10909 P 11453 P 11482 P 11518 O 17430 PO
10929 P 11454 P 11483 O 11519 O 19155 P
10941 P 11455 P 11485 P 11520 P 19164 PO
11008 S 11456 P 11486 P 11521 P 19383 P
11112 S 11457 P 11488 P 11522 P 19609 P
11125 P 11460 P 11489 P 11523 S 19610 P
11170 P 11461 P 11491 P 11524 P 19903 P
11172 P 11462 P 11493 FP 11525 P 19904 PO
11175 P 11463 P 11497 S 11526 P 19906 P
11419 P 11464 P 11498 P 11527 19912 P
11420 P 11465 P 11499 O 11528 P 19934 P
11421 P 11467 P 11500 P 11529 19940 PO
11422 O 11468 P 11501 O 11532 P 19942 O
11424 O 11469 P 11502 P 11533 P 19949 P
11428 S 11470 P 11503 P 11535 PO 19950 P
11429 O 11471 P 11505 P 12468 P 19954 O
11430 P 11472 P 11506 P 12802 P 20076
11431 P 11473 P 11507 P 13777 P 20077 P
11432 S 11474 P 11509 P 13796 P 20078 P
11434 P 11475 S 11510 P 14546 S 20248 O
11441 O 11476 P 11511 P 15124 P 22349 P
11444 P 11477 11512 O 16130 O 22766 P
11445 P 11478 11513 P 16133 F 23021 F
11446 P 11479 P 11515 P 16136 O 23029 S
11450 P 11480 P 11516 O 16142 P 23032 S

Secondary: Monographs
10132 O 11076 P 13612 O 16007 FP 19063 PO
10133 O 11095 O 13618 P 16132 O 19389 P
10139 P 11106 O 14337 P 16788 PO 19590 P
10141 O 11110 P 14369 O 16902 FP 19597 FP
10158 O 11135 O 14370 O 16996 S 19611 P
10165 O 11884 P 14520 17006 P 19909 P
10167 O 11885 P 14846 FP 17127 P 19922 P
10488 P 12440 PO 14885 P 17350 FP 20244 P
10894 P 12525 P 14908 FP 17360 P 20690 P
10960 FP 12795 O 15113 P 18003 FP 21108 FP
10994 P 12849 P 15294 P 18225 P 21435 O
11003 P 13420 FP 15550 O 18236 P 21948 P
11069 O 13602 P 16002 FP

Secondary: Inclusions
10912 P 11157 P 14393 O 15911 P 19914 S
10915 P 11158 P 14880 PO 16032 PO 19952 P
10916 P 11159 P 15906 P 16085 FP 20118 O
10919 P 11989 P 15907 P 16851 P 20120 O
11079 P 12559 P 15909 P 19593 PO 23014 S
11156 P 14325 P

Secondary: Journal Articles
10312 O 11148 P 14531 P 17592 P 19924
10901 S 11645 P 15211 P 18197 P 19936 F
10913 P 11648 P 15282 S 18230 P 19941 S
10939 P 12078 S 16030 P 18336 P 20073 P
10954 P 12129 P 16043 19061 S 21430 F
10955 13586 P 16084 P 19183 P 21560 S
10968 P 14076 P 16147 PO 19607 P 22312
10991 P 14441 S 16149 O 19900 O 22761 O
11118 P 14519 P 16832 S 19902 O 22846

13 Elite and Official Religion
社會領導階層與官定之宗教信仰
国教及び上層階級の宗教

1644-1842

Primary 11536 O 11557 P 16185 P 22398 O
10044 O 11541 P 11563 P 18936 P 22520 P
10580 O 11545 P 11569 PO 18948 P 22578 O
10652 O 11555 P 11571 P 21661 PO 22637 P

Second. 10036 O 12179 S 18891 P 22033 P
10008 S 10050 O 12189 P 18904 P 22537 P
10020 PO 10535 P 13812 18916 P 22590 O
10022 O 10542 P 14156 O 20563 S 22619 PO
10026 O 10590 P 14197 P 21643 PO 22865 S
10027 O 11675 O 14210 P 21644 P 22880
10032 O

1644-1911

Primary 11544 S 11560 P 14191 PO 20149 S
10001 O 11546 P 11561 PO 16192 P 21163 FP
10014 O 11547 O 11562 PO 16194 O 21437 P
10029 PO 11548 O 11564 S 16206 PO 21627
10550 P 11549 P 11566 S 16221 PO 21642 FP
11538 11550 FP 11568 PO 18421 P 21656 P
11539 FP 11552 P 11570 P 18848 P 21657 P
11540 O 11556 P 11572 PO 18880 P 21697 PO
11542 FP 11558 PO 11573 PO 18927 PO 21703
11543 S 11559 P 11574 PO 18946 PO 21709 P

Second. 11677 S 16190 FP 20002 P 21669 S
10012 P 12197 P 16196 P 20545 FP 21696 P
10042 PO 12941 PO 16200 PO 21173 O 22024 P
10053 P 14167 P 16207 P 21269 22036 P
10505 P 14201 P 16217 FP 21300 S 22054 P
10573 S 15327 PO 18862 P 21610 F 22056 P
10574 P 15341 O 18873 PO 21612 P 22061 P
10586 15743 O 18890 S 21630 P 22394 PO
11194 O 16161 PO 18910 21641 FP 22414 S
11198 P 16162 PO 18945 P 21645 P 22551 P
11203 P 16189 FP 19992 S

1842-1911

Primary 11551 O 14163 PO 16211 O 19719 P
10043 O 11553 O 15347 PO 16219 O 19779 P
10509 O 11554 O 15710 18857 O 20544 F
10611 O 11565 O 15749 PO 18859 P 21260 PO
11537 11567 P 16186 O 18911 O 22588 P

Second. 10519 P 16159 O 18924 PO 21624 O
10019 PO 10531 P 16169 O 18926 O 21980 O
10024 O 11245 PO 16183 O 19740 O 22037 P
10030 O 13804 P 16187 O 20258 O 22051 P
10031 O 13853 P 16220 PO 20540 O 22530 P
10041 14157 O 17974 O 20557 O 22562 O
10048 O 14566 PO 18096 P 20559 O 22564 P
10052 P 14601 O 18378 O 20579 O 22572 O
10059 O 15317 O 18430 P 21264 O 22580 PO
10513 PO 15355 O 18471 S 21621 O

1842-1928
(including 1644-1928)

Primary 11578 P 11589 P 16235 O 16241 O
10069 O 11579 P 11590 PO 16236 O 16242 O
10082 PO 11581 PO 11591 16237 O 16243 O
11575 F 11583 P 11592 PO 16238 O 16244 O
11576 F 11584 O 16230 O 16239 O 16281 P
11577 F 11587 P 16232 FP 16240 O 18958 P

18960 po 18983 fp 21742 s 21774 21794 o
18961 p 21723 po 21752 po 21791 po 21798 p
18980 o 21735 po

Second. 16228 po 16276 o 19793 p 22083 p
10255 o 16234 f 18957 o 20618 po 22085 p
10713 p 16247 po 18959 o 20619 o 22108 p
11247 p 16261 s 18962 po 21788 p 22112 p
11298 p 16264 po 18978 po 22001 p 22123 p
14214 po 16273 o

1911-1928

Primary 11597 po 11600 p 19000 p 21455 o
11594 o 11599 po 18997 po

Second. 19001 po 19010 f 19024 o 21378 o
16285 19002 po 19013 o 19028 o 22179 o
18700 o

1911-1949
(including 1644-1949, 1842-1949)

Primary 11586 fp 11596 p 18988 fp 21761 p
11580 p 11588 fp 11598 p 21724 p 22102 po
11582 po 11593 p 11601 p 21746 22129 p
11585 s 11595 p 15372 o 21750 po

Second. 16272 po 18981 p 20615 o 21804 p
10759 p 16282 s 18989 fp 21363 21821 o
11258 p 16300 o 19006 o 21447 po 21992 p
14215 s 18149 p 19964 p 21718 o 22006 s
15370 o 18544 p 20012 po 21740 p 22170 p
16255 s 18953 o 20166 o 21771 po 22893 o
16271 po

1928-1949

Primary 22010 p

Second. 10827 po 15416 o 15773 p 16294 o
20639 s

1928-1972
(incl. 1644-1972, 1842-1972, 1911-1972)

Primary 11606 s 11612 p 19033 p 19056
10120 s 11607 p 11613 p 19042 po 21467 s
10891 s 11608 s 11614 p 19046 p 21851 o
11602 p 11609 p 11615 p 19047 p 21860 o
11603 po 11610 po 11616 s 19048 p 21868 p
11604 s 11611 po 16343 p 19049 p 22193
11605 o

Second. 14272 p 19029 19052 p 21477 s
10110 po 16329 s 19036 p 19054 f 21843 po
10113 16331 p 19038 p 20994 o 22015 p
10124 s 16332 p 19040 21412 p 22216 s
10126 o 16335 p 19041 21421 o 22231 p
10259 p 16336 p 19043 p 21428 o 22234 p
11855 s 16341 p 19050 21476 s

1949-1972

Primary 11625 p 11636 o 11647 p 16077 o
10173 o 11626 s 11637 p 11648 p 16356 p
10978 o 11627 f 11638 o 11649 po 18280 p
11617 po 11628 p 11639 p 11650 p 19057 p
11618 po 11629 p 11640 p 11651 fp 19059 s
11619 p 11630 p 11641 p 11652 fp 19060
11620 o 11631 p 11642 p 11653 p 19063 po
11621 p 11632 11643 s 11654 p 19069 po
11622 p 11633 p 11644 po 12811 o 22749 p
11623 p 11634 s 11645 p 15267 p 23044 s
11624 p 11635 po 11646 po

Second. 10168 o 11883 o 18232 p 19067 o
10134 o 10170 o 14370 o 18272 p 20668 o
10150 o 11135 o 15575 o 18842 p 21563 po
10155 p 11147 16352 s 19058 s 22335 p
10164 o 11174 p 17995 o

14 National Economy and Economic Planning
全國經濟及經濟計劃
国家経済及び経済計画

1644-1842

Primary 10045 o 11675 o 12901 p 20563 s
10007 o 10552 p 11680 p 13134 s 21284 p
10008 s 10561 o 11682 p 15582 p 22619 po
10033 o 10651 p 12189 p 15752 o 22874 p
10044 o

Second. 10036 o 10627 p 11010 p 22779 p
10015 o 10618 p 10643 po 13621 po 22876 s
10027 o 10626 p

1644-1911

Primary 10060 po 10582 po 11672 po 13458 p
10004 po 10277 p 11194 o 11676 s 13482 p
10010 p 10325 po 11655 po 11677 s 14159 p
10016 o 10329 po 11656 s 12193 po 18526 s
10037 10333 p 11663 o 12201 p 19210
10042 po 10437 p 11664 12933 p 20257
10053 p 10441 p 11666 p 12947 p 21263 p
10058 po 10560 p 11667 p 12948 p 21276 p

Second. 13456 p 14091 15658 p 21291 p
10187 po 13457 p 14454 p 18421 p 21709 p
10252 13459 p 15044 s 21288 p 22058 p
12929 p 14088 p 15130 s

1842-1911

Primary 10510 p 11660 p 12593 po 13811 o
10003 o 10511 p 11661 p 12601 o 14164 p
10017 o 10516 po 11662 12880 p 14400 o
10041 10536 s 11665 p 12888 po 15924 po
10047 o 10564 p 11668 o 12894 o 18073 p
10048 o 10640 po 11669 12899 o 18378 o
10055 o 10641 o 11670 p 12905 o 18387 p
10061 o 10650 po 11671 o 12920 o 18430 p
10062 po 10660 o 11673 p 12926 o 18504 p
10063 o 10677 p 11674 s 12934 o 18511 p
10064 o 11186 po 11678 p 13452 21287 p
10065 o 11657 po 11679 p 13627 p 22568 p
10330 p 11658 o 11681 o 13801 s 22631 s
10331 s 11659 p

Second. 10056 o 12580 po 15126 s 20596 o
10011 o 10318 o 12616 f 16186 o 21261 p
10013 o 10323 o 12921 o 17974 o 21652 o
10021 o 10509 o 12922 p 18090 o 22074 p
10030 o 10538 p 13486 p 18408 s 22556 po
10031 o 10607 p 13631 s 18515 s 22623 p
10040 o 12577 p 14100 o 20036 p 22771 p
10049 po

1842-1928
(including 1644-1928)

Primary 11691 p 11713 p 13163 s 13681 p
10068 s 11697 p 11717 p 13164 fp 13688 p
10073 11698 p 11718 13168 s 14109 p
10076 s 11701 11719 o 13187 p 16261 s
10338 p 11702 p 12215 p 13487 p 18555
10340 po 11703 p 12222 p 13500 po 20618 po
10342 o 11705 po 12229 p 13508 p 22076 s
10348 o 11708 s 12233 p 13511 p 22644 o
10698 p 11709 12951 po 13518 p 22650 p
11683 o 11710 12953 po 13520 p 22922 s
11686 p 11711 s 13147 p 13662 p

Second. 12224 s 13502 p 13692 p 19215 o
10072 s 12226 s 13515 p 14113 p 22079 p
10077 o 12620 p 13646 s 15132 p 22101 p
10287 p 12655 s 13667 s 15133 s 22131 po
10709 p 13493 p 13686 p 18540 22907 s
10712 s 13498 s

1911-1928

Primary 10374 s 10750 p 11729 p 11734 p
10094 o 10380 po 10835 p 11730 o 11736 p
10106 p 10381 p 11345 p 11731 11737
11749 p 11790 s 11814 p 12349 o 15692 p
11754 p 11794 p 11816 s 12355 s 19229 o
11766 po 11802 o 11817 13538 o 19248 o
11780 p 11809 p 11828 s 13737 o 19512 p
11783 p 11812 p 11831 13738 p 22698 o
11784 p 11813 p 12327 p 14122 o

Second. 12717 p 13536 p 17272 p 18653 p
10099 o 12732 p 13741 p 17879 o 18709 p
10209 fp 12745 o 13937 fp 17939 o 18710 p
10369 o 13032 p 14408 p 18579 o 19242 o
10769 p 13248 p 14410 18597 po 19462
11026 p 13267 fp 14493 p 18610 o 19534 p
12361 p

1911-1949
(including 1644-1949, 1842-1949)

Primary: Monographs
10070 p 10812 p 11715 p 12674 p 13676 p
10097 o 11685 s 11716 p 12675 po 13701 s
10104 o 11687 p 11756 p 12682 p 13755 p
10107 p 11689 p 11825 po 13037 p 13901 o
10341 p 11690 p 11839 p 13176 p 14640 po
10346 s 11692 p 12218 p 13222 p 14703 s
10349 s 11694 po 12257 fp 13255 s 15674 po
10364 fp 11696 s 12270 p 13261 p 18722 o
10370 p 11699 s 12271 p 13290 p 18759 p
10375 p 11704 p 12328 p 13291 s 20620 po
10725 p 11707 p 12631 p 13516 po 22109 s
10745 po 11712 fp 12638 p 13535 p 22660 po
10781 p 11714 p

Primary: Inclusions
10295 po 11695 11721 p 11786 p 13259 p
10453 s 11700 s 11746 p 11840 p 18537 s
10694 p 11720 po 11747 fp 13242 p 18556
11688 s

Primary: Journal Articles
10717 po 11773 o 11824 o 13153 s 15669 p
10719 11776 11832 s 13154 s 18673 p
11684 p 11779 p 11836 s 13173 po 22098 p
11693 p 11795 o 11837 o 13731 p 22167 p
11706 p 11801 p 12334 p 14740 o 22651 s
11726 s 11810 p 12634 p 15142 p 22665 s
11735 11815 s 12681

Second. 10776 po 13570 p 14736 p 18619 s
10074 p 11263 po 13673 p 15063 s 18651 s
10079 po 11290 p 13682 p 15071 p 18674 p
10080 12227 p 13687 p 15137 18711 o
10083 po 12293 s 13725 p 15585 s 18768 s
10090 o 12303 fp 13727 p 15586 p 19218
10253 p 12372 p 14428 f 15675 p 19240 po
10288 s 12641 p 14455 s 17190 po 19241
10696 p 12650 s 14457 p 17248 f 22006 s
10700 po 12662 s 14486 p 18123 p 22095 p
10706 po 13232 p 14495 p 18561 o 22646 p
10715 p 13491 po 14496 p 18562 s 22785 s
10718 s 13517 p 14686 p 18571 s 22787 s
10726 13561 p 14694 p 18588 p 22923 fp
10759 p

1928-1949

Primary: Monographs
10092 o 11748 p 11804 p 12291 s 13708 po
10103 po 11750 s 11805 p 12331 p 13743 po
10105 fp 11752 fp 11807 p 12345 o 13744 po
10108 p 11760 po 11808 s 12358 p 13760 po
10365 11767 po 11822 p 12708 s 13761 po
10792 o 11777 p 11823 p 13025 po 15067 po
10813 p 11782 o 11829 p 13039 o 17228 p
10827 po 11785 fp 11830 o 13042 s 18114 p
11724 p 11793 p 11833 p 13549 p 18142 p
11732 p 11796 p 11834 fp 13556 p 18717 p
11740 p 11797 p 11841 po 13704 po 22718
11745 p 11799 p

Primary: Inclusions
10747 o 11753 o 11819 12326 s 18712 p
11741 p 11769 po 11838 o 13571 po 18763 s
11751 p 11775 12269 p 14435 o

Primary: Journal Articles
10296 10816 f 11725 p 11733 p 11742
10357 s 11722 11727 11738 o 11743
10358 s 11723 p 11728 s 11739 p 11744 o

11755 P 11772 O 11803 O 12276 O 13263 P
11757 P 11774 11806 S 12290 P 13279 P
11758 S 11778 P 11811 P 12301 S 13280 P
11759 O 11781 S 11818 P 12360 P 13555 P
11761 P 11787 O 11820 S 12983 S 13559 P
11762 P 11788 S 11821 S 13013 P 14117 P
11763 P 11789 11826 P 13018 S 15154 P
11764 P 11791 P 11827 PO 13028 PO 18684
11765 S 11792 P 11835 13223 O 19568 S
11768 S 11798 12263 13234 P 19629 P
11770 11800 P 12266 P 13236 P 22715 S
11771 O

SECOND. 12277 O 13564 P 13909 O 18159 O
10101 O 12342 P 13565 PO 13912 O 18629 P
10443 P 12689 13705 PO 13960 S 18701 P
10452 S 12730 PO 13711 P 14248 P 18707 O
10746 O 12738 13714 S 15150 18761 P
10748 O 13257 P 13735 P 15155 20639 S
10758 P 13265 FP 13748 O 15773 P 22169 P
10761 O 13286 P 13750 FP 16054 P 22714 P
10796 P 13550 P 13903 S 17297 PO 22722 P
10819 P 13560 P

1928-1972
(incl. 1644-1972, 1842-1972, 1911-1972)

PRIMARY: MONOGRAPHS
10111 S 10882 P 11863 P 13311 P 16737 P
10113 10888 S 11864 FP 13314 P 16740 FP
10114 P 11044 PO 11869 P 13315 P 16741 P
10120 S 11045 FP 11872 PO 13764 P 16742 P
10123 O 11391 P 11874 P 14513 P 16747 P
10125 P 11393 P 11876 P 15085 P 18170 P
10129 S 11845 P 11877 S 15090 O 18172 P
10214 P 11846 P 11878 S 15158 S 18185 P
10382 P 11848 PO 12375 P 15161 P 18312 P
10385 FP 11849 P 12380 P 15163 S 18795 P
10386 F 11850 P 12420 P 15168 18817 PO
10387 S 11852 P 12426 P 15172 PO 19092 P
10392 P 11855 S 12770 S 15174 P 19285 P
10395 FP 11857 P 12776 P 15175 FP 21392 PO
10396 S 11858 P 13050 P 15181 P 21904 FP
10852 P 11860 P 13306 P 15600 P 22219 P
10855 FP 11862 P 13308 P 15614 P 22740 P

PRIMARY: INCLUSIONS
10389 S 11859 P 11875 P 15188 P 19087 P
11842 P 11861 P 12395 P 15799 O 22221 S
11844 O 11865 P 15170 17955 S 22287 P
11847 S

PRIMARY: JOURNAL ARTICLES
10393 S 11854 P 12398 P 14126 18821 S
10863 P 11856 P 12410 S 15087 P 19084 P
10877 P 11866 P 12771 P 15162 P 19582 P
11034 P 11867 P 13294 P 15173 O 20474 P
11054 P 11868 S 13297 FP 15471 P 22239 S
11843 P 11870 S 13312 P 15874 P 22947 P
11851 P 11871 S 13765 P 18790 P 23007 P
11853 S 11873 P

SECOND. 10870 P 13986 P 18786 P 22183 P
10110 PO 10881 P 14001 P 18797 S 22189
10115 O 10883 S 14413 P 18802 P 22209 S
10118 O 10885 PO 14414 P 18804 PO 22212 P
10119 S 10891 S 15088 P 18807 22224 P
10122 S 11035 O 15159 P 18809 S 22229 P
10124 S 11042 P 15169 P 18810 22233 PO
10127 12384 P 15180 18812 22238 P
10217 S 12765 P 15182 P 18819 P 22255 P
10220 P 12773 P 15187 S 19860 22282 P
10260 O 12774 PO 15194 21414 FP 22815 P
10853 PO 12777 P 15698 P 21476 S 22950 S
10854 S 13293 P 16335 P 21847 P 22954 P
10858 S 13295 P 16748 P 21855 S 22988 S
10859 P 13316 P 17895 O 21882 P

1949-1972

PRIMARY: MONOGRAPHS
10132 O 10149 O 10172 PO 10424 P 10431 FP
10134 O 10153 O 10173 O 10425 P 10432 P
10139 P 10154 P 10177 O 10426 FP 10435 FP
10140 O 10159 O 10263 P 10427 FP 10460 P
10142 P 10161 O 10399 P 10428 FP 10487 P
10143 O 10167 O 10407 P 10429 FP 10498 P
10148 P 10168 O 10415 PO 10430 FP 10503 P
10894 P 11928 P 12044 P 12434 F 13584 P
10895 O 11939 S 12054 P 12475 PO 13588 P
10943 PO 11946 P 12060 P 12515 P 13589 P
10997 P 11948 P 12062 S 12519 P 13594 P
11076 P 11949 P 12069 P 12524 FP 13597 S
11087 O 11952 P 12070 P 12525 P 13602 P
11106 O 11955 P 12071 P 12532 PO 13614 P
11138 F 11962 PO 12076 P 12552 P 13788 P
11883 O 11970 P 12082 P 12562 P 14066 FP
11884 P 11975 P 12086 12811 O 14153 PO
11885 P 11980 PO 12090 O 12849 P 14296 P
11889 P 11984 P 12096 P 12853 O 14416 P
11891 P 11988 P 12102 O 13070 P 14522 P
11894 O 11995 P 12109 P 13078 P 14882 S
11897 PO 11996 P 12114 S 13104 P 15123 O
11901 O 11998 P 12118 P 13105 P 15249 P
11903 O 12000 P 12123 P 13113 FP 15260 P
11905 P 12001 P 12148 P 13118 P 15294 P
11906 P 12002 P 12149 P 13336 P 17381 P
11907 12003 P 12150 P 13338 P 17395 P
11909 P 12005 P 12154 13339 P 17993 P
11912 P 12008 FP 12157 13344 S 18299 P
11917 P 12014 12158 PO 13366 P 19166 P
11919 O 12015 P 12163 P 13389 P 19302 P
11920 P 12019 P 12166 P 13399 P 22291 P
11921 P 12027 P 12173 P 13420 FP 22318 P
11922 O 12029 P 12174 PO 13432 P 22322 P
11925 P 12039 P 12175 P 13579 P 22760 O
11927 S

PRIMARY: INCLUSIONS
10137 P 11888 11990 P 12132 P 13444 P
10138 P 11911 S 12009 P 12147 P 13601 P
10147 P 11914 12010 P 12151 O 13605 P
10151 S 11916 S 12017 P 12156 P 13779 P
10163 P 11918 P 12020 P 12159 S 14043 P
10176 P 11929 S 12041 S 12160 S 14138 P
10178 P 11940 P 12042 P 12165 P 14521 P
10179 P 11942 P 12043 P 12168 P 15101 P
10414 S 11951 P 12045 P 12176 P 15217 P
10433 S 11959 PO 12047 P 12444 P 15233 P
10434 S 11960 P 12055 P 12449 P 15259
10468 P 11965 P 12074 S 13327 PO 19290 P
10469 P 11968 S 12088 P 13330 P 21486 O
10493 O 11969 P 12092 P 13337 P 21921 P
10915 P 11974 S 12101 S 13408 P 21955 P
10993 P 11978 PO 12107 P 13413 P 22290 P
11447 P 11989 P 12121 P 13417 O 22356 P
11887 P

PRIMARY: JOURNAL ARTICLES
10225 P 11896 PO 11964 P 12028 P 12080 P
10238 P 11898 P 11966 P 12030 PO 12081 P
10249 P 11899 11967 12031 P 12083 P
10305 P 11900 S 11971 P 12032 P 12084 P
10403 S 11902 S 11972 O 12033 P 12085 PO
10408 P 11904 P 11973 P 12034 P 12087 S
10418 P 11908 P 11976 O 12035 P 12089 P
10467 P 11910 S 11977 P 12036 P 12091 S
10473 P 11913 P 11979 PO 12037 P 12093 P
10476 S 11915 P 11981 P 12038 O 12094 P
10490 P 11923 O 11982 P 12040 P 12095 P
10491 P 11924 P 11983 P 12046 S 12097 S
10496 P 11926 P 11985 P 12048 PO 12098 P
10502 PO 11930 P 11986 P 12049 PO 12099 P
10901 S 11931 P 11987 P 12050 P 12100 FP
10905 P 11932 P 11991 P 12051 P 12103 P
10910 P 11933 P 11992 P 12052 S 12104 P
10911 P 11934 P 11993 S 12053 P 12105 P
10933 P 11935 S 11994 P 12056 P 12106 P
10939 P 11936 11997 P 12057 P 12108 P
10957 P 11937 11999 P 12058 P 12110 P
10984 O 11938 S 12004 P 12059 P 12111 P
10987 P 11941 P 12006 FP 12061 P 12112 PO
11009 P 11943 P 12007 P 12063 P 12113 S
11059 S 11944 P 12011 P 12064 S 12115 P
11505 P 11945 P 12012 P 12065 P 12116 P
11879 P 11947 P 12013 P 12066 P 12117 P
11880 P 11950 S 12016 P 12067 12119 S
11881 S 11953 P 12018 P 12068 P 12120 P
11882 P 11954 P 12021 P 12072 P 12122 PO
11886 P 11956 P 12022 S 12073 P 12124 O
11890 S 11957 PO 12023 S 12075 P 12125 P
11892 11958 O 12024 S 12077 S 12126 P
11893 PO 11961 P 12025 P 12078 S 12127 S
11895 PO 11963 P 12026 P 12079 P 12128 S
12129 P 12164 P 13320 P 13615 P 16783 PO
12130 12167 S 13321 P 13616 P 16829 P
12131 O 12169 P 13322 P 13771 P 16884 S
12133 P 12170 S 13332 S 13782 P 17596 P
12134 P 12171 P 13347 S 13784 P 18246 P
12135 P 12172 P 13349 P 13785 P 18269 P
12136 P 12177 S 13355 P 13790 O 18297 P
12137 P 12445 O 13358 S 13791 P 19107 S
12138 P 12457 P 13363 S 13792 19301 P
12139 P 12460 P 13385 PO 14060 P 19312 P
12140 P 12472 P 13391 P 14148 19314 P
12141 P 12511 P 13407 FP 14149 P 19316 P
12142 P 12533 S 13425 FP 14332 P 19321 P
12143 P 12539 P 13427 PO 14333 P 19374 P
12144 P 12561 O 13429 P 14814 P 19375 P
12145 P 13063 P 13433 15211 P 19673 P
12146 P 13068 P 13439 P 15212 O 21922 P
12152 P 13084 P 13575 PO 15228 P 22302 P
12153 P 13089 P 13580 P 15244 P 22323 P
12155 O 13106 O 13591 S 15247 P 22328 P
12161 P 13108 O 13599 P 15262 22352 S
12162 P 13115 P 13604 P 15620 P 22768 P

SECONDARY: MONOGRAPHS
10145 O 11096 P 13443 P 14955 FP 15890 P
10150 O 11144 O 13449 P 14974 PO 16898 S
10152 O 11437 P 13585 P 15031 P 18225 P
10155 P 11496 P 13590 P 15033 P 18296
10157 O 12439 P 13593 P 15202 P 19069 PO
10162 O 12795 O 13618 P 15230 P 19135 P
10180 O 12841 P 13773 P 15234 P 19291 P
10464 P 13079 FP 13775 P 15235 P 20314 P
10479 P 13080 P 13795 P 15237 P 20328 P
10488 P 13119 P 14139 O 15245 PO 20334 FP
10962 13325 S 14144 P 15248 P 20496 PO
10978 O 13353 P 14311 P 15258 P 21124 PO
10994 P 13384 P 14322 P 15550 O 21570 FP
11003 P 13397 P 14874 FP 15615 P 22293 S
11061 O 13440 P 14885 P 15888 P 22298 P
11092 S

SECONDARY: INCLUSIONS
10244 P 12479 13121 P 13583 P 18293 P
10499 P 12484 P 13333 P 14326 FP 18343 FP
10898 FP 12506 P 13334 P 14880 PO 20698 O
11063 PO 12548 P 13335 P 14901 P 21934 P
11134 PO 12798 P 13393 15303 FP 22327 P
11173 12877 13430 P 15847 O 22336 P
11435 P 13072 P 13435 P 18290 P 23028 S
11531

SECONDARY: JOURNAL ARTICLES
10230 P 11155 P 13405 PO 15198 P 18234 P
10231 P 11169 13410 15199 18326 P
10241 PO 11446 P 13428 P 15200 P 18327 S
10251 11468 P 13438 S 15204 19188 S
10266 S 11503 P 13587 P 15216 S 19323 P
10897 P 11510 P 13592 P 15220 P 19326 PO
10902 P 11511 P 13608 P 15227 P 19414 P
10903 P 12451 O 13611 P 15238 P 19470 S
10913 P 12483 P 13780 P 15253 P 20374 P
10942 12806 O 13789 P 15275 PO 21960 S
10958 P 13071 P 13793 O 15290 22294 P
10959 S 13075 P 14154 O 15845 P 22300 P
10967 P 13077 P 14303 S 15893 F 22306 P
10983 S 13109 O 14417 F 16019 P 22312
10986 P 13116 14526 P 16038 P 22329 P
11004 P 13348 P 14532 P 16830 22345 O
11066 O 13354 P 14537 P 16990 P 22361 P
11093 P 13364 P 14898 P 17388 P 22376 P
11112 S 13379 P 14920 P 17781 P 22382 S
11116 P 13401 S 15098 PO 18190 P 23039 P

14.1 AGRARIAN ECONOMY
農業 農業

1644-1842
PRIMARY 12179 S 12189 P 12207 PO 17160 P
10026 O 12183 P 12190 P 12890 O 22057 P
10320 P 12184 P 12198 P 13856 22577 P

SECOND. 10045 O 10626 P 11680 P 14422 P
10033 O 10542 P 11010 P 14096 S 14423 P

15037 P 17145 P 21644 P 22034 P 22559 O
15043 P 20582 P 21676 P 22552 S 22619 PO
17144 P

1644-1911

Primary 11667 P 12199 P 12923 P 14420 P
10014 O 12185 P 12200 P 12947 P 14421 P
10066 S 12188 S 12201 P 13475 P 15130 S
10437 P 12193 PO 12203 P 13482 P 16213 S
10441 P 12194 PO 12205 13483 P 20038 P
11572 PO 12196 S 12206 PO 13859 S 21263 P
11664 12197 P

Second. 11015 P 12941 PO 13484 P 16049 P
10001 O 11220 P 12948 P 14176 18405 S
10520 P 11226 P 13128 P 15044 S 18526 S
10560 P 11564 S 13465 P 15047 P 19747 P
10664 S 12578 O

1842-1911

Primary 12180 PO 12191 F 13124 O 13831 P
11665 P 12181 O 12192 S 13131 O 17179 O
11671 O 12182 O 12195 P 13471 P 20034 PO
11674 S 12186 P 12202 P 13486 P 20036 P
12178 O 12187 O 12204 O

Second. 10334 O 12582 O 18436 P 20766 P
10017 O 10438 S 12921 O 18461 P 22047 P
10018 PO 11013 PO 12934 O 18479 O 22066 P
10035 O 11014 P 13473 P 18504 P 22580 PO
10038 O 11681 O 15038 P 19751 O 22599 O
10041 12569 O 17149 P 19775 O 22771 P
10055 O 12570 O 18409 P 20540 O 22879 S

1842-1928
(including 1644-1928)

Primary 11711 S 12216 P 12224 S 13163 S
10291 P 12208 12219 S 12225 O 13503 P
10355 P 12211 P 12220 P 12226 S 15052 FP
10701 P 12214 P 12221 P 12229 P 20049 P
11282 P 12215 P 12222 P 12233 P 21502
11686 P

Second. 10697 S 12643 S 13511 P 15051 S
10068 S 10713 P 12949 P 13514 O 20618 PO
10085 PO 11287 P 13151 P 13874 P 22079 P
10348 O 11697 P 13172 P 15050 O 22112 P
10354 P 11717 P 13494 P

1911-1928

Primary 12240 S 12306 P 12357 S 14432 P
10089 O 12247 S 12316 P 12361 P 14434 P
10360 O 12249 P 12319 FP 12362 P 15072 FP
10363 FP 12253 F 12320 12363 PO 17760 O
10371 F 12254 FP 12324 S 12366 O 17873 PO
11736 P 12268 P 12327 P 12368 O 18609 O
11790 S 12273 FP 12340 S 12711 O 18733 P
11802 O 12274 O 12346 P 13006 P 18782 P
11814 P 12280 P 12349 O 13284 P 19450 P
11816 S 12284 12353 S 13738 P 19455 P
12234 S 12300 P 12355 S 14425 P 19462
12236 S 12302 P

Second. 11754 P 13248 P 18709 P 19448 P
10374 S 12747 O 13531 P 18725 P 19453 P
10756 S 12749 O 13717 S 18757 O 19459
11730 O 12997 S 15692 P 18772 P 19534 P
11737 13027 P 15694 P 19445 P 19558
11749 P

1911-1949
(including 1644-1949, 1842-1949)

Primary: Monographs
10074 P 11825 PO 12270 P 12372 P 15674 PO
10337 P 12218 P 12271 P 12992 P 16106 P
10341 P 12227 P 12295 S 13041 P 17763 PO
10379 P 12230 P 12297 P 13250 P 18619 S
10812 P 12231 P 12303 FP 13288 P 18780 P
10828 P 12232 PO 12308 P 13572 P 19457 P
11689 P 12241 P 12317 PO 13715 P 20067 P
11707 P 12257 FP 12328 P 14436 S 20643 P
11714 P 12264 FP 12367 P 15668 S 22787 S
11756 P 12267 FP 12371 P

Primary: Inclusions
10078 S 12213 S 12293 S 12341 O 19637 O
10353 S 12228 P 12338 P 12370 P

Primary: Journal Articles
10192 S 12223 P 12304 P 12959 S 15081 O
11684 P 12251 S 12305 P 12989 15669 P
11735 12252 S 12307 P 13198 P 15677 P
11776 12259 F 12322 P 13492 P 18673 P
11815 S 12282 P 12325 P 14424 P 19073 S
11824 O 12283 P 12334 P 14428 F 19444 P
12209 P 12285 12335 S 14431 P 19458
12210 FP 12286 S 12344 FP 14433 S 20063 P
12212 S 12288 P 12350 P 14751 FP 22171 S
12217 S 12296 P 12351 P 15048 S 22784 P

Secondary: Monographs
10083 PO 10749 13037 P 17979 P 18752 P
10088 O 11685 S 13516 PO 18123 P 18783 P
10351 S 11704 P 13887 P 18543 S 19071 P
10370 P 11716 P 14116 P 18562 S 20068 P
10448 P 12638 P 15063 S 18585 O 20620 PO
10706 PO 12675 PO 15678 P 18598 O 22144 P
10726 12684 FP 17869 PO 18636 P 22805 O
10745 PO

Secondary: Inclusions
10093 O 11720 PO 15049 17032 F 18571 S
11688 S 13703 S 15666 S 18558 S 18645 S
11700 S 13878 P

Secondary: Journal Articles
10198 S 12648 S 13205 15082 O 19463 P
10347 P 12681 13252 S 15687 O 20045 P
10717 PO 12998 P 13281 P 16225 20057 P
11693 P 13011 P 13731 P 18580 P 22098 P
11779 P 13166 S 14456 P 18714 P 22791 S
11832 S 13180 P 15060 O 18726 P

1928-1949

Primary: Monographs
10361 S 11830 O 12309 P 12345 O 12708 S
11745 P 12256 F 12310 P 12348 PO 13271 P
11750 S 12260 P 12312 P 12358 P 13736 P
11777 P 12281 P 12331 P 12359 O 15077 FP
11793 P 12291 S 12336 P 12364 P 17092 P
11797 P 12298 P 12339 PO 12369 FP 19707 O
11808 S

Primary: Inclusions
10377 S 12269 P 12326 S 12352 P 18632 P
10378 S 12272 S 12333 P 14435 O 22928 O
12261 P 12294 12337 P

Primary: Journal Articles
10451 S 12246 P 12279 P 12323 O 12976
11762 P 12248 P 12287 P 12329 P 12978 P
11764 P 12250 S 12289 S 12330 O 13018 S
11768 S 12255 FP 12290 P 12332 P 13256 O
11821 S 12258 12292 S 12342 P 14426 S
12235 12262 F 12299 S 12343 P 15069 P
12237 S 12263 12301 S 12347 P 15154 P
12238 P 12265 S 12311 P 12354 O 17247
12239 P 12266 P 12313 P 12356 P 18627 P
12242 12275 P 12314 P 12360 P 19629 P
12243 P 12276 O 12315 P 12365 P 19635 O
12244 P 12277 O 12318 12373 F 20064 P
12245 12278 P 12321 S 12972

Secondary: Monographs
10105 FP 11760 PO 13042 S 18603 O 18766 P
10452 S 11804 P 13761 PO 18608 O 19074 O
10796 P 11805 P 13903 S 18656 P 19638 S
10806 O 11807 P 13928 O 18660 P 19640 P
10813 P 11829 P 15059 FP 18717 P 20639 S
10839 O 11834 FP 18114 P 18750 O 22714 P

Secondary: Inclusions
11775 13258 P 18761 P 19399 O 21225 F
13257 P 18307 P 18763 S 20647 F 22146 P

Secondary: Journal Articles
10443 P 11743 12984 S 13548 P 15681
10454 F 11744 O 12994 13550 P 17304 S
10786 P 11761 P 13014 P 13960 S 18682 P
10798 O 11763 P 13194 15055 P 18684
11331 P 11770 13207 15078 P 18718 S
11728 S 11788 S 13223 O 15083 O 19636 O
11739 P 11798 13234 P 15590 P 20624 O

1928-1972
(incl. 1644-1972, 1842-1972, 1911-1972)

Primary: Monographs
10115 O 11848 PO 12378 P 12402 S 12783 FP
10126 O 11849 P 12379 P 12412 P 13304 P
10214 P 11850 P 12380 P 12414 P 14127 P
10395 FP 11852 P 12383 P 12420 P 18801 P
10396 S 11860 P 12384 P 12421 O 19078 P
10397 S 11864 FP 12386 P 12423 19092 P
11047 P 11874 P 12387 PO 12424 P 19650 PO
11845 P 11876 P 12399 FP 12426 P 22233 PO
11846 P 12375 P 12401 P 12770 S

Primary: Inclusions
10389 S 12377 PO 12397 S 12415 P 18802 P
11042 P 12390 P 12406 P 12416 19087 P
11859 P 12394 P 12407 S 12422 S 21894 S
11875 P 12395 P 12408 P 15189 O 22282 P
12376 S 12396 P

Primary: Journal Articles
10455 O 12388 O 12404 S 12419 P 14440 S
11041 P 12389 P 12405 P 12425 P 14515 O
11384 P 12391 P 12409 P 12775 P 15608 S
11870 S 12392 P 12410 S 13300 P 19081 P
12374 P 12393 P 12411 P 13302 P 19084 P
12381 12398 P 12413 P 14130 P 19091 S
12382 P 12400 P 12417 S 14438 S 19469 O
12385 P 12403 P 12418 FP 14439 P 19654 PO

Secondary: Monographs
10120 S 10893 S 12767 15174 P 18187 P
10124 S 11035 O 13308 P 15175 FP 18796 O
10125 P 11390 P 13311 P 15176 O 18809 S
10129 S 11391 P 15085 P 15181 P 18812
10386 F 11857 P 15158 S 15614 P 18817 PO
10862 P 11858 P 15161 P 15977 P 21904 FP
10870 P 11872 PO 15163 S 18172 P 22204 P
10888 S 11877 S 15171 FP 18185 P 22991 S
10890 P 11878 S 15172 PO

Secondary: Inclusions
10215 P 14129 15188 P 18825 P 20981 P
11865 P 15170 18807 20957 P 21893 P
13305 P 15185 S

Secondary: Journal Articles
10221 P 11386 P 15088 P 19034 O 22183 P
10390 S 11868 S 17947 S 19076 PO 22239 S
11034 P 13294 P 18821 S 19086 P 22994 S
11054 P 14262 P 18835 S 19982 S 23007 P

1949-1972

Primary: Monographs
10130 O 11906 P 12148 P 12475 PO 12850 P
10140 O 11909 P 12154 12485 P 13070 P
10148 P 11912 P 12158 PO 12487 PO 13328 O
10150 O 11920 P 12166 P 12508 P 13399 P
10157 O 11921 P 12428 P 12515 P 13610 P
10170 O 11925 P 12429 P 12519 P 13769 P
10172 PO 11939 S 12434 F 12522 FP 15100 P
10232 P 11946 P 12436 P 12523 P 15258 P
10399 P 11949 P 12439 P 12524 FP 18232 P
10400 11955 P 12440 PO 12525 P 19122 P
10415 PO 11962 PO 12441 P 12528 P 19132 P
10423 P 11970 P 12442 P 12532 PO 19133 PO
10424 P 11980 PO 12446 P 12535 P 19134 P
10429 FP 12000 P 12453 P 12544 O 19135 P
10431 FP 12003 P 12456 PO 12552 P 19181 P
10432 P 12015 P 12461 O 12562 P 19194 P
10435 FP 12044 P 12463 P 12563 P 19203 P
10503 P 12060 P 12464 P 12564 P 20502 O
10906 P 12096 P 12467 P 12787 P 22293 S
11891 P 12102 O 12469 P 12843 S 22318 P
11903 O 12123 P

Primary: Inclusions
10147 P 11989 P 12455 P 12538 P 13097 P
10227 P 12041 S 12459 PO 12540 P 13101 P
10250 PO 12088 P 12462 P 12541 P 14451 S
10410 S 12107 P 12476 P 12542 P 15099 P
10412 12156 P 12479 12543 P 15107 P
10484 P 12432 S 12484 P 12547 P 15210 S
11887 P 12437 12506 P 12548 P 15885
11929 S 12444 P 12507 P 12557 P 15895
11942 P 12447 P 12510 P 12559 P 18280 P
11960 P 12449 P 12536 P 13064 P 19101 P
11969 P 12454 S 12537 13088 P 19104

19129 P 19162 19182 19198 P 21129 F
19149 O 19170 S 19190 P 19202 P 21947 P

Primary: Journal Articles
10241 PO 12098 P 12466 S 12512 P 13400 S
10417 P 12100 FP 12468 P 12513 P 14441 S
10462 FP 12104 P 12470 P 12514 P 14444 P
10476 S 12105 P 12471 P 12516 14450 P
10480 P 12110 P 12472 P 12517 P 14452 P
10489 S 12111 P 12473 P 12518 O 14845 P
10502 PO 12112 PO 12474 P 12520 14873 O
10925 P 12119 S 12477 P 12521 P 15098 PO
11070 P 12120 P 12478 P 12526 P 15102 P
11085 P 12125 P 12480 P 12527 P 15104 P
11097 PO 12127 S 12481 S 12529 P 15292 P
11503 P 12128 S 12482 P 12530 P 17778 P
11896 PO 12130 12483 P 12531 P 18269 P
11898 P 12139 P 12486 P 12533 S 19096 P
11902 S 12141 P 12488 P 12534 P 19097 PO
11913 P 12145 P 12489 P 12539 P 19102 S
11931 P 12162 P 12490 P 12545 P 19107 S
11936 12167 S 12491 P 12546 P 19121 P
11944 P 12427 P 12492 P 12549 P 19124 P
11953 P 12430 P 12493 P 12550 PO 19128 O
11954 P 12431 O 12494 P 12551 PO 19130 P
11956 P 12433 O 12495 P 12553 P 19136 O
12004 P 12435 FP 12496 P 12554 P 19137 P
12006 FP 12438 P 12497 P 12555 P 19150 P
12022 S 12443 P 12498 P 12556 S 19169 PO
12023 S 12445 O 12499 P 12558 P 19174 P
12030 PO 12448 P 12500 P 12560 P 19175 P
12031 P 12450 P 12501 P 12561 O 19183 P
12038 O 12451 O 12502 P 13055 P 19187 S
12050 P 12452 P 12503 P 13056 P 19189 P
12061 P 12457 P 12504 P 13073 P 19392 P
12064 S 12458 O 12505 P 13086 S 19470 S
12083 P 12460 P 12509 P 13087 P 21241 P
12091 S 12465 S 12511 P 13383 P 21548 O
12097 S

Secondary: Monographs
10132 O 10177 O 11180 P 12082 P 14990 P
10133 O 10240 P 11437 P 12849 P 14999 O
10136 O 10402 FP 11534 P 13104 P 15123 O
10139 P 10407 P 11884 P 13117 P 15249 P
10141 O 10425 P 11889 P 13118 P 15267 P
10144 O 10426 FP 11894 O 13318 P 15273 P
10153 O 10427 FP 11897 PO 13344 S 15830 O
10156 O 10430 FP 11901 O 13579 P 15856 O
10158 O 10460 P 11907 13593 P 17395 P
10159 O 10477 P 11917 P 13603 P 18225 P
10161 O 10498 P 11928 P 13773 P 18842 P
10162 O 10931 P 12005 P 13795 P 19166 P
10167 O 10937 PO 12019 P 14329 P 21948 P
10168 O 10970 P 12039 P 14369 O 22322 P
10169 O 10978 O 12071 P 14943 O 22375 PO
10174 O 11106 O

Secondary: Inclusions
10137 P 10493 O 11974 S 12165 P 15217 P
10138 P 10930 P 11990 P 13058 P 15233 P
10163 P 10988 FP 12009 P 13066 P 19146 P
10178 P 10993 P 12010 P 13330 P 19199 P
10313 P 11447 P 12042 P 13444 P 20081 P
10404 S 11888 12043 P 14325 P 20306 P
10405 S 11911 S 12055 P 14448 P 21066 P
10406 S 11916 S 12074 S 14521 P 21067 F
10485 P 11918 P 12132 P 15209 P 21911 P
10486 P 11940 P 12151 O

Secondary: Journal Articles
10225 P 11879 P 11972 O 12065 P 12134 P
10231 P 11886 P 11986 P 12066 P 12140 P
10315 P 11890 S 11987 P 12073 P 12161 P
10403 S 11893 PO 11991 P 12075 P 12169 P
10408 P 11895 PO 11992 P 12077 S 12171 P
10472 P 11900 S 11993 S 12080 P 12794 O
10482 P 11908 P 11994 P 12084 P 13063 P
10490 P 11910 S 11997 P 12087 S 13089 P
10897 P 11915 P 12013 P 12089 P 13094 P
10901 S 11924 P 12016 P 12094 P 13096 P
11058 P 11930 P 12021 P 12095 P 13108 O
11086 O 11933 P 12025 P 12103 P 13322 P
11099 P 11934 P 12026 P 12113 S 13349 P
11124 P 11937 12052 S 12115 P 13354 P
11169 11945 P 12058 P 12126 P 13371 P
11421 P 11958 O 12059 P 12131 O 13388 P
11460 P 11966 P 12063 P 12133 P 13391 P
13401 S 13796 P 15216 S 19145 P 21029 FP
13407 FP 14443 P 15228 P 19156 P 21917 P
13424 P 14449 FP 15231 S 19168 PO 21960 S
13426 PO 14547 P 15244 P 19176 P 22309 P
13427 PO 14916 P 15247 P 19188 S 22345 O
13596 S 15020 P 17388 P 19388 P 22766 P
13608 P 15103 P 17809 O 19673 P 22838 S
13771 P 15109 P 18213 PO 19934 P 22839 P
13791 P 15122 P 18234 P 20521 P

14.2 Transport and Communications
交通　交通

1644-1842

Primary 12583 P 12609 P 13469 P 21676 P
10005 O 12591 P 12614 P 13835 P 22590 O
10045 O 12596 O 12619 P 20549 O 22619 PO
10580 O
Second. 10020 PO 12930 P 15037 P 21675 P
10008 S 10039 O 13812 15923 O 22578 O
10015 O 11680 P

1644-1911

Primary 10576 S 12574 PO 12612 P 13808 P
10014 O 10577 P 12578 O 12948 P 16213 S
10028 PO 12572 P 12587 P 13459 P 21677 FP
10437 P 12573 P 12602 P
Second. 10333 P 12193 PO 13457 P 18384 P
10010 P 10441 P 12203 P 14623 20595 PO
10016 O 10664 S 12913 P 15751 21695 S
10029 PO 10678 P 12940 S 18098 P 22866 P
10329 PO 11672 PO

1842-1911

Primary: Monographs
10011 O 11657 PO 12590 P 12601 O 13804 P
10047 O 12567 P 12593 PO 12606 P 14092 PO
10064 O 12569 O 12595 P 12611 P 18074 P
10318 O 12570 O 12597 O 12613 P 22568 P
10330 P 12575 P 12598 PO 12915 S 22575 P
10331 S 12576 PO 12599 P 13461 P 22599 O
10660 O 12580 PO 12600 P 13466 P 22602 P

Primary: Inclusions
10642 PO 12592 O 12944 PO 19365 P 22525 O
12589 O 12617 O 18370 P

Primary: Journal Articles
10323 O 12577 P 12588 P 12610 P 13833 P
10581 P 12579 O 12594 O 12615 P 13840 O
12178 O 12581 P 12603 PO 12616 F 15045 O
12565 O 12582 O 12604 PO 12618 S 18402 P
12566 O 12584 O 12605 O 12879 PO 18909 O
12568 P 12585 O 12607 P 12936 PO 20596 O
12571 O 12586 P 12608

Second. 10598 O 12896 P 14164 P 20540 O
10002 O 10611 O 12918 P 14174 P 20590 PO
10013 O 10614 P 12922 P 14399 P 20605 O
10017 O 10650 PO 13122 S 14584 PO 20722 P
10018 PO 11185 PO 13125 P 15038 P 21265 P
10038 O 11245 PO 13464 P 15333 O 21287 P
10041 11658 O 13805 P 17137 PO 22025 P
10054 O 11670 P 13810 P 18075 O 22027 P
10061 O 11673 P 13839 O 18472 P 22052 P
10065 O 11681 O 13849 P 18487 P 22594 O
10536 S 12180 PO 13853 P 18492 PO 22617 PO
10544 P 12893 PO 13861 S 18494 P 22625 P
10553 P 12894 O 13866 O 19686 O

1842-1928
(including 1644-1928)

Primary 10698 P 12624 PO 12644 PO 12666 P
10067 O 10722 P 12625 P 12646 O 12667 S
10081 PO 11697 P 12626 PO 12653 P 12669 P
10255 O 11710 12632 PO 12654 P 12670
10338 P 12620 P 12640 FP 12655 S 12671 O
10354 P 12622 P 12643 S 12663 P 12673 O
12677 P 12949 P 13497 P 20618 PO 22092 P
12679 13155 P 13520 P 22089 P 22117 P
12680 P 13188 S 18103 P
Second. 12963 PO 13876 15755 21327 P
10085 PO 13152 PO 13883 18102 O 21340 P
10348 O 13177 P 13885 S 18560 P 21350 P
11686 P 13182 S 15050 O 18970 O 22127 P
11691 P 13489 P 15052 FP 20182 P 22134 P
12950 P 13495 PO 15132 P 20616 O 22643 S
12957 O 13663 S 15134 P 21311 O 22670
12958 P

1911-1928

Primary 12363 PO 12707 P 12725 12756 O
10106 P 12688 12709 P 12728 O 12758 S
10363 FP 12690 P 12711 O 12732 P 13006 P
10447 12691 P 12715 O 12737 P 13012 P
11730 O 12693 12716 12741 P 13213 S
11737 12701 S 12717 P 12745 O 15683 PO
11766 PO 12704 P 12718 12746 P 15770 O
11780 P 12705 P 12722 O 12747 O 15781
12349 O 12706 P 12724 P 12749 O 22181 FP
Second. 11790 S 14411 P 17272 P 19545 P
10360 O 11794 P 14492 P 17575 O 19558
10372 12324 S 14497 FP 17760 O 19560 P
10374 S 12975 PO 15145 PO 17873 PO 19562 O
10768 PO 13202 P 15148 P 18601 P 19570 P
10778 O 13266 S 15393 18625 P 22141 P
10838 P 13277 F 15422 O 18757 O 22177 P
11736 P 13962 P 15692 P 19402 S 22690 P
11749 P 14410 15694 P

1911-1949
(including 1644-1949, 1842-1949)

Primary: Monographs
10107 P 11825 PO 12647 P 12682 P 13144 P
10341 P 12629 PO 12657 PO 12684 FP 13251 P
10684 O 12630 P 12658 PO 12687 S 13701 S
10732 P 12631 P 12660 P 12714 PO 14238 P
10812 P 12633 S 12674 P 12721 S 14694 P
11687 P 12637 PO 12675 PO 12757 P 19245 O
11692 P 12638 P 12676 S 12759 S 21321 P
11715 P

Primary: Inclusions
10344 11786 P 12650 S 12678 13189 P
10366 12649 12651 S 12731 O

Primary: Journal Articles
12621 P 12641 P 12661 S 12683 S 12740 O
12623 S 12642 P 12662 S 12685 P 12750 P
12627 12645 P 12664 PO 12686 P 12960 S
12628 O 12648 S 12665 PO 12695 S 12961 P
12634 P 12652 12668 P 12699 13011 P
12635 12656 12672 O 12733 P 15082 O
12636 12659 P 12681 12739 S 15669 P
12639 P

Second. 11735 13156 P 15668 S 18699 P
10282 11776 13233 PO 15674 PO 19397 O
10337 P 11815 S 13504 S 15676 FP 19705 P
10343 11840 P 13873 O 15687 O 21322 S
10346 S 12210 FP 13901 O 15954 S 21367 O
10353 S 12232 PO 14231 P 16407 P 21766 P
10706 PO 12328 P 14409 18119 P 22133 PO
10717 PO 12995 14436 S 18120 P 22656
10724 S 12998 P 14456 P 18543 S 22694 O
11370 P 13000 S 14660 P 18557 P 22789 S
11707 P 13037 P 15049 18645 S 22791 S
11714 P 13153 S 15081 O 18661 P

1928-1949

Primary 11834 FP 12712 P 12738 12983 S
10098 O 12689 12713 P 12742 P 13040 O
10108 P 12692 P 12719 12743 13265 FP
10377 S 12694 12720 12744 O 13285 O
10378 S 12696 P 12723 P 12748 P 13720 P
11023 O 12697 P 12726 F 12751 P 14464 P
11032 P 12698 P 12727 S 12752 P 14504 S
11724 P 12700 P 12729 P 12753 P 15059 FP
11767 PO 12702 S 12730 PO 12754 P 19260 P
11772 O 12703 O 12734 O 12755 P 19263 S
11774 12708 S 12735 O 12760 21465 O
11777 P 12710 S 12736

14.3 COMMERCE AND SERVICES

商業　　商業

13740 P 16675 P 17763 PO 20067 P 20934 P
13759 P 16977 O 18131 P 20068 P 22133 PO
15642 FP 17274 FP 19245 O 20643 P 22666 S
16405 P

Secondary: Inclusions
10078 S 10353 S 11840 P 14409 17447 P
10288 S 11688 S 13224 FP 15387 PO 19075 PO
10343 11700 S 13225 FP 16621 FP 19279 F
10344 11747 FP 13226 FP

Secondary: Journal Articles
10352 P 12739 S 13283 P 15954 S 17222 O
11706 P 13138 13504 S 16115 P 17229 P
11726 S 13140 13672 P 16572 P 17256 FP
11815 S 13142 13678 P 16951 PO 17283 P
12322 P 13146 P 13749 P 17034 FP 17440 S
12642 P 13153 S 14759 O 17035 FP 19235 P
12662 S 13204 15142 P 17039 F 19432 P
12665 PO 13206 15764 PO 17206 O 20054 P
12672 O 13233 PO 15765 S 17208 O

1928-1949

Primary 12287 P 12981 13026 PO 13729 F
11335 P 12315 P 12983 S 13028 PO 13758 F
11348 S 12326 S 12984 S 13030 PO 16583
11722 12343 P 12986 O 13033 P 16948 O
11723 P 12345 O 12991 F 13035 16980 P
11738 O 12360 P 12994 13036 P 17062 F
11739 P 12708 S 13003 P 13038 P 17089 FP
11770 12723 P 13009 O 13039 O 17093 PO
11807 P 12727 S 13013 P 13040 O 17096 P
12235 12971 O 13014 P 13042 S 17098 F
12242 12972 13018 S 13194 17099 F
12243 P 12976 13020 FP 13207 17212 O
12244 P 12977 O 13022 F 13223 O 17246 O
12245 12978 P 13024 O 13229 P 19239 F
12278 P 12980 O 13025 PO 13708 PO 19260 P

Secondary: Monographs
11808 S 12339 PO 13565 PO 13957 PO 16650 F
11823 P 12348 PO 13704 PO 13958 PO 17245 P
11833 P 12712 P 13718 P 13959 PO 17277 F
11834 FP 12730 PO 13760 PO 15965 P 17484 FP
12281 P 12751 P 13761 PO 16431 FP 17858 O
12336 P 13289 P

Secondary: Inclusions
16620 FP 16622 FP 16623 FP 17732 F 18712 P
19258 19264 F

Secondary: Journal Articles
10358 S 12238 P 13210 O 16569 17059 F
10451 S 12246 P 13236 P 16571 P 17100 F
11308 P 12258 13237 P 16575 17220
11728 S 12265 S 13256 O 16577 17305 PO
11742 12276 O 13263 P 16586 P 17465 O
11762 P 12318 13566 O 16587 18107 P
11768 S 12347 P 14500 P 16588 18136 S
11788 S 12726 F 15084 16957 F 19234 P
11800 P 12752 P 16422 16967 PO 19238 O
11818 P 13195 16432 PO 17046 19270 O
11835 13196 O 16448 O 17053 FP 22161 P

1928-1972
(incl. 1644-1972, 1842-1972, 1911-1972)

Primary 12422 S 13050 P 13311 P 17323 P
10259 P 13043 P 13051 P 13574 P 19285 P
11850 P 13044 S 13052 P 15601 P 19286 O
11860 P 13045 13053 FP 15794 FP 20662 S
11863 P 13046 P 13054 P 15795 P 22209 S
12384 P 13047 P 13305 P 16727 FP 22723 O
12408 P 13048 F 13306 P 17318 P 22724 P
12414 P 13049 P

Second. 11872 PO 13304 P 14415 P 16729 FP
10111 S 12390 P 13313 P 15087 P 17317 S
10214 P 12400 P 13315 P 15458 PO 19033 P
10393 S 12417 S 13762 P 15461 P 21426 P
11041 P 12774 PO 13766 P 15469 P 22732 FP
11044 PO 12781 P 13989 P 15789 22740 P
11868 S 12783 FP 14130 P 15810 FP

1949-1972

Primary: Monographs
10232 P 13070 P 13081 P 13113 FP 13120 PO
11946 P 13076 P 13104 P 13117 P 13593 P
12118 P 13078 P 13105 P 13118 P 16825 FP
12442 P 13079 FP 13107 O 13119 P 19338 P
13065 P 13080 P 13112 P

Primary: Inclusions
12101 S 13066 P 13088 P 13101 P 13357 S
12147 P 13067 13097 P 13102 P 13613 P
13058 P 13072 P 13098 P 13111 P 15538 P
13059 F 13082 13099 P 13121 P 17106 P
13064 P 13085 P 13100 P

Primary: Journal Articles
10408 P 13060 P 13077 P 13094 P 13116
11503 P 13061 13083 F 13095 P 13771 P
12457 P 13062 13084 P 13096 P 15845 P
12471 P 13063 P 13086 S 13103 P 16497 P
12474 P 13068 P 13087 P 13106 O 16829 P
12499 P 13069 P 13089 P 13108 O 17121 P
12870 13071 P 13090 P 13109 O 17374 P
13055 P 13073 P 13091 P 13110 P 19330
13056 P 13074 P 13092 P 13114 O 22761 O
13057 PO 13075 P 13093 P 13115 P

Secondary: Monographs
10172 PO 11906 P 12166 P 13440 P 15890 P
10424 P 11949 P 12515 P 13443 P 16463 P
10470 P 12000 P 12562 P 13612 O 16777 P
11113 P 12001 P 12845 P 13773 P 16816 F
11440 P 12039 P 12862 13795 P 17350 FP
11889 P 12054 P 13343 S 14419 P 17360 P
11891 P 12086 13344 S 14522 P 18354 O
11897 PO 12148 P 13399 P 15553 PO 19302 P
11905 P 12149 P

Secondary: Inclusions
10414 S 11960 P 12159 S 14068 P 19332 P
10993 P 11978 PO 12540 P 15990 P 19333 P
11063 PO 12042 P 12541 P 16037 FP 19334 P
11447 P 12088 P 12542 P 17110 20306 P
11929 S 12092 P 12543 P 19331 P 21066 P

Secondary: Journal Articles
10492 O 12033 P 12430 P 13391 P 15620 P
11097 PO 12049 PO 12478 P 13398 P 16499 S
11473 P 12066 P 12480 P 13450 O 16501 P
11910 S 12080 P 12482 P 13575 PO 16823 S
11915 P 12091 S 12486 P 13607 P 17390 P
11933 P 12095 P 12490 P 13609 PO 17738 O
11953 P 12115 P 12511 P 13616 P 18326 P
11985 P 12125 P 12531 P 13770 P 18336 P
12004 P 12126 P 12555 P 13776 P 19128 O
12006 FP 12133 P 12558 P 13790 O 19183 P
12007 P 12139 P 12816 P 13793 O 19310 P
12013 P 12141 P 13332 S 14446 P 21104 O
12016 P 12145 P 13358 S 15111 O 22345 O
12032 P 12162 P 13364 P 15124 P

14.4 Industrial Economy
工業 工業

1644-1842

Primary 10656 P 12909 P 13132 P 17160 P
10026 O 12179 S 12928 P 13134 S
Second. 12878 O 14096 S 17173 P

1644-1911

Primary 11664 13128 P 13477 P 14454 P
11656 S 12206 PO 13136 P
Second. 11663 O 12578 O 13458 P 18098 P
10066 S 11676 S 12612 P 13846 P 21297 P

1842-1911

Primary 11673 P 12924 O 13126 O 13133 P
10054 O 12571 O 13122 S 13127 O 13135 S
11659 P 12879 PO 13123 P 13129 P 13137
11660 P 12888 PO 13124 O 13130 P 13452
11665 P 12898 O 13125 P 13131 O 13849 P
14400 O 17149 P 17161 P 17167 P 22569 P
14453 O 17151 O 17162 P 17179 O 22596 P
15126 S 17152 PO

Second. 11670 P 12880 P 14164 P 18370 P
10034 S 11671 O 12894 O 14187 P 18412 FP
10055 O 12195 P 12905 O 14396 P 19365 P
10330 P 12570 O 12912 S 14584 PO 21287 P
10511 P 12597 O 12918 P 15128 S 21302 O
10650 PO 12610 P 12920 O 15718 PO 22572 O

1842-1928
(including 1644-1928)

Primary 12208 13151 P 13168 S 13185 P
10255 O 12667 S 13152 PO 13169 P 13187 P
10340 PO 12950 P 13155 P 13170 P 13188 S
10355 P 13141 P 13161 P 13172 P 13191 P
11282 P 13143 P 13163 S 13177 P 19478
11686 P 13145 P 13164 FP 13182 S 20049 P
11711 S 13147 P 13165 13183 O 22650 P
11713 P 13149 PO 13167 S

Second. 10348 O 12669 P 14458 P 19475
10067 O 10697 S 12956 P 15951 19481 P
10081 PO 11697 P 13497 P 17630 P 22089 P
10291 P 11718 13663 S 17757 P 22134 P
10338 P 12226 S 13874 P 19219 S 22643 S

1911-1928

Primary 11814 P 13244 PO 13282 PO 19242 O
11729 P 11816 S 13245 13284 P 19256 O
11730 O 12280 P 13248 P 14119 S 19512 P
11731 12975 PO 13254 P 14411 P 19517 FP
11766 PO 13202 P 13260 P 14470 O 19558
11780 P 13209 O 13266 S 14497 FP 19562 O
11794 P 13213 S 13267 FP 17272 P 20455
11802 O 13220 FP 13272 P 18733 P 20904 FP
11809 P 13238 13277 F

Second. 11737 14468 P 14511 19496 P
10091 O 11790 S 14476 PO 15148 P 19515 O
10363 FP 12349 O 14485 PO 15413 O 19534 P
10374 S 12988 PO 14492 P 18596 PO 20209 P
10744 12997 S 14493 P 18654 P 20222 S
10833 14115 P 14498 P 19278 P 22162 P
11736 P 14465 14502 O 19489 O

1911-1949
(including 1644-1949, 1842-1949)

Primary: Monographs
11692 P 12295 S 13184 P 13222 P 13290 P
11707 P 13144 P 13190 P 13232 P 13291 S
11714 P 13158 FP 13211 S 13250 P 14491 P
11715 P 13171 P 13212 PO 13251 P 14496 P
11825 PO 13175 P 13214 PO 13255 S 20643 P
12230 P 13176 P 13217 P 13261 P 22109 S
12241 P 13178 P 13218 P 13288 P

Primary: Inclusions
10353 S 13150 FP 13189 P 13226 FP 14406 P
11700 S 13156 P 13224 FP 13242 P 14455 S
11786 P 13162 S 13225 FP 13259 P 14495 P
11840 P 13179 P

Primary: Journal Articles
11795 O 13148 P 13186 P 13239 S 13709 P
11801 P 13153 S 13192 P 13246 P 13871
12351 P 13154 S 13198 P 13247 14456 P
12623 S 13157 P 13201 13252 S 14505 P
12642 P 13159 P 13204 13253 P 17229 P
12645 P 13160 O 13205 13268 S 17248 F
12990 13166 S 13206 13269 P 19221
13138 13173 PO 13208 13270 P 19576 P
13139 O 13174 P 13227 P 13281 P 19577 P
13140 13180 P 13231 P 13283 P 22098 P
13142 13181 PO 13233 PO 13292 PO 22171 S
13146 P

Secondary: Monographs
10337 P 10745 PO 11756 P 13689 S 18543 S
10341 P 10781 P 11839 P 13759 P 18783 P
10345 FP 10828 P 12371 P 13945 P 19476 P
10370 P 11685 S 12372 P 14508 P 19551 P
10448 P 11687 P 12638 P 14510 PO 19559 PO
10725 P 11699 S 12721 S 15140 O 22133 PO
10726 11704 P 13535 P 15678 P 22694 O

SECONDARY: INCLUSIONS
10093 O 10254 P 11688 S 11720 PO 18558 S

SECONDARY: JOURNAL ARTICLES
10717 PO 11815 S 12683 S 14481 P 19235 P
11693 P 11832 S 12685 P 14482 P 19432 P
11706 P 11837 O 12686 P 14503 S 19473 S
11726 S 12285 12995 15585 S 19561 P
11735 12634 P 13019 P 15669 P 20390 S
11773 O 12639 P 13685 P 16584 P 22651 S
11776 12648 S 13731 P 18157 P 22665 S
11779 P 12681 14477 P

1928-1949

PRIMARY: MONOGRAPHS
10101 O 11777 P 13219 P 13271 P 13720 P
11740 P 11793 P 13228 P 13285 O 14471 P
11745 P 11808 S 13243 P 13286 P 14478 FP
11760 PO 11834 FP 13249 S 13289 P 17238 P
11767 PO 12359 O 13265 FP

PRIMARY: INCLUSIONS
12986 O 13241 S 13257 P 13258 P

PRIMARY: JOURNAL ARTICLES
10451 S 11821 S 13203 P 13236 P 13278 PO
11722 11827 PO 13207 13237 P 13279 P
11723 P 12994 13210 O 13240 P 13280 P
11725 P 13003 P 13215 P 13256 O 13287 O
11739 P 13193 13216 P 13262 O 14480 P
11762 P 13194 13221 O 13263 P 14500 P
11764 P 13195 13223 O 13264 15154 P
11765 S 13196 O 13229 P 13273 O 16586 P
11770 13197 P 13230 O 13274 O 19224 O
11772 O 13199 P 13234 P 13275 P 19226 P
11774 13200 P 13235 O 13276 P

SECOND. 11753 O 11823 P 13751 P 18718 S
10103 PO 11761 P 11830 O 13919 P 18750 O
10105 FP 11763 P 11838 O 13928 O 19484 O
10443 P 11775 12318 14490 P 19568 S
10799 PO 11778 P 12752 P 14501 P 19572 P
10806 O 11789 12978 P 14763 O 19573 P
10813 P 11797 P 12984 S 15070 O 20219 P
11724 P 11798 13035 15150 21818 O
11728 S 11800 P 13042 S 17281 PO 21819 O
11733 P 11804 P 13549 P 17303 S 22161 P
11741 P 11805 P 13719 P 18307 P 22720 PO
11744 O 11807 P

1928-1972
(incl. 1644-1972, 1842-1972, 1911-1972)

PRIMARY 11854 P 13294 P 13306 P 14013 P
10115 O 11856 P 13295 P 13307 P 14415 P
10126 O 11860 P 13296 P 13308 P 14512 P
10389 S 11863 P 13297 FP 13309 P 14513 P
10392 P 11864 FP 13298 P 13310 P 14515 O
10394 FP 11870 S 13299 13311 P 15180
10396 S 11873 P 13300 P 13312 P 15181 P
11845 P 11874 P 13301 FP 13313 P 15600 P
11846 P 11875 P 13302 P 13314 P 19285 P
11848 PO 11876 P 13303 P 13315 P 19583 P
11849 P 12375 P 13304 P 13316 P 21416 O
11851 P 12770 S 13305 P 13574 P 21844 P
11852 P 13293 P

SECOND. 11048 S 12416 15161 P 17315 P
10120 S 11391 P 12774 PO 15163 S 18172 P
10125 P 11843 P 13049 P 15172 PO 18185 P
10129 S 11857 P 13989 P 15175 FP 18801 P
10261 S 11858 P 14262 P 15471 P 18807
10382 P 11859 P 14518 15614 P 18821 S
10385 FP 11868 S 14783 P 15644 S 19582 P
10386 F 11872 PO 14795 P 15697 FP 20957 P
10387 S 11878 S 15085 P 15698 P 20973 P
10395 FP 12386 P 15087 P 15806 P 21473 PO
10397 S 12390 P 15088 P 16726 P 21904 FP
10870 P 12414 P 15158 S 16740 FP 22947 P
10888 S

1949-1972

PRIMARY: MONOGRAPHS
10136 O 10399 P 10429 FP 11161 P 11903 O
10139 P 10415 PO 10431 FP 11884 P 11906 P
10148 P 10424 P 10432 P 11891 P 11909 P
10150 O 10427 FP 11095 O 11897 PO 11912 P
11920 P 12015 P 12849 P 13366 P 13449 P
11921 P 12027 P 13317 P 13384 P 13584 P
11925 P 12039 P 13318 P 13389 P 14829 O
11927 S 12044 P 13324 PO 13397 P 14835 S
11928 P 12060 P 13325 S 13399 P 14874 FP
11939 S 12102 O 13328 O 13415 P 15273 P
11946 P 12114 S 13329 P 13420 FP 15830 O
11949 P 12123 P 13336 P 13432 P 16777 P
11955 P 12157 13338 P 13437 17395 P
11962 PO 12158 PO 13339 P 13440 P 18232 P
11970 P 12163 P 13343 S 13442 P 19291 P
11980 PO 12166 P 13344 S 13443 P 19302 P
11995 P 12175 P 13345 P 13446 19338 P
12000 P 12475 PO 13353 P 13447 P 19595 S
12003 P 12843 S 13361 P 13448 P 20502 O
12005 P 12845 P 13365 S

PRIMARY: INCLUSIONS
10147 P 11960 P 13330 P 13390 P 13417 O
10163 P 11969 P 13333 P 13392 O 13419 P
10269 P 11990 P 13334 P 13393 13430 P
10410 S 12041 S 13335 P 13394 P 13435 P
10468 P 12156 P 13337 P 13396 P 13436 P
10484 P 12159 S 13341 O 13402 P 13441 O
10485 P 12449 P 13351 P 13403 O 13444 P
11887 P 12548 P 13352 P 13408 P 14523 P
11916 S 12877 13357 S 13411 P 15210 S
11942 P 13319 P 13362 P 13413 P 19324 FP
11959 PO 13327 PO 13387 P 13416

PRIMARY: JOURNAL ARTICLES
10465 P 12097 S 13323 PO 13383 P 14417 F
11097 PO 12098 P 13326 O 13385 PO 14418 PO
11896 PO 12100 FP 13331 S 13386 P 14519 P
11898 P 12103 P 13332 S 13388 P 14532 P
11902 S 12104 P 13340 P 13391 P 14533 S
11915 P 12105 P 13342 P 13395 P 14538 S
11926 P 12106 P 13346 P 13398 P 14547 P
11930 P 12110 P 13347 S 13400 S 14845 P
11931 P 12111 P 13348 P 13401 S 16824
11934 P 12112 PO 13349 P 13404 PO 17352 O
11935 S 12117 P 13350 O 13405 PO 17368 O
11936 12120 P 13354 P 13406 P 17403
11943 P 12122 PO 13355 P 13407 FP 17809 O
11944 P 12130 13356 P 13409 P 18269 P
11953 P 12138 P 13358 S 13410 19289 S
11954 P 12139 P 13359 P 13412 P 19310 P
11956 P 12141 P 13360 P 13414 S 19311
11957 PO 12143 P 13363 S 13418 P 19312 P
11983 P 12145 P 13364 P 13421 P 19315 P
11987 P 12146 P 13367 13422 19317 P
11992 P 12161 P 13368 P 13423 19321 P
11997 P 12162 P 13369 P 13424 P 19323 P
12004 P 12167 S 13370 P 13425 FP 19326 PO
12006 FP 12170 S 13371 P 13426 PO 19327 P
12007 P 12172 P 13372 P 13427 PO 19330
12022 S 12431 O 13373 P 13428 P 19601 P
12023 S 12486 P 13374 P 13429 P 19667 P
12030 PO 12492 P 13375 P 13431 O 20250
12031 P 12502 P 13376 P 13433 21039 P
12038 O 12518 O 13377 P 13434 21090
12048 PO 12818 P 13378 P 13438 S 21097 P
12050 P 13106 O 13379 P 13439 P 21914
12061 P 13320 P 13380 P 13445 P 21917 P
12063 P 13321 P 13381 P 13450 O 21975 PO
12066 P 13322 P 13382 P 14024 S 21979 P
12083 P

SECONDARY: MONOGRAPHS
10132 O 10435 FP 11984 P 12564 P 15123 O
10144 O 10470 P 11998 P 12787 P 15245 PO
10153 O 10477 P 12019 P 12862 15267 P
10156 O 10488 P 12069 P 13104 P 15285 O
10157 O 10498 P 12071 P 13113 FP 15890 P
10158 O 10503 P 12082 P 13117 P 16898 S
10159 O 10978 O 12096 P 13120 PO 17381 P
10161 O 11069 O 12148 P 13579 P 17990 P
10167 O 11106 O 12149 P 13602 P 18842 P
10168 O 11113 P 12150 P 13612 O 19166 P
10170 O 11138 F 12174 PO 14066 FP 19296 O
10172 PO 11889 P 12428 P 14419 P 19594
10177 O 11894 O 12434 F 14520 19668 P
10407 P 11901 O 12441 P 14522 P 21108 FP
10425 P 11905 P 12485 P 14535 P 21936 O
10426 FP 11907 12528 P 14549 P 22322 P
10428 FP 11917 P 12532 PO 14990 P 22375 PO
10430 FP 11975 P 12544 O

SECONDARY: INCLUSIONS
10178 P 11911 S 12042 P 12462 P 18343 FP
10414 S 11918 P 12055 P 12559 P 19331 P
10463 P 11929 S 12074 S 12788 P 19332 P
10486 P 11940 P 12088 P 13064 P 19333 P
10493 O 11965 P 12092 P 14138 P 19334 P
10930 P 11974 S 12101 S 14325 P 21146 P
10988 FP 12009 P 12132 P 14521 P 21958 P
10993 P 12010 P 12165 P 15233 P 21964 P
11447 P 12017 P 12454 S 17106 P 22357 FP
11888

SECONDARY: JOURNAL ARTICLES
10225 P 11958 O 12095 P 12797 P 16836 P
10251 11966 P 12113 S 12872 16864 S
10265 P 11972 O 12115 P 13063 P 17007 P
10311 P 11986 P 12124 O 13069 P 17388 P
10403 S 11991 P 12125 P 13089 P 18213 PO
10408 P 11993 S 12127 S 13091 P 19169 PO
10416 S 11994 P 12131 O 13116 19183 P
10472 P 12011 P 12133 P 13580 P 19303 P
10489 S 12013 P 12134 P 13607 P 19304 P
11085 P 12016 P 12135 P 13609 PO 19316 P
11086 O 12021 P 12136 P 13616 P 19328 P
11114 S 12025 P 12140 P 13784 P 19375 P
11130 P 12026 P 12142 P 13790 O 19377 P
11879 P 12034 P 12144 P 13791 P 19388 P
11886 P 12058 P 12169 P 14518 P 19410 P
11890 S 12059 P 12171 P 14526 P 19606 P
11893 PO 12065 P 12460 P 14546 S 19610 P
11900 S 12073 P 12472 P 15020 P 19673 P
11904 P 12075 P 12478 P 15124 P 20669 P
11908 P 12080 P 12498 P 15228 P 21548 O
11910 S 12084 P 12521 P 15244 P 21957 O
11913 P 12087 S 12531 P 15620 P 22309 P
11924 P 12089 P 12561 O 16006 P 22766 P
11933 P 12091 S 12790 P 16079 P 22838 S
11937 12094 P

14.5 STATE REVENUE AND EXPENDITURE

國家財政　国家財政

1644-1842

PRIMARY 10542 P 12198 P 13472 P 22057 P
10033 O 10561 O 13467 P 13814 S 22578 O
10533 PO 10652 O 13469 P 15043 P

SECOND. 10626 P 12189 P 13830 P 18470 P
10008 S 10643 PO 12207 PO 13856 21279 P
10020 PO 10654 P 12596 O 14183 P 22034 P
10039 O 10672 P 12928 P 14401 P 22552 S
10522 P 11680 P 12930 P 16517 P 22590 O

1644-1911

PRIMARY 11672 PO 13451 P 13474 P 13629 PO
10524 P 12185 P 13456 P 13475 P 13637 P
10525 P 12574 PO 13457 P 13476 P 13842 P
10574 P 12602 P 13458 P 13477 P 14201 P
10577 P 12923 P 13459 P 13482 P 14211 P
10655 P 12932 P 13462 P 13483 P 21291 P
11656 S 12947 P 13465 P 13484 P

SECOND. 10576 S 11667 P 13859 S 21259 P
10010 P 10582 PO 12587 P 14093 P 21283 P
10014 O 10609 P 12913 P 14175 S 21293 P
10016 O 10615 P 12929 P 14397 P 22531 P
10053 P 10669 P 12933 P 18526 S 22548 S
10187 PO 11015 P 12940 S 19347 PO 22558 P
10441 P 11241 P 13136 P 20038 P 22567 P
10505 P 11243 P 13622 P 20041 O 22581 P
10520 P 11664 13638 P 20595 PO

1842-1911

PRIMARY 12187 O 13454 P 13464 P 13473 P
10038 O 12594 O 13455 P 13466 P 13478 P
10544 P 12896 P 13460 P 13468 O 13479 P
10658 O 13452 13461 P 13470 P 13480 PO
11679 P 13453 S 13463 P 13471 P 13481 P

13485 P 15924 PO 18364 P 18450 P 20034 PO
13486 P 16525 P 18436 P 19775 O 22625 P
13627 P 16530 P

Second. 10587 PO 11014 P 14164 P 18461 P
10011 O 10601 O 11186 PO 14584 PO 18504 P
10034 S 10607 P 11191 PO 15038 P 18511 P
10052 P 10611 O 11657 PO 16093 O 20036 P
10065 O 10619 P 11673 P 16371 PO 21287 P
10331 S 10636 P 12186 P 16383 PO 22047 P
10334 O 10637 12893 PO 16394 P 22549 P
10511 P 10650 PO 12894 O 17407 PO 22575 P
10518 P 10653 P 12897 PO 17550 PO 22586 P
10519 P 10660 O 12906 P 18090 O 22594 O
10536 S 10662 P 13804 P 18379 PO 22641 P
10562 P 10665 P 13828 P 18422 O 22771 P
10584 O 11013 PO 13869 P

1842-1928
(including 1644-1928)

Primary 13152 PO 13495 PO 13505 O 13515 P
11270 P 13487 P 13497 P 13506 P 13518 P
11705 PO 13488 13498 S 13508 P 13519 P
12225 O 13489 P 13499 P 13510 S 13520 P
12229 P 13490 P 13500 PO 13511 P 13522 P
12950 P 13493 P 13502 P 13513 P 13523 P
12963 PO 13494 P 13503 P 13514 O 13882 O

Second. 10728 P 12224 S 13874 P 16267 O
10085 PO 11702 P 12640 FP 13881 P 17758 P
10196 P 12215 P 12957 O 14214 PO 19789 P
10291 P 12216 P 12968 PO 14628 FP 21347 P
10695 P 12220 P 13663 S 14658 P 22652 P
10713 P 12221 P 13674 FP 14700 P

1911-1928

Primary 13032 P 13531 P 13547 P 13569 O
10380 PO 13244 PO 13536 P 13552 O 13699 PO
12268 P 13526 P 13538 O 13553 PO 13962 P
13005 P 13527 P 13539 P 13558 P 18621 O
13008 P 13530 P 13542 PO 13563 PO

Second. 11766 PO 12987 14714 P 18743 P
10769 P 11817 13717 S 18129 FP 19278 P
10785 P 12273 FP 13979 P 18144 P 22708 O
10844 P 12346 P 14432 P 18579 O

1911-1949
(including 1644-1949, 1842-1949)

Primary 12267 FP 13509 P 13537 FP 13653 P
10684 O 12307 P 13512 P 13543 P 13685 P
10694 P 12629 PO 13516 PO 13546 S 13716 P
10702 O 12675 PO 13517 P 13554 14640 PO
10707 P 13171 P 13521 PO 13557 P 14751 FP
10721 13491 PO 13525 P 13561 P 16613 FP
10732 P 13492 P 13529 P 13562 PO 16675 P
10790 P 13496 P 13532 P 13568 P 17032 F
11706 P 13501 S 13533 P 13570 P 18154 P
11773 O 13504 S 13535 P 13572 P 21363
11839 P 13507 P

Second. 11694 PO 12350 P 13687 P 18131 P
10078 S 11726 S 12627 13701 S 18304 P
10688 P 11779 P 12647 P 13755 P 18585 O
10719 11837 O 12658 PO 13901 O 18598 O
10720 P 12212 S 12665 PO 13920 P 18673 P
10724 S 12227 P 12682 P 13977 P 18722 O
10725 P 12232 PO 13148 P 14231 P 18745 O
10739 P 12259 F 13158 FP 14508 P 19072 F
10781 P 12264 FP 13160 O 16123 FP 19458
10791 P 12293 S 13204 16550 P 20934 P
10807 P 12303 FP 13222 P 16551 P 21368 O
10812 P 12325 P 13652 P 16561 S 21805 P
11689 P 12328 P 13657 S 16639 P 22717 P
11693 P 12334 P 13668 O 17763 PO 22785 S

1928-1949

Primary 11827 PO 13524 P 13544 PO 13551 P
11738 O 11833 P 13528 P 13545 P 13555 P
11760 PO 11841 PO 13534 S 13548 P 13556 P
11769 PO 12248 P 13540 P 13549 P 13559 P
11778 P 13040 O 13541 P 13550 P 13560 P
13564 P 13567 13718 P 14738 20064 P
13565 PO 13571 PO 13734 S 17846 F 22701
13566 O 13708 PO 13886 P

Second. 10839 O 12243 P 13014 P 13761 PO
10758 P 11733 P 12262 F 13018 S 14121 O
10760 P 11740 P 12275 P 13210 O 14239 O
10789 P 11742 12277 O 13704 PO 14712 P
10801 11743 12311 P 13719 P 17570 O
10809 11750 S 12314 P 13723 O 18659 O
10816 F 11764 P 12326 S 13739 18682 P
10817 PO 11767 PO 12331 P 13756 P 18684
10836 PO 11806 S 12360 P 13760 PO 18712 P

1928-1972
(incl. 1644-1972, 1842-1972, 1911-1972)

Primary 10855 FP 11047 P 13573 S 13762 P
10114 P 10890 P 11865 P 13574 P 16741 P
10214 P 10893 S

Second. 11850 P 12385 P 12781 P 16742 P
10125 P 11856 P 12388 O 13049 P 16745 P
10299 P 11858 P 12396 P 13990 19033 P
11036 P 11863 P 12412 P 15174 P 19286 O
11041 P 11873 P 12419 P 15180 21877 S
11054 P 12379 P 12426 P 16740 FP 22740 P

1949-1972

Primary 13080 P 13584 P 13596 S 13608 P
11071 P 13081 P 13585 P 13597 S 13609 PO
11961 P 13088 P 13586 P 13598 P 13610 P
11988 P 13575 PO 13587 P 13599 P 13611 P
12039 P 13576 P 13588 P 13600 P 13612 O
12052 S 13577 P 13589 P 13601 P 13613 P
12053 P 13578 P 13590 P 13602 P 13614 P
12054 P 13579 P 13591 S 13603 P 13615 P
12442 P 13580 P 13592 P 13604 P 13616 P
12515 P 13581 P 13593 P 13605 P 13617 F
13063 P 13582 P 13594 P 13606 P 13618 P
13073 P 13583 P 13595 P 13607 P 13772 P

Second. 11943 P 12147 P 13068 P 14443 P
10138 P 11964 P 12161 P 13070 P 14885 P
10492 O 11969 P 12443 P 13087 P 16481 PO
11063 PO 11991 P 12451 O 13093 P 16829 P
11076 P 12006 FP 12459 PO 13321 P 18232 P
11109 S 12017 P 12468 P 13333 P 18327 S
11150 P 12032 P 12475 PO 13355 P 18842 P
11154 P 12047 P 12490 P 13776 P 19199 P
11906 P 12086 12511 P 13785 P 19374 P
11912 P 12092 P 12529 P 13789 P 19470 S
11923 O 12097 S 12559 P 14133 O 21563 PO
11925 P 12136 P 12562 P

14.6 Financial, Monetary, and Credit Systems
金融、貨幣及信託制度
金融、貨幣及び信用制度

1644-1842

Primary 13621 PO 13625 P 13632 P 22040 P

Second. 10522 P 10643 PO 12878 O 14401 P
22619 PO

1644-1911

Primary 13619 P 13626 P 13633 P 13639 S
12931 PO 13620 P 13628 S 13637 P 13640 P
12948 P 13622 P 13629 PO 13638 P 13641 P
13465 P 13623 P 13630 S

Second. 11220 P 11676 S 14397 P 21259 P
10053 P 11239 P 12612 P 18526 S 21263 P
10582 PO 11664 12933 P 19347 PO 21291 P
10655 P 11672 PO 14201 P 20042 P

1842-1911

Primary 11670 P 12880 P 12920 O 13624 P
10023 O 12590 P 12914 P 13463 P 13627 P
13631 S 13635 14092 PO 15333 O 18388 P
13634 O 13636 PO 15126 S 17550 PO 19344 S

Second. 11186 PO 12613 P 13481 P 14399 P
10003 O 11657 PO 12895 P 13486 P 17167 P
10013 O 11658 O 12911 P 13799 PO 18365 O
10017 O 11669 12918 P 13826 P 18370 P
10065 O 12566 O 12934 O 13840 O 19206 PO
10581 P 12568 P 13122 S 13847 P 19365 P
10642 PO 12607 P 13471 P 14395 P 21302 O
10650 PO 12611 P 13478 P 14396 P 22641 P
11185 PO

1842-1928
(including 1644-1928)

Primary 13147 P 13648 O 13665 P 13686 P
10722 P 13167 S 13656 P 13666 P 13688 P
11698 P 13168 S 13658 PO 13667 S 13690 O
11702 P 13497 P 13660 P 13670 PO 13692 P
11703 P 13520 P 13661 P 13674 FP 19219 S
11705 PO 13642 P 13662 P 13675 O 22643 S
12653 P 13644 P 13663 S 13681 P 22650 P
13145 P 13646 S 13664 P 13683 PO

Second. 11717 P 12669 P 13493 P 13523 P
10695 P 12211 P 12963 PO 13498 S 14112 P
10734 O 12215 P 13151 P 13502 P 15052 FP
11248 P 12222 P 13152 PO 13510 S 18540
11691 P 12655 S 13155 P 13511 P 22652 P
11701 12663 P 13165 13518 P

1911-1928

Primary 13539 P 13712 13733 PO 13745 P
11794 P 13697 O 13713 13737 O 13746 P
12327 P 13699 PO 13717 S 13738 P 13753 P
12985 PO 13706 S 13726 O 13741 P 14411 P
13536 P 13707 O

Second. 11754 P 12709 P 14410 19281
10752 O 12268 P 13006 P 14434 P 19430
10756 S 12346 P 13209 O 18144 P 19450 P
10768 PO 12362 P 13563 PO 19225 20463 F
11729 P 12693 14115 P 19255 PO 22698 O
11731 12707 P 14407 P 19265 O

1911-1949
(including 1644-1949, 1842-1949)

Primary: Monographs
10828 P 13010 P 13659 P 13687 P 13727 P
11313 P 13517 P 13668 O 13689 S 13740 P
11344 P 13570 P 13669 P 13691 P 13755 P
11369 P 13649 P 13673 P 13701 S 13759 P
11687 P 13650 P 13676 P 13710 P 14436 S
11839 P 13651 P 13679 S 13715 P 19705 P
12317 PO 13652 P 13680 P 13716 P 20068 P
12372 P 13653 P 13682 P 13725 P 21363
12629 PO 13654 PO

Primary: Inclusions
10694 P 13657 S 13703 S 13724 P

Primary: Journal Articles
11773 O 13501 S 13672 P 13698 P 13749 P
11779 P 13557 P 13677 P 13702 P 13757 P
12210 FP 13643 O 13678 P 13709 P 14424 P
12334 P 13645 P 13684 S 13730 P 17229 P
12961 P 13647 13685 P 13731 P 17283 P
13019 P 13655 O 13694 P 13747 P 17443 S
13146 P 13671 PO

Second. 11714 P 12633 S 13222 P 18120 P
10688 P 11756 P 12637 PO 13507 P 18154 P
10707 P 11824 O 12639 P 13516 PO 18304 P
10719 11832 S 12648 S 13535 P 18585 O
10724 S 11837 O 12650 S 13543 P 18714 P
10732 P 12212 S 12695 S 13546 S 19246 O
10790 P 12227 P 12714 PO 13977 P 19271 P
10791 P 12230 P 12731 O 15669 P 19458
10815 12257 FP 12962 S 16106 P 20057 P
11684 P 12264 FP 12964 P 16675 P 20067 P
11692 P 12267 FP 13000 S 17032 F 20886 O
11694 PO 12270 P 13144 P 17448 P 21368 O
11696 S 12293 S 13156 P 17464 FP 22098 P
11699 S 12630 P 13159 P 17485 P 22785 S
11704 P 12631 P 13211 S

1928-1949

Primary 11841 PO 13695 P 13722 13748 O
11331 P 12310 P 13696 P 13723 O 13750 FP
11724 P 12313 P 13700 13728 O 13751 P
11745 P 12358 P 13704 PO 13729 F 13752 S
11750 S 12723 P 13705 PO 13732 13754 P
11762 P 12730 PO 13708 PO 13734 S 13756 P
11778 P 13042 S 13711 P 13735 P 13758 F
11791 P 13228 P 13714 S 13736 P 13760 PO
11807 P 13286 P 13718 P 13739 13761 PO
11822 P 13551 P 13719 P 13742 P 16417 P
11827 PO 13571 PO 13720 P 13743 PO 17238 P
11833 P 13693 P 13721 P 13744 PO

Second. 11743 12321 S 13236 P 16609 P
10741 P 11748 P 12331 P 13237 P 17245 P
10746 O 11761 P 12360 P 13249 S 17570 O
10758 P 11764 P 12373 F 13262 O 18114 P
10813 P 11806 S 12702 S 13263 P 18659 O
10819 P 11818 P 12738 13275 P 18684
10827 PO 11821 S 13020 FP 13541 P 18717 P
10836 PO 11823 P 13026 PO 13548 P 19262 PO
11335 P 11830 O 13030 PO 13556 P 19276 P
11723 P 11835 13036 P 13565 PO 19638 S
11733 P 12269 P 13040 O 13919 P 21465 O
11738 O 12289 S 13203 P 14427 P 22681 FP
11740 P 12291 S 13230 O 15074 F 22720 PO
11742 12314 P 13234 P 15394 O 22928 O

1928-1972
(incl. 1644-1972, 1842-1972, 1911-1972)

Primary 13762 P 13765 P 13767 P 21877 S
11857 P 13763 PO 13766 P 16740 FP 22732 FP
11877 S 13764 P

Second. 11865 P 12420 P 14440 S 18817 PO
11044 PO 11873 P 13053 FP 15600 P 19286 O
11846 P 12383 P 13308 P 16742 P 19585 P
11851 P 12384 P 14127 P 18801 P 20475 O
11852 P 12419 P 14130 P

1949-1972

Primary 13062 13768 P 13779 P 13790 O
10498 P 13078 P 13769 P 13780 P 13791 P
11893 PO 13080 P 13770 P 13781 O 13792
11962 PO 13420 FP 13771 P 13782 P 13793 O
11988 P 13584 P 13772 P 13783 P 13794 P
11991 P 13587 P 13773 P 13784 P 13795 P
12005 P 13601 P 13774 O 13785 P 13796 P
12053 P 13607 P 13775 P 13786 13797
12054 P 13608 P 13776 P 13787 O 14153 PO
12098 P 13609 PO 13777 P 13788 P 18343 FP
12147 P 13614 P 13778 P 13789 P

Second. 12059 P 12150 P 13085 P 13615 P
10132 O 12060 P 12151 O 13105 P 14533 S
10951 P 12101 S 12154 13336 P 15109 P
11085 P 12106 P 12427 P 13338 P 15115 P
11440 P 12134 P 12439 P 13355 P 18326 P
11903 O 12136 P 12441 P 13428 P 19122 P
11905 P 12138 P 12469 P 13575 PO 19129 P
11912 P 12139 P 12470 P 13580 P 19135 P
11959 PO 12142 P 12524 FP 13583 P 19175 P
11987 P 12143 P 13065 P 13599 P 19302 P
11992 P 12144 P 13068 P 13604 P 19310 P
12007 P 12149 P 13069 P 13605 P 19314 P

15 The Military

軍事 軍事

1644-1842

Primary 10590 P 13822 P 13865 P 18470 P
10008 S 10593 P 13829 P 13868 P 18476 S
10020 PO 10626 P 13830 P 14156 O 19441 P
10027 O 10643 PO 13832 P 15043 P 20558 S
10051 P 10651 P 13835 P 15662 P 20563 S
10320 P 13812 13836 O 15752 O 21279 P
10526 S 13813 P 13837 P 16517 P 22559 O
10529 P 13814 S 13855 17524 P 22590 O
10542 P 13815 P 13856 17530 P 22629 P
10552 P 13817 P 13864 P 18418 22878 P

Second. 10522 P 11675 O 18478 S 22511 O
10005 O 10528 P 12189 P 18864 S 22521 S
10007 O 10533 PO 13621 PO 19440 P 22555 O
10022 O 10534 O 14562 P 21278 P 22577 P
10032 O 10561 O 15310 O 21644 P 22578 O
10044 O 10654 P 18475 P 21712 P 22585 P
10050 O 11010 P 18477 S 22057 P 22619 PO

1644-1911

Primary 11015 P 13842 P 15334 PO 18862 P
10001 O 11241 P 13844 P 15729 PO 18915 FP
10325 PO 13808 P 13846 P 18098 P 21259 P
10329 PO 13819 PO 13859 S 18421 P 21283 P
10577 P 13824 P 13863 P 18493 PO 21690 PO
10608 P 13834 P 13867 P 18523 22531 P
10616 13838 14201 P 18526 S 22565
10644 PO 13841 O

Second. 10586 14102 P 16389 PO 21276 P
10004 PO 10596 S 14176 17531 P 21293 P
10010 P 10638 P 14555 P 17541 P 21300 S
10029 PO 10674 S 14575 P 18366 P 21713 PO
10042 PO 11655 PO 14627 P 18459 O 22058 P
10046 O 11677 S 15320 PO 18890 S 22394 PO
10053 P 12578 O 15322 O 18937 P 22507 S
10058 PO 13458 P 15665 P 20762 O 22516
10560 P 13459 P 15727 PO 21269 22639 P
10574 P 13622 P 15742 PO 21270 PO 22866 P

1842-1911

Primary: Monographs
10013 O 13804 P 13870 P 18376 P 20565 PO
10038 O 13807 P 14195 P 18390 P 20576 PO
10052 P 13811 O 14584 PO 18409 P 20578 O
10519 P 13828 P 15311 O 18412 FP 20749 O
10562 P 13831 P 15355 O 18430 P 21265 P
10587 PO 13847 P 17143 P 18461 P 21287 P
10653 P 13849 P 17161 P 18492 PO 22576 O
11657 PO 13858 P 17529 P 18511 P 22580 PO
13125 P 13861 S 17549 O 18524 P 22584 S
13802 P 13866 O 18077 P 18871 PO 22594 O
13803 PO

Primary: Inclusions
10650 PO 13806 O 13843 O 13848 P 18429 P
11017 O 13816 P 13845 O 18370 P 21267 P
11673 P 13823 P

Primary: Journal Articles
10575 P 13809 P 13833 P 13857 P 18365 O
10663 P 13810 P 13839 O 13860 P 18399 PO
13479 P 13818 P 13840 O 13862 P 18441 PO
13798 P 13820 O 13850 P 13869 P 18446 P
13799 PO 13821 O 13851 O 15731 O 18463 P
13800 S 13825 P 13852 O 17539 PO 22571 P
13801 S 13826 P 13853 P 17545 O 22642 P
13805 P 13827 P 13854 O 17556

Secondary: Monographs
10025 O 10631 P 15350 O 18387 P 18509 P
10040 O 10660 O 15930 P 18388 P 18922 O
10047 O 10677 P 16377 O 18422 O 21264 O
10048 O 11681 O 16395 O 18438 P 21286 P
10056 O 12921 O 17532 O 18442 P 22067 O
10059 O 13455 P 18089 P 18447 O 22513 PO
10061 O 14155 S 18092 P 18448 PO 22561 P
10331 S 14164 P 18364 P 18449 O 22562 O
10516 PO 14178 P 18371 P 18454 PO 22572 O
10539 P 14204 PO 18375 P 18466 O 22614
10551 P 14207 P 18378 O 18490 P 22615 O
10566 P 14560 P 18379 PO 18494 P 22617 PO
10598 O 15345 O 18382 P 18496 P 22623 P
10611 O 15347 PO 18386 P 18498 PO

Secondary: Inclusions
10334 O 12617 O 15753 O 18452 P 18525 P
10510 P 13471 P 16920 O 18513 O 19365 P
10601 O 14212 P 18073 P 18515 S 21299 P
10639 O 14400 O 18445 P 18521 S 22522 O
12589 O 15359 O

Secondary: Journal Articles
10185 P 10661 S 12898 O 14163 PO 15732 O
10530 10675 P 12924 O 14571 P 15735 O
10553 P 11014 P 13129 P 14612 S 16525 P
10563 11185 PO 13135 S 15126 S 16908 O
10572 11209 P 14162 P 15128 S 17162 P
17523 P 18094 S 18411 P 19438 P 22608 P
17548 O 18363 O 18435 O 20588 O 22641 P
17625 O 18381 P 18460 P 22506 O 22771 P
18090 O 18398 P 18471 S 22554 P

1842-1928
(including 1644-1928)

Primary 10708 P 12215 P 13872 13883
10067 O 10713 P 12624 PO 13874 P 13884 PO
10073 10727 PO 12663 P 13876 13885 S
10082 PO 10734 O 12963 PO 13881 P 18563 O
10085 PO 10735 S 13497 P 13882 O 21319 P
10695 P 11583 P

Second. 11260 P 18533 PO 18560 P 21775
10072 S 11708 S 18540 18566 S 21798 P
10076 S 13147 P 18542 P 18956 PO 22110 P
10077 O 13489 P 18549 PO 20795 O 22131 PO
10697 S 13493 P 18551 PO 21328 P 22650 P
10698 P 13505 O 18552 P 21355 O 22657 S
10699 PO 14109 P 18555 21723 PO 22669 S
10712 S 14403 P

1911-1928

Primary 13896 PO 13937 P 13979 P 18655 P
10106 P 13905 PO 13938 P 13981 P 18665 O
10753 O 13906 PO 13947 P 17562 P 18697 PO
10766 P 13910 O 13950 S 17567 O 18727 P
10769 P 13913 13953 O 18126 P 18742 P
10811 P 13918 O 13955 O 18609 O 18772 P
10834 P 13921 S 13956 O 18611 P 18775 P
10844 P 13922 P 13962 P 18615 19448 P
11737 13925 P 13966 P 18621 O 19456 P
13530 P 13927 P 13971 18644 P 19511 O
13538 O 13929 O 13972 O 18654 P 21377 O
13889 P 13931 O 13976 P

Second. 15151 O 18579 O 18713 O 18784
10091 O 15780 O 18582 O 18725 P 19442 PO
10744 17571 O 18596 PO 18729 P 19454 FP
10750 P 17982 P 18616 18733 P 19503 FP
10752 O 18110 P 18617 P 18734 P 19550 O
10768 PO 18115 P 18618 P 18743 P 19825 O
10778 O 18129 FP 18653 P 18757 O 20107 S
10785 P 18144 P 18664 O 18764 O 20893 F
10802 18148 P 18669 P 18765 21456 O
10820 S 18152 P 18700 O 18777 P 22678 O
11377 S 18156 P 18704 O 18779 P 22680 O
14119 S 18160 P 18706 O 18782 P 22708 O
14122 O

1911-1949
(including 1644-1949, 1842-1949)

Primary 10781 P 13911 P 18143 O 18732 P
10107 P 10791 P 13916 P 18157 P 18745 O
10684 O 11689 P 13920 P 18303 P 18759 P
10688 P 11699 S 13940 P 18309 S 19463 P
10694 P 13871 13945 P 18534 PO 21320
10700 PO 13873 O 13948 O 18574 P 21324 P
10706 PO 13875 S 13949 O 18585 O 21345 P
10715 P 13877 PO 13968 O 18593 PO 21367 O
10718 S 13878 P 13977 P 18619 S 21368 O
10719 13879 P 13980 P 18635 P 21381 P
10726 13880 PO 18119 P 18636 P 22135 P
10729 P 13887 P 18120 P 18674 P 22152 P
10743 P 13901 O 18137 S 18726 P 22666 S

Secondary: Monographs
10079 PO 12629 PO 17754 P 18588 P 20160 PO
10696 P 12684 FP 18104 P 18598 O 20166 O
10702 O 14217 P 18123 P 18685 P 20210 P
10724 S 14219 PO 18140 O 18699 P 20820 O
10725 P 14508 P 18147 P 18711 O 21321 P
10749 14677 P 18154 P 18730 P 21354 PO
10759 P 14685 O 18535 P 18741 PO 21359 P
10776 PO 15136 O 18536 P 18756 21373 P
10782 PO 15156 O 18545 PO 18767 O 22648 PO
10803 P 15377 P 18554 P 18768 S 22655 O
11258 P 15674 PO 18557 P 18780 P 22660 PO
11336 P 16055 PO 18562 S 18783 P 22694 O
11696 S 17561 O 18567 O 19551 P 22939 P
11714 P

16.1 ELITE STRATA

社會領導階層　　エリート階層

18082 s 18090 o 18435 o 18500 p 22029 p
18083 p 18094 s 18467 o 18520 p 22515 p
18084 p 18097 p 18472 p 20145 p 22634 p
18085 p 18398 p 18497 p

Secondary: Monographs
10018 po 10679 o 18075 o 18492 po 21260 po
10038 o 11665 p 18076 p 18854 po 22028 p
10043 o 12593 po 18077 p 18859 p 22052 p
10055 o 12601 o 18364 p 18872 p 22067 o
10065 o 12611 p 18409 p 18925 o 22513 po
10544 p 12910 p 18412 fp 20036 p 22568 p
10587 po 13125 p 18416 p 20255 po 22580 po
10594 po 13455 p 18458 p 20540 o 22594 o
10611 o 13461 p 18461 p 20559 o 22602 p
10619 p 13847 p 18466 o 20716 o 22605 p
10636 p 14560 p 18485 p

Secondary: Inclusions
10510 p 10610 o 18079 p 20564 o 22025 p
10549 s 10612 o 18080 p 21267 p 22065 p
10555 p 11244 o 18081 s 21274 p 22399 s
10601 o 18078 p

Secondary: Journal Articles
10530 12898 o 14564 o 18440 p 21261 p
10547 s 13486 p 14571 p 18460 p 21652 o
10569 13839 o 14572 po 18504 p 22037 p
10647 p 13851 o 14615 o 19614 o 22049 p
10663 p 13852 o 15045 o 19779 p 22063 p
10670 o 13853 p 17162 p 20139 22400 o
11191 po 13854 o 17167 p 20544 f 22569 p
11238 p 13869 p 18402 p 21169 po 22771 p
11661 p 14399 p

1842-1928
(including 1644-1928)

Primary 13882 o 14227 p 18540 21350 p
10708 p 13883 14228 o 18546 po 21355 o
10713 p 13884 po 14229 18560 p 21361 p
10731 po 14214 po 14232 p 18572 o 21785 p
11270 p 14216 s 14651 s 18980 o 22077 p
11590 po 14221 15133 s 20177 p 22083 p
11711 s 14222 s 15134 p 21337 po 22086 s
13688 p 14224 po 18533 po 21340 p 22099 p

Second. 11581 po 14661 p 21311 o 22082 p
10067 o 11587 p 18102 o 21318 p 22092 p
10073 12222 p 18106 p 21319 p 22097 p
10697 s 13151 p 18552 p 21338 p 22108 p
10699 po 13155 p 18563 o 21346 p 22112 p
10703 p 13170 p 18569 po 21504 o 22118 p
10716 p 13881 p 18991 p 21723 po 22121 p
10722 p 14108 s 20608 p 21765 po 22128 p
10727 po 14635 o 20619 o 21769 22657 s
10734 o 14638 p 21184 p 21793 p 22658 s
11291 p 14646 p 21306 p 22078 p 22663 s
11292 po 14658 p 21310 p 22079 p 22670
11579 p

1911-1928

Primary 14251 p 18148 p 21460 p 22153 p
11599 po 15075 o 18996 o 21461 p 22160 p
14234 o 15145 po 18999 o 21506 o 22174 p
14237 p 15153 20466 21807 o 22684 p
14243 15157 p 21365 o 21809 p 22690 p
14250 18144 p 21378 o 21825 p 22804 s

Second. 13905 po 15152 18610 o 20462 fp
10094 o 13910 o 17941 o 18616 21455 o
10766 p 13913 17982 p 18621 o 21456 o
10769 p 13956 o 18152 p 18625 p 22156 p
10838 p 14434 p 18579 o 18649 p 22159 p
11319 o 14727 p 18586 p 18782 p 22177 p
11597 po 14752 p 18597 po 18997 po 22680 o
11814 p 14767 p 18600 s 19002 po 22689 p
12361 p 15144 p 18601 p 19459 22691 p
13539 p 15148 p

1911-1949
(including 1644-1949, 1842-1949)

Primary 10705 s 11320 p 12657 po 14215 s
10074 p 10711 p 12212 s 13875 s 14217 p
10078 s 10725 p 12252 s 13880 po 14218 po
10690 p 10791 p 12264 fp 14107 p 14219 po
10702 o 10845 p 12307 p 14213 p 14220 p

14223 p 14247 p 17754 p 18571 s 21359 p
14225 o 14648 18104 p 18635 p 21459 p
14226 p 14670 p 18120 p 18689 p 21758 p
14230 p 14740 o 18147 p 19835 f 21764 p
14231 p 14753 p 18154 p 20012 po 21787 po
14238 p 15049 18536 p 21321 p 22668 p
14242 p 15140 o 18557 p 21325 p 22679 s
14245 15156 o 18562 s 21357 p 22694 o
14246 p 15947 o

Secondary: Monographs
10289 fp 10793 p 18137 s 20615 o 21766 p
10684 o 11279 p 18545 po 20826 p 21826 p
10707 p 11289 p 18598 o 21354 po 22091 p
10715 p 11336 p 18990 po 21362 o 22102 po
10718 s 11692 p 19617 p 21363 22135 p
10726 12271 p 19964 p 21370 o 22144 p
10729 p 14681 po 20009 s 21444 p 22666 s
10776 po 14684 p 20431 p 21447 po 22672 p
10781 p 15674 po 20432 p 21761 p 22939 p

Secondary: Inclusions
10694 p 12678 14406 p 18631 21332 p
10730 o 13878 p 15139 21303 p 21747 p
11700 s 13977 p 16105 21309 p 22000 p
12228 p 14405 17933 p 21326 p 22924 p
12370 p

Secondary: Journal Articles
10710 s 12335 s 18162 p 19463 p 22098 p
10736 s 13159 p 19393 p 21322 s 22120 s
10762 p 14710 p 19444 p 21725 p 22170 p
11773 o 15137 19458 21792 s 22786 p
12217 s

1928-1949

Primary 10797 f 14233 p 14248 p 18640 s
10740 s 10805 p 14235 p 14249 p 18641 s
10741 p 10839 o 14236 p 14426 s 18647 p
10760 p 11030 p 14239 o 14427 p 18648 p
10761 o 11032 p 14240 o 14762 p 18677 p
10780 p 12255 fp 14241 p 17569 18681 p
10796 p 12373 f 14244 p 18133 p 18691 p

Second. 11830 o 13893 o 18136 s 18683 p
10096 o 12248 p 13894 o 18307 p 18688 o
10758 p 12261 p 13897 p 18584 o 18707 o
10806 o 12290 p 13957 po 18599 p 18747 po
10813 p 12298 p 13958 po 18603 o 20449 p
10817 po 12310 p 13959 po 18637 20461 p
10826 o 12312 p 13983 p 18659 o 20849 p
10827 po 12313 p 14124 p 18663 p 20895 f
11028 p 12332 p 14733 po 18675 p 21812
11765 s 12352 p 14749 po 18678 p 22146 p
11800 p 12360 p 14763 o 18679 p 22710 o
11806 s 12729 p 18111 p 18682 p 22714 p
11822 p 13888 o 18125 po

1928-1972
(incl. 1644-1972, 1842-1972, 1911-1972)

Primary: Monographs
10124 s 14015 o 14292 p 19405 p 21412 p
10855 fp 14258 p 14293 s 20960 p 21414 fp
10857 o 14263 p 14795 p 20973 p 21417 p
10870 p 14264 p 15175 fp 21392 po 21422 o
11040 po 14269 p 18164 p 21401 p 21423 p
11052 fp 14274 p 18176 p 21404 p 21471 p
11855 s 14278 p 18178 fp 21407 s 21887 p
14002 p 14279 po 18182 p 21410 fp 22486 po
14010 s 14285 p 18827 o

Primary: Inclusions
10856 s 14254 14280 p 15185 s 21870 s
10866 fp 14255 p 14281 p 15186 s 21871 p
11613 p 14261 p 14288 p 18802 p 21880 p
12772 p 14268 p 14289 s 18811 21898 po
13993 p 14275 p 14290 p 19404 p 22238 p
13999 p 14276 p 14788 p 21858 p 22267 p

Primary: Journal Articles
10846 12405 p 14259 p 14267 p 14277
10864 s 14252 14260 p 14270 p 14282 s
11033 s 14253 p 14262 p 14271 p 14283 s
11404 s 14256 14265 s 14272 p 14284
12389 p 14257 s 14266 p 14273 p 14286 p

14287 s 18171 p 20471 s 21408 p 22245
14291 p 18184 f 21387 s 21473 po 22815 p
14777 p

Secondary: Monographs
10111 s 11048 s 15171 fp 21400 p 22190 p
10112 s 12378 p 15174 p 21415 p 22198 o
10114 p 12387 po 15176 o 21416 o 22202 p
10852 p 12414 p 15191 po 21419 p 22206 p
10858 s 13049 p 18804 po 21420 po 22210 p
10862 p 13986 p 18817 po 21424 p 22225 s
10871 p 14513 p 18834 p 21467 s 22251 p
10882 p 14780 p 19036 p 21476 s 22268 p
10888 s 14783 p 19092 p 21853 p 22728 o
11036 p 15163 s 20109 p 21873 p 22740 p
11044 po 15168 20473 p

Secondary: Inclusions
10122 s 14019 s 16745 p 19659 p 21409
10847 s 14781 p 18167 p 19709 p 21470 s
11612 p 14794 p 18799 p 19880 s 21877 s
12396 p 15165 s 18825 p 21388 p 22197 p
13995 p 15170 19087 p 21394 o 22272 p
14000 p 16340 s

Secondary: Journal Articles
10872 p 11602 p 18166 s 19081 p 22014
10880 p 11851 p 18174 p 20280 p 22216 s
10884 o 12391 p 18177 p 21398 p 22218 s
11037 p 12398 p 18797 s 21403 s 22227 s
11038 p 14412 s 18803 21829 p 22276 p
11054 p 14414 p 18813 p 21830 s 22278 s
11396 p 15162 p 18815 p 21846 p 22286 p
11402 p 15979 p 18830 p 21849 s

1949-1972

Primary: Monographs
10464 p 11160 p 14316 s 14387 p 15248 p
10937 po 13449 p 14322 p 14835 s 15258 p
10960 fp 14047 p 14329 p 14885 p 15267 p
10961 p 14055 p 14334 p 14910 p 18212 p
10989 p 14296 p 14337 p 14974 po 18225 p
10999 14299 p 14364 p 15025 p 18264 p
11003 p 14301 p 14369 o 15202 p 18272 p
11094 p 14305 p 14370 o 15214 po 18298 p
11096 p 14309 p 14378 p 15234 p 18324 po
11107 p 14310 14384 p 15237 p 21594 s
11110 p 14311 p 14385 p 15245 po 22339 p
11113 p

Primary: Inclusions
10171 s 11128 p 14326 fp 14379 p 17642 p
10463 p 11174 p 14327 p 14380 p 18189 p
10469 p 11484 p 14328 p 14390 p 18196 p
10916 p 13408 p 14330 fp 14391 p 18206 p
10946 p 14082 p 14336 p 14393 o 18282 p
10993 p 14297 s 14343 p 14394 p 21911 p
11002 14300 p 14344 p 14945 p 21958 p
11065 po 14302 p 14363 p 14964 o 21962 p
11072 p 14304 p 14372 p 15287 p 21964 p
11073 p 14324 p 14374 15296 p 22321 p
11126 p 14325 p 14377 17638 p 22827 p

Primary: Journal Articles
10307 p 14298 po 14341 p 14367 o 15269 s
10902 p 14303 s 14342 14368 o 15277
10913 p 14306 p 14345 s 14371 p 15282 s
10967 p 14307 p 14346 p 14373 p 15290
10996 p 14308 p 14347 p 14375 p 16144 p
11001 p 14312 p 14348 p 14376 p 18198 p
11056 o 14313 p 14349 p 14381 p 18202 p
11075 p 14314 p 14350 p 14382 p 18203 p
11093 p 14315 14351 p 14383 p 18207 p
11108 p 14317 p 14352 p 14386 p 18210 p
11123 p 14318 p 14353 p 14388 p 18211 p
11133 p 14319 p 14354 p 14389 p 18217 p
11139 p 14320 p 14355 p 14392 p 18226 p
11141 s 14321 p 14356 p 14814 p 18248 p
11145 p 14323 s 14357 14886 p 18250 p
11149 o 14331 p 14358 p 14937 p 18256 p
11166 p 14332 p 14359 p 14991 fp 18257 p
11485 p 14333 p 14360 p 15015 p 18258 p
12078 s 14335 s 14361 p 15018 p 18266 p
12131 o 14338 p 14362 p 15196 p 18292 p
14294 p 14339 s 14365 p 15211 p 18318 o
14295 p 14340 p 14366 p 15255 18339 p

19168 PO 20490 P 21918 P 21979 P 22347 P
19366 S 21075 O 21939 P 22314 P 22757 P
19410 P 21573 F 21940 P

SECONDARY: MONOGRAPHS
10135 O 11104 P 14828 P 15830 O 20244 P
10136 O 11135 O 14871 P 16148 FP 20314 P
10139 P 11138 F 14908 FP 17993 P 20496 PO
10150 O 11168 P 14943 O 18232 P 21009 FP
10161 O 11514 P 14969 P 18236 P 21569 P
10162 O 11639 P 14976 P 18277 P 21570 FP
10165 O 12442 P 14979 PO 18279 S 21579 PO
10174 O 12515 P 14990 P 18296 21936 O
10481 P 12523 P 15017 P 18341 P 21951 P
10895 O 12524 FP 15022 P 18345 P 22291 P
10906 P 12791 P 15023 FP 18350 P 22293 S
10908 P 12836 P 15033 P 19166 P 22296 P
10938 P 12839 FP 15205 O 19390 P 22299 P
10945 P 12864 P 15230 P 19422 P 22304 P
10970 P 14033 P 15235 P 19594 22305 P
11005 P 14077 P 15240 O 19595 S 22324 P
11088 14139 O 15260 P 19597 FP 22350 P
11092 S 14144 P 15543 O

SECONDARY: INCLUSIONS
10898 FP 13387 P 15281 S 18340 P 21947 P
11007 P 14146 F 15299 P 19129 P 21959 P
11083 P 14151 P 17644 F 19290 P 22290 P
11134 PO 14906 P 18000 P 19407 P 22313 P
11632 15203 P 18209 P 20121 P 22336 P
11634 S 15222 P 18241 P 20491 P 22380 P
12510 P 15223 P 18293 P 21432 P 22857 S
13058 P 15224 P 18294 S 21913 P

SECONDARY: JOURNAL ARTICLES
10166 O 11453 P 14920 P 15292 P 19378 P
10305 P 11642 P 14959 P 15295 P 19386 P
10501 P 11976 O 14968 P 16864 S 19414 P
10897 P 12098 P 14971 P 17992 P 19596 P
10911 P 12099 P 14993 P 17996 P 20237 O
10924 P 12100 FP 14997 P 18195 P 21096 O
10925 P 12821 P 15201 S 18199 P 21914
10927 12848 P 15208 P 18220 P 21919 P
10928 P 13425 FP 15213 O 18221 P 21953 P
10935 P 14029 P 15219 P 18223 P 21956 P
10941 P 14038 15220 P 18227 P 21961 P
10981 P 14064 P 15225 P 18235 P 21968 P
11068 P 14073 P 15227 P 18238 P 22022 P
11084 P 14076 P 15253 P 18259 P 22289 P
11091 P 14152 P 15263 P 18262 P 22316 P
11116 P 14813 P 15264 P 18265 P 22344 P
11122 P 14822 O 15265 18276 P 22377 P
11136 P 14832 P 15268 18338 P 22836 S
11165 P 14834 P 15276 P 19370 P 22843 P
11169 14897 P 15288 P 19377 P 23021 F
11419 P 14902 P 15289 P

16.2 THE BOURGEOISIE

商人及市民階級

商人及び市民階級

1644-1842

PRIMARY 10654 P 12909 P 14401 P

SECOND. 11680 P 17145 P 19350 P 22885 S
10005 O 12928 P 17160 P 21676 P

1644-1911

PRIMARY 10622 P 12927 12933 P 14397 P
10621 S 11667 P 12929 P 13637 P 20725 PO

SECOND. 10664 S 11676 S 14201 P 20606 P
10006 S 10671 S 13456 P 17147 P 21276 P
10042 PO 11656 S 13629 PO 18007 S 22628
10060 PO 11672 PO 14093 P 18012 P

1842-1911

PRIMARY 12615 P 14395 P 14399 P 19204 O
10548 P 13133 P 14396 P 14400 O 19206 PO
11661 P 13455 P 14398 18017 O 19717 P
12565 O

SECOND. 10566 P 12938 PO 18079 P 18458 P
10272 10677 P 13129 P 18088 P 19344 S
10510 P 11658 O 13463 P 18301 S 22568 P
10544 P 12593 PO 13624 P 18416 P 22613 S
10553 P 12922 P 13811 O

1842-1928
(including 1644-1928)

PRIMARY 13170 P 14402 P 14404 P 19219 S
12949 P 13688 P 14403 P

SECOND. 11691 P 13168 S 13686 P 19478
10067 O 12624 PO 13191 P 13876 19789 P
10085 PO 12950 P 13500 PO 14693 FP 20793 O
10727 PO 12957 O 13646 S 15133 S 22663 S
11291 P 13155 P

1911-1928

PRIMARY 12985 PO 14122 O 14410 18127 S
10835 P 13220 FP 14407 P 14411 P 18628 P
11734 P 14115 P 14408 P 15148 P 19281
11783 P

SECOND. 13738 P 15145 PO 18625 P 19512 P
10750 P 13746 P 17982 P 18642 19526
11024 P 13889 P 18115 P 19225 19527
13005 P 13905 PO 18308 P 19359 S 19562 O
13284 P 14484 18601 P 19430

1911-1949
(including 1644-1949, 1842-1949)

PRIMARY 14405 14409 19353 S 21348 O
10088 O 14406 P 17283 P 19354 P

SECOND. 11692 P 13159 P 15954 S 19432 P
10289 FP 11700 S 13176 P 17190 PO 20826 P
11263 PO 12668 P 13643 O 18543 S 21333 O
11334 S 12961 P 13668 O 18699 P 21363
11684 P 13000 S 13679 S 19218 22133 PO
11687 P 13144 P 14231 P 19356 22171 S

1928-1949

PRIMARY 18128 P 18136 S

SECOND. 11822 P 14490 P 18659 O 19573 P
10813 P 11830 O 15150 18718 S 19574 P
10826 O 14244 P 18130 P 19565 O 22161 P
11761 P 14474 FP 18146 P

1928-1972
(incl. 1644-1972, 1842-1972, 1911-1972)

PRIMARY 12375 P 14413 P 14415 P 19286 O
11855 S 14412 S 14414 P 19285 P 21416 O

SECOND. 11860 P 15162 P 18038 FP 21830 S
10214 P 11877 S 15179 S 18188 P 21877 S
10885 PO 13049 P 17322 19030 P 22221 S
11040 PO 14269 P 17955 S 21392 PO 22251 P
11846 P 15090 O

1949-1972

PRIMARY 11069 O 14416 P 15025 P 18327 S
10463 P 11142 P 14417 F 15279 O 19294 P
10464 P 11150 P 14418 PO 18049 F 19326 PO
10913 P 12067 14419 P 18263 FP 19338 P
10923 F 13408 P 14969 P

SECOND. 11088 12045 P 14364 P 18064 O
10135 O 11113 P 12070 P 14369 O 18222 P
10140 O 11440 P 12094 P 14378 P 18254 P
10165 O 11453 P 12111 P 14814 P 18276 P
10172 PO 11885 P 13069 P 14824 P 18842 P
10457 P 11901 O 13071 P 14999 O 19302 P
10481 P 11937 13366 P 15022 P 19312 P
10483 P 11943 P 13420 FP 15123 O 19330
10494 11962 PO 13776 P 15228 P 21482 F
10495 S 11976 O 14149 P 15248 P 22760 O
10500 P 12024 S 14154 O 15295 P 22838 S
11063 PO

16.3 THE PEASANTRY

農民階級 農民階級

1644-1842

PRIMARY 12190 P 13814 S 14096 S 14422 P
14423 P

SECOND. 10542 P 12198 P 16185 P 22563 P
10526 S 12189 P 15043 P 19440 P

1644-1911

PRIMARY 12188 S 12201 P 14420 P 14421 P
10001 O 12197 P 13484 P

SECOND. 10664 S 12199 P 20606 P 21709 P
10006 S 12193 PO 13859 S 21439 P 22565
10066 S 12196 S 16049 P

1842-1911

PRIMARY 10440 O 14087 S 18429 P 18451 S
10063 O 12186 P 16525 P 18431 P 22067 O

SECOND. 11662 14160 P 18482 20766 P
10017 O 12187 O 16530 P 18494 P 22399 S
10035 O 12192 S 18388 P 18504 P 22605 P
10438 S 13805 P 18461 P 19751 O 22879 S
10642 PO

1842-1928
(including 1644-1928)

PRIMARY 10291 P 11698 P 11711 S 12211 P
12624 PO 14105 S

SECOND. 11713 P 12233 P 15670 P 20430 P
10084 PO 12225 O 13147 P 18540 21502
11581 PO 12229 P 13163 S 20049 P

1911-1928

PRIMARY 12361 P 14425 P 18733 P 19459
12268 P 12363 PO 14429 S 19445 P 19461 P
12274 O 13738 P 14432 P 19448 P 20455
12302 P 13925 P 14434 P 19455 P 22162 P
12346 P 14123 P

SECOND. 12306 P 13929 O 18148 P 19443
10445 O 12340 S 14468 P 18161 O 19450 P
10744 12362 P 15054 P 18592 P 19453 P
11754 P 12366 O 15076 S 18617 P 19462
11784 P 12368 O 15683 PO 18646 P 20197 O
11814 P 13531 P 15694 P 18778 P 21208 F
12249 P 13889 P 17760 O 18782 P 21456 O
12273 FP 13896 PO 17873 PO

1911-1949
(including 1644-1949, 1842-1949)

PRIMARY 12227 P 12317 PO 14436 S 18605 S
10078 S 12252 S 12341 O 15049 18783 P
10088 O 12264 FP 14424 P 17979 P 19444 P
10192 S 12271 P 14428 F 18571 S 19447
10446 O 12303 FP 14431 P 18585 O 19458
12212 S 12307 P 14433 S

SECOND. 12232 PO 13011 P 16549 P 18705 P
10083 PO 12257 FP 13250 P 16551 P 18711 O
10285 PO 12259 F 13715 P 17032 F 18768 S
10364 FP 12270 P 13731 P 17933 P 18780 P
10726 12282 P 13880 PO 18154 P 19457 P
10791 P 12286 S 13887 P 18545 PO 19463 P
10828 P 12304 P 13920 P 18580 P 20009 S
11689 P 12322 P 14456 P 18587 S 20204 P
11704 P 12334 P 15588 P 18635 P 21320
11735 12335 S 15669 P 18645 S 21368 O
12213 S 12370 P 15674 PO 18657 O 22168 P
12217 S 12759 S 15677 P 18673 P 22171 S
12228 P 12961 P 16105 18699 P

1928-1949

PRIMARY 10839 O 12248 P 12289 S 12311 P
10096 O 11752 FP 12255 FP 12291 S 12312 P
10827 PO 11834 FP 12256 F 12310 P 12313 P

12321 s 14426 s 14430 s 18660 P 19638 s
12360 P 14427 P 14435 O 18712 P 20190 P

Second. 11763 P 12301 s 14124 P 18637
10451 s 11788 s 12314 P 14248 P 18672 P
10796 P 11792 P 12326 s 15053 P 18718 s
10806 O 12239 P 12333 P 15067 PO 18763 s
10821 s 12261 P 12348 PO 15154 P 18766 P
11723 P 12269 P 12352 P 15682 19464 P
11743 12279 P 12358 P 18307 P 21227 s
11745 P 12290 P 13042 s 18577 O 21228 F
11750 s 12298 P 13894 O 18632 P 22166 P
11762 P

1928-1972

(incl. 1644-1972, 1842-1972, 1911-1972)

Primary 12392 P 12424 P 14515 O 18835 s
10391 P 12393 P 14127 P 15170 19086 P
11861 P 12401 P 14437 P 15187 s 19091 s
12374 P 12403 P 14438 s 16739 P 19092 P
12385 P 12412 P 14439 P 16741 P 21859 P
12389 P 12419 P 14440 s 17947 s

Second. 12386 P 12783 FP 15873 19469 O
10118 O 12387 PO 13986 P 15875 P 19650 PO
10121 O 12388 O 14126 16745 P 19880 s
10124 s 12391 P 15085 P 18799 P 20226 PO
10862 P 12395 P 15087 P 18804 PO 20993 s
10884 O 12396 P 15088 P 18816 P 21420 PO
11844 O 12397 s 15163 s 19078 P 21853 P
11846 P 12398 P 15168 19081 P 22197 P
11866 P 12413 P 15178 19083 P 22221 s
11877 s 12425 P 15179 s 19084 P 22250 P
12378 P 12426 P 15190 19087 P 22265 P
12379 P

1949-1972

Primary 12456 PO 14443 P 14525 P 19135 P
10462 FP 12467 P 14444 P 14543 O 19137 P
10465 P 12479 14445 P 15109 P 19141 P
10477 P 12488 P 14446 P 15115 P 19150 P
10492 O 12525 P 14447 P 15122 P 19168 PO
11003 P 12531 P 14448 P 15209 P 19169 PO
11124 P 12535 P 14449 FP 18280 P 19176 P
12027 P 12552 P 14450 P 18842 P 19183 P
12111 P 14150 P 14451 s 19104 19198 P
12439 P 14441 s 14452 P 19128 O 20247 P
12451 O 14442 P

Secondary: Monographs
10136 O 11005 P 12076 P 13104 P 18324 PO
10140 O 11092 s 12096 P 13579 P 19122 P
10148 P 11106 O 12442 P 14139 O 19133 PO
10153 O 11897 PO 12453 P 14364 P 19662 P
10161 O 11903 O 12515 P 14416 P 20502 O
10167 O 11912 P 12519 P 14828 P 21948 P
10172 PO 11996 P 12523 P 14999 O 22291 P
10487 P 12060 P 12562 P 15112 P 22293 s
10937 PO 12070 P 13070 P 15113 P 22298 P
10970 P

Secondary: Inclusions
10486 P 12510 P 13066 P 19129 P 19199 P
11176 P 12536 P 14151 P 19149 O 19202 P
12151 O 12547 P 15293 19170 s 20491 P
12459 PO 12559 P 18000 P 19182 21486 O
12507 P 13058 P 18837 P 19190 P

Secondary: Journal Articles
10472 P 12050 P 12511 P 14834 P 17782 P
10489 s 12128 s 12529 P 15114 PO 18252 P
10496 P 12131 O 12534 P 15213 O 18338 P
10502 PO 12171 P 12546 P 15231 s 19124 P
10933 P 12450 P 12549 P 15246 s 19187 s
10972 P 12452 P 13056 P 15247 P 19189 P
11056 O 12458 O 13073 P 15275 PO 19375 P
11058 P 12468 P 13089 P 15292 P 19471 P
11097 PO 12473 P 13370 P 16822 P 20237 O
11460 P 12482 P 13596 s 16864 s 20521 P
11915 P 12483 P 14149 P 16885 P 21015 O
11943 P 12489 P 14154 O 17778 P 21557
12004 P 12496 P 14830 P

16.4 The Working Class

勞工階級 労働者階級

1644-1842

Primary □
Second. 13469 P 17160 P 17174 P

1644-1911

Primary 14454 P
Second. □

1842-1911

Primary 14087 s 14453 O
Second. 11662 13130 P 14400 O 18435 O
10272 12616 F 13133 P

1842-1928

(including 1644-1928)

Primary 13164 FP 14458 P 19477 PO 19480 P
10076 s 13169 P 19474 19478 19481 P
11698 P 14113 P 19475
Second. 10291 P 11718 13876 20049 P
10077 O 10293 s 12646 O 18540 20430 P
10081 PO 11713 P 13163 s 19219 s 22117 P
10085 PO 11717 P 13168 s

1911-1928

Primary 14476 PO 14497 FP 18630 P 19546 P
13254 P 14483 PO 14498 P 18708 19558
14115 P 14484 14502 O 18733 P 19562 O
14122 O 14485 PO 14507 P 19256 O 19563
14123 P 14487 s 14511 19500 P 19575
14462 s 14488 15062 O 19512 P 20222 s
14465 14489 s 18110 P 19517 FP 20904 FP
14468 P 14492 P 18625 P 19527 22160 P
14469 s 14493 P 18628 P 19534 P 22162 P
14470 O
Second. 13277 F 18161 O 19242 O 19536
10091 O 13284 P 18308 P 19281 19545 P
10445 O 13950 s 18592 P 19483 19548 P
10744 15057 FP 18596 PO 19496 P 19552
11024 P 15066 s 18597 PO 19502 P 19554 P
11754 P 15073 P 18617 P 19504 P 19570 P
11766 PO 15076 s 18642 19515 O 20197 O
11831 15157 P 18646 P 19520 O 20209 P
13213 s 15694 P 18762 P 19526 20455
13238 15867 P 18778 P 19531 O 22159 P
13267 FP 17873 PO

1911-1949

(including 1644-1949, 1842-1949)

Primary 14466 P 14494 P 15156 O 19542
10446 O 14473 O 14495 P 18580 P 19551 P
13184 P 14475 FP 14496 P 18739 P 19559 PO
13920 P 14477 P 14503 s 18768 s 19561 P
14455 s 14479 PO 14505 P 18783 P 19576 P
14456 P 14481 P 14508 P 19473 s 19577 P
14457 P 14482 P 14509 P 19476 P 20187 P
14460 s 14486 P 14510 PO 19492 P 20390 s
14463 P 14491 P 15080 P 19532
Second. 13142 13214 PO 15140 O 18635 P
10346 s 13158 FP 13242 P 15669 P 18711 O
10828 P 13162 s 13247 17266 s 19358 P
11694 PO 13175 P 13252 s 17283 P 19539 P
11721 P 13176 P 13261 P 18157 P 20161 P
11726 s 13179 P 13270 P 18529 20178 PO
11735 13180 P 13291 s 18543 s 20204 P
11824 O 13189 P 13731 P 18598 O 20643 P
11836 s 13211 s 13887 P 18605 s 22168 P
12651 s 13212 PO 15063 s

1928-1949

Primary 11834 FP 14459 P 14467 P 14474 FP
10449 O 13278 PO 14461 P 14471 P 14478 FP
10451 s 13751 P 14464 P 14472 O 14480 P
14490 P 14504 s 18668 s 19568 s 20190 P
14499 s 14506 F 19224 O 19571 P 20201 P
14500 P 15070 O 19484 O 19572 P 20219 P
14501 P 17245 P 19544 P 19704 P 22161 P

Second. 11767 PO 13275 P 18130 P 19487 P
10103 PO 11826 P 13289 P 18141 P 19488 P
10297 O 13199 P 13704 PO 18146 P 19525 s
10775 PO 13223 O 15064 s 18632 P 19565 O
10821 s 13229 P 15154 P 18672 P 19573 P
11725 P 13230 O 17211 19485 P 19574 P
11739 P 13264

1928-1972

(incl. 1644-1972, 1842-1972, 1911-1972)

Primary 14512 P 14515 O 19582 P 22238 P
10456 P 14513 P 15088 P 19585 P 22250 P
14437 P 14514 15181 P 22213 P

Second. 11866 P 13303 P 14438 s 20226 PO
10122 s 11874 P 13311 P 15085 P 20978 O
10882 P 12770 s 13314 P 15087 P 22224 P
10885 PO 13294 P 14413 P 15873 22265 P
11860 P 13302 P 14415 P 15875 P

1949-1972

Primary 13415 P 14529 P 14543 O 18842 P
10465 P 13774 O 14530 P 14544 F 19291 P
10472 P 14516 s 14531 P 14545 P 19590 P
10477 P 14517 O 14532 P 14546 s 19597 FP
10487 P 14518 P 14533 s 14547 P 19598 FP
10492 O 14519 P 14534 O 14548 P 19600 P
10496 P 14520 14535 P 14549 P 19602 P
11114 s 14521 P 14536 P 14874 FP 19606 P
11920 P 14522 P 14537 P 15112 P 19611 P
11943 P 14523 P 14538 s 15113 P 19668 P
12027 P 14524 P 14539 P 15114 PO 20250
12825 P 14525 P 14540 P 15115 P 20502 O
12831 P 14526 P 14541 P 15117 P 20521 P
13353 P 14527 P 14542 P 15231 s 21108 FP
13412 P 14528 P

Secondary: Monographs
10148 P 11903 O 13339 P 14305 P 18324 PO
10153 O 11912 P 13343 s 14943 O 19338 P
10172 PO 11949 P 13344 s 15123 O 19594
10174 O 12003 P 13345 P 15205 O 19595 s
10488 P 12076 P 13361 P 15245 PO 19662 P
10500 P 12163 P 13432 P 15248 P 20244 P
11003 P 12532 PO 13442 P 15856 O 21482 F
11106 O 13104 P 13443 P 15890 P 22298 P
11113 P 13338 P 13768 P 18232 P 22760 O
11884 P

Secondary: Inclusions
10486 P 13403 O 15105 P 17792 P 19608 P
12045 P 13416 15233 P 19290 P 21486 O
13387 P 13419 P 15270 P 19588 P 21589 P
13390 P 14302 P 15287 P 19589 P

Secondary: Journal Articles
10265 P 11915 P 13342 P 15247 P 19592 P
10457 P 11954 P 13355 P 15915 P 19596 P
10467 P 12004 P 13364 P 17782 P 19599 P
10474 P 12024 s 13368 P 17809 O 19601 P
10494 12048 PO 13386 P 18222 P 19609 P
10495 s 12122 PO 13391 P 19307 FP 19610 P
10933 P 12171 P 13406 P 19315 P 19667 P
10969 P 12531 P 13445 P 19317 P 21015 O
10972 P 12854 O 14417 F 19321 P 22309 P
11097 PO 13320 P 14830 P 19327 P 22761 O
11533 P 13323 PO 15228 P 19377 P 22851 s
11908 P

17 National and Higher Education

全國教育及高等教育
国民教育及び高等教育

1644-1842

Primary 10033 o 14557 p 14570 p 14599 p
10008 s 10045 o 14559 o 14580 s 20558 s
10020 po 10526 s 14562 p 14585 s 21278 p
10022 o

Second. 10552 p 14096 s 20571 o 22033 p
10007 o 10627 p 15310 o 21277 p 22034 p
10027 o 10651 p 17140 po 21661 po 22048 p
10044 o 10654 p 18877 p 21679 p 22398 o
10507 p 11010 p 20563 s

1644-1911

Primary 10646 14208 s 14575 p 14617 p
10029 po 10676 p 14553 14582 po 14621 po
10532 11194 o 14555 p 14594 fp 14623
10557 p 13451 p 14558 p 14596 p 14627 p
10559 po 14093 p 14567 14598 p 20414 p
10599 p 14097 p 14569 p 14602 po 21682 p

Second. 10574 p 14158 p 16049 p 20124 po
10004 po 10583 s 14159 p 16918 20769 po
10006 s 10586 14189 s 18098 p 21276 p
10010 p 10624 p 14191 po 18459 o 21439 p
10014 o 10664 s 14193 p 18862 p 21625 s
10053 p 10669 p 14202 s 18876 o 22045
10058 po 11241 p 14205 p 18919 p 22053 p
10505 p 11243 p 15313 po 18930 po 22056 p
10560 p 11558 po 15320 po 18937 p 22528 p
10568 o 11663 o 15322 o 19210 22620
10573 s 13458 p 15327 po 19695 p

1842-1911

Primary: Monographs
10002 o 10519 p 14574 o 14622 p 18378 o
10025 o 10566 p 14584 po 14626 p 18854 po
10030 o 10660 o 14588 po 15315 o 20126 s
10043 o 13870 p 14592 p 16374 po 20579 o
10054 o 14554 po 14597 o 16375 po 20749 o
10055 o 14556 p 14600 18075 o 22530 p
10062 po 14560 p 14619 po 18077 p

Primary: Inclusions
10610 o 14583 po 14601 o 14604 o 15314 s
14400 o 14591 po 14603 o 14624 o 22525 o
14579 p

Primary: Journal Articles
10553 p 14565 po 14586 o 14609 po 14620 s
10668 p 14566 po 14587 p 14610 p 14625
11215 p 14568 o 14589 po 14611 15126 s
13840 o 14571 p 14590 o 14612 s 15129 o
14550 p 14572 po 14593 p 14613 p 18866 p
14551 o 14573 o 14595 s 14614 o 18893 p
14552 o 14576 p 14605 p 14615 o 18899 p
14561 p 14577 o 14606 po 14616 p 19686 o
14563 14578 s 14607 p 14618 p 21628 o
14564 o 14581 po 14608 p

Secondary: Monographs
10003 o 10611 o 14164 p 17143 p 20559 o
10018 po 10614 p 14171 o 17151 o 21260 po
10021 o 10653 p 14187 p 18074 p 21262 o
10024 o 10677 p 14195 p 18092 p 21264 o
10031 o 11657 po 15307 o 18376 p 21265 p
10034 s 11658 o 15319 o 18387 p 21272 p
10038 o 11678 p 15321 o 18412 fp 21287 p
10049 po 12567 p 15325 o 18487 p 21302 o
10052 p 12569 o 15328 p 18490 p 21603 p
10059 o 12597 o 15713 18494 p 22027 p
10064 o 13125 p 15744 o 18908 o 22074 p
10065 o 13461 p 16090 o 18914 o 22562 o
10331 s 13804 p 16167 o 18932 po 22572 o
10551 p 13807 p 16186 o 19751 o 22599 o
10594 po 13847 p 16376 po 20128 o 22612 p
10598 o 14155 s 17019 po 20137 o

Secondary: Inclusions
10639 o 13823 p 16915 f 18525 p 19721 po
10658 o 16526 o 18370 p 19365 p 20786 po
11673 p

Secondary: Journal Articles
10063 o 11659 p 14161 o 15352 o 22029 p
10530 12615 p 14163 po 15629 o 22037 p
10536 s 12924 o 14186 p 15746 o 22038 po
10591 o 13135 s 14199 18093 p 22041 p
10649 o 13820 o 15312 o 20130 o 22604 p
10663 p 13839 o 15335 o 21261 p 22859 o
11209 p 13853 p 15348 o 21652 o

1842-1928
(including 1644-1928)

Primary 14638 p 14667 p 14697 o 20182 p
10068 s 14639 s 14668 o 14700 p 20430 p
10081 po 14642 p 14673 p 14701 o 20790 po
11591 14643 p 14674 o 15944 p 20798 o
13151 p 14644 p 14676 s 18560 p 21318 p
14628 fp 14646 p 14682 p 18987 p 21335 p
14631 o 14651 s 14683 s 20169 fp 21355 o
14632 o 14658 p 14689 p 20170 p 22110 p
14633 o 14661 p 14690 p 20174 p 22140 p
14634 f 14662 o 14693 fp 20179 p 22644 o
14635 o 14666 p

Second. 13155 p 16938 f 20795 o 21765 po
10069 o 13187 p 17630 p 20800 o 21774
10077 o 13881 p 18546 po 21305 o 21785 p
10084 po 13885 s 18551 po 21334 o 22002 p
10697 s 14214 po 18949 po 21337 po 22083 p
10698 p 14224 po 18951 o 21340 p 22112 p
10699 po 14229 18971 s 21342 p 22116 p
10708 p 14232 p 18980 o 21346 p 22118 p
11292 po 15132 p 18991 p 21352 o 22131 po
11587 p 15373 p 19697 p 21361 p 22670
11683 o 15388 s 20005 s 21453 o 22675 p
11703 p 15938 p 20177 p 21504 o 22676 o
12229 p 16261 s 20183 p

1911-1928

Primary 14705 p 14735 p 14767 p 19639 p
13913 14708 o 14741 o 14775 p 20202
13921 s 14711 p 14742 fp 15145 po 20438 f
13929 o 14714 p 14743 f 15407 fp 20463 f
13937 p 14720 o 14745 o 16424 po 20464 p
13947 p 14724 p 14748 o 17562 p 20467 p
13953 o 14725 p 14752 p 17842 f 20865 o
13955 o 14726 po 14758 po 18110 p 21462 o
14250 14727 p 14765 18992 fp 22707 p
14704 p 14731 o

Second. 13896 po 15450 f 18775 p 20222 s
10091 o 13906 po 15786 o 18778 p 20462 fp
10094 o 13972 o 16664 po 18997 po 20465 p
10099 o 14122 o 17614 o 19012 o 20468
10106 p 14237 p 17843 o 19503 fp 20832 fp
10381 p 14243 17856 f 19699 o 20932 o
10757 po 14251 p 18115 p 19825 o 21218 f
10778 o 15075 o 18596 po 20196 o 22162 p
11026 p 15143 p 18654 p 20211 o 22181 fp
11345 p 15151 o 18655 p 20213 o 22708 o
11377 s 15427 o

1911-1949
(including 1644-1949, 1842-1949)

Primary: Monographs
10074 p 14636 14670 p 14694 p 15428 o
10102 o 14637 p 14671 p 14695 s 16423 po
10104 o 14640 po 14675 po 14696 p 18952 p
10690 p 14647 p 14677 p 14698 p 19006 o
10781 p 14649 p 14678 s 14699 p 20204 p
11263 po 14650 s 14679 p 14703 s 20823 po
11586 fp 14652 po 14681 po 14719 o 20826 p
11601 p 14654 p 14684 p 14723 po 21308 o
11690 p 14655 p 14685 o 14728 f 21325 p
12230 p 14656 p 14686 p 14736 p 21359 p
14215 s 14657 p 14687 po 14753 p 21370 o
14219 po 14659 p 14688 p 14761 o 21457 p
14231 p 14665 po 14691 p 14770 o 22679 s
14629 po 14669 p 14692 p 14772 22805 o

Primary: Inclusions
10093 o 14645 p 14680 o 14715 p 14773
19637 o 20194 o

Primary: Journal Articles
10705 s 14653 o 14706 o 14751 fp 20192 o
11020 14660 p 14710 p 14759 o 20819 o
11029 p 14663 14722 o 14776 p 20827 po
14630 po 14664 s 14729 p 18964 p 22105 o
14641 o 14672 po 14734 p 19397 o 22150 s
14648 14702 14740 o 19835 f

Secondary: Monographs
10079 po 11839 p 15140 o 18988 fp 21321 p
10097 o 12317 po 15376 fp 18993 po 21363
10107 p 12638 p 15382 p 19617 p 21368 o
10349 s 13873 o 15384 po 19964 p 21444 p
10356 po 13880 po 15446 p 20160 po 21447 po
10706 po 13911 p 15941 p 20161 p 22006 s
10711 p 13916 p 15945 p 20162 p 22102 po
10725 p 13945 p 17095 o 20166 o 22132 p
10732 p 14217 p 17869 po 20173 s 22135 p
10759 p 14223 p 18120 p 20208 o 22654 p
10791 p 14230 p 18123 p 20431 p 22674 p
10812 p 14238 p 18154 p 20615 o 22706 o
11274 p 14457 p 18759 p 20791 p 22717 p
11595 p 14486 p 18969 p 20886 o

Secondary: Inclusions
10694 p 16105 18645 s 19965 p 21316 f
13878 p 18558 s 18745 o 20176

Secondary: Journal Articles
10717 po 12661 s 14456 p 15950 s 19833 fp
11267 s 13537 fp 15137 18303 p 20168
11810 p 14225 o 15764 po 19014 p 20804 po
11837 o 14226 p 15940 s 19618 p 20825
12623 s 14424 p

1928-1949

Primary 14713 o 14747 o 14769 p 20212 p
10092 o 14716 p 14749 po 14771 f 20437 o
10098 o 14717 o 14750 f 14774 fp 20440 o
10103 po 14718 po 14754 po 16058 p 20445 o
10105 fp 14721 po 14755 o 16063 p 20456 o
10740 s 14730 o 14756 16420 po 20458 o
10792 o 14732 p 14757 po 16432 po 20459 o
10816 f 14733 po 14760 po 17863 po 20841
11765 s 14737 p 14762 p 17872 p 21814 o
11782 o 14738 14763 o 19003 fp 21819 o
14240 o 14739 f 14764 o 19022 f 21820 s
14707 po 14744 p 14766 fp 19640 p 22711 p
14709 o 14746 o 14768 p 20189 p 22928 o
14712 p

Secondary: Monographs
10101 o 13888 o 15434 o 16054 p 20436 o
10108 p 13891 o 15437 po 17613 f 20444 p
10783 o 13928 o 15438 p 17632 o 20447 f
10799 po 13959 po 15439 p 18584 o 20863 o
10823 p 14121 o 15440 p 18647 p 20869 p
10836 po 15150 15441 p 18707 o 20923 po
11752 fp 15394 o 15443 p 18716 o 20926 po
11777 p 15409 p 15444 p 18717 p 21366 o
11834 fp 15416 o 15640 f 18746 o 21818 o
12256 f 15429 f 15965 p 18750 o 22714 p
13039 o 15431 p 15971 p 19018 fp 22720 po

Secondary: Inclusions
11753 o 18307 p 20443 p 20901 o 21225 f
13974 po 19823 o 20896 fp 20908 o 21508 f

Secondary: Journal Articles
10298 s 11772 o 15448 f 18679 p 20895 f
10357 s 13221 o 16443 o 19622 s 20900 po
10742 p 13941 p 16974 o 19629 p 20943 o
10767 o 14233 p 17868 f 19700 o 21812
10808 p 14244 p 18133 p 20441 p 22693 o
10809 14506 f 18150 p 20450 p 22797 o
10843 o 15155 18658 o 20831 p 22798 o
11028 p 15423 18677 p

1928-1972
(incl. 1644-1972, 1842-1972, 1911-1972)

Primary 11039 s 14778 o 14782 p 14786 po
10126 o 13308 p 14779 s 14783 p 14787 p
10859 p 14255 p 14780 p 14784 o 14788 p
10863 p 14777 p 14781 p 14785 po 14789 s

14790 P 14800 P 14810 18041 P 21404 P
14791 14801 P 14811 P 19652 P 21413 O
14792 P 14802 P 14812 P 19659 P 21421 O
14793 P 14803 P 15172 PO 20472 P 21472 S
14794 P 14804 15472 P 20475 O 21529 PO
14795 P 14805 S 15614 P 20962 FP 21874 P
14796 PO 14806 P 15799 O 20973 P 21879 P
14797 P 14807 O 15806 P 20978 O 22198 O
14798 FP 14808 P 17312 O 20981 P 22271 P
14799 O 14809 O 17895 O 20988 O 22740 P

SECONDARY: MONOGRAPHS

10110 PO 11606 S 15191 PO 18172 P 21407 S
10114 P 11607 P 15452 PO 18178 FP 21412 P
10120 S 11614 P 15454 P 18809 S 21467 S
10121 O 11855 S 15458 PO 18817 PO 21532 O
10123 O 12383 P 15459 PO 19033 P 21538 FP
10124 S 12770 S 15461 P 19035 PO 21847 P
10301 FP 13986 P 15468 O 19045 P 21900 P
10382 P 14013 P 15469 P 19053 P 21904 FP
10852 P 14015 O 15613 P 19583 P 22224 P
10853 PO 14018 S 15789 20229 P 22229 P
10855 FP 14020 FP 16729 FP 20231 PO 22474 P
10871 P 15158 S 17315 P 20954 FP 22724 P
10882 P 15161 P 17322 20960 P 22733 P
10888 S 15163 S 17956 P 20963 P 22736 PO
11045 FP 15181 P 18170 P 21392 PO 22806 P

SECONDARY: INCLUSIONS

10866 FP 15611 PO 19040 21898 PO 22816 P
12415 P 17635 P 19709 P 22221 S 22820 P
15187 S 18807 20975 P

SECONDARY: JOURNAL ARTICLES

10384 P 14256 15182 P 19030 P 20990
10872 P 14257 S 15193 S 19034 O 21536
11034 P 14259 P 15471 P 19581 21829 P
11054 P 14262 P 15646 P 19651 S 22189
11602 P 14291 P 16739 P 19656 P 22223 P
11866 P 14415 P 17580 O 19857 O 22812 S
13295 P 14515 O 17648 O 19898 O 22814 S
13992 P 15173 O 18171 P 20471 S

1949-1972

PRIMARY: MONOGRAPHS

10130 O 14825 FP 14921 P 15017 P 17799 FP
10154 P 14828 P 14940 P 15022 P 18061 O
10159 O 14829 O 14942 P 15023 FP 18350 P
10162 O 14833 P 14943 O 15024 FP 18362 O
10164 O 14835 S 14944 P 15025 P 19292 F
10167 O 14836 PO 14949 O 15027 P 19670 P
10175 O 14846 FP 14951 P 15028 P 20484 P
10464 P 14853 P 14955 FP 15029 P 20492 P
10481 P 14860 P 14962 P 15031 P 20496 PO
10894 P 14871 P 14969 P 15033 P 20522 FP
10895 O 14874 FP 14972 P 15034 P 20526 P
10997 P 14882 S 14974 PO 15267 P 20527 O
11105 P 14885 P 14976 P 15273 P 21009 FP
11135 O 14887 F 14979 PO 15501 O 21103 O
11894 O 14889 FP 14983 F 15523 FP 21124 PO
12082 P 14890 P 14990 P 15568 P 21433 O
12123 P 14894 P 14992 FP 15828 O 21563 PO
12532 PO 14899 P 14995 FP 15830 O 21578 O
12811 O 14903 P 14999 O 15898 FP 21937 P
13328 O 14908 FP 15002 FP 16457 O 22296 P
13420 FP 14909 P 15006 O 17006 P 22753 O
14384 P 14910 P 15007 P 17779 P 22831 P

PRIMARY: INCLUSIONS

10463 P 14850 P 14893 P 14970 O 15035 PO
10469 P 14851 P 14895 O 14973 P 15538 P
10497 P 14852 P 14901 P 14975 P 18344 F
11065 PO 14856 14905 P 14977 P 20491 P
12852 PO 14858 P 14906 P 14987 PO 21050 PO
13394 P 14859 P 14913 P 14994 PO 21549 O
14330 FP 14864 PO 14945 P 15000 P 21912 P
14816 P 14876 P 14946 PO 15001 P 21913 P
14821 P 14878 PO 14947 O 15005 P 21964 P
14831 PO 14880 PO 14957 PO 15011 P 21965 P
14838 PO 14888 O 14958 P 15012 21978 P
14839 F 14891 P 14964 O 15013 22762 S
14840 P 14892 P 14967 P 15014 O 22857 S
14844 O

PRIMARY: JOURNAL ARTICLES

10495 S 10942 11932 P 12085 PO 14360 P
10896 O 11152 P 11944 P 12802 P 14813 P
10933 P 11171 P 11976 O 12814 PO 14814 P
14815 O 14872 PO 14929 P 14986 P 19067 O
14817 O 14873 O 14930 P 14988 O 19410 P
14818 P 14875 O 14931 P 14989 P 19414 P
14819 14877 O 14932 P 14991 FP 19660 P
14820 O 14879 O 14933 P 14993 P 19665 P
14822 O 14881 O 14934 P 14996 O 19682 P
14823 P 14883 P 14935 P 14997 P 20479 O
14824 P 14884 P 14936 P 14998 P 20497 F
14826 O 14886 P 14937 P 15003 O 20501 P
14827 P 14896 F 14938 O 15004 P 20513 P
14830 P 14897 P 14939 PO 15008 O 20515 P
14832 P 14898 P 14941 P 15009 O 20521 P
14834 P 14900 P 14948 O 15010 PO 20531 PO
14837 O 14902 P 14950 O 15015 P 20666
14841 O 14904 S 14952 P 15016 O 21000
14842 P 14907 O 14953 P 15018 P 21011 O
14843 P 14911 O 14954 P 15019 P 21015 O
14845 P 14912 O 14956 P 15020 P 21048 PO
14847 S 14914 14959 P 15021 O 21084 O
14848 P 14915 P 14960 O 15026 O 21096 O
14849 P 14916 P 14961 PO 15030 O 21113 O
14854 FP 14917 P 14963 O 15032 PO 21123 O
14855 O 14918 O 14965 P 15206 O 21478 F
14857 O 14919 S 14966 O 15252 O 21943 P
14861 O 14920 P 14968 P 15579 O 21979 P
14862 P 14922 O 14971 P 16069 O 22311
14863 P 14923 P 14978 PO 16759 O 22346 P
14865 PO 14924 P 14980 O 16812 F 22369 P
14866 O 14925 P 14981 F 17329 O 22828 S
14867 S 14926 P 14982 O 17330 O 22833 P
14868 P 14927 P 14984 P 17636 O 22836 S
14869 P 14928 P 14985 O 18065 O 22852 FP
14870 O

SECONDARY: MONOGRAPHS

10132 O 11106 O 12475 PO 15483 P 18330 PO
10133 O 11107 P 12564 P 15486 FP 18341 P
10135 O 11113 P 12839 FP 15491 F 18345 P
10136 O 11138 F 12845 P 15499 PO 18355 O
10141 O 11161 P 12864 P 15506 O 19063 PO
10143 O 11168 P 13324 PO 15509 O 19069 PO
10144 O 11180 P 13449 P 15511 O 19408 PO
10149 O 11496 P 14139 O 15518 P 19422 P
10152 O 11619 P 14144 P 15519 O 19590 P
10153 O 11654 P 14305 P 15526 O 19594
10155 P 11883 O 14311 P 15530 F 20335 P
10156 O 11884 P 14322 P 15543 O 20368 F
10168 O 11901 O 14329 P 15549 P 20478 F
10170 O 11906 P 14337 P 15550 O 20502 O
10174 O 11920 P 14369 O 15553 PO 20503 O
10177 O 11922 O 14370 O 15575 O 20507 P
10180 O 11975 P 14378 P 15617 F 21037 F
10240 P 11995 P 14522 P 15888 P 21061 P
10415 PO 12003 P 14544 F 15890 P 21434 O
10421 FP 12008 FP 14549 P 15901 F 21570 FP
10470 P 12015 P 15123 O 16013 P 21574 FP
10937 PO 12027 P 15214 PO 16016 O 21594 S
10960 FP 12070 P 15230 P 16495 P 21936 O
10994 P 12071 P 15248 P 16798 FP 22291 P
10999 12109 P 15249 P 16806 F 22293 S
11003 P 12149 P 15254 O 16858 PO 22339 P
11005 P 12150 P 15285 O 16902 FP 22375 PO
11061 O 12158 PO 15294 P 17990 P 22749 P
11069 O 12175 P 15297 O 17995 O 22764 O
11087 O 12434 F 15481 O 18324 PO 22769 O
11104 P 12441 P

SECONDARY: INCLUSIONS

10137 P 11959 PO 14363 P 17642 P 21038 F
10138 P 11974 S 15215 17808 O 21066 P
10147 P 12009 P 15217 P 19407 P 21073 P
10151 S 12010 P 15243 O 19409 P 21099 F
10163 P 12017 P 15271 O 19413 P 21105 P
10176 P 12506 P 15291 P 19418 P 21148 O
10178 P 12788 P 15485 F 19421 P 21154 O
10179 P 12801 P 15497 P 19423 O 21486 O
10468 P 12875 P 15578 P 19424 P 21934 P
10930 P 13408 P 15817 19598 FP 21958 P
10946 P 13436 P 15917 P 20495 P 21977 P
11131 P 14030 P 16035 P 20528 P 22290 P
11162 P 14146 F 16357 F 20530 P 22379 O
11176 P 14151 P 16893 F 21025 P 23053 O
11484 P 14343 P

SECONDARY: JOURNAL ARTICLES

10233 P 10501 P 11001 P 11070 P 11086 O
10420 10986 P 11057 O 11085 P 11097 PO
11114 S 14134 FP 15852 FP 19366 S 21112 F
11177 P 14143 P 15912 P 19368 S 21122 O
11478 14148 16017 P 19377 P 21250 P
11505 P 14323 S 16026 S 19417 O 21550 F
11956 P 14351 P 16030 P 19683 F 21561 F
11961 P 14352 P 16036 P 19902 O 21572 O
11963 P 14452 P 16135 O 19936 F 21918 P
11981 P 15197 O 16458 O 20239 O 21919 P
12011 P 15200 P 16472 O 20250 21924 S
12038 O 15211 P 16481 PO 20476 P 21940 P
12058 P 15212 O 16485 S 20488 P 21956 P
12061 P 15213 O 16502 O 20489 O 21957 O
12129 P 15231 S 16839 P 20490 P 21961 P
12153 P 15255 16874 O 20511 P 21963 O
12431 O 15289 P 17332 O 20514 P 22023 F
12445 O 15302 O 17502 O 20520 P 22292 P
12518 O 15477 O 17592 P 20668 O 22300 P
12534 P 15478 O 17597 P 20678 O 22314 P
12817 P 15480 O 17996 P 21013 P 22365 O
12847 S 15492 O 18002 P 21043 P 22376 P
13355 P 15510 O 18051 O 21047 P 22757 P
13406 P 15512 O 18254 P 21058 PO 22845 S
13422 15516 O 18271 F 21075 O 22854 O
13425 FP 15563 PO 19065 PO 21077 P 22855 O
13431 O 15618 PO 19068 O 21081 P 22856
13580 P 15620 P 19158 P 21106 O 23058 O
14024 S

18 NATIONAL WELFARE AND LIVING STANDARDS

全國性福利及生活水準
国民の福祉及び生活水準

1644-1842

PRIMARY 12890 O 15037 P 15043 P

SECOND. 10039 O 12198 P 17160 P 22578 O
10007 O 10542 P 13868 P 21284 P 22590 O
10036 O 11541 P 14156 O 22577 P

1644-1911

PRIMARY 12197 P 15044 S 16196 P 20285 P
10046 O 12587 P 15046 P 19687 P 20591 PO
10577 P 15040 P 15047 P 19695 P 20745 O
11194 O

SECOND. 10520 P 14159 P 20560 P 21263 P
10004 PO 10525 P 15130 S 20761 P 21269
10029 PO 10599 P 18526 S 20769 PO 21283 P
10437 P 11655 PO 18930 PO 20788 S 22531 P

1842-1911

PRIMARY 12582 O 15039 P 18893 P 20726 F
10055 O 12921 O 15041 P 18925 O 20729 O
10641 O 13811 O 15042 O 19613 20749 O
10642 PO 15036 O 15045 O 20258 O 20766 P
10670 O 15038 P 18077 P

SECOND. 10660 O 12894 O 18398 P 19957 O
10024 O 10677 P 13471 P 18429 P 20710 O
10035 O 11013 PO 13831 P 18430 P 20714 O
10056 O 11659 P 13866 O 18436 P 20721 O
10057 O 11665 P 14095 O 18449 O 20782 S
10065 O 11668 O 15129 O 18452 P 21265 P
10440 O 11673 P 16907 PO 18504 P 22534 P
10516 PO 12569 O 18375 P 18511 P 22556 PO
10610 O 12593 PO 18378 O 19719 P 22623 P
10640 PO

1842-1928
(including 1644-1928)

PRIMARY 12216 P 15051 S 19477 PO 20798 O
11711 S 12220 P 15052 FP 19480 P 21504 O
12211 P 15050 O 18980 O

SECOND. 10291 P 12666 P 16261 S 19789 P
10067 O 10293 S 13151 P 17758 P 20049 P
10076 S 11270 P 13164 FP 18971 S 20294 PO
10077 O 12214 P 13520 P 19478 20790 PO
10284 P 12215 P 13688 P 19479 20800 O
10287 P 12233 P 14458 P 19481 P

1911-1928

Primary 14476 PO 15057 FP 15075 O 19517 FP
10094 O 14487 S 15061 S 15076 S 20222 S
10381 P 14488 15062 O 17760 O 20837 PO
13712 14493 P 15065 P 17873 PO 20877 P
13962 P 14497 FP 15066 S 19256 O 20902 PO
14462 S 14502 O 15072 FP 19504 P 20932 O
14465 15054 P 15073 P 19514 P 20942 O
14469 S

Second. 12718 14511 19001 PO 20211 O
10089 O 12749 O 14741 O 19512 P 20455
10209 FP 13209 O 14767 P 19546 P 20635 PO
10445 O 13531 P 15147 P 19547 PO 20832 FP
10769 P 14118 18601 P 19558 20865 O
12306 P 14434 P 18654 P 19562 O 20866 O
12320 14483 PO 18710 P 19567 21456 O
12349 O 14492 P 18743 P 20209 P 21506 O
12366 O 14507 P 18764 O

1911-1949
(including 1644-1949, 1842-1949)

Primary 12223 P 14482 P 15048 S 19559 PO
10079 PO 12307 P 14491 P 15049 19576 P
10102 O 13920 P 14495 P 15060 O 19577 P
10370 P 14111 O 14496 P 15063 S 19705 P
10448 P 14424 P 14505 P 15071 P 20302 FP
10453 S 14457 P 14508 P 15080 P 20813 P
11690 P 14479 PO 14509 P 15081 O 20826 P
11773 O 14481 P 14510 PO 15082 O 20827 PO

Secondary: Monographs
10104 O 12257 FP 13291 S 15586 P 20178 PO
10191 PO 12264 FP 13715 P 15674 PO 20204 P
10379 P 12267 FP 13727 P 17869 PO 20614 P
10684 O 12270 P 13755 P 18585 O 20806 PO
10700 PO 12297 P 13880 PO 18588 P 20822 PO
10726 12328 P 14219 PO 18759 P 20823 PO
10732 P 12631 P 14436 S 18988 FP 21325 P
10812 P 12684 FP 14466 P 19240 PO 21459 P
11699 S 12759 S 14486 P 19245 O 22095 P
11716 P 13158 FP 14649 P 19358 P 22133 PO
11756 P 13184 P 14686 P 19476 P 22655 O
11839 P 13212 PO 14694 P 19551 P 22666 S
12218 P 13250 P 14703 S 19644 PO 22694 O
12227 P 13261 P 15140 O 20067 P 22805 O

Secondary: Inclusions
12213 S 12293 S 12341 O 12650 S 13242 P
13657 S 19637 O

Secondary: Journal Articles
10195 P 13233 PO 15669 P 19014 P 20187 P
11735 13247 15677 P 19221 20261 S
11779 P 14433 S 16309 O 19397 O 20939 O
11824 O 14456 P 16549 P 19458 22098 P
12217 S 14477 P 16550 P 19463 P 22105 O
12252 S 14494 P 17283 P 19532 22171 S
12296 P 14503 S 18304 P 19542 22665 S
12623 S

1928-1949

Primary 12278 P 15053 P 15083 O 20393 O
10296 12291 S 15055 P 15084 20398 PO
10298 S 12310 P 15056 P 15681 20652 F
10451 S 12311 P 15058 P 17245 P 20831 P
10452 S 12321 S 15059 FP 19484 O 20834 P
10454 F 12359 O 15064 S 19544 P 20841
10839 O 13018 S 15067 PO 19572 P 20848
11748 P 14461 P 15068 O 19573 P 20926 PO
11752 FP 14467 P 15069 P 19623 PO 20944 PO
11829 P 14471 P 15070 O 19636 O 21465 O
12248 P 14474 FP 15074 F 19638 S 22714 P
12250 S 14480 P 15077 FP 19704 P 22715 S
12256 F 14490 P 15078 P 19707 O 22720 PO
12277 O 14500 P 15079 20219 P

Secondary: Monographs
10096 O 11724 P 11807 P 14501 P 20190 P
10100 O 11740 P 12348 PO 14774 FP 20639 S
10101 O 11750 S 13704 PO 15150 20871 P
10105 FP 11760 PO 13708 PO 17297 PO 20880 PO
10806 O 11777 P 13909 O 18142 P 20940 S
10821 S 11804 P 13951 O 18608 O 22710 O
10827 PO 11805 P 14478 FP 18717 P 22718
10836 PO

Secondary: Inclusions
10377 S 10747 O 15682 20212 P 20435 O
20647 F 20896 FP

Secondary: Journal Articles
10297 O 11028 P 11821 S 14124 P 18141 P
10368 11372 P 12313 P 14427 P 18150 P
10443 P 11742 12360 P 14464 P 18754 S
10444 O 11762 P 13223 O 14472 O 19574 P
10760 P 11763 P 13275 P 16567 P 19629 P
10761 O 11788 S 13567 17278 P 20300 F
10801 11806 S 13899 S 18133 P 20445 O
10816 F 11820 S

1928-1972
(incl. 1644-1972, 1842-1972, 1911-1972)

Primary 11845 P 12779 P 15089 S 20226 PO
10126 O 11846 P 15085 P 15090 O 20991 PO
10214 P 12402 S 15086 15091 P 20993 S
10393 S 12419 P 15087 P 19035 PO 21413 O
10455 O 12423 15088 P 19583 P 21529 PO
11844 O

Second. 11852 P 12424 P 15875 P 20962 FP
10115 O 11857 P 12426 P 16745 P 20966 O
10122 S 11862 P 12767 17947 S 20967 P
10220 P 11864 FP 13049 P 18172 P 20973 P
10386 F 11874 P 13050 P 18799 P 20978 O
10389 S 12379 P 13986 P 18817 PO 20979 S
10456 P 12384 P 14015 O 18827 O 20990
10852 P 12386 P 14258 P 19033 P 21391 S
10882 P 12389 P 14515 O 19078 P 21840 S
10883 S 12392 P 14778 O 19581 21855 S
11035 O 12394 P 15173 O 19582 P 21885 S
11044 PO 12395 P 15175 FP 19585 P 21894 S
11842 P 12406 P 15181 P 20662 S 22490 S
11848 PO 12414 P 15195 P 20953 PO 22740 P
11851 P 12420 P 15873 20960 P

1949-1972

Primary: Monographs
10130 O 10460 P 11901 O 12811 O 15112 P
10132 O 10488 P 12003 P 13070 P 15113 P
10139 P 10500 P 12070 P 13107 O 15115 P
10141 O 10503 P 12090 O 13120 PO 15123 O
10144 O 10895 O 12109 P 13769 P 15509 O
10145 O 11106 O 12434 F 14520 19597 FP
10149 O 11138 F 12463 P 14544 F 20502 O
10154 P 11144 O 12524 FP 14549 P 21103 O
10162 O 11894 O 12535 P 15100 P 21124 PO
10402 FP 11897 PO 12544 O

Primary: Inclusions
12042 P 14525 P 15107 P 15121 P 20495 P
13058 P 15099 P 15118 P 15215 20504 P
13066 P 15101 P 15119 P 15271 O 21148 O
13098 P 15105 P 15120 P

Primary: Journal Articles
10471 P 12171 P 14546 S 15109 P 20362 P
10472 P 12427 P 14872 PO 15110 P 21014
10475 P 12431 O 15092 P 15111 O 21043 P
10476 S 12458 O 15093 P 15114 PO 21045 P
10494 12465 S 15094 P 15116 O 21047 P
11147 12480 P 15095 P 15117 P 21058 PO
11164 F 12517 P 15096 P 15122 P 21082 P
11881 S 13060 P 15097 P 15124 P 21084 O
11924 P 13091 P 15098 PO 15231 S 21104 O
11932 P 13096 P 15102 P 18214 S 21107 O
12012 P 13596 S 15103 P 20243 P 21113 O
12040 P 13782 P 15104 P 20248 O 21142 O
12058 P 14516 S 15106 P 20250 22745 O
12155 O 14529 P 15108 P

Secondary: Monographs
10135 O 10180 O 11095 O 11980 PO 12150 P
10136 O 10232 P 11654 P 11988 P 12154
10150 O 10263 P 11883 O 12008 FP 12157
10152 O 10423 P 11884 P 12015 P 12173 P
10153 O 10466 P 11891 P 12019 P 12175 P
10156 O 10477 P 11906 P 12027 P 12428 P
10159 O 10894 P 11912 P 12039 P 12436 P
10167 O 10908 P 11920 P 12071 P 12439 P
10168 O 10978 O 11921 P 12082 P 12467 P
10172 PO 10997 P 11949 P 12096 P 12485 P
10173 O 11076 P 11952 P 12123 P 12564 P
10174 O 11087 O 11962 PO 12148 P 12787 P
12843 S 13597 S 14972 P 18061 O 20328 P
12853 O 13772 P 14990 P 18232 P 20335 P
13117 P 14522 P 15205 O 18277 P 20690 P
13118 P 14524 P 15260 P 19122 P 20700 P
13328 O 14535 P 15273 P 19135 P 20996 FP
13336 P 14828 P 15294 P 19590 P 21484 F
13420 FP 14829 O 16155 O 19594 22322 P
13432 P 14853 P 16788 PO 19595 S 22749 P
13584 P 14885 P 16844 P 20247 P 22769 O

Secondary: Inclusions
10137 P 11940 P 12538 P 14542 P 19587 O
10176 P 11959 PO 12548 P 15217 P 19589 P
10178 P 11989 P 13097 P 15885 19608 P
10179 P 11990 P 13101 P 15917 P 20999 P
10250 PO 12043 P 13390 P 16840 P 21025 P
10915 P 12132 P 13444 P 18290 P 21125 P
10920 P 12151 O 14138 P 19101 P 21146 P
11887 P 12447 P 14539 P 19170 S 21147
11914 12479 14540 P 19202 P 21153 S
11916 S 12506 P 14541 P 19418 P 21486 O
11918 P 12536 P

Secondary: Journal Articles
10225 P 11953 P 12457 P 14536 P 20370 P
10231 P 11957 PO 12460 P 14543 O 20405 O
10233 P 11961 P 12491 P 14814 P 20498 P
10238 P 11963 P 12496 P 14827 P 20520 P
10241 PO 11976 O 12518 O 15290 20696 O
10243 P 12022 S 12526 P 15918 P 21007 O
10265 P 12023 S 12549 P 16481 PO 21008 F
10316 P 12038 O 12555 P 16854 S 21012 O
10457 P 12052 S 12827 P 16864 S 21040 PO
10459 FP 12056 P 13073 P 16885 P 21057 S
10465 P 12059 P 13077 P 16896 P 21075 O
10491 P 12098 P 13087 P 18297 P 21085 S
10496 P 12100 FP 13094 P 19057 P 21090
10502 PO 12119 S 13103 P 19061 S 21094 O
11071 P 12125 P 13109 O 19137 P 21096 O
11155 P 12138 P 13575 PO 19169 PO 21102 O
11483 O 12145 P 13608 P 19175 P 21106 O
11882 P 12152 P 13774 O 19410 P 21123 O
11886 P 12170 S 14152 P 19599 P 21143 O
11895 PO 12430 P 14445 P 19600 P 21158
11896 PO 12443 P 14446 P 19606 P 21245 P
11943 P 12448 P 14519 P 20329 O 21248 P
11947 P 12451 O

19 Modernization and Directed Social Change
近代化運動及社會改革
近代化及び社会改革

1644-1842

Primary □
Second. 11682 P

1644-1911

Primary 10560 P 10681 P 13846 P 15130 S
15131 18510 P

Second. 10644 PO 11676 S 18930 PO 22780 P
10554 P 11241 P 13859 S 22053 P

1842-1911

Primary 11660 P 15125 S 18077 P 18395 P
10553 P 13125 P 15126 S 18092 P 18508 P
10555 P 13135 S 15127 P 18365 O 18515 S
10564 P 13831 P 15128 S 18369 P 18525 P
10566 P 13853 P 15129 O 18378 O 22037 P
10587 PO 14204 PO

Second. 11669 18079 P 18450 P 22042 P
10055 O 13470 P 18388 P 18460 P 22574 P
10504 O 14578 S 18409 P 18487 P 22575 P
10516 PO 15311 O 18414 S 18517 P 22623 P
10614 P 16921 P 18416 P 21267 P 22631 S
10660 O 18076 P 18429 P 21606 P 22771 P

1842-1928
(including 1644-1928)

PRIMARY 13151 P 15135 20798 O 21453 O
10071 O 14112 P 15138 21307 O 22076 S
10073 15132 P 18530 P 21311 O 22094 S
10699 PO 15133 S 18566 S 21319 P 22131 PO
11708 S 15134 P 18980 O

SECOND. 12950 P 18960 PO 21736 PO 22118 P
10072 S 13168 S 20430 P 21768 S 22128 P
10698 P 16256 O 20433 P 22079 P 22644 O
10709 P 18551 PO 21318 P 22083 P 22675 P
11709 18569 PO 21723 PO 22106 22902 S

1911-1928

PRIMARY 15147 P 15786 O 18720 S 20462 FP
11734 P 15148 P 18127 S 18725 P 20465 P
13921 S 15151 O 18579 O 18733 P 21464 P
15143 P 15152 18601 P 19000 P 22162 P
15144 P 15153 18630 P 19402 S 22708 O
15145 PO 15157 P 18665 O 20448 P 22804 S
15146 PO

SECOND. 14119 S 18615 19445 P 20222 S
10833 14511 18708 19453 P 22164 P
10838 P 18138 P 19229 O 20193 P 22931 S
10844 P 18582 O

1911-1949
(including 1644-1949, 1842-1949)

PRIMARY 10729 P 15141 18631 20432 P
10070 P 13017 P 15142 P 18714 P 21367 O
10079 PO 13291 S 15156 O 18745 O 21368 O
10083 PO 14652 PO 18143 O 18752 P 21826 P
10104 O 15136 O 18537 S 18756 22088 P
10352 P 15137 18543 S 19218 22095 P
10700 PO 15139 18558 S 20161 P 22105 O
10715 P 15140 O 18561 O 20431 P

SECOND. 13231 P 14719 O 18722 O 22006 S
10087 O 13255 S 18140 O 19447 22096 S
10693 P 13649 P 18535 P 19643 P 22102 PO
10714 S 13880 PO 18536 P 20934 P 22109 S
10718 S 13920 P 18545 PO 21324 P 22133 PO
10739 P 14116 P 18559 P 21330 O 22145 P
11289 P 14223 P 18574 P 21360 P 22173 P
11586 FP 14684 P 18619 S 21457 P 22651 S
11699 S 14699 P 18698 P 21459 P 22653 S
12661 S

1928-1949

PRIMARY 13909 O 15154 P 18659 O 19638 S
10767 O 14117 P 15155 18750 O 21366 O
11028 P 15149 S 18136 S 19625 S 22683 S
13262 O 15150 18658 O 19636 O

SECOND. 11752 FP 13970 O 18690 P 20855 O
10760 P 11765 S 14771 F 18723 P 22688 S
10813 P 12266 P 15438 P 18744 O 22711 P
10832 O 13919 P 17945 O 20440 O 22714 P
11744 O

1928-1972
(incl. 1644-1972, 1842-1972, 1911-1972)

PRIMARY: MONOGRAPHS
10112 S 11614 P 15158 S 15174 P 16456 F
10113 11846 P 15161 P 15175 FP 18795 P
10124 S 11848 PO 15163 S 15176 O 18796 O
10125 P 11849 P 15166 15181 P 19082 PO
10853 PO 11852 P 15168 15191 PO 21395 PO
10858 S 11872 PO 15169 P 15192 O 21420 PO
11045 FP 13308 P 15171 FP 15460 FP 22225 S
11052 FP 14274 P 15172 PO 15476 F 22275 P

PRIMARY: INCLUSIONS
12772 P 15165 S 15184 15189 O 21836
14275 P 15170 15185 S 15195 P 22231 P
14289 S 15177 S 15186 S 15456 P 22238 P
15160 P 15180 15187 S 18807 22264 P
15164 P 15183 PO 15188 P

PRIMARY: JOURNAL ARTICLES
11868 S 15162 P 15173 O 15179 S 15190
15159 P 15167 S 15178 15182 P 15193 S
15194 18793 18826 S 22213 P 22222 S
15474 O 18797 S 21864 S 22218 S 22245
18790 P 18821 S 22186

SECOND. 12412 P 14788 P 19655 P 22193
10109 12426 P 15452 PO 20472 P 22203 P
10121 O 13304 P 18180 P 20473 P 22212 P
10849 P 13986 P 18182 P 21404 P 22237 S
10868 S 14001 P 18186 P 21406 P 22249 P
10873 P 14002 P 18312 P 21418 O 22251 P
10877 P 14020 FP 18801 P 21473 PO 22256 P
10879 O 14258 P 18804 PO 21835 S 22268 P
10883 S 14278 P 18808 P 21844 P 22278 S
11039 S 14279 PO 18809 S 21847 P 22472 S
11054 P 14285 P 18819 P 21871 P 22730 P
12387 PO 14414 P 19035 PO 21878 S 22740 P
12394 P 14437 P 19087 P 22189 23007 P
12397 S 14513 P 19467 S 22191 P

1949-1972

PRIMARY: MONOGRAPHS
10134 O 11949 P 15214 PO 15260 P 16013 P
10136 O 12002 P 15230 P 15267 P 16031 P
10145 O 12008 FP 15234 P 15273 P 17995 O
10150 O 12114 S 15235 P 15279 O 18236 P
10164 O 12154 15237 P 15283 O 19939 F
10931 P 12440 PO 15240 O 15285 O 19953 F
10938 P 12791 P 15241 S 15294 P 20496 PO
11092 S 13420 FP 15245 PO 15297 O 20503 O
11104 P 14309 P 15248 P 15304 O 22291 P
11883 O 14369 O 15249 P 15501 O 22299 P
11897 PO 14962 P 15250 P 15553 PO 22325 P
11919 O 15202 P 15254 O 15572 FP 22750 O
11920 P 15205 O 15258 P

PRIMARY: INCLUSIONS
11634 S 15210 S 15233 P 15287 P 17997 P
11965 P 15215 15243 O 15291 P 22290 P
11969 P 15217 P 15259 15293 22313 P
12009 P 15222 P 15270 P 15296 P 22336 P
13444 P 15223 P 15271 O 15298 P 22342 P
14390 P 15224 P 15281 S 15299 P 22364 P
15203 P 15229 P 15286 15303 FP 22754 P
15209 P

PRIMARY: JOURNAL ARTICLES
10976 P 15201 S 15239 P 15275 PO 17996 P
10979 S 15204 15242 15276 P 18001 O
11915 P 15206 O 15244 P 15277 18190 P
11933 P 15207 15246 S 15278 18195 P
11941 P 15208 P 15247 P 15280 S 18216 P
11994 P 15211 P 15251 P 15282 S 18229 P
12012 P 15212 O 15252 O 15284 P 18237 P
12051 P 15213 O 15253 P 15288 P 18238 P
12080 P 15216 S 15255 15289 P 18243 P
12091 S 15218 P 15256 P 15290 18338 P
12472 P 15219 P 15257 P 15292 P 20476 P
14041 P 15220 P 15261 P 15295 P 20485 O
14136 O 15221 15262 15300 20489 O
14340 P 15225 P 15263 P 15301 P 21487
14452 P 15226 P 15264 P 15302 O 21548 O
14917 P 15227 P 15265 15512 O 22292 P
15196 P 15228 P 15266 S 15620 P 22306 P
15197 O 15231 S 15268 15845 P 22312
15198 P 15232 15269 S 16772 F 22328 P
15199 15236 P 15272 O 17590 P 22361 P
15200 P 15238 P 15274 PO 17656 O

SECONDARY: MONOGRAPHS
10132 O 11003 P 12563 P 15509 O 21569 P
10133 O 11061 O 12811 O 16347 O 21948 P
10155 P 11094 P 13432 P 18324 PO 22305 P
10161 O 11105 P 14033 P 19062 O 22318 P
10167 O 11154 P 14310 19166 P 22326 S
10168 O 11901 O 14871 P 19919 P 22350 P
10223 P 11922 O 14943 O 20080 P 22367 P
10947 P 12102 O 15486 FP 20492 P 22769 O
10978 O 12475 PO

SECONDARY: INCLUSIONS
10313 P 11530 PO 12121 P 15014 O 19170 S
10410 S 11951 P 14150 P 15101 P 21955 P
10930 P 11978 PO 14302 P 15558 P 23035 O
11433 PO 11990 P 14363 P 18358 F 23051 O

SECONDARY: JOURNAL ARTICLES
10311 P 10936 P 11001 P 11483 O 11497 S
10403 S 10998 S 11148 P 11493 FP 11930 P
11944 P 13391 P 14536 P 17908 O 19406 O
11979 PO 13406 P 14813 P 18218 P 19599 P
11987 P 13428 P 14814 P 18222 P 19673 P
11999 P 14073 P 15913 O 18233 P 20531 PO
12050 P 14140 P 16006 P 18262 P 21960 S
12099 P 14335 S 16038 P 18273 P 22294 P
12129 P 14349 P 16808 O 19102 S 22314 P
12431 O 14350 P 16856 PO 19159 P 22382 S
12529 P 14441 S 17335 PO 19368 S 23039 P
12546 P

20 LOCAL COMMUNITIES AS TOTAL SYSTEMS
地方社區整體研究
地方共同体全般

1644-1842

PRIMARY 10027 O 15305 O 15306 O 15310 O
15343 O

SECONDARY: *Not used*

1644-1911

PRIMARY 15320 PO 15334 PO 15581 O 17816 P
10327 P 15322 O 15341 O 15743 O 17920 O
14101 S 15323 O 15346 P 15935 P 18920 FP
15313 PO 15327 PO 15353 PO 16173 P 20762 O
15318 O 15331 P 15354 P

SECONDARY: *Not used*

1842-1911

PRIMARY 15312 O 15335 O 15355 O 15735 O
10011 O 15314 S 15336 O 15356 O 16090 O
10021 O 15315 O 15337 O 15357 O 16201 O
10064 O 15316 O 15338 P 15358 O 16377 O
12881 PO 15317 O 15339 O 15359 O 16384 FP
12882 PO 15319 O 15340 FP 15360 O 16397 O
12884 PO 15321 O 15342 O 15361 O 16510 P
12885 PO 15324 O 15344 O 15362 O 16915 F
12886 PO 15325 O 15345 O 15363 O 17551 S
12887 PO 15326 O 15347 PO 15364 O 17918 O
12902 O 15328 P 15348 O 15365 O 17931 O
15307 O 15329 O 15349 O 15366 O 18075 O
15308 O 15330 FP 15350 O 15367 O 18889 O
15309 O 15332 O 15351 O 15368 FP 20573 O
15311 O 15333 O 15352 O 15726 O

SECONDARY: *Not used*

1842-1928
(including 1644-1928)

PRIMARY 15371 PO 15379 O 15388 S 16109 PO
12951 PO 15373 P 15381 P 15389 PO 18951 O
14634 F 15374 F 15383 O 15390 O 20260 O
15369 PO 15378 F

SECONDARY: *Not used*

1911-1928

PRIMARY 15397 O 15413 O 15445 O 16680 O
10752 O 15400 F 15418 F 15450 F 17871 FP
14758 PO 15402 F 15422 O 15771 O 18764 O
15393 15403 F 15425 O 16630 F 19454 FP
15395 O 15407 FP 15427 O 16669 PO

SECONDARY: *Not used*

1911-1949
(including 1644-1949, 1842-1949)

PRIMARY 15375 O 15386 15449 O 16402 FP
10083 PO 15376 FP 15387 PO 15624 O 16624 FP
10086 PO 15377 P 15391 PO 15759 P 17036 FP
10356 PO 15380 15408 F 15761 P 17094 F
11582 PO 15382 P 15420 PO 15764 PO 17444 FP
15370 O 15384 PO 15428 O 15945 P 22706 O
15372 O 15385 PO 15446 P 15946 FP

SECONDARY: *Not used*

1928-1949

Primary 15409 p 15426 s 15440 p 17852 o
10804 o 15410 o 15429 f 15441 p 17854 f
14750 f 15411 p 15430 p 15442 p 17868 f
15392 o 15412 o 15431 p 15443 p 17940 f
15394 o 15414 po 15432 f 15444 p 18663 p
15396 o 15415 po 15433 o 15447 f 20262 f
15398 o 15416 o 15434 o 15448 f 20873 fp
15399 f 15417 o 15435 o 15640 f 22454 f
15401 o 15419 o 15436 f 15957 o 22704 o
15404 o 15421 o 15437 po 15965 p 22713 f
15405 f 15423 15438 p 15970 p 22721 p
15406 f 15424 f 15439 p 17073 s

Secondary: *Not used*

1928-1972
(incl. 1644-1972, 1842-1972, 1911-1972)

Primary 15455 fp 15463 fp 15470 s 15977 p
11846 p 15456 p 15464 p 15471 p 16456 f
11859 p 15457 p 15465 po 15472 p 17313 o
15191 po 15458 po 15466 o 15473 f 17984 o
15451 fp 15459 po 15467 po 15474 o 19082 po
15452 po 15460 fp 15468 o 15475 o 19090 fp
15453 15461 p 15469 p 15476 f 19972 fp
15454 p 15462 fp

Secondary: *Not used*

1949-1972

Primary: Monographs
10136 o 15495 p 15520 p 15557 o 16354 f
10161 o 15498 o 15523 fp 15560 fp 16457 o
10173 o 15499 po 15524 o 15565 o 16495 p
10421 fp 15501 o 15526 o 15567 o 16763 o
11939 s 15504 f 15527 o 15568 p 17386 fp
12434 f 15505 f 15530 f 15569 17589 f
12441 p 15506 o 15537 p 15570 p 19663 po
12508 p 15507 p 15543 o 15571 o 19737 fp
15205 o 15508 o 15544 o 15572 fp 19990 fp
15481 o 15509 o 15545 o 15575 o 20018 f
15482 o 15511 o 15547 p 15576 o 20236 f
15483 p 15513 po 15548 p 15824 fp 20367 f
15486 fp 15515 fp 15549 p 16012 p 20411 o
15488 p 15517 f 15550 o 16031 p 20699 o
15491 f 15518 p 15553 po 16046 po 22291 p
15493 o 15519 o

Primary: Inclusions
15485 f 15521 f 15542 15987 f 19152 o
15489 p 15532 o 15546 f 16037 fp 19198 p
15497 p 15538 p 15558 p 19108 p 19200 o
15500 o 15539 p 15578 p 19138 p

Primary: Journal Articles
12511 p 15510 o 15551 o 15580 p 17428 o
14862 p 15512 o 15552 o 15984 o 17620 f
15232 15514 o 15554 o 16027 o 17677 o
15477 o 15516 o 15555 o 16038 p 17776 o
15478 o 15522 o 15556 o 16041 p 17965 f
15479 o 15525 o 15559 p 16464 o 19098 o
15480 o 15528 p 15561 16757 o 19151 p
15484 f 15529 o 15562 o 16762 o 19156 p
15487 o 15531 o 15563 po 16772 f 19171 p
15490 o 15533 f 15564 p 16839 p 19179 p
15492 o 15534 o 15566 o 16846 o 19340 o
15494 p 15535 p 15573 f 16897 o 22340 p
15496 15536 o 15574 f 17335 po 22343 p
15502 o 15540 p 15577 o 17380 o 22767 o
15503 o 15541 o 15579 o

Secondary: *Not used*

21 Regional and Local Population

地方人口　地方人口

1644-1842

Primary 15582 p
Second. 17024 o 22619 po

1644-1911

Primary 15581 o 22510 p
Second. 11677 s 15661 s 16515 p 17921 o
10327 p 12948 p 15742 po 17816 p 18862 p
10333 p 14088 p 15927 p 17920 o 18915 fp
11015 p

1842-1911

Primary 12897 po 15584 p 16382 o 18925 o
10317 o 15356 o 15738 f 16391 o 20600 o
11679 p 15583 o 16371 po 17922 o
Second. 12580 po 15748 o 16384 fp 16915 f
10017 o 12924 o 15750 o 16386 o 16926 o
10035 o 15328 p 15924 po 16390 o 17025 o
10064 o 15359 o 15933 p 16398 o 17551 s
10328 o 15361 o 16372 po 16510 p 18438 p
10330 p 15718 po 16374 po 16533 o 18852 po
11657 po 15720 o 16375 po 16538 o 20551 o
11658 o 15739 f 16376 po 16909 o 20583 o
11678 p 15740 o

1842-1928
(including 1644-1928)

Primary 11686 p 16553 fp 16558 f
Second. 10354 p 12214 p 15381 p 16406 p
10292 p 11710 12221 p 15667 s 16552 o
10340 po 12211 p 12670 16403 p 16938 f

1911-1928

Primary 11812 p 15593 po 16433 fp 17871 fp
10207 p 15400 f 15595 s 16643 fp 21206 p
10363 fp 15450 f 15690 p 16695 f 21208 f
Second. 12975 po 15403 f 16426 p 16644 fp
10294 p 13209 o 15686 p 16591 f 16669 po
10381 p 13244 po 16424 po 16594 f 18992 fp
11828 s

1911-1949
(including 1644-1949, 1842-1949)

Primary 11716 p 15586 p 15592 fp 15668 s
10341 p 15380 15587 fp 15597 p 15678 p
10362 p 15382 p 15588 p 15599 p 21204 p
11690 p 15585 s 15589 s
Second. 11712 fp 15391 po 15761 p 16557 fp
10200 p 11715 p 15642 fp 15763 o 16624 fp
10337 p 12286 s 15669 p 15766 s 16675 p
10345 fp 12322 p 15676 fp 15945 p 17036 fp
10719 12687 s 15679 fp 16410 p 18981 p
10725 p 14640 po 15684 p 16423 po 18993 po
10751 p 15377 p 15689 p 16449 po 20622 p
11684 p 15387 po 15691 p 16556 fp 22660 po
11706 p

1928-1949

Primary 15594 f 15641 f 16430 p 19850 f
15590 p 15596 f 16064 fp 16604 o 21210 fp
15591 p 15598 fp 16422 17761 o 21216 f
Second. 11787 o 15399 f 16427 o 16686 o
10357 s 11797 p 15409 p 16431 fp 16973 fp
10361 s 11823 p 15437 po 16435 p 17872 p
10368 12256 f 15440 p 16437 o 17875 o
10378 s 12292 s 15773 p 16599 fp 17883 fp
11722 12309 p 15776 o 16606 f 19846 p
11723 p 12708 s 15777 o 16646 f 21213 fp
11732 p 14712 p 16062 p 16647 o 21520 o

1928-1972
(incl. 1644-1972, 1842-1972, 1911-1972)

Primary 15471 p 15605 p 15612 p 16747 p
10395 fp 15472 p 15606 p 15613 p 16751 s
11844 o 15600 p 15607 p 15614 p 21231 p
11878 s 15601 p 15608 s 15698 p 21233 fp
13297 fp 15602 15609 p 15805 po 21234 p
15457 p 15603 p 15610 p 16727 fp 21235 p
15463 fp 15604 p 15611 po 16739 p
Second. 10301 fp 10385 fp 10392 p 10855 fp
10214 p 10382 p 10387 s 10398 fp 10874 p
12414 p 15467 po 15974 fp 17101 fp 19980 fp
13313 p 15695 p 16726 p 17103 fp 21232 fp
15455 fp 15696 f 16736 p 17956 p 21827 fp
15456 p 15697 fp 16743 19090 fp 21854 po
15461 p 15874 p 16745 p 19975 fp 22732 fp
15465 po

1949-1972

Primary 15517 f 15620 p 15625 p 15890 p
10413 p 15615 p 15621 f 15647 p 15917 p
10427 fp 15616 f 15622 p 15822 po 16869 f
10431 fp 15617 f 15623 p 15829 po 17961 fp
14134 fp 15618 po 15624 p 15861 p 21254 p
15491 f 15619 p

Secondary: Monographs
10401 f 10432 p 14874 fp 16493 p 17001 f
10402 fp 10435 fp 15518 p 16495 p 17002 fp
10415 po 10436 p 15520 p 16786 f 17350 fp
10421 fp 11138 f 15655 fp 16787 fp 17387 p
10424 p 12003 p 15708 fp 16827 p 19153 f
10426 fp 12157 15850 fp 16841 po 20018 f
10428 fp 12434 f 16348 f 16871 f 20681 f
10429 fp 12522 fp 16354 f 16872 fp 20682 p
10430 fp 14549 p 16463 p 16898 s

Secondary: Inclusions
10176 p 10993 p 12020 p 15837 o 16003 f
10179 p 11959 po 15497 p 15843 o 18290 p
10269 p 12017 p 15820 po 15859 fp 20409 o

Secondary: Journal Articles
10264 p 12152 p 15842 p 16758 o 17109 f
10310 p 15477 o 15852 fp 16762 o 17680 f
11964 p 15492 o 15903 f 16819 f 17685 f
12106 p 15502 o 16042 f 16839 p 19057 p
12136 p 15533 f 16499 s 16856 po 20320 fp
12146 p 15577 o 16504 16894 o 20338 f

21.1 Regional Urbanization and City Population

地方性都市化及都市人口
地方の都市化及び都市人口

1644-1842

Primary 10032 o 15725 s 17822 o 22590 o
Second. 15310 o 17024 o 17657 o 19429 p
20549 o

1644-1911

Primary 10333 p 15626 o 15627 p 18933
Second. 12907 o 15322 o 15334 po 17021 o
10188 p 12948 p 15323 o 15754 o 18464 p
12578 o 15313 po 15327 po 16379 po 20762 o

1842-1911

Primary 15628 p 15716 o 16506 o 18852 po
12889 o 15629 o 15723 o 16906 o 20590 po
15308 o 15630 o 15730 o 16934 o 22582 o
15325 o 15710 16370 po 17546 o
Second. 12884 po 15714 o 16390 o 17169 o
10035 o 12888 po 15737 p 16537 o 17535 o
10321 o 12916 o 15746 o 16908 o 18372
10324 o 12919 po 15749 po 16909 o 19719 p
10330 p 12936 po 16374 po 16915 f 20542 o
11232 fp 12937 po 16375 po 16928 o 20706 o
11658 o 15356 o 16376 po 16932 o 20735 o
12570 o 15357 o 16377 o 17019 po 20773 f

1842-1928
(including 1644-1928)

Primary 15633 po 17560 p
Second. 12663 p 12969 po 15951 17191 f
11710 12951 po 14224 po 16403 p 17412 p
12214 p 12953 po 15373 p 16552 o 18967 o

21.1 Regional Urbanization

1911-1928

PRIMARY 15425 O 15690 P 15786 O 16945 O
15395 O 15636 P 15768 O

SECOND. 12717 P 15413 O 16413 O 17696 PO
10207 P 12725 15769 O 16424 PO 17856 F
10363 FP 12988 PO 15770 O 16436 PO 20883 S
11749 P 15407 FP 15780 O 17221

1911-1949
(including 1644-1949, 1842-1949)

PRIMARY 15588 P 15637 P 15642 FP 15766 S
15446 P 15631 P 15638 O 15678 P 15946 FP
15586 P 15632 P 15639 O 15764 PO 21821 O

SECOND. 10791 P 15693 P 16405 P 16941 P
10200 P 12674 P 15756 S 16407 P 17030 FP
10337 P 15377 P 15765 S 16421 18953 O
10341 P 15382 P 15948 P 16423 PO 19006 O
10364 FP 15669 P 16401 FP 16562 S 20622 P
10366 15684 P 16402 FP 16633 FP 21204 P
10375 P

1928-1949

PRIMARY 11803 O 15447 F 15635 P 15869 F
10206 P 15431 P 15594 F 15640 F 19846 P
10832 O 15432 F 15634 P 15641 F

SECOND. 15430 P 15776 O 15957 O 17863 PO
10368 15438 P 15778 O 16430 P 19270 O
11777 P 15439 P 15779 O 16438 P 19834 F
15404 O 15441 P 15782 O 16440 O 20885 P
15417 O 15442 P 15784 PO 16448 O 20890 PO
15429 F 15774 15788 O 16596 F 21205 P

1928-1972
(incl. 1644-1972, 1842-1972, 1911-1972)

PRIMARY 15602 15644 S 15794 FP 16454 S
10301 FP 15608 S 15645 P 15796 S 17323 P
10384 P 15609 P 15646 P 15805 PO 19885 P
10387 S 15613 P 15698 P 15810 FP 21234 P
15467 PO 15614 P 15793 FP 15811 P 21235 P
15471 P 15643 FP

SECOND. 11878 S 15610 P 15803 S 16752 P
10382 P 13297 FP 15612 P 15806 P 16753 PO
10385 FP 15454 P 15697 FP 15808 17312 O
10386 F 15458 PO 15789 16342 PO 17318 P
10392 P 15472 P 15791 S 16726 P 17946 O
10395 FP 15473 F 15795 P 16729 FP 20658 F
10398 FP 15600 P 15798 P 16731 21232 FP
11389 P 15606 P 15799 O 16751 S

1949-1972

PRIMARY 15647 P 15653 S 15828 O 17386 FP
10264 P 15648 P 15654 FP 15832 O 17392 O
10269 P 15649 S 15655 FP 15852 FP 17911 O
15568 P 15650 P 15822 PO 15858 P 20677 O
15617 F 15651 P 15824 FP 16491 F 21254 P
15620 P 15652 P 15827 P 17350 FP 21575 FP

SECOND. 10434 S 14939 PO 15823 F 17642 P
10230 P 10435 FP 15499 PO 15834 PO 17961 FP
10241 PO 10436 P 15538 P 15835 O 17963 F
10268 P 10479 P 15569 15838 F 17994 FP
10401 F 10993 P 15616 F 15842 P 19932 F
10424 P 12003 P 15621 F 15861 P 19933 FP
10426 FP 12008 FP 15623 P 15913 O 20334 FP
10427 FP 12069 P 15624 P 16347 O 20409 O
10428 FP 12152 P 15702 S 16469 P 20676 P
10429 FP 12434 F 15708 FP 16492 P 20678 O
10430 FP 12474 P 15812 O 17001 F 20685 P
10431 FP 13332 S 15813 F 17368 O 20695 PO
10432 P 13395 P 15821 P

21.2 Regional and Local Geographic Mobility
地方性流動遷移
地域間又は地域内人口移動

1644-1842

PRIMARY 15657 15662 P 15663 P 15664 P

SECOND. 10626 P 16514 P 19959 P 22577 P
10552 P 13812 18470 P 21279 P 22627 S

1644-1911

PRIMARY 15658 P 15660 15665 P 19718 P
14101 S 15659 PO 15661 S

SECOND. 10674 S 12201 P 15936 P 17921 O
10325 PO 11015 P 15353 PO 16379 PO 22531 P
10327 P 11677 S 15742 PO 17520 PO

1842-1911

PRIMARY 15325 O 15368 FP 15656 O 15932 O
17553 P 18438 P

SECOND. 13799 PO 16375 PO 17025 O 17925 O
12180 PO 15723 O 16376 PO 17540 O 17928 PO
12888 PO 15728 O 16399 O 17547 P 20542 O
12937 PO 16374 PO 16929 O 17924 P

1842-1928
(including 1644-1928)

PRIMARY 15633 PO 15670 P 15673 O 17934 S
10354 P 15667 S 15671 O

SECOND. 11686 P 11697 P 16553 FP 18950 O
10340 PO 11691 P 12211 P

1911-1928

PRIMARY 15686 P 15692 P 16643 FP 16968 P
15683 PO 15690 P 15694 P

SECOND. 11749 P 16644 FP 16961 P 17611 O
10363 FP 16424 PO 16695 F 17231 O 17717 PO
10381 P 16429 P

1911-1949
(including 1644-1949, 1842-1949)

PRIMARY 15586 P 15669 P 15677 P 15687 O
10337 P 15597 P 15672 O 15678 P 15689 P
10345 FP 15599 P 15674 PO 15679 FP 15691 P
15376 FP 15666 S 15675 P 15684 P 15693 P
15585 S 15668 S 15676 FP 15685 P 17298 P

SECOND. 11712 FP 15588 P 15763 O 19444 P
10195 P 11714 P 15637 P 15766 S 19561 P
10341 P 11715 P 15639 O 15945 P 21204 P
10364 FP 11716 P 15642 FP 16423 PO 22655 O
10375 P 11825 PO 15758 PO 16941 P 22662
10719 12674 P 15761 P 17721 P 22682 O
11684 P 15446 P

1928-1949

PRIMARY 12310 P 15681 15688 P 17854 F
11785 FP 15432 F 15682 17838 O 17860 O
12292 S 15680 S

SECOND. 12248 P 16422 16681 O 19850 F
10796 P 12309 P 16425 F 17416 O 20451 O
10827 PO 13970 O 16435 P 17417 O 21216 F
11031 P 15053 P 16606 F 17664 F 22129 P
11745 P 15436 F 16607 O 17883 FP 22693 O
11755 P 15594 F 16635 P 19011 F 22718
11797 P 15776 O

1928-1972
(incl. 1644-1972, 1842-1972, 1911-1972)

PRIMARY 15451 FP 15645 P 15696 F 17318 P
10393 S 15600 P 15646 P 15697 FP 17949 P
10398 FP 15614 P 15695 P 15698 P 19858 F

SECOND. 10387 S 11052 FP 15455 FP 15464 P
10385 FP 10874 P 12382 P 15461 P 15467 PO
15468 O 15789 16731 17635 P 21232 FP
15470 S 15791 S 16739 P 17954 21233 FP
15471 P 15795 P 16740 FP 17985 FP 21234 P
15604 P 15798 P 16751 S 17988 S 21235 P
15608 S 15805 PO 16752 P 18314 P 21534 F
15610 P 15873 17103 FP 19863 F 21827 FP
15612 P 16729 FP 17323 P 19972 FP 22724 P

1949-1972

PRIMARY 15620 P 15705 P 16485 S 19939 F
10479 P 15699 F 15706 F 17372 P 20488 P
11085 P 15700 O 15707 FP 17678 P 20491 P
11161 P 15701 P 15708 FP 18339 P 20512 P
15292 P 15702 S 15709 S 18360 P 21575 FP
15571 O 15703 FP 15822 PO 19910 F 22768 P
15615 P 15704 FP 16078 P

SECOND. 14391 P 15820 PO 17350 FP 21009 FP
10176 P 14868 P 15821 P 17386 FP 21048 PO
10233 P 14929 P 15850 FP 17592 P 21054 O
10415 PO 15291 P 15858 P 17645 O 21055 O
10428 FP 15546 F 15861 P 17646 P 21056 O
10482 P 15555 O 15876 P 17961 FP 21115 O
10957 P 15578 P 15892 P 17963 F 21139 O
11099 P 15616 F 15989 F 18245 P 21151 O
11130 P 15617 F 16072 P 18332 P 21236 F
11148 P 15622 P 16134 F 18361 P 21244 FP
11926 P 15623 P 16354 F 20119 O 21478 F
11985 P 15624 P 16463 P 20409 O 21584 O
12146 P 15625 P 16477 P 20676 P 21928 P
12513 P 15647 P 16493 P 20688 O 22754 P
14347 P 15648 P 16813 PO 20695 PO

21.3 Microecology and Particular Settlements
市鎮村舍聚落研究
地域社会生態学及び居住形態

1644-1842

PRIMARY 15711 O 15725 S 16369 O 20563 S
10627 P 15722 O 15752 O

SECOND. 10039 O 15305 O 18013 P 19959 P
10027 O 11536 O 15306 O 18936 P 22619 PO

1644-1911

PRIMARY 15323 O 15729 PO 15751 20545 FP
10333 P 15327 PO 15741 P 15754 O 20548 S
11542 FP 15627 P 15742 PO 17148 PO 21677 FP
15313 PO 15665 P 15743 O 18865 PO 22510 P
15322 O 15727 PO 15745 PO

SECOND. 10674 S 15353 PO 17921 O 20762 O
10004 PO 12193 PO 15354 P 17927 FP 21610 F
10060 PO 15318 O 17021 O 18915 FP 21695 S
10325 PO 15320 PO 17028 P 20090 PO 22409 P
10582 PO 15334 PO

1842-1911

PRIMARY: MONOGRAPHS
10328 O 15713 15734 O 15929 O 20578 O
10330 P 15721 O 15736 O 16187 O 20726 F
13804 P 15726 O 15740 O 16383 PO 20760 F
15311 O 15728 O 15744 O 17169 O 20773 F
15361 O 15733 O 15749 PO 18075 O

PRIMARY: INCLUSIONS
10334 O 15715 O 15750 O 16371 PO 16927 O
10335 O 15716 O 15753 O 16526 O 17138 O
10336 O 15717 O 16166 O 16915 F 20551 O
12897 PO 15719 O 16370 PO 16925 PO 22522 O
15366 O

PRIMARY: JOURNAL ARTICLES
10278 O 15357 O 15720 O 15732 O 15746 O
10319 S 15710 15723 O 15735 O 15747 O
12584 O 15712 S 15724 P 15737 P 15748 O
15348 O 15714 O 15730 O 15738 F 16047 O
15356 O 15718 PO 15731 O 15739 F 16373 O

21.4 Regional Labor Force and Local Division of Labor
地方勞動力及職業分化
地方労働力及び職業分化

15861 P 16036 P 16498 P 17337 O 19163 FP
15995 O 16083 F 16829 P 17798 O 19195 F
16004 O 16145 P 17124 O 19102 S 19340 O
16015 P 16458 O 17129 P 19125 P 19586 O
16026 S 16476 O 17130 PO 19158 P 20345 F
16027 O 16481 PO 17329 O

22 Local Political Systems

地方政治制度 地方政治制度

1644-1842

Primary 10512 PO 15310 O 15923 O 16517 P
10507 P 10533 PO 15582 P

Second. 10561 O 10672 P 15711 O 17408 PO
10039 O 10626 P 14096 S 16507 PO 19958 O
10529 P 10651 P 15664 P 16529 P 22555 O

1644-1911

Primary 14158 P 15931 O 15936 P 17541 P
10525 P 15334 PO 15934 P 16049 P 18519 P
10603 P 15863 P 15935 P 16379 PO 22510 P
12948 P 15927 P

Second. 10674 S 14167 P 15341 O 18405 S
10042 PO 11015 P 14189 S 15626 O 18464 P
10058 PO 11243 P 14201 P 16543 PO 18865 PO
10567 S 12573 P 15318 O 17021 O 21709 P
10621 S 12612 P 15322 O 17542 P 22531 P
10628 S 14093 P 15323 O

1842-1911

Primary 15307 O 15921 P 15933 P 17551 S
10019 PO 15316 O 15922 O 16094 P 17973 PO
10513 PO 15340 FP 15924 PO 16398 O 18393 O
10519 P 15351 O 15925 P 16912 O 18394 PO
10601 O 15360 O 15926 P 17025 O 18922 O
10670 O 15368 FP 15928 P 17411 P 20550 O
10679 O 15716 O 15929 O 17522 O 22522 O
12187 O 15919 PO 15930 P 17544 P 22612 P
14207 P 15920 P 15932 O 17547 P 22632 P

Secondary: Monographs
10021 O 13455 P 15721 O 17019 PO 18490 P
10048 O 13858 P 16090 O 17176 PO 18491 O
10062 PO 14092 PO 16374 PO 17409 FP 18496 P
10064 O 14160 P 16375 PO 17553 P 18889 O
10551 P 15309 O 16376 PO 17662 O 21265 P
10677 P 15336 O 16384 FP 18387 P 22067 O
11678 P 15338 P 16394 P 18428 P 22074 P
12570 O 15347 PO 16516 P 18449 O 22595 P
12595 P 15350 O 16536 O 18461 P

Secondary: Inclusions
10510 P 14395 P 15359 O 17526 P 17626 O
19721 PO 22523 O

Secondary: Journal Articles
10326 PO 11186 PO 15352 O 17170 O 18488 P
10514 P 11659 P 15365 O 17178 O 20281 O
10518 P 14177 O 15731 O 17410 PO 21438 PO
10538 P 14199 15737 P 17533 FP 22041 P
10572 15312 O 16510 P 18401 P 22517 O
10606 P 15335 O 16511 O 18404 P 22546 P
10648 O 15337 O 16540 O 18456 O 22570 P
11181 F 15348 O

1842-1928
(including 1644-1928)

Primary 15374 F 15943 P 16052 P 18956 PO
10084 PO 15388 S 15944 P 16406 P 20260 O
10196 P 15937 P 15951 16563 O 22673 P
10685 P 15938 P 15952 O 17560 P

Second. 11705 PO 14224 PO 17559 P 19789 P
10082 PO 11711 S 15373 P 17630 P 20006 PO
10716 P 12211 P 15383 O 17631 PO 20389 PO
11260 P 12666 P 15390 O 18983 FP 20802 PO
11270 P 13163 S 15673 O 18987 P 21347 P
11271 PO 13881 P 16108 PO 19219 S 21355 O
11295 P 14222 S 16109 PO

1911-1928

Primary 15397 O 15418 F 15972 O 19449 P
10840 S 15403 F 15966 FP 16433 FP 20883 S
11364 P 15407 FP 15969 S 19363

Second. 13925 P 16424 PO 18126 P 19558
10768 PO 13979 P 16643 FP 18709 P 20875 O
10769 P 14758 PO 17566 O 18734 P 20897 O
12368 O 15425 O 17611 O 19442 PO 22680 O
12747 O 15450 F 17760 O 19524 P 22802 FP
13905 PO 15593 PO 17848 O 19547 PO

1911-1949
(including 1644-1949, 1842-1949)

Primary 15449 O 15946 FP 15956 P 17444 FP
11019 P 15632 P 15947 O 15959 P 17572 O
13977 P 15674 PO 15948 P 15961 FP 18588 P
14223 P 15762 P 15949 P 15964 P 19355 FP
15382 P 15939 P 15950 S 16113 S 19630 P
15384 PO 15940 S 15953 P 16408 FP 19632 S
15387 PO 15941 P 15954 S 17052 PO 19962 S
15420 PO 15942 P 15955 P 17095 O 21312 F
15446 P 15945 P

Second. 11690 P 16407 P 18119 P 19006 O
10083 PO 13512 P 16409 P 18121 P 19257 P
10366 14106 16410 P 18157 P 19576 P
10688 P 14509 P 16423 PO 18536 P 19619 O
10707 P 14636 16449 PO 18567 O 19963 P
10711 P 15377 P 16550 P 18585 O 20063 P
10776 PO 15385 PO 16559 P 18622 O 21313 F
10790 P 15391 PO 16561 S 18726 P 21314 F
10795 P 15408 F 17036 FP 18730 P 21315 F
10828 P 15672 O 17094 F 18732 P 21369 F
10845 P 16053 P 17694 PO 18759 P 22682 O
11267 S 16402 FP 17979 P 18981 P

1928-1949

Primary 14754 PO 15441 P 15968 P 18667 FP
10760 P 15399 F 15443 P 15970 P 18682 P
10789 P 15406 F 15444 P 15971 P 18690 P
10830 P 15410 O 15957 O 16054 P 18694 F
10831 P 15411 P 15958 O 16061 P 18746 O
10842 P 15421 O 15960 FP 16063 P 18751 S
13891 O 15433 O 15962 O 16430 P 19011 F
13974 PO 15434 O 15963 P 17570 O 19243 P
14117 P 15437 PO 15965 P 17613 F 20898 PO
14239 O 15438 P 15967 P 18643 F 22677 O

Second. 12291 S 15436 F 17891 O 19629 P
10101 O 12331 P 16060 O 18118 P 19638 S
10103 PO 13909 O 16064 FP 18305 P 19642 S
10747 O 13934 P 16420 PO 18307 P 19648 O
10754 S 13969 O 16972 FP 18647 P 20844 F
10764 O 15392 O 17062 F 18678 P 20876 PO
10774 PO 15405 F 17063 F 18684 20930 O
10794 P 15409 P 17564 O 18703 O 22161 P
10796 P 15412 O 17707 O 18749 O 22169 P
10818 P 15414 PO 17709 F 19018 FP 22681 FP
10836 PO 15424 F 17849 O 19280 O 22704 O
10837 PO 15429 F 17863 PO 19555 FP 22715 S
11031 P

1928-1972
(incl. 1644-1972, 1842-1972, 1911-1972)

Primary 11054 P 15460 FP 15978 FP 17985 FP
10261 S 11391 P 15473 F 15979 P 17987 P
10851 P 12379 P 15476 F 15980 P 17988 S
10870 P 12389 P 15973 P 15981 F 19085 O
10873 P 12391 P 15974 FP 15982 19970 FP
10887 PO 12426 P 15975 P 16128 FP 19971
11036 P 15455 FP 15976 PO 17635 P 21426 P
11052 FP 15459 PO 15977 P

Second. 10880 P 12418 FP 15461 P 16746 FP
10113 10886 P 12424 P 15468 O 17772 O
10216 P 10888 S 13046 P 15470 S 17897 F
10383 S 10890 P 14129 15474 O 17899 O
10391 P 11042 P 14131 15791 S 17953 P
10855 FP 11848 PO 14256 15807 P 18178 FP
10872 P 12375 P 14515 O 15811 P 18312 P
10874 P 12378 P 15174 P 16334 PO 18809 S
10875 P 12380 P 15185 S 16451 19077 P
10876 12383 P 15192 O 16454 S 19080 F
10877 P 12405 P 15451 FP 16735 P 19081 F
19082 PO 19650 PO 19975 FP 21410 FP 22227 S
19090 FP 19873 S 20475 O 21538 FP 22724 P

1949-1972

Primary: Monographs
10306 PO 12524 FP 15537 P 16007 FP 16887 F
10894 P 14329 P 15544 O 16011 P 17593 PO
10904 F 15258 P 15549 P 16012 P 18277 P
10931 P 15481 O 15557 O 16013 P 19100 P
10953 P 15483 P 15560 FP 16016 O 19105 FP
10960 FP 15488 P 15567 O 16022 O 19122 P
10962 15495 P 15568 P 16029 S 19131 P
10994 P 15507 P 15572 FP 16031 P 19153 F
10997 P 15513 PO 15991 P 16046 PO 19922 P
11006 P 15520 P 15992 P 16072 P 20079 P
11094 P 15524 O 15993 P 16139 O 20492 P
11496 P 15526 O 16001 S 16148 FP 20681 F
12002 P 15530 F 16002 FP 16488 PO 22375 PO

Primary: Inclusions
11458 P 15990 P 16032 PO 16769 P 19148 O
15542 15996 P 16033 PO 17642 P 19154 P
15546 F 15998 O 16035 P 17643 P 19989 F
15578 P 16003 F 16037 FP 17644 F 20683 FP
15987 F 16028 FP 16496 FP 18290 P

Primary: Journal Articles
10897 P 15983 O 16015 P 16041 P 17115 P
10923 F 15984 O 16017 P 16042 F 17130 PO
10964 P 15985 O 16018 P 16043 17428 O
10965 P 15986 O 16019 P 16044 F 17502 O
10973 P 15988 P 16020 P 16045 P 17620 F
11468 P 15989 F 16021 P 16079 P 17624 O
11626 S 15994 P 16023 O 16081 P 17673 P
11957 PO 15995 O 16024 O 16133 F 17905 P
12077 S 15997 O 16025 P 16134 F 18221 P
14447 P 15999 P 16026 S 16479 P 18273 P
15496 16000 O 16027 O 16482 O 19099 P
15502 O 16004 O 16030 P 16792 P 19123 P
15514 O 16005 P 16034 P 16801 F 19126 P
15534 O 16006 P 16036 P 16811 F 19142 P
15551 O 16008 F 16038 P 16850 P 19144 P
15580 P 16009 P 16039 P 17107 P 19158 P
15835 O 16010 FP 16040 P 17112 P 22340 P
15900 F 16014 S

Secondary: Monographs
10228 PO 12485 P 15519 O 16771 F 19135 P
10432 P 14153 PO 15523 FP 16773 PO 19679 FP
10906 P 14301 P 15543 O 16788 PO 19737 FP
10937 PO 14337 P 15545 O 16794 F 20018 F
10943 PO 15241 S 15565 O 16798 FP 20236 F
10970 P 15491 F 15570 P 16816 F 20272 FP
11076 P 15493 O 16070 P 16872 FP 20496 PO
11143 P 15498 O 16132 O 16902 FP 20503 O
12082 P 15501 O 16354 F 17012 P 20694 F
12123 P 15504 F 16457 O 17913 P 21009 FP
12440 PO 15515 FP 16473 P 18264 P 22291 P
12441 P 15517 F 16493 P 18289 P 22318 P
12442 P 15518 P 16495 P 19095 P 22322 P
12475 PO

Secondary: Inclusions
10912 P 14138 P 17638 P 19104 19945 FP
10916 P 14300 P 17683 F 19116 O 21065 O
10917 P 14363 P 17971 F 19165 F 21105 P
10921 15229 P 17999 P 19170 S 21150 F
10930 P 15497 P 18284 P 19173 S 22290 P
10988 FP 15539 P 18285 P 19182 22762 S
11002 16471 P 18286 P 19190 P 23035 O
12121 P 16851 P 18287 P 19191 O 23036 O
12459 PO 16877 P 18322 O 19192 O 23051 O
13058 P 17376 O 19094 O 19593 PO 23053 O
14135 P 17519

Secondary: Journal Articles
10239 P 11108 P 12431 O 15829 PO 16894 O
10411 P 11124 P 12452 P 15831 P 17384 O
10483 P 11441 O 12551 PO 15845 P 17425 O
10502 PO 11464 P 12555 P 15896 P 17430 PO
10900 11488 P 13093 P 15914 F 17606 O
10910 P 11493 FP 15236 P 16135 O 17916 O
10924 P 11511 P 15280 S 16153 P 17992 P
10926 S 11896 PO 15533 F 16760 O 17996 P
10929 P 11992 P 15540 P 16791 18204 P
10939 P 12100 FP 15559 P 16812 F 18243 P
10983 S 12129 P 15564 P 16874 O 18261 P
10992 PO 12427 P 15574 F 16879 F 18351 P

19102 S 19156 P 19185 20024 F 20677 O
19107 S 19157 P 19188 S 20082 O 21068 O
19125 P 19160 P 19197 F 20497 F 21122 O
19140 P 19169 PO 19325 O 20674 F 22368 P
19151 P 19179 P 19340 O

22.1 LOCAL POLITICAL AND SOCIAL CONTROLS

地方統治及社會控制

地方の政治的社会的統制

1644-1842

PRIMARY □

SECOND. 10672 P 12890 O 14096 S 15663 P
16517 P

1644-1911

PRIMARY 16049 P

SECOND. 11243 P 14158 P 16379 PO 18518 P
10646 12923 P 15346 P 17541 P 18519 P
10676 P 14101 S 15863 P 17542 P 20090 PO
11015 P

1842-1911

PRIMARY 15583 O 16048 PO 17535 O 18434 P
12919 PO 15920 P 16050 O 17689 P 19720 O
14199 15925 P 16051 O 17812 O 20702 O
15340 FP 15928 P 16086 O 18382 P 22047 P
15366 O 16047 O 16536 O

SECOND. 14400 O 16091 P 17411 P 18438 P
10513 PO 15316 O 16374 PO 17521 O 18465 O
10514 P 15325 O 16375 PO 17533 FP 18498 PO
10606 P 15345 O 16376 PO 17544 P 18859 P
10658 O 15350 O 16516 P 17553 P 18926 O
10677 P 15357 O 16539 O 18390 P 22557 O
10679 O 15361 O 16933 O 18404 P 22587 P
11186 PO 15919 PO 16934 O 18411 P 22595 P
12937 PO 15932 O 17139 O

1842-1928
(including 1644-1928)

PRIMARY 15937 P 16052 P 16101 O 16406 P

SECOND. 15943 P 17691 PO 18573 O 20389 PO
14668 O 15944 P 17758 P 20048 P 21998 P
15388 S 16227 P 18022 O

1911-1928

PRIMARY 15395 O 19453 P 19509 P 19533 P
10840 S 18596 PO 19490 PO

SECOND. 15966 FP 17578 P 17844 O 19498 P
11026 P 15969 S 17717 PO 18748 P 19499 P
13906 PO 16424 PO 17836 O 19449 P 22700 P
15450 F

1911-1949
(including 1644-1949, 1842-1949)

PRIMARY 12965 P 15959 P 16055 PO 21729 P
11021 PO 15384 PO 16053 P 18981 P

SECOND. 15377 P 15942 P 16423 PO 17423 P
10093 O 15387 PO 15946 FP 16559 P 17444 FP
10707 P 15420 PO 15949 P 16561 S 18162 P
11019 P 15642 FP 15955 P 16562 S 18304 P
11336 P 15762 P 15956 P 16612 FP 18534 PO
11382 FP 15941 P 16123 FP 17239 18732 P
14215 S

1928-1949

PRIMARY 15960 FP 16060 O 16430 P 18667 FP
13974 PO 16054 P 16061 P 16659 PO 18671 O
14754 PO 16056 F 16062 P 17573 O 18695 O
14762 P 16057 P 16063 P 18305 P 18746 O
15438 P 16058 P 16064 FP 18643 F 18749 O
15442 P 16059 P 16065 P 18658 O 21515 F

SECOND. 15067 PO 15436 F 15963 P 18703 O
10747 O 15394 O 15440 P 15971 P 19629 P
10760 P 15399 F 15443 P 16709 19638 S
11027 S 15426 S 15444 P 16718 F 19702 P
12360 P 15434 O 15870 PO 17613 F 21215 FP

1928-1972
(incl. 1644-1972, 1842-1972, 1911-1972)

PRIMARY 12426 P 15978 FP 16068 O 19081 P
10851 P 14440 S 15981 F 16128 FP 20475 O
11036 P 15459 PO 16066 O 17635 P 21421 O
12379 P 15470 S 16067 O 19077 P 21428 O
12418 FP 15474 O

SECOND. 15456 P 15976 PO 17894 P 19975 FP
10383 S 15466 O 16126 S 17895 O 20657 PO
10855 FP 15613 P 16343 P 18178 FP 20982 O
11051 15973 P 17586 P 19086 P 21426 P
11052 FP 15974 FP 17615 O 19859 FP 21538 FP
11383 P 15975 P 17648 O 19970 FP 22724 P
12378 P

1949-1972

PRIMARY: MONOGRAPHS
10953 P 15524 O 16076 P 18003 FP 20505 PO
10960 FP 15572 FP 16077 O 18289 P 20527 O
10962 16001 S 16139 O 19100 P 21433 O
11006 P 16029 S 17012 P 19131 P 22747 O
11143 P 16031 P 17593 PO 19591 O 22750 O
14337 P 16070 O 17647 P 19922 P 22763 O
15488 P 16071 FP 17674 P 20503 O 22764 O
15517 F 16072 P

PRIMARY: INCLUSIONS
11079 P 15293 16035 P 16075 P 17358 O
11127 FP 15578 P 16037 FP 16085 FP 17640 P
11443 FP 15990 P 16074 O 16994 O 19154 P
13058 P

PRIMARY: JOURNAL ARTICLES
10973 P 15986 O 16080 S 16850 P 17996 P
12529 P 16014 S 16081 P 17008 P 18335 O
14817 O 16034 P 16082 P 17597 P 19065 PO
15197 O 16038 P 16083 F 17653 O 19099 P
15496 16069 O 16084 P 17659 O 19157 P
15516 O 16073 P 16143 F 17660 P 19186 P
15535 P 16078 P 16153 P 17679 P 20117 FP
15580 P 16079 P 16781 P 17912 F 21115 O
15984 O

SECONDARY: MONOGRAPHS
10906 P 14329 P 15549 P 16011 P 17588 P
10943 PO 15100 P 15553 PO 16012 P 17909 P
10994 P 15482 O 15560 FP 16046 PO 17995 O
11094 P 15483 P 15617 F 16148 FP 18362 O
11514 P 15495 P 15991 P 16347 O 19291 P
11651 FP 15508 O 15992 P 16794 F 19713 P
12429 P 15537 P 15993 P 16841 PO 20496 PO
12524 FP 15543 O 16002 FP 16887 F 20682 P
13769 P 15544 O 16007 FP 16902 FP 22755 O

SECONDARY: INCLUSIONS
11162 P 15987 F 16997 19192 O 20667 P
11487 P 16028 FP 17340 P 19200 O 21019 O
13392 O 16033 PO 17644 F 19202 P 21026 O
15107 P 16769 P 19108 P 19319 21141 O
15303 FP 16833 P 19152 O 19661 O 22357 FP
15521 F 16851 P

SECONDARY: JOURNAL ARTICLES
10967 P 15533 F 16145 P 17606 O 19102 S
11089 P 15534 O 16478 O 17620 F 19103 O
11170 P 15551 O 16481 PO 17636 O 19125 P
11441 O 15559 P 16482 O 17637 O 19159 P
12458 O 15579 O 16831 O 17654 O 19169 PO
12513 P 15827 P 16835 P 17677 O 19179 P
12808 P 15845 P 16854 S 17678 P 19340 O
13055 P 15877 FP 16879 F 17780 O 19471 P
14516 S 16005 P 17130 PO 17901 O 19671 P
14938 O 16010 FP 17331 O 17916 O 20479 O
15008 O 16018 P 17335 PO 17994 FP 20516 P
15477 O 16020 P 17369 18327 S 21056 O
15512 O 16023 O 17403 18351 P 21114 O
15528 P 16030 P 17594 P 19057 P 22303 P
15531 O 16135 O

22.2 CUSTOMARY LAW AND DISPUTE RESOLUTION

習慣法及仲裁解決

慣習法及び紛争の解決

1644-1842

PRIMARY 15722 O 16087 P 16100 P 20035 P

SECOND. 13469 P 15752 O 19429 P 22577 P
10022 O 14183 P 17408 PO 19958 O 22635 P
10672 P 14401 P 18468 PO

1644-1911

PRIMARY 15931 O 17542 P 19748 PO 20591 PO
11243 P 16049 P 18862 P 19754 PO 20769 PO
12941 PO 16088 P 19744 20285 P 21988 P
13628 S 16098

SECOND. 11195 P 12193 PO 18384 P 19769 P
10004 PO 11197 P 12935 18459 O 19772 P
10006 S 11210 P 13484 P 18464 P 19774 P
10016 O 11211 P 14098 P 18519 P 20033 P
10441 P 11218 P 14102 P 18915 FP 20037 PO
10559 PO 11222 P 15320 PO 19209 O 20038 P
10582 PO 11227 P 15331 P 19210 20089 P
10603 P 11239 P 15661 S 19346 P 20135 PO
10616 11246 O 17816 P 19755 PO 20762 O
10666 P

1842-1911

PRIMARY 16048 PO 16099 P 18456 O 20039 O
10025 O 16086 O 16521 O 18490 P 20084 O
10056 O 16089 P 17409 FP 18509 P 20254 P
10059 O 16090 O 17521 O 18522 P 20748 O
10679 O 16091 P 17525 O 18892 P 21177 O
11181 F 16092 P 17532 O 18906 O 22532 P
12946 PO 16093 O 17548 O 18911 O 22564 P
15328 P 16094 P 17608 18922 O 22587 P
15721 O 16095 O 18390 P 19765 O 22595 P
15928 P 16096 O 18434 P 19773 PO 22600 P
15933 P 16097 O 18453 P 19778 PO 22623 P

SECONDARY: MONOGRAPHS
10019 PO 14195 P 15364 O 16910 PO 20578 O
10023 O 14584 PO 15368 FP 16912 O 20590 PO
10031 O 15316 O 15733 O 17688 O 20715 O
10043 O 15321 O 15744 O 17812 O 20782 S
10055 O 15338 P 15930 P 18378 O 22542 O
10061 O 15340 FP 16187 O 18455 S 22586 P
10275 P 15344 O 16374 PO 18491 O 22599 O
10587 PO 15351 O 16375 PO 18875 O 22601 O
10660 O 15355 O 16376 PO 18932 PO 22605 P
10677 P 15362 O 16377 O 20258 O 22612 P
11678 P 15363 O 16395 O 20287 P 22615 O
12593 PO

SECONDARY: INCLUSIONS
10658 O 11244 O 14395 P 16526 O 17550 PO
18486 P 19742 O

SECONDARY: JOURNAL ARTICLES
10273 P 14177 O 17811 O 19759 PO 22527 O
11187 PO 15348 O 17973 PO 19760 PO 22545 P
11188 P 15629 O 18440 P 19762 S 22557 O
11190 P 15862 O 18878 O 19777 O 22566 P
11192 P 16911 O 18928 O 20130 O 22570 P
12594 O 17162 P 19208 P 20290 O 22573 P
12937 PO 17540 O 19344 S 22400 O 22597 P
14094 17689 P 19694 O

1842-1928
(including 1644-1928)

PRIMARY 15388 S 16102 O 16109 PO 20047 P
11261 P 15389 PO 16103 FP 16110 P 20048 P
11305 P 15864 P 16108 PO 16267 O 21996 P
13882 O 16101 O

SECOND. 10734 O 11292 PO 14214 PO 16554 P
10071 O 11270 P 11303 S 15138 16563 O
10292 P 11271 PO 11705 PO 15378 F 17559 P
10695 P 11275 PO 12963 PO 15943 P 17691 PO
10713 P 11280 P 13522 P 15944 P 17981 P

18022 o 19715 20389 po 21504 o 22669 s
19215 o 20175 p 21311 o 22001 p 22673 p
19477 po

1911-1928

Primary 16114 p 18697 po 19966 o 22678 o
11026 p 16121 o 19514 p 20462 fp 22700 p
11356 p 16122 o 19546 p

Second. 11766 po 16296 o 19360 f 19558
10778 o 12747 o 16424 po 19450 p 19841 o
11324 p 14407 p 16963 o 19460 f 19842 p
11329 p 15143 p 18126 p 19509 p 20213 o
11352 o 15407 fp 18617 p 19533 p 22680 o
11353 p 15966 fp 18621 o

1911-1949
(including 1644-1949, 1842-1949)

Primary 12965 p 15955 p 16120 p 20061 p
10707 p 13691 p 16104 s 16123 fp 20063 p
11255 p 15375 o 16105 18541 s 20067 p
11262 p 15632 p 16106 p 18548 o 20068 p
11264 p 15941 p 16107 p 18550 p 20265 o
11265 o 15942 p 16111 s 19701 p 21313 f
11336 p 15945 p 16112 s 19782 p 21994
11369 p 15948 p 16113 s 19799 p 22667 p
11382 fp 15950 s 16115 p

Second. 11368 p 15959 p 19556 p 20046 p
10078 s 12303 fp 16055 po 19577 p 20264 o
10104 o 12370 p 16423 po 19727 s 21308 o
10702 o 12372 p 16663 p 19785 p 21312 f
10738 p 13491 po 17193 fp 19792 p 21314 f
11251 p 13749 p 17444 fp 19801 p 21315 f
11252 s 14219 po 18558 s 19840 o 21368 o
11272 p 14479 po 18585 o 19964 p 21501 s
11273 14734 p 18622 o 20009 s 21728
11293 p 15428 o 18636 p 20010 p 22457 f
11311 15762 p 18953 o 20013 p 22654 p
11333 p 15946 fp 19245 o 20045 p

1928-1949

Primary 15960 fp 16117 p 17416 o 19267 p
11346 p 15971 p 16118 f 18643 f 19702 p
15394 o 16057 p 16119 p 18746 o 20453 p
15430 p 16060 o 16430 p 18994 o 20940 s
15431 p 16116 o 16619 f

Second. 11340 p 15410 o 15965 p 18717 p
10096 o 11380 o 15411 p 16672 f 18751 s
10100 o 11381 p 15423 17415 o 19011 f
10754 s 11767 po 15434 o 18028 o 19555 fp
10804 o 13040 o 15441 p 18682 p 19813 p
10839 o 13965 o 15957 o 18707 o 22681 fp
11326 po 14478 fp 15963 p 18716 o 22710 o
11331 p 15399 f

1928-1972
(incl. 1644-1972, 1842-1972, 1911-1972)

Primary 11407 s 15981 f 17581 19891 p
10301 fp 11415 po 16068 o 19042 po 20069 po
11044 po 11605 o 16124 fp 19077 p 20662 s
11388 p 12378 p 16125 p 19089 f 21196 f
11396 p 14514 16126 s 19859 fp 21426 p
11398 p 15452 po 16127 s 19874 p 21529 po
11402 p 15461 p 16128 fp 19878 po 22736 po

Second. 11412 p 15643 fp 19710 p 21410 fp
10110 po 11414 p 15645 p 19873 s 21416 o
10114 p 11418 p 15973 p 19887 p 21421 o
10117 po 11607 p 15974 fp 19892 p 21538 fp
10865 p 12405 p 15979 p 19894 fp 21853 p
11036 p 15173 o 16451 19897 p 22198 o
11051 15192 o 16454 s 19975 fp 22238 p
11383 p 15455 fp 17313 o 20071 p 22264 p
11386 p 15463 fp 17615 o 20113 o 22728 o
11390 p 15466 o 18820 o 20114 o 22732 fp
11405 s 15468 o 18832 20115 s 22735 s
11408 p 15470 s 19039 20231 po 22740 p
11410 p 15474 o 19053 p 20663 p

1949-1972

Primary: Monographs
11076 p 14033 p 16138 p 16146 f 16841 po
11138 f 15550 o 16139 o 16148 fp 19713 p
11514 p 16076 p 16140 p 16150 p 22744 o
11534 p 16132 o 16141 p 16155 o

Primary: Inclusions
11442 fp 11494 p 15209 p 16075 p 17971 f
11443 fp 11530 po 15908 p 16152 o 21432 p
11487 p 14302 p 16032 po 17638 p

Primary: Journal Articles
11071 p 11501 o 16134 f 16149 o 19925 f
11150 p 12531 p 16135 o 16151 p 19950 p
11424 o 15225 p 16136 o 16153 p 19954 o
11441 o 15989 f 16137 po 16154 p 20499 p
11455 p 15999 p 16142 p 16345 o 20516 p
11460 p 16082 p 16143 f 16855 o 20517 f
11467 p 16129 16144 p 17592 p 20532 p
11477 16130 o 16145 p 19383 p 21588 f
11493 fp 16131 o 16147 po 19912 p 22021 p
11499 o 16133 f

Secondary: Monographs
10135 o 14139 o 15572 fp 17593 po 20244 p
10139 p 15214 po 15575 o 17748 o 20478 f
10263 p 15230 p 15992 p 18003 fp 20503 o
10938 p 15245 po 15993 p 18277 p 20522 fp
10945 p 15254 o 16007 fp 18299 p 20680 f
10960 fp 15481 o 16013 p 19591 o 21569 p
10994 p 15493 o 16071 fp 19737 fp 21578 o
11423 p 15508 o 16077 o 19738 f 22500 o
11439 p 15526 o 16887 f 19917 p 22747 o
11466 p 15568 p 17006 p 20236 f 22751 o
11495 p

Secondary: Inclusions
11134 po 14363 p 15987 f 18219 p 18349 p
12801 p 15222 p 16033 po 18346 p 18843 o
13058 p 15243 o 16035 p 18347 p 20081 p
13099 p 15291 p 16085 fp 18348 p 20120 o
14147 p 15296 p

Secondary: Journal Articles
10465 p 11431 p 12555 p 15534 o 17623 o
10929 p 11445 p 12825 p 15552 o 17639 p
10951 p 11456 p 12831 p 16027 o 17660 p
10955 11483 o 13093 p 16038 p 17912 f
11090 s 11485 p 13106 o 16044 f 18245 p
11118 p 11486 p 13354 p 16355 p 19942 o
11121 p 11488 p 14531 p 16472 o 20488 p
11170 p 11527 15196 p 16792 p 20523 p
11419 p 11529 15514 o 17000 p 22496 f
11422 o 11915 p 15533 f 17430 po 23021 f

23 Folk Religion

民間之宗教信仰 民間宗教

1644-1842

Primary 16218 o 18014 p 22405 o 22420 p
16185 p 16223 p 18916 p

Second. 11675 o 17657 o 18864 s 20558 s
10020 po 12179 s 17820 o 18897 p 20563 s
10022 o 15305 o 18013 p 18935 p 21661 po
10580 o 15306 o 18476 s 18936 p 22555 o
11536 o 15310 o 18478 s

1644-1911

Primary 16171 po 16194 o 16389 po 18939 po
10582 po 16173 p 16196 p 18010 p 19776 fp
11542 fp 16175 o 16200 po 18493 po 20545 fp
11544 s 16179 o 16204 p 18849 po 21610 f
11550 fp 16181 o 16206 po 18853 po 21613
11558 po 16184 p 16207 p 18865 po 21617 p
11562 po 16188 p 16208 po 18867 p 21627
12193 po 16189 fp 16212 o 18881 o 21645 p
15322 o 16190 fp 16213 s 18902 po 22394 po
16161 po 16191 16217 fp 18910 22409 p
16162 po 16192 p 16221 po 18927 po 22414 s
16163 po 16193 po

Second. 10014 o 10046 o 10550 p 11194 o
10012 p 10028 po 10058 po 10560 p 11539 fp
11556 p 15927 p 18900 po 20149 s 21612 p
11570 p 16049 p 18915 fp 20284 p 21641 fp
11574 po 16542 po 18920 fp 20285 p 21642 fp
12941 po 17920 o 18945 p 20720 po 21651 o
15318 o 18012 p 19748 po 20741 p 21656 p
15320 po 18507 p 19755 po 20769 po 21697 po
15354 p 18879 p 19992 s 21183 po 22059 p
15729 po 18886 p 20083 p 21437 p 22386 p
15743 o 18890 s

1842-1911

Primary: Monographs
10049 po 15364 o 16167 o 16219 o 18872 p
10057 o 15367 o 16169 o 16378 o 18889 o
10318 o 15726 o 16183 o 16396 o 18903 p
15316 o 15744 o 16186 o 17662 o 18932 po
15317 o 16158 o 16187 o 18491 o 21990 o
15336 o 16164 s 16210 o 18856 o 22383 po
15361 o

Primary: Inclusions
16165 o 16166 o 16203 o 16526 o 17626 o
21606 p

Primary: Journal Articles
15583 o 16170 o 16197 o 16215 o 18894 o
15629 o 16172 o 16198 po 16216 o 20384 o
15735 o 16174 o 16199 po 16220 po 20569 o
15862 o 16176 o 16201 o 16222 o 20592
16156 o 16177 o 16202 f 16224 o 21689 o
16157 o 16178 o 16205 16934 o 22400 o
16159 o 16180 o 16209 o 17535 o 22408 o
16160 f 16182 o 16211 o 18471 s 22412 o
16168 o 16195 p 16214 p 18473 o

Secondary: Monographs
10002 o 13866 o 15360 o 18908 o 21286 p
10018 po 14584 po 15362 o 19719 p 21624 o
10047 o 14597 o 16090 o 20003 o 21980 o
10048 o 15321 o 17649 o 20128 o 22026 p
10055 o 15325 o 18364 p 20137 o 22067 o
10056 o 15332 o 18379 po 20275 o 22562 o
10059 o 15338 p 18447 o 20379 o 22599 o
10064 o 15350 o 18455 s 20579 o 22615 o
12569 o 15355 o 18852 po 20782 s 22623 p

Secondary: Inclusions
10658 o 15358 o 15753 o 20279 o 22618 o
14400 o 15359 o 19720 o

Secondary: Journal Articles
11565 o 16935 o 18504 p 19343 s 20777 o
13801 s 17689 p 18845 o 19746 po 21162 o
14590 o 17924 p 18884 o 19759 po 21171 o
15308 o 17925 o 18907 o 20254 p 21182
15348 o 17926 o 18923 p 20542 o 22384 o
15365 o 17928 po 18926 o 20544 f 22397 fp
16508 o 18301 s 18934 o 20746 o 22582 o
16540 o 18383 p

1842-1928
(including 1644-1928)

Primary 16232 fp 16247 po 16268 po 21186 s
11575 f 16233 f 16250 o 16269 s 21719 p
11577 f 16234 f 16252 po 16273 o 21723 po
11581 po 16235 o 16254 p 16275 o 21742 s
11683 o 16236 o 16256 o 16276 o 21755 p
15374 f 16237 o 16257 o 16277 p 21772 s
15378 f 16238 o 16259 fp 16281 p 21774
15379 o 16239 o 16260 o 16284 o 21782 p
15383 o 16240 o 16261 s 18570 p 21791 po
15673 o 16241 o 16262 p 18957 o 21798 p
16226 po 16242 o 16264 po 18959 o 21799 o
16227 p 16243 o 16265 o 18966 o 22422 fp
16228 po 16244 o 16266 o 18983 fp 22423 po
16230 o 16245 o 16267 o 20005 s 22443 p
16231 fp 16246 o

Second. 16552 o 20008 s 21502 21779 o
10069 o 17691 po 20291 o 21504 o 21781 s
10071 o 17981 p 20618 po 21735 po 21784 fp
11583 p 18532 o 20619 o 21739 p 21794 o
11589 p 18968 po 20795 o 21752 po 21998 p
11591 18978 po 20802 po 21754 p 22001 p
12963 po 20006 po 21189 po 21765 po 22658 s
16103 fp 20007 o 21307 o

1911-1928

1911-1949
(including 1644-1949, 1842-1949)

1928-1949

1928-1972
(incl. 1644-1972, 1842-1972, 1911-1972)

1949-1972

24 LOCAL ECONOMIC SYSTEMS
地方經濟 地方経済

1644-1842

1644-1911

1842-1911

1842-1928
(including 1644-1928)

1911-1928

1911-1949
(including 1644-1949, 1842-1949)

1928-1949

1928-1972
(incl. 1644-1972, 1842-1972, 1911-1972)

1949-1972

15846 F 16028 FP 16886 F 17680 F 19157 P
15854 O 16036 P 17012 P 17684 P 19184 PO
15894 O 16083 F 17107 P 17913 P 19185
15896 P 16139 O 17328 O 17917 P 19291 P
15910 O 16152 O 17344 O 18289 P 19336 O
15999 P 16786 F 17384 O 18333 O 19943 F
16002 FP 16795 P 17391 P 18354 O 20024 F
16019 P 16873 FP 17502 O 19110 O 20074 FP
16027 O 16874 O 17639 P 19156 P 22500 O

24.1 Local Agrarian Economies

地方農業 地方農業

1644-1842

Primary 15657 16369 O 16514 P 16518 O
13814 S 15663 P 16507 PO 16517 P 16529 P

Second. 15306 O 17173 P 18470 P 22627 S
10032 O 16218 O 17822 O 20536 O

1644-1911

Primary 15660 16515 P 16524 O 17153 PO
15334 PO 15661 S 16519 S 16542 PO 17627 P
15354 P 15665 P 16523 O 16543 PO 17816 P
15659 PO

Second. 11663 O 15346 P 15658 P 17175 P
10327 P 12907 O 15353 PO 15863 P 19718 P

1842-1911

Primary 15340 FP 16505 O 16525 P 16537 O
10319 S 15358 O 16506 O 16526 O 16538 O
10321 O 15584 P 16508 O 16527 O 16539 O
10330 P 15656 O 16509 FP 16528 O 16540 O
10668 P 15718 PO 16510 P 16530 P 16541 P
11232 FP 15726 O 16511 O 16531 O 16544 P
11678 P 15750 O 16512 O 16532 O 16911 O
12919 PO 15862 O 16513 O 16533 O 17137 PO
12924 O 16048 PO 16516 P 16534 PO 17169 O
13126 O 16383 PO 16520 O 16535 PO 17662 O
15328 P 16394 P 16521 O 16536 O 20573 O
15330 FP 16399 O 16522 O

Second. 15314 S 16220 PO 16928 O 17930 O
10278 O 15317 O 16222 O 16929 O 18868 PO
10332 O 15351 O 16376 PO 16930 O 18875 O
10566 P 15355 O 16380 O 16932 O 18889 O
11181 F 15368 FP 16384 FP 16935 O 19746 PO
11659 P 15715 O 16388 O 17156 PO 20254 P
11679 P 15717 O 16396 O 17159 O 20537 P
12904 O 15732 O 16912 O 17409 FP 20542 O
12908 P 15744 O 16915 F 17410 PO 20556 O
12912 S 15747 O 16920 O 17411 P 20583 O
12925 PO 15753 O 16922 O 17547 P 22522 O
14554 PO 15926 P 16923 O 17548 O 22553 O
15308 O 15928 P 16926 O 17817 O 22618 O

1842-1928
(including 1644-1928)

Primary 16103 FP 16552 O 16558 F 17441 PO
10340 PO 16406 P 16553 FP 16563 O 20047 P
12221 P 16546 S 16554 P 17189 O 20048 P
15673 O 16548 O 16555 PO

Second. 12663 P 15864 P 16403 P 17191 F
11683 O 15667 S 16261 S 16404 O 19726 O
12214 P

1911-1928

Primary 16573 16630 F 16667 F 16699 F
10380 PO 16578 16642 F 16669 PO 16712 F
12319 FP 16579 P 16643 FP 16680 O 16968 P
12993 FP 16582 16644 FP 16684 O 17067 O
13277 F 16589 F 16645 F 16685 P 17068 P
16419 O 16590 F 16648 O 16687 F 17257 O
16445 O 16591 F 16651 O 16691 P 17306 FP
16565 16593 F 16657 P 16692 F 19442 PO
16566 16594 F 16664 PO 16695 F 20641 F
16568 P 16627 O

Second. 15413 O 16412 16961 P 17873 PO
10294 P 15418 F 16426 P 17213 P 19259 P
12253 F 15595 S 16433 FP 17482 O 19449 P
12254 FP 15686 P 16436 PO 17848 O 19455 P
12979 O 15768 O 16442 P 17871 FP 20645 F
12988 PO 15769 O 16945 O

1911-1949
(including 1644-1949, 1842-1949)

Primary 16415 16562 S 16633 FP 17239
11746 P 16545 FP 16572 P 16639 P 17241 P
11747 FP 16547 S 16581 16660 P 17274 FP
15672 O 16549 P 16584 P 16663 P 17282
15679 FP 16550 P 16605 P 16668 P 17298 P
15761 P 16551 P 16611 P 16671 O 17307 S
15763 O 16556 FP 16612 FP 16675 P 17460 FP
16120 P 16557 FP 16613 FP 16689 O 17666 FP
16299 F 16559 P 16614 O 17050 P 17832 O
16408 FP 16560 FP 16621 FP 17065 O 19213 P
16410 P 16561 S 16624 FP

Second. 11795 O 16977 O 17474 P 19618 P
10345 FP 11837 O 17029 FP 17769 P 19619 O
10700 PO 13179 P 17079 FP 18131 P 19632 S
10707 P 15408 F 17095 O 18534 PO 19962 S
10725 P 15599 P 17234 S 18622 O 20612 FP
10781 P 15691 P 17260 F 18732 P 22452 FP
11588 FP 16449 PO 17444 FP 18981 P 22466 O
11726 S 16976 PO 17456 O 18989 FP

1928-1949

Primary: Monographs
11760 PO 16431 FP 16628 O 16710 P 17858 O
15406 F 16598 F 16636 PO 16711 P 17872 P
15409 P 16608 F 16637 P 16717 F 17891 O
16061 P 16609 P 16640 PO 17091 F 18643 F
16062 P 16617 PO 16650 F 17846 F 18746 O
16425 F

Primary: Inclusions
12272 S 16623 FP 16681 O 16718 F 17417 O
15957 O 16626 PO 16690 FP 16721 O 17462 O
16607 O 16631 F 16693 FP 17057 O 17634
16618 F 16638 PO 16694 O 17287 O 17665
16619 F 16658 O 16709 17295 O 17854 F
16620 FP 16661 O 16714 F 17415 O 17860 O
16622 FP 16666 F

Primary: Journal Articles
10368 16575 16610 P 16670 O 16705 F
10767 O 16576 16615 O 16672 F 16706 F
11722 16577 16616 PO 16673 O 16707 F
11723 P 16580 16625 F 16674 P 16708 F
12255 FP 16583 16629 P 16676 F 16713 F
12354 O 16585 P 16632 F 16677 F 16715 O
13203 P 16586 P 16634 O 16678 F 16716 F
13541 P 16587 16635 P 16679 O 16719 F
15426 S 16588 16641 PO 16682 F 16720 F
15772 O 16592 F 16646 F 16683 PO 16722 F
16411 FP 16595 F 16647 O 16686 O 16723 F
16422 16596 F 16649 O 16688 O 17046
16432 PO 16597 F 16652 F 16696 17211
16443 O 16599 FP 16653 FP 16697 F 17258 O
16564 16600 F 16654 F 16698 F 17664 F
16567 P 16601 FP 16655 FP 16700 F 17667 F
16569 16602 F 16656 FP 16701 F 17668 F
16570 16603 P 16659 PO 16702 F 17847 O
16571 P 16604 O 16662 F 16703 F 17875 O
16574 P 16606 F 16665 FP 16704 F

Second. 14427 P 15785 O 17458 F 18695 O
10816 F 14771 F 16063 P 17461 F 18703 O
11753 O 15398 O 16065 P 17479 FP 18712 P
11769 PO 15414 PO 16418 F 17484 FP 18749 O
11789 15415 PO 16427 O 17492 PO 19633 O
11818 P 15421 O 16435 P 17663 F 19728 F
12256 F 15432 F 16437 O 17825 P 19823 O
12294 15434 O 16438 P 17845 O 20198 F
12991 F 15440 P 16448 O 17849 O 20262 F
13221 O 15442 P 16450 P 17868 F 20840 F
13287 O 15598 FP 16957 F 18305 P 22453 F
13540 P 15773 P 16966 O 18595 P 22693 O
13965 O 15777 O 17418 FP 18690 P 22701
13974 PO 15779 O

1928-1972
(incl. 1644-1972, 1842-1972, 1911-1972)

Primary 15192 O 16727 FP 16741 P 17774 FP
10382 P 15457 P 16728 P 16742 P 17897 F
10385 FP 15459 PO 16729 FP 16743 19077 P
10387 S 15463 FP 16730 16744 P 19079 F
10392 P 15469 P 16731 16745 P 19080 F
10882 P 15697 FP 16732 O 16746 FP 19082 PO
11843 P 15797 FP 16733 P 16747 P 19085 O
11851 P 15802 FP 16734 P 16748 P 19088 F
11856 P 15811 P 16735 P 16749 O 19089 F
11873 P 15975 P 16736 P 16750 F 19090 FP
12400 P 16456 F 16737 P 16751 S 19466 F
13053 FP 16724 16738 FP 16752 P 19864 FP
13301 FP 16725 F 16739 P 16753 PO 19970 FP
13313 P 16726 P 16740 FP 17579 O 21827 FP
13315 P

Second. 13300 P 15600 P 16452 PO 17949 P
10301 FP 13312 P 15601 P 17312 O 17989 S
10303 P 15451 FP 15606 P 17313 O 19980 FP
10398 FP 15452 PO 15800 O 17320 P 21393 O
10455 O 15455 FP 15808 17424 P 21428 O
10855 FP 15464 P 15810 FP 17669 FP 22724 P
11863 P 15470 S 16068 O 17895 O 22732 FP
13052 P 15471 P 16127 S 17896 F

1949-1972

Primary: Monographs
10401 F 15518 P 16776 P 16825 FP 16892 F
10421 FP 15523 FP 16777 P 16826 F 16898 S
10428 FP 15524 O 16778 P 16827 P 16899 P
12069 P 15527 O 16782 16841 PO 16902 FP
12150 P 15850 FP 16785 F 16844 P 17128 F
12157 15991 P 16786 F 16845 F 17647 P
12175 P 15992 P 16787 FP 16849 FP 17681 F
13079 FP 15993 P 16788 PO 16852 O 17910 F
13112 P 16046 PO 16790 P 16858 PO 17913 P
15002 FP 16070 O 16794 F 16865 F 17963 F
15481 O 16077 O 16795 P 16866 F 19095 P
15483 P 16457 O 16797 P 16867 F 19105 FP
15493 O 16488 PO 16798 FP 16868 F 19110 O
15495 P 16495 P 16800 O 16869 F 19131 P
15499 PO 16756 O 16806 F 16870 F 19153 F
15504 F 16763 O 16814 F 16871 F 19184 PO
15505 F 16768 P 16816 F 16872 FP 19663 PO
15507 P 16771 F 16818 F 16886 F 19737 FP
15511 O 16773 PO 16820 F 16887 F 20080 P
15515 FP

Primary: Inclusions
11959 PO 16461 O 16802 16853 O 17382 O
13102 P 16462 O 16803 O 16860 O 17683 F
15539 P 16465 O 16804 F 16862 19093 P
15819 F 16466 O 16821 O 16875 O 19115 F
15820 PO 16468 P 16833 P 16877 P 19117 O
15847 O 16474 O 16838 P 16881 O 19127 O
15883 16484 PO 16840 P 16883 F 19154 P
15884 16769 P 16842 O 16891 F 19165 F
15894 O 16779 16848 P 16893 F 19167 O
15899 O 16799 16851 P 16900 O 19200 O
15910 O

Primary: Journal Articles
10416 S 15878 F 16765 O 16811 F 16850 P
11130 P 15886 S 16766 O 16812 F 16854 S
11926 P 15896 P 16767 F 16813 PO 16855 O
11985 P 15985 O 16770 O 16815 O 16856 PO
12106 P 16000 O 16772 F 16817 16857 F
12135 P 16017 P 16774 O 16819 F 16859 P
12143 P 16458 O 16775 O 16822 P 16861
12146 P 16459 F 16780 P 16823 S 16863 P
12152 P 16460 P 16781 P 16824 16864 S
15272 O 16476 O 16783 PO 16828 P 16873 FP
15477 O 16477 P 16784 O 16829 P 16874 O
15502 O 16503 P 16789 P 16830 16876 P
15503 O 16504 16791 16831 O 16878 O
15510 O 16754 O 16792 P 16832 S 16879 F
15525 O 16755 O 16793 16834 O 16880 O
15528 P 16757 O 16796 16835 P 16882 O
15534 O 16758 O 16801 F 16836 P 16884 S
15562 O 16759 O 16805 S 16837 P 16885 P
15564 P 16760 O 16807 P 16839 P 16888 O
15577 O 16761 O 16808 O 16843 S 16889
15813 F 16762 O 16809 P 16846 O 16890 FP
15814 O 16764 O 16810 PO 16847 O 16894 O

16895 o 17327 o 17677 o 19158 p 19186 p
16896 p 17329 o 17685 f 19159 p 19196
16897 o 17373 p 19098 o 19163 fp 19375 p
16901 f 17518 p 19125 p 19164 po 20072 f
17107 p 17671 o 19126 p 19177 p 20671 o
17130 po 17675 f 19151 p 19185 21046 o

SECONDARY: MONOGRAPHS
10436 p 12149 p 15498 o 15572 fp 17674 p
10904 f 12174 po 15519 o 15655 fp 17779 p
11105 p 12475 po 15520 p 15890 p 17995 o
11138 f 13081 p 15530 f 15897 o 19100 p
11143 p 13113 fp 15543 o 16001 s 19309 p
11161 p 13602 p 15545 o 16031 p 19679 fp
11651 fp 15482 o 15549 p 16463 p 20079 p
11905 p 15486 fp 15553 po 17387 p 20236 f
11984 p 15488 p 15557 o 17588 p 22749 p
12070 p 15491 f 15565 o 17589 f

SECONDARY: INCLUSIONS
11173 15843 o 17347 o 19094 o 19152 o
12017 p 15849 o 17355 p 19106 p 19180 o
13059 f 15885 17365 p 19109 o 19191 o
14839 f 15895 17376 o 19113 o 19192 o
14946 po 15908 p 17400 o 19114 o 19193 o
15500 o 15998 o 17646 p 19116 o 21141 o
15521 f 17110 17787 o 19118 o 21152 o
15542 17122 o 17793 o 19147 o 21905 f
15818 p 17343 o 17971 f 19148 o

SECONDARY: JOURNAL ARTICLES
10461 p 15490 o 15857 p 17007 p 17908 o
10939 p 15496 15880 o 17326 o 17966 o
11904 p 15516 o 15882 17330 o 18297 p
11964 p 15529 o 15887 f 17332 o 18335 o
12011 p 15535 p 15900 f 17334 o 19140 p
12037 p 15551 o 15983 o 17353 o 19160 p
12083 p 15554 o 15984 o 17393 o 19179 p
12136 p 15555 o 16005 p 17620 f 19195 f
12137 p 15573 f 16009 p 17623 o 19672 o
12144 p 15574 f 16470 p 17670 o 20082 o
13083 f 15620 p 16478 o 17678 p 20686 fp
13450 o 15815 o 16480 fp 17680 f 21029 fp
14815 o 15829 po 16498 p 17682 p 21254 p
14996 o 15845 p 16499 s 17789 o 21906 f
15478 o 15852 fp 16992 17901 o 22301 p
15479 o 15853 o

24.2 LOCAL TRANSPORT AND COMMUNICATIONS
地方交通 地方交通

1644-1842

PRIMARY □

SECOND. 15306 o 16218 o 16529 p 17172 s
11675 o 15722 o 16514 p 17140 po

1644-1911

PRIMARY 15353 po 15729 po 16918 16924 o
17148 po 17927 fp

SECOND. 15327 po 15626 o 15741 p 17627 p
12907 o 15334 po 15627 p 16524 o 20153 o
15313 po 15341 o 15727 po 17028 p 20548 s
15318 o 15346 p

1842-1911

PRIMARY: MONOGRAPHS
10321 o 16376 po 16910 po 16928 o 20578 o
10328 o 16377 o 16912 o 16933 o 22542 o
15367 o 16383 po 16913 o 18491 o 22553 o
15713 16384 fp 16914 o 18889 o 22612 p
16375 po 16395 o 16917 o

PRIMARY: INCLUSIONS
10332 o 15717 o 16915 f 16926 o 16930 o
12943 po 15753 o 16920 o 16927 o 16931 o
13126 o 16512 o 16925 po 16929 o 17554 po
15715 o

PRIMARY: JOURNAL ARTICLES
10319 s 11679 p 12882 po 12885 po 12892 o
11660 p 12881 po 12884 po 12887 po 12912 s
12919 po 15862 o 16905 p 16919 o 17025 o
12937 po 16390 o 16906 o 16921 p 17548 o
15308 o 16392 o 16907 po 16922 o 17919 o
15712 s 16399 o 16908 o 16923 o 20542 o
15718 po 16508 o 16909 o 16932 o 21438 po
15731 o 16903 p 16911 o 16934 o 22539 p
15732 o 16904 p 16916 o 16935 o

SECONDARY: MONOGRAPHS
10317 o 15332 o 15734 o 17141 p 18498 po
10566 p 15339 o 15740 o 17143 p 18524 p
10653 p 15340 fp 15929 o 17158 o 18875 o
14157 o 15345 o 16378 o 17161 p 20565 po
14187 p 15349 o 16381 o 17169 o 20579 o
15316 o 15362 o 16388 o 17662 o 20600 o
15319 o 15721 o 16396 o 18490 p

SECONDARY: INCLUSIONS
10324 o 15750 o 16371 po 20551 o 22618 o
15366 o 16166 o 16539 o 22523 o

SECONDARY: JOURNAL ARTICLES
10274 o 12917 po 15312 o 16092 p 18087 p
10668 p 12924 o 15335 o 16373 o 18453 p
11659 p 12925 po 15342 o 16393 po 18895 o
12883 po 12936 po 15365 o 17159 o 20541 o
12889 o 12939 o 15583 o 17410 po 22506 o
12891 o 12942 o 15748 o 17533 fp 22604 p
12916 o 15129 o 16047 o 17817 o

1842-1928
(including 1644-1928)

PRIMARY 12966 po 15670 p 16553 fp 17182 po
10340 po 13872 16403 p 16938 f 18956 po
12953 po 15633 po 16552 o

SECOND. 13522 p 15767 o 17560 p 19219 s
10708 p 15381 p 15944 p 17630 p 20795 o
12954 po 15389 po 16404 o 17661 p 22673 p
12969 po 15673 o 16563 o

1911-1928

PRIMARY 15413 o 16944 p 16961 p 18026 p
12974 p 15872 o 16945 o 16963 o 20633 o
12979 o 16419 o 16950 o 16968 p 20914 o
13001 o 16445 o 16958 o 16971 o

SECOND. 15143 p 16578 17066 p 17878 o
11594 o 15427 o 16594 f 17232 po 18773 p
12749 o 15690 p 16643 fp 17243 o 18992 fp
12988 po 15769 o 16648 o 17253 p 19511 o
13007 po 15775 f 16651 o 17265 p 19516 s
13538 o 16413 o 16669 po 17713 fp 21816 p
13713 16436 po 16691 p 17848 o 22445 o
14743 f 16447 o 17051 p 17856 f

1911-1949
(including 1644-1949, 1842-1949)

PRIMARY 13015 p 16940 o 16953 p 17094 f
10343 15385 po 16941 p 16959 17095 o
10352 p 15765 s 16942 po 16962 o 17234 s
10725 p 16410 p 16943 16976 po 17857 f
11706 p 16421 16947 fp 16977 o 18019
11837 o 16936 p 16951 po 16978 o 19228 f
12684 fp 16937 fp 16952 p 17052 po 19523 f
12699 16939 o

SECOND. 12649 15679 fp 16401 fp 17054 fp
10086 po 13019 p 15689 p 16405 p 17186 fp
10339 o 13150 fp 15756 s 16407 p 17208 o
10344 13224 fp 15758 po 16408 fp 17260 f
10345 fp 13227 p 15759 p 16449 po 18981 p
10366 15377 p 15761 p 16621 fp 19394 p
11020 15380 15762 p 16668 p 19620 fp
11588 fp 15384 po 15766 s 17030 fp 22801 o
11795 o 15599 p 16400 p

1928-1949

PRIMARY 16061 p 16954 p 16965 f 16973 fp
10368 16062 p 16955 p 16966 o 16974 o
11025 p 16443 o 16956 fp 16967 po 16975 p
13221 o 16946 o 16957 f 16969 o 16979 o
15404 o 16948 o 16960 s 16970 o 16980 p
15417 o 16949 o 16964 o 16972 fp 22460 o
15773 p

SECOND. 13974 po 16063 p 16649 o 17473 f
10358 s 14712 p 16064 fp 16715 o 17667 f
10767 o 15394 o 16307 f 17043 o 17732 f
10831 p 15409 p 16418 f 17062 f 17838 o
11031 p 15437 po 16422 17072 f 17849 o
11722 15688 p 16431 fp 17082 o 17858 o
11753 o 15772 o 16432 po 17091 f 18694 f
11769 po 15774 16441 o 17225 po 19258
11787 o 15778 o 16597 f 17242 f 19264 f
11789 15784 po 16598 f 17261 p 19555 fp
12991 f 15870 po 16599 fp 17267 o 19648 o
13196 o 15971 p 16622 fp 17273 f 20863 o
13235 o 16057 p 16640 po

1928-1972
(incl. 1644-1972, 1842-1972, 1911-1972)

PRIMARY 10398 fp 16738 fp 16984 fp 17103 fp
10382 p 15469 p 16981 fp 16985 p 17954
10385 fp 15789 16982 po 16986 fp 22724 p
10387 s 15792 fp 16983 p 16987 s

SECOND. 13301 fp 15697 fp 15805 po 15811 p
10392 p 15452 po 15793 fp 15806 p 16732 o
10394 fp 15461 p 15794 fp 15807 p 17892 p
11044 po 15467 po 15802 fp 15810 fp 18313 p
13051 p 15472 p

1949-1972

PRIMARY 16472 o 16996 s 17006 p 17015 o
10904 f 16878 o 16997 17007 p 17016 o
10977 po 16988 o 16998 po 17008 p 17017 o
11959 po 16989 o 16999 o 17009 p 17365 p
12150 p 16990 p 17000 p 17010 p 18321 o
12157 16991 f 17001 f 17011 o 19679 fp
15651 p 16992 17002 fp 17012 p 20308 f
15817 16993 p 17003 p 17013 p 20347 f
15836 16994 o 17004 p 17014 p 20668 o
15877 fp 16995 p 17005 o

SECONDARY: MONOGRAPHS
10175 o 12174 po 15616 f 16786 f 20688 o
10306 po 13079 fp 15655 fp 16787 fp 20699 o
10401 f 15254 o 15708 fp 16800 o 21552 f
10421 fp 15481 o 15850 fp 16871 f 21574 fp
11080 p 15482 o 16007 fp 17362 p 22500 o
11138 f 15518 p 16076 p 17386 fp 22747 o
12069 p 15519 o 16139 o 20018 f 22755 o
12149 p 15520 p 16495 p 20368 f

SECONDARY: INCLUSIONS
12017 p 15497 p 15854 o 16075 p 17376 o
12863 p 15650 p 15859 fp 16484 po 20323 o
14844 o 15844 15860 o 16799 20697 p
15303 fp 15847 o 15884

SECONDARY: JOURNAL ARTICLES
11926 p 15478 o 15841 o 16489 o 19125 p
12135 p 15492 o 15845 p 16796 19325 o
12136 p 15563 po 15852 fp 16836 p 19671 p
13083 f 15579 o 15857 p 16837 p 20330 f
13095 p 15620 p 15989 f 16839 p 20346 f
14817 o 15647 p 16042 f 17616 p 20351 f
15263 p 15822 po 16135 o 17749 o 20352 f
15302 o 15832 o 16458 o 18836 f 21020 f
15477 o 15838 f 16477 p 19065 po

24.3 LOCAL COMMERCE AND SERVICES
地方商業 地方商業

1644-1842

PRIMARY 12928 p 17140 po 17408 po 22627 s
12901 p 17024 o 17173 p 17658 p

SECOND. 15305 o 17144 p 17820 o 19205 p
10580 o 15722 o 17172 s 17822 o 22511 o

1644-1911
Primary 12913 P 12948 P 17021 O 17028 P
17652 O 19209 O
Second. 13629 PO 15627 P 16049 P 17627 P
10327 P 15334 PO 15729 PO 17147 P 19346 P
10333 P 15626 O 15743 O 17175 P 19351 P
12947 P

1842-1911
Primary 15726 O 16380 O 17020 O 17608
10321 O 15735 O 16392 O 17022 PO 17662 O
12580 PO 15737 P 16505 O 17023 O 20538 S
12889 O 15747 O 16534 PO 17025 O 20540 O
12893 PO 15753 O 16917 O 17026 O 20557 O
12902 O 15929 O 16926 O 17027 O 20585 O
12916 O 16187 O 16934 O 17158 O 21655 O
12944 PO 16373 O 17018 PO 17533 FP 22508 O
15365 O 16378 O 17019 PO
Second. 15345 O 15925 P 16531 O 17176 PO
10319 S 15355 O 16048 PO 16539 O 17431 P
10334 O 15359 O 16381 O 16541 P 17548 O
11181 F 15361 O 16387 O 16912 O 18889 O
11679 P 15363 O 16390 O 16913 O 19207 O
12180 PO 15367 O 16395 O 16920 O 19343 S
12903 O 15710 16396 O 16927 O 20535 O
12908 P 15712 S 16399 O 16933 O 20550 O
12919 PO 15717 O 16511 O 16935 O 20556 O
15311 O 15734 O 16513 O 17137 PO 20580 O
15314 S 15740 O 16516 P 17152 PO 20601 O
15329 O 15744 O 16522 O 17167 P 22047 P
15339 O

1842-1928
(including 1644-1928)
Primary 12954 PO 15371 PO 15633 PO 17661 P
12952 PO 12958 P 15390 O 17191 F 17824 P
12953 PO 12969 PO
Second. 12955 PO 15767 O 16103 FP 17560 P
12208 13170 P 15864 P 16406 P 17981 P

1911-1928
Primary 15769 O 16664 PO 17067 O 17268 O
12253 F 15770 O 16687 F 17068 P 17611 O
12993 FP 16413 O 17041 P 17085 O 19231 O
13006 P 16433 FP 17048 P 17221 19266 P
13029 S 16442 P 17051 P 17253 P 19360 F
15422 O 16648 O 17055 O 17254 P 20631 O
15450 F 16657 P 17066 P
Second. 15413 O 16582 16691 P 19248 O
12988 PO 16121 O 16593 F 16712 F 19251 P
12997 S 16412 16627 O 17223 19259 P
13001 O 16434 P 16642 F 17270 F 19359 S
13012 P 16445 O 16645 F 17296 O 19560 P
13260 P 16447 O 16684 O 17713 FP 20635 PO
13713 16566 16685 P 17877 F 20641 F

1911-1949
(including 1644-1949, 1842-1949)
Primary 16547 S 17034 FP 17065 O 17234 S
10352 P 16584 P 17035 FP 17069 F 17298 P
11706 P 16675 P 17036 FP 17075 F 17309 F
12367 P 16936 P 17037 P 17076 FP 17457 P
12992 P 16937 FP 17038 P 17079 FP 17464 FP
13037 P 16947 FP 17039 F 17080 17474 P
15763 O 17029 FP 17044 P 17083 F 19246 O
16400 P 17030 FP 17049 F 17094 F 19247 P
16405 P 17031 FP 17050 P 17095 O 19426
16408 FP 17032 F 17052 PO 17186 FP 20620 PO
16410 P 17033 FP 17054 FP 17187 FP
Second. 12989 15384 PO 16613 FP 17256 FP
10344 12998 P 15428 O 16621 FP 17307 S
10351 S 12999 S 15954 S 16633 FP 17463 FP
10717 PO 13000 S 15961 FP 16671 O 17467 O
11588 FP 13041 P 16401 FP 16939 O 17487 F
11689 P 13150 FP 16415 17184 FP 17666 FP
11747 FP 13504 S 16449 PO 17185 FP 17723 P
12271 P 15372 O 16551 P 17239 18673 P
12371 P 15382 P 16562 S 17241 P 19240 PO
19257 P 19644 PO 20643 P 21314 F 22462 F
19273 O 20612 FP 20836 O 22441 P 22463 O
19275 P

1928-1949
Primary 16656 FP 17059 F 17078 F 17096 P
12977 O 16678 F 17060 P 17081 O 17097 F
12991 F 16713 F 17061 F 17082 O 17098 F
13022 F 17040 O 17062 F 17084 F 17099 F
15417 O 17042 17063 F 17086 F 17100 F
15419 O 17043 O 17064 F 17087 P 17212 O
15436 F 17045 F 17070 F 17088 P 17252 F
16313 O 17046 17071 F 17089 FP 17471 O
16444 P 17047 O 17072 F 17090 P 17651 O
16598 F 17053 FP 17073 S 17091 F 17826 P
16603 P 17056 P 17074 F 17092 P 19280 O
16607 O 17057 O 17077 F 17093 PO 20624 O
16653 FP 17058 P
Secondary: Monographs
11740 P 15411 P 16438 P 17249 P 19243 P
11748 P 15430 P 16636 PO 17273 F 19555 FP
12298 P 15432 F 16650 F 17484 FP 19640 P
12339 PO 16418 F 16710 P 17846 F 20262 F
13704 PO 16425 F 17238 P 17872 P 20870 P
13708 PO
Secondary: Inclusions
10747 O 16620 FP 16623 FP 16681 O 17462 O
13030 PO 16622 FP 16626 PO 17295 O 17730 O
15962 O
Secondary: Journal Articles
11742 15435 O 16441 O 17300 F 17492 PO
12245 15779 O 16446 P 17301 F 17667 F
12246 P 16427 O 16448 O 17304 S 17852 O
12265 S 16428 O 16450 P 17305 PO 18033 FP
12289 S 16435 P 16672 F 17310 O 18694 F
12321 S 16437 O 16683 PO 17473 F 19227
13014 P 16439 P 17209 O 17477 O 19362 F
13223 O 16440 O 17250 PO 17483 O 22704 O
15392 O

1928-1972
(incl. 1644-1972, 1842-1972, 1911-1972)
Primary 13046 P 17101 FP 17103 FP 17323 P
12408 P 15470 S 17102 FP
Second. 13044 S 15455 FP 16451 19284 P
10391 P 13045 15459 PO 16455 S 19650 PO
10393 S 13049 P 15463 FP 16456 F 19858 F
11859 P 15087 P 15792 FP 16729 FP 19970 FP
12400 P 15192 O 15793 FP 16747 P 20663 P
12414 P 15452 PO 15794 FP 17892 P

1949-1972
Primary 15845 P 17111 17125 O 19093 P
12442 P 16472 O 17112 P 17126 F 19160 P
12513 P 16473 P 17113 P 17127 P 19167 O
13071 P 16483 F 17114 P 17128 F 19288
13075 P 16486 P 17115 P 17129 P 19299 O
13083 F 16497 P 17116 F 17130 PO 19309 P
13089 P 16847 O 17117 F 17131 19431 O
13092 P 17104 O 17118 F 17374 P 20268 F
13095 P 17105 17119 O 17379 P 20272 FP
13105 P 17106 P 17120 P 17401 P 20688 O
13109 O 17107 P 17121 P 17511 P 20699 O
13114 O 17108 F 17122 O 17514 P 21144 O
13117 P 17109 F 17123 O 17618 F 21157 O
15555 O 17110 17124 O 17917 P 23045 O
15651 P
Secondary: Monographs
10172 PO 13399 P 15544 O 16826 F 18354 O
10975 P 14153 PO 15828 O 16827 P 19105 FP
11903 O 15260 P 15897 O 16858 PO 19302 P
11946 P 15483 P 16013 P 16867 F 19738 F
12475 PO 15491 F 16348 F 16869 F 20681 F
12487 PO 15506 O 16773 PO 17655 F 21063 P
12853 O 15507 P 16797 P 17963 F 21574 FP
13070 P 15513 PO 16816 F 17995 O 22764 O
13112 P 15543 O
Secondary: Inclusions
10414 S 13100 P 15990 P 16848 P 17404 P
13064 P 15485 F 16035 P 16877 P 17646 P
13082 15859 FP 16838 P 16893 F 17683 F
13099 P
Secondary: Journal Articles
10461 P 15211 P 16355 P 16850 P 17902 O
12012 P 15529 O 16470 P 16863 P 17912 F
12511 P 15531 O 16482 O 17333 S 18069 O
13055 P 15541 O 16499 S 17369 18327 S
13061 15822 PO 16501 P 17394 O 19159 P
13074 P 15838 F 16767 F 17428 O 19294 P
13789 P 16345 O 16807 P 17516 F 20668 O

24.4 Local Industry
地方工業 地方工業

1644-1842
Primary 16529 P 17145 P 17172 S 17174 P
15306 O 17140 PO 17160 P 17173 P 19211 P
16507 PO 17144 P 17171 P
Second. 10036 O 12183 P 13856 20582 P
10022 O 10552 P 12878 O 16369 O 21675 P
10033 O 11675 O

1644-1911
Primary 15327 PO 17148 PO 17163 O 17175 P
10006 S 16519 S 17153 PO 17165 PO 20595 PO
12201 P 17147 P
Second. 12572 P 15313 PO 15346 P 21677 FP
10001 O 12907 O 15318 O 15729 PO 21705 PO
10322 12941 PO 15331 P 21263 P

1842-1911
Primary 16506 O 17135 P 17152 PO 17168 O
11665 P 16509 FP 17136 P 17154 O 17169 O
12580 PO 16513 O 17137 PO 17155 FP 17170 O
12925 PO 16534 PO 17138 O 17156 PO 17176 PO
13123 P 16539 O 17139 O 17157 P 17177 O
13127 O 16541 P 17141 P 17158 O 17178 O
13130 P 16911 O 17142 O 17159 O 17179 O
16187 O 16913 O 17143 P 17161 P 17180 O
16378 O 16934 O 17146 PO 17162 P 17662 O
16380 O 17132 17149 P 17164 P 18491 O
16390 O 17133 17150 F 17166 O 20760 F
16393 PO 17134 17151 O 17167 P 22612 P
16395 O
Second. 12891 O 15713 16392 O 16928 O
10031 O 12908 P 15734 O 16508 O 17022 PO
10061 O 12915 S 15737 P 16512 O 17431 P
10319 S 12920 O 15747 O 16520 O 17548 O
10321 O 12936 PO 15750 O 16522 O 17817 O
10330 P 12937 PO 15753 O 16908 O 18852 PO
10331 S 13122 S 15929 O 16912 O 18875 O
10440 O 14554 PO 16374 PO 16914 O 20551 O
11679 P 15325 O 16381 O 16915 F 20590 PO
11681 O 15332 O 16384 FP 16917 O 22553 O
12879 PO 15363 O 16387 O 16926 O 22599 O
12889 O 15364 O 16388 O 16927 O 22618 O

1842-1928
(including 1644-1928)
Primary 13177 P 17182 PO 17191 F 17691 PO
11683 O 13872 17183 P 17194 PO 19220 P
13164 FP 16404 O 17189 O 17661 P
Second. 12222 P 13161 P 15633 PO 16938 F
10077 O 12663 P 13163 S 15864 P 17981 P
10338 P 12951 PO 13191 P 16101 O 18956 PO
11698 P 12955 PO 13522 P 16406 P 20618 PO
11713 P 12966 PO 15369 PO 16552 O 22673 P
11717 P 12969 PO 15381 P 16563 O

1911-1928
Primary 14434 P 16657 P 17199 P 17210
13260 P 15422 O 16691 P 17202 P 17213 P
13277 F 15770 O 17197 17203 O 17215 P

17216 P 17231 O 17263 O 17286 O 17696 PO
17217 P 17232 PO 17265 P 17292 O 17705
17218 P 17243 O 17268 O 17294 O 17713 FP
17221 17253 P 17270 F 17296 O 17720 F
17223 17254 P 17272 P 17306 FP 19360 F
17224 O 17257 O 17284 O 17650 O

SECOND. 13976 P 16433 FP 16961 P 17876 F
10094 O 14468 P 16434 P 16963 O 18582 O
10294 P 15393 16436 PO 17717 PO 19490 PO
11730 O 15445 O 16447 O 17722 O 19491
11734 P 15781 16582 17724 P 19547 PO
11766 PO 16412 16651 O 17836 O 19558
11784 P 16419 O 16684 O 17843 O 19578 S
11794 P 16424 PO 16692 F 17861 O 20392 S
12979 O 16426 P 16945 O 17874 S 20947 O
13238

1911-1949
(including 1644-1949, 1842-1949)

PRIMARY 15961 FP 17190 PO 17241 P 17290 P
11756 P 16401 FP 17192 17244 O 17298 P
13037 P 16405 P 17193 FP 17248 F 17307 S
13150 FP 16407 P 17200 P 17251 F 17309 F
13180 P 16415 17201 17256 FP 17694 PO
13181 PO 17030 FP 17204 17260 F 17716 F
13212 PO 17054 FP 17206 O 17266 S 19075 PO
13224 FP 17181 17208 O 17271 O 19216 P
13225 FP 17184 FP 17222 O 17274 FP 19233 F
13226 FP 17185 FP 17229 P 17276 P 19356
13242 P 17186 FP 17234 S 17280 S 19523 F
13250 P 17187 FP 17237 O 17282 20617 FP
15765 S 17188 O 17239 17283 P

SECOND. 13205 15759 P 16939 O 19257 P
10339 O 13218 P 15762 P 16951 PO 19273 O
10343 13281 P 15766 S 17037 P 19458
10366 14456 P 15948 P 17050 P 19486 P
11704 P 14508 P 16400 P 17094 F 19556 P
11795 O 15049 16421 17736 P 19566 P
11824 O 15372 O 16423 PO 17869 PO 19644 PO
12257 FP 15380 16572 P 18622 O 20276 O
12271 P 15384 PO 16584 P 18722 O 20390 S
12297 P 15408 F 16621 FP 18732 P 20620 PO
12675 PO 15446 P 16624 FP 18981 P 22651 S
12992 P 15599 P 16633 FP 19217 P 22665 S
13162 S 15758 PO 16668 P

1928-1949

PRIMARY: MONOGRAPHS
10096 O 16417 P 17228 P 17249 P 17291 S
14771 F 16425 F 17236 PO 17261 P 17297 PO
15409 P 16980 P 17238 P 17262 O 17725 FP
16061 P 17225 PO 17240 F 17273 F 20199 O
16062 P 17226 PO 17245 P 17277 F

PRIMARY: INCLUSIONS
12986 O 16607 O 17281 PO 17287 O 17295 O
17308 O

PRIMARY: JOURNAL ARTICLES
10358 S 17196 P 17230 O 17264 F 17300 F
11723 P 17198 17233 O 17267 O 17301 F
11743 17205 17235 F 17269 O 17302 S
12980 O 17207 P 17242 F 17275 O 17303 S
13194 17209 O 17246 O 17278 P 17304 S
13280 P 17211 17247 17279 F 17305 PO
13287 O 17212 O 17250 PO 17285 O 17310 O
15772 O 17214 O 17252 F 17288 O 17706 O
16411 FP 17219 P 17255 O 17289 O 17715 P
16444 P 17220 17258 O 17293 P 19261 F
16569 17227 O 17259 O 17299 O 19270 O
17195 P

SECONDARY: MONOGRAPHS
10101 O 12339 PO 15965 P 17709 F 19640 P
11740 P 12359 O 16063 P 17728 F 19648 O
11745 P 13040 O 16431 FP 17846 F 19707 O
11748 P 15430 P 16650 F 17872 P 20195 FP
11750 S 15431 P 16710 P 19268 F 20862 F
11767 PO 15442 P 16711 P 19555 FP 20915 F
12291 S 15773 P 17091 F 19638 S 20919 F
12298 P 15871 F

SECONDARY: INCLUSIONS
11769 PO 13241 S 16623 FP 19823 O 20200 O
11819 16622 FP 19267 P

SECONDARY: JOURNAL ARTICLES
10767 O 13003 P 16427 O 16571 P 17483 O
11722 13223 O 16428 O 16583 17703 F
11742 13566 O 16435 P 16588 17707 O
11768 S 15404 O 16437 O 16603 P 17726 P
11770 15774 16440 O 16635 P 17731 O
11778 P 15777 O 16443 O 16672 F 17734 FP
12977 O 15778 O 16446 P 17064 F 17868 F
12978 P 16422 16448 O 17087 P 17875 O
12981

1928-1972
(incl. 1644-1972, 1842-1972, 1911-1972)

PRIMARY 15469 P 17312 O 17317 S 17322
10398 FP 15789 17313 O 17318 P 17323 P
11845 P 15810 FP 17314 P 17319 O 17772 O
13299 15811 P 17315 P 17320 P 18313 P
15458 PO 16451 17316 P 17321 P 19283 F
15466 O 17311 O

SECOND. 11876 P 14809 O 15794 FP 17580 O
10301 FP 12375 P 15085 P 16068 O 17895 O
10382 P 12383 P 15173 O 16452 PO 17985 FP
10392 P 12386 P 15191 PO 16454 S 19078 P
11854 P 12419 P 15192 O 16455 S 19284 P
11859 P 12422 S 15459 PO 16736 P 20976 PO
11860 P 13043 P 15465 PO 16750 F 22947 P
11864 FP 13294 P 15474 O 16751 S 22991 S
11875 P 13300 P 15600 P 16753 PO

1949-1972

PRIMARY: MONOGRAPHS
10172 PO 15511 O 15560 FP 16493 P 17362 P
10421 FP 15518 P 16012 P 16756 O 17381 P
11912 P 15519 O 16070 O 16806 F 17386 FP
12027 P 15527 O 16457 O 17350 FP 17387 P
14153 PO 15537 P 16473 P 17360 P 17395 P
15481 O 15550 O 16486 P 17361 P 17741 O
15482 O

PRIMARY: INCLUSIONS
13396 P 17336 P 17347 O 17366 O 17404 P
15532 O 17338 O 17349 FP 17376 O 17405 O
15651 P 17339 O 17354 F 17378 O 17406 O
15847 O 17340 P 17355 P 17382 O 17747
16474 O 17341 O 17356 P 17396 O 19298 O
16487 PO 17343 O 17357 P 17397 O 19339 O
16494 P 17345 O 17358 O 17400 O 19341 F
16862 17346 O 17365 P 17402 O

PRIMARY: JOURNAL ARTICLES
12482 P 16476 O 17329 O 17369 17394 O
13320 P 16477 P 17330 O 17370 P 17398 P
13364 P 16480 FP 17331 O 17371 P 17399 P
13373 P 16497 P 17332 O 17372 P 17401 P
13374 P 16501 P 17333 S 17373 P 17403
13375 P 16503 P 17334 O 17374 P 17654 O
13377 P 16504 17335 PO 17375 O 17738 O
13378 P 16754 O 17337 O 17377 O 17739 P
13404 PO 16758 O 17342 O 17379 P 17740 O
15478 O 16761 O 17344 O 17380 O 17749 O
15522 O 16807 P 17348 P 17383 O 17750
15536 O 16839 P 17351 F 17384 O 17806 O
15563 PO 16894 O 17352 O 17385 FP 17810 O
15815 O 17016 O 17353 O 17388 P 19305 P
15833 PO 17113 P 17359 O 17389 O 19308 P
16004 O 17324 O 17363 17390 P 19313 F
16015 P 17325 O 17364 17391 P 19335 P
16079 P 17326 O 17367 P 17392 O 20477 O
16458 O 17327 O 17368 O 17393 O 20668 O
16470 P 17328 O

SECONDARY: MONOGRAPHS
10141 O 12015 P 13344 S 15547 P 16463 P
10149 O 12069 P 13384 P 15548 P 16488 PO
10401 F 12150 P 15100 P 15553 PO 16763 O
10429 FP 12157 15297 O 15565 O 16771 F
11105 P 12158 PO 15483 P 15572 FP 16786 F
11651 FP 12429 P 15498 O 15828 O 16800 O
11891 P 12434 F 15506 O 15850 FP 16844 P
11897 PO 12475 PO 15507 P 15897 O 16845 F
11903 O 12485 P 15508 O 15901 F 16869 F
11946 P 12532 PO 15513 PO 15991 F 17779 P
11955 P 12853 O 15517 F 15993 P 17907 O
12003 P 13338 P 15520 P 16016 O 17913 P
12005 P 13343 S 15543 O 16046 PO 17995 O
19095 P 19291 P 19922 P 20505 PO 21574 FP
19105 FP 19292 F 19953 F 20694 F 22749 P
19131 P 19302 P 20074 FP 20699 O 22755 O
19184 PO

SECONDARY: INCLUSIONS
11173 13419 P 15844 16484 PO 19200 O
11960 P 13441 O 15859 FP 16877 P 19319
12042 P 15485 F 15998 O 16997 19337 O
12092 P 15500 O 16461 O 17744 O 19605 O
13334 P 15542 16462 O 17802 O 20238 O
13352 P 15817 16465 O 17914 O 20416
13403 O 15836 16483 F 19172 O

SECONDARY: JOURNAL ARTICLES
10166 O 13349 P 15857 P 16770 O 18335 O
10461 P 13354 P 15878 F 16774 O 19125 P
10492 O 13409 P 15886 S 16775 O 19126 P
11097 PO 13426 PO 15983 O 16863 P 19159 P
11895 PO 14417 F 15995 O 16879 F 19185
11902 S 14817 O 15997 O 16992 19196
12012 P 14960 O 16000 O 17107 P 19297 O
12048 PO 14961 PO 16006 P 17123 O 19306 O
12066 P 15272 O 16009 P 17129 P 19318 O
12083 P 15292 P 16034 P 17513 P 19431 O
12111 P 15480 O 16478 O 17618 F 19586 O
12112 PO 15502 O 16489 O 17653 O 19712 O
12427 P 15503 O 16498 P 17656 O 20673 P
12458 O 15562 O 16499 S 17751 O 20679 O
12498 P 15649 S 16500 17775 O 20998 O
12526 P 15829 PO 16759 O 17902 O 21041 O
12533 S 15832 O 16764 O 17994 FP 21254 P
13095 P 15834 PO 16765 O 18069 O

24.5 LOCAL REVENUE AND EXPENDITURE
地方財政　地方財政

1644-1842

PRIMARY 17408 PO 19429 P 19436 P
SECOND. 13472 P 19205 P

1644-1911

PRIMARY 15346 P 15354 P 15863 P
SECOND. 16049 P 17028 P 18464 P 18518 P
15661 S 16543 PO 18427 P

1842-1911

PRIMARY 15732 O 16375 PO 16922 O 17410 PO
11232 FP 15921 P 16376 PO 16923 O 17411 P
13455 P 15930 P 16394 P 17407 PO 18087 P
15340 FP 16374 PO 16538 O 17409 FP

SECOND. 15328 P 15933 P 16526 O 17146 PO
10668 P 15365 O 16093 O 16532 O 19343 S
12903 O 15584 P 16387 O 16535 PO 20537 P
12937 PO 15726 O 16510 P 16536 O 20556 O
13463 P 15928 P

1842-1928
(including 1644-1928)

PRIMARY 13500 PO 13522 P 17412 P 17560 P
SECOND. 13508 P 15943 P 16403 P 16554 P
12663 P 15388 S 15944 P 16546 S 22673 P
12958 P

1911-1928

PRIMARY 16424 PO 17413 P 17421 P 17422 O
19442 PO
SECOND. 13906 PO 16963 O 17066 P 20635 PO
13029 S 16685 P 16971 O

1911-1949
(including 1644-1949, 1842-1949)

PRIMARY 13529 P 16423 PO 17423 P 17444 FP
13525 P 15762 P 16559 P
SECOND. 15639 O 15959 P 17029 FP 17456 O
12992 P 15942 P 16408 FP 17032 F 17832 O
12998 P 15945 P 16556 FP 17181 18589 P
13512 P 15946 FP 16557 FP 17184 FP 18732 P
15380 15950 S 16612 FP 17185 FP 19216 P
15382 P 15955 P 16614 O 17251 F 21315 F
15408 F

1928-1949

PRIMARY 16438 P 17414 FP 17417 O 17419 P
15406 F 16721 O 17415 O 17418 FP 17420 P
15960 FP 16723 F 17416 O
SECOND. 15957 O 16636 PO 17209 O 18595 P
13566 O 15965 P 16638 PO 17214 O 18643 F
13974 PO 15971 P 16701 F 17240 F 18695 O
15409 P 16056 F 16955 P 17663 F 19702 P
15431 P 16062 P 17062 F 17860 O 20062 P
15434 O 16601 FP 17082 O 17885 F 20870 P
15437 PO 16619 F

1928-1972
(incl. 1644-1972, 1842-1972, 1911-1972)

PRIMARY 17424 P
SECOND. 10880 P 15470 S 15974 FP 16735 P
10301 FP 13046 P 15797 FP 15976 PO

1949-1972

PRIMARY 16887 F 17426 O 17428 O 17430 PO
16083 F 17425 O 17427 P 17429 P 17512 PO
SECOND. 16009 P 16494 P 17360 P 19167 O
13112 P 16013 P 16769 P 17674 P 19713 P
15518 P 16028 FP 16771 F 17682 P 19990 FP
15568 P 16075 P 16851 P 17684 P 20075 P
15882 16465 O 16859 P 18354 O 20694 F
15889 P 16487 PO 17004 P 19153 F 21063 P
15900 F 16490 O

24.6 Local Finance, Money, and Credit
地方金融、貨幣及信託制度
地方金融、貨幣及び信用制度

1644-1842

PRIMARY 17408 PO 19205 P
SECOND. 15752 O 19211 P

1644-1911

PRIMARY 15863 P 17434 P
SECOND. 13641 P 19209 O

1842-1911

PRIMARY 17431 P 17433 P 17436 O 17438 PO
16374 PO 17432 O 17435 P 17437 PO 17439 O
17411 P
SECOND. 15355 O 16393 PO 17132 20578 O
10682 O 15926 P 16511 O 17410 PO 21266 O
11232 FP 16373 O 16908 O 19207 O 22542 O
12917 PO 16375 PO 16913 O 19343 S 22589 P
12942 O 16384 FP

1842-1928
(including 1644-1928)

PRIMARY 13662 P 13692 P 16553 FP 17441 PO
SECOND. 12966 PO 15952 O 16546 S 17183 P
12954 PO 13670 PO 16103 FP 16938 F 17692 P
12955 PO 15390 O

1911-1928

PRIMARY 16645 F 17468 O 17482 O 18607 O
13260 P 16699 F 17469 O 17486 S 19251 P
13717 S 17449 17470 F 17488 O 19259 P
16424 PO 17452 O 17478 P 17489 PO 19553
16642 F
SECOND. 16433 FP 16644 FP 17221 18126 P
13029 S 16445 O 16664 PO 17223 19231 O
15393 16593 F 17048 P 17265 P 20631 O
15422 O 16630 F 17085 O 17848 O 20641 F

1911-1949
(including 1644-1949, 1842-1949)

PRIMARY 17033 FP 17445 S 17460 FP 17666 FP
15382 P 17052 PO 17446 PO 17463 FP 19217 P
15948 P 17186 FP 17447 P 17464 FP 19257 P
16405 P 17229 P 17448 P 17467 O 19273 O
16421 17440 S 17450 17474 P 19282 P
16423 PO 17442 FP 17456 O 17485 P 19426
16675 P 17443 S 17457 P 17487 F 22463 O
16947 FP 17444 FP 17459 P 17491 P
SECOND. 13710 P 16613 FP 17038 P 19075 PO
11746 P 13725 P 16624 FP 17054 FP 19240 PO
11747 FP 15060 O 16639 P 17192 19632 S
12998 P 15446 P 17029 FP 17307 S 19962 S
12999 S 15945 P 17030 FP 19071 P 20276 O
13533 P 16120 P 17037 P 19073 S 22805 O
13668 O 16612 FP

1928-1949

PRIMARY 17417 O 17461 F 17473 F 17481 FP
11031 P 17451 P 17462 O 17475 P 17483 O
11760 PO 17453 O 17465 O 17476 P 17484 FP
16681 O 17454 O 17466 O 17477 O 17490 O
17074 F 17455 17471 O 17479 FP 17492 PO
17088 P 17458 F 17472 P 17480 P 19280 O
SECOND. 15971 P 16626 PO 17060 P 17634
10767 O 16061 P 16661 O 17063 F 17663 F
10831 P 16425 F 16694 O 17086 F 17845 O
11743 16431 FP 16703 F 17098 F 17849 O
12272 S 16441 O 16716 F 17236 PO 17860 O
12977 O 16444 P 16722 F 17279 F 19227
15074 F 16601 FP 17046 17300 F 19244
15960 FP 16602 F 17053 FP 17301 F 19508 O
15965 P 16619 F 17056 P 17418 FP

1928-1972
(incl. 1644-1972, 1842-1972, 1911-1972)

PRIMARY 13767 P 16735 P 17494 PO 17495 PO
13046 P 16451 17493 P
SECOND. 15469 P 15981 F 16729 FP 19284 P
12409 P 15797 FP 16455 S 16747 P 21426 P
15455 FP 15978 FP 16456 F 17323 P 22724 P
15467 PO

1949-1972

PRIMARY 17429 P 17503 17511 P 17519
15900 F 17496 O 17504 P 17512 PO 17618 F
16463 P 17497 O 17505 17513 P 17683 F
16483 F 17498 O 17506 P 17514 P 17900 P
16489 O 17499 F 17507 F 17515 PO 19296 O
16492 P 17500 O 17508 P 17516 F 19309 P
17124 O 17501 O 17509 O 17517 O 20268 F
17127 P 17502 O 17510 PO 17518 P
SECOND. 15574 F 16501 P 17002 FP 19140 P
12511 P 15882 16790 P 17116 F 19155 P
13057 PO 15998 O 16797 P 17126 F 19195 F
13083 F 16026 S 16816 F 17129 P 19990 FP
13112 P 16083 F 16857 F 17336 P 20072 F
14153 PO 16472 O 16858 PO 17367 P 20074 FP
15504 F 16473 P 16872 FP 17379 P 20272 FP
15515 FP 16490 O 16873 FP 17426 O 20681 F
15533 F 16495 P 16887 F 17963 F 22764 O
15537 P 16500 16893 F

25 Feuds, Banditry, and Local Paramilitary Units
械鬥、盜賊及地方武力
械鬥、匪賊行為及び地方の保安組織

1644-1842

PRIMARY 13830 P 13865 P 17530 P 19441 P
10626 P 13836 O 15663 P 17555 O 19958 O
10651 P 13855 17524 P 17557 P 22563 P
13815 P 13864 P 17528 P
SECOND. 13822 P 16517 P 19959 P 21712 P
10032 O 13835 P 17657 O 21277 P 22398 O
10526 S 13868 P 18418 21279 P 22635 P
10618 P 14166 P 18475 P 21685 P 22776 P
12901 P 16514 P 19440 P

1644-1911

PRIMARY 13841 O 17531 P 18464 P 18919 P
10625 P 13844 P 17541 P 18518 P 21259 P
11015 P 16049 P 17542 P 18519 P 21271 O
13824 P 17520 PO 18427 P 18523 22531 P
SECOND. 10638 P 15334 PO 18459 O 18890 S
10010 P 12193 PO 15354 P 18489 18941 FP
10060 PO 12940 S 15727 PO 18526 S 21269
10276 13838 16379 PO 18527 P 21270 PO
10325 PO 13863 P 17434 P 18853 PO 21276 P
10327 P 14093 P 18366 P 18862 P 22558 P
10329 PO 15313 PO 18384 P 18865 PO 22592 P
10616 15318 O 18421 P 18876 O

1842-1911

PRIMARY: MONOGRAPHS
15324 O 17543 P 18454 PO 18861 P 22591 PO
15929 O 17549 O 18455 S 18868 PO 22594 O
15930 P 17553 P 18461 P 18924 PO 22595 P
16376 PO 18376 P 18490 P 20128 O 22600 P
16377 O 18390 P 18509 P 21287 P 22601 O
17411 P 18412 FP 18511 P 22584 S 22612 P
17529 P 18422 O 18524 P 22589 P 22617 PO
17532 O 18438 P
PRIMARY: INCLUSIONS
11244 O 17544 P 17554 PO 18374 P 18445 P
13471 P 17550 PO 17558 O 18400 P 18452 P
13816 P 17551 S 17610 P 18410 P 21281 P
17526 P
PRIMARY: JOURNAL ARTICLES
11668 O 17525 O 17545 O 18393 O 19957 O
12891 O 17527 P 17546 O 18394 PO 22538 P
13826 P 17533 FP 17547 P 18404 P 22545 P
13853 P 17534 O 17548 O 18434 P 22554 P
15128 S 17535 O 17552 O 18440 P 22566 P
15735 O 17536 O 17556 18456 O 22570 P
15921 P 17537 O 18087 P 18463 P 22582 O
17521 O 17538 O 18300 O 18465 O 22607 P
17522 O 17539 PO 18363 O 18488 P 22642 P
17523 P 17540 O 18381 P
SECONDARY: MONOGRAPHS
10544 P 13811 O 15355 O 18442 P 21265 P
10566 P 13847 P 15360 O 18466 O 21280 O
10631 P 13858 P 15368 FP 18491 O 21302 O
10677 P 14164 P 16374 PO 18492 PO 21655 O
11657 PO 14207 P 16375 PO 18494 P 22513 PO
11671 O 15038 P 16394 P 18496 P 22532 P
12569 O 15316 O 16520 O 18871 PO 22556 PO
12595 P 15340 FP 16912 O 18903 P 22586 P
12601 O 15349 O 18089 P 18947 S 22615 O
13807 P 15351 O 18388 P 20137 O
SECONDARY: INCLUSIONS
10639 O 15753 O 16927 O 18513 O 22522 O
13843 O 16094 P 18377 O 22399 S 22618 O
15359 O 16920 O 18392 P 22508 O
SECONDARY: JOURNAL ARTICLES
10511 P 15737 P 16934 O 18094 S 18471 S
10536 S 15738 F 17025 O 18372 18483 P
12584 O 15919 PO 17811 O 18397 S 18497 P
13869 P 15925 P 17924 P 18403 O 18851 O
15357 O 15928 P 17973 PO 18411 P 18892 P
15583 O 16392 O 18016 O 18435 O 19344 S

26 LOCAL SOCIAL STRATIFICATION AND MOBILITY

地方社會之階層與流動

地方の社会階層及びその流動性

16134 F 17643 P 19153 F 19946 FP 20524 FP
16457 O 17675 F 19201 P 20074 FP 21433 O
16466 O 17913 P 19737 FP 20326 F 21583 F
16486 P 17961 FP 19918 F 20359 F 21598 F
16865 F 19116 O 19933 FP 20360 F 22753 O
16893 F 19117 O 19939 F 20425 F 22758 F
16991 F

26.1 The Local Elite

地方領導階層

地方エリート階層

1644-1842

Primary 15923 O 17657 O

Second. 10652 O 17822 O 19211 P 20043 P
10512 PO 16369 O 18014 P

1644-1911

Primary 14596 P 15626 O 16049 P 17627 P
10525 P 15318 O 15931 O

Second. 14158 P 16217 FP 17542 P 18915 FP
10616 15320 PO 16389 PO 18519 P 18940 P
14093 P 15354 P 17541 P 18865 PO 18945 P

1842-1911

Primary 16094 P 17544 P 17626 O 18490 P
15357 O 16201 O 17547 P 17628 O 18875 O
15925 P 16912 O 17610 P 17629 P 22632 P
15926 P 17143 P 17625 O

Second. 15324 O 16220 PO 18438 P 20578 O
10675 P 15350 O 16378 O 18491 O 20579 O
10679 O 15351 O 16391 O 18509 P 20758 O
11681 O 15361 O 16394 P 18859 P 21168 O
14160 P 15629 O 17411 P 18868 PO 21258
14161 O 15721 O 17526 P 18922 O 21655 O
14177 O 15733 O 17533 FP 20093 O 21707 P
14207 P 15735 O 17553 P 20550 O 22570 P
14597 O 15924 PO 18390 P 20557 O 22589 P
15317 O 15929 O

1842-1928
(including 1644-1928)

Primary 15373 P 15943 P 15944 P 17630 P
17631 PO 21305 O

Second. 15388 S 15390 O 17559 P 18951 O
14676 S 15389 PO 16546 S 17560 P 19726 O

1911-1928

Primary 15395 O 18669 P

Second. 15143 P 18126 P 19449 P 19460 F
12741 P 15966 FP 19021 O 19454 FP 22696 O
13925 P 16685 P

1911-1949
(including 1644-1949, 1842-1949)

Primary 16053 P 16675 P 21312 F 21316 F
15940 S 16612 FP 21308 O 21315 F 21369 F
15947 O

Second. 15632 P 16120 P 16613 FP 20210 P
11336 P 15762 P 16410 P 18589 P 21313 F
14215 S 15953 P 16559 P 19619 O 21344 O
15372 O 16104 S

1928-1949

Primary 15960 FP 17613 F 17634 17889 F
14771 F 16722 F 17632 O 17830 P 18751 S
15957 O 17492 PO 17633 F 17866 F 20450 P

Second. 15406 F 16714 F 17854 F 19649 O
10783 O 15430 P 16718 F 17867 F 20262 F
14124 P 16059 P 17664 F 18643 F 20436 O
14739 F 16602 F 17846 F 18749 O 20458 O
15394 O 16709

1928-1972
(incl. 1644-1972, 1842-1972, 1911-1972)

Primary 16735 P 19969 O 19985 O 20994 O
15974 FP 16746 FP 19970 FP 19986 O 22733 P
15981 F 17635 P

Second. 10856 S 15456 P 16725 F 20475 O
10117 PO 10872 P 16128 FP 17615 O 21426 P
10851 P 12405 P 16333 PO 17953 P 22724 P

1949-1972

Primary 15916 O 16902 FP 17641 O 18357 P
11080 P 15989 F 17588 P 17642 P 19100 P
14363 P 16020 P 17606 O 17643 P 19111 O
14866 O 16028 FP 17636 O 17644 F 19112 O
14970 O 16044 F 17637 O 17645 O 19161 O
15014 O 16071 FP 17638 P 17646 P 19675 O
15304 O 16080 S 17639 P 17647 P 20998 O
15488 P 16792 P 17640 P 18330 PO 22303 P
15572 FP

Second. 14938 O 16018 P 16851 P 18362 O
10166 O 14946 PO 16069 O 16859 P 19131 P
11002 14960 O 16070 O 16872 FP 19142 P
11094 P 14962 P 16075 P 16888 O 19165 F
11493 FP 15254 O 16133 F 17383 O 19197 F
14300 P 15291 P 16148 FP 17620 F 19200 O
14301 P 15485 F 16347 O 17679 P 19679 FP
14816 P 15507 P 16478 O 17802 O 20497 F
14819 15545 O 16771 F 17996 P 20524 FP
14839 F 15560 FP 16811 F 18070 O 21431 F
14877 O 15913 O 16835 P 18329 P 22291 P
14888 O 15992 P 16850 P 18355 O 23046 P

26.2 Businessmen

商人及市民　　商人及び市民

1644-1842

Primary 17408 PO 17658 P 18013 P 19429 P
17173 P 17657 O 17820 O

Second. 10546 P 15722 O 16218 O 17144 P
19211 P 19436 P

1644-1911

Primary 17652 O 19437 P

Second. 14093 P 17175 P 18519 P 19434 P
13841 O 15743 O 17434 P 19351 P

1842-1911

Primary 17020 O 17176 PO 17548 O 18490 P
15355 O 17141 P 17431 P 17629 P 21257
16092 P 17158 O 17432 O 17649 O

Second. 15359 O 16913 O 19693 P 20601 O
12600 P 15926 P 17155 FP 19716 P 20775 O
15308 O 15929 O 17167 P 19742 O 21258
15324 O 16187 O 17608 20579 O 22589 P
15344 O 16910 PO

1842-1928
(including 1644-1928)

Primary 15864 P 17559 P 17661 P 17690 P

Second. 11683 O 15390 O 15943 P 16108 PO
10292 P 12954 PO 15633 PO 15944 P 22423 PO
10340 PO 12955 PO

1911-1928

Primary 16945 O 17831 F 19231 O 20631 O
16292 O 17650 O 18126 P 19511 O

Second. 16442 P 17611 O 19360 F 19498 P
12993 FP 17286 O 17876 F 19427 P 19507 P
13966 P 17294 O 17877 F 19490 PO 19538 O
15143 P 17306 FP 19248 O

1911-1949
(including 1644-1949, 1842-1949)

Primary 17054 FP 17186 FP 17446 PO 17459 P
19217 P 21314 F

Second. 16299 F 17187 FP 18571 S 21384 O
15372 O 16624 FP 17251 F 21315 F 22457 F
15953 P

1928-1949

Primary 17071 F 17864 F 17890 F 19258
16672 F 17651 O 17865 F 18032 O 19261 F
17063 F

Second. 16317 O 17288 O 17863 PO 20262 F
15417 O 16979 O 17414 FP 17888 F 20644 F
15960 FP 17249 P 17715 P 18036 O

1928-1972
(incl. 1644-1972, 1842-1972, 1911-1972)

Primary 16068 O 17648 O 21393 O

Second. 15973 P 17314 P 17316 P 20994 O
22724 P

1949-1972

Primary 16070 O 17646 P 17655 F 17660 P
15891 P 16075 P 17653 O 17656 O 20272 FP
15901 F 17116 F 17654 O 17659 O

Second. 15511 O 16991 F 17617 F 19292 F
12475 PO 16083 F 17370 P 18327 S 19341 F
13083 F 16135 O 17516 F 18354 O 22755 O
14417 F 16347 O

26.3 Peasants

農民　　農民

1644-1842

Primary □

Second. 16369 O 16507 PO 17822 O 20558 S

1644-1911

Primary □

Second. 15661 S 17028 P 17541 P 17627 P
17816 P 17927 FP

1842-1911

Primary 16399 O 16513 O 16538 O 17662 O
18437 P 19746 PO

Second. 16094 P 16509 FP 16526 O 18016 O
14597 O 16220 PO 16516 P 16527 O 18390 P
15311 O 16394 P 16522 O 17411 P 18455 S
15358 O

1842-1928
(including 1644-1928)

Primary 15378 F 16553 FP 17559 P 18980 O

Second. 10340 PO 16546 S 16554 P 17560 P
22423 PO

1911-1928

Primary 16642 F 16692 F 19449 P 19460 F
16573 16645 F 17881 FP 19454 FP 20641 F
16591 F 16685 P

Second. 16445 O 16657 P 17871 FP 19455 P
13260 P 16565 16699 F 18611 P 19456 P
13925 P 16578 16712 F 18669 P 19490 PO
15686 P 16590 F 17486 S 19451 O 20185 O
15775 F 16630 F

1911-1949
(including 1644-1949, 1842-1949)

PRIMARY 16612 FP 16675 P 17666 FP 19619 O
16053 P 16613 FP 17274 FP 17769 P 19632 S
16299 F 16624 FP 17460 FP 17832 O 22430 O
16309 O 16671 O

SECOND. 16120 P 16633 FP 17456 O 20210 P
10356 PO 16321 O 16639 P 17561 O 20629 O
11746 P 16322 F 16942 PO 18534 PO 21344 O
15391 PO 16410 P 17065 O 18589 P 22452 FP
16104 S 16562 S 17423 P 18622 O

1928-1949

PRIMARY 16598 F 16672 F 17664 F 17840 F
13891 O 16601 FP 16673 O 17665 17841 F
15405 F 16629 P 16693 FP 17667 F 17845 O
15426 S 16632 F 16707 F 17668 F 17846 F
15957 O 16636 PO 17492 PO 17825 P 18035 O
16065 P 16661 O 17663 F 17830 P 20198 F
16311 F

SECOND. 16618 F 16696 17418 FP 18643 F
12272 S 16628 O 16706 F 17458 F 18667 FP
13970 O 16637 P 16709 17479 FP 18690 P
14124 P 16638 PO 16714 F 17481 FP 18746 O
15421 O 16653 FP 16721 O 17613 F 18749 O
15434 O 16659 PO 16948 O 17854 F 19633 O
15772 O 16662 F 17045 F 17860 O 19649 O
16059 P 16666 F 17057 O 17868 F 19850 F
16325 O 16690 FP 17250 PO 18305 P 22453 F
16602 F 16694 O 17262 O

1928-1972
(incl. 1644-1972, 1842-1972, 1911-1972)

PRIMARY 15799 O 16735 P 17895 O 18791 P
15192 O 15978 FP 16746 FP 17897 F 19085 O
15453 16724 17669 FP

SECOND. 15697 FP 16733 P 17586 P 19080 F
13048 F 15977 P 16736 P 17896 F 19889 F
15191 PO 16456 F 17424 P 19077 P 19970 FP
15464 P 16725 F 17580 O 19079 F 22481 O
15466 O 16728 P

1949-1972

PRIMARY 15573 F 16882 O 17673 P 17971 F
14996 O 15991 P 16886 F 17674 P 19093 P
15232 15992 P 16890 FP 17675 F 19100 P
15478 O 15993 P 16893 F 17676 F 19110 O
15488 P 16013 P 16899 F 17677 O 19140 P
15493 O 16031 P 16902 FP 17678 P 19154 P
15494 P 16072 P 17120 P 17679 P 19167 O
15505 F 16083 F 17606 O 17680 F 19177 P
15517 F 16145 P 17620 F 17681 F 19184 PO
15525 O 16813 PO 17624 O 17682 P 19197 F
15528 P 16834 O 17639 P 17683 F 19679 FP
15543 O 16847 O 17670 O 17684 P 20080 P
15544 O 16869 F 17671 O 17685 F 20241 O
15545 O 16872 FP 17672 F 17905 P 20701 F
15558 P

SECONDARY: MONOGRAPHS
10175 O 15524 O 16763 O 16866 F 17913 P
14153 PO 15549 P 16771 F 16867 F 18289 P
15297 O 15567 O 16787 FP 16868 F 19095 P
15491 F 16001 S 16794 F 16871 F 19922 P
15501 O 16011 P 16797 P 17588 P 20079 P
15506 O 16046 PO 16820 F 17741 O 20503 O
15507 P 16071 FP 16852 O 17910 F 20699 O
15508 O

SECONDARY: INCLUSIONS
15894 O 16804 F 16877 P 19114 O 19148 O
15990 P 16821 O 16881 O 19116 O 19161 O
15996 P 16842 O 17638 P 19117 O 19165 F
16461 O 16851 P 17640 P 19138 P 19172 O
16468 P 16860 O 17793 O 19147 O 19661 O
16803 O

SECONDARY: JOURNAL ARTICLES
10461 P 15516 O 15877 FP 16478 O 16815 O
13083 F 15531 O 15880 O 16759 O 16835 P
14922 O 15552 O 15886 S 16792 P 16850 P
15510 O 15559 P 15887 F 16801 F 16855 O
15512 O 15814 O 15999 P 16805 S 16859 P
16873 FP 17616 F 17801 O 19151 P 19672 O
16888 O 17645 O 19099 P 19156 P 20072 F
16894 O 17790 O 19142 P 19195 F 21017 F
17326 O 17795 O 19144 P 19664 O 22767 O
17329 O

26.4 WORKERS
勞工　　労働者

1644-1842

PRIMARY □

SECOND. 15305 O 17173 P

1644-1911

PRIMARY 17687 P

SECOND. □

1842-1911

PRIMARY 15629 O 17176 PO 17686 O 17688 O
17689 P 18410 P

SECOND. 15344 O 16397 O 17143 P 21655 O
10278 O 16166 O 17141 P 17178 O

1842-1928
(including 1644-1928)

PRIMARY 17690 P 17691 PO 17692 P 17693 P
17824 P

SECOND. 11683 O 16403 P 17630 P 19220 P

1911-1928

PRIMARY 17705 17722 O 17874 S 19509 P
16944 P 17711 P 17724 P 17876 F 19510 P
17268 O 17712 P 17727 O 17877 F 19511 O
17695 O 17713 FP 17828 F 17887 F 19557 P
17696 PO 17714 O 17835 F 18582 O 19578 S
17697 P 17717 PO 17836 O 19490 PO 20216 F
17700 P 17719 O 17842 F 19499 P 20392 S
17701 P 17720 F 17861 O 19506 P 20394 P
17702 F

SECOND. 17213 P 17263 O 17886 F 19533 P
10840 S 17215 P 17270 F 18611 P 19538 O
13260 P 17216 P 17284 O 18618 P 20185 O
13966 P 17217 P 17286 O 19495 F 20434 O
15143 P 17218 P 17294 O 19498 P 20850 F
15445 O 17221 17306 FP 19507 P 22164 P
17199 P 17232 PO 17611 O 19524 P

1911-1949
(including 1644-1949, 1842-1949)

PRIMARY 17274 FP 17723 P 17827 P 19486 P
15961 FP 17694 PO 17733 P 17869 PO 19523 F
17193 FP 17716 F 17736 P 17880 P 19556 P
17251 F 17721 P

SECOND. 15950 S 17185 FP 17298 P 19492 P
13150 FP 16947 FP 17187 FP 18534 PO 19566 P
13224 FP 17054 FP 17237 O 19006 O 19579 P
15632 P 17184 FP 17244 O 19216 P 20622 P
15866

1928-1949

PRIMARY 17704 P 17728 F 17834 F 19505 P
15871 F 17706 O 17729 F 17839 19555 FP
16063 P 17707 O 17730 O 17863 PO 20195 FP
16065 P 17708 P 17731 O 17864 F 20217 F
16417 P 17709 F 17732 F 17868 F 20642 F
17235 F 17710 F 17734 FP 17870 F 20862 F
17273 F 17715 P 17735 P 17888 F 20915 F
17698 O 17718 P 17737 O 19267 P 20919 F
17699 P 17725 FP 17833 F 19269 FP 22460 O
17703 F 17726 P

SECOND. 15437 PO 16979 O 17230 O 17262 O
14478 FP 15868 P 17205 17242 F 17275 O
15409 P 15965 P 17219 P 17249 P 17289 O
15430 P 16974 O 17220 17250 PO 17300 F
17302 S 17310 O 19268 F 19497 F 20644 F
17305 PO 17838 O 19270 O 19564 20951 O

1928-1972
(incl. 1644-1972, 1842-1972, 1911-1972)

PRIMARY 15192 O 16068 O 17311 O

SECOND. 15466 O 17316 P 17580 O 18313 P
14809 O 15810 FP 17318 P 17586 P 18820 O
15191 PO 16451

1949-1972

PRIMARY 17326 O 17742 F 17750 19297 O
10461 P 17331 O 17743 P 17751 O 19306 O
14527 P 17358 O 17744 O 17752 F 19325 O
15478 O 17383 O 17745 P 17805 O 19336 O
15506 O 17497 O 17746 PO 17914 O 19680 O
15560 FP 17738 O 17747 18060 F 20673 P
15915 P 17739 P 17748 O 19293 O 21035 O
16471 P 17740 O 17749 O 19295 O 21574 FP
16487 PO 17741 O

SECOND. 15531 O 16152 O 17372 P 19318 O
10175 O 15532 O 16458 O 17375 O 19322 P
10936 P 15537 P 16469 P 17380 O 19339 O
11173 15538 P 16480 FP 17389 O 19341 F
14819 15543 O 16894 O 17393 O 19586 O
14922 O 15556 O 16991 F 17593 PO 19593 PO
14947 O 15569 17327 O 17802 O 19605 O
14960 O 15578 P 17329 O 17806 O 20477 O
15254 O 15651 P 17332 O 17904 O 20497 F
15302 O 15891 P 17336 P 17994 FP 20503 O
15303 FP 15913 O 17340 P 17995 O 20679 O
15482 O 15916 O 17357 P 19291 P 20694 F
15501 O 15997 O 17361 P 19305 P 20699 O
15508 O 16075 P 17367 P 19308 P 21037 F
15518 P 16135 O

27 ELEMENTARY AND VOCATIONAL EDUCATION
初等教育及職業補習教育
初等教育及び補習教育

1644-1842

PRIMARY 17753 O

SECOND. 20043 P 20418 P 21279 P

1644-1911

PRIMARY 20157 O

SECOND. 19692 PO

1842-1911

PRIMARY 14556 P 15360 O 19612 20138 O
20275 O 21273

SECOND. 15340 FP 15735 O 20258 O 20380 O
14590 O 15349 O 15925 P 20379 O 20385 O
15338 P

1842-1928
(including 1644-1928)

PRIMARY 15374 F 17755 P 17756 S 17757 P
17758 P 19726 O

SECOND. 16101 O 19220 P 20006 PO 22423 PO
15378 F 17631 PO 19616 S 21342 P

1911-1928

PRIMARY 17760 O 17764 O 17770 P 19641
17759 P 17762 P 17768 P 17771 P 19646 O

SECOND. 15403 F 17871 FP 19645 P 20947 O
13976 P 15771 O 19001 PO 20207 O 21365 O
14429 S 16593 F 19021 O 20218 O 21816 P
15400 F 17306 FP

1911-1949
(including 1644-1949, 1842-1949)

PRIMARY 17754 P 17769 P 19619 O 19631 P
15408 F 17763 PO 18981 P 19620 FP

SECOND. 14629 PO 17721 P 19643 P 20845 F
10086 PO 15384 PO 18021 PO 19644 PO 20946 F
12328 P 15961 FP 19233 F 19962 S 20949 F
13212 PO 16549 P 19257 P 19963 P 21330 O
14238 P 16624 FP 19615 PO 20210 P 21384 O
14496 P 17444 FP 19632 S 20264 O

1928-1949

PRIMARY 15415 PO 17761 O 17767 F 19648 O
15399 F 15430 P 17765 O 19633 O 20199 O
15414 PO 16414 O 17766 FP 19638 S 20221 O

SECOND. 15424 F 16057 P 17308 O 20200 O
11724 P 15426 S 16062 P 17718 P 20262 F
12269 P 15436 F 16617 PO 17891 O 20396 O
12310 P 15447 F 16626 PO 19621 O 20451 O
14474 FP 15596 F 16662 F 19649 O 20843 F
15405 F 15598 FP 17245 P 19702 P 20844 F
15406 F 15957 O 17278 P 20195 FP 20930 O
15410 O 16056 F 17287 O

1928-1972
(incl. 1644-1972, 1842-1972, 1911-1972)

PRIMARY 16732 O 17772 O 17773 F 17774 FP
19655 P 19658 P

SECOND. 15470 S 17311 O 19466 F 20428 O
12403 P 16733 P 17313 O 19970 FP 21417 P
15463 FP 16746 FP 19090 FP 19975 FP 22724 P

1949-1972

PRIMARY 17777 O 17789 O 17801 O 19662 P
14526 P 17778 P 17790 O 17802 O 19668 P
14840 P 17779 P 17791 P 17803 O 19671 P
15035 PO 17780 O 17792 P 17804 P 19679 FP
15482 O 17781 P 17793 O 17805 O 20407 P
15544 O 17782 P 17794 O 17806 O 20410 F
15891 P 17783 17795 O 17807 P 20416
16899 P 17784 17796 PO 17808 O 20419 O
17358 O 17785 P 17797 PO 17809 O 20426 FP
17670 O 17786 P 17798 O 17810 O 21562 O
17775 O 17787 O 17799 FP 17907 O 22755 O
17776 O 17788 F 17800 O 19597 FP

SECOND. 15508 O 15861 P 16760 O 19673 P
12427 P 15517 F 15889 P 16784 O 19678 P
12429 P 15521 F 15893 F 16824 19713 P
12485 P 15522 O 15989 F 17382 O 19990 FP
12528 P 15533 F 16009 P 17395 P 20249 F
13415 P 15545 O 16034 P 17745 P 20425 F
14535 P 15557 O 16046 PO 17748 O 20699 O
14957 PO 15577 O 16074 O 18003 FP 21118
15292 P 15621 F 16076 P 19309 P 21122 O
15478 O 15655 FP 16348 F 19667 P 22296 P
15479 O 15827 P

1842-1911

PRIMARY 17549 O 17815 O 18914 O 20705 O
10328 O 17609 O 17817 O 18926 O 20707 O
15307 O 17688 O 17818 O 20281 O 20711 O
15629 O 17811 O 17819 O 20282 O 20754 O
15720 O 17812 O 17821 O 20557 O 20758 O
16380 O 17813 O 17823 O 20583 O 20771 O
17026 O 17814 O 18444 O 20704 O 20773 F

SECONDARY: MONOGRAPHS
11681 O 15349 O 16377 O 17649 O 20565 PO
15315 O 15350 O 16378 O 18390 P 20579 O
15316 O 15355 O 16910 PO 18447 O 20590 PO
15321 O 15361 O 16912 O 18491 O 20713 O
15328 P 15744 O 16913 O 18889 O 20760 F
15344 O 15749 PO 17141 P 18906 O 22542 O
15345 O 15930 P 17158 O 18922 O 22612 P
15347 PO 16187 O

SECONDARY: INCLUSIONS
15358 O 15715 O 15753 O 16166 O 16920 O
15359 O 15717 O 16048 PO 16915 F 22523 O
15366 O

SECONDARY: JOURNAL ARTICLES
10274 O 15739 F 16399 O 19691 O 20702 O
15342 O 15862 O 16540 O 19694 O 20748 O
15357 O 15928 P 16906 O 20541 O 20764 O
15723 O 15932 O 17170 O 20542 O 20765 O
15730 O 16220 PO 17919 O 20567 O 21266 O
15735 O 16398 O 18300 O

1842-1928
(including 1644-1928)

PRIMARY 11683 O 17691 PO 17824 P 20795 O

SECOND. 15373 P 15864 P 16546 S 17690 P
10292 P 15374 F 15938 P 16553 FP 18956 PO
10340 PO 15388 S 15943 P 16555 PO 18960 PO
12953 PO 15389 PO 16101 O 16938 F 20006 PO
14224 PO 15673 O 16108 PO 17191 F 20802 PO
14634 F

1911-1928

PRIMARY 16695 F 17829 P 17859 O 17884 O
13029 S 17482 O 17831 F 17861 O 17886 F
13277 F 17611 O 17835 F 17862 O 17887 F
13976 F 17614 O 17836 O 17871 FP 19490 PO
15407 FP 17696 PO 17842 F 17873 PO 19511 O
15872 O 17697 P 17843 O 17874 S 19538 O
16122 O 17705 17844 O 17876 F 20627 F
16589 F 17713 FP 17848 O 17877 F 20883 S
16590 F 17717 PO 17851 S 17878 O 20889 F
16593 F 17719 O 17853 F 17879 O 20938 P
16594 F 17722 O 17855 F 17881 FP 20947 O
16685 P 17828 F 17856 F 17882 O 21517 O

SECOND. 16445 O 17263 O 19454 FP 20468
10294 P 16591 F 17566 O 19455 P 20626 F
15393 16627 O 17695 O 19516 S 20645 F
15413 O 16630 F 17712 P 19641 20868 F
15769 O 16645 F 17720 F 20103 O 20878 F
15771 O 16664 PO 18126 P 20216 F 20891 O
15865 P 17203 O 18697 PO 20296 O 20897 O
15966 FP 17221 18992 FP 20392 S 20914 O
16296 O 17232 PO 19364 O 20394 P 22802 FP
16413 O 17253 P

1911-1949
(including 1644-1949, 1842-1949)

PRIMARY 15961 FP 16953 P 17733 P 17869 PO
15376 FP 16409 P 17193 FP 17827 P 17880 P
15382 P 16556 FP 17666 FP 17832 O 19619 O
15408 F 16624 FP 17694 PO 17850 S 19632 S
15762 P 16668 P 17721 P 17857 F 20166 O
15866 16941 P 17723 P

SECOND. 15391 PO 15950 S 17192 17444 FP
10751 P 15420 PO 15959 P 17234 S 17460 FP
11747 FP 15428 O 16547 S 17237 O 17463 FP
13224 FP 15761 P 16557 FP 17239 17736 P
13537 FP 15941 P 16560 FP 17244 O 17769 P
15372 O 15942 P 16612 FP 17274 FP 18953 O
15377 P 15945 P 17029 FP 17282 18976 FP
15384 PO 15946 FP 17033 FP 17307 S 18993 PO
15387 PO 15948 P 17095 O 17309 F 19006 O
19014 P 19644 PO 20622 P 20912 P 22457 F
19233 F 20098 O 20791 P 20946 F 22654 P
19523 F 20106 O 20845 F 20949 F

1928-1949

PRIMARY: MONOGRAPHS
10804 O 15432 F 16064 FP 17728 F 17891 O
13970 O 15434 O 16418 F 17846 F 19648 O
15059 FP 15437 PO 16425 F 17849 O 19827 F
15394 O 15439 P 16628 O 17858 O 20644 F
15409 P 15869 F 17708 P 17863 PO 20863 O
15424 F 15965 P 17709 F 17872 P 20873 FP
15430 P 15971 P 17718 P 17883 FP

PRIMARY: INCLUSIONS
15074 F 16661 O 17845 O 17860 O 20910 O
16420 PO 17732 F 17854 F

PRIMARY: JOURNAL ARTICLES
10767 O 17058 P 17825 P 17864 F 19700 O
14717 O 17096 P 17826 P 17865 F 19703 O
15410 O 17097 F 17830 P 17866 F 20451 O
15412 O 17098 F 17833 F 17867 F 20642 F
15419 O 17250 PO 17834 F 17868 F 20843 F
15423 17633 F 17837 O 17870 F 20844 F
16422 17663 F 17838 O 17875 O 20846 O
16632 F 17668 F 17839 17885 F 20885 P
16662 F 17703 F 17840 F 17888 F 20890 PO
16708 F 17704 P 17841 F 17889 F 20894 O
16720 F 17707 O 17847 O 17890 F 20921 F
17045 F 17715 P 17852 O 19621 O 20945 O
17047 O

SECONDARY: MONOGRAPHS
10783 O 15405 F 15640 F 17725 FP 20199 O
11031 P 15406 F 15871 F 17729 F 20221 O
12256 F 15429 F 16063 P 18749 O 20396 O
13040 O 15431 P 16417 P 19555 FP 20436 O
13964 O 15438 P 16617 PO 19633 O 20862 F
14478 FP 15441 P 16717 F 19649 O 20919 F
14750 F 15443 P 17262 O 19846 P 20923 PO
14771 F 15444 P 17632 O 20195 FP

SECONDARY: INCLUSIONS
15870 PO 16666 F 16709 17479 FP 19280 O
16065 P 16690 FP 16721 O 17665 20198 F
16607 O 16693 FP 17416 O 18703 O 20872 F
16658 O 16694 O 17417 O 19022 F 20887 O

SECONDARY: JOURNAL ARTICLES
13022 F 16599 FP 17100 F 18658 O 20916 P
13038 P 16601 FP 17207 P 19622 S 20925 F
14474 FP 16602 F 17418 FP 19624 O 20937 F
15398 O 16686 O 17667 F 19834 F 20944 PO
15433 O 16713 F 17710 F 20637 F 20951 O
15447 F 16964 O 17726 P 20840 F 21210 FP
15448 F 16969 O 17734 FP 20851 S 21212 F
15868 P 16974 O 17737 O 20882 F 21230 F
16432 PO 17074 F 17943 O 20898 PO 21510 F
16443 O 17089 FP 18595 P

1928-1972
(incl. 1644-1972, 1842-1972, 1911-1972)

PRIMARY 15469 P 17313 O 17896 F 20657 PO
10301 FP 15472 P 17669 FP 17897 F 20663 P
13048 F 15607 P 17772 O 17898 O 20982 O
15192 O 15796 S 17892 P 17899 O 20994 O
15459 PO 16451 17893 O 20403 P 21231 P
15466 O 16455 S 17894 P 20475 O 22736 PO
15468 O 17311 O 17895 O

SECOND. 15458 PO 15981 F 16749 O 19082 PO
12387 PO 15460 FP 16068 O 17312 O 20224 O
14809 O 15461 P 16728 P 17615 O 20658 F
15191 PO 15467 PO 16729 FP 18788 O 20964 PO
15452 PO 15789 16734 P 19077 P 21393 O
15457 P 15975 P 16747 P 19080 F

1949-1972

PRIMARY: MONOGRAPHS
15297 O 15518 P 15545 O 15828 O 17676 F
15482 O 15519 O 15550 O 16768 P 17745 P
15491 F 15526 O 15553 PO 16771 F 17907 O
15499 PO 15530 F 15560 FP 16800 O 17909 P
15501 O 15537 P 15575 O 16887 F 17910 F
15506 O 15543 O 15621 F 17350 FP 17911 O

28 Local Welfare and Living Standards
地方福利及生活水準
地方の福祉及び生活水準

1644-1842

PRIMARY 15306 O 16369 O 17820 O 17822 O

SECOND. 10652 O 15305 O 15310 O 16507 PO
20043 P 20558 S

1644-1911

PRIMARY 15743 O 17816 P 19692 PO 20762 O
15320 PO 17687 P 19688 P

SECOND. 15346 P 16542 PO 17165 PO 18862 P
15313 PO 16049 P 16543 PO

29 REGIONAL AND SUBETHNIC VARIATION
習俗方言等等地域性差異
習俗方言等の地域的差異

30 VOLUNTARY ASSOCIATIONS & FORMAL ORGANIZATION IN GENERAL
組織原理及會社團體通論
組織原理及び社会団体一般

1911-1949
(including 1644-1949, 1842-1949)

PRIMARY 10086 PO 15384 PO 17979 P 17980 P
19357 FP

SECOND. 16104 S 18149 P 19218 19962 S
10781 P 16309 O 18544 P 19355 FP 20214 O
12623 S 17036 FP 18619 S 19358 P 22939 P
14698 P 18119 P 18745 O

1928-1949

PRIMARY 15448 F 17228 P 18118 P 18750 O
19640 P 19702 P

SECOND. 14762 P 15441 P 17570 O 19270 O
13909 O 15438 P 15443 P 18117 P 19362 F
14249 P 15439 P 15968 P 18647 P 20873 FP
14754 PO 15440 P 16290 O 18660 P

1928-1972
(incl. 1644-1972, 1842-1972, 1911-1972)

PRIMARY 14256 15470 S 17985 FP 17989 S
11045 FP 14292 P 16330 P 17986 P 18311 PO
11052 FP 15181 P 16343 P 17987 P 19284 P
14015 O 15183 PO 17984 O 17988 S 22016 S
14131

SECOND. 11607 P 15981 F 18809 S 21469
10117 PO 11862 P 16128 FP 18832 21476 S
10123 O 13986 P 16332 P 19650 PO 21830 S
10125 P 15171 FP 16335 P 19734 O 22199 P
10127 15472 P 18313 P 19978 FP 22238 P
10851 P 15980 P 18795 P 20417 O

1949-1972

PRIMARY 15233 P 16082 P 17997 P 18263 FP
10131 F 15258 P 17386 FP 17998 P 19420
10967 P 15287 P 17990 P 17999 P 19713 P
10975 P 15303 FP 17991 S 18000 P 19714 P
11006 P 15495 P 17992 P 18001 O 19737 FP
11083 P 15540 P 17993 P 18002 P 20236 F
11111 P 16003 F 17994 FP 18003 FP 20272 FP
14297 S 16007 FP 17995 O 18004 F 21579 PO
14331 P 16027 O 17996 P 18251 P 22307 PO

SECOND. 12012 P 15221 16034 P 19607 P
10154 P 12082 P 15280 S 16354 F 19931 P
10900 12839 FP 15291 P 16496 FP 20268 F
10911 P 14040 FP 15509 O 17646 P 20426 FP
10913 P 14084 P 15530 F 18208 P 20484 P
10935 P 14142 P 15537 P 18232 P 21012 O
10941 P 14144 P 15560 FP 18284 P 22021 P
11003 P 14329 P 15563 PO 18285 P 22304 P
11067 FP 14337 P 15568 P 18286 P 22337
11076 P 14343 P 15655 FP 18287 P 22361 P
11120 P 14345 S 15813 F 18320 P 22746 P
11144 O 14853 P 15845 P 18340 P 23035 O
11154 P 14872 PO 15852 FP 19595 S 23051 O
11179 P 14950 O 15912 P

31 Social Organization of Recreation

娯樂組織　娯楽組織

1644-1842

PRIMARY 16218 O 18011 P 18013 P 18014 P
22511 O

SECOND. 10026 O 11675 O 15305 O 17657 O
22398 O

1644-1911

PRIMARY 18005 18007 S 18012 P 18015 O
16194 O 18006 P 18010 P

SECOND. 10016 O 14208 S 17975 O 21276 P
10001 O 10058 PO 15313 PO 19718 P 21691 PO
10014 O 10550 P 15327 PO

1842-1911

PRIMARY 16156 O 18016 O 20259 O 20579 O
10025 O 16219 O 18017 O 20279 O 22397 FP
10641 O 18008 O 20093 O 20382 O 22601 O
15364 O 18009 O 20258 O

SECOND. 10611 O 15363 O 18445 P 20557 O
10002 O 14157 O 15367 O 19686 O 20559 O
10003 O 15308 O 15630 O 19751 O 20578 O
10024 O 15317 O 16090 O 20254 P 20749 O
10030 O 15325 O 16526 O 20379 O 21980 O
10038 O 15338 P 16533 O 20381 O 22067 O
10043 O 15355 O 16915 F 20385 O 22599 O
10059 O 15360 O 17410 PO

1842-1928
(including 1644-1928)

PRIMARY 14701 O 15390 O 18022 O 19697 P
14214 PO 15374 F 16246 O 18024 PO 21346 P

SECOND. 16267 O 18983 FP 21504 O 21798 P
10082 PO 16938 F 21331 O

1911-1928

PRIMARY 15407 FP 16121 O 18025 18026 P
20468

SECOND. 15418 F 17720 F 20107 S 20434 O
10838 P 16593 F 19825 O 20273 O 20463 F
15403 F 17614 O 20103 O

1911-1949
(including 1644-1949, 1842-1949)

PRIMARY 18020 S 18027 P 18034 O 20609 PO
14698 P 18021 PO 18029 F 19354 P 21348 O
18018 O 18023 PO 18030 F 20106 O 21459 P
18019

SECOND. 15372 O 17036 FP 20612 FP 21351 P
10083 PO 15384 PO 17448 P 20615 O 21359 P
10104 O 15408 F 18622 O 20623 PO 22004 P
10807 P 15446 P 19245 O 21325 P 22452 FP
15370 O

1928-1949

PRIMARY 18028 O 18032 O 18035 O 18037
15414 PO 18031 O 18033 FP 18036 O 21527 F

SECOND. 14762 P 15417 O 16295 F 19638 S
10098 O 14774 FP 15448 F 16313 O 19702 P
11724 P 15394 O 15773 P 16432 PO 20447 F
13970 O 15404 O 16058 P 16979 O 20461 P
14750 F 15405 F 16060 O 19396 P 22455 F
14754 PO 15415 PO 16116 O

1928-1972
(incl. 1644-1972, 1842-1972, 1911-1972)

PRIMARY 14285 P 18039 O 18043 P 18315
11046 P 15458 PO 18040 O 18044 P 19659 P
12782 P 16332 P 18041 P 18045 21395 PO
14264 P 18038 FP 18042 PO 18046 O

SECOND. 14269 P 15466 O 17895 O 20661
10118 O 14293 S 15468 O 17985 FP 21428 O
10120 S 14808 P 15469 P 17989 S 21874 P
11033 S 14809 O 15981 F 18170 P 22473 S
12766 P 15189 O 16334 PO 18827 O 22480 F
12772 P 15452 PO 17615 O 20223 O 22485 S
12783 FP 15460 FP 17892 P 20224 O 22493 S
14263 P

1949-1972

PRIMARY 18049 F 18056 P 18063 O 18070 O
10175 O 18050 O 18057 P 18064 O 18071 P
11139 P 18051 O 18058 P 18065 O 18072 P
11151 P 18052 P 18059 P 18066 P 20272 FP
12810 O 18053 O 18060 F 18067 O 20668 O
14351 P 18054 P 18061 O 18068 O 22504 P
18047 PO 18055 P 18062 O 18069 O 23054 S
18048 F

SECONDARY: MONOGRAPHS
10132 O 10145 O 10174 O 11003 P 11096 P
10143 O 10149 O 10894 P 11061 O 11105 P
11113 P 15481 O 15828 O 19713 P 20688 O
11178 P 15482 O 16007 FP 19714 P 20699 O
11885 P 15493 O 18263 FP 19738 F 21063 P
11901 O 15498 O 18362 O 19990 FP 21124 PO
12849 P 15501 O 19105 FP 20249 F 21484 F
14369 O 15511 O 19590 P 20484 P 22500 O
14829 O 15526 O 19594 20502 O 22750 O
14999 O 15549 P 19595 S 20522 FP 22755 O
15205 O 15550 O 19663 PO

SECONDARY: INCLUSIONS
11072 P 11078 P 12858 P 12861 P 15817
11073 P 11128 P 12859 P 14844 O 21486 O
11077 P 11617 PO 12860 P 15243 O

SECONDARY: JOURNAL ARTICLES
12518 O 15839 O 16362 PO 18338 P 21010 PO
12848 P 16017 P 17751 O 19158 P 21591 P
15487 O 16135 O 17994 FP 19938 F 22292 P

32 Political Parties

政黨　政党

1644-1842

PRIMARY 10626 P

SECOND. 10552 P

1644-1911

PRIMARY 10557 P 11235 P 14555 P 18098 P
10541 S 10667 P 11241 P

SECOND. 13838 14206 P 21300 S 22068 P
10540 S 14205 P 21288 P 22058 P 22558 P
12933 P

1842-1911

PRIMARY 12615 P 18080 P 18093 P 21272 P
10508 P 14186 P 18081 S 18094 S 21680 P
10547 S 14187 P 18082 S 18095 22025 P
10555 P 14556 P 18083 P 18096 P 22029 P
10556 P 15127 P 18084 P 18097 P 22037 P
10558 P 17411 P 18085 P 18099 P 22046 P
10606 P 18073 P 18086 P 18100 P 22060 P
10631 P 18074 P 18087 P 18457 P 22069 P
10640 PO 18075 O 18088 P 18469 P 22073 P
10662 P 18076 P 18089 P 18517 P 22074 P
10677 P 18077 P 18090 O 19365 P 22571 P
11191 PO 18078 P 18091 P 21265 P 22625 P
11209 P 18079 P 18092 P

SECOND. 10619 P 12921 O 18872 P 22027 P
10510 P 10630 PO 17523 P 20254 P 22039 P
10530 10637 18388 P 21260 PO 22049 P
10537 P 10645 P 18487 P 21264 O 22542 O
10538 P 12611 P 18520 P 21436 P 22607 P
10548 P

1842-1928
(including 1644-1928)

PRIMARY 11285 P 18102 O 18533 PO 22076 S
10686 P 11297 PO 18103 P 18542 P 22079 P
10713 P 14109 P 18105 18551 PO 22127 P
11247 P 15944 P 18106 P 18991 P 22128 P
11260 P 18101 P

SECOND. 10733 O 14232 P 18555 21338 P
10076 S 10735 S 18563 O 21343 P
10695 P 11269 S 14634 F 21361 P
10697 S 11291 P 14693 FP 19474 22097 P
10698 P 11708 S 15134 P 19475 22117 P
10703 P 11718 15373 P 19477 PO 22118 P
10709 P 12644 PO 15390 O 21304 P 22657 S
10712 S 13508 P 18540 21306 P
18552 P 21337 PO

1911-1928

PRIMARY 10844 P 13921 S 15143 P 18122 P
10106 P 11375 P 13927 P 17567 O 18126 P
10757 PO 11377 S 13955 O 17982 P 18127 S
10777 P 13889 P 13962 P 18109 18129 FP
10778 O 13896 PO 13979 P 18110 P 18138 P
10834 P 13905 PO 14114 18115 P 18144 P

18148 P 18163 P 18713 O 18774 P 19500 P
18152 P 18579 O 18724 P 18777 P 19512 P
18153 P 18596 PO 18742 P 18779 P 19534 P
18156 P 18616 18757 O 18782 P 20211 O
18160 P 18649 P 18765 18784 22689 P
18161 O 18670 S

SECOND. 11816 S 13971 18620 P 19502 P
10750 P 12741 P 13972 O 18654 P 19503 FP
10779 13016 P 14119 S 18706 O 19526
10785 P 13906 PO 14468 P 18720 S 19558
10811 P 13929 O 14752 P 18725 P 22165 FP
10835 P 13931 O 16122 O 18748 P 22180 P
10838 P 13937 P 18601 P 18764 O 22678 O
10840 S 13938 P 18602 P 19450 P 22684 P
11349 P 13953 O 18615 19459 22934 S
11376 P 13966 P

1911-1949

(including 1644-1949, 1842-1949)

PRIMARY 10828 P 14703 S 18137 S 18545 PO
10107 P 11029 P 14753 P 18140 O 18562 S
10689 11257 P 15139 18143 O 18565 S
10693 P 11289 P 15140 O 18147 P 18626 P
10696 P 11699 S 15156 O 18149 P 18685 P
10700 PO 12307 P 18104 P 18151 21324 P
10718 S 13887 P 18108 P 18154 P 21354 PO
10724 S 13911 P 18119 P 18155 P 21373 P
10739 P 13916 P 18120 P 18157 P 22080 P
10743 P 13945 P 18121 P 18162 P 22095 P
10776 PO 13977 P 18123 P 18303 P 22150 S
10782 PO 14238 P 18131 P 18304 P 22672 P
10815 14670 P 18132 S 18309 S

SECONDARY: MONOGRAPHS
10090 O 12271 P 15955 P 18732 P 21321 P
10346 S 12676 S 18534 PO 18752 P 21325 P
10715 P 13880 PO 18535 P 18756 21359 P
10793 P 14217 P 18536 P 18759 P 21362 O
10803 P 14219 PO 18557 P 18767 O 21459 P
11263 PO 14223 P 18598 O 18780 P 22091 P
11279 P 14479 PO 18635 P 19457 P 22135 P
11290 P 14496 P 18661 P 19476 P 22144 P
11336 P 14678 S 18699 P 20431 P 22648 PO
11601 P 14686 P 18722 O 20442 P 22666 S
11690 P 14692 P 18730 P 20653 O 22939 P

SECONDARY: INCLUSIONS
10078 S 13920 P 18645 S 21303 P 21326 P
12678 18571 S 18745 O 21309 P 21332 P

SECONDARY: JOURNAL ARTICLES
10762 P 18591 S 18698 P 19542 22171 S
12325 P 18651 S 19463 P 20454 P 22656
18587 S

1928-1949

PRIMARY 12314 P 18114 P 18142 P 18761 P
10103 PO 12331 P 18116 P 18145 P 19464 P
10741 P 13888 O 18117 P 18146 P 19626 P
10748 O 13893 O 18118 P 18150 P 20184
10780 P 13909 O 18124 FP 18158 PO 20440 O
10798 O 13919 P 18125 PO 18159 O 20443 P
10813 P 13932 P 18128 P 18584 O 20444 P
10814 P 13975 PO 18130 P 18603 O 20450 P
10819 P 14248 P 18133 P 18629 P 21372 O
10826 O 16054 P 18134 P 18656 P 22157 P
10839 O 16056 F 18135 S 18672 P 22169 P
11341 P 18107 P 18136 S 18675 P 22681 FP
11367 P 18111 P 18139 P 18707 O 22695 P
11765 S 18112 O 18141 P 18712 P 22699 P
11806 S 18113 O

SECOND. 10830 P 13934 P 18613 P 19623 PO
10096 O 10831 P 13942 P 18663 P 20437 O
10101 O 11327 P 13943 O 18677 P 20449 P
10108 P 11328 PO 13954 O 18681 P 21371 O
10742 P 11338 P 14235 P 18687 O 22143 P
10758 P 11343 P 15154 P 18701 P 22176 P
10771 11738 O 15394 O 18717 P 22683 S
10773 P 11788 S 15957 O 18718 S 22688 S
10786 P 11841 PO 15967 P 18754 S 22702 P
10789 P 13902 O 16119 P 18755 P 22710 O
10796 P 13907 P 16430 P 18766 P 22714 P
10797 F 13912 O 17565 O 19571 P 22720 PO
10804 O 13923 P 17735 P 19573 P 22942 S
10805 P 13926 O 18612 P

1928-1972

(incl. 1644-1972, 1842-1972, 1911-1972)

PRIMARY: MONOGRAPHS
10124 S 11605 O 15169 P 18185 P 21400 P
10129 S 11614 P 15175 FP 18186 P 21405 P
10850 PO 11872 PO 15176 O 18187 P 21412 P
10853 PO 12387 PO 15191 PO 18312 P 21414 FP
10855 FP 14002 P 15806 P 18792 P 21419 P
10882 P 14258 P 15980 P 18804 PO 21425 P
10883 S 14278 P 18164 P 18809 S 21427 PO
10885 PO 14279 PO 18170 P 18812 21538 FP
10887 PO 14292 P 18172 P 18817 PO 22196 P
10888 S 15158 S 18176 P 18822 P 22229 P
11035 O 15161 P 18178 FP 18823 S 22235 P
11052 FP 15163 S 18182 P 20473 P 22251 P
11393 P 15168 18183 P

PRIMARY: INCLUSIONS
10856 S 14280 P 15186 S 18181 21877 S
13999 P 14281 P 17955 S 18808 P 22247 O
14261 P 14288 P 18167 P 18811 22267 P
14275 P 15164 P 18180 P

PRIMARY: JOURNAL ARTICLES
10848 P 14272 P 18166 S 18177 P 18806 P
10849 P 14291 P 18168 P 18179 P 18814 P
10880 P 14413 P 18169 P 18184 F 18815 P
11037 P 15182 P 18171 P 18188 P 18830 P
11417 P 15979 P 18173 P 18311 PO 20474 P
12391 P 17987 P 18174 P 18789 P 21390 P
14262 P 18165 P 18175 P 18803

SECONDARY: MONOGRAPHS
10125 P 11391 P 15174 P 18834 P 21466 P
10126 O 11848 PO 15181 P 19583 P 21847 P
10128 O 13997 15192 O 19899 P 22203 P
10851 P 14001 P 15459 PO 20231 PO 22224 P
10852 P 14006 P 15460 FP 21392 PO 22225 S
10858 S 14012 P 15973 P 21395 PO 22250 P
10865 P 14014 P 17311 O 21406 P 22260 P
10873 P 14018 S 17615 O 21410 FP 22273 P
10890 P 14020 FP 18313 P 21420 PO 22734 O
11040 PO 14274 P 18796 O 21422 O 22950 S
11044 PO 14285 P 18810 21424 P 22954 P
11048 S 15166 18819 P

SECONDARY: INCLUSIONS
10119 S 14276 P 15188 P 21858 P 22209 S
10866 FP 14290 P 18799 P 21893 P 22234 P
11612 P 15160 P 18825 P 21898 PO 22236 P
11613 P 15170 18833 P 22197 P 22272 P
13995 P 15185 S 20472 P 22205 S

SECONDARY: JOURNAL ARTICLES
10877 P 14004 P 14414 P 18797 S 22201 P
11039 S 14008 P 14415 P 18813 P 22213 P
11402 P 14260 P 14438 S 18829 S 22228 P
11404 S 14270 P 15167 S 21397 P 22245
11408 P 14271 P 15178 21408 P 22265 P
11602 P 14282 S 16128 FP 21426 P 22274 S
11866 P 14283 S 17986 P 22189 22280 P

1949-1972

PRIMARY: MONOGRAPHS
10173 O 11168 P 14951 P 17913 P 18289 P
10177 O 11179 P 15202 P 17990 P 18296
10180 O 11437 P 15214 PO 17993 P 18298 P
10894 P 14033 P 15234 P 18212 P 18299 P
10938 P 14037 P 15235 P 18224 P 18319 P
10970 P 14047 P 15237 P 18225 P 18324 PO
10975 P 14077 P 15245 PO 18232 P 20314 P
10994 P 14309 P 15248 P 18236 P 20328 P
10999 14316 S 15250 P 18263 FP 20505 PO
11076 P 14329 P 15254 O 18264 P 22291 P
11094 P 14384 P 15285 O 18272 P 22298 P
11113 P 14385 P 15294 P 18277 P 22299 P
11132 14387 P 15304 O 18279 S 22324 P
11154 P 14416 P 15856 O 18283 P 22375 PO
11160 P 14885 P 16071 FP

PRIMARY: INCLUSIONS
10147 P 14324 P 15233 P 17638 P 18209 P
10930 P 14326 FP 15287 P 17644 F 18219 P
11083 P 14336 P 15291 P 18000 P 18240 P
11942 P 15203 P 15299 P 18189 P 18241 P
11965 P 15222 P 15485 F 18196 P 18242 P
12121 P 15223 P 16035 P 18206 P 18280 P
14138 P 15224 P 16769 P 18208 P 18281 FP
18282 P 18287 P 18334 P 19369 P 22290 P
18284 P 18290 P 18340 P 20524 FP 22313 P
18285 P 18293 P 18343 FP 20698 O 22321 P
18286 P 18294 S 18344 F

PRIMARY: JOURNAL ARTICLES
10900 14073 P 15295 P 18223 P 18265 P
10905 P 14076 P 16481 PO 18226 P 18266 P
10913 P 14081 P 17596 P 18227 P 18267 P
10924 P 14303 S 17775 O 18228 P 18268 P
10928 P 14307 P 17992 P 18229 P 18269 P
10933 P 14317 P 17998 P 18230 P 18270
10935 P 14319 P 18190 P 18231 P 18271 F
10940 P 14320 P 18191 P 18233 P 18273 P
10955 14333 P 18192 O 18234 P 18274 P
10958 P 14345 S 18193 PO 18235 P 18275 P
10965 P 14346 P 18194 P 18237 P 18276 P
10976 P 14355 P 18195 P 18238 P 18278 S
10979 S 14357 18197 P 18239 P 18288 P
10980 P 14367 O 18198 P 18243 P 18291 P
10983 S 14381 P 18199 P 18244 18292 P
10992 PO 14383 P 18200 P 18245 P 18295 P
11098 P 14386 P 18201 P 18246 P 18297 P
11108 P 15196 P 18202 P 18247 P 18316 P
11114 S 15198 P 18203 P 18248 P 18329 P
11121 P 15206 O 18204 P 18249 P 18335 O
11129 15208 P 18205 P 18250 P 18353 P
11136 P 15211 P 18207 P 18251 P 19169 PO
11452 P 15219 P 18210 P 18252 P 19183 P
11533 P 15220 P 18211 P 18253 P 19370 P
11900 S 15226 P 18213 PO 18254 P 19379 P
11941 P 15236 P 18214 S 18255 P 19596 P
11981 P 15244 P 18215 P 18256 P 20374 P
12037 P 15251 P 18216 P 18257 P 20476 P
12078 S 15255 18217 P 18258 P 20501 P
12099 P 15256 P 18218 P 18259 P 20521 P
12116 P 15257 P 18220 P 18260 P 22303 P
12117 P 15263 P 18221 P 18261 P 22344 P
12129 P 15282 S 18222 P 18262 P 22374 P

SECONDARY: MONOGRAPHS
10134 O 11514 P 12813 P 15267 P 19338 P
10152 O 11639 P 12864 P 15493 O 19390 P
10164 O 11883 O 13366 P 15507 P 19595 S
10169 O 11897 PO 14053 P 15544 O 19597 FP
10960 FP 11919 O 14144 P 15553 PO 19922 P
10961 P 11922 O 14153 PO 16029 S 20478 F
10989 P 12008 FP 14296 P 16070 O 20492 P
10997 P 12015 P 14299 P 16072 P 20496 PO
11003 P 12027 P 14305 P 16148 FP 21433 O
11005 P 12044 P 14322 P 16150 P 21585 O
11006 P 12082 P 14334 P 16347 O 21594 S
11092 S 12086 14835 S 17779 P 22304 P
11110 P 12109 P 14962 P 17995 O 22325 P
11138 F 12123 P 15230 P 18003 FP 22326 S
11178 P 12523 P 15240 O 19069 PO 22339 P
11180 P 12524 FP 15241 S 19100 P 22747 O
11496 P 12811 O 15260 P 19135 P

SECONDARY: INCLUSIONS
10131 F 11435 P 14147 P 14945 P 17646 P
10137 P 11443 FP 14325 P 14977 P 17997 P
10151 S 11451 P 14330 FP 15101 P 18325 P
10163 P 11458 P 14343 P 15229 P 19111 O
10171 S 11459 P 14344 P 15243 O 19165 F
10918 P 11637 P 14363 P 15281 S 19290 P
10919 P 11959 PO 14372 P 15286 19324 FP
10920 P 13058 P 14374 15296 P 19373 P
10946 P 13097 P 14380 P 15987 F 20530 P
10993 P 13413 P 14393 O 16075 P 21916 P
11007 P 14054 P 14394 P 17640 P 22358 P
11077 P 14082 P 14448 P 17642 P 22380 P
11433 PO 14146 F 14888 O 17643 P

SECONDARY: JOURNAL ARTICLES
10897 P 10966 P 11122 P 11650 P 14042 P
10899 PO 10967 P 11177 P 12028 P 14044 P
10901 S 10969 P 11430 P 12040 P 14067 P
10907 P 10977 PO 11444 P 12057 P 14132 P
10910 P 10986 P 11453 P 12111 P 14149 P
10914 P 11009 P 11456 P 12153 P 14294 P
10923 F 11058 P 11457 P 12549 P 14295 P
10925 P 11070 P 11493 FP 12842 O 14308 P
10926 S 11093 P 11515 P 12848 P 14313 P
10936 P 11097 PO 11522 P 13069 P 14315
10949 S 11109 S 11525 P 13346 P 14318 P
10956 PO 11112 S 11532 P 13429 P 14331 P
10959 S 11116 P 11626 S 14041 P 14332 P

14338 P 15227 P 16027 O 18360 P 20489 O
14339 S 15238 P 16129 18361 P 20490 P
14342 15239 P 16792 P 19099 P 20514 P
14353 P 15242 17130 PO 19139 P 20520 P
14365 P 15246 S 17383 O 19150 P 20997 O
14371 P 15252 O 17597 P 19294 P 20998 O
14375 P 15253 P 17620 F 19305 P 21548 O
14388 P 15261 P 17636 O 19371 P 21560 S
14417 F 15265 17902 O 19376 P 22328 P
14532 P 15277 17991 S 19378 P 22330 P
14814 P 15278 17994 FP 19382 P 22337
15197 O 15290 17996 P 19386 P 22345 O
15199 15302 O 18328 P 19387 P 22361 P
15200 P 15540 P 18331 P 19599 P 22370 P
15201 S 15994 P 18337 P 19610 P 22382 S
15218 P 16014 S 18352 P 20479 O 22759
15225 P 16018 P 18359 S 20485 O 22838 S

32.1 State or Party Control of Organized Groups

政府或政黨對於組織團體之控制

政府又は政党による組織団体の統制

1644-1842

Primary 11541 P 17173 P
Second. 10552 P 17822 O 19350 P 22590 O
10033 O 13812 18425 P

1644-1911

Primary 17541 P
Second. 13844 P 17975 O 18526 S 22866 P
13838 14617 P 18391 P 19437 P

1842-1911

Primary 14565 PO 18301 S 18436 P 18479 O
10631 P 18300 O 18407 O 18467 O
Second. 14592 P 18073 P 18437 P 19349 P
10062 PO 14593 P 18087 P 18453 P 19438 P
10630 PO 17523 P 18370 P 18457 P 21260 PO
14396 P 17540 O 18392 P 18521 S 22514 P
14571 P 17973 PO 18433 P 19343 S 22571 P

1842-1928

(including 1644-1928)

Primary 12666 P 15938 P 18531 S
Second. 13646 S 15944 P 19477 PO 19697 P
12663 P 14109 P 17981 P 19479 22137 S
13187 P 14693 FP 19215 O

1911-1928

Primary 14752 P 18582 O 18709 P 19501 P
11026 P 18306 O 18655 P 19448 P 19530
13947 P 18308 P 18669 P 19455 P 19533 P
13950 S 18310 P 18670 S
Second. 14484 18654 P 19427 P 19546 P
10750 P 15147 P 18724 P 19454 FP 19548 P
10769 P 15148 P 18725 P 19502 P 19558
10844 P 18115 P 18734 P 19503 FP 19570 P
12346 P 18122 P 18735 P 19504 P 19639 P
12741 P 18148 P 18742 P 19506 P 20465 P
13260 P 18586 P 18764 O 19510 P 20466
13906 PO 18592 P 18774 P 19545 P 22162 P
13931 O 18649 P 18775 P

1911-1949

(including 1644-1949, 1842-1949)

Primary 14753 P 18149 P 18309 S 18732 P
13945 P 15140 O 18303 P 18547 PO 19561 P
14677 P 18121 P 18304 P 18645 S 22654 P
14679 P
Second. 10700 PO 13980 P 14655 P 14695 S
10446 O 11290 P 14238 P 14656 P 14715 P
10689 13537 FP 14479 PO 14665 PO 14736 P
10696 P 13911 P 14496 P 14681 PO 14761 O
14770 O 18143 O 18768 S 19435 P 19532
18119 P 18544 P 19216 P 19444 P 19542
18120 P 18650 P 19358 P 19476 P 19559 PO
18137 S 18714 P 19398 S 19519 O 19630 P

1928-1949

Primary 13923 P 18134 P 18668 S 19572 P
11030 P 16061 P 18302 O 18692 P 19573 P
11725 P 16064 FP 18305 P 18766 P 19574 P
13030 PO 18111 P 18307 P 19270 O 20443 P
13904 P 18125 PO 18606 P 19525 S 20460 O
Second. 14478 FP 16659 PO 18581 P 19537
10103 PO 14501 P 17047 O 18643 F 19540
10796 P 14718 PO 17715 P 18660 P 19565 O
10799 PO 14749 PO 17767 F 18703 O 19625 S
10821 S 14762 P 18112 O 19280 O 19626 P
11343 P 14764 O 18117 P 19396 P 20437 O
11732 P 14771 F 18118 P 19493 P 20444 P
11838 O 15441 P 18124 FP 19494 P 20458 O
13943 O 16058 P 18135 S 19508 O 22714 P
13965 O 16430 P

1928-1972

(incl. 1644-1972, 1842-1972, 1911-1972)

Primary 12418 FP 14270 P 17986 P 18315
10855 FP 13986 P 14285 P 18171 P 18797 S
10883 S 13991 P 14777 P 18179 P 18798 P
10885 PO 13992 P 14788 P 18186 P 19077 P
11033 S 14000 P 14798 FP 18187 P 19092 P
11035 O 14001 P 14808 P 18311 PO 19286 O
11042 P 14006 P 15978 FP 18312 P 20960 P
11391 P 14263 P 15979 P 18313 P 22738 P
11408 P 14268 P 17584 P 18314 P
Secondary: Monographs
10850 PO 14002 P 15158 S 18176 P 20473 P
10852 P 14010 S 15169 P 18178 FP 20475 O
10887 PO 14014 P 15980 P 18810 21395 PO
11036 P 14015 O 15981 F 18817 PO 21414 FP
11052 FP 14258 P 17313 O 18822 P 21416 O
11053 O 14264 P 17315 P 19082 PO 21538 FP
11390 P 14269 P 17586 P 19083 P 21853 P
11852 P 14292 P 17772 O 19285 P 22190 P
11862 P 14512 P 17985 FP 19466 F 22217 P
11872 PO 14784 O 18041 P 19468 F 22233 PO
12379 P 14786 PO 18172 P 19583 P 22250 P
13314 P 14797 P
Secondary: Inclusions
10856 S 13993 P 15183 PO 18180 P 20472 P
10874 P 13999 P 18043 P 18181 22236 P
11043 P 14017 18045 19080 F 22247 O
Secondary: Journal Articles
10848 P 14003 P 17987 P 18789 P 19031 P
11034 P 14005 P 18044 P 18800 P 19287 P
11055 S 14259 P 18166 S 18824 19582 P
12391 P 14787 P 18174 P 18829 S 22188 P
12784 P 16128 FP 18188 P

1949-1972

Primary: Monographs
10931 P 12845 P 15230 P 18061 O 18362 O
10962 12876 P 15260 P 18212 P 19166 P
11076 P 13105 P 15511 O 18264 P 19184 PO
11094 P 14037 P 15570 P 18272 P 19338 P
11096 P 14040 FP 16013 P 18277 P 19422 P
11101 FP 14047 P 16016 O 18319 P 19594
11138 F 14055 P 17015 O 18324 PO 19595 S
11161 P 14299 P 17387 P 18330 PO 19597 FP
11437 P 14337 P 17588 P 18341 P 19668 P
11651 FP 14853 P 17674 P 18345 P 20507 P
11885 P 15006 O 17990 P 18350 P 21433 O
11975 P 15007 P 17993 P 18354 O 21928 P
12523 P 15017 P 18003 FP 18355 O 22764 O
Primary: Inclusions
10898 FP 14913 P 17643 P 18285 P 18343 FP
11063 PO 15217 P 17644 F 18286 P 18344 F
11100 P 15296 P 17646 P 18287 P 18346 P
11131 P 15485 F 18208 P 18322 O 18347 P
12863 P 15990 P 18240 P 18325 P 18348 P
14302 P 16075 P 18241 P 18334 P 18349 P
14391 P 16769 P 18284 P 18340 P 18356 P
18358 F 19290 P 19332 P 19605 O 21916 P
19094 O 19324 FP 19333 P 19608 P 22857 S
19113 O 19331 P 19334 P
Primary: Journal Articles
10897 P 14064 P 18054 P 18329 P 19310 P
10941 P 14073 P 18059 P 18331 P 19330
10951 P 14081 P 18066 P 18332 P 19386 P
11067 FP 14360 P 18072 P 18333 O 19410 P
11142 P 14362 P 18192 O 18335 O 19596 P
11155 P 14417 F 18226 P 18336 P 19599 P
11431 P 14832 P 18227 P 18337 P 19600 P
11444 P 14881 O 18247 P 18338 P 19606 P
11482 P 14950 O 18254 P 18339 P 19607 P
11515 P 14959 P 18271 F 18342 P 20490 P
12028 P 14985 O 18276 P 18351 P 20497 F
12040 P 15200 P 18316 P 18352 P 20514 P
12497 P 15208 P 18317 P 18353 P 20520 P
12802 P 15845 P 18318 O 18357 P 20533 P
12815 P 16081 P 18320 P 18359 S 20997 O
12847 S 16082 P 18321 O 18360 P 21431 F
12874 S 16135 O 18323 P 18361 P 21968 P
13069 P 16784 O 18326 P 19168 PO 22369 P
13346 P 17639 P 18327 S 19169 PO 22825
14061 P 17645 O 18328 P
Secondary: Monographs
10136 O 12485 P 14385 P 15544 O 19133 PO
10140 O 12563 P 14828 P 15572 FP 19135 P
10150 O 12791 P 14871 P 15897 O 19288
10167 O 12813 P 14885 P 16029 S 19291 P
10177 O 12836 P 14899 P 16070 O 19296 O
10232 P 12849 P 14909 P 16071 FP 19367 P
10464 P 12864 P 14942 P 16150 P 19389 P
10944 P 13070 P 14962 P 16996 S 19408 PO
10960 FP 13104 P 14969 P 17381 P 19590 P
10961 P 13117 P 14974 PO 17587 P 19611 P
10994 P 13775 P 15025 P 18224 P 20079 P
11423 P 14053 P 15028 P 18279 S 20484 P
11627 F 14065 P 15029 P 18283 P 20506 P
11946 P 14077 P 15034 P 18298 P 20526 P
11980 PO 14310 15214 PO 19063 PO 21435 O
11998 P 14322 P 15241 S 19100 P 22291 P
12086 14329 P 15294 P 19110 O 22296 P
12109 P 14364 P 15507 P 19122 P 22753 O
12441 P 14370 O 15524 O 19131 P 22831 P
12442 P 14378 P
Secondary: Inclusions
10138 P 14049 P 16035 P 18294 S 19598 FP
10178 P 14054 P 16037 FP 19109 O 19603 P
10917 P 14138 P 17005 O 19116 O 20486 P
10930 P 14327 P 17122 O 19119 O 20530 P
11007 P 14363 P 17345 O 19162 20693 O
11065 PO 14816 P 17396 O 19193 O 21064 O
11079 P 14821 P 17638 P 19200 O 21146 P
11083 P 14905 P 17783 19295 O 21911 P
11126 P 14906 P 17792 P 19298 O 21913 P
11127 FP 14970 O 17793 O 19299 O 21947 P
11163 S 15001 P 17914 O 19300 PO 21962 P
11176 P 15014 O 17999 P 19336 O 21965 P
11435 P 15203 P 18209 P 19369 P 21978 P
11637 P 15209 P 18219 P 19373 P 22290 P
12101 S 15224 P 18281 FP 19588 P 22357 FP
12799 P 15293 18293 P 19589 P 22754 P
13408 P 16028 FP
Secondary: Journal Articles
10465 P 11485 P 14029 P 14847 S 15564 P
10491 P 11493 FP 14041 P 14848 P 15831 P
10899 PO 11513 P 14042 P 14849 P 15999 P
10900 11626 S 14045 P 14857 O 16036 P
10901 S 11650 P 14052 P 14866 O 16044 F
10909 P 11895 PO 14076 P 14897 P 16083 F
10923 F 11902 S 14083 P 14898 P 16142 P
10952 O 11937 14136 O 14912 O 16459 F
10955 11943 P 14307 P 14941 P 16801 F
11008 S 12012 P 14323 S 14952 P 16807 P
11070 P 12018 P 14347 P 14984 P 16879 F
11139 P 12034 P 14352 P 14997 P 17324 O
11147 12036 P 14358 P 15198 P 17325 O
11148 P 12049 PO 14382 P 15219 P 17331 O
11149 O 12098 P 14418 PO 15239 P 17342 O
11150 P 12129 P 14441 S 15274 PO 17384 O
11170 P 12477 P 14518 P 15289 P 17502 O
11177 P 12529 P 14526 P 15295 P 17597 P
11453 P 12796 P 14545 P 15302 O 17738 O
11476 P 13391 P 14827 P 15551 O 17778 P

17781 P 18288 P 19307 FP 19414 P 20672 O
17996 P 18291 P 19311 19420 21043 P
17998 P 18836 F 19312 P 19471 P 21048 PO
18050 O 18840 19315 P 19592 P 21591 P
18052 P 19057 P 19317 P 19601 P 21909 P
18064 O 19099 P 19318 O 19609 P 21918 P
18067 O 19107 S 19323 P 19675 O 21969 P
18195 P 19156 P 19328 P 20476 P 22328 P
18205 P 19159 P 19370 P 20482 22768 P
18245 P 19160 P 19382 P 20501 P 22855 O
18255 P 19164 PO 19385 P 20513 P 23021 F
18273 P 19294 P 19412 P

32.2 ANTI-STATE ASSOCIATIONS

反叛集團　反国家的な団体

1644-1842

PRIMARY 17530 P 18462 18476 S 19439 S
13813 P 18418 18468 PO 18477 S 19440 P
13830 P 18420 S 18470 P 18478 S 19441 P
13856 18424 P 18474 P 18514 P 21686 P
14181 P 18425 P 18475 P

SECOND. 10618 P 11571 P 18916 P 21279 P
10032 O 10626 P 14156 O 21277 P 22521 S
10552 P 11557 P 16517 P

1644-1911

PRIMARY 18367 18426 P 18503 18890 S
10046 O 18384 P 18427 P 18507 P 18940 P
10644 PO 18385 18443 S 18510 P 21259 P
10664 S 18391 P 18459 O 18516 P 21270 PO
12572 P 18396 S 18464 P 18518 P 21300 S
13838 18405 S 18480 P 18519 P 22059 P
14175 S 18406 P 18489 18523 22531 P
17541 P 18419 P 18493 PO 18526 S 22565
17975 O 18421 P 18495 PO 18527 P 22592 P
17977 PO 18423 PO 18501 PO 18880 P 22866 P
18366 P

SECOND. 10586 13859 S 15353 PO 18930 PO
10010 P 10603 P 14167 P 16217 FP 21271 O
10053 P 10667 P 14176 17976 21276 P
10276 11544 S 14189 S 18853 PO 21629 P
10327 P 11574 PO 14206 P 18876 O 21988 P
10505 P 12940 S 14555 P 18921 O 22620
10541 S 13834 P 15320 PO 18927 PO 22633 P

1842-1911

PRIMARY: MONOGRAPHS
10043 O 15929 O 18408 S 18458 P 18868 PO
10059 O 15930 P 18409 P 18461 P 18871 PO
10065 O 16090 O 18412 FP 18466 O 20576 PO
10566 P 16378 O 18415 O 18484 P 21262 O
10587 PO 16394 P 18416 P 18485 P 21286 P
10631 P 17532 O 18422 O 18487 P 22026 P
10660 O 18089 P 18428 P 18490 P 22066 P
10679 O 18364 P 18430 P 18491 O 22532 P
12570 O 18371 P 18436 P 18492 PO 22556 PO
13802 P 18375 P 18438 P 18494 P 22562 O
13831 P 18376 P 18442 P 18496 P 22572 O
13847 P 18378 O 18447 O 18498 PO 22584 S
13866 O 18379 PO 18448 PO 18502 P 22589 P
14171 O 18382 P 18449 O 18506 P 22595 P
14174 P 18386 P 18450 P 18508 P 22605 P
14187 P 18387 P 18454 PO 18509 P 22615 O
14195 P 18388 P 18455 S 18511 P 22617 PO
15307 O 18390 P 18457 P 18524 P 22623 P
15749 PO

PRIMARY: INCLUSIONS
10642 PO 18368 P 18410 P 18452 P 20429 O
14087 S 18370 P 18414 S 18486 P 21274 P
14395 P 18373 S 18417 P 18513 O 21281 P
14400 O 18374 P 18429 P 18515 S 21606 P
17526 P 18377 O 18431 P 18521 S 22065 P
17550 PO 18389 P 18433 P 18525 P 22399 S
17551 S 18392 P 18437 P 18528 P 22884 S
18079 P 18400 P 18445 P

PRIMARY: JOURNAL ARTICLES
11014 P 18082 S 18402 P 18456 O 18500 P
12186 P 18094 S 18403 O 18460 P 18504 P
12588 P 18363 O 18404 P 18463 P 18505 P
13486 P 18365 O 18407 O 18465 O 18512 P
13805 P 18369 P 18411 P 18467 O 18517 P
13851 O 18372 18413 P 18469 P 18520 P
13852 O 18380 18432 P 18471 S 18522 P
13860 P 18381 P 18434 P 18472 P 18899 P
15357 O 18383 P 18435 O 18473 O 19438 P
16530 P 18393 O 18439 O 18479 O 20136 O
17523 P 18394 PO 18440 P 18481 22062 P
17525 O 18395 P 18441 PO 18482 22538 P
17533 FP 18397 S 18444 O 18483 P 22593 O
17535 O 18398 P 18446 P 18488 P 22641 P
17536 O 18399 PO 18451 S 18497 P 22771 P
17537 O 18401 P 18453 P 18499 S 22774 P

SECONDARY: MONOGRAPHS
10003 O 13858 P 17549 O 18872 P 21302 O
10516 PO 14178 P 17553 P 18922 O 22028 P
11231 P 14584 PO 17688 O 18943 P 22591 PO
12580 PO 15362 O 17974 O 19349 P 22594 O
12921 O 16395 O 18074 P 20749 O 22602 P
13485 P 17529 P 18854 PO 21287 P 22614
13811 O 17543 P

SECONDARY: INCLUSIONS
10510 P 12617 O 14203 P 18073 P 21436 P
10549 S 13471 P 14212 P 18078 P 22025 P
10639 O 13816 P 15333 O 18081 S 22518 P
10650 PO 13823 P 16099 P 21299 P 22533 S
11017 O 14180 S 16927 O 21301 P 22618 O
11244 O 14190 P 17558 O

SECONDARY: JOURNAL ARTICLES
10009 P 13827 P 15629 O 17547 P 21615 S
10536 S 13833 P 15731 O 17552 O 21689 O
10563 13840 O 15747 O 18300 O 22039 P
10675 P 13853 P 15921 P 19693 P 22554 P
11662 13869 P 17527 P 20139 22571 P
11668 O 14199 17534 O 20566 PO 22604 P
13801 S 15126 S 17545 O 21491 S 22775 S
13826 P

1842-1928
(including 1644-1928)

PRIMARY 13876 18532 O 18569 PO 21327 P
10067 O 13881 P 18533 PO 18570 P 21328 P
10073 14221 18540 18572 O 21342 P
10085 PO 14403 P 18542 P 18573 O 21347 P
10687 P 15388 S 18546 PO 18956 PO 21349 PO
10699 PO 16267 O 18549 PO 18962 PO 21355 O
10712 S 17559 P 18551 PO 19475 22076 S
10727 PO 17560 P 18552 P 19479 22078 P
10733 O 17630 P 18553 P 20430 P 22079 P
10734 O 17693 P 18555 20433 P 22092 P
11260 P 17981 P 18560 P 21304 P 22104 P
11708 S 18101 P 18563 O 21306 P 22131 PO
11709 18530 P 18566 S 21307 O 22137 S
12663 P 18531 S 18568 21310 P

SECOND. 11592 PO 14113 P 18991 P 21350 P
10068 S 11705 PO 14222 S 19477 PO 21352 O
10071 O 11718 14404 P 19478 21504 O
10076 S 12216 P 15134 P 20182 P 22086 S
10686 P 12963 PO 15373 P 21311 O 22094 S
10695 P 13147 P 15944 P 21317 P 22118 P
10713 P 13505 O 18102 O 21337 PO 22121 P
10728 P 13882 O 18105 21339 P 22127 P
10735 S 13883 18971 S 21340 P 22128 P
11269 S 13885 S 18980 O 21343 P 22134 P
11297 PO 14108 S 18987 P 21346 P 22644 O
11590 PO 14112 P

1911-1928

PRIMARY: MONOGRAPHS
10769 P 17614 O 18597 PO 18646 P 18709 P
10833 18148 P 18609 O 18649 P 18710 P
13896 PO 18163 P 18610 O 18653 P 18720 S
13905 PO 18306 O 18617 P 18654 P 18725 P
13906 PO 18579 O 18620 P 18655 P 18727 P
13927 P 18582 O 18621 O 18664 O 18733 P
13956 O 18592 P 18630 P 18700 O 18735 P
15147 P 18596 PO 18639 P 18708 18748 P
18753 O 18782 P 19455 P 19534 P 22162 P
18760 19445 P 19502 P 20455 22708 O
18764 O 19453 P 19517 FP 20465 P

PRIMARY: INCLUSIONS
10750 P 18310 P 18662 P 18743 P 18778 P
13889 P 18600 S 18665 O 18765 18784
13921 S 18601 P 18669 P 18771 P 19456 P
13955 O 18602 P 18670 S 18773 P 19459
14251 P 18611 P 18704 O 18774 P 19460 F
17567 O 18615 18713 O 18775 P 19500 P
17571 O 18616 18734 P 18776 P 19546 P
17578 P 18618 P 18742 P 18777 P 19550 O
18110 P 18628 P

PRIMARY: JOURNAL ARTICLES
11024 P 18607 O 18724 P 19446 P 19522
12724 P 18623 18729 P 19448 P 19554 P
13922 P 18625 P 18757 O 19449 P 19570 P
13981 P 18642 18762 P 19450 P 20452 P
14484 18644 P 18769 P 19461 P 20457 O
15146 PO 18652 F 18772 P 19462 20466
18156 P 18697 PO 18779 P 19498 P 22159 P
18586 P 18706 O 19025 PO 19501 P 22163 P
18590 P 18719 P 19442 PO 19509 P 22181 FP
18594 O

SECOND. 13925 P 17575 O 19518 O 22141 P
10744 13929 O 17696 PO 19520 O 22148 S
10752 O 13950 S 18138 P 19527 22149 S
10766 P 13953 O 18152 P 19528 22153 P
10768 PO 13966 P 18161 O 19536 22160 P
10802 13971 18308 P 19547 PO 22165 FP
10834 P 13972 O 19451 O 19548 P 22172 P
10838 P 14114 19452 S 19557 P 22177 P
10844 P 14119 S 19454 FP 19578 S 22180 P
11783 P 14122 O 19490 PO 21377 O 22689 P
11784 P 14123 P 19499 P 21378 O 22690 P
11831 14468 P 19503 FP 21382 O 22696 O
12361 P 14711 P 19507 P 21385 22931 S
12747 O 15145 PO 19510 P 21824 P 22934 S
13913 15780 O

1911-1949
(including 1644-1949, 1842-1949)

PRIMARY: MONOGRAPHS
10079 PO 15136 O 18547 PO 18650 P 18767 O
10700 PO 15140 O 18550 P 18657 O 18768 S
10715 P 15156 O 18554 P 18661 P 18780 P
10718 S 16409 P 18557 P 18674 P 18783 P
10729 P 16639 P 18559 P 18685 P 19006 O
10749 18104 P 18562 S 18699 P 20204 P
10803 P 18120 P 18567 O 18711 O 21320
11596 P 18123 P 18583 S 18722 O 21354 PO
11699 S 18140 O 18585 O 18730 P 21362 O
13880 PO 18147 P 18588 P 18732 P 21368 O
13887 P 18155 P 18598 O 18739 P 22088 P
13911 P 18534 PO 18614 P 18740 S 22095 P
13945 P 18535 P 18619 S 18741 PO 22173 P
14116 P 18536 P 18622 O 18752 P 22648 PO
14219 PO 18543 S 18635 P 18756 22655 O
14247 P 18544 P 18636 P 18759 P 22666 S
14703 S 18545 PO

PRIMARY: INCLUSIONS
13878 P 18539 P 18565 S 18631 21309 P
13920 P 18541 S 18571 S 18633 P 21326 P
18108 P 18556 18589 P 18645 S 21332 P
18119 P 18558 S 18605 S 18745 O 22662
18537 S 18561 O 18626 P 21303 P

PRIMARY: JOURNAL ARTICLES
10815 18548 O 18593 PO 18715 P 21351 P
12325 P 18564 S 18651 S 18726 P 22119
14246 P 18574 P 18673 P 18728 P 22167 P
15142 P 18575 18686 P 19447 22168 P
17980 P 18578 O 18689 P 19458 22171 S
18304 P 18580 P 18698 P 19463 P 22175 P
18529 18587 S 18705 P 19561 P 22665 S
18538 P 18591 S 18714 P 20454 P

SECONDARY: MONOGRAPHS
10086 PO 10696 P 10781 P 11601 P 12965 P
10090 O 10724 S 10791 P 11694 PO 13877 PO
10104 O 10725 P 11258 P 11704 P 13916 P
10349 S 10739 P 11290 P 12271 P 13980 P
10375 P 10759 P 11336 P 12631 P 14215 S
10684 O 10776 PO 11586 FP 12676 S 14217 P

14223 P 17694 PO 20431 P 21359 P 22646 P
14231 P 18143 O 20432 P 21367 O 22667 P
14496 P 18154 P 20615 O 21373 P 22672 P
14652 PO 19476 P 20934 P 21380 O 22679 S
14692 P 19551 P 21308 O 21459 P 22694 O
15377 P 19617 P 21324 P 22102 PO 22717 P
15939 P 19962 S 21345 P 22144 P 22939 P
16123 FP

Secondary: Inclusions
10078 S 13948 O 14242 P 21353 O 22130 P
10694 P 13949 O 15141

Secondary: Journal Articles
10719 12335 S 16415 19542 22150 S
10743 P 13879 P 18157 P 20187 P 22430 O
10755 O 13940 P 19473 S 21323 P 22656
10790 P 15391 PO 19532 22105 O 22686
11706 P

1928-1949

Primary: Monographs
10100 O 14241 P 18643 F 18702 O 18755 P
10796 P 14762 P 18647 P 18707 O 18766 P
10819 P 15434 O 18656 P 18716 O 18781 O
10827 PO 16637 P 18659 O 18717 P 20190 P
11732 P 18118 P 18660 P 18723 P 20444 P
13892 O 18145 P 18666 P 18736 PO 20458 O
13895 P 18577 O 18667 FP 18744 O 21379 O
13903 S 18584 O 18687 O 18746 O 22158 P
13930 P 18603 O 18690 P 18747 PO 22699 P
13963 P 18608 O 18696 O 18749 O 22712 O
13975 PO 18629 P 18701 P 18750 O 22718

Primary: Inclusions
10746 O 18146 P 18612 P 18688 O 18761 P
12713 P 18305 P 18632 P 18703 O 18763 S
14236 P 18307 P 18671 O 18712 P 21372 O
14248 P 18604 S 18672 P 18731 P 22146 P
18113 O 18606 P 18683 P 18751 S 22166 P

Primary: Journal Articles
10786 P 15967 P 18634 P 18680 PO 18758 P
11028 P 16058 P 18637 18681 P 18770 P
12279 P 17735 P 18638 S 18682 P 19464 P
12290 P 18130 P 18640 S 18684 19537
12311 P 18135 S 18641 S 18691 P 19568 S
13897 P 18136 S 18648 P 18692 P 19571 P
13899 S 18141 P 18658 O 18693 O 19574 P
13919 P 18150 P 18663 P 18694 F 20441 P
13932 P 18576 S 18668 S 18695 O 20470
13933 P 18581 P 18675 P 18718 S 22695 P
13934 P 18595 P 18676 P 18721 O 22702 P
13935 P 18599 P 18677 P 18737 S 22703 PO
13978 P 18613 P 18678 P 18738 P 22715 S
14249 P 18624 P 18679 P 18754 S 22941 P
14427 P 18627 P

Secondary: Monographs
10096 O 11785 FP 13902 O 13983 P 17577 O
10103 PO 11799 P 13923 P 14754 PO 17613 F
10758 P 11807 P 13954 O 15394 O 18114 P
10780 P 13040 O 13957 PO 15436 F 18142 P
10813 P 13760 PO 13959 PO 15437 PO 22681 FP
10814 P 13891 O 13961 S 16063 P 22710 O
10839 O 13894 O 13965 O 16064 FP 22714 P
11327 P 13898 P 13969 O 16119 P

Secondary: Inclusions
10747 O 13942 P 13946 O 13982 O 15957 O
16416 O 22683 S

Secondary: Journal Articles
10798 O 12332 P 14707 PO 18159 O 20453 P
10826 O 12360 P 17064 F 19505 P 20894 O
11023 O 13890 O 17565 O 19540 21371 O
11030 P 13907 P 17569 19564 21376 O
11738 O 14233 P 17574 S 19572 P 22010 P
11762 P 14239 O 18116 P 19573 P 22176 P
11788 S 14426 S 18128 P 20446 P 22721 P
11800 P 14499 S 18139 P 20449 P 22942 S
12314 P 14500 P

1928-1972
(incl. 1644-1972, 1842-1972, 1911-1972)

Primary: Monographs
10111 S 10120 S 10124 S 10850 PO 10858 S
10114 P 10121 O 10129 S 10853 PO 10883 S
10888 S 15168 18792 P 18820 O 21414 FP
13984 P 15174 P 18794 P 18822 P 21420 PO
13986 P 15176 O 18795 P 18823 S 21424 P
13989 P 15191 PO 18796 O 18827 O 21425 P
13997 17615 O 18801 P 18834 P 21853 P
14002 P 17895 O 18804 PO 20231 PO 22204 P
14012 P 18170 P 18809 S 21392 PO 22229 P
14020 FP 18172 P 18810 21400 P 22251 P
14278 P 18185 P 18812 21405 P 22724 P
14279 PO 18186 P 18817 PO 21406 P 22734 O
15158 S 18187 P 18819 P 21412 P 22991 S
15161 P

Primary: Inclusions
14011 O 16066 O 18808 P 21840 S 22236 P
14255 P 16067 O 18811 21848 S 22238 P
14288 P 18167 P 18825 P 22191 P 22247 O
14289 S 18180 P 18832 22192 P 22256 P
15185 S 18798 P 18833 P 22197 P 22263 P
15186 S 18799 P 20472 P 22209 S 22267 P
15187 S 18802 P 21388 P 22234 P 22272 P
15188 P 18807 21394 O

Primary: Journal Articles
10391 P 18165 P 18791 P 18818 P 21389 P
10880 P 18166 S 18793 18821 S 21397 P
13294 P 18169 P 18797 S 18824 21830 S
14003 P 18175 P 18800 P 18826 S 21849 S
14004 P 18177 P 18803 18828 FP 21864 S
14414 P 18785 P 18805 18829 S 21865 P
14415 P 18786 P 18806 P 18830 P 21883 P
15159 P 18787 S 18813 P 18831 P 22189
15167 S 18788 O 18814 P 18835 S 22213 P
15178 18789 P 18815 P 19467 S 22215 S
15182 P 18790 P 18816 P 19469 O 22729 P
17580 O

Secondary: Monographs
10112 S 11849 P 15166 19043 P 22182 P
10113 11858 P 15171 FP 19053 P 22196 P
10126 O 11860 P 15175 FP 19583 P 22203 P
10128 O 12387 PO 15192 O 20473 P 22210 P
10303 P 12426 P 15458 PO 20994 O 22224 P
10855 FP 13762 P 15468 O 21395 PO 22225 S
10887 PO 13991 P 15806 P 21410 FP 22235 P
10890 P 14006 P 16068 O 21413 O 22250 P
10891 S 14010 S 16328 O 21418 O 22260 P
11035 O 14018 S 16343 P 21419 P 22268 P
11040 PO 14258 P 17311 O 21422 O 22273 P
11044 PO 14274 P 18164 P 21466 P 22486 PO
11048 S 14285 P 18176 P 21476 S 22728 O
11391 P 14292 P 18312 P 21538 FP 22740 P
11393 P 14512 P 18313 P 21847 P 22950 S
11605 O 14513 P 19033 P 21900 P 22954 P
11607 P

Secondary: Inclusions
10119 S 14276 P 18045 19404 P 21859 P
11042 P 14281 P 18181 19585 P 21885 S
11612 P 14290 P 19046 P 21409 21892 S
11613 P 15164 P 19047 P 21831 P 21893 P
13988 F 15165 S 19048 P 21842 P 22205 S
14129 15184 19049 P 21858 P 22221 S
14254 15799 O 19087 P

Secondary: Journal Articles
10848 P 12411 P 15474 O 21403 S 22248 P
10849 P 14008 P 16336 P 21408 P 22255 P
10877 P 14126 17949 P 21473 PO 22257 P
10881 P 14271 P 17987 P 21846 P 22261 P
11054 P 14413 P 18168 P 21851 O 22265 P
11403 PO 14514 19084 P 22199 P 22274 S
11417 P 15173 O 19085 O 22201 P 22276 P
11871 S 15179 S 20471 S 22208 P 22280 P
12391 P 15190 21390 P 22220 P 22281 P
12398 P 15194 21391 S 22245 22947 P
12403 P

1949-1972

Primary 15239 P 18346 P 18356 P 18840
11138 F 16083 F 18347 P 18836 F 18841 O
11167 P 16135 O 18348 P 18837 P 18842 P
11483 O 16152 O 18349 P 18838 P 18843 O
11626 S 17012 P 18355 O 18839 P 20494 P
11885 P 17593 PO

Second. 10931 P 10998 S 11112 S 11147
10170 O 10984 O 11070 P 11121 P 11168 P
11486 P 15217 P 16471 P 17902 O 20502 O
11534 P 15228 P 17589 F 18220 P 21907 P
12813 P 15294 P 17598 P 18277 P 22318 P
13069 P 16078 P 17602 19591 O

33 Religious Sects and Associations
宗教派別及組織
宗教各派及び組織

1644-1842

Primary 15923 O 18882 O 18916 P 19439 S
11541 P 18863 P 18891 P 18935 P 20563 S
11545 P 18864 S 18897 P 18936 P 21686 P
11557 P 18870 P 18904 P 18948 P 22555 O
15752 O 18877 P 18905 P

Second. 11563 P 15722 O 21284 P 22560 S
10044 O 11571 P 17657 O 22520 P 22637 P
10045 O 12190 P 18420 S 22550 P 22865 S
10580 O 15343 O

1644-1911

Primary 16217 FP 18862 P 18898 PO 18939 PO
10046 O 17520 PO 18865 PO 18900 PO 18940 P
11542 FP 18391 P 18867 P 18901 PO 18941 FP
11556 P 18406 P 18869 PO 18902 PO 18944 PO
11562 PO 18480 P 18873 PO 18910 18945 P
11570 P 18493 PO 18876 O 18913 P 18946 PO
11574 PO 18495 PO 18879 P 18915 FP 20547 FP
12572 P 18846 P 18880 P 18917 PO 21170 P
14167 P 18847 PO 18881 O 18919 P 21270 PO
15044 S 18848 P 18885 PO 18920 FP 21642 FP
16190 FP 18849 PO 18886 P 18921 O 21657 P
16192 P 18853 PO 18887 FP 18927 PO 21697 PO
16196 P 18855 O 18888 P 18930 PO 21709 P
16200 PO 18858 P 18890 S 18933 21716
16206 PO 18860 P 18896 PO 18937 P 22866 P

Second. 11544 S 16171 PO 18405 S 21300 S
10010 P 11549 P 16179 O 18519 P 21627
10016 O 11550 FP 16181 O 19695 P 21639 P
10028 PO 13838 16184 P 19752 P 21641 FP
10060 PO 15327 PO 16189 FP 20124 PO 21668 P
10582 PO 16049 P 16191 20548 S 21703
10644 PO 16161 PO 17977 PO 21259 P 22068 P
11194 O 16162 PO 18396 S 21271 O

1842-1911

Primary: Monographs
10031 O 16169 O 18871 PO 18922 O 21298 O
10049 PO 16187 O 18872 P 18924 PO 21624 O
10611 O 16210 O 18875 O 18925 O 21655 O
11567 P 18852 PO 18889 O 18931 F 22530 P
12567 P 18854 PO 18903 P 18932 PO 22556 PO
15363 O 18856 O 18906 O 18943 P 22595 P
15721 O 18859 P 18908 O 18947 S 22615 O
15733 O 18861 P 18914 O 20578 O 22630 P
16158 O 18868 PO

Primary: Inclusions
10510 P 18377 O 18513 O 18874 P 22523 O
22525 O

Primary: Journal Articles
11014 P 18372 18884 O 18923 P 21622 P
14565 PO 18380 18892 P 18926 O 21652 O
15348 O 18500 P 18893 P 18928 O 22029 P
15710 18844 O 18894 O 18929 O 22517 O
15731 O 18845 O 18895 O 18934 O 22526 P
15732 O 18850 P 18899 P 18938 O 22545 P
16159 O 18851 O 18907 O 18942 O 22564 P
16201 O 18857 O 18909 O 19686 O 22566 P
16216 O 18866 P 18911 O 20544 F 22583 PO
17973 PO 18878 O 18912 O 20557 O 22607 P
18300 O 18883 O 18918 O

Secondary: Monographs
10018 PO 10056 O 10566 P 12921 O 15038 P
10025 O 10062 PO 10631 P 14178 P 15307 O
10034 S 10064 O 10660 O 14204 PO 15319 O
10041 10321 O 12569 O 14597 O 15344 O

15349 O 16388 O 18436 P 20385 O 22553 O
15361 O 16520 O 18438 P 20716 O 22572 O
15364 O 16910 PO 18449 O 21286 P 22591 PO
15930 P 16912 O 18491 O 21621 O 22594 O
16183 O 18371 P 19751 O 21980 O 22601 O
16186 O 18378 O 20137 O 22383 PO 22623 P
16219 O 18387 P 20138 O

SECONDARY: INCLUSIONS
16512 O 16526 O 17626 O 18073 P 18521 S
22588 P 22618 O

SECONDARY: JOURNAL ARTICLES
10440 O 16222 O 18439 O 19344 S 22534 P
14571 P 16392 O 18441 PO 19696 O 22540 P
14586 O 17545 O 18471 S 19775 O 22554 P
15747 O 17924 P 18473 O 20254 P 22593 O
16160 F 18301 S 18483 P 20596 O 22597 P
16220 PO 18394 PO 18497 P 21628 O

1842-1928
(including 1644-1928)

PRIMARY 18950 O 18962 PO 18975 P 18987 P
11578 P 18951 O 18966 O 18977 P 18991 P
11592 PO 18956 PO 18967 O 18978 PO 20619 O
15369 PO 18957 O 18968 PO 18980 O 21331 O
16227 P 18958 P 18970 O 18982 P 21754 P
17981 P 18959 O 18971 S 18983 FP 21788 P
18102 O 18960 PO 18972 P 18985 PO 22001 P
18949 PO 18961 P 18974 PO

SECOND. 11583 P 16226 PO 20179 P 21784 FP
10081 PO 11591 16231 FP 20618 PO 21794 O
10697 S 13882 O 16252 PO 21355 O 22077 P
10713 P 14673 P 16257 O 21742 S 22110 P
11270 P 14676 S 16276 O 21760 P 22140 P
11579 P 15388 S 19219 S 21782 P

1911-1928

PRIMARY 19000 P 19012 O 19023 O 20469 F
10838 P 19001 PO 19013 O 19024 O 21462 O
18992 FP 19002 PO 19016 O 19025 PO 21816 P
18996 O 19005 O 19017 O 19027 P 22696 O
18997 PO 19009 19020 O 19028 O 22707 P
18999 O 19010 F 19021 O 19699 O

SECOND. 12747 O 16950 O 18700 O 20462 FP
10089 O 14711 P 17842 F 20107 S 21456 O
10106 P 14720 O 18596 PO 20434 O 22445 O
11594 O 15075 O 18697 PO

1911-1949
(including 1644-1949, 1842-1949)

PRIMARY 14694 P 18575 18976 FP 19008 O
10083 PO 14698 P 18952 P 18979 PO 19014 P
10087 O 14759 O 18953 O 18981 P 19618 P
10104 O 16229 PO 18954 O 18984 S 21383 F
10356 PO 16271 PO 18955 FP 18986 21770 P
11585 S 16279 P 18963 O 18988 FP 21797 P
11586 FP 16309 O 18964 P 18989 FP 21822 P
11595 P 17448 P 18965 O 18990 PO 22654 P
11596 P 17935 18969 P 18993 PO 22667 P
11601 P 17980 P 18973 P 19006 O 22682 O
14652 PO 18544 P

SECOND. 14629 PO 16409 P 20208 O 21804 P
10107 P 14655 P 16689 O 20791 P 22009 P
10339 O 14772 17256 FP 20820 O 22102 PO
10725 P 15372 O 18545 PO 20823 PO 22441 P
11593 P 16270 O 18558 S 21363 22694 O
12325 P 16282 S 19620 FP 21750 PO 22706 O
12660 P 16300 O 20205 O

1928-1949

PRIMARY 16289 FP 18995 O 19011 F 19026 F
10108 P 16304 F 18998 O 19015 O 20221 O
14760 PO 16315 O 19003 FP 19018 FP 20436 O
15414 PO 18595 P 19004 O 19019 O 20896 FP
15773 P 18994 O 19007 O 19022 F 22714 P

SECOND. 15409 P 15448 F 16297 O 16307 F
10806 O 15415 PO 16058 P 16302 F 16312 O
13899 S 15416 O 16290 O 16305 F 16314 F
16317 O 16631 F 19638 S 20461 P 22719 O
16325 O 16718 F 19649 O 20873 FP 22720 PO
16628 O 18658 O 19700 O

1928-1972
(incl. 1644-1972, 1842-1972, 1911-1972)

PRIMARY 15163 S 19032 P 19043 P 19053 P
11602 P 15454 P 19033 P 19044 P 19054 F
11603 PO 15475 O 19034 O 19045 P 19055 FP
11604 S 16335 P 19035 PO 19046 P 19056
11605 O 16339 FP 19036 P 19047 P 19709 P
11607 P 16343 P 19037 P 19048 P 21477 S
11609 P 17985 FP 19038 P 19049 P 21860 O
11610 PO 18828 FP 19039 19050 21900 P
11611 PO 19029 19040 19051 F 22205 S
14266 P 19030 P 19041 19052 P 22972 P
14798 FP 19031 P 19042 PO

SECOND. 15086 16332 P 19090 FP 21892 S
10111 S 15191 PO 16341 P 19886 S 22727 P
10120 S 15466 O 17953 P 20231 PO 22733 P
14004 P 16328 O 18804 PO 21392 PO 22991 S
14784 O 16331 P 18827 O 21468

1949-1972

PRIMARY 11633 P 15566 O 19060 19068 O
10145 O 11636 O 16361 F 19061 S 19069 PO
11617 PO 11643 S 16365 P 19062 O 19070 F
11618 PO 11644 PO 17994 FP 19063 PO 20251 O
11621 P 11648 P 18068 O 19064 FP 20529 F
11625 P 11651 FP 19057 P 19065 PO 21199 P
11626 S 11652 FP 19058 S 19066 O 21910 P
11629 P 11654 P 19059 S 19067 O

SECOND. 11622 P 12129 P 16354 F 21554 O
10141 O 11627 F 15205 O 16357 F 21593 PO
10155 P 11635 PO 15504 F 16358 F 21925 F
10164 O 11645 P 15518 P 16360 FP 22760 O
10170 O 11647 P 16345 O 16362 PO 22764 O
10937 PO 11649 PO 16348 F 16363 S 23027 O
11619 P 11885 P

34.1 AGRICULTURAL ASSOCIATIONS AND COOPERATIVES

農業生産組織 農業生産組織

1644-1842

PRIMARY □

SECOND. 12183 P 13814 S

1644-1911

PRIMARY □

SECOND. 12196 S 16049 P

1842-1911

PRIMARY 17978 O

SECOND. 15360 O 16516 P 20254 P

1842-1928
(including 1644-1928)

PRIMARY □

SECOND. 11686 P 12233 P 20006 PO 21738 O
10338 P 12229 P 19715

1911-1928

PRIMARY 17760 O 19259 P 19461 P

SECOND. 15418 F 16593 F 17231 O 19455 P
12363 PO 15450 F 16685 P 19251 P 19641
14497 FP 16591 F

1911-1949
(including 1644-1949, 1842-1949)

PRIMARY 12293 S 17763 PO 19072 F 19233 F
12227 P 12372 P 17979 P 19073 S 19257 P
12257 FP 16668 P 19071 P 19075 PO 19705 P
12271 P

SECOND. 12223 P 15063 S 16621 FP 18645 S
10088 O 12230 P 15408 F 17444 FP 18732 P
10700 PO 12317 PO 15679 FP 17769 P 19240 PO
10812 P 12328 P 16408 FP 18585 O 19282 P
11747 FP 12334 P 16550 P 18622 O 19457 P
12212 S 13703 S 16561 S

1928-1949

PRIMARY 15406 F 17462 O 19243 P 19638 S
15154 P 16420 PO 17891 O 19280 O 19648 O
15405 F 16626 PO 19074 O

SECOND. 11807 P 15414 PO 16432 PO 17667 F
10796 P 11829 P 15415 PO 16574 P 17872 P
11740 P 12263 15421 O 16598 F 18307 P
11741 P 12310 P 15433 O 16617 PO 19227
11750 S 12314 P 15439 P 16620 FP 19244
11769 PO 12331 P 15441 P 17071 F 19635 O
11793 P 13221 O 15443 P 17092 P 19649 O
11798 13750 FP 16430 P

1928-1972
(incl. 1644-1972, 1842-1972, 1911-1972)

PRIMARY 12397 S 15977 P 19079 F 19087 P
10391 P 12403 P 15978 FP 19080 F 19088 F
10852 P 12424 P 16732 O 19081 P 19089 F
12375 P 12426 P 16736 P 19082 PO 19090 FP
12379 P 14440 S 16748 P 19083 P 19091 S
12388 O 14515 O 19076 PO 19084 P 19092 P
12391 P 15456 P 19077 P 19085 O 19284 P
12394 P 15975 P 19078 P 19086 P 19466 F

SECONDARY: MONOGRAPHS
10125 P 11393 P 12380 P 15460 FP 17985 FP
10126 O 11845 P 12383 P 15466 O 18170 P
10396 S 11846 P 13308 P 15476 F 18172 P
10853 PO 11848 PO 13766 P 15614 P 18178 FP
10855 FP 11849 P 15085 P 15980 P 18312 P
10888 S 11852 P 15090 O 16068 O 18827 O
11047 P 11857 P 15175 FP 16456 F 19468 F
11048 S 11862 P 15181 P 16729 FP 21416 O
11391 P 11874 P 15192 O 16747 P 22210 P

SECONDARY: INCLUSIONS
11042 P 12396 P 12415 P 15170 22221 S
11859 P 12406 P 12422 S 15185 S 22282 P
11861 P 12407 S 14129 16744 P

SECONDARY: JOURNAL ARTICLES
11041 P 12400 P 12425 P 16751 S 18821 S
11851 P 12413 P 14260 P 17312 O 20402 S
12374 P 12418 FP 14439 P 18786 P 22239 S
12393 P 12419 P 16735 P 18797 S 22738 P

1949-1972

PRIMARY: MONOGRAPHS
11906 P 12552 P 15549 P 16457 O 19135 P
11998 P 12563 P 15557 O 16798 FP 19153 F
12003 P 12564 P 15567 O 17674 P 19166 P
12015 P 14153 PO 15570 P 18004 F 19178 O
12029 P 15258 P 15889 P 19095 P 19181 P
12123 P 15260 P 15991 P 19100 P 19184 PO
12429 P 15483 P 15992 P 19105 FP 19194 P
12439 P 15488 P 15993 P 19110 O 19201 P
12441 P 15493 O 16001 S 19122 P 19203 P
12456 PO 15495 P 16011 P 19131 P 19408 PO
12464 P 15507 P 16013 P 19132 P 20079 P
12467 P 15523 FP 16046 PO 19133 PO 20080 P
12475 PO 15544 O 16070 O 19134 P

PRIMARY: INCLUSIONS
12176 P 14451 S 16468 P 19106 P 19116 O
12459 PO 15217 P 16803 O 19108 P 19117 O
12506 P 15539 P 17519 19109 O 19118 O
12536 P 15542 18322 O 19111 O 19119 O
12559 P 15558 P 19093 P 19112 O 19120 O
14138 P 15987 F 19094 O 19113 O 19127 O
14442 P 15990 P 19101 P 19114 O 19129 P
14448 P 15996 P 19104 19115 F 19138 P

34.2 Business Organization
商業組織 商業組織

1644-1842

1644-1911

1842-1911

1842-1928
(including 1644-1928)

1911-1928

1911-1949
(including 1644-1949, 1842-1949)

1928-1949

1928-1972
(incl. 1644-1972, 1842-1972, 1911-1972)

1949-1972

Primary: Monographs
10172 PO 12475 PO 13773 P 17350 FP 19296 O
11061 O 12795 O 14153 PO 18354 O 19302 P
11903 O 13107 O 14419 P 19288 19309 P
11906 P 13119 P 16488 PO 19291 P 19338 P
11998 P 13336 P 16493 P 19292 F 20075 P
12442 P 13399 P

Primary: Inclusions
11063 PO 16997 17747 19324 FP 19339 O
11494 P 17005 O 19290 P 19329 O 19341 F
12092 P 17122 O 19293 O 19331 P 19587 O
13333 P 17126 F 19295 O 19332 P 19593 PO
13403 O 17396 O 19298 O 19333 P 19605 O
13416 17646 P 19299 O 19334 P 20268 F
16075 P 17742 F 19300 PO 19336 O 20424 F
16893 F 17746 PO 19319 19337 O

Primary: Journal Articles
10951 P 13378 P 17401 P 19304 P 19318 O
11142 P 13398 P 17499 F 19305 P 19320 F
11150 P 13789 P 17501 O 19306 O 19321 P
12018 P 13790 O 17516 F 19307 FP 19322 P
12028 P 14417 F 17654 O 19308 P 19323 P
12111 P 14418 PO 18327 S 19310 P 19325 O
12816 P 14911 O 18359 S 19311 19326 PO
13071 P 15997 O 19156 P 19312 P 19327 P
13075 P 16894 O 19289 S 19313 F 19328 P
13083 F 17116 F 19294 P 19314 P 19330
13106 O 17335 PO 19297 O 19315 P 19335 P
13108 O 17370 P 19301 P 19316 P 19340 O
13326 O 17384 O 19303 P 19317 P 19342 O
13364 P

Secondary: Monographs
10145 O 12158 PO 13432 P 15560 FP 17395 P
10150 O 12166 P 13437 15568 P 17963 F
10895 O 12793 P 13584 P 15890 P 17990 P
10962 12849 P 13612 O 15897 O 19594
11094 P 13078 P 13787 O 16016 O 19668 P
11423 P 13104 P 14520 16790 P 19939 F
11894 O 13105 P 14549 P 16902 FP 20272 FP
11897 PO 13339 P 14829 O 17002 FP 21009 FP
11980 PO 13366 P 15123 O 17006 P 21575 FP
11995 P 13384 P 15260 P 17127 P 22322 P
12082 P 13415 P 15501 O 17386 FP 22500 O
12109 P 13420 FP 15511 O 17387 P

Secondary: Inclusions
11942 P 13082 13387 P 15233 P 17349 FP
12010 P 13085 P 13392 O 15916 O 17397 O
12017 P 13098 P 13396 P 16862 17802 O
12045 P 13100 P 13413 P 17110 17914 O
12168 P 13335 P 13435 P 17336 P 18358 F
13059 F 13341 O 14138 P 17346 O 21486 O

Secondary: Journal Articles
10492 O 11966 P 13370 P 15913 O 17385 FP
10910 P 12012 P 13381 P 16010 FP 17391 P
10913 P 12034 P 13412 P 16873 FP 17393 O
10923 F 12036 P 13423 16988 O 17403
11505 P 12085 PO 13445 P 17123 O 17653 O
11515 P 12089 P 13771 P 17125 O 18002 P
11895 PO 12099 P 13776 P 17131 18321 O
11937 13092 P 13785 P 17348 P 19155 P
11944 P 13346 P 15838 F 17372 P 19171 P
11954 P

34.3 Guilds

舊式行會 ギルド

1644-1842

Primary 12901 P 19205 P 19350 P
Second. 10526 S 14401 P 17173 P

1644-1911

Primary 19210 19346 P 19351 P 19695 P
11672 PO 19345 P 19347 PO
Second. 10582 PO 14397 P 17976 18367
10058 PO 11243 P 17975 O 18012 P 21709 P
10560 P 13629 PO

1842-1911

Primary 17432 O 19343 S 19348 O 19716 P
17176 PO 18301 S 19344 S 19349 P 19717 P
Second. 10598 O 12894 O 14396 P 17137 PO
10019 PO 10682 O 12898 O 15712 S 17662 O
10023 O 11223 S 12938 PO 16089 P 18490 P
10024 O 12180 PO 12946 PO 16092 P 19206 PO
10048 O 12600 P 13839 O 16187 O 22607 P
10566 P 12889 O

1842-1928
(including 1644-1928)

Primary 11698 P 13163 S 13670 PO 17692 P
19352 O 19715
Second. 11250 P 13187 P 17824 P 19477 PO
10068 S 11260 P 13520 P 17981 P 19478
10069 O 11708 S 16403 P 18024 PO 19481 P
10073 12233 P 17690 P 18546 PO 21774
10084 PO

1911-1928

Primary 15407 FP 19248 O 19361 19364 O
10294 P 17696 PO 19359 S 19363 19558
13029 S 17717 PO 19360 F
Second. 13277 F 14468 P 19281 19514 P
10768 PO 14115 P 14476 PO 19430 19517 FP
11794 P 14118 17712 P 19483 19549
12985 PO 14407 P 17713 FP 19506 P 20631 O
13220 FP 14408 P 18609 O

1911-1949
(including 1644-1949, 1842-1949)

Primary 14508 P 19354 P 19356 19358 P
13672 P 17283 P 19355 FP 19357 FP 19644 PO
14486 P 19353 S
Second. 11707 P 13291 S 15446 P 19473 S
10083 PO 11712 FP 13668 O 17190 PO 19542
10086 PO 12684 FP 14455 S 17467 O 19561 P
10097 O 12961 P 14496 P 18529 21348 O
10446 O 12965 P 14510 PO 19072 F 22006 S
10707 P 13233 PO 14652 PO 19245 O 22109 S
11689 P 13242 P 15375 O 19432 P

1928-1949

Primary 19362 F
Second. 12983 S 17062 F 18117 P 19623 PO
10444 O 13279 P 17240 F 19555 FP 19703 O
10451 S 15436 F 17471 O 19574 P 20262 F
11745 P 16431 FP 17725 FP

1928-1972
(incl. 1644-1972, 1842-1972, 1911-1972)

Primary □
Second. 15469 P 17322 17989 S 19583 P
11855 S 16343 P 17985 FP 18795 P 21473 PO

1949-1972

□

35 Veterans Associations and the Military in Society

退伍軍人組織及軍人之社會活動
在郷軍人会及び軍人の社会活動

1644-1842

Primary 12190 P 12207 PO 13868 P
Second. 13469 P

1644-1911

Primary 16515 P 17542 P 18519 P 21263 P
Second. 10441 P 13863 P 15863 P 17541 P
17976 22866 P

1842-1911

Primary 19365 P
Second. 13818 P 15731 O 18433 P 18486 P
13803 PO 13852 O 17535 O 18436 P 18508 P

1842-1928
(including 1644-1928)

Primary 12215 P 12663 P
Second. 11686 P 13874 P 18533 PO 18555
10734 O 13503 P 17630 P

1911-1928

Primary 13905 PO 13966 P 18308 P 18697 PO
10769 P 13925 P 13979 P 18601 P 18742 P
13699 PO 13950 S 18144 P 18669 P 19451 O
13896 PO 13962 P
Second. 13955 O 17567 O 18654 P 19455 P
13929 O 15148 P 18602 P 18655 P

1911-1949
(including 1644-1949, 1842-1949)

Primary 10791 P 17423 P 18309 S 18544 P
Second. 10729 P 11699 S 15672 O 18728 P
19561 P

1928-1949

Primary 15406 F
Second. 13970 O 17576 P 18660 P 18781 O
11028 P 16058 P 18145 P 18717 P 19626 P
13039 O 17238 P 18595 P

1928-1972
(incl. 1644-1972, 1842-1972, 1911-1972)

Primary 13986 P 14000 P 14006 P 17585 P
10880 P 13998 P 14001 P 15979 P
Second. 13991 P 15175 FP 18829 S 21415 P
10456 P 13993 P 15697 FP 20474 P 22219 P
10863 P 13999 P 17584 P 20475 O 22229 P
11613 P 14281 P 18801 P 21400 P 22991 S

1949-1972

Primary 14054 P 16150 P 19372 P 19383 P
10905 P 14056 P 16836 P 19373 P 19384 P
10930 P 14078 P 17597 P 19374 P 19385 P
10963 P 14084 P 18228 P 19375 P 19386 P
10970 P 14332 P 18235 P 19376 P 19387 P
11005 P 15211 P 18337 P 19377 P 19388 P
11099 P 15223 P 19366 S 19378 P 19389 P
11160 P 15229 P 19367 P 19379 P 19390 P
12011 P 15238 P 19368 S 19380 P 19391 P
12116 P 15243 O 19369 P 19381 P 19392 P
14033 P 15290 19370 P 19382 P 22297 P
14044 P 16018 P 19371 P

Secondary: Monographs
10152 O 12791 P 15235 P 16071 FP 20506 P
10173 O 13336 P 15237 P 16800 O 20507 P
10175 O 14037 P 15245 PO 17588 P 20526 P
10960 FP 14047 P 15250 P 18264 P 21434 O
11076 P 14053 P 15254 O 18298 P 22299 P
11132 14055 P 15267 P 18299 P 22325 P
11161 P 14139 O 15486 FP 18319 P 22339 P
11996 P 14910 P 15501 O 20478 F 22375 PO
12150 P 15202 P

Secondary: Inclusions
10147 P 14048 S 14363 P 15287 P 18219 P
10171 S 14082 P 14380 P 15578 P 18290 P
10916 P 14138 P 15209 P 17378 O 21432 P
10993 P 14302 P 15222 P 17601 P 22336 P
14031 P 14326 FP 15233 P 18189 P 22754 P
14046 P 14344 P 15270 P

Secondary: Journal Articles
10316 P 12141 P 14362 P 15984 O 18336 P
10418 P 12153 P 14528 P 15985 O 18342 P
10902 P 12825 P 14830 P 16083 F 19139 P
10907 P 12831 P 14834 P 17383 O 19316 P
10924 P 13438 S 14868 P 17590 P 19317 P
10926 S 14021 15199 17599 P 19412 P
10942 14041 P 15239 P 17620 F 19599 P
10966 P 14060 P 15247 P 17996 P 20520 P
10967 P 14061 P 15255 18190 P 21045 P
11115 P 14142 P 15261 P 18217 P 21077 P
11116 P 14303 S 15263 P 18227 P 22292 P
11452 P 14314 P 15265 18259 P 22370 P
11941 P 14317 P 15268 18260 P 22374 P
11981 P 14320 P 15282 S 18326 P 22768 P
12037 P 14331 P

36.1 Elite and Professional Associations
社會領導階層與專門職業之會社
エリート及び専門職業者の団体

1644-1842
Primary □
Second. 21685 P 22776 P

1644-1911
Primary 14205 P 16918
Second. 18098 P 20769 PO

1842-1911
Primary 10551 P 14601 O 18076 P
Second. 14174 P 18092 P 18409 P 22606 P
13858 P 14556 P 18095 22029 P

1842-1928
(including 1644-1928)
Primary 17981 P 22079 P
Second. 14228 O 18102 O 19715 20790 PO
21343 P

1911-1928
Primary 14704 P 19402 S
Second. 18127 S 19265 O 22153 P

1911-1949
(including 1644-1949, 1842-1949)
Primary 19393 P 19397 O 19400 O 21459 P
11263 PO 19394 P 19398 S 19630 P 22801 O
14218 PO 19395 S
Second. 14223 P 18304 P 20823 PO 21321 P
10717 PO 14231 P 18661 P 20826 P 22091 P
14217 P

1928-1949
Primary 19396 P 19399 O 19401 O 21818 O
Second. 11757 P 14762 P 20450 P 22797 O
10103 PO 14241 P 14763 O 20926 PO 22928 O
11724 P 14721 PO 19635 O 21819 O

1928-1972
(incl. 1644-1972, 1842-1972, 1911-1972)
Primary 14271 P 18045 19404 P 20960 P
10892 P 14277 19403 19405 P 21904 FP
Second. 14259 P 18043 P 20990 21902 P
11038 P 14264 P 18315 21392 PO 22188 P
11398 P 14268 P 20954 FP 21399 P 22806 P
12386 P 14269 P 20957 P 21412 P 22816 P
12415 P 14270 P 20959 P 21471 P 22817 O
12764 S 14293 S 20981 P 21887 P 22820 P
14252 14792 P

1949-1972
Primary 15016 O 19408 PO 19418 P 21096 O
11073 P 15030 O 19409 P 19419 21909 P
11145 P 15273 P 19410 P 19420 21913 P
13408 P 16020 P 19411 O 19421 P 21918 P
14299 P 18277 P 19412 P 19422 P 21936 O
14358 P 18341 P 19413 P 19423 O 21979 P
14835 S 18345 P 19414 P 19424 P 22840 O
14964 O 18350 P 19415 O 19425 P 22850 O
14990 P 19406 O 19416 O 21053 O 22857 S
15007 P 19407 P 19417 O
Second. 12801 P 14853 P 18357 P 21937 P
10175 O 12836 P 14879 O 19309 P 21947 P
10417 P 13381 P 14886 P 19666 P 21961 P
10463 P 13394 P 14969 P 20272 FP 21962 P
10464 P 13411 P 15017 P 20996 FP 21963 O
10481 P 13436 P 15031 P 21025 P 21964 P
10975 P 13449 P 15212 O 21048 PO 21968 P
11104 P 14305 P 16460 P 21050 PO 21977 P
11107 P 14327 P 16798 FP 21073 P 21978 P
11117 P 14352 P 16858 PO 21092 FP 22327 P
11126 P 14364 P 17972 S 21146 P 22831 P
11946 P 14378 P 17990 P 21911 P 22836 S
12447 P 14844 O 18263 FP 21912 P 22839 P
12485 P

36.2 Employers Associations
商業雇主之社團　　雇用者団体

1644-1842
Primary 19429 P 19436 P
Second. 14401 P

1644-1911
Primary 17434 P 19209 O 19347 PO 19434 P
19437 P
Second. 19345 P

1842-1911
Primary 14396 P
Second. 17409 FP 19208 P 19349 P 19717 P
13122 S 17689 P 19343 S 19365 P 22606 P
16092 P 18490 P

1842-1928
(including 1644-1928)
Primary □
Second. 12955 PO 14404 P 17661 P 19715
10084 PO 13644 P 15944 P 19472 22131 PO
11708 S

1911-1928
Primary 11734 P 14408 P 16319 O 18126 P
19427 P 19430
Second. 11345 P 15407 FP 17306 FP 18609 O
10091 O 11784 P 15450 F 17449 19281
10381 P 13209 O 16114 P 17696 PO 19512 P
10750 P 14122 O 16442 P 18310 P 19553

1911-1949
(including 1644-1949, 1842-1949)
Primary 17459 P 19426 19432 P 19435 P
Second. 11712 FP 13171 P 17054 FP 17491 P
10257 12965 P 13242 P 17251 F 19358 P
10717 PO 12998 P 13250 P 17274 FP 19561 P
11368 P 13037 P 13679 S 17464 FP 19840 O
11699 S 13140 14409

1928-1949
Primary 13279 P
Second. 12727 S 17291 S 19258 19272 P
10831 P 12980 O 18117 P 19267 P 19555 FP
11031 P 16587 19238 O

1928-1972
(incl. 1644-1972, 1842-1972, 1911-1972)
Primary 19433 P
Second. 12764 S 13053 FP 14413 P 14415 P
19286 O

1949-1972
Primary 19428 P 19431 O
Second. 16135 O 17990 P 19302 P 20272 FP
14549 P 16473 P 17994 FP 19593 PO 22764 O
16075 P

36.3 Peasant Associations and Movements
農民協會及農民運動
農民団体及び農民運動

1644-1842
Primary 13813 P 19439 S 19440 P 19441 P
21686 P
Second. 18477 S

1644-1911
Primary 17977 PO 18391 P
Second. 16049 P 18526 S 22866 P

1842-1911
Primary 13860 P 16530 P 18463 P 19438 P
Second. 16089 P 18370 P 18430 P 18452 P
13831 P 17411 P 18382 P 18436 P

1842-1928
(including 1644-1928)
Primary 12211 P 14109 P 14112 P 17560 P
Second. 11698 P 11708 S 12233 P 18102 O

1911-1928
Primary 18697 PO 19443 19451 O 19459
18161 O 18708 19445 P 19452 S 19460 F
18609 O 18743 P 19446 P 19453 P 19461 P
18654 P 18757 O 19448 P 19454 FP 19462
18655 P 18782 P 19449 P 19455 P 19503 FP
18669 P 19442 PO 19450 P 19456 P 19504 P
Second. 13906 PO 14497 FP 18615 18777 P
12268 P 13925 P 17486 S 18616 18779 P
12302 P 13927 P 18115 P 18644 P 18784
12346 P 13950 S 18310 P 18709 P 19259 P
13896 PO 14251 P 18582 O 18725 P 20455
13905 PO 14429 S 18602 P 18742 P 22162 P

1911-1949
(including 1644-1949, 1842-1949)
Primary 16550 P 18588 P 18780 P 19458
10078 S 16639 P 18645 S 19444 P 19463 P
12325 P 18571 S 18673 P 19447 21320
13715 P 18583 S 18752 P 19457 P 22173 P
14116 P
Second. 12232 PO 17463 FP 18626 P 18722 O
10446 O 12257 FP 17763 PO 18636 P 18728 P
10749 12259 F 18120 P 18674 P 18745 O
10791 P 12271 P 18121 P 18686 P 19355 FP
10812 P 12296 P 18304 P 18699 P 19632 S
11336 P 12317 PO 18545 PO 18711 O 20210 P
12223 P 15156 O 18578 O 18715 P 22805 O
12227 P 16123 FP 18605 S

1928-1949
Primary 12311 P 18604 S 18663 P 19464 P
12279 P 18577 O 18660 P 18690 P 19465 F

SECOND. 12310 P 14426 S 16637 P 18643 F
10792 O 12348 PO 15426 S 18305 P 18755 P
11346 P 13970 O 16430 P 18603 O 19074 O

1928-1972
(incl. 1644-1972, 1842-1972, 1911-1972)

PRIMARY 12413 P 18819 P 19467 S 21840 S
12391 P 12418 FP 19085 O 19468 F 21853 P
12394 P 16729 FP 19466 F 19469 O 21885 S
12403 P 18791 P

SECOND. 12396 P 14256 18185 P 19081 P
10391 P 12401 P 14278 P 18794 P 19092 P
11391 P 12412 P 15168 18795 P 21389 P
11874 P 12424 P 15460 FP 18810 21393 O
12378 P 12426 P 15980 P 18834 P 21420 PO
12379 P 12767 16736 P 18835 S 22203 P
12383 P 13766 P 16747 P 19077 P 22251 P
12387 PO 14127 P 17989 S

1949-1972

PRIMARY 15510 O 16902 FP 19107 S 19470 S
10489 S 16798 FP 17127 P 19124 P 19471 P
10904 F 16858 PO 17683 F 19189 P 21486 O
10950 O 16889

SECOND. 12464 P 15517 F 16833 P 19177 P
10159 O 12477 P 15530 F 17907 O 19178 O
11423 P 12480 P 15545 O 18263 FP 19184 PO
11916 S 12518 O 16071 FP 18323 P 19194 P
12064 S 12549 P 16760 O 19110 O 19201 P
12070 P 14447 P 16769 P 19133 PO 20236 F
12173 P 14965 P 16771 F 19134 P 21907 P
12442 P 15002 FP 16810 PO 19135 P 22318 P
12458 O 15491 F

36.4 LABOR UNIONS AND THE LABOR MOVEMENT

工會及勞工運動
労働組合及び労働運動

1644-1842

PRIMARY □
SECOND. 12901 P

1644-1911

PRIMARY □
SECOND. 14454 P 19347 PO

1842-1911

PRIMARY 13122 S
SECOND. 17689 P

1842-1928
(including 1644-1928)

PRIMARY 19474 19477 PO 19479 19481 P
19472 19475 19478 19480 P

SECOND. 11713 P 13520 P 14458 P 18102 O
10348 O 13149 PO 13884 PO 17691 PO 22092 P
11708 S 13164 FP 14113 P 17693 P 22131 PO
11711 S 13169 P

1911-1928

PRIMARY: MONOGRAPHS
11812 P 17717 PO 18655 P 19517 FP 19534 P
13016 P 18161 O 18708 19520 O 19558
14497 FP 18308 P 19490 PO 19524 P 19578 S
15073 P 18582 O 19502 P 19533 P 20209 P
15143 P 18654 P 19503 FP

PRIMARY: INCLUSIONS
14468 P 17571 O 19500 P 19526 19557 P
14476 PO 17696 PO 19504 P 19546 P 19562 O
14492 P 17712 P 19511 O 19550 O 19563
15148 P

PRIMARY: JOURNAL ARTICLES
15065 P 19495 F 19514 P 19535 P 19552
16122 O 19496 P 19515 O 19536 19553
17700 P 19498 P 19516 S 19538 O 19554 P
18623 19499 P 19518 O 19541 O 19560 P
18642 19501 P 19522 19543 O 19567
18757 O 19506 P 19527 19545 P 19569
19482 P 19507 P 19528 19547 PO 19570 P
19483 19509 P 19529 19548 P 19575
19489 O 19510 P 19530 19549 19580 P
19491 19512 P 19531 O

SECOND. 14123 P 15062 O 18596 PO 18725 P
10106 P 14251 P 15145 PO 18597 PO 18733 P
10445 O 14407 P 17268 O 18601 P 18764 O
10840 S 14408 P 17294 O 18602 P 18778 P
13277 F 14469 S 17719 O 18609 O 18779 P
13284 P 14483 PO 17720 F 18611 P 20222 S
13906 PO 14484 18115 P 18617 P 20457 O
13927 P 14487 S 18127 S 18625 P 22159 P
13966 P 14489 S 18129 FP 18665 O 22162 P
14114 14502 O 18310 P 18709 P 22678 O
14122 O 14511 18592 P 18720 S

1911-1949
(including 1644-1949, 1842-1949)

PRIMARY 14503 S 19006 O 19519 O 19559 PO
11824 O 14508 P 19358 P 19523 F 19561 P
12965 P 14510 PO 19473 S 19532 19566 P
14473 O 17251 F 19476 P 19539 P 19576 P
14479 PO 18583 S 19486 P 19542 19577 P
14486 P 18739 P 19492 P 19551 P 19579 P
14496 P 18752 P 19513 19556 P

SECOND. 13162 S 14482 P 17193 FP 18557 P
10079 PO 13184 P 14491 P 17274 FP 18605 S
10086 PO 13233 PO 14505 P 17694 PO 18635 P
10107 P 13242 P 14509 P 17721 P 18636 P
10446 O 13261 P 14703 S 17733 P 18674 P
10729 P 13887 P 15156 O 17869 PO 18711 O
10749 13968 O 15384 PO 17880 P 18715 P
10791 P 14116 P 15446 P 18120 P 18722 O
10828 P 14457 P 17054 FP 18121 P 18780 P
11712 FP 14463 P 17184 FP 18157 P 18783 P
11716 P 14466 P 17185 FP 18304 P 19356
13158 FP 14475 FP 17190 PO 18534 PO 20204 P

1928-1949

PRIMARY 18693 O 19494 P 19540 19572 P
10101 O 19267 P 19497 F 19544 P 19573 P
13275 P 19268 F 19505 P 19555 FP 19574 P
14472 O 19484 O 19508 O 19564 19704 P
14478 FP 19485 P 19521 19565 O 20190 P
14501 P 19487 P 19525 S 19568 S 20195 FP
16974 O 19488 P 19537 19571 P 22161 P
17718 P 19493 P

SECOND. 11750 S 14500 P 17725 FP 18603 O
10103 PO 11830 O 16417 P 17728 F 18668 S
10108 P 14461 P 17047 O 17735 P 18717 P
10792 O 14471 P 17300 F 17863 PO 18755 P
10821 S 14474 FP 17704 P 18118 P 20470
11031 P 14480 P 17710 F 18130 P 21379 O
11732 P 14499 S 17715 P

1928-1972
(incl. 1644-1972, 1842-1972, 1911-1972)

PRIMARY 18313 P 19581 19583 P 19585 P
14415 P 18810 19582 P 19584 P 22724 P
14513 P

SECOND. 14512 P 17318 P 18795 P 21412 P
10114 P 14514 17580 O 18819 P 21414 FP
11052 FP 15089 S 17615 O 18820 O 22224 P
11845 P 15168 17985 FP 18833 P 22239 S
11862 P 15172 PO 17989 S 19031 P 22250 P
11874 P 15468 O 18185 P 21388 P 22945 S
14258 P 15875 P 18187 P 21397 P 22991 S

1949-1972

PRIMARY 12819 P 14536 P 14542 P 15889 P
10488 P 14518 P 14539 P 14549 P 16075 P
11114 S 14519 P 14540 P 15124 P 16469 P
11506 P 14528 P 14541 P 15231 S 17745 P
17748 O 19589 P 19595 S 19601 P 19607 P
17990 P 19590 P 19596 P 19602 P 19608 P
19291 P 19591 O 19597 FP 19603 P 19609 P
19307 FP 19592 P 19598 FP 19604 O 19610 P
19586 O 19593 PO 19599 P 19605 O 19611 P
19587 O 19594 19600 P 19606 P 21486 O
19588 P

SECOND. 11885 P 14526 P 15489 P 18263 FP
10141 O 11909 P 14527 P 15532 O 18323 P
10145 O 11912 P 14529 P 15578 P 18324 PO
10159 O 11943 P 14531 P 16078 P 18354 O
10465 P 12000 P 14534 O 16135 O 18841 O
10473 P 12018 P 14535 P 16471 P 19297 O
10894 P 12518 O 14545 P 16485 S 19321 P
10895 O 13328 O 14546 S 16486 P 19667 P
10960 FP 13353 P 14965 P 16493 P 20521 P
10975 P 13391 P 14974 PO 17336 P 20673 P
10997 P 13768 P 14984 P 17383 O 21015 O
11094 P 14138 P 15105 P 17497 O 21085 S
11095 O 14364 P 15263 P 17744 O 22318 P
11142 P 14516 S 15294 P 17994 FP 22339 P
11423 P 14517 O 15482 O 18003 FP

37 EDUCATIONAL ASSOCIATIONS AND MOVEMENTS

教育團體及教育運動
教育団体及び教育運動

1644-1842

PRIMARY □
SECOND. 17753 O

1644-1911

PRIMARY □
SECOND. 14555 P 14558 P 19695 P

1842-1911

PRIMARY 14556 P 16907 PO 19612 19613
19614 O 21603 P

SECOND. 14566 PO 14583 PO 14618 P 18490 P
14187 P 14577 O 14613 P 18487 P 21302 O

1842-1928
(including 1644-1928)

PRIMARY 19616 S 19697 P 20182 P

SECOND. 14628 FP 14697 O 18949 PO 21335 P
10067 O 14634 F 15944 F 18977 P 21340 P
11591 14674 O 18102 O 18987 P 22110 P
14224 PO 14693 FP

1911-1928

PRIMARY 17760 O 19641 19647 O 20207 O
10838 P 19627 O 19645 P 19699 O 22160 P
13976 P 19639 P 19646 O

SECOND. 14720 O 15145 PO 17759 P 17938
10091 O 14724 P 15153 17842 F 19013 O
11597 PO 14735 P 17695 O 17843 O 19402 S
11783 P 14765

1911-1949
(including 1644-1949, 1842-1949)

PRIMARY 14695 S 17869 PO 19620 FP 19632 S
11586 FP 14719 O 19615 PO 19628 P 19637 O
14223 P 14723 PO 19617 P 19630 P 19643 P
14656 P 17754 P 19618 P 19631 P 19644 PO
14678 S 17763 PO 19619 O

SECOND. 14647 P 14688 P 15408 F 20845 F
10781 P 14653 O 14691 P 16550 P 20909 O
11601 P 14660 P 14694 P 16639 P 20946 F
12740 O 14670 P 14696 P 17463 FP 20949 F
14238 P 14677 P 14772 17769 P 21321 P
14640 PO 14681 PO 14776 P 19257 P

1928-1949

Primary 17872 P 19624 O 19635 O 19649 O
10760 P 17891 O 19625 S 19636 O 19704 P
11724 P 19074 O 19626 P 19638 S 20189 P
12331 P 19621 O 19629 P 19640 P 20444 P
16694 O 19622 S 19633 O 19642 S 22714 P
17238 P 19623 PO 19634 O 19648 O

Second. 14754 PO 17245 P 20200 O 20841
10105 FP 14760 PO 17278 P 20443 P 20843 F
14733 PO 14774 FP 17761 O 20450 P 20844 F
14738 16054 P 18111 P 20451 O 20896 FP
14749 PO 16617 PO 19003 FP 20458 O 20910 O
14750 F

1928-1972
(incl. 1644-1972, 1842-1972, 1911-1972)

Primary 19081 P 19652 P 19655 P 19658 P
14779 S 19650 PO 19653 P 19656 P 19659 P
14808 P 19651 S 19654 PO 19657 P 20402 S
19035 PO

Second. 14784 O 14802 P 15799 O 19709 P
10855 FP 14785 PO 14803 P 17772 O 20961 PO
12403 P 14792 P 14804 17897 F 21404 P
14255 P 14800 P 15193 S 18827 O 21874 P
14780 P 14801 P 15614 P 19031 P

1949-1972

Primary 14965 P 18318 O 19668 P 19678 P
10904 F 14974 PO 19587 O 19669 O 19679 FP
10950 O 14986 P 19660 P 19670 P 19680 O
11117 P 14999 O 19661 O 19671 P 19681 P
12864 P 16009 P 19662 P 19672 O 19682 P
14362 P 16852 O 19663 PO 19673 P 19683 F
14526 P 17645 O 19664 O 19674 O 19684 P
14914 17793 O 19665 P 19675 O 21124 PO
14931 P 18003 FP 19666 P 19676 P 21562 O
14959 P 18004 F 19667 P 19677 P

Second. 14823 P 14905 P 14969 P 17795 O
11453 P 14827 P 14906 P 15017 P 17810 O
12123 P 14828 P 14910 P 15028 P 18061 O
12845 P 14865 PO 14913 P 15557 O 19063 PO
14325 P 14872 PO 14919 S 15908 P 20486 P
14347 P 14878 PO 14947 O 16005 P 20521 P
14359 P 14890 P 14951 P 16070 O 20530 P
14813 P 14894 P 14952 P 16858 PO 21150 F

38 Organized Philanthropy and Mutual-Aid Societies

慈善團體及互助組織

慈善団体及び共済組合

1644-1842

Primary 20043 P

Second. □

1644-1911

Primary 19687 P 19688 P 19692 PO 19695 P
20285 P

Second. 15318 O 17975 O 17977 PO 21172 P
11574 PO 15346 P 17976 19347 PO

1842-1911

Primary 17433 P 19344 S 19689 O 19693 P
12569 O 17812 O 19685 O 19690 O 19694 O
15735 O 18407 O 19686 O 19691 O 19696 O

Second. 15036 O 16187 O 17811 O 18490 P
10047 O 15041 P 17410 PO 17924 P 19343 S
10049 PO 15348 O 17439 O 18380 20258 O
10059 O 15717 O 17608 18436 P 20282 O
10271 O 16186 O 17629 P 18437 P 22523 O
13853 P

1842-1928
(including 1644-1928)

Primary 15944 P 17981 P 18102 O 19697 P
19698 O

Second. 11703 P 17691 PO 20182 P 20389 PO
11698 P 16103 FP 18949 PO 20294 PO 20800 O

1911-1928

Primary 17843 O 17862 O 17879 O 19699 O
15061 S 17848 O 17873 PO 17884 O 20832 FP
17720 F

Second. 15418 F 17842 F 19256 O 20186 O
13717 S 16630 F 17877 F 19259 P 20462 FP
15407 FP 17470 F 19251 P

1911-1949
(including 1644-1949, 1842-1949)

Primary 15060 O 17980 P 19701 P 20160 PO
14698 P 15949 P 18952 P 19705 P 20934 P

Second. 12684 FP 14770 O 17979 P 19964 P
10104 O 12965 P 15672 O 18547 PO 20302 FP
11368 P 13673 P 15679 FP 18964 P 20827 PO
12227 P 13679 S 16309 O 19233 F 22655 O
12257 FP 14665 PO 17445 S 19282 P

1928-1949

Primary 19640 P 19703 O 19707 O 20461 P
17047 O 19700 O 19704 P 19708 O 20833 P
17849 O 19702 P 19706 O 20398 PO 22714 P

Second. 12298 P 16432 PO 19621 O 20393 O
10092 O 13748 O 16607 O 19629 P 20844 F
10100 O 15078 P 16716 F 19638 S 20910 O
10108 P 15448 F 17228 P 19649 O 20926 PO
11372 P 16057 P 17484 FP 20184

1928-1972
(incl. 1644-1972, 1842-1972, 1911-1972)

Primary 15086 15981 F 17894 P 19034 O
19709 P 19710 P

Second. 11869 P 16335 P 17985 FP 19857 O
11851 P 15454 P 17984 O 19053 P 21529 PO

1949-1972

Primary 15120 P 16044 F 19711 FP 19714 P
10304 F 15121 P 17909 P 19712 O 20272 FP
15118 P 16010 FP 17994 FP 19713 P 20664 P
15119 P 16023 O 19587 O

Second. 12173 P 15498 O 16482 O 19590 P
10312 O 13780 P 15835 O 16773 PO 20667 P
11467 P 15105 P 15998 O 17990 P 21014
12128 S 15491 F 16076 P 19428 P 21550 F

39 Associations Based on Common Place of Origin

鄉誼組織　同鄉組織

1644-1842

Primary 17173 P

Second. 18014 P

1644-1911

Primary 17976 18396 S 19347 PO 19718 P

Second. 10333 P 10571 17541 P 19351 P
19695 P

1842-1911

Primary 15925 P 17973 PO 19343 S 19349 P
19716 P 19717 P

Second. 12894 O 15629 O 16526 O 17689 P
10551 P 14396 P 16187 O 16908 O 18490 P

1842-1928
(including 1644-1928)

Primary 17981 P 19715

Second. 10073 10084 PO 15944 P 19352 O
19477 PO

1911-1928

Primary 14468 P 19360 F

Second. 10766 P 13029 S 17983 O 18144 P
19281 19363

1911-1949
(including 1644-1949, 1842-1949)

Primary 19357 FP

Second. 10086 PO 14409 14475 FP 17190 PO
19561 P

1928-1949

Primary □

Second. 10297 O 11031 P 12727 S 19270 O
19704 P

1928-1972
(incl. 1644-1972, 1842-1972, 1911-1972)

Primary 17985 FP

Second. 10259 P 15973 P 17956 P 17984 O

1949-1972

Primary 17994 FP

Second. 10304 F 15913 O 20272 FP

40 Kinship Systems in General

親屬制度通論　親族制度一般

1644-1842

Primary 10020 PO 10027 O 16185 P 22619 PO

Second. □

1644-1911

Primary 11203 P 15320 PO 19723 F 20144 P
10006 S 11655 PO 18010 P 19763 P 20154 P
11194 O 12193 PO 19722 P 20022 P 21982 P

Second. 10608 P 11243 P 19748 PO 20548 S
10028 PO 11183 P 14088 P 19772 P 22639 P
10037 11211 P 16379 PO 19992 S

1842-1911

Primary 15325 O 16526 O 19721 PO 20287 P
10003 O 15360 O 19719 P 20088 F 20590 PO
10041 16183 O 19720 O 20130 O 21980 O
11662

Second. 10056 O 16910 PO 18852 PO 20155 O
10034 S 10057 O 17551 S 20141 O 21265 P
10048 O 11230 P 17974 O

1842-1928
(including 1644-1928)

Primary 11250 P 19726 O 20005 S 22644 O
10084 PO 16226 PO 19795 P 21798 P

Second. 11261 P 11719 O 17981 P 21998 P
10067 O 11709 15379 O 18024 PO

1911-1928

Primary 15418 F 19826 P 19841 O

Second. 10094 O 14758 PO 20107 S 20215 O
10089 O 10778 O 15397 O

1911-1949
(including 1644-1949, 1842-1949)

PRIMARY 11029 P 19785 P 20013 P 21344 O
10070 P 19218 19802 PO 20025 P 21761 P
10074 P 19724 19806 P 20053 P 22004 P
10086 PO 19725 P 19816 FP 21330 O 22682 O
10093 O 19727 S 19963 P

SECOND. 14650 S 19964 P 21308 O 22006 S
10080 15679 FP 20009 S 21740 P 22457 F
10104 O 18976 FP 20057 P 21997 P 22923 FP
11382 FP 19357 FP 20160 PO

1928-1949

PRIMARY 19728 F 19810 P 19847 FP 22713 F
14430 S 19729 F 19813 P 20066 P

SECOND. 15150 15399 F 15424 F 15426 S
15640 F 20262 F

1928-1972
(incl. 1644-1972, 1842-1972, 1911-1972)

PRIMARY 19055 FP 19735 S 19882 19975 FP
10110 PO 19730 S 19736 S 19888 S 19980 FP
10117 PO 19731 S 19862 P 19892 P 20017 F
14126 19732 P 19868 S 19899 P 20069 PO
15451 FP 19733 S 19869 S 19973 FP 21467 S
15463 FP 19734 O 19871 S

SECOND. 16335 P 19972 FP 20231 PO 21532 O
10846 19872 P 19978 FP 20234 PO 22187 S
14127 P 19971 20227 P 21466 P 22198 O

1949-1972

PRIMARY 15515 FP 19738 F 20249 F 21546 F
11103 P 17675 F 19905 P 21201 O 21556 F
15504 F 18048 F 19990 FP 21483 FP 21574 FP
15505 F 19737 FP 20236 F

SECOND. 10155 P 15530 F 15709 S 19070 F
10134 O 12427 P 15560 FP 16496 FP 20248 O
10154 P

41 MARRIAGE AND THE FAMILY
婚姻與家庭 婚姻と家庭

1644-1842

PRIMARY 10585 P 11536 O 19741 O 20035 P
20558 S

SECOND. 10036 O 10654 P 15923 O 21278 P
10007 O 10045 O 12198 P 20040 S 21644 P
10026 O 10512 PO 14085 P 20563 S 22578 O
10032 O 10652 O 14096 S 20571 O

1644-1911

PRIMARY 14196 P 19750 FP 19767 PO 19992 S
11203 P 18915 FP 19752 P 19768 P 20044 P
11218 P 19722 P 19754 PO 19769 P 20096 P
11220 P 19723 F 19755 PO 19770 S 20135 PO
11221 P 19743 PO 19756 O 19771 S 20144 P
11568 PO 19744 19757 19772 P 20149 S
11672 PO 19747 P 19763 P 19774 P 20570 O
14090 P 19748 PO 19766 O 19776 FP 21982 P

SECOND. 11195 P 16184 P 20002 P 20157 O
10001 O 11211 P 16188 P 20020 P 20720 PO
10012 P 11212 16208 PO 20022 P 21163 FP
10014 O 11222 P 17520 PO 20083 P 21172 P
10016 O 11226 P 18010 P 20089 P 21440 O
10042 PO 11243 P 18421 P 20092 P 21657 P
10046 O 14098 P 18862 P 20123 21703
10060 PO 14099 P 18890 S 20124 PO 21981 O
10276 14102 P 18933 20131 PO 21983 P
10560 P 15044 S 18940 P 20150 22390 P
11194 O 16098 19960 PO 20154 P

1842-1911

PRIMARY 10030 O 11230 P 15317 O 15336 O
10002 O 10038 O 11232 FP 15321 O 15338 P
10018 PO 10682 O 15314 S 15330 FP 15358 O
15367 O 19739 O 19759 PO 19778 PO 20259 O
15749 PO 19740 O 19760 PO 19779 P 20282 O
17608 19742 O 19761 O 19780 P 20379 O
17821 O 19745 19762 S 19996 PO 20385 O
17973 PO 19746 PO 19764 O 20085 P 20539 O
18908 O 19749 O 19765 O 20125 O 21264 O
19719 P 19751 O 19773 PO 20130 O 21652 O
19720 O 19753 P 19775 O 20137 O 22067 O
19721 PO 19758 O 19777 O 20142 O 22397 FP

SECONDARY: MONOGRAPHS
10013 O 10062 PO 14182 FP 16186 O 20275 O
10017 O 10562 P 14195 P 17176 PO 20576 PO
10019 PO 10598 O 14592 P 17649 O 20716 O
10024 O 12580 PO 15311 O 18449 O 21280 O
10035 O 12902 O 15325 O 18511 P 21990 O
10041 12920 O 15744 O 20138 O 22066 P
10047 O 14157 O 16090 O 20258 O 22580 PO
10049 PO 14178 P 16167 O 20274 O 22589 P
10059 O

SECONDARY: INCLUSIONS
11223 S 17978 O 20279 O 20564 O 21664 O

SECONDARY: JOURNAL ARTICLES
10009 P 13840 O 17625 O 20088 F 21168 O
10531 P 14094 17818 O 20129 O 21181 O
10648 O 14163 PO 17925 O 20139 21266 O
11188 P 15932 O 18301 S 20141 O 22047 P
11189 P 16089 P 18398 P 20541 O 22403 P
11204 P 16096 O 19994 O 21160 PO 22541 O
11662 16214 P

1842-1928
(including 1644-1928)

PRIMARY 16250 O 19791 P 20005 S 21305 O
10071 O 16267 O 19793 P 20051 P 21307 O
10082 PO 16275 O 19794 P 20175 P 21311 O
11248 P 19726 O 19795 P 20177 P 21355 O
15138 19784 P 19797 PO 20182 P 21453 O
15378 F 19789 P 19803 PO 20389 PO 21798 P
16103 FP 19790 PO 19805

SECOND. 11275 PO 15374 F 18974 PO 21337 PO
10069 O 11581 PO 15379 O 20100 21502
10081 PO 11683 O 15390 O 20163 P 21504 O
10084 PO 11698 P 16226 PO 20169 FP 21781 S
10255 O 12211 P 16252 PO 20179 P 21996 P
10348 O 12225 O 16277 P 20181 P 21998 P
10704 S 12963 PO 16552 O 20430 P 22002 P
11250 P 13163 S 18022 O 20798 O 22131 PO
11260 P 14214 PO 18024 PO 21189 PO

1911-1928

PRIMARY 17876 F 19825 O 19851 O 20213 O
15403 F 19811 P 19826 P 19852 P 20648 F
16593 F 19812 O 19841 O 19856 O 21208 F
17855 F 19818 FP 19842 P 20107 S 21218 F
17856 F

SECOND. 15061 S 16695 F 20215 O 21207 F
10089 O 15450 F 17720 F 20220 P 21223 F
11316 P 16121 O 17871 FP 20266 PO 21226 F
11363 P 16591 F 17877 F 20462 FP 21365 O
13029 S 16594 F 17887 F 20463 F 21525 O
13277 F 16644 FP 19255 PO 20633 O 22445 O
14429 S 16664 PO 19277 P 20938 P

1911-1949
(including 1644-1949, 1842-1949)

PRIMARY: MONOGRAPHS
11263 PO 17869 PO 19828 PO 20159 PO 20276 O
11344 P 19796 P 19836 F 20160 PO 20432 P
15376 FP 19801 P 19839 PO 20162 P 20615 O
15408 F 19802 PO 19840 O 20166 O 20623 PO
15428 O 19804 P 19854 P 20178 PO 20653 O
15449 O 19806 P 19962 S 20204 P 21330 O
15586 P 19816 FP 19964 P 20205 O 21384 O
15955 P 19819 P 20013 P 20208 O 21821 O
16104 S 19824 PO 20050 S 20210 P 21994
16123 FP

PRIMARY: INCLUSIONS
19724 19727 S 19786 19788 FP 20298 F

PRIMARY: JOURNAL ARTICLES
10199 P 19785 P 19809 19837 S 20104 O
16112 S 19787 19821 P 19843 S 20192 O
16278 O 19792 P 19829 S 19848 F 21209 S
19781 19798 P 19832 P 19853 P 21744 P
19782 P 19799 P 19833 FP 20028 S 21763
19783 S 19800 P 19835 F

SECONDARY: MONOGRAPHS
10070 P 12303 FP 17274 FP 20302 FP 21375 O
10079 PO 13880 PO 17721 P 20614 P 21380 O
10086 PO 14686 P 17979 P 20886 O 21443 F
10088 O 14687 PO 18544 P 21325 P 21444 P
10097 O 14703 S 18722 O 21333 O 21457 P
10205 P 15372 O 19246 O 21359 P 21729 P
10349 S 15446 P 20025 P 21362 O 21761 P
10718 S 15674 PO 20053 P 21367 O 22004 P
11317 P 16624 FP 20161 P 21368 O 22109 S
12230 P 17193 FP 20173 S 21370 O 22432 P

SECONDARY: INCLUSIONS
10295 PO 14405 16299 F 19965 P 20621
11252 S 15386 18029 F 20176 20654
14220 P 16271 PO 18558 S 20292 S

SECONDARY: JOURNAL ARTICLES
10195 P 11334 S 17036 FP 19353 S 20168
10710 S 11382 FP 17054 FP 19967 P 20857 O
11262 P 16107 P 17880 P 20010 P 22430 O
11264 P 16310 F 19014 P 20055 P 22456

1928-1949

PRIMARY 15596 F 19808 P 19831 P 20212 P
11362 P 15598 FP 19810 P 19834 F 20221 O
12291 S 16118 F 19813 P 19838 S 20262 F
14750 F 16631 F 19814 P 19844 O 20436 O
15399 F 16632 F 19815 P 19845 S 20439 P
15405 F 16672 F 19817 O 19846 P 20639 S
15410 O 17667 F 19820 F 19847 FP 21213 FP
15426 S 17761 O 19822 F 19849 F 21214 F
15436 F 17868 F 19823 O 19850 F 21215 FP
15447 F 19729 F 19827 F 19855 S 21217 P
15448 F 19807 O 19830 F 20199 O 21366 O

SECOND. 15150 16311 F 19011 F 20642 F
10098 O 15394 O 16317 O 19362 F 20863 O
10206 P 15406 F 16662 F 19640 P 20921 F
10297 O 15414 PO 17458 F 20015 F 21225 F
10298 S 15431 P 17613 F 20062 P 21229 P
11308 F 15432 F 17632 O 20066 P 21508 F
11372 P 15434 O 17665 20184 21511 F
11752 FP 15594 F 17833 F 20188 O 21512 F
12256 F 15640 F 17834 F 20190 P 21513 F
12298 P 15641 F 17854 F 20203 O 21522 O
12358 P 15869 F 17872 P 20206 O 21527 F
14117 P 16289 FP 17943 O 20217 F 22455 F
14430 S

1928-1972
(incl. 1644-1972, 1842-1972, 1911-1972)

PRIMARY 19733 S 19869 S 19884 P 19898 O
11387 P 19734 O 19870 19885 P 19899 P
11388 P 19736 S 19871 S 19886 S 19975 FP
11400 P 19857 O 19872 P 19887 P 19978 FP
11403 PO 19858 F 19873 S 19888 S 20070 FP
11414 P 19859 FP 19874 P 19889 F 20226 PO
15180 19860 19875 P 19890 S 20229 P
15189 O 19861 P 19876 19891 P 20231 PO
15463 FP 19862 P 19877 P 19892 P 20232 O
17103 FP 19863 F 19878 PO 19893 P 20234 PO
17956 P 19864 FP 19879 P 19894 FP 20235 O
19090 FP 19865 P 19880 S 19895 FP 20428 O
19730 S 19866 P 19881 PO 19896 FP 21393 O
19731 S 19867 P 19882 19897 P 21538 FP
19732 P 19868 S 19883 P

SECONDARY: MONOGRAPHS
10113 11036 P 15460 FP 16456 F 20475 O
10115 O 11045 FP 15470 S 17897 F 20658 F
10117 PO 11053 O 15472 P 17953 P 20994 O
10120 S 11390 P 15476 F 19970 FP 21413 O
10126 O 11391 P 15613 P 20069 PO 21416 O
10214 P 15171 FP 16068 O 20109 P 21422 O
10888 S 15192 O 16343 P 20224 O 21862 S
11035 O

41 Marriage and the Family

Secondary: Inclusions
10216 P 15611 PO 20111 S 20472 P 22016 S
11399 P 15645 P 20228 P 20661 22476 P
12772 P 19974 P 20233 S 20995 FP 22479 P
13048 F 19979 P 20303 P 21196 F 22490 S
15473 F 20017 F

Secondary: Journal Articles
11386 P 15471 P 17949 P 20227 P 21541 P
11402 P 15475 O 17984 O 20230 S 21543 O
11412 P 15646 P 19735 S 20304 F 21545 O
14126 16125 P 19973 FP 21472 S 21868 P
14130 P 16127 S 19980 FP 21473 PO 22014
15451 FP 17669 FP 19985 O 21533 S 22015 P

1949-1972

Primary: Monographs
10141 O 16013 P 19917 P 19946 FP 20421 F
14983 F 16348 F 19918 F 19953 F 20422 F
15491 F 16354 F 19919 P 20236 F 20522 FP
15515 FP 17963 F 19920 20244 P 21037 F
15517 F 19738 F 19922 P 20249 F 21484 F
15544 O 19905 P 19931 P 20360 F 21579 PO
15621 F 19909 P 19933 FP 20368 F 21946 O
15708 FP 19910 F 19939 F

Primary: Inclusions
11447 P 19901 F 19928 P 19951 FP 20427 F
14135 P 19911 P 19930 P 19952 P 21581 FP
15215 19913 S 19935 F 20121 P 22762 S
15271 O 19914 S 19945 FP 20326 F 23034 O
16003 F 19915 P

Primary: Journal Articles
15232 19906 P 19929 F 19947 F 20359 F
15887 F 19907 O 19932 F 19948 P 20363 P
16036 P 19908 P 19934 P 19949 P 21237 FP
16137 PO 19912 P 19936 F 19950 P 21243 FP
17118 F 19916 F 19937 F 19954 O 21250 P
17622 F 19921 P 19938 F 19955 F 21564 F
19145 P 19923 P 19940 PO 19956 P 21567 F
19900 O 19924 19941 S 20072 F 21568 F
19902 O 19925 F 19942 O 20237 O 21580 F
19903 P 19926 P 19943 F 20242 P 21584 O
19904 PO 19927 P 19944 P

Secondary: Monographs
10136 O 10263 P 15526 O 18048 F 20503 O
10139 P 11135 O 15549 P 19132 P 20527 O
10140 O 11437 P 15550 O 19679 FP 20694 F
10144 O 12090 O 15567 O 19737 FP 21249 FP
10145 O 13584 P 15617 F 19990 FP 21546 F
10149 O 14133 O 15707 FP 20074 FP 21563 PO
10152 O 14990 P 16001 S 20075 P 21575 FP
10153 O 15483 P 16132 O 20247 P 21577 FP
10155 P 15505 F 16869 F 20328 P 21578 O
10157 O 15506 O 16886 F 20334 FP 21586 F
10164 O 15508 O 16902 FP 20411 O 22018 F
10165 O 15509 O 16991 F 20426 FP 22769 O
10177 O 15511 O 17386 FP

Secondary: Inclusions
10229 P 16035 P 20081 P 20321 F 20683 FP
11443 FP 16893 F 20267 F 20480 P 21251 P
15558 P 17971 F 20306 P 20495 P 21556 F
15843 O 19138 P

Secondary: Journal Articles
11060 P 15878 F 20239 O 20370 P 21240 P
11071 P 15913 O 20240 P 20376 P 21244 FP
11421 P 15914 F 20313 P 20377 F 21481 F
11467 P 16038 P 20317 F 20378 F 21483 FP
11958 O 16130 O 20318 O 20407 P 21487
12131 O 16772 F 20329 O 20520 P 21547 O
12146 P 17803 O 20331 P 20529 F 21576 F
12167 S 17966 O 20345 F 21137 21590 P
15574 F 18071 P 20358 F 21202 O 22301 P
15620 P 20073 P 20361 P 21238 P 22494 F
15827 P 20077 P

42 Lineages and Clanship
氏族及譜系 氏族及び系譜

1644-1842
Primary 18014 P 18905 P 19958 O 19959 P
20043 P
Second. 10512 PO 13868 P

1644-1911
Primary 14088 P 15927 P 19695 P 19961 PO
11243 P 15331 P 16049 P 19960 PO 21203 P
Second. 14159 P 17541 P 19747 P 20135 PO
10016 O 14168 P 17607 P 19766 O 21709 P
10597 S 14208 S 18519 P 19769 P 22780 P
11203 P 16217 FP 19688 P 20022 P 22886 S
14093 P

1842-1911
Primary 15925 P 17533 FP 17973 PO 19777 O
19957 O
Second. 14161 O 15330 FP 16089 P 18438 P
10682 O 14178 P 15338 P 16537 O 18449 O
11232 FP 14182 FP 15735 O 17547 P 19719 P
12187 O 15314 S 15932 O 17610 P 19720 O

1842-1928
(including 1644-1928)
Primary 20006 PO
Second. 11698 P 16103 FP 19793 P 20005 S
10084 PO 15138 17191 F 19795 P 20260 O
10291 P 15374 F 17560 P 19805

1911-1928
Primary 19966 O
Second. 18144 P 19460 F

1911-1949
(including 1644-1949, 1842-1949)
Primary 19785 P 19963 P 19965 P 19968 O
15375 O 19828 PO 19964 P 19967 P 21384 O
15955 P 19962 S
Second. 10718 S 16559 P 19727 S 20013 P
10078 S 14687 PO 17036 FP 19836 F 20050 S
10086 PO 15376 FP 17980 P 19837 S 21770 P
10693 P 15449 O 18571 S 20009 S 22441 P
10707 P 16104 S 19463 P

1928-1949
Primary 18671 O 19838 S
Second. 14430 S 15447 F 17613 F 20015 F
12291 S 14750 F 15596 F 19823 O 20262 F
14117 P 15406 F 16631 F

1928-1972
(incl. 1644-1972, 1842-1972, 1911-1972)
Primary 17988 S 19970 FP 19976 S 19982 S
15455 FP 19858 F 19971 19977 S 19983 F
15473 F 19868 S 19972 FP 19978 FP 19984 S
15800 O 19877 P 19973 FP 19979 P 19985 O
17102 FP 19880 S 19974 P 19980 FP 19986 O
17984 O 19969 O 19975 FP 19981 FP
Second. 15476 F 17953 P 19864 FP 19882
15451 FP 15797 FP 17956 P 19866 P 19888 S
15462 FP 15974 FP 19732 P 19869 S 19891 P
15463 FP 16332 P 19735 S 19873 S 20017 F
15464 P 16456 F 19736 S 19875 P 20235 O
15470 S 17949 P 19862 P

1949-1972
Primary 17961 FP 19987 F 19989 F 20018 F
16003 F 19737 FP 19988 S 19990 FP 20024 F
16354 F 19939 F
Second. 17675 F 19163 FP 19943 F 21546 F
15505 F 17683 F 19738 F 19944 P 21575 FP
15535 P 17971 F 19913 S 20236 F 21966 F
16353 S 17994 FP 19927 P 21250 P 22021 P
17618 F 18263 FP 19933 FP

43 Ancestor Worship
祖先崇祀 祖先崇拝

1644-1842
Primary 21165 PO 21985 P
Second. 10652 O 14156 O 18936 P 22520 P
10020 PO 11563 P 18904 P 21278 P 22590 O
10561 O 12198 P

1644-1911
Primary 16192 P 19993 P 19999 PO 21656 P
10006 S 19748 PO 19995 P 20002 P 21710 P
15353 PO 19991 19997 20545 FP 22386 P
16188 P 19992 S 19998 PO 21167 FP
Second. 11559 P 16191 19767 PO 21437 P
10004 PO 11568 PO 16217 FP 19770 S 21627
10010 P 11574 PO 16221 PO 19776 FP 21633 P
10029 PO 12941 PO 18012 P 19960 PO 21642 FP
10046 O 13838 18855 O 20022 P 21657 P
10586 14191 PO 18867 P 20149 S 21693 S
11539 FP 16163 PO 18915 FP 20762 O 21981 O
11547 O 16171 PO 18927 PO 21163 FP 21982 P
11548 O 16181 O 19723 F 21172 P 21983 P
11550 FP 16189 FP 19750 FP 21173 O 22024 P
11556 P 16190 FP 19763 P 21290 P

1842-1911
Primary 16164 S 19994 O 20001 PO 21175 O
10002 O 16170 O 19996 PO 20003 O 21182
10024 O 19720 O 20000 PO 20036 P 21624 O
15744 O 19777 O
Second. 14195 P 15735 O 19719 P 21166 O
10009 P 15307 O 16169 O 19721 PO 21171 O
10030 O 15311 O 16180 O 19739 O 21176 P
10038 O 15317 O 16186 O 19746 PO 21260 PO
10049 PO 15321 O 16195 P 19751 O 21621 O
10052 P 15333 O 16222 O 20128 O 21689 O
10059 O 15336 O 17813 O 20137 O 22038 PO
11223 S 15337 O 17928 PO 20274 O 22383 PO
12593 PO 15351 O 17929 O 20544 F 22397 FP
13840 O 15364 O 18903 P 21162 O 22556 PO
14178 P 15710 18932 PO

1842-1928
(including 1644-1928)
Primary 16268 PO 20004 S 20006 PO 20008 S
11581 PO 16277 P 20005 S 20007 O 21788 P
Second. 14214 PO 18959 O 20610 P 21502
10069 O 16252 PO 18968 PO 20618 PO 21723 PO
10082 PO 16260 O 18983 FP 20619 O 21779 O
11589 P 16267 O 19790 PO 21187 O 21791 PO
13152 PO 16269 S 19793 P 21318 P 22001 P
13163 S 18024 PO 19805 21453 O 22443 P

1911-1928
Primary 20014 O
Second. 15422 O 17614 O 19856 O 21195 PO
11599 PO 16285 19818 FP 19966 O 21365 O
14708 O 16320 F 19852 P 20273 O 22469 O

1911-1949
(including 1644-1949, 1842-1949)
Primary 19828 PO 20010 P 20013 P 21744 P
15955 P 19962 S 20011 S 20050 S 21997 P
16263 PO 19963 P 20012 PO 20302 FP 22441 P
16298 O 20009 S
Second. 11585 S 16258 S 16280 19724
10070 P 14215 S 16271 PO 17979 P 19725 P
10088 O 16248 S 16278 O 17980 P 19816 FP

19829 s 20614 P 21718 O 21773 P 21994
19968 O 20623 PO 21750 PO 21804 P 22005
20046 P 21333 O 21761 P 21821 O 22102 PO
20611 s 21499 s

1928-1949

PRIMARY 19729 F 19847 FP 20015 F

SECOND. 16290 O 16315 O 20199 O 21191 O
12291 s 16311 F 16317 O 20639 s 21194 O
14750 F 16312 O 19846 P 21190 O 21520 O
15410 O

1928-1972
(incl. 1644-1972, 1842-1972, 1911-1972)

PRIMARY 19733 s 19969 O 19975 FP 20016 P
11610 PO 19735 s 19973 FP 19986 O 20017 F
15800 O

SECOND. 16332 P 19736 s 19970 FP 19983 F
11614 P 16336 P 19875 P 19972 FP 20070 FP
15463 FP 16343 P 19882 19976 s 21862 s
16329 s 19090 FP 19896 FP 19978 FP 21868 P
16330 P 19731 s

1949-1972

PRIMARY 11492 PO 16348 F 20018 F 21966 F

SECOND. 16352 s 19913 s 19989 F 21484 F
11467 P 16353 s 19918 F 19990 FP 21932 F
14133 O 16354 F 19925 F 21198 F 21946 O
15505 F 16359 F 19943 F 21250 P 22500 O
15515 FP 19070 F 19947 F

44 Kin Terms and Relationships

親屬關係及稱呼
親属関係及び称呼

1644-1842

PRIMARY □

SECOND. 10050 O 11536 O

1644-1911

PRIMARY 19722 P 19960 PO 20020 P 20022 P
20030 O

SECOND. 11218 P 19752 P 19774 P 20042 P
10634 O 14189 s 19763 P 20033 P 20044 P
11195 P 16098 19766 O

1842-1911

PRIMARY 19759 PO 20032 P

SECOND. 10682 O 16908 O 17158 O 19720 O
21648 P

1842-1928
(including 1644-1928)

PRIMARY □

SECOND. 19784 P 19797 PO 20181 P 21996 P
15138 19790 PO 20175 P

1911-1928

PRIMARY 19856 O

SECOND. 18144 P 19826 P

1911-1949
(including 1644-1949, 1842-1949)

PRIMARY 19839 PO 20025 P 20027 s 21185 P
19828 PO 20023 P 20026 O 20028 s 22682 O
19836 F

SECOND. 16053 P 19962 s 20063 P 20276 O
10086 PO 19816 FP 20046 P 20160 PO 21367 O
14219 PO 19854 P 20053 P 20208 O 21384 O
15376 FP

1928-1949

PRIMARY 19362 F 20021 F

SECOND. 14430 s 15405 F 20262 F

1928-1972
(incl. 1644-1972, 1842-1972, 1911-1972)

PRIMARY 19880 s 19980 FP 20031 s 21533 s
19090 FP 19973 FP 20019 O

SECOND. 19731 s 19869 s 19979 P 21196 F
11387 P 19859 FP 19870 19982 s 21470 s
15460 FP 19861 P 19888 s 20235 O 21541 P
19730 s 19864 FP 19899 P 20401 P 21850 F

1949-1972

PRIMARY 10304 F 19910 F 19916 F 19939 F
20024 F 20029 F

SECOND. 17618 F 19913 s 19953 F 20427 F
11074 P 17622 F 19924 20076 21201 O
12131 O 19110 O 19925 F 20272 FP 21579 PO
15515 FP 19737 FP

45 Property and Inheritance

財產及繼承 財産及び相続

1644-1842

PRIMARY 12189 P 12198 P 20035 P 20040 s
20043 P

SECOND. 11680 P 13472 P 13868 P 21279 P

1644-1911

PRIMARY 11203 P 19754 PO 20038 P 20042 P
10524 P 17627 P 20033 PO 20041 O 20044 P
10632 P 19722 P 20037 PO

SECOND. 11211 P 11672 PO 15130 s 19770 s
11195 P 11220 P 13484 P 17816 P 19772 P
11197 P 11239 P 14159 P 19769 P 21709 P

1842-1911

PRIMARY 12187 O 16536 O 19719 P 20036 P
11232 FP 16535 PO 17407 PO 20034 PO 20039 O

SECOND. 11204 P 14163 PO 15336 O 17978 O
10513 PO 11223 s 15314 s 15933 P 19775 O
10531 P 11662 15321 O 16538 O 20279 O
10601 O 14157 O 15328 P 17409 FP 22573 P

1842-1928
(including 1644-1928)

PRIMARY 12225 O 19789 P 20047 P 20049 P
12215 P 16103 FP 20006 PO 20048 P 20051 P

SECOND. 10354 P 11299 P 16108 PO 19795 P
10082 PO 11248 P 12229 P 16267 O 20175 P
10084 PO 11250 P 12233 P 16403 P 21798 P
10291 P 11275 PO 13506 P

1911-1928

PRIMARY 12361 P 16579 P 19852 P 20060 P
12306 P 14434 P 16594 F 20056

SECOND. 11363 P 12988 PO 16644 FP 19826 P
11316 P 11813 P 15450 F 16685 P 20463 F
11356 P 12363 PO 16429 P 19277 P 20648 F

1911-1949
(including 1644-1949, 1842-1949)

PRIMARY 16112 s 19963 P 20050 s 20057 P
11333 P 16613 FP 19964 P 20052 P 20061 P
11344 P 18722 O 20013 P 20053 P 20063 P
11689 P 19819 P 20045 P 20054 P 20067 P
12370 P 19821 P 20046 P 20055 P 20068 P
16106 P 19828 PO

SECOND. 11263 PO 11313 P 12231 P 13496 P
10078 s 11264 P 12212 s 12350 P 13749 P
10364 FP 11309 PO 12228 P 13491 PO 14734 P
15376 FP 16560 FP 19724 19804 P 19967 P
15449 O 16675 P 19785 P 19839 PO 20160 PO
15762 P 17290 P 19787 19848 F 20162 P
16104 s 17763 PO 19792 P 19854 P 20614 P
16107 P 17979 P 19798 P 19962 s 22133 PO
16115 P 19271 P 19799 P

1928-1949

PRIMARY 12290 P 15405 F 20058 P 20064 P
11332 P 12298 P 15426 s 20059 s 20065 P
11362 P 12313 P 19831 P 20062 P 20066 P

SECOND. 11335 P 13548 P 16425 F 19729 F
11307 s 12311 P 15596 F 16632 F 19810 P
11331 P 12331 P 15965 P 16641 PO

1928-1972
(incl. 1644-1972, 1842-1972, 1911-1972)

PRIMARY 12409 P 16735 P 19893 P 20069 PO
11389 P 14413 P 19731 s 19970 FP 20070 FP
11400 P 16127 s 19870 19983 F 20071 P
12398 P 16456 F 19878 PO

SECOND. 13294 P 16746 FP 19867 P 19979 P
10214 P 14130 P 19033 P 19877 P 19980 FP
10893 s 14415 P 19084 P 19882 20017 F
11386 P 14515 O 19090 FP 19883 P 20657 PO
11387 P 15463 FP 19730 s 19890 s 21196 F
11399 P 15476 F 19733 s 19892 P 22199 P
11855 s 15975 P 19859 FP 19899 P 22474 P
11866 P 16337 O 19862 P 19975 FP 23007 P
12404 s 16736 P 19863 F 19976 s

1949-1972

PRIMARY 15858 P 19160 P 20074 FP 20079 P
11447 P 15882 19177 P 20075 P 20080 P
11473 P 16132 O 19912 P 20076 20081 P
11492 PO 16859 P 19918 F 20077 P 20082 O
12056 P 16890 FP 20072 F 20078 P 20697 P
15838 F 19155 P 20073 P

SECOND. 13584 P 15820 PO 17683 F 19931 P
11421 P 13596 s 15831 P 19063 PO 19934 P
11423 P 13796 P 15887 F 19123 P 19939 F
11440 P 14141 s 15995 O 19129 P 19942 O
11464 P 14418 PO 16036 P 19159 P 19943 F
11467 P 14419 P 16038 P 19164 PO 19949 P
11526 P 14442 P 16488 PO 19171 P 19954 O
11530 PO 15483 P 16861 19179 P 20018 F
12077 s 15495 P 16863 P 19193 O 20268 F
12166 P 15507 P 16872 FP 19195 F 20368 F
12442 P 15517 F 16883 F 19340 O 20683 FP
12456 PO 15539 P 17110 19375 P 20684 P
12525 P 15542 17675 F 19737 FP 22299 P
12536 P 15564 P 17680 F 19910 F 22764 O

46 Sex

性 性

1644-1842

PRIMARY □

SECOND. 10005 O 14156 O 14166 P 18013 P
20133 P 20719 PO

1644-1911

PRIMARY 20086 s 20090 PO 20095 PO 20154 P
20083 P 20089 P 20092 P 20096 P 21440 O

SECOND. 19722 P 20150 20730 P 20769 PO
11195 P 19772 P 20156 P 20741 P 21172 P
18012 P 19774 P 20284 P 20761 P 21300 s
18366 P 20135 PO

1842-1911

PRIMARY 17625 O 20085 P 20088 F 20093 O
16907 PO 20084 O 20087 O 20091 O 20094

SECOND. 18008 O 20125 O 20380 O 20729 O
14163 PO 18461 P 20130 O 20716 O 20760 F
17689 P 19773 PO 20141 O 20723 O 20782 s

1842-1928
(including 1644-1928)

Primary 18022 o 20097 p 20099 p 20100
20182 p

Second. 15390 o 19803 po 20180 po 21346 p
15373 p 19791 p 20008 s 20181 p 21355 o

1911-1928

Primary 20102 po 20103 o 20107 s 20108 po
20866 o 20911 p

Second. 15143 p 15407 fp 17844 o 19818 fp

1911-1949
(including 1644-1949, 1842-1949)

Primary 20098 o 20104 o 20159 po 20796 o
10730 o 20101 s 20106 o 20172 f 21500 s
16123 fp

Second. 19008 o 19968 o 20298 f 21370 o
15674 po 19798 p 20178 po 20623 po 21443 f
17193 fp 19799 p 20205 o 20939 o 21516 o
18029 f 19839 po 20208 o 21330 o 22004 p
18989 fp

1928-1949

Primary 20105 20206 o 21522 o

Second. 18643 f 20921 f 21511 f 21513 f
16116 o 19729 f 21366 o 21512 f 21519 o
16118 f 19827 f 21508 f

1928-1972
(incl. 1644-1972, 1842-1972, 1911-1972)

Primary 19894 fp 20110 po 20114 o 21542 s
19710 p 19895 fp 20111 s 20115 s 22016 s
19734 o 19896 fp 20112 o 20225 p 22474 p
19880 s 20109 p 20113 o 21537 p 22479 p

Second. 19736 s 19881 po 20304 f 21428 o
10117 po 19861 p 19889 f 20969 p 21529 po
15466 o 19872 p 20229 p 21395 po 21544 s
15468 o 19873 s 20231 po 21416 o 21869 s
19732 p

1949-1972

Primary 20118 o 20121 p 20317 f 20688 o
19911 p 20119 o 20122 f 20331 p 22494 f
20116 o 20120 o 20237 o 20335 p 22500 o
20117 fp

Second. 15205 o 19909 p 20334 fp 21556 f
10152 o 15215 19914 s 20411 o 21563 po
10153 o 15271 o 19928 p 20503 o 21582 p
10165 o 16132 o 19947 f 21092 fp 21584 o
10173 o 18048 f 19951 fp 21138 f 21590 p
11443 fp 18071 p 19990 fp 21483 fp 22020 p
14943 o 19738 f 20249 f 21484 f 22769 o

47 Female Roles and Male-Female Differences

婦女地位及男女分別

女性の地位及び男女の区別

1644-1842

Primary 10005 o 20132 p 20133 p

Second. 15711 o 20558 s 21686 p 22578 o
10036 o 15722 o 20563 s 22511 o 22590 o
10044 o 17145 p 20571 o 22559 o 22619 po

1644-1911

Primary 19772 p 20131 po 20150 20157 o
18946 po 20086 s 20134 p 20152 o 20158 p
19723 f 20089 p 20135 po 20153 o 20285 p
19763 p 20090 po 20144 p 20154 p 20762 o
19766 o 20123 20147 p 20156 p 21300 s
19768 p 20124 po 20149 s

Second. 11239 p 15729 po 19695 p 21163 fp
10001 o 11672 po 16163 po 19743 po 21172 p
10004 po 12572 p 16184 p 19752 p 21276 p
10006 s 12941 po 17920 o 19755 po 21440 o
10012 p 14098 p 18010 p 19770 s 21634 p
10029 po 14103 18421 p 20044 p 21657 p
10046 o 14167 p 18459 o 20083 p 21981 o
10441 p 14621 po 18855 o 20095 po 21982 p
10560 p 15323 o 18930 po 20284 p 22409 p
11218 p 15327 po 18937 p 20730 p 22419 o
11220 p

1842-1911

Primary 17930 o 20128 o 20141 o 20274 o
10024 o 18481 20129 o 20142 o 20275 o
10668 p 19751 o 20130 o 20143 20282 o
14092 po 19994 o 20136 o 20145 p 20559 o
14157 o 20085 p 20137 o 20146 o 20715 o
15333 o 20088 f 20138 o 20148 o 20728 o
15347 po 20125 o 20139 20151 o 21178 o
15367 o 20126 s 20140 o 20155 o 22395 o
16907 po 20127 p

Secondary: Monographs
10013 o 10660 o 15363 o 18378 o 20540 o
10017 o 13811 o 15364 o 18449 o 20576 po
10019 po 14178 p 15721 o 18508 p 20583 o
10023 o 14182 fp 15744 o 18511 p 20716 o
10025 o 14204 po 15749 po 18908 o 21260 po
10030 o 14597 o 16167 o 18932 po 21262 o
10031 o 14626 p 16183 o 19765 o 21265 p
10047 o 15317 o 17608 20087 o 22066 p
10049 po 15321 o 17649 o 20094 22542 o
10054 o 15360 o 17662 o 20258 o 22580 po
10061 o 15361 o 17974 o 20379 o 22599 o
10611 o 15362 o 18077 p 20385 o 22601 o
10631 p

Secondary: Inclusions
13130 p 18525 p 20259 o 21174 o 22523 o
14087 s 19721 po 20288 po 22508 o 22525 o
18008 o 19742 o 20605 o

Secondary: Journal Articles
10009 p 14590 o 17535 o 19746 po 20581 o
11014 p 14612 s 17813 o 19761 o 20601 o
11188 p 15312 o 17919 o 19775 o 20602 o
11189 p 15335 o 18016 o 19778 po 21160 po
11662 15348 o 18441 po 19780 p 21628 o
13839 o 15735 o 18463 p 19996 po 21652 o
14163 po 15747 o 19696 o 20290 o 22047 p
14566 po 16530 p 19745 20380 o 22541 o
14577 o

1842-1928
(including 1644-1928)

Primary 20163 p 20174 p 20180 po 20388
16261 s 20165 f 20175 p 20181 p 20389 po
16275 o 20167 s 20177 p 20182 p 20607 o
18022 o 20169 fp 20179 p 20183 p 21781 s
19803 po 20170 p

Second. 13163 s 15134 p 19480 p 20790 po
10068 s 13164 fp 16103 fp 19481 p 20798 o
10069 o 14105 s 17560 p 19784 p 21305 o
10081 po 14216 s 17691 po 19789 p 21307 o
10340 po 14458 p 18102 o 19791 p 21358 o
11250 p 14628 fp 18956 po 19793 p 21453 o
11581 po 14689 p 19475 19805 22123 p
11683 o 14690 p 19477 po 20430 p 22423 po

1911-1928

Primary 20185 o 20202 20215 o 20296 o
15403 f 20186 o 20207 o 20216 f 20866 o
17727 o 20193 p 20209 p 20218 o 21365 o
19812 o 20196 o 20211 o 20220 p 21382 o
20103 o 20197 o 20213 o 20222 s 21385
20107 s

Second. 14493 p 14775 p 16121 o 17705
10091 o 14497 fp 15061 s 16971 o 17717 po
11316 p 14502 o 15073 p 17213 p 17724 p
11730 o 14507 p 15075 o 17292 o 17760 o
13029 s 14720 o 15143 p 17612 p 17771 p
14469 s 14727 p 15145 po 17614 o 17879 o
14476 po 14758 po 15865 p 17696 po 17939 o
17941 o 18617 p 19506 p 19842 p 20648 f
17942 o 18621 o 19515 o 19851 o 20865 o
18115 p 18664 o 19517 fp 20108 po 20911 p
18126 p 18700 o 19546 p 20455 21456 o
18310 p 18992 fp 19811 p 20462 fp 21462 o
18596 po 19017 o 19825 o 20463 f 22708 o
18597 po 19281

1911-1949
(including 1644-1949, 1842-1949)

Primary 19799 p 20162 p 20178 po 20210 p
10088 o 19804 p 20164 fp 20187 p 20214 o
14219 po 19824 po 20166 o 20191 po 20261 s
14629 po 19836 f 20168 20192 o 20276 o
14650 s 19839 po 20171 f 20194 o 20297 o
14772 20101 s 20172 f 20204 p 20796 o
19246 o 20159 po 20173 s 20205 o 21330 o
19644 po 20160 po 20176 20208 o 21370 o
19798 p 20161 p

Secondary: Monographs
10070 p 14509 p 15428 o 18993 po 21344 o
10079 po 14510 po 15586 p 19006 o 21359 p
10104 o 14647 p 15674 po 19476 p 21362 o
10356 po 14654 p 15675 p 19551 p 21384 o
11263 po 14655 p 16104 s 19643 p 21443 f
11690 p 14656 p 16123 fp 19796 p 21444 p
13184 p 14657 p 16279 p 19816 fp 21457 p
13880 po 14659 p 17193 fp 19819 p 21761 p
14215 s 14681 po 17274 fp 19854 p 21821 o
14466 p 14688 p 17694 po 19962 s 21994
14479 po 14694 p 17869 po 20623 po 22004 p
14491 p 14696 p 18585 o 20823 po 22432 p
14508 p 14770 o 18622 o 20826 p 22666 s

Secondary: Inclusions
13242 p 15592 fp 20292 s 20654 21211 p
14645 p 19788 fp 20298 f

Secondary: Journal Articles
14424 p 17256 fp 19792 p 20010 p 20939 o
14481 p 17716 f 19832 p 20063 p 21341 p
16112 s 18021 po 19833 fp 20106 o 21500 s
16310 f 19577 p 19837 s 20912 p 22430 o
17054 fp 19725 p 19853 p

1928-1949

Primary 16311 f 20184 20200 o 20221 o
10092 o 17238 p 20188 o 20201 p 20300 f
13969 o 17868 f 20189 p 20203 o 20301 f
14459 p 19007 o 20190 p 20206 o 20436 o
14478 fp 19703 o 20195 fp 20212 p 20439 p
14766 fp 19823 o 20198 f 20217 f 21366 o
15414 po 19838 s 20199 o 20219 p 21376 o
15436 f

Second. 14471 p 15871 f 18608 o 21214 f
10451 s 14718 po 16058 p 18643 f 21215 fp
10742 p 14750 f 16116 o 19572 p 21217 p
10792 o 14764 o 16672 f 19704 p 21225 f
10797 f 14774 fp 17297 po 19729 f 21229 p
11331 p 15398 o 17308 o 19810 p 21379 o
11372 p 15404 o 17665 19822 f 21508 f
11724 p 15410 o 17667 f 19845 s 21513 f
12291 s 15415 po 17715 p 19850 f 21522 o
12358 p 15434 o 17718 p 20456 o 21527 f
13039 o 15448 f 17729 f 20855 o 21528 f
13279 p 15598 fp 17734 fp 20856 o 22704 o
13928 o 15641 f 17863 po 20861 p 22712 o
13970 o 15869 f 17945 o 21213 fp

1928-1972
(incl. 1644-1972, 1842-1972, 1911-1972)

Primary 19869 s 20109 p 20226 po 20232 o
11414 p 19870 20114 o 20227 p 20233 s
15471 p 19873 s 20115 s 20228 p 20234 po
19710 p 19875 p 20223 o 20229 p 20235 o
19732 p 19896 fp 20224 o 20230 s 21417 p
19866 p 19899 p 20225 p 20231 po 21542 s

Secondary: Monographs
10115 o 10885 po 14015 o 15192 o 17313 o
10117 po 11045 fp 14285 p 15459 po 17894 p
10120 s 11862 p 14513 p 15460 fp 17895 o
10123 o 11864 fp 15090 o 16068 o 18172 p
10852 p 14012 p 15171 fp 16740 fp 19045 p

19082 PO 19881 PO 19975 FP 21197 FP 21466 P
19858 F 19883 P 20475 O 21392 PO 21900 P
19859 FP 19886 S 20659 O 21395 PO 22488 S
19862 P 19892 P 20994 O 21412 P

SECONDARY: INCLUSIONS
11400 P 19734 O 19890 S 20303 P 22479 P
15799 O 19867 P 19979 P 20657 PO 22485 S
19733 S 19877 P 20111 S

SECONDARY: JOURNAL ARTICLES
10848 P 16739 P 19860 19891 P 20304 F
11388 P 18171 P 19872 P 19894 FP 20403 P
11403 PO 19031 P 19885 P 20112 O 21234 P
15698 P 19730 S 19889 F

1949-1972

PRIMARY 15617 F 19922 P 20239 O 20250
10141 O 15881 O 19925 F 20240 P 20251 O
10159 O 17990 P 19931 P 20241 O 20411 O
10166 O 17995 O 19933 FP 20242 P 20422 F
10470 P 19712 O 19942 O 20243 P 20423 F
11061 O 19738 F 19946 FP 20244 P 20519 F
12131 O 19900 O 19949 P 20245 O 21086 P
14369 O 19901 F 20116 O 20246 O 21137
15297 O 19908 P 20236 F 20247 P 21202 O
15501 O 19909 P 20237 O 20248 O 21250 P
15513 PO 19918 F 20238 O 20249 F 22500 O
15522 O 19920

SECONDARY: MONOGRAPHS
10133 O 10975 P 15294 P 16012 P 19919 P
10136 O 11180 P 15482 O 16013 P 19953 F
10140 O 11883 O 15486 FP 16771 F 20328 P
10145 O 11894 O 15493 O 17386 FP 20503 O
10149 O 11901 O 15505 F 17745 P 20522 FP
10153 O 12003 P 15509 O 17748 O 20527 O
10156 O 12090 O 15517 F 17909 P 20688 O
10160 O 12109 P 15526 O 17961 FP 21009 FP
10161 O 12123 P 15544 O 18061 O 21124 PO
10180 O 12525 P 15545 O 18263 FP 21433 O
10226 P 13768 P 15549 P 18362 O 21563 PO
10263 P 14520 15567 O 19153 F 21575 FP
10464 P 14544 F 15575 O 19595 S 22747 O
10487 P 14999 O 15576 O 19905 P 22760 O
10488 P 15115 P 15890 P 19917 P 22763 O
10895 O

SECONDARY: INCLUSIONS
10499 P 19911 P 19952 P 20326 F 21099 F
15215 19914 S 20081 P 20427 F 21246 P
15271 O 19915 P 20121 P 20504 P 21556 F
15546 F 19951 FP 20269 F 20701 F 21597 F
19138 P

SECONDARY: JOURNAL ARTICLES
10242 P 15903 F 18051 O 19936 F 21237 FP
10491 P 15913 O 18069 O 19943 F 21483 FP
11142 P 15984 O 18071 P 19944 P 21548 O
14526 P 16004 O 19057 P 19954 O 21564 F
14545 P 16130 O 19606 P 19955 F 21565 F
14814 P 16482 O 19906 P 19956 P 21566 F
14872 PO 16772 F 19912 P 20072 F 21571 F
14998 P 16855 O 19921 P 20318 O 21583 F
15021 O 17331 O 19923 P 20324 F 21584 O
15231 S 17369 19924 20377 F 21598 F
15232 17383 O 19926 P 20407 P 22301 P
15561 17994 FP 19934 P 21092 FP 22770 F
15878 F

48 NON-KIN INTERPERSONAL RELATIONSHIPS

非親屬關係 非親族関係

1644-1842

PRIMARY 10618 P 14422 P 20571 O 22578 O

SECOND. 10026 O 10032 O 20558 S 22776 P

1644-1911

PRIMARY 14090 P 14104 P 14198 S 20256
10004 PO 14099 P 14184 P 17975 O 20257

SECOND. 10680 P 14102 P 18495 PO 21300 S
10042 PO 11220 P 14569 P 20042 P 21657 P
10557 P 11655 PO 16217 FP 20414 P 21988 P
10568 O 14098 P

1842-1911

PRIMARY 14094 20032 P 20254 P 20259 O
10038 O 14157 O 20252 P 20255 PO 20572 F
10551 P 15338 P 20253 O 20258 O 22541 O

SECOND. 14177 O 17535 O 20088 F 22395 O
10636 P 15364 O 18086 P 20138 O 22400 O
10679 O 16096 O 18914 O 20565 PO 22556 PO
14171 O 16183 O 19751 O 21260 PO

1842-1928
(including 1644-1928)

PRIMARY 14105 S 19797 PO 20260 O 21998 P

SECOND. 11250 P 20099 P 20182 P 21996 P
10082 PO 16275 O 20100 20795 O 22002 P
11248 P 18570 P

1911-1928

PRIMARY 10766 P 17983 O 18144 P 20263
20266 PO 21456 O

SECOND. 13979 P 19229 O 19558 19826 P
20463 F 22469 O

1911-1949
(including 1644-1949, 1842-1949)

PRIMARY 17980 P 20053 P 20264 O 22003 P
16104 S 18544 P 20261 S 20265 O 22006 S

SECOND. 18303 P 19836 F 21359 P 21994
12252 S 18976 FP 19840 O 21367 O 22004 P
15428 O 19218 20067 P 21375 O 22457 F
17857 F 19781 21330 O 21384 O 22463 O
18018 O 19821 P 21333 O 21806 S 22694 O
18104 P 19828 PO

1928-1949

PRIMARY 15150 15434 O 19625 S 20262 F

SECOND. 13964 O 16294 O 18035 O 20217 F
10098 O 15641 F 16979 O 19261 F 20456 O
13951 O

1928-1972
(incl. 1644-1972, 1842-1972, 1911-1972)

PRIMARY 15464 P 20019 O 21533 S 21538 FP
21543 O 22016 S

SECOND. 17313 O 19051 F 19978 FP 21422 O
11053 O 17772 O 19055 FP 19980 FP 21423 P
15462 FP 17984 O 19734 O 20475 O 21467 S
15470 S 18805 19859 FP 20661 22014
16128 FP 18820 O 19861 P 20994 O 22017 S
17102 FP

1949-1972

PRIMARY 17616 F 20267 F 20271 F 21575 FP
10135 O 17958 F 20268 F 20272 FP 21933 F
14146 F 17971 F 20269 F 20355 F 21948 P
15508 O 19738 F 20270 O 21570 FP 22020 P
16133 F 19951 FP

SECOND. 15574 F 18263 FP 20425 F 21547 O
10162 O 16137 PO 18362 O 20517 F 21556 F
11064 PO 16348 F 19070 F 20997 O 21579 PO
11101 FP 16902 FP 19911 P 21480 O 21585 O
12549 P 17126 F 19946 FP 21481 F 21586 F
15505 F 17803 O 20081 P 21483 FP 22018 F
15515 FP 17959 FP 20236 F 21484 F 22303 P
15561 18048 F 20249 F 21546 F

50 LIFE CYCLE AND AGE GRADING

生命周期及年齡

生命周期及び年齡

1644-1842

PRIMARY 21278 P

SECOND. 13621 PO 16087 P

1644-1911

PRIMARY 11202 P 15927 P 18915 FP 19692 PO
10029 PO 12193 PO 17920 O 19688 P 21290 P
10604 P

SECOND. 10028 PO 18518 P 19992 S 20741 P
10006 S 11194 O 18865 PO 20124 PO 20761 P
10014 O 18459 O 19695 P 20154 P 22409 P

1842-1911

PRIMARY 17625 O 20130 O 20275 O 20559 O
14092 PO 18871 PO 20137 O 20279 O 20782 S
14608 P 19751 O 20138 O 20287 P 22556 PO
15317 O 20091 O 20274 O 20386 O

SECOND. 14178 P 15348 O 18922 O 20155 O
10041 15321 O 15349 O 19694 O 20258 O
10057 O 15330 FP 17689 P 19719 P 20557 O
10062 PO 15347 PO

1842-1928
(including 1644-1928)

PRIMARY 14214 PO 16226 PO 20618 PO 22437 F

SECOND. 10082 PO 18956 PO 18971 S 20182 P
21335 P 21798 P

1911-1928

PRIMARY 20273 O

SECOND. 15061 S 17877 F 20938 P 21207 F
10778 O 15073 P 19818 FP 21206 P

1911-1949
(including 1644-1949, 1842-1949)

PRIMARY 19816 FP 20208 O 20302 FP 21375 O
18990 PO 19839 PO 20276 O 20623 PO 22694 O

SECOND. 15675 P 17721 P 19840 O 20801 P
10200 P 15678 P 17979 P 19843 S 20912 P
11382 FP 15685 P 19006 O 19964 P 22004 P
12303 FP 16123 FP 19615 PO 20292 S 22457 F
15446 P 16405 P 19836 F 20622 P 22706 O

1928-1949

PRIMARY 15415 PO 15640 F 16311 F 17613 F
19827 F 22455 F

SECOND. 18608 O 19729 F 20449 P 21520 O
15598 FP 18643 F 19834 F 21213 FP 21522 O
17664 F 18750 O 20212 P 21229 P 22713 F
17854 F

1928-1972
(incl. 1644-1972, 1842-1972, 1911-1972)

PRIMARY 10123 O 19873 S 20231 PO 20401 P
10117 PO 14515 O 19896 FP 20278 S 22733 P
10118 O 19732 P 20226 PO 20280 P

SECOND. 15089 S 15695 P 19090 FP 21232 FP
11045 FP 15171 FP 16727 FP 19860 21233 FP
14280 P 15176 O 17635 P 19872 P 21234 P
14285 P 15471 P 18164 P 19880 S 21529 PO
14290 P 15612 P 19035 PO 19899 P 22486 PO
14777 P 15613 P 19085 O 20474 P

1949-1972

PRIMARY 15515 FP 15900 F 19948 P 20277 O
10136 O 15545 O 16348 F 19990 FP 21242 FP
15504 F 15557 O 19933 FP 20249 F 21244 FP
15509 O 15890 P

50 Life Cycle and Age Grading

Secondary: Monographs
10165 o 15505 F 19738 F 20368 F 21482 F
10180 o 15560 FP 19939 F 20421 F 21489 o
10226 P 15617 F 19946 FP 20522 FP 21563 PO
10470 P 16139 o 20236 F 21037 F 21570 FP
11095 o 18003 FP 20341 F 21108 FP 21575 FP
14974 PO 19597 FP 20366 P 21249 FP 22755 o
15486 FP

Secondary: Inclusions
10244 P 15105 P 17640 P 17744 o 20081 P
14330 FP 16075 P 17644 F 19945 FP 20427 F

Secondary: Journal Articles
10242 P 15480 o 19683 F 20340 F 21020 F
11108 P 15618 PO 19908 P 20342 F 21030 F
11913 P 15709 s 19956 P 20343 F 21145 F
12131 o 15878 F 20309 F 20351 F 21238 P
14318 P 16458 o 20312 F 20364 F 21240 P
15096 P 17497 o 20320 FP 20517 F 21250 P
15292 P 17776 o 20338 F 21008 F

51 Reproduction

生殖 生殖

1644-1842

Primary □
Second. 20719 PO

1644-1911

Primary 19776 FP 20284 P 20286 P 20730 P
19767 PO 20154 P 20285 P

Second. 16190 FP 20083 P 20761 P 20788 s
10060 PO 17920 o 20144 P 20762 o 21172 P
11568 PO 19772 P 20720 PO 20769 PO 22390 P
11574 PO 19992 s 20745 o

1842-1911

Primary 20282 o 20287 P 20289 o 20379 o
20085 P 20283 o 20288 PO 20290 o 20380 o
20281 o

Second. 15351 o 20137 o 20593 o 21980 o
10003 o 19721 PO 20274 o 20778 o 21990 o
10019 PO 19775 o 20275 o 20782 s 22067 o
10024 o 19996 PO 20540 o 20783 o 22395 o
10047 o 20125 o 20541 o 21264 o 22397 FP
15307 o 20130 o 20565 PO 21664 o 22556 PO
15338 P

1842-1928
(including 1644-1928)

Primary 20291 o 20293 P 20294 PO 20295 o
Second. 15379 o 15390 o 16267 o 21781 s

1911-1928

Primary 19818 FP 20296 o 20837 PO 20917 o
21219 F
Second. 14429 s 15403 F 20273 o

1911-1949
(including 1644-1949, 1842-1949)

Primary 20297 o 20299 F 20822 PO 21220 F
20292 s 20298 F 20302 FP

Second. 19802 PO 20801 P 20886 o 21344 o
10191 PO 20205 o 20812 P 20939 o 21808 F
15428 o 20276 o 20826 P

1928-1949

Primary 20637 F 20930 o 21217 P 21224 F
20300 F 20839 o 21212 F 21221 FP 21230 F
20301 F 20876 PO

Second. 16294 o 20829 o 20952 PO 21229 P
10105 FP 16295 F 20835 o 21215 FP 21366 o
15414 PO 16311 F 20869 P 21216 F 22455 F
15436 F 18608 o

1928-1972
(incl. 1644-1972, 1842-1972, 1911-1972)

Primary 20229 P 20304 F 20403 P 20961 PO
10218 P 20303 P 20305 P

Second. 16337 o 19889 F 20661 20991 PO
15191 PO 19866 P 19896 FP 20969 P 21233 FP
15471 P 19872 P 19974 P 20983 PO 21234 P
15600 P

1949-1972

Primary: Monographs
20249 F 20335 P 20360 F 20368 F 21009 FP
20314 P 20341 F 20366 P 20411 o 21086 P
20328 P 20347 F 20367 F 20996 FP 21249 FP
20334 FP

Primary: Inclusions
20306 P 20323 o 20337 o 20356 P 20372 F
20319 F 20326 F 20339 o 20371 P 21253 P
20321 F

Primary: Journal Articles
10233 P 20316 F 20338 F 20355 F 20376 P
10236 P 20317 F 20340 F 20357 s 20377 F
13086 s 20318 o 20342 F 20358 F 20378 F
14896 F 20320 FP 20343 F 20359 F 21104 o
15618 PO 20322 F 20344 F 20361 P 21132 P
19948 P 20324 F 20345 F 20362 P 21136 F
20307 F 20325 s 20346 F 20363 P 21137
20308 F 20327 P 20348 P 20364 F 21236 F
20309 F 20329 o 20349 s 20365 P 21238 P
20310 F 20330 F 20350 o 20369 21244 FP
20311 F 20331 P 20351 F 20370 P 21247 P
20312 F 20332 F 20352 F 20373 P 21250 P
20313 P 20333 FP 20353 o 20374 P 21252 PO
20315 PO 20336 F 20354 s 20375 P 21571 F

Second. 10251 15240 o 19905 P 21045 P
10143 o 10410 s 15271 o 19906 P 21061 P
10156 o 10482 P 15292 P 19914 s 21065 o
10168 o 10502 PO 15504 F 19932 F 21068 o
10173 o 11103 P 15517 F 19933 FP 21084 o
10223 P 11892 15519 o 19944 P 21121 o
10225 P 11956 P 15550 o 20074 FP 21131 FP
10229 P 11959 PO 15615 P 20121 P 21237 FP
10230 P 12090 o 15655 FP 20405 o 21241 P
10240 P 12129 P 15852 FP 21010 PO 21243 FP
10241 PO 12155 o 16858 PO 21013 P 21248 P
10242 P 12175 P 17780 o 21014 21251 P
10243 P 12530 P 17916 o 21030 F 23034 o

52 Infancy and Childhood

嬰兒及童年 嬰児及び幼年

1644-1842

□

1644-1911

Primary 18015 o

Second. 18493 PO 19769 P 20154 P 20732 P
10029 PO 19688 P 20044 P 20285 P 21682 P
11220 P 19692 PO 20135 PO 20730 P 22414 s
16171 PO 19768 P

1842-1911

Primary 20279 o 20381 o 20385 o 20579 o
19696 o 20289 o 20382 o 20386 o 20710 o
19721 PO 20379 o 20383 o 20387 F 21266 o
20138 o 20380 o 20384 o 20420 o 22397 FP

Second. 14603 o 16167 o 19694 o 20259 o
10003 o 15308 o 17819 o 20085 P 20274 o
10062 PO 15338 P 17974 o 20125 o 20275 o
10185 P 15348 o 18009 o 20137 o 20283 o
11228 o 15350 o 18441 PO 20148 o 22384 o
14163 PO 15361 o 18868 PO 20155 o 22573 P

1842-1928
(including 1644-1928)

Primary 17691 PO 20388 20389 PO 20391 P

Second. 16252 PO 18971 s 20005 s 21305 o
10069 o 16260 o 19795 P 20177 P 21307 o
10084 PO 16277 P 19805 20618 PO 21342 P
14113 P

1911-1928

Primary 17836 o 20392 s 20905 o 22448 o
17727 o 20222 s 20394 P

Second. 15073 P 17717 PO 19256 o 20273 o
11316 P 15403 F 17724 P 19546 P 20648 F
13277 F 17614 o 17873 PO 19811 P 21365 o
14476 PO 17696 PO 17879 o 19826 P 21456 o
14483 PO

1911-1949
(including 1644-1949, 1842-1949)

Primary 20204 P 20297 o 20395 F 21443 F
16322 F 20261 s 20390 s 21330 o

Second. 15063 s 19785 P 20098 o 20454 P
13242 P 15961 FP 19802 PO 20166 o 20623 PO
13880 PO 16248 s 19816 FP 20187 P 20822 PO
14481 P 17716 F 19824 PO 20205 o 21344 o
14491 P 19476 P 19828 PO 20208 o 21384 o
14509 P 19577 P 19836 F 20298 F 21729 P
14510 PO 19781 19839 PO 20299 F 22452 FP

1928-1949

Primary 20201 P 20396 o 20399 F 20881 P
14459 P 20219 P 20397 F 20400 o 20952 PO
19827 F 20393 o 20398 PO 20858 F 21212 F

Second. 13969 o 16295 F 20190 P 20637 F
10451 s 14478 FP 17839 20195 FP 20876 PO
10775 PO 15410 o 17863 PO 20199 o 21217 P
11834 FP 15414 PO 19702 P 20200 o 21221 FP
12291 s 15424 F 19813 P 20221 o 21519 o
13928 o

1928-1972
(incl. 1644-1972, 1842-1972, 1911-1972)

Primary 19730 s 20114 o 20304 F 20401 P
20402 s 20403 P

Second. 17894 P 19873 s 20226 PO 20991 PO
10117 PO 19710 P 19877 P 20235 o 20995 FP
11045 FP 19732 P 19895 FP 20955 P 21529 PO
16328 o 19872 P 19896 FP 20966 o 21542 s

1949-1972

Primary 20249 F 20409 o 20427 F 21250 P
12131 o 20269 F 20410 F 20482 21551 F
14831 PO 20404 F 20411 o 20996 FP 21586 F
15035 PO 20405 o 20412 F 21010 PO 21590 P
16348 F 20406 o 20413 o 21040 PO 21933 F
17788 F 20407 P 20415 F 21069 F 22758 F
17796 PO 20408 F 20425 F 21122 o

Second. 15479 o 17589 F 20077 P 20693 o
10133 o 15495 P 17780 o 20081 P 20699 o
10895 o 15501 o 17797 PO 20237 o 21042 o
11095 o 15522 o 17808 o 20238 o 21049 F
13768 P 15537 P 17909 P 20242 P 21050 PO
14824 P 15544 o 18061 o 20247 P 21089 F
14943 o 15570 P 19673 P 20250 21137
14953 P 15828 o 19711 FP 20353 o 21138 F
14974 PO 15991 P 19713 P 20416 21158
15008 o 15993 P 19900 o 20421 F 21247 P
15118 P 16012 P 19903 P 20422 F 21255 F
15119 P 16034 P 19915 P 20499 F 21568 F
15120 P 16457 o 19945 FP 20687 s 21576 F
15121 P 16482 o 19951 FP 20688 o 22500 o
15252 o 17331 o

53 Socialization
教養化育　社会化

1644-1842
Primary 20418 P 21278 P
Second. 21279 P

1644-1911
Primary 10029 PO 14569 P 20154 P 20414 P
Second. 11194 O 19768 P 20135 PO 20144 P
20157 O 20284 P

1842-1911
Primary 17625 O 19751 O 20255 PO 20379 O
20420 O
Second. 16934 O 20130 O 20381 O 20386 O
10018 PO 17689 P 20258 O 20382 O 20602 O
15367 O 17819 O 20275 O 20383 O 20748 O
15629 O 17974 O 20380 O 20385 O 21280 O

1842-1928
(including 1644-1928)
Primary □
Second. 12957 O 19726 O 20005 S 21305 O
21775 22001 P

1911-1928
Primary □
Second. 15786 O 21365 O 22708 O

1911-1949
(including 1644-1949, 1842-1949)
Primary 19816 FP 19964 P 21443 F
Second. 18783 P 20101 S 20264 O 21516 O
11586 FP 18989 FP 20164 FP 20395 F 22456
15449 O 19354 P 20172 F 20820 O 22458 F
16283 PO 19828 PO 20208 O 21370 O 22706 O
17980 P 19839 PO

1928-1949
Primary 20396 O 21522 O
Second. 15077 FP 19729 F 20639 S 21519 O
12291 S 18671 O 19827 F 21512 F 22461 F

1928-1972
(incl. 1644-1972, 1842-1972, 1911-1972)
Primary 19895 FP 20417 O 21538 FP 22198 O
10110 PO 20110 PO 20428 O 21540 S
Second. 19875 P 20224 O 21472 S 21542 S
18039 O 19881 PO 20656 P 21535 P 21543 O
19732 P 19894 FP 20991 PO 21536

1949-1972
Primary 20419 O 20424 F 21124 PO 21576 F
17780 O 20421 F 20425 F 21555 F 21579 PO
17804 P 20422 F 20426 FP 21560 S 21594 S
20415 F 20423 F 20427 F 21570 FP 22755 O
20416
Second. 14369 O 16013 P 19951 FP 21546 F
10143 O 15252 O 17958 F 19990 FP 21552 F
10149 O 15275 PO 18061 O 20249 F 21557
11061 O 15486 FP 18068 O 20411 O 21563 PO
11894 O 15504 F 18277 P 20499 P 21581 FP
14059 F 16007 FP 19918 F 20519 F 22831 P
14133 O 16008 F 19945 FP 20534 P

54 Adolescence and Youth
青春期及青年　青春期及び青年

1644-1842
Primary 21278 P
Second. □

1644-1911
Primary □
Second. 11220 P 20086 S 21682 P

1842-1911
Primary 18453 P 20275 O 20385 O 21280 O
10516 PO 18487 P 20379 O 20429 O 22604 P
18412 FP 19686 O
Second. 14174 P 18088 P 18494 P 20129 O
10642 PO 14551 O 18370 P 18525 P 20155 O
12191 F 14593 P 18375 P 18854 PO 20382 O
12588 P 15360 O 18411 P 19365 P 20602 O
14087 S 16092 P 18433 P 20085 P 22606 P
14164 P 17158 O 18490 P 20091 O 22613 S

1842-1928
(including 1644-1928)
Primary 18991 P 19698 O 20433 P 21453 O
18102 O 19697 P 20430 P 21355 O
Second. 14683 S 18560 P 21335 P 22131 PO
10081 PO 15134 P 18967 O 21346 P 22644 O
10085 PO 15135 20182 P 22117 P 22657 S
14674 O 17560 P

1911-1928
Primary 18999 O 20220 P 20455 20465 P
15143 P 19455 P 20434 O 20457 O 20466
15145 PO 19490 PO 20438 F 20462 FP 20467 P
15148 P 19699 O 20448 P 20463 F 20468
17575 O 19812 O 20452 P 20464 P 20469 F
Second. 14735 P 18115 P 19013 O 22141 P
10091 O 15144 P 18308 P 19023 O 22149 S
10094 O 15147 P 18310 P 19024 O 22156 P
12741 P 15152 18597 PO 19027 P 22160 P
14251 P 16971 O 18601 P 19506 P 22164 P
14476 PO 17611 O 18616 19546 P 22165 FP
14493 P 17612 P 18654 P 19826 P 22181 FP
14711 P 17713 FP 18773 P 21365 O 22690 P
14720 O 17722 O 18778 P 21462 O

1911-1949
(including 1644-1949, 1842-1949)
Primary 14698 P 19006 O 20194 O 20432 P
13920 P 14740 O 19968 O 20261 S 20442 P
14231 P 18558 S 20098 O 20431 P 20454 P
14685 O 18783 P 20192 O
Second. 14665 PO 14736 P 18303 P 19836 F
10791 P 14671 P 14761 O 18534 PO 19839 PO
12965 P 14675 PO 14770 O 18557 P 20205 O
13887 P 14680 O 15953 P 18614 P 20615 O
14466 P 14696 P 17049 F 18631 21344 O
14649 P 14715 P 18119 P 19816 FP 21370 O
14653 O 14723 PO 18120 P 19828 PO 22009 P

1928-1949
Primary 18717 P 20441 P 20449 P 20459 O
11826 P 20435 O 20443 P 20450 P 20460 O
13969 O 20436 O 20444 P 20451 O 20461 P
14233 P 20437 O 20445 O 20453 P 20470
14757 PO 20439 P 20446 P 20456 O 21374 O
15394 O 20440 O 20447 F 20458 O 22695 P
Second. 14459 P 16063 P 18746 O 21509 F
10100 O 14733 PO 17709 F 18747 PO 21528 F
11372 P 14760 PO 17718 P 19261 F 22699 P
13891 O 14762 P 18118 P 19700 O 22711 P
13970 O 14771 F 18707 O 20221 O 22712 O
13974 PO 16058 P

1928-1972
(incl. 1644-1972, 1842-1972, 1911-1972)
Primary 16332 P 19899 P 20472 P 20474 P
11047 P 17313 O 20471 S 20473 P 20475 O
15175 FP 17895 O
Second. 14279 PO 14812 P 18827 O 21386 F
10117 PO 14289 S 15161 P 19466 F 21420 PO
10852 P 14785 PO 15459 PO 19709 P 21858 P
10853 PO 14786 PO 15471 P 19875 P 22229 P
10887 PO 14790 P 17772 O 19889 F 22238 P
10888 S 14792 P 18172 P 20226 PO 22251 P
11052 FP 14795 P 18312 P 20979 S 22724 P
14274 P 14810 18809 S

1949-1972
Primary: Monographs
10180 O 14962 P 17990 P 20492 P 20526 P
10945 P 14974 PO 18324 PO 20496 PO 20527 O
10970 P 15214 PO 18330 PO 20502 O 21434 O
12864 P 15235 P 18355 O 20503 O 21944 F
14139 O 15245 PO 18362 O 20505 PO 22339 P
14364 P 15250 P 19069 PO 20506 P 22375 PO
14885 P 15267 P 19922 P 20507 P 22747 O
14910 P 15297 O 20478 F 20522 FP 22755 O
14921 P 16155 O 20484 P
Primary: Inclusions
10930 P 15223 P 15578 P 20424 F 20504 P
14151 P 15224 P 16357 F 20480 P 20524 FP
14328 P 15229 P 17595 P 20486 P 20528 P
14525 P 15243 O 19109 O 20491 P 20530 P
14840 P 15270 P 19928 P 20495 P 21549 O
15222 P 15298 P 19935 F
Primary: Journal Articles
10146 S 16131 O 20479 O 20508 F 20529 F
10305 P 16135 O 20481 P 20509 P 20531 PO
10316 P 16137 PO 20482 20510 P 20532 P
10907 P 16151 P 20483 P 20511 P 20533 P
10936 P 17014 P 20485 O 20512 P 20534 P
14830 P 17328 O 20487 P 20513 P 21478 F
14877 O 17617 F 20488 P 20514 P 21479 F
14926 P 17641 O 20489 O 20515 P 21481 F
14929 P 18227 P 20490 P 20516 P 21561 F
15021 O 18271 F 20493 P 20517 F 21567 F
15226 P 18329 P 20494 P 20518 F 21588 F
15236 P 18332 P 20497 F 20519 F 21599 F
15263 P 19371 P 20498 P 20520 F 21600 F
15302 O 19712 O 20499 P 20521 P 22023 F
15705 P 20476 P 20500 P 20523 P 22844 P
16073 P 20477 O 20501 P 20525 F
Secondary: Monographs
10162 O 14033 P 15230 P 15550 O 21433 O
10975 P 14309 P 15237 P 16071 FP 21552 F
11092 S 14416 P 15240 O 16139 O 21563 PO
11094 P 14825 FP 15248 P 16150 P 21569 P
11096 P 14894 P 15254 O 16457 O 22018 F
11113 P 14909 P 15283 O 16798 FP 22296 P
11132 14951 P 15304 O 17745 P 22299 P
11179 P 14992 FP 15482 O 17995 O 22325 P
12109 P 15002 FP 15501 O 18003 FP 22750 O
12158 PO 15007 P 15519 O 18060 F 22751 O
12791 P 15017 P 15544 O 18061 O 22753 O
12839 FP 15202 P 15545 O 18299 P 22760 O
13328 O 15205 O
Secondary: Inclusions
10147 P 14393 O 14994 PO 18285 P 19945 FP
10410 S 14852 P 15209 P 18286 P 19952 P
11634 S 14880 PO 15287 P 18287 P 20121 P
11637 P 14905 P 15291 P 18344 F 20371 P
12009 P 14906 P 15538 P 18837 P 21099 F
12010 P 14958 P 17638 P 19113 O 21432 P
14147 P 14967 P 18219 P 19369 P 22754 P
14302 P 14977 P 18284 P
Secondary: Journal Articles
10465 P 11148 P 14452 P 15018 P 15246 S
10905 P 11452 P 14814 P 15196 P 15247 P
10933 P 11623 P 14917 P 15197 O 15252 O
10969 P 11972 O 14923 P 15198 P 15256 P
10979 S 12116 P 14938 O 15200 P 15274 PO
10986 P 14044 P 14966 O 15206 O 15275 PO
11057 O 14063 P 14981 F 15218 P 15276 P
11098 P 14143 P 14996 O 15219 P 15277
11142 P 14331 P 15008 O 15244 P 15282 S

15292 P 17781 P 18216 P 19936 F 21565 F
15295 P 17794 O 18217 P 19937 F 21566 F
15918 P 17803 O 18228 P 19947 F 21573 F
15984 O 17959 FP 18243 P 20666 21587 P
16010 FP 18068 O 18323 P 20687 S 21593 PO
17000 P 18197 P 19376 P 21431 F 21925 F
17590 P 18198 P 19592 P 21480 O 22308 P
17596 P 18202 P 19673 P 21488 P 22344 P
17606 O 18214 S 19926 P 21557 22770 F
17777 O

55 Living Routines
生活起居 日常生活

1644-1842
Primary 10045 O 15722 O 20555 O 20587 P
10005 O 10580 O 16369 O 20558 S 20719 PO
10007 O 14210 P 16507 PO 20563 S 22511 O
10032 O 15305 O 17140 PO 20571 O 22590 O
10036 O 15306 O 20536 O 20582 P 22619 PO
10039 O 15310 O 20549 O 20586 PO

Second. 10050 O 12183 P 16087 P 22398 O
10015 O 10522 P 12900 P 16218 O 22505 P
10026 O 10590 P 14156 O 16518 O 22559 O
10027 O 10627 P 15711 O 17160 P 22578 O
10044 O 11675 O 15752 O 17657 O

1644-1911
Primary 14191 PO 17927 FP 20560 P 20597 P
10001 O 15320 PO 18862 P 20568 P 20599 S
10016 O 15353 PO 19756 O 20570 O 20604 O
10028 PO 15626 O 20156 P 20574 PO 20606 P
10058 PO 15743 O 20545 FP 20589 P 20762 O
10060 PO 15754 O 20547 FP 20591 PO 21610 F
10441 P 16523 O 20548 S 20594 PO 21677 FP
11568 PO 16524 O 20554 P 20595 PO 21705 PO
12941 PO 17165 PO

Second. 11194 O 14582 PO 17175 P 19776 FP
10006 S 11203 P 15313 PO 18005 20730 P
10014 O 11573 PO 15318 O 18846 P 20732 P
10042 PO 12205 15327 PO 18869 PO 20769 PO
10046 O 12935 15334 PO 18915 FP 21300 S
10252 13824 P 15729 PO 18917 PO 21634 P
10276 13841 O 15931 O 18940 P 21639 P
10550 P 14208 S 16206 PO 19748 PO 21651 O
10568 O 14454 P 16213 S 19755 PO

1842-1911
Primary: Monographs
10002 O 15324 O 16516 P 20385 O 20578 O
10003 O 15325 O 16520 O 20538 S 20579 O
10018 PO 15338 P 18906 O 20539 O 20583 O
10024 O 15350 O 19751 O 20540 O 20590 PO
10025 O 15355 O 20138 O 20546 F 20600 O
10035 O 15361 O 20255 PO 20552 O 20721 O
12569 O 15364 O 20258 O 20556 O 20766 P
13811 O 15630 O 20274 O 20559 O 20773 F
14157 O 15721 O 20275 O 20565 PO 22067 O
15317 O 16187 O 20379 O 20576 PO 22599 O
15321 O 16388 O

Primary: Inclusions
11013 PO 15753 O 16526 O 20550 O 20564 O
15333 O 16048 PO 19742 O 20551 O 20605 O
15358 O 16166 O 20279 O

Primary: Journal Articles
14177 O 19746 PO 20557 O 20581 O 20603 O
15308 O 20130 O 20561 O 20584 O 20705 O
15348 O 20146 O 20562 O 20585 O 20710 O
15747 O 20148 O 20566 PO 20588 O 20711 O
16391 O 20535 O 20567 O 20592 20728 O
16538 O 20537 P 20569 O 20593 O 20748 O
16934 O 20541 O 20572 F 20596 O 20754 O
17142 O 20542 O 20573 O 20598 O 21652 O
17689 P 20543 O 20575 O 20601 O 22385 O
17815 O 20544 F 20577 O 20602 O 22541 O
17922 O 20553 O 20580 O

Secondary: Monographs
10013 O 12182 O 15349 O 16917 O 20140 O
10019 PO 12580 PO 15360 O 16928 O 20716 O
10021 O 12601 O 15363 O 17176 PO 20781 O
10031 O 12888 PO 15367 O 18075 O 20782 S
10034 S 12894 O 15713 18491 O 21262 O
10047 O 12902 O 15726 O 18875 O 21264 O
10048 O 13804 P 15734 O 18889 O 21298 O
10049 PO 14164 P 15744 O 18922 O 22530 P
10056 O 15038 P 15749 PO 18925 O 22553 O
10059 O 15307 O 16090 O 19765 O 22556 PO
10061 O 15309 O 16167 O 20125 O 22594 O
10062 PO 15316 O 16378 O 20137 O 22601 O
10317 O 15347 PO 16522 O

Secondary: Inclusions
10332 O 12191 F 16929 O 17138 O 22395 O
10612 O 13845 O 16931 O 17609 O 22522 O
10639 O 15359 O 17027 O 19721 PO 22618 O
10642 PO 16539 O

Secondary: Journal Articles
10274 O 15710 16537 O 17930 O 20756 O
10278 O 15730 O 16919 O 17931 O 20770 O
10323 O 15731 O 17818 O 18363 O 20780 O
11181 F 16197 O 17918 O 18918 O 20784 O
12582 O 16380 O 17919 O 20088 F 21266 O
12594 O 16390 O 17925 O 20129 O 22388 O
15356 O 16399 O 17926 O 20709 O 22400 O
15365 O 16527 O 17928 PO 20747 22415 O
15629 O 16528 O 17929 O

1842-1928
(including 1644-1928)

Primary 15379 O 19726 O 20610 P 20618 PO
12211 P 15767 O 20607 O 20613 FP 20619 O
12624 PO 16254 P 20608 P 20616 O 21504 O
14214 PO 16552 O

Second. 15374 F 16228 PO 16553 FP 20795 O
10071 O 15390 O 16250 O 16938 F 20821 O
10082 PO 15633 PO 16252 PO 18950 O 21305 O
11270 P 15673 O 16256 O 18974 PO 21502
12220 P 16101 O 16267 O 20167 S 21760 P
12957 O 16226 PO 16404 O 20180 PO 22644 O

1911-1928
Primary 16121 O 17856 F 20628 O 20645 F
10094 O 16445 O 17871 FP 20630 O 20648 F
10359 O 16945 O 17877 F 20631 O 20649 O
12985 PO 17614 O 19818 FP 20633 O 20655 F
14726 PO 17713 FP 19825 O 20634 O 20832 FP
14743 F 17828 F 20273 O 20635 PO 20852 O
15403 F 17853 F 20626 F 20640 O 22469 O
15775 F 17855 F 20627 F 20641 F

Second. 13896 PO 17566 O 18621 O 20468
10091 O 14429 S 17611 O 18764 O 20837 PO
10106 P 15400 F 17720 F 19248 O 20865 O
10363 FP 15771 O 17831 F 19442 PO 20938 P
11594 O 15780 O 17843 O 19841 O 20942 O
12236 S 16593 F 17873 PO 19851 O 21195 PO
12349 O 16695 F 17886 F 20056 21365 O
12363 PO 17203 O 17887 F 20103 O 21455 O
12728 O 17268 O 17939 O 20455

1911-1949
(including 1644-1949, 1842-1949)

Primary 15760 O 20208 O 20620 PO 20654
10351 S 16547 S 20261 S 20621 20934 P
12317 PO 16624 FP 20276 O 20622 P 21344 O
13250 P 16633 FP 20609 PO 20623 PO 21787 PO
13281 P 17290 P 20611 S 20625 FP 21821 O
15370 O 17307 S 20612 FP 20629 O 22425 P
15372 O 17869 PO 20614 P 20643 P 22446 O
15391 PO 18018 O 20615 O 20646 S 22694 O
15428 O 18990 PO 20617 FP 20653 O

Second. 12241 P 14491 P 15961 FP 17260 F
10102 O 12341 O 14505 P 16120 P 17721 P
10107 P 12367 P 14508 P 16123 FP 17857 F
10295 PO 12759 S 15080 P 16278 O 17980 P
10345 FP 13011 P 15082 O 16299 F 18954 O
10356 PO 13184 P 15376 FP 16421 18976 FP
10684 O 14111 O 15449 O 16550 P 18981 P
11588 FP 14479 PO 15756 S 17049 F 18989 FP
19577 P 21330 O 21745 22452 FP 22706 O
20204 P 21384 O 21750 PO 22457 F 22805 O
20812 P 21443 F 21771 PO 22682 O 22932 S
20820 O

1928-1949
Primary 15077 FP 16670 O 20624 O 20644 F
10098 O 15079 16974 O 20632 F 20647 F
10105 FP 15396 O 17261 P 20636 S 20650 O
11031 P 15410 O 17667 F 20637 F 20651 S
12291 S 15416 O 19817 O 20638 O 20652 F
12971 O 15424 F 19823 O 20639 S 20896 FP
14750 F 15437 PO 19827 F 20642 F 20919 F
15074 F 16116 O 20199 O

Second. 13964 O 16431 FP 17837 O 20064 P
10298 S 15399 F 16599 FP 17858 O 20195 FP
10376 O 15409 P 16616 PO 17863 PO 20198 F
10758 P 15414 PO 16672 F 17868 F 20212 P
11764 P 15419 O 16709 17888 F 20451 O
11768 S 15434 O 16972 FP 17889 F 20855 O
12278 P 15435 O 17084 F 17890 F 20862 F
12281 P 15448 F 17089 FP 17945 O 20873 FP
12348 PO 15773 P 17097 F 18584 O 20894 O
12358 P 15869 F 17098 F 18608 O 20910 O
13274 O 16305 F 17264 F 18643 F 20937 F
13891 O 16311 F 17297 PO 18746 O 21366 O
13928 O 16317 O 17729 F 19261 F 22453 F
13951 O 16425 F 17730 O 19729 F 22455 F
13959 PO

1928-1972
(incl. 1644-1972, 1842-1972, 1911-1972)

Primary 15468 O 17669 FP 20657 PO 20662 S
10301 FP 15601 P 17898 O 20658 F 20663 P
12783 FP 15790 S 17956 P 20659 O 20989 F
15452 PO 15798 P 20417 O 20660 F 21428 O
15463 FP 16727 FP 20656 P 20661 22490 S

Second. 12402 S 15807 P 19466 F 20979 S
10117 PO 12419 P 15808 19896 FP 20982 O
10397 S 13986 P 15809 O 20070 FP 20994 O
11035 O 15189 O 16332 P 20109 P 21413 O
11045 FP 15459 PO 16342 PO 20224 O 21417 P
11845 P 15475 O 16456 F 20226 PO 21422 O
11864 FP 15697 FP 16732 O 20231 PO 21529 PO
11869 P 15796 S 16749 O 20304 F 21532 O
12386 P 15799 O 19035 PO 20958 22736 PO
12391 P

1949-1972
Primary: Monographs
10135 O 15509 O 16146 F 20236 F 20694 F
10144 O 15526 O 16347 O 20244 P 20699 O
10169 O 15543 O 17362 P 20680 F 20700 P
12544 O 15553 PO 17386 FP 20681 F 21063 P
13113 FP 15575 O 17963 F 20682 P 22500 O
15205 O 15621 F 17995 O 20688 O 22747 O
15504 F 15824 FP 19738 F 20690 P 22755 O

Primary: Inclusions
13101 P 15843 O 15860 O 20675 P 20697 P
15653 S 15844 20409 O 20683 FP 20698 O
15817 15854 O 20667 P 20684 P 20701 F
15837 O 15859 FP 20670 O 20693 O

Primary: Journal Articles
11097 PO 15821 P 17351 F 20668 O 20679 O
11924 P 15827 P 17368 O 20669 P 20685 P
12155 O 15835 O 17677 O 20671 O 20686 FP
15122 P 15841 O 17901 O 20672 O 20687 S
15492 O 15851 O 19907 O 20673 P 20689 P
15529 O 15914 F 20243 P 20674 F 20691 P
15531 O 16005 P 20664 P 20676 P 20692 P
15555 O 16036 P 20665 F 20677 O 20695 PO
15563 PO 16482 O 20666 20678 O 20696 O
15574 F

Secondary: Monographs
10130 O 10150 O 10421 FP 11920 P 13107 O
10133 O 10152 O 10427 FP 12002 P 13120 PO
10139 P 10154 P 10931 P 12003 P 13336 P
10140 O 10156 O 11087 O 12019 P 14153 PO
10141 O 10162 O 11095 O 12149 P 14544 F
10145 O 10175 O 11135 O 12150 P 14983 F
10149 O 10399 P 11901 O 12461 O 15112 P

15115 P 15524 O 15993 P 17907 O 20249 F
15483 P 15537 P 16012 P 17917 P 20411 O
15486 FP 15544 O 16348 F 18362 O 20478 F
15493 O 15545 O 16359 F 19153 F 20505 PO
15495 P 15570 P 16457 O 19590 P 20527 O
15501 O 15571 O 16492 P 19905 P 21484 F
15506 O 15655 FP 16798 FP 19920 21575 FP
15508 O 15828 O 16800 O 19922 P 21594 S
15513 PO 15848 P 16826 F 19933 FP 21936 O
15518 P 15856 O 16902 FP 19953 F 22750 O
15519 O 15991 P 17350 FP 19990 FP 22769 O
15523 FP 15992 P 17512 PO

SECONDARY: INCLUSIONS
10898 FP 15648 P 15996 P 17340 P 20238 O
12506 P 15836 15998 O 19138 P 20410 F
13102 P 15849 O 16471 P 19299 O 21065 O
14852 P 15881 O 16883 F 19951 FP

SECONDARY: JOURNAL ARTICLES
12031 P 14872 PO 15842 P 16472 O 19164 PO
12131 O 15477 O 15852 FP 16491 F 19406 O
12431 O 15494 P 15853 O 16498 P 19906 P
12518 O 15496 15995 O 16501 P 19955 F
12520 15503 O 15997 O 16808 O 20072 F
13060 P 15510 O 15999 P 16874 O 21010 PO
13091 P 15516 O 16015 P 17383 O 21024 F
13096 P 15522 O 16026 S 17637 O 21059 S
13347 S 15525 O 16034 P 17738 O 21106 O
14529 P 15536 O 16038 P 17905 P 21149 F
14543 O 15554 O 16069 O 17906 P 21254 P
14848 P 15556 O 16149 O 17908 O 21560 S
14862 P 15562 O 16345 O 19144 P 22023 F

56 ILLNESS AND MEDICINE

疾病及醫療　　疾病及び医療

1644-1842

PRIMARY 20582 P 20719 PO 20740 P 21644 P
16223 P 20703 O 20733 PO 20742 O 22874 P

SECOND. 10045 O 15722 O 17160 P 22512 P
10005 O 11675 O 15752 O 21646 S 22555 O
10036 O 14156 O 16218 O 22398 O 22619 PO
10044 O 15306 O

1644-1911

PRIMARY 20708 20738 PO 20751 PO 20774
16171 PO 20717 P 20739 O 20752 PO 20776 PO
16184 P 20720 PO 20741 P 20761 P 20785 P
16204 P 20725 PO 20743 PO 20762 O 20787 P
19692 PO 20730 P 20744 S 20763 PO 20788 S
20090 PO 20732 P 20745 O 20769 PO 21671 P
20284 P 20736 P 20750 PO 20772 P 22882 P
20591 PO 20737 P

SECOND. 10276 12941 PO 16193 PO 19992 S
10016 O 10560 P 15313 PO 17148 PO 21634 P
10029 PO 10582 PO 15327 PO 18876 O 21713 PO
10042 PO 11199 P 16189 FP 19688 P 22417 PO
10046 O 12206 PO 16190 FP

1842-1911

PRIMARY: MONOGRAPHS
10018 PO 15728 O 20540 O 20726 F 20773 F
10031 O 16374 PO 20713 O 20731 O 20781 O
12569 O 17169 O 20715 O 20749 O 20782 S
15039 P 18925 O 20716 O 20760 F 21298 O
15355 O 20287 P 20721 O 20766 P

PRIMARY: INCLUSIONS
10612 O 20786 PO 22508 O

PRIMARY: JOURNAL ARTICLES
14095 O 20593 O 20711 O 20728 O 20754 O
15723 O 20702 O 20712 O 20729 O 20755 PO
17689 P 20704 O 20714 O 20734 O 20756 O
17815 O 20705 O 20718 O 20735 O 20757 O
17819 O 20706 O 20722 P 20746 O 20758 O
18893 P 20707 O 20723 O 20747 20759 O
20553 O 20709 O 20724 PO 20748 O 20764 O
20584 O 20710 O 20727 O 20753 O 20765 O
20767 P 20771 O 20778 O 20783 O 21490 O
20768 O 20775 O 20779 O 20784 O 21689 O
20770 O 20777 O 20780 O 21178 O

SECOND. 12883 PO 16378 O 19694 O 20575 O
10002 O 15041 P 16915 F 19696 O 20581 O
10003 O 15325 O 17558 O 19742 O 21262 O
10019 PO 15330 FP 17818 O 19760 PO 21621 O
10023 O 15362 O 18494 P 19996 PO 21664 O
10024 O 15365 O 18524 P 20000 PO 22384 O
10025 O 15713 18854 PO 20087 O 22415 O
10038 O 15718 PO 18875 O 20088 F 22525 O
10047 O 15726 O 18899 P 20143 22534 P
10059 O 15730 O 18908 O 20258 O 22542 O
10061 O 16090 O 18914 O 20279 O 22556 PO
10064 O 16178 O 18947 S 20380 O 22599 O
11181 F 16375 PO 19693 P 20567 O 22617 PO
11678 P

1842-1928
(including 1644-1928)

PRIMARY 18987 P 20795 O 20805 O 20814 S
14682 P 20789 P 20798 O 20807 S 20821 O
16252 PO 20790 PO 20800 O 20809 PO 20824 P
18956 PO 20793 O 20802 PO 20811 S 21721 O

SECOND. 15374 F 16267 O 19726 O 21781 S
10071 O 15381 P 16277 P 19797 PO 21790 PO
11683 O 16245 O 16404 O 21342 P 21791 PO
12954 PO 16256 O 18971 S 21752 PO 22644 O
12957 O 16260 O 18983 FP 21760 P

1911-1928

PRIMARY 20635 PO 20875 O 20902 PO 20922 F
10106 P 20832 FP 20877 P 20903 PO 20924 F
10359 O 20837 PO 20878 F 20904 FP 20931 O
14708 O 20850 F 20883 S 20905 O 20932 O
14725 P 20852 O 20884 O 20907 O 20933 O
16308 O 20854 F 20888 F 20911 P 20938 P
16424 PO 20865 O 20889 F 20914 O 20942 O
17722 O 20866 O 20891 O 20917 O 20947 O
17873 PO 20867 P 20893 F 20920 F 21525 O
18992 FP 20868 F 20897 O

SECOND. 17614 O 17871 FP 20107 S 20645 F
14462 S 17727 O 17878 O 20222 S 20648 F
14720 O 17842 F 18596 PO 20455 21223 F
15407 FP 17843 O 18664 O 20631 O 22445 O
17566 O 17848 O 19517 FP

1911-1949
(including 1644-1949, 1842-1949)

PRIMARY 20791 P 20810 O 20823 PO 20909 O
10107 P 20792 PO 20812 P 20825 20912 P
10191 PO 20794 P 20813 P 20826 P 20918 O
14111 O 20796 O 20815 PO 20827 PO 20934 P
16279 P 20797 P 20816 P 20836 O 20939 O
16423 PO 20799 O 20817 P 20845 F 20946 F
17561 O 20801 P 20818 PO 20857 O 20949 F
17869 PO 20803 P 20819 O 20864 F 21344 O
18952 P 20804 PO 20820 O 20879 P 21499 S
20208 O 20806 PO 20822 PO 20886 O 22431 S
20298 F 20808 PO

SECOND. 15376 FP 16557 FP 18993 PO 20623 PO
10104 O 15384 PO 16959 19619 O 20625 FP
10353 S 15428 O 17049 F 19632 S 21375 O
10356 PO 15586 P 17721 P 20172 F 21500 S
10717 PO 15940 S 18759 P 20276 O 21750 PO
10732 P 15945 P 18964 P 20299 F 22435 O
13901 O 15946 FP 18969 P 20622 P 22462 F
13945 P 16274 O 18981 P

1928-1949

PRIMARY: MONOGRAPHS
10105 FP 14730 O 20839 O 20870 P 20919 F
10108 P 15067 PO 20855 O 20871 P 20923 PO
11724 P 15077 FP 20862 F 20873 FP 20926 PO
14121 O 15437 PO 20863 O 20880 PO 20940 S
14721 PO 20835 O 20869 P 20915 F

PRIMARY: INCLUSIONS
14746 O 20848 20896 FP 20910 O 21508 F
20652 F 20872 F 20901 O 20913 F 21515 F
20834 P 20887 O 20908 O 21507 F 21526 F

PRIMARY: JOURNAL ARTICLES
14717 O 20840 F 20860 P 20900 PO 20943 O
14766 FP 20841 20861 P 20906 F 20944 PO
14768 P 20842 F 20874 F 20916 P 20945 O
15404 O 20843 F 20876 PO 20921 F 20948 O
15596 F 20844 F 20881 P 20925 F 20950 F
16294 O 20846 O 20882 F 20927 F 20951 O
19624 O 20847 PO 20885 P 20928 F 20952 PO
20828 O 20849 P 20890 PO 20929 O 21224 F
20829 O 20851 S 20892 F 20930 O 21510 F
20830 O 20853 F 20894 O 20935 O 21511 F
20831 P 20856 O 20895 F 20936 F 21512 F
20833 P 20858 F 20898 PO 20937 F 21520 O
20838 O 20859 F 20899 F 20941 O 21524 F

SECOND. 13891 O 16290 O 17667 F 19629 P
10767 O 15078 P 16297 O 17707 O 19827 F
11372 P 15409 P 16311 F 17718 P 20639 S
11753 O 15414 PO 16314 F 17849 O 20644 F
11761 P 15419 O 16683 PO 17852 O 21210 FP
11777 P 15431 P 16972 FP 17945 O 21216 F
11834 FP 15436 F 16979 O 19022 F 21513 F
12281 P 16117 P 17238 P 19626 P 22453 F
12310 P

1928-1972
(incl. 1644-1972, 1842-1972, 1911-1972)

PRIMARY 20958 20970 P 20981 P 20992
14792 P 20959 P 20971 P 20982 O 20993 S
14799 O 20960 P 20972 P 20983 PO 20994 O
16326 PO 20961 PO 20973 P 20984 P 20995 FP
16339 FP 20962 FP 20974 P 20985 P 21197 FP
20403 P 20963 P 20975 P 20986 S 21231 P
20662 S 20964 PO 20976 PO 20987 P 21413 O
20953 PO 20965 O 20977 PO 20988 O 21529 PO
20954 FP 20966 O 20978 O 20989 P 21534 F
20955 P 20967 P 20979 S 20990 21544 S
20956 P 20968 P 20980 P 20991 PO 21545 O
20957 P 20969 P

SECOND. 14805 S 15472 P 17313 O 20304 F
10110 PO 15089 S 15600 P 17895 O 20656 P
10126 O 15090 O 15603 P 19039 21537 P
10218 P 15454 P 15614 P 19043 P 21884 P
11044 PO 15458 PO 15698 P 19045 P 22736 PO
11603 PO 15461 P 15973 P 19053 P 22740 P
12383 P 15466 O 15981 F 19650 PO 22818 S
14778 O 15469 P 16337 O

1949-1972

PRIMARY: MONOGRAPHS
10141 O 15550 O 21009 FP 21063 P 21103 O
10173 O 16146 F 21036 21086 P 21108 FP
11087 O 16798 FP 21037 F 21093 O 21124 PO
12149 P 20996 FP 21061 P 21098 P 21131 FP
15501 O 21003 P 21062 P 21100 21578 O
15506 O

PRIMARY: INCLUSIONS
19421 P 21025 P 21064 O 21105 P 21146 P
19945 FP 21026 O 21065 O 21117 PO 21147
20371 P 21031 F 21066 P 21119 O 21148 O
20670 O 21033 21067 F 21125 P 21150 F
20999 P 21038 F 21070 P 21126 P 21152 O
21001 O 21042 O 21073 P 21127 P 21153 S
21004 21050 PO 21087 O 21128 P 21154 O
21019 O 21053 O 21088 O 21129 F 22379 O
21023 P 21060 O 21099 F 21141 O

PRIMARY: JOURNAL ARTICLES
10249 P 20353 O 21013 P 21035 O 21057 S
11097 PO 20364 F 21014 21039 P 21058 PO
14870 O 20378 F 21015 O 21040 PO 21059 S
14896 F 20405 O 21016 F 21041 O 21068 O
14907 O 20686 FP 21017 F 21043 P 21069 F
14936 P 20997 O 21018 F 21044 P 21071 S
14948 O 20998 O 21020 F 21045 P 21072 O
14968 P 21000 21021 S 21046 O 21074 O
14985 O 21002 O 21022 O 21047 P 21075 O
14988 O 21005 F 21024 F 21048 PO 21076 P
15292 P 21006 O 21027 O 21049 F 21077 P
17330 O 21007 O 21028 P 21051 F 21078 P
17332 O 21008 F 21029 FP 21052 O 21079 P
17916 O 21010 PO 21030 F 21054 O 21080 P
19669 O 21011 O 21032 F 21055 O 21081 P
20122 F 21012 O 21034 O 21056 O 21082 P

21083 F 21102 O 21118 21138 F 21157 O
21084 O 21104 O 21120 O 21139 O 21158
21085 S 21106 O 21121 O 21140 PO 21202 O
21089 F 21107 O 21122 O 21142 O 21252 PO
21090 21109 O 21123 O 21143 O 21550 F
21091 F 21110 P 21130 F 21144 O 21561 F
21092 FP 21111 21132 P 21145 F 21572 O
21094 O 21112 F 21133 F 21149 F 21583 F
21095 O 21113 O 21134 O 21151 O 21584 O
21096 O 21114 O 21135 F 21155 F 21600 F
21097 P 21115 O 21136 F 21156 F 22841 P
21101 PO 21116 O 21137

Secondary: Monographs
10130 O 14544 F 15520 P 16141 P 20411 O
10133 O 14885 P 15526 O 16816 F 20680 F
10139 P 15249 P 15545 O 16852 O 20699 O
10140 O 15482 O 15568 P 16858 PO 21579 PO
10149 O 15498 O 15575 O 17745 P 22291 P
12003 P 15504 F 15655 FP 17963 F 22500 O
12082 P 15508 O 15856 O 19663 PO 22747 O
12123 P 15509 O 15888 P 19711 FP 22755 O
14520 15518 P 15993 P 20018 F 22831 P

Secondary: Inclusions
10147 P 13102 P 15485 F 16035 P 20339 O
12447 P 15215 15817 19425 P 21246 P

Secondary: Journal Articles
10166 O 15478 O 16368 F 19417 O 20674 F
10985 P 15516 O 16754 O 19925 F 20687 S
11164 F 15533 F 16759 O 19950 P 21560 S
11932 P 15618 PO 16856 PO 20250 21571 F
12112 PO 15852 FP 17329 O 20318 O 21580 F
12129 P 16009 P 17331 O 20329 O 21582 P
14817 O 16010 FP 17497 O 20362 P 21590 P
14930 P 16017 P 17636 O 20666 21599 F
14956 P 16030 P 17738 O 20668 O 21917 P
15111 O 16036 P 17903 P

57 Death Practices

死亡及喪葬 死亡及び葬祭

1644-1842

Primary 11536 O 20571 O 21165 PO
Second. 10036 O 11675 O 18936 P 21985 P
10007 O 10044 O 14599 P 20549 O 22420 P
10020 PO 10050 O 15722 O 20563 S 22609 O
10027 O 10580 O 15752 O 21644 P 22619 PO
10032 O 10652 O 16218 O

1644-1911

Primary 18915 FP 19776 FP 20002 P 21170 P
11568 PO 19748 PO 19991 20762 O 21172 P
15743 O 19752 P 19992 S 21163 FP 21173 O
16181 O 19772 P 19998 PO 21167 FP 21183 PO
16190 FP
Second. 11203 P 16171 PO 18933 19993 P
10001 O 11542 FP 16184 P 18941 FP 19997
10016 O 11550 FP 16188 P 18944 PO 20022 P
10029 PO 11574 PO 16189 FP 19688 P 20144 P
10046 O 11655 PO 16192 P 19692 PO 20545 FP
10060 PO 15320 PO 17977 PO 19695 P 20548 S
10559 PO 15341 O 18853 PO 19722 P 20570 O
10582 PO 15353 PO 18862 P 19723 F 20591 PO
10604 P 15626 O 18881 O 19754 PO 20769 PO
11194 O 15754 O 18885 PO 19756 O 22390 P
11195 P 16161 PO 18927 PO 19763 P 22394 PO

1842-1911

Primary 15348 O 20003 O 21169 PO 21180 O
10024 O 16164 S 21159 P 21171 O 21181 O
10059 O 16197 O 21160 PO 21174 O 21182
12569 O 18075 O 21161 O 21175 O 21652 O
14095 O 19721 PO 21162 O 21176 P 22384 O
14590 O 19739 O 21164 O 21177 O 22397 FP
15308 O 19765 O 21166 O 21178 O 22556 PO
15347 PO 20000 PO 21168 O 21179 O

Secondary: Monographs
10003 O 10018 PO 10031 O 10047 O 10061 O
10017 O 10019 PO 10041 10049 PO 10062 PO
11678 P 15360 O 16378 O 20255 PO 20766 P
12902 O 15364 O 16522 O 20258 O 20781 O
13866 O 15367 O 18856 O 20274 O 20782 S
15038 P 15713 18868 PO 20275 O 21621 O
15039 P 15726 O 18903 P 20540 O 21624 O
15317 O 15734 O 18906 O 20546 F 21980 O
15319 O 15749 PO 20128 O 20579 O 21990 O
15325 O 16186 O 20137 O 20721 O 22594 O
15355 O 16187 O 20138 O 20749 O

Secondary: Inclusions
12589 O 15753 O 20279 O 21301 P 21648 P
21664 O

Secondary: Journal Articles
12566 O 17535 O 19777 O 20544 F 20754 O
14163 PO 17625 O 19996 PO 20557 O 21623 O
15629 O 18301 S 20130 O 20575 O 21689 O
16195 P 18365 O 20148 O 20593 O 22400 O
16390 O 18918 O 20541 O 20722 P 22412 O
17525 O 19690 O 20542 O 20746 O 22415 O

1842-1928
(including 1644-1928)

Primary 16252 PO 18959 O 21184 P 21187 O
15378 F 16267 O 20008 S 21186 S 21189 PO
16250 O 16275 O 20182 P
Second. 16103 FP 16276 O 20004 S 21355 O
10082 PO 16228 PO 16277 P 20175 P 21361 P
11683 O 16245 O 16552 O 20616 O 21791 PO
12211 P 16260 O 18570 P 20618 PO 21798 P
14214 PO 16266 O 19784 P 20811 S 22001 P
15374 F 16269 S 19803 PO 20821 O 22443 P
15379 O

1911-1928

Primary 19818 FP 20220 P 21195 PO
Second. 15403 F 16296 O 17856 F 20273 O
11356 P 15425 O 17614 O 17871 FP 20631 O
11363 P 15786 O 17844 O 20266 PO 22445 O
14758 PO 16121 O

1911-1949
(including 1644-1949, 1842-1949)

Primary 16298 O 20011 P 21185 P 21192
15428 O 19809 20623 PO 21188 F 21744 P
16271 PO 19962 S
Second. 16323 F 19799 P 20298 F 21729 P
10684 O 16942 PO 19816 FP 20299 F 21740 P
12684 FP 18673 P 20010 P 20621 21750 PO
15372 O 18976 FP 20013 P 20653 O 21773 P
15385 PO 18989 FP 20025 P 20813 P 22435 O
15408 F 19014 P 20053 P 21315 F 22441 P
16248 S 19245 O 20205 O 21344 O 22456
16263 PO 19725 P 20208 O 21375 O 22694 O
16300 O 19798 P 20276 O 21384 O

1928-1949

Primary 19708 O 21190 O 21193 O 21194 O
16315 O 19729 F 21191 O
Second. 15424 F 16297 O 17945 O 20873 FP
10098 O 15426 S 16301 F 19702 P 20923 PO
11762 P 15431 P 16311 F 20639 S 21520 O
15410 O 16060 O 16628 O 20858 F 22455 F
15414 PO 16290 O 16979 O 20870 P

1928-1972
(incl. 1644-1972, 1842-1972, 1911-1972)

Primary 16342 PO 20017 F 20304 F 21196 F
21197 FP 21850 F
Second. 15645 P 16343 P 19896 FP 20965 O
10110 PO 15796 S 19043 P 19970 FP 21475 P
10397 S 16328 O 19732 P 20016 P 22733 P
15457 P 16330 P 19873 S 20226 PO 22736 PO
15472 P 16332 P 19892 P 20234 PO

1949-1972

Primary 21063 P 21198 F 21199 P 21200 O
21201 O 21202 O
Second. 15526 O 17497 O 20018 F 21556 F
11150 P 15544 O 19070 F 20072 F 21597 F
11467 P 15546 F 19713 P 20249 F 21946 O
15504 F 16132 O 19913 S 20668 O 21966 F
15505 F 16348 F 19925 F 21483 FP 22494 F
15515 FP 16354 F

58 Fertility and Mortality

繁殖率及死亡率
出生率及び死亡率

1644-1842

Primary 22057 P
Second. 10045 O

1644-1911

Primary 19747 P 21203 P
Second. 10184 P 11542 FP 14088 P 20286 P

1842-1911

Primary 20281 O 20710 O 20729 O 20735 O
Second. 11678 P 15039 P 15328 P 20713 O
10271 O 14605 P 15041 P 20130 O 22522 O

1842-1928
(including 1644-1928)

Primary 10194 P
Second. 10190 P 15051 S

1911-1928

Primary 20655 F 21207 F 21218 F 21223 F
15395 O 21206 P 21208 F 21219 F 21226 F
Second. 16591 F 17873 PO 20877 P 20904 FP
14462 S 16664 PO 20222 S 20883 S 21378 O
15400 F 17871 FP

1911-1949
(including 1644-1949, 1842-1949)

Primary 10199 P 15585 S 21204 P 21220 F
10193 S 12303 FP 15586 P 21209 S 22793 O
10195 P 15446 P 20302 FP 21211 P
Second. 10202 S 12328 P 15382 P 15959 P
10191 PO 10205 P 13676 P 15408 F 19833 FP
10197 P 10345 FP 14424 P 15637 P 20803 P
10198 S 11690 P 15071 P 15678 P 22682 O
10200 P 11706 P 15376 FP

1928-1949

Primary 19834 F 21210 FP 21216 F 21225 F
11750 S 19850 F 21212 F 21217 P 21227 S
12256 F 20842 F 21213 FP 21221 FP 21228 F
15634 P 20844 F 21214 F 21222 S 21229 P
15640 F 20846 O 21215 FP 21224 F 21230 F
17943 O 21205 P
Second. 14117 P 15594 F 19846 P 20890 PO
10204 S 15077 FP 15596 F 20300 F 20898 PO
11752 FP 15404 O 17664 F 20869 P 20926 PO
12277 O 15431 P 17667 F 20871 P 20936 F
12310 P 15432 F 19624 O 20876 PO 20937 F
12311 P 15437 PO 19638 S 20885 P 20952 PO
12358 P 15447 F 19640 P

1928-1972
(incl. 1644-1972, 1842-1972, 1911-1972)

Primary 10220 P 15646 P 19974 P 21232 FP
10210 P 10302 P 15698 P 20303 P 21233 FP
10211 P 15600 P 15874 P 20994 O 21234 P
10212 P 15607 P 17323 P 21231 P 21235 P
10218 P 15611 PO 19873 S

SECOND. 11845 P 15090 O 15608 S 16745 P
10214 P 11848 PO 15471 P 15610 P 16747 P
10215 P 11856 P 15472 P 15613 P 19090 FP
10301 FP 11859 P 15601 P 15614 P 19885 P
10387 S 12426 P 15603 P 15695 P 20403 P
10393 S 12772 P 15604 P 15798 P 20661
10396 S 13297 FP 15605 P 16727 FP 20991 PO
11844 O 13308 P

1949-1972

PRIMARY 10241 PO 20324 F 21237 FP 21247 P
10223 P 10242 P 20328 P 21238 P 21248 P
10224 P 10243 P 20334 FP 21239 F 21249 FP
10225 P 10244 P 20341 F 21240 P 21250 P
10226 P 10263 P 20360 F 21241 P 21251 P
10228 PO 10502 PO 20361 P 21242 FP 21252 PO
10229 P 11913 P 20366 P 21243 FP 21253 P
10231 P 12431 O 20368 F 21244 FP 21254 P
10232 P 15568 P 20377 F 21245 P 21255 F
10234 P 19932 F 21009 FP 21246 P 21256 P
10236 P 20314 P 21236 F

SECONDARY: MONOGRAPHS
10136 O 11903 O 14874 FP 16348 F 19910 F
10172 PO 11912 P 14983 F 16354 F 19933 FP
10173 O 11955 P 15115 P 16463 P 20075 P
10240 P 11975 P 15491 F 16869 F 20996 FP
10432 P 12019 P 15615 P 16898 S 21037 F
10487 P 12071 P 15617 F 17386 FP 21061 P
10498 P 13420 FP 15708 FP 17961 FP 21124 PO
10937 PO 13584 P 15890 P 19905 P 21131 FP
11884 P 14520

SECONDARY: INCLUSIONS
10147 P 11959 PO 15622 P 20321 F 20683 FP
10227 P 12009 P 15624 P 20323 O 20999 P
10250 PO 12017 P 15648 P 20326 F 21127 P
10469 P 12160 S 20306 P 20339 O 21150 F
10478 P 15217 P 20319 F 20371 P

SECONDARY: JOURNAL ARTICLES
10230 P 12119 S 15619 P 20345 F 20695 PO
10235 P 12136 P 15918 P 20346 F 21010 PO
10238 P 12152 P 20317 F 20348 P 21047 P
10248 P 12530 P 20318 O 20352 F 21083 F
10251 12558 P 20320 FP 20357 S 21084 O
10264 P 13086 S 20325 S 20362 P 21121 O
10305 P 14134 FP 20327 P 20363 P 21122 O
10462 FP 15114 PO 20330 F 20369 21132 P
11936 15577 O 20338 F 20370 P 21137
11947 P 15618 PO 20340 F 20375 P

59 LIFE HISTORIES AND BIOGRAPHIES

生活史及傳記 生活史及び伝記

1644-1842

PRIMARY 11569 PO 21282 P 21295 21679 P
10585 P 21277 P 21284 P 21296 P 21685 P
10617 P 21278 P 21292 S 21631 P 22772 P
10651 P 21279 P 21294 P 21670 P 22776 P
SECOND. 10626 P 10672 P 14210 P 22071 P

1644-1911

PRIMARY 18366 P 21269 21288 P 21297 P
10633 P 18421 P 21270 PO 21289 P 21300 S
14093 P 18507 P 21271 O 21290 P 21609 P
14206 P 21259 P 21276 P 21291 P 22058 P
14555 P 21263 P 21283 P 21293 P 22558 P
18012 P 21268 P 21285 P
SECOND. 18858 P 20134 P 21659 P 22621 P
18098 P 18876 O 20147 P 22531 P 22866 P
18523 20022 P 21620 P

1842-1911

PRIMARY 14164 P 14203 P 18428 P 20140 O
10511 P 14174 P 14204 PO 18447 O 20155 O
10551 P 14178 P 17543 P 18494 P 21257
10631 P 14180 S 18074 P 18500 P 21258
14155 S 14182 FP 18375 P 20139 21260 PO
21261 P 21267 P 21275 P 21287 P 21302 O
21262 O 21272 P 21280 O 21298 O 21491 S
21264 O 21273 21281 P 21299 P 21648 P
21265 P 21274 P 21286 P 21301 P 22074 P
21266 O
SECOND. 14190 P 18092 P 18472 P 22069 P
10636 P 14396 P 18370 P 18509 P 22072
10653 P 15127 P 18381 P 18511 P 22518 P
10661 S 15926 P 18412 FP 19614 O 22535 P
11238 P 17143 P 18413 P 21680 P 22589 P
11244 O 17523 P 18442 P 22027 P 22602 P
14157 O 17526 P 18454 PO 22029 P 22618 O
14161 O 18086 P 18461 P

1842-1928

(including 1644-1928)

PRIMARY 21305 O 21329 O 21343 P 21448 P
10722 P 21306 P 21331 O 21346 P 21450 P
13151 P 21307 O 21334 O 21347 P 21765 PO
14229 21310 P 21335 P 21349 PO 21793 P
14676 S 21311 O 21336 P 21350 P 22077 P
17661 P 21317 P 21337 PO 21352 O 22110 P
18533 PO 21318 P 21338 P 21355 O 22112 P
18540 21319 P 21339 P 21356 P 22117 P
18560 P 21327 P 21340 P 21358 O 22118 P
18563 O 21328 P 21342 P 21361 P 22137 S
21304 P
SECOND. 12214 P 18103 P 21786 P 22099 P
10068 S 13881 P 18572 O 22086 S 22104 P
10708 P 14232 P 19220 P 22093 P 22136 P
10712 S 16938 F 21785 P 22094 S

1911-1928

PRIMARY 21365 O 21378 O 21385 22164 P
19825 O 21377 O 21382 O 22141 P 22172 P
SECOND. 13956 O 18600 S 21809 P 22174 P
10106 P 18129 FP 18639 P 22155 P 22181 FP
10766 P 18579 O 18773 P 22165 FP 22708 O

1911-1949

(including 1644-1949, 1842-1949)

PRIMARY: MONOGRAPHS
10706 PO 18104 P 20432 P 21348 O 21375 O
10729 P 18534 PO 21308 O 21354 PO 21380 O
10759 P 18557 P 21320 21359 P 21381 P
10781 P 18559 P 21321 P 21360 P 21384 O
13880 PO 18567 O 21324 P 21362 O 21444 P
14223 P 18661 P 21325 P 21363 21495 S
14231 P 18988 FP 21330 O 21367 O 22009 P
14238 P 20166 O 21333 O 21368 O 22091 P
14247 P 20173 S 21344 O 21370 O 22135 P
15449 O 20210 P 21345 P 21373 P 22672 P

PRIMARY: INCLUSIONS
14242 P 21312 F 21315 F 21332 P 21369 F
21303 P 21313 F 21316 F 21353 O 22107 P
21309 P 21314 F 21326 P 21357 P

PRIMARY: JOURNAL ARTICLES
14213 P 14710 P 18689 P 21322 S 21351 P
14226 P 15940 S 18728 P 21323 P 21383 F
14246 P 18303 P 20171 F 21341 P 22090 P
14660 P
SECOND. 13968 O 16123 FP 19630 P 22120 S
10107 P 13977 P 18622 O 19631 P 22168 P
10688 P 14218 PO 18979 PO 19644 PO 22648 PO
10694 P 14245 18990 PO 20159 PO 22668 P
10791 P 15136 O 19620 FP 21766 P

1928-1949

PRIMARY 13893 O 21366 O 21372 O 21376 O
10100 O 17613 F 21371 O 21374 O 21379 O
10758 P 21364 P
SECOND. 14241 P 18731 P 19642 S 22681 FP
10108 P 18638 S 18736 PO 22157 P 22710 O
10780 P 18679 P 19396 P

1928-1972

(incl. 1644-1972, 1842-1972, 1911-1972)

PRIMARY 21386 F 21399 P 21412 P 21425 P
11038 P 21387 S 21400 P 21413 O 21426 P
11053 O 21388 P 21401 P 21414 FP 21427 PO
14262 P 21389 P 21402 21415 P 21428 O
14273 P 21390 P 21403 S 21416 O 21471 P
14279 PO 21391 S 21404 P 21417 P 22197 P
14288 P 21392 PO 21405 P 21418 O 22210 P
17580 O 21393 O 21406 P 21419 P 22224 P
18173 P 21394 O 21407 S 21420 PO 22235 P
18816 P 21395 PO 21408 P 21421 O 22268 P
18827 O 21396 S 21409 21422 O 22274 S
18834 P 21397 P 21410 FP 21423 P 22276 P
20223 O 21398 P 21411 S 21424 P 22811
20994 O
SECOND. 14271 P 15466 O 19404 P 21537 P
10124 S 14276 P 15612 P 19405 P 21541 P
10128 O 14291 P 17953 P 19985 O 21545 O
10883 S 14293 S 18042 PO 20109 P 22200 P
11052 FP 14790 P 18791 P 20112 O 22273 P
13985 P 15175 FP 18796 O 20224 O 22809 P
14002 P 15453 19054 F 21534 F 22954 P
14020 FP

1949-1972

PRIMARY 14388 P 20478 F 21430 F 21433 O
11057 O 15237 P 20503 O 21431 F 21434 O
11110 P 18266 P 20508 F 21432 P 21435 O
14343 P 20116 O 21429 P
SECOND. 12156 P 14341 P 16368 F 19371 P
10139 P 12524 FP 14346 P 16478 O 20249 F
10927 14073 P 14353 P 17643 P 20511 P
10989 P 14296 P 14381 P 18205 P 20527 O
11080 P 14300 P 14392 P 18207 P 21569 P
11091 P 14336 P 15984 O 18836 F 21582 P
11106 O 14339 S 15985 O

60 IDEA SYSTEMS AND VALUES IN GENERAL

觀念及價值體系通論

観念及び価値体系一般

1644-1842

PRIMARY 10027 O 18420 S 21277 P 22048 P
10005 O 10036 O 18936 P 21278 P 22057 P
10007 O 10050 O 20418 P 21673 P 22064 P
10020 PO 10051 P 20563 S 21711 P 22603 P
10022 O 11563 P
SECOND. 10044 O 13812 18882 O 22590 O
10026 O 11682 P 16185 P

1644-1911

PRIMARY 10559 PO 16163 PO 21439 P 21688 P
10006 S 11239 P 18366 P 21440 O 21698 P
10010 P 11558 PO 18459 O 21441 S 21710 P
10028 PO 11572 PO 20144 P 21617 P 22068 P
10042 PO 14208 S 20720 PO 21668 P 22528 P
10046 O 15327 PO 21437 P 21677 FP 22558 P
10550 P
SECOND. 12193 PO 15931 O 18930 PO 21270 PO
10001 O 12941 PO 16918 19752 P 21660 S
10060 PO 14189 S 18098 P 19992 S 21694 S
10646 14627 P 18917 PO 20124 PO 22024 P
11542 FP 15131

1842-1911

PRIMARY 10062 PO 15319 O 18504 P 21436 P
10002 O 10064 O 15321 O 18871 PO 21438 PO
10003 O 11662 15350 O 18872 P 21624 O
10025 O 13821 O 16183 O 18932 PO 22042 P
10030 O 13853 P 16210 O 18943 P 22556 PO
10041 14606 PO 17142 O 20000 PO 22572 O
10049 PO 15308 O 18084 P 20128 O 22580 PO
10059 O 15316 O 18433 P 20590 PO 22605 P

SECOND. 11658 O 17689 P 20088 F 20583 O
10017 O 14092 PO 17974 O 20252 P 20596 O
10024 O 14155 S 18376 P 20287 P 21178 O
10047 O 15333 O 18378 O 20379 O 21980 O
10063 O 15347 PO 18852 PO 20544 F 22535 P
10317 O 15749 PO

1842-1928
(including 1644-1928)

PRIMARY 18551 PO 21446 P 21749 P 22082 P
10075 18570 P 21448 P 21754 P 22103
10082 PO 18983 FP 21450 P 21775 22110 P
10713 P 21318 P 21451 P 21779 O 22118 P
11261 P 21337 PO 21453 O 21782 P 22123 P
11592 PO 21340 P 21504 O 21786 P 22128 P
14661 P 21361 P 21736 PO 21791 PO 22140 P
15133 S 21445 O 21741 P 21801 P 22423 PO
SECOND. 12233 P 17756 S 21350 P 22644 O
10698 P 14646 P 18024 PO 21798 P 22675 P
11291 P 17631 PO 20618 PO 22136 P

1911-1928

PRIMARY 12741 P 19016 O 21460 P 22007 S
10094 O 14408 P 19402 S 21461 P 22011 O
10099 O 15144 P 21455 O 21462 O 22148 S
10778 O 15145 PO 21456 O 21464 P 22690 P
11356 P 17612 P
SECOND. 14122 O 19248 O 20438 F 22689 P
10765 S 19027 P 19639 P 22156 P 22691 P
10833

1911-1949
(including 1644-1949, 1842-1949)

PRIMARY 14245 19393 P 21452 P 21766 P
10079 PO 14247 P 19394 P 21454 21771 PO
10083 PO 14672 PO 20159 PO 21457 P 22000 P
10086 PO 14692 P 20166 O 21458 P 22004 P
10349 S 14699 P 20432 P 21459 P 22005
10684 O 14719 O 21357 P 21492 P 22006 S
10782 PO 16104 S 21442 P 21493 P 22009 P
11267 S 17979 P 21443 F 21494 P 22129 P
11317 P 18538 P 21444 P 21718 O 22170 P
11368 P 18557 P 21447 PO 21737 P 22178 P
14223 P 18588 P 21449 21761 P 22679 S
14238 P 19245 O
SECOND. 13017 P 18752 P 21325 P 22095 P
10087 O 14652 PO 20164 FP 21516 O 22107 P
10088 O 15674 PO 20621 21796 S 22130 P
11598 P 18544 P 21308 O 21821 O 22457 F

1928-1949

PRIMARY 15149 S 19625 S 20436 O 21465 O
10105 FP 16054 P 19626 P 21463 F 22010 P
12710 S 19003 FP
SECOND. 13964 O 14739 F 20206 O 20872 F
10098 O 13969 O 18158 PO 20451 O 22719 O
11332 P

1928-1972
(incl. 1644-1972, 1842-1972, 1911-1972)

PRIMARY 14284 20959 P 21477 S 22189
10110 PO 14513 P 21404 P 21529 PO 22202 P
10117 PO 14777 P 21466 P 21536 22205 S
10118 O 15168 21467 S 21538 FP 22206 P
10120 S 15170 21468 21832 22207 P
11403 PO 15171 FP 21469 21835 S 22225 S
11409 S 15174 P 21470 S 21844 P 22245
11613 P 15455 FP 21471 P 21855 S 22249 P
13986 P 18786 P 21472 S 21880 P 22284 S
14263 P 19405 P 21473 PO 21881 P 22288 P
14266 P 20225 P 21474 P 21887 P 22474 P
14274 P 20226 PO 21475 P 22012 P 22726 S
14277 20661 21476 S 22013 P
SECOND. 10129 S 14293 S 18805 20984 P
10112 S 10864 S 14412 S 19053 P 21900 P
10124 S 11038 P 15090 O 19899 P 22743 P
10125 P 11045 FP 15473 F 20417 O 22954 P
10126 O 14289 S 18793 20475 O

1949-1972

PRIMARY 14361 P 17675 F 21479 F 21556 F
10135 O 14370 O 17959 FP 21480 O 21563 PO
10149 O 14872 PO 18048 F 21481 F 21577 FP
10154 P 14886 P 19919 P 21482 F 21579 PO
10166 O 15226 P 19935 F 21483 FP 21591 P
11060 P 15273 P 19937 F 21484 F 21919 P
11072 P 15304 O 19953 F 21485 P 21932 F
11103 P 16031 P 20270 O 21486 O 21967 O
11105 P 16132 O 20521 P 21487 22023 F
11641 P 16850 P 20522 FP 21488 P 22354 P
12131 O 16902 FP 21478 F 21489 O 22763 O
12869 P
SECOND. 11144 O 14898 P 15826 F 21103 O
10150 O 11145 P 14908 FP 16496 FP 21549 O
10160 O 14148 14986 P 17597 P 21575 FP
11006 P 14310 15576 O 17803 O 21585 O
11076 P 14871 P 15825 F 17804 P 21951 P
11096 P

61 PERSONALITY AND BEHAVIORAL PROCESSES
人格及行爲
パーソナリティ及び行為

1644-1842

PRIMARY 10623 P 11682 P 12619 P 13829 P
14156 O 20418 P
SECOND. 14166 P 15306 O 16218 O 20571 O
21278 P 21295

1644-1911

PRIMARY 10624 P 18855 O 20256 21441 S
22528 P
SECOND. 11199 P 17920 O 18933 20154 P
10006 S 13819 PO 17927 FP 20092 P 21613
10277 P 14184 P 18919 P 20149 S

1842-1911

PRIMARY 11231 P 16526 O 18435 O 21286 P
10057 O 14564 O 17535 O 21260 PO 21490 O
10272 15338 P 18398 P 21267 P 21491 S
10440 O 15357 O
SECOND. 13858 P 16909 O 18926 O 20716 O
10054 O 15126 S 16928 O 19761 O 20766 P
10064 O 15309 O 17649 O 20127 P 21265 P
10569 15316 O 17973 PO 20130 O 21648 P
10607 P 15337 O 17978 O 20143 21652 O
10640 PO 15717 O 18500 P 20259 O 22043 P
10670 O 16176 O 18512 P 20274 O 22067 O
12580 PO 16512 O 18528 P 20559 O 22601 O

1842-1928
(including 1644-1928)

PRIMARY 16552 O 21339 P 21503 P 21504 O
11719 O 21337 PO 21502
SECOND. 10704 S 18533 PO 21319 P 21996 P
10071 O 12654 P 20097 P 21346 P 22103
10287 P 12963 PO 20099 P 21349 PO 22902 S
10355 P

1911-1928

PRIMARY 20263 20902 PO 21456 O 21517 O
10091 O 20463 F 20903 PO 21506 O 21525 O
17942 O 20469 F 21365 O 21514 S 22008 O
SECOND. 13976 P 17983 O 19281 22174 P
10094 O 15395 O 18706 O 21195 PO 22179 O
12268 P

1911-1949
(including 1644-1949, 1842-1949)

PRIMARY 14245 19447 20276 O 21443 F
10102 O 19245 O 19727 S 20825 21449
21492 P 21495 S 21498 21501 S 22004 P
21493 P 21496 S 21499 S 21516 O 22666 S
21494 P 21497 P 21500 S 21806 S
SECOND. 16251 O 19556 P 20432 P 22005
10070 P 17869 PO 19828 PO 20939 O 22006 S
10295 PO 18752 P 20164 FP 21323 P 22432 P
10684 O 18976 FP 20172 F 21359 P 22463 O
14219 PO 19006 O 20204 P 21444 P 22655 O
14242 P 19246 O 20264 O 21718 O 22667 P
14246 P 19271 P 20265 O 21808 F 22932 S
14247 P 19398 S 20302 FP

1928-1949

PRIMARY 19729 F 21508 F 21515 F 21523 F
10780 P 20921 F 21509 F 21518 P 21524 F
14760 PO 20935 O 21510 F 21519 O 21526 F
17632 O 21463 F 21511 F 21520 O 21527 F
17943 O 21505 F 21512 F 21521 F 21528 F
18158 PO 21507 F 21513 F 21522 O 22693 O
18723 P
SECOND. 14472 O 17868 F 19261 F 20642 F
10096 O 15399 F 18606 P 20189 P 20863 O
12291 S 15410 O 18750 O 20212 P 20873 FP
13892 O 17854 F 19003 FP 20436 O 22166 P
14241 P

1928-1972
(incl. 1644-1972, 1842-1972, 1911-1972)

PRIMARY 15183 PO 21386 F 21533 S 21540 S
11053 O 17950 FP 21472 S 21534 F 21541 P
11615 P 19894 FP 21475 P 21535 P 21542 S
13987 P 19978 FP 21529 PO 21536 21543 O
13988 F 20475 O 21530 FP 21537 P 21544 S
14011 O 20955 P 21531 F 21538 FP 21545 O
14269 P 20995 FP 21532 O 21539 F 22216 S
SECOND. 14264 P 16337 O 20657 PO 22233 PO
11616 S 14415 P 18825 P 20662 S 22266 P
12394 P 14513 P 19036 P 21863 S 22474 P
13991 P 15474 O 19732 P 22223 P 22727 P
14009 P 15981 F

1949-1972

PRIMARY: MONOGRAPHS
10139 P 14305 P 21552 F 21574 FP 21585 O
10150 O 15481 O 21554 O 21575 FP 21586 F
10161 O 20522 FP 21563 PO 21577 FP 21594 S
10164 O 21433 O 21569 P 21578 O 22018 F
10477 P 21546 F 21570 FP 21579 PO 22831 P
11101 FP

PRIMARY: INCLUSIONS
14059 F 21119 O 21562 O 21596 O 21927 F
19911 P 21549 O 21581 FP 21597 F 22357 FP
19951 FP 21556 F 21589 P

PRIMARY: JOURNAL ARTICLES
10998 S 20519 F 21555 F 21571 F 21591 P
11102 S 20523 P 21557 21572 O 21592 F
11140 O 21016 F 21558 F 21573 F 21593 PO
11650 P 21102 O 21559 F 21576 F 21595 F
14376 P 21478 F 21560 S 21580 F 21598 F
14824 P 21483 FP 21561 F 21582 P 21599 F
15252 O 21547 O 21564 F 21583 F 21600 F
18273 P 21548 O 21565 F 21584 O 21960 S
19936 F 21550 F 21566 F 21587 P 22354 P
20122 F 21551 F 21567 F 21588 F 22847 O
20271 F 21553 F 21568 F 21590 P

SECONDARY: MONOGRAPHS
10399 P 16077 O 19933 FP 20492 P 21944 F
10970 P 17995 O 20080 P 20694 F 22350 P
11534 P 18289 P 20367 F 20996 FP 22755 O
13420 FP 18324 PO 20421 F 21131 FP 22763 O
14040 FP 18362 O 20422 F 21928 P 22769 O
14065 P 19738 F 20426 FP 21932 F

SECONDARY: INCLUSIONS
11065 PO 12009 P 15271 O 17746 PO 22373
11176 P 12010 P 15904 17793 O 22762 S
11530 PO 14945 P 15906 P 20267 F

SECONDARY: JOURNAL ARTICLES
10900 11097 PO 11623 P 14822 O 15295 P
11068 P 11142 P 12085 PO 14959 P 15559 P
11075 P 11172 P 14347 P 14991 FP 16044 F

62 COGNITION

認知 認知

1644-1842

1644-1911

1842-1911

1842-1928

(including 1644-1928)

1911-1928

1911-1949

(including 1644-1949, 1842-1949)

1928-1949

1928-1972
(incl. 1644-1972, 1842-1972, 1911-1972)

PRIMARY: MONOGRAPHS
10117 PO 19975 FP 21399 P 21847 P 21887 P
11395 P 20401 P 21401 P 21853 P 21891 P
14809 O 20953 PO 21466 P 21862 S 21900 P
15171 FP 20976 PO 21467 S 21863 S 21904 FP
16343 P 20985 P 21476 S 21869 S 22474 P
19033 P 20987 P 21532 O 21873 P 22740 P
19044 P 20991 PO 21838 P 21874 P 22809 P
19657 P

PRIMARY: INCLUSIONS
10262 21831 P 21856 21877 S 21892 S
12415 P 21836 21858 P 21878 S 21893 P
14789 S 21840 S 21859 P 21880 P 21894 S
16338 PO 21842 P 21870 S 21881 P 21898 PO
16342 PO 21843 PO 21871 P 21882 P 21901 S
20017 F 21845 P 21872 P 21885 S 21902 P
21468 21848 S 21876 P 21889 P 22739 P
21828 P 21854 PO

PRIMARY: JOURNAL ARTICLES
11608 S 18828 FP 21833 O 21860 O 21895
11871 S 19054 F 21834 P 21861 P 21896 P
12411 P 19656 P 21835 S 21864 S 21897 S
13047 P 20304 F 21837 P 21865 P 21899
14259 P 20971 P 21839 S 21866 P 21903 S
14282 S 20990 21841 P 21867 P 22222 S
15193 S 21473 PO 21844 P 21868 P 22223 P
15643 FP 21530 FP 21846 P 21875 P 22246 S
15807 P 21541 P 21849 S 21879 P 22470 S
16326 PO 21542 S 21850 F 21883 P 22471 F
16327 PO 21827 FP 21851 O 21884 P 22487
16333 PO 21829 P 21852 P 21886 P 22824 S
16337 O 21830 S 21855 S 21888 22984 S
16341 P 21832 21857 P 21890 P 22998 S
18039 O

SECONDARY: MONOGRAPHS
10113 15163 S 19403 20992 22196 P
10115 O 15797 FP 19870 21404 P 22202 P
10852 P 16748 P 19978 FP 21413 O 22217 P
11848 PO 17952 S 20960 P 21471 P 22229 P
11855 S 17953 P 20963 P 21475 P 22486 PO
12386 P 18819 P 20973 P 21538 FP 22733 P
12783 FP 19078 P 20982 O 22185 S 22806 P

SECONDARY: INCLUSIONS
15177 S 17320 P 20981 P 22016 S 22236 P
16334 PO 19037 P 22013 P 22192 P 22287 P
16340 S 19866 P

SECONDARY: JOURNAL ARTICLES
11055 S 14273 P 19051 F 20965 O 22288 P
11387 P 14807 O 19052 P 20969 P 22726 S
11409 S 15790 S 19865 P 22015 P 22949
11414 P 15801 O 19889 F 22227 S 22990 S
11415 PO 16329 S 20016 P 22241 P 22995 S
11602 P 16749 O 20956 P 22286 P 23007 P
14256 19032 P

1949-1972

PRIMARY: MONOGRAPHS
10464 P 15033 P 19131 P 21928 P 21948 P
11113 P 16354 F 19422 P 21932 F 21949 P
13446 16359 F 20018 F 21936 O 21950 P
13449 P 16360 FP 20996 FP 21937 P 21951 P
14835 S 18062 O 21569 P 21944 F 22305 P
14871 P 18345 P 21570 FP 21946 O 22831 P
14990 P 19063 PO

PRIMARY: INCLUSIONS
11163 S 19425 P 21913 P 21931 P 21964 P
11448 P 20670 O 21916 P 21934 P 21965 P
11638 O 21596 O 21920 S 21947 P 21971 O
13408 P 21905 F 21921 P 21952 P 21977 P
14964 O 21907 P 21923 P 21955 P 21978 P
19407 P 21910 P 21927 F 21958 P 22335 P
19409 P 21911 P 21929 P 21959 P 22503 S
19424 P 21912 P 21930 O 21962 P 22829 P

PRIMARY: JOURNAL ARTICLES
11117 P 14392 P 17964 P 19925 F 21908 O
11618 PO 14900 P 18329 P 20515 P 21909 P
11899 15813 F 19057 P 21113 O 21914
13401 S 16019 P 19068 O 21485 P 21915 S
13433 16344 O 19410 P 21555 F 21917 P
14359 P 16364 F 19415 O 21906 F 21918 P
21919 P 21940 P 21960 S 21973 P 22338 P
21922 P 21941 P 21961 P 21974 O 22365 O
21924 S 21942 P 21963 O 21975 PO 22496 F
21925 F 21943 P 21966 F 21976 22502 P
21926 O 21945 21967 O 21979 P 22830 S
21933 F 21953 P 21968 P 22022 P 22842 P
21935 P 21954 P 21969 P 22316 P 22843 P
21938 P 21956 P 21970 P 22330 P 22848 O
21939 P 21957 O 21972 P 22337 23043 S

SECONDARY: MONOGRAPHS
10139 P 12429 P 14974 PO 16348 F 21100
10145 O 12525 P 14976 P 17589 F 21489 O
10154 P 13324 PO 15273 P 18061 O 21546 F
10159 O 14299 P 15505 F 18341 P 22304 P
10175 O 14378 P 15509 O 18350 P 22500 O
10481 P 14833 P 15515 FP 19408 PO 22746 P
10970 P 14921 P 15526 O 19679 FP

SECONDARY: INCLUSIONS
11072 P 11951 P 13436 P 19418 P 22363 P
11078 P 12447 P 15296 P 21038 F 22827 P
11174 P 12799 P 15546 F 21198 F 22837 S
11632 13387 P 16848 P 22321 P 22857 S
11647 P 13394 P 19413 P 22342 P

SECONDARY: JOURNAL ARTICLES
10417 P 12458 O 14814 P 17962 O 22023 F
10420 12534 P 14980 O 19070 F 22310 P
11091 P 13425 FP 15814 O 19414 P 22317 P
11146 P 13427 PO 16351 F 21005 F 22320 P
11631 P 13431 O 16352 S 21006 O 22347 P
11645 P 14023 P 16361 F 21035 O 22361 P
11935 S 14028 P 16365 P 21094 O 22825
12119 S 14348 P 16460 P 21199 P 22839 P
12427 P 14358 P

63 ETHICS
倫理 倫理

1644-1842

PRIMARY 14166 P 21985 P 22776 P

SECOND. 10652 O 12198 P 16100 P 20043 P
10033 O 11010 P 12619 P 16369 O 21279 P
10507 P 11555 P 13621 PO 17753 O 21685 P
10585 P 11563 P 14580 S 17822 O 22387 P
10623 P 11569 PO 15752 O 18478 S

1644-1911

PRIMARY 18862 P 20256 21642 FP 21981 O
10520 P 18879 P 21293 P 21657 P 21982 P
11195 P 18887 FP 21608 P 21666 S 21983 P
11219 P 19993 P 21609 P 21697 PO 21984
14169 P 20134 P 21639 P 21703 21986 P
18006 P 20147 P 21641 FP 21709 P 21988 P

SECOND. 11233 S 18367 19748 PO 21440 O
10053 P 11235 P 18384 P 19771 S 21616 P
10525 P 11243 P 18849 PO 20037 PO 21626 PO
10559 PO 11556 P 18867 P 20042 P 21627
10573 S 11562 PO 18881 O 20090 PO 21668 P
10615 P 11655 PO 18901 PO 20092 P 21688 P
10657 P 14208 S 18902 PO 20095 PO 21710 P
10680 P 14569 P 18921 O 20135 PO 22045
11183 P 14596 P 18927 PO 20154 P 22054 P
11184 P 15931 O 18944 PO 20414 P 22056 P
11203 P 16184 P 19687 P 20762 O 22059 P
11207 S 16190 FP 19695 P 21172 P 22390 P
11218 P 16192 P 19723 F 21437 P 22620
11224 P 17975 O

1842-1911

PRIMARY 16214 P 18479 O 20255 PO 21987 O
10551 P 17548 O 18859 P 20258 O 21989 P
10649 O 17625 O 19721 PO 21622 P 21990 O
11213 P 17978 O 19996 PO 21980 O 22066 P
13811 O 18461 P

SECOND. 10607 P 13124 O 15314 S 16089 P
10023 O 10679 O 13803 PO 15316 O 16165 O
10025 O 11188 P 13840 O 15319 O 16224 O
10041 11205 O 14556 P 15325 O 16526 O
10504 O 11206 O 14590 O 15744 O 18086 P
18467 O 20085 P 20252 P 21491 S 22067 O
18524 P 20088 F 20722 P 21649 P 22072
19761 O 20125 O 20723 O 22026 P 22530 P
20001 PO 20130 O 20766 P 22043 P 22564 P
20032 P 20137 O 21174 O 22047 P 22599 O
20036 P 20143 21490 O

1842-1928
(including 1644-1928)

PRIMARY 19805 21340 P 21993 P 22002 P
11590 PO 20005 S 21356 P 21995 P 22082 P
14635 O 20163 P 21450 P 21996 P 22100 S
16281 P 21331 O 21723 PO 21998 P 22140 P
18978 PO 21338 P 21991 PO 22001 P 22437 F

SECOND. 13688 P 17981 P 20181 P 21503 P
10067 O 14227 P 19215 O 20182 P 21736 PO
10731 PO 14642 P 19795 P 20795 O 21782 P
11261 P 14676 S 20047 P 21329 O 21791 PO
11284 S 15138 20097 P 21446 P 21793 P
11298 P 15378 F 20100 21451 P 22118 P
11305 P 16110 P 20179 P 21502 22123 P
11583 P 16226 PO

1911-1928

PRIMARY 19009 20266 PO 20907 O 22008 O
12985 PO 20108 PO 20463 F 22007 S 22011 O
16121 O

SECOND. 15425 O 19017 O 20263 21365 O
10094 O 16320 F 19024 O 20273 O 21825 P
11356 P 19001 PO 19281 20466 22147 P
11817 19002 PO 19825 O 20467 P 22179 O
15145 PO

1911-1949
(including 1644-1949, 1842-1949)

PRIMARY 17979 P 20264 O 21494 P 22003 P
10102 O 18989 FP 20292 S 21796 S 22004 P
10710 S 19644 PO 21330 O 21992 P 22005
11596 P 19725 P 21359 P 21994 22006 S
14657 P 19800 P 21443 F 21997 P 22009 P
15955 P 19816 FP 21457 P 21999 P 22102 PO
16104 S 19964 P 21493 P 22000 P 22126 P
16251 O

SECOND. 11598 P 19271 P 20823 PO 21725 P
10080 14111 O 19829 S 20886 O 21728
10711 P 14687 PO 19836 F 21308 O 21746
11029 P 14699 P 20013 P 21309 P 21750 PO
11255 P 16272 PO 20050 S 21357 P 21761 P
11263 PO 16283 PO 20162 P 21442 P 21806 S
11264 P 17443 S 20176 21452 P 22080 P
11267 S 17754 P 20204 P 21459 P 22132 P
11321 P 18162 P 20265 O 21498 22463 O
11323 P 19217 P 20297 O 21499 S 22655 O
11586 FP 19246 O 20302 FP 21722 O

1928-1949

PRIMARY 15416 O 19634 O 20439 P 22010 P
15150 17632 O 20206 O 20839 O

SECOND. 16060 O 19003 FP 19827 F 21379 O
10105 FP 16312 O 19015 O 20066 P 21463 F
11752 FP 16325 O 19018 FP 20189 P 21823 P
12729 P 18133 P 19074 O 20212 P 22467 F
14774 FP 18692 P 19625 S

1928-1972
(incl. 1644-1972, 1842-1972, 1911-1972)

PRIMARY 19035 PO 21856 22014 22199 P
15184 19861 P 21881 P 22015 P 22286 P
16343 P 19867 P 21896 P 22016 S 22472 S
19032 P 19978 FP 22012 P 22017 S 22479 P
19033 P 21470 S 22013 P 22187 S

SECOND. 11611 PO 16128 FP 20019 O 21197 FP
11386 P 11846 P 17313 O 20227 P 21404 P
11388 P 14001 P 17950 FP 20229 P 21407 S
11397 P 14127 P 18794 P 20304 F 21467 S
11409 S 14273 P 19735 S 20657 PO 21468
11414 P 14283 S 19866 P 20661 21472 S
11416 16126 S 19894 FP 20955 P 21539 F
11608 S 16127 S 20017 F 20971 P 21540 S

21867 P 21900 P 22247 O 22284 S 22480 F
21871 P 21901 S 22273 P 22474 P 22743 P
21891 P

1949-1972

Primary 14389 P 19908 P 21546 F 22020 P
10145 O 14998 P 19936 F 21570 FP 22021 P
11443 FP 18053 O 20267 F 21579 PO 22022 P
11451 P 18358 F 20270 O 21925 F 22023 F
11623 P 19905 P 20426 FP 22018 F 22331 P
11653 P 19906 P 21484 F 22019 P

Second. 11986 P 16351 F 19921 P 21909 P
10997 P 14370 O 16357 F 19938 F 21927 F
11073 P 14991 FP 16756 O 19951 FP 21933 F
11096 P 15099 P 17589 F 20240 P 21944 F
11120 P 15123 O 17622 F 20271 F 22300 P
11153 O 15221 17653 O 20500 P 22317 P
11424 O 15489 P 18048 F 20527 O 22330 P
11442 FP 15495 P 18241 P 20530 P 22337
11477 15509 O 18279 S 21433 O 22341 P
11509 P 15550 O 18354 O 21481 F 22378 P
11654 P 15553 PO 19909 P 21594 S 22755 O
11902 S 16082 P 19919 P 21595 F

64 Ideology and the Great Tradition

正統思想及意識型態

正統思想及びイデオロギー

1644-1842

Primary 11010 P 18478 S 22040 P 22057 P
10027 O 11569 PO 21679 P 22048 P 22064 P
10051 P 12198 P 21686 P 22050 S 22071 P
10507 P 14086 P 22033 P 22055 P 22075 P
10526 S 16100 P 22034 P

Second. 10672 P 12901 P 20132 P 22555 O
10020 PO 11011 P 14197 P 20418 P 22560 S
10033 O 11555 P 14210 P 21278 P 22585 P
10039 O 11557 P 17408 PO 21661 PO 22637 P
10579 P 11563 P 18470 P 21673 P 22640 P
10623 P 11682 P 18948 P 21985 P 22880
10626 P 12619 P 19439 S 22520 P 22885 S
10654 P

1644-1911

Primary 11195 P 14170 P 21642 FP 22054 P
10053 P 11198 P 14205 P 21678 P 22056 P
10505 P 11203 P 14569 P 21982 P 22058 P
10520 P 11219 P 15044 S 21986 P 22059 P
10550 P 11224 P 18526 S 22024 P 22061 P
10573 S 11235 P 18930 PO 22035 S 22068 P
10586 11243 P 19998 PO 22036 P 22070
10597 S 11539 FP 20414 P 22044 P 22528 P
10624 P 11540 O 21293 P 22045 22551 P
10628 S 11552 P 21441 S 22053 P 22633 P
10680 P 12572 P 21630 P

Second. 11233 S 14189 S 18480 P 21659 P
10012 P 11241 P 14198 S 18493 PO 21666 S
10029 PO 11538 14201 P 18519 P 21693 S
10557 P 11549 P 14202 S 18880 P 21710 P
10574 P 11550 FP 14397 P 19687 P 21983 P
10615 P 11559 P 14555 P 20256 21984
10633 P 11564 S 14567 20548 S 22394 PO
10666 P 11664 15130 S 21163 FP 22524 P
10667 P 11667 P 15320 PO 21288 P 22548 S
10681 P 12197 P 16171 PO 21300 S 22565
11016 S 12929 P 16221 PO 21608 P 22581 P
11183 P 14093 P 17541 P 21619 P 22639 P
11207 S 14167 P 18391 P 21620 P 22866 P
11225 S 14184 P 18459 O 21657 P

1842-1911

Primary: Monographs
10024 O 11567 P 15749 PO 18375 P 18461 P
10619 P 14160 P 16186 O 18387 P 18487 P
10677 P 14174 P 16394 P 18430 P 18494 P
11230 P 14178 P 18092 P 18457 P 18511 P
20540 O 22028 P 22052 P 22067 O 22074 P
22026 P 22031 P 22066 P 22073 P 22530 P
22027 P 22046 P

Primary: Inclusions
18073 P 18417 P 21275 P 22025 P 22060 P
18368 P 18429 P 21301 P 22030 P 22065 P
18392 P 18437 P 21648 P 22051 P 22518 P

Primary: Journal Articles
10504 O 14590 O 18460 P 22038 PO 22062 P
10682 O 18083 P 18469 P 22039 P 22063 P
11014 P 18094 S 18472 P 22041 P 22069 P
11669 18096 P 18482 22042 P 22072
12588 P 18100 P 21680 P 22043 P 22535 P
12615 P 18363 O 22029 P 22047 P 22604 P
14561 P 18395 P 22032 P 22049 P 22634 P
14566 PO 18451 S 22037 P

Secondary: Monographs
10031 O 10660 O 14195 P 18089 P 18508 P
10034 S 10679 O 14207 P 18099 P 18859 P
10049 PO 11193 P 14556 P 18388 P 21272 P
10539 P 13831 P 14597 O 18412 FP 21286 P
10544 P 13849 P 15362 O 18416 P 21655 O
10551 P 13858 P 18074 P 18436 P 22572 O
10587 PO 14155 S 18076 P 18442 P 22591 PO
10631 P 14187 P 18077 P

Secondary: Inclusions
10510 P 14190 P 18374 P 18528 P 21436 P
10555 P 14203 P 18389 P 19365 P 21606 P
10610 O 18081 S 18410 P 21267 P 22533 S
10662 P 18370 P

Secondary: Journal Articles
10531 P 14162 P 18082 S 18402 P 18522 P
10537 P 14571 P 18086 P 18404 P 18911 O
10663 P 14572 PO 18090 O 18413 P 18934 O
11209 P 14612 S 18365 O 18471 S 22543 P
11238 P 16525 P 18369 P 18505 P 22607 P
13818 P 17523 P 18401 P 18517 P

1842-1928

(including 1644-1928)

Primary: Monographs
10069 O 18103 P 21336 P 22082 P 22111 P
10697 S 18105 21342 P 22087 P 22112 P
11587 P 18540 21349 PO 22089 P 22114 P
13511 P 18551 PO 21352 O 22094 S 22117 P
14113 P 18983 FP 21361 P 22099 P 22118 P
14635 O 19697 P 21765 PO 22101 P 22127 P
15134 P 19726 O 22002 P 22106 22128 P
17661 P 20004 S 22076 S 22110 P 22131 PO
18102 O 21306 P 22079 P

Primary: Inclusions
14232 P 21317 P 21446 P 22092 P 22113 P
15135 21343 P 22078 P 22108 P 22137 S

Primary: Journal Articles
10704 S 18101 P 22077 P 22103 22123 P
10708 P 18546 PO 22083 P 22104 P 22134 P
11298 P 18961 P 22085 P 22115 P 22136 P
11579 P 20167 S 22086 S 22116 P 22138 P
11591 21451 P 22093 P 22121 P 22139
12224 S 21453 O 22097 P 22122 P 22140 P
14651 S 21996 P 22100 S

Second. 11261 P 14228 O 18555 21347 P
10067 O 11270 P 14701 O 18566 S 21450 P
10073 11284 S 15133 S 18991 P 21504 O
10342 O 11286 P 15938 P 19481 P 21736 PO
10695 P 11581 PO 16247 PO 20005 S 21738 O
10699 PO 11592 PO 16257 O 20169 FP 21783 P
10703 P 11713 P 16281 P 20608 P 21788 P
10709 P 13152 PO 17560 P 21304 P 21795 P
10716 P 13489 P 17630 P 21318 P 21993 P
10727 PO 13882 O 18106 P 21319 P 21995 P
10731 PO 14105 S 18533 PO 21327 P 22902 S
11260 P 14109 P 18542 P 21346 P 22907 S

1911-1928

Primary 12268 P 15786 O 18161 O 18615
10757 PO 12320 17571 O 18310 P 18617 P
10838 P 12724 P 18109 18586 P 18628 P
11597 PO 14243 18122 P 18592 P 18639 P
11599 PO 15148 P 18126 P 18597 PO 18646 P
11790 S 15153 18138 P 18601 P 18719 P
18720 S 18784 21824 P 22156 P 22174 P
18725 P 18997 PO 22141 P 22159 P 22177 P
18753 O 19000 P 22142 P 22160 P 22179 O
18757 O 19402 S 22147 P 22162 P 22180 P
18773 P 19503 FP 22148 S 22163 P 22181 FP
18777 P 19534 P 22149 S 22164 P 22689 P
18778 P 19550 O 22153 P 22165 FP 22708 O
18779 P 20448 P 22154 22172 P 22927 S
18782 P 20462 FP 22155 P

Second. 13947 P 18110 P 18662 P 19453 P
10089 O 13953 O 18115 P 18670 S 19490 PO
10750 P 13955 O 18127 S 18700 O 19500 P
10769 P 13962 P 18129 FP 18709 P 19526
10777 P 13976 P 18148 P 18733 P 19552
10820 S 14119 S 18152 P 18735 P 19570 P
10834 P 14237 P 18579 O 18742 P 20220 P
10844 P 14735 P 18590 P 18760 20457 O
11376 P 15143 P 18596 PO 18762 P 21815 P
11600 P 15144 P 18602 P 18775 P 22685 P
13906 PO 15145 PO 18618 P 18776 P 22690 P
13913 15152 18620 P 19445 P 22707 P
13921 S 15157 P 18649 P 19448 P 22804 S
13927 P 17982 P 18654 P 19449 P 22931 S
13937 P 18026 P 18655 P

1911-1949

(including 1644-1949, 1842-1949)

Primary: Monographs
10070 P 11290 P 18137 S 18768 S 22088 P
10087 O 11598 P 18535 P 18783 P 22091 P
10088 O 11694 PO 18545 PO 19617 P 22095 P
10690 P 12271 P 18557 P 19964 P 22102 PO
10693 P 14231 P 18559 P 20204 P 22109 S
10696 P 14247 P 18614 P 20615 O 22125 P
10718 S 14508 P 18619 S 21345 P 22132 P
10726 14654 P 18635 P 21360 P 22133 PO
10729 P 14681 PO 18661 P 21444 P 22135 P
10782 PO 14687 PO 18674 P 21457 P 22144 P
10793 P 14692 P 18711 O 21459 P 22151 P
10803 P 14699 P 18730 P 21758 P 22173 P
10828 P 15140 O 18752 P 21994 22787 S

Primary: Inclusions
10694 P 18558 S 18633 P 21767 P 22129 P
11265 O 18605 S 18745 O 22081 S 22130 P
13259 P 18626 P 19628 P 22096 S 22649 P
15139 18631 21309 P 22107 P

Primary: Journal Articles
10710 S 15137 21724 P 22119 22167 P
10714 S 18162 P 21725 P 22120 S 22168 P
10738 P 18574 P 21748 S 22124 P 22170 P
11580 P 18593 PO 22080 P 22126 P 22171 S
12251 S 18698 P 22084 P 22145 P 22175 P
12325 P 18705 P 22090 P 22150 S 22178 P
12335 S 21351 P 22098 P 22152 P 22656
14225 O 21452 P 22105 O

Secondary: Monographs
10074 P 11707 P 17979 P 18636 P 20432 P
10079 PO 12227 P 18104 P 18685 P 20801 P
10700 PO 13901 O 18120 P 18722 O 20820 O
10706 PO 14116 P 18123 P 18739 P 20823 PO
10715 P 14215 S 18143 O 18741 PO 20826 P
10776 PO 14223 P 18147 P 18756 21321 P
10807 P 14238 P 18155 P 18759 P 21324 P
10845 P 14640 PO 18534 PO 18780 P 21354 PO
11263 PO 14677 P 18536 P 18979 PO 21368 O
11279 P 14684 P 18543 S 19806 P 21447 PO
11289 P 14686 P 18547 PO 20050 S 21740 P
11317 P 14696 P 18562 S 20053 P 22646 P
11336 P 14723 PO 18567 O 20161 P 22648 PO
11586 FP 15136 O 18583 S 20210 P 22679 S
11699 S 16104 S 18598 O 20431 P

Secondary: Inclusions
10093 O 13878 P 14645 P 18537 S 21332 P
10453 S 13977 P 14680 O 18556 21747 P
11695 14242 P 18119 P 18571 S 21804 P

Secondary: Journal Articles
10689 13875 S 14710 P 18578 O 21737 P
10736 S 13940 P 14729 P 18580 P 21992 P
11262 P 14110 P 18121 P 18651 S 22668 P
11296 S 14245 18149 P 18714 P 22786 P
11585 S 14246 P 18151 18728 P 22788 S
11773 O 14648 18157 P 21442 P 22943 S

1928-1949

PRIMARY 14762 P 18632 P 18692 P 21823 P
10783 O 16637 P 18647 P 18718 S 22143 P
10827 PO 18114 P 18648 P 18723 P 22146 P
11028 P 18124 FP 18660 P 18731 P 22157 P
11337 P 18135 S 18663 P 18738 P 22158 P
11338 P 18307 P 18666 P 18755 P 22161 P
12332 P 18606 P 18672 P 19625 S 22166 P
13894 O 18608 O 18676 P 19642 S 22169 P
13898 P 18627 P 18677 P 20444 P 22176 P
14248 P

SECONDARY: MONOGRAPHS
10100 O 10842 P 13903 S 18125 PO 18747 PO
10105 FP 11327 P 13969 O 18134 P 18749 O
10758 P 11752 FP 13983 P 18659 O 18750 O
10799 PO 11830 O 14241 P 18696 O 18766 P
10806 O 11834 FP 14744 P 18736 PO 21194 O
10814 P 13895 P 14754 PO 18744 O 21379 O
10819 P 13902 O 15970 P 18746 O 22714 P
10836 PO

SECONDARY: INCLUSIONS
12326 S 13982 O 18305 P 18612 P 18763 S
13974 PO 14236 P 18604 S 18761 P 21372 O

SECONDARY: JOURNAL ARTICLES
10741 P 11765 S 15154 P 18658 O 19568 S
10810 P 13897 P 17569 18668 S 19623 PO
11023 O 14235 P 18117 P 18675 P 19634 O
11032 P 14240 O 18128 P 18682 P 22010 P
11312 P 14249 P 18159 O 18691 P 22715 S
11341 P 14427 P 18599 P 18695 O 22935 P
11367 P 14755 O 18613 P 18737 S 22938 P
11378 O 15149 S 18638 S 18754 S 22941 P

1928-1972
(incl. 1644-1972, 1842-1972, 1911-1972)

PRIMARY: MONOGRAPHS
10113 13984 P 18795 P 21853 P 22225 S
10115 O 13991 P 18796 O 21862 S 22229 P
10124 S 14014 P 18812 21891 P 22233 PO
10125 P 14258 P 18817 PO 22182 P 22235 P
10850 PO 14264 P 18819 P 22185 S 22243 P
10865 P 14269 P 18822 P 22190 P 22249 P
10883 S 14274 P 20960 P 22194 P 22250 P
10887 PO 14285 P 21400 P 22196 P 22251 P
10891 S 14780 P 21401 P 22198 O 22260 P
11045 FP 14783 P 21404 P 22202 P 22268 P
11046 P 14795 P 21405 P 22203 P 22269 P
11053 O 15166 21406 P 22204 P 22271 P
11391 P 15168 21419 P 22206 P 22273 P
11393 P 15171 FP 21420 PO 22207 P 22275 P
11614 P 15980 P 21424 P 22210 P 22277 P
11848 PO 17952 S 21466 P 22217 P 22486 PO
11855 S 18172 P 21471 P 22219 P 22809 P
11862 P 18178 FP 21476 S 22224 P 22991 S
11872 PO 18185 P

PRIMARY: INCLUSIONS
10127 18802 P 21885 S 22221 S 22256 P
10859 P 18807 21893 P 22230 P 22258 P
11042 P 18808 P 21898 PO 22231 P 22263 P
11043 P 18825 P 22191 P 22232 P 22264 P
14790 P 19659 P 22192 P 22234 P 22267 P
14794 P 21831 P 22195 P 22236 P 22272 P
15164 P 21848 S 22197 P 22237 S 22282 P
15170 21871 P 22205 S 22238 P 22283 P
15195 P 21876 P 22209 S 22244 P 22287 P
18043 P 21881 P 22212 P 22247 O 22737
18045

PRIMARY: JOURNAL ARTICLES
10116 S 14262 P 18786 P 21536 22184 P
10848 P 14265 S 18787 S 21541 P 22186
10849 P 14283 S 18789 P 21837 P 22187 S
10864 S 14291 P 18797 S 21841 P 22188 P
11033 S 14413 P 18806 P 21846 P 22189
11034 P 14414 P 18816 P 21849 S 22193
11388 P 14415 P 18830 P 21857 P 22199 P
11413 P 15178 19469 O 21865 P 22200 P
11602 P 15179 S 19651 S 21867 P 22201 P
11608 S 15182 P 19656 P 21868 P 22208 P
11610 PO 16452 PO 19658 P 21879 P 22211 P
14130 P 17986 P 21397 P 21883 P 22213 P
14256 18165 P 21403 S 22012 P 22214
14260 P 18177 P 21472 S 22183 P 22215 S
22216 S 22239 S 22253 P 22266 P 22284 S
22218 S 22240 P 22254 S 22270 P 22285 P
22220 P 22241 P 22255 P 22274 S 22286 P
22222 S 22242 P 22257 P 22276 P 22288 P
22223 P 22245 22259 P 22278 S 22735 S
22226 P 22246 S 22261 P 22279 P 22994 S
22227 S 22248 P 22262 P 22280 P 23008 S
22228 P 22252 P 22265 P 22281 P

SECONDARY: MONOGRAPHS
10111 S 12424 P 15161 P 18804 PO 21412 P
10114 P 12780 P 15163 S 18809 S 21415 P
10123 O 13986 P 15169 P 18810 21421 O
10128 O 13997 15172 PO 19035 PO 21422 O
10851 P 14001 P 15174 P 19082 PO 21423 P
10853 PO 14002 P 15175 FP 19285 P 21425 P
10893 S 14012 P 15977 P 19286 O 21467 S
11052 FP 14015 O 16343 P 19655 P 21532 O
11395 P 14018 S 17772 O 19657 P 21539 F
11398 P 14020 FP 18041 P 19732 P 21847 P
11603 PO 14263 P 18170 P 19899 P 21873 P
11605 O 14278 P 18176 P 20473 P 21874 P
11846 P 14279 PO 18182 P 21395 PO 21887 P
11849 P 14293 S 18312 P 21407 S 22734 O
11857 P 14513 P 18792 P 21410 FP 22740 P
12379 P 15158 S 18801 P

SECONDARY: INCLUSIONS
10119 S 14268 P 15160 P 19404 P 21840 S
10122 S 14275 P 15177 S 19866 P 21856
10847 S 14281 P 15185 S 19871 S 21859 P
11612 P 14781 P 15186 S 19873 S 21870 S
12394 P 14788 P 15187 S 20472 P 21872 P
12772 P 14800 P 15188 P 21388 P 21877 S
14000 P 14801 P 15982 21394 O 21894 S
14131 14802 P 18799 P 21468 21901 S
14255 P 14803 P 18833 P 21836 22739 P

SECONDARY: JOURNAL ARTICLES
10383 S 11417 P 14272 P 18166 S 19868 S
10393 S 11615 P 14277 18168 P 19875 P
10846 12374 P 14282 S 18169 P 19891 P
10854 S 12391 P 14284 18175 P 20227 P
10868 S 13992 P 14286 P 18188 P 21535 P
10877 P 14003 P 14438 S 18311 PO 21830 S
10881 P 14005 P 14777 P 18790 P 21835 S
11038 P 14016 15159 P 18800 P 21851 O
11054 P 14252 15162 P 18814 P 22726 S
11383 P 14253 P 15167 S 18826 S 22727 P
11386 P 14257 S 15190 18831 P 22984 S
11408 P 14267 P 16128 FP 19467 S 23007 P
11416 14270 P 18044 P

1949-1972

PRIMARY: MONOGRAPHS
10132 O 11132 14329 P 15241 S 20484 P
10134 O 11135 O 14370 O 15248 P 20496 PO
10142 P 11144 O 14387 P 15249 P 21124 PO
10144 O 11178 P 14416 P 15254 O 21563 PO
10153 O 11180 P 14828 P 15260 P 21569 P
10160 O 11639 P 14853 P 15279 O 21948 P
10161 O 11646 PO 14871 P 15283 O 22291 P
10168 O 11897 PO 14903 P 15294 P 22293 S
10175 O 11922 O 14943 O 15507 P 22296 P
10180 O 12002 P 14951 P 15545 O 22298 P
10938 P 12027 P 14974 PO 15549 P 22299 P
10970 P 12082 P 14976 P 15553 PO 22304 P
10994 P 12086 14990 P 17995 O 22305 P
10997 P 12109 P 15025 P 18277 P 22318 P
11061 O 12158 PO 15028 P 18299 P 22322 P
11081 P 12791 P 15029 P 19062 O 22324 P
11088 13420 FP 15034 P 19069 PO 22325 P
11092 S 14139 O 15205 O 19367 P 22326 S
11096 P 14296 P 15214 PO 19905 P 22339 P
11104 P 14299 P 15230 P 19919 P 22350 P
11111 P 14305 P 15234 P 20314 P 22367 P
11113 P 14322 P 15235 P 20426 FP 22375 PO

PRIMARY: INCLUSIONS
10244 P 11508 P 12045 P 14363 P 15296 P
10930 P 11617 PO 13387 P 14448 P 17971 F
11007 P 11634 S 14046 P 14880 PO 17999 P
11163 S 11637 P 14057 P 15005 P 18206 P
11174 P 11638 O 14138 P 15101 P 18242 P
11176 P 11942 P 14325 P 15203 P 18281 FP
11426 P 11965 P 14327 P 15233 P 18282 P
11451 P 11978 PO 14328 P 15281 S 19290 P
19928 P 22290 P 22335 P 22358 P 22373
20480 P 22313 P 22336 P 22359 22378 P
21907 P 22319 P 22342 P 22360 22379 O
21916 P 22321 P 22356 P 22363 P 22380 P
21931 P 22327 P 22357 FP 22364 P 22827 P
21947 P

PRIMARY: JOURNAL ARTICLES
10896 O 12113 S 15247 P 19159 P 22328 P
10933 P 12153 P 15257 P 19322 P 22329 P
10934 S 12164 P 15266 S 19323 P 22330 P
10968 P 12561 O 15268 20348 P 22331 P
11070 P 13063 P 15275 PO 20349 S 22332 P
11082 P 13090 P 15280 S 20476 P 22333 P
11084 P 13386 P 15282 S 21097 P 22334 P
11091 P 14029 P 15289 P 21151 O 22337
11098 P 14074 P 15295 P 21488 P 22338 P
11116 P 14140 P 15540 P 21548 O 22340 P
11119 P 14143 P 16027 O 21557 22341 P
11129 14148 16080 S 21591 P 22343 P
11146 P 14149 P 16082 P 21919 P 22344 P
11155 P 14154 O 16352 S 21938 P 22345 O
11177 P 14308 P 16832 S 21940 P 22346 P
11453 P 14313 P 17119 O 21941 P 22347 P
11481 P 14331 P 17645 O 21942 P 22348 P
11511 P 14353 P 17660 P 21961 P 22349 P
11513 P 14354 P 18002 P 21970 P 22351 P
11515 P 14356 P 18066 P 22289 P 22352 S
11525 P 14371 P 18190 P 22292 P 22353
11533 P 14444 P 18194 P 22294 P 22354 P
11623 P 14824 P 18197 P 22295 22355 P
11624 P 14834 P 18211 P 22297 P 22361 P
11631 P 14847 S 18213 PO 22300 P 22362 P
11642 P 14857 O 18214 S 22301 P 22365 O
11645 P 14862 P 18216 P 22302 P 22366 P
11650 P 14884 P 18217 P 22303 P 22368 P
11900 S 14898 P 18222 P 22306 P 22369 P
11937 14902 P 18250 P 22307 PO 22370 P
11941 P 14927 P 18252 P 22308 P 22371 P
11973 P 14930 P 18265 P 22309 P 22372 P
11979 PO 15004 P 18268 P 22310 P 22374 P
11986 P 15018 P 18269 P 22311 22376 P
12024 S 15020 P 18276 P 22312 22377 P
12025 P 15032 PO 18278 S 22314 P 22381 P
12040 P 15199 18339 P 22315 22382 S
12075 P 15200 P 18352 P 22316 P 22838 S
12093 P 15216 S 18353 P 22317 P 22852 FP
12095 P 15220 P 19067 O 22320 P 23044 S
12108 P 15238 P 19150 P 22323 P

SECONDARY: MONOGRAPHS
10133 O 11883 O 14066 FP 15481 O 19110 O
10135 O 11889 P 14153 PO 15495 P 19131 P
10140 O 11894 O 14309 P 15517 F 19135 P
10141 O 11919 O 14310 15524 O 19302 P
10155 P 11920 P 14311 P 15543 O 19422 P
10164 O 11939 S 14337 P 15575 O 19662 P
10165 O 11949 P 14364 P 16029 S 19920
10170 O 11955 P 14384 P 16046 PO 19922 P
10173 O 11970 P 14829 O 16071 FP 20079 P
10477 P 12001 P 14874 FP 16077 O 20247 P
10931 P 12014 14885 P 16347 O 20328 P
10937 PO 12123 P 14899 P 17012 P 20478 F
10960 FP 12439 P 14910 P 17647 P 20492 P
11003 P 12441 P 14921 P 17674 P 20505 PO
11006 P 12467 P 14942 P 17804 P 20526 P
11076 P 12519 P 14962 P 18212 P 21579 PO
11094 P 12523 P 14969 P 18225 P 21585 O
11101 FP 12524 FP 15017 P 18232 P 21594 S
11105 P 12525 P 15031 P 18236 P 21949 P
11107 P 12552 P 15237 P 18264 P 21950 P
11160 P 12562 P 15240 O 18272 P 22746 P
11436 P 12813 P 15245 PO 18279 S 22747 O
11437 P 12839 FP 15258 P 18289 P 22750 O
11439 P 14033 P 15267 P 18298 P 22753 O
11622 P 14047 P 15297 O 18319 P 22769 O
11625 P 14055 P 15304 O 18324 PO 22831 P

SECONDARY: INCLUSIONS
10147 P 11458 P 13417 O 14913 P 15243 O
11072 P 11484 P 14054 P 14946 PO 15286
11073 P 11530 PO 14068 P 14957 PO 15303 FP
11083 P 11633 P 14304 P 14958 P 16075 P
11100 P 11914 14390 P 14964 O 17340 P
11128 P 12121 P 14850 P 15217 P 17640 P
11443 FP 12156 P 14856 15222 P 17997 P
11447 P 12840 P 14906 P 15223 P 18000 P

18189 P 18241 P 19104 20081 P 21432 P
18196 P 18293 P 19129 P 20306 P 21959 P
18208 P 18294 S 19162 20491 P 22837 S
18209 P 18344 F 19915 P 20698 O 22857 S

SECONDARY: JOURNAL ARTICLES
10225 P 11977 P 14443 P 15984 O 19414 P
10243 P 11983 P 14538 S 16020 P 19596 P
10249 P 12050 P 14814 P 16874 O 19599 P
10305 P 12064 S 14826 O 16890 FP 19607 P
10467 P 12068 P 14827 P 17590 P 19678 P
10496 P 12077 S 14841 O 17596 P 19682 P
10897 P 12084 P 14845 P 17778 P 19906 P
10902 P 12098 P 14849 P 17781 P 19908 P
10909 P 12100 FP 14869 P 17916 O 19926 P
10911 P 12105 P 14872 PO 17992 P 19941 S
10925 P 12116 P 14881 O 17998 P 20248 O
10941 P 12117 P 14886 P 18052 P 20327 P
10958 P 12129 P 14912 O 18056 P 20370 P
10974 P 12431 O 14931 P 18067 O 20374 P
10987 P 12472 P 14937 P 18072 P 20481 P
10995 P 12481 S 14941 P 18191 P 20485 O
11009 P 12529 P 14950 O 18198 P 20494 P
11067 FP 12808 P 14959 P 18200 P 20497 F
11068 P 12821 P 14965 P 18205 P 20520 P
11074 P 12835 P 15009 O 18207 P 20521 P
11085 P 13360 P 15010 PO 18226 P 20529 F
11136 P 13401 S 15019 P 18227 P 20533 P
11149 O 13405 PO 15201 S 18237 P 21055 O
11153 O 13425 FP 15226 P 18238 P 21056 O
11431 P 14021 15227 P 18249 P 21092 FP
11445 P 14026 P 15236 P 18262 P 21114 O
11446 P 14035 S 15244 P 18270 21115 O
11452 P 14067 P 15246 S 18275 P 21429 P
11461 P 14076 P 15251 P 18316 P 21560 S
11465 P 14141 S 15253 P 18317 P 21909 P
11477 14152 P 15261 P 18321 O 21935 P
11482 P 14294 P 15264 P 18335 O 21945
11493 FP 14303 S 15276 P 18337 P 21968 P
11497 S 14306 P 15277 18342 P 21969 P
11522 P 14321 P 15278 18357 P 21973 P
11532 P 14323 S 15284 P 18836 F 22748 P
11618 PO 14335 S 15288 P 18838 P 22825
11621 P 14340 P 15292 P 19130 P 22828 S
11628 P 14352 P 15301 P 19168 PO 22844 P
11640 P 14362 P 15478 O 19183 P 22847 O
11648 P 14367 O 15494 P 19189 P 22848 O
11879 P 14382 P 15512 O 19195 F 22850 O
11902 S 14383 P 15559 P 19308 P 22854 O
11950 S 14389 P 15580 P 19366 S 23056 P
11954 P 14392 P

65 FOLKLORE AND LITTLE TRADITIONS
民俗 民間伝承

1644-1842
PRIMARY 16185 P 20719 PO 22391 P 22405 O
14166 P 18476 S 22387 P 22398 O 22420 P
SECOND. 16223 P 18424 P 19439 S 21681 S
12184 P 18014 P 18468 PO 19441 P 21711 P

1644-1911
PRIMARY 16194 O 19755 PO 22386 P 22410 PO
11568 PO 16196 P 19776 FP 22390 P 22411 O
15313 PO 18006 P 20574 PO 22392 O 22414 S
16171 PO 18010 P 20769 PO 22394 PO 22417 PO
16181 O 18012 P 21612 P 22396 P 22418 P
16184 P 18406 P 21613 22402 22419 O
16188 P 18865 PO 21640 PO 22409 P 22592 P
SECOND. 16162 PO 16208 PO 18910 20570 O
10012 P 16189 FP 16221 PO 18939 PO 20708
10014 O 16190 FP 16542 PO 18946 PO 20720 PO
10046 O 16191 16924 O 19743 PO 20725 PO
12194 PO 16192 P 17153 PO 19991 20730 P
12578 O 16193 PO 18005 20134 P 20739 O
12941 PO 16200 PO 18396 S 20149 S 20751 PO
14093 P 16204 P 18421 P 20154 P 20774
15323 O 16206 PO 18867 P 20285 P 21167 FP
15745 PO 16207 P 18902 PO 20568 P 21172 P

21611 FP 21645 P 21668 P 21691 PO 21982 P
21617 P 21667 P 21677 FP 21696 P 22059 P

1842-1911
PRIMARY 16396 O 20782 S 22388 O 22404 O
10018 PO 17649 O 21176 P 22389 O 22406 O
10023 O 17662 O 21621 O 22393 O 22407 O
10061 O 18856 O 21664 O 22395 O 22408 O
16090 O 18875 O 21689 O 22397 FP 22412 O
16198 PO 20274 O 21987 O 22399 S 22413 P
16199 PO 20275 O 22383 PO 22400 O 22415 O
16220 PO 20288 PO 22384 O 22401 O 22416 O
16222 O 20383 O 22385 O 22403 P
SECOND. 15726 O 16219 O 18894 O 20581 O
10043 O 15733 O 16224 O 18914 O 20603 O
10048 O 16156 O 16538 O 18929 O 20715 O
10056 O 16170 O 16917 O 19719 P 20749 O
10271 O 16172 O 17137 PO 19751 O 20753 O
10660 O 16180 O 17930 O 19778 PO 20759 O
12902 O 16182 O 18016 O 19957 O 20777 O
15317 O 16183 O 18017 O 20003 O 20778 O
15332 O 16186 O 18374 P 20088 F 21160 PO
15336 O 16187 O 18383 P 20381 O 21182
15349 O 16201 O 18415 O 20382 O 21273
15360 O 16202 F 18452 P 20539 O 21683 P
15362 O 16205 18456 O 20553 O 21990 O
15367 O 16211 O 18491 O 20561 O 22583 PO
15583 O 16214 P 18889 O

1842-1928
(including 1644-1928)
PRIMARY 16247 PO 16275 O 21189 PO 22421 S
11576 F 16250 O 16276 O 21720 O 22422 FP
11581 PO 16252 PO 16277 P 21760 P 22423 PO
12624 PO 16254 P 18024 PO 21774 22437 F
15378 F 16256 O 20004 S 21781 S 22438 O
15379 O 16259 FP 20291 O 21789 P 22439 O
16227 P 16260 O 20295 O 21798 P 22442 PO
16228 PO 16264 PO 20824 P 21801 P 22443 P
16245 O 16267 O
SECOND. 16238 O 16266 O 20391 P 21739 P
10071 O 16239 O 16268 PO 20619 O 21751 O
10076 S 16240 O 16273 O 20790 PO 21752 PO
11710 16241 O 16284 O 20798 O 21765 PO
15374 F 16242 O 18103 P 20807 S 21772 S
15390 O 16243 O 18959 O 21187 O 21784 FP
16103 FP 16244 O 18966 O 21307 O 21791 PO
16230 O 16246 O 18978 PO 21719 P 21799 O
16235 O 16261 S 18980 O 21723 PO 21993 P
16236 O 16262 P 19795 P 21735 PO 22661
16237 O 16265 O 20099 P

1911-1928
PRIMARY 16308 O 20273 O 22447 O 22468 P
14758 PO 16319 O 22445 O 22448 O 22469 O
15147 P
SECOND. 15775 F 19818 FP 20631 O 21455 O
12728 O 16285 19851 O 20640 O 21456 O
15418 F 16320 F 20107 S 20884 O 21811 O

1911-1949
(including 1644-1949, 1842-1949)
PRIMARY 17049 F 20654 22425 P 22441 P
10339 O 18019 20794 P 22426 P 22446 O
15372 O 18027 P 20810 O 22427 S 22452 FP
16225 18029 F 21188 F 22428 FP 22456
16248 S 18548 O 21344 O 22429 PO 22457 F
16249 P 20101 S 21375 O 22430 O 22458 F
16253 FP 20265 O 21500 S 22431 S 22459 F
16258 S 20276 O 21722 O 22432 P 22462 F
16270 O 20298 F 21726 22433 S 22463 O
16271 PO 20299 F 21740 P 22434 O 22464 F
16274 O 20395 F 21750 PO 22435 O 22466 O
16279 P 20612 FP 21777 O 22436 22792 S
16283 PO 20614 P 22424 22440 O 22801 O
16298 O
SECOND. 13875 S 16229 PO 16300 O 16323 F
10356 PO 13877 PO 16263 PO 16310 F 16408 FP
11582 PO 15370 O 16278 O 16318 O 16547 S
12684 FP 15428 O 16288 S 16322 F 16962 O

16977 O 18589 P 20792 PO 20857 O 21759 O
17260 F 18622 O 20797 P 21330 O 21762
17460 FP 19354 P 20801 P 21370 O 21763
17980 P 20176 20804 PO 21731 P 21773 P
18020 S 20208 O 20818 PO 21733 P 21808 F
18030 O 20611 S 20826 P 21737 P 22000 P
18547 PO 20617 FP 20836 O 21745 22679 S

1928-1949
PRIMARY 16301 F 18671 O 21810 O 22454 F
10096 O 16303 FP 20203 O 21813 P 22455 F
15773 P 16311 F 20397 F 22444 O 22460 O
16290 O 16314 F 20399 F 22449 F 22461 F
16291 O 18032 O 20632 F 22450 F 22465 F
16294 O 18033 FP 20856 O 22451 F 22467 F
16295 F 18036 O 20873 FP 22453 F
SECOND. 16312 O 19820 F 20199 O 21190 O
13969 O 16315 O 19822 F 20639 S 21216 F
15405 F 16317 O 19827 F 20835 O 21511 F
16060 O 16949 O 19830 F 20839 O 21519 O
16289 FP 19261 F 19847 FP 20858 F 21520 O
16307 F 19729 F

1928-1972
(incl. 1644-1972, 1842-1972, 1911-1972)
PRIMARY 18794 P 22470 S 22478 FP 22486 PO
16328 O 18820 O 22471 F 22479 P 22487
16329 S 18832 22472 S 22480 F 22488 S
16330 P 19865 P 22473 S 22481 O 22489 S
16332 P 19889 F 22474 P 22482 P 22490 S
16335 P 20656 P 22475 P 22483 S 22491 P
16337 O 20992 22476 P 22484 S 22492 P
16750 F 21869 S 22477 P 22485 S 22493 S
18038 FP 21889 P
SECOND. 16336 P 19032 P 20401 P 21532 O
11403 PO 16338 PO 19090 FP 20661 21838 P
11610 PO 16339 FP 19859 FP 20953 PO 21853 P
11869 P 16341 P 19870 20962 FP 21862 S
12783 FP 17950 FP 19896 FP 20965 O 21887 P
15469 P 17956 P 20109 P 20973 P 22995 S
15799 O 18798 P 20304 F 20987 P

1949-1972
PRIMARY 16354 F 17971 F 21905 F 22498 F
14996 O 16355 P 18048 F 21906 F 22499 P
15505 F 16356 P 18049 F 21949 P 22500 O
16132 O 16363 S 20518 F 21950 P 22501 O
16346 F 16366 F 21005 F 22494 F 22502 P
16348 F 16367 F 21138 F 22495 F 22503 S
16349 F 17675 F 21596 O 22496 F 22504 P
16353 S 17963 F 21598 F 22497 F 22849 P
SECOND. 15504 F 17351 F 20018 F 21483 FP
11105 P 15526 O 17623 O 20236 F 21489 O
11151 P 15573 F 18061 O 20249 F 21556 F
11619 P 16359 F 18070 O 21003 P 21908 O
11976 O 16360 FP 19738 F 21045 P 21946 O
14133 O 16362 PO 19950 F 21237 FP 21948 P
14351 P 16763 O

66 SELF-CONCEPTION IN RELATION TO OUTSIDERS
「華夷」「中外」之分辨及對異族之観念
「華夷」「中外」等異民族に対する観念

1644-1842
PRIMARY 12901 P 15752 O 21712 P 22544 P
10036 O 13829 P 16218 O 22071 P 22550 P
10522 P 13832 P 17657 O 22398 O 22552 S
10535 P 13835 P 18863 P 22505 P 22555 O
10580 O 13837 P 18936 P 22511 O 22559 O
10626 P 13856 18948 P 22512 P 22560 S
10651 P 13865 P 20586 PO 22519 S 22563 P
11541 P 14156 O 21279 P 22520 P 22577 P
11545 P 15306 O 21661 PO 22521 S 22578 O
11571 P 15722 O 21685 P 22537 P 22585 P

22590 O 22609 O 22626 P 22635 P 22640 P
22598 P 22611 P 22627 S 22636 P 22878 P
22603 P 22619 PO 22629 P 22637 P

SECOND. 10528 P 13812 18425 P 21284 P
10005 O 10529 P 13813 P 18470 P 21292 S
10020 PO 10533 PO 13814 S 18478 S 21294 P
10027 O 10542 P 13822 P 18904 P 21604 P
10032 O 10552 P 13855 19205 P 21643 PO
10044 O 10593 P 13864 P 19429 P 21672 P
10045 O 10673 P 14585 S 20555 O 22034 P
10051 P 11012 P 15664 P 21277 P 22865 S
10526 S 11563 P 17555 O 21278 P 22874 P
10527 P 12900 P 18418

1644-1911

PRIMARY: MONOGRAPHS
10010 P 10560 P 15320 PO 18876 O 21288 P
10016 O 10644 PO 16389 PO 18919 P 21300 S
10028 PO 10674 S 18098 P 18930 PO 21659 P
10042 PO 11015 P 18405 S 18937 P 22531 P
10046 O 12941 PO 18459 O 18945 P 22558 P
10058 PO 13458 P 18464 P 19209 O 22567 P
10325 PO 13824 P 18519 P 19752 P 22620
10329 PO 13841 O 18860 P 21285 P

PRIMARY: INCLUSIONS
10006 S 14176 22507 S 22548 S 22592 P
10603 P 17520 PO 22516 22565 22628
12940 S 18443 S 22547 22581 P 22639 P
13859 S

PRIMARY: JOURNAL ARTICLES
10589 P 14575 P 20785 P 21714 P 22551 P
10664 S 15660 21283 P 22058 P 22579 S
11197 P 15742 PO 21619 P 22510 P 22610 S
11210 P 16918 21620 P 22524 P 22621 P
11543 S 17920 O 21658 P 22528 P 22633 P
13838 18493 PO 21699 P 22529 P 22638 O
13867 P

SECOND. 11568 PO 13808 P 15665 P 20574 PO
10004 PO 11655 PO 13819 PO 15931 O 20594 PO
10053 P 11667 P 13834 P 18384 P 21259 P
10505 P 11672 PO 13846 P 18523 21269
10557 P 12572 P 14175 S 18526 S 21601 P
10571 12913 P 14555 P 18847 PO 21671 P
10586 12931 PO 15131 18915 FP 21716
10625 P 12935 15323 O 19434 P 22059 P
10638 P 13128 P 15353 PO 19437 P 22394 PO
10671 S 13457 P 15581 O 19769 P 22864 S
11241 P 13629 PO 15659 PO 19774 P 22866 P
11556 P 13637 P 15661 S 19998 PO 22887 S

1842-1911

PRIMARY: MONOGRAPHS
10017 O 13470 P 16388 O 18868 PO 22553 O
10019 PO 13803 PO 16536 O 18872 P 22556 PO
10034 S 13811 O 16910 PO 18875 O 22561 P
10047 O 14155 S 17529 P 18889 O 22562 O
10055 O 14160 P 17532 O 18903 P 22568 P
10056 O 14164 P 18364 P 18914 O 22572 O
10065 O 14178 P 18371 P 18922 O 22575 P
10275 P 14187 P 18375 P 18924 PO 22576 O
10519 P 14195 P 18378 O 18943 P 22580 PO
10544 P 14584 PO 18409 P 18947 S 22584 S
10566 P 15038 P 18412 FP 20128 O 22586 P
10611 O 15309 O 18416 P 20540 O 22589 P
10614 P 15316 O 18422 O 20552 O 22591 PO
10631 P 15338 P 18428 P 20559 O 22594 O
10653 P 15350 O 18430 P 20565 PO 22595 P
10665 P 15351 O 18436 P 20579 O 22599 O
10677 P 15355 O 18484 P 20600 O 22600 P
11567 P 15361 O 18485 P 20716 O 22601 O
11657 PO 15364 O 18487 P 21265 P 22602 P
11658 O 15721 O 18490 P 22026 P 22605 P
11681 O 15733 O 18491 O 22074 P 22612 P
12569 O 15744 O 18502 P 22509 O 22614
12570 O 15929 O 18511 P 22513 PO 22615 O
12590 P 16183 O 18524 P 22530 P 22617 PO
12601 O 16375 PO 18854 PO 22532 P 22623 P
12611 P 16376 PO 18859 P 22536 P 22630 P
12918 P 16387 O 18861 P 22542 O 22631 S
12921 O

PRIMARY: INCLUSIONS
10334 O 14604 O 18368 P 19365 P 22522 O
10510 P 15359 O 18370 P 20564 O 22523 O
10639 O 15715 O 18429 P 21436 P 22525 O
11013 PO 16929 O 18433 P 21707 P 22533 S
12589 O 17554 PO 18486 P 22508 O 22588 P
14190 P 18073 P 18525 P 22518 P 22618 O
14395 P 18080 P 18874 P

PRIMARY: JOURNAL ARTICLES
10009 P 15921 P 18850 P 22515 P 22573 P
10530 16091 P 18851 O 22517 O 22574 P
10563 16092 P 18866 P 22526 P 22582 O
10581 P 16380 O 18878 O 22527 O 22583 PO
10663 P 16382 O 18892 P 22534 P 22587 P
10683 16511 O 18895 O 22535 P 22593 O
11238 P 16935 O 18911 O 22538 P 22596 P
11662 17522 O 18928 O 22539 P 22597 P
12566 O 17533 FP 18942 O 22540 P 22604 P
12584 O 17535 O 19614 O 22541 O 22606 P
12607 P 17538 O 19693 P 22543 P 22607 P
12618 S 17546 O 20148 O 22545 P 22608 P
12898 O 17552 O 20596 O 22546 P 22613 S
13124 O 18083 P 20780 O 22549 P 22616 P
13799 PO 18094 S 22029 P 22554 P 22622 P
13839 O 18369 P 22032 P 22557 O 22624 P
14561 P 18403 O 22039 P 22564 P 22625 P
14613 P 18453 P 22042 P 22566 P 22632 P
15127 P 18483 P 22049 P 22569 P 22634 P
15128 S 18488 P 22506 O 22570 P 22641 P
15129 O 18497 P 22514 P 22571 P 22642 P
15348 O

SECONDARY: MONOGRAPHS
10025 O 12606 P 15307 O 17688 O 20034 PO
10043 O 12911 P 15324 O 18077 P 20126 S
10049 PO 12914 P 15332 O 18092 P 20274 O
10064 O 12920 O 15339 O 18379 PO 20275 O
10271 O 13461 P 15362 O 18382 P 20379 O
10321 O 13464 P 15367 O 18386 P 20576 PO
10328 O 13485 P 15726 O 18387 P 20583 O
10508 P 13802 P 15728 O 18408 S 20715 O
10539 P 13831 P 15740 O 18438 P 20731 O
10587 PO 13847 P 15749 PO 18449 O 20749 O
10645 P 13849 P 15930 P 18450 P 20781 O
10660 O 13858 P 16169 O 18454 PO 21260 PO
10679 O 13866 O 16378 O 18455 S 21262 O
11230 P 14092 PO 16395 O 18461 P 21264 O
11231 P 14174 P 16513 O 18492 PO 21286 P
11665 P 14182 FP 16520 O 18494 P 21298 O
11678 P 14204 PO 16913 O 18496 P 21302 O
12567 P 14209 P 16914 O 18852 PO 21603 P
12593 PO 14554 PO 17151 O 18908 O 21624 O
12597 O 14560 P 17161 P 18925 O 22027 P
12598 PO 14592 P 17409 FP 18932 PO 22868 S
12600 P 14597 O 17543 P 19719 P

SECONDARY: INCLUSIONS
10332 O 13468 O 15753 O 17431 P 18513 O
10650 PO 14203 P 16920 O 17526 P 18515 S
11017 O 15358 O 16926 O 17978 O 20551 O
11245 PO 15366 O 16927 O 18088 P 21299 P
12191 F 15716 O 17138 O 18392 P 21301 P
12934 O 15717 O 17139 O 18452 P 21648 P

SECONDARY: JOURNAL ARTICLES
10272 12916 O 14612 S 17556 18471 S
10273 P 12937 PO 14616 P 17625 O 18482
10278 O 12938 PO 15042 O 17931 O 18500 P
10326 PO 13137 15045 O 17973 PO 18504 P
10536 S 13460 P 15126 S 18086 P 18512 P
10538 P 13800 S 15583 O 18087 P 18517 P
10547 S 13821 O 15714 O 18095 18522 P
10569 13840 O 15718 PO 18096 P 18893 P
10668 P 13850 P 15720 O 18300 O 18899 P
10675 P 13851 O 15731 O 18365 O 18918 O
10682 O 13853 P 15738 F 18372 18938 O
11189 P 14162 P 16390 O 18395 P 20281 O
11240 P 14177 O 16530 P 18398 P 20711 O
11661 P 14399 P 16531 O 18404 P 20727 O
11668 O 14551 O 16905 P 18407 O 21438 PO
12579 O 14552 O 16911 O 18434 P 21615 S
12581 P 14566 PO 16919 O 18435 O 21680 P
12585 O 14571 P 17023 O 18440 P 21689 O
12610 P 14573 O 17142 O 18444 O 22069 P
12879 PO 14578 S 17521 O 18456 O 22389 O
12891 O 14593 P 17523 P 18465 O 22771 P
12912 S 14610 P 17540 O

1842-1928
(including 1644-1928)

PRIMARY: MONOGRAPHS
10067 O 12222 P 15373 P 18991 P 22106
10069 O 12653 P 15389 PO 20004 S 22110 P
10076 S 12655 S 15937 P 20294 PO 22118 P
10081 PO 12663 P 15952 O 20790 PO 22131 PO
10085 PO 12957 O 16108 PO 20795 O 22644 O
10338 P 12963 PO 16109 PO 20802 PO 22650 P
10712 S 13147 P 17630 P 21311 O 22652 P
11270 P 13163 S 18553 P 21336 P 22657 S
11291 P 13505 O 18960 PO 21342 P 22658 S
11578 P 14224 PO 18968 PO 21361 P 22664 P
11705 PO 14404 P 18972 P 22087 P 22669 S
11709 14683 S 18987 P 22089 P 22673 P

PRIMARY: INCLUSIONS
10290 P 15673 O 18555 22643 S 22661
14216 S 18533 PO 18971 S

PRIMARY: JOURNAL ARTICLES
10691 15671 O 22077 P 22663 S 22675 P
11260 P 21785 P 22086 S 22670 22676 O
14682 P

SECONDARY: MONOGRAPHS
10068 S 13502 P 14112 P 18958 P 21350 P
10077 O 13511 P 14214 PO 18962 PO 21355 O
10695 P 13513 P 14661 P 19697 P 21450 P
10727 PO 13519 P 15134 P 19726 O 21504 O
11299 P 13520 P 15369 PO 20182 P 21723 PO
11587 P 13523 P 15388 S 20430 P 21786 P
11703 P 13674 FP 15938 P 20798 O 21788 P
11708 S 13683 PO 16256 O 21304 P 21791 PO
12624 PO 13876 16277 P 21307 O 22076 S
12950 P 13882 O 18102 O 21335 P 22082 P
13152 PO 13883 18530 P 21337 PO 22112 P
13155 P 13884 PO 18540 21346 P 22117 P
13165 13885 S 18552 P 21349 PO 22423 PO
13489 P 14109 P 18956 PO

SECONDARY: INCLUSIONS
10073 14232 P 15135 20433 P 21769
11284 S 14674 O 19475 21317 P 22092 P

SECONDARY: JOURNAL ARTICLES
10354 P 11717 P 13167 S 15138 19219 S
10687 P 12225 O 13487 P 15951 19352 O
10728 P 12626 PO 13648 O 17412 P 19715
10734 O 12679 14632 O 17559 P 21318 P
11259 PO 12954 PO 14673 P 18546 PO 22093 P
11579 P 12969 PO 15050 O 18961 P 22097 P
11592 PO 13161 P 15132 P 18967 O 22139

1911-1928

PRIMARY 13905 PO 18129 FP 18762 P 22181 FP
10091 O 13925 P 18160 P 18764 O 22678 O
10099 O 13950 S 18308 P 19013 O 22680 O
10768 PO 14411 P 18590 P 19021 O 22684 P
10838 P 14468 P 18596 PO 19249 PO 22685 P
10844 P 14497 FP 18601 P 19277 P 22689 P
11024 P 14511 18620 P 19490 PO 22690 P
11345 P 14731 O 18649 P 19499 P 22691 P
11358 P 15148 P 18652 F 19501 P 22696 O
11734 P 15157 P 18653 P 19580 P 22698 O
11812 P 17770 P 18654 P 20865 O 22700 P
12741 P 18110 P 18664 O 22141 P 22705
12747 O 18126 P 18706 O 22148 S 22707 P
12996 P 18127 S 18719 P 22149 S 22708 O
13896 PO

SECONDARY: MONOGRAPHS
10106 P 15145 PO 18306 O 18709 P 19825 O
10381 P 15407 FP 18582 O 18725 P 20462 FP
11783 P 17566 O 18597 PO 19012 O 20463 F
11790 S 17575 O 18609 O 19455 P 21456 O
13016 P 17614 O 18610 O 19517 FP 21825 P
13962 P 18138 P 18621 O 19534 P 22172 P
15073 P 18148 P 18630 P 19639 P 22179 O
15143 P 18161 O 18655 P

SECONDARY: INCLUSIONS
10750 P 15153 18628 P 18774 P 19454 FP
11828 S 16712 F 18662 P 18775 P 19511 O
13260 P 18026 P 18670 S 18776 P 19557 P
13889 P 18602 P 18734 P 18778 P 19562 O
13953 O 18618 P 18771 P 18992 FP 21815 P
13955 O

Secondary: Journal Articles

10359 o 12756 o 17268 o 19023 o 20914 o
10369 o 13913 17292 o 19509 p 21809 p
10766 p 13981 p 18156 p 19512 p 22155 p
10784 p 14726 po 18586 p 19553 22163 p
10835 p 15593 po 18757 o 20060 p 22180 p
11597 po 15780 o 18769 p 20452 p 22934 s
11600 p 15969 s

1911-1949

(including 1644-1949, 1842-1949)

Primary: Monographs

10097 o 12965 p 15674 po 20173 s 22654 p
10684 o 13144 p 15941 p 20791 p 22655 o
10702 o 13521 po 15945 p 20823 po 22660 po
10725 p 13676 p 15948 p 20886 o 22666 s
10759 p 13880 po 18547 po 20934 p 22667 p
11266 p 14652 po 18619 s 21325 p 22672 p
11293 p 14670 p 18622 o 21373 p 22674 p
11304 p 14679 p 18969 p 22133 po 22679 s
11317 p 14685 o 18981 p 22645 s 22682 o
11336 p 14692 p 18993 po 22646 p 22692 o
11586 fp 14694 p 19217 p 22647 p 22694 o
11601 p 15376 fp 19246 o 22648 po 22706 o
11696 s 15377 p 19801 p 22653 s 22717 p
12630 p

Primary: Inclusions

10080 11700 s 15386 19279 f 22659
10295 po 13532 p 18558 s 22649 p 22662
11695 13878 p 18984 s

Primary: Journal Articles

10719 15940 s 18157 p 22119 22665 s
10743 p 15950 s 18580 p 22150 s 22668 p
11684 p 17229 p 18686 p 22651 s 22671
13554 18121 p 21778 s 22656 22686
15137

Secondary: Monographs

10074 p 12674 p 14719 o 18562 s 20813 p
10079 po 12676 s 14728 f 18583 s 20822 po
10087 o 13222 p 14736 p 18635 p 20826 p
10102 o 13570 p 14761 o 18674 p 21321 p
10104 o 13659 p 15063 s 18685 p 21333 o
10107 p 13740 p 15136 o 18722 o 21344 o
10201 s 13873 o 15140 o 18730 p 21359 p
10345 fp 13887 p 15156 o 18739 p 21360 p
10346 s 13901 o 15382 p 18780 p 21368 o
10700 po 13916 p 15586 p 18952 p 21381 p
10706 po 14219 po 15638 o 18988 fp 21444 p
10715 p 14231 p 15668 s 18989 fp 21447 po
10726 14509 p 15939 p 19006 o 21457 p
10729 p 14510 po 16407 p 19008 o 21459 p
10803 p 14650 s 16409 p 19551 p 21718 o
11595 p 14655 p 17572 o 19620 fp 21758 p
11692 p 14665 po 17979 p 19705 p 21796 s
11712 fp 14671 p 18137 s 20166 o 22009 p
11714 p 14681 po 18143 o 20204 p 22088 p
11715 p 14684 p 18534 po 20276 o 22132 p
12629 po 14688 p 18535 p 20431 p 22905 o
12631 p 14696 p 18545 po 20432 p 22939 p
12637 po 14703 s 18557 p

Secondary: Inclusions

10288 s 14645 p 18561 o 18745 o 22005
11252 s 14680 o 18605 s 20621 22081 s
12731 o 15946 fp 18626 p 21303 p 22096 s
13920 p 16671 o 18633 p 21326 p 22462 f
14106 17052 po 18645 s 21767 p 22924 p
14406 p 17282

Secondary: Journal Articles

10285 po 13148 p 15391 po 18593 po 19561 p
10689 13159 p 15632 p 18698 p 19576 p
10815 14660 p 15676 fp 18705 p 19618 p
11267 s 14663 15964 p 18714 p 20054 p
11288 14710 p 16668 p 18715 p 21494 p
11726 s 14759 o 17474 p 18964 p 22098 p
11824 o 14776 p 17936 19014 p 22105 o
11836 s 15081 o 18019 19221 22120 s
13017 p 15082 o 18303 p 19236 p 22171 s
13146 p

1928-1949

Primary: Monographs

10096 o 11823 p 13958 po 18608 o 22710 o
10098 o 13891 o 13959 po 18707 o 22711 p
10100 o 13895 p 15965 p 20456 o 22712 o
10452 s 13914 p 16119 p 21374 o 22714 p
10758 p 13928 o 17577 o 22681 fp 22718
10821 s 13951 o 18142 p 22688 s 22719 o
11031 p 13952 o 18145 p 22699 p 22720 po
11732 p 13957 po 18584 o

Primary: Inclusions

13974 po 18612 p 18672 p 22677 o 22683 s
18146 p 18632 p 18712 p

Primary: Journal Articles

10786 p 13934 p 18141 p 20441 p 22702 p
10787 p 13941 p 18150 p 20446 p 22703 po
11023 o 14117 p 18302 o 20449 p 22704 o
11728 s 14499 s 18581 p 20450 p 22709 p
11755 p 14500 p 18595 p 22687 po 22713 f
11826 p 17735 p 18677 p 22693 o 22715 s
12265 s 17943 o 18758 p 22695 p 22716 p
13919 p 18107 p 19011 f 22697 22721 p
13924 o 18116 p 19573 p 22701 22722 p
13933 p

Secondary: Monographs

10103 po 11740 p 13963 p 16980 p 20206 o
10108 p 11748 p 13964 o 17846 f 20436 o
10783 o 13039 o 13969 o 17858 o 20444 p
10796 p 13743 po 13970 o 17945 o 20458 o
10804 o 13750 fp 13975 po 18660 p 20835 o
10806 o 13756 p 15067 po 18666 p 20839 o
10813 p 13760 po 15416 o 18690 p 20863 o
10814 p 13893 o 15438 p 18717 p 20926 po
10819 p 13894 o 15439 p 18747 po 21366 o
10827 po 13902 o 16417 p 20199 o 21379 o
10839 o 13903 s 16628 o

Secondary: Inclusions

14760 po 17043 o 18688 o 18763 s 20435 o
16065 p 17766 fp 18731 p 19022 f 21372 o

Secondary: Journal Articles

10741 p 11821 s 14233 p 16647 o 18737 s
11312 p 12263 14427 p 16688 o 18738 p
11337 p 12266 p 14755 o 16966 o 18995 o
11761 p 12311 p 15149 s 17573 o 19572 p
11762 p 13197 p 15396 o 17576 p 19574 p
11764 p 13215 p 15401 o 18648 p 20453 p
11791 p 13890 o 16606 f 18658 o 21364 p

1928-1972

(incl. 1644-1972, 1842-1972, 1911-1972)

Primary: Monographs

10110 po 12778 p 17615 o 19045 p 22728 o
10111 s 13049 p 17772 o 19053 p 22730 p
10114 p 14274 p 17985 fp 20475 o 22731 s
10128 o 14792 p 18183 p 20973 p 22732 fp
10303 p 15174 p 18801 p 21404 p 22733 p
11044 po 15461 p 19039 22210 p 22734 o
11606 s 15468 o 19043 p 22225 s 22736 po
11607 p 17311 o 19044 p 22724 p 22740 p
11611 po

Primary: Inclusions

10874 p 17635 p 19040 22192 p 22739 p
14129 18799 p 21892 s 22209 s 22743 p
15799 o 19029 21901 s 22737

Primary: Journal Articles

10863 p 14266 p 21839 s 22245 22735 s
11041 p 15193 s 21844 p 22723 o 22738 p
11412 p 15194 21861 p 22725 p 22741
11416 16735 p 21899 22726 s 22742 p
11602 p 18806 p 22189 22727 p 22807 s
14004 p 19584 p 22208 p 22729 p

Secondary: Monographs

10124 s 11605 o 14279 po 15458 po 18187 p
10129 s 11848 po 14512 p 15460 fp 18794 p
10850 po 11857 p 14783 p 15806 p 18795 p
10858 s 12770 s 14786 po 15810 fp 18804 po
10879 o 13762 p 15158 s 15976 po 18812
10885 po 13991 p 15161 p 16732 o 18817 po
10887 po 13997 15163 s 17895 o 18819 p
10890 p 14015 o 15166 18041 p 18822 p
11393 p 14018 s 15168 18042 po 18827 o
11603 po 14263 p 15191 po 18172 p 19078 p

19650 po 21401 p 21422 o 21873 p 22243 p
19858 f 21410 fp 21424 p 21887 p 22260 p
20473 p 21414 fp 21425 p 22185 s 22474 p
20960 p 21416 o 21467 s 22206 p 22486 po
20962 fp 21417 p 21847 p 22233 po 22991 s
20994 o 21421 o 21853 p

Secondary: Inclusions

10216 p 14280 p 16331 p 20111 s 21871 p
10261 s 14782 p 18808 p 20975 p 22205 s
11392 p 15186 s 18832 20981 p 22238 p
12772 p 15188 p 19709 p 21848 s 22817 o

Secondary: Journal Articles

10877 p 15159 p 18803 21386 f 22214
10878 s 15178 18821 s 21469 22216 s
11386 p 15179 s 18826 s 21473 po 22218 s
11401 po 16751 s 18830 p 21835 s 22246 s
14277 17581 19034 o 21846 p 22288 p
14284 18314 p 19653 p 21855 s 22483 s
14779 s 18786 p 19710 p 21865 p

1949-1972

Primary: Monographs

10134 o 11646 po 15304 o 20699 o 22750 o
10135 o 11654 p 15506 o 21574 fp 22751 o
10156 o 11883 o 15543 o 22375 po 22753 o
10162 o 12008 fp 15856 o 22500 o 22755 o
10165 o 12070 p 18354 o 22744 o 22760 o
10175 o 12109 p 19062 o 22746 p 22763 o
11135 o 14943 o 19302 p 22747 o 22764 o
11154 p 15123 o 20505 po 22749 p 22769 o
11627 f 15205 o

Primary: Inclusions

10179 p 14851 p 14852 p 20267 f 21549 o
22754 p 22762 s

Primary: Journal Articles

10310 p 12122 po 16008 f 21481 f 22759
10312 o 12129 p 16135 o 22317 p 22761 o
10939 p 14044 p 16478 o 22745 o 22765 p
11099 p 14072 p 17600 o 22748 p 22766 p
11649 po 14814 p 17602 22752 o 22767 o
11892 15269 s 17958 f 22756 p 22768 p
11954 p 15274 po 18220 p 22757 p 22770 f
12011 p 15620 p 18245 p 22758 f

Secondary: Monographs

10130 o 10172 po 11144 o 14974 po 19063 po
10132 o 10174 o 11625 p 15297 o 19069 po
10133 o 10401 f 11885 p 15493 o 19422 p
10140 o 10421 fp 11894 o 15524 o 19591 o
10142 p 10427 fp 12002 p 15526 o 20272 fp
10144 o 10937 po 12027 p 15572 fp 20502 o
10145 o 10978 o 12123 p 15828 o 20688 o
10149 o 10989 p 12811 o 15830 o 21563 po
10150 o 10997 p 13366 p 16132 o 21570 fp
10153 o 11003 p 14305 p 16786 f 21578 o
10159 o 11087 o 14369 o 16787 fp 21585 o
10164 o 11094 p 14829 o 16798 fp 21936 o
10168 o 11106 o 14885 p 16806 f 21937 p
10170 o 11113 p 14921 p 17589 f

Secondary: Inclusions

10163 p 11484 p 13408 p 15497 p 21486 o
10918 p 11942 p 14324 p 16357 f 21920 s
10919 p 12121 p 14393 o 17808 o 21934 p
10921 13333 p 15101 p 18340 p 21958 p
11007 p 13357 s 15243 o 20081 p 23034 o

Secondary: Journal Articles

10411 p 11645 p 14877 o 18228 p 21548 o
10911 p 12116 p 14879 o 18352 p 21560 s
10922 p 12117 p 14938 o 19067 o 21967 o
10941 p 12131 o 15008 o 19068 o 21973 p
10950 o 12153 p 15266 s 19187 s 21975 po
10957 p 12431 o 16042 f 19392 p 22023 f
11112 s 12505 p 16839 p 19599 p 22306 p
11114 s 12797 p 16859 p 20520 p 22316 p
11129 12851 p 16894 o 20521 p 22365 o
11446 p 13106 o 17596 p 20529 f 22374 p
11453 p 13401 s 17653 o 20668 o 22828 s
11500 p 14039 p 17749 o 21096 o 22834 po
11533 p 14367 o 17780 o 21134 o 22852 fp
11636 o 14826 o 18222 p 21487

70 Chinese Scholars of Chinese Society
華人研究中國社會
中国人学者による中国社会研究

1644-1842

Primary 19440 p 22772 p 22776 p 22779 p
11011 p 21700 s 22773 p

Second. 10552 p 11682 p 12190 p 21679 p
22637 p

1644-1911

Primary 21289 p 21702 s 22777 p 22781 p
10681 p 21632 p 21716 22780 p 22866 p
21276 p 21678 p 22053 p

Second. 11234 p 15863 p 20154 p 21619 p
11202 p 13859 s 15935 p

1842-1911

Primary 22399 s 22771 p 22775 s 22860 po
19438 p 22518 p 22774 p 22778

Second. 15128 s 18092 p 18414 s 21299 p
10569 16525 p 18375 p 18463 p 22543 p
13858 p 18079 p 18382 p 18506 p 22634 p
13860 p

1842-1928
(including 1644-1928)

Primary 16110 p 21361 p 21765 po 21769
22111 p

Second. 14105 s 21318 p 21757 s 21793 p
11261 p 20047 p 21723 po

1911-1928

Primary 14741 o 22802 fp 22804 s

Second. 18719 p 22142 p

1911-1949
(including 1644-1949, 1842-1949)

Primary 21357 p 22783 s 22789 s 22796 s
10717 po 21743 p 22784 p 22791 s 22801 o
12270 p 21747 p 22785 s 22792 s 22803 s
14678 s 21792 s 22786 p 22793 o 22805 o
18651 s 21803 p 22787 s 22794 22916 s
19397 o 22782 p 22788 s 22795 o 22932 s
19637 o

Second. 13217 p 14641 o 19393 p 22660 po
11264 p 14231 p 16255 s 22432 p 22679 s
11693 p

1928-1949

Primary 17734 fp 22790 o 22798 o 22800 o
10095 o 19399 o 22797 o 22799 o 22928 o
13018 s

Second. 13943 o 17839 18634 p 19401 o
22940 o

1928-1972
(incl. 1644-1972, 1842-1972, 1911-1972)

Primary 21402 21872 p 22477 p 22816 p
10862 p 21830 s 21876 p 22489 s 22817 o
10892 p 21831 p 21877 s 22493 s 22818 s
11858 p 21840 s 21878 s 22806 p 22819 s
11871 s 21841 p 21882 p 22807 s 22820 p
12411 p 21845 p 21887 p 22808 o 22821 o
12785 s 21846 p 21891 p 22809 p 22822 o
14256 21847 p 21892 s 22810 s 22823 s
14267 p 21853 p 21893 p 22811 22824 s
14270 p 21857 p 21894 s 22812 s 22954 p
18800 p 21858 p 21902 p 22813 p 22961 s
20970 p 21865 p 21903 s 22814 s 22964 s
21392 po 21866 p 22288 p 22815 p 23007 p

Second. 17951 s 19657 p 21898 po 22475 p
10211 p 17953 p 21848 s 22193 22487
10220 p 18791 p 21859 p 22223 p 22951 s
12410 s 19079 f 21864 s 22244 p 22970 s
15452 po 19403 21885 s 22473 s 22978 s

1949-1972

Primary 21921 p 22335 p 22835 p 22848 o
11471 p 21923 p 22378 p 22836 s 22849 p
12801 p 21929 p 22756 p 22837 s 22850 o
14378 p 21931 p 22825 22838 s 22851 s
14871 p 21935 p 22826 22839 p 22852 fp
14912 o 21954 p 22827 p 22840 o 22853
17964 p 21956 p 22828 s 22841 p 22854 o
17972 s 21959 p 22829 p 22842 p 22855 o
19411 o 21968 p 22830 s 22843 p 22856
21102 o 21972 p 22831 p 22844 p 22857 s
21910 p 21973 p 22832 s 22845 s 22858 o
21916 p 21976 22833 p 22846 23042 po
21920 s 22327 p 22834 po 22847 o 23058 o

Second. 14299 p 15016 o 20319 f 21934 p
10235 p 14327 p 15511 o 20333 fp 21942 p
10313 p 14343 p 15517 f 20361 p 21979 p
10467 p 14522 p 19414 p 20372 f 22350 p
11482 p 14841 o 19416 o 21009 fp 23011 o
13408 p 15015 p 19922 p 21907 p 23032 s
14135 p

71 Non-Chinese Scholars of Chinese Society
外人研究中國社會
外国人学者による中国社会研究

1644-1842

Primary 22872 p 22875 p 22878 p 22883
10552 p 22874 p 22876 s 22880 22885 s
22865 s

Second. 10533 po 11563 p 11682 p 18425 p
22773 p

1644-1911

Primary 11677 s 22866 p 22871 s 22887 s
11198 p 21678 p 22869 s 22882 p 22888 s
11225 s 22864 s 22870 s 22886 s

Second. 10681 p 11208 p 13859 s 17927 fp
10669 p 11016 s 11234 p 14089 s 21441 s

1842-1911

Primary 22859 o 22862 s 22868 s 22879 s
18914 o 22860 po 22863 o 22873 o 22881 s
22771 p 22861 o 22867 s 22877 p 22884 s

Second. 13860 p 18079 p 18382 p 19438 p
10663 p 16931 o 18375 p 18506 p 20601 o

1842-1928
(including 1644-1928)

Primary 22423 po 22898 s 22911 o 22919 s
11589 p 22889 22902 s 22912 o 22920 s
11709 22895 s 22904 s 22915 s 22922 s
21742 s 22896 s 22907 s

Second. 11275 po 12221 p 14105 s 14402 p
14403 p 15952 o

1911-1928

Primary 22927 s 22930 s 22934 s 22944 o
22804 s 22929 s 22931 s

Second. 12361 p 18764 o 19500 p

1911-1949
(including 1644-1949, 1842-1949)

Primary 18651 s 22784 p 22805 o 22892 s
10195 p 19637 o 22788 s 22890 22893 o
16112 s 22651 s 22793 o 22891 22894 s
22897 22906 s 22914 p 22923 fp 22933 s
22899 s 22908 22916 s 22924 p 22936 s
22900 22909 22917 s 22925 s 22937 o
22901 22910 s 22918 22926 p 22939 p
22903 s 22913 s 22921 22932 s 22943 s
22905 o

Second. 11693 p 18564 s 22660 po 22785 s
10193 s 13217 p 19801 p 22679 s 22787 s
10337 p 16255 s 21776 p

1928-1949

Primary 22928 o 22938 p 22941 p 22942 s
22797 o 22935 p 22940 o

Second. 19399 o 20873 fp 22799 o

1928-1972
(incl. 1644-1972, 1842-1972, 1911-1972)

Primary: Monographs
10862 p 22950 s 22962 s 22982 p 22991 s
11858 p 22954 p 22974 s 22985 o 23003 s
22819 s 22961 s 22978 s 22986

Primary: Inclusions
21878 s 22813 p 22945 s 22956 s 22997 s
23002 p

Primary: Journal Articles
10869 p 22951 s 22967 s 22981 s 22996
10878 s 22952 o 22968 s 22983 22998 s
11049 22953 s 22969 22984 s 22999
12411 p 22955 p 22970 s 22987 s 23000 s
18800 p 22957 s 22971 s 22988 s 23001 s
21403 s 22958 p 22972 p 22989 23004 s
21903 s 22959 s 22973 s 22990 s 23005 s
22812 s 22960 s 22975 22992 p 23006 s
22946 o 22963 s 22976 s 22993 s 23007 p
22947 p 22964 s 22977 s 22994 s 23008 s
22948 s 22965 s 22979 s 22995 s 23009 o
22949 22966 22980 s

Second. 11869 p 17951 s 21859 p 21901 s
10116 s 12410 s 17953 p 21864 s 22493 s
10211 p 14267 p 19035 po 21871 p 22733 p
10216 p 15166 21842 p

1949-1972

Primary 23015 s 23027 o 23038 o 23049
10982 23016 o 23028 s 23039 p 23050 s
10998 s 23017 23029 s 23040 f 23051 o
12046 s 23018 s 23030 o 23041 o 23052 o
13414 s 23019 o 23031 s 23042 po 23053 o
15280 s 23020 23032 s 23043 s 23054 s
22835 p 23021 f 23033 s 23044 s 23055
23010 s 23022 s 23034 o 23045 o 23056 p
23011 o 23023 s 23035 o 23046 p/ 23057
23012 s 23024 s 23036 o 23047 23058 o
23013 23025 o 23037 23048 s 23059 o
23014 s 23026 s

Second. 11973 p 14339 s 17972 s 19988 s
11531 14297 s 14343 p 19416 o 20333 fp

72 Bibliography
書目　書誌

1644-1842

Primary 12190 p 17173 p 22875 p

Second. 12198 p 16517 p 21686 p 22779 p
10552 p 13132 p 18891 p 21700 s

1644-1911

Primary 10325 po 10635 p 11234 p 11666 p
16519 s 22866 p

Second. 11241 p 16389 po 18920 fp 20776 po
10333 p 12201 p 18421 p 18930 po 21659 p
10574 p 12572 p 18519 p 18937 p 22781 p
10667 p 15729 po 18915 fp 20741 p

Geographic Index

A subject index to entries, arranged by geographic region and showing historical era and type of place

地理索引

款目内容索引、依地理區域排列、並示歷史時代及城鄉類別

地理索引

地区別並びに時代、都市郷村の区別を示す解題索引

"Primary" and "Secondary" (or "Second.") refer to the relative usefulness of the entry for the subject in question. Open squares indicate that the Bibliography lacks entries so classified. Letter suffixes indicate historical era: T (Traditional) for before 1911, R (Republican) for 1911–1949, C (Contemporary) for after 1949. Italic number suffixes are Type-of-place codes (see p. xxxvii or the back end-papers). The structure of this index is described fully on p. xli.

10 Chinese Society in General

中國社會通論 中国社会一般

Geographic China Broadly Conceived

Primary 10045 T *2* 10106 R *2* 10853 TRC*2*
10001 T *2* 10048 T *2* 10107 R *2* 10854 TRC*1*
10004 T *2* 10052 T *2* 10108 R *2* 10891 TRC*1*
10008 T *2* 10053 T *2* 10111 TRC*2* 11709 TR *2*
10010 T *2* 10058 T *2* 10113 TRC*2* 12233 TR *2*
10013 T *2* 10060 T *2* 10114 TRC*2* 12941 T *2*
10014 T *2* 10070 TR *2* 10117 TRC*2* 13812 T *2*
10015 T *1* 10073 TR *2* 10118 RC*2* 14126 TRC*2*
10016 T *2* 10074 TR *2* 10119 TRC*2* 15044 T *2*
10017 T *2* 10075 TR *2* 10129 TRC*2* 15185 TRC*2*
10022 T *2* 10076 TR *2* 10139 C*2* 18409 T *2*
10024 T *2* 10077 TR *2* 10144 C*2* 21855 TRC*2*
10025 T *2* 10082 TR *2* 10162 C*2* 22877 T *1*
10026 T *2* 10085 TR *2* 10177 C*2* 22886 T *1*
10032 T *2* 10093 R *2* 10331 T *2* 22984 TRC*1*
10034 T *2* 10096 R *2* 10560 T *2* 22995 TRC*2*
10042 T *2* 10100 R *2* 10611 T *2* 22996 TRC*2*

Secondary: *Not used*

Mainland China

Primary: Monographs
10002 T *2* 10072 TR *2* 10130 C*2* 10173 C*2*
10003 T *2* 10079 TR *2* 10132 C*2* 10180 C*2*
10005 T *2* 10081 TR *2* 10133 C*2* 10349 TR *2*
10007 T *2* 10083 TR *2* 10134 C*2* 10712 TR *2*
10011 T *2* 10086 TR *2* 10135 C*2* 10715 TR *2*
10019 T *2* 10088 R *2* 10136 C*2* 10778 R *2*
10020 T *2* 10089 R *2* 10140 C*2* 10883 TRC*2*
10023 T *2* 10090 R *2* 10142 C*2* 10893 TRC*2*
10029 T *2* 10092 R *2* 10143 C*2* 11003 C*2*
10030 T *2* 10094 R *2* 10145 C*2* 11689 TR *2*
10035 T *2* 10097 R *2* 10148 C*2* 12963 TR *2*
10036 T *2* 10098 R *2* 10149 C*2* 14119 R *2*
10039 T *2* 10099 R *2* 10150 C*2* 15006 C*2*
10041 T *2* 10101 R *2* 10152 C*2* 15150 R *2*
10043 T *2* 10103 R *2* 10153 C*2* 15241 C*2*
10044 T *2* 10104 R *2* 10154 C*2* 15509 C*2*
10047 T *2* 10105 R *2* 10155 C*2* 18170 RC*2*
10049 T *2* 10110 TRC*2* 10156 C*2* 18585 R *2*
10055 T *2* 10112 TRC*2* 10157 C*2* 18661 R *2*
10059 T *2* 10115 RC*2* 10159 C*2* 18722 R *2*
10061 T *2* 10120 TRC*2* 10160 C*2* 20639 R *2*
10062 T *2* 10121 RC*2* 10164 C*2* 21476 TRC*2*
10065 T *2* 10123 RC*2* 10165 C*2* 22644 TR *2*
10067 TR *2* 10124 TRC*2* 10167 C*2* 22648 TR *2*
10068 TR *2* 10125 RC*2* 10168 C*2* 22734 RC*2*
10069 TR *2* 10126 RC*2* 10169 C*2* 22950 TRC*2*
10071 TR *2* 10128 TRC*2* 10172 C*2*

Primary: Inclusions
10012 T *2* 10080 TR *2* 10131 C*1* 11459 C*1*
10037 T *2* 10109 TRC*1* 10147 C*2* 18556 TR *1*
10051 T *2* 10122 RC*2* 10151 C*2* 21930 C*2*
10078 TR *2* 10127 TRC*2* 10171 C*2* 22287 RC*1*

Primary: Journal Articles
10009 T *2* 10166 C*2* 10869 TRC*1* 21474 TRC*2*
10033 T *2* 10233 C*2* 11049 TRC*1* 22246 TRC*2*
10063 T *2* 10342 TR *2* 11054 TRC*2* 22663 TR *2*
10084 TR *2* 10347 TR *2* 15132 TR *2* 23007 TRC*1*
10095 R *1* 10532 T *1* 15133 TR *2* 23018 C*1*
10146 C*2* 10846 TRC*1* 15204 C*1*

Secondary: *Not used*

The Eighteen Provinces

Primary 10054 T *2* 10138 C*2* 10175 C*2*
10006 T *2* 10056 T *2* 10141 C*2* 11061 C*2*
10018 T *2* 10087 R *2* 10158 C*2* 11667 T *2*
10021 T *2* 10091 R *2* 10161 C*2* 19245 R *2*
10027 T *2* 10102 R *2* 10170 C*2* 21786 TR *1*
10038 T *2* 10116 TRC*1* 10174 C*2* 22923 TR *2*
10050 T *2*

Secondary: *Not used*

North China Broadly Conceived

Primary 10040 T *2* 10057 T *1* 10064 T *2*
10066 T *2*

Secondary: *Not used*

Manchuria

Primary 10163 C*2* 11677 T *2*

Secondary: *Not used*

Northern China

Primary 10178 C*2*

Secondary: *Not used*

Northwestern China and Frontier Regions

Primary 10176 C*2*

Secondary: *Not used*

South China Broadly Conceived

Primary 10028 T *2* 10031 T *2* 10046 T *2*
10137 C*2* 10593 T *1*

Secondary: *Not used*

East Central China

□

Central Yangtze Provinces

□

Southwestern China

Primary 10179 C*2*

Secondary: *Not used*

Southeastern China

□

Taiwan Only

Not applicable

Hong Kong and Macau Only

Not applicable

11 National Population

全國人口 国民総人口

Geographic China Broadly Conceived

Primary 10202 TR *1* 10215 RC*2* 10276 T *2*
10060 T *2* 10204 R *1* 10216 TRC*2* 10329 T *2*
10076 TR *2* 10207 R *2* 10217 RC*2* 10346 TR *2*
10186 T *1* 10210 TRC*2* 10220 TRC*2* 10367 R *2*
10188 T *2* 10211 TRC*1* 10221 RC*2* 12160 C*2*
10197 TR *2* 10212 RC*1* 10222 TRC*2* 12759 R *2*
10200 TR *2*

Second. 10107 R *2* 10386 RC*2* 12019 C*2*
10008 T *2* 10108 R *2* 10396 TRC*2* 12416 RC*2*
10010 T *2* 10113 TRC*2* 10397 TRC*2* 12957 TR *2*
10026 T *2* 10129 TRC*2* 10432 C*2* 15126 T *2*
10042 T *2* 10277 T *2* 10526 T *2* 15161 TRC*2*
10048 T *2* 10284 TR *1* 10586 T *1* 18919 T *1*
10052 T *2* 10286 TR *1* 11317 R *1* 20306 C*2*
10073 TR *2* 10328 T *2* 11665 T *2* 22578 T *2*
10093 R *2* 10363 R *2* 11709 TR *2* 22922 TR *1*
10106 R *2* 10377 R *2* 11859 TRC*2*

Mainland China

Primary: Monographs
10035 T *2* 10223 C*2* 10338 TR *2* 12218 TR *2*
10044 T *2* 10226 C*2* 10424 C*2* 12303 R *2*
10136 C*2* 10228 C*2* 10425 C*2* 15652 C*2*
10191 TR *2* 10232 C*2* 10498 C*2* 20302 R *2*
10201 TR *2* 10240 C*2* 11752 R *2* 20328 C*2*
10214 TRC*2* 10330 T *2* 12173 C*2*

Taiwan Only
PRIMARY 10307 c1
SECOND. □

Hong Kong and Macau Only
PRIMARY 10306 c2 16002 c2 20120 c3
10301 rc2 10312 c3 19990 c8 21254 c2
10304 c3 15489 c3
SECOND. 15621 c4 17893 rc2 19929 c2
15611 trc2 15646 trc3 17899 rc2 20683 c3
15617 c2 15827 c4 17911 c3 22723 trc4
15618 c2 16491 c3

11.3 Macroecology and Settlement Patterns
全域性區位分佈及聚落型態
巨視的社会生態学及び定住様式

Geographic China Broadly Conceived
PRIMARY 10329 t 2 10377 r 2 10432 c2
10004 t 2 10331 t 2 10384 trc4 11853 trc2
10052 t 2 10336 t 2 10386 rc2 11859 trc2
10197 tr 2 10346 tr 2 10389 trc2 12416 rc2
10221 rc2 10361 r 2 10396 trc2 17036 tr 7
10259 trc4 10363 r 2 10397 trc2 18852 t 2
10261 trc4 10367 r 2 10407 c2 21855 trc2
10328 t 2
SECOND. 10217 rc2 12201 t 7 12629 tr 2
10118 rc2 10263 c2 12232 tr 7 13856 t 2
10119 trc2 10277 t 2 12348 r 2 20563 t 2
10129 trc2 12160 c2 12401 rc7

Mainland China
PRIMARY 10365 r 2 10413 c2 12434 c2
10062 t 2 10372 r 2 10414 c2 12556 c2
10201 tr 2 10374 r 2 10418 c2 12708 r 2
10260 rc2 10379 r 8 10419 c1 12765 trc4
10269 c4 10383 rc2 10420 c2 13006 r 2
10303 trc1 10390 rc2 10422 c2 13298 rc2
10320 t 2 10391 rc2 10424 c2 13311 trc2
10330 t 2 10393 trc2 10425 c2 13349 c2
10334 t 2 10399 c2 10433 c2 13410 c3
10338 tr 2 10400 c8 10890 trc2 13440 c2
10342 tr 2 10403 c2 11878 rc2 15756 tr 4
10347 tr 2 10405 c2 11880 c2 16014 c2
10349 tr 2 10408 c2 12295 r 2 16196 t 2
10352 tr 7 10409 c2 12302 r 2 16335 trc2
10353 tr 2 10410 c2 12323 r 8 18699 r 2
10355 tr 2 10411 c2 12399 trc8 19453 r 2
10360 r 2 10412 c2
SECOND. 10967 c2 12422 rc7 14659 tr 2
10039 t 2 10990 c1 12486 c2 15741 t 3
10086 tr 2 11815 r 2 12524 c2 15845 c7
10224 c2 11906 c2 12776 trc2 18862 t 2
10227 c2 11929 c2 12877 c2 18992 r 2
10228 c2 11947 c2 12949 tr 2 19121 c7
10230 c2 12256 r 7 13182 tr 2 20302 r 2
10255 tr 2 12324 r 8 13307 rc3 20690 c3
10257 r 4 12341 r 8 13393 c2 21465 r 2
10264 c2 12362 r 8 13432 c2 21677 t 2
10709 tr 4 12392 rc7 14127 rc2 22791 r 2
10905 c4 12415 rc2 14131 trc2

The Eighteen Provinces
PRIMARY 10350 tr 2 12345 r 2 15781 r 2
10209 r 2 10351 tr 7 12509 c8 15895 c8
10258 r 4 10371 r 8 12675 tr 2 16935 t 2
10322 t 2 10373 r 7 14101 t 2 17145 t 2
10333 t 2 10376 r 2 14217 tr 2 18645 r 7
10335 t 2 11784 r 2 15047 t 2 21897 trc2
10348 tr 2
SECOND. 11735 r 2 13801 t 2 15954 tr 5
10006 t 2 12827 c8 13925 r 2 17937 tr 2
10050 t 2 12890 t 2 14117 r 2

North China Broadly Conceived
PRIMARY 10404 c2 10450 r 2 11869 trc2
10343 tr 4 10417 c8 10452 r 2 12369 r 2
10370 r 2 10423 c7 10454 r 8 22660 tr 2
10402 c8 10435 c2 10455 rc8
SECOND. 10302 trc2 10476 c2 10580 t 2
12469 c8 12728 r 2

Manchuria
PRIMARY 10378 r 2 11797 r 2 15679 tr 7
10337 tr 2 10381 r 2 11825 r 2 15692 r 2
10340 tr 2 10398 trc2 13012 r 2 16434 r 7
10341 tr 2 10421 c2 15669 tr 2 16929 t 2
10354 tr 2 10428 c2 15676 tr 2 16961 r 2
10356 r 2 11671 t 2 15678 tr 2 17024 t 2
10364 r 2
SECOND. 12643 tr 2 15585 tr 2 16383 t 2
11732 r 2 12687 tr 2 15588 tr 2

Northern China
PRIMARY 10319 t 2 10388 rc2 15883 c8
10317 t 2 10380 r 2 10431 c2 16928 t 2
SECOND. 16926 t 2

Northwestern China and Frontier Regions
PRIMARY 10415 c2 16751 trc2 16927 t 2
10332 t 2 10427 c2 16752 trc2 16957 r 2
10369 r 2 12857 c2 16786 c2 16984 trc2
10375 r 2 13332 c2 16896 c8 22732 trc2
10401 c2 15603 rc2
SECOND. 12003 c2 15667 tr 8 22738 rc2
10863 trc2 12330 r 8 15696 rc2 22754 c2
11686 tr 2 15609 rc2 16422 r 2

South China Broadly Conceived
PRIMARY 10344 tr 4 12297 r 7 16386 t 8
10289 tr 2 10366 r 3 12522 c8 16689 r 2
10323 t 2 10406 c2 12680 tr 2 17947 rc2
10326 t 2 10434 c2 12843 c2
SECOND. 16930 t 2

East Central China
PRIMARY 10321 t 2 10339 tr 2 10362 r 1
10368 r 2 10430 c2
SECOND. 12157 c2 12420 rc7

Central Yangtze Provinces
PRIMARY 10324 t 2 10395 trc2 13395 c4
16393 t 2
SECOND. 16526 t 2

Southwestern China
PRIMARY 10382 trc2 15740 t 2 16931 t 2
10318 t 2 10429 c2 16640 r 2 16932 t 2
10358 r 2 15413 r 2 16787 c2 18922 t 2
10359 r 2
SECOND. 16443 r 2 22552 t 8

Southeastern China
PRIMARY 10357 r 2 10426 c2 16552 tr 2
10327 t 2 10392 trc2 12069 c2 17025 t 2
SECOND. 15334 t 2 16391 t 2 16558 tr 7
17547 t 2

Taiwan Only
PRIMARY 10385 rc2 10416 c2 15825 c2
10325 t 2 10387 trc2 10436 c2 15826 c2
10345 tr 2 10394 rc2 15792 trc5 16726 trc2
SECOND. 13083 c2 15698 trc2 16347 c2
11844 trc2 13297 rc2 15917 c2 21233 rc2
12106 c2

Hong Kong and Macau Only
□

11.4 National Labor Force & Occupational Differentiation
全國勞動力及職業分化
国民総労働力及び職業分化

Geographic China Broadly Conceived
PRIMARY 10445 r 2 10447 r 3 20160 tr 2
10261 trc4 10446 r 2 14475 r 2 20222 r 3
10438 t 7
SECOND. 10407 c2 11892 c2 14145 c2
10053 t 2 10432 c2 12233 tr 2 14465 r 5
10217 rc2 11045 rc2 13129 t 5 19546 r 3
10263 c2 11384 trc2 14098 t 2 20463 r 3
10284 tr 1 11694 tr 2 14102 t 2 21904 rc2
10386 rc2

Mainland China
PRIMARY: MONOGRAPHS
10448 r 2 10488 c2 11912 c2 14793 rc1
10460 c8 10498 c2 11996 c2 14882 c2
10464 c4 10500 c4 12086 c2 14885 c1
10466 c7 10503 c2 12109 c2 14969 c2
10470 c4 11752 r 2 12423 trc7 15025 c2
10477 c2 11783 r 2 12787 c2 15028 c2
10479 c4 11864 rc2 13336 c2 15085 rc2
10481 c2 11874 rc2 13365 c2 19389 c1
10487 c2 11894 c2 14522 c2 22293 c2
PRIMARY: INCLUSIONS
10441 t 2 10469 c2 10493 c2 13444 c2
10453 r 2 10478 c2 10497 c2 14147 c2
10456 rc2 10484 c2 10499 c2 14967 c2
10463 c4 10485 c2 12010 c2 15293 c7
10468 c2 10486 c2 12415 rc2
PRIMARY: JOURNAL ARTICLES
10251 c2 10472 c2 10495 c4 12448 c7
10308 c2 10473 c2 10496 c2 12504 c7
10440 t 2 10474 c2 10501 c2 12521 c2
10442 r 2 10480 c2 10502 c7 13233 r 2
10451 r 2 10482 c2 11172 c2 13295 rc4
10457 c1 10483 c5 11963 c2 14259 rc4
10459 c2 10489 c7 11967 c2 14532 c2
10461 c2 10490 c2 11992 c2 14813 c1
10462 c7 10491 c2 12084 c2 14814 c4
10465 c2 10492 c2 12119 c2 21250 c2
10467 c2 10494 c3 12431 c2
SECONDARY: MONOGRAPHS
10154 c2 11906 c2 13308 rc2 17757 tr 4
10157 c2 11920 c2 13328 c2 18185 rc2
10240 c2 11928 c2 13353 c2 18225 c2
10338 tr 2 11949 c2 13384 c2 18617 r 2
10906 c2 11962 c2 13945 r 2 18647 r 2
10999 c1 11980 c2 13986 trc2 18708 r 2
11101 c2 12000 c2 14258 rc2 18720 r 2
11689 tr 2 12044 c2 14310 c5 18733 r 2
11754 r 2 12054 c2 14337 c2 19551 r 2
11756 r 2 12096 c2 14378 c4 19583 rc4
11812 r 2 12173 c2 14736 r 4 19655 rc2
11845 rc2 12358 r 2 14828 c2 19668 c5
11848 rc2 12525 c2 14833 c1 20314 c2
11849 trc2 12535 c2 14853 c2 20484 c2
11852 rc2 12853 c2 15022 c1 20837 r 2
11862 rc2 13104 c2 15112 c2 21677 t 2
11891 c2
SECONDARY: INCLUSIONS
10254 tr 2 12009 c2 13327 c1 15071 r 2
10295 r 2 12042 c2 13435 c2 15303 c2
11002 c2 12156 c2 14043 c1 19198 c2
11176 c2 12159 c2 14138 c2 19409 c1
11847 rc2 13097 c2 14880 c2 20228 rc2
11989 c2 13259 r 2 14901 c1 20371 c2
SECONDARY: JOURNAL ARTICLES
10236 c2 11717 tr 2 11947 c2 12167 c2
10238 c2 11814 r 2 11987 c2 12170 c4
10246 c1 11815 r 2 12004 c2 12177 c2
10260 rc2 11854 rc2 12012 c2 12425 trc8
10305 c2 11895 c2 12059 c2 12774 rc2
10311 c2 11913 c2 12094 c2 12961 tr 2
10896 c2 11932 c2 12120 c2 13056 c7
11022 r 2 11941 c2 12141 c2 13109 c2
11093 c1 11944 c2 12153 c2 13115 c2

13149 TR 2 13433 C2 14832 C1 19145 C7
13197 R 3 14028 C1 14897 C1 19473 TR 4
13263 R 2 14141 C2 14920 C1 21047 C1
13320 C1 14446 C2 14959 C2 21914 C1
13321 C4 14612 T 2 14971 C2 22239 RC2
13426 C2 14827 C2 18580 R 2 22839 C2
13427 C2

The Eighteen Provinces

Primary 10443 R 2 14250 R 1 19350 T 4
10205 R 2 10444 R 2 14456 TR 2 20178 TR 2
10437 T 2 10449 R 2 14493 R 4 20193 R 2
10439 T 1 11784 R 2 15080 R 2 22067 T 2
Second. 12573 T 2 12933 T 2 20144 T 1
11735 R 2 12794 C2 13153 TR 2 20606 T 2
12247 R 7 12827 C8 14424 TR 7 21225 R 7

North China Broadly Conceived

Primary 10450 R 2 10455 RC8 10475 C2
10370 R 2 10452 R 2 10458 C8 10476 C2
10423 C7 10454 R 8 10471 C2 12421 RC7
Second. 10302 TRC2 10577 T 1 17873 R 2

South China Broadly Conceived

Primary □
Second. 10289 TR 2 11729 R 2 18463 T 2

12 National Political System and Bureaucracy

政制及吏治

政治制度及び官僚制

Geographic China Broadly Conceived

Primary: Monographs
10008 T 2 10573 T 1 10865 TRC3 18450 T 2
10010 T 2 10586 T 1 10891 TRC1 18492 T 2
10013 T 2 10611 T 2 11241 T 2 18540 TR 2
10014 T 2 10614 T 1 11250 TR 1 18542 TR 2
10016 T 2 10615 T 2 11418 RC1 18579 R 2
10017 T 2 10619 T 1 11858 TRC2 18687 R 2
10022 T 2 10626 T 2 12629 TR 2 18700 R 2
10026 T 2 10634 T 1 12657 TR 4 18801 TRC2
10042 T 2 10645 T 1 12957 TR 2 18809 RC2
10048 T 2 10657 T 1 13762 TRC1 18871 T 2
10053 T 2 10665 T 1 13812 T 2 18936 T 2
10058 T 2 10684 TR 2 13841 T 4 18937 T 2
10060 T 2 10700 TR 2 13876 TR 2 19503 R 2
10082 TR 2 10707 TR 2 14155 T 2 20615 TR 2
10085 TR 2 10713 TR 2 14156 T 2 21262 T 2
10111 TRC2 10716 TR 1 14167 T 2 21279 T 2
10113 TRC2 10773 R 1 14174 T 3 21302 T 2
10114 TRC2 10803 R 2 14193 T 1 21350 TR 3
10129 TRC2 10804 R 3 14627 T 1 21467 TRC1
10329 T 2 10806 R 2 15158 TRC2 22586 T 3
10526 T 2 10823 R 1 15161 TRC2 22657 TR 1
10539 T 1 10828 R 2 15166 TRC2 22672 TR 1
10541 T 1 10850 RC1 15174 TRC2 22681 R 3
10550 T 1 10853 TRC2 18077 T 2 22740 TRC2
10557 T 1 10862 TRC2 18125 R 1 22866 T 2
10560 T 2

Primary: Inclusions
10073 TR 2 10646 T 4 13856 T 2 20418 T 1
10220 TRC2 10866 RC3 13878 TR 2 21712 T 2
10510 T 2 10892 TRC2 15185 TRC2 22578 T 2
10596 T 1 11556 T 1 18073 T 2 22588 T 1
10627 T 2 11673 T 2 18558 TR 2

Primary: Journal Articles
10534 T 2 10666 T 2 10875 RC1 15130 T 2
10537 T 1 10681 T 1 11278 TR 1 15194 TRC2
10553 T 1 10704 TR 2 11544 T 1 18549 TR 3
10564 T 2 10714 TR 1 12679 TR 1 21296 T 1
10585 T 1 10736 TR 1 13950 R 2 21377 R 2
10617 T 1 10741 R 1 13985 RC1 22024 T 1
10618 T 1 10854 TRC1 14089 T 1 22080 TR 1
10655 T 1 10860 TRC1 14184 T 1 22085 TR 1
10663 T 2 10864 RC1 14211 T 1 22345 C2
10664 T 2 10867 RC2

Secondary: Monographs
10004 T 2 11857 TRC2 17572 R 3 21342 TR 2
10015 T 1 12575 T 2 18102 TR 2 21347 TR 2
10034 T 2 12593 T 2 18375 T 2 21349 TR 1
10045 T 2 12598 T 2 18379 T 1 21392 TRC2
10070 TR 2 12730 R 1 18409 T 2 21404 TRC1
10076 TR 2 12918 T 4 18494 T 2 21412 RC2
10077 TR 2 12965 TR 4 18511 T 2 21425 TRC5
10100 R 2 13502 TR 1 18514 T 2 21427 TRC1
10106 R 2 13627 T 2 18534 TR 2 21435 C2
10107 R 2 13658 TR 3 18545 TR 2 21538 TRC2
10108 R 2 13824 T 2 18560 TR 2 21579 C2
10259 TRC4 13844 T 1 18707 R 2 21847 TRC2
10331 T 2 13846 T 2 18764 R 2 21904 RC2
10346 TR 2 13873 TR 2 18904 T 2 22074 T 2
11047 RC2 13916 R 2 20050 TR 2 22082 TR 1
11257 TR 1 14215 TR 2 20083 T 1 22095 TR 2
11270 TR 4 14951 C2 20659 TRC4 22101 TR 1
11317 R 1 15136 TR 2 20960 TRC2 22555 T 2
11665 T 2 15773 R 2 21269 T 2 22594 T 2
11692 TR 2 15956 TR 2 21276 T 2 22629 T 2
11703 TR 2 16068 RC2 21291 T 2 22631 T 1
11709 TR 2 16376 T 2 21306 TR 2 22650 TR 3
11841 R 2 17531 T 1

Secondary: Inclusions
10210 TRC2 12940 T 1 14097 T 2 20563 T 2
12190 T 2 13571 R 2 14248 R 2 22779 T 1
12589 T 2 13705 R 2 14621 T 1 22919 TR 1
12922 T 3 13848 T 1 18368 T 1

Secondary: Journal Articles
10186 T 1 12898 T 4 15044 T 2 22515 T 3
10384 TRC4 13106 C4 15126 T 2 22634 T 1
11296 TR 1 13497 TR 4 16128 TRC2 22640 T 1
11384 TRC2 13717 R 2 18489 T 1 22651 TR 2
12188 T 2 13733 R 4 18786 TRC2 22886 T 1
12223 TR 7 13747 R 3 21327 TR 2 22984 TRC1
12585 T 2 14185 T 1 21855 TRC2

Mainland China

Primary: Monographs
10005 T 2 10574 T 1 10758 R 4 10938 C4
10011 T 2 10587 T 2 10765 R 1 10943 C2
10019 T 2 10599 T 2 10768 R 4 10944 C1
10020 T 2 10600 T 4 10769 R 2 10947 C1
10029 T 2 10613 T 1 10778 R 2 10948 C1
10030 T 2 10631 T 2 10779 R 1 10953 C2
10035 T 2 10640 T 4 10780 R 1 10960 C2
10036 T 2 10643 T 1 10782 R 1 10961 C1
10039 T 2 10654 T 3 10785 R 1 10962 C4
10041 T 2 10660 T 2 10793 R 1 10970 C2
10043 T 2 10667 T 1 10795 R 4 10975 C2
10044 T 2 10669 T 1 10799 R 2 10978 C2
10047 T 2 10672 T 2 10807 R 1 10994 C2
10049 T 2 10676 T 2 10811 R 1 10997 C2
10062 T 2 10677 T 2 10812 R 2 10999 C1
10067 TR 2 10686 TR 1 10813 R 2 11000 C4
10072 TR 2 10688 TR 2 10814 R 2 11003 C2
10079 TR 2 10690 TR 1 10819 R 2 11005 C2
10088 R 2 10692 TR 1 10820 R 1 11006 C2
10089 R 2 10693 TR 1 10821 R 2 11036 TRC7
10090 R 2 10695 TR 2 10833 R 2 11048 TRC2
10098 R 2 10696 TR 1 10836 R 4 11087 C3
10101 R 2 10697 TR 2 10837 R 2 11094 C2
10103 R 2 10698 TR 2 10838 R 4 11104 C2
10104 R 2 10702 TR 2 10842 R 4 11183 T 1
10120 TRC2 10703 TR 4 10844 R 4 11193 T 1
10125 RC2 10706 TR 2 10845 R 1 11194 T 2
10132 C2 10709 TR 4 10851 RC2 11230 T 1
10133 C2 10711 TR 4 10858 TRC2 11235 T 1
10149 C2 10712 TR 2 10870 RC2 11243 T 2
10153 C2 10715 TR 2 10871 TRC1 11258 TR 1
10155 C2 10718 TR 2 10873 TRC2 11263 TR 1
10156 C2 10720 TR 1 10879 RC3 11279 TR 1
10165 C2 10721 TR 2 10883 TRC2 11289 TR 1
10167 C2 10724 TR 4 10885 RC4 11290 TR 1
10168 C2 10726 TR 2 10887 TRC2 11291 TR 2
10508 T 3 10727 TR 3 10888 TRC2 11297 TR 2
10516 T 2 10729 TR 2 10890 TRC2 11364 R 1
10519 T 4 10732 TR 2 10893 TRC2 11368 R 2
10548 T 2 10733 TR 2 10894 C1 11375 R 1
10551 T 4 10737 TR 1 10895 C2 11376 R 1
10558 T 1 10739 TR 1 10906 C2 11377 R 1
10559 T 4 10749 R 2 10931 C2 11393 TRC2
10562 T 1 10757 R 1 10937 C2 11496 C1
11699 TR 2 13945 R 2 18106 TR 2 18701 R 1
11702 TR 2 13961 R 1 18114 R 2 18717 R 2
11705 TR 2 13986 TRC2 18118 R 4 18720 R 2
11718 TR 2 14001 RC1 18120 R 2 18722 R 2
11724 R 2 14020 RC2 18123 R 2 18725 R 2
11745 R 2 14053 C1 18134 R 2 18760 R 2
11812 R 2 14093 T 2 18140 R 4 18804 TRC2
11829 R 2 14109 TR 2 18143 R 2 18817 RC2
11830 R 2 14164 T 2 18144 R 2 19390 C2
11872 RC2 14178 T 2 18154 R 2 19453 R 2
11885 C2 14179 T 1 18164 RC3 19719 T 2
11906 C2 14181 T 4 18170 RC2 20328 C2
12475 C2 14219 TR 2 18176 RC1 20492 C3
12524 C2 14230 TR 1 18178 RC2 21260 T 2
12532 C2 14231 TR 4 18264 C2 21265 T 2
12619 T 1 14329 C2 18277 C2 21363 TR 4
12795 C5 14385 C2 18296 C1 21373 R 1
12950 TR 2 14396 T 2 18298 C2 21422 TRC2
12963 TR 2 14478 R 3 18312 RC2 21644 T 2
13290 R 2 14599 T 2 18324 C2 22071 T 1
13353 C2 14637 TR 1 18378 T 2 22131 TR 2
13447 C2 14753 R 1 18387 T 2 22202 TRC1
13458 T 2 14754 R 2 18430 T 2 22260 RC1
13511 TR 2 15007 C4 18454 T 2 22269 RC1
13539 R 3 15163 RC2 18458 T 1 22572 T 2
13680 TR 1 15237 C2 18551 TR 2 22644 TR 2
13847 T 1 15241 C2 18563 TR 4 22655 TR 3
13858 T 2 15294 C2 18585 R 2 22658 TR 1
13882 TR 2 15938 TR 2 18588 R 2 22689 R 1
13896 R 2 16071 C2 18596 R 2 22714 R 2
13905 R 2 16148 C5 18610 R 2 22734 RC2
13928 R 2 17974 T 3 18629 R 2 22991 TRC2
13930 R 1 18098 T 3

Primary: Inclusions
10012 T 2 10694 TR 2 11458 C2 17644 C2
10037 T 2 10723 TR 2 11459 C1 17997 C1
10122 RC2 10750 R 2 11531 C1 18088 T 2
10506 T 1 10800 R 1 11617 C1 18112 R 3
10521 T 4 10847 TRC1 11978 C1 18119 R 2
10542 T 2 10856 RC2 12101 C2 18293 C2
10549 T 2 10859 TRC1 12168 C2 18343 C2
10554 T 1 10912 C2 13532 R 4 18370 T 2
10555 T 1 10915 C2 13859 T 2 18515 T 2
10561 T 2 10916 C2 14096 T 2 18533 TR 2
10579 T 1 10917 C2 14208 T 2 18555 TR 2
10597 T 1 10918 C4 14302 C3 18571 TR 2
10601 T 2 10919 C2 14344 C1 18601 R 2
10603 T 2 10920 C2 14372 C1 18799 RC2
10610 T 4 10930 C2 14562 T 1 18802 RC2
10616 T 2 10946 C3 14601 T 3 19324 C4
10624 T 1 10988 C2 15160 TRC1 19365 T 2
10637 T 3 10993 C2 15186 RC1 21432 C3
10642 T 2 11002 C2 15259 C2 22033 T 1
10650 T 2 11007 C1 15296 C1 22108 TR 1
10658 T 4 11010 T 2 15298 C3 22191 RC2
10659 T 4 11245 T 1 15314 T 2 22192 RC2
10662 T 2 11295 TR 1 17642 C2 22548 T 1
10671 T 3 11451 C1

Primary: Journal Articles
10033 T 2 10545 T 1 10691 TR 1 10775 R 2
10225 C2 10567 T 4 10699 TR 1 10777 R 1
10296 R 2 10571 T 1 10705 TR 1 10784 R 1
10383 RC2 10572 T 2 10710 TR 1 10786 R 2
10411 C2 10575 T 1 10717 TR 2 10788 R 4
10422 C2 10578 T 3 10722 TR 3 10789 R 5
10504 T 2 10583 T 1 10728 TR 1 10794 R 2
10509 T 4 10589 T 1 10731 TR 4 10802 R 1
10512 T 2 10604 T 1 10734 TR 2 10805 R 2
10513 T 4 10605 T 3 10738 TR 1 10808 R 1
10515 T 3 10609 T 1 10740 R 1 10809 R 2
10517 T 4 10620 T 2 10742 R 1 10810 R 1
10518 T 4 10621 T 4 10743 R 2 10815 R 1
10520 T 1 10622 T 5 10744 R 2 10817 R 1
10523 T 1 10628 T 2 10748 R 2 10818 R 4
10524 T 2 10629 T 2 10753 R 1 10822 R 1
10527 T 1 10633 T 1 10754 R 2 10826 R 2
10530 T 2 10635 T 1 10755 R 1 10829 R 1
10531 T 3 10648 T 4 10762 R 3 10834 R 2
10532 T 1 10649 T 4 10763 R 1 10835 R 4
10535 T 1 10661 T 2 10764 R 2 10846 TRC1
10536 T 2 10678 T 1 10766 R 2 10848 RC2
10538 T 1 10683 T 1 10771 R 4 10849 RC2
10540 T 1 10687 TR 1 10772 R 2 10861 RC1
10543 T 1 10689 TR 1 10774 R 2 10868 RC1

Secondary: Monographs

Secondary: Inclusions

Secondary: Journal Articles

The Eighteen Provinces

Primary: Monographs

Primary: Inclusions

Primary: Journal Articles

Secondary: Monographs

Secondary: Inclusions

Secondary: Journal Articles
10209 R *2* 12666 TR *3* 15662 T *2* 21295 T *1*
11187 T *1* 13813 T *2* 15751 T *4* 21473 TRC*2*
11215 T *4* 13879 TR *1* 15954 TR *5* 21678 T *2*
11224 T *1* 13938 R *2* 15960 R *2* 21883 TRC*1*
11319 R *1* 14090 T *1* 18083 T *1* 21996 TR *1*
11359 R *1* 14091 T *2* 18085 T *4* 22044 T *1*
11536 T *3* 14117 R *2* 18149 R *1* 22045 T *1*
11656 T *2* 14172 T *1* 18432 T *1* 22218 RC*1*
11725 R *2* 14188 T *1* 18546 TR *2* 22514 T *1*
11798 R *2* 14218 TR *4* 18679 R *2* 22603 T *1*
12573 T *2* 14225 TR *1* 20090 T *3* 22761 C*3*
12584 T *2* 14226 TR *1* 20257 T *1* 22776 T *2*
12664 TR *1* 14590 T *2* 21282 T *3*

North China Broadly Conceived

Primary 10825 R *2* 11727 R *1* 18493 T *2*
10066 T *2* 10827 R *2* 11791 R *2* 18678 R *2*
10577 T *1* 10830 R *2* 13810 T *2* 18682 R *2*
10580 T *2* 10907 C*3* 13832 T *2* 20549 T *2*
10679 T *2* 10936 C*3* 13962 R *2* 21287 T *2*
10792 R *2* 10969 C*3* 14210 T *2* 22562 T *3*
10798 R *2* 10989 C*5* 16119 R *2*

Second. 13954 R *2* 17028 T *5* 21292 T *2*
10040 T *2* 14195 T *3* 18146 R *2* 22532 T *2*
10064 T *2* 15324 T *2* 18160 R *3* 22584 T *2*
10454 R *8* 15752 T *2* 18307 R *2* 22623 T *2*
12577 T *2* 16430 R *2* 18732 R *2* 22695 R *2*

Manchuria

Primary 10719 TR *1* 10911 C*2* 12663 TR *2*
10163 C*2* 10745 R *2* 11015 T *2* 13147 TR *2*
10364 R *2* 10787 R *3* 11337 R *1* 13500 TR *2*
10581 T *1* 10796 R *2* 11732 R *2* 15936 T *2*
10582 T *2* 10824 R *2* 11777 R *2* 15995 C*2*
10647 T *1* 10852 RC*2* 11826 R *2* 20813 TR *2*
10685 TR *2* 10886 TRC*1* 12248 R *2*

Second. 11785 R *2* 13557 R *1* 16657 R *2*
11671 T *2* 11823 R *2* 13917 R *2* 17838 R *2*
11677 T *2* 11825 R *2* 15181 RC*2* 18739 R *2*
11691 TR *2* 12280 R *2* 15287 C*2* 20795 TR *2*
11712 TR *2* 13039 R *4* 15659 T *2* 22693 R *2*
11714 TR *2* 13258 R *2* 15680 R *2* 22718 R *1*
11715 TR *2*

Northern China

Primary 10606 T *3* 10941 C*3* 16903 T *3*
10178 C*2* 10607 T *3* 10945 C*3* 17570 R *2*
10505 T *3* 10612 T *3* 10977 C*3* 18092 T *3*
10514 T *2* 10644 T *2* 10996 C*3* 18235 C*3*
10528 T *3* 10652 T *3* 14163 T *3* 18398 T *2*
10529 T *3* 10673 T *3* 14182 T *3* 18467 T *3*
10547 T *3* 10730 TR *3* 14197 T *3* 20128 T *3*
10556 T *3* 10747 R *2* 14204 T *3* 20464 R *3*
10565 T *3* 10776 R *2* 14570 T *3* 20505 C*3*
10570 T *3* 10781 R *2* 14625 T *3* 20557 T *3*
10576 T *1* 10783 R *2* 15075 R *8* 20579 T *3*
10584 T *3* 10797 R *3* 15373 TR *3* 21169 T *3*
10591 T *3* 10816 R *2* 15538 C*2* 21293 T *3*
10595 T *3* 10898 C*3* 15958 R *3* 22747 C*2*
10598 T *2*

Second. 15452 TRC*2* 18868 T *2* 20479 C*3*
11568 T *3* 17334 C*2* 18990 TR *3* 20559 T *3*
11782 R *2* 18286 C*2* 19442 R *8* 20608 TR *3*
13974 R *2* 18348 C*2* 19452 R *2* 21278 T *3*
14157 T *3* 18422 T *3* 19779 T *3* 22612 T *2*
15037 T *2* 18498 T *3* 19825 R *3* 22617 T *2*

Northwestern China and Frontier Regions

Primary 10876 TRC*1* 12037 C*2* 22598 T *4*
10369 R *2* 10921 C*4* 13799 T *1* 22616 T *1*
10725 TR *2* 10922 C*1* 16517 T *2* 22732 TRC*2*
10759 R *2* 10939 C*2* 16647 R *2* 22749 C*2*
10863 TRC*2* 10957 C*1* 18340 C*2* 22754 C*2*
10874 TRC*2* 11582 TR *3* 22531 T *2* 22765 C*2*

Second. 13814 T *2* 16912 T *2* 20601 T *2*
10375 R *2* 15811 TRC*2* 17527 T *1* 21364 R *2*
11099 C*2* 16628 R *2* 18749 R *2* 22642 T *4*
12747 R *2* 16633 R *2* 18864 T *1* 22698 R *2*

South China Broadly Conceived

Primary 10641 T *2* 14262 RC*2* 18421 T *2*
10031 T *2* 10832 R *3* 15239 C*1* 18766 R *2*
10593 T *1* 11744 R *2* 17982 R *2* 19984 TRC*1*
10632 T *1* 12578 T *2* 18129 R *3* 21294 T *1*
10636 T *1* 13869 T *2* 18137 R *1* 22664 TR *4*

Second. 12920 T *4* 17543 T *2* 18455 T *2*
11014 T *2* 13881 TR *2* 18376 T *2* 18459 T *2*
11772 R *2* 13889 R *2* 18386 T *2* 18471 T *1*
12245 R *2* 15749 T *3* 18412 T *2* 18779 R *2*
12383 RC*2* 15928 T *2* 18449 T *2* 18875 T *2*
12680 TR *2* 16092 T *4*

East Central China

Primary 11552 T *1* 15924 T *2* 17162 T *3*
10751 R *2* 13544 R *2* 16394 T *2* 17411 T *2*
10770 R *3* 14161 T *2* 16525 T *8* 17646 C*2*
10801 R *4* 15254 C*3* 16908 T *2* 22539 T *2*
10841 R *3* 15291 C*3*

Second. 15727 T *3* 16943 R *2* 19069 C*3*
11121 C*2* 15744 T *2* 17161 T *3* 19566 R *3*
12157 C*2* 16113 TR *3* 17858 R *2* 19706 R *3*
13802 T *2* 16559 TR *2* 18466 T *2* 22536 T *3*
14606 T *3* 16638 R *2*

Central Yangtze Provinces

Primary 15155 R *2* 17539 T *2* 17630 TR *4*
18091 T *3* 18667 R *7*

Second. 13908 R *3* 15469 TRC*2* 18703 R *2*
20820 TR *2*

Southwestern China

Primary 10746 R *4* 13801 T *2* 18089 T *2*
10179 C*2* 10767 R *2* 14171 T *3* 18131 R *2*
10566 T *2* 10790 R *2* 14750 R *2* 18365 T *3*
10639 T *2* 10791 R *2* 15270 C*2* 18381 T *2*
10651 T *2* 13538 R *2* 15716 T *3* 18491 T *2*

Second. 13221 R *2* 18287 C*2* 18892 T *3*
11679 T *2* 15957 R *2* 18349 C*2* 18922 T *2*
12601 T *2* 16443 R *2* 18475 T *2* 22597 T *3*
12924 T *2*

Southeastern China

Primary 10708 TR *2* 11675 T *2* 15742 T *2*
10511 T *2* 10756 R *2* 14326 C*3* 16062 R *2*
10522 T *3* 10840 R *3* 15359 T *2* 16389 T *2*
10552 T *2* 10843 R *3* 15485 C*2* 17545 T *2*
10588 T *3* 10855 RC*2* 15497 C*2* 17657 T *3*
10625 T *1* 10935 C*1* 15725 T *5* 20894 R *2*
10668 T *2*

Second. 15334 T *2* 16839 C*2* 18488 T *5*
10271 T *4* 15735 T *2* 17151 T *3* 18742 R *2*
11683 TR *2* 15780 R *3* 17524 T *3* 18775 R *3*
13798 T *3* 15923 T *3* 17559 TR *2* 19371 C*2*
13808 T *3* 16218 T *2* 18428 T *3* 21271 T *2*
13854 T *1* 16396 T *2* 18483 T *2* 22398 T *4*
15263 C*2* 16530 T *2*

Taiwan Only

Primary 10923 C*3* 11109 C*1* 15439 R *2*
10325 T *2* 10950 C*2* 11134 C*1* 15441 R *2*
10638 T *1* 10955 C*1* 11417 RC*1* 15442 R *2*
10653 T *2* 10956 C*4* 11524 C*1* 15582 T *2*
10674 T *2* 10958 C*1* 11663 T *2* 16025 C*2*
10675 T *2* 10959 C*2* 11678 T *2* 16043 C*2*
10857 TRC*2* 10983 C*2* 14367 C*1* 16129 C*2*
10882 RC*2* 10984 C*2* 15351 T *2* 18263 C*2*
10904 C*2* 10985 C*3* 15369 TR *2* 18290 C*2*
10908 C*1* 11019 TR *2* 15438 R *2* 19769 T *2*
10914 C*1* 11044 RC*2*

Second. 12070 C*2* 15874 TRC*1* 18981 TR *2*
11108 C*1* 12078 C*1* 16729 RC*2* 20334 C*2*
11138 C*2* 13673 TR *4* 16812 C*2* 21009 C*2*
11166 C*1* 14224 TR *2* 16858 C*2* 22646 TR *2*
11232 T *2* 14549 C*4* 16898 C*2* 22741 TRC*2*
11690 TR *2* 15437 R *2* 18297 C*2* 22759 C*1*
12008 C*2* 15471 RC*2* 18650 R *1*

Hong Kong and Macau Only

Not applicable

12.1 State Controls of the Populace

政治控制　国家の大衆統制

Geographic China Broadly Conceived

Primary 10664 T *2* 11164 C*2* 18470 T *2*
10053 T *2* 10700 TR *2* 11328 R *1* 18786 TRC*2*
10096 R *2* 10704 TR *2* 11646 C*1* 18809 RC*2*
10139 C*2* 10854 TRC*1* 12233 TR *2* 20306 C*2*
10144 C*2* 11035 RC*2* 12401 RC*7* 20934 R *3*
10162 C*2* 11038 RC*2* 12772 TRC*2* 21279 T *2*
10526 T *2* 11045 RC*2* 13828 T *1* 21712 T *2*
10564 T *2* 11047 RC*2* 16186 T *2* 22645 TR *1*
10618 T *1* 11150 C*4* 18468 T *1*

Secondary: Monographs
10013 T *2* 10806 R *2* 13873 TR *2* 18707 R *2*
10048 T *2* 10828 R *2* 14113 TR *2* 18801 TRC*2*
10070 TR *2* 10853 TRC*2* 14694 TR *4* 19752 T *1*
10113 TRC*2* 10891 TRC*1* 15161 TRC*2* 20213 R *3*
10114 TRC*2* 11222 T *1* 15166 TRC*2* 20560 T *1*
10129 TRC*2* 11241 T *2* 15174 TRC*2* 20662 TRC*1*
10177 C*2* 11257 TR *1* 15175 RC*2* 20954 TRC*1*
10263 C*2* 11270 TR *4* 18299 C*2* 20960 TRC*2*
10277 T *2* 11301 TR *1* 18511 T *2* 21434 C*2*
10329 T *2* 11418 RC*1* 18514 T *2* 21435 C*2*
10586 T *1* 11708 TR *2* 18540 TR *2* 21538 TRC*2*
10615 T *2* 12439 C*8* 18542 TR *2* 21579 C*2*
10626 T *2* 12654 TR *4* 18579 R *2* 22002 TR *1*
10707 TR *2* 12957 TR *2* 18687 R *2* 22629 T *2*
10713 TR *2* 13811 T *2* 18700 R *2*

Secondary: Inclusions
10093 R *2* 13856 T *2* 18079 T *1* 20111 TRC*2*
10210 TRC*2* 14248 R *2* 18417 T *1* 20418 T *1*
10220 TRC*2* 15185 TRC*2* 18443 T *2* 22477 RC*1*
12678 TR *2* 17933 TR *1* 19546 R *3* 22813 TRC*1*

Secondary: Journal Articles
10186 T *1* 10860 TRC*1* 14098 T *2* 22024 T *1*
10663 T *2* 11213 T *2* 14102 T *2* 22284 TRC*1*
10666 T *2* 11278 TR *1* 14126 TRC*2* 22515 T *3*
10714 TR *1* 13017 R *3* 22014 TRC*1* 22984 TRC*1*

Mainland China

Primary: Monographs
10072 TR *2* 11027 R *2* 11534 C*2* 15176 RC*2*
10115 RC*2* 11036 TRC*7* 11783 R *2* 15214 C*2*
10140 C*2* 11040 RC*4* 11848 RC*2* 15230 C*2*
10148 C*2* 11046 RC*1* 11849 TRC*2* 15235 C*2*
10150 C*2* 11048 TRC*2* 11883 C*2* 15237 C*2*
10152 C*2* 11052 RC*2* 11894 C*2* 15241 C*2*
10155 C*2* 11053 RC*2* 12001 C*2* 15260 C*2*
10157 C*2* 11069 C*2* 12082 C*2* 15267 C*2*
10159 C*2* 11076 C*2* 12453 C*7* 15279 C*2*
10165 C*2* 11081 C*1* 12524 C*2* 15294 C*2*
10169 C*2* 11087 C*3* 12525 C*2* 15509 C*2*
10303 TRC*1* 11088 C*4* 12780 RC*2* 15980 RC*2*
10466 C*7* 11092 C*2* 12839 C*2* 16054 R *7*
10477 C*2* 11094 C*2* 13572 R *1* 16055 R *2*
10488 C*2* 11095 C*2* 14258 RC*2* 18172 RC*2*
10548 T *2* 11096 C*2* 14264 RC*1* 18178 RC*2*
10692 TR *1* 11101 C*2* 14269 RC*4* 18185 RC*2*
10758 R *4* 11104 C*2* 14293 RC*3* 18225 C*2*
10799 R *2* 11105 C*2* 14299 C*2* 18232 C*2*
10807 R *1* 11106 C*2* 14305 C*4* 18312 RC*2*
10836 R *4* 11107 C*4* 14311 C*1* 18387 T *2*
10844 R *4* 11110 C*1* 14322 C*1* 18551 TR *2*
10885 RC*4* 11111 C*1* 14364 C*2* 18647 R *2*
10888 TRC*2* 11113 C*4* 14369 C*2* 18659 R *2*
10890 TRC*2* 11132 C*2* 14370 C*2* 18725 R *2*
10893 TRC*2* 11144 C*2* 14378 C*4* 18755 R *2*
10937 C*2* 11154 C*1* 14396 T *2* 18783 R *2*
10938 C*4* 11160 C*2* 14416 C*2* 18822 TRC*2*
10943 C*2* 11168 C*2* 14419 C*2* 18842 C*2*
10953 C*2* 11178 C*2* 14535 C*4* 19166 C*2*
10970 C*2* 11179 C*1* 14684 TR *1* 19732 RC*2*
10975 C*2* 11180 C*2* 14783 RC*2* 19899 TRC*2*
10994 C*2* 11195 T *1* 14885 C*1* 19905 C*2*
11000 C*4* 11243 T *2* 14976 C*1* 19931 C*1*
11003 C*2* 11336 R *2* 15017 C*2* 20244 C*2*
11006 C*2* 11390 RC*2* 15090 RC*2* 20328 C*2*
11011 T *1* 11391 RC*2* 15123 C*2* 20496 C*2*
11021 TR *2* 11495 C*1* 15171 TRC*2* 20926 R *2*

The Eighteen Provinces

North China Broadly Conceived

Primary 11028 r 2 18747 r 1 22660 tr 2
10798 r 2 18307 r 2 21109 c4

Second. 10825 r 2 13548 r 2 18493 t 2
10066 t 2 10827 r 2 14751 r 2 18509 t 2
10314 c2 10969 c3 18371 t 2 18731 r 2
10679 t 2

Manchuria

Primary 11015 t 2 11162 c2 15181 rc2
10796 r 2 11032 r 4 11345 r 2 15664 t 2
10852 rc2 11051 rc2 11834 r 2

Second. 11337 r 1 15670 tr 2 19876 rc2
10354 tr 2 13039 r 4 15911 c2 20813 tr 2
10647 t 1 15287 c2 18181 rc1 22506 t 2
10719 tr 1 15665 t 7 18702 r 2

Northern China

Primary 11080 c3 11765 r 1 18498 t 3
10747 r 2 11135 c3 12860 c2 21554 c3
10776 r 2 11158 c2 14735 r 2 22577 t 2
10781 r 2 11173 c2 18348 c2 22712 r 7

Second. 10816 r 2 16142 c3 20464 r 3
10505 t 3 14330 c3 18330 c3 21438 t 3
10565 t 3 14802 rc2 20435 r 3 22374 c3

Northwestern China and Frontier Regions

Primary 11079 c2 11147 c2 18245 c2
10759 r 2 11099 c2 11161 c2 22698 r 2
10874 trc2 11130 c2 12011 c2 22749 c2
11050 rc2 11131 c1 14080 c1

Second. 10939 c2 18340 c2 22732 trc2
10176 c2 15620 c2 22662 tr 1

South China Broadly Conceived

Primary 11014 t 2 11017 t 4 15205 c2
18459 t 2

Second. 17581 trc1 18421 t 2 18577 r 2
18766 r 2 21117 c2

East Central China

Primary 11121 c2 14393 c2 15291 c3
11025 r 3 12911 t 1 14925 c3 17646 c2

Second. 10801 r 4 16831 c7 18487 t 2

Central Yangtze Provinces

Primary 15155 r 2 18531 tr 2

Second. 13541 r 7 17630 tr 4 18726 r 2

Southwestern China

Primary 10791 r 2 11159 c2 12861 c2
18089 t 2 18349 c2

Second. 10179 c2 10746 r 4 14803 rc2
15909 c2 22552 t 8

Southeastern China

Primary 12069 c2 15485 c2 17589 c2
11127 c5 13906 r 2 15572 c2 20525 c2
11143 c2

Second. 16389 t 2 16530 t 2 17913 c2
17949 trc7

Taiwan Only

Primary 11059 c2 11138 c2 16745 trc8
10914 c1 11090 c1 11166 c1 17955 rc1
10955 c1 11108 c1 11521 c2 18981 tr 2
11019 tr 2 11109 c1 15439 r 2 21488 c1
11020 tr 2 11134 c1 16261 tr 2 22646 tr 2
11044 rc2

Second. 11500 c1 16151 c1 18824 rc1
10325 t 2 11502 c1 16550 tr 8 19769 t 2
10857 trc2 14367 c1 18290 c2 20335 c1
10959 c2 14796 rc2 18297 c2 22735 trc2
11417 rc1 15586 tr 2 18650 r 1 22741 trc2

Hong Kong and Macau Only

Primary 11031 r 2

Second. ☐

12.2 National Legal System
司法制度 司法制度

Geographic China Broadly Conceived

Primary: Monographs
10008 t 2 11257 tr 1 12260 r 8 20051 tr 1
10014 t 2 11261 tr 1 15956 tr 2 20053 tr 1
10017 t 2 11270 tr 4 16186 t 2 20160 tr 2
10615 t 2 11293 tr 1 18308 r 3 20162 tr 1
10707 tr 2 11299 tr 3 19752 t 1 20934 r 3
10716 tr 1 11301 tr 1 19763 t 1 21698 t 1
10828 r 2 11304 tr 1 19772 t 1 22567 t 1
11222 t 1 11317 r 1 19774 t 1 22650 tr 3
11241 t 2 11385 rc1 19859 trc2 22652 tr 3
11250 tr 1 11418 rc1 20025 tr 1

Primary: Inclusions
11328 r 1 11411 rc1 12190 t 2 12801 c2
17696 r 3 18541 tr 2

Primary: Journal Articles
10666 t 2 11264 tr 1 14007 rc1 19879 trc1
10714 tr 1 11278 tr 1 14098 t 2 19940 c1
10875 rc1 11296 tr 1 14102 t 2 20044 t 1
11199 t 1 11384 trc2 15065 r 4 22080 tr 1
11207 t 1 11387 trc1 16128 trc2 22085 tr 1
11210 t 1 11403 trc1 17494 trc1 22515 t 3
11213 t 2 11404 rc1 18301 t 4 22742 rc1
11216 t 1 11415 trc1 19762 t 1 23000 trc1
11228 t 3 11555 t 1 19771 t 1 23021 c2
11242 t 1

Secondary: Monographs
10001 t 2 10823 r 1 13828 t 1 19755 t 1
10004 t 2 10850 rc1 13844 t 1 20050 tr 2
10013 t 2 10865 trc3 14175 t 1 20231 rc2
10016 t 2 10891 trc1 14627 t 1 20285 t 1
10025 t 2 11045 rc2 15158 trc2 20540 t 2
10034 t 2 11603 trc1 15161 trc2 20590 t 3
10042 t 2 11605 rc2 15311 t 2 21279 t 2
10060 t 2 11692 tr 2 17691 tr 2 21350 tr 3
10070 tr 2 12201 t 7 17981 tr 2 21425 trc5
10082 tr 2 12657 tr 4 18077 t 2 21435 c2
10085 tr 2 12764 trc3 18379 t 1 21467 trc1
10106 r 2 12901 t 2 18409 t 2 21788 tr 1
10107 r 2 12941 t 2 18494 t 2 22056 t 1
10108 r 2 12947 t 2 18511 t 2 22580 t 2
10113 trc2 12957 tr 2 18547 tr 2 22586 t 3
10139 c2 13025 r 4 18579 r 2 22594 t 2
10526 t 2 13457 t 3 18871 t 2 22629 t 2
10573 t 1 13649 tr 2 18943 t 1 22666 tr 2
10626 t 2 13676 tr 4 19481 tr 3 22720 r 3
10657 t 1 13811 t 2 19503 r 2 22866 t 2
10684 tr 2 13812 t 2

Secondary: Inclusions
10646 t 4 14248 r 2 18558 tr 2 21712 t 2
12370 r 7 18368 t 1 19871 trc1 22578 t 2
13571 r 2 18527 t 2 20222 r 3

Secondary: Journal Articles
10279 t 1 10736 tr 1 13763 trc2 20108 r 3
10618 t 1 13672 tr 5 20085 t 2 22624 t 1
10704 tr 2 13733 r 4

Mainland China

Primary: Monographs
10019 t 2 10692 tr 1 10944 c1 11219 t 1
10023 t 2 10703 tr 4 10953 c2 11230 t 1
10035 t 2 10711 tr 4 10997 c2 11235 t 1
10044 t 2 10765 r 1 11006 c2 11243 t 2
10047 t 2 10768 r 4 11027 r 2 11258 tr 1
10059 t 2 10778 r 2 11036 trc7 11263 tr 1
10413 c2 10782 r 1 11183 t 1 11266 tr 1
10559 t 4 10793 r 1 11193 t 1 11274 tr 4
10574 t 1 10799 r 2 11194 t 2 11279 tr 1
10600 t 4 10807 r 1 11195 t 1 11282 tr 1
10640 t 4 10842 r 4 11202 t 1 11283 tr 2
10660 t 2 10851 rc2 11203 t 2 11289 tr 1
11290 tr 1 11376 r 1 13105 c2 19719 t 2
11291 tr 2 11377 r 1 13491 tr 1 19732 rc2
11292 tr 1 11381 r 1 13535 r 2 19789 tr 2
11294 tr 1 11390 rc2 13650 tr 5 19796 tr 1
11297 tr 2 11391 rc2 13740 r 3 19801 tr 1
11300 tr 1 11393 trc2 13755 r 4 19804 tr 1
11305 tr 1 11395 trc1 13759 r 3 19806 tr 1
11307 r 1 11398 rc2 14201 t 4 19819 r 1
11313 r 1 11423 c1 14471 r 1 19826 r 1
11318 r 1 11427 c1 14479 r 2 19854 r 1
11323 r 1 11436 c1 14509 r 3 19862 trc1
11324 r 1 11437 c2 15073 r 2 19883 rc2
11325 r 1 11438 c1 15963 r 3 19892 rc1
11327 r 1 11439 c1 15966 r 3 19905 c2
11336 r 2 11440 c2 16123 r 2 19931 c1
11342 r 1 11495 c1 16148 c5 20034 t 2
11344 r 1 11496 c1 16637 r 7 20036 t 2
11348 r 1 11514 c2 18647 r 2 20065 r 1
11356 r 1 11534 c2 19042 rc1 20066 r 1
11358 r 1 11586 tr 2 19222 tr 4 20067 r 2
11362 r 1 11622 c1 19252 r 1 20068 r 2
11364 r 1 11672 t 4 19275 r 1 20107 r 2
11365 r 1 12271 r 7 19276 r 1 20175 tr 1
11368 r 2 12378 rc8 19277 r 4 20226 trc2
11369 r 2 12676 tr 1 19457 r 7 21172 t 2
11371 r 2 13004 r 1 19476 tr 2 21585 c2
11375 r 1

Primary: Inclusions
10554 t 1 11321 r 1 11458 c2 15105 c4
10561 t 2 11329 r 1 11459 c1 18516 t 2
10601 t 2 11379 r 1 11484 c1 19279 r 4
10723 tr 2 11392 trc1 11487 c2 19866 trc2
10918 c4 11397 trc1 11490 c1 19873 rc2
11120 c2 11399 rc1 11494 c2 19884 rc1
11223 t 1 11425 c1 11504 c1 19893 rc1
11244 t 2 11426 c1 11508 c1 19915 c1
11245 t 1 11433 c1 11530 c2 19930 c2
11248 tr 1 11435 c2 11531 c1 20071 trc1
11252 tr 1 11442 c2 12396 rc8 20081 c2
11256 tr 1 11443 c2 12510 c8 20228 rc2
11265 tr 2 11447 c1 14455 tr 4 20292 tr 2
11284 tr 1 11448 c1 14878 c3 21066 c2
11295 tr 1 11449 c1 15043 t 2 23050 c1
11303 tr 1 11451 c1

Primary: Journal Articles
10084 tr 2 11204 t 1 11286 tr 1 11374 r 1
10518 t 4 11205 t 1 11287 tr 2 11378 r 1
10531 t 3 11206 t 1 11288 tr 1 11380 r 4
10689 tr 1 11208 t 1 11298 tr 1 11382 r 2
10738 tr 1 11211 t 1 11302 tr 1 11383 trc1
10762 r 3 11212 t 1 11306 tr 1 11386 trc1
10763 r 1 11214 t 1 11308 r 1 11388 trc2
10764 r 2 11217 t 1 11309 r 1 11394 rc1
10771 r 4 11218 t 1 11310 r 1 11396 trc1
10774 r 2 11220 t 1 11311 r 1 11401 rc1
10775 r 2 11221 t 1 11312 r 1 11402 trc1
10809 r 2 11225 t 2 11314 r 1 11405 rc1
10818 r 4 11226 t 1 11315 r 1 11406 trc2
10829 r 1 11227 t 1 11316 r 1 11407 trc1
10868 rc1 11233 t 1 11320 r 1 11408 rc1
10897 c2 11234 t 1 11322 r 1 11409 trc1
10909 c1 11236 t 1 11326 r 1 11410 trc2
10929 c2 11238 t 3 11330 r 1 11412 trc1
11008 c1 11239 t 1 11331 r 1 11413 rc1
11026 r 2 11240 t 1 11332 r 1 11414 trc1
11112 c1 11247 tr 1 11333 r 1 11416 trc1
11125 c1 11249 tr 1 11334 r 4 11419 c1
11170 c2 11251 tr 1 11338 r 1 11420 c4
11172 c2 11253 tr 1 11341 r 1 11421 c2
11175 c2 11254 tr 1 11343 r 1 11422 c1
11181 t 2 11255 tr 1 11347 r 1 11424 c1
11182 t 1 11259 tr 1 11349 r 1 11428 c1
11184 t 1 11260 tr 2 11352 r 1 11429 c2
11186 t 4 11262 tr 1 11353 r 1 11430 c1
11188 t 1 11267 tr 1 11355 r 1 11431 c1
11189 t 1 11268 tr 4 11357 r 1 11432 c1
11190 t 1 11269 tr 1 11360 r 1 11434 c1
11191 t 1 11271 tr 1 11361 r 1 11441 c2
11192 t 4 11272 tr 1 11363 r 1 11444 c1
11196 t 4 11273 tr 1 11366 r 1 11445 c1
11197 t 1 11275 tr 1 11367 r 1 11446 c1
11198 t 1 11277 tr 1 11370 r 1 11450 c1
11200 t 1 11281 tr 1 11372 r 1 11452 c2
11201 t 1 11285 tr 1 11373 r 1 11453 c2

The Eighteen Provinces

North China Broadly Conceived

Manchuria

Northern China

Northwestern China and Frontier Regions

South China Broadly Conceived

East Central China

Central Yangtze Provinces

☐

Southwestern China

Southeastern China

Taiwan Only

Hong Kong and Macau Only

13 Elite and Official Religion
社會領導階層與官定之宗教信仰
国教及び上層階級の宗教

Geographic China Broadly Conceived

Primary 11555 T 1 16186 T 2 21742 TR 1
10001 T 2 11556 T 1 16192 T 1 21746 TR 1
10014 T 2 11603 TRC1 16281 TR 1 21750 TR 1
10082 TR 2 11605 RC2 18936 T 2 22102 TR 2
10550 T 1 11608 TRC1 21467 TRC1 22578 T 2
10611 T 2 11619 C2 21656 T 1 22588 T 1
10891 TRC1 11646 C1 21703 T 1 22637 T 1
11544 T 1 16185 T 2

Second. 10573 T 1 18700 R 2 21412 RC2
10008 T 2 10586 T 1 18891 T 2 21477 TRC2
10022 T 2 10713 TR 2 18904 T 2 21641 T 1
10024 T 2 12941 T 2 19036 TRC2 21718 TR 1
10026 T 2 13812 T 2 19052 TRC1 21740 TR 1
10032 T 2 14156 T 2 20540 T 2 21788 TR 1
10042 T 2 14167 T 2 20563 T 2 22001 TR 1
10048 T 2 14215 TR 2 20615 TR 2 22015 TRC1
10052 T 2 15773 R 2 20619 TR 2 22024 T 1
10053 T 2 16217 T 7 20994 TRC5 22056 T 1
10113 TRC2 16273 TR 1 21173 T 2 22085 TR 1
10259 TRC4 18544 TR 1 21269 T 2 22580 T 2

Mainland China

Primary: Monographs
10029 T 2 11581 TR 2 11620 C1 18980 TR 2
10043 T 2 11586 TR 2 11622 C1 18988 TR 2
10044 T 2 11587 TR 4 11625 C2 19033 TRC1
10069 TR 2 11588 TR 2 11627 C2 19042 RC1
10120 TRC2 11595 R 1 11639 C1 19063 C2
10173 C2 11596 R 1 11643 C2 19719 T 2
10978 C2 11598 R 1 11651 C2 21163 T 7
11540 T 4 11601 R 2 11654 C2 21260 T 2
11545 T 1 11606 RC1 12811 C2 21437 T 1
11562 T 1 11607 TRC1 15267 C2 21657 T 1
11563 T 4 11611 RC1 16343 TRC2 21723 TR 1
11569 T 5 11614 RC1 18927 T 1 21798 TR 1
11578 TR 1

Primary: Inclusions
11550 T 2 11612 RC1 11637 C1 19000 R 1
11566 T 4 11613 RC1 11638 C2 19056 RC1
11574 T 1 11617 C1 11647 C1 21709 T 2
11589 TR 1 11632 C1 11653 C1 21774 TR 2
11590 TR 1 11633 C1 18280 C2 22129 TR 1
11604 RC1 11634 C1

Primary: Journal Articles
10509 T 4 11593 R 1 11631 C1 18848 T 2
11543 T 1 11600 R 1 11635 C1 18961 TR 1
11546 T 4 11602 RC1 11636 C1 19057 C2
11549 T 1 11609 RC2 11640 C1 19059 C1
11557 T 1 11610 TRC1 11641 C1 19060 C1
11558 T 4 11615 RC1 11642 C1 21724 TR 1
11559 T 4 11616 RC1 11644 C1 21735 TR 1
11560 T 2 11618 C3 11645 C1 21752 TR 1
11572 T 2 11623 C1 11648 C3 21794 TR 1
11580 TR 1 11624 C2 11649 C2 21860 RC1
11583 TR 2 11626 C2 11650 C1 21868 TRC1
11585 TR 1 11628 C2 11652 C2 22010 R 1
11591 TR 1 11629 C2 16356 C1 23044 C1
11592 TR 1 11630 C2

Secondary: Monographs
10019 T 2 10519 T 4 18272 C1 21363 TR 4
10020 T 2 10574 T 1 18378 T 2 21447 TR 2
10030 T 2 11194 T 2 18430 T 2 21476 TRC2
10036 T 2 11203 T 2 18842 C2 21563 C1
10041 T 2 11258 TR 1 18862 T 2 21624 T 2
10059 T 2 11855 TRC2 18945 T 2 21644 T 2
10110 TRC2 11883 C2 18959 TR 2 21771 TR 1
10124 TRC2 14201 T 4 18978 TR 1 21821 R 2
10126 RC2 14370 C2 18989 TR 2 21980 T 4
10134 C2 15575 C4 19038 RC1 22006 R 1
10150 C2 16189 T 2 20166 TR 2 22112 TR 2
10155 C2 16332 TRC1 20258 T 2 22179 R 1
10164 C2 16335 TRC2 20618 TR 2 22530 T 1
10168 C2 17974 T 3 20639 R 2 22572 T 2
10255 TR 2 18232 C2 21300 T 2 22619 T 2

Secondary: Inclusions
10012 T 2 14601 T 3 19040 TRC2 22051 T 1
10542 T 2 16282 TR 1 21643 T 1 22108 TR 1
11174 C2 19010 R 2 21804 TR 1 22231 TRC1
11245 T 1 19028 R 1 21843 TRC1 22234 RC2
12197 T 7 19029 TRC1 22033 T 1 22335 C1

Secondary: Journal Articles
10513 T 4 14566 T 2 19058 C2 22037 T 1
10531 T 3 16196 T 2 19067 C1 22054 T 1
10535 T 1 16255 TR 1 19793 TR 1 22061 T 1
11198 T 1 16272 TR 2 19992 T 1 22123 TR 1
11247 TR 1 16285 R 1 20545 T 2 22216 TRC1
11298 TR 1 16294 R 1 21378 R 2 22551 T 1
12189 T 2 16329 TRC2 21669 T 1 22564 T 2
13853 T 4 16336 TRC1 21696 T 1 22893 TR 1
14272 RC1 18873 T 1 21992 TR 1

The Eighteen Provinces

Primary 11571 T 1 18948 T 1 21627 T 1
11536 T 3 11579 TR 1 19046 RC1 21642 T 1
11539 T 2 11621 C3 19047 RC1 21697 T 1
11564 T 3 16211 T 2 20149 T 1 21761 TR 1
11567 T 2 18859 T 2 20544 T 2 21791 TR 1
11570 T 1 18880 T 1 21455 R 5 22193 TRC1

Second. 16200 T 2 19001 R 2 21645 T 1
10027 T 2 16207 T 1 19002 R 5 22036 T 1
10050 T 2 16247 TR 2 19024 R 4 22083 TR 1
10170 C2 16264 TR 2 19964 TR 1 22170 R 1
10590 T 5 16271 TR 2 20002 T 1 22414 T 1
12179 T 2 16276 TR 1 20668 C2 22537 T 1
13804 T 2 17995 C2 21610 T 2 22590 T 3
15327 T 3 18149 R 1 21612 T 1 22865 T 3
16161 T 2 18916 T 2 21630 T 1 22880 T 1
16183 T 2

North China Broadly Conceived

Primary 10580 T 2 18960 TR 2

Second. 14210 T 2 16352 C8 22394 T 2
10827 R 2 16169 T 2 18953 TR 2 22562 T 3

Manchuria

Primary □

Second. 11677 T 2 15743 T 3 19050 RC1

Northern China

Primary 11573 T 3 15372 TR 3 16239 TR 3
10652 T 3 11575 TR 3 15710 T 2 16240 TR 3
11537 T 3 11576 TR 8 16206 T 2 16241 TR 3
11538 T 3 11577 TR 3 16219 T 3 16242 TR 3
11541 T 2 11584 TR 3 16221 T 4 16243 TR 3
11542 T 8 11594 R 2 16230 TR 3 16244 TR 3
11547 T 3 11597 R 3 16232 TR 7 18946 T 3
11548 T 3 11599 R 3 16235 TR 3 18958 TR 3
11551 T 3 14163 T 3 16236 TR 3 19048 RC1
11565 T 4 14191 T 5 16237 TR 3 19779 T 3
11568 T 3 15347 T 3 16238 TR 3 22520 T 3

Second. 15341 T 2 16234 TR 7 20012 TR 2
10505 T 3 15355 T 2 18096 T 3 20557 T 3
11135 C3 15370 TR 3 18910 T 1 20559 T 3
14157 T 3 15416 R 3 18957 TR 3 20579 T 3
14197 T 3 16220 T 2 19740 T 3 21264 T 3
14214 TR 3 16228 TR 8

Northwestern China and Frontier Regions

Primary 11582 TR 3 18911 T 2 21851 RC8
22749 C2

Second. 11147 C2 18890 T 2 19041 RC2
10759 R 2 16331 TRC1 18924 T 2

South China Broadly Conceived

Primary 15749 T 3 18421 T 2

Second. 10031 T 2 16159 T 2 18471 T 1
19006 R 4 19054 RC2

East Central China

Primary 11554 T 3 18857 T 4 19069 C3
11552 T 1 11561 T 3 18983 TR 3 21661 T 1
11553 T 7

Second. 16162 T 7 18926 T 3 21621 T 1

Central Yangtze Provinces

□

Southwestern China

Primary 16077 C2 19049 RC1

Second. 16300 R 2 18962 TR 1

Southeastern China

Primary 16194 T 3 18997 R 3 22398 T 4

Second. 16187 T 3 16341 TRC7 19043 TRC2
11675 T 2 16190 T 2 19013 R 3 21428 RC2
15317 T 2

Taiwan Only

Primary □

Second. 16261 TR 2 18981 TR 2 21421 RC3

Hong Kong and Macau Only

□

14 National Economy and Economic Planning
全國經濟及經濟計劃
国家経済及び経済計画

Geographic China Broadly Conceived

Primary: Monographs
10004 T 2 10139 C2 11708 TR 2 13662 TR 4
10008 T 2 10177 C2 11709 TR 2 13676 TR 4
10010 T 2 10263 C2 11766 R 2 13688 TR 2
10016 T 2 10277 T 2 11767 R 2 13704 R 2
10017 T 2 10329 T 2 11839 R 2 13708 R 2
10042 T 2 10331 T 2 11841 R 2 13811 T 2
10045 T 2 10346 TR 2 11857 TRC2 15158 TRC2
10048 T 2 10386 RC2 11858 TRC2 15161 TRC2
10053 T 2 10396 TRC2 11921 C2 15174 TRC2
10058 T 2 10407 C2 12019 C2 15175 RC2
10060 T 2 10432 C2 12118 C1 18299 C2
10070 TR 2 10560 T 2 12201 T 7 18511 T 2
10076 TR 2 11045 RC2 12233 TR 2 20620 TR 2
10106 R 2 11657 T 4 12328 R 7 21276 T 2
10107 R 2 11665 T 2 12593 T 2 21392 TRC2
10108 R 2 11687 TR 2 12901 T 2 21904 RC2
10111 TRC2 11692 TR 2 12947 T 2 22109 TR 2
10113 TRC2 11694 TR 2 13025 R 4 22631 T 1
10114 TRC2 11703 TR 2 13222 R 2 22650 TR 3
10129 TRC2 11704 TR 2 13627 T 2 22740 TRC2

Primary: Inclusions
10073 TR 2 11720 TR 2 12160 C2 14400 T 4
10389 TRC2 11859 TRC2 12934 T 2 18073 T 2
10510 T 2 11960 C2 13571 R 2 20563 T 2
11673 T 2 12147 C1

Primary: Journal Articles
10564 T 2 11779 R 2 13106 C4 15162 TRC2
11669 T 3 11853 TRC2 13154 TR 2 22651 TR 2
11682 T 1 11867 TRC2 13168 TR 4 22665 TR 2
11738 R 2 11892 C2 14126 TRC2 22922 TR 1
11770 R 2 13028 R 2

Second. 10287 TR 2 12224 TR 1 13705 R 2
10013 T 2 10288 TR 1 12439 C8 13748 R 2
10015 T 1 10618 T 1 12548 C2 13793 C2
10074 TR 2 10626 T 2 12730 R 1 14113 TR 2
10077 TR 2 10627 T 2 12922 T 3 14248 R 2
10118 RC2 10700 TR 2 13457 T 3 14694 TR 4
10119 TRC2 10853 TRC2 13502 TR 1 15044 T 2
10162 C2 10854 TRC1 13517 TR 1 15063 R 2
10217 RC2 10891 TRC1 13667 TR 1 15126 T 2
10220 TRC2 11035 RC2 13692 TR 4 15130 T 2

15194 TRC2 18707 R 2 21291 T 2 22101 TR 1
15773 R 2 18711 R 2 21847 TRC2 22189 RC1
16186 T 2 18786 TRC2 21855 TRC2 22345 c2
17272 R 2 18809 RC2 22074 T 2 22779 T 1
18540 TR 2 18810 RC2 22095 TR 2 22907 TR 1
18579 R 2 19534 R 2

MAINLAND CHINA

PRIMARY: MONOGRAPHS

10003 T 2 11740 R 2 12027 c2 13389 c2
10007 T 2 11745 R 2 12029 c1 13399 c2
10041 T 2 11748 R 2 12039 c2 13420 c2
10044 T 2 11750 R 2 12044 c2 13432 c2
10047 T 2 11752 R 2 12054 c2 13458 T 2
10055 T 2 11754 R 2 12060 c2 13482 T 2
10061 T 2 11756 R 2 12062 c2 13508 TR 2
10062 T 2 11760 R 2 12071 c2 13511 TR 2
10065 T 2 11783 R 2 12076 c2 13516 TR 2
10068 TR 2 11790 R 2 12082 c2 13518 TR 1
10092 R 2 11793 R 2 12086 c2 13520 TR 2
10094 R 2 11794 R 5 12090 c2 13535 R 2
10097 R 2 11796 R 1 12096 c2 13549 R 2
10103 R 2 11799 R 2 12102 c2 13556 R 1
10104 R 2 11804 R 2 12109 c2 13579 c2
10105 R 2 11805 R 2 12114 c1 13584 c2
10120 TRC2 11807 R 2 12123 c2 13588 c3
10123 RC2 11812 R 2 12148 c2 13589 c2
10125 RC2 11822 R 2 12154 c2 13594 c2
10132 c2 11829 R 2 12158 c2 13597 c1
10134 c2 11830 R 2 12163 c2 13614 c2
10140 c2 11833 R 1 12166 c2 13681 TR 3
10142 c2 11845 RC2 12173 c2 13701 R 1
10143 c2 11846 RC2 12218 TR 2 13743 R 2
10148 c2 11848 RC2 12222 TR 7 13744 R 2
10149 c2 11849 TRC2 12229 TR 7 13755 R 4
10153 c2 11850 TRC2 12257 R 7 13760 R 2
10154 c2 11852 RC2 12270 R 7 13761 R 2
10159 c2 11855 TRC2 12271 R 7 13788 c1
10167 c2 11860 RC2 12291 R 7 13901 R 2
10168 c2 11862 RC2 12331 R 7 14066 c2
10172 c2 11864 RC2 12355 R 2 14109 TR 2
10173 c2 11872 RC2 12358 R 2 14122 R 3
10214 TRC2 11874 RC2 12375 RC2 14153 c2
10330 T 2 11876 RC2 12380 RC7 14164 T 2
10338 TR 2 11877 RC2 12426 RC7 14296 c2
10349 TR 2 11878 RC2 12434 c2 14416 c2
10365 R 2 11883 c2 12475 c2 14513 TRC2
10399 c2 11884 c2 12515 c7 14522 c2
10424 c2 11885 c2 12519 c8 14640 TR 2
10425 c2 11889 c2 12524 c2 14703 TR 2
10460 c8 11891 c2 12525 c2 14882 c2
10487 c2 11894 c2 12532 c2 15085 RC2
10498 c2 11897 c2 12552 c2 15090 RC2
10503 c2 11901 c2 12562 c7 15123 c2
10516 T 2 11903 c2 12631 TR 2 15163 RC2
10640 T 4 11906 c2 12638 TR 2 15168 TRC2
10660 T 2 11907 c2 12674 TR 2 15172 TRC2
10677 T 2 11909 c2 12708 R 2 15249 c2
10698 TR 2 11912 c2 12776 TRC2 15260 c2
10812 R 2 11917 c2 12811 c2 15294 c2
10813 R 2 11919 c2 12849 c2 17228 R 5
10888 TRC2 11920 c2 12853 c2 17381 c5
10894 c1 11922 c2 13042 R 2 17395 c2
10895 c2 11927 c2 13050 RC2 17993 c2
10943 c2 11928 c2 13070 c2 18114 R 2
10997 c2 11939 c2 13078 c1 18142 R 2
11076 c2 11946 c2 13104 c2 18170 RC2
11087 c3 11948 c1 13105 c2 18172 RC2
11106 c2 11949 c2 13118 c2 18185 RC2
11194 T 2 11952 c1 13163 TR 2 18312 RC2
11391 RC2 11955 c2 13164 TR 4 18378 T 2
11393 TRC2 11962 c2 13176 TR 3 18387 T 2
11672 T 4 11970 c2 13187 TR 4 18430 T 2
11685 TR 2 11980 c2 13261 R 5 18526 T 2
11689 TR 2 11988 c2 13290 R 2 18717 R 2
11698 TR 2 11995 c2 13291 R 4 18722 R 2
11699 TR 2 11996 c2 13308 RC2 18759 R 2
11702 TR 2 11998 c2 13311 TRC2 18795 TRC2
11705 TR 2 12000 c2 13314 RC1 18817 RC2
11707 TR 2 12001 c2 13336 c2 19092 RC8
11710 TR 5 12002 c2 13338 c2 19166 c2
11713 TR 2 12005 c2 13339 c4 19248 R 4
11718 TR 2 12014 c2 13344 c2 19285 RC5
11724 R 2 12015 c2 13366 c4 19302 c5
20618 TR 2 22291 c2 22322 c2 22619 T 2
22219 RC2 22318 c2 22568 T 3 22644 TR 2

PRIMARY: INCLUSIONS

10037 T 2 11838 R 2 12043 c2 13417 c2
10147 c2 11840 R 3 12045 c2 13444 c2
10151 c2 11842 RC2 12047 c1 13601 c2
10295 R 2 11847 RC2 12055 c2 13605 c2
10414 c2 11861 RC7 12074 c1 13779 c1
10433 c2 11865 RC2 12088 c2 14043 c1
10441 T 2 11875 RC2 12092 c2 14138 c2
10453 R 2 11887 c2 12101 c2 14435 R 2
10468 c2 11888 c2 12107 c2 14521 c2
10469 c2 11911 c2 12121 c2 15101 c2
10493 c2 11914 c1 12132 c2 15170 RC2
10561 T 2 11916 c2 12156 c2 15188 RC2
10650 T 2 11918 c2 12159 c2 15217 c2
10694 TR 2 11929 c2 12165 c2 15233 c2
10750 R 2 11940 c2 12168 c2 15259 c2
10915 c2 11942 c2 12176 c7 15799 RC2
10993 c2 11951 c1 12269 R 8 18537 TR 2
11447 c1 11965 c2 12326 R 2 18555 TR 2
11674 T 7 11968 c2 12395 RC2 18556 TR 1
11688 TR 2 11969 c2 12444 c7 19087 RC8
11700 TR 2 11974 c2 12449 c2 19290 c4
11711 TR 2 11978 c1 13242 R 5 21486 c2
11721 R 2 11989 c2 13259 R 2 21921 c1
11741 R 1 11990 c2 13327 c1 21955 c1
11751 R 3 12009 c2 13330 c2 22221 RC2
11775 R 2 12010 c2 13337 c4 22287 RC1
11786 R 2 12041 c2 13408 c4 22290 c2
11819 R 1 12042 c2 13413 c4 22356 c1

PRIMARY: JOURNAL ARTICLES

10033 T 2 11764 R 2 11937 c2 12034 c2
10063 T 2 11768 R 2 11938 c2 12035 c2
10225 c2 11773 R 2 11941 c2 12036 c2
10238 c2 11774 R 2 11943 c2 12040 c2
10249 c2 11778 R 2 11944 c2 12046 c1
10296 R 2 11788 R 2 11945 c2 12048 c4
10305 c2 11792 R 2 11947 c2 12049 c2
10342 TR 2 11800 R 2 11950 c1 12050 c2
10374 R 2 11801 R 4 11953 c2 12051 c1
10393 TRC2 11802 R 2 11954 c2 12052 c2
10403 c2 11806 R 2 11956 c1 12053 c2
10408 c2 11809 R 2 11957 c2 12056 c2
10418 c2 11810 R 2 11958 c2 12057 c2
10467 c2 11811 R 1 11961 c2 12058 c2
10473 c2 11813 R 2 11963 c2 12059 c2
10490 c2 11814 R 2 11966 c2 12061 c2
10491 c2 11815 R 2 11967 c2 12063 c2
10496 c2 11817 R 2 11971 c2 12064 c2
10502 c7 11820 R 2 11972 c2 12065 c2
10536 T 2 11831 R 2 11973 c2 12066 c2
10717 TR 2 11835 R 2 11976 c2 12067 c1
10835 R 4 11836 R 1 11977 c1 12068 c1
10877 RC2 11854 RC2 11979 c2 12072 c1
10901 c2 11866 RC2 11981 c2 12073 c2
10905 c4 11868 RC2 11982 c1 12075 c2
10910 c1 11870 TRC2 11983 c1 12077 c2
10933 c2 11871 TRC2 11986 c2 12080 c2
10987 c2 11879 c2 11987 c2 12081 c1
11009 c1 11880 c2 11991 c2 12083 c2
11034 RC2 11881 c2 11992 c2 12084 c2
11054 TRC2 11882 c2 11993 c2 12085 c2
11186 T 4 11886 c2 11994 c2 12087 c2
11505 c2 11890 c2 11997 c2 12089 c2
11661 T 4 11893 c1 11999 c2 12091 c2
11662 T 2 11895 c2 12004 c2 12093 c1
11664 T 2 11896 c2 12006 c2 12094 c2
11666 T 2 11898 c1 12007 c4 12095 c2
11676 T 2 11899 c1 12012 c2 12097 c2
11680 T 2 11900 c2 12013 c2 12098 c2
11693 TR 2 11902 c2 12016 c2 12099 c1
11701 TR 1 11908 c2 12018 c4 12100 c2
11717 TR 2 11910 c2 12021 c2 12103 c2
11730 R 2 11913 c2 12022 c2 12104 c2
11733 R 2 11915 c2 12023 c2 12105 c1
11734 R 3 11923 c1 12024 c4 12108 c1
11736 R 2 11924 c2 12025 c2 12110 c2
11742 R 2 11930 c2 12026 c2 12111 c2
11743 R 2 11931 c2 12028 c4 12112 c2
11757 R 2 11932 c2 12030 c2 12113 c2
11761 R 2 11933 c2 12031 c2 12115 c2
11762 R 2 11935 c2 12032 c2 12116 c2
11763 R 2 11936 c2 12033 c2 12117 c2
12119 c2 12445 c7 13429 c4 15247 c2
12120 c2 12457 c2 13433 c2 15262 c2
12122 c2 12460 c2 13439 c2 17596 c2
12124 c2 12472 c2 13452 T 2 18246 c2
12125 c2 12511 c7 13487 TR 1 18269 c2
12126 c2 12533 c1 13555 R 1 18504 T 2
12127 c2 12539 c8 13575 c2 18673 R 7
12128 c2 12561 c2 13580 c1 18684 R 2
12129 c2 12634 TR 2 13591 c2 18790 RC2
12130 c2 12681 TR 2 13599 c1 18821 RC2
12131 c2 12771 RC1 13604 c2 19084 RC8
12133 c2 12880 T 5 13615 c1 19107 c7
12134 c2 12983 R 2 13616 c1 19229 R 5
12138 c2 13018 R 7 13737 R 3 19312 c4
12139 c2 13063 c2 13738 R 2 19314 c1
12140 c2 13068 c2 13765 RC1 19316 c4
12141 c2 13084 c2 13771 c2 19321 c4
12145 c2 13089 c2 13782 c2 19374 c2
12153 c2 13108 c2 13784 c4 19512 R 4
12161 c2 13115 c2 13785 c4 19568 R 3
12162 c2 13134 T 2 13790 c1 19582 RC3
12164 c2 13234 R 2 13791 c2 19629 R 2
12167 c2 13236 R 4 13792 c2 19673 c2
12169 c1 13263 R 2 14060 c2 20474 RC2
12170 c4 13279 R 2 14148 c2 21263 T 2
12171 c2 13280 R 4 14149 c2 21284 T 2
12172 c2 13294 RC2 14332 c2 21922 c1
12177 c2 13320 c1 14333 c1 22098 TR 2
12189 T 2 13321 c4 14740 R 2 22167 R 2
12215 TR 2 13322 c2 14814 c4 22239 RC2
12263 R 2 13347 c4 15087 RC2 22302 c1
12266 R 2 13349 c2 15142 R 2 22323 c7
12276 R 2 13363 c1 15154 R 2 22328 c2
12334 R 8 13385 c2 15173 RC2 22352 c2
12349 R 2 13391 c2 15211 c2 22874 T 1
12360 R 7 13407 c2 15212 c2 22947 RC1
12398 RC8 13425 c5 15228 c2 23007 TRC1
12410 TRC2 13427 c2 15244 c2

SECONDARY: MONOGRAPHS

10011 T 2 11092 c2 13775 c2 18588 R 2
10030 T 2 11096 c2 13795 c2 18597 R 4
10036 T 2 11144 c2 13903 R 2 18610 R 2
10049 T 2 11263 TR 1 13909 R 2 18619 R 2
10072 TR 2 11290 TR 1 13937 R 2 18629 R 2
10079 TR 2 11437 c2 13986 TRC2 18653 R 2
10083 TR 2 11496 c1 14001 RC1 18674 R 2
10090 R 2 12227 TR 7 14139 c2 18701 R 1
10099 R 2 12303 R 2 14144 c1 18709 R 2
10101 R 2 12372 R 2 14311 c1 18710 R 1
10110 TRC2 12384 RC2 14322 c1 18768 R 2
10115 RC2 12795 c5 14457 TR 3 18804 TRC2
10124 TRC2 12921 T 2 14486 R 2 18812 RC2
10145 c2 13080 c1 14496 R 5 18819 RC2
10150 c2 13119 c1 14686 TR 1 19135 c7
10152 c2 13232 R 4 14736 R 4 19240 R 2
10155 c2 13316 TRC4 14885 c1 19291 c2
10157 c2 13325 c2 14974 c2 20036 T 2
10180 c2 13353 c2 15033 c1 20314 c2
10464 c4 13384 c2 15150 R 2 20328 c2
10479 c4 13397 c4 15169 RC2 20496 c2
10488 c2 13440 c2 15202 c2 20639 R 2
10643 T 1 13443 c2 15230 c2 21124 c3
10696 TR 1 13449 c1 15234 c2 21288 T 1
10706 TR 2 13456 T 2 15235 c2 21414 RC2
10709 TR 4 13491 TR 1 15237 c2 21476 TRC2
10712 TR 2 13498 TR 1 15245 c2 21570 c1
10715 TR 2 13536 R 1 15248 c2 22006 R 1
10718 TR 2 13565 R 1 15258 c7 22079 TR 2
10726 TR 2 13570 R 1 15550 c2 22131 TR 2
10758 R 4 13585 c1 16054 R 7 22224 RC2
10769 R 2 13590 c2 16335 TRC2 22229 RC2
10819 R 2 13593 c2 17190 TR 5 22233 RC2
10858 TRC2 13682 TR 2 17297 R 2 22293 c2
10870 RC2 13687 TR 1 17895 RC2 22298 c2
10883 TRC2 13711 R 4 17974 T 3 22556 T 2
10885 RC4 13725 R 3 18123 R 2 22714 R 2
10962 c4 13727 R 1 18225 c2 22787 TR 2
10978 c2 13735 R 1 18296 c1 22950 TRC2
10994 c2 13750 R 2 18408 T 1 22954 TRC1
11003 c2 13773 c2 18562 TR 2

SECONDARY: INCLUSIONS

10080 TR 2 10244 c2 11010 T 2 11435 c2
10122 RC2 10499 c2 11042 RC2 11531 c1
10127 TRC2 10859 TRC1 11063 c3 12293 R 8

12479 C2 13335 C2 15187 RC7 21709 T 2
12484 C8 13393 C2 15303 C2 21882 TRC1
12506 C2 13430 C2 18293 C2 21934 C1
12620 TR 2 13435 C2 18343 C2 22169 R 2
12650 TR 2 13583 C2 18515 T 2 22209 TRC1
12798 C1 14455 TR 4 18561 TR 2 22212 RC2
12877 C2 14495 R 5 18571 TR 2 22238 RC4
13072 C1 14880 C2 18761 R 2 22282 RC2
13121 C2 14901 C1 18802 RC2 22327 C1
13257 R 2 15071 R 2 18807 TRC2 22336 C1
13333 C2 15180 TRC1 20698 C2 23028 C2
13334 C5

Secondary: Journal Articles
10230 C2 12773 RC1 14154 C2 18159 R 2
10231 C2 12774 RC2 14303 C1 18190 C2
10241 C2 12777 TRC1 14408 R 3 18234 C2
10251 C2 12806 C4 14410 R 4 18326 C1
10253 TR 4 12929 T 4 14413 RC4 18327 C2
10260 RC2 13071 C2 14414 RC4 18651 R 2
10266 C3 13075 C2 14417 C3 18797 RC1
10509 T 4 13077 C2 14428 R 7 19188 C7
10538 T 1 13109 C2 14526 C3 19215 TR 5
10748 R 2 13116 C5 14532 C2 19218 TR 1
10881 RC1 13248 R 2 14537 C4 19242 R 3
10897 C2 13293 TRC4 14898 C1 19323 C2
10902 C2 13295 RC4 14920 C1 19326 C4
10903 C1 13348 C7 15088 RC2 19414 C4
10913 C4 13354 C2 15098 C7 19462 R 7
10942 C2 13364 C2 15132 TR 2 19470 C8
10967 C2 13379 C2 15133 TR 2 19860 TRC1
10986 C2 13401 C2 15137 TR 1 20374 C1
11004 C1 13405 C2 15159 RC1 21652 T 2
11026 R 2 13410 C3 15182 RC1 21960 C2
11066 C2 13428 C4 15198 C2 22058 T 1
11093 C1 13438 C2 15199 C2 22183 TRC1
11112 C1 13486 T 1 15200 C2 22255 RC2
11116 C2 13493 TR 2 15204 C1 22294 C1
11155 C2 13515 TR 1 15216 C2 22300 C1
11169 C2 13550 R 2 15220 C2 22306 C1
11446 C1 13561 R 2 15227 C1 22312 C1
11468 C1 13587 C2 15238 C2 22329 C2
11503 C2 13592 C1 15253 C2 22361 C1
11510 C1 13608 C7 15275 C2 22376 C1
11511 C1 13611 C1 15290 C2 22382 C2
12226 TR 2 13631 T 1 15845 C7 22722 R 2
12277 R 2 13686 TR 4 16019 C2 22771 T 2
12342 R 8 13714 R 2 16038 C2 22785 TR 1
12361 R 7 13741 R 5 17388 C2 22815 RC1
12451 C7 13780 C2 17781 C1 22876 T 1
12483 C8 13789 C2 17879 R 3 22988 TRC1
12662 TR 2 13960 R 2 18090 T 3 23039 C1
12765 TRC4

The Eighteen Provinces

Primary 11731 R 4 12155 C2 13223 R 2
10138 C2 11735 R 2 12193 T 8 13255 R 2
10161 C2 11758 R 1 12345 R 2 13731 R 2
10333 T 2 11759 R 2 12675 TR 2 14117 R 2
10348 TR 2 11771 R 1 12682 TR 6 14159 T 1
10437 T 2 11776 R 2 12770 TRC2 15067 R 2
11655 T 1 11784 R 2 12933 T 2 19210 T 2
11656 T 2 11798 R 2 12948 T 2 19301 C2
11667 T 2 11816 R 2 13037 R 2 20257 T 1
11681 T 2 11824 R 2 13153 TR 2 22076 TR 1
11719 TR 1 11934 C2 13173 TR 4 22760 C3
11725 R 2 12151 C2

Second. 10252 T 2 13267 R 3 14454 T 2
10021 T 2 10443 R 2 13621 T 4 14493 R 4
10027 T 2 10761 R 4 13646 TR 3 17248 R 2
10056 T 2 11061 C2 13912 R 2 19241 R 2
10187 T 1 12738 R 4 14091 T 2 21261 T 2
10209 R 2 12745 R 2 14100 T 2 22923 TR 2

North China Broadly Conceived

Primary 10827 R 2 11791 R 2 15752 T 2
10064 T 2 11727 R 1 11821 R 2 18712 R 7
10370 R 2 11728 R 2 11869 TRC2 21287 T 2
10435 C2 11737 R 2 11925 C2 22660 TR 2
10476 C2 11780 R 2 12290 R 8 22715 R 2
10792 R 2

Second. 10452 R 2 12616 T 2 13286 R 4
10040 T 2 12577 T 2 12655 TR 2 22623 T 2

Manchuria

Primary 11671 T 2 11777 R 2 12327 R 2
10163 C2 11677 T 2 11781 R 2 12926 T 2
10340 TR 2 11684 TR 2 11785 R 2 13013 R 2
10341 TR 2 11691 TR 2 11797 R 2 13039 R 4
10364 R 2 11695 TR 1 11803 R 2 13147 TR 2
10381 R 2 11696 TR 2 11808 R 2 13355 C4
10428 C2 11697 TR 2 11818 R 2 13500 TR 2
10582 T 2 11712 TR 2 11823 R 2 13559 R 2
10719 TR 1 11714 TR 2 11825 R 2 15181 RC2
10745 R 2 11715 TR 2 11826 R 2 15614 RC2
10852 RC2 11716 TR 2 11827 R 2 15669 TR 2
10911 C2 11732 R 2 11832 R 2 15674 TR 2
11345 R 2 11749 R 2 11834 R 2 15692 R 2
11670 T 4 11755 R 2 12301 R 7 22718 R 1

Second. 12732 R 2 13265 R 2 15585 TR 2
10796 R 2 12841 C2 13560 R 1 15847 C2
12641 TR 2 13032 R 2 13564 R 1 20596 T 2
12717 R 4

Northern China

Primary 10431 C2 10816 R 2 11782 R 2
10178 C2 10747 R 2 11765 R 1 12905 T 2
10380 R 2 10781 R 2

Second. 10607 T 3 10776 R 2 10898 C3
11173 C2 12689 R 4

Northwestern China and Frontier Regions

Primary 10863 TRC2 11926 C2 13358 C2
10176 C2 10939 C2 12003 C2 15620 C2
10375 R 2 10957 C1 12011 C2 19375 C2
10415 C2 11686 TR 2 12037 C2 22698 R 2
10427 C2 11722 R 2 13332 C2 22768 C2
10725 TR 2 11787 R 2

Second. 10369 R 2 10759 R 2

South China Broadly Conceived

Primary 10641 T 2 11744 R 2 12894 T 2
10137 C2 11658 T 2 11772 R 2 12920 T 4
10434 C2 11729 R 2 12888 T 2 18763 R 2

Second. 10323 T 2 13459 T 2 18421 T 2
10031 T 2 12580 T 2 17939 R 2

East Central China

Primary 11746 R 2 12038 C2 12420 RC7
10430 C2 11747 R 2 12157 C2 15924 T 2
11739 R 2 11769 R 2

Second. 19069 C3

Central Yangtze Provinces

Primary 10395 TRC2 11723 R 2 11726 R 2
11795 R 2

Second. 15155 R 2

Southwestern China

Primary 10429 C2 11753 R 2 12951 TR 2
10179 C2 10651 T 2 11789 R 2 13538 R 2
10358 R 2 11679 T 2 12601 T 2 13801 T 2
10382 TRC2 11706 TR 2 12899 T 2

Second. 10318 T 2 10746 R 4 16990 C2

Southeastern China

Primary 10511 T 2 11675 T 2 11837 R 2
10357 R 2 10552 T 2 11683 TR 2 12069 C2
10392 TRC2 10855 RC2 11828 R 2 12953 TR 2
10426 C2 11668 T 2

Second. 14088 T 2 14326 C3

Taiwan Only

Primary 11138 C2 11851 TRC2 11975 C2
10325 T 2 11659 T 2 11856 RC2 11984 C2
10385 RC2 11660 T 2 11863 RC2 11985 C2
10387 TRC2 11663 T 2 11873 RC2 12008 C2
10882 RC2 11678 T 2 11904 C2 12017 C2
10984 C2 11690 TR 2 11905 C2 12020 C1
11044 RC2 11843 RC2 11959 C2 12070 C2
11059 C2 11844 TRC2 11964 C2 12078 C1
12079 C1 12149 C2 13315 RC2 16740 TRC2
12106 C2 12150 C2 13602 C2 16741 TRC8
12135 C2 12152 C2 13764 RC2 16742 TRC2
12136 C2 12174 C2 15471 RC2 16747 RC2
12137 C2 12175 C2 15582 T 2 16783 C7
12142 C2 13113 C2 15600 TRC2 16829 C7
12143 C2 13297 RC2 15874 TRC1 16884 C2
12144 C2 13306 TRC4 16261 TR 2 17955 RC1
12146 C2 13312 RC2 16737 TRC8 18297 C2

Second. 13673 TR 4 15658 T 2 16748 RC2
10958 C1 14874 C2 15675 TR 2 16830 C8
10959 C2 14955 C2 15698 TRC2 16898 C2
10983 C2 15031 C1 15888 C2 18290 C2
11134 C1 15586 TR 2 15890 C2 20334 C2
13079 C2 15615 C2 15893 C2 22646 TR 2
13618 C1

Hong Kong and Macau Only

Not applicable

14.1 Agrarian Economy

農業　農業

Geographic China Broadly Conceived

Primary 11921 C2 12281 R 2 12439 C8
10014 T 2 11960 C2 12294 R 2 12461 C7
10026 T 2 12184 T 8 12310 R 8 12478 C2
10074 TR 2 12188 T 2 12328 R 7 12495 C2
10361 R 2 12190 T 2 12348 R 2 12548 C2
10363 R 2 12196 T 7 12364 R 7 12947 T 2
10377 R 2 12201 T 7 12367 R 2 12989 R 2
10389 TRC2 12202 T 2 12370 R 7 13124 T 2
10396 TRC2 12203 T 2 12377 RC8 13856 T 2
10397 TRC2 12223 TR 7 12390 TRC2 15048 TR 2
10432 C2 12224 TR 1 12394 RC7 15130 T 2
10828 R 2 12232 TR 7 12401 RC7 18801 TRC2
11047 RC2 12233 TR 2 12408 TRC2 19650 RC2
11384 TRC2 12238 R 2 12409 RC7 19654 RC7
11665 T 2 12246 R 2 12416 RC2 20643 R 2
11859 TRC2 12260 R 8 12417 RC2

Second. 10438 T 7 12934 T 2 18409 T 2
10001 T 2 10560 T 2 12941 T 2 18558 TR 2
10017 T 2 10626 T 2 12997 R 1 18809 RC2
10045 T 2 10664 T 2 13194 R 2 19534 R 2
10085 TR 2 10713 TR 2 13465 T 2 19982 TRC8
10093 R 2 10806 R 2 13494 TR 2 20306 C2
10129 TRC2 10862 TRC2 13717 R 2 20540 T 2
10139 C2 11035 RC2 13878 TR 2 20620 TR 2
10144 C2 11704 TR 2 15044 T 2 20766 T 2
10162 C2 11720 TR 2 15063 R 2 20981 TRC2
10177 C2 11770 R 2 15158 TRC2 21904 RC2
10215 RC2 11779 R 2 15161 TRC2 22345 C2
10221 RC2 11857 TRC2 15174 TRC2 22559 T 2
10386 RC2 11858 TRC2 15175 RC2 22580 T 2
10407 C2 12019 C2 15185 TRC2

Mainland China

Primary: Monographs
10089 R 2 11282 TR 1 11906 C2 12166 C2
10115 RC2 11689 TR 2 11909 C2 12182 T 8
10126 RC2 11707 TR 2 11912 C2 12218 TR 2
10130 C2 11745 R 2 11920 C2 12222 TR 7
10140 C2 11750 R 2 11939 C2 12227 TR 7
10148 C2 11756 R 2 11946 C2 12229 TR 7
10150 C2 11790 R 2 11949 C2 12230 TR 2
10157 C2 11793 R 2 11955 C2 12241 R 2
10172 C2 11830 R 2 11962 C2 12254 R 8
10214 TRC2 11845 RC2 11970 C2 12256 R 7
10232 C2 11846 RC2 11980 C2 12257 R 7
10291 TR 2 11848 RC2 12000 C2 12264 R 7
10355 TR 2 11849 TRC2 12015 C2 12267 R 8
10360 R 2 11850 TRC2 12044 C2 12268 R 8
10379 R 8 11852 RC2 12060 C2 12270 R 7
10399 C2 11860 RC2 12096 C2 12271 R 7
10400 C8 11864 RC2 12102 C2 12291 R 7
10424 C2 11874 RC2 12123 C2 12295 R 2
10503 C2 11876 RC2 12148 C2 12298 R 7
10812 R 2 11891 C2 12154 C2 12302 R 2
10906 C2 11903 C2 12158 C2 12303 R 2

14873 c4 16213 T 1 19637 R 2 21502 TR 8
15072 R 8 18609 R 2 20063 R 8 22057 T 2
15885 c8 19122 c8 21129 c8 22928 R 2
15895 c8 19458 R 8

SECOND. 11681 T 2 13223 R 2 17144 T 2
10018 T 2 11798 R 2 13703 R 2 17145 T 2
10038 T 2 11934 c2 13731 R 2 17869 R 2
10138 c2 12151 c2 14422 T 8 18405 T 2
10141 c2 12675 TR 2 14456 TR 2 18436 T 2
10158 c2 12767 TRC2 15038 T 2 18461 T 2
10161 c2 12794 c2 15047 T 2 18645 R 7
10174 c2 12948 T 2 15049 TR 2 19071 R 7
10348 TR 2 13037 R 2 15051 TR 2 19747 T 2
10351 TR 7 13128 T 2 15055 R 7 20057 R 7
10443 R 2 13151 TR 2 15830 c2 21225 R 7
10839 R 2 13166 TR 2 16049 T 2 21676 T 2
11564 T 3

North China Broadly Conceived

PRIMARY 10476 c2 12290 R 8 12505 c8
10066 T 2 11821 R 2 12354 R 8 12972 R 2
10417 c8 11925 c2 12369 R 2 14751 R 2
10423 c7 12234 R 8 12421 RC7 15081 R 2
10435 c2 12235 R 2 12463 c8 17873 R 2
10455 RC8 12274 R 8 12469 c8 18627 R 8

SECOND. 10454 R 8 12998 R 2 15694 R 2
10370 R 2 10798 R 2 13548 R 2 18307 R 2
10402 c8 11728 R 2 15082 R 2 18682 R 2
10404 c2 11737 R 2 15681 R 8 18750 R 2
10452 R 2 12582 T 2

Manchuria

PRIMARY 11825 R 2 12301 R 7 12382 RC8
10337 TR 2 12180 T 2 12309 R 8 12406 RC8
10341 TR 2 12211 TR 8 12315 R 2 13271 R 2
10378 R 2 12248 R 2 12321 R 7 13304 RC2
11671 T 2 12280 R 2 12322 R 7 14431 R 7
11684 TR 2 12285 R 2 12327 R 2 15668 TR 2
11714 TR 2 12286 R 8 12329 R 8 15669 TR 2
11777 R 2 12287 R 7 12338 R 8 15674 TR 2
11797 R 2 12292 R 2 12351 R 2 15677 TR 7
11808 R 2 12300 R 7

SECOND. 11749 R 2 13014 R 2 15181 RC2
10163 c2 11832 R 2 13205 R 2 15590 R 8
10354 TR 2 11834 R 2 13252 R 3 15614 RC2
10745 R 2 12643 TR 2 13258 R 2 15678 TR 2
10796 R 2 12648 TR 2 13281 R 2 15687 R 2
11015 T 2 12984 R 2 13514 TR 8 15692 R 2
11697 TR 2 13011 R 2 14129 RC2 16225 TR 8
11716 TR 2

Northern China

PRIMARY 10431 c2 12353 R 7 12542 c7
15077 R 2 22577 T 2

SECOND. 10178 c2 15037 T 2 15083 R 2
20624 R 2

Northwestern China and Frontier Regions

PRIMARY 11686 TR 2 12330 R 8 12407 RC8
10415 c2 12003 c2 12368 R 8

SECOND. 10427 c2 11099 c2 12747 R 2
15666 TR 8

South China Broadly Conceived

PRIMARY 12258 R 2 12437 c7 12992 R 2
12181 T 2 12265 R 2 12522 c8 13256 R 2
12186 T 7 12297 R 7 12775 TRC2 13471 T 2
12191 T 2 12357 R 8 12843 c2 17179 T 2
12245 R 2 12383 RC2

SECOND. 12569 T 2 13887 R 2 18766 R 2
10137 c2 12570 T 2 14262 RC2 18772 R 2
10406 c2 12578 T 2 15078 R 2 19399 R 2
11014 T 2 12684 TR 2 17947 RC2 19448 R 2
11744 R 2 13207 R 2 18763 R 2 21029 c2

East Central China

PRIMARY 12038 c2 12420 RC7

SECOND. 10430 c2 11739 R 2

Central Yangtze Provinces

PRIMARY 10395 TRC2 19450 R 7

SECOND. 18726 R 2

Southwestern China

PRIMARY 10429 c2 12543 c7

SECOND. 22552 T 8

Southeastern China

PRIMARY 12428 c2 15608 TRC2

SECOND. 10426 c2 10756 R 2 13305 TRC1

Taiwan Only

Not applicable

Hong Kong and Macau Only

Not applicable

14.2 Transport and Communications

交通 交通

Geographic China Broadly Conceived

PRIMARY 11384 TRC2 12609 T 1 12679 TR 1
10014 T 2 11657 T 4 12611 T 1 12692 R 3
10045 T 2 11687 TR 2 12624 TR 2 12730 R 1
10106 R 2 11692 TR 2 12627 TR 1 12759 R 2
10107 R 2 11766 R 2 12629 TR 2 12764 TRC3
10108 R 2 11767 R 2 12632 TR 1 12772 TRC2
10259 TRC4 11853 TRC2 12654 TR 4 12785 TRC3
10261 TRC4 12575 T 2 12657 TR 4 12801 c2
10331 T 2 12576 T 4 12658 TR 1 13144 TR 2
10363 R 2 12585 T 2 12660 TR 4 13189 TR 2
10377 R 2 12589 T 2 12661 TR 4 13461 T 4
10432 c2 12593 T 2 12665 TR 1 13497 TR 4
10447 R 3 12598 T 2 12677 TR 2 14694 TR 4
10684 TR 2 12600 T 3 12678 TR 2 23042 c1

SECONDARY: MONOGRAPHS
10008 T 2 10614 T 1 13873 TR 2 20994 TRC5
10010 T 2 10865 TRC3 13876 TR 2 21350 TR 3
10013 T 2 11841 R 2 14174 T 3 21392 TRC2
10015 T 1 11921 c2 14951 c2 21399 TRC2
10016 T 2 12019 c2 15134 TR 4 21412 RC2
10017 T 2 12203 T 2 15158 TRC2 21904 RC2
10085 TR 2 12232 TR 7 17272 R 2 22027 T 4
10129 TRC2 12328 R 7 18042 TRC2 22127 TR 1
10139 c2 12348 R 2 18102 TR 2 22133 TR 2
10144 c2 12918 T 4 18492 T 2 22594 T 2
10329 T 2 12957 TR 2 18494 T 2 22694 R 3
10346 TR 2 13049 TRC2 18560 TR 2 22720 R 3
10361 R 2 13457 T 3 18970 TR 4 22728 RC2
10396 TRC2 13574 TRC2 19650 RC2 22740 TRC2
10397 TRC2 13762 TRC1 20540 T 2 22819 TRC1
10407 c2 13812 T 2 20590 T 3 22866 T 2
10611 T 2

SECONDARY: INCLUSIONS
10389 TRC2 12416 RC2 15422 R 4 21902 TRC2
11673 T 2 12922 T 3 19861 RC1 22578 T 2
11859 TRC2 12940 T 1 20595 T 3 22690 R 3
12294 R 2 14248 R 2

SECONDARY: JOURNAL ARTICLES
10553 T 1 12495 c2 14399 T 4 21695 T 2
10664 T 2 13274 R 2 21327 TR 2 23021 c2

Mainland China

PRIMARY: MONOGRAPHS
10005 T 2 10660 T 2 11874 RC2 12637 TR 1
10011 T 2 10698 TR 2 12363 R 8 12638 TR 2
10047 T 2 10732 TR 2 12572 T 3 12640 TR 2
10067 TR 2 10812 R 2 12590 T 2 12653 TR 1
10081 TR 2 11101 c2 12597 T 2 12674 TR 2
10098 R 2 11113 c4 12599 T 2 12676 TR 1
10255 TR 2 11178 c2 12606 T 2 12701 R 1
10330 T 2 11179 c1 12619 T 1 12708 R 2
10338 TR 2 11710 TR 5 12631 TR 2 12712 R 2
10424 c2 11724 R 2 12633 TR 2 12714 R 1
12721 R 2 12812 c2 13006 R 2 19263 R 4
12742 R 1 12813 c2 13213 R 7 20492 c3
12751 R 2 12836 c4 13251 R 2 20618 TR 2
12757 R 4 12839 c2 13285 R 5 21321 TR 2
12763 TRC2 12845 c4 13336 c2 21395 RC2
12776 TRC2 12846 c1 13440 c2 21465 R 2
12778 TRC1 12849 c2 13520 TR 2 21677 T 2
12780 RC2 12850 c8 13701 R 1 22089 TR 2
12783 TRC2 12853 c2 14066 c2 22117 TR 2
12787 c2 12856 c1 14364 c2 22568 T 3
12791 c1 12862 c2 14808 RC2 22575 T 1
12793 c2 12864 c1 15059 R 2 22599 T 2
12795 c5 12876 c2 18103 TR 1 22602 T 1
12811 c2 12915 T 2 18324 c2 22619 T 2

PRIMARY: INCLUSIONS
10410 c2 12650 TR 2 12792 c2 12865 c2
10642 T 2 12651 TR 5 12798 c1 12868 c2
11176 c2 12673 TR 3 12799 c1 12871 c2
11786 R 2 12719 R 2 12803 c2 12875 c2
11989 c2 12720 R 2 12805 c4 12877 c2
12159 c2 12727 R 2 12840 c2 18370 T 2
12617 T 4 12731 R 2 12844 c2 19365 T 2
12620 TR 2 12782 RC2 12852 c3 22525 T 2
12649 TR 2 12788 c2 12863 c4

PRIMARY: JOURNAL ARTICLES
10722 TR 3 12659 TR 1 12771 RC1 12826 c4
11023 R 2 12662 TR 2 12773 RC1 12828 c1
11062 c2 12668 TR 2 12774 RC2 12829 c1
11471 c1 12669 TR 2 12777 TRC1 12830 c1
11730 R 2 12671 TR 2 12779 TRC1 12831 c2
11774 R 2 12681 TR 2 12781 TRC2 12832 c2
12138 c2 12685 TR 4 12784 RC2 12833 c2
12178 T 2 12686 TR 1 12786 c1 12834 c1
12349 R 2 12688 R 3 12789 c1 12835 c1
12565 T 4 12690 R 2 12790 c2 12837 c2
12566 T 2 12691 R 2 12796 c1 12838 c2
12568 T 2 12694 R 2 12797 c2 12847 c2
12583 T 2 12695 R 1 12800 c2 12848 c1
12586 T 1 12696 R 4 12802 c2 12851 c1
12588 T 1 12697 R 1 12804 c2 12854 c2
12591 T 1 12698 R 2 12806 c4 12855 c1
12594 T 2 12700 R 2 12807 c2 12872 c2
12596 T 2 12702 R 2 12808 c7 12873 c1
12603 T 4 12703 R 2 12809 c2 12874 c1
12604 T 4 12707 R 4 12810 c1 12949 TR 2
12605 T 3 12709 R 2 12814 c2 12961 TR 2
12607 T 1 12710 R 3 12815 c1 12983 R 2
12608 T 2 12711 R 2 12816 c4 13840 T 2
12610 T 4 12729 R 1 12817 c2 14024 c1
12621 TR 1 12733 R 1 12818 c2 14464 R 5
12622 TR 1 12739 R 2 12819 c3 14855 c2
12623 TR 4 12744 R 2 12820 c4 15292 c2
12625 TR 1 12748 R 1 12821 c2 18402 T 1
12634 TR 2 12749 R 2 12822 c2 19592 c3
12635 TR 1 12750 R 1 12823 c2 22371 c1
12636 TR 1 12760 R 3 12824 c2 22748 c1
12644 TR 4 12762 TRC1 12825 c3 22836 c2
12656 TR 1 12765 TRC4

SECONDARY: MONOGRAPHS
10002 T 2 11707 TR 2 13277 R 2 15052 TR 2
10020 T 2 11745 R 2 13289 R 2 15168 TRC2
10029 T 2 11790 R 2 13328 c2 15176 RC2
10039 T 2 11794 R 5 13343 c2 15508 c2
10041 T 2 11804 R 2 13442 c7 17226 R 2
10061 T 2 11829 R 2 13464 T 3 17245 R 5
10065 T 2 11845 RC2 13489 TR 3 17575 R 2
10101 R 2 11850 TRC2 13849 T 4 17760 R 7
10135 c2 11864 RC2 13861 T 1 17895 RC2
10165 c2 11876 RC2 13883 TR 2 18075 T 2
10360 R 2 11878 RC2 13885 TR 1 18098 T 3
10425 c2 11955 c2 13901 R 2 18120 R 2
10481 c2 11996 c2 13957 R 2 18543 TR 2
10706 TR 2 12015 c2 13959 R 2 18557 TR 2
10724 TR 4 12148 c2 14133 c3 18608 R 2
10768 R 4 12154 c2 14164 T 2 18661 R 2
10778 R 2 12339 R 2 14231 TR 4 18699 R 2
10821 R 2 12414 TRC2 14299 c2 19390 c2
10838 R 4 12434 c2 14369 c2 19405 TRC3
10890 TRC2 12524 c2 14436 R 7 19558 R 2
10970 c2 12950 TR 2 14497 R 2 19652 RC2
11052 RC2 12963 TR 2 14522 c2 19657 RC1
11180 c2 13125 T 2 14584 T 2 19704 R 3
11440 c2 13152 TR 2 14809 RC2 19705 R 2
11672 T 4 13182 TR 2 14974 c2 19732 RC2

20182 TR 2 21311 TR 2 21471 TRC1 22052 T 4
20502 C2 21367 R 2 21766 TR 1 22273 RC2
20996 C2 21406 RC2 21819 R 2 22350 C1
21265 T 2 21420 TRC2 21887 TRC2 22769 C2

Secondary: Inclusions
10147 C2 11775 R 2 13430 C2 19562 R 4
10353 TR 2 11840 R 3 13435 C2 19666 C1
10405 C2 11916 C2 13663 TR 4 20605 T 2
10412 C2 11918 C2 14000 TRC1 21964 C2
10441 T 2 11940 C2 14068 C2 21977 C2
10493 C2 11990 C2 14327 C4 21978 C2
10650 T 2 12449 C2 14411 R 4 22025 T 1
11077 C2 13099 C2 14492 R 3 22336 C1
11126 C2 13156 TR 2 15333 T 3 22357 C2
11128 C1 13257 R 2 18119 R 2 22643 TR 1
11245 T 1 13330 C2 18601 R 2 23046 C1
11741 R 1 13357 C3

Secondary: Journal Articles
10296 R 2 12277 R 2 13839 T 2 19230 R 1
10372 R 2 12324 R 8 13853 T 4 19289 C4
10374 R 2 12445 C7 13994 TRC1 19321 C4
10536 T 2 12486 C2 14312 C2 19391 C1
10678 T 1 12518 C2 14410 R 4 19396 R 2
10717 TR 2 12534 C2 14499 R 3 19402 R 4
11117 C4 12896 T 3 14506 R 2 19572 R 2
11370 R 1 12995 R 1 14623 T 1 20490 C2
11513 C1 13000 R 2 15050 TR 2 20616 TR 2
11525 C2 13108 C2 15132 TR 2 21043 C2
11680 T 2 13122 T 4 15790 TRC2 21322 TR 1
11736 R 2 13177 TR 4 17008 C2 22134 TR 2
11757 R 2 13202 R 3 18047 C1 22276 RC2
11815 R 2 13233 R 2 18107 R 2 22292 C2
11835 R 2 13278 R 2 18198 C1 22300 C1
12023 C2 13303 RC3 18273 C2 22344 C2
12048 C4 13348 C7 18338 C7 22625 T 2
12103 C2 13422 C4 18384 T 1 22656 TR 1
12126 C2 13433 C2 18625 R 3 22766 C1
12139 C2 13495 TR 2 18757 R 2 22789 TR 1
12140 C2 13504 TR 4 19128 C7 22791 R 2
12244 R 2

The Eighteen Provinces

Primary 12664 TR 1 12745 R 2 13469 T 2
10437 T 2 12666 TR 3 12754 R 4 13804 T 2
12567 T 2 12667 TR 3 12758 R 1 14092 T 2
12573 T 2 12675 TR 2 12767 TRC2 14238 R 3
12574 T 2 12682 TR 6 12770 TRC2 14504 R 2
12584 T 2 12683 TR 2 12794 C2 14779 TRC2
12587 T 2 12699 R 3 12827 C8 15781 R 2
12592 T 2 12704 R 4 12858 C2 16213 T 1
12602 T 2 12705 R 4 12859 C2 18074 T 2
12612 T 2 12706 R 4 12869 C3 18909 T 2
12615 T 3 12713 R 3 12936 T 4 19245 R 2
12639 TR 2 12718 R 2 12948 T 2 21676 T 2
12642 TR 2 12724 R 4 13155 TR 4 22092 TR 3
12646 TR 2 12738 R 4 13188 TR 2 22181 R 3
12652 TR 1 12740 R 2 13466 T 2 22590 T 3

Second. 11776 R 2 13866 T 2 18645 R 7
10018 T 2 11798 R 2 14121 R 2 18676 R 1
10038 T 2 11934 C2 14456 TR 2 19397 R 2
10054 T 2 12151 C2 14660 TR 2 19545 R 4
10138 C2 12193 T 8 15038 T 2 19570 R 2
10161 C2 12210 TR 8 15049 TR 2 19686 T 3
10174 C2 12930 T 2 15111 C2 20489 C3
10333 T 2 13037 R 2 15145 R 4 20699 C2
10348 TR 2 13107 C3 15148 R 4 21340 TR 3
10544 T 3 13153 TR 2 15203 C3 21675 T 1
11185 T 2 13266 R 2 15751 T 4 22177 R 3
11681 T 2 13566 R 2 15954 TR 5 22760 C3
11735 R 2 13805 T 2 18472 T 4

North China Broadly Conceived

Primary 11780 R 2 12655 TR 2 12737 R 4
10064 T 2 12571 T 1 12693 R 4 12753 R 4
10402 C8 12577 T 2 12715 R 2 12944 T 2
10435 C2 12582 T 2 12722 R 2 15082 R 2
10577 T 1 12616 T 2 12728 R 2 19260 R 2
10580 T 2 12630 TR 1 12734 R 2 20549 T 2
11737 R 2

Second. 10404 C2 10454 R 8 11821 R 2
10343 TR 4 10452 R 2 11728 R 2 12913 T 5
12998 R 2 14409 R 2 15694 R 2 21287 T 2
13810 T 2 14762 R 2 16119 R 2 22141 R 3
13962 R 2 15081 R 2 17873 R 2

Manchuria

Primary 11825 R 2 12687 TR 2 12841 C2
10341 TR 2 11834 R 2 12716 R 4 13011 R 2
10354 TR 2 12595 T 2 12717 R 4 13012 R 2
10378 R 2 12641 TR 2 12732 R 2 13265 R 2
10581 T 1 12643 TR 2 12736 R 4 13720 R 2
11032 R 4 12645 TR 2 12743 R 2 15669 TR 2
11697 TR 2 12648 TR 2 12746 R 2 15683 R 2
11715 TR 2 12663 TR 2 12752 R 4 20596 T 2
11777 R 2 12670 TR 2 12755 R 4

Second. 11691 TR 2 12893 T 2 15676 TR 2
10337 TR 2 11714 TR 2 13035 R 3 15687 R 2
10428 C2 11749 R 2 13240 R 2 15692 R 2
10824 R 2 11808 R 2 15668 TR 2 19237 R 1
11335 R 1 12180 T 2 15674 TR 2 19560 R 2
11670 T 4 12292 R 2

Northern China

Primary 12689 R 4 12842 C3 15045 T 2
10388 RC2 12725 R 4 12860 C2 15770 R 4
10576 T 1 12741 R 3

Second. 12958 TR 3 15083 R 2 22617 T 2
10431 C2 15037 T 2 15755 TR 3 22750 C3
10598 T 2

Northwestern China and Frontier Regions

Primary 12747 R 2 12768 RC1 12857 C2
12726 R 2 12766 RC2 12769 RC1

Second. 10427 C2 13358 C2 22754 C2
10415 C2 11686 TR 2 15393 R 2

South China Broadly Conceived

Primary 12578 T 2 12647 TR 2 12843 C2
10028 T 2 12579 T 2 12672 TR 2 12879 T 2
10323 T 2 12580 T 2 12680 TR 2 12960 TR 1
10344 TR 4 12581 T 2 12684 TR 2 13040 R 4
10366 R 3 12613 T 2 12723 R 2 13459 T 2
11772 R 2 12618 T 3 12756 R 2 13833 T 2
12569 T 2 12628 TR 2 12775 TRC2 13835 T 1
12570 T 2

Second. 10406 C2 12894 T 2 15078 R 2
10137 C2 11658 T 2 14262 RC2 15205 C2

East Central China

Primary ☐

Second. 10430 C2 12038 C2 12420 RC7
16407 TR 3 18487 T 2

Central Yangtze Provinces

Primary ☐

Second. 10395 TRC2 12975 R 2

Southwestern China

Primary 10318 T 2 12601 T 2 12626 TR 2
12735 R 2 12861 C2

Second. 10429 C2 17137 T 2

Southeastern China

Primary 12614 T 1 12870 C3 13808 T 3

Second. 10282 TR 3 10426 C2 15923 T 3
20722 T 4

Taiwan Only

Primary 12866 C4

Second. ☐

Hong Kong and Macau Only

Primary 12761 RC1 12867 C3 13043 RC3
16991 C4

Second. 22670 TR 1

14.3 Commerce and Services
商業 商業

Geographic China Broadly Conceived

Primary 12593 T 2 13017 R 3 13661 TR 1
10015 T 1 12759 R 2 13023 R 1 13676 TR 4
10017 T 2 12895 T 1 13025 R 4 13698 R 3
10022 T 2 12898 T 4 13028 R 2 13708 R 2
10026 T 2 12900 T 1 13033 R 1 15063 R 2
10042 T 2 12901 T 2 13049 TRC2 17142 T 3
10052 T 2 12902 T 3 13054 RC1 17531 T 1
10259 TRC4 12918 T 4 13106 C4 19217 TR 3
10586 T 1 12922 T 3 13111 C1 19219 TR 2
11270 TR 4 12934 T 2 13124 T 2 19717 T 2
11665 T 2 12940 T 1 13178 TR 3 20620 TR 2
11738 R 2 12941 T 2 13194 R 2 20662 TRC1
11770 R 2 12947 T 2 13461 T 4 21291 T 2
12118 C1 12957 TR 2 13574 TRC2 22555 T 2
12147 C1 12965 TR 4 13622 T 2 22586 T 3
12201 T 7 12989 R 2 13629 T 2 22614 T 3
12367 R 2 12997 R 1 13636 T 2 22705 R 1
12408 TRC2 13010 R 1

Second. 12478 C2 13704 R 2 20643 R 2
10111 TRC2 12575 T 2 13718 R 1 20832 R 2
10288 TR 1 12624 TR 2 13762 TRC1 20934 R 3
10363 R 2 12665 TR 1 13793 C2 22133 TR 2
10447 R 3 12730 R 1 13856 T 2 22345 C2
10614 T 1 13138 TR 2 13876 TR 2 22515 T 3
10663 T 2 13140 TR 4 14395 T 2 22561 T 1
11210 T 1 13142 TR 3 14399 T 4 22567 T 1
11293 TR 1 13144 TR 2 15937 TR 3 22578 T 2
11704 TR 2 13171 TR 2 16977 R 2 22594 T 2
11960 C2 13457 T 3 17272 R 2 22618 T 2
12202 T 2 13465 T 2 18470 T 2 22620 T 1
12238 R 2 13505 TR 4 20306 C2 22629 T 2
12246 R 2 13627 T 2 20560 T 1 22650 TR 3
12281 R 2 13649 TR 2 20576 T 2 22652 TR 3
12348 R 2 13662 TR 4 20591 T 3 22666 TR 2
12390 TRC2 13672 TR 5 20594 T 3 22740 TRC2
12417 RC2 13688 TR 2 20595 T 3 22866 T 2

Mainland China

Primary: Monographs
10232 C2 12906 T 1 13050 RC2 13470 T 4
10698 TR 2 12910 T 1 13065 C1 13518 TR 1
11313 R 1 12914 T 3 13070 C2 13523 TR 1
11348 R 1 12915 T 2 13076 C2 13542 R 2
11369 R 2 12921 T 2 13078 C1 13593 C2
11698 TR 2 12923 T 2 13080 C1 13666 TR 2
11707 TR 2 12950 TR 2 13104 C2 13689 TR 1
11790 R 2 12963 TR 2 13105 C2 13725 R 3
11807 R 2 12967 TR 1 13117 C2 17190 TR 5
11850 TRC2 12970 TR 2 13118 C2 17241 R 2
11860 RC2 12985 R 2 13119 C1 19222 TR 4
11946 C2 13004 R 1 13120 C2 19232 R 3
12218 TR 2 13006 R 2 13158 TR 2 19248 R 4
12384 RC2 13008 R 3 13217 R 3 19277 R 4
12414 TRC2 13015 R 4 13284 R 2 19281 R 5
12442 C7 13029 R 2 13311 TRC2 19285 RC5
12631 TR 2 13041 R 2 13456 T 2 19286 RC5
12708 R 2 13042 R 2 13464 T 3 19338 C5

Primary: Inclusions
11248 TR 1 13064 C2 13099 C2 13613 C2
12101 C2 13066 C2 13100 C2 14405 TR 4
12326 R 2 13067 C2 13101 C2 14406 TR 4
12422 RC7 13072 C1 13121 C2 14495 R 5
12617 T 4 13085 C2 13357 C3 22209 TRC1
12727 R 2 13088 C2 13532 R 4 22643 TR 1
13058 C7 13097 C2

Primary: Journal Articles
10408 C2 12471 C2 12949 TR 2 13003 R 2
10524 T 2 12474 C2 12956 TR 2 13018 R 7
10621 T 4 12499 C7 12961 TR 2 13020 R 2
11503 C2 12568 T 2 12964 TR 1 13026 R 2
12243 R 2 12594 T 2 12973 R 3 13027 R 2
12244 R 2 12668 TR 2 12982 R 1 13031 R 1
12278 R 1 12880 T 5 12983 R 2 13036 R 1
12343 R 2 12896 T 3 12990 R 2 13047 RC1
12344 R 2 12916 T 5 12994 R 2 13055 C2
12360 R 7 12929 T 4 12995 R 1 13056 C7
12457 C2 12945 T 1 13000 R 2 13060 C1

13061 c2 13087 c2 13110 c2 15066 R 2
13062 c2 13089 c2 13114 c2 15845 c7
13063 c2 13090 c2 13115 c2 16948 R 2
13068 c2 13091 c2 13116 c5 17121 c2
13069 c4 13092 c2 13180 TR 2 17135 T 1
13071 c2 13093 c2 13220 R 2 17374 c7
13073 c2 13094 c2 13244 R 2 19236 R 1
13074 c2 13095 c2 13253 R 2 19330 c3
13075 c2 13096 c2 13487 TR 1 19344 T 5
13077 c2 13103 c3 13771 c2 19359 R 3
13084 c2 13108 c2 14397 T 4 19435 R 4
13086 c2 13109 c2 14410 R 4 20566 T 4

SECONDARY: MONOGRAPHS

10007 T 2 11897 c2 12862 c2 13761 R 2
10011 T 2 11906 c2 13163 TR 2 13766 RC2
10019 T 2 11949 c2 13164 TR 4 13773 c2
10035 T 2 12000 c2 13172 TR 2 13795 c2
10068 TR 2 12001 c2 13250 R 2 13882 TR 2
10069 TR 2 12039 c2 13251 R 2 13883 TR 2
10083 TR 2 12054 c2 13272 R 2 13957 R 2
10172 c2 12086 c2 13289 R 2 13958 R 2
10214 TRC2 12148 c2 13343 c2 13959 R 2
10330 T 2 12166 c2 13344 c2 13989 RC1
10338 TR 2 12222 TR 7 13399 c2 14419 c2
10360 R 2 12241 R 2 13440 c2 14522 c2
10424 c2 12257 R 7 13443 c2 15553 c2
10470 c4 12270 R 7 13458 T 2 15741 T 3
10706 TR 2 12336 R 2 13482 T 2 17245 R 5
10715 TR 2 12339 R 2 13491 TR 1 17760 R 7
10768 R 4 12372 R 2 13535 R 2 17763 R 2
10820 R 1 12515 c7 13565 R 1 18987 TR 2
11113 c4 12562 c7 13570 R 1 19033 TRC1
11440 c2 12599 T 2 13612 c5 19302 c5
11689 TR 2 12606 T 2 13664 TR 1 19789 TR 2
11702 TR 2 12633 TR 2 13669 TR 1 20067 R 2
11705 TR 2 12637 TR 1 13674 TR 2 20068 R 2
11718 TR 2 12638 TR 2 13680 TR 1 20582 T 2
11754 R 2 12712 R 2 13701 R 1 20618 TR 2
11833 R 1 12714 R 1 13716 R 1 21644 T 2
11872 RC2 12751 R 2 13740 R 3 22162 R 2
11889 c2 12783 TRC2 13759 R 3 22575 T 1
11891 c2 12845 c4 13760 R 2 22669 TR 1

SECONDARY: INCLUSIONS

10078 TR 2 11700 TR 2 13131 T 2 18601 R 2
10334 T 2 11840 R 3 14068 c2 19279 R 4
10353 TR 2 11929 c2 14411 R 4 19332 c2
10414 c2 11978 c1 15990 c7 19333 c3
10993 c2 12042 c2 16037 c3 21066 c2
11013 T 2 12088 c2 17110 c7 22507 T 1
11063 c3 12092 c2 17317 RC2 22548 T 1
11447 c1 12159 c2 18452 T 2 22581 T 1
11688 TR 2 12197 T 7

SECONDARY: JOURNAL ARTICLES

10033 T 2 12007 c4 12531 c2 13616 c1
10352 TR 7 12013 c2 12555 c7 13624 T 1
10372 R 2 12016 c2 12558 c2 13631 T 1
10374 R 2 12032 c2 12610 T 4 13644 TR 3
10393 TRC2 12033 c2 12662 TR 2 13678 TR 5
10451 R 2 12049 c2 12739 R 2 13738 R 2
10492 c2 12066 c2 12774 RC2 13741 R 5
11041 RC2 12080 c2 12781 TRC2 13749 R 5
11097 c2 12091 c2 12816 c4 13776 c4
11190 T 1 12095 c2 13122 T 4 13790 c1
11308 R 1 12115 c2 13145 TR 4 13853 T 4
11373 R 1 12125 c2 13161 TR 2 14130 TRC2
11473 c1 12126 c2 13177 TR 4 14402 TR 4
11676 T 2 12133 c2 13202 R 3 14407 R 3
11717 TR 2 12139 c2 13204 R 2 14415 RC4
11742 R 2 12141 c2 13206 R 2 14420 T 7
11762 R 2 12145 c2 13210 R 4 14446 c2
11768 R 2 12162 c2 13233 R 2 14500 R 4
11788 R 2 12220 TR 2 13236 R 4 14759 R 4
11800 R 2 12226 TR 2 13237 R 4 15084 R 2
11802 R 2 12236 R 2 13238 R 3 15087 RC2
11815 R 2 12276 R 2 13263 R 2 15124 c1
11817 R 2 12284 R 7 13283 R 2 15128 T 4
11835 R 2 12318 R 2 13364 c2 15142 R 2
11868 RC2 12400 RC7 13391 c2 15787 R 3
11910 c2 12430 c7 13398 c4 17149 T 2
11915 c2 12480 c2 13452 T 2 17283 R 5
11933 c2 12482 c2 13504 TR 4 18107 R 2
11953 c2 12486 c2 13575 c2 18136 R 4
12004 c2 12490 c7 13607 c1 18326 c1
12006 c2 12511 c7 13609 c1 18336 c2

19128 c7 19235 R 1 20054 TR 1 22161 R 4
19183 c2 19278 R 1 20589 T 2 22540 T 1
19204 T 4 19310 c3 21104 c1 22700 R 3
19234 R 1 19613 T 1

THE EIGHTEEN PROVINCES

PRIMARY 12927 T 1 12978 R 2 13455 T 5
11656 T 2 12928 T 2 13022 R 2 13645 TR 4
11667 T 2 12930 T 2 13037 R 2 13758 R 2
11731 R 4 12933 T 2 13107 c3 14401 T 5
11776 R 2 12935 T 1 13151 TR 2 17096 R 2
11824 R 2 12936 T 4 13155 TR 4 17098 R 2
12204 T 2 12938 T 3 13160 TR 2 17099 R 6
12242 R 2 12946 T 1 13188 TR 2 17145 T 2
12345 R 2 12948 T 2 13191 TR 3 19239 R 5
12878 T 2 12959 TR 2 13223 R 2 21655 T 5
12890 T 2 12962 TR 3 13267 R 3 22761 c3
12909 T 2 12976 R 2 13288 R 2

SECOND. 12541 c7 13637 T 2 17144 T 2
10091 R 2 12587 T 2 13804 T 2 17484 R 2
10102 R 2 12642 TR 2 15111 c2 18405 T 2
10322 T 2 13128 T 2 15148 R 4 19212 T 4
10333 T 2 13153 TR 2 15951 TR 3 19245 R 2
10525 T 2 13212 R 2 15954 TR 5 19265 R 3
11185 T 2 13460 T 3 15965 R 3 19345 T 4
12195 T 2 13466 T 2 16114 R 4 19432 TR 4
12208 TR 2 13468 T 3 16115 R 1 21672 T 1
12253 R 2 13469 T 2 17034 TR 2 22057 T 2
12347 R 2 13521 TR 3 17059 R 4 22137 TR 2
12371 R 2 13566 R 2 17100 R 6 22537 T 1
12540 c7

NORTH CHINA BROADLY CONCEIVED

PRIMARY 12913 T 5 12998 R 2 19225 R 4
11780 R 2 12944 T 2 13021 R 3 19260 R 2
12235 R 2 12972 R 2 13024 R 2

SECOND. 11728 R 2 12722 R 2 15752 T 2
10343 TR 4 12582 T 2 12728 R 2 17658 T 4
10577 T 1 12655 TR 2 14409 R 2 18712 R 7

MANCHURIA

PRIMARY 12746 R 2 13001 R 3 13039 R 4
10337 TR 2 12892 T 5 13005 R 5 13082 c2
11335 R 1 12893 T 2 13007 R 3 13098 c2
11671 T 2 12925 T 2 13011 R 2 13229 R 7
11684 TR 2 12926 T 2 13012 R 2 13281 R 2
11697 TR 2 12968 TR 2 13013 R 2 14431 R 7
11715 TR 2 12969 TR 2 13014 R 2 16383 T 2
12285 R 2 12984 R 2 13032 R 2 16657 R 2
12287 R 7 12988 R 2 13035 R 3 19266 R 2
12315 R 2 12999 R 3

SECOND. 11818 R 2 12663 TR 2 16951 R 3
10341 TR 2 11823 R 2 12670 TR 2 16961 R 2
10354 TR 2 11834 R 2 12752 R 4 16967 R 3
11015 T 2 12180 T 2 13146 TR 2 17068 R 2
11670 T 4 12300 R 7 13304 RC2 17229 R 4
11691 TR 2 12322 R 7 16442 R 2 17265 R 3
11716 TR 2 12327 R 2 16448 R 2 17305 R 2
11749 R 2 12595 T 2 16691 R 7 17478 R 3
11808 R 2 12643 TR 2

NORTHERN CHINA

PRIMARY 12958 TR 3 12991 R 2 17062 R 2
12903 T 4 12966 TR 3 12993 R 2 17141 T 5
12905 T 2 12971 R 2 13002 R 3 17181 TR 2
12907 T 2 12974 R 2 13034 R 2 17197 R 3
12917 T 4 12979 R 2 15538 c2 17223 R 3
12931 T 3 12986 R 3 16578 R 2 17627 T 2
12939 T 3

SECOND. 15373 TR 3 16403 TR 2 17053 R 5
10319 T 2 15626 T 2 16536 T 2 17221 R 2
10380 R 2 15789 TRC2 16568 R 2 17277 R 3
12542 c7 15810 TRC2 16575 R 2 17409 T 2
12725 R 4 15952 TR 2 17039 TR 2 19331 c2
15328 T 2 16379 T 2 17046 R 2 22577 T 2

NORTHWESTERN CHINA AND FRONTIER REGIONS

PRIMARY 11722 R 2 12981 R 3 13019 R 2
13044 RC2 13045 RC2

SECOND. 13358 c2 15393 R 2 16431 R 2
10759 R 2 13799 T 1 15620 c2 16957 R 2
12726 R 2 15322 T 3 15673 TR 7 22732 TRC2
13332 c2 15323 T 4 16422 R 2

SOUTH CHINA BROADLY CONCEIVED

PRIMARY 12579 T 2 12891 T 2 13030 R 2
10366 R 3 12580 T 2 12894 T 2 13040 R 4
11658 T 2 12618 T 3 12897 T 2 13207 R 2
11729 R 2 12647 TR 2 12920 T 4 13729 R 3
12245 R 2 12723 R 2 12960 TR 1 13757 R 3
12297 R 7 12879 T 2 12987 R 3 17038 TR 2
12578 T 2 12888 T 2 12992 R 2 18463 T 2

SECOND. 12265 R 2 13195 R 2 18449 T 2
10046 T 2 12569 T 2 13256 R 2 19238 R 3
10289 TR 2 12672 TR 2 15726 T 2 20538 T 3
10344 TR 4 12680 TR 2 16650 R 2 21426 TRC3
12258 R 2 12684 TR 2 18377 T 2 22664 TR 4

EAST CENTRAL CHINA

PRIMARY 12911 T 1 13009 R 3 16980 R 3
10321 T 2 12955 TR 3 13139 TR 2 17212 R 2
11739 R 2 12977 R 3 16407 TR 3 17246 R 3
11746 R 2 12980 R 2 16922 T 2 19206 T 4
12904 T 2

SECOND. 16571 R 2 17213 R 2 17732 R 3
11747 R 2 16587 R 2 17220 R 2 17858 R 2
13224 R 4 16588 R 2 17222 R 3 18354 c3
13225 R 2 16620 R 2 17274 R 2 19075 R 2
13226 R 2 16621 R 2 17306 R 2 19258 R 3
15346 T 2 16622 R 2 17431 T 3 19264 R 3
15764 TR 3 16623 R 2 17434 T 2 22536 T 3
15765 TR 3 17035 TR 2 17440 TR 3 22696 R 3
16569 R 2 17208 R 2 17465 R 3

CENTRAL YANGTZE PROVINCES

PRIMARY 12942 T 3 13522 TR 2 16393 T 2
11723 R 2 12943 T 2 15445 R 3 16583 R 2
11795 R 2 12975 R 2 16381 T 3 19072 R 2

SECOND. 15129 T 2 16405 TR 3 16586 R 2
11726 R 2 15469 TRC2 16432 R 2 17172 T 3
14187 T 2 15642 R 2 16572 R 2 17206 R 2

SOUTHWESTERN CHINA

PRIMARY 12919 T 2 13209 R 2 16372 T 2
11679 T 2 12924 T 2 13538 R 2 16913 T 2
12889 T 2 12932 T 2 13801 T 2 17089 R 2
12899 T 2 12951 TR 2 16370 T 2 17106 c3
12912 T 2 13038 R 2 16371 T 2 17182 TR 7

SECOND. 12543 c7 16404 TR 2 19270 R 2
10318 T 2 12626 TR 2 16675 R 7 19334 c2
10358 R 2 13196 R 2 17137 T 2 20537 T 2
10566 T 2 15413 R 2 17146 T 7 22508 T 2
11706 TR 2 15748 T 2 18131 R 2

SOUTHEASTERN CHINA

PRIMARY 12885 T 2 12954 TR 3 16218 T 2
11675 T 2 12886 T 2 12996 R 3 16387 T 2
11683 TR 2 12887 T 2 13016 R 3 16505 T 2
12870 c3 12908 T 2 13305 TRC1 16923 T 2
12881 T 3 12952 TR 3 15359 T 2 18438 T 2
12883 T 2 12953 TR 2 15371 TR 2 19429 T 3
12884 T 2

SECOND. 15718 T 2 17191 TR 2 18427 T 5
10327 T 2 16507 T 2 17256 R 2 19209 T 3
15334 T 2 16514 T 2 17390 c2 19434 T 3
15364 T 3 16577 R 2 17738 c3 22678 R 3
15458 TRC2

TAIWAN ONLY

PRIMARY 13079 c2 13113 c2 15794 TRC3
11863 RC2 13081 c7 13306 TRC4 16727 RC2
13052 RC2 13083 c2 15601 RC2 16825 c7
13053 TRC2 13102 c2 15657 T 2 16829 c7
13059 c2 13112 c2 15658 T 2

HONG KONG AND MACAU ONLY

14.4 INDUSTRIAL ECONOMY

工業 工業

GEOGRAPHIC CHINA BROADLY CONCEIVED

MAINLAND CHINA

PRIMARY: MONOGRAPHS

PRIMARY: INCLUSIONS

PRIMARY: JOURNAL ARTICLES

SECONDARY: MONOGRAPHS

SECONDARY: INCLUSIONS

SECONDARY: JOURNAL ARTICLES

12956 TR 2 14482 R 1 17303 R 2 19496 R 4
12995 R 1 14490 R 3 17388 C2 19561 R 3
13063 C2 14498 R 3 18157 R 2 19568 R 3
13069 C4 14502 R 2 18213 C2 19572 R 2
13089 C2 14503 R 2 18718 R 2 19573 R 3
13091 C2 14511 R 2 18821 RC2 19582 RC3
13116 C5 14518 C4 19169 C2 19606 C3
13580 C1 14526 C3 19183 C2 19610 C3
13607 C1 14546 C1 19235 R 1 19673 C2
13609 C1 15020 C2 19278 R 1 20390 TR 3
13616 C1 15070 R 4 19303 C7 20669 C4
13685 TR 4 15087 RC2 19304 C1 21548 C2
13784 C4 15088 RC2 19316 C4 21957 C3
13790 C1 15124 C1 19328 C4 22134 TR 2
13791 C2 15128 T 4 19377 C2 22161 R 4
13919 R 2 15228 C2 19388 C2 22309 C1
14115 R 3 15244 C2 19410 C4 22766 C1
14458 TR 3 15644 RC3 19473 TR 4 22838 C2
14477 R 3 16006 C3 19484 R 3 22947 RC1
14481 R 2 16079 C7

The Eighteen Provinces

Primary 12770 TRC2 13167 TR 4 13275 R 3
10054 T 2 12909 T 2 13173 TR 4 13288 R 2
10656 T 2 12928 T 2 13188 TR 2 13709 R 4
11656 T 2 13128 T 2 13190 TR 1 14454 T 2
11725 R 2 13130 T 2 13191 TR 3 14456 TR 2
11731 R 4 13143 TR 3 13212 R 2 14480 R 4
11816 R 2 13151 TR 2 13223 R 2 14505 R 2
11934 C2 13153 TR 2 13254 R 2 14829 C2
12179 T 2 13155 TR 4 13255 R 2 15830 C2
12208 TR 2 13160 TR 2 13266 R 2 17248 R 2
12642 TR 2 13166 TR 2 13267 R 3 19577 R 3
12667 TR 3

Second. 11798 R 2 13731 R 2 17173 T 2
10091 R 2 12195 T 2 13751 R 1 17281 R 2
10158 C2 12371 R 2 14485 R 3 18654 R 2
10161 C2 12612 T 2 14493 R 4 19432 TR 4
10170 C2 12639 TR 2 14514 RC4 19489 R 4
10348 TR 2 12683 TR 2 14763 R 3 19515 R 3
10443 R 2 12878 T 2 15148 R 4 21297 T 2
11735 R 2 12978 R 2 15951 TR 3 21473 TRC2
11776 R 2

North China Broadly Conceived

Primary 11780 R 2 11821 R 2 11925 C2
12571 T 1 13286 R 4

Second. 10435 C2 11737 R 2 18750 R 2
10066 T 2 11728 R 2 18307 R 2 21287 T 2
10370 R 2

Manchuria

Primary 12280 R 2 13229 R 7 13281 R 2
10163 C2 12351 R 2 13230 R 3 13304 RC2
10340 TR 2 12645 TR 2 13240 R 2 13309 RC2
11714 TR 2 13146 TR 2 13249 R 2 13355 C4
11715 TR 2 13147 TR 2 13252 R 3 13362 C4
11777 R 2 13174 TR 2 13258 R 2 13396 C4
11808 R 2 13186 TR 2 13265 R 2 13720 R 2
11825 R 2 13205 R 2 13269 R 2 15181 RC2
11827 R 2 13215 R 1 13271 R 2 17229 R 4
11834 R 2 13219 R 4 13276 R 3 19311 C3

Second. 11671 T 2 12648 TR 2 15585 TR 2
10337 TR 2 11697 TR 2 12752 R 4 15614 RC2
10341 TR 2 11797 R 2 12984 R 2 15669 TR 2
10428 C2 11823 R 2 12988 R 2 15678 TR 2
10745 R 2 11832 R 2 13035 R 3 17315 RC3
11670 T 4 12285 R 2

Northern China

Primary 10431 C2 11765 R 1 12986 R 3
13126 T 2 13441 C5

Second. 10178 C2 10781 R 2 12905 T 2
15806 TRC3 19331 C2

Northwestern China and Frontier Regions

Primary 11161 C2 11926 C2 13332 C2
10415 C2 11686 TR 2 12003 C2 13358 C2
10427 C2 11722 R 2 13299 RC4

Second. 12011 C2 15620 C2 17007 C2
10725 TR 2 13019 R 2 16836 C2 19375 C2
11130 C2

South China Broadly Conceived

Primary 12879 T 2 13195 R 2 13403 C4
11729 R 2 12888 T 2 13207 R 2 17167 T 3
11772 R 2 13123 T 2 13208 R 3 17179 T 2
12843 C2 13192 R 7 13256 R 2

Second. 12578 T 2 12920 T 4 18412 T 2
11744 R 2 12894 T 2 14262 RC2 19296 C3
12570 T 2

East Central China

Primary 13139 TR 2 13225 R 2 17161 T 3
11739 R 2 13150 TR 5 13226 R 2 17162 T 3
12038 C2 13193 R 2 13326 C3 22596 T 3
12157 C2 13224 R 4 13392 C5

Second. 10430 C2

Central Yangtze Provinces

Primary 11795 R 2 13227 R 2 16586 R 2
11723 R 2 12975 R 2 13395 C4

Second. 10395 TRC2 11726 R 2 14187 T 2
17630 TR 4

Southwestern China

Primary 12924 T 2 13209 R 2 13287 R 2
10429 C2 13196 R 2 13221 R 2

Second. 11753 R 2 12912 T 2 17106 C3
10382 TRC2 11789 R 2 15413 R 2 19334 C2
11706 TR 2

Southeastern China

Primary 10392 TRC2 13203 R 2 13305 TRC1
17151 T 3

Second. 10511 T 2 12069 C2 15718 T 2
10426 C2 11837 R 2 12428 C2 16584 R 2

Taiwan Only

Primary 11959 C2 13235 R 2 13445 C4
10394 RC2 12106 C2 13297 RC2 13450 C2
11659 T 2 12143 C2 13301 RC2 14874 C2
11660 T 2 12146 C2 13306 TRC4 15600 TRC2
11851 TRC2 12175 C2 13312 RC2 16777 C2
11856 RC2 13137 T 2 13313 RC2 16824 C2
11863 RC2 13179 TR 2 13315 RC2 21039 C1
11873 RC2

Second. 11904 C2 12144 C2 15697 TRC2
10345 TR 2 11905 C2 12149 C2 15698 TRC2
10385 RC2 11975 C2 12150 C2 15890 C2
10387 TRC2 11984 C2 12174 C2 16726 TRC2
10416 C2 12017 C2 13113 C2 16740 TRC2
11138 C2 12135 C2 13602 C2 16864 C2
11663 T 2 12136 C2 14549 C4 16898 C2
11843 RC2 12142 C2 15471 RC2 21108 C7

Hong Kong and Macau Only

□

14.5 State Revenue and Expenditure

國家財政 国家财政

Geographic China Broadly Conceived

Primary 12629 TR 2 13497 TR 4 13627 T 2
10114 TRC2 12947 T 2 13502 TR 1 13629 T 2
10655 T 1 13171 TR 2 13505 TR 4 13708 R 2
10684 TR 2 13457 T 3 13517 TR 1 13718 R 1
10707 TR 2 13461 T 4 13554 R 3 13762 TRC1
11047 RC2 13462 T 1 13571 R 2 14211 T 1
11270 TR 4 13465 T 2 13573 RC1 18450 T 2
11738 R 2 13481 T 1 13574 TRC2 21291 T 2
11839 R 2 13485 T 1 13617 C3 22578 T 2
11841 R 2 13494 TR 2

Second. 10713 TR 2 12658 TR 1 18379 T 1
10008 T 2 11150 C4 12665 TR 1 18470 T 2
10010 T 2 11241 T 2 12940 T 1 18511 T 2
10014 T 2 11657 T 4 12957 TR 2 18579 R 2
10016 T 2 11673 T 2 13049 TRC2 20595 T 3
10034 T 2 11694 TR 2 13222 R 2 20934 R 3
10052 T 2 11766 R 2 13622 T 2 21279 T 2
10053 T 2 11767 R 2 13638 T 1 21347 TR 2
10085 TR 2 11779 R 2 13652 TR 3 21368 R 2
10331 T 2 11858 TRC2 13704 R 2 22567 T 1
10611 T 2 12147 C1 13717 R 2 22586 T 3
10615 T 2 12224 TR 1 13828 T 1 22594 T 2
10619 T 1 12232 TR 7 13856 T 2 22652 TR 3
10626 T 2 12328 R 7 14175 T 1 22740 TRC2
10665 T 1 12627 TR 1 15174 TRC2

Mainland China

Primary: Monographs
10214 TRC2 13008 R 3 13513 TR 4 13585 C1
10574 T 1 13080 C1 13516 TR 2 13588 C3
10702 TR 2 13152 TR 2 13518 TR 1 13589 C2
10721 TR 2 13456 T 2 13519 TR 1 13590 C2
10732 TR 2 13458 T 2 13520 TR 2 13593 C2
10890 TRC2 13464 T 3 13523 TR 1 13594 C2
10893 TRC2 13470 T 4 13535 R 2 13597 C1
11672 T 4 13472 T 1 13536 R 1 13603 C8
11705 TR 2 13473 T 1 13539 R 3 13610 C7
11760 R 2 13482 T 2 13542 R 2 13612 C5
11833 R 1 13489 TR 3 13543 R 1 13614 C2
11988 C2 13491 TR 1 13546 R 1 13653 TR 1
12039 C2 13496 TR 1 13549 R 2 13716 R 1
12054 C2 13498 TR 1 13556 R 1 13734 R 3
12229 TR 7 13499 TR 1 13563 R 1 13772 C1
12267 R 8 13503 TR 2 13565 R 1 13882 TR 2
12268 R 8 13506 TR 3 13570 R 1 14201 T 4
12442 C7 13507 TR 1 13572 R 1 14640 TR 2
12515 C7 13508 TR 2 13579 C2 18154 R 2
12923 T 2 13510 TR 1 13581 C1 20034 T 2
12950 TR 2 13511 TR 2 13584 C2 21363 TR 4
12963 TR 2

Primary: Inclusions
10542 T 2 13088 C2 13582 C2 13606 C2
10561 T 2 13532 R 4 13583 C2 13613 C2
10658 T 4 13552 R 4 13601 C2 15043 T 2
10694 TR 2 13576 C1 13605 C2 17032 TR 7
11865 RC2 13577 C2

Primary: Journal Articles
10033 T 2 13467 T 1 13528 R 1 13592 C1
10524 T 2 13474 T 1 13530 R 1 13596 C7
11071 C2 13476 T 1 13531 R 2 13598 C1
11773 R 2 13477 T 2 13533 R 2 13599 C1
11778 R 2 13480 T 1 13534 R 8 13600 C2
11961 C2 13483 T 1 13545 R 1 13604 C2
12052 C2 13484 T 2 13547 R 1 13607 C1
12053 C2 13486 T 1 13550 R 2 13608 C7
12185 T 8 13487 TR 1 13553 R 2 13609 C1
12187 T 8 13488 TR 2 13555 R 1 13611 C1
12307 R 7 13490 TR 1 13561 R 2 13615 C1
12594 T 2 13492 TR 8 13562 R 4 13616 C1
12896 T 3 13493 TR 2 13567 R 1 13685 TR 4
13063 C2 13495 TR 2 13569 R 4 13842 T 1
13073 C2 13501 TR 1 13575 C2 13886 R 4
13244 R 2 13504 TR 4 13578 C1 14738 R 2
13451 T 1 13509 TR 1 13580 C1 19775 T 2
13452 T 2 13515 TR 1 13587 C2 20064 R 2
13453 T 1 13526 R 1 13591 C2 22625 T 2

Secondary: Monographs
10011 T 2 10724 TR 4 11850 TRC2 13668 TR 4
10020 T 2 10739 TR 1 11906 C2 13674 TR 2
10039 T 2 10758 R 4 11912 C2 13687 TR 1
10065 T 2 10769 R 2 12086 C2 13701 R 1
10125 RC2 10785 R 1 12227 TR 7 13719 R 4
10291 TR 2 10807 R 1 12264 R 7 13755 R 4
10519 T 4 10812 R 2 12303 R 2 13756 R 1
10562 T 1 10836 R 4 12331 R 7 13760 R 2
10587 T 2 10844 R 4 12379 RC7 13761 R 2
10643 T 1 11036 TRC7 12412 RC7 13874 TR 1
10654 T 3 11076 C2 12426 RC7 13901 R 2
10660 T 2 11154 C1 12475 C2 14093 T 2
10669 T 1 11243 T 2 12562 C7 14133 C3
10672 T 2 11689 TR 2 12640 TR 2 14164 T 2
10688 TR 2 11702 TR 2 12906 T 1 14231 TR 4
10695 TR 2 11740 R 2 13070 C2 14508 R 3
10720 TR 1 11750 R 2 13158 TR 2 14584 T 2

14658 TR 2 18144 R 2 18722 R 2 20036 T 2
14700 TR 2 18232 C2 18842 C2 21259 T 2
14885 C1 18526 T 2 19033 TRC1 21563 C1
16123 R 2 18585 R 2 19286 RC5 22575 T 1
17758 TR 2 18598 R 2 19789 TR 2 22717 R 2
17763 R 2 18659 R 2

Secondary: Inclusions
10078 TR 2 11969 C2 13136 T 7 15180 TRC1
10334 T 2 12047 C1 13333 C2 17550 T 2
10441 T 2 12092 C2 13657 TR 1 18745 R 2
10601 T 2 12216 TR 7 13663 TR 4 19199 C7
10637 T 3 12293 R 8 13859 T 2 21877 RC3
10650 T 2 12326 R 2 13920 R 2 22034 T 2
10662 T 2 12396 RC8 13977 R 2 22548 T 1
11013 T 2 12459 C7 14628 TR 2 22581 T 1
11063 C3 12559 C2

Secondary: Journal Articles
10196 TR 2 11923 C1 12419 RC7 14183 T 2
10492 C2 11943 C2 12443 C7 14239 R 7
10518 T 4 11991 C2 12451 C7 14397 T 4
10520 T 1 12006 C2 12468 C2 14443 C7
10536 T 2 12032 C2 12490 C7 16481 C7
10609 T 1 12097 C2 12511 C7 18090 T 3
10728 TR 1 12161 C2 12529 C7 18304 R 2
10789 R 5 12189 T 2 12596 T 2 18327 C2
10809 R 2 12215 TR 2 12781 TRC2 18504 T 2
10817 R 1 12220 TR 2 12929 T 4 18673 R 7
11041 RC2 12221 TR 2 13018 R 7 18684 R 2
11054 TRC2 12243 R 2 13068 C2 19278 R 1
11186 T 4 12259 R 7 13087 C2 19374 C2
11191 T 1 12262 R 2 13093 C2 19470 C8
11664 T 2 12273 R 7 13148 TR 1 20038 T 7
11680 T 2 12277 R 2 13204 R 2 20041 T 1
11693 TR 2 12311 R 7 13210 R 4 21283 T 2
11733 R 2 12314 R 8 13321 C4 21805 TR 1
11742 R 2 12325 R 2 13723 R 2 22047 T 2
11743 R 2 12334 R 8 13739 R 1 22549 T 1
11764 R 2 12350 R 8 13776 C4 22771 T 2
11806 R 2 12360 R 7 13785 C4 22785 TR 1
11817 R 2 12388 RC7 13789 C2

The Eighteen Provinces

Primary 12574 T 2 13469 T 2 13551 R 1
10038 T 2 12602 T 2 13475 T 8 13566 R 2
10525 T 2 12675 TR 2 13478 T 2 13637 T 2
10533 T 2 13455 T 5 13521 TR 3 18364 T 2
10544 T 3 13460 T 3 13524 R 1 18436 T 2
11656 T 2 13463 T 5 13527 R 2 18621 R 3
12198 T 8 13466 T 2 13529 R 3 22057 T 2
12225 TR 8 13468 T 3

Second. 12346 R 8 13804 T 2 16093 T 2
10138 C2 12385 RC8 13830 T 2 18461 T 2
10187 T 1 12587 T 2 13979 R 2 19347 T 3
10760 R 2 12682 TR 6 13990 TRC1 19458 R 8
10839 R 2 12928 T 2 14121 R 2 22558 T 2
11667 T 2 12930 T 2 14401 T 5 22590 T 3
12207 T 2 12933 T 2 14432 R 8 22641 T 2
12212 TR 2 13160 TR 2 15038 T 2 22708 R 3
12275 R 8

North China Broadly Conceived

Primary 10577 T 1 13548 R 2 13962 R 2
14751 R 2 17846 R 7

Second. 12913 T 5 18712 R 7 21287 T 2
11925 C2 18682 R 2 18743 R 7

Manchuria

Primary 13032 R 2 13557 R 1 13564 R 1
11827 R 2 13500 TR 2 13558 R 2 13568 R 1
12248 R 2 13512 TR 2 13559 R 2 13699 R 3
13005 R 5 13514 TR 8 13560 R 1

Second. 11015 T 2 12968 TR 2 13355 C4
10582 T 2 12893 T 2 13014 R 2 16383 T 2
10719 TR 1

Northern China

Primary 10380 R 2 10652 T 3 13525 R 3
13537 R 4

Second. 10607 T 3 14214 TR 3 17570 R 2
10505 T 3 10781 R 2 14712 R 2 18422 T 3
10576 T 1 10816 R 2 17407 T 8 21293 T 3
10584 T 3

Northwestern China and Frontier Regions

Primary 13814 T 2 22701 R 2

Second. 10725 TR 2 16517 T 2 22531 T 2

South China Broadly Conceived

Primary 13040 R 4 13459 T 2 13471 T 2

Second. 11014 T 2 12894 T 2 13869 T 2
10299 TRC3 12186 T 7 12897 T 2 13881 TR 2
10636 T 1 12647 TR 2 12987 R 3 18129 R 3

East Central China

Primary 11769 R 2 13540 R 2 13544 R 2
15924 T 2 16525 T 8

Second. 10801 R 4 14714 R 1 16394 T 2

Central Yangtze Provinces

Primary 13479 T 1 13522 TR 2 13541 R 7

Second. 11726 R 2 16639 R 7 19072 R 2

Southwestern China

Primary 11679 T 2 12932 T 2 13538 R 2
10790 R 2 11706 TR 2 13454 T 1 16675 R 7

Second. 10791 R 2 16267 TR 2 16371 T 2
18131 R 2 22552 T 8

Southeastern China

Primary 10855 RC2 16530 T 2 16613 R 7

Second. 10511 T 2 10522 T 3 11837 R 2

Taiwan Only

Primary 13586 C1 13602 C2 16741 TRC8
13081 C7 13595 C1 13618 C1

Second. 11863 RC2 12136 C2 16740 TRC2
10653 T 2 11873 RC2 16550 TR 8 16742 TRC2
11109 C1 11964 C2 16551 TR 7 16745 TRC8
11856 RC2 12017 C2 16561 TR 2 16829 C7

Hong Kong and Macau Only

□

14.6 Financial, Monetary, and Credit Systems

金融、貨幣及信託制度
金融、貨幣及び信用制度

Geographic China Broadly Conceived

Primary 13517 TR 1 13658 TR 3 13710 R 3
10828 R 2 13571 R 2 13661 TR 1 13717 R 2
11687 TR 2 13619 T 2 13662 TR 4 13718 R 1
11703 TR 2 13622 T 2 13665 TR 1 13730 R 1
11779 R 2 13625 T 1 13667 TR 1 13733 R 4
11839 R 2 13627 T 2 13672 TR 5 13742 R 1
11841 R 2 13629 T 2 13676 TR 4 13747 R 3
11857 TRC2 13630 T 1 13683 TR 1 13748 R 2
12147 C1 13633 T 1 13688 TR 2 13762 TRC1
12310 R 8 13636 T 2 13692 TR 4 13763 TRC2
12629 TR 2 13638 T 1 13698 R 3 13793 C2
12730 R 1 13642 TR 3 13704 R 2 15126 T 2
13010 R 1 13649 TR 2 13705 R 2 18388 T 2
13168 TR 4 13652 TR 3 13707 R 3 19219 TR 2
13465 T 2 13656 TR 4 13708 R 2 22650 TR 3
13497 TR 4

Second. 10017 T 2 10655 T 1 10741 R 1
10013 T 2 10053 T 2 10707 TR 2 11657 T 4
11669 T 3 12895 T 1 14112 TR 1 21291 T 2
11692 TR 2 12918 T 4 14395 T 2 21302 T 2
11694 TR 2 12934 T 2 14399 T 4 21368 R 2
11704 TR 2 13144 TR 2 17448 TR 1 22652 TR 3
11738 R 2 13222 R 2 18540 TR 2 22681 R 3
12439 C8 13481 T 1 18801 TRC2 22720 R 3
12611 T 1 13502 TR 1 20463 R 3

Mainland China

Primary: Monographs
10023 T 2 12590 T 2 13668 TR 4 13744 R 2
10498 C2 12653 TR 1 13669 TR 1 13750 R 2
11313 R 1 12914 T 3 13674 TR 2 13755 R 4
11344 R 1 12985 R 2 13680 TR 1 13756 R 1
11369 R 2 13042 R 2 13681 TR 3 13759 R 3
11698 TR 2 13078 C1 13682 TR 2 13760 R 2
11702 TR 2 13080 C1 13687 TR 1 13761 R 2
11705 TR 2 13228 R 3 13689 TR 1 13766 RC2
11724 R 2 13420 C2 13690 TR 5 13768 C1
11745 R 2 13520 TR 2 13691 TR 2 13769 C7
11750 R 2 13536 R 1 13701 R 1 13772 C1
11794 R 5 13539 R 3 13706 R 1 13773 C2
11807 R 2 13570 R 1 13711 R 4 13775 C2
11822 R 2 13584 C2 13715 R 8 13778 C2
11833 R 1 13614 C2 13716 R 1 13787 C2
11877 RC2 13641 T 2 13719 R 4 13788 C1
11962 C2 13650 TR 5 13725 R 3 13795 C2
11988 C2 13651 TR 2 13727 R 1 14153 C2
12005 C2 13653 TR 1 13734 R 3 14436 R 7
12054 C2 13654 TR 4 13735 R 1 17238 R 2
12317 R 7 13659 TR 4 13736 R 7 19705 R 2
12358 R 2 13664 TR 1 13740 R 3 20068 R 2
12372 R 2 13666 TR 2 13743 R 2 21363 TR 4

Primary: Inclusions
10694 TR 2 13675 TR 1 14411 R 4 18343 C2
13601 C2 13779 C1 15333 T 3 21877 RC3
13657 TR 1 13794 C1 17550 T 2 22643 TR 1
13663 TR 4

Primary: Journal Articles
10722 TR 3 13609 C1 13693 R 2 13774 C4
11331 R 1 13620 T 1 13694 R 2 13776 C4
11762 R 2 13623 T 1 13695 R 2 13780 C2
11773 R 2 13624 T 1 13696 R 1 13781 C1
11778 R 2 13626 T 1 13702 R 1 13782 C2
11893 C1 13628 T 8 13712 R 1 13783 C2
11991 C2 13631 T 1 13714 R 2 13784 C4
12053 C2 13632 T 3 13723 R 2 13785 C4
12098 C2 13639 T 2 13737 R 3 13786 C1
12313 R 8 13643 TR 5 13738 R 2 13789 C2
12334 R 8 13644 TR 3 13739 R 1 13790 C1
12880 T 5 13648 TR 4 13741 R 5 13791 C2
12961 TR 2 13660 TR 2 13745 R 1 13792 C2
13062 C2 13670 TR 3 13746 R 4 13796 C1
13145 TR 4 13677 TR 1 13749 R 5 13797 C1
13501 TR 1 13678 TR 5 13753 R 4 17283 R 5
13587 C2 13684 TR 1 13765 RC1 19344 T 5
13607 C1 13685 TR 4 13771 C2 22040 T 1
13608 C7 13686 TR 4

Secondary: Monographs
10003 T 2 11912 C2 13152 TR 2 15115 C2
10065 T 2 12060 C2 13165 TR 7 16106 TR 2
10132 C2 12154 C2 13211 R 2 17245 R 5
10643 T 1 12222 TR 7 13308 RC2 17485 R 2
10688 TR 2 12227 TR 7 13336 C2 18114 R 2
10695 TR 2 12230 TR 2 13338 C2 18120 R 2
10724 TR 4 12257 R 7 13498 TR 1 18144 R 2
10732 TR 2 12264 R 7 13507 TR 1 18154 R 2
10758 R 4 12267 R 8 13510 TR 1 18526 T 2
10768 R 4 12268 R 8 13511 TR 2 18585 R 2
10813 R 2 12270 R 7 13516 TR 2 18659 R 2
10819 R 2 12291 R 7 13518 TR 1 18717 R 2
10836 R 4 12331 R 7 13523 TR 1 18817 RC2
11440 C2 12384 RC2 13535 R 2 19135 C7
11672 T 4 12441 C2 13543 R 1 19246 R 5
11699 TR 2 12524 C2 13546 R 1 19276 R 1
11740 R 2 12631 TR 2 13556 R 1 19281 R 5
11748 R 2 12633 TR 2 13563 R 1 19286 RC5
11754 R 2 12637 TR 1 13565 R 1 19302 C5
11756 R 2 12714 R 1 13847 T 1 19638 R 7
11830 R 2 12963 TR 2 14127 RC2 20067 R 2
11846 RC2 13006 R 2 14201 T 4 21259 T 2
11852 RC2 13065 C1 14396 T 2 21465 R 2
11903 C2 13105 C2 15052 TR 2 22619 T 2

Secondary: Inclusions
10642 T *2* 12269 R *8* 13156 TR *2* 17032 TR *7*
10650 T *2* 12293 R *8* 13583 C*2* 18370 T *2*
11248 TR *1* 12650 TR *2* 13605 C*2* 19129 C*8*
11865 RC*2* 12731 R *2* 13977 R *2* 19365 T *2*
12101 C*2* 13085 C*2* 15074 R *7* 19585 RC*4*

Secondary: Journal Articles
10734 TR *2* 12134 C*2* 13026 R *2* 14130 TRC*2*
10815 R *1* 12138 C*2* 13036 R *1* 14397 T *4*
10951 C*3* 12139 C*2* 13068 C*2* 14407 R *3*
11085 C*2* 12215 TR *2* 13069 C*4* 14410 R *4*
11186 T *4* 12289 R *7* 13122 T *4* 14434 R *7*
11220 T *1* 12314 R *8* 13159 TR *2* 14440 RC*8*
11239 T *1* 12360 R *7* 13234 R *2* 14533 C*4*
11664 T *2* 12362 R *8* 13236 R *4* 15109 C*7*
11676 T *2* 12419 RC*7* 13237 R *4* 18304 R *2*
11701 TR *1* 12427 C*7* 13262 R *4* 18326 C*1*
11717 TR *2* 12470 C*8* 13263 R *2* 18684 R *2*
11733 R *2* 12566 T *2* 13428 C*4* 18714 R *2*
11742 R *2* 12568 T *2* 13486 T *1* 19175 C*8*
11743 R *2* 12607 T *1* 13493 TR *2* 19255 R *4*
11761 R *2* 12669 TR *2* 13575 C*2* 19271 R *4*
11764 R *2* 12695 R *1* 13580 C*1* 19310 C*3*
11806 R *2* 12702 R *2* 13599 C*1* 19314 C*1*
11835 R *2* 12707 R *4* 13604 C*2* 19430 R *4*
11987 C*2* 12709 R *2* 13615 C*1* 20042 T *1*
11992 C*2* 12964 TR *1* 13840 T *2* 21263 T *2*
12007 C*4* 13000 R *2* 13919 R *2* 22098 TR *2*
12059 C*2* 13020 R *2* 14115 R *3* 22785 TR *1*

The Eighteen Provinces

Primary 13621 T *4* 13671 TR *1* 13732 R *1*
12210 TR *8* 13635 T *1* 13679 TR *5* 13751 R *1*
12948 T *2* 13637 T *2* 13703 R *2* 13752 R *4*
13167 TR *4* 13645 TR *4* 13709 R *4* 13758 R *2*
13463 T *5* 13646 TR *3* 13724 R *3* 14092 T *2*
13551 R *1* 13647 TR *1* 13731 R *2* 14424 TR *7*

Second. 12346 R *8* 12962 TR *3* 19262 R *1*
10752 R *3* 12373 R *7* 13151 TR *2* 19265 R *3*
11185 T *2* 12612 T *2* 13155 TR *4* 19347 T *3*
11731 R *4* 12639 TR *2* 13275 R *3* 19458 R *8*
11824 R *2* 12738 R *4* 13478 T *2* 20057 R *7*
12151 C*2* 12878 T *2* 14401 T *5* 22641 T *2*
12212 TR *2* 12933 T *2* 19122 C*8* 22928 R *2*

North China Broadly Conceived

Primary 11791 R *2* 13286 R *4*

Second. 12469 C*8* 12655 TR *2* 13548 R *2*
10827 R *2* 12630 TR *1* 12693 R *4* 19225 R *4*
11821 R *2*

Manchuria

Primary 13146 TR *2* 13655 TR *2* 13720 R *2*
11670 T *4* 13147 TR *2* 13697 R *4* 13722 R *1*
11827 R *2* 13557 R *1* 13699 R *3* 13728 R *1*
12327 R *2* 13634 T *2* 13700 R *1* 17229 R *4*

Second. 11684 TR *2* 11823 R *2* 12663 TR *2*
10581 T *1* 11691 TR *2* 11832 R *2* 13230 R *3*
10582 T *2* 11696 TR *2* 12211 TR *8* 13249 R *2*
10719 TR *1* 11714 TR *2* 12321 R *7* 13355 C*4*
11335 R *1* 11818 R *2* 12648 TR *2* 15669 TR *2*

Northern China

Primary 12931 T *3* 13640 T *5* 13754 R *2*

Second. 14427 R *2* 15394 R *2* 17570 R *2*

Northwestern China and Frontier Regions

Primary 13019 R *2* 13713 R *2* 22732 TRC*2*

Second. 13799 T *1* 13826 T *1* 22698 R *2*

South China Broadly Conceived

Primary 12723 R *2* 12920 T *4* 13729 R *3*
13757 R *3* 17443 TR *2*

Second. 12383 RC*2* 13030 R *2* 13471 T *2*
11658 T *2* 12613 T *2* 13040 R *4* 17167 T *3*
11729 R *2*

East Central China

Primary 13721 R *2* 13726 R *3* 16417 R *3*

Second. 12911 T *1* 17464 R *4* 20886 R *3*
12420 RC*7* 16609 R *7* 19206 T *4*

Central Yangtze Provinces

Primary □

Second. 11723 R *2* 13541 R *7* 19450 R *7*

Southwestern China

Primary □

Second. 10790 R *2* 13209 R *2* 18365 T *3*
10746 R *4* 10791 R *2* 16675 R *7* 20475 RC*4*

Southeastern China

Primary □

Second. 10522 T *3* 10756 R *2* 11837 R *2*
13203 R *2*

Taiwan Only

Primary 13673 TR *4* 13764 RC*2* 13770 C*4*
13777 C*1* 16740 TRC*2*

Second. 11905 C*2* 12142 C*2* 12150 C*2*
11044 RC*2* 11959 C*2* 12143 C*2* 13053 TRC*2*
11851 TRC*2* 12106 C*2* 12144 C*2* 15600 TRC*2*
11873 RC*2* 12136 C*2* 12149 C*2* 16742 TRC*2*

Hong Kong and Macau Only

Primary 13767 RC*3*

Second. □

15 The Military

軍事 軍事

Geographic China Broadly Conceived

Primary: Monographs
10001 T *2* 10806 R *2* 13877 TR *2* 18801 TRC*2*
10008 T *2* 11241 T *2* 13902 R *2* 18809 RC*2*
10013 T *2* 11657 T *4* 13916 R *2* 18871 T *2*
10052 T *2* 12624 TR *2* 13997 RC*2* 20576 T *2*
10082 TR *2* 13718 R *1* 14156 T *2* 21279 T *2*
10085 TR *2* 13811 T *2* 14951 C*2* 21368 R *2*
10106 R *2* 13812 T *2* 15175 RC*2* 21425 TRC*5*
10107 R *2* 13824 T *2* 15191 RC*2* 21427 TRC*1*
10108 R *2* 13828 T *1* 15311 T *2* 22559 T *2*
10111 TRC*2* 13841 T *4* 18077 T *2* 22580 T *2*
10329 T *2* 13844 T *1* 18409 T *2* 22594 T *2*
10526 T *2* 13846 T *2* 18492 T *2* 22629 T *2*
10626 T *2* 13864 T *2* 18511 T *2* 22666 TR *2*
10684 TR *2* 13873 TR *2* 18534 TR *2* 22728 RC*2*
10700 TR *2* 13876 TR *2* 18707 R *2* 22740 TRC*2*
10713 TR *2*
21366 R *2* 22555 T *2* 22650 TR *3* 22694 R *3*
21392 TRC*2* 22561 T *1* 22657 TR *1* 22720 R *3*
21412 RC*2* 22614 T *3* 22681 R *3* 22866 T *2*
21467 TRC*1*

Primary: Inclusions
10073 TR *2* 13856 T *2* 13966 R *2* 18470 T *2*
11673 T *2* 13878 TR *2* 18418 T *1* 20563 T *2*
13848 T *1*

Primary: Journal Articles
10663 T *2* 13855 T *2* 13985 RC*1* 18303 R *2*
13497 TR *4* 13867 T *4* 14007 RC*1* 21377 R *2*
13825 T *1* 13950 R *2*

Secondary: Monographs
10004 T *2* 10539 T *1* 14155 T *2* 18540 TR *2*
10010 T *2* 10560 T *2* 14560 T *3* 18542 TR *2*
10022 T *2* 10586 T *1* 14627 T *1* 18545 TR *2*
10025 T *2* 10611 T *2* 15136 TR *2* 18560 TR *2*
10042 T *2* 10803 R *2* 15158 TRC*2* 18579 R *2*
10048 T *2* 10804 R *3* 15161 TRC*2* 18687 R *2*
10053 T *2* 10850 RC*1* 15174 TRC*2* 18700 R *2*
10058 T *2* 10853 TRC*2* 15345 T *3* 18711 R *2*
10076 TR *2* 10891 TRC*1* 17531 T *1* 18741 R *2*
10077 TR *2* 11605 RC*2* 18125 R *1* 18764 R *2*
10096 R *2* 11708 TR *2* 18375 T *2* 18937 T *2*
10100 R *2* 12629 TR *2* 18379 T *1* 19503 R *2*
10113 TRC*2* 13505 TR *4* 18388 T *2* 20160 TR *2*
10114 TRC*2* 13622 T *2* 18442 T *4* 21269 T *2*
10331 T *2* 13762 TRC*1* 18494 T *2* 21276 T *2*

Secondary: Inclusions
10032 T *2* 12589 T *2* 18478 T *1* 18566 TR *1*
10510 T *2* 14248 R *2* 18525 T *2* 21712 T *2*
10596 T *1* 14400 T *4* 18558 TR *2* 22578 T *2*
10892 TRC*2* 18073 T *2*

Secondary: Journal Articles
10534 T *2* 13129 T *5* 18111 R *1* 21408 TRC*2*
10553 T *1* 14102 T *2* 18549 TR *3* 21855 TRC*2*
10714 TR *1* 15126 T *2* 20588 T *2* 22345 C*2*
12898 T *4* 15194 TRC*2* 21328 TR *2*

Mainland China

Primary: Monographs
10020 T *2* 13858 T *2* 13991 RC*1* 18563 TR *4*
10067 TR *2* 13861 T *1* 14001 RC*1* 18585 R *2*
10092 R *2* 13868 T *2* 14002 RC*2* 18603 R *2*
10101 R *2* 13870 T *1* 14006 RC*2* 18608 R *2*
10103 R *2* 13874 TR *1* 14010 RC*2* 18619 R *2*
10126 RC*2* 13880 TR *2* 14012 RC*2* 18629 R *2*
10128 TRC*2* 13882 TR *2* 14013 RC*1* 18635 R *2*
10180 C*2* 13883 TR *2* 14014 RC*1* 18636 R *2*
10519 T *4* 13884 TR *2* 14015 RC*1* 18647 R *2*
10562 T *1* 13885 TR *1* 14018 TRC*2* 18655 R *2*
10587 T *2* 13888 R *2* 14020 RC*2* 18656 R *2*
10643 T *1* 13893 R *2* 14033 C*2* 18674 R *2*
10688 TR *2* 13896 R *2* 14037 C*2* 18744 R *2*
10695 TR *2* 13898 R *2* 14040 C*1* 18759 R *2*
10706 TR *2* 13901 R *2* 14047 C*1* 18792 RC*2*
10715 TR *2* 13903 R *2* 14053 C*1* 18817 RC*2*
10718 TR *2* 13905 R *2* 14055 C*1* 18819 RC*2*
10726 TR *2* 13909 R *2* 14065 C*1* 18827 RC*2*
10727 TR *3* 13914 R *2* 14066 C*2* 18862 T *2*
10729 TR *2* 13923 R *1* 14077 C*1* 18915 T *2*
10769 R *2* 13927 R *2* 14201 T *4* 19389 C*1*
10811 R *1* 13928 R *2* 14329 C*2* 19390 C*2*
10813 R *2* 13930 R *1* 14584 T *2* 20496 C*2*
10844 R *4* 13937 R *2* 15235 C*2* 20506 C*1*
10888 TRC*2* 13945 R *2* 15279 C*2* 20558 T *2*
10893 TRC*2* 13951 R *2* 15285 C*4* 20749 T *2*
11053 RC*2* 13957 R *2* 17588 C*8* 21259 T *2*
11689 TR *2* 13958 R *2* 18098 T *3* 21265 T *2*
11699 TR *2* 13959 R *2* 18120 R *2* 21320 TR *2*
11849 TRC*2* 13961 R *1* 18126 R *3* 21324 TR *2*
11949 C*2* 13963 R *2* 18142 R *2* 21345 TR *2*
12783 TRC*2* 13965 R *2* 18143 R *2* 21367 R *2*
12963 TR *2* 13969 R *2* 18145 R *2* 21381 R *1*
13125 T *2* 13970 R *2* 18172 RC*2* 21414 RC*2*
13328 C*2* 13975 R *2* 18309 R *3* 21415 RC*1*
13807 T *1* 13980 R *1* 18312 RC*2* 21420 TRC*2*
13819 T *1* 13984 RC*1* 18319 C*1* 22135 TR *2*
13847 T *1* 13986 TRC*2* 18430 T *2* 22217 RC*2*
13849 T *4* 13989 RC*1* 18526 T *2* 22710 R *2*

Primary: Inclusions
10051 T *2* 13971 R *2* 14032 C*2* 15043 T *2*
10542 T *2* 13977 R *2* 14043 C*1* 18000 C*2*
10616 T *2* 13982 R *1* 14046 C*1* 18119 R *2*
10650 T *2* 13987 TRC*2* 14048 C*1* 18325 C*1*
10694 TR *2* 13988 RC*1* 14049 C*1* 18370 T *2*
13296 RC*3* 13993 RC*2* 14050 C*1* 18429 T *2*
13806 T *3* 13995 RC*1* 14054 C*1* 18615 R *2*
13823 T *2* 13996 TRC*2* 14057 C*1* 18632 R *2*
13834 T *2* 13998 RC*1* 14059 C*1* 18672 R *2*
13859 T *2* 13999 RC*1* 14068 C*2* 18745 R *2*
13865 T *2* 14000 TRC*1* 14069 C*1* 18825 RC*2*
13904 R *2* 14011 RC*2* 14071 C*1* 19373 C*1*
13920 R *2* 14017 RC*1* 14082 C*1* 22169 R *2*
13942 R *2* 14019 RC*1* 14147 C*2* 22319 C*1*
13946 R *2* 14022 C*1* 14261 RC*1* 22379 C*2*
13948 R *2* 14030 C*2* 14325 C*2* 22565 T *2*
13949 R *2* 14031 C*2* 14380 C*1* 22878 T *1*

Primary: Journal Articles
10320 T *2* 10933 C*2* 12314 R *8* 13821 T *1*
10575 T *1* 10966 C*2* 13530 R *1* 13829 T *1*
10734 TR *2* 10974 C*3* 13555 R *1* 13838 T *2*
10743 R *2* 10995 C*1* 13800 T *3* 13839 T *2*
10753 R *1* 11148 C*2* 13809 T *1* 13840 T *2*
10766 R *2* 11583 TR *2* 13815 T *2* 13842 T *1*
10786 R *2* 11768 R *2* 13817 T *1* 13850 T *1*
10834 R *2* 12215 TR *2* 13818 T *1* 13851 T *1*

13852 T 3 14025 C1 14078 C1 18680 R 1
13853 T 4 14026 C1 14079 C1 19366 C1
13863 T 1 14027 C1 14081 C1 19368 C1
13871 TR 2 14028 C1 14083 C1 19376 C3
13875 TR 1 14029 C1 14084 C2 19377 C2
13886 R 4 14034 C1 14312 C2 19378 C1
13897 R 8 14035 C1 14314 C1 19380 C2
13899 R 2 14036 C2 15226 C2 19381 C2
13915 R 1 14038 C1 15236 C2 19382 C1
13919 R 2 14039 C1 18107 R 2 19383 C2
13926 R 7 14041 C2 18141 R 2 19384 C2
13932 R 2 14042 C1 18157 R 2 19385 C1
13933 R 2 14044 C2 18198 C1 19386 C3
13936 R 1 14045 C1 18227 C2 19391 C1
13939 R 1 14051 C1 18233 C4 19392 C2
13940 R 2 14052 C1 18317 C1 19463 R 2
13943 R 2 14056 C1 18320 C1 19464 R 7
13944 R 2 14060 C2 18328 C1 20476 C2
13960 R 2 14061 C1 18331 C1 20521 C2
13992 RC1 14062 C1 18342 C1 21283 T 2
13994 TRC1 14063 C2 18353 C2 21398 TRC1
14003 RC1 14064 C1 18446 T 1 21690 T 1
14004 TRC2 14067 C1 18476 T 1 21830 TRC2
14005 RC1 14070 C1 18574 R 2 22152 R 8
14008 RC2 14072 C1 18593 R 2 22213 RC2
14009 TRC2 14073 C1 18599 R 2 22697 R 2
14016 TRC1 14074 C1 18624 R 1 22721 R 2
14021 C1 14075 C1 18648 R 1 22722 R 2
14023 C1 14076 C1 18663 R 2 22941 R 2
14024 C1

Secondary: Monographs

10005 T 2 11107 C4 15176 RC2 18653 R 2
10007 T 2 11144 C2 15214 C2 18659 R 2
10029 T 2 11160 C2 15234 C2 18660 R 2
10044 T 2 11258 TR 1 15237 C2 18666 R 1
10047 T 2 11336 R 2 15241 C2 18685 R 2
10059 T 2 11377 R 1 15250 C3 18699 R 2
10061 T 2 11614 RC1 15294 C2 18701 R 1
10072 TR 2 11724 R 2 15297 C2 18723 R 1
10079 TR 2 11748 R 2 15856 C2 18725 R 2
10105 R 2 11752 R 2 16054 R 7 18730 R 2
10120 TRC2 11807 R 2 16055 R 2 18733 R 2
10123 RC2 11830 R 2 16071 C2 18755 R 2
10124 TRC2 11894 C2 16395 T 2 18767 R 2
10125 RC2 11922 C2 17311 RC2 18768 R 2
10134 C2 11928 C2 17313 RC2 18780 R 2
10142 C2 12001 C2 17586 RC2 18782 R 2
10155 C2 12102 C2 17754 TR 1 18783 R 2
10156 C2 12811 C2 17993 C2 18796 RC2
10157 C2 12849 C2 18041 TRC2 18812 RC2
10159 C2 12921 T 2 18104 TR 2 18822 TRC2
10303 TRC1 13042 R 2 18114 R 2 19551 R 2
10516 T 2 13432 C2 18123 R 2 20107 R 2
10551 T 4 13449 C1 18134 R 2 20166 TR 2
10574 T 1 13458 T 2 18140 R 4 20226 TRC2
10631 T 2 13489 TR 3 18144 R 2 20444 R 2
10654 T 3 13743 R 2 18147 R 1 20492 C3
10660 T 2 13760 R 2 18148 R 2 20926 R 2
10677 T 2 13761 R 2 18154 R 2 21286 T 1
10696 TR 1 14109 TR 2 18158 R 2 21300 T 2
10697 TR 2 14119 R 3 18170 RC2 21321 TR 2
10698 TR 2 14122 R 3 18176 RC1 21354 TR 2
10702 TR 2 14133 C3 18187 RC2 21355 TR 2
10712 TR 2 14144 C1 18232 C2 21373 R 1
10724 TR 4 14164 T 2 18236 C1 21400 RC2
10749 R 2 14178 T 2 18264 C2 21405 TRC1
10758 R 4 14219 TR 2 18272 C1 21410 TRC2
10768 R 4 14278 RC2 18277 C2 21417 TRC2
10778 R 2 14279 RC2 18324 C2 21418 RC2
10782 R 1 14292 RC2 18378 T 2 21424 TRC2
10785 R 1 14309 C1 18387 T 2 21563 C1
10820 R 1 14334 C1 18454 T 2 21569 C1
10858 TRC2 14478 R 3 18535 TR 1 21644 T 2
10883 TRC2 14508 R 3 18536 TR 2 21723 TR 1
10931 C2 14512 RC2 18551 TR 2 21798 TR 1
10961 C1 14677 TR 1 18552 TR 1 22131 TR 2
10994 C2 14685 TR 2 18554 TR 1 22203 RC2
10997 C2 14721 R 2 18557 TR 2 22210 TRC2
10999 C1 14733 R 2 18562 TR 2 22251 RC2
11005 C2 14809 RC2 18567 TR 2 22260 RC1
11006 C2 14835 C2 18588 R 2 22268 RC1
11027 R 2 14999 C2 18596 R 2 22291 C2
11052 RC2 15156 R 2 18598 R 2 22296 C2
11096 C2 15168 TRC2 18617 R 2 22304 C1

22572 T 2 22648 TR 2 22669 TR 1 22939 R 2
22585 T 1 22655 TR 3 22699 R 3 22954 TRC1
22619 T 2

Secondary: Inclusions

10078 TR 2 12650 TR 2 17997 C1 19365 T 2
10151 C2 12868 C2 18110 R 2 19369 C1
10334 T 2 14138 C2 18180 RC1 20698 C2
10463 C4 14176 T 2 18280 C2 21372 R 2
10561 T 2 14212 T 1 18334 C1 21958 C1
10601 T 2 14275 RC2 18452 T 2 22000 TR 1
10750 R 2 14276 RC1 18515 T 2 22130 TR 2
10800 R 1 14288 RC2 18521 T 5 22146 R 2
10946 C3 14343 C1 18533 TR 2 22166 R 2
11010 T 2 14374 C1 18555 TR 2 22191 RC2
11042 RC2 14394 C1 18571 TR 2 22256 RC1
11425 C1 14562 T 1 18606 R 1 22263 RC7
11435 C2 15141 TR 1 18616 R 2 22290 C2
11458 C2 15170 RC2 18626 R 2 22313 C1
11613 RC1 15188 RC2 18761 R 2 22507 T 1
11968 C2 15217 C2 18799 RC2 22516 T 1
12617 T 4 17601 C2 19087 RC8 22639 T 1

Secondary: Journal Articles

10185 T 2 11642 C1 15242 C1 18591 R 2
10253 TR 4 11693 TR 2 15256 C1 18677 R 2
10422 C2 12129 C2 15276 C1 18714 R 2
10451 R 2 12164 C2 15277 C2 18729 R 1
10459 C2 12169 C1 15288 C2 18754 R 1
10530 T 2 12189 T 2 15292 C2 18757 R 2
10572 T 2 12635 TR 1 15295 C4 18789 RC2
10661 T 2 12748 R 1 15967 R 2 18800 TRC2
10699 TR 1 13135 T 4 15979 RC4 18813 RC1
10744 R 2 13377 C2 17278 R 5 18816 RC2
10755 R 1 13493 TR 2 17574 R 2 18818 RC7
10762 R 3 13591 C2 17585 RC2 18829 RC2
10802 R 1 14162 T 1 17599 C1 19370 C1
10808 R 1 14249 R 1 17603 C1 19374 C2
10809 R 2 14271 RC2 17987 RC2 19387 C1
10826 R 2 14338 C1 18090 T 3 19440 T 2
10848 RC2 14340 C1 18094 T 3 19447 R 7
10900 C2 14345 C1 18116 R 3 19467 RC7
10901 C2 14353 C1 18136 R 4 20446 R 1
10905 C4 14357 C1 18150 R 1 20514 C2
10927 C1 14362 C2 18159 R 2 20531 C3
10928 C1 14375 C1 18166 RC1 21390 RC2
10932 C1 14381 C1 18171 RC1 21775 TR 1
10967 C2 14403 TR 2 18184 RC1 21806 R 1
10979 C4 14536 C3 18202 C1 22058 T 1
10981 C1 14612 T 2 18207 C1 22105 TR 2
10986 C2 14759 R 4 18215 C1 22119 TR 2
11022 R 2 15070 R 4 18216 C1 22168 R 2
11030 R 2 15128 T 4 18234 C2 22171 R 2
11054 TRC2 15137 TR 1 18237 C2 22248 RC1
11066 C2 15151 R 2 18261 C4 22308 C1
11086 C2 15196 C2 18267 C1 22312 C1
11097 C2 15200 C2 18273 C2 22554 T 1
11098 C2 15208 C2 18304 R 2 22608 T 1
11260 TR 2 15218 C2 18359 C1 22686 R 1
11267 TR 1 15219 C2 18435 T 2 22702 R 1
11405 RC1 15220 C2 18460 T 2 22771 T 2
11464 C1 15238 C2 18477 T 2 22955 TRC2

The Eighteen Provinces

Primary 13831 T 2 13934 R 2 18609 R 2
10027 T 2 13836 T 4 13938 R 2 18621 R 3
10038 T 2 13843 T 4 13952 R 2 18654 R 2
10590 T 5 13845 T 1 13956 R 4 18679 R 2
10608 T 2 13860 T 2 13979 R 2 18727 R 2
10735 TR 1 13866 T 2 13990 TRC1 18834 RC2
10839 R 2 13879 TR 1 15662 T 2 19441 T 2
13804 T 2 13890 R 2 17143 T 3 20565 T 2
13805 T 2 13911 R 2 18399 T 2 21267 T 2
13813 T 2 13912 R 2 18441 T 2 21319 TR 2
13827 T 1 13922 R 2 18461 T 2 22590 T 3
13830 T 2 13925 R 2 18523 T 2

Second. 11655 T 1 14555 T 1 18382 T 2
10050 T 2 11681 T 2 16058 R 2 18445 T 2
10056 T 2 12411 TRC8 16920 T 2 18448 T 4
10091 R 2 12683 TR 2 17541 T 7 18513 T 2
10158 C2 13455 T 5 18115 R 2 18578 R 2
10533 T 2 13621 T 4 18152 R 1 18604 R 7
10563 T 3 14207 T 2 18346 C2 18638 R 2
10752 R 3 14217 TR 2 18347 C2 18645 R 7
11185 T 2 14225 TR 1 18364 T 2 18676 R 1
11209 T 1 14236 R 2 18366 T 2 18683 R 2

18713 R 2 19243 R 7 21473 TRC2 22615 T 2
18756 R 1 19458 R 8 21883 TRC1 22641 T 2
18765 R 1 20489 C3 22057 T 2 22680 R 3
18777 R 2 21389 RC2 22067 T 2 22708 R 3
18784 R 2 21456 R 2 22110 TR 1

North China Broadly Conceived

Primary 13935 R 2 16430 R 2 18732 R 2
10577 T 1 13954 R 2 18146 R 2 18747 R 1
11737 R 2 13962 R 2 18390 T 2 20578 T 2
13810 T 2 13976 R 2 18493 T 2 21287 T 2
13832 T 2 13978 R 2 18682 R 2 22584 T 2
13894 R 2 14195 T 3 18716 R 2 22695 R 2
13918 R 2 15752 T 2 18731 R 2

Second. 16119 R 2 18664 R 2 22394 T 2
10040 T 2 17564 R 2 18669 R 7 22511 T 2
10792 R 2 17577 R 2 18688 R 2 22562 T 3
10827 R 2 18160 R 3 18712 R 7 22623 T 2
10936 C3 18371 T 2 18738 R 1 22660 TR 2
10969 C3 18496 T 2 18743 R 7 22715 R 2
13548 R 2 18509 T 2 18750 R 2

Manchuria

Primary 10824 R 2 12663 TR 2 13907 R 4
10719 TR 1 11015 T 2 13837 T 7 13917 R 2
10796 R 2

Second. 11785 R 2 15691 R 2 20795 TR 2
10163 C2 11826 R 2 17548 T 7 22506 T 2
11677 T 2 11834 R 2 18356 C2 22693 R 2
11695 TR 1 13147 TR 2 18581 R 2 22718 R 1
11696 TR 2 15665 T 7 18715 R 2 22719 R 3
11714 TR 2 15674 TR 2

Northern China

Primary 10783 R 2 13974 R 2 17569 R 8
10529 T 3 13803 T 2 14427 R 2 17570 R 2
10644 T 2 13891 R 2 15355 T 2 19456 R 2
10747 R 2 13910 R 2 17529 T 3 22576 T 2
10781 R 2 13964 R 7 17556 T 3

Second. 15394 R 2 18422 T 3 20762 T 3
10528 T 3 16056 R 8 18498 T 3 21264 T 3
10598 T 2 16059 R 8 18658 R 7 21278 T 3
10776 R 2 16377 T 2 19438 T 7 21293 T 3
14163 T 3 17532 T 2 19442 R 8 21359 TR 3
14204 T 3 17625 T 3 19825 R 3 22577 T 2
15014 C3 18092 T 3 20436 R 3 22617 T 2
15320 T 3 18348 C2 20479 C3 22712 R 7
15347 T 3 18398 T 2 20505 C3 22747 C2

Northwestern China and Frontier Regions

Primary 13826 T 1 15729 T 2 18749 R 2
13799 T 1 13895 R 2 16517 T 2 19375 C2
13814 T 2 13981 R 1 18584 R 4 22531 T 2
13822 T 7 14080 C1 18697 R 2 22642 T 4

Second. 10922 C1 16628 R 2 18890 T 2
10725 TR 2 15322 T 3 18706 R 5 18956 TR 2
10759 R 2 15350 T 2 18864 T 1 22732 TRC2
10863 TRC2 15753 T 2

South China Broadly Conceived

Primary 13881 TR 2 13968 R 2 18463 T 2
10593 T 1 13887 R 2 13972 R 2 18524 T 2
10832 R 3 13889 R 2 13973 R 2 18613 R 1
11017 T 4 13892 R 2 17567 R 2 18721 R 8
13040 R 4 13929 R 2 18137 R 1 18763 R 2
13833 T 2 13941 R 3 18376 T 2 18772 R 2
13835 T 1 13955 R 2 18412 T 2 18781 R 8
13869 T 2 13967 R 8 18421 T 2 19448 R 2

Second. 13459 T 2 18447 T 2 18779 R 2
10046 T 2 13471 T 2 18449 T 2 21299 T 2
11014 T 2 15205 C2 18459 T 2 22513 T 2
11772 R 2 17982 R 2 18471 T 1 22521 T 1
12578 T 2 18129 R 3 18577 R 2 22522 T 2
12684 TR 2 18386 T 2 18766 R 2

East Central China

Primary 13900 R 3 17161 T 3 19511 R 3
10770 R 3 13924 R 3 17549 T 2 22571 T 2
13802 T 2 15731 T 2 17565 R 2

Second. 15732 T 2 16908 T 2 18466 T 2
10751 R 2 15930 T 3 17162 T 3 19069 C3
15377 TR 3 16417 R 3 17735 R 3 19550 R 3
15727 T 3 16525 T 8 18363 T 2

Central Yangtze Provinces

Primary 13820 T 2 13983 R 7 18703 R 2
13479 T 1 13908 R 3 17539 T 2 18726 R 2
13816 T 4 13931 R 2 18644 R 2
Second. 17576 R 2 18704 R 2 20494 C4
15155 R 2 18411 T 3 18751 R 7 20820 TR 2
17561 TR 2 18582 R 2 20210 R 2 21041 C3

Southwestern China

Primary 10791 R 2 13801 T 2 17562 R 2
10651 T 2 13538 R 2 13857 T 2 18365 T 3
Second. 12924 T 2 17613 R 7 18381 T 2
10566 T 2 14571 T 4 17632 R 3 18475 T 2
10639 T 2 15270 C2 18089 T 2 18922 T 2
10790 R 2 17267 R 2 18349 C2

Southeastern China

Primary 13862 T 1 13953 R 3 17589 C2
10552 T 2 13872 TR 6 15334 T 2 18611 R 2
10708 TR 2 13906 R 2 16064 R 2 18665 R 3
13798 T 3 13913 R 4 17524 T 3 18742 R 2
13808 T 3 13921 R 2 17530 T 2 18775 R 3
13854 T 1 13947 R 4 17545 T 2
Second. 15497 C2 16839 C2 19371 C2
10522 T 3 15499 C2 17523 T 3 19454 R 7
10855 RC2 15735 T 2 17571 R 3 20493 C3
11675 T 2 15742 T 2 18156 R 1 20893 R 3
14575 T 3 15763 TR 2 18438 T 2 20894 R 2
15263 C2 15780 R 3 18490 T 2 21270 T 2
15310 T 3 16389 T 2 18618 R 3 22678 R 3
15359 T 2 16477 C2 18734 R 2

Taiwan Only

Primary 10325 T 2 10653 T 2 10882 RC2
12008 C2 14058 C1
Second. 10958 C1 12150 C2 15562 C2
10638 T 1 11109 C1 14367 C1 16347 C2
10674 T 2 11138 C2 14955 C2 17907 C7
10675 T 2 12078 C1 15554 C2 18297 C2
10955 C1

Hong Kong and Macau Only

Primary □
Second. 11031 R 2 16139 C3 20688 C2

16 Social Stratification and Mobility
社會階層及社會流動
社会階層及びその流動性

Geographic China Broadly Conceived

Primary 11857 TRC2 15185 TRC2 19534 R 2
10001 T 2 11867 TRC2 16185 T 2 20009 TR 1
10004 T 2 12201 T 7 18073 T 2 20010 TR 2
10060 T 2 12233 TR 2 18368 T 1 20050 TR 2
10113 TRC2 13856 T 2 18409 T 2 20101 TR 1
10117 TRC2 14089 T 1 18414 T 1 20152 T 2
10144 C2 14095 T 3 18525 T 2 21276 T 2
10177 C2 14097 T 2 18539 TR 2 21392 TRC2
10263 C2 14098 T 2 18541 TR 2 21411 TRC2
10346 TR 2 14102 T 2 18545 TR 2 21412 RC2
10539 T 1 14112 TR 1 18719 R 2 21467 TRC1
10560 T 2 14113 TR 2 18741 R 2 21853 TRC2
10823 R 1 14126 TRC2 18764 R 2 22109 TR 2
10891 TRC1 14145 C2 18786 TRC2 22265 RC2
11045 RC2 14166 T 1 18801 TRC2 22640 T 1
11704 TR 2 14951 C2 18809 RC2 22886 T 1
11709 TR 2 15130 T 2
Second. 10015 T 1 10082 TR 2 10541 T 1
10010 T 2 10024 T 2 10119 TRC2 10564 T 2
10014 T 2 10034 T 2 10261 TRC4 10854 TRC1
10864 RC1 15044 T 2 20463 R 3 22095 TR 2
11035 RC2 15134 TR 4 20540 T 2 22189 RC1
11047 RC2 15174 TRC2 20543 T 1 22214 TRC1
11199 T 1 15283 C2 20588 T 2 22225 TRC2
11387 TRC1 18388 T 2 21368 R 2 22476 TRC2
11708 TR 2 18489 T 1 21404 TRC1 22580 T 2
12188 T 2 18542 TR 2 21538 TRC2 22588 T 1
12665 TR 1 18558 TR 2 21712 T 2 22779 T 1
12772 TRC2 18566 TR 1 21718 TR 1 22780 T 1
13812 T 2 19353 TR 2 21847 TRC2 22922 TR 1
14193 T 1 20085 T 2 22056 T 1 22995 TRC2
14600 T 1 20109 TRC2 22088 TR 1

Mainland China

Primary: Monographs
10019 T 2 11707 TR 2 14139 C2 18720 R 2
10041 T 2 11748 R 2 14144 C1 18722 R 2
10086 TR 2 11862 RC2 14153 C2 18725 R 2
10089 R 2 11872 RC2 14206 T 1 18730 R 2
10097 R 2 11894 C2 14278 RC2 18768 R 2
10125 RC2 12000 C2 14364 C2 18795 TRC2
10133 C2 12002 C2 14370 C2 18819 RC2
10134 C2 12044 C2 14513 TRC2 19132 C7
10143 C2 12082 C2 15085 RC2 19655 RC2
10145 C2 12096 C2 15553 C2 20258 T 2
10149 C2 12123 C2 17974 T 3 20492 C3
10154 C2 12154 C2 18142 R 2 21821 R 2
10155 C2 12267 R 8 18145 R 2 21891 TRC1
10159 C2 12375 RC2 18185 RC2 22089 TR 2
10172 C2 12378 RC8 18387 T 2 22144 R 2
10811 R 1 12811 C2 18526 T 2 22179 R 1
10893 TRC2 13163 TR 2 18543 TR 2 22219 RC2
10994 C2 13884 TR 2 18598 R 2 22250 RC2
11003 C2 14093 T 2 18617 R 2 22260 RC1
11076 C2 14109 TR 2 18619 R 2 22318 C2
11180 C2 14114 R 2 18655 R 2 22375 C2
11203 T 2 14116 R 2 18699 R 2 22619 T 2
11336 R 2 14119 R 2 18708 R 2 22655 TR 3
11393 TRC2 14122 R 3 18709 R 2 22734 RC2
11689 TR 2 14127 RC2 18717 R 2 22991 TRC2
11699 TR 2 14133 C3

Primary: Inclusions
10012 T 2 14135 C2 15222 C2 18745 R 2
10147 C2 14138 C2 15296 C1 18799 RC2
10295 R 2 14146 C2 15982 TRC2 18808 TRC2
10453 R 2 14147 C2 17147 T 2 19365 T 2
10662 T 2 14150 C2 18370 T 2 20504 C2
10930 C2 14151 C2 18452 T 2 21211 R 2
11531 C1 14232 TR 1 18521 T 5 21767 TR 1
11700 TR 2 14405 TR 4 18537 TR 2 21859 TRC1
11842 RC2 14958 C2 18555 TR 2 22146 R 2
11965 C2 15043 T 2 18561 TR 2 22221 RC2
14096 T 2 15101 C2 18571 TR 2 22238 RC4
14120 R 2 15170 RC2 18615 R 2 22256 RC1
14123 R 2 15177 TRC2 18616 R 2 22282 RC2
14131 TRC2 15217 C2 18633 R 2

Primary: Journal Articles
10033 T 2 12215 TR 2 14154 C2 18826 TRC1
10296 R 2 12325 R 2 14173 T 1 18830 RC2
10408 C2 12468 C2 14256 RC2 19218 TR 1
10754 R 2 14085 T 1 14331 C2 19377 C2
10826 R 2 14094 T 2 14536 C3 19561 R 3
10848 RC2 14099 T 1 14822 C2 19921 C2
10884 RC2 14103 T 1 14920 C1 19926 C1
10913 C4 14105 TR 2 15084 R 2 20196 R 1
10971 C1 14110 TR 2 15087 RC2 20197 R 2
10981 C1 14111 TR 2 15198 C2 20476 C2
10987 C2 14115 R 3 15200 C2 20531 C3
11054 TRC2 14128 RC2 15212 C2 21284 T 2
11089 C2 14130 TRC2 15247 C2 22047 T 2
11460 C7 14132 C2 15262 C2 22149 R 2
11662 T 2 14136 C2 15512 C2 22183 TRC1
11814 R 2 14137 C2 18157 R 2 22255 RC2
11900 C2 14140 C1 18276 C4 22292 C2
11976 C2 14141 C2 18304 R 2 22330 C1
12012 C2 14142 C1 18504 T 2 22331 C1
12040 C2 14143 C2 18714 R 2 22332 C1
12116 C2 14148 C2 18754 R 1 22333 C2
12129 C2 14149 C2 18757 R 2 22844 C7
12189 T 2 14152 C1 18806 RC2 22955 TRC2

Secondary: Monographs
10002 T 2 10043 T 2 10079 TR 2 10115 RC2
10011 T 2 10044 T 2 10094 R 2 10120 TRC2
10030 T 2 10072 TR 2 10101 R 2 10157 C2
10169 C2 12412 RC7 15260 C2 20169 TR 2
10173 C2 12424 RC7 15294 C2 20496 C2
10180 C2 12456 C8 15550 C2 20837 R 2
10477 C2 12525 C2 16335 TRC2 21103 C2
10643 T 1 12631 TR 2 17190 TR 5 21325 TR 2
10749 R 2 12985 R 2 17757 TR 4 21459 R 4
10769 R 2 13420 C2 18114 R 2 21476 TRC2
10778 R 2 13520 TR 2 18134 R 2 21705 T 1
10883 TRC2 13536 R 1 18144 R 2 21826 R 2
11000 C4 13579 C2 18147 R 1 21869 TRC1
11006 C2 13584 C2 18158 R 2 22066 T 2
11069 C2 13589 C2 18172 RC2 22079 TR 2
11087 C3 13761 R 2 18178 RC2 22106 TR 1
11094 C2 13868 T 2 18186 RC1 22128 TR 1
11101 C2 13901 R 2 18187 RC2 22131 TR 2
11195 T 1 13928 R 2 18212 C1 22158 R 2
11368 R 2 13969 R 2 18430 T 2 22162 R 2
11534 C2 14179 T 1 18588 R 2 22182 RC2
11740 R 2 14258 RC2 18629 R 2 22196 RC1
11756 R 2 14274 TRC2 18630 R 2 22203 RC2
11790 R 2 14329 C2 18653 R 2 22210 TRC2
11793 R 2 14334 C1 18661 R 2 22229 RC2
11807 R 2 14378 C4 18710 R 1 22235 RC2
11848 RC2 14584 T 2 18752 R 2 22268 RC1
11883 C2 14599 T 2 18753 R 2 22293 C2
11980 C2 14650 TR 1 18759 R 2 22299 C2
11998 C2 14703 TR 2 18760 R 2 22322 C2
12015 C2 14754 R 2 18827 RC2 22326 C1
12109 C2 14974 C2 19062 C2 22367 C1
12158 C2 15147 R 4 19092 RC8 22644 TR 2
12222 TR 7 15150 R 2 19135 C7 22648 TR 2
12268 R 8 15156 R 2 19517 R 3 22658 TR 1
12303 R 2 15169 RC2 19597 C2 22950 TRC2
12379 RC7 15235 C2 19719 T 2 22954 TRC1
12380 RC7

Secondary: Inclusions
10080 TR 2 14336 C1 18281 C2 21893 RC2
10131 C1 14363 C2 18429 T 2 21894 TRC2
10499 C2 14391 C2 18515 T 2 21907 C1
10561 T 2 14455 TR 4 18626 R 2 21916 C2
10694 TR 2 14628 TR 2 18761 R 2 22034 T 2
11002 C2 14850 C2 18802 RC2 22078 TR 2
11245 T 1 14856 C2 18807 TRC2 22148 R 2
11443 C2 14967 C2 19974 TRC2 22192 RC2
11451 C1 15195 RC2 20480 C2 22247 RC1
11459 C1 17644 C2 20698 C2 22264 RC1
11914 C1 17997 C1 21848 TRC2 22321 C3
11978 C1 18110 R 2 21871 TRC1 22357 C2
14208 T 2 18119 R 2 21872 TRC1 22358 C1
14220 TR 1 18180 RC1 21885 TRC2 22363 C2
14328 C2

Secondary: Journal Articles
10166 C2 11986 C2 15206 C2 19722 T 1
10249 C2 12053 C2 15236 C2 19868 TRC1
10710 TR 1 12063 C2 15253 C2 19908 C1
10786 R 2 12279 R 8 15255 C2 19927 C2
10881 RC1 12311 R 7 15284 C2 20148 T 2
10901 C2 12332 R 2 15967 R 2 20271 C1
10991 C1 12362 R 8 16038 C2 20441 R 2
11001 C1 12392 RC7 16907 T 4 20485 C4
11034 RC2 12472 C2 18018 TR 1 20490 C2
11058 C7 12929 T 4 18021 TR 4 20501 C2
11070 C2 12949 TR 2 18136 R 4 21837 RC2
11115 C2 13567 R 1 18168 RC1 22084 TR 1
11153 C2 13818 T 1 18177 RC2 22105 TR 2
11155 C2 14038 C1 18190 C2 22120 TR 1
11171 C2 14257 RC4 18214 C1 22161 R 4
11212 T 1 14366 C1 18253 C2 22186 RC2
11240 T 1 14414 RC4 18288 C1 22199 TRC1
11383 TRC1 14434 R 7 18311 RC1 22213 RC2
11413 RC1 14447 C7 18316 C1 22216 TRC1
11430 C1 14488 R 2 18332 C2 22220 RC1
11446 C1 14557 T 1 18369 T 1 22246 TRC2
11452 C2 14566 T 2 18574 R 2 22306 C1
11486 C2 14777 TRC1 18692 R 1 22312 C1
11493 C2 14872 C2 18698 R 2 22346 C2
11511 C1 14898 C1 18789 RC2 22362 C1
11813 R 2 14917 C2 18790 RC2 22366 C1
11871 TRC2 14959 C2 19215 TR 5 22932 R 2
11937 C2 14986 C1 19366 C1 22947 RC1
11941 C2 15003 C3 19471 C7 22988 TRC1
11947 C2 15132 TR 2 19647 R 2 22994 TRC1

THE EIGHTEEN PROVINCES

PRIMARY 14087 T 2 14121 R 2 18765 R 1
10091 R 2 14090 T 1 14124 R 7 18784 R 2
10141 C2 14091 T 2 14207 T 2 20092 T 2
10158 C2 14092 T 2 14489 R 3 20478 C2
10161 C2 14100 T 2 15830 C2 20606 T 2
10170 C2 14101 T 2 18436 T 2 21473 TRC2
10507 T 2 14104 T 1 18602 R 2 21482 C4
10682 T 2 14107 TR 1 18609 R 2 21761 TR 1
12385 RC8 14108 TR 1 18642 R 4 22137 TR 2
13831 T 2 14117 R 2 18654 R 2 22760 C3
14086 T 1 14118 R 4 18713 R 2 22885 T 2

SECOND. 13621 T 4 18756 R 1 20284 T 1
10027 T 2 14401 T 5 19349 T 3 20287 T 1
10038 T 2 14493 R 4 19446 R 2 20604 T 2
10050 T 2 14656 TR 2 19528 R 2 20728 T 4
10333 T 2 15131 T 1 19839 R 1 21678 T 2
10533 T 2 18012 T 2 20144 T 1 22004 R 1
12198 T 8 18382 T 2 20193 R 2 22009 R 2
12207 T 2 18431 T 7 20223 RC2 22076 TR 1
12212 TR 2 18590 R 3 20256 T 1 22923 TR 2
12869 C3

NORTH CHINA BROADLY CONCEIVED

PRIMARY 12290 R 8 18433 T 2 20716 T 2
22141 R 3

SECOND. 11737 R 2 13548 R 2 20539 T 4
22660 TR 2

MANCHURIA

PRIMARY 10796 R 2 11732 R 2 14129 RC2
15674 TR 2

SECOND. 10341 TR 2 11785 R 2 15181 RC2

NORTHERN CHINA

PRIMARY 22577 T 2

SECOND. 10652 T 3 11135 C3 14791 RC3
21359 TR 3

NORTHWESTERN CHINA AND FRONTIER REGIONS

PRIMARY 14106 TR 2 16517 T 2

SECOND. ☐

SOUTH CHINA BROADLY CONCEIVED

PRIMARY 14125 TRC7 17947 RC2 18412 T 2
18763 R 2

SECOND. 12580 T 2 18463 T 2 18670 R 2
21865 TRC2

EAST CENTRAL CHINA

PRIMARY ☐

SECOND. 18487 T 2 19069 C3

CENTRAL YANGTZE PROVINCES

PRIMARY 11726 R 2 18704 R 2

SECOND. 13820 T 2

SOUTHWESTERN CHINA

PRIMARY 14571 T 4

SECOND. 13209 R 2 18089 T 2 21892 TRC2

SOUTHEASTERN CHINA

PRIMARY 10275 T 2 10298 R 2 14088 T 2
22398 T 4

SECOND. 14772 R 3 20722 T 4

TAIWAN ONLY

PRIMARY 14134 C2 16740 TRC2 21008 C2
11134 C1 15471 RC2 17989 TRC2 22735 TRC2

SECOND. 15709 C2 18877 T 2 19938 C2
20334 C2 21484 C2

HONG KONG AND MACAU ONLY

☐

16.1 ELITE STRATA

社會領導階層　　エリート階層

GEOGRAPHIC CHINA BROADLY CONCEIVED

PRIMARY: MONOGRAPHS

10022 T 2 11270 TR 4 15134 TR 4 21302 T 2
10053 T 2 12657 TR 4 15175 RC2 21337 TR 2
10074 TR 2 13688 TR 2 18375 T 2 21350 TR 3
10526 T 2 14155 T 2 18388 T 2 21392 TRC2
10557 T 1 14156 T 2 18494 T 2 21404 TRC1
10573 T 1 14166 T 1 18540 TR 2 21412 RC2
10615 T 2 14167 T 2 18560 TR 2 22027 T 4
10626 T 2 14174 T 3 18904 T 2 22056 T 1
10645 T 1 14175 T 1 19752 T 1 22074 T 2
10657 T 1 14193 T 1 20960 TRC2 22586 T 3
10713 TR 2 14215 TR 2 21276 T 2 22637 T 1
11241 T 2 14627 T 1 21279 T 2 22694 R 3

PRIMARY: INCLUSIONS

10646 T 4 14097 T 2 14222 TR 4 15185 TRC2
10866 RC3 14203 T 1 14248 R 2 22578 T 2
12772 TRC2 14216 TR 1 14621 T 1 22690 R 3

PRIMARY: JOURNAL ARTICLES

10537 T 1 14184 T 1 14266 TRC1 21408 TRC2
10741 R 1 14185 T 1 14284 TRC1 22160 R 1
10864 RC1 14211 T 1 14648 TR 1 22515 T 3
11404 RC1 14244 R 4 18082 T 3 22634 T 1

SECONDARY: MONOGRAPHS

10001 T 2 11665 T 2 18409 T 2 21467 TRC1
10096 R 2 11692 TR 2 18492 T 2 21579 C2
10111 TRC2 12310 R 8 18545 TR 2 21853 TRC2
10114 TRC2 12593 T 2 18579 R 2 22082 TR 1
10139 C2 12611 T 1 18707 R 2 22102 TR 2
10162 C2 13049 TRC2 18919 T 1 22206 TRC1
10541 T 1 13461 T 4 19036 TRC2 22225 TRC2
10560 T 2 14560 T 3 20009 TR 1 22559 T 2
10611 T 2 14567 T 1 20109 TRC2 22580 T 2
10619 T 1 14594 T 2 20540 T 2 22594 T 2
10634 T 1 15174 TRC2 20615 TR 2 22657 TR 1
10684 TR 2 15191 RC2 20619 TR 2 22666 TR 2
10707 TR 2 16185 T 2 20769 T 4 22672 TR 1
10716 TR 1 18077 T 2 20826 TR 2 22728 RC2
10806 R 2 18102 TR 2 21306 TR 2 22740 TRC2
10862 TRC2 18125 R 1

SECONDARY: INCLUSIONS

10073 TR 2 12190 T 2 16340 TRC1 21332 TR 1
10510 T 2 12370 R 7 17933 TR 1 21338 TR 1
10596 T 1 12678 TR 2 18079 T 1 22065 T 1
11556 T 1 13878 TR 2 20563 T 2

SECONDARY: JOURNAL ARTICLES

10617 T 1 12898 T 4 18891 T 2 21619 T 1
10663 T 2 14399 T 4 19614 T 3 22014 TRC1
10666 T 2 14710 R 1 20152 T 2 22886 T 1
10736 TR 1 15162 TRC2 21318 TR 1 23021 C2
11038 RC2 18111 R 1

MAINLAND CHINA

PRIMARY: MONOGRAPHS

10023 T 2 11011 T 1 14164 T 2 14296 C2
10124 TRC2 11040 RC4 14178 T 2 14299 C2
10464 C4 11052 RC2 14179 T 1 14305 C4
10508 T 3 11094 C2 14181 T 4 14309 C1
10548 T 2 11096 C2 14189 T 4 14310 C5
10551 T 4 11107 C4 14201 T 4 14311 C1
10559 T 4 11110 C1 14206 T 1 14316 C1
10640 T 4 11113 C4 14209 T 1 14322 C1
10643 T 1 11160 C2 14219 TR 2 14329 C2
10654 T 3 11855 TRC2 14223 TR 2 14334 C1
10669 T 1 12264 R 7 14230 TR 1 14337 C2
10672 T 2 13449 C1 14231 TR 4 14364 C2
10677 T 2 13858 T 2 14241 R 2 14369 C2
10690 TR 1 13880 TR 2 14247 R 1 14370 C2
10702 TR 2 13882 TR 2 14258 RC2 14378 C4
10711 TR 4 13883 TR 2 14263 RC1 14384 C1
10780 R 1 13884 TR 2 14264 RC1 14385 C2
10845 R 1 14002 RC2 14269 RC4 14387 C3
10870 RC2 14010 RC2 14274 TRC2 14396 T 2
10937 C2 14015 RC1 14278 RC2 14556 T 2
10960 C2 14047 C1 14279 RC2 14584 T 2
10961 C1 14055 C1 14285 TRC1 14592 T 1
10999 C1 14093 T 2 14292 RC2 14670 TR 4
11003 C2 14160 T 2 14293 RC3 14753 R 1
14795 RC2 18120 R 2 18647 R 2 21422 TRC2
14835 C2 18144 R 2 18827 RC2 21423 RC2
14885 C1 18147 R 1 18980 TR 2 21459 R 4
14910 C2 18148 R 2 19405 TRC3 21461 R 1
14974 C2 18154 R 2 20177 TR 2 21471 TRC1
15025 C2 18164 RC3 20414 T 1 21594 C1
15140 TR 2 18176 RC1 20558 T 2 21644 T 2
15156 R 2 18178 RC2 20973 TRC1 21758 TR 1
15202 C2 18182 RC2 21265 T 2 21825 R 1
15214 C2 18212 C1 21288 T 1 21887 TRC2
15234 C2 18225 C2 21300 T 2 22031 T 1
15237 C2 18264 C2 21321 TR 2 22046 T 1
15245 C2 18272 C1 21325 TR 2 22071 T 1
15248 C2 18298 C2 21355 TR 2 22099 TR 2
15258 C7 18324 C2 21361 TR 1 22339 C2
15267 C2 18526 T 2 21401 RC3 22486 RC8
17754 TR 1 18536 TR 2 21407 TRC3 22530 T 1
18098 T 3 18557 TR 2 21410 TRC2 22572 T 2
18099 T 1 18562 TR 2 21414 RC2 22599 T 2
18104 TR 2 18635 R 2 21417 TRC2 22679 R 2

PRIMARY: INCLUSIONS

10051 T 2 13408 C4 14302 C3 18189 C2
10078 TR 2 13993 RC2 14304 C1 18196 C1
10171 C2 13999 RC1 14324 C1 18206 C2
10463 C4 14082 C1 14325 C2 18282 C1
10469 C2 14096 T 2 14327 C4 18533 TR 2
10506 T 1 14176 T 2 14328 C2 18571 TR 2
10597 T 1 14190 T 1 14336 C1 18802 RC2
10616 T 2 14208 T 2 14343 C1 18811 RC2
10642 T 2 14212 T 1 14344 C1 19404 RC3
10658 T 4 14220 TR 1 14363 C2 21357 TR 1
10671 T 3 14221 TR 1 14372 C1 21460 R 3
10856 RC2 14227 TR 1 14374 C1 21709 T 2
10916 C2 14232 TR 1 14377 C1 21858 RC1
10946 C3 14242 R 1 14379 C1 21870 RC1
10993 C2 14251 R 2 14380 C1 21871 TRC1
11002 C2 14254 TRC1 14390 C1 21880 TRC1
11065 C1 14255 RC1 14391 C2 21898 RC1
11072 C2 14261 RC1 14394 C1 21911 C1
11073 C4 14268 RC3 14579 T 1 21958 C1
11126 C2 14275 RC2 14788 RC2 21962 C3
11128 C1 14276 RC1 14945 C3 21964 C2
11174 C2 14280 RC2 14964 C1 22033 T 1
11484 C1 14281 RC1 15153 R 3 22238 RC4
11590 TR 1 14288 RC2 15186 RC1 22267 RC1
11613 RC1 14289 RC4 15296 C1 22321 C3
11711 TR 2 14290 RC1 17638 C2 22827 C1
12197 T 7 14297 C1 17642 C2

PRIMARY: JOURNAL ARTICLES

10504 T 2 12131 C2 14271 RC2 14348 C1
10509 T 4 12189 T 2 14272 RC1 14350 C1
10517 T 4 12255 R 7 14282 RC1 14351 C2
10518 T 4 12307 R 7 14283 TRC1 14352 C1
10520 T 1 12405 TRC2 14286 RC1 14353 C1
10524 T 2 13484 T 2 14287 RC1 14354 C2
10538 T 1 13840 T 2 14291 RC1 14355 C1
10540 T 1 13875 TR 1 14294 C1 14356 C1
10543 T 1 14162 T 1 14295 C1 14357 C1
10604 T 1 14165 T 3 14298 C1 14358 C1
10605 T 3 14173 T 1 14303 C1 14359 C2
10622 T 5 14177 T 2 14306 C1 14360 C3
10661 T 2 14183 T 2 14307 C1 14361 C1
10705 TR 1 14192 T 1 14308 C1 14362 C2
10731 TR 4 14198 T 1 14312 C2 14365 C1
10740 R 1 14202 T 1 14313 C1 14366 C1
10805 R 2 14205 T 4 14314 C1 14371 C1
10846 TRC1 14213 TR 1 14315 C1 14373 C2
10902 C2 14229 TR 1 14317 C1 14375 C1
10913 C4 14233 R 3 14318 C1 14376 C1
10967 C2 14235 R 1 14319 C1 14381 C1
11001 C1 14239 R 7 14321 C1 14382 C3
11030 R 2 14240 R 1 14323 C1 14383 C1
11033 RC1 14243 R 3 14331 C2 14386 C4
11056 C8 14245 R 4 14332 C2 14389 C1
11075 C1 14246 R 1 14333 C1 14392 C3
11093 C1 14249 R 1 14335 C1 14420 T 7
11123 C1 14252 RC3 14338 C1 14423 T 7
11133 C3 14253 RC1 14339 C1 14426 R 8
11139 C1 14256 RC2 14340 C1 14566 T 2
11141 C3 14257 RC4 14341 C1 14569 T 2
11145 C4 14259 RC4 14342 C1 14608 T 1
11149 C1 14260 RC2 14345 C1 14651 TR 1
11320 R 1 14265 RC1 14346 C1 14740 R 2
11485 C1 14267 RC1 14347 C2 14777 TRC1

14814 C4 18133 R 1 18435 T 2 21785 TR 1
14886 C4 18171 RC1 18648 R 1 21809 R 1
14937 C1 18184 RC1 18677 R 2 21918 C2
14991 C2 18198 C1 18689 R 1 21939 C1
15015 C1 18202 C1 18691 R 7 21940 C1
15128 T 4 18203 C1 19168 C2 21979 C4
15133 TR 2 18207 C1 19366 C1 22077 TR 2
15157 R 4 18210 C3 19410 C4 22153 R 1
15196 C2 18211 C4 20145 T 3 22174 R 1
15211 C2 18217 C4 20466 R 4 22245 TRC1
15255 C2 18226 C2 20471 TRC1 22314 C2
15269 C1 18248 C1 20490 C2 22347 C1
15277 C2 18250 C1 21075 C2 22529 T 3
15282 C1 18256 C1 21378 R 2 22621 T 1
15290 C2 18257 C1 21387 TRC2 22668 TR 1
16144 C2 18258 C1 21439 T 2 22757 C1
18084 T 1 18266 C3 21506 R 3 22804 R 4
18090 T 3 18292 C1 21764 TR 1 22815 RC1
18094 T 3 18339 C2

Secondary: Monographs

10005 T 2 11639 C1 15023 C2 21346 TR 2
10007 T 2 11672 T 4 15033 C1 21354 TR 2
10036 T 2 11822 R 2 15163 RC2 21363 TR 4
10039 T 2 11830 R 2 15168 TRC2 21400 RC2
10043 T 2 12222 TR 7 15171 TRC2 21415 RC1
10055 T 2 12271 R 7 15176 RC2 21416 RC2
10065 T 2 12298 R 7 15230 C2 21419 RC2
10067 TR 2 12312 R 8 15235 C2 21420 TRC2
10094 R 2 12378 RC8 15260 C2 21424 TRC2
10112 TRC2 12387 RC8 16148 C5 21444 TR 1
10135 C2 12414 TRC2 17993 C2 21447 TR 2
10136 C2 12442 C7 18075 T 2 21476 TRC2
10150 C2 12515 C7 18106 TR 2 21504 TR 2
10165 C2 12523 C8 18232 C2 21569 C1
10481 C2 12524 C2 18236 C1 21570 C1
10574 T 1 12619 T 1 18277 C2 21657 T 1
10587 T 2 12791 C1 18279 C1 21723 TR 1
10600 T 4 12836 C4 18296 C1 21766 TR 1
10667 T 1 12839 C2 18341 C3 21826 R 2
10676 T 2 12864 C1 18345 C4 21873 TRC3
10697 TR 2 12910 T 1 18350 C1 21936 C3
10703 TR 4 13125 T 2 18416 T 4 21951 C1
10715 TR 2 13482 T 2 18458 T 1 22028 T 1
10718 TR 2 13539 R 3 18552 TR 1 22052 T 4
10726 TR 2 13847 T 1 18563 TR 4 22053 T 1
10727 TR 3 13888 R 2 18597 R 4 22079 TR 2
10729 TR 2 13893 R 2 18598 R 2 22091 TR 1
10758 R 4 13905 R 2 18603 R 2 22112 TR 2
10769 R 2 13957 R 2 18610 R 2 22118 TR 1
10793 R 1 13958 R 2 18649 R 1 22128 TR 1
10813 R 2 13959 R 2 18659 R 2 22135 TR 2
10838 R 4 13986 TRC2 18782 R 2 22144 R 2
10858 TRC2 14033 C2 18804 TRC2 22156 R 1
10871 TRC1 14077 C1 18817 RC2 22190 RC2
10888 TRC2 14139 C2 18854 T 1 22198 TRC2
10895 C2 14144 C1 18991 TR 4 22202 TRC1
10906 C2 14513 TRC2 19092 RC8 22210 TRC2
10938 C4 14599 T 2 19166 C2 22251 RC2
10970 C2 14617 T 4 19390 C2 22268 RC1
11005 C2 14638 TR 2 19422 C3 22291 C2
11036 TRC7 14658 TR 2 19594 C4 22293 C2
11048 TRC2 14661 TR 1 19595 C4 22296 C2
11088 C4 14681 TR 1 19597 C2 22299 C2
11092 C2 14684 TR 1 19617 TR 2 22304 C1
11104 C2 14727 R 3 20036 T 2 22305 C1
11168 C2 14733 R 2 20244 C2 22324 C2
11194 T 2 14749 R 2 20255 T 1 22350 C1
11202 T 1 14780 RC1 20314 C2 22568 T 3
11243 T 2 14783 RC2 20431 TR 4 22602 T 1
11279 TR 1 14828 C2 20432 TR 2 22605 T 2
11289 TR 1 14871 C2 20461 R 1 22609 T 3
11291 TR 2 14943 C2 20462 R 2 22658 TR 1
11292 TR 1 14969 C2 20473 RC2 22689 R 1
11336 R 2 14976 C1 20496 C2 22710 R 2
11514 C2 14990 C2 21259 T 2 22714 R 2
11581 TR 2 15017 C2 21260 T 2 22939 R 2
11587 TR 4 15022 C1 21311 TR 2

Secondary: Inclusions

10037 T 2 10601 T 2 11007 C1 11634 C1
10122 RC2 10603 T 2 11010 T 2 11700 TR 2
10441 T 2 10610 T 4 11083 C1 12228 TR 2
10521 T 4 10659 T 4 11244 T 2 12261 R 7
10549 T 2 10694 TR 2 11612 RC1 12352 R 8
10555 T 1 10847 TRC1 11632 C1 12396 RC8

12510 C8 15170 RC2 18858 T 1 21913 C1
13058 C7 15222 C2 19087 RC8 21947 C2
13170 TR 2 15223 C2 19129 C8 21959 C1
13387 C1 15224 C2 19290 C4 22000 TR 1
13859 T 2 15281 C1 19407 C1 22025 T 1
13977 R 2 15299 C2 19459 R 7 22048 T 1
13995 RC1 17644 C2 19659 RC2 22050 T 1
14000 TRC1 17941 R 2 19709 TRC3 22078 TR 2
14019 RC1 18000 C2 19880 TRC2 22108 TR 1
14146 C2 18078 T 1 20121 C2 22146 R 2
14151 C2 18081 T 1 20491 C2 22197 RC2
14405 TR 4 18167 RC1 21303 TR 2 22272 RC1
14406 TR 4 18209 C2 21326 TR 2 22290 C2
14562 T 1 18241 C2 21388 TRC2 22313 C1
14767 R 1 18293 C2 21394 RC1 22336 C1
14781 TRC1 18294 C1 21409 TRC2 22380 C1
14794 TRC2 18601 R 2 21432 C3 22548 T 1
14906 C2 18616 R 2 21747 TR 1 22857 C2
15139 TR 2 18631 R 2 21793 TR 1 22878 T 1
15152 R 3 18799 RC2 21877 RC3 22924 TR 1
15165 TRC1 18825 RC2

Secondary: Journal Articles

10166 C2 12100 C2 15253 C2 20280 TRC1
10305 C2 12217 TR 2 15264 C2 20545 T 2
10501 C2 12313 R 8 15265 C2 20554 T 1
10530 T 2 12332 R 2 15268 C1 20587 T 1
10532 T 1 12360 R 7 15276 C1 20849 R 2
10583 T 1 12361 R 7 15288 C2 21283 T 2
10589 T 1 12391 RC7 15289 C2 21284 T 2
10609 T 1 12398 RC8 15292 C2 21290 T 1
10699 TR 1 12729 R 1 15295 C4 21322 TR 1
10710 TR 1 12821 C2 15934 T 2 21398 TRC1
10722 TR 3 12848 C1 15979 RC4 21403 RC1
10734 TR 2 13159 TR 2 17992 C2 21441 T 1
10762 R 3 13425 C5 17996 C2 21609 T 1
10766 R 2 13451 T 1 18136 R 4 21652 T 2
10817 R 1 13476 T 1 18162 R 1 21653 T 1
10826 R 2 13486 T 1 18166 RC1 21725 TR 1
10872 TRC2 13839 T 2 18174 RC1 21792 TR 1
10880 RC2 13851 T 1 18177 RC2 21812 R 1
10884 RC2 13852 T 3 18195 C2 21829 TRC1
10897 C2 13853 T 4 18199 C2 21830 TRC2
10924 C3 13897 R 8 18221 C2 21846 TRC1
10925 C2 14029 C1 18223 C1 21849 TRC1
10927 C1 14038 C1 18227 C2 21914 C1
10928 C1 14064 C1 18238 C2 21919 C2
10981 C1 14073 C1 18259 C1 21953 C1
11037 RC1 14076 C1 18262 C1 21956 C1
11054 TRC2 14152 C1 18265 C1 21961 C2
11068 C1 14412 RC1 18276 C4 21968 C3
11084 C1 14414 RC4 18338 C7 22037 T 1
11091 C1 14434 R 7 18402 T 1 22049 T 1
11116 C2 14564 T 4 18460 T 2 22063 T 1
11122 C1 14572 T 2 18504 T 2 22097 TR 1
11136 C1 14752 R 1 18599 R 2 22098 TR 2
11165 C1 14813 C1 18625 R 3 22120 TR 1
11169 C2 14822 C2 18663 R 2 22121 TR 1
11191 T 1 14832 C1 18675 R 2 22159 R 2
11238 T 3 14834 C2 18797 RC1 22216 TRC1
11396 TRC1 14897 C1 18803 RC1 22227 TRC1
11402 TRC1 14902 C1 18813 RC1 22276 RC2
11419 C1 14920 C1 18815 RC2 22278 RC1
11453 C2 14959 C2 18830 RC2 22289 C1
11602 RC1 14968 C2 19081 RC8 22316 C1
11642 C1 14971 C2 19370 C1 22344 C2
11661 T 4 14993 C1 19377 C2 22377 C1
11664 T 2 14997 C2 19378 C1 22400 T 2
11676 T 2 15137 TR 1 19386 C3 22528 T 1
11680 T 2 15144 R 2 19393 TR 1 22569 T 2
11773 R 2 15201 C1 19414 C4 22633 T 1
11800 R 2 15208 C2 19440 T 2 22636 T 1
11806 R 2 15213 C2 19444 R 7 22663 TR 2
11814 R 2 15219 C2 19463 R 2 22771 T 2
11976 C2 15220 C2 19596 C4 22786 TR 1
12098 C2 15225 C2 19768 T 2 22836 C2
12099 C1 15227 C1 20237 C2 22843 C1

The Eighteen Provinces

Primary 10623 T 3 12212 TR 2 14107 TR 1
10056 T 2 10680 T 3 12252 R 8 14158 T 2
10322 T 2 10760 R 2 12373 R 7 14159 T 1
10525 T 2 10761 R 4 12389 RC8 14168 T 2
10546 T 3 10839 R 2 12615 T 3 14169 T 1
10608 T 2 11016 T 2 13836 T 4 14170 T 1

14172 T 1 14250 R 1 18083 T 1 21295 T 1
14180 T 2 14273 RC3 18085 T 4 21297 T 2
14188 T 1 14277 TRC3 18097 T 1 21340 TR 3
14199 T 2 14300 C3 18448 T 4 21365 R 3
14200 T 1 14301 C3 18472 T 4 21473 TRC2
14207 T 2 14388 C3 18520 T 1 21679 T 4
14217 TR 2 14578 T 1 18546 TR 2 21807 R 4
14218 TR 4 15018 C2 18681 R 2 22029 T 3
14225 TR 1 15049 TR 2 18948 T 1 22083 TR 1
14226 TR 1 15145 R 4 18999 R 3 22086 TR 1
14236 R 2 15931 T 4 19835 R 3 22558 T 2
14237 R 3 15947 TR 2 21272 T 2 22684 R 1
14238 R 3 18074 T 2 21277 T 2 22776 T 2

Secondary: Monographs

10018 T 2 13155 TR 4 18076 T 3 21370 R 2
10038 T 2 13455 T 5 18364 T 2 21455 R 5
10161 C2 13637 T 2 18461 T 2 21456 R 2
10174 C2 13956 R 4 18621 R 3 21685 T 2
10544 T 3 14555 T 1 18834 RC2 21761 TR 1
10594 T 1 15240 C3 18859 T 2 21765 TR 1
11667 T 2 15543 C2 19441 T 2 22057 T 2
12198 T 8 15830 C2 19964 TR 1 22067 T 2
13151 TR 2 18012 T 2 21362 TR 3 22680 R 3

Secondary: Inclusions

10252 T 2 18080 T 2 21310 TR 1 22177 R 3
14763 R 3 18683 R 2 21319 TR 2 22399 T 2
15148 R 4 20776 T 2 22036 T 1 22691 R 3
15203 C3 21267 T 2 22092 TR 3 22773 T 2
16105 TR 2 21309 TR 2

Secondary: Journal Articles

10568 T 4 12933 T 2 18679 R 2 21096 C4
10569 T 2 14091 T 2 19002 R 5 21261 T 2
10590 T 5 14101 T 2 19458 R 8 21700 T 1
10670 T 4 14108 TR 1 20139 T 1 22045 T 1
11319 R 1 14124 R 7 20449 R 4 22170 R 1
11579 TR 1 18152 R 1 20544 T 2 22218 RC1
12335 R 2 18586 R 2 20606 T 2 22286 TRC1
12909 T 2 18637 R 2 20895 R 3

North China Broadly Conceived

Primary 14195 T 3 14762 R 2 21287 T 2
10989 C5 14210 T 2 18497 T 2 21787 TR 3

Second. 12290 R 8 18678 R 2 18872 T 2
10066 T 2 13894 R 2 18682 R 2 20716 T 2
10679 T 2 15752 T 2 18688 R 2 21292 T 2
10827 R 2 18307 R 2 18747 R 1 22394 T 2
11028 R 2

Manchuria

Primary 10796 R 2 11032 R 4 15287 C2

Second. 10647 T 1 10911 C2 15674 TR 2
10582 T 2 10852 RC2 12248 R 2

Northern China

Primary 14157 T 3 14228 TR 2 17569 R 8
10505 T 3 14163 T 3 14234 R 3 18092 T 3
10591 T 3 14182 T 3 14270 RC3 18398 T 2
10598 T 2 14191 T 5 14320 C3 18467 T 3
10607 T 3 14194 T 2 14330 C3 18946 T 3
10673 T 3 14196 T 3 14427 R 2 20012 TR 2
10797 R 3 14197 T 3 14551 T 3 20140 T 3
10996 C3 14204 T 3 14570 T 3 21264 T 3
11599 R 3 14214 TR 3 15075 R 8 21359 TR 3

Second. 10781 R 2 11597 R 3 19779 T 3
10529 T 3 10898 C3 11765 R 1 20559 T 3
10547 T 3 10941 C3 13910 R 2 20608 TR 3
10612 T 3 10945 C3 14615 T 2 21169 T 3
10652 T 3 11135 C3 15045 T 2 21278 T 3
10730 TR 3 11541 T 2 18235 C3 21293 T 3
10776 R 2 11568 T 3 18990 TR 3

Northwestern China and Frontier Regions

Primary 10725 TR 2 13814 T 2 18318 C8
18996 R 2

Second. 18220 C1 18584 R 4 22531 T 2
16517 T 2 18340 C2 18890 T 2

SOUTH CHINA BROADLY CONCEIVED

PRIMARY 10632 T 1 18500 T 2 18641 R 2
10031 T 2 14262 RC2 18572 TR 2

SECOND. 13881 TR 2 18137 R 1 18485 T 4
10289 TR 2 15205 C2 18412 T 2 21294 T 1
10636 T 1 17167 T 3 18421 T 2 22513 T 2
13869 T 2 17982 R 2

EAST CENTRAL CHINA

PRIMARY 14161 T 2 14393 C2 16525 T 8
18487 T 2

SECOND. 14646 TR 3 18466 T 2 21661 T 1
14635 TR 5 17162 T 3 18600 R 3

CENTRAL YANGTZE PROVINCES

PRIMARY 14186 T 4 14187 T 2 17554 T 4

SECOND. 13983 R 7

SOUTHWESTERN CHINA

PRIMARY 10791 R 2 14349 C1 18640 R 4
10566 T 2 14171 T 3 18089 T 2

SECOND. 12601 T 2 14571 T 4 18925 T 2

SOUTHEASTERN CHINA

PRIMARY 10708 TR 2 13798 T 3 14326 C3
10522 T 3 10855 RC2 14088 T 2 21573 C3

SECOND. 13854 T 1 18569 TR 3 21274 T 1
10552 T 2 13913 R 4 18997 R 3 21769 TR 3
10935 C1 15263 C2 21184 TR 5 22022 C1

TAIWAN ONLY

PRIMARY 10675 T 2 11166 C1 14367 C1
10307 C1 10857 TRC2 12078 C1 14368 C1
10653 T 2 11108 C1 14224 TR 2

SECOND. 11134 C1 14908 C4 16864 C2
10882 RC2 11138 C2 14979 C3 18440 T 1
10908 C1 11851 TRC2 16745 TRC8 21009 C2
11044 RC2

HONG KONG AND MACAU ONLY

PRIMARY □

SECOND. 20564 T 8 22670 TR 1

16.2 THE BOURGEOISIE

商人及市民階級

商人及び市民階級

GEOGRAPHIC CHINA BROADLY CONCEIVED

PRIMARY 13688 TR 2 14400 T 4 19353 TR 2
11150 C4 14395 T 2 19219 TR 2 19717 T 2
13133 T 4 14399 T 4

SECOND. 11687 TR 2 13144 TR 2 18301 T 4
10042 T 2 11692 TR 2 13168 TR 4 18308 R 3
10060 T 2 12593 T 2 13629 T 2 19478 TR 4
10085 TR 2 12624 TR 2 13811 T 2 20826 TR 2
10272 T 3 12922 T 3 13876 TR 2 21276 T 2
10510 T 2 12957 TR 2 14244 R 4 21333 TR 2
10553 T 1 13049 TRC2 15162 TRC2 21392 TRC2
10664 T 2 13129 T 5 18079 T 1 22133 TR 2

MAINLAND CHINA

PRIMARY 11734 R 3 14122 R 3 14412 RC1
10088 R 2 11783 R 2 14396 T 2 14413 RC4
10463 C4 11855 TRC2 14397 T 4 14414 RC4
10464 C4 12067 C1 14398 T 3 14415 RC4
10548 T 2 12375 RC2 14402 TR 4 14416 C2
10621 T 4 12565 T 4 14403 TR 2 14417 C3
10622 T 5 12929 T 4 14404 TR 3 14418 C4
10654 T 3 12949 TR 2 14405 TR 4 14419 C2
10835 R 4 12985 R 2 14406 TR 4 14969 C2
10913 C4 13170 TR 2 14407 R 3 15025 C2
11069 C2 13220 R 2 14408 R 3 15279 C2
11142 C4 13408 C4 14410 R 4 17283 R 5
11661 T 4 14115 R 3 14411 R 4 18128 R 4
18136 R 4 19204 T 4 19286 RC5 19338 C5
18327 C2 19281 R 5 19294 C5 20725 T 2
18628 R 2 19285 RC5 19326 C4 21416 RC2

SECONDARY: MONOGRAPHS
10005 T 2 11263 TR 1 13420 C2 15150 R 2
10067 TR 2 11291 TR 2 13456 T 2 15248 C2
10135 C2 11440 C2 13668 TR 4 17160 T 2
10140 C2 11672 T 4 13905 R 2 17190 TR 5
10165 C2 11822 R 2 14093 T 2 18416 T 4
10172 C2 11830 R 2 14201 T 4 18458 T 1
10214 TRC2 11846 RC2 14231 TR 4 18543 TR 2
10481 C2 11860 RC2 14269 RC4 18659 R 2
10500 C4 11877 RC2 14364 C2 18699 R 2
10677 T 2 11885 C2 14369 C2 18842 C2
10727 TR 3 11901 C2 14378 C4 19302 C5
10813 R 2 11962 C2 14693 TR 4 19789 TR 2
10885 RC4 12950 TR 2 14999 C2 21363 TR 4
11040 RC4 13176 TR 3 15022 C1 22251 RC2
11088 C4 13284 R 2 15090 RC2 22568 T 3
11113 C4 13366 C4 15123 C2

SECONDARY: INCLUSIONS
10671 T 3 11700 TR 2 18088 T 2 19562 R 4
10750 R 2 12045 C2 18601 R 2 21877 RC3
11063 C3 17147 T 2 19526 R 3 22221 RC2

SECONDARY: JOURNAL ARTICLES
10457 C1 12111 C2 14814 C4 19312 C4
10483 C5 12668 TR 2 14824 C2 19330 C3
10494 C3 12961 TR 2 15133 TR 2 19344 T 5
10495 C4 13000 R 2 15179 RC2 19359 R 3
10826 R 2 13069 C4 15228 C2 19430 R 4
11024 R 4 13071 C2 15295 C4 19512 R 4
11334 R 4 13159 TR 2 18064 C3 19565 R 3
11453 C2 13624 T 1 18130 R 3 19573 R 3
11676 T 2 13643 TR 5 18188 RC2 19574 R 3
11680 T 2 13686 TR 4 18222 C2 21830 TRC2
11761 R 2 13738 R 2 18254 C2 22161 R 4
11937 C2 13746 R 4 18276 C4 22171 R 2
11943 C2 13776 C4 18625 R 3 22613 T 1
11976 C2 14149 C2 18718 R 2 22663 TR 2
12024 C4 14154 C2 19030 RC4 22838 C2
12094 C2 14490 R 3 19218 TR 1

THE EIGHTEEN PROVINCES

PRIMARY 12927 T 1 13637 T 2 18017 T 3
11667 T 2 12933 T 2 14401 T 5 18127 R 3
12615 T 3 13455 T 5 15148 R 4 19354 TR 4
12909 T 2

SECOND. 13463 T 5 17322 TRC2 19527 R 4
10006 T 2 13646 TR 3 18007 T 1 20606 T 2
10544 T 3 13679 TR 5 18012 T 2 20793 TR 5
11656 T 2 14474 R 3 18115 R 2 21482 C4
12928 T 2 14484 R 4 18642 R 4 21676 T 2
12938 T 3 15145 R 4 19350 T 4 22628 T 3
13155 TR 4 15954 TR 5 19356 TR 4 22760 C3
13191 TR 3 17145 T 2 19432 TR 4 22885 T 2

NORTH CHINA BROADLY CONCEIVED

PRIMARY 14409 R 2 21348 TR 3

SECOND. 18038 TRC5 18146 R 2 19225 R 4

MANCHURIA

PRIMARY □

SECOND. 11684 TR 2 11691 TR 2 13005 R 5
13500 TR 2

NORTHERN CHINA

□

NORTHWESTERN CHINA AND FRONTIER REGIONS

□

SOUTH CHINA BROADLY CONCEIVED

PRIMARY □

SECOND. 10289 TR 2 11658 T 2 13889 R 2
17982 R 2

EAST CENTRAL CHINA

PRIMARY 19206 T 4

SECOND. □

CENTRAL YANGTZE PROVINCES

□

SOUTHWESTERN CHINA

PRIMARY □

SECOND. 10566 T 2

SOUTHEASTERN CHINA

□

TAIWAN ONLY

PRIMARY 10923 C3 18049 C3 18263 C2

SECOND. 12070 C2 17955 RC1

HONG KONG AND MACAU ONLY

□

16.3 THE PEASANTRY

農民階級 農民階級

GEOGRAPHIC CHINA BROADLY CONCEIVED

PRIMARY 10446 R 2 12201 T 7 12439 C8
10001 T 2 12188 T 2 12310 R 8 12624 TR 2
10096 R 2 12190 T 2 12401 RC7

SECOND. 10828 R 2 14126 TRC2 18711 R 2
10017 T 2 10862 TRC2 14248 R 2 19650 RC2
10118 RC2 11704 TR 2 14468 R 2 20009 TR 1
10285 TR 2 12196 T 7 16185 T 2 20766 T 2
10438 T 7 12232 TR 7 17933 TR 1 21368 R 2
10445 R 2 12233 TR 2 18388 T 2 21557 C2
10526 T 2 12348 R 2 18494 T 2 21853 TRC2
10664 T 2 12370 R 7 18540 TR 2 22265 RC2
10806 R 2 12759 R 2 18545 TR 2

MAINLAND CHINA

PRIMARY: MONOGRAPHS
10088 R 2 12271 R 7 12525 C2 18783 R 2
10291 TR 2 12291 R 7 12535 C2 18842 C2
10477 C2 12302 R 2 12552 C7 19092 RC8
11003 C2 12303 R 2 14127 RC2 19135 C7
11698 TR 2 12312 R 8 14436 R 7 19445 R 7
11752 R 2 12317 R 7 15115 C2 19455 R 8
12027 C2 12363 R 8 17979 TR 7 19638 R 7
12227 TR 7 12412 RC7 18585 R 2 20247 C7
12256 R 7 12424 RC7 18660 R 2 20455 R 2
12264 R 7 12456 C8 18733 R 2 22162 R 2
12268 R 8 12467 C7

PRIMARY: INCLUSIONS
10078 TR 2 14123 R 2 14525 C2 18571 TR 2
11711 TR 2 14150 C2 15170 RC2 18605 R 2
11861 RC7 14435 R 2 15187 RC7 19104 C7
12197 T 7 14442 C7 15209 C7 19198 C2
12341 R 8 14448 C7 18280 C2 19459 R 7
12479 C2 14451 C7 18429 T 2 21859 TRC1
14096 T 2

PRIMARY: JOURNAL ARTICLES
10063 T 2 12360 R 7 14421 T 8 14445 C7
10192 TR 2 12361 R 7 14423 T 7 14446 C2
10391 RC2 12374 RC7 14426 R 8 14447 C7
10440 T 2 12392 RC7 14428 R 7 14449 C7
10462 C7 12393 RC8 14429 R 8 14450 C7
10465 C2 12403 RC7 14430 R 8 14452 C7
10492 C2 12419 RC7 14434 R 7 14515 RC2
11124 C7 12451 C7 14437 RC2 15109 C7
12111 C2 12488 C7 14438 RC2 15122 C7
12255 R 7 12531 C2 14439 RC7 18835 RC8
12289 R 7 13484 T 2 14440 RC8 19086 RC7
12307 R 7 13738 R 2 14441 C7 19091 RC7
12311 R 7 14105 TR 2 14443 C7 19128 C7
12313 R 8 14420 T 7 14444 C7 19137 C7

19141 C7 19169 C2 19183 C2 19447 R 7
19150 C2 19176 C8 19444 R 7 19461 R 8
19168 C2

Secondary: Monographs
10035 T 2 11897 C2 13104 C2 18699 R 2
10083 TR 2 11903 C2 13163 TR 2 18768 R 2
10121 RC2 11912 C2 13250 R 2 18780 R 2
10124 TRC2 11996 C2 13579 C2 18782 R 2
10136 C2 12060 C2 13715 R 8 18804 TRC2
10140 C2 12076 C2 13880 TR 2 19078 RC8
10148 C2 12096 C2 13896 R 2 19083 RC7
10153 C2 12229 TR 7 13986 TRC2 19133 C7
10167 C2 12257 R 7 14139 C2 19453 R 2
10172 C2 12270 R 7 14160 T 2 19457 R 7
10487 C2 12298 R 7 14364 C2 19662 C2
10726 TR 2 12358 R 2 14416 C2 19751 T 2
10821 R 2 12378 RC8 14828 C2 20049 TR 2
10937 C2 12379 RC7 14999 C2 20204 R 2
10970 C2 12386 RC2 15085 RC2 20226 TRC2
11005 C2 12387 RC8 15112 C2 20430 TR 2
11092 C2 12426 RC7 15113 C2 20502 C2
11106 C2 12442 C7 15163 RC2 21320 TR 2
11581 TR 2 12453 C7 15168 TRC2 21420 TRC2
11689 TR 2 12515 C7 17760 R 7 21948 C2
11713 TR 2 12519 C8 18148 R 2 22250 RC2
11745 R 2 12523 C8 18154 R 2 22291 C2
11750 R 2 12562 C7 18161 R 2 22293 C2
11754 R 2 12783 TRC2 18324 C2 22298 C2
11846 RC2 13042 R 2 18617 R 2 22605 T 2
11877 RC2 13070 C2 18635 R 2

Secondary: Inclusions
10486 C2 12397 RC7 15293 C7 19182 C7
10542 T 2 12459 C7 15682 R 2 19190 C7
10642 T 2 12507 C7 17032 TR 7 19199 C7
11176 C2 12510 C8 18000 C2 19202 C7
12213 TR 7 12536 C7 18632 R 2 19880 TRC2
12228 TR 2 12547 C7 18672 R 2 20491 C2
12261 R 7 12559 C2 18799 RC2 21486 C2
12269 R 8 13058 C7 18837 C2 21709 T 2
12326 R 2 13066 C2 19087 RC8 22166 R 2
12333 R 7 13859 T 2 19129 C8 22197 RC2
12352 R 8 13920 R 2 19149 C7 22221 RC2
12395 RC2 14151 C2 19170 C7 22565 T 2
12396 RC8 15043 T 2

Secondary: Journal Articles
10084 TR 2 12192 T 2 12534 C2 18252 C2
10451 R 2 12199 T 8 12546 C7 18338 C7
10472 C2 12217 TR 2 12549 C8 18504 T 2
10489 C7 12239 R 7 12961 TR 2 18580 R 2
10496 C2 12249 R 7 13056 C7 18587 R 1
10502 C7 12259 R 7 13073 C2 18673 R 7
10744 R 2 12273 R 7 13089 C2 18705 R 2
10884 RC2 12279 R 8 13370 C2 18718 R 2
10933 C2 12282 R 8 13531 R 2 18816 RC2
10972 C2 12304 R 2 13596 C7 19081 RC8
11056 C8 12306 R 8 14149 C2 19084 RC8
11058 C7 12314 R 8 14154 C2 19124 C8
11097 C2 12334 R 8 14830 C2 19187 C8
11460 C7 12362 R 8 14834 C2 19189 C7
11662 T 2 12388 RC7 15076 R 2 19440 T 2
11743 R 2 12391 RC7 15087 RC2 19462 R 7
11762 R 2 12398 RC8 15088 RC2 19463 R 2
11763 R 2 12413 RC7 15114 C2 19464 R 7
11788 R 2 12425 TRC8 15154 R 2 19469 RC2
11792 R 2 12450 C8 15178 TRC2 19471 C7
11814 R 2 12452 C7 15179 RC2 20197 R 2
11866 RC2 12458 C7 15190 RC2 20237 C2
11915 C2 12468 C2 15213 C2 20521 C2
11943 C2 12473 C7 15231 C2 20993 RC8
12004 C2 12482 C2 15246 C2 21015 C2
12050 C2 12483 C8 15247 C2 21227 R 8
12128 C2 12489 C7 15275 C2 21439 T 2
12131 C2 12496 C7 15292 C2 22168 R 2
12171 C2 12511 C7 17778 C7 22171 R 2
12187 T 8 12529 C7 17782 C2 22879 T 8
12189 T 2

The Eighteen Provinces

Primary 12389 RC8 14425 R 7 18431 T 7
10839 R 2 13925 R 2 14432 R 8 18451 T 2
12212 TR 2 14087 T 2 14433 R 8 19458 R 8
12252 R 8 14422 T 8 14543 C2 20190 R 2
12346 R 8 14424 TR 7 15049 TR 2 22067 T 2
12385 RC8

Second. 12335 R 2 16049 T 2 18778 R 2
10006 T 2 12340 R 8 16105 TR 2 19122 C8
10161 C2 12366 R 7 18461 T 2 20606 T 2
11735 R 2 13731 R 2 18482 T 2 21208 R 8
11784 R 2 13805 T 2 18592 R 2 21228 R 8
12151 C2 14124 R 7 18637 R 2 21456 R 2
12193 T 8 14456 TR 2 18645 R 7 21502 TR 8
12198 T 8 15054 R 7 18657 R 7 22399 T 2
12225 TR 8 15067 R 2

North China Broadly Conceived

Primary 10827 R 2 12274 R 8 18712 R 7
Second. 12290 R 8 15694 R 2 18307 R 2
10066 T 2 13894 R 2 17873 R 2

Manchuria

Primary 11834 R 2 12211 TR 8 12248 R 2
12321 R 7 14431 R 7
Second. 12301 R 7 15053 R 7 15674 TR 2
10364 R 2 12322 R 7 15588 TR 2 15677 TR 7
10796 R 2 13011 R 2 15669 TR 2 15683 R 2
12286 R 8 13147 TR 2 15670 TR 2 15873 RC2

Northern China

Primary 14427 R 2
Second. ☐

Northwestern China and Frontier Regions

Primary 13814 T 2
Second. 12368 R 8 19375 C2

South China Broadly Conceived

Primary 12186 T 7 17947 RC2 19448 R 2
Second. 13889 R 2 18577 R 2 18763 R 2
13887 R 2 13929 R 2 18646 R 2 18766 R 2

East Central China

Primary 16525 T 8
Second. ☐

Central Yangtze Provinces

Primary ☐
Second. 11723 R 2 19443 R 8 19450 R 7

Southwestern China

Primary ☐
Second. 10791 R 2

Southeastern China

Primary ☐
Second. 16530 T 2 22563 T 2

Taiwan Only

Primary 16739 TRC8 16741 TRC8
Second. 15875 RC2 16745 TRC8 16864 C2
11844 TRC2 16549 TR 7 16822 C8 16885 C8
12070 C2 16551 TR 7

Hong Kong and Macau Only

☐

16.4 The Working Class

勞工階級　労働者階級

Geographic China Broadly Conceived

Primary 14468 R 2 19478 TR 4 19546 R 3
10076 TR 2 14475 R 2 19481 TR 3 19559 R 5
10446 R 2 14476 R 3 19500 R 4 20222 R 3
14113 TR 2 14491 R 3 19534 R 2 22160 R 1
14465 R 5 19475 TR 4

Second. 11694 TR 2 13189 TR 2 18540 TR 2
10077 TR 2 11766 R 2 13704 R 2 18711 R 2
10085 TR 2 11767 R 2 13876 TR 2 19219 TR 2
10272 T 3 13133 T 4 13950 R 2 19554 R 3
10346 TR 2 13142 TR 3 14400 T 4 20209 R 3
10445 R 2 13168 TR 4 15063 R 2 20643 R 2
10828 R 2 13175 TR 2 18308 R 3 22265 RC2

Mainland China

Primary: Monographs
10477 C2 14478 R 3 14535 C4 19477 TR 4
10487 C2 14479 R 2 15112 C2 19480 TR 3
11698 TR 2 14483 R 4 15113 C2 19517 R 3
11920 C2 14486 R 2 15115 C2 19551 R 2
12027 C2 14496 R 5 15156 R 2 19558 R 2
13164 TR 4 14497 R 2 17245 R 5 19590 C4
13169 TR 3 14501 R 4 18630 R 2 19597 C2
13184 TR 2 14508 R 3 18708 R 2 19611 C4
13353 C2 14509 R 3 18733 R 2 19668 C5
13415 C4 14510 R 4 18768 R 2 19704 R 3
14122 R 3 14512 RC2 18783 R 2 20219 R 3
14457 TR 3 14513 TRC2 18842 C2 20502 C2
14466 R 3 14520 C3 19291 C2 22162 R 2
14470 R 4 14522 C2 19476 TR 2 22250 RC2
14471 R 1 14524 C2

Primary: Inclusions
10456 RC2 14495 R 5 18110 R 2 19563 R 5
13920 R 2 14521 C2 18628 R 2 19585 RC4
14123 R 2 14523 C4 19256 R 3 19598 C4
14455 TR 4 14525 C2 19562 R 4 22238 RC4
14492 R 3

Primary: Journal Articles
10451 R 2 14487 R 4 14533 C4 19512 R 4
10465 C2 14488 R 2 14534 C3 19532 R 4
10472 C2 14490 R 3 14536 C3 19542 R 4
10492 C2 14498 R 3 14537 C4 19544 R 2
10496 C2 14499 R 3 14538 C1 19561 R 3
11114 C4 14500 R 4 14545 C5 19568 R 3
11943 C2 14502 R 2 14546 C1 19571 R 3
12825 C3 14503 R 2 14547 C2 19572 R 2
12831 C2 14506 R 2 14548 C1 19576 R 3
13278 R 2 14511 R 2 15070 R 4 19582 RC3
13412 C4 14515 RC2 15088 RC2 19600 C3
13774 C4 14516 C4 15114 C2 19602 C4
14115 R 3 14517 C4 15117 C4 19606 C3
14437 RC2 14518 C4 15231 C2 20187 R 2
14453 T 4 14519 C3 18580 R 2 20201 R 4
14458 TR 3 14526 C3 18625 R 3 20250 C3
14460 R 2 14527 C4 18668 R 4 20390 TR 3
14464 R 5 14528 C2 19224 R 7 20521 C2
14473 R 2 14529 C4 19473 TR 4 20904 R 3
14477 R 3 14530 C4 19474 TR 4 22161 R 4
14481 R 2 14531 C5 19484 R 3 22213 RC2
14482 R 1 14532 C2

Secondary: Monographs
10081 TR 2 12076 C2 13345 C7 18597 R 4
10103 R 2 12163 C2 13361 C2 18598 R 2
10148 C2 12532 C2 13432 C2 18617 R 2
10153 C2 13104 C2 13442 C7 18635 R 2
10172 C2 13158 TR 2 13443 C2 19281 R 5
10291 TR 2 13163 TR 2 13768 C1 19338 C5
10488 C2 13176 TR 3 14305 C4 19358 TR 3
10500 C4 13211 R 2 14943 C2 19520 R 3
10821 R 2 13213 R 7 15073 R 2 19594 C4
10885 RC4 13214 R 4 15085 RC2 19595 C4
11003 C2 13261 R 5 15123 C2 19662 C2
11106 C2 13277 R 2 15140 TR 2 20049 TR 2
11113 C4 13284 R 2 15245 C2 20161 TR 3
11713 TR 2 13289 R 2 15248 C2 20204 R 2
11718 TR 2 13291 R 4 15856 C2 20226 TRC2
11754 R 2 13311 TRC2 17160 T 2 20244 C2
11860 RC2 13314 RC1 18161 R 2 20430 TR 2
11874 RC2 13338 C2 18232 C2 20455 R 2
11884 C2 13339 C4 18324 C2 22117 TR 2
11903 C2 13343 C2 18543 TR 2 22224 RC2
11912 C2 13344 C2 18596 R 2 22298 C2
11949 C2

Secondary: Inclusions
10122 RC2 12651 TR 5 13390 C2 15105 C4
10486 C2 13162 TR 4 13416 C4 15233 C2
11721 R 2 13242 R 5 13419 C3 17174 T 2
12045 C2 13387 C1 14302 C3 17792 C2

18605 R 2 19290 C4 19589 C4 21486 C2
18632 R 2 19526 R 3 19608 C4 21589 C5
18672 R 2 19588 C4

SECONDARY: JOURNAL ARTICLES
10265 C2 12122 C2 14830 C2 19321 C4
10297 R 2 12171 C2 15057 R 2 19327 C3
10457 C1 12531 C2 15064 R 3 19377 C2
10467 C2 12854 C2 15066 R 2 19485 R 3
10474 C2 13180 TR 2 15076 R 2 19496 R 4
10494 C3 13199 R 4 15087 RC2 19525 R 3
10495 C4 13238 R 3 15154 R 2 19531 R 4
10744 R 2 13247 R 7 15157 R 4 19539 R 3
10775 R 2 13264 R 4 15228 C2 19565 R 3
10933 C2 13270 R 3 15247 C2 19573 R 3
10972 C2 13294 RC2 15915 C2 19574 R 3
11024 R 4 13302 RC1 17283 R 5 19592 C3
11097 C2 13303 RC3 17782 C2 19596 C4
11533 C1 13320 C1 17809 C2 19599 C4
11662 T 2 13323 C4 18130 R 3 19601 C4
11717 TR 2 13342 C7 18141 R 2 19609 C1
11831 R 2 13364 C2 18157 R 2 19610 C3
11836 R 1 13368 C2 18222 C2 19667 C3
11866 RC2 13386 C4 18435 T 2 20197 R 2
11908 C2 13391 C2 18762 R 4 21015 C2
11915 C2 13406 C3 19242 R 3 22159 R 2
11954 C2 14413 RC4 19307 C2 22168 R 2
12004 C2 14415 RC4 19315 C4 22309 C1
12024 C4 14417 C3 19317 C2 22851 C4
12048 C4 14438 RC2

THE EIGHTEEN PROVINCES

PRIMARY 14462 R 3 14489 R 3 14540 C2
10449 R 2 14463 R 3 14493 R 4 14543 C2
13254 R 2 14467 R 3 14494 R 2 15062 R 2
13751 R 1 14469 R 3 14504 R 2 15080 R 2
14087 T 2 14472 R 3 14505 R 2 19527 R 4
14454 T 2 14474 R 3 14507 R 4 19575 R 2
14456 TR 2 14480 R 4 14514 RC4 19577 R 3
14459 R 3 14484 R 4 14539 C2 20190 R 2
14461 R 4 14485 R 3

SECOND. 12770 TRC2 18592 R 2 19545 R 4
10091 R 2 13130 T 2 18642 R 4 19570 R 2
10174 C2 13212 R 2 18778 R 2 20178 TR 2
10293 TR 2 13223 R 2 19483 R 4 20978 RC2
11725 R 2 13267 R 3 19487 R 3 21482 C4
11735 R 2 13275 R 3 19488 R 3 22760 C3
11824 R 2 13469 T 2 19515 R 3 22761 C3
12646 TR 2 13731 R 2 19536 R 4

NORTH CHINA BROADLY CONCEIVED

PRIMARY □

SECOND. 10969 C3 12616 T 2 15694 R 2
17873 R 2 18146 R 2

MANCHURIA

PRIMARY 11834 R 2 15181 RC2 18739 R 2

SECOND. 13230 R 3 15287 C2 15873 RC2
11826 R 2 13252 R 3 15669 TR 2 17266 R 2
13229 R 7 13355 C4 15867 R 2 19548 R 3

NORTHERN CHINA

PRIMARY 14541 C2 19492 R 3

SECOND. □

NORTHWESTERN CHINA AND FRONTIER REGIONS

PRIMARY □

SECOND. 12003 C2

SOUTH CHINA BROADLY CONCEIVED

PRIMARY □

SECOND. 13403 C4 13887 R 2 15205 C2
18646 R 2

EAST CENTRAL CHINA

PRIMARY □

SECOND. 11739 R 2 18529 TR 2 19552 R 3

CENTRAL YANGTZE PROVINCES

PRIMARY □

SECOND. 11726 R 2 19504 R 2

SOUTHWESTERN CHINA

PRIMARY 14542 C2

SECOND. 15270 C2 17211 R 2

SOUTHEASTERN CHINA

PRIMARY □

SECOND. 19502 R 3

TAIWAN ONLY

PRIMARY 14544 C5 14549 C4 14874 C2
21108 C7

SECOND. 10882 RC2 13179 TR 2 13445 C4
15875 RC2 15890 C2

HONG KONG AND MACAU ONLY

□

17 NATIONAL AND HIGHER EDUCATION

全國教育及高等教育

国民教育及び高等教育

GEOGRAPHIC CHINA BROADLY CONCEIVED

PRIMARY 14559 T 1 14696 TR 1 16423 R 2
10008 T 2 14560 T 3 14698 TR 1 16424 R 2
10022 T 2 14567 T 1 14699 TR 1 18077 T 2
10025 T 2 14594 T 2 14709 R 2 18560 TR 2
10045 T 2 14600 T 1 14710 R 1 20445 R 2
10074 TR 2 14620 T 1 14720 R 2 20463 R 3
10093 R 2 14621 T 1 14766 R 3 20790 TR 4
10162 C2 14627 T 1 14798 TRC2 20826 TR 2
10526 T 2 14648 TR 1 14811 RC1 20827 TR 3
10553 T 1 14654 TR 2 14812 RC1 20981 TRC2
10557 T 1 14657 TR 2 14903 C1 21318 TR 1
10646 T 4 14672 TR 1 14951 C2 21404 TRC1
14097 T 2 14676 TR 3 15126 T 2 21472 TRC1
14215 TR 2 14679 TR 1 16374 T 2 22740 TRC2
14400 T 4 14694 TR 4 16375 T 2

SECONDARY: MONOGRAPHS
10004 T 2 10823 R 1 18707 R 2 21337 TR 2
10010 T 2 10853 TRC2 18809 RC2 21342 TR 2
10014 T 2 11045 RC2 18919 T 1 21366 R 2
10024 T 2 11241 T 2 18937 T 2 21368 R 2
10034 T 2 11619 C2 18969 TR 2 21392 TRC2
10052 T 2 11657 T 4 19503 R 2 21412 RC2
10053 T 2 11703 TR 2 20005 TR 1 21434 C2
10058 T 2 11839 R 2 20160 TR 2 21467 TRC1
10077 TR 2 13461 T 4 20162 TR 1 21538 TRC2
10106 R 2 13873 TR 2 20173 TR 1 21603 T 3
10107 R 2 13916 R 2 20213 R 3 21847 TRC2
10108 R 2 14155 T 2 20231 RC2 21904 RC2
10114 TRC2 14193 T 1 20615 TR 2 22002 TR 1
10144 C2 15158 TRC2 20769 T 4 22027 T 4
10177 C2 15161 TRC2 20954 TRC1 22056 T 1
10331 T 2 15191 RC2 20960 TRC2 22074 T 2
10560 T 2 16186 T 2 20963 TRC1 22102 TR 2
10573 T 1 16376 T 2 21262 T 2 22474 TRC1
10586 T 1 16938 TR 2 21276 T 2 22620 T 1
10611 T 2 18494 T 2 21302 T 2 22720 R 3
10614 T 1

SECONDARY: INCLUSIONS
10627 T 2 13878 TR 2 19699 R 3 20786 T 2
10866 RC3 18525 T 2 20222 R 3 20832 R 2
11673 T 2 18558 TR 2 20563 T 2 22816 RC1
12801 C2 18971 TR 2

SECONDARY: JOURNAL ARTICLES
10384 TRC4 12661 TR 4 22189 RC1 22812 RC1
10663 T 2 14244 R 4 22604 T 3 23058 C1
10664 T 2 18303 R 2

MAINLAND CHINA

PRIMARY: MONOGRAPHS
10002 T 2 14231 TR 4 14736 R 4 18061 C2
10020 T 2 14384 C1 14744 R 1 18075 T 2
10029 T 2 14553 T 1 14749 R 2 18350 C1
10030 T 2 14556 T 2 14753 R 1 18378 T 2
10043 T 2 14574 T 2 14754 R 2 18854 T 1
10055 T 2 14584 T 2 14774 R 3 18952 TR 2
10062 T 2 14588 T 1 14780 RC1 18987 TR 2
10068 TR 2 14592 T 1 14783 RC2 19639 R 1
10081 TR 2 14599 T 2 14793 RC1 19640 R 7
10092 R 2 14617 T 4 14795 RC2 19652 RC2
10098 R 2 14619 T 1 14797 RC1 19670 C1
10103 R 2 14622 T 1 14808 RC2 20169 TR 2
10104 R 2 14626 T 1 14809 RC2 20170 TR 1
10105 R 2 14637 TR 1 14810 TRC1 20179 TR 1
10126 RC2 14638 TR 2 14828 C2 20182 TR 2
10130 C2 14640 TR 2 14833 C1 20204 R 2
10154 C2 14642 TR 1 14835 C2 20414 T 1
10159 C2 14647 TR 2 14853 C2 20430 TR 2
10164 C2 14650 TR 1 14871 C2 20484 C2
10167 C2 14652 TR 2 14882 C2 20492 C3
10464 C4 14655 TR 1 14885 C1 20496 C2
10481 C2 14658 TR 2 14899 C1 20526 C2
10519 T 4 14659 TR 2 14909 C1 20558 T 2
10559 T 4 14661 TR 1 14910 C2 20749 T 2
10599 T 2 14669 TR 1 14921 C1 20798 TR 2
10660 T 2 14670 TR 4 14942 C2 20823 TR 4
10676 T 2 14677 TR 1 14943 C2 20962 RC2
10690 TR 1 14678 TR 3 14969 C2 20973 TRC1
10894 C1 14681 TR 1 14974 C2 21103 C2
10895 C2 14683 TR 1 14976 C1 21124 C3
10997 C2 14684 TR 1 14990 C2 21308 TR 2
11105 C2 14685 TR 2 14999 C2 21325 TR 2
11194 T 2 14686 TR 1 15006 C2 21335 TR 1
11263 TR 1 14687 TR 2 15007 C4 21355 TR 2
11586 TR 2 14688 TR 1 15017 C2 21457 R 1
11601 R 2 14691 TR 1 15022 C1 21563 C1
11894 C2 14692 TR 1 15023 C2 21819 R 2
12082 C2 14693 TR 4 15025 C2 21874 RC2
12123 C2 14695 TR 1 15028 C2 21937 C2
12230 TR 2 14700 TR 2 15029 C1 22198 TRC2
12532 C2 14703 TR 2 15033 C1 22271 RC1
12811 C2 14718 R 1 15034 C1 22296 C2
13308 RC2 14719 R 4 15172 TRC2 22530 T 1
13328 C2 14721 R 2 15267 C2 22644 TR 2
13420 C2 14723 R 2 15273 C2 22679 R 2
13870 T 1 14724 R 1 16457 C2 22711 R 1
13937 R 2 14727 R 3 17779 C2 22805 R 2
14093 T 2 14730 R 5 17895 RC2 22831 C2
14219 TR 2 14733 R 2 18041 TRC2

PRIMARY: INCLUSIONS
10463 C4 14689 TR 1 14880 C2 18110 R 2
10469 C2 14690 TR 1 14901 C1 18992 R 2
10497 C2 14715 R 2 14905 C2 19003 R 2
10610 T 4 14760 R 1 14906 C2 19659 RC2
10859 TRC1 14767 R 1 14913 C2 20189 R 1
11065 C1 14773 R 2 14945 C3 20202 R 4
12852 C3 14781 TRC1 14957 C2 20212 R 2
13394 C1 14788 RC2 14958 C2 20472 RC3
14208 T 2 14789 TRC1 14964 C1 20491 C2
14255 RC1 14790 RC2 14967 C2 20988 RC2
14562 T 1 14794 TRC2 14973 C2 21050 C3
14579 T 1 14821 C2 14975 C2 21529 TRC3
14591 T 2 14840 C2 14977 C2 21682 T 2
14601 T 3 14850 C2 15001 C2 21912 C2
14603 T 2 14851 C1 15005 C1 21913 C1
14628 TR 2 14852 C4 15011 C1 21964 C2
14643 TR 1 14856 C2 15012 C4 21965 C2
14645 TR 1 14864 C1 15013 C2 21978 C2
14667 TR 1 14876 C2 15314 T 2 22525 T 2
14674 TR 2 14878 C3 15799 RC2 22857 C2

PRIMARY: JOURNAL ARTICLES
10033 T 2 11591 TR 1 14557 T 1 14595 T 1
10495 C4 11932 C2 14558 T 1 14598 T 1
10532 T 1 11944 C2 14564 T 4 14605 T 1
10705 TR 1 11976 C2 14565 T 4 14607 T 1
10740 R 1 12085 C2 14566 T 2 14608 T 1
10896 C2 12802 C2 14569 T 2 14611 T 4
10933 C2 12814 C2 14572 T 2 14612 T 2
10942 C2 13451 T 1 14576 T 1 14613 T 1
11039 RC1 13840 T 2 14580 T 1 14614 T 2
11152 C1 14240 R 1 14589 T 1 14618 T 1
11171 C2 14360 C3 14593 T 1 14623 T 1

14631 TR 4 14822 C2 14923 C1 18893 T 2
14633 TR 4 14823 C2 14924 C2 18964 TR 2
14644 TR 1 14824 C2 14926 C2 19067 C1
14651 TR 1 14827 C2 14927 C4 19410 C4
14653 TR 4 14830 C2 14928 C3 19414 C4
14662 TR 3 14832 C1 14929 C2 19660 C2
14663 TR 1 14834 C2 14930 C2 19665 C1
14664 TR 1 14837 C1 14931 C2 19682 C1
14666 TR 5 14842 C3 14932 C2 20174 TR 1
14673 TR 1 14843 C2 14933 C2 20437 R 3
14697 TR 2 14845 C2 14934 C1 20438 R 1
14702 TR 1 14847 C1 14935 C2 20501 C2
14704 R 2 14848 C1 14936 C1 20515 C2
14706 R 2 14849 C1 14937 C1 20521 C2
14707 R 2 14855 C2 14941 C1 20531 C3
14708 R 3 14857 C2 14948 C1 20666 C3
14713 R 2 14862 C7 14952 C2 20819 TR 1
14716 R 1 14863 C2 14953 C1 20841 R 1
14722 R 1 14867 C1 14954 C2 20865 R 2
14726 R 2 14868 C2 14956 C2 21011 C4
14729 R 2 14869 C7 14959 C2 21015 C2
14734 R 1 14870 C2 14965 C2 21113 C3
14738 R 2 14872 C2 14968 C2 21123 C2
14740 R 2 14883 C3 14971 C2 21462 R 1
14741 R 3 14884 C3 14984 C2 21814 R 1
14742 R 1 14886 C4 14986 C1 21820 R 1
14747 R 2 14897 C1 14991 C2 21879 RC1
14752 R 1 14898 C1 14993 C1 21943 C3
14759 R 4 14900 C2 14997 C2 21979 C4
14765 R 3 14902 C1 14998 C1 22105 TR 2
14768 R 3 14907 C2 15003 C3 22140 TR 1
14769 R 3 14912 C4 15004 C1 22150 R 5
14775 R 3 14914 C1 15008 C3 22311 C1
14776 R 1 14915 C1 15015 C1 22346 C2
14777 TRC1 14916 C2 15020 C2 22369 C1
14778 RC2 14917 C2 15032 C2 22828 C1
14787 TRC2 14918 C4 15206 C2 22833 C1
14813 C1 14919 C1 15252 C2 22836 C2
14814 C4 14920 C1 18866 T 1 22852 C1
14818 C2

Secondary: Monographs
10003 T 2 10799 R 2 12229 TR 7 14370 C2
10007 T 2 10812 R 2 12256 R 7 14378 C4
10044 T 2 10836 R 4 12317 R 7 14457 TR 3
10049 T 2 10871 TRC1 12434 C2 14486 R 2
10059 T 2 10888 TRC2 12441 C2 14522 C2
10065 T 2 10937 C2 12475 C2 15123 C2
10069 TR 2 10960 C2 12564 C2 15140 TR 2
10079 TR 2 10994 C2 12597 T 2 15150 R 2
10094 R 2 10999 C1 12638 TR 2 15163 RC2
10097 R 2 11003 C2 12839 C2 15214 C2
10099 R 2 11005 C2 12845 C4 15230 C2
10101 R 2 11069 C2 12864 C1 15248 C2
10110 TRC2 11087 C3 13125 T 2 15249 C2
10120 TRC2 11104 C2 13187 TR 4 15285 C4
10121 RC2 11106 C2 13324 C7 15294 C2
10123 RC2 11107 C4 13449 C1 15297 C2
10124 TRC2 11113 C4 13458 T 2 15434 R 7
10132 C2 11168 C2 13807 T 1 15483 C7
10133 C2 11180 C2 13847 T 1 15486 C7
10135 C2 11243 T 2 13880 TR 2 15506 C2
10136 C2 11274 TR 4 13885 TR 1 15509 C2
10143 C2 11292 TR 1 13888 R 2 15519 C2
10149 C2 11377 R 1 13896 R 2 15549 C7
10152 C2 11496 C1 13928 R 2 15550 C2
10153 C2 11587 TR 4 13945 R 2 15553 C2
10155 C2 11595 R 1 13959 R 2 15575 C4
10156 C2 11606 RC1 13986 TRC2 15938 TR 2
10168 C2 11607 TRC1 14013 RC1 15971 R 4
10180 C2 11614 RC1 14015 RC1 16013 C7
10240 C2 11654 C2 14018 TRC2 16054 R 7
10349 TR 2 11752 R 2 14020 RC2 17095 R 7
10470 C4 11855 TRC2 14122 R 3 17140 T 2
10551 T 4 11883 C2 14139 C2 17990 C2
10574 T 1 11884 C2 14144 C1 18098 T 3
10654 T 3 11901 C2 14164 T 2 18120 R 2
10669 T 1 11906 C2 14189 T 4 18123 R 2
10677 T 2 11920 C2 14223 TR 2 18154 R 2
10697 TR 2 11922 C2 14230 TR 1 18170 RC2
10698 TR 2 11995 C2 14305 C4 18172 RC2
10706 TR 2 12015 C2 14311 C1 18178 RC2
10711 TR 4 12027 C2 14322 C1 18324 C2
10732 TR 2 12071 C2 14329 C2 18341 C3
10757 R 1 12109 C2 14337 C2 18345 C4
10778 R 2 12158 C2 14369 C2 18387 T 2

18551 TR 2 19594 C4 21265 T 2 22118 TR 1
18596 R 2 19617 TR 2 21321 TR 2 22131 TR 2
18647 R 2 19697 TR 3 21346 TR 2 22135 TR 2
18655 R 2 19751 T 2 21361 TR 1 22162 R 2
18717 R 2 20124 T 4 21363 TR 4 22224 RC2
18746 R 2 20137 T 2 21407 TRC3 22229 RC2
18759 R 2 20161 TR 3 21444 TR 1 22291 C2
18817 RC2 20166 TR 2 21447 TR 2 22293 C2
18862 T 2 20177 TR 2 21504 TR 2 22339 C2
18980 TR 2 20229 RC1 21570 C1 22375 C2
18988 TR 2 20431 TR 4 21594 C1 22572 T 2
18991 TR 4 20444 R 2 21818 R 2 22599 T 2
19033 TRC1 20462 R 2 21900 TRC2 22674 TR 1
19035 TRC2 20465 R 3 21936 C3 22714 R 2
19063 C2 20502 C2 22006 R 1 22717 R 2
19422 C3 20926 R 2 22053 T 1 22769 C2
19583 RC4 21260 T 2 22112 TR 2 22806 TRC1
19590 C4

Secondary: Inclusions
10147 C2 13823 T 2 18951 TR 2 20896 R 2
10151 C2 14030 C2 19040 TRC2 20975 TRC1
10468 C2 14096 T 2 19365 T 2 21025 C2
10624 T 1 14146 C2 19407 C1 21066 C2
10658 T 4 14151 C2 19409 C1 21073 C2
10694 TR 2 14232 TR 1 19413 C1 21105 C2
10930 C2 14251 R 2 19418 C1 21148 C3
10946 C3 14343 C1 19421 C4 21486 C2
11010 T 2 14363 C2 19424 C1 21774 TR 2
11176 C2 15187 RC7 19598 C4 21898 RC1
11484 C1 15215 C2 19709 TRC3 21934 C1
11974 C2 15217 C2 19721 T 2 21958 C1
12009 C2 15271 C7 19965 TR 2 21977 C2
12010 C2 16035 C4 20176 TR 1 22033 T 1
12415 RC2 17642 C2 20443 R 1 22034 T 2
12506 C2 18370 T 2 20495 C2 22048 T 1
12788 C2 18745 R 2 20528 C1 22221 RC2
12875 C2 18807 TRC2 20530 C1 22290 C2
13408 C4 18949 TR 2 20571 T 1 22379 C2
13436 C2

Secondary: Journal Articles
10063 T 2 12445 C7 15212 C2 20490 C2
10084 TR 2 12518 C2 15213 C2 20511 C2
10233 C2 12534 C2 15231 C2 20514 C2
10420 C2 12623 TR 4 15255 C2 20520 C2
10501 C2 12817 C2 15289 C2 20831 R 1
10530 T 2 12847 C2 15512 C2 20932 R 3
10536 T 2 13135 T 4 16026 C3 20943 R 2
10583 T 1 13295 RC4 16036 C7 20990 TRC1
10649 T 4 13406 C3 16481 C7 21013 C2
10699 TR 1 13422 C4 17597 C2 21043 C2
10717 TR 2 13425 C5 17996 C2 21047 C1
10742 R 1 13431 C3 18002 C2 21058 C1
10808 R 1 13580 C1 18051 C1 21075 C2
10809 R 2 13839 T 2 18093 T 4 21077 C2
10872 TRC2 13853 T 4 18133 R 1 21081 C1
10986 C2 13992 RC1 18150 R 1 21106 C2
11001 C1 14024 C1 18171 RC1 21250 C2
11026 R 2 14143 C2 18254 C2 21439 T 2
11034 RC2 14148 C2 18677 R 2 21536 TRC1
11054 TRC2 14202 T 1 19014 R 2 21652 T 2
11057 C2 14205 T 4 19030 RC4 21785 TR 1
11070 C2 14229 TR 1 19034 RC2 21812 R 1
11085 C2 14233 R 3 19158 C7 21829 TRC1
11086 C2 14243 R 3 19366 C1 21918 C2
11097 C2 14256 RC2 19368 C1 21919 C2
11114 C4 14257 RC4 19377 C2 21924 C1
11177 C1 14259 RC4 19417 C2 21940 C1
11267 TR 1 14291 RC1 19581 RC4 21956 C1
11478 C1 14323 C1 19622 R 7 21957 C3
11505 C2 14351 C2 19629 R 2 21961 C2
11558 T 4 14352 C1 19651 TRC1 21963 C4
11602 RC1 14415 RC4 19656 RC1 22037 T 1
11810 R 2 14452 C7 19700 R 2 22038 T 1
11866 RC2 14506 R 2 20130 T 2 22041 T 2
11956 C1 14515 RC2 20168 TR 1 22223 RC2
11961 C2 15132 TR 2 20196 R 1 22292 C2
11963 C2 15137 TR 1 20211 R 4 22300 C1
11981 C2 15151 R 2 20250 C3 22314 C2
12058 C2 15173 RC2 20441 R 2 22365 C2
12061 C2 15182 RC1 20468 R 2 22376 C1
12129 C2 15193 TRC1 20471 TRC1 22528 T 1
12153 C2 15200 C2 20476 C2 22675 TR 1
12431 C2 15211 C2 20488 C2 22676 TR 1

22757 C1 22814 RC1 22854 C1 22856 C3
22797 R 2 22845 C1 22855 C1 22859 T 1
22798 R 1

The Eighteen Provinces

Primary 14656 TR 2 14838 C3 19397 R 2
10054 T 2 14660 TR 2 14873 C4 19637 R 2
10102 R 2 14671 TR 4 14875 C2 19686 T 3
10175 C2 14680 TR 4 14980 C3 19835 R 3
11029 R 1 14725 R 1 14982 C3 20126 T 5
11215 T 4 14746 R 3 15016 C3 20192 R 3
13151 TR 2 14755 R 3 15018 C2 20459 R 2
14250 R 1 14756 R 3 15030 C3 20513 C3
14555 T 1 14763 R 3 15035 C3 20978 RC2
14568 T 2 14779 TRC2 15145 R 4 21048 C2
14578 T 1 14800 RC2 15501 C2 21096 C4
14583 T 3 14801 RC2 15830 C2 21370 R 2
14590 T 2 14826 C3 16058 R 2 22110 TR 1
14639 TR 1 14829 C2 17842 R 2 22928 R 2
14649 TR 3 14831 C3

Secondary: Monographs
10018 T 2 13804 T 2 16806 C7 19210 T 2
10021 T 2 13911 R 2 17143 T 3 19695 T 2
10027 T 2 14121 R 2 17322 TRC2 19964 TR 1
10038 T 2 14158 T 2 17614 R 2 20478 C2
10091 R 2 14159 T 1 17869 R 2 20503 C2
10141 C2 14217 TR 2 17995 C2 21272 T 2
10170 C2 14238 R 3 18074 T 2 21277 T 2
10174 C2 15327 T 3 18115 R 2 21305 TR 4
10507 T 2 15446 R 3 18654 R 2 21340 TR 3
10594 T 1 15511 C2 18930 T 2 21679 T 4
11061 C2 15543 C2 19012 R 2 21765 TR 1
12567 T 2 15965 R 3 19018 R 7 22132 TR 1
12770 TRC2 16049 T 2 19053 TRC2 22708 R 3
13155 TR 4

Secondary: Inclusions
10006 T 2 16105 TR 2 18778 R 2 20908 R 3
10138 C2 17808 C3 19423 C3 21225 R 7
15243 C2 18645 R 7 19823 R 7

Secondary: Journal Articles
10568 T 4 14456 TR 2 20489 C3 21261 T 2
11209 T 1 15478 C2 20668 C2 21334 TR 2
12615 T 3 18546 TR 2 20800 TR 3 21453 TR 1
14199 T 2 18679 R 2 20825 TR 3 22029 T 3
14225 TR 1 19618 R 7 20895 R 3 22045 T 1
14226 TR 1 19833 R 2 20900 R 3 22083 TR 1
14237 R 3 19902 C3 21122 C2 22116 TR 4
14424 TR 7 20450 R 2 21218 R 2 22181 R 3

North China Broadly Conceived

Primary 10792 R 2 14751 R 2 14762 R 2
15428 R 7 16063 R 2

Second. 14195 T 3 18750 R 2 21287 T 2
10064 T 2 18307 R 2 18914 T 2 22562 T 3
11028 R 2 18716 R 2

Manchuria

Primary 14804 RC1 14988 C2 15614 RC2

Second. 10852 RC2 13039 R 4 16974 R 4
10163 C2 11162 C2 13355 C4 17315 RC3
10356 R 2 11345 R 2 15181 RC2 20795 TR 2
10381 R 2 11777 R 2 15335 T 3 22654 TR 2
10421 C2 11834 R 2 16915 T 2 22693 R 2

Northern China

Primary 14615 T 2 14938 C3 16759 C7
10781 R 2 14625 T 3 14946 C7 17636 C3
10816 R 2 14632 TR 3 14947 C3 18065 C3
11135 C3 14641 TR 3 14950 C3 18344 C3
11765 R 1 14701 TR 3 14962 C2 18362 C3
11782 R 2 14712 R 2 14985 C3 20440 R 3
14330 C3 14717 R 4 14996 C7 20458 R 3
14550 T 3 14731 R 3 15009 C3 20464 R 3
14551 T 3 14735 R 2 15010 C3 20467 R 3
14570 T 3 14757 R 2 15014 C3 20479 C3
14573 T 3 14785 TRC2 15021 C3 20497 C2
14582 T 3 14791 RC3 15407 R 3 20527 C3
14585 T 3 14802 RC2 15538 C2 20579 T 3
14587 T 4 14816 C3 15806 TRC3 21278 T 3
14602 T 3 14877 C3 15828 C3 21359 TR 3
14604 T 3 14881 C3 16069 C3 22753 C3
14610 T 3 14888 C6

NORTHWESTERN CHINA AND FRONTIER REGIONS

SOUTH CHINA BROADLY CONCEIVED

EAST CENTRAL CHINA

CENTRAL YANGTZE PROVINCES

SOUTHWESTERN CHINA

SOUTHEASTERN CHINA

TAIWAN ONLY

HONG KONG AND MACAU ONLY

18 NATIONAL WELFARE AND LIVING STANDARDS

全國性福利及生活水準

国民の福祉及び生活水準

GEOGRAPHIC CHINA BROADLY CONCEIVED

MAINLAND CHINA

PRIMARY: MONOGRAPHS

PRIMARY: INCLUSIONS

PRIMARY: JOURNAL ARTICLES

SECONDARY: MONOGRAPHS

10836 R 4 12227 TR 7 14219 TR 2 19033 TRC1
10883 TRC2 12257 R 7 14258 RC2 19078 RC8
10894 C1 12264 R 7 14436 R 7 19135 C7
10978 C2 12267 R 8 14466 R 3 19240 R 2
10997 C2 12270 R 7 14478 R 3 19358 TR 3
11076 C2 12379 RC7 14483 R 4 19476 TR 2
11087 C3 12384 RC2 14486 R 2 19551 R 2
11095 C2 12386 RC2 14501 R 4 19558 R 2
11654 C2 12414 TRC2 14522 C2 19590 C4
11699 TR 2 12424 RC7 14524 C2 19594 C4
11724 R 2 12426 RC7 14535 C4 19595 C4
11740 R 2 12436 C7 14686 TR 1 19644 R 2
11750 R 2 12467 C7 14703 TR 2 19719 T 2
11756 R 2 12485 C2 14774 R 3 19789 TR 2
11760 R 2 12564 C2 14828 C2 20049 TR 2
11804 R 2 12631 TR 2 14853 C2 20067 R 2
11805 R 2 12787 C2 14885 C1 20204 R 2
11807 R 2 12853 C2 14990 C2 20247 C7
11848 RC2 13050 RC2 15140 TR 2 20294 TR 2
11852 RC2 13117 C2 15147 R 4 20328 C2
11862 RC2 13118 C2 15150 R 2 20455 R 2
11864 RC2 13158 TR 2 15260 C2 20614 TR 2
11874 RC2 13164 TR 4 15273 C2 20639 R 2
11883 C2 13184 TR 2 15294 C2 20690 C3
11884 C2 13250 R 2 17160 T 2 20700 C2
11891 C2 13261 R 5 17297 R 2 20721 T 2
11906 C2 13291 R 4 17758 TR 2 20782 T 1
11912 C2 13328 C2 18061 C2 20806 TR 1
11920 C2 13336 C2 18142 R 2 20823 TR 4
11949 C2 13420 C2 18172 RC2 20940 R 2
11952 C1 13432 C2 18232 C2 20953 TRC1
11962 C2 13520 TR 2 18277 C2 20962 RC2
11980 C2 13584 C2 18378 T 2 20966 RC2
11988 C2 13597 C1 18430 T 2 20973 TRC1
12015 C2 13715 R 8 18526 T 2 20996 C2
12027 C2 13727 R 1 18585 R 2 21265 T 2
12039 C2 13755 R 4 18588 R 2 21325 TR 2
12071 C2 13772 C1 18608 R 2 21459 R 4
12082 C2 13868 T 2 18710 R 1 22322 C2
12096 C2 13880 TR 2 18717 R 2 22556 T 2
12123 C2 13909 R 2 18759 R 2 22655 TR 3
12148 C2 13951 R 2 18817 RC2 22710 R 2
12154 C2 13986 TRC2 18827 RC2 22769 C2
12173 C2 14015 RC1 18988 TR 2 22805 R 2
12218 TR 2

Secondary: Inclusions

10122 RC2 12043 C2 13444 C2 19562 R 4
10250 C2 12132 C2 13657 TR 1 19585 RC4
10456 RC2 12213 TR 7 14138 C2 19589 C4
10542 T 2 12293 R 8 14492 R 3 19608 C4
10610 T 4 12341 R 8 14767 R 1 20212 R 2
10915 C2 12395 RC2 15195 RC2 20647 R 7
10920 C2 12447 C2 15217 C2 20896 R 2
11013 T 2 12479 C2 15682 R 2 20999 C1
11842 RC2 12506 C2 18429 T 2 21025 C2
11887 C2 12536 C7 18452 T 2 21146 C1
11914 C1 12538 C8 18601 R 2 21153 C2
11916 C2 12650 TR 2 18799 RC2 21486 C2
11918 C2 13097 C2 19101 C7 21840 TRC2
11940 C2 13101 C2 19170 C7 21885 TRC2
11989 C2 13242 R 5 19202 C7 21894 TRC2
11990 C2 13390 C2 19418 C1

Secondary: Journal Articles

10195 TR 2 11483 C2 12056 C2 12451 C7
10225 C2 11742 R 2 12059 C2 12457 C2
10231 C2 11762 R 2 12098 C2 12460 C2
10233 C2 11763 R 2 12100 C2 12491 C7
10238 C2 11788 R 2 12119 C2 12496 C7
10241 C2 11806 R 2 12125 C2 12518 C2
10243 C1 11820 R 2 12138 C2 12526 C7
10265 C2 11882 C2 12145 C2 12549 C8
10297 R 2 11886 C2 12170 C4 12555 C7
10316 C2 11895 C2 12214 TR 2 12623 TR 4
10440 T 2 11896 C2 12215 TR 2 12749 R 2
10457 C1 11943 C2 12217 TR 2 13073 C2
10459 C2 11947 C2 12306 R 8 13077 C2
10465 C2 11953 C2 12313 R 8 13087 C2
10491 C2 11957 C2 12320 R 7 13094 C2
10496 C2 11961 C2 12349 R 2 13103 C3
10502 C7 11963 C2 12360 R 7 13109 C2
10520 T 1 11976 C2 12392 RC7 13233 R 2
11071 C2 12022 C2 12430 C7 13247 R 7
11155 C2 12023 C2 12443 C7 13531 R 2
11372 R 1 12052 C2 12448 C7 13567 R 1
13575 C2 15290 C2 19532 R 4 21007 C2
13608 C7 16309 R 2 19542 R 4 21012 C2
13774 C4 16481 C7 19574 R 3 21040 C1
13899 R 2 16907 T 4 19581 RC4 21057 C2
14152 C1 17278 R 5 19582 RC3 21075 C2
14434 R 7 17283 R 5 19599 C4 21085 C2
14445 C7 18133 R 1 19600 C3 21090 C4
14446 C2 18141 R 2 19606 C3 21094 C1
14458 TR 3 18150 R 1 19629 R 2 21102 C3
14464 R 5 18304 R 2 20187 R 2 21106 C2
14477 R 3 18504 T 2 20211 R 4 21123 C2
14503 R 2 18754 R 1 20370 C2 21143 C2
14511 R 2 19014 R 2 20405 C1 21158 C7
14515 RC2 19057 C2 20498 C2 21248 C2
14519 C3 19137 C7 20520 C2 21263 T 2
14536 C3 19169 C2 20761 T 1 21283 T 2
14741 R 3 19175 C8 20788 T 1 21284 T 2
14778 RC2 19221 TR 3 20865 R 2 21506 R 3
14814 C4 19410 C4 20866 R 4 22098 TR 2
14827 C2 19463 R 2 20939 R 3 22105 TR 2
15173 RC2 19512 R 4 20990 TRC1 22171 R 2

The Eighteen Provinces

Primary 14461 R 4 15046 T 2 15080 R 2
10102 R 2 14462 R 3 15047 T 2 15111 C2
10141 C2 14467 R 3 15049 TR 2 15118 C2
10670 T 4 14469 R 3 15051 TR 2 15119 C2
10839 R 2 14474 R 3 15054 R 7 19514 R 2
12155 C2 14480 R 4 15055 R 7 19577 R 3
12250 R 2 14493 R 4 15058 R 1 19695 T 2
12587 T 2 14505 R 2 15062 R 2 20393 R 2
12890 T 2 15036 T 2 15067 R 2 20726 T 2
13107 C3 15038 T 2 15072 R 8 20729 T 2
14424 TR 7

Second. 12366 R 7 14494 R 2 19479 TR 2
10056 T 2 12389 RC8 14507 R 4 19637 R 2
10174 C2 12666 TR 3 14539 C2 20178 TR 2
10209 R 2 12718 R 2 14540 C2 20190 R 2
10293 TR 2 12767 TRC2 14543 C2 20300 R 3
10437 T 2 12827 C8 14649 TR 3 20329 C2
10443 R 2 13151 TR 2 14829 C2 20696 C4
10444 R 2 13212 R 2 15885 C8 20800 TR 3
10525 T 2 13223 R 2 16155 C2 20822 TR 4
10760 R 2 13275 R 3 17869 R 2 20978 RC2
10761 R 4 13831 T 2 18436 T 2 20979 TRC1
11655 T 1 13866 T 2 18654 R 2 21096 C4
11735 R 2 14118 R 4 18930 T 2 21125 C2
11824 R 2 14124 R 7 19001 R 2 21391 TRC1
12151 C2 14159 T 1 19122 C8 21456 R 2
12198 T 8 14433 R 8 19245 R 2 22534 T 1
12252 R 8 14456 TR 2 19397 R 2 22590 T 3
12296 R 8 14472 R 3 19458 R 8

North China Broadly Conceived

Primary 10455 RC8 12463 C8 15082 R 2
10370 R 2 10471 C2 12582 T 2 15681 R 8
10402 C8 10475 C2 13962 R 2 17873 R 2
10452 R 2 10476 C2 15041 T 2 22715 R 2
10454 R 8 10577 T 1 15081 R 2

Second. 10827 R 2 11821 R 2 20714 T 2
10057 T 1 11028 R 2 18743 R 7 22623 T 2
10423 C7

Manchuria

Primary 12211 TR 8 12321 R 7 15053 R 7
10381 R 2 12248 R 2 13098 C2 20813 TR 2

Second. 12406 RC8 15677 TR 7 20871 R 2
10852 RC2 15181 RC2 15873 RC2 20967 RC2
11716 TR 2 15669 TR 2 19547 R 4 22718 R 1
11777 R 2 15674 TR 2

Northern China

Primary 15039 T 1 15075 R 8 15083 R 2
15037 T 2 15045 T 2 15077 R 2 15120 C2

Second. 10816 R 2 14541 C2 20880 R 2
10178 C2 11541 T 2 18398 T 2 22577 T 2
10747 R 2 14427 R 2 20435 R 3

Northwestern China and Frontier Regions

Primary 11147 C2 12003 C2 15086 RC2

Second. 10176 C2 16896 C8 22531 T 2
22749 C2

South China Broadly Conceived

Primary 10641 T 2 15068 R 2 20848 R 2
10046 T 2 15042 T 2 15078 R 2 20944 R 1

Second. 12684 TR 2 13471 T 2 18449 T 2
10137 C2 12843 C2 15205 C2 19957 T 7
12297 R 7 12894 T 2 17947 RC2 21147 C8
12569 T 2

East Central China

Primary □

Second. 10368 R 2 10801 R 4 12038 C2
12157 C2 12420 RC7

Central Yangtze Provinces

Primary 19504 R 2

Second. 15129 T 2 16567 R 7

Southwestern China

Primary 15121 C2 18925 T 2

Second. 10179 C2 13209 R 2 14542 C2

Southeastern China

Primary 10298 R 2 21413 RC3

Second. 11668 T 2 12428 C2 20261 R 1

Taiwan Only

Primary 11844 TRC2 14549 C4 15095 C1
11138 C2 12070 C2 15091 RC2 15106 C2
11690 TR 2 14544 C5 15093 C1 21084 C2

Second. 12152 C2 16550 TR 8 18297 C2
10882 RC2 12175 C2 16745 TRC8 19061 C1
10908 C1 14972 C1 16788 C7 19587 C4
11044 RC2 15586 TR 2 16840 C8 20335 C1
11659 T 2 15875 RC2 16844 C7 21008 C2
11851 TRC2 15917 C2 16854 C7 21245 C1
11959 C2 15918 C2 16864 C2 21484 C2
12008 C2 16261 TR 2 16885 C8 22490 RC2
12150 C2 16549 TR 7 18290 C2

Hong Kong and Macau Only

□

19 Modernization and Directed Social Change

近代化運動及社會改革

近代化及び社会改革

Geographic China Broadly Conceived

Primary 11045 RC2 15158 TRC2 18077 T 2
10070 TR 2 11708 TR 2 15161 TRC2 18525 T 2
10073 TR 2 12772 TRC2 15162 TRC2 18558 TR 2
10113 TRC2 13017 R 3 15166 TRC2 18566 TR 1
10553 T 1 13846 T 2 15174 TRC2 18579 R 2
10560 T 2 14112 TR 1 15175 RC2 21366 R 2
10564 T 2 15126 T 2 15185 TRC2 21368 R 2
10681 T 1 15130 T 2 15191 RC2 22088 TR 1
10700 TR 2 15134 TR 4 15194 TRC2 22095 TR 2
10853 TRC2 15136 TR 2 15283 C2 22225 TRC2

Second. 12394 RC7 18388 T 2 20222 R 3
10614 T 1 12661 TR 4 18409 T 2 20934 R 3
10714 TR 1 13168 TR 4 18414 T 1 21318 TR 1
11241 T 2 13649 TR 2 18450 T 2 21404 TRC1
11669 T 3 14699 TR 1 18545 TR 2 21835 TRC1
11682 T 1 15311 T 2 18801 TRC2 21844 TRC2
11709 TR 2 18079 T 1 18809 RC2 21847 TRC2

20 Local Communities as Total Systems

地方社區整體研究

地方共同体全般

15488 C7 15519 C2 15567 C7 16046 C2
15495 C2 15524 C7 15570 C2 16457 C2
15506 C2 15537 C4 15575 C4 17313 RC2
15507 C7 15549 C7 15970 R 4 18075 T 2
15508 C2 15550 C2 15977 RC7 19082 RC7
15509 C2 15553 C2 16012 C4 22291 C2
15513 C4 15560 C4 16031 C7

Primary: Inclusions
15314 T 2 15558 C7 18951 TR 2 19138 C7
15333 T 3 16037 C3 19108 C7 19198 C2
15542 C7

Primary: Journal Articles
12511 C7 15528 C7 16038 C2 19151 C7
14862 C7 15540 C7 16041 C7 19156 C7
15232 C7 15551 C7 16173 T 4 22340 C2
15398 R 7 15559 C7 16897 C7 22343 C7
15494 C7 15564 C7 17335 C2 22721 R 2
15496 C7 15580 C2 18663 R 2 22767 C2
15512 C2 16027 C2

Secondary: *Not used*

The Eighteen Provinces

Primary 15306 T 2 15478 C2 15935 T 2
10021 T 2 15327 T 3 15501 C2 15965 R 3
10027 T 2 15375 TR 2 15511 C2 19098 C7
10161 C2 15400 R 8 15527 C7 20411 C2
10752 R 3 15446 R 3 15531 C2 20699 C2
14101 T 2 15470 RC7 15543 C2

Secondary: *Not used*

North China Broadly Conceived

Primary 10064 T 2 15324 T 2 15428 R 7
15433 R 2

Secondary: *Not used*

Manchuria

Primary 15532 C4 16397 T 5 16915 T 2
10356 R 2 15569 C3 16510 T 2 17551 T 2
10421 C2 15743 T 3 16669 R 8 17852 R 3
15335 T 3 16384 T 2 16680 R 8

Secondary: *Not used*

Northern China

Primary 15384 TR 4 15452 TRC2 16846 C7
15320 T 3 15389 TR 3 15459 RC7 17094 R 6
15328 T 2 15390 TR 3 15460 RC7 17428 C7
15336 T 2 15394 R 2 15475 RC8 17444 TR 8
15338 T 7 15395 R 3 15477 C7 17620 C7
15341 T 2 15397 R 7 15502 C7 17677 C7
15342 T 3 15399 R 7 15510 C7 17871 R 7
15347 T 3 15403 R 8 15516 C7 17918 T 8
15352 T 3 15406 R 8 15525 C7 17940 R 7
15355 T 2 15407 R 3 15534 C7 18920 T 2
15360 T 7 15408 R 2 15538 C2 19152 C7
15362 T 7 15410 R 8 15548 C3 19171 C7
15366 T 3 15414 R 8 15557 C7 19200 C7
15367 T 2 15415 R 8 15561 C3 19340 C3
15370 TR 3 15416 R 3 15565 C7 20260 TR 8
15372 TR 3 15417 R 3 15759 TR 3 20762 T 3
15373 TR 3 15435 R 3 16201 T 6 22454 R 7
15378 TR 7 15449 R 7 16377 T 2 22704 R 3
15383 TR 2 15450 R 7 16762 C7 22706 R 6

Secondary: *Not used*

Northwestern China and Frontier Regions

Primary 15350 T 2 15421 R 8 15544 C8
11582 TR 3 15386 TR 2 15453 RC8 15545 C8
15322 T 3 15391 TR 2 15492 C2 22713 R 5
15323 T 4 15393 R 2

Secondary: *Not used*

South China Broadly Conceived

Primary 15205 C2 15332 T 2 15361 T 2
15726 T 2 17931 T 7

Secondary: *Not used*

East Central China

Primary 15377 TR 3 15474 RC3 15764 TR 3
15307 T 3 15388 TR 3 15480 C2 15771 R 7
15313 T 2 15396 R 3 15493 C7 15946 TR 3
15315 T 3 15402 R 8 15503 C7 16109 TR 3
15318 T 3 15404 R 3 15517 C8 16402 TR 3
15346 T 2 15405 R 7 15535 C8 16624 R 7
15348 T 3 15426 R 7 15552 C2 17380 C3
15354 T 2 15429 R 3 15556 C3 17816 T 7
15357 T 3 15430 R 3 15577 C7 17868 R 7
15368 T 7 15431 R 3 15578 C3 20262 R 2
15374 TR 8 15432 R 2 15761 TR 7

Secondary: *Not used*

Central Yangtze Provinces

Primary 15445 R 3 15498 C2 16757 C7
15412 R 3 15469 TRC2 15523 C7 16763 C2
15427 R 3 15481 C2 16090 T 2 17776 C7

Secondary: *Not used*

Southwestern China

Primary 15356 T 2 15425 R 3 15640 R 2
12951 TR 2 15365 T 2 15436 R 6 15957 R 2
14634 TR 3 15379 TR 3 15522 C3 17854 R 2
14750 R 2 15392 R 6 15579 C3 18889 T 2
15308 T 5 15401 R 2 15581 T 2 20573 T 7
15316 T 2 15413 R 2 15638 R 2 20873 R 7
15326 T 7 15424 R 7

Secondary: *Not used*

Southeastern China

Primary 15334 T 2 15420 R 3 15572 C2
10327 T 2 15337 T 5 15423 R 2 15576 C5
12881 T 3 15339 T 3 15447 R 3 15735 T 2
12884 T 2 15344 T 3 15448 R 3 15984 C7
12885 T 2 15349 T 2 15456 RC7 15987 C7
12886 T 2 15353 T 2 15458 TRC2 16464 C4
12887 T 2 15358 T 8 15476 RC8 16630 R 8
14758 R 2 15359 T 2 15479 C8 16839 C2
15305 T 2 15364 T 3 15485 C2 17073 R 4
15310 T 3 15371 TR 2 15497 C2 17589 C2
15312 T 3 15376 TR 2 15499 C2 17920 T 7
15317 T 2 15385 TR 2 15500 C7 19179 C7
15319 T 3 15418 R 8 15547 C3 19454 R 7
15321 T 2 15419 R 6

Secondary: *Not used*

Taiwan Only

Primary 15443 R 2 15515 C8 16772 C8
15351 T 2 15444 R 2 15521 C8 17386 C4
15369 TR 2 15457 RC2 15530 C7 17984 RC2
15437 R 2 15471 RC2 15533 C7 19090 RC8
15438 R 2 15472 RC2 15554 C2 19663 C7
15439 R 2 15490 C2 15562 C2 19737 C8
15440 R 2 15491 C7 15568 C3 20018 C8
15441 R 2 15504 C8 16354 C8 20236 C8
15442 R 2 15505 C8 16495 C2 20367 C3

Secondary: *Not used*

Hong Kong and Macau Only

Primary 15409 R 2 15473 TRC2 15555 C2
12882 T 2 15411 R 7 15484 C3 15563 C4
15325 T 3 15451 TRC7 15487 C2 15566 C8
15329 T 3 15454 TRC3 15489 C3 15571 C3
15330 T 7 15455 TRC7 15514 C2 15573 C8
15331 T 8 15461 TRC2 15518 C2 15574 C8
15340 T 7 15462 TRC7 15520 C2 15824 C4
15343 T 4 15463 TRC7 15526 C3 15945 TR 2
15380 TR 2 15464 TRC8 15529 C2 16456 TRC7
15381 TR 2 15465 TRC8 15536 C4 17965 C2
15382 TR 3 15467 TRC3 15541 C2 19972 TRC7
15387 TR 2 15468 TRC3 15546 C7 19990 C8

Secondary: *Not used*

21 Regional and Local Population

地方人口 地方人口

Geographic China Broadly Conceived

Primary 10207 R 2 10363 R 2 21204 TR 2
Second. 10361 R 2 16374 T 2 16424 R 2
10017 T 2 10432 C2 16375 T 2 16938 TR 2
10200 TR 2 11657 T 4 16376 T 2 17036 TR 7
10328 T 2 15773 R 2 16423 R 2 18852 T 2

Mainland China

Primary 11812 R 2 15589 TR 1 19850 R 8
10413 C2 11878 RC2 15619 C1
Second. 10330 T 2 12256 R 7 18862 T 2
10035 T 2 10424 C2 12414 TRC2 18915 T 2
10214 TRC2 10993 C2 12434 C2 18992 R 2
10264 C2 11710 TR 5 12708 R 2 19057 C2
10269 C4 12214 TR 2 13244 R 2 22619 T 2
10310 C1 12221 TR 2 14640 TR 2

The Eighteen Provinces

Primary 15400 R 8 15622 C2 15623 C2
21208 R 8
Second. 10333 T 2 16591 R 7 21213 R 2
10294 R 2 12948 T 2 16894 C2

North China Broadly Conceived

Primary 16430 R 2 16695 R 7
Second. 10064 T 2 10402 C8 10435 C2
16973 R 2 22660 TR 2

Manchuria

Primary 15588 TR 2 15602 RC2 15690 R 2
10341 TR 2 15590 R 8 15614 RC2 16433 R 2
11716 TR 2 15595 R 2 15668 TR 2 16553 TR 7
15583 T 8 15597 R 2 15678 TR 2 16643 R 7
15585 TR 2 15599 R 2
Second. 11684 TR 2 12687 TR 2 16426 R 2
10337 TR 2 11712 TR 2 15661 T 8 16427 R 7
10340 TR 2 11715 TR 2 15669 TR 2 16435 R 7
10354 TR 2 11732 R 2 15676 TR 2 16437 R 2
10378 R 2 11797 R 2 15679 TR 7 16449 R 2
10381 R 2 11823 R 2 15684 R 2 16510 T 2
10398 TRC2 12211 TR 8 15686 R 2 16644 R 8
10421 C2 12286 R 8 15689 R 2 16669 R 8
10428 C2 12292 R 2 15691 R 2 16915 T 2
10719 TR 1 12309 R 8 15776 R 2 17024 T 2
11015 T 2 12322 R 7 16384 T 2 17551 T 2
11677 T 2 12670 TR 2 16406 TR 2

Northern China

Primary 15450 R 7 15596 R 7 17871 R 7
10317 T 2 15594 R 2 15624 C2 21206 R 1
10431 C2
Second. 15502 C7 16538 T 8 16762 C7
14712 R 2 15903 C7 16556 TR 8 16909 T 2
15328 T 2 15933 T 2 16557 TR 8 16926 T 2
15399 R 7 16390 T 2 16594 R 8 17685 C7
15403 R 8 16403 TR 2 16758 C7 19153 C8
15477 C7

Northwestern China and Frontier Regions

Primary 15603 RC2 15609 RC2 16422 R 2
10427 C2 15604 RC1 15620 C2 16751 TRC2
11686 TR 2
Second. 11722 R 2 15696 RC2 16647 R 2
10176 C2 11787 R 2 15777 R 2 16686 R 8
10401 C2 12003 C2 16431 R 2 16786 C2
10415 C2 15391 TR 2 16515 T 8 18993 R 2
10725 TR 2 15492 C2 16606 R 8 22732 TRC2
10874 TRC2 15667 TR 8

South China Broadly Conceived

Primary 12897 T 2
Second. 12580 T 2 16410 TR 8 17883 R 7
11658 T 2 15361 T 2 17875 R 2 17956 TRC2
12522 c8 16386 T 8

East Central China

Primary 15584 T 2 15592 R 2 21210 R 7
10362 R 1 15587 TR 2 16604 R 8 21216 R 7
15517 c8 15591 R 2 20600 T 2
Second. 12157 c2 15761 TR 7 16533 T 2
10368 R 2 15377 TR 3 15837 c7 16624 R 7
10430 c2 15577 c7 15843 c7 17680 c7
10751 R 2 15720 T 2 15924 T 2 17816 T 7

Central Yangtze Provinces

Primary 10395 TRC2 17761 R 7
Second. 11723 R 2 12975 R 2 15642 R 2

Southwestern China

Primary 15581 T 2 15625 c2 16371 T 2
11679 T 2 15593 R 2 15641 R 2 18925 T 2
15356 T 2 15598 R 7 15738 T 7
Second. 13209 R 2 16372 T 2 16787 c2
10179 c2 15739 T 2 16504 c2 17872 R 7
10382 TRC2 15740 T 2 16599 R 7 19846 R 3
10429 c2 15748 T 2 16646 R 8 20551 T 3
11706 TR 2 15750 T 2 16675 R 7 20583 T 2
12924 T 2

Southeastern China

Primary 16064 R 2 16391 T 2 22510 T 2
15608 TRC2 16382 T 2 16558 TR 7
Second. 11828 R 2 15763 TR 2 17025 T 2
10292 TR 4 14088 T 2 16062 R 2 17387 c2
10327 T 2 15359 T 2 16398 T 2 17920 T 7
10357 R 2 15456 RC7 16552 TR 2 17921 T 2
10392 TRC2 15497 c2 16736 RC7 18438 T 2
10426 c2 15718 T 2 16839 c2 19975 TRC7
10855 RC2 15742 T 2 16841 c8 20338 c1

Taiwan Only

Primary 15582 T 2 15615 c2 16739 TRC8
11690 TR 2 15586 TR 2 15647 c3 16747 RC2
11844 TRC2 15600 TRC2 15698 TRC2 16869 c7
13297 RC2 15601 RC2 15822 c3 17922 T 2
14134 c2 15605 TRC2 15861 c2 17961 c2
15457 RC2 15606 RC2 15890 c2 21231 TRC2
15471 RC2 15607 TRC2 15917 c2 21233 RC2
15472 RC2 15612 RC2 16727 RC2 21235 TRC2
15491 c7 15613 RC2
Second. 12146 c2 15852 c2 16872 c7
10345 TR 2 12152 c2 15874 TRC1 16898 c2
10385 RC2 13313 RC2 16003 c7 17101 TRC7
10387 TRC2 14549 c4 16042 c2 17103 TRC7
10436 c2 14874 c2 16354 c8 18290 c2
11138 c2 15437 R 2 16495 c2 18981 TR 2
11678 T 2 15440 R 2 16726 TRC2 19090 RC8
11959 c2 15533 c7 16743 RC8 19980 TRC8
11964 c2 15655 c2 16745 TRC8 20018 c8
12017 c2 15695 RC2 16819 c8 20320 c2
12020 c1 15697 TRC2 16827 c7 21232 TRC2
12106 c2 15708 c2 16856 c7 21520 R 2
12136 c2 15766 TR 4 16871 c7

Hong Kong and Macau Only

Primary 15610 TRC2 15618 c2 15829 c2
15380 TR 2 15611 TRC2 15621 c4 21234 RC2
15382 TR 3 15616 c2 15805 TRC2 21254 c2
15463 TRC7 15617 c2
Second. 15467 TRC3 15945 TR 2 17109 c7
10301 RC2 15518 c2 15974 TRC2 17350 c5
15381 TR 2 15520 c2 16348 c7 20409 c2
15387 TR 2 15820 c2 16463 c2 20622 TR 2
15409 R 2 15842 c2 16493 c3 20681 c2
15455 TRC7 15850 c2 16499 c2 20682 c2
15461 TRC2 15859 c2 17001 c2 21827 TRC7
15465 TRC8 15927 T 7 17002 c2 21854 RC8

21.1 Regional Urbanization and City Population

地方性都市化及都市人口

地方の都市化及び都市人口

Geographic China Broadly Conceived

Primary 10032 T 2 10384 TRC4 15645 TRC3
18852 T 2 20590 T 3
Second. 10363 R 2 16375 T 2 16424 R 2
10188 T 2 10386 RC2 16376 T 2 17696 R 3
10200 TR 2 10432 c2 16423 R 2 21204 TR 2
10207 R 2 16374 T 2

Mainland China

Primary 10264 c2 15644 RC3 15832 c4
10206 R 2 10269 c4 15652 c2 21821 R 2
Second. 10424 c2 12214 TR 2 15756 TR 4
10035 T 2 10479 c4 12434 c2 15799 RC2
10230 c2 10993 c2 12474 c2 17368 c2
10241 c2 11710 TR 5 12674 TR 2 17642 c2
10268 c4 11878 RC2 12916 T 5 19719 T 2
10330 T 2

The Eighteen Provinces

Primary 10333 T 2 15446 R 3 15631 TR 3
15723 T 3 22590 T 3
Second. 12948 T 2 15623 c2 15951 TR 3
12936 T 4 15327 T 3 15823 c3 21205 R 3

North China Broadly Conceived

Primary □
Second. 10435 c2 16430 R 2 18953 TR 2
20549 T 2

Manchuria

Primary 15602 RC2 15637 R 4 15678 TR 2
11803 R 2 15614 RC2 15639 R 2 15690 R 2
15588 TR 2
Second. 11777 R 2 15684 R 2 16436 R 3
10337 TR 2 12663 TR 2 15693 R 2 16440 R 2
10341 TR 2 12717 R 4 15737 T 3 16448 R 2
10364 R 2 12969 TR 2 15774 R 3 16562 TR 2
10398 TRC2 12988 R 2 15776 R 2 16915 T 2
10428 c2 15569 c3 15778 R 3 17024 T 2
11749 R 2 15669 TR 2

Northern China

Primary 15627 T 3 15768 R 2 15828 c3
15395 R 3 15636 R 3 15786 R 3 16906 T 2
15594 R 2 15710 T 2 15810 TRC2 17392 c3
15626 T 2 15730 T 3
Second. 15538 c2 15791 TRC3 16413 R 4
10431 c2 15624 c2 15806 TRC3 16909 T 2
12725 R 4 15746 T 3 15812 c5 16928 T 2
12907 T 2 15754 T 2 16377 T 2 17221 R 2
15373 TR 3 15769 R 5 16379 T 2 17856 R 3
15407 R 3 15770 R 4 16390 T 2 18967 TR 3
15417 R 3 15789 TRC2 16403 TR 2 20762 T 3

Northwestern China and Frontier Regions

Primary 15609 RC2 15620 c2 15811 TRC2
Second. 10427 c2 15322 T 3 16751 TRC2
10375 R 2 12003 c2 15323 T 4 16752 TRC2
10401 c2 13332 c2 16633 R 2 18372 T 4

South China Broadly Conceived

Primary 10832 R 3 16934 T 2
Second. 11658 T 2 12578 T 2 15749 T 3
10366 R 3 12570 T 2 12888 T 2 19006 R 4
10434 c2

East Central China

Primary 15632 TR 3 15764 TR 3 15946 TR 3
15431 R 3 15634 R 3 15869 R 3 22582 T 3
15432 R 2 15635 R 3
Second. 15404 R 3 16401 TR 4 17863 R 3
10321 T 2 15429 R 3 16402 TR 3 18464 T 3
10368 R 2 15430 R 3 16407 TR 3 19834 R 4
10430 c2 15765 TR 3 16908 T 2 20685 c3
15313 T 2 15788 R 3 17030 TR 4 20883 R 3
15357 T 3 15948 TR 3 17412 TR 3 20885 R 3
15377 TR 3

Central Yangtze Provinces

Primary 15642 R 2
Second. 10324 T 2 10395 TRC2 13395 c4
16405 TR 3 17312 RC2

Southwestern China

Primary 15629 T 2 15641 R 2 18933 T 4
12889 T 2 15633 TR 3 15716 T 3 19846 R 3
15308 T 5 15638 R 2 16370 T 2 19885 RC2
15425 R 3 15640 R 2
Second. 12919 T 2 15784 R 2 17535 T 4
10382 TRC2 12951 TR 2 15957 R 2 19270 R 2
10429 c2 15356 T 2 16596 R 2 20735 T 3
10791 R 2 15413 R 2 16932 T 2 20890 R 4

Southeastern China

Primary 15628 T 3 15725 T 5 17560 TR 2
15447 R 3 15630 T 3 16945 R 2 21575 c3
15608 TRC2 15651 c4 17546 T 3
Second. 15310 T 3 15780 R 3 17191 TR 2
10392 TRC2 15334 T 2 15782 R 3 17657 T 3
10426 c2 15458 TRC2 16421 R 3 19429 T 3
12069 c2 15499 c2 16537 T 2 20542 T 2
12884 T 2 15714 T 3 16552 TR 2 20706 T 4
12953 TR 2 15779 R 2 17021 T 3

Taiwan Only

Primary 15613 RC2 15698 TRC2 15852 c2
10387 TRC2 15647 c3 15766 TR 4 16506 T 2
15471 RC2 15650 c3 15793 TRC3 17386 c4
15568 c3 15654 c2 15794 TRC3 17822 T 2
15586 TR 2 15655 c2 15822 c3 21235 TRC2
Second. 14224 TR 2 15606 RC2 16726 TRC2
10385 RC2 15438 R 2 15612 RC2 16729 RC2
10436 c2 15439 R 2 15697 TRC2 17169 T 2
11232 T 2 15441 R 2 15708 c2 17961 c2
12008 c2 15442 R 2 15861 c2 20334 c2
12152 c2 15472 RC2 16347 c2 21232 TRC2
13297 RC2 15600 TRC2

Hong Kong and Macau Only

Primary 15646 TRC3 15824 c4 17350 c5
10301 RC2 15648 c4 15827 c4 17911 c3
15325 T 3 15649 c3 15858 c2 20677 c3
15467 TRC3 15653 c4 16454 TRC3 21234 RC2
15617 c2 15796 TRC2 16491 c3 21254 c2
15643 RC2 15805 TRC2 17323 TRC3
Second. 15795 TRC3 16342 TRC3 17963 c2
11389 TRC2 15798 RC4 16438 R 2 17994 c2
12937 T 3 15803 TRC3 16469 c3 19932 c3
14939 c3 15808 TRC2 16492 c2 19933 c3
15382 TR 3 15813 c2 16731 RC2 20409 c2
15454 TRC3 15821 c4 16753 TRC2 20622 TR 2
15473 TRC2 15834 c4 16941 TR 2 20658 RC3
15610 TRC2 15835 c3 17001 c2 20676 c3
15616 c2 15838 c3 17019 T 3 20678 c3
15621 c4 15842 c2 17318 RC3 20695 c3
15702 c2 15913 c3 17946 TRC2 20773 T 2

21.2 Regional and Local Geographic Mobility

地方性流動遷移

地域間又は地域内人口移動

Geographic China Broadly Conceived

Mainland China

The Eighteen Provinces

North China Broadly Conceived

Manchuria

Northern China

Northwestern China and Frontier Regions

South China Broadly Conceived

East Central China

Central Yangtze Provinces

Southwestern China

Southeastern China

Taiwan Only

Hong Kong and Macau Only

21.3 Microecology and Particular Settlements

市鎮村舍聚落研究

地域社会生態学及び居住形態

Geographic China Broadly Conceived

Mainland China

The Eighteen Provinces

North China Broadly Conceived

Manchuria

Northern China

Northwestern China and Frontier Regions

Primary 15673 TR 7 15811 TRC2 16927 T 2
15322 T 3 15729 T 2 15857 C2 17376 C2
15323 T 4 15753 T 2 16431 R 2 20601 T 2
15393 R 2 15777 R 2 16800 C7 22701 R 2

Second. 15672 TR 7 16633 R 2 16912 T 2
10332 T 2 16306 R 8 16749 RC8 18956 TR 2
11686 TR 2 16606 R 8 16751 TRC2 19818 R 7
15350 T 2

South China Broadly Conceived

Primary 15361 T 2 15726 T 2 17138 T 2
10344 TR 4 15721 T 2 15749 T 3 17931 T 7
10366 R 3 15722 T 2 15775 R 2 22522 T 2
12897 T 2

Second. 12618 T 3 16914 T 2 17947 RC2
12569 T 2 13833 T 2 16930 T 2

East Central China

Primary 15720 T 2 15764 TR 3 15853 C7
10339 TR 2 15727 T 3 15765 TR 3 15854 C7
15313 T 2 15728 T 3 15771 R 7 15929 T 3
15348 T 3 15731 T 2 15772 R 2 15946 TR 3
15357 T 3 15732 T 2 15788 R 3 17667 R 7
15388 TR 3 15744 T 2 15837 C7 17892 TRC3
15404 R 3 15745 T 3 15843 C7 18865 T 2
15632 TR 3 15761 TR 7 15844 C3

Second. 15354 T 2 16484 C7 17898 RC3
10801 R 4 15930 T 3 16709 R 8 18013 T 2
11553 T 7 16113 TR 3 16980 R 3 18465 T 3
11554 T 3 16401 TR 4 17030 TR 4 20685 C3
15307 T 3 16402 TR 3 17052 R 3 22409 T 2
15318 T 3 16407 TR 3 17662 T 7

Central Yangtze Provinces

Primary 15642 R 2 15712 T 3 15884 C8
16526 T 2 20056 R 3

Second. 12943 T 2 17554 T 4 19726 TR 7
20275 T 4

Southwestern China

Primary 15641 R 2 15740 T 2 16371 T 2
15356 T 2 15715 T 2 15748 T 2 16528 T 8
15413 R 2 15716 T 3 15750 T 2 19846 R 3
15598 R 7 15717 T 2 15784 R 2 20551 T 3
15633 TR 3 15738 T 7 16166 T 2 20735 T 3
15640 R 2 15739 T 2 16370 T 2

Second. 16425 R 7 17854 R 2 19742 T 2
10359 R 2 16512 T 2 17926 T 7 20584 T 4
10382 TRC2 16618 R 8 18491 T 2 20645 R 7
10639 T 2 16787 C2 18922 T 2 22508 T 2
15957 R 2

Southeastern China

Primary 15734 T 2 15782 R 3 17813 T 3
10278 T 2 15735 T 2 15819 C7 17919 T 5
15458 TRC2 15742 T 2 15840 C7 18063 C2
15711 T 3 15763 TR 2 16187 T 3 20706 T 4
15714 T 3 15779 R 2 16919 T 2 20757 T 3
15718 T 2 15780 R 3 17533 T 7 22510 T 2
15725 T 5

Second. 15371 TR 2 15628 T 3 17921 T 2
10392 TRC2 15418 R 8 15987 C7 18906 T 3
15305 T 2 15420 R 3 16341 TRC7 19975 TRC7
15312 T 3 15447 R 3 16479 C2 20770 T 3
15334 T 2 15485 C2 17021 T 3 20894 R 2
15353 T 2 15547 C3 17560 TR 2 21033 C3
15359 T 2

Taiwan Only

Primary 15766 TR 4 15822 C3 15918 C2
15605 TRC2 15785 R 7 15825 C2 16611 R 2
15647 C3 15792 TRC5 15826 C2 17101 TRC7
15654 C2 15793 TRC3 15848 C4 17103 TRC7
15655 C2 15794 TRC3 15852 C2 17169 T 2
15697 TRC2 15816 C8 15861 C2 19973 TRC8

Second. 10345 TR 2 10674 T 2 13137 T 2
10325 T 2 10385 RC2 11678 T 2 13297 RC2
14224 TR 2 15568 C3 16506 T 2 17961 C2
15457 RC2 15615 C2 17922 T 2 17984 RC2

Hong Kong and Macau Only

Primary 15798 RC4 15824 C4 16453 RC2
15461 TRC2 15800 TRC8 15827 C4 16491 C3
15536 C4 15802 TRC2 15829 C2 16814 C8
15563 C4 15803 TRC3 15833 C4 16880 C7
15621 C4 15805 TRC2 15834 C4 16925 T 3
15646 TRC3 15808 TRC2 15835 C3 19969 TRC8
15653 C4 15809 TRC8 15838 C3 19970 TRC7
15719 T 2 15813 C2 15842 C2 20622 TR 2
15724 T 3 15814 C7 15850 C2 20677 C3
15758 TR 3 15815 C8 15858 C2 20688 C2
15795 TRC3 15818 C8 15859 C2 20695 C3
15796 TRC2 15820 C2 15981 RC3 20773 T 2
15797 TRC7 15821 C4

Second. 15611 TRC2 17350 C5 19985 TRC7
10301 RC2 15643 RC2 17362 C2 20075 C2
11389 TRC2 15649 C3 17593 C3 20657 RC3
13051 RC3 15702 C2 17626 T 4 20667 C4
15329 T 3 16032 C2 17911 C3 20674 C3
15382 TR 3 16348 C7 17946 TRC2 20694 C3
15451 TRC7 16862 C7 17963 C2 20697 C3
15463 TRC7 16941 TR 2 17985 RC2 21254 C2
15467 TRC3 17261 R 2 19959 T 7 21574 C3
15520 C2 17321 RC5 19972 TRC7 21854 RC8

21.4 Regional Labor Force and Local Division of Labor

地方勞動力及職業分化

地方労働力及び職業分化

Geographic China Broadly Conceived

Primary 15877 C8 21204 TR 2

Second. 11164 C2 15645 TRC3 17696 R 3
10407 C2 15539 C7 16522 T 2

Mainland China

Primary 15882 C7 15915 C2 16837 C8
10479 C4 15886 C7 16768 C7 16863 C7
15483 C7 15896 C7

Second. 15537 C4 16037 C3 17760 R 7
10338 TR 2 15570 C2 16145 C7 17779 C2
11105 C2 15831 C7 16481 C7 19014 R 2
11118 C2 16004 C8 16690 R 8 19077 RC7
11730 R 2 16012 C4 17129 C6 19102 C7
12504 C7 16015 C4 17130 C7 19110 C8
12749 R 2 16026 C3 17297 R 2 19125 C7
14478 R 3 16027 C2 17341 C2 19158 C7
15495 C2 16036 C7 17588 C8 19184 C8
15528 C7

The Eighteen Provinces

Primary 15864 TR 2 15885 C8 15895 C8
15906 C2 15907 C2

Second. 15119 C2 15623 C2 16591 R 7
15118 C2 15446 R 3 15767 TR 4 17301 R 7

North China Broadly Conceived

Primary 12505 C8

Second. 10435 C2 12469 C8 15656 T 2
16695 R 7

Manchuria

Primary 15614 RC2 15873 RC2 16397 T 5
10341 TR 2 15669 TR 2 15911 C2 17689 T 7
10354 TR 2 15737 T 3 15914 C7 19538 R 2
15585 TR 2 15867 R 2

Second. 12211 TR 8 15690 R 2 17263 R 6
10337 TR 2 12687 TR 2 15995 C2 17294 R 4
10428 C2 13229 R 7 16429 R 2 19111 C8
11712 TR 2 15677 TR 7 16439 R 5 19195 C7
11716 TR 2 15678 TR 2 17244 R 7 20654 R 2

Northern China

Primary 15880 C8 15903 C7 16475 C7
11173 C2 15883 C8 15904 C8 16857 C7
15866 R 3 15894 C7 15908 C2 17878 R 8
15868 R 3 15900 C7 15910 C8 19180 C8
15872 R 7

Second. 15594 R 2 17158 T 3 19112 C8
14214 TR 3 15596 R 7 17187 TR 7 19192 C7
14712 R 2 15789 TRC2 17652 T 3 19211 T 7
15037 T 2 15851 C3 17687 T 3 19340 C3
15120 C2 16408 TR 7 17856 R 3 19497 R 3
15328 T 2 16476 C2 17862 R 2 19586 C3
15403 R 8 16513 T 8 17871 R 7 20238 C3
15450 R 7 16692 R 8 17877 R 3 20693 C2
15502 C7 16696 R 8 17882 R 8 21508 R 3
15538 C2 17054 R 3 17896 RC7 22747 C2

Northwestern China and Frontier Regions

Primary 15899 C8 16431 R 2

Second. 13332 C2 15386 TR 2 22682 R 2
11161 C2 14764 R 5 16786 C2

South China Broadly Conceived

Primary 15870 R 2

Second. 15078 R 2

East Central China

Primary 15871 R 3 16468 C7 17649 T 5
12420 RC7 15881 C3 17176 T 2 17719 R 3
15869 R 3 15892 C3 17242 R 3

Second. 15432 R 2 17207 R 4 17728 R 3
12038 C2 15587 TR 2 17667 R 7 19556 R 3
15313 T 2 16458 C2 17725 R 3 19834 R 4
15429 R 3 16624 R 7

Central Yangtze Provinces

Primary 15863 T 2 15884 C8

Second. 16393 T 2 17337 C3 17798 C6
11726 R 2 16405 TR 3 17343 C7

Southwestern China

Primary 15633 TR 3 15909 C2 16482 C3
10358 R 2 15862 T 2 15916 C7 17854 R 2
15629 T 2 15897 C2

Second. 15121 C2 16425 R 7 17613 R 7
10382 TRC2 15625 C2 16618 R 8 17888 R 3
12626 TR 2 15640 R 2 16675 R 7 19827 R 6
12735 R 2 16083 C2 17105 C3 20873 R 7

Southeastern China

Primary 11683 TR 2 15865 R 3 17615 RC2
11675 T 2 15447 R 3 16874 C7

Second. 15456 RC7 17345 C5 19148 C7
10855 RC2 15458 TRC2 17387 C2 20185 R 2
12069 C2 17329 C2 18438 T 2 21575 C3

Taiwan Only

Primary 15704 C8 15889 C2 15918 C2
14874 C2 15874 TRC1 15890 C2 16870 C7
14955 C2 15875 RC2 15893 C2 16871 C7
15031 C1 15878 C2 15898 C4 17619 C2
15586 TR 2 15879 C2 15902 C2 17621 C3
15600 TRC2 15887 C8 15912 C2 21009 C2
15701 C2 15888 C2 15917 C2 21577 C3
15703 C2

Second. 12020 C1 15472 RC2 15794 TRC3
10345 TR 2 12106 C2 15533 C7 15825 C2
10436 C2 12142 C2 15568 C3 15826 C2
10908 C1 12143 C2 15605 TRC2 15852 C2
11528 C2 12144 C2 15612 RC2 15861 C2
11690 TR 2 12146 C2 15613 RC2 16727 RC2
11843 RC2 13313 RC2 15650 C3 16729 RC2
11851 TRC2 13315 RC2 15655 C2 16829 C7
11863 RC2 14058 C1 15685 R 1 16840 C8
11985 C2 14134 C2 15695 RC2 16858 C2
12008 C2 14846 C1 15698 TRC2 16898 C2
12017 C2 15437 R 2 15707 C2 17681 C8

17799 c4 19939 c2 20334 c2 21231 TRC2
19163 c8 20236 c8 20345 c2 21233 RC2

Hong Kong and Macau Only

Primary 15618 c2 15905 c3 17718 R 2
14961 c3 15646 TRC3 15913 c3 17745 c2
14995 c3 15876 c3 16456 TRC7 17810 c2
15024 c3 15891 c3 16469 c3 19593 c2
15617 c2 15901 c3 17617 c3 21574 c3
Second. 15621 c4 16463 c2 17350 c5
10301 RC2 15802 TRC2 16473 c2 17626 T 4
10304 c3 15813 c2 16486 c3 19918 c3
14889 c2 15827 c4 16487 c2 19946 c2
14992 c3 15829 c2 16498 c2 19953 c3
15409 R 2 15850 c2 17001 c2 19969 TRC8
15411 R 7 15858 c2 17002 c2 20522 c3
15455 TRC7 15859 c2 17012 c3 20667 c4
15518 c2 16002 c2 17124 c2 20680 c3
15616 c2 16438 R 2 17318 RC3 21234 RC2

22 Local Political Systems

地方政治制度 地方政治制度

Geographic China Broadly Conceived

Primary 10261 TRC4 15937 TR 3 15956 TR 2
16128 TRC2 17572 R 3
Second. 10626 T 2 15174 TRC2 18809 RC2
10042 T 2 10707 TR 2 15185 TRC2 19219 TR 2
10048 T 2 10716 TR 1 15539 c7 19524 R 3
10058 T 2 10828 R 2 16374 T 2 19650 RC2
10082 TR 2 10875 RC1 16375 T 2 21347 TR 2
10113 TRC2 11270 TR 4 16376 T 2 21538 TRC2
10216 TRC2 14167 T 2 16423 R 2 22074 T 2
10432 c2 14222 TR 4 16424 R 2 22555 T 2
10510 T 2 14395 T 2 17036 TR 7 22681 R 3

Mainland China

Primary: Monographs
10019 T 2 11391 RC2 15560 c4 16029 c7
10519 T 4 11496 c1 15567 c7 16031 c7
10842 R 4 12002 c2 15762 TR 3 16046 c2
10851 RC2 12379 RC7 15938 TR 2 16054 R 7
10870 RC2 12426 RC7 15955 TR 8 16072 c7
10873 TRC2 12524 c2 15959 R 3 16148 c5
10887 TRC2 14223 TR 2 15963 R 3 16488 c7
10894 c1 14329 c2 15966 R 3 17095 R 7
10931 c2 14754 R 2 15970 R 4 18277 c2
10953 c2 15258 c7 15971 R 4 18588 R 2
10960 c2 15434 R 7 15977 RC7 18746 R 2
10962 c4 15483 c7 15980 RC2 19100 c7
10994 c2 15488 c2 15991 c7 19105 c7
10997 c2 15495 c2 15992 c7 19131 c7
11006 c2 15507 c7 15993 c7 19922 c7
11036 TRC7 15513 c4 16001 c7 20079 c7
11052 RC2 15524 c7 16011 c7 20492 c3
11094 c2 15537 c4 16012 c4 22375 c2
11364 R 1 15549 c7 16013 c7 22673 TR 4
Primary: Inclusions
10601 T 2 15542 c7 15996 c7 17642 c2
10603 T 2 15978 RC7 16028 c2 17644 c2
11458 c2 15982 TRC2 16035 c4 19154 c8
13977 R 2 15990 c7 16037 c3
Primary: Journal Articles
10084 TR 2 14239 R 7 16014 c2 17107 c7
10196 TR 2 14447 c7 16015 c4 17112 c7
10512 T 2 15496 c7 16018 c2 17130 c7
10513 T 4 15551 c7 16019 c2 17673 c7
10789 R 5 15580 c2 16020 c7 17905 c7
10897 c2 15934 T 2 16021 c7 17987 RC2
10964 c2 15967 R 2 16026 c3 18221 c2
10965 c2 15968 R 2 16027 c2 18273 c2
10973 c7 15975 RC7 16034 c4 19099 c8
11054 TRC2 15979 RC4 16036 c7 19123 c7
11468 c1 15994 c7 16038 c2 19126 c7
11626 c2 15997 c4 16039 c7 19142 c7
11957 c2 15999 c7 16040 c7 19144 c7
12077 c2 16004 c8 16041 c7 19158 c7
12187 T 8 16005 c7 16079 c7 19363 R 3
12391 RC7 16006 c3 16081 c2 22340 c2
Secondary: Monographs
10039 T 2 11243 T 2 14189 T 4 18567 TR 2
10062 T 2 11705 TR 2 14201 T 4 18585 R 2
10083 TR 2 11848 RC2 14337 c2 18647 R 2
10101 R 2 12082 c2 14509 R 3 18709 R 2
10103 R 2 12123 c2 15192 RC2 18730 R 2
10228 c2 12291 R 7 15241 c2 18759 R 2
10551 T 4 12331 R 7 15309 T 2 18987 TR 2
10672 T 2 12375 RC2 15519 c2 19077 RC7
10677 T 2 12378 RC8 15570 c2 19082 RC7
10688 TR 2 12380 RC7 16070 c2 19095 c7
10711 TR 4 12424 RC7 16457 c2 19135 c7
10768 R 4 12440 c7 16516 T 7 19257 R 7
10769 R 2 12441 c2 17760 R 7 19558 R 2
10795 R 4 12442 c7 17848 R 2 19638 R 7
10836 R 4 12475 c2 17849 R 2 19789 TR 2
10837 R 2 12485 c2 17979 TR 7 20496 c2
10845 R 1 13163 TR 2 18118 R 4 21265 T 2
10888 TRC2 13858 T 2 18126 R 3 21355 TR 2
10890 TRC2 13905 R 2 18178 RC2 21410 TRC2
10906 c2 13909 R 2 18264 c2 22291 c2
10937 c2 13969 R 2 18289 c7 22318 c2
10943 c2 14093 T 2 18312 RC2 22322 c2
10970 c2 14153 c2 18387 T 2 22595 T 5
11076 c2 14160 T 2 18536 TR 2
Secondary: Inclusions
10561 T 2 11711 TR 2 16877 c7 19280 R 2
10912 c2 12121 c2 17519 c7 19721 T 2
10916 c2 12459 c7 17638 c2 19873 RC2
10917 c2 13058 c7 17999 c2 19945 c2
10930 c2 14096 T 2 18119 R 2 21105 c2
10988 c2 14131 TRC2 19104 c7 21150 c2
11002 c2 14135 c2 19170 c7 21709 T 2
11042 RC2 14138 c2 19182 c7 22169 R 2
11295 TR 1 14363 c2 19190 c7 22290 c2
Secondary: Journal Articles
10239 c2 10924 c3 12452 c7 18261 c4
10383 RC2 10926 c5 12551 c8 18351 c2
10391 RC2 10929 c2 12555 c7 18401 T 2
10411 c2 10992 c2 13093 c2 18684 R 2
10483 c5 11124 c7 14177 T 2 19081 RC8
10502 c7 11181 T 2 14256 RC2 19102 c7
10518 T 4 11186 T 4 14515 RC2 19107 c7
10538 T 1 11260 TR 2 15236 c2 19125 c7
10567 T 4 11267 TR 1 15280 c2 19140 c7
10572 T 2 11271 TR 1 15540 c7 19151 c7
10621 T 4 11441 c2 15559 c7 19156 c7
10628 T 2 11464 c1 15564 c7 19157 c8
10648 T 4 11488 c2 15807 TRC3 19160 c7
10754 R 2 11493 c2 15831 c7 19169 c2
10764 R 2 11511 c1 15845 c7 19185 c7
10774 R 2 11896 c2 15896 c7 19188 c7
10794 R 2 11992 c2 16053 TR 2 19576 R 3
10818 R 4 12100 c2 16153 c2 19629 R 2
10872 TRC2 12129 c2 17992 c2 22041 T 2
10877 RC2 12405 TRC2 17996 c2 22161 R 4
10880 RC2 12418 RC7 18157 R 2 22227 TRC1
10900 c2 12427 c7 18204 c2 22368 c3
10910 c1 12431 c2 18243 c2

The Eighteen Provinces

Primary 12389 RC8 15935 T 2 16049 T 2
10507 T 2 12948 T 2 15947 TR 2 17541 T 7
10525 T 2 14117 R 2 15951 TR 3 17973 T 2
10533 T 2 14158 T 2 15954 TR 5 19122 c8
10670 T 4 14207 T 2 15960 R 2 19243 R 7
10760 R 2 15446 R 3 15965 R 3 19630 R 2
10831 R 3 15931 T 4 15969 R 3 19632 R 7
Second. 13979 R 2 16894 c2 19018 R 7
10021 T 2 14092 T 2 17542 T 8 19963 TR 2
12573 T 2 14199 T 2 17631 TR 8 20063 R 8
12612 T 2 14300 c3 17916 c2 20503 c2
12666 TR 3 14301 c3 18284 c2 21122 c2
13455 T 5 15470 RC7 18285 c2 22067 T 2
13925 R 2 15501 c2 18405 T 2 22680 R 3
13934 R 2 15543 c2 18461 T 2

North China Broadly Conceived

Primary 15433 R 2 16430 R 2 18690 R 7
10679 T 2 16063 R 2 18682 R 2 19011 R 2
10830 R 2
Second. 18307 R 2 18622 R 2 18732 R 2
10064 T 2 18496 T 2 18678 R 2 22715 R 2
17564 R 2

Manchuria

Primary 15936 T 2 16406 TR 2 16801 c8
10685 TR 2 15995 c2 16433 R 2 17551 T 2
15674 TR 2
Second. 12595 T 2 15737 T 3 16643 R 7
10796 R 2 13512 TR 2 15914 c7 16879 c8
10886 TRC1 14129 RC2 16384 T 2 17566 R 8
11015 T 2 15335 T 3 16449 R 2 19547 R 4
12211 TR 8 15664 T 2 16510 T 2

Northern China

Primary 15410 R 8 15952 TR 2 17428 c7
13891 R 2 15449 R 7 15958 R 3 17444 TR 8
13974 R 2 15459 RC7 15988 c8 17522 T 7
15360 T 7 15460 RC7 16016 c3 17570 R 2
15384 TR 4 15502 c7 16023 c3 17620 c7
15397 R 7 15534 c7 16379 T 2 18643 R 8
15399 R 7 15557 c7 16408 TR 7 19153 c8
15403 R 8 15900 c7 16563 TR 8 20260 TR 8
15406 R 8 15933 T 2 16850 c7 22612 T 2
15407 R 3 15942 TR 3 17115 c4 22632 T 3
Second. 15390 TR 3 17409 T 2 19619 R 7
10514 T 2 15408 R 2 17410 T 2 19642 R 7
10529 T 3 15414 R 8 17526 T 8 19648 R 7
10606 T 3 15450 R 7 17611 R 3 20281 T 5
10747 R 2 15565 c7 17891 R 7 20497 c2
10776 R 2 15626 T 2 17953 TRC3 20844 R 2
15336 T 2 15791 TRC3 18286 c2 20930 R 3
15338 T 7 16536 T 2 18456 T 7 21065 c7
15341 T 2 16760 c8 19094 c8 21438 T 3
15347 T 3 16791 c8 19192 c7 22546 T 3
15352 T 3 17062 R 2 19340 c3 22704 R 3
15373 TR 3 17094 R 6 19442 R 8 22802 R 7
15383 TR 2 17384 c7

Northwestern China and Frontier Regions

Primary 15544 c8 16912 T 2 19355 TR 2
15421 R 8 16517 T 2 18956 TR 2
Second. 12747 R 2 15545 c8 17376 c2
10874 TRC2 14106 TR 2 15672 TR 7 17772 RC7
10876 TRC1 15322 T 3 15673 TR 7 18749 R 2
10921 c4 15323 T 4 15811 TRC2 19080 RC7
10939 c2 15350 T 2 16735 RC8 22531 T 2
12368 R 8 15391 TR 2 16972 R 2 22682 R 2

South China Broadly Conceived

Primary 15928 T 2 15986 c3 16061 R 2
21426 TRC3 22522 T 2
Second. 12383 RC2 15721 T 2 18449 T 2
10326 T 2 12570 T 2 16410 TR 8 19006 R 4
10366 R 3 13881 TR 2

East Central China

Primary 15924 T 2 15948 TR 3 16094 T 2
15307 T 3 15929 T 3 15950 TR 3 16113 TR 3
15368 T 7 15930 T 3 15953 TR 3 17052 R 3
15374 TR 8 15939 TR 3 15961 R 3 17411 T 2
15388 TR 3 15943 TR 3 15964 R 3 18393 T 2
15578 c3 15944 TR 3 15983 c2 20883 R 3
15632 TR 3 15946 TR 3 15985 c7 20898 R 3
15921 T 3
Second. 15731 T 2 16559 TR 2 18404 T 3
15318 T 3 16060 R 3 17176 T 2 18464 T 3
15348 T 3 16108 TR 3 17606 c7 18865 T 2
15377 TR 3 16109 TR 3 17662 T 7 18983 TR 3
15405 R 7 16394 T 2 17694 TR 3 19116 c8
15429 R 3 16402 TR 3 17707 R 3 19555 R 3
15474 RC3 16407 TR 3 17709 R 3 20875 R 3
15493 c7 16409 TR 3 17863 R 3 20876 R 2
15517 c8

Central Yangtze Provinces

Primary 15919 T 3 17502 c7 18667 R 7
15481 c2 15998 c7 17643 c3 18751 R 7
15863 T 2

22.1 LOCAL POLITICAL AND SOCIAL CONTROLS

地方統治及社會控制

地方の政治的社会的統制

17553 T 7 18022 TR 3 18748 R 3 19975 TRC7
17578 R 3 18438 T 2 19179 C7 21141 C7
17615 RC2 18518 T 2 19449 R 2 22557 T 3
17901 C7 18519 T 2 19499 R 3

Taiwan Only

Primary 15442 R 2 18981 TR 2 20702 T 3
15438 R 2 16066 TRC1 19065 C2 21421 RC3
Second. 15521 C8 16561 TR 2 16854 C7
11019 TR 2 15533 C7 16794 C8 16887 C8
15440 R 2 15613 RC2 16833 C8 16902 C7
15443 R 2 16007 C3 16851 C7 17544 T 2
15444 R 2 16347 C2

Hong Kong and Macau Only

Primary 15981 RC3 16139 C3 17635 RC3
15340 T 7 16057 R 2 17012 C3 19591 C2
15920 T 3 16067 TRC1 17593 C3 20117 C4
15925 T 7 16076 C2
Second. 15973 TRC2 16126 TRC3 19970 TRC7
12937 T 3 15974 TRC2 16135 C3 20389 TR 3
15325 T 3 15976 TRC2 17894 RC2 20516 C4
15387 TR 2 16002 C2 17909 C2 20657 RC3
15617 C2 16010 C2 17994 C2 20667 C4
15827 C4 16030 C2 19702 R 2 20682 C2
15941 TR 3 16033 C3 19713 C2 22724 RC2
15949 TR 3

22.2 Customary Law and Dispute Resolution

習慣法及仲裁解決

慣習法及び紛争の解決

Geographic China Broadly Conceived

Primary 11415 TRC1 16127 TRC2 20285 T 1
10025 T 2 11605 RC2 16128 TRC2 20591 T 3
10707 TR 2 12941 T 2 18541 TR 2 20662 TRC1
11150 C4 12965 TR 4 19546 R 3 20769 T 4
11261 TR 1 16068 RC2 19859 TRC2 21988 T 1
11264 TR 1 16104 TR 7
Second. 11270 TR 4 16376 T 2 19897 TRC1
10004 T 2 11293 TR 1 16423 R 2 20009 TR 1
10016 T 2 11418 RC1 16424 R 2 20010 TR 2
10022 T 2 11766 R 2 17691 TR 2 20089 T 1
10096 R 2 11767 R 2 17981 TR 2 20213 R 3
10100 R 2 12370 R 7 18299 C2 20231 RC2
10114 TRC2 12593 T 2 18468 T 1 20590 T 3
10117 TRC2 12801 C2 18558 TR 2 21368 R 2
10139 C2 13106 C4 18707 R 2 21538 TRC2
10263 C2 14098 T 2 19039 TRC2 21853 TRC2
10666 T 2 14102 T 2 19727 TR 1 22001 TR 1
10713 TR 2 14395 T 2 19755 T 1 22586 T 3
10804 R 3 15363 T 2 19759 T 1 22681 R 3
10865 TRC3 15645 TRC3 19762 T 1 22728 RC2
11210 T 1 16374 T 2 19772 T 1 22740 TRC2
11222 T 1 16375 T 2 19774 T 1 23021 C2

Mainland China

Primary: Monographs
10059 T 2 11514 C2 15971 R 4 19042 RC1
11076 C2 11534 C2 16103 TR 2 19077 RC7
11243 T 2 12378 RC8 16106 TR 2 20067 R 2
11305 TR 1 13691 TR 2 16123 R 2 20068 R 2
11336 R 2 13882 TR 2 16148 C5 20462 R 2
11356 R 1 14033 C2 18550 TR 1 20940 R 2
11369 R 2 15550 C2 18746 R 2 22595 T 5
11398 RC2 15955 TR 8 18862 T 2 22667 TR 1
Primary: Inclusions
11265 TR 2 11494 C2 15209 C7 17638 C2
11442 C2 11530 C2 16110 TR 2 21432 C3
11443 C2 14302 C3 16124 RC2 21529 TRC3
11487 C2
Primary: Journal Articles
11026 R 2 11262 TR 1 11402 TRC1 11455 C4
11071 C2 11382 R 2 11407 TRC1 11460 C7
11181 T 2 11388 TRC2 11424 C1 11477 C1
11255 TR 1 11396 TRC1 11441 C2 11493 C2
11499 C2 16096 T 1 19383 C2 20453 R 3
11501 C4 16100 T 1 19701 R 1 20499 C2
12531 C2 16112 TR 1 19799 TR 1 20532 C2
13628 T 8 16144 C2 19891 TRC1 22021 C2
15225 C2 16145 C7 19950 C1 22564 T 2
15999 C7 16149 C3 20061 R 1 22587 T 3
16082 C1 16153 C2 20254 T 2 22700 R 3
16089 T 2 16154 C2
Secondary: Monographs
10019 T 2 11324 R 1 15434 R 7 18915 T 2
10023 T 2 11368 R 2 15466 RC2 19477 TR 4
10043 T 2 11381 R 1 15508 C2 19558 R 2
10055 T 2 11390 RC2 15575 C4 19801 TR 1
10061 T 2 11423 C1 15762 TR 3 19892 RC1
10071 TR 2 11439 C1 15959 R 3 20013 TR 1
10104 R 2 11495 C1 15963 R 3 20135 T 1
10110 TRC2 11607 TRC1 15966 R 3 20175 TR 1
10135 C2 11705 TR 2 15992 C7 20244 C2
10559 T 4 12303 R 2 15993 C7 20258 T 2
10587 T 2 12372 R 2 16013 C7 20782 T 1
10660 T 2 12963 TR 2 16055 R 2 21308 TR 2
10672 T 2 13491 TR 1 16071 C2 21311 TR 2
10677 T 2 13965 R 2 16395 T 2 21410 TRC2
10695 TR 2 14139 C2 17313 RC2 21416 RC2
10702 TR 2 14219 TR 2 18003 C2 21504 TR 2
10778 R 2 14478 R 3 18126 R 3 21569 C1
10938 C4 14479 R 2 18277 C2 22198 TRC2
10960 C2 14584 T 2 18378 T 2 22599 T 2
10994 C2 15192 RC2 18585 R 2 22605 T 2
11036 TRC7 15214 C2 18617 R 2 22669 TR 1
11195 T 1 15230 C2 18636 R 2 22673 TR 4
11292 TR 1 15245 C2 18717 R 2 22710 R 2
Secondary: Inclusions
10078 TR 2 11303 TR 1 15296 C1 19873 RC2
10441 T 2 11329 R 1 16035 C4 20071 TRC1
10603 T 2 13058 C7 16085 C4 20081 C2
10616 T 2 13099 C2 17550 T 2 20115 TRC2
10658 T 4 14147 C2 18219 C2 22238 RC4
11244 T 2 14363 C2 18832 TRC1 22264 RC1
11252 TR 1 15222 C2
Secondary: Journal Articles
10465 C2 11331 R 1 11915 C2 18384 T 1
10734 TR 2 11333 R 1 12405 TRC2 18928 T 2
10738 TR 1 11352 R 1 12555 C7 19208 T 1
10754 R 2 11353 R 1 12594 T 2 19215 TR 5
10929 C2 11380 R 4 12825 C3 19344 T 5
10951 C3 11383 TRC1 12831 C2 19715 TR 2
11118 C2 11386 TRC1 13093 C2 19760 T 1
11170 C2 11405 RC1 13354 C2 19777 T 1
11188 T 1 11408 RC1 13484 T 2 19785 TR 1
11190 T 1 11410 TRC2 13749 R 5 19792 TR 1
11192 T 4 11412 TRC1 14094 T 2 19813 R 1
11197 T 1 11414 TRC1 14177 T 2 19842 R 1
11211 T 1 11419 C1 14183 T 2 20038 T 7
11218 T 1 11422 C1 14407 R 3 20045 TR 1
11227 T 1 11431 C1 14531 C5 20046 TR 1
11239 T 1 11445 C1 14734 R 1 20130 T 2
11251 TR 1 11456 C2 15138 TR 2 20488 C2
11271 TR 1 11483 C2 15173 RC2 20523 C2
11272 TR 1 11485 C1 15196 C2 21501 TR 2
11273 TR 1 11486 C2 15979 RC4 21728 TR 1
11275 TR 1 11488 C2 16027 C2 22400 T 2
11311 R 1 11527 C1 16038 C2 22573 T 1
11326 R 1 11529 C1 17000 C3

The Eighteen Provinces

Primary 15960 R 2 16107 TR 1 19754 T 1
10056 T 2 16048 T 2 16114 R 4 19765 T 2
11346 R 2 16049 T 2 16115 R 1 19954 C2
12946 T 1 16093 T 2 16155 C2 20035 T 1
14514 RC4 16098 T 7 17542 T 8 20063 R 8
15375 TR 2 16099 T 7 19514 R 2 20265 R 1
15864 TR 2 16102 TR 1 19744 T 1 21996 TR 1
15931 T 4 16105 TR 2
Second. 14401 T 5 18346 C2 20037 T 1
10006 T 2 15243 C2 18347 C2 20287 T 1
10839 R 2 15470 RC7 18621 R 3 20290 T 2
11187 T 1 15733 T 2 19053 TRC2 20478 C2
11246 T 1 15965 R 3 19210 T 2 20503 C2
11280 TR 1 16355 C2 19245 R 2 22527 T 3
12193 T 8 17748 C3 19577 R 3 22615 T 2
12935 T 1 17912 C2 19942 C2 22680 R 3
13469 T 2 17973 T 2 19964 TR 1

North China Broadly Conceived

Primary 16430 R 2 18509 T 2 22532 T 2
10679 T 2 18390 T 2 20748 T 2 22623 T 2
16119 R 2
Second. 15752 T 2 18716 R 2 19011 R 2
14195 T 3 18622 R 2 18953 TR 2 20578 T 2
15428 R 7 18682 R 2

Manchuria

Primary 16120 R 2 17525 T 2 17548 T 7
20047 TR 2
Second. 15661 T 8 17688 T 2 20715 T 3
10582 T 2 17540 T 2 17689 T 7 22654 TR 2
11051 RC2

Northern China

Primary 15933 T 2 16130 C2 18456 T 7
15328 T 2 15942 TR 3 16136 C3 18643 R 8
15389 TR 3 16087 T 3 16142 C3 18994 R 3
15394 R 2 16101 TR 3 17409 T 2 20084 T 1
15452 TRC2 16111 TR 1 17532 T 2 21177 T 7
15908 C2 16121 R 3 18434 T 1
Second. 15378 TR 7 16563 TR 8 20762 T 3
10945 C3 15399 R 7 17444 TR 8 22457 R 3
14214 TR 3 15407 R 3 17639 C7 22577 T 2
15320 T 3 15410 R 8 17811 T 7 22612 T 2
15338 T 7 15534 C7 18348 C2 22747 C2
15355 T 2 16296 R 2 19360 R 3 22751 C3
15362 T 7 16377 T 2

Northwestern China and Frontier Regions

Primary 17416 R 2 18697 R 2 18911 T 2
20048 TR 8 21196 RC2
Second. 12747 R 2 16672 R 7 16912 T 2
18245 C2 22732 TRC2

South China Broadly Conceived

Primary 15722 T 2 16092 T 4 17581 TRC1
15721 T 2 15928 T 2 16855 C8 21426 TRC3
Second. 16910 T 4 18486 T 2 19894 TRC2
10031 T 2 18455 T 2 18875 T 2 22601 T 2
13040 R 4 18459 T 2

East Central China

Primary 15950 TR 3 16108 TR 3 18453 T 3
15388 TR 3 16060 R 3 16109 TR 3 18522 T 3
15430 R 3 16075 C3 16113 TR 3 19267 R 3
15431 R 3 16086 T 3 16122 R 3 19748 T 2
15632 TR 3 16091 T 3 16345 C3 22744 C3
15948 TR 3 16094 T 2 16521 T 8
Second. 15474 RC3 15946 TR 3 18028 R 3
11121 C2 15493 C7 16663 R 7 18464 T 3
15143 R 3 15552 C2 17162 T 3 18932 T 4
15254 C3 15744 T 2 17193 TR 3 19509 R 3
15291 C3 15930 T 3 17660 C3 19533 R 3
15348 T 3 15943 TR 3 17812 T 7 19555 R 3
15368 T 7 15944 TR 3 17816 T 7 19556 R 3

Central Yangtze Provinces

Primary 16090 T 2 16150 C3 19966 R 2
Second. 15481 C2 18751 R 7 19460 R 8
13522 TR 2 16526 T 2 19450 R 7 19694 T 3

Southwestern China

Primary 16267 TR 2 18548 TR 1 18922 T 2
16118 R 2 16619 R 8 18892 T 3 21313 TR 2
Second. 16077 C2 18491 T 2 21315 TR 2
15316 T 2 16911 T 2 19742 T 2 22542 T 2
15629 T 2 16963 R 4 21312 TR 4 22570 T 3
15862 T 2 17415 R 8 21314 TR 4 22597 T 3
15957 R 2 18349 C2

Southeastern China

Primary 16143 C2 18906 T 3 20039 T 1
16095 T 3 16841 C8 19773 T 1 20069 TRC1
16097 T 3 17521 T 7 19778 T 3 22678 R 3
16116 R 4 18490 T 2

TAIWAN ONLY

HONG KONG AND MACAU ONLY

23 FOLK RELIGION

民間之宗教信仰 民間宗教

GEOGRAPHIC CHINA BROADLY CONCEIVED

MAINLAND CHINA

THE EIGHTEEN PROVINCES

NORTH CHINA BROADLY CONCEIVED

MANCHURIA

NORTHERN CHINA

NORTHWESTERN CHINA AND FRONTIER REGIONS

SOUTH CHINA BROADLY CONCEIVED

EAST CENTRAL CHINA

CENTRAL YANGTZE PROVINCES

SOUTHWESTERN CHINA

24.1 LOCAL AGRARIAN ECONOMIES

地方農業 地方農業

GEOGRAPHIC CHINA BROADLY CONCEIVED

MAINLAND CHINA

THE EIGHTEEN PROVINCES

NORTH CHINA BROADLY CONCEIVED

MANCHURIA

NORTHERN CHINA

NORTHWESTERN CHINA AND FRONTIER REGIONS

SOUTH CHINA BROADLY CONCEIVED

EAST CENTRAL CHINA

CENTRAL YANGTZE PROVINCES

SOUTHWESTERN CHINA

15715T 2 16932T 2 18131 R 2 20583T 2
15717T 2 17159T 2 18889T 2 20645 R 7
15897 C2 17479 R 7 20537T 2 20840 R 8
16404TR 2 17663 R 7

Southeastern China

Primary 16507T 2 16616 R 8 16779 C7
10392TRC2 16514T 2 16630 R 8 16781 C7
10668T 2 16518T 7 16634 R 8 16792 C7
12069 C2 16530T 2 16660 R 7 16798 C2
13203 R 2 16537T 2 16670 R 8 16839 C2
15334T 2 16552TR 2 16679 R 8 16841 C8
15358T 8 16558TR 7 16684 R 7 16874 C7
15499 C2 16564 R 7 16687 R 2 16888 C8
15718T 2 16577 R 2 16697 R 8 17329 C2
15763TR 2 16579 R 8 16712 R 7 17665 R 7
15819 C7 16580 R 7 16736 RC7 17671 C7
16000 C7 16581 R 2 16764 C7 17847 R 7
16017 C2 16584 R 2 16769 C2 17913 C2
16062 R 2 16607 R 2 16774 C7 19115 C8
16477 C2 16613 R 7 16775 C7 19165 C8
16505T 2

Second. 15479 C8 17156T 7 19109 C8
10278T 2 15500 C7 17191TR 2 19113 C8
10327T 2 15572 C2 17353 C2 19148 C7
10855 RC2 15779 R 2 17365 C2 19179 C7
11143 C2 15984 C7 17387 C2 19449 R 2
11683TR 2 16218T 2 17547T 2 19962TR 7
11837 R 2 16396T 2 17589 C2 20082 C7
12908T 2 16480 C2 17901 C7 20542T 2
14815 C7 16923T 2 17930T 7 21141 C7
15317T 2 16945 R 2 17949TRC7 21393 RC2
15353T 2 16976 R 2 18695 R 2 21428 RC2
15418 R 8

Taiwan Only

Primary: Monographs
10385 RC2 16725 RC8 16794 C8 16871 C7
10387TRC2 16726TRC2 16795 C8 16872 C7
10882 RC2 16727 RC2 16797 C7 16886 C7
11232T 2 16729 RC2 16818 C7 16887 C8
11678T 2 16730TRC8 16820 C7 16892 C8
12150 C2 16733TRC8 16825 C7 16898 C2
12175 C2 16737TRC8 16826 C7 16899 C8
13053TRC2 16740TRC2 16827 C7 16902 C7
13079 C2 16741TRC8 16844 C7 17128 C7
13112 C2 16742TRC2 16845 C7 17169T 2
13301 RC2 16747 RC2 16849 C8 17681 C8
13315 RC2 16748 RC2 16852 C8 17774 RC7
15002 C2 16771 C8 16858 C2 17897 RC8
15504 C8 16776 C8 16865 C7 17910 C7
15505 C8 16777 C2 16866 C8 19090 RC8
15515 C8 16778 C8 16867 C7 19466 RC7
15697TRC2 16785 C8 16868 C8 19663 C7
16495 C2 16788 C7 16869 C7 19737 C8
16710 R 2 16790 C8 16870 C7 19864 RC8
16711 R 2

Primary: Inclusions
11959 C2 16734 RC7 16821 C7 16851 C7
13102 C2 16743 RC8 16833 C8 16883 C7
16544T 8 16745TRC8 16840 C8 16891 C8

Primary: Journal Articles
10416 C2 16506T 2 16789 C8 16854 C7
11843 RC2 16549TR 7 16810 C7 16856 C7
11851TRC2 16550TR 8 16811 C8 16864 C2
11856 RC2 16551TR 7 16812 C2 16873 C7
11873 RC2 16554TR 7 16817 C7 16884 C2
11985 C2 16561TR 2 16819 C8 16885 C8
12106 C2 16610 R 8 16822 C8 16889 C7
12135 C2 16611 R 2 16823 C7 16901 C8
12143 C2 16651 R 2 16824 C2 17518 C7
12146 C2 16674 R 8 16828 C8 17675 C2
12152 C2 16728TRC7 16829 C7 19079 RC8
13313 RC2 16739TRC8 16830 C8 19088 RC8
15457 RC2 16746 RC8 16832 C8 19089 RC8
15562 C2 16772 C8 16834 C8 19163 C8
15657T 2 16780 C8 16843 C8 20072 C7
15878 C2 16783 C7

Second. 11659T 2 11964 C2 12137 C2
10345TR 2 11663T 2 11984 C2 12144 C2
10436 C2 11863 RC2 12017 C2 12149 C2
10904 C2 11904 C2 12070 C2 12174 C2
11138 C2 11905 C2 12136 C2 13052 RC2
13059 C2 15440 R 2 15606 RC2 17669 RC8
13081 C7 15442 R 2 15655 C2 17822T 2
13083 C2 15471 RC2 15658T 2 17989TRC2
13113 C2 15490 C2 15785 R 7 18297 C2
13179TR 2 15491 C7 15852 C2 18981TR 2
13312 RC2 15521 C8 15887 C8 19679 C7
13450 C2 15530 C7 15890 C2 19980TRC8
13602 C2 15554 C2 16009 C7 20236 C8
14554T 2 15600TRC2 16261TR 2 20686 C2
15351T 2 15601 RC2 17424 RC8 22627T 7

Hong Kong and Macau Only

Primary 15814 C7 16799 C8 16876 C8
15330T 7 15820 C2 16805 C8 16878 C3
15340T 7 15850 C2 16813 C8 16880 C7
15409 R 2 16456TRC7 16814 C8 16893 C7
15463TRC7 16529T 7 16815 C7 17683 C8
15518 C2 16731 RC2 16816 C2 17963 C2
15797TRC7 16753TRC2 16838 C7 19970TRC7
15802TRC2 16767 C7 16848 C7 21046 C8
15813 C2 16773 C2 16862 C7 21827TRC7

Second. 15573 C8 15926T 7 17966 C2
10301 RC2 15574 C8 16438 R 2 17971 C8
15451TRC7 15800TRC8 16463 C2 19309 C2
15455TRC7 15808TRC2 16498 C2 21254 C2
15464TRC8 15815 C8 16499 C2 21905 C8
15520 C2 15818 C8 17320TRC7 21906 C8
15529 C2 15829 C2 17623 C2 22724 RC2
15555 C2

24.2 Local Transport and Communications
地方交通　地方交通

Geographic China Broadly Conceived

Primary 15877 C8 16376T 2 16949 R 2
10328T 2 16375T 2 16938TR 2 16977 R 2
15773 R 2

Second. 16539T 7 19219TR 2 22618T 2
15345T 3 16715 R 2 22604T 3

Mainland China

Primary 16907T 4 16993 C7 17014 C4
10352TR 7 16948 R 2 17000 C3 17095 R 7
13015 R 4 16969 R 2 17008 C2 20914 R 2
16395T 2 16992 C7

Second. 15303 C2 15845 C7 17848 R 2
10086TR 2 15482 C2 15971 R 4 17849 R 2
11588TR 2 15519 C2 16524T 2 18773 R 2
12649TR 2 15741T 3 16837 C8 18992 R 2
12749 R 2 15756TR 4 17140T 2 19125 C7
12863 C4 15762TR 3 17260 R 2 19671 C7
12916T 5 15807TRC3 17661TR 2 22673TR 4
13095 C2 15832 C4

The Eighteen Provinces

Primary 16920T 2 16962 R 3 20668 C2
12699 R 3 16935T 2 19228 R 3 22553T 2
16508T 2 16944 R 3

Second. 15306T 2 15841 C3 20565T 2
10175 C2 15327T 3 17143T 3 20699 C2
10831 R 3 15478 C2 17749 C2 21816 R 2
12936T 4 15767TR 4 20548T 2 22801 R 3

North China Broadly Conceived

Primary 10343TR 4 16973 R 2 17017 C1
20578T 2

Second. 16063 R 2 16732 RC2 17028T 5
20541T 2

Manchuria

Primary 16383T 2 16951 R 3 17013 C2
10340TR 2 16384T 2 16961 R 2 17234 R 2
10398TRC2 16553TR 7 16967 R 3 17548T 7
12892T 5 16915T 2 16968 R 2 17857 R 2
13001 R 3 16929T 2 16974 R 4 19523 R 2
15670TR 2 16939TR 2 16997 C4

Second. 15583T 8 15778 R 3 17066 R 7
10421 C2 15599 R 2 15847 C2 17253 R 5
12925T 2 15679TR 7 16436 R 3 17265 R 3
12969TR 2 15688 R 2 16449 R 2 17838 R 2
12988 R 2 15689 R 2 16643 R 7 20795TR 2
13007 R 3 15690 R 2 16669 R 8 22506T 2
15335T 3 15774 R 3 16691 R 7

Northern China

Primary 15713T 2 16904T 5 16956 R 2
10319T 2 15789TRC2 16906T 2 16966 R 2
10977 C3 15817 C3 16909T 2 16975 R 4
12966TR 3 15836 C3 16926T 2 17005 C3
12974 R 2 15872 R 7 16928T 2 17094 R 6
12979 R 2 16377T 2 16936TR 3 17148T 2
13126T 2 16390T 2 16940TR 2 17927T 2
15367T 2 16403TR 2 16950 R 2 21438T 3
15417 R 3 16903T 3 16953 R 2 22612T 2

Second. 15366T 3 16047T 4 17410T 2
10317T 2 15384TR 4 16373T 3 17627T 2
11080 C3 15389TR 3 16408TR 7 17713 R 3
11594 R 2 15394 R 2 16413 R 4 17817T 2
12907T 2 15452TRC2 16563TR 8 17856 R 3
12917T 4 15477 C7 16578 R 2 17878 R 8
12939T 3 15626T 2 16594 R 8 18313TRC3
12991 R 2 15627T 3 17054 R 3 18498T 3
13974 R 2 15759TR 3 17062 R 2 19394 R 3
14157T 3 15769 R 5 17141T 5 19620 R 2
14712 R 2 15806TRC3 17158T 3 19648 R 7
15341T 2 15810TRC2 17186TR 2 20579T 3
15342T 3 15860 C3 17273 R 3 22747 C2
15362T 7

Northwestern China and Frontier Regions

Primary 15753T 2 16912T 2 16984TRC2
10332T 2 16399T 7 16927T 2 16994 C8
10725TR 2 16445 R 7 16957 R 2 17007 C2
15729T 2 16738 RC2 16972 R 2 18956TR 2

Second. 13713 R 2 15811TRC2 16786 C2
10401 C2 14844 C2 15857 C2 16800 C7
11722 R 2 15302 C3 16307 R 8 16836 C2
11787 R 2 15492 C2 16422 R 2 17043 R 2
11926 C2 15620 C2 16431 R 2 17376 C2
13019 R 2 15673TR 7

South China Broadly Conceived

Primary 16410TR 8 16917T 2 16964 R 2
12684TR 2 16910T 4 16930T 2 16979 R 2
16061 R 2 16914T 2 16934T 2 20633 R 2
16392T 5

Second. 15332T 2 15870 R 2 17225 R 2
10344TR 4 15721T 2 16092T 4 18524T 2
10366 R 3 15722T 2 16378T 2 18875T 2
12891T 2 15775 R 2 16388T 2

East Central China

Primary 15731T 2 16922T 2 16980 R 3
10321T 2 15732T 2 16937TR 5 17015 C4
10368 R 2 15765TR 3 16943 R 2 17052 R 3
11025 R 3 16905T 3 16946 R 2 18026 R 3
12157 C2 16908T 2 16947 R 2 18321 C3
15404 R 3 16921T 3 16978 R 3 22539T 2

Second. 15727T 3 16484 C7 17667 R 7
10274T 3 15761TR 7 16621 R 2 17732 R 3
10339TR 2 15772 R 2 16622 R 2 17858 R 2
11769 R 2 15844 C3 16668 R 7 17892TRC3
13150TR 5 15854 C7 16796 C7 18453T 3
13224 R 4 15929T 3 17030TR 4 19258 R 3
15143 R 3 15944TR 3 17051 R 4 19264 R 3
15254 C3 16075 C3 17161T 3 19511 R 3
15313T 2 16401TR 4 17208 R 2 19555 R 3
15318T 3 16407TR 3 17232 R 3 20600T 2
15346T 2 16418 R 2 17242 R 2 22755 C3
15377TR 3 16458 C2 17662T 7

Central Yangtze Provinces

Primary 12943T 2 15469TRC2 15712T 3
17554T 4

Second. 11795 R 2 13227 R 2 14187T 2
10324T 2 12942T 3 13522TR 2 14743 R 3

Southwestern China

Southeastern China

Taiwan Only

Hong Kong and Macau Only

24.3 Local Commerce and Services

地方商業　地方商業

Geographic China Broadly Conceived

Mainland China

The Eighteen Provinces

North China Broadly Conceived

Manchuria

Northern China

Northwestern China and Frontier Regions

South China Broadly Conceived

East Central China

Central Yangtze Provinces

Southwestern China

Primary 16653 R 2 17061 R 3 17088 R 3
11706 TR 2 16675 R 7 17063 R 3 17089 R 2
12889 T 2 16678 R 2 17064 R 2 17090 R 3
15365 T 2 16713 R 7 17070 R 7 17091 R 7
15436 R 6 17031 TR 5 17071 R 7 17105 C3
15633 TR 3 17044 R 3 17072 R 5 17106 C3
16444 R 3 17045 R 7 17082 R 7 19299 C3
16598 R 7 17058 R 3 17086 R 7 22508 T 2
16648 R 7

Second. 15740 T 2 16511 T 7 17872 R 7
11679 T 2 15897 C2 16531 T 7 18694 R 2
12919 T 2 16425 R 7 16683 R 2 18889 T 2
15392 R 6 16441 R 3 16913 T 2 19362 R 6
15413 R 2 16447 R 5 17137 T 2 20550 T 3
15717 T 2 16482 C3 17473 R 3 21314 TR 4

Southeastern China

Primary 15651 C4 16607 R 2 17073 R 4
12952 TR 3 15735 T 2 16687 R 2 17191 TR 2
12953 TR 2 15763 TR 2 17021 T 3 17268 R 3
12954 TR 3 16187 T 3 17022 T 3 17408 T 3
15371 TR 2 16505 T 2 17025 T 2 17533 T 7
15419 R 6 16584 R 2 17055 R 3 19209 T 3

Second. 15359 T 2 16613 R 7 17270 R 4
10327 T 2 15485 C2 16684 R 7 17560 TR 2
12908 T 2 15734 T 2 16712 R 7 17820 T 3
15305 T 2 15779 R 2 16933 T 5 19205 T 3
15334 T 2 16387 T 2 17209 R 2 19346 T 4
15339 T 3 16396 T 2 17256 R 2

Taiwan Only

Primary 17103 TRC7 17127 C2 19247 R 3
13083 C2 17117 C2 17128 C7 20268 C6
17101 TRC7 17118 C7 17618 C5 22627 T 7

Second. 15794 TRC3 16747 RC2 16867 C7
13112 C2 15822 C3 16797 C7 16869 C7
15491 C7 16551 TR 7 16826 C7 17822 T 2
15792 TRC5 16710 R 2 16827 C7 19738 C7
15793 TRC3 16729 RC2 16858 C2

Hong Kong and Macau Only

Primary 16497 C2 17116 C8 17608 T 3
13046 TRC2 17019 T 3 17124 C2 17917 C2
15555 C2 17026 T 3 17126 C3 19309 C2
16400 TR 4 17093 R 4 17323 TRC3 19431 C3
16472 C3 17102 TRC7 17379 C2 20272 C7
16473 C2 17108 C7 17511 C1 20688 C2
16483 C5 17109 C7 17514 C1 23045 C2
16486 C3

Second. 15925 T 7 16773 C7 17963 C2
15329 T 3 15962 R 3 16816 C2 19207 T 3
15382 TR 3 16348 C7 16838 C7 19858 RC7
15411 R 7 16438 R 2 16848 C7 19970 TRC7
15455 TRC7 16451 RC3 16893 C7 20663 RC3
15463 TRC7 16455 RC2 17333 C3 20681 C2
15529 C2 16456 TRC7 17394 C3 20870 R 2
15541 C2 16499 C2 17516 C7 21063 C2
15838 C3 16501 C2 17655 C3 21574 C3
15859 C2 16767 C7 17683 C8 22441 TR 7

24.4 Local Industry

地方工業 地方工業

Geographic China Broadly Conceived

Primary 13127 T 2 16539 T 7 17691 TR 2
10096 R 2 13194 R 2 17142 T 3 17696 R 3
11665 T 2 13404 C2 17165 T 2 20595 T 3
12201 T 7 15422 R 4 17272 R 2

Second. 11859 TRC2 16068 RC2 19217 TR 3
10001 T 2 11960 C2 16374 T 2 19490 R 2
10022 T 2 12941 T 2 16423 R 2 20200 R 2
10077 TR 2 13856 T 2 16424 R 2 20590 T 3
10331 T 2 14468 R 2 16522 T 2 20620 TR 2
11704 TR 2 15191 RC2 16938 TR 2 22618 T 2
11766 R 2 15363 T 2 17981 TR 2 22651 TR 2
11767 R 2 15773 R 2 18852 T 2 22665 TR 2
11770 R 2

Mainland China

Primary: Monographs
10172 C2 15482 C2 17140 T 2 17260 R 2
11756 R 2 15519 C2 17160 T 2 17291 R 2
11845 RC2 15537 C4 17190 TR 5 17297 R 2
11912 C2 15550 C2 17226 R 2 17311 RC2
12027 C2 15560 C4 17228 R 5 17313 RC2
13164 TR 4 16012 C4 17238 R 2 17316 RC2
13250 R 2 16070 C2 17241 R 2 17381 C5
13277 R 2 16395 T 2 17245 R 5 17395 C2
14153 C2 16457 C2 17249 R 7 17661 TR 2
15466 RC2

Primary: Inclusions
13242 R 5 17157 T 5 17314 RC2 17355 C7
13260 R 2 17174 T 2 17317 RC2 17404 C7
17147 T 2 17192 TR 2 17341 C2 19216 TR 2
17152 T 2

Primary: Journal Articles
11743 R 2 13378 C4 17247 R 2 17369 C3
12482 C2 14434 R 7 17255 R 7 17370 C2
13177 TR 4 16004 C8 17278 R 5 17371 C7
13180 TR 2 16015 C4 17280 R 2 17373 C7
13181 TR 4 16079 C7 17283 R 5 17374 C7
13280 R 4 16470 C2 17289 R 2 17388 C2
13320 C1 16503 C7 17303 R 2 17389 C4
13364 C2 16807 C7 17304 R 2 17391 C2
13373 C2 17113 C7 17335 C2 17401 C2
13374 C2 17135 T 1 17352 C3 17403 C2
13375 C2 17149 T 2 17368 C2 19305 C3
13377 C2

Secondary: Monographs
10036 T 2 11955 C2 13338 C2 17895 RC2
10061 T 2 12005 C2 13343 C2 18722 R 2
10094 R 2 12015 C2 13344 C2 19078 RC8
10101 R 2 12158 C2 13384 C2 19095 C7
10149 C2 12222 TR 7 14508 R 3 19105 C7
10330 T 2 12257 R 7 14809 RC2 19131 C7
10338 TR 2 12271 R 7 15085 RC2 19184 C8
11105 C2 12291 R 7 15100 C7 19257 R 7
11651 C2 12298 R 7 15192 RC2 19291 C2
11698 TR 2 12339 R 2 15297 C2 19302 C5
11713 TR 2 12359 R 2 15483 C7 19558 R 2
11740 R 2 12375 RC2 15506 C2 19638 R 7
11745 R 2 12386 RC2 15507 C7 19640 R 7
11748 R 2 12429 C7 15508 C2 19644 R 2
11750 R 2 12434 C2 15513 C4 19707 R 7
11794 R 5 12475 C2 15553 C2 19922 C7
11860 RC2 12485 C2 15762 TR 3 20582 T 2
11864 RC2 12532 C2 15991 C7 20618 TR 2
11876 RC2 12572 T 3 15993 C7 21677 T 2
11891 C2 12853 C2 16046 C2 21705 T 1
11897 C2 12915 T 2 16488 C7 22599 T 2
11903 C2 13163 TR 2 17717 R 3 22673 TR 4
11946 C2 13218 R 2 17779 C2 22991 TRC2

Secondary: Inclusions
11819 R 1 12422 RC7 13334 C5 15542 C7
11875 RC2 13162 TR 4 13352 C2 16877 C7
12042 C2 13241 R 7 13419 C3 19284 RC2
12092 C2

Secondary: Journal Articles
10033 T 2 12048 C4 13294 RC2 16770 C7
10166 C2 12066 C2 13300 TRC2 16863 C7
10440 T 2 12083 C2 13349 C2 16992 C7
10461 C2 12111 C2 13354 C2 17107 C7
10492 C2 12112 C2 13409 C2 17129 C6
11097 C2 12419 RC7 13426 C2 17902 C3
11717 TR 2 12427 C7 14417 C3 18335 C2
11730 R 2 12458 C7 15173 RC2 19125 C7
11734 R 3 12498 C2 15292 C2 19126 C7
11742 R 2 12526 C7 15747 T 2 19159 C7
11768 R 2 12533 C1 15832 C4 19185 C7
11778 R 2 13003 R 2 15886 C7 19273 R 2
11854 RC2 13095 C2 15997 C4 20390 TR 3
11895 C2 13122 T 4 16006 C3 21263 T 2
11902 C2 13161 TR 2 16034 C4 22947 RC1
12012 C2 13238 R 3 16452 RC2

The Eighteen Provinces

Primary 15306 T 2 16806 C7 17153 T 2
10006 T 2 15327 T 3 16894 C2 17173 T 2
13037 R 2 15478 C2 17143 T 3 17175 T 2
13130 T 2 15511 C2 17144 T 2 17198 R 5
13212 R 2 15527 C7 17145 T 2 17233 R 7
17236 R 2 17287 R 2 17322 TRC2 19356 TR 4
17248 R 2 17301 R 7 17741 C2 20668 C2
17257 R 2 17308 R 2 17749 C2 20760 T 2
17281 R 2

Second. 12878 T 2 15446 R 3 17869 R 2
10141 C2 12936 T 4 15543 C2 17995 C2
10294 R 2 12978 R 2 15781 R 2 19458 R 8
10322 T 2 13191 TR 3 15864 TR 2 19491 R 4
11681 T 2 13223 R 2 15965 R 3 19823 R 7
11784 R 2 13566 R 2 16369 T 2 20699 C2
11824 R 2 14456 TR 2 16478 C2 20976 TRC1
12183 T 8 15049 TR 2 16508 T 2 21675 T 1
12675 TR 2 15272 C2 17861 R 3 22553 T 2

North China Broadly Conceived

Primary 16380 T 7 17307 R 7

Second. 13976 R 2 17846 R 7 18732 R 2
10343 TR 4 16063 R 2 18622 R 2

Manchuria

Primary 16691 R 7 17265 R 3 17327 C2
10398 TRC2 17229 R 4 17266 R 2 17340 C7
10421 C2 17230 R 3 17286 R 3 17346 C3
12925 T 2 17231 R 8 17294 R 4 17348 C8
13396 C4 17234 R 2 17298 R 2 17383 C3
15532 C4 17244 R 7 17302 R 2 17716 R 5
15847 C2 17253 R 5 17305 R 2 19298 C4
16509 T 2 17254 R 2 17310 R 4 19523 R 2
16657 R 2 17263 R 6 17315 RC3

Second. 16384 T 2 16440 R 2 16997 C4
12663 TR 2 16406 TR 2 16446 R 3 17050 R 3
12969 TR 2 16426 R 2 16448 R 2 17483 R 3
13205 R 2 16427 R 7 16462 C7 17548 T 7
13281 R 2 16428 R 2 16879 C8 19196 C7
15599 R 2 16433 R 2 16915 T 2 19318 C3
15737 T 3 16434 R 7 16939 TR 2 19547 R 4
15774 R 3 16435 R 7 16951 R 3 20276 R 4
15778 R 3 16436 R 3 16961 R 2 20416 C2
15995 C2 16437 R 2

Northern China

Primary: Monographs
15789 TRC2 17184 TR 3 17262 R 2 17720 R 4
15810 TRC2 17185 TR 3 17273 R 3 18313 TRC3
16513 T 8 17240 R 7 17277 R 3 19360 R 3
17141 T 5 17251 R 3 17713 R 3 22612 T 2
17158 T 3

Primary: Inclusions
12986 R 3 17239 R 7 17347 C2 17397 C7
16474 C7 17282 R 7 17382 C8 17400 C2
17166 T 3 17338 C8 17396 C7 19339 C7

Primary: Journal Articles
15770 R 4 17197 R 3 17264 R 8 17384 C7
16390 T 2 17199 R 3 17271 R 3 17392 C3
16476 C2 17200 R 3 17288 R 3 17393 C2
16519 T 2 17201 R 4 17292 R 2 17650 R 3
16758 C7 17202 R 4 17300 R 5 17705 R 3
16761 C2 17204 R 3 17309 R 2 17715 R 3
17054 R 3 17215 R 3 17319 RC3 17740 C7
17148 T 2 17218 R 3 17325 C7 17750 C3
17171 T 3 17221 R 2 17331 C3 17806 C3
17180 T 8 17223 R 3 17334 C2 19211 T 7
17181 TR 2 17224 R 3 17342 C2 20477 C2
17186 TR 2 17252 R 3 17375 C3 20617 TR 3
17187 TR 7

Second. 15565 C7 16692 R 8 17843 R 3
10319 T 2 15713 T 2 16759 C7 17876 R 3
11173 C2 15759 TR 3 16765 C7 17914 C7
12907 T 2 15817 C3 16926 T 2 18069 C3
12966 TR 3 15828 C3 16928 T 2 19172 C7
12979 R 2 15836 C3 17094 R 6 19200 C7
13441 C5 16016 C3 17123 C3 19337 C3
15372 TR 3 16101 TR 3 17731 R 7 19586 C3
15384 TR 4 16412 R 7 17736 R 3 19648 R 7
15408 R 2 16465 C7 17751 C3 20238 C3
15459 RC7 16563 TR 8 17802 C3 20505 C3
15502 C7 16582 R 2 17817 T 2 20947 R 3
15548 C3

24.5 Local Revenue and Expenditure

SECOND. 15518 c2 16494 c3 19990 c8
10301 RC2 15797 TRC7 16955 R 2 20062 R 2
12937 T 3 15945 TR 2 17004 c2 20075 c2
13046 TRC2 15974 TRC2 17360 c2 20694 c3
15380 TR 2 15976 TRC2 19702 R 2 20870 R 2
15382 TR 3 16487 c2 19713 c2 21063 c2
15409 R 2 16490 c3

24.6 Local Finance, Money, and Credit

地方金融、貨幣及信託制度

地方金融、貨幣及び信用制度

Geographic China Broadly Conceived

PRIMARY 13717 R 2 16424 R 2 17494 TRC1
13662 TR 4 16374 T 2 17448 TR 1 19217 TR 3
13692 TR 4 16423 R 2

SECOND. 13710 R 3 16375 T 2 17060 R 3
12409 RC7 15422 R 4 16938 TR 2

Mainland China

PRIMARY 17460 R 7 17486 R 8 19251 R 2
11760 R 2 17472 R 8 17492 R 7 19257 R 7
13260 R 2 17481 R 2 17507 c7 19273 R 2
17441 TR 2 17482 R 7 17519 c7 19280 R 2
17456 R 7 17485 R 2 17666 R 8

SECOND. 13670 TR 3 15978 RC7 18126 R 3
11743 R 2 13725 R 3 16026 c3 19073 R 8
12272 R 8 14153 c2 16103 TR 2 19140 c7
12511 c7 15060 R 2 16612 R 7 19155 c7
13029 R 2 15074 R 7 17129 c6 19240 R 2
13533 R 2 15537 c4 17192 TR 2 19284 RC2
13641 T 2 15882 c7 17848 R 2 19343 T 4
13668 TR 4 15971 R 4 17849 R 2 22805 R 2

The Eighteen Provinces

PRIMARY 17445 TR 1 17484 R 2 19282 R 2
17439 T 1 17461 R 7 19259 R 7 22463 R 1

SECOND. 15960 R 2 17098 R 2 19244 R 7
10682 T 2 15965 R 3 17236 R 2 19632 R 7
10831 R 3 16602 R 8 17301 R 7 21266 T 2
15446 R 3 16626 R 7 19071 R 7

North China Broadly Conceived

PRIMARY □

SECOND. 12998 R 2 15752 T 2 17307 R 7
19231 R 3 20578 T 2

Manchuria

PRIMARY 17229 R 4 17478 R 3 17490 R 3
16553 TR 7 17455 R 4 17483 R 3 17500 c3
16642 R 7 17471 R 5 17488 R 4 17501 c7
16645 R 7 17477 R 3 17489 R 4

SECOND. 16433 R 2 17056 R 6 19195 c7
12999 R 3 16546 TR 7 17085 R 2 20276 R 4
16120 R 2 16644 R 8 17265 R 3 20641 R 7
16384 T 2

Northern China

PRIMARY 17444 TR 8 17451 R 7 17469 R 7
15900 c7 17446 TR 3 17463 R 7 17470 R 7
16699 R 7 17449 R 3 17468 R 8 17497 c3
17186 TR 2 17450 R 4

SECOND. 16661 R 7 17221 R 2 17692 TR 3
12917 T 4 16703 R 8 17223 R 3 17845 R 8
12966 TR 3 16857 c7 17300 R 5 17860 R 7
15355 T 2 17046 R 2 17410 T 2 19211 T 7
15390 TR 3 17053 R 5 17418 R 8 19227 R 7
15952 TR 2 17054 R 3 17634 R 7 20631 R 3
16373 T 3

Northwestern China and Frontier Regions

PRIMARY 16681 R 2 16735 RC8 17417 R 2
17474 R 2

SECOND. 15393 R 2 16431 R 2 16445 R 7
16664 R 7 16716 R 8

South China Broadly Conceived

PRIMARY 17443 TR 2 19296 c3

SECOND. 16061 R 2 17038 TR 2 21426 TRC3

East Central China

PRIMARY 17431 T 3 17454 R 3 17466 R 3
15948 TR 3 17432 T 3 17457 R 3 17467 R 3
16947 R 2 17434 T 2 17458 R 8 17475 R 3
17033 TR 7 17438 T 2 17459 R 3 17476 R 3
17052 R 3 17440 TR 3 17462 R 7 17487 R 3
17074 R 6 17442 TR 5 17464 R 4 17491 R 3
17411 T 2 17452 R 3 17465 R 3 19426 R 3

SECOND. 16593 R 7 17030 TR 4 19075 R 2
11746 R 2 16624 R 7 17037 TR 3 19508 R 3
11747 R 2 16694 R 8 17048 R 3 22589 T 2
12955 TR 3 16908 T 2 17183 TR 2 22764 c3
12977 R 3 17029 TR 2

Central Yangtze Provinces

PRIMARY 15863 T 2 16405 TR 3 17498 c7
17502 c7

SECOND. 15469 TRC2 16393 T 2 17132 T 3
12942 T 3 15998 c7 16639 R 7

Southwestern China

PRIMARY 17088 R 3 17473 R 3 17480 R 2
16675 R 7 17437 T 3 17479 R 7

SECOND. 16441 R 3 16619 R 8 17086 R 7
10767 R 2 16444 R 3 16722 R 7 17279 R 4
16083 c2 16511 T 7 16913 T 2 17663 R 7
16425 R 7 16601 R 7 17063 R 3 22542 T 2

Southeastern China

PRIMARY 17408 T 3 17453 R 3 19205 T 3
16421 R 3 17436 T 3 18607 R 3

SECOND. 12954 TR 3 16613 R 7 16630 R 8
19209 T 3 19962 TR 7

Taiwan Only

PRIMARY 17505 c1 17618 c5 20268 c6
17127 c2 17518 c7 17900 c1

SECOND. 15515 c8 16790 c8 16873 c7
11232 T 2 15533 c7 16797 c7 16887 c8
13083 c2 16495 c2 16858 c2 20072 c7
13112 c2 16729 RC2 16872 c7 20074 c2
15504 c8 16747 RC2

Hong Kong and Macau Only

PRIMARY 16492 c2 17499 c3 17513 c3
11031 R 2 17124 c2 17503 c3 17514 c1
13046 TRC2 17429 c3 17504 c1 17515 c3
13767 RC3 17433 T 7 17506 c3 17516 c7
15382 TR 3 17435 T 3 17508 c1 17517 c3
16451 RC3 17447 TR 3 17509 c3 17683 c8
16463 c2 17493 TRC1 17510 c3 19309 c2
16483 c5 17495 RC3 17511 c1 19553 R 3
16489 c3 17496 c3 17512 c3

SECOND. 15981 RC3 16816 c2 17379 c2
13057 c3 16455 RC2 16893 c7 17426 c3
15455 TRC7 16456 TRC7 17002 c2 17963 c2
15467 TRC3 16472 c3 17116 c8 19207 T 3
15574 c8 16473 c2 17126 c3 19990 c8
15797 TRC7 16490 c3 17323 TRC3 20272 c7
15926 T 7 16500 c2 17336 c3 20681 c2
15945 TR 2 16501 c2 17367 c3 22724 RC2

25 Feuds, Banditry, and Local Paramilitary Units

械鬥、盜賊及地方武力

械鬥、匪賊行為及び地方の保安組織

Geographic China Broadly Conceived

PRIMARY 13864 T 2 16104 TR 7 18540 TR 2
10287 TR 2 13902 R 2 16376 T 2 18794 TRC2
10626 T 2 13916 R 2 17531 T 1 18919 T 1
13824 T 2 13966 R 2 17572 R 3 21374 R 3
13841 T 4 13997 RC2 18511 T 2 21434 c2
13844 T 1 15191 RC2 18534 TR 2 22594 T 2
13855 T 2

SECOND. 10853 TRC2 18388 T 2 19982 TRC8
10010 T 2 11328 R 1 18418 T 1 20615 TR 2
10032 T 2 11411 RC1 18442 T 4 21269 T 2
10060 T 2 11657 T 4 18489 T 1 21276 T 2
10096 R 2 12624 TR 2 18492 T 2 21279 T 2
10100 R 2 12901 T 2 18494 T 2 21302 T 2
10106 R 2 12940 T 1 18527 T 2 21306 TR 2
10107 R 2 13811 T 2 18547 TR 2 21337 TR 2
10108 R 2 14166 T 1 18809 RC2 21347 TR 2
10114 TRC2 15174 TRC2 18871 T 2 21366 R 2
10276 T 2 15175 RC2 18947 T 2 21425 TRC5
10300 TRC2 16374 T 2 18971 TR 2 21712 T 2
10329 T 2 16375 T 2 19475 TR 4 21853 TRC2
10526 T 2 16423 R 2 19490 R 2 22586 T 3
10618 T 1 16424 R 2 19503 R 2 22593 T 2
10700 TR 2 17696 R 3 19534 R 2 22618 T 2
10803 R 2 18306 R 2 19978 TRC2 22694 R 3

Mainland China

PRIMARY 14020 RC2 17588 c8 18660 R 2
10749 R 2 14033 c2 17590 c3 18717 R 2
10766 R 2 15128 T 4 17591 c1 18746 R 2
10769 R 2 15209 c7 17594 c7 18791 TRC7
10967 c2 15238 c2 17596 c2 18825 RC2
11244 T 2 15434 R 7 17597 c2 18991 TR 4
12783 TRC2 15483 c7 17599 c1 19380 c2
13815 T 2 15495 c2 17601 c2 19447 R 7
13853 T 4 15524 c7 17603 c1 20518 c2
13865 T 2 16123 R 2 17604 c1 21259 T 2
13899 R 2 16145 c7 17605 c1 21320 TR 2
13926 R 7 17550 T 2 18120 R 2 21381 R 1
13942 R 2 17574 R 2 18304 R 2 22152 R 8
13969 R 2 17575 R 2 18452 T 2 22554 T 1
13977 R 2 17584 RC1 18454 T 2 22591 T 1
13982 R 1 17585 RC2 18589 R 8 22595 T 5
13996 TRC2 17586 RC2 18598 R 2 22655 TR 3
14001 RC1 17587 c1 18608 R 2 22721 R 2
14012 RC2

SECONDARY: MONOGRAPHS
10071 TR 2 13858 T 2 15570 c2 19132 c7
10101 R 2 13868 T 2 15977 RC7 19184 c8
10123 RC2 13882 TR 2 16013 c7 19240 R 2
10214 TRC2 13896 R 2 16046 c2 19390 c2
10631 T 2 13909 R 2 18114 R 2 19551 R 2
10677 T 2 13927 R 2 18126 R 3 19597 c2
10695 TR 2 13951 R 2 18134 R 2 19638 R 7
10697 TR 2 13965 R 2 18154 R 2 19644 R 2
10706 TR 2 13991 RC1 18309 R 3 20137 T 2
10712 TR 2 14002 RC2 18526 T 2 20182 TR 2
10715 TR 2 14006 RC2 18535 TR 1 20204 R 2
10718 TR 2 14014 RC1 18551 TR 2 20526 c2
10782 R 1 14018 TRC2 18557 TR 2 21265 T 2
10811 R 1 14037 c2 18567 TR 2 21307 TR 2
10819 R 2 14040 c1 18585 R 2 21308 TR 2
10888 TRC2 14055 c1 18588 R 2 21311 TR 2
11036 TRC7 14093 T 2 18617 R 2 21345 TR 2
11053 RC2 14139 c2 18655 R 2 21373 R 1
11132 c2 14164 T 2 18674 R 2 21400 RC2
11160 c2 14278 RC2 18685 R 2 21414 RC2
11689 TR 2 14329 c2 18759 R 2 21420 TRC2
11872 RC2 14733 R 2 18767 R 2 22203 RC2
12230 TR 2 14754 R 2 18768 R 2 22217 RC2
12412 RC7 15052 TR 2 18783 R 2 22375 c2
13328 c2 15235 c2 18842 c2 22556 T 2
13489 TR 3 15506 c2 18853 T 2 22669 TR 1
13807 T 1 15553 c2 18862 T 2 22710 R 2
13847 T 1

26 Local Social Stratification and Mobility

地方社會之階層與流動

地方の社会階層及びその流動性

Second. 15403 R 8 17309 R 2 19825 R 3
13964 R 7 15459 RC7 17522 T 7 20140 T 3
13974 R 2 15502 C7 17628 T 3 20762 T 3
14881 C3 15534 C7 17855 R 3 20938 R 3
15021 C3 15754 T 2 17856 R 3 21273 T 2
15338 T 7 15900 C7 19117 C8 21330 TR 7
15397 R 7 15903 C7 19153 C8 22753 C3

Northwestern China and Frontier Regions

Primary □

Second. 15673 TR 7 16399 T 7 19080 RC7
19233 R 7

South China Broadly Conceived

Primary □

Second. 15721 T 2 15726 T 2 20821 TR 2
22601 T 2

East Central China

Primary 15944 TR 3 17943 R 3 19703 R 3
15143 R 3 17612 R 3 18392 T 2 20262 R 2
15346 T 2 17784 C7 19268 R 3

Second. 15584 T 2 17694 TR 3 20103 R 3
15354 T 2 16416 R 3 17812 T 7 21210 R 7
15374 TR 8 16466 C7 18013 T 2 21216 R 7
15493 C7 16631 R 7 19116 C8 21433 C2

Central Yangtze Provinces

Primary 16629 R 7 17630 TR 4 18703 R 2

Second. 15523 C7 17643 C3 20379 T 4
15481 C2 16636 R 7 20199 R 7

Southwestern China

Primary 16425 R 7 17663 R 7 19270 R 2
15436 R 6 17613 R 7 17854 R 2 19729 R 6
15581 T 2 17624 C2 17885 R 3 20583 T 2
16083 C2

Second. 15308 T 5 16077 C2 20573 T 7
13038 R 2 15424 R 7 16118 R 2 22517 T 2
14750 R 2

Southeastern China

Primary 17589 C2 18518 T 2 19348 T 3
15456 RC7 17607 T 2 18734 R 2 19975 TRC7
15476 RC8 17615 RC2 18742 R 2 21575 C3
15630 T 3

Second. 15447 R 3 15984 C7 19840 R 2
14970 C3 15448 R 3 15987 C7 19962 TR 7
15353 T 2 15500 C7 16552 TR 2 20006 TR 8
15364 T 3 15572 C2 16712 R 7 20524 C3
15418 R 8 15780 R 3 17913 C2 21393 RC2
15419 R 6 15782 R 3 18488 T 5 22545 T 4

Taiwan Only

Primary 17610 T 8 17622 C3 20344 C3
15472 RC2 17616 C8 17743 C2 20368 C2
15504 C8 17618 C5 17984 RC2 20421 C2
16771 C8 17619 C2 18004 C7 21030 C7
16902 C7 17621 C3 19910 C3 21577 C3

Second. 16007 C3 17961 C2 20326 C4
15505 C8 16134 C8 19737 C8 20360 C3
15530 C7 16865 C7 19939 C2 20425 C3
15615 C2 17675 C2 20074 C2 21583 C8
15708 C2

Hong Kong and Macau Only

Primary 15876 C3 17623 C2 19953 C3
10301 RC2 16496 C2 17963 C2 19972 TRC7
14597 T 2 17608 T 3 17966 C2 20522 C3
15489 C3 17617 C3 17985 RC2

Second. 16456 TRC7 19898 RC3 20663 RC3
15455 TRC7 16486 C3 19918 C3 21197 RC2
15574 C8 16893 C7 19933 C3 21598 C3
15981 RC3 16991 C4 19946 C2 21827 TRC7
16044 C3 19710 TRC3 20359 C3 22758 C3

26.1 The Local Elite

地方領導階層

地方エリート階層

Geographic China Broadly Conceived

Primary 20994 TRC5

Second. 14215 TR 2 16104 TR 7 16217 T 7
10117 TRC2 14676 TR 3 16128 TRC2

Mainland China

Primary 16053 TR 2 17638 C2 17647 C7
14363 C2 16071 C2 17640 C8 19100 C7
15488 C7 16612 R 7 17641 C3 21308 TR 2
16020 C7 17492 R 7 17642 C2 22303 C1
16028 C2 17588 C8 17644 C2

Second. 11493 C2 16018 C2 18940 T 1
10166 C2 12405 TRC2 16070 C2 18945 T 2
10512 T 2 14093 T 2 16148 C5 18951 TR 2
10616 T 2 14160 T 2 16835 C7 19021 R 2
10851 RC2 14177 T 2 17679 C7 19131 C7
10856 RC2 15507 C7 17996 C2 19142 C7
10872 TRC2 15560 C4 18014 T 7 19649 R 7
11002 C2 15762 TR 3 18126 R 3 22291 C2
11094 C2 15966 R 3 18589 R 8 23046 C1
11336 R 2 15992 C7 18915 T 2

The Eighteen Provinces

Primary 15947 TR 2 17143 T 3 20450 R 2
10525 T 2 15960 R 2 17631 TR 8 21305 TR 4
15931 T 4 16049 T 2

Second. 14207 T 2 16369 T 2 17542 T 8
11681 T 2 14300 C3 16478 C2 18070 C4
13925 R 2 14301 C3 16602 R 8 18859 T 2
14124 R 7 15733 T 2 17541 T 7 21655 T 5
14158 T 2

North China Broadly Conceived

Primary 18669 R 7

Second. 15324 T 2 18390 T 2 20578 T 2
10679 T 2 17846 R 7 18509 T 2

Manchuria

Primary 19111 C8

Second. 16120 R 2 16546 TR 7 17383 C3

Northern China

Primary 15626 T 2 17634 R 7 18330 C3
11080 C3 16080 C3 17636 C3 18357 C3
15014 C3 16201 T 6 17639 C7 19112 C8
15304 C3 17625 T 3 17645 C2 19161 C7
15373 TR 3 17627 T 2 17830 R 7 22632 T 3
15395 R 3 17628 T 3

Second. 15372 TR 3 17526 T 8 19211 T 7
10652 T 3 15389 TR 3 17620 C7 19619 R 7
10783 R 2 15390 TR 3 17802 C3 20436 R 3
12741 R 3 15394 R 2 17953 TRC3 20458 R 3
14816 C3 15406 R 8 18329 C3 20497 C2
14877 C3 16059 R 8 18355 C3 20557 T 3
14888 C6 16069 C3 18362 C3 20579 T 3
14938 C3 16220 T 2 18643 R 8 20758 T 3
14946 C7 16685 R 7 18868 T 2 21344 TR 2
14962 C2 16850 C7 19200 C7 21431 C2
15320 T 3

Northwestern China and Frontier Regions

Primary 14771 R 7 16735 RC8 16912 T 2

Second. 15350 T 2 15545 C8 16859 C8
18749 R 2

South China Broadly Conceived

Primary 18875 T 2

Second. 15361 T 2 15721 T 2 16378 T 2
16410 TR 8 21426 TRC3

East Central China

Primary 15357 T 3 16094 T 2 17637 C3
14866 C3 15943 TR 3 17606 C7 17646 C2
15318 T 3 15944 TR 3

Second. 15354 T 2 16075 C3 18865 T 2
14161 T 2 15388 TR 3 16394 T 2 20043 T 8
14739 R 3 15430 R 3 16559 TR 2 20262 R 2
14819 C3 15632 TR 3 16709 R 8 21258 T 3
14960 C3 15924 T 2 16714 R 7 21707 T 3
15143 R 3 15929 T 3 16718 R 8 22589 T 2
15254 C3 15953 TR 3 17411 T 2 22696 R 3
15291 C3

Central Yangtze Provinces

Primary 17630 TR 4 17643 C3 18751 R 7

Second. 19460 R 8 19726 TR 7 20210 R 2

Southwestern China

Primary 16722 R 7 17866 R 3 21315 TR 2
15916 C7 17613 R 7 17889 R 3 21316 TR 2
15957 R 2 17632 R 3 21312 TR 4 21369 R 2
16675 R 7 17633 R 3

Second. 17664 R 8 18491 T 2 20550 T 3
14839 C2 17854 R 2 18922 T 2 21313 TR 2
15629 T 2 17867 R 3 20475 RC4 22570 T 3

Southeastern China

Primary 15923 T 3 17657 T 3 19675 C8
14970 C3 16792 C7 18490 T 2 20998 C2
15572 C2 17547 T 2

Second. 16391 T 2 17560 TR 2 19449 R 2
15317 T 2 16613 R 7 17615 RC2 19454 R 7
15456 RC7 16888 C8 18438 T 2 20093 T 3
15485 C2 17533 T 7 18519 T 2 20524 C3
15735 T 2 17553 T 7 19165 C8 21168 T 3
16389 T 2 17559 TR 2 19197 C8

Taiwan Only

Primary 16746 RC8 16902 C7 17544 T 2
17610 T 8

Second. 16133 C8 16771 C8 16872 C7
10675 T 2 16347 C2 16811 C8 17822 T 2
15351 T 2 16725 RC8 16851 C7 19679 C7

Hong Kong and Macau Only

Primary 15974 TRC2 17626 T 4 19970 TRC7
14596 T 8 15981 RC3 17629 T 3 19985 TRC7
15925 T 7 15989 C7 17635 RC3 19986 TRC8
15926 T 7 16044 C3 19969 TRC8 22733 TRC3
15940 TR 3

Second. 14597 T 2 15913 C3 16333 RC8
22724 RC2

26.2 Businessmen

商人及市民　商人及び市民

Geographic China Broadly Conceived

Primary 16068 RC2 19217 TR 3

Second. 12600 T 3 13841 T 4 13966 R 2
19490 R 2 20994 TRC5

Mainland China

Primary 16070 C2 17661 TR 2 18126 R 3

Second. 17249 R 7 18327 C2 19351 T 4
12475 C2 17314 RC2 18571 TR 2 19427 R 3
14093 T 2 17316 RC2 19248 R 4 22423 TR 7
14417 C3 17370 C2

The Eighteen Provinces

Primary 15864 TR 2 17173 T 2

Second. 10546 T 3 15511 C2 15960 R 2
17144 T 2 17175 T 2

NORTH CHINA BROADLY CONCEIVED

PRIMARY 17658 T 4 19231 R 3
SECOND. 15324 T 2 16317 R 2

MANCHURIA

PRIMARY 17548 T 7
SECOND. 15743 T 3 17286 R 3 19538 R 2
10340 TR 2 16442 R 2 17294 R 4

NORTHERN CHINA

PRIMARY 17141 T 5 17650 R 3 17831 R 3
15355 T 2 17158 T 3 17652 T 3 18032 R 3
17020 T 3 17186 TR 2 17659 C3 20631 R 3
17054 R 3 17446 TR 3 17690 TR 3
SECOND. 17187 TR 7 17715 R 3 19360 R 3
12993 R 2 17251 R 3 17876 R 3 20579 T 3
15372 TR 3 17288 R 3 17877 R 3 20775 T 7
15390 TR 3 17414 R 4 18036 R 3 22457 R 3
15417 R 3 17611 R 3 19211 T 7

NORTHWESTERN CHINA AND FRONTIER REGIONS

PRIMARY 16672 R 7
SECOND. 16299 R 7 20601 T 2

SOUTH CHINA BROADLY CONCEIVED

PRIMARY 16092 T 4
SECOND. 15722 T 2 16910 T 4 16979 R 2
17167 T 3 21384 R 2

EAST CENTRAL CHINA

PRIMARY 17432 T 3 17651 R 3 17660 C3
16075 C3 17459 R 3 17653 C3 18013 T 2
16292 R 3 17646 C2 17654 C3 19258 R 3
17176 T 2 17648 RC3 17656 C3 19511 R 3
17431 T 3 17649 T 5
SECOND. 15953 TR 3 17434 T 2 20262 R 2
12955 TR 3 16108 TR 3 17863 R 3 20644 R 3
15143 R 3 16624 R 7 18354 C3 21258 T 3
15929 T 3 17155 T 3 19498 R 3 22589 T 2
15943 TR 3 17306 R 2 19507 R 3 22755 C3
15944 TR 3

CENTRAL YANGTZE PROVINCES

☐

SOUTHWESTERN CHINA

PRIMARY 17071 R 7 17865 R 3 19261 R 3
17063 R 3 17864 R 3 17890 R 3 21314 TR 4
SECOND. 15633 TR 3 16913 T 2 19742 T 2
15308 T 5 16083 C2 17888 R 3 21315 TR 2

SOUTHEASTERN CHINA

PRIMARY 17559 TR 2 18490 T 2 19437 T 3
16945 R 2 17657 T 3 19429 T 3 21393 RC2
17408 T 3 17820 T 3
SECOND. 12954 TR 3 16187 T 3 19434 T 3
10292 TR 4 15344 T 3 16218 T 2 19436 T 3
11683 TR 2 15359 T 2 18519 T 2 19716 T 4

TAIWAN ONLY

PRIMARY ☐
SECOND. 13083 C2 16347 C2 19292 C3

HONG KONG AND MACAU ONLY

PRIMARY 15901 C3 17629 T 3 20272 C7
15891 C3 17116 C8 17655 C3 21257 T 3
SECOND. 16135 C3 17608 T 3 19693 T 3
15926 T 7 16991 C4 17617 C3 22724 RC2
15973 TRC2 17516 C7 19341 C3

26.3 PEASANTS

農民 農民

GEOGRAPHIC CHINA BROADLY CONCEIVED

PRIMARY ☐
SECOND. 15311 T 2 16104 TR 7 18534 TR 2
15191 RC2 15877 C8 16522 T 2 19490 R 2

MAINLAND CHINA

PRIMARY 15993 C7 17460 R 7 17905 C7
15192 RC2 16013 C7 17492 R 7 18791 TRC7
15232 C7 16031 C7 17666 R 8 18980 TR 2
15488 C7 16053 TR 2 17673 C7 19100 C7
15494 C7 16072 C7 17674 C7 19110 C8
15528 C7 16145 C7 17678 C7 19140 C7
15558 C7 16309 R 2 17679 C7 19154 C8
15799 RC2 16612 R 7 17682 C7 19167 C7
15978 RC7 16693 R 7 17684 C7 19177 C8
15991 C7 16847 C7 17769 R 7 19184 C8
15992 C7 17120 C7 17895 RC2 20080 C7
SECOND. 15559 C7 16860 C7 19099 C8
10461 C2 15567 C7 16877 C7 19138 C7
12272 R 8 15886 C7 16948 R 2 19142 C7
13260 R 2 15977 RC7 17456 R 7 19144 C7
13970 R 2 15990 C7 17481 R 2 19151 C7
14153 C2 15996 C7 17486 R 8 19156 C7
15297 C2 15999 C7 17586 RC2 19455 R 8
15434 R 7 16001 C7 17588 C8 19649 R 7
15466 RC2 16011 C7 17638 C2 19850 R 8
15506 C2 16046 C2 17640 C8 19922 C7
15507 C7 16071 C2 18289 C7 20079 C7
15508 C2 16516 T 7 18589 R 8 20558 T 2
15512 C2 16637 R 7 18746 R 2 22423 TR 7
15524 C7 16690 R 8 19077 RC7 22452 R 2
15549 C7 16835 C7 19095 C7 22767 C2

THE EIGHTEEN PROVINCES

PRIMARY 15543 C2 16890 C7 19632 R 7
15478 C2 16591 R 7 18437 T 2
SECOND. 15501 C2 16602 R 8 17741 C2
10175 C2 15531 C2 16894 C2 20503 C2
13925 R 2 16369 T 2 17541 T 7 20699 C2
14124 R 7 16478 C2

NORTH CHINA BROADLY CONCEIVED

PRIMARY 17846 R 7
SECOND. 17028 T 5 18390 T 2 18669 R 7
16659 R 7 17423 R 7 18622 R 2 18690 R 7

MANCHURIA

PRIMARY 16553 TR 7 16645 R 7 20641 R 7
16065 R 2 16642 R 7 17881 R 8
SECOND. 15686 R 2 16562 TR 2 17795 C7
10340 TR 2 16120 R 2 16657 R 2 17801 C8
10356 R 2 16509 T 2 16801 C8 19195 C7
15661 T 8 16546 TR 7 17065 R 7

NORTHERN CHINA

PRIMARY 16538 T 8 16692 R 8 17830 R 7
13891 R 2 16573 R 7 17620 C7 17832 R 8
14996 C7 16632 R 8 17639 C7 17845 R 8
15378 TR 7 16661 R 7 17672 C7 19093 C7
15525 C7 16671 R 2 17677 C7 19619 R 7
16311 R 8 16673 R 8 17685 C7 20701 C7
16513 T 8 16685 R 7
SECOND. 16696 R 8 17645 C2 19117 C8
15510 C7 16699 R 7 17790 C8 19147 C8
15516 C7 16706 R 8 17793 C8 19161 C7
15880 C8 16759 C7 17860 R 7 19172 C7
15894 C7 16850 C7 17871 R 7 19451 R 7
16059 R 8 16881 C7 17896 RC7 19456 R 2
16220 T 2 17057 R 7 17927 T 2 19633 R 7
16322 R 8 17262 R 2 18016 T 2 19664 C8
16565 R 7 17418 R 8 18643 R 8 21344 TR 2
16578 R 2 17627 T 2 19114 C8

NORTHWESTERN CHINA AND FRONTIER REGIONS

PRIMARY 15545 C8 16672 R 7 20198 R 8
15453 RC8 16299 R 7 16735 RC8 22430 TR 8
15544 C8 16399 T 7
SECOND. 16445 R 7 16859 C8 19672 C8
15391 TR 2 16628 R 2 18749 R 2 19889 RC8
15421 R 8 16633 R 2 19080 RC7 22453 R 8
16321 R 8 16803 C7 19661 C7 22481 RC8
16325 R 8 16804 C8

SOUTH CHINA BROADLY CONCEIVED

PRIMARY ☐
SECOND. 15775 R 2 16410 TR 8 16855 C8
18455 T 2

EAST CENTRAL CHINA

PRIMARY 15517 C8 17606 C7 17680 C7
15405 R 7 16624 R 7 17662 T 7 17825 R 7
15426 R 7 16724 RC8 17667 R 7 19746 T 8
15493 C7 17274 R 2 17670 C7
SECOND. 16461 C7 16709 R 8 17458 R 8
11746 R 2 16468 C7 16714 R 7 17816 T 7
15552 C2 16638 R 2 16721 R 8 17868 R 7
15772 R 2 16662 R 7 17250 R 7 19116 C8
16094 T 2 16666 R 7 17326 C2 20629 R 8
16394 T 2 16694 R 8 17411 T 2

CENTRAL YANGTZE PROVINCES

PRIMARY 16629 R 7 16636 R 7 16882 C7
19460 R 8 20241 C8
SECOND. 16763 C2 17580 RC2 18667 R 7
16526 T 2 16842 C7 18305 R 7 20210 R 2
16639 R 7 17561 TR 2

SOUTHWESTERN CHINA

PRIMARY 16601 R 7 17663 R 7 17841 R 7
15957 R 2 16675 R 7 17664 R 8 18035 R 6
16083 C2 16707 R 8 17668 R 2 19085 RC7
16598 R 7 17624 C2 17840 R 7
SECOND. 16618 R 8 17045 R 7 17613 R 7
16527 T 8 16653 R 2 17479 R 7 17854 R 2
16590 R 8 16787 C2

SOUTHEASTERN CHINA

PRIMARY 17559 TR 2 17671 C7 19449 R 2
16613 R 7 17665 R 7 19197 C8 19454 R 7
SECOND. 16712 R 7 16942 TR 2 18611 R 2
14922 C2 16736 RC7 17329 C2 19148 C7
15358 T 8 16792 C7 17560 TR 2 19165 C8
16507 T 2 16888 C8 17913 C2 20185 R 2
16630 R 8

TAIWAN ONLY

PRIMARY 16869 C7 16902 C7 17681 C8
15505 C8 16872 C7 17669 RC8 17897 RC8
16746 RC8 16886 C7 17675 C2 19679 C7
16834 C8 16899 C8 17676 C8
SECOND. 16728 TRC7 16851 C7 17424 RC8
13083 C2 16733 TRC8 16852 C8 17616 C8
15491 C7 16771 C8 16866 C8 17822 T 2
15697 TRC2 16794 C8 16867 C7 17910 C7
15887 C8 16797 C7 16868 C8 19079 RC8
16554 TR 7 16820 C7 16871 C7 20072 C7
16725 RC8 16821 C7 16873 C7 21017 C7

HONG KONG AND MACAU ONLY

PRIMARY 15573 C8 16813 C8 16893 C7
17683 C8 17971 C8
SECOND. 15464 TRC8 16456 TRC7 16815 C7
13048 RC2 15814 C7 16805 C8 19970 TRC7
14597 T 2

26.4 Workers

劳工　劳働者

Geographic China Broadly Conceived

Primary 16068 RC2 17691 TR 2 17696 R 3 19490 R 2

Second. 13966 R 2 15191 RC2 18534 TR 2 19524 R 3

Mainland China

Primary 15192 RC2 15915 C2 17712 R 3
10461 C2 15506 C2 17311 RC2 17717 R 3
14527 C4 15560 C4 17695 R 3 21035 C2

Second. 15466 RC2 17249 R 7 19216 TR 2
13260 R 2 15482 C2 17289 R 2 19291 C2
14478 R 3 15508 C2 17316 RC2 19305 C3
14809 RC2 15537 C4 17389 C4 19322 C1
15303 C2 15997 C4 17586 RC2 20434 R 2

The Eighteen Provinces

Primary 17711 R 3 17749 C2 17869 R 2
15478 C2 17741 C2 17842 R 2 20642 R 2
16944 R 3 17748 C3 17861 R 3

Second. 15543 C2 17173 T 2 20503 C2
10175 C2 15965 R 3 17995 C2 20699 C2
15501 C2 16894 C2 19564 R 2 21655 T 5
15531 C2 17143 T 3

North China Broadly Conceived

Primary 16063 R 2

Second. 10936 C3

Manchuria

Primary 17688 T 2 17723 R 3 19505 R 3
16065 R 2 17689 T 7 19293 C3 19523 R 2
17383 C3 17716 R 5 19336 C2

Second. 17230 R 3 17298 R 2 17340 C7
15532 C4 17244 R 7 17302 R 2 17838 R 2
15569 C3 17263 R 6 17305 R 2 17904 C3
16397 T 5 17286 R 3 17310 R 4 19318 C3
16974 R 4 17294 R 4 17327 C2 19538 R 2

Northern China

Primary 17692 TR 3 17721 R 7 17751 C3
17251 R 3 17697 R 3 17727 R 3 17824 TR 3
17273 R 3 17702 R 3 17730 R 3 17828 R 3
17331 C3 17705 R 3 17731 R 7 17876 R 3
17497 C3 17713 R 3 17736 R 3 17877 R 3
17687 T 3 17715 R 3 17740 C7 17914 C7
17690 TR 3 17720 R 4 17750 C3 20216 R 3

Second. 17141 T 5 17262 R 2 18313 TRC3
11173 C2 17184 TR 3 17300 R 5 19339 C7
14947 C3 17185 TR 3 17375 C3 19492 R 3
15538 C2 17187 TR 7 17393 C2 19497 R 3
15810 TRC2 17199 R 3 17611 R 3 19579 R 2
15866 R 3 17215 R 3 17802 C3 19586 C3
15868 R 3 17218 R 3 17806 C3 20477 C2
16403 TR 2 17221 R 2 17886 R 3 20497 C2
17054 R 3

Northwestern China and Frontier Regions

Primary 17235 R 5

Second. 15302 C3 20679 C3

South China Broadly Conceived

Primary □

Second. 16979 R 2 19006 R 4

East Central China

Primary 17274 R 2 17699 R 3 17709 R 3
15871 R 3 17326 C2 17701 R 3 17710 R 3
15961 R 3 17358 C3 17703 R 3 17714 R 3
16417 R 3 17693 TR 3 17704 R 3 17719 R 3
17176 T 2 17694 TR 3 17706 R 3 17722 R 3
17193 TR 3 17698 R 3 17707 R 3 17724 R 3
17725 R 3 17827 R 3 17880 R 3 19555 R 3
17726 R 3 17833 R 3 17887 R 3 19556 R 3
17728 R 3 17834 R 3 18410 T 3 19680 C3
17732 R 3 17835 R 3 19267 R 3 20195 R 3
17733 R 3 17836 R 3 19269 R 3 20392 R 3
17734 R 3 17839 R 3 19295 C3 20394 R 3
17735 R 3 17863 R 3 19486 R 3 20862 R 3
17737 R 3 17868 R 7 19509 R 3 20915 R 3
17747 C3 17870 R 3 19510 R 3 20919 R 3
17805 C3 17874 R 3 19511 R 3

Second. 15950 TR 3 17242 R 3 19498 R 3
13150 TR 5 16075 C3 17250 R 7 19507 R 3
13224 R 4 16458 C2 17275 R 3 19533 R 3
14819 C3 16947 R 2 17306 R 2 19566 R 3
14960 C3 17213 R 2 17332 C2 19605 C3
15143 R 3 17216 R 3 17372 C3 20644 R 3
15254 C3 17217 R 3 17380 C3 20850 R 3
15430 R 3 17219 R 3 19220 TR 4 20951 R 3
15556 C3 17220 R 2 19268 R 3 21037 C3
15578 C3 17232 R 3 19308 C3 22164 R 3
15632 TR 3

Central Yangtze Provinces

Primary 17746 C5 18582 R 2 19578 R 7

Second. 15445 R 3 17205 R 3 17580 RC2 17630 TR 4

Southwestern China

Primary 17729 R 3 17888 R 3 22460 R 7
15629 T 2 17864 R 3 20217 R 3

Second. 15916 C7 16166 T 2 17178 T 8 19270 R 2

Southeastern China

Primary 17686 T 3 17738 C3 19506 R 3
17268 R 3 17700 R 3 19499 R 3 19557 R 4

Second. 15305 T 2 17237 R 2 18611 R 2
10278 T 2 15344 T 3 17270 R 4 18618 R 3
10840 R 3 15651 C4 17284 R 7 19495 R 3
11683 TR 2 16480 C2 17329 C2 20185 R 2
14922 C2

Taiwan Only

Primary 17743 C2 17752 C2 20673 C2

Second. 15437 R 2

Hong Kong and Macau Only

Primary 17718 R 2 17745 C2 19306 C2
16471 C2 17739 C3 18060 C2 19325 C3
16487 C2 17742 C3 19297 C3 21574 C3
17708 R 4 17744 C4

Second. 16152 C3 17357 C2 18820 TRC3
15409 R 2 16451 RC3 17361 C7 19341 C3
15518 C2 16469 C3 17367 C3 19593 C2
15891 C3 16991 C4 17593 C3 20622 TR 2
15913 C3 17318 RC3 17994 C2 20694 C3
16135 C3 17336 C3

27 Elementary and Vocational Education

初等教育及職業補習教育

初等教育及び補習教育

Geographic China Broadly Conceived

Primary □

Second. 12328 R 7 20418 T 1 21342 TR 2
12310 R 8 20200 R 2 21279 T 2

Mainland China

Primary 17754 TR 1 17762 R 1 17770 R 1
14526 C3 17755 TR 2 17763 R 2 17771 R 1
14556 T 2 17757 TR 4 17764 R 2 17777 C2
14840 C2 17758 TR 2 17766 R 2 17778 C7
15482 C2 17759 R 2 17768 R 1 17779 C2
17753 T 1 17760 R 7 17769 R 7 17781 C1
17782 C2 17804 C1 19641 R 8 19671 C7
17785 C1 17807 C2 19655 RC2 20157 T 1
17792 C2 17809 C2 19658 RC2 20221 R 2
17796 C2 19597 C2 19662 C2 20407 C2
17803 C2 19638 R 7 19668 C5

Second. 14429 R 8 17311 RC2 19644 R 2
10086 TR 2 14496 R 5 17313 RC2 19645 R 1
11724 R 2 14535 C4 17395 C2 19649 R 7
12269 R 8 14957 C2 18003 C2 19667 C3
12403 RC7 15292 C2 18021 TR 4 19673 C2
12427 C7 15508 C2 19021 R 2 19678 C1
12429 C7 16034 C4 19257 R 7 20258 T 2
12485 C2 16046 C2 19615 TR 2 21417 TRC2
12528 C2 17245 R 5 19616 TR 1 22296 C2
13415 C4 17278 R 5 19643 R 2 22423 TR 7

The Eighteen Provinces

Primary 17756 TR 7 17808 C3 19646 R 2
15035 C3 17767 R 2 19631 R 2

Second. 15400 R 8 17308 R 2 19963 TR 2
13212 R 2 15470 RC7 17631 TR 8 20699 C2
14238 R 3 15478 C2 17748 C3 21122 C2
14474 R 3 16626 R 7 19001 R 2 21365 R 3
14590 T 2 17287 R 2 19632 R 7 21816 R 2

North China Broadly Conceived

Primary 16732 RC2 17797 C3

Second. 13976 R 2

Manchuria

Primary 17795 C7 17801 C8 20416 C2
17789 C8 17800 C2 20410 C7

Second. 21118 C4

Northern China

Primary 15415 R 8 17793 C8 19620 R 2
15360 T 7 17773 RC7 17802 C3 19633 R 7
15399 R 7 17780 C3 17806 C3 19648 R 7
15408 R 2 17790 C8 19619 R 7 21273 T 2
15414 R 8

Second. 15557 C7 17444 TR 8 20845 R 7
15338 T 7 15596 R 7 17721 R 7 20930 R 3
15378 TR 7 16056 R 8 17871 R 7 20946 R 7
15384 TR 4 16101 TR 3 17891 R 7 20947 R 3
15403 R 8 16760 C8 20218 R 3 20949 R 7
15406 R 8 16784 C7 20843 R 7 21330 TR 7
15410 R 8 17382 C8 20844 R 2

Northwestern China and Frontier Regions

Primary 15544 C8 17772 RC7

Second. 15545 C8 19233 R 7 20380 T 7

South China Broadly Conceived

Primary □

Second. 21384 R 2

East Central China

Primary 16414 R 8 17765 R 3 17805 C3
15374 TR 8 17358 C3 17783 C2 22755 C3
15430 R 3 17670 C7 17784 C7

Second. 15577 C7 16624 R 7 20043 T 8
15405 R 7 15771 R 7 16662 R 7 20195 R 3
15426 R 7 15961 R 3 17306 R 2 20207 R 3
15517 C8 16593 R 7 19220 TR 4 20262 R 2

Central Yangtze Provinces

Primary 17787 C7 19726 TR 7 20199 R 7
17761 R 7 17798 C6 20138 T 2 20275 T 4
17776 C7 19612 T 4

Second. 16617 R 7 19621 R 7 20210 R 2
20379 T 4

Southwestern China

Primary □

Second. 15436 R 6 15598 R 7 20396 R 8
15424 R 7 15522 C3 15957 R 2

SOUTHEASTERN CHINA

PRIMARY 17775 c7

SECOND. 15479 c8 19692 T 3 20006 TR 8
14629 TR 4 15735 T 2 19962 TR 7 20385 T 5
15349 T 2 16062 R 2 19975 TRC7 20451 R 7
15447 R 3 16074 c7

TAIWAN ONLY

PRIMARY 17786 c2 17907 c7 19679 c7
16899 c8 17794 c3 18981 TR 2 21562 c3
17774 RC7 17799 c4

SECOND. 15861 c2 16549 TR 7 19090 RC8
15521 c8 15889 c2 16733 TRC8 19466 RC7
15533 c7 15893 c2 16746 RC8 20249 c7
15655 c2 16009 c7 16824 c2 20425 c3

HONG KONG AND MACAU ONLY

PRIMARY 17788 c3 17810 c2 20426 c2
15891 c3 17791 c1 20419 c3

SECOND. 15925 T 7 17718 R 2 19970 TRC7
15340 T 7 15989 c7 17745 c2 19990 c8
15463 TRC7 16057 R 2 19309 c2 20428 RC3
15621 c4 16076 c2 19702 R 2 22724 RC2
15827 c4 16348 c7 19713 c2

28 LOCAL WELFARE AND LIVING STANDARDS

地方福利及生活水準

地方の福祉及び生活水準

GEOGRAPHIC CHINA BROADLY CONCEIVED

PRIMARY 10804 R 3 17696 R 3 20994 TRC5
10328 T 2 17691 TR 2 19490 R 2

SECOND. 15191 RC2 16938 TR 2 18976 TR 2
10162 c2 15345 T 3 17165 T 2 20590 T 3
11164 c2 16068 RC2

MAINLAND CHINA

PRIMARY 15519 c2 17313 RC2 17905 c7
13029 R 2 15537 c4 17369 c3 19108 c7
13277 R 2 15550 c2 17482 R 7 19138 c7
13970 R 2 15553 c2 17666 R 8 19140 c7
15059 R 2 15560 c4 17682 c7 19154 c8
15074 R 7 15575 c4 17684 c7 19700 R 2
15192 RC2 15762 TR 3 17717 R 3 19945 c2
15297 c2 15971 R 2 17848 R 2 20166 TR 2
15434 R 7 16015 c4 17849 R 2 20282 T 2
15466 RC2 16036 c7 17879 R 3 20403 RC2
15482 c2 16768 c7 17895 RC2 21150 c2
15506 c2 17311 RC2 17902 c3

SECONDARY: MONOGRAPHS
11144 c2 15549 c7 16031 c7 19184 c8
12256 R 7 15567 c7 16488 c7 19455 R 8
12387 RC8 15570 c2 17095 R 7 19644 R 2
12475 c2 15938 TR 2 17460 R 7 19649 R 7
14478 R 3 15959 R 3 17769 R 7 19922 c7
14809 RC2 15966 R 3 18126 R 3 20080 c7
15483 c7 15991 c7 18862 T 2 20221 R 2
15486 c7 15992 c7 19077 RC7 20224 RC2
15507 c7 15993 c7 19082 RC7 20558 T 2
15513 c4 16013 c7 19105 c7 21103 c2
15524 c7

SECONDARY: INCLUSIONS
15542 c7 16690 R 8 17695 R 3 19167 c7
15990 c7 16693 R 7 17712 R 3 19280 R 2
16612 R 7 17192 TR 2 18992 R 2

SECONDARY: JOURNAL ARTICLES
14519 c3 16004 c8 19014 R 2 20468 R 2
15398 R 7 16005 c7 19103 c7 20692 c4
15496 c7 16027 c2 19156 c7 20765 T 2
15580 c2 16041 c7 19157 c8 20914 R 2
15882 c7 16808 c7 19158 c7 21035 c2
15975 RC7 16969 R 2 19364 R 4 21142 c2
15997 c4 17120 c7 19622 R 7 22301 c2
15999 c7 17130 c7 19641 R 8 22767 c2

THE EIGHTEEN PROVINCES

PRIMARY 16369 T 2 17842 R 2 17916 c2
15111 c2 16478 c2 17861 R 3 19632 R 7
15306 T 2 17096 R 2 17869 R 2 19688 T 2
15501 c2 17098 R 2 17908 c2 20642 R 2
15543 c2 17614 R 2 17912 c2 20699 c2
15965 R 3

SECOND. 15531 c2 16591 R 7 20098 TR 3
10175 c2 15723 T 3 16602 R 8 20503 c2
10294 R 2 15864 TR 2 16920 T 2 20565 T 2
11681 T 2 16048 T 2 17100 R 6 20760 T 2
13022 R 2 16049 T 2 17741 c2 21266 T 2
14474 R 3 16355 c2 17748 c3 21489 c2
15527 c7 16560 TR 2

NORTH CHINA BROADLY CONCEIVED

PRIMARY 16380 T 7 17846 R 7 18914 T 2
13976 R 2 16695 R 7 17873 R 2

SECOND. 17307 R 7 18953 TR 2 20541 T 2
15428 R 7 18390 T 2 18960 TR 2 20748 T 2
15433 R 2 18595 R 7 19920 c2 20964 RC2
16063 R 2

MANCHURIA

PRIMARY 17688 T 2 17857 R 2 19538 R 2
15743 T 3 17723 R 3 17881 R 8 20672 c7
15914 c7 17838 R 2 17904 c3 20795 TR 2
15995 c2 17852 R 3

SECOND. 16627 R 7 17244 R 7 19195 c7
10340 TR 2 16645 R 7 17253 R 5 19523 R 2
10421 c2 16801 c8 17263 R 6 20410 c7
16065 R 2 16915 T 2 17327 c2 20416 c2
16546 TR 7 16974 R 4 17340 c7 22654 TR 2
16553 TR 7 17234 R 2 17566 R 8

NORTHERN CHINA

PRIMARY: MONOGRAPHS
15320 T 3 16594 R 8 17871 R 7 19648 R 7
15394 R 2 17713 R 3 17877 R 3 20527 c3
15407 R 3 17721 R 7 17886 R 3 20762 T 3
15408 R 2 17824 TR 3 17891 R 7 20938 R 3
15459 RC7 17855 R 3 19619 R 7 20982 RC3
15828 c3 17856 R 3

PRIMARY: INCLUSIONS
15817 c3 16475 c7 17845 R 8 19114 c8
15860 c3 16661 R 7 17860 R 7 20693 c2
15872 R 7 17609 T 3 17914 c7 21064 c7
15910 c8

PRIMARY: JOURNAL ARTICLES
14717 R 4 16953 R 2 17828 R 3 18444 T 2
15410 R 8 17047 R 4 17829 R 3 20281 T 5
15510 c7 17497 c3 17830 R 7 20557 T 3
15516 c7 17611 R 3 17831 R 3 20754 T 3
15561 c3 17687 T 3 17832 R 8 20758 T 3
15866 R 3 17697 R 3 17843 R 3 20843 R 7
15880 c8 17705 R 3 17844 R 3 20844 R 2
15900 c7 17715 R 3 17853 R 7 20846 R 2
15903 c7 17751 c3 17862 R 2 20889 R 3
16556 TR 8 17811 T 7 17876 R 3 20921 R 3
16632 R 8 17817 T 2 17878 R 8 20947 R 3
16685 R 7 17819 T 3 17882 R 8 21083 c2
16762 c7 17823 T 2 17896 RC7 21517 R 3
16846 c7

SECONDARY: MONOGRAPHS
10652 T 3 15389 TR 3 16557 TR 8 19178 c8
10783 R 2 15406 R 8 16782 c8 19633 R 7
11135 c3 15452 TRC2 17141 T 5 20216 R 3
13964 R 7 15460 RC7 17158 T 3 20436 R 3
15328 T 2 15565 c7 17262 R 2 20505 c3
15347 T 3 15789 TRC2 17463 R 7 20579 T 3
15355 T 2 15942 TR 3 17720 R 4 20923 R 3
15372 TR 3 16016 c3 17736 R 3 22612 T 2
15373 TR 3 16101 TR 3 19153 c8 22753 c3
15384 TR 4 16377 T 2

SECONDARY: INCLUSIONS
15366 T 3 17282 R 7 19172 c7 20238 c3
15538 c2 17802 c3 19192 c7 21031 c8
16474 c7 19093 c7 19193 c7 21065 c7
16658 R 8 19152 c7 19200 c7 21099 c4
17239 R 7

SECONDARY: JOURNAL ARTICLES
13537 R 4 16759 c7 17636 c3 20764 T 3
14881 c3 16761 c2 17672 c7 20845 R 7
15342 T 3 16766 c8 17685 c7 20868 R 3
15477 c7 16850 c7 17690 TR 3 20937 R 2
15525 c7 16906 T 2 18658 R 7 20946 R 7
15730 T 3 17221 R 2 18788 RC8 20949 R 7
15769 R 5 17309 R 2 19340 c3 21134 c3
15868 R 3 17384 c7 19406 c3 21230 R 3
16220 T 2 17418 R 8 19624 R 7 21510 R 3
16296 R 2 17428 c7 20626 R 8 22457 R 3
16413 R 4 17444 TR 8 20637 R 3 22802 R 7

NORTHWESTERN CHINA AND FRONTIER REGIONS

PRIMARY 16422 R 2 16800 c7 17837 R 2
15545 c8 16628 R 2 17772 RC7 17859 R 2

SECOND. 15753 T 2 16717 R 7 18749 R 2
10401 c2 16399 T 7 16749 RC8 18956 TR 2
14771 R 7 16445 R 7 16912 T 2 18993 R 2
15350 T 2 16555 TR 8 17416 R 2 19080 RC7
15391 TR 2 16664 R 7 17417 R 2 19233 R 7
15393 R 2 16686 R 8 18697 R 2 20198 R 8
15673 TR 7

SOUTH CHINA BROADLY CONCEIVED

PRIMARY 17097 R 3 17875 R 2 17883 R 7

SECOND. 15870 R 2 16547 TR 7 18447 T 2
13040 R 4 15928 T 2 16910 T 4 19006 R 4
15361 T 2 15986 c3 16964 R 2 20944 R 1
15749 T 3 16378 T 2

EAST CENTRAL CHINA

PRIMARY 17549 T 2 17821 T 7 17880 R 3
15307 T 3 17637 c3 17825 R 7 17887 R 3
15430 R 3 17680 c7 17826 R 3 17892 TRC3
15432 R 2 17694 TR 3 17827 R 3 17898 RC3
15720 T 2 17703 R 3 17833 R 3 18926 T 3
15869 R 3 17704 R 3 17834 R 3 19511 R 3
15961 R 3 17707 R 3 17835 R 3 19703 R 3
16122 R 3 17709 R 3 17836 R 3 20644 R 3
16409 TR 3 17719 R 3 17839 R 3 20883 R 3
16418 R 2 17722 R 3 17850 R 3 20885 R 3
16593 R 7 17728 R 3 17851 R 3 21026 c3
16624 R 7 17732 R 3 17858 R 2 21037 c3
16662 R 7 17733 R 3 17863 R 3 21152 c2
16668 R 7 17812 T 7 17868 R 7 21154 c3
17193 TR 3 17816 T 7 17870 R 3 22755 c3
17250 R 7 17818 T 8 17874 R 3

SECOND. 15552 c2 16694 R 8 17943 R 3
10274 T 3 15556 c3 16709 R 8 19555 R 3
10751 R 2 15744 T 2 16721 R 8 19834 R 4
11747 R 2 15761 TR 7 17029 TR 2 20043 T 8
13224 R 4 15771 R 7 17033 TR 7 20103 R 3
15313 T 2 15837 c7 17074 R 6 20195 R 3
15315 T 3 15844 c3 17207 R 4 20392 R 3
15346 T 2 15871 R 3 17232 R 3 20394 R 3
15357 T 3 15881 c3 17274 R 2 20851 R 3
15374 TR 8 15930 T 3 17326 c2 20862 R 3
15377 TR 3 15943 TR 3 17649 T 5 20882 R 2
15388 TR 3 15946 TR 3 17667 R 7 20898 R 3
15405 R 7 15948 TR 3 17710 R 3 20919 R 3
15429 R 3 15950 TR 3 17725 R 3 20925 R 7
15431 R 3 16108 TR 3 17726 R 3 20951 R 3
15493 c7 16417 R 3 17734 R 3 21210 R 7
15503 c7 16666 R 7 17737 R 3 21433 c2
15517 c8

CENTRAL YANGTZE PROVINCES

PRIMARY 15884 c8 16720 R 8 19191 c7
15412 R 3 15998 c7 17884 R 2 19621 R 7
15469 TRC2 16420 R 2

SECOND. 16432 R 2 17312 RC2 20199 R 7
14817 c2 16617 R 7 17337 c3 20241 c8
15481 c2 17170 T 3 18703 R 2 20802 TR 3
15523 c7 17203 R 4 19694 T 3 20878 R 2

SOUTHWESTERN CHINA

PRIMARY 15629 T 2 16589 R 8 17045 R 7
10767 R 2 16425 R 7 16590 R 8 17058 R 3
15424 R 7 16482 c3 16708 R 8 17633 R 3

17663 R 7 17865 R 3 17890 R 3 20711 T 3
17668 R 2 17866 R 3 19827 R 6 20771 T 7
17815 T 5 17867 R 3 20475 RC4 20863 R 2
17840 R 7 17872 R 7 20583 T 2 20873 R 7
17841 R 7 17885 R 3 20627 R 2 20890 R 4
17854 R 2 17888 R 3 20704 T 3 20910 R 7
17864 R 3 17889 R 3 20707 T 2

Second. 16166 T 2 17106 C3 19846 R 3
13038 R 2 16443 R 2 17479 R 7 20396 R 8
14634 TR 3 16540 T 2 17632 R 3 20645 R 7
14750 R 2 16542 T 8 17729 R 3 20840 R 8
15316 T 2 16543 T 2 18300 T 2 20872 R 6
15413 R 2 16599 R 7 18333 C3 20887 R 7
15640 R 2 16601 R 7 18491 T 2 20916 R 3
15715 T 2 16713 R 7 18889 T 2 21212 R 3
15717 T 2 16913 T 2 18922 T 2 22523 T 2
15739 T 2 17089 R 2 19022 R 2 22542 T 2
15862 T 2 17105 C3

Southeastern China

Primary 16781 C7 17847 R 7 20945 R 2
11683 TR 2 16874 C7 17901 C7 20997 C2
15376 TR 2 16888 C8 17913 C2 20998 C2
15419 R 6 17738 C3 19692 T 3 21001 C8
15423 R 2 17813 T 3 20451 R 7 21033 C3
15499 C2 17814 T 3 20705 T 4 21141 C7
16064 R 2 17820 T 3 20894 R 2

Second. 15458 TRC2 16798 C2 19691 T 3
10292 TR 4 15479 C8 17191 TR 2 20006 TR 8
12953 TR 2 15735 T 2 17237 R 2 20106 R 3
15305 T 2 15865 R 3 17353 C2 20296 R 2
15310 T 3 15932 T 8 17589 C2 20542 T 2
15321 T 2 16187 T 3 17615 RC2 20567 T 3
15344 T 3 16398 T 2 17665 R 7 20791 TR 3
15349 T 2 16480 C2 17775 C7 20891 R 5
15358 T 8 16507 T 2 17919 T 5 20897 R 3
15359 T 2 16607 R 2 18906 T 3 20912 R 1
15420 R 3 16630 R 8 19165 C8 21149 C2
15447 R 3 16774 C7 19179 C7 21393 RC2
15448 R 3 16775 C7 19454 R 7 21575 C3

Taiwan Only

Primary 15607 TRC2 17897 RC8 19663 C7
15437 R 2 16771 C8 17900 C1 19711 C2
15439 R 2 16887 C8 17903 C1 20074 C2
15472 RC2 17669 RC8 17907 C7 20686 C2
15491 C7 17676 C8 17910 C7 21009 C2
15530 C7 17822 T 2 17915 C2 21231 TRC2
15562 C2

Second. 15568 C3 16852 C8 19065 C2
10985 C3 15707 C2 16869 C7 19163 C8
14224 TR 2 15708 C2 16871 C7 19679 C7
15438 R 2 15822 C3 16872 C7 19910 C3
15441 R 2 15878 C2 16873 C7 19955 C7
15443 R 2 16042 C2 16886 C7 20018 C8
15444 R 2 16495 C2 16901 C8 20368 C2
15457 RC2 16728 TRC7 16902 C7 20702 T 3
15515 C8 16729 RC2 17386 C4 21051 C3
15521 C8 16734 RC7 17743 C2 21561 C2
15533 C7 16747 RC2 17961 C2 21572 C1
15554 C2 16797 C7

Hong Kong and Macau Only

Primary 15913 C3 17708 R 4 20663 RC3
10301 RC2 15989 C7 17718 R 2 20664 C3
10312 C3 16451 RC3 17745 C2 20678 C3
13048 RC2 16455 RC2 17893 RC2 20680 C3
15382 TR 3 16471 C2 17894 RC2 20683 C3
15409 R 2 16483 C5 17899 RC2 20688 C2
15468 TRC3 16489 C3 17906 C3 20694 C3
15484 C3 16494 C3 17909 C2 20695 C3
15518 C2 16893 C7 17911 C3 20773 T 2
15526 C3 16941 TR 2 17917 C2 21059 C3
15621 C4 17026 T 3 19714 C4 21550 C3
15700 C4 17350 C5 20409 C2 21578 C3
15796 TRC2 17592 C3 20657 RC3 22736 TRC2

Second. 15461 TRC2 15617 C2 15981 RC3
11031 R 2 15467 TRC3 15824 C4 16002 C2
14890 C2 15487 C2 15835 C3 16010 C2
14894 C2 15520 C2 15876 C3 16139 C3
14939 C3 15529 C2 15941 TR 3 16152 C3
15387 TR 2 15555 C2 15945 TR 2 16487 C2
16490 C3 17429 C3 19990 C8 20697 C3
16492 C2 17593 C3 20324 C3 20713 T 2
16805 C8 17739 C3 20622 TR 2 21005 C7
16991 C4 19325 C3 20658 RC3 21101 C3
17002 C2 19516 R 3 20667 C4 21254 C2
17012 C3 19712 C3 20674 C3 21574 C3
17336 C3 19933 C3 20682 C2

29 Regional and Subethnic Variation

習俗方言等等地域性差異
習俗方言等の地域的差異

Geographic China Broadly Conceived

Primary 10300 TRC2 17951 RC2 18852 T 2
10032 T 2 10363 R 2 17972 C2 20096 T 2
10262 TRC3 17933 TR 1

Second. 12772 TRC2 17036 TR 7 20010 TR 2
10026 T 2 13812 T 2 18024 TR 1 20109 TRC2
10075 TR 2 14166 T 1 18511 T 2 20152 T 2
10287 TR 2 15134 TR 4 18969 TR 2 20592 T 1
10336 T 2 15363 T 2 19913 C2 21855 TRC2
10526 T 2 16185 T 2 19982 TRC8 22555 T 2
10684 TR 2 16977 R 2 19983 TRC7 22580 T 2
11317 R 1

Mainland China

Primary 16277 TR 2 17952 TRC2 19850 R 8
10420 C2 16907 T 4 17960 C1 20618 TR 2
10549 T 2 17932 TR 1 17964 C1 20651 R 4
10890 TRC2 17935 TR 1 18853 T 2 21644 T 2
13815 T 2 17936 TR 1 18915 T 2 21948 C2
14135 C2 17938 R 1 18951 TR 2 22599 T 2
15508 C2 17941 R 2 18973 TR 3 22649 TR 1
15741 T 3 17942 R 2 18992 R 2 22656 TR 1
15747 T 2 17948 TRC1 19657 RC1 22661 TR 2
15756 TR 4

Second. 10616 T 2 15079 R 2 19799 TR 1
10003 T 2 10768 R 4 15790 TRC2 19950 C1
10020 T 2 10895 C2 15955 TR 8 20292 TR 2
10061 T 2 10967 C2 16103 TR 2 21265 T 2
10098 R 2 11626 C2 16332 TRC1 21286 T 1
10123 RC2 11654 C2 16395 T 2 21311 TR 2
10135 C2 12422 RC7 17260 R 2 21874 RC2
10154 C2 12434 C2 18043 RC4 21924 C1
10334 T 2 12963 TR 2 18862 T 2 21949 C1
10338 TR 2 12970 TR 2 18941 T 2 22066 T 2
10342 TR 2 13853 T 4 19517 R 3 22432 TR 1
10349 TR 2 13882 TR 2 19656 RC1 22737 TRC1
10353 TR 2 14828 C2 19665 C1 22771 T 2
10360 R 2 14943 C2 19666 C1 22874 T 1

The Eighteen Provinces

Primary 17937 TR 2 17962 C2 18011 T 4
10350 TR 2 17945 R 2 17967 C1 18012 T 2
14207 T 2 17950 TRC1 17968 C1 20548 T 2
16252 TR 2

Second. 10294 R 2 14101 T 2 18930 T 2
10027 T 2 10333 T 2 15327 T 3 20146 T 2
10175 C2 10335 T 2 17631 TR 8 20607 TR 1
10209 R 2 12675 TR 2 18385 T 1 21213 R 2

North China Broadly Conceived

Primary 22660 TR 2

Second. 10064 T 2 16063 R 2

Manchuria

Primary □

Second. 16315 R 3

Northern China

Primary 17927 T 2 17953 TRC3 20632 R 3
17918 T 8 17940 R 7 17969 C1 22454 R 7

Second. 17625 T 3 19847 R 7 20015 R 3
20273 R 3

Northwestern China and Frontier Regions

Primary 18864 T 1 22462 R 7

Second. 15350 T 2 17527 T 1 18890 T 2
22701 R 2

South China Broadly Conceived

Primary 15726 T 2 17931 T 7 17947 RC2
14125 TRC7 17189 TR 2 17939 R 2 17956 TRC2
15361 T 2 17923 T 2 17944 R 2 19957 T 7
15721 T 2 17929 T 7

Second. 13833 T 2 15722 T 2 16930 T 2
10028 T 2 15332 T 2 16061 R 2 18421 T 2
10289 TR 2 15663 T 8 16386 T 8 20561 T 2
12894 T 2

East Central China

Primary 15318 T 3 17667 R 7 17943 R 3

Second. 15346 T 2 17816 T 7 22696 R 3

Central Yangtze Provinces

Primary □

Second. 19726 TR 7

Southwestern China

Primary 10318 T 2 17926 T 7 17970 C1

Second. 15716 T 3 18845 T 4 21892 TRC2
13801 T 2 18394 T 2 20873 R 7

Southeastern China

Primary 16175 T 7 17921 T 2 17949 TRC7
10270 T 7 17547 T 2 17925 T 7 17959 C2
10292 TR 4 17553 T 7 17928 T 7 18950 TR 2
11143 C2 17615 RC2 17930 T 7 19981 TRC7
15353 T 2 17919 T 5 17934 TR 2 22392 T 7
15932 T 8 17920 T 7

Second. 15447 R 3 16180 T 3 18876 T 2
10278 T 2 15448 R 3 16270 TR 2 20386 T 7
10327 T 2 15572 C2 16387 T 2 20891 R 5
12069 C2 15718 T 2 16552 TR 2 21480 C2
14758 R 2 15735 T 2 16919 T 2 21781 TR 1
15305 T 2 15742 T 2 16923 T 2 22455 R 2
15349 T 2 16064 R 2 17025 T 2 22510 T 2
15376 TR 2 16074 C7 18438 T 2

Taiwan Only

Primary 17169 T 2 17954 RC2 17961 C2
15887 C8 17922 T 2 17955 RC1 21484 C2
16347 C2

Second. 16226 TR 2 19980 TRC8 21487 C1
10325 T 2 16365 C2 19989 C3 21932 C1
10345 TR 2 17103 TRC7 20072 C7 21946 C7
10882 RC2 19737 C8 21237 C2 22735 TRC2
15861 C2 19973 TRC8

Hong Kong and Macau Only

Primary 17623 C2 17958 C7 17966 C2
15462 TRC7 17924 T 7 17963 C2 17971 C8
15546 C7 17946 TRC2 17965 C2 19959 T 7
15574 C8 17957 C7

Second. 15699 C7 16126 TRC3 19858 RC7
15331 T 8 15797 TRC7 16328 TRC2 19943 C8
15451 TRC7 15809 TRC8 16346 C6 21555 C2
15463 TRC7 15926 T 7 16893 C7 21827 TRC7
15464 TRC8 15989 C7 17683 C8 22494 C2

30 Voluntary Associations & Formal Organization in General

組織原理及會社團體通論

組織原理及び社会団体一般

Geographic China Broadly Conceived

Primary 17975 T 2 17981 TR 2 18407 T 2
10541 T 1 17976 T 2 18102 TR 2 21579 C2
11045 RC2 17980 TR 1 18301 T 4 22016 TRC1
11708 TR 2

Second. 16128 TRC2 18809 RC2 20213 R 3
10117 TRC2 16185 T 2 19650 RC2 21469 TRC2
14193 T 1 17036 TR 7 19717 T 2 22160 R 1
14698 TR 1 18544 TR 1 19978 TRC2 22886 T 1
16104 TR 7

Mainland China

Primary 14297 C1 17977 T 2 18002 C2
10084 TR 2 14331 C2 17978 T 2 18003 C2
10086 TR 2 14599 T 2 17979 TR 7 18118 R 4
10131 C1 15183 RC1 17986 RC1 18144 R 2
10769 R 2 15233 C2 17987 RC2 18251 C1
10967 C2 15258 C7 17990 C2 18311 RC1
10975 C2 15303 C2 17991 C2 18380 T 1
11006 C2 15495 C2 17992 C2 19284 RC2
11052 RC2 15540 C7 17993 C2 19343 T 4
11083 C1 16027 C2 17996 C2 19420 C4
11111 C1 16082 C1 17997 C1 19640 R 7
14015 RC1 16343 TRC2 17998 C1 20042 T 1
14131 TRC2 17228 R 5 17999 C2 20254 T 2
14256 RC2 17441 TR 2 18000 C2 22307 C1
14292 RC2 17974 T 3 18001 C2

Secondary: Monographs
10055 T 2 11154 C1 14853 C2 18795 TRC2
10081 TR 2 11179 C1 15171 TRC2 19358 TR 3
10123 RC2 11607 TRC1 15509 C2 19480 TR 3
10125 RC2 11862 RC2 15537 C4 19595 C4
10154 C2 12082 C2 15560 C4 19931 C1
10551 T 4 12839 C2 15980 RC2 20484 C2
10667 T 1 13909 R 2 16332 TRC1 21265 T 2
10768 R 4 13986 TRC2 16335 TRC2 21476 TRC2
10778 R 2 14040 C1 18232 C2 22304 C1
10851 RC2 14144 C1 18551 TR 2 22585 T 1
11003 C2 14329 C2 18619 R 2 22746 C1
11076 C2 14337 C2 18647 R 2 22939 R 2
11144 C2 14754 R 2 18660 R 2

Secondary: Inclusions
10037 T 2 14343 C1 18745 R 2 19256 R 3
10127 TRC2 18119 R 2 18832 TRC1 22238 RC4
11120 C2 18208 C2

Secondary: Journal Articles
10342 TR 2 14084 C2 15845 C7 20214 R 2
10766 R 2 14142 C1 15968 R 2 21012 C2
10900 C2 14205 T 4 16034 C4 21830 TRC2
10913 C4 14249 R 1 16309 R 2 21998 TR 1
11067 C1 14345 C1 18320 C1 22021 C2
11190 T 1 14872 C2 18479 T 2 22199 TRC1
11316 R 1 15221 C1 19218 TR 1 22337 C1
12012 C2 15280 C2 19607 C3 22361 C1
12623 TR 4

The Eighteen Provinces

Primary 14493 R 4 15145 R 4 15470 RC7
17973 T 2 17995 C2

Second. 10680 T 3 14159 T 1 18149 R 1
10525 T 2 12938 T 3 16252 TR 2 18284 C2
10569 T 2 13979 R 2 17541 T 7 18285 C2
10608 T 2 14100 T 2 18117 R 4 18621 R 3

North China Broadly Conceived

Primary 10057 T 1 18750 R 2

Second. 14762 R 2

Manchuria

Primary 15181 RC2 15287 C2

Second. 10911 C2

Northern China

Primary 15360 T 7 15384 TR 4 19357 TR 3

Second. 14950 C3 17570 R 2 18313 TRC3
10781 R 2 15373 TR 3 18286 C2 20417 RC2
10941 C3

Northwestern China and Frontier Regions

Primary □

Second. 18340 C2 19355 TR 2

South China Broadly Conceived

Primary 17982 R 2

Second. 11658 T 2

East Central China

Primary 15143 R 3

Second. 15291 C3 16290 R 8 17646 C2
19023 R 3

Central Yangtze Provinces

Primary □

Second. 19726 TR 7

Southwestern China

Primary □

Second. 16267 TR 2 18287 C2 19270 R 2
19362 R 6 20873 R 7

Southeastern China

Primary 15317 T 2 15448 R 3

Second. 10935 C1 16052 TR 3 19962 TR 7

Taiwan Only

Primary 16330 TRC2 17988 RC2 18263 C2
16003 C7 17386 C4 17989 TRC2 19737 C8
16007 C3 17984 RC2 18004 C7 20236 C8

Second. 15441 R 2 15568 C3 15912 C2
15438 R 2 15443 R 2 15655 C2 16354 C8
15439 R 2 15472 RC2 15852 C2 20268 C6
15440 R 2 15530 C7

Hong Kong and Macau Only

Primary 17994 C2 19713 C2 20272 C7
17985 RC2 19702 R 2 19714 C4

Second. 15813 C2 16496 C2 23035 C2
15563 C4 15981 RC3 20426 C2 23051 C1

31 Social Organization of Recreation

娛樂組織 娯楽組織

Geographic China Broadly Conceived

Primary 10025 T 2 14698 TR 1 18024 TR 1
18039 TRC1 18042 TRC2

Second. 10058 T 2 12772 TRC2 17448 TR 1
10001 T 2 10082 TR 2 15363 T 2 17975 T 2
10014 T 2 10118 RC2 15773 R 2 20463 R 3
10016 T 2 10550 T 1 16938 TR 2 20615 TR 2
10024 T 2 10611 T 2 17036 TR 7 21276 T 2
10026 T 2

Mainland China

Primary 16246 TR 1 18045 TRC4 18058 C2
11046 RC1 16332 TRC1 18047 C1 18059 C2
11139 C1 18014 T 7 18051 C1 18061 C2
11151 C1 18018 TR 1 18052 C2 18062 C2
12782 RC2 18020 TR 2 18053 C4 18064 C3
12810 C1 18021 TR 4 18054 C2 18071 C1
14264 RC1 18041 TRC2 18055 C1 18072 C1
14285 TRC1 18043 RC4 18056 C3 18315 RC4
14351 C2 18044 RC1 18057 C2 19659 RC2
19697 TR 3 20259 T 1 20468 R 2 21395 RC2
20258 T 2 20382 T 1 21346 TR 2 21459 R 4

Secondary: Monographs
10002 T 2 11003 C2 14774 R 3 19751 T 2
10003 T 2 11096 C2 14808 RC2 20107 R 2
10030 T 2 11105 C2 14809 RC2 20224 RC2
10043 T 2 11113 C4 14999 C2 20461 R 1
10059 T 2 11178 C2 15466 RC2 20484 C2
10083 TR 2 11724 R 2 15482 C2 20502 C2
10098 R 2 11885 C2 15549 C7 20623 TR 2
10104 R 2 11901 C2 15550 C2 20749 T 2
10120 TRC2 12783 TRC2 17895 RC2 21124 C3
10132 C2 12849 C2 18170 RC2 21325 TR 2
10143 C2 13970 R 2 18827 RC2 21504 TR 2
10145 C2 14263 RC1 19105 C7 21691 T 2
10149 C2 14269 RC4 19590 C4 21798 TR 1
10807 R 1 14293 RC3 19594 C4 21874 RC2
10838 R 4 14369 C2 19595 C4 21980 T 4
10894 C1 14754 R 2 19638 R 7 22599 T 2

Secondary: Inclusions
11072 C2 11078 C2 14208 T 2 20661 TRC1
11073 C4 11128 C1 15189 RC2 21486 C2
11077 C2 11617 C1 20434 R 2 22473 RC2

Secondary: Journal Articles
11033 RC1 19158 C7 21010 C2 22292 C2
12518 C2 19396 R 2 21351 TR 1 22452 R 2
12848 C1 20254 T 2 21591 C2 22493 RC2
18338 C7

The Eighteen Provinces

Primary 18006 T 1 18012 T 2 18070 C4
10175 C2 18007 T 1 18015 T 1 19354 TR 4
16156 T 1 18010 T 1 18017 T 3 20609 TR 1
18005 T 1 18011 T 4 18037 R 1 20668 C2

Second. 14829 C2 15839 C3 20223 RC2
10038 T 2 15243 C2 16058 R 2 20612 TR 2
10174 C2 15327 T 3 17614 R 2 20699 C2
11061 C2 15446 R 3 18445 T 2 22004 R 1
12858 C2 15501 C2 19245 R 2 22067 T 2
12859 C2 15511 C2 19686 T 3

North China Broadly Conceived

Primary 18038 TRC5 21348 TR 3 22511 T 2

Second. 14762 R 2 18622 R 2 20578 T 2

Manchuria

Primary □

Second. 16915 T 2

Northern China

Primary 16121 R 3 18032 R 3 18066 C3
14214 TR 3 16219 T 3 18033 R 3 18068 C3
14701 TR 3 18009 T 3 18036 R 3 18069 C3
15390 TR 3 18016 T 2 18050 C3 20579 T 3
15407 R 3 18027 R 7 18065 C3 22397 T 3
15414 R 8 18029 R 8

Second. 15384 TR 4 15817 C3 19825 R 3
12860 C2 15394 R 2 15828 C3 20273 R 3
14157 T 3 15403 R 8 16295 R 3 20381 T 2
15338 T 7 15408 R 2 16313 R 3 20557 T 3
15355 T 2 15415 R 8 17410 T 2 20559 T 3
15360 T 7 15417 R 3 17720 R 4 21359 TR 3
15367 T 2 15452 TRC2 17751 C3 22485 TRC2
15370 TR 3 15460 RC7 18362 C3 22750 C3
15372 TR 3

Northwestern China and Frontier Regions

Primary □

Second. 12766 RC2 14844 C2

South China Broadly Conceived

Primary 10641 T 2 18030 R 3 18034 R 3
22601 T 2

Second. 15205 C2 16979 R 2 19718 T 2

East Central China

Primary 18013 T 2 18026 R 3 18046 RC2
15374 TR 8 18023 TR 8 18028 R 3 18067 C3
18008 T 3 18025 R 3

Second. 15493 C7 16593 R 7 20103 R 3
15313 T 2 16060 R 3 17892 TRC3 21331 TR 1
15404 R 3 16533 T 2 18983 TR 3 22755 C3
15405 R 7

Central Yangtze Provinces

Primary □

Second. 15481 C2 16090 T 2 16526 T 2
15469 TRC2 15498 C2 16432 R 2 20379 T 4

Southwestern China

Primary 18035 R 6 18040 TRC2

Second. 12861 C2 14750 R 2 15308 T 5
16267 TR 2 20447 R 3

Southeastern China

Primary 16194 T 3 18048 C3 20106 R 3
15364 T 3 16218 T 2 18063 C2 21527 R 1
15458 TRC2 18022 TR 3 20093 T 3

Second. 15418 R 8 16116 R 4 21428 RC2
11675 T 2 15448 R 3 17615 RC2 22398 T 4
15305 T 2 15630 T 3 17657 T 3 22455 R 2
15317 T 2 16017 C2 20385 T 5 22480 RC1

Taiwan Only

Primary 18019 TR 2 18049 C3 22504 C1

Second. 17989 TRC2 19738 C7 20249 C7
16007 C3 18263 C2 19938 C2 21484 C2
16362 C1 19663 C7

Hong Kong and Macau Only

Primary 18031 R 4 18060 C2 20272 C7
20279 T 1 23054 C3

Second. 15981 RC3 19702 R 2 20522 C3
15325 T 3 16135 C3 19713 C2 20688 C2
15468 TRC3 16334 TRC2 19714 C4 21063 C2
15487 C2 17985 RC2 19990 C8 22500 C3
15526 C3 17994 C2

32 Political Parties

政黨 政党

Geographic China Broadly Conceived

Primary 10853 TRC2 18077 T 2 18809 RC2
10106 R 2 11035 RC2 18079 T 1 19500 R 4
10107 R 2 11241 T 2 18082 T 3 19534 R 2
10129 TRC2 11257 TR 1 18102 TR 2 21412 RC2
10177 C2 11605 RC2 18105 TR 2 21425 TRC5
10541 T 1 13916 R 2 18111 R 1 21427 TRC1
10557 T 1 14248 R 2 18125 R 1 21538 TRC2
10626 T 2 14951 C2 18299 C2 22074 T 2
10700 TR 2 15158 TRC2 18303 R 2 22080 TR 1
10713 TR 2 15161 TRC2 18542 TR 2 22095 TR 2
10741 R 1 15175 RC2 18545 TR 2 22127 TR 1
10828 R 2 15191 RC2 18579 R 2 22672 TR 1
10850 RC1 18073 T 2 18707 R 2 22681 R 3

Second. 11328 R 1 15185 TRC2 21332 TR 1
10076 TR 2 11404 RC1 16128 TRC2 21337 TR 2
10096 R 2 11708 TR 2 18388 T 2 21338 TR 1
10108 R 2 11738 R 2 18534 TR 2 21392 TRC2
10119 TRC2 11841 R 2 18540 TR 2 21408 TRC2
10346 TR 2 12611 T 1 18687 R 2 21847 TRC2
10510 T 2 12678 TR 2 18764 R 2 22027 T 4
10537 T 1 13902 R 2 18810 RC2 22189 RC1
10619 T 1 13966 R 2 19475 TR 4 22225 TRC2
10645 T 1 13997 RC2 19503 R 2 22265 RC2
10773 R 1 14468 R 2 20231 RC2 22345 C2
10803 R 2 15134 TR 4 20653 R 2 22657 TR 1
10804 R 3 15166 TRC2 21304 TR 2 22666 TR 2
10865 TRC3 15174 TRC2 21306 TR 2 22720 R 3
10866 RC3

Mainland China

Primary: Monographs
10103 R 2 11699 TR 2 15856 C2 18296 C1
10124 TRC2 11872 RC2 15980 RC2 18298 C2
10173 C2 12331 R 7 16054 R 7 18309 R 3
10180 C2 12387 RC8 16071 C2 18312 RC2
10508 T 3 13888 R 2 17990 C2 18319 C1
10558 T 1 13893 R 2 17993 C2 18324 C2
10631 T 2 13896 R 2 18075 T 2 18457 T 1
10640 T 4 13905 R 2 18098 T 3 18551 TR 2
10667 T 1 13909 R 2 18099 T 1 18562 TR 2
10677 T 2 13927 R 2 18103 TR 1 18596 R 2
10686 TR 1 13945 R 2 18104 TR 2 18603 R 2
10693 TR 1 13975 R 2 18106 TR 2 18629 R 2
10696 TR 1 14002 RC2 18114 R 2 18649 R 1
10718 TR 2 14033 C2 18118 R 4 18656 R 2
10724 TR 4 14037 C2 18120 R 2 18685 R 2
10739 TR 1 14047 C1 18123 R 2 18782 R 2
10757 R 1 14077 C1 18126 R 3 18792 RC2
10778 R 2 14109 TR 2 18134 R 2 18804 TRC2
10780 R 1 14114 R 2 18140 R 4 18812 RC2
10782 R 1 14258 RC2 18142 R 2 18817 RC2
10813 R 2 14278 RC2 18143 R 2 18822 TRC2
10814 R 2 14279 RC2 18144 R 2 18823 RC2
10819 R 2 14292 RC2 18145 R 2 18991 TR 4
10844 R 4 14309 C1 18147 R 1 20314 C2
10883 TRC2 14316 C1 18148 R 2 20328 C2
10885 RC4 14329 C2 18154 R 2 20444 R 2
10887 TRC2 14384 C1 18155 R 2 20473 RC2
10888 TRC2 14385 C2 18158 R 2 21265 T 2
10894 C1 14387 C3 18161 R 2 21324 TR 2
10938 C4 14416 C2 18163 R 1 21354 TR 2
10970 C2 14556 T 2 18164 RC3 21373 R 1
10975 C2 14670 TR 4 18170 RC2 21400 RC2
10994 C2 14703 TR 2 18172 RC2 21405 TRC1
10999 C1 14753 R 1 18176 RC1 21414 RC2
11052 RC2 14885 C1 18178 RC2 21419 RC2
11076 C2 15140 TR 2 18182 RC2 22046 T 1
11094 C2 15156 R 2 18183 RC1 22073 T 1
11113 C4 15163 RC2 18185 RC2 22079 TR 2
11132 C2 15168 TRC2 18186 RC1 22128 TR 1
11154 C1 15169 RC2 18187 RC2 22196 RC1
11160 C2 15176 RC2 18212 C1 22229 RC2
11168 C2 15202 C2 18224 C2 22235 RC2
11179 C1 15214 C2 18225 C2 22251 RC2
11235 T 1 15234 C2 18232 C2 22291 C2
11289 TR 1 15235 C2 18236 C1 22298 C2
11297 TR 2 15237 C2 18264 C2 22299 C2
11375 R 1 15245 C2 18272 C1 22324 C2
11377 R 1 15248 C2 18277 C2 22375 C2
11393 TRC2 15250 C3 18279 C1 22689 R 1
11437 C2 15285 C4 18283 C1 22699 R 3
11614 RC1 15294 C2 18289 C7

Primary: Inclusions
10147 C2 15164 RC1 18189 C2 18672 R 2
10555 T 1 15186 RC1 18196 C1 18761 R 2
10662 T 2 15222 C2 18206 C2 18808 TRC2
10856 RC2 15223 C2 18208 C2 18811 RC2
10930 C2 15224 C2 18209 C2 19365 T 2
11083 C1 15233 C2 18219 C2 19369 C1
11942 C2 15299 C2 18240 C1 19626 R 2
11965 C2 16035 C4 18241 C2 20443 R 1
12121 C2 17638 C2 18242 C7 20698 C2
13977 R 2 17644 C2 18280 C2 21372 R 2
13999 RC1 18000 C2 18281 C2 21877 RC3
14138 C2 18078 T 1 18282 C1 22025 T 1
14261 RC1 18081 T 1 18293 C2 22060 T 1
14275 RC2 18088 T 2 18294 C1 22169 R 2
14280 RC2 18108 R 1 18334 C1 22247 RC1
14281 RC1 18110 R 2 18343 C2 22267 RC1
14288 RC2 18112 R 3 18533 TR 2 22290 C2
14324 C1 18119 R 2 18616 R 2 22313 C1
14336 C1 18167 RC1 18626 R 2 22321 C3
15139 TR 2 18180 RC1

Primary: Journal Articles
10689 TR 1 10880 RC2 10976 C1 11191 T 1
10743 R 2 10900 C2 10979 C4 11247 TR 1
10748 R 2 10905 C4 10980 C2 11260 TR 2
10777 R 1 10913 C4 10992 C2 11285 TR 1
10815 R 1 10924 C3 11037 RC1 11341 R 1
10826 R 2 10928 C1 11098 C2 11367 R 1
10834 R 2 10933 C2 11114 C4 11452 C2
10848 RC2 10940 C1 11129 C1 11533 C1
10849 RC2 10965 C2 11136 C1 11806 R 2
11900 C2 17992 C2 18201 C1 18268 C1
11941 C2 17998 C1 18202 C1 18269 C2
11981 C2 18084 T 1 18203 C1 18270 C1
12099 C1 18086 T 1 18204 C2 18273 C2
12116 C2 18090 T 3 18205 C1 18274 C2
12117 C2 18093 T 4 18207 C1 18275 C1
12129 C2 18094 T 3 18210 C3 18276 C4
12307 R 7 18095 T 3 18211 C4 18278 C1
12314 R 8 18100 T 1 18213 C2 18288 C1
12391 RC7 18101 TR 3 18214 C1 18291 C1
13919 R 2 18107 R 2 18215 C1 18292 C1
13932 R 2 18109 R 3 18216 C1 18304 R 2
14073 C1 18116 R 3 18217 C4 18311 RC1
14076 C1 18122 R 1 18218 C1 18316 C1
14081 C1 18124 R 2 18221 C2 18335 C2
14272 RC1 18128 R 4 18222 C2 18353 C2
14291 RC1 18130 R 3 18223 C1 18469 T 1
14303 C1 18132 R 1 18226 C2 18517 T 1
14307 C1 18133 R 1 18227 C2 18675 R 2
14317 C1 18135 R 4 18228 C2 18724 R 1
14319 C1 18136 R 4 18229 C1 18757 R 2
14333 C1 18139 R 1 18230 C1 18789 RC2
14345 C1 18141 R 2 18231 C3 18803 RC1
14346 C1 18150 R 1 18233 C4 18806 RC2
14355 C1 18151 R 1 18234 C2 18814 RC1
14357 C1 18157 R 2 18237 C2 18815 RC2
14381 C1 18159 R 2 18238 C2 18830 RC2
14383 C1 18162 R 1 18239 C1 19169 C2
14386 C4 18165 RC1 18243 C2 19183 C2
14413 RC4 18166 RC1 18244 C2 19370 C1
15182 RC1 18168 RC1 18246 C2 19379 C2
15196 C2 18169 RC1 18247 C1 19464 R 7
15198 C2 18171 RC1 18248 C1 19512 R 4
15206 C2 18173 RC2 18249 C1 19596 C4
15208 C2 18174 RC1 18250 C1 20184 R 1
15211 C2 18175 TRC1 18251 C1 20211 R 4
15219 C2 18177 RC2 18252 C2 20374 C1
15220 C2 18179 RC1 18253 C2 20474 RC2
15226 C2 18184 RC1 18254 C2 20476 C2
15236 C2 18188 RC2 18255 C1 20501 C2
15244 C2 18190 C2 18256 C2 20521 C2
15251 C1 18191 C1 18257 C1 21390 RC2
15255 C2 18192 C2 18258 C2 21680 T 1
15256 C1 18193 C1 18259 C1 22037 T 1
15257 C1 18194 C1 18260 C2 22069 T 2
15282 C2 18195 C2 18261 C4 22150 R 5
15295 C4 18197 C1 18262 C1 22157 R 1
15979 RC4 18198 C1 18265 C1 22303 C1
16481 C7 18199 C2 18266 C3 22344 C2
17596 C2 18200 C2 18267 C1 22625 T 2
17987 RC2

Secondary: Monographs
10090 R 2 11006 C2 12523 C8 14496 R 5
10101 R 2 11040 RC4 12524 C2 14678 TR 3
10125 RC2 11048 TRC2 12676 TR 1 14686 TR 1
10126 RC2 11092 C2 12811 C2 14692 TR 1
10128 TRC2 11110 C1 12813 C2 14693 TR 4
10134 C2 11178 C2 12864 C1 14835 C2
10152 C2 11180 C2 12921 T 2 15192 RC2
10164 C2 11263 TR 1 13366 C4 15230 C2
10169 C2 11279 TR 1 13508 TR 2 15241 C2
10548 T 2 11290 TR 1 13880 TR 2 15260 C2
10695 TR 2 11291 TR 2 13923 R 1 15267 C2
10697 TR 2 11327 R 1 13937 R 2 15507 C7
10698 TR 2 11336 R 2 14001 RC1 15553 C2
10703 TR 4 11376 R 1 14006 RC2 15955 TR 8
10709 TR 4 11391 RC2 14012 RC2 16029 C7
10712 TR 2 11496 C1 14014 RC1 16070 C2
10715 TR 2 11514 C2 14018 TRC2 16072 C7
10733 TR 2 11601 R 2 14020 RC2 16148 C5
10758 R 4 11639 C1 14053 C1 17311 RC2
10779 R 1 11718 TR 2 14119 R 2 17779 C2
10785 R 1 11848 RC2 14144 C1 18003 C2
10793 R 1 11883 C2 14153 C1 18535 TR 1
10811 R 1 11897 C2 14206 T 1 18536 TR 2
10838 R 4 11919 C2 14219 TR 2 18552 TR 1
10851 RC2 11922 C2 14223 TR 2 18557 TR 2
10858 TRC2 12015 C2 14274 TRC2 18563 TR 4
10873 TRC2 12027 C2 14285 TRC1 18598 R 2
10890 TRC2 12044 C2 14296 C2 18635 R 2
10960 C2 12082 C2 14299 C2 18661 R 2
10961 C1 12086 C2 14305 C4 18699 R 2
10997 C2 12109 C2 14322 C1 18701 R 1
11003 C2 12123 C2 14334 C1 18717 R 2
11005 C2 12271 R 7 14479 R 2 18720 R 2

18722 R 2 19558 R 2 21406 RC2 22224 RC2
18725 R 2 19583 RC4 21410 TRC2 22250 RC2
18730 R 2 19595 C4 21420 TRC2 22260 RC1
18752 R 2 19597 C2 21422 TRC2 22273 RC2
18755 R 2 19899 TRC2 21424 TRC2 22304 C1
18759 R 2 19922 C7 21459 R 4 22325 C2
18767 R 2 20431 TR 4 21466 TRC1 22326 C1
18780 R 2 20442 R 3 21585 C2 22339 C2
18796 RC2 20492 C3 21594 C1 22648 TR 2
18819 RC2 20496 C2 22068 T 1 22688 R 1
19100 C7 21260 T 2 22091 TR 1 22710 R 2
19135 C7 21288 T 1 22117 TR 2 22714 R 2
19338 C5 21300 T 2 22118 TR 1 22734 RC2
19390 C2 21321 TR 2 22135 TR 2 22939 R 2
19457 R 7 21325 TR 2 22144 R 2 22950 TRC2
19476 TR 2 21361 TR 1 22203 RC2 22954 TRC1
19477 TR 4 21395 RC2

SECONDARY: INCLUSIONS
10078 TR 2 13097 C2 14945 C3 19290 C4
10131 C1 13413 C4 14977 C2 19324 C4
10151 C2 13920 R 2 15101 C2 19373 C1
10171 C2 13942 R 2 15160 TRC1 19459 R 7
10637 T 3 13971 R 2 15170 RC2 19526 R 3
10750 R 2 13995 RC1 15188 RC2 20472 RC3
10918 C4 14054 C1 15281 C1 20530 C1
10919 C2 14082 C1 15286 C2 21303 TR 2
10920 C2 14146 C2 15296 C1 21326 TR 2
10946 C3 14147 C2 17640 C8 21436 T 1
10993 C2 14232 TR 1 17642 C2 21858 RC1
11007 C1 14276 RC1 17997 C1 21893 RC2
11077 C2 14290 RC1 18325 C1 21898 RC1
11433 C1 14325 C2 18555 TR 2 21916 C2
11435 C2 14343 C1 18571 TR 2 22197 RC2
11443 C2 14344 C1 18601 R 2 22205 TRC1
11451 C1 14363 C2 18612 R 2 22209 TRC1
11458 C2 14372 C1 18615 R 2 22234 RC2
11459 C1 14374 C1 18745 R 2 22236 TRC1
11612 RC1 14380 C1 18799 RC2 22272 RC1
11613 RC1 14394 C1 18825 RC2 22358 C1
11637 C1 14448 C7 18833 RC1 22380 C1
13058 C7

SECONDARY: JOURNAL ARTICLES
10530 T 2 11493 C2 14313 C1 16018 C2
10538 T 1 11515 C1 14315 C1 16027 C2
10540 T 1 11522 C1 14318 C1 17130 C7
10742 R 1 11525 C2 14331 C2 17597 C2
10762 R 3 11532 C1 14332 C2 17902 C3
10771 R 4 11602 RC1 14338 C1 17986 RC1
10786 R 2 11626 C2 14339 C1 17991 C2
10789 R 5 11650 C1 14342 C1 17996 C2
10805 R 2 11788 R 2 14353 C1 18328 C1
10835 R 4 11866 RC2 14365 C1 18331 C1
10877 RC2 12028 C4 14371 C1 18337 C1
10897 C2 12040 C2 14375 C1 18352 C1
10899 C1 12057 C2 14414 RC4 18359 C1
10901 C2 12111 C2 14415 RC4 18360 C2
10910 C1 12153 C2 14417 C3 18361 C2
10925 C2 12325 R 2 14438 RC2 18587 R 1
10926 C5 12549 C8 14532 C2 18591 R 2
10949 C1 12644 TR 4 14752 R 1 18651 R 2
10966 C2 12848 C1 14814 C4 18663 R 2
10967 C2 13069 C4 15154 R 2 18677 R 2
10986 C2 13346 C5 15167 RC2 18698 R 2
11009 C1 13429 C4 15178 TRC2 18718 R 2
11039 RC1 13838 T 2 15199 C2 18754 R 1
11058 C7 13926 R 7 15200 C2 18797 RC1
11070 C2 13943 R 2 15201 C1 18813 RC1
11093 C1 14004 TRC2 15218 C2 18829 RC2
11097 C2 14008 RC2 15225 C2 19099 C8
11112 C1 14041 C2 15227 C1 19139 C7
11116 C2 14042 C1 15238 C2 19150 C2
11122 C1 14044 C2 15242 C1 19294 C5
11177 C1 14067 C1 15246 C2 19305 C3
11269 TR 1 14132 C2 15252 C2 19376 C3
11338 R 1 14149 C2 15253 C2 19378 C1
11343 R 1 14205 T 4 15261 C1 19382 C1
11349 R 1 14235 R 1 15265 C2 19386 C3
11402 TRC1 14260 RC2 15277 C2 19387 C1
11408 RC1 14271 RC2 15278 C2 19463 R 2
11430 C1 14282 RC1 15290 C2 19474 TR 4
11444 C1 14283 TRC1 15540 C7 19542 R 4
11453 C2 14294 C1 15967 R 2 19571 R 3
11456 C2 14295 C1 15994 C7 19573 R 3
11457 C1 14308 C1 16014 C2 19599 C4

19610 C3 21548 C2 22180 R 2 22337 C1
19623 R 4 21560 C1 22201 RC1 22361 C1
20254 T 2 22039 T 1 22213 RC2 22370 C1
20437 R 3 22049 T 1 22228 RC1 22382 C2
20454 R 1 22058 T 1 22245 TRC1 22656 TR 1
20485 C4 22097 TR 1 22274 RC1 22702 R 1
20490 C2 22143 R 1 22280 RC1 22838 C2
20514 C2 22165 R 1 22328 C2 22934 R 1
20520 C2 22171 R 2 22330 C1 22942 R 1
21397 RC2 22176 R 1

THE EIGHTEEN PROVINCES

PRIMARY 15127 T 1 18117 R 4 18713 R 2
10839 R 2 15203 C3 18127 R 3 18765 R 1
11029 R 1 18074 T 2 18138 R 3 18774 R 2
11209 T 1 18076 T 3 18149 R 1 18777 R 2
12615 T 3 18080 T 2 18152 R 1 18784 R 2
13911 R 2 18083 T 1 18153 R 1 20450 R 2
13979 R 2 18085 T 4 18284 C2 21272 T 2
14238 R 3 18097 T 1 18285 C2 22029 T 3
14555 T 1 18115 R 2 18565 TR 2 22076 TR 1

SECOND. 13938 R 2 18645 R 7 20489 C3
10630 T 3 14217 TR 2 18654 R 2 21309 TR 2
10735 TR 1 14388 C3 18681 R 2 21343 TR 2
10831 R 3 15240 C3 18756 R 1 21362 TR 3
11816 R 2 15243 C2 18834 RC2 22558 T 2
12933 T 2 17995 C2 20449 R 4 22683 R 2
13912 R 2 18520 T 1 20478 C2 22684 R 1
13934 R 2 18602 R 2

NORTH CHINA BROADLY CONCEIVED

PRIMARY 13962 R 2 18160 R 3 22695 R 2
10798 R 2 18146 R 2 18712 R 7

SECOND. 10936 C3 13954 R 2 18732 R 2
10830 R 2 10969 C3 16119 R 2 18872 T 2
10907 C3 10989 C5 16430 R 2

MANCHURIA

PRIMARY 15287 C2 18181 RC1

SECOND. 10796 R 2 13907 R 4 17383 C3
10163 C2 10852 RC2 15181 RC2 19111 C8

NORTHERN CHINA

PRIMARY 11765 R 1 18092 T 3 18329 C3
10547 T 3 14320 C3 18096 T 3 18344 C3
10556 T 3 15304 C3 18235 C3 20440 R 3
10606 T 3 15806 TRC3 18286 C2 20505 C3
10776 R 2 16056 R 8 18295 C3 22374 C3

SECOND. 14330 C3 15394 R 2 20479 C3
10797 R 3 14888 C6 15459 RC7 21264 T 3
10977 C3 14962 C2 15460 RC7 21359 TR 3
12741 R 3 15197 C3 17620 C7 21371 R 3
12842 C3 15373 TR 3 17636 C3 22747 C2
14270 RC3 15390 TR 3 18313 TRC3

NORTHWESTERN CHINA AND FRONTIER REGIONS

PRIMARY 12037 C2 18220 C1 18245 C2
18340 C2 18584 R 4

SECOND. 15302 C3 15544 C8 18706 R 5

SOUTH CHINA BROADLY CONCEIVED

PRIMARY 13955 R 2 17982 R 2 18137 R 1
13887 R 2 14262 RC2 18113 R 3 18670 R 2
13889 R 2 17567 R 2 18129 R 3 18779 R 2

SECOND. 13929 R 2 15239 C1 18766 R 2
10137 C2 13972 R 2 18613 R 1 21426 TRC3

EAST CENTRAL CHINA

PRIMARY 15143 R 3 15291 C3 17411 T 2
11121 C2 15254 C3 15944 TR 3 22571 T 2

SECOND. 16075 C3 17646 C2 19069 C3
14393 C2 16122 R 3 17735 R 3 21433 C2
15493 C7 17565 R 2 18487 T 2

CENTRAL YANGTZE PROVINCES

PRIMARY 14186 T 4 14187 T 2 18091 T 3

SECOND. 13931 R 2 15229 C3 16150 C3
17643 C3 19450 R 7

SOUTHWESTERN CHINA

PRIMARY 18087 T 4 18089 T 2 18131 R 2
18287 C2

SECOND. 14634 TR 3 15957 R 2 22542 T 2

SOUTHEASTERN CHINA

PRIMARY 14326 C3 17775 C7 18271 C3
10855 RC2 15263 C2 17913 C2 18742 R 2
10935 C1 15485 C2 18156 R 1 20524 C3
13921 R 2 16769 C2

SECOND. 13953 R 3 18620 R 3 20997 C2
10552 T 2 15987 C7 18748 R 3 20998 C2
10840 R 3 16792 C7 19165 C8 22607 T 2
13016 R 3 17523 T 3 19371 C2 22678 R 3
13906 R 2 17615 RC2 19502 R 3

TAIWAN ONLY

PRIMARY 10983 C2 14367 C1 18263 C2
10882 RC2 11108 C1 17955 RC1 18290 C2
10955 C1 11417 RC1 18121 R 2 18297 C2
10958 C1 12078 C1

SECOND. 10959 C2 11690 TR 2 16129 C2
10914 C1 11044 RC2 11959 C2 16347 C2
10923 C3 11109 C1 12008 C2 22759 C1
10956 C4 11138 C2

HONG KONG AND MACAU ONLY

PRIMARY □

SECOND. 15973 TRC2 17994 C2

32.1 STATE OR PARTY CONTROL OF ORGANIZED GROUPS

政府或政黨對於組織團體之控制

政府又は政党による組織団体の統制

GEOGRAPHIC CHINA BROADLY CONCEIVED

PRIMARY 14798 TRC2 18303 R 2 18407 T 2
11035 RC2 18111 R 1 18306 R 2 18547 TR 2
13950 R 2 18125 R 1 18308 R 3 20960 TRC2
14679 TR 1 18301 T 4

SECOND. 13812 T 2 18073 T 2 19559 R 5
10177 C2 13844 T 1 18544 TR 1 21435 C2
10446 R 2 15158 TRC2 18764 R 2 21538 TRC2
10700 TR 2 16128 TRC2 18810 RC2 21853 TRC2
10850 RC1 17975 T 2 19503 R 2 22866 T 2
11150 C4 17981 TR 2 19546 R 3 23021 C2

MAINLAND CHINA

PRIMARY: MONOGRAPHS
10631 T 2 13991 RC1 15260 C2 18324 C2
10883 TRC2 14001 RC1 15570 C2 18341 C3
10885 RC4 14006 RC2 15938 TR 2 18345 C4
10931 C2 14037 C2 16013 C7 18350 C1
10962 C4 14040 C1 17588 C8 18655 R 2
11076 C2 14047 C1 17674 C7 18709 R 2
11094 C2 14055 C1 17990 C2 19077 RC7
11096 C2 14263 RC1 17993 C2 19092 RC8
11101 C2 14285 TRC1 18003 C2 19166 C2
11391 RC2 14299 C2 18061 C2 19184 C8
11437 C2 14337 C2 18134 R 2 19286 RC5
11651 C2 14677 TR 1 18186 RC1 19338 C5
11885 C2 14753 R 1 18187 RC2 19422 C3
12523 C8 14808 RC2 18212 C1 19455 R 8
12845 C4 14853 C2 18264 C2 19594 C4
12876 C2 15006 C2 18272 C1 19595 C4
13105 C2 15007 C4 18277 C2 19597 C2
13923 R 1 15017 C2 18309 R 3 19668 C5
13945 R 2 15140 TR 2 18312 RC2 21928 C2
13986 TRC2 15230 C2 18319 C1

PRIMARY: INCLUSIONS
11042 RC2 14268 RC3 15296 C1 18241 C2
11063 C3 14302 C3 15978 RC7 18310 R 2
11100 C1 14391 C2 15990 C7 18315 RC4
12863 C4 14788 RC2 17644 C2 18325 C1
13904 R 2 14913 C2 18208 C2 18334 C1
14000 TRC1 15217 C2 18240 C1 18343 C2

32.2 Anti-State Associations

反叛集團　反国家的な団体

The Eighteen Provinces

North China Broadly Conceived

Manchuria

Northern China

Northwestern China and Frontier Regions

South China Broadly Conceived

East Central China

Central Yangtze Provinces

Southwestern China

Southeastern China

Taiwan Only

Hong Kong and Macau Only

33 Religious Sects and Associations
宗教派別及組織
宗教各派及び組織

Geographic China Broadly Conceived
Primary 16229 TR 2 18923 T 1 19032 TRC1
10108 R 2 17448 TR 1 18936 T 2 19036 TRC2
10510 T 2 17980 TR 1 18937 T 2 19039 TRC2
10611 T 2 17981 TR 2 18943 T 1 19044 TRC2
11556 T 1 18102 TR 2 18947 T 2 19052 TRC1
11603 TRC1 18480 T 2 18968 TR 2 19055 TRC2
11605 RC2 18495 T 2 18969 TR 2 19699 R 3
14167 T 2 18544 TR 1 18970 TR 4 20563 T 2
14266 TRC1 18828 TRC1 18971 TR 2 20619 TR 2
14694 TR 4 18852 T 2 18972 TR 2 21383 R 2
14698 TR 1 18871 T 2 18975 TR 1 21477 TRC2
14798 TRC2 18886 T 1 18976 TR 2 21754 TR 1
15044 T 2 18888 T 1 18979 TR 2 21788 TR 1
15363 T 2 18891 T 2 18982 TR 1 22001 TR 1
15773 R 2 18900 T 1 18984 TR 1 22555 T 2
16158 T 2 18902 T 1 18995 R 2 22866 T 2
16192 T 1 18904 T 2 19016 R 2 22972 TRC1
16217 T 7 18919 T 1
Second. 11270 TR 4 18396 T 2 21750 TR 1
10010 T 2 11544 T 1 18545 TR 2 21760 TR 1
10016 T 2 11619 C2 18558 TR 2 22102 TR 2
10025 T 2 12190 T 2 18700 R 2 22560 T 1
10034 T 2 12660 TR 4 19219 TR 2 22588 T 1
10045 T 2 14676 TR 3 19752 T 1 22593 T 2
10060 T 2 14720 R 2 20231 RC2 22594 T 2
10106 R 2 15191 RC2 21392 TRC2 22618 T 2
10107 R 2 16179 T 1 21639 T 1 22637 T 1
10111 TRC2 16186 T 2 21641 T 1 22694 R 3
10713 TR 2 18073 T 2 21703 T 1 22720 R 3
10806 R 2 18301 T 4 21742 TR 1

Mainland China
Primary: Monographs
10049 T 2 11643 C2 18915 T 2 19038 RC1
10083 TR 2 11651 C2 18927 T 1 19042 RC1
10104 R 2 11654 C2 18940 T 1 19062 C2
10145 C2 12572 T 3 18945 T 2 19063 C2
10838 R 4 14652 TR 2 18952 TR 2 20221 R 2
11545 T 1 15163 RC2 18959 TR 2 21624 T 2
11562 T 1 16210 T 2 18974 TR 1 21657 T 1
11578 TR 1 16335 TRC2 18978 TR 1 21797 TR 1
11586 TR 2 16343 TRC2 18980 TR 2 21900 TRC2
11595 R 1 18391 T 7 18987 TR 2 22530 T 1
11596 R 1 18849 T 1 18988 TR 2 22556 T 2
11601 R 2 18853 T 2 18989 TR 2 22595 T 5
11607 TRC1 18854 T 1 18991 TR 4 22667 TR 1
11611 RC1 18862 T 2 19033 TRC1 22714 R 2
11625 C2 18867 T 2 19035 TRC2
Primary: Inclusions
11574 T 1 18879 T 1 18992 R 2 19056 RC1
11604 RC1 18885 T 2 19000 R 1 19709 TRC3
11617 C1 18896 T 2 19003 R 2 20896 R 2
11633 C1 18944 T 1 19010 R 2 21709 T 2
14760 R 1 18949 TR 2 19028 R 1 21910 C1
16289 R 4 18951 TR 2 19029 TRC1 22205 TRC1
17935 TR 1 18977 TR 1 19037 TRC1 22525 T 2
18858 T 1 18986 TR 1 19040 TRC2
Primary: Journal Articles
11557 T 1 14565 T 4 18961 TR 1 19057 C2
11585 TR 1 14759 R 4 18963 TR 1 19058 C2
11592 TR 1 16196 T 2 18964 TR 2 19059 C1
11602 RC1 16309 R 2 18973 TR 3 19060 C1
11609 RC2 18380 T 1 19009 R 2 19067 C1
11610 TRC1 18848 T 2 19014 R 2 20469 R 4
11618 C3 18866 T 1 19020 R 1 21170 T 1
11626 C2 18873 T 1 19021 R 2 21462 R 1
11629 C2 18893 T 2 19025 R 1 21652 T 2
11636 C1 18897 T 1 19030 RC4 21716 T 1
11644 C1 18928 T 2 19031 RC2 21860 RC1
11648 C3 18938 T 1 19034 RC2 22564 T 2
11652 C2 18941 T 2
Secondary: Monographs
10041 T 2 10062 T 2 10089 R 2 10155 C2
10044 T 2 10081 TR 2 10120 TRC2 10164 C2
10631 T 2 14178 T 2 19638 R 7 20823 TR 4
10660 T 2 14655 TR 1 19649 R 7 21259 T 2
10697 TR 2 15466 RC2 19751 T 2 21286 T 1
10937 C2 16189 T 2 19886 TRC1 21300 T 2
11194 T 2 16332 TRC1 20107 R 2 21355 TR 2
11563 T 4 17977 T 2 20124 T 4 21363 TR 4
11622 C1 18378 T 2 20137 T 2 21980 T 4
11627 C2 18387 T 2 20179 TR 1 22068 T 1
11885 C2 18596 R 2 20461 R 1 22572 T 2
12921 T 2 18804 TRC2 20462 R 2 22591 T 1
13882 TR 2 18827 RC2 20618 TR 2 22991 TRC2
Secondary: Inclusions
11550 T 2 16282 TR 1 20434 R 2 21804 TR 1
11647 C1 18521 T 5 21468 TRC1
Secondary: Journal Articles
10440 T 2 12129 C2 16257 TR 1 21593 C1
11549 T 1 12325 R 2 18439 T 1 21794 TR 1
11583 TR 2 13838 T 2 19344 T 5 22077 TR 2
11591 TR 1 13899 R 2 19700 R 2 22140 TR 1
11593 R 1 14004 TRC2 19775 T 2 22540 T 1
11635 C1 14673 TR 1 20254 T 2 22554 T 1
11645 C1 15747 T 2 21284 T 2 22727 TRC1
11649 C2 16184 T 1

The Eighteen Provinces
Primary 18859 T 2 18999 R 3 19686 T 3
10087 R 2 18869 T 3 19001 R 2 20544 T 2
11567 T 2 18870 T 3 19002 R 5 20547 T 2
11570 T 1 18874 T 2 19008 R 2 21199 C7
11621 C3 18880 T 1 19012 R 2 21642 T 1
12567 T 2 18881 T 2 19017 R 2 21655 T 5
15733 T 2 18882 T 1 19018 R 7 21686 T 2
16200 T 2 18907 T 7 19024 R 4 21697 T 1
16271 TR 2 18909 T 2 19027 R 2 21816 R 2
16279 TR 1 18916 T 2 19046 RC1 21822 R 1
17973 T 2 18917 T 2 19047 RC1 22029 T 3
18406 T 1 18930 T 2 19053 TRC2 22615 T 2
18513 T 2 18948 T 1 19439 T 1 22630 T 2
18850 T 3 18985 TR 3 19618 R 7
Second. 15327 T 3 16276 TR 1 21627 T 1
10018 T 2 16049 T 2 17842 R 2 22009 R 2
10056 T 2 16058 R 2 18405 T 2 22110 TR 1
10141 C2 16161 T 2 18436 T 2 22534 T 1
10170 C2 16171 T 1 18441 T 2 22553 T 2
11571 T 1 16183 T 2 19695 T 2 22760 C3
11579 TR 1 16191 T 1 20548 T 2 22865 T 3
15038 T 2 16252 TR 2 21456 R 2

North China Broadly Conceived
Primary 18493 T 2 18914 T 2 19011 R 2
15752 T 2 18595 R 7 18953 TR 2 20578 T 2
16169 T 2 18872 T 2 18960 TR 2 21622 T 1
Second. 16317 R 2 18497 T 2 21784 TR 7
10064 T 2 18371 T 2 20716 T 2 22623 T 2
10580 T 2

Manchuria
Primary 10356 R 2 16315 R 3 18942 T 5
19050 RC1 22654 TR 2
Second. 10582 T 2 20596 T 2 22719 R 3

Northern China
Primary 18068 C3 18920 T 2 18990 TR 3
11541 T 2 18846 T 3 18921 T 1 18994 R 3
11542 T 8 18847 T 3 18931 T 3 18998 R 3
15414 R 8 18856 T 3 18939 T 7 19007 R 2
15475 RC8 18868 T 2 18946 T 3 19048 RC1
15710 T 2 18887 T 8 18954 TR 8 20436 R 3
16201 T 6 18894 T 8 18957 TR 3 20557 T 3
16206 T 2 18905 T 3 18958 TR 3 21298 T 2
16216 T 3 18910 T 1 18965 TR 8 21770 TR 3
16304 R 3 18913 T 3 18967 TR 3 22583 T 4
Second. 15416 R 3 16305 R 2 19620 R 2
10644 T 2 16160 T 8 16314 R 8 20205 R 2
11594 R 2 16219 T 3 16950 R 2 21554 C3
14204 T 3 16220 T 2 17953 TRC3 22383 T 2
15075 R 8 16222 T 8 18420 T 4 22520 T 3
15372 TR 3 16231 TR 7 18658 R 7 22706 R 6
15415 R 8

Northwestern China and Frontier Regions
Primary 18911 T 2 18955 TR 3 18996 R 2
18372 T 4 18924 T 2 18956 TR 2 19041 RC2
18864 T 1 18935 T 2 18993 R 2 22682 R 2
18890 T 2
Second. 15086 RC2 16331 TRC1 16912 T 2
10725 TR 2 16307 R 8 16628 R 2 18697 R 2
12747 R 2 16325 R 8

South China Broadly Conceived
Primary 15721 T 2 18377 T 2 18898 T 8
10031 T 2 16159 T 2 18500 T 2 19006 R 4
10046 T 2 16339 TRC2 18875 T 2 19054 RC2
11014 T 2
Second. 15205 C2 16392 T 5 18449 T 2
10028 T 2 15361 T 2 16520 T 2 18471 T 1
12569 T 2 15722 T 2 16689 R 2 20208 R 2
14784 RC3 16388 T 2 16910 T 4 22601 T 2

East Central China
Primary 18857 T 4 18932 T 4 19015 R 3
15348 T 3 18865 T 2 18934 T 7 19023 R 3
15731 T 2 18883 T 8 18966 TR 8 19069 C3
15732 T 2 18884 T 8 18983 TR 3 20251 C3
16227 TR 4 18918 T 3 19004 R 8 21331 TR 1
18575 R 8 18926 T 3 19005 R 3 22696 R 3
18855 T 2
Second. 15930 T 3 16345 C3 18473 T 3
10321 T 2 16162 T 7 16409 TR 3 21621 T 1
10339 TR 2 16290 R 8 16631 R 7 21628 T 7
15307 T 3 16297 R 3 16718 R 8 22764 C3
15388 TR 3

Central Yangtze Provinces
Primary 18895 T 4 18912 T 2
Second. 16526 T 2 20138 T 2 20820 TR 2
22445 R 1

Southwestern China
Primary 18889 T 2 18933 T 4 19026 R 2
17520 T 2 18892 T 3 18962 TR 1 19049 RC1
18300 T 2 18922 T 2 19019 R 8 22517 T 2
18845 T 4 18925 T 2 19022 R 2 22523 T 2
18861 T 4 18929 T 7
Second. 16300 R 2 16512 T 2 20873 R 7
10566 T 2 16302 R 4 18394 T 2 21892 TRC2
14571 T 4 16312 R 2 18491 T 2 22597 T 3

Southeastern China
Primary 18860 T 2 18906 T 3 21270 T 2
15923 T 3 18863 T 1 18950 TR 2 22526 T 3
16187 T 3 18876 T 2 18997 R 3 22545 T 4
16190 T 2 18878 T 2 19013 R 3 22566 T 3
18844 T 1 18899 T 2 19043 TRC2 22607 T 2
18851 T 7 18901 T 2 19045 TRC2 22707 R 3
Second. 15344 T 3 16341 TRC7 18519 T 2
14586 T 4 15349 T 2 17256 R 2 20385 T 5
14629 TR 4 15364 T 3 17545 T 2 20791 TR 3
14711 R 3 15448 R 3 17657 T 3 21271 T 2
14772 R 3 16181 T 2 18438 T 2 22550 T 4
15319 T 3 16270 TR 2 18483 T 2

Taiwan Only
Primary 16365 C2 18908 T 2 19064 C2
15369 TR 2 18877 T 2 18981 TR 2 19065 C2
16361 C8 18903 T 2 19061 C1 19068 C2
Second. 16354 C8 16360 C4 19090 RC8
15504 C8 16357 C3 16362 C1 21925 C3
16226 TR 2 16358 C3 16363 C1 23027 C2

Hong Kong and Macau Only
Primary 17985 RC2 19051 TRC2 19070 C3
15454 TRC3 17994 C2 19066 C3 20529 C3
15566 C8
Second. 15409 R 2 16348 C7 19696 T 3
14597 T 2 15518 C2 17626 T 4 22441 TR 7
15343 T 4 16328 TRC2 17924 T 7 22733 TRC3

34.1 Agricultural Associations and Cooperatives

農業生產組織 農業生産組織

Geographic China Broadly Conceived

Primary 12394 rc7 12439 c8 15539 c7
Second. 10700 tr 2 12223 tr 7 15175 rc2
10144 c2 10853 trc2 12233 tr 2 15185 trc2
10162 c2 11047 rc2 12310 r 8 16068 rc2
10177 c2 11857 trc2 12328 r 7 18786 trc2
10396 trc2 11859 trc2 13793 c2 20306 c2
10432 c2 12196 t 7 15063 r 2

Mainland China

Primary: Monographs
11906 c2 12475 c2 16001 c7 19105 c7
11998 c2 12552 c7 16011 c7 19110 c8
12015 c2 12563 c7 16013 c7 19131 c7
12029 c1 12564 c2 16046 c2 19132 c7
12123 c2 14153 c2 16070 c2 19133 c7
12227 tr 7 15258 c7 16457 c2 19134 c8
12257 r 7 15260 c2 17674 c7 19135 c7
12271 r 7 15483 c7 17760 r 7 19166 c2
12372 r 2 15488 c7 17763 r 2 19181 c8
12375 rc2 15495 c2 17979 tr 7 19184 c8
12379 rc7 15507 c7 19074 r 7 19194 c8
12424 rc7 15549 c7 19077 rc7 19201 c7
12426 rc7 15567 c7 19078 rc8 19203 c7
12429 c7 15570 c2 19082 rc7 19257 r 7
12441 c2 15977 rc7 19083 rc7 19638 r 7
12456 c8 15991 c7 19092 rc8 19705 r 2
12464 c8 15992 c7 19095 c7 20079 c7
12467 c7 15993 c7 19100 c7 20080 c7

Primary: Inclusions
12176 c7 14451 c7 19101 c7 19170 c7
12293 r 8 15217 c2 19104 c7 19182 c7
12397 rc7 15542 c7 19108 c7 19190 c7
12459 c7 15558 c7 19129 c8 19198 c2
12506 c2 15978 rc7 19138 c7 19199 c7
12536 c7 15990 c7 19146 c7 19202 c7
12559 c2 15996 c7 19149 c7 19280 r 2
14138 c2 17519 c7 19154 c8 19284 rc2
14442 c7 17978 t 2 19162 c7 21486 c2
14448 c7 19087 rc8 19167 c7

Primary: Journal Articles
10391 rc2 15228 c2 19081 rc8 19145 c7
10490 c2 15494 c7 19084 rc8 19150 c2
10502 c7 15496 c7 19086 rc7 19151 c7
11085 c2 15559 c7 19091 rc7 19155 c7
11937 c2 15564 c7 19096 c8 19156 c7
12040 c2 15831 c7 19097 c8 19157 c8
12111 c2 15882 c7 19099 c8 19158 c7
12388 rc7 15886 c7 19102 c7 19159 c7
12391 rc7 15975 rc7 19103 c7 19160 c7
12403 rc7 15999 c7 19107 c7 19164 c7
12443 c7 16004 c8 19121 c7 19168 c2
12445 c7 16005 c7 19123 c7 19169 c2
12451 c7 16770 c7 19124 c8 19174 c7
12458 c7 16807 c7 19125 c7 19175 c8
12477 c7 16808 c7 19126 c7 19176 c8
12483 c8 16835 c7 19128 c7 19177 c8
12486 c2 16861 c7 19130 c7 19183 c2
12497 c2 16863 c7 19136 c7 19185 c7
12501 c7 17130 c7 19137 c7 19187 c8
12511 c7 17673 c7 19139 c7 19188 c7
12529 c7 17684 c7 19140 c7 19189 c7
12549 c8 17778 c7 19141 c7 19461 r 8
14440 rc8 18338 c7 19142 c7 21045 c2
14449 c7 19073 r 8 19143 c7 21548 c2
14515 rc2 19076 rc8 19144 c7 22306 c1
15154 r 2

Secondary: Monographs
10088 r 2 10159 c2 10487 c2 11096 c2
10125 rc2 10164 c2 10503 c2 11106 c2
10126 rc2 10165 c2 10812 r 2 11391 rc2
10130 c2 10167 c2 10888 trc2 11393 trc2
10134 c2 10172 c2 10895 c2 11423 c1
10143 c2 10232 c2 10937 c2 11437 c2
10145 c2 10338 tr 2 11048 trc2 11440 c2
10150 c2 10425 c2 11092 c2 11496 c1
10152 c2 10477 c2 11094 c2 11651 c2
11740 r 2 12002 c2 13105 c2 16031 c7
11750 r 2 12071 c2 13117 c2 16488 c7
11793 r 2 12082 c2 13308 rc2 16516 t 7
11807 r 2 12086 c2 13584 c2 16768 c7
11829 r 2 12109 c2 13750 r 2 17092 r 7
11845 rc2 12154 c2 13766 rc2 17769 r 7
11846 rc2 12158 c2 13769 c7 18003 c2
11848 rc2 12173 c2 13773 c2 18170 rc2
11849 trc2 12229 tr 7 13795 c2 18172 rc2
11852 rc2 12230 tr 2 14139 c2 18178 rc2
11862 rc2 12317 r 7 14497 r 2 18264 c2
11874 rc2 12331 r 7 15085 rc2 18312 rc2
11883 c2 12363 r 8 15090 rc2 18585 r 2
11884 c2 12380 rc7 15100 c7 18827 rc2
11885 c2 12440 c7 15123 c2 19063 c2
11894 c2 12453 c7 15192 rc2 19240 r 2
11897 c2 12485 c2 15248 c2 19455 r 8
11901 c2 12487 c7 15294 c2 19457 r 7
11903 c2 12515 c7 15297 c2 19649 r 7
11909 c2 12519 c8 15466 rc2 19922 c7
11920 c2 12524 c2 15482 c2 21416 rc2
11939 c2 12535 c2 15506 c2 22210 trc2
11946 c2 12544 c2 15509 c2 22291 c2
11949 c2 12562 c7 15519 c2 22318 c2
11962 c2 12811 c2 15524 c7 22322 c2
11980 c2 13070 c2 15980 rc2 22375 c2
12000 c2 13104 c2 16029 c7

Secondary: Inclusions
10410 c2 12010 c2 12507 c7 17640 c8
10993 c2 12092 c2 12557 c8 18280 c2
11042 rc2 12121 c2 13066 c2 18293 c2
11447 c1 12396 rc8 13088 c2 18358 c2
11741 r 1 12415 rc2 13097 c2 20081 c2
11861 rc7 12422 rc7 15099 c7 22221 rc2
11888 c2 12462 c7 15107 c2 22282 rc2
11942 c2 12479 c2 15170 rc2 22290 c2
11965 c2 12484 c8 17110 c7

Secondary: Journal Articles
10241 c2 12140 c2 13056 c7 16079 c7
10462 c7 12162 c2 13322 c2 16145 c7
10489 c7 12263 r 2 13596 c7 17107 c7
10492 c2 12314 r 8 13608 c7 17131 c7
10925 c2 12334 r 8 14148 c2 17335 c2
11041 rc2 12374 rc7 14260 rc2 17373 c7
11056 c8 12393 rc8 14439 rc7 17507 c7
11503 c2 12400 rc7 14445 c7 17597 c2
11944 c2 12413 rc7 14824 c2 17905 c7
11945 c2 12418 rc7 14862 c7 18269 c2
11954 c2 12419 rc7 14984 c2 18335 c2
11957 c2 12425 trc8 15098 c7 18797 rc1
12006 c2 12430 c7 15122 c7 18821 rc2
12012 c2 12472 c2 15232 c7 19251 r 2
12056 c2 12473 c7 15528 c7 19635 r 7
12089 c2 12480 c2 15551 c7 19641 r 8
12097 c2 12482 c2 15580 c2 19673 c2
12100 c2 12493 c7 15845 c7 19715 tr 2
12103 c2 12494 c2 15896 c7 20254 t 2
12110 c2 12500 c7 15994 c7 20402 rc2
12112 c2 12516 c7 16020 c7 20521 c2
12120 c2 12518 c2 16036 c7 22239 rc2
12128 c2 12526 c7 16040 c7 22301 c2
12138 c2 13055 c2 16041 c7 22323 c7
12139 c2

The Eighteen Provinces

Primary
16626 r 7 16894 c2 19098 c7 19243 r 7
16890 c7 19071 r 7 19122 c8 19259 r 7

Second. 12212 tr 2 15527 c7 19244 r 7
10138 c2 12540 c7 15543 c2 19282 r 2
10161 c2 12541 c7 16049 t 2 20668 c2
11798 r 2 13703 r 2 16591 r 7 21489 c2
12155 c2 15478 c2 16806 c7 21738 tr 2
12183 t 8 15511 c2 18645 r 7

North China Broadly Conceived

Primary 16732 rc2
Second. 15433 r 2 16744 rc7 18622 r 2
10435 c2 16430 r 2 18307 r 2 18732 r 2

Manchuria

Primary 10852 rc2 16879 c8 19111 c8
19195 c7 19196 c7
Second. 14129 rc2 15679 tr 7 16801 c8
10796 r 2 15181 rc2 15914 c7 17231 r 8
12406 rc8 15614 rc2 15995 c2 20672 c7

Northern China

Primary 16850 c7 19114 c8 19172 c7
15406 r 8 17672 c7 19117 c8 19178 c8
15477 c7 17677 c7 19118 c7 19180 c8
15502 c7 17891 r 7 19147 c8 19186 c8
15557 c7 19093 c7 19152 c7 19192 c7
15903 c7 19094 c8 19153 c8 19193 c7
16760 c8 19106 c8 19161 c7 19200 c7
16766 c8 19112 c8 19171 c7 19648 r 7
Second. 15904 c8 16765 c7 17382 c8
12542 c7 16408 tr 7 16782 c8 17444 tr 8
15360 t 7 16474 c7 16791 c8 17620 c7
15408 r 2 16475 c7 16857 c7 17685 c7
15414 r 8 16574 r 7 16875 c7 17793 c8
15415 r 8 16685 r 7 16900 c8 19227 r 7
15450 r 7 16759 c7 17334 c2 22747 c2
15460 rc7 16762 c7

Northwestern China and Frontier Regions

Primary 15544 c8 19080 rc7 19233 r 7
12003 c2 16803 c7 19119 c8 19661 c7
Second. 13814 t 2 16751 trc2 16994 c8
11130 c2 15421 r 8 16786 c2 18340 c2
11161 c2 15545 c8 16804 c8 19375 c2
11686 tr 2 16735 rc8 16836 c2 22738 rc2
12407 rc8

South China Broadly Conceived

Primary □
Second. 10137 c2 12383 rc2 16855 c8

East Central China

Primary 16468 c7 17462 r 7 19075 r 2
15405 r 7 16668 r 7 17680 c7 19116 c8
15493 c7
Second. 15535 c8 16466 c7 16621 r 2
11747 r 2 15577 c7 16593 r 7 16793 c8
11769 r 2 15985 c7 16620 r 2 17667 r 7
15480 c2

Central Yangtze Provinces

Primary 16420 r 2 19072 r 2 19127 c8
15523 c7 16757 c7 19120 c8 19191 c7
Second. 16617 r 7 16842 c7 17502 c7
16432 r 2 16754 c7 17312 rc2 17776 c7
16459 c8 16802 c8 17498 c7 20241 c8

Southwestern China

Primary 18322 c7 19085 rc7
Second. 12543 c7 16598 r 7 17071 r 7
10179 c2 13221 r 2 16787 c2 17872 r 7

Southeastern China

Primary 16764 c7 19109 c8 19179 c7
15456 rc7 16774 c7 19113 c8 19197 c8
15984 c7 16781 c7 19115 c8 19408 c2
15987 c7 16798 c2 19148 c7 20082 c7
16736 rc7 16874 c7 19165 c8
Second. 15476 rc8 16479 c2 16888 c8
10855 rc2 15479 c8 16775 c7 17671 c7
12069 c2 15572 c2 16779 c7 17913 c2
15418 r 8 16017 c2 16792 c7 20006 tr 8

Taiwan Only

Primary 18004 c7 19089 rc8 19173 c7
15889 c2 19079 rc8 19090 rc8 19466 rc7
16748 rc2 19088 rc8 19163 c8
Second. 12008 c2 15439 r 2 15515 c8
10904 c2 13079 c2 15441 r 2 15530 c7
11851 trc2 15002 c2 15443 r 2 15533 c7

16003 c7 16797 c7 16833 c8 17127 c2
16550 TR 8 16810 c7 16852 c8 19468 RC7
16561 TR 2 16824 c2 16854 c7 19679 c7
16729 RC2 16828 c8 16858 c2 19737 c8
16747 RC2 16832 c8 16873 c7

Hong Kong and Macau Only

Primary □
Second. 16456 TRC7 17985 RC2 19309 c2

34.2 Business Organization

商業組織 商業組織

Geographic China Broadly Conceived

Primary 12600 T 3 13762 TRC1 19217 TR 3
11150 c4 12692 R 3 14399 T 4 19219 TR 2
11250 TR 1 13106 c4 16068 RC2 20111 TRC2
12593 T 2 13717 R 2 18301 T 4

Second. 11839 R 2 13622 T 2 15363 T 2
10074 TR 2 11857 TRC2 13652 TR 3 17691 TR 2
10111 TRC2 12233 TR 2 13676 TR 4 17696 R 3
10117 TRC2 12409 RC7 13688 TR 2 19481 TR 3
10510 T 2 13049 TRC2 13692 TR 4 19534 R 2
11035 RC2 13138 TR 2 13704 R 2 19546 R 3
11270 TR 4 13144 TR 2 13708 R 2 19559 R 5
11692 TR 2 13168 TR 4 14468 R 2 19717 T 2
11703 TR 2 13574 TRC2 14475 R 2 20620 TR 2

Mainland China

Primary: Monographs
10172 c2 13119 c1 17190 TR 5 19246 R 5
11313 R 1 13169 TR 3 17226 R 2 19248 R 4
11344 R 1 13187 TR 4 17228 R 5 19252 R 1
11672 T 4 13284 R 2 17238 R 2 19257 R 7
11740 R 2 13308 RC2 17241 R 2 19263 R 4
11794 R 5 13314 RC1 17245 R 5 19275 R 1
11903 c2 13336 c2 17249 R 7 19276 R 1
11906 c2 13399 c2 17291 R 2 19277 R 4
11998 c2 13641 T 2 17297 R 2 19281 R 5
12442 c7 13666 TR 2 17311 RC2 19285 RC5
12475 c2 13668 TR 4 17313 RC2 19286 RC5
12606 T 2 13740 R 3 17316 RC2 19291 c2
12631 TR 2 13766 RC2 17441 TR 2 19302 c5
12712 R 2 13773 c2 17460 R 7 19338 c5
12795 c5 14153 c2 17661 TR 2 19480 TR 3
12985 R 2 14419 c2 19222 TR 4 19517 R 3
13004 R 1 14496 R 5 19232 R 3 19789 TR 2
13029 R 2 16488 c7 19240 R 2 22006 R 1

Primary: Inclusions
11063 c3 13260 R 2 17472 R 8 19284 RC2
11494 c2 13333 c2 19216 TR 2 19290 c4
12092 c2 13416 c4 19256 R 3 19324 c4
13156 TR 2 14455 TR 4 19279 R 4 19332 c2
13162 TR 4 17192 TR 2 19280 R 2 19333 c3
13170 TR 2

Primary: Journal Articles
10880 RC2 13648 TR 4 19215 TR 5 19294 c5
10951 c3 13678 TR 5 19218 TR 1 19303 c7
11142 c4 13749 R 5 19221 TR 3 19304 c1
12018 c4 13789 c2 19224 R 7 19305 c3
12028 c4 13790 c1 19226 R 2 19307 c2
12111 c2 14398 T 3 19229 R 5 19310 c3
12565 T 4 14417 c3 19230 R 1 19312 c4
12605 T 3 14418 c4 19234 R 1 19314 c1
12690 R 2 14460 R 2 19235 R 1 19315 c4
12691 R 2 15997 c4 19236 R 1 19316 c4
12816 c4 17278 R 5 19242 R 3 19317 c2
13000 R 2 17289 R 2 19249 R 3 19321 c4
13071 c2 17335 c2 19250 R 1 19322 c1
13075 c2 17370 c2 19251 R 2 19323 c2
13108 c2 17401 c2 19253 R 4 19326 c4
13149 TR 2 17482 R 7 19254 R 4 19327 c3
13216 R 1 18327 c2 19255 R 4 19328 c4
13233 R 2 18359 c1 19271 R 4 19330 c3
13364 c2 19156 c7 19272 R 1 19344 T 5
13378 c4 19204 T 4 19273 R 2 19351 T 4
13398 c4 19208 T 1 19278 R 1 20054 TR 1
13643 TR 5 19214 TR 1 19289 c4

Secondary: Monographs
10067 TR 2 11846 RC2 13105 c2 14520 c3
10069 TR 2 11849 TRC2 13250 R 2 14687 TR 2
10103 R 2 11852 RC2 13261 R 5 15123 c2
10145 c2 11864 RC2 13339 c4 15192 RC2
10150 c2 11874 RC2 13366 c4 15260 c2
10654 T 3 11894 c2 13384 c2 15560 c4
10702 TR 2 11897 c2 13415 c4 17395 c2
10758 R 4 11980 c2 13420 c2 17485 R 2
10895 c4 11995 c2 13432 c2 17717 R 3
10962 c4 12082 c2 13437 c2 17974 T 3
11094 c2 12109 c2 13456 T 2 17990 c2
11194 T 2 12158 c2 13520 TR 2 18187 RC2
11263 TR 1 12166 c2 13584 c2 18783 R 2
11348 R 1 12230 TR 2 13612 c5 19476 TR 2
11423 c1 12271 R 7 13654 TR 4 19594 c4
11689 TR 2 12375 RC2 13659 TR 4 19640 R 7
11698 TR 2 12590 T 2 13690 TR 5 19644 R 2
11705 TR 2 12757 R 4 13743 R 2 19668 c5
11707 TR 2 12793 c2 13750 R 2 19707 R 7
11745 R 2 12849 c2 13787 c2 21416 RC2
11748 R 2 12950 TR 2 14122 R 3 22322 c2
11756 R 2 13041 R 2 14164 T 2 22568 T 3
11793 R 2 13078 c1 14396 T 2 22805 R 2
11807 R 2 13104 c2 14513 TRC2

Secondary: Inclusions
11248 TR 1 12727 R 2 13413 c4 17147 T 2
11399 RC1 13085 c2 13435 c2 17157 T 5
11840 R 3 13100 c2 14138 c2 17174 T 2
11942 c2 13242 R 5 14406 TR 4 17314 RC2
12010 c2 13257 R 2 14495 R 5 17317 RC2
12045 c2 13335 c2 15187 RC7 18358 c2
12168 c2 13341 c4 15233 c2 21486 c2
12197 T 7 13387 c1 17110 c7

Secondary: Journal Articles
10440 T 2 12089 c2 13381 c4 18684 R 2
10492 c2 12099 c1 13412 c4 19155 c7
10910 c1 12318 R 2 13423 c4 19352 TR 2
10913 c4 12566 T 2 13693 R 2 19430 R 4
11186 T 4 12568 T 2 13771 c2 19435 R 4
11190 T 1 12623 TR 4 13776 c4 19473 TR 4
11309 R 1 12635 TR 1 13785 c4 19572 R 2
11316 R 1 12668 TR 2 14397 T 4 19629 R 2
11505 c2 12702 R 2 14410 R 4 19635 R 7
11515 c1 12982 R 1 14413 RC4 19715 TR 2
11730 R 2 13092 c2 14415 RC4 20042 T 1
11895 c2 13134 T 2 14481 R 2 20058 R 1
11937 c2 13159 TR 2 15060 R 2 20201 R 4
11944 c2 13177 TR 4 15151 R 2 20214 R 2
11954 c2 13180 TR 2 17131 c7 20904 R 3
11966 c2 13270 R 3 17283 R 5 21540 RC1
12012 c2 13279 R 2 17391 c2 22098 TR 2
12034 c2 13280 R 4 17403 c2 22161 R 4
12036 c2 13346 c5 17492 R 7 22239 RC2
12085 c2 13370 c2 18002 c2

The Eighteen Provinces

Primary 16115 R 1 19228 R 3 19274 R 1
11061 c2 16894 c2 19239 R 5 19282 R 2
12878 T 2 17080 R 7 19241 R 2 19301 c2
12938 T 3 17236 R 2 19244 R 7 19345 T 4
13107 c3 17308 R 2 19245 R 2 19349 T 3
13155 TR 4 19210 T 2 19259 R 7 19356 TR 4
13166 TR 2 19212 T 4 19262 R 1 19527 R 4
13212 R 2 19223 R 3 19265 R 3 20793 TR 5
13637 T 2

Second. 12946 T 1 15501 c2 17248 R 2
10546 T 3 12962 TR 3 15511 c2 17301 R 7
11185 T 2 13037 R 2 16114 R 4 17484 R 2
11776 R 2 13151 TR 2 17143 T 3 17869 R 2
12253 R 2 13275 R 3 17144 T 2 17973 T 2
12683 TR 2 14474 R 3 17145 T 2 19577 R 3
12909 T 2 14480 R 4 17173 T 2 22463 R 1
12927 T 1 14505 R 2 17175 T 2 22628 T 3
12930 T 2 14829 c2

North China Broadly Conceived

Primary 14409 R 2 19225 R 4 19260 R 2
12998 R 2 17846 R 7 19231 R 3

Second. 11780 R 2 16430 R 2 17028 T 5
17658 T 4

Manchuria

Primary 17310 R 4 17857 R 2 19311 c3
11716 TR 2 17315 RC3 19237 R 1 19318 c3
13258 R 2 17501 c7 19266 R 2 19329 c3
16446 R 3 17689 T 7 19293 c3 19336 c2
16997 c4 17716 R 5 19298 c4 19523 R 2
17244 R 7

Second. 12180 T 2 13082 c2 16120 R 2
10852 RC2 12315 R 2 13098 c2 17346 c3
11345 R 2 12595 T 2 13396 c4 17348 c8
11691 TR 2 12641 TR 2 15181 RC2 19547 R 4
11712 TR 2 13005 R 5

Northern China

Primary 17252 R 3 17450 R 4 18313 TRC3
17005 c3 17262 R 2 17451 R 7 19211 T 7
17053 R 5 17300 R 5 17463 R 7 19227 R 7
17054 R 3 17309 R 2 17468 R 8 19288 c3
17122 c7 17319 RC3 17469 R 7 19331 c2
17141 T 5 17384 c7 17713 R 3 19337 c3
17186 TR 2 17396 c7 17721 R 7 19339 c7
17187 TR 7 17446 TR 3 17736 R 3 19340 c3
17251 R 3

Second. 15770 R 4 17200 R 3 17802 c3
11782 R 2 16016 c3 17240 R 7 17877 R 3
12991 R 2 16671 R 2 17277 R 3 17914 c7
12993 R 2 17020 T 3 17282 R 7 19171 c7
13640 T 5 17047 R 4 17393 c2 19357 TR 3
15416 R 3 17062 R 2 17397 c7 19579 R 2
15450 R 7 17123 c3 17705 R 3 19642 R 7
15768 R 2 17199 R 3 17720 R 4 22612 T 2

Northwestern China and Frontier Regions

Primary 17235 R 5 17293 R 3 19233 R 7

Second. 22682 R 2

South China Broadly Conceived

Primary 13403 c4 17225 R 2 19287 TRC3
12992 R 2 17167 T 3 19238 R 3 19296 c3
13030 R 2

Second. 12894 T 2 13123 T 2 17443 TR 2
12265 R 2 12920 T 4 15722 T 2 21426 TRC3
12647 TR 2

East Central China

Primary 17193 TR 3 17714 R 3 19268 R 3
13224 R 4 17213 R 2 17747 c3 19269 R 3
13326 c3 17274 R 2 18354 c3 19295 c3
15961 R 3 17434 T 2 19206 T 4 19300 c3
16075 c3 17440 TR 3 19213 TR 7 19308 c3
16292 R 3 17442 TR 5 19220 TR 4 19319 c3
16559 TR 2 17464 R 4 19258 R 3 19555 R 3
16937 TR 5 17467 R 3 19264 R 3 19605 c3
17162 T 3 17646 c2 19267 R 3 20262 R 2
17176 T 2 17654 c3

Second. 15948 TR 3 17125 c3 17732 R 3
13139 TR 2 16603 R 2 17250 R 7 17863 R 3
13193 R 2 16620 R 2 17372 c3 18321 c3
13226 R 2 16621 R 2 17462 R 7 19075 R 2
13392 c5 16622 R 2 17653 c3 20838 R 3
15430 R 3 16641 R 8 17694 TR 3 20884 R 3
15474 RC3 16947 R 2

Central Yangtze Provinces

Primary 17746 c5 19072 R 2

Second. 11723 R 2 16411 R 2 17132 T 3
17203 R 4 20210 R 2

Southwestern China

Primary 17063 R 3 19261 R 3 19299 c3
13209 R 2 17480 R 2 19270 R 2 19334 c2

Second. 15897 c2 17064 R 2 17163 T 8
15436 R 6 15916 c7 17146 T 7

Southeastern China

Primary 15376 TR 2 17191 TR 2 17270 R 4
15364 T 3 17151 T 3 17268 R 3 17436 T 3

19205 T 3 19429 T 3 19436 T 3 19840 R 2
19209 T 3 19434 T 3 19437 T 3 21268 T 3
19342 C3

Second. 16187 T 3 17256 R 2 19506 R 3
10292 TR 4 16988 C3 17387 C2 21575 C3
10522 T 3 17164 T 3 17453 R 3 22398 T 4
15317 T 2 17237 R 2 18022 TR 3 22887 T 3

Taiwan Only

Primary 19247 R 3 19320 C4 20268 C6
13083 C2 19292 C3 19587 C4 20424 C3
14911 C4 19313 C2

Second. 13315 RC2 15890 C2 17006 C4
10923 C3 13445 C4 16790 C8 17127 C2
12017 C2 13673 TR 4 16873 C7 17386 C4
13059 C2 14549 C4 16902 C7 19939 C2
13312 RC2 15351 T 2 16983 TRC4 21009 C2
13313 RC2 15568 C3

Hong Kong and Macau Only

Primary 17133 T 2 19207 T 3 19325 C3
16493 C3 17350 C5 19283 RC3 19335 C2
16893 C7 17499 C3 19297 C3 19341 C3
17116 C8 17516 C7 19306 C2 19593 C2
17126 C3 17742 C3 19309 C2 20075 C2

Second. 16451 RC3 17336 C3 17963 C2
15325 T 3 16862 C7 17349 C2 20272 C7
15838 C3 17002 C2 17385 C3 20663 RC3
15913 C3 17276 R 8 17495 RC3 22500 C3
16010 C2

34.3 Guilds

舊式行會　　ギルド

Geographic China Broadly Conceived

Primary 13672 TR 5 18301 T 4 19717 T 2
12901 T 2 17696 R 3 19353 TR 2

Second. 10560 T 2 12898 T 4 17976 T 2
10024 T 2 10707 TR 2 12965 TR 4 17981 TR 2
10048 T 2 11250 TR 1 13629 T 2 18024 TR 1
10058 T 2 11708 TR 2 14468 R 2 19478 TR 4
10073 TR 2 12233 TR 2 14476 R 3 19481 TR 3
10446 R 2 12600 T 3 17975 T 2 22109 TR 2
10526 T 2

Mainland China

Primary 14486 R 2 19344 T 5 19363 R 3
11672 T 4 14508 R 3 19351 T 4 19364 R 4
11698 TR 2 17283 R 5 19352 TR 2 19558 R 2
13029 R 2 17717 R 3 19358 TR 3 19644 R 2
13163 TR 2 19248 R 4 19359 R 3 19715 TR 2
13670 TR 3 19343 T 4 19361 R 3

Second. 11707 TR 2 13668 TR 4 18795 TRC2
10019 T 2 11745 R 2 13839 T 2 19281 R 5
10023 T 2 11794 R 5 14115 R 3 19430 R 4
10068 TR 2 11855 TRC2 14396 T 2 19473 TR 4
10069 TR 2 12961 TR 2 14397 T 4 19477 TR 4
10083 TR 2 12983 R 2 14407 R 3 19517 R 3
10084 TR 2 12985 R 2 14408 R 3 19542 R 4
10086 TR 2 13187 TR 4 14455 TR 4 19561 R 3
10097 R 2 13220 R 2 14496 R 5 19574 R 3
10451 R 2 13233 R 2 14510 R 4 19583 RC4
10768 R 4 13242 R 5 14652 TR 2 19623 R 4
11223 T 1 13277 R 2 16089 T 2 21709 T 2
11243 T 2 13279 R 2 16343 TRC2 21774 TR 2
11260 TR 2 13291 R 4 17190 TR 5 22006 R 1
11689 TR 2 13520 TR 2 17712 R 3

The Eighteen Provinces

Primary 19345 T 4 19350 T 4 19356 TR 4
10294 R 2 19347 T 3 19354 TR 4 19695 T 2
19210 T 2 19349 T 3

Second. 12938 T 3 14401 T 5 17173 T 2
10444 R 2 12946 T 1 15375 TR 2 17322 TRC2
10682 T 2 14118 R 4 15446 R 3 18012 T 2
18117 R 4 18609 R 2 19432 TR 4 19514 R 2
18367 T 2 19245 R 2 19483 R 4 21473 TRC2
18546 TR 2

North China Broadly Conceived

Primary □

Second. 21348 TR 3

Manchuria

Primary □

Second. 10582 T 2 11712 TR 2 12180 T 2
17471 R 5

Northern China

Primary 15407 R 3 17692 TR 3 19357 TR 3
19360 R 3

Second. 17062 R 2 17690 TR 3 17824 TR 3
10598 T 2 17240 R 7 17713 R 3 20631 R 3
16403 TR 2

Northwestern China and Frontier Regions

Primary 19355 TR 2

Second. 16431 R 2

South China Broadly Conceived

Primary □

Second. 12684 TR 2 12894 T 2 16092 T 4

East Central China

Primary 17176 T 2 17432 T 3

Second. 17725 R 3 19549 R 3 19703 R 3
17467 R 3 18529 TR 2 19555 R 3 20262 R 2
17662 T 7 19206 T 4

Central Yangtze Provinces

Primary □

Second. 15469 TRC2 15712 T 3 19072 R 2

Southwestern China

Primary 19362 R 6

Second. 10566 T 2 12889 T 2 15436 R 6
17137 T 2

Southeastern China

Primary 19205 T 3 19346 T 4 19348 T 3
19716 T 4

Second. 16187 T 3 18490 T 2 19506 R 3
22607 T 2

Taiwan Only

Primary □

Second. 17989 TRC2

Hong Kong and Macau Only

Primary □

Second. 17985 RC2

35 Veterans Associations and the Military in Society

退伍軍人組織及軍人之社會活動

在郷軍人会及び軍人の社会活動

Geographic China Broadly Conceived

Primary 12190 T 2 13950 R 2 13966 R 2
18308 R 3 18544 TR 1

Second. 17976 T 2 18801 TRC2 22866 T 2
15175 RC2 18299 C2 21434 C2

Mainland China

Primary 14001 RC1 18144 R 2 19379 C2
10769 R 2 14006 RC2 18228 C2 19380 C2
10880 RC2 14033 C2 18309 R 3 19381 C2
10905 C4 14044 C2 18337 C1 19382 C1
10930 C2 14054 C1 18601 R 2 19383 C2
10963 C1 14056 C1 19365 T 2 19384 C2
10970 C2 14078 C1 19366 C1 19385 C1
11005 C2 14084 C2 19367 C2 19386 C3
11160 C2 14332 C2 19368 C1 19387 C1
12116 C2 15211 C2 19369 C1 19388 C2
12215 TR 2 15223 C2 19370 C1 19389 C1
13868 T 2 15238 C2 19372 C3 19390 C2
13896 R 2 15290 C2 19373 C1 19391 C1
13905 R 2 15979 RC4 19374 C2 19392 C2
13986 TRC2 16018 C2 19376 C3 21263 T 2
13998 RC1 17585 RC2 19377 C2 22297 C2
14000 TRC1 17597 C2 19378 C1

Secondary: Monographs
10152 C2 13991 RC1 15267 C2 19455 R 8
10173 C2 14037 C2 15486 C7 20506 C1
10729 TR 2 14047 C1 16071 C2 20526 C2
10960 C2 14053 C1 17238 R 2 21400 RC2
11076 C2 14055 C1 17588 C8 21415 RC1
11132 C2 14139 C2 18145 R 2 22219 RC2
11699 TR 2 14910 C2 18264 C2 22229 RC2
11996 C2 15202 C2 18298 C2 22299 C2
12791 C1 15235 C2 18319 C1 22325 C2
13336 C2 15237 C2 18655 R 2 22339 C2
13503 TR 2 15245 C2 18660 R 2 22375 C2
13874 TR 1 15250 C3 18717 R 2 22991 TRC2
13970 R 2

Secondary: Inclusions
10147 C2 13999 RC1 14344 C1 18189 C2
10171 C2 14031 C2 14363 C2 18219 C2
10441 T 2 14046 C1 14380 C1 18533 TR 2
10456 RC2 14048 C1 15209 C7 18555 TR 2
10916 C2 14082 C1 15222 C2 19626 R 2
10993 C2 14138 C2 15233 C2 21432 C3
11613 RC1 14281 RC1 17601 C2 22336 C1
13993 RC2 14302 C3

Secondary: Journal Articles
10316 C2 13438 C2 14868 C2 18326 C1
10418 C2 13818 T 1 15199 C2 18336 C2
10734 TR 2 13852 T 3 15247 C2 18342 C1
10902 C2 13863 T 1 15255 C2 18728 R 2
10924 C3 14021 C1 15261 C1 18829 RC2
10926 C5 14041 C2 15265 C2 19139 C7
10942 C2 14060 C2 15268 C1 19316 C4
10966 C2 14061 C1 15282 C1 19317 C2
10967 C2 14142 C1 17584 RC1 19412 C2
11115 C2 14303 C1 17590 C3 19561 R 3
11116 C2 14314 C1 17599 C1 19599 C4
11452 C2 14317 C1 17996 C2 20474 RC2
11941 C2 14331 C2 18190 C2 20520 C2
11981 C2 14362 C2 18217 C4 21045 C2
12141 C2 14528 C2 18227 C2 21077 C2
12153 C2 14830 C2 18259 C1 22292 C2
12825 C3 14834 C2 18260 C2 22370 C1
12831 C2

The Eighteen Provinces

Primary 12207 T 2 13925 R 2 13979 R 2
15243 C2 17542 T 8

Second. 15148 R 4 17541 T 7 18602 R 2
10175 C2 15501 C2 18436 T 2 18654 R 2
13469 T 2 16058 R 2 18508 T 2 20478 C2

North China Broadly Conceived

Primary 13962 R 2 17423 R 7 18669 R 7

Second. 10907 C3 11028 R 2 18433 T 2
18595 R 7

Manchuria

Primary 12663 TR 2 13699 R 3

Second. 13039 R 4 15287 C2 17383 C3

Northern China

Primary 15406 R 8 18235 C3 19451 R 7

Second. 13803 T 2 14320 C3 17620 C7
20507 C3 22374 C3

Northwestern China and Frontier Regions

Primary 12011 c2 16836 c2 19375 c2
11099 c2 16515 T 8 18697 R 2

Second. 11686 TR 2 15672 TR 7 22754 c2
10863 TRC2 12037 c2 16800 c7 22768 c2
11161 c2

South China Broadly Conceived

Primary □

Second. 13955 R 2 17567 R 2 18781 R 8
13929 R 2 15239 c1 18486 T 2

East Central China

Primary □

Second. 15254 c3 15578 c3 15731 T 2
15985 c7 17378 c8

Central Yangtze Provinces

Primary 15229 c3 16150 c3

Second. 15863 T 2 17576 R 2 17630 TR 4

Southwestern China

Primary 10791 R 2

Second. 15270 c2 16083 c2 17535 T 4
20475 RC4

Southeastern China

Primary 18519 T 2 18742 R 2 19371 c2

Second. 14326 c3 15263 c2 15984 c7

Taiwan Only

Primary □

Second. 12150 c2 15697 TRC2 18290 c2

Hong Kong and Macau Only

□

36.1 Elite and Professional Associations

社會領導階層與專門職業之會社
エリート及び専門職業者の団体

Geographic China Broadly Conceived

Primary 10892 TRC2 17981 TR 2 19403 RC2
20960 TRC2 21904 RC2

Second. 17972 c2 20826 TR 2 21412 RC2
11038 RC2 18102 TR 2 20954 TRC1 21902 TRC2
12764 TRC3 18409 T 2 20981 TRC2 22816 RC1
12801 c2 20769 T 4 21392 TRC2 22817 TRC2
14174 T 3 20790 TR 4 21399 TRC2

Mainland China

Primary 14990 c2 19404 RC3 19422 c3
10551 T 4 15007 c4 19405 TRC3 19424 c1
11073 c4 15273 c2 19407 c1 19425 c1
11145 c4 16020 c7 19409 c2 21053 c2
11263 TR 1 18045 TRC4 19410 c4 21459 R 4
13408 c4 18277 c2 19412 c2 21818 R 2
14205 T 4 18341 c3 19413 c1 21909 c1
14271 RC2 18345 c4 19414 c4 21913 c1
14299 c2 18350 c1 19415 c3 21918 c2
14358 c1 19393 TR 1 19417 c2 21936 c3
14601 T 3 19396 R 2 19418 c1 21979 c4
14704 R 2 19398 R 1 19420 c4 22079 TR 2
14835 c2 19400 R 2 19421 c4 22857 c2
14964 c1 19402 R 4

Secondary: Monographs
10103 R 2 11107 c4 12485 c2 14231 TR 4
10464 c4 11398 RC2 12836 c4 14241 R 2
10481 c2 11724 R 2 13449 c1 14264 RC1
10975 c2 11946 c2 13858 T 2 14269 RC4
11104 c2 12386 RC2 14223 TR 2 14293 RC3
14305 c4 14969 c2 20926 R 2 21887 TRC2
14364 c2 15017 c2 20996 c2 21937 c2
14378 c4 17990 c2 21321 TR 2 22091 TR 1
14556 T 2 18098 T 3 21471 TRC1 22806 TRC1
14721 R 2 18661 R 2 21819 R 2 22831 c2
14853 c2 20823 TR 4

Secondary: Inclusions
10463 c4 14268 RC3 21025 c2 21947 c2
11126 c2 14327 c4 21050 c3 21962 c3
12415 RC2 18043 RC4 21073 c2 21964 c2
12447 c2 18315 RC4 21146 c1 21977 c2
13394 c1 19666 c1 21911 c1 21978 c2
13411 c4 20957 TRC2 21912 c2 22327 c1
13436 c2

Secondary: Journal Articles
10717 TR 2 14886 c4 19715 TR 2 21968 c3
11117 c4 15212 c2 20959 RC1 22153 R 1
11757 R 2 16460 c2 20990 TRC1 22188 RC1
13381 c4 18095 T 3 21092 c2 22797 R 2
14252 RC3 18304 R 2 21961 c2 22836 c2
14259 RC4 19635 R 7 21963 c4 22839 c2
14352 c1

The Eighteen Provinces

Primary 15030 c3 19401 R 3 21096 c4
14218 TR 4 18076 T 3 19423 c3 22801 R 3
14277 TRC3 19395 R 4 19630 R 2 22850 c3
15016 c3 19397 R 2

Second. 18127 R 3 21048 c2 22029 T 3
10175 c2 19265 R 3 21343 TR 2 22776 T 2
14217 TR 2 20450 R 2 21685 T 2 22928 R 2
14763 R 3

North China Broadly Conceived

Primary □

Second. 10417 c8 14762 R 2

Manchuria

□

Northern China

Primary 19394 R 3 19406 c3 19411 c3

Second. 14228 TR 2 14270 RC3 18092 T 3
18357 c3

Northwestern China and Frontier Regions

Primary □

Second. 14844 c2

South China Broadly Conceived

Primary 19399 R 2

Second. □

East Central China

□

Central Yangtze Provinces

Primary □

Second. 14792 TRC3

Southwestern China

□

Southeastern China

Primary 19408 c2

Second. 16798 c2 22606 T 3

Taiwan Only

Primary 19419 c1 22840 c3

Second. 14879 c3 15031 c1 16858 c2
18263 c2 22820 RC1

Hong Kong and Macau Only

Primary 16918 T 4 19416 c3

Second. 19309 c2 20272 c7

36.2 Employers Associations

商業雇主之社團　　雇用者団体

Geographic China Broadly Conceived

Primary □

Second. 12764 TRC3 13140 TR 4 17696 R 3
11708 TR 2 12965 TR 4 13171 TR 2 19717 T 2

Mainland China

Primary 14396 T 2 18126 R 3 19430 R 4
11734 R 3 14408 R 3 19427 R 3 19435 R 4
13279 R 2

Second. 13122 T 4 17291 R 2 19302 c5
10084 TR 2 13242 R 5 17661 TR 2 19343 T 4
10257 R 4 13250 R 2 17990 c2 19358 TR 3
10717 TR 2 13644 TR 3 18310 R 2 19365 T 2
10750 R 2 14122 R 3 19208 T 1 19512 R 4
11368 R 2 14404 TR 3 19272 R 1 19561 R 3
11699 TR 2 14413 RC4 19281 R 5 19715 TR 2
12727 R 2 14415 RC4 19286 RC5 22131 TR 2

The Eighteen Provinces

Primary 19347 T 3 19432 TR 4

Second. 11784 R 2 14401 T 5 18609 R 2
10091 R 2 13037 R 2 16114 R 4 19345 T 4
10831 R 3 13679 TR 5 18117 R 4 19349 T 3

North China Broadly Conceived

Primary □

Second. 12998 R 2 14409 R 2

Manchuria

Primary □

Second. 10381 R 2 11345 R 2 11712 TR 2
16442 R 2 17689 T 7

Northern China

Primary □

Second. 15450 R 7 17251 R 3 17449 R 3
15407 R 3 17054 R 3 17409 T 2

Northwestern China and Frontier Regions

□

South China Broadly Conceived

Primary □

Second. 16092 T 4 19238 R 3

East Central China

Primary 16319 R 3 17434 T 2 17459 R 3
19426 R 3

Second. 16075 c3 17464 R 4 19267 R 3
12955 TR 3 16587 R 2 17491 R 3 19555 R 3
12980 R 2 17274 R 2 19258 R 3 22764 c3
15944 TR 3 17306 R 2

Central Yangtze Provinces

□

Southwestern China

Primary □

Second. 13209 R 2

Southeastern China

Primary 19209 T 3 19429 T 3 19434 T 3
19436 T 3 19437 T 3

Second. 18490 T 2 19472 TR 5 19840 R 2
22606 T 3

Taiwan Only

Primary □

Second. 13053 TRC2 14549 C4

Hong Kong and Macau Only

Primary 19428 C3 19431 C3 19433 TRC3

Second. 16135 C3 17994 C2 19593 C2
11031 R 2 16473 C2 19553 R 3 20272 C7

36.3 Peasant Associations and Movements

農民協會及農民運動

農民団体及び農民運動

Geographic China Broadly Conceived

Primary 12394 RC7 14112 TR 1 19503 R 2
21853 TRC2

Second. 12232 TR 7 12401 RC7 18711 R 2
10446 R 2 12233 TR 2 13950 R 2 18794 TRC2
11708 TR 2 12310 R 8 18102 TR 2 18810 RC2
12223 TR 7 12348 R 2 18545 TR 2 22866 T 2

Mainland China

Primary 18161 R 2 18791 TRC7 19461 R 8
10078 TR 2 18391 T 7 18819 RC2 19462 R 7
10489 C7 18571 TR 2 19107 C7 19463 R 2
12279 R 8 18588 R 2 19124 C8 19464 R 7
12311 R 7 18655 R 2 19189 C7 19467 RC7
12325 R 2 18660 R 2 19440 T 2 19469 RC2
12391 RC7 18663 R 2 19444 R 7 19470 C8
12403 RC7 18673 R 7 19445 R 7 19471 C7
12413 RC7 18708 R 2 19447 R 7 21320 TR 2
12418 RC7 18752 R 2 19453 R 2 21486 C2
13715 R 8 18757 R 2 19455 R 8 21840 TRC2
14109 TR 2 18780 R 2 19457 R 7 21885 TRC2
14116 R 2 18782 R 2 19459 R 7 22173 R 2
17977 T 2

Secondary: Monographs
10159 C2 12412 RC7 16123 R 2 19074 R 7
10749 R 2 12424 RC7 16637 R 7 19077 RC7
10812 R 2 12426 RC7 17486 R 8 19092 RC8
11336 R 2 12442 C7 17763 R 2 19110 C8
11391 RC2 12464 C8 18120 R 2 19133 C7
11423 C1 13766 RC2 18185 RC2 19134 C8
11698 TR 2 13896 R 2 18430 T 2 19135 C7
11874 RC2 13905 R 2 18526 T 2 19184 C8
12173 C2 13927 R 2 18603 R 2 19194 C8
12227 TR 7 13970 R 2 18636 R 2 19201 C7
12257 R 7 14127 RC2 18674 R 2 20455 R 2
12268 R 8 14278 RC2 18699 R 2 21420 TRC2
12271 R 7 14497 R 2 18709 R 2 22162 R 2
12302 R 2 15156 R 2 18722 R 2 22203 RC2
12317 R 7 15168 TRC2 18725 R 2 22251 RC2
12378 RC8 15980 RC2 18755 R 2 22318 C2
12379 RC7 16071 C2 18795 TRC2 22805 R 2
12387 RC8

Secondary: Inclusions
11916 C2 18310 R 2 18605 R 2 18626 R 2
12396 RC8 18370 T 2 18615 R 2 18745 R 2
14251 R 2 18452 T 2 18616 R 2 21907 C1

Secondary: Journal Articles
10391 RC2 12518 C2 14447 C7 18477 T 2
12064 C2 12549 C8 14965 C2 18728 R 2
12259 R 7 14256 RC2 16089 T 2 18835 RC8
12458 C7 14426 R 8 18304 R 2 19081 RC8
12477 C7 14429 R 8 18323 C2 19177 C8
12480 C2

The Eighteen Provinces

Primary 18604 R 7 18654 R 2 19446 R 2
13813 T 2 18609 R 2 19439 T 1 19458 R 8
13860 T 2 18645 R 7 19441 T 2 21686 T 2
18583 R 2

Second. 13831 T 2 18436 T 2 18834 RC2
11346 R 2 13925 R 2 18578 R 2 19259 R 7
12296 R 8 16049 T 2 18602 R 2 19632 R 7
12346 R 8 18115 R 2 18777 R 2 21389 RC2
12767 TRC2 18382 T 2 18784 R 2

North China Broadly Conceived

Primary 18669 R 7 18690 R 7 18743 R 7

Second. 10792 R 2 16430 R 2

Manchuria

Primary 12211 TR 8

Second. 18715 R 2

Northern China

Primary 19438 T 7 19451 R 7 19456 R 2
15510 C7 19442 R 8 19452 R 2

Second. 15460 RC7 16760 C8 17463 R 7
18643 R 8 19178 C8

Northwestern China and Frontier Regions

Primary 18697 R 2

Second. 15545 C8 19355 TR 2

South China Broadly Conceived

Primary 18463 T 2 18577 R 2 19448 R 2

Second. 12383 RC2 18779 R 2

East Central China

Primary □

Second. 15426 R 7 15517 C8 17411 T 2

Central Yangtze Provinces

Primary 16639 R 7 19443 R 8 19450 R 7
19460 R 8 19504 R 2

Second. 18305 R 7 18582 R 2 18644 R 2
20210 R 2

Southwestern China

Primary 19085 RC7 19465 R 7

Second. 10791 R 2

Southeastern China

Primary 16530 T 2 16798 C2 17560 TR 2
19449 R 2 19454 R 7

Second. 16736 RC7 18686 R 2 21393 RC2
13906 R 2 16769 C2 18742 R 2

Taiwan Only

Primary 16550 TR 8 16889 C7 19466 RC7
10904 C2 16729 RC2 16902 C7 19468 RC7
10950 C2 16858 C2 17127 C2

Second. 15530 C7 16833 C8 18121 R 2
12070 C2 16747 RC2 17907 C7 18263 C2
15002 C2 16771 C8 17989 TRC2 20236 C8
15491 C7 16810 C7

Hong Kong and Macau Only

Primary 17683 C8

Second. □

36.4 Labor Unions and the Labor Movement

工會及勞工運動

労働組合及び労働運動

Geographic China Broadly Conceived

Primary 18308 R 3 19490 R 2 19546 R 3
12965 TR 4 18810 RC2 19500 R 4 19554 R 3
14468 R 2 19475 TR 4 19503 R 2 19559 R 5
14476 R 3 19478 TR 4 19524 R 3 19567 R 4
15065 R 4 19481 TR 3 19534 R 2 19584 RC3
17696 R 3 19482 R 3 19543 R 3 20209 R 3

Second. 10446 R 2 14475 R 2 18711 R 2
10106 R 2 10828 R 2 14491 R 3 18764 R 2
10107 R 2 11708 TR 2 17691 TR 2 20222 R 3
10108 R 2 12901 T 2 18102 TR 2 21412 RC2
10114 TRC2 13966 R 2 18534 TR 2 22945 RC4
10445 R 2 14113 TR 2

Mainland China

Primary: Monographs
10101 R 2 14508 R 3 18752 R 2 19558 R 2
10488 C2 14510 R 4 19291 C2 19583 RC4
11812 R 2 14513 TRC2 19358 TR 3 19590 C4
14478 R 3 15073 R 2 19476 TR 2 19594 C4
14479 R 2 17717 R 3 19477 TR 4 19595 C4
14486 R 2 17990 C2 19480 TR 3 19597 C2
14496 R 5 18161 R 2 19517 R 3 19611 C4
14497 R 2 18655 R 2 19520 R 3 19704 R 3
14501 R 4 18708 R 2 19551 R 2

Primary: Inclusions
14492 R 3 19562 R 4 19588 C4 19603 C4
17712 R 3 19563 R 5 19589 C4 19608 C4
19526 R 3 19585 RC4 19598 C4 21486 C2

Primary: Journal Articles
11114 C4 18757 R 2 19539 R 3 19582 RC3
12819 C3 19307 C2 19542 R 4 19592 C3
13122 T 4 19473 TR 4 19544 R 2 19596 C4
14415 RC4 19474 TR 4 19561 R 3 19599 C4
14473 R 2 19484 R 3 19565 R 3 19600 C3
14503 R 2 19485 R 3 19568 R 3 19601 C4
14518 C4 19494 R 4 19571 R 3 19602 C4
14519 C3 19496 R 4 19572 R 2 19606 C3
14528 C2 19512 R 4 19573 R 3 19607 C3
14536 C3 19521 R 3 19574 R 3 19609 C1
15124 C1 19525 R 3 19576 R 3 19610 C3
15231 C2 19531 R 4 19581 RC4 22161 R 4
18623 R 3 19532 R 4

Secondary: Monographs
10079 TR 2 11909 C2 14483 R 4 18636 R 2
10086 TR 2 11912 C2 14509 R 3 18674 R 2
10103 R 2 12000 C2 14512 RC2 18709 R 2
10145 C2 13158 TR 2 14535 C4 18717 R 2
10159 C2 13164 TR 4 14703 TR 2 18720 R 2
10729 TR 2 13169 TR 3 14974 C2 18722 R 2
10749 R 2 13184 TR 2 15156 R 2 18725 R 2
10821 R 2 13261 R 5 15168 TRC2 18733 R 2
10894 C1 13277 R 2 15172 TRC2 18755 R 2
10895 C2 13284 R 2 15294 C2 18780 R 2
10960 C2 13328 C2 15482 C2 18783 R 2
10975 C2 13353 C2 17190 TR 5 18795 TRC2
10997 C2 13520 TR 2 18003 C2 18819 RC2
11052 RC2 13768 C1 18118 R 4 20204 R 2
11094 C2 13884 TR 2 18120 R 2 21379 R 2
11095 C2 13927 R 2 18185 RC2 21414 RC2
11423 C1 14114 R 2 18187 RC2 22131 TR 2
11713 TR 2 14116 R 2 18324 C2 22162 R 2
11750 R 2 14122 R 3 18557 TR 2 22224 RC2
11830 R 2 14258 RC2 18596 R 2 22250 RC2
11845 RC2 14364 C2 18597 R 4 22318 C2
11862 RC2 14457 TR 3 18603 R 2 22339 C2
11874 RC2 14466 R 3 18617 R 2 22991 TRC2
11885 C2 14471 R 1 18635 R 2

Secondary: Inclusions
11711 TR 2 14123 R 2 15105 C4 18605 R 2
13162 TR 4 14138 C2 18310 R 2 18833 RC1
13242 R 5 14251 R 2 18601 R 2 21388 TRC2

Secondary: Journal Articles
10465 C2 11142 C4 12018 C4 13149 TR 2
10473 C2 11943 C2 12518 C2 13233 R 2

13391 C2 14516 C4 14984 C2 19667 C3
14407 R 3 14517 C4 15089 RC2 20457 R 2
14408 R 3 14526 C3 18130 R 3 20470 R 4
14458 TR 3 14527 C4 18157 R 2 20521 C2
14482 R 1 14529 C4 18304 R 2 21015 C2
14487 R 4 14531 C5 18323 C2 21085 C2
14499 R 3 14534 C3 18625 R 3 21397 RC2
14500 R 4 14545 C5 18668 R 4 22159 R 2
14502 R 2 14546 C1 19031 RC2 22239 RC2
14511 R 2 14965 C2 19321 C4

The Eighteen Provinces

Primary 18642 R 4 19514 R 2 19540 R 2
11824 R 2 18654 R 2 19515 R 3 19545 R 4
13275 R 3 19479 TR 2 19518 R 4 19564 R 2
14472 R 3 19483 R 4 19527 R 4 19569 R 4
14539 C2 19487 R 3 19528 R 2 19570 R 2
14540 C2 19488 R 3 19530 R 4 19575 R 2
15148 R 4 19489 R 4 19536 R 4 19577 R 3
17748 C3 19491 R 4 19537 R 2 20190 R 2
18583 R 2 19513 R 3

Second. 14474 R 3 15145 R 4 18602 R 2
10141 C2 14480 R 4 15446 R 3 18609 R 2
10348 TR 2 14484 R 4 17869 R 2 18778 R 2
14454 T 2 14489 R 3 18115 R 2 19347 T 3
14461 R 4 14505 R 2 18127 R 3 19356 TR 4
14463 R 3 14514 RC4 18592 R 2 22092 TR 3
14469 R 3 15062 R 2

North China Broadly Conceived

Primary 19580 R 3
Second. 10792 R 2

Manchuria

Primary 19505 R 3 19538 R 2 19548 R 3
16974 R 4 19523 R 2 19547 R 4 19560 R 2
18739 R 2

Second. 11732 R 2 17294 R 4 17689 T 7
11712 TR 2 15532 C4 17383 C3 18715 R 2
11716 TR 2

Northern China

Primary 17251 R 3 19492 R 3 19579 R 2
14541 C2 18313 TRC3 19497 R 3 19586 C3

Second. 17054 R 3 17300 R 5 17720 R 4
15384 TR 4 17184 TR 3 17497 C3 17721 R 7
17047 R 4 17185 TR 3 17715 R 3

Northwestern China and Frontier Regions

□

South China Broadly Conceived

Primary 19006 R 4
Second. 13887 R 2 13968 R 2 18129 R 3
18779 R 2

East Central China

Primary 19486 R 3 19519 R 3 19552 R 3
15143 R 3 19498 R 3 19522 R 3 19555 R 3
16075 C3 19507 R 3 19529 R 3 19556 R 3
16122 R 3 19508 R 3 19533 R 3 19566 R 3
18693 R 3 19509 R 3 19535 R 3 19605 C3
19267 R 3 19510 R 3 19549 R 3 20195 R 3
19268 R 3 19511 R 3 19550 R 3

Second. 17274 R 2 17719 R 3 17735 R 3
15578 C3 17693 TR 3 17725 R 3 17863 R 3
16078 C3 17694 TR 3 17728 R 3 17880 R 3
16417 R 3 17704 R 3 17733 R 3 18354 C3
17193 TR 3 17710 R 3

Central Yangtze Provinces

Primary 18582 R 2 19504 R 2 19578 R 7
Second. 17580 RC2

Southwestern China

Primary 14542 C2
Second. 10791 R 2

Southeastern China

Primary 19472 TR 5 19499 R 3 19506 R 3
13016 R 3 19493 R 4 19501 R 3 19541 R 3
17571 R 3 19495 R 3 19502 R 3 19557 R 4
17700 R 3

Second. 15263 C2 17615 RC2 18665 R 3
10840 R 3 17268 R 3 18611 R 2 22678 R 3
13906 R 2

Taiwan Only

Primary 14549 C4 15889 C2 19587 C4
Second. 15875 RC2 17989 TRC2 18121 R 2
18263 C2 20673 C2

Hong Kong and Macau Only

Primary 17718 R 2 19553 R 3 19604 C3
11506 C3 17745 C2 19591 C2 22724 RC2
16469 C3 19516 R 3 19593 C2

Second. 16471 C2 17318 RC3 17994 C2
11031 R 2 16485 C4 17336 C3 18820 TRC3
15468 TRC3 16486 C3 17744 C4 18841 C3
15489 C3 16493 C3 17985 RC2 19297 C3
16135 C3

37 Educational Associations and Movements

教育團體及教育運動
教育団体及び教育運動

Geographic China Broadly Conceived

Primary 19650 RC2 19654 RC7 21603 T 3
19614 T 3 19653 RC1 19699 R 3 22160 R 1

Second. 14720 R 2 18111 R 1 21302 T 2
14694 TR 4 14951 C2 20200 R 2 21404 TRC1
14696 TR 1 18102 TR 2

Mainland China

Primary: Monographs
10838 R 4 14808 RC2 19617 TR 2 19657 RC1
11586 TR 2 14974 C2 19625 R 1 19662 C2
11724 R 2 14999 C2 19638 R 7 19668 C5
12331 R 7 17238 R 2 19639 R 1 19670 C1
12864 C1 17754 TR 1 19640 R 7 19674 C2
14223 TR 2 17760 R 7 19643 R 2 19697 TR 3
14556 T 2 17763 R 2 19644 R 2 19704 R 3
14678 TR 3 18003 C2 19645 R 1 20182 TR 2
14695 TR 1 19035 TRC2 19649 R 7 20444 R 2
14719 R 4 19074 R 7 19652 RC2 21124 C3
14723 R 2 19615 TR 2 19655 RC2 22714 R 2

Primary: Inclusions
19626 R 2 19628 R 2 19659 RC2 19666 C1
20189 R 1

Primary: Journal Articles
11117 C4 19081 RC8 19636 R 7 19671 C7
14362 C2 19613 T 1 19641 R 8 19673 C2
14526 C3 19616 TR 1 19647 R 2 19676 C2
14914 C1 19622 R 7 19651 TRC1 19677 C2
14931 C2 19623 R 4 19656 RC1 19678 C1
14959 C2 19627 R 2 19658 RC2 19681 C2
14965 C2 19629 R 2 19660 C2 19682 C1
14986 C1 19634 R 2 19665 C1 19684 C1
16907 T 4 19635 R 7 19667 C3 20402 RC2

Secondary: Monographs
10067 TR 2 14681 TR 1 14780 RC1 17769 R 7
10105 R 2 14688 TR 1 14828 C2 18061 C2
11601 R 2 14691 TR 1 14910 C2 18827 RC2
11783 R 2 14693 TR 4 14969 C2 18987 TR 2
12123 C2 14724 R 1 15017 C2 19063 C2
12845 C4 14733 R 2 15028 C2 19257 R 7
14640 TR 2 14749 R 2 16054 R 7 21321 TR 2
14647 TR 2 14754 R 2 16070 C2 21335 TR 1
14670 TR 4 14774 R 3 17245 R 5 21874 RC2
14677 TR 1

Secondary: Inclusions
14255 RC1 14628 TR 2 14760 R 1 14905 C2
14325 C2 14674 TR 2 14878 C3 14906 C2
14913 C2 17938 R 1 19709 TRC3 20530 C1
15153 R 3 18949 TR 2 20443 R 1 20896 R 2
15799 RC2 18977 TR 1 20486 C2 21150 C2
17695 R 3 19003 R 2

Secondary: Journal Articles
11453 C2 14618 T 1 14827 C2 17753 T 1
11591 TR 1 14653 TR 4 14872 C2 17759 R 2
12403 RC7 14697 TR 2 14919 C1 19031 RC2
14347 C2 14738 R 2 14952 C2 19402 R 4
14359 C2 14765 R 3 15193 TRC1 20521 C2
14558 T 1 14776 R 1 16005 C7 20841 R 1
14566 T 2 14813 C1 17278 R 5 20961 RC2
14613 T 1 14823 C2

The Eighteen Provinces

Primary 14779 TRC2 19630 R 2 19637 R 2
10760 R 2 17869 R 2 19631 R 2 19646 R 2
14656 TR 2 19618 R 7 19632 R 7

Second. 14555 T 1 14801 RC2 20450 R 2
10091 R 2 14583 T 3 15145 R 4 21340 TR 3
12740 R 2 14660 TR 2 17842 R 2 22110 TR 1
14238 R 3 14800 RC2 19695 T 2

North China Broadly Conceived

Primary 13976 R 2
Second. □

Manchuria

Primary 19669 C7
Second. 14804 RC1 15614 RC2 17795 C7

Northern China

Primary 17891 R 7 19624 R 7 19648 R 7
17645 C2 19619 R 7 19633 R 7 19664 C8
17793 C8 19620 R 2 19642 R 7

Second. 14802 RC2 17463 R 7 20845 R 7
10781 R 2 14947 C3 17843 R 3 20909 R 2
11597 R 3 15408 R 2 20458 R 3 20946 R 7
14735 R 2 15557 C7 20843 R 7 20949 R 7
14785 TRC2 15908 C2 20844 R 2

Northwestern China and Frontier Regions

Primary 18318 C8 19661 C7 19672 C8
Second. 17772 RC7

South China Broadly Conceived

Primary □
Second. 14784 RC3

East Central China

Primary 16694 R 8 19680 C3 20207 R 3
Second. 15944 TR 3 18487 T 2

Central Yangtze Provinces

Primary 19612 T 4 19621 R 7
Second. 14577 T 3 16617 R 7 17761 R 7
14187 T 2 14792 TRC3 16639 R 7

Southwestern China

Primary 17872 R 7
Second. 14634 TR 3 14750 R 2 14803 RC2
20910 R 7

Southeastern China

Primary 19675 C8
Second. 10855 RC2 14772 R 3 18490 T 2
19013 R 3 20451 R 7

Taiwan Only

Primary 16009 C7 19587 C4 19679 C7
10904 C2 16852 C8 19663 C7 21562 C3
10950 C2 18004 C7

Second. 14224 TR 2 14865 C1 16550 TR 8
16858 C2 17897 RC8

Hong Kong and Macau Only

Primary 19683 c3

Second. 14890 c2 14894 c2 17810 c2

38 Organized Philanthropy and Mutual-Aid Societies

慈善團體及互助組織

慈善団体及び共済組合

Geographic China Broadly Conceived

Primary 17981 TR 2 19687 T 1 20285 T 1
14698 TR 1 18102 TR 2 19699 R 3 20832 R 2
17980 TR 1 18407 T 2 20160 TR 2 20934 R 3

Second. 12965 TR 4 17691 TR 2 18547 TR 2
10100 R 2 13717 R 2 17975 T 2 20186 R 3
10108 R 2 13748 R 2 17976 T 2 20827 TR 3
11703 TR 2 16186 T 2

Mainland China

Primary 18952 TR 2 19700 R 2 19709 TRC3
15060 R 2 19034 RC2 19701 R 1 20398 R 1
15061 R 3 19344 T 5 19704 R 3 20461 R 1
17848 R 2 19640 R 7 19705 R 2 20833 R 4
17849 R 2 19697 TR 3 19707 R 7 22714 R 2
17879 R 3

Second. 12227 TR 7 17990 c2 20184 R 1
10047 T 2 12257 R 7 18380 T 1 20258 T 2
10049 T 2 12298 R 7 18949 TR 2 20282 T 2
10059 T 2 13780 c2 18964 TR 2 20294 TR 2
10092 R 2 13853 T 4 19251 R 2 20302 R 2
10104 R 2 15105 c4 19256 R 3 20462 R 2
11368 R 2 16103 TR 2 19343 T 4 20926 R 2
11372 R 1 16309 R 2 19590 c4 21014 c2
11574 T 1 16335 TRC2 19629 R 2 21172 T 2
11698 TR 2 17228 R 5 19638 R 7 21529 TRC3
12128 c2 17977 T 2 19649 R 7 22655 TR 3
12173 c2 17979 TR 7 20182 TR 2

The Eighteen Provinces

Primary 15119 c2 19688 T 2 19698 TR 4
15118 c2 19686 T 3 19695 T 2

Second. 17445 TR 1 18437 T 2 19347 T 3
13679 TR 5 17484 R 2 19053 TRC2 19964 TR 1
15036 T 2 17842 R 2 19259 R 7 20393 R 2
17439 T 1 18436 T 2 19282 R 2 20800 TR 3

North China Broadly Conceived

Primary 17873 R 2

Second. 11869 TRC2 15041 T 2

Manchuria

Primary □

Second. 15679 TR 7

Northern China

Primary 16023 c3 17720 R 4 17862 R 2
15120 c2 17047 R 4 17843 R 3 19708 R 8

Second. 17410 T 2 17811 T 7 19857 RC3
15407 R 3 17470 R 7 17877 R 3 20844 R 2

Northwestern China and Frontier Regions

Primary 15086 RC2

Second. 15672 TR 7 16716 R 8 19233 R 7

South China Broadly Conceived

Primary 12569 T 2

Second. 12684 TR 2 14770 R 3 15078 R 2

East Central China

Primary 17812 T 7 19690 T 3 19706 R 3
15944 TR 3 19689 T 7 19703 R 3 20043 T 8

Second. 14665 TR 3 15318 T 3 15346 T 2
15348 T 3

Central Yangtze Provinces

Primary 17884 R 2 19694 T 3

Second. 15498 c2 15998 c7 16432 R 2
19621 R 7

Southwestern China

Primary 15121 c2

Second. 15717 T 2 16482 c3 20910 R 7
22523 T 2

Southeastern China

Primary 15735 T 2 19691 T 3 19692 T 3

Second. 15418 R 8 16187 T 3 16630 R 8
10271 T 4 15448 R 3 16607 R 2 18490 T 2

Taiwan Only

Primary 19587 c4 19711 c2

Second. 11851 TRC2 13673 TR 4 15491 c7
17984 RC2

Hong Kong and Macau Only

Primary 16044 c3 19685 T 2 19712 c3
10304 c3 17433 T 7 19693 T 3 19713 c2
15949 TR 3 17894 RC2 19696 T 3 19714 c4
15981 RC3 17909 c2 19702 R 2 20272 c7
16010 c2 17994 c2 19710 TRC3 20664 c3

Second. 15835 c3 17608 T 3 19428 c3
10312 c3 16057 R 2 17629 T 3 20389 TR 3
11467 c1 16076 c2 17924 T 7 20667 c4
15454 TRC3 16773 c7 17985 RC2 21550 c3

39 Associations Based on Common Place of Origin

鄉誼組織　同鄉組織

Geographic China Broadly Conceived

Primary 14468 R 2 17976 T 2 17981 TR 2
18396 T 2 19717 T 2

Second. 10073 TR 2 10259 TRC4 14475 R 2

Mainland China

Primary 19343 T 4 19715 TR 2

Second. 10571 T 1 17190 TR 5 19352 TR 2
10084 TR 2 10766 R 2 18014 T 7 19363 R 3
10086 TR 2 12727 R 2 18144 R 2 19477 TR 4
10297 R 2 13029 R 2 19281 R 5 19561 R 3
10551 T 4 14396 T 2 19351 T 4 19704 R 3

The Eighteen Provinces

Primary 17173 T 2 17973 T 2 19347 T 3
19349 T 3

Second. 10333 T 2 17541 T 7 19695 T 2

North China Broadly Conceived

Primary □

Second. 14409 R 2

Manchuria

Primary □

Second. 17689 T 7

Northern China

Primary 19357 TR 3 19360 R 3

Second. □

Northwestern China and Frontier Regions

□

South China Broadly Conceived

Primary 19718 T 2

Second. 12894 T 2 17956 TRC2

East Central China

Primary □

Second. 15944 TR 3 16908 T 2

Central Yangtze Provinces

Primary □

Second. 16526 T 2

Southwestern China

Primary □

Second. 15629 T 2 19270 R 2

Southeastern China

Primary 19716 T 4

Second. 16187 T 3 18490 T 2

Taiwan Only

Primary □

Second. 17984 RC2

Hong Kong and Macau Only

Primary 15925 T 7 17985 RC2 17994 c2

Second. 10304 c3 11031 R 2 15913 c3
15973 TRC2 20272 c7

40 Kinship Systems in General

親屬制度通論　親族制度一般

Geographic China Broadly Conceived

Primary 14126 TRC2 19735 TRC1 20017 TRC1
10070 TR 2 16185 T 2 19763 T 1 20025 TR 1
10074 TR 2 19055 TRC2 19802 TR 2 20053 TR 1
10093 R 2 19727 TR 1 19871 TRC1 20088 T 3
10117 TRC2 19730 TRC1 19888 TRC2 20590 T 3
11250 TR 1 19733 TRC1 20005 TR 1 21467 TRC1

Second. 11709 TR 2 18976 TR 2 20155 T 2
10034 T 2 17981 TR 2 19772 T 1 20160 TR 2
10048 T 2 18024 TR 1 19978 TRC2 20231 RC2
11261 TR 1 18852 T 2 20009 TR 1 21740 TR 1

Mainland China

Primary 14430 R 8 19785 TR 1 19899 TRC2
10003 T 2 19218 TR 1 19795 TR 1 19905 c2
10020 T 2 19719 T 2 19806 TR 1 20013 TR 1
10041 T 2 19720 T 8 19810 R 1 20066 R 1
10084 TR 2 19721 T 2 19813 R 1 20130 T 2
10086 TR 2 19722 T 1 19816 R 2 20154 T 1
10110 TRC2 19724 TR 1 19826 R 1 21798 TR 1
11103 c1 19728 R 8 19862 TRC1 21980 T 4
11194 T 2 19731 TRC1 19868 TRC1 21982 T 2
11203 T 2 19732 RC2 19869 RC2 22619 T 2
11662 T 2 19736 TRC1 19892 RC1 22644 TR 2

Second. 10778 R 2 14650 TR 1 20248 c2
10037 T 2 10846 TRC1 15150 R 2 21265 T 2
10067 TR 2 11183 T 1 15560 c4 21308 TR 2
10080 TR 2 11211 T 1 16335 TRC2 21466 TRC1
10089 R 2 11230 T 1 17974 T 3 21998 TR 1
10094 R 2 11243 T 2 19872 RC1 22006 R 1
10104 R 2 11382 R 2 19992 T 1 22187 TRC1
10134 c2 12427 c7 20107 R 2 22198 TRC2
10154 c2 14127 RC2 20227 RC1 22639 T 1
10155 c2

The Eighteen Provinces
PRIMARY 11655 T 1 19963 TR 2 20287 T 1
10006 T 2 12193 T 8 20022 T 1 21761 TR 1
10027 T 2 16183 T 2 20144 T 1 22004 R 1
11029 R 1 18010 T 1
SECOND. 10608 T 2 19964 TR 1 20548 T 2
10056 T 2 11719 TR 1 20057 R 7 22923 TR 2

North China Broadly Conceived
PRIMARY □
SECOND. 10057 T 1

Manchuria
PRIMARY □
SECOND. 15679 TR 7 17551 T 2 20141 T 4

Northern China
PRIMARY 15360 T 7 19847 R 7 21344 TR 2
15320 T 3 19723 T 4 21330 TR 7
SECOND. 15397 R 7 15399 R 7 16379 T 2
19357 TR 3 22457 R 3

Northwestern China and Frontier Regions
PRIMARY 22682 R 2 22713 R 5
SECOND. □

South China Broadly Conceived
PRIMARY □
SECOND. 10028 T 2 16910 T 4

East Central China
PRIMARY □
SECOND. 15426 R 7 19748 T 2 20262 R 2

Central Yangtze Provinces
PRIMARY 16526 T 2 19726 TR 7
SECOND. □

Southwestern China
PRIMARY 19729 R 6
SECOND. 15379 TR 3 15424 R 7 15640 R 2

Southeastern China
PRIMARY 15418 R 8 18048 C3 19975 TRC7
20069 TRC1
SECOND. 14088 T 2 14758 R 2 20215 R 3
20234 TRC2

Taiwan Only
PRIMARY 16226 TR 2 19973 TRC8 21201 C8
15504 C8 17675 C2 19980 TRC8 21483 C2
15505 C8 19737 C8 20236 C8 21556 C2
15515 C8 19738 C7 20249 C7
SECOND. 15530 C7 15709 C2

Hong Kong and Macau Only
PRIMARY 15325 T 3 15451 TRC7 15463 TRC7
19990 C8 21574 C3
SECOND. 16496 C2 19070 C3 19971 TRC8
19972 TRC7

41 Marriage and the Family
婚姻與家庭　婚姻と家庭

Geographic China Broadly Conceived
PRIMARY 19727 TR 1 19755 T 1 19774 T 1
10082 TR 2 19730 TRC1 19759 T 1 19800 TR 1
10585 T 1 19733 TRC1 19762 T 1 19802 TR 2
11387 TRC1 19743 T 1 19763 T 1 19859 TRC2
11403 TRC1 19750 T 1 19771 T 1 19861 RC1
16104 TR 7 19752 T 1 19772 T 1 19870 TRC1
19871 TRC1 19978 TRC2 20085 T 2 20235 TRC2
19879 TRC1 19996 T 2 20096 T 2 20615 TR 2
19881 TRC1 20005 TR 1 20160 TR 2 20653 R 2
19888 TRC2 20044 T 1 20162 TR 1 21366 R 2
19897 TRC1 20050 TR 2 20213 R 3 21538 TRC2
19913 C2 20051 TR 1 20231 RC2 21579 C2
19940 C1

Secondary: Monographs
10001 T 2 10117 TRC2 15311 T 2 20173 TR 1
10013 T 2 10139 C2 16068 RC2 20463 R 3
10014 T 2 10144 C2 16186 T 2 20576 T 2
10016 T 2 10177 C2 18024 TR 1 20994 TRC5
10017 T 2 10263 C2 18511 T 2 21333 TR 2
10024 T 2 10560 T 2 18544 TR 1 21337 TR 2
10026 T 2 11035 RC2 20025 TR 1 21368 R 2
10042 T 2 11045 RC2 20053 TR 1 21703 T 1
10045 T 2 11222 T 1 20083 T 1 22002 TR 1
10060 T 2 11250 TR 1 20089 T 1 22109 TR 2
10070 TR 2 11317 R 1 20109 TRC2 22580 T 2
10113 TRC2 12902 T 3

Secondary: Inclusions
10032 T 2 18558 TR 2 20111 TRC2 22016 TRC1
10216 TRC2 19979 TRC1 20306 C2 22476 TRC2
12772 TRC2 20017 TRC1 20563 T 2 22578 T 2
15645 TRC3

Secondary: Journal Articles
10276 T 2 14126 TRC2 19353 TR 2 20181 TR 1
10704 TR 2 15044 T 2 19735 TRC1 21472 TRC1
11264 TR 1 16127 TRC2 20010 TR 2 22014 TRC1
14098 T 2 17036 TR 7 20088 T 3 22015 TRC1
14102 T 2 18301 T 4

Mainland China
Primary: Monographs
10002 T 2 19751 T 2 19892 RC1 20204 R 2
10030 T 2 19789 TR 2 19899 TRC2 20221 R 2
10071 TR 2 19794 TR 1 19905 C2 20226 TRC2
11203 T 2 19795 TR 1 19909 C2 20229 RC1
11230 T 1 19796 TR 1 19919 C1 20244 C2
11263 TR 1 19801 TR 1 19922 C7 20432 TR 2
11344 R 1 19803 TR 2 19931 C1 20558 T 2
11362 R 1 19804 TR 1 20013 TR 1 20623 TR 2
11672 T 4 19806 TR 1 20107 R 2 20639 R 2
12291 R 7 19810 R 1 20135 T 1 20648 R 2
15955 TR 8 19816 R 2 20137 T 2 21307 TR 2
16013 C7 19819 R 1 20159 TR 2 21311 TR 2
16103 TR 2 19826 R 1 20166 TR 2 21355 TR 2
16123 R 2 19854 R 1 20175 TR 1 21798 TR 1
18915 T 2 19862 TRC1 20177 TR 2 21821 R 2
19719 T 2 19883 RC2 20182 TR 2 21982 T 2
19732 RC2 19886 TRC1

Primary: Inclusions
11248 TR 1 19721 T 2 19867 TRC1 19928 C2
11447 C1 19724 TR 1 19873 RC2 19930 C2
14135 C2 19731 TRC1 19877 TRC1 19945 C2
15180 TRC1 19736 TRC1 19880 TRC2 19951 C3
15189 RC2 19767 T 1 19884 RC1 19952 C2
15215 C2 19788 TR 1 19893 RC1 20121 C2
15271 C7 19850 R 8 19914 C1 20212 R 2
15314 T 2 19855 R 1 19915 C1 20259 T 1
19720 T 8 19866 TRC2

Primary: Journal Articles
10199 TR 2 19775 T 2 19832 R 1 19934 C1
11218 T 1 19777 T 1 19842 R 1 19941 C1
11220 T 1 19780 T 1 19852 R 1 19944 C1
11221 T 1 19783 TR 1 19853 R 1 19948 C2
11388 TRC2 19784 TR 1 19860 TRC1 19949 C1
11414 TRC1 19785 TR 1 19868 TRC1 19950 C1
15138 TR 2 19790 TR 1 19869 RC2 19992 T 1
15232 C7 19791 TR 1 19872 RC1 20130 T 2
16036 C7 19792 TR 1 19875 TRC2 20232 RC1
16112 TR 1 19793 TR 1 19891 TRC1 20237 C2
19145 C7 19798 TR 1 19903 C1 20242 C2
19722 T 1 19799 TR 1 19906 C2 20282 T 2
19741 T 1 19809 R 1 19908 C1 20363 C2
19745 T 1 19811 R 1 19921 C2 20439 R 4
19753 T 1 19813 R 1 19923 C1 21209 R 1
19757 T 1 19814 R 1 19924 C1 21250 C2
19760 T 1 19821 R 1 19926 C1 21652 T 2
19766 T 1 19831 R 1 19927 C2 21744 TR 1
19768 T 2

Secondary: Monographs
10007 T 2 10255 TR 2 14592 T 1 20161 TR 3
10019 T 2 10349 TR 2 14686 TR 1 20169 TR 2
10035 T 2 10562 T 1 14687 TR 2 20179 TR 1
10036 T 2 10654 T 3 14703 TR 2 20224 RC2
10041 T 2 10718 TR 2 14990 C2 20247 C7
10047 T 2 10888 TRC2 15150 R 2 20258 T 2
10049 T 2 11036 TRC7 15171 TRC2 20302 R 2
10059 T 2 11053 RC2 15192 RC2 20328 C2
10062 T 2 11194 T 2 15434 R 7 20430 TR 2
10069 TR 2 11195 T 1 15483 C7 20462 R 2
10079 TR 2 11243 T 2 15506 C2 20614 TR 2
10081 TR 2 11390 RC2 15508 C2 20798 TR 2
10086 TR 2 11391 RC2 15509 C2 21163 T 7
10088 R 2 11437 C2 15549 C7 21172 T 2
10089 R 2 11581 TR 2 15550 C2 21325 TR 2
10097 R 2 11698 TR 2 15567 C7 21367 R 2
10098 R 2 11752 R 2 16001 C7 21416 RC2
10115 RC2 12090 C2 16277 TR 2 21422 TRC2
10120 TRC2 12230 TR 2 16343 TRC2 21444 TR 1
10126 RC2 12256 R 7 17979 TR 7 21457 R 1
10136 C2 12298 R 7 18722 R 2 21504 TR 2
10140 C2 12303 R 2 18862 T 2 21563 C1
10145 C2 12358 R 2 18940 T 1 21644 T 2
10149 C2 12963 TR 2 18974 TR 1 21657 T 1
10152 C2 13029 R 2 19132 C7 21862 TRC1
10153 C2 13163 TR 2 19246 R 5 21981 T 1
10155 C2 13277 R 2 19277 R 4 22066 T 2
10157 C2 13584 C2 19640 R 7 22131 TR 2
10164 C2 13880 TR 2 20066 R 1 22432 TR 1
10165 C2 14133 C3 20124 T 4 22769 C2
10214 TRC2 14178 T 2 20154 T 1

Secondary: Inclusions
10012 T 2 14220 TR 1 19974 TRC2 20472 RC3
10229 C1 14405 TR 4 20081 C2 20480 C2
10295 R 2 15558 C7 20176 TR 1 20495 C2
11223 T 1 16035 C4 20228 RC2 20571 T 1
11252 TR 1 16289 R 4 20233 RC2 20661 TRC1
11399 RC1 17978 T 2 20292 TR 2 21189 TR 2
11443 C2 19138 C7 20303 RC2 21251 C1
14096 T 2 19965 TR 2

Secondary: Journal Articles
10009 T 2 11316 R 1 16038 C2 20188 R 1
10084 TR 2 11334 R 4 16089 T 2 20227 RC1
10195 TR 2 11363 R 1 16096 T 1 20230 TRC2
10206 R 2 11372 R 1 16184 T 1 20240 C1
10297 R 2 11382 R 2 16214 T 1 20313 C2
10512 T 2 11386 TRC1 17803 C2 20318 C2
10531 T 3 11402 TRC1 18071 C1 20331 C2
10648 T 4 11412 TRC1 19014 R 2 20361 C2
10710 TR 1 11421 C2 19255 R 4 20370 C2
11060 C2 11662 T 2 19967 R 1 20376 C1
11071 C2 11958 C2 19994 T 1 20407 C2
11188 T 1 12131 C2 20040 T 8 20520 C2
11189 T 1 12167 C2 20055 TR 1 20720 T 1
11204 T 1 13840 T 2 20073 C1 21137 C1
11211 T 1 14085 T 1 20077 C1 21160 T 1
11212 T 1 14094 T 2 20123 T 2 21541 RC1
11226 T 1 14099 T 1 20131 T 2 21868 TRC1
11260 TR 2 14130 TRC2 20157 T 1 21998 TR 1
11262 TR 1 14429 R 8 20163 TR 1 22047 T 2
11275 TR 1 14430 R 8 20168 TR 1 22301 C2
11308 R 1 15061 R 3 20184 R 1

The Eighteen Provinces
PRIMARY 19754 T 1 19836 R 2 20125 T 2
10018 T 2 19765 T 2 19838 R 1 20144 T 1
10038 T 2 19781 TR 1 19839 R 1 20149 T 1
10141 C2 19797 TR 2 19843 R 8 20178 TR 2
10682 T 2 19805 TR 1 19845 R 2 20192 R 3
11536 T 3 19808 R 2 19848 R 2 21208 R 8
14090 T 1 19812 R 3 19900 C3 21213 R 2
16278 TR 1 19815 R 3 19902 C3 21214 R 7
17869 R 2 19823 R 7 19942 C2 21218 R 2
17973 T 2 19829 R 1 19954 C2 21305 TR 4
19744 T 1 19833 R 2 19964 TR 1 21453 TR 1
19747 T 2 19835 R 3 20035 T 1 22067 T 2
SECOND. 15470 RC7 18010 T 1 20190 R 2
10205 R 2 15511 C2 20002 T 1 20329 C2
10348 TR 2 16098 T 7 20022 T 1 20411 C2
12198 T 8 16107 TR 1 20092 T 2 20503 C2
12225 TR 8 16252 TR 2 20100 TR 1 20642 R 2
14117 R 2 16271 TR 2 20139 T 1 21207 R 8
15446 R 3 16591 R 7 20150 T 1 21225 R 7

21226 R 3 21370 R 2 21502 TR 8 21996 TR 1
21266 T 2 21380 R 2 21525 R 1 22004 R 1
21362 TR 3 21440 T 1 21761 TR 1 22390 T 2
21365 R 3 21473 TRC2 21983 T 1

North China Broadly Conceived

Primary 15428 R 7 19920 C2 20539 T 4
Second. 16317 R 2 19011 R 2 20541 T 2
14195 T 3 16695 R 7 19960 T 1 20716 T 2

Manchuria

Primary 19828 R 8 19876 RC2 20104 R 8
20276 R 4
Second. 15674 TR 2 16644 R 8 20654 R 2
12211 TR 8 15914 C7 20141 T 4 21229 R 2

Northern China

Primary 15408 R 2 19723 T 4 19857 RC3
11568 T 3 15410 R 8 19739 T 1 19907 C8
14196 T 3 15449 R 7 19740 T 3 20142 T 2
15336 T 2 15596 R 7 19758 T 3 20205 R 2
15338 T 7 16250 TR 3 19776 T 2 20436 R 3
15367 T 2 16632 R 8 19779 T 3 21217 R 3
15378 TR 7 17855 R 3 19825 R 3 21264 T 3
15399 R 7 17856 R 3 19847 R 7 21330 TR 7
15403 R 8 17876 R 3 19851 R 2 22397 T 3
Second. 15450 R 7 17721 R 7 21223 R 3
10598 T 2 15460 RC7 17871 R 7 21278 T 3
10652 T 3 15475 RC8 17877 R 3 21359 TR 3
11135 C3 15594 R 2 17953 TRC3 21375 R 3
14157 T 3 16121 R 3 18029 R 8 21508 R 3
14163 T 3 16130 C2 18398 T 2 21511 R 3
14182 T 3 16310 R 4 20015 R 3 21512 R 3
14214 TR 3 16311 R 8 20206 R 3 21513 R 3
15372 TR 3 16594 R 8 20527 C3 21664 T 3
15390 TR 3 17054 R 3 20921 R 3 21729 TR 7
15394 R 2 17625 T 3 20938 R 3 22456 R 1
15406 R 8 17720 R 4 21181 T 2 22541 T 3
15414 R 8

Northwestern China and Frontier Regions

Primary 16672 R 7 19822 R 2 20298 R 7
15544 C8 19818 R 7 19889 RC8
Second. 16299 R 7 20304 RC2 21196 RC2
15386 TR 2 16664 R 7 20621 TR 1 22430 TR 8
15620 C2 18890 T 2 20857 R 1

South China Broadly Conceived

Primary 17956 TRC2 19894 TRC2 21384 R 2
15749 T 3 19764 T 2 20208 R 2
Second. 12580 T 2 18421 T 2 20274 T 3
10046 T 2 12920 T 4 18449 T 2 20633 R 2

East Central China

Primary 16631 R 7 19746 T 8 19844 R 3
15405 R 7 17667 R 7 19748 T 2 20262 R 2
15426 R 7 17821 T 7 19807 R 3 21037 C3
15517 C8 17868 R 7 19834 R 4 21215 R 7
16593 R 7
Second. 15869 R 3 17458 R 8 17880 R 3
15374 TR 8 16624 R 7 17649 T 5 17887 R 3
15431 R 3 16662 R 7 17818 T 8 17943 R 3
15432 R 2 17176 T 2 17833 R 3 20886 R 3
15744 T 2 17193 TR 3 17834 R 3 22589 T 2
15843 C7 17274 R 2

Central Yangtze Provinces

Primary 19726 TR 7 20199 R 7 20379 T 4
17761 R 7 19820 R 8 20210 R 2
Second. 20129 T 6 20220 R 3 22445 R 1
16090 T 2 20138 T 2 20275 T 4

Southwestern China

Primary 16118 R 2 19817 R 3 19846 R 3
14750 R 2 16267 TR 2 19827 R 6 19849 R 2
15436 R 6 19729 R 6 19830 R 8 19885 RC2
15598 R 7 19742 T 2
Second. 17520 T 2 17872 R 7 20475 RC4
15379 TR 3 17613 R 7 18933 T 4 20863 R 2
15640 R 2 17632 R 3 19362 R 6 21280 T 5
15641 R 2 17854 R 2 20217 R 3 21990 T 1

Southeastern China

Primary 15447 R 3 19773 T 1 19975 TRC7
15317 T 2 15448 R 3 19778 T 3 20234 TRC2
15321 T 2 19749 T 7 19840 R 2 20385 T 5
15358 T 8 19756 T 2 19865 TRC1 20570 T 1
15376 TR 2 19761 T 7 19962 TR 7 21393 RC2
Second. 16208 T 2 18048 C3 21527 R 1
10298 R 2 16552 TR 2 20069 TRC1 21575 C3
11683 TR 2 17665 R 7 20215 R 3 21781 TR 1
15476 RC8 17925 T 7 21168 T 3 22403 T 1
15923 T 3 17949 TRC7 21413 RC3 22455 R 2
15932 T 8 18022 TR 3 21522 R 1 22479 TRC8
16188 T 1

Taiwan Only

Primary 19090 RC8 19935 C3 20421 C2
11232 T 2 19738 C7 19936 C3 20422 C8
15491 C7 19769 T 2 19937 C3 20427 C2
15515 C8 19782 TR 2 19938 C2 21237 C2
15586 TR 2 19863 RC2 19939 C2 21243 C2
15708 C2 19864 RC8 19955 C7 21484 C2
15887 C8 19890 TRC2 19956 C2 21564 C3
16003 C7 19895 RC8 20072 C7 21567 C2
16354 C8 19896 TRC8 20236 C8 21568 C3
17103 TRC7 19910 C3 20249 C7 21580 C3
17118 C7 19911 C2 20326 C4 21581 C3
17622 C3 19916 C8 20360 C3 21584 C3
18908 T 2 19925 C8 20368 C2 21946 C7
Second. 16869 C7 20074 C2 21249 C1
12146 C2 16886 C7 20317 C7 21481 C3
15471 RC2 16902 C7 20321 C1 21483 C2
15472 RC2 17386 C4 20334 C2 21487 C1
15505 C8 17669 RC8 20345 C2 21545 RC1
15613 RC2 17897 RC8 20377 C8 21556 C2
15707 C2 17984 RC2 20378 C3 21577 C3
15878 C2 19679 C7 20995 RC2 21590 C3
16167 T 2 19737 C8 21238 C2 22018 C4
16226 TR 2 19973 TRC8 21240 C2 22490 RC2
16772 C8 19980 TRC8

Hong Kong and Macau Only

Primary 17608 T 3 19904 C1 19947 C3
11400 TRC1 17963 C2 19912 C2 19953 C3
14983 C3 19824 R 2 19917 C3 20070 TRC8
15330 T 7 19858 RC7 19918 C3 20359 C3
15463 TRC7 19874 TRC2 19929 C2 20389 TR 3
15621 C4 19878 TRC1 19932 C3 20428 RC3
16137 C3 19887 RC1 19933 C3 20522 C3
16275 TR 2 19898 RC3 19943 C8 22762 C2
16348 C7 19901 C7 19946 C2 23034 C2
Second. 15827 C4 19990 C8 20658 RC3
11467 C1 15913 C3 20062 R 2 20683 C3
13048 RC2 16125 TRC2 20075 C2 20694 C3
15325 T 3 16132 C2 20239 C3 21202 C3
15451 TRC7 16456 TRC7 20267 C3 21244 C2
15473 TRC2 16893 C7 20279 T 1 21547 C3
15526 C3 16991 C4 20358 C2 21576 C3
15574 C8 17966 C2 20426 C2 21578 C3
15611 TRC2 17971 C8 20529 C3 21586 C3
15617 C2 19970 TRC7 20564 T 8 22494 C2
15646 TRC3 19985 TRC7

42 Lineages and Clanship

氏族及譜系 氏族及び系譜

Geographic China Broadly Conceived

Primary 19978 TRC2 19979 TRC1 19982 TRC8
19983 TRC7
Second. 17036 TR 7 19913 C2 20050 TR 2
10016 T 2 17980 TR 1 20005 TR 1 20235 TRC2
10707 TR 2 19727 TR 1 20009 TR 1 22780 T 1
16104 TR 7 19735 TRC1 20017 TRC1 22886 T 1
16217 T 7 19888 TRC2

Mainland China

Primary 19777 T 1 19877 TRC1 19965 TR 2
11243 T 2 19785 TR 1 19880 TRC2 19967 R 1
15955 TR 8 19868 TRC1 19961 T 1 19974 TRC2
18014 T 7
Second. 12291 R 7 18144 R 2 19869 RC2
10078 TR 2 13868 T 2 18571 TR 2 19873 RC2
10084 TR 2 14093 T 2 19463 R 2 19875 TRC2
10086 TR 2 14178 T 2 19719 T 2 19891 TRC1
10291 TR 2 14208 T 2 19720 T 8 19927 C2
10512 T 2 14430 R 8 19732 RC2 19944 C1
10597 T 1 14687 TR 2 19736 TRC1 20013 TR 1
10693 TR 1 15138 TR 2 19766 T 1 20135 T 1
10718 TR 2 15314 T 2 19793 TR 1 21250 C2
11203 T 2 16089 T 2 19795 TR 1 21709 T 2
11698 TR 2 16103 TR 2 19862 TRC1 22021 C2
12187 T 8 16332 TRC1 19866 TRC2

The Eighteen Provinces

Primary 16049 T 2 19695 T 2 19963 TR 2
15375 TR 2 17973 T 2 19838 R 1 19964 TR 1
Second. 14168 T 2 19688 T 2 19823 R 7
10682 T 2 15470 RC7 19747 T 2 19836 R 2
14117 R 2 17541 T 7 19805 TR 1 20022 T 1
14159 T 1

North China Broadly Conceived

Primary 19960 T 1
Second. □

Manchuria

Primary 19828 R 8
Second. □

Northern China

Primary 18905 T 3
Second. 15406 R 8 17953 TRC3 20260 TR 8
14182 T 3 15449 R 7 20015 R 3 21770 TR 3
15338 T 7 15596 R 7

Northwestern China and Frontier Regions

Primary 18671 R 7
Second. □

South China Broadly Conceived

Primary 19957 T 7 19976 TRC8 19977 TRC1
19984 TRC1 21384 R 2
Second. 17956 TRC2 18449 T 2

East Central China

Primary 20043 T 8
Second. 15374 TR 8 16559 TR 2 20262 R 2
14161 T 2 15535 C8 16631 R 7

Central Yangtze Provinces

Primary 19966 R 2
Second. 19460 R 8

Southwestern China

Primary □
Second. 14750 R 2 17613 R 7

Southeastern China

Primary 19958 T 7 19975 TRC7 20006 TR 8
14088 T 2 19962 TR 7 19981 TRC7 21203 T 1
17533 T 7 19968 R 8 19987 C8
Second. 15735 T 2 17547 T 2 18438 T 2
15376 TR 2 15932 T 8 17560 TR 2 18519 T 2
15447 R 3 16537 T 2 17607 T 2 21575 C3
15476 RC8 17191 TR 2 17949 TRC7

Taiwan Only

Primary 17984 RC2 19939 C2 19989 C3
16003 C7 17988 RC2 19973 TRC8 20018 C8
16354 C8 19737 C8 19980 TRC8 20024 C8
17961 C2

Second. 17610 T 8 18263 C2 19769 T 2
11232 T 2 17618 C5 19163 C8 19864 RC8
15505 C8 17675 C2 19738 C7 20236 C8

Hong Kong and Macau Only

Primary 15925 T 7 19969 TRC8 19985 TRC7
15331 T 8 15927 T 7 19970 TRC7 19986 TRC8
15455 TRC7 17102 TRC7 19971 TRC8 19988 C8
15473 TRC2 19858 RC7 19972 TRC7 19990 C8
15800 TRC8 19959 T 7

Second. 15464 TRC8 16456 TRC7 19933 C3
15330 T 7 15797 TRC7 17683 C8 19943 C8
15451 TRC7 15974 TRC2 17971 C8 21966 C8
15462 TRC7 16353 C7 17994 C2 22441 TR 7
15463 TRC7

43 Ancestor Worship

祖先崇祀　　祖先崇拝

Geographic China Broadly Conceived

Primary 19993 T 1 20005 TR 1 20017 TRC1
10024 T 2 19995 T 1 20009 TR 1 20050 TR 2
16192 T 1 19996 T 2 20010 TR 2 21656 T 1
19733 TRC1 19998 T 1 20016 TRC1 21788 TR 1
19735 TRC1

Second. 14156 T 2 18904 T 2 21173 T 2
10004 T 2 14215 TR 2 18936 T 2 21318 TR 1
10010 T 2 15311 T 2 18968 TR 2 21333 TR 2
10052 T 2 15422 R 4 19750 T 1 21689 T 2
10070 TR 2 16186 T 2 19763 T 1 21718 TR 1
10082 TR 2 16217 T 7 19913 C2 21750 TR 1
10586 T 1 16248 TR 1 19978 TRC2 22001 TR 1
11556 T 1 16258 TR 1 19983 TRC7 22024 T 1
12593 T 2 17980 TR 1 20619 TR 2 22102 TR 2
12941 T 2 18024 TR 1 21171 T 3

Mainland China

Primary 19720 T 8 20001 T 2 20302 R 2
10002 T 2 19777 T 1 20007 TR 1 20545 T 2
11581 TR 2 19992 T 1 20008 TR 1 21165 T 1
11610 TRC1 19994 T 1 20011 TR 2 21182 T 1
15955 TR 8 19999 T 1 20013 TR 1 21624 T 2
16263 TR 2 20000 T 1 20036 T 2 21744 TR 1
16277 TR 2

Secondary: Monographs
10020 T 2 13163 TR 2 18959 TR 2 21172 T 2
10029 T 2 14133 C3 19719 T 2 21260 T 2
10030 T 2 14178 T 2 19751 T 2 21437 T 1
10049 T 2 16189 T 2 19816 R 2 21657 T 1
10059 T 2 16332 TRC1 20137 T 2 21723 TR 1
10069 TR 2 16343 TRC2 20614 TR 2 21821 R 2
10088 R 2 17979 TR 7 20618 TR 2 21862 TRC1
11563 T 4 18867 T 2 20623 TR 2 21981 T 1
11614 RC1 18915 T 2 20639 R 2 21982 T 2
12291 R 7 18927 T 1 21163 T 7 22556 T 2
13152 TR 2

Secondary: Inclusions
10561 T 2 11589 TR 1 19721 T 2 19736 TRC1
11223 T 1 15333 T 3 19724 TR 1 19767 T 1
11550 T 2 16269 TR 1 19731 TRC1 21804 TR 1
11574 T 1

Secondary: Journal Articles
10009 T 2 16320 R 2 20046 TR 1 21499 TR 1
11559 T 4 16329 TRC2 20610 TR 1 21633 T 1
11585 TR 1 16336 TRC1 20611 TR 2 21693 T 1
13838 T 2 19790 TR 1 21190 R 2 21779 TR 1
13840 T 2 19793 TR 1 21195 R 2 21868 TRC1
14708 R 3 19852 R 1 21250 C2 22038 T 1
16285 R 1 19875 TRC2 21290 T 1 22469 R 1

The Eighteen Provinces

Primary 19963 TR 2 19997 T 1 20004 TR 1
10006 T 2 19991 T 1 20002 T 1

Second. 16271 TR 2 20149 T 1 21627 T 1
10038 T 2 16278 TR 1 20544 T 2 21642 T 1
11539 T 2 16280 TR 2 21162 T 2 21761 TR 1
12198 T 8 17614 R 2 21166 T 2 21773 TR 1
16171 T 1 18012 T 2 21365 R 3 21791 TR 1
16191 T 1 19805 TR 1 21453 TR 1 21983 T 1
16195 T 1 19829 R 1 21502 TR 8 22590 T 3
16252 TR 2 20022 T 1

North China Broadly Conceived

Primary □

Second. 14195 T 3 16169 T 2 16317 R 2
16352 C8 19960 T 1

Manchuria

Primary 19828 R 8

Second. 16315 R 3

Northern China

Primary 19847 R 7 20012 TR 2 20015 R 3

Second. 14214 TR 3 19723 T 4 21187 TR 2
10652 T 3 15336 T 2 19739 T 1 21191 R 2
11547 T 3 15410 R 8 19776 T 2 21278 T 3
11548 T 3 15710 T 2 20128 T 3 22383 T 2
11568 T 3 16221 T 4 20273 R 3 22397 T 3
11599 R 3 16222 T 8 20762 T 3 22520 T 3
14191 T 5 16311 R 8 21176 T 1

Northwestern China and Frontier Regions

Primary 16170 T 7

Second. 19818 R 7 22005 R 1

South China Broadly Conceived

Primary 21175 T 2

Second. 10046 T 2 17929 T 7 19976 TRC8
20274 T 3

East Central China

Primary 15744 T 2 19748 T 2 20003 T 5

Second. 16290 R 8 18932 T 4 19746 T 8
15307 T 3 18855 T 2 18983 TR 3 21621 T 1

Central Yangtze Provinces

Primary □

Second. 19966 R 2 20199 R 7

Southwestern China

Primary 16268 TR 1 19729 R 6

Second. 16260 TR 2 16312 R 2 21194 R 4
14750 R 2 16267 TR 2 19846 R 3

Southeastern China

Primary 16188 T 1 19975 TRC7 20014 R 3
15353 T 2 19962 TR 7 20006 TR 8 21167 T 3
16164 T 3

Second. 15364 T 3 16180 T 3 17813 T 3
15317 T 2 15735 T 2 16181 T 2 17928 T 7
15321 T 2 16163 T 3 16190 T 2 19968 R 8
15337 T 5

Taiwan Only

Primary 19973 TRC8 20018 C8

Second. 16330 TRC2 19090 RC8 21484 C2
15351 T 2 16354 C8 19896 TRC8 21520 R 2
15505 C8 16359 C2 19925 C8 21932 C1
15515 C8 18903 T 2 19989 C3 21946 C7

Hong Kong and Macau Only

Primary 16298 R 8 19969 TRC8 21966 C8
11492 C3 16348 C7 19986 TRC8 22441 TR 7
15800 TRC8

Second. 19070 C3 19970 TRC7 20070 TRC8
11467 C1 19918 C3 19972 TRC7 21198 C8
15463 TRC7 19943 C8 19990 C8 22500 C3
16353 C7 19947 C3

44 Kin Terms and Relationships

親屬關係及稱呼

親属関係及び称呼

Geographic China Broadly Conceived

Primary 19759 T 1 20025 TR 1 20031 TRC1

Second. 19774 T 1 19913 C2 20160 TR 2
10634 T 1 19859 TRC2 19979 TRC1 20181 TR 1
11387 TRC1 19861 RC1 19982 TRC8 20235 TRC2
19730 TRC1 19870 TRC1 20044 T 1 21579 C2
19752 T 1 19888 TRC2 20053 TR 1 21850 TRC2
19763 T 1

Mainland China

Primary 19722 T 1 19880 TRC2 21185 TR 1

Second. 14430 R 8 19784 TR 1 19924 C1
10086 TR 2 15138 TR 2 19790 TR 1 20042 T 1
11074 C2 16053 TR 2 19816 R 2 20046 TR 1
11195 T 1 18144 R 2 19826 R 1 20076 C1
11218 T 1 19110 C8 19854 R 1 20175 TR 1
12131 C2 19720 T 8 19869 RC2 21367 R 2
14189 T 4 19731 TRC1 19899 TRC2 21541 RC1
14219 TR 2 19766 T 1

The Eighteen Provinces

Primary 19836 R 2 19839 R 1 20021 R 4
20022 T 1 20027 R 1

Second. 11536 T 3 19797 TR 2 21648 T 1
10050 T 2 16098 T 7 20063 R 8 21996 TR 1
10682 T 2

North China Broadly Conceived

Primary 19960 T 1

Second. □

Manchuria

Primary 19828 R 8

Second. 20276 R 4

Northern China

Primary □

Second. 15460 RC7 17158 T 3

Northwestern China and Frontier Regions

Primary 22682 R 2

Second. 21196 RC2

South China Broadly Conceived

Primary □

Second. 20208 R 2 21384 R 2

East Central China

Primary □

Second. 15405 R 7 16908 T 2 20262 R 2

Central Yangtze Provinces

□

Southwestern China

Primary 19362 R 6

Second. □

Southeastern China

Primary 20029 C1

Second. 15376 TR 2 19962 TR 7 20033 T 3

Taiwan Only
Primary 19910 c3 19939 c2 19980 trc8
19090 rc8 19916 c8 19973 trc8 20024 c8
Second. 17622 c3 19864 rc8 20427 c2
15515 c8 19737 c8 19925 c8 21201 c8
17618 c5

Hong Kong and Macau Only
Primary 10304 c3
Second. 19953 c3 20272 c7

45 Property and Inheritance
財産及繼承 財産及び相続

Geographic China Broadly Conceived
Primary 16127 trc2 20044 t 1 20051 tr 1
12370 r 7 19870 trc1 20050 tr 2 20053 tr 1
12409 rc7 19983 trc7
Second. 12233 tr 2 19733 trc1 20162 tr 1
10082 tr 2 15130 t 2 19772 t 1 20463 r 3
11250 tr 1 15539 c7 19859 trc2 21279 t 2
11264 tr 1 16104 tr 7 19979 trc1 22133 tr 2
11299 tr 3 16337 trc1 20017 trc1 22474 trc1
11387 trc1 19730 trc1 20160 tr 2

Mainland China
Primary 12361 r 7 19821 r 1 20055 tr 1
10524 t 2 12398 rc8 19831 r 1 20058 r 1
11203 t 2 14413 rc4 19852 r 1 20061 r 1
11332 r 1 14434 r 7 19893 rc1 20064 r 2
11333 r 1 15882 c7 20013 tr 1 20065 r 1
11344 r 1 16103 tr 2 20034 t 2 20066 r 1
11362 r 1 16106 tr 2 20036 t 2 20067 r 2
11447 c1 16112 tr 1 20038 t 7 20068 r 2
11473 c1 18722 r 2 20040 t 8 20071 trc1
11689 tr 2 19155 c7 20041 t 1 20073 c1
12056 c2 19160 c7 20042 t 1 20076 c1
12187 t 8 19177 c8 20045 tr 1 20077 c1
12189 t 2 19719 t 2 20046 tr 1 20078 c2
12215 tr 2 19722 t 1 20049 tr 2 20079 c7
12298 r 7 19731 trc1 20052 tr 1 20080 c7
12306 r 8 19789 tr 2 20054 tr 1 20081 c2
12313 r 8 19819 r 1

Secondary: Monographs
10214 trc2 12229 tr 7 15483 c7 19826 r 1
10291 tr 2 12331 r 7 15495 c2 19854 r 1
10893 trc2 12363 r 8 15507 c7 19862 trc1
11195 t 1 12442 c7 15762 tr 3 19883 rc2
11263 tr 1 12456 c8 16488 c7 19892 rc1
11307 r 1 12525 c2 17763 r 2 19899 trc2
11313 r 1 13472 t 1 17979 tr 7 19931 c1
11356 r 1 13491 tr 1 19033 trc1 20175 tr 1
11423 c1 13496 tr 1 19063 c2 20614 tr 2
11440 c2 13506 tr 3 19277 r 4 20648 r 2
11672 t 4 13584 c2 19795 tr 1 21798 tr 1
11855 trc2 13868 t 2 19804 tr 1 22299 c2
12166 c2 14419 c2 19810 r 1

Secondary: Inclusions
10078 tr 2 11530 c2 15542 c7 19724 tr 1
10601 t 2 12228 tr 2 17110 c7 19867 trc1
11223 t 1 12536 c7 17978 t 2 19877 trc1
11248 tr 1 14442 c7 19129 c8 21709 t 2
11399 rc1 15314 t 2

Secondary: Journal Articles
10084 tr 2 11363 r 1 12404 trc8 15564 c7
10513 t 4 11386 trc1 13294 rc2 15831 c7
10531 t 3 11421 c2 13484 t 2 15975 rc7
11197 t 1 11464 c1 13596 c7 16036 c7
11204 t 1 11526 c1 13749 r 5 16038 c2
11211 t 1 11662 t 2 13796 c1 16861 c7
11220 t 1 11680 t 2 14130 trc2 16863 c7
11239 t 1 11813 r 2 14141 c2 19084 rc8
11275 tr 1 11866 rc2 14415 rc4 19123 c7
11309 r 1 12077 c2 14418 c4 19159 c7
11316 r 1 12311 r 7 14515 rc2 19164 c7
11331 r 1 12350 r 8 14734 r 1 19271 r 4
19775 t 2 19798 tr 1 19949 c1 22573 t 1
19785 tr 1 19799 tr 1 19967 r 1 23007 trc1
19792 tr 1 19934 c1 22199 trc1

The Eighteen Provinces
Primary 16890 c7 19964 tr 1 20057 r 7
12198 t 8 19754 t 1 20035 t 1 20059 r 1
12225 tr 8 19963 tr 2 20037 t 1 20063 r 8
Second. 14159 t 1 16115 r 1 19848 r 2
12212 tr 2 15965 r 3 16560 tr 2 19942 c2
12231 tr 7 16107 tr 1 19839 r 1 19954 c2

North China Broadly Conceived
Primary 12290 r 8
Second. 13548 r 2

Manchuria
Primary 19828 r 8 20047 tr 2
Second. 11335 r 1 15995 c2 16644 r 8
10354 tr 2 12988 r 2 16429 r 2 19195 c7
10364 r 2

Northern China
Primary 16536 t 2 17407 t 8 20060 r 3
16535 t 8 16594 r 8 17627 t 2
Second. 15449 r 2 16403 tr 2 17409 t 2
14157 t 3 15450 r 7 16538 t 8 19171 c7
14163 t 3 15596 r 7 16632 r 8 19193 c7
15328 t 2 15933 t 2 16685 r 7 19340 c3
15336 t 2

Northwestern China and Frontier Regions
Primary 16735 rc8 16859 c8 20048 tr 8
Second. 19375 c2 21196 rc2

South China Broadly Conceived
Primary 10632 t 1
Second. 19976 trc8

East Central China
Primary 15405 r 7 15426 r 7 20043 t 8
Second. 16108 tr 3 17290 r 3 17816 t 7
15517 c8 16641 r 8 17680 c7 22764 c3

Central Yangtze Provinces
Primary 20056 r 3
Second. □

Southwestern China
Primary □
Second. 16267 tr 2 16425 r 7 16675 r 7
19729 r 6

Southeastern China
Primary 16613 r 7 20033 t 3 20069 trc1
16579 r 8 20006 tr 8 20039 t 1 20082 c7
Second. 15376 tr 2 16736 rc7 19962 tr 7
15321 t 2 15476 rc8 19179 c7 19975 trc7

Taiwan Only
Primary 11232 t 2 20072 c7 20074 c2
Second. 17675 c2 19863 rc2 19980 trc8
15887 c8 19090 rc8 19890 trc2 20018 c8
16746 rc8 19737 c8 19910 c3 20268 c6
16872 c7 19769 t 2 19939 c2 20368 c2
16883 c7

Hong Kong and Macau Only
Primary 15838 c3 19878 trc1 20062 r 2
11389 trc2 15858 c2 19912 c2 20070 trc8
11400 trc1 16132 c2 19918 c3 20075 c2
11492 c3 16456 trc7 19970 trc7 20697 c3
Second. 15820 c2 20279 t 1 20683 c3
11467 c1 17683 c8 20657 rc3 20684 c3
15463 trc7 19943 c8

46 Sex
性 性

Geographic China Broadly Conceived
Primary 20088 t 3 20108 r 3 20225 trc1
20083 t 1 20089 t 1 20109 trc2 22016 trc1
20085 t 2 20096 t 2 20111 trc2 22474 trc1
20086 t 1 20101 tr 1 20172 tr 1
Second. 19772 t 1 20180 tr 1 20769 t 4
10117 trc2 19774 t 1 20181 tr 1 20969 trc1
14156 t 2 19861 rc1 20231 rc2 21366 r 2
14166 t 1 19881 trc1 20719 t 1 21544 rc2

Mainland China
Primary 20105 r 1 20154 t 1 20331 c2
16123 r 2 20107 r 2 20159 tr 2 20796 tr 1
16907 t 4 20110 trc1 20182 tr 2 20866 r 4
19880 trc2 20115 trc2 20237 c2 21500 tr 1
20102 r 5 20121 c2
Second. 18989 tr 2 19951 c3 21092 c2
10005 t 2 19722 t 1 20008 tr 1 21172 t 2
10152 c2 19732 rc2 20130 t 2 21300 t 2
10153 c2 19736 trc1 20133 t 1 21346 tr 2
10165 c2 19791 tr 1 20135 t 1 21355 tr 2
10173 c2 19798 tr 1 20229 rc1 21395 rc2
11195 t 1 19799 tr 1 20623 tr 2 21416 rc2
11443 c2 19803 tr 2 20723 t 4 21529 trc3
14943 c2 19872 rc1 20741 t 1 21563 c1
15215 c2 19873 rc2 20761 t 1 21869 trc1
15271 c7 19909 c2 20782 t 1 22020 c1
15466 rc2 19914 c1 20939 r 3 22769 c2
18071 c1 19928 c2

The Eighteen Provinces
Primary 20094 t 3 20097 tr 1 20100 tr 1
20090 t 3 20095 t 3 20098 tr 3 21440 t 1
20092 t 2
Second. 19839 r 1 20284 t 1 20760 t 2
18012 t 2 20125 t 2 20411 c2 21370 r 2
18366 t 2 20150 t 1 20503 c2 21519 r 1
18461 t 2 20156 t 1 20729 t 2 22004 r 1
19008 r 2 20178 tr 2 20730 t 1

North China Broadly Conceived
Primary □
Second. 20716 t 2

Manchuria
Primary 20104 r 8
Second. 15674 tr 2 17689 t 7 20141 t 4

Northern China
Primary 17625 t 3 20091 t 3 20206 r 3
10730 tr 3 20084 t 1 20116 c3
Second. 15407 r 3 20205 r 2 21511 r 3
14163 t 3 17844 r 3 20921 r 3 21512 r 3
15373 tr 3 18029 r 8 21330 tr 7 21513 r 3
15390 tr 3 18643 r 8 21508 r 3

Northwestern China and Frontier Regions
Primary □
Second. 19818 r 7 19889 rc8 20298 r 7
20304 rc2 20380 t 7

South China Broadly Conceived
Primary 19894 trc2 21537 rc2
Second. 15205 c2 20208 r 2

East Central China
Primary 20087 t 3 20103 r 3 20112 rc3
Second. 15143 r 3 17193 tr 3 18008 t 3
18013 t 2

47 Female Roles and Male-Female Differences

婦女地位及男女分別

女性の地位及び男女の区別

18956 TR *2* 19889 RC*8* 20380 T *7* 20856 R *1*
18993 R *2* 20298 R *7* 20601 T *2* 22430 TR *8*
19822 R *2* 20304 RC*2*

South China Broadly Conceived

Primary 20208 R *2* 20274 T *3* 21376 R *2*
21382 R *2*

Second. 15361 T *2* 17939 R *2* 19006 R *4*
10031 T *2* 15721 T *2* 18421 T *2* 19894 TRC*2*
10046 T *2* 15722 T *2* 18449 T *2* 20855 R *2*
11014 T *2* 15749 T *3* 18459 T *2* 21384 R *2*
14770 R *3* 16855 C*8* 18463 T *2* 22601 T *2*

East Central China

Primary 19703 R *3* 20136 T *4* 20207 R *3*
15881 C*3* 20103 R *3* 20195 R *3* 20251 C*3*
17868 R *7*

Second. 15871 R *3* 17694 TR *3* 20087 T *3*
15143 R *3* 17193 TR *3* 17724 R *3* 20112 RC*3*
15348 T *3* 17213 R *2* 17734 R *3* 20581 T *3*
15404 R *3* 17274 R *2* 17863 R *3* 21215 R *7*
15493 C*7* 17612 R *3* 18008 T *3* 21433 C*2*
15517 C*8* 17649 T *5* 18855 T *2* 21528 R *3*
15592 R *2* 17662 T *7* 18932 T *4* 21628 T *7*
15744 T *2* 17667 R *7* 19746 T *8* 22409 T *2*
15869 R *3*

Central Yangtze Provinces

Primary 20138 T *2* 20210 R *2* 20241 C*8*
20129 T *6* 20199 R *7* 20220 R *3* 20275 T *4*

Second. 14577 T *3* 20379 T *4*

Southwestern China

Primary 15436 R *6* 15522 C*3* 20217 R *3*

Second. 16971 R *2* 19742 T *2* 20583 T *2*
14750 R *2* 17535 T *4* 19885 RC*2* 22508 T *2*
15598 R *7* 17729 R *3* 20456 R *3* 22523 T *2*
15641 R *2* 19729 R *6* 20475 RC*4* 22542 T *2*
16482 C*3*

Southeastern China

Primary 18022 TR *3* 20185 R *2* 20296 R *2*
10668 T *2* 20151 T *1* 20215 R *3* 20297 R *2*
14629 TR *4* 20153 T *3* 20234 TRC*2* 21385 R *2*
14772 R *3* 20183 TR *2* 20261 R *1* 21781 TR *1*
17930 T *7*

Second. 15711 T *3* 17665 R *7* 19975 TRC*7*
11683 TR *2* 15735 T *2* 17813 T *3* 20106 R *3*
14758 R *2* 15865 R *3* 17919 T *5* 20385 T *5*
15312 T *3* 15984 C*7* 17920 T *7* 20911 R *3*
15317 T *2* 16116 R *4* 19045 TRC*2* 20912 R *1*
15321 T *2* 16163 T *3* 19506 R *3* 21522 R *1*
15364 T *3* 16530 T *2* 19761 T *7* 21527 R *1*
15448 R *3* 17256 R *2* 19778 T *3* 21575 C*3*
15576 C*5* 17560 TR *2* 19962 TR *7* 22479 TRC*8*

Taiwan Only

Primary 19738 C*7* 20236 C*8* 20422 C*8*
15471 RC*2* 19896 TRC*8* 20246 C*1* 20423 C*8*
16261 TR *2* 19925 C*8* 20249 C*7*

Second. 16739 TRC*8* 19936 C*3* 21483 C*2*
11690 TR *2* 16740 TRC*2* 19955 C*7* 21556 C*2*
14544 C*5* 16771 C*8* 19956 C*2* 21564 C*3*
15505 C*8* 16772 C*8* 20072 C*7* 21565 C*3*
15586 TR *2* 17386 C*4* 20269 C*1* 21566 C*3*
15675 TR *2* 17961 C*2* 20326 C*4* 21571 C*3*
15698 TRC*2* 18263 C*2* 20377 C*8* 21583 C*8*
15878 C*2* 18908 T *2* 20427 C*2* 21584 C*3*
15890 C*2* 19890 TRC*2* 21009 C*2* 22770 C*3*
16167 T *2* 19911 C*2* 21237 C*2*

Hong Kong and Macau Only

Primary 19824 R *2* 19946 C*2* 20389 TR *3*
15617 C*2* 19901 C*7* 20114 TRC*3* 20519 C*3*
16275 TR *2* 19918 C*3* 20194 R *3* 21202 C*3*
19710 TRC*3* 19933 C*3* 20239 C*3* 22500 C*3*
19712 C*3*

Second. 15526 C*3* 17608 T *3* 17894 RC*2*
11400 TRC*1* 15546 C*7* 17718 R *2* 17909 C*2*
14597 T *2* 15913 C*3* 17745 C*2* 17994 C*2*
19696 T *3* 19943 C*8* 20657 RC*3* 21234 RC*2*
19858 RC*7* 19953 C*3* 20688 C*2* 21597 C*3*
19912 C*2* 20324 C*3* 21197 RC*2* 21598 C*3*
19917 C*3* 20522 C*3*

48 Non-Kin Interpersonal Relationships

非親屬關係　　非親族関係

Geographic China Broadly Conceived

Primary 14184 T *1* 17980 TR *1* 21538 TRC*2*
10004 T *2* 16104 TR *7* 18544 TR *1* 22016 TRC*1*
10618 T *1* 17975 T *2* 20053 TR *1* 22578 T *2*

Second. 14098 T *2* 18976 TR *2* 21333 TR *2*
10026 T *2* 14102 T *2* 19055 TRC*2* 21467 TRC*1*
10032 T *2* 16128 TRC*2* 19859 TRC*2* 21579 C*2*
10042 T *2* 16217 T *7* 19861 RC*1* 21988 T *1*
10082 TR *2* 18303 R *2* 19978 TRC*2* 22002 TR *1*
10162 C*2* 18495 T *2* 20088 T *3* 22014 TRC*1*
10557 T *1* 18570 TR *1* 20463 R *3* 22694 R *3*
11250 TR *1* 18805 TRC*1* 20994 TRC*5*

Mainland China

Primary 14146 C*2* 19951 C*3* 20571 T *1*
10135 C*2* 14198 T *1* 20254 T *2* 20572 T *1*
10551 T *4* 15150 R *2* 20255 T *1* 21570 C*1*
10766 R *2* 15434 R *7* 20258 T *2* 21948 C*2*
14094 T *2* 15508 C*2* 20259 T *1* 21998 TR *1*
14099 T *1* 18144 R *2* 20270 C*1* 22006 R *1*
14105 TR *2* 19625 R *1* 20271 C*1* 22020 C*1*

Second. 16096 T *1* 19821 R *1* 21367 R *2*
10098 R *2* 16294 R *1* 19826 R *1* 21422 TRC*2*
11053 RC*2* 17313 RC*2* 20042 T *1* 21423 RC*2*
11064 C*1* 17803 C*2* 20067 R *2* 21585 C*2*
11101 C*2* 18018 TR *1* 20081 C*2* 21657 T *1*
11220 T *1* 18086 T *1* 20182 TR *2* 21806 R *1*
11248 TR *1* 18104 TR *2* 20414 T *1* 22303 C*1*
12549 C*8* 19218 TR *1* 20558 T *2* 22400 T *2*
13951 R *2* 19229 R *5* 20661 TRC*1* 22469 R *1*
14177 T *2* 19558 R *2* 21260 T *2* 22556 T *2*
14569 T *2* 19751 T *2* 21300 T *2*

The Eighteen Provinces

Primary 14104 T *1* 20256 T *1* 20265 R *1*
10038 T *2* 14422 T *8* 20257 T *1* 21456 R *2*
14090 T *1* 19797 TR *2*

Second. 13979 R *2* 19836 R *2* 22004 R *1*
10568 T *4* 15470 RC*7* 20100 TR *1* 22395 T *2*
10680 T *3* 16183 T *2* 20565 T *2* 22463 R *1*
11655 T *1* 19781 TR *1* 21996 TR *1* 22776 T *2*
12252 R *8*

North China Broadly Conceived

Primary ☐

Second. 10679 T *2* 15428 R *7* 18914 T *2*

Manchuria

Primary 20253 T *1*

Second. 17857 R *2* 19828 R *8* 20795 TR *2*

Northern China

Primary 14157 T *3* 15338 T *7* 20260 TR *8*
22541 T *3*

Second. 15561 C*3* 21330 TR *7* 21375 R *3*
13964 R *7* 18362 C*3* 21359 TR *3* 22457 R *3*

Northwestern China and Frontier Regions

Primary ☐

Second. 17772 RC*7*

South China Broadly Conceived

Primary ☐

Second. 10636 T *1* 16979 R *2* 21384 R *2*

East Central China

Primary 20262 R *2*

Second. ☐

Central Yangtze Provinces

Primary ☐

Second. 20138 T *2*

Southwestern China

Primary ☐

Second. 17535 T *4* 19261 R *3* 20456 R *3*
14171 T *3* 18035 R *6* 20217 R *3* 20475 RC*4*
15641 R *2*

Southeastern China

Primary 20252 T *4* 20261 R *1* 21575 C*3*

Second. 17959 C*2* 19840 R *2* 21480 C*2*
15364 T *3* 18048 C*3* 20997 C*2*

Taiwan Only

Primary 17616 C*8* 20268 C*6* 20355 C*8*
16133 C*8* 19738 C*7* 20269 C*1*

Second. 18263 C*2* 20249 C*7* 21483 C*2*
15505 C*8* 19911 C*2* 20425 C*3* 21484 C*2*
15515 C*8* 19980 TRC*8* 20517 C*4* 21556 C*2*
16902 C*7* 20236 C*8* 21481 C*3* 22018 C*4*
17984 RC*2*

Hong Kong and Macau Only

Primary 15464 TRC*8* 17958 C*7* 17971 C*8*
20267 C*3* 20272 C*7*

Second. 16275 TR *2* 18820 TRC*3* 19946 C*2*
15462 TRC*7* 16348 C*7* 19051 TRC*2* 21547 C*3*
15574 C*8* 17102 TRC*7* 19070 C*3* 21586 C*3*
16137 C*3* 17126 C*3*

50 Life Cycle and Age Grading

生命周期及年齡

生命周期及び年齢

Geographic China Broadly Conceived

Primary 10117 TRC*2* 10118 RC*2* 18871 T *2*
20231 RC*2* 22694 R *3*

Second. 10082 TR *2* 11045 RC*2* 20155 T *2*
10014 T *2* 10200 TR *2* 18971 TR *2*

Mainland China

Primary 14608 T *1* 19873 RC*2* 20302 R *2*
10029 T *2* 15509 C*2* 19948 C*2* 20618 TR *2*
10123 RC*2* 18915 T *2* 20130 T *2* 20623 TR *2*
10136 C*2* 19732 RC*2* 20137 T *2* 20782 T *1*
10604 T *1* 19751 T *2* 20226 TRC*2* 21290 T *1*
11202 T *1* 19816 R *2* 20280 TRC*1* 22556 T *2*
14515 RC*2*

Second. 14285 TRC*1* 17644 C*2* 20124 T *4*
10041 T *2* 14290 RC*1* 17979 TR *7* 20154 T *1*
10062 T *2* 14318 C*1* 18003 C*2* 20182 TR *2*
10165 C*2* 14777 TRC*1* 18164 RC*3* 20212 R *2*
10180 C*2* 14974 C*2* 18608 R *2* 20258 T *2*
10226 C*2* 15061 R *3* 19035 TRC*2* 20292 TR *2*
10242 C*2* 15073 R *2* 19597 C*2* 20474 RC*2*
10244 C*2* 15089 RC*2* 19615 TR *2* 20741 T *1*
10470 C*4* 15096 C*1* 19719 T *2* 20761 T *1*
10778 R *2* 15105 C*4* 19860 TRC*1* 20801 TR *1*
11095 C*2* 15171 TRC*2* 19872 RC*1* 21250 C*2*
11194 T *2* 15176 RC*2* 19880 TRC*2* 21335 TR *1*
11382 R *2* 15292 C*2* 19899 TRC*2* 21529 TRC*3*
11913 C*2* 15486 C*7* 19908 C*1* 21563 C*1*
12131 C*2* 15560 C*4* 19945 C*2* 21570 C*1*
12303 R *2* 16123 R *2* 19992 T *1* 21798 TR *1*
14178 T *2* 17640 C*8* 20081 C*2* 22486 RC*8*
14280 RC*2*

THE EIGHTEEN PROVINCES

PRIMARY 12193 T 8 14092 T 2 19688 T 2
19839 R 1 20287 T 1

SECOND. 19695 T 2 20449 R 4 21482 C4
10006 T 2 19836 R 2 21207 R 8 21489 C2
13621 T 4 19843 R 8 21213 R 2 22004 R 1
15446 R 3 19964 TR 1

NORTH CHINA BROADLY CONCEIVED

PRIMARY □

SECOND. 10057 T 1 18750 R 2

MANCHURIA

PRIMARY 20276 R 4

SECOND. 15678 TR 2 17689 T 7 21229 R 2

NORTHERN CHINA

PRIMARY 15900 C7 20091 T 3 20559 T 3
14214 TR 3 16311 R 8 20273 R 3 21278 T 3
15415 R 8 17625 T 3 20277 C7 21375 R 3
15557 C7 18990 TR 3

SECOND. 17497 C3 18643 R 8 21206 R 1
14330 C3 17721 R 7 20557 T 3 22457 R 3
15347 T 3 17877 R 3 20938 R 3 22706 R 6
16087 T 3

NORTHWESTERN CHINA AND FRONTIER REGIONS

PRIMARY 15545 C8 22437 TR 2

SECOND. 18956 TR 2 19818 R 7 22713 R 5

SOUTH CHINA BROADLY CONCEIVED

PRIMARY 20208 R 2 20274 T 3

SECOND. 10028 T 2 18459 T 2 19006 R 4

EAST CENTRAL CHINA

PRIMARY □

SECOND. 16075 C3 19834 R 4 22409 T 2
15348 T 3 16458 C2 21037 C3 22755 C3
15480 C2 18865 T 2

CENTRAL YANGTZE PROVINCES

PRIMARY 20138 T 2 20275 T 4

SECOND. 16405 TR 3 17776 C7 19694 T 3

SOUTHWESTERN CHINA

PRIMARY 15640 R 2 17613 R 7 19827 R 6

SECOND. 17664 R 8 18922 T 2 19729 R 6
15598 R 7 17854 R 2 19085 RC7

SOUTHEASTERN CHINA

PRIMARY 15317 T 2 17920 T 7 19692 T 3
20386 T 7 22455 R 2

SECOND. 18518 T 2 20912 R 1 21522 R 1
15321 T 2 19840 R 2 21145 C2 21575 C3
15349 T 2 20338 C1

TAIWAN ONLY

PRIMARY 15515 C8 16226 TR 2 20249 C7
15504 C8 15890 C2 19896 TRC8

SECOND. 15878 C2 20341 C3 21008 C2
11108 C1 16727 RC2 20342 C3 21020 C2
15471 RC2 19090 RC8 20343 C3 21030 C7
15505 C8 19738 C7 20351 C2 21108 C7
15612 RC2 19939 C2 20364 C3 21232 TRC2
15613 RC2 19956 C2 20366 C1 21233 RC2
15675 TR 2 20236 C8 20368 C2 21238 C2
15685 R 1 20312 C2 20421 C2 21240 C2
15695 RC2 20320 C2 20427 C2 21249 C1
15709 C2 20340 C3 20517 C4 21520 R 2

HONG KONG AND MACAU ONLY

PRIMARY 19933 C3 20279 T 1 21244 C2
15927 T 7 19990 C8 21242 C3 22733 TRC3
16348 C7

SECOND. 16139 C3 19683 C3 20522 C3
15330 T 7 17635 RC3 19946 C2 20622 TR 2
15617 C2 17744 C4 20309 C2 21234 RC2
15618 C2

51 REPRODUCTION

生殖　生殖

GEOGRAPHIC CHINA BROADLY CONCEIVED

PRIMARY 20085 T 2 20285 T 1 20291 TR 1
20295 TR 1 20306 C2

SECOND. 15191 RC2 19996 T 2 20769 T 4
10024 T 2 16337 TRC1 20083 T 1 20826 TR 2
10060 T 2 19772 T 1 20540 T 2 20969 TRC1
11892 C2 19802 TR 2 20719 T 1 21366 R 2

MAINLAND CHINA

PRIMARY 20292 TR 2 20348 C2 20375 C2
10218 RC2 20294 TR 2 20349 C1 20376 C1
10233 C2 20302 R 2 20356 C2 20403 RC2
10236 C2 20303 RC2 20361 C2 20837 R 2
13086 C2 20305 RC1 20362 C2 20961 RC2
19767 T 1 20313 C2 20363 C2 20996 C2
19948 C2 20314 C2 20365 C2 21086 C1
20154 T 1 20318 C2 20370 C2 21104 C1
20229 RC1 20325 C2 20371 C2 21137 C1
20282 T 2 20327 C1 20373 C1 21250 C2
20286 T 2 20328 C2 20374 C1 21253 C1
20288 T 1 20331 C2

SECOND. 10251 C2 19775 T 2 20761 T 1
10003 T 2 10410 C2 19866 TRC2 20782 T 1
10019 T 2 10482 C2 19872 RC1 20788 T 1
10047 T 2 10502 C7 19905 C2 20801 TR 1
10105 R 2 11103 C1 19906 C2 20939 R 3
10143 C2 11574 T 1 19914 C1 20983 RC1
10156 C2 11956 C1 19944 C1 20991 TRC2
10168 C2 12090 C2 19974 TRC2 21010 C2
10173 C2 12129 C2 19992 T 1 21013 C2
10191 TR 2 12530 C2 20121 C2 21014 C2
10223 C2 14429 R 8 20130 T 2 21045 C2
10225 C2 15271 C7 20137 T 2 21172 T 2
10229 C1 15292 C2 20405 C1 21241 C2
10230 C2 15519 C2 20593 T 1 21248 C2
10240 C2 15550 C2 20661 TRC1 21251 C1
10241 C2 16294 R 1 20720 T 1 21980 T 4
10242 C2 18608 R 2 20745 T 2 22556 T 2
10243 C1 19721 T 2

THE EIGHTEEN PROVINCES

PRIMARY 20290 T 2 20329 C2 20730 T 1
20284 T 1 20300 R 3 20411 C2 20822 TR 4
20287 T 1 20301 R 1

SECOND. 17916 C2 20565 T 2 22390 T 2
12155 C2 20125 T 2 21121 C2 22395 T 2
15240 C3 20144 T 1 22067 T 2

NORTH CHINA BROADLY CONCEIVED

PRIMARY □

SECOND. 15428 R 7 20541 T 2 20835 R 2

MANCHURIA

PRIMARY □

SECOND. 20276 R 4 21229 R 2

NORTHERN CHINA

PRIMARY 20315 C3 21217 R 3 21221 R 3
19776 T 2 20353 C3 21219 R 3 21224 R 3
20281 T 5 20637 R 3 21220 R 3 21230 R 3
20293 TR 1 20930 R 3

SECOND. 15414 R 8 20273 R 3 21264 T 3
11568 T 3 16295 R 3 20762 T 3 21344 TR 2
15338 T 7 16311 R 8 20952 R 3 21664 T 3
15390 TR 3 17780 C3 21065 C7 22397 T 3
15403 R 8 20205 R 2

NORTHWESTERN CHINA AND FRONTIER REGIONS

PRIMARY 19818 R 7 20298 R 7 20299 R 8
20304 RC2 20380 T 7

SECOND. 19889 RC8 21808 R 8

SOUTH CHINA BROADLY CONCEIVED

PRIMARY 20289 T 2

SECOND. 20274 T 3

EAST CENTRAL CHINA

PRIMARY 20876 R 2 21136 C3 21252 C3

SECOND. 15307 T 3 15517 C8 20886 R 3
21215 R 7 21216 R 7

CENTRAL YANGTZE PROVINCES

PRIMARY 20379 T 4

SECOND. 20275 T 4 20829 R 7

SOUTHWESTERN CHINA

PRIMARY 20839 R 3 21212 R 3

SECOND. 15379 TR 3 15436 R 6 16267 TR 2
21990 T 1

SOUTHEASTERN CHINA

PRIMARY 20296 R 2 20338 C1 20917 R 4
20283 T 3 20297 R 2 20357 C2

SECOND. 17920 T 7 20783 T 4 22455 R 2
16190 T 2 20778 T 3 21781 TR 1

TAIWAN ONLY

PRIMARY 20326 C4 20344 C3 20368 C2
14896 C3 20330 C2 20345 C2 20369 C2
20249 C7 20332 C3 20346 C2 20372 C3
20307 C2 20333 C3 20347 C1 20377 C8
20308 C3 20334 C2 20351 C2 20378 C3
20311 C2 20335 C1 20352 C2 21009 C2
20312 C2 20336 C2 20354 C1 21132 C1
20316 C2 20337 C2 20355 C8 21236 C8
20317 C7 20339 C2 20360 C3 21238 C2
20319 C2 20340 C3 20364 C3 21247 C2
20320 C2 20341 C3 20366 C1 21249 C1
20321 C1 20342 C3 20367 C3 21571 C3
20322 C2 20343 C3

SECOND. 15504 C8 16858 C2 21084 C2
11959 C2 15600 TRC2 19896 TRC8 21131 C2
12175 C2 15615 C2 20074 C2 21233 RC2
15351 T 2 15655 C2 21030 C7 21237 C2
15471 RC2 15852 C2 21068 C2 21243 C2

HONG KONG AND MACAU ONLY

PRIMARY 20310 C2 20350 C2 20359 C3
15618 C2 20323 C2 20358 C2 21244 C2
20309 C2 20324 C3

SECOND. 19933 C3 21061 C2 23034 C2
19932 C3 20869 R 2 21234 RC2

52 INFANCY AND CHILDHOOD

嬰兒及童年　嬰児及び幼年

GEOGRAPHIC CHINA BROADLY CONCEIVED

PRIMARY 17691 TR 2 19730 TRC1 20222 R 3
20710 T 2

SECOND. 14491 R 3 19802 TR 2 20200 R 2
10117 TRC2 15063 R 2 20005 TR 1 20235 TRC2
11045 RC2 16248 TR 1 20044 T 1 20285 T 1
11228 T 3 17696 R 3 20085 T 2 20955 RC2
14113 TR 2 18971 TR 2 20155 T 2 21342 TR 2
14476 R 3 19546 R 3

MAINLAND CHINA

PRIMARY 19721 T 2 20219 R 3 20390 TR 3
12131 C2 20201 R 4 20382 T 1 20391 TR 1
17796 C2 20204 R 2 20383 T 1 20398 R 1

20402 RC2 20407 C2 20996 C2 21040 C1
20403 RC2 20482 C2 21010 C2 21250 C2
20405 C1

SECONDARY: MONOGRAPHS
10003 T 2 14478 R 3 16277 TR 2 20154 T 1
10029 T 2 14483 R 4 16457 C2 20166 TR 2
10062 T 2 14509 R 3 17717 R 3 20177 TR 2
10069 TR 2 14510 R 4 17974 T 3 20221 R 2
10133 C2 14943 C2 18061 C2 20226 TRC2
10895 C2 14974 C2 19476 TR 2 20247 C7
11095 C2 15073 R 2 19732 RC2 20618 TR 2
12291 R 7 15495 C2 19795 TR 1 20623 TR 2
13277 R 2 15537 C4 19816 R 2 20648 R 2
13768 C1 15570 C2 19826 R 1 20966 RC2
13880 TR 2 15991 C7 20135 T 1 20991 TRC2
13928 R 2 15993 C7 20137 T 2 21307 TR 2
13969 R 2 16012 C4

SECONDARY: INCLUSIONS
13242 R 5 19877 TRC1 19951 C3 21050 C3
14603 T 2 19915 C1 20081 C2 21529 TRC3
19256 R 3 19945 C2 20259 T 1 21682 T 2
19873 RC2

SECONDARY: JOURNAL ARTICLES
10084 TR 2 15008 C3 19872 RC1 20454 R 1
10185 T 2 15252 C2 19903 C1 20499 C2
10451 R 2 16034 C4 20077 C1 20687 C1
10775 R 2 17879 R 3 20148 T 2 20732 T 1
11220 T 1 19673 C2 20187 R 2 21137 C1
11316 R 1 19768 T 2 20237 C2 21158 C7
14481 R 2 19785 TR 1 20242 C2 22452 R 2
14824 C2 19811 R 1 20250 C3 22573 T 1
14953 C1 19813 R 1

THE EIGHTEEN PROVINCES

PRIMARY 15035 C3 20393 R 2 21122 C2
14459 R 3 18015 T 1 20411 C2 21266 T 2
14831 C3 20388 TR 1 20420 T 1
SECOND. 17808 C3 19839 R 1 20822 TR 4
15118 C2 18441 T 2 19900 C3 21305 TR 4
15119 C2 19577 R 3 20098 TR 3 21365 R 3
15501 C2 19688 T 2 20125 T 2 21456 R 2
16171 T 1 19781 TR 1 20190 R 2 21519 R 1
16252 TR 2 19805 TR 1 20699 C2 22414 T 1
17614 R 2 19836 R 2 20730 T 1

NORTH CHINA BROADLY CONCEIVED

PRIMARY □
SECOND. 17797 C3 17873 R 2 18493 T 2

MANCHURIA

PRIMARY 20410 C7
SECOND. 11834 R 2 17716 R 5 19828 R 8
20416 C2 21255 C3

NORTHERN CHINA

PRIMARY 20384 T 3 20406 C3 21069 C3
16322 R 8 20395 R 3 20413 C3 21330 TR 7
17727 R 3 20397 R 7 20579 T 3 22397 T 3
20381 T 2 20400 R 8 20952 R 3
SECOND. 15828 C3 18868 T 2 20693 C2
14163 T 3 16295 R 3 20205 R 2 21042 C7
15120 C2 17331 C3 20238 C3 21217 R 3
15338 T 7 17780 C3 20273 R 3 21221 R 3
15403 R 8 17819 T 3 20353 C3 21344 TR 2
15410 R 8 18009 T 3 20637 R 3 21729 TR 7
15414 R 8

NORTHWESTERN CHINA AND FRONTIER REGIONS

PRIMARY 20304 RC2 20380 T 7 20399 R 7
20858 R 8
SECOND. 15350 T 2 15544 C8 20298 R 7
20299 R 8

SOUTH CHINA BROADLY CONCEIVED

PRIMARY 20289 T 2 20387 T 4
SECOND. 15361 T 2 20208 R 2 20274 T 3
21384 R 2

EAST CENTRAL CHINA

PRIMARY 17836 R 3 20392 R 3 20394 R 3
SECOND. 17724 R 3 17863 R 3 20876 R 2
15348 T 3 17839 R 3 20195 R 3 22384 T 2
15961 R 3

CENTRAL YANGTZE PROVINCES

PRIMARY 20138 T 2 20379 T 4
SECOND. 19694 T 3 20199 R 7 20275 T 4

SOUTHWESTERN CHINA

PRIMARY 19827 R 6 20396 R 8 20881 R 2
21212 R 3 22448 R 8
SECOND. 15308 T 5 15522 C3 16482 C3
15121 C2 15424 R 7 16260 TR 2

SOUTHEASTERN CHINA

PRIMARY 20261 R 1 20297 R 2 20385 T 5
20386 T 7 20905 R 8
SECOND. 15479 C8 17589 C2 19692 T 3
20283 T 3

TAIWAN ONLY

PRIMARY 20412 C1 20425 C3 21551 C1
20249 C7 20415 C1 20427 C2 21590 C3
20269 C1
SECOND. 19895 RC8 20422 C8 21089 C8
16167 T 2 19896 TRC8 20995 RC2 21247 C2
19711 C2 20421 C2 21049 C3 21568 C3
19769 T 2

HONG KONG AND MACAU ONLY

PRIMARY 19696 T 3 20389 TR 3 20409 C2
16348 C7 20114 TRC3 20404 C3 21586 C3
17788 C3 20279 T 1 20408 C4 22758 C3
SECOND. 17909 C2 19713 C2 21138 C3
16328 TRC2 19702 R 2 19824 R 2 21576 C3
17894 RC2 19710 TRC3 20688 C2 22500 C3

53 SOCIALIZATION

教養化育　社会化

GEOGRAPHIC CHINA BROADLY CONCEIVED

PRIMARY 20418 T 1 21538 TRC2 21579 C2
SECOND. 19881 TRC1 20172 TR 1 21472 TRC1
12957 TR 2 20005 TR 1 20656 TRC1 21557 C2
17980 TR 1 20101 TR 1 21279 T 2 22001 TR 1
18039 TRC1 20164 TR 1

MAINLAND CHINA

PRIMARY 19751 T 2 20255 T 1 21560 C1
10029 T 2 19816 R 2 20414 T 1 21570 C1
10110 TRC2 20110 TRC1 21124 C3 21594 C1
14569 T 2 20154 T 1 21540 RC1 22198 TRC2
17804 C1
SECOND. 15252 C2 19768 T 2 20383 T 1
10143 C2 15275 C2 19875 TRC2 20499 C2
10149 C2 15486 C7 19945 C2 20534 C4
11194 T 2 16013 C7 19951 C3 20639 R 2
11586 TR 2 17974 T 3 20130 T 2 20991 TRC2
11894 C2 18061 C2 20135 T 1 21536 TRC1
12291 R 7 18277 C2 20157 T 1 21563 C1
14059 C1 18783 R 2 20224 RC2 21775 TR 1
14133 C3 18989 TR 2 20258 T 2 22831 C2
14369 C2 19732 RC2 20382 T 1

THE EIGHTEEN PROVINCES

PRIMARY 19964 TR 1 20420 T 1
SECOND. 19839 R 1 20411 C2 21370 R 2
10018 T 2 20144 T 1 21305 TR 4 21519 R 1
11061 C2 20284 T 1 21365 R 3 22708 R 3
19354 TR 4

NORTH CHINA BROADLY CONCEIVED

PRIMARY □
SECOND. 20748 T 2

MANCHURIA

PRIMARY 20416 C2
SECOND. 17689 T 7 19828 R 8

NORTHERN CHINA

PRIMARY 17625 T 3 17780 C3 20417 RC2
21278 T 3
SECOND. 15786 R 3 20395 R 3 22458 R 8
15077 R 2 17819 T 3 20602 T 3 22461 R 3
15367 T 2 18068 C3 21512 R 3 22706 R 6
15449 R 7 20381 T 2 22456 R 1

NORTHWESTERN CHINA AND FRONTIER REGIONS

PRIMARY □
SECOND. 18671 R 7 20380 T 7

SOUTH CHINA BROADLY CONCEIVED

PRIMARY □
SECOND. 16934 T 2 19894 TRC2 20208 R 2

EAST CENTRAL CHINA

PRIMARY 22755 C3
SECOND. □

CENTRAL YANGTZE PROVINCES

PRIMARY 20379 T 4
SECOND. 19726 TR 7 20275 T 4 20820 TR 2

SOUTHWESTERN CHINA

PRIMARY 20396 R 8
SECOND. 15629 T 2 19729 R 6 19827 R 6
21280 T 5

SOUTHEASTERN CHINA

PRIMARY 21522 R 1
SECOND. 20385 T 5 20386 T 7

TAIWAN ONLY

PRIMARY 20421 C2 20423 C8 20425 C3
19895 RC8 20422 C8 20424 C3 20427 C2
20415 C1
SECOND. 15504 C8 16007 C3 20249 C7
21552 C3 21581 C3

HONG KONG AND MACAU ONLY

PRIMARY 20419 C3 20426 C2 20428 RC3
21555 C2 21576 C3
SECOND. 16008 C3 17958 C7 19918 C3
19990 C8 20519 C3

54 ADOLESCENCE AND YOUTH

青春期及青年　青春期及び青年

GEOGRAPHIC CHINA BROADLY CONCEIVED

PRIMARY 18102 TR 2 19699 R 3 21374 R 3
11047 RC2 18558 TR 2 20445 R 2 21434 C2
14698 TR 1 19490 R 2 20463 R 3 22604 T 3
15175 RC2
SECOND. 14696 TR 1 18308 R 3 20085 T 2
10085 TR 2 14720 R 2 18375 T 2 20086 T 1
10100 R 2 14812 RC1 18494 T 2 20155 T 2
10117 TRC2 14951 C2 18525 T 2 20615 TR 2
10162 C2 15134 TR 4 18534 TR 2 21557 C2
10853 TRC2 15161 TRC2 18560 TR 2 22160 R 1
12965 TR 4 15283 C2 18707 R 2 22657 TR 1
14174 T 3 18299 C2 18809 RC2 22690 R 3
14476 R 3 18303 R 2 19546 R 3

MAINLAND CHINA

PRIMARY: MONOGRAPHS

10180 C2 15214 C2 18783 R 2 20462 R 2
10516T 2 15235 C2 18991TR 4 20465 R 3
10970 C2 15245 C2 19455 R 8 20473 RC2
12864 C1 15250 C3 19697TR 3 20484 C2
13969 R 2 15267 C2 19899TRC2 20492 C3
14139 C2 15297 C2 19922 C7 20496 C2
14231TR 4 16332TRC1 20430TR 2 20502 C2
14364 C2 17313 RC2 20431TR 4 20506 C1
14685TR 2 17575 R 2 20432TR 2 20526 C2
14885 C1 17895 RC2 20442 R 3 21355TR 2
14910 C2 17990 C2 20444 R 2 22339 C2
14921 C1 18324 C2 20455 R 2 22375 C2
14974 C2 18717 R 2 20461 R 1

PRIMARY: INCLUSIONS

10930 C2 15222 C2 20434 R 2 20491 C2
13920 R 2 15223 C2 20443 R 1 20495 C2
14151 C2 15224 C2 20472 RC3 20504 C2
14328 C2 15298 C3 20480 C2 20528 C1
14525 C2 19928 C2 20486 C2 20530 C1
14840 C2 20433TR 3

PRIMARY: JOURNAL ARTICLES

10146 C2 20437 R 3 20474 RC2 20510 C2
10305 C2 20438 R 1 20476 C2 20511 C2
10316 C2 20439 R 4 20481 C1 20512 C2
14233 R 3 20441 R 2 20482 C2 20514 C2
14740 R 2 20446 R 1 20483 C1 20515 C2
14830 C2 20452 R 1 20485 C4 20518 C2
14926 C2 20453 R 3 20487 C2 20520 C2
14929 C2 20454 R 1 20488 C2 20521 C2
15226 C2 20457 R 2 20490 C2 20523 C2
15236 C2 20466 R 4 20498 C2 20531 C3
15705 C2 20468 R 2 20499 C2 20532 C2
17014 C4 20469 R 4 20500 C1 20533 C2
17641 C3 20470 R 4 20501 C2 20534 C4
18227 C2 20471TRC1 20508 C2 22844 C7
18332 C2

SECONDARY: MONOGRAPHS

10081TR 2 14164T 2 15248 C2 20182TR 2
10094 R 2 14274TRC2 15482 C2 20221 R 2
10887TRC2 14279 RC2 15519 C2 20226TRC2
10888TRC2 14309 C1 15550 C2 21335TR 1
10975 C2 14416 C2 16071 C2 21346TR 2
11052 RC2 14466 R 3 16457 C2 21420TRC2
11092 C2 14683TR 1 18003 C2 21563 C1
11094 C2 14723 R 2 18061 C2 21569 C1
11096 C2 14733 R 2 18118 R 4 22117TR 2
11113 C4 14736 R 4 18120 R 2 22131TR 2
11132 C2 14795 RC2 18172 RC2 22156 R 1
11179 C1 14810TRC1 18312 RC2 22229 RC2
12109 C2 14909 C1 18557TR 2 22251 RC2
12158 C2 15007 C4 18597 R 4 22296 C2
12791 C1 15017 C2 18746 R 2 22299 C2
12839 C2 15147 R 4 18827 RC2 22325 C2
13328 C2 15202 C2 18854T 1 22644TR 2
13970 R 2 15230 C2 19816 R 2 22699 R 3
14033 C2 15237 C2 19826 R 1 22711 R 1

SECONDARY: INCLUSIONS

10147 C2 14715 R 2 15209 C7 19365T 2
10410 C2 14760 R 1 17638 C2 19369 C1
10642T 2 14790 RC2 18088T 2 19709TRC3
11634 C1 14852 C4 18119 R 2 19945 C2
11637 C1 14880 C2 18219 C2 19952 C2
12009 C2 14905 C2 18310 R 2 20121 C2
12010 C2 14906 C2 18370T 2 20371 C2
14147 C2 14958 C2 18601 R 2 21432 C3
14251 R 2 14967 C2 18616 R 2 21682T 2
14289 RC4 14977 C2 18631 R 2 21858 RC1
14302 C3 15135TR 3 18773 R 2 22238 RC4
14674TR 2 15152 R 3 18837 C2

SECONDARY: JOURNAL ARTICLES

10465 C2 11452 C2 14653TR 4 15219 C2
10905 C4 11623 C1 14814 C4 15244 C2
10933 C2 11972 C2 14917 C2 15246 C2
10979 C4 12116 C2 14923 C1 15247 C2
10986 C2 12588T 1 15008 C3 15252 C2
11057 C2 14044 C2 15144 R 2 15256 C1
11098 C2 14063 C2 15196 C2 15275 C2
11142 C4 14143 C2 15198 C2 15276 C1
11148 C2 14331 C2 15200 C2 15277 C2
11220T 1 14452 C7 15206 C2 15282 C1
11372 R 1 14593T 1 15218 C2 15292 C2
15295 C4 18202 C1 19592 C3 21462 R 1
17000 C3 18214 C1 19673 C2 21587 C1
17590 C3 18216 C1 19700 R 2 21593 C1
17596 C2 18217 C4 19875TRC2 22149 R 2
17777 C2 18228 C2 19926 C1 22165 R 1
17781 C1 18243 C2 20382T 1 22308 C1
17803 C2 18323 C2 20666 C3 22344 C2
18197 C1 19376 C3 20687 C1 22613T 1
18198 C1

THE EIGHTEEN PROVINCES

PRIMARY 19686T 3 20429T 3 20489 C3
15145 R 4 19698TR 4 20449 R 4 20503 C2
15148 R 4 19812 R 3 20450 R 2 20509 C3
15243 C2 20098TR 3 20459 R 2 20513 C3
16155 C2 20192 R 3 20478 C2 21453TR 1
18999 R 3

SECOND. 15018 C2 18285 C2 20979TRC1
10091 R 2 15240 C3 18654 R 2 21365 R 3
14087T 2 15501 C2 18778 R 2 21370 R 2
14459 R 3 16058 R 2 19024 R 4 21386 RC3
14493 R 4 17995 C2 19027 R 2 22009 R 2
14649TR 3 18115 R 2 19836 R 2 22181 R 3
14671TR 4 18284 C2 19839 R 1 22760 C3
14680TR 4

NORTH CHINA BROADLY CONCEIVED

PRIMARY 10907 C3 10936 C3 22695 R 2

SECOND. 14762 R 2 18433T 2 22141 R 3
10969 C3 16063 R 2 18747 R 1

MANCHURIA

PRIMARY 11826 R 2

SECOND. 10852 RC2 15287 C2 19828 R 8

NORTHERN CHINA

PRIMARY 16073 C3 20440 R 3 20479 C3
10945 C3 18329 C3 20448 R 3 20497 C2
14757 R 2 18330 C3 20458 R 3 20505 C3
14877 C3 18355 C3 20460 R 3 20507 C3
14962 C2 18362 C3 20464 R 3 20527 C3
15021 C3 20435 R 3 20467 R 3 21278T 3
15394 R 2 20436 R 3 20477 C2 22747 C2

SECOND. 15197 C3 17713 R 3 21099 C4
12741 R 3 15274 C3 18068 C3 21344TR 2
13891 R 2 15304 C3 18286 C2 21431 C2
13974 R 2 15360T 7 18344 C3 21509 R 3
14551T 3 15459 RC7 18967TR 3 22712 R 7
14735 R 2 15538 C2 20091T 3 22750 C3
14785TRC2 17049 R 3 20205 R 2 22751 C3
14938 C3 17158T 3 20602T 3 22753 C3
14996 C7 17611 R 3

NORTHWESTERN CHINA AND FRONTIER REGIONS

PRIMARY 15302 C3

SECOND. 15544 C8 17772 RC7 22754 C2
14771 R 7 15545 C8 19889 RC8

SOUTH CHINA BROADLY CONCEIVED

PRIMARY 18412T 2 19006 R 4

SECOND. 13887 R 2 15205 C2 18614 R 2
12191T 2 14770 R 3 16092T 4

EAST CENTRAL CHINA

PRIMARY 15578 C3 18487T 2 22755 C3
15143 R 3 18453T 3 19069 C3

SECOND. 14966 C3 17606 C7 19023 R 3
14393 C2 15254 C3 17612 R 3 21433 C2
14665TR 3 15291 C3 17709 R 3 21528 R 3
14675TR 3 15953TR 3 17722 R 3 22164 R 3
14786TRC3

CENTRAL YANGTZE PROVINCES

PRIMARY 17328 C2 20275T 4 20494 C4
15229 C3 20220 R 3 20379T 4

SECOND. 14792TRC3 16150 C3 18411T 3
20129T 6

SOUTHWESTERN CHINA

PRIMARY 15270 C2 20447 R 3 20456 R 3
20475 RC4 21280T 5

SECOND. 10791 R 2 16971 R 2 18287 C2
19261 R 3

SOUTHEASTERN CHINA

PRIMARY 19371 C2 20385T 5 20524 C3
15263 C2 19968 R 8 20451 R 7 20525 C2
18271 C3 20261 R 1 20493 C3 21479 C2
19109 C8

SECOND. 16798 C2 19013 R 3 21480 C2
14711 R 3 17560TR 2 19113 C8 21573 C3
14761 R 7 17959 C2 19506 R 3 22606T 3
15984 C7 18490T 2

TAIWAN ONLY

PRIMARY 20424 C3 21561 C2 21600 C3
16151 C1 20517 C4 21567 C2 21944 C3
16357 C3 21478 C2 21588 C3 22023 C3
19935 C3 21481 C3 21599 C2

SECOND. 15918 C2 19937 C3 21566 C3
14981 C3 17794 C3 21488 C1 21925 C3
14994 C2 19466 RC7 21552 C3 22018 C4
15002 C2 19936 C3 21565 C3 22770 C3
15471 RC2

HONG KONG AND MACAU ONLY

PRIMARY 17595 C3 20194 R 3 20522 C3
16131 C3 17617 C3 20516 C4 20529 C3
16135 C3 19712 C3 20519 C3 21549 C3
16137 C3

SECOND. 14992 C3 17718 R 2 19947 C3
14825 C3 16010 C2 17745 C2 22724 RC2
14894 C2 16139 C3 18060 C2

55 LIVING ROUTINES

生活起居 日常生活

GEOGRAPHIC CHINA BROADLY CONCEIVED

PRIMARY 12941T 2 20590T 3 20653 R 2
10001T 2 13811T 2 20591T 3 20656TRC1
10016T 2 17142T 3 20592T 1 20659TRC4
10024T 2 17165T 2 20594T 3 20662TRC1
10025T 2 20540T 2 20595T 3 20710T 2
10032T 2 20543T 1 20615TR 2 20719T 1
10045T 2 20560T 1 20619TR 2 20766T 2
10058T 2 20563T 2 20620TR 2 20832 R 2
10060T 2 20576T 2 20635 R 2 20934 R 3
10144 C2 20588T 2 20643 R 2 22694 R 3
12624TR 2

SECOND. 10397TRC2 13274 R 2 20180TR 1
10013T 2 10550T 1 13824T 2 20231 RC2
10014T 2 10627T 2 13841T 4 20756T 2
10015T 1 10684TR 2 14156T 2 20769T 4
10026T 2 11035 RC2 14491 R 3 20994TRC5
10034T 2 11045 RC2 15363T 2 21262T 2
10042T 2 11270TR 4 15773 R 2 21366 R 2
10048T 2 12019 C2 16522T 2 21634T 2
10082TR 2 12281 R 2 16539T 7 21639T 1
10106 R 2 12348 R 2 16938TR 2 21750TR 1
10107 R 2 12367 R 2 17980TR 1 21760TR 1
10117TRC2 12461 C7 18764 R 2 22559T 2
10139 C2 12759 R 2 18976TR 2 22578T 2
10162 C2 12900T 1 19755T 1 22594T 2
10276T 2 12902T 3 20088T 3 22618T 2
10363 R 2 12957TR 2 20109TRC2

MAINLAND CHINA

PRIMARY: MONOGRAPHS

10002T 2 10094 R 2 12544 C2 16516T 7
10003T 2 10098 R 2 12783TRC2 17140T 2
10005T 2 10105 R 2 12985 R 2 18862T 2
10007T 2 10135 C2 13250 R 2 19751T 2
10035T 2 10169 C2 15509 C2 20244 C2
10036T 2 12291 R 7 15553 C2 20255T 1
10039T 2 12317 R 7 15575 C4 20258T 2

17669 RC8 19738 C7 20673 C2 20989 RC2
17922 T 2 20236 C8 20686 C2 22490 RC2

SECOND. 15655 C2 16550 TR 8 19896 TRC8
10345 TR 2 15697 TRC2 16826 C7 19955 C7
12149 C2 15848 C4 16883 C7 20072 C7
12150 C2 15852 C2 16902 C7 20249 C7
13102 C2 16167 T 2 17907 C7 21024 C3
14544 C5 16226 TR 2 18981 TR 2 21484 C2
15554 C2 16359 C2 19466 RC7 22023 C3
15562 C2

HONG KONG AND MACAU ONLY

PRIMARY 15821 C4 20622 TR 2 20678 C3
10301 RC2 15824 C4 20650 R 7 20680 C3
11031 R 2 15827 C4 20657 RC3 20681 C2
15325 T 3 15835 C3 20658 RC3 20682 C2
15463 TRC7 15859 C2 20663 RC3 20683 C3
15468 TRC3 16146 C2 20664 C3 20684 C3
15526 C3 17261 R 2 20665 C7 20688 C2
15529 C2 17362 C2 20667 C4 20694 C3
15555 C2 17963 C2 20670 C1 20695 C3
15563 C4 20279 T 1 20674 C3 20697 C3
15574 C8 20409 C2 20675 C4 20773 T 2
15621 C4 20552 T 3 20676 C3 21063 C2
15653 C4 20564 T 8 20677 C3 22500 C3
15798 RC4

SECOND. 15808 TRC2 16491 C3 19933 C3
14983 C3 15809 TRC8 16492 C2 19953 C3
15409 R 2 15842 C2 16498 C2 19990 C8
15518 C2 16342 TRC3 16501 C2 20070 TRC8
15536 C4 16348 C7 17350 C5 21059 C3
15571 C3 16456 TRC7 17512 C3 21254 C2
15648 C4 16471 C2 17906 C3 22736 TRC2
15796 TRC2 16472 C3 17917 C2

56 ILLNESS AND MEDICINE

疾病及醫療　疾病及び医療

GEOGRAPHIC CHINA BROADLY CONCEIVED

PRIMARY 20710 T 2 20787 T 1 20934 R 3
10106 R 2 20717 T 1 20790 TR 4 20954 TRC1
10107 R 2 20719 T 1 20792 TR 1 20955 RC2
10108 R 2 20737 T 1 20803 TR 2 20956 TRC1
14095 T 3 20740 T 1 20805 TR 1 20960 TRC2
14766 R 3 20756 T 2 20807 TR 1 20963 TRC1
16374 T 2 20759 T 1 20811 TR 1 20969 TRC1
16423 R 2 20766 T 2 20815 TR 4 20974 TRC1
16424 R 2 20769 T 4 20824 TR 1 20981 TRC2
20540 T 2 20774 T 1 20826 TR 2 20992 TRC1
20591 T 3 20777 T 1 20827 TR 3 20994 TRC5
20635 R 2 20779 T 4 20832 R 2 21544 RC2
20662 TRC1 20785 T 4 20861 R 4 21689 T 2
20703 T 1 20786 T 2

SECOND. 11603 TRC1 18947 T 2 20656 TRC1
10016 T 2 12281 R 2 18969 TR 2 21262 T 2
10024 T 2 12310 R 8 18971 TR 2 21342 TR 2
10025 T 2 12941 T 2 19039 TRC2 21579 C2
10042 T 2 12957 TR 2 19650 RC2 21634 T 2
10045 T 2 14156 T 2 19996 T 2 21750 TR 1
10139 C2 14720 R 2 20088 T 3 21760 TR 1
10276 T 2 16274 TR 1 20143 T 1 22512 T 1
10560 T 2 16337 TRC1 20172 TR 1 22555 T 2
11164 C2 16375 T 2 20222 R 3 22740 TRC2
11199 T 1 18494 T 2

MAINLAND CHINA

PRIMARY: MONOGRAPHS
10105 R 2 18987 TR 2 20823 TR 4 20996 C2
10173 C2 20582 T 2 20837 R 2 21003 C7
10191 TR 2 20721 T 2 20926 R 2 21036 C2
11087 C3 20743 T 1 20940 R 2 21086 C1
11724 R 2 20749 T 2 20953 TRC1 21098 C1
14721 R 2 20763 T 1 20962 RC2 21100 C1
14730 R 5 20782 T 1 20966 RC2 21103 C2
15506 C2 20798 TR 2 20973 TRC1 21124 C3
15550 C2 20801 TR 1 20983 RC1 21644 T 2
18952 TR 2 20806 TR 1 20991 TRC2

PRIMARY: INCLUSIONS
18992 R 2 20957 TRC2 21050 C3 21119 C4
19421 C4 20975 TRC1 21053 C2 21146 C1
19945 C2 20984 TRC1 21066 C2 21148 C3
20371 C2 20988 RC2 21067 C8 21150 C2
20652 R 2 20999 C1 21070 C2 21153 C2
20814 TR 1 21023 C2 21073 C2 21529 TRC3
20834 R 2 21025 C2 21105 C2 22379 C2
20896 R 2

PRIMARY: JOURNAL ARTICLES
10249 C2 20752 T 1 20943 R 2 21076 C2
11097 C2 20761 T 1 20959 RC1 21077 C2
14111 TR 2 20765 T 2 20961 RC2 21078 C5
14708 R 3 20767 T 1 20965 TRC3 21079 C7
14768 R 3 20788 T 1 20970 TRC1 21080 C2
14870 C2 20794 TR 1 20971 TRC1 21081 C1
14907 C2 20796 TR 1 20972 TRC1 21082 C2
14936 C1 20797 TR 1 20990 TRC1 21085 C2
14948 C1 20799 TR 3 20993 RC8 21090 C4
14968 C2 20810 TR 1 21006 C3 21091 C8
15292 C2 20816 TR 1 21007 C2 21092 C2
16184 T 1 20817 TR 1 21010 C2 21094 C1
16223 T 1 20819 TR 1 21011 C4 21097 C2
16294 R 1 20831 R 1 21012 C2 21102 C3
16308 R 2 20833 R 4 21013 C2 21104 C1
18893 T 2 20841 R 1 21014 C2 21106 C2
20403 RC2 20849 R 2 21015 C2 21107 C2
20405 C1 20852 R 2 21021 C1 21110 C1
20553 T 5 20860 R 3 21027 C1 21111 C2
20593 T 1 20865 R 2 21028 C2 21113 C3
20720 T 1 20866 R 4 21034 C2 21123 C2
20723 T 4 20867 R 1 21035 C2 21137 C1
20725 T 2 20877 R 2 21040 C1 21142 C2
20732 T 1 20902 R 3 21043 C2 21143 C2
20733 T 1 20903 R 3 21044 C2 21158 C7
20736 T 1 20904 R 3 21045 C2 21499 TR 1
20738 T 1 20914 R 2 21047 C1 21671 T 1
20741 T 1 20929 R 1 21052 C2 22841 C1
20745 T 2 20932 R 3 21057 C2 22874 T 1
20750 T 1 20939 R 3 21058 C1 22882 T 1
20751 T 1 20942 R 3 21075 C2

SECONDARY: MONOGRAPHS
10002 T 2 10130 C2 15508 C2 18854 T 1
10003 T 2 10133 C2 15509 C2 19517 R 3
10005 T 2 10140 C2 15575 C4 20107 R 2
10019 T 2 10149 C2 15856 C2 20258 T 2
10023 T 2 10732 TR 2 15993 C7 20455 R 2
10029 T 2 12082 C2 16189 T 2 20623 TR 2
10036 T 2 12123 C2 16277 TR 2 20639 R 2
10044 T 2 13901 R 2 17160 T 2 20648 R 2
10047 T 2 13945 R 2 17238 R 2 21790 TR 1
10059 T 2 14520 C3 17313 RC2 22291 C2
10061 T 2 14885 C1 17848 R 2 22556 T 2
10071 TR 2 15090 RC2 17849 R 2 22599 T 2
10104 R 2 15249 C2 17895 RC2 22619 T 2
10110 TRC2 15466 RC2 18596 R 2 22644 TR 2
10126 RC2 15482 C2 18759 R 2 22831 C2

SECONDARY: INCLUSIONS
10147 C2 12206 T 2 16035 C4 20000 T 1
10218 RC2 12447 C2 19425 C1 21646 T 1
10353 TR 2 15215 C2 19626 R 2 22525 T 2

SECONDARY: JOURNAL ARTICLES
10166 C2 14930 C2 19760 T 1 21500 TR 1
10717 TR 2 14956 C2 19950 C1 21560 C1
11181 T 2 15089 RC2 19992 T 1 21752 TR 1
11372 R 1 16036 C7 20250 C3 21884 TRC1
11761 R 2 16245 TR 1 20318 C2 21917 C2
11932 C2 18964 TR 2 20362 C2 22417 T 1
12112 C2 19417 C2 20666 C3 22435 TR 1
12129 C2 19629 R 2 20687 C1 22818 RC1
14778 RC2

THE EIGHTEEN PROVINCES

PRIMARY 16204 T 1 20729 T 2 20818 TR 2
10018 T 2 16252 TR 2 20730 T 1 20822 TR 4
10141 C2 16279 TR 1 20739 T 1 20825 TR 3
14121 R 2 17869 R 2 20742 T 2 20864 R 3
14725 R 1 17916 C2 20760 T 2 20895 R 3
14746 R 3 20090 T 3 20772 T 1 20899 R 8
15067 R 2 20284 T 1 20776 T 2 20900 R 3
15501 C2 20287 T 1 20789 TR 1 20907 R 4
15723 T 3 20726 T 2 20793 TR 5 20908 R 3
16171 T 1 20728 T 4 20800 TR 3 20941 R 1

20976 TRC1 20986 TRC1 21121 C2 21129 C8
20978 RC2 21048 C2 21122 C2 21525 R 1
20979 TRC1 21096 C4 21125 C2 21721 TR 4
20980 TRC1 21120 C2 21126 C2 22431 TR 1

SECOND. 15478 C2 19632 R 7 20625 R 1
10038 T 2 17614 R 2 19688 T 2 20668 C2
14462 R 3 17842 R 2 19797 TR 2 20699 C2
15111 C2 17945 R 2 20329 C2 21791 TR 1
15306 T 2 19053 TRC2 20411 C2 22534 T 1
15327 T 3

NORTH CHINA BROADLY CONCEIVED

PRIMARY 20716 T 2 20835 R 2 20977 TRC2
17873 R 2 20748 T 2 20964 RC2 21109 C4
20714 T 2 20780 T 2

SECOND. 15041 T 2 15752 T 2 18914 T 2
10064 T 2 15428 R 7 18664 R 2

MANCHURIA

PRIMARY 20731 T 3 20871 R 2 21055 C7
14988 C2 20795 TR 2 20967 RC2 21056 C2
17689 T 7 20813 TR 2 21004 C6 21118 C4
19669 C7 20836 R 7 21054 C8 21151 C8
20715 T 3

SECOND. 11777 R 2 16915 T 2 20276 R 4
10356 R 2 11834 R 2 17566 R 8 20575 T 4
10582 T 2 15614 RC2 17852 R 3 21246 C3

NORTHERN CHINA

PRIMARY 20775 T 7 20930 R 3 21087 C7
10612 T 3 20781 T 2 20931 R 3 21099 C4
14717 R 4 20842 R 7 20937 R 2 21127 C2
14985 C3 20843 R 7 20938 R 3 21134 C3
15039 T 1 20844 R 2 20946 R 7 21139 C7
15077 R 2 20845 R 7 20947 R 3 21140 C3
15355 T 2 20846 R 2 20949 R 7 21157 C3
15596 R 7 20847 R 7 20952 R 3 21178 T 2
17819 T 3 20868 R 3 20982 RC3 21224 R 3
19624 R 7 20880 R 2 21018 C3 21298 T 2
20353 C3 20888 R 2 21019 C7 21344 TR 2
20709 T 2 20889 R 3 21031 C8 21507 R 3
20718 T 4 20909 R 2 21042 C7 21508 R 3
20727 T 4 20913 R 3 21060 C7 21510 R 3
20754 T 3 20921 R 3 21064 C7 21511 R 3
20758 T 3 20922 R 3 21065 C7 21512 R 3
20762 T 3 20923 R 3 21069 C3 21515 R 3
20764 T 3 20928 R 3 21083 C2 21526 R 3

SECOND. 15817 C3 17331 C3 19619 R 7
13891 R 2 16256 TR 3 17497 C3 20631 R 3
15362 T 7 16311 R 8 17636 C3 21223 R 3
15384 TR 4 16314 R 8 17721 R 7 21375 R 3
15407 R 3 16557 TR 8 17727 R 3 21513 R 3
15414 R 8 16759 C7 17843 R 3 21664 T 3
15516 C7 17049 R 3 17871 R 7 22617 T 2
15713 T 2 17148 T 2 17878 R 8 22747 C2
15730 T 3

NORTHWESTERN CHINA AND FRONTIER REGIONS

PRIMARY 20856 R 1 20859 R 8 20958 RC1
18956 TR 2 20857 R 1 20927 R 7 20968 RC7
20298 R 7 20858 R 8

SECOND. 15603 RC2 20299 R 8 22453 R 8
12003 C2 16972 R 2 20304 RC2 22462 R 7
15545 C8 18993 R 2 20380 T 7

SOUTH CHINA BROADLY CONCEIVED

PRIMARY 20208 R 2 20821 TR 2 20944 R 1
10031 T 2 20724 T 2 20848 R 2 21029 C2
12569 T 2 20734 T 2 20855 R 2 21117 C2
16339 TRC2 20747 T 4 20901 R 2 21147 C8

SECOND. 15078 R 2 16378 T 2 18875 T 2
10046 T 2 15722 T 2 16979 R 2 21537 RC2
12383 RC2 15726 T 2 18524 T 2

EAST CENTRAL CHINA

PRIMARY 17332 C2 20850 R 3 20876 R 2
15404 R 3 17722 R 3 20851 R 3 20879 R 3
15728 T 3 20830 R 3 20862 R 3 20882 R 2
17330 C2 20838 R 3 20875 R 3 20883 R 3

20884 R 3 20919 R 3 21000 C7 21133 C3
20885 R 3 20924 R 3 21022 C7 21136 C3
20886 R 3 20925 R 7 21026 C3 21152 C2
20898 R 3 20935 R 3 21037 C3 21154 C3
20915 R 3 20936 R 3 21115 C8 21252 C3
20918 R 3 20951 R 3 21116 C7

Second. 16290 R 8 17818 T 8 21210 R 7
15313 T 2 16297 R 3 18983 TR 3 21216 R 7
15374 TR 8 17558 T 2 20087 T 3 21621 T 1
15431 R 3 17667 R 7 20581 T 3 22384 T 2
15946 TR 3 17707 R 3 20644 R 3 22755 C3
16178 T 8

Central Yangtze Provinces

Primary 20802 TR 3 20878 R 2 21041 C3
14682 TR 1 20820 TR 2 20920 R 3 21072 C7
14792 TRC3 20829 R 7 21002 C7 21144 C6
17561 TR 2 20854 R 3

Second. 15498 C2 16754 C7 19726 TR 7
14817 C2 16090 T 2 19694 T 3 22445 R 1
15469 TRC2

Southwestern China

Primary 20735 T 3 20872 R 6 20916 R 3
10359 R 2 20771 T 7 20873 R 7 20933 R 2
17815 T 5 20804 TR 3 20874 R 3 20948 R 3
18925 T 2 20808 TR 2 20881 R 2 20950 R 3
20584 T 4 20809 TR 2 20887 R 7 21114 C7
20704 T 3 20839 R 3 20890 R 4 21128 C2
20707 T 2 20840 R 8 20910 R 7 22508 T 2
20711 T 3 20863 R 2

Second. 15436 R 6 16683 R 2 19827 R 6
10767 R 2 16260 TR 2 19022 R 2 20645 R 7
11753 R 2 16267 TR 2 19742 T 2 22542 T 2
15365 T 2 16404 TR 2

Southeastern China

Primary 20768 T 1 20893 R 3 20998 C2
16798 C2 20770 T 3 20894 R 2 21001 C8
19692 T 3 20778 T 3 20897 R 3 21033 C3
20705 T 4 20783 T 4 20905 R 8 21095 C3
20706 T 4 20784 T 5 20906 R 4 21130 C2
20712 T 3 20791 TR 3 20911 R 3 21141 C7
20722 T 4 20828 R 3 20912 R 1 21145 C2
20744 T 3 20853 R 8 20917 R 4 21149 C2
20746 T 3 20891 R 5 20945 R 2 21413 RC3
20755 T 2 20892 R 3 20997 C2 21490 T 3
20757 T 3

Second. 15458 TRC2 16218 T 2 19043 TRC2
11675 T 2 15485 C2 16959 R 3 19045 TRC2
11683 TR 2 15718 T 2 17329 C2 20567 T 3
12883 T 2 16017 C2 17738 C3 21781 TR 1
12954 TR 3 16190 T 2 18876 T 2 22398 T 4
15376 TR 2 16193 T 3 18899 T 2 22415 T 2
15419 R 6

Taiwan Only

Primary 20995 RC2 21051 C3 21156 C1
12149 C2 21008 C2 21068 C2 21231 TRC2
14799 RC3 21009 C2 21071 C1 21520 R 2
14896 C3 21016 C1 21074 C3 21524 R 1
15437 R 2 21017 C7 21084 C2 21534 RC2
17169 T 2 21020 C2 21089 C8 21545 RC1
20364 C3 21024 C3 21108 C7 21561 C2
20378 C3 21030 C7 21131 C2 21572 C1
20686 C2 21032 C1 21132 C1 21583 C8
20702 T 3 21039 C1 21135 C2 21584 C3
20753 T 1 21049 C3 21155 C2 21600 C3
20989 RC2

Second. 15568 C3 16852 C8 19925 C8
10985 C3 15586 TR 2 16856 C7 20018 C8
11044 RC2 15600 TRC2 16858 C2 20339 C2
11678 T 2 15655 C2 17903 C1 21571 C3
13102 C2 15698 TRC2 18908 T 2 21580 C3
14544 C5 15852 C2 18981 TR 2 21582 C3
15472 RC2 15888 C2 19663 C7 21590 C3
15504 C8 16009 C7 19711 C2 21599 C2
15533 C7 16368 C8

Hong Kong and Macau Only

Primary 20869 R 2 21061 C2 21112 C3
16146 C2 20870 R 2 21062 C3 21138 C3
16326 TRC2 21005 C7 21063 C2 21197 RC2
20122 C3 21038 C3 21088 C3 21202 C3
20670 C1 21046 C8 21093 C2 21550 C3
20713 T 2 21059 C3 21101 C3 21578 C3
20773 T 2

Second. 15518 C2 16010 C2 19693 T 3
14805 TRC3 15520 C2 16030 C2 19696 T 3
15325 T 3 15526 C3 16117 R 2 20279 T 1
15330 T 7 15618 C2 16141 C2 20622 TR 2
15381 TR 2 15940 TR 3 16816 C2 20674 C3
15409 R 2 15945 TR 2 17718 R 2 20680 C3
15454 TRC3 15973 TRC2 17745 C2 22500 C3
15461 TRC2 15981 RC3 17963 C2 22736 TRC2

57 Death Practices

死亡及喪葬 死亡及び葬祭

Geographic China Broadly Conceived

Primary 19752 T 1 20017 TRC1 21173 T 2
10024 T 2 19772 T 1 21171 T 3 21850 TRC2
14095 T 3 19998 T 1

Second. 12902 T 3 19913 C2 20653 R 2
10001 T 2 15645 TRC3 19993 T 1 20766 T 2
10016 T 2 16186 T 2 19996 T 2 20769 T 4
10017 T 2 16192 T 1 20010 TR 2 20811 TR 1
10032 T 2 16248 TR 1 20016 TRC1 21689 T 2
10060 T 2 16522 T 2 20025 TR 1 21740 TR 1
10082 TR 2 18301 T 4 20053 TR 1 21750 TR 1
10397 TRC2 18570 TR 1 20540 T 2 22001 TR 1
10684 TR 2 18936 T 2 20563 T 2 22594 T 2
11150 C4 18976 TR 2 20591 T 3 22694 R 3
12589 T 2 19763 T 1

Mainland China

Primary 20000 T 1 21163 T 7 21185 TR 1
10059 T 2 20008 TR 1 21164 T 2 21189 TR 2
18075 T 2 20011 TR 2 21165 T 1 21190 R 2
18915 T 2 20182 TR 2 21170 T 1 21195 R 2
18959 TR 2 20571 T 1 21172 T 2 21652 T 2
19721 T 2 20623 TR 2 21182 T 1 21744 TR 1
19809 R 1 21160 T 1 21183 T 2 22556 T 2
19992 T 1

Secondary: Monographs
10003 T 2 10559 T 4 18927 T 1 20618 TR 2
10007 T 2 11194 T 2 18989 TR 2 20639 R 2
10019 T 2 11195 T 1 19732 RC2 20721 T 2
10020 T 2 11203 T 2 19803 TR 2 20749 T 2
10029 T 2 11356 R 1 19816 R 2 20782 T 1
10036 T 2 14599 T 2 19892 RC1 21355 TR 2
10041 T 2 16103 TR 2 20013 TR 1 21361 TR 1
10044 T 2 16189 T 2 20137 T 2 21624 T 2
10047 T 2 16277 TR 2 20175 TR 1 21644 T 2
10049 T 2 16332 TRC1 20226 TRC2 21798 TR 1
10061 T 2 16343 TRC2 20255 T 1 21980 T 4
10062 T 2 17977 T 2 20258 T 2 22609 T 3
10098 R 2 18853 T 2 20546 T 2 22619 T 2
10110 TRC2 18862 T 2

Secondary: Inclusions
11550 T 2 16263 TR 2 18885 T 2 19873 RC2
11574 T 1 16269 TR 1 18944 T 1

Secondary: Journal Articles
10604 T 1 18673 R 7 19798 TR 1 20593 T 1
11363 R 1 18941 T 2 19799 TR 1 20616 TR 2
11762 R 2 19014 R 2 20130 T 2 20965 TRC3
12566 T 2 19722 T 1 20148 T 2 22400 T 2
16184 T 1 19777 T 1 20545 T 2 22435 TR 1
16245 TR 1 19784 TR 1

The Eighteen Provinces

Primary 16271 TR 2 21159 T 1 21186 TR 2
11536 T 3 19765 T 2 21162 T 2 21193 R 3
14590 T 2 19991 T 1 21166 T 2 21199 C7
16252 TR 2 20002 T 1

Second. 10027 T 2 11655 T 1 15038 T 2
10018 T 2 10050 T 2 13866 T 2 16161 T 2
16171 T 1 19245 R 2 20022 T 1 21623 T 2
16195 T 1 19688 T 2 20144 T 1 21648 T 1
16276 TR 1 19695 T 2 20544 T 2 21773 TR 1
17614 R 2 19754 T 1 20548 T 2 21791 TR 1
17945 R 2 19997 T 1 20668 C2 22390 T 2
18881 T 2 20004 TR 1 21301 T 1

North China Broadly Conceived

Primary 15428 R 7

Second. 10580 T 2 15752 T 2 20541 T 2
20549 T 2 22394 T 2

Manchuria

Primary 15743 T 3 16315 R 3

Second. 12211 TR 8 20276 R 4 20813 TR 2
10582 T 2 17525 T 2 20575 T 4 22412 T 2

Northern China

Primary 19708 R 8 21169 T 3 21181 T 2
11568 T 3 19739 T 1 21174 T 3 21187 TR 2
15347 T 3 19776 T 2 21176 T 1 21188 TR 3
15378 TR 7 20762 T 3 21177 T 7 21191 R 2
16250 TR 3 21161 T 2 21178 T 2 22397 T 3

Second. 15403 R 8 16323 R 8 20273 R 3
10652 T 3 15408 R 2 16390 T 2 20557 T 3
11542 T 8 15410 R 8 17497 C3 20579 T 3
14163 T 3 15414 R 8 17625 T 3 20631 R 3
14214 TR 3 15626 T 2 17844 R 3 20754 T 3
15039 T 1 15713 T 2 17856 R 3 20781 T 2
15320 T 3 15754 T 2 17871 R 7 20923 R 3
15341 T 2 15786 R 3 18856 T 3 21344 TR 2
15355 T 2 16121 R 3 18868 T 2 21375 R 3
15360 T 7 16228 TR 8 19723 T 4 21664 T 3
15367 T 2 16296 R 2 20128 T 3 21729 TR 7
15372 TR 3 16311 R 8 20205 R 2 22456 R 1

Northwestern China and Frontier Regions

Primary 19818 R 7 20304 RC2 21196 RC2

Second. 15753 T 2 20298 R 7 20621 TR 1
15544 C8 16628 R 2 20299 R 8 20858 R 8

South China Broadly Conceived

Primary 12569 T 2 21175 T 2

Second. 15722 T 2 16378 T 2 20274 T 3
10031 T 2 15726 T 2 16979 R 2 20821 TR 2
10046 T 2 15749 T 3 20208 R 2 21384 R 2
12684 TR 2

East Central China

Primary 16197 T 3 20003 T 5 22384 T 2
15348 T 3 19748 T 2 21180 T 1

Second. 15431 R 3 16290 R 8 19690 T 3
15374 TR 8 16060 R 3 16297 R 3 21621 T 1
15426 R 7 16266 TR 1 18918 T 3

Central Yangtze Provinces

Primary 20220 R 3

Second. 20138 T 2 20275 T 4 22445 R 1

Southwestern China

Primary 15308 T 5 16267 TR 2 19729 R 6
21192 R 1 21194 R 4

Second. 15629 T 2 17535 T 4 20873 R 7
15379 TR 3 16260 TR 2 18365 T 3 21315 TR 2
15424 R 7 16300 R 2 18933 T 4 21990 T 1
15425 R 3 16301 R 1

Southeastern China

Primary 16190 T 2 21167 T 3 21179 T 2
16164 T 3 19962 TR 7 21168 T 3 21184 TR 5
16181 T 2

Second. 15317 T 2 15385 TR 2 16218 T 2
11675 T 2 15319 T 3 15734 T 2 16552 TR 2
11683 TR 2 15353 T 2 16187 T 3 16942 TR 2
14758 R 2 15364 T 3 16188 T 1 18906 T 3

21290 T 1 21387 TRC2 21403 RC1 22058 T 1
21322 TR 1 21390 RC2 21429 C1 22077 TR 2
21341 TR 2 21396 RC1 21430 C2 22274 RC1
21351 TR 1 21397 RC2 21448 TR 1 22276 RC2
21378 R 2 21398 TRC1 21609 T 1

Secondary: Monographs
10068 TR 2 12524 C2 18098 T 3 21569 C1
10124 TRC2 14002 RC2 18103 TR 1 21766 TR 1
10128 TRC2 14020 RC2 18454 T 2 22071 T 1
10672 T 2 14241 R 2 18796 RC2 22099 TR 2
10688 TR 2 14293 RC3 19405 TRC3 22273 RC2
10712 TR 2 14296 C2 19644 R 2 22602 T 1
10780 R 1 14396 T 2 20134 T 2 22648 TR 2
10883 TRC2 15466 RC2 20159 TR 2 22710 R 2
11052 RC2 16123 R 2 20224 RC2 22954 TRC1
11106 C2

Secondary: Inclusions
10694 TR 2 14190 T 1 14336 C1 18773 R 2
11244 T 2 14232 TR 1 14790 RC2 18858 T 1
12156 C2 14276 RC1 18370 T 2 19404 RC3
13977 R 2

Secondary: Journal Articles
10661 T 2 14339 C1 19396 R 2 22120 TR 1
10766 R 2 14341 C1 20511 C2 22155 R 1
10927 C1 14346 C1 21541 RC1 22157 R 1
11091 C1 14353 C1 21620 T 1 22165 R 1
11238 T 3 14381 C1 21680 T 1 22168 R 2
12214 TR 2 14392 C3 21785 TR 1 22174 R 1
14073 C1 18086 T 1 21809 R 1 22200 RC2
14245 R 4 18205 C1 22069 T 2 22621 T 1
14271 RC2 18207 C1 22093 TR 1 22668 TR 1
14291 RC1 18791 TRC7 22104 TR 1

The Eighteen Provinces

Primary 20171 TR 2 21309 TR 2 21389 RC2
13151 TR 2 20223 RC2 21310 TR 1 21391 TRC1
14180 T 2 20478 C2 21319 TR 2 21648 T 1
14226 TR 1 20503 C2 21323 TR 1 21679 T 4
14238 R 3 21261 T 2 21334 TR 2 21685 T 2
14273 RC3 21266 T 2 21340 TR 3 21765 TR 1
14388 C3 21267 T 2 21343 TR 2 22009 R 2
14555 T 1 21272 T 2 21356 TR 2 22090 TR 3
14660 TR 2 21277 T 2 21362 TR 3 22107 TR 1
18012 T 2 21282 T 3 21365 R 3 22110 TR 1
18074 T 2 21295 T 1 21370 R 2 22137 TR 2
18366 T 2 21297 T 2 21380 R 2 22558 T 2
18834 RC2 21301 T 1 21386 RC3 22776 T 2
20139 T 1 21305 TR 4

Second. 18413 T 2 18736 R 2 22029 T 3
13956 R 4 18461 T 2 19630 R 2 22072 T 1
14218 TR 4 18472 T 4 19631 R 2 22086 TR 1
14300 C3 18523 T 2 20022 T 1 22094 TR 2
15127 T 1 18638 R 2 20147 T 1 22181 R 3
16478 C2 18639 R 3 21786 TR 1 22708 R 3
17143 T 3 18679 R 2

North China Broadly Conceived

Primary 21287 T 2 21292 T 2 21348 TR 3
22141 R 3

Second. 10989 C5 14210 T 2 18509 T 2
18622 R 2 18731 R 2

Manchuria

□

Northern China

Primary 19825 R 3 21278 T 3 21359 TR 3
10781 R 2 20116 C3 21293 T 3 21371 R 3
14182 T 3 20140 T 3 21298 T 2 21375 R 3
14204 T 3 21264 T 3 21330 TR 7 21431 C2
15449 R 7 21273 T 2 21344 TR 2 21631 T 8

Second. 17526 T 8 18990 TR 3 19642 R 7
11080 C3 17953 TRC3 19620 R 2 20527 C3
14157 T 3 18092 T 3

Northwestern China and Frontier Regions

Primary 10759 R 2 21364 R 2
Second. 15453 RC8 22531 T 2

South China Broadly Conceived

Primary 18447 T 2 21294 T 1 21382 R 2
14262 RC2 18500 T 2 21299 T 2 21384 R 2
17543 T 2 18507 T 3 21339 TR 2 21426 TRC3
18421 T 2 21275 T 1 21376 R 2

Second. 13968 R 2 18572 TR 2 21537 RC2
10636 T 1 18129 R 3 19054 RC2 22535 T 3
13881 TR 2 18412 T 2

East Central China

Primary 21329 TR 1 21433 C2 22164 R 3
21258 T 3 21331 TR 1 21670 T 3

Second. 15985 C7 19220 TR 4 22589 T 2
14161 T 2 18600 R 3 20112 RC3

Central Yangtze Provinces

Primary 17580 RC2 20210 R 2 21352 TR 2
Second. 17643 C3

Southwestern China

Primary 21280 T 5 21314 TR 4 21316 TR 2
10651 T 2 21312 TR 4 21315 TR 2 21369 R 2
17613 R 7 21313 TR 2

Second. 10791 R 2 18381 T 2

Southeastern China

Primary 21268 T 3 21274 T 1 21393 RC2
10511 T 2 21270 T 2 21281 T 1 21413 RC3
18428 T 3 21271 T 2 21385 R 2 21428 RC2

Second. 10708 TR 2 15984 C7 17523 T 3
18876 T 2 19371 C2

Taiwan Only

Primary 21421 RC3

Second. 15612 RC2 20249 C7 21545 RC1
10653 T 2 16368 C8 21534 RC2 21582 C3

Hong Kong and Macau Only

Primary 15940 TR 3 21257 T 3
Second. 15926 T 7 18836 C3 19985 TRC7

60 Idea Systems and Values in General
觀念及價値體系通論
観念及び価値体系一般

Geographic China Broadly Conceived

Primary 14266 TRC1 20563 T 2 21754 TR 1
10010 T 2 14284 TRC1 20590 T 3 21835 TRC1
10022 T 2 14672 TR 1 21318 TR 1 21844 TRC2
10025 T 2 14699 TR 1 21337 TR 2 21855 TRC2
10042 T 2 15174 TRC2 21404 TRC1 22013 TRC1
10075 TR 2 16104 TR 7 21467 TRC1 22082 TR 1
10082 TR 2 17142 T 3 21469 TRC2 22178 R 1
10117 TRC2 18570 TR 1 21472 TRC1 22189 RC1
10118 RC2 18786 TRC2 21477 TRC2 22206 TRC1
10550 T 1 18871 T 2 21538 TRC2 22225 TRC2
10684 TR 2 18936 T 2 21579 C2 22284 TRC1
10713 TR 2 18943 T 1 21688 T 1 22474 TRC1
11261 TR 1 19016 R 2 21698 T 1 22580 T 2
11317 R 1 20225 TRC1 21718 TR 1 22690 R 3
11403 TRC1 20418 T 1

Second. 10864 RC1 14155 T 2 20088 T 3
10001 T 2 11038 RC2 14627 T 1 20164 TR 1
10017 T 2 11045 RC2 16185 T 2 21350 TR 3
10024 T 2 11682 T 1 18024 TR 1 21660 T 1
10026 T 2 12233 TR 2 18544 TR 1 22024 T 1
10060 T 2 12941 T 2 18805 TRC1 22095 TR 2
10129 TRC2 13017 R 3 18852 T 2 22136 TR 1
10646 T 4 13812 T 2 19752 T 1

Mainland China

Primary: Monographs
10002 T 2 10559 T 4 17979 TR 7 21504 TR 2
10003 T 2 10778 R 2 18551 TR 2 21563 C1
10005 T 2 10782 R 1 18557 TR 2 21617 T 1
10007 T 2 11105 C2 18588 R 2 21624 T 2
10020 T 2 11356 R 1 19405 TRC3 21677 T 2
10030 T 2 11368 R 2 19625 R 1 21711 T 1
10036 T 2 11563 T 4 19919 C1 21741 TR 1
10041 T 2 13986 TRC2 20159 TR 2 21749 TR 1
10049 T 2 14223 TR 2 20166 TR 2 21766 TR 1
10059 T 2 14247 R 1 20226 TRC2 21771 TR 1
10062 T 2 14263 RC1 20432 TR 2 21887 TRC2
10079 TR 2 14274 TRC2 21361 TR 1 22006 R 1
10083 TR 2 14370 C2 21437 T 1 22068 T 1
10086 TR 2 14513 TRC2 21444 TR 1 22118 TR 1
10094 R 2 14661 TR 1 21447 TR 2 22128 TR 1
10099 R 2 14692 TR 1 21450 TR 2 22202 TRC1
10105 R 2 14719 R 4 21457 R 1 22207 TRC1
10110 TRC2 15168 TRC2 21459 R 4 22249 TRC1
10120 TRC2 15171 TRC2 21461 R 1 22423 TR 7
10135 C2 15273 C2 21465 R 2 22556 T 2
10149 C2 16031 C7 21466 TRC1 22572 T 2
10154 C2 16054 R 7 21471 TRC1 22605 T 2
10349 TR 2 16210 T 2 21476 TRC2 22679 R 2

Primary: Inclusions
10051 T 2 19626 R 2 21460 R 3 22000 TR 1
11072 C2 20000 T 1 21468 TRC1 22048 T 1
11613 RC1 20661 TRC1 21486 C2 22129 TR 1
14208 T 2 21357 TR 1 21529 TRC3 22148 R 2
15170 RC2 21436 T 1 21880 TRC1 22205 TRC1
19003 R 2 21458 R 1 21881 TRC1

Primary: Journal Articles
10166 C2 14361 C1 21439 T 2 21832 TRC1
11060 C2 14408 R 3 21441 T 1 21919 C2
11103 C1 14777 TRC1 21445 TR 1 21967 C1
11239 T 1 14872 C2 21448 TR 1 22007 R 1
11267 TR 1 14886 C4 21451 TR 1 22010 R 1
11409 TRC1 15133 TR 2 21452 TR 1 22011 R 1
11558 T 4 15144 R 2 21462 R 1 22012 RC1
11572 T 2 15226 C2 21464 R 1 22042 T 1
11592 TR 1 18084 T 1 21474 TRC2 22103 TR 1
11641 C1 18504 T 2 21485 C1 22123 TR 1
11662 T 2 19393 TR 1 21492 TR 1 22140 TR 1
12131 C2 19402 R 4 21536 TRC1 22245 TRC1
12710 R 3 20270 C1 21591 C2 22288 RC1
13821 T 1 20521 C2 21736 TR 1 22354 C1
13853 T 4 20720 T 1 21775 TR 1 22528 T 1
14245 R 4 20959 RC1 21779 TR 1 22726 TRC3

Second. 11144 C2 15333 T 3 20984 TRC1
10044 T 2 11145 C4 17597 C2 21103 C2
10047 T 2 11291 TR 2 17803 C2 21308 TR 2
10063 T 2 11332 R 1 17804 C1 21325 TR 2
10088 R 2 11598 R 1 17974 T 3 21585 C2
10098 R 2 13969 R 2 18098 T 3 21798 TR 1
10112 TRC2 14122 R 3 18158 R 2 21821 R 2
10124 TRC2 14148 C2 18378 T 2 21900 TRC2
10125 RC2 14189 T 4 18752 R 2 21951 C1
10126 RC2 14289 RC4 18793 RC1 21980 T 4
10150 C2 14293 RC3 19248 R 4 22130 TR 2
10160 C2 14310 C5 19639 R 1 22156 R 1
10698 TR 2 14412 RC1 19899 TRC2 22644 TR 2
10765 R 1 14652 TR 2 19992 T 1 22675 TR 1
10833 R 2 14871 C2 20124 T 4 22689 R 1
11006 C2 14898 C1 20438 R 1 22743 RC1
11076 C2 14986 C1 20618 TR 2 22954 TRC1
11096 C2 15090 RC2

The Eighteen Provinces

Primary 16183 T 2 21455 R 5 21791 TR 1
10006 T 2 18366 T 2 21456 R 2 22004 R 1
10027 T 2 18538 TR 1 21463 R 1 22009 R 2
10050 T 2 19245 R 2 21473 TRC2 22057 T 2
12869 C3 20144 T 1 21482 C4 22064 T 1
14238 R 3 21277 T 2 21489 C2 22110 TR 1
14277 TRC3 21340 TR 3 21673 T 1 22170 R 1
15145 R 4 21440 T 1 21761 TR 1 22558 T 2
15149 R 1 21453 TR 1 21786 TR 1 22603 T 1
15327 T 3

Second. 12193 T 8 15131 T 1 17631 TR 8
10087 R 2 14092 T 2 15931 T 4 17756 TR 7

18882 T 1 19027 R 2 20544 T 2 22590 T 3
18917 T 2 19053 TRC2 21796 TR 1 22691 R 3
18930 T 2 20287 T 1 22107 TR 1

North China Broadly Conceived

Primary 10064 T 2 18433 T 2 18872 T 2
Second. □

Manchuria

Primary □
Second. 15674 TR 2 17689 T 7 20596 T 2
22719 R 3

Northern China

Primary 16850 C7 20128 T 3 21438 T 3
12741 R 3 18420 T 4 20436 R 3 22763 C3
15304 C3 19394 R 3 21278 T 3
Second. 13964 R 7 20206 R 3 21178 T 2
10317 T 2 15347 T 3 20417 RC2 22457 R 3
11542 T 8

Northwestern China and Frontier Regions

Primary 15350 T 2 22005 R 1
Second. 20621 TR 1

South China Broadly Conceived

Primary 10028 T 2 10046 T 2 18459 T 2
Second. 11658 T 2 15749 T 3 18376 T 2
22535 T 3

East Central China

Primary 14606 T 3 17612 R 3 18932 T 4
18983 TR 3
Second. 14646 TR 3 14739 R 3

Central Yangtze Provinces

Primary □
Second. 20379 T 4

Southwestern China

Primary 15308 T 5 15316 T 2
Second. 20475 RC4 20583 T 2 20872 R 6

Southeastern China

Primary 15321 T 2 17959 C2 21479 C2
15319 T 3 16163 T 3 18048 C3 21480 C2
Second. 15576 C5 20252 T 4 20451 R 7
21270 T 2 21575 C3

Taiwan Only

Primary 19937 C3 21484 C2 21577 C3
16902 C7 21478 C2 21487 C1 21932 C1
17675 C2 21481 C3 21488 C1 22023 C3
19935 C3 21483 C2 21556 C2
Second. 14908 C4 15825 C2 15826 C2

Hong Kong and Macau Only

Primary 15455 TRC7 16132 C2 19953 C3
20522 C3
Second. 15473 TRC2 16496 C2 16918 T 4
21549 C3

61 Personality and Behavioral Processes

人格及行爲

パーソナリティ及び行為

Geographic China Broadly Conceived

Primary 10272 T 3 14156 T 2 19978 TRC2
10139 C2 11682 T 1 19727 TR 1 20418 T 1
20463 R 3 21472 TRC1 21544 RC2 21579 C2
20955 RC2 21491 T 1 21557 C2 22666 TR 2
21337 TR 2 21538 TRC2
Second. 12394 RC7 18919 T 1 20662 TRC1
10070 TR 2 12654 TR 4 18976 TR 2 20766 T 2
10096 R 2 14166 T 1 19036 TRC2 21349 TR 1
10277 T 2 14184 T 1 20127 T 2 21613 T 1
10287 TR 2 15126 T 2 20143 T 1 21718 TR 1
10684 TR 2 16337 TRC1 20164 TR 1 22043 T 1
10704 TR 2 18528 T 1 20172 TR 1 22474 TRC1
11199 T 1

Mainland China

Primary 14059 C1 20523 C2 21548 C2
10150 C2 14245 R 4 20902 R 3 21560 C1
10164 C2 14269 RC4 20903 R 3 21563 C1
10440 T 2 14305 C4 21102 C3 21569 C1
10477 C2 14376 C1 21119 C4 21570 C1
10624 T 1 14564 T 4 21260 T 2 21585 C2
10780 R 1 14760 R 1 21286 T 1 21587 C1
10998 C1 14824 C2 21441 T 1 21589 C5
11053 RC2 15183 RC1 21492 TR 1 21591 C2
11101 C2 15252 C2 21495 TR 1 21593 C1
11102 C1 17942 R 2 21499 TR 1 21594 C1
11140 C2 18158 R 2 21500 TR 1 21806 R 1
11615 RC1 18273 C2 21501 TR 2 21960 C2
11650 C1 18435 T 2 21504 TR 2 22216 TRC1
12619 T 1 18723 R 1 21506 R 3 22354 C1
13829 T 1 19447 R 7 21529 TRC3 22357 C2
13987 TRC2 19951 C3 21536 TRC1 22528 T 1
13988 RC1 20271 C1 21540 RC1 22831 C2
14011 RC2 20469 R 4 21541 RC1 22847 C1

Secondary: Monographs
10071 TR 2 13858 T 2 18752 R 2 21346 TR 2
10094 R 2 13991 RC1 19246 R 5 21444 TR 1
10355 TR 2 14040 C1 19281 R 5 21928 C2
10399 C2 14065 C1 19732 RC2 22006 R 1
10640 T 4 14219 TR 2 20080 C7 22179 R 1
10970 C2 14241 R 2 20154 T 1 22233 RC2
11534 C2 14247 R 1 20204 R 2 22350 C1
12268 R 8 14264 RC1 20302 R 2 22432 TR 1
12291 R 7 14513 TRC2 20432 TR 2 22655 TR 3
12963 TR 2 15309 T 2 20492 C3 22667 TR 1
13420 C2 18289 C7 20996 C2 22769 C2
13819 T 1 18324 C2 21265 T 2

Secondary: Inclusions
10295 R 2 14242 R 1 18606 R 1 20259 T 1
11065 C1 14945 C3 18825 RC2 20571 T 1
11176 C2 15271 C7 19003 R 2 22166 R 2
11530 C2 17978 T 2 20189 R 1 22373 C1
12009 C2 18533 TR 2 20212 R 2 22902 TR 1
12010 C2

Secondary: Journal Articles
10900 C2 14415 RC4 20130 T 2 21652 T 2
11068 C1 14822 C2 20488 C2 22103 TR 1
11075 C1 14959 C2 20500 C1 22174 R 1
11097 C2 14991 C2 20501 C2 22223 RC2
11142 C4 15295 C4 20508 C2 22266 RC1
11172 C2 15559 C7 20518 C2 22306 C1
11616 RC1 16251 TR 8 20521 C2 22310 C1
11623 C1 17389 C4 20534 C4 22727 TRC1
12085 C2 17998 C1 20939 R 3 22841 C1
14009 TRC2 19271 R 4 21021 C1 22851 C4
14246 R 1 19366 C1 21195 R 2 22932 R 2
14347 C2 19398 R 1

The Eighteen Provinces

Primary 11719 TR 1 21267 T 2 21502 TR 8
10091 R 2 17950 TRC1 21365 R 3 21519 R 1
10102 R 2 19245 R 2 21386 RC3 21525 R 1
10161 C2 20256 T 1 21456 R 2 22004 R 1
10623 T 3 20825 TR 3 21463 R 1
Second. 15906 C2 20149 T 1 21319 TR 2
10006 T 2 17869 R 2 20265 R 1 21323 TR 1
10054 T 2 17973 T 2 20642 R 2 21648 T 1
10569 T 2 17995 C2 20668 C2 21996 TR 1
10670 T 4 19900 C3 21122 C2 22067 T 2
14472 R 3 20092 T 2 21295 T 1 22463 R 1
15306 T 2 20097 TR 1

North China Broadly Conceived

Primary 10057 T 1
Second. 10064 T 2 13976 R 2 18750 R 2
20716 T 2

Manchuria

Primary 20276 R 4 22693 R 2
Second. 19828 R 8 21151 C8

Northern China

Primary 21508 R 3 21512 R 3 21523 R 3
15338 T 7 21509 R 3 21513 R 3 21526 R 3
18398 T 2 21510 R 3 21515 R 3 21531 RC3
20921 R 3 21511 R 3 21517 R 3 21554 C3
21507 R 3
Second. 15904 C8 17793 C8 20559 T 3
10607 T 3 16073 C3 17927 T 2 21278 T 3
15395 R 3 16909 T 2 18362 C3 21359 TR 3
15399 R 7 16928 T 2 20436 R 3 22763 C3
15410 R 8 17780 C3

Northwestern China and Frontier Regions

Primary □
Second. 18706 R 5 21808 R 8 22005 R 1

South China Broadly Conceived

Primary 19894 TRC2 21339 TR 2 21537 RC2
Second. 13892 R 2 18512 T 3 20274 T 3
12580 T 2 18500 T 2 19006 R 4 22601 T 2

East Central China

Primary 17943 R 3 20935 R 3 21528 R 3
15357 T 3 18855 T 2 21433 C2
Second. 17649 T 5 18926 T 3 22755 C3
15474 RC3 17868 R 7 19556 R 3

Central Yangtze Provinces

Primary 15481 C2 16526 T 2
Second. 17746 C5

Southwestern China

Primary 17535 T 4 17632 R 3 19729 R 6
20475 RC4
Second. 16077 C2 18933 T 4 20863 R 2
15316 T 2 16512 T 2 19261 R 3 20873 R 7
15717 T 2 17854 R 2

Southeastern China

Primary 21490 T 3 21527 R 1 21575 C3
16552 TR 2 21522 R 1 21573 C3
Second. 16176 T 2 17920 T 7 20525 C2
15337 T 5 16218 T 2 19761 T 7

Taiwan Only

Primary 21534 RC2 21566 C3 21583 C8
19911 C2 21545 RC1 21567 C2 21584 C3
19936 C3 21551 C1 21568 C3 21588 C3
20995 RC2 21552 C3 21571 C3 21590 C3
21016 C1 21553 C1 21572 C1 21592 C3
21478 C2 21556 C2 21577 C3 21595 C2
21483 C2 21561 C2 21580 C3 21599 C2
21518 R 3 21562 C3 21581 C3 21600 C3
21520 R 2 21564 C3 21582 C3 22018 C4
21524 R 1 21565 C3
Second. 19738 C7 20421 C2 21932 C1
16368 C8 19937 C3 20422 C8 21944 C3
16772 C8 20367 C3 21131 C2 22496 C1
17794 C3

Hong Kong and Macau Only

Primary 21547 C3 21558 C3 21586 C3
11231 T 1 21549 C3 21574 C3 21596 C1
20122 C3 21550 C3 21576 C3 21597 C3
20519 C3 21555 C2 21578 C3 21598 C3
20522 C3

SECOND. 19933 C3 20426 C2 20694 C3
15981 RC3 20267 C3 20657 RC3 22762 C2
16044 C3

62 COGNITION

認知 認知

GEOGRAPHIC CHINA BROADLY CONCEIVED

PRIMARY: MONOGRAPHS
10004 T 2 18979 TR 2 21613 T 1 21751 TR 1
10010 T 2 19044 TRC2 21626 T 2 21760 TR 1
10016 T 2 19755 T 1 21634 T 2 21788 TR 1
10048 T 2 20083 T 1 21641 T 1 21847 TRC2
10077 TR 2 20463 R 3 21656 T 1 21853 TRC2
10117 TRC2 20619 TR 2 21659 T 1 21904 RC2
16192 T 1 20769 T 4 21698 T 1 22001 TR 1
18480 T 2 20774 T 1 21703 T 1 22474 TRC1
18495 T 2 20826 TR 2 21718 TR 1 22637 T 1
18501 T 2 21399 TRC2 21740 TR 1 22740 TRC2
18968 TR 2 21467 TRC1 21750 TR 1 22809 TRC1
18975 TR 1 21603 T 3

PRIMARY: INCLUSIONS
10093 R 2 21660 T 1 21902 TRC2 22779 T 1
10262 TRC3 21712 T 2 22777 T 1 22780 T 1
10627 T 2 21754 TR 1 22778 T 1 22931 R 1
20017 TRC1 21803 TR 1

PRIMARY: JOURNAL ARTICLES
10681 T 1 20181 TR 1 21702 T 1 21890 TRC1
11207 T 1 21602 T 2 21742 TR 1 21903 TRC1
11216 T 1 21619 T 1 21743 TR 1 22136 TR 1
11608 TRC1 21636 T 1 21746 TR 1 22471 TRC1
15126 T 2 21639 T 1 21835 TRC1 22512 T 1
16337 TRC1 21649 T 1 21844 TRC2 22626 T 2
18039 TRC1 21658 T 1 21850 TRC2 22984 TRC1
18828 TRC1 21688 T 1 21855 TRC2 22998 RC1
18923 T 1 21689 T 2 21857 TRC1 23043 C1
18982 TR 1 21695 T 2 21875 TRC1

SECONDARY: MONOGRAPHS
10014 T 2 11293 TR 1 16186 T 2 20719 T 1
10045 T 2 11692 TR 2 16229 TR 2 20790 TR 4
10058 T 2 12184 T 8 16281 TR 1 20815 TR 4
10070 TR 2 12902 T 3 18700 R 2 20960 TRC2
10074 TR 2 12957 TR 2 18904 T 2 20963 TRC1
10113 TRC2 13175 TR 2 18976 TR 2 20992 TRC1
10139 C2 13688 TR 2 19403 RC2 21279 T 2
10550 T 1 14167 T 2 19870 TRC1 21404 TRC1
10557 T 1 14657 TR 2 19978 TRC2 21538 TRC2
10560 T 2 14696 TR 1 20009 TR 1 22002 TR 1
10611 T 2 14698 TR 1 20053 TR 1 22082 TR 1
11270 TR 4 15773 R 2

SECONDARY: INCLUSIONS
11556 T 1 18073 T 2 20981 TRC2 22578 T 2
12589 T 2 18373 T 1 22013 TRC1 22896 TR 1
16340 TRC1 20703 T 1 22016 TRC1

SECONDARY: JOURNAL ARTICLES
10564 T 2 18407 T 2 20016 TRC1 20969 TRC1
11387 TRC1 18468 T 1 20180 TR 1 21318 TR 1
11415 TRC1 18489 T 1 20737 T 1 21491 T 1
13629 T 2 18900 T 1 20759 T 1 22015 TRC1
14648 TR 1 18995 R 2 20787 T 1 22634 T 1
14710 R 1 19032 TRC1 20807 TR 1 22912 TR 1
16179 T 1 19052 TRC1 20811 TR 1 22917 TR 1
17036 TR 7 19993 T 1 20827 TR 3 22995 TRC2
18396 T 2 19996 T 2 20956 TRC1

MAINLAND CHINA

PRIMARY: MONOGRAPHS
10003 T 2 12970 TR 2 14990 C2 19063 C2
10036 T 2 13132 T 1 15033 C1 19131 C7
10049 T 2 13152 TR 2 15171 TRC2 19422 C3
10068 TR 2 13446 C5 16343 TRC2 19657 RC1
10464 C4 13449 C1 18062 C2 20546 T 2
10672 T 2 14164 T 2 18345 C4 20614 TR 2
11113 C4 14642 TR 1 18853 T 2 20782 T 1
11263 TR 1 14677 TR 1 18862 T 2 20801 TR 1
11395 TRC1 14693 TR 4 18867 T 2 20953 TRC1
11563 T 4 14809 RC2 18927 T 1 20991 TRC2
11581 TR 2 14835 C2 18959 TR 2 20996 C2
12967 TR 1 14871 C2 19033 TRC1 21163 T 7
21321 TR 2 21691 T 2 21821 R 2 21949 C1
21401 RC3 21705 T 1 21825 R 1 21950 C1
21437 T 1 21711 T 1 21826 R 2 21951 C1
21444 TR 1 21723 TR 1 21838 TRC2 21981 T 1
21466 TRC1 21741 TR 1 21862 TRC1 22068 T 1
21476 TRC2 21749 TR 1 21869 TRC1 22073 T 1
21504 TR 2 21758 TR 1 21873 TRC3 22091 TR 1
21569 C1 21766 TR 1 21874 RC2 22112 TR 2
21570 C1 21771 TR 1 21887 TRC2 22147 R 1
21617 T 1 21772 TR 1 21891 TRC1 22151 R 1
21624 T 2 21790 TR 1 21900 TRC2 22305 C1
21632 T 1 21797 TR 1 21928 C2 22432 TR 1
21644 T 2 21798 TR 1 21936 C3 22602 T 1
21657 T 1 21818 R 2 21937 C2 22772 T 2
21677 T 2 21819 R 2 21948 C2 22831 C2
21681 T 1

PRIMARY: INCLUSIONS
10441 T 2 21643 T 1 21858 RC1 21921 C1
11163 C1 21646 T 1 21859 TRC1 21923 C1
11265 TR 2 21663 T 1 21870 RC1 21929 C1
11448 C1 21682 T 2 21871 TRC1 21930 C2
11550 T 2 21709 T 2 21872 TRC1 21931 C1
11590 TR 1 21739 TR 1 21876 RC1 21934 C1
11638 C2 21747 TR 1 21877 RC3 21947 C2
12197 T 7 21753 TR 1 21878 TRC1 21952 C1
12415 RC2 21767 TR 1 21880 TRC1 21955 C1
13408 C4 21774 TR 2 21881 TRC1 21958 C1
14096 T 2 21780 TR 2 21882 TRC1 21959 C1
14645 TR 1 21793 TR 1 21885 TRC2 21962 C3
14789 TRC1 21802 TR 1 21889 TRC1 21964 C2
14964 C1 21804 TR 1 21893 RC2 21965 C2
16203 T 1 21815 R 1 21894 TRC2 21977 C2
16269 TR 1 21817 R 1 21898 RC1 21978 C2
18944 T 1 21831 RC1 21901 TRC1 22034 T 2
19407 C1 21836 TRC1 21907 C1 22108 TR 1
19409 C1 21840 TRC2 21910 C1 22335 C1
19424 C1 21842 TRC1 21911 C1 22548 T 1
19425 C1 21843 TRC1 21912 C2 22661 TR 2
19721 T 2 21845 TRC1 21913 C1 22739 TRC1
21468 TRC1 21848 TRC2 21916 C2 22829 C1
21606 T 1 21856 TRC1 21920 C1

PRIMARY: JOURNAL ARTICLES
10440 T 2 19415 C3 21722 TR 1 21866 TRC1
10513 T 4 19656 RC1 21724 TR 1 21867 TRC1
10622 T 5 19961 T 1 21725 TR 1 21868 TRC1
11117 C4 20382 T 1 21728 TR 1 21879 RC1
11233 T 1 20515 C2 21732 TR 1 21884 TRC1
11298 TR 1 20545 T 2 21734 TR 2 21886 RC1
11560 T 2 20720 T 1 21735 TR 1 21899 TRC1
11618 C3 20732 T 1 21736 TR 1 21909 C1
11871 TRC2 20741 T 1 21744 TR 1 21914 C1
11899 C1 20788 T 1 21748 TR 1 21915 C1
13047 RC1 20794 TR 1 21752 TR 1 21917 C2
13401 C2 20810 TR 1 21755 TR 1 21918 C2
13433 C2 20819 TR 1 21757 TR 1 21919 C2
14259 RC4 20971 TRC1 21759 TR 2 21922 C1
14282 RC1 20990 TRC1 21764 TR 1 21924 C1
14359 C2 21113 C3 21775 TR 1 21926 C1
14392 C3 21182 T 1 21777 TR 1 21935 C1
14566 T 2 21290 T 1 21779 TR 1 21938 C1
14651 TR 1 21485 C1 21785 TR 1 21939 C1
14706 R 2 21499 TR 1 21789 TR 1 21940 C1
14740 R 2 21541 RC1 21792 TR 1 21941 C1
14900 C2 21604 T 1 21794 TR 1 21942 C1
15050 TR 2 21609 T 1 21795 TR 1 21943 C3
15128 T 4 21620 T 1 21805 TR 1 21945 C1
15137 TR 1 21633 T 1 21806 R 1 21953 C1
15193 TRC1 21640 T 1 21809 R 1 21954 C1
15757 TR 2 21647 T 1 21812 R 1 21956 C1
15807 TRC3 21652 T 2 21814 R 1 21957 C3
16019 C2 21653 T 1 21820 R 1 21960 C2
16184 T 1 21665 T 1 21823 R 1 21961 C2
16224 T 1 21669 T 1 21824 R 1 21963 C4
16255 TR 1 21671 T 1 21829 TRC1 21967 C1
16308 R 2 21680 T 1 21830 TRC2 21968 C3
16320 R 2 21683 T 1 21832 TRC1 21969 C1
17964 C1 21684 T 1 21834 TRC1 21970 C1
18086 T 1 21687 T 1 21837 RC2 21972 C1
18476 T 1 21690 T 1 21839 TRC1 21973 C1
18963 TR 1 21693 T 1 21841 TRC1 21974 C1
19009 R 2 21696 T 1 21846 TRC1 21975 C3
19057 C2 21699 T 1 21849 TRC1 21976 C1
19400 R 2 21714 T 1 21860 RC1 21979 C4
19410 C4 21716 T 1 21864 TRC1 21992 TR 1
22035 T 1 22330 C1 22502 C1 22786 TR 1
22140 TR 1 22337 C1 22621 T 1 22824 TRC1
22157 R 1 22338 C1 22636 T 1 22830 C1
22222 TRC1 22365 C2 22771 T 2 22842 C1
22223 RC2 22436 TR 1 22781 T 1 22843 C1
22246 TRC2 22440 TR 1 22782 TR 3 22848 C1
22316 C1 22487 RC7 22783 TR 1 22874 T 1

SECONDARY: MONOGRAPHS
10002 T 2 12525 C2 15273 C2 20743 T 1
10041 T 2 12783 TRC2 15509 C2 20749 T 2
10043 T 2 12963 TR 2 16246 TR 1 20763 T 1
10105 R 2 13125 T 2 17260 R 2 20798 TR 2
10115 RC2 13163 TR 2 17763 R 2 20973 TRC1
10145 C2 13213 R 7 17770 R 1 21100 C1
10154 C2 13324 C7 17952 TRC2 21260 T 2
10159 C2 13511 TR 2 18061 C2 21471 TRC1
10481 C2 13882 TR 2 18103 TR 1 22031 T 1
10559 T 4 13898 R 2 18341 C3 22046 T 1
10718 TR 2 14160 T 2 18350 C1 22071 T 1
10782 R 1 14209 T 1 18746 R 2 22099 TR 2
10970 C2 14231 TR 4 18819 RC2 22131 TR 2
11243 T 2 14299 C2 18849 T 1 22185 TRC1
11258 TR 1 14378 C4 18974 TR 1 22196 RC1
11305 TR 1 14574 T 2 18978 TR 1 22202 TRC1
11356 R 1 14650 TR 1 18989 TR 2 22217 RC2
11562 T 1 14670 TR 4 18991 TR 4 22229 RC2
11569 T 5 14681 TR 1 19078 RC8 22304 C1
11587 TR 4 14692 TR 1 19697 TR 3 22486 RC8
11588 TR 2 14727 R 3 19707 R 7 22605 T 2
11596 R 1 14749 R 2 19719 T 2 22619 T 2
11689 TR 2 14833 C1 19751 T 2 22674 TR 1
11848 RC2 14921 C1 20294 TR 2 22746 C1
11855 TRC2 14974 C2 20431 TR 4 22787 TR 2
12386 RC2 14976 C1 20462 R 2 22806 TRC1
12429 C7 15163 RC2

SECONDARY: INCLUSIONS
10554 T 1 12799 C1 19010 R 2 22192 RC2
10671 T 3 13387 C1 19037 TRC1 22236 TRC1
10723 TR 2 13394 C1 19413 C1 22287 RC1
11072 C2 13436 C2 19418 C1 22321 C3
11078 C2 14176 T 2 19866 TRC2 22342 C1
11174 C2 14601 T 3 19999 T 1 22363 C2
11574 T 1 14760 R 1 20814 TR 1 22649 TR 1
11632 C1 15177 TRC2 21357 TR 1 22827 C1
11647 C1 15296 C1 21986 T 1 22837 C1
11951 C1 16289 R 4 21991 TR 1 22857 C2
12206 T 2 18885 T 2 22051 T 1 22924 TR 1
12447 C2 18986 TR 1

SECONDARY: JOURNAL ARTICLES
10199 TR 2 13632 T 3 20610 TR 1 22120 TR 1
10420 C2 13899 R 2 20611 TR 2 22227 TRC1
10834 R 2 14023 C1 20725 T 2 22241 TRC1
11055 TRC1 14028 C1 20733 T 1 22288 RC1
11091 C1 14213 TR 1 20738 T 1 22310 C1
11146 C1 14256 RC2 20761 T 1 22317 C1
11225 T 2 14348 C1 20767 T 1 22320 C1
11262 TR 1 14358 C1 20797 TR 1 22347 C1
11334 R 4 14613 T 1 20902 R 3 22361 C1
11409 TRC1 14663 TR 1 20903 R 3 22396 T 1
11414 TRC1 14814 C4 20965 TRC3 22408 T 1
11546 T 4 15790 TRC2 21006 C3 22417 T 1
11559 T 4 16172 T 1 21035 C2 22435 TR 1
11602 RC1 16214 T 1 21094 C1 22524 T 1
11631 C1 16223 T 1 21170 T 1 22573 T 1
11645 C1 16272 TR 2 21183 T 2 22668 TR 1
11664 T 2 16329 TRC2 21190 R 2 22726 TRC3
11935 C2 16460 C2 21500 TR 1 22774 T 1
12119 C2 18866 T 1 22007 R 1 22788 TR 1
12427 C7 19020 R 1 22042 T 1 22825 C1
12458 C7 19242 R 3 22054 T 1 22839 C2
12534 C2 19402 R 4 22055 T 1 22949 TRC1
13425 C5 19414 C4 22070 T 1 22990 TRC1
13427 C2 20001 T 2 22105 TR 2 23007 TRC1
13431 C3

THE EIGHTEEN PROVINCES

PRIMARY: MONOGRAPHS
10038 T 2 16252 TR 2 20284 T 1 21645 T 1
10056 T 2 16279 TR 1 20976 TRC1 21655 T 5
15327 T 3 18870 T 3 21340 TR 3 21672 T 1
16161 T 2 18916 T 2 21455 R 5 21673 T 1
16183 T 2 19008 R 2 21456 R 2 21675 T 1
16247 TR 2 20097 TR 1 21642 T 1 21676 T 2

21679 T 4 21715 T 1 21765 TR 1 21791 TR 1
21685 T 2 21738 TR 2 21786 TR 1 21796 TR 1
21697 T 1 21761 TR 1

Primary: Inclusions
10602 T 3 21612 T 1 21662 T 1 22463 R 1
14169 T 1 21630 T 1 21686 T 2 22628 T 3
14763 R 3 21648 T 1 22177 R 3 22773 T 2
16105 TR 2

Primary: Journal Articles
11579 TR 1 20603 T 1 21623 T 2 21773 TR 1
12205 T 8 20730 T 1 21627 T 1 21778 TR 1
12411 TRC8 20742 T 2 21629 T 2 21807 R 4
14639 TR 1 20789 TR 1 21635 T 1 21816 R 2
14660 TR 2 21297 T 2 21651 T 1 21822 R 1
16207 T 1 21356 TR 2 21678 T 2 21883 TRC1
19024 R 4 21473 TRC2 21700 T 1 21897 TRC2
19439 T 1 21610 T 2 21720 TR 1 21983 T 1
20149 T 1 21611 T 2 21721 TR 4 22083 TR 1
20388 TR 1 21615 T 1 21768 TR 1 22090 TR 3
20544 T 2

Second. 16171 T 1 19001 R 2 21463 R 1
10175 C2 16191 T 1 19017 R 2 21489 C2
10351 TR 7 16200 T 2 19781 TR 1 21502 TR 8
11536 T 3 16204 T 1 20002 T 1 21519 R 1
11539 T 2 16254 TR 1 20150 T 1 21525 R 1
11567 T 2 16264 TR 2 20547 T 2 22045 T 1
11719 TR 1 16271 TR 2 20548 T 2 22086 TR 1
12179 T 2 16276 TR 1 20604 T 2 22116 TR 4
12675 TR 2 16280 TR 2 20612 TR 2 22170 R 1
12948 T 2 16508 T 2 20739 T 1 22286 TRC1
13155 TR 4 17153 T 2 20776 T 2 22390 T 2
14226 TR 1 17767 R 2 20793 TR 5 22414 T 1
14273 RC3 17962 C2 20818 TR 2 22418 T 1
14555 T 1 18432 T 1 21166 T 2 22419 T 1
14980 C3 18506 T 2 21186 TR 2 22431 TR 1
15149 R 1 18869 T 3 21199 C7 22433 TR 1
15767 TR 4 18881 T 2

North China Broadly Conceived

Primary 18634 R 2 21622 T 1 21787 TR 3
16169 T 2 19011 R 2 21784 TR 7

Second. 14195 T 3 16352 C8 20578 T 2
10417 C8 15752 T 2 18493 T 2 22394 T 2

Manchuria

Primary 20795 TR 2

Second. 15743 T 3 16315 R 3 20715 T 3
10852 RC2 16202 T 2 20577 T 3 22412 T 2
11032 R 4

Northern China

Primary 16232 TR 7 18939 T 7 21264 T 3
11538 T 3 16233 TR 8 18954 TR 8 21344 TR 2
12931 T 3 16293 R 3 19007 R 2 21511 R 3
14214 TR 3 16295 R 3 20273 R 3 21631 T 8
14551 T 3 16310 R 4 20381 T 2 21664 T 3
15416 R 3 17049 R 3 20436 R 3 21729 TR 7
15786 R 3 18009 T 3 20608 TR 3 21770 TR 3
16228 TR 8 18329 C3 20631 R 3 22456 R 1
16231 TR 7

Second. 15801 TRC3 17020 T 3 20015 R 3
10505 T 3 15872 R 7 17817 T 2 20559 T 3
11568 T 3 16160 T 8 17953 TRC3 20727 T 4
11573 T 3 16201 T 6 18658 R 7 20758 T 3
11597 R 3 16206 T 2 18856 T 3 20775 T 7
13891 R 2 16216 T 3 18887 T 8 20982 RC3
14163 T 3 16219 T 3 18920 T 2 21178 T 2
14228 TR 2 16234 TR 7 18921 T 1 21181 T 2
15320 T 3 16304 R 3 18946 T 3 21187 TR 2
15338 T 7 16311 R 8 19776 T 2 21188 TR 3
15367 T 2 16314 R 8 19851 R 2 21278 T 3
15395 R 3 16323 R 8 20012 TR 2 21330 TR 7
15626 T 2

Northwestern China and Frontier Regions

Primary 13822 T 7 20304 RC2 21808 R 8
21851 RC8 22453 R 8

Second. 16749 RC8 20298 R 7 20927 R 7
16170 T 7 18955 TR 3 20601 T 2 22429 TR 8
16299 R 7 19818 R 7 20858 R 8 22467 R 8
16628 R 2 19889 RC8

South China Broadly Conceived

Primary 16182 T 2 18471 T 1 19399 R 2
10031 T 2 18030 R 3 19054 RC2 21865 TRC2
16159 T 2 18449 T 2

Second. 15722 T 2 18500 T 2 20734 T 2
12580 T 2 16917 T 2 18512 T 3 22026 T 1
15361 T 2 18386 T 2 20274 T 3 22601 T 2
15721 T 2 18459 T 2

East Central China

Primary 16290 R 8 21621 T 1 21670 T 3
15744 T 2 18026 R 3 21628 T 7 21707 T 3
16178 T 8 21331 TR 1 21661 T 1

Second. 16197 T 3 19005 R 3 20886 R 3
11561 T 3 17662 T 7 19015 R 3 20918 R 3
14807 RC3 18466 T 2 19746 T 8 21180 T 1
15346 T 2 18487 T 2 20003 T 5 21216 R 7
15348 T 3 18884 T 8 20535 T 3 21329 TR 1
15374 TR 8 18934 T 7

Central Yangtze Provinces

Primary 16090 T 2

Second. 18912 T 2

Southwestern China

Primary 16312 R 2 21618 T 7 21892 TRC2
15326 T 7 20839 R 3 21810 R 2 22448 R 8
16287 R 1 20873 R 7

Second. 16302 R 4 19729 R 6 20809 TR 2
13209 R 2 18889 T 2 19830 R 8 20872 R 6
16268 TR 1 18962 TR 1 20804 TR 3 21192 R 1
16301 R 1 19026 R 2 20808 TR 2 22542 T 2

Southeastern China

Primary 16190 T 2 19975 TRC7 21811 R 3
15319 T 3 16288 R 2 20722 T 4 22022 C1
16174 T 8 16338 TRC7 21769 TR 3 22398 T 4
16181 T 2 16341 TRC7 21781 TR 1 22415 T 2

Second. 16208 T 2 19209 T 3 21179 T 2
13808 T 3 16265 TR 3 19408 C2 21184 TR 5
15317 T 2 16270 TR 2 19865 TRC1 21413 RC3
15735 T 2 16924 T 2 20014 R 3 22385 T 1
16188 T 1 17589 C2 20712 T 3 22403 T 1
16193 T 3 18901 T 2 21167 T 3 22566 T 3

Taiwan Only

Primary 16364 C7 20018 C8 21944 C3
16354 C8 19068 C2 21925 C3 21946 C7
16359 C2 19925 C8 21932 C1 22496 C1
16360 C4

Second. 16351 C3 16748 RC2 20753 T 1
15505 C8 16361 C8 19679 C7 22023 C3
15515 C8 16365 C2

Hong Kong and Macau Only

Primary 16327 TRC2 21555 C2 21906 C8
15643 RC2 16333 RC8 21596 C1 21908 C3
15813 C2 16342 TRC3 21827 TRC7 21966 C8
16298 R 8 16344 C7 21854 RC8 21971 C1
16326 TRC2 20670 C1 21905 C8 22503 C1

Second. 15814 C7 17320 TRC7 21038 C3
14597 T 2 16334 TRC2 19051 TRC2 21198 C8
15526 C3 16348 C7 19070 C3 22500 C3
15546 C7 16848 C7 21005 C7 22733 TRC3
15797 TRC7

63 Ethics

倫理 倫理

Geographic China Broadly Conceived

Primary 19800 TR 1 21338 TR 1 22013 TRC1
11213 T 2 19861 RC1 21579 C2 22014 TRC1
13811 T 2 19978 TRC2 21639 T 1 22015 TRC1
14166 T 1 19993 T 1 21641 T 1 22016 TRC1
14657 TR 2 19996 T 2 21703 T 1 22082 TR 1
16104 TR 7 20005 TR 1 21988 T 1 22100 TR 1
16281 TR 1 20108 R 3 22001 TR 1 22102 TR 2
19032 TRC1 20463 R 3 22002 TR 1 22126 TR 1

Second. 13688 TR 2 19771 T 1 21491 T 1
10025 T 2 14676 TR 3 20017 TRC1 21626 T 2
10053 T 2 14699 TR 1 20050 TR 2 21649 T 1
10573 T 1 16127 TRC2 20085 T 2 21688 T 1
10585 T 1 16128 TRC2 20088 T 3 21746 TR 1
10615 T 2 16192 T 1 20143 T 1 21750 TR 1
10657 T 1 17975 T 2 20162 TR 1 22043 T 1
11207 T 1 17981 TR 2 20181 TR 1 22056 T 1
11261 TR 1 18478 T 1 20766 T 2 22059 T 1
11264 TR 1 18794 TRC2 20955 RC2 22080 TR 1
11555 T 1 18902 T 1 21279 T 2 22284 TRC1
11556 T 1 19217 TR 3 21404 TRC1 22474 TRC1
11608 TRC1 19687 T 1 21467 TRC1 22620 T 1
13124 T 2 19735 TRC1 21472 TRC1

Mainland China

Primary: Monographs
10145 C2 16343 TRC2 19644 R 2 21570 C1
10551 T 4 17979 TR 7 19816 R 2 21657 T 1
11195 T 1 18053 C4 19905 C2 21723 TR 1
11219 T 1 18862 T 2 20134 T 2 21980 T 4
11596 R 1 18978 TR 1 20255 T 1 21981 T 1
12985 R 2 18989 TR 2 20258 T 2 21982 T 2
15150 R 2 19033 TRC1 21450 TR 2 22006 R 1
15955 TR 8 19035 TRC2 21457 R 1 22066 T 2

Primary: Inclusions
11443 C2 17978 T 2 20292 TR 2 21986 T 1
11451 C1 18358 C2 21709 T 2 21989 T 1
11590 TR 1 18879 T 1 21856 TRC1 21991 TR 1
11653 C1 19721 T 2 21881 TRC1 22000 TR 1
15184 RC2 19867 TRC1

Primary: Journal Articles
10520 T 1 18479 T 2 21609 T 1 22019 C1
10649 T 4 19009 R 2 21992 TR 1 22020 C1
10710 TR 1 19634 R 2 21993 TR 1 22021 C2
11623 C1 19906 C2 21998 TR 1 22140 TR 1
14389 C1 19908 C1 22007 R 1 22187 TRC1
14998 C1 20163 TR 1 22010 R 1 22199 TRC1
16214 T 1 20270 C1 22011 R 1 22331 C1
16251 TR 8 20439 R 4 22012 RC1

Secondary: Monographs
10023 T 2 11598 R 1 18849 T 1 20302 R 2
10041 T 2 11611 RC1 18867 T 2 20414 T 1
10067 TR 2 11654 C2 18927 T 1 20823 TR 4
10094 R 2 11752 R 2 19074 R 7 21172 T 2
10105 R 2 11846 RC2 19246 R 5 21308 TR 2
10559 T 4 12619 T 1 19281 R 5 21379 R 2
10711 TR 4 14001 RC1 19625 R 1 21407 TRC3
10997 C2 14127 RC2 19795 TR 1 21437 T 1
11096 C2 14370 C2 19909 C2 21459 R 4
11183 T 1 14556 T 2 19919 C1 21594 C1
11203 T 2 14642 TR 1 20013 TR 1 21825 R 1
11235 T 1 14687 TR 2 20036 T 2 21891 TRC1
11243 T 2 14774 R 3 20066 R 1 21900 TRC2
11263 TR 1 15123 C2 20135 T 1 22118 TR 1
11305 TR 1 15495 C2 20137 T 2 22147 R 1
11323 R 1 15509 C2 20154 T 1 22179 R 1
11356 R 1 15550 C2 20179 TR 1 22273 RC2
11562 T 1 15553 C2 20182 TR 2 22530 T 1
11563 T 4 17313 RC2 20204 R 2 22599 T 2
11569 T 5 17754 TR 1 20229 RC1 22655 TR 3
11586 TR 2 18279 C1

Secondary: Inclusions
10080 TR 2 11397 TRC1 16110 TR 2 19951 C3
11010 T 2 11442 C2 16165 T 3 20176 TR 1
11073 C4 14208 T 2 18241 C2 20189 R 1
11120 C2 14227 TR 1 18944 T 1 20212 R 2
11284 TR 1 15099 C7 19003 R 2 20530 C1
11321 R 1 15314 T 2 19866 TRC2 20661 TRC1

21357 TR 1 21871 TRC1 22247 RC1 22387 T 1
21468 TRC1 21901 TRC1 22378 C1 22743 RC1
21793 TR 1

SECONDARY: JOURNAL ARTICLES
10033 T 2 11583 TR 2 17753 T 1 21452 TR 1
10504 T 2 11817 R 2 18086 T 1 21499 TR 1
10731 TR 4 11902 C2 18133 R 1 21540 RC1
11153 C2 11986 C2 18162 R 1 21722 TR 1
11184 T 1 12729 R 1 18384 T 1 21725 TR 1
11188 T 1 13840 T 2 18692 R 1 21728 TR 1
11205 T 1 14111 TR 2 19215 TR 5 21736 TR 1
11206 T 1 14283 TRC1 19271 R 4 21806 R 1
11218 T 1 14569 T 2 19921 C2 21823 R 1
11233 T 1 14580 T 1 20001 T 2 21867 TRC1
11255 TR 1 14991 C2 20042 T 1 21909 C1
11267 TR 1 15138 TR 2 20130 T 2 22047 T 2
11298 TR 1 15221 C1 20227 RC1 22054 T 1
11386 TRC1 16082 C1 20240 C1 22123 TR 1
11388 TRC2 16089 T 2 20271 C1 22300 C1
11409 TRC1 16100 T 1 20466 R 4 22317 C1
11414 TRC1 16184 T 1 20500 C1 22330 C1
11416 TRC1 16224 T 1 20723 T 4 22337 C1
11424 C1 16272 TR 2 20971 TRC1 22341 C1
11477 C1 16320 R 2 21451 TR 1 22564 T 2
11509 C1

THE EIGHTEEN PROVINCES

PRIMARY 19805 TR 1 21356 TR 2 21996 TR 1
10102 R 2 19964 TR 1 21642 T 1 22004 R 1
14169 T 1 20147 T 1 21697 T 1 22009 R 2
18006 T 1 20256 T 1 21796 TR 1 22286 TRC1
18461 T 2 20907 R 4 21983 T 1 22776 T 2
18859 T 2 21340 TR 3

SECOND. 15931 T 4 19836 R 2 21463 R 1
10507 T 2 16369 T 2 20037 T 1 21502 TR 8
10525 T 2 17950 TRC1 20090 T 3 21627 T 1
10623 T 3 18367 T 2 20092 T 2 21685 T 2
10680 T 3 18881 T 2 20095 T 3 21761 TR 1
11029 R 1 19001 R 2 20097 TR 1 21791 TR 1
11224 T 1 19002 R 5 20100 TR 1 22045 T 1
11655 T 1 19017 R 2 20125 T 2 22067 T 2
12198 T 8 19018 R 7 20265 R 1 22072 T 1
13621 T 4 19024 R 4 21309 TR 2 22132 TR 1
14273 RC3 19695 T 2 21365 R 3 22390 T 2
14590 T 2 19829 R 1 21440 T 1 22463 R 1
15145 R 4

NORTH CHINA BROADLY CONCEIVED

PRIMARY 21622 T 1
SECOND. 10679 T 2 15752 T 2

MANCHURIA

PRIMARY 17548 T 7
SECOND. 20047 TR 2 20795 TR 2

NORTHERN CHINA

PRIMARY 17625 T 3 21293 T 3 21359 TR 3
15416 R 3 18887 T 8 21330 TR 7 21987 T 3
16121 R 3 20206 R 3

SECOND. 15378 TR 7 19825 R 3 20527 C3
10607 T 3 18467 T 3 20273 R 3 20762 T 3
10652 T 3 18921 T 1 20467 R 3 21174 T 3
13803 T 2 19723 T 4

NORTHWESTERN CHINA AND FRONTIER REGIONS

PRIMARY 22005 R 1 22437 TR 2
SECOND. 16325 R 8 20304 RC2 22467 R 8

SOUTH CHINA BROADLY CONCEIVED

PRIMARY □
SECOND. 17443 TR 2 18524 T 2 19894 TRC2
22026 T 1

EAST CENTRAL CHINA

PRIMARY 14635 TR 5 21331 TR 1
SECOND. 17653 C3 19748 T 2 21329 TR 1
15744 T 2 18354 C3 20043 T 8 21433 C2
16060 R 3 19015 R 3 20886 R 3 22755 C3

CENTRAL YANGTZE PROVINCES

PRIMARY □
SECOND. 16526 T 2 16756 C2

SOUTHWESTERN CHINA

PRIMARY 17632 R 3 20839 R 3 21990 T 1
SECOND. 15316 T 2 15425 R 3 16312 R 2
19827 R 6

SOUTHEASTERN CHINA

PRIMARY 22022 C1 22479 TRC8
SECOND. 17589 C2 19761 T 7 20722 T 4
15319 T 3 18048 C3 20252 T 4 21490 T 3
16190 T 2 18901 T 2 20297 R 2 22480 RC1

TAIWAN ONLY

PRIMARY 19936 C3 21484 C2 21925 C3
22018 C4 22023 C3
SECOND. 16357 C3 19938 C2 21595 C2
16226 TR 2 17622 C3 21481 C3 21944 C3
16351 C3 17822 T 2

HONG KONG AND MACAU ONLY

PRIMARY 20267 C3 20426 C2
SECOND. 15325 T 3 16126 TRC3 21197 RC2
14596 T 8 15489 C3 20657 RC3

64 IDEOLOGY AND THE GREAT TRADITION

正統思想及意識型態

正統思想及びイデオロギー

GEOGRAPHIC CHINA BROADLY CONCEIVED

PRIMARY: MONOGRAPHS
10024 T 2 11646 C1 18494 T 2 22027 T 4
10053 T 2 11694 TR 2 18511 T 2 22056 T 1
10070 TR 2 14113 TR 2 18540 TR 2 22074 T 2
10113 TRC2 14174 T 3 18545 TR 2 22082 TR 1
10144 C2 14654 TR 2 18711 R 2 22088 TR 1
10526 T 2 14699 TR 1 19503 R 2 22095 TR 2
10550 T 1 14903 C1 19534 R 2 22101 TR 1
10573 T 1 14951 C2 20540 T 2 22102 TR 2
10586 T 1 15134 TR 4 20615 TR 2 22109 TR 2
10619 T 1 15166 TRC2 20960 TRC2 22114 TR 1
10803 R 2 15283 C2 21306 TR 2 22127 TR 1
10828 R 2 16186 T 2 21342 TR 2 22133 TR 2
10850 RC1 18102 TR 2 21349 TR 1 22206 TRC1
10865 TRC3 18105 TR 2 21404 TRC1 22225 TRC2
10891 TRC1 18299 C2 21853 TRC2 22809 TRC1
11045 RC2 18375 T 2 22002 TR 1

PRIMARY: INCLUSIONS
14248 R 2 18478 T 1 22030 T 1 22081 TR 1
18073 T 2 18558 TR 2 22059 T 1 22237 TRC1
18368 T 1 21317 TR 1 22065 T 1 22518 T 1
18417 T 1

PRIMARY: JOURNAL ARTICLES
10704 TR 2 19998 T 1 22080 TR 1 22178 R 1
10714 TR 1 21472 TRC1 22085 TR 1 22189 RC1
10864 RC1 21557 C2 22100 TR 1 22214 TRC1
11608 TRC1 21857 TRC1 22115 TR 1 22265 RC2
11669 T 3 22024 T 1 22126 TR 1 22284 TRC1
12224 TR 1 22032 T 1 22136 TR 1 22345 C2
15044 T 2 22043 T 1 22139 TR 1 22604 T 3
18719 R 2 22062 T 1 22160 R 1 22634 T 1
18786 TRC2

SECONDARY: MONOGRAPHS
10034 T 2 10716 TR 1 12439 C8 15158 TRC2
10074 TR 2 10806 R 2 12901 T 2 15161 TRC2
10100 R 2 10853 TRC2 13902 R 2 15174 TRC2
10111 TRC2 11241 T 2 13997 RC2 15175 RC2
10114 TRC2 11261 TR 1 14155 T 2 16104 TR 7
10539 T 1 11270 TR 4 14167 T 2 16281 TR 1
10557 T 1 11317 R 1 14215 TR 2 18077 T 2
10615 T 2 11603 TRC1 14567 T 1 18125 R 1
10626 T 2 11605 RC2 14696 TR 1 18388 T 2
10700 TR 2 11857 TRC2 15136 TR 2 18442 T 4
18480 T 2 18810 RC2 21304 TR 2 21740 TR 1
18534 TR 2 18979 TR 2 21347 TR 2 21788 TR 1
18542 TR 2 19481 TR 3 21368 R 2 21847 TRC2
18547 TR 2 19490 R 2 21412 RC2 22555 T 2
18579 R 2 19687 T 1 21425 TRC5 22637 T 1
18700 R 2 20005 TR 1 21467 TRC1 22740 TRC2
18741 R 2 20050 TR 2 21579 C2 22866 T 2
18801 TRC2 20053 TR 1 21659 T 1 22907 TR 1
18809 RC2 20826 TR 2

SECONDARY: INCLUSIONS
10073 TR 2 13878 TR 2 18528 T 1 20418 T 1
10093 R 2 14203 T 1 18566 TR 1 21332 TR 1
10119 TRC2 15185 TRC2 19500 R 4 22560 T 1
10510 T 2 18389 T 1 19871 TRC1 22690 R 3
12394 RC7 18470 T 2 20306 C2 22931 R 1
12772 TRC2

SECONDARY: JOURNAL ARTICLES
10537 T 1 11038 RC2 14648 TR 1 21318 TR 1
10663 T 2 11207 T 1 14710 R 1 21327 TR 2
10666 T 2 11296 TR 1 15130 T 2 21619 T 1
10681 T 1 11555 T 1 15162 TRC2 21835 TRC1
10736 TR 1 11682 T 1 16128 TRC2 22640 T 1
10741 R 1 14184 T 1 18082 T 3 22984 TRC1
10854 TRC1 14284 TRC1

MAINLAND CHINA

PRIMARY: MONOGRAPHS
10069 TR 2 11639 C1 15028 C2 18782 R 2
10088 R 2 11790 R 2 15029 C1 18783 R 2
10115 RC2 11848 RC2 15034 C1 18795 TRC2
10124 TRC2 11855 TRC2 15140 TR 2 18796 RC2
10125 RC2 11862 RC2 15168 TRC2 18812 RC2
10132 C2 11872 RC2 15171 TRC2 18817 RC2
10134 C2 11897 C2 15214 C2 18819 RC2
10142 C2 11922 C2 15230 C2 18822 TRC2
10153 C2 12002 C2 15234 C2 19062 C2
10160 C2 12027 C2 15235 C2 19367 C2
10168 C2 12082 C2 15241 C2 19617 TR 2
10180 C2 12086 C2 15248 C2 19625 R 1
10677 T 2 12109 C2 15249 C2 19697 TR 3
10690 TR 1 12158 C2 15260 C2 19905 C2
10693 TR 1 12268 R 8 15279 C2 19919 C1
10696 TR 1 12271 R 7 15294 C2 20204 R 2
10697 TR 2 12572 T 3 15507 C7 20314 C2
10718 TR 2 12791 C1 15549 C7 20414 T 1
10726 TR 2 13420 C2 15553 C2 20444 R 2
10729 TR 2 13511 TR 2 15980 RC2 20462 R 2
10757 R 1 13898 R 2 16637 R 7 20484 C2
10782 R 1 13984 RC1 17661 TR 2 20496 C2
10793 R 1 13991 RC1 17952 TRC2 21124 C3
10838 R 4 14014 RC1 18103 TR 1 21336 TR 1
10883 TRC2 14139 C2 18114 R 2 21345 TR 2
10887 TRC2 14160 T 2 18126 R 3 21360 TR 2
10938 C4 14178 T 2 18161 R 2 21361 TR 1
10970 C2 14231 TR 4 18172 RC2 21400 RC2
10994 C2 14247 R 1 18178 RC2 21401 RC3
10997 C2 14258 RC2 18185 RC2 21405 TRC1
11046 RC1 14264 RC1 18277 C2 21406 RC2
11053 RC2 14269 RC4 18387 T 2 21419 RC2
11081 C1 14274 TRC2 18430 T 2 21420 TRC2
11088 C4 14285 TRC1 18457 T 1 21424 TRC2
11092 C2 14296 C2 18526 T 2 21444 TR 1
11096 C2 14299 C2 18535 TR 1 21457 R 1
11104 C2 14305 C4 18551 TR 2 21459 R 4
11111 C1 14322 C1 18557 TR 2 21466 TRC1
11113 C4 14329 C2 18559 TR 1 21471 TRC1
11132 C2 14370 C2 18597 R 4 21476 TRC2
11144 C2 14387 C3 18608 R 2 21563 C1
11178 C2 14416 C2 18617 R 2 21569 C1
11180 C2 14508 R 3 18619 R 2 21758 TR 1
11195 T 1 14681 TR 1 18635 R 2 21862 TRC1
11203 T 2 14687 TR 2 18647 R 2 21891 TRC1
11219 T 1 14692 TR 1 18660 R 2 21948 C2
11230 T 1 14780 RC1 18661 R 2 21982 T 2
11235 T 1 14783 RC2 18666 R 1 22028 T 1
11243 T 1 14795 RC2 18674 R 2 22031 T 1
11290 TR 1 14828 C2 18720 R 2 22046 T 1
11391 RC2 14853 C2 18723 R 1 22052 T 4
11393 TRC2 14871 C2 18725 R 2 22053 T 1
11540 T 4 14943 C2 18730 R 2 22066 T 2
11569 T 5 14974 C2 18752 R 2 22068 T 1
11587 TR 4 14976 C1 18753 R 2 22071 T 1
11598 R 1 14990 C2 18755 R 2 22073 T 1
11614 RC1 15025 C2 18768 R 2 22079 TR 2

15160 TRC1 18208 C2 19404 RC3 21836 TRC1
15177 TRC2 18209 C2 19526 R 3 21840 TRC2
15186 RC1 18241 C2 19866 TRC2 21856 TRC1
15187 RC7 18293 C2 19873 RC2 21859 TRC1
15188 RC2 18294 C1 19915 C1 21870 RC1
15217 C2 18370 T 2 20081 C2 21872 TRC1
15222 C2 18533 TR 2 20472 RC3 21877 RC3
15223 C2 18537 TR 2 20491 C2 21894 TRC2
15286 C2 18555 TR 2 20698 C2 21901 TRC1
15303 C2 18556 TR 1 21372 R 2 21959 C1
15982 TRC2 18571 TR 2 21388 TRC2 22533 T 1
17640 C8 18612 R 2 21394 RC1 22548 T 1
17997 C1 18761 R 2 21432 C3 22565 T 2
18000 C2 18799 RC2 21436 T 1 22581 T 1
18081 T 1 18833 RC1 21468 TRC1 22639 T 1
18110 R 2 19104 C7 21606 T 1 22739 TRC1
18119 R 2 19129 C8 21747 TR 1 22837 C1
18189 C2 19162 C7 21804 TR 1 22857 C2
18196 C1 19365 T 2 21815 R 1 22902 TR 1

Secondary: Journal Articles

10033 T 2 11557 T 1 14245 R 4 15288 C2
10225 C2 11559 T 4 14246 R 1 15292 C2
10243 C1 11585 TR 1 14249 R 1 15301 C1
10249 C2 11592 TR 1 14252 RC3 15494 C7
10305 C2 11600 R 1 14253 RC1 15512 C2
10342 TR 2 11615 RC1 14257 RC4 15559 C7
10383 RC2 11618 C3 14267 RC1 15580 C2
10393 TRC2 11628 C2 14272 RC1 16020 C7
10467 C2 11640 C1 14282 RC1 16257 TR 1
10496 C2 11648 C3 14286 RC1 17590 C3
10531 T 3 11664 T 2 14294 C1 17596 C2
10633 T 1 11773 R 2 14303 C1 17778 C7
10689 TR 1 11879 C2 14306 C1 17781 C1
10699 TR 1 11902 C2 14321 C1 17992 C2
10731 TR 4 11950 C1 14323 C1 17998 C1
10777 R 1 11954 C2 14335 C1 18044 RC1
10810 R 1 11977 C1 14340 C1 18052 C2
10834 R 2 11983 C1 14352 C1 18056 C3
10846 TRC1 12050 C2 14362 C2 18072 C1
10868 RC1 12064 C2 14382 C3 18086 T 1
10877 RC2 12068 C1 14383 C1 18090 T 3
10881 RC1 12077 C2 14389 C1 18128 R 4
10897 C2 12084 C2 14392 C3 18151 R 1
10902 C2 12098 C2 14397 T 4 18157 R 2
10909 C1 12100 C2 14438 RC2 18159 R 2
10925 C2 12105 C1 14443 C7 18166 RC1
10974 C3 12116 C2 14538 C1 18168 RC1
10987 C2 12117 C2 14572 T 2 18169 RC1
10995 C1 12129 C2 14612 T 2 18175 TRC1
11009 C1 12374 RC7 14729 R 2 18188 RC2
11023 R 2 12391 RC7 14777 TRC1 18191 C1
11054 TRC2 12431 C2 14814 C4 18198 C1
11067 C1 12472 C2 14827 C2 18200 C2
11068 C1 12481 C8 14845 C2 18205 C1
11074 C2 12529 C7 14849 C1 18207 C1
11085 C2 12808 C7 14869 C7 18226 C2
11136 C1 12821 C2 14872 C2 18227 C2
11149 C1 12835 C1 14886 C4 18237 C2
11153 C2 12929 T 4 14912 C4 18238 C2
11225 T 2 13360 C4 14931 C2 18249 C1
11233 T 1 13401 C2 14937 C1 18262 C1
11238 T 3 13405 C2 14941 C1 18270 C1
11260 TR 2 13425 C5 14959 C2 18275 C1
11262 TR 1 13818 T 1 14965 C2 18311 RC1
11286 TR 1 13875 TR 1 15133 TR 2 18316 C1
11312 R 1 13897 R 8 15144 R 2 18317 C1
11341 R 1 13940 R 2 15154 R 2 18335 C2
11367 R 1 13992 RC1 15157 R 4 18337 C1
11378 R 1 14003 RC1 15159 RC1 18342 C1
11383 TRC1 14005 RC1 15167 RC2 18369 T 1
11386 TRC1 14016 TRC1 15190 RC2 18401 T 2
11408 RC1 14021 C1 15201 C1 18402 T 1
11416 TRC1 14026 C1 15226 C2 18505 T 4
11431 C1 14035 C1 15227 C1 18517 T 1
11445 C1 14067 C1 15236 C2 18580 R 2
11446 C1 14076 C1 15244 C2 18599 R 2
11452 C2 14105 TR 2 15246 C2 18651 R 2
11461 C1 14110 TR 2 15251 C1 18668 R 4
11465 C1 14141 C2 15253 C2 18675 R 2
11477 C1 14152 C1 15261 C1 18691 R 7
11482 C1 14162 T 1 15264 C2 18714 R 2
11493 C2 14198 T 1 15276 C1 18728 R 2
11522 C1 14202 T 1 15277 C2 18737 R 1
11532 C1 14235 R 1 15278 C2 18754 R 1
11549 T 1 14240 R 1 15284 C2 18762 R 4

18790 RC2 19682 C1 21429 C1 22685 R 1
18800 TRC2 19868 TRC1 21560 C1 22726 TRC3
18814 RC1 19875 TRC2 21620 T 1 22727 TRC1
18826 TRC1 19891 TRC1 21693 T 1 22748 C1
18831 RC1 19906 C2 21736 TR 1 22786 TR 1
18838 C2 19908 C1 21795 TR 1 22788 TR 1
19130 C7 19926 C1 21830 TRC2 22804 R 4
19168 C2 19941 C1 21909 C1 22825 C1
19183 C2 20227 RC1 21935 C1 22828 C1
19189 C7 20248 C2 21945 C1 22844 C7
19366 C1 20327 C1 21968 C3 22847 C1
19414 C4 20370 C2 21969 C1 22848 C1
19467 RC7 20374 C1 21973 C1 22854 C1
19568 R 3 20457 R 2 21992 TR 1 22935 R 1
19596 C4 20481 C1 21993 TR 1 22938 R 1
19599 C4 20485 C4 22010 R 1 22941 R 2
19607 C3 20520 C2 22524 T 1 22943 R 1
19623 R 4 20521 C2 22543 T 1 23007 TRC1
19634 R 2 20533 C2 22668 TR 1 23056 C1
19678 C1 21092 C2

The Eighteen Provinces

Primary: Monographs

10027 T 2 11567 T 2 18930 T 2 22067 T 2
10087 R 2 12198 T 8 19964 TR 1 22076 TR 1
10161 C2 17995 C2 20004 TR 1 22094 TR 2
10175 C2 18138 R 3 21642 T 1 22110 TR 1
10507 T 2 18461 T 2 21679 T 4 22132 TR 1
11061 C2 18592 R 2 21765 TR 1 22708 R 3
11539 T 2 18639 R 3 22057 T 2

Primary: Inclusions

10680 T 3 18777 R 2 21343 TR 2 22064 T 1
14086 T 1 18778 R 2 21630 T 1 22092 TR 3
14170 T 1 18784 R 2 21648 T 1 22107 TR 1
15148 R 4 21301 T 1 21686 T 2 22137 TR 2
15203 C3 21309 TR 2 22036 T 1 22177 R 3
18437 T 2

Primary: Journal Articles

10116 TRC1 15018 C2 21678 T 2 22086 TR 1
10682 T 2 18083 T 1 21883 TRC1 22090 TR 3
11224 T 1 18451 T 2 21996 TR 1 22116 TR 4
11579 TR 1 18472 T 4 22029 T 3 22170 R 1
12335 R 2 18482 T 2 22044 T 1 22181 R 3
12615 T 3 18546 TR 2 22045 T 1 22193 TRC1
12724 R 4 18586 R 2 22072 T 1 22218 RC1
14225 TR 1 18676 R 1 22083 TR 1 22286 TRC1
14590 T 2 21453 TR 1

Second. 14800 RC2 18127 R 3 18859 T 2
10141 C2 14801 RC2 18149 R 1 18880 T 1
10170 C2 14826 C3 18152 R 1 18948 T 1
10544 T 3 14829 C2 18413 T 2 19439 T 1
10623 T 3 15145 R 4 18436 T 2 19570 R 2
11016 T 2 15149 R 1 18508 T 2 20256 T 1
11209 T 1 15240 C3 18578 R 2 20478 C2
11564 T 3 15243 C2 18583 R 2 20548 T 2
11621 C3 15478 C2 18590 R 3 21267 T 2
11667 T 2 15543 C2 18602 R 2 21272 T 2
13831 T 2 16171 T 1 18604 R 7 21319 TR 2
14207 T 2 16247 TR 2 18638 R 2 21655 T 5
14236 R 2 16890 C7 18654 R 2 21673 T 1
14237 R 3 17541 T 7 18662 R 3 21738 TR 2
14238 R 3 17916 C2 18735 R 4 21983 T 1
14277 TRC3 18074 T 2 18736 R 2 22850 C3
14555 T 1 18076 T 3 18756 R 1 22880 T 1
14680 TR 4 18115 R 2 18776 R 1 22885 T 2
14755 R 3 18117 R 4

North China Broadly Conceived

Primary 13894 R 2 18307 R 2 18738 R 1
10827 R 2 14762 R 2 18627 R 8 22141 R 3
11028 R 2 16352 C8 18731 R 2

Second. 14195 T 3 18682 R 2 19920 C2
10679 T 2 14210 T 2 18747 R 1 22394 T 2
13962 R 2 18493 T 2 18750 R 2 22715 R 2
13976 R 2

Manchuria

Primary 11337 R 1 21151 C8

Second. 11695 TR 1 18739 R 2 21055 C7
10911 C2 11834 R 2 19195 C7 21056 C2
11032 R 4 17340 C7

Northern China

Primary 11597 R 3 17645 C2 19642 R 7
10505 T 3 11599 R 3 18066 C3 20448 R 3
10783 R 2 15786 R 3 18092 T 3 21293 T 3
11135 C3 16080 C3 18096 T 3 22374 C3

Second. 14270 RC3 15009 C3 18658 R 7
10776 R 2 14427 R 2 15010 C3 20497 C2
10941 C3 14701 TR 3 15304 C3 20505 C3
11497 C3 14735 R 2 15320 T 3 20608 TR 3
11538 T 3 14802 RC2 15362 T 7 21278 T 3
11765 R 1 14881 C3 16221 T 4 22520 T 3
13974 R 2 14946 C7 17569 R 8 22747 C2
14197 T 3 14950 C3 18344 C3 22750 C3
14228 TR 2 14962 C2 18357 C3 22753 C3

Northwestern China and Frontier Regions

Primary 15545 C8

Second. 13895 R 2 17772 RC7 18749 R 2
18911 T 2 21851 RC8

South China Broadly Conceived

Primary 15749 T 3 18646 R 2 21865 TRC2
11014 T 2 18137 R 1 18779 R 2 22026 T 1
14262 RC2 18614 R 2 21275 T 1 22535 T 3
15205 C2

Second. 18129 R 3 18471 T 1 18763 R 2
10031 T 2 18374 T 2 18613 R 1 18766 R 2
13955 R 2 18412 T 2 18670 R 2 19448 R 2
17982 R 2 18459 T 2

East Central China

Primary 15254 C3 18392 T 2 19069 C3
11552 T 1 16394 T 2 18487 T 2 19550 R 3
14561 T 3 17660 C3 18983 TR 3 22164 R 3
14635 TR 5 18363 T 2

Second. 16525 T 8 18404 T 3 19308 C3
15019 C3 18026 R 3 18410 T 3 19552 R 3
15143 R 3 18067 C3 18522 T 3 21115 C8
15517 C8 18321 C3 18934 T 7 21661 T 1
16075 C3

Central Yangtze Provinces

Primary 19726 TR 7 21352 TR 2

Second. 15481 C2 20210 R 2 20494 C4
13983 R 7 17630 TR 4 20220 R 3 20820 TR 2
14187 T 2 18305 R 7

Southwestern China

Primary ☐

Second. 14803 RC2 18089 T 2 21114 C7
14571 T 4 16077 C2 18365 T 3 21194 R 4

Southeastern China

Primary 10708 TR 2 17571 R 3 18997 R 3

Second. 13953 R 3 17560 TR 2 18742 R 2
13906 R 2 15984 C7 18519 T 2 18775 R 3
13913 R 4 16874 C7 18618 R 3 19449 R 2
13921 R 2 17408 T 3 18620 R 3 22607 T 2
13947 R 4 17523 T 3 18695 R 2 22707 R 3

Taiwan Only

Primary 16832 C8 21488 C1 22735 TRC2

Second. 14367 C1 16347 C2 21421 RC3
10958 C1 14874 C2 18121 R 2 22646 TR 2
11417 RC1 15031 C1

Hong Kong and Macau Only

Primary 17971 C8 20426 C2

Second. 14597 T 2 14841 C1 17012 C3
18836 C3 20529 C3

65 FOLKLORE AND LITTLE TRADITIONS
民俗　民間伝承

66 SELF-CONCEPTION IN RELATION TO OUTSIDERS
「華夷」「中外」之分辨及對異族之觀念
「華夷」「中外」等異民族に対する観念

18972 TR 2 21285 T 3 22567 T 1 22652 TR 3
19039 TRC2 21342 TR 2 22580 T 2 22657 TR 1
19044 TRC2 21374 R 3 22586 T 3 22666 TR 2
19217 TR 3 21404 TRC1 22594 T 2 22672 TR 1
19490 R 2 21659 T 1 22614 T 3 22681 R 3
19752 T 1 22074 T 2 22620 T 1 22694 R 3
20173 TR 1 22133 TR 2 22629 T 2 22720 R 3
20540 T 2 22225 TRC2 22631 T 1 22728 RC2
20790 TR 4 22555 T 2 22637 T 1 22730 TRC1
20934 R 3 22559 T 2 22645 TR 1 22740 TRC2
21279 T 2 22561 T 1 22650 TR 3

PRIMARY: INCLUSIONS

10290 TR 2 14216 TR 1 18525 T 2 22560 T 1
10510 T 2 14395 T 2 18558 TR 2 22578 T 2
12589 T 2 14468 R 2 18971 TR 2 22588 T 1
12940 T 1 18073 T 2 18984 TR 1 22618 T 2
13856 T 2 18368 T 1 21712 T 2 22690 R 3
13878 TR 2 18443 T 2 22518 T 1

PRIMARY: JOURNAL ARTICLES

10663 T 2 14266 TRC1 22032 T 1 22626 T 2
10664 T 2 15194 TRC2 22189 RC1 22634 T 1
11210 T 1 18719 R 2 22512 T 1 22638 T 1
11892 C2 19584 RC3 22515 T 3 22640 T 1
12898 T 4 19614 T 3 22579 T 4 22651 TR 2
13124 T 2 20785 T 4 22593 T 2 22665 TR 2
13554 R 3 21619 T 1 22604 T 3 22705 R 1
13867 T 4 21658 T 1 22611 T 1 22742 RC1
13950 R 2 21844 TRC2 22624 T 1

SECONDARY: MONOGRAPHS

10004 T 2 11692 TR 2 14560 T 3 20576 T 2
10025 T 2 11703 TR 2 14696 TR 1 20826 TR 2
10045 T 2 11708 TR 2 15063 R 2 20960 TRC2
10053 T 2 11857 TRC2 15134 TR 4 20994 TRC5
10074 TR 2 12593 T 2 15136 TR 2 21262 T 2
10077 TR 2 12598 T 2 15158 TRC2 21269 T 2
10106 R 2 12600 T 3 15161 TRC2 21302 T 2
10107 R 2 12624 TR 2 15166 TRC2 21304 TR 2
10108 R 2 12629 TR 2 15191 RC2 21333 TR 2
10129 TRC2 12900 T 1 17572 R 3 21337 TR 2
10144 C2 13222 R 2 18042 TRC2 21349 TR 1
10328 T 2 13457 T 3 18077 T 2 21350 TR 3
10346 TR 2 13461 T 4 18102 TR 2 21366 R 2
10526 T 2 13485 T 1 18306 R 2 21368 R 2
10539 T 1 13502 TR 1 18379 T 1 21425 TRC5
10557 T 1 13683 TR 1 18450 T 2 21467 TRC1
10586 T 1 13762 TRC1 18492 T 2 21603 T 3
10645 T 1 13812 T 2 18494 T 2 21718 TR 1
10700 TR 2 13846 T 2 18534 TR 2 21788 TR 1
10803 R 2 13864 T 2 18540 TR 2 21847 TRC2
10804 R 3 13873 TR 2 18545 TR 2 21853 TRC2
10806 R 2 13876 TR 2 18794 TRC2 22027 T 4
10850 RC1 13902 R 2 18852 T 2 22082 TR 1
11241 T 2 13916 R 2 18904 T 2 22088 TR 1
11299 TR 3 13997 RC2 19534 R 2 22206 TRC1
11603 TRC1 14112 TR 1 19650 RC2 22474 TRC1
11605 RC2 14174 T 3 19774 T 1 22866 T 2
11665 T 2 14175 T 1 20463 R 3 22905 TR 3

SECONDARY: INCLUSIONS

10032 T 2 12772 TRC2 18478 T 1 21317 TR 1
10073 TR 2 12934 T 2 19475 TR 4 22059 T 1
10216 TRC2 14203 T 1 20111 TRC2 22081 TR 1
10261 TRC4 18418 T 1 20594 T 3 22817 TRC2
10288 TR 1 18470 T 2 20981 TRC2 22864 T 1
11556 T 1

SECONDARY: JOURNAL ARTICLES

10272 T 3 13629 T 2 18303 R 2 21318 TR 1
10285 TR 2 13855 T 2 18407 T 2 21469 TRC2
10741 R 1 14284 TRC1 18786 TRC2 21689 T 2
12585 T 2 14399 T 4 18995 R 2 21835 TRC1
12679 TR 1 14710 R 1 19219 TR 2 21855 TRC2
13017 R 3 15126 T 2 19653 RC1 22139 TR 1
13106 C4 17142 T 3 19998 T 1 22214 TRC1

MAINLAND CHINA

PRIMARY: MONOGRAPHS

10019 T 2 10097 R 2 10165 C2 10758 R 4
10036 T 2 10098 R 2 10303 TRC1 10768 R 4
10047 T 2 10099 R 2 10338 TR 2 10821 R 2
10055 T 2 10110 TRC2 10519 T 4 10838 R 4
10065 T 2 10128 TRC2 10631 T 2 10844 R 4
10067 TR 2 10134 C2 10677 T 2 11154 C1
10069 TR 2 10135 C2 10702 TR 2 11266 TR 1
10081 TR 2 10156 C2 10712 TR 2 11291 TR 2
11336 R 2 14160 T 2 18653 R 2 22572 T 2
11358 R 1 14164 T 2 18854 T 1 22575 T 1
11545 T 1 14178 T 2 18945 T 2 22585 T 1
11578 TR 1 14274 TRC2 18987 TR 2 22591 T 1
11586 TR 2 14404 TR 3 18991 TR 4 22595 T 5
11601 R 2 14497 R 2 19062 C2 22599 T 2
11606 RC1 14584 T 2 19246 R 5 22602 T 1
11607 TRC1 14652 TR 2 19277 R 4 22605 T 2
11611 RC1 14670 TR 4 19302 C5 22609 T 3
11627 C2 14683 TR 1 19801 TR 1 22619 T 2
11654 C2 14685 TR 2 20294 TR 2 22644 TR 2
11705 TR 2 14692 TR 1 20823 TR 4 22648 TR 2
11812 R 2 14943 C2 20973 TRC1 22653 TR 1
11883 C2 15123 C2 21265 T 2 22655 TR 3
12109 C2 15309 T 2 21288 T 1 22658 TR 1
12222 TR 7 15506 C2 21300 T 2 22667 TR 1
12590 T 2 15856 C2 21311 TR 2 22669 TR 1
12653 TR 1 17311 RC2 21325 TR 2 22673 TR 4
12778 TRC1 17770 R 1 21336 TR 1 22674 TR 1
12921 T 2 18098 T 3 21361 TR 1 22679 R 2
12963 TR 2 18126 R 3 21373 R 1 22688 R 1
13163 TR 2 18142 R 2 22071 T 1 22689 R 1
13458 T 2 18145 R 2 22087 TR 1 22692 R 1
13470 T 4 18183 RC1 22089 TR 2 22699 R 3
13880 TR 2 18378 T 2 22106 TR 1 22710 R 2
13896 R 2 18416 T 4 22118 TR 1 22711 R 1
13905 R 2 18430 T 2 22131 TR 2 22714 R 2
13914 R 2 18484 T 1 22210 TRC2 22717 R 2
13928 R 2 18596 R 2 22375 C2 22731 TRC1
13951 R 2 18608 R 2 22530 T 1 22734 RC2
13957 R 2 18619 R 2 22556 T 2 22746 C1
13958 R 2 18649 R 1 22568 T 3 22769 C2
13959 R 2

PRIMARY: INCLUSIONS

10080 TR 2 14852 C4 19040 TRC2 22548 T 1
10295 R 2 15799 RC2 19279 R 4 22565 T 2
10334 T 2 18110 R 2 19365 T 2 22581 T 1
10603 T 2 18370 T 2 21436 T 1 22639 T 1
11013 T 2 18429 T 2 21901 TRC1 22643 TR 1
11700 TR 2 18533 TR 2 22148 R 2 22649 TR 1
13532 R 4 18555 TR 2 22192 RC2 22659 TR 1
13859 T 2 18601 R 2 22209 TRC1 22661 TR 2
13865 T 2 18612 R 2 22507 T 1 22737 TRC1
14176 T 2 18632 R 2 22516 T 1 22739 TRC1
14190 T 1 18672 R 2 22525 T 2 22743 RC1
14411 R 4 18799 RC2 22533 T 1 22878 T 1
14851 C1 19029 TRC1 22547 T 1

PRIMARY: JOURNAL ARTICLES

10009 T 2 14072 C1 20865 R 2 22608 T 1
10310 C1 14499 R 3 21283 T 2 22613 T 1
10530 T 2 14500 R 4 21620 T 1 22621 T 1
10535 T 1 14511 R 2 21699 T 1 22625 T 2
10589 T 1 14613 T 1 21714 T 1 22633 T 1
10683 T 1 14814 C4 21785 TR 1 22636 T 1
10691 TR 1 15128 T 4 21839 TRC1 22656 TR 1
10743 R 2 15137 TR 1 21899 TRC1 22663 TR 2
10786 R 2 15157 R 4 22039 T 1 22668 TR 1
11023 R 2 15193 TRC1 22042 T 1 22671 TR 1
11024 R 4 15269 C1 22049 T 1 22675 TR 1
11041 RC2 18094 T 3 22058 T 1 22676 TR 1
11197 T 1 18107 R 2 22077 TR 2 22685 R 1
11238 T 3 18116 R 3 22119 TR 2 22686 R 1
11260 TR 2 18141 R 2 22149 R 2 22687 R 4
11412 TRC1 18150 R 1 22150 R 5 22697 R 2
11416 TRC1 18157 R 2 22208 TRC1 22700 R 3
11543 T 1 18369 T 1 22245 TRC1 22702 R 1
11602 RC1 18580 R 2 22317 C1 22703 R 1
11649 C2 18652 R 3 22505 T 1 22709 R 1
11662 T 2 18677 R 2 22524 T 1 22721 R 2
11734 R 3 18758 R 1 22528 T 1 22722 R 2
11954 C2 18762 R 4 22529 T 3 22725 TRC1
12122 C2 18806 RC2 22540 T 1 22726 TRC3
12129 C2 18866 T 1 22543 T 1 22727 TRC1
12566 T 2 18928 T 2 22544 T 3 22729 RC1
12607 T 1 19021 R 2 22549 T 1 22745 C2
13829 T 1 19249 R 3 22551 T 1 22748 C1
13838 T 2 19573 R 3 22554 T 1 22756 C1
13839 T 2 20148 T 2 22564 T 2 22757 C1
13919 R 2 20441 R 2 22569 T 2 22766 C1
13933 R 2 20446 R 1 22573 T 1 22767 C2
14004 TRC2 20586 T 4 22587 T 3 22807 TRC1
14044 C2

SECONDARY: MONOGRAPHS

10005 T 2 12572 T 3 14736 R 4 19697 TR 3
10020 T 2 12597 T 2 14783 RC2 19705 R 2
10043 T 2 12606 T 2 14885 C1 19719 T 2
10044 T 2 12631 TR 2 14921 C1 20034 T 2
10049 T 2 12637 TR 1 14974 C2 20166 TR 2
10068 TR 2 12674 TR 2 15073 R 2 20182 TR 2
10079 TR 2 12676 TR 1 15140 TR 2 20204 R 2
10103 R 2 12811 C2 15156 R 2 20430 TR 2
10104 R 2 12914 T 3 15163 RC2 20431 TR 4
10124 TRC2 12950 TR 2 15168 TRC2 20432 TR 2
10130 C2 13152 TR 2 15297 C2 20444 R 2
10132 C2 13165 TR 7 15524 C7 20462 R 2
10133 C2 13366 C4 15938 TR 2 20473 RC2
10140 C2 13464 T 3 16277 TR 2 20502 C2
10142 C2 13489 TR 3 16395 T 2 20749 T 2
10145 C2 13511 TR 2 17575 R 2 20798 TR 2
10149 C2 13513 TR 4 17895 RC2 20926 R 2
10150 C2 13519 TR 1 17979 TR 7 20962 RC2
10153 C2 13520 TR 2 18041 TRC2 21259 T 2
10159 C2 13523 TR 1 18143 R 2 21260 T 2
10164 C2 13570 R 1 18148 R 2 21286 T 1
10168 C2 13659 TR 4 18161 R 2 21307 TR 2
10172 C2 13674 TR 2 18172 RC2 21321 TR 2
10201 TR 2 13740 R 3 18187 RC2 21335 TR 1
10508 T 3 13743 R 2 18387 T 2 21346 TR 2
10587 T 2 13750 R 2 18408 T 1 21355 TR 2
10660 T 2 13756 R 1 18454 T 2 21360 TR 2
10695 TR 2 13760 R 2 18526 T 2 21379 R 2
10706 TR 2 13819 T 1 18530 TR 2 21381 R 1
10715 TR 2 13847 T 1 18535 TR 1 21401 RC3
10726 TR 2 13849 T 4 18552 TR 1 21410 TRC2
10727 TR 3 13858 T 2 18557 TR 2 21414 RC2
10729 TR 2 13882 TR 2 18562 TR 2 21416 RC2
10813 R 2 13883 TR 2 18597 R 4 21417 TRC2
10814 R 2 13884 TR 2 18610 R 2 21422 TRC2
10819 R 2 13885 TR 1 18630 R 2 21424 TRC2
10858 TRC2 13893 R 2 18635 R 2 21444 TR 1
10879 RC3 13901 R 2 18655 R 2 21447 TR 2
10885 RC4 13903 R 2 18660 R 2 21450 TR 2
10887 TRC2 13963 R 2 18666 R 1 21457 R 1
10890 TRC2 13969 R 2 18674 R 2 21459 R 4
10937 C2 13970 R 2 18685 R 2 21504 TR 2
10978 C2 13975 R 2 18709 R 2 21563 C1
10997 C2 13991 RC1 18717 R 2 21570 C1
11003 C2 14015 RC1 18722 R 2 21585 C2
11087 C3 14018 TRC2 18725 R 2 21624 T 2
11094 C2 14109 TR 2 18730 R 2 21723 TR 1
11106 C2 14209 T 1 18780 R 2 21758 TR 1
11113 C4 14219 TR 2 18795 TRC2 21825 R 1
11144 C2 14231 TR 4 18804 TRC2 21873 TRC3
11230 T 1 14263 RC1 18812 RC2 21887 TRC2
11393 TRC2 14279 RC2 18817 RC2 21936 C3
11563 T 4 14305 C4 18819 RC2 21937 C2
11587 TR 4 14369 C2 18822 TRC2 22112 TR 2
11595 R 1 14509 R 3 18827 RC2 22117 TR 2
11625 C2 14510 R 4 18915 T 2 22172 R 2
11672 T 4 14512 RC2 18952 TR 2 22179 R 1
11740 R 2 14592 T 1 18988 TR 2 22185 TRC1
11748 R 2 14650 TR 1 18989 TR 2 22233 RC2
11783 R 2 14655 TR 1 19063 C2 22243 TRC1
11790 R 2 14661 TR 1 19078 RC8 22260 RC1
11848 RC2 14681 TR 1 19422 C3 22423 TR 7
11885 C2 14684 TR 1 19455 R 8 22486 RC8
11894 C2 14688 TR 1 19517 R 3 22868 T 1
12002 C2 14703 TR 2 19551 R 2 22939 R 2
12027 C2 14719 R 4 19639 R 1 22991 TRC2
12123 C2

SECONDARY: INCLUSIONS

10051 T 2 12731 R 2 15135 TR 3 18808 TRC2
10542 T 2 13260 R 2 15153 R 3 18832 TRC1
10650 T 2 13333 C2 15186 RC1 18992 R 2
10671 T 3 13357 C3 15188 RC2 19562 R 4
10750 R 2 13408 C4 17766 R 2 19709 TRC3
10918 C4 13834 T 2 17978 T 2 20081 C2
10919 C2 13920 R 2 18088 T 2 20433 TR 3
11007 C1 14232 TR 1 18452 T 2 20975 TRC1
11245 T 1 14280 RC2 18515 T 2 21303 TR 2
11252 TR 1 14324 C1 18561 TR 2 21326 TR 2
11284 TR 1 14406 TR 4 18605 R 2 21372 R 2
11392 TRC1 14645 TR 1 18626 R 2 21486 C2
11484 C1 14674 TR 2 18628 R 2 21643 T 1
11942 C2 14760 R 1 18633 R 2 21767 TR 1
12121 C2 15101 C2 18745 R 2 21815 R 1

21848 TRC2 21934 C1 22096 TR 1 22238 RC4
21871 TRC1 21958 C1 22205 TRC1 22924 TR 1
21920 C1 22034 T 2

SECONDARY: JOURNAL ARTICLES

10411 C2 12131 C2 15266 C1 19715 TR 2
10527 T 1 12153 C2 17596 C2 20054 TR 1
10536 T 2 12263 R 2 17936 TR 1 20452 R 1
10538 T 1 12266 R 2 18086 T 1 20453 R 3
10571 T 1 12311 R 7 18095 T 3 20520 C2
10687 TR 1 12431 C2 18222 C2 20521 C2
10689 TR 1 12610 T 4 18228 C2 20914 R 2
10728 TR 1 12797 C2 18352 C1 21284 T 2
10734 TR 2 12851 C1 18384 T 1 21548 C2
10766 R 2 12916 T 5 18395 T 1 21560 C1
10784 R 1 13148 TR 1 18435 T 2 21604 T 1
10815 R 1 13159 TR 2 18504 T 2 21671 T 1
10835 R 4 13161 TR 2 18517 T 1 21680 T 1
10877 RC2 13197 R 3 18593 R 2 21716 T 1
10878 TRC1 13401 C2 18648 R 1 21809 R 1
11012 T 1 13487 TR 1 18698 R 2 21846 TRC1
11112 C1 13648 TR 4 18705 R 2 21967 C1
11114 C4 13800 T 3 18714 R 2 21973 C1
11129 C1 13821 T 1 18737 R 1 21975 C3
11189 T 1 13840 T 2 18757 R 2 22069 T 2
11240 T 1 13850 T 1 18803 RC1 22093 TR 1
11259 TR 1 13851 T 1 18821 RC2 22097 TR 1
11267 TR 1 13853 T 4 18826 TRC1 22098 TR 2
11288 TR 1 14039 C1 18830 RC2 22105 TR 2
11312 R 1 14162 T 1 18893 T 2 22120 TR 1
11386 TRC1 14177 T 2 18938 T 1 22155 R 1
11401 RC1 14233 R 3 18961 TR 1 22163 R 1
11446 C1 14566 T 2 18964 TR 2 22171 R 2
11453 C2 14593 T 1 19014 R 2 22180 R 2
11533 C1 14612 T 2 19034 RC2 22216 TRC1
11592 TR 1 14663 TR 1 19067 C1 22246 TRC2
11600 R 1 14673 TR 1 19187 C8 22288 RC1
11636 C1 14726 R 2 19221 TR 3 22306 C1
11645 C1 14759 R 4 19236 R 1 22316 C1
11661 T 4 14776 R 1 19352 TR 2 22365 C2
11717 TR 2 15008 C3 19392 C2 22771 T 2
11761 R 2 15050 TR 2 19512 R 4 22828 C1
11762 R 2 15132 TR 2 19561 R 3 22834 C1
11764 R 2 15138 TR 2 19572 R 2 22852 C1
11836 R 1 15159 RC1 19574 R 3 22874 T 1
12116 C2 15178 TRC2 19576 R 3 22934 R 1
12117 C2 15179 RC2 19599 C4

THE EIGHTEEN PROVINCES

PRIMARY 15306 T 2 18874 T 2 22534 T 1
10006 T 2 15543 C2 18930 T 2 22537 T 1
10056 T 2 15733 T 2 18948 T 1 22553 T 2
10091 R 2 15965 R 3 19053 TRC2 22558 T 2
10175 C2 16183 T 2 20004 TR 1 22574 T 2
10544 T 3 16478 C2 20449 R 4 22590 T 3
10563 T 3 16935 T 2 20450 R 2 22603 T 1
11567 T 2 18080 T 2 20565 T 2 22615 T 2
11571 T 1 18083 T 1 20699 C2 22628 T 3
11681 T 2 18127 R 3 21685 T 2 22630 T 2
12584 T 2 18364 T 2 21778 TR 1 22641 T 2
13521 TR 3 18405 T 2 22029 T 3 22680 R 3
13925 R 2 18436 T 2 22086 TR 1 22683 R 2
13934 R 2 18502 T 2 22110 TR 1 22684 R 1
13952 R 2 18590 R 3 22181 R 3 22691 R 3
14117 R 2 18654 R 2 22514 T 1 22708 R 3
15038 T 2 18850 T 3 22519 T 1 22760 C3
15127 T 1 18859 T 2 22527 T 3 22761 C3
15148 R 4

SECONDARY: MONOGRAPHS

10027 T 2 13831 T 2 17614 R 2 20822 TR 4
10087 R 2 13866 T 2 17945 R 2 21277 T 2
10102 R 2 14092 T 2 18138 R 3 21456 R 2
10170 C2 14555 T 1 18382 T 2 21672 T 1
10174 C2 14671 TR 4 18461 T 2 21786 TR 1
10839 R 2 14829 C2 18583 R 2 21791 TR 1
11667 T 2 15067 R 2 18609 R 2 21796 TR 1
12567 T 2 15145 R 4 18621 R 3 22009 R 2
12770 TRC2 15830 C2 19008 R 2 22076 TR 1
13155 TR 4 15931 T 4 19012 R 2 22132 TR 1
13637 T 2 16806 C7 20126 T 5

SECONDARY: INCLUSIONS

13468 T 3 15243 C2 17808 C3 18523 T 2
14680 TR 4 16920 T 2 18513 T 2 18602 R 2
18645 R 7 18776 R 1 21301 T 1 22092 TR 3
18662 R 3 18778 R 2 21648 T 1 22865 T 3
18774 R 2

SECONDARY: JOURNAL ARTICLES

10533 T 2 13460 T 3 15149 R 1 18586 R 2
10569 T 2 13813 T 2 15951 TR 3 18769 R 3
10682 T 2 13890 R 2 15969 R 3 19618 R 7
11579 TR 1 14277 TRC3 16894 C2 20668 C2
11655 T 1 14578 T 1 17573 R 2 21096 C4
11824 R 2 14660 TR 2 17749 C2 21386 RC3
12225 TR 8 14755 R 3 17973 T 2 21473 TRC2
12935 T 1 14779 TRC2 18425 T 1 21615 T 1
12938 T 3 14826 C3 18482 T 2 22218 RC1
13128 T 2 15131 T 1 18546 TR 2 22389 T 1
13167 TR 4

NORTH CHINA BROADLY CONCEIVED

PRIMARY 16380 T 7 18664 R 2 22141 R 3
10452 R 2 17577 R 2 18712 R 7 22511 T 2
10580 T 2 18146 R 2 18872 T 2 22532 T 2
11728 R 2 18160 R 3 18914 T 2 22562 T 3
12630 TR 1 18371 T 2 18960 TR 2 22584 T 2
12655 TR 2 18433 T 2 19011 R 2 22623 T 2
13832 T 2 18493 T 2 19580 R 3 22660 TR 2
14195 T 3 18497 T 2 20716 T 2 22695 R 2
15752 T 2 18595 R 7 20780 T 2 22715 R 2
16119 R 2 18622 R 2

SECOND. 12505 C8 16169 T 2 18731 R 2
10064 T 2 12913 T 5 16732 RC2 18738 R 1
10679 T 2 13894 R 2 17846 R 7 18747 R 1
10827 R 2 13962 R 2 18496 T 2 20835 R 2
10989 C5 15081 R 2 18688 R 2 21292 T 2
11791 R 2 15082 R 2 18690 R 7 22394 T 2
11821 R 2 15324 T 2

MANCHURIA

PRIMARY 11696 TR 2 13837 T 7 20596 T 2
10581 T 1 11732 R 2 14129 RC2 20795 TR 2
10719 TR 1 11755 R 2 15674 TR 2 22506 T 2
10787 R 3 11823 R 2 16929 T 2 22654 TR 2
11015 T 2 11826 R 2 17229 R 4 22693 R 2
11345 R 2 12663 TR 2 18581 R 2 22718 R 1
11684 TR 2 13147 TR 2 18942 T 5 22719 R 3
11695 TR 1

SECOND. 11712 TR 2 15659 T 2 17566 R 8
10163 C2 11714 TR 2 15661 T 8 17688 T 2
10354 TR 2 11715 TR 2 15664 T 2 18715 R 2
10381 R 2 12969 TR 2 15665 T 7 18739 R 2
10421 C2 13039 R 4 15668 TR 2 20276 R 4
10796 R 2 13146 TR 2 15676 TR 2 20715 T 3
10911 C2 13215 R 1 16065 R 2 20731 T 3
11337 R 1 15583 T 8 17540 T 2 20813 TR 2

NORTHERN CHINA

PRIMARY 15338 T 7 18868 T 2 22610 T 3
10644 T 2 15355 T 2 20128 T 3 22612 T 2
11135 C3 15373 TR 3 20505 C3 22617 T 2
11541 T 2 15389 TR 3 20559 T 3 22632 T 3
12741 R 3 15952 TR 2 20579 T 3 22704 R 3
13803 T 2 16536 T 2 22509 T 7 22706 R 6
13891 R 2 17522 T 7 22520 T 3 22712 R 7
13974 R 2 17529 T 3 22541 T 3 22747 C2
14604 T 3 17532 T 2 22546 T 3 22750 C3
14731 R 3 17552 T 3 22576 T 2 22751 C3
15274 C3 18403 T 2 22577 T 2 22753 C3
15304 C3 18422 T 3 22583 T 4 22763 C3
15320 T 3

SECOND. 14427 R 2 15806 TRC3 17780 C3
10505 T 3 14551 T 3 15810 TRC2 18092 T 3
10528 T 3 14573 T 3 15828 C3 18096 T 3
10529 T 3 14585 T 3 16256 TR 3 18398 T 2
10547 T 3 14610 T 3 16390 T 2 18434 T 1
10673 T 3 14632 TR 3 16513 T 8 18444 T 2
10783 R 2 14877 C3 16671 R 2 18456 T 7
10941 C3 14938 C3 16926 T 2 18658 R 7
11568 T 3 15045 T 2 16966 R 2 18847 T 3
11597 R 3 15362 T 7 17282 R 7 18958 TR 3
12931 T 3 15366 T 3 17292 R 2 18967 TR 3
13964 R 7 15367 T 2 17409 T 2 19620 R 2
14182 T 3 15407 R 3 17526 T 8 19825 R 3
14204 T 3 15416 R 3 17556 T 3 20060 R 3
14214 TR 3 15460 RC7 17625 T 3 20206 R 3
20281 T 5 20727 T 4 21278 T 3 21359 TR 3
20435 R 3 20781 T 2 21298 T 2 21438 T 3
20436 R 3 21134 C3 21344 TR 2 22374 C3
20458 R 3 21264 T 3

NORTHWESTERN CHINA AND FRONTIER REGIONS

PRIMARY 15350 T 2 18584 R 4 22682 R 2
10725 TR 2 15386 TR 2 18706 R 5 22698 R 2
10759 R 2 15620 C2 18911 T 2 22701 R 2
10863 TRC2 15660 T 7 18924 T 2 22713 R 5
10874 TRC2 15671 TR 7 18993 R 2 22732 TRC2
10939 C2 15673 TR 7 22531 T 2 22738 RC2
11099 C2 16735 RC8 22598 T 4 22749 C2
12011 C2 17772 RC7 22616 T 1 22754 C2
12747 R 2 18220 C1 22642 T 4 22765 C2
13799 T 1 18245 C2 22662 TR 1 22768 C2
13895 R 2 18302 R 2

SECOND. 13822 T 7 16628 R 2 17474 R 2
10332 T 2 13981 R 1 16647 R 2 18340 C2
10369 R 2 14106 TR 2 16751 TRC2 18372 T 4
10401 C2 14782 RC1 16786 C2 18956 TR 2
10427 C2 15323 T 4 16859 C8 20621 TR 1
10921 C4 15391 TR 2 16927 T 2 21364 R 2
10922 C1 15753 T 2 17023 T 6 22005 R 1
10957 C1 16331 TRC1 17043 R 2 22462 R 7
13814 T 2 16606 R 8

SOUTH CHINA BROADLY CONCEIVED

PRIMARY 13835 T 1 16910 T 4 22026 T 1
10028 T 2 13941 R 3 18129 R 3 22513 T 2
10046 T 2 15205 C2 18412 T 2 22521 T 1
11658 T 2 15361 T 2 18459 T 2 22522 T 2
12265 R 2 15721 T 2 18485 T 4 22535 T 3
12569 T 2 15722 T 2 18486 T 2 22592 T 1
12570 T 2 16092 T 4 18524 T 2 22601 T 2
12618 T 3 16388 T 2 18875 T 2 22664 TR 4

SECOND. 12920 T 4 16914 T 2 18500 T 2
10326 T 2 13887 R 2 17138 T 2 18512 T 3
10593 T 1 13889 R 2 17543 T 2 18670 R 2
11017 T 4 13955 R 2 17581 TRC1 18763 R 2
12191 T 2 15042 T 2 17931 T 7 18771 R 3
12579 T 2 15332 T 2 18137 R 1 19006 R 4
12581 T 2 15726 T 2 18386 T 2 20274 T 3
12756 R 2 15749 T 3 18449 T 2 21294 T 1
12879 T 2 16378 T 2 18455 T 2 21299 T 2
12891 T 2 16520 T 2 18471 T 1 21865 TRC2

EAST CENTRAL CHINA

PRIMARY 15950 TR 3 18487 T 2 22582 T 3
13924 R 3 16091 T 3 20600 T 2 22589 T 2
14561 T 3 16108 TR 3 20886 R 3 22596 T 3
15348 T 3 16109 TR 3 21661 T 1 22696 R 3
15377 TR 3 17735 R 3 21707 T 3 22716 R 3
15744 T 2 17943 R 3 22536 T 3 22744 C3
15921 T 3 18354 C3 22538 T 3 22755 C3
15929 T 3 18453 T 3 22539 T 2 22764 C3
15948 TR 3 18464 T 3 22571 T 2

SECOND. 15396 R 3 16417 R 3 18026 R 3
10321 T 2 15493 C7 16668 R 7 18392 T 2
12911 T 1 15632 TR 3 16905 T 3 18404 T 3
13802 T 2 15720 T 2 16980 R 3 18465 T 3
14393 C2 15728 T 3 17052 R 3 18522 T 3
14552 T 3 15731 T 2 17161 T 3 18918 T 3
14665 TR 3 15930 T 3 17412 TR 3 18932 T 4
14728 R 4 15939 TR 3 17431 T 3 19023 R 3
14786 TRC3 15946 TR 3 17555 T 3 19069 C3
15143 R 3 15964 R 3 17653 C3 19509 R 3
15307 T 3 16407 TR 3 17858 R 2 19511 R 3
15388 TR 3 16409 TR 3

CENTRAL YANGTZE PROVINCES

PRIMARY 14792 TRC3 17554 T 4 18895 T 4
14187 T 2 15129 T 2 17630 TR 4 20802 TR 3
14682 TR 1

SECOND. 17576 R 2 19726 TR 7 20275 T 4
11726 R 2 18582 R 2 20199 R 7 20379 T 4

SOUTHWESTERN CHINA

PRIMARY 10566 T 2 10651 T 2 15316 T 2
10179 C2 10639 T 2 12601 T 2 15715 T 2

66 Self-Conception

16511 T 7 18861 T 4 20475 RC4 22542 T 2
17520 T 2 18889 T 2 21892 TRC2 22552 T 8
17535 T 4 18892 T 3 22508 T 2 22570 T 3
17538 T 2 18922 T 2 22517 T 2 22597 T 3
18491 T 2 20456 R 3 22523 T 2 22677 R 2

Second. 15638 R 2 16911 T 2 19022 R 2
10359 R 2 15716 T 3 16913 T 2 20551 T 3
12626 TR 2 15717 T 2 17139 T 2 20574 T 2
12912 T 2 15738 T 7 18087 T 4 20583 T 2
14571 T 4 15740 T 2 18300 T 2 20711 T 3
14616 T 3 16531 T 7 18365 T 3 20839 R 3
15401 R 2 16688 R 8 18925 T 2 20863 R 2
15581 T 2 16787 C2 18962 TR 1 22483 TRC8
15593 R 2

Southeastern China

Primary 17533 T 7 18860 T 2 22526 T 3
10275 T 2 17546 T 3 18863 T 1 22545 T 4
10522 T 3 17615 RC2 18876 T 2 22550 T 4
12996 R 3 17657 T 3 18878 T 2 22557 T 3
14575 T 3 17920 T 7 19013 R 3 22563 T 2
15359 T 2 18428 T 3 19043 TRC2 22566 T 3
15364 T 3 18483 T 2 19045 TRC2 22606 T 3
15376 TR 2 18488 T 5 19209 T 3 22607 T 2
15742 T 2 18490 T 2 19499 R 3 22622 T 3
16218 T 2 18519 T 2 19501 R 3 22635 T 1
16382 T 2 18620 R 3 20791 TR 3 22647 TR 1
16387 T 2 18686 R 2 22398 T 4 22678 R 3
16389 T 2 18851 T 7 22510 T 2 22707 R 3

Second. 13953 R 3 16798 C2 18734 R 2
10271 T 4 14761 R 7 16839 C2 18775 R 3
10273 T 4 15339 T 3 16919 T 2 18899 T 2
10278 T 2 15353 T 2 17151 T 3 19205 T 3
10552 T 2 15358 T 8 17268 R 3 19429 T 3
10625 T 1 15458 TRC2 17521 T 7 19434 T 3
10668 T 2 15497 C2 17523 T 3 19437 T 3
11668 T 2 15572 C2 17559 TR 2 19454 R 7
11828 R 2 15714 T 3 17589 C2 19557 R 4
12954 TR 3 15718 T 2 18156 R 1 20555 T 3
13016 R 3 15780 R 3 18438 T 2 21769 TR 3
13808 T 3 16530 T 2 18618 R 3 22887 T 3
13913 R 4 16712 R 7

Taiwan Only

Primary 12070 C2 18981 TR 2 22735 TRC2
10325 T 2 14224 TR 2 21481 C3 22741 TRC2
10653 T 2 15351 T 2 22600 T 2 22752 C5
10674 T 2 18121 R 2 22627 T 7 22759 C1
11044 RC2 18903 T 2 22646 TR 2 22770 C3
12008 C2

Second. 13137 T 2 15439 R 2 18908 T 2
10345 TR 2 14367 C1 15586 TR 2 19068 C2
10638 T 1 14554 T 2 16042 C2 19769 T 2
10675 T 2 14879 C3 16357 C3 21421 RC3
10950 C2 15369 TR 2 18019 TR 2 21487 C1
11500 C1 15438 R 2 18440 T 1 22023 C3
11678 T 2

Hong Kong and Macau Only

Primary 16008 C3 19693 T 3 22670 TR 1
10312 C3 16135 C3 20267 C3 22723 TRC4
11031 R 2 16918 T 4 20552 T 3 22724 RC2
15461 TRC2 17600 C4 20564 T 8 22733 TRC3
15468 TRC3 17602 C3 21549 C3 22736 TRC2
15940 TR 3 17635 RC3 21574 C3 22758 C3
15941 TR 3 17958 C7 22500 C3 22762 C2
15945 TR 2 17985 RC2

Second. 15526 C3 19591 C2 20529 C3
11231 T 1 15976 TRC2 19710 TRC3 20688 C2
12937 T 3 16132 C2 19858 RC7 21578 C3
14597 T 2 18314 TRC4 20272 C7 23034 C2
15382 TR 3 19553 R 3

70 Chinese Scholars of Chinese Society

華人研究中國社會

中国人学者による中国社会研究

Geographic China Broadly Conceived

Primary 21402 TRC1 22518 T 1 22817 TRC2
10681 T 1 21702 T 1 22777 T 1 22819 TRC1
10862 TRC2 21743 TR 1 22778 T 1 22821 RC1
10892 TRC2 21803 TR 1 22779 T 1 22822 RC1
11858 TRC2 21847 TRC2 22780 T 1 22826 C1
12785 TRC3 21853 TRC2 22799 R 1 22860 T 1
12801 C2 21857 TRC1 22809 TRC1 22866 T 2
17972 C2 21902 TRC2 22812 RC1 22964 RC2
21276 T 2 21903 TRC1 22813 TRC1 23042 C1
21392 TRC2 22477 RC1 22816 RC1 23058 C1

Second. 11682 T 1 18414 T 1 22634 T 1
10211 TRC1 12190 T 2 18719 R 2 22637 T 1
10220 TRC2 17951 RC2 19403 RC2 22970 TRC1
11261 TR 1 18079 T 1 21318 TR 1 23011 C1
11264 TR 1 18375 T 2 21619 T 1

Mainland China

Primary: Monographs
11011 T 1 21361 TR 1 22111 TR 1 22811 TRC1
12270 R 7 21632 T 1 22772 T 2 22831 C2
14378 C4 21887 TRC2 22787 TR 2 22954 TRC1
14678 TR 3 21891 TRC1 22805 R 2 22961 TRC1
14871 C2 22053 T 1 22806 TRC1

Primary: Inclusions
16110 TR 2 21876 RC1 21916 C2 22327 C1
21357 TR 1 21877 RC3 21920 C1 22335 C1
21747 TR 1 21878 TRC1 21921 C1 22378 C1
21831 RC1 21882 TRC1 21923 C1 22827 C1
21840 TRC2 21893 RC2 21929 C1 22829 C1
21845 TRC1 21894 TRC2 21931 C1 22837 C1
21858 RC1 21910 C1 21959 C1 22857 C2
21872 TRC1

Primary: Journal Articles
10095 R 1 21954 C1 22791 R 2 22834 C1
10717 TR 2 21956 C1 22792 R 1 22836 C2
11471 C1 21968 C3 22793 R 1 22838 C2
11871 TRC2 21972 C1 22794 R 1 22839 C2
13018 R 7 21973 C1 22795 R 1 22841 C1
14256 RC2 21976 C1 22796 R 1 22842 C1
14267 RC1 22288 RC1 22797 R 2 22843 C1
14741 R 3 22489 RC1 22798 R 1 22844 C7
14912 C4 22493 RC2 22803 R 1 22845 C1
17964 C1 22756 C1 22804 R 4 22846 C3
18651 R 2 22771 T 2 22807 TRC1 22847 C1
18800 TRC2 22774 T 1 22810 RC1 22848 C1
19440 T 2 22775 T 1 22814 RC1 22849 C1
20970 TRC1 22781 T 1 22815 RC1 22851 C4
21102 C3 22782 TR 3 22818 RC1 22852 C1
21289 T 1 22783 TR 1 22823 TRC1 22853 C1
21716 T 1 22784 TR 2 22824 TRC1 22854 C1
21792 TR 1 22785 TR 1 22825 C1 22855 C1
21830 TRC2 22786 TR 1 22828 C1 22856 C3
21841 TRC1 22788 TR 1 22830 C1 22916 TR 1
21846 TRC1 22789 TR 1 22832 C1 22932 R 2
21866 TRC1 22790 R 1 22833 C1 23007 TRC1
21935 C1

Second. 14135 C2 20154 T 1 22142 R 1
10235 C2 14231 TR 4 20361 C2 22223 RC2
10313 C2 14299 C2 21723 TR 1 22244 TRC1
10467 C2 14327 C4 21757 TR 1 22350 C1
11202 T 1 14343 C1 21793 TR 1 22432 TR 1
11234 T 1 14522 C2 21848 TRC2 22473 RC2
11482 C1 15015 C1 21859 TRC1 22475 RC1
11693 TR 2 15128 T 4 21864 TRC1 22487 RC7
12410 TRC2 16255 TR 1 21885 TRC2 22543 T 1
13217 R 3 18791 TRC7 21898 RC1 22679 R 2
13408 C4 19393 TR 1 21907 C1 22940 R 2
13858 T 2 19414 C4 21934 C1 22951 TRC1
13859 T 2 19657 RC1 21942 C1 22978 TRC1
13943 R 2 19922 C7 21979 C4 23032 C1
14105 TR 2

The Eighteen Provinces

Primary 21678 T 2 22773 T 2 22801 R 3
12411 TRC8 21700 T 1 22776 T 2 22850 C3
19397 R 2 21765 TR 1 22800 R 2 22928 R 2
19637 R 2 22399 T 2

Second. 15016 C3 18382 T 2 21679 T 4
10569 T 2 15511 C2 18506 T 2 22193 TRC1
13860 T 2 15935 T 2 19401 R 3

North China Broadly Conceived

Primary □

Second. 18634 R 2 22660 TR 2

Manchuria

Primary □

Second. 20047 TR 2

Northern China

Primary 14270 RC3 19411 C3 19438 T 7
22802 R 7

Second. 14641 TR 3 15452 TRC2 17953 TRC3
18092 T 3

Northwestern China and Frontier Regions

□

South China Broadly Conceived

Primary 19399 R 2 21865 TRC2

Second. 18463 T 2 21299 T 2

East Central China

Primary 17734 R 3

Second. 15517 C8 16525 T 8 17839 R 3

Central Yangtze Provinces

Primary □

Second. 15863 T 2

Southwestern China

Primary 21892 TRC2

Second. □

Southeastern China

Primary 21769 TR 3

Second. 10552 T 2

Taiwan Only

Primary 22808 RC1 22820 RC1 22835 C1
22840 C3 22858 C1

Second. 19079 RC8 20319 C2 20333 C3
20372 C3 21009 C2

Hong Kong and Macau Only

Primary □

Second. 14841 C1 19416 C3

Local-Systems Index

An index to entries, arranged by geographic region, type of place, and nature of sources and showing historical era

地方索引

依地理區域、城鄉類別、及資料性質排列、並示歷史時代

地方索引

地区別、都市郷村別、資料の来源別並びに時代を示す索引

Type-of-place subcategories are subdivided by Sources code only when the number of entry numbers exceeds 28. Open squares indicate that the Bibliography lacks entries so classified. Letter suffixes indicate historical era: T (Traditional) for before 1911, R (Republican) for 1911–1949, C (Contemporary) for after 1949. The structure of this index is described fully on p. xli.

1.1 Geographic China Broadly Conceived

廣義的地理中國

地理上の中国全土

1 Place Irrelevant or Type of Place Unspecified

See Historical Index

2 Urban *and* Rural

Field Research

10386 RC 11164 C 16938 TR 21383 R
21850 TRC 23021 C

Primary Sources: Monographs

10010 T 11703 TR 14113 TR 18969 TR
10052 T 11704 TR 14167 T 18972 TR
10053 T 11839 R 14654 TR 19036 TRC
10070 TR 11857 TRC 14657 TR 19044 TRC
10074 TR 11858 TRC 14951 C 19534 R
10106 R 11921 C 15161 TRC 19717 T
10107 R 12019 C 15174 TRC 20109 TRC
10108 R 12203 T 15773 R 20127 T
10114 TRC 12233 TR 15956 TR 20643 R
10139 C 12281 R 16185 T 20766 T
10200 TR 12367 R 17272 R 20826 TR
10207 R 12575 T 17981 TR 20960 TRC
10263 C 12901 T 18077 T 21276 T
10277 T 12947 T 18299 C 21279 T
10407 C 13049 TRC 18375 T 21291 T
10432 C 13144 TR 18388 T 21304 TR
10560 T 13171 TR 18409 T 21306 TR
10615 T 13175 TR 18450 T 21342 TR
10626 T 13222 R 18480 T 21347 TR
10707 TR 13494 TR 18494 T 21399 TRC
10713 TR 13574 TRC 18511 T 21412 RC
10803 R 13619 T 18514 T 21634 T
10828 R 13622 T 18542 TR 21847 TRC
10862 TRC 13627 T 18553 TR 21853 TRC
11047 RC 13649 TR 18560 TR 22074 T
11241 T 13688 TR 18794 TRC 22095 TR
11619 C 13824 T 18801 TRC 22629 T
11665 T 13846 T 18904 T 22740 TRC
11687 TR 13864 T 18936 T 22866 T
11692 TR 13916 R 18937 T
14248 R 18470 T 18539 TR 21712 T
14395 T 18525 T 20306 C 21902 TRC
14468 R 18527 T 20981 TRC 22476 TRC
18073 T

Primary Sources: Inclusions

10188 T 10222 TRC 11859 TRC 12772 TRC
10197 TR 10290 TR 11960 C 12801 C
10210 TRC 10510 T 12190 T 13189 TR
10215 RC 10627 T 12390 TRC 13878 TR
10216 TRC 10892 TRC 12408 TRC 13966 R
10220 TRC 11673 T 12548 C 14097 T

Primary Sources: Journal Articles

10221 RC 11867 TRC 15162 TRC 20955 RC
10287 TR 12202 T 18303 R 21204 TR
10564 T 12238 R 18719 R 21327 TR
10663 T 12246 R 18786 TRC 21328 TR
10666 T 12478 C 18891 T 21408 TRC
10867 RC 12495 C 20010 TR 21844 TRC
11038 RC 12677 TR 20085 T 22265 RC
11213 T 13465 T 20096 T 22491 TRC
11384 TRC 14098 T 20803 TR 22626 T
11779 R 14102 T

Field Research *and* Primary Sources

10363 R 14798 TRC 19055 TRC 20832 R
11045 RC 15175 RC 19503 R 21538 TRC
14145 C 16128 TRC 19859 TRC 21904 RC
14475 R 18976 TR 19978 TRC 22478 TRC
14594 T

Personal Observation: Monographs

10001 T 10162 C 15311 T 20540 T
10013 T 10177 C 15363 T 20615 TR
10014 T 10328 T 16068 RC 20619 TR
10016 T 10611 T 16158 T 20653 R
10017 T 10684 TR 16186 T 21262 T
10022 T 10806 R 16522 T 21302 T
10024 T 11035 RC 16949 R 21333 TR
10025 T 11605 RC 16977 R 21366 R
10026 T 12957 TR 18102 TR 21368 R
10045 T 13811 T 18306 R 21434 C
10048 T 13873 TR 18579 R 21435 C
10077 TR 13902 R 18687 R 22555 T
10096 R 14156 T 18700 R 22559 T
10100 R 14720 R 18707 R 22594 T
10118 RC 15136 TR 18711 R 22728 RC
10144 C 15283 C 18764 R

Personal Observation: Inclusions

10032 T 12589 T 19016 R 22578 T
10093 R 12934 T 20200 R 22618 T
10336 T 13748 R 20235 TRC 22817 TRC

Personal Observation: Journal Articles

10445 R 13274 R 18995 R 20756 T
10446 R 13793 C 20152 T 21173 T
10534 T 14709 R 20155 T 21377 R
11738 R 16715 R 20445 R 21689 T
12585 T 17975 T 20588 T 22345 C
13124 T 18407 T 20710 T 22593 T
13127 T

Primary Sources *and* Personal Observation

10004 T 12598 T 16375 T 18979 TR
10042 T 12624 TR 16376 T 19490 R
10058 T 12629 TR 16423 R 19650 RC
10060 T 12941 T 16424 R 19802 TR
10082 TR 13028 R 17165 T 19996 T
10085 TR 13292 R 17691 TR 20160 TR
10117 TRC 13404 C 18042 TRC 20231 RC
10285 TR 13571 R 18423 T 20576 T
10329 T 13629 T 18492 T 20620 TR
10700 TR 13636 T 18495 T 20635 R
10853 TRC 13704 R 18501 T 20786 T
11694 TR 13705 R 18534 TR 21337 TR
11720 TR 13708 R 18545 TR 21392 TRC
11766 R 13763 TRC 18547 TR 21579 C
11767 R 13877 TR 18741 R 21626 T
11841 R 15191 RC 18852 T 22102 TR
12348 R 16229 TR 18871 T 22133 TR
12593 T 16374 T 18968 TR 22580 T

Secondary Sources, Well Documented

10008 T 10664 T 15130 T 20050 TR
10034 T 10704 TR 15158 TRC 20111 TRC
10076 TR 11708 TR 15185 TRC 20563 T
10111 TRC 11853 TRC 16127 TRC 21411 TRC
10119 TRC 12160 C 17951 RC 21477 TRC
10129 TRC 12188 T 17972 C 21544 RC
10217 RC 12417 RC 18396 T 21602 T
10300 TRC 12759 R 18443 T 21695 T
10331 T 13154 TR 18541 TR 21855 TRC
10346 TR 13717 R 18558 TR 22109 TR
10361 R 13950 R 18809 RC 22225 TRC
10367 R 14155 T 18947 T 22651 TR
10377 R 14215 TR 18971 TR 22665 TR
10389 TRC 15044 T 19219 TR 22666 TR
10396 TRC 15048 TR 19353 TR 22899 TR
10397 TRC 15063 R 19888 TRC 22964 RC
10526 T 15126 T 19913 C 22995 TRC

Unsupported or Poorly Documented

See Geographic Index

3 Narrowly Urban: Large Cities Only

Field Research

13617 C 20088 T 20463 R

Primary Sources

10865 TRC 13457 T 14491 R 19481 TR
11299 TR 13642 TR 14560 T 19482 R
12600 T 13652 TR 15645 TRC 19524 R
12692 R 13698 R 15937 TR 19546 R
12922 T 13710 R 17060 R 19554 R
13017 R 13747 R 18308 R 19584 RC
13178 TR 14174 T 19217 TR 20209 R

20934 R 21603 T 22604 T 22652 TR
21285 T 22515 T 22650 TR 22690 R
21350 TR 22586 T

Field Research *and* Primary Sources

10866 RC 14766 R 22681 R

Personal Observation

10804 R 15345 T 19614 T 21171 T
11228 T 17142 T 19699 R 21374 R
12902 T 17572 R 20186 R 22694 R
13707 R 19543 R 20213 R 22905 TR
14095 T

Primary Sources *and* Personal Observation

13658 TR 18549 TR 20591 T 20827 TR
14476 R 20108 R 20594 T 22720 R
17696 R 20590 T 20595 T

Secondary Sources, Well Documented

12764 TRC 12785 TRC 14676 TR 18082 T
20222 R

Unsupported or Poorly Documented

See Geographic Index

4 Urban, Including Smaller Cities and Hsien Capitals

Field Research

□

Primary Sources

10259 TRC 12965 TR 13692 TR 15134 TR
10384 TRC 13133 T 13867 T 18442 T
11150 C 13461 T 14244 R 19500 R
11270 TR 13497 TR 14399 T 20785 T
12654 TR 13656 TR 14694 TR 20861 R
12660 TR 13662 TR 15065 R 22027 T
12918 T 13676 TR

Field Research *and* Primary Sources

□

Personal Observation

12898 T 13841 T 15422 R 20659 TRC
13106 C 14400 T 18970 TR 20779 T
13505 TR

Primary Sources *and* Personal Observation

11657 T 12657 TR 13733 R 20790 TR
12576 T 13025 R 20769 T 20815 TR

Secondary Sources, Well Documented

10261 TRC 13168 TR 18301 T 22945 RC
12661 TR 14222 TR 22579 T

Unsupported or Poorly Documented

See Geographic Index

5 Broadly Urban: Cities *and* Market Towns

13129 T 13672 TR 14465 R 19559 R
20994 TRC 21425 TRC

6 Market Towns Only

□

7 Broadly Rural: Villages *and* Market Towns

10438 T 12328 R 12409 RC 16217 T
12196 T 12364 R 12461 C 16539 T
12201 T 12370 R 13243 R 17036 TR
12223 TR 12394 RC 15539 C 19654 RC
12232 TR 12401 RC 16104 TR 19983 TRC

8 Narrowly Rural: Villages Only

12184 T 12310 R 12439 C 19982 TRC
12260 R 12377 RC 15877 C

1.2 Mainland China

中國大陸　中国大陆

1 Place Irrelevant or Type of Place Unspecified

See Historical Index

2 Urban *and* Rural

Field Research

11181 T 14146 C 18358 C 20648 R
11627 C 14506 R 19010 R 20652 R
12262 R 16320 R 20508 C 21150 C
12434 C 17260 R 20518 C 21430 C
13277 R 17644 C 20546 T

Primary Sources: Monographs

10125 RC 11243 T 12002 C 13218 R
10142 C 11291 TR 12005 C 13250 R
10148 C 11336 R 12015 C 13251 R
10154 C 11368 R 12027 C 13272 R
10155 C 11369 R 12039 C 13284 R
10214 TRC 11371 R 12044 C 13289 R
10223 C 11390 RC 12054 C 13290 R
10226 C 11391 RC 12060 C 13308 RC
10232 C 11393 TRC 12071 C 13311 TRC
10240 C 11398 RC 12076 C 13318 C
10291 TR 11437 C 12082 C 13329 C
10330 T 11440 C 12096 C 13336 C
10338 TR 11514 C 12109 C 13338 C
10355 TR 11534 C 12123 C 13353 C
10399 C 11601 R 12148 C 13361 C
10413 C 11625 C 12163 C 13384 C
10424 C 11654 C 12166 C 13389 C
10425 C 11689 TR 12173 C 13399 C
10448 R 11698 TR 12218 TR 13432 C
10477 C 11702 TR 12230 TR 13440 C
10481 C 11707 TR 12241 R 13443 C
10487 C 11713 TR 12302 R 13447 C
10488 C 11724 R 12336 R 13456 T
10498 C 11740 R 12358 R 13458 T
10503 C 11745 R 12372 R 13482 T
10548 T 11748 R 12375 RC 13503 TR
10599 T 11754 R 12384 RC 13508 TR
10631 T 11756 R 12386 RC 13511 TR
10672 T 11783 R 12414 TRC 13520 TR
10676 T 11793 R 12441 C 13535 R
10677 T 11799 R 12485 C 13549 R
10688 TR 11804 R 12525 C 13579 C
10695 TR 11805 R 12528 C 13584 C
10698 TR 11807 R 12535 C 13589 C
10715 TR 11812 R 12564 C 13590 C
10729 TR 11822 R 12590 T 13593 C
10732 TR 11829 R 12599 T 13594 C
10769 R 11845 RC 12606 T 13614 C
10812 R 11846 RC 12631 TR 13641 T
10813 R 11849 TRC 12638 TR 13651 TR
10814 R 11850 TRC 12674 TR 13666 TR
10819 R 11852 RC 12712 R 13682 TR
10851 RC 11860 RC 12751 R 13691 TR
10870 RC 11862 RC 12763 TRC 13766 RC
10873 TRC 11874 RC 12776 TRC 13773 C
10890 TRC 11876 RC 12780 RC 13775 C
10906 C 11884 C 12787 C 13778 C
10931 C 11885 C 12793 C 13795 C
10953 C 11889 C 12813 C 13858 T
10970 C 11891 C 12849 C 13868 T
10975 C 11906 C 12876 C 13898 R
10994 C 11909 C 12923 T 13914 R
10997 C 11912 C 12950 TR 13927 R
11003 C 11917 C 12970 TR 13937 R
11005 C 11920 C 13006 R 13945 R
11006 C 11928 C 13041 R 13963 R
11076 C 11946 C 13050 RC 13986 TRC
11094 C 11949 C 13070 C 14002 RC
11096 C 11955 C 13076 C 14006 RC
11104 C 11970 C 13104 C 14012 RC
11105 C 11988 C 13105 C 14033 C
11160 C 11995 C 13117 C 14037 C
11168 C 11996 C 13118 C 14093 T
11178 C 11998 C 13125 T 14109 TR
11180 C 12000 C 13172 TR 14116 R
11203 T 12001 C 13184 TR 14127 RC
14160 T 15980 RC 18725 R 21324 TR
14164 T 16106 TR 18730 R 21325 TR
14178 T 16277 TR 18733 R 21345 TR
14223 TR 16335 TRC 18752 R 21346 TR
14241 R 16343 TRC 18755 R 21360 TR
14258 RC 17160 T 18759 R 21400 RC
14274 TRC 17238 R 18780 R 21406 RC
14278 RC 17241 R 18782 R 21417 TRC
14292 RC 17316 RC 18783 R 21419 RC
14296 C 17395 C 18792 RC 21423 RC
14299 C 17485 R 18795 TRC 21424 TRC
14329 C 17586 RC 18819 RC 21450 TR
14337 C 17661 TR 18822 TRC 21644 T
14364 C 17758 TR 18842 C 21826 R
14385 C 17779 C 18862 T 21838 TRC
14396 T 17990 C 18867 T 21874 RC
14416 C 17993 C 18945 T 21887 TRC
14419 C 18041 TRC 18952 TR 21900 TRC
14486 R 18104 TR 18987 TR 21928 C
14512 RC 18106 TR 19166 C 21937 C
14513 TRC 18114 R 19291 C 21948 C
14522 C 18120 R 19367 C 21982 T
14524 C 18123 R 19390 C 22066 T
14556 T 18134 R 19453 R 22079 TR
14599 T 18142 R 19476 TR 22089 TR
14638 TR 18144 R 19551 R 22099 TR
14647 TR 18145 R 19617 TR 22112 TR
14658 TR 18148 R 19643 R 22117 TR
14659 TR 18154 R 19652 RC 22135 TR
14700 TR 18155 R 19655 RC 22144 R
14783 RC 18170 RC 19662 C 22158 R
14795 RC 18172 RC 19705 R 22162 R
14808 RC 18182 RC 19719 T 22172 R
14828 C 18185 RC 19732 RC 22173 R
14853 C 18187 RC 19789 TR 22182 RC
14871 C 18224 C 19883 RC 22190 RC
14910 C 18225 C 19899 TRC 22203 RC
14942 C 18232 C 19905 C 22204 RC
14969 C 18264 C 19909 C 22210 TRC
14990 C 18277 C 20036 T 22217 RC
15017 C 18298 C 20049 TR 22219 RC
15025 C 18312 RC 20067 R 22224 RC
15028 C 18387 T 20068 R 22229 RC
15073 R 18430 T 20134 T 22235 RC
15085 RC 18530 TR 20177 TR 22250 RC
15112 C 18536 TR 20182 TR 22251 RC
15113 C 18557 TR 20204 R 22273 RC
15115 C 18588 R 20244 C 22291 C
15169 RC 18617 R 20314 C 22296 C
15202 C 18629 R 20328 C 22298 C
15230 C 18630 R 20430 TR 22299 C
15234 C 18635 R 20432 TR 22318 C
15235 C 18636 R 20444 R 22322 C
15237 C 18647 R 20473 RC 22324 C
15248 C 18653 R 20484 C 22325 C
15249 C 18655 R 20526 C 22339 C
15260 C 18656 R 20582 T 22605 T
15267 C 18660 R 20614 TR 22714 R
15273 C 18661 R 20700 C 22717 R
15294 C 18674 R 21172 T 22772 T
15495 C 18685 R 21259 T 22831 C
15570 C 18699 R 21265 T 22926 TR
15652 C 18709 R 21321 TR 22939 R
15938 TR 18717 R

Primary Sources: Inclusions

10012 T 10499 C 11078 C 11965 C
10051 T 10542 T 11120 C 11969 C
10147 C 10603 T 11126 C 11989 C
10190 TR 10662 T 11167 C 11990 C
10218 RC 10694 TR 11174 C 12009 C
10224 C 10750 R 11176 C 12010 C
10227 C 10912 C 11435 C 12042 C
10244 C 10915 C 11458 C 12043 C
10254 TR 10916 C 11487 C 12045 C
10313 C 10917 C 11494 C 12055 C
10441 T 10919 C 11721 R 12088 C
10456 RC 10920 C 11786 R 12092 C
10468 C 10930 C 11842 RC 12107 C
10469 C 10993 C 11865 RC 12121 C
10478 C 11010 T 11875 RC 12132 C
10484 C 11042 RC 11887 C 12156 C
10485 C 11043 RC 11918 C 12165 C
10486 C 11072 C 11940 C 12168 C
10497 C 11077 C 11942 C 12228 TR

12395 RC
12415 RC
12447 C
12449 C
12506 C
12559 C
12620 TR
12782 RC
12788 C
12792 C
12803 C
12840 C
12844 C
12868 C
12871 C
12875 C
13064 C
13066 C
13085 C
13088 C
13097 C
13099 C
13100 C
13101 C
13121 C
13156 TR
13170 TR
13185 TR
13257 R
13259 R
13260 R
13319 C
13330 C
13333 C
13335 C
13352 C
13390 C
13430 C
13435 C
13436 C
13444 C
13577 C
13582 C
13583 C
13601 C
13605 C
13606 C
13613 C
13823 T
13834 T
13865 T
13904 R
13920 R
13942 R
13977 R
13987 TRC
13993 RC
14030 C
14031 C
14032 C
14068 C
14123 R
14135 C
14138 C
14147 C
14150 C
14151 C
14251 R
14275 RC
14280 RC
14288 RC
14325 C
14328 C
14363 C
14391 C
14521 C
14525 C
14715 R
14788 RC
14790 RC
14794 TRC
14821 C
14840 C
14850 C
14876 C
14905 C
14906 C
14913 C
14958 C
14967 C
14973 C
14975 C
14977 C
15001 C
15043 T
15071 R
15101 C
15107 C
15188 RC
15195 RC
15217 C
15222 C
15223 C
15224 C
15233 C
15299 C
16110 TR
17147 T
17174 T
17314 RC
17601 C
17638 C
17642 C
17792 C
17807 C
17999 C
18000 C
18088 T
18110 R
18119 R
18189 C
18206 C
18208 C
18209 C
18219 C
18241 C
18280 C
18293 C
18310 R
18370 T
18429 T
18452 T
18516 T
18601 R
18612 R
18626 R
18628 R
18632 R
18633 R
18672 R
18761 R
18773 R
18798 RC
18799 RC
18802 RC
18808 TRC
18825 RC
18837 C
19198 C
19216 TR
19284 RC
19332 C
19365 T
19626 R
19628 R
19659 RC
19866 TRC
19928 C
19930 C
19952 C
19965 TR
19974 TRC
20081 C
20121 C
20212 R
20228 RC
20303 RC
20356 C
20371 C
20480 C
20486 C
20491 C
20495 C
20504 C
20834 R
20957 TRC
21023 C
21025 C
21066 C
21070 C
21073 C
21105 C
21211 R
21303 TR
21326 TR
21388 TRC
21682 T
21709 T
21893 RC
21912 C
21916 C
21947 C
21964 C
21965 C
21977 C
21978 C
22034 T
22078 TR
22130 TR
22146 R
22166 R
22169 R
22191 RC
22192 RC
22197 RC
22212 RC
22234 RC
22282 RC
22290 C
22363 C

PRIMARY SOURCES: JOURNAL ARTICLES

10009 T
10185 T
10195 TR
10196 TR
10199 TR
10206 R
10225 C
10230 C
10231 C
10233 C
10235 C
10236 C
10237 C
10238 C
10239 C
10242 C
10247 C
10248 C
10249 C
10264 C
10265 C
10281 TR
10305 C
10308 C
10309 C
10311 C
10315 C
10316 C
10320 T
10347 TR
10391 RC
10408 C
10411 C
10418 C
10442 R
10461 C
10465 C
10467 C
10472 C
10473 C
10474 C
10480 C
10482 C
10490 C
10491 C
10496 C
10501 C
10524 T
10620 T
10629 T
10743 R
10766 R
10786 R
10794 R
10805 R
10834 R
10848 RC
10849 RC
10872 TRC
10877 RC
10880 RC
10897 C
10902 C
10925 C
10929 C
10933 C
10964 C
10965 C
10966 C
10967 C
10972 C
10980 C
10986 C
10987 C
11022 R
11026 R
11030 R
11034 RC
11041 RC
11054 TRC
11060 C
11070 C
11071 C
11074 C
11085 C
11089 C
11098 C
11115 C
11116 C
11118 C
11137 C
11148 C
11155 C
11170 C
11171 C
11172 C
11175 C
11260 TR
11287 TR
11388 TRC
11410 TRC
11421 C
11452 C
11453 C
11456 C
11486 C
11488 C
11503 C
11505 C
11525 C
11560 T
11583 TR
11609 RC
11624 C
11628 C
11629 C
11630 C
11666 T
11680 T
11693 TR
11717 TR
11733 R
11736 R
11757 R
11761 R
11762 R
11763 R
11764 R
11778 R
11792 R
11800 R
11809 R
11810 R
11813 R
11814 R
11854 RC
11866 RC
11879 C
11880 C
11882 C
11886 C
11908 C
11913 C
11915 C
11924 C
11930 C
11931 C
11932 C
11933 C
11941 C
11943 C
11944 C
11945 C
11947 C
11953 C
11954 C
11961 C
11963 C
11966 C
11971 C
11973 C
11981 C
11986 C
11987 C
11991 C
11992 C
11994 C
11997 C
11999 C
12004 C
12012 C
12013 C
12016 C
12021 C
12025 C
12026 C
12031 C
12032 C
12033 C
12034 C
12035 C
12036 C
12040 C
12050 C
12053 C
12056 C
12057 C
12058 C
12059 C
12061 C
12063 C
12065 C
12066 C
12073 C
12075 C
12080 C
12083 C
12084 C
12089 C
12094 C
12095 C
12098 C
12103 C
12104 C
12110 C
12111 C
12115 C
12116 C
12117 C
12120 C
12125 C
12126 C
12129 C
12133 C
12134 C
12138 C
12139 C
12140 C
12141 C
12145 C
12153 C
12161 C
12162 C
12164 C
12171 C
12172 C
12189 T
12214 TR
12215 TR
12220 TR
12221 TR
12243 R
12244 R
12266 R
12304 R
12325 R
12332 R
12343 R
12405 TRC
12457 C
12460 C
12468 C
12471 C
12472 C
12474 C
12480 C
12482 C
12486 C
12492 C
12494 C
12497 C
12498 C
12502 C
12513 C
12517 C
12521 C
12530 C
12531 C
12534 C
12558 C
12568 T
12583 T
12634 TR
12668 TR
12669 TR
12690 R
12691 R
12698 R
12700 R
12709 R
12781 TRC
12784 RC
12790 C
12797 C
12802 C
12817 C
12818 C
12821 C
12822 C
12823 C
12824 C
12831 C
12832 C
12833 C
12949 TR
12956 TR
12961 TR
13003 R
13027 R
13055 C
13063 C
13068 C
13071 C
13073 C
13074 C
13075 C
13077 C
13084 C
13087 C
13089 C
13090 C
13091 C
13092 C
13093 C
13094 C
13095 C
13096 C
13110 C
13115 C
13157 TR
13159 TR
13161 TR
13180 TR
13198 R
13234 R
13248 R
13253 R
13263 R
13279 R
13283 R
13294 RC
13298 RC
13300 TRC
13322 C
13340 C
13349 C
13354 C
13359 C
13364 C
13368 C
13370 C
13371 C
13372 C
13373 C
13374 C
13375 C
13376 C
13377 C
13379 C
13382 C
13383 C
13388 C
13391 C
13409 C
13421 C
13424 C
13439 C
13477 T
13484 T
13493 TR
13531 R
13533 R
13550 R
13561 R
13587 C
13600 C
13604 C
13660 TR
13693 R
13694 R
13695 R
13738 R
13771 C
13780 C
13782 C
13783 C
13789 C
13791 C
13815 T
13919 R
13932 R
13933 R
13940 R
14004 TRC
14008 RC
14009 TRC
14036 C
14041 C
14044 C
14060 C
14063 C
14084 C
14110 TR
14128 RC
14130 TRC
14132 C
14137 C
14143 C
14149 C
14183 T
14260 RC
14271 RC
14312 C
14331 C
14332 C
14347 C
14351 C
14354 C
14359 C
14362 C
14373 C
14403 TR
14437 RC
14446 C
14481 R
14528 C
14532 C
14547 C
14569 T
14704 R
14729 R
14787 TRC
14818 C
14823 C
14824 C
14827 C
14830 C
14834 C
14843 C
14845 C
14863 C
14868 C
14900 C
14916 C
14917 C
14924 C
14926 C
14929 C
14930 C
14931 C
14932 C
14933 C
14935 C
14952 C
14954 C
14956 C
14959 C
14965 C
14968 C
14971 C
14984 C
14997 C
15020 C
15056 R
15069 R
15087 RC
15088 RC
15102 C
15103 C
15132 TR
15142 R
15144 R
15154 R
15196 C
15198 C
15200 C
15208 C
15211 C
15218 C
15219 C
15220 C
15225 C
15226 C
15228 C
15236 C
15238 C
15244 C
15247 C
15253 C
15264 C
15284 C
15288 C
15289 C
15292 C
15580 C
15705 C
15757 TR
15915 C
15934 T
15967 R
15968 R
16018 C
16019 C
16038 C
16053 TR
16081 C
16084 C
16089 T
16144 C
16153 C
16154 C
16196 T
16460 C
16470 C
17008 C
17121 C
17149 T
17370 C
17388 C
17391 C
17401 C
17585 RC
17596 C
17597 C
17755 TR
17759 R
17782 C
17987 RC
17992 C
17996 C
18002 C
18052 C
18054 C
18057 C
18058 C
18059 C
18107 R
18141 R
18157 R
18173 RC
18177 RC
18188 RC
18190 C
18195 C
18199 C
18200 C
18204 C
18221 C
18222 C
18226 C
18227 C
18228 C
18234 C
18237 C
18238 C
18243 C
18246 C
18252 C
18253 C
18254 C
18260 C
18269 C
18273 C
18274 C
18304 R
18323 C
18332 C
18336 C
18339 C
18351 C
18353 C
18360 C
18361 C
18401 T
18460 T
18504 T
18574 R
18580 R
18599 R
18663 R
18675 R
18677 R
18698 R
18705 R
18714 R
18728 R
18789 RC
18790 RC
18800 TRC
18806 RC
18815 RC
18816 RC
18830 RC
18838 C
18839 C
18848 T
18893 T
18964 TR
19014 R
19031 RC
19057 C
19150 C
19183 C
19226 R
19251 R
19317 C
19323 C
19374 C
19377 C
19379 C
19380 C
19381 C
19383 C
19384 C
19388 C
19392 C
19396 R
19412 C
19440 T
19463 R
19544 R
19572 R
19629 R
19658 RC
19660 C
19673 C
19676 C
19677 C
19681 C
19768 T
19875 TRC
19906 C
19921 C
19927 C
19948 C
20011 TR
20064 R
20078 C
20187 R
20242 C
20243 C
20254 T
20286 T
20313 C
20331 C
20348 C
20361 C
20362 C
20363 C
20365 C
20370 C
20375 C
20403 RC
20407 C
20441 R
20474 RC
20476 C
20487 C
20488 C
20490 C
20498 C
20499 C
20501 C
20510 C
20511 C
20512 C
20514 C
20515 C
20520 C
20521 C
20523 C
20532 C
20533 C
20589 T
20849 R
20877 R
21013 C
21028 C
21043 C
21044 C
21045 C
21076 C
21077 C
21080 C
21082 C
21097 C
21241 C
21248 C
21250 C
21263 T
21283 T
21284 T
21341 TR
21390 RC
21397 RC
21439 T
21474 TRC
21591 C
21734 TR
21837 RC
21917 C
21918 C
21919 C
21961 C
22021 C
22041 T
22047 T
22069 T
22077 TR
22098 TR
22134 TR
22159 R
22167 R
22168 R
22180 R
22200 RC
22213 RC
22223 RC
22252 RC
22255 RC
22259 RC
22262 RC
22276 RC
22281 RC
22292 C
22297 C
22301 C
22314 C
22328 C
22329 C
22333 C
22340 C
22344 C
22346 C
22349 C
22351 C
22564 T
22569 T
22625 T
22721 R
22722 R
22771 T
22784 TR
22839 C
22875 T
22941 R
22955 TRC

FIELD RESEARCH *and* PRIMARY SOURCES: MONOGRAPHS

10105 R
10960 C
11052 RC
11101 C
11586 TR
11588 TR
11651 C
11752 R
11864 RC
12303 R
12524 C
12640 TR
12783 TRC
12839 C
13158 TR
13420 C
13674 TR
13750 R
14020 RC
14066 C
14497 R
15023 C
15052 TR
15059 R
15171 TRC
16071 C
16103 TR
16123 R
16189 T
18003 C
18178 RC
18915 T
18988 TR
18989 TR
19597 C
19816 R
20169 TR
20302 R
20462 R
20962 RC
20996 C
21410 TRC
21414 RC
21677 T

FIELD RESEARCH *and* PRIMARY SOURCES: INCLUSIONS

10988 C
11442 C
11443 C
11550 T
14628 TR
15303 C
16028 C
16124 RC

17481 R 18343 C 19945 C 21780 TR
17766 R 18992 R 20896 R 22357 C
18281 C 19003 R

Field Research *and* Primary Sources: Journal Articles

10459 C 12100 C 14991 C 19307 C
11382 R 12344 R 15057 R 20545 T
11493 C 13020 R 18124 R 21092 C
11652 C 13220 R 18941 T 22452 R
12006 C 13407 C

Personal Observation: Monographs

10002 T 10159 C 14139 C 18722 R
10003 T 10160 C 14369 C 18744 R
10005 T 10164 C 14370 C 18746 R
10007 T 10165 C 14574 T 18753 R
10011 T 10167 C 14685 TR 18767 R
10023 T 10168 C 14809 RC 18796 RC
10030 T 10169 C 14943 C 18827 RC
10035 T 10173 C 14999 C 18959 TR
10036 T 10180 C 15006 C 18980 TR
10039 T 10255 TR 15090 RC 19062 C
10043 T 10360 R 15123 C 19674 C
10044 T 10660 T 15140 TR 19751 T
10047 T 10702 TR 15156 R 20137 T
10055 T 10733 TR 15176 RC 20166 TR
10059 T 10778 R 15192 RC 20221 R
10061 T 10895 C 15279 C 20224 RC
10065 T 10978 C 15297 C 20258 T
10067 TR 11053 RC 15309 T 20502 C
10069 TR 11069 C 15466 RC 20556 T
10071 TR 11095 C 15482 C 20721 T
10088 R 11106 C 15506 C 20749 T
10089 R 11144 C 15508 C 20798 TR
10090 R 11194 T 15509 C 20966 RC
10092 R 11830 R 15519 C 21103 C
10094 R 11883 C 15550 C 21307 TR
10097 R 11894 C 15856 C 21308 TR
10098 R 11901 C 16070 C 21311 TR
10099 R 11903 C 16210 T 21355 TR
10101 R 11919 C 16395 T 21367 R
10104 R 11922 C 16457 C 21379 R
10115 RC 12090 C 17311 RC 21416 RC
10121 RC 12102 C 17313 RC 21418 RC
10123 RC 12359 R 17575 R 21422 TRC
10126 RC 12544 C 17848 R 21465 R
10128 TRC 12597 T 17849 R 21504 TR
10130 C 12811 C 17895 RC 21585 C
10132 C 12853 C 18061 C 21624 T
10133 C 12921 T 18062 C 21818 R
10134 C 13328 C 18075 T 21819 R
10135 C 13787 C 18143 R 21821 R
10136 C 13882 TR 18161 R 22198 TRC
10140 C 13888 R 18378 T 22446 R
10143 C 13893 R 18567 TR 22572 T
10145 C 13901 R 18585 R 22599 T
10149 C 13909 R 18598 R 22644 TR
10150 C 13928 R 18603 R 22710 R
10152 C 13951 R 18608 R 22734 RC
10153 C 13965 R 18610 R 22769 C
10156 C 13969 R 18659 R 22805 R
10157 C 13970 R

Personal Observation: Inclusions

10334 T 13417 C 17341 C 20698 C
10493 C 13946 R 17941 R 20988 RC
10561 T 13948 R 17942 R 21053 C
10601 T 13949 R 17978 T 21353 TR
11244 T 14011 RC 18561 TR 21372 R
11265 TR 14435 R 18745 R 21486 C
11638 C 14603 T 18951 TR 21930 C
11838 R 14674 TR 19280 R 22379 C
12731 R 15189 RC 20434 R 22525 T
13131 T 15799 RC 20605 T

Personal Observation: Journal Articles

10033 T 10734 TR 11057 C 11512 C
10063 T 10748 R 11066 C 11518 C
10166 C 10764 R 11086 C 11519 C
10260 RC 10772 R 11140 C 11730 R
10297 R 10826 R 11153 C 11773 R
10342 TR 10884 RC 11429 C 11802 R
10440 T 10896 C 11441 C 11958 C
10492 C 10952 C 11483 C 11972 C
10504 T 11023 R 11499 C 11976 C

12124 C 14177 T 17081 R 20318 C
12131 C 14473 R 17289 R 20457 R
12178 T 14502 R 17368 C 20616 TR
12276 R 14515 RC 17764 R 20745 T
12277 R 14614 T 17777 C 20765 T
12349 R 14697 TR 17803 C 20852 R
12431 C 14706 R 17809 C 20865 R
12518 C 14713 R 18001 C 20914 R
12561 C 14740 R 18159 R 20943 R
12566 T 14747 R 18192 C 21007 C
12594 T 14778 RC 18335 C 21012 C
12596 T 14822 C 18435 T 21015 C
12671 TR 14855 C 18479 T 21034 C
12703 R 14857 C 18757 R 21035 C
12711 R 14870 C 18928 T 21052 C
12744 R 14907 C 19021 R 21075 C
12749 R 15050 TR 19034 RC 21106 C
12807 C 15060 R 19273 R 21107 C
12809 C 15151 R 19352 TR 21123 C
12837 C 15173 RC 19400 R 21142 C
12838 C 15206 C 19417 C 21143 C
12854 C 15212 C 19469 RC 21164 T
13108 C 15213 C 19627 R 21190 R
13109 C 15252 C 19634 R 21378 R
13114 C 15512 C 19647 R 21548 C
13273 R 15747 T 19700 R 21652 T
13723 R 16027 C 19775 T 21759 TR
13839 T 16209 T 20130 T 22105 TR
13840 T 16308 R 20148 T 22365 C
13943 R 16309 R 20197 R 22400 T
13944 R 16523 T 20214 R 22745 C
14111 TR 16524 T 20237 C 22767 C
14136 C 16948 R 20248 C 22797 R
14154 C 16969 R 20282 T 22940 R

Primary Sources *and* Personal Observation: Monographs

10019 T 11962 C 14584 T 18853 T
10020 T 11980 C 14640 TR 19035 TRC
10029 T 12158 C 14652 TR 19063 C
10049 T 12339 R 14687 TR 19240 R
10062 T 12475 C 14721 R 19615 TR
10079 TR 12532 C 14723 R 19644 R
10081 TR 12812 C 14733 R 19803 TR
10083 TR 12963 TR 14749 R 20034 T
10086 TR 12985 R 14754 R 20159 TR
10103 R 13120 C 14974 C 20226 TRC
10110 TRC 13152 TR 15172 TRC 20294 TR
10172 C 13516 TR 15214 C 20496 C
10191 TR 13542 R 15245 C 20618 TR
10228 C 13743 R 15553 C 20623 TR
10516 T 13744 R 16046 C 20837 R
10587 T 13760 R 16055 R 20926 R
10706 TR 13761 R 17140 T 20991 TRC
10799 R 13880 TR 17226 R 21260 T
10837 R 13884 TR 17297 R 21354 TR
10887 TRC 13896 R 17441 TR 21395 RC
10937 C 13905 R 17763 R 21420 TRC
10943 C 13957 R 17977 T 21447 TR
11021 TR 13958 R 18158 R 21691 T
11297 TR 13959 R 18324 C 22131 TR
11581 TR 13975 R 18454 T 22233 RC
11705 TR 14153 C 18551 TR 22375 C
11760 R 14219 TR 18596 R 22556 T
11848 RC 14279 RC 18804 TRC 22619 T
11872 RC 14479 R 18817 RC 22648 TR
11897 C

Primary Sources *and* Personal Observation: Inclusions

10250 C 11530 C 16263 TR 18885 T
10295 R 12206 T 17152 T 18896 T
10642 T 12865 C 17550 T 18949 TR
10650 T 14591 T 17796 C 19721 T
10723 TR 14880 C 18533 TR 21189 TR
11013 T 14957 C

Primary Sources *and* Personal Observation: Journal Articles

10084 TR 11062 C 11957 C 12774 RC
10241 C 11097 C 11979 C 12814 C
10512 T 11406 TRC 12030 C 13026 R
10717 TR 11572 T 12049 C 13149 TR
10774 R 11649 C 12085 C 13233 R
10775 R 11895 C 12112 C 13244 R
10992 C 11896 C 12122 C 13278 R

13385 C 14572 T 16452 RC 20131 T
13405 C 14707 R 17335 C 20191 R
13426 C 14726 R 18213 C 20725 T
13427 C 14872 C 18593 R 20961 RC
13495 TR 15032 C 19168 C 21010 C
13553 R 15114 C 19169 C 21183 T
13575 C 15275 C 20001 T 21195 R
14566 T 16272 TR

Secondary Sources, Well Documented: Monographs

10068 TR 11643 C 13163 TR 18543 TR
10072 TR 11685 TR 13182 TR 18562 TR
10112 TRC 11699 TR 13211 R 18619 R
10120 TRC 11750 R 13325 C 18720 R
10124 TRC 11790 R 13343 C 18768 R
10201 TR 11855 TRC 13344 C 18823 RC
10349 TR 11877 RC 13365 C 20107 R
10697 TR 11878 RC 13903 R 20558 T
10712 TR 11927 C 14010 RC 20639 R
10718 TR 11939 C 14018 TRC 20940 R
10821 R 12062* C 14119 R 21300 T
10858 TRC 12295 R 14703 TR 21476 TRC
10883 TRC 12355 R 14835 C 22293 C
10888 TRC 12633 TR 14882 C 22679 R
10893 TRC 12708 R 15163 RC 22787 TR
11027 R 12721 R 15241 C 22950 TRC
11048 TRC 12915 T 17291 R 22991 TRC
11092 C 13029 R 17952 TRC 23003 TRC
11283 TR 13042 R 18526 T

Secondary Sources, Well Documented: Inclusions

10078 TR 11711 TR 13859 T 20115 TRC
10122 RC 11847 RC 14096 T 20233 RC
10151 C 11911 C 14208 T 20292 TR
10171 C 11916 C 15177 TRC 21153 C
10353 TR 11929 C 15210 C 21840 TRC
10405 C 11968 C 15314 T 21848 TRC
10410 C 11974 C 17317 RC 21885 TRC
10414 C 12041 C 18515 T 21894 TRC
10433 C 12101 C 18537 TR 22148 R
10453 R 12159 C 18571 TR 22221 RC
10549 T 12326 R 18605 R 22473 RC
10856 RC 12376 RC 19873 RC 22857 C
11688 TR 12650 TR 19880 TRC 23028 C
11700 TR 12727 R

Secondary Sources, Well Documented: Journal Articles

10146 C 11900 C 12983 R 16014 C
10192 TR 11902 C 13000 R 16329 TRC
10198 TR 11910 C 13086 C 17280 R
10245 C 11935 C 13134 T 17303 R
10374 R 11938 C 13268 R 17304 R
10383 RC 11993 C 13331 C 17574 R
10390 RC 12022 C 13400 C 17991 C
10393 TRC 12023 C 13401 C 18020 TR
10403 C 12052 C 13438 C 18327 C
10409 C 12064 C 13591 C 18397 T
10422 C 12077 C 13639 T 18477 T
10451 R 12087 C 13714 R 18591 R
10536 T 12091 C 13899 R 18651 R
10628 T 12097 C 13960 R 18718 R
10661 T 12113 C 14105 TR 18821 RC
10754 R 12119 C 14141 C 18829 RC
10889 TRC 12127 C 14438 RC 19058 C
10901 C 12128 C 14460 R 19869 RC
11225 T 12167 C 14503 R 20230 TRC
11626 C 12177 C 14612 T 20325 C
11676 T 12217 TR 15066 R 20402 RC
11768 R 12226 TR 15076 R 20611 TR
11788 R 12236 R 15089 RC 21057 C
11806 R 12410 TRC 15133 TR 21085 C
11815 R 12556 C 15167 RC 21387 TRC
11820 R 12662 TR 15179 RC 21501 TR
11868 RC 12702 R 15216 C 21830 TRC
11870 TRC 12739 R 15231 C 21960 C
11871 TRC 12800 C 15246 C 22149 R
11881 C 12804 C 15280 C 22171 R
11890 C 12847 C 15790 TRC 22215 RC

1.2 Mainland China

Primary Sources: Monographs

10466 C 12453 C 15991 C 19077 RC
11036 TRC 12467 C 15992 C 19083 RC
12222 TR 12508 C 15993 C 19095 C
12227 TR 12515 C 16011 C 19100 C
12229 TR 12552 C 16013 C 19131 C
12270 R 12562 C 16031 C 19132 C
12271 R 12563 C 16054 R 19135 C
12298 R 13345 C 16072 C 19201 C
12308 R 13442 C 16516 T 19203 C
12331 R 13610 C 16637 R 19257 R
12379 RC 13736 R 16768 C 19445 R
12380 RC 13769 C 17092 R 19457 R
12412 RC 15100 C 17249 R 19640 R
12424 RC 15258 C 17647 C 19922 C
12426 RC 15483 C 17674 C 20079 C
12429 C 15488 C 17769 R 20080 C
12436 C 15507 C 17979 TR 20247 C
12442 C 15549 C 18289 C 21003 C
12446 C 15977 RC 18391 T

Primary Sources: Inclusions

11861 RC 12507 C 15558 C 19101 C
12176 C 12536 C 15990 C 19108 C
12197 T 12547 C 15996 C 19138 C
12216 TR 13058 C 16877 C 19146 C
12261 R 13136 T 16993 C 19190 C
12333 R 14442 C 17355 C 19199 C
12444 C 14448 C 17404 C 19202 C
12462 C 15099 C 18242 C 22263 RC
12476 C 15209 C

Primary Sources: Journal Articles

10352 TR 12501 C 15564 C 18338 C
10973 C 12504 C 15831 C 18673 R
11058 C 12511 C 15845 C 18691 R
11124 C 12512 C 15896 C 18791 TRC
11460 C 12526 C 15975 RC 18818 RC
12209 TR 12529 C 15994 C 19086 RC
12239 R 12546 C 15999 C 19121 C
12249 R 12553 C 16005 C 19123 C
12307 R 12555 C 16020 C 19125 C
12311 R 12808 C 16021 C 19126 C
12356 R 13056 C 16036 C 19130 C
12360 R 13246 R 16039 C 19137 C
12361 R 13310 RC 16040 C 19139 C
12365 R 13342 C 16041 C 19140 C
12374 RC 13348 C 16079 C 19141 C
12391 RC 13369 C 16145 C 19142 C
12392 RC 13418 C 16503 C 19143 C
12400 RC 13608 C 16807 C 19144 C
12403 RC 14420 T 16835 C 19145 C
12413 RC 14423 T 16863 C 19151 C
12419 RC 14434 R 17107 C 19155 C
12427 C 14439 RC 17112 C 19156 C
12430 C 14443 C 17113 C 19158 C
12438 C 14444 C 17114 C 19159 C
12443 C 14445 C 17120 C 19160 C
12448 C 14447 C 17371 C 19174 C
12452 C 14450 C 17373 C 19189 C
12473 C 14452 C 17374 C 19303 C
12477 C 14862 C 17594 C 19444 R
12488 C 14869 C 17673 C 19464 R
12489 C 15108 C 17678 C 19471 C
12490 C 15109 C 17679 C 19671 C
12491 C 15122 C 17682 C 20038 T
12493 C 15494 C 17684 C 21079 C
12496 C 15528 C 17778 C 22323 C
12499 C 15540 C 17905 C 22343 C
12500 C 15559 C 18014 T 22844 C

Field Research *and* Primary Sources

10462 C 12273 R 15978 RC 17460 R
12255 R 12418 RC 16612 R 19105 C
12257 R 14449 C 16693 R 21163 T
12264 R 15486 C

Personal Observation

12388 RC 15271 C 16770 C 17255 R
12433 C 15398 R 16808 C 17456 R
12445 C 15434 R 16847 C 17482 R
12451 C 15524 C 16860 C 17760 R
12458 C 15551 C 16897 C 19074 R
13926 R 15567 C 17095 R 19103 C
14239 R 15855 C 17119 C 19128 C
19136 C 19167 C 19635 R 19649 R
19149 C 19224 R 19636 R 19707 R

Primary Sources *and* Personal Observation

10502 C 12487 C 16481 C 19082 RC
12317 R 13282 R 16488 C 19133 C
12440 C 13324 C 17130 C 19164 C
12459 C 15098 C 17492 R 22423 TR

Secondary Sources, Well Documented

10489 C 12422 RC 14441 C 19102 C
11674 T 12465 C 14451 C 19107 C
12213 TR 12466 C 15187 RC 19170 C
12237 R 13018 R 15886 C 19188 C
12240 R 13213 R 16001 C 19467 RC
12289 R 13241 R 16029 C 19622 R
12291 R 13596 C 19091 RC 19638 R
12397 RC 14436 R

Unsupported or Poorly Documented

See Geographic Index

8 Narrowly Rural: Villages Only

Field Research

19728 R 19850 R 21067 C 21091 C

Primary Sources: Monographs

10379 R 12464 C 13715 R 19134 C
10460 C 12519 C 15955 TR 19181 C
12268 R 12523 C 17588 C 19194 C
12312 R 12850 C 19078 RC 19455 R
12378 RC 13603 C 19092 RC

Primary Sources: Inclusions

12269 R 12484 C 17472 R 19087 RC
12352 R 12510 C 17640 C 19129 C
12396 RC 12538 C 18589 R 19154 C
12455 C 12557 C

Primary Sources: Journal Articles

10208 R 12342 R 12539 C 19081 RC
12185 T 12350 R 12545 C 19084 RC
12199 T 12362 R 12549 C 19096 C
12279 R 12393 RC 12554 C 19099 C
12282 R 12398 RC 12560 C 19124 C
12283 R 12425 TRC 13492 TR 19157 C
12288 R 12450 C 13897 R 19175 C
12306 R 12470 C 14421 T 19176 C
12313 R 12483 C 15104 C 19177 C
12314 R 12503 C 15110 C 19461 R
12316 R 12514 C 16837 C 22152 R
12334 R 12527 C

Field Research *and* Primary Sources

12254 R 12267 R 12319 R 12399 TRC
16690 R 17666 R

Personal Observation

11056 C 12323 R 16251 TR 19720 T
12182 T 12341 R 19110 C 20640 R
12187 T 16004 C

Primary Sources *and* Personal Observation

12363 R 12550 C 19076 RC 19184 C
12387 RC 12551 C 19097 C 22486 RC
12456 C

Secondary Sources, Well Documented

12192 T 12402 RC 14429 R 19187 C
12219 TR 12404 TRC 14430 R 19470 C
12251 R 12454 C 14440 RC 20040 T
12272 R 12481 C 17486 R 20993 RC
12293 R 13534 R 18835 RC 21227 R
12299 R 13628 T 19073 R 22879 T
12324 R 14426 R

Unsupported or Poorly Documented

See Geographic Index

1.3 The Eighteen Provinces
本部十八省 本土十八省

1 Place Irrelevant or Type of Place Unspecified

See Historical Index

2 Urban *and* Rural

Field Research

12253 R 17767 R 20171 TR 20726 T
13022 R 17842 R 20478 C 20760 T
13758 R 17912 C 20544 T 21218 R
17098 R 19836 R 20642 R 21610 T
17248 R 19848 R

Primary Sources: Monographs

10205 R 13637 T 18074 T 19053 TRC
10333 T 13804 T 18115 R 19441 T
10437 T 13830 T 18364 T 19631 R
10507 T 13831 T 18366 T 19695 T
10525 T 13911 R 18382 T 19963 TR
11567 T 13925 R 18436 T 20092 T
11667 T 14158 T 18461 T 20190 R
11784 R 14207 T 18502 T 21272 T
12371 R 14217 TR 18506 T 21277 T
12567 T 14656 TR 18508 T 21676 T
12587 T 15038 T 18592 R 21685 T
12948 T 15080 R 18654 R 22009 R
13037 R 16049 T 18727 R 22057 T
13151 TR 17145 T 18834 RC 22558 T
13288 R 17173 T 18859 T 22630 T
13466 T 18012 T 18916 T

Primary Sources: Inclusions

10138 C 14236 R 17144 T 18777 R
10294 R 14454 T 17175 T 18778 R
11156 C 14539 C 18080 T 18874 T
11157 C 14540 C 18284 C 21125 C
12195 T 14800 RC 18285 C 21126 C
12858 C 14801 RC 18346 C 21267 T
12859 C 15118 C 18347 C 21309 TR
12928 T 15119 C 18437 T 21319 TR
13130 T 15622 C 18445 T 21343 TR
13469 T 15623 C 18602 R 21686 T
13979 R 15906 C 18683 R 22773 T
14168 T 15907 C 18774 R

Primary Sources: Journal Articles

10443 R 13128 T 15047 T 19630 R
10608 T 13254 R 15662 T 19688 T
10656 T 13478 T 15864 TR 19747 T
10701 TR 13527 R 15935 T 19808 R
10760 R 13731 R 16058 R 20193 R
11346 R 13805 T 16355 C 20450 R
11725 R 13813 T 17096 R 20606 T
11934 C 13860 T 18413 T 21261 T
12200 T 13922 R 18426 T 21297 T
12347 R 13934 R 18586 R 21356 TR
12573 T 13938 R 18679 R 21389 RC
12602 T 14117 R 18681 R 21629 T
12612 T 14456 TR 19027 R 21678 T
12639 TR 14494 R 19282 R 21816 R
12642 TR 14505 R 19301 C 22390 T
12909 T 14660 TR 19446 R 22574 T
12930 T 15018 C 19514 R 22641 T
12933 T 15046 T 19570 R 22776 T
12978 R

Field Research *and* Primary Sources

10209 R 16560 TR 19833 R 21213 R
11539 T 17034 TR 20547 T 21611 T
15960 R 17484 R 20612 TR 22923 TR

Personal Observation: Monographs

10021 T 10141 C 11681 T 15306 T
10027 T 10158 C 12345 R 15501 C
10038 T 10161 C 12745 R 15511 C
10050 T 10170 C 13866 T 15543 C
10054 T 10174 C 13912 R 15733 T
10056 T 10175 C 13952 R 15830 C
10087 R 10348 TR 14100 T 16155 C
10091 R 10839 R 14121 R 16183 T
10102 R 11061 C 14829 C 16369 T

1.4 North China Broadly Conceived

廣義的中國北方 中国北部一般

1.4 North China Broadly Conceived

Personal Observation

10040 T 12734 R 16169 T 18953 TR
10064 T 13024 R 16317 R 20541 T
10580 T 13894 R 16732 RC 20549 T
10679 T 13918 R 17564 R 20578 T
10792 R 13954 R 17577 R 20630 R
10798 R 15081 R 18622 R 20714 T
10825 R 15082 R 18664 R 20716 T
12582 T 15324 T 18688 R 20748 T
12715 R 15433 R 18716 R 20780 T
12722 R 15656 T 18750 R 20835 R
12728 R 15752 T 18914 T 22511 T

Primary Sources *and* Personal Observation

10827 R 18493 T 20964 RC 22394 T
12944 T 18960 TR 20977 TRC 22660 TR
17873 R

Secondary Sources, Well Documented

10066 T 10476 C 12655 TR 22584 T
10404 C 11728 R 21292 T 22715 R
10452 R 11821 R

Unsupported or Poorly Documented

See Geographic Index

3 Narrowly Urban: Large Cities Only

10907 C 14195 T 19580 R 21787 TR
10936 C 17797 C 20598 T 22141 R
10969 C 18160 R 21348 TR 22562 T
13021 R 19231 R

4 Urban, Including Smaller Cities and Hsien Capitals

10343 TR 12753 R 17658 T 20539 T
12693 R 13286 R 19225 R 21109 C
12737 R

5 Broadly Urban: Cities *and* Market Towns

10989 C 12913 T 15783 R 17028 T
18038 TRC

6 Market Towns Only

□

7 Broadly Rural: Villages *and* Market Towns

10423 C 16659 R 17423 R 18690 R
12421 RC 16695 R 17846 R 18712 R
15428 R 16744 RC 18595 R 18743 R
16380 T 17307 R 18669 R 21784 TR

8 Narrowly Rural: Villages Only

10402 C 10458 C 12354 R 15681 R
10417 C 12234 R 12463 C 16352 C
10454 R 12274 R 12469 C 16585 R
10455 RC 12290 R 12505 C 18627 R

1.5 South China Broadly Conceived

廣義的中國南方 中国南部一般

1 Place Irrelevant or Type of Place Unspecified

See Geographic Index

2 Urban *and* Rural

Field Research

12191 T 15775 R 16650 R 19054 RC

Primary Sources

10137 C 13459 T 17543 T 18524 T
11014 T 13471 T 17944 R 18614 R
11729 R 13833 T 17956 TRC 18646 R
12383 RC 13869 T 17982 R 18766 R
12581 T 13881 TR 18374 T 18772 R
12613 T 13887 R 18376 T 18779 R
12647 TR 13889 R 18386 T 19448 R
12680 TR 14262 RC 18400 T 19718 T
12723 R 15078 R 18421 T 21299 T
12775 TRC 15928 T 18463 T 21339 TR
12992 R 16061 R 18486 T 21537 RC
13123 T 17038 TR 18500 T 21865 TRC

Field Research *and* Primary Sources

10289 TR 12684 TR 16339 TRC 18412 T
19894 TRC 21029 C

Personal Observation

10031 T 13929 R 16914 T 18875 T
10046 T 13955 R 16917 T 19399 R
10323 T 13968 R 16930 T 19764 T
10641 T 13972 R 16934 T 20208 R
11658 T 13973 R 16964 R 20289 T
11744 R 15042 T 16979 R 20561 T
11772 R 15068 R 17138 T 20633 R
12181 T 15205 C 17179 T 20734 T
12569 T 15332 T 17189 TR 20821 TR
12570 T 15361 T 17567 R 20855 R
12578 T 15721 T 17875 R 20901 R
12579 T 15722 T 17923 T 21175 T
12628 TR 15726 T 17939 R 21376 R
12672 TR 16159 T 18377 T 21382 R
12756 R 16182 T 18447 T 21384 R
12891 T 16378 T 18449 T 22444 R
12894 T 16388 T 18459 T 22522 T
13256 R 16520 T 18572 TR 22601 T
13892 R 16689 R 18577 R

Primary Sources *and* Personal Observation

10028 T 12879 T 13030 R 20724 T
10326 T 12888 T 15870 R 21117 C
12580 T 12897 T 17225 R 22513 T

Secondary Sources, Well Documented

10406 C 12843 C 18455 T 18670 R
10434 C 17443 TR 18641 R 18763 R
12265 R 17947 RC

Unsupported or Poorly Documented

See Geographic Index

3 Narrowly Urban: Large Cities Only

Field Research

13729 R 17097 R

Primary Sources

10299 TRC 17167 T 18771 R 21426 TRC
13757 R 18507 T 19287 TRC 22535 T
13941 R 18512 T

Field Research *and* Primary Sources

18129 R

Personal Observation

10832 R 15986 C 18113 R 19296 C
14770 R 18030 R 19238 R 20274 T
14784 RC 18034 R

Primary Sources *and* Personal Observation

15749 T

Secondary Sources, Well Documented

12618 T 20538 T

Unsupported or Poorly Documented

See Geographic Index

4 Urban, Including Smaller Cities and Hsien Capitals

10344 TR 13403 C 18485 T 20387 T
11017 T 16092 T 18499 T 20747 T
12920 T 16910 T 19006 R 22664 TR
13040 R 17150 T

5 Broadly Urban: Cities *and* Market Towns

16392 T

6 Market Towns Only

□

7 Broadly Rural: Villages *and* Market Towns

12186 T 14125 TRC 16592 R 17929 T
12297 R 16534 T 16677 R 17931 T
12437 C 16547 TR 17883 R 19957 T
13192 R

8 Narrowly Rural: Villages Only

12357 R 16386 T 17177 T 18898 T
12522 C 16410 TR 18721 R 19976 TRC
13967 R 16576 R 18781 R 21147 C
15663 T 16855 C

2.0 Manchuria

東北地區 東北地区又は満州

1 Place Irrelevant or Type of Place Unspecified

10581 T 11695 TR 13568 R 18181 RC
10719 TR 13215 R 13700 R 19050 RC
10886 TRC 13557 R 13722 R 19237 R
11335 R 13560 R 13728 R 20253 T
11337 R 13564 R 14804 RC 22718 R

2 Urban *and* Rural

Field Research

16202 T 16915 T 17857 R 19523 R

Primary Sources: Monographs

10337 TR 11714 TR 12663 TR 15678 TR
10341 TR 11715 TR 12841 C 15692 R
10381 R 11716 TR 13147 TR 17068 R
10796 R 11732 R 13271 R 17254 R
10852 RC 11777 R 13304 RC 18739 R
11015 T 11797 R 13720 R 20813 TR
11345 R 11823 R 15181 RC 20871 R
11691 TR 12327 R 15614 RC 22654 TR
11697 TR 12595 T 15664 T

Primary Sources: Inclusions

10163 C 13258 R 15911 C 20967 RC
11162 C 13309 RC 16065 R 21229 R
11749 R 15597 R 18356 C

Primary Sources: Journal Articles

10354 TR 12645 TR 13240 R 15690 R
10685 TR 12732 R 13269 R 15691 R
10911 C 12746 R 13281 R 15936 T
11684 TR 13011 R 13512 TR 16510 T
11755 R 13012 R 13559 R 16657 R
11826 R 13013 R 15588 TR 16961 R
12248 R 13014 R 15669 TR 18581 R
12280 R 13032 R 15670 TR 18715 R
12315 R 13146 TR 15688 R 19266 R
12351 R 13174 TR 15689 R 19560 R
12641 TR 13186 TR

Field Research *and* Primary Sources

10364 R 11712 TR 11834 R 15676 TR
10428 C 11785 R 13265 R 16509 T

Personal Observation

10824 R 15687 R 17525 T 19538 R
11671 T 16929 T 17688 T 20596 T
11803 R 16939 TR 17838 R 20795 TR
13655 TR 17024 T 18702 R 22693 R
13917 R

Primary Sources and Personal Observation

10340 TR 11825 R 12893 T 15683 R
10582 T 11827 R 13500 TR 16383 T
10745 R 12180 T 15674 TR 17305 R

Secondary Sources, Well Documented

10378 R 11832 R 12984 R 15680 R
11677 T 12292 R 13249 R 17266 R
11696 TR 12643 TR 15585 TR 17302 R
11781 R 12648 TR 15595 R 17551 T
11808 R 12687 TR 15668 TR 18576 R

Unsupported or Poorly Documented

11051 RC 12743 R 14129 RC 19876 RC
12285 R 13082 C 15602 RC 20654 R
12670 TR 13205 R 15873 RC

3 Narrowly Urban: Large Cities Only

10787 R 13252 R 17265 R 19548 R
12999 R 13276 R 17477 R 20731 T
13035 R 13699 R 17904 C 22719 R
13230 R

4 Urban, Including Smaller Cities and Hsien Capitals

11032 R 12736 R 13219 R 17229 R
11670 T 12752 R 13355 C 17310 R
12716 R 12755 R 13697 R 17455 R
12717 R 13039 R 13907 R 19547 R

5 Broadly Urban: Cities and Market Towns

13005 R 17253 R 17471 R 17716 R
18942 T

6 Market Towns Only

17056 R

7 Broadly Rural: Villages and Market Towns

12287 R 13229 R 16434 R 16645 R
12300 R 14431 R 16553 TR 17065 R
12301 R 15053 R 16627 R 17340 C
12321 R 15677 TR 16642 R 17568 R
12322 R 15679 TR 16643 R 20641 R

8 Narrowly Rural: Villages Only

12211 TR 12338 R 15583 T 16644 R
12286 R 12382 RC 15590 R 16669 R
12309 R 12406 RC 16225 TR 17231 R
12329 R 13514 TR

2.1 Heilungkiang

黑龍江 黑龍江

1 Place Irrelevant or Type of Place Unspecified

☐

2 Urban and Rural

10356 R 12968 TR 15639 R 15995 C
10398 TRC 12969 TR 15684 R 16120 R
11818 R 13634 T 15686 R 16384 T
12925 T 15287 C 15776 R 16406 TR
16429 R 16440 R 17327 C 21056 C
16433 R 16448 R 17540 T 22506 T
16437 R 16449 R

3 Narrowly Urban: Large Cities Only

15778 R 16436 R 17852 R 19329 C
21255 C

4 Urban, Including Smaller Cities and Hsien Capitals

15532 C 16974 R 19298 C 20575 T

5 Broadly Urban: Cities and Market Towns

12892 T

6 Market Towns Only

☐

7 Broadly Rural: Villages and Market Towns

13837 T 16450 R 17066 R 19669 C
15914 C 16546 TR 17067 R 20836 R
16435 R 16691 R 17244 R 21055 C

8 Narrowly Rural: Villages Only

15661 T 16879 C 17566 R 21054 C
16755 C 17348 C 17789 C 21151 C
16801 C

2.2 Kirin

吉林 吉林

1 Place Irrelevant or Type of Place Unspecified

☐

2 Urban and Rural

10421 C 15599 R 16442 R 17298 R
12926 T 15659 T 16968 R 17800 C
12988 R 16426 R 17085 R 20416 C
13558 R 16428 R

3 Narrowly Urban: Large Cities Only

15774 R 17050 R 17421 R 17490 R
16315 R 17230 R 17422 R 17723 R
16446 R 17286 R 17478 R 19311 C
16951 R 17346 C 17483 R 21246 C
16967 R

4 Urban, Including Smaller Cities and Hsien Capitals

15637 R 20141 T 21118 C

5 Broadly Urban: Cities and Market Towns

16397 T 16439 R

6 Market Towns Only

17263 R 21004 C

7 Broadly Rural: Villages and Market Towns

15665 T 16427 R 16462 C 17548 T
19196 C

8 Narrowly Rural: Villages Only

☐

2.3 Liaoning

遼寧 遼寧

1 Place Irrelevant or Type of Place Unspecified

10647 T 11237 T

2 Urban and Rural

13098 C 15847 C 16562 TR 19336 C
14988 C 15867 R 17013 C 20047 TR
15693 R 16385 T 17234 R 22412 T

3 Narrowly Urban: Large Cities Only

13001 R 15737 T 17500 C 19505 R
13007 R 15743 T 19293 C 20577 T
15335 T 17315 RC 19318 C 20715 T
15569 C 17383 C

4 Urban, Including Smaller Cities and Hsien Capitals

13362 C 16997 C 17488 R 20276 R
13396 C 17294 R 17489 R

5 Broadly Urban: Cities and Market Towns

☐

6 Market Towns Only

☐

7 Broadly Rural: Villages and Market Towns

17501 C 17689 T 17795 C 19195 C
20410 C 20672 C

8 Narrowly Rural: Villages Only

16680 R 17801 C 17881 R 19111 C
19828 R 20104 R

3.0 Inner Mongolia

(including 3.1-4, Jehol, Chahar, Suiyuan, or Ningsia only)

內蒙古 内蒙古

1 Place Irrelevant or Type of Place Unspecified

10876 TRC 11131 C 12769 RC 18220 C
22662 TR

2 Urban and Rural

Field Research

16786 C 22437 TR

Primary Sources

10375 R 11686 TR 17474 R 22738 RC
10874 TRC 12003 C 18245 C 22754 C
11099 C 15603 RC

Field Research and Primary Sources

10427 C 16972 R 19355 TR

3.0 Inner Mongolia

Personal Observation
11787 R 16681 R 17417 R 18911 T
15492 C 17043 R 18302 R

Primary Sources *and* Personal Observation
15391 TR 18924 T

Secondary Sources, Well Documented
□

Unsupported or Poorly Documented
11050 RC 13045 RC 15086 RC 19041 RC
11722 R 14106 TR 15393 R

3 Narrowly Urban: Large Cities Only
11582 TR 12981 R 18955 TR

4 Urban, Including Smaller Cities and Hsien Capitals
□

5 Broadly Urban: Cities *and* Market Towns
22713 R

6 Market Towns Only
17023 T

7 Broadly Rural: Villages *and* Market Towns
15660 T 15672 TR 16399 T 19080 RC
15671 TR 15673 TR 16445 R 20968 RC

8 Narrowly Rural: Villages Only
12330 R 15421 R 16303 R 22429 TR
12368 R 15666 TR 16306 R 22466 R
12407 RC 15667 TR 16307 R

4.0 Northwest and Far West
(including 4.3-5, Sinkiang, Tsinghai, or Tibet only)

西北地區及西部邊境

西北地区及び西部辺境

1 Place Irrelevant or Type of Place Unspecified
10922 C 13981 R 16331 TRC 20857 R
10957 C 14080 C 18864 T 20958 RC
12768 RC 14782 RC 20621 TR 22005 R
13799 T 15604 RC 20856 R 22616 T
13826 T

2 Urban *and* Rural

Field Research
10401 C 15696 RC 20304 RC 21196 RC
12726 R 19822 R 20660 RC

Primary Sources
10176 C 11161 C 15811 TRC 19375 C
10725 TR 11926 C 15857 C 21364 R
10759 R 12011 C 16517 T 22531 T
10863 TRC 12037 C 16752 TRC 22749 C
10939 C 12766 RC 16836 C 22765 C
11079 C 13019 R 17007 C 22768 C
11130 C 15620 C 18340 C

Field Research *and* Primary Sources
16633 R 22732 TRC

Personal Observation
10332 T 12857 C 16912 T 22682 R
10369 R 15753 T 16927 T 22698 R
12747 R 16647 R 20601 T

Primary Sources *and* Personal Observation
10415 C 15729 T

Secondary Sources, Well Documented
13044 RC 13332 C 13358 C 13814 T
16751 TRC 18890 T

Unsupported or Poorly Documented
11147 C 13713 R 15386 TR 22701 R

3 Narrowly Urban: Large Cities Only
□

4 Urban, Including Smaller Cities and Hsien Capitals
10921 C 13299 RC 22598 T 22642 T

5 Broadly Urban: Cities *and* Market Towns
□

6 Market Towns Only
□

7 Broadly Rural: Villages *and* Market Towns
13822 T 17351 C 20298 R 20927 R
16672 R 18671 R 20399 R 22462 R
16800 C

8 Narrowly Rural: Villages Only
16321 R 16809 C 20198 R 21808 R
16515 T 16859 C 20299 R 22453 R
16606 R 16896 C 20858 R 22467 R
16686 R 19889 RC 20859 R 22481 RC
16735 RC

4.1 Shensi

陝西　　陕西

1 Place Irrelevant or Type of Place Unspecified
17527 T

2 Urban *and* Rural
13895 R 15609 RC 16738 RC 18956 TR
14844 C 16422 R 16984 TRC 18993 R
15350 T 16628 R 18749 R

3 Narrowly Urban: Large Cities Only
15302 C 17087 R 20679 C

4 Urban, Including Smaller Cities and Hsien Capitals
18584 R

5 Broadly Urban: Cities *and* Market Towns
17235 R 18706 R

6 Market Towns Only
□

7 Broadly Rural: Villages *and* Market Towns
16656 R 16717 R 16803 C 19233 R

8 Narrowly Rural: Villages Only
15453 RC 16555 TR 16994 C 20634 R
15544 C 16716 R 18318 C 21851 RC
15545 C 16804 C 19119 C 22430 TR

4.2 Kansu

甘肅　　甘肃

1 Place Irrelevant or Type of Place Unspecified
□

2 Urban *and* Rural
15777 R 17376 C 17859 R 18935 T
16431 R 17416 R 18697 R 18996 R
16957 R 17837 R

3 Narrowly Urban: Large Cities Only
14820 C 15322 T 17293 R

4 Urban, Including Smaller Cities and Hsien Capitals
15323 T 18372 T

5 Broadly Urban: Cities *and* Market Towns
14764 R

6 Market Towns Only
□

7 Broadly Rural: Villages *and* Market Towns
14771 R 16299 R 17772 RC 19818 R
16170 T 16664 R 19661 C 20380 T

8 Narrowly Rural: Villages Only
15899 C 16325 R 16749 RC 16750 RC
19672 C 20048 TR

5.0 Northern China

華北地區　　華北地区

1 Place Irrelevant or Type of Place Unspecified
10576 T 15039 T 17969 C 19048 RC
20293 TR

2 Urban *and* Rural

Field Research
21083 C

Primary Sources
10178 C 13754 R 15120 C 18348 C
11158 C 14541 C 15624 C 19331 C
11541 T 14802 RC 15908 C 21127 C
12860 C 15037 T 18286 C 22577 T

Field Research *and* Primary Sources
10388 RC 10431 C 15077 R

Personal Observation

10598 T 14615 T 17292 R 20417 RC
11782 R 15045 T 17393 C 20624 R
12971 R 15083 R 17532 T 20709 T
12979 R 15367 T 18403 T 21298 T
13891 R 15626 T 18444 T 21344 TR
14228 TR 16926 T 19007 R

Primary Sources and Personal Observation

10380 R 14194 T 20880 R 22617 T
10776 R 14757 R 22383 T

Secondary Sources, Well Documented

19452 R

Unsupported or Poorly Documented

☐

3 Narrowly Urban: Large Cities Only

14573 T 19825 R 21359 TR 21531 RC
16295 R 20632 R 21509 R

4 Urban, Including Smaller Cities and Hsien Capitals

11565 T 12689 R 12725 R 12903 T
15770 R 22583 T

5 Broadly Urban: Cities and Market Towns

15812 C 20281 T

6 Market Towns Only

16051 T

7 Broadly Rural: Villages and Market Towns

12353 R 15360 T 17428 C 21729 TR
12542 C 16408 TR 21177 T 22454 R
13964 R 16699 R

8 Narrowly Rural: Villages Only

15406 R 16059 R 16625 R

5.1 Hopei

河北 河北

1 Place Irrelevant or Type of Place Unspecified

20084 T 21176 T 22456 R

2 Urban and Rural

Field Research

12991 R 17039 TR 20497 C 20888 R
15408 R 17062 R 20844 R 21431 C
15594 R 17309 R

Primary Sources

10514 T 14962 C 16568 R 18398 T
14712 R 15538 C 16953 R 19579 R

Field Research and Primary Sources

12993 R 15810 TRC 16956 R 17186 TR

Personal Observation

13910 R 16130 C 17645 C 20846 R
15341 T 16761 C 20142 T 20909 R
15355 T 16906 T 20381 T 21161 T
15394 R 16966 R 20477 C 21191 R
15754 T 17334 C 20585 T 22576 T
15768 R 17570 R 20693 C 22747 C

Primary Sources and Personal Observation

13034 R 13803 T 15452 TRC 16379 T
20012 TR

Secondary Sources, Well Documented

☐

Unsupported or Poorly Documented

15710 T 15789 TRC 16578 R 16582 R
17221 R

3 Narrowly Urban: Large Cities Only

Field Research

10797 R 17828 R 20889 R 21508 R
11575 TR 17831 R 20913 R 21510 R
11577 TR 17855 R 20921 R 21511 R
15846 C 17856 R 20922 R 21512 R
16304 R 17876 R 20928 R 21513 R
16316 R 17877 R 21018 C 21515 R
17049 R 17886 R 21069 C 21523 R
17069 R 18344 C 21219 R 21526 R
17083 R 19360 R 21220 R 22449 R
17251 R 19497 R 21223 R 22457 R
17252 R 20015 R 21224 R 22459 R
17273 R 20216 R 21230 R 22461 R
17277 R 20395 R 21507 R 22464 R
17702 R 20637 R

Primary Sources: Monographs

10505 T 15548 C 17692 TR 18958 TR
10607 T 15627 T 17736 R 20467 R
10945 C 15806 TRC 17824 TR 20507 C
11080 C 15942 TR 18092 T 20938 R
12958 TR 17529 T 18313 TRC 21278 T

Primary Sources: Inclusions

12741 R 14816 C 20464 R

Primary Sources: Journal Articles

10528 T 14270 RC 17215 R 18357 C
10529 T 14320 C 17218 R 19394 R
10556 T 14570 T 17413 R 19492 R
10565 T 14610 T 17687 T 19779 T
10570 T 15636 R 17690 TR 20448 R
10595 T 15868 R 17697 R 20608 TR
10606 T 16073 C 17715 R 20691 C
10673 T 16087 T 17829 R 21256 C
10941 C 16142 C 18066 C 21293 T
10996 C 16903 T 18096 T 22374 C
13002 R 16936 TR 18235 C 22426 TR
13525 R 17171 T 18295 C 22520 T
14196 T 17199 R 18329 C 22546 T
14197 T 17200 R

Field Research and Primary Sources

10898 C 17054 R 18033 R 20617 TR
14182 T 17184 TR 19357 TR 21221 R
14330 C 17185 TR 20613 TR 22397 T
15407 R 17713 R

Personal Observation: Monographs

10584 T 16121 R 18856 T 20579 T
10652 T 16219 T 20128 T 20631 R
11135 C 16250 TR 20140 T 20762 T
14157 T 16256 TR 20206 R 21264 T
15304 C 17158 T 20273 R 21375 R
15370 TR 18032 R 20436 R 21554 C
15372 TR 18036 R 20440 R 22750 C
15390 TR 18355 C 20458 R 22751 C
15416 R 18362 C 20527 C 22753 C
15828 C 18422 T 20559 T 22763 C
16101 TR

Personal Observation: Inclusions

10612 T 15014 C 17730 R 20435 R
10730 TR 15366 T 17802 C 20536 T
11229 T 15958 R 19337 C 21174 T
12986 R 17166 T 20091 T 21664 T
14604 T 17609 T 20238 C 21987 T
14947 C

Personal Observation: Journal Articles

10591 T 14551 T 14950 C 15760 TR
11547 T 14632 TR 15009 C 15786 R
11548 T 14641 TR 15021 C 15801 TRC
11551 T 14701 TR 15197 C 15851 C
11584 TR 14731 R 15342 T 16023 C
12842 C 14877 C 15395 R 16069 C
12939 T 14881 C 15435 R 16136 C
14234 R 14938 C 15730 T 16230 TR
16235 TR 17331 C 18050 C 20413 C
16236 TR 17375 C 18065 C 20460 R
16237 TR 17497 C 18068 C 20479 C
16238 TR 17552 T 18069 C 20557 T
16239 TR 17611 R 18467 T 20628 R
16240 TR 17625 T 18957 TR 20754 T
16241 TR 17628 T 18994 R 20758 T
16242 TR 17636 C 19406 C 20764 T
16243 TR 17650 R 19411 C 20930 R
16244 TR 17652 T 19586 C 20931 R
16293 R 17659 C 19740 T 20947 R
16313 R 17751 C 19758 T 21134 C
16373 T 17780 C 19857 RC 21157 C
17020 T 17806 C 20116 C 21371 R
17123 C 17819 T 20353 C 21517 R
17271 R 17843 R 20384 T 22541 T
17288 R 17844 R 20406 C 22704 R
17319 RC 18009 T

Primary Sources and Personal Observation

10977 C 14163 T 15320 T 18498 T
11568 T 14204 T 15347 T 18946 T
11573 T 14214 TR 15389 TR 20315 C
11597 R 14582 T 16198 T 20505 C
11599 R 14602 T 16199 T 20952 R
12931 T 15010 C 17446 TR 21169 T
12966 TR 15274 C 18330 C 21438 T

Secondary Sources, Well Documented

10547 T 14585 T 16080 C 22610 T
11497 C 15791 TRC 20599 T

Unsupported or Poorly Documented

11537 T 15561 C 17197 R 17705 R
11538 T 15755 TR 17204 R 17750 C
14625 T 15817 C 17556 T 19288 C
14791 RC 15866 R

4 Urban, Including Smaller Cities and Hsien Capitals

12917 T 16047 T 17414 R 20718 T
13537 R 17115 C 17450 R 21099 C
14717 R 17202 R 17720 R

5 Broadly Urban: Cities and Market Towns

14191 T 15769 R 17053 R 17141 T
17300 R

6 Market Towns Only

16201 T 22706 R

7 Broadly Rural: Villages and Market Towns

Field Research

15399 R 17240 R 17853 R 20843 R
15450 R 17470 R 17896 RC 20845 R
15596 R 17620 C 20701 C 20946 R
16234 TR 17773 RC 20842 R 20949 R

Primary Sources

16574 R 17639 C 18027 R 19211 T
17451 R 17830 R 19093 C

Field Research and Primary Sources

15460 RC 16232 TR 17463 R 22802 R
16231 TR 17187 TR 17871 R

Personal Observation

15397 R 16758 C 17534 T 19192 C
15502 C 16759 C 17677 C 19193 C
15510 C 16762 C 17731 R 19339 C
15516 C 16784 C 17740 C 19619 R
15525 C 16846 C 17891 R 19624 R
15565 C 16853 C 17914 C 19648 R
15849 C 16881 C 18456 T 20277 C
15872 R 17122 C 18658 R 21019 C
15894 C 17325 C 19118 C 21064 C
16465 C 17397 C 19152 C 21065 C
16474 C 17469 R 19161 C 21139 C
16661 R 17522 T

3 Narrowly Urban: Large Cities Only

14646 TR 22536 T 22596 T

4 Urban, Including Smaller Cities and Hsien Capitals

10801 R 14728 R 19206 T 19834 R
20136 T

5 Broadly Urban: Cities *and* Market Towns

□

6 Market Towns Only

□

7 Broadly Rural: Villages *and* Market Towns

12420 RC 16595 R 17812 T

8 Narrowly Rural: Villages Only

16521 T 16525 T 16700 R 17818 T

6.1 Kiangsu

江蘇　江蘇

1 Place Irrelevant or Type of Place Unspecified

14714 R 21621 T

2 Urban *and* Rural

Field Research
15432 R 16418 R 20882 R

Primary Sources
13802 T 15591 R 17183 TR 22409 T
15346 T 16094 T 17646 C 22539 T
15354 T 16394 T 18013 T 22589 T
15584 T 16559 TR

Field Research *and* Primary Sources
11747 R 15587 TR 16623 R 17029 TR
13226 R 16621 R 16947 R 17035 TR

Personal Observation
12980 R 15720 T 16908 T 17549 T
13139 TR 15731 T 17212 R 17558 T
14393 C 15732 T 17258 R 18363 T
14668 TR 15772 R 17330 C 22401 T
15552 C 16458 C 17332 C

Primary Sources *and* Personal Observation
16638 R 18865 T 19075 R 19748 T
20876 R

Secondary Sources, Well Documented
□

Unsupported or Poorly Documented
10368 R 12157 C 13193 R 17134 T
17783 C

3 Narrowly Urban: Large Cities Only

Field Research
14739 R 17487 R 17870 R 20915 R
15429 R 17709 R 17887 R 20919 R
15869 R 17710 R 19264 R 20924 R
15871 R 17728 R 19268 R 20936 R
17075 R 17732 R 20644 R 21037 C
17077 R 17833 R 20850 R 21136 C
17084 R 17834 R 20862 R 21528 R
17242 R 17835 R

Primary Sources: Monographs
11025 R 15930 T 16409 TR 17459 R
14732 R 15939 TR 16417 R 17892 TRC
15143 R 15944 TR 16980 R 18464 T
15377 TR 15948 TR 17037 TR 19533 R
15430 R 15953 TR 17161 T 19556 R
15431 R 16407 TR 17457 R 20879 R

Primary Sources: Inclusions
15291 C 15943 TR 18026 R 21670 T
15578 C 16075 C 18410 T 21707 T
15892 C 17431 T 19267 R

Primary Sources: Journal Articles
10841 R 17048 R 17693 TR 19308 C
14561 T 17162 T 17699 R 19486 R
14705 R 17195 R 17701 R 19498 R
14925 C 17196 R 17704 R 19507 R
15019 C 17217 R 17724 R 19509 R
15632 TR 17219 R 17726 R 19510 R
15634 R 17290 R 17733 R 19535 R
15635 R 17372 C 17735 R 19566 R
15921 T 17412 TR 17826 R 20394 R
15964 R 17475 R 17827 R 20685 C
16078 C 17476 R 17880 R 20885 R
16091 T 17491 R 18404 T 22164 R
16905 T 17612 R 18453 T 22538 T
16921 T 17660 C 18522 T 22716 R
17041 R

Field Research *and* Primary Sources
15946 TR 17155 T 17734 R 19555 R
15961 R 17193 TR 19269 R 20195 R
16402 TR 17725 R

Personal Observation: Monographs
15254 C 15728 T 18354 C 22744 C
15307 T 15929 T 20087 T 22755 C
15315 T 16050 T 20886 R 22764 C
15318 T 16060 R 22696 R

Personal Observation: Inclusions
15881 C 18008 T 19550 R 19680 C
16416 R 19508 R 19605 C 21154 C
17358 C 19511 R

Personal Observation: Journal Articles
10274 T 16197 T 17637 C 18918 T
11554 T 16292 R 17648 RC 18926 T
12977 R 16297 R 17651 R 19015 R
13009 R 16319 R 17653 C 19023 R
13326 C 16345 C 17654 C 19519 R
13726 R 16502 C 17656 C 19690 T
13900 R 17040 R 17698 R 19703 R
13924 R 17125 C 17706 R 19706 R
14552 T 17168 T 17707 R 19807 R
14748 R 17222 R 17714 R 19844 R
14807 RC 17227 R 17719 R 20103 R
14866 C 17246 R 17722 R 20112 RC
14960 C 17269 R 17737 R 20207 R
14963 C 17275 R 17765 R 20251 C
14966 C 17324 C 17805 C 20830 R
15357 T 17380 C 17836 R 20838 R
15396 R 17432 T 17898 RC 20875 R
15404 R 17452 R 17943 R 20884 R
15474 RC 17454 R 18028 R 20918 R
15556 C 17465 R 18067 C 20935 R
15788 R 17466 R 18473 T 20951 R
16086 T 17467 R 18693 R 22582 T
16122 R 17555 T

Primary Sources *and* Personal Observation
12955 TR 15727 T 17052 R 19300 C
14609 T 15764 TR 17694 TR 20898 R
14665 TR 16108 TR 17863 R 21252 C
14675 TR 16109 TR 19069 C

Secondary Sources, Well Documented
15388 TR 16113 TR 17851 R 20392 R
15765 TR 17440 TR 17874 R 20851 R
15950 TR 17850 R 18600 R 20883 R

Unsupported or Poorly Documented
10770 R 17042 R 19258 R 19529 R
11350 R 17747 C 19319 C 19549 R
14819 C 17839 R 19426 R 19552 R
15844 C 18025 R 19522 R 21258 T

4 Urban, Including Smaller Cities and Hsien Capitals

13224 R 16401 TR 17076 R 19220 TR
16227 TR 17051 R 17464 R

5 Broadly Urban: Cities *and* Market Towns

20003 T

6 Market Towns Only

□

7 Broadly Rural: Villages *and* Market Towns

Field Research
15405 R 16662 R 17667 R 20925 R
16631 R 16714 R 17868 R 21216 R

Primary Sources
15761 TR 16605 R 16668 R 17816 T
17825 R 19213 TR

Field Research *and* Primary Sources
15368 T 17033 TR 17079 R 21210 R
21215 R

Personal Observation
11553 T 15843 C 16895 C 17821 T
15503 C 15853 C 17295 R 19689 T
15577 C 15854 C 17462 R 21116 C
15771 R 16466 C 17606 C 21628 T
15837 C 16831 C

Primary Sources *and* Personal Observation
16484 C

Secondary Sources, Well Documented
15426 R

Unsupported or Poorly Documented
17784 C 21000 C

8 Narrowly Rural: Villages Only

15374 TR 16641 R 16724 RC 19116 C
15402 R 16718 R 16793 C 20043 T
15517 C 16721 R 17402 C 20629 R
16414 R

6.2 Anhwei

安徽　安徽

1 Place Irrelevant or Type of Place Unspecified

11552 T

2 Urban *and* Rural

10751 R 15924 T 17858 R 20262 R
21152 C

3 Narrowly Urban: Large Cities Only

18321 C 18983 TR 20581 T 21133 C

4 Urban, Including Smaller Cities and Hsien Capitals

17015 C 18857 T

5 Broadly Urban: Cities *and* Market Towns

13392 C 14635 TR

7.3 Kiangsi
江西　江西

1 Place Irrelevant or Type of Place Unspecified
13479 T　22445 R

2 Urban and Rural
11726 R　16411 R　16583 R　17312 RC
11795 R　16415 R　16586 R　17580 RC
13522 TR　16420 R　16763 C　19966 R
15155 R　16432 R

3 Narrowly Urban: Large Cities Only
14743 R　17170 T　17172 T　17296 R
17344 C

4 Urban, Including Smaller Cities and Hsien Capitals
17203 R

5 Broadly Urban: Cities and Market Towns
☐

6 Market Towns Only
17798 C　21144 C

7 Broadly Rural: Villages and Market Towns
13541 R　16639 R　18305 R　19621 R
13983 R　16842 C　18751 R　19726 TR
15998 C　17761 R　19191 C　20829 R
16617 R　17776 C　19578 R　21072 C
16629 R

8 Narrowly Rural: Villages Only
20241 C

8.0 Southwestern China
西南地區　西南地区

1 Place Irrelevant or Type of Place Unspecified
16287 R　17970 C　19049 RC

2 Urban and Rural

Field Research
☐

Primary Sources
10179 C　14542 C　15909 C　18349 C
10651 T　14803 RC　17562 R　19334 C
11159 C　15121 C　18089 T　21128 C
12861 C　15625 C　18287 C

Field Research and Primary Sources
10429 C　16787 C

Personal Observation
10318 T　15356 T　16911 T　18925 T
12601 T　15629 T　16913 T　22523 T
12735 R　15750 T　16931 T　22542 T
12899 T　16512 T

Primary Sources and Personal Observation
17137 T

Secondary Sources, Well Documented
21892 TRC

Unsupported or Poorly Documented
16504 C

3 Narrowly Urban: Large Cities Only
☐

4 Urban, Including Smaller Cities and Hsien Capitals
☐

5 Broadly Urban: Cities and Market Towns
☐

6 Market Towns Only
☐

7 Broadly Rural: Villages and Market Towns
12543 C　15738 T　17146 T　17926 T

8 Narrowly Rural: Villages Only
16646 R　22552 T

8.1 Szechwan
(including Sikang)
四川　四川

1 Place Irrelevant or Type of Place Unspecified
13454 T　16268 TR　16301 R　18548 TR
21990 T

2 Urban and Rural

Field Research
14750 R　16596 R　17668 R　19026 R
14839 C　16678 R　18694 R　19849 R
15739 T　17064 R　19022 R　20627 R
16083 C

Primary Sources
10382 TRC　10791 R　13038 R　17480 R
10566 T　11706 TR　15270 C　18475 T
10790 R　12932 T　16990 C　20537 T

Field Research and Primary Sources
16653 R　17089 R

Personal Observation
10359 R　15717 T　16312 R　18532 TR
11753 R　15740 T　16404 TR　18889 T
12889 T　15862 T　16419 R　19742 T
13196 R　15897 C　16443 R　20583 T
13287 R　15957 R　17139 T　20863 R
13538 R　16166 T　17243 R　21810 R
15365 T　16260 TR　17624 C　22517 T
15401 R　16267 TR　18040 TRC　22677 R
15413 R　16300 R

Primary Sources and Personal Observation
15784 R　16543 T　16683 R　20808 TR
16371 T　16640 R　20574 T　20809 TR

Secondary Sources, Well Documented
10358 R　16960 R

Unsupported or Poorly Documented
17211 R

3 Narrowly Urban: Large Cities Only

Field Research
14634 TR　17864 R　17888 R　20447 R
17061 R　17865 R　17889 R　20874 R
17063 R　17866 R　17890 R　20950 R
17473 R　17867 R　19261 R　21212 R
17633 R　17885 R

Primary Sources
16444 R　17088 R　17106 C　22570 T
17044 R　17090 R　18892 T　22597 T
17058 R

Field Research and Primary Sources
☐

Personal Observation
14171 T　15716 T　19299 C　20704 T
14745 R　16482 C　19817 R　20711 T
15379 TR　18333 C　20456 R　20735 T
15522 C　18573 TR　20551 T　20839 R
15579 C

Primary Sources and Personal Observation
14630 TR　17437 T　20804 TR

Secondary Sources, Well Documented
☐

Unsupported or Poorly Documented
17105 C

4 Urban, Including Smaller Cities and Hsien Capitals
16302 R　17535 T　18845 T　20475 RC
17279 R　18087 T　18861 T　20584 T

5 Broadly Urban: Cities and Market Towns
16447 R　17031 TR　17072 R　17366 C
21280 T

6 Market Towns Only
15392 R　15436 R　18035 R　19827 R

7 Broadly Rural: Villages and Market Towns

Field Research
16598 R　16713 R　17070 R　17663 R
16654 R　16722 R　17071 R　17840 R
16701 R　16965 R　17086 R　17841 R
16704 R　17045 R　17091 R　19465 R

Primary Sources
16635 R　16675 R　17872 R

Field Research and Primary Sources
15598 R　16599 R　16601 R　16655 R
16665 R　17479 R

Personal Observation
15916 C　17011 C　18929 T　20910 R
16548 TR　17082 R　20887 R　22460 R

Primary Sources and Personal Observation
☐

Secondary Sources, Well Documented
☐

Unsupported or Poorly Documented
17210 R

8 Narrowly Rural: Villages Only
16527 T　16597 R　16707 R　17415 R
16528 T　16600 R　16708 R　19019 R
16542 T　16649 R　16723 R　20396 R
16589 R　16652 R　17163 T　20840 R
16590 R　16698 R　17178 T

8.2 Yunnan
雲南　雲南

1 Place Irrelevant or Type of Place Unspecified
18962 TR

2 Urban and Rural
Field Research
15640 R　16118 R　21313 TR　21316 TR
15641 R　17854 R　21315 TR　21369 R

Primary Sources
11679 T　13857 T　18131 R　18381 T
19885 RC

Field Research and Primary Sources
□

Personal Observation
10639 T　15638 R　16932 T　18491 T
12924 T　15715 T　16970 R　18922 T
13209 R　15748 T　17159 T　19270 R
13221 R　16077 C　17267 R　20707 T
15316 T　16168 T　17538 T　20933 R
15581 T　16916 T　18300 T　22508 T

Primary Sources and Personal Observation
12626 TR　12951 TR　16372 T　18394 T
12919 T　15593 R　17520 T

Secondary Sources, Well Documented
12912 T　13801 T

Unsupported or Poorly Documented
11789 R

3 Narrowly Urban: Large Cities Only
14616 T　16441 R　18365 T　20550 T
15425 R　17632 R　19846 R　20916 R
15633 TR　17729 R　20217 R　20948 R

4 Urban, Including Smaller Cities and Hsien Capitals
10746 R　16963 R　20890 R　21312 TR
14571 T　18933 T　21194 R　21314 TR

5 Broadly Urban: Cities and Market Towns
15308 T　17815 T

6 Market Towns Only
19362 R　19729 R　20872 R

7 Broadly Rural: Villages and Market Towns
15326 T　16648 R　19085 RC　20873 R
15424 R　17182 TR　20573 T　21618 T
16425 R　17194 TR　20645 R　22388 T
16467 C　17613 R　20771 T　22447 R
16511 T

8 Narrowly Rural: Villages Only
16618 R　16619 R　17664 R　19830 R
22448 R

8.3 Kweichow
貴州　貴州

1 Place Irrelevant or Type of Place Unspecified
14349 C　21192 R

2 Urban and Rural
10767 R　16370 T　16540 T　16971 R
20881 R

3 Narrowly Urban: Large Cities Only
□

4 Urban, Including Smaller Cities and Hsien Capitals
18640 R　18770 R

5 Broadly Urban: Cities and Market Towns
□

6 Market Towns Only
□

7 Broadly Rural: Villages and Market Towns
16531 T　18322 C　21114 C

8 Narrowly Rural: Villages Only
16688 R　22483 TRC

9.0 Southeastern China
華南地區　華南地区

1 Place Irrelevant or Type of Place Unspecified
10625 T　20029 C　21274 T　22403 T
12614 T　20069 TRC　21281 T　22480 RC
13305 TRC　20261 R　21522 R　22495 C
13854 T　20338 C　21781 TR　22635 T
19865 TRC　20768 T　22022 C

2 Urban and Rural
Field Research
17589 C　21479 C

Primary Sources
10275 T　10708 TR　16514 T　18490 T
10327 T　12428 C　17390 C　18860 T
10511 T　14088 T　17530 T　19045 TRC
10552 T　16062 R　18438 T

Field Research and Primary Sources
10426 C　15376 TR　16064 R　16190 T
16798 C　17959 C

Personal Observation
15305 T　16396 T　17615 RC　21271 T
15349 T　16945 R　18063 C　21428 RC
15359 T　17237 R　18950 TR　21480 C
16387 T　17353 C　20297 R　22415 T
16391 T

Primary Sources and Personal Observation
13906 R　16507 T　20234 TRC　21270 T
14758 R　16998 C　20755 T

Secondary Sources, Well Documented
10298 R　10756 R　11828 R　15608 TRC
20357 C

Unsupported or Poorly Documented
□

3 Narrowly Urban: Large Cities Only
10280 T　15339 T　18569 TR　19692 T
10282 TR　15344 T　18607 R　21413 RC
10522 T　15923 T　18997 R　21573 C
12870 C　17657 T　19501 R　21575 C
12996 R　17813 T　19502 R　22606 T
13016 R　18048 C　19506 R

4 Urban, Including Smaller Cities and Hsien Capitals
10271 T　10292 TR　19557 R　22398 T
10273 T　14629 TR　20722 T　22550 T

5 Broadly Urban: Cities and Market Towns
15725 T　17919 T　18427 T　19472 TR
20385 T

6 Market Towns Only
□

7 Broadly Rural: Villages and Market Towns
10270 T　17533 T　19962 TR　19981 TRC
16338 TRC　17949 TRC　19975 TRC　20386 T
16558 TR

8 Narrowly Rural: Villages Only
17563 R　19987 C　22479 TRC

9.1 Kwangsi
廣西　広西

1 Place Irrelevant or Type of Place Unspecified
22647 TR

2 Urban and Rural
10357 R　12953 TR　17545 T　20894 R
11668 T　15423 R　18686 R　22510 T
11837 R　16530 T

3 Narrowly Urban: Large Cities Only
13798 T　20828 R

4 Urban, Including Smaller Cities and Hsien Capitals
15651 C

5 Broadly Urban: Cities and Market Towns
16933 T

6 Market Towns Only
□

7 Broadly Rural: Villages and Market Towns
17665 R　18851 T　21141 C

8 Narrowly Rural: Villages Only
16634 R　19675 C　20853 R

13764 RC 15586 TR 15890 C 16748 RC
15438 R 15600 TRC 16330 TRC 16777 C
15439 R 15613 RC 16495 C 17127 C
15440 R 15615 C 16710 R 18877 T
15441 R 15675 TR 16711 R 18903 T
15442 R 15695 RC 16726 TRC 18981 TR
15443 R 15701 C 16742 TRC 22600 T
15444 R 15888 C 16747 RC 22646 TR
15472 RC 15889 C

Primary Sources: Inclusions
12017 C 15601 RC 15875 RC 18290 C
13102 C 15606 RC 15917 C 19911 C
13179 TR 15612 RC 17544 T 20989 RC
15091 RC 15658 T 17786 C

Primary Sources: Journal Articles
10675 T 12106 C 15457 RC 17743 C
11019 TR 12135 C 15471 RC 18121 R
11521 C 12136 C 15582 T 18297 C
11528 C 12137 C 15605 TRC 19769 T
11659 T 12142 C 15607 TRC 19782 TR
11660 T 12143 C 15698 TRC 19956 C
11843 RC 12144 C 15861 C 20673 C
11851 TRC 12146 C 15902 C 21231 TRC
11856 RC 12152 C 15912 C 21235 TRC
11873 RC 13052 RC 15918 C 21238 C
11904 C 13312 RC 16025 C 21240 C
11964 C 13313 RC 16365 C 21247 C
11985 C 15106 C 16611 R

Field Research *and* Primary Sources
10345 TR 14134 C 15852 C 20334 C
10385 RC 14874 C 16727 RC 20686 C
10394 RC 14955 C 16729 RC 20995 RC
11232 T 15002 C 16740 TRC 21009 C
12008 C 15654 C 17961 C 21131 C
13053 TRC 15655 C 18263 C 21232 TRC
13079 C 15697 TRC 19064 C 21233 RC
13113 C 15703 C 19711 C 21237 C
13297 RC 15707 C 20074 C 21243 C
13301 RC 15708 C 20320 C 21483 C

Personal Observation
10857 TRC 14949 C 16506 T 19068 C
10950 C 15351 T 16651 R 20337 C
10984 C 15490 C 17169 T 20339 C
11663 T 15554 C 17822 T 21068 C
11844 TRC 15562 C 17922 T 21084 C
13235 R 16022 C 17984 RC 21520 R
13450 C 16167 T 18908 T 23027 C
14895 C 16347 C

Primary Sources *and* Personal Observation
10325 T 14224 TR 14994 C 16226 TR
11044 RC 14554 T 15369 TR 16858 C
11959 C 14796 RC 15437 R 19065 C
12174 C

Secondary Sources, Well Documented
10387 TRC 11059 C 16884 C 17989 TRC
10416 C 15709 C 16898 C 19890 TRC
10674 T 16261 TR 16987 RC 22490 RC
10959 C 16561 TR 17988 RC 22735 TRC
10983 C 16864 C

Unsupported or Poorly Documented
See Geographic Index

3 Narrowly Urban: Large Cities Only

Field Research
10923 C 19936 C 20367 C 21566 C
14896 C 19937 C 20372 C 21568 C
14981 C 19989 C 20378 C 21571 C
16351 C 20308 C 20424 C 21580 C
16357 C 20332 C 20425 C 21588 C
16358 C 20340 C 21024 C 21592 C
17621 C 20341 C 21049 C 21600 C
17622 C 20342 C 21051 C 21925 C
18049 C 20343 C 21481 C 21944 C
19292 C 20344 C 21552 C 22023 C
19910 C 20360 C 21564 C 22497 C
19935 C 20364 C 21565 C 22770 C

Primary Sources
10985 C 15647 C 19247 R 21582 C
15568 C 15650 C 21518 R 21590 C

Field Research *and* Primary Sources
15793 TRC 15794 TRC 16007 C 20333 C
21577 C 21581 C

Personal Observation
14799 RC 17794 C 21074 C 21584 C
14879 C 20119 C 21421 RC 22840 C
16024 C 20702 T 21562 C

Primary Sources *and* Personal Observation
14979 C 15822 C

Secondary Sources, Well Documented
16996 C

Unsupported or Poorly Documented
See Geographic Index

4 Urban, Including Smaller Cities and Hsien Capitals

10956 C 14858 C 15898 C 17799 C
12866 C 14908 C 16360 C 19320 C
13306 TRC 14911 C 16983 TRC 19587 C
13445 C 15026 C 16999 C 20326 C
13673 TR 15766 TR 17006 C 20517 C
13770 C 15848 C 17386 C 22018 C
14549 C

5 Broadly Urban: Cities *and* Market Towns

14544 C 15792 TRC 17618 C 22752 C

6 Market Towns Only

20268 C

7 Broadly Rural: Villages *and* Market Towns

Field Research
15491 C 16845 C 16886 C 19738 C
15530 C 16865 C 17118 C 19955 C
15533 C 16867 C 17128 C 20072 C
16003 C 16869 C 17910 C 20249 C
16364 C 16870 C 18004 C 20317 C
16818 C 16871 C 19466 RC 21017 C
16820 C 16883 C 19468 RC 21030 C
16826 C

Primary Sources
13081 C 16551 TR 16797 C 16844 C
16009 C 16554 TR 16827 C 16851 C
16088 T 16728 TRC 16829 C 17518 C
16549 TR 16734 RC

Field Research *and* Primary Sources
16825 C 16902 C 17103 TRC 19679 C
16872 C 16986 TRC 17774 RC 21108 C
16873 C 17101 TRC

Personal Observation
15785 R 16350 C 16821 C 17907 C
21946 C

Primary Sources *and* Personal Observation
16783 C 16788 C 16810 C 16856 C
19663 C

Secondary Sources, Well Documented
16823 C 16854 C 19173 C 22627 T

Unsupported or Poorly Documented
See Geographic Index

8 Narrowly Rural: Villages Only

Field Research
15504 C 15887 C 16361 C 16772 C
15505 C 16133 C 16368 C 16785 C
15521 C 16134 C 16725 RC 16794 C
15816 C 16354 C 16771 C 16811 C
16819 C 17616 C 19916 C 20377 C
16866 C 17676 C 19925 C 20422 C
16868 C 17681 C 20018 C 20423 C
16887 C 17897 RC 20024 C 21089 C
16891 C 19079 RC 20236 C 21236 C
16892 C 19088 RC 20355 C 21583 C
16901 C 19089 RC

Primary Sources
16544 T 16739 TRC 16789 C 16840 C
16550 TR 16741 TRC 16790 C 16885 C
16610 R 16745 TRC 16795 C 16899 C
16674 R 16776 C 16822 C 17424 RC
16733 TRC 16778 C 16828 C 17610 T
16737 TRC 16780 C 16833 C

Field Research *and* Primary Sources
15515 C 17669 RC 19737 C 19896 TRC
15704 C 19090 RC 19864 RC 19973 TRC
16746 RC 19163 C 19895 RC 19980 TRC
16849 C

Personal Observation
16834 C 16852 C 21201 C

Primary Sources *and* Personal Observation
□

Secondary Sources, Well Documented
16832 C 16843 C

Unsupported or Poorly Documented
See Geographic Index

9.5 Hong Kong and Macau

香港及澳門 香港及び澳門

1 Place Irrelevant or Type of Place Unspecified

See Geographic Index

2 Urban *and* Rural

Field Research
13048 RC 16146 C 19051 TRC 20681 C
14887 C 16816 C 19929 C 20773 T
15473 TRC 17001 C 20309 C 21555 C
15616 C 17963 C 20310 C 22494 C
15617 C 17965 C 20358 C 22498 C
15813 C 18060 C

Primary Sources
11031 R 15945 TR 16955 R 19309 C
11340 R 15973 TRC 16985 TRC 19335 C
11389 TRC 16030 C 17003 C 19702 R
11466 C 16057 R 17004 C 19713 C
13046 TRC 16076 C 17009 C 19874 TRC
14890 C 16117 R 17261 R 19912 C
14891 C 16125 TRC 17357 C 20062 R
14892 C 16141 C 17360 C 20075 C
14893 C 16438 R 17362 C 20622 TR
14894 C 16463 C 17379 C 20682 C
15381 TR 16471 C 17398 C 20869 R
15409 R 16473 C 17399 C 20870 R
15461 TRC 16492 C 17419 R 21061 C
15518 C 16497 C 17718 R 21063 C
15520 C 16498 C 17745 C 21234 RC
15610 TRC 16501 C 17894 RC 21254 C
15842 C 16941 TR 17909 C 22724 RC
15858 C 16954 R 17917 C

Field Research *and* Primary Sources
10301 RC 15859 C 17002 C 19946 C
14889 C 15974 TRC 17349 C 20426 C
15643 RC 16002 C 17985 RC 21197 RC
15802 TRC 16010 C 17994 C 21244 C
15850 C 16496 C

Personal Observation
14597 T 15555 C 17124 C 17899 RC
15487 C 15719 T 17425 C 17946 TRC
15514 C 16132 C 17623 C 17966 C
15529 C 16275 TR 17810 C 19306 C
15541 C 16328 TRC 17893 RC 19591 C

3 Narrowly Urban: Large Cities Only

4 Urban, Including Smaller Cities and Hsien Capitals

5 Broadly Urban: Cities and Market Towns

6 Market Towns Only

7 Broadly Rural: Villages and Market Towns

8 Narrowly Rural: Villages Only

□

AUTHOR INDEXES
AND GENERAL INDEX

Author Index

編著者姓名索引

著者姓名索引

An alphabetical index of personal authors, editors, compilers, and reviewers, showing variant names

著者、編纂者、書評作者姓名索引、依羅馬拚音字母排列、並示筆名別號

'著者、編者名索引
（ＡＢＣ順、別名を含む）

Authors whose names are identical (or identical in romanized form) are distinguished by birth and death dates or publication dates. Oriental names are of the surname-first form where no comma follows the surname. To eliminate cross-references, all pertinent entry numbers are listed after each variant form of an author's name. Alphabetization rules are specified on p. lxiii.

A

A Sheng 17892
A-shen 17892
Aagaard, Johannes 21843
Abbatucci, *Dr.* 20705
Abbott, Kenneth Albert 21546
Abe Munemitsu 14821 19660
Abeel, David 15305
Abegg, Lily 11883 13873 14822 21718
Abel, Clarke 15306
Abel, Theodora Mead 21505
Abend, Hallett Edward 13888
Aborigine 19685
Abramson, Manuil Moiseevich 11726 18109
Adam, Kenneth 16989
Adams, George Burton 18006
Adams, Inez 12209
Adams, John B- 19770
Adams, Ruth 14964 15271 19167 21148
Addison, James Thayer 20004
Adie, William Andrew Charles 15199 19366
Adlakha, Arjun L- 21242
Adler, Marcus Nathan 18846
Adler, Solomon 11884 12090
Adolph, Paul Ernest 20835
Adolph, William Henry 14706 17224 20625 20626
Adrianovskii, A- 11885
Adshead, Samuel Adrian Miles 10536 12949 12950 13454 20537 22507
Adzharov, A- 14114
Adzhimamudova, V- S- 18026
Afanas'ev, A- G- 12741 13260 14411 14468 15148 18026 22092 22141
Afanas'evskii, Evgenii Aleksandrovich 10382 16990
Afanas'yevskiy, Yevgeniy Aleksandrovich 10382 16990
Agapov, Evgenii 10743 11727
Agassi, Joseph 15330 15473 15546 15876 16494 16496 17595 17635 20267 20419 20657 20663 20664 21059 21549
Agassi, Judith Buber 15876 20664
Agnew, Mary Caldwell 20627
Agostinoni, Emidio 14553
Aguirre, 20296
Ahern, Emily Martin 20018
Ahlers, John 13210 17454
Ahmad, S- H- 15200
Ahn, Byung-joon 22290 22291
Ai Kang 17005
Aiaks, ——— 13487
Aijmer, Lars Göran 15451 20016 21827
Aingreville, Pacifique-Marie d' 21162
Aird, John Shields 10210 10223 10224 10225 10226 10235 20306
Airey, Willis Thomas Goodwin 17311
Akatova, Tat'iana Nikolaevna 13889 14468 18110 19499 19500 19501 19502 22945
Akers-Jones, David 19969
Akhmatov, Iv—— 19444
Akramovskaia, V- 14469
Alabaster, Chaloner 17018
Alabaster, Ernest 11183 11184
Albrecht, A- 18713
Albrecht, Dietmar 15201 20476
Alderfer, Evan B- 13143
Aleksandrenko, G- 19289
Aleksandrov, G- I- 13700
Alekseenko, Ivan Pimenovich 20953
Alekseev, Vasilii Mikhailovich 11819 12333 21719 22142 22383 22422 22423
Alekseeva, N- M- 22946
Alenkovich, A- A- 12445
Alexeiev, Basil M. 11819 12333 21719 22142 22383 22422 22423
Alimov, A- 18556
Alin, V- N- 16225
Alisjabana, Sutan Takdir 21470
Alitto, Susan Biele 14823
Allain, R- 16506
Allan, Charles Wilfrid 22438
Allen, Andrew 17440
Allen, Bernard M- 13802
Allen, Charles Laurel 16991
Allen, Edwin Joseph, Jr. 21003
Allen, George Cyril 13144
Allen, Nathan 20538
Allen, Richard V- 18189
Alley, Rewi 15421 15479 15480 15481 15482 15983 15984 15985 16414 16457 16458 16754 16755 16756 16757 16758 16759 16760 16761 16762 16763 16764 16765 16766 17225 17226 17227 17255 17312 17313 17326 17327 17328 17329 17330 17331 17332 17579 17580 17670 17772 17776 17777 20477 20915
Allman, Norwood Francis 12982
Allom, Thomas 10001
Almond, Gabriel Abraham 23012
Al'skii, M- 10744 13488 13531 19503
Altree, Wayne 12623
Álvarez, José María 15369 16226
Álvarez del Vayo, Julio 10130 10895
Alvarez Semedo, F- 13836
Amann, Gustav 18577 18578 18579
Amaury, E- G- 15712
Ament, William S- 17918
An Hsüan-hung 21004
An, Tai Sung 14021 15202
An, Thomas S. 14021 15202
An Tze-wen 10896 18192
An Tzu-wen 10896 18192
An, Yung-Jui 12701
An, Yü-kun 11307
An Yü-k'un 11307
Anan'eva, M- I- 22825
Anastas'eva, T- N- 14824
Anderson, Adelaide Mary 17691 17836
Anderson, Dick 15986
Anderson, Eugene Newton, Jr. 14125 15813 15814 16346 16767 17957 17958 19987 20665 21005 21547 21905 21906 22494
Anderson, Flavia Giffard 18366
Anderson, G- L- 21666
Anderson, George E- 17686
Anderson, James Norman Dalrymple 11400 19930
Anderson, John 17520 22508
Anderson, Luther 20628
Anderson, Malcolm P- 12178
Anderson, Marja Lisa 20665 21005
Anderson, Mary Raleigh 14629
Anderson, Maurice John 14825
Anderson, Walfred Albin 19466
Andō Hikotarō 15452 19406
Andors, Stephen Paul 16054 19290
Andreev, M- G- 14105 16415 17611
Andreichik, A- 19504
Andrew, Geoffrey Clement 14826
Andrew, George Findlay 13643 17837
Andrews, Carol Corder 19445
Anelli, Emilio 22509
Ang Tian-se 21647
Anna 20187
Anschel, Kurt R- 19173
Anshen, Ruth Nanda 19788 19914
Ansley, Clive 15203
Antelava, N- V- 21006
Antoine, R- 17137
Antonini, Paul 15307
Antonov, Konstantin Vladimirovich 22076
Anuchin, Vsevolod Aleksandrovich 10337

Aoki Shinichi 11886
Aoki Shin'ichi 11886
Aparnikova, TS- 11422
Appleton, Sheldon Lee 11059 17959 21478 21479 21480
Arai Yoshirō 17732
Araki, Mitsutaro 13701
Araki Mitsutarō 13701
Ardant, Philippe 10897 11060
Arditi, Lazzaro 17838
Ardsheal 10504
Arendt, Carl 20539
Arens, M- 11728
Arens, Richard 14707 14827 14828
Ariëns Kappers, Cornelis Ubbo 14708
Ariga, Kizaemon 19724
Arkus, R- S- 11729 13145 13532 22643
Arkush, Ralph David 14295 22077
Arlington, Lewis Charles 10684 15370 20388 20607 20789 21720 21721
Arlt, Gustave O- 22450
Armand, Adolphe 20540
Armbruster, Frank E- 14022
Armerding, Hudson Taylor 18952
Armstrong, Alexander 10317
Armstrong, John Paul 17228
Arnault, Jacques 21548
Arndt, Paul 10453 14455 14495
Arnold, Julean Herbert 11730 11731 14470 14554
Arnol'dov, L- V- 10087 10088
Arsen'ev, Vladimir Klavdievich 20836
Arsent'ev, Aleksandr Ivanovich 14829
Arssenjew, W. 20836
Arturov, O- A- 22947
Asakawa Kenji 12429 13318 13769 16768
Ashbrook, Arthur Garwood, Jr. 11887 11888
Ashchepkov, Evgenii Andreevich 21486
Ashdown, John 14517
Ashmore, William 17521
Ashton, John 13319
Asiaticus, pub. 1928 20807
Asiaticus, pub. 1930s 12702 13890
Aske, Sigurd 18993
Aslett, Michael 15815
Aspberg, Johan 22470
Astaf'ev, Gennadii Vasil'evich 13294 13295 13320 13321 13322 22826
Athenoux, André 11603
Atkinson, Robert Llewellyn Peter 16981
Attatucci, *Dr.* 20706
Atterbury, Marguerite 19650
Atwood, Elaine Spalding 22386
Au, Lewis Li-tang 12788
Auboyer, Jeannine 22890
Auclair, Marcelle 19900
Audemard, Louis 12624
Augenstein, Bruno Wilhelm 14023
Avarin, Vladimir IAkovlevich 11732 11733 13146 13147 15204 17229 18580 18785
Avdoshchenkov, A- IA- 17455 19505
Avenarius, G- G- 12625 12983 12984 13644 13645 14402 14407 17230 19359 19715 22024
Averink, Annie 16070
Awarin, W. 11732 11733 13146 13147 15204 17229 18580 18785
Axilrod, Eric 11889 22182
Aya, Roderick 15187 15281
Ayers, Thomas William 10536 14518 14555 19394 19506 19507 21429
Aymard, Am—— 15308
Ayraud, *Dr.* 20707
Ayscough, Florence Wheelock 16227 20159 20608 21455 22444

B

Baber, Edward Colborne 10318
Babić, Blagoje 11890
Bach, A- H- 19716
Backhouse, Edmund Trelawney 10505 21260
Bacon, C- A- 19228 20838
Bady, Paul 14830 22292
Bagwell, May 20195
Baikov, Nikolai Apollonovich 17231
Bain, Harry Foster 13211
Bainbridge, Oliver 18847
Baird, George Burleigh 17812
Baker, Dwight Condo 16228
Baker, Gilbert 17632
Baker, Hugh David Roberts 19901 19970 19971 19972 19988 21198
Baker, John Earl 10067 12703 15060 16102 19229
Baker, O- E- 12249
Baker, Timothy Danforth 21008 21009 21155
Bakulin, A- B- 18582
Balandier, Georges 14325
Balazs, Etienne 10109 10151 10506 10507 10846 10847 11656 12341 14412 17933 18786 20228
Balconi, Lorenzo Maria 18953
Bales, William Leslie 21259
Balet, Jean Cyprien 10745
Balfour, Frederic Henry 18367
Balfour, Marshall Coulter 10191
Balfour, S- F- 19959
Ball, James Dyer 10002 10003 16158
Ball, Samuel 16507
Ballande, Charles Adolphe 16906
Balme, Harold 20790
Baltzer, Franz 12704 12705 12706 12707
Band, Claire 13891
Band, William 13891
Bandyopadhyaya, Kalyani 13056
Banks, Mike 22723
Banno, Masataka 10508 22899 22948
Banu, Ion 22183
Bao Chiao-ming 12708 15789
Bao TSziao-min 12708 15789
Barandov, G- V- 18583
Baranov, Ippolit Gavrilovich 10685 12709 12985 16285 19230 19231 19427
Baranov, M- IA- 14831
Barbedette, F- 17813
Barcata, Louis 11061 15205
Barclay, George Watson 10204 15586 15615
Bard, Emile 10004
Bardhan, Pranab K- 12430
Barendsen, Robert Dale 14832 14833 14836 17778 17779
Baret, L- 20541
Barker, Aldred Farrer 13212
Barker, Curtis H- 21585
Barker, Kenneth Crookes 13212
Barker, M- 16275
Barkman, Charles P- 17232
Barnes, Arthur Alison Stuart 13803
Barnes, George G- 22644
Barnes, Hugh 16060
Barnes, Joseph 22659
Barnett, Arthur Doak 10131 10304 10746 10747 10898 10899 10900 11062 11063 11064 11065 11066 11067 11891 12986 13057 13058 13323 13575 14296 15105 15484 15485 15877 15957 15958 15987 15990 16075 16416 17043 17643 17644 18047 18112 18113 18193 18305 18307 18311 18645 18836 19096 19097 19508 20435 21386 22256 22287 22677 23013 23046
Barnett, Irving 12375
Barnett, Kenneth Myer Arthur 15616 15617 17946 21828
Barnett, Robert Warren 11892 16417
Barnett, S- A- 19968
Barnett, William Kester 20236
Barr, John S- 17707 19700
Barrett, David D- 18584
Barrett, Edward F- 21856
Barrett, John 14453
Barrow, John 10005 22578
Barry, Arthur John 12566
Barrymaine, Norman 22744
Barthélemy, *Marquis* de 10509
Bartke, Wolfgang 18164
Bartoli, Henri 12431
Barton, Shirley 17313
Bartsch, Günter 22184
Bartz, Fritz 17947
Bashford, James Whitford 10068
Basil, George Chester 20839
Bassett, Beulah E- 21722
Bastid, Marianne 10510 10750 14556 14834 15206 15207 18073 18370 18601 19365
Bastid, Paul 17902
Bates, Miner Searle 10748 11593 11604 14709 15141 15869 16418 19029 19040 19058 22949
Bau, Mingchien Joshua 10686
Baudrit, A- 20297
Bauer, Heinrich Wilhelm 13213
Bauer, Wolfgang 20401 21466 21829 22185
Baum, Richard Dennis 15208 15209 15988 16071 16072 17638 17639 18194 18195 22293 22294
Bayer-Dortmund, Hans 11893
Bays, Daniel Henry 10511 16769 18074 18751
Bazhenov, Ivan Ivanovich 13324
Bazin, Antoine Pierre Louis 10512 10513 10627 12179 14557 14558 15919 18848
Beach, Harlan Page 21991
Beal, Edwin George, Jr. 10536 13455
Beal, John Robinson 18803
Beal, Samuel 18849
Beasley, William Gerald 10506 21357 21747 22773
Beauvais, Jean Joseph 22510
Bechtoldt, Heinrich 18787
Becker, Pierre Emile 17522
Beckmann, George Michael 15158 15210
Beckmann, Johannes 10356 19030
Bedeski, Robert Edward 10848 13985 18114 22143
Beech, Joseph 14630 16419
Beer, Patrice de 10749
Beh, Yu 13770
Behayhel, G- 20542
Behling, Thomas George 17588
Behme, F- 15713
Behr, Edward 21428
Behrens, ——— 20708
Behrman, S- J- 20321
Behrsing, Siegfried 19438
Bel, Raymond 16945
Bel'chenko, A- T- 12626 12881 12882 12883 12884 12885 12886 12887 12951 12952 12953 12954 15371 17182
Belden, Jack 13892 18585 18788
Beliakova, Anna Mikhailovna 11423
Bell, Francis Hayley 22678
Bell, John 22511
Bell, Mark Sever 13804
Bellet, Daniel 13122
Bellotti, Felice 16347
Belov, Evgenii Aleksandrovich 10687 18368 18369 18530 18531 19446
Bender, Peter L- 19902
Bendix, Reinhard 14117

C

D

E

F

G

H

I

J

K

L

M

Ma, Chao-chun 19477
Ma Ch'ao-chün 19477
Ma Ch'ao-sheng 13788
Ma, Chia-chi 21247
Ma Chieh 13255 19263
Ma Chien 19014
Ma Fei-hai 19680
Ma Feng-ch'en 22577
Ma Feng-chou 16845
Ma Feng-hua 11865 12053 12054 12055 12517
Ma, Fengchow C. 16845
Ma Hai-te 21092
Ma Hai-teh 21092
Ma, Herbert Han-pao 10875
Ma Hsiang 21377
Ma Hsiang-yun 16484
Ma Hsiang-yung 16484
Ma Hsiu-chung 17123
Ma Hsiung-fan 16994
Ma, James Chao-seng 13788
Ma, John T. 14954 23042
Ma Jung-li 16438
Ma, Ming-to 15610
Ma Pao-shan 17382
Ma, Ronald A. 16438
Ma Shih-tu 21376
Ma Sian 21377
Ma Ta 12198
Ma Ta-jen 14954 23042
Ma, Te-chih 18092
Ma T'ien-shui 19319
Ma Tseng-hsiang 13015
Ma, Tsie 13255 19263
Ma TSy-ian' 18697
Ma Tz'u-yen 18697
Ma, W. H. 10801
Ma Wen-huan 10801
Ma Yin-ch'u 10238 12048 12049 13473 13737
Ma-Ta 12198
Maas, Gerard 16070
McAleavy, Henry 10802 11400 11401 13628 16112 19930 21285 21341 21417
Macartney, George 22578
McCall, Davy H- 19220
McCarthy, J- P- 22757
McCartney, James Lincoln 20902 20903
Macciocchi, Maria Antonietta 17995
McClelland, David Clarence 21535
McCloy, Thomas 14094
McClure, Floyd Alonzo 13256 16670 17284 17285
McColl, Robert William 10422 18698 18699
McCormick, Elsie 17859
McCormick, Frederick 18454 20616
McCoy, William John, Jr. 17965 20029
MacCulloch, John Arnott 21739
McCune, Shannon 15778
McCusker, Henry F-, Jr. 14955
McCutcheon, James M- 22579
McDonald, Angus 23043
Macdonald, J- H- 18908
MacDonald, James 14363 22336
McDouall, J- C- 19887
McDougall, Colin 20172
MacDougall, Colina 16846 16847 17750 19157
McDowell, S- Garrett 14956
Mace, David Robert 19881
Mace, Vera 19881
McFarlane, Bruce 12050 12158
MacFarlane, Charles 18455
MacFarquhar, Emily 11132
MacFarquhar, Roderick Lemonde 11074 11133 12051 12098 12480 12842 13391 13947 14067 14252 14271 14364 14365 14897 14898 15975 17778 17986 18207 18268 18329 19126 19414 20271 22188 22361
MacGowan, Daniel Jerome 11227 17550 19347 20750 20751 20752 21170 22404
Macgowan, John 10038 15344 19721
MacInnis, Donald Earl 11633 11634 20451
Macintyre, John 16202
Mackay, Alan 21678
MacKay, George Leslie 18908 20753
MacKenzie, D- J- M- 21093
MacKenzie, Donald Alexander 21772
MacKenzie, Norman 18832
Mackerras, Colin Patrick 10164 18011 18012 18013
Mackie, John Milton 21286
MacKinnon, Stephen Robert 10722 21287
MacLean, Archibald 10606
Maclellan, J- W- 15929
McMorran, C- Ian 22057
MacNair, Harley Farnsworth 10290 10800 10803 11720 11838 12269 14680 15075 16263 17854 18745 20652 20848 20901 22081 22129
Macrae, John T- 12052
Macridis, Roy Constantine 11007
McWade, Robert W- 17164
Maddox, Patrick Gaynor 16059
Madian, A- L- 22337
Madian, Marcia Dunn 19931
Mad'iar, Liudvig Ignat'evich 11704 12222 12325 12961 13738
Madrolle, Claudius 15742 15763 16389 16919 17025
Mäding, Klaus 20069 21574
Maeker, V- 20913 21507 21508 21515 21526
Mänchen-Helfen, Otto 14119 19458
Magalhães, Gabriel de 10039
Magnenoz, Robert 22158 22233
Magrini, Luciano 18700
Mah, Feng-hwa 11865 12053 12054 12055 12517
Mai Te-chih 18092
Mai Wen-shao 12059
Main, Idabelle Lewis 17765 17766 20169
Maiorova, T- G- 22947
Maison, Emile 22580
Maitland, Charles Titterton 17722 20904
Mak Shiu Hung 16848
Makino, Tatsumi 19882
Maklakov, A- 12056 12057 15088
Malcolm, Howard 17820
Malden, William 14366
Malenbaum, Wilfred 12058
Malitskii, V- S- 17286 17723
Mallett, Richard David 18701
Mallory, Walter Hampton 15052 17482
Malon, Sesil' 14497 18306
Malone, Carroll Brown 14191 16695 22802
Malone, Cecil John L'Estrange 14497 18306
Maloney, Joan M- 15294
Mamaev, I- 10076 19459
Mamaeva, R- 12326
Mancall, Mark 10955 11134 11964 14367 14368 17551 18824 22581 22735
Mandalian, T- 19478
Mangin, Ignace 18456
Mangold, Rudolf 13178
Mankiewicz, R- H- 19435
Manly, Grace Edna 22460
Mann, Albert Burwell 10607
Mann, Felix 20983 21094
Mannnerheim, Carl Gustaf Emil 10040
Mao, Cho-ting 13549 13550
Mao Cho-t'ing 13549 13550
Mao Ch'ün 15651
Mao, James C. T. 13549 13550
Mao Tse-tung 13948 13949 14120 18561 18703 18704 19460 22263
Mao, W. P. 20317
Mao Wen-ping 20317
Mao, Yu-kang 16849
Mao Yü-kang 16849
Maquenne, Paul 13401
Marakuev, Aleksandr Vasil'evich 12327
Marakuev, V- N- 10041
Marakulin, V- 17421
March, Andrew Lee 21773
March, Benjamin 18032
Marchant, Leslie Ronald 17532 22664
Marchisio, Hélène 12403 16850 19158
Marchisio, Joseph 21956
Marcks, Erich 21267 21319
Marcuse, Jacques 10165
Maresca, François-Xavier 22582
Margouliès, Georges 14755
Mari, Benito 17287
Mark, Max 18705
Mark, Shelley Muin 12059
Markham, James Walter 12772
Markham, John 16390
Markushevich, Aleksei I- 12852 14831 14838 14957 15035 17796 17797 17808
Marquart, Jakob 20205
Marsh, Robert Mortimer 10608 10609 14145 14192 14193 17621 17622
Marsh, Susan Han 22250
Marsouin, Jacques 11135
Marsouin, Thérèse 11135
Martello, Tullio 14600
Martin, Bernard 21342
Martin, Charles Ernest 10182 11228 14095 17165 19759 19760 19998 20090 20143 20287 20585 20754 20755 20756 21171 21172 21173 22583
Martin, Christopher 22584
Martin, Ilse 20617 22461
Martin, Louis Auguste 20144
Martin, Robert Montgomery 10042
Martin, William 10804
Martin, William Alexander Parsons 10043 10610 10611 14194 14601 14602 14603 14604 16203 17552 18909 19999 21662 21663 21986 21987
Martini, G- B- de 15044
Martini, Martin 13836
Martinson, Harold H- 21418
Martynov, Aleksandr Aleksandrovich 14010 18269
Martynov, K- A- 15967
Maryański, Andrzej 10217
Mas, *Dr.* 20757
Masi, Edoarda 22251
Masip, Jaime P- 19761
Maslennikov, Viacheslav Aleksandrovich 11799 11800 11801 11866 11867 12060 13772 18141 18142
Masliakov, Vasilii Nikolaevich 12843
Mason, Isaac 18974
Maspero, Henri 12199 16204 16271 21774
Masserman, Jules H- 20995
Masson, J- 21925
Mast, Herman William, III 10805 22117 22164 22165
Masters, R- E- L- 20110
Masubuchi, Tatsuo 22988
Masui, Tsuneo 13671
Mateer, Calvin Wilson 18910
Mateos, Fernando 11635 22338
Matgioï 14201 18479 18480 18923
Matheson, Donald 19721
Mathews, Thomas Jay 15270
Mathos, Michael 22749

N

T

Treadgold, Donald Warren 11073 11442 12101 13444 18180 18358
Treat, Payson Jackson 22716
Tregear, Thomas Refoy 10396 10432 15642 15850 16941
Tremanns, Johann M- 19851
Trenerry, Deborah 17398 17399
Tretchikov, Nikolai G- 11716
Tretiak, Daniel 10996 22768
Tret'iak, Pod"esaul 12616
Tret'iakov, Sergei Mikhailovich 17614 21355
Tretjakow, Sergej 17614 21355
Treudley, Mary Bosworth 15436
Treutlein, Theodore E- 22626
Trewartha, Glenn Thomas 10221 10258 12356 12357 15954 16697
Tricht-Kessing, E- E- van 20233
Trifonov, V- 13429
Trillat, Jean-Jacques 18068
Trinidad, Ruben F- 13618
Trippner, Josef 16749 20399 20660 20927 22467
Trittel, Walter 12677
Trivière, Léon 11648 11649 18357 19183
Troitskii, I- A- 11737
Trolliet, Pierre 16041
Trotskii, Lev 18713 18756 18765 18784
Trotsky, Leon 18713 18756 18765 18784
Trott, Lamarr B- 16880
Trumbull, Robert 10180
Tryon, Carol Gillespie 19389
TSagolov, A- 13703
Tsai Chiao 20652
Tsai, Chutung 11240
TSai Khe-sen' 18757
Tsai, Mark 14691
Tsai, Pao-tien 14806
Tsai, Tsong Wang 19852
Tsai, Yung-mei 15912
Ts'ai Cheng-ya 17733 17734 17880 19566
Ts'ai Ch'iao 20652
Ts'ai Ho-sen 18757
Ts'ai Jen-yü 14691
Ts'ai, Ju-sheng 20928
Ts'ai Tsung-huang 19852
Ts'ai Tun-ming 11411
Ts'ai, Yung-ch'un 21194
Ts'ai Yung-hui 12449
TSan IU-chuan 20990
Tsang, Chiu-sam 14692 15005 15006
Tsang Wei-t'ing 16881
Ts'ang Yu-ch'uang 20990
Tsao Ching 14083
Tsao, J. 15621
Tsao, Kai-fu 18514
Tsao, Li Yieni 20155
Tsao Lien-en 13567 15677 20929
Tsao Meng-chun 20248
Tsao, T. C. 13430
Tsao Ting-chüan 21139
Tsao Ting-ming 17366
TSao TSziui-zhu 13793
Tsao, W. Y. 10828 16100 19891
Tsao, Y. S. 19706 20429
Ts'ao Chu-ju 13793
Ts'ao, Ignatius J. H. 21970 22276 22371
Ts'ao Jih-ch'ang 21589
Ts'ao Lien-en 13567 15677 20929
Ts'ao Sung-yeh 18023 22428
Ts'ao Ting-chüan 21139
Ts'ao T'ing-ming 17366
Ts'ao Wen-yen 10828 16100 19891
Ts'ao Yang-ko 19336
Ts'ao Ying-huan 16014 19132
Ts'ao, Yung-ho 22627
Ts'ao Yün-hsiang 19706 20429
Tsay, Queenie 20295
Tschang, Wen-hsi 12231
Tscharner, Eduard Horst von 22921
Tschepe, Albert 18939
Tschou, Tso-Tschun 10666 11241
Tse, N. Q. 15913
Tse, Tsan-tai 18569
TSelishchev, M- 11831
Tsen Tsonming 14506
Tseng Chao-sen 14692 15005 15006
Tseng Chao-yang 22277
Tseng Chieh 17400
Tseng, Chieh-hsin 13113
Tseng Chien 19337
Tseng Chin-ch'un 19480
Tseng Chung-ming 14506
Tseng, Edward C. 22277
Tseng, H. P. 12678
Tseng Hsi-ching 17015
Tseng Hsiu-fu 18186 18758
Tseng Huan-chiu 13755
Tseng, Ju-Pai 11293
Tseng Kien 19337
Tseng, Kuo-cheng 13315
Tseng, Lily 20930
Tseng Ling 13795
Tseng, P. S. 20176
Tseng Pao-sun 20176
Tseng San 22854
Tseng T'ien-yü 13656
Tseng T'ung-ch'un 13284
Tseng Wen-ching 13432
Tseng, Wen-Shing 16368 21590
Tseng Yu-hao 22132
Tseng Yuan 19106
Tseng Yung-hsien 18295
Tseng Yüan 19106
Ts'eng Hsi-ch'ing 17015
Tsenhungsiang 18611 19518 19519 19565
Tseo, Cheng-se 13687
Tseung, F. I. 21971
Tsha, T. Y. 17733 17734 17880 19566
Tsiang, Chieh 12358
Tsiang, Kuen 22133
Tsiang, S. C. 13794
Tsiang, Tingfu Fuller 19436 22179
TSiba, T. 17881
Tsien, Josiane 19609
Tsien Tai 10667
Tsien Tche-hao 10997 11525 11526 15007 19609
Tsien, Ts'uen-Hsuin 15193
Ts'ien Siang-suen 17037
Tsing, Chin-chun 19480
Tsing Tung-chun 13284
Tsiui Vei-to 18602
Tso, Ernest 20931
Tso, S. K. Sheldon 14507 19481
Tso, S. W. 20279
Tson, Hauin-kio 13755
Tsou Jung 14190
Tsou Ssu-i 13033
Tsou, Stanley Szu-yee 13033
Tsou, Tang 10603 10859 10998 11043 11951 12041 13977 15165 15295 15296 17997 19734 22359 22364 22380 23006
Tsou Wei-tsai 16882
Tsou Yu-ning 21141
Tsu Chwan-hwai 17035 17083 17084
Tsu Djenchow 11294
Tsu, François Xavier 17667
Tsu Min-yi 20819 20932
Tsu, Raphael 13431
Tsu, Y. Y. 19695 21794 21795
Tsuda Sōkichi 21454
TSuda, Sookichi 21454
Tsü, Kwoh-mo 22673
Tsui, R. T. 16698 16699 16700 16701 16702 16703 16704 16705 16706 16707 16708
Tsui, Shu-chin 18156 22180
Tsui, Tseng-ti 16600
Tsui, Young-chi 16883 16884 16885 16886 16887
Ts'ui Shu-ch'in 18156 22180
Ts'ui Yung-chi 16883 16884 16885 16886 16887
Ts'ui Yü-chün 16698 16699 16700 16701 16702 16703 16704 16705 16706 16707 16708
Tsukamoto, Zenryu 18986 19052
Tsukamoto Zenryū 18986 19052
Tsung Han 17129
Tsung, Tien 20234
Tsur, Nyok-Ching 17176
Tsuzuki, J. 20780
TSvetkov, P- 13136
TSzan' TSzi-pyi 11527
TSzen Lin 13795
TSzen San' 22854
TSzen Siu-fu 18186 18758
TSzen Ven'-tszin 13432
TSzen'-Fo-ta 12267 18598 19511
TSzian Chun-fan 22134
TSzian Di 13860
TSzin' Sin'-chzhun 20991 21142
Tu Chi-yuan 16709
Tu Chih-yüan 16709
Tu, Ching-I 21356
Tu Ling 11164
Tu Shu-ying 15998
Tu Tien-feng 15851
Tu, Wei-ming 10037 10252 21696
Tu, Yuan-li 20080
T'u Huai-ying 11524
T'u T'ien-feng 15851
Tuan, Chi-hsien 20377
Tuan I-fu 10397 21897
Tuan, Yi-fu 10397 21897
Tuan-mu Chung 12402
Tuden, Arthur 14145 19989
Tulaev, A- IA- 14807
Tulisov, M- 11516
Tun Li-chen 16219
Tung, C. Y. 13186
Tung, Chi-ping 21433
Tung, Constantine 21591
Tung Hsien-kuang 21425
Tung Lin 10887
Tung Mong-sheng 10732
Tung Pi 13496
Tung, Robert 16084 17660
Tung, Samuel C. H. 12750
Tung, Ta-lin 19184
Tung, William L. 10887
Tung-li 13973
T'ung Meng-sheng 10732
Tuohy, Frank 15008
Turner, F- B- 17882
Turner, Victor W- 19989
Tutaev, A- G- 11832
Tuzhilin, Aleksandr Vasil'evich 10062 10668
Twanmo, Chong 12402
Twanmoh, Chien-ming 20177
Twinem, Paul de Witt 19024
Twiss, George Ransom 14693
Twitchett, Denis Crispin 20043 21357 21648 22780 22999 23000
Tyau, Min-ch'ien T. Z. 10081 10103 10829 11295
Tyler, William Ferdinand 13882
Tyzack, David 13137
Tzeng, John Jenn 17774

U

U Bao-kan 15009
U Chan-chzhen' 19949
U IUi-chzhan 15010 18572

V

W

Y

Z

Institutional Author Index

An alphabetical index of corporate authors, editors, and compilers

編著者機關名稱索引

機關團體編著者名稱索引、依羅馬拚音字母排列

編纂機関名索引

編纂機関団体名索引（ＡＢＣ順）

Entries for nested agencies begin with the name of the body at the highest level and proceed down through the hierarchy to the agency in question; lower-level units are cross-referenced to the highest-level body. Entries for agencies of national and colonial governments begin with the English name of the country or colony. Those for agencies of provincial and municipal governments in China begin with the Post Office form of the name of the province or municipality.

A

A-ch'eng chi tien ch'i ch'ang wei yüan hui: *see* Chung-kuo kung ch'an tang
A-ch'eng Relay Instrument Factory Committee: *see* Chinese Communist Party
Academia Sinica 19403
Administrative Office: *see* Shanghai
Admiralty: *see* Great Britain
Agricultural Census Committee: *see* Taiwan
Agricultural, Cultural, and Educational Investigation Group: *see* Hua-chung Normal College
Agricultural Economics Research Office: *see* China Agricultural Sciences Institute
Agriculture Division: *see* United Nations
Agro-economic Unit: *see* Shantung Provincial Economic Research Institute
Ajia keizai kenkyūjo 12428
Ajia no yume dōjinkai 12763 12787
Ajia seikai gakkai 14821
Akademiia nauk SSSR 10227 10930 12121 14138 18633
——. Geograficheskoe obshchestvo SSSR. Vostochnaia komissiia 22484 22919
——. Institut Dal'nego Vostoka 11458 11842 15101 18808 19659
——. Institut geografii 22806
——. Institut kitaevedeniia 11965 13889 14913 18043 18045 18110 18315 18670 18712 18763 22221 22236
——. Institut mezhdunarodnogo rabochego dvizheniia 18628 18632 18662 18672
——. Institut narodov Azii 10542 11674 13129 13133 13814 13837 13859 13929 13953 13955 13972 14422 15043 17157 17174 17567 18079 18368 18373 18389 18414 18417 18429 18470 18478 18531 19500 22033 22065 22148 22518 22588 22878
——. Institut vostokovedeniia 12190 12741 13260 14411 14468 15148 18026 18374 18392 18431 18433 18437 18669 18798 19456 21686 21840 21848 21877 21885 21892 21893 21894 21898 21907 21916 22092 22141 22221 22592
Akademiia pedagogicheskikh nauk RSFSR 12852 14831 14838 14957 15035 17796 17797 17808
All-China Federation of Trade Unions 19590
All-China Society of Nurses 14778
Amerasia Staff 18111
American Council: *see* Institute of Pacific Relations
American National Red Cross. Commission to China 15059
An-shan Municipal Committee: *see* Chinese Communist Party
An-shan shih wei yüan hui: *see* Chung-kuo kung ch'an tang
Anti-Cobweb Club 11683
Antituberculosis Assn. of China 21007
Asia Office: *see* World Confederation of Organizations of the Teaching Profession
Asian Peoples' Anti-Communist League 13984 15483 17587 19095 19367
Assn. for Asian Political-Economic Studies 14821
Assn. for the Advancement of Public Health in China 20837

B

Bank of China. Head Office. Research Dept. 13710
Biuro Tikhookeanskoi kon"iunktury: *see* Dal'ne-Vostochnyi krai
Board of Customs Control: *see* China [Ch'ing]
Bōei kenshūjo: *see* Japan
Bōeichō: *see* Japan
Bureau of Accounting and Statistics: *see* Taiwan
Bureau of Agriculture, Forestry and Irrigation: *see* Peking
Bureau of Foreign Trade: *see* China [Republic]
Bureau of Social Affairs: *see* Shanghai
Bureau of Statistics: *see* Liaoning

C

Canton Advertising and Commission Agency 16421
Canton Branch: *see* China [People's Republic]
Center for International Affairs: *see* Harvard U.
Central Committee: *see* Chinese Communist Party
Central Political-Judicial Cadres School. Institute of Civil Law Research 11440
——. Institute of Criminal Law Research 11439
Central Shansi District Committee: *see* Chinese Communist Party
Centre d'étude des pays de l'Est: *see* Université libre de Bruxelles
Centre national pour l'étude des pays à régime communiste 11449 11638 11647 12459 13327 14135 14880
Chambre de commerce de Lyon 12897 12943 13636 15715 15716 15717 15750 16166 16370 16371 16372 16512 16534 16925 17137 17138 17139 17146 17152 17437 19742 20550 20551 22522 22523
Chao-yüan Hsien: *see* Heilungkiang
Chao-yüan hsien cheng fu: *see* Heilungkiang
Chekiang. Chia-shan Hsien Antiepidemic Station. Revolutionary Leading Group 21022
——. Chien she t'ing 16609
——. Reconstruction Dept. 16609
Cheng chih ching chi hsüeh chiao yen shih: *see* Hu-pei ta hsüeh
Cheng ts'e yen chiu shih: *see* Chung-kuo kung ch'an tang
Ch'eng shih chien she. Editorial Dept. 15817
——. Pien chi pu 15817
Ch'eng shih chien she chü: *see* Shanghai
Chi-lin sheng wei yüan hui: *see* Chung-kuo kung ch'an tang
Chi-lin shih fan ta hsüeh. Ti li hsi 16462
Chia-shan Hsien Antiepidemic Station: *see* Chekiang
Chiang-hsi jih pao. Shang-jao chi che chan 17798
Chiao t'ung pu: *see* China [Republic]
Chiao yü pu: *see* China [Republic]
Chiao yü t'ing: *see* Fukien
Chiao-ho Hsien: *see* Hopei
Chiao-ho hsien cheng fu: *see* Hopei
Chien chu hsi: *see* T'ien-chin ta hsüeh
Chien chu kung ch'eng pu: *see* China [People's Republic]
Chien she t'ing: *see* Chekiang *or* Taiwan
Chih sha kung tso tui: *see* Chung-kuo k'o hsüeh yüan

D

E

F

G

H

I

J

K

L

M

N

O

P

R

S

T

——. Lao tung li tiao ch'a yen chiu so 17752
——. Liang shih chü 13112
——. Min cheng t'ing 15613
——. ——. Ti cheng chü 16865
——. Nung lin t'ing 16866 16867 16868 17128
——. Nung yeh p'u ch'a wei yüan hui 16869 16870 16871
——. She hui ch'u 14544
——. Wei sheng ch'u 21131
Taiwan [Sōtokufu] 11678
Teng-feng hsien: *see* Honan
Teng-feng hsien cheng fu: *see* Honan
Tetsudōin: *see* Japan
Ti cheng chü: *see* Taiwan
Ti chih ti li hsi: *see* Lan-chou ta hsüeh
Ti i ch'i che chih tsao ch'ang wei yüan hui: *see* Chung-kuo kung ch'an tang
Ti li hsi: *see* Chi-lin shih fan ta hsüeh, Chung-shan ta hsüeh, Shih-chia-chuang shih fan hsüeh yüan, *or* Ta-lien shih fan hsüeh yüan
Ti li yen chiu so: *see* Chung-kuo k'o hsüeh yüan
Tiao ch'a tsu: *see* China [People's Republic], Chung-kuo jen min ta hsüeh, Chung-kuo kung ch'an tang, Chung-kuo nung yeh k'o hsüeh yüan, Honan, Kwangsi, *or* Kwangtung
T'ieh tao pu: *see* China [People's Republic]
Tien hsin kuan li chü: *see* China [Republic]
T'ien-chin ta hsüeh. Chien chu hsi. Hsiao-chan kuei hua tsu 15849
Tientsin. No. 42 Middle School Revolutionary Committee 17806
——. Ssu shih erh chung ko ming wei yüan hui 17806
Tientsin U. Dept. of Architecture. Hsiao-chan Planning Group 15849
Tōyō bunko. Kindai Chūgoku kenkyū iinkai 19449
Trade and Finance Office: *see* China [People's Republic]
Ts'ai cheng pu: *see* China [People's Republic] *or* China [Republic]
Ts'ai cheng wei yüan hui: *see* Chung-kuo kung ch'an tang
Ts'ai mao pan kung shih: *see* China [People's Republic]
Ts'ai mao pu: *see* Chung-kuo kung ch'an tang
Tsingtao Medical College Hospital. Dept. of General Surgery 21140
Tsung kuan li ch'u: *see* Chung-kuo yin hang
Tsung li ya men: *see* China [Ch'ing]
Tsung shui wu ssu shu: *see* China [Republic]
Tsungli Yamen: *see* China [Ch'ing]
Tung pei chü: *see* Chung-kuo kung ch'an tang
T'ung chi chü: *see* Liaoning
T'ung chi k'o: *see* China [Republic]
T'ung chi kung tso. Documents Office 10248
——. Tzu liao shih 10248
T'ung chi kung tso t'ung hsün. Documents Office 10499
——. Tzu liao shih 10499
T'ung chi yen chiu ch'u pan she. Documents Office 17684
——. Tzu liao shih 17684
T'ung hsün tsu: *see* Kiangsi
T'ung shang hai kuan: *see* China [Republic]
Tzu liao shih: *see T'ung chi kung tso, T'ung chi kung tso t'ung hsün, or T'ung chi yen chiu* ch'u pan she

U

U.S.S.R. Ministerstvo vneshnei torgovli. Nauchno-issledovatel'skii kon"iunkturnyi institut 12015 12132
U.S.S.R. Academy of Sciences. Institute of the Peoples of Asia 22148
Union Research Institute 10137 10138 10163 10176 10178 10179 10915 10916 10917 10918 10919 10920 10946 11072 11077 11078 11126 11128 11174 11490 11918 12107 12484 12507 12536 12792 12803 12844 12863 12871 13066 13085 13099 13100 13121 13333 13334 13335 13390 13582 13583 13605 13606 13613 14030 14031 14032 14394 14905 14906 15001 15099 15107 15222 15223 15224 15497 18206 18208 18209 18241 18837 19146 19202 19588 19589 19603 19608 20486 20530 21387 21394 21911 21912 21913 21965 21977 21978 22827
United Nations. Dept. of Economic and Social Affairs 10497
——. Economic Commission for Asia and the Far East 12146
——. ——. Research and Planning Division 11873 16497
——. ——. Research and Statistics Division 12133
——. ——. Secretariat 12134 12135 12136 12137 12138 12139 12140 12141 12142 12143 12144 12145 16498 16499 16500 16501
——. Educational, Scientific and Cultural Organization 12865 12866 12867 14858 14859 14891 14892 14893 14987 17786 17791 17807 20910
——. ——. Regional Office for Education in Asia 14895
——. ——. Secretariat 15011 15012 15013
——. Food and Agriculture Organization 14771
——. ——. Agriculture Division 12146
——. Relief and Rehabilitation Administration 12359 13285 19707
——. Secretariat 11528
U.S. Central Intelligence Agency 10500 12147 12148
U.S. Congress. House of Representatives. Committee on Un-American Activities 11167
——. Joint Economic Committee 10224 10463 10468 11887 11888 11974 11990 11993 12009 12010 12043 12095 12147 12168 12432 12462 12506 12771 12868 13319 13351 13352 13408 13419 13435 13794 14043 14967 15259 20306 21964 22356 23028 23047
——. Senate. Committee on Foreign Relations 11168
——. ——. Committee on Government Operations. Subcommittee on National Policy Machinery 18296
——. ——. ——. Subcommittee on National Security Staffing and Operations 10999
——. ——. Judiciary Committee 12713
U.S. Dept. of State 18108
U.S. Joint Publications Research Service 10499 11173 11914 11940 12437 12537 12538 13067 13098 13341 13362 13392 13393 13396 13403 13416 13441 13587 14017 14816 14821 14839 14844 14878 14888 14946 14947 14970 15098 15114 15500 15651 15817 15836 15837 15843 15844 15849 15854 15860 15881 15904 15916 15998 16074 16468 16474 16475 16779 16802 16803 16804 16842 16875 16900 16994 16997 17005 17013 17105 17106 17110 17122 17155 17314 17341 17343 17345 17346 17347 17358 17365 17396 17397 17400 17405 17519 17746 17747 17783 17784 17787 17802 17914 18242 18843 19093 19106 19111 19112 19114 19115 19120 19161 19172 19180 19191 19293 19295 19298 19299 19300 19319 19329 19336 19339 19605 19680 19867 20238 20245 20410 20416 20693 20701 20999 21001 21004 21014 21019 21026 21031 21033 21042 21053 21060 21064 21065 21067 21087 21099 21117 21129 21141 21147 21152 21154 21246 21253 21255 21580 22131
U.S. Library of Congress. Orientalia Division 21276
U.S. Mutual Security Mission to China 12149 12150
United States National Board: *see* Y.W.C.A.
U.S. Office of Naval Operations 15437 15438 15439 15440 15441 15442 15443 15444 16710 16711
U.S. Office of Strategic Services. Research and Analysis Branch 10830 10831 11833 11834 12751 13286 16061 16062 16063 16064 16972 16973
United States Testing Co. Shanghai International Testing House 17306
U.S. War Dept. 13861
——. General Staff. Military Intelligence Division 18759
Université libre de Bruxelles. Institut de sociologie Solvay. Centre d'étude des pays de l'Est 10244 11449 11638 11647 12459 13327 14135 14880 22282
U. of Hong Kong. Dept. of Chinese 15343 16099
U. of Nanking. College of Agriculture and Forestry. Dept. of Agricultural Economics 17883
U. of Washington. Far Eastern and Russian Institute 10456 10874 10876 10886 10921 11050 11051 11079 11131 11162 12406 12407 12766 12768 12769 12782 13044 13045 13082 13299 13309 14106 14129 14131 14782 14804 15086 15386 15602 15603 15604 15873 15911 16331 16744 17317 17960 18181 18340 18356 19041 19050 19284 19585 19876 20621 20654 20661 20958 20967 20968 22005 22662
Urban Construction Bureau: *see* Shanghai
Urban Council: *see* Hong Kong
Urban Services Dept.: *see* Hong Kong

V

Visiting group to the Wei-hsing commune: *see* Shanghai College of Social Science
Vostochnaia komissiia: *see* Akademiia nauk SSSR
Vostochno-sibirskii otdel: *see* Imperatorskoe russkoe geograficheskoe obshchestvo
Vsesoiuznaia torgovaia palata 13532

W

Wai chiao pu: *see* China [Republic]
Walter Hines Page School of International Relations: *see* Johns Hopkins U.

Wang-ssu commune: *see* Hopei
Wang-ssu jen min kung she: *see* Hopei
War History Office: *see* Senshishitsu
Wei sheng chiao yen tsu: *see* Shen-yang i hsüeh yüan
Wei sheng ch'u: *see* Honan *or* Taiwan
Wei sheng fang i chan: *see* Peking
Wei sheng hsi: *see* Pei-ching i hsüeh yüan
Wei sheng kung tso shih tien kung tso tsu: *see* Hopei
Wei-hsing Commune: *see* Honan
Wei-hsing jen min kung she: *see* Honan
Wei-hsing jen min kung she ts'an kuan t'uan: *see* Shang-hai she hui k'o hsüeh yüan
Wen chiao chü: *see* Honan
Wen chiao kung tso tsu: *see* Chung-kuo kung ch'an tang
Wen chiao wei sheng pu: *see* Honan
Wen Yu Huei Society 11302
Wing On Fire Commission: *see* Hong Kong
Work Section: *see* Jui-chin Hsien Women's Federation
Work Team: *see* China [People's Republic], Chinese Communist Party, *or* New Democratic Youth League
Worker– People's Liberation Army Mao Tse-tung Thought Propaganda Team: *see* Shenyang Medical College
World Assn. for Adult Education 19645
World Confederation of Organizations of the Teaching Profession. Asia Office 15023
Write-up Team: *see* China [People's Republic] *or* Liaoning
Wu-han pan shih ch'u: *see* China [People's Republic]
Wu-han pu tui: *see* Chung-kuo jen min chieh fang chün
Wu-yüan Hsien: *see* Kiangsi
Wu-yüan hsien cheng fu: *see* Kiangsi
Wuhan Branch: *see* China [People's Republic]
Wuhan Unit: *see* People's Liberation Army

Y

Yang P'u Cotton Spinning, Weaving, and Dyeing Factory of Shanghai Work-Study Technical School 17805
Yeh chin kung yeh pu: *see* China [People's Republic]
Yen-shou Hsien: *see* Heilungkiang
Yen-t'ai Special District: *see* Shantung
Yen-t'ai ti ch'ü cheng fu: *see* Shantung
Yenching U. Dept. of Sociology and Social Work 15450
Ying-shan Hsien Committee: *see* Chinese Communist Party
Ying-shan hsien wei yüan hui: *see* Chung-kuo kung ch'an tang
Yomiuri Shimbun Staff 10180
Yu cheng kuan li chu: *see* China [Republic]
Yu chuan pu: *see* China [Republic]
Yü Hsien Committee: *see* Chinese Communist Party
Yü hsien wei yüan hui: *see* Chung-kuo kung ch'an tang
Yü-chiang Antischistosomiasis Station 21072
Yü-chiang Hsien: *see* Kiangsi
Yü-lin chuan ch'ü cheng fu: *see* Kwangsi
Yü-lin Special District: *see* Kwangsi
Yüeh chung ch'ü kung tso wei yüan hui: *see* Chung-kuo kung ch'an chu i ch'ing nien t'uan
Yün shu kan pu kung tso hsün lien pan chiang i pien chi wei yüan hui: *see* China [People's Republic]
Y.W.C.A. Industrial Dept. 20222
——. United States National Board. Education and Research Division 20222

General Index

An alphabetical index of selected topics, terms, events, and proper names, with references to coding categories and to the analytical indexes as well as to particular entries

綜合索引

選錄題材、名稱、事件及專用名詞索引、注明主題標碼分類及各別類目

総合索引

トピック、名称及び事件並びにコード分類別及び項目番号を示す索引（ＡＢＣ順）

References to code numbers show prefix S for Subject codes, G for Geographic codes, and P for Type-of-place codes. Entry numbers are listed only for title mentions. When title mentions exceed 30, entry numbers are omitted in favor of page references to relevant subcategories in the Bibliography. References to analytical indexes give the page number on which the relevant subcategory begins.

A

Abortion, see S51. In titles of 20287 20288 20375.
Academia Sinica, see S36.1. In titles of 19401 19403 19419.
Academic institutions, see S17.
Academic societies, S36.1.
Academies, military, see S15. In titles of 13913 13947 13953. *See also* Whampoa Academy.
Academies, scholarly, see S17.
  Hanlin. In titles of 14570 14599.
  Imperial (*Kuo-tzu-chien*). In titles of 14558 14582 14601.
  Traditional (*shu-yüan*). In titles of 14550 14563.
Academies, scientific, see S36.1. In titles of 18341 19411 19412 19421 19422.
Accountants and accounting. For accountants, see S16.2; for accounting in government, S14.5/24.5; for accounting in banks, S14.6/24.6; for accounting in business, S34.2. In titles of 13787 17446 19265 19314.
Actors, see S31.
Acupuncture, see S56. In titles of 20808 20812 20974 20983 21023 21100.
Administration, S12/22. For administration of particular fields, see code for field, e.g. for economic administration, S14; for educational administration, S17; for health, S56. Generic title mentions not listed; for title mentions of levels of administration, see below.
  Civil (public) administration. In titles of 10528 10619 10670 10788 13160 13812 15941.
  Local administration. In titles of 10732 16039.
  Municipal administration. In title of 10658.
  Provincial administration. In titles of 10709 10751 10843 10855 11417.
  See also Government.
Adolescence, S54. *See* Youth.
Adopted daughters-in-law, see S41. In title of 19894.
Adoption, see S41. In titles of 19750 19754 19781 19783 19797 19896 20044 20051.
Adult education. *See under* Education.
Adultery, see S46. In titles of 20084 20105.
Advertising, see S34.2. In titles of 19228 19230 19263.
Age grading, S50.
Aged persons, see S50.
Agrarian movements, S36.3.
Agricultural associations, S34.1.
Agricultural cooperatives. *See under* Cooperatives.
Agricultural producers' cooperatives. *See under* Cooperatives.
Agriculture, S14.1/24.1. For agricultural production, farm management, land use, irrigation, S14.1/24.1; for agricultural associations and cooperatives, S34.1; for agricultural extension, S37. Generic title mentions not listed; for title mentions of specific terms, see below.
  Agricultural capital. *See under* Capital.
  Agricultural collectivization. In titles of 12559 19124 19132 19146 19149 19201.
  Agricultural cooperativization. In title of 19077.
  Agricultural labor and workers. In titles of 14421 14422 14433 17664 17665 19444 20198.
  Agricultural loans. In title of 13769.
  Agricultural management. In titles of 16666 16690.
  Agricultural policy. In titles of 12276 12395 12511 12562 14444.
  Agricultural technology. In title of 17793.
  Agricultural zoning. In title of 10401.
  See also Animal husbandry, Crops, Fertilizers, *and* Implements.
Air force, see S15. In title of 14069.
Alchemy, see S62. In titles of 21646 21662 21760.
All-China Democratic Women's Association. See S47, 1949–1972, indexed at p. 601; see also pp. 426–427.
All-China Federation of Labor. See S36.4, 1911–1928, indexed at p. 595; see also pp. 396–400. In titles of 19520 19562 19611.
Alumni associations, see S37.
Amoy. See G9.3: P3, indexed at p. 725. In titles of 12879 15353 15779 16188 16387 16392 16976 17537 17711 20283 21167 21168.
Amoy island. See G9.2: P2, indexed at p. 725.
Amur basin/region/valley. See G2.0. In titles of 10398 13837 15661 15776 16434 16546 16657 17024 20836.
Amur river. See G2.0.
Ancestor worship (Ancestral cult, Cult of the Dead), S43. In titles of 19991–19995 19998 19999 20002 20004 20006–20118 *passim* 21171 21187 21194 21198.
Ancestral halls, see S43.
Ancestral trusts, see S45.
An-ch'ing. See G6.2: P3, indexed at p. 721. In title of 18983.
Anhwei, G6.2. Also for East Central China
[Anhwei]
  poss. incl. Anhwei, G6.0. For Anhwei in Local-Systems Index, p. 721.
Animal husbandry, see S14.1/24.1. In titles of 12407 16620–16623 16744 16786 16787. *See also* Cattle, Eggs, Livestock, Pigs, *and* Wool.
Annual round of festivities, see S23. In titles of 16170 16188 16219.
An-shan. To 1928, see G2.3: P4, indexed at p. 717; after 1928, see G2.3: P3, indexed at p. 717. In title of 19293.
Anti-Ch'ing movement, see S32.2. In titles of 10552 17530 21848. *For Han Chinese opposition to Manchus, see also* Anti-Manchu movement.
Anti-Christian. *See under* Christianity.
Anti-foreign movements/anti-foreignism, see S66. In titles of 18485 18486 22528 22545 22554 22591 22605 22711.
Anti-Manchu movement, see S66. In titles of 18429 18478 21892 22518 22592 22633. *For the anti-dynastic movement, see also* Anti-Ch'ing movement.
Anti-missionary. *See under* Missionaries.
Anti-state associations, S32.2.
Anti-tax movements, see S14.5/24.5.
An-tung. To 1911, see G2.3: P4, indexed at p. 717; after 1911, see G2.3: P3, indexed at p. 717.
Appeals (judicial), see S12.2. In titles of 11351 11462.
Apprentices/apprenticeship, see S34.2. In titles of 19261 19306.
Arbitration, see S12.2/22.2. In title of 16114.
Archaeology, see S70. In title of 22814.
Architecture, see S55. In titles of 10001 15851 20544 20545 20546 20548 20599 20605 20610 20628 20649 20691.
Armaments, see S15. For armaments industry, see S14.4/24.4. *See also* Weaponry.
Armed forces, see S15/25. *See also* Air force, Army, Militia, *and* Navy.
Army, see S15/25. Generic title mentions not listed. Title mentions of particular armies: Anhwei, 13869; Black Flag, 17543 21281; Eighth Route, 13964; Ever-Victorious, 18524 22571; Green Standard, 13863; Huai, 13858; National Revolutionary, 13889 13929; New, 13818 13819 18412; New Fourth, 13890 13892 13930 13933 13967; Nien, 13860 18509; Red (pre-1949 Communist), 13904 13923 13936 13963 13965 13968 13973 13983 14012 18636 18726 22941; Workers and Peasants Revolutionary, 13857 13881. *See also* People's Liberation Army.

[Court (Imperial)]
18092 20140 20554 21269 22519 22520 22524 22544 22610 22611.
Courts (judicial), see S12.2/22.2. In titles of 11175 11215 11231 11264 11268 11300 11306 11315 11401 11405 11422 11438 11444 11445 11461 11463 11466 11495 11501 11513 11518 11534 12946 16091 16108 16109 16114 16154 19798. *See also* Judicial/judiciary *and* Trials.
Craftsmen, see S16.2/26.2.
Credit, S14.6/24.6. Title mentions not listed. Most titles occur on pp. 151–158, 308–312.
Credit cooperatives. *See under* Cooperatives.
Crime, see S12.2/22.2. In titles of 11216 11382 11411 11504 16123 16147 20105.
Criminal code, see S12.2/22.2. In titles of 11352 11372. *See also* Law.
Criminal law. *See under* Law.
Criminals, see S12.2/22.2. In title of 11227.
Crops. For cultivation, see S14.1/24.1; for marketing and prices, S14.3/24.3. Title mentions not listed. Most titles occur on pp. 93–108, 121–131, 269–286, 291–295. *See also* Cotton, Fruit, Grain, Rice, Sugar, Tea, Tobacco, *and* Wheat.
Crop-watching societies, see S34.1.
Cuisine, see S55.
Cultural Revolution. See S15/25 (military aspects); S19 (movements for directed social change); S32 (party rectification); S54 (youth movement), 1949–1972, indexed at pp. 560, 581, 568, 587, 603; see also pp. 167–169, 314–315, 215–219, 339–343, 436–438. Title mentions not listed. *See also* Red Guards.
Culture. In general and in the sense of ideation, S60. Elite culture, S64; folk culture, S65. Cultural variation associated with regions and ethnicity, S29; with class, S16/26.
Currency. *See* Money.
Currency laws. *See under* Law.
Curricula. *See under* Education.
Customary law. *See under* Law.
Customs. Customary practices in general, S50, S55, and S65; in business, S34.2. Customary law, S22.2. For specific customs see specific S codes, S41 for marriage customs, S57 for funeral customs, etc. *See also* Customs duties *and* Maritime customs.
Customs administration. *See* Maritime customs.
Customs duties, see S14.5/24.5. In titles of 13171 13489 13490 13521 13559.

D

Dairen. To 1911, see G2.3: P4, indexed at p. 717; after 1911, see G2.3: P3, indexed at p. 717. In titles of 12893 13001. *See also* Lü-ta.
Dams. For flood-control, see S11.4/21.4; for irrigation, S14.1/24.1; for electrical power, S14.4/24.4. *See also* Flood control, Hydroelectricity, Irrigation, *and* Water conservancy.
Day-care centers, see S52. *See also* Child-care centers.
Death practices, S57. *See* Burials *and* Funerals.
Debts, see S14.6/24.6.
Private debts. In title of 19205.
Public (national) debt. In titles of 13495 13502 13509 13510 13518 13526.
December Ninth Incident (1935). See S54, 1928–1949, indexed at p. 603; see also pp. 434–436.
December Ninth Movement (1935–). In title of 21858.
Deeds (property), see S45. In titles of 20036 20038.
Defense (military), see S15/25. In titles of 13808 13825 13954 14043 17542 17735 22571.
Deities, see S23. Title mentions not listed. Most titles occur on pp. 254–263. *See also* City gods, Kitchen God, *and* Ma-tsu.
Demeaned peoples, see S16/26.
Democratic League. See S32, 1928–1949, indexed at p. 587; see also pp. 335–338. In title of 18133.
Democratic parties, see S32. In title of 18276.
Demons. For religious aspects, see S23; for folklore, S65. In titles of 16210 16266 21621 22389 22420 22462.
Dentistry, see S56. In title of 20804.
Department stores. For commercial aspects, see S24.3; for business organization, S34.2. In titles of 17123 17125 19288 19342.
Depression. For economic depression, see S14/24; see specific S14/24 codes for depression in various sectors of the economy. In titles of 12986 13019 13042 13236 13237 13744.
Development. Refer to specific S codes whose first digit is 1: S14 for economic development, S14.4 for industrial development, S17 for educational development, etc.
Dialect associations, see S39.
Dialects and dialectology, see S29. In titles of 17932 17944 17949 17951 17965 17972 19847.
Diet, see S55. In titles of 20605 20626 20627 20636 20637 20644 20655 20670 20687.
Dikes. For flood-control, see S11.4/21.4; for irrigation, S14.1/24.1. In title of 15863. *See also* Flood control *and* Irrigation.
Disasters and disaster relief, see S18/28. *See also* Droughts, Famine, Floods, Natural calamities and disasters, *and* Relief work.
Disease, see S56. Title mentions not listed. Most titles occur on pp. 444–462.
Divination, see S62. In titles of 20810 21618 21640 21781 21811 21869.
Divorce, see S41. In titles of 19745 19804 19807 19811 19814 19815 19826 19831 19904 19930 19942 19949.
Divorce laws. *See under* Laws.
Doctors (medical), see S56. In titles of 11087 17561 20353 20725 20734 20775 20802 20855 20865 20982 20997 21000 21075 21120 22882.
Downward transfer (*hsia-fang*). As a means of control, S22.1/32.1; as a form of migration, S21.2. In title of 21928.
Drama, see S31. In titles of 14701 18006 18011 18021 18043 18045.
Dream of the Red Chamber. In titles of 14110 14265 18357.
Dreams, see S61. In titles of 21483 21530 21556 21808.
Dress, see S55. In titles of 20543 20605.
Drinking, see S55.
Droughts, see S18/28. In titles of 15046 15047 15108. *See also* Natural calamities and disasters.

E

East Central China, G6.0. Recurs as a subheading in the Geog. Index and appears in the Local-Systems Index at p. 720.
Eating, see S55. In titles of 13096 20543.
Ecology, see S11.3/21.3. In titles of 10338 12556 15797 16196 16780 18645 22552.
Economic geography, see S11.3/21.3. In titles of 10319 10321 10340 10341 10346 10348 10357 10358 10365 10374 10375 10380 10381 10382 10392 10395 10398 10416 10421 10424 10426–10432 10435 12643 15810 16449.
Economy. For general treatments of economic structure, economic development, and economic planning, see S14. For general treatments of particular sectors of the
[Economy]
economy, see S14.1 (agrarian), S14.2 (transport), S14.3 (commercial), S14.4 (industrial), S14.5 (fiscal), S14.6 (financial). For local economic systems, see corresponding S codes whose first digit is 2. For economic theories, see S64. Generic title mentions not listed; for title mentions of some particular terms, see below.
Economic development. Title mentions not listed.
Economic history. In titles of 11666 11667 11680 11691 11693 11857 11858 11706 11870 17155 21805 21882 21921 22779 22988.
Economic planning. In titles of 11741 11893 11852 11909 11995 12093 12103 12108 12119 13779.
Economic policies. In titles of 11171 11661 11744 11836 11839 11840 11887 11888 12016 12050 12094 12098 12099 12144 12153 13458 14333 14537 16487.
Economic reconstruction. In titles of 11669 11727 11752 11759 11774 11838 12154 12296 17891.
Economic theories. In titles of 11889 22239.
Economics. Title mentions not listed.
Education. In general, S17. For kindergarten, compulsory, elementary, and vocational education, see S27; for secondary, professional, and higher education, S17; for adult, community, fundamental, rural, and mass education, S37; for educational associations and movements, S37; for educational subjects that cut across levels, such as curricula and textbooks, S17; for informal education and socialization, S53. Title mentions of types of education are given below.
Adult education. In titles of 19615 19645 19655 19678 19683.
Audio-visual education. In title of 14732.
Compulsory education. In titles of 14884 17767.
Curricula. In titles of 14764 14895 14903 17756 17770 22369.
Elementary education. In titles of 14838 17753–17756 17762 17770 17781 17789 17797 17801 20416 21586.
Higher education. Title mentions not listed. Most titles occur on pp. 188–208.
Mass education. In titles of 19619 19643 19646 19658 19671 19682.
Rural education. In titles of 17763 17766 17795.
Secondary education. In titles of 14664 14667 14686 14864 14934 14935 14944 15034.
Teachers education. In titles of 14644 14732 14806.
Textbooks. In titles of 12852 14895 21879 22674 22711.
Vocational education. In titles of 17757 17759 17764 17771 17774 17799 17810.
See also Schools, Students, *and* Teachers.
Eggs. For production, see S14.1/24.1; for marketing, S14.3/24.3; for processing, S14.4/24.4. In titles of 12991 13288 17277.
Elections, see S12/22. In titles of 10851 10992 16024 16025.
Electricity/electric-power industry, see S14.4/24.4. In titles of 13200 13319 13330 13340 13371 13390 13393 13443 17339.
Electronics/electrical manufacturing industry. In titles of 13178 13292 13394 13419 13422.
Elementary education and schools, S27. *See also* Education *and* Schools.
Elites, S16.1/26.1. For elite associations, see S36.1. Title mentions not listed. Most titles occur on pp. 173–182, 316–317. *See also* Cadres, Gentry, Intellectuals, Landlords, Magistrates, Officials, Scholar-offi-

[Elites]
cials, Scientists, Teachers, *and* Technicians.
Embassy, see S66. In titles of 15306 15355 16369 22505 22511 22519 22537 22544 22559 22576 22578 22603 22619.
Emigration, see S11.2/21.2. For overseas emigration, see S11.2.
Overseas emigration. In titles of 15376 19990.
Rural emigration. In title of 15682.
See also Immigration *and* Migration.
Employers associations, S36.2.
Employment. In general and cross-sectoral, see S11.4/21.4; of agricultural workers, S16.3/26.3; of blue-collar workers, S16.4/26.4; of professionals, S16.1/26.1; of white-collar workers, S16.2/26.2. In titles of 10468 10478 10479 10501 13264 14433 14522 14995 15869 15879 15889 15892 15905 16739 17752 20415. *See also* Unemployment.
Enterprises. For company organization, see S34.2; for commercial enterprises, S14.3/24.3; for financial enterprises, S14.6/24.6. Generic title mentions not listed; for title mentions of particular types of enterprises, see below.
Capitalist enterprises. In title of 18693.
Commercial enterprises. In titles of 16937 16947 17442 17464.
Joint public-private enterprises. In title of 19337.
Private enterprise. In titles of 19310 19313.
State-run enterprises. In titles of 13789 19296.
Entertainment, see S31.
Epidemics, see S56. In titles of 16146 16339 20704 20705 20706 20709 20727 20770 20780 20794 20840 20871 20872 20916 20979 21018 21031 21049 21051 21107 21130 21145 21600.
Eroticism, see S46. In titles of 20083 20089 20097 20110 22016.
Ethics, see S63. In titles of 13124 17979 18459 20907 21642 21709 21981 21984 21986 21991 21996 22001 22007 22010 22012.
Ethnicity/ethnic groups, see S29. In title of 22770.
Ethnocentrism, see S66.
Ethnology, see S70. In titles of 22783 22795 22817.
Etiquette, see S48. In titles of 19229 20032 20258 20266 20270.
Eunuchs. In titles of 10607 10612 10730 20092 20095.
Examination system. As a system for bureaucratic recruitment, see S12; as an academic institution, S17. In titles of 10557 10599 10610 10690 14097 14562 14576 14579 14611 14627 14635 14637. *See also* Bureaucracy *and* Civil service.
Examination Yüan, see S12.
Executive Yüan, see S12.
Expenditures (governmental), see S14.5/24.5. In titles of 13453 13479 13524 13528 13530 13533 13537 13555.
Exports, see S14.3/24.3. In titles of 12238 12243 12327 12345 12355 13000 13195 13315 16514 17172 17190 17367 19232.
Extraterritoriality, see S12.2. In titles of 11210 11266 11270 11291 11293 19279 22717.

F

Face, see S48.
Factories. *See under* Industry.
Factory laws. *See under* Law.
Fairs, see S24.3. In titles of 17018 17081 17111.
Family, S41. For family division, S45 in respect to property arrangements, S41 to social arrangements. For "familism" when broadly conceived, S40. Title mentions not listed. Most titles occur on pp. 407–415.
Family budgets. *See under* Budgets.
Family law. *See under* Law.
Family planning, see S51. In titles of 20307 20318–20322 20326 20329 20330 20332–20338 20346 20355 20358 20359 20366 20367 20372 21068. *See also* Birth control.
Famines, see S18/28. In titles of 12779 13094 15036 15038 15039 15041 15042 15051 15052 15060 15072 15075 15081 15100 16695 17811 17812 17818 17848 17849 17862 17873 17878 17882 17884 19705. *See also* Natural calamities and disasters.
Farmers, S16.3/26.3. *See* Peasants.
Farmers associations, see S36.3. In titles of 19466 19468. *See also* Peasant associations.
Farmland, see S14.1/24.1. In titles of 12221 16663 16705 16857. *See also* Land.
Farmland-rent reduction, see S14.1/24.1. In title of 16663.
Farms, see S14.1/24.1. For farm economy, farm income, farm management, farm size and farming methods, S14.1/24.1; for farm families, farm households, farm labor, and farm workers, S16.3/26.3; for collective farms and state farms, S34.1. Generic title mentions not listed; for title mentions of particular terms, see below.
Collective farms. In titles of 19118 19139 19140.
Farm economy. In titles of 12525 16591 16899.
Farm families. In titles of 12256 19738.
Farm households. In titles of 12239 16869 17825.
Farm labor and workers. In titles of 14425 15053 15701.
Farm management. In titles of 12352 16699 16708 17910.
State farms. In titles of 16835 16879 19078 19136 19137.
Fate, see S62.
Fei Hsiao-t'ung, 1910–. In title of 14267.
Female, S47. Generic title mentions not listed; for title mentions of particular terms, see below.
Female labor and workers. In titles of 20198 20217 20219.
See also Feminist movement *and* Women.
Female roles, see S47.
Feminist movement. See S47, 1911–1949, indexed at p. 600; see also pp. 425–426. In titles of 20145 20184 20191.
Feng Yü-hsiang, 1882–1948. In titles of 13962 13976 18160 21266.
Feng Yu-lan. *See* Fung Yu-lan.
Feng-shui, see S62. In titles of 15643 21602 21610 21623 21626 21651 21689 21779 21780 21810 21827. *See also* Geomancy.
Fengtien (province renamed Liaoning in 1928), G2.3. Also for Manchuria poss. incl. Fengtien, G2.0; for N. China poss. incl. Fengtien, G1.4. In Local-Systems Index see 2.3 Liaoning, p. 717.
Fertility, S58. In titles of 14896 19932 19948 20324 20349 20360 20365 20368 21211 21229 21237–21250 *passim*.
Fertilizer. In titles of 12437 12454 12492 13081 13318 13399 13450 16687 16804 16823 17080.
Festivals, see S23. In titles of 11564 16163 16164 16180 16185 16193 16195 16198 16199 16209 16211 16215 16247 16253 16273 16288 16315 16316 16332 16345 20014. *See also* Annual round of festivities *and* Lunar New Year.
Feuds, see S25.
Fictive kinship, see S48.
Filial piety, see S63. In titles of 19735 19800 19993 19996 21997.
Films, see S31. In titles of 18042 18056 18057 18064 18071 21527 23054.
Finance, S14.6/24.6. For financiers, see S16.2/26.2. General title mentions not listed; for title mentions of some particular types of finance, see below.
Agricultural financing. In titles of 16790 16813.
Financial institutions. In titles of 17442 17464.
Industrial financing. In titles of 11794 13784.
First Five-Year Plan. *See under* Five-year plans.
First Revolutionary Civil War. *See under* Revolutionary civil wars.
Fiscal administration, S14.5/24.5. Title mentions not listed. *See also* Bonds, Budgets, Customs duties, Expenditures, Maritime customs, Public debt, Revenues, *and* Taxes.
Fishermens associations, see S36.3.
Fishing, see S14.1/24.1. Fishermen, see S16.3/26.3.
Fishermen. In titles of 15573 16893 17667 17947 17971.
Fishing. In titles of 12193 12265 12294 12417 12432 12494 12495 16213 16516 16575 16615 16622 16623 16711 16715 16816 16862 17900 19090.
Five-Anti Campaign (1951–52). See S12.1/22.1 (political and ideological controls), S16.2/26.2 (businessmen), and S34.2 (reform of business firms), 1949–1972, indexed at pp. 548, 573, 564, 582, 593. In titles of 10913 11063 11142 11150 16075.
Five-year plans. See S14, 1949–1972, indexed at p. 552; see also pp. 81–93.
First Five-Year Plan (1953–1957). In titles of 11882 11918 12031 13429 21058.
Second Five-Year Plan (1958–1962). In titles of 11882 11943 12029 12526.
Third Five-Year Plan (1963–1967). In titles of 11898 12169.
Flood control and prevention, see S11.4/21.4.
Floods, see S18/28. In titles of 15046 15047 15050 15055 15056 15067 15068 15069 15078 15082 15108 17852 17882 17883. *See also* Natural calamities and disasters.
Flour. For marketing, see S14.3/24.3; for manufacture, S14.4/24.4. In titles of 17201 17265 20660.
Folklore, folk art, folk songs, folk tales, etc., S65.
Folk arts. In titles of 22386 22423.
Folk beliefs. In titles of 22388 22447 22490 22501.
Folk literature. In title of 22495.
Folk songs. In titles of 22430 22452 22494 22502.
Folklore. Title mentions not listed. Most titles occur on pp. 513–518.
Foochow. See G9.3: P3, indexed at p. 725. In titles of 10278 13879 14772 15782 16193 16194 16265 16958 17151 17436 17453 18899 20770 21811 22557 22566.
Food. For food production, S14.1/24.1; for food supply and rationing, S14.3/24.3; for food preparation and consumption, S55. Generic title mentions not listed; for title mentions of particular terms, see below.
Food consumption. In titles of 13064 15079 16727 20646.
Food distribution. In titles of 17672.
Food production. In titles of 12376 12435 12446 12474 12512 12514 13064 16727 16783 16842.
Food supply. In titles of 12218 12422 12890 15601.

G

H

I

J

K

L

M

N

O

P

R

[Rectification campaigns]
18250 18267 18275 18291 18316 18329 18330 18692 20535.
Red and expert schools. *See under* Schools.
Red Cross Society. For activities, see S18/28; for society itself, S38. In titles of 15059 19706.
Red Gang, see S32.2. In title of 18565.
Red Guards. See S54, 1949–1972, indexed at p. 603; see also pp. 436–438. In titles of 14288 15226 15297 16073 17000 17014 17606 19371 20474 20476 20478 20485 20493 20496 20498 20501 20507 20509 20532 20534 21434 21557.
Red Spear Society, see S32.2. In titles of 18575 18637 18743 19442 19455 19456.
Reform movement of 1898. See S32, 1842–1911, indexed at p. 586; see also pp. 334–335. In titles of 14186 18076 18077 18080 18085 18086 18091 18092 18098 18099 22046 22069 22542.
Regional clubs, S39.
Regional planning, see S11.3.
Regions. For regional administrative units, whether extra- or subprovincial, S11.3. For regional planning, S11.3 for extra-provincial macroregions, S21.3 for subprovincial microregions. For treatments of particular subjects at the level of extra-provincial macroregions, refer to S codes whose first digit is 1 rather than 2 with these exceptions: 21 (population), 21.1 (urbanization), 21.3 (geographic mobility), and 21.4 (labor force). For particular macroregions, see G2.0, G3.0, etc., through G9.0. For treatments of particular subjects at the level of subprovincial microregions, refer to S codes whose first digit is 2 rather than 1 with these exceptions: 12 (political system), 12.2 (law), and 14.5 (fiscal affairs).
Relief work, see S18/28. In titles of 10065 15038 15060 15061 15075 15081 17811 17812 17878.
Religion. For elite, official, and state cults and religion, see S13; for folk religion, S23; for religious sects including Buddhism, Christianity, Islam, and Taoism as formal religions, S33; for state control and state-sponsored religious organizations, S13; for theology, S62; for religious movements and anti-religious movements, S33. Title mentions not listed. *See also* Buddhism, Catholic church, Christianity, Deities, Islam, Lamaism, Missionaries, Monasteries, Official cults, Protestant churches, State cult, *and* Taoism.
Religious organizations, S33.
Remittances, see S14.6/24.6. From overseas Chinese, in title of 13617.
Rents. For agricultural land, see S14.1/24.1; for urban land and housing, S45. In titles of 12267 12272 12312 16861 16876 16890 20658.
Reproduction, S51. In titles of 19833 20341 20377.
Research. For news of research by Chinese scholars, see S70; by non-Chinese scholars, S71; for research on specific topics, see Subject code for particular topic.
Research institutes, see S36.1. In title of 19408.
Resist-America Aid-Korea campaign (1951–1953). See S12.1, 1949–1972, indexed at p. 548. In titles of 11154 22746.
Retirement, see S50. In titles of 10604 17599.
Return-to-the-village movements, see S21.2.
Revenues (government), see S14.5/24.5. In titles of 13093 13244 13453 13459 13462 13463 13473 13477 13524 13528 13570 13612 17427.
Revive China Society. *See* Hsing-Chung Hui.
Revolts. Anti-state, S32.2; anti-tax, S24.5;

[Revolts]
student, S54; for military aspects, see S15/25. In titles of 17411 17535 17539 18372 18413 18474 18686 20479 20531.
Revolution of 1911. See S15/25 (military aspects) and S32.2 (anti-state rebellions), 1842–1911, indexed at pp. 559, 580, 589; see also pp. 158–161, 312–313, 346–353. Title mentions not listed.
Revolutionary bases. For anti-state aspects, see S32.2; for government of bases, S22. In titles of 18763 18775.
Revolutionary civil wars. See S15 (military history) and S32.2 (Communist movement), 1911–1949, indexed at pp. 559, 589; see also pp. 162–167, 355–364.
First Revolutionary Civil War (1924–1927). In titles of 13906 18727 19499. *See also* Peasant movement *and* Labor movement.
Third Revolutionary Civil War (1945–1949). In titles of 10786 12290 15967 18629.
Revolutionary committees. See S12/22, 1949–1972, indexed at p. 547, 572; see also pp. 41–45, 248–250. In titles of 10907 10922 10924 10926 10927 10937 10968 11005 18298 19372.
Revolutionary movements/organizations, see S32.2.
Rice. For cultivation and production, see S14.1/24.1; for tribute rice, S14.2/24.2; for marketing, prices, and trade, S14.3/24.3.
Rice cultivation and production. In titles of 12209 12367 12759 16653 16734 16813 16815 16818 16820 16827 16838 17910 19088 19089.
Rice marketing, trade. In titles of 12977 13053 17072.
Rice prices. In title of 17044.
Rice-planting songs (*yang-ko*), see S65. In title of 18044.
Rickshaws. As a means of transport, see S14.2/24.2; for rickshaw men, S16.4/26.4. In titles of 16944 17695 17697.
Riddles, see S65. In titles of 20397 22466 22467.
Riots, see S25; anti-foreign, S66. In titles of 16094 17593 17595 17602 18861 18892 22554 22566 22570 22591 22593 22595 22597 22630.
Rites of passage, see S50.
Ritual adoption, see S48.
River control. For flood control, see S11.4/21.4; for irrigation, S14.1/24.1.
Roads, see S14.2/24.2. In titles of 12609 12620 12650 12682 12694 12735 12742 12744 12828 12854 12979 16344 16958 16960 16965 16970 16971 17878. *See also* Highways *and* Transportation.
Rotating-credit societies, see S24.6. In titles of 17438 17439 17441 17445 17470 17486 17494 17499 17505.
Rural. For rural communities, S20; the rural economy, S24.1; rural politics, S22; rural associations, S34.1 and 36.3; rural reconstruction and community education, S37; rural-urban migration, S21.3. *See also under* Agriculture, Communes, Peasants, *and* Villages. Use Type-of-place codes: P8 for narrowly rural (villages only), P7 for broadly rural (including market towns) and rural in the immediate vicinity of cities, P2 for rural-urban contrasts. P codes are shown as italic letter suffixes in the Geog. Index and as subheadings in the Local-Systems Index.
Rural education. *See under* Education.
Rural electrification, see S14.4/24.4. In title of 13330.
Rural emigration. *See under* Emigration.
Rural industry and industrialization. *See under* Industry.

S

Salaries. In general and cross-sectoral, see S11.4/21.4; for bureaucrats and professionals, S16.1/26.1; for white-collar workers, S16.2/26.2. In titles of 10457 17633. *See also* Wages.
Salt. For government administration, salt monopoly, salt tax, see S14.5/24.5; for salt industry, S14.4/24.4; for salt lands, S14.1/24.1; for salt merchants, S16.2/26.2; for salt producers, S16.4/26.4.
Salt administration/monopoly. In titles of 12928 12930 12932 12950 13160 13452 13515.
Salt industry. In titles of 13136 13244 17181 17209 17210 17243 17276 17299 19213.
Salt merchants. In titles of 12909 12933.
Salt tax. In titles of 13244 13477 13535 13574.
Sampans, see S14.2/24.2. In titles of 12684 12727 17732 19264. *See also* Junks, Steamships, *and* Transportation.
Sanitation, see S56. In titles of 20704 20760 20877 20897 20958 20967 20968 20989 21087 21125–21129 21143.
Savings, see S14.6/24.6. In titles of 11861 13696 13697 17470 17505 17683 20332.
Scholar-officials, see S16.1/26.1. In titles of 18083 22558. *See also* Gentry, Magistrates, *and* Officials.
Scholars of Chinese society. Native Chinese, S70; non-Chinese, S71. In titles of 10594 14170 14182 14257 17631 21298 21340 22872.
Schools. Elementary, S27; *i-hsüeh*, S27; kindergarten, S27; normal, S17; Red and expert, S17/27; secondary, S17; *shu-yüan*, S17; *ssu-shu*, S27; vocational, S27. Title mentions of types of schools are given below.
Elementary schools. Title mentions not listed. Most titles occur on pp. 321–324. See also S52 for elementary-school students.
Kindergartens. In title of 20410. See also S52 for kindergarten children.
Middle schools. In titles of 10501 14666 14728 14747 14820 14885 17778 17783 17784 17790 17798 21099. See also S54 for middle-school students.
Normal schools. In titles of 14638 14644 14922.
Red and expert schools. In titles of 14321 14375 14946 15028 17787 22294.
Vocational schools. In title of 15898.
See also Education, Students, Teachers, *and* Universities.
Science, S62. For medical sciences, see S56; for natural science, S62; for social science, S70. For education in scientific fields, S17; for scientific academies, institutes, and societies, S36.1.
Science (general title mentions). Title mentions not listed. Most titles occur on pp. 480–496.
Education in sciences. In title of 15019.
Medical science. In titles of 19421 20981 20996 21036 21050 21081.
Natural sciences. In titles of 12447 19413 20814 21626 21812 21912 21917 21977 22512.
Nuclear science. In titles of 14013 21959.
Scientific academies, institutes, and societies. In titles of 11553 18341 19411 19412 19415 19421 19422 21918.
Social sciences. In titles of 22223 22789 22798 22837 22845 22996 23033 23047.
Scientists, see S11.4. In titles of 10463 10464 10481 14259 14304 14358 14373 14382 14814 17641 22828.
Second Five-Year Plan. *See under* Five-year plan.
Secondary education and schools, S17. *See also under* Education *and* Schools.